KT-424-813

Debrett's Distinguished People of Today

HM THE QUEEN AND HRH PRINCE PHILIP
(Tim Graham Picture Library, London)

Debrett's Distinguished People of Today

Edited by
Patricia Ellis

Senior Editor
David Williamson

Published by
DEBRETT'S PEERAGE LIMITED
73/77 Britannia Road · PO BOX 357 · London · SW6 2JY

ISBN 1 870520 02 5

Debrett's Distinguished People of Today 1989
Published by Debrett's Peerage Limited
73/77 Britannia Road · PO Box 357 · London · SW6 2JY

Printed in England

Data and computer typesetting prepared by Morton Computer Services Limited, Scarborough, Yorks.

Printed by Redwood Burn Limited, Trowbridge, Wiltshire and Ebenezer Baylis and Son Limited, Worcester. Bound by Hartnolls Limited, Bodmin, Cornwall.

CONTENTS

FOREWORD BY THE DUKE OF NORFOLK, KG, GCVO, CB, CBE, MC.

As a Patron of Debrett, it gives me great pleasure to be able to commend the second edition of this useful book of reference which has now become, I am glad to report, an annual publication for the first time this year. The first edition, with 25,000 entrants, achieved instant acceptance, prompting the Editors to expand into wider fields of entrants, adding a further 10,000 names of those who have distinguished themselves in their profession or calling.

A feature of *Debrett's Distinguished People of Today* is the inclusion of specially commissioned articles and I was particularly interested to read that on the work of the College of Arms by Hubert Chesshyre, the Chester Herald.

Debrett's Distinguished People of Today is a mine of useful information on our contemporaries—men and women of every calling, who have made their mark in public life and whose names frequently appear in the media. This should ensure that each annual edition will retain its value as a source of biographical information for very many years to come, and will no doubt become a serious alternative to a certain other well-known biographical reference book!

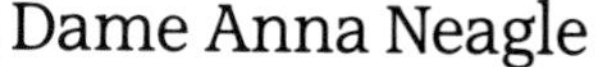

Dame Anna Neagle

Kenneth More

Anna Galica

Ray Kennedy

INTRODUCTION

This, the second edition of *Debrett's Distinguished People of Today* contains some 35,000 entries, approximately 10,000 of which have been added since the first edition. Of course, not all entrants from the 1988 edition have graduated to this edition, some having died during the past twelve months and others, in accordance with our editorial policy, having been deleted if it is considered that their distinction has somewhat waned.

In our quest to produce the definitive biographical reference book we have opened our pages to a wide variety of fields of human endeavour and have expanded existing ones to mirror the changes which are taking place socially, professionally, culturally, economically and commercially in Britain today.

We have included a full list of the Royal Warrant Holders for the first time and have also commissioned several excellent articles. David Williamson, senior editor at Debrett and author of numerous books on the Royal Family and the Royal Families of Europe, has penned an informative and illuminating piece on the Dukedom of York. The witty newspaper columnist Craig Brown has committed to paper for us some characteristically amusing thoughts on distinction. Hubert Chesshyre, LVO, Chester Herald of Arms, has provided us with a most fascinating article on the history and work of the College of Arms, and Lesley Abdela, freelance journalist and founder of the 300 Group investigates the proportion of women in various areas of British life and presents us with some interesting statistics in her article 'Distinguished Women of Today'.

For their help in compiling and editing this edition I would like to thank in particular, David Williamson for his patient guidance, Charles Kidd for his advice on Peerage and sundry matters and Jonathan Parker who did all the difficult and disagreeable tasks that nobody else wanted to do. Finally, for their editorial assistance I would like to express my utmost gratitude to Jeremy Bradford, Sara Cremer, Juliet Hime, Michelle Jacques, Francesca Johnson, Helen Kedie, Daniel Lyons, Gary McPake, Brian O'Grady, Michael Rodrigue, Simon Shackleton, Devinder Sidhu and Bill Williamson.

PATRICIA ELLIS

THE ROYAL FAMILY

For full details see *Debrett's Peerage and Baronetage*

HER MAJESTY THE QUEEN, Elizabeth Alexandra Mary; style in the United Kingdom: Elizabeth II, by The Grace of God, of The United Kingdom of Great Britain and Northern Ireland and of Her Other Realms and Territories Queen, Head of The Commonwealth, Defender of The Faith; crowned at Westminster Abbey 2 June 1953; celebrated her Silver Jubilee 1977; er da of His Majesty King George VI (d 6 Feb 1952) and of Lady Elizabeth Angela Marguerite Bowes-Lyon (HM Queen Elizabeth The Queen Mother, *qv*), da of 14 Earl of Strathmore and Kinghorne; *b* 21 April 1926; *m* 20 Nov 1947, HRH The Prince Philip, Duke of Edinburgh, KG, KT, OM, GBE, PC, *qv*; 3 s, 1 da (*see below*); *Heirs*, HRH The Prince of Wales, *qv*; Lord High Adm of the United Kingdom; Col-in-Chief: Life Guards, Blues and Royals (Royal Horse Gds and 1 Dragoons), Royal Scots Dragoon Gds (Carabiniers and Greys), 16/5 Queen's Royal Lancers, Royal Tank Regt, RE, Grenadier Gds, Coldstream Gds, Scots Gds, Irish Gds, Welsh Gds, Royal Welch Fus, Queen's Lancashire Regt, Argyll and Sutherland Highlanders (Princess Louise's), Royal Green Jackets, RAOC, Queen's Own Mercian Yeo, Duke of Lancaster's Own Yeo, Corps of Royal Mil Police, Corps of Royal Canadian Engrs, Canadian Forces Mil Engrs Branch, King's Own Calgary Regt, Royal 22e Regt, Govr-Gen's Foot Gds. Canadian Grenadier Gds, Le Regiment de la Chaudière, Royal New Brunswick Regt, 48 Highlanders of Canada, Argyll and Sutherland Highlanders of Canada (Princess Louise's), Royal Canadian Ordnance Corps, Malawi Rifles; Capt-Gen; RA, HAC, Combined Cadet Force, Royal Canadian Artillery, Royal Malta Artillery; Air Cdre-in-Chief: RAuxAF, RAF Regt, Royal Observer Corps, Royal Canadian Air Force Aux; Hon Air Cdre RAF Marham, Cmdt-in-Chief RAF Coll Cranwell, Hon Cmmr Royal Canadian Mounted Police, Master of the Merchant Navy and Fishing Fleets, Head Civil Defence Corps and Nat Hosp Service Reserve; Sovereign of all British Orders of Knighthood, Order of Merit, Royal Order of Victoria and Albert, Order of Crown of India, Order of Companions of Honour, Distinguished Service Order, Imperial Service Order, Order of Canada; Sovereign Head of Order of Hosp of St John of Jerusalem, Order of Australia, The Queen's Service Order of NZ; patron Royal Coll of Physicians Edinburgh and Victoria League for Cwlth Friendship; FRS 1947; Residences: Buckingham Palace, London SW1A 1AA; Windsor Castle, Berkshire; Balmoral Castle, Aberdeenshire; Sandringham House, Norfolk.

EDINBURGH, HRH 1 Duke of; HRH The Prince Philip; KG (1947), KT (1952), OM (1968), GBE (mil 1953), PC (1951, Canada 1957); cr Baron Greenwich, of Greenwich, Co London, Earl of Merioneth, and Duke of Edinburgh (UK 1947); naturalized a British subject and adopted surname of Mountbatten 1947; granted title, style and attribute of Royal Highness 1947; granted style and titular dignity of a Prince of UK 1957; only s of HRH Prince Andrew of Greece and Denmark, GCVO (d 1944), by HRH Princess (Victoria) Alice Elizabeth Julia Marie, RRC (d 1969), da of 1 Marquess of Milford Haven; *b* 10 June 1921; *Educ* Cheam Sch; Salem, Baden; Gordonstoun; RNC Dartmouth; *m* 20 Nov 1947, HM Queen Elizabeth II, *qv*; 3 s, 1 da; 1939-45 War, Mediterranean Fleet (Home Waters) and with British Pacific Fleet in SE Asia and Pacific (despatches, Greek War Cross; 1939-45, Atlantic, Africa, Burma (with Pacific rosette), and Italy Stars; War Medal 1939-45 (with oak leaf) and French Croix de Guerre (with Palm); a personal ADC to HM King George VI 1948; Field Marshal; Capt-Gen RM; Col-in-Chief: Queen's Royal Irish Hussars, Duke of Edinburgh's Royal Regt (Berks and Wilts), Queen's Own Highlanders (Seaforth and Camerons), REME, Intelligence Corps, Army Cadet Force, Royal Canadian Regt, Seaforth Highlanders of Canada, Cameron Highlanders of Ottawa, Queen's Own Cameron Highlanders of Canada, Royal Canadian Army Cadets; Col Grenadier Gds; Hon Col: Edinburgh and Heriot-Watt Univs OTC, Trinidad and Tobago Regt; *Navy:* Adm of the Fleet; Sea Cadet Corps, Royal Canadian Sea Cadets; Marshal of the RAF; Air Cdre-in-Chief: ATC, Royal Canadian Air Cadets; Hon Air Cdre RAF Kinloss; Cmdt-in-Ch and Extra Master Merchant Navy; memb cncl Duchy of Cornwall 1952-, Ranger of Windsor Great Park 1952-, Lord High Steward of Plymouth 1960-; chllr of univs: Salford 1967-71, Wales 1948-, Edinburgh 1952-, Cambridge 1977-; master bench Inner Temple 1954-, elder bro Trinity House 1952, (master 1969-; hon bro Hull 1953-); pres: Amateur Athletic Bd 1952-, Cwlth Games Fedn 1955-, Br Sportsman's Club 1958-, Central Cncl of Physical Recreation 1951-, City & Guilds of London Inst 1951-, ESU of Cwlth 1952-, Guards' Polo Club 1955-, RAS of Cwlth 1958-, Royal Household Cricket Club 1953-, Royal Merchant Navy Sch 1952-, RSA 1952-, World Wild Life Fund British Nat Appeal 1961-; third pres Int Wild Life Fund 1981-; Royal pres Soc of Friends of St George's and Descendants of KGs 1948-; patron and trustee Duke of Edinburgh's Award, chm Duke of Edinburgh's Ctee for Queen's Awards to Industry 1965-; patron UK branch Soc d'Entr'aide of Legion of Honour; Adm and Cdre Royal Yacht Sqdn 1961-68; Adm of Yacht Clubs: House of Lords, Royal Motor, Royal Southern, Bar, Dart, Royal Gibraltar, RNSA, Royal Yacht Club of Victoria (Australia) and of Great Navy State of Nebraska USA; King George VI Coronation Medal 1937, Queen Elizabeth II Coronation Medal 1953; Grand Master and First or Princ Kt of Order of British Empire 1953; FRS 1951.

HM QUEEN ELIZABETH THE QUEEN MOTHER; Lady Elizabeth Angela Marguerite, *née* Bowes-Lyon; Lady of the Order of the Garter (1936), Lady of the Order of the Thistle (1937), CI (1931), GCVO (1937), GBE (1927); da of 14 Earl of Strathmore and Kinghorne, KG, KT, GCVO, TD, JP, DL (d 1944) and Nina Cecilia, GCVO (d 1938), da of Rev Charles William Frederick Cavendish-Bentinck (gs of 3 Duke of Portland, who was twice Prime Minister during King George III's reign); *b* 4 Aug 1900: *m* 26 April 1923, HM King George VI (d 6 Feb 1952); 2 da (HM The Queen and HRH The Princess Margaret, *qqv*); Col-in-Chief: 1 Queen's Dragoon Gds, The Queen's Own Hussars, 9/12 Royal Lancers (Prince of Wales's), King's Regt, Royal Anglian Regt, Light Inf, The Black Watch (Royal Highland Regt), RAMC, The Black Watch (Royal Highland Regt) of Canada, The Toronto Scottish Regt, Canadian Forces Medical Services; Hol Col: Royal Yeo, London Scottish (Gordon Highlanders) (TA), Univ of London Contingent OTC; Cmdt-in-Chief: WRNS, WRAC, RAF Central Flying Sch, WRAF, Nursing Corps and Divs St John Ambulance Bde; hon member of Lloyd's; pres British Red Cross Soc 1937-52, since when dep pres; pres Royal Highland and Agric Soc 1963-64; Gold Albert Medal of RSA 1952; Grand Master Royal Victorian Order 1937; pres Univ Coll of Rhodesia and Nyasaland 1957-70, chllr London Univ 1955-81, first chllr Dundee Univ 1967; bencher Middle Temple 1944 (tres 1949); hon fellow London Univ, and of King's Coll London; FRS; appointed Lord Warden and Admiral of the Cinque Ports and Constable of Dover Castle (the first woman to hold this office) 1978; received Royal Victorian Chain 1937; Grand Cross of Legion of Honour; GCStJ; *Residences:* Clarence House, London SW1A 1BA; Royal Lodge, Windsor Great Park, Berks; Birkhall, Ballater, Aberdeenshire; Castle of Mey, Caithness-shire

WALES, HRH The Prince of; HRH Prince Charles Philip Arthur George; KG (1958, invested and installed 1968), KT (1977), GCB and Great Master of Order of the Bath (1975), AK, QSO, PC 1977; cr Prince of Wales and Earl of Chester 1958 (invested 1969); also Duke of Cornwall and Rothesay, Earl of Carrick and Baron of Renfrew, Lord of the Isles and Great Steward of Scotland; eldest s and h of HM Queen Elizabeth II, *qv*; *b* 14 Nov 1948; *Educ* Cheam Sch; Gordonstoun; Geelong GS Australia; Trinity Coll Cambridge (MA, Polo Half-Blue), Univ Coll of Wales, Aberystwyth; Bar of Gray's Inn 1974 (hon bencher 1975); *m* 29 July 1981, Lady Diana Spencer (*see* Wales, HRH The Princess of); 2s (*see below*); *Heir,* HRH Prince William of Wales, *qv*; Col-in-Chief: The Royal Regt of Wales (24/41 Foot) 1960-, The Cheshire Regt 1977-, The Gordon Highlanders 1977-, Lord Strathcona's Horse (Royal Canadian) Regt 1977-, The Parachute Regt 1977-, The Royal Regt of Canada 1977-, 2 King Edward VII Own Goorkhas 1977-, The Royal Winnipeg Rifles 1977-; personal ADC to HM 1973-; Col Welsh Guards 1974-; Cdr RN 1976-, Wing Cdr RAF 1976-; Hon Air Cdre RAF Brawdy 1977-; Col-in-Chief Air Reserves Gp of Air Cmd in Canada 1977-, pres: Soc of Friends St George's and Descendants of KG's 1975-, United World Colls 1978-, The Prince's Trust 1975-; Cdre Royal Thames Yacht Club 1974-, High Steward Royal Borough of Windsor and Maidenhead 1974-; chm: Queen's Silver Jubilee Trust 1978-, The Prince of Wales' Ctee for Wales 1971-; chllr The Univ of Wales 1976-, memb bd Cwlth Devpt Corpn 1979-; patron: The Press Club, Transglobe Expedition, Welsh National Opera, Royal Sch for the Blind, Mary Rose Trust; author of The Old Man of Lochnagar; Coronation Medal 1953, Queen's Silver Jubilee Medal 1977; *Residences:* Kensington Palace, London W8 4PU; Highgrove House, Doughton, Tetbury, Glos GL8 8TG

WALES, HRH The Princess of; Lady Diana Frances, *née* Spencer; 3 da of 8 Earl Spencer, LVO, DL (*see main text*) and (first wife) Hon Mrs Shand Kydd (*see main text*); *b* 1 July 1961; *Educ* Riddlesworth Hall; West Heath; Switzerland; *m* 29 July 1981, HRH The Prince of Wales, *qv*; 2s (*see below*); former kindergarten teacher

WALES, HRH Prince William of; Prince William Arthur Philip Louis; s and h of HRH The Prince of Wales, *qv*; *b* 21 June 1982

WALES, HRH Prince Henry (Harry) of; Prince Henry Charles Albert David; yr s of HRH The Prince of Wales, *qv*; *b* 15 Sept 1984.

YORK, HRH The Duke of; The Prince Andrew Albert Christian Edward; CVO (1979); *cr* Baron Killyleagh, Earl of Inverness, and Duke of York (UK 1986); 2 s of HM The Queen; *b* 19 Feb 1960; *Educ* Gordonstoun, Lakefield Coll Sch Ontario, RNC Dartmouth; Lieut RN, served S Atlantic Campaign 1982 as helicopter pilot HMS *Invincible*; personal ADC to HM The Queen 1984; *m* 23 July 1986, Sarah Margaret Ferguson (*see* York, HRH The Duchess of). *Residence:* Buckingham Palace, London SW1A 1AA

YORK, HRH The Duchess of; Sarah Margaret, *née* Ferguson; da of Maj Ronald Ivor Ferguson, The Life Guards, and his 1 w, Susan Mary, *née* Wright (now Mrs Hector Barrantes); *b* 15 Oct 1959; *Educ* Hurst Lodge Sunningdale, Queen's Secretarial Coll London; *m* 23 July 1986, HRH The Duke of York, *qv*.

YORK, HRH Princess Beatrice of; Princess Beatrice Elizabeth Mary; da of HRH The Duke of York; *b* 8 Aug 1988

HRH The Prince Edward Antony Richard Louis; CVO (1989); 3 and yst s of HM The Queen; *b* 10 March 1964; *Educ* Gordonstoun; Jesus Coll Cambridge; former house tutor and jr master Wanganui Collegiate Sch NZ; 2 Lieut RM 1983; *Residence:* Buckingham Palace, London SW1A 1AA

HRH THE PRINCESS ROYAL; Princess Anne Elizabeth Alice Louise; GCVO (1974); declared Princess Royal 13 June 1987; o da of HM The Queen; *b* 15 Aug 1950; *Educ* Benenden Sch; *m* 14 Nov 1973, Capt Mark Anthony Peter Phillips, CVO, ADC (P) (*see main text*); 1 s, 1 da (*see below*); Col-in-Chief: 14/20 King's Hussars, Worcs and Sherwood Foresters Regt (29/45 Foot) and 8 Canadian Hussars (Princess Louise's), Royal Corps of Signals, Canadian Forces Communications and Electronics Branch, Grey and Simcoe Foresters Militia; Ch Cmdt WRNS, Hon Air Cdre RAF Lyneham; pres: Save The Children Fund, British Acad of Film and Television Arts, WRNS Benevolent Trust, Windsor Horse Trials, Royals Sch for Daughters of Offrs of RN and RM (Haslemere); patron: Assoc of WRNS, Communications and Electronics Assoc, Riding for the Disabled Assoc, Jersey Wildlife Trust, R Corps of Signals Assoc, Royal Corps of Signals Instn, Breast Cancer Research Trust, Save the Children Action Group, Army and RA Hunter Trials, Gloucester and N Avon Fedn of Young Farmers' Clubs, Horse of the Year Ball, Benenden Ball; vice-patron British Show Jumping Assoc; Cmdt-in-Ch St John Ambulance and Nursing Cadets; chllr London Univ 1981-, *Residence:* Gatcombe Park, Minchinhampton, Stroud, Glos GL6 9AT

PHILLIPS, Peter Mark Andrew; s of HRH The Princess Royal, *qv*; *b* 15 Nov 1977

PHILLIPS, Zara Anne Elizabeth; da of HRH The Princess Royal, *qv*; *b* 15 May 1981

SNOWDON, HRH The Princess Margaret, Countess of; HRH Princess Margaret Rose; CI (1947), GCVO (1953); yr da of His late Majesty King George VI and Lady Elizabeth Angela Marguerite Bowes-Lyon (HM Queen Elizabeth The Queen Mother, *qv*); *b* 21 Aug 1930; *m* 6 May 1960 (m dis 1978), 1 Earl of Snowdon, GCVO (*see main text*); 1 s, 1 da (*see below*); Col-in-Chief: Royal Highland Fus (Princess Margaret's Own Glasgow and Ayrshire Regt), 15/19 King's Royal Hussars, Princess Louise Fus, Highland Fus of Canada, QARANC; Dep Col-in-Chief Royal Anglian Regt, Hon Air Cdre RAF Coningsby, chllr Univ of Keele; pres: Barnado's Scottish Children's League, Victoria League, Sunshine Homes and Schs for Blind Children (Royal Nat Inst for the Blind), Royal Ballet, NSPCC (and Royal Scottish Soc), Dockland Settlements, Friends of the Elderly and Gentlefolk's Help, Invalid Children's Aid Assoc (also chm cncl), Sadler's Wells Fndn, English Folk Dance and Song Soc, Horder Centres for Arthritics, Girl Guides Assoc, RASE; patron: Princess Margaret Rose Hosp Edinburgh, Royal Coll of Nursing, Nat Cncl of Nurses of UK, London Festival Ballet, Tenovus (Inst of Cancer Research); bencher Lincoln's Inn and tres 1967; Grand Pres of St John Ambulance Assoc and Bde, hon memb and patron of Grand Antiquity Soc of Glasgow; CStJ; *Residence* Kensington Palace, London W8 4PU

LINLEY, Viscount; David Albert Charles Armstrong-Jones; s of HRH The Princess Margaret and s and h of 1 Earl of Snowdon (*see main text*); *b* 3 Nov 1961; *Educ* Bedales; John Makepeace Sch of Woodcraft, Beaminster, Dorset.

ARMSTRONG-JONES, Lady Sarah Frances Elizabeth; da of HRH The Princess Margaret and 1 Earl of Snowdon (*see main text*); *b* 1 May 1964; *Educ* Bedales.

GLOUCESTER, HRH 2 Duke of; HRH Prince Richard Alexander Walter George; GCVO (1974); also Earl of Ulster and Baron Culloden (both UK 1928); 2 but only surv s of HRH the late Prince Henry, 1 Duke of Gloucester (d 1974, 3 s of King George V) and HRH Princess Alice, Duchess of Gloucester, *qv*; *b* 26 Aug 1944; *Educ* Eton, Magdalene Coll Cambridge (MA, Dip Arch); *m* 8 July 1972, Birgitte Eva, DStJ (Col-in-Ch Royal Army Educational Corps; pres: London Region WRVS, Royal Alexander and Albert Sch, Cambridge House; patron: Asthma Research Cncl, Bobath Centre), da of Asger Preben Wissing Henriksen, lawyer, of Odense, Denmark, and his 1 w, Vivian, da of late Waldemar Oswald Van Deurs, whose name she assumed; 1 s, 2 da (*see below*); *Heir* s, Earl of Ulster, *qv*; *Career* RIBA, FSA, FRSA; Col-in-Chief: The Gloucestershire Regt 1975-, Royal Pioneer Corps 1977-; Hon Col Royal Monmouthshire RE (Militia) 1977-; pres: Inst of Advanced Motorists 1971-, Cancer Research Campaign 1973-, Nat Assoc of Boy's Clubs 1974-, British Consultants Bureau 1978-, E England Agric Soc 1979-; vice-pres British Leprosy Relief Assoc 1971-; patron: ASH 1974-, Victorian Soc 1976-, Bulldog Manpower Services 1976; ranger of Epping Forest 1975-; Grand Prior Order of St John of Jerusalem 1975-; KStJ; *Residences* Kensington Palace, London W8 4PU; Barnwell Manor, Peterborough, Cambs PE8 5PJ

ULSTER, Earl of ; Alexander Patrick Gregers Richard; s and h of HRH 2 Duke of Gloucester, GCVO, *qv*; *b* 24 Oct 1974.

WINDSOR, Lady Davina Elizabeth Alice Benedikte; er da of HRH 2 Duke of Gloucester, GCVO, *qv*; *b* 19 Nov 1977.

WINDSOR, Lady Rose Victoria Birgitte Louise; yr da of HRH 2 Duke of Gloucester, GCVO, *qv*; *b* 1 March 1980.

GLOUCESTER, HRH Princess Alice, Duchess of; Lady Alice Christabel, *née* Montagu Douglas Scott; GCB (1975), CI (1937), GCVO (1948), GBE (1937); 3 da of 7 Duke of Buccleuch and Queensberry, KT, GCVO, JP (d 1935), and Lady Margaret Alice, *née* Bridgeman (d 1954), 2 da of 4 Earl of Bradford; *b* 25 Dec 1901; *Educ* St James's Sch W Malvern, Paris; *m* 6 Nov 1935, HRH Prince Henry William Frederick Albert, KG, KT, KP, GCB, GCMG, GCVO, 1 Duke of Gloucester (d 10 June 1974, 3 s of King George V); 1 s (*see above*) and 1 s decd (HRH Prince William, who was killed in an aeroplane accident 28 Aug 1972); Air Marshal WRAF; Col-in-Chief: KOSB, Royal Hussars, RCT; Dep Col-in-Chief Royal Anglian Regt; memb cncl British Red Cross Soc; Dep Cmdt-in-C Nursing Corps and Divs of St John Ambulance Bde 1937-; GCStJ; *Residences* Kensington Palace, London W8 4PU; Barnwell Manor, Peterborough, Cambs PE8 5PJ

KENT, HRH 2 Duke of; Prince Edward George Nicholas Paul Patrick; KG (1985), GCMG (1967), GCVO (1960); also Earl of St Andrews and Baron Downpatrick (both UK 1934); er s of HRH 1 Duke of Kent, KG, KT, GCMG, GCVO, PC (killed on active service 25 Aug 1942, 4 s of King George V), and HRH Princess Marina, CI, GCVO, GBE (d 27 Aug 1968), yst da of HRH late Prince Nicholas of Greece and Denmark; *b* 9 Oct 1935; *Educ* Eton; Switzerland; RMA Sandhurst; *m* 8 June 1961, Katharine Lucy Mary, GCVO (1977) (Controller-Cmdt WRAC and Hon Maj-Gen; Col-in-Chief Army Catering Corps, Hon Col Yorks Volunteers TAVR, chllr Leeds Univ), only da of late Sir William Arthington Worsley, 4 Bt; 2 s, 1 da (*see below*); Maj-Gen (ret) Royal Scots Dragoon Gds; Col-in-Chief: Royal Regt of Fusiliers, Devonshire and Dorset Regt; Col Scots Gds, personal ADC to HM 1966-, GSO II E Cmd 1966-68, company instr RMA Sandhurst 1968-70, cmd C Sqdn Royal Scots Greys 1970-71; Grand Master United Grand Lodge Freemasons of England and Grand Master Order of St Michael and St George; pres: Wellington Coll, Cwlth War Graves Cmmn. Scout Assoc, Technician Educn Cncl; vice-chm British Overseas Trade Bd 1976-; chllr Surrey Univ 1977-; dir British Insulated Callender's Cables 1981-; *Residences* York House, St James's Palace, London SW1A 1BQ; Anmer Hall, King's Lynn, Norfolk PE31 6RW

ST ANDREWS, Earl of; George Philip Nicholas Windsor; er s, and h or HRH 2 Duke of Kent, KG, GCMG, GCVO, *qv*; *b* 26 June 1962; *Educ* Eton, and Downing Coll Camb; *m* 9 Jan 1988, Sylvana, da of Max Tomaselli; 1 s (Lord Downpatrick *b* 2 Dec 1988).

WINDSOR, Lord Nicholas Charles Edward Jonathan; 2 s of HRH 2 Duke of Kent, KG, GCMG, GCVO, *qv*; *b* 25 July 1970.

WINDSOR, Lady Helen Marina Lucy; da of HRH 2 Duke of Kent, KG, GCMG, GCVO, *qv*; b 28 April 1964.

KENT, HRH Prince Michael of; Prince Michael George Charles Franklin; 2 s of HRH 1 Duke of Kent (killed on active service 1942); *b* 4 July 1942; *Educ* Eton, RMA Sandhurst; *m* 30 June 1978, Baroness Marie Christine Agnes Hedwig Ida, da of late Baron Günther Hubertus von Reibnitz, and formerly wife of Thomas Troubridge, yr bro of Sir Peter Troubridge, 6 Bt; 1 s, 1 da (*see below*); Maj Royal Hussars to 1981; foreign attaché liaison sec MOD 1968-70, UN Force Cyprus 1971, Defence Intelligence Service 1974-76, Army Recruiting Directorate 1976-78, GSO Defence Intelligence Staff 1978-81; pres: British Bobsleigh Assoc 1977-, Soc of Genealogists, Inst of Motor Industry 1978-, Royal Patriotic Fund Corpn 1980-, Soldiers', Sailors' and Airmen's Families Assoc 1982-; Cwlth pres Royal Lifesaving Soc; memb: RAC British Motor Sports Cncl, British Olympic Assoc 1977-, HAC; *Residences* Kensington Palace, London W8 4PU; Nether Lypiatt Manor, Stroud, Glos GL6 7LS

WINDSOR, Lord Frederick Michael George David Louis; o s of HRH Prince Michael of Kent, *qv*; *b* 6 April 1979.

WINDSOR, Lady Gabriella (Ella) Marina Alexandra Ophelia; o da of HRH Prince Michael of Kent, *qv*; *b* 23 April 1981.

HRH Princess Alexandra, the Hon Lady Ogilvy; HRH Princess Alexandra Helen Elizabeth Olga Christabel; GCVO (1960); da of HRH 1 Duke of Kent (killed on active service 1942); *b* 25 Dec 1936; *Educ* Heathfield, Paris; *m* 24 April 1963, Hon Sir Angus Ogilvy, KCVO (*see main text*), 2 s of 12 Earl of Airlie, KT GCVO, MC; 1 s, 1 da (*see below*); Col-in-Chief: 17/21 Lancers, Queen's Own Rifles of Canada, The King's Own Border Regt, The Canadian Scottish Regt (Princess Mary's); Dep Col-in-Chief LI, Dep Hon Col Royal Yeo TAVR, Air Chief Cmdt Princess Mary's RAF Nursing Service; Hon Cmdt-Gen: Royal Hong Kong Police Force, Royal Hong Kong Aux Police Force; pres: Royal Commonwealth Soc for the Blind. Children's Country Holidays Fund, Queen Alexandra's House Assoc, Star and Garter Home for Disabled Sailors, Soldiers and Airmen, Alexandra Day, British Sch at Rome, Royal Humane Soc; vice-pres British Red Cross Soc; chllr: Lancaster Univ 1964-, Univ of Mauritius 1974-, Hon FRCPS, Hon FRCOG, Hon FFA RCS; *Residences* Thatched House Lodge, Richmond Park, Surrey; 22 Friary Court, St James's Palace, London SW1A 1BQ

OGILVY, James Robert Bruce; o s of HRH Princess Alexandra and Hon Sir Angus Ogilvy, KCVO, *qqv*; *b* 29 Feb 1964. *(See main text)*

OGILVY, Marina Victoria Alexandra; o da of HRH Princess Alexandra and Hon Sir Angus Ogilvy, KCVO, *qqv*; *b* 31 July 1966.

For other members of the Royal Family, the Earl of Harewood, KBE, the Hon Gerald Lascelles, the Duke of Fife, Captain Alexander Ramsay of Mar and Lady May Abel Smith, see their entries in the main body of the work.

THEIR ROYAL HIGHNESSES THE DUKE AND DUCHESS OF YORK
(Tim Graham Picture Library, London)

THE DUKEDOM OF YORK

The birth on 8 August 1988 of HRH Princess Beatrice of York, the first child of Their Royal Highnesses the Duke and Duchess of York and the fifth grandchild of HM The Queen, was an occasion of much joy to the Royal Family and throughout the Commonwealth. Not only is the little Princess the first to be born since the birth of her aunt Princess Anne in 1950, but she is the first member of the Royal Family to bear the style or designation 'of York' since it was borne by her grandmother the Queen and her great-aunt Princess Margaret prior to their father's accession to the throne in December 1936.

The honour of York, unlike the other royal dukedoms, has always been a royal one, if we discount the Earldom of York conferred on William of Aumale by King Stephen in 1138 as a reward for his part in the Battle of the Standard which defeated the invading Scots. William was not very keen on this English title it seems and soon dropped it. He died without male issue in 1179. There is some suggestion that Richard *Coeur de Lion* intended to bestow the Earldom of York on his nephew Otto of Saxony, but nothing came of it, and it was not until 6 August 1385 that the Dukedom of York was conferred for the first time by King Richard II on his uncle Edmund of Langley, Earl of Cambridge, the fifth son of King Edward III, in the course of an expedition to Scotland. The new Duke was invested in Parliament at Westminster in October and the following month received a grant of one thousand pounds a year to support the dignity of his Dukedom. He died in 1402 and was succeeded by his eldest son Edward as 2nd Duke of York. On Edward's death without issue in 1415, the Dukedom passed to his nephew Richard, who became 3rd Duke. Famous as the leader of the Yorkists against the Lancastrians in the Wars of the Roses, Richard succeeded in getting himself publicly proclaimed as heir to the throne in November 1460, only to be ignominiously defeated and killed at Wakefield on 30 December by Queen Margaret and the Lancastrians. His severed head, crowned with a paper crown, was set up on Micklegate Bar, York. A little over a month later the tables were turned by Richard's son Edward, 4th Duke of York, at the Battle of Mortimer's Cross. Edward then advanced to London, where he was proclaimed King as Edward IV on 4 March 1461 and the first creation of the Dukedom of York thereby merged in the Crown.

Thirteen years later the Dukedom was re-created on 28 May 1474 in favour of Edward's second son Richard, a child of nine months. The little Duke made an equally precocious marriage at the tender age of four to the great Mowbray heiress Anne, only daughter of the 4th Duke of Norfolk. Almost a year older than her husband, the Duchess of York succumbed to some childish ailment and died in November 1481 at the age of eight. Her widower lived on to become one of the 'little Princes in the Tower' whose eventual fate has become such a matter of controversy.

The Dukedom of York was next conferred on Prince Henry, the second son of King Henry VII on 31 October 1494, but when he was created Prince of Wales in 1504 after the death of his elder brother Arthur, the patent of his creation as Duke of York was declared void by Parliament. It is hardly necessary to add that Henry was to gain fame and notoriety as King Henry VIII.

The next Duke of York was the future King Charles I, who received the Dukedom on 6 January 1605, being the second son of King James I. On the death of his elder brother Henry in 1612 he became Duke of Cornwall and Rothesay and was created Prince of Wales and Earl of Chester in November 1616, but this time no cancellation of the York Dukedom was deemed necessary, and when Charles succeeded his father in 1625 the Dukedom again merged in the Crown. By now it had come to be regarded as the traditional title for the second born son of the sovereign and Charles's second surviving (though actually third born) son James was designated Duke of York on the day of his birth, 14 October 1633, and so proclaimed at his baptism a month later, although he was not formally so created until January 1644. In 1685 he succeeded to the throne as King James II and the Dukedom merged in the Crown.

The next Duke of York was the brother, rather than the son, of a sovereign, being Ernest Augustus, Prince-Bishop of Osnabrück, the only surviving brother of King George I, who created him Duke of York and Albany and Earl of Ulster on 5 July 1716. He died unmarried on 14 August 1728, but three years before he died a Jacobite Dukedom of York had been created by the titular King James III in favour of his second son Henry, later to be known as 'Cardinal York' and eventually as 'King Henry IX' by his followers.

The titles which George I had conferred on his brother were re-conferred by King George II on his grandson Edward Augustus, the second son of Frederick, Prince of Wales on 1 April 1760. The Duke became heir-presumptive to his brother King George III in October the same year and retained that position until the birth of the King's first son in August 1762. Edward made his career in the navy and was promoted Admiral of the Blue in 1766 at the age of twenty-seven. The following year he was cruising in the Mediterranean when he fell ill with 'malignant fever.' He was put ashore at Monaco, where the Prince accommodated him in his palace and provided every medical attention, but sadly he died there on 17 September 1767. The room in which he died is still known as the 'York Chamber' and shown to all visitors to the Princely Palace. Edward was unmarried and his Dukedom became extinct on his death.

On 27 November 1784 King George III conferred the titles which his late brother had held on his second son, the 21 year old Prince Frederick. Frederick had been elected Prince-Bishop of Osnabrück at the age of six months, a position which it will be recalled had also been held by one of his predecessors in the Dukedom. He is the 'Grand Old Duke of York' of the nursery rhyme and had a long army career, not untouched by scandal and charges of corruption, ending up as Commander-in-Chief. On his elder brother's accession to the throne as King George IV in 1820, he became heir-presumptive and remained such until his death in 1827. He had married a Prussian Princess, but they had no children and she led an eccentric existence surrounded by pet dogs and monkeys. On her death, several years before that of the Duke, she was buried at her own request in a very modest grave in Weybridge Churchyard, only distinguished by the royal coronets surmounting the railings which surround it.

Queen Victoria departed from precedent in the choice of ducal title conferred on her second son, Prince Alfred, who became Duke of Edinburgh. Perhaps she felt the reputation of her uncle Frederick was not one to perpetuate in people's minds by a revival of his title. However, she did create her grandson Prince George, second (but by then only surviving) son of her eldest son, Baron Killarney, Earl of Inverness and Duke of York on 24 May 1892. On his father's accession as King Edward VII in 1901, Prince George automatically succeeded to the Dukedoms of Cornwall and Rothesay as well, and for some months, until he was created Prince of Wales, was known as Duke of Cornwall and York. On his accession to the throne as King George V in 1910, all his titles merged in the Crown.

On 3 June 1920, King George V created his second son, Prince Albert, Duke of York, Earl of Inverness and Baron Killarney (the same titles he himself had held). He ascended the throne as King George VI on the abdication of his brother King Edward VIII in December 1936, when his titles merged in the Crown until the Dukedom was re-created in favour of HRH The Prince Andrew nearly fifty years later.

There have been fourteen Dukes of York (not counting the Jacobite one) and eleven separate creations of the dignity. Only in the first creation was there a succession of Dukes before the title merged in the Crown or became extinct. Six Dukes of York have succeeded to the throne, three others were at one time Heirs-Presumptive but never succeeded, and five (including the present holder) have pursued naval careers. The birth of a son (or sons) to Their Royal Highnesses in the future will ensure that we may look forward to a succession of Dukes of York stemming from the Royal Family.

DAVID WILLIAMSON

THE ORDER OF SUCCESSION

The first twenty-five persons in line of succession to the throne

HRH The Prince of Wales
HRH Prince William of Wales
HRH Prince Henry of Wales
HRH The Duke of York
HRH Princess Beatrice of York
HRH The Prince Edward
HRH The Princess Royal
Peter Phillips
Zara Phillips
HRH The Princess Margaret, Countess of Snowdon
Viscount Linley
Lady Sarah Armstrong-Jones
HRH The Duke of Gloucester
Earl of Ulster
Lady Davina Windsor
Lady Rose Windsor
HRH The Duke of Kent

(NB Earl of St Andrews would be next in line but for his marriage to a Roman Catholic)

Lord Downpatrick
Lord Nicholas Windsor
Lady Helen Windsor

(NB HRH Prince Michael of Kent would be next in line but for his marriage to a Roman Catholic. His rights are, however, transmitted to his two children who follow)

Lord Frederick Windsor
Lady Gabriella Windsor
HRH Princess Alexandra, the Hon Mrs Angus Ogilvy
James Ogilvy
Marina Ogilvy

THE ROYAL HOUSEHOLDS

THE QUEEN'S HOUSEHOLD

Lord Chamberlain, The Earl of Airlie, KT, GCVO, PC
Lord Steward, Vacant
Master of the Horse, The Earl of Westmorland, KCVO
Mistress of the Robes, The Duchess of Grafton, GCVO
Lords in Waiting, Lt-Col the Lord Charteris of Amisfield, GCB, GCVO, OBE, QSO, PC (Permanent); The Lord Maclean, KT, GCVO, KBE (Permanent); The Lord Somerleyton; The Viscount Boyne; The Viscount Long; The Earl of Dundee; The Earl of Arran; The Lord Strathclyde; The Lord Henley
Captain, Gentlemen at Arms, The Lord Denham, PC
Captain, Yeoman of the Guard, The Viscount Davidson
Treasurer of the Household, David Hunt, MBE, MP
Comptroller of the Household, Tristan Garel-Jones, MP
Vice-Chamberlain of the Household, Robert Durrant, MP
Ladies of the Bedchamber, The Countess of Airlie, CVO; The Lady Farnham
Extra Lady of the Bedchamber, The Countess of Cromer, CVO; The Marchioness of Abergavenny, DCVO
Women of the Bedchamber, Hon Mary Morrison, DCVO; Lady Susan Hussey, DCVO: Mrs John Dugdale, DCVO; The Lady Elton
Extra Women of the Bedchamber, Mrs John Woodroffe, CVO; Lady Rose Baring, DCVO; Mrs Michael Wall, DCVO; Lady Abel Smith, DCVO; Mrs Robert de Pass
Equerries, Lt- Col Blair Stewart-Wilson, CVO; Cdr Timothy Laurence, RN
Temporary Equerry, Capt Hon Richard Margesson
Private Secretary, The Rt Hon Sir William Heseltine, GCVO, KCB, AC
Deputy Private Secretary, Robert Fellowes, CB, LVO
Assistant Private Secretary, Kenneth Scott, CMG
Chief Clerk, Mrs Graham Coulson, MVO
Press Secretary, Robin Janvrin, LVO
Deputy Press Secretary, John Haslam, LVO
Assistant Press Secretaries, Richard Arbiter; Geoffrey Crawford
Deputy Keeper and Deputy Treasurer, John Parsons
Defence Services Secretary, Rear Adm David Allen, CBE
Keeper of the Privy Purse and Treasurer to The Queen, Major Shane Blewitt, CVO
Chief Accountant and Paymaster, Frank Mintram, LVO
Personnel Officer, Gordon Franklin, LVO
High Almoner, The Bishop of St Albans (The Rt Rev John Taylor, MA, BTh)
Secretary, Royal Almonry, Peter Wright, CVO
Master of the Household, Rear Admiral Sir Paul Greening, KCVO
Deputy Master of the Household, Lt-Col Blair Stewart-Wilson, CVO
Chief Clerk, Alan Hancock, MVO
Comptroller, Lord Chamberlain's Office, Lt- Col George West, CVO
Assistant Comptroller, LCO, Lt-Col Malcolm Ross, OBE
Secretary, LCO, John Titman, CVO
Marshal of the Diplomatic Corps, Lt-Gen Sir John Richards, KCB
Vice-Marshal of the Diplomatic Corps, Roger Hervey, CMG
Assistant Marshals of the Diplomatic Corps, Stanley Martin, LVO; Clive Almond, OBE
Secretary, Central Chancery of the Orders of Knighthood, Maj-Gen Desmond Rice, CVO, CBE
Crown Equerry, Lt-Col Seymour Gilbart-Denham
Superintendent, Royal Mews, Major Albert Smith, MBE
Master of The Queen's Music, Malcolm Williamson, CBE, AO
Poet Laureate, Edward Hughes, OBE
Gentlemen at Arms: Lieutenant, Major David Jamieson, VC
Clerk of the Cheque and Adjutant, Major Thomas St Aubyn
Yeomen of the Guard: Lieutenant, Colonel Alan Pemberton, CVO, MBE
Clerk of the Cheque and Adjutant, Col Greville Tufnell
Clerk of the Closet, The Rt Rev John Bickersteth, MA
Deputy Clerk of the Closet, The Rev Canon Anthony Caesar, LVO, MA, MusB, FRCO
Dean of the Chapels Royal, The Bishop of London, PC (The Rt Rev and Rt Hon Graham Leonard)
Sub-Dean of the Chapels Royal, The Rev Canon Anthony Caesar, LVO, MA, MusB, FRCO
Head of the Medical Household and Physician, Dr Anthony Dawson, MD, FRCP
Apothecary to The Queen, Dr Nigel Southward, LVO, MA, MB, BChir, MRCP
Serjeant Surgeon, William Slack, MCh, FRCS
Windsor Castle: Constable and Governor, Admiral Sir David Halifax, KCB, KBE
Superintendent, Major Barrie Eastwood, MBE
Director of the Royal Collection and Surveyor of the Queen's Works of Art, Sir Geoffrey de Bellague, KCVO, FSA
Surveyor of The Queen's Pictures, Christopher Lloyd
Librarian, Royal Library, Oliver Everett, LVO
Heralds and Pursuivants, see HER MAJESTY'S OFFICERS OF ARMS

HOUSEHOLD OF QUEEN ELIZABETH THE QUEEN MOTHER

Apothecary to the Household, Dr Nigel Southward, LVO, MA, MB BChir, MRCP
Clerk Comptroller to the Household, Malcolm Blanch, LVO
Comptroller, Captain Sir Alastair Aird, KCVO
Equerries, Lt-Col Sir Martin Gilliat, GCVO, MBE; Major Sir Ralph Anstruther, Bt, KCVO, MC; Major Raymond Seymour, LVO
Temporary Equerry, Captain Giles Bassett
Mistress of the Robes, The Dowager Duchess of Abercorn, GCVO
Ladies of the Bedchamber, The Dowager Viscountess Hambleden, DCVO; The Lady Grimthorpe, CVO
Women of the Bedchamber, The Dowager Lady Fermoy, DCVO, OBE; Mrs Patrick Campbell-Preston, CVO; Lady Elizabeth Basset, CVO; Lady Angela Oswald
Lord Chamberlain, The Earl of Dalhousie, KT, GCVO, GBE, MC
Page of Honour, Viscount Lumley
Press Secretary, Major John Griffin, CVO
Private Secretary, Lt-Col Sir Martin Gilliat, GCVO, MBE
Apothecary to the Household at Royal Lodge, Windsor, Dr John Briscoe, MA, MB, BChir, MRCGP, DObst, RCOG
Treasurer, Major Sir Ralph Anstruther, Bt, KCVO, MC

HOUSEHOLD OF THE PRINCE PHILIP, DUKE OF EDINBURGH

Chief Clerk and Accountant to the Household, Vernon Jewell, MVO
Equerry, Major Sir Guy Acland, Bt, RHA
Temporary Equerries, Capt James Fraser; Capt Alastair Rogers, RN
Private Secretary and Treasurer, Brian McGrath,CVO

HOUSEHOLD OF THE PRINCE AND PRINCESS OF WALES

Apothecary to the Household, Dr Michael Linnett, OBE, MB, BS, FRCGP
Equerry to The Prince of Wales, Major Christopher Lavender
Equerry to The Princess of Wales, Cdr Alastair Watson, RN
Temporary Equerry to The Prince of Wales, Capt Rupert Cockcroft
Lady in Waiting and Assistant Private Secretary to The Princess of Wales, Miss Anne Beckwith-Smith
Extra Ladies in Waiting, Mrs George West; Viscountess Campden; Mrs Max Pike; Miss Alexandra Loyd; Hon Mrs Vivian Baring
Private Secretary and Treasurer to The Prince and Princess of Wales, Sir John Riddell, Bt
Deputy Private Secretary to The Prince of Wales, David Wright
Assistant Private Secretary and Comptroller to The Prince of Wales, Cdr Richard Aylard, RN

HOUSEHOLD OF THE DUKE AND DUCHESS OF YORK

Ladies in Waiting, Mrs John Spooner; Mrs John Floyd
Extra Lady in Waiting (temporary), Miss Lucy Manners
Equerry, Capt William McLean, Coldstream Guards
Private Secretary and Equerry, Lt-Col Sean O'Dwyer, Irish Guards

HOUSEHOLD OF THE PRINCE EDWARD

Private Secretary and Equerry, Lt-Col Sean O'Dwyer, Irish Guards

HOUSEHOLD OF THE PRINCESS ROYAL

Ladies in Waiting, Mrs Richard Carew Pole, LVO; Hon Mrs Legge-Bourke LVO; Mrs Malcolm Wallace; Mrs Timothy Holderness-Roddam; Mrs Charles Ritchie
Extra Ladies in Waiting, Mrs Andrew Feilden, LVO; Miss Victoria Legge-Bourke, LVO; Mrs Malcolm Innes, LVO; The Countess of Lichfield
Private Secretary, Lt-Col Peter Gibbs
Assistant Private Secretary, Hon Mrs Louloudis

HOUSEHOLD OF THE PRINCESS MARGARET, COUNTESS OF SNOWDON

Apothecary to the Household, Dr Nigel Southward, LVO, MA, MB, BChir, MRCP
Comptroller, Major the Lord Napier and Ettrick, CVO
Equerry, Major the Lord Napier and Ettrick, CVO
Extra Ladies in Waiting, Lady Elizabeth Cavendish, LVO; Lady Aird, LVO; Mrs Robin Benson, LVO; Hon Mrs Wills, LVO; Mrs Jane Stevens; Lady Juliet Townsend, LVO; The Lady Glenconner; Hon Mrs Whitehead, LVO; The Countess Alexander of Tunis; Mrs Charles Vyvyan
Personal Secretary, Miss Muriel Murray Brown, CVO
Private Secretary, Major the Lord Napier and Ettrick, CVO

HOUSEHOLD OF PRINCESS ALICE, DUCHESS OF GLOUCESTER

Apothecary to the Household, Dr Nigel Southward, LVO, MA, MB, BChir, MRCP
Clerk Comptroller, Mrs Gordon Franklin
Comptroller, Maj Nicholas Barne
Equerry, Maj Nicholas Barne
Extra Equerry, Lt-Col Sir Simon Bland, KCVO
Ladies in Waiting, Dame Jean Maxwell-Scott, DCVO; Mrs Michael Harvey
Private Secretary, Maj Nicholas Barne

HOUSEHOLD OF THE DUKE AND DUCHESS OF GLOUCESTER

Apothecary to the Household, Dr Nigel Southward, LVO, MA, MB, BChir, MRCP
Clerk Comptroller, Mrs Gordon Franklin
Comptroller, Maj Nicholas Barne
Equerry, Maj Nicholas Barne
Extra Equerry, Lt-Col Sir Simon Bland, KCVO
Ladies in Waiting, Mrs Michael Wigley, LVO; Mrs Euan McCorquodale; Mrs Howard Page; The Lady Camoys (temporary)
Extra Lady in Waiting, Miss Jennifer Thomson
Assistant Private Secretary to the Duchess of Gloucester, Miss Suzanne Marland
Private Secretary, Maj Nicholas Barne

HOUSEHOLD OF THE DUKE AND DUCHESS OF KENT

Apothecary to the Household, Dr Nigel Southward, LVO, MA, MB, BChir, MRCP
Clerk Comptroller, Mrs Henry Gow
Temporary Equerry, Capt Charles Page
Ladies in Waiting, Mrs Alan Henderson, CVO; Mrs David Napier, LVO; Miss Sarah Partridge
Extra Lady in Waiting, Mrs Peter Wilmot-Sitwell
Private Secretary, Andrew Palmer, CMG, CVO

HOUSEHOLD OF PRINCE AND PRINCESS MICHAEL OF KENT

Ladies in Waiting, Hon Mrs Leatham; Miss Anne Frost
Personal Secretary to Prince Michael of Kent, Miss Sally Cox
Personal Secretary to Princess Michael of Kent, Miss Emma Kitchener

HOUSEHOLD OF PRINCESS ALEXANDRA, THE HON LADY OGILVY

Extra Equerry, Major Peter Clarke, CVO
Lady in Waiting, Lady Mary Mumford, CVO
Extra Ladies in Waiting, Mrs Peter Afia; Lady Mary Colman; Hon Lady Rowley
Private Secretary and Extra Lady in Waiting, Miss Mona Mitchell, CVO

THE QUEEN'S HOUSEHOLD IN SCOTLAND

Hereditary Lord High Constable, The Earl of Erroll
Hereditary Master of the Household, The Duke of Argyll
Hereditary Standard Bearer for Scotland, The Earl of Dundee
Hereditary Bearer of the National Flag of Scotland, The Earl of Lauderdale
Hereditary Keepers:-
Holyrood, The Duke of Hamilton and Brandon
Falkland, Ninian Crichton-Stuart
Stirling, The Earl of Mar and Kellie
Dunstaffnage, The Duke of Argyll
Dunconnel, Sir Fitzroy Maclean, Bt, CBE
Keeper of Dumbarton Castle, Brig A S Pearson, CB, DSO, OBE, MC, TD
Governor of Edinburgh Castle, Lt-Gen Sir John MacMillan, KCB
Dean of the Order of the Thistle, The Very Rev Prof J McIntyre, CVO, MA, DD, DLitt, FRSE, DHL
Dean of the Chapel Royal, Very Rev Prof R A S Barbour, MC, MA, DD
Physicians in Scotland, Dr Peter Brunt, MD, FRCP; Dr Alexander Muir, MD, FRCPEdin
Surgeons in Scotland, Jetmund Engeset, ChM, FRCS; Ian Macleod, BSc, MD, ChB, FRCS
Apothecary to the Household at Balmoral, Dr Douglas Glass, MB, ChB
Apothecary to the Household at the Palace of Holyrood, Dr Henry Gebbie, MB, ChB, MRCGP
Royal Company of Archers:
Capt-Gen and Gold Stick for Scotland, Col the Lord Clydesmuir, KT, CB, MBE, TD
Adjutant, Major Hon Lachlan Maclean
Heralds and Pursuivants, see HER MAJESTY'S OFFICERS OR ARMS

HER MAJESTY'S OFFICERS OF ARMS

ENGLAND

College of Arms, Queen Victoria Street, London EC4V 4BT

EARL MARSHAL

His Grace the Duke of Norfolk, KG, GCVO, CB, CBE, MC

KINGS OF ARMS

Garter-Sir (Alexander) Colin Cole, KCVO, TD, FSA
Clarenceux-Sir Anthony Richard Wagner, KCB, KCVO, DLitt, FSA
Norroy and Ulster-John Philip Brooke Brooke-Little, CVO, FSA

HERALDS

York (and Registrar)-Conrad Marshall John Fisher Swan, CVO, PhD, FSA
Chester-David Hubert Boothby Chesshyre, LVO, FSA
Windsor-Theobald David Mathew
Lancaster-Peter Llewellyn Gwynn-Jones
Somerset-Thomas Woodcock
Richmond-Patric Laurence Dickinson

PURSUIVANTS

Portcullis-Peter Brotherton Spurrier
Bluemantle-Terence David McCarthy
Rouge Croix-Henry Edgar Paston-Bedingfeld
Rouge-Dragon-Timothy Hugh Stewart Duke

HERALDS EXTRAORDINARY

Norfolk-George Drewry Squibb, LVO, QC, FSA
Wales-Major Francis Jones, CVO, TD, FSA, DL
New Zealand-Phillippe Patrick O'Shea
Surrey (and Earl Marshal's Secretary)-Sir Walter John George Verco, KCVO
Beaumont-Francis Sedley Andrus, LVO
Arundel-Rodney Onslow Dennys, CVO, OBE, FSA
Maltravers-John Martin Robinson, DPhil, FSA

SCOTLAND

Court of the Lord Lyon , HM New Register House, Edinburgh

THE RT HON THE LORD LYON KING OF ARMS

Malcolm Rognvald Innes of Edingight, CVO, WS, FSA Scot

HERALDS

Albany-John Alexander Spens, RD, WS
Rothesay-Sir Crispin Agnew of Lochnaw, Bt
Ross-Charles John Burnett, FSA Scot

PURSUIVANTS

Kintyre-John Charles Grossmith George,FSA Scot
Unicorn-Alastair Lorne Campbell of Airds, yr, FSA Scot

PURSUIVANTS OF EARLS

(Not forming part of Her Majesty's Household)
Pursuivants to the Earl of Erroll and the Countess of Mar
Slains-Peter Drummond-Murray of Mastrick (Pursuivant to the Earl of Erroll)
Garioch-David Gordon Allen d'Aldecamb Lumsden of Cushnie (Pursuivant to the Countess of Mar)

THE COLLEGE OF ARMS Photograph by Gary McPake

THE WORK OF THE COLLEGE OF ARMS

The College of Arms, near St. Paul's Cathedral in the City of London, is the home of the English heralds and the official registry of English, Welsh, Northern Irish and Commonwealth arms and pedigrees.

In the early Middle Ages heralds were responsible for the conduct of tournaments or jousts at which the knights were identified by the colourful devices painted on their shields. The heralds had to recognise these emblems and soon began recording them and eventually granting and confirming them on behalf of the Sovereign. True heraldry, described by Sir Anthony Wagner as "the systematic use of hereditary devices centred on the shield" emerged as a system in Europe towards the middle of the twelfth century, but the English heralds were not incorporated until 1484 when King Richard III gave them a house called Coldharbour in the City of London where they could meet together and keep their records. This was lost after the Battle of Bosworth in 1485 and it was only in 1555 that they were given their current Charter by Queen Mary Tudor and a house on the site which they still occupy today. The original structure was destroyed in the Fire of London in 1666 and the present building of mellow red brick around a cobbled courtyard was completed towards the end of the seventeenth century.

Since 1555 the College has been a corporation of 13 Officers of Arms, all members of the Royal Household, appointed by Letters Patent under the Great Seal on the recommendation of the Duke of Norfolk as hereditary Earl Marshal of England. The corporation consists of three Kings of Arms (Garter, Clarenceux and Norroy & Ulster), six heralds (Chester, Lancaster, Richmond, Somerset, Windsor and York) and four Pursuivants (Bluemantle, Portcullis, Rouge Croix and Rouge Dragon). All receive only nominal salaries from the Crown and are therefore in effect self-employed consultants in heraldry, genealogy and ceremonial.

There are several categories of records, one of the most important being the heraldic visitations which were started by King Henry VIII in 1530 when he instructed the Kings of Arms to visit their provinces and record the arms and pedigrees of the gentry. These surveys continued until 1689 so that most counties were visited several times in the course of the 16th and 17th centuries. Another major category consists of the records of grants and confirmations of arms from the Middle Ages to the present day.

Arms are a form of property and there are two ways by which an individual can establish a legal right to them. One is to prove and register at the College a legitimate descent in the male line from an ancestor to whom arms were previously granted or allowed and the other is to apply for a new grant (see below). Those hoping for an instant coat of arms may be disappointed as there is no such thing as a "coat of arms for a surname". Many families of the same surname may bear different arms whilst others of that name may have no right to any arms at all.

The Heralds and Pursuivants take it in turn to be Officer in Waiting for a week at a time, which means dealing with all the letters, telephone calls and visitors received during that week. Members of the public who are not acquainted with an individual herald should therefore address their enquiries to the Officer in Waiting who will advise them what he can do to help and at what cost. Thereafter the enquirer becomes the client of that Officer and should continue to deal with him, as each herald runs his own practice rather like a doctor or a barrister.

The first step in any enquiry is often a search in the Official Registers of the College in order to ascertain whether any arms or pedigrees may already be on record for the client's family. For this purpose the officer concerned will need to be given as much information about the family as is already known, preferably in the form of a narrative pedigree or chart including as far as possible full names, occupations, religious denomination and dates and places of birth, marriage and death. He will then quote a fee for a preliminary investigation and once this has been paid he will make the necessary searches and compile his report. This may take several weeks if there is other work in hand and it may even be disappointing if it turns out that the crest on the family silver was adopted by a Victorian ancestor who had no right to it!

As the College is not supported by the State like a museum or public library and furthermore as the Record Room is small and the indexes are complex it is not possible for members of the public to make searches themselves. However once an initial investigation has been made they are welcome to come and inspect any relevant entries which have come to light. They may also call at the College on any weekday between 10 and 4 o'clock in order to consult the Officer in Waiting or simply to look at the impressive entrance hall known as the Earl Marshal's Court. This is a fine panelled room containing a throne enclosed by wooden railings and designed for sessions of the ancient Court of Chivalry which still exists to settle heraldic disputes but has only met once since the eighteenth century. The court room is hung with banners and portraits, and there is a desk at which heraldic books and other items may be purchased.

Many people who apply to the College are not necessarily seeking to establish a right to arms for themselves. They may simply wish to have some arms identified which appear on a painting or a ring or a piece of furniture, silver or porcelain. For this purpose the College maintains a set of pictorial indexes known as Ordinaries and these are used not only to identify existing arms but also to test the distinctiveness of new designs.

The College Registers also contain numerous pedigrees which have been entered simply to preserve the results of genealogical research irrespective of any entitlement to arms. The heralds developed their skills as genealogists during the course of the Visitations and are happy to undertake such work today. Sometimes the purpose is to try and establish a right to arms or a title of nobility but often the object is simply to trace someone's ancestry out of interest, regardless of how many skeletons may be found in the cupboard! People are less bashful about such things nowadays and many Australians who used to be ashamed of a convict ancestor are now rather proud if they can find one.

If details of an enquirer's ancestry are not already to be found in the College Records or Collections the officer concerned will recommend a programme of research in outside sources such as the Principal Probate Registry (for modern wills), the General Register Office (for births, deaths and marriages since 1837), the nineteenth century census returns and the parish registers. He will ask for a sum of money on account and will report on progress from time to time, though it is never possible to guarantee successful results in detective work of this nature, particularly if the surname is a common one, or an ancestor guilty of an indiscretion has taken steps to cover his tracks.

Once a pedigree has been pursued as far as the client requires, it can be entered in the College Records though in order to preserve the integrity of these it must first be submitted in draft form to two Examiners who are generally Officers of Arms who have had no part in its compilation. They will work carefully through it in order to satisfy themselves that it is correct in every detail. The work of the member of the family who submits and signs the pedigree is normally acceptable for details back to his or her grandparents but beyond that point documentary evidence has to be produced in support of each and every item. Once the examination is complete the pedigree can go forward to the Registrar in order to be engrossed by hand in the official records of the College. The purpose of recording a pedigree in this way is to create a permanent and official record of the family genealogy and in some cases to establish a right by descent to a coat of arms or to a Peerage or Baronetcy.

If an enquirer cannot establish a right to existing arms he or she may apply for new arms to be granted. This is effected in England by Letters Patent under the hands and seals of the Kings of Arms to whom this function has long been delegated by the Sovereign. A grant of Arms is a form of honour but an ususual one in that it has to be applied for and paid for. The Kings of Arms are only allowed to make grants to "eminent men", an expression which is taken to include women and corporate bodies. A case for the applicant's eligibility must therefore be established before a grant can proceed. There are no hard and fast rules but a personal petition is likely to be favourably entertained if the applicant has received some honour or decoration from the Crown, held a commission in the armed forces, gained a university degree or professional qualification, made a worthwhile contribution to national or local affairs, charitable causes and so on. In the case of corporate bodies grants are made to local authorities, universities, schools and colleges and to major professional or charitable institutions. As for commercial enterprises these are required to be of national standing and reasonably long established, to be leaders in their field and financially sound and to perform some function which is beneficial to the life of the nation.

Any herald may act as the agent for a grant of arms though it is the Kings of Arms who will sign and seal the Patent at the end of the operation. Once the candidate's eligibility has been established he must submit a Memorial (or formal petition) to the Earl Marshal. This will be prepared by the agent who will send it to his client for signature and then forward it to the Earl Marshal together with the fees, which are payable in advance.

The next stage is to settle the design of the proposed arms and the agent will start by asking his client whether he has any ideas of his own. He may compile a list of some five or ten items to which some allusion could be made in the design. Suitable items would be the applicant's place of birth, his school, university, company, regiment, professional career, recreational activities, favourite shapes and colours and even household pets. Reference could be made to the occupations and places of residence of his paternal or maternal ancestors, to his wife, his children and so on. However the symbolism of the design is a private matter between the grantee and his agent and is not recited in the grant itself.

Once the agent has worked out a provisional design he makes searches to ensure that it is distinctive and if so he orders an approval sketch. When this has been accepted by the grantee and the Kings of Arms he instructs an artist to make a start on the Letters Patent by which the arms will be granted. This is an elaborate vellum document which has to go through a great many processes as well as taking its turn with others (some 200 grants are completed in the course of an average year) and several months will elapse before it is finally signed and sealed. However once the design has been agreed in principle by the Kings of Arms the grantee is at liberty to make use of it and the agent will be happy to supply quotations for drawings or paintings for specific purposes, such as a finely illuminated library painting on strained vellum to hang on the wall, a black and white line drawing for letterheads, a bookplate design or a drawing of the crest or shield for a signet ring or cufflinks. Many modern corporations like to display their arms on a banner, and a simple heraldic badge can make an attractive alternative to a company logo for those who appreciate the time-honoured symbolism of heraldry.

The College is fortunate in having the services of several highly skilled herald painters and scriveners who maintain a tradition of craftsmanship dating back to the middle ages. Apart from painting and engrossing grants of arms and pedigrees they are sometimes called upon to prepare illuminated certificates, illustrated pedigree books, designs for monuments and even to depict a King of Arms in an initial letter or the tools of a trade, or animals, birds or flowers in the border of a patent of arms. In addition there is a conservation and bookbinding department which is sometimes able to undertake work for institutions outside the College of Arms which have important collections of books and manuscripts.

Although the Officers of Arms spend most of their time working for their clients they still have certain ceremonial duties deriving from their conduct of tournaments in the Middle Ages. They participate in State Ceremonies under the direction of the Earl Marshal, wearing their distinctive uniform of the tabard embroidered with the Royal Arms. They took part in the funeral of Sir Winston Churchill in 1965 and the Investiture of the Prince of Wales in 1969 and they are regularly on parade at the State Opening of Parliament and the Garter Ceremony in Windsor. Garter King of Arms has special duties in relation to peers of the realm. He has to settle their titles and conduct their formal introduction in the House of Lords. Peers and Knights Grand Cross are entitled to add supporters to their arms (figures which support the shield like the Lion and the Unicorn in the Royal Arms) and this privilege is extended to important corporate bodies.

Several Officers of Arms are well known as authors and lecturers and the College has its own museum in the Tower of London. The College library includes copies of the Irish records formerly preserved in Dublin Castle, and the English heralds maintain contact with the Lord Lyon King of Arms in Edinburgh and with other heraldic authorities all over the world. Much use is made of the latest genealogical records published in microfiche by the Mormon Church and there is even a provision whereby honorary arms may be granted to distinguished Americans who have proved and recorded a male line descent from an ancestor who was once a subject of the British Crown.

HUBERT CHESSHYRE

GENERAL TABLE OF PRECEDENCE

The Queen.
The Duke of Edinburgh.
The Prince of Wales.
Prince William of Wales.
Prince Henry of Wales.
The Duke of York.
Prince Edward.
Cousins of the Sovereign (according to the seniority of their fathers).
Archbishop of Canterbury.
Lord High Chancellor.
Archbishop of York.
The Prime Minister.
Lord High Treasurer (no such office exists at present).
Lord President of the Council.
The Speaker of the House of Commons.
Lord Privy Seal.
Ambassadors and High Commissioners.

Above all Peers of their own degree:
Lord Great Chamberlain.
Lord High Constable (no such office exists at present).
Earl Marshal (Duke of Norfolk).
Lord High Admiral (office held by H.M. the Queen).
Lord Steward of the Household (Duke of Northumberland).
Lord Chamberlain of the Household.

Master of the Horse (Earl of Westmorland).
Dukes of England.
Dukes of Scotland (none created since 1707).
Dukes of Great Britain (1707–1801).
Duke of Leinster (being the only Irish Duke existing at the time of the union).
Dukes of the United Kingdom (created since 1801).
Eldest sons of Dukes of the Blood Royal (when they are not brothers, grandsons, uncles, or nephews of the reigning sovereign).
Marquess of Cholmondeley (as Lord Great Chamberlain).
Marquesses of England (marq. of Winchester).
__________ Scotland (none created after 1707).
__________ Great Britain (1707–1801).
__________ Ireland (created before 1801).
__________ the United Kingdom (created since 1801).
Eldest sons of Dukes.
Earls of England (anterior to 1707).
______ Scotland (none created after 1707).
______ Great Britain (1707–1801).
______ Ireland (created before 1801).
______ the United Kingdom (created since 1801).
Younger sons of Dukes of the Blood Royal (when they are not brothers, grandsons, uncles or nephews of the reigning sovereign).
Eldest sons of Marquesses.
Younger sons of Dukes.
Viscounts of England (visc. Hereford).
_________ Scotland (anterior to 1707).
_________ Great Britain (1707–1801).
_________ Ireland (anterior to 1801).
_________ the United Kingdom (created since 1801).
Eldest sons of Earls.
Younger sons of Marquesses.
Bishop of London.
_______ Durham.
_______ Winchester.
English Bishops (according to date of consecration).
Bishops Suffragan (according to date of consecration).
Secretary of State (if a baron).
Barons of England.
Barons of Scotland (none created since 1707).
_______ Great Britain (1707–1801).
_______ Ireland (anterior to 1801).
_______ the United Kingdom (created since 1801).
Lords of Appeal in Ordinary.
Commissioners of the Great Seal (those persons who execute the office of Lord High Chancellor when it happens to be vacant).
Treasurer of the Household.
Comptroller of the Household.
Vice-Chamberlain of the Household.
Secretary of State (when not a baron).
Eldest sons of Viscounts.
Younger sons of Earls.
Eldest sons of Barons.
Knights of the Garter.
Privy Councillors.
Chancellor of the Exchequer.
____________ Duchy of Lancaster.
Lord Chief Justice.
Master of the Rolls.
President of the Family Division.
Lords Justices of Appeal, ranking according to date of appointment.
Judges of the High Court of Justice, ranking according to date of appointment
Vice-Chancellor of the County Palatine of Lancaster.
Younger sons of Viscounts.
____________ Barons.
Younger sons of Life Peers.
Baronets.
Knights of the Thistle.
Knights Grand Cross of the Bath.
Knights Grand Commanders of the Star of India.
Knights Grand Cross of St. Michael and St. George.
Knights Grand Commanders of the Order of the Indian Empire.
Knights Grand Cross of the Royal Victorian Order.
Knights Grand Cross of the Order of the British Empire.
Knights Commanders of the Bath.
Knights Commanders of the Star of India.
Knights Commanders of St. Michael and St. George.
Knights Commanders of the Order of the Indian Empire.
Knights Commanders of the Royal Victorian Order.
Knights Commanders of the Order of the British Empire.
Knights Bachelor.
Official Referees of the Supreme Court of Judicature.
Circuit Judges.
County Court Judges of England and Wales.
Masters in Chancery.
Master of Court of Protection.
Companions of the Bath.
Companions of the Star of India.
Companions of St. Michael and St. George.
Companions of the Indian Empire.
Commanders of the Royal Victorian Order.
Commanders of the Order of the British Empire.
Companions of the Distinguished Service Order.
Lieutenants of the Royal Victorian Order.
Officers of the Order of the British Empire.
Companions of the Imperial Service Order.
Eldest sons of the younger sons of Peers.
Eldest sons of Baronets.
Eldest sons of Knights of the Garter.
Eldest sons of Knights, according to the precedence of their fathers.
Members of the Royal Victorian Order.
Members of the Order of the British Empire.
Younger sons of Baronets.
Younger sons of Knights.
Esquires.
Gentlemen.

RELATIVE RANK AND PRECEDENCE IN THE NAVY, ARMY AND AIR FORCE.

Navy	Army	Air Force
Admiral of the Fleet	Field Marshal	Marshal of the RAF
Admiral	General	Air Chief Marshal
Vice Admiral	Lieutenant-General	Air Marshal
Rear Admiral	Major-General	Air Vice-Marshal
Commodore	Brigadier	Air Commodore
Captain	Colonel	Group Captain
Commander	Lieutenant-Colonel	Wing Commander
Lieutenant Commander	Major	Squadron Leader
Lieutenant	Captain	Flight Lieutenant
Sub Lieutenant	Lieutenant	Flying Officer
Commissioned Officers from Warrant Rank	Second Lieutenant	Pilot Officer

PRECEDENCE AMONG LADIES.

The daughter of a peer does not lose her own rank should she marry a person not a peer, but if she marries a peer her title and precedence are merged in his, *e.g.*, if the daughter of a duke marries a baron, she takes the rank of a baroness. Maids of Honour* to the Queen Regnant, the Queen Consort, or the Queen Dowager, who are not the daughters of peers, are styled Honourable for life. The widow of a peer, baronet or knight who re-marries does not retain any title or precedence acquired from her previous husband, but may do so only by courtesy. A dowager peeress or the widow of a baronet, while a widow, takes precedence of the wife of the living holder of the title. The divorced wife of a peer or baronet derives no rank or precedence from her former husband but unless she remarries usually retains the title with her christian or forename prefixed (e.g. Mary, Lady Jones). Official rank and precedence is not communicable to the wife, but the wife of a lord mayor has precedence derived from her husband's office.

The Queen.
The Queen Mother.
The Princess of Wales.
The Duchess of York.
The Princess Royal.
Sister of the Sovereign.
Wives of the Sovereign's uncles.
Wives of the Sovereign's cousins.
Cousin of the Sovereign.
The Prime Minister.
Duchesses of England.
__________ Scotland.
__________ Great Britain.
__________ Ireland.
__________ the United Kingdom.
Wives of the eldest sons of Dukes of the Blood Royal.
Marchionesses (in the same order as the Duchesses).
Wives of the eldest sons of Dukes.
Daughters of Dukes (while unmarried, or when married to commoners).
Countesses (in the same order as the Duchesses).
Wives of the younger sons of Dukes of the Blood Royal.
Wives of the eldest sons of Marquesses.
Daughters of Marquesses (while unmarried or when married to commoners).
Wives of the younger sons of Dukes.
Viscountesses (in the same order as the Duchesses).
Wives of the elder sons of Earls.
Daughters of Earls (while unmarried, or when married to commoners).
Wives of younger sons of Marquesses.
Baronesses (in the same order as the Duchesses).
Wives of the eldest sons of Viscounts.
Daughters of Viscounts (while unmarried or when married to a commoner).
Wives of the younger sons of Earls.
Wives of the eldest sons of Barons.
Daughters of Barons (if unmarried, or when married to a commoner).
Maids of Honour.
Wives of Knights of the Garter.
Privy Councillors (Women).
Wives of the younger sons of Viscounts.Wives of the younger sons of Barons.
Daughters of Lords of Appeal.
Wives of the sons of Legal Life Peers.
Wives of Baronets (according to the dates of creation of titles held by their husbands).
Wives of Knights of the Thistle.
Dames Grand Cross of St. Michael and St. George.
Dames Grand Cross of the Royal Victorian Order.
Dames Grand Cross of the Order of the British Empire.
Wives of Knights Grand Cross of the Bath.
Wives of Knights Grand Commanders of the Star of India.
Wives of Knights Grand Cross of St. Michael and St. George.
Wives of Knights Grand Commanders of the Indian Empire.
Wives of Knights Grand Cross of the Royal Victorian Order.
Wives of Knights Grand Cross of the Order of the British Empire.
Dames Commanders of the Bath.
Dames Commanders of St. Michael and St. George.
Dames Commanders of the Royal Victorian Order.
Dames Commanders of the Order of the British Empire.
Wives of Knights Commanders of the Bath.
Wives of Knights Commanders of the Star of India.
Wives of Knights Commanders of St. Michael and St. George.
Wives of Knights Commanders of the Indian Empire.
Wives of Knights Commanders of the Royal Victorian Order.
Wives of Knights Commanders of the Order of the British Empire.
Wives of Knights Bachelor.
Commanders of St. Michael and St. George.
Commanders of the Royal Victorian Order.
Commanders of the Order of the British Empire.
Wives of Commanders and Companions of the Orders of the Bath, the Star of India, St. Michael and St. George, Indian Empire, Royal Victorian Order, and the British Empire.
Wives of Companions of the Distinguished Service Order.
Lieutenants of the Royal Victorian Order.
Officers of the Order of the British Empire.
Wives of Lieutenants of the Royal Victorian Order.
Wives of Officers of the Order of the British Empire.
Companions of the Imperial Service Order.
Wives of Companions of the Imperial Service Order.
Wives of the eldest sons of the younger sons of Peers.
Daughters of the younger sons of Peers.
Wives of the eldest sons of Baronets.
Daughters of Baronets.
Wives of the eldest sons of Knights of the Garter.
Wives of the eldest sons of Knights Bachelor.
Daughters of Knights Bachelor.
Members of the Royal Victorian Order.
Members of the Order of the British Empire.
Wives of members of the Royal Victorian Order.
Wives of members of the Order of the British Empire.
Wives of the Younger sons of Baronets.
Wives of the younger sons of Knights.
Wives of the eldest sons of Knights of the Garter.
Wives of the eldest sons of Knights Bachelor.
Daughters of Knights Bachelor.
Members of the Fifth class of the Royal Victorian Order.
Members of the Order of the British Empire.
Wives of the members of the Fifth Class of the Royal Victorian Order.
Wives of members of the British Empire.
Wives of the younger sons of Baronets.
Wives of the younger sons of Knights.

*No Maids of Honour have been appointed since the reign of King George V and it must be assumed that the dignity has now lapsed and seems unlikely to be revived.

POSITION OF LETTERS AFTER THE NAME

The abbreviations 'Bt' or 'Bart' (for a Baronet) and 'Esq', if applicable, precede all other letters.

The series of other letters are grouped either by regulations or by custom as follows:

1. Orders and Decorations conferred by the Crown.

2. Appointments in the following order, Privy Counsellor, Aide de Camp to Her Majesty, Honorary Physician to The Queen, Honorary Surgeon to The Queen, Honorary Dental Surgeon to The Queen, Honorary Nursing Sister to The Queen, and Honorary Chaplain to The Queen, viz, PC, ADC, QHP, QHS, QHDS, QHNS and QHC.

3. Queen's Counsel, Justice of the Peace and Deputy Lieutenant, viz. QC, JP and DL.

4. University Degrees.

5. (a) Religious Orders.
   (b) Medical Qualifications.

6. (a) Fellowships of Learned Societies,
   (b) Royal Academicians and Associates,
   (c) Fellowships, Memberships, etc., of Professional Institutions, Associations, etc.,
   (d) Writers to the Signet.

7. Member of Parliament, viz. MP

8. Membership of one of the Armed Forces, such as RN or RAF.

The following notes are given for guidance.

It is important to keep the group order, even if the individual series of letters in Groups 4, 5 and 6 present difficulties. For further details see the appropriate section.

The nature of the correspondence determines which series of letters should normally be included under Groups 4, 5 and 6. For instance, when writing a professional letter to a doctor of medicine one would normally add more medical qualifications than in a social letter.

On a formal list all the appropriate letters are usually included after each name.

Those who have letters signifying Crown Honours and Awards are usually given only the principal letters in Groups 3, 4 and 5 (e.g. MD, FRCS, FRS).

A peer who is a junior officer in the Armed Forces, is not usually addressed by his Service rank in social correspondence, unless he so wishes, or a letter is forwarded to him at a Service address or club.

1. ORDERS AND DECORATIONS

All the appropriate letters are obligatory in correspondence and lists. The order is laid down for Knights, Dames and others.

They are addressed according to their rank, with the appropriate letters after their name in order of precedence. The use of all these letters is obligatory, e.g John Brown, Esq, CBE, MVO, TD.

The recipient is allowed to use the appropriate letters for the Order from the date of announcement in the 'London Gazette'.

Those promoted within the same Order of Chivalry do not continue to show the letters of the lower class of that Order, e.g. if Brigadier John Smith, OBE, is promoted to CBE he is addressed as Brigadier John Smith, CBE, the OBE being dropped.

Precedence of letters

The full list of honours and awards in order of precedence *of letters* of given below. A baronet has the letters Bt or Bart immediately after the name, and before any letters which signify honours.

It should be noted the VC and GC have precedence of *all* letters signifying Orders (including Knightly grades therein), Decorations and Medals.

The Order of Merit (OM) and Companion of Honour (CH) are important honours which bestow no title on the holder. The letters OM follow GCB, and CH follow GBE.

Some people prefer PC after KG since that is its correct position in order of precedence.

Victoria Cross	VC
George Cross	GC
Knight of the Garter	KG
Knight of the Thistle	KT
Knight/Dame Grand Cross of the Order of the Bath	GCB
Order of Merit	OM
Knight Grand Commander of the Star of India	GCSI
Knight/Dame Grand Cross of the Order of St Michael and St George	GCMG
Knight Grand Commander of the Indian Empire	GCIE
Knight/Dame Grand Cross of the Royal Victorian Order	GCVO
Knight/Dame Grand Cross of the British Empire	GBE
Companion of Honour	CH
Knight Commander of the Bath	KCB
Dame Commander of the Bath	DCB
Knight Commander of the Star of India	KCSI
Knight Commander of St Michael and St George	KCMG
Dame Commander of St Michael and St George	DCMG
Knight Commander of the Indian Empire	KCIE
Knight Commander of the Royal Victorian Order	KCVO
Dame Commander of the Royal Victorian Order	DCVO
Knight Commander of the British Empire	KBE
Dame Commander of the British Empire	DBE
Companion of the Order of the Bath	CB
Companion of the Order of the Star of India	CSI
Companion of the Order of St Michael and St George	CMG
Companion of the Order of the Indian Empire	CIE
Commander of the Royal Victorian Order	CVO
Commander of the Order of the British Empire	CBE
Distinguished Service Order	DSO
Lieutenant of the Royal Victorian Order	LVO
Officer of the Order of the British Empire	OBE
Imperial Service Order	ISO
Member of the Royal Victorian Order	MVO
Member of the Order of the British Empire	MBE
Indian Order of Merit (Military)	IOM
Royal Red Cross	RRC
Distinguished Service Cross	DSC
Military Cross	MC
Distinguished Flying Cross	DFC
Air Force Cross	AFC
Associate, Royal Red Cross	ARRC
Order of British India	OBI
Distinguished Conduct Medal	DCM
Conspicuous Gallantry Medal	CGM
George Medal	GM
Distinguished Conduct Medal of the Royal West African Frontier Force and the King's African Rifles	DCM
Indian Distinguished Service Medal	IDSM
Distinguished Service Medal	DSM
Military Medal	MM
Distinguished Flying Medal	DFM
Air Force Medal	AFM
Medal for Saving Life at Sea	SGM
Indian Order of Merit (Civil)	IOM
Colonial Police Medal for Gallantry	CPM
Queen's Gallantry Medal	QGM
British Empire Medal	BEM
King's Police Medal	KPM
King's Police and Fire Service Medal	KPFSM
Queen's Police Medal	QPM
Queen's Fire Service Medal	QFSM
Colonial Police Medal for Meritorious Service	CPM
Meritorious Service Medal	MSM
Army Emergency Reserve Decoration	ERD
Volunteer Officer's Decoration	VD
Territorial Decoration	TD
Efficiency Decoration	ED

Decoration for Officers of the Royal Naval Reserve	RD
Decoration for Officers of the Royal Naval Volunteer Reserve	VRD
Air Efficiency Award	AE
Canadian Forces Decoration	CD

ORDER OF CANADA

The formation of the Order of Canada was announced in 1967.

The Order, of which the Queen is Sovereign, is divided into the following grades according to its last revised constitution:

CG Companion of the Order of Canada, with precedence after VC and GC before all other letters.
OC Officer of the Order of Canada, with precedence after CC.
CM Member of the Order of Canada, with precedence after OC.

The Cross of Valour, The Star of Courage and The Medal of Bravery have no letters.

ORDER OF AUSTRALIA

The Order of Australia was established in 1975.

The Order, of which The Queen is Sovereign, consists of a General Division and a Military Division and is divided into the following classes:

AK Knight of the Order of Australia, with precedence after the Order of Merit.
AD Dame of Order of Australia, with the same precedence as Knight of the Order of Australia.
AC Companion of the Order of Australia, with precedence after Knight Grand Cross of the Order of the British Empire.
AO Officer of the Order of Australia, with precedence after the Knight Bachelor.
AM Member of the Order of Australia, with precedence after the Distinguished Service Order.
OAM Medal of the Order of Australia, with precedence after the Royal Red Cross (2nd class).

THE QUEEN'S SERVICE ORDER OF NEW ZEALAND

This order was established in 1975. The Order, of which The Queen is Sovereign, is divided into two parts, for Community Service and for Public Services.

There are two divisions:

QSO Companions of The Queen's Service Order, with precedence after Officer of the Order of the British Empire.
QSM The Queen's Service Medal, with precedence after Queen's Gallantry Medal, and before British Empire Medal.

2. PRIVY COUNSELLORS AND APPOINTMENTS TO THE QUEEN

For peers the letters PC are obligatory. For other Privy Counsellors, 'Rt Hon' before the name is sufficient identification. As the other appointments to the Crown (QHP, QHS, etc.) are held for a limited period only, they are not always used by recipients.

3. UNIVERSITY DEGREES

Doctorates in the faculties of Divinity and Medicine (DD, MD) and Masters degrees in the latter (eg MS) are given in all correspondence. Other divinity degrees (eg BD) are sometimes included.

Other degrees in medicine (e.g. MB, BS) are sometimes included, especially in professional correspondence, but if one progresses in the same degree only the higher is given.

Doctorates in other faculties are sometimes given, especially if the correspondence concerns the particular profession or subject (e.g. LLD, DSc). Alternatively, except for surgeons, the envelope may be addressed as 'Doctor' before his name, without giving his (or her) degrees.

Other degrees are seldom, and MA and BA never, used in social correspondence, but they are generally included in a formal list.

4. (a) RELIGIOUS ORDERS

Letters for members of religious communities, when used, should be included, e.g. SJ. Some Members of the Order of St. Benedict do not normally use the letters OSB as the prefix of 'Dom' or 'Dame' is held to be a sufficient identification.

(b) MEDICAL QUALIFICATIONS

Fellowships are given in all correspondence (e.g. FRCP, FRCS)

Other qualifications are sometimes given, especially those which are the highest held. They are usually included when writing professionally.

When all letters signifying qualifications are included, as for example in a nominal list, they should appear in the following order. (*Note:* Fellows and Members of each category precede the next category):

Medicine
Surgery (except MRCS)
Obstetrics, Gynaecology and other specialities
Qualifying diplomas (e.g. MRCS, LRCP)
Other diplomas (e.g. DPH, DObst, RCOG)

In practice, a maximum of three series of letters including MD (see Group 3 above) is usually sufficient in ordinary correspondence (e.g. MD, MS, FRCS).

5. (a) FELLOWSHIPS OF LEARNED SOCIETIES

Fellowships fall into two categories:

(a) honorific, i.e. nomination by election,
(b) nomination by subscription.

Normally only honorific fellowships are used in social correspondence (e.g. FRS, FBA). Fellowships by subscription are generally restricted to correspondence concerning the same field of interest, e.g. a writer to a Fellow of the Zoological Society on the subject of zoology will include FZS after the name.

There is no recognized order for placing these letters. Strictly speaking, they should be arranged according to the date of foundation or incorporation of the societies concerned, but some hold that those with a Royal Charter should precede others.

In practice the following is usually adhered to:

(1) Where one society is indisputably of greater importance than another, the letters may be placed in that order; or alternatively the fellowship of the junior society may be omitted.
(2) If such precedence cannot be determined, the letters may be placed in order of conferment. Where this is not known, they may be placed in alphabetical order.
(3) Where a fellow is pre-eminent in a particular subject, his fellowship of a society connected with this interest may either be placed first, or his other fellowships omitted.

The following are some of the principal learned societies, with their dates of incorporation:

Fellow of The Royal Society	FRS	1662
Fellow of The Society of Antiquaries	FSA	1707
Fellow of The Royal Society of Edinburgh	FRSE	1783
Fellow of The Royal Society of Literature	FRSL	1823
Fellow of The British Academy	FBA	1901

Presidents of some societies have special letters to signify their appointment, e.g. The President of the Royal Society has PRS after his name, but these letters are only used within the particular society.

The Royal Society of Literature bestows an award limited to ten recipients, the Companion of Literature. The letters CLit are placed before the Fellowship.

(b) ROYAL ACADEMY OF ARTS, THE ROYAL SCOTTISH ACADEMY, ETC.

It is not suggested that Royal Academicians yield in precedence to fellows of learned societies. In practice the two lists do not coincide.

The President and Past Presidents are indicated as follows:

President of the Royal Academy	PRA
Past President of the Royal Academy	PPRA
President of the Royal Scottish Academy	PRSA
Past President of the Royal Scottish Academy	PPRSA

Royal Academicians and Associates are included as follows:

Royal Academician	RA
Royal Scottish Academician	RSA
Associate of the Royal Academy	ARA
Associate of the Royal Scottish Academy	ARSA

Similarly with other Academies, e.g. President Royal Hibernian Academy (PRHA) and Academicians (RHA).

Honorary Academicians and Associates do not normally use the relevant letters.

(c) FELLOWSHIPS AND MEMBERSHIPS OF PROFESSIONAL INSTITUTIONS, ASSOCIATIONS, ETC.

These letters are usually restricted to correspondence concerning the particular profession.

It is not suggested that professional societies as such yield precedence to learned societies, but in point of fact the two groups do not coincide to any great extent. Most of the senior learned societies which elect fellows are senior in age and importance to the professional. Those whose fellowships are by subscription are generally only used in the particular field of interest. For example, if Mr. John Smith is a Chartered Engineer and a Fellow of the Royal Historical Society, he would normally be described professionally as John Smith, Esq, CEng, FIMechE. When corresponding on historical subjects he is normally described as John Smith, Esq, FRHistS. If both series of letters are placed after his name, it is usual to place first those which concern the particular function or subject.

As there is no recognized order for placing qualifications awarded by different bodies, a recipient usually places these letters on headed paper, business cards, etc. in order of importance to his particular profession.

The Engineering Council

The Engineering Council was granted a Royal Charter in 1981. The object of the Council is to advance the education and training of engineers and technologists, and to promote the science and practice of engineering for the public benefit. The Engineering Council accredits engineering academic courses and training programmes in the UK and registers qualified engineers.

There are 47 Professional Engineering Institutions which are Nominated bodies of The Engineering Council and which work closely with the Council in the qualification and registration areas. Of these 47 Professional Institutions, 17 are chartered. The Engineering Council, through its Board for Engineers' Registration, determines the standards and criteria for the education, training and levels of experience by which Chartered Engineers, Incorporated Engineers and Engineering Technicians may be registered, enabling them to use the designatory letters CEng, IEng, and EngTech respectively. Chartered Engineers must be in membership of a nominated Chartered Engineering Institution, or an institution affiliated body.

The designatory letters CEng, denoting Chartered Engineer, follow immediately after an individual's name and decorations and are followed in turn by the letters F (Fellow) or M (Member) identifying him with the particular institution(s) to which he belongs. Thus J Smith, Esq, OBE, CEng, FICE, MIMechE, is a Chartered Engineer who is a Fellow of the Institution of Civil Engineers and a Member of the Institution of Mechanical Engineers.

The nominated Bodies which are also Chartered Engineering Institutions are: Royal Aeronautical Society, Institution of Civil Engineers, Institution of Chemical Engineers, Institution of Electrical Engineers, Institute of Energy, Institution of Gas Engineers, Institute of Marine Engineers, Institution of Mechanical Engineers, Institute of Metals, Institution of Mining Engineers, Institution of Mining and Metallurgy, Royal Institution of Naval Architects, Institution of Production Engineers, Institution of Structural Engineers, Institute of Measurement and Control, Chartered Institution of Building Services Engineers and the British Computer Society (The BCS is subject to a transitional period).

Chartered Societies of the Land

Three chartered societies of the land, viz.:

The Royal Institution of Chartered Surveyors
The Chartered Land Agents' Society
The Chartered Auctioneers' and Estate Agents' Institute

united in June 1970 to become the Royal Institution of Chartered Surveyors. Fellows and Professional Associates respectively have the letters FRICS and ARICS.

Incorporated Society of Valuers and Auctioneers

The Incorporated Society of Auctioneers and Landed Property Agents united in April 1968 with The Valuers Institution to form The Incorporated Society of Valuers and Auctioneers, with the letters FSVA and ASVA.

(d) WRITERS TO THE SIGNET

It is customary for the letters WS to follow the name after University degrees and those which signify Fellowship or Membership of a Society or Institution, despite the fact that the WS Society (an ancient Society of Solicitors in Scotland) is frequently considerably older than many Institutions. This is a way of indicating the profession. It is not customary for the letters WS to be used socially.

6. APPOINTMENTS

The letters MP are always shown for a Member of Parliament.

The letters QC are always shown for a Queen's Counsel including a County Court Judge, but not a High Court Judge.

The letters JP for a Justice of the Peace and DL for a Deputy Lieutenant may be included *in that order.* In practice they are often omitted for a peer, or for one with several honours and awards.

Note: There is no official abbreviation for a Lord-Lieutenant, HM Lieutenant or a Vice-Lieutenant.

7. MEMBERSHIP OF ONE OF THE ARMED FORCES

Royal Navy.—The letters 'RN' (or 'Royal Navy', which this Service prefers) are placed after the names of serving officers of and below the rank of Captain. They are also placed after the names of retired Captains, Commanders, and Lieutenant-Commanders where they are prefixed by Naval rank. The letters RNR are likewise used by officers of the Royal Naval Reserve.

Army.—The appropriate letters which signify a Regiment or Corps may be placed after the name for officers on the active list of and below the rank of Lieutenant-Colonel, but are often omitted in social correspondence. These letters are not used for retired officers.

Corps have letter abbreviations (e.g. RE, RAMC, RAOC, RAPC). Most regiments are written in full.

Royal Air Force.—The letters RAF are placed after serving and retired officers, except for Marshals of The Royal Air Force. Officers above the rank of Group Captain do not often use these letters. Similarly with RAFVR.

Royal Marines.—The letters 'RM' (or 'Royal Marines' which some officers prefer) are placed after the names of serving and retired officers of and below the rank of Lieutenant-Colonel. Similarly RMR (Royal Marines Reserve).

FORMS OF ADDRESSING PERSONS OF TITLE

Ecclesiastical and Services prefixes of rank are written before other titles. A High Officer of State of an official holding an important office, should be addressed by his official title when the communication refers to official business.

Eldest Sons of Dukes, Marquesses, and Earls bearing courtesy titles should not be styled "The Rt. Hon." or "The" unless they themselves are Peers of Members of the Privy Council.

Formal conclusions to letters to Peers. The style "I am, my Lord, Your obedient servant" may be used (as applicable), but "Yours faithfully" and "Yours truly" are now more customarily adopted, except for letters to Members of the Royal Family. After the Lambeth Conference 1968 under the guidance of the Archbishop of Canterbury, a simplified form of address for the Clergy of the Church of England was announced.

Commanders, Companions, Officers or Members of any Order and recipiants of Decorations and Medals are addressed according to their rank and are entitled to place the recognised initials after their names in the following order:—VC, GC, OM, VA, CI, CH, CB, CSI, CMG, CIE, CVO, CBE, DSO, LVO, (4th class), OBE, QSO, ISO, MVO (5th class), MBE, RRC, DSC, MC, DFC, AFC, ARRC, DCM, CGM, GM, DSM, MM, DFM, AFM, SGM, CPM (for Gallantry), QGM, BEM, KPM, KPFSM, QPM, QFSM, CPM (for Meritorious Service), ERD, TD, ED, RD, VRD, AE, CD.

Succession to hereditary titles. By custom those who have succeeded to peerages and baronetcies are not so addressed until after their predecessor's funeral.

New honours. Knights and Dames of Orders of Chivalry may use their style of "Sir" and "Dame" and the appropriate letters after their names, and Knights Bachelor their style of "Sir" immediately their honours have been announced. Other recipients of honours may also use the appropriate letters. Peers may use their titles after the patent of creation has passed the Great Seal, when their respective Peerage titles will be anounded.

Full details of forms of address are included in DEBRETT'S CORRECT FORM.

Air Efficiency Award.—The Air Efficiency Award, introduced in 1942 to recognize meritorious Service in the Royal Auxiliary Air Force and the RAFVR, since 1975 officers including retired officers who have received the Award may place AE after their names.

Albert Medal.—In Oct. 1971, The Queen approved the exchange by which holders of the Albert Medal (AM) receive the George Cross. See George Cross.

Ambassador (British).—LETTERS—.—*Superscription.* (When in the country to which he is accredited only). "His Excellency [preceding all other ranks and titles], HM Ambassador to ______." *Commencement,* "Sir" or socially according to rank. *Conclusion,* "I have the honour to be Sir, Your Excellency's obedient servant." PERSONAL ADDRESS, "Your Excellency."

Ambassador's Wife. She is not entitled to the style "Her Excellency" and is referred to and addressed by name or conversationally as the Ambassadress.

Archbishop.—LETTERS.—*Superscription,* "The Most Rev. The Lord Archbishop of ______," *Commencement,* "Dear Archbishop."PERSONAL ADDRESS, "Your Grace" or "Archbishop." On retirement from office he reverts to the style of Bishop.

Archbishop's Wife.—As the Wife of an Esquire.

Archdeacon.—LETTERS.—*Superscription,* "The Venerable the Archdeacon of [Ely]." *Commencement,* "Dear Archdeacon." The prefix of the Venerable is not retained after retirement unless the title of Archdeacon Emeritus has been conferred.

Baron.—LETTERS.—*Superscription,* "The Right Hon. the Lord ______" or socially "The Lord ______." *Commencement,* "My Lord" or socially "Dear Lord ______." PERSONAL ADDRESS, ""My Lord."

Baroness.—LETTERS.—*Superscription,* if a Baroness in her own right "The Right Hon. the Baroness ______." or socially "The Baroness ______," or "The Right Hon. the Lady ." or "The Lady" ______." If the wife of a Baron "The Rights Hon. the Lady ______," or socially "The Lady ______." *Commencement,* "Madam" or socially "Dear Lady ______." PERSONAL ADDRESS, "Madam." [See also Barons Widow.]

***If a Baroness in her own right marry a commoner and has issue, the children have the same rank and are addressed as if their father were a Baron.

Baronet.—LETTERS.—*Superscription,* "Sir [Charles] ______ Bt." (The abbreviation "Bart." is also sometimes used). *Commencement,* "Sir." PERSONAL ADDRESS, "Sir" or socially "Dear Sir [Charles] Smith" or "Dear Sir [Charles]."

Baronet's Widow.—*Same as Baronet's Wife* if present baronet is unmarried. For widows where present incumbent of the title is married "Dowager"]. As to re-marriage, see "Widows."

Baronet's Wife.—LETTERS.—*Superscription,* if the daughter (i) of a commoner. "Lady ______"; (ii) of a Baron or a Viscount, "The Hon. Lady ______"; (iii) of an Earl, a Marquess, or a Duke, "Lady [Emily] ______." *Commencement,* "Madam.", or socially, "Dear Lady ______." PERSONAL ADDRESS, "Madam."

Baron's Daughter.—LETTERS.—*Superscription,* if married (i) to an esquire, "The Hon. Mrs. ______"; (ii) to a knight, or a baronet, "The Hon. Lady ______"; (iii) to the son of an Baron, or Viscount, or to the younger son of an Earl, "The Hon. Mrs. ______," or if her husband has a married brother. "The Hon. Mrs. [William] ______"; (iv) to the younger son of a Marquess or a Duke, "Lady [Henry] ______." If unmarried, "The Hon. [Mary] ______"; (v) to the eldest son of a Duke, Marquess, or Earl by his courtesy title. [See also under "Duke's Daughter."] *Commencement,* "Madam." PERSONAL ADDRESS, "Madam," or socially if married to an esquire, "Dear Mrs. ______," or according to her husband's rank if a Peer.

Baron's Son.—LETTERS.—*Superscription,* "The Hon. [John] ______." *Commencement,* "Sir." PERSONAL ADDRESS, "Sir." or socially "Dear Mr. ______." See also "Master of ______.".

Baron's Son's Widow.—*Same as Baron's Son's Wife* so long as she remains a widow. As to re-marriage, see "Widows."

Baron's Son's Wife.—LETTERS.—*Superscription,* "The Hon. Mrs. [Edward] ______," but if the daughter (i) of a Viscount of Baron "The Hon. Mrs. ______," (ii) of an Earl, a Marquess, or a Duke, "Lady [Ellen]." [See also under "Duke's Daughter." *Commencement,* "Madam," or socially, if her father an esquire "Dear Mrs ______" or according to her father's rank, if a Peer. PERSONAL ADDRESS, "Madam."

Baron's Widow.—*Same as Baroness* if present Baron is unmarried. For widows where present incumbent of title is married [see "Dowager"]. As to re-marriage, see "Widows."

Bishop (Diocesan).—LETTERS.—*Superscription,* "The Rt. Rev. the Lord Bishop of ______," *Commencement,* "Dear Bishop."

Bishop (Commonwealth, Church Overseas, Irish, Scottish Episcopal, Suffragan and Welsh).—LETTERS.—*Superscription,* "The Right Rev. the Bishop of ______." Exceptions, The Bishop of Meath (Premier Bishop of Ireland), and the Primus of Scotland, who are styled "Most Rev." *Commencement,* "Dear Bishop."

(Bishop retired).—Letters commence "Dear Bishop," and are addressed "The Right Rev. [John Smith] DD."

Bishop's Wife.—As wife of Esquire.

Cabinet Ministers.—Are Invariably Privy Counsellors, which see.

Canon-—LETTERS.—*Superscription,* "The Rev. Canon [John Smith]." *Commencement,* "Dear Canon, " or "Dear Canon [Smith]." On retirement from office he reverts to the style of other clergy unless he has been appointed a Canon Emeritus.

Chairman of Scottish Land Court, as for Lord of Session.

Circuit Judge.—See "Judge, Circuit."

Clergy.—LETTERS.—*Superscription,* "The Rev. John ______." *Commencement,* "Dear Mr. (Smith)" or "Dear Father Smith." PERSONAL ADDRESS, "Sir." The Reverend precedes any title: The Rev. the Hon. It is *incorrect* to write "The Hon. and Rev." or "The Rev. *Mr.* " Christian name or initals should always be shown.

Consuls [British].—LETTERS.—*Superscription,* " ______, Esq. HM ['Consul-General,' 'Consul,' or 'Vice-Consul,' as the case may be] ______," In other respects as an Esquire.

Countess.—LETTERS.—*Superscription,* "The Rt. Hon. the Countess of ______," or socially "The Countess of ______," In other respects, as Baroness. [See also "Earl's Widow."] *Commencement,* formally "Madam," socially "Dear Lady ______." If a Countess in her own right marries a gentleman of lesser degree than herself, and has issue, the children would have same rank and are addressed as if their father were an Earl.

Dames of Orders of Chivalry prefix "Dame" to their Christian names, adding the initials "GCB," "GCMG," "GCVO," "GBE" "DCB," "DCMG." "DCVO," or "DBE," as the case may be, after the surname. *Commencement,* formally "Madam" or socially "Dear Dame Edith ______" or "Dear Dame Edith." PERSONAL ADDRESS, "Dame Edith.

Dean.—LETTERS.—*Superscription,* "The Very Rev. The Dean of ______." *Commencement,* "Dear Dean." PERSONAL ADDRESS, ""Sir." The prefix of "The Very Rev." is not retained on retirement.

Degrees.—Those with doctorates of any faculty may be addressed by the appropriate abbreviations after their names, following those of orders, decorations and medals conferred by the Crown. DD should always be included. Masters' and bachelors' degrees are not used in social correspondence. The order of letters signifying doctorates and degrees depends on the individual university which confers them.

Deputy Lieutenant.—The letters DL are usually put after name. They follow JP.

Divorced Ladies. When a lady is divorced she loses any precedence which she gained by marriage. With regard to divorced Peeresses, the College of Arms, acting on an opinion of the Lord Chancellor, has long held that such persons cannot claim the privileges or status of Peeresses which they derived from their husbands. Divorced Peeresses are not summoned to a Coronation as Peeresses. The above remarks apply to ladies who have divorced their husbands as well as to those who have been divorced.

The correct style and description of divorced ladies who have not remarried, nor have taken steps to resume their maiden name with the prefix of Mrs, is as follows:

The former wife of a Peer or courtesy Peer,—Mary, Viscountess ______.

The former wife of a Baronet or Knight,—Mary, Lady ______.

The divorced wife of an "Honourable,"—The Hon. Mrs. John ______, or alternatively she may prefer to be known as Mrs. Mary ______.

The divorced wife of a younger son of a Duke or Marquess,—Lady John ______,

The divorced wife of an untitled gentleman,—Mrs. Mary ______ initials.

Dowager Lady is addressed according to her rank. Immediately a peer, or a baronet, marries, the widow of the previous incumbent of the title becomes "The Dowager"; but if there is more than one widow living or previous incumbents of a title, use must be made of the Christian name as a distinction, since the style of Dowager belongs to the senior of the widows for her lifetime. This prefix, however, is very much less used than formerly, use of the Christian name generally being preferred. In such cases ladies are addressed as Right Hon. [Mary] Countess of ______"; or socially as "[Mary], Countess of ______," etc., etc., if a peeress; or, as Ellen, Lady ______," if a Baronet's widow.

Duchess.—LETTERS.—*Superscription,* "Her Grace the Duchess of ______," or socially "The Duchess of ______." *Commencement,* formally "Madam," or socially "Dear Duchess of ______" or "Dear Duchess."

PERSONAL ADDRESS, "Your Grace." [See also "Duke's Widow," and for "Duchess of the Blood Royal" see "Princess."]

Duke.—LETTERS.—*Superscription,* "His Grace the Duke of ______" or socially "The Duke of ______." The very formal style of "The Most Noble" is now rarely used. *Commencement,* "My Lord Duke," "Dear Duke of ______," or [more usual) "Dear Duke." PERSONAL ADDRESS, "Your Grace." [For "Duke of the Blood Royal" see "Prince."]

Duke's Daughter.—LETTERS.—*Superscription,* "Lady [Henrietta] ______." *Commencement,* "Madam," or socially "Dear Lady Henrietta ______" or "Dear Lady Henrietta." PERSONAL ADDRESS, "Madam."

*** If the daughter of a Duke, a Marquess, or an Earl marry a Peer she is addressed according to the rank of her husband. If she marry the eldest son of a Duke, Marquess of Earl she is known by her husband's courtesy title, but if the daughter of a *Duke* or *Marquess* marry the eldest son of an Earl she is sometimes addressed by the courtesy title of her husband, but she may revert to the style of Lady [Mary] Stavordale, i.e. her own title, followed by her husband's courtesy title. His surname must never be used. This form is invariably used by such ladies after divorce.

There is no authority for the practice of styling the daughters of Dukes, Marqueses, and Earls, " The Lady [Henrietta] ______."

Duke's Eldest Son, assumes by courtesy a secondary title of his father, and is addressed personally as if he were a Peer without 'The Most Hon.' or 'The Rt. Hon.' *Superscription,* "Marquess of ______" (or as title adopted may be).

Duke's Eldest Son, assumes by courtesy a secondary title of his father, and is addressed personally as if he were a Peer without 'The Most Hon.' or 'The Rt. Hon.' *Superscription,* "Marquess of ______" (or as title adopted may be).

Duke's Eldest Son's Daughter is by courtesy addressed as if her father were a Peer.

Duke's Eldest Son's Eldest Son assumed by courtesy the third title of his grandfather, and is addressed personally as if he were a peer provided such courtesy title is the title of a Peerage vested in his grandfather. *Superscription,* "The Earl of ______" or "Lord ______" (or as title adopted may be).

Duke's Eldest Son's Younger Son is by courtesy addressed as if his father were a Peer.

Duke's Eldest Son's Widow, *Same as Duke's Eldest Sons's Wife* so long as she remains a widow. As to re-marriage, see "Widow."

Duke's Eldest Son's Wife is known by his courtesy title, and is addressed personally as peeress without 'The Most Hon.' or 'The Rt. Hon.'

Duke's Widow, *same as Duchess* if present Duke is unmarried. For widows where present incumbent of title is married [see "Dowager"]. As to re-marriage, see "Widows."

Duke's Younger Son.—LETTERS.—*Superscription,* "Lord [Robert] ______." *Commencement,* formally "My Lord," or socially "Dear Lord Robert ______," or "Dear Lord Robert." PERSONAL ADDRESS, "My Lord."

Duke's Younger Son's Widow, *same as Duke's Younger Son's Wife.* As to re-marriage, see "Widows."

Duke's Younger Son's Wife.—LETTERS.—*Superscription,* "Lady [Thomas] ______." *Commencement,* "Madam,'" or socially "Dear Lady Thomas ______," or "Dear Lady Thomas."

Earl.—LETTERS.—*Superscription,* "The Right Hon. the Earl of ______," or socially "The Earl of ______." In other respects as Baron.

Earl's Daughter, *same as Duke's Daughter.*

Earl's Eldest Son bears by courtesy a lesser (usually the second) title of his father, and is addressed as if he were a Peer but without 'The Rt., Hon., *Superscription,* "Viscount ______."

Earl's Eldest Son's Daughter is by courtesy addressed as if her father were a Peer.

Earl's Eldest Son's Son is by courtesy addressed as if his father were a Peer. [If a Scottish Earldom, the eldest may be addressed as "The Master of ______." *See Master.]*

Earl's Eldest Son's Widow, *same as Eldest son's Wife* so long as she remains a widow. As to re-marriage, see "Widows."

Earl's Eldest Son's Wife is usually known by his courtesy title (for exception see under "Duke's Daughter"), and is addressed personally as if a Peeress but without. The Rt. Hon.'

Earl's Widow, *same as Countess if* present Earl is unmarried. For widows where present incumbent of the title is married [see "Dowager"].

Earl's Wife.—See "Countess."

Earl's Younger Son, *same as Baron's Son.*

Earl's Younger Son's Widow, *same as Baron's Son's Wife.*

Earl's Younger Son's Wife, *same as Baron's Son's Wife.*

Edward Medal.—In Oct. 1971, The Queen approved the exchange by which holders of the Edward Medal (EM) receive the George Cross. (see George Cross).

Esquire.—LETTERS.—*Superscription,* "[Edward] ______, Esq." *Commencement, "Sir."* PERSONAL ADDRESS, *"Sir."*

Esquire's Widow, *same as Esquire's Wife.*She continues to use her late husband's christian name unless she re-marries. e.g. Mrs John Smith *not* Mrs Mary Smith.

Esquire's Wife.—*Superscription.* "Mrs [Egerton]," or "Mrs [John Egerton]." The former style is applicable if she is the wife of the head of the family, provided that there is no senior widow living, who retains the style for life or until re-marriage. —LETTERS.—*Commencement,* "Madam." PERSONAL ADDRESS, "Madam."

Fire Service Medals.—See Police Medals.

George Cross. The letters GC take precedence after VC, and before all other honours and decorations.

Governor of a Country within the British Commonwealth is styled "His Excellency" [preceding all other ranks and titles] while aetually administering a Government and within its boundary (also an officer administering in his absence). If the Governor has not been knighted he is styled "His Excellency Mr. John Smith." Esquire should not be used with H.E.

Governor-General.—The style of His Excellency precedes all other titles and ranks, and is used while actually administering a Government and within the territory administered. —LETTERS.—*Superscription,* "His Excellency [Sir John] ______, Governor- General of ______" (also an officer administering in his absence). In other respects as for Governor.

Governor-General's Wife.—The style of "Her Excellency" has, since 1924, been confined to the wives of the Govs.-Gen. of Countries of the Commonwealth within the country administered by her husband.

Governor's Wife.—She is not accorded the style of "Her Excellency."

Grandchildren of Peers.—If the eldest son of a peer predeceases his father and the grandson succeeds to the peerage held by his grandfather, a Royal Warrant is necessary (when such succession has eventuated) to grant to his younger brothers and his sisters, the "rank, title, place, pre-eminence, and precedence" which would have been due to them if their father had survived to inherit the Peerage.

High Commissioner.—*Superscription,* His Excellency [preceding all other ranks, and titles] the High Commissioner for ______." Otherwise as for an Ambassador.

"Honourable" in Commonwealth Countries. The title of "Honourable" is borne *for life* by all Members of the Queen's Privy Council in Canada, Member of the Canadian Senate and Premiers and Lieutenant-Governors of Canadian Provinces, and of the Executive Councils of the Commonwealth of Australia and of the States of Victoria and Tasmania. In Canada the title of "Honourable" is borne *during office* by the following categories of Judges in Canada—Judges of Supreme and Exchequer Courts of Canada the Chief Justices and Judges of the Supreme Courts of Ontario, Nova Scotia, New Brunswick, Alberta and Newfoundland, the Court of Queens's Bench and the Superior Court of Quebec, the Court of Appeal and the Court of Queen's Bench of Manitoba and Saskatchewan, the Court of Appeal and the Supreme Court of British Columbia, the Supreme Court of Judicature of Prince Edward Island, and the Territorial Courts of NW Territories and Yukon Territory. They are eligible to be personally recommended by the Governor General for Her Majesty's permission to retain the title on retirement. Also in Commonwealth countries all Members of Executive Councils, all Members of Legislative Councils (other than Legislative Councils of Provinces of Canada), and by the Speaker of the Lower House of the Legislatures. It is also used locally by Members of the Executive and Legislative Councils of territories not possessing Responsible Government. The following in Commonwealth Countries are eligible to be recommended to retain the title of "Honourable" on retirement. Executive Councillors who have served for at least three years as Ministers or one year as Prime Minister; Presidents of Senates and Legislative Councils and Speakers of Legislative Assemblies on quitting office after having served three years in their respective offices: Senators and Members of the Legislative Councils on retirement or resignation after a continuous service of not less than ten years.
[*See also* Judges in Commonwealth and Overseas Territories]

Invitations. When sent jointly to married couples at their home address, the envelope should always be addressed to the wife.

Judge of City of London Court, as for Circuit Judge.

Judge in Commonwealth and Overseas Territories.—The title of "The Right Honourable" is borne for life by the Chief Justice of Canada. The title of "Honourable" during tenure of office is borne by Chief Justices and Judges of the High Court of Australia, and the Supreme Courts of New South Wales, Vic., Queensland, S. Aust., W. Aust., Tasmania, NZ, and the Judges of the Supreme and Exchequer Courts, and the Chief Justices and Judges of certain other Courts in the provinces of Canada; also such Chief Justices and Judges of those Courts as may be specially permitted to bear it after retirement. *Superscription,* "The Hon. the Chief Justice," or "The Hon. Mr. Justice ______." Judges of the Supreme Courts in Commonwealth Countries are styled "The Honourable."

Judge, Circuit.—For the various appointments see Table of General Precedence.—LETTERS.—*Superscription,* "His Honour Judge ______." - PERSONAL ADDRESS—"Sir", but when on the Bench, "Your Honour." The prefix of "His Honour," but not "Judge," is retained after retirement from office, but personal address as "Judge" or "Judge Brown" may be continued unofficially in retirement.

Judge of High Court.—LETTERS.—*Superscription,* (official) "The Hon. Mr. Justice ______." (private) "Sir John ______." *Commencement,* "Sir." PERSONAL ADDRESS, "Sir," but when on the Bench, "My Lord," or, "Your Lordship." See also "Lord Chief Justice of England," "Master of the Rolls," "Lord Justice of Appeal," and "Lord of Appeal in Ordinary."

Judges of High Court, Ladies.—LETTERS.—*Superscription,* (official) "The Hon. Mrs, Justice ______" (private) "Dame Mary Smith" ______," *Commencement,* "Madam." PERSONAL ADDRESS, "Madam," but when on the Bench "My Lady" or "Your Ladyship.

Justice of the Peace.—PERSONAL ADDRESS.—When on the Bench, "Your Worship," and in other respects as an Esquire. The letters JP are usually put after name.

Knight Bachelor.—LETTERS.—*Superscription,* "Sir [George] ______." In other respects same as Baronet. The letters KB should *not* be used.

Knight's Wife, *same as Baronet's Wife.* The wife of a clergyman of the Church of England who receives a Knighthood of an Order of Chivalry but consequently not the accolade, retains the style of "Mrs. ______."

Knight of an Order of Chivalry, *same as Knight Bachelor,* but adding to the superscription the recognised letters of the Order, such as "GCB," or "KCB". Clergymen of the Church of England and Honorary Knights do not receive the accolade, and consequently are addressed by the letters of the Orders but not the prefix "Sir."

Knight's Widow, *same as Knight's Wife* so long as she remains a widow. As to re-marriage, see "Widows."

Lady (untitled). See Esquire's wife and widow. Of unmarried daughters, the eldest of the senior generation is styled "Miss [Egerton]." A younger daughter is addressed as "Miss [Helen Egerton]."

Lady Mayoress. See "Lord Mayor's Wife."

Lieutenant-Governor.—Isle of Man, Jersey and Guernsey, as for Governor. The style of a Lt.-Gov. of a Canadian Province is "*The Hon.*"(borne for life).

Life Peer.—He is addressed as for an hereditary peer.—See "Baron."

Life Peer's Son.—See "Baron's son."

Life Peer's Daughter.—See "Baron's daughter."

Life Peeress. See "Baroness."

Life Peeress in her own right. She is addressed as for an hereditary peeress. See "Baroness."

Lord, in Peerage of Scotland.—See "Baron."

Lord Advocate.—LETTERS.—*Superscription,* "The Rt. Hon. the Lord Advocate," or, "The Rt. Hon. [George] ______." In other respects as an esquire. [The prefix of Rt. Hon. is not retained after retirement from office, unless a Member of the Privy Council.]

Lord Chancellor.—LETTERS.—*Superscription,* "The R. Hon. the Lord High Chancellor." In other respects as a peer according to his rank.

Lord Chief Justice.—LETTERS.—*Superscription,* "The Lord Chief Justice of England," or "To the Right Hon. Lord ______, Lord Chief Justice of England." In other respects as a Judge, except when of noble rank, when he is addressed according to his degree.

Lord High Commissioner to General Assembly of Church of Scotland.—LETTERS.—*Superscription,* "To His Grace the Lord High Commissioner." *Commencement,* "Your Grace." PERSONAL ADDRESS, "Your Grace."

Lord Justice Clerk and Lord Justice General.—See Lord of Session, but addressed as "The Rt. Hon. the Lord Justice Clerk and the Rt. Hon. the Lord Justice General."

Lord Justice of Appeal.—LETTERS.—*Superscription,* "The Right Hon. Lord Justice ______," or "To the Right Hon. Sir [Robert] ______." In other respects as a Judge of High Court.

Lord Mayor.—LETTERS.— The Lord Mayors of London, York, Belfast, and Cardiff have the privilege of being styled "The Rt. Hon."; and permission to use this style has also been granted to the Lord Mayors of Sydney (NSW), Melbourne (Vic.), Adelaide (S. Aust.), Perth (W. Aust.), Brisbane (Queensland), and Hobart (Tasmania). *Superscription,* "The Rt. Hon. the Lord Mayor of ______." or "[Henry ______,] The Rt. Hon. Lord Mayor of ______," [The prefix of Right Hon. is not retained after retirement from office. [See also "Lord Provost."]. *Commencement,* "My Lord," or less formally, "Dear Lord Mayor." *Superscription* for other Lord Mayors "The Right Worshipful the Lord Mayor of ______."

Lord Mayor's Wife or Lady Mayoress.—LETTERS.—*Superscription,* "The Lady Mayoress." In other respects as Knight's of Esquire's wife.

Lord of Appeal-in-Ordinary.—See *Baron.*

Lord of Session, Scottish.—LETTERS.—*Superscription,* "The Hon. Lord ______." In other respects as a Baron, but children have no courtesy styles. See also Lord Justice Clerk and Lord Justice General.

Lord of Session's Wife or Widow.—LETTERS.—*Superscription,* "Lady ______." In other respects as Baron's wife.

Lord Provost.—LETTERS.—*Superscription,* The Lord Provosts of Edinburgh and Glasgow are addressed as "The Rt. Hon. the Lord Provost," while in office. The prefix may be placed before the name of the holder in the case of the Lord Provost of Edinburgh. In other respects as a Baron. The Lord Provost of Perth, Dundee and Aberdeen are styled "The Lord Provosts of ______."

Lord Provost's Wife. Same as the wife of an Esquire. The style of Lady Provost is incorrect.

Marchioness.—LETTERS.—*Superscription,* "The Most Hon. the Marchioness of ______," or socially, "The Marchioness of ______." In other respects as Baroness. [See also "Marquess's Widow."]

Marquess.—LETTERS.—*Superscription,* "The Most Hon. the Marquess of ______," or less formally, "The Marquess of ______." In other respects as Baron.

Marquess's Daughter, *same as Duke's Daughter.*

Marquess's Eldest Son, *same as Duke's Eldest Son. Superscription,* "Earl of ______" (or as title adopted may be).

Marquess's Eldest Son's Daughter is by courtesy addressed as if her father were a peer.

Marquess's Eldest Son's Eldest Son, *same as Duke's Eldest Son. Superscription,* "Viscount ______" (or as title adopted may be).

Marquess's Eldest Son's Younger Son is by courtesy addressed as if his father were a Peer, viz. "The Hon. ______."

Marquess's Eldest Son's Widow, *same as Duke's Eldest Son's Widow.*

Marquess's Eldest Son's Wife is known by his courtesy title, and is addressed personally as a peeress without 'The Rt. Hon.'

Marquess's Widow, *same as Marchioness,* if present Marquess is unmarried. For widows where present incumbent of title is married [see "Dowager"]. As to re-marriage see "Widows."

Marquess's Younger Son, *same as Duke's Younger Son.*

Marquess's Younger Son's Widow, *same as Duke's Younger Son's Wife,* As to re-marriage, see "Widows."

Marquess's Younger Son's Wife, *same as Duke's Younger Son's Wife.*

Master.—This title is borne in the *Peerage of Scotland* by the heir apparent or presumptive of a Peer. It is also used *by courtesy* by the eldest son of a Peer by courtesy. In the case of the heir apparent, "Master" is normally used by the eldest son of a Viscount and Lord, as the heirs of the senior grades of the Peerage normally use a courtesy title. He is styled "The Master of ______" (the appropriate title will be found under the Peerage article). If the heir be a woman, she is officially designated "The Mistress of ______" but this title is seldom used. A Master's wife is styled "The Hon. Mrs. [Donald Campbell"] or according to her husband's rank.

Master of the Rolls.—LETTERS.—*Superscription,* "The Right Hon. the Master of the Rolls," or "The Right Hon. ______, according to his rank." *Commencement,* as "Judge." PERSONAL ADDRESS, "Sir," but when on the Bench, "My Lord," or "Your Lordship."

Mayor (whether man or woman).—LETTERS.—*Superscription,* (if Mayor of a City), "The Right Worshipful the Mayor of ______" (if a Mayor of a Borough or Town Mayor. "The Worshipful the Mayor of ______." *Commencement,* "Sir (or Madam)." In other respects as an Esquire or an Esquire's wife. The form "Dear Mr. Mayor" may be used for a man or woman.

Members of the Executive and Legislative Councils.—See Honourable in Commonwealth Countries.

Members of Parliament.—According to rank, but adding the initials "MP" after title or name and honours.

Military Officers.—See "Naval, Military, and Air Force Officers."

Minister of the Crown.—If a Privy Counsellor, see that section, otherwise see Member of Parliament or Grade of Peerage. The social form of "Dear Secretary of State," or "Dear Minister" may be used if the matter concerns the Department.

Moderator of the General Assembly of Church of Scotland. By Order in Council the Moderator has precedence in Scotland and at Court functions immediately after Bishops of the Church of England, and while in office is addressed as "Rt. Rev." Former Moderators, "Very Rev."

Naval, Military, and Air Force Officers.—Professional rank should always precede any titles, *e.g.,* "Adm. (the Right Hon.) the Earl of ______," "Gen. the (Right Hon.) Lord ______," "Air-Marshal Sir ," but Lieutenants in the Army, Flying Officers and Pilot Officers in the Air Force are addressed by their social and not their professional rank, *e.g.,* "The Hon. Benjamin ______, Irish Guards," "George ______, Esq., 11th Hussars," or "William ______, Esq., RAF."

Peers and Peeresses by courtesy. —As commoners they are not addressed as "Rt. Hon." or "The" but "Viscount [Brown]" or appropriate title.

Police and Fire Service Medals. The letters KPM, KPFSM, QPM, QFSM and CPM are now placed after the name. If the Colonial Police Medal were awarded for gallantry the letters CPM are placed before BEM, and if for meritorious service after QFSM (see paragraph 4 at beginning of section).

Prebendary.—As for Canon, but substituting the word Prebendary for Canon.

Prime Minister, The.—See Privy Counsellors. The social form of "Dear (Mr.) Prime Minister" may be used if the matter concerns his office.

Prince.—LETTERS.—*Superscription,* (i) the son of a Sovereign "His Royal Highness The Prince [Edward]": (ii) other Princes "His Royal Highness Prince [Michael of Kent]"; (iii) Duke "His Royal Highness The Duke of [Gloucester]." *Commencement,* "Sir," *Conclusion,* "I have the honour to be, Sir. Your Royal Highness's most humble and obedient servant." - PERSONAL ADDRESS, "Your Royal Highness," and henceforward as "Sir." [See also Royal Family.]

Princess.—LETTERS.—*Superscription,* (i) the daughter of a Sovereign "Her Royal Highness The Princess [Royal]"; (ii) other Princesses "Her Royal Highness Princess [Alexandra], the Hon. Mrs. Angus Ogilvy"; (iii) Duchess "Her Royal Highness The Duchess of [Kent]." *Commencement,* "Madam." *Conclusion,* "I have the honour to be, Madam, Your Royal Highness's most humble and obedient servant." PERSONAL ADDRESS, "Your Royal Highness." and henceforward as "Ma'am." [See also Royal Family.]

Privy Counsellors, also spelt PRIVY COUNCILLORS.,—LETTERS.—*Superscription,* "The Right Hon. ______," but if a peer then as such, followed by the letters "PC," *after* all Orders and Decorations. *Commencement, &c.,* according to the rank of the individual. Privy Counsellors of Northern Ireland, which are no longer created, are entitled to the prefix of Right Hon. and are included in this section. Members of the Privy Council of Canada are entitled to the style of "Hon." for life. *Commencement,* as for Esquire or appropriate rank.

Privy Counsellors, Wives of.—They enjoy no special style or precedence as such.

Provost.—As for Dean, but substituting the word Provost for Dean.

Queen Mother.—LETTERS.—*Superscription,* for formal and state documents, "Her Gracious Majesty Queen Elizabeth The Queen Mother," otherwise "Her Majesty Queen Elizabeth The Queen Mother." *Commencement,* as for the Queen Regnant. *Conclusion,* "I have the honour to remain, Madam, Your Majesty's most humble and obedient servant." PERSONAL ADDRESS, as for the Queen Regnant.

Queen Regnant.—LETTERS.—*Superscription,* for formal and state documents. "The Queen's Most Excellent Majesty." otherwise "Her Majesty The Queen," *Commencement,* "Madam," or "May it please your Majesty." *Conclusion,* "I have the honour to remain Madam, Your Majesty's most humble and obedient servant." PERSONAL ADDRESS, "Your Majesty," and henceforth as "Ma'am."

Queen's Counsel.—LETTERS.—*Superscription,* " ______ Esq., QC." In other respects as an Esquire. The letters are used after the name by Circuit Judges, but not by High Court Judges.

Rt. Honourable.—This prefix is borne by Privy Counsellors of Great Britain and Northern Ireland, the Governor General of Canada, and Prime Minister and Chief Justice of Canada *for life*; by Earls, Viscounts and Barons: (except peers by courtesy) their wives and widows; and certain Lord Mayors (see Lord Mayors), and Provosts of Edinburgh and Glasgow (see Lord Provosts), and the Chairman of Greater London Council *while in office.*

Royal Dukes. —See "Prince."

Royal Family.—On Dec. 11th, 1917, it was ordained that "The children of any Sovereign of the United Kingdom and the children of the sons of any such Sovereign and the eldest living son of the eldest son of the Prince of Wales, shall have and at all times hold and enjoy the style, title, or attribute of Royal Highness with their titular dignity of Prince or Princess prefixed to their respective Christian names, or with their other titles of honour; and that the grandchildren of the sons of any such Sovereign in the direct male line (save only the eldest living son of the eldest son of the Prince of Wales) shall have the style and title enjoyed by the children of Dukes." [See also "Queen Regnant," "Queen Mother." "Prince," and "Princess."]

Rural Deans. No special form of address.

Secretary of State. See "Minister of the Crown" and "Privy Counsellors."

Sovereign, The.—See "Queen Regnant."

Titles just announced.—See paragraph at commencement of this section.

Trinity House, Elder Brethren of are entitled to be called "Captain," with precedence after Naval Captains.

Victoria Cross.—The letters VC take precedence of all other honours and decorations.

Viscount.—LETTERS.—*Superscription,* "The Right Hon. The Viscount ______," or socially "The Viscount ______." In other respects as Baron.

Viscountess.—LETTERS.—*Superscription,* "The Right Hon. The Viscountess ______." or socially, "The Viscountess." In other respects as Baroness and Baron's widow. [See also "Viscount's Widow"].

Viscount's Son, and his Wife or Widow *same* as Baron's.

Viscount's Daughter, *same as Baron's.*

Viscount's Widow, *same as Viscountess* if present Viscount is unmarried. For widows where present incumbent of title is married [see "Dowager"]. As to re-marriage, see "Widows."

Wales, Prince of. See "Prince" and "Royal Family."

Widows.—A Widow who re-marries *loses* any title or precedence she gained by her previous marriage, and is not recognised as having any claim to bear the title of her deceased husband, *e.g.:* at a coronation or other State ceremonial, the widow of a peer would not be summoned as a peeress if she had subsequently married a commoner; and, if having espoused a peer of lesser degree than her former husband, she would only be recognised by the rank acquired by her last marriage. [See also Esquire's Widow.]

THOUGHTS ON DISTINCTION

Quite a few years ago, I had an enjoyable job working on the Atticus column of the Sunday Times. The greater part of the year seemed to be spent preparing for our Christmas lunch party, to which we planned to invite half-a-dozen or so distinguished people to tell them the joyous news that they had been selected for the long-awaited Atticus Christmas lunch, to take place in a dining-room at London Zoo.

After a week on the phone, it dawned on me that one of the distinguishing marks of distinguished people is that they have no interest in lunching with complete strangers. Nevertheless, we eventually managed to pressurise an odd selection of people into attendance. John Gross, the distinguished man of letters, sat next to Willie Rushton, the distinguished cartoonist; James Fenton, the distinguished poet, sat next to Molly Parkin, the distinguished writer of cheap fiction; and Colonel Blashford Snell, the distinguished wayfarer, sat next to Mary O'Hara, the distinguished harpist. Finally, we gained acceptances from the distinguished first person in the London telephone directory, a Mrs Aal, and from the distinguished last person in the London telephone directory, a Mr Zzitz.

It was, to be frank, a rather awkward occasion. No-one seemed to be quite sure why they were there, and we found it hard to remember the exact reason for inviting them. The sound of knife and fork clattering on plate was interrupted only by the distant sound of the trumpeting of elephants, the baying of wolves and, in the quieter moments, the slither of snakes. None of us could think of anything to say. Distinction, it emerged, is no great leveller. Even Mrs Aal and Mr Zzitz, who were at least distinguished in the same field, albeit at opposite ends of the same field, seemed to have little in common. Mrs Aal, I remember, worked in a picture gallery in Bond Street, while Mr Zzitz, who had taken the trouble to change his name by deed poll so as to merit his distinction, ran a bicycle shop in Stoke Newington. After a spirited opening, in which they discussed the advantages and disadvantages of being so placed in the London telephone directory, their conversation seemed to flag. After coffee, during which the tinkle of spoons was accompanied by the whooping honks of sea-lions being fed, the distinguished company quickly dispersed, still visibly wondering why they had been there at all. We never again organised an Atticus lunch, at Christmas or at any other time.

In many ways, 'Debrett's Distinguished People of Today' is like a vast, hardcover version of that fateful lunch. Within these pages are disc-jockeys and politicians, public relations consultants and aristocrats, sportsmen and writers of blank verse. There is even a Mr Aalders and a Mrs Zvegintzov, one a QC, the other an Hon. But Debrett's Distinguished People of Today has two great advantages over our ill-conceived lunch party. First, it had invited 35,000 or so distinguished people compared to our own paltry eight. Second, there is no obligation to entertain all or any of them to lunch. As with that excellent magazine, 'Country Life', one can snoop without having to offer an explanation, one can view without adopting the pretence of possible purchase.

While browzing through the house advertisements in 'Country Life', I find that my mind attacks each property in three distinct stages. I begin by imagining that I have lived there for some years, and know it well. Then I look for a prize. Finally, I stare hard at the photograph in search of shortcomings just out of shot—a deluxe development of executive-style luxury homes just over the garden wall, perhaps, or a fully refurbished nuclear power station sited within easy walking distance of the kitchen. I find this swift cycle of fantasy—from believing I own the property to thanking goodness that I don't, and all in three seconds—relaxing. Browzing through 'Debrett's Distinguished People of Today', I find that my mind works in much the same way.

First, I imagine that I am in some way related to the particular Distinguished Person, and know him well. Then my eye glances up and down his entry in an attempt to assess his worth. Does he have a London address and a country address? Is his country property a Manor, an Old Vicarage or—woe!—a New Vicarage? How many effortless directorships does he have? How many honours and awards? And then I arrive at the final stage, peering for the shortcomings that lie just a little bit off the page. What became of that first wife? Aren't those recreations rather too dull, or rather too arch? What dreadful deeds were perpetrated during those five unchronicled years? Was there, perhaps, a spell in prison? Why did he achieve no higher rank during his period in the Forces? And—ooh!—middle name! How very often a Distinguished Person, replete with honours and medals, books published and awards conferred, is let down by his middle name! One has only to think of Sir Terence ORBY Conran, Michael Ray DIBDIN Heseltine or Paddy DURHAM Ashdown to realise how fragile is the skein of worldly distinction. (Incidentally, I wonder whether, statistically, more Distinguished People have embarrassing middle names than Undistinguished People, and, if so, whether they were driven to the attainment of distinction through that most motivating of emotions, embarrassment?).

There are, of course, other, less pernickety, ways of reading 'Debrett's Distinguished People of Today'. In these days when so many works of contemporary fiction tend to concentrate on a few hours in the life of a solitary character, those few hours usually ending in bitterness and despair, it is reassuring to be able to turn to a work with a cast of over 35,000 leading characters, all of them seeming to live happy, straightforward lives, choc-a-bloc with healthy recreations, fresh-faced families and responsible positions on important committees. Thirty five thousand happy endings! It seems almost too good to be true.

Until twenty years ago, the question most often asked when two strangers met at a party was 'Where do you live?' Now, it is 'What do you do?' Debrett's nicely answers both questions. In my experience, the longer the reply to the latter question, the less distinguished the speaker. When I was young and starry-eyed, I used to be impressed by people I met at parties who would reel off a list of film, book, marketing, experimental drama and television projects on which they were working, but I now realise that with failure comes volubility, and that with distinction comes reticence. By and large, Debrett's is as true-to-life as ever, and those who brag of a mountain of distinctions are likely, on closer investigation, to be among the least distinguished. Certainly, a great many failed Conservative candidates seem to award themselves more lines than the Prime Minister, and those who have failed a number of times tend to outdo those who have failed only once or twice.

Some professions are more distinguished than others. There are, I note, few dentists in Debrett's. Why this should be, I do not know—perhaps the editors suffered traumas at the hands of that profession many years ago—but, once again, I must observe that it echoes life itself. Dentists have long occupied an awkward slot in the British social order, and at times it has seemed that a Distinguished Dentist of Today would be as hard to find as a Distinguished Estate Agent of Today or a Distinguished Quiz Show Compère of Today. I am reminded of my distinguished father-in-law's first day as a member of The Traveller's Club. The man next to him lowered his newspaper, declared 'I am a dentist. No-one speaks to me. That's the way I like it', and then resumed his reading. It seems just as well, then, that Debrett's should turn a blind eye to such a standoffish, not to say threatening, profession.

One of the great merits of 'Debrett's Distinguished People of Today' is that it is not afraid to expel those who, for whatever reason, have not come up to scratch. No longer can the cricketer saunter through a season confident that his name will not be excised; no longer can the poet toss off some sloppy scansion and expect to remain included; no longer can the politician perpetrate deeds most foul believing that, like the portrait of Dorian Gray, his untarnished image will remain intact. This is all to the good if society's standards are to be upheld, but I can't help wishing that all the bad hats, slug-a-beds and ne'erdowells who have forfeited their positions might be celebrated in a companion volume. I feel sure that 'Debrett's Extinguished People of Today' would sell like hot cakes.

CRAIG BROWN

ROLL OF THE BRITISH ASSOCIATION OF THE SOVEREIGN MILITARY ORDER OF MALTA

The Sovereign Military Order of St John of Jerusalem of Rhodes and of Malta, to give the full title, may have its roots in Jerusalem prior to the capture of that city in 1099 by the first Crusade. In 1113 Pope Paschal II made the brethren an independent order under its Master. When the kingdom of Jerusalem fell in 1291 the Order settled briefly in Cyprus before conquering Rhodes. Rhodes was taken from them by the Turks after an epic siege in 1522 and the Order was given Malta by the Holy Roman Emperor Charles V in 1530. Malta fell to Napoleon in 1798 and the Grand Magistry is now settled in Rome.

The British Association represents the former Grand Priory of England and was established in 1875. It has close and friendly relations with the Most Venerable Order of St John of Jerusalem which was established in England in the nineteenth century and received a Royal Charter in 1888.

The Order of Malta is a religious order and the Knights of Justice make the usual monastic vows of chastity, poverty and obedience. They, and the Knights of Obedience who make a special promise, are drawn from the ranks of the Knights of Honour and Devotion and the Knights of Grace and Devotion. The Knights of Honour and Devotion are required to prove their nobility either by demonstrating that their sixteen great-great-grandparents were noble or that their four grandparents came of families noble in the male line for 200 years. An alternative proof is nobility in the male line for 300 years. The Knights of Grace and Devotion need only prove nobility in the male line for 100 years. The Knights of Magistral Grace do not need genealogical qualifications but must be of outstanding merit and service to the Order. Nobility is defined as the lawful possession of arms which must have been on record either at the College of Arms or at the Court of the Lord Lyon for the period demanded by the statutes of the Order.

The official roll of the Order does not show military rank or membership of other orders and decorations. There is no recognised way of showing membership of the Order of Malta and letters such as KM are not used by members of the British Association.*

THE PRINCE AND GRAND MASTER

His Most Eminent Highness Fra' Andrew Bertie

HIS EXCELLENCY THE PRESIDENT

Sir Peter Hope, KCMG, TD
Knight Grand Cross of Honour and Devotion

THE VICE-PRESIDENT

The Lord Craigmyle
Knight Grand Cross of Obedience

THE CHANCELLOR

Peter Drummond-Murray of Mastrick
Slains Pursuivant of Arms
Knight Grand Cross of Obedience

THE TREASURER

J A W Jennings, Esq, JP
Knight of Grace and Devotion

THE HOSPITALLER

N J I Stourton, Esq, OBE
Knight of Honour and Devotion

BAILIFF GRAND CROSS OF JUSTICE

His Excellency The Venerable Bailiff Fra' Anthony Furness

KNIGHTS OF JUSTICE IN SOLEMN VOWS

Fra' Ewen Cameron

KNIGHT OF JUSTICE IN SIMPLE VOWS

R M Festing, Esq

BAILIFFS GRAND CROSS OF OBEDIENCE

The Earl of Gainsborough
Major-General The Viscount Monckton of Brenchley, CB, OBE, MC, DL

KNIGHTS GRAND CROSS OF OBEDIENCE

Peter Drummond-Murray of Mastrick, Slains Pursuivant of Arms
The Lord Craigmyle

KNIGHTS OF OBEDIENCE

F J P Crichton-Stuart Esq, TD, JP
Major N G H Holdich
John F Power, Esq, MBE, JP, DL
Lt Cdr John Bedells, JP, RN
J C G George, Esq, Kintyre Pursuivant of Arms
J W de Gaynesford, Esq
Cecil Humphery-Smith, Esq
A G L Turner, Esq
Dr Peter Wren, VRD, JP, DL
Walter Stewart Fothringham, Esq
T M Carter, Esq, JP, DL
Capt G M Salvin

BAILIFF GRAND CROSS OF HONOUR AND DEVOTION

His Eminence Gordon Cardinal Gray
His Excellency Sir Peter Hope, KCMG, TD

KNIGHTS GRAND CROSS OF HONOUR AND DEVOTION

Gervase Elwes, Esq
J C W Riddell, Esq
Lt-Col H J G Weld, MC, DL
Count Joseph Czernin

KNIGHTS OF HONOUR AND DEVOTION

Major-General The Duke of Norfolk, KG, GCVO, CB, CBE, MC
The Lord Mowbray and Stourton, CBE
The Marquess of Lothian, KCVO
Lt-Col A B Constable-Maxwell, MBE, MC
E W Trafford, Esq
H R Tempest, Esq, DL
Lt-Col A J E Cranstoun of that Ilk, MC
Michael Dormer, Esq
C Stafford Northcote, Esq, OBE
Christopher Scott of Gala
Peregrine Bertie, Esq
Anthony Hornyold, Esq
J G Elwes, Esq
Gerald E H N de Trafford, Esq
Major-Gen Lord Michael Fitzalan-Howard, GCVO, CB, CBE, MC, DL
Count de Lalanne Mirrlees
Wing Cdr M H Constable-Maxwell, DSO, DFC, RAF rtd
Col Sir J W Weld, OBE, TD
Count Charles de Salis
Henry Crichton-Stuart, Esq
P O R Bridgeman, Esq, TD, DL
Major J F Arbuthnott
J H O Bridgeman, Esq
Sir William H Lawson, Bt, DL
Sir Philip de Zulueta
H I and R H The Archduke Geza of Austria-Hungary
D H L Nugent, Esq
Col The Lord Clifford of Chudleigh, OBE, DL
Major Niall Crichton-Stuart
Col David Stirling, DSO, OBE
Sir Ian Fraser, CBE, MC
P de V Beauclerk-Dewar, Esq, RD, JP
The Earl of Lisburne
The Hon Christopher Monckton
The Earl of Iddesleigh
Major Trappes-Lomax, JP
C H J Weld, Esq
Brig The Lord Lovat, DSO, MC, TD, JP
The Count de Salis
Henry Bedingfeld, Esq, Rouge Croix Pursuivant of Arms
Nicholas Elwes, Esq
Gen Sir J D Mostyn, KCB, CBE
J R R A Nevill, Esq
Jonathan Elwes, Esq
A J Fraser von Wartburg, Esq
Nigel Stourton, Esq, OBE
The Lord Talbot of Malahide, DL
Sir Paul Grey, KCMG
J V Monckton, Esq
D B E Belson, Esq
Henry Hornyold-Strickland, Esq
Martin Elwes, Esq
Sir Michael Maxwell-Scott, Bt
The Hon John Vaughan
Jeremy Hope, Esq
Conrad Swan, Esq, MVO, York Herald of Arms
David Lumsden of Cushnie, Garioch Pursuivant of Arms
Sir Bernard de Hoghton, Bt
Francis Trappes-Lomax, Esq
Capt The Lord Clifford
Prince Rupert zu Loewenstein
A H Stafford Northcote, Esq, JP
The Hon John Jolliffe
George Hope of Luffness
The Lord Carbery
The Lord Vaux of Harrowden
John Chichester-Constable, Esq, GM
Peter Prideaux-Brune, Esq
James Drummond-Murray, Esq
Andrew Festing, Esq
The Hon Richard Norton
Peter Constable-Maxwell, Esq
M C R Monteith, Esq
William Charlton, Esq
The Hon Andrew Fraser
The Hon James Stourton
Desmond FitzGerald, Esq
Rory More O'Ferrall, Esq.
John C F Prideaux-Brune, Esq
Major Count von Merveldt
Edward Stourton, Esq
Charles Cavenagh-Mainwaring, Esq
Don Victor Franco de Baux
Peregrine Fellowes, Esq
Major Michael Festing, JP
Merlin Dormer, Esq
Matthew Wauchope, Esq
Col Andrew Parker Bowles, OBE
P A Scrope, Esq
C H Petre, Esq
P A C Wauchope, Esq
Col Michael Dewar
P J Stirling, Esq
Andrew Swan, Esq

DAME GRAND CROSS OF HONOUR AND DEVOTION

Lady Jean Bertie

DAMES OF HONOUR AND DEVOTION

The Hon Mrs Woodruff
Mrs Geoffrey Elwes
Lady Maureen Fellowes
Lady Kelly
Mrs Laurence Cave
Baroness von Twickel
Mrs J C de F Sleeman
Mrs J C W Riddell
Mrs Philip Kerr
Mrs P M Blundell-Brown
Mrs Gervase Elwes
The Viscountess Monckton of Brenchley
The Countess of Lisburne
Miss Theresa Weld-Blundell
The Hon Mrs Bird
Mrs J C G George
Mrs Sandars
Lady Hilda Swan
Lady Grey
Mrs Montieth
Mrs Michael Dormer
Lady Gadsden
Lady Celestria Noel
Lady Maria Pridden
Mrs Miles Huntington-Whiteley
Countess de Serego della Scala
The Hon Mrs Edward Ward
Princess Rupert zu Loewenstein, JP
Mrs Alexander McEwan
Lady Keswick
Mrs S M Stewart

GRAND CROSS CONVENTUAL CHAPLAINS "ad honorem"

The Most Rev Maurice Couve de Murville, Archbishop of Birmingham
The Most Rev Keith O'Brien,
Archbishop of St Andrews and Edinburgh
The Rt Rev Mgr A N Gilbey

CONVENTUAL CHAPLAINS "ad honorem"

The Rev Dom E M Phillips, OSB
The Rt Rev Bishop Gordon Wheeler
The Rev D C Braithwaite-Young

KNIGHTS GRAND CROSS OF GRACE AND DEVOTION

Lt Col R C M Monteith, OBE, MC, TD, JP, DL
J P B Brooke-Little, Esq, CVO, Norroy and Ulster King of Arms

KNIGHTS OF GRACE AND DEVOTION

The Lord Buxton of Alsa
The Viscount Sidmouth
Captain Andrew Duncan, OBE
Adrian Stokes, Esq
Capt A F M Beeley
David Bune, Esq
Wilfrid J Ward, Esq
Lt-Col Robert A Cambell of Altries
N A Maxwell-Lawford, Esq
O W Ainscough, Esq
Philip Ogilvie, Esq
Charles Hargrove, Esq, OBE
Desmond Seward, Esq
The Hon Lord Brand
Anthony Jennings, Esq, JP
P R Loyd, Esq
Major Raonuill Ogilvie
Philip King, Esq
Michael Callender, Esq
H J Grisewood, Esq, CBE
Charles Wright, Esq
Ian Scott, Esq
Major General J H S Bowring, CB, OBE, MC
S D Lawson, Esq
Julian Lawson, Esq
R D Hartley-Russell, Esq
John Carleton-Paget, Esq

DAMES OF GRACE AND DEVOTION

Lady Tomkins
Mrs John de Gaynesford

CHAPLAINS OF MAGISTRAL OBEDIENCE

The Rev Michael Hollings, MC
The Rev J Alastair Russell, CF, STL
The Rev John Ramsay
The Rev Dom Fabian Cowper, OSB
The Very Rev Michael Scott Napier
The Rev Dom Stephen Ortiger, OSB
The Rev Dom Raphael Appleby, OSB
The Rev Dom Philip Jebb, OSB
The Rev Anthony Conlon
The Rev and Hon Dom Piers Grant-Ferris, OSB
The Very Rev Canon Maurice O'Leary
The Rev Peter Knott, SJ
The Rev Mark Turnham Elvins
The Rt Rev Bishop Crispian Hollis
The Rt Rev Vincent Logan, Bishop of Dunkeld
The Rev George Francis Davidson, OSB

KNIGHT GRAND CROSS OF MAGISTRAL GRACE WITH RIBAND

The Lord Harvington, AE, PC

KNIGHT GRAND CROSS OF MAGISTRAL GRACE

Brigadier M Gordon-Watson, OBE, MC

KNIGHTS OF MAGISTRAL GRACE

Major Sir Paul Makins, Bt
Sir Noel Moynihan
Captain W Eric Brockman, CBE, RN
Francis Arthur D'Abreu, Esq, ERD
Major Sir Patrick H B Wall, MC, VRD, RM, MP
Wing Commander M M Kane, MBE, RAF
Brigadier Sir Geoffrey Hardy-Roberts, KCVO, CB, CBE
W G Eagleton, Esq
Bruce Todd, Esq, TD
The Lord Forte of Ripley
Denis J Barlow, Esq
Charles G Gaggero, Esq, OBE, JP
The Lord Rawlinson of Ewell, PC
Dr Jonathan Riley-Smith
Dr Karl Eibenschuetz-Keplinger
Sir Harold Hood, Bt, TD
M W Rapinet, Esq
J R A Fox, Esq
Michael H Kelleher, Esq
Seweryn Lukas, Esq
Kenneth Wagg, Esq, TD
Dr T C Taylor
Michael Bonn, Esq
Col and Alderman Sir Ronald Laurence Gardner-Thorpe, GBE, TD
Dr D P J McCarthy, TD
Alfred Marnau, Esq
Brigadier D K Neville
Col M J Campbell-Lamerton

DAMES OF MAGISTRAL GRACE

The Lady Harvington
Miss Ann Ryan
Lady Gardner-Thorpe

DONATS OF DEVOTION, FIRST CLASS

Bernard C Owens, Esq
J D P Keegan, Esq

DONATS OF DEVOTION, SECOND CLASS

Samuel Dunlop, Esq
J M C Robinson, Esq, Fitzalan Pursuivant of Arms Extraordinary
H A Bond, Esq

MEMBER OF THE ORDER

Attached to the British Association

KNIGHT OF MAGISTRAL GRACE

Sir Etienne Dupuch, OBE

LONDON CLUBS

American	95 Piccadilly, W1	01-499 2303
Army and Navy	36 Pall Mall, SW1	01-930 9721
Anglo-Belgian	60 Knightsbridge, SW1	01-235 2121
Arts	40 Dover Street, W1	01-499 8581
Athenaeum	107 Pall Mall, SW1	01-930 4843
Beefsteak	9 Irving Street, WC2	01-930 5722
Boodle's	28 St James's Street, SW1	01-930 7166
Brooks's	St James's Street SW1	01-499 0072
Buck's	18 Clifford Street, W1	01-734 6896
Caledonian	9 Halkin Street, SW1	01-235 5162
Canning	42 Half Moon Street, W1	01-499 5163
Carlton	69 St James's Street, SW1	01-493 1168
Cavalry and Guards'	127 Piccadilly, W1	01-499 1261
City of London	19 Old Broad Street, EC2	01-588 7991
East India, Devonshire, Sports and Public Schools	16 St James's Square, SW1	01-930 1000
Eccentric	9 Ryder Street, SW1	01-930 6133
Farmers	3 Whitehall Court, SW1	01-930 3557
Flyfishers'	24a Old Burlington Street, W1	01-629 6776
Garrick	15 Garrick Street WC2	01-836 1737
Gresham	15 Abchurch Lane, EC4	01-629 7231
Hurlingham	Ranelagh Gardens SW6	01-736 8411
Lansdowne	9 Fitzmaurice Place, Berkeley Square, W1	01-629 7200
MCC (Marylebone Cricket Club)	Lord's Cricket Ground, NW8	01-286 3649
National Liberal	1 Whitehall Place, SW1	01-930 9871
Naval and Military	94 Piccadilly, W1	01-499 5163
New Cavendish	44 Great Cumberland Place, W1	01-262 5536
Oriental	Stratford House, Stratford Place, W1	01-629 5126
Portland	42 Half Moon Street, W1	01-499 1523
Pratt's	14 Park Place, SW1	01-493 0397
Queen's	Palliser Road, W14	01-385 3421
Reform	104 Pall Mall, SW1	01-930 9374
Royal Air Force	128 Piccadilly, W.1.	01-499 3456
Royal Automobile	89-91 Pall Mall, SW1	01-930 2345
Royal Over-Seas League	Over-Seas House, St James's Street, SW1	01-408 0214
Royal Thames Yacht	60 Knightsbridge, SW1	01-235 2121
St Stephen's	34 Queen Anne's Gate, SW1	01-222 1382
Savile	69 Brook Street, W1	01-629 5462
Ski Club of Great Britain	118 Eaton Square, SW1	01-235 4711
Travellers'	106 Pall Mall, W1	01-930 8688
Turf	5 Carlton House Terrace, SW1	01-930 8555
United Oxford & Cambridge University	71 Pall Mall, SW1	01-930 4152
University Women's	2 Audley Square, South Audley Street, W1	01-499 6478
White's	37 St James's Street, SW1	01-493 6671

CLUBS OUTSIDE LONDON

Caledonian	32 Abercromby Place, Edinburgh 3	031 557 2675
Jockey	High Street, Newmarket	0638 663101
Kildare St and University	17 St Stephen's Green, Dublin 2	0001 76 65 23
Ladies Club	29 Queensferry Road, Edinburgh 2	031 225 8002
Leander	Henley-on-Thames	04912 3665
Manchester	50 Spring Gardens, Manchester	061 834 7678
New	86 Princess Street, Edinburgh 2	031 226 4881
Northern Counties	Hood Street, Newcastle-upon-Tyne	0632 326611
Puffin's	c/o Martin's, 70 Rose Street North, Edinburgh	031 225 3106
Royal and Ancient	St Andrews	0334 72112
Royal Irish Automobile	34 Glasgow Street, Dublin 2	001 77 06 68
Royal Scottish Automobile	11 Blythswood Square, Glasgow 2	041 221 3850
Royal Yacht Squadron	Cowes, Isle of Wight	0983 292743
Stephen's Green	9 St Stephen's Green North, Dublin	0001 77 47 44
Ulster	48 High Street, Belfast	0232 230355
Ulster Reform	4 Royal Avenue, Belfast	0232 23411
Western	32 Royal Exchange Square, Glasgow 1	041 221 2016
Yorkshire	17 Museum Street, York	0904 24116

DISTINGUISHED WOMEN OF TODAY

Last year Debrett highlighted and welcomed the way Her Majesty The Queen had opened up the Orders of the Garter and Thistle to women. Before this, these had been exclusively male honours.

This year, in line with the policy of awarding due recognition to women, Debrett is including this selective summary of women's progress.

British Politics

The year 1989 marks the seventieth anniversary of the first woman MP, Lady Astor, taking her seat in the House of Commons, yet Britain has one of the lowest proportions of women in Parliament of all European countries. In Scandinavian countries between a quarter and a third of Members of Parliament are women.

The 1987 General Election returned a record total of 41 women to Parliament from 5 political parties.

Betty Boothroyd, MP, is a Deputy Speaker of the House of Commons, only the second woman in that post. Ms Diane Abbott has become Britain's first black woman Member of Parliament. Although 41 women MPs is a record number of women in the House, it is still only 6% of the 650 MPs elected.

On the other hand, Britain's first woman Prime Minister, the Rt Hon Mrs Margaret Thatcher, PC, MP, is still very much at the helm after 10 years at 10 Downing Street. There have been rumours for the past 10 years she may soon add a woman to her Cabinet. Baroness Young is the only woman to have served in Mrs Thatcher's Cabinet, in the early 1980s. Since her departure from Cabinet to become the first woman board member of Marks and Spencer it has remained an all-male body, with the exception of the Prime Minister herself, by contrast with Norway where almost half the Cabinet is female.

Honours

Women are still lacking in the upper echelons of the Honours Lists. Since Conservative Prime Minister Harold Macmillan introduced the Life Peerages Act in 1958, women have only appeared at a ratio of one woman to eight men. There are now 357 life peers of whom 46 are women. In the three Honours Lists from New Year 1987 to New Year 1989, 43 men were given life peerages and just 4 women, Baroness Oppenheim-Barnes, Baroness Hart of South Lanark, Baroness Blackstone and Baroness Blatch.

There are in total 66 women out of 1,188 members of the House of Lords.

In addition to the overwhelming number of male hereditary peers, 26 seats are reserved for the Bishops of the Church of England, though women in the United Kingdom still cannot be ordained priests or consecrated bishops.

Whether we want to reform it, abolish it or keep it, the House of Lords is Britain's upper legislative chamber. For the time being, as constituted, it plays an important part in initiating, investigating, and amending the laws of the land. Such specialist committees of the Lords as the European Committee act as a link between Britain and the European Community.

Members of the House of Lords have individual platforms outside the Palace of Westminster for their voices to be heard.

Happily, when women do get into the Upper Chamber they are treated more equally than in any other institution in the land. Both on party benches and on cross-benches, they are readily promoted and respected. Baroness Seear, former Leader of the Liberal Peers, states 'I can honestly say I have never been in a place that treats you better on male-female equality. And that includes the London School of Economics where I've lectured for years.'

Although HM The Queen actually bestows honours, almost all the names on the New Year and Birthday Honours Lists are suggested by Number 10. It is time the criteria for choosing those who would be of value to the country in the Upper Chamber and on the Public Appointments Committees broadened out, reflecting the very considerable changes taking place in women's contribution to Britain's public and commercial life.

Public Bodies

Women make up 19% of the approximately 44,000 places on public bodies. Some of these posts are both nominated and appointed by Government Departments, noted for the 'old boy' network. Other names are selected from nominations put forward to Government by such outside bodies as trade unions, farmers' organisations, industry, and local authorities, filling posts ranging from the Board of Trustees of the Imperial War Museum or The British Tourist Authority to St Patrick's Training School Management Board, Northern Ireland. A woman was recently appointed Director of The Victoria and Albert Museum. There is a precedent in public appointments for a fair balance of women and men. Magistrates in Britain, are selected from appropriate men and women on virtually a 50/50 basis.

The Law

In the past 70 years women have broken through into many areas of public life, professions, the media, academe, and the business world. Nevertheless, important areas of national life remain overwhelmingly male. Lord Justice Butler-Sloss is the first woman High Court Judge appointed to the 27-member Court of Appeal. There are no women among the 10 members of the House of Lords Appelate Committee, the Highest Court in the land. Now that Dame Rose Heilbron has retired, Dame Margaret Booth is the only woman out of 81 High Court Judges. There are only 17 women out of 404 Circuit Judges. However, more women than men now apply to become solicitors and an equal number of women and men are applying to the bar to become barristers. The number of women judges is expected to increase in the next 10 to 15 years.

Universities

In the academic field although 17% of full-time adademic staff in universities are women, only 3% are professors.

Medicine

In the medical arena, Professor Lesley Rees has recently been appointed the first woman Dean of a large London Hospital, St Bartholomew's. Well over half of community health doctors, a quarter of hospital doctors, and one in five general practitioners are women. Nearly half of all medical students are female. For economic and domestic reasons, many of these women students fail to enter the high prestige medical posts with the result only 2% of surgeons are female.

The Civil Service

Forty-eight per cent of the non-industrial Civil Service are women but they make up only 5% of the top 3 grades. Assistant Chief Scientific Officer Margaret Bourne is the first woman grade 3 at the Ministry of Defence. The numbers of women at grades just below top grades are slowly improving, doubling to 9% since 1982.

Fleet Street

In the traditionally chauvinistic press and media world there are now 3 national newspapers—The People, The News of the World and The Sunday Mirror—with women editors, Wendy Henry, Pat Chapman and Eve Pollard.

The BBC and ITV

On the BBC's important 11-seat Board of Governors there are 2 women, Miss P D James, OBE and Lady Parkes, JP. Pat Ewing has just been appointed controller of the new BBC Radio 5 network but there is a dearth of women in the senior ranks of the BBC. The second highest person at Channel 4 TV is Liz Forgan, Director of Programmes.

Commerce

The boardrooms of Britain are still predominantly male though all but one of the major clearing banks now have at least one woman on their main boards. Only one building society has a woman at its head. However, demographic changes are taking place which will ensure employers recognise a need for many more skilled women employees at all levels. The critical mass of women is moving up the ranks and it is now estimated that 25% of middle management are women.

In many respects 1989 offers a hopeful picture. Advances by women in commercial and public life have certainly been made. The 'critical' mass in politics may almost have been reached where it is no longer unusual to choose women for winnable Parliamentary seats. Many young people in Britain have never known a male Prime Minister at Downing Street. The number of women entrepreneurs ('wenties') is a striking feature of Britain's commercial life. Laws on training, child care, parental leave, part-time working and equality of opportunity promulgated in Brussels will have a profound effect on the advances made by women in Britain which Debrett will hope to highlight as 1992 approaches and Britain becomes more fully integrated into the European Community.

LESLEY ABDELA

LIFE PEERS AND LAW LORDS
*LAW LORDS

Baron Ackner
Baron Alexander of Potterhill
Baron Alexander of Weedon
Baron Allen of Abbeydale
Baron Alport
Baron Annan
Baron Ardwick
Baron Armstrong of Ilminster
Baron Ashby
Baron Aylestone

Baron Balniel (Earl of Crawford)
Baron Bancroft
Baron Banks
Baron Barber
Baron Barnett
Baron Bauer
Baron Beaumont of Whitley
Baron Bellwin
Baron Beloff
Baron Benson
Baron Bernstein
Baron Blake
Baron Blanch
Baron Blease
Baron Boardman
Baron Bonham-Carter
Baron Boston of Faversham
Baron Bottomley
Baron Bowden
Baron Boyd Carpenter
Baron Bramall
*Baron Brandon of Oakbrook
*Baron Bridge of Harwich
Baron Briggs
*Baron Brightman
Baron Brimelow
Baron Brookes
Baron Brooks of Tremorfa
Baron Broxbourne
Baron Bruce of Donington
Baron Bruce-Gardyne
Baron Bullock
Baron Butterworth
Baron Buxton of Alsa

Baron Caccia
Baron Cameron of Lochbroom
Baron Campbell of Alloway
Baron Campbell of Croy
Baron Campbell of Eskan
Baron Caradon
Baron Carmichael of Kelvingrove
Baron Carr of Hadley
Baron Carter
Baron Carver
Baron Cayzer
Baron Chalfont
Baron Chapple
Baron Charteris of Amisfield
Baron Chelmer
Baron Chitnis
Baron Cledwyn of Penrhos
Baron Cockfield
Baron Coggan
Baron Collison
Baron Constantine of Stanmore
Baron Craigton
Baron Crohan
*Baron Cross of Chelsea
Baron Cudlipp

Baron Dacre of Glanton
Baron Dainton
Baron Davies of Penrhys
Baron Dean of Beswick
Baron Deedes
Baron Delfont
*Baron Denning
*Baron Devlin
Baron Diamond
Baron Donald of Lymington
Baron Donaldson of Kingsbridge
Baron Donoghue

Baron Eden of Winton
*Baron Edmund-Davies
Baron Elliott of Morpeth
Baron Elworthy
*Baron Elwyn Jones
Baron Elystan Morgan
Baron Emslie
Baron Ennals
Baron Evans of Claughton
Baron Ezra

Baron Fanshawe of Richmond
Baron Ferrier
Baron Fitt
Baron Fletcher
Baron Flowers
Baron Foot
Baron Forte
Baron Franks
Baron Fraser of Kilmorack

Baron Gallacher
Baron Galpern
Baron Gardiner
Baron Gibson
Baron Gibson-Watt
Baron Glenamara
*Baron Goff of Chieveley
Baron Goodman
Baron Goold
Baron Gormley
Baron Grade
Baron Graham of Edmonton
Baron Granville of Eye
Baron Gray of Contin
Baron Greene of Harrow Weald
Baron Greenhill of Harrow
Baron Gregson
Baron Grey of Naunton
*Baron Griffiths
Baron Grimond

Baron Hailsham of St Marylebone
Baron Hanson
Baron Harmar-Nicholls
Baron Harris of Greenwich
Baron Harris of High Cross
Baron Hartwell

Baron Harvey of Prestbury
Baron Harvington
Baron Hatch of Lusby
Baron Henderson of Brompton
Baron Heycock
Baron Hill of Luton
Baron Hill-Norton
Baron Hirshfield
Baron Holderness
Baron Home of the Hirsel
Baron Hooson
Baron Houghton of Sowerby
Baron Howie of Troon
Baron Hughes
Baron Hunt
Baron Hunt of Tanworth
Baron Hunter of Newington
Baron Hutchinson of Lullington

Baron Ingrow
Baron Irvine of Lairg
Baron Irving of Dartford

Baron Jacques
Baron Jakobovits
Baron James of Rusholme
*Baron Jauncey of Tullichettle
Baron Jenkins of Putney
Baron John-Mackie
Baron Johnston of Rockport

Baron Kaberry of Adel
Baron Kadoorie
Baron Kagan
Baron Kahn
Baron Kearton
Baron Keith of Castleacre
*Baron Keith of Kinkel
*Baron Kilbrandon
*Baron Kimball
Baron King of Wartnaby
Baron King-Hall
Baron Kings Norton
Baron Kirkhill
Baron Kissin

*Baron Lane
Baron Leatherland
Baron Leonard
Baron Lever of Manchester
Baron Lewin
Baron Lloyd of Hampstead
Baron Lloyd of Kilgerran
Baron Lovell-Davies
Baron Lowry

Baron McAlpine of Moffat
Baron McAlpine of West Green
Baron Macaulay of Bragar
Baron McCarthy
Baron McCluskey
Baron McFadzean
Baron McFadzean of Kelvinside
Baron McIntosh of Haringey
Baron MacKay of Clashfern
Baron Mackenzie-Stuart
Baron Mackie of Benshie
Baron Maclean
Baron MacLehose of Beoch
Baron MacLeod of Fuinary
Baron Mais

Baron Marsh
Baron Marshall of Goring
Baron Marshall of Leeds
Baron Matthews
Baron Maude of Stratford-upon-Avon
Baron Mayhew
Baron Mellish
Baron Miles
Baron Mishcon
Baron Molloy
Baron Molson
Baron Moore of Wolvercote
Baron Morris of Grasmere
Baron Morton of Shuna
Baron Moyola
Baron Mulley
Baron Murray of Epping Forest
Baron Murray of Newhaven
Baron Murton of Lindisfarne

Baron Normand
Baron Northfield
Baron Nugent of Guildford

Baron O' Brien of Lothbury
*Baron Oliver of Aylmerton
Baron Olivier
Baron O' Neill of The Maine
Baron Oram
Baron Orr-Ewing

Baron Paget of Northampton
Baron Parry
*Baron Pearce
Baron Penney
Baron Pennock
Baron Perry of Walton
Baron Peston
Baron Peyton of Yeovil
Baron Pitt of Hampstead

Baron Plowden
Baron Plumb
Baron Plummer of St Marylebone
Baron Porritt
Baron Pritchard
Baron Prys-Davies

Baron Quinton

Baron Rawlinson of Ewell
Baron Rayne
Baron Rayner
Baron Rees-Mogg
Baron Reigate
Baron Reilly
Baron Renton
Baron Rhodes
Baron Richardson
Baron Richardson of Duntisbourne
Baron Robens of Woldingham
Baron Roll of Ipsden
*Baron Roskill
Baron Ross of Marnock
Baron Ryder of Eaton Hastings

Baron Sainsbury
Baron Sainsbury of Preston Candover
Baron Saint Brides
*Baron Salmon

Baron Sanderson of Bowden
Baron Scanlon
*Baron Scarman
Baron Schon
Baron Seebohm
Baron Shackleton
Baron Shawcross
Barn Sieff of Brimpton
Baron Simon of Glaisdaile
Baron Smith
Baron Soper
Baron Stallard
Baron Stevens of Ludgate
Baron Stewart of Fulham
Baron Stodart of Leaston
Baron Stoddart of Swindon
Baron Stokes
Baron Stonham
Baron Strauss
Baron Swann

Baron Tanlaw
Baron Taylor of Blackburn
Baron Taylor of Gryfe
Baron Taylor of Hadfield
Baron Taylor of Mansfield
*Baron Templeman
Baron Thomas of Swynnerton
Baron Thomson of Monifieth
Baron Thorneycroft
Baron Todd
Baron Tordoff
Baron Trafford
Baron Tranmire

Baron Underhill

Baron Vinson

Baron Wallace of Campsie
Baron Wallace of Coslany
Baron Walston
Baron Watkins
Baron Wedderburn of Charlton
Baron Weidenfeld
Baron Weinstock
Baron Wells-Pestell
Baron Whaddon
Baron Wigoder
*Baron Wilberforce
Baron Williams of Elvel
Baron Willis
Baron Wilson of Langside
Baron Wilson of Rivaulx
Baron Winstanley
Baron Winterbottom
Baron Wolfson
Baron Wyatt of Weeford

Baron Young of Dartington
Baron Young of Graffham

Baron Zuckerman

LIFE PEERESSES

Baroness Airey of Abingdon

Baroness Bacon
Baroness Birk
Baroness Blackstone
Baroness Blatch
Baroness Brooke of Ystradfellte
Baroness Burton of Coventry

Baroness Carnegy of Lour
Baroness Cox

Baroness David
Baroness Delacourt-Smith of Alteryn
Baroness Denington

Baroness Elles
Baroness Elliot of Harwood
Baroness Ewart-Biggs

Baroness Faithfull
Baroness Falkender
Baroness Fisher of Rednal

Baroness Gaitskell
Baroness Gardner of Parkes

Baroness Hooper
Baroness Hylton-Foster

Baroness Jeger

Baroness Llewelyn-Davies of Hastoe

Baroness McFarlane of Llandaff
Baroness MacLoed of Borve

Baroness Nicol

Baroness Oppenheim-Barnes

Baroness Phillips
Baroness Pike
Baroness Platt of Writtle

Baroness Robson of Kiddington
Baroness Ryder of Warsaw

Baroness Seear
Baroness Serota
Baroness Sharples
Baroness Stedman

Baroness Turner of Camden
Baroness Trumpington

Baroness Vickers

Baroness Warnock
Baroness White

Baroness Young

ROYAL WARRANTS OF APPOINTMENT TO HER MAJESTY QUEEN ELIZABETH II

DEPARTMENT OF HER MAJESTY's PRIVY PURSE

List of Tradesmen in the Department of Her Majesty's Privy Purse permitted to style themselves "By Appointment to Her Majesty The Queen" or "By Appointment to Her Majesty Queen Elizabeth II" and entitling them to display the Royal Arms, but not to fly the Royal Standard. The word "Royal" should not be used without first advising the Secretary, Royal Household Tradesmen's Warrants Committee.

Name	Description	Address
Abbey Rose Gardens	Rose Growers and Nurserymen	Burnham
Aberdeen Coal	Coal Merchants	Aberdeen
Ainsworths Homoeopathic Pharmacy	Chemists	London
Allan & Davidson	Interior Decorators and Painting Contractors	Aberdeen
Allen and Neale (Chemists) Ltd.	Chemists	Heacham, Norfolk
Amies, Hardy Ltd	Dressmakers	London
Anglia Telecomms Limited	Suppliers of Radio Telecommunications and Associated Services	March
Angus Chain Saw Service	Horticultural Engineers	Lawton, by Arbroath
APV Vent-Axia Limited	Suppliers of Unit Ventilation Equipment	Crawley
Archibald, James L. & Sons, Ltd.	Cabinetmakers and Upholsterers	Aberdeen
Ardleigh Swift Ltd.	Manufacturers of Agricultural Machinery	Ardleigh
Armitage Brothers, PLC	Pet Food Manufacturers	Nottingham
Armstrong Addison & Co Ltd.	Suppliers of Preserved Timber Fencing	Sunderland
Army & Navy Stores, Ltd	Suppliers of Household and Fancy Goods	London
Asprey PLC	Goldsmiths, Silversmiths and Jewellers	London
Atco Limited	Manufacturers of Motor Mowers	Stowmarket
BBC Fire Protection Ltd	Purveyors of Fire Protection Systems	Norwich
BICC Pyrotenax Ltd.	Manufacturers and Suppliers of Electric Cable	Hebburn
BOCM Silcock Ltd.	Suppliers of Cattle Foods	Basingstoke
BP Oil Ltd.	Purveyors of Motor Spirit	London
BACO-Compak (Norfolk) Ltd.	Waste Disposal Contractors	Bawsey
Bamford, J. C. Excavators, Ltd.	Manufacturers of Construction and Agricultural Equipment	Rocester
Barbour J. and Sons Ltd.	Manufacturers of Waterproof and Protective Clothing	South Shields
Barnhams Electrical Co. Ltd.	Electrical Contractor	Fakenham
Barrow Hepburn Equipment Ltd	Manufacturers of Royal Maundy Purses	London
Barton & Gant	Suppliers of Agro-Chemicals and Fertilisers	King's Lynn
Bartram Mowers Ltd.	Suppliers of Horticultural Equipment	Norwich
Belling & Co. Ltd.	Manufacturers of Electrical Appliances	Enfield
Bennett-Levy, Valerie M.	Supplier of Nosegays	Haslemere
Bennett, R. S. & Co. Ltd.	Suppliers of Agricultural Machinery and Farm Equipment	Downham Market
Bennett & Fountain PLC	Suppliers of Electrical Equipment	London
Benney, Gerald	Goldsmith and Silversmith	Beenham
Bentley, Joseph, Ltd.	Suppliers of Horticultural Chemicals	Barrow-on-Humber
Berkshire Air and Hydraulics Ltd.	Suppliers of Hydraulic Hose Assemblies	Windsor
Berthoud Limited	Manufacturers of Agricultural Crop Sprayers	King's Lynn
Bestobell Service Co. Ltd.	Maintenance Engineers	Taplow
Billings & Edmonds, Ltd.	Tailors and Outfitters	London
Blackhall, William	Tailor and Outfitter	Tarland
Blooms of Bressingham Limited	Suppliers of Hardy Nursery Stock	Diss
Blue Circle Industries PLC	Cement Manufacturers	London
Boiler Mantenance and Plumbing Repairs	Boiler Service Engineer	Newmarket
Bonk and Company Limited	Suppliers of Multifuel Heating Appliances and Chimney Systems	Inverness
Booker Seeds Limited	Seedsmen	Sleaford
Boots Co. PLC, The	Manufacturing Chemists	Nottingham
Boots The Chemists, Ltd.	Chemists	Nottingham
Bowden, M. D.	Newsagent	Dersingham
Bridger & Kay Ltd.	Postage Stamp Dealer	London
Bridon Fibres Limited	Manufacturers of Agricultural Twine	Doncaster
Brintons, Ltd.	Carpet Manufacturers	Kidderminster
British Olivetti Limited	Manufacturers of Office Equipment	London
Bruce, Simon Limited	Catering Equipment Consultants and Suppliers	Norwich
Buckley, Anthony & Constantine Ltd.	Photographers	London
Burberrys Ltd.	Weatherproofers	London
Burgess, Ben and Company	Suppliers of Agricultural Machinery	Norwich
Bynoth, H. C.	Roofing Contractor	King's Lynn
Calders Limited	Suppliers of Diamond Braced Field Gates	Brandon, Suffolk
Caleys (Cole Brothers Ltd.)	Suppliers of Household and Fancy Goods	Windsor
Callander, R. F.	Drystane Dyker	Finzean
Calman Links (Trading) Ltd.	Furriers	London
Calor Gas Ltd.	Suppliers of Liquefied Petroleum Gas	Slough
Car-Men Supplies Limited	Supplies of Agricultural and Industrial Equipment	Corby
Carters Tested Seeds Ltd.	Seedsmen	Llangollen

Case International	Manufacturers of Agricultural Machinery	Doncaster
Cash, J. & J., Ltd.	Manufacturers of Woven Name Tapes	Coventry
Cassie, Alistair	TV Suppliers and Engineer	Ballater
Cassie, William C.	Pianoforte Tuner	Aberdeen
Century Oils Limited	Suppliers of Agricultural and Horticultural Lubricant	Stoke-on-Trent
Chafer, J. W. Ltd.	Suppliers of Agricultural Chemicals	Doncaster
Charrington-Hargreaves	Suppliers of Fuel Oils	Bishops Stortford
Charringtons Solid Fuel	Coal Merchants	Huntingdon
Chase, W. D. (Builder)	Builder and Contractor	King's Lynn
Child, G. E. & Son Ltd.	Electrical Contractor	King's Lynn
Chubb Alarms Ltd.	Installers of Intruder Alarms	Walton-on-Thames
Chubb & Son's Lock and Safe Co., Ltd.	Patent Lock and Safe Makers	Feltham
Ciba-Geigy Agrochemicals	Manufacturers of Crop Protection Chemicals	Cambridge
Clark, A. A. Ltd.	Automobile Engineers	Windsor
Coalite Building Supplies	Suppliers of Building Materials	King's Lynn
Cocker, James & Sons	Suppliers of Roses	Aberdeen
Coe, C. & C. (Bircham) Limited	Haulage Contractors	Bircham, King's Lynn
Collie, Peter S.	Suppliers of Game Food	Aberdeen
Collingwood of Bond Street Limited	Jewellers and Silversmiths	London
Colt, W. H. Son & Co. Ltd.	Suppliers of Pre-Fabricated Timber Framed Houses	Bethersden, Ashford
Coopers Animal Health Limited	Manufacturers of Animal Health and Hygiene Products	Crewe
Countrywear	Field Sports Outfitter	Ballater
Cox, Harold & Sons (Jewellers), Ltd.	Jewellers	Windsor
C. P. & B. (Haulage) Ltd.	Suppliers of Woodshavings	Diss
Crawford, Robert H. & Son	Suppliers of Agricultural Machinery	Boston, Lincolnshire
Crompton Parkinson Ltd.	Manufacturers of Electrical Lamps	Northampton
Crossley Ferguson	Suppliers of Building Materials	Stockon-on-Tees
Crown Berger Europe Limited	Manufacturers of Paints and Wallcoverings	Darwen
Culford Fencing Limited	Suppliers of Specialist Fencing	Bury St. Edmunds
Cyclax Ltd.	Manufacturers of Beauty Preparations	London
Dacrylate Paints Limited	Manufacturers of Paint Varnishes and Emulsions	Kirkby-in-Ashfield
Dale, Frank H. Ltd.	Suppliers of Farm Buildings and Tubular Equipment	Leominster
Dalgety Agriculture Ltd.	Manufacturers of Animal Feeds	Bristol
Dalton Supplies Ltd.	Manufacturers of Animal Identification Equipment	Nettlebed
Daniel, Neville Ltd.	Hairdressers	London
Darby Nursery Stock Ltd..	Suppliers of Ornamental Shrubs and Trees	Thetford
Day, Thomas Motors Ltd.	Motor Vehicle Suppliers	Fleet
Deas, John. D. and Company Limited	Suppliers of Kitchen Equipment	Glasgow
Deere, John Ltd.	Suppliers of Agriculture Equipment	Nottingham
Delamore, R. Ltd.	Suppliers of Chrysanthemum Stock	Wisbech
Dennison PLC	Suppliers of Gift Wrapping Material	Watford
D.E.R. Ltd.	Suppliers of Television Receivers	Chertsey
Devlin Stuart Ltd.	Goldsmith and Jeweller	London
Dilloway, P. W. Ltd.	Agricultural Engineers	Swindon
Dobbie & Co., Ltd.	Seedsmen and Nurserymen	Lasswade
Dodson and Horrell Limited	Horse Feed Manufacturers	Kettering
Double Paul Nurseries Limited	Tree Nurseryman	Ipswich
Dow Agriculture	Suppliers of Agricultural Insecticides, Fungicides and Foliar Feeds.	Hitchin
Drake & Fletcher, Ltd.	Manufacturers of Agricultural Spraying Machinery	Maidstone
Driscoll	Tailors	Eastbourne
Dunhill, Alfred, Ltd.	Suppliers of Smokers' Requisites	London
Dynatron Radio Ltd.	Manufacturers of Television and Radiogramophones	West Molesey
Eastern Counties Farmers Ltd.	Suppliers of Agricultural Products	Ipswich
Edmondson, R. C. Ltd.	Suppliers of Motor Vehicles and Agricultural Machinery	Fakenham
Edwardes (Camberwell) Ltd.	Suppliers of Mopeds	London
Eldernell Vehicles	Suppliers of Agricultural Vehicles	Peterborough
Elliott, Thomas, Ltd.	Suppliers of Fertilisers and Peat	Hayes, Kent
Ellis and McHardy Oils	Oil Distributors	Aberdeen
Elsoms Seeds Ltd.	Seedsmen	Spalding
En-tout-cas plc	Manufacturers of Tennis Courts	Leicester
Equiform Nutrition Ltd.	Suppliers of Equine Vitamin Supplements and Feed Additives.	Grimsby
Eutectic-Castolin	Supplier of Maintenance Welding Materials	Feltham
Ewers, D. and G. Pet Supplies	Bird Seed Supplier	Windsor
Express Lift Co., Ltd.	Manufacturers and Suppliers of Passenger Lifts	Northampton
FMC Corporation (U.K.) Limited	Suppliers of Pea Harvesting Equipment	Fakenham
FSL Bells, Ltd.	Manufacturers of Animal Feed Supplements	Corsham
FARGRO Ltd.	Horticultural Sundriesmen	Littlehampton
Farm Health Limited	Suppliers of Animal Health, Dairy Hygiene and Nutritional Products	Alton
Farmwork Services (Eastern) Ltd.	Agricultural and Spraying Contractors	Holbeach
Fen Ditching Company	Land Drainage Contractors	Wisbech
Fisons PLC	Manufacturers of Horticultural Products	Ipswich
Fleming, John & Co. Ltd.	Timber Merchants	Aberdeen

Forces Help Society and Lord Roberts Workshops, The	Manufacturers of Fancy Goods	London
Fosroc Ltd.—Timber Treatments Division	Manufacturers of Wood Preservatives	Marlow
Fossitt and Thorne	Tyre Distributors and Service	Boston, Lincolnshire
Fox, Frederick Ltd.	Milliner	London
Fraser, G. R., & Co.	Printers and Stationers	Aberdeen
Frasers, Edinburgh	House Furnishers	Edinburgh
Fyfe, John, Limited	Supplier of Quarry and Concrete Products	Aberdeen
Gallyon & Sons, Ltd.	Gunsmiths	Norwich
Gascoigne Milking Equipment Ltd.	Milking Machine Manufacturers	Reading
Gates Rubber Company Limited, The	Manufacturers of Waterproof Rubber Footwear	Dumfries
General Trading Co. (Mayfair) Ltd., The	Suppliers of Fancy Goods	London
Gibbons, Stanley Limited	Philatelists	London
Gibbs, J. Ltd.	Suppliers of Agricultural Machinery and Implements	Feltham
Gibson Saddlers Ltd.	Suppliers of Racing Colours	Newmarket
Gilbertson & Page Ltd.	Manufacturer of Dog and Game Food	Colney Heath
Gladwell, H. G. & Sons Limited	Millers and Agricultural Merchants	Ipswich
Goodyear, Edward Ltd.	Florist	London
Grugeon, Peter Studio	Photographer	Reading
Guardian Window Co., Ltd.	Manufacturers and Suppliers of Double Glazing	King's Lynn
Halcyon Days Ltd	Suppliers of Objets d'Art	London
Hall and Tawse Scotland Limited	Building Contractors	Northfield
Hallam (E. C. Engineering, Leicester) Ltd.	Manufacturers of Construction Machinery	Leicester
Hamblin, Theodore Ltd.	Opticians	London
Hamleys of Regent Street Ltd.	Toy and Sports Merchants	London
Hardie, R. G. & Co.	Bagpipe Makers	Glasgow
Hardy Brothers, Ltd.	Silversmiths	Sydney
Hardy Minnis	Mercers of Woollen Cloth	Stroud
Harris, L. G. & Co. Ltd.	Manufacturers of Paint Brushes and Painters Tools	Stoke Prior
Hartnell, Norman, Ltd	Dressmakers	London
Hatchards	Booksellers	London
Hayters PLC	Manufacturers of Agricultural Machinery	Bishop's Stortford
Haythornthwaite & Sons, Ltd.	Manufacturers of Grenfell Garments	Burnley
Heaton, Wallace Limited	Suppliers of Photographic Equipment	London
Henderson, J. & W. Ltd. Paint and Wallpaper Division	Suppliers of Paint and Wallpaper	Aberdeen
Hilleshög (United Kingdom) Limited	Seed Suppliers	Docking
Hillier Nurseries (Winchester) Ltd.	Nurserymen and Seedsmen	Ampfield
Hilling Woodshavings	Suppliers of Baled Woodshavings	Tushingham
Holme Park Game Hatcheries	Suppliers of Stock Game	Wokingham
Horrockses Fashions, Ltd.	Dressmakers	Milton Keynes
Horse Requisites Newmarket Ltd.	Suppliers of Equine Products	Newmarket
Houseman (Burnham) Ltd.	Specialists in Water Treatment Services	Burnham, Buckinghamshire
Humber Fertilisers Limited	Fertiliser Manufacturers	Hull
Hydro Fertilizers Limited	Manufacturers of Agricultural Fertilisers	Ipswich
I.R.S. Ltd.	Sign and Notice Manufacturer	Swaffham
Imperial Business Equipment Ltd.	Suppliers of Typewriters	London
ICI Agrochemicals	Manufacturers of Crop Protection Chemicals	Haslemere
ICI Fertilisers	Manufacturers of Fertilisers	Cleveland
ICI Seeds UK Limited	Seedsmen	Boston, Lincolnshire
Institution Supplies (Leeds) Ltd.	Manufacturers of Luggage Trolleys and Accessories	Leeds
James, Cornelia Ltd.	Glove Manufacturer	Brighton
James and Son (Grain Merchants) Ltd.	Suppliers of Animal Feeding Stuffs	London
John, C. (Rare Rugs) Ltd.	Suppliers of Carpets	London
Johnson Brothers	Manufacturers of Ceramic Tableware	Stoke-on-Trent
Johnson, Herbert (Bond Street) Ltd.	Hatters	London
Jollye, Leonard F. (Brookmans Park), Ltd.	Forage Merchant	Enfield
Kango Ltd.	Suppliers of Electrical Equipment	London
Kardex Systems (UK) Limited	Manufacturers of Office Machines and Equipment	London
Kemira Fertilisers	Manufacturers of Agricultural Fertilisers	Chester
Kerner-Greenwood & Co. Ltd.	Manufacturer of Waterproofing Material	Mansfield
Kidd Farm Machinery Ltd.	Manufacturers of Farm Machinery	Devizes
Kilian & Crisp (Great Baddow) Ltd.	Suppliers of Horticultural Chemicals	Great Baddow
Kilian, H. Ltd.	Manufacturer of Horticultural Packaging	Great Baddow
King, John K. & Sons, Ltd.	Seedsmen	Coggeshall
Kinloch Anderson	Tailors and Kiltmakers	Edinburgh
Knight, Peter (Beaconsfield) Ltd.	Suppliers of Interior Furnishings	Beaconsfield
Knight, Peter (Esher) Ltd.	Suppliers of Fancy Goods and Lighting	Esher
Kodak, Ltd.	Manufacturers of Photographic Supplies	Hemel Hempstead
LEP (Bloodstock) Ltd.	International Bloodstock Forwarders	Newmarket
Lambert, James & Sons, Ltd.	Suppliers of Building Materials	Snettisham
Lambourn Racehorse Transport Limited	Horse Transport Contractors	Lambourn
Langton, W. E.	Suppliers of Milking Machine Components	Coventry

Latham, James PLC	Wood Merchants	London
Latter, G. P. and Company (Engineers) Limited	General Engineers	Windsor
Launer, S. & Co. (London) Ltd.	Manufacturers of Handbags	Croydon
Leech, Ken Trees	Fruit Tree Nurserymen	Bulmer Tye Sudbury
Lewis East Ltd.	Manufacturers of Stationery	Leicester
Leyland DAF Ltd.	Manufacturers of Commercial Vehicles	Preston
Leyland Paint Company, The	Supplier of Decorative Paints	Batley
Lidstone, Midwinter Limited	Suppliers of Animal Feed, Seed, Fertiliser and Crop Protection Chemicals.	Newbury
Lilliman and Cox, Ltd.	Dry Cleaners	London
Lillywhites, Ltd.	Outfitters	London
Lincolnshire Drainage Co. Ltd.	Drainage Contractors	Boston
Lindisposables Limited	Suppliers of Cleaning and Catering Disposable Products	Boston
Lister Shearing Equipment Limited	Manufacturers of Animal Health Care Products	Gloucester
Lock, S., Ltd.	Embroiderers	London
London Brick Company Limited	Brick Makers	Bedford
Longmire, Paul, Ltd.	Supplier of Jewellery and Leather Goods	London
Luda Pet Food Limited	Dog and Game Food Manufacturers	Louth
Lusher, W. S. & Sons, Ltd.	Building Contractor	Norwich
M.K. Electric Limited	Manufacturers of Electrical Equipment	London
Malloch, P.D.	Suppliers of Shooting and Fishing Equipment	Perth
Mann, Egerton & Co. Ltd.	Automobile Engineers	Norwich
Marley Building Systems Limited	Building Manufacturers and Constructors	Godalming
Marley Floors Ltd.	Suppliers of Floor Tiles	Maidstone
Marley Roof Tile Co. Ltd., The	Suppliers of Roof Tiles	Sevenoaks
Massey Ferguson (U.K.) Ltd.	Manufacturers of Agricultural Machinery	London
Maxwell, Henry & Co. Ltd.	Bootmakers	London
May & Baker Ltd.	Manufacturers of Agricultural Herbicides	Dagenham
May, H. (Ascot) Ltd.	Automobile Engineers	Ascot
McArthur Group Limited	Suppliers of Fencing, Wire Products and Ironmongery	Bristol
Meadham and Rampton	Builders	Kingsclere
Merryweather & Sons, Ltd.	Fire Engineers	Hyde, Cheshire
Meyer and Mortimer, Ltd.	Military Outfitters	London
Mill Feed Company Limited, The	Mobile Compounders and Suppliers of Animal Feed	Lincoln
Minns Bros. Ltd.	Builders	Sedgeford, Hunstanton
Mirman, Simone	Milliner	London
Mobil Oil Co., Ltd.	Suppliers of Petroleum Fuels and Lubricants	London
Moir, W.	Clock Repairer	Aberdeen
Morris, Green Machinery (Sussex) Ltd.	Manufacturers of Agricultural Machinery	Worthing
Mowlem, John & Co., PLC	Building Contractors	Brentford
Murkett Brothers, Ltd.	Suppliers of Motor Vehicles	Huntington
Murray, J. & D.	Chemists	Ballater
NCR Limited	Suppliers of Electronic Accounting Systems	London
NDS Animal Feeds	Suppliers of Dogfood	Nairn
NEI International Combustion Ltd.	Cochran Boilermakers	Annan
NRS Limited	Manufacturers of Refrigerating Machinery	Newbury
National Foaling Bank	Supplier of Foster Mares for Orphan Foals	Newport, Shropshire
Netlon Ltd.	Manufacturers of Plastic Mesh	Blackburn
Newey & Eyre Ltd.	Suppliers of Industrial and Domestic Electrical Equipment	Edgbaston
Nickerson Seeds Ltd.	Seed Merchants	Lincoln
Norfolk Seeds Ltd.	Seedsmen	Fakenham
Norfolk Steel Stockholders Ltd.	Suppliers of Steel Products	King's Lynn
Northern Heating Supplies Limited	Suppliers of Central Heating Equipment	Aberdeen
Notcutts Nurseries Ltd.	Nurserymen	Woodbridge
Nu-way Ltd.	Manufacturers of Combustion Equipment	Droitwich
O'Hanlon & Co. Ltd., Wm.	Suppliers of Window Shade Fabrics	Manchester
Office International (Eastern Counties) Limited	Supplies of Office Stationery and Equipment	King's Lynn
Olympia Business Machines Co. Ltd.	Suppliers of Office Equipment	London
Page, J. & E. (Sales) Ltd.	Florist	London
Papworth Industries	Travel Goods Makers	Cambridge
Parker Pen UK Ltd.	Manufacturers of Pens, Pencils and Ink	Newhaven
Patman of Cambridge	Clock Repairer	Cambridge
Pattrick and Thompsons Limited	Timber Merchants	King's Lynn
Pauls Agriculture Ltd.	Manufacturers of Animal Feeding Stuffs	Ipswich
Peden International Transport Limited	Bloodstock Shipping Agents	Newbury
Pedigree Petfoods	Manufacturers of Canned Dog Food	Melton Mowbray
Pertwee Holdings Limited	Suppliers of Horticultural Chemicals	Colchester
Pilkington Glass Ltd.	Manufacturers and Suppliers of Glass	St. Helens
Planned Maintenance Painting Limited	Painter and Decorator	Glasgow
Plaspak (UK) Ltd.	Polyethylene Film and Bag Manufacturers	Swindon
Pleyer and Morton Limited	Manufacturers of Equine Products and Equipment	Telford
Pratt & Leslie Jones Ltd.	Suppliers of Fancy Goods	Windsor

Price, Arthur & Co. Ltd.	Cutlers and Silversmiths	Lichfield
Pringle, J.	Motor Engineer	Ballater
Pringle of Scotland, Limited	Manufacturers of Knitted Garments	Hawick
Protim Services Ltd.	Damp Proofing and Timber Treatment Specialists	Hayes
Purdey, James & Sons, Ltd.	Gun and Cartridge Makers	London
Rank Xerox Ltd.	Manufacturers and Suppliers of Xerographic Copying Equipment and Materials	Marlow
Ransoms Sims and Jeffries, PLC	Manufacturers of Agricultural and Horticultural Machinery	Ipswich
Rayne, H. & M. Ltd.	Shoemakers and Handbag Manufacturers	London
Redmayne, S. Ltd.	Tailors	Wigton
Reekie Engineering Ltd.	Suppliers of Agricultural Machinery	Arbroath
Reid, Ben & Co. Ltd.	Nurserymen and Seedsmen	Aberdeen
Remploy Ltd.	Manufacturers of Knitwear	London
Rentokil, Ltd.	Pest Control and Timber Preservation Services and Products	Felcourt
Rexel Business Machines Limited	Manufacturers of Security Shredding Machines	Aylesbury
Rexel Limited	Suppliers of Office Equipment	Aylesbury
Rigby, John & Co. (Gunmakers) Ltd.	Rifle and Cartridge Makers	London
Rigby and Peller	Corsetières	Croydon
Riverside Garage	Automobile and Electrical Engineers	Ballater
Roberts Radio Co., Ltd.	Radio Manufacturers	West Molesey
Rony	Belt Maker	London
Ross Breeders Ltd.	Suppliers of Ross Live Poultry	Newbridge, Midlothian
Rowe, Frank	Suppliers of Chrysanthemum Stock	Wellington, Somerset
Royal Albert Limited	Manufacturers of Paragon Fine Bone China	Stoke-on-Trent
Royal British Legion Poppy Factory Ltd., The	The Royal British Legion Poppy Manufacturers and Supplier of Rosettes	Richmond
Russell, Gordon Ltd.	Manufacturers of Furniture	Broadway
Sanderson, Arthur & Sons Ltd.	Suppliers of Wallpapers, Paints and Fabrics	Uxbridge
Sanderson (Forklifts) Limited	Manufacturers of Material Handling Equipment	Skegness
Savory & Moore, Ltd.	Chemists	Leighton Buzzard
Schering Agrochemicals Limited	Manufacturers of Agrochemicals	Hauxton
Scottish Agricultural Industries PLC	Manufacturers of Fertilisers and Seeds	Edinburgh
Securicor Ltd.	Express Parcel Carriers	Sutton
Sellers, Derek Home Choose Carpets Limited	Carpet and Floor Covering Supplier	Ingoldisthorpe
Semex (UK) Sales Ltd.	Suppliers of Cattle Breeding Services	Dalrymple, Ayrshire
Simmonds Brothers and Sons Limited	Building Contractor	London
Simpson (Piccadilly) Ltd.	Outfitters	London
Smith, James (Scotland Nurseries), Ltd.	Nurserymen	Matlock
Smith, W. and Son, Ltd.	Seedsmen and Nurserymen	Aberdeen
Smythson, Frank	Stationers	London
Solignum Ltd.	Manufacturers of Wood Preservatives	Crayford
Southern Tree Surgeons Ltd.	Tree Surgeons	Crawley
Sovereign Chemical Industries Limited	Building Material Manufacturers	Barrow-in-Furness
Spencer (Aberdeen) PLC	Manufacturers of Paints and Putties	Aberdeen
Spey Pheasantries	Suppliers of Ex Laying Pheasants and Pheasant Poults	Grantown-on-Spey
Spink & Son, Ltd.	Medallists	London
Spratt's Patent Ltd.	Suppliers of Dog Foods	New Moldon
Stanton Hope, Ltd.	Suppliers of Forestry Equipment	Laindon
Star Horse Transport	Horse Transporter	Ely
Steinway & Sons	Pianoforte Manufacturers	London
Stenner of Tiverton Ltd.	Manufacturers and Suppliers of Sawmilling Machinery	Tiverton
Store Design Ltd.	Shopfitters	Dunfermline
Stuart, A. G. Limited	Suppliers of Timber Buildings	Insch
Suttons Seeds Ltd.	Seedsmen	Torquay
Tate, Anthony	Chemist	London
Taylor O. A. & Sons Bulbs Ltd.	Bulb Growers	Holbeach
Technoproof, Ltd.	Roofing Contractors	Newbury
Thwaites and Reed Ltd.	Turret Clockmakers	Hastings
Thomas, Ian	Dressmaker	London
Thorn Lighting Ltd.	Manufacturers of Electric Lamps	Enfield
Timber, H. G. Ltd.	Suppliers of Timber Products	Hayes
Valentines of Dundee Ltd.	Suppliers of Christmas Cards and Calendars	Dundee
Vitax Limited	Manufacturers of Fertilisers and Insecticides	Skelmersdale
Wallace, Cameron & Co., Ltd.	Manufacturers and Suppliers of Ultraplast First Aid Dressings	Glasgow
Wartski Ltd	Jewellers	London
Weatherill, Bernard, Ltd.	Riding Clothes Outfitters and Livery Tailors	London
West Norfolk Super Lime Company, Ltd.	Suppliers and Distributors of Agricultural Lime	Hillington, King's Lynn
Wigg & Plowright—Dalgety Engineers Ltd.	Suppliers of Agricultural Machines	Fakenham
Wilder, John (Agricultural) Ltd.	Suppliers of Agricultural Machinery	Wallingford, Oxon
Wilson, William & Co. (Aberdeen) Ltd.	Suppliers of Plumbing, Electrical and Building Materials	Aberdeen
Wimpey Asphalt Ltd.	Road Surfacing Contractors	London
Witney Blanket Co., Ltd.	Bedding Manufacturers	Gateshead
Wood, William & Son, Ltd.	Garden Contractors and Horticultural Builders	Taplow
Wright, Rain Ltd.	Manufacturers of Irrigation Equipment	Ringwood

ROYAL WARRANTS OF APPOINTMENT TO HER MAJESTY QUEEN ELIZABETH II

DEPARTMENT OF THE MASTER OF THE HOUSEHOLD

List of Tradesmen in the Department of the Master of the Household permitted to style themselves "By Appointment to Her Majesty The Queen" or "By Appointment to Her Majesty Queen Elizabeth II" and entitling them to display the Royal Arms, but not to fly the Royal Standard. The word "Royal" should not be used without first advising the Secretary, Royal Household Tradesmen's Warrants Committee.

Name	Description	Address
Abels of Watton Limited	Removals and Storage Contractor	Thetford
Aberdeen Meat Marketing Ltd.	Suppliers of Beef and Lamb	Banchory
Afia Carpets Limited	Carpet Suppliers	London
Agma PLC	Manufacturers of Cleaning and Hygiene Products	Northumberland
Airwick (UK) Limited	Manufacturers of Airwick	Hull
Angostura Bitters (Dr. J. G. B. Siegert & Sons), Ltd.	Manufacturers of Angostura Aromatic Bitters	Trinidad
Ardath Tobacco Co., Ltd.	Suppliers of Cigarettes	London
Arden, Elizabeth, Ltd.	Manufacturers of Cosmetics	London
Armstrong World Industries Ltd.	Manufacturers of Floor Covering	Uxbridge
"At-A-Glance" Calendar Company Limited	Calendar Manufacturers	London
Baker G. P. and J. Ltd.	Suppliers of Furnishing Fabrics and Wallcoverings	High Wycombe
Balls Albert (King's Lynn) Ltd.	Wholesale Fish and Shellfish Merchant	King's Lynn
Barnard and Westwood Limited	Printers and Stationers	London
Bartholomew, John & Son Ltd.	Suppliers of Maps	Edinburgh
Bass Brewing Ltd.	Brewers	Burton-on-Trent
Baxter, G. G. Ltd.	Suppliers of Pork Sausages	Birchington-on-Sea
Baxter, James & Son	Purveyors of Potted Shrimps	Morecambe
Baxter, W. A., & Sons Ltd.	Fruit Canners	Fochabers
Beecham Products	Suppliers of Lucozade and Shloer	Brentford
Bendicks (Mayfair), Ltd.	Manufacturers of Chocolates	Winchester
Benoist, V. Ltd.	Purveyors of Table Delicacies	London
Benson & Hedges Limited	Tobacconists	London
Berkel Ltd.	Manufacturers of Slicing Machines	Leicester
Berry Bros. & Rudd, Ltd.	Wine and Spirit Merchants	London
Black & Edgington Hire Ltd.	Tent and Flag Makers	London
Bollom, J. W. & Co. Ltd. Trading as Henry Flack Ltd.	Manufacturers of French Polishes and Lacquers	Beckenham
Booth's Distilleries Limited	Gin Distillers	London
Brentfords	Bedlinen Suppliers	Cramlington, Northumberland
British Sugar plc	Manufacturers of Sugar	Peterborough
British Van Heusen Company Ltd., The	Shirt Makers	Taunton
Broadwood, John & Sons Ltd.	Pianoforte Manufacturers	Milton Keynes
Bronnley, H. & Co., Ltd	Toilet Soap Makers	London
Brooks W. & Son (UYC Foods Ltd.)	Purveyors of Frozen Food	London
Bryant & May Ltd.	Match Manufacturers	High Wycombe
Buchanan, James & Co., Ltd.	Scotch Whisky Distillers	London
Bulmer, H. P. Limited	Cider Makers	Hereford
Burgess, John & Son, Ltd.	Manufacturers of Pastes and Condiment Sauces	London
Burton Son & Saunders, Ltd.	Manufacturers of Fondant	Ipswich
Bury Cooper Whitehead Ltd.	Felt and Carpet Manufacturers	Bury
C.P.C. (United Kingdom) Ltd.	Manufacturers of Corn Oil and Cornflour	Esher
Cadbury Limited	Cocoa and Chocolate Manufacturers	Bournville
Campbell Brothers	Purveyors of Meat and Poultry	Edinburgh
Campbell George and Sons (Fishmongers) Ltd.	Suppliers of Fish and Poultry	Edinburgh
Carlsberg Brewery Ltd.	Suppliers of Lager Beer	Northampton
Carnell, J. W. Limited	Coach Hirers	Sutton Bridge, Spalding
Carr's of Carlisle Ltd.	Biscuit Manufacturers	Carlisle
Castle Pharmacy	Pharmaceutical Chemists	Windsor
Cerebos	Suppliers of Table Salt and Pepper	London
Chalmers, David Limited	Fruit and Vegetable Supplier	Elgin
Champagne J. Bollinger, S.A.	Purveyors of Champagne	Ay-Champagne
Champagne Heidsieck & Co. Monopole, S.A.	Purveyors of Champagne	Reims
Champagne Lanson Pere et Fils	Purveyors of Champagne	Reims
Champagne Louis Roederer	Purveyors of Champagne	Reims
Champagne Moet & Chandon	Purveyors of Champagne	Epernay
Charbonnel et Walker Ltd.	Chocolate Manufacturers	London
Clare House Limited	Suppliers of Lampshades and Fittings	London
Clyde Canvas Goods & Structures Ltd. (Trading as Purvis Equipments).	Manufacturer and Hirer of Marquees	Leith
Coca-Cola Great Britain Limited	Suppliers of Soft Drinks	London

Cole and Son (Wallpapers) Ltd.	Suppliers of Wallpapers	London
Coloroll Carpets Limited	Carpet Manufacturers	Kidderminster
Colmans of Norwich	Manufacturers of Mustard and Sauces	Norwich
Cooper, Frank, Ltd.	Marmalade Manufacturers	Esher
Cope & Timmins Ltd.	Brass Finishers and Spring Makers	London
Corney & Barrow Limited	Wine Merchants	London
County Window Cleaning & Steam Carpet Beating Company, The	Window Cleaners	Reading
Crawford, D. S. (Catering)	Caterers	Edinburgh
Crawford, William & Sons, Ltd.	Biscuit Manufacturers	Edinburgh
Cromessol Company Limited	Manufacturers and Suppliers of Disinfectants and Detergents	Glasgow
Cross Paperware Ltd.	Manufacturers of Disposable Tableware	Dunstable
Crosse and Blackwell	Purveyors of Preserved Provisions	Croydon
Darville & Son, Ltd.	Grocers	Windsor
Davies, Bruce Limited	Fruit and Vegetable Merchant	London
—Trading as Robert Bruce		
De Blank, Justin (Provisions) Ltd.	Baker	London
Dewar, John & Sons, Ltd.	Scotch Whisky Distillers	Perth
Dewhurst J. H. Ltd.	Butcher	London
Dobbins, J. T. Limited	Suppliers of Household Cleaning Materials	Liverpool
Domecq (U.K.) Ltd.	Suppliers of Domecq Sherry	London
Donaldson, Andrew, Ltd.	Suppliers of Fish and Ice	King's Lynn
Drew, Clark & Co. Ltd.	Manufacturers of Ladders	London
Dubois Chemicals Ltd.	Suppliers of Dishwashing Compounds and Controls	Wembley
Early's of Witney PLC	Manufacturers of Blankets	Witney
Electrolux Ltd.	Suppliers of Suction Cleaners and Floor Polishers	Luton
Express Foods Group Ltd.	Dairy Suppliers South	Ruislip
Fenland Laundries Limited	Launderers and Cleaners	Skegness
Ferrari, S. & Sons (Soho), Ltd.	Suppliers of Kitchen Equipment	London
Findlater Mackie Todd & Co. Ltd.	Wine and Spirit Merchants	London
Findus	Suppliers of Frozen Food	Croydon
Fitch and Sons, Limited	Provision Merchants	London
Floris, J. Ltd.	Perfumers	London
Footsure South Eastern Limited	Safety Footware Supplier	London
Fortnum & Mason PLC	Grocers and Provision Merchants	London
Foster, John & Co. Ltd.	Suppliers of Furnishing Fabrics	London
Frigicold Limited	Suppliers of Freezer Ware Packaging	Shipley, West Yorkshire
Gainsborough Silk Weaving Co. Ltd., The	Manufacturers of Furnishing Fabrics	Chilton, Sudbury
Gaskell Textiles Ltd.	Manufacturers of Carpet Underlays	Bacup
Gaunt, J. R, and Son Ltd.	Ribbon Suppliers	Birmingham
Gaymer, William, & Son Ltd.	Cyder Manufacturers	Attleborough
Givan's Irish Linen Stores Limited	Linen Drapers	London
Gloag, Matthew & Son Ltd.	Scotch Whisky Blenders	Perth
Goddard, J. & Sons, Ltd.	Manufacturers of Silver and Metal Polishes	Camberley
Goldenlay Eggs Ltd.	Supplier of Eggs	Drighlington
Goode, Thomas & Co. Ltd.	Suppliers of China and Glass	London
Gray, James & Son (Ironmongers & Electricians) Ltd.	Suppliers of Cleaning Materials	Edinburgh
Guinness PLC	Brewers	London
H.P. Foods Limited	Manufacturers of HP Sauces	Market Harborough
Hamilton & Inches Ltd.	Silversmiths and Clock Specialists	Edinburgh
Harris, C. & T. (Calne) Limited	Manufacturers of Bacon and Sausages	London
Harrods Ltd.	Suppliers of Provisions and Household Goods	London
Harvey, John & Sons Ltd	Wine Merchants	Bristol
Hawker, James, & Co. Ltd.	Purveyors of Sloe Gin	Wokingham
Heal and Son Ltd.	Upholsterers and Suppliers of Bedding	London
Heering, Peter F.	Purveyors of Cherry Heering	Haslev, Denmark
Heinz, H. J., Company Ltd.	Purveyors of Heinz Products	Hayes, Middlesex
Higgins, H. R. (Coffee-man) Ltd.	Coffee Merchants	London
Hill Brush Co. (Mere), The	Manufacturers of Household Brushware	Mere
Hill Thomson & Co. Ltd.	Scotch Whisky Distillers	Edinburgh
Hine, Thomas & Co.	Suppliers of Cognac	Jarnac, France
Hodgkiss H. and Son Limited	Fishmonger	Windsor
Hooper Struve & Co. Ltd.	Mineral Water Manufacturers	Chelmsford
Hoover PLC	Manufacturers of Vacuum Cleaners and Laundry Equipment	Merthyr Tydfil, South Wales
Horne Brothers PLC	Livery Tailors	London
Hunter and Hyland Limited	Suppliers of Curtain Rails and Upholstery Fittings	Leatherhead
Huntley & Palmers Ltd.	Biscuit Manufacturers	Reading
Hyams & Cockerton Ltd.	Purveyors of Fruits and Vegetables	London
Hypnos Limited	Upholsterers and Bedding Manufacturers	Princes Risborough
Idris Ltd.	Manufacturers of Mineral Water and Fruit Beverages	Chelmsford
Ind Coope Ltd.	Brewers of Ale and Lager	London
Jacob & Co., W. & R. (Liverpool) Ltd.	Biscuit Manufacturers	Liverpool

Jaeggi, Leon & Sons, Ltd.	Suppliers of Catering Utensils and Equipment	London
Jenners, Princes Street, Edinburgh, Limited	Suppliers of Furnishing Materials	Edinburgh
Jet Carpet Cleaners Ltd.	Carpet Cleaners	Uxbridge
Johnson Wax Ltd.	Manufacturers of Wax Polishes, Cleaner and Hygiene Products	Camberley
Jones, Yarrell & Co., Ltd.	Newsagents	London
Justerini & Brooks Ltd.	Wine Merchants	London
Kellogg Company of Great Britain Limited	Purveyors of Cereals	Manchester
Kennerty Farm Dairies Ltd.	Suppliers of Milk and Dairy Products	Aberdeen
Kent, G. B. and Sons PLC	Brush Makers	Hemel Hempstead
Kirkness & Gorie	Supplier of Honey	Kirkwall
Kleen-Way (Berkshire) Co.	Chimney Sweepers	Bracknell
Knight's Gallery	Mount Cutters and Picture Framers	Luton
Knowles & Sons (Fruiterers), Ltd.	Purveyors of Fruit and Vegetables	Aberdeen
Krug, Vins, Fins de Champagne S.A.	Purveyors of Champagne	Reims
Lampitt, Henry, Ltd.	Suppliers of Hardware	London
Lansing Bagnall Ltd.	Manufacturers of Industrial Trucks	Basingstoke
Lea & Perrins Ltd.	Purveyors of Worcestershire Sauce	Worcester
Leith, G. & Son	Bakers and Confectioners	Ballater
Lever Brothers Limited	Soap and Detergent Makers	Kingston-upon-Thames
Lidstone, John	Butchers	London
Lingwood Richard A.	Gold Leaf Manufacturer	South Ruislip
Lister & Co. plc	Manufacturers of Furnishing Fabrics	Bradford
Lyons Bakery Ltd.	Manufacturers of Cakes	London
Lyons, J. & Co. Ltd.	Caterers	Alperton, Middlesex
Lyons Maid Ltd.	Manufacturers of Ice Cream	Greenford, Middlesex
M. & R.—Martini & Rossi Ltd.	Suppliers of Martini Vermouth	London
John Mackaness	Maker and Supplier of Charcoal	Northampton
Mackay Hugh plc	Manufacturers of Wilton Carpeting	Durham
Magnolia Manufacturing Ltd.	Manufacturers of Picture Frame Mouldings	Loughborough
Manns & Norwich Brewery Ltd.	Brewers	Northampton
Marsh & Baxter, Ltd.	Suppliers of York Ham	Northallerton
Martin & Son Edinburgh Ltd (Trading as Martin & Frost)	Interior Furnishing Specialist	Edinburgh
McCarthy, D. & F. Ltd.	Fruit and Vegetable Merchants	Norwich
McVitie & Price Ltd.	Biscuit Manufacturers	Edinburgh
Mappin & Webb Ltd.	Silversmiths	London
Mattessons Wall's Limited	Suppliers of Sausages and Meat Pies	Banbury
Mayfair Trunks Limited	Suppliers of Luggage	London
Medway Sacks	Suppliers of Domestic Refuse Sacks	Maidstone
Melroses Limited	Purveyors of Tea and Coffee	Edinburgh
Milevac Scientific Glass Ltd.	Manufacturers of Vacuum Flasks	Halstead
Minton Limited	China Manufacturers	Stoke-on-Trent
Modern Fibre Glass Products Ltd.	Manufacturers of Fibre Glass Carrying Cases	Tonbridge
Morny Limited	Manufacturers of Soap	London
Mumm, G. H. & Cie	Purveyors of Champagne	Paris
Myland, John Limited	Manufacturers of French Polish, Stains and Wax Polish	London
Nairobi Coffee & Tea Co. Ltd.	Coffee Merchants	Watford
Nestlé Company Ltd., The	Manufacturers of Instant Coffee	Croydon
Newbery, Henry & Co. Ltd.	Suppliers of Furnishing Trimmings	London
Norprint Ltd.	Manufacturers of Baggage Labels	Boston, Lincolnshire
North, James & Sons Ltd.	Suppliers of Safety Footwear	Hyde
Office Cleaning Services Ltd.	Cleaning Contractor	Sanderstead
Parry Tyzack Limited	Supplier of Hand Tools and Portable Electric Tools	London
Pears, A. & F. Ltd.	Soap Manufacturers	London
Peek, Frean & Co. Ltd.	Biscuit Manufacturers	London
Percheron, H. A. Ltd.	Suppliers of Furnishing Fabrics	London
Picreator Enterprises Ltd.	Supplier of Products for Restoration and Conservation	London
Pilgrim Payne & Co. Ltd.	Cleaners of Soft Furnishings and Carpets	London
Pinneys of Scotland, Ltd.	Purveyors of Smoked Salmon	Dumfries
Plastona (John Waddington) Ltd.	Manufacturers of Disposable Plates	Leeds
Porter Nicholson	Upholsterers' Warehousemen	London
Preedy J. and Sons Limited	Supplier of Glass Table Tops	London
Prestat Ltd.	Purveyors of Chocolates	London
Price's Patent Candle Company Ltd.	Candlemakers	London
Procter and Gamble Limited	Manufacturers of Soap and Detergents	Newcastle upon Tyne
Quaker Oats Limited	Suppliers of Quaker Products	Southall
R & L Packaging	Suppliers of Plastic Bags	London
Rawlings, H. D. Ltd.	Mineral Water Manufacturers	Chelmsford
Reckitt & Colman, Products Ltd. (see Colmans of Norwich).		
Reckitt & Colman Pharmaceutical Division	Manufacturers of Antiseptics	Hull
Renshaw, John F. & Company Ltd.	Purveyors of Almond Products	Mitcham

Ridgways	Tea Merchants	London
Robertson, James & Sons Preserve Manufacturers Ltd.	Preserve Manufacturers	Manchester
Roger & Gallett SA	Manufacturers of Soap	Paris
Rose, L., & Co. Ltd.	Suppliers of Lime Juice Cordial	London
Ross, John Jnr. (Aberdeen) Limited	Fish Merchants and Curers	Aberdeen
Royal Brierley Crystal Ltd.	Suppliers of Table Glassware	Brierley Hill, West Midlands
Royal Doulton Limited	Manufacturers of China	Stoke-on-Trent
H. & L. Russell Ltd.	Manufacturers of Garment Hangers	London
Russell, Donald Limited	Supplier of Meat and Poultry	Inverurie
Ryvita Company Limited, The	Manufacturers of Crispbreads	Poole
SDL Limited	Manufacturers of Sewing Machines	Basingstoke
Saccone & Speed Ltd.	Wine Merchants	London
St. Ivel, Ltd.	Suppliers of Butter and Cheese	Swindon
Sandeman, Geo. G. Sons & Co. Ltd.	Wine Merchants	London
Sanderson, William & Son Ltd.	Scotch Whisky Distillers	London
Savoy Hotel Coffee Department, The	Suppliers of Coffee	London
Schweppes International Limited	Soft Drink Manufacturers	London
Scoles, R. F. & J.	Butchers	London
Scott Limited	Manufacturer of Disposable Tissues	Dersingham
Scottish & Newcastle Breweries plc	Brewers	East Grinstead
Sekers Fabrics, Ltd.	Manufacturers of Furnishing Fabrics	Edinburgh
Sharp, Edward & Sons Ltd.	Confectioners	London
Sharwood, J. A. & Co. Ltd.	Manufacturers of Chutney and Purveyors of Indian Curry Powder	Maidstone
Shaw, Elizabeth, Ltd.	Manufacturers of Confectionery	London
Sheridan H. M.	Purveyor of Meat and Poultry	Bristol
Shirras, Laing & Co. Ltd.	Ironmongers	Ballater
Sinclair Melson Designs Limited	Upholsterers	Aberdeen
Sleepeezee Limited	Bedding Manufacturers	Feltham
Slumberland Ltd.	Bedding Manufacturers	London
Smith, Tom Group, Ltd.	Suppliers of Christmas Crackers	Oldham
Spink R. R. and Sons	Fishmongers	Norwich
Spode	Manufacturers of China	Arbroath
Sproston, W. F., Ltd.	Suppliers of Fish	Stoke-on-Trent
St. Jude's Laundry	Launderers	London
Staples & Co., Ltd.	Manufacturers of Bedsteads and Bedding	Edinburgh
Stewart, J. & G. Ltd.	Suppliers of Scotch Whisky	Huntingdon
Still, W. M. & Sons, Ltd.	Manufacturers of Kitchen Equipment	Edinburgh
Stoddard, Carpets Limited	Carpet Manufacturers	Hastings
Strachan, George, Ltd.	General Merchants	Johnstone, Scotland
Sturtevant Engineering Co., Ltd.	Manufacturers of Vacuum Cleaners	Crathie
Swindle, Clive Restorations	Porcelain Restorer	Brighton
Sycamore Laundry & Dry Cleaners (Leman Brothers)	Launderers and Dry Cleaners	Westerham, Kent
Szell, Michael Limited	Suppliers of Furnishing Fabrics	London
Tanqueray, Gordon, & Co. Ltd.	Gin Distillers	London
Tate & Lyle PLC	Sugar Refiners	London
Telephone Rentals plc	Suppliers of Dictograph Telephones	London
Temple & Crook Ltd.	Suppliers of Brushes and Hardware	Milton Keynes
Terry, Joseph & Sons	Confectionery Manufacturer	London
Thermos Ltd.	Manufacturers of Vacuum Vessels	York
Thresher & Glenny Limited	Shirtmakers	London
Tissunique, Ltd.	Suppliers of Furnishing Fabrics	London
Turner, G. J. & Co. (Trimmings) Ltd.	Manufacturers of Furnishing Trimmings	London
Twining, R. & Co. Ltd.	Tea and Coffee Merchants	London
Unigate Dairies Limited	Suppliers of Dairy Produce	London
Van den Berghs	Manufacturers of Margarine	London
Vantona International Linen Co. Ltd.	Suppliers of Linen	Burgess Hill
Veuve Clicquot-Ponsardin	Purveyors of Champagne	London
Vileda Limited	Suppliers of Nonwoven Cleaning Materials	Reims
Vitopan Limited	Suppliers of Mopping Equipment	Cleckheaton
Waddington's Playing Card Co., Ltd.	Manufacturers of Playing Cards	Sanderstead
Walker, H. & T. Ltd.	Suppliers of Canned Foods	Leeds
Walker, John & Sons, Ltd.	Scotch Whisky Distillers	Sevenoaks
Walley Ltd.	Suppliers of Crockery and Glassware	London
Warner Fabrics plc	Suppliers of Silks and Furnishings Fabrics	Grays
Watney Truman Limited	Brewers	London
Weetabix Ltd.	Manufacturers of Breakfast Cereals	London
Western Quilters Limited	Quilters	Burton Latimer
Whitbread & Co., PLC	Brewers	London
Whitbread Wessex	Purveyors of Beers, Spirits and Mineral Waters	London
White Horse Distillers Limited	Scotch Whisky Distillers	Portsmouth
White, John, Footwear Ltd.	Footwear Manufacturers	Glasgow
		Wellingborough

Whitworths Ltd.	Manufacturers of Provisions and Dried Fruit	Wellingborough
Whytock & Reid	Decorators and Furnishers	Edinburgh
Wilkin & Sons, Ltd.	Jam and Marmalade Manufacturers	Tiptree
Wilkinson, R. and Son.	Glass Restorers	London
Wilson, Andrew & Sons Ltd.	Catering Equipment Hirers	Edinburgh
Wilton Royal Carpet Factory Limited, The	Carpet Manufacturers	Wilton
Windsor Glass Company Ltd.	Glass Merchants	Windsor
Wolsey Division, Courtaulds Clothing Brands Ltd.	Manufacturers of Hosiery and Knitwear	Leicester
Woodhouse Hume Ltd.	Suppliers of Meat and Poultry	London
Worcester Royal Porcelain Co., The	Manufacturers of China and Porcelain	Worcester
Yardley & Co. Ltd.	Manufacturers of Soap	London

ROYAL WARRANTS OF APPOINTMENT TO HER MAJESTY QUEEN ELIZABETH II

LORD CHAMBERLAIN'S OFFICE

List of Tradesmen in the Lord Chamberlain's Office permitted to style themselves "By Appointment to Her Majesty The Queen" or "By Appointment to Her Majesty Queen Elizabeth II" and entitling them to display the Royal Coat of Arms, but not to fly the Royal Standard. The word "Royal" should not be used without first advising the Secretary, Royal Household Tradesmen's Warrants Committee.

Name	Description	Address
Alden & Blackwell (Eton) Ltd.	Booksellers	Windsor
Alliance Engraving & Lettering Co. Ltd.	Engravers	Bristol
Atlantis Paper Company Ltd.	Fine Art and Archival Suppliers	London
Barcham Green & Co. Ltd.	Hand-Made Papermakers	Maidstone
Beam Office Equipment Limited	Photocopying Oxford, Suppliers of Photocopying Equipment	Thame
Berol Ltd.	Manufacturers of Writing Instruments	King's Lynn
Burn, James International	Suppliers of Office Binding Equipment	Esher
Carter, W. F. & Sons Ltd.	Coach Hirers	Maidenhead
Carvers and Gilders	Carvers, Gilders and Restorers	London
Collings, Denis Vere	Calligrapher	New Barnet
Compton, J., Sons & Webb, Ltd.	Uniform Makers	London
Connelly Bros. (Curriers) Ltd.	Leather Tanners and Curriers	London
Conservation Resources (UK) Limited	Manufacturers of Archival Storage Material	Cowley
Cooper, A. C., Ltd.	Fine Art Photographers	London
Cooper, A. C. (Colour) Ltd.	Fine Art Colour Photographers	London
Dege, J & Sons Limited	Tailors	London
Ede & Ravenscroft, Ltd.	Robe Makers	London
Farris, Charles Ltd.	Chandlers	London
Firmin & Sons plc	Button Makers	London
Garrad & Co., Ltd	Goldsmiths and Crown Jewellers	London
Greenaway-Harrison Ltd.	Printers	London
Harrild, W. L. and Partners Ltd.	Suppliers of Bookbinding Equipment	London
Harris, Aubrey Ltd.	Suppliers of Printing and Stationery	London
Hewit, J, & Sons Ltd.	Manufacturers of Leather	Edinburgh
Hill, William, & Son, and Norman & Beard, Ltd.	Organ Builders	London
IBM United Kingdom Limited	Suppliers of Electric and Electronic Typewriters	Portsmouth
Maggs Bros. Ltd.	Purveyors of Rare Books and Manuscripts	London
Petersfield Bookshop	Picture Framer and Supplier of Art Materials	Petersfield
Phoenix Fine Art	Suppliers of Fine Art Services	London
Plan Conservation Limited	Restorer of Drawings	Windsor
Plowden & Smith Limited	Restorer of Fine Arts Objects	London
Polybags Limited	Polythene Bagmakers	Greenford
Rogers, T. & Co. (Packers) Ltd.	Packers and Transporters of Works of Art	London
Ryder, G. and Company Limited	Specialist Box Makers	Milton Keynes
Securicor Cleaning, Ltd.	Office Cleaning Contractors	Walton-on-Thames
Skinner A. E. & Company	Jewellers and Silversmiths	London
Stothers & Hardy (Henley) Ltd.	Manufacturers of Computer Software	Henley-on-Thames
Swann: Heddon-on-the-Wall	Cabinet Maker	Newcastle-upon-Tyne
Tortoiseshell and Ivory House Ltd., The	Restorers of Objets D'Art	London
Toye, Kenning & Spencer Ltd.	Suppliers of Gold and Silver Laces, Insignia and Embroidery	London
Unisys Limited	Suppliers of Computer Systems	London
Walker, J. W. & Sons Ltd.	Pipe Organ Tuners and Builders	Brandon
Watkins & Watson Ltd.	Organ Blower Manufacturers	Wareham
Watts & Company Limited	Ecclesiastical Furnishers	London
Wiggins, Arnold & Sons Ltd.	Picture Frame Makers	London
Wilkinson Sword Ltd.	Sword Cutlers	High Wycombe
Wilson & Son	Piano and Harpisichord Tuners	Edinburgh

ROYAL WARRANTS OF APPOINTMENT TO HER MAJESTY QUEEN ELIZABETH II

ROYAL MEWS DEPARTMENT

List of Tradesmen in the Royal Mews Department permitted to style themselves "By Appointment to Her Majesty The Queen" or "By Appointment to Her Majesty Queen Elizabeth II" and entitling them to display the Royal Arms, but not to fly the Royal Standard. The word "Royal" should not be used without first advising the Secretary, Royal Household Tradesmen's Warrants Committee.

Name	Description	Address
Allen J. A. & Co. (The Horseman's Bookshop) Limited	Suppliers of Equine and Equestrian Literature	London
Anstee & Company, Ltd.	Forage Merchants	London
Arnolds Veterinary Products Limited	Suppliers of Equine Veterinary Pharmaceuticals	Leighton Buzzard
Asbridge, James (Greenwich) Ltd.	Repairer and Painter of Horse Drawn Vehicles	London
Austin Rover Group Ltd.	Manufacturers of Rover Cars & Austin Cars	Coventry
Betts and Broughton	Suppliers of Safety Footwear	Sutton-in-Ashfield
Birr, H. H.	Suppliers of Riding Clothing	Leicester
British Nova Works Ltd.	Manufacturers of Floor Maintenance Products and Waxes	Southall
Bullens Limited	Road Transport Contractors	Borehamwood
Campbell, Smith & Co. Ltd.	Decorators	London
Car Care Products Group	Supplier of Vehicle Polishes and Cleaners	Liphook
Carpenter, J. W., Ltd.	Suppliers of Cleaning Stores	Thame
Carr & Day & Martin Ltd.	Manufacturers of Saddlery Care Products and Weatherproof County Clothing	Gt. unmow
Castrol Limited	Manufacturers of Motor Lubricants	Swindon
Champion Sparking Plug Co., Ltd.	Suppliers of Sparking Plugs	Upton, Wirral
Chapman, Albert E. Limited	Upholsterers	London
Chubb Fire Ltd.	Manufacturers of Chubb Fire Extinguishers	Sunbury-on-Thames
Coppermill Limited	Manufacturers of Industrial Cleaning Cloths	London
Croford Coachbuilders Ltd.	Wheelwright and Coachbuilders	Ashford
Curzon, G. E.	Forage Merchants	Wraybury
D & H Horse Feeds	Horse Feed Supplier	Cirencester
Day Son and Hewitt Limited	Manufacturers of Veterinary Products	Lancaster
Eastern Counties Leather PLC	Manufacturers of Chamois Leather	Cambridge
Esso Petroleum Company, Ltd.	Purveyors of Motor Spirit	London
Forbo-Nairn Ltd.	Manufacturers of Floor Covering	Kircaldy
Ford Motor Company, Ltd.	Motor Vehicle Manufacturers	Brentwood
Frames Rickards Ltd.	Road Transport Contractors	Brentford
Francis, G. C.	Heraldic Artist	North Lancing
Gardiner & Co.	Suppliers of Protective Clothing	London
Gidden, W. & H. Ltd.	Saddlers	London
Gieves & Hawkes Ltd.	Livery and Military Tailors	London
Gliddons Gloves & Leatherwear Ltd.	Suppliers of Gloves	Yeovil
Godfrey Davis Europcar Ltd.	Motor Vehicle Hirers	London
Harvey, Matthew & Co. Ltd.	Bitmakers	Walsall
Hawkins, G. T. Ltd.	Riding Footwear Manufacturers	Northampton
Henleys (London) Limited	Coachbuilders	London
Hutton, E. H. (Coachbuilders) Ltd.	Manufacturer and Repairer of Horseboxes	Melton Mowbray
Incorporated Association for Promoting the General Welfare of the Blind, The	Suppliers of Stable Mats, etc, and Renovators of Mattresses	London
Jaguar Cars Limited	Supplier of Motor Cars	Coventry
Jeyes' Group PLC	Manufacturers of Hygiene Products	Thetford
K Shoes Limited	Bootmakers	Kendal
Keep, John T. & Sons Ltd.	Paint Manufacturer	London
Kenning London	Motor Car Distributors	London
Land Rover UK Ltd.	Manufacturers of Land Rovers and Range Rovers	Solihull
Lobb, John Limited	Bootmaker	London
Lucas, Joseph, Ltd.	Manufacturers of Electrical Equipment	Birmingham
Luxford, Keith (Saddlery) Ltd.	Saddlers, Horse Clothiers and Harness Makers	Teddington
McArthur Gray (Stamford) Ltd.	Suppliers of Shoeing Iron and Farriers' Equipment	Stamford, Lincolnshire
Mason, Joseph, PLC	Manufacturers of Coach Paints	Derby
Metropolitan Window Cleaning Co., Ltd.	Window Cleaners	London
"Mordax" Studs Ltd.	Makers of "Mordax" Studs	Burnley
National Benzole Co., Ltd.	Suppliers of Motor Spirit	London
Newsham, Stuart Photography	Photographer	Stourport-on-Severn
North, W. A. & Son	Forage Merchants	Bourne
Offord, Gordon J.	Coachbuilders	Thames Ditton
Owen, Charles & Co. (Bow) Ltd.	Protective Headwear Manufacturer	London
Parker, F. & Sons Ltd.	Suppliers of Garden Materials	Bagshot
Patey, S. (London) Ltd.	Manufacturers of Hats	London
Pettifer, Thomas & Co. Ltd.	Manufacturers of Animal Health and Nutrition Products	Barking

Plessey Company, PLC, The	Suppliers of Car Radios	Ilford
Poole, Henry, & Company (Savile Row) Ltd.	Livery Outfitters	London
Pratt, Jeffery A.	Supplier of Animal Health and Veterinary Products	Rickmansworth
Reckitt Household Products	Manufacturers of Air Fresheners, Polishes and Cleaners and Laundry Products	Hull
Redwood and Feller	Tailors	London
Rolls Royce Motor Cars Limited	Motor Car Manufacturers	Crewe
Scottish Midland Co-operative Society Limited	Coach Painters	Edinburgh
Sandicliffe Garage Ltd.	Suppliers of Motor Horse Boxes and Automobile Engineers	Stapleford
Sandicliffe of Stapleford (see Sandicliffe Garage Ltd.).		
Shell U.K. Ltd.	Purveyors of Motor Spirit	London
S. P. Tyres U.K. Limited	Motor Vehicle Tyre Suppliers	Birmingham
Sleigh, W. L. Ltd.	Motor Vehicle Hirers	Edinburgh
Sturgess, Walter E. & Sons Ltd.	Suppliers of Horse and Carriage Conveyances	Leicester
Swaine, Adeney, Brigg & Sons, Ltd.	Whip and Glove Makers	London
Tropical Plants Display Ltd.	Installers and Maintainers of Plant Displays	London
Turner-Bridgar	Saddler and Harness Maker	Goring-on-Thames
Vauxhall Motors, Ltd.	Motor Vehicle Manufacturers	Luton
Westway, Mark & Son	Manufacturers of Horse Forage	Marldon, Devon

Buckingham Palace
1st January 1989

Airlie, Lord Chamberlain

ROYAL WARRANTS OF APPOINTMENT TO HER MAJESTY QUEEN ELIZABETH THE QUEEN MOTHER

LIST of Tradesmen who hold Warrants of Appointment to Queen Elizabeth The Queen Mother, from the Lord Chamberlain to Her Majesty, permitted to style themselves "By Appointment" to Her Majesty, with authority to display Her Majesty's Arms, but not to fly Her Majesty's Standard. The word "Royal" should not be used without first advising the Secretary, Royal Household Tradesmen's Warrants Committee.

Name	**Description**	**Address**
Ackerman's Chocolates Ltd.	Confectioners	London
Addis Limited	Suppliers of Plastic Housewares	Hertford
Ainsworths Homeopathic Pharmacy	Chemist	London
Amor, Albert Ltd.	Suppliers of Fine Porcelain	London
Aquascutum, Limited	Makers of Weatherproof Garments	London
Arden, Elizabeth, Ltd.	Manufacturers of Cosmetics	London
Army and Navy Stores, Ltd.	Suppliers of Household and Fancy Goods	London
Asprey and Co., PLC	Jewellers	London
'At-A-Glance' Calendar Company Limited, The	Calendar Manufacturers	London
Avon Tyres Limited	Tyre Manufacturers	Melksham
Bandaville Ltd.	Conveyors of Motor Vehicles	London
Bass Brewing Ltd.	Brewers	Burton upon Trent
Baxter, G. G. Ltd.	Suppliers of Pork Sausages	Birchington-on-Sea
Baxter, James & Son	Purveyors of Potted Shrimps	Morecambe
Baxter, W. A. & Sons, Ltd.	Purveyor of Scottish Specialities	Fochabers
Begg, Graham Limited	Radio and Television Suppliers	Wick, Caithness
Benney, Gerald	Goldsmith, Silversmith and Enameller	Beenham
Benoist, V. Ltd.	Purveyors of General Groceries	London
Black & Edgington Hire Ltd.	Flag Makers	London
Brannam, C. H., Limited	Pottery Makers	Barnstable
Bremner, F. & J.	Haulage Contractors	Castletown, Caithness
British Cable Services Ltd.	Suppliers of Rediffusion	Guildford
Broadwood, John & Sons, Ltd.	Pianoforte Tuner	Milton Keynes
Bronnley, H. & Co., Ltd.	Toilet Soap Makers	London
Brooks, W., & Son (UYC Foods Ltd.)	Purveyors of Fruit and Quick Frozen Foods	London
Budgens	Grocers	Ruislip
Burley's Newsagents	Newsagent and Tobacconist	Englefield Green
Cadbury, Ltd.	Cocoa and Chocolate Manufacturers	Bourneville, Birmingham
Caithness Glass PLC	Glassmakers	Wick, Caithness
Caleys (Cole Bros. Ltd.)	Suppliers of Household and Fancy Goods and Millinery	Windsor
Calman Links (Trading) Ltd.	Furriers	London
Calor Gas Limited	Suppliers of Liquefied Petroleum Gas	Datchet, Slough
Campbell & Co.	Tweed Mercers	Beauly
Carrington & Company, Limited	Jewellers and Silversmiths	London
Carters (J. & A.), Ltd.	Invalid Furniture Manufacturers	Westbury Wiltshire
Carters Tested Seeds Ltd.	Seedsmen	Llangollen
Cartier Ltd.	Jewellers and Goldsmiths	London
Cassie, Alistair	Television supplier and Engineer	Ballater

Castrol, Ltd.	Purveyors of Motor Lubricants	Swindon
Chapman & Frearson Limited	Suppliers of Protein Balancers, Vitamin and Mineral Supplements.	Grimsby
Chess, Mary Ltd.	Perfumers	London
Collingwood of Bond Street Limited	Jewellers	London
Coombs & Sons (Guildford) Ltd.	Suppliers of Motor Cars	Guildford
Corner Fruit Shop, The	Fruiterer and Greengrocer	Thurso
Corney and Barrow Limited	Wine Merchants	London
Cox, Harold & Sons Jewellers Ltd.	Clockmakers and Silversmiths	Windsor
Cromessol Co. Ltd.	Manufacturers and Suppliers of Disinfectants and Detergents	Glasgow
Crosse & Blackwell	Purveyors of Preserved Provisions	Croydon
Daimler Cars	See BL Cars Ltd.	
DER Limited	Suppliers of Television Receivers	Chertsey
Dettlyn Limited trading as Egham Mower Service	Suppliers of Horticultural Machinery	Egham
Dipre, D., & Son	Cutlery Servicers, Knifegrinders and Suppliers of Kitchen Equipment	London
Dreamland Appliances PLC	Manufacturers of Electric Blankets	Hythe
Dunnet, John	Agricultural Contractor	Seater
Ede & Ravenscroft Ltd.	Robemakers	London
Egham Animal Food Supplies	Corn and Animal Feed Merchants	Egham
Emmetts Store	Curers and Suppliers of Sweet Pickled Hams	Peasenhall
Farris, Charles Ltd.	Candlemakers	London
Findus	Suppliers of Frozen Foods	Croydon
Firmin & Sons Ltd.	Button Makers	London
Forces Help Society and Lord Roberts Workshops, The	Furniture Makers	London
Ford Motor Co. Ltd.	Motor Vehicle Manufacturers	Brentwood
Ford Oliver, Ltd.	Decorators	London
Fortnum & Mason, PLC	Suppliers of Leather and Fancy Goods	London
Foster, John & Co.	Suppliers of Furnishing Fabrics	London
Fox's Biscuits Limited	Biscuit Manufacturers	Bately
Frederick, John, Ltd.	Carpet Cleaners	London
Garrard & Co. Ltd.	Jewellers and Silversmiths	London
General Trading Co. (Mayfair) Ltd., The	Suppliers of Fancy Goods	London
Gestetner Limited	Suppliers of Reprographic Office Equipment	London
Gibson Saddlers Ltd.	Suppliers of Racing Colours	Newmarket
Goddard, J. and Sons Ltd.	Manufacturers of Silver and Metal Polishes	Camberley
Goode, Thomas & Co. Ltd.	Suppliers of Glass and China	London
Goodyear, Edward, Ltd	Florist	London
Green Stage Ltd.	Suppliers of Musks Sausages	Newmarket
Greenaway-Harrison Ltd.	Printers	London
Grover Clyne	Carpet and Vinyl Floor Covering Supplier	Wick
H. P. Foods Ltd.	Manufacturers of H. P. Sauces and Canned Foods	Market Harborough
Haggart, P. & J. Ltd.	Tartan and Woollen Manufacturers	Aberfeldy
Halcyon Days Ltd.	Suppliers of Objets d'Art	London
Hall, Matthew Mechanical and Electrical Engineers Ltd.	Building Services Engineers	London
Hamblin, Theodore, Ltd.	Opticians	London
Hancocks and Co. (Jewellers) Ltd.	Goldsmiths and Silversmiths	London
Hardy Minnis	Mercers of Woollen Cloth	Stroud
Harris Aubrey Limited	Suppliers of Stationery and Office Equipment	London
Harris, D. R. & Company, Limited	Chemist	London
Harrods, Limited	Suppliers of China, Glass and Fancy Goods	London
Hartnell, Norman, Limited	Dressmakers	London
Harvey Nichols & Company, Limited	Drapers	London
Hatchards	Booksellers	London
Heaton, Wallace Ltd.	Suppliers of Photographic Equipment	London
Hillier Nurseries (Winchester) Ltd.	Nurserymen and Seedsmen	Winchester
Holt, Ray (Land Drainage) Ltd.	Land Draining Contractors	Thurso
Hoover PLC	Suppliers of Vacuum Cleaners	Merthyr Tydfil, South Wales
Hubbard Refrigeration Ltd.	Suppliers of Automatic Ice making Machines	Woodbridge
Huntley & Palmers Ltd.	Biscuit and Cake Manufacturers	Reading
Hypnos Limited	Upholsterers and Bedding Manufacturers	Princes Risborough
Idris Ltd	Manufacturers of Fruit Beverages	Chelmsford
Jacob, W. & R. & Co. (Liverpool) Ltd.	Biscuit Manufacturers	Liverpool
Jaguar Cars	Manufacturers of Daimler and Jaguar Cars	Coventry
Jeyes Group plc	Manufacturers of Hygiene Products	Thetford
Johnson Brothers	Manufacturers of Ceramic Tableware	Stoke-on-Trent
Johnson Wax, Ltd.	Manufacturers of Wax Polishes, Cleaner and Hygiene Products	Camberley
Jones, Peter	Draper and Furnisher	London
Jones, Yarrell & Co., Ltd.	Newsagents	London
K Shoes Limited	Bootmakers	Kendal
Kleen-Way (Berkshire) Co.	Chimney Sweepers	Bracknell
Knight, J. W. (Fisheries) Ltd.	Fishmonger and Poulterer	Virginia Water

Knowles & Sons (Fruiterers) Ltd.	Fruiterers and Greengrocers	Aberdeen
Land Rover UK Ltd.	Manufacturers of Land Rovers	Solihull
Lang Brothers Ltd.	Scotch Whisky Distillers	Glasgow
Leigh, G. & Son	Bakers and Confectioners	Ballater
Lentheric, Ltd.	Manufacturers of Perfumery Products	Camberley
Lever Brothers Limited	Soap and Detergent Makers	Kingston-upon-Thames
Levy, M. (London Wall) Ltd.	Fruiterers and Greengrocers	London
Leyland Cars	See BL Cars Ltd.	
Liberty PLC	Silk Mercers	London
Lidstone, John	Butchers	London
Lilliman and Cox, Ltd.	Dry Cleaners	London
Longmire Paul Limited	Supplier of Silver and Presentation Gifts	London
Lyons, J. & Co. Ltd.	Caterers	Alperton, Middlesex
McCallum & Craigie Ltd.	Suppliers of Lan-Air-Cel Blankets	Huddersfield
M & R—Martini & Rossi Ltd.	Suppliers of Brandy and Martini Vermouth	London
Mattessons Wall's Limited	Suppliers of Sausages and Meat Pies	Banbury
Maurice & Robert	Hairdressers	London
Mayfair Trunks Ltd.	Suppliers of Luggage	London
Mayfair Window Cleaning Co., Ltd.	Window Cleaners	London
Menzies, John & Co. PLC	Booksellers	Edinburgh
Milne John & Sons	Clockmaker	Wick, Caithness
Mirman, Simone	Milliner	London
Morny, Ltd	Manufacturers of Soap	London
Mowbray, A. R. & Co. Ltd.	Suppliers of Fine Bindings	London
Moyses Stevens Ltd.	Florists	London
Murray, J. & D.	Chemists	Ballater
NRS Limited	Manufacturers of Refrigerating Machinery	Newbury
Nairobi Coffee and Tea Company, Ltd., The	Coffee Merchants	Watford
National Benzole Co., Ltd.	Suppliers of Motor Spirit	London
Nestlé Company Limited, The	Manufacturers of Nestlé Products	Croydon
Papworth Industries	Trunk and Cabinet Makers	Cambridge
Parker's	Saddlers	Horsham
Paxton & Whitfield Ltd.	Cheesemongers	London
Pears, A. F. Ltd.	Soap Manufacturers	London
Peek, Frean & Co. Ltd.	Biscuit Manufacturers	London
Petrie E.	Painters and Decorators	Thurso
Philips, S. J., Ltd.	Antique Dealers	London
Phonotas Services Ltd.	Telephone Cleaners and Sterilisers	Tunbridge Wells
Pratt & Leslie Jones Ltd.	Suppliers of China, Glass and Fancy Goods	Windsor
Premier Brands UK Limited	Manufacturers of Christmas Puddings	Birmingham
Pringle John	Suppliers of Motor Spirit, Oil and Accessories	Ballater
Pringle, of Scotland Ltd.	Manufacturers of Knitted Garments	Hawick
Procter & Gamble, Ltd.	Manufacturers of Soaps, Detergents and Shortening	Newcastle-upon-Tyne
Prowse, Keith & Company Limited	Theatre Ticket Agents	London
RTC Mechanical Services Ltd.	Heating Equipment Engineers	Ewell
Rayne, H, and M., Ltd.	Shoemakers and Handbag Manufacturers	London
Reid C. J. (Eton)	Chemist	Eton
Renshaw, John F. & Co. Ltd.	Purveyors of Almond Products	Mitcham
Reynier, J. B. Limited	Wine Merchants	London
Ridgways	Tea and Coffee Merchants	London
Roberts Radio	Manufacturers and Suppliers of Radio Receivers	West Molesey, Surrey
Robertsons of Tain Limited	Supplier of Agricultural and Horticultural Machinery	Tain
Rowntree PLC	Makers of Table Jellies	York
Royal Albert Limited	Manufacturers of Paragon Fine Bone China	Stoke-on-Trent
Royal British Legion Disabled Men's Industries Ltd., The	Makers of Leather and Fancy Goods	Maidstone
Royal Crown Derby Porcelain Co., Ltd	Manufacturers of Fine Bone China	Derby
Royal Hotel (Caithness) Ltd. The	Victuallers and Vintners	Thurso
Rudolf	Milliner	London
Russell, Gordon, Limited	Suppliers of Furniture and Furnishings	Broadway
Sanderson, Wm. & Son, Ltd.	Scotch Whisky Distillers	London
Savory & Moore, Ltd.	Chemists	Leighton Buzzard
Scott Limited	Manufacturers of Disposable Tissues	East Grinstead
Schweppes International Ltd.	Soft Drink Manufacturers	London
Scott's Fish Shop	Cheesemonger	Kirkwall
Semex (UK Sales) Limited	Supplier of Cattle Breeding Services	Dalrymple, Ayrshire
Sharp, Edward, & Sons Ltd.	Suppliers of Confectionery and Confectionery Novelties	Maidstone
Sheridan, H. M.	Purveyor or Meat and Poultry	Ballater
Ships Wheel, The	Furniture and Picture Restorer	Thurso
Sleigh, W. L., Ltd.	Motor Vehicle Hirers	Edinburgh
Slumberland, Limited	Bedding Manufacturers	Oldham
Smith, H. Allen Ltd.	Wine Cooper and Merchant	London
Smith, Tom Group Ltd.	Suppliers of Christmas Crackers	Norwich

Smith, W. & Son Ltd.	Seedsmen and Nurserymen	Aberdeen
Sparkes, John, Ltd.	Antiquaries of Chinese Art	London
Spink R. R. and Sons	Fishmongers	Arbroath
Sproston W. F. Ltd.	Fishmongers	London
Steiner Products	Cosmeticians	London
Steven, James L.	Plumbing and Heating Engineer	Wick, Caithness
Stoppes J. & Sons Ltd.	Bakers and Confectioners	Egham
Stowells of Chelsea	Wine and Spirit Merchants	Dorking
Strachan, George Ltd.	General Merchants	Crathie
Suttons Seeds Ltd.	Seedsmen	Torquay
Swaine, Adeney, Brigg & Sons, Limited	Umbrella Makers	London
Sycamore Laundry & Dry Cleaners (Leaman Brothers)	Launderers and Dry Cleaners	London
Tanqueray Gordon and Company Limited	Gin Distillers	London
Telephone Rentals PLC	Suppliers of Dictograph Telephones	Milton Keynes
Thomas, J. Rochelle Inc.	Dealers in Works of Art	Hamilton, Bermuda
Thomas Window Cleaning	Window Cleaner	Englefield Green
Thomson, Donald	Grocer	Castletown, Caithness
Thorn Lighting Limited	Manufacturers of Electric Lamps	Enfield
Thresher & Gleny, Ltd.	Shirtmakers	London
Trianco, Redfyre, Ltd	Manufacturers of Domestic Boilers	Sheffield
Twining, R. & Co., Ltd.	Tea and Coffee Merchants	London
Unigate Dairies (London) Ltd.	Suppliers of Dairy Produce	London
Valentines of Dundee, Ltd.	Suppliers of Christmas Cards and Calendars	Dundee, Scotland
Vernons Electrical Limited	Electrical Engineers	Sunningdale
Veuve Clicquot-Ponsardin	Purveyors of Champagne	Reims
Wallace, Cameron, & Co., Ltd.	Manufacturers of Ultraplast First Aid Dressings	Glasgow
Want, Albert & Co., Ltd.	Suppliers of Household Hardware and Garden Sundries	Englefield Green
Wartski Ltd.	Jewellers	London
Watmough, Ken	Fishmonger	Aberdeen
Weatherill, Bernard, Ltd.	Livery Tailors	London
Weetabix Limited	Manufacturers of Breakfast Cereals	Burton Latimer
West, R. & C.	Greengrocer and Fruiterer	Sunningdale
Whitbread Fremlins	Brewers	Maidstone
Whitworths Ltd.	Processors and Packers of Food Products	Wellingborough
Wholesale Fittings, PLC, The	Suppliers of Electrical Equipment	Dagenham
Wicks, E. J.	Saddler	Lambourn
Wiggins, Arnold and Sons, Limited	Picture Frame Makers	London
Wolsey Division, Courtaulds Clothing Brands Limited	Manufacturers of Hosiery and Knitwear	Leicester
Wood, William & Son. Ltd.	Garden Contractors and Horticultural Builders	Taplow
Woodhouse Hume Ltd.	Suppliers of Meat and Poultry	London
Worham, Antony, Ltd.	Suppliers of Tudor Queen Hams and Tongues	London
Yardley and Co., Ltd.	Perfumers and Manufacturers of Soap	London

Clarence House, St. James's,
1st January 1989

Dalhousie, Lord Chamberlain to Queen Elizabeth The Queen Mother

ROYAL WARRANTS OF APPOINTMENT TO HIS ROYAL HIGHNESS THE DUKE OF EDINBURGH

LIST of Tradesmen who hold Warrants of Appointment to His Royal Highness The Duke of Edinburgh, permitted to style themselves "By Appointment" and entitling them to display The Duke of Edinburgh's Arms but not to fly His Royal Highness's Standard. The word "Royal" should not be used without first advising the Secretary, Royal Household Tradesmen's Warrants Committee.

Name	Description	Address
Allen, J. A. & Co. (The Horseman's Bookshop) Ltd.	Equine and Equestrian Bookseller	London
Artistic Iron Products	Carriage Builder	Newark
Ashley and Blake Ltd.	Shirtmakers	Manchester
Autoscan Limited	Manufacturers of Power Filing Systems	London
Barbour, J. & Sons, Ltd.	Manufacturers of Waterproof and Protective Clothing	South Shields
Beken of Cowes, Ltd.	Marine Photographers	Cowes, I.W.
Benney, Gerald	Goldsmith and Silversmith	Beenham
BOS Software Ltd.	Computer Software Manufacturers	London
British Equipment Co. Ltd.	Suppliers of Office Machinery	Warlingham
Buckley, Anthony & Constantine Ltd.	Photographers	London
Ede & Ravenscroft Ltd.	Robe Makers	London
Gates Rubber Company Limited, The	Manufacturers of Waterproof Rubber Footwear	Dumfries
General Trading Co. (Mayfair), Ltd.	Suppliers of Fancy Goods	London
Gieves and Hawkes Ltd.	Naval Tailors and Outfitters	London
Goodyear, Edward	Florist	London
Grant, Pat	Hairdresser	Aberdeen
Greenaway-Harrison Ltd.	Printers	London
Halcyon Days	Supplier of Objets d'Art	London
Hamblin, Theodore Ltd.	Opticians	London
Harrods Ltd.	Outfitters	London
Hatchards	Booksellers	London
Heaton, Wallace Limited	Suppliers of Photographic Equipment	London
Holland & Holland Ltd.	Rifle Makers	London
Jekmoth Ltd.	Manufacturers of Garment Bags and Wardrobe Accessories	Watton
Johns & Pegg Ltd.	Military Tailors	London
Jones, Yarrell & Co., Ltd.	Newsagents	London
Kardex Systems (UK) Ltd.	Manufacturers of Office Equipment	London
Kinlock Anderson Limited	Tailors and Kiltmakers	Edinburgh
Land Rover (UK) Limited	Vehicle Manufacturers	Solihull
Lobb, John Limited	Bootmakers	London
Lock, James & Co., Ltd.	Hatters	London
Longmire, Paul Limited	Supplier of Jewellery and Presentation Gifts	London
Lyle and Scott Limited	Manufacturers of Underwear and Knitwear	Hawick
Penhaligon's Ltd.	Manufacturers of Toilet Requisites	London
Philips Electronic and Associated Industries Limited	Suppliers of Electrical Goods	London
Purdey, James & Sons Ltd.	Gunmakers	London
Savory & Moore Ltd.	Chemists	Leighton Buzzard
Simpson (Piccadilly) Ltd.	Outfitters	London
Spink & Son Ltd.	Medallists	London
Stephens Brothers Ltd.	Shirt Makers and Hosier	London
Sycamore Laundry & Dry Cleaners (Leman Brothers)	Launderers and Dry Cleaners	London
Trivector Systems International Limited	Computer Supplier	Sandy, Bedfordshire
Weatherill, Bernard Limited	Livery Tailors	London
Wilkinson Sword Ltd.	Sword Cutlers	High Wycombe

Buckingham Palace
1st January 1989

Brian McGrath, Treasurer to The Duke of Edinburgh

ROYAL WARRANTS OF APPOINTMENT TO HIS ROYAL HIGHNESS THE PRINCE OF WALES

LIST of Tradesmen who hold Warrants of Appointment to The Prince of Wales, permitted to style themselves "By Appointment to His Royal Highness", and entitling them to display The Prince of Wales Badge of Three Feathers but not to display The Prince of Wales's Arms or fly His Royal Highness's Standard. The word "Royal" should not be used without first advising the Secretary, Royal Household Tradesmen's Warrants Committee.

Name	Description	Address
Anderson and Sheppard Limited	Tailors	London
Asprey and Co. plc	Jewellers Goldsmiths and Silversmiths	London
Aston Martin Lagonda Ltd.	Motor Car Manufacturer and Repairer	Newport Pagnell
Atco Limited	Manufacturers of Motor Mowers	Stowmarket
Australian Dried Fruits (Europe) Limited	Purveyors of Dried Fruits	London
Barbour, J. & Sons Limited	Manufacturers of Waterproof and Protective Clothing	South Shields
Bennett & Fountain plc	Suppliers of Electrical Equipment	London
Benney, Gerald	Goldsmith and Silversmith	Beenham
Benoist, V. Ltd.	Purveyors of Fine Foods and General Groceries	London
Bradfield Garages Limited	Automobile Engineers and Suppliers of Motor Fuel	Tetbury
Bronnley H., and Company Limited	Toilet Soap Makers	London
Collingwood of Bond Street Limited	Jewellers and Silversmiths	London
Corgi Hosiery Limited	Knitwear and Hosiery Manufacturer	Ammanford
Corney and Barrow Ltd.	Wine Merchants	London
Crerar, Robert	Gold and Silversmith	Cellardyke
DER Limited	Suppliers of Television Receivers	Chertsey
Dipre, D. & Sons	Suppliers of Kitchen and Catering Equipment	London
Ede & Ravenscroft Limited	Robemakers	London
Eximious Limited	Manufacturers of Monogrammed Accessories	London
Farlow, C. and Co. Ltd.	Suppliers of Fishing Tackle and Waterproof Clothing	London
Findus	Suppliers of Frozen Foods	Croydon
Five Trees Garden Centre and Nursery Limited	Supplier of Gardening Materials	Tetbury
Floris, J. Limited	Manufacturers of Toilet Preparations	London
Ford Motor Co. Ltd.	Motor Vehicle Manufacturers	Brentford
General Trading Company (Mayfair) Ltd., The	Supplier of Fancy Goods	London
Gieves & Hawkes Limited	Tailors and Outfitters	London
Goode, Thomas & Co. Ltd.	Suppliers of China and Glass	London
Goodyear, Edward Ltd.	Florist	London
Grugeon, Peter Studio	Photographer	Reading
Halcyon Days	Supplier of Objets d'Art	London
Hall, Frank (Market Harborough) Ltd.	Tailors	Market Harborough
Hardy, House of Ltd.	Manufacturers of Fishing Tackle	Alnwick
Harris, Aubrey Limited	Suppliers of Stationery and Office Equipment	London
Harris Office Systems, Office Systems Division	Suppliers of Dictation Equipment	Winnersh
Harrods Ltd.	Outfitters and Saddlers	London
Harvey Nichols and Company Ltd.	Suppliers of Household and Fancy Goods	London
Hatchards	Booksellers	London
Heaton, Wallace Ltd.	Suppliers of Photographic Equipment	London
Hyams & Cockerton Ltd.	Purveyors of Fruit and Vegetables	London
IBM United Kingdom Ltd.	Suppliers of Typewriters and Word Processing Equipment	Portsmouth
Jaguar Cars Limited	Supplier of Motor Cars	Coventry
Johns & Pegg Limited	Tailors	London
Johnson Herbert (Bond Street) Ltd.	Hatters	London
Jones, Peter	Draper and Furnisher	London
Jones Yarrell & Company Limited	Newsagents	London
Kenning London	Motor Car Distributors	London
Kinloch Anderson Limited	Tailors and Kiltmakers	Edinburgh
Knowles and Sons (Fruiterers) Ltd.	Purveyors of Fruit and Vegetables	Aberdeen
Land-Rover UK Limited	Motor Vehicle Manufacturers	Solihull
Leigh, George & Son	Bakers and Confectioners	Ballater
Lilliman & Cox Ltd.	Dry Cleaners	London
Lobb, John Ltd.	Bootmakers	London
Luxford, Keith (Sadlery) Ltd.	Saddlers and Horse Clothiers	Teddington
Lyons J. & Company Ltd.	Caterers	Alperton, Middlesex
Mann Egerton and Company Limited	Suppliers of Bentley Motor Cars and Automobile Engineers	Leicester
Mappin & Webb Limited	Silversmiths	London
Metropolitan Window Cleaning Company Limited	Window Cleaners	London
Murray J. & D.	Chemists	Ballater
Nicoll, B. (Shops) Limited	Fishmongers	Aberdeen
North, W. A. & Son	Forage Merchants	Bourne
Paintons	Greengrocer and Florist	Tetbury

Palmer, David, Building Contractors Limited	Building Contractors	Chippenham
Penhaligon's Limited	Manufacturers of Toilet Requisites	London
Poplak, Dudley Limited	Interior Designers	London
Pratt, Jeffery A.	Suppliers of Animal Health and Veterinary Products	Rickmansworth
Price, Arthur and Company Limited	Cutlers and Silversmiths	Lichfield
Purdey, James & Sons Ltd.	Gun and Cartridge Makers	London
Rank Xerox Limited	Manufacturers and Suppliers of Xerographic Equipment and Materials	Marlow
Roberts Radio Co. Ltd.	Manufacturers and Suppliers of Radio Receivers	West Molesey, Surrey
Royal Brierley Crystal Ltd.	Suppliers of Crystal Table Glassware	Brierley Hill, W. Midlands
Royal Doulton Limited	Manufacturers of Fine Bone China	Stoke-on-Trent
Russells of Tetbury	Dry Cleaners	Tetbury
Salter, J. & Son	Manufacturers of Polo Sticks	Aldershot
Sandicliffe Garage Limited	Suppliers of Motor Horseboxes and Automobile Engineers	Nottingham
Savory and Moore Limited	Chemists	Leighton Buzzard
Sheridan H. M.	Purveyor of Meat and Poultry	Ballater
Simpson (Piccadilly) Ltd.	Outfitters	London
Sleepeezee Ltd.	Bedding Manufacturers	London
Sleigh, W. L., Ltd.	Motor Vehicle Hirers	Edinburgh
Smith, Tom, Group Limited	Christmas Cracker Manufacturer	Norwich
Spink and Son Ltd.	Medallists	London
Sproston W. F. Ltd.	Suppliers of Fish	London
Start-rite Shoes Limited	Shoemakers	Norwich
Stephens Brothers Limited	Hosier	London
Strachan George Ltd.	General Merchants	Aboyne
Swaine Adeney Brigg & Sons Limited	Suppliers of Leather Goods	London
Sycamore Laundry & Dry Cleaners (Leman Brothers)	Launderers	London
Tate, Anthony	Chemist	London
Telephone Rentals PLC	Suppliers of Loudspeaking Telephones	Bletchley
Tricker, R. E., Limited	Shoe Manufacturers	Northampton
Turnbull & Asser Limited	Shirtmakers	London
Vantona International Linen Company Limited	Suppliers of Bed and Table Linen	London
Wallace, Cameron & Co, Ltd.	Manufacturers and Suppliers of Ultraplast First Aid Dressings	Glasgow
Wartski Limited	Jewellers	London
Woodhouse Hume Ltd.	Supplier of Meat and Poultry	London

St. James's Palace,
1st January 1989

John Riddell, Treasurer to the Prince of Wales

THE 1988 BIRTHDAY HONOURS LIST

As published in the Supplement to The London Gazette of Friday, 10th June 1988

CENTRAL CHANCERY OF THE ORDERS OF KNIGHTHOOD

CENTRAL CHANCERY OF
THE ORDERS OF KNIGHTHOOD

ST. JAMES'S PALACE, LONDON S.W.1

11th June 1988

THE QUEEN has been graciously pleased, on the occasion of the Celebration of Her Majesty's Birthday, to signify her intention of conferring Peerages of the United Kingdom for Life upon the undermentioned:

LIFE PEERS

To be Barons:

Robert Scott ALEXANDER, Q.C., Judge of the Courts of Appeal of Jersey and Guernsey. Chairman, Panel on Take-overs and Mergers.
Professor Sir (William) John (Hughes) BUTTERFIELD, O.B.E., former Regius Professor of Physic, University of Cambridge.
The Honourable Lord Alexander John Mackenzie Stuart, MACKENZIE STUART, President, Court of Justice, European Communities, Luxembourg.
Sir William REES-MOGG, Chairman, The Arts Council of Great Britain.

THE QUEEN has been graciously pleased, on the occasion of the Celebration of Her Majesty's Birthday, to declare that the undermentioned shall be sworn of Her Majesty's Most Honourable Privy Council:

PRIVY COUNSELLORS

John Ambrose COPE, M.P., Member of Parliament, Northavon. Minister of State, Department of Employment.
The Honourable Peter Hugh MORRISON, M.P., Member of Parliament, City of Chester. Minister of State, Department of Energy.

CENTRAL CHANCERY OF THE ORDERS OF KNIGHTHOOD

ST. JAMES'S PALACE, LONDON S.W.1

11th June 1988

THE QUEEN has been graciously pleased, on the occasion of the Celebration of Her Majesty's Birthday, to signify her intention of conferring the Honour of Knighthood upon the undermentioned:

KNIGHTS BACHELOR

Christopher John Elinger BALL, Chairman, National Advisory Body for Public Sector Higher Education.
Anthony Richard BARROWCLOUGH, Q.C., Parliamentary Commissioner for Administration and Health Service Commissioner for England, Wales and Scotland.
Harrison (Harry) BIRTWISTLE, Composer.
John Derek Richardson BRADBEER, O.B.E., T.D., President, The Law Society.
Colin Michael CHANDLER, Head of Defence Export Services, Ministry of Defence.
Alcon Charles COPISAROW. For public services.
John Muir DRINKWATER, Q.C. For political and public service.
Nicholas Hardwick FAIRBAIRN, Q.C., M.P. For political service.
Antony George Anson FISHER, A.F.C. For political and public service.
William Gerald GOLDING, C.B.E., Author.
Graham John HILLS, Principal and Vice-Chancellor, University of Strathclyde.
Peter Fenwick HOLMES, M.C., Chairman, Shell Transport and Trading Company plc.
Peter Michael IMBERT, Q.P.M., Commissioner, Metropolitan Police.
Aaron KLUG. For services to Molecular Biology.
John (Jack) LAYDEN, Chairman, Association of Metropolitan Authorities.
Robert Michael Conal McNAIR-WILSON, M.P. For political service.
Hilary Duppa (Hal) MILLER, M.P. For political service.
Peter North MILLER, lately Chairman, Lloyds.
John Godolphin QUICKE, C.B.E., D.L. For public service and services to Agriculture.
Edward RAYNE, C.V.O. Chairman, British Fashion Council.
Charles Hugh REECE. For services to Science and Technology.
William Vernon Stephen SECCOMBE, Chairman, South Western Regional Health Authority.
Cyril SMITH, M.B.E., M.P. For political and public service.
Kerry ST JOHNSTON, lately President, General Council of British Shipping.
Reo Argiros STAKIS, Chairman, The Reo Stakis Organisation.
John Heydon Romaine STOKES, M.P. For political service.
William George MacKenzie SUTHERLAND, Q.P.M., Chief Constable, Lothian and Borders Police.
Keith Vivian THOMAS, President, Corpus Christi College, Oxford. For services to the Study of History.
Alexander Cuthbert TURNBULL, C.B.E., Nuffield Professor of Obstetrics and Gynaecology, University of Oxford.
Norman Edward WAKEFIELD, Chairman and Chief Executive, Y J Lovell (Holdings) plc.
Dennis Murray WALTERS, M.B.E., M.P. For political service.
Neil Gowanloch WESTBROOK, C.B.E. For political and public service.
Philip William WILKINSON, Deputy Chairman, National Westminster Bank.

DIPLOMATIC SERVICE AND OVERSEAS LIST

KNIGHTS BACHELOR

LEE Quo-wei, C.B.E., J.P. For public and community services in Hong Kong.
Alfred Joseph VASQUEZ. C.B.E., Q.C. For public services in Gibraltar.

CENTRAL CHANCERY OF THE ORDERS OF KNIGHTHOOD

ST. JAMES'S PALACE, LONDON S.W.1

11th June 1988

THE QUEEN has been graciously pleased, on the occasion of the Celebration of Her Majesty's Birthday, to give orders for the following promotions in, and appointments to, the Most Honourable Order of the Bath.

ORDER OF THE BATH (MILITARY DIVISION)

MINISTRY OF DEFENCE (NAVY DEPARTMENT)

K.C.B.

To be an Ordinary Member of the Military Division of the Second Class, or Knight Commander, of the said Most Honourable Order:

Vice Admiral John Cunningham Kirkwood SLATER, L.V.O.

C.B.

To be Ordinary Members of the Military Division of the Third Class, or Companions, of the said Most Honourable Order:

Rear Admiral Roger Charles DIMMOCK.
Surgeon Rear Admiral Trevor Richard Walker HAMPTON, Q.H.P.

MINISTRY OF DEFENCE (ARMY DEPARTMENT)

G.C.B.

To be an Ordinary Member of the Military Division of the First Class, or Knight Grand Cross, of the said Most Honourable Order:

General Sir John CHAPPLE, K.C.B., C.B.E., A.D.C. Gen. (410821), Colonel 2nd King Edward VII's Own Gurkha Rifles (The Sirmoor Rifles).

K.C.B.

To be Ordinary Members of the Military Division of the Second Class, or Knights Commanders, of the said Most Honourable Order:

Lieutenant General John Richard Alexander MACMILLAN, C.B.E. (431870), late The Gordon Highlanders, Colonel Commandant The Scottish Division.

Lieutenant General Charles John WATERS, C.B.E. (445998), Colonel The Gloucestershire Regiment.

C.B.

To be Ordinary Members of the Military Division of the Third Class, or Companions, of the said Most Honourable Order:

Major General Bryan Morris BOWEN (437553), late Royal Army Pay Corps.

Major General Patrick Guy BROOKING, M.B.E. (448524), late 5th Royal Inniskilling Dragoon Guards.

Major General David Bryan Hall COLLEY, C.B.E. (433082), Colonel Commandant Royal Corps of Transport.

Major General Charles Gordon CORNOCK, M.B.E. (451215), Colonel Commandant Royal Regiment of Artillery.

Major General Anthony John SHAW, C.B., Q.H.P. (449523), late Royal Army Medical Corps.

Major General Colin Terry SHORTIS, C.B.E. (426767), Colonel Commandant The Prince of Wales's Division, Colonel The Devonshire and Dorset Regiment.

Major General Stephen Robert Anthony STOPFORD, M.B.E. (437176), late The Royal Scots Dragoon Guards (Carabiniers and Greys).

MINISTRY OF DEFENCE—AIR FORCE DEPARTMENT

K.C.B.

To be an Ordinary Member of the Military Division of the Second Class, or Knight Commander, of the said Most Honourable Order:

Air Marshal Kenneth William HAYR, C.B. C.B.E., A.F.C*, Royal Air Force.

C.B.

To be Ordinary Members of the Military Division of the Third Class, or Companions, of the said Most Honourable Order:

Air Vice-Marshal Richard Anthony MASON, C.B.E., Royal Air Force.

Air Vice-Marshal Michael George SIMMONS, A.F.C., Royal Air Force.

Air Vice-Marshal David WHITTAKER, M.B.E., Royal Air Force.

ORDER OF THE BATH (CIVIL DIVISION)

G.C.B.

To be an Ordinary Member of the Civil Division of the First Class, or Knight Grand Cross, of the said Most Honourable Order:

Sir Clive Anthony WHITMORE, K.C.B., C.V.O., Permanent Under Secretary of State, Home Office.

K.C.B

To be Ordinary Members of the Civil Division of the Second Class, or Knights Commanders, of the said Most Honourable Order:

Peter Lewis GREGSON, C.B., Permanent Under Secretary of State, Department of Energy.

Richard Anthony LLOYD JONES, C.B., Permanent Secretary, Welsh Office.

C.B.

To be Ordinary Members of the Civil Division of the Third Class, or Companions, of the said Most Honourable Order:

Professor Ronald Leslie BELL, Director-General, Agricultural Development and Advisory Service; Chief Scientific Adviser, Ministry of Agriculture, Fisheries and Food.

William Joseph BOHAN, Assistant Under Secretary of State, Home Office.

(John) Michael BRIDGEMAN, Chief Registrar of Friendly Societies and Industrial Assurance Commissioner.

John St Leger BROCKMAN, Solicitor to the Department of Health and Social Security, and Registrar General to the Office of Population Censuses and Surveys.

Harold Granville Terence Payne DOYNE-DITMAS, Under Secretary, Minister of Defence.

William Hugh JACK, Permanent Secretary, Department of Agriculture, Northern Ireland.

Iain Smith MACDONALD, Chief Medical Officer, Scottish Home and Health Department.

James Alexander Mackintosh MacKENZIE, lately Chief Road Engineer, Scottish Development Department.

James Stephen MASON, Parliamentary Counsel, Office of the Parliamentary Counsel.

Nicholas Jeremy MONCK, Deputy Secretary, H.M. Treasury.

Robin MOUNTFIELD, Deputy Secretary, Department of Trade and Industry.

John Tregarthen MURLEY, Foreign and Commonwealth Office.

Bernard POLLARD, lately Deputy Secretary and Director General (Technical), Board of Inland Revenue.

Peter Graham SMITH, Under Secretary, Ministry of Defence.

CENTRAL CHANCERY OF THE ORDERS OF KNIGHTHOOD

ST. JAMES'S PALACE, LONDON S.W.1

11th June 1988

THE QUEEN has been graciously pleased, on the occasion of the Celebration of Her Majesty's Birthday, to give orders for the following promotions in and appointments to the Most Distinguished Order of Saint Michael and Saint George:

C.M.G.

To be Ordinary Members of the Third Class, or Companions, of the said Most Distinguished Order:

Ronald Frank Robert DEARE, Grade 5, Overseas Development Administration.

Anthony David LOEHNIS, Executive Director, The Bank of England.

DIPLOMATIC SERVICE AND OVERSEAS LIST

G.C.M.G.

To be an Ordinary Member of the First Class, or Knight Grand Cross, of the said Most Distinguished Order:

The Right Honourable Peter Alexander Rupert, Baron CARRINGTON, K.G., C.H., K.C.M.G., M.C., Secretary-General, North Atlantic Treaty Organisation, Brussels.

K.C.M.G.

To be Ordinary Members of the Second Class, or Knights Commanders, of the said Most Distinguished Order:

Rodric Quentin BRAITHWAITE, C.M.G., Foreign and Commonwealth Office.

Alan Ewen DONALD, C.M.G., H.M. Ambassador, Peking.

John Rodney JOHNSON, C.M.G., British High Commissioner, Nairobi.

James MELLON, C.M.G., H.M. Consul-General and Director-General of Trade and Investment, New York.

C.M.G.

To be Ordinary Members of the Third Class, or Companions, of the said Most Distinguished Order:

Adrian John BEAMISH, H.M. Ambassador, Lima.
John Kenneth Elliott BROADLEY, H.M. Ambassador, Holy See.
Juliet Jeanne d'Auvergne Mrs. CAMPBELL, H.M. Ambassodor, Luxembourg.
Mark ELLIOTT, H.M. Ambassodor, Tel Aviv.
John Donald GARNER, L.V.O., H.M. Consul-General, Houston.
Michael John Carlisle GLAZE, H.M. Ambassador, Luanda.
Paul Emil HEIM, lately Registrar, European Court of Justice, Luxembourg.
Roger William HORRELL, O.B.E., Foreign and Commonwealth Office.
Alexander David KNOX, lately Vice-President, IBRD, New York.
Christopher John Rome MEYER, Foreign and Commonwealth Office.
David Purvis SMALL, M.B.E., British High Commissioner, Georgetown.
Veronica Evelyn Mrs. SUTHERLAND, H.M. Ambassador, Abidjan.

CENTRAL CHANCERY OF
THE ORDERS OF KNIGHTHOOD

ST. JAMES'S PALACE, LONDON S.W.1

11 June 1988

The QUEEN has been graciously pleased, on the occasion of the Celebration of Her Majesty's Birthday, to make the following promotions in, and appointments to, the Royal Victorian Order:

ROYAL VICTORIAN ORDER

G.C.V.O.

To be a Knight Grand Cross:

The Right Honourable Sir William Frederick Payne HESELTINE, K.C.B., K.C.V.O., A.C.

K.C.V.O.

To be Knights Commanders:

Colonel Robert Andrew St. George MARTIN, O.B.E.
Lieutentant-Colonel William Bertram SWAN, C.B.E., T.D.

C.V.O.

To be Commanders:

Eric HOPWOOD, O.B.E.
Michael MACLAGAN.
Brian Henry McGRATH.
William Richard Michael OSWALD, L.V.O.
Colonel Alan Brooke PEMBERTON, M.B.E.
Derek Roy WATERS, L.V.O.

L.V.O.

To be Lieutenants:

The Honourable Elizabeth Shan Josephine, Mrs LEGGE-BOURKE.
David Hubert Boothby CHESSHYRE.
John Cregg FENNELL.
Jean, Mrs. MAITLAND, M.V.O.
Anthony Stuart POOLE.
Group Captain Joseph Léon Gabriel TASCHEREAU, C.D., D.F.C., R.C.A.F. (Retd.)
Commander Christopher Robin TUFFLEY, Royal Navy.

M.V.O.

To be Members:

Miss Sheena Mary FERGUS.
Inspector Brian Cecil HOWES, Metropolitan Police.
Major Leslie Bertie Fitzroy MARSHAM.
Captain Roger McCLOSKY.
Dona, Mrs. MOWBRAY.
Warrant Officer (Seaman) Ellis Victor NORRELL, R.V.M., (J882555R), Royal Navy.

Superintendent Harold PARKINSON, Norfolk Constabulary.
Frederick George WAITE, R.V.M.
Sarah, Mrs. WARBURTON.

CENTRAL CHANCERY OF
THE ORDERS OF KNIGHTHOOD

ST. JAMES'S PALACE, LONDON S.W.1

11th June 1988

The QUEEN has been graciously pleased, on the occasion of the Celebration of Her Majesty's Birthday, to award the Royal Victorian Medal (Silver) to the undermentioned:

ROYAL VICTORIAN MEDAL (SILVER)

R.V.M.

Christopher Frederick BIGGS.
Divisional Sergeant-Major William Edward BRAMMER.
Corporal of Horse Edward George Reginald CHARLETT (22516123), Life Guards.
Percival COTTRELL.
Band Colour Sergeant Richard Cameron James GRANGER, (Q003923V), Royal Marines.
Graham John HARROD.
Roy Thomas William HOWLING
Lance Sergeant Ronald John LEWIS, (22831128), Welsh Guards.
Trevor MACE.
Corporal of Horse Douglas Clifford Frederick PREECE, (22026779), Blues and Royals.
James RUTT.
E1950220 Chief Technician Peter Clive SOAR, Royal Air Force.
A8080938 Chief Technician David TURNOCK, Royal Air Force.

CENTRAL CHANCERY OF
THE ORDERS OF KNIGHTHOOD

ST. JAMES'S PALACE, LONDON S.W.1

11th June 1988

The QUEEN has been graciously pleased, on the occasion of the Celebration of Her Majesty's Birthday, to give orders for the following promotions in, and appointments to, the Most Excellent Order of the British Empire:

ORDER OF THE BRITISH EMPIRE (MILITARY DIVISION)

MINISTRY OF DEFENCE (NAVY DEPARTMENT)

K.B.E.

To be an Ordinary Knight Commander of the Military Division of the said Most Excellent Order:
Surgeon Vice Admiral Geoffrey James MILTON-THOMPSON, Q.H.P.

C.B.E.

To be Ordinary Commanders of the Military Division of the said Most Excellent Order:

Captain Peter John ERSKINE, A.D.C., Royal Navy.
Captain Neil Erskine RANKIN, Royal Navy.
Captain Michael Edward SOUTHGATE, Royal Navy.

O.B.E.

To be Ordinary Officers of the Military Division of the said Most Excellent Order:

Commander Edgar Walter ANDREW, Royal Navy.
Commander Andrew Nigel BAIRD, Royal Navy.
Commander Joseph Louis BALLANTINE, R.D., Royal Naval Reserve.
Commander Christopher James CLAY, Royal Navy.
Lieutenant Colonel Timothy Kendall COURTENAY, Royal Marines.
Commander Anthony John Talbot EDDISON, Royal Navy.
Major (Local Lieutenant Colonel) Malcolm Loudoun Adair MACLEOD, Royal Marines.
Commander Geoffrey George MEEKUMS, Royal Navy.
Reverend Father John Joseph O'FARRELL, R.D., Royal Naval Reserve.
Commander Martin Herbert RHODES, Royal Navy.
Commander Michael Dewell SIZELAND, Royal Navy.

M.B.E.

To be Ordinary Members of the Military Division of the said Most Excellent Order:

Lieutenant Commander Phillip John Wheler BUSH, Royal Navy.
Lieutenant Colin Donald CARTER, Royal Navy.
Lieutenant Commander Edward Albert CHAMBERS, Royal Navy.
Warrant Officer (Seaman) Kan Fu CHUNG.
Lieutenant Commander David John CRINGLE, Royal Navy.
Warrant Officer (Master-at-Arms) Michael John Anan DULSON.
Lieutenant Commander John Vivian HARRIS, Royal Naval Reserve.
Lieutenant Commander John William HICKS, Royal Navy.
Lieutenant Commander Roy William LAMBERT, Royal Navy.
Lietenant Commander (SCC) Geoffrey PRESHNER, Royal Naval Reserve.
Lieutenant Jeremy Richard TOWNLEY, Royal Navy.
Lieutenant David Thomas WALKER, Royal Marines.
Lieutenant Mark Edward Charles WALTON, Royal Navy.
Warrant Officer (Communications Technician) Michael WILKINSON.
Lieutenant Commander Ronald Leslie YERRILL, Royal Navy.

MINISTRY OF DEFENCE (ARMY DEPARTMENT)

C.B.E.

To be Ordinary Commanders of the Military Division of the said Most Excellent Order:

Colonel David Leslie BURDEN (476891), late Royal Army Ordnance Corps.
Brigadier Raphael Christopher Joseph DICK (436305), late Royal Tank Regiment.
Brigadier Peter Royson DUFFELL, O.B.E., M.C. (466356), late 2nd King Edward VII's Own Gurkha Rifles (The Sirmoor Rifles).
Brigadier Michael Arthur GARDNER (445862), late Corps of Royal Electrical and Mechanical Engineers.
Colonel Harold Edward Dunstan GRIFFITHS, T.D. (424908), late Royal Army Medical Corps, Territorial Army.
Brigadier Mary Brigid Teresa HENNESSY, M.B.E., R.R.C., Q.H.N.S. (461076), Queen Alexandra's Royal Army Nursing Corps.
Bridadier Robert George LONG, O.B.E., M.C. (448172), Colonel The Royal Hampshire Regiment.
Colonel David John Ralls, O.B.E., D.F.C. (472605), late Army Air Corps.
Brigadier Michael John WILKES, O.B.E. (467647), late Royal Regiment of Artillery.

O.B.E.

To be Ordinary Officers of the Military Division of the said Most Excellent Order:

Lieutenant Colonel James Graham ALDOUS (473528), The Royal Regiment of Fusiliers.
Lieutenant Colonel David Arnold Kellett BIGGART, M.B.E. (481643), The Royal Regiment of Fusiliers.
Lieutenant Colonel (Quartermaster) Robert Cecil EDGER, M.B.E. (485037), The Royal Regiment of Wales (24th/41st Foot).
Lieutenant Colonel Christopher David GALE, T.D. (476219), Royal Corps of Signals, Teritorial Army.
Lieutenant Colonel (Electrical Mechanical Assistant Engineer) Ian Alexander GARROW (488675), Corps of Royal Electrical and Mechanical Engineers.
Lieutenant Colonel Anthony Edward HEMESLEY (457178), The Queen's Lancashire Regiment.
Lieutenant Colonel Richard John HEYWOOD, M.B.E. (474385), Coldstream Guards.
Lieutenant Colonel Edward Richard HOLMES, T.D. (483098), Wessex Regiment, Territorial Army.
Lieutenant Colonel William Barry HUGHES-JONES (464455), Corps of Royal Military Police.
Lieutenant Colonel Anthony William KINGABY (493080), Royal Regiment of Artillery.
Lieutenant Colonel Robert Michael McGHIE (483967), The Queen's Regiment.
Lieutenant Colonel Peter John RUSSELL-JONES (485821), Corps of Royal Engineers.
Lieutenant Colonel Eric Henry SAMBELL (483546), Royal Corps of Signals.
Acting Colonel Michael Joseph Forster SHEFFIELD, T.D., D.L. (438754), Army Cadet Force, Territorial Army.
Acting Colonel Kenneth Richard SMITH (475912), Army Cadet Force, Territorial Army.
Lieutenant Colonel John Michael THORN (482854), The Duke of Wellington's Regiment (West Riding).
The Reverend Christopher Charles TOMLINSON, Chaplain to the Forces 2nd Class (493827), Royal Army Chaplains' Department.
Lieutenant Colonel George Dennis Sommerville TRUELL, M.B.E. (365912), Royal Regiment of Artillery.

M.B.E.

To be Ordinary Members of the Military Division of the said Most Excellent Order:

Captain Jeremy Wilfred Lloyd Shepherdson AVERY (508765), The Parachute Regiment, Territorial Army.
Major (Quartermaster) Ronald Thomas BEVAN (506231), 2nd King Edward VII's Own Gurkha Rifles (The Sirmoor Rifles).
22462406 Warrant Officer Class 2 Livingstone BOYD, Royal Regiment of Artillery, Territorial Army.
24034340 Warrant Officer Class 1 Arthur Grahame BRADSHAW, Army Catering Corps.
Major Andrew John BRIGGS (478491), Royal Corps of Signals.
Major (Quartermaster) Harry Roy BURNETT (500916), The Light Infantry.
Major (Quartermaster) Ronald Cecil COLEMAN (501458), Royal Regiment of Artillery.
Major Stewart James CROWE (491433), Royal Army Ordnance Corps.
Major Michael John DENT (503659), Royal Corps of Signals.
Major Anthony Paul DOMEISEN (486635), The Royal Anglian Regiment.
Major Anthony Harrison DOUGLAS (495505), Corps of Royal Engineers.
Major Roger Alan DUDIN (485718), Corps of Royal Engineers.

Major Graham Richard ELLIOT (485721), Royal Corps of Signals.
Captain (Quartermaster) Clifton Luther FIELDS (515033), Royal Regiment of Artillery.
22082248 Warrant Officer Class 2 Ronald GORDON, Royal Army Pay Corps, Territorial Army.
Major John Richard IBBOTSON (505050), The Parachute Regiment.
Captain Thomas Edwin HALL (489624), Royal Corps of Signals, Territorial Army.
Major John Richard IBBOTSON (505050), The Parachute Regiment.
24211547 Warrant Officer Class 1 Stephen Francis JOSEPH, Corps of Royal Electrical and Mechanical Engineers.
Captain Bernard Francis KANE (500141), Mercian Volunteers, Territorial Army.
Major John Seumas KERR (495356), Royal Army Ordnance Corps.
Major Gerald David KNEALE (498172), Royal Corps of Transport.
Major Graeme Cameron Maxwell LAMB (495192), Queen's Own Highlanders (Seaforth and Camerons).
Major Gerard Courtney MIDDLETON (479430), Royal Regiment of Artillery.
Captain John Frederick MILWARD (487247), The Royal Anglian Regiment, Territorial Army.
Major Robert James MOORE (499486), Royal Corps of Signals, Territorial Army.
Major John Barry MORGAN (507798), Royal Army Ordnance Corps.
Major Michael Duncan Arthur MORRIS (485789), Royal Regiment of Artillery.
Captain Alan William Martin PETCH, T.D. (473596), The Royal Anglian Regiment, Territorial Army.
Major David Michael Gurney RANDALL (437145), Royal Corps of Transport.
22661878 Warrant Officer Class 2 Alan John SLADE, Royal Regiment of Artillery.
24069783 Warrant Officer Class 1 Terence Charles SPICER, Royal Corps of Signals.
Major (Quartermaster) William Roger STAFFORD (505566), The Duke of Edinburgh's Royal Regiment (Berkshire and Wiltshire).
The Reverend Herbert Edward STEED, Chaplain to the Forces 3rd Class (457810), Royal Army Chaplains' Department, Territorial Army.
Captain (Electrical Mechanical Assistant Engineer) John TAYLOR (512337), Corps of Royal Electrical and Mechanical Engineers.
Captain (Quartermaster) Harold Alwyn Vibert TONEY (518504), The Royal Irish Rangers (27th (Inniskilling) 83rd and 87th).
Major Garth Jon WHITTY (503967), Corps of Royal Engineers.
Major Aldwin James Glendinning WIGHT, M.C. (501023), Welsh Guards.
24085177 Warrant Officer Class 2 Oliver Nicholas Bogle WILLMOTT, Corps of Royal Engineers.
Captain Barrie Edward WRIGHT (520443). Royal Tank Regiment.

OVERSEAS AWARD

M.B.E.

To be an Ordinary Member of the Military Division of the said Most Excellent Order:

Major John Joseph BENTO, The Bermuda Regiment.

MINISTRY OF DEFENCE—AIR FORCE DEPARTMENT

C.B.E.

To be Ordinary Commanders of the Military Division of the said Most Excellent Order:

Air Commodore William Henry CROYDON, O.B.E., Royal Air Force.
Group Captain David Francis Layton EDWARDS, Royal Air Force.
Air Commodore Ian Ross LINDSAY, Royal Air Force.
Air Commodore Robert Lawrence REID, O.B.E., Royal Air Force (Retd.)

O.B.E.

To be Ordinary Officers of the Military Division of the said Most Excellent Order:

Wing Commander David Christopher BROWN (4335265), Royal Air Force.
Wing Commander Leslie HAKIN (4256441), Royal Air Force.
Wing Commander Ian Rowland HILL (5200882), Royal Air Force.
Wing Commander Timothy John JOHNS (208755), Royal Air Force Volunteer Reserve (Training).
Wing Commander Graham Fearon McMELLIN(2619363), Royal Air Force.
Wing Commander Ronald George NAILER (609393), Royal Air Force.
Wing Commander Leslie Winston POYNTER (4335207), Royal Air Force.
Wing Commander Anthony Francis SHORT (4335224), Royal Air Force.
Wing Commander Trevor George SIDEBOTTOM (5200966), Royal Air Force.
Wing Commander Graeme Campbell SMITH, A.F.C. (5200231), Royal Air Force.
Wing Commander Neil Alexander INNES-SMITH (2410992), Royal Air Force.

M.B.E.

To be Ordinary Members of the Military Division of the said Most Excellent Order:

Squadron Leader Nicholas Robert CHANDLER (5204435), Royal Air Force.
Squadron Leader John Sutherland DOUGLAS (4232150), Royal Air Force.
Squadron Leader John Geoffrey ELLIOTT (608743), Royal Air Force.
Squadron Leader Brynmor EVANS (1922868), Royal Air Force.
Warrant Officer David Andrew GUY (X3526147), Royal Air Force.
Warrant Officer David John HELSON (F0592503), Royal Air Force.
Flight Lieutenant Willie HUGGINS (592298), Royal Air Force (Retd.)
Squadron Leader Eric James Alfred HUGHES (40667588), Royal Air Force.
Squadron Leader George Everritt HUNTLEY (2761985), Royal Air Force Volunteer Reserve (Training).
Flight Lieutenant Erhard Walter JUNGMAYR (5205162), Royal Air Force.
Warrant Officer Robert Harvey KEAY (A1932610), Royal Air Force.
Squadron Leader James Robert LEES (8022808), Royal Air Force.
Squadron Leader Richard Charles MOORE (8022778), Royal Air Force.
Squadron Leader Glenn Stewart PEARSON (4280764), Royal Air Force.
Squadron Leader Stuart Luff PIERCE (4094714), Royal Air Force.
Warrant Officer Ian REEVES (S1923847), Royal Air Force.
Warrant Officer Robert Lewis SEMPLE (H4133243), Royal Air Force.
Warrant Officer Alexander Murray SIMPSON, B.E.M. (H1941660), Royal Air Force.
Flight Lieutenant Brian Turner STOCKMAN (4075680), Royal Air Force.
Warrant Officer Keith John TEESDALE, A.F.M. (B4153188), Royal Air Force.
Warrant Officer Edward Alan TOINTON (Q4074319), Royal Air Force.
Squadron Leader John McMillan TWEEDLEY (1926529), Royal Air Force.
Squadron Leader David Charles VASS (8025130), Royal Air Force.
Squadron Leader Richard Stafford WATERS (5203066), Royal Air Force.
Reverend (Squadron Leader) Ivan John WESTON (5203496), Royal Air Force.
Warrant Officer Robert Bewley WREN (G4237895), Royal Air Force.

ORDER OF THE BRITISH EMPIRE (CIVIL DIVISION)

G.B.E.

To be an Ordinary Knight Grand Cross of the Civil Division of the said Most Excellent Order:

Sir Kenneth BERRILL, K.C.B., lately Chairman, Securities and Investments Board.

D.B.E.

To be Ordinary Dames Commanders of the Civil Division of the said Most Excellent Order:

Miss Beryl Elizabeth GREY, C.B.E. (Mrs. Svenson). For services to the London Festival Ballet and the Royal Academy of Dancing.
Miss Rosalinde HURLEY (Mrs. Gortvai), Chairman, The Medicines Commission; Professor of Microbiology, University of London.

K.B.E.

To be an Ordinary Knight Commander of the Civil Division of the said Most Excellent Order:

Sir (John) Robin IBBS, Director, Lloyds Bank plc; Adviser to the Prime Minister on Efficiency and Effectiveness in Government.

C.B.E.

To be Ordinary Commanders of the Civil Division of the said Most Excellent Order:

Miss Aileen Kirkpatrick ADAMS, Dean, Faculty of Anaesthetists Royal College of Surgeons.
Peter Dobson ALLEN, Managing Director, Operations, Strip Products Group, British Steel Corporation.
Brian Cecil ARTHUR, Chief Inspector, H.M. Inspectorate of Schools, Department of Education and Science.
John Charles BASS, Director of Research, The Plessey Company plc.
Edward John BAVISTER, Chairman, John Brown Engineers and Constructors Limited.
Professor John Kenneth Anthony BLEASDALE, lately Director, Institute of Horticultural Research, Agriculture and Food Research Council.
Dennis Galt BOYD, Chief Conciliation Officer, Advisory, Conciliation and Arbitration Service.
Michael Dennis BRYANT, Actor.
John David Keith BURTON, H.M. Coroner, Western District, Greater London; Secretary, Coroners' Society, England and Wales.
Patrick Alfred CALDWELL-MOORE, O.B.E. For services to Astronomy.
John Cyril CHAPLIN, Group Director, Safety Regulation Group, Civil Aviation Authority.
Francis Ian CHAPMAN, Chairman and Chief Executive, William Collins plc.
Barton James CLARKE, Chairman and Managing Director, Racal Radar Defence Systems. For services to Export.
Samuel Laurence Harrison CLARKE. For services to Collaborative Research in Information Technology.
Timothy Francis CLEMENT-JONES. For political service.
Geoffrey John CLEVERDON. For political and public service.
John Ernest CLOUT, Leader, North Yorkshire County Council.
Herbert Evan CORNISH, Chairman, Lin Pac Group Limited.
Elizabeth Crawford Gallagher, Mrs. GRAGHILL, lately Assistant Secretary, Scottish Development Department.
Edward Brandwood CUNNINGHAM, Director, Planning and Projects, Scottish Development Agency.
James Gresham DAVIS, Chairman, International Maritime Industries Forum.
Hugh Arnold Freeman DUDLEY, Professor of Surgery, St. Mary's Hospital.
Brian EDWARDS, Regional General Manager, Trent Regional Health Authority.
Noreen Louisa, Mrs. EDWARDS, O.B.E., T.D., D.L., Chairman, Gwynedd Health Authority.
Frederick Ernest ELLIOTT. For services to the National Farmers' Union.
Donald FORSTER, lately Chairman, Merseyside Development Corporation.
Wallace Stewart FOULDS, Tennent Professor of Ophthalmology, University of Glasgow.
John GADD, lately Regional Chairman, North Thames, British Gas plc.
Nicol Spence GALBRAITH, Director, Communicable Disease Surveillance Centre, Public Health Laboratory Service.
Derek Stanley GORDON, O.B.E., Consultant Neuro-Surgeon, Royal Victoria Hospital, Belfast.
Ian David GRANT, President National Farmers' Union, Scotland.
Professor Edward Thomas HALL. For scientific services to Archaeology.
Dennis John HATFIELD, Chief Education Officer, Trafford.
Gordon Drummond John HAY, Chairman, Stoddard Holdings plc.
Robert Colquhoun HAY, President, Industrial Tribunals, Scotland.
William Ross HENDERSON, T.D. For political service.
Stanley Thomas Keck HESTER, lately Director of Audit, Ministry of Agriculture, Fisheries and Food.
Werner Wolfgang HEUBUCK, O.B.E., Managing Director, Ulsterbus Limited and Citybus Limited.
Colonel William Peter HOWELLS, O.B.E., T.D., D.L., Chairman, Wales Territorial Auxiliary and Volunteer Association.
Pamela May, Mrs. HUDSON-BENDERSKY, Regional Nursing Director, North West Thames Regional Health Authority.
Thomas HUNTER, Convenor, Borders Regional Council.
Francis Brian Appleton IRVING. For political and public service.
Professor Robert Barr JACK. For services to the Legal Profession in Scotland.
Professor Anthony KELLY. For services to Science and Engineering; Vice Chancellor, University of Surrey.
Patrick Gerard Joseph KINDER, General Manager, Eastern Health and Social Services Board.
Frederick John KINGDOM, Deputy Leader, West Glamorgan County Council.
Gavin Harry LAIRD, General Secretary, Amalgamated Engineering Union.
Philip Michael LEE, Grade 4 Department of Transport.
His Honour Arthur Christian LUFT, lately First Deemster and Clerk of the Rolls and Deputy Governor, Isle of Man.
Katharine Elizabeth, Mrs. LUMSDEN, D.L. For political and public service.
John Alexander Rose MacPHAIL, O.B.E., Chairman, The Scotch Whisky Association.
Norman Alastair Duncan MACRAE, Deputy Editor, The Economist.
Peter MASON, Foreign and Commonwealth Office.
Miss (Margaret) Valerie MASTERSON (Mrs. March), Opera and Concert Singer.
Keith Desmond McDOWALL, lately Deputy Director-General, Confederation of British Industry.
George Roy Colquhoun McDOWELL, Chairman of the Board, The British Standards Institution.
Kenneth Allan Glen MILLER, Director General, The Engineering Council.
Commander Denis Woolnough MILLS, R.N. (Retd.), O.B.E., D.S.C. For political and public service.
Kenneth MOSES, Technical Director, British Coal Corporation.
David Fairlie MYLES. For political and public service.
Charles Allen OAKLEY. For public service in the West of Scotland.
Gareth OWEN, Principal, University College of Wales, Aberystwyth.
Henry Richard OWEN, M.B.E., Grade 5, Department of Trade and Industry.
John William PENYCATE, Chairman Yvonne Arnaud Theatre.
Michael John PRICE. For political and public service.
John Charles RAMSDEN. For political and public service.
Alfred Graham RAPER, lately Chief Executive and Deputy Chairman, Davy Corporation plc.
John David RENDLE, lately Managing Director, Shell Tankers (UK) Limited.
John David Benbow RICHARDSON, M.C., President, Northern Rent Assessment Panel.
Eric Frederick ROGERS, Deputy Chairman, Occupational Pensions Board.
James Cecil Cumine RUSSELL, M.B.E. For political and public service.
Colin SAMPSON, Q.P.M., Chief Constable, West Yorkshire Police.
Charles Robert SCAIFE, National Chairman, The Royal British Legion.
Professor John Parsons SHILLINGFORD, Medical Director, British Heart Foundation.
Keith Alexander SKINNER, Senior Principal Inspector of Taxes, Board of Inland Revenue.
William Leggat SMITH, M.C., T.D., D.L. For public service in Glasgow.

William Lawrence SOUTH, Technical Director, Philips Electronic and Associated Industries Limited.
Professor Colin Raymond William SPEDDING, Director, Centre for Agricultural Strategy, Reading University.
Colin STANSFIELD SMITH, County Architect, Hampshire County Council.
Frederick Alistair STONE, lately Clerk and Chief Executive Surrey County Council.
Michael Anthony STOTHERS, Chairman, William Steward Group.
William Henry STRAWSON, D. L., Chairman, Institute of Plant Science Research.
Norman Frederick SUSSMAN, O.B.E., Joint Managing Director, L.S. and J. Sussman Limited.
Arthur Cecil TAYLOR, Chairman, Newcastle Health Authority.
Miss Wendy Ann TAYLOR, Sculptor.
John Harry TEE, Assistant Secretary, Board of Customs and Excise.
William James UTTLEY-MOORE, Chairman and Managing Director, Computing Devices plc.
Arthur Burton WELLER, Chairman, Britain-Australia Bicentennial Schooner Trust.
Reginald Alfred, Baron WELLS-PESTELL. For Services to Parliamentary Committees.
Alan WICKS, Organist and Director of Music, Canterbury Cathedral.
John Meredith WILLIAMS, Chairman, Welsh Development Agency.
Dennis James WILLMOTT, Q.F.S.M., lately Chief Fire Officer, Merseyside Fire Brigade.
Reginald George WOODMAN, Grade 4, Ministry of Defence.
Group Captain John Basil WRAY, R.A.F., (Retd.) D.F.C. For political service.
John Mickelthwaite WRAY, Assistant Secretary, Department of Health and Social Security.
Peter WRIGHT, O.B.E., Chief Constable, South Yorkshire Police.

O.B.E.

To be Ordinary Officers of the Civil Division of the said Most Excellent Order:

Eric Martin ABBOTT, Grade 6, Ministry of Agriculture, Fisheries and Food.
Anne Maureen, Mrs. ACLAND, Chairman of Council, Queen's Nursing Institute.
Eric Edward ALLEY. For services to Civil Defence.
Kenneth Michael BAKER, Managing Director, Durr Limited.
Thomas Anthony BALL, lately Senior Catering Adviser, Department of Education and Science.
Anthony Kenneth BARBOUR. For services to Environmental Science.
Andrew BARR, Member, South of Scotland Electricity Board.
Miss Joyce Anne BEAK, Chief Nursing Officer, Tunbridge Wells Health Authority.
Dennis Henry Caleb BENNETT, Head Teacher, Cyfarthfa Comprehensive School, Merthyr Tydfil, Mid Glamorgan.
Alan Winstan BOND, Deputy Director, London Chamber of Commerce.
Professor Thomas Geoffrey BOOTH, lately President, Pharmaceutical Society of Great Britain.
Professor Richard John BROOK, lately Head of Department of Ceramics, University of Leeds.
Charles Harry BROOKS, Director, Hawker Siddeley International Ltd. For services to Export.
Professor Raymond Victor BROOKS. For services to research into drug usage in Sport.
Greta Mary, Mrs. BROWN. For political and public service.
Lionel Neville BROWN, Professor of Comparative Law, University of Birmingham; Member, Council on Tribunals.
Miss Marian Phyllis BULL, Chief Administrative Nursing Officer, Mid Glamorgan Health Authority.
Anthony Winston BURTON, Director, The Planning Exchange.
Sister Hannah CALLAGHAN (Sister Mary Perpetua), Sister Superior, St. Anthony's Hospital, Sutton, Surrey.
John Alexander CALVERT. For political and public service.
Romayne Winifred, Mrs. CARSWELL, Deputy Chairman, Independent Commission for Police Complaints for Northern Ireland.
Kenneth James Herbert CARTER, Principal, Ministry of Defence.
Jack Morgan CHAPMAN, Principal, West Kent College of Further Education, Tonbridge, Kent.
Miss Claire Helen CHOVIL, Head of School Broadcasting (Radio), British Broadcasting Corporation.
William John CHRISTIE. For services to Farming and Conservation.
Captain Peter COBB, R.N. (Retd.), Secretary, United Kingdom Branch, Commonwealth Parliamentary Association.
Miss Audrey Towl COLLINS, President, Women's Cricket Association.
Peter James CONCHIE, Director, Business Development, Space and Communications Division, British Aerospace plc.
Miss Anne Valerie COWIE (Mrs. Harvey), Director, Labour Relations and Legal Department, Royal College of Nursing.
Anthony Bernard COYLE, Leader of the Council, Wigan Metropolitan Borough Council.
John Burton CROWTHER, Principal, John Crowther and Associates.
Raymond Charles CURRY, T.D. For political and public service.
John David Scott CURTIS, Chairman, Standing Conference on Crime Prevention, Home Office.
Barrie Randel DAREWSKI, Secretary, Osteopathic Educational Foundation.
Gerald Hill DAVID, Chairman and Managing Director, Aerial Facilities Limited.
Susan Elizabeth, Mrs. DAVIES, Director, The Photographers, Gallery Limited.
Michael Henry DAVIS, Grade 6, Department of Transport.
William Henry DEAKIN. For services to County Planning particularly in Kent.
Alexander Patrick Cuming DICKSON, Director, Dickson Nurseries Limited, County Down, Northern Ireland.
Kenneth DUDLEY, lately Director-General, Campden Food Preservation Research Association.
Anthony John Hast DURHAM, Deputy Chairman, Cambridge Newspapers Limited.
James Millar ECKFORD, General Manager, Ayrshire and Arran Health Board.
Robert Leadam EDDISON, Actor.
Felicity Clare, Mrs. EDWARDS, lately Senior Employment Medical Adviser, Rehabilitation, Health and Safety Executive.
Nancy, Mrs. ELLIOTT, Senior Inspector, Primary Education, Newcastle-upon-Tyne Local Education Authority.
Maurice Alfred ELWOOD, lately Principal Scientific Officer, Ministry of Defence.
David Eurof EVANS, Site General Manager, Amersham International plc, Cardiff.
Alan FENWICK, Grade 7, Overseas Development Administration.
Miss Barbara Mary FEWSTER (Mrs. Wilkinson), Associate Director, The Royal Ballet School.
Brigadier Richard Harry FISHER, M.B.E., M.C., Vice-President, County Durham Branch, Soldiers' Sailors' and Airmen's Families Association.
John Allan FLEMING, Consultant Veterinary Adviser to the Royal Air Force.
Keith FOX, Chairman and Managing Director, Blackwood Bros. Limited, Kilmarnock.
Captain John Lionel FRANCIS, D.L. For political and public service.
Harry FRITH, Chairman of Trustee Directors, Pilots' National Pension Fund Trust Company Limited.
John Charles GALE, lately Principal Professional and Technology Officer, Ministry of Defence.
Thomas Noel Cheney GARFIT, lately Member, Process Plant and Engineering Construction, Economic Development Committee.
Peter Harry GAYWARD, Director of Finance, University of Liverpool.
Alan Johnston GIBSON, lately President, Institute of Chartered Accountants in Ireland.
John Eifion GOSS, Headteacher, Broadway Comprehensive School, Birmingham.
Daphne Jasmine Elliot, Mrs. GOULD, Headteacher, Mulberry School, Tower Hamlets, Inner London Education Authority.
The Reverend William Robert Nelson GRAY, lately Executive Producer, Religious Programmes, Scottish Television plc.
Norma Lea, Mrs. GREEN. For political service.
Professor Peter Arthur GREEN, Dean, Faculty of Art and Design, Middlesex Polytechnic.

Lionel Harry GRUNDY, Deputy Chief Constable, Wiltshire Constabulary.
John Philip HALL, Principal, Board of Customs and Excise.
Miss Martha HAMILTON (Mrs. Steedman), lately Headmistress, St. Leonards School, St. Andrews.
Thomas Allingham HAMILTON, Principal, Glengormley High School, County Antrim.
Elizabeth Ivy, Her Grace the Dowager Duchess of HAMILTON and BRANDON, D.L. For services to the Lamp of Lothian Collegiate Trust.
Bernard HAMMOND, manager, Test Division, Southern Electricity Board.
Leonard HARRIS, Director, Central Area, British Coal Corporation.
Harold HASSAL. For services to the community in Cheshire.
Pamela Norah Elizabeth, Mrs. HAWTON. For political and public service.
Mary Xenia, Lady HENDERSON. For services to British Fashion Design.
Stuart HENDY, Partner, Faulkner-Brown, Hendy, Watkinson Stoner.
Beresford Ivan HENRY, Co-ordinator and Company Secretary, Handsworth Employment Scheme.
James HENRY, Chairman and Managing Director, Henry Brothers (Magherafelt) Limited.
Frank Norry HOGG, Principal, Welsh College of Librarianship.
Anthony David HOPKINS, Chairman and Managing Director, Delta Sound Limited.
Jadwiga, Mrs. HOWELLS, Grade 7, Department of the Environment.
Miss Janet Latta Picken HUNTER, Consultant Paediatrician, Grimsby Hospital Group.
Maria Luisa, Countess of IDDESLEIGH, D.L., President, Devon Branch, The British Red Cross Society.
Mary (Marie) Isabella, Mrs. JACK, Principal, The Arts Educational Trust School, Tring, Hertfordshire.
Robert Hugh JACKSON, M.C., Medical Consultant, Child Accident Prevention Trust.
Brian JARMAN, General Medical Practitioner; Professor of Primary Care, St. Mary's Hospital Medical School.
Elgar Spencer JENKINS, Leader, Bath City Council.
Michael David JENNER, Process Innovation Manager, Mullard Limited.
Geoffrey Arthur JENNINGS, Leader, Brentwood District Council.
John Anthony William JENNINGS. For services to the Catholic Fund for Overseas Development.
William Maurice JOHNSTON, M.B.E., Assistant Chief Constable, Royal Ulster Constabulary.
Roy Charles JONES, Principal, Department of the Environment.
Vincent KANE. For services to Broadcasting in Wales.
Miss Olga KENNARD. For services to Scientific Research on the Structure of Biological Molecules.
Noel KIRTON, Chairman, Cleveland Area Manpower Board.
Eddie (Elias George) KULUKUNDIS. For services to Sport.
Peter Edmund LAKE, Head of Department of Reproductive Physiology, Institute of Animal Physiology and Genetics Research, Edinburgh, Agricultural and Food Research Council.
Professor David LAYTON. For services to Science Education.
Miss Daphne Orynthia LEARMONT, lately Nursing Officer, Department of Health and Social Security.
Norman William LEE, County Engineer and Surveyor, Avon.
Jonathan Andrew LEITCH, Deputy Managing Director, Dynamics Division, Stevenage, British Aerospace plc.
The Honourable Robin William LEWIS, Managing Director, Physiological Instrumentation Limited, Whitland, Dyfed.
Leonard Arthur George LINDEN, Production and Engineering Director, Negretti Aviation Limited.
John Walter LLOYD, Director, Regional Pain Relief Unit, Oxford.
James LOGAN, lately Vice-Chairman, Scottish Arts Council.
Eric James MACFARLANE, Principal, Queen Mary's Sixth Form College, Basingstoke, Hampshire.
Peter MALCOLMSON, Director of Social Work, Shetland Islands Council
William MARTIN, Chief Executive, Coventry Churches Housing Association.
Jeffery George MATHIESON, Deputy City Surveyor, Corporation of London.
David Edward Moore MAXWELL, Principal, Clondermot High School, Londonderry.
Edward Fredrick MAY, Director, Schlumberger Industries (Sangamo-Metering).
William McEWAN, Director Scottish School of Non-Destructive Testing, Paisley College of Technology.
Andrew McKIBBIN, Consultant, Erne Hospital, Enniskillen, Northern Ireland.
John Francis Valentine McMURRAY, Principal, Department of Health and Social Services, Northern Ireland.
James McWILLIAM, Chairman, Highland Health Board.
John William Marc MESTON, Controller, Occupational Safety and Hygiene, Rank Hovis McDougall.
Major Peter Victor MOORE (Retd.). For services to Rural Conservation.
Henry John NASH, Chairman, Firsteel Manufacturing Limited.
George Henry NEAL. For services to the mentally handicapped.
Jesse Richard NEW, Executive Director, Personnel, Marshall of Cambridge (Engineering) Limited.
Sir Iain Andrew NOBLE Bt. For services to Gaelic Language and Culture.
Ian David NUSSEY, Manager, Warwick Development Group, IBM United Kingdom Limited.
Egil Robert ORSKOV, Senior Principal Scientific Officer, Rowett Research Institute, Aberdeen.
Miss Joan OWENS, Principal, Northern Ireland Office.
Henry Anthony PAWSON. For services to Angling.
George Walter PEKAREK, General Manager, Commercial, Albright and Wilson Limited.
Thomas Heydon PENSON. For political and public service.
Ray Buchanan, Mrs. PIGOTT. For political service.
Harold PINDER. For political and public service.
Derek Edward PIPE, Senior Principal, Board of Inland Revenue.
Raymond Arthur PITTOCK, Grade 7, The Patent Office.
Derrick James Branscomb PLATT, Chairman, Eastbourne Health Authority and Eastbourne Association of Voluntary Service.
Miss Jennifer POLAND, Director, Unit of Veterinary Continuing Education, Royal Veterinary College.
Colin Harold POTHECARY, Partner, MRM Partnership, Consulting Engineers.
Dawson PRICE, Principal Establishment Officer, London Headquarters, United Kingdom Atomic Energy Authority.
Canon William Frederick REID, lately Secretary, Church of England Hospital Chaplaincies Council.
John Alistair RIDDELL, General Practitioner, Glasgow.
Richard Frank RIMMER, lately Deputy Managing Director, YARD Limited, Glasgow.
Julian Mervyn ROBERTS, Consultant Psychiatrist, St James' Hospital, Leeds, and High Royds' Hospital, Menston.
Robert William Kelly Cupples ROGERSON, Chairman, Committee on Access for Scotland.
Daniel Clive Thomas ROWLANDS. For services to Rugby Union Football.
Robert William RUSSELL, Principal Professional and Technology Officer, Ministry of Defence.
Douglas Cecil RUSTOM, D.F.C., Executive Secretary, Association of International Courier and Express Services.
William John SAINT, Chief Executive, North West Europe, BP Petroleum Development Limited.
Gordon Ramsay SCOTT. For services to Tropical Veterinary Medicine.
Laurence Alfred SCUDDER, Senior Principal, Home Office.
Mortimer (Tim) SHAPLEY. For services to Mobility for the Disabled.
Terence John SIGGS, Deputy Assistant Commissioner, Metropolitan Police.
Allen SIMMEN, Principal, Scottish Home and Health Department.
Frank Alexander SIMS, Chief Executive, Pell Frischmann Consultants Limited.
Francis William SLEEMAN, Inspector (P), Board of Inland Revenue.
Eric Watson SMITH, Industrial Relations Director, Yarrow Shipbuilders Limited.
Margaret Watson, Mrs. SMITH. For political and public service.
Maurice George SMITH, Chairman, Knights Association of Christian Youth Clubs, Lambeth.

Thomas SMITH, Managing Director, Thomas Smith and Sons (Kirkoswald) Limited.
Thomas Peter SNAPE, General Secretary, Secondary Heads' Association.
Kenneth George Edwin SPINK. For political and public service.
Roger Charlton SPOOR. For services to the community in Newcastle-upon-Tyne.
The Reverend Brother Cornelius (John) SREENAN, lately Head, St Boniface's College, Plymouth.
John Robin STAYT, lately Chief Commissioner, The Scout Association.
James STEWART, Member, Fire Authority for Northern Ireland.
John Barry Bingham STEWART, Member, Scottish Agricultural Wages Board.
Miss Patricia Creswick STOCKEN. For political service.
Martin William SUTHERS. For political and public service.
Merrick Wentworth TAYLOR, Deputy Chairman and Managing Director, Motor Panels Coventry Limited.
John Hedly Brian TEW, External Professor of Economics, Loughborough University. For public service.
Archibald Grahame THOMSON, Director, Scottish Daily Newspaper Society.
William Paterson Loudoun THOMSON, Rector, Kirkwall Grammar School, Orkney.
Sydney Frederick TONGUE, lately Chief Executive, Wrexham Maelor Borough Council.
Major Alexander TRIMMER R.E. (Retd.), Secretary, Quantity Surveyors Division, Royal Institution of Chartered Surveyors.
Geoffrey Wensly TROTTER, Chairman, London Taxi Board.
Donald Alexander Gordon TROUP. For services to Agriculture and Land Agency.
John Oliver Warrillow TUNNELL, Leader, Scottish Chamber Orchestra.
Robert John TYLER, President, National Federation of Meat Traders.
Joseph Michael VALDES SCOTT, Chief Executive, Latin America Trade Advisory Group. For services to Export.
Julia Colleen, Mrs. VEALE, Member, Prison Service Board of Visitors, H.M. Prison, Channings Wood.
Rita Joyce, Mrs. WAITE, Area Organiser, East Midlands, Women's Royal Voluntary Service.
Joseph WALKER, Senior Director, Walkers Shortbread Limited, Aberlour.
Captain Brian Owen WALPOLE, General Manager, Concorde, British Airways plc.
Robert Gordon WEAVER, Chief Executive, Fisheries Conservancy Board, Northern Ireland.
Trevor Hugh WEBB. For political and public service.
Major Geoffrey Hildred WEBB-BOWEN (Retd.) D.L., lately Chairman, Stoke-on-Trent Advisory Committee on Justices of the Peace. For services to the Magistracy.
Professor John Roger WEBSTER, lately Chairman, Post Office User's Council and Advisory Committee on Telecommunications, Wales.
Michael John David WESTBROOK, Jazz Musician and Composer.
Alan Rogers WHITEHEAD, Inspector (SP), Board of Inland Revenue.
Frederick George WILCOX, lately Special Projects Manager, Commercial Department, Devonport Management Limited.
David Cranston WILLIAMS, Chairman, Area Manpower Board, Dyfed and West Glamorgan, Manpower Services Commission.
John Brinley WILLIAMS, lately Managing Director, Associated British Ports; Director, Associated British Ports Holdings plc.
John James Hiam WILSON, Director, Frederick Hiam Limited, Bury St Edmunds, Suffolk.
Winifred Mary, Mrs. WILSON, Chairman, Children Nationwide Research Fund.
Phoebe Madeline, Mrs. WINCH. For political service.
Cecil Douglas WOODWARD, Director, Fire Protection Association.

M.B.E.

To be Ordinary Members of the Civil Division of the said Most Excellent Order:

Donald ALLEN. For services to the community in Sittingbourne, Kent.
Rosa Anna, Mrs. ALLEN, Freelance Interpreter and Translator.
Jack Deighton APPLEBY, Divisional Surveyor, Durham County Council.
Pauline Winifred, Mrs. ARMITAGE, Area Principal for Adult Education, Adult Education Centre, Swinton, Manchester.
Donald ATTWOOD, Divisional Director, Paper, Printing, Packaging Industries Research Association.
Miss Kay BALL DODD, Civilian Medical Practitioner, North East District.
Miss Pamela Grace Blundell BANKART, Commercial Consultant, John Brown plc. For services to Export.
Brenda Anne, Mrs. BARNES, Secretary, Devon County Association for the Blind.
George BARR. For services to the Ayrshire Branch, Multiple Sclerosis Society.
Eric Tom BEAUCHAMP, Assistant Secretary, Biscuit, Cake, Chocolate and Confectionery Alliance.
Clifford Douglas BEDFORD. For political service.
John Robert BELL, Executive Officer, Board of Customs and Excise.
Kenneth Ridley BELL, Chief Executive, Ken Bell (International) Limited. For services to Export.
Bernard Charles BERESFORD, Local Officer II, Department of Health and Social Security.
Raghubir Sain BERRY, Collector, Board of Inland Revenue.
Norman Wilfred BESWICK, lately Librarian, Institute of Education Library, University of London.
Leslie Albert BIGGS, Chief Estimator, Marconi Radar Systems Limited, Chelmsford.
Bernard BIRN, Chairman, Southend-on-Sea Music Club.
Anthony BOLTON. For services to the Scout Association, Greater London.
Thomas George BOOBYER. For political service.
The Reverend Peter John BOWES. For services to the Ark Housing Association.
Denys Webster BRADFIELD, Secretary, National Federation of Fishmongers.
Charles Noel BRANNIGAN, Chief Officer, Northern Ireland Airports Constabulary.
Denise Jessie, Mrs. BRETT. For services to the Leukaemia and Cancer Children's Fund, Scotland.
Kenneth Albert BRIXEY, lately Stores Officer B, H.M. Stationery Office.
James Ignatius BROCKIE, Estate Forestry Manager, Hamilton District Council.
Miss Winifred Annie BROMHEAD, Administrative Officer, Department of Employment.
Cecil Ernest BROWN, Deputy Leader, Kettering Borough Council.
Dorothy, Mrs. BROWN, Chairman, Bristol Visual and Environmental Group.
John BROWN. For services to the community in Bedlington, Northumberland.
Ada Margaret, Mrs. BRYAN, Tax Officer, Higher Grade, Board of Inland Revenue.
Douglas Henry BRYANT. For services to the Ulster Savings Movement.
Miss Patricia BRYDEN. Registrar, Births, Deaths and Marriages, Gretna.
Major Clifford Fordyce BURKE (Retd.), lately Superintendent, Forth District Salmon Fishery Board.
Gerard BURNS, Clerk and Chief Executive, Fermanagh District Council.
John BUTCHER, Deputy Chief Executive, Director of Administration and Secretary, Footwear Technology Centre, Shoe and Allied Trades Research Association.
Miss Diana Frances BUTLER, lately Research Assistant, Cabinet Office.
Martha Grant, Mrs. CALDER, Area Organiser, East of Scotland, King George's Fund for Sailors.
Major Allan John CAMERON (Retd.), D.L., Member, Ross and Cromarty District Council.
Miss Elizabeth Rae CAMERON, Principal Nursing Officer, British Airways plc.
Jean Blair, Mrs. CAMPBELL, Headteacher, Glendale Primary School, Glasgow.
Justin James CARTWRIGHT. For political service.
Peter CAVE, Senior Manager, Head of Refit and Build Analysis, Naval Electronics & Space Division, Filton, British Aerospace plc.
Annie Morfina, Mrs. CHALMERS. For political service.
Thomas CHALMERS, lately Senior Executive Officer, Scottish Office.

Miss Joyce Ivy Evelyn CHAPMAN, Social Worker, Norfolk Social Services Department.
Walter Robert CHAPMAN, lately Senior Executive Officer, Manpower Services Commission.
Eric Douglas MacDonald CHEYNE, Foreign and Commonwealth Office.
Lenin Basil CHRISTODOULIDES, General Production Manager and Safety Officer, Carless Solvents, Harwich.
John Geoffrey CLARKE, lately Chief Housing Officer, Stratford-on-Avon District Council.
Eric William COLLINS, A.E. For public service and service to the community in Richmondshire.
Cyril James COOPER, General Secretary, English Schools Cricket Association.
Morigue, Mrs. CORNWELL, Mobility Centre Superintendent, Banstead Place, Banstead, Surrey.
Owen John CORRIGAN, Senior Executive Officer, Ministry of Defence.
Dorothy, Mrs. CRAYFORD, Primary School Teacher, Co-ordinator for Mathematics and Science, Wybers Wood First School, Grimsby.
Maurice Anthony CURRAN, Higher Professional and Technology Officer, Department of the Environment.
Joan, Mrs. DARBYSHIRE, Headteacher, Model Village Primary School, Shirebrook, Derbyshire.
David John DAVIES, lately Head of Technical Services, South Wales Area, British Coal Corporation.
Miss Laura Jane DAVIES. For services to Women's Golf.
Maldwyn DAVIES, Export Marketing Director, Dowty Mining Equipment Limited. For services to Export.
William Daniel (Danny) DAVIES, President, Llanybydder Branch, The Royal British Legion.
Steve DAVIS. For services to Snooker.
Margaret Winifred, Mrs. DAVOLL, Local Officer II, Department of Health and Social Security.
Alan DEY, Chief Superintendent, Northumbria Police.
John DINSMORE, Manager, Londonderry Office, Belfast Telegraph.
Ronald Albert DOLBEAR, lately Dockmaster, Babcock-Thorn Limited, Rosyth.
Jack William DONOVAN, lately Higher Professional and Technology Officer, Ministry of Agriculture, Fisheries and Food.
Anthony Paul DOYLE. For services to Cycling.
Michael William DUGMORE, Administrative Officer, Department of Health and Social Security.
Peter Harry DUKE, Principal Lecturer, Youth and Community Work, Leicester Polytechnic.
Alison Zoe, Mrs. EDMONDS, Headteacher, Denbigh Infant School, Luton, Bedfordshire.
Richard Foster EDWARD-COLLINS, Chairman, War Pensions Committee, Cornwall and Isles of Scilly.
Miss Joan Evelyn ELLIOTT, lately Secretary, Joint Examination Board for Orthopaedic Nursing.
John Malcolm ELLIOTT, Managing Director, EBAC Limited.
Miss Mildred EMMETT, Group Fire Control Officer, Greater Manchester Fire Service.
Colin George James EMMINS. For political and public service.
Miss Joan Olive ESSEN, Administrative Assistant, Board of Inland Revenue.
David Sydney Endle EVANS, Auxiliary Lieutenant, Royal Naval Auxiliary Service.
Maurice Leslie EVANS, Higher Professional and Technology Officer, Ministry of Defence.
Miss Sylvia Emmeline EVANS, Headteacher, Oldford Nursery and Infants School, Powys.
Frederick Walter EVE, lately General Manager, Standard Telephones and Cables plc, Treforest, Mid Glamorgan.
Susan Mary, Mrs. EVERSHED, D.L. Member, Chichester Health Authority; Chairman, Mental Handicap Planning Group.
Margaret Joan, Mrs. FARRER, Payroll Supervisor, SERCO Limited.
Roy Stanley FAULCONBRIDGE, Finance Manager, Lucas Industrial Components Limited.
Keith Anthony FERRIN. For political and public service.
George FISHER, lately Senior Nurse, Clinical and Managerial Mental Handicap Services, Strathmartine Hospital, Dundee.
Diana Mary, Mrs. FISHWICK, Member, South West Area Museum Council.
Alfred Henry Frank FOOKS, Organiser, Agriculture and Allied Trades Group, Transport and General Workers' Union.
William Frederick FORMAN, Member, Bournemouth Borough Council.
Emmanuel FRANKS, Restaurateur, Caterer and Retailer.
Frederic Bertin GENTLE, Senior Executive Officer, Office of Population Censuses and Surveys.
Margaret Joan, Mrs. GEOGHEGAN, Chairman, Hospice for Rochdale Appeal.
John Arthur GEORGE. For services to agriculture in Wales.
Geoffrey Alfred George GIBBONS, Secretary, Isle of Wight Association of Local Councils.
Alec Alfred GIBSON. For services to the community in Tamworth, Staffordshire.
Mary Scott, Mrs. GINNELLY, Senior Personal Secretary, Lord Chancellor's Department.
Miss Jean Doris GLASSBERG, lately Bursar, Ilford County High School, London Borough of Redbridge.
Miss Eileen Edith GLEADLE-RICHARDS, Staff Offficer, Grade II, Gloucestershire Branch, St John Ambulance Brigade.
Terence James GOLDRICK, Director, Engineering and Consultancy, Freight Transport Association Limited.
Elizabeth Davidson, Mrs. GOODHEW, Keeper of Education, Horniman Museum and Library.
Margaret Glenis, Mrs. GOODYEAR, Higher Executive Officer, Department of Education and Science.
Miss Heather St Clair GORDON, Head Occupational Therapist, Southern General Hospital, Glasgow.
Robert Wilson GRAHAM, Inspector, Metropolitan Police.
Jack GRIME. For services to the community in Lancashire.
Francis Estlin Christopher GRUNDY. For services to the Magistracy.
James Ross GUY, Member, Derry City Council.
Cecil Robson HALL, Chief Engineer, Resinous Chemicals Limited.
Miss Audrey HANDBURY, Health Visitor and Fieldwork Teacher, Milton Keynes Health Authority.
Michael HARDCASTLE, Writer of Children's books.
Jack Vincent HARDING, Head of Department, Mechanical and Motor Vehicle Engineering, Kingston College of Further Education.
Derek HARPER, lately Deputy Clerk to the Justices, Manchester.
Geoffrey Farrar HARPER. For political service.
Kenneth William HARRIS, Distribution Manager, Rugby Portland plc.
Luke Daniel HASSON, Owner and Managing Director, Austin & Co Limited, Londonderry.
James Angus HATFIELD. For charitable services and services to Yachting.
William Henry HAYDEN. For services to the community in Watford, Hertfordshire.
Miss Sally HAYNES, Vice-President, British Paraplegic Sports Society.
Barbara Barnes, Mrs. HELSBY, Chairman, Halton Arts, Widnes.
Miss Maura Christina Evelyn HENDERSON, Staff Officer, Department of Health and Social Services, Northern Ireland.
Unity Brogan, Mrs. HENRY, Director of Student Services, Dundee College of Technology.
James HEPBURN, Inspector, Fife Constabulary.
Miss Aleen Mary HERDMAN. For voluntary services in Northern Ireland.
Henry Michael HESSION, lately Chief Commandant, Norfolk Special Constabulary.
Mary Elizabeth Catherine, Mrs. HITCHCOCK, Senior Personal Secretary, Ministry of Defence.
Keith Gordon HODSON, Executive Director, Hawk (USA), Military Aircraft Division, Kingston upon Thames, British Aerospace plc.
Miss Dora Emily HOEHNS-HENSCHEL, Director, Midwifery Services, Camberwell Health Authority.
Philip Oliver HOLMES, lately Senior Professional and Technology Officer, Ministry of Defence.
Bryan HOLTON, Technical and Development Director, D. Anderson and Son Limited.
Thomas HOOD, Chief Superintendent, Royal Ulster Constabulary.
Frank HOWARD. For political and public service.
William Forster HUDSON, lately Administrative Officer, Department of Health and Social Security.
Miss Nerys Myfanwy HUGHES, District Physiotherapist, Clwyd Health Authority.
Doreen, Mrs HUNT, Senior Executive Officer, Ministry of Defence.

Maurice Vyvyan INGRAM, Chairman, Executive Committee Fish Farming, National Farmers' Union, England and Wales.
Anthony Woof JACKSON, Director and Company Secretary, Thompson and Jackson Limited, Lancaster.
Charles William JACOB. For services to charitable and educational organisations in Wales.
Miss Evelyn Audrey Ker JAMES, General Secretary, Scottish Headquarters, Girl Guides Association.
Terry John JARRETT, lately Senior Executive Officer, National Institute of Medical Research, Medical Research Council.
Miss Pamela Mary JOHNSON, Diabetes Liaison Health Visitor, Ipswich.
Raymond Leslie JOHNSON. For services to the Employment of the Disabled.
Ian Alexander JOHNSTONE, Higher Professional and Technology Officer, Commonwealth War Graves Commission.
David JONES, President, Durham Aged Mineworkers' Homes Association.
Frederick JORDAN, Chairman, Stockton Branch, The Royal Air Force Association.
Eric Maclean KEAN, lately Member, Edinburgh District Couuncil.
Gladys Joan, Mrs. KEANE, Service Welfare Adviser, The Light Division Depot, Shrewsbury, Women's Royal Voluntary Service.
Richard KEARTON, Manager, Personnel and Administration, Humber Refinery, Conoco Limited.
Thomas Peter KEIGHLEY. For political and public service.
Mary Patricia, Mrs. KENDRICK, lately Principal Scientific Officer, Hydraulics Research Limited.
Doreen Violet, Mrs. KENYON, Member, National Council, National Association of Victim's Support Schemes.
Leonard Arthur KETCHER, Higher Executive Officer, House of Lords.
Gwendoline Vera, Mrs. KIMBER, Administrative Officer, The Patent Office.
David KINGHORN, Deputy Head, Scott Sutherland School of Architecture, Aberdeen.
Anthony KIRTON, lately Superintendent, Surrey Constabulary.
Gwendoline Iris, Mrs. KITE, lately Ward Sister, Powick Hospital, Worcester and District Health Authority.
Alexander Wilson LAMBE, Safety and Administrative Officer, Federation of Building and Civil Engineering Contractors, Northern Ireland.
Miss Joan LAMBERT, Shorthand Typist, Bedfordshire Police.
Alfred Whiteman LAWRENCE. For services to the Bedfordshire Branch, Soldiers' Sailors' and Airmen's Families Association.
Patricia Caroline, Mrs. LESTER, Fabric and Fashion Designer, Patricia Lester Ltd., Abergavenny, Gwent.
Dennis Edward LEWIS, Commercial Director, Flight Refuelling Aviation Limited.
Lewis Islwyn LEWIS, Staff Oficer, Board of Inland Revenue.
Dennis William LITHGOW, lately Head of Training Operations, South Eastern Electricity Board.
Charles William LITTLE, Regional Director, Greater London & Home Counties Branch, The Forces Help Society and Lord Roberts Workshops.
Brian Gordon LOCK, lately Head of Engineering, Local Radio.
Richard LOWRY, Finance and Administration Officer, Research and Development Engineering Research Station, British Gas plc.
Alexander LOWSON. For services to Industry, Arbroath.
Agnes McDonald, Mrs. LYLE. For services to Scouting and the community in Hawick.
Miss Eileen Mairi MacCOLL, General Practitioner, Killin, Perthshire.
Isobel Duncan, Mrs. MacKENZIE. For services to Scottish Women's Rural Institute.
Robert Douglas MATTEN. For political service.
Rachel Sylvia Clegg, Mrs. MATTHEWS, Emergency Services, Bedford, Women's Royal Voluntary Service.
Miss Doreen MAUDE, lately Drawing Office Services Supervisor, David Brown Gear Industries Limited.
Thomas Walter Aitken McBAIN. For services to the fishing industry.
Isabella Frances, Mrs. McCALL, lately Chairman, Calvay Housing Co-operative Limited, Glasgow.
Miss Eileen McCARTHY, lately Executive Officer, Department of Health and Social Security.
Mary Elizabeth, Mrs. McGEOUGH, lately Nursing Officer, Hamilton.
Betty, Mrs. McINNES. For political service.
Miss Kinn Hamilton McINTOSH. For services to the Girl Guides Association.
Margaretta, Mrs. McINTYRE. For services to the Parents and Friends of Muckamore Abbey Special Care Hospital, Northern Ireland.
William McKERRELL, General Practitioner, Clachan Seil, Argyll.
Ronald Hugh McKIE, Consultant, Royal Institute of British Architects Publications Limited.
Joseph McLEAN. For political service.
Miss Diana McMAHON, Programme Director, Industry Matters.
James Ossian Lamont McNEILAGE. For political service.
Sheelagh Margaret Mary, Mrs. McRANDAL, Partner, Fergus Gilligan Consulting Engineers.
Edward William McWILLIAMS. For services to the Boys' Brigade.
Robert MEGRAW. For voluntary services to youth.
Miss Merle MELFORD-COLEGATE, Welfare Officer, the Royal Star and Garter Home, Richmond, Surrey.
Robert Lawrence METCALFE, Chairman, Brighton and Hove Co-ordinating Committee, Duke of Edinburgh's Award Scheme.
Freda, Mrs. MIDDLETON, Chairman, National Schizophrenia Fellowship, Scotland.
Sydney MILLAR. For services to Rugby Union Football.
Mary Kathleen, Mrs. MILLER, Vice-President and Hospital Liaison Officer, South Glamorgan Branch, The British Red Cross Society.
Thomas MOFFAT, Chairman, Durham Small Business Club.
Alan Ernest MOLE, Technical Director, Kent Messenger Group.
Christopher Philip Streatfield MORLEY, Marketing and Export Director, Matbro Limited.
Isabella McGregor Steel, Mrs. MORRISON, Nursing Officer, Community, Lothian Health Board.
Kenneth MORT, Local Officer I, Department of Health and Social Security.
Arthur MOSELEY, Chairman and Managing Director, Moseley (Holdings) Limited. For services to Export.
Frederick Claude MOUNTIER, Chairman, Voluntary Services Association, Redbridge.
Hugh Sutherland MUNRO, Senior Executive Officer, Department of Health and Social Security.
Miss Marian Gaye MURDOCH, Director, British Invisible Exports Council.
Alan MURPHY, General Medical Practitioner; Lecturer in General Practice, University of Nottingham.
Andrew Steel MURRAY. For services to the community in Creetown, Wigtownshire.
Terence Patrick NEALON, Director, Caradon Curran Ltd., Cardiff.
Mary, Mrs. NEESON. For services to the National Deaf Children's Society, Scotland.
John Edward Brian NEWMAN, Japanese Programme Organiser, External Broadcasting, British Broadcasting Corporation.
Margaret Mary, Mrs. NEWTON, Executive Officer, Home Office.
John Simpson NOBLE, General Medical Practitioner; Vice-Chairman, Family Practitioner Committee, Northumberland.
Gerald Patrick NOONE, Principal Technical Development Officer, Severn Trent Water Authority.
Gerald NUGENT, lately Senior Executive Officer, Department for National Savings.
Gerald O'NEILL, General Manager, Plessey Telecommunications Limited, Ballynahinch, Co. Down.
Miss Moira Helen ORD. For services to Netball.
Michael Patrick O'SULLIVAN, Exploration Manager, Wytch Farm Development, British Petroleum Exploration.
Glynn Meirion OWEN, Chief Physicist, University Hospital of Wales, Cardiff.
Robert Ivor OWEN, Executive Officer, Ministry of Defence.
John Francis OXLEY, Senior Operating Department Assistant, Princess Alexandra Hospital, Harlow, Essex.
Jane Ann, Mrs. PACKHAM, Casualty Sister, Erne Hospital, Enniskillen.
Pamela Maurice, Mrs. PARKER, Secretary, Devon Branch, Council for the Protection of Rural England.
Margaret Mary, Mrs. PARR, Vice Chairman, Blackpool Wyre and Fylde Health Authority.
Mary Diana, Mrs. PAULINE, Senior Primary Education Adviser, Mid Glamorgan Education Authority.

Miss Gloria Sheena PEARSON, Press Officer, Southern Region, British Railways.
Eric PENSON, Senior Professional and Technology Officer, Department of Transport.
Desmond Charles PERRIS, Director, W. A. Perris and Sons Ltd.
John Wharne PICKERING, Chairman, Crawley Training Association.
Michael Stanley PIKE, Chief Superintendent, H.M. Inspectorate of Constabulary.
Miss Danuta Stanislava PNIEWSKA, lately Local Officer I, Department of Health and Social Security.
Richard Edward REUBERSON. For political service.
Derek John RICE, Tax Officer, Higher Grade, Board of Inland Revenue.
David RICHARDS, Chief Superintendent, Metropolitan Police.
Russell RICHARDSON, Managing Director, Cross Gates Carriage Works, Optare Limited, Leeds.
Roydon Bircham RICHMOND, Managing Director, H. R. Richmond Limited (Epsom Coaches).
Miss Norah Kathleen RIDDINGTON, Member, Electricity Consumers' Council.
Peter Sanderson ROBERTS, Director of Trading Standards, Leicestershire County Council.
Miss Beryl Christine ROBINSON, District Nurse, Okehampton, Devon.
Harold Edwin ROBINSON, lately President National Society of Allotment and Leisure Gardens Limited.
John Wilfred ROE, Director of Housing, Bolton Metropolitan Borough Council.
Muriel Ellen, Mrs. ROGERS. For political and public service.
Dennis Charles ROOS, Manager, Hunterston 'A' Nuclear Power Station.
Betty, Mrs. ROOT, Director, Reading and Language Information Centre, University of Reading.
Audrey Wilhelmina, Mrs. ROSE. For political service.
Peter Lambert RUSSELL, V.R.D., Business Counsellor, Small Business Division, Scottish Development Agency.
Captain David Vivian RUSTED, Senior Master, Marine Department, Shell UK Oil.
Miss Lotte SAHLMANN, Medical Officer, Sheiling Curative Schools, Camphill Trust Community.
William Munce SAULTERS, Deputy Chief Vehicle Examiner, Department of the Environment, Northern Ireland.
George Copeland SAUNDERS, Law Correspondent, The Scotsman.
Joan Henderson, Mrs. SCOTT, Assistant, Chairman's Department; Organiser, Scotland, Welfare for the Disabled, Women's Royal Voluntary Service.
Ronald Malcolm SCOTT, Managing Director, M.S.A. (Britain) Limited, Coatbridge.
James SHAW, Inspector, Board of Inland Revenue.
Malcolm John SHAW, lately Chief Superintendent, H.M. Inspectorate of Constabulary.
Miss Vera Rosaline SHEPHERD, Chief Typing Managing, Health and Safety Executive.
Gertrude (Trudie), Mrs. SHEPPARD, Organiser, Newent Centre for Disabled and Gloucestershire Association for the Disabled.
Maurice Lea SHERWIN. For services to agriculture in Cheshire.
Stanley SHORROCK, Chairman, Shorrock plc.
David Cyril SHORT. For political and public service.
John SIMMONITE, Director, Mosely and District Churches Housing Association Limited.
Thomas George SINCLAIR, Chief Superintendent, Royal Ulster Constabulary.
Ajit SINGH, lately Chairman, Kingston Group for Racial Understanding.
William SKELTON, Chairman, Merseyside Drugs Council.
Charles McDowell SMITH, Platoon Commander, Wigtownshire, Home Service Force.
Mary Elizabeth, Mrs. SMITH. For services to handicapped children.
Seymour James Louvain SOUTHWOOD. For services to Boys' Clubs, Wales.
John Henry STACY, Security Officer, National Maritime Museum.
Walter STAINROD, Regional Collector, Board of Inland Revenue.
James Edward STANSFIELD, Higher Executive Officer, Board of Customs and Excise.
John Arthur Charles STEVENS, lately Senior Professional and Technology Officer, Ministry of Defence.
Neville George Joseph Herbert STIFF. For political service.
Eileen, Mrs. STUDDY, Volunteer Worker, Chelmsford, Citizen's Advice Bureau.
James William SUTTON, Purchasing Manager, Shotton Paper Company Limited.
Marjorie, Mrs. SWAINSTON. For political and public service.
Frank Leslie SYLVESTER, 'B' Clerk, Devon Army Cadet Force; Secretary, Exeter Branch, Coldstream Guards Association.
Kenneth Ernest TAPPENDEN, Chief Superintendent, Kent Constabulary.
Ernest William Edward TAYLOR, Assistant Inspector, Fire Services Inspectorate.
Nancy Barbara, Mrs. TAYLOR, lately Document Interpreter, Cabinet Office.
Peter Branston TAYLOR. For services to agriculture in Wales.
James Roland TEW, Member, National Executive Committee, Motor Neurone Disease Association.
Miss Adrienne Mary Laetitia THIRKELL, Junior Administrator, British College of Optometrists.
Reginald William Tudor THORP. For services to the National Trust in the Farne Islands.
William TIMYM, Sculptor.
David Crabtree TINNISWOOD. For services to Industry and Education, North East Lancashire.
Henry Fenwick TOWNSEND, Higher Executive Officer, Department of Employment.
Gordon Maurice TREVETT, Chief Engineer, Greater Manchester Police.
John Jeffery TURNER, lately Company Secretary, Federation of Agricultural Co-operatives (UK) Limited.
Anthony Michael TYNAN, Curator, The Hancock Museum, Newcastle upon Tyne.
Arnold ULLMAN, Senior Professional and Technology Officer, Department of the Environment.
Joyce Ceridwen. Mrs, URCH, Senior Nurse, Brynhyryd Hospital, Forden, Welshpool, Powys.
Bhanu Arjan VADGAMA, Administration Officer, The Insolvency Service.
Ian Alistair Ward VANCE, Director, Navigation Systems, Radio and Microwave, Standard Telephones and Cables plc.
Judith Anne, Mrs. VERDON, Managing Director, ISA Controls Limited.
Miss Drucilla Joy VESTRY, Director, Royal Docks Area Team, London Dockyards Development Corporation.
Arthur Roy WADD, Senior Probation Officer, Nottinghamshire.
John James WALKLEY. For services to Music in Gloucestershire and Worcestershire.
Henry WATSON, Senior Executive Officer, Manpower Services Commission.
David WATT, Member, Chemistry, Pharmacy and Standards Sub Committee; Committee on Safety of Medicines and British Pharmacopoeia Committees.
Thomas Fraser WATT. For services to the Chartered Institute of Transport, Scotland.
Samuel Herbert WATTERSON. Director, S. H. Watterson (Engineering) Limited.
Henry John WELLINGS, Annunciator Superintendent, House of Commons.
Elizabeth Peternel, Mrs. WELLS, Curator and Director, Museum of Ancient Instruments, Royal College of Music.
Donald Aldred WHITEHEAD, Managing Director, VSW Scientific Instruments Limited. For services to Export.
Miss Daphne June WHITMORE, Deputy Headteacher, Hugh Christie Secondary School, Tonbridge, Kent.
Jean Gertrude, Mrs. WHITTON, lately Headteacher, Mill Rythe First School, Hayling Island, Hampshire.
Miss Eunice Freda WILLIAMS (Mrs. Fuller), Nursing Sister, Gynaecology, Outpatients Department, Royal Free Hospital.
Miss Heather WILLIAMS. For services to the community in Cumbria.
Hugh Griffith WILLIAMS, Controller Operations, Western Counters Territory, Birmingham, The Post Office.
Lyndon David WILLIAMS, For political and public service.
Maurice Charles WILLIAMS, General Manager, Devon Industrial Services.

Frederick Roy WILLIS, Vice-Chairman, Civilian Committee, Tiverton, Sea Cadet Corps Unit.
Albert James WOOD, Production Manager, Trebor plc.
Marilynn Beryl, Mrs. WOOD, Enrolled Nurse, Ear, Nose and Throat Unit, Portsmouth and South East Hampshire Health Authority.
Reginald James WYATT, Senior Scientific Officer, British Geological Survey, Natural Environment Research Council.
David Frank YOUNG, Chairman, Continental Microwave (Holdings) plc. For services to Export.

DIPLOMATIC SERVICE AND OVERSEAS LIST

K.B.E.

To be an Ordinary Knight Commander of the Civil Division of the said Most Excellent Order:

Derek Maxwell MARCH, C.B.E., British High Commissioner, Kampala.

C.B.E.

To be Ordinary Commanders of the Civil Division of the said Most Excellent Order:

Harold Royrie Mansfield BROCK, Financial Secretary, Bermuda.
Alan John CARTER, I.S.O., J.P., Director of Immigration, Hong Kong.
Anthony William Thomas HUDSON. For services to British commercial interests in the Far East.
Alec IBBOTT, British High Commissioner, Banjul.
William PURVES, D.S.O., J.P. For public and community services in Hong Kong.
Harold Theodore ROWLANDS, O.B.E., Financial Secretary, Falkland Islands.
Miss Maria TAM Wai-chu, O.B.E., J.P. For public services in Hong Kong.

O.B.E.

To be Ordinary Officers of the Civil Division of the said Most Excellent Order:

Alistair Peter ASPREY, A.E., J.P. For public services in Hong Kong.
Jeffrey Christopher ASTWOOD. For public services in Bermuda.
William David BROWN, British Council Representative, Kuwait.
Brian George John CANTY, Deputy Governor, Bermuda.
Edward Graham Mellish CHAPLIN, lately Head of Chancery, British Interest Section, Tehran.
Dr CHIU Hin-Kwong, J.P. For public and community services in Hong Kong.
George William CLARKE, lately Adviser, Statistical Office, Commission of the EC, Brussels.
Dr Geoffrey Roy COURTS, lately British Council Deputy Representative, Nigeria.
Roger Kenneth EVE. For services to British commercial interests in Maryland, USA.
Michael Derek FORD. For services to British commercial interests in Belgium.
Dr Victor FUNG Kwok-king. For Public and community services in Hong Kong.
Nicholas Lawrence GORTON. For services to British aviation interests in Frankfurt.
Geoffrey Gordon HARDWICKE. For services to British commercial interests in Bangladesh.
Simon Robert Mark HEATHCOTE, Foreign and Commonwealth Office.
Leslie HODGSON. For services to British commercial and community interests in Nigeria.
Robin Anthony JOWIT. For services to British commercial and community interests in Lisbon.
Jeremy LONG, First Secretary (Administration), H.M. Embassy, Islamabad.
John Frederick MATTHEWS. For services to British commercial and community interests in Sao Paulo.
Miss Ann Eliza Alfreda MEADE, Permanent Secretary and Chief Establishment Officer, Montserrat.
Howard Andrew Clive MORRISON, lately Chief Magistrate, Fiji.
Robert Vivian PEARCE. For services to British commercial interests in Japan.
Ivor Jon RAWLINSON, H.M. Consul, Florence.
David Frederick Charles RIDGWAY, lately Chargé d'Affaires, H.M. Embassy, San Salvador.
Francis Xavier ROONEY, lately Puisne Judge, Fiji.
Professor Patricia Mary SHAW DE URDIALES. For services to English studies in Spain.
Harvey Nolan James SMITH, English Language Teaching Adviser (British Council), Government of Mali.
William Arthur TINCEY, lately First Secretary (Commercial), British High Commission, Nairobi.
Dennis TING Hok-Shou, J.P. For public and commmunity services in Hong Kong.
John Baird TYSON, M.C. For services to education in Nepal.
Edward Bevan WAIDE, lately Resident Representative, IBRD, New Delhi.
Miss Jean Margaret WATSON. For nursing and welfare services to lepers in East Africa and Malaysia.
Norman Charles WESTON. For services to British commercial and community interests in Colombia.
John Michael WOOD, M.B.E. For services to education in Kenya.
Robert Hamilton WRIGHT. For services to the British community in Calcutta.

M.B.E.

To be Ordinary Members of the Civil Division of the said Most Excellent Order:

George Anwar ARIDA, Honorary British Consul, Tripoli, Lebanon.
James Martin BIRKBECK. For services to British commercial and community interests in Peru.
Thomas MacLaren BLAIR, Chief Quantity Surveyor, Housing Department, Hong Kong.
Margaret Genevieve, Mrs. BORDE, Clerk of the Legislative Council, British Virgin Islands.
Gilbert CALLEJA. For services to the British community in Rio de Janeiro.
Helene Patricia Mrs. CARIDIS, lately British Consul, Corfu.
David Osborne CLARKE. For services to the British community in Aden.
Maud Amara Mrs. DE KEREKRETHY. For services to the British community in Rio de Janeiro.
Joan Annie Enrica Mrs. DIAZ, Secretary, HM Embassy, Guatemala City.
John Charles EDWARDS. For services to the British community in Salalah, Oman.
Miss Marion FANG Sum-suk, J.P. For services to the disabled in Hong Kong.
Angela Mrs. GARCIA SAINZ. For services to the British community in Mexico City.
Henry Maurice GREGSON. For services to British tourists in France.
Nigel Bathurst HANKIN. For services to the British community in New Delhi.
Olive Ethelma Mrs. HODGE. For services to the community in Anguilla.
Douglas Charles HULME. For services to British commercial and community interests in Jedda.
John Michael JAQUES. For services to Anglo-Jordanian relations in Amman.
Phillipine Hare Mrs. LAWSON. For services to the British community in Paris.
Louis Joseph LOMBARD. For services to the community in Gibraltar.
Nathan MA Ning-hei, J.P. For public and community services in Hong Kong.
John Ellis PALFREY, English Language Adviser (British Council), Government of the Congo.

Stephen PROCTER. For services to the British community in Jedda.
Miss Jacqueline Bryony Lucy PULLINGER. For welfare services to the community in Hong Kong.
Peter David Sydney RADFORD, Commercial Assistant, HM Embassy, Paris.
Donald Joseph RAINS. For services to British commercial interests in Morocco.
Paul Andrew RAMSAY, lately Senior Visa Officer, British Interests Section, Tehran.
Everet Ferdinand ROMNEY. For services to the community in Anguilla.
Diana Bryant, Mrs. ROSENBERG, lately Librarian, Juba University, Sudan.
SO Yan-kin, Student Adviser, Hong Kong Government Office, London.
Robert SOUTHERN. For services to British tourism interests in Canada.
David Paul SPENCER, lately Second Secretary, HM Embassy, Aden.
Dr Elizabeth Ruth SWAIN. For medical and welfare services to the community in Zambia.
Nylon Leonard TSO, Q.P.M., C.P.M. For public services in Hong Kong.
Frances Violet Mrs. WALFORD. For services to the British community in Lisbon.
Keith Wallis WARREN. For services to the community in Mozambique.

CENTRAL CHANCERY OF
THE ORDERS OF KNIGHTHOOD

ST. JAMES'S PALACE, LONDON S.W.1

11th June 1988

The QUEEN has been graciously pleased, on the occasion of the Celebration of Her Majesty's Birthday, to give orders for the following appointments to the Imperial Service Order:

I.S.O.

To be Companions of the Order:

HOME CIVIL SERVICE

William Arthur ASTILL, Inspector (P), Board of Inland Revenue.
Trevor David BADHAM, Audit Manager, National Audit Office.
Thomas Royston BERRY, Principal Scientific Officer, Ministry of Defence.
Donald George CARTER, Principal Professional and Technology Officer, Ministry of Defence.
Cecil William CHADWICK, Grade 7, Department of Health and Social Security.
William CHAPPELL, Chief Clerk, Newcastle Crown Court, Lord Chancellor's Department.
Ralph George Busby COX, T.D., Principal, Department of Health and Social Security.
Anthony Robert DOBSON, Principal, Ministry of Defence.
Alistair Greig DODDS, Principal, Department of Employment.
James EWING, Principal Professional and Technology Officer, Ministry of Defence.
Geoffrey Ward HARRISON, Principal Collector, Board of Inland Revenue.
Miss Jean Corisande HOWLISTON, Principal, Department of the Environment.
Gerald Lionel JOHNSTON, Principal Professional and Technical Officer, Department of the Environment, Northern Ireland.
Bernard LYONS, Official Receiver (B), The Insolvency Service.
Arthur Inman PROCTER, Inspector (SP), Board of Inland Revenue.
Arthur Wilson SCRUTON, Foreign and Commonwealth Office.
Ernest Harold Matthew SEAWARD, Grade 7, Manpower Services Commission.
Harry SIMPSON, Inspector (P), Board of Inland Revenue.
Roy SMITH, Senior Principal, Board of Customs and Excise.
Reginald Bryce SNOW, Principal, Home Office.
Robert Kirby WEST, Principal Accountant, Scottish Office.
Rita Gwendoline Mrs. WOODLEY, Grade 7, Ministry of Agriculture, Fisheries and Food.

DIPLOMATIC SERVICE AND OVERSEAS LIST

Joseph Charles Anthony HAMMOND, Commmissioner for Labour, Hong Kong.
John WINFIELD, J.P., Senior Assistant Director of Education, Hong Kong.

CENTRAL CHANCERY OF
THE ORDERS OF KNIGHTHOOD

ST. JAMES'S PALACE, LONDON S.W.1

11th June 1988

The QUEEN has been graciously pleased, on the occasion of the Celebration of Her Majesty's Birthday, to approve the award of the British Empire Medal (Military Division) to the undermentioned:

BRITISH EMPIRE MEDAL (MILITARY DIVISION)

B.E.M.

MINISTRY OF DEFENCE (NAVY DEPARTMENT)

Charge Chief Marine Engineering Artificer (P) Ian ALDRED, M913836T.
Chief Petty Officer (Mine Warfare) Lee John BARNETT, D053744R.
Chief Petty Officer Steward DAVID DEADY, D105452D.
Chief Radio Supervisor Colin Edward DREWETT, D096172R.
Chief Petty Officer Writer Graeme Ross Kilday FERNIE, D081846Q.
Band Colour Sergeant Alan Reginald FLOOK, Royal Marines, Q003943F.
Chief Petty Officer Air Engineering Artificer (R) James Brodie HOLMES, D091957N.
Chief Petty Officer Marine Engineering Artificer Kenneth Peter HOUSE, D985584V.
Chief Petty Officer (Acting Local Charge Chief) Air Engineering Artificer (WL) David Edward KNOTT, D206102C.
Charge Chief Marine Engineering Artificer (P) Brian Richard LINGHAM, D060122A.
Charge Chief Communications Technician John Brian McCORMICK, D098502H.
Sergeant (Local Colour Sergeant) Alexander Henry Geddes McLEOD, Royal Marines, P019033M.
Chief Petty Officer (Operations) (Missile) Robert Thomas NORMAN, D105454L.
Charge Chief Marine Engineering Artificer (P) Charles William OLIVER, D070724P.
Acting Chief Petty Officer (Operations) (Missile) Robert Thomas John SEARLE, J975679U.
Chief Petty Officer Stores Accountant Brian SMITH, D099753S.
Chief Petty Officer Weapon Engineering Artificer Nigel SNAPE, D101124A.
Chief Petty Officer Stores Accountant Richard Charles WHALE, D113696G.
Colour Sergeant Andrew Frederick WREY, Royal Marines, P017729H.
Charge Chief Air Engineering Artificer (M) Eric Francis YOUNG, F944478T.

MINISTRY OF DEFENCE (ARMY DEPARTMENT)

24352048 Staff Sergeant David Neil ALCROFT, The Royal Highland Fusiliers (Princess Margaret's Own Glasgow and Ayrshire Regiment).
W0455714 Sergeant SUSAN Anne ALDERSON, Women's Royal Army Corps.
24233851 Staff Sergeant Kingsley Charles AUGUSTUS, Corps of Royal Engineers.
24211676 Staff Sergeant Keith BATH, Army Air Corps.
24136634 Staff Sergeant Richard Langrish BIRD, Corps of Royal Electrical and Mechanical Engineers.

24264343 Staff Sergeant Bernard Trevor BIRLEY, Corps of Royal Electrical and Mechanical Engineers.
23265007 Lance Sergeant Henry BOND, Welsh Guards.
24173096 Staff Sergeant John Anthony BRADBURN, The Queen's Own Mercian Yeomanry, Territorial Army.
24295069 Sergeant Fredrick Victor BROADHURST, Corps of Royal Electrical and Mechanical Engineers.
24118877 Sergeant Walter BROWNE, 5th Royal Inniskilling Dragoon Guards.
23908641 Staff Sergeant Phillip Frederick BUTLER, Welsh Guards.
24283995 Corporal Derek CARMAN, Royal Corps of Signals.
24164833 Staff Sergeant Ronald Michael CARTER, Grenadier Guards.
24344952 Staff Sergeant Thomas Gerard CASSIDY, Corps of Royal Electrical and Mechanical Engineers.
24319044 Staff Sergeant Graham John CHAMBERS, Royal Army Ordnance Corps.
24339159 Staff Sergeant Royston CHARLES, Army Physical Training Corps.
24257019 Staff Sergeant John Henry CLORLEY, Royal Army Ordnance Corps.
23691811 Sergeant Christopher Dennis COADY, Royal Regiment of Artillery, Territorial Army.
24271482 Corporal Michael David COURTNAGE, The Queen's Regiment, Territorial Army.
23721788 Sergeant Eric Blair CRAIG, The 4th (Volunteer) Battalion Royal Irish Rangers (27 (Inniskilling) 83rd and 87th (The North Irish Militia)), Territorial Army.
24398394 Corporal Allan Morris CRICKMORE, Corps of Royal Military Police.
24259801 Staff Sergeant Christopher Alan CUNNINGHAM, Corps of Royal Engineers.
24060016 Staff Sergeant Michael William DANIELS, Corps of Royal Electrical and Mechanical Engineers.
24182212 Staff Sergeant Peter Joseph DAVIS, Army Physical Training Corps.
24160774 Staff Sergeant Richard John DOREY, Corps of Royal Engineers.
24625250 Corporal Richard John DOWNES, Corps of Royal Military Police.
24298076 Staff Sergeant John William DOWNIE, The Light Infantry.
23987931 Sergeant Edward Nugent DUFFY, Royal Army Ordnance Corps.
2424709 Staff Sergeant Philip Oral ECCLES, Army Physical Training Corps.
24257077 Corporal Paul EMERSON, Royal Corps of Signals.
24084941 Staff Sergeant Terence FINLAY, The Cheshire Regiment.
24414198 Sergeant Anthony Ethelbert FRANKLIN, Royal Army Ordnance Corps.
24080089 Staff Sergeant Ian FRIEND, Royal Army Pay Corps, Territorial Army.
24087249 Staff Sergeant David Michael GAFFNEY, Royal Corps of Signals.
24074281 Staff Sergeant Keith Douglas GODBEER, The King's Regiment.
21160086 Sergeant HUKUMBAHADUR THAPA, 7th Duke of Edinburgh's Own Gurkha Rifles.
W0454127 Staff Sergeant Honour June JAEGER, Women's Royal Army Corps.
24143782 Staff Sergeant Raymond JASPER, The Royal Welch Fusiliers.
24138335 Staff Sergeant Donald KEY, Royal Regiment of Artillery.
24032176 Staff Sergeant Philip KING, Army Physical Training Corps.
24041738 Sergeant Martin John LEAPER, Royal Tank Regiment.
24282073 Sergeant Robert Brynmor LEWIS, The Parachute Regiment.
24225587 Sergeant Michael MASON, The King's Own Royal Border Regiment.
24108453 Sergeant David Andrew McCURDY, Corps of Royal Engineers.
24391283 Corporal Douglas Collins MURRAY, Royal Corps of Transport.
24463347 Staff Sergeant John Henry Albert NEEDHAM, The Royal Green Jackets.
W0469765 Staff Sergeant Maureen Malone O'DONNELL, Intelligence Corps, Territorial Army.
24103877 Staff Sergeant Bromley Paul O'HARE, The Parachute Regiment.
24251479 Sergeant Christopher Malcolm PASCOE, Corps of Royal Engineers.
24204569 Staff Sergeant Keith PENDLETON, Royal Army Ordnance Corps.
W0459749 Sergeant Linda Karen RICHARDS, Women's Royal Army Corps.
24352633 Corporal Alexander ROBERTSON, The Black Watch (Royal Highland Regiment).
24596319 Lance Corporal Robert Denzil ROBINSON, Royal Army Ordnance Corps.
23180242 Sergeant John Ronald ROGERS, Royal Army Pay Corps, Territorial Army.
23203808 Corporal James Edwin SANSOM, Army Catering Corps, Territorial Army.
24195901 Staff Sergeant John SHARKEY, Royal Corps of Signals.
24340229 Corporal Robert Barrie SINCLAIR, Army Catering Corps.
24532819 Staff Sergeant Paul Arthur SWEATMAN, The Queen's Regiment, Territorial Army.
23517316 Sergeant William Fred TAYLOR, The Light Infantry, Territorial Army.
24092028 Sergeant Arthur Duncan THOMSON, Royal Army Ordnance Corps.
24171917 Sergeant Kevin Michael TOBIN, Intelligence Corps.
23966424 Staff Sergeant Terence David WALKER, Royal Corps of Signals.
23867017 Staff Sergeant John William WARD, The Green Howards (Alexandra, Princess of Wales's Own Yorkshire Regiment).
24147563 Staff Sergeant Stephen WARD, Army Physical Training Corps.
22902560 Sergeant Anthony Edward WILSON, Army Catering Corps, Territorial Army.
24373712 Lance Bombardier Ronald WYNN, Royal Regiment of Artillery.

(B.E.M.—MILITARY DIVISION)
MINISTRY OF DEFENCE (AIR FORCE DEPARTMENT)

Q8077757 Flight Sergeant Denis Ronald ALLEN, Royal Air Force Regiment.
Y4272305 Sergeant Reginald ALLSOPP, Royal Air Force.
Q8076223 Flight Sergeant Alan BARNETT, Royal Air Force.
W4241163 Flight Sergeant Clive Leslie BRUTON, Royal Air Force Regiment.
E4257064 Flight Sergeant Peter CURZON, Royal Air Force.
A8001161 Sergeant Alan Victor DURRANT, Royal Air Force.
L4281028 Sergeant George Gerald EDWARDS, Royal Air Force.
A0685604 Flight Sergeant Martin EVERSFIELD, Royal Air Force.
W4276916 Flight Sergeant Norman GRAY, Royal Air Force.
Q8082288 Chief Technician Peter Stanley GREGSON, Royal Air Force.
Y1947222 Flight Sergeant Thomas Robert GREY, Royal Air Force.
G8095750 Corporal Kenneth William HALL, Royal Air Force.
G4283187 Chief Technician John Charles HEARSE, Royal Air Force.
R4244338 Flight Sergeant Eric Stephen HELSDON, Royal Air Force.
T0687548 Flight Sergeant Thomas Allan JOHNSTON, Royal Air Force.
J4288600 Sergeant Michael John KING, Royal Air Force.
V0688240 Flight Sergeant Alfred Thompson McKAY, Royal Air Force.
Q8068880 Sergeant Stephen Charles NICHOLSON, Royal Air Force.
G1941382 Flight Sergeant Patrick Joseph O'NEILL, Royal Air Force.
D1960468 Flight Sergeant Stephen Charles PATEY, Royal Air Force.
G1942139 Flight Sergeant Peter Alan SNITCH, Royal Air Force.
H4291568 Flight Sergeant David TAPPIN, Royal Air Force.
G8093131 Flight Sergeant Peter Owen Stephen TUCKER, Royal Air Force.
R1938655 Chief Technician Robert Anthony YOUNG, Royal Air Force.

THE QUEEN has been graciously pleased, on the occasion of the Celebration of Her Majesty's Birthday, to approve the award of the British Empire Medal (Civil Division) to the undermentioned:

BRITISH EMPIRE MEDAL (CIVIL DIVISION)

B.E.M.

UNITED KINGDOM

Colin William ANDERSON, Constable, Metropolitan Police.
Peter Blair ANDERSON, Constable, Northern Constabulary.
William Low ANDERSON, Senior Inspector, Military Knitware, Remploy Limited.
Kenneth Frederick Bywater ASTLE, Toolmaker, Nottingham, Royal Ordnance plc.
Norman ATKINS, Chief Naval Auxiliaryman, Royal Naval Auxiliary Service.
Peggy Rose, Mrs. BATHOLOMEW, Foster Parent, East Sussex County Council.
Barbara, Mrs. BEARDS, Member, Truro, Women's Royal Voluntary Service.
William Moffat BEATTIE, Frameworker, Hogg of Hawick.
Edith Ann Clark, Mrs. BELL, Caretaker, Territorial Army Centre, 39 Signal Regiment (V), Dundee.
Leonard Walter BETTS, Component Engineering Supervisor, Marconi Space Systems Limited.
Frederick John BILLING, Convenor, Amalgamated Engineering Union, GEC Large Machines Limited.
James McAleece BINNIE, Postal Executive 'D', Royal Mail Letters, Edinburgh, The Post Office.
James Walter BISHOP, Roadman, West Sussex County Council
William Blair BLACK, Loading and Size Supervisor, Wm. Sommerville and Son plc, Penicuik.
Dorothy Lucy, Mrs. BOLTON, Leader, Cheadle Animal Welfare Society and for services to the community.
Norman BOULTON, Sub Officer, Mid-Glamorgan Fire Service.
Gerard Micheal BOWKER, Engineering Powerplants and Components Superintendent, British Midland Airways.
William Robert BOWMAN, lately Commandant, Clydebank Detachment, British Red Cross Society.
Ronald George Weston BREWER, Workshops Manager, Space and Communications Division, British Aerospace plc.
James Harvey BROOMHEAD, lately Constable, H.M. Inspectorate of Constabulary.
Elizabeth, Mrs BROWN, Foster Parent, Bolton County Council.
John Richard BRYANT, Training Supervisor, Knotterbridge Training Centre for Roadmen, Devon County Council.
William Henry BULLOCK, Shunter, Ministry of Defence.
John Albert BULPIT, Constable, Greater Manchester Police.
John Richard BYARD, "Specials" Foreman, Butterley Brick Ltd. For services to Export.
Miss Winifred Ora CARSE, Transport Organiser, Northumberland and Tyneside, Women's Royal Voluntary Service.
Miss Dorothy Myrtle CHANT. For services to the Blood Transfusion Service in Southport.
Barry CLARKE, Station Officer, Dorset Fire Brigade.
Ewart Edward CLARKE. For services to the blind in Redditch.
Ernest CLYDE, Sub-Officer, Fire Authority for Northern Ireland.
Norman Walter COBB, Chief Steward I, Ministry of Defence.
Peter Daniel CODD, Leading Street Sweeper, Westminster City Council.
David Henry Grahame COLES, Construction Manager, Balfour Beatty Power Construction Limited.
Leonard Eugene COLWELL, Professional and Technology Officer, Ministry of Defence.
Lawrence Frederick COOKE, Auxiliary Coastguard, Reporting Section, Pett Level, Sussex.
Reginald James COOPER. For services to the community in Langbank, Renfrewshire.
Albert George COX, For services to Bowls in Kent.
Alec Lionel CROSS, Foreman (Ganger), Anglian Water.
Audrey Alice, Mrs. CRUST, Telephonist, 10 Downing Street.
Patrick CURRY, Head Porter, Erne Hospital, Enniskillen.
James Victor Harris DAVIDSON, Glassblower, Wear Glass Works, Corning Limited.
Miss Eileen Winifred DAVIES, lately Plant Assistant, Oswestry Water Treatment Plant, North West Water Authority.
Leonard Frank DAVIES, Assistant Technician, Stores, London Midland Region, British Railways.
Oswald DAVIES, Cadet Superintendent, Bro Ddyfi Division, St John Ambulance Brigade.
Susan Florence, Mrs. DAWSON, Psychiatric Unit Representative for the League of Friends, Sutton Hospital, Surrey.
James DENMAN, Wire Mill Superintendent, Briden Limited.
Hilda, Mrs. DIXON, School Crossing Patrol, Salford District Council.
James McGonnell DOBSON, Works Manager, A. Monk and Company plc.
William Ronald DOCKERILL, Messenger, Home Office.
Charles Bernard DODWELL, Senior Usher, North Devon Magistrates' Court.
Robert Marshall DUNCAN, Service Engineer, Scotland, British Gas plc.
Francis EDWARD, Head Carver, The Savoy Hotel, London WC2.
Dorothy, Mrs. EDWARDS, Supplies Officer, Clwyd Branch, The British Red Cross Society.
Clifford Joseph ELLIS. For services to the fishing industry in the North East.
Sidney ELLIS. For services to the League of Friends, Morriston Hospital, Swansea.
Cyril Charles EVANS, Graphics Officer, Ministry of Defence.
Leslie EVANS, Constable, South Wales Constabulary.
Rita, Mrs. EVERETT, Office Keeper IA, Department of Health and Social Security.
Gordon David FARMER, Sub Officer, East Sussex Fire Brigade.
James Eric FORREST. For services to youth in Todmorden, West Yorkshire.
John Harrison FOSTER, Sub Postmaster, Westgate TSO, Grantham, Corby Counters District, The Post Office.
Leslia William John FROST, Secretary, RAF Regiment, South East Asia Command Association.
Philip GARNER, lately International Exchange Consultant, Bath City Council.
Henry Charles GEERE, Supervising Instructional Officer 1, Ministry of Defence.
Albert Kenneth GEORGE, lately Process and General Supervisory C, Ministry of Defence.
John Philip GERRISH, General Foreman, Southern Electricity Board.
John GIBBONS, Section Inspector, Liverpool Section, British Waterways Board.
William Robert GILBERT, lately Prison Officer, Northern Ireland Prison Service.
Eleanor May, Mrs. GILKS. lately Home Help, Warwickshire County Council.
Arthur Henry GODDARD, Professional and Technology Officer, Ministry of Defence.
Andrew Gage GRAHAM, Plant Operator, Department of Agriculture, Northern Ireland.
Kenneth William GRANTHAM, Engineer, Inspection Department, Marconi Space Systems Limited.
Mary, Mrs. GRAVES. For services to the Patients' Library Organisation, Maidstone Hospital, Kent.
Lawrence GRAY, Joiner, Swan Hunter Limited.
Alan GREEN, Railman, Eastern Region, British Railways.
Glyn HAINES, Craftsman Overhead Lines, South Eastern Electricity Board.
John Duckworth HALL, Civilian Instructor, No. 341 (Preston) Squadron, Air Training Corps.
Robert Hugh HAMILL, Electrician, BP Chemicals Limited.
Marjorie Elsie, Mrs. HAMMOND, lately Foster Parent, Suffolk.
Francis Bernard HAND, District Superintendent, Permanent Way Division, Civil Engineering Department, London Underground Limited.
Dorothy Joyce, Mrs. HARRIS. For services to the community in Welwyn Garden City, Hertfordshire.
John HART, Section Officer, Durham Special Constabulary.
Sidney George HAWKINS, Warden, Grand Western Canal, Devon County Council.
Norman Frederick HIDE, Foreign and Commonwealth Office.

Florence Beatty, Mrs. HIGGINS, lately Foster Parent, Folkestone.
Norman Edwin HOBBS, Shipwright, Ministry of Defence.
John HODGSON, Traffic Checker, International Paint.
Annalena, Mrs. HOGG. For services to the Women's Royal Voluntary Service in Roxburghshire.
Ronald Walter HOILE. For services to the League of Friends, Chadwell Heath Hospital, Essex.
Edmund HOUGHTON. For services to the community in Hayfield, Derbyshire.
Averial Suzanne, Mrs. HOWELL, Member, Saxmundham, Suffolk, Women's Royal Voluntary Service.
John Thomas HUGHES, Observer Llanrhaeadr Post, No. 17 Group, Royal Observer Corps.
John William HUGHES, Governor Grade V, H.M. Prison Bedford.
William HUGHES, Steel Worker, Pallion Shipyard. North East Shipbuilders Limited.
Eric Herbert HYDE, Foreman, Merthyr Tydfil Institute for the Blind.
John Charles JACK, lately Staff Instructor, Loretto School, Edinburgh, Combined Cadet Force.
Peter William JARVIS, Station Officer, Norfolk Fire Service.
Thomas Chapman JENKINSON. For services to the fishing industry at Filey.
Frederick John Thomas JONES, Leading Ambulanceman, Gwynedd Health Authority.
Henry William JUDD, District Service Officer, Southern, British Gas plc.
Mary Butler, Mrs. MEADE-KING. For services to the Phobic Club in Plymouth.
William Henry Richard KING, County Treasurer, Lincolnshire, The Royal British Legion.
John LARKIN, Technical Officer, Northern Ireland Housing Executive.
Thomas LAURIE, Professional and Technical Officer, National Engineering Laboratory, Department of Trade and Industry.
Brian Ronald LEE, Detective Constable, Sussex Police.
Norman LEE, Technical Officer, Lancashire and Cumbria District, British Telecommunications plc.
Frank LEICESTER, lately Colliery Overman, Bickershaw Complex, Western Area, British Coal Corporation.
Brian Joseph LE MAR, lately Clerk of Works, Canterbury Cathedral.
Ralph Stanley LINHAM, Chairman, Glastonbury Club, The Royal British Legion.
William Laurence LITHERLAND, Caretaker, Range High School, Sefton Local Education Authority.
Kathleen Margaret, Mrs. LITTLE, Nursing Auxiliary, Accident and Emergency Department, Harringey Health Authority.
Myra, Mrs. LLOYD, Transport Organiser, South West England, Women's Royal Voluntary Service.
George Fraser LOW, Marshman, Glenfiddich Distillery, William Grant and Sons Limited.
Marjorie Frances, Mrs. LYALL, Chairwoman, Thrift Shop, Rheindahlen Garrison.
Susan Williamson, Mrs. McARTHUR. For services to Music.
Beatrice Margaret, Mrs. MACEY, Administrative Assistant (Transportation), County Surveyors Department, Avon County Council.
Robert McGOWAN, General Packer, Remploy Aintree Factory.
Francis Patrick McHUGH, lately Prison Officer, Northern Ireland Prison Service.
Thomas Henry McIVOR, Store-keeper and Clerk, Eastern Health and Social Services Board.
Evan Fraser MACKENZIE, Sub Postmaster, Burghead, Morayshire, The Post Office.
John McMULLAN, Stores Officer D, Ministry of Defence.
Reginald William MAGEE, Security Foreman, Northern Ireland Electricity.
Hilda Helen, Mrs. MAIDMENT, Chairman, The Brook General Hospital Body Scanner Appeal.
Frederick William MANN, Master Weaver, Edinburgh Tapestry Company Limited.
Arnot MANSON, Fire Protection and Safety Officer, Clyde Port Authority.
Francis MARGRAVE, Mobility Officer for Blind People, Essex County Council.
Tom MARSDEN, lately Driver, East Yorkshire Motor Services Limited.
Betty Margaret, Mrs. MARSH, Auxiliary Nurse, Dudley Road Hospital, West Birmingham Health Authority.
Peter Miller MARTIN, Sub-Divisional Officer, South Yorkshire Special Constabulary.
Eric Henry MASTERS, Senior Ranger, Forestry Commission.
John Lindsay MATHEWSON, Constable, Humberside Police.
Richard John Vaudin MAUGER, Sub Officer, Guernsey States Fire Brigade.
Alfred MAWHINNEY, lately Chief Electronic Technician, Royal Victoria Hospital, Belfast.
William MAXWELL, Convenor, General, Municipal, Boilermakers and Allied Trades Union, Sellafield Site, British Nuclear Fuels Limited.
Gordon DAVID MAYHEW, Senior Administrative Assistant, Suffolk Constabulary.
Miss Irene MAYKELS, Driver, Government Car Service. Department of the Environment.
Miss Patricia Amy MINCHINTON, Cartographic Draughtsman, Ordnance Survey.
Malcolm MORLEY, Sergeant, Greater Manchester Police.
George Gordon Wyllie MORRISON, Reserve Constable, Royal Ulster Constabulary.
Henry MORRISON, Senior Supervisor, Harland and Wolff plc.
James Andrew MORRISON, Sergeant, Royal Ulster Constabulary.
James Auld MORRISON, Craft Supervisor, Department of the Environment, Northern Ireland.
Ernest William MUNRO, Governor Grade V, H.M. Prison Noranside.
Gwen, Mrs. MURDIN. For services to the community in Higham Ferrers, Northamptonshire.
John Forbes MURRAY, Supervising Bailiff I, Middlesborough Group of Courts.
James George NEISH, Station Officer, H.M. Coastguard, Department of Transport.
Harold NELSON. For services to Cycling.
Robert Watson OPRAY, Constable, Metropolitan Police.
Edward Cyril ORR, Constable, Royal Ulster Constabulary.
David Henry PARMEE, Chief Observer, Woodvale Post, No. 21 Group, Royal Observer Corps.
Henry Swan PATERSON, Safety and Training Officer, Barony Colliery, Scottish Area, British Coal Corporation.
Leonard Charles PATTEN, lately Coxswain, Newhaven Lifeboat, Royal National Lifeboat Institution.
Keith Charles PENTLOW, Stores Supervisor, Unilever Research, Colworth Laboratory.
John Walter PILBEAM, Sergeant, Warwickshire Constabulary.
Ivor Derek QUICKENDEN, Craftsman, Ministry of Defence.
Anthony Michael John QUINN, Process and General Supervisor, Ministry of Agriculture, Fisheries and Food.
Joseph RANNACHAN, Senior Foreman, Outside Labour Force, A and W Fullarton Limited, Glasgow.
Sydney Norman John RAPSON, Air Frame Engine Fitter, Ministry of Defence.
Arthur RAVENHILL, Governor Grade IV, H.M. Prison Gartree.
Geoffrey William REEKS. For services to Cricket in Bedfordshire.
Rose Taylor, Mrs. REID. For services to the League of Friends, Peterhead Cottage Hospital.
Mary Katherine, Mrs. RICE. For services to the community in Newcastle, Co. Down.
Anthony Ernest RICHES, Stores Supervisory Officer Grade C, Metropolitan Police.
Donald Ross RIDDELL, Leader, Highland Strathspey and Reel Society.
Margaret Elizabeth, Mrs. ROBINSON. For services to the Lincolnshire Agricultural Society.
Peter Kenneth James ROBINSON, Chief Observer, Farnsfield Post, No. 8 Group, Coventry, Royal Observer Corps.
Watson RUTHVEN, Chargehand Painter, Scottish Development Department.
Eleanor, Mrs. SANKEY. For services to the League of Friends, Winwick Hospital, Cheshire.
Miss Ellen Crake SCOTT, Linen Room Supervisor, Cherry Knowle Hospital, Sunderland Health Authority.
SHAO Chun Kar, Laundry Contractor, H.M.S. Ark Royal.
William SINCLAIR, Treasurer, Wick Harbour Trust.
Alan George SMITH, Milkman, Express Dairies.
David Edward SMITH, Fitter, George Wimpey plc.

George Frederic SMITH, Driver and Clerk, Gloucester County Libraries.
John Frederick Raymond SMITH, Constable, Staffordshire Police.
Edward STAFFORD, Assistant Works Superindent, City of Newcastle upon Tyne.
Bridget O'Niel, Mrs. STENHOUSE, Quality Control Supervisor, Patons and Baldwins Limited, Alloa.
Frederick Hall STEWART, lately Professional and Technology Officer, Ministry of Defence.
Samuel STITT, Site Engineer, Lambeg Industrial Research Association.
Christopher STRAIN, lately Process and General Supervisory D, Ministry of Defence.
Janet Louise, Mrs. STUCKE, Organiser, Greenwich District Hospital Shop, Women's Royal Voluntary Service.
Beatrice Sarah, Mrs. STURGESS Honorary Firewoman (Cleaner), Cambridgeshire Fire Service.
Edwin SWAINE, Instructor, Wakefield, Sea Cadet Corps Unit.
Esther Martin, Mrs. TAYLOR, Chef, British Broadcasting Corporation, Belfast.
Geoffrey William TAYLOR, Professional and Technology Officer, Commonwealth War Graves Commission.
Gordon THAIN, Marine Service Officer III, Ministry of Defence.
Frank Herbert THISTLETON, Driver, Eastern Region, British Railways.
Royston Noel THOMAS, Production Manager, Alfred Reader and Company Limited.
Ronald THOMPSON, Senior Dock Foreman, Immingham Dock Associated British Ports.
Peggy, Mrs TIMMS, Deputy County Organiser, Warwickshire, Women's Royal Voluntary Service.
Doreen, Mrs. TULIP, First Aid and Nursing Group Leader, Durham County Branch, The British Red Cross Society.
George Reginald TURBUTT, Glass Planning and Estimating Engineer, Pilkington plc.
John Bryan TUTHILL, Superintendent, Anglian Water Authority.
Alfred Henry UNDERWOOD, Caretaker, Raglan Barracks, Newport, Territorial Auxiliary and Volunteer Reserve Association.
Henry VALENTINE, Civilian Instructional Officer Grade III, H.M. Prison Bristol.
Sidney VAUGHAN. For services to the community in Ormesby, Cleveland.
Edward John VINEY, Seaman, Pilot Launch Crew, Isle of Wight Pilot Vessel Service.
Miss Jemima Mearns WALKER, lately Administrator, Denburn Health Centre, Aberdeen.
John WALKER, Driver, London Midland Region, British Railways.
Basil WARNE, lately Works Supervisor Surrey County Council.
Charles Hubert WEBB, Professional and Technology Officer, Ministry of Defence.
Frederick John WEIR, Courtkeeper, Omagh Courthouse, Co. Tyrone.
Roy James WELLS, Observer, Cranbrook Post, No. 1 Group, Royal Observer Corps.
Anthony WEST, Installation Manager (Northern) Engineering and General Equipment Ltd.
Joan, Mrs. WESTLAND, Supervisor of Government Telephonists, Department of the Environment.
Eric Bruce WHITE, Instructor, Operative Training Centre, George Wimpey plc.
Margaret, Mrs. WHITE, lately Commandant, Stanley Company (Glasgow), St. Andrew's Ambulance Corps.
Alexander WHYTE, Sub-Officer, Highlands and Islands Fire Brigade.
Donald Alexander WILSON, Freight Supervisor, Scottish Region, British Railways.
Lawrence Arthur WILSON, lately Site Agent, William Sindall plc.
Miss Mary Anna Chapman WILSON. For services to agriculture in County Fermanagh.
Willaim WOOD, Electrician, Vickers Shipbuilding and Engineering Limited.
Albert Edward WRIGHT, Foreign and Commonwealth Office.
Fredrick Baden Horace WRIGHT, Electrical Fitter, Eastern Electricity Board.
Alexander YOUNG, lately Chief Clerk Officer, H.M. Prison Inverness.
Allan McNasser YOUNG, Professional and Technology Officer, Department of the Environment.
Thomas David YOUNG, Governor Grade IV, H.M. Prison Camp Hill.

OVERSEAS TERRITORIES

CHUNG Wun-ching, Butcher Class I, Urban Services Department, Hong Kong.
James COLLINS. For services to Agriculture in Montserrat.
George GASKIN, Third Officer, Fire Service, Gibraltar.
Miss Lydia HENRICH, Executive Officer, Housing Department, Gibraltar.
KAN Kong-Lam, Chief Customs Officer, Customs and Excise Service, Hong Kong.
KWOK Bing-chau, Senior Clerical Officer, Buildings and Lands Department, Hong Kong.
LAM Shun-pung, Transport Supervisor, Government Land Transport Agency, Hong Kong.
Victoria, Mrs. LOMBARD, Headteacher, St Mary's First School, Gibraltar.
James THOMPSON, Senior Motor Vehicle Examiner, Police Department, Hong Kong.
TSOI Kwing-hi, Senior Clerical Officer, Medical and Health Department, Hong Kong.
Sau-ha Cheung, Mrs. TSOI, Staff Midwife, Medical and Health Department, Hong Kong.
WONG Kai-chiu, lately Senior Foreman, Urban Services Department, Hong Kong.

MINISTRY OF DEFENCE
WHITEHALL, LONDON S.W.1

11th June 1988

THE QUEEN has been graciously pleased, on the occasion of the Celebration of Her Majesty's Birthday, to give orders for the following appointments to the Royal Red Cross:

ROYAL RED CROSS

MINISTRY OF DEFENCE (NAVY DEPARTMENT)

A.R.R.C.

To be an Ordinary Associate of the Royal Red Cross, Second Class.

Superintending Nursing Officer Judith Claire BROWN, Queen Alexandra's Royal Naval Nursing Service.

MINISTRY OF DEFENCE (ARMY DEPARTMENT)

R.R.C.

To be Ordinary Members of the Royal Red Cross, First Class:

Lieutenant Colonel Elizabeth Jane CAMPBELL (498549), Queen Alexandra's Royal Army Nursing Corps, Territorial Army.
Lieutenant Colonel Sylvia SCOTT (482642), Queen Alexandra's Royal Army Nursing Corps.

A.R.R.C.

To be Ordinary Associates of the Royal Red Cross, Second Class:

Major Susan Elizabeth DALY (497906), Queen Alexandra's Royal Army Nursing Corps.
Lieutenant Colonel Dorothy GOLDING, T.D. (497234), Queen Alexandra's Royal Army Nursing Corps, Territorial Army.
Major Ann KERR (492417), Queen Alexandra's Royal Army Nursing Corps.
Major Joyce WIDEMAN (500233), Queen Alexandra's Royal Army Nursing Corps.

MINISTRY OF DEFENCE (AIR FORCE DEPARTMENT)

R.R.C.

To be an Ordinary Member of the Royal Red Cross, First Class:

Group Captain Elizabeth Angela Innes SANDISON, A.R.R.C. (408108), Princess Mary's Royal Air Force Nursing Service.

A.R.R.C.

To be Ordinary Associates of the Royal Red Cross, Second Class:

Squadron Leader Anthony Charles Wesley COX (594310), Princess Mary's Royal Air Force Nursing Service.
Squadron Leader Janet EDMUNDS-JONES (407876), Princess Mary's Royal Air Force Nursing Service.

MINISTRY OF DEFENCE WHITEHALL, S.W.I

11th June 1988

The QUEEN has been graciously pleased, on the occasion of the Celebration of Her Majesty's Birthday, to approve the award of the Air Force Cross to the undermentioned:

AIR FORCE CROSS

A.F.C.

MINISTRY OF DEFENCE (NAVY DEPARTMENT)

Lieutenant Commander Phillip Anthony Robertson HARRALL, Royal Navy.
Lieutenant Commander Nigel Geoffrey HENNELL, Royal Navy.

MINISTRY OF DEFENCE (AIR FORCE DEPARTMENT)

Squadron Leader Russell George BRAITHWAITE (4230269), Royal Air Force.
Wing Commander Jeremy Andrew KING (4231703), Royal Air Force.
Squadron Leader Martin Buckwell STONER (608909), Royal Air Force.
Wing Commander Denys Andrew WILLIAMS (4232127), Royal Air Force.

HOME OFFICE QUEEN ANNE'S GATE, LONDON S.W.1

11th June 1988

The QUEEN has been graciously pleased, on the occasion of the Celebration of Her Majesty's Birthday, to approve the award of The Queen's Police Medal for Distinguished Service to the undermentioned.

QUEEN'S POLICE MEDAL

Q.P.M.

ENGLAND AND WALES

Philip Henry CORBETT, Commander, Metropolitan Police.
Lance CORNISH, Detective Superintendent, Port of London Authority Police.
Bernard DREW, Assistant Chief Constable, West Mercia Constabulary.
Jefferson Edward EASTON, Chief Superintendent, Greater Manchester Police.
Walter Raymond GIRVEN, Deputy Chief Constable, Dorset Police.
Peter HAYES, Deputy Chief Constable, South Yorkshire Police.
Michael HORNBY, Detective Sergeant, West Midlands Police.
Robert William JACKSON, Superintendent, Nottinghamshire Constabulary.
Gordon Reginald LLOYD, Commander, Metropolitan Police.
Gordon McMURCHIE, Assistant Chief Constable, Northumbria Police.
Frank Herbert MORRITT, Assistant Chief Constable, North Yorkshire Police.
David Joseph O'DOWD, Chief Constable, Northamptonshire Police.
Brian John PHILLIPS, Assistant Chief Constable, Devon and Cornwall Constabulary.
David John POLKINGHORNE, lately Commander, Metropolitan Police.
John Peter ROBINSON, Commander, Metropolitan Police.
William Derick SPALTON, Inspector, Lincolnshire Police.
Beston WAKELY, Chief Superintendent, Wiltshire Constabulary.
Neville YARWOOD, lately Detective Sergeant, Merseyside Police.

NORTHERN IRELAND

Sir John HERMON, O.B.E., Chief Constable, Royal Ulster Constabulary.
John Niall HOWE, Superintendent, Royal Ulster Constabulary.

HONG KONG

Gordon JACK, C.P.M., Assistant Commissioner of Police, Hong Kong.
SO Lai-yin, C.P.M., Assistant Commissioner of Police, Hong Kong.

SCOTTISH OFFICE ST. ANDREW'S HOUSE EDINBURGH

11th June 1988

The QUEEN has been graciously pleased, on the occasion of the Celebration of Her Majesty's Birthday, to approve the award of The Queen's Police Medal for Distinguished Service to the undermentioned:

QUEEN'S POLICE MEDAL

Q.P.M.

SCOTLAND

Robert Carter CUNNINGHAM, Assistant Chief Constable, Strathclyde Police.
Donald Kerr MILLAR, Chief Superintendent, Lothian and Borders Police.

HOME OFFICE QUEEN ANNE'S GATE, LONDON S.W.1

11th June 1988

The QUEEN has been graciously pleased, on the occasion of the Celebration of Her Majesty's Birthday, to approve the award of The Queen's Fire Service Medal for Distinguished Service to the undermentioned:

QUEEN'S FIRE SERVICE MEDAL

Q.F.S.M.

ENGLAND AND WALES

Frank BOOTH, Assistant Chief Officer, Army Fire Service.
William Wilson DUNLOP, Deputy Chief Officer, Tyne and Wear Fire Brigade.
James GURNEY, Deputy Assistant Chief Officer, London Fire Brigade.
Frank Nicholson HIGGINS, Deputy Chief Officer, Bedfordshire Fire Service.
Alan McANDREW, Divisional Officer II, Suffolk Fire Service.
Francis George WILTON, Chief Officer, Avon Fire Service.
Henry Edward WRIGHT, Chief Officer, South Yorkshire County Fire Service.

HONG KONG

LAM Chek-yuen, C.P.M., Chief Fire Officer, Hong Kong.

SCOTTISH OFFICE ST. ANDREW'S HOUSE EDINBURGH

11th June 1988

The QUEEN has been graciously pleased, on the occasion of the Celebration of Her Majesty's Birthday, to approve the award of The Queen's Fire Service Medal for Distinguished Service to the undermentioned:

QUEEN'S FIRE SERVICE MEDAL

Q.F.S.M.

SCOTLAND

Clive Benson HALLIDAY, Firemaster, Strathclyde Fire Brigade.

FOREIGN AND COMMONWEALTH OFFICE
DOWNING STREET, LONDON, S.W.1

11th June 1988

THE QUEEN has been graciously pleased, on the occasion of the Celebration of Her Majesty's Birthday, to approve the award of the Colonial Police and Fire Service Medal for Meritorious Service to the undermentioned:

COLONIAL POLICE AND FIRE SERVICE MEDAL

C.P.M.

Colin Malcolm BAKER, Superintendent, Royal Hong Kong Police Force.
Thomas Albert BARNES, Senior Superintendent, Royal Hong Kong Police Force.
CHAN Siu-chik, Chief Inspector, Royal Hong Kong Police Force.
CHEUNG Chi-keung, Senior Superintendent, Royal Hong Kong Police Force.
CHEUNG King-tim, Station Sergeant, Royal Hong Kong Police Force.
HO Hon-kwan, Principal Fireman, Hong Kong Fire Services.
James HO Kwok-chuen, Senior Divisional Officer, Hong Kong Fire Services.
IU Yee-hung, Superintendent, Royal Hong Kong Police Force.
KWOK Ping-tong, Station Sergeant, Royal Hong Kong Police Force.
LAI Wun-wing, Chief Inspector, Royal Hong Kong Police Force.
LAU Chun-sang, Station Sergeant, Royal Hong Kong Police Force.
LEE Wai, Principal Fireman, Hong Kong Fire Services.
LI Kam-chuen, Station Sergeant, Royal Hong Kong Police Force.
Peter MAGINNIS, Superintendent, Gibraltar Police Force.
MAK Kwok-kuen, Chief Inspector, Royal Hong Kong Police Force.
PUN Ying-kuen, Sergeant, Royal Hong Kong Police Force.
Robert Charles TOAL, Senior Superintendent, Royal Hong Kong Police Force.
YIP Kwok-keung, Senior Superintendent, Royal Hong Kong Police Force.

MINISTRY OF DEFENCE WHITEHALL, LONDON, S.W.1

11th June 1988

THE QUEEN has been graciously pleased, on the occasion of the Celebration of Her Majesty's Birthday, to approve the award of The Queen's Commendation for Valuable Service in the Air to the undermentioned:

QUEEN'S COMMENDATION FOR VALUABLE SERVICE IN THE AIR

MINISTRY OF DEFENCE (AIR FORCE DEPARTMENT)

Squadron Leader Thomas Leonard BOYLE (8026463), Royal Air Force.
Squadron Leader William George COUPAR (584305), Royal Air Force.
Squadron Leader Denis Edwin HERRETT (1920484), Royal Air Force.
Flight Lieutenant Malcolm John Andrew MACDONALD (2621178), Royal Air Force.
Squadron Leader Nigel David Alan MADDOX (8026221), Royal Air Force.
Flight Lieutenant Ian George Leslie MALIN (8026345), Royal Air Force.
Squadron Leader Ian MORTIMER (5202579), Royal Air Force.
Squadron Leader Christopher Mark NICKOLS (5202730), Royal Air Force.
Flight Lieutenant Malcolm John REEVES (8023123), Royal Air Force.
Squadron Leader Frank Lester TURNER (8026176), Royal Air Force.
Squadron Leader Jeremy Richard WOODS (5202028), Royal Air Force.

THE 1989 NEW YEAR HONOURS LIST

As published in the Supplement to The London Gazette of Friday, 30th December 1988
CENTRAL CHANCERY OF THE ORDERS OF KNIGHTHOOD

THE QUEEN has been graciously pleased, to signify her intention of conferring Peerages of the United Kingdom for Life upon the undermentioned:

LIFE PEERS

To be a Baroness:

The Right Honourable Sally, Mrs. OPPENHEIM-BARNES, Chairman, National Consumer Council.

To be Barons:

Professor Sir Jack LEWIS, Professor of Chemistry, University of Cambridge; Chairman, Commission on Environmental Pollution..
Sir John (Davan) SAINSBURY, Chairman, J. Sainsbury plc.

CENTRAL CHANCERY OF
THE ORDERS OF KNIGHTHOOD

ST. JAMES'S PALACE, LONDON SW1

31st December 1988

THE QUEEN has been graciously pleased to declare that the undermentioned shall be sworn of Her Majesty's Most Honourable Privy Council:

PRIVY COUNSELLORS

Jeremy John Durham (Paddy) ASHDOWN, M.P., Leader Social and Liberal Democratic Party; Member of Parliament Yeovil.
(Bernard Harold) Ian (Halley) STEWART, M.P., Minister of State Northern Ireland Office; Member of Parliament North Hertfordshire.
David Garro, Baron TREFGARNE, Minister of State Ministry of Defence.

CENTRAL CHANCERY OF
THE ORDERS OF KNIGHTHOOD

ST. JAMES'S PALACE, LONDON SW1

31st December 1988

THE QUEEN has been graciously pleased to signify her intention of conferring the Honour of Knighthood upon the undermentioned:

KNIGHTS BACHELOR

David ALLIANCE, C.B.E., Chief Executive, Coats Viyella plc.
Derek Sydney BIRLEY, Vice-Chancellor, The University of Ulster.
John BOARDMAN, Lincoln Professor of Classical Archaeology and Art; Fellow, Lincoln College, University of Oxford.
The Right Honourable Leon BRITTAN, Q.C. For political service.
Professor Bryan Victor CARSBERG, Director General, Office of Telecommunications.
Peter Grenville CAZALET, Deputy Chairman, The British Petroleum Company plc.
Robert COWAN, Chairman, Highlands and Islands Development Board.
Cyril Humphrey CRIPPS, D.L. For political and public service.
Judson Graham DAY, Chairman and Chief Executive, The Rover Group plc.
Evelyn Robert Adrian de ROTHSCHILD, Chairman, N.M. Rothschild and Sons Ltd.
Reginald Derek Henry DOYLE, C.B.E., Her Majesty's Chief Inspector of Fire Services.
Graham Newman EYRE, Q.C. For services to the London Airports Authority.
Hugh FISH, C.B.E., lately Chairman, Natural Environment Research Council.
Peter Walter GIBBINGS, Chairman, Anglia Television Group plc; lately Chairman, Guardian and Manchester Evening News.
William Howard GOODHART, Q.C. For political and public service.
Matthew Dean GOODWIN, C.B.E. For political service.
Arthur Alfred HILL, C.B.E. For political and public service.
Brian John HILL, Chairman and Chief Executive, Higgs and Hill Group plc.
Ian Charter MacLAURIN, Chairman, Tesco plc.
Edward Michael OGDEN, Q.C., Chairman, Criminal Injuries Compensation Board.
Geoffrey OWEN, Editor, The Financial Times.
Eduardo Luigi PAOLOZZI, C.B.E., Sculptor.
William Jeremy Masefield SHELTON, M.P. For political service.
Alfred Joseph SHEPPERD, Chairman and Chief Executive, Wellcome plc.
Charles Eric STROUD, lately Professor of Child Health, King's College School of Medicine and Dentistry.
Christopher Stephen WATES, Chairman, The English Industrial Estates Corporation; Chairman, Wates Building Group Ltd.
William Henry Nairn WILKINSON, Chairman, Nature Conservancy Council.

CENTRAL CHANCERY OF
THE ORDERS OF KNIGHTHOOD

ST. JAMES'S PALACE, LONDON SW1

31st December 1988

THE QUEEN has been graciously pleased to give orders for the following promotions in, and appointments to, the Most Honourable Order of the Bath:

ORDER OF THE BATH (MILITARY DIVISION)

MINISTRY OF DEFENCE (NAVY DEPARTMENT)

G.C.B.

To be an Ordinary Member of the Military Division of the First Class, or Knight Grand Cross, of the said Most Honourable Order:

Admiral Sir Julian OSWALD, K.C.B.

K.C.B.

To be an Ordinary Member of the Military Division of the Second Class, or Knight Commander, of the said Most Honourable Order:

Vice Admiral John Beverley KERR.

C.B.

To be Ordinary Members of the Military Division of the Third Class, or Companions, of the said Most Honourable Order:

Rear Admiral Anthony Mansfeldt NORMAN.
Rear Admiral David Robert SHERVAL.

MINISTRY OF DEFENCE (ARMY DEPARTMENT)

K.C.B.

To be an Ordinary Member of the Military Division of the Second Class, or Knight Commander of the said Most Honourable Order:

Lieutenant General Charles Edward Webb JONES, C.B.E. (448994), Colonel Commandant 3rd Battalion The Royal Green Jackets, Colonel Commandant Royal Army Educational Corps.

C.B.

To be Ordinary Members of the Military Division of the Third Class, or Companions, of the said Most Honourable Order:

Major General Paul Donald ALEXANDER, M.B.E. (439931), late Royal Corps of Signals.
Major General John David Graham PANK (459052), Colonel the Light Infantry.
Major General Robert SCOTT, Q.H.S. (450391), late Royal Army Medical Corps.
Major General Christopher TYLER (437190), late Corps of Royal Electrical and Mechanical Engineers.
Major General Robert William WARD, M.B.E. (443583), late 1st The Queen's Dragoon Guards.

MINISTRY OF DEFENCE (AIR FORCE DEPARTMENT)

G.C.B.

To be an Ordinary Member of the Military Division of the First Class, or Knight Grand Cross, of the said Most Honourable Order.

Air Chief Marshal Sir Patrick HINE, K.C.B., Royal Air Force.

K.C.B.

To be an Ordinary Member of the Military Division of the Second Class, or Knight Commander, of the said Most Honourable Order:

Air Marshal Thomas Henry STONOR, Royal Air Force.

C.B.

To be Ordinary Members of the Military Division of the Third Class, or Companions, of the said Most Honourable Order:

Air Vice-Marshal Richard Christopher ALLERTON, Royal Air Force.
Air Vice-Marshal Kenneth Archibald CAMPBELL, Royal Air Force.
Air Vice-Marshal Peter HOWARD, O.B.E., Royal Air Force (Retired).

ORDER OF THE BATH (CIVIL DIVISION)

G.C.B.

To be an Ordinary Member of the Civil Division of the First Class, or Knight Grand Cross, of the said Most Honourable Order:

Sir Peter Edward MIDDLETON, K.C.B., Permanent Secretary, H.M. Treasury.

K.C.B.

To be Ordinary Members of the Civil Division of the Second Class, or Knights Commanders, of the said Most Honourable Order:

Anthony Michael William BATTISHILL, Chairman, Board of Inland Revenue.
Christopher Walter FRANCE, C.B., Permanent Secretary, Department of Health.

C.B.

To be Ordinary Members of the Civil Division of the Third Class, or Companions, of the said Most Honourable Order:

Robert Morrison AINSCOW, Deputy Secretary, Overseas Development Administration.
Miss Sandra Pauline BURNS, Parliamentary Counsel, Office of the Parliamentary Counsel.
Christopher Hugh COSSHAM, Senior Assistant Director, Department of the Director of Public Prosecutions, Northern Ireland.
Miss Patricia Ann Cox, lately Under Secretary, Scottish Home and Health Department.
Miss Zelma Ince DAVIES, Under Secretary, Department of Health and Social Services, Northern Ireland.
Roger Garnett LAVELLE, Deputy Secretary, Cabinet Office.
William Frederick MUMFORD, Grade 3, Ministry of Defence.
Ronald Martin OLIVER, R.D., Deputy Chief Medical Officer, Department of Health.
Jeffrey William PRESTON, Deputy Secretary, Welsh Office.
Peter Vivian Henworth SMITH, Solicitor, Board of Customs and Excise.
Anthony William STEPHENS, C.M.G., Deputy Secretary, Northern Ireland Office.
Neville TAYLOR, lately Director General, Central Office of Information.
George Morton WEDD, Grade 3, Department of the Environment.
Roland Hewlett WIDDOWS, Presiding Special Commissioner of Income Tax.
Roy WILLIAMS, Deputy Secretary, Department of Trade and Industry.
John WOOD, Director, Serious Fraud Office.

CENTRAL CHANCERY OF
THE ORDERS OF KNIGHTHOOD

ST. JAMES'S PALACE, LONDON SW1

31st December 1988

THE QUEEN has been graciously pleased to give orders for the following promotions in, and appointments to, the Most Distinguished Order of Saint Michael and Saint George:

C.M.G.

To be an Ordinary Member of the Third Class, or Companion, of the said Most Distinguished Order:

James Bowen THOMAS, Grade 5, Ministry of Defence.

DIPLOMATIC SERVICE AND OVERSEAS LIST

G.C.M.G.

To be an Ordinary Member of the First Class, or Knight Grand Cross, of the said Most Distinguished Order:

Sir Crispin TICKELL, K.C.V.O. United Kingdom Permanent Representative to the United Nations, New York.

K.C.M.G.

To be Ordinary Members of the Second Class, or Knights Commanders, of the said Most Distinguished Order:

Arthur John COLES, C.M.G., British High Commissioner, Canberra.
Nicholas Maxted FENN, C.M.G., H.M. Ambassador, Dublin.
Robin William RENWICK, C.M.G., H.M. Ambassador, Pretoria.
Arthur Desmond WATTS, C.M.G., Q.C. Legal Adviser, Foreign and Commonwealth Office.
The Right Reverend Robert Wilmer WOODS, K.C.V.O., Prelate of the Order of Saint Michael and Saint George.

C.M.G.

To be Ordinary Members of the Third Class, or Companions, of the said Most Distinguished Order:

James Nicholas ALLAN, C.B.E., H.M. Ambassador, Maputo.
David BEATTIE, United Kingdom Deputy Permanent Representative to NATO, Brussels.
John BROWN, Deputy Consul-General and Director of Trade Development, New York.
Michael Francis DALY, H.M. Ambassador, San José.
Stephen Peter DAY, H.M. Ambassador, Tunis.
Peter John GOULDEN, Foreign and Commonwealth Office.
Michael John LLEWELLYN SMITH, Minister, H.M. Embassy, Paris.
Ian Warren MACKLEY, Chargé d'Affaires, H.M. Embassy, Kabul.
Jeremy Fell MATHEWS, J.P., Attorney-General, Hong Kong.
David Joseph MOSS, Foreign and Commonwealth Office.
Michael Jacques THOMPSON, O.B.E., Foreign and Commonwealth Office.
Terence Courtney WOOD, Minister, H.M. Embassy, Rome.

CENTRAL CHANCERY OF
THE ORDERS OF KNIGHTHOOD

ST. JAMES'S PALACE, LONDON SW1

31st December 1988

THE QUEEN has been graciously pleased to make the following promotions in, and appointments to, the Royal Victorian Order:

D.C.V.O

To be a Dame Commander:

Mary Elizabeth, Mrs. HEDLEY-MILLER, C.B.

K.C.V.O.

To be Knights Commanders:

Charles Annand FRASER, C.V.O.
Hon. Angus James Bruce OGILVY
Colonel Hon. Gordon William Nottage PALMER, O.B.E., T.D.
Wing Commander Kenneth Maxwell STODDART, A.E.

C.V.O.

To be Commanders:

Ronald William ABBOTT, C.B.E
Trevor Edwin CHINN.
Denys Michael Gwilym KING.
Sir (Robert) Andrew MORRITT.
Nigel Leonard WICKS, C.B.E.
Lieutenant-Colonel Blair Aubyn STEWART-WILSON, L.V.O

L.V.O.

To be Lieutenants:

Jeffrey Bertram CACKETT, M.V.O.
Colonel Charles Herbert Kenneth CORSAR, O.B.E., T.D., D.L.
Elizabeth Anne, Mrs. GRIFFITHS, M.V.O.
John Oswald HITCHINGS, M.V.O.
Celia, Mrs. INNES.
Charles QUANT, M.B.E., J.P.

M.V.O.

To be Members:

Susan, Mrs. BENJAMIN.
Cyril DAVIDSON.
Cyril Sidney DICKMAN, R.V.M.
David Nawton GRIMSTON.
Miss Sandra KOLLER.
Michael Trevor PARKER.
Michael Hugh Lacey WARNES.
Thomas Archibald Stark WICKS.
Miss Bridget Anne WRIGHT.

CENTRAL CHANCERY OF
THE ORDERS OF KNIGHTHOOD

ST. JAMES'S PALACE, LONDON SW1

31st December 1988

THE QUEEN has been graciously pleased to award a Bar to the Royal Victorian Medal (Silver) to the undermentioned:

BAR TO THE ROYAL VICTORIAN MEDAL (SILVER)

William Edward ROWE, R.V.M.

CENTRAL CHANCERY OF
THE ORDERS OF KNIGHTHOOD

ST. JAMES'S PALACE, LONDON SW1

31st December 1988

THE QUEEN has been graciously pleased to award the Royal Victorian Medal (Silver) to the undermentioned:

ROYAL VICTORIAN MEDAL (SILVER)

R.V.M.

Dobrinka, Mrs. BAMBIC.
Grenville Leslie Victor BATTERBEE.
Geoffrey Howard BORTON.
F8105711 Chief Technician Michael BROWN, Royal Air Force.
Stanley Walter BUTLER.
George William COOKE.
J4290707 Chief Technician Alan GIBSON, Royal Air Force.
Police Constable Dennis William GOLDSMITH, Metropolitan Police.
Kenneth Reginald MAYNARD.
Arthur Jeffrey NUNN.
Vincent PAYNE.
Sergeant Allan Ritson PETERS, Metropolitan Police.
Chief Petty Officer Marine Engineering Mechanic (Mechanical) Stephen James TURNER, (D140964F), Royal Navy.
Kevan Barry YOXALL.

CENTRAL CHANCERY OF
THE ORDERS OF KNIGHTHOOD

ST. JAMES'S PALACE, LONDON SW1

31st December 1988

THE QUEEN has been graciously pleased to make the following promotions in, and appointments to, the Most Excellent Order of the British Empire:

ORDER OF THE BRITISH EMPIRE (MILITARY DIVISION)

MINISTRY OF DEFENCE (NAVY DEPARTMENT)

K.B.E.

To be an Ordinary Knight Commander of the Military Division of the said Most Excellent Order:

Vice Admiral Norman Ross Dutton KING.

C.B.E.

To be Ordinary Commanders of the Military Division of the said Most Excellent Order:

Commodore Ian Affleck Warden BERRY, R.D.*, D.L., Royal Naval Reserve.
Captain Geoffrey Alan EADES, A.D.C., Royal Navy.
Surgeon Commodore Raymond RADFORD, Q.H.S., Royal Navy.

O.B.E.

To be Ordinary Officers of the Military Division of the said Most Excellent Order:

Commander Geoffrey Douglas Simon BRYANT, Royal Navy.
Commander William John BURLING, Royal Navy.
Commander Maurice Edgar COOK, Royal Navy.
Chief Officer Margaret Hope GOSSE, Women's Royal Naval Service.
Commander Keith Alfred HARRIS, Royal Navy.
Commander Ian Rhoderick HEWITT, Royal Navy.
Lieutenant Colonel Gordon Douglas Birdwood KEELAN, Royal Marines.
Commander Gilbert Ian MAYES, Royal Navy.
Commander Adrian MUNNS, Royal Navy.
Commander Alan John SPRUCE, Royal Navy.
Commander Mark STANHOPE, Royal Navy.

M.B.E.

To be Ordinary Members of the Military Division of the said Most Excellent Order:

Lieutenant Commander Ian Adams CAMPBELL, Royal Navy.
Warrant Officer Anthony Frederick James COLBOURNE.
Lieutenant (now Lieutenant Commander) John Andrew CONNELL, Royal Navy.
Warrant Officer Norman Barry COOKE.
Warrrant Officer 1 Graham James DEAR, Royal Marines.
Warrant Officer John Henry FLETCHER.
Lieutenant Commander (SCC) Leslie HACKETT, Royal Naval Reserve.
Lieutenant Commander Christopher John LISHMAN, Royal Navy.
Lieutenant Commander Thomas McCRIMMON, Royal Navy
Lieutenant Commander Michael Richard MOORE, Royal Navy.
Warrant Officer Henry PAGE.
Captain Christopher Leonard TAYLOR, Royal Marines.
Warrant Officer Anna Jane WEEKS, Women's Royal Naval Service.
Lieutenant Commander John WILSON, Royal Navy.

MINISTRY OF DEFENCE (ARMY DEPARTMENT)

C.B.E.

To be Ordinary Commanders of the Military Division of the said Most Excellent Order:

Brigadier John Alexander James Pooler BARR (466324), late Corps of Royal Engineers.
Brigadier Eric COULTHARD, Q.H.D.S. (431090), late Royal Army Dental Corps.
Brigadier Henry John HICKMAN, O.B.E. (460866), Royal Pioneer Corps.
Colonel Noel Henry PETERS (476747), late Royal Army Medical Corps.
Brigadier Michael Francis Linton SHELLARD (453551), late Royal Regiment of Artillery.
Brigadier Michael Robert TOPPLE, A.D.C. (433254), late Royal Corps of Signals.
The Right Reverend Monsignor John Noctor WILLIAMS, Chaplain To The Forces 1st Class (482672), Royal Army Chaplains' Department.

O.B.E.

To be Ordinary Officers of the Military Division of the said Most Excellent Order:

Lieutenant Colonel Alaistair Michael CUMMING (470048), The Gordon Highlanders.
Lieutenant Colonel Charles Robert Knowles DEAN (480282), 14th/20th King's Hussars.
Lieutenant Colonel Peter David GARDNER (477414), The Duke of Wellington's Regiment (West Riding).
Lieutenant Colonel Charles Alan Colin HERON (485743), The Worcestershire and Sherwood Foresters Regiment (29th/45th Foot).
Lieutenant Colonel William James HURRELL (483937), 17th/21st Lancers.
Lieutenant Colonel Stuart JARDINE (437095), Corps of Royal Engineers.
Lieutenant Colonel Christopher David MACKENZIE-BEEVOR (491496), 1st The Queen's Dragoon Guards.
Lieutenant Colonel William James MARSHALL, M.B.E., T.D., D.L. (468108), Royal Corps of Transport, Territorial Army.
Lieutenant Colonel David Robin Dare NEWELL (469425), The Worcestershire and Sherwood Foresters Regiment (29th/45th Foot), Territorial Army.
Acting Lieutenant Colonel Hugh George Lyon PLAYFAIR (455556), Combined Cadet Force, Territorial Army.
Acting Lieutenant Colonel Edward Hugh Frere SAWBRIDGE (460627), Combined Cadet Force, Territorial Army.
Lieutenant Colonel David Harold Andrew SHEPHARD (476633), The Queen's Regiment.
Lieutenant Colonel Rupert Nigel Clayton SMALES (470154), Corps of Royal Engineers.
Lieutenant Colonel Roger John THEIS, M.B.E. (453058), Corps of Royal Military Police.
Lieutenant Colonel Norman Jan Piet WALKER, T.D. (493387), Royal Army Medical Corps, Territorial Army.
Lieutenant Colonel Evelyn John WEBB-CARTER (481893), Grenadier Guards.
Lieutenant Colonel Alasdair Allan WILSON (484058), Corps of Royal Engineers.

M.B.E.

To be Ordinary Members of the Military Division of the said Most Excellent Order:

Captain Ian Colin AMBROSE (524248), Corps of Royal Military Police.
Major Stephen ASHBY (482681), The Prince of Wales's Own Regiment of Yorkshire.
Major James BABINGTON-SMITH (510928), Intelligence Corps.
Major James Edgar BATTYE (486027), The Parachute Regiment, Territorial Army.
Captain Brian Walter BELL (518217), 1st The Queen's Dragoon Guards.
Acting Major John Geoffrey BREWER (464581), Army Cadet Force, Territorial Army.
Major Frank Derek BURGOYNE, T.D. (482589), Corps of Royal Engineers, Territorial Army.
Captain Raymond Norman BUTCHER (520125), Corps of Royal Engineers.
Captain Eileen CARTER, T.D. (470192), Women's Royal Army Corps, Territorial Army.
LS 22205508 Warrant Officer Class 2 Jack Alan CLARKE, The Blues and Royals (Royal Horse Guards and 1st Dragoons).
Captain Harry DENNISON (512350), Royal Tank Regiment.
Acting Major John Grant DOW (433959), Combined Cadet Force, Territorial Army.
Major Samuel Murray DRENNAN, D.F.C. (503656), Army Air Corps.
WO429977 Warrant Officer Class 1 Elaine FARRAND, Women's Royal Army Corps.
Major Henry Edward FLEMING (465487), Royal Army Ordnance Corps.
22527485 Warrant Officer Class 1 James William GOSSIP, Royal Corps of Transport, Territorial Army.
Captain Stephen John Derek HARRISON (509212), Royal Tank Regiment.
Captain David HENRY (491945), Royal Corps of Signals, Territorial Army.
Major Graham William HODGSON, T.D. (493846), Corps of Royal Engineers, Territorial Army.
24176581 Warrant Officer Class 2 Robert Stephen HUGHES, Royal Army Ordnance Corps.
Major Richard James JACKSON (499187), The Royal Anglian Regiment.
Captain Murdo Alexander MACDONALD (510969), Queen's Own Highlanders (Seaforth and Camerons).
Major George Taylor NEIL (506675), 17th/21st Lancers.
Captain Martin NICOL (516980), Royal Corps of Signals.
Captain Peter Stanley OAKLEY (512300), The King's Regiment.
Major Nicholas John Walter PARSONS (495449), Coldstream Guards.
Major Colin McFall PEEBLES (488475), Corps of Royal Engineers.
Major Richard John POPE, T.D. (437567), Royal Monmouthshire Royal Engineers (Militia), Territorial Army.
Captain Philip Andrew PRATLY (503901), Royal Corps of Signals.
Captain David Craigie RODGER, T.D. (475887), Corps of Royal Engineers, Territorial Army.
22484651 Warrant Officer Class 2 Ronald Arthur ROWE, Royal Regiment of Artillery.
Captain Michael John SEALE, B.E.M. (512311), The Parachute Regiment.
Major James SHARP (506597), The Gordon Highlanders.
Major William Francis SHUTTLEWOOD (489211), 2nd King Edward VII's Own Gurkha Rifles (The Sirmoor Rifles).
Captain Stuart Frank SIBLEY (519336), The Blues and Royals (Royal Horse Guards and 1st Dragoons).
Captain Robert William SILK (522697), Corps of Royal Military Police.
Major Duncan Leslie SMITH, T.D. (478915), Royal Corps of Signals, Territorial Army.

The Reverend David Arthur TICKNER, Chaplain To The Forces 3rd Class (498759), Royal Army Chaplains' Department.
Major John WADDINGTON (487057), Corps of Royal Engineers.
Lieutenant Michael Joseph WINSTANLEY (529207), The Cheshire Regiment.
Major Malcolm David WOOD (495263), Royal Army Ordnance Corps.
Major Ronald Bruce Hayward YOUNG (472655), Royal Regiment of Artillery.

OVERSEAS AWARD

M.B.E.

To be an Ordinary Member of the Military Division of the said Most Excellent Order:

Major Francis Robert MULLENS, E.D., The Royal Hong Kong Regiment (The Volunteers).

MINISTRY OF DEFENCE (AIR FORCE DEPARTMENT)

G.B.E.

To be an Ordinary Knight Grand Cross of the Military Division of the said Most Excellent Order:

Air Chief Marshal Sir David HARCOURT-SMITH, K.C.B., D.F.C., Royal Air Force.

K.B.E.

To be an Ordinary Knight Commander of the Military Division of the said Most Excellent Order:

Air Marshal Frank Martyn HOLROYD, C.B., Royal Air Force.

C.B.E.

To be Ordinary Commanders of the Military Division of the said Most Excellent Order:

Air Commodore John Frederick BOON, Royal Air Force.
Air Commodore David EMMERSON, A.F.C., Royal Air Force.
Group Captain Edward David FRITH, A.F.C.*, Royal Air Force (retired).
Air Commodore Joan HOPKINS, O.B.E., Women's Royal Air Force.
Group Captain John Holt SPENCER, A.F.C., Royal Air Force.

O.B.E.

To be Ordinary Officers of the Military Division of the said Most Excellent Order:

Wing Commander Eric BANKS, M.B.E. (4040326), Royal Air Force.
Wing Commander Keith BICHARD (607461), Royal Air Force.
Wing Commander William Michael Nigel CROSS (608149), Royal Air Force.
Wing Commander Patrick Charles John HERBERT (4230712), Royal Air Force.
Wing Commander Thomas Joseph HINDMARSH (4232219), Royal Air Force.
Wing Commander Ian Walter LINDSEY (208047), Royal Air Force Volunteer Reserve (Training).
Reverend (Wing Commander) Duncan Alexander Fraser MACLENNAN (507803), Royal Air Force.
Wing Commander Roy James SPRINGETT (2617738), Royal Air Force.
Wing Commander Nigel John SUDBOROUGH (4233248), Royal Air Force.
Wing Commander Christopher George WINSLAND (608655), Royal Air Force.
Wing Commander Jeffrey YOUNG (5201766), Royal Air Force.

M.B.E.

To be Ordinary Members of the Military Division of the said Most Excellent Order:

Squadron Leader Michael Kenneth ALLPORT (608455), Royal Air Force.
Master Aircrew Michael Allen John ANDERSON (S1943187), Royal Air Force.
Warrant Officer John Wilkins BEALE, B.E.M. (Q4115543), Royal Air Force.
Master Aircrew David Francis CLARKSON (U0683186), Royal Air Force.
Flight Lieutenant Andrew Geoffrey COHEN (5203846), Royal Air Force.
Squadron Leader Robert Bourke CUNNINGHAM (5202843), Royal Air Force.
Warrant Officer Brian GRINDROD (J1932912), Royal Air Force.
Flight Lieutenant Eric HAYES (1922443), Royal Air Force.
Squadron Leader Nigel Morrell HUCKINS (5201058), Royal Air Force.
Squadron Leader James Llyn JOHN (582609), Royal Air Force.
Flight Lieutenant Denys Gilbert KINSELLA (193051), Royal Air Force Volunteer Reserve.
Squadron Leader David Anthony Ian FITZGERALD-LOMBARD (8022672), Royal Air Force.
Squadron Leader Dennis Arthur LONGDEN (4257056), Royal Air Force.
Flight Lieutenant Michael James McCLEAVE (209347), Royal Air Force Volunteer Reserve (Training).
Squadron Leader Gary Graham MARTIN (8023061), Royal Air Force.
Squadron Leader Gwendoline Peggy PARIS (2655858), Women's Royal Auxiliary Air Force (Retired).
Warrant Officer Brian PROCTOR (R1935853), Royal Air Force.
Squadron Leader John Lawrence SHAW (4081448), Royal Air Force (Retired).
Flight Lieutenant (now Squadron-Leader) Alan Alfred SOUTH (5201975), Royal Air Force.
Flight Lieutenant (now Squadron-Leader) Alan James SWAN, Q.G.M., (685685), Royal Air Force.
Squadron Leader Paul Royston THOMAS (5202367), Royal Air Force.
Warrant Officer Robert Lindsay THOMSON, B.E.M., (E4256158), Royal Air Force.
Squadron Leader Christopher John TRIGG (5202334), Royal Air Force.
Warrant Officer David Gordon UMPLEBY (C1930324), Royal Air Force.
Squadron Leader Phillip John WILCOCK (8026115), Royal Air Force.
Warrant Officer Edward Marcus WILLIS (H0588559), Royal Air Force.

ORDER OF THE BRITISH EMPIRE (CIVIL DIVISION)

D.B.E.

To be Ordinary Dames Commanders of the Civil Division of the said most Excellent Order:

Miss Audrey Caroline EMERTON. For services to nursing.
Miss Janet Evelyn FOOKES, M.P. For political service.
Margaret Louise, Mrs. FRY, O.B.E. For political and public service.

K.B.E.

To be Ordinary Knights Commanders of the Civil Division of the said Most Excellent Order:

Edward Alexander JOHNSTON, C.B., Government Actuary.
Peter Keith LEVENE, Chief of Defence Procurement, Ministry of Defence.
Sir David Chilton PHILLIPS, Professor of Molecular Biophysics, University of Oxford; Chairman, Advisory Board for the Research Council.
Ian Pelham TODD, President, Royal College of Surgeons.

C.B.E.

To be Ordinary Commanders of the Civil Division of the said Most Excellent Order:

Peter Hugh ALEXANDER. For political and public service.
Thomas Boaz ALLEN, Opera Singer.
John Graeme ANDERSON, Executive Deputy Chairman, Northern Engineering Industries plc.
Alec Walter BARBOUR, President, Board of Governors, East of Scotland College of Agriculture.
Brian James BEEDHAM, Foreign Editor, The Economist.
David John BINNS, General Manager, Warrington and Runcorn Development Corporation.
Donald BISHOP, M.C., Chairman, Study Team on Professional Liability in the Construction Industry.
Alastair Kenneth Lamond BLACK, D.L., Under Sheriff, Greater London.
Peter Leahy BONFIELD, Chairman and Managing Director, ICL Ltd.
Peter Derek CARR, Regional Director, Northern Region Employment Service, Department of Employment.
Victor CHAMBERS, lately Chief Executive, Ulster Bank Ltd.
George CHARLTON, Q.P.M., Chief Constable, Norfolk Constabulary.
Robert William COZENS, Q.P.M., lately Director, Police Requirements Support Unit, Home Office.
John Alister DAVIDSON, Director, Confederation of British Industry, Scotland.
Denis Fitzgerald DESMOND, Chairman, Desmond and Sons Ltd.
Patrick Lancaster DONOVAN, Chairman and Managing Director, Allied Mills Ltd.
Professor Ronald Philip DORE, Director, Japan-Europe Industry Research Centre, Imperial College, University of London.
Norman Gordon Edward DUNLOP, Finance Director, British Airways plc.
Gerard Howard FAIRTLOUGH, Chief Executive, Celltech Group plc.
Frank FITZGERALD, Board Member and Managing Director, Technical, British Steel Corporation plc.
Kenneth Peter FOGGO, Partner, Arup Associates.
Brian Leslie FULLER, Q.F.S.M., Chief Fire Officer, West Midlands Fire Service.
Derrick John FULLER, Grade 4, Ministry of Agriculture, Fisheries and Food.
Norman GASH, Historian. Emeritus Professor, University of St. Andrews.
John Glen Mackay GAU, Independent Television Producer.
Lester Joseph GEORGE, President, Manchester Chamber of Commerce and Industry.
Donald Henry GRATTAN. For services to education; Chairman, Council for Educational Technology.
Roy William GRAVENOR, Production and Human Resources Director, Royal Mint.
Leslie Leonard GREEN, lately Director, Daresbury Laboratory, Science and Engineering Research Council.
William Thomas GREER, Director of Sewerage, Strathclyde Regional Council.
Richard Langton GREGORY, lately Professor of Neuropsychology and Director of Brain Perception Laboratory, University of Bristol.
Professor Anthony Gordon GUEST, Q.C. For services to the Department of Trade and Industry on the United Nations Commission on International Trade Law.
Cyril Keith GULLAND, lately Deputy Chief Scientific Officer, Ministry of Defence.
Donald Philip HARDING. For political and public service.
Maurice Graham HARDY, President and Chief Operating Officer, Pall Corporation; Chairman and Managing Director, Pall Europe Ltd.
Aubrey Edward HARPER, Chairman, Board of Governors, Paisley College of Technology.
Philip Rowland Francis HARRIS, Head of Division, Network Operations Services Department, British Telecommunications plc.
John David Jayne HAVARD, Secretary, British Medical Association.
John Malcolm HAYLES, Director of Finance, British Nuclear Fuels plc.
David William St. John HEATH. For political and public service.
Peter David Nelson HEDDERWICK, Managing Director, Aircraft Division, Marshall of Cambridge.
Richard HIGGINS, Grade 5, Department of Trade and Industry.
Arnold Quinney HITCHCOCK, lately Chairman, Potato Marketing Board.
John Warwick, Baron HIVES. For political service.
John HODDELL, Deputy Chairman, Chartered Trust plc.
Christopher Jarvis Haley HOGWOOD, Director, Academy of Ancient Music.
Michael De Courcy Fraser HOLROYD, Literary Biographer.
Brian Howard HORD. For political service.
Caryl Lois, Mrs. HUBBARD, lately Chairman, Contemporary Arts Society.
Ian Stuart HUTCHESON, Chairman and Chief Executive, Acatos and Hutcheson plc.
Ralph ILEY, Joint Managing Director, Cookson Group plc.
Sydney Carol JACKSON, Assistant Secretary, Northern Ireland Office.
Professor Andrew Michael JAFFE, Director, Fitzwilliam Museum, Cambridge.
Angus Norman JOHNSTON, Chairman, Central Council of Probation Committees.
Betty Joan, Lady JOHNSTON, Chairman, Girls Public Day School Trust.
Willaim Albert Morgan JONES, Superintending Valuer, Board of Inland Revenue.
John MacGregor Kendall KENDALL-CARPENTER. For services to Rugby Union.
Elihu LAUTERPACHT, Q.C., Director, Research Centre for International Law, University of Cambridge.
Douglas McColl MACINNES. For political and public service.
David Drury MACKLIN, lately Chief Executive, Devon County Council.
Reginald Arthur Edward MAGEE, lately President, Royal College of Surgeons in Ireland.
John Peter MASON. For political and public service.
Timothy Lewis MAY, T.D., D.L., Chairman, Territorial Auxiliary and Volunteer Reserve Association, Eastern Wessex.
Raymond Arthur McCABE, Managing Director, John Brown Engineering Ltd., Clydebank. For services to Export.
Marshall MEEK, Chairman, Marine Technology Board; lately Deputy Chairman, British Maritime Technology Ltd.
George Albert MOORE. For political and public service.
David Cornelius MORLEY, lately Professor of Tropical Child Health, Institute of Child Health, University of London.
Duncan Kirkbride NICHOL, Regional General Manager, Mersey Regional Health Authority.
Reginald Fred NORMAN, Managing Director, Ciba-Geigy plc; Chairman, British Crop Protection Council.
Peter Machin NORTH, Chairman, Road Traffic Law Review.
John Frederick Corfield OLNEY, Treasurer Valuer, HM Treasury.
John Edward OWEN, Deputy Receiver, Metropolitan Police.
David Bruce PATTULLO, Chief Executive, Bank of Scotland.
Alan Ernest Alfred READ, Professor of Medicine and Director of Medical Professorial Unit, University of Bristol.
Ian William RICHARDSON, Actor.
David Edward ROBERTS. For political service.
Gordon ROBERTS, lately Grade 5, Treasury Solicitor's Department.
Philip Michael ROSE, Managing Director, Butterley Brick Ltd; Chairman, Building Materials Export Group.
Albert Muir Galloway RUSSELL, Q.C., Sheriff, Aberdeen Sheriff Court, Scottish Courts Administration.
Michael Edward Wylie SAMUELSON, Vice-President, National Association for Maternal and Child Welfare.
Norman Keith SCOTT, Chairman, Building Design Partnership.
David Aitken SHAW, Professor of Clinical Neurology, University of Newcastle upon Tyne.
Michael SHEPHERD, lately Professor of Epidemiological Psychiatry, Institute of Psychiatry, University of London.
Peter Geoffrey SHEPHERD, Chairman, West Sussex County Council.
Alexander SHERLOCK, M.E.P. For political service.
James Cadzow SMITH, Chairman, Eastern Electricity Board.
Robert Carr SMITH, Director, Kingston Polytechnic.
Frederick Richard STALLARD, D.L. For political and public service.
Charles Walter SUCKLING, Member, Royal Commission on Environmental Pollution.
Monty SUMRAY, Chairman and Managing Director, FII Group plc.

Stanley THOMSON, lately President, Chartered Association of Certified Accountants.
Alan Walker TYSON. Fellow, All Souls College, Oxford. For services to Musicology.
Geoffrey Henry WHALEN, Managing Director, Peugeot Talbot Motor Company Ltd.
Robert Brian WILLIAMSON, lately Chairman, London International Financial Futures Exchange.
Arthur Brian WILSON, The Chief Commoner, Corporation of London.
Olgierd Cecil ZIENKIEWICZ, lately Professor and Head of Department, Civil Engineering, University of Wales.

O.B.E.

To be Ordinary Officers of the Civil Division of the said Most Excellent Order:

Clifford Raymond ALDERTON, Chairman and Managing Director, J. Picard and Company, Seed Merchants Ltd.
Hugh Doig ARCHBOLD, Project Manager, H.M.S. Sheffield and H.M.S. Coventry, Swan Hunter Ltd.
Miss Catherine Archibald ASHER, Chairman, National Board for Nursing, Midwifery and Health Visiting for Scotland.
Elsie, Mrs ASHLEY. For political and public service.
Diana Clare, Mrs. BANKS. For political and public service.
Ronald Bernard BARNES, lately Headmaster, Great Stony Special School, Chipping Ongar, Essex.
Richard Henry Howard BARR, Chairman, Centrax Ltd.
Patrick Haydon BARRY, lately Chairman, Joint Contracts Tribunal.
Peter Markendale BILLAM, Director, Plant Engineering, Central Electricity Generating Board.
Neil Cathcart BLACK, Principal Oboeist, English Chamber Orchestra.
Miss Bridget Marilyn BLOOM, Correspondent, Financial Times.
Miss Nancy Margetts BRADFIELD, (Mrs. Sayer). For services to the history of costume design.
Miss Margaret Anne BRAIN (Mrs. Wheeler), lately Chief Administrative Nursing Officer, South Glamorgan Health Authority.
Richard David BRIERS, Actor.
Professor Mary BROMLY, Head, School of Fashion, Newcastle Polytechnic.
Peter Walding BRYANN, County Planning Officer, West Sussex County Council; Chairman, Technical Liaison Group, South East Regional Planning Conference.
Morris BURDON, Director, Engineering Employers' Association of South Lancashire, Cheshire and North Wales.
Michael John BURKE, Principal Scientific Officer, Ministry of Defence.
Colin Middleton CAMPBELL, Director, Bookers Sugar Company Ltd.
William CHALLINOR. For political and public service.
Michael Bernard John CLARKE, lately National Co-ordinator of Regional Crime Squads.
Miss Julia CLEMENTS, (Lady Seton), International floral art judge. For charitable services.
Gerald CLEREHUGH, Director of Technology, Headquarters, British Gas plc.
John (Louis) Brunel COHEN, Chairman, "Not Forgotten" Association.
Bryan Thomas Alfred COLLINS, Q.F.S.M., Chief Fire Officer, Humberside Fire Brigade.
John Charles COLLINS, Grade 6, Department of the Environment.
Roy Eric COXON, Consulting Engineer; for services to dam engineering.
Sean Coleman CURRAN, Director, Standard Telephones and Cables, Northern Ireland, Ltd.
Leonard Frank CURTIS, lately National Park Officer, Exmoor National Park.
Professor Anthony Ralph CUSENS, Head of Civil Engineering Department, University of Leeds; Transport and Road Research Laboratory Visitor.
Peter Wilton CUSHING, Actor.
Iain Leonard DALE, Chief Executive, Dale Electric International plc. For services to Export.
Ronald DARRINGTON. For services to the community in Wakefield, West Yorkshire.
Colonel John Patrick DAVEY, T.D., D.L., Association Vice-Chairman (Military) East Anglia, Territorial Auxiliary and Volunteer Reserve Association.
Ronald Walter DAY, Trading Director, Navy, Army and Air Force Institutes, London.
John Barrie DENTON. For services to the Ockenden Venture.
Francis William DICK, Director of Coaching, British Amateur Athletic Board.
James DICKSON, D.L., Leader, Woodspring District Council.
John Thomson DICKSON, Assistant Chief Constable Strathclyde Police.
Frank Pool DILKES, Chairman, West Bromwich Building Society.
Alan Aubrey DOBSON, V.R.D., Chairman, Nottingham Sea Cadet Corps Unit.
Richard David Allan DODDS. For services to Hockey.
Professor John Wharry DUNDEE. For services to Medicine in Northern Ireland.
Richard David DUNDERDALE, Principal Collector, Board of Inland Revenue.
Alastair Barr DUNLOP. For political and public service.
Colonel Peter Arthur William George DURRANT (Retd.), Grade 7, Foreign and Commonwealth Office.
William Albert George EASTON, lately Principal, Southgate Technical College.
Andrew John EBERLEIN, lately Head, Major Hazards and Environment Co-ordination, Shell U.K. Ltd.
Albert Charles EDWARDS. For political and public service.
John Trevor EGGINTON, A.F.C., lately Chief Test Pilot, Westland Helicopters Ltd.
Charles William ELLIS, Chairman, Grampian Health Board.
John Colin EVANS, Headmaster, Sir Thomas Picton Comprehensive School, Haverfordwest, Dyfed.
Edward Charles Richard FAWCETT. For services to the National Trust.
Robin Leaper FENTON. For political and public service.
Leonard FERGUSON, M.B.E., lately Director of Housing Management, Scottish Special Housing Association.
Professor Francis FISH, Dean, the School of Pharmacy, University of London.
Michael John FITZHERBERT-BROCKHOLES, D.L. For public service in Lancashire.
William Bailey FOSTER, lately Principal, Plymouth College of Further Education.
Ian Ross FRASER, Rector, Inverness Royal Academy.
Peter Robert FRAZER, Deputy Director-General, Take-Over Panel.
Aleksa GAVRILOVIC, lately Technical Director, GEC Transmission and Distribution Group.
Roger GIBBS, Grade 7, Ministry of Defence.
William Fulton GILLESPIE, T.D., D.L. For public service in Northern Ireland.
John Smylie Dixon GILMORE, Alderman, Belfast City Council.
John GOODWIN, Managing Director, St. Regis Harvesting Company; Chairman, Forest Windblow Action Group.
Thomas Talbot Anthony GORSUCH, Director of Research and Quality Control, Colmans of Norwich; Member, Food Advisory Committee.
Ronald Edgar GRANGER, President, Export Credit Insurance Comprehensive Guarantees Group.
Barboura Patricia, Mrs. GRANT, Joint Managing Director, Norfrost Limited, Castletown.
William GREENWOOD, Assistant Director, Curriculum, Wigan Local Education Authority.
Owen GREGORY, Consultant Mining Surveyor; Member, Black Country Limestone Advisory Panel.
Anthony Fitzhardinge GUETERBOCK. For services to the Construction Industry.
Henry Edward GUMBEL, Consultant, Willis Faber Group plc.
Alexander Derek Gower GUNN, Director, University Health Service, University of Reading.
Miss Hester Mary HALLAWAY, Principal, Trinity and All Saints' College, Horsforth, Leeds.
Christopher Michael HANN, lately Senior Pigs and Poultry Adviser, Ministry of Agriculture, Fisheries and Food.
Christopher HANNINGTON. For political and public service.
James Francis HANRATTY, lately Medical Director, St. Joseph's Hospice, Hackney.

Gladys Rose, Mrs. HARDING, Deputy President, Bedfordshire Branch, The British Red Cross Society.
Alan George HARRIS, Grade 7, Laboratory of the Government Chemist.
Margaret Valerie, Mrs. HARRISON, Senior Consultant, Home Start Consultancy.
Alan John HARVEY, Leader, Rochford District Council.
Edward Walter HAYDON, Executive Commissioner and Administration Secretary, The Scout Association.
John Francis Alexander HEATH-STUBBS, Poet.
Richard David HENSHELL, Chairman, PAFEC Ltd.
George Kenneth Frank HOLDEN, M.C., T.D., Honorary Chairman, West Midlands Central Branch, Soldiers', Sailors' and Airmen's Families Association.
Robert HOLSTEAD, Chief Surveyor, Department of Transport.
Hywell HUGHES. For sevices to Agriculture in Wales.
Irma Ann, Mrs. HULKS, Chief Architect, Kent County Council.
Alan David HUNT, Senior Principal, Ministry of Defence.
Norman Murray Crawford ISHAM, Superintending Architect, Department of the Environment.
Patricia, Mrs. JEFFERY. For political and public service.
Gregory Warwick JOHNSON. For political and public service.
Albert Joseph KEELING, Counselling Adviser, North West Region, Small Firms Service.
Miss Penelope Anne Constance KEITH, (Mrs. Timpson), Actress.
Miss Joy Adelaide Mabel KINSLEY, Grade I, H.M. Prison, Brixton.
Thomas LAURIE. For services to the Arts in Scotland.
Peter Urquhart LAWSON, Director of Agriculture, Angus Marts, Forfar.
Francis LEDWIDGE, Chairman, Northern Ireland Fishery Harbour Authority.
Robert Derrick LITTLEWOOD, Superintendent of Works, York Minster.
Arthur Llewellyn LLOYD, Chairman, Advisory Committee on Justices of the Peace, Birmingham.
Roy LUFF, Managing Director, Aluminium Corporation Ltd., Dolgarrog, Gwynedd.
Malcolm MACDONALD, Director of Environmental Health, Falkirk District Council.
Donald Gordon MACINTYRE. For services to Education in Northern Ireland.
Felix Aloysius MACKLE, Northern Secretary, Irish National Teachers' Organisation.
Timothy Hugh MACNAMARA. For political and public service.
Andrew Reginald Sprake MARSH, Grade 7, National Physical Laboratory.
Laurence MARTINDALE, lately Principal, Luton Sixth Form College.
Richard Moreton MAWDITT, Secretary and Registrar, University of Bath.
Gordon Malcolm McCOOMBE, Principal Professional and Technology Officer, Ministry of Defence.
John Lindsay McGAVIGAN, Chairman, John McGavigan and Company Ltd., Kirkintilloch. For services to Export.
David Henry Harold METCALFE, Professor and Head of Department of General Practice, Manchester University Medical School.
Patrick James MOORE, Commercial Development Manager, P & O Containers Ltd.
Joseph MOUNSEY, B.E.M., Q.P.M., lately Assistant Chief Constable, Lancashire Constabulary.
Elizabeth Jane, Mrs. NICOLL. For services to the Tayside Region Girls' Brigade.
Annette, Mrs. NOSKWITH. For political and public service.
Patrick Charles Kenneth O'FERRALL, General Manager, Total Minatome Oil and Gas, United Kingdom.
George Thomas OGLANBY, lately General Manager, Lincoln Division, Anglian Water Authority.
Robert Henry O'HANLON, Q.P.M., Chairman, National Road Safety Committee, Royal Society for the Prevention of Accidents.
Neil Buchanan OSBORN, Director of Works, Commonwealth War Graves Commission.
Denis Peter OWEN, Headteacher, Thurnscoe Comprehensive School, Barnsley.
John Hefin OWEN. For services to Medicine in Wales.
Bernard Harold Michael PALMER, Editor, The Church Times.
Nigel Webb PALMER, Managing Director, C. W. Pittard and Company Ltd.
Arnold John PARKINSON, lately Member, West Midlands Regional Health Authority.
Hugh Charles PARKMAN, Chairman, Parkman Group Consulting Engineers.
Charles Jellis PATON, Controller, Resource Operations, British Broadcasting Corporation (Television).
Derek James PATTERSON. For services to the community in Berkshire.
John Edmund PEARSON, Clerk to the Liverpool Justices.
Miss Mary Kate PENN, Director, Sino British Trade Council. For services to Export.
Major Thomas Hope PERKINS, (Retd.), lately Chief Administrative Officer, Women's Royal Voluntary Service.
Norman PIMBLETT. For services to the St. John Ambulance Brigade, Merseyside.
Domingos Joseph Diago Teodoro PINTO, Consultant Surgeon, General Surgery, Tyrone County Hospital.
Charles Walter John PLEDGER. For services to the Royal British Legion.
William PLEETH, Cellist.
Rosemary Patricia Nova, Mrs. POCKLEY. For political and public service.
Christopher Leslie POLLARD. For services to Industry and Tourism in Wales.
Peter Henry PRIESTLEY, Senior Education Officer and Regional Psychologist, Lothian Region.
Cahal RAMSEY, M.B.E., Assistant Chief Constable, Royal Ulster Constabulary.
Daniel REID, Director, Communicable Diseases Scotland Unit, Ruchill Hospital, Glasgow.
Derek Woodhouse ROBERTS, Principal Engineer, Sir William Halcrow and Partners, Consulting Engineers.
Bernard ROBINSON, Director and Chief Executive, Tallent Engineering Ltd.
Bryan Allinson ROBSON, Principal, Department of Social Security.
William Taylor ROBSON, President, Northern Ireland Association of Boys' Clubs.
James Malcolm RODGER. For services to the Glasgow and West of Scotland Committee, National Press Fund.
John Frank ROGERS, Director of Quality Assurance and Chief Nursing Adviser, Hull Health Authority.
Jenifer Bernice, Mrs. ROSENBERG, Managing Director, J. & J. Fashions Ltd.
Miss Winifred Ida ROUSE, Director, International Social Service of Great Britain.
Vera, Mrs. ROZSA-NORDELL, Singing Teacher and Consultant, Guildhall School of Music and Drama.
Roy SANDERSON, Managing Director, Sanderson (Forklifts) Ltd.
David Robert SHADBOLT, Principal, Worcester College of Higher Education.
Thomas SHARPLES, Executive Director, Design, Military Aircraft Division, Warton Unit, British Aerospace plc.
Ronald Archibald SHEPHERD, Manager, Education Training and Personnel Services, Ford Motor Company.
Geoffrey SHILLITO, Director, Trent International Centre for School Technology, Nottinghamshire.
Alan SHOTLIFF. For political and public service.
Robert William SKELTON, lately Keeper, Indian Department, Victoria and Albert Museum.
Alec Luke SMITH, Divisional Manager, Basic Research Group, Unilever Research.
Dennis Clayton SMITH, Principal Consultant, Plessey Research Ltd.
Derek Randall SMITH, Engineering Director, National Nuclear Corporation Ltd.
James Patrick SMITH, Editor, Journal of Advanced Nursing.
Jack Richard SPEYER. For political service.
Michael Alexander SPRACKLEN. For services to Rowing.
Trevor Ferguson SPROTT, Director of Planning, Grampian Regional Council.
John Wilson STEEL, H.M. Inspector of Schools, Department of Education and Science.
John Hamish Maitland STEIN, Export Sales Director, GR-Stein Refractories Ltd., Linlithgow. For services to Export.

Margaret Jessie, Mrs. TAYLOR, lately Headteacher, Whalley Range Girls' School, Manchester.
Robert Richard TAYLOR, M.B.E., D.L., Managing Director, Birmingham Airport.
James Bernard TERRY, Principal Inspector, Health and Safety Executive, Department of Employment.
John Husband THOMAS, lately Regional Chairman, Wales Region, Air Training Corps.
John Paul TRISELIOTIS, Director of Social Work Education, University of Edinburgh.
Ralph TUCK. For political and public service.
Eric McKenzie TURNER, Director and General Manager, P.& O Ferries Ltd (Orkney and Shetland Services), Aberdeen.
Terence Dudley TURNER. For services to Pharmacy in Wales.
James WADDELL, Chairman, Manchester, Salford and Trafford Committee for the Employment of Disabled People.
Derek WADDINGTON, City Housing Officer, Birmingham City Council.
Ernest John Munro WALKER, Secretary, Scottish Football Association.
John Harley WALLACE, Director, Home Division, OXFAM.
Frank Edwin WARBOYS, lately Senior Chief Fingerprint Officer, Metropolitan Police.
Thelma Evelyn, Mrs. WEBB, lately Deputy Commissioner, Bedfordshire, St. John Ambulance.
David Brian WHITAKER. For services to Hockey.
John Honour WILLMER, Farmer, Clanfield, West Oxfordshire.
John Grant William WOODRUFF, Director, Public Affairs, British Railways Board.
Alan Herbert YENDLE, First Class Valuer, Board of Inland Revenue.
Miss Wendy Ann FRANKS, lately Health Visitor Co-ordinator, Islington.
Hugh Donald George FRASER, Q.P.M. For services to the Scottish Chamber of Safety.
Gordon Percival FRENCH, In-Service Support Manager, Electronic Warfare Division, Marconi Defence Systems Ltd.
Doreen Sylvia, Mrs. GILMOUR, Community Mental Handicap Nurse, Stockport District Authority.
Thomas Mason GLEDHILL, Welfare Officer, Cheshire Constabulary.
Neville Edmund GOSS. For services to Motor Cycling.
Robert Anthony GRAHAM, Assistant Chief Officer, Greater Manchester Fire Service.
Miss Constance Patricia GRAND, lately Senior Personal Secretary, Cabinet Office.
Lawrence Love GREEN, lately Senior Regional Secretary, Scotland and North East England, National Union of Seamen.
Edward Gerald GREGORY, Deputy County Director & Head of Branch Training Department, West Yorkshire County Branch, The British Red Cross Society.
Edna, Mrs. GRIFFITHS, lately Personal Secretary, Board of Inland Revenue.
Hugh John GULLIVER. For political and public service.
Chris Alexander HALLAM. For services to Paraplegic Sports.
Wright Whiteley HAMER, Chairman, Civilian Management Committee, Huddersfield Sea Cadet Corps Unit.
Sylvester John HARDWICKE, Chairman, Westminster and District Street Traders' Association. For services to the community.
William Henry HARE. For services to Rugby Union Football.
Leonard Edward George HARPER, lately National Secretary, Road Haulage Association.
Miss Dorothy Jean HARRIS, Director of Nursing Services, South Derbyshire Health Authority.
Ian Hamilton HARRISON, lately Director, Leicestershire Association for the Disabled.
Miss Rosemary Ellen HARRISON, Collector, Higher Grade, Board of Inland Revenue.
William Kingsley HARTLEY. For services to the Disabled in Cheshire.
Juliet Anne, Mrs. HAYDEN, lately Schools Liaison Officer, Association of British Insurers.
John George HAYTON, lately Director and General Manager, West Kent Water Company.
Miss Bridget Almina Suzanne HEATON-ARMSTRONG. For services to the community and for charitable services.
Edward HEBBLETHWAITE, Secretary, Scarborough, Bridlington, Hull and District Branch, British Limbless Ex-Servicemen's Association.
William James HENDERSON, Head of the Electron Microscope Unit, Tenovus Institute for Cancer Research, University Hospital of Wales, Cardiff.
Betty, Mrs. HOLMES, Chairman, Old Basing Parish Council, Hampshire.
Antony Trevor HOOPER, Senior Executive Officer, Board of Customs and Excise.
William Edmund James HOOPER, Vice-Chairman, British Beekeeping Association.
Stanley HORSLEY, Senior Professional and Technology Officer, Department of the Environment.
Robert HOWARD, Civilian Operating Room Assistant (Anaesthetics), Royal Naval Hospital, Haslar.
Derrick HUNTER, Managing Director, Taylor Hitec Ltd.
James David Kinahan HURFORD, Project Architect, Percy Thomas Partnership.
Harold HUTCHINSON, Chief Executive, Road Transport Industry Training Board, Northern Ireland.
Louisa, Mrs. HUTCHINSON, Committee Member and former Chairman, Darlington Branch, National Society for the Prevention of Cruelty to Children.
Isobel May, Mrs. INGRAM, lately Principal, Sandbrook Nursery School, Belfast.
Frederick George Ernest IRWIN, Director, Ove Arup and Partners, Consulting Engineers.
Stuart IRWIN, Director, Central Lancashire Engineering Employers' Association.
Miss Muriel Agnes JACKMAN, Secretary, League of Friends of the Grimsby Hospitals.
Cecil Albert JAMES. For services to Youth. General Secretary, Catholic Youth Service.
James Clemence JAMES, Chairman, North Eastern Sea Fisheries Committee.
Margaret Anne, Mrs. JAYCOCK, Community Midwife, Charlotte Keel Health Centre, Bristol.
Eric Godfrey JEANS, Works and Production Manager, Gowllands Ltd.
John Morgan JEREMY, Counsellor, Small Firms Service, Reading.
Thomas William Malcolm JOHN, Assistant Divisional Officer, South Glamorgan Fire Service.
Elizabeth Marion Elsie, Mrs. JOHNSON, Education Advisers' Co-ordinating Officer, London Borough of Hounslow.
Peter JOHNSON, Managing Director, Saltire Knitwear Ltd., Kilwinning.
William JOHNSON, lately Department Manager, Inspection and Instrumentation, Swinden Laboratories, British Steel plc.
James Alexander JOHNSTON, Superintendent, Fife Constabulary.
David Haydn JONES. For services to Agriculture in Wales.
Shankar Janardan JOSHI, Executive Officer, Board of Customs and Excise.
Dorothy Leonara, Mrs. KAVANAGH, County Adviser for Primary Education, Oxfordshire.
Miss Myra Evelyn KELLY, lately Matron, Ramsey Cottage Hospital, Isle of Man.
Mary, Mrs. KENNEDY, Administrative Officer, Department of the Environment.
Christopher Robin KIMBER, lately Chief Executive and General Secretary, Society of Licensed Victuallers.
Brian Michael KING, Higher Executive Officer, Department of Social Security.
Derek Antony KNIBBS, lately Manager, Personnel and Quality, Rank Xerox Ltd.
Derek Birchell LANE, Superintendent, Avon and Somerset Constabulary.
Helen Maeve, Mrs. LANIGAN WOOD, Curator, Fermanagh County Museum.
Lieutenant Commander Dennis LARKINS, Retd., Retired Officer II, Ministry of Defence.
Lancelot LAYCOCK, Volunteer Member, Kirkman and Rural Fylde, Citizens' Advice Bureau.
Ronald Geoffrey Stentiford LELEUX, Inspector (S), Board of Inland Revenue.
Evan LEWIS, General Secretary and Chief Executive Officer, Farmers' Union of Wales.

Gerwyn James LEWIS, Director, Welsh Division, National Farmers' Union.
George Frederick LINDOP. For services to Rugby Football League.
Miriam Jean, Mrs. LONG, Executive Officer, Lord Chancellor's Department.
William Douglas MacCONNACHIE, lately Area Wayleave Officer, North of Scotland Hydro-Electric Board.
Jean, Mrs. MACGREGOR, Director of Nurse Education Northallerton Health Authority.
Miss Avril Calder MACKIE. For services to the mentally handicapped in Glasgow.
Mary Elizabeth, Mrs. MACPHERSON, Headteacher, Balbardie Primary School, Bathgate, West Lothian.
George Millikin MALCOLM, Higher Executive Officer, Dounreay, United Kingdom Atomic Energy Authority.
Joseph MALLOCH, President, Orkney Fisheries Association.
Roger Norris MANNS. For voluntary services to the Nene Valley Railway.
Robert Arthur John MARSHMAN, Finishing Manager, Western Board Ltd, Treforest, Mid-Glamorgan.
Kathleen Rose, Mrs. MARTIN, Head, Blackburn Minority Ethnic Group Support-Service, Lancashire.
Alan MARTINDALE, Deputy Secretary, Yorkshire Agricultural Society.
Miss Lilias Elizabeth MASON, lately Senior Professional and Technology Officer, Ministry of Defence.
Pauline Kathleen Eleanor, Mrs. MATEER. For services to the Board of Visitors, Her Majesty's Prison, Belfast.
Miss Florence MATTHEWS, Administrative Officer, Department of Health.
John Joseph McAFEE, Chief Superintendent, Royal Ulster Constabulary.
James McCLATCHEY, Forest Education and Public Relations Officer, Department of Agriculture, Northern Ireland.
Doreen, Mrs. McCRAW, lately Finance Officer, Middlesex Probation Service.
James Craig McFADZEAN, Chairman, Lapwing Lodge Scout Training and Activity Centre, Paisley.
Denis McGRATH, Nursing Officer, Ards Hospital, County Down.
Michael Mackay McINTYRE. For services to Yachting.
Miss Clare McKERNAN, District Manager, Northern Ireland Housing Executive.
James Graham McKINNEY, Senior Business Adviser, North Yorkshire Development Commission.
William Gibb McKINNON, Regional Catering Officer, Home Office.
Robert McKNIGHT, Area Maintenance Manager, Ayrshire and Arran Health Board.
Benjamin McLEAN, Head of Department of Fabrication and Services Engineering, Telford College, Edinburgh.
Mary Katherine, Mrs. McSORLEY, Chairman, Magherafelt District Council.
Brenda Sharp, Mrs. McSTRAVOCK, Ward Sister, Acute Male Medical and Geriatric, Southport and Formby District Health Authority.
Keith MEIKLE-JANNEY, Chief Service Engineer; Manager, Product Support Rolls Royce and Associates Ltd.
George Watson MIDDLETON, lately General Practitioner, Dyfed. For services to the community.
Charles Keith MILLMAN, General Dental Practitioner.
Duncan MILLS, Chairman, Loch Lomond Park Authority.
Alexander Hugh Bruce MITCHELL. For services to the housing construction industry in Scotland.
Edna, Mrs. MITCHELL, President, Family Contact Line, Altrincham.
Miss Janet Evelin Louise MOORES. For services to Glyndebourne.
Abraham MORGAN, President, North Monmouthshire Society for Mentally Handicapped Children.
Marilyn, Mrs. MORGAN, Speech Therapist, Mid-Glamorgan Health Authority.
Charles William MOXON, Owner, C. W. Moxon Ltd.
Henry Farrow MUDD, Founder Director, Alpha Records. For services to English Church Music.
William MUIR, Principal Medical Laboratory Scientific Officer, Scottish National Blood Transfusion Service.
Peter George NEESON, Divisional Officer, Fire Authority for Northern Ireland.
Robert Bradshaw NEILLY, lately Deputy Chairman, Equal Opportunities Commission for Northern Ireland.
Miss Mary NEWLAND, Advisory Teacher, Primary Art and Design, Inner London Education Authority.
Miss Avril Gladys NEWSAM, General Practitioner, Edinburgh.
Edward George NORMAN, Partner, The House of Darts. For services to Export.
Kenneth Roy NORMAN, lately Sub-Commissioner of Pilotage and Chairman, District Pilotage Committee, Trinity House.
Audrey Mary, Mrs. NORTH. For political service.
Thomas O'NEILL, lately Superintendent Radiographer, Nottinghamshire Health Authority.
James ORMEROD, lately Collector, Higher Grade, Board of Inland Revenue.
Henry Frederick OVERY, Chairman of Trustees, Hospice-care Service, East Hertfordshire.
Miss Hazel Mary PAGET, Secretary to the Chairman, The Electricity Council.
Muriel Aileen, Mrs. PALMER. For services to the community in Swindon.
Sybil, Mrs. PATERSON. For services to The British Red Cross Society.
Arthur PATTISON, Inspector, Northumbria Police.
Philip George PAYNE, lately Project Manager, Eastern Region, British Railways.
Miss Agnes PEET. For public service in Wigan.
William David PIGOTT, lately Administrative Officer, Ministry of Defence.
Roy PIZZEY, Chief Inspector, Greater Manchester Police.
Barbara Jane, Mrs. PORTER. For political and public service.
John Brian Vasey PORTER, Chairman, Cumbria Committee for the Employment of Disabled People.
Gordon Kenneth PRESTON, Chief Building Services Engineer, Newcastle City Council.
Anthony Francis PRICE, Senior Executive Officer, Department of Employment.
Major John PRITCHARD-GORDON. For political and public service.
Thomas RALSTON, Scientific Officer, National Engineering Laboratory.
Neville Anthony RENDALL, lately Research and Development Adviser, Shell UK Exploration and Production.
Stanley David RENDELL, Inspector (T), Board of Inland Revenue.
Christopher John RENNARD. For political service.
Robert Frederick RIDGEON, Agricultural Economist, Cambridge University.
Henry ROBERTS, lately Headteacher, Buckley County Primary School, Padeswood Road, Buckley, Clwyd.
James ROBINSON. For services to Schools' Football.
Joyce Hannah, Mrs. ROBINSON. For services to the mentally handicapped in Cardiff.
George William ROBSON, Senior Press Photographer, Ripon Gazette.
Roland Herbert ROGERS. For services to the community in Norfolk.
David ROLLO, Engineering Manager, Fields Aircraft Services Ltd.
Miss Norma Alexandra RONALD. For services to Her Majesty's Institution, Cornton Vale.
John Vesey ROOME, Senior Traffic Examiner, Department of Transport.
Denis ROONEY, lately Member, Northern Ireland Construction Industry Advisory Council.
George Albert ROSE, Field Support Engineer, Woodford, British Aerospace plc.
Mary Teresa Edina, Mrs. ROSE, Head Teacher, Troon County Primary School, Cornwall.
Olga, Mrs. ROWE. For political and public service.
David Keith ROWLANDS, Assistant Secretary, Wales, Territorial Auxiliary and Volunteer Reserve Association.
Alexander Anderson RUBIE, Member, Cunninghame District Council.
Miss Patricia Joan RYAN, Administrative Officer, Export Credits Guarantee Department.
Graham Henry SALMON. For services to Sport for the visually handicapped.
Mary Caroline Vera, Mrs. SANSBURY. For services to the community in Bristol.
Gerald Edmund SAUNDERS, Publisher, "Draper's Record" and "Men's Wear" International Thomson Publishing Ltd.

Desmond Percy SCARLE, lately Assistant Treasurer, Revenue, Waveney District Council.
Charlotte Ivy, Mrs. SCOTT-DINGLE, lately Chairman, East Dorset Community Health Council; Vice-Chairman, League of Friends, Royal Victoria Hospital.
Jean, Mrs SELLARS. For services to the community in Farnborough, Hampshire.
Dennis SHEPPERD, Assistant Manager, Employee Relations, Devonport Management Ltd.
Anna, Mrs. SIMPSON, Unit Personnel Officer, Psychiatric and Mental Handicap Unit, Tayside Health Board.
Olive Mary, Mrs. SIMPSON, Typing Manager, Department of Social Security.
John Stephen SKELTON, Letter-cutter and Sculptor.
Margaret Evelyn, Mrs. SLATER. For political and public service.
Joan May, Mrs. SMITH, lately Higher Executive Officer, Advisory Conciliation and Arbitration Service.
John Henry Williams SMITH, Professional Officer, London and South East Region, Regional Advisory Council for Further Education.
Royden James Carter SMITH, lately Municipal Correspondent, Birmingham Evening Mail.
William Todd SOUTAR, lately Director, Scottish and Northern Ireland Plumbing Employers' Federation.
Alistair Caie SPENCE, Station Officer, Fire Prevention, Grampian Fire Brigade.
Sylvia Audrey, Mrs. SPENCER, Manager, Sumlock Calculating Services Ltd., Nottingham.
Norman SPURR, Printing House Manager, West Yorkshire Police.
David Raymon John STAGG, Amenity Verderer, Verderers Court, New Forest.
Lilian Margaret Helen, Mrs. STEMBRIDGE, Caseworker, Royal Air Force Kinloss Branch, Soldiers', Sailors' and Airmen's Families Association.
Miss Frances Anne STENHOUSE, lately Senior Executive Officer, Scottish Development Department.
Donald George STOVEY, lately General Manager, The Victory (Services) Association Ltd.
Michael STRODE. For services to Chailey Heritage, Handicapped Children's Pilgrimage Trust.
Miss Rosemary Ropner STROYAN. For services to the disabled.
Robin Hugh SURGEONER. For services to Sport for the disabled.
David Scott SUTHERLAND, lately Senior Executive Officer, Employment Service, Department of Employment.
Aurelio Aldo Joseph TARQUINI, lately Catering Manager, BP Oil Ltd.
Leonard TASKER, Founder Member, Coventry Enterprise Club. For services to the Disabled in Coventry.
Constance Jean, Mrs. TAYLOR, Headteacher, Pennyburn Primary School, Kilwinning.
Frederick Charles Hector TAYLOR, Member, Panel of Flying Instructor Examiners, Civil Aviation Authority.
Miss Margaretha Anne TAYLOR, Foreign and Commonwealth Officer.
Arnold Watson TOMALIN, lately Senior Information Officer, Agricultural and Food Research Council.
Philip Michael John TOMBLESON, General Medical Practitioner; Chief Examiner, Royal College of General Practitioners.
Miss Nicola Pauline Marie TRAHAN, lately Health Visitor, Soldiers', Sailors' and Airmen's Families Association, SHAPE.
John Broderick TUCKEY. For services to the National Executive Council, Royal British Legion.
Derek Frederick Thomas TUNN-CLARKE, Q.P.M. For services to the community in Reigate, Surrey.
Ronald Charles TURNER. For political and public service.
Philip Bryn VAILE. For services to Yachting.
Theodora Phoebe, Mrs. WAINWRIGHT, Vice-President, Surrey Branch, The British Red Cross Society.
Charles Gordon WASHINGTON, Chairman, Eaves Brook Housing Association.
Hugh Thomas WATKINS, Administrator, Gwent Family Practitioner Committee.
Miss Margaret Elizabeth WATSON, lately Nursing Sister, National Westminster Bank Residential Staff Training College.
Miss Rosemary Lilian WATT, Administrator, Architectural Heritage Fund.
Cecilia Monica, Mrs. WAUGH, Vice-Chairman, Kingston and Richmond, Family Practitioner Committee.
William John WEBB, Superintendent, Royal Ulster Constabulary.
Peter WHELDON. For services to the Fruit Growing Industry.
Michael John WHITCHER. For political service.
Monica Violet, Mrs. WHITE. For services to The National Autistic Society.
Robert Walter WHITE, Senior Professional and Technology Officer, Ministry of Defence.
Miss Violet Gertrude Lilian WHITE, Midwifery and Paediatric Service Manager and Director of Nursing Services, Harrow Health Authority.
Rex WHITTA, Head Ranger, Forestry Commission.
William Ernest WILKINS, Member, Humberside County Council.
Patricia Anne, Mrs. WILLIAMS. For political and public service.
Josephine Joy, Mrs. WINNIFRITH, Deputy Chairman, South Eastern Electricity Consultative Council.
Rodney John WINTER, lately Chief Inspector, Sussex Police.
John Barry Blake WOOD, lately Chief Medical Laboratory Scientific Officer, Swindon Health Authority.
Miss Margaret Jean WOODFIELD. For political service.
Miss Muriel Pamela WOODS, Export Services Manager, Chamberlain Phipps International Ltd. For services to Export.
James Arthur WRIGHT, Principal Administrative Officer, Department of Highways and Transportation, Cheshire County Council.
William John Alan WRIGHT, Chairman, Police Federation for Northern Ireland.
Carroll William WYNNE, Chairman, Belfast Charitable Society.

DIPLOMATIC SERVICE AND OVERSEAS LIST

G.B.E.

To be an Ordinary Knight Grand Cross of the Civil Division of the said Most Excellent Order:

Sir Sze-yuen CHUNG, C.B.E., J.P. For public service in Hong Kong.

D.B.E.

To be an Ordinary Dame Commander of the Civil Division of the said Most Excellent Order:

Miss Lydia DUNN, C.B.E., J.P. For public service in Hong Kong.

C.B.E.

To be Ordinary Commanders of the Civil Division of the said Most Excellent Order:

Richard Radford BEST, M.B.E., lately Deputy British High Commissioner, Kaduna.
Joseph James GAGGERO. For services to commerce in Gibraltar.
John Anthony Forrestal HAILWOOD, O.B.E. For services to British commercial interests in the Eastern Caribbean.
Dr HO Kam-fai, O.B.E., J.P. For public and community services in Hong Kong.
HU Fa-kuang, O.B.E., J.P. For public and community services in Hong Kong.
Adrian Ditchburn JOHNSON, British Council Representative, Malaysia.
LI Ka-shing, J.P. For services to commerce and the community in Hong Kong.
Bernard Herbert Gordon MILLS, lately Director of UNRWA Affairs, Gaza.
Edwin MIRVISH, O.C. For services to the Theatre.
Ian Joseph SIMS. For services to British commercial interests and to the community in South Africa.
Michael Douglas SYMINGTON. For services to British commercial and community interests in Portugal.

O.B.E.

To be Ordinary Officers of the Civil Division of the said Most Excellent Order:

Thomas Clive ALMOND, lately H.M. Ambassador, Brazzaville.
Michael Thomas Smallwood BLICK, Administrator, Ascension Island.
Cyril Donald BRADSHAW. For services to British commercial interests in Japan.
Percival Austin BRAMBLE. For public and community services in Montserrat.
Simon Michael Jeremy BUTLER-MADDEN, Foreign and Commonwealth Office.
Charles Richard CLARKE. For services to British commercial and community interests in Nigeria.
Professor Dafydd Meurig Emrys EVANS, J.P. For services to the Faculty of Law, University of Hong Kong.
Marvie Elton GEORGES, Deputy Governor, British Virgin Islands.
Michael John HARDIE, First Secretary (Administration), British High Commission, Lagos.
William Dickson HEWETSON. For services to British commercial and community interests in Dubai.
Tudor JACKSON. For services to legal training in Kenya.
Roland Edouard Vincent Michael KING. For services to British commercial interests in France.
Donald Peter LINES, J.P. For public and community services in Bermuda.
Geoffrey Colin LIVESEY, First Secretary (Commercial), H.M. Embassy, Havana.
Professor MA CHUNG Ho-kei. For services to medical education in Hong Kong.
John MAYATT, British Council Representative, Tanzania.
Henry Michael Pearson MILES, J.P. For services to commerce and aviation in Hong Hong.
William Smith MILLAR. For services to British commercial and community interests in Liberia.
Peter John Reeve MOLLER, For services to British commercial interests in Kenya.
Professor Denys MORGAN. For services to education and the community in Zambia.
John Nisbet MORTON. For services to British commercial and community interests in Uruguay.
Raymond Scudamore NEWBERRY, British Council Representative, Australia.
Dr. NIP Kam Fan, J.P., Director of Civil Engineering Services, Hong Kong.
Leo Edmund O'KEEFFE. For services to English language teaching in Zambia.
David James PEATE, First Secretary and Consul, H.M. Embassy, Brussels.
Major Robert John PELIZA, E.D. For public service in Gibraltar.
William Eden POOL, lately a Head of Division, EC Commission, Brussels.
Peter POON Wing-cheung, M.B.E., J.P. For public service in Hong Kong.
John RAWSON. For services to British commercial interests in Connecticut, USA.
Colonel Brian Sinclair READ. For services to British commercial engineering interests in the USA.
Francis Joseph SAVAGE, First Secretary (Consular), British High Commission, Lagos.
Thomas Julian Durrant SHEPHERD. For services to British commercial interests in California.
David John SPILLER, First Secretary (Library and Books), British Council, India.
Charles THOMPSON, British High Commissioner, Tarawa.
Roderick James TOLLEY. For services to British commercial and community interests in Penang.
Thomas Robert Henry Stratford TUITE, M.B.E., Consul, British Consulate, Malaga.
Duncan Huson WALKER. For services to British commercial interests in Barcelona.

M.B.E.

To be Ordinary Members of the Civil Division of the said Most Excellent Order:

Ann Hilary, Mrs. ALLAN, Commercial Officer, British Consulate-General, Montreal.
The Reverend Father Gerard Augustine AVERY. For services to the British community in North East Nigeria.
Muriel, Mrs. BARRON, Head of Passport Section, British Consulate-General, Dusseldorf.
Timothy BENJAMIN. For services to road safety research in France.
Ronald Ballantyne BLANCHE, Assistant Director of Audit, Hong Kong.
Miss Evelyn Lucy BROWN. For welfare services to the British community in Santiago.
Robert Kenneth BROWN, Senior Assistant Commissioner, Royal Hong Kong Police Force.
Denise Frances Farquharson, Mrs. BRYAN. For services to Anglo-American educational co-operation.
Charles James Kinloch CAMPBELL. For welfare services to children in India.
Alan John CARNE, lately Third Secretary, H.M. Embassy, Havana.
Alphonso CASSELL. For services to musical entertainment in Montserrat.
CHAN Cheuk-sang, Staff Officer, Auxiliary Medical Services, Hong Kong.
Janet Fulton, Mrs. CHUBB. For welfare services to the community in Kenya.
Miss Morag Henderson CLARK. For welfare services to children in Turkey.
Brian CLISSOLD. For services to English language teaching in North Yemen.
John Richard David COWELL. For services to British ex-servicemen in Hamburg.
Robert Wade CROWTHER. For services to the British community in Cyprus.
Christopher Robin DE KRETSER. For services to British commercial and community interests in Kaduna, Nigeria.
Edwin Ernest GARTH, P.S.A. Clerk, H.M. Embassy, Bahrain.
Marion, Mrs. GENTLE. For services to medical training in Oman.
The Reverend John Noel Keith GIBSON. For services to education and the community in the British Virgin Islands.
Miss Norma Fay GRIMSHAW, Personal Assistant to H.M. Consul-General, Sydney.
Hugh Palmer HAILE, Head of Property Section, British High Commission, Nicosia.
Dr. Robert John HART. For medical services to the community in Bangladesh.
HUI Chun-Keung, C.P.M., J.P. For community services in Hong Kong.
Michael Robin JACKSON. For services to Anglo-American relations in California.
Mona Natalie, Mrs. JACKSON, Clerk to the Executive Council, Cayman Islands.
John Michael JAMES. For welfare services to the community in Ethiopia.
Adrian John JENKYN. For services to British commercial and community interests in Tokyo.
Derek Alexander KINGSTON, Senior Engineer, Fire Services Department, Hong Kong.
LEE Sai-hei, Senior Superintendent, Urban Services Department, Hong Kong.
Pamela Elizabeth, Mrs. McNEIL. For welfare services to the community in Jamaica.
Norman MATTIN, Section Head, Operations Department, ICAC, Hong Kong.
Victor Katsuro MIHARA. For services to education and the community in Kobe, Japan.
Miss Margaret MUNDAY, Personal Secretary, H.M. Embassy, Maputo.
NG Cho-yi, Chief Immigration Officer, Immigration Service, Hong Kong.
Dr. Robert PARSONS. For welfare services to children in Sri Lanka.
Miss Eileen PLATTS. For nursing and welfare services to the community in India.

Miss Yvonne Jean POLLITT, Personal Assistant to the British High Commissioner, Dar es Salaam.
Miss Laura Adeline Mary QUARTARA, Registry Clerk, Administration Section, H.M. Embassy, Paris.
Maureen, Mrs. REED. For services to the British community in Brussels.
Francis, Mrs. SALINIE, Library and Books Officer, British Council, Paris.
David James SIMM. For services to electric power development in Bangladesh.
Thomas SLATER. For services to education in Madrid.
The Reverend Dr. Goodwin Campbell SMITH, J.P. For services to education and the community in Bermuda.
Oswald Arthur SMITH, Electricity Commissioner, Turks and Caicos Islands.
Norman Richard Prescott SPEED. For services to British commercial and community interests in Casablanca.
Margaret Ruth Denholm, Mrs. TAYLOR. For services to the British community in Paris.
Kenneth Thomas WALLACE, D.F.C., Assistant Representative, British Council, Canada.
Miss Christine Mary WALLOND, lately Personal Secretary to the Vice-President of the EC, Brussels.
John WARDER. For services to the British community in Ikeja, Nigeria.
Doris Katherine, Mrs. WEBB. For welfare services to the community in Karnataka State, India.
Leonard Richard WILLIAMS. For services to British ex-servicemen in Switzerland.

CENTRAL CHANCERY OF
THE ORDERS OF KNIGHTHOOD

ST. JAMES'S PALACE, LONDON SW1

31st December 1988

The QUEEN has been graciously pleased to give orders for the following appointments to the Imperial Service Order:

I.S.O.

To be Companions of the Order:

HOME CIVIL SERVICE

Miss Audrey BEGGS, Principal, Police Authority for Northern Ireland.
Kenneth Frank BURNS, Secretary, Queen's Award Office.
James Alexander DONALDSON, Principal, Department of Finance and Personnel, Northern Ireland.
Douglas DUNCAN, Inspector(P), Board of Inland Revenue.
George Barron DUNCAN, lately Grade II, H.M. Young Offenders' Institution, Polmont, Scottish Home and Health Deparment.
Brian Stuart EVERNESS, Chief Examiner, Board of Inland Revenue.
William GAMBLE, Assistant Accountant General, Department of Education and Science.
Graham George GODDARD, lately Grade 7, Department of Social Security.
Vincent James GREEN, Grade 7, Department of Health.
John Hill HARDING, lately Principal Professional and Technology Officer, Ministry of Defence.
Alexander Eaton HENDRY, lately Deputy Collector, Board of Customs and Excise.
Henry HUNTER, Principal, Department of Employment.
Ronald Charles LANE, Principal Scientific Officer, Ministry of Defence.
Leslie Brian LINLEY, Grade 7, Ministry of Agriculture, Fisheries and Food.
Peter Henry MAJOR, Principal, Department of Employment.
Peter John McINTOSH, Inspector (SP), Board of Inland Revenue.
Gilbert Alfred PAUL-CLARK, Senior Chief Examiner, Department of Energy.
Murdoch McLean SKELLY, Senior Principal Scientific Officer, Ministry of Defence.
John Hicklin SMITH, Grade 6, Prison Service Industries and Farms, Home Office.
Leslie Harold STONE, Grade 7, Department of the Environment.
George William THOMPSON, Principal, Ministry of Defence.
Stanley VARNAM, Inspector (SP), Board of Inland Revenue.

DIPLOMATIC SERVICE AND OVERSEAS LIST

Derek HOGAN, Secretary, Examinations Authority, Hong Kong.
Alexander Lamont PURVES, J.P., Director of Urban Services, Hong Kong.
Michael John SMITH, J.P., Deputy Director of Government Supplies, Hong Kong.

CENTRAL CHANCERY OF
THE ORDERS OF KNIGHTHOOD

ST. JAMES'S PALACE, LONDON SW1

31st December 1988

The QUEEN has been graciously pleased to approve the award of the British Empire Medal (Military Division) to the undermentioned:

BRITISH EMPIRE MEDAL (MILITARY DIVISION)

B.E.M.

MINISTRY OF DEFENCE (NAVY DEPARTMENT)

Acting Charge Chief Weapon Engineering Artificer Stephen Paul BEARD, D073847A.
Chief Wren Writer (P) Veronica Ann BELL, W122630P.
Chief Radio Supervisor Thomas David BOOTH, D086036X.
Master-at-Arms Desmond BRIGGS, D094569X.
Acting Chief Petty Officer Weapon Engineering Artificer Peter DERBYSHIRE, D133429M.
Colour Sergeant Clive Ernest EVANS, Royal Marines, P023572L.
Chief Petty Officer (Operations) (Missile) Colin EVANS, D078182G.
Charge Chief Communications Technician Peter John HOSFORD, D119312P.
Chief Wren Quarters Assistant Margaret Theresa LEDINGHAM-FOX, W131356S.
Chief Air Engineering Mechanic (WL) Nigel Edward MALCOLM, D128892W.
Chief Petty Officer (Seaman) Kenneth John PETERS, D078243W.
Bugler Alan John PINER, Royal Marines, P013682B.
Chief Petty Officer Writer Norman Graham PRIOR, D124742N.
Chief Medical Technician William Frederick Davies SAMPSON, M960828D.
Chief Petty Officer (Seaman) (Careers Service) Barry Leonard STOKES, J957134Y.
Chief Wren (Degaussing) Heather Olwen TAYLOR, Women's Royal Naval Reserve, W990338T.
Charge Chief Communications Technician David Kenneth Frank THOMAS, D188366R.
Acting Chief Petty Officer Physical Trainer Thomas WALLACE, D092630D.
Chief Petty Officer Air Engineering Artificer (M) Raymond Eric WEDLAKE, F977939D.
Chief Petty Officer Electrician (Air) (Careers Service) Bruce WISELY, F908405T.

MINISTRY OF DEFENCE (ARMY DEPARTMENT)

24067696 Bombardier Robert John ADAMS, Royal Regiment of Artillery.
W 0405408 Private Yvonne Edna BALMENT, Women's Royal Army Corps.
LS 23545074 Staff Sergeant Colin Arnold BELL, Royal Corps of Signals.
24010024 Staff Sergeant William John BOGIE, Royal Corps of Signals.
24086860 Sergeant Malcolm Roy BONE, The Duke of Lancaster's Own Yeomanry, Territorial Army.
23871188 Corporal David Columbus Hayter BROWN, Royal Army Ordnance Corps.
24269434 Staff Sergeant Richard John BURNS, Royal Horse Artillery.
24327449 Corporal Stuart Fraser CAMERON, Corps of Royal Engineers, Territorial Army.
24101276 Staff Sergeant George Ian CARR, The King's Own Scottish Borderers.
HK 18264700 Staff Sergeant Miu Kei CHAN, Hong Kong Military Service Corps/Intelligence Corps.
24398320 Corporal John Norman CHAPMAN, Royal Corps of Signals.

24259678 Corporal of Horse Ronald CLARKE, The Life Guards.
24328637 Sergeant Steven Robert DAVIES, Corps of Royal Engineers.
242073766 Bombardier Stephen DORRAINE, Royal Regiment of Artillery.
24152652 Sergeant Richard Martin ELIAS, The Queen's Royal Irish Hussars.
23657399 Staff Sergeant William Edwin FRAME, Officers Training Corps, Territorial Army.
24383088 Staff Sergeant Kenneth Michael GALE, Corps of Royal Engineers.
2411878 Staff Sergeant Kevin John GREENSLADE, Army Air Corps.
24241377 Corporal Alan GREENWOOD, Royal Corps of Transport.
LS 22998091 Corporal Gilbert Terence HAGUE, Royal Pioneer Corps.
24253831 Staff Sergeant David Michael HAINES, Royal Army Medical Corps.
24265892 Staff Sergeant Gordon Arthur Pake HUGHES, Corps of Royal Engineers.
24081181 Lance Corporal Michael John JONES, The Royal Regiment of Wales (24th/41st Foot).
24364627 Sergeant Roy JONES, The Royal Regiment of Wales, (24th/41st Foot).
24278261 Staff Sergeant Walter Stewart Farquharson KENNEDY, Corps of Royal Engineers.
24153818 Staff Sergeant Gordon George LAING, The Gordon Highlanders.
24118960 Sergeant James LAVERY, 1st The Queen's Dragoon Guards.
24152867 Sergeant Colin Sydney LE CLERCQ, Army Catering Corps.
24182798 Staff Sergeant Allan Michael LILLINGTON, Royal Regiment of Artillery.
24141822 Sergeant Stephen Harold LIVERSAGE, Welsh Guards.
24213483 Staff Sergeant Philip Edward LYDON, The Cheshire Regiment.
24366865 Sergeant Robert MALLON, The Royal Irish Rangers (27th (Inniskilling) 83rd and 87th).
24543208 Corporal Gerard John McFADYEN, Royal Army Ordnance Corps.
22271132 Staff Sergeant James Anthony McGILLOWAY, Royal Army Medical Corps, Territorial Army.
24326153 Staff Sergeant Edward Mervyn MIDDLETON, The Parachute Regiment.
22480177 Staff Sergeant Jack MILEHAM, Royal Corps of Signals, Territorial Army.
24443488 Corporal Terence Andrew MONERY, 1st The Queen's Dragoon Guards.
W 0423187 Staff Sergeant Christine MUIR, Women's Royal Army Corps.
23228704 Staff Sergeant Ole Anton NELSON-GIRTCHEN, Army Catering Corps, Territorial Army.
24118257 Sergeant Robert Charles PENFOLD, The Royal Hussars (Prince of Wales's Own).
24152374 Staff Sergeant John William PHILLIPS, Royal Corps of Transport.
24413798 Sergeant Ian Geoffrey PILLING, Corps of Royal Electrical and Mechanical Engineers.
24267713 Sergeant Neil Ward PORTER, Royal Corps of Transport.
24184540 Corporal Norman PRITCHARD, The Royal Welch Fusiliers, Territorial Army.
21160389 Sergeant RAMESHBAHADUR GURUNG, 2nd King Edward VII's Own Gurkha Rifles (The Sirmoor Rifles).
24099870 Sergeant Harry RICHARDSON, The Light Infantry.
24262345 Staff Sergeant Ian Solomon ROBERTS, The Royal Green Jackets.
24227590 Staff Sergeant Tony ROBINSON, The Queen's Regiment.
24346604 Sergeant Kenneth Bryan ROGERSON, Royal Corps of Transport.
21161295 Rifleman RUKMAN GURUNG, 6th Queen Elizabeth's Own Gurkha Rifles.
24038793 Staff Sergeant Douglas William SCOTT, Royal Corps of Signals.
W 0433874 Private Maureen SIBERT, Women's Royal Army Corps.
24060063 Staff Sergeant Graham Thomas SMITH, Corps of Royal Electrical and Mechanical Engineers.
24344524 Sergeant John William Steven SMITH, Army Catering Corps.
24561516 Sergeant Peter Francis SMYTH, Royal Corps of Signals, Territorial Army.
24218166 Sergeant Bernard Neil STAINTHORPE, Corps of Royal Engineers.
24008236 Staff Sergeant Peter STILL, Corps of Royal Electrical and Mechanical Engineers.
24069513 Staff Sergeant Brian George TANNER, Royal Corps of Signals.
24293678 Staff Sergeant Kenneth William THOMSON, The Argyll and Sutherland Highlanders (Princess Louise's).
24445630 Sergeant David John TOWNLEY, The Royal Green Jackets, Territorial Army.
24080304 Corporal Raymond David WALKER, Royal Tank Regiment.
24088719 Corporal Patrick WEBB, The Duke of Edinburgh's Royal Regiment (Berkshire and Wiltshire).
23895827 Sergeant James William WELLS, Royal Corps of Signals.
24343628 Staff Sergeant David Michael WHITELOCK, Corps of Royal Electrical and Mechanical Engineers.
23500096 Corporal Peter John WILSON, The Royal Regiment of Fusiliers.
LS 22838833 Staff Sergeant George WINTERBOTTOM, The Royal Regiment of Fusiliers.

MINISTRY OF DEFENCE (AIR FORCE DEPARTMENT)

K8099211 Sergeant Ian ARUNDEL, Royal Air Force.
F8103700 Flight Sergeant Anthony John ASHWOOD, Royal Air Force.
H1944972 Chief Technician Michael William BEALES, Royal Air Force.
N1948516 Chief Technician Peter James BLEI, Royal Air Force.
K1936871 Flight Sergeant Eric BOWDEN, Royal Air Force.
R4268666 Flight Sergeant Malcolm Sidney BROWNE, Royal Air Force.
K1941824 Flight Sergeant Peter John Robertson BRUSBY, Royal Air Force.
M0688762 Flight Sergeant Bruce CAIN, Royal Air Force.
D4283329 Flight Sergeant Samuel William Joseph CHAMBERLAIN, Royal Air Force.
X4250200 Flight Sergeant Peter William COOK, Royal Air Force.
F0684244 Flight Sergeant Raymond Alfred FREESTONE, Royal Air Force.
N2553237 Flight Sergeant Peter HAGAN, Royal Air Force.
R8038015 Flight Sergeant (now Warrant Officer) Edna HILDITCH, Women's Royal Air Force.
L4172935 Flight Sergeant Terence John HOLMES, R.V.M., Royal Air Force.
C8097213 Chief Technician Nicholas John JAMES, Royal Air Force.
Q1960378 Corporal Ward Hugh LIDDLE, Royal Air Force.
R4273322 Flight Sergeant Victor William Bonnar McLAREN, Royal Air Force.
E8110886 Corporal Arthur Edward MORRALL, Royal Air Force.
L8008799 Chief Technician (now Flight Sergeant) Brian James MULHOLLAND, Royal Air Force.
Q8115108 Flight Sergeant Francis Eric PENDER, Royal Air Force.
D1934597 Flight Sergeant James Joseph ROMER, Royal Air Force.
V1943896 Sergeant Clifford SHEPHERDSON, Royal Air Force.
Q8090749 Flight Sergeant Thomas Martin STEIN, Royal Air Force Regiment.
R0589095 Flight Sergeant Trevor Norman WELBY, Royal Air Force.

OVERSEAS AWARD

BRITISH EMPIRE MEDAL (MILITARY DIVISION)

B.E.M.

Flight Sergeant Edward Vincent LAU, Royal Hong Kong Auxiliary Air Force.

BRITISH EMPIRE MEDAL (CIVIL DIVISION)

B.E.M.

UNITED KINGDOM

Robert Barry ADAMSON, Constable, Lancashire Constabulary.
Bashir AHMED, Arabic Typist and Translator, Foreign and Commonwealth Office.
James Paton ALLISON, lately Station Warden, Royal Air Force Lossiemouth, Ministry of Defence.
Leslie Gerald ALLUM, Foreman, Manor Farm, Grazeley, Reading.
Thomas Kell ANDERSON, Security Officer, Foreign and Commonwealth Office.
Sybil Joyce Louise, Mrs. ANDREWS, Observer (W), No 3 Group, Oxford, Royal Observer Corps.
Frederick ARKWRIGHT, For services to the community in Wigan, Lancashire.
Samuel James ARMOUR, Constable, Royal Ulster Constabulary.
Alma, Mrs. BAILEY, Foster Mother, Mid-Glamorgan County Council Social Services Department.
Eric Edward BAKER, Senior Railman, London Midland Region, British Railways.
Arthur Alan BARLOW, For services to charity in Stoke-on-Trent, Staffordshire.
James Barrie BARRIE, Secretary and Treasurer Manchester Branch, Regimental Asssociation.
James Scott BARTLET, Sergeant, Grampian Police.
Anthony Trevor BASTABLE, Manager, Families Shop, Blandford Camp, NAAFI., Dorset.
Benjamin Louis William BATTIE, Master Class IV Harbour Service, Port of London Authority.
Monica, ELizabeth, Mrs. BECK, For services to the Northern General Hospital League of Friends.
Margaret Ann, Mrs. BEESTON, For services to the community in Gateshead, Tyne and Wear.
John Edward BERRY, Fingerprint Officer, Hertfordshire Constabulary.
Reginald Cecil BLISSETT, Senior Meter Inspector, West Midlands British Gas plc.
Harold William BOOKER, Process and General Supervisory 'C' Ministry of Defence.
Miss Hilary Halden BOURNE. For services to the community in Ditchling, Sussex.
Miss Joanna Leeson BOURNE. For services to the community in Ditchling, Sussex.
Reginald Kenneth BRADDICK. For sporting and charitable services to the City of Cardiff.
Rosalind May, Mrs. BRAIN. For services to the community in Yarnton, Oxfordshire.
Leslie BRAMLEY, Day Foreman, Scunthorpe Works, General Steels Group, British Steel plc.
Gudrun, Mrs. BRISBANE, lately Housing Clerk, Soest Station West Germany, Ministry of Defence.
Peter James BROWN, Forest Craftsman, Forestry Commission.
Walter David BUCKLE, lately Truck Operator, Hythe Terminal, Esso.
John James BURNS, Sub-Officer, Fire Authority for Northern Ireland.
Frank Evered CALVERT, Gravure Printer, Coloroll Group plc.
Donald CAMERON. For services to the Glasgow Council on Alcohol.
Robert Frederick John CANN. For services to folk music.
Morley Eric CASTLE, Principal Engineer, Design Ofice, Marconi Space Systems Ltd.
Miss Emily Maud CATLIN. For services to the community in Godstone, Surrey.
Gordon Harold CHEER, Chargehand I, Engineering Services Branch, United Kingdom Atomic Energy Authority, Winfrith.
Arthur Kay CLAYTON. For services to English Heritage.
Arthur Frederick CLEMENTS, Senior Head Gardener, Commonwealth War Graves Commission.
Lewis Leslie Newman COBB. For services to the 250 (Halifax) Squadron Air Training Corps.
Mary, Mrs. COLES. For services to the community in Melton Mowbray, Leicestershire.
George Thomas COX. For services to the community in Leeds.
Norman CRAVEN, Chargehand Fitter, Merseyside Transport Ltd.
Keith Frederick CRIPPS, Works Manager, K.S. Paul Products Ltd.
James Geoffrey DALLAS, Foreman, Hiram Walker & Sons (Scotland) plc.
Eric James DAVIES, Engineering Foreman, Merseyside and North Wales Electricity Board.
Evan Bertie DAVIES, Storekeeper, Remploy Brynamman Factory.
Thomas Trevor DINGLE, Bridge Foreman, Cornwall County Council.
Norman George DODDS, Permanent Way Section Supervisor, London Midland Region, British Railways.
Hilda May, Mrs. DREW. For services to the Patients League King George Hospital.
Andrew Alexander DUNCAN. For services to the community in Saltcoats, Ayrshire.
Walter George DUNCAN, Foreman, John Wood Group plc.
Aubrey BURTON-DURHAM, Pilot, Sealink Harbours Ltd., Newhaven.
Edna Mary, Mrs. EATWELL. For services to the National Spinal Injuries Centre, Stoke Mandeville Hospital.
Stanley EGERTON, Sergeant, Greater Manchester Police.
Terence Raymond EVES, Chargehand Craftsman, Ministry of Defence.
Thomas Alan FAULDS. For services to the Auxiliary Coastguard Service, Isle of Whithorn, Wigtownshire.
Dennis FELLOWS, Constable, Derbyshire Constabulary.
Edward George FENN, Caretaker, Chartered Institute of Management Accountants.
Norman James FERGUSSON, Course Superintendent, Royal Troon Golf Club.
Margaret, Mrs. FLINT, Deputy Metropolitan Organiser, Manchester, Women's Royal Voluntary Service.
Victor John FORDHAM, Constable, Metropolitan Police.
David George FRANKCOM, Driver, Shell International.
Evelyn Mary, Mrs. FROMHOLD, Member, Basildon, Women's Royal Voluntary Service.
Michael Anthony GAITENS, lately Prison Officer Grade VI, H.M. Prison, Greenock.
Allan William GAULT, Sergeant, North Yorkshire Police.
Hugh McClelland GILMORE, Sergeant, Royal Ulster Constabulary.
Phyllis Gwendolin, Mrs. GOLCH. For voluntary services to the British Red Cross Society, Gloucester.
John Samuel GOLDSMITH, Ganger, Omagh District Council.
James Bernard GOODWIN, Sub Officer, West Midlands Fire Service.
Lawrence GOSLING, Masonry Manager, Quibell and Son Ltd.
Cyril GRACEY, Mortician, Johnson and Company.
Thomas Duffy GRAHAM, Driver, Scottish Region, British Railways.
Rita, Mrs. GREEN, Nursing Auxiliary, Hull Maternity Hospital.
James GRIERSON, Shepherd, Slongaber, Dumfries.
Donald GRIGOR, Driver, Ministry of Defence.
Kathleen, Mrs. HAMER. For services to the Huddersfield Sea Cadet Corps Unit.
Montague HAND, President, West Sussex Council of the Fire Services National Benevolent Fund.
Peter Howell HANDLER, Site Superintendent, Victor Works, Lucas Aerospace.
John Tolhurst HANDOVER, Royal Automobile Club, Service Patrol.
George Dennis Charles HANDY, Bus Driver Powick Hospital, Worcester and District Health Authority.
Samuel HANNA, Head Porter, Belfast City Hospital.
Miss Winifred Stuart HARDIE. For services to the Edinburgh Branch, Parkinson's Disease Society.
George William HARRISON. For services to the welfare of ex-Servicemen and women.
Roger Ernest HAYES, Vice President, Island of Jersey Band.
Evelyn Diane, Mrs. HEWSON, Supervisor, Office and Print Services, The Chartered Institute of Building.
Annie, Mrs. HODSON, lately Chief Reprographics Officer, Ministry of Defence.
Richard Alan HOILE, Constable, Devon and Cornwall Constabulary.
Frank HOMER, Leading Hand, Stainless Steel Division, British Steel plc.
Dorothy Winifred, Mrs. HOOD, Meals-on-Wheels Organiser, Penarth, Women's Royal Voluntary Service.
William HOPPER. For services to the Royal British Legion, Scarborough.
John Edward HOUSLEY, Foreman, Nottingham Royal Ordnance plc.

Kenneth HOWARTH, Sewing Machinist, Woodfield Industries Sheltered Workshop.
Emrys HUGHES, Forest Craftsman, Forestry Commission, Wales.
Raymond John Frederick ILES, lately Process and General Supervisory 'C', Ministry of Defence.
Annie, Mrs. JACKSON. For services to the community in Bolton, Lancashire.
Alan Lawrence JEFFREYS, Constable, Lothians and Borders Police.
George Kenneth JEFFS, lately Coxswain Assistant Mechanic, Barmouth Lifeboat, Royal National Lifeboat Institution.
Derek Edward Charles JOHNS, Joiner, Ministry of Defence.
John JOHNSTON, Prison Officer, Northern Ireland Prison Service.
Cyril Rhys JONES, Prison Officer Grade IV, H.M. Prison, Brixton.
Glyn JONES, lately Prison Officer Grade IV, H.M. Youth Custody Centre, Portland.
Idris JONES, Skilled Turner, Ministry of Defence.
Margaret Ann, Mrs. JONES, Auxiliary Postwoman, Swansea Head Office.
William Oswald JONES, Caretaker, Ysgol Mair Primary School, Rhyl, Clwyd.
William JORDAN, Security Guard, Department of Economic Development, Northern Ireland.
Christopher Laurence JOYCE, Detective Constable, West Midlands Police.
Jacqueline Nellie, Mrs. KEEN, lately School Crossing Patrol, Manchester City Council.
Francis Patrick KELLY, Constable, Merseyside Police.
John James KENNEDY, Senior Traffic Warden, Police Authority for Northern Ireland.
Ronald John KENNEDY, Driver, Eastern Region, British Railways.
Mona, Mrs. KIRBY, Chief Reprographics Officer, Department of Trade and Industry.
William Jess KNOX, Manager, Auchinleck Talbot Junior Football Club.
David Henry LAWTHER, Senior Driver, South Eastern Education and Library Board.
George LEGG, lately Truck Operator, Avonmouth Terminal, Esso.
Brian LEONARD, Field Support Engineer, Basildon General Electric Company Sensors Ltd.
Claude LEWIS. For services to cricket.
Edward LIDDLE, Constable, Sussex Police.
Sidney Charles Williamson LONGSTAFFE. For services to animal welfare, Newcastle-upon-Tyne.
George Robert LOWER, Inspector of Works, Brian Colquhoun and Partners.
Michael LYONS, Constable, Hampshire Constabulary.
Hugh Alexander MACKENZIE. For services to the community in Achateny, Argyllshire.
James Angus MACLEAN, School Crossing Attendant Newtonmore, Inverness-shire.
Wilson Ronald MADDOCKS, Constable, Kent Constabulary.
Thomas Swanston MALTMAN, Harbour Master, Eyemouth, Berwickshire.
Victor Albert Charles MARSH, Coxswain Mechanic, Swanage Lifeboat, Royal National Lifeboat Institution.
Miss Audrey MARSHALL, Constable, Humberside Police.
Edward Younger MARSHALL. For services to Edenhall Hospital, Musselburgh.
William Dawson MARSTON, Chief Warder, National Gallery.
Leslie MAW. For services to music and the community of Kirkbymoorside, York.
James McCAFFERTY. For services to music in Livingston, West Lothian.
Albert James Daniel McCALL, Senior Engineering Foreman, London Electricity Board.
Arthur McCALLION, Forestry Supervisor, Department of Agriculture, Northern Ireland.
Hugh McCLYMONT, Attendant Lightkeeper, Northern Lighthouse Board.
Barbara, Mrs. McDONALD, lately County Food Organiser, East Sussex, Women's Royal Voluntary Service.
William Campbell McILROY, Supervisor, Michelin Tyre plc.
George McKEE. For services to the Royal National Institute for the Blind.
Hazlett Campbell McKEOWN, Constable, Royal Ulster Constabulary.
Norah, Mrs. McKEVER, Government Telephonist, Board of Customs and Excise.
Doris Ivy, Mrs. McQUEEN, Emergency Services, Devon, Women's Royal Voluntary Service.
James Alexander Graham McSPORRAN. For services to the community in Gigha, Argyll.
Shirley Victoria, Mrs. MILES. For services to swimming in the Isle of Wight.
James Michael MILLAR. For services to the St. Andrew's Ambulance Corps in Fife.
Catherine, Mrs. MILLER, Controlling Supervisor, Department of Social Security.
Geoffrey Ronald MILLS, Superintendent AB Machine Shop Dynamics Division, British Aerospace plc.
Rosalie Ann, Mrs. MITCHELL, Leading Reprographics Operator, Ministry of Defence.
Irene Gwendoline, Mrs. MOON. For services to the Friends of Maida Vale Hospital.
Michael William MORREL, Constable, Nottinghamshire Constabulary.
Kenneth George MOXHAM, Chargehand Carpenter, Ministry of Defence.
William Edward Denis OLIVER, Driver, Government Car Service, Department of the Environment.
Malcolm Howe PADLEY. For services to the Peak Park Joint Planning Board.
Fernley Edgar PALMER, Senior Storekeeper, Ministry of Defence.
Ralph Stanley PARTNER, Prison Officer Grade VIII (Trades Officer) H.M. Prison, Standford Hill.
Christabel, Mrs. PATTERSON. For services to the community in Maryport, Cumbria.
Elsa Mary, Mrs. PEARCE. For services to the League of Remembrance.
Colin John PIDDUCK, lately Special Services Officer, South Western British Gas plc.
Arthur Ralph POINTER, lately Senior Gatekeeper, Bank of England.
Sidney Charles POMEROY, Administrative Assistant, Cleansing Department, Corporation of London.
George David POPE. For services to the Campbeltown Sea Cadet Corps Unit.
Maurice POWELL, Chargehand, Metropolitan Police.
Mary, Mrs. PRICE. For services to the community in Ammanford, Dyfed.
Ronald William PRICE, Chargehand Instrument Mechanic, Risley Laboratory, United Kingdom Atomic Energy Authority.
Miss Kathleen Christiana PRICKETT. For musical services to the Queen Elizabeth Military Hospital, Woolwich.
Gwendoline May, Mrs. PROUT. For services to disabled people in Exeter, Devon.
Emmeline Mary, Mrs. PUGH, lately Head of Print Room, Medical Research Council.
Leslie Alfred QUANTRILL, lately Postman, Albury, Guildford, The Post Office.
Selwyn John REECE, Heavy Goods Vehicle Class I Driver, Bassett Group of Companies.
William Frederick Thomas RIBBONS. For services to Association Football in Norwich.
Dennis Percival ROACH. For services to swimming in Wales.
Jacqueline Mary, Mrs. ROBERTS. For services to the Weston Super Mare Sea Cadet Corps Unit.
Thomas James ROBERTS, Agricultural Training Board Instructor, Sheep Handling Skills.
Alfred ROBINSON. For services to the community in East Halton, South Humberside.
John Barrie ROBINSON, Station Officer, West Yorkshire Fire Service.
John Martin RODGERS, Public Relation Officer, St. John Ambulance Brigade.
Jeanne Irene, Mrs. ROLFE, Foster Mother, Avon, Somerset County Council.
Bertram Reginald ROOKE, Senior Head Gardener, Commonwealth War Graves Commission.
Herbert ROSE. For services to the 2527 (Lawnswood) Squadron Air Training Corps.

Horace SANKEY, Grade 1 Underground Fitter, Donisthorpe and Rawdon Colliery, Central Area, British Coal.
Gertrude Nancy, Mrs. SAWYER, Personal Assistant, Coal Trade Benevolent Association.
Miss Violet May SCOTT, Cap Spinner, Joseph Horsfall and Sons Ltd.
Miss Elizabeth SHORT, Head Receptionist and Telephonist, Institute of Mechanical Engineers.
Anne, Mrs. SIMPSON, Quality Control Manageress, Lismona Wear Ltd.
William John SISLEY, Postman, Guildford Letter District Office, The Post Office.
Frederick William SMART, lately for services to the Coventry Branch, Soldiers' Sailors' and Airmen's Families Association.
Harriet, Mrs. SMITH. For services to the blind in Wales.
Peter Dent SMITH, Observer Crew 1, No 9 Group, Dorset Royal Observer Corps.
Martin Trevor SMITHURST, Senior Shop Steward, Electrical Electronic Telecommunication and Plumbing Union, Anglesey Aluminium Metals Ltd.
Michael SPEAR, Experimental Worker I, Ministry of Defence.
Harold William Charles STANDING, Bus Driver, Alder Valley South Ltd.
Doris, Mrs. STEARN, School Crossing Patrol, Cambridgeshire County Council.
Michael Wilfred STEEL, Water Controller, Southern Water Authority.
Kenneth James STENNER, Divisional Superintendent, Avon St. John Ambulance Brigade.
Kenneth STEPHENS, Service Technician, North Western British Gas plc.
Raymond STEVENSON, Chief Carver, Jaycee Furniture (Brighton) Ltd. for services to export.
John Cameron STODDART, Chargehand Craftsman, Ministry of Defence.
William Richard STONEBRIDGE, Foreman, Central Repair Depot, Gloucestershire County Council.
John Richard STUART, Prison Officer, Grade VIII, H.M. Prison, Peterhead.
May, Mrs. TALBOT. For services to the community in Horton Kirby, Kent.
Judith Selina, Mrs. TAYLOR. For services to the Guide Dogs for the Blind Association in Derbyshire.
Raymond Daniel TEFT, Station Officer H.M. Coastguard Department of Transport.
Horace Reginald THELWELL, Voluntary Motorcycle Training Instructor, Wirral.
Julia Lousia Kate, Mrs. THURSTON, Member, Wallington, Women's Royal Voluntary Service.
Major Ben Howard TINTON. For services to the Woolwich (The Royal Anglian Regiment) Military Hospital.
Miss Breidge Gertrude TREANOR, Matron, Mitchell House Special School, Belfast.
William Thomas TUCKER, lately Centre Leader, Fallingbostel, West Germany Young Women's Christian Association.
Frederick Thomas TURNER, Chargehand Maintenance Engineer, Royal Marsden Hospital.
Kenneth John VINE, Supervisor, Grouting and Anchors, Cementation Piling and Foundations Ltd.
Gerald Newman VINEY. For voluntary services to the community in Hulme.
Michael WADE, lately Supervising Usher IV, Lord Chancellor's Department.
Peter WALDEN, Insurance Secretary, Lancing Scout Association.
Harry WALKER. For services to the St Ninian's Old Folk's Association, Stirling.
Mavis Noreen, Mrs. WALLBANK. For services to the community in Denby, Derby.
Irene, Mrs. WARD-THOMPSON, Branch Secretary, Durham Branch, The British Red Cross Society.
Christopher John WARREN, Constable, Metropolitan Police.
Eric WARRINGTON, lately District Adviser, Catering, Macclesfield Health Authority.
Pamela Margaret, Mrs. WASYLYK, Chief Paperkeeper, Department of Trade and Industry.
John Edward WATERS, Driver, London Midland Region, British Railways.
Peter WEST, Instructional Officer I, H.M. Prison, Ashwell.
George WESTLE, Lately Support Manager III, Lord Chancellor's Department.
Stanley Hubert Cecil WESTON, Postman, North West London Letter District Office, The Post Office.
Miss Effie Marjorie WHITEHEAD, Centre Organiser and Branch Industrial Training Officer Humberside Branch, The British Red Cross Society.
Gordon WHITTAKER. For services to the Salford Division Soldiers', Sailors' and Airmen's Families Association.
James Copland WHYTE, Building Inspector, Scottish Special Housing Association.
Anthony Ernest David WILLIAMS. For services to the No 1148 (Penarth) Squadron Air Training Corps.
Peter Edward WILLIAMS, Painting Foreman, West Midlands British Gas plc.
Vivian Frank Llewellyn WILLIAMS, Prison Officer Grade V, H.M. Prison, Littlehey.
Frederick John WILLIAMSON, lately Worcester City Centre Organiser, Hereford and Worcester Branch, The British Red Cross Society.
Jack WILMINGTON, Museum Warder V, H.M. Tower of London.
Miss Doreen WILSON, Examinations Secretary, The Chartered Institution of Building Services Engineering..
Harry Hunter WILSON, Sub Officer, Cumbria Fire Service.
John McArthy WOLFE, Milk Roundsman, Unigate Dairies.
Miss Beryl Margaret WRIGHT, Technical Assistant, Anglian Water Authority, Norwich.

OVERSEAS TERRITORIES

Jimmy FUNG Yuen Sum, Gatechecker, Public Works Department, Hong Kong.
Alma Jean, Mrs. HARDING, Registrar, Safe Care Registry, Government Secretariat, Hong Kong.
HO Ping-chiu, Chief Supervisor, Auxiliary Medical Services, Hong Kong.
LAU Wing-kan, Chief Customs Officer, Customs and Excise Service, Hong Kong.
LEE Kam-lun, Senior Clerical Officer, Island Regional Headquarters, Hong Kong.
LEE Tim-sang, Senior Inspector, Regional Transport Inspectorate, Hong Kong.
MA Chung, Supervisory Foreman, Housing Department, Hong Kong.
Joseph NG Mau-fai, Manager, Linen Production Unit, Medical and Health Department, Hong Kong.
Miss Lola O'HOY, Personal Secretary Grade 1, Industry Department, Hong Kong.
Julio PONS. For community services in Gibraltar.
TSE Kwok-fu, Controller, Civil Aid Services Band, Hong Kong.

MINISTRY OF DEFENCE WHITEHALL, LONDON SW1

31st December 1988

THE QUEEN has been graciously pleased to give orders for the following promotions in, and appointments to, the Royal Red Cross:

ROYAL RED CROSS

MINISTRY OF DEFENCE (NAVY DEPARTMENT)

A.R.R.C.

To be Ordinary Associates of the Royal Red Cross, Second Class:

Superintending Nursing Officer Anne Patricia GAUGHAN, Queen Alexandra's Royal Naval Nursing Service.
Senior Nursing Officer Kathryn McCARTHY, Queen Alexandra's Royal Naval Nursing Service.

MINISTRY OF DEFENCE (ARMY DEPARTMENT)

R.R.C.

To be Ordinary Members of the Royal Red Cross, First Class:

Lieutenant Colonel Carolyn Margaret AYERS (481229), Queen Alexandra's Royal Army Nursing Corps.
Lieutenant Colonel Hilary Stephanie DIXON-NUTTALL, A.R.R.C. (473186), Queen Alexandra's Royal Army Nursing Corps.
Colonel Jill Margaret FIELD, A.R.R.C. (454251), Queen Alexandra's Royal Army Nursing Corps.

A.R.R.C.

To be Ordinary Associates of the Royal Red Cross, Second Class:

Major Tessa Ann BROUGHTON (501139), Queen Alexandra's Royal Army Nursing Corps.
Major Patricia Anne FRIEND (511223), Queen Alexandra's Royal Army Nursing Corps, Territorial Army.
23935274 Staff Sergeant Derek Alfred GEORGE, Royal Army Medical Corps.

MINISTRY OF DEFENCE (AIR FORCE DEPARTMENT)

A.R.R.C.

To be an Ordinary Associate of the Royal Red Cross, Second Class:

Squadron Leader Rosalie Ann REID (408852), Princess Mary's Royal Air Force Nursing Service.

MINISTRY OF DEFENCE
WHITEHALL, LONDON SW1

31st December 1988

THE QUEEN has been graciously pleased to approve the award of the Air Force Cross to the undermentioned:

AIR FORCE CROSS

A.F.C.

MINISTRY OF DEFENCE (NAVY DEPARTMENT)

Lieutenant Commander Andrew Campbell Thomson TAIT, Royal Navy.

MINISTRY OF DEFENCE (AIR FORCE DEPARTMENT)

Squadron Leader Stephen CALTON (8025287), Royal Air Force.
Flight Lieutenant Raymond St. George CARPENTER (4131609), Royal Air Force.
Squadron Leader Paul Sydney DIXON (507870), Royal Air Force.
Wing Commander (now Group Captain) Ian Michael STEWART (5201156), Royal Air Force.
Squadron Leader Frederick Ian WELCH (4081438), Royal Air Force.

MINISTRY OF DEFENCE
WHITEHALL, LONDON S.W.1

31st December 1988

THE QUEEN has been graciously pleased to approve the award of the Air Force Medal to the undermentioned:

AIR FORCE MEDAL

A.F.M.

MINISTRY OF DEFENCE (ARMY DEPARTMENT)

24338024 Staff Sergeant Robert John ODDIE, Army Air Corps.

HOME OFFICE QUEEN ANNE'S GATE, LONDON SW1

31st December 1988

THE QUEEN has been graciously pleased to approve the award of The Queen's Police Medal for Distinguished Service to the undermentioned:

QUEEN'S POLICE MEDAL

Q.P.M.

ENGLAND AND WALES

Anthony John BECK, Constable, Norfolk Constabulary.
John Stuart BENNION, Deputy Chief Constable, Hertfordshire Constabulary.
Frederick BLOOR, lately Chief Superintendent, Staffordshire Police.
Michael Charles CRONIN, lately Chief Superintendent, Dyfed-Powys Police.
Henri Harman EXTON, Sergeant, Greater Manchester Police.
Alan Grahame FRY, Commander, Metropolitan Police.
Ronald HADFIELD, Chief Constable, Nottinghamshire Constabulary.
Eric Denwood HUMPHREY, Commander, Metropolitan Police.
Terence Arthur Louis LAMBERT, Chief Superintendent, Suffolk Constabulary.
Jeremy John PLOWMAN, Commander, Metropolitan Police.
Francis Frederick READ, Chief Inspector, Thames Valley Police.
James SHARPLES, Deputy Chief Constable, Merseyside Police.
Donald SHAW, Assistant Chief Constable, West Yorkshire Police.
Cenydd Golyddan Price THOMAS, Chief Superintendent, South Wales Constabulary.
Peter David TOPPING, lately Detective Chief Superintendent, Greater Manchester Police.
John Arthur WESELBY, Deputy Chief Constable, Derbyshire Constabulary.
Frederick Thomas WILSON, Assistant Chief Constable, Durham Constabulary.
Alan William YOUNG, lately Deputy Assistant Commissioner, Metropolitan Police.

NORTHERN IRELAND

Noel George BOONE, Sergeant, Royal Ulster Constabulary.
Cecil SCOTT, Superintendent, Royal Ulster Constabulary.

HONG KONG

William CHAN Kang-po, Chief Superintendent, Royal Hong Kong Auxiliary Police Force.
LEE Lam-chuen, C.P.M., Assistant Commissioner, Royal Hong Kong Police Force.

GIBRALTAR

Joseph Louis CANEPA, Commissioner of Police, Gibraltar.

SCOTTISH OFFICE ST. ANDREW'S HOUSE, EDINBURGH

31st December 1988

THE QUEEN has been graciously pleased to approve the award of the Queen's Police Medal for Distinguished Service to the undermentioned:

QUEEN'S POLICE MEDAL

Q.P.M.

SCOTLAND

George Albert ESSON, Deputy Chief Constable, Grampian Police.
John Harling MARTINDALE, Chief Superintendent, Strathclyde Police.
John Archibald MacLEAN, Sergeant, Northern Constabulary.

HOME OFFICE QUEEN ANNE'S GATE, LONDON SW1

31st December 1988

THE QUEEN has been graciously pleased to approve the award of the Queen's Fire Service Medal for Distinguished Service to the undermentioned:

QUEEN'S FIRE SERVICE MEDAL

Q.F.S.M.

ENGLAND AND WALES

Ronald JENKINS, Divisional Officer III, Cheshire Fire Brigade.
Terence William MALPASS, Chief Officer, Durham County Fire Brigade.
John Robert PEARSON, Chief Officer, Hampshire Fire Service.
John WEDDELL, Deputy Chief Officer, Northumberland Fire and Rescue Service.
James Henry WINDSOR, Chief Officer, West Glamorgan Fire Brigade.

CAYMAN ISLANDS

Kirkland Hencliffe NIXON, M.B.E., Chief Fire Officer, Cayman Islands.

HONG KONG

WOO, Kwan-kuen, C.P.M., Chief Fire Officer, Hong Kong Fire Services.

FOREIGN AND COMMONWEALTH OFFICE
DOWNING STREET, LONDON SW1

31st December 1988

THE QUEEN has been graciously pleased to approve the award of the Colonial Police and Fire Service Medal for Meritorious Service to the undermentioned:

COLONIAL POLICE AND FIRE SERVICE MEDAL

C.P.M.

CHAN Tit-kin, Senior Superintendent, Royal Hong Kong Police Force.
CHEUNG Fook-leung, Superintendent, Royal Hong Kong Police Force.
Justin CUNNINGHAM, Senior Superintendent, Royal Hong Kong Police Force.
Donald Ellis GRIFFITHS, Senior Superintendent, Royal Hong Kong Police Force.
HSU King-ping, Senior Divisional Officer, Hong Kong Fire Services.
Ian Frank LACY-SMITH, Senior Superintendent, Royal Hong Kong Police Force.
LEUNG Koon-tung, Principal Fireman, Hong Kong Fire Services.
LEUNG Kwong-ling, Principal Fireman, Hong Kong Fire Serices.
LEUNG Pak-shing, Station Sergeant, Royal Hong Kong Police Force.
LI Tung, Chief Inspector, Royal Hong Kong Police Force.
LIP Chung-wai, Station Sergeant, Royal Hong Kong Police Force.
Dennis Leslie SHACKLETON, Senior Superintendent, Royal Hong Kong Police Force.
Robert Thomas SULLIVAN, Chief Inspector, Royal Hong Kong Police Force.
Peter James THOMPSON, Senior Superintendent, Royal Hong Kong Police Force.
Thomas THOMSON, Senior Superintendent, Royal Hong Kong Police Force.
Matthew Vincent WALSH, Senior Superintendent, Royal Hong Kong Police Force.
YUEN kam-chi, Principal Fireman, Hong Kong Fire Services.

MINISTRY OF DEFENCE, WHITEHALL, LONDON SW1

31st December 1988

THE QUEEN has been graciously pleased to approve the award of the Queen's Commendation for Valuable Service in the Air to the undermentioned:

QUEEN'S COMMENDATION FOR VALUABLE SERVICE IN THE AIR

MINISTRY OF DEFENCE (NAVY DEPARTMENT)

Lieutenant Commander John BEATTIE, Royal Navy.

MINISTRY OF DEFENCE (ARMY DEPARTMENT)

24114928 Warrant Officer Class I James Stephen LAWTON, Army Air Corps.

MINISTRY OF DEFENCE (AIR FORCE DEPARTMENT)

Master Aircrew Francis Hugh GRAHAM (M1939918), Royal Air Force.
Squadron Leader Kenneth Robert McCALLUM (8024911), Royal Air Force.
Squadron Leader Graham Douglas MAGEE (8025761), Royal Air Force.
Squadron Leader Michael James METCALF (8025815), Royal Air Force.
Squadron Leader Eric George NORBURY (608574), Royal Air Force.
Flight Lieutenant David John PARKER (5067685) Royal Air Force.
Wing Commander (now Group Captain) Brian Edward Allen PEGNALL (608582) Royal Air Force.
Squadron Leader Alan POTTER (585107), Royal Air Force.
Flight Lieutenant (now Squadron Leader) John Richards POTTER (4230949), Royal Air Force.
Squadron Leader Timothy Raymond WATTS (8025733), Royal Air Force.
Flight Lieutenant Eric Alexander WEALLEANS (8026708), Royal Air Force.

CENTRAL CHANCERY OF
THE ORDERS OF KNIGHTHOOD

ST. JAMES'S PALACE, LONDON SW1

31st December 1988

THE QUEEN has been graciously pleased to approve the award of the Queen's Commendation for Valuable Service in the Air to the undermentioned:

QUEEN'S COMMENDATION FOR VALUABLE SERVICE IN THE AIR

UNITED KINGDOM

Laurence James BUIST, Managing Pilot of British Aerospace, 146 Fleet, Dan-Air Services, Gatwick Airport.
Keith Hill CHADBOURN, lately Senior Test Pilot, Westland Helicopters Ltd.
Anthony John HAWKES, Senior Experimental Test Pilot, Manchester, British Aerospace plc.

ABBREVIATIONS

A

AA Automobile Association; Anti-Aircraft; Architectural Association
AAAS American Association for the Advancement of Science
AACCA Associate of Association of Certified & Corporate Accountants
AACI Accredited Appraiser, Canadian Institute
AADipl Diploma, Architectural Association
A&AEE Aeroplane and Armament Experimental Association
AAF Auxiliary Air Force
AAFCE Allied Air Forces Central Europe
AAG Assistant Adjutant-General
AAI Association of Chartered Auctioneers' and Estate Agents' Institute
AALPA Associate of Incorporated Auctioneers & Landed Property Agents
AAM Association of Assistant Mistresses in Secondary Schools
AAMC Australian Army Medical Corps
AA&QMG Asssistant Adjutant & Quarter-Master-General
AASA Associate of Australian Society of Accountants
AASC Australian Army Service Corps
AASF Advanced Air Striking Force
AB Bachelor of Arts (USA); Able-bodied Seaman
ABA Associate of British Archaeological Association; Antiquarian Booksellers' Association
ABIBA Associate of the British Institute of Brokers Association
ABIM Associate of British Institute of Management
ABOD Advance Base Ordnance Depot
ABPS Associate of the British Psychological Society
ABTA Association of British Travel Agents
AC Companion of the Order of Australia
ACA Associate of the Institute of Chartered Accountants
Acad Academy
ACARD Advisory Council for Applied Research and Development
ACAS Advisory, Conciliation and Arbitration Service
ACBSI Associate, Chartered Building Societies Institute
ACC Association of County Councils
ACCM Advisory Council for the Church's Ministry
ACCS Associate of the Corporation of Secretaries
AcDipEd Academic Diploma in Education
ACDS Assistant Chief of Defence Staff
ACE Association of Consulting Engineers
ACF Army Cadet Force
ACG Assistant Chaplain General
ACGI Associate of City & Guilds of London Institute
ACGS Assistant Chief of General Staff
ACIArb Associate, Chartered Institute of Arbitrators
ACIB Associate, Chartered Institute of Bankers
ACII Associate of Chartered Insurance Institute
ACIS Associate of Chartered Institute of Secretaries
ACMA Associate, Institute of Cost and Management Accountants
ACNS Assistant Chief of Naval Staff
ACommA Associate, Society of Commercial Accountants
ACORD Advisory Committee on Research and Development
ACOS Assistant Chief of Staff
ACOST Advisory Council on Science and Technology
ACRE Action with Rural Communities in England
ACS American Chemical Society
ACSEA Allied Command SE Asia
ACT Australian Capital Territory; Australian College of Theology
Actg Acting
ACTT Association of Cinematograph, Television and Allied Technicians
ACVO Assistant Chief Veterinary Officer
ACWA Associate of Institute of Cost and Works Accountants
AD Corps Army Dental Corps
ADAS Agricultural Development and Advisory Service (MAFF)
ADC Aide-de-Camp
ADC(P) Personal Aide-de-Camp to HM The Queen
ADGB Air Defence of Great Britain
ADGMS Assistant Director-General of Medical Services
Adj Adjutant
Adj-Gen Adjutant-General
Adm Admiral
Admin Administration; Administrative; Administrator
ADMS Assistant Director of Medical Services
Admty Admiralty
ADNI Assistant Director of Naval Intelligence
ADOS Assistant Director of Ordnance Service
ADP Automatic Data Processing
ADPR Assistant Director Public Relations
ADS&T Assistant Director of Supplies and Transport
Adv-Gen Advocate-General
Advsr Adviser
Advsy Advisory
ADVS Assistant Director of Veterinary Services
AE Air Efficiency Award (see AEA)
AEA Air Efficiency Award; Atomic Energy Authority
AEAF Allied Expeditionary Air Force
AEC Agricultural Executive Committee
AED Air Efficiency Decoration
AEF Amalgamated Union of Engineering and Foundry Workers
AEM Air Efficiency Medal
AER Army Emergency Reserve
AERE Atomic Energy Research Establishment
AEU Amalgamated Engineering Union
AF Air Force
AFAIM Associate Fellow of the Australian Institute of Management
AFC Air Force Cross; Association Football Club
AFCENT Allied Forces Central Europe
Affrs Affairs
AFHQ Allied Force Headquarters
AFI Associate of the Faculty of Insurance
AFIMA Associate Fellow, Institute of Mathematics and its applications
AFM Air Force Medal
AFOM Associate, Faculty of Occupational Medicine
AFRAeS Fellow of the Royal Aeronautical Society
AFRC Agricultural and Food Research Council
AFS Auxiliary Fire Service
AFV Armoured Fighting Vehicles
AG Attorney-General
Agent-Gen Agent-General
AGI Artistes Graphiques Internationales
AGRA Association of Genealogists and Record Agents
Agric Agriculture, Agricultural
AHA Area Health Authority
AHQ Army Head Quarters
AHSM Associate, Institute of Health Services Management
AIA American Institute of Architects; Associate, Institute of Actuaries: Association of International Artists
AIAA Associate of the Institute of Administrative Accountants
AIAC Associate of the Institute of Company Accountants
AIB Associate of Institute of Bankers
AIBD Associate, Institute of British Decorators
AICA Associate Member Commonwealth Institute of Accountants
AICE Associate, Institute of Civil Engineers
AIChor Associate of the Institute of Choreography
AICS Associate of the Institute of Chartered Shipbuilders
AIEE Associate of the Institution of Electrical Engineers
AIF Australian Imperial Forces
AIG Adjutant-Inspector-General
AIIA Associate of the Institute of Industrial Administration
AIL Associate, Institute of Linguists
AIM Associate of the Institution of Metallurgists
AIMarE Associate of the Institute of Marine Engineers
AINA Associate of the Institute of Naval Architects
AInstM Associate Member of the Institute of Marketing
AInstP Associate of the Institute of Physics
AInstT Associate, Institute of Taxation
AIPM Associate of the Institute of Personnel Management
Air Cdre Air Commodore
AIT Associate, Institute of Taxation
AIYL Association of International Young Lawyers
aka Also known as
AKC Associate, King's College London
ALA Associate, Library Association
ALAS Associate Member of Chartered Land Agent's Society
ALFSEA Allied Land Forces South East Asia
ALI Argyll Light Infantry; Associate, Landscape Institute
Alta Alberta (Canada)
AM Member of the Order of Australia; Albert Medal; Master of the Arts (USA); Alpes Maritimes
AMA Associate, Museum Association; Association of Metropolitan Authorities
Ambass Ambassador
AMBIM Associate Member of the British Institute of Management
AMCT Associate, Manchester College of Technology
AMDEA Associate of Manufacturers of Domestic and Electrical Appliances
AMEC Association of Management Education for Clinicians

AMEME Association of Mining Electrical and Mechanical Engineers
AMF Australian Military Forces
AMGOT Allied Military Government Occupied Territory
AMIBE Associate Member of the Institution of British Engineers
AMICE Associate Member of the Institution of Civil Engineers
AMIChemE Associate Member of Chemical Engineers
AMIED Associate Member of the Institution of Engineering Designers
AMIEE Associate Member of the Institution of Electrical Engineers
AMIMechE Associate Member of the Institution of Mechanical Engineers
AMIMinE Associate Member of the Institution of Mining Engineers
AMInstNA Associate Member of the Institution of Naval Architects
AMIPE Associate Member of the Institution of Production Engineers
AMIStructE Associate Member, Institute of Structural Engineers
AMP Air Ministry Personnel; (Harvard Business School) Advanced Management Programme
AMPC Auxiliary Military Pioneer Corps
AMRAes Associate Member, Royal Aeronautical Society
AMS Army Medical Service; Assistant Military Secretary
AMSIA Associate Member, Society of Investment Analysts
AMTPI Associate of the Town Planning Institution
ANU Australian National University
AO Air Officer; Officer of the Order of Australia
AOA Air Officer in Charge in Administration
AOC Air Officer Commanding
AOC-in-C Air Officer Commanding-in-Chief
AOD Army Ordnance Department
AOEng Air Officer Engineering
AOER Army Officers' Emergency Reserve
AOM Air Officer Maintenance
APA American Psychiatric Association
APEX Association of Professional, Executive, Clerical and Computer Staffs
APM Assistant Provost Marshal
Appt Appointment
APRA Association of Political Risks Analysts
APS American Physical Society
AQ Administration and Quartering
AQMG Assistant Quarter-Master General
ARA Associate of the Royal Academy of the Arts
ARAD Associate, Royal Academy of Dancing
ARAeS Associate of the Royal Aeronautical Society
ARAM Associate of the Royal Academy of Music
ARBA Associate of the Royal Society of British Artists
ARBS Associate of the Royal Society of British Sculptors
ARC Agricultural Research Council
ARCA Associate of Royal College of Art
ARCA (Lond) Associate of the Royal Academy of Arts
ARCM Associate of the Royal College of Music
ARCO Associate of the Royal College of Organists
ARCS Associate, Royal College of Science
ARCUK Architects' Registration Council of the UK
ARCVS Associate of the Royal College of Veterinary Surgeons
ARE Associate, Royal Society of Painters-Etchers and Engravers
ARELS Association of Recognised English Language Schools
ARIAS Associate, Royal Incorporation of Architects in Scotland
ARIBA Associate of the Royal Institute of British Artists
ARIC Associate of the Royal Institute of Chemistry
ARICS Associate of the Royal Institution of Chartered Surveyors
ARINA Associate of the Royal Institution of Naval Architects
ARMCM Associate, Royal Manchester College of Music
Armd Armoured
ARP Air Raid Precautions
ARPS Associate of the Royal Photographic Society
ARRC Associate of the Royal Red Cross
ARSA Associate of the Royal Scottish Academy
ARSM Associate of the Royal School of Mines
ARTC Associate of the Royal Technical College
ARWS Associate of the Royal Society of Painters in Water Colours
ASA Associate Member of the Society of Actuaries; Australian Society of Accountants
ASAA Associate of the Society of Incorporated Accountants
ASC Army Service Corps
ASCAP American Society of Composers, Authors and Publishers
ASD Armament Supply Department
ASF Associate of the Institute of Shipping and Forwarding Agents
A&SH Argyll and Sutherland Highlanders
ASIA Associate, Society of Investment Analysts
ASIAD Associate, Society of Industrial Artists and Designers
ASLIB Association of Special Libraries and Information Bureau
ASME American Society of Mechanical Engineers; Association for Study of Medical Education
ASO Air Staff Officer
assas assassinated
Assoc Association; Associate; Associated
Assoc InstT Associate of the Institute of Transport
Asst Assistant
Assur Assurance
ASTMS Association of Scientific, Technical and Managerial Staff
ASVO Association of State Veterinary Officers
ATA Air Transport Auxiliary
ATAF Allied Tactical Air Force
ATC Air Training Corps
ATD Art Teachers' Diploma
ATI Associate, Textile Institute
ATII Associate Member, Institute of Taxation
ATO Ammunitions Technical Officer
ATOA Taxi Operators Association
ATS Auxiliary Territorial Service
AUEW Amalgamated Union of Engineering Workers
Aust Australian, Australia
Authy Authority
Aux Auxiliary
Ave Avenue
AVR Army Volunteer Reserve
AWRE Atomic Weapons Research Establishment
AWS Graduate of Air Warfare Course

B

b Born
BA Bachelor of Arts; British Airways
BAC British Aircraft Corporation
BADA British Antique Dealers Association
BAFO British Air Forces Occupation
BAFSEA British Air Forces South East Asia
BAFTA British Academy of Film and Television Arts
BAI Baccalarius in Arte Ingeniaria
BAIE British Association of Industrial Editors
BAIPA British Airline Pilots Association
BAO Bachelor of Obstetrics
BAOMS British Association of Oral and Maxillo-Facial Surgeons
BAOR British Army of the Rhine
BARC British Automobile Racing Club
BArch Bachelor of Architecture
Barr Barrister
Bart's St Bartholomew's Hospital
BAS Bachelor in Agricultural Science
BASc Bachelor of Applied Science
Batty Battery
BAUA Business Aviation Users Association
BBA British Banker's Association
BBC British Broadcasting Corporation
BBS Bachelor of Social Sciences (USA)
BC British Columbia
BCE Bachelor of Civil Engineering
BCh or BChir Bachelor of Surgery
BCL Bachelor in Civil Law
BCOF British Commonwealth Occupation Force in Japan
BCom Bachelor of Commerce
BCS Bengal Civil Service
BCU British Canoe Union
BD Bachelor in Divinity
Bd Board
BDA British Dental Association
Bdcast(ing) Broadcast(ing)
Bde Brigade
BDS Bachelor of Dental Surgery
BE Bachelor of Engineering
BEA British European Airways Corporation
BEAMA Federation of British Electrotechnical and Allied Manufacturers Association
BEcon Bachelor of Economics
BEd Bachelor of Education
BEE Bachelor of Electrical Engineering
BEF British Expeditionary Force
BEM British Empire Medal
BEng Bachelor of Engineering
BETRO British Export Trade Organisation
BFI British Film Institute
BFME British Forces Middle East
BFPO British Forces Post Office
BFSS British Field Sports Society
BGGS Brigadier-General, General Staff
BGS Brigadier, General Staff
BHS British Horse Society

BHy Bachelor of Hygiene
BIBA British Insurance Brokers Association
BICC British Insulated Callender's Cables
BIEE British Institute of Energy Economics
BIM British Institute of Management
BJSM British Joint Service Mission
BL Bachelor of Law; British Leyland
BLA British Army of Liberation
Bldgs Buildings
BLESMA British Limbless Ex-servicemens' Association
BLitt Bachelor of Letters
BM Bachelor of Medicine (Oxford); Brigade Major
BMA British Medical Association
BMH British Military Hospital
BMus Bachelor of Music
Bn Battalion
BNAF British North Africa Force
BNC Brasenose (College)
BNES British Nuclear Energy Society
BNF British Nuclear Fuels
BNFL British Nuclear Fuels Ltd
BNSC British National Space Centre
BNurs Bachelor of Nursing
BOA British Olympic Association
BOAC British Overseas Airways Corporation
BOT Board of Trade
BOTB British Overseas Trade Board
BP British Petroleum
BPharm Bachelor of Pharmacy
BPIF British Printing Industries Federation
Br British
BR British Railways
BRCS British Red Cross Society
BRDC British Racing Drivers' Club
Brig Brigadier
bro brother
BS Bachelor of Surgery
BSAC British Sub Aqua Club
BSc Bachelor of Science
BSC British Steel Corporation
BSI British Standards Institution
Bt Baronet
BT British Telecom
BTA British Troops in Austria; British Tourist Authority
Bt-Col Brevet-Colonel
Btcy Baronetcy
BTEC Business and Technicians Education Council
Btss Baronetess
BVA British Veterinary Association
BWI British West Indies
BWM British War Medal
BWS Member of the British Watercolour Society

C

c circa
C Conservative
C of C Chamber of Commerce
C of E Church of England
CA Chartered Accountant; County Alderman
CAA Civil Aviation Authority
CAB Citizens Advice Bureau
CACTM Central Advisory Council of Training for the Ministry
CAMC Canadian Army Medical Corps
CAMRA Campaign for Real Ale
Cantab Of Cambridge University
Capt Captain
CARE Cottage and Rural Enterprises
CAS Chief of Air Staff
Cav Cavalry
CB Companion of the Order of the Bath
CBA Council for British Archaeology
CBC County Borough Council
CBE Commander of the Order of the British Empire
CBI Confederation of British Industry
CBIM Companion, British Institute of Management
CBiol Chartered Biologist
CBIREE Companion, British Institute of Radio and Electronic Engineers
CC County Council: Companion of the Order of Canada; Cricket Club
CCA County Councils' Association
CCAB Consultative Committee of Accounting Bodies
CCBE Consultative Council of European Bars and Law Societies (Commission Consultative des Barreaux de la Communant Européene)
CCC Corpus Christi College; County Cricket Club
CCF Combined Cadet Force
CCG(BE) Control Commission, Germany (British Element)
CChem Chartered Chemist
CCIBS Companion, Chartered Institute of Building Services
CCncllr County Councillor
CCO Conservative Central Office
CCPR Central Council of Physical Recreation
CCRE Commander Corps of Royal Engineers
CCRA Commander Corps, Royal Artillery
CCRSigs Commander Corps of Royal Signals
CCS Casualty Clearing Station
CD Civil Defence; Canadian Forces Decoration
CDipAF Certified Diploma in Accounting and Finance
Cdr Commander
Cdre Commodore
CDS Chief of Defence Staff
CE Chief Engineer
CEDEP Centre Européen d'Education Permanente
CEFIC Counseil Européen des Federations de L'Industrie Chimique
CEGB Central Electricity Generating Board
CEI Council of Engineering Institutions
CEng Chartered Engineer
CERN Conseil (now Organisation) Européenne pour la Recherche Nucléaire
CertEd Certificate of Education
CF Chaplain to the Forces
CFM Canadian Forces Medal
CFS Central Flying School
CGA Country Gentleman's Association
CGIA City and Guilds of London Insignia Awards Association
CGLI City and Guilds of the London Institute
CGS Chief of the General Staff
CH Companion of Honour
ChB Bachelor of Surgery
ChCh Christ Church (Oxford)
Chem Chemical
Chev Chevalier
Chllr Chancellor
Chm Chairman
ChM Mastery of Surgery
ChStJ Chaplain of the Order of St John of Jerusalem
CI Order of the Crown of India; Channel Islands
CIArb Chartered Institute of Arbitrators
CIBS Chartered Institute of Building Services
CIBSE Chartered Institution of Building Services Engineers
CICeram Companion, Institute of Ceramics
CICHE Committee for International Co-operation in Higher Education
CID Criminal Investigation Department
CIE Companion of the Order of the Indian Empire
CIEE Companion, Institution of Electrical Engineers
CIGS Chief of the Imperial General Staff
CIMarE Companion of the Institute of Marine Engineers
CIMechE Companion of the Institution of Mechanical Engineers
C-in-C Commander-in-Chief
CIPFA Chartered Institute of Public Finance and Accountancy
CIPM Companion, Institute of Personnel Managers
CIRIA Construction Industry Research and Information Association
CIT Chartered Institute of Transport
CJ Chief Justice
Cl Class
CLA Country Landowners' Association
CLitt Companion of the Royal Society of Literature
CLP Constituency Labour Party
CM Member of the Order of Canada; Master of Surgery
Cmd Commanded; command
Cmdg Commanding
Cmdt Commandant
CMF Commonwealth Military Forces; Central Mediterranean Force
CMG Companion of the Order of St Michael and St George
Cmmn Commission
cmmnd Commissioned
Cmmr Commissioner
CMO Chief Medical Officer
CMP Corps of Military Police
CMS Church Missionary Society
CNAA Council for National Academic Awards
Cncl Council
Cncllr Councillor
CND Campaign for Nuclear Disarmament

Cnsllr Counsellor
CO Commanding Officer
Co Company; County
Co L Coalition Liberal
COD Communications and Operations Department (FO)
C of C Chamber of Commerce
C of E Church of England
COGS Chief of General Staff
COI Central Office of Information
Col Colonel
Coll College
Com Communist
COMMET Council of Mechanical and Metal Trade Associations
Comp Comprehensive
Conf Conference
Confedn Confederation
Conn Connecticut
Cons Conservative
Conslt Consultant
consltg consulting
contrib Contributor, contributed, contribution
Co-op Co-Operative
corp corporate
Corpl Corporal
Corpn Corporation
Corr Correspondent
COS Chief of Staff
COSIRA Council for Smaller Industries in Rural Areas
cous cousin
CPC Conservative Political Centre
CPhys Chartered Physicist
CPM Colonial Police Medal
CPRE Council for the Protection of Rural England
CPRS Central Policy Review Staff
CPS Canadian Pacific Steamships
CPU Commonwealth Press Union
cr created
CRA Commander Royal Artillery
CRAC Careers Research and Advisory Council
CRAeS Companion, Royal Aeronautical Society
CRC Community Relations Commission
CRD Conservative Research Department
CRE Commanding Royal Engineers
CRMP Corps of Royal Military Police
CRO Commonwealth Relations Office
CS Clerk to the Signet
CSA Commonwealth Society of Artists; Chair Schools Association
CSD Civil Service Department; Chartered Society of Designers
CSERB Computer Systems and Electronics Requirements Board
CSI Companion of the Order of the Star of India; Council for the Securities Industries
CSIR Council for Scientific and Industrial Research
CSIRO Commonwealth Scientific and Industrial Research Organisation
CSO Chief Signal Officer; Chief Staff Officer; Chief Scientific Officer
CStJ Commander of the Order of St John of Jerusalem
CSTI Council of Science and Technology Institutes
CSV Community Service Volunteers
Ct court
Ctee Committee
CText Chartered Textile Technologist
Ctory Consistory (Court)
ctr creator
CU Cambridge University
CUBC Cambridge University Boat Club
CUF Common Universities Fund
CUP Cambridge University Press
CVCP Committee of Vice-Chancellors and Principals of the UK
CVO Commander of the Royal Victorian Order
Cwlth Commonwealth

D

d Died, death
da Daughter
DA Diploma in Anaesthetics; Diploma in Art
DA & QMG Deputy-Adjutant and Quartermaster-General
DAA & QMG Deputy Assistant-Adjutant and Quartermaster-General
DAAG Deputy-Assistant-Adjutant-General
D & ADA Designers & Art Directors' Association
DACG Deputy Assistant Chaplain General
DADGMS Deputy Assistant Director General of Medical Services
DADMS Deputy Assistant Director Medical Services
DADR Deputy Assistant Director of Remounts
DAD Deputy-Assistant Director
DADST Deputy Assistant Director of Supplies and Transport
DAG Deputy-Adjutant-General
DAMS Deputy-Assistant Military Secretary
DAPM Deputy Assistant Provost Marshall
DAPS Director of Army Postal Services
DAQMG Deputy-Assistant-Quartermaster-General
DBA Doctor of Business Administration
DBE Dame Commander of the British Empire
DC District Council
DCAS Deputy Chief of Air Staff
DCB Dame Commander Order of the Bath
DCGS Deputy Chief of General Staff
DCH Diploma in Child Health
DCL Doctor of Civil Law
DCLI Duke of Cornwall's Light Infantry
DCM Distinguished Conduct Medal
DCMG Dame Commander Order of St Michael and St George
DCMS Deputy Commissioner Medical Services
DCSO Deputy Chief Scientific Officer
DCVO Dame Commander Royal Victorian Order
DD Doctor in Divinity
DDDS Deputy Director of Dental Services
DDME Deputy Director Mechanical Engineering
DDMS Deputy Director of Medical Services
DDO Diploma in Dental Orthopaedics
DDOS Deputy Director of Ordnance Services
DDPS Deputy Director of Personal Services
DDR Deputy Director of Remounts
DDS Doctor of Dental Surgery; Director of Dental Services
DDS & T Deputy Director Supplies and Transport
DDSD Deputy Director of Staff Duties
DDVS Deputy-Director of Veterinary Services
DDWE & M Deputy Director of Works, Electrical and Mechanical
decd deceased
DEd Doctor of Education
Def Defence
Del Delegate
Delgn Delegation
DEM Diploma in Education Management
DEME Director of Electrical and Mechanical Engineering
DEng Doctor of Engineering
Dep Deputy
Dep-Adv-Gen Deputy-Advocate-General
Dep-Sec Deputy Secretary
Dept Department
DES Department of Education and Science
DèsL Docteur ès Lettres
DesRCA Designer of the Royal College of Art
Devpt Development
DFA Doctor of Fine Arts
DFC Distinguished Flying Cross
DFH Diploma of the Faraday House
DG Director General
DGAMS Director-General of Army Medical Services
DGCStJ Dame Grand Cross of the Order of St John of Jerusalem
DGMS Director-General of Medical Services
DGStJ Dame of Grace of the Order of St John of Jerusalem
DH Doctor of Humanities
DHA District Health Authority
DHMSA Diploma in the History of Medicine (Society of Apothecaries)
DHQ District Headquarters
DHSS Department of Health and Social Security
DHy Doctor of Hygiene
DIC Diploma of the Imperial College
DIH Diploma in Industrial Health
Dio Diocese
Dip Diploma; Diplomatic
DipAD Diploma in Arts and Design
DipAg Diploma in Agriculture
Dip Arch Diploma in Architecture
DipBA Diploma in Business Administration
DipCAM Diploma in Communication, Advertising and Marketing of the CAM Foundation
DipCD Diploma in Civic Design
DipED Diploma in Education
DipHA Diploma in Hospital Administration
DipOrthMed Diploma in Orthopaedic Medicine
DipTP Diploma in Town Planning
Dir Director
dis dissolved (marriage)

Dist	District
Div	Division
Divnl	Divisional
DJAG	Deputy Judge Advocate General
DJStJ	Dame of Justice of the Order of St John of Jerusalem
DL	Deputy-Lieutenant for the County of
DLC	Diploma Loughborough College
DLI	Durham Light Infantry
DLitt	Doctor of Letters
DLit	Doctor of Literature
DLO	Diploma in Larynology and Otology
DM	Doctor of Medicine
DMD	Doctor in Dental Medicine
DME	Director of Mechanical Engineering
DMGO	Divisional Machine Gun Officer
DMI	Director Military Intelligence
DMJ	Diploma in Medical Jurisprudence
DMO & I	Director Military Operations and Intelligence
DMRD	Diploma in Medical Radiological Diagnosis
DMRE	Diploma in Medical Radiology and Electrology
DMS	Director of Medical Services
DMSI	Director of Management and Support Intelligence
DMT	Director of Military Training
DMus	Doctor of Music (Oxford)
DNI	Director of Naval Intelligence
DNO	Director of Naval Ordnance
DO	Diploma in Ophthalmology; Divisional Officer
DOAE	Defence Operational Analysis Establishment
DObstRCOG	Diploma Royal College of Obstetricians and Gynaecologists
DOC	District Officer Commanding
DOE	Department of Environment
DOI	Dept of Industry
DOMS	Diploma in Ophthalmic Medicine
DOR	Director of Operational Requirements
DOS	Director of Ordnance Services
DPA	Diploma in Public Administration
DPH	Diploma in Public Health
DPhil	Doctor of Philosophy
DPL	Director of Pioneers and Labour
DPM	Diploma in Psychological Medicine
DPMO	Deputy Principal Medical Officer
DPR	Director of Public Relations
DPS	Director of Personal Services
DQMG	Deputy Quartermaster-General
DRC	Diploma of the Royal College of Science and Technology, Glasgow
DRVO	Deputy Regional Veterinary Officer
DS	Directing Staff
DS & T	Director of Supplies and Transport
DSAC	Defence Scientific Advisory Committee
DSAO	Diplomatic Service Administration Office
DSC	Distinguished Service Cross
DSc	Doctor of Science
DSD	Director of Staff Duties
DSIR	Department of Scientific and Industrial Research
DSM	Distinguished Service Medal (United States of America)
DSO	Companion of the Distinguished Service Order
dsp	*decessit sine prole* (died without issue)
DSP	Docteur en Sciences Politiques (Montreal)
DSSC	Doctor of Social Science
DStJ	Dame of Grace of the Order of St John of Jerusalem
DS & T	Director of Supplies and Transport
DTech	Doctor of Technology
DTh	Doctor of Theology
DTI	Dept of Trade and Industry
DTM & H	Diploma in Tropical Medicine and Hygiene
DTp	Dept of Transport
DUniv	Doctor of the University
DVFS	Director, Veterinary Field Services
DVM	Doctor of Veterinary Medicine
DVO	Divisional Veterinary Officer
DVS	Director of Veterinary Services
DVSM	Diploma of Veterinary State Medicine

E

E	East; Earl; England
EASA	Ecclesiastical Architects and Surveyors Association
EBU	European Broadcasting Union
EC	European Commission
ECGD	Export Credit Guarantee Department
Econ	Economic
Ed	Editor; editorial
ED	Efficiency Decoration; European Democratic (Group)
EDC	Economic Development Committee
EDG	European Democratic Group (UK Conservative Group, European Parliament)
edn	edition
educnl	educational
Educn	education
EETPU	Electrical, Electronic, Telecommunication and Plumbing Union
EFTA	European Free Trade Association
EIU	Economist Intelligence Unit
eld	eldest
EMS	Emergency Medical Service
Eng	English; England
Engr	Engineer
Engrg	Engineering
ENO	English National Opera
ENSA	Entertainments National Services Association
ENT	Ear, Nose and Throat
er	elder
ERD	Emergency Reserve Decoration
ESRC	Economic and Social Research Council
Estab	Established; establishment
ESU	English-Speaking Union
Eur Ing	European Engineer
Euro	European
Exec	Executive
Expdn	Expedition
Ext	Extinct; extension

F

f	father
FA	Football Association
FAA	Fellow of the Australian Academy of Science
FAAAS	Fellow, American Academy of Arts & Sciences
FAAV	Fellow, Central Association of Agricultural Valuers
FACC	Fellow, American College of Cardiology
FACCA	Fellow of the Association of Certified and Corporate Accountants
FACD	Fellow, American College of Dentristry
FACE	Fellow, Australian College of Education
FACOG	Fellow, American College of Obstetricians and Gynaecologists
FACP	Fellow, American College of Physicians
FACS	Fellow, American College of Surgeons
FACVT	Fellow, American College of Veterinary Toxicology
FAES	Fellow of the Audio Engineering Society
FAI	Fellow of the Chartered Auctioneers' and Estate Agents' Institute
FAIA	Fellow, American Institute of Architects
FAIM	Fellow of the Australian Institute of Management
FAIP	Fellow, of the Australian Institute of Physics
FAIRE	Fellow of the Australian Institute of Radio Engineers
FALPA	Fellow of the Incorporated Auctioneers and Land Property Agents
FAMEME	Fellow, Association of Mining, Electrical and Mechanical Engineers
FAMI	Fellow of the Australian Marketing Institute
FAMS	Fellow of the Ancient Monuments Society
FANY	First Aid Nursing Yeomanry
FAO	Food and Agricultural Organisation
FAPM	Fellow of the Association of Project Managers
FARELF	Far East Land Forces
FAS	Fellow, Antiquarian Society
FASA	Fellow of the Australian Society of Accountants
FASCE	Fellow of the American Society of Civil Engineers
FBA	Fellow of the British Academy
FBCO	Fellow of British College of Opticians
FBCS	Fellow, British Computer Society
FBHI	Fellow of the British Horological Institute
FBI	Federation of British Industries
FBIBA	Fellow of the British Insurance Brokers Association
FBIEE	Fellow of the British Institute of Energy Economists
FBIM	Fellow of the British Institute of Management
FBIPP	Fellow of the British Institute of Professional Photographers
FBIS	Fellow of the British Interplanetary Society
FBKSTS	Fellow, British Kinematograph, Sound and Television Society
FBOA	Fellow of the British Optical Association
FBPsS	Fellow, British Psychological Society
FBSI	Fellow of the Boot and Shoe Industry
FC	Football Club
FCA	Fellow of the Institute of Chartered Accountants
FCAI	Fellow of the Canadian Aeronautical Institute
FCAM	Fellow, Communications Advertising & Marketing Educational Foundation
FCBSI	Fellow of the Chartered Building Societies Institute

FCCA	Fellow of the Association of Certified and Corporate Accountants
FCCS	Fellow of the Corporation of Certified Secretaries
FCDA	Fellow of the Company Directors Association of Australia
FCEC	Federation of Civil Engineering Contractors
FCFA	Fellow of the Cookery and Food Association
FCGI	Fellow, City and Guilds of London Institute
FCIA	Fellow, Corporation of Insurance Agents
FCIArb	Fellow, Chartered Institute of Arbitrators
FCIB	Fellow of the Corporation of Insurance Brokers; Fellow, Chartered Institute of Bankers
FCIBS	Fellow, Chartered Institution of Building Services
FCIBSE	Fellow, Chartered Institution of Building Service Engineers
FCII	Fellow of the Chartered Insurance Institute
FCIOB	Fellow, Chartered Institute of Building
FCIS	Fellow of the Chartered Institute of Secretaries
FCIT	Fellow of the Chartered Institute of Transport
FCMA	Fellow, Institute of Cost and Management Accountants
FCO	Foreign and Commonwealth Office
FCOG	Fellow of the College of Obstetrics and Gynaecology
FCommA	Fellow of the Society of Commercial Accountants
FCP	Fellow, College of Preceptors
FCPS	Fellow of the College of Physicians and Surgeons
FCS	Fellow of the Chemical Society
FCSD	Fellow, Chartered Society of Designers
FCSVA	Fellow, Corporate Society of Valuers and Auctioneers
FCT	Fellow of the Institute of Corporate Treasurers
FCWA	Fellow of the Institute of Cost and Works Accountants
FDR	Federalische Deutsche Republik
FDS	Fellow in Dental Surgery
FDSRCS	Fellow in Dental Surgery Royal College of Surgeons of England
FEAF	Far East Air Force
Fed	Federal
Fedn	Federation
FEIS	Fellow of the Educational Institute of Scotland
Fell	Fellow
FEng	Fellow, Fellowship of Engineering
FES	Fellow of the Entomological Society
FFA	Fellow of the Faculty of Actuaries (Scotland)
FFARACS	Fellow, Faculty of Anaesthetists Royal Australian College of Surgeons
FFARCS	Fellow of the Faculty of Anaesthetists, Royal College of Surgeons
FFARCSI	Fellow, Faculty of Anaesthetists Royal College of Surgeons of Ireland
FFAS	Fellow of the Faculty of Architects and Surveyors
FFB	Fellow of the Faculty of Building
FFCM	Fellow, Faculty of Community Medicine
FFDRCSI	Fellow, Faculty of Dentistry, Royal College of Surgeons in Ireland
FFHom	Fellow, Faculty of Homeopathy
FFR	Fellow of the Faculty of Radiologists
FGA	Fellow of the Gemmological Association
FGS	Fellow of the Geological Society
FGSM	Fellow, Guildhall School of Music
FHA	Fellow, Institute of Health Service Administrators
FHCIMA	Fellow of the Hotel Catering and Institutional Management Association
FHKIE	Fellow, Hong Kong Institute of Engineers
FHSM	Fellow, Institute of Health Service Managers
FIA	Fellow, Institute of Actuaries; Fédération Internationale de L'Automobile
FIAAS	Fellow Architect Member of the Incorporated Association of Architects and Surveyors
FIAC	Fellow, Institute of Company Accountants
FIAeS	Fellow of the Institute of Aeronautical Sciences
FIAgrE	Fellow, Institution of Agricultural Engineers
FIAL	Fellow, International Institute of Arts and Letters
FIAM	Fellow, International Academy of Management
FIArb	Fellow of the Institute of Arbitration
FIAS	Fellow, Institute of Aeronautical Sciences (US)
FIB	Fellow of the Institute of Bankers
FIBiol	Fellow, Institute of Biology
FIBM	Fellow, Institute of Builders' Merchants
FIBScot	Fellow of the Institute of Bankers in Scotland
FICA	Fellow of the Institute of Chartered Accountants in England and Wales
FICAS	Fellow, Institute of Chartered Accountants in Scotland
FICD	Fellow of the Institute of Civil Defence
FICE	Fellow of the Institution of Civil Engineers
FICeram	Fellow, Institute of Ceramics
FICFor	Fellow, Institute of Chartered Foresters
FIChemE	Fellow of the Institution of Chemical Engineers
FICM	Fellow, Institute of Credit Management
FICS	Fellow of the Institute of Chartered Shipbrokers
FICSA	Fellow of the Institute of Chartered Secretaries and Administrators
FID	Fellow of the Institute of Directors
FIE(Aust)	Fellow, Institution of Engineers, Australia
FIEE	Fellow of the Institution of Electrical Engineers
FIEEE	Fellow, Institution of Electrical and Electronics Engineers (New York)
FIERE	Fellow of the Institution of Electronics and Radio Engineers
FIEx	Fellow, Institute of Export
FIFM	Fellow, Institute of Fisheries Management
FIFor	Fellow, Institute of Forestry
FIFST	Fellow of Food Science and Technology
FIGD	Fellow, Institute of Grocery Distribution
FIGE	Fellow, Institute of Gas Engineers
FIGeol	Fellow, Institute of Geology
FIHE	Fellow, Institute of Health Education
FIHort	Fellow of the Institute of Horticulture
FIHospE	Fellow, Institute of Hospital Engineering
FIHT	Fellow, Institute of Highways and Transportation
FIHVE	Fellow, Institution of Heating and Ventilating Engineers
FIIM	Fellow, Institute of Industrial Managers
FIInfSc	Fellow, Institute of Information Scientists
FIInst	Fellow of the Imperial Institute
FIL	Fellow of the Institute of Linguists
FILA	Fellow of the Institute of Landscape Architects
FILDM	Fellow, Institute of Logistics and Distribution Management
FilDr	Doctor of Philosophy
FIM	Fellow, Institute of Metals (formerly Institution of Metallurgists)
FIMA	Fellow of the Institute of Mathematics and its Applications
FIMarE	Fellow, Institute of Marine Engineers
FIMBRA	Financial Intermediaries, Managers and Brokers Regulatory Association
FIMC	Fellow, Institute of Management Consultants
FIMechE	Fellow of the Institution of Mechanical Engineers
FIMFT	Fellow, Institute of Maxillo-Facial Technology
FIMH	Fellow, Institute of Materials Handling; Fellow, Institute of Military History
FIMI	Fellow, Institute of Motor Industry
FIMinE	Fellow, Institute of Mining Engineers
FIMIT	Fellow, Institute of Musical Instrument Technology
FIMLS	Fellow, Institute of Medical and Laboratory Sciences
FIMM	Fellow, Institution of Mining and Metallurgy
FIMT	Fellow of the Institute of the Motor Trade
FIMTA	Fellow of the Institute of Municipal Treasurers & Accountants
Fin	Finance; financial
FInstAA	Fellow of the Institute of Administrative Accountants
FInstAM	Fellow, Institute of Administrative Management
FInstCES	Fellow of the Institution of Civil Engineering Surveyors
FInstCS	Fellow, Institute of Chartered Secretaries
FInstD	Fellow, Institute of Directors
FInstF	Fellow of Institute of Fuel
FinstFF	Fellow, Institute of Freight Forwarders
FInst GasE	Fellow, Institution of Gas Engineers
FInstGeol	Fellow Institute of Geologists
FInstHE	Fellow, Institution of Highway Engineers
FInstLEx	Fellow, Institute of Legal Executives
FInstM	Fellow, Institute of Marketing
FInstMC	Fellow, Institute of Measurement and Control
FInstMSM	Fellow of the Institute of Marketing and Sales Management
FInstP	Fellow of the Institute of Physics
FInstPet	Fellow of the Institute of Petroleum
FInstPI	Fellow, Institute Patentees (Incorporated)
FInstPS	Fellow, Institute of Purchasing and Supply
FInstSMM	Fellow, Institute of Sales and Marketing Management
FINucE	Fellow of the Institute of Nuclear Engineers
FIOA	Fellow, Institute of Acoustics
FIOB	Fellow, Institute of Building
FIOP	Fellow of the Institute of Printing
FIOSc	Fellow of the Institute of Optical Science
FIP	Fellow, Australian Institute of Petroleum
FIPA	Fellow of the Institute of Public Administration; Fellow of the Institute of Practitioners in Advertising
FIPHE	Fellow of the Institution of Public Health Engineers
FIPI	Fellow, Institute of Professional Investigators
FIPM	Fellow, Institute of Personnel Management
FIPR	Fellow of the Institute of Public Relations
FIProdE	Fellow of the Institute of Production Engineers
FIPS	Fellow, Institute of Purchasing and Supply
FIQ	Fellow, Institute of Quarrying
FIRE	Fellow of the Institution of Radio Engineers
FIRI	Fellow of the Institution of the Rubber Industry
FISE	Fellow of the Institute of Sanitary Engineers
FIStructE	Fellow, Institution of Structural Engineers
FITA	Fellow, International Archery Federation
FITD	Fellow, Institute of Training and Development

FIWEM Fellow, Institution of Water and Environmental Management
FIWES Fellow, Institute of Water Engineers and Scientists
FIWSc Fellow, Institute of Wood Science
FJI Fellow, Institute of Journalists
FKC Fellow, King's College London
FLA Fellow, Library Association
FLAS Fellow, Land Agents Society
FLCM Fellow, London College of Music
FLI Fellow, Landscape Institute
FLIA Fellow, Life Assurance Association
FLS Fellow, Linnean Society
Flt Flight
Flt Lt Flight Lieutenant
FM Field Marshal
FMA Fellow of the Museums' Association
FMS Fellow, Institute of Management Services; Fellow, Institute of Medical Society; Fellow, Manorial Society
FNAEA Fellow, National Association of Estate Agents
Fndn Foundation
Fndr Founder
FNI Fellow, Nautical Institute
FNIAB Fellow, National Institute of Agricultural Botany
FO Foreign Office
FOR Fellowship of Operational Research
For Foreign
FPC Family Practitioner Committee
FPCA Fellow of Practising and Commercial Accountants
FPhS(Eng) Fellow, Philosophical Society of England
FPMI Fellow, Pensions Management Institute
FPRI Fellow, Plastics and Rubber Institute
FPS Fellow of Philological Society of Great Britain
Fr France
FRACDS Fellow, Royal Australian College of Dental Surgeons
FRACP Fellow of the Royal Australasian College of Physicians
FRACS Fellow of the Royal Australasian College of Surgeons
FRAeS Fellow, Royal Aeronautical Society
FRAgS Fellow, Royal Agricultural Societies
FRAI Fellow of the Royal Anthropological Institute
FRAIC Fellow, Royal Architectural Institute of Canada
FRAM Fellow of the Royal Academy of Music
FRAS Fellow of the Royal Astronomical Society; Fellow, Royal Asiatic Society
FRBS Fellow of the Royal Botanic Society; Fellow of the Royal Society of British Sculptors
FRCAA Fellow of the Royal Cambrian Academy of Art
FRCGP Fellow, Royal College of General Practitioners
FRCM Fellow of the Royal College of Music
FRCN Fellow, Royal College of Nursing
FRCO Fellow of the Royal College of Organists
FRCOG Fellow of the Royal College of Obstetricians and Gynaecologists
FRCP Fellow of the Royal College of Physicians
FRCPA Fellow, Royal College of Pathologists of Australia
FRCPath Fellow, Royal College of Pathologists
FRCPE Fellow of the Royal College of Physicians of Edinburgh
FRCPG Fellow, Royal College of Physicians, Glasgow
FRCPS Fellow of the Royal College of Physicians and Surgeons (Glasgow)
FRCPsych Fellow, Royal College of Psychiatrists
FRCR Fellow, Royal College of Radiologists
FRCS Fellow of the Royal College of Surgeons; Fellow of the Royal C'wlth Society (formerly Royal Empire Soc)
FRCSEd Fellow, Royal College of Surgeons Edinburgh
FRCSI Fellow, Royal College of Surgeons in Ireland
FRCVS Fellow, Royal College of Veterinary Surgeons
FREconS Fellow of the Royal Economic Society
FREntS Fellow of the Royal Entomological Society
FRG Federal Republic of Germany
FRGS Fellow of the Royal Geographical Society
FRHistS Fellow of the Royal Historical Society
FRHS Fellow of the Royal Horticultural Society
FRIA Fellow, Royal Institute of Arbitrators
FRIAS Fellow of the Royal Incorporation of Architects in Scotland
FRIBA Fellow of the Royal Institute of British Architects
FRIC Fellow of the Royal Institute of Chemistry
FRICS Fellow of the Royal Institution of Chartered Surveyors
FRIN Fellow of the Royal Institute of Navigation
FRINA Fellow of the Royal Institution of Naval Architects
FRIPH Fellow of the Royal Institute of Public Health
FRMetS Fellow of the Royal Meteorological Society
FRMIA Fellow of the Retail Management Institute of Australia
FRMS Fellow of the Royal Microscopical Society
FRNCM Fellow, Royal Northern College of Music
FRNS Fellow of the Royal Numismatic Society
FRPS Fellow of the Royal Photographic Society
FRPSL Fellow of the Royal Philatelic Society, London
FRS Fellow of the Royal Society
FRSA Fellow of the Royal Society of Arts
FRSAIre Fellow of the Royal Society of Antiquaries of Ireland
FRSAMD Fellow Royal Scottish Academy of Music and Drama
FRSC Fellow of the Royal Society of Canada
FRSCM Fellow, Royal School of Church Music
FRSE Fellow of the Royal Society of Edinburgh
FRSGS Fellow of the Royal Scottish Geographical Society
FRSH Fellow of the Royal Society of Health
FRSL Fellow of the Royal Society of Literature
FRSM Fellow of the Royal Society of Medicine
FRSNZ Fellow, Royal Society of New Zealand
FRSTM & H Fellow, Royal Society of Tropical Medicine and Health
FRTPI Fellow, Royal Town Planning Institute
FRTS Fellow, Royal Television Society
FRVA Fellow of the Rating and Valuation Association
FRZS Scot Fellow of the Royal Zoological Society of Scotland
FSA Fellow of the Society of Antiquaries
FSAA Fellow of the Society of Incorporated Accountants and Auditors
FSAE Fellow, Society of Arts Education
FSAS Fellow of the Society of Antiquaries, Scotland
FSE Fellow of Society of Engineers
FSF Fellow of the Institute of Shipping and Forwarding Agents
FSG Fellow of the Society of Genealogists
FSI Fellow, Royal Institution of Chartered Surveyors (*see also* FRICS)
FSIA Fellow of the Society of Industrial Artists
FSLAET Fellow, Society of Licensed Aircraft Engineers and Technologists
FSLGD Fellow, Society for Landscape and Garden Designs
FSS Fellow of the Royal Statistical Society
FSScA Fellow of the Society of Science and Art, of London
FSTD Fellow, Society of Typographic Designers
FSUT Fellow, Society for Underwater Technology
FSVA Fellow, Society of Valuers and Auctioneers
FTC Flying Training Command
FTCL Fellow of Trinity College of Music, London
FTI Fellow of the Textile Institute
FTII Fellow, Institute of Taxation
FTS Fellow of the Tourism Society
Fus Fusiliers
FVI Fellow, Valuers Institution
FWA Fellow, World Academy of Arts and Sciences
FZS Fellow of the Zoological Society

G

g great
Ga Georgia (USA)
GAA Gaelic Athletic Association
GAMTA General Aviation Manufacturers' Association
GATT General Agreement on Tariffs and Trade
G&MWU General and Municipal Workers' Union
GB Great Britain
GBA Governing Bodies Association
GBE Knight of the Grand Cross of the British Empire
GBSM Graduate, Birmingham and Midland Institute School of Music
GC George Cross; Grand Cross; Golf Club
GCB Knight Grand Cross of the Bath
GCH Knight Grand Cross of Hanover
GCHQ Government Communications Headquarters
GCIE Knight/Dame Grand Commander of the Indian Empire
GCMG Knight/Dame Grand Cross of St Michael and St George
GCON Grand Cross, Order of the Niger
GCSI Knight Grand Commander of the Star of India
GCStJ Bailiff or Dame Grand Cross of the Order of St John of Jerusalem
GCVO Knight or Dame of the Grand Cross of the Royal Victorian Order
gda granddaughter
gdns gardens
Gds Guards
GDR German Democratic Republic
Gds Guards
Gen General
Ger Germany
gf grandfather
ggda great granddaughter (and so forth)
ggs great grandson (and so forth)
GHQ General Headquarters
GIMechE Graduate Institution of Mechanical Engineers

GLC Greater London Council
GM George Medal
gm grandmother
GMB Great Master of the Bath
GMBATU General Municipal Boilermakers and Allied Trade Unions
GMC General Medical Council
GMIE Grand Master of the Indian Empire
GMMG Grand Master of St Michael and St George
GMSI Grand Master of the Star of India
GMWU General Municipal Workers Union
gn great nephew; great niece
GO Grand Officier (de la Légion d'Honneur)
GOC-in-C General Officer Commanding- in-Chief
Govr Governor
Govt Government
GP General Practitioner
Gp Group
Gp Capt Group Captain
GPDST Girls' Public Day School Trust
GPO General Post Office
Gr Grove
GRCM Graduate of the Royal College of Music
GRSM Graduate of the Royal Schools of Music
GS General Staff; Grammar School
gs grandson
GSM General Service Medal; Guildhall School of Music and Drama
GSO General Staff Officer
Gt Great
Gtr Greater
Guy's Guy's Hospital
GWR Great Western Railway

H

h heir
ha heir apparent
HA Historical Association
HAA Heavy Anti-Aircraft
HAC Honourable Artillery Company
HBM His/Her Britannic Majesty
hc honoris causa
HCF Hon Chaplain to the Forces
HCITB Hotel and Catering Industry Training Board
HDip in Ed Honorary Diploma in Education
HE His Excellency
HG Homeguard
HESIN Higher Education Support for Industry in the North
HG Homeguard
HH His/Her Highness
HHA Historic Houses Association
HHD Doctor of Humanities (US)
High Cmmr High Commissioner
HIH His/Her Imperial Highness
HIllH His/Her Illustrious Highness
HIM His/Her Imperial Majesty
Hist Historical
HKIA Member, Hong Kong Institute of Architects
Hldgs Holdings
HLI Highland Light Infantry
HMC Headmasters' Conference; Hospital Management Committee
HMEH His Most Emminent Highness
HMHS Her Majesty's Hospital Ship
HMOCS Her Majesty's Overseas Civil Service
HMS Her Majesty's Ship
HMSO Her Majesty's Stationery Office
HNC Higher National Certificate
HND Higher National Diploma
Hon Honourable; Honour (Judges); Honorary
Hons Honours
Hort Horticultural
Hosp Hospital
hp heir presumptive
HRE Holy Roman Empire
HRH His/Her Royal Highness
HRI Hon Member of the Royal Institute of Painters in Water Colours
HRSA Hon Member Royal Scottish Academy
HS High School
HSE Health and Safety Executive
HSH His/Her Serene Highness
husb husband
HVCert Health Visitors Certificate

I

I Ireland
IA Indian Army
IACP International Association of Chiefs of Police (USA)
IAEA International Atomic Energy Agency
IAF Indian Air Force; Indian Auxiliary Force
IAMC Indian Army Medical Corps
IAOC Indian Army Ordnance Corps
IAOMS International Association of Oral and Maxillo-Facial Surgeons
IAP Institute of Analysts and Programmers
IAPS Incorporated Association of Preparatory Schools
IARO Indian Army Reserve of Officers
IAS Indian Administrative Service
IASC Indian Army Service Corps
IATA International Air Transport Association
IATEEL International Association of Teachers of English as a Foreign Language
IBA Independent Broadcasting Authority
IBPA International Bridge Players Association
IBRD International Bank for Reconstruction and Devpt (World Bank)
IBRO International Brain Research Organisation
i/c in charge of
ICA Institute of Contemporary Arts
ICE Institute of Civil Engineers
ICAEW Institute of Chartered Accountants of England and Wales
ICF International Canoe Federation
ICFC Industrial and Commercial Finance Corporation
ICI Imperial Chemical Industries
ICL International Computers Ltd
ICOM International Council of Museums
ICS Indian Civil Service
ICSID International Council of Societies of Industrial Design
idc has completed a course at, or served for a year on the staff, of The Imperial Defence Coll
IDC Imperial Defence College
IDS Institute of Development Studies
IEE Institution of Electrical Engineers
IEF Indian Expeditionary Force
IFC International Finance Corporation
IFLA International Federation of Library Associations
IFPA Industrial Fire Protection Association
IG Instructor in Gunnery
IIEP International Institute for Educational Planning
IIM Institution of Industrial Managers
IISS International Institute of Strategic Studies
ILEA Inner London Education Authority
ILO International Labour Office
ILP Independent Labour Party
IMA International Music Association
IMCB International Management Centre Buckingham
IMRO Investment Management Regulatory Organisation
IMS Indian Medical Service; International Military Services
IMechE Institution of of Mechanical Engineers
IMF International Monetary Fund
Imp Imperial
Inc Incorporated
incl include; including
Ind Independent
Indust Industry
Industl Industrial
Industs Industries
Inf Infantry
Info Information
INSEAD Institut Européen d'Administration des Affaires
Inspr Inspector
Inst Institute
Instn Institution
Instr Instructor
Insur Insurance
Int International
Investmt Investment
IOD Institute of Directors
IOM Isle of Man
IOW Isle of Wight
IPA Institute of Practioneers in Advertising
IPFA Chartered Institute of Public Finance and Accountancy
IPHE Institution of Public Health Engineers
IPM Institute of Personnel Management
IPPA Independent Programme Producers' Association
IProdE Institute of Production Engineers
IPS Indian Political Service

Ir Irish
IRA Irish Republican Army
IRE Indian Corps of Royal Engineers
IRN Independant Radio News
Is Island(s)
ISBA Incorporated Society of British Advertisers
ISC Indian Staff Corps; Imperial Service College
ISCO Independent Schools Careers Organisation
ISI International Statistical Institute
ISIS Independent Schools Information Service
ISM Imperial Service Medal; Incorporated Society of Musicians (member/associate)
ISO Imperial Service Order
ISOCARP International Society of City and Regional Planning
ISPP International Society of Political Psychology
IStructE Institution of Structural Engineers
ITA Independent Television Authority
ITN Independent TV News
ITV Independent Television
IUCN International Union for the Conservation of Nature and Natural Resources
IY Imperial Yeomanry

J

JAG Judge Advocate General
JCD Doctor of Canon Law (Juris Canonici Doctor)
Jcl Licentiate of Canon Law
JD Doctor of Jurisprudence
JDipMA Joint Diploma in Management Accounting Services
jl/s journal/s
JP Justice of the Peace
jr junior
JSM Johan Seita Mahkota (Malaysia)
jssc Qualified at Joint Services Staff College
Jt Joint
jtly jointly

K

k killed
ka killed in action
KAR King's African Rifles
KASG Knightly Association of St George the Martyr
KBE Knight Commander of the Order of the British Empire
KC King's Counsel
KCB Knight Commander of the Order of the Bath
KCH King's College Hospital
KCIE Knight Commander of the Order of the Indian Empire
KCMG Knight Commander of the Order of St Michael and St George
KCS King's College School
KCSG Knight Commander of St Gregory
KCSI Knight Commander of the Star of India
KCVO Knight Commander of the Royal Victorian Order
KDG King's Dragoon Guards
KEH King Edward's Horse Regiment
KG Knight of the Order of the Garter
KGStJ Knight of Grace, Order of St John of Jerusalem *(see also* KSEJ)
KGVO King George V's Own
KHC Honorary Chaplain to the King
KHDS Honorary Dental Surgeon to the King
KHP Honorary Physician to the King
KHS Honorary Surgeon to the King
K-i-H Kaisar-i-Hind
KJStJ Knight of Justice, Order of St John of Jerusalem
KMN Kesatria Mangku Negara (Malaysian Decoration)
KORR King's Own Royal Regiment
KOSB King's Own Scottish Borderers
KOYLI King's Own Yorkshire Light Infantry
KP Knight of the Order of St Patrick
KPFSM King's Police and Fire Service Medal
KPM King's Police Medal
KRI King's Royal Irish
KRRC King's Royal Rifle Corps
KSG Knight of St Gregory
KSLI King's Shropshire Light Infantry
KStJ Knight of the Order of St John of Jerusalem
KT Knight of the Order of the Thistle
kt knighted (Knight Bachelor)

L

L Labour
LA Los Angeles
La Louisiana
LAA Light Anti-Aircraft
Lab Labour
LAC Leading Aircraftsman
LACOTS Local Authorities Co-ordination of Trading Standards Committee
LACSAB Local Authorities' Conditions of Service Advisory Board
LAH Licentiate of Apothecaries Hall, Dublin
LAMDA London Academy of Music and Dramatic Art
LBC London Broadcasting Co
LCC London County Council
LCDS London Contemporary Dance Studio
LCDT London Contemporary Dance Theatre
LCJ Lord Chief Justice
LCP Licentiate of the College of Preceptors
Ldr Leader
LDS Licentiate in Dental Surgery
LDV Local Defence Volunteers
LEA Local Education Authority
LEB London Electricity Board
lectr lecturer
Legve Legislative
LesL Licenciees Lettres
LF Land Forces
LFAA Look first, ask afterwards
LG Life Guards
LGSM Licentiate, Guildhall School of Music and Drama
LH Light Horse
LI Light Infantry
Lib Liberal
LIBC Lloyd's Insurance Brokers' Committee
Lieut Lieutenant
Lit Literature
LittD Doctor of Letters (Cambridge & Dublin)
LLA Lady Literate in Arts
LLB Bachelor of Laws
LLCM Licentiate London College of Music
LLD Doctor of Laws
LLM Master of Laws
LM Licentiate in Midwifery
LMCC Licentiate of Medical Council of Canada
LMH Lady Margarate Hall (Oxford)
LMSSA Licentiate in Medicine and Surgery, Society of Apothecaries
LMTPI Legal Member of the Town Planning Institute
LNER London and North East Railway
LPTB London Passenger Transport Board
LRAM Licentiate of the Royal Academy of Music
LRCP Licentiate of the Royal College of Physicians
LRCPE Licentiate, Royal College of Physicians Edinburgh
LRCSE Licentiate, Royal College of Surgeons Edinburgh
LRFPS Licentiate of the Royal Faculty of Physicians and Surgeons (Glasgow)
LRIBA Licentiate of the Royal Institute of British Architects
LSA Licentiate of the Society of Apothecaries
LSE London School of Economics
LSHTM London School of Hygiene and Tropical Medicine
LSO London Symphony Orchestra
LTCL Licentiate, Trinity College of Music, London
Lt-Col Lieutenant-Colonel
Ltcy Lieutenancy
Lt-Gen Lieutenant-General
LTh Licentiate in Theology
LU Liberal Unionist
LVO Lieutenant of the Royal Victorian Order
LWT London Weekend Television

M

m married, marriage
m dis marriage dissolved
MA Master of Arts; Military Assistant
MAAF Mediterranean Allied Air Forces
MACE Member, Association of Conference Executives
MAFF Ministry of Agriculture, Fisheries and Food
MAI Master of Engineering

MAIAA Member, American Institute of Aeronautics and Astronautics
Maj Major
Maj-Gen Major-General
mangr manager
Mans Mansions
MAOT Member of the Association of Occupational Therapists
MAP Ministry of Aircraft Production
MArch Master of Architecture
Marq Marquess
MASAE Member, American Society of Agricultural Engineers
MASCE Member, American Society of Civil Engineers
Mass Massachusetts (US)
MB Bachelor of Medicine
MBA Master of Business Administration
MBAE Member, British Academy of Experts
MBCS Member, British Computer Society
MBE Member of the Order of the British Empire
MBEDA Member, Bureau of European Designers
MBHI Member of the British Horological Institute
MBII Member of the British Institute of Innkeeping
MBIM Member of the British Institute of Management
MBKS Member, British Kinematograph Society
MBOU Member, British Ornithologists' Union
MBSG Member British Society of Gastroenterology
MC Military Cross
MCAM Member, Institute of Communications, Advertising and Marketing
MCB Master of Clinical Biochemistry
MCC Marylebone Cricket Club; Metropolitan County Council
MCD Master of Civic Design
MCFA Member of the Cookery and Food Association
MChir Master in Surgery
MCIOB Member Chartered Institute of Building
MCIT Member of the Chartered Institute of Transport
MCom Master of Commerce
MConsE Member Association of Consulting Engineers
MCOphth Member, College of Ophthalmologists (formerly Faculty of Ophthalmologists, FacOpth, and Ophthalmic Society of UK, OSUK)
MCP Member of Colonial Parliament
MCPath Member of the College of Pathologists
MCPS Member, College of Physicians and Surgeons
MCSD Member Chartered Society of Designers
MCSP Member of the Chartered Society of Physiotherapy
MCT Member, Association of Corporate Treasurers
MD Doctor of Medicine
md managing director
MDC Metropolitan District Council
MDes Master of Design
MDS Master of Dental Surgery
ME Middle East
MEAF Middle East Air Force
MEC Member, Executive Council
MECAS Middle East Centre for Arab Studies
MEd Master of Education
Med Medical; medicine; Mediterranean
MEF Mediterranean Expeditionary Force
MEIC Member of the Engineering Institute of Canada
MELF Middle East Land Forces
memb member
Meml Memorial
MEP Member of the European Parliament
Met Metropolitan
MFA Ministry of Foreign Affairs
MFARCS Member of the Faculty of Anaesthetists, Royal College of Surgeons
MFCM Member, Faculty of Community Medicine
MFH Master of Fox Hounds
MFOM Member, Faculty of Occupational Medicine
mfr/mfrg manufacturer/manufacturing
MGC Machine Gun Corps
MGDS RCS Member in General Dental Surgery, Royal College of Surgeons
MGGS Major-General General Staff
Mgmnt Management
MGO Master General of the Ordnance
Mgr Monsignor
MGRA Major-General Royal Artillery
MH Military Hospital
MHCIMA Member, Hotel Catering and Institutional Management Association
MHK Member of the House of Keys (IOM)
MHR Member of the House of Representatives
MI Military Intelligence
MIAeE Member, Institute of Aeronautical Engineers
MIBE Member of the Institution of British Engineers
MIBG Member, Institute of British Geographers
MIBiol Member, Institute of Biology
MICAS Member of the Institute of Chartered Accountants of Scotland
MICE Member, Institution of Civil Engineers
MICEI Member, Institution of Civil Engineers of Ireland
MICFM Member of the Institute of Charity Fund-Raising Managers
MIChemE Member of the Institution of Chemical Engineers
MIConsE Member Institute of Consulting Engineers
MIEA Member of the Institution of Engineers, Australia
MIED Member, Institution of Engineering Design
MIEE Member of the Institution of Electrical Engineers
MIEEE Member, Institute of Electrical and Electronics Engineers (NY)
MIEI Member of the Institute of Engineering Inspection
MIERE Member of the Institution of Electronic and Radio Engineers
MIES Member of the Institution of Engineers and Shipbuilders in Scotland
MIEx Member of the Institute of Export
MIFA Member, Institute of Field Archaeologists
MIH Member of the Institute of Housing
MIHT Member, Institute of Highways and Transportation
MIL Member, Institute of Linguists
Mil Military
MILE Member of the Institution of Locomotive Engineers
MIM Member, Institution of Metallurgists
MIMarE Member of the Institute of Marine Engineers
MIMC Member of the Institute of Management Consultants; Corporate Member of the Institute of Measurement and Control
MIMCE Member of the Institute of Municipal and County Engineers
MIME,MInstME Member of the Institution of Mining Engineers
MIMechE Member of the Institution of Mechanical Engineers
MIMI Member of the Institute of the Motor Industry
MIMM Member of the Institution of Mining & Metallurgy
Min Minister
MIngF Member, Danish Engineers' Association
Miny Ministry
MInstD Member of the Institute of Directors
MInstE Member, Institute of Energy
MInstGasE Member of the Institution of Gas Engineers
MInstHE Member of the Institution of Highway Engineers
MInstM Member of the Institute of Marketing
MInstMet Member of the Institute of Metals
MInstP Member of the Institute of Physics
MInst Pet Member of the Institute of Petroleum
MInstPS Member, Institute of Purchasing and Supply
MInstW Member of the Institution of Welding
MINucE Member of the Institution of Nuclear Engineers
MIOB Member of the Institute of Building
MIPA Member of the Institution of Practitioners in Advertising
MIPharmM Member, Institute of Pharmacy Management
MIPHE Member of the Institute of Public Health Engineers
MIPM Member of the Institute of Personnel Management
MIPR Member of the Institute of Public Relations
MIProdE Member of the Institution of Production Engineers
MIQ Member, Institute of Quarrying
MIRE Member of the Institution of Royal Engineers
MIS Member of the Institute of Statisticians
MISA Member, Institute of South African Architects
MISI Member of the Iron and Steel Institute
Miss Mississipi (USA)
MIStructE Member of the Institution of Structural Engineers
MIT Massachusetts Institute of Technology (USA)
MITD Member, Institute of Training and Development
MIWE Member of the Institution of Water Engineers
MJI Member of the Institute of Journalists
MJInstE Member of the Junior Engineers Institute
Mktg Marketing
MLA Member, Legislative Assembly; Modern Language Association; Master in Landscape Architecture
MLC Member of the Legislative Council
MLitt Master of Literature
MLO Military Liaison Officer
MM Military Medal
MMC Monopolies and Mergers Commission
MMechE Master of Mechanical Engineering
MMIM Member, Malaysian Institute of Management
MN Merchant Navy
MNECInst Member, North East Coast Institution of Engineers and Shipbuilders
MNI Member, Nautical Institute
MNZIE Member of the New Zealand Institution of Engineers
Mo Missouri (USA)

MO Medical Officer
MOD Ministry of Defence
Mod Modern
MOH Medical Officer of Health
MOI Ministry of Information
MOP Ministry of Power
MOS Ministry of Supply
MP Member of Parliament
MPBW Ministry of Public Building and Works
MPhil Master of Philosophy
MPRISA Member of the Public Relations Institute of South Africa
MPS Member of the Pharmaceutical Society of Great Britain
MR Master of the Rolls
MRAC Member of the Royal Agricultural College
MRAD Member of the Royal Academy of Dancing
MRAeS Member, Royal Aeronautical Society
MRAS Member of the Royal Asiatic Society
MRC Medical Research Council
MRCGP Member, Royal College of General Practitioners
MRCOG Member of the Royal College of Obstetricians and Gynaecologists
MRCP Member of the Royal College of Physicians
MRCPsych Member, Royal College of Psychiatrists
MRCS Member of the Royal College of Surgeons
MRCVS Member of the Royal College of Veterinary Surgeons
MRI Member Royal Institution
MRIA Member of the Royal Irish Academy
MRIBA Member of the Royal Institute of British Architects
MRIC Member, Royal Institute of Chemistry
MRICS Member of the Royal Institution of Chartered Surveyors
MRIN Member of the Royal Institute of Navigation
MRINA Member of the Royal Institution of Naval Architects
MRO Member of the Register of Osteopaths
MRS Market Research Society
MRSH Member of the Royal Society of Health
MRST Member of the Royal Society of Teachers
MRTPI Member of the Royal Town Planning Institute
MRUSI Member of the Royal United Service Institution
MRVA Member, Rating and Valuation Association
MS Master of Surgery; Manuscript; Master of Science (US)
MSAE Member Society of Automotive Engineers (US)
MSC Manpower Services Commission
MSc Master of Science
MScL Member, Society of Construction Law
MSE Member of the Society of Engineers
MSIA Member of the Society of Industrial Artists
MSIAD Member of the Society of Industrial Artists and Designers
MSM Meritorious Service Medal
MSST Member of the Society of Surveying Technicians
MTB Motor Torpedo Boat
MTG Member of the Translators' Guild
MTh Master of Theology
MTPI Member, Town Planning Institute
MTTA Machine Tool Trades Association
MusB Bachelor of Music
MusD Doctor of Music (Cambridge and Durham)
MusM Master of Music
MV Motor Vessel
Mvmnt Movement
MVO Member, Royal Victorian Order
MW Master of Wine
MWB Metropolitan Water Board
MWeldI Member, Welding Institute
MY Motor Yacht

N

N Nationalist; North
n nephew
NA Naval Attaché
NAAFI Navy, Army and Air Force Institutes
NABC National Association of Boys' Clubs
NAC National Agriculture Centre
NADFAS National Association of Decorative and Fine Arts Societies
NAG Northern Army Group
NAHT National Association of Head Teachers
NALGO National and Local Government Officers' Association
NAO National Audit Office
NAPM National Association of Paper Merchants
Nat National
Nat Lib National Liberal
NATCS National Air Traffic Control Services
NATFHE National Association of Teachers in Further and Higher Education
NATO North Atlantic Treaty Organisation
NBL National Book League
NBPI National Board for Prices and Incomes
NC Nautical College
NCA National Certificate of Agriculture
NCB National Coal Board
NCCI National Committee for Commonwealth Immigrants
NCCL National Council for Civil Liberties
NCLC National Council of Labour Colleges
NCO Non-commissioned officer
NCVO National Council for Voluntary Organisation
NDA National Diploma in Agriculture
NDC National Defence College
NDD National Diploma in Dairying; National Diploma in Design
NEAC New English Art Club
NEAF Near East Air Force
NEC National Executive Committee
NEDC National Economic Development Council
NEDO National Economic Development Office
NERC Natural Environment Research Council
NFL National Football League
NFS National Fire Service
NFU National Farmers' Union
NFWI National Federation of Women's Institutes
NGW Nice Glass of Water
NHS National Health Service
NI Northern Ireland
NICS Northern Ireland Civil Service
NID Naval Intelligence Department
NIESR National Institute of Economic and Social Research
NILP Northern Ireland Labour Party
NJ New Jersey (USA)
NLF National Liberal Federation
N'mberland Northumberland
NMCU National Metrological Coordinating Unit Committee
NP Notary Public
NRA National Rifle Association
NRDC National Research Development Corporation
ns Graduate of the Royal Naval Staff College, Greenwich
NS Nova Scotia
NSocIs Member Societé des Ingenieurs et Scientifiques de France
NSW New South Wales
NT National Theatre
NTDA National Trade Development Association
NUGMW National Union of General and Municipal Workers
NUI National University of Ireland
NUJ National Union of Journalists
NUM National Union of Mineworkers
NUPE National Union of Public Employees
NUR National Union of Railwaymen
NUS National Union of Students
NUT National Union of Teachers
NWFP North West Frontier Province
NY New York
NYBG New York Botanical Garden
NYC New York City
NZ New Zealand
NZEF New Zealand Expeditionary Force

O

o only
O & O Oriental and Occidental Steamship Co
OA Officier d'Académie
OB Order of Barbados
OBE Officer of the Order of the British Empire
OC Officer Commanding; Officer of the Order of Canada
OCF Officiating Chaplain to the Forces
OCS Officer Cadet School
OCTU Officer Cadet Training Unit
ODA Overseas Development Administration
ODI Overseas Development Institute
ODM Ministry of Overseas Development
OECD Organisation for Economic Co-operation and Development
OEEC Organisation for European Economic Co-operation
OER Officers' Emergency Reserve
Offr Officer
OFMCap Order of Friars Minor Capuchin (Franciscan)
OFS Orange Free State
OFT Office of Fair Trading
OIC Officer in Charge
OJ Order of Jamaica
OM Order of Merit

O & M Organisation and Method
OMC Oxford Military College
ON Order of the Nation (Jamaica)
Oppn Opposition
Ops Operations
OR Order of Roraima (Guyana)
Orch Orchestra
Orgn Organisation
OSB Order of St Benedict
OSNC Orient Steam Navigation Company
OSRD Office of Scientific Research and Development
OStJ Officer of the Order of St John of Jerusalem
OTC Officers' Training Corps
OUBC Oxford University Boat Club
OUDS Oxford University Dramatic Society
OUP Oxford University Press

P

pa per annum
Pa Pennsylvania (USA)
PA Personal Assistant
pac Passed final exam of advanced class Military College of Science
Paiforce Palestine and Iraq Force
PAO Prince Albert's Own
Parl Parliament
Parly Parliamentary
PBWS President, British Watercolour Society
PC Privy Councillor; Peace Commissioner (Ireland)
PCC Parochial Church Council
PDSA People's Dispensary for Sick Animals
PDTC Professional Dancers' Teaching College
PE Procurement Executive
PEI Prince Edward Island
PEN Poets, Playwrights, Editors, Essayists, Novelists Club
PEng Registered Professional Engineer (Canada)
PEP Political and Economic Planning
Perm Permanent
PGA Professional Golf Association
PGCE Post Graduate Certificate of Education
PHAB Physically Handicapped and Able Bodied
PhD Doctor of Philosophy
PhL Licentiate of Philosophy
PID Political Intelligence Department
PIRA Paper Industries Research Association
PLA Port of London Authority
PLC, plc Public Limited Company
Plen Plenipotentiary
PLP Parliamentary Labour Party
PM Prime Minister
PMG Postmaster-General
PMN Pangilma Mangku Negara (Malaysia)
PMO Principal Medical Officer
Pmr Paymaster
PMRAFNS Princess Mary's Royal Air Force Nursing Service
PNEU Parents' National Educational Union
PNG Papua New Guinea
PO Pilot Officer; Post Office
POD Personnel Operations Department
POEU Post Office Engineering Union
Poly Polytechnic
P & OSNCo Peninsular and Oriental Steam Navigation Company
post grad post graduate
POUNC Post Office Users' National Council
POW Prisoner of War
PPE Philosophy, Politics and Economics (Oxford University)
PPRA Past President of the Royal Academy
PPS Parliamentary Private Secretary
PR Public Relations
PRA President of the Royal Academy
PRE President of the Royal Society of Painters, Etchers and Engravers
Preb Prebendary
Prep Preparatory
Pres President
prev previously
Princ Principal
PRO Public Relations Officer; Public Records Office
Prodn Production
Prodr Producer
Prods Products
Prof Professor
prog/s programme/s
Prov Provost; Provincial
PRS President of Royal Society
psa Graduate of RAF Staff College
PSA President of the Society of Antiquaries; Property Services Agency
psc Staff College Graduate
PSD Petty Session Division
psm Certificate of the Royal Military School of Music
PSM President of the Society of Miniaturists
PSNC Pacific Steam Navigation Society
PSO Principal Staff Officer
pt part
PT Physical Training
PTE Passenger Transport Executive
ptnr partner
pt/t part time
Pty Proprietary; Party
Pub Public
Pubns Publications
PWD Public Works Department
PWO Prince of Wales's Own

Q

QAIMNS Queen Alexandra's Imperial Military Nursing Service
QALAS Qualified Associate of Land Agents' Society
QARANC Queen Alexandra's Royal Army Nursing Corps
QC Queen's Counsel
QFSM Queen's Fire Service Medal for Distinguished Service
QGM Queens Gallantry Medal
QHC Honorary Chaplain to The Queen
QHDS Honorary Dental Surgeon to The Queen
QHNS Honorary Nursing Sister to The Queen
QHP Honorary Physician to The Queen
QHS Honorary Surgeon to The Queen
Qld Queensland
QMAAC Queen Mary's Army Auxiliary Corps
QMC Queen Mary College (London)
QMG Quartermaster-General
QO Qualified Officer
QOH Queen's Own Hussars
QPM Queen's Police Medal
qqv Qua Vide (which see-plural)
QRIH Queen's Royal Irish Hussars
QS Quarter Sessions
QSM Queen's Service Medal (NZ)
QSO Queen's Service Order (NZ)
qv Quod Vide (which see)

R

(R) Reserve
R & A Royal and Ancient (St Andrews) Club
R & D Research and Development
R of O Reserve of Officers
RA Royal Artillery; Royal Academician
RAAF Royal Australian Air Force
RAAMC Royal Australian Army Medical Corps
RAC Royal Armoured Corps; Royal Automobile Club; Royal Agricultural College
RACGP Royal Australian College of General Practitioners
RACP Royal Australasian College of Physicians
RACS Royal Australasian College of Surgeons
RADA Royal Academy of Dramatic Art
RADC Royal Army Dental Corps
RAE Royal Australian Engineers; Royal Aircraft Establishment
RAEC Royal Army Educational Corps
RAeS Royal Aeronautical Society
RAF Royal Air Force
RAFA Royal Air Force Association
RAFO Reserve of Air Force Officers
RAFRO Royal Air Force Reserve of Officers
RAFVR Royal Air Force Volunteer Reserve
RAI Royal Anthropological Institute
RAIA Royal Australian Institute of Architects
RAIC Royal Architectural Institute of Canada
RAM (member of) Royal Academy of Music
RAMC Royal Army Medical Corps
RAN Royal Australian Navy
RANR Royal Australian Naval Reserve
RANVR Royal Australian Naval Volunteer Reserve
RAOC Royal Army Ordnance Corps

RAPC Royal Army Pay Corps
RARO Regular Army Reserve of Officers
RAS Royal Agricultural Society; Royal Astronomical Society; Royal Asiatic Society
RASC Royal Army Service Corps (now RCT)
RASE Royal Agricultural Society of England
RAuxAF Royal Auxiliary Air Force
RAVC Royal Army Veterinary Corps
RB Rifle Brigade
RBA Royal Society of British Artists
RBC Royal British Colonial Society of Artists
RBK & C Royal Borough of Kensington and Chelsea
RBS Royal Society of British Sculptors
RC Roman Catholic
RCA Royal College of Art
RCAC Royal Canadian Armoured Corps
RCAF Royal Canadian Air Force
RCAMC Royal Canadian Army Medical Corps
RCDS Royal College of Defence Studies
RCGP Royal College of General Practitioners
RCHA Royal Canadian Horse Artillery
RCM Royal College of Music
RCN Royal Canadian Navy
RCNC Royal Corps of Naval Constructors
RCNR Royal Canadian Naval Reserve
RCNVR Royal Canadian Naval Volunteer Reserve
RCO Royal College of Organists
RCOG Royal College of Obstetricians and Gynaecologists
RCP Royal College of Physicians, London
RCPath Royal College of Pathologists
RCPE(d) Royal College of Physicians, Edinburgh
RCPSGlas Royal College of Physicians and Surgeons, Glasgow
RCPI Royal College of Physicians in Ireland
RCPsych Royal College of Psychiatrists
RCR Royal College of Radiologists
RCS Royal College of Surgeons of England; Royal Corps of Signals; Royal College of Science
RCSE(d) Royal College of Surgeons of Edinburgh
RCSI Royal College of Surgeons in Ireland
RCT Royal Corps of Transport
RCVS Royal College of Veterinary Surgeons
Rd Road
RD Royal Naval Reserve Officers' Decoration; Rural Dean
RDA Royal Defence Academy
RDC Rural District Council
RDF Royal Dublin Fusiliers
RDI Royal Designer for Industry (RSA)
RE Royal Engineers; Fellow, Royal Society of Painter-Etchers and Engravers
Rear-Adm Rear-Admiral
Rec Recorder
Reg Regular
Regnl Regional
Regt Regiment
Regtl Regimental
Rels Relations
REME Royal Electrical and Mechanical Engineers
REngDes Registered Engineering Designer
Rep Representative
Repub Republic(an)
RERO Royal Engineers Reserve of Officers
Res Reserve; Research; Resident
RES Royal Empire Soc (Now Royal Commonwealth Soc)
ret retired
Rev Reverend
RFA Royal Field Artillery
RFC Royal Flying Corps; Rugby Football Club
RFU Rugby Football Union
RGA Royal Garrison Artillery
RGI Royal Glasgow Institute of Fine Arts
RGS Royal Geographic Society
RHA Royal Horse Artillery; Royal Hibernian Academy; Regional Health Authority
RHB Regional Hospital Board
RHF Royal Highland Fusiliers
RHG Royal Horse Guards
RHR Royal Highland Regiment
RHS Royal Horticultural Society
RI Royal Institute of Painters in Water Colours; Rhode Island
RIAI Royal Institute of Architects of Ireland
RIAS Royal Incorporation of Architects in Scotland
RIASC Royal Indian Army Service Corps
RIBA Royal Institute of British Architects
RIC Royal Irish Constabulary
RICS Royal Institute of Chartered Surveyors
RIF Royal Irish Fusiliers
RIIA Royal Institute of International Affairs
RIM Royal Indian Marine
RIN Royal Indian Navy
RINA Royal Institute of Naval Architects
RINVR Royal Indian Navy Volunteer Reserve
RIOP Royal Institute of Oil Painters
RIPA Royal Institute of Public Administration
RIPH & H Royal Institute of Public Health and Hygiene
RIR Royal Irish Rifles
RL Retired List
RLSS Royal Life Saving Society
Rlwy Railway
RM Royal Marines
RMA Royal Military Academy; Royal Marine Artillery
RMC Royal Military College, Sandhurst (now Royal Military Academy)
RMCS Royal Military College of Science
RMFVR Royal Marine Forces Volunteer Reserve
RMLI Royal Marine Light Infantry
RMO Resident Medical Officer
RMP Royal Military Police
RMR Royal Marine Reserve
RMS Royal Meterological Society
RN Royal Navy
RNAS Royal Naval Air Service
RNC Royal Nautical College; Royal Naval College
RNCM (Member of) Royal Northern College of Music
RND Royal Naval Division
RNEC Royal Naval Engineering College
RNIB Royal National Institute for the Blind
RNID Royal National Institute for the Deaf
RNLI Royal National Lifeboat Institution
RNR Royal Naval Reserve
RNSA Royal Naval Sailing Association
RNSD Royal Naval Store Depot
RNVR Royal Naval Volunteer Reserve
RNVSR Royal Naval Volunteer Supplementary Reserve
RNZADC Royal New Zealand Army Dental Corps
RNZAF Royal New Zealand Air Force
RNZN Royal New Zealand Navy
RNZNVR Royal New Zealand Naval Volunteer Reserve
ROC Royal Observer Corps
ROI Royal Institute of Painters in Oils
ROSPA Royal Society for the Prevention of Accidents
R of O Reserve of Officers
RP Member of the Royal Society of Portrait Painters
RPC Royal Pioneer Corps
RPO Royal Philharmonic Orchestra
RPS Royal Photographic Society
RR Royal Regiment
RRAF Royal Rhodesian Air Force
RRC Royal Red Cross
RRF Royal Regiment of Fusiliers
RSA Royal Scottish Academician; Royal Society of Arts
RSAA Royal Society for Asian Affairs
RSAC Royal Scottish Automobile Club
RSAMD Royal Scottish Academy of Music and Drama (Diploma of)
RSBA Royal Society of British Artists
RSC Royal Shakespeare Co; Royal Society of Canada
RSE Royal Society of Edinburgh
RSF Royal Scots Fusiliers
RSL Royal Society of Literature; Returned Services League of Australia
RSM Royal Society of Medicine; Regimental Sergeant Major
RSMA Royal Society of Marine Artists
RSME Royal School of Military Engineers
RSPB Royal Society for the Protection of Birds
RSPCA Royal Society for the Prevention of Cruelty to Animals
RSPP Royal Society of Portrait Painters
RSRE Royal Signals and Radar Establishment
RSS Royal Statistical Society
RSSPCC Royal Scottish Society for the Prevention of Cruelty to Children
RSW Royal Scottish Water Colours Society
Rt Hon Right Honourable
Rt Rev Right Reverend
RTC Royal Tank Corps
RTO Railway Transport Officer
RTPI Royal Town Planning Institute
RTR Royal Tank Regiment
RTS Royal TV Society
RUC Royal Ulster Constabulary

RUFC Rugby Union Football Club
RUI Royal University of Ireland
RUKBA Royal United Kingdom Beneficent Association
RUR Royal Ulster Regiment
RUSI Royal United Services Institute
RVC Royal Veterinary College
RVO Regional Veterinary Officer
RWA Member, Royal West of England Academy
RWAFF Royal West African Frontier Force
RWAR Royal West African Regiment
RWF Royal Welch Fusiliers
RWS Member, Royal Society of Painters in Water Colours
RYA Royal Yachting Association
RYS Royal Yacht Squadron
RZS Royal Zoological Society

S

s son
S South; Scotland/Scottish (Peerages)
SA South Africa; South Australia; Sociéte Anonyme
SAAF South African Air Force
sac Qualified at Small Arms Technical Long Course
SAC Senior Aircraftsman
SACEUR Supreme Allied Commander Europe
SACLANT Supreme Allied Commander Atlantic
SACSEA Supreme Allied Commander, S E Asia
SADG Societé des Architectes Diplomés par le Gouvernement
Salop (now) Shropshire
SAS Special Air Service
Sask Saskatchewan
SASO Senior Air Staff Officer
SATRO Science & Technology Regional Organisation
SBAC Society of British Aircraft Constructors, now Society of British Aerospace Companies
SBNO Senior British Naval Officer
SBStJ Serving Brother of the Order of St John of Jerusalem
SC Sailing Club
ScD Doctor of Science (Cambridge and Dublin)
SCF Senior Chaplain to the Forces
SCGB Ski Club of Great Britain
Sch School
Sci Science
SCI Society of Chemical Engineering
SCL Student in Civil Law
SCM State Certified Midwife
Scot Scottish; Scotland
SCUA Scottish Conservative Unionist Association
SDLP Social Democratic and Labour Party
SEAC South East Asia Command
SEATAG South East Asia Trade Advisory Group
Sec Secretary
Secdy Secondary
Sec-Gen Secretary-General
Sen Senator
SEN State Enrolled Nurse
sep separated
SERC Science and Engineering Research Council
SERT Society of Electronic and Radio Technicians
Serv Service
SFInstE Senior Fellow Institute of Energy
SFTA Society of Film and Television Arts
SG Solicitor-General
SGM Sea Gallantry Medal
Sgt Sergeant
SHA Secondary Heads Association
SHAEF Supreme Headquarters, Allied Expeditionary Force
SHAPE Supreme Headquarters, Allied Powers Europe
SHHD Scottish Home and Health Department
SIAD Society of Industrial Artists and Designers
sis sister
SJ Society of Jesus (Jesuits)
SLD Social and Liberal Democrats
SLDP Social, Liberal and Democratic Party
slr solicitor
SM Service Medal of the Order of Canada; Master of Science (USA); Member, Society of Miniaturists
SME School of Military Engineering
SMMT Society of Motor Manufacturers and Traders
SMN Seri Maharaja Mangku Negara (Malaysia)
SMO Senior Medical Officer; Sovereign Military Order
SMOM Sovereign Military Order of Malta
SNO Senior Naval Officer
SNP Scottish Nationalist Party
SNTS Society for New Testament Studies
SO Scottish Office; Staff Officer
SOAS School of Oriental and African Studies
Soc Society
SOE Special Operations Executive
SOGAT Society of Graphical and Allied Trades
Som Somerset
SOTS Society for Old Testament Studies
Sov Sovereign
sp sine prole (without issue)
Sp Spain; Spanish
SPCK Society for Promoting Christian Knowledge
SPG Society for the Propagation of the Gospel
SPNM Society for the Promotion of New Music
SPSO Senior Personnel Staff Officer
SPTL Society of Public Teaching of Law
Sq Square
Sqdn Squadron
Sqdn Ldr Squadron Leader
sr senior
SR Special Reserve; Southern Railway; Southern Region
SRC Science Research Council
SRHE Society for Research in Higher Education
SRN State Registered Nurse
SRO Supplementary Reserve of Officers
SSA Society of Scottish Artists
SSAFA Soldiers', Sailors', and Airmen's Families' Association
SSC Solicitor, Supreme Court (Scotland)
SSEES School of Slavonic and East European Studies
SSO Senior Supply Officer
SSRC Social Science Research Council
SSStJ Serving Sister of the Order of St John of Jerusalem
STA Society of Technical Analysts
STC Senior Training Corps
STD Doctor of Sacred Theology
STh Scholar in Theology
STL Licenciate of Sacred Theology
STM Master of Sacred Theology
STSO Senior Technical Staff Officer
Subalt Subaltern
Subs Submarines (RN)
Subsid Subsidiary
Subst Substitute
suc succeeded
Sup Supérieure
Supp Supplementary
Supt Superintendent
Surgn Surgeon
Survg Surviving
SWB South Wales Borderers
SWET Society of West End Theatres

T

TA Territorial Army
TA & VR Territorial and Army Volunteer Reserve
TA & VRA Territorial and Army Volunteer Reserve Association
TAA Territorial Army Association; Tropical Agriculture Association
TAF Tactical Air Force
T&AFA Territorial and Auxiliary Forces Association
TANS Territorial Army Nursing Service
TARO Territorial Army Reserve of Officers
Tas Tasmania
Tbnl Tribunal
TC Order of Trinity Cross (Trinidad and Tobago)
TCCB Test and County Cricket Board
TD Territorial Officers' Decoration; Teachta Dala (member of the Dail Parliament of Eire)
Tech Technical
Technol Technology; Technological
TEM Territorial Efficiency Medal
Temp Temporary
TES Times Educational Supplement
TF Territorial Force
TGWU Transport and General Workers' Union
Theol Theological
ThM Master of Theology

TLS Times Literary Supplement
TMA Theatre Managers Association
Tport Transport
Transfd Transferred
TRE Telecommunications Research Establishment
Treasy Treasury
Tres Treasurer
Trg Training
TRH Their Royal Highnesses
Trin Trinity College
Tst Trust
Tstee Trustee
TUC Trades Union Congress
TV Television

U

U Unionist
UAR United Arab Republic
UC University College
UCCA Universities Central Council on Admissions
UCH University College Hospital
UCL University College London
UCLA University of California at Los Angeles
UCNW University College of North Wales
UCS University College School
UCW University College of Wales
UDC Urban District Council
UDF Union Defence Force; Ulster Defence Force
UDR Ulster Defence Regiment
UDS United Drapery Stores
UDUP Ulster Democratic Unionist Party
UEA University of East Anglia
UFO Unidentified Flying Object
UGC University Grants Committee
UHS University High School
UK United Kingdom
UKAEA United Kingdom Atomic Energy Authority
UKLF United Kingdom Land Forces
UMDS United Medical and Dental Schools
UMIST University of Manchester Institute of Science and Technology
UN United Nations
UNA United Nations Association
unc uncle
UNCTAD United Nations Commission for Trade and Development
UNESCO United Nations Educational, Scientific and Cultural Organisation
UNFAO United Nations Food and Agricultural Organisation
UNICE Union des Industries de la Communauté Européenne
UNICEF United Nations International Children's Emergency Fund
UNIDROIT Institut International pour l'Unification du Droit Privé
Univ University
UNO United Nations Organisation
UNRRA United Nations Relief and Rehabilitation Administration
UP Uttar Pradesh; United Provinces; United Presbyterian
UPNI Unionist Party of Northern Ireland
US United States
USA United States of America
USAF United States Air Force
USDAW Union of Shop, Distributive and Allied Workers
USMC United States Military College
USN United States Navy
USNR United States Naval Reserve
USSR Union of Soviet Socialist Republics
UTC University Training Corps

V

v versus (against)
V & A Victoria and Albert (Museum)
VA Lady of the Order of Victoria and Albert
Va Virginia
VAD Voluntary Aid Detachment
VAT Value Added Tax
VBF Veterinary Benevolent Fund
VC Victoria Cross
VCAS Vice-Chief of the Air Staff
VCC Vintage Car Club
VD Volunteer Officers' Decoration (now VRD)
VDC Volunteer Defence Corps
Ven Venerable
Very Rev Very Reverend
Vet Veterinary
Visc Viscount
VM Victory Medal
VMH Victoria Medal of Honour (Royal Horticultural Society)
VO Veterinary Officer
Vol Volunteer
VRD Volunteer Reserve Officers' Decoration
VSCC Vintage Sports Car Club
VSO Voluntary Service Overseas

W

W West
w wife
WA Western Australia
WAAF Women's Auxiliary Air Force (now WRAF)
WEA Worker's Educational Association
WFN World Fund for Nature, see World Wildlife Fund
WFTU World Federation of Trade Unions
WHO World Health Organisation
WI West Indies
wid widow
WIPO World Intellectual Property Organisation
Wm William
WNO Welsh National Opera
WNSM Welsh National School of Medicine
WO War Office
WR West Riding
WRAC Women's Royal Army Corps
WRAF Women's Royal Air Force
WRNR Women's Royal Naval Reserve
WRNS Women's Royal Naval Service
WRVS Women's Royal Voluntary Service (formerly WVS)
WS Writer to the Signet
WVS Women's Voluntary Service
WWI First World War
WWII Second World War
WWF World Wildlife Fund

Y

Yeo Yeomanry
YC Yacht Club
YHA Youth Hostels' Association
YMCA Young Men's Christian Association
yr younger
yst youngest
YWCA Young Women's Christian Association

AALDERS, Michael Laurence; s of Prof Laurence Aalders (d 1980), and Kathleen, *née* O'Callaghan; *b* 25 Sept 1944; *Educ* St Ignatius Sch London; *m* 24 Sept 1966, Evelyn Juliet Victoria, da of Pierino Appi (d 1988); 1 s (Dominic Michael b 1972), 1 da (Siobhan Evelyn b 1969); *Career* co fndr Aalders & Marchant Advertising Ltd 1968-82, co fndr and dir The Travel Business Ltd 1978; co fndr and chm: The Grayling Co Ltd (PR) 1981, Westminster Strategy Ltd; ptnr Badger Antiques; *Recreations* sailing, skiing; *Clubs* Savile; *Style*— Michael Aalders, Esq; 86 Grange Rd, London W5 (☎ 01 579 5072); 4 Bedford Square, London WC1 (☎ 01 255 1100, car tel 0860 310 369)

AARONOVITCH, David Morris; s of Dr Sam Aaronovitch, of 100 Chetwynd Road, London NW5, and Lavender Geraldine Janet, *née* Walmsley; *b* 8 July 1954; *Educ* William Ellis Sch London, Balliol Coll Oxford, Univ of Manchester (BA); *Career* prodr Weekend World LWT 1984-87 (researcher 1982-84), ed On The Record BBC 1988-; pres Nat Union of Students 1980-82; *Recreations* cinema (particularly Soviet film), literature; *Style*— David Aaronovitch, Esq; 29 Countess Rd, London NW5 2XH (☎ 01 485 6515); BBC Studios, Lime Grove, London W12 (☎ 01 576 7927)

AARONS, John Iulius Emile; s of Jacob Henry Aarons (d 1945), of Hampstead, and Esther, *née* Cohen (d 1975); *b* 12 August 1936; *Educ* Kent Coll Canterbury, St John's Coll Cambridge (BA, MA), Sch of Mil Survey Newbury; *m* 14 Jan 1962, Maureen (Mo) Finley; 1s (Matthew David Edward b Aug 1969), 3 da (Emma Julia b June 1963, Sarah Annabel b Jan 1965, Olivia Rachel b Sept 1967); *Career* surveyor Directorate of Overseas Surveys 1959-63, systems analyst London Boroughs Organs and Methods Ctee 1963-65, conslt CEIR 1965-67, data processing mangr Wates Ltd 1967-71, systems analyst The Stock Exchange 1971, dir Inter Market Projects 1987; parent govr Montpelier Middle Sch 1975-80; *Books* The Useless Land (with Claudio Vita Finzi); *Recreations* squash, sculling, etymology; *Style*— John Aarons, Esq; 8 Winscombe Cres, London W5 1AZ (☎ 01 997 7961); The Stock Exchange, Throgmorton St, London EC2N 1HP (☎ 01 588 2355)

AARONSON, Graham Raphael; QC (1982); s of Jack Aaronson (d 1973), of London, and Dora, *née* Franks; *b* 31 Dec 1944; *Educ* City of London Sch, Trinity Hall Cambridge (MA); *m* 12 Sept 1967, Linda Esther, da of Maj William Smith, of Oxford; 2 s (Oran b 1968, Avi b 1974), 1 da (Orit b 1970); *Career* barr Middle Temple 1966; md Worldwide Plastics Development Ltd 1973-77; fndr Standford Grange Rehabilitation Centre for Ex- Offenders; dir Tax Law Reforms Israel 1986-; *Recreations* photography; *Style*— Graham Aaronson, Esq, QC; Queen Elizabeth Building, Temple, London EC4Y 9BS (☎ 01 353 0551, fax 01 353 1927, telex 8951414)

AARONSON, (Edward) John; *b* 16 August 1918; *m* ; 2 s (Michael John, Robin Hugh); *Career* dir: Wanborough Studios Ltd, Camlab Ltd; chm: Equity Recoveries Ltd, Ws F C Bonhoem & Sons Ltd, Montpelier Properties Ltd, Sharepar Ltd, The Reject Shop Ltd; FCA, FInstD; *Recreations* family, music, literature, economic and financial affairs, swimming; *Clubs* Reform, IOD; *Style*— Jack Aaronson, Esq; c/o Equities Recoveries Ltd, Bushey House, Upper Wanborough, nr Swindon, Wilts SN4 0BZ

AARVOLD, His Hon Sir Carl Douglas; OBE (1945), TD (1950), DL (Surrey 1973); s of late Ole Peter Aarvold, and late J M Aarvold, of Highnam, West Hartlepool; *b* 7 June 1907; *Educ* Durham Sch, Emmanuel Coll Cambridge; *m* 1934, Noeline Etrenne, da of Arthur James Hill (d 1935), of Denton Park, Yorks, and gda of Sir James Hill, 1 Bt (d 1935); 3 s; *Career* barr Inner Temple 1932, N Eastern Circuit, rec of Pontefract 1951-54, judge of the Mayor's and City of London Ct 1954-59, common Sgt City of London 1959-64; chm: Inner London Probations Ctee 1965-75, City of London QS, Home Sec's Advsy Bd on Restricted Patients 1978-, RAC 1978-81, statutory ctee Pharmaceutical Soc of GB 1981-86; pres: Central Cncl of Probation Ctees 1968-75; pres Lawn Tennis Assoc 1962 -81, Hon LLD Dalhousie 1962, Hon DLC Durham 1965, hon fell Cambridge; kt 1968; *Style*— His Hon Sir Carl Aarvold, OBE, TD, DL; The Coach House, Crabtree Lane, Westhumble, Dorking, Surrey RH5 6BQ (☎ 0306 882 771)

ABBADO, Claudio; *b* 26 June 1933; *Educ* Conservatorio G Verdi Milan, Musical Acad Vienna; 2 s, 1 da; *Career* musical dir: La Scala Milan 1968-86, London Symphony Orch 1979-86, Euro Community Youth Orch 1977-, GMJO, Chicago Symphony; princ conductor Vienna Philharmonic 1971-, music dir Vienna State Opera 1986; GMD town of Vienna 1987; *Style*— Claudio Abbado, Esq; Staatsoper, A-1010 Vienna, Austria

ABBEY, Henry William; s of John George Abbey (d 1936); *b* 9 April 1925; *Educ* Dulwich; *m* 1950, Kathleen, da of Thomas Adair (d 1978); 5 children; *Career* served RN Aust and Far East as telegraphist; chartered secretary; chm Joint Promotions 1972, dep md William Hill Orgn 1984- (asst md 1980-84); dir: Riley plc 1970-, Champion Individual Odds Ltd, William Hill Leisure Ltd, Joint Promotions Ltd, Dale Martin Promotions Ltd and various other sporting, leisure and entertainment related cos; member of Lloyds, ACIS; *Recreations* bridge, golf, literature, theatre; *Style*— Henry Abbey, Esq; 111Heath Drive, Sutton, Surrey (☎ 01 642 2928); William Hill Organization; 19 Valentine Place, London SE1 8QW

ABBOTT, Sir Albert Francis; CBE (1974); s of late Albert Victor Abbott, and Diana Abbott; *b* 10 Dec 1913; *Educ* Mt Martin Secdy Sch Qld; *m* 1941, Gwendoline Joyce, *née* Maclean; 2 s, 4 da; *Career* served RAAF 1942-46; cane farmer; pres sub-branch Mackay RSL 1960-65 (Mackay District pres 1965-74, Qld State pres 1974-); Mayor City of Mackay Qld 1970; memb Picture Theatre and Films Cmmn 1976, Local Govt Grants Cmmn 1977; pres: Qld Local Govt Assoc 1983, Aust Council Local Govt Assoc 1987; kt 1981; *Style*— Sir Albert Abbott, CBE; 2 Tudor Court, Mackay, Qld 4740, Australia

ABBOTT, Hon Anthony C; PC (Canada); s of Hon Douglas Charles Abbott, PC, QC (d 1987), and his 1 w, Mary Winifred, *née* Chisholm (d 1980); *b* 26 Nov 1930; *Educ* Bishop's Univ Lennoxville (BA), Osgoode Hall Toronto (LLB); *m* 1955, Naomi Siddall Smith; 3 s; *Career* lawyer; Canadian Federal MP (Lib) 1974-79, min of Consumer & Corporate Affairs, min of National Revenue; dir: Debrett's Business History Research Ltd, JDE Consulting Ltd, Pickfoods Ltd; business conslt 1979-; *Style*— The Hon Tony Abbott, PC; 54 Hyde Street, Winchester, Hants SO23 7DY

ABBOTT, Derek Francis; s of Jesse Abbott, of Effingham, Surrey, and Rosetta Daisy Abbott (d 1975); *b* 12 August 1935; *Educ* Brockley County GS; *m* 1; 2 s, 2 da; m 2, 1982, Ruth Janet; *Career* chief exec: Mace Mktg Services Ltd Gp 1983-, Mace-Wavy Line Mktg Services; chm Wavy Line Grocers Ltd, dir Booker Belmont Hldgs; *Recreations* golf; *Clubs* Gatton Manor Golf (Surrey); *Style*— Derek Abbott, Esq; Beech Lawns, Outdowns, Effingham, Surrey; Marketing Services Ltd, 276 High St, Langley, Slough SL3 8HD (☎ 0753 43 840)

ABBOTT, Maj John (Lancelot) Stutely; s of Rev Reginald Francis Stutely Abbott (d 1956), of Sussex, and Minnie Reffell (d 1960); *b* 11 May 1913; *m* 1, 19 June 1937, Araminta Barbara (d 1980), da of Henry Langhorne (d 1970), of Sussex; 1 s (Timothy John Stutely b 1938); m 2, 18 Oct 1985, Olwen Sandra; *Career* RE UK and NW Europe (despatches 1944), ret Maj 1947; practising civil engr 1939, dir Trendells Ltd (family firm of printers) 1981; *Recreations* sailing, coursing, breeding wild fowl; *Style*— Maj Lancelot Abbott; Masons, Old Way, Ilminster, Somerset TA19 9EU (☎ 0460 54123)

ABBOTT, John William; s of William Charles Abbott, of Broxbourn, Herts, and Gladys Louise, *née* Baker; *b* 15 April 1943; *Educ* SW Ham Tech Sch; *m* 27 March 1965, Shelia, da of Francis Stephen Stanbrook; 1 s (Steven John b 18 Feb 1969), 1 da (Tina Dawn b 10 Feb 1966); *Career* Freedom City of London 1979, Liveryman Worshipful Co of Builders Merchants; memb Inst Builders Merchants; *Recreations* golf; *Clubs* Romford GC; *Style*— John Abbott, Esq; 85 Links Ave, Gidea Park, Romford, Essex RM2 6NH (☎ 0708 751 02); 1-7 Whalebone Lane South, Dagenham, Essex RM8 1AH (☎ 01 595 2128, fax 01 595 1658)

ABBOTT, Reginald James; s of James Joseph Abbott (d 1907), of Norbury, London, and Adeline Mary, *née* Kipling (d 1932); *b* 2 June 1902; *Educ* London Univ; *m* 16 June 1928, Margaret Ivy (d 1975), da of Ernest Sebire (d 1930), of Newmarket, Melbourne, Aust; 1 s (Geoffrey James Kipling b 20 June 1934); *Career* Marconi Int Marine Radio Communications Co, seconded Admty 1920-24; concerned with commercial element radio-TV experiments with Baird 1924-32, Aust 1933, commercial devpt TV 1934-60, res and experiment serv LP records MI (ix) 1940-44, govt business Europe 1950-60, admin sec Nat Playing Fields Assoc London 1962-73, chm educn ctee Nat Cncl Social Serv 1968-73, vice chm co supplying charities 1963-89; cncl memb and hon advsy offr local and co sports assocs; Liveryman Worshipful Co Drapers 1934; *Recreations* travel; *Style*— Reginald Abbott, Esq; Chillon, 40 Tongdean Rd, Hove BN3 6QE

ABBOTT, Roderick Evelyn; s of Stuart Evelyn Abbott, OBE, of Cambridge, and Jocelyn, *née* Niemeyer; *b* 16 April 1938; *Educ* Rugby, Merton Coll Oxford (BA); *m* 22 June 1963, Elizabeth, da of Dr Neil McLean; 3 da (Nicola b 1964, Mary b 1966, Melissa b 1972); *Career* Nat Serv 1956-58 RCS (2 Lt 1957), TA Oxford Univ 1958-62 (Lt 1959); Bd of Trade 1962-71, FCO 1971-73; EEC Cmmn: DG external relations 1973-, dep head of mission Geneva 1975-79, dir DG external relations 1982-; sec SE Econ Planning Cncl 1966-68; *Style*— Roderick Abbott, Esq; EEC Commission, Rue De La Loi 200, 1049 Brussels, Belgium

ABBOTT, Ronald William; CVO (1989) CBE (1979); s of Edgar Abbott (d 1956); *b* 18 Jan 1917; *Educ* St Olaves and St Saviour's GS; *m* 1, 1948, Hilda Mary (d 1972), da of William George Clarke (d 1918); 2 da (Mary Elaine b 1949, Christine Margaret b 1956); m 2, 1973, Barbara Constance, da of Gilbert Hugh Clough (d 1961); *Career* conslt actuary; sr ptnr of Bacon & Woodrow 1972-81; memb: Inst of Actuaries 1966-74 (itm tres 1971-73), Industrial Soc 1964-84, Pensions Management Inst 1977-81 (vice-pres 1978-80); chm Occupational Pensions Bd 1982-87 (dep chm 1973-82); memb of Ct Worshipful Co Ironmongers (master 1986-87); FIA, ASA, FPHI, FRSA; *Recreations* music, theatre; *Clubs* Royal Automobile; *Style*— Ronald W Abbott, Esq; 43 Rottingdeam Place, Falmer Rd, Rottingdean, E Sussex (☎ 0273 303302) Empire House, St Martins-Le-Grand, London EC1A 4ED (☎ 01 600 2747)

ABDELA, His Hon Judge; Jack Samuel Ronald; TD (1948), QC (1966); s of Joseph Abdela (d 1953), of Manchester, and Dorothy Abdela; *b* 9 Oct 1913; *Educ* Manchester GS, Milton Sch Bulawayo, Fitzwilliam Coll Cambridge (MA); *m* 1942, Enid Hope, da of Edgar Dodd Russell (d 1950), of London; 1 s (and 1 s decd); *Career* Lt-Col, served UK, NW Europe WW II; barr Gray's Inn 1935, judge Central Criminal Court 1970-86; Liveryman Worshipful Co of Painter Stainers; *Recreations* swimming, tennis, gardening; *Clubs* Savage; *Style*— His Honour Judge Abdela, TD, QC; Tall Trees Cottage, Shipton Under Wychwood, Oxfordshire OX7 6DB (☎ 0993 831520)

ABDELA, Lesley Julia; da of Frederick Abdela (d 1985), and Henrietta, *née* Hardy (d 1959); Abdela family were shipbuilders in nineteenth century at Manchester Ship Canal (vessels for Amazon rubber trade), and Brimscombe, Stroud, Glos (for river tug boats). From the 1930s, Henrietta and Frederick Abdela built successful catering and frozen food companies; *b* 17 Nov 1945; *Educ* Glendower London, Queen Anne's Caversham, Châtelard Sch Les Avants Switzerland, Queen's Coll Harley St, Hammersmith Coll of Art, London Sch of Printing; *m* 1972 (m dis); 1 s (Nicholas b 1973); *Career* advertising exec Royds London, researcher House of Commons 1976-77, stood for Parl (Lib) in Herts East 1979, fndr all-Party 300 Gp for Women in

Politics 1980, US Leader Grant visiting Washington DC, LA, Seattle 1983, studied Third World by residence in the Gambia 1984-86; sr ptnr Eyecatcher Journalism, television and radio broadcaster on politics and travel; *Books* Women in Politics (1989); *Recreations* travel, painting, desert agriculture; *Style*— Ms Lesley Abdela; Harper's Marsh, King's Saltern, Lymington, Hampshire

ABDULRAHMAN-AL-HELAISSI; GCVO; *Style*— Abdulrahman-Al-Helaissi, GCVO; c/o Ministry of Foreign Affairs, Riyadh, Saudi Arabia

ABDY, Sir Valentine Robert Duff; 6 Bt (UK 1850), of Albyns, Essex; s of Sir Robert Abdy, 5 Bt (d 1976), and Lady Diana (d 1967), *née* Bridgeman, da of 5 Earl of Bradford; *b* 11 Sept 1937; *Educ* Eton; *m* 1971 (m dis 1982), Mathilde, da of Etienne Coche de la Ferté; 1 s (Robert); *Heir* s, Robert Etienne Eric Abdy b 22 Feb 1978; *Career* set up (with Peter Wilson) Sotheby's first office abroad in Paris and Munich; first rep Smithsonian Inst (Washington DC) in Europe 1983-; *Clubs* Jockey (Paris), The Travellers (Paris); *Style*— Sir Valentine Abdy, Bt; Newton Ferrers, Callington, Cornwall; 13 Villa Molitor, 75016 Paris, France; Clos Du Petit Bois, St Martins, Guernsey CI

ABEL, Hyman; s of Harry Abel (d 1972), and late Rosa Abel; *b* 6 Nov 1921; *Educ* Queen Elizabeth's GS Blackburn, Liverpool Univ, Leeds Univ, Manchester Univ (MEd), Birkbeck Coll Univ of London, Inst of Educn Univ of London (MSc), NW London Univ (DSc); *m* 1 Jan 1957, Dr Rhoda Anne Doreen, da of late Dr Michael J Fenton, of London; *Career* occupational and counselling pyschologist; dep head of maths Leggatts Sch Watford Herts 1969-86; chm Jewish Students' Soc, Birbeck Coll, memb Student Union Cncl, memb bd Deputies of Br Jews (Union of Jewish Students) respresenting students, hon Life memb of Liverpool Jewish Students' Soc, memb Br Psychological Soc; *Recreations* travel, attending conferences, further academic achievements; *Style*— Dr Hyman Abel; 41 Ashbourne Avenue, Temple Fortune, London NW11 0DT (☎ 01 455 9571)

ABEL, Julian David; s of David John Abel, and Heather Diana, *née* Ingram; *b* 10 April 1961; *Educ* St Dunstan's Coll Catford, LSE (BSc); *m* 15 Feb 1986, Donna Christine, da of Christopher Byrne (d 1988); 1 s (Christopher David b 1988); *Career* portfolio mangr CIN Mgmnt Ltd (Br Coal Pension Fund) 1986- (investmt analyst 1984-86); *Recreations* sailing, squash, sub-aqua diving ; *Style*— Julian Abel, Esq; CN Management Ltd, PO Box 10 Hobart House, Grosbenor Place, London SW1X 7AD, (☎ 245 6911, fax 389 2822, telex 883 770 Ginman G)

ABEL SMITH, David Francis; s of Sir Alexander Abel Smith (d 1978), of Quenington Old Rectory, Cirencester, Glos, and Elizabeth, *née* Morgan (d 1948); *b* 3 Feb 1940; *Educ* Gordonstoun; *m* 18 Nov 1982, Lucy Marie, da of Col Bryce Muir Knox, MC, TD (Lord Lt of Ayr and Arran); *Career* The Delta Gp plc 1961-82 (exec dir 1974-82); md Benjamin Priest Gp plc 1983-; memb Quenington Parish Cncl 1987-; Freeman City of London, memb Worshipful Co of Fishmongers; *Recreations* foxhunting; *Clubs* Buck's, Pratt's; *Style*— David Abel Smith, Esq; Quenington Old Rectory, Cirencester, Glos GL7 5BN (☎ 028 575 358); Benjamin Priest Gp plc, PO Box 38, Warley, W Mids B64 63W (☎ 0384 66501, fax 0384 64578)

ABEL SMITH, Lady; Henriette Alice; DCVO (1977, CVO 1964), JP (Tunbridge Wells 1955, Glos 1971); o da of Cdr Francis Charles Cadogan, RN (d 1970), and Ruth Evelyn, *neé* Howard (d 1962); *b* 6 June 1914; *m* 1, 4 Sept 1939, Sir Anthony Frederick Mark Palmer, 4 Bt (ka 1941); 1 s (Sir Mark Palmer, 5 Bt, *qv*), 1 da; m 2, 17 Feb 1953, Sir Alexander Abel Smith, KCVO, TD, JP (d 1980); 1 s, 1 da; *Career* Lady-in-Waiting to HM The Queen 1949-; *Style*— Lady Abel Smith, DCVO, JP; The Garden House, Quenington, Cirencester, Glos (☎ Coln St Aldwyns 231)

ABEL SMITH, Col Sir Henry; KCMG (1961), KCVO (1950), DSO (1945), DL (Berks 1953); s of Francis Abel Smith, DL (d 1908), of Wilford House, Notts, and Madeline St Maur (d 1951), 4 da of late Rev Henry Seymour, Rector of Holme Pierrepoint; *b* 8 Mar 1900; *Educ* Eton, RMC Sandhurst; *m* 24 Oct 1931, Lady May, *qv*, o da of Earl of Athlone, KG, GCB, GCMG, GCVO, DSO, PC (d 1957), and HRH Princess Alice, Countess of Athlone, VA, GCVO, GBE (d 1981); 1 s (Richard Abel Smith, *qv*), 2 da (Anne b 1932, Elizabeth b 1936); *Career* joined RHG 1919, Capt 1930, Maj 1934, Lt-Col 1944, Col 1946; Hon Cdre RAF; ADC to Earl of Athlone (when govr-gen and CIC S Africa) 1928-31, govr of Queensland 1958-66, administrator Australian Commonwealth 1965; KStJ 1958, Kt Order of Orange-Nassau with swords (Netherlands); Hon LLD Qld Univ; *Recreations* hunting, shooting, fishing, polo; *Clubs* Turf; *Style*— Col Sir Henry Abel Smith, KCMG, KCVO, DSO, DL; Barton Lodge, Winkfield, Windsor, Berks (☎ 0344 882632)

ABEL SMITH, Lady Mary Elisabeth; *née* Carnegie; da of late 10 Earl of Southesk; *b* 4 Mar 1899; *m* 1932, Vice Adm Sir (Edward Michael) Conolly Abel Smith, GCVO, CB, *qv*; 1 s, 1 da; *Style*— Lady Mary Abel Smith; Ashiestiel, Galashiels, Selkirkshire 089 685 214)

ABEL SMITH, Lady May Helen Emma; *née* Cambridge; o da of 1 Earl of Athlone, KG, GCB, GCMG, GCVO, DSO, PC (d 1957), and HRH Princess Alice, Countess of Athlone, VA, GCVO, GBE (d 1981); ggda of Queen Victoria and last surv gggda of King George III; *b* 23 Jan 1906; *m* 24 Oct 1931, Col Sir Henry Abel Smith, KCMG, KCVO, DSO, DL, *qv*; 1 s, 2 da; *Career* styled HSH Princess May of Teck until 1917; CStJ; *Style*— Lady May Abel Smith; Barton Lodge, Winkfield, Windsor, Berks (☎ 0344 882632)

ABEL SMITH, Ralph Mansel; o s of Thomas Abel Smith, JP (d 1983), of Woodhall Park, Watton-at-Stone, Hertford, and Alma Mary Agatha, *née* de Falbe; *b* 11 Dec 1946; *Educ* Eton; *m* 17 July 1985, Alexandra Clare Ragnhild, da of Maj Ian Stuart Rae Bruce, MC (d 1967), of Highfield, Bells Yew Green, Sussex; *Career* landowner and farmer; chm: Herts/Middx Branch CLA 1981-86, Herts Co Award Liaison Panel of Duke of Edinburghs Award Scheme 1976-81; patron of livings: Watton-at-Stone, Sacombe, Bramfield with Stapleford, Bengeo; High Sheriff Herts 1984-85; memb: E Herts Dist Cncl 1976-83, Herts CC 1985-; life govr: Haileybury, Imperial Serv Coll 1985-; *Recreations* shooting, fishing, music, classical architecture; *Clubs* Bucks, Pratt's, Turf; *Style*— Ralph Abel Smith, Esq; Woodhall Park, Watton-at-Stone, Hertford; Cambusmore Lodge, Dornoch, Sutherland

ABEL SMITH, Richard Francis; DL; s of Col Sir Henry Abel Smith, KCMG, KCVO, DSO, DL, *qv*; *b* 11 Oct 1933; *Educ* Eton, Sandhurst, RAC Cirencester; *m* 1960, Marcia, da of Maj-Gen Sir Douglas Kendrew, KCMG, CB, CBE, DSO (d 1989); 1 da (*see* Hon Hubert Beaumont); *Career* RHG (Blues): Escort Cdr and ADC to Govrs of Cyprus 1957-60, instr RMA Sandhurst 1960-63, ret; co cmmr for Scouts (Notts) 1966-75, cmd Sherwood Rangers Sqdn, Royal Yeo Regt 1967-69 (Hon Col 1979); High Sheriff Notts 1978; chm Sports Aid Fndn East Midlands 1979-; farmer; *Recreations* shooting, fishing, riding; *Clubs* Farmers', Army and Navy; *Style*— Col Richard Abel Smith, DL; Blidworth Dale, Ravenshead, Nottingham NG15 9AL (☎ 0623 792241)

ABEL-SMITH, Lionel; s of Brig Gen Lionel Abel Abel-Smith, DSO (d 1946), of London, gs of Abel Smith of Woodhall Park, and Frances, da of Gen Sir Harry Calvert 1 Bt, and Genevieve Lilac Walsh (d 1980); landed gentry (family assumed additional surname of Abel 1922); *b* 1 Sept 1924; *Educ* Haileybury, Merton Coll Oxford (MA); *Career* RNVR 1943-47, Flag Lt to Adm Sir Victor Crutchley VC (Flag Offr Gibraltar) 1946-47; called to Bar Lincolns Inn 1950, practiced Chancery Bar 1950-63; farmer in Sussex 1964; *Recreations* amateur cellist; *Clubs* MCC, Henley; *Style*— Lionel Abel-Smith, Esq; Groves, Peasmarsh, Rye, Sussex (☎ 079 721 338)

ABELES, Sir (Emil Herbert) Peter; s of late Alexander Abel and Mrs Anna Deakin; *b* 25 April 1924; *Educ* Budapest; *m* 1969, Katalin Ottilia, da of late Arthur Fischer; 2 da; *Career* fndr Alltrans Ltd 1950 (taken over by Thomas Nationwide Tport 1967); md and dep chm: Thomas Nationwide Tport 1967-, Seatainer Terminals 1971-, Tasman Union 1971-; dir: Acme World Shipping Pty Ltd 1975, Speedy Communications Pty Ltd 1979-; jt chief exec Ansett Tport Industs Ltd 1979- (dir 1972-, jt chm 1982-); kt 1972; *Style*— Sir Peter Abeles; 6 Queens Ave, Vaucluse, NSW 2030, Australia

ABELL, Sir Anthony Foster; KCMG (1952, CMG 1950); 2 s of George Foster Abell, JP, of Foxcote Manor, Andoversford, Glos (d 1946); bro of Sir George Abell, *qv*; *b* 11 Dec 1906; *Educ* Repton, Magdalen Coll Oxford; *Career* joined Colonial Admin Service Nigeria 1929, govr and Cdr in Chief Sarawak 1950-59, high cmmr Brunei 1950-58; Gentleman Usher of the Blue Rod in Order of St Michael and St George 1972-79; *Style*— Sir Anthony Abell, KCMG; Gavel House, Wherwell, Andover, Hants (☎ 026 474 216)

ABELL, (John) David; s of Leonard Abell; *b* 15 Dec 1942; *Educ* Leeds Univ, LSE; *m* 1967 (m dis 1977), Anne Priestley; 3 s; *Career* former md BL Commercial Vehicles, former chm and md Leyland Vehicles Ltd; chm and chief exec Suter plc 1981-; *Style*— David Abell, Esq; The Old Rectory, Branston-by-Belvoir, Grantham, Lincs

ABELL, John Norman; s of Sir George Edmund Brackenbury Abell, KCIE, OBE, of Whittonditch House, Ramsbury, Wilts, *qv*, and Susan, *née* Norman-Butler; *b* 18 Sept 1931; *Educ* Marlborough, Worcester Coll Oxford (MA); *m* 17 Nov 1957, Mora Delia, da of Anthony George Clifton-Brown, of Rome, Italy (d 1984); 2 s (Martin b 1962, Antony b 1964), 1 da (Sarah b 1959); *Career* 2 Lt 1 Bn Rifle Brigade 1950-51; Wood Gundy Inc 1955-82 (vice chm 1978-82), pres Wood Gundy New York 1966-72, chm and chief exec offr Orion Royal Bank Ltd 1982-85; appted rep for Canadian Govt on Massey Fergusson refinancing 1980; dir: Echo Bay Mines Ltd 1982-, Varity Corpn 1983-, Minerals Resources Corpn Ltd 1984-, Slough Estates Canada Ltd 1986-; vice chm Wood Gundy Inc Toronto Canada 1986-; memb Securities and Investmt Bd 1985-86; govr Toronto Stock Exchange; *Recreations* tennis, shooting, fishing; *Clubs* Toronto, York, India House, Boodle's; *Style*— John N Abell, Esq; Foxcote Farm, Hillsburgh, Ontario, Canada (☎ 510 8554595); 63 Warwick Square, London SW1; Wood Gundy Inc, Royal Trust Tower, Toronto Dominion Centre, Toronto, Ontario, Canada (☎ 416 869 6930)

ABER, Prof Geoffrey Michael; s of David Aber (d 1988), of Leeds, and Hilda, *née* Madeloff (d 1982); *b* 19 Feb 1928; *Educ* Leeds GS, Leeds Univ (MB, ChB, MD), Birmingham Univ (PhD); *m* 27 June 1964, Eleanor Maureen, da of Gerald Christopher Harcourt; 1 s (Mark Barrington b 1967), 1 da (Alison Jane b 1965); *Career* Lt and Capt RAMC 1954-56; house physician Brompton Hosp 1957-68, res fell McGill Univ Montreal 1959-60, sr registrar Queen Elizabeth Hosp Brimingham 1960-64, Wellcome sr res fell and hon sr lectr Birmingham Univ 1964-65, conslt physician North Staffs Hosp Centre 1965-, prof and advsr clinical res Dept Postgrad Med Univ of Keele 1979-82, prof renal med and head Dept Postgrad Med Univ of Keele 1982-; MRCP (memb cncl 1984-87); *Recreations* music, sport, motor cars; *Style*— Professor Geoffrey Aber; Greenleaves, Seabridge Lane, Westlands, Newcastle, Staffs (☎ 0782 613 692); Dept of Postgraduate Medicine, Univ of Keele, Thornburrow Drive, Hartshill, Stoke-on-Trent, Staffs ST5 5BG (☎ 0782 49144 ext 4047, fax 0782 613 847, telex 36113 UNKLIB G)

ABERCONWAY, 3 Baron (1911 UK); Sir Charles Melville McLaren; 3 Bt (UK 1902), JP (Denbigh 1946); eld s of 2 Baron Aberconway, CBE (d 1953), and Christabel (d 1974), da of Sir Melville Macnaghten, CB; *b* 16 April 1913; *Educ* Eton, New Coll Oxford (BA); *m* 1, 1941 (m dis 1949), Deirdre, da of John Knewstub; 1 s, 2 da; m 2, 1949, Ann, o da of Mrs Alexander Lindsay Aymer, of New York, and formerly w of Maj Robert Lee Bullard III; 1 s; *Heir* s, Hon (Henry) Charles McLaren, *qv*; *Career* barr 1937; chm: John Brown & Co Ltd 1953-78 (pres 1978-85), Sheepbridge Engrg 1961-79, English China Clays 1963-84 (pres 1984-); dep chm: Sun Alliance & London Insur Co Ltd until 1985, Westland plc 1979-85; pres RHS 1961-84 (pres emeritus 1984-); cmmr-gen Int Garden Festival of Liverpool 1984; dir Nat Garden Festival Stoke on Trent 1986; High Sheriff of Denbighshire 1950; hon fell Inst of Horticulture 1985; *Recreations* gardening, travel; *Style*— The Rt Hon The Lord Aberconway, JP; 25 Egerton Terrace, London SW3 (☎ 01 589 4369); Bodnant, Tal-y-Cafn, N Wales (☎ 0492 650 200)

ABERCORN, 5 Duke of (I 1868); Sir James Hamilton; 15 Bt (I 1660) ; also Lord Paisley (S 1578), Lord Abercorn (S 1603), Earl of Abercorn and Lord Paisley, Hamilton, Mountcastell, and Kilpatrick (S 1606), Baron of Strabane (I 1617), Baron Mountcastle and Viscount Strabane (I 1701), Viscount Hamilton (GB 1785), Marquess of Abercorn (GB 1790 - title in House of Lords), and Marquess of Hamilton (I 1868); s of 4 Duke of Abercorn (d 1979) and Kathleen Mary, Dowager Duchess of Abercorn, GCVO, *née* Crichton, *qv*; *b* 4 July 1934; *Educ* Eton, RAC Cirencester; *m* 1966, Alexandra Anastasia, da of Lt-Col Harold Pedro Phillips (d 1980), of Checkendon Court, nr Reading, also sis of Duchess of Westminster and gda through her m, Georgina, of late Sir Harold Wernher, 3 Bt, GCVO, TD, DL, by his w, late Lady Zia, CBE, *née* Countess Anastasia Mikhailovna (er da of HIH Grand Duke Mikhail Mikhailovitch of Russia, himself gs of Tsar Nicholas I); 2 s (Marquess of Hamilton, Lord Nicholas b 1979), 1 da (Lady Sophie b 1973), *qv*; *Heir* s, Marquess of Hamilton, *qv*; *Career* 2 Lt Grenadier Gds; MP (UU) Fermanagh and S Tyrone 1964-70; dir Local Enterprise Devpt Unit 1971-77; memb: Cncl of Europe 1968-70, Economic and Social Ctee EEC 1973-78; pres RUKBA 1979-; dir: NI Industrial Devpt Bd 1982-, Northern Bank Ltd 1970-, NI Regional Bd Nationwide Building Soc 1971-; pres The Building Societies Assoc 1976; chm Templeton Investment Mgmnt Ltd 1985-; High Sheriff Co Tyrone 1970, Ld Lt Co Tyrone; *Recreations* shooting; *Clubs* Brooks's; *Style*— His

Grace The Duke of Abercorn, DL; Barons Court, Omagh, Co Tyrone, N Ireland BT78 4EZ (☎ 066 26 61470); Baronscourt Estate Office, Omagh, Co Tyrone (☎ 06626 61683, fax 06626 62059

ABERCORN, Dowager Duchess of; Lady Mary Kathleen; *née* Crichton; GCVO (1982, DCVO 1969); da of Viscount Crichton, MVO, DSO (ka 1914, s and h of 4 Earl of Erne, KP, PC, sometime MP Enniskillen), and Lady Mary Grosvenor, da of 1 Duke of Westminster; raised to rank of Earl's da 1920; *b* 8 July 1905; *m* 1928, 4 Duke of Abercorn (d 1979); 2 s (*see* 5 Duke of Abercorn), 1 da; *Career* Mistress of the Robes to HM Queen Elizabeth The Queen Mother 1964-; *Style—* Her Grace The Dowager Duchess of Abercorn, GCVO; Barons Court, Omagh, Co Tyrone, N Ireland

ABERCROMBIE, Prof David; s of Lascelles Abercrombie (d 1938), of North Moreton, Didcot, and Catherine, *née* Gatkin (d 1909); *b* 19 Dec 1967; *Educ* Leeds GS, Leeds Univ, UCL, Sorbonne Paris; *m* 31 Aug 1944, Mary, da of Eugene Marble (d 1973), of Carmel, California; *Career* asst English lectr LSE 1934-38, lectr Inst of English Studies Athens 1938-40, English lectr Cairo Univ 1940-45, English lectr LSE 1945-47; phonetics lectr: Leeds Univ 1947-48, Edinburgh Univ 1948-51 (sr lectr 1951-57, reader 1957-63, prof 1964-80); lectr in phonetics and linguistics Glasgow Univ 1980-81; *Recreations* cricket; *Style—* Prof David Abercrombie; 13 Grosvenor Crescent, Edinburgh EH12 5EL (☎ 031 337 4864)

ABERCROMBIE, (George) Forbes; s of George Francis Abercrombie, VRD, RNVR (d 1978), and Marie, *née* Underhill; *b* 28 Mar 1935; *Educ* Charterhouse, Gonville and Caius Coll Cambridge, St Bartholomew's Hosp Med Coll (MA, MD); *m* 15 August 1959, Jennifer Elizabeth Dormer, da of Richard Valentine Dormer Kirby (d 1957); 2 s (John Forbes b 1961, Colin Francis b 1963); *Career* conslt urological surgn St Mary's Hosp Portsmouth 1971-; cncl memb Br Assoc of Urological Surgns 1984-87, memb Int Urologica Soc; Liveryman Worshipful Co of Apothecaries 1964 (former memb Livery Ctee); FRCS; *Recreations* golf, salmon fishing, chess; *Style—* Forbes Abercrombie, Esq; Church House, Catherington Lane, Catherington, Hants PO8 0TE (☎ 0705 597 676)

ABERCROMBY, Sir Ian George; 10 Bt (NS 1636), of Birkenbog, Banffshire; s of Robert Ogilvie Abercromby, gs of 5 Bt; suc kinsman 1972; *b* 30 June 1925; *Educ* Lancing, Bloxham Sch; *m* 1, 1950 (m dis 1957), Joyce Beryl, da of Leonard Griffiths; m 2, 1959, Fanny Mary (Molly), da of Dr Graham Udale-Smith, of Sitio Litre, Puerto de la Cruz, Tenerife; 1 da; m 3, 1976, Diana Marjorie, da of Horace Geoffrey Cockell, and wid of Capt Ian Charles Palliser Galloway; *Style—* Sir Ian Abercromby, Bt; c/o National Westminster Bank, 224 King's Rd, London SW3

ABERDARE, 4 Baron (UK 1873); Morys George Lyndhurst Bruce; PC (1974), KBE (1984), DL (Dyfed 1985); s of 3 Baron Aberdare, GBE (d 1957) ; *b* 16 June 1919; *Educ* Winchester, New Coll Oxford; *m* 1946, (Maud Helen) Sarah, da of Sir John Dashwood, 10 Bt, CVO (d 1966); 4 s; *Heir* s, Hon Alastair Bruce; *Career* Welsh Guards 1939-46; min of State DHSS 1970-74, min without portfolio 1974, chm Ctees House of Lords 1976-; chm: Albany Life Assurance 1975-, Metlife (UK) Ltd 1986-; The Football Tst; pres: YMCA of Wales, Tennis and Rackets Assoc, Kidney Research Unit for Wales Fndn; Hon LLD Wales 1985; GCStJ Prior for Wales Order of St John of Jerusalem; *Books* The Story of Tennis, Willis Faber Book of Tennis and Rackets; *Recreations* real tennis, rackets; *Clubs* Lansdowne, MCC, All England Lawn Tennis, Queen's; *Style—* The Rt Hon the Lord Aberdare, KBE, DL; 32 Elthiron Rd, London SW6 4BW (☎ 01 736 0825)

ABERDEEN, Bishop of (RC) 1977-; Rt Rev Mario Joseph Conti; s of Louis Conti and Josephine Panicali; *b* 1934; *Educ* St Marie's Convent Sch, Springfield Elgin, Blairs Coll Aberdeen, Pontifical Gregorian Univ Rome (STL, PhL); *Career* formerly parish priest (jointly) St Joachim's, Wick and St Anne's Thurso; chm Scottish Catholic Heritage Cmmn, pres Nat Cmmn for Christian Doctrine and Unity; Commendatore of the Order of Merit (Italy); memb of (Roman) Secretariat for Promotion of Christian Unity; *Style—* The Rt Rev Mario Conti, Bishop of Aberdeen; Bishop's House, 156 King's Gate, Aberdeen AB2 6BR (☎ 0224 319154)

ABERDEEN AND ORKNEY, Bishop of, 1978-; Rt Rev Frederick Charles Darwent; JP; s of Samuel Darwent (d 1957), and Edith Emily, *née* Malcolm (d 1968); *b* 20 April 1927; *Educ* Warbreck Sch Liverpool, Ormskirk GS, Wells Theol Coll; *m* 1, 1949, Edna Lilian (d 1981), da of David Waugh and Lily Elizabeth, *née* McIndoe; 2 da (twin); m 2, 1983, Mrs Roma Evelyn Fraser, elder da of John Michie and Evelyn, *née* Stephen; *Career* served with Royal Inniskilling Fusiliers 1945-48; banker Williams Deacon's (later Williams and Glyn's, now merged with Royal Bank of Scotland) 1943-61; deacon 1963, priest 1964; former rector of Strichen, New Pitsligo, Fraserburgh; Canon of St Andrew's Cathedral Aberdeen 1971, dean of Aberdeen and Orkney 1973-78; Hon LTh St Mark's Inst of Theology, Burgess of Guild of the City of Aberdeen 1985; *Recreations* amateur stage (acting and producing), music (especially jazz), calligraphy; *Clubs* The Club of Deir (Aberdeenshire), Rotary International; *Style—* The Rt Rev the Bishop of Aberdeen and Orkney, JP; 107 Osborne Place, Aberdeen AB2 4DD (☎ (0224) 646497); Diocesan Office, 16 Crown Terrace, Aberdeen AB1 2HD (☎ (0224) 580172)

ABERDEEN AND TEMAIR, 6 Marquess of (UK 1916); Sir Alastair Ninian John Gordon; 14 Bt (NS 1642); also 12 Earl of Aberdeen (S 1682), Lord Haddo, Methlic, Tarves, and Kellie (S 1682), Viscount Formartine (S 1782), Viscount Gordon (UK 1814), and Earl of Haddo (UK 1916); s of 3 Marquess of Aberdeen and Temair, DSO (d 1972), by his 1 w, Cecile, da of George Drummond (ggggs of Andrew Drummond, yr bro of 4 Viscount Strathallan and fndr of Messrs Drummond, the bankers) by Elizabeth (da of Rev Frederick Norman and Lady Adeliza Manners, da of 5 Duke of Rutland); suc er bro 5 Marquess of Aberdeen and Temair 1984; *b* 20 July 1920; *Educ* Harrow; *m* 1950, Anne, da of Lt-Col Gerald Barry, MC (s of William Barry, JP, 4 s of Sir Francis Barry, 1 Bt, by William's w Lady Grace Murray, MBE, da of 7 Earl of Dunmore) and Lady Margaret Pleydell-Bouverie, da of 5 Earl of Radnor; 1 s, 2 da; *Heir* s, Earl of Haddo, *qv*; *Career* served WW II Capt Scots Gds; painter; memb Int Assoc of Art Critics; chm Arts Club 1966-76; memb Bach Choir 1939-82; *Recreations* music, people; *Clubs* Arts, MCC, Puffin's; *Style—* The Most Hon the Marquess of Aberdeen and Temair; Quicks Green, Ashamptstead, Berks RG8 8SN (☎ Upper Basildon 331)

ABERDEEN AND TEMAIR, Marchioness of; Anne; da of Lt-Col Gerald Barry, MC (s of William Barry, JP, 4 s of Sir Francis Barry, 1 Bt, by William's w Lady Grace Murray, MBE, da of 7 Earl of Dunmore) who married, 1923, Lady Margaret Pleydell-Bouverie, da of 5 Earl of Radnor; *b* 28 April 1924; *Educ* Godolphin Sch Salisbury, Chapin Sch New York; *m* 1950, Marquess of Aberdeen and Temair, *qv*; 1 s, 2 da; *Career* potter; fell of Morgan Library NY; *Recreations* gardening; *Style—* The Most Hon the Marchioness of Aberdeen and Temair; Quicks Green, Ashampstead, Berkshire RG8 8SN

ABERDEEN AND TEMAIR, June, Marchioness of; (Beatrice Mary) June Gordon; MBE (1971), DL (Aberdeenshire 1971); da of late Arthur Paul Boissier (d 1953); *b* 29 Dec 1913; *Educ* Southlands Sch Harrow, RCM; *m* 29 April 1939, 4 Marquess of Aberdeen and Temair, CBE, TD (d 1974); 2 adopted s, 2 adopted da; *Career* musical dir and conductor Haddo House Choral and Operatic Soc 1945-, dir Haddo House Arts Centre; chm: Scottish Children's League 1969, Advsy Cncl Scottish Opera; Hon LLD Aberdeen 1968, DStJ 1977, FRSE 1983, FRCM 1967, FRSM, ARCM; *Style—* The Most Hon June, Marchioness of Aberdeen and Temair, MBE, DL; Haddo House, Aberdeen AB4 0ER (☎ Tarves 216)

ABERDEEN AND TEMAIR, Margaret, Marchioness of; Margaret Gladys; ARRC (1941), JP, DL (E Sussex); da of late Lt-Col Reginald Munn, CMG; *b* 26 April 1907; *m* 1949, as his 2 w, 3 Marquess of Aberdeen and Temair, DSO (d 1972); *Career* chm E Grinstead UDC 1953-54 and 1960-61, pres Sussex Counties Branch BRCS 1975-80, chm Soc of Friends of Ashdown Forest, govr Ardingly Coll; *Clubs* Royal Ashdown Forest Golf; *Style—* The Most Hon Margaret, Marchioness of Aberdeen and Temair, ARRC, JP, DL; Sycamore Cottage, Forest Row, Sussex RH18 5BE

ABERDOUR, Dr Kenneth Robert; s of Kenneth Aberdour (d 1965), of Chelmsford, and Jennie May Titilah (d 1986); *b* 9 Mar 1927; *Educ* Trinity GS N London, St Georges Hosp Med Sch, Univ of London (MB); *m* 17 Sept 1960, Jean Rosemary, da of Philip Henry Hardy (d 1977), of Chelmsford; 1 s (Robert b 1964), 1 da (Rosemary b 1961); *Career* conslt radiologist and memb Mid Essex Health Authy 1962; radiologist: The London Clinic, Springfield Med Centre Chelmsford; FRCP, FRCR; *Recreations* gardening, walking; *Style—* Dr Kenneth R Aberdour; The Old Rectory, Wickham Bishops, Witham, Essex CM8 3LA (☎ 0621 891597); Broomfield Hosp, Chelmsford, Essex (☎ 0245 440761)

ABERDOUR, Lord; (John) Stewart Sholto Douglas; s and h of 21 Earl of Morton, *qv*; *b* 17 Jan 1952; *Educ* Dunrobin Castle Sch, Aberdeen Univ; *m* 20 July 1985, Amanda K, yr da of David J M Mitchell, of Castle St, Kirkcudbright; 1 s (Hon John David, Master of Aberdour b 28 May 1986); *Career* ptnr Dalmahoy Farms; *Style—* Lord Aberdour; Haggs Farm, Kirknewton, Midlothian

ABERGAVENNY, 5 Marquess of (UK 1876); John Henry Guy Nevill; KG (1974), OBE (1945), JP (Sussex 1948); also Baron Abergavenny (E 1450 as Baron Bergavenny; 14 Baron, who held the title 1724-45, was the first to be styled Lord Abergavenny), Viscount Nevill, Earl of Abergavenny (both GB 1784), and Earl of Lewes (UK 1876); s of 4 Marquess of Abergavenny (d 1954); *b* 8 Nov 1914; *Educ* Eton, Trinity Coll Cambridge; *m* 1938, Patricia (*see* Abergavenny, Marchioness of); 3 da (and 1 s and 1 da decd); *Heir* nephew, Guy Nevill; *Career* 2 Lt LG 1935, Maj 1942, served N W Europe (despatches), temp Lt-Col 1945, ret 1946; Hon Col Kent and Co of London Yeo 1948-62, Ald E Sussex CC 1954-62; tstee Ascot Authy 1952-82, former HM Representative at Ascot; pres Royal Agric Soc of England 1967 (dep pres 1968 and 1972), former pres Royal Assoc of Br Dairy Farmers and of Assoc of Agric, pres Br Horse Soc 1970-71, memb Nat Hunt Ctee (former Sr Steward), former vice-chm Turf Bd; Lord-Lt of E Sussex 1974- (Vice-Lt of Sussex 1970-74, DL Sussex 1955), Chllr of Order of the Garter 1977-, pres Cncl of Order of St John Sussex 1975- (KStJ 1976); chm: Lloyds Bank Property Co Ltd, Lloyds Bank S E Regional Bd; dir: Lloyds Bank plc, Lloyds Bank UK Management, Massey-Ferguson Hldgs Ltd (ret 1985), Whitbread Investment Co Ltd, Br Equestrian Promotions Ltd, ret; *Clubs* White's; *Style—* The Most Hon The Marquess of Abergavenny, KG, OBE, JP; Eridge Park, Tunbridge Wells, Kent TN3 9JT (☎ 27378); Flat 2, 46 Pont St, London SW1 (☎ 01 581 3967)

ABERGAVENNY, Marchioness of; (Mary) Patricia; DCVO (1981, CVO 1970); da of late Lt-Col John Fenwick Harrison, RHG, and Hon Margery, da of 3 Baron Burnham, DSO; *b* 1915; *m* 1938, 5 Marquess of Abergavenny, *qv*; 3 da (and 1 s and 1 da decd); *Career* Lady of the Bedchamber to HM The Queen 1966- (an Extra Lady of the Bedchamber 1960-66); *Style—* The Most Hon The Marchioness of Abergavenny, DCVO; Eridge Park, Tunbridge Wells, Kent TN3 9JT (☎ 0892 27378); Flat 2, 46 Pont St, London SW1 (☎ 01 581 3967)

ABERNETHY, (William) Leslie; CBE (1972); s of Robert Abernethy (d 1956), and Margaret, *née* Pickup (d 1935); *b* 10 June 1910; *Educ* Darwen GS; *m* 1937, Irene, da of Walter Holden (d 1968); 1 s (David); *Career* dep county tres Derbyshire CC 1945-48, tres Newcastle-upon-Tyne Regnl Hosp Bd 1948-50; dep comptroller LCC 1956-64 (asst comptroller 1950-56), tres GLC 1964-72, comptroller of Fin Services GLC 1972-73; managing tstee Municipal Mutual Insur Ltd 1973-1987; dir: Municipal Life Assur Ltd, Municipal Gen Insur Ltd, MLA Unit Tst Mgmnt Ltd, OQS Property Mgmnt Ltd, OQS Property Devpt Ltd 1978-87; memb cncl Chartered Inst of Pub Finance and Accountancy until 1973; FCA; IPFA; *Clubs* Nat Liberal; *Style—* Leslie Abernethy, Esq, CBE£; 6 Ballakeyll, Colby, Isle of Man (☎ 0624 832792)

ABIDI, Vilayat Husain; s of Bahadar Husain Abidi (d 1985), of 2a Link St, Defence Housing Soc, Karachi, Pakistan, and Bilquees, *née* Begum; *b* 10 Dec 1934; *Educ* Centenial HS of Christian Coll Lucknow India, Karachi Univ Pakistan (BA); *m* 1, 1960 (m dis 1965), Farhat, da of S F Meerza SQA; 2 s (Ali b 1963, Asad b 1964); m 2, Jawahir, da of Syed Mohammed Siddick (d 1964), of Mecca, Saudi Arabia; *Career* Grindlays Bank 1951-59; sr vice pres (formerly offr mangr & vice pres) United Bank Ltd Pakistan 1960-75, Union Bank Ltd Karachi 1969-71; vice-chm and gen mangr United Bank of Lebanon and Pakistan SAL Beirut 1971-75, gen mangr Bank of Credit and Commerce Int Lebanon SAL 1977-80, for BCCI SA on the bd of dirs of Iran Arab Bank Tehran 1975-79, regnl gen mangr BCCI UK 1980-88, dir BCCI Gilbratar 1980-88; governing memb Business in the Community; *Clubs* RAC; *Style—* Vilayat Abidi, Esq; Beechcroft, Manor House Drive, Brondesbury Park, London NW6 7DD (☎ 01 459 5939); Bank of Credit and Commerce Int, 100 Leadenhall St, London EC3A 3AD (☎ 01 283 8566, fax 01 623 4635, car 0860 324 864, telex 892251)

ABINGDON, Earl of; *see*: Lindsey and Abingdon, Earl of

ABINGER, 8 Baron (UK 1835); James Richard Scarlett; DL (Essex 1968); s of 7 Baron Abinger, DSO (d 1943); *b* 28 Sept 1914; *Educ* Eton, Magdalene Coll Cambridge; *m* 1957, Isla Carolyn, niece of Sir Henry Rivett-Carnac, 7 Bt, and da of late Vice Adm J W Rivett-Carnac, CB, CBE, DSC; 2 s; *Heir* s, Hon James Scarlett, *qv*; *Career* Hon Lt-Col RA, served France and India, ret 1947; sits as Conservative in

House of Lords; farmer and co dir; vice pres Byron Soc, former chm Keats-Shelley Meml Soc, memb exec ctee CPRE, pres Mid Anglia Centre Nat Tst; former govr ESU; served Halstead Rural and Braintree Dist Cncls; KStJ; *Recreations* field sports; *Clubs* Carlton, RAC; *Style—* The Rt Hon the Lord Abinger, DL; Clees Hall, Bures, Suffolk (☎ 0787 227227)

ABNEY-HASTINGS, Lady Clare Louise; da of Countess of Loudoun, *qv* and (3 husb), Peter Abney-Hastings; *b* 8 Dec 1958; *Style—* Lady Clare Abney-Hastings

ABNEY-HASTINGS, Hon Frederick James; s of Countess of Loudoun, *qv* and (2 husb), Capt Gilbert Greenwood (d 1951); *b* 29 Jan 1949; *Style—* The Hon Frederick Abney-Hastings

ABRAHAM, Sir Edward Penley; CBE (1973); s of Albert Penley Abraham, and Mary, *née* Hearn; *b* 10 June 1913; *Educ* King Edward VI Sch Southampton, Queen's Coll Oxford (MA, DPhil, hon fell 1973); *m* 1939, Asbjörg Harung, of Bergen Norway; 1 s; *Career* fell Lincoln Coll Oxford 1948-80, hon fell 1980-; prof chemical pathology Oxford 1964-80; hon fell: Linacre Coll Oxford 1976, Lady Margaret Hall Oxford 1978, Wolfson Coll Oxford 1982, St Peter's Coll Oxford 1983; Royal Medal 1973 and Mullard Medal and Prize 1980 of the Royal Soc; Chemical Soc Award in Medicinal Chemistry 1975; Hon DSc: Exeter 1980, Oxon 1984; foreign hon memb American Academy of Arts and Scis (1983), Int Soc of Chemotherapy Award (1983); FRS; kt 1980; *Publications* Biochemistry of Some Peptide and Steroid Antibiotics (1957), Biosynthesis and Enzymic Hydrolysis of Penicillins and Cephalosporina (1974), medical and scientific jls on penicillins, cephalosperms and other substances with biological activity; *Clubs* Athenaeum; *Style—* Sir Edward Abraham, CBE; Badger's Wood, Bedwells Heath, Boars Hill, Oxford (☎ 0865 735395); Sir William Dunn School of Pathology, Oxford (☎ 0865 275500)

ABRAHAM, Maj-Gen (Sutton) Martin O'Heguerty; CB (1973), MC (1942, and bar 1943); s of Capt Edgar Gaston Furtado Abraham, CB, late ICS (d 1955), and Ruth Eostre, da of Rev Gerald S Davies, master of the Charterhouse, London; *b* 26 Jan 1919; *Educ* Eton, Trinity Coll Cambridge (BA); *m* 1950, Iona Margaret, da of Sir John Stirling, KT, MBE; 2 s, 1 da; *Career* dir of combat Devpt MOD 1968-71, chief of jt servs liaison orgn BAOR 1971-73, FO Balanced Force Reductions in Europe 1973-76; sec Bedford Coll London Univ 1976-82 (govr 1983-85); Col 9/12 Royal Lancers 1978-82; *Style—* Maj-Gen Martin Abraham, CB, MC; c/o Hoare & Co, 37 Fleet St, London EC4 (☎ 01 353 4522)

ABRAHAM, Neville Victor; s of Solomon Abraham (d 1987), and Sarah Raphael; *b* 22 Jan 1937,Calcutta; *Educ* Brighton Coll, LSE (BSc); *Career* sr princ Board of Trade and parly sec Minister of State 1963-71; corporate policy advsr Whitehead Consulting Gp 1971-76; fndr chm and md Amis du Vin Gp and Les Amis du Vin Ltd 1974-86; visiting lecturer at leading business schools 1974-83; gp exec dir Kennedy Brookes plc 1984-86, dep chm Creative Business Communications plc 1986-, chm and chief exec Lakebird Leisure Ltd 1986-; *Books* Big Business and Government: The New Disorder (1974); *Recreations* music, gardening, walking; *Clubs* RAC; *Style—* Neville Abraham, Esq; 83 Gloucester Terrace, London W2 3HB; 37 Dean St, London W1 (☎ 01 439 2925)

ABRAHAMS, Allan Rose; CMG (1962); s of late Frank Abrahams, of Kingston, Jamaica; *b* 29 Nov 1908; *Educ* Jamaica Coll Jamaica; *m* 1948, Norma Adeline, da of Cecil Neita; 1 s, 2 da; *Career* civil servant 1927-64; co dir; *Style—* Allan Abrahams, Esq, CMG; 20 Widcombe Rd, Kingston 6, Jamaica (☎ 78214)

ABRAHAMS, Maj (Sidney) Anthony George; TD; s of Anthony Claude Walter Abrahams, of Goldsmith Bldg, Temple, London, and Laila, *née* Myking; *b* 30 Oct 1951; *Educ* Bedford Sch, Coll of Law; *m* 6 Oct 1979, Kathryn Helen Anne, da of Humphrey John Patrick Chetwynd-Talbot, of South Warnborough, Basingstoke, Hants; 1 s (Thomas b 1985), 1 da (Annika b 1983); *Career* cmmnd 1976 Maj 1984, 4 Bn Royal Green Jackets (V); admitted slr 1978, Wade-Gery and Brackenbury 1980-84, Alexander Farr and Son 1984-88, Wade Gery Farr 1988-; Freeman City of London 1985; memb Worshipful Co Glaziers 1985, memb Law Soc; *Recreations* TA, squash, food and drink; *Style—* Maj Anthony Abrahams, TD; Corner Cottage, Brook End, Keysoe, Beds MK44 2HP (☎ 0234 708 631); Wade Gery Farr, 30-32 Bromham Rd, Bedford MK40 2QD (☎ 0234 273 273, fax 0234 532 110, telex 265871 MONREF G)

ABRAHAMS, Gerald Milton; CBE (1967); s of Isidor Abrahams (d 1943); *b* 20 June 1917; *Educ* Westminster; *m* 1, 1946, Doris, da of late Mark Cole, of Brookline, Mass, USA; 2 da; m 2, 1972, Mrs Marianne Wilson, da of late David Kay, of London; *Career* Maj Br Army WW II, HAC, RHA, served Greece, W Desert and Ceylon; chm and md Aquascutum Gp plc and associated cos 1947-; memb: Br Menswear Guild (chm 1959-61 and 1964-66), cncl CBI 1965-, Br Nat Export Cncl Ctee for Exports to Canada 1965-70, Consumer Goods Ctee Export Cncl for Europe, Clothing Export Cncl (chm 1966-70, vice pres 1970-), Economic Devpt Ctee for Clothing Indust 1966-69, Clothing Manufacturers' Fedn of GB 1960-82 (chm Exec Cncl 1965-66), North American Advsy Gp BOTB 1978-86 (vice chm 1983-86), Br Clothing Indust Assoc 1982-87; FRSA 1972, CBIM 1979; *Recreations* swimming, golf; *Clubs* Buck's; *Style—* Gerald Abrahams, Esq, CBE; c/o Aquascutum Group plc, 100 Regent St, London W1A 2AQ (☎ 01 734 6090, telex 264426 fax 01 734 0726)

ABRAHAMS, Henry; s of Joseph Henry Abrahams (d 1938), of Leeds, and Florence, *née* Towers (d 1942); *b* 14 Oct 1964; *Educ* Leeds GS, Crawford Coll Berks, Business Sch London; *m* 1, 21 July 1935 (m dis 15 June 1942), Miriam orse Marion, da of Henry Silbert, of London; m 2, 23 July 1946, Grete, da of Peter Anton Johannes Bork; 2 da (Carol Rosalind (Mrs Le Vay Laurnece), Janet Barbara (Mrs Gluckstein); *Career* industrialist; co fndr A W Securities (mfrs of carpets, plastics, coated fabrics); farmer 1946-59; underwriting memb of Lloyds; ret 1973; supporter of charities and funds through The Henry and Grete Abrahams Charitable Fndn; donations incl: 2 day centres at Israeli hosps, library of med Tel Aviv Univ, paediatric high dependency unit St Mary's Hosp Paddington; created Nurses Endowment Fund; Freeman City of London 1985, memb Worshipful Co of Upholders 1985; Hon PhD Tel Univ 1986; *Recreations* salmon and sea trout fishing, tennis, golf, chess, bridge, travel; *Style—* Henry Abrahams, Esq; 23 Chelwood House, Gloucester Square, London W2 2SY (☎ 01 262 4742)

ABRAHAMS, Ian John; s of Michael Leonard Abrahams (d 1950), and Gertrude Maud, *née* Clavering (d 1983); *b* 23 Nov 1921; *Educ* The Hall Sch Hampstead, Westminster, Pembroke Coll Cambridge (BA, MA); *m* 1, 9 Sept 1947 (m dis 1979), Jill Maude, da of the late Leslie Koppenhagen, of London; 1 s (Michael b 1950), 1 da (Penelope (Mrs Madden) b 1951); m 2, Ruth Daponte, da of the late J Hulme-Smith, of Poonah, India; 2 step da (Susan (Mrs Leigh-Wood) b 1948, Sarah b 1957); *Career* WWII 1941-45, Lt RNVR served MTB after injury courtesy tour USA for RN; chm and chief exec Temple Varnish Co Ltd 1952-53, jt md Ripolin Ltd 1953-55, dir Amalgamated Investment Property Co Ltd 1955-64, chm & chief exec TV Int Ltd 1964-80, Crown Int Prodns Ltd 1969-80, chm TV Applications Ltd 1967-80, Video Communications Ltd 1967-80, dir Crown Cassette Communications Ltd 1967-80, chm Radio Orwell Ltd, chief exec Interservice (Med) Ltd; dir Consumer & Video Hldgs Ltd, chm Monmouth Film Production Ltd 1985-88, Chelsea Cable Co Ltd 1984-; vice pres Br Acad of Songwriters, Composers and Authors 1970-, govr: Contemporary Dance Theatre 1971-84, Hall Sch Hampstead; tv and film: Ivor Novello Awards at the Talk of the Town 1972, A month in the Country 1976, Pictures at an Exhibition with Emerson, Lake and Palmer 1978, Tribute to Her Majesty (with John Mills) 1986; Capt Cambridge Univ Boxing 1947-48; *Recreations* music, reading, cinema; *Clubs* Hawks (Cambridge); *Style—* Ian Abrahams, Esq

ABRAHAMS, Keith Elias; s of Percy Abel (d 1944), of Birmingham, and Esther, *née* Blanckensee (d 1939); *b* 7 Sept 1905; *Educ* Malvern; *m* 22 July 1941, Winifred Margaret, da of James McDougal Cowper (d 1940), of Edinburgh; 2 s (Timothy b 1942, Jonathan b 1949); *Career* stockbroker; Major KOSB 1939-45, NW Frontier India 1941-43, Burma campaign 1943-45; chm Birmingham Stock Exchange 1969-71; Freeman City of London 1965, memb Worshipful Co of Clockmakers 1965; *Recreations* fly fishing, golf; *Style—* Keith E Abrahams, Esq; Wynnat's Edge, Pen-y-Bryn, Mynytho, Pwllheli, Gwynedd LL53 7SE (☎ 0758 740 481)

ABRAMS, Dr Mark Alexander; s of Abram Abrams (d 1952), of Enfield, Middx, and Anne, *née* Jackson (d 1955); *b* 27 April 1906; *Educ* Latymer Sch, London Univ (BSc, PhD); *m* 1, 1931 (m dis 1951), Una Strugnell; 1 s (Philip d 1982), 1 da (Evelyn); m 2, 1951, Jean, da of Frederick Bird (d 1974), of Newtown, Connecticut, USA; 1 da (Sarah); *Career* political intelligence dept FO 1941-46; res dir London Press Exchange 1946-70; dir: res unit Social Sci Res Cncl 1971-77, res unit Age Concern Eng 1977-; *Recreations* listening to music; *Clubs* Civil Service; *Style—* Dr Mark Abrams; 12 Pelham Sq, Brighton BN1 4ET (☎ 0273 684573); 60 Pitcairn Rd, Mitcham, Surrey CR4 3LL

ABRAMS, Dr Michael Ellis; s of Sam Philip Abrams, OBE (d 1964), and Ruhamah Emmie, *née* Glieberman; *b* 17 Sept 1932; *Educ* King Edwards Sch Birmingham, Univ of Birmingham (MB, ChB, BSc); *m* 1962, Rosalind June, da of Nathan Beckman (d 1970); 3 s (Jonathan, Jeremy, Nathan), 1 da (Rebecca); *Career* dep chief med offr DHSS; FRCP, FFCM; *Recreations* beachcombing; *Style—* Dr Michael Abrams; DH, Richmond House, Whitehall, London SW1A 2NS

ABRAMSON, Sidney; CMG (1979); s of Jacob Abramson (d 1951), of 31 Cadogan St, London, and Rebecca, *née*Cohen (d 1956); *b* 14 Sept 1921; *Educ* Emanuel Sch London, Queen's Coll Oxford (BA,MA); *m* 15 Dec 1946 (m dis 1958), Lerine, da of Hyman Freedman; 2 s (John b 1947, Richard b 1952); m 2, 1960, Violet Ellen, da of Frederick William Eatley (d 1959); *Career* Interservice Bureau Colombo 1943-46; served BOT (later Dept of Trade) 1950-63 and 1965-81, under sec 1972-81; memb UK Delgn to: OEEC Paris 1957-59, EFTA Geneva 1960; GATT Secretariat Geneva 1963-65; *Recreations* gardening, music; *Style—* Sidney Abramson, Esq, CMG; 75a Holden Rd, London N12 7DP (☎ 01 445 1264)

ABSE, Dr Dannie; s of Rudolf Abse (d 1964), of Cardiff, and Kate, *née* Shepherd (d 1981); bro of Leo Abse, *qv*; *b* 22 Sept 1923; *Educ* St Illtyds Coll Cardiff, Univ of Wales Cardiff, King's Coll London, Westminster Hosp London; *m* 4 Aug 1951, Joan, da of John Mercer, of St Helens, Lancs; 1 s (Jesse David b 1958), 2 da (Keren Danielle b 1953, Susanna Ruth b 1957); *Career* RAF 1951-54, Sqdn Ldr i/c chest clinic, Central Med Estab London; poet, playwright and novelist; sr fell of humanities Princeton Univ 1973-74, pres Poetry Soc 1979-; MRCS, LRCP, FRSL; poetry: After Every Thing Green (1948), Walking Under Water (1952), Tenants of the House (1957), Poems Golders Green (1962), A Small Desperation (1968), Funland and Other Poems (1973), Collected Poems (1977), Way Out in the Centre (1981), Ask the Bloody Horse (1986), White Coat, Purple Coat (1989); prose: Ash on a Young Man's Sleeve (1954), Journals from the Ant-Heap (1986); novels: Some Corner of an English Field (1957), O Jones, O Jones (1970); autobiography: A Poet in the Family (1974), A Strong Dose of Myself (1983); plays: House of Cowards (1960), The Dogs of Pavlov (1969), Pythagoras (1976), Gone in January (1978); *Style—* Dr Dannie Abse; c/o The Poetry Society, 21 Earls Court Sq, London SW1

ABSE, Leo; s of Rudolph Abse, of Cardiff, and Kate, *née* Shepherd; *b* 22 April 1917; *Educ* LSE; *m* 1955, Marjorie, *née* Davies; 1 s, 1 da; *Career* slr; MP (Lab): Pontypool 1958-1983, Torfaen 1983-87 ; *Style—* Leo Abse, Esq; 54 Strand-on-the-Green, London W4 (☎ 01 994 1166)

ACFIELD, David Laurence; s of Robert Douglas Acfield, of Chelmsford, Essex, and Ena Violet Acfield; *b* 24 July 1947; *Educ* Brentwood Sch, Christs Coll Cambridge (MA); *m* 1973, Helen Mary, da of David Joseph Bradford, of Hutton, Essex; 2 da (Clare b 1977, Rosemary b 1982); *Career* wine & spirit rep; BBC TV summarizer (cricket); Save & Prosper Group Ltd; Olympic fencer (sabre 1968 and 1972), Br Sabre Champion 1969, 1970, 1971, and 1972; cricketer Essex CCC 1966-87, cricket and fencing blue Cambridge; *Recreations* birdwatching, wine, films; *Clubs* MCC, Old Brentwoods, Incogniti; *Style—* David Acfield, Esq; 48 The Furlongs, Ingatestone, Essex; Essex CCC

ACHESON, Prof (Ernest) Donald; KBE (1986); s of Malcolm King Acheson, MC, and Dorothy Josephine, *née* Rennoldson; *b* 17 Sept 1926; *m* Barbara Mary, *née* Castle; 1 s, 5 da; *Career* chief med offr: Dept of Health, DES, Home Off 1984; *Style—* Prof Sir Donald Acheson, KBE; Richmond House, 79 Whitehall, London SW1A 2NS

ACHESON, John Francis; s of Jack Francis Acheson (d 1972); *b* 5 Jan 1921; *Educ* Dulwich; *m* 1, 1942, Mary; 2 children; m 2, 1964, Patricia; 2 children; *Career* served WWII Capt 27 Lancers in Africa and Italy; banker; Coutts & Co (ret 1985); non exec dir Methuem (LUA) Ltd; *Recreations* philology, opera; *Clubs* City Livery, IOD; *Style—* John Acheson, Esq; Blackthorn Cottage, Highfield Rd, West Byfleet, Surrey KT14 6QX (☎ 093 23 43646)

ACHESON, Hon Patrick Bernard Victor Montagu; s of 5 Earl of Gosford, MC (d 1954), and Caroline Mildred Carter, Countess of Gosford (d 1965); unc and hp of 7 Earl of Gosford; *b* 4 Feb 1915; *Educ* Harrow, Trinity Coll Cambridge (BA), Harvard (MBA); *m* 1946, Judith, da of Frederick B Bate, of Waterford, Virginia, USA (d 1970); 3 s, 2 da; *Career* Int Bank for Reconstruction and Devpt 1947-65, pres Culligan Water Conditioning Corpn of N Virginia 1966-80; *Recreations* golf, tennis, gardening; *Clubs*

Loudoun Golf; *Style*— The Hon Patrick Acheson; Box 71, Waterford, Va 22190, USA (☎ 703 882 3259)

ACHESON, Prof Roy Malcolm; s of Malcolm King Acheson, MC, MD, (d 1962), of Carrickfergus, Co Antrim, and Dorothy Josephine, *née* Rennoldson (d 1976); *b* 18 August 1921; *Educ* Merchiston Castle Sch Edinburgh, Trinity Coll Dublin (BA, MA, ScD), Brasenose Coll and Radcliffe Infirm Oxford (BA, MA, BM, BCh, DM, MD, ScD); *m* 16 March 1950, Fiona Marigo, da of Wing Cdr Vincent O'Brien, RAF (d 1950), of Altrincham, Ches; 2 s (Malcolm b 1950, Vincent Rennoldson b 1960), 1 da (Marigo Fiona b 1963); *Career* enlisted WWII RAC (N Irish Horse) 1942, active serv Algeria and Tunisia, cmmnd RMC Sandhurst 1944, rejoined N Irish Horse, active serv Italy, discharged Lt 1946; prof community med Cambridge Univ 1976-88 (emeritus prof and fell Churchill Coll 1988-); memb: Cambridge Health Authy 1986-88, GMC, TGDC; Hon MA Yak; FRCP, FFOM 1984, FFCM (vice pres 1986-); *Books* Health, Society and Medicine: An Introduction to Community Medicine (with S Hagard, 1985), Costs and Benefits of the Heart Transplant Programmes at Harefield and Papworth Hospitals (with M Buxton, N Caine, S Gibson and B O'Brien, 1985); author and ed many scientific texts and papers; *Recreations* choral singing, occasional bird watching, golf; *Clubs* Utd Oxford and Cambridge Univ, Gog Magog GC; *Style*— Prof Roy Acheson; 8 Kingston St, Cambridtge CB1 2NU (☎ 0223 315596); Churchill Coll, Cambridge CB3 ODS (☎ 0223 336000)

ACKERMAN, Bruce Trevor; s of Gustave Ackerman (d 1966), of Cape Town, South Africa, and Freda, *née* Kahanovitz; *b* 28 Dec 1907; *Educ* Diocesan Coll Cape Town, Cape Town Univ (BA, MBA); *m* 9 Feb 1972, Patricia Anne, da of Norman Guy; *Career* dir: German Smaller Co's Investment Tst plc 1985-, Lloyds Merchant Bank Ltd 1985-, First Spanish Investment Tst plc 1988-, Portugal Fund Ltd 1988-; md Lloyds Investment Mangrs Ltd 1985-; *Recreations* sport, music, classic cars, travel; *Style*— Bruce Ackerman, Esq; Investment Managers Ltd, 40 Queen Victoria Street, London EC4 (☎ 01 600 4500)

ACKERMAN, Wing Cdr (John) Darral; OBE (1965, MBE 1945); s of Mathew Joliffe (d 1951), of Masterton, NZ, and Phyllis Phoebe, *née* Pearse (d 1962); *b* 6 July 1921; *Educ* Lansdowne Sch Wairarapa, Dannevirke and Levin HS, Victoria Coll Wellington; *m* 22 April 1946, Jean Kathleen, da of Howard Brown (d 1948), of Bramley, Hants; 2 s (Howard b 1947, Neil b 1950); *Career* RNZAF 1940-46, coastal cmd Atlantic 1942-45, (despatches 1943); RAF 1946-74, Bomber Cmd 1948-52; Miny of Supply 1952-58 and 1961-64; UK Mission USA 1958-61, Cyprus 1965-68; md Seahorse Sails Ltd 1975-; Half Ton Cup Sailing Championships 1971 and 1973; Queen's Commendation 1958; *Recreations* sailing (racing and cruising); *Clubs* RAF, RAF Yacht; *Style*— Wing Cdr Darral Ackerman, OBE; 7 Apple Grove, Aldwick Bay, Bognor Regis, W Sussex PO21 4NB (☎ 0243 262311); Seahorse Sails South Ltd, Birdham Pool, Birdham, nr Chichester, W Sussex PO20 7BB (☎ 0243 512195)

ACKERS, Godfrey Lloyd; s of George Lloyd Ackers, OBE (d 1966), and Sylvia Ruth, *née* Tilly (d 1969); *b* 10 August 1926; *Educ* King's Sch Canterbury, Trinity Coll Oxford (BA, MA); *m* 4 June 1955, Wendy Bettina, da of William Hunters Lobb (d 1963); 2 s (Jeremy b 1957, Timothy b 1959), 1 da (Penelope b 1966); *Career* served RNVR Lt 1944-48; ptnr: Sir M MacDonald & Ptnrs (dir 1976-86), Sir M MacDonald Assocs 1977-85, Sir M MacDonald & Ptnrs (Africa) 1980-86, Associated Consultants & Ptnrs (Khartoum) 1984-87; dir Cambridge Educn Cnslts Ltd 1984-87; conslt Sir M MacDonald & Ptnrs 1986-; memb: Arbitration Advsy Bd Inst of Civil Engrs, Client/ Conslts Relationship Ctee, Fédération Int des ingénieurs Conseils 1987-; dir Sir M MacDonald Ltd 1976-87; CEng, FICE, MIWEM, FCIArb; *Recreations* sculling, sailing, Dartmoor; *Style*— Godfrey Ackers, Esq; 26 Kings Orchard, Bridgetown, Totnes, S Devon TQ9 5BX (☎ 0803 866193, fax 0803 867350)

ACKERS, James George; s of James Ackers, and Vera Harriet, *née* Edwards; *b* 20 Oct 1935; *Educ* Oundle, LSE; *m* 1, 1959, Judith Ann Locket; 1 s, 1 da; m 2, 1972, Enid Lydia Silverthorne; *Career* contested (C) Walsall N 1959; former vice chm Bow Group; chm and md Ackers Jarrett Ltd, chm Ackers Jarrett Leasing Ltd; memb Monopolies and Mergers Cmmn 1981-; chm West Midlands RHA 1982-; chm nat cncl Assoc of Br Chambers of Commerce 1984- (formerly dep chm), former chm West Midlands Chambers of Industry and Commerce; *Style*— James Ackers, Esq; 21A Greycoat Gdns, Greycoat St, London SW1

ACKLAM, David Ian; s of Ronald Bernard Acklam, of Ashfield Lane, Milnrow, Rochdale, and Edith, *née* Billington; *b* 10 Sept 1953; *Educ* Hulme GS, Birmingham Poly (BA); *m* 3 Sept 1977, Maureen, da of Edward Taylor (d 1985), of William Street, Accrington; 2 da (Jennifer Louise b 1983, Emma Elizabeth b 1988); *Career* solicitor; *Recreations* golf, squash; *Clubs* Accrington and District Round Table, Rotary Accrington; *Style*— David I Acklam, Esq; 28 Mosedale Drive, Burnley, Lancs (☎ 0282 54382; 28 Warner Street, Accrington, Lancs (☎ 0254 872272)

ACKLAND, Joss (Sidney Edmond Jocelyn); s of Maj Sidney Norman Ackland (d 1981), and Ruth Izod (d 1957); *b* 29 Feb 1928; *Educ* Dame Alice Owens Sch, Central Sch of Speech Training and Dramatic Art; *m* 18 Aug 1951, Rosemary Jean, da of Capt Robert Hunter Kirkcalchy (d 1954); 2 s (Toby b 1966; Paul b 1953 d 1982), 5 da (Melanie b 1952, Antonia b 1956, Penelope b 1958, Samantha b 1962, Kirsty b 1963); *Career* actor; The Hasty Heart Aldwych 1945, Jorrocks 1967, Hotel in Amsterdam 1968-69, Mitch in A Streetcar Named Desire 1974, Frederick in A Littel Night Music 1975-76, The Madras House 1977, Peron in Evita 1978, Falstaff in Henry IV pts 1 and 2 (opening production at RSC's Barbican theatre), Captain Hook and Mr Darling in Peter Pan RSC 1982 (roles repeated in musical version Aldwych 1985), Jean Seberg NT 1983, Pack of Lies 1984; films incl: The Three Musketeers 1973, Royal Flash 1975, Lady Jane 1984, Don Masino in The Sicilian 1986, Jock Delves Broughton in White Mischief 1987, the Colonel in To Kill a Priest 1988, Arjen Rudd in Play Dirty (Lethal Weapon 2); TV incl: Mr Barrett in The Barrets of Wimpole Street 1983, CS Lewis in Shadowlands, the Colonel in The Colonel's Lady 1986, Queenie (US mini-series) 1987, Goering in The Man Who Lived at the Ritz (US-French mini-series) 1988, Theodore Carter in The Quiet Conspiracy 1988; memb: Drug Help Line, Amnesty Int, Covent Garden Community Assoc; *Books* I Must Be in There Somewhere (autobiography 1989); *Recreations* writing, painting, watching movies, bringing up children; *Clubs* Garrick; *Style*— Joss Ackland, Esq; c/o Michael Anderson, ICM Ltd, 388/396 Oxford St, London W1N 9HE (☎ 01 629 8080)

ACKLAND-SNOW, Mr Brian Percy; s of Frank Whittlesey Ackland - Snow (d 1974), and Ivy Jesse Byway; *b* 31 Mar 1940; *Educ* Harrow Sch of Art; *m* 24 Sept 1960, Carol Avis, da of James Eli Dunsby (d 1963); 1 s (Andrew b 1961), 1 da (Amanda b 1963); *Career* production designer and art director; films incl: Death on the Nile, McVicar, Superman III, Room with a View (BAFTA award for production design, Academy Award for art direction), Maurice, Man in the Brown Suit, Without a Clue, The Secret Garden; memb: BAFTA, ALTT; *Recreations* historical architecture, archaeology; *Style*— Brian Ackland-Snow, Esq; Quarry Edge, Cookham Dean, Berks (☎ 06284 3387); CCA Management 4 Ct Lodge, 48 Sloane Sq, London (☎ 01 730 8857)

ACKNER, Baron (Life Peer UK 1986), of Sutton, Co of W Sussex; Desmond James Conrad Ackner; PC (1980), QC (1961); s of Dr Conrad Ackner, of Yew Tree House, Jordans, Beaconsfield, Bucks, and Rhoda Ackner; *b* 18 Sept 1920; *Educ* Highgate, Clare Coll Cambridge (hon fell 1983); *m* 1946, Joan Ackner, JP (memb Local Govt Boundary Cmmn 1981-87), da of late John Evans, JP, and wid of K B Spence; 1 s, 1 da, 1 adopted step da; *Career* served WW II RA and Admiralty Naval Law Branch; barr 1945, recorder of Swindon 1962-71, high court judge (Queen's Bench) 1971-80; judge Jersey and Guernsey Courts of Appeal 1967-71; presiding judge W Circuit 1976-79, Lord Justice of Appeal 1980-86; chm Gen Cncl Bar 1968-70 (memb 1957-, hon tres 1964-66, vice chm 1966-68); pres Senate of Inns of Court and Bar 1980-82; chm Law Advsy Ctee Br Cncl 1981-; dep tres Middle Temple 1983 (tres 1984), created Lord of Appeal in Ordinary 1986; *Style*— The Rt Hon Lord Ackner, PC; 7 Rivermill, 151 Grosvenor Rd, London SW1 (☎ 01 821 8068); Browns House, Sutton, Petworth, W Sussex (☎ 079 87 206)

ACKNER, Hon Martin Stewart; o s of Baron Ackner, PC (Life Peer), *qv*; *b* 1951,; *Educ* Oundle, Birmingham Univ (BSc); *m* 1983, Janet, da of late C W Williamson; *Style*— The Hon Martin Ackner; Lands Farm, W Anstey, S Molton, Devon

ACKROYD, Sir John Robert Whyte; 2 Bt (UK 1956), of Dewsbury, W Riding of Yorks; s of Sir Cuthbert Lowell Ackroyd, 1 Bt (d 1973), of Bromley, Kent; *b* 2 Mar 1932; *Educ* Bradfield, Worcester Coll Oxford (MA); *m* 1956, Jennifer Eileen McLeod, da of Henry George Stokes Bishop (d 1977), of Stow-on-the-Wold, Glos; 2 s (Timothy b 1958, Andrew b 1961), 2 da (Jane b 1957, Kate b 1963,); *Heir* s, Timothy Robert Whyte Ackroyd b 7 Oct 1958; *Career* Sword of Honour Mons OCS and cmmnd 2 Lt RA, served Jordan 1951-52 (ed Jordan 1978, in celebration of Silver Jubilee of HM King Hussein); memb Lloyd's, chm and md Ackroyd Underwriting Agencies Ltd 1978-, EPAR 1969-75, served under Maj-Gen L D Grand; dir Martingdale Prodns Ltd; vice pres Bromley Symphony Orch, patron of LISA; memb cncl RCM 1980 (hon sec 1986-), hon sec Pilgrims of GB 1965, churchwarden St Mary-Le-Bow Cheapside (Bow Bells); Freeman of City of London, Liveryman Worshipful Co Carpenters; FRCM 1988, FRSA 1989; *Recreations* music, theatre, travel; *Clubs* Garrick, Oxford Union (life memb); *Style*— Sir John Ackroyd, Bt; 25 Princedale Road, Holland Park, London W11 4NW (☎ 01 727 5465)

ACKROYD, Peter; s of Graham Ackroyd, and Audrey, *née* Whiteside; *b* 5 Oct 1949; *Educ* Clare Coll Cambridge, Yale Univ; *Career* lit ed Spectator 1971 (managing ed 1977-81); full time writer Somerset Maugham Prize 1984, Guardian Fiction Award 1985, Whithead Prize for Best Biography 1984/85; Fell RSL; *poetry* London Lickpenny (1973), Country Life (1978), The Diversions of Purley (1987); *biography* Ezra Pound and His World (1980), T S Eliot (1984); *novels* The Great Fire of London (1982), The Last Testament of Oscar Wilde (1983), Hawkmoor (1985), Chatterton (1987); *Style*— Peter Ackroyd, Esq; 43 Doughty Street, London WC1N 2LF

ACKROYD, Rev Prof Peter Runham; s of Rev Jabez Robert Ackroyd (d 1978), and Winifred, *née* Brown (d 1971); *b* 15 Sept 1917; *Educ* Harrow, Downing, Trinity Coll Cambridge (MA, PhD), London Univ (BD, MTh, DD); *m* 1940, Evelyn Alice, da of William Young Nutt (d 1926); 2 s (William, Simon), 3 da (Jane, Jenny, Sarah); *Career* clerk in Holy Orders 1957; lectr: Leeds Univ 1948-52, Cambridge 1952-61; Samuel Davidson prof of Old Testament Studies King's Coll London 1961-82 (emeritus 1982-); visiting prof: Lutheran Sch of Theology Chicago 1967 and 1976, Univ of Toronto 1972, Univ of Notre Dame Indiana 1982, Emory Univ Atlanta 1984; special lectures: Selwyn Lectures New Zealand 1970, Haskell Lectures Oberlin Ohio 1984; foreign sec 1987-; editor Book List Soc for Old Testament Study 1967-73, pres Soc for Old Testament Study 1972; editor Palestine Exploration Quarterly 1972-86; chm: cncl Br Sch of Archaeology in Jerusalem 1980-84; chm Palestine Exploration Fund 1986; *Books Incl:* Exile and Restoration (1968), Israel under Babylon and Persia (1970), I and II Samuel (1971, 1977), I, II Chronicles, Ezra, Nehemiah (1973), Doors of Perception (1978), Studies in the Religious Tradition of the Old Testament (1987); *Recreations* music, reading; *Style*— The Rev Prof Peter R Ackroyd; Lavender Cottage, Middleton, Saxmundham, Suffolk IP17 3NQ (☎ 072 873 458)

ACKROYD, Timothy Robert Whyte; s of Sir John Robert Whyte Ackroyd Bt, of 25 Princedale Rd, London, and Lady Jennifer Eileen MacLeod, *née* Bishop; *b* 7 Oct 1958; *Educ* Bradfield, LAMDA; *Career* actor; theatre inc: Agamemnon (nomination Most Promising Newcomer award West End Theatre Critics) 1976, On Approval 1979, Much Ado About Nothing 1980, A Month in the Country 1981, Man and Superman 1982, A Sleep of Prisoners 1983, Pygmalion 1984, Another Country 1986, No Sex Please - We're British 1987, Black Coffee 1988, The Reluctante Debutante 1989; films and tv incl: Jack Be Nimble 1979, Martin Luther - Heretic 1983, Creator 1984 (Hollywood), Man and Superman 1985, That Has Such People In It 1987; dir Martingale Productions 1985-; hon memb Theatre of Comedy; Freeman City of London, Liveryman Worshipful Co Carpenters; *Recreations* rugby, literature, history, sumo wrestling; *Clubs* MCC; *Style*— Timothy Ackroyd, Esq; Flat 4, 33 Chepstow Rd, London W2 5BP (☎ 01 727 3364)

ACLAND, Sir Antony Arthur; GCMG (1986, KCMG 1982, CMG 1976), KCVO (1976); s of Brig Peter Bevil Edward Acland, OBE, MC, TD, *qv*; *b* 12 March 1930; *Educ* Eton, Ch Ch Oxford (MA); *m* 1, 6 Nov 1956, (Clare) Anne (d 1984), da of F R Verdon (d 1960), of Liverpool, and Sidbury, Devon; 2 s (Simon b 27 March 1958, Nicholas b 6 Feb 1960), 1 da (Katharine b 30 June 1965); m 2, 28 July 1987, Mrs Jennifer Joyce McGougan, da of Col R Dyke, OBE (d 1976), of Bicton, Devon; *Career* HM Foreign Service; UK Mission to UN 1962-66, head Chancery UK Mission Geneva 1966-68, head Arabian Dept 1970-72, PPS to Foreign Sec 1972-75; ambass: Luxembourg 1975-77, Spain 1977-80; dep under-sec FCO 1980-82, head HM Diplomatic Serv and perm under-sec FCO 1982-86; ambass Washington USA 1986-; Hon LLD (Exeter) ; *Recreations* riding, gardening, country pursuits; *Clubs* Brooks's; *Style*— Sir Antony Acland, GCMG, KCVO; c/o Foreign and Commonwealth Office, Downing St, London SW1; 40 Cambridge St, London SW1

ACLAND, Lt Col Arthur William; MC (1971), OBE (1945), TD (1940); eld s of Col Alfred Dyke Acland (d 1937), and Beatrice Danvers, *née* Smith (d 1942) (see

Hambleden); *b* 20 Nov 1897; *Educ* Eton, RMC; *m* Dec 1926, Violet Gwendolen Grimston, da of Rev Canon The Hon Robert Grimston (d 1984); 3 s (David Alfred b 1929, Martin Edward b 1932, Charle Robert b 1937); *Career* Grenadier Gds 1916-22, Royal Devon Yeo 1922-40, Cmd W Somerset Yeo 1940-43, Grenadier Gds 1944-45; WWI France wounded twice 1916-18, WWII G1 Welfare France; md W H Smith & Son 1924-64; OStJ; *Recreations* shooting, sailing; *Clubs* Guards, Royal Yacht Squadron; *Style*— Lt-Col Arthur Acland, MC, OBE, TD; Yeomans, 4 Queens Rd, Cowes, Isle of Wight PO31 8BQ (☎ 0983 293345)

ACLAND, David Alfred; s of Lt-Col Arthur William Acland, OBE, MC, of Cowes, IOW, and Violet Gwendolen, *née* Grimston; *b* 21 Oct 1929; *Educ* Eton, Ch Ch Oxford (MA); *m* 19 Oct 1960, Serena Elizabeth, da of late Cyril Hugh Kleinwort; 1 s (Harry Alexander b 1963), 1 da (Lucy Henrietta b 1962); *Career* 2 Lt XI Hussars (PAO) 1947-49; chm: Barclays de Zoete Wedd Asset Mgmnt Ltd, Barclays de Zoete Wedd Investmt Mgmnt, Electric & General Investmt Co plc; vice-chm Barclays de Zoete Wedd Property Investmt Mgmnt; dir: Barclays Financial Services Ltd, Barclays Bank SA (Switzerland), Kleinwort Overseas Investmt Trust plc; vice-pres RNLI; *Recreations* sailing, hunting, tennis; *Clubs* Royal Yacht Squadron; *Style*— David Acland, Esq; Seal House, 1 Swan Lane, London EC4R 3UD (☎ 01 623 7777, fax 01 621 9411, telex 9413073)

ACLAND, Maj Sir (Christopher) Guy (Dyke); 6 Bt (UK 1890), of St Mary Magdalen Oxford; s of Sir Antony Acland, 5 Bt (d 1983) and Margaret, Lady Acland, *qv*; *b* 24 Mar 1946; *Educ* Allhallows Sch, RMA Sandhurst; *m* 1971, Christine Mary Carden, da of John William Brodie Waring, of Isle of Wight; 2 s (Alexander b 1973, Hugh b 1976); *Heir* s, Alexander John Dyke b 29 May 1973; *Career* Maj RHA; Equerry to HRH The Duke of Edinburgh; *Recreations* sailing, fishing, shooting; *Clubs* Royal Artillery Yacht (RAYC); *Style*— Maj Sir Guy Acland, Bt

ACLAND, John Dyke; s and h of Sir Richard Acland, 15 Bt; *b* 13 May 1939; *Educ* Clifton, Magdalene Coll Cambridge (BA, MSc), Univ of West Indies; *m* 1961, Virginia, da of Roland Forge, of The Grange, Barnold-le-Beck, Lincs; 2 s, 1 da; *Style*— John Acland, Esq; Sprydon, Broadclyst, Devon (☎ 039 282 412)

ACLAND, Maj-Gen Sir John Hugh Bevil; KCB (1980), CBE (1978), DL (Devon 1983); s of Brig Peter Acland, and bro of Sir Antony Acland, KCMG, KCVO, *qqv*; *b* 26 Nov 1928; *Educ* Eton; *m* 1953, Myrtle, da of Brig Alastair Crawford (d 1978), of Stirlingshire; 1 s (Peter), 1 da (Victoria); *Career* enlisted Scots Gds 1946, cmmnd Scots Gds 1948, served with 1 or 2 Bn in Malaya, Cyprus, Egypt, Germany, Kenya, Zanzibar and NI 1949-70, equerry to HRH the Duke of Gloucester 1957-59, Staff Coll 1959, Bde Maj 4 Gds Armd Bde 1964-66, CO 2 Bn Scots Gds 1968-71, Col and BGS MOD 1972-75, Cmd Land Forces Cyprus 1976-78, GOC SW Dist 1978-81, Cdr Monitoring Force S Rhodesia and mil advsr to govr 1979-80, ret 1982; Hon Col: Exeter Univ OTC 1980-, Royal Devon Yeo 1983-, Royal Wessex Yeo 1989-; pres Devon RBL 1982-; dir Allied Vintners 1982-; govr Allhallows Sch 1982-; memb Dartmoor Nat Park Auth 1986; chm: Gallant Ordnance 1986-, SW Regnl Working Party on Alcohol 1987-; memb Steering Ctee for Schs Health Educn Unit Exeter Univ 1987-; *Recreations* fly-fishing, arboriculture, destroying vermin; *Clubs* MCC, Blue Seal; *Style*— Maj-Gen Sir John Acland, KCB, CBE, DL; Feniton Court, Honiton, Devon

ACLAND, Lady; Katherine Wilder; da of John Davies Ormond, of Hawkes Bay, NZ; *m* 1935, Sir (Hugh) John Dyke Acland, KBE, JP, sometime MP in NZ (d 1981, himself eld s of Sir Hugh Thomas Dyke Acland, CMG, CBE, who was in his turn gs of Sir Thomas Dyke Acland, 10 Bt, of Columb John); 3 s (John, Mark, Simon), 3 da (Audrey, Evelyn, Sarah); *Style*— Lady Acland; Mount Peel, Peel Forest, South Canterbury, New Zealand

ACLAND, Margaret, Lady; Margaret Joan; da of late Maj Nelson Rooke, HLI, of Badminton; *m* 15 July 1944, as his 2 w, Sir Antony Guy Acland, 5 Bt (d 1983); 1 s (6 Bt, *qv*), 1 da; *Style*— Margaret, Lady Acland; Merrie Cottage, Queens Rd, Freshwater, Isle of Wight

ACLAND , Martin Edward; JP (Herts 1964); s of Lt-Col Arthur Acland, OBE, MC, TD, of Cowes; *b* 31 July 1932; *Educ* Eton; *m* 1956, (Anne) Maureen, *qv* da of late Stanley Ryder Runton, of Ilkley, Yorks; 3 s; *Career* formerly 2 Lt 11 Hussars; dir: Mercantile Credit 1970-84, Alexander Hldgs plc 1985-87, Redfearn Nat Glass 1985-88, Cambridge Corporate Consultants Ltd 1985-; UK dir of Christian Children's Fund; memb Legal Aid Bd 1988; High Sheriff Herts 1978-79; *Recreations* shooting, gun-dog training, sailing; *Clubs* Royal Yacht Sqdn, Seaview Yacht; *Style*— Martin Acland, Esq, JP; Standon Green End, Ware, Herts (☎ 0920 438 233)

ACLAND, (Anne) Maureen; *née* Runton; OBE (1988); da of Stanley Ryder Runton (d 1983), of Ilkley, W Yorkshire, and Kathleen Ryder Runton, CBE, *née* Carter (d 1975); *b* 3 Oct 1934; *Educ* private in England and Paris; *m* 22 Sept 1956, Martin Edward Acland, s of Lt-Col Arthur William Acland, MC, OBE; 3 s (Michael Christopher Dyke b 1958, Richard Arthur Dyke b 1962, Peter Edward Dyke b 1964); *Career* FO 1954-56; memb: cncl St John Herts 1970, London Choral Soc 1970-78 (cncl 1973-78); Co organiser Herts Nat Gardens Scheme 1971-87, pres and tstee Herts Nursing Tst 1975, chm Queen's Nursing Inst 1978, memb Nat Cncl Nat Gardens Scheme 1978, vice-pres and exec ctee Dist Nursing Assoc UK 1979, memb cncl and grants ctee Nation's Fund for Nurses 1980, tstee Kytes Settlement for Disabled Ex-Servicemen, Open Section RSM 1982 (cncl 1985-); dep co cmmr St John Ambulance Herts 1983-87, chapter-gen Order of St John London 1987, Cdr St John Ambulance Herts 1987, chm Nat Florence Nightingale Memorial ctee 1988, memb cncl Br Holistic Assoc 1987, assoc tstee Florence Nightingale Museum Tst 1988; FRSA, MRSH, LRAM; Offr of the Venerable Order of St John; *Recreations* country life, music, gardening, the arts (creative, performing and spectator), tennis, designing and making things; *Clubs* Seaview YC, RSM; *Style*— Mrs Martin Acland, OBE; Standon Green End, near Ware, Hertfordshire SG11 1BN (☎ 0920 438 527)

ACLAND, Brig Peter Bevil Edward; OBE (1945), MC (1941), TD (1948), JP (Devon 1962), DL (1948); s of Col Alfred Dyke Acland, CBE, TD, JP (d 1937), and Hon Beatrice Smith, da of Viscountess Hambleden; *b* 9 July 1902; *Educ* Eton, ChCh Oxford (MA); *m* 1927, Bridget Susan, da of late Canon Herbert Barnett; 2 s (Sir Antony Acland, GCMG, KCVO, Maj-Gen Sir John Acland, KCB, CBE, *qqv*); *Career* Sudan Political Serv 1924-40; served WWII Abyssinia, N Africa, Aegean (wounded, despatches), Brig 1945, cmd Devon Yeo 1947-51, Hon Col 1952-68; farmer 1946-80; chm Devon Agric Exec Ctee 1948-58, chm T and AF Assoc Devon 1960-67; High Sheriff 1961, Vice Lt Devon 1962-78; *Style*— Brig Peter Acland, OBE, MC, TD, JP, DL; Little Court, Feniton, Honiton, Devon (☎ 0404 850202)

ACLAND, Sir Richard Thomas Dyke; 15 Bt (E 1678, with precedency from 1644), of Columb-John, Devon; s of Rt Hon Sir Francis Dyke Acland, 14 Bt, PC, MP (Richmond, N Yorks), JP, DL (d 1939); *b* 26 Nov 1906; *Educ* Rugby, Balliol Coll Oxford; *m* 1936, Anne Stella, da of Robert G Alford (d 1937), of Chelsea; 3 s; *Heir* s, John Dyke Acland; *Career* MP (Lib and subsequently Cwlth) Barnstaple 1939-45, MP (Lab) Gravesend 1947-55; teacher Wandsworth Comprehensive Sch 1955-59, lectr St Luke's Coll Exeter 1960-74; *Style*— Sir Richard Acland, Bt; College, Broadclyst, Exeter

ACLAND-HOOD, (Alexander) William; *see*: Fuller-Acland-Hood

ACLOQUE, Hon Mrs (Camilla Anne Bronwen); *née* Scott-Ellis; da of 9 Baron Howard de Walden and 5 Baron Seaford, and his 1 w, Countess Irene Harrach (d 1975); *b* 1 April 1947; *Educ* Convent of the Sacred Heart Woldingham Surrey; *m* 1971, Guy, s of John Acloque (d 1971), of Reigate, Surrey; 1 s, 2 da (twin); *Career* co-heiress to Barony of Howard de Walden; *Style*— The Hon Mrs Acloque; Alderley Grange, Wotton-under-Edge, Glos (☎ 0453 842161)

ACRES, Dr Douglas Ian; s of Syndey Herbert Acres, MBE (d 1952), of Benfleet, Essex, and Hilda Emily (d 1979), *née* Chatton; *b* 21 Nov 1924; *Educ* Westcliff HS, Borland's Victoria, London Hosp Med Coll; *m* 17 Sept 1949, Joan Marjorie, da of Charles William Bloxham (d 1966), of Benfleet, Essex; 3 da (Mary b 1952, Jane b 1955, Elizabeth b 1957); *Career* RAF med branch 1951-53 Acting Sqdn-Ldr, vice pres med bd, Air Crew Selection Centre Hornchurch; AOC's Commendation and Vote of Thanks OStJ East Coast flood disaster 1953; house surgeon and casualty registrar King George Hosp Ilford 1949-51, GP 1953-84; MD Remploy Ltd 1962-, med correspondent, SE Essex Evening Echo 1967-, med advsr, Congregation Fedn 1985-; memb and chm pub health ctee Benfleet UDC 1960-65; chm: Essex Cncl on Alcoholism 1981-86, governing body King John Sch Thundersley 1971-, Rochford Bench 1974-84 (memb since 1958); pres Essex Branch Nat Assoc Probation Officers 1983-; memb Lord Chancellor's Essex Advsy Ctee 1973-84, chm cncl Magistrates' Assoc 1984-87; memb: ctee on Mentally Abnormal Offenders 1972-75, int dept ctee on alcoholism 1975-78, Parole Board 1984-87; Freedom City of London, Liveryman, Society of Apothecaries 1968; MRCS, LRCP 1949, MRCEP 1968, DMJ (CLIN) 1968; *Books articles and chapters on* medico-legal matters since 1968; *Clubs* Royal Society of Medicine; *Style*— Dr Douglas Acres, CBE, DL; Thundersley Lodge, Runnymede Chase, Thundersley, Benfleet, Essex SS7 3DB (☎ 0268 793241)

ACTON, Daphne, Dowager Lady; Daphne; *née* Strutt; o da of 4 Baron Rayleigh, JP, DL (d 1947), and his 1 w, Lady Mary Hilda Clements (d 1919), 2 da of 4 Earl of Leitrim; *b* 5 Nov 1911; *m* 25 Nov 1931, 3 Baron Acton, CMG, MBE, TD (d 1989); 5 s, 6 da (1 decd); *Style*— The Dowager Lady Acton; Marcham Priories, Nr Abingdon, Oxon OX13 6NT (☎ 0865 391260)

ACTON, Sir Harold Mario Mitchell; CBE (1965); s of Arthur Mario Acton, and Hortense, *née* Mitchell; *b* 5 July 1904; *Educ* Eton, Ch Ch Oxford (BA); *Career* served WW II RAF, seconded to SHAEF (Paris) 1944; lectured in English literature Peking National Univ and Normal Coll; author; vice chm Br Inst of Florence; Grand Offr of the Italian Republic; Hon DLitt New York; FRSL; kt 1974; *Recreations* baiting Philistines; *Clubs* Savile; *Style*— Sir Harold Acton, CBE; Villa La Pietra, Florence, Italy (☎ 496 156)

ACTON, 4 Baron Acton (UK 1869); Sir Richard Gerald Lyon-Dalberg-Acton; 11 Bt (E 1644); also a Patrician of Naples; patron of one living (but being a Roman Catholic cannot present); eldest s of 3 Baron Acton, CMG, MBE, TD (d 1989), and Hon Daphne, *née* Strutt, da of 4 Baron Rayleigh; *b* 30 July 1941; *Educ* St George's Coll Salisbury Rhodesia, Trinity Coll Oxford; *m* 1, 28 Aug 1965, Hilary Juliet Sarah (d 1973), 2 da of Dr Osmond Laurence Charles Cookson, of Perth, WA; 1 s (Hon John Charles Ferdinand Harold); *m* 2, 1974 (m dis 1987), Judith Garfield, da of the Hon Garfield Todd, of Hokonu Ranch, P O Dadaya, Rhodesia (formerly PM of S Rhodesia); m 3, 19 March 1988, Patricia, o da of late M Morey Nassif, of 115 34th Street, South East, Cedar Rapids, Iowa 53403, USA; *Heir* s, Hon John Charles Ferdinand Harold Lyon-Dalberg-Acton b 19 Aug 1966; *Career* barr Inner Temple 1976; dir Coutts & Co 1971-74; *Style*— The Rt Hon the Lord Acton; Marcham Priory, nr Abingdon, Oxon

ACTON, William Antony; s of late William Acton; *b* 8 April 1904; *Educ* Eton, Trinity Coll Cambridge; *m* 1932, Joan, da of Hon Francis Pearson; 1 da; *Career* served with Treasury 1939-45, thereafter banker; High Sheriff London 1955; *Clubs* White's; *Style*— William Acton, Esq; PO Box 31, Poste Restante, Corfu, Greece (☎ 91 236)

ADAM; *see*: Forbes-Adam

ADAM, Beverley Ann; da of Clement Alfred Adam, and Nora Margaret, *née* Willis; *b* 11 Feb 1953; *Educ* King George V Sch Hong Kong, Warwick Univ (LLB); *m* 16 April 1977, Graham Robert Starling, s of Arthur Ewart Starling, MBE; 2 s (Gareth b 20 April 1982, Sean b 12 Dec 1985); *Career* slr Linklater & Paines; memb Worshipful Co of City of London Slrs; memb Law Soc; *Style*— Miss Beverley Adam; Linklaters & Paines, Barrington House, 59-67 Gresham St, London EC2V 7JA (☎ 01 606 7080, fax 01 606 5113, telex 884349)

ADAM, David Lionel; TD (1950); s of Cdr Lionel Stuart Moncrieffe Adam, RN (d 1955), of Hythe, Kent; *b* 15 Oct 1915; *Educ* Christ's Hosp; *m* 1945, Marjorie Diana, da of Gerald Sharpe (d 1972), of Charlwood, Surrey; 2 s (Nigel, James); *Career* served WWII, Maj, Middle East; CA; managing ptnr Mann Judd and Co 1968-75; *Recreations* walking; *Clubs* Naval and Military; *Style*— David Adam, Esq, TD; The Grange, Ruckinge, Ashford, Kent (☎ 023 373 2400)

ADAM, (David Stuart) Gordon; s of James Adam RCNC (d 1973), and Florence Victoria, *née* Kilpatrick (d 1970); *b* 21 Dec 1927; *Educ* Upper Canada Coll, Queen's Univ Belfast (LLB), Trinity Hall Cambridge (MA, LLB), Harvard Business Sch (AMP); *m* 4 Sept 1965, Rosanne, da of William Watson (d 1979), of Ardlamont; 2 s (James b 1966, Alastair b 1972), 1 da (Alexandra b 1968); *Career* WO 1952-53; barr 1951; Barclays Bank: joined 1954, gen mangr 1968, dir Barclays Bank UK 1977-87, dep chm Tst Co Ltd 1977-82; chm Int Tst Gp 1983-; cncl chm Wycombe Abbey Sch 1981; *Clubs* Boodle's, Kandahar; *Style*— Gordon Adam, Esq; Mulberry Hill, Wendover, Bucks; Quinta dos Ciprestes, Sta Barbara de Nexe, Portugal; 54 Lombard Street, London EC3P 3AH (☎ 01 626 1567)

ADAM, Dr Gordon Johnston; MEP; (Lab) Northumbria 1979; s of John Craig Adam (d 1969), and Deborah Armstrong, *née* Johnston; *b* 28 Mar 1934; *Educ* Leeds Univ (BSc, PhD); *m* 1973, Sarah Jane, da of John Seely; 1 s (John Duncan b 1979); *Career* mining engr NCB 1959-79; dep ldr North Tyneside Met Borough Cncl 1975-80, memb Northern Econ Planning Cncl 1974-79; vice chm Euro Parliaments Energy, Res and

Technol Ctee 1984-; *Style*— Dr Gordon Adam, MEP; 2 Queens Rd, Whitley Bay, Tyne and Wear (☎ 091 2528616); office: 10 Coach Rd, Wallsend, Tyne and Wear NE28 6JA (☎ 091 2635838)

ADAM, James; s of James Wheelan Hudson Adam (d 1948), of Troon, and Mary Ann Reid, *née* Polland; *b* 12 Jan 1937; *Educ* Marr Coll Troon; *m* 30 Sept 1967 (m dis), Janet Elizabeth; *Career* CA James Adam & Co; fell Inst of Chartered Accountants of Scotland 1961; *Recreations* golf, Robert Burns, Al Jolson Soc; *Clubs* Troon (Portland), Irvine Burns; *Style*— James Adam, Esq; 39A Titchfield Road, Troon KA10 6AN (☎ 0294 314018); 151 High Street, Irvine KA12 8AD (☎ 0294 76386)

ADAM, Nigel David; s of Maj David Lionel Adam, TD, of The Grange, Ruckinge, Ashford, Kent, and Marjorie Diana, *née* Sharpe; *b* 7 April 1946; *Educ* The King's Sch Canterbury, St Andrews Univ (MA); *m* 29 Aug 1987, Katherine, da of Edward Neil McMillan, of 41 Grapevine Rd, Wenham, Massachusetts, USA; *Career* corr Reuters Europe 1971-78, US ed Euromoney New York 1981-83, dep ed Euromoney London 1983-85, ed Business Magazine 1985-86, managing ed Cornhill Pubns Ltd 1987-; contributor to magazines incl: The Banker, American Banker, International Management; *Recreations* tennis, squash, cricket, backgammon; *Clubs* RAC; *Style*— Nigel Adam, Esq; Tudor Lodge, Compton Bassett, Calne, Wiltshire SN11 8RA (☎ 0249 816796); 124 Great Portland St, London W1N 5PG (☎ 01 436 4417)

ADAMS; *see*: Small-Adams

ADAMS, Dr Aileen Kirkpatrick; CBE (1988); da of Dr Joseph Adams, MC (d 1985), of Sheffield, and Agnes, *née* Munro (d 1983); *b* 5 Sept 1923; *Educ* Farringtons Sch Chislehurst Kent, Sheffield Univ (MB, ChB), Cambridge Univ (MA); *Career* clinical fell Massachesetts Gen Hosp Boston USA 1955-57, first asst Nuffield Dept of Anaesthetics Oxford 1957-59, conslt anaesthetist Addenbrooke's Hosp Cambridge 1960-84, sr lectr Lagos Univ Med Sch Nigeria 1963-64, assoc lectr Univ of Cambridge 1977-84, dean Faculty of Anaesthetists RCS 1985-88; examiner: Clinical Pharmacology Cambridge Univ 1977-80, Final FFARCS 1979-82; dining memb Trinity Hall Cambridge; hon memb Assoc of Anaesthetists of GB and Ireland 1989 (hon sec 1970-72, vice-pres 1976-78), memb ed bd Anaesthetists 1972-85; pres: Soc of Anaesthetists of SW Region, East Anglian Assoc of Anaesthetists 1983-85; cncl memb RCS 1982-84 and 1985-88; Hon MA Cambridge Univ 1977; Hon FFA SA 1987, RSM (pres anaesthetics section 1985-86), FRCS 1988, FFARCS 1954; *Recreations* choral singing, hill walking, skiing, natural history; *Style*— Dr Aileen Adams, CBE

ADAMS, Air Vice-Marshal Alexander Annan; CB (1957), DFC (1944); s of Capt Norman Anderson Adams, of Durham; *b* 14 Nov 1908; *Educ* Beechmont Sevenoaks, Switzerland, Austria; *m* 1933, Eileen Mary, da of William Charles O'Neill, of Dublin; 1 s, (and 1 da decd); *Career* cmmnd RAF 1930, Pilot 54 Fighter Sqdn RAF 1931-33, flying instr 1933-35, Asst Air Attaché Berlin 1937-39, Intelligence Missions 1940-42, cmd 49 Lancaster Sqdn 1943-44, RAF Station Binbrook 1948-50, NATO Standing Gp Washington 1951-53, Air Attaché Bonn 1955, MOD 1956, COS FEAF 1957-59; Hawker Siddeley Aviation 1961-66; dir Mental Health Fndn 1970-77; *Books* Passing Experiences (1980); *Recreations* painting; *Clubs* RAF; *Style*— Air Vice-Marshal Alexander Adams, CB, DFC; 31 Saffrons Court, Compton Palace Rd, Eastbourne, East Sussex BN21 1DX

ADAMS, Alfred William David; s of Alfred Adams (d 1928), and Louisa, *née* West (d 1945); *b* 2 April 1905; *Educ* St Lukes Sch, Kingston Tech Coll; *m* 1, 4 Aug 1934 (m dis 1977), Barbara Edith, da of Harold George Ely (d 1960); 1 s (Graham David b 1935), 1 da (Sylvia Lorraine Barbara b 1944); m 2, 1978, Jaqueline Andre Tudor-Pole; *Career* WWII Upper Thames Patrol HG 1940-41, entertainments offr 51 East Surrey Regt 1941-43; unit controller Miny of Transport 1943-51; memb Union Fraternelle Franco Britannique (Br Section) 1951- (pres 1975-); md: Adams Bros Ltd 1926-52, Adams & Adams Ltd 1936-, George Bristow Ltd 1942-52, Adams Randall Ltd 1970-82; dir Adfin Ltd 1963-; memb New Malden Rotary Club 1954, fndr memb Mitre Club with Sir John Boyd-Carpenter Lord Marchwood 1956; Liveryman Worshipful Co of Clockmakers 1976; MIMI 1936, FIMM 1962, FGEM 1988; Membre Honourable de la ville D'Eleu dit Lovette 1980, Medciile de Merite de la Ville 'Henin Beaumont 1977, Medaitte de Merite de la Ville d'Arras 1984; *Recreations* veteran Rolls Royces, veteran car rallies; *Clubs* Rolls Royce Euthusiasts, ex Monte Carlo Rally Br Competitors; *Style*— Alfred Adams, Esq; 31 Anglers Reach, Grove Road, Surbiton, Surrey KT6 4EX (☎ 01 399 0401); Mon Desir, Coney Six, East Wittering, Chichester, W Sussex PO20 8DL (☎ 0243 671 234); Adams House, Dickerage Lane, New Malden, Surrey KT3 3SF (☎ 01 949 1121)

ADAMS, Prof Anthony Peter; s of Sqdn-Ldr Henry William John Adams (d 1986), and Winifred Louise, *née* Brazenor; *b* 17 Oct 1936; *Educ* Epsom Coll, Univ of London (MB BS, PhD); *m* 30 Sept 1961 (m dis 1972), Martha Jill Vearncombe, da of Herbert William Davis (d 1985), of Yeovil, Somerset; 2 s (Christopher b 1963, Paul b 1965); m 2, 12 May 1973, Veronica Rosemary, da of Raymond Ashley John, of Maidenhead, Berks; 1 s (Adrian b 1979), 1 da (Jenny b 1975); *Career* conslt anaesthetist and clinical lectr Nuffield Dept of Anaesthetics Oxford 1969-79; prof of anaesthetics Univ of London at Utd Med and Dental Schs of Guy's and St Thomas's Hosps 1979-; hon conslt anaesthetist Guy's Hosp 1979-; examiner: RCVS 1986-, Univ of the W Indies 1986-, FFARCS 1974-86; senator Euro Acad of Anaesthesiology 1985- (academician 1981-), regnl advsr in anaesthetics SE Thames 1980-88, memb exec ctee Anaesthetic Res Soc 1983-, conslt SE Asia WHO 1982, memb educn res ctee Assoc Anaesthetist GBI 1987-88; visiting professorships inc: Univ of Texas 1983, John Hopkins Hosp Baltimore 1983, Univ of Yale 1984, Univ of Zimbabwe 1985, Univ of W Ontario 1985; memb: Shabbington Parish Cncl 1977-79, bd of govrs Sutton HS for Girls 1988-; FFARCS; *Books* Principles and Practice of Blood - Gas Analysis (jtly 1979, 1982), Intensive Care (jtly 1984), Emergency Anaesthesea (jtly 1986), Recent Advances in Anaesthesia (jtly 1985, 1989); *Recreations* cinema, croquet, tennis, badger watching; *Clubs* Royal Soc of Medicine; *Style*— Prof Anthony Adams; Dept Anaesthetics, Guy's Hospital, London SE1 9RT (☎ 01 407 7600)

ADAMS, Barbara Georgina; *née* Bishop; da of Charles Bishop (d 1980), and Ellaline, *née* Cowdrey (d 1972); *b* 19 Feb 1945; *Educ* Godolphin & Latymer GS, Univ of London (Dip Archaeology), Univ of London (Cert Geology); *m* 27 Sept 1967, Robert Frederick, s of Frederick Adams (ka 1943); *Career* sci asst entomology and sub-dept of anthrolpology Br Museum of Nat History 1962-65, curator Petrie Museum of Egyptian Archaeology 1984- (asst 1965-75, asst curator 1975-84); memb: London Fedn of Museums and Art Galleries, London Museum Consultative Ctee; active memb Lib pty, candidate for GLC 1982; memb: EES, IAE, Palaeopathology Assoc; *Books* Ancient Hierakonpolis (1974), The Koptos Lions (1984), The Fort Cemetery at Hierakonpolis (1987), ed Shire Egyptology series; *Recreations* geology, film, countryside, museums and galleries; *Style*— Mrs Barbara Adams; Petrie Museum of Egyptian Archaeology, University Coll London, Gower St, London WC1E 6BT (☎ 01 387 7050, ext 2882)

ADAMS, Bernard Charles; s of Charles Willoughby Adams (d 1963), of Ryde, IOW, and Emily Alice, *née* Ambrose (d 1950); *b* 29 Oct 1915; *Educ* King James I Sch IOW; *m* 1942, Marjorie Barrett, da of William Henry Frederick Weller (d 1918), of Barnoldswick, Yorks; 3 da (Jane, Gillian d 1983, Catherine d 1973); *Career* TA 1938-39, served WWII 57 Wessex Heavy Anti-Aircraft Regt RA, Battle of Britain defence of Portsmouth and Southampton, 107 HAA Regt (Mobile) RA in UK, France (Normandy), Belgium, Holland, Germany, Capt RA (despatches); architect, sr architect Derbyshire CC 1951-54, asst county architect Kent CC 1954-59, dep county architect Herts CC 1959-60, county architect Somerset CC 1960-80; vice pres RIBA 1970-72 (memb cncl 1963-69 and 1970-76); chm: SW regnl cncl RIBA 1972-74, Structure of the Profession Study RIBA 1976-79; pres: County Architects' Soc 1973-74 (vice pres 1971-73), Soc of Chief Architects of Local Authorities (SCALA) 1975-76 (vice pres 1974-75, hon memb 1983-); memb: Nat Consultative Cncl for the Building and Civil Engrg Industs 1974-80, Bd of Architectural Studies Univ of Bristol 1964-74; architect advsr to Assoc of County Councils 1971-80, fndr chm Architects' Ctee Consortium for Method Building 1961-68; fndr memb Taunton Theatre Tst 1972 (memb Tst Ctee 1972-, chm 1986-), RIBA Architecture Award 1970 (Commendation 1974), Heritage Year Award (European Architectural Heritage Year) 1975, Civic Awards 1962-68 and 1971 (Commendation 1965); ARIBA, FRIBA, FRSA; *Books* contributor to journal of the RIBA and other professional journals; *Recreations* arts, theatre, languages; *Style*— Bernard Adams, Esq; Meadowside, Wild Oak Lane, Trull, Taunton, Somerset TA3 7JT (☎ 0823 272 485)

ADAMS, Lady Celia Anne; *née* Fortescue; da (by 1 m) of 7 Earl Fortescue, *qv*; *b* 30 Dec 1957; *m* 10 Dec 1988, David A S Adams, yst s of Dr M S Adams, of Seaview, Isle of Wight

ADAMS, Prof Colin Wallace Maitland; s of Sidney Ewart Adams (d 1958), of The Old Rectory, Hawkwell, Essex, and Gladys Alathea Fletcher, *née* Keddie (d 1970); *b* 17 Feb 1928; *Educ* Oundle, Christs Coll Cambridge (MA, MD), London Hospital Medical Coll, London Univ (DSc); *m* 16 May 1953, Anne, da of Ernest William Brownhill (d 1933), of Squirrel Cottage, Mere, Knutsford, Cheshire; 1s (Richard James Maitland b 1958); *Career* Freedom res fell London Hosp 1955-58, visiting scientist Nat Inst of Health Bethesda USA 1960-61, reader in experimental pathology Guy's Hosp Med Sch 1962-65, conslt pathologist Guy's Hosp 1962, Sir William Dunn prof of pathology Guy's Hosp Med Sch 1965; chm div of pathology Utd Med Dental Schs of Guy's and St Thomas' Hosps London Univ 1984-87; conslt ed Arterosclerosis (Elsevier) 1984- (sr ed 1966-83); former memb: Cncl Int Arterosclerosis Soc, Cncl Int Cardiology Soc; memb advsy panel DHSS Ctee on Diet & Vascular Disease; FRCP, FRCPath; *Books* Neurohistochemistry (1965), Vascular Histochemistry (1967), Research on Multiple Sclerosis (1972), Multiple Sclerosis (jointly 1983, new edn 1989), Colour Atlas of Multiple Sclerosis & Other Demyclinating Diseases (1988); *Style*— Prof Colin Adams; The Priory, Braxted Rd, Tiptree, Essex CO5 0QB (☎ 0621 818446); Division of Pathology, United Medical & Dental Schs of Guy's and St Thomas' Hospitals, Guys Campus, London Bridge SE1 9RT (☎ 01 470 7600); Neuropathology Laboratory, Runwell Hospital, Wickford, Essex (☎ 0268 735555)

ADAMS, Air Cdre Cyril Douglas; CB (1948), OBE (1942); s of Lionel Lincoln Adams (d 1940), of Penn Hall, Parlestrone, Dorset, and Blanche Annie, *née* Meatyard (d 1960); *b* 18 Sept 1897; *Educ* Parkstone GS; *m* 1, 1927, Doris Mary (d 1957), da of Edward LeBrocq, of Highfield, Jersey, CI; 1 s (Robin), 1 da (Tamaris); m 2, 1959 (m dis 1968), Joan Ramsay, da of Cdr William Ramsay-Fairfax, CMG, DSO, RN (d 1946); m 3, 1968, Mrs Kate Edna Webster; *Career* served WW I, cmmnd RFC 1918, staff and flying duties Halton 1918-27, Sqdn Leader CO 15 Sqdn Abingdon 1936-38, Staff HQ Bomber Cmd 1938, CO 38 Sqdn 1938-39, served WW II (Egypt, Palestine, India), Staff Offr No 3 Gp 1939-40, Station Cdr Kembline, Oakington, Abingdon 1940-44, Base Cdr Marston Moor and N Laffenham 1944, AOA Air HQ Delhi 1944-45, Base Cdre Bombay 1945-46, Air Cdre No 2 Royal Indian Air Force 1945-47, No 85 Gp Germany 1947-50, ret; *Recreations* golf, tapestry, rugby, cricket (represented RAF); *Clubs* Barton on Sea Golf; *Style*— Air Cdre Cyril Adams, CB. OBE; Flat 6, Solent Pines, Milford on Sea (☎ Lymington 43754);

ADAMS, David Howard; s of Capt Bernard Adams, RA (d 1982), of Manchester, and Eve, *née* Glass (d 1987); *b* 15 Nov 1943; *Educ* Manchester GS; *m* 22 June 1969, Zoë Adams, da of Victor Joseph Dwek, of Manchester; 2 da (Gisele b 1970, Zanine b 1975); *Career* dir Henry Cooke Lumsden plc 1975, int chief exec Henry Cooke Gp plc 1988; past chm: Manchester Stock Exchange, Inst for Fiscal Studies North West; ctee memb: Whitworth Art Gallery Centenary Appeal, Umist Millenium Ctee; memb Worshipful Co of Chartered Accountants 1978; FCA 1967, FRSA 1988; *Recreations* acting, reading, trying to get fit; *Style*— David Adams, Esq; 1 King Street, Manchester M60 3AH (☎ 061 834 2332, fax as phone, car tel 0836 600714, telex 667783)

ADAMS, Hon Mrs (Eileen Esther); *née* Handcock; da of late 7 Baron Castlemaine; *b* 14 Nov 1931; *m* 1959, Flt Lt Terence Frank Adams, RAF (ret), s of late Joseph Adams, of Wolverhampton; 2 s (Patrick b 1960, Niall b 1968), 1 da (Siobhan b 1962); *Clubs* RAF; *Style*— The Hon Mrs Adams; c/o National Westminster Bank, 851 Gleadless Rd, Sheffield S12 2LG

ADAMS, Hon Lady; Hon (Mary) Elizabeth; *née* Lawrence; da of 3 Baron Trevethin and (1) Oaksey, DSO, TD, PC (d 1971), and Marjorie, *née* Robinson; *b* 20 Nov 1922; *m* 1954, Sir Philip George Doyne Adams, KCMG, *qv*; 2 s, 2 da; *Style*— The Hon Lady Adams; 78 Sussex Sq, London W2

ADAMS, Lady; Esther Marie Ottilie; *née* Overdyck; *m* 1980, as his 2 w, Sir Maurice Edward Adams, KBE (d 1982), sometime Civil Engineer in Chief to Admiralty; *Style*— Lady Adams; 32 Cavendish Ave, Ealing, London W13 (☎ 01 998 2376)

ADAMS, Prof (John) Frank; s of William Frederick Adams (d 1980), of London, and Jean Mary, *née* Baines (d 1967); *b* 5 Nov 1930; *Educ* Bedford Sch, Trinity Coll Cambridge (BA, MA, PhD, ScD); *m* 13 Dec 1953, Grace Rhoda, da of late Charles Benjamin Carty ; 1 s (Adrian b 1960), 3 da (Alice b 1958, Lucy b 1964, Katy b 1965) ; *Career* RE 1948-49; jr lectr Oxford 1955-56, res fell Trinity Coll Cambridge 1955-58, asst lectr Cambridge and dir studies in mathematics Trinity Hall 1958-61, reader Manchester Univ 1962-64 (Fielden prof 1964-71), Lowndean prof of astronomy and geometry and professorial fell Trinity Coll Cambridge 1970-; memb mathematics ctee Sci and Engrg Res Cncl; Hon DSc Heidelberg 1986; FRS, foreign assoc Nat Acad of Sci USA, foreign memb Royal Danish Acad of Sci & Letters; *Books* Stable Homotopy Theory (1966), Lectures on Lie Groups (1969), Algebraic Topology (1972), Stable Homotopy and Generalised Homology (1974), Infinite Loop Spaces (1978); *Recreations* walking, climbing, enamel; *Style*— Prof Frank Adams; DPMMS, 16 Mill Lane, Cambridge CB2 1SB (☎ 0223 337999)

ADAMS, (Gerard) Gerry; MP (Provisional Sinn Fein) Belfast West 1983-; *Educ* St Mary's GS Belfast; *Career* vice pres Provisional Sinn Fein 1978-, elected (W Belfast) N Ireland Assembly 1982; *Style*— Gerry Adams, Esq, MP; House of Commons, London SW1A 0AA

ADAMS, Haldane George; s of George Edward (d 1952), of Paignton, Devon, and Gwendoline Ivy, *née* Hill (d 1988); *b* 12 Mar 1932; *Educ* King Edward VI Sch Devon; *m* 13 June 1953, Doreen Margaret, da of Maj F A Monaghan of Emsworth, Hants; 1 s (Stephen b 1953); *Career* cmmnd Lt Light Inf Somerset 1950-53; gen mangr office supplies IBM S Africa 1969-75, mktg dir Koroes Nordic Ltd 1975-, md Keymax Int Ltd 1988-; chm of govrs Nazeing Park Sch Essex, chm Thaxted Branch Cons Assoc, vice-chm Charity for Physically Handicapped Thaxted Essex; memb IOD 1977; *Recreations* sailing, golf; *Style*— Haldane Adams, Esq; Drive House, Watling Lane, Thaxted, Essex (☎ 0371 830 854); Kaymax Int Ltd, West Rd, Templefields, Harlow, Essex CM20 2AL (☎ 0279 20411, fax 0279 44550, telex 81456)

ADAMS, Jennifer; *née* Crisp; da of Arthur Roy Thomas Crisp, and Joyce Muriel, *née* Davey; *b* 1 Feb 1948; *Educ* City of London Sch, IPRA Staff Coll; *m* 21 Sept 1968, Terence William Adams; *Career* supt Central Royal Parks 1983-; FILAM, Dip PRA, FI Hort; *Clubs* Soroptimists' International; *Style*— Mrs Jennifer Adams; Central Royal Parks, The Storeyard, Hyde Park, London W2 2UH

ADAMS, John Douglas Richard; s of Gordon Arthur Richard Adams (d in enemy hands 1944), and Marjorie Ethel Adams, *née* Ongley (d 1983); *b* 19 Mar 1940; *Educ* Watford GS, Durham Univ (LLB); *m* 12 April 1966, Anne Easton, da of Robert Easton Todd (d 1967); 2 da (Katharine b 1975, Caroline b 1978); *Career* called to the Bar Lincoln's Inn 1968; lectr in law: Univ of Newcastle upon Tyne 1963-71, UCL 1971-78; also practised at the Revenue Bar until 1978; special commnr of Income Tax 1978-82; current office registrar of Civil Appeals 1982-; hon lectr St Edmund Hall Oxford 1975-; *Publications* International Taxation of Multinational Enterprises (with J Whalley, 1977), Supreme Court Practice (ed 1985 and 1988 editions), Atkin's Court Forms (1984), Chitty & Jacob's Queen's Bench Forms (1987); *Recreations* music, walking, dining; *Style*— John Adams, Esq; Royal Courts of Justice, Strand, London WC2A 2LL (☎ 01 936 6017)

ADAMS, Rear Adm John Harold; CB (1967), LVO (1957); s of H V Adams (d 1938), of Alnmouth, Northumberland; *b* 19 Dec 1918; *Educ* Glenalmond; *m* 1, 1943 (m dis 1961), Mary, da of Arthur Parker, of London; 1 s (decd); m 2, 1961, Ione Eadie, MVO, JP, da of late Col James Alister Eadie, DSO, TD; 2 s, 2 da; *Career* joined RN 1936, served WW II (despatches), Lt 1941, Lt Cmdr 1949, Cdr 1951, Capt 1957, Rear Adm 1966, asst Chief Naval Staff (policy) 1966-68, ret; dir Paper Industry Trg Bd and Employers Fedn of Papermakers 1968-74, dir-gen Br Paper and Bd Indust Fedn 1974-83; md DUO (UK) Ltd (Interview Guidance) 1983-; FIPM; *Recreations* photography, fishing; *Clubs* Army and Navy; *Style*— Rear Adm John Adams, CB, LVO; The Oxdrove House, Burghclere, Newbury, Berks (☎ 063 527 385)

ADAMS, John Kenneth; o child of late Thomas John Adams, and Mabel, *née* Jarvis; *b* 3 June 1915; *Educ* City of Oxford Sch, Balliol Coll Oxford; *m* 1944, Margaret, o child of late Edward Claude Fortescue, of Banbury, Oxon; *Career* served WW II RAFVR; Country Life: joined 1946, asst ed 1952, dep ed 1956, ed 1958-73, editorial dir 1959-73; ret; *Style*— J K Adams, Esq; 95 Alleyn Pk, W Dulwich, London SE21 8AA (☎ 01 693 1736)

ADAMS, John Trevor; s of Fl Lt Claude Walter Adams (d 1985), of Wembley, Middx, and Ann Fletcher Gordon, *née* Taylor; *b* 2 April 1936; *Educ* UCS; *m* 6 July 1963, Elizabeth Mary, da of Montague William Lacey (d 1981), of Lytham, Lancs; 1 s (David John b 1968), 1 da (Caroline Mary b 1965); *Career* Nat Serv RASC 1954-56; articled to Temple Gothard 1957-63, audit sr Shipley Blackburn Sutton & Co 1963-68, tax sr Arthur Andersen 1966-68, tax sr and tax ptnr Josolyne Miles and Cassleton Elliot 1968-71, ptnr Clark Whitehill 1972-; FCA 1964; *Recreations* rugby, cricket, badminton, music, fine art; *Style*— John Adams, Esq; 4 Grove Rd, Northwood, Middx HA6 2AP (☎ 09274 24933); 25 New St Square, London EC4 (☎ 01 353 1577, fax 01 583 1720, telex 887422)

ADAMS, Maj Kenneth Galt; CVO (1979); s of William Adams, OBE (d 1949), of the Limes, Ranskill, Retford, Notts, and Christina Elisabeth, *née* Hall (d 1948); *b* 6 Jan 1920; *Educ* Doncaster GS, Lambeth (MA); *m* 23 Dec 1988, Sally, da of late Col John Middleton, of Fleet, Hants, and widow of Douglas Long; *Career* RASC 1940-59: cmmnd Cairo 1941, WWII served ME and N Africa, DADST WO 1946-48, co cdr Kenya 1949-51, DAA & QMG Aldershot 1952, Staff Coll Camberley 1953, DA & QMG HQ Northern Cmd 1954-56, sr instr RASC 1956-59; mangr Proprietors of Hays Wharf Ltd 1960-61 (dir 1966-70), dir Hays Wharf Ltd 1962-70, dir of studies St Georges House Windsor Castle 1969-76; Comimo fell St George's House 1976-79; Royal Soc of Arts 1979; Indust fell Comimo Fndn 1987-; vice chm Archbishops Cncl on Evangelism 1965-77, chm Industl Christian Fellowship 1977-86, patron Nat Soc for Christian Standards in Soc 1985-; FCIT 1980, CBIM 1975, FMS 1970, FRSA 1979; *Recreations* reading, walking my dog; *Clubs* Army and Navy; *Style*— Maj Kenneth Adams, CVO; St George's Lodge, 8 Datchet Rd, Windsor, Berks SL4 1QE (☎ 0753 869 708)

ADAMS, Hon Mrs (Marjorie Heather); *née* Davies; JP (1963); yr da of 1 Baron Darwen (d 1950), and Kathleen, *née* Brown (d 1964); *b* 27 Oct 1923; *Educ* Queen Mary's Sch Lytham, Ayton Sch, The Mount Sch York, Rachel McMillan Training Coll; *m* 9 Aug 1944, Frederick Joseph Adams, CBE, s of late Joseph Stephen Adams; 1 s (Christopher Stephen b 1946); *Recreations* painting; *Style*— The Hon Mrs Adams, JP; 2 Beaumont Close, Belper, Derbyshire DE5 OED; 4 Redwood Close, Boverton, Llantwit Major, S Glamorgan CF6 9UT

ADAMS, Surgeon Rear Admiral Maurice Henry; CB (1965); s of Henry Adams, of Belfast, and Dorothea, *née* Whitehouse; *b* 16 July 1908; *Educ* Queen's Univ Belfast (MB BCh, DOMS); *m* 1938, Kathleen Mary, da of William J Hardy, of Belfast; 1 s (Brian), 2 da (Moya, Patricia); *Career* RN Med Serv 1932-66; *Style*— Surgeon Rear Admiral Maurice Adams, CB; Canberra, Rock, Wadebridge, Cornwall PL27 6LF

ADAMS, Michael Robert; s of Walter Adams (d 1978), of London, and Dorothy May, *née* Masters (1980); *b* 23 Sept 1923; *m* 15 June 1946, Margaret Steven, da of Douglas Carruth Stevenson (d 1977), of Wimbledon; 2 s (Robert Douglas b 7 May 1948, Ian Colin b 10 Oct 1954); *Career* WW II Fl Lt RAF 1939-47; insurance broker 1947-82, memb Lloyds, dep chm Sedgewicks Ltd 1979-82, chm Lloyds Insurance Brokers Ctee 1975- 76; chm numerous farming ctees, dep chm Horsley Probus Club; Freeman City of London, fndr memb Worshipful Co of Insurers; memb ACII; *Recreations* farming, travel; *Style*— Michael Adams, Esq; Crocknorth Farm, East Horsley, Surrey KT24 5TG (☎ 048 653325)

ADAMS, Murray; s of Frank Adams (d 1950), of Mansfield, Vic, Australia; *b* 15 July 1919; *Educ* Trinity GS Melbourne; *m* 1946, Ethne Margot Maplesden, da of Brig William Henry Scott, CMG, DSO (d 1959); 1 s, 2 da; *Career* Fl Lt RAAF North Africa, Italy, UK, Netherlands 1940 (despatches 1945); mangr Nat Safety Cncl of Australia (Qld Div) 1966-73, state dir 1973-84; memb Consumer Affairs Cncl Qld 1981-; *Recreations* tennis; *Clubs* United Service (pres 1984-85); *Style*— Murray Adams, Esq; 16 Lohe St, Indooroopilly, Qld 4068, Australia (☎ (07) 870 2816)

ADAMS, (Adrian) Neil; s of Alfred Cyril Adams, of 144 Dovehouse Drive, Wellesbourne, Warwicks, and Jean, *née* Wrighley; *b* 27 Sept 1958; *m* 27 Aug 1984, Alison Louise, da of Alan Charles Walker; 1 s (Ashley Neil James); *Career* 8 times Br Open Judo Champion, European Title holder 1979, 1980, 1983, 1984, 1985, 2 Olympic Silver medals, World Champion 1981;; *Books* A Life in Judo (1985), Olympic Judo (Tachiwaza) standing, Olympic judo (Newaza) Groundwork, The Neil Adams Guide to Better Judo 1987-88; *Style*— Neil Adams, Esq; The Neil Adams Club, Kenpas Highway, Coventry, Warwics, (☎ 01 771 3795)

ADAMS, Prof Norman Edward Albert; s of Albert Henry Adams, and Elizabeth Winifred Rose Adams; *b* 9 Feb 1927; *Educ* Junior Sch Edgware, Harrow Art Sch, Royal Coll of Art (MA); *m* 1947, Anna Theresa, da of George Baesden Butt (d 1963); 2 s (Jacob, Benjamin); *Career* artist, painter; prof of fine art Univ of Newcastle upon Tyne 1981-; prof of painting and keeper of the Royal Academy 1986-; freelance artist (solo exhibitions) murals St Anselms Church Kennington London 1970, Stations of the Cross Our Lady of Lourdes Milton Keynes 1975, decor for Ballet Covent Garden and Sadler's Wells; RA, ARCA, ARA; *Recreations* art, music, literature; *Style*— Professor Norman Adams; 284 Butts, Horton-in-Ribblesdale, Settle, N Yorks (☎ (072 96) 284); Royal Academy of Arts, Piccadilly, London W1 (☎ 01 734 9052)

ADAMS, Sir Philip George Doyne; KCMG (1969, CMG 1959); s of Dr George Basil Doyne Adams (d 1957), and Arline Maud, *née* Dodgson (d 1986); *b* 17 Dec 1915; *Educ* Lancing, Ch Ch Oxford (MA); *m* 1954, Hon (Mary) Elizabeth, *qv*; 2 s (Geoffrey b 1957, Justin b 1961), 2 da (Lucy b 1955, Harriet b 1959); *Career* HM Consular and Diplomatic Serv 1939-75: ambass to Jordan 1966-70, dep sec Cabinet Office 1971-72, ambass to Egypt 1973-75; dir Ditchley Fndn 1977-82; *Clubs* Brooks's; *Style*— Sir Philip Adams, KCMG; 78 Sussex Sq, London W2 (☎ 01 262 1547); The Malt House, Ditchley, Enstone, Oxon (☎ 060 872 679)

ADAMS, Richard Borlase; CBE (1982); s of James Elwin Cokayne Adams (d 1961), and Susan Mercer, *née* Porter; *b* 9 Sept 1921; *Educ* Winchester, Trinity Coll Oxford; *m* 1951, Susan Elizabeth, da of Col Ronald Streeter Lambert, MC (d 1976); 2 s (Christopher, Jeremy), 1 da (Jill); *Career* served WW II with Rifle Bde Middle East and Italy; chm Islay Kerr & Co Ltd Singapore 1963-66; chm Br India Steam Navigation Co Ltd 1970-84 (dir 1966, md 1969), chief exec P & O 1981-84 (dir 1970-, dep md 1974, md 1979-84), dir Clerical Med and Gen Life Assur Soc 1975; *Recreations* gardening, tennis, golf; *Clubs* Oriental; *Style*— Richard Adams, Esq, CBE; Beacon House, Bethersden, Ashford, Kent TN26 3AE (☎ 023 382 247)

ADAMS, Richard George; s of Evelyn George Beadon Adams, and Lilian Rosa, *née* Button; *b* 9 May 1920; *Educ* Bradfield, Worcester Coll Oxford (MA); *m* 1949, (Barbara) Elizabeth Acland; 2 da (Juliet, Rosamond); *Career* Nat Serv 1940-46; entered Civil Service 1948, ret 1974; writer in residence: Univ of Florida 1975, Hollins Coll Virginia; author; pres RSPCA 1980-82; FRSL; *Books* Watership Down (1972, filmed 1978), Shardik (1974), The Plague Dogs (1977, filmed 1982), The Iron Wolf (1980, short stories), The Girl in a Swing (1980), Voyage Through The Antarctic (1982, travel book), Maia (1984), The Bureaucats (1985), Nature Diary (1985), contributed to and edited Occasional Poets anthology (1986), The Legend of Te Tuna (narrative poem, 1986) Traveller (1988); *Clubs* MCC; *Style*— Richard Adams, Esq; 26 Church St, Whitchurch, Hants, RG28 7AR

ADAMS, Richard Hugh MacGregor; MBE (1989); s of Ronald Shaw Adams (d 1974), of Gosforth, Newcastle-on-Tyne, and Elizabeth Frances Mary Carew-Hunt, *née* Hunter; *b* 7 Nov 1945; *Educ* Harrow; *m* 1, 19 April 1969 (m dis 1980), Sally Hazel; 1 da (Lucy b 1973); m 2, 25 Sept 1985, Susan Jane, da of George Gray, of Richmond, N Yorks; 1 s (Jack b 1988), 1 da (Rosie b 1985); *Career* md Shaws Biscuits Ltd 1970, chm and md Northumbrian Fine Foods plc 1986; chm: Sunwheel Foods Ltd 1987, Danish Natural Foods 1987; *Recreations* sport, tennis, squash, jogging; *Clubs* Northumberland Lawn Tennis and Squash Rackets; *Style*— Richard Adams, Esq, MBE; Longshaws Mill, Netherwitton, Morpeth, Northumberland; 27 Brandling Place South, Newcastle-upon-Tyne 2 (☎ 067 072 291); Northumbrian Fine Foods PLC, Dukesway, Team Valley, Gateshead, Tyne and Wear NE11 OQP (☎ 091 482 2611, fax 491 0826, telex 53346)

ADAMS, (John) Roderick Seton; s of George Adams (d 1980), of Edinburgh, and Winifred, *née* Wilson; *b* 29 Feb 1936; *Educ* Whitgift Sch, Trinity Coll Cambridge (MA); *m* 1965, (Pamela) Bridget, da of Rev David Edmund Rice, MC (d 1978), of Hexham; 3 s (Robert b 1966, James b 1967, John b 1973); *Career* 2 Lt Seaforth Highlanders 1954-56, Capt Parachute Regt 1960-66; barr Inner Temple 1962, in practice 1968-, rec Crown Ct 1980-; *Recreations* music, fishing; *Style*— Roderick Adams, Esq; 78 South Croxted Rd, Dulwich, London SE21 8BD (☎ 01 670 4130); 6 Pump Court, Temple, London EC4 (☎ 01 583 6013); Melness House, Sutherland (☎ 084 756255)

ADAMS, William Horace; s of David Horace Adams (d 1965), and Patience Adams, *née* Dixon (d 1963); *b* 15 August 1925; *Educ* Stamford Sch, Oakham Sch; *m* 1947, Joan, da of James Pugh (d 1960); 2 s, 2 da; *Career* chartered surveyor; pres Br Chapter Int Real Est Fndn (FIABCI) 1982-83, chm RICS Continental Euro Branch, pres Arbitration and Conciliation Cncl FIABCI 1982-; chm Waterglade plc 1987-, dir Property Intelligence Ltd 1984-; conslt: Security Pacific Nat Bank 1984-, Privatbanken and others; *Recreations* golf; *Clubs* RAC; *Style*— William H Adams, Esq; Lavender

Cottage, Walton Street, Walton on the Hill, Surrey HT20 7RR (☎ Tadworth 3163); Security Pacific National Bank, 4 Broadgate, London EC2M 7LE

ADAMSON, Sir (William Owen) Campbell; o s of late John Adamson, of Kinross; *b* 26 June 1922; *Educ* Rugby, Corpus Christi Cambridge; *m* 1, 1945 (m dis 1984), Gilvray, da of Dr William Allan, of Baildon, Yorks; 2 s, 2 da; m 2, 1984, Mrs J (Mimi) Lloyd-Chandler; *Career* with Richard Thomas & Baldwins and Steel Co of Wales 1947-69; former memb: BBC Advsy Ctee, NEDC, SSRC, Design Cncl, Industl Soc Cncl, and formerly vice chm Nat Savings Ctee for England and Wales; dir-gen CBI 1969-76; chm: Abbey Nat Bldg Soc 1978-, Revertex Chems 1978-81, Renold Ltd 1982-86 (dir 1976-, dep chm 1981-82); dir: Imperial Gp 1976-86, Yule Catto to 1982, Lazard Bros 1976-87, Doulton and Co 1977-83, Tarmac plc 1980-; vice pres Inst Manpower Studies 1982-; govr Rugby Sch; kt 1976; *Books* various tech pubns; *Recreations* walking, music; *Clubs* Naval and Military; *Style—* Sir Campbell Adamson; Abbey House, Baker St, London NW1 (☎ 01 486-5555)

ADAMSON, Donald; JP (City of London 1983); s of Donald Adamson, (d 1982), of Lymm, Cheshire, and Hannah Mary, *née* Booth; *b* 30 Mar 1939; *Educ* Manchester GS, Magdalen Coll Oxford and Univ of Paris (MA, MLitt, DPhil); *m* 24 Sept 1966, Helen Freda, da of Frederick Percival Griffiths (d 1970), of Mossley Hill, Liverpool; 2 s (Richard b 1970, John b 1971); *Career* Lycée Louis-Le-Grand Paris 1964-65, J Walter Thompson Co Ltd 1965-67, princ lectr Goldsmiths' Coll London 1977 (lectr 1969, sr lectr 1970), visiting fell Wolfson Coll Cambridge 1989; judge Museum of the Year Awards 1979-83, memb exec ctee Nat Heritage; Freeman City of London 1969, Liveryman Worshipful Co of Haberdashers Co 1976; FSA 1979, FRSL 1983; Chevalier Ordre des Palmes Academiques France 1986, Companion of the First Class Order of the Orthodox Hospitallers Cyprus 1986-; Lord of the Manor at Dodmore Kent, OStJ 1985,; *Books* The Genesis of Le Cousin Pons (1966), Dusty Heritage A National Policy for Museums and Libraries (1971), The House of Nell Gwyn (jtly 1974), A Rescue Policy for Museums (1980), Balzac Illusions Perdues (1981), Les Romantiques Francais devant la Pienture Espagnole (1985, two trans of Balyac novels); *Recreations* genealogy, heraldry, local history, windsurfing; *Clubs* Beefsteak, City Livery; *Style—* Dr Donald Adamson; Dodmore House, The Street, Meopham, Kent DA13 OAJ; Topple Cottage, Polperro, Cornwall PL13 2RS; Goldsmiths' Coll, New Cross, London SE14 6NW (☎ 01 692 7171, fax 469)

ADAMSON, Hamish Cristopher; s of John Adamson (d 1985), of Perth, and Denise, *née* Colman-Sadd; *b* 17 Sept 1935; *Educ* Stonyhurst, Lincoln Coll Oxford (MA); *Career* slr 1961; Law Soc: memb, asst sec 1966-81, sec Law Reform and Int Relations 1981-87, dir Int 1987-; sec UK Delegation cncl of Bars and Law Soc's of Euro Community 1981-, exec sec Cwlth Lawyers 1983-; *Books* The Solicitors Act 1974 (1975); *Recreations* plants, books, travel; *Style—* Hamish Adamson, Esq; 133 Hartington Road, London SW8 2EY (☎ 01 720 4406); The Law Society, 113 Chancery Lane, London WC2A 1PL (☎ 01 242 1067, fax 01 242 4059522, telex 261 203)

ADAMSON, Iain Beaton; s of late Alexander Adamson, MBE, journalist and playwright, and late Matilda Beaton Adamson; descendant of noted braggart who fought on both sides in American Civil War, whose son wrote first book on teaching swimming; *b* 22 August 1928; *Educ* Glasgow Academy, Univ of Paris (Political Science Diploma); *m* 17 Feb 1962, Zita Mary, da of late Vincent Russell James; 1 s (Rory Beaton b 1966), 2 da (Kirstie b 1962, Zita b 1964); *Career* author and foreign corr; served Seaforth Highlanders, Malay Regt and Ghurkha Rifles in Malaya 1948; journalist with: Glasgow Herald org, Scottish Daily Express Glasgow, Daily Mirror London, Santa Monica Outlook USA; foreign corr, France, Germany, Spain, USA; md: Iain Adamson & Prtnrs, public relations in London, Bristol, Italy; The London Art Coll leisure study Coll Gp; former TV spokesman for Consumer Cncl; contributor to many journals and newspapers in UK, USA, Canada, Australia, New Zealand; *Books* author of various biographies including The Old Fox, A Man of Quality, The Great Detective, (Military Histories) The Forgotten Men (instruction), Profitable Art; *Recreations* travel, eating; *Style—* Iain Adamson, Esq; Maggs House, Bristol BS8 1QX (☎ 0272 266531, fax 0272 211594)

ADAMSON, Norman Joseph; CB (1981), QC (Scot 1979); s of Joseph Adamson, of Glasgow, and Lily, *née* Thorrat; *b* 29 Sept 1930; *Educ* Hillhead HS, Glasgow Univ (MA, LLB); *m* 1961, Patricia Mary, er da of Walter Scott Murray Guthrie, of Edinburgh; 4 da; *Career* advocate (Scotland) 1957, barr Gray's Inn 1959; parly draughtsman and legal sec Lord Advocate's Dept London 1965-, legal sec to Lord Advocate and first parly draughtsman for Scotland 1979-; Elder of Church of Scotland; *Style—* Norman Adamson, Esq, CB, QC; Whiteways, White Lane, Guildford, Surrey (☎ 0483 65301); Lord Advocate's Chambers, 10 Great College St, Westminster, London SW1 (☎ 01 276 6836)

ADAMSON, Paul Malcolm; s of Ivan Adamson (d 1967), and Marjorie, *née* Doughty (d 1974); *b* 21 June 1932; *Educ* Epsom Coll; *m* 15 Feb 1958, Olive, da of Albert Edward Studd: 1 s (Toby Seth Alexander b 1963), 1 da (Isobel Adamson b 1960); *Career* Nat Serv RAF 1950-52, Adjt Corpl Far East Air Force Malaya 1951-52; Chartered Bank of India Australia and China (London), Bank of Br W Africa (Ghana, W Africa), Bank of the North (Karo, Nigeria), United Bank for Africa (Lagos, Nigeria), Browning Arms Co (Montreal, Canada), US Steel (London); Outward Bound Tst Eskdale Cumbria; hon memb 3 Bn and 5 Bn Offrs Mess Ghana Regt (5 Bn disbanded following mutiny in Congo 1961), hon memb Dagomba Tribe of N Territories Ghana 1960; AIBDip (lapsed); *Books* many articles in various sporting pubns, many letters in local press; *Recreations* shootin', fishing, travelling, drinkin', snipin' at BNFL; *Clubs* MLAGB, BASC, CGA, RAC, GSPAssoc; *Style—* Paul Adamson, Esq; Richmond Cottage, Eskdale, Cumbria; 2 Randle How Cottages, Eskdale, Cumbria (☎ 09403 281); Outward Bound Eskdale, Eskdale Green, Holmrook, Cumbria CA19 1TE (☎ 09403 293)

ADAMSON, Stephen James Lister; s of James Lister Adamson (d 1985), and Helen Galloway Begg Adamson (d 1980); *b* 10 July 1942; *Educ* John Lyon Sch, Harrow; *m* 20 May 1972, Elizabeth Margaret, da of John Leslie Tunley (d 1965), of Heswall, Cheshire; 3 s (Neil b 15 Feb 1974, Stuart b 25 Jan 1977, Ross b 19 March 1981); *Career* CA 1966, ptnr Arthur Young 1978, vice pres Insolvency Practitioners Assoc 1988-(memb 1978-); chm Virginia Water Prep Sch; memb Faringdon Ward Club 1988; FIPA 1978; *Recreations* fishing, golf, theatre; *Clubs* Inst of Dirs; *Style—* Stephen Adamson, Esq; Englewood, Ridgemead Rd, Englefield Green, Surrey; Arthur Young, Rolls Hse, 7 Rolls Bldgs, Fetter La, London, EC4A 1NH (☎ 01 831 7130, fax 01 405 2147, telex 888604-262973 AYLO)

ADAMSON, Lt-Col William John Campbell; TD, JP (1951), DL (Angus 1971); s of Capt W Adamson (ka 1915; gn through his m, Norah, da of Rt Hon James Campbell, PC, MP, of Rt Hon Sir Henry Campbell-Bannerman, Liberal PM 1905-08), of Careston Castle, Brechin; *b* 13 Mar 1914; *Educ* Eton, Trinity Coll Oxford (MA); *m* 1947, Margaret Josephine, da of James Helme (d 1972); 2 s, 3 da; *Career* served WW II, Lt-Col Black Watch RHR (wounded); memb Royal Co of Archers (Queen's Body Guard for Scotland); md Careston Estates; memb CC Angus for 24 years, Hon Sheriff Angus: FRICS; *Recreations* farming, foreign travel, shooting; *Style—* Lt-Col William Adamson, TD, JP, DL; Careston Castle, Brechin, Angus (☎ 035 63 242); Craig Lodge, Glenprosen (☎ 057 54 314); Nathro Lodge, Lethnot

ADBURGHAM, (Marjorie Vere) Alison; da of Dr Arthur Norman Haig, MD (d 1938), of Yeovil, Somerset, and Agnes Isobel, *née* Stephenson (d 1958); *b* 28 Jan 1912; *Educ* Roedean; *m* 22 Aug 1936, Myles Ambrose Adburgham; 2 s (Thurstan Haig b 1938, Roland Faulkner b 1945), 2 da (Carolyn Ashton b 1941, Jocelyn Alison b 1943); *Career* staff feature writer and fashion editor the Guardian 1954-73; *Books* A Punch History of Manners and Modes (1961), Shops and Shopping 1900-14 (1964, second ed 1981), View of Fashion (1966), Women in Print - Writing Women & Women's Magazines from the Restoration to Victoria (1972), Liberty's - A Biography of a Shop (1975), Shopping in Style - London from the Restoration to Edwardian Elegance (1979), Silver Fork Society - Fashionable Life and Literature 1814 to 1840 (1983); *Clubs* Univ Women's; *Style—* Mrs Alison Adburgham; Tredore Cottage, Little Petherick, Wadebridge, Cornwall PL27 7QT (☎ 0841 540 362)

ADCOCK, Andrew John; s of Reay Stanley Adcock, of Underbarrow, Westmoreland, and Elizabeth, *née* Sadler; *b* 10 Sept 1953; *Educ* Kendal GS, Magdalene Coll Cambridge (MA); *m* 17 Sept 1977, Maya (Jessie Maria), da of Maj (Charles) Peter S Ligertwood, of Bagborough, Somerset; 2 s (Oliver William b 1981, Tobias Henry b 1985), 1 da (Amabel Cecilia b 1983); *Career* with Hoare Govett Ltd (Stockbrokers) 1975-87, Prolific Gp plc 1987-; memb Stock Exchange; *Recreations* tennis, shooting; *Style—* Andrew Adcock, Esq; 19 Crieff Road, London SW18 (☎ 01 874 8792); 222 Bishopsgate, London EC2M 4JS (☎ 01 247 6544)

ADCOCK, Sir Robert Henry; CBE (1941), DL (Lancs 1951); s of Henry Adcock (d 1937), of Polesworth, Warwickshire; *b* 27 Sept 1899; *Educ* Atherstone Warwicks; *m* 1927, Mary Hannah, da of Robert Kay Wadsworth (d 1952), of Handforth Hall, Cheshire; 1 s, 2 da; *Career* slr; asst slr Manchester 1923, asst clerk Notts CC 1927, sr asst slr Manchester 1929, dep town clerk Manchester 1931, town clerk Manchester 1939, clerk of CC Lancs 1944-60, clerk of the peace Lancs and of Lancs Ltcy; kt 1950; *Recreations* golf; *Style—* Sir Robert Adcock, CBE, DL; Summer Place, Rock End, Torquay, Devon (☎ 0803 22775)

ADCOCK, Robert Wadsworth; DL (1978); s of Sir Robert Adcock, CBE, DL, *qv*, of Summer Place, Rock End, Torquay, and Mary Hannah, *née* Wadsworth; *b* 2 Dec 1932; *Educ* Rugby, Manchester Univ; *m* 26 Oct 1957, Valerie Colston, da of Col Stanley Robins, MBE, IA (d 1974), of Hereford; 1 s (Robert Charles b 20 Nov 1961), 1 da (Olivia Charlotte (twin)); *Career* slr; asst slr: Lancs CC 1955-56, Manchester CC; sr slr Berks CC 1959-63, asst clerk then dep clerk Northumberland CC, chief exec Essex CC 1976- (dep chief exec 1970-76); clerk of Essex Lieutenancy 1976-; ACC: advsr Police Ctee 1976-, offrs advsy Gp 1983- (chm 1987-), hon sec assoc of co chief execs 1983-, chm offrs advsy panel SE Regnl Planning Conference 1984-88; *Recreations* gardening, ornithology; *Style—* Robert Adcock, Esq, DL; The Christmas Cottage, Gt Sampford, Saffron Walden, Essex (☎ 079 986 363); Essex County Council, County Hall, Chelmsford, Essex (☎ 0245 492 211, ext 20011, fax 0245 352 710, telex 995910)

ADDERLEY, Hon James Nigel Arden; er s and h of 7 Baron Norton, OBE; *b* 2 June 1947; *Educ* Downside; *m* 1971, Jacqueline Julie, da of Guy W Willett, of Alderney; 1 s (Edward James Arden b 1982), 1 da (Olivia Fleur Elizabeth b 1979); *Career* FCA 1970; *Recreations* skiing, music; *Style—* The Hon James Adderley; 50 Adam and Eve Mews, Kensington High St, London W8 6UJ

ADDERLEY, Gp Capt Hon Michael Charles; AFC and bar, OBE (1960); s of 6 Baron Norton (d 1961); *b* 8 April 1917; *Educ* Radley, Sidney Sussex Coll Cambridge; *m* 1953, Margrethe Ann (d 1986); 3 s, 1 da; *Career* Group Capt RAF (ret); served 1939-45 War, Malaya 1949-51 (King's Commendation), Korea 1951-52 (American DFC, Bronze Star and Air Medal), Woomera 1957-59, Air Attaché British Embassy Prague 1963-65; *Style—* Group Capt the Hon Michael Adderley, AFC, OBE; 23 Welham Rd, Norton, Malton, Yorks YO17 9DS

ADDERLEY, Hon Nigel John; s of 7 Baron Norton, OBE; *b* 30 Mar 1950; *Educ* Downside, RMA Sandhurst; *Career* Capt Life Gds; *Style—* The Hon Nigel Adderley

ADDINGTON, Alexandra, Baroness; Alexandra Patricia; yr da of late Norman Ford Millar; *m* 1961 (m dis 1974), 5 Baron Addington (d 1982); 2 s, 2 da; *Style—* Alexandra, Lady Addington; 9/11 Chalk Hill Rd, Norwich NR1 1SL

ADDINGTON, 6 Baron (UK 1887); Dominic Bryce Hubbard; s of 5 Baron Addington (d 1982), and Alexandra, Baroness Addington, *qv*; *b* 24 August 1963; *Educ* Hewett Sch, Norwich City Coll, Univ of Aberdeen; *Heir* bro, Hon Michael Hubbard, *qv*; *Recreations* rugby football; *Clubs* National Liberal; *Style—* The Rt Hon the Lord Addington; 9/11 Chalk Hill Rd, Norwich NR1 1SL

ADDINGTON, Hon Elizabeth Clare; da of late 6 Viscount Sidmouth; *b* 4 August 1928; *Style—* The Hon Elizabeth Addington; Coachmans Cottage, Pewsey, Wilts

ADDINGTON, Hon Gurth Louis Francis; s of late 6 Viscount Sidmouth; *b* 26 Feb 1920; *Educ* Downside, BNC Oxford (MA); *m* 1950, Patience Gillian, da of late Col L E Travers, RE; 3 s, 6 da (inc 2 sets twins); *Career* served Flying Offr RAF (aircrew) 1939-45 in Italy and M East; *Style—* The Hon Gurth Addington; 11 Edwin St, Fairlight, NSW 2094, Australia

ADDINGTON, Hon Hiley William Dever; s of late 6 Viscount Sidmouth; *b* 31 Oct 1917; *m* 1942, Brenda Swanney, da of late Robert Charles Wallace, CMG, sometime princ of Queen's Univ Kingston, Canada; 2 s, 1 da; *Career* Lt-Cdr RN (ret); sometime chief engr Imp Oil Ltd and conslt Exxon Corpn; *Style—* The Hon Hiley Addington; 1688 Mills St, Sarnia, Ontario, Canada

ADDINGTON, Hon Jeremy Francis; s of 7 Viscount Sidmouth; *b* 29 July 1947; *Educ* Ampleforth; *m* 1970, Grete, *née* Henningsen, of Randers, Denmark; 1 s, 1 da; *Style—* The Hon Jeremy Addington; Herskind Sondergaard, Praestbrovej 14, Herskind, 8464 Galten, Denmark

ADDINGTON, Lt-Col Hon Leslie Richard Bagnall; DFC (1951); 5 s of 6 Viscount Sidmouth; *b* 20 Sept 1923; *Educ* Downside; *m* 1955, Anne, da of Capt Trevor Hume (d 1968), and Sybil, sis of late Sir Maurice Lacy, 2 Bt; 2 s (William b 1956, Richard b 1958), 2 da (Sarah b 1961, Alice b 1964); *Career* served RA 1941-71 Far East, ret as Lt-Col; CO Essex Yeo 1965-66 and 100 (Yeo) FD Regt 1967-68; *Clubs* Army and Navy; *Style*— Lt-Col The Hon Leslie Addington, DFC; Polebridge, Sutton Veny, Warminster, Wilts BA12 7AL (☎ 0985 40202)

ADDINGTON, Hon Thomas Raymond Casamajor; MC; s of late 6 Viscount Sidmouth; *b* 7 Jan 1919; *Educ* Downside; *m* 1947, Veronique (d 1970), da of Emile Wirtz, of Antwerp, Belgium; 3 s, 4 da; *Career* Maj RHA (ret), War with Commandos 1939-45; *Style*— The Hon Thomas Addington, MC; Highway Farm, nr Calne, Wilts

ADDISON, Lt-Col Archibald Randall George; MBE (1971); s of George Anthony Walter Addison (d 1947), and Sheila Mary, *née* Davidson (d 1985); paternal gf was Maj-Gen George Henry Addison, CB, CMG, DSO; maternal g uncle was Dr Randall Thomas Davidson, Archbishop of Canterbury 1903-28; *b* 3 Oct 1933; *Educ* Wellington, RMA Sandhurst; *m* 11 May 1974, Susan Primrose, da of Prof Reginald Victor Jones, CB, CBE, of 8 Queens Terrace, Aberdeen, and former w of Dr John Thomas Parente, of New York; 1 step s (John Addison formerly Parente b 1965), 1 step da (Gigina Addison, formerly Parente b 1964); *Career* cmmnd The Royal Scots 1954, served Suez Canal Zone, Cyprus, Port Said, Berlin 1954-58, seconded Trucial Oman Scouts 1960-64, served with RS Radfan, Aden 1964-65, Staff Coll 1966, HQ 52 Lowland Div 1967-68, served with Royal Scots, BAOR, N Ireland 1968-71, seconded Abu Dhabi 1971-73, Staff Appt Belize 1975-77, 1982-83; cmd TA Bn Edinburgh 1979-82, ret 1987; re-employed by MOD in Retired Offr appt; *Recreations* gardening, reading; *Clubs* Northern (Aberdeen); *Style*— Lt-Col Archibald Addison, MBE; The Veldt, Monikie, Angus

ADDISON, Edward Norman; OBE (1987); *b* 28 May 1918; *Educ* Real Gymnasium Vienna; *m* 1 May 1945, Patricia, *née* Saint; 2 da (Vivien b 1946, Jacqueline b 1949); *Career* WWII Army 1940-46; fndr and chm The Addison Tool Co Ltd 1956-; pres MTTA 1985-86, chm COMMET 1986-87, pres Comité Européen de Liason des Importateurs de Machines-Outils 1977-80; FRSA 1988; *Recreations* race horse owner; *Style*— Edward Addison, Esq, OBE; The Addison Tool Co Ltd, Westfields Rd, London W3 0RE (☎ 01 993 1661, fax 01 993 8767, telex 934 211 ADSON G)

ADDISON, Hon (Jacqueline Faith); *née* Addison; da of 2 Viscount Addison (d 1976), and Brigit Helen Christine, *née* Williams (d 1980); *b* 2 Mar 1944; *Educ* Chichester HS for Girls, King's Coll London (BA), Univ of Strathclyde (Dip Lib); *m* 1966 (m dis 1985), Jeremy Warren Payne, s of Cecil Warren Payne (d 1973), of Old Bursledon, Hants; 3 da (Katy Josephine b 1972, Christina Meriel b 1975, Anna Isabella b 1978); *Career* librarian; *Style*— The Hon Jacqueline Addison; 16A Bright's Crescent, Edinburgh EH9 2DB (☎ 031 667 6528); Reiach & Hall, Architects & Planners, 6 Darnaway Street, Edinburgh EH3 6BG (☎ 031-225-8444)

ADDISON, Hon Mrs (Jacqueline Faith); *née* Addison; er da of 2 Viscount Addison (d 1976), and Brigit Helen Christine, *née* Williams (d 1980); *b* 2 March 1944; *m* 8 Oct 1966, Jeremy Warren Payne, yr s of Cecil Warren Payne, of Old Bursledon, Hants; 3 da (Katy Josephine b 1972, Christina Meriel b 1975, Anna Isabella b 1978); *Style*— The Hon Mrs Payne; 16a Brights Crescent, Edinburgh EH9 2DB

ADDISON, Joseph; CBE (1967); s of Francis Lacy Addison (d 1914); *b* 30 May 1912; *Educ* Eton, Trinity Coll Cambridge; *m* 1938, Wendy Blyth, JP, da of Cecil (Bill) Payn (d 1959), of Durban; 1 s (Michael), 1 da (Jill (Mrs Whiteley)) ; *Career* WWII Maj Queen's Royal Regt; admitted slr 1936; Linklaters & Paines 1933-46; legal advsr to Anglo-Iranian Oil Co Ltd 1946-54, gen mangr Iranian Oil Participants Ltd 1955-71, chm London Policy Gp of Int Oil Indust 1971; Order of TAJ Iran 1971; *Style*— Joseph Addison, Esq, CBE; The Weir House, Alresford, Hants (☎ 0962 732 320)

ADDISON, Kenneth George; OBE (1978); s of Herbert George Addison, and Ruby, *née* Leathers; *b* 1 Jan 1923; *Educ* Felixstowe GS; *m* 1945, Maureen Newman; 1 s, 1 da; *Career* dep chief gen mangr Sun Alliance & London Insur Gp 1976-84 (dir 1971-); FCIS, FCII (pres 1980), FIArb (pres 1968-69); *Style*— Kenneth Addison, Esq, OBE; Ockley, 13 Hillcroft Ave, Purley, Surrey (☎ 01 660 2793); Sun Alliance Insur Group, Bartholomew Lane, London EC2N 2AB (☎ 01 588 2345)

ADDISON, 3 Viscount (UK 1945); Michael Addison; s of 1 Viscount Addison, KG, PC, sometime MP Shoreditch and Swindon (d 1951); suc er bro, 2 Viscount Addison, 1976; *b* 12 April 1914; *Educ* Hele's Sch Exeter, Balliol Coll Oxford; *m* 1936, Kathleen, da of late Rt Rev and Rt Hon William Wand, KCVO, DD, formerly 110 Bp of London; 1 s, 2 da; *Heir* s, Hon William Addison; *Career* Civil Service 1935-65; polytechnic lecturer 1966-76; memb Royal Inst Public Admin Assoc of Teachers of Management; *Style*— The Rt Hon The Viscount Addison; Old Stables, Maplehurst, Horsham, W Sussex (☎ 040 376 298)

ADDISON, Terry Robert; s of Keith Roy Addison (d 1982), and Dorothy Phyllis, *née* Hind (d 1969); *b* 27 Dec 1932; *Educ* Hinckley GS Leics, Leicester Coll of Art, Royal Coll of Art London (DesRCA); *m* 4 Oct 1958, Anne Jennifer (d 1982), da of Percival White (d 1947); 2 s (Scott b 1961, Ben b 1961), 1 da (Elizabeth b 1970); *Career* Nat Service IRHA, BAOR; interior design conslt; ptnr YRM Architects 1960-78; own practice: Addison Associates 1978-, Addison Design Pte Ltd Singapore 1983-, AM Associates 1982-; associate practice: Addison Sutphin Boston Mass 1982-, Addison Larson Chicago Ill 1987-; dir: Development & Investment Co, Adsul Ltd 1986-; fell Soc of Artists and Designers; *Recreations* piano, squash; *Clubs* IOD; *Style*— Terry R Addison, Esq; 10 Stukeley Street, London WC2 (☎ 01 405 0491, fax 242 3892, telex 896691 TLXIR G); car telephone 0836 209 715

ADDISON, Hon William Matthew Wand; s and h of 3 Viscount Addison; *b* 13 June 1945; *Educ* King's Sch Bruton, Essex Inst of Agric; *m* 1970, Joanna Mary, da of John Dickinson, of Blyborough Grange, Lincs; 1 s, 2 da; *Style*— The Hon William Addison; Kingerby Hall, Market Rasen, Lincs (☎ 067 382 255)

ADDISON, Sir William Wilkinson; JP (1949), DL (Essex 1973); s of Joseph Addison, of Bashall Eaves; *b* 4 April 1905; *m* 1929, Phoebe, da of Robert Dean, of Rimington, W Yorks; *Career* Verderer Epping Forest 1957-; chm cncl Magistrates Assoc 1970-76; FSA, FRHistS; kt 1974;; *Books* Local Styles of the English Parish Church (1982), Farmhouses in the English Landscape (1986); *Style*— Sir William Addison, JP, DL; Ravensmere, Epping, Essex (☎ 78 73439)

ADEANE, Hon (George) Edward; CVO (1985); s of Baron Adeane, GCB, GCVO, PC (Life Peer) (d 1984), and Helen, Baroness Adeane, *qv*; *b* 4 Oct 1939; *Educ* Eton, Magdalene Coll Cambridge (MA); *Career* barr Middle Temple 1962; page of honour to HM The Queen 1954-56; private sec to: HRH The Prince of Wales 1979-85, HRH The Princess of Wales 1984-85; *Style*— The Hon Edward Adeane, CVO; B4 Albany, Piccadilly, London W1 (☎ 01 734 9410)

ADEANE, Baroness; Helen; *née* Chetwynd-Stapylton; da of late Richard Chetwynd-Stapylton; *b* 16 Jan 1916; *m* 1939, Baron Adeane, GCB, GCVO, PC, (Life Peer) (d 1984); 1 s (The Rt Hon Edward *qv*), 1 da (d 1952); *Style*— Lady Adeane; 22 Chelsea Square, London SW3 6LF

ADENEY, (Howard) Martin; s of Rev Arthur Webster Adeney, and Edith Marjorie, *née* Blagden (d 1987); *b* 7 Sept 1942; *Educ* Monkton Combe Sch, Queens Coll Cambridge (BA); *m* 18 Dec 1971, Ann Valerie, *née* Corcoran; 2 s (William Edward b 3 Sept 1973, Thomas Henry b 7 June 1976), 1 step s (Samuel John Stanton Moore b 29 April 1963); *Career* reporter Guardian 1965-77 (Labour corr 1972-77), feature writer Colombo Pubn Bureau 1968-69, industl corr Sunday Telegraph 1978-82, industl ed BBC TV 1982- (Labour corr 1978-82); memb Westminster City Cncl 1971-74; *Books* The Miners Strike: Loss With Limit (with John Lloyd, 1986), The Motormakers: The Turbulent History of Britain's Car Industry (1988); *Recreations* walking, garden labouring; *Style*— Martin Adeney, Esq; BBC TV Centre, Wood Lane, London W12 7RJ

ADEY, (Arthur) Victor; s of Arthur Fredrick and Pollie Adey; *b* 2 May 1912; *Educ* Wolverhampton Sec Sch; *m* 1936, Kathleen Mary Lewis; 1 s, 1 da; *Career* chm Mercantile Credit 1997-; dir: Barclays Bank Int 1979-, Ampex Corp (US) 1973-; *Recreations* fishing, gardening; *Style*— Victor Adey, Esq; Rosemount, Burtons Lane, Chalfont St Giles, Bucks HP8 4BN (☎ 024 04 2160)

ADIE, Jack Jesson; CMG (1962); s of Percy James Adie (d 1948), and Marion Adie, *née* Sharp (d 1957); *b* 1 May 1913; *Educ* Shrewsbury, Magdalen Coll Oxford (BA); *m* 1940, Patricia (d 1978), da of William McLoughlin; 1 s (Peter), 2 da (Susan, Jane); *Career* entered Colonial Admin Serv 1938; served in Zanzibar 1938-48 (on military serv 1940-42 in Kenya Regt, KAR and Occupied Territory Admin), private sec to the Sultan, Priv sec to the Br Resident, sr asst sec; seconded to Colonial Office 1949-51; asst sec Kenya 1951; sec for: Educn and Labour Kenya 1952, Educ, Labour and Lands 1954; act min 1955-56; chief sec Barbados 1957; perm sec for: Forest Devpt, Game and Fisheries Kenya April-Dec 1958, Agric, Animal Husbandry and Water Resources; chm: African Land Devpt Bd 1958-59, and Central Housing Bd 1959-60, Housing, Common Services Probation and Approved Schs 1960-61, Labour and Housing 1961-62; perm sec for Labour 1962-63; ret 1964; contributor East Africa Annual; temp princ min of Overseas Devpt 1964-69; Order of Brilliant Star of Zanzibar (4th class) 1947, Coronation Medal 1953; *Recreations* opera, travel; *Style*— J J Adie, Esq; 3 Braemar, Kersfield Road, Putney, London SW15 3HG (☎ 01 789 8301)

ADIE, Rt Rev Michael Edgar; *see*: Guildford, Bishop of

ADLAM, (Avis) Marjorie; OBE (1981); da of Richard Michael Charles Collins, of Suffolk, and Milly Elizabeth Rolfe (d 1958); *b* 17 Jan 1913; *Educ* Thetford GS for Girls, UC Southampton (BA); *m* 8 April 1939, Bernard Stephen Adlam (d 1976), s of Walter Adlam (d 1962); 3 s (Simon b 1941, Nicholas b 1945 *qv*, Martin b 1946); *Career* teacher -1939; JP 1952-83, ex Bench chm Magistrates Assoc, Co rep on cncl of Probation and After Care (branch chm 1953-85); Hunts, Mid Anglia and Cambs Police Authy 1954-83; Bd of Visitors Gaynes Hall Borstal 1973-85; Liveryman Worshipful Co of Spectacle Makers 1986; *Recreations* gardening, lacemaking, needlework; *Style*— Mrs Marjorie Adlam, OBE; The Walnuts, Hail Weston, nr St Neots, Huntingdon, Cambs (☎ Huntingdon 72209)

ADLAM, Nicholas Rolfe; s of Bernard Stephen Adlam (d 1976), of The Walnuts, Hail Weston, St Neots, Cambs, and Avis Marjorie, *née* Collins, OBE, *qv*; *b* 1 Oct 1945; *Educ* Kimbolton Sch; *m* 10 April 1971, Heather Miranda, da of George May (d 1974), of Thatch Cottage, Wyboston, Beds; *Career* chm: Gordon, Watts & Co Ltd 1981, B S Adlam & Co Ltd 1977; md: Cavingston Properties Ltd, Cavingston Ltd, Wincomblee Estates Ltd 1988-; dir (non-exec) Omnibus Workspace Ltd: Freeman City of London 1967, Liveryman Worshipful Co of Spectacle Makers 1971 (Freeman 1966), memb Guild of Freeman of the City of London 1969 ; *Recreations* horse-racing, travelling, reading balance sheets; *Clubs* E India, RAC; *Style*— Nicholas R Adlam Esq; 109 Kingsway, Holborn, London, WC2B 6PP (☎ 01 405 8372, telex 22693, fax 01 405 4525

ADLER, John James; JP (Chelmsford 1987); s of Cdr Alan Adler, RNVR (d 1966); *b* 16 Sept 1935; *Educ* Felsted; *m* 1962, Hilary Anne, da of Reginald Drew, of Essex; 2 s (Michael b 1962, Harry b 1970), 2 da (Fiona b 1964, Julia b 1967); *Career* chm: Cadogan Investments 1970- (md 1966), Tobacco Trade Benevolent Assoc 1977-82; A Oppenheimer & Co 1979-; chm: medical academic unit Broomsfield Hosp, Eastern Cos Rugby Referees; chm bd visitors HM Prison Chelmsford 1985-87 (now ordinary member); *Recreations* squash, sailing (Albacore 'Phee Anna'), rugby refereeing; *Clubs* City Livery, Thorpe Bay Yacht; *Style*— John Adler, Esq; c/o A Oppenheimer & Co, 20 Vanguard Way, Shoeburyness, Southend-on- Sea, Essex (☎ 0702 297 785, fax 0702 294 225, telex 99 453)

ADLER, Larry (Lawrence Cecil); s of Louis Adler and Sadie Hack; *b* 10 Feb 1914; *Educ* Baltimore City Coll; *m* 1, 1938 (m dis 1961), Eileen Walser; 1 s, 2 da; m 2, 1969 (m dis 1977), Sally Cline; 1 da; *Career* mouth organist; journalist and critic, contrib: Sunday Times, Spectator, New Statesman, Harpers and Queen, Boardroom London Theatre Visitor, Jazz Express, London After Dark (restuarant critic); fell Yale Univ; *Books* Jokes and How to Tell Them (1963), It Ain't Necessarily So (Collin 1985); *Recreations* tennis,journalism, food critic; *Clubs* Paddington Tennis; *Style*— Larry Adler, Esq; c/o MBA Literary Agents Ltd, 45 Fitzroy Street, London W1P 5HR

ADLER, Prof Michael William; s of Gerhard Adler, and Hella, *née* Hildergard; *b* 12 June 1939; *Educ* Middlesex Hosp Med Sch (MB BS); *m* 1, (m dis 1978) Susan Jean Burnett; m 2, 23 June 1979, Karen Hope Dunnell, da of Richard Henry Williamson (d 1984); 2 da (Zoe b 1980, Emma b 1982); *Career* house offr and registrar in med Middx, Centl Middx and Whittington Hosps 1965-69; lectr St Thomas' Hosp Med Sch 1970-75, sr lectr Middx Hosp Med Sch 1975-79, prof of genito urinary med Middx Hosp Med Sch 1979-; MRC: memb res advsy gp on epidemiological studies of sexually transmitted dieases 1975-80, working pty to co-ordinate lab studies on the gonococcus 1979-83, working pty on AIDS 1981-87 sub ctee theapeutic studies 1985-87, ctee epidemiological studies on AIDS 1985, ctee on clinical studies of prototype vaccines against AIDS 1987; Jt Ctee of Higher Med Trg: memb advsy ctee on genito urinary med 1981-86, sec 1982-83, chm 1984-86; memb EC working gp on AIDS 1985-, chm RCP ctee on Genito Urinary Med 1987- (memb 1981-); advsr Parly All Pty Ctee on AIDs 1987-; tstee and dir Nat AIDS Tst 1987-, dir AIDS Policy Unit 1988-; memb: cncl med soc for study of venereal diseases; DHSS: memb expert advsy gp AIDS

1984-, gp on health care workers 1987, chief scientists advsr res liaison gp (Child Health) 1985, exec ctee Int Union against Venereal Diseases 1986-, BMA AIDS Working Pty 1986-; advsr in venereology WHO 1983-; MRCM, FFCM, FRCP, MRCP; *Books* ABC of Sexually Transmitted Diseases (1984), ABC of AIDS (1987); jt fdr ed AIDS (bi monthly jl 1986-); *Recreations* yoga, jogging; *Style*— Prof Michael Adler; Academic Dept of Genito Urinary Medicine, James Pringle House, The Middlesex Hospital, London W1N 8AA (☎ 01 380 9146)

ADLEY, James Anthony; s of John Gordon Adley, and Valerie Elizabeth Rose, *née* Goodman; *b* 7 June 1956; *Educ* Uppingham, Stanmore Coll Middx; *m* 29 March 1981, Ruth Beverley, da of Sidney Middleburgh; 1 da (Natasha b 1985); *Career* dir: Charles Sydney Assur Cnslts Ltd, Charles Sydney (Gen Cnslts) Ltd; memb FIMBRA, Chartered Insur Inst; contributor on assur matters to leading specialist magazines; *Recreations* writing, music; *Style*— James A Adley, Esq; c/o Charles Sydney Assurance Conslts Ltd, Boundary House, Turner Road, Edgware, Middx (☎ 01 951 0336)

ADLEY, Robert James; MP (C) Christchurch 1983-; s of Harry and Marie Adley, of Hove, Sussex; *b* 2 Mar 1935; *Educ* Uppingham; *m* 1961, Jane Elizabeth, da of Wilfrid Pople (d 1966), of Burnham, Somerset; 2 s (Simon b 1964, Rupert b 1967); *Career* MP (C): Bristol NE 1970-74, Christchurch and Lymington 1974-83; chm: All-Party Parly Tourism Gp; chm: Br-Hungarian Parly Gp, Br-Chinese Parly Gp; dir and marketing conslt Cwlth Holiday Inns of Canada Ltd; memb Nat Cncl for Br Hotels, Restaurants and Caterers Assoc; fndr and first chm Brunel Soc, tstee Brunel Engrg Centre Tst; patron SS GB Project; ctee memb Nat Railway Museum, York; *Books* British Steam in Camera Colour (1979), In Search of Steam (1981), The Call of Steam (1982), To China for Steam (1983), All Change Hong Kong (1984), In praise of Steam (1985), Wheels (1987), Covering My Tracks (1988); *Style*— Robert Adley, Esq, MP; c/o House of Commons, London SW1A 0AA

ADMANI, Dr (Abdul) Karim; OBE (1987), JP (1974); s of Haji Razzak Admani (d 1954), of Palitana, India, and Hajiani Rahima Admani; *b* 19 Sept 1934; *Educ* Gujrat Univ (BSc), Karachi Univ (MB, BS), London Univ 1968; *m* Seema, da of Charles Robson (d 1947), of South Shields; 1 s (Nadim b 1969), 1 da (Nilofer b 1971); *Career* conslt physician with special interest in the elderly; teacher Health Authority 1970-, clinical lectr Sheffield Medical Sch 1972-; dir: Ranmoor Grange Nursing Home Ltd 1975-80, Overseas Doctors Assoc in the UK Ltd 1976- (chm 1981-), Sunningdale Yorks Ltd 1983-; county pres BRCS (S Yorks) 1982-; memb: exec ctee for Racial Equality in Sheffield 1972- (chm 1978-), exec ctee BMA Sheffield 1974- Gen Medical Cncl in UK 1979-, central ctee Hosp Medical Services in UK 1979-, exec ctee Age Concern Sheffield 1982-; memb editorial bd: Pakistan Medical Bulletin 1974-, Medi-Scene 1981-, ODA News Review 1985-; pres: Muslim Cncl of Sheffield, Rotherham and Dists 1978-, Union of Pakistani Orgns in UK and Europe 1979-; magistrate City of Sheffield 1974-; DTM&H (Eng), MRCP, FRCP; *Publications* Guidance for Overseas Doctors in National Health Service in UK (ed 1982); *Recreations* tennis, table tennis, snooker, chess; *Clubs* Abbeydale Rotary, Liberal, Medico-Chirurgical Soc; *Style*— Dr Karim Admani, OBE, JP; 1 Derriman Glen, Silverdale Rd, Sheffield S11 9LQ (☎ 0742 360465); Northern General Hospital, Barnsley Rd, Sheffield (☎ 0742 387253)

ADOCK, Robert Wadsworth; DL 1978; s of Sir Robert Adock CBE DL, of Torquay, and Mary Hannah, *née* Wadsworth, of Handforth Hall, Cheshire; *b* 29 Dec 1932; *Educ* Rugby, Manchester Univ; *m* 26 Oct 1957, Valerie Colston, da of Col Stanley Robins MBE (Indian Army) (d 1974), of Hereford; 1 s (Robert Charles 1961), 1 da (Olivia Charlotte 1961); *Career* asst slr Lancs CC 1955-56, asst slr Manchester CC 1956-59, sen slr Berks CC 1959-63, asst clerk (later dept clerk) Northumberland CC 1963-70, dept chief exec Essex CC 1970-76, chief exec Essex CC 1976-, clerk of Essex Lieutenancy 1976-; assoc of County Cncls: advsr Police Ctee 1976-83, advsr Policy Ctee 1983-, memb Officers Adv GP 1983-,chm Officers Adv GP 1987; hon sec Assoc of County Chief Exec 1983-, chm Officers Adv Panel SE Reg Planning Conf 1984-88; *Recreations* gardening, ornithology; *Style*— Robert Adock, Esq, DL; The Christmas Cottage, Great Sampford, Saffron Walden, Essex (☎ Gt Sampford 363); Essex County Council, County Hall, Chelmsford, Essex (☎ 0245 492211 ext: 20011, fax 0245 352710, telex 995910)

ADOLFSSON, (Eva Lisbeth) Kristina; da of Kurt Egon Adolfsson, and Siv Ingegärd, *née* Larsson; *b* 7 June 1959; *Educ* Katedralskolan Faculty of Arts Lund Sweden; *Career* corr for Kvällsposten London 1980-85, prodr Swedish TV 1984-85, critic and columnist Expressen 1986-, ed art magazine Slitz 1987-, broadcaster Swedish Radio 1988-; *Recreations* music, clubbing; *Clubs* Publicistklubben (Sweden); *Style*— Ms Kristina Adolfsson; 164 Camberwell New Road, London SE5 0RR (☎ 01 582 5387)

ADOLPH, Dr Moir Patrick Nelham; s of William Edgar Leonard Adolph (d 1959), of London, and Bridget, *née* Honan (d 1981); *b* 8 Mar 1931; *Educ* Clongowes Wood Coll Naas Co Kildare Eire, Univ Coll Dublin, Nat Univ of Ireland (HB, BCh, BAO), Royal Coll of Physicians & Surgeons (D Ad Med), London Univ (MSc); *m* 17 June 1961, Yvette Mary, da of Donald Hayes; 3 s (William Patrick, Richard Vincent, Christopher Justin); *Career* Unit MO and sr MO RAF 1962, RAF Inst of Aviation Med 1971, Occupational Med Advsr to Princ MO HQ RAF Support Cmd, Offr i/c Envirnomental Health Team RAF Halton, Staff MO advsr to Dir of Health & res 1978, Specialist in Aviation and Occupational Med to Royal Saudi Air Force, MO in res Civil Service 1988; Freeman City of London 1960, Liveryman Worshipful Co of Gold and Silver Wyre Drawers 1960; MFOM; *Recreations* bridge, golf, snowskiing; *Style*— Dr Patrick Adolph; Hope Cotage, 12 Hope Lane, Upper Hale, Farnham, Surrey GU9 0HYP (☎ 0252 721 463)

ADRIAN, 2 Baron (UK 1955); Richard Hume Adrian; s of 1 Baron Adrian, OM (d 1977), and Hester, *née* Pinsent, DBE, BEM (d 1966); *b* 16 Oct 1927; *Educ* Westminster, Trinity Coll Cambridge (MA, MB, BChir, MD); *m* 1967, Lucy, da of Alban Caroe, of Campden Hill Sq, London W8; *Career* Capt RAMC, Nat Ser 1952-54; prof of Cell Physiology Cambridge 1978-; master Pembroke Coll Cambridge 1981-, tstee Br Museum 1979-; vice-chllr Cambridge Univ 1985-87; memb American Philosophical Soc; FRS, FRCP; *Style*— The Rt Hon the Lord Adrian, FRS; The Master's Lodge, Pembroke College, Cambridge (☎ 0223 65862); Umgeni, Cley, Holt, Norfolk (☎ 0263 740597)

ADRIEN; *see*: Latour-Adrien

ADYE, John Anthony; s of Maj Arthur Francis Capel Adye RA (ka 1940), and Hilda Marjorie, *née* Elkes (d 1971); *b* 24 Oct 1939; *Educ* Leighton Park Sch Reading, Lincoln Coll Oxford (MA); *m* 9 Sept 1961, Anne Barbara, da of Dr John Alfred Aeschlimann, of Montclair, NJ, USA; 2 s (Timothy b 1964, Nicholas b 1967), 1 da (Elizabeth b 1966); *Career* joined GCHQ 1963, princ 1968; Br Embassy Washington 1973-75, Nat Def Coll 1975-76, asst sec 1977-83; under sec (princ estab and princ fin offr) GCHQ 1983-; *Clubs* Naval and Military; *Style*— John Adye, Esq; Government Communications HQ, Prior's Rd, Cheltenham, Glos

AGA KHAN (IV), HH The; Prince Karim; s of late Prince Aly Khan, and Hon Joan, *née* Yarde-Buller (now Viscountess Camrose), da of 3 Baron Churston, MVO, OBE; gs of HH Rt Hon the Aga Khan (III), GCSI, GCIE, GCVO (d 1957); *b* 13 Dec 1936; *Educ* Le Rosey, Harvard; *m* 1969, Sarah Frances (Sally), o da of Lt-Col A E Croker Poole, and former w of Lord James Crichton-Stuart, s of 5 Marquess of Bute; 2 s (Prince Rahim b 1971, Prince Hussain b 1974), 1 da (Princess Zahra b 1970); *Career* Spiritual Leader and Imam of Ismaili Muslims, granted title HH by HM The Queen 1957, and HRH by late Shah of Iran 1959; *Style*— His Highness the Aga Khan

AGAR, Lady Caroline Amy Cora; da of 4 Earl of Normanton (d 1933); *b* 11 July 1899; *Style*— Lady Caroline Agar; Little Park, Ibsley, Ringwood, Hants BH24 3PP

AGAR, Hon Mark Sidney Andrew; s of 5 Earl of Normanton (d 1967), and Lady Fiona (d 1985), da of 4 Marquess Camden; *b* 2 Sept 1948; *Educ* Gordonstoun; *m* 1, 1973 (m dis 1979), Rosemary, da of Maj Philip Marnham; m 2, 8 Feb 1985, Arabella Clare, da of John Gilbert Gilbey (d 1982), and formerly w of Thomas Charles Blackwell; 1 s (Max John Andrew b 6 April 1986); *Career* Lt Blues and Royals; farmer and landowner (1200 acres); *Style*— The Hon Mark Agar; Inholmes, Woodlands St Mary, Newbury, Berks

AGBIM, Osita Godfrey; s of Felix Agbim (d 1956) and Amodo Agbim (d 1981); *b* 26 June 1932; *Educ* CKC Coll Nigeria, Univ Coll Dublin; *m* 20 Aug 1960, Beatrice, da of James Okafor (d 1977); 3 s (Raymond b 1961, Stephen b 1963, Anthony b 1966), 1 da (Claire b 1977); *Career* consultant surgeon; consultant to the Nigeria High Commission London; *Recreations* jogging; *Style*— Osita Agbim, Esq; 17 Grosvenor Gdns, London NW11 (☎ 01 458 1995), 92 Harley Street, London W1

AGGETT, Ms Valerie (Mrs John Grenier); da of James William Cocksey (d 1986); *b* 15 Dec 1950; *Educ* Bury GS, Durham Univ (BA), Coll of Law Guildford; *m* 1 (m dis), Mr Aggett; m 2, 1981, John Allan Genier, s of Rev George Arthur Grenier (d 1973); 1 step s, 1 step da; *Career* slr; princ and md The HLT Group Ltd 1976- (Queen's Award for Export 1982); *Recreations* motor cruising, tennis, interior design, fashion; *Clubs* RAC, Reform, Queens; *Style*— Ms Valerie Aggett; The HLT Group Ltd Tutors, 200 Greyhound Rd, London W14 9RY (☎ 01 385 3377); Plovers, Ruck Lane, Horsmonden, Kent

AGGETT, William John Percy; s of Reginald Percy Aggett (d 1969), of Wallington, Surrey, and Mary Elizabeth, *née* Parsons (d 1969); *b* 16 Jan 1922; *Educ* John Roan's Sch Blackheath London, St Lukes' Coll Exeter; *m* 22 Oct 1949, Hilary Mary (d 1986), da of Brig Dougal Campbell McPherson, MBE (d 1955), of Woolwich; 2 s (Francis John Percy b 1951, Richard Thomas Henry b 1953); *Career* Lt RA 1942-44, Maj The Devonshire Regt, (E Africa, Europe) 1944-58; asst teacher Archbishop Temple's Sch Lambeth 1958-63; headmaster St Michael and All Angel's Sch Camberwell 1963-70; headmaster The Archbishop Michael Ramsey Sch Camberwell 1971-81; gen sec London Headquarters Assoc 1969-72; memb: various ctees ILEA 1963-75, Southwark Diocesan Bd of Educn; pres London Branch Devonshire Regt Old Comrades Assoc 1979-86, tres The Neroche Soc 1983-86; FRGS; *Recreations* mediaeval art, biography, country sports; *Style*— William J P Aggett, Esq; Crosslands, Currey Rivel, nr Langport, Somerset TA10 0JE (☎ 0458 251 662)

AGIUS, Marcus Ambrose Paul; s of Lt-Col Alfred Victor Louis Benedict Agius, MC, TD (d 1969), and Ena Eleanora, *née* Hueffer; *b* 22 July 1946; *Educ* St George's Coll Weybridge, Trinity Hall Camb (MA), Harvard Business Sch (MBA); *m* 1971, Kate Juliette, da of Maj Edmund Leopold de Rothschild, TD, of Hants; 2 da (Marie-Louise Eleanor b 1977, Lara Sophie Elizabeth b 1980); *Career* merchant banker; md Lazard Bros & Co Ltd 1985- (dir 1981-85); non exec dir: Carless Capel & Leonard plc, Exbury Gardens Ltd; *Recreations* gardening, tennis, shooting, skiing, cinema; *Clubs* White's; *Style*— Marcus A P Agius, Esq; Lazard Bros & Co Ltd, 21 Moorfields, London EC2P 2HT (☎ 01 588 2721, telex 886438, fax 01 628 2485)

AGLIONBY, His Hon Judge; Francis John; s of Francis Basil and Marjorie Wycliffe Aglionby; *b* 17 May 1932; *Educ* Charterhouse, Corpus Christi Coll Oxford; *m* 1967, Susan Victoria Mary Vaughan; 1 s, 1 da; *Career* barr Inner Temple 1956, rec of Crown Ct 1975-80, bencher Inner Temple 1976, chllr: Birmingham Diocese 1971-, Portsmouth Diocese 1978-, circuit judge (SE) 1980-; *Clubs* Brooks's; *Style*— His Hon Judge Aglionby; 36 Bark Place, London W2 4AT (☎ 01 229 7303)

AGNEW, Hon Mrs; Hon Agneta Joanna Middleton; *née* Campbell; yr da (by 1 m) of Baron Campbell of Eskan (Life Peer); *b* 18 Oct 1944; *m* 21 Oct 1966 (m dis 1985), Jonathan Geoffrey William Agnew, er s of late Sir Geoffrey William Gerald Agnew; 1 s (and 1 s decd), 2 da; *Style*— The Hon Mrs Agnew; Flat 1, 30 Pond Place, London SW3 6QP

AGNEW, Sir (John) Anthony Stuart; 4 Bt (UK 1895), of Great Stanhope St, St George, Hanover Sq, Co London; s of Maj Sir John Stuart Agnew, 3 Bt (d 1957); *b* 25 July 1914; *Heir* bro, Maj (George) Keith Agnew; *Style*— Sir Anthony Agnew, Bt; c/o Blackthorpe Farm, Rougham, Bury St Edmunds, Suffolk

AGNEW, (Alexander James) Blair; s of James Percival Agnew, DL, LLD, CA Derclach and Jessie Blair, *née* Anderson (d 1978), of Racecourse Road, Ayr; *b* 6 Oct 1935; *Educ* Rugby; *m* 1958, Gillian Margaret, da of Maj W D Gray-Newton, of Little Court, Warboys, Cambs, 2 s (Blair, Angus), 1 da (Caroline); *Career* regular offr Royal Scots Fus then Royal Highland Fus 1954-65 (Capt); stockbroker, chm Penney Easton & Co, memb of cncl of Stock Exchange 1979-85; CBIM; *Recreations* gardening, walking; *Clubs* Army and Navy, Western (Glasgow); *Style*— Blair Agnew, Esq; Drumbarr, Ayr KA6 6BN (☎ (0292) 41312); Penney Easton & Co, PO Box 112, 24 George Square, Glasgow G2 1EB (☎ 041 248 2911; telex 777967, code 390)

AGNEW, Hon Mrs Clare Rosalind; *née* Dixon; da of 2 Baron Glentoran, KBE, by his w, Lady Diana Mary Wellesley, eld da of 3 Earl Cowley (d 1919); *b* 15 Nov 1937; *m* 1965 (m dis 1980), as his 2 w, Rudolph Ion Joseph Agnew, *qv*; 1 s, 1 da; *Style*— The Hon Mrs Clare Agnew; 35 St Peter's Sq, London W6 9NW

AGNEW, Sir (William) Godfrey; KCVO (1965, CVO 1953), CB (1975); s of Lennox Edelsten Agnew (d 1968), of Tunbridge Wells, and Elsie Blyth, *née* Nott (d 1972); *b* 11 Oct 1913; *Educ* Tonbridge Sch; *m* 1, 1939, Ruth Mary (d 1962), da of late Capt Charles Joseph Henry O'Hara Moore, CVO, MC, and late Lady Dorothie, da of 9 Earl of Denbigh and Desmond, GCVO, and Hon Cecilia Clifford (da of 8 Baron Clifford of Chudleigh); 3 s, 3 da (*see* Richard J H Pollen, the Hon Jonathan Davies); m 2, 1965,

Lady (Nancy Veronica) Tyrwhitt, wid of Adm Sir St John Tyrwhitt, 2 Bt, KCB, DSO, DSC; 2 step s, 1 step da; *Career* serv WWII Surrey and Sussex Yeo and RA attaining rank of Maj; slr 1935, joined Pub Tstee Off 1936; dep sec Cabinet Off 1972-74, clerk Privy Cncl 1953-74 (dep clerk 1951-53, sr clerk 1946-51); memb Bd Hon Tutors Cncl Legal Educn Univ of West Indies 1973-; chm: Sembal Tst 1966-73, Lady Clare Ltd 1970-87 (dir 1948-87); vice-chm Sun Life Assurance Soc 1983-84 (dir 1974-84); dir: Seaway Shipping Agencies Ltd 1971-80, Seaway Hldgs Ltd 1971-80, Artagen Properties 1976-80, Sun Life Properties 1980-84; conslt: Cncl Engrg Institutions 1974-79, Univ Coll Cardiff and Univ of Wales Inst of Sciences and Technology 1982-84; Hon FIMechE, Hon FIMunE, Hon FCIBS, FICE; *Clubs* Army and Navy, Swinley Forest Golf, Rye Golf; *Style*— Sir Godfrey Agnew, KCVO, CB; Pinehurst, Friary Road, South Ascot, Berks SL5 9HD

AGNEW, Ian Hervey; s of Peter Graeme Agnew, of The Old House, Manaccan, nr Helston, Cornwall, and Mary Diana, *née* Hervey; *b* 19 August 1941; *Educ* Stowe, London Sch of Printing & Graphic Arts (Admin Dipl); *m* 4 April 1964, Amanda Barbara, da of Maj A W Read, of Inns of Court Regiment, Water Hall Farm, Ifield Wood, Crawley, Sussex (ka 1944); 2 s (Mark b 1966, Jonathan b 1968); *Career* Mil Serv Lt Inns of Court and City Yeomany Regt TA 1962-68; printer 1961-72 Bradbury Agnew and Co London (Publishers of Punch); dir subsidiary cos 1968-72; md Flarepath Printers Ltd 1972-75; proprietor of Edgebury Press (printers) 1978-; dir Iris Fund for Prevention of Blindness London 1987-; *Recreations* shooting, skiing, motor racing (hill climbing classic f3 car); *Style*— Ian Agnew, Esq; Oak Lodge, Ifield Wood, Crawley, Sussex RH11 0LE (☎ 0293 22255); Edgebury Press, 104A Green Street, Eastbourne, Sussex (☎ 0323 20810)

AGNEW, Jonathan Geoffrey William; s of late Sir Geoffrey Agnew, and Hon Doreen, da of 1 Baron Jessel, CB, CMG; *b* 30 July 1941; *Educ* Eton, Trinity Coll Cambridge (MA); *m* 1966 (m dis 1985), Hon Agneta Joanna Middleton, *qv*, da of Baron Campbell of Eskan; 1 s (and 1 s decd), 2 da; *Career* md Morgan Stanley Int (London) and Morgan Stanley & Co Inc (New York) 1977-82; fin conslt 1983-86; chm: Kleinwort Benson Securities Ltd 1987-; chief exec Kleinwort Benson Gp plc, chm Kleinwort Benson Ltd 1988- dir: Thos Agnew and Sons Ltd, Int Financial Markets Trading Ltd; *Clubs* White's, Automobile (Paris); *Style*— Jonathan Agnew, Esq; 51E Eaton Sq, London SW1W 9BE (☎ 01 235 7589)

AGNEW, Jonathan Herbert; s of David Quentin Hope Agnew (d 1976), and Janet May Dilkes, *née* Malden (d 1981); *b* 7 Nov 1933; *Educ* Clifton; *m* 17 May 1958, (Mary) Mollie Kathleen, (d 1982) da of Brig Stannus Grant Fraser, MC (d 1980) 2 s (George b 26 Feb 1962, Michael 22 Oct 1965), 1 da (Susan b 11 May 1963); *Career* RNR Submarines; deck offr Merchant Navy 1952-69, cargo mangr OCL 1970-80, dir Macgregor Ports and Harbours 1980-81, self employed cargo Res Consulting 1981-; press offr local MS Soc; co organiser Blackwater Folk Club; *Books* Container Stowage, A Practical Approach (co-author, 1972), Thomas Stowage (co-author 1983); *Recreations* sailing, music (bagpipes); *Clubs* Army & Navy; *Style*— Jonathan Agnew, Esq; 3 Birthwhistle St, Gatehouse of Fleet, Scotland; 11 Ulting Lane, Langford, Maldon, Essex (☎ 0621 55447, fax 0621 56819, telex 995548 LEDA G)

AGNEW, Hon Mrs (Joyce Violet); *née* Godber; er da of 1 and last Baron Godber (d 1976) and Baroness Godber, *qv*; *b* 23 June 1917; *m* 27 Jan 1937, Andrew Agnew, s of late Sir Andrew Agnew, of Glenlee Park, New Galloway, Kirkcudbright; 3 da; *Style*— The Hon Mrs Agnew; Sweethaws Farm, Crowborough, Sussex TN6 3SS (☎ 0892 655045); Garheugh, Port William, Wigtownshire (☎ 058 15 235)

AGNEW, Maj (George) Keith; TD, JP; s of Maj Sir John Stuart Agnew, 3 Bt (d 1957); hp of bro, Sir (John) Anthony Stuart Agnew, 4 Bt; *b* 25 Nov 1918; *Educ* Rugby, Trinity Coll Cambridge; *m* 1948, Baroness Anne Merete Louise, yr da of Baron Johann Schaffalitzky de Muckadell, of Rodkilde, Fyn, Denmark; 2 s; *Career* Maj Suffolk Yeo (Res); landowner, farmer, forester; *Style*— Maj Keith Agnew, TD, JP; Blackthorpe Farm, Rougham, Bury St Edmunds, Suffolk

AGNEW, Sir Peter Garnett; 1 Bt (UK 1957), of Clendry, Co Wigtown; s of Charles Agnew, of Knutsford (n of Sir William Agnew, 1 Bt, JP, of London, *see* Sir Anthony Agnew, 4 Bt); *b* 9 July 1900; *Educ* Repton; *m* 1, 1928, Enid Frances (d 1982), da of Henry Boan, of Perth, W Australia; 1 s; m 2, 1984 (m dis 1987), Mrs Julie Marie Watson; *Heir* s, Quentin Agnew-Somerville; *Career* Cdr RN served China Station, Mediterranean, N Sea; MP (C) Camborne 1931-50 and S Worcs 1955-66, Cons whip 1945-50; ADC to govr Jamaica 1927-28; memb Church Assembly 1935-65, church cmmr for E 1948-68, tstee Historic Churches Preservation Trust 1968-; KASG; *Recreations* travel; *Clubs* Carlton, Buck's; *Style*— Sir Peter Agnew, Bt; 2 Smith Sq, London SW1P 3HS (☎ 01 222 7179)

AGNEW, Peter Graeme; MBE (1946); s of late Alan Graeme Agnew; *b* 7 April 1914; *Educ* Stowe, Trinity Coll Cambridge; *m* 1937, Mary Diana, *née* Hervey; 2 s, 2 da; *Career* served WW II Wing-Cdr; dep chm Bradbury Agnew & Co (proprietors of Punch) 1969-83 (joined 1937); *Style*— Peter Agnew, Esq, MBE; The Old House, Manaccan, Helston, Cornwall TR12 6HR (☎ 032 623 468)

AGNEW, Stephen William; s of Maj, Sir John Agnew, 3 Bt, TD, JP DL (d 1957), and Kathleen, *née* White (d 1971); bro of Sir Anthony Agnew, 4 bt, *qv*; *b* 31 July 1921; *Educ* Rugby, Trinity Coll Cambridge; *m* 1, 28 June 1947 (m dis 1966), Elizabeth, da of James Brooks Close, of Grey Walls, Aldeburgh, Suffolk; 6 s (Stuart b 30 Aug 1949, Bolton b 21 Oct 1950, Jim b 12 April 1953, Stephen b 5 Dec 1954, Theodore b 17 Jan 1961, St John b 25 Feb 1964), 1 da (Margaret (Mrs Gurney) b 12 Jan 1952), m 2, Adene Leona Cookson, yst da of Vincent J Brady, DSC (d 1967), of Manly, NSW; *Career* served WWII 7 Queen's Own Hussars, Lt, Middle East and Italy 1942-46, wounded Sept 1944, invalided out Feb 1946; md Farming Cos in Norfolk 1963-, local dir Sun Alliance and London Insur Gp 1964-85, chm Rogate Farms Pty Ltd NSW 1983-87, dir Aust Regnl Offices Pty Ltd 1988-, Sydney, chm: Cawston Coll 1964-71, Norfolk and Norwich Marriage Guidance Cncl 1978-85; memb High Steward Ctee Norwich Cathedral 1962-80, gen cmmr Income Tax 1964-; *Recreations* hunting, shooting, music; *Clubs* Cavalry and Guards', Union (Sydney), Norfolk (Norwich), Rotary (Sydney); *Style*— Stephen Agnew, Esq; Oulton Hall, Norwich, Norfolk (☎ 026 387 237)

AGNEW OF LOCHNAW, Sir Crispin Hamlyn; 11 Bt (NS 1629), of Lochnaw, Wigtownshire; Chief of the Name of Agnew; s of Sir Fulque Melville Gerald Noel Agnew of Lochnaw, 10 Bt (d 1975), and Swanzie, da of Maj Esme Nourse Erskine, CMG, MC (descended from the Earls of Buchan), late Consular Serv; *b* 13 May 1944; *Educ* Uppingham, RMA Sandhurst; *m* 27 Aug 1980, Susan Rachel Strang, da of Jock Strang Steel (2 s of Sir Samuel Strang Steel of Philiphaugh, 1 Bt, TD, DL, and Hon Vere Cornwallis, 2 da of 1 Baron Cornwallis) and Lesley (da of Lt-Col Sir John Graham of Larbert, 3 Bt, VC, OBE, by Rachel, 5 da of Col Sir Alexander Sprot of Stravithie, 1 Bt, CMG); 2 da (Isabel b 1984, Emma b 1986); *Heir* cous, Dr Andrew Agnew; *Career* Maj RHF (ret 1981); Advocate 1982; Slains Pursuivant of Arms to the Lord High Constable of Scotland (The Earl of Erroll) 1978-81, Unicorn Pursuivant of Arms 1981-86, Rothesay Herald of Arms 1986-; ldr of expeditions to: Greenland 1968, Patagonia 1972, Api Himal 1980; memb of expeditions to Greenland 1966, Antarctica 1970, Nuptse Himal 1975, Everest 1976; *Recreations* mountaineering, yachting (yacht 'Pippa's Song'), heraldry, genealogy; *Clubs* Army and Navy; *Style*— Sir Crispin Agnew of Lochnaw, Bt; 6 Palmerston Rd, Edinburgh EH9 1TN (☎ 031 667 4970)

AGNEW-SOMERVILLE, Hon Mrs (Margaret April Irene); *née* Drummond of Megginch; 3 and yst da of 15 Baron Strange (d 1982), to which Barony she was co-heiress with her sisters; *b* 3 April 1939; *m* 1963, Quentin Charles Somerville Agnew-Somerville, *qv*; *Style*— The Hon Mrs Agnew-Somerville; Mount Auldyn House, Jurby Rd, Ramsey, IOM (☎ 0624 813724)

AGNEW-SOMERVILLE, Quentin Charles Somerville; s and h of Sir Peter Agnew, 1 Bt, *qv* (assumed by Royal Licence 1950 additional surname of Somerville after that of Agnew, and the arms of Somerville quarterly with those of Agnew, on succeeding to the Somerville estate of his maternal unc by m, 2 and last Baron Athlumney, who d 1929, leaving a widow, Margery, da of Henry Boan and sis of Enid, Quentin's mother); *b* 8 Mar 1929; *Educ* RNC Dartmouth; *m* 1963, Hon Margaret Drummond, *qv*, da of 15 Baron Strange and Violet (da of Sir Robert Buchanan-Jardine, 2 Bt); 1 s, 2 da; *Career* Sub Lt RN to 1950, when invalided from service; co dir; *Style*— Quentin Agnew-Somerville, Esq; Mount Auldyn House, Jurby Rd, Ramsey, IOM (☎ 0624 813724)

AGUTTER, David Jeremy; s of Albert Thomas George Agutter, of Bushey, Herts, and Joyce Winship, *née* Kirkland; *b* 23 Sept 1948; *Educ* Watford GS, Cental London Poly (BA); *m* 10 April 1981, Barbara Anne, da of George Archer Whiting (d 1984); 2 s (Thomas James b 1982, Mark Jonathan b 1984); *Career* ptnr Shears and Ptnrs 1972-80, princ David Agutter and Co 1980-, chief exec Falstaff Taverns Ltd 1987-, dir Town Centre Leisure Ltd 1987-; chm Dunstable Football; FCA 1971; *Recreations* sports; *Style*— David Agutter, Esq; Loudwater Cottage, Loudwater Lane, Chorleywood, Rickmansworth, Herts; 28 Portland Place, London W1N 3DF (☎ 01 631 1022, fax 01 323 4763)

AGUTTER, Richard Devenish; s of Anthony Tom Devenish Agutter (d 1960), and Joan Hildegarde Sabiné, *née* Machen (now Mrs Fleming); *b* 17 Sept 1941; *Educ* Marlborough; *m* 29 June 1968, Lesley Anne, da of Kenneth Alfred Ballard, MC, of Giles Barn Cottage, Horsted Keynes, Sussex; 3 s (Rupert William Devenish b 3 Nov 1972, Tom Alexander Devenish b 17 July 1975, Giles Edward Devenish b 6 April 1979); *Career* CA 1964, articled WT Walton & Sons 1960; Peat Marwick McLintock (formerly Peat Marwick Mitchell): joined 1964, ptnr 1977, currently ldr UK mergers and acquisitions; memb City No 1 Ctee (Lord Mayor's Advsy Ctee); Liveryman: Worshipful Co of Goldsmiths, Worshipful Co of Chartered Accountants; ACA 1964 (currently Fell); *Recreations* sailing, tennis, gardening; *Clubs* City Livery; *Style*— Richard Agutter, Esq; Great Frenches Park, Snow Hill, Crawley Down, West Sussex RH10 3EE (☎ 0342 716 816); Peat Marwick McLintock, 1 Puddle Dock, London EC4V 3PD (☎ 01 236 8000, fax 01 329 6101, car tel 0860 718 531)

AH-CHUEN, Sir Moi Lin Jean (Etienne); s of Jean George Ah-Chuen and Li Choi; *b* 22 Feb 1911; *Educ* St Jean Baptiste de La Salle, Chinese HS Mauritius; *m* 1929, Jeanne Hau Man Mui; 5 s, 6 da; *Career* MLA Mauritius 1948-76, Mauritius Govt delgn to UN 1974 and 1976, Cwlth Parly Assoc Mauritius 1948-, Min Local Govt Mauritius 1969-76; chm Chue Wing & Co 1977-; vice-chm Mauritius Union Assur Co 1948-; pres Chinese Cultural Centre 1968-; kt 1980; *Style*— Sir Jean Ah-Chuen; 5 Reverend Lebrun St, Rose Hill, Mauritius (☎ 4-3804)

AHEARNE, Stephen James; s of James Joseph Ahearne (d 1972), and Phyllis Eva, *née* Grigsby; *b* 7 Sept 1939; *Educ* St Ignatius Coll London; *m* 24 April 1965, Janet Elizabeth, da of Jack Ronald Edwards; 2 s (Jeremy b 1966, Thomas b 1968); *Career* CA; md BP Denmark 1978-81; dir: BP chemicals Int 1981-86, BP Exploration, BP Coal, BP Int 1986-, gp controller BP plc 1986-; *Recreations* tennis, gardening; *Style*— Stephen J Ahearne, Esq; Canonfylde, Stebbing, Essex (☎ 037186 236); British Petroleum plc, Britannic House, Moor Lane, London EC2 (☎ 01 920 7320)

AHERN, Most Rev John James; *see*: Cloyne, Bishop (RC) of

AHRENDS, Prof Peter; s of Steffen Bruno Ahrends, and Margarete Maria Sophie Ahrends; *b* 30 April 1933; *Educ* Architectural Assoc, Sch of Architecture, (Dip RIBA); *m* 1954, Elizabeth Robertson; 2 da; *Career* architect: Steffen Ahrends & Ptnrs Johannesburg 1957-58, Dennys Lasdun & Ptnrs/Julian Keable & Ptnrs 1958-60; fndr ptnr and dir of Ahrends Burton & Koralek 1961, princ works incl: Trinity Coll Dublin, Berkeley Library 1972, Arts Faculty Bldg 1979, Residential Bldg Keble Coll 1976, Templeton Coll Oxford 1969-88, Nebenzahl House Jerusalem 1972, warehouse and showroom for Habitat Wallingford, factory for Cummins Engines Shotts, J Sainsbury Canterbury Supermarket 1984, Retail HQ W H Smith Swindon 1985, Kingston Department Store John Lewis, St Marys Hospital Newport IOW, Heritage Centre Dover, stations for extension Docklands railway prof of Architecture Bartlett Sch of Architecture & Planning Univ Coll London 1986; *Clubs* Architectural Assoc; *Style*— Professor Peter Ahrends; 7 Chalcot Rd, London NW1 8LH (fax 01 722 5445)

AHRENS, Christine; da of Jacob Ahrens, and Gesa, *née* Bey; *b* 12 Dec 1961; *Educ* Humanistisches Gymnasium Hamburg, Coldwainers Col (Dip SIAD); *Career* shoe designer; designed for films: A View to a Kill, Absolute Beginners; first winter collection 1985, exhibited New York, Milan, Paris 1987-88; made shoes for such designers as: Ally Cappelino, Jasper Conran, David Fielden, Joe-Casely-Hayford; exhibited with London Designer Collections 1988; *Style*— Ms Christine Ahrens; 11 Old Compton Street, London W1 5PH (☎ 01 287 1752)

AIKEN, Joan Delano; da of Conrad Potter Aiken and Jessie McDonald Aiken; *b* 4 Sept 1924; *Educ* privately, Wychwood Sch Oxford; *m* 1, 7 July 1945 (d 1955), s of Albert Brown (d 1953); 1 s (John b 1949), 1 da (Elizabeth b 1951); m 2, 2 Sep 1976, Julius Goldstein; *Career* worked BBC 1942-43, librarian UN Information Ctee 1943-49 sub ed and features ed Argosy magazine 1955-60, copywriter J Watter Thompson London; author stories and plays; Guardian award for Children's Literature 1969, mystery writers of America Edgar Allan Poe Award 1972, Lewis Carroll Shelf Award 1962; childrens books; adult pubns; memb: Soc of Authors, Writers Guild, Mystery Writers of America; *Books* children's books: All You've Ever Wanted (1953), The Kingdom and the Cave (1960), Balck Hearts in Battersea (1964), The Whispering Mountain Cape (1968), Armitage, Armitage, Fly Away Home (1970), Smoke From Cromwell's Time (1970), The Kingdom Under the Sea (1971), A Harp of Fishbones (1972), Winterthing (play) (1972), The Mooncusser's Daughter (1933), The Escaped Black Mamba (1973), Tales of Arabel's Raven (1974), Tale of a One-Way Street (1978), The Skin Spinners (poems) (1976), A Bundle of Nerves (1976), The Faithless Lollybird (1977), Mice and Mendelson (1978), Street (1979), Mortimer's Portrait on Glass (1982), Bridle the Wind Cape (1983), Moritmer's Cross (1983), Up the Chimney Down (stories) (1984), The Last Slice of Rainbow (stories) (1985), Dido and Pa Cape (1986), The Teeth of the Gale Cape (1988), The Erl King's Daughter (1988), Voices Hippo (1988); adult pubns: The Silence of Herondale (1964), The Fortune Hunters (1965), Hate Begins at Home (1967), The Embroidered Sunset (1970), Died on a Rainy Sunday (1972), Castle Barebane (1976), The Smile of the Stranger (1978), The Weeping Ash (1980), A Whisper in the Night (1982), The Way to Write for Children (1982), Foul Matter (1983), Mansfield Revisited (1985), Blackground (1989); *Recreations* walking, gardening, listening to music, looking at art, travel; *Style*— Ms Joan Aiken; c/o A M Heath and Co Ltd, 79 St Martins Lane, London WC2N 4AA

AIKEN, Air Chief Marshal Sir John Alexander Carlisle; KCB (1973, CB 1967); s of Thomas Leonard and Margaret Aiken; *b* 22 Dec 1921; *Educ* Birkenhead Sch; *m* 1948, Pamela Jane, da of late H F W Bartlett, of Brook Lodge, Stock, Essex; 1 s, 1 da; *Career* joined RAF 1941, C-in-C NEAF 1973-76; air memb for Personnel 1976-78, dir-gen Intelligence MOD 1978-81; pres RAF Assoc 1984-; memb cncl Chatham House 1984-85 and 1987-88; *Recreations* skiing, walking; *Clubs* Royal Air Force; *Style*— Air Chief Marshal Sir John Aiken, KCB; 128 Piccadilly, London W1V 0PY

AIKENS, Richard John Pearson; s of Maj Basil Aikens (d 1983), and Jean Eleonor, *née* Pearson; *b* 28 August 1948; *Educ* Norwich Sch, St John's Coll Cambridge (MA); *m* 3 March 1979, Penelope Anne Hartley, da of Hartley Baker (d 1961); 2 s (Christopher b 1979, Nicholas b 1981), 2 step da (Jessica b 1964, Anna b 1966); *Career* barr 1973, practice 1974- (now at 1 Brick Court, Temple); jnr cnsl to the crown common law 1981-86; memb Supreme Ct Rules Ctee 1984-88; govr Sedbergh Sch 1988-; *Books* contributing Bullen and Leake on Pleadings and Practice (13 edn, ed); *Recreations* music, the country; *Clubs* Leander; *Style*— Richard Aikens, Esq; 1 Brick Court, Temple, London EC4 (☎ 01 583 0777)

AIKIN, Olga Lindholm (Mrs J M Driver); *née* Daly; da of Sidney Richard Daly, of Buckley, Clwyd, and Lilian May, *née* Lindholm (d 1966); *b* 10 Sept 1934; *Educ* Ilford Co HS for Girls, LSE (LLB), King's Coll London, London Business Sch;; *m* 1, 1959 (m dis 1979), Ronald Sidney Aikin; 1 da (Gillian); m 2, 1982, John Michael Driver; 1 step da (Katie); *Career* barr Gray's Inn 1956; lectr: King's Coll London 1956-59, LSE 1959- 70, London Business Sch 1971-; cncl memb ACAS 1982-, dir-gen law div Lion Int 1985-;; *Recreations* collecting cookery books and glass; *Style*— Mrs Olga Aikin; 22 St Lukes Rd, London W11 1DP (☎ 01 727 9791);

AILESBURY, Jean, Marchioness of; Jean Frances Margaret; *née* Wilson; da of John Addison Wilson, of Bodicote, Banbury, Oxon; *m* 1, Sqdn Ldr Richard Williamson, MBE, RAF (decd); m 2, 20 Feb 1950, as his 3 w, 7 Marquess of Ailesbury (d 1974); 1 s (Lord Charles Brudenell-Bruce, *qv*); *Style*— The Most Hon Jean, Marchioness of Ailesbury; Bel au Vent, St Lawrence, Jersey

AILESBURY, 8 Marquess of (UK 1821); Sir Michael Sydney Cedric Brudenell-Bruce; 14 Bt (E 1611); also Baron Brudenell (E 1628), Earl of Cardigan (E 1661), Baron Bruce (GB 1746), Earl of Ailesbury (GB 1776), and Earl Bruce and Viscount Savernake (both UK 1821); 30 Hereditary Warden of Savernake Forest; s of 7 Marquess of Ailesbury (d 1974); *b* 31 Mar 1926; *Educ* Eton; *m* 1, 1952 (m dis 1961), Edwina, da of Lt-Col Sir Edward Wills, 4 Bt; 1 s, 2 da; m 2, 1963 (m dis 1974), Juliet, da of Hilary Kingsford; 2 da; m 3, 1974, Caroline, da of the late Cdr Owen Wethered, JP, DL, RN, and former w of Simon Romilly; *Heir* s, Earl of Cardigan; *Career* late Lt RHG (reserve); memb London Stock Exchange 1954-; *Style*— The Most Hon the Marquess of Ailesbury; Stable Block, Tottenham House, Marlborough, Wilts

AILSA, 7 Marquess of (UK 1831); Archibald David Kennedy; OBE (1968), DL (Ayrshire); also Lord Kennedy (S 1452), Earl of Cassillis (S 1509), and Baron Ailsa (UK 1806); s of Capt 6 Marquess of Ailsa (d 1957); *b* 3 Dec 1925; *Educ* Pangbourne Nautical Coll; *m* 1954, Mary, da of late John Burn, of Amble, Northumberland; 2 s, 1 da; *Heir* s, Earl of Cassillis; *Career* formerly Lt Scots Gds, Lt-Col Royal Scots Fusiliers (TA), Hon Col Ayrshire Bn ACF 1980-, Patron IOM Rly Soc 1978-, chm Scottish Assoc of Boys Clubs 1978-82; *Clubs* New (Edinburgh), Carlton; *Style*— The Most Hon the Marquess of Ailsa, OBE, DL; Cassillis Castle, Maybole, Ayrshire KA19 7JN

AINGER, David William Dawson; TD (1969); s of Rev John Dawson Ainger (d 1987, Lt Cdr RN), of Weston Super Mare, and Frieda Emily, *née* Brand; *b* 10 Mar 1935; *Educ* Marlborough, Oxford Univ (MA), Cornell Univ; *m* 25 July 1964, Elizabeth Ann, da of Albert William Lewis, of 19a Granard Rd, London SW12; 3 s (William b 1969, Luke b 1972, Ruairidh b 1980), 2 da (Katharine b 1966, Siobhan b 1976); *Career* Nat Serv 2 Lt RE 1953-55, AER and TAVR RE and RCT 1955-69; barr Lincoln's Inn 1961, visiting lectr in law Southampton Univ 1961-71; *Style*— David Ainger, Esq, TD; 4 Northampton Park, London N1 2PJ (☎ 01 226 1401); 8 Stone Buildings, Lincoln's Inn, London WC2A 3TA (☎ 01 242 5002, fax 01 831 9188, telex 268072)

AINLEY, Sir (Alfred) John; MC (1940); only s of late Rev Alfred Ainley, of Cockermouth, Cumberland; *b* 10 May 1906; *Educ* St Bees Sch, Corpus Christi Coll Oxford; *m* 1935, Mona Sybil (d 1981), da of Sidney Wood, of Bromborough, Cheshire; 1 s, 2 da; *Career* barr 1928, chief justice Kenya 1963-68, chm Industl Tbnls 1972-76; kt 1957; *Style*— Sir John Ainley, MC; Horrock Wood, Watermillock, Penrith, Cumbria (☎ Watermillock 268)

AINSLIE, David Galbraith; s of Patrick David Lafone Ainslie, of Aynhoe Park, Aynho, nr Banbury, Oxon, and Agnes Ursula, *née* Galbraith; *b* 13 Oct 1947; *Educ* Wellington, Pembroke Coll Cambridge (MA); *Career* slr 1972 Dawson & Co, ptnr Lovell White & King 1981-83 (joined 1976) Towry Law & Co Ltd (independent fin advsrs) 1983; dir: Towry Law Tstee Co Ltd 1984, Towry Law Advsy Servs Ltd 1985, Towry Law & Co Ltd 1987; memb: UK Falkland Islands Ctee 1973-, exec ctee Falkland Islands Assoc 1977-; tstee UK Falkland Islands Tst 1981-; memb Law Soc 1971-; Freeman City of London, Liveryman Worshipful Co of Haberdashers 1971; *Books* Practical Tax Planning with Precedents (contrib 1987); *Recreations* fishing, shooting, flying; *Style*— David Ainslie, Esq; The Old Bakehouse, Hampstead Norreys, Nr Newbury, Berks RG16 0TE (☎ 0635 201 355); Towry Law Group, Towry Law House, 57 High St, Windsor, Berks SL4 1LX (☎ 0753 868 244, fax 0753 859 719, telex 847 894 Towlaw)

AINSLIE, John Bernard (Jack); OBE (1983); s of Capt Charles Bernard Ainslie, MC, (d 1937), of Lissadian, Sth Ascot, Berks, and Eileen, *née* Hollway (d 1962); *b* 2 August 1921; *Educ* Harrow, Trinity Coll Oxford; *m* 21 April 1951, Shelagh Lillian, da of Thomas Lawrence Forbes, (d 1976), of Chilbolton Cottage, Chilbolton, Stockbridge, Hants; 1 s (Andrew b 1952), 3 da (Sarah b 1952, Serena b 1957, Teresa b 1959); *Career* WWII 1941-46, cmmnd to Royal Berks Regt 1942 serving in the UK and NW Europe till 1945, 2nd Royal Lincolns 1945-46, capt, served NW Europe, Egypt and Palestine; farmed in ptnrship at Mildenhall Marlborough 1951-, md Gale and Ainslie Ltd; dir Progressive Pig Producers Ltd, N Wilts Cereals; formerly chm Ridgeway Grain, vice-chm Gp Cerial Serv's; memb exec ctee Community Concl for Wilts (former chm), memb Mildenhall parish cncl (former chm), contested Lib Derives 1974 and 79; Euro Lib Candidate: Upper Thames 1979, Wilts 1984; memb Wilts cc 1964-, (chm Educn Ctee 1973-77, ldr Lib Gp 1964-85, chm 1985-); VP Acre, memb Acc exec 1985-, memb Burnham Ctee 1985-87; FRAgS; *Recreations* music, drama, gardening; *Clubs* Farmers; *Style*— Jack Ainslie, Esq; Pennings, Mildenhall, Marlborough, Wilts SN8 2LT (☎ 0672 53477); Church Farm, Mildenhall, Marlborough, Wilts SN8 2LU (☎ 0672 52385)

AINSLIE, Michael Lewis; s of George L Ainslie, 100 Netherland Lane, Baysmont, Box 21, Kingsport, Tennessee 37660 and Jean Clare, *née* Waddell; *b* 12 May 1943; *Educ* Vanderbilt Univ (BA), Harvard Business Sch where he was a J Spencer Lover Fellow (MBA); *m* 1, 11 Dec 1971, Lucy Scardino; 1 s (Michael Loren b 28 June 1974); m 2, 13 Dec 1986, Suzanne H Braga; *Career* Assoc McKinsey & Co, NYC1968-71; pres Palmas de Mar, PR 1971-75; sr vice-pres C O O N-Ren Corp Cincinnati, 1975-80; pres National Tst for Historic Preservation, Washington DC 1980-84; pres CEO Southeby's Hldgs, Inc 1984-; *Recreations* tennis, golf; *Clubs* Metropolitain, Washington DC, River Club NYC, Buck's, Queen's; *Style*— Michael L Ainslie, Esq; 150 East 73rd Street, New York 10021, NY; Sotheby's Holdings Inc, 1334 York Avenue, New York 10021, NY

AINSWORTH, Anita, Lady; Anita Margaret Ann; da of Harold Arthur Lett, of Co Wexford; *m* 1946, as his 2 w, Sir John Ainsworth, 3 Bt (d 1981); *Style*— Anita, Lady Ainsworth; Carraphuca, Shankill, Co Dublin, Eire

AINSWORTH, Anthony Thomas Hugh; s and h of Sir David Ainsworth, 4 Bt; *b* 30 Mar 1962; *Educ* Harrow; *Career* Lt Royal Hussars (PWO) 1982-85; *Style*— Anthony Ainsworth, Esq

AINSWORTH, Sir (Thomas) David; 4 Bt (UK 1916); s of Sir Thomas Ainsworth, 2 Bt, by his 2 w, Marie, da of Compton Domvile; suc half-bro, Sir John Ainsworth, 3 Bt, 1981; *b* 22 August 1926; *Educ* Eton; *m* 1957, Sarah Mary, da of Lt-Col Hugh Carr Walford, 17/21 Lancers (ka 1941); 2 s (Anthony, Charles b 1966), 2 da (Serena b 1958, Tessa b 1959); *Heir* s, Anthony Thomas Hugh Ainsworth; *Recreations* shooting, fishing; *Style*— Sir David Ainsworth, Bt; 80 Elm Park Gdns, London SW10; Ashley House, Wootton, nr Woodstock, Oxon (☎ 0993 811650)

AINSWORTH, Mavis; da of Reginald Frederick Davenport (d 1967), of Totley, Sheffield, and Wilhelmina, *née* Mynette; *b* 6 Sept 1931; *Educ* Univ of London (BA, PGCE), Univ of Illinois (MA 1959); *m* 8 Aug 1953, Stanley Ainsworth, s of late Andrew Rutherford Ainsworth, of Heaton Chapel, Stockport; 2 s (Jonathan Grieve b 1960, Quentin Paul b 1961); *Career* head English Dept, Totley Thornbridge Coll of Educn Sheffield 1969-76; head English Dept, Sheffield City Poly 1976-87; dean Faculty of Cultured Studies, Wiol Poly wide responsibility for initial and in service teacher training 1987-; *Recreations* theatre, travel, visiting London; *Style*— Mrs Mavis Ainsworth; 139 Dore Rd, Dore, Sheffield S17 3NF; Dean of Cultural Studies, Sheffield City Poly, Psalter Lane, Sheffield S11 8UZ (☎ 0742 556101, telex 54680 SHPOLY6, fax 758019)

AINSWORTH, (Edward) Peter Richard; s of Edward Ainsworth (d 1955), of Sale, Cheshire, and Sara Katharina, *née* Healey (d 1962); *b* 31 July 1932; *Educ* Manchester GS; *m* 12 Aug 1959, Moira Josephine, da of Albert Grant, of Manchester; 4 s (Michael b 1980, Timothy b 1982, John b 1984, Mark b 1987); *Career* accountant; FCA; *Recreations* sailing (cruising and racing), skiing, golf; *Clubs* Royal Mersey Yacht, Budworth Sailing, Trearddur Bay Sailing; *Style*— Peter Ainsworth, Esq; Quinta, Hawley Lane, Hale, Altrincham, Cheshire; Ashfield House, Ashfield Road, Cheadle, Cheshire

AINSWORTH, Robert David; *b* 10 Dec 1949; *Educ* Dudley GS, Leeds Univ (BA); *m* 31 July 1971, Alison Elizabeth; 1 da (Rachel b 1976), 1 s (Colin b 1978); *Career* company dir, gp fin dir: The Phoenix Timber Gp plc 1986-, Palma Gp plc 1982-86, FCA; *Recreations* golf, squash; *Style*— Robert D Ainsworth, Esq; Turner House, Station Rd, Elsenham, Bishops Stortford, Herts CM22 6LA; Rainham House, New Rd, Rainham, Essex RM13 8RJ (☎ 04027 21100, fax 04027 23505)

AINSWORTH, William Robert; s of William Murray Ainsworth (d 1964), of Stockton-on-Tees, Co Durham, and Emma Laura MAry, *née* Easley (d 1981); *b* 24 June 1935; *Educ* Holy Trinity Sch Stockton on Tees, Stockton GS, Durham Univ Sch of Architecture (BArch); *m* 7 Nov 1959, Sylvia Vivian, da of Norman Brown, of Buenos Aires, Argentina, S America; 3 da (Graciela Glenn b 1960, Anita Susan b 1964, Lucia Emma b 1977); *Career* chartered architect, designer and urban planner, fndr ptnr Ainsworth Spark Assocs 1963- (completed over 2500 projects throughout UK and Europe for local, nat and int cos; working tours of: S America, USA, and Europe; visiting studio tutor Sch of Architecture Newcastle upon Tyne 1961-63; external examiner: Sch of Architecture, Coll of Arts and Technol Newcastle; RIBA: chm Northern Region 1972-73, fndr chm Nat Ctee for Environmental Educn 1977, dir Bd of Servs Ltd London, memb and vice pres Nat Cncl 1980-82, hon librarian Br Architectural Library 1987-; initiator of World Day of Architecture in UK; chm: Sculpture Tst Northern Arts (fndr) 1981-, Northumberland and Durham Lord's Taverners; FRIBA 1967, MCSD 1977, IOB 1980, FRSA 1985; *Recreations* cricket, golf, gardening, reading, painting (water colours); *Clubs* Art (London), Northumberland GC; *Style*— William Ainsworth, Esq; 1 Edgewood, Darras Hall, Ponteland, Newcastle upon Tyne; Summerhill House (Ainsowrth Spark Associates), 9 Summerhill Terrace, Newcastle upon Tyne NE4 6EB (☎ 091 232 3434, fax 091 261 0628, telex 537533)

AIRD, Capt Sir Alastair Sturgis; KCVO (1984, CVO 1977, LVO 1969); s of Col Malcolm Aird (d 1965); *b* 14 Jan 1931; *Educ* Eton, RMA Sandhurst; *m* 1963, Fiona Violet, LVO (1980), da of Lt-Col Ririd Myddelton (d 1988); 2 da (Caroline b 1964,

Henrietta b 1966); *Career* cmmnd 9 Queen's Royal Lancers 1951, Adjutant 1956-59, ret 1964; equerry to Queen Elizabeth The Queen Mother 1960-63, asst private aec 1964-74, comptroller to Queen Elizabeth The Queen Mother 1974-; *Recreations* shooting, fishing, tennis; *Style*— Capt Sir Alastair Aird, KCVO; 31B St James's Palace, London SW1 (☎ 01 839 6700)

AIRD, Sir (George) John; 4 Bt (UK 1901), of Hyde Park Terrace, Paddington, Co London; s of Col Sir John Renton Aird, 3 Bt, MVO, MC, JP, DL (d 1973), sometime Extra Equerry to King George VI and to HM The Queen, of Forest Lodge, Windsor Great Park, by his w, Lady Priscilla, *née* Heathcote-Drummond-Willoughby, yr da of 2 Earl of Ancaster; *b* 30 Jan 1940; *Educ* Eton, Ch Ch Oxford (MA), Harvard (MBA); *m* 1968, Margaret Elizabeth, da of Sir John Muir, 3 Bt, TD, DL; 1 s, 2 da (Rebecca b 1970, Belinda b 1972); *Heir* s, James John Aird b 12 June 1978; *Career* page of honour to HM 1955-57; MICE 1965; engineer Sir Alexander Gibb & Partners 1961-65; mangr John Laing & Co 1967-69; chm and md Sir John Aird & Co 1969-; *Recreations* skiing, farming; *Clubs* White's; *Style*— Sir John Aird, Bt; Grange Farm, Evenlode, Moreton-in-Marsh, Glos GL56 0NT (☎ 0608 50607)

AIRD, Lady Priscilla; *née* Heathcote-Drummond-Willoughby; yr da of 2 Earl of Ancaster, GCVO, TD, JP, DL (d 1951); co-heiress to Barony of niece, Baroness Willoughby de Eresby, *qv*; *b* 29 Oct 1909; *m* 1939, Col Sir John Renton Aird, 3 Bt, MVO, MC, Gren Gds (d 1973); 1 s, 3 da; *Style*— Lady Priscilla Aird; Wingrove House, Chipping Campden, Glos

AIREDALE, 4 Baron (UK 1907); Sir Oliver James Vandeleur Kitson; 4 Bt (UK 1886); s of 3 Baron Airedale, DSO, MC (d 1958); *b* 22 April 1915; *Educ* Eton, Trinity Coll Cambridge; *Career* sits as Lib Peer; Maj The Green Howards; barr Inner Temple 1941; dep chm Ctees House of Lords 1961-, dep speaker 1962-; *Clubs* Royal Cwlth Soc; *Style*— The Rt Hon the Lord Airedale; Ufford Hall, Stamford, Lincs

AIREY, Lady; Bridget Georgina; da of Col Hon Thomas Eustace Vesey (d 1946, bro of 5 Viscount de Vesci) and Lady Cecily Browne (da of 5 Earl of Kenmare and a Lady-in-Waiting to HRH Duchess of Gloucester 1947-51, Woman of the Bedchamber to HM Queen Mary 1951-53); *b* 6 Feb 1915; *m* 1947, as his 2 w, Lt-Gen Sir Terence Airey, KCMG, CB, CBE (d 1983, Cdr Br Forces Hong Kong 1952-54); *Style*— Lady Airey; The White Cottage, Busgay Rd, Hempnall, Norwich, Norfolk NR15 2NG (☎ 050 842 214)

AIREY, Clifford; s of Maj William Airey, REME (d 1986), of Preston, Lancashire, and Ellen, *née* Hogg (d 1974); *b* 16 Jan 1939; *Educ* British Army Schools Overseas, Liverpool Univ, Manchester Univ; *m* 1, 23 Jan 1960 (m dis 1980), Maureen, *née* Fowler; 1 s (Shawn James b 1965), 2 da (Dawn Elizabeth b 1960, Rachel Louise b 1967); m 2, 1982, Gina Margarita, *née* Kingdon, 2 s (Sebastian Jon b 1983, Clifford Lloyd 1985), 1 da (Dominique Ellen b 1984); *Career* res ptnr Jubb & Partners Consulting Engrs 1964-73; sr ptnr Airey and Coles Consulting Engineers 1973-; sr lectr Plymouth Poly 1967-70; former chm Inst of Structural Engrs; CEng, FIStructE, MConsE, FFB; *Recreations* fly fishing, sailing, shooting, stamp and coin collecting; *Clubs* Plymouth Philatelic Soc, Dart Sailing; *Style*— Clifford Airey, Esq; 8 Whiteford Rd, Mannamead, Plymouth (☎ 0752 266 456); Kirkby Lodge, Portland Square Lane North, Plymouth, Devon (☎ 0752 229 119/0752 227 983, fax 0752 222 115)

AIREY, John Fritjof; s of Philip Wainwright Airey, of Cumbria, and Anna-Lisa, *née* Fornander; *b* 3 May 1942; *Educ* Rossall Sch, Regent St Poly (sch of mod lang); *m* 14 Sept 1968 (m dis 1981), Jane (d 1984); 2 s (James b 1972, Alexander b 1973); *Career* travel, writer, ed British Travel News 1971-79; *Books* Cotswolds Walks With a Point; *Recreations* walking, photography, travel; *Clubs* British Guild of Travel Writers; *Style*— John F Airey, Esq; 2 Rosemary Court, Fortune Green Rd, Hampstead, London NW6 1UA (☎ 01 794 5387)

AIREY, Wendy Helen; da of Edward Docherty (d 1976), of Woodfield, Lasswade, Scotland, and Elizabeth Craig, *née* Ross; *b* 26 Jan 1963; *Educ* St Margaret's Sch for Girls, Royal Scottish Acad of Music & Drama (DRSAMD), Univ of Glasgow (MSc); *m* 7 May 1988, Timothy Charles Airey, s of Frank L Airey, of Craigmount Ave North, Barnton, Edinburgh; *Career* princ Turin Opera House 1984, singer and presenter RAI 1984-85, French Art Song Concerts in Paris, Milan and Atlanta 1985, advent concert soloist St Peter's Rome 1987 given many charity concerts in Scotland especially for Marie Curie Cancer Fndn; *Recreations* horse riding, polo, swimming; *Clubs* Carlton; *Style*— Mrs W H Airey; Freelance Singer, 16B Fettes Row, Edinburgh, EH3 6RH (☎031-556-3272)

AIREY OF ABINGDON, Baroness (Life Peer UK 1979); Diana Josceline Barbara Neave Airey; da of Thomas Giffard, MBE, JP, of Chillington, Staffs (descended from Osbern de Bolebec, Sire de Longueville, *temp* Richard 'Sans Peur' Duke of Normandy, who d 960 and whose sister-in-law, Aveline, Osbern married), and Angela, eld da and co-heir of Sir William Trollope, 10 Bt; *b* 7 July 1919; *m* 1942, Airey Neave, DSO, OBE, MC, TD, MP (assassinated 1979; gggs of Sir Thomas Neave, 2 Bt); 2 s, 1 da; *Career* with Foreign Office and Polish Miny of Info London WW II, thereafter supported husb politically; memb North Atlantic Assembly; trustee: Dorneywood Trust, Imperial War Museum 1985-, Stansted Park Fndn; Freeman City of London; FRSA; *Recreations* reading, opera, theatre; *Style*— The Rt Hon Baroness Airey of Abingdon; House of Lords, London SW1A 0AA

AIRLIE, 13 Earl of (S 1639); Sir David George Coke Patrick Ogilvy; PC (1984), DL (Angus 1964), KT (1985) GCVO (1984); also Lord Ogilvy of Airlie (S 1491) and Lord Ogilvy of Alyth and Lintrathen (S 1639); s of 12 Earl of Airlie, KT, GCVO, MC (d 1968), and Lady Alexandra Coke (d 1984), da of 3 Earl of Leicester; *b* 17 May 1926; *Educ* Eton; *m* 1952, Virginia Fortune, CVO (1982; vice-pres Women of the Year, Lady in Waiting to HM The Queen 1976-), da of John Ryan, of Newport, RI, USA; 3 s (David (Lord Ogilvy), Bruce b 1959, Patrick b 1965), 3 da (Doune b 1953, Jane b 1953, Elizabeth b 1965); *Heir* s, Lord Ogilvy; *Career* Lt Scots Gds 1944; Capt ADC to High Cmmr and C-in-C Austria 1947-48, Malaya 1948-49, resigned cmmn 1950; tres Scouts Assoc 1962-86; Ensign Royal Co of Archers (Queen's Body Guard for Scotland) 1975-; chm: Schroders 1977-84, Ashdown Investment Trust to 1982 (also resigned directorship); chm Gen Accident Fire & Life Assur Corpn 1987-; dir: J Henry Schroder Wagg & Co 1961-84 (chm 1973-77), Scottish & Newcastle Breweries 1969-83, Royal Bank of Scotland Gp 1983-; Lord Chamberlain of the Queen's Household 1984-; govr Nuffield Hospitals 1984-; tstee: Tate Gallery, fine Arts Cmmn; CStJ 1981; kt 1985; *Clubs* White's; *Style*— The Rt Hon The Earl of Airlie, KT, GCVO, PC, DL; Cortachy Castle, Kirriemuir, Angus (☎ Cortachy 231); 5 Swan Walk, London SW3 4JJ (☎ 01 352 0296); Lord Chamberlain's Office, St James's Palace, London SW1 (☎ 01 930 3007)

AIRS, Graham John; s of George William Laurence Airs, of Northampton, and Marjorie, *née* Lewis (d 1967); *b* 8 August 1953; *Educ* Newport GS Essex, Emmanuel Coll Cambridge (BA, MA, LLB); *m* 4 April 1981, Stephanie Annette, da of William Henry Marshall; *Career* admitted slr 1978, ptnr Airs Dickinson 1980-84, Slaughter & May (1976-80, asst slr 1984-87) 1987-; memb Law Soc, AInstT; *Books* Tolley's Tax Planning (chapter on tax losses published annually); *Style*— Graham Airs, Esq; 35 Basinghall St, London EC2V 5DB (☎ 01 600 1200, fax 01 726 0038, 01 600 0289, telex 883486, 888926)

AISHER, Sir Owen Arthur; s of late Owen Aisher, of Branksome Park, Poole; *b* 28 May 1900; *m* 1921, Ann Allingham; 2 s, 2 da; *Career* life pres Marley Tile Companies; Yachtsman of the Year 1958; pres: RYA 1970-75, Little Ship Club; adm: Island Sailing Club, Royal Ocean Racing Club 1969-75; kt 1981; *Style*— Sir Owen Aisher

AITCHISON, Sir Charles Walter de Lancey; 4 Bt (UK 1938), of Lemmington, Co Northumberland; s of Sir Stephen Charles de Lancey Aitchison, 3 Bt (d 1958); *b* 27 May 1951; *m* 1984, Susan, yr da of late Edward Ellis, of Hest Bank, Lancs; 1 s (Rory), 1 da (Tessa); *Heir* s, Rory Edward de Lancey; *Career* late Lt 15/19 KRH; co dir: De Lancey Lands Ltd, Walter Wilson Ltd; *Recreations* fishing; *Style*— Sir Charles Aitchison, Bt; Kirkharle Manor, Harle, Newcastle-upon-Tyne, Tyne and Wear

AITCHISON, Craigie Ronald John; yr s of Rt Hon Lord Aitchison, PC, KC, LLD (Scottish Lord of Session, Lord Justice-Clerk and Lord Advocate Scotland under Ramsay MacDonald; noted for never losing a case involving an indictment on a capital charge when defending); yr bro of Raymund Craigie Aitchison, the writer; *b* 13 Jan 1926; *Educ* Slade Sch of Fine Art; *Career* painter; various one-man shows: Beaux Art, Marlborough Fine Art Galleries, Compass (Glasgow), Rutland, Artis Monte-Carlo Albermarle Gallery, Basil Jacobs, Knoedler; works in: Tate, Scottish National Gallery of Modern Art, Arts Cncl of GB, National Gallery of Australia (Melbourne); ARA 1988; *Style*— Craigie Aitchison, Esq; Montecastelli San Gusme, Siena, Italy; 32 St Mary's Gdns, London SE11 (☎ 01 582 3708)

AITCHISON, (Stephen) Edward; s of Sir Stephen Charles de Lancey Aitchison, 3 Bt (d 1958); hp of bro, Sir Charles Aitchison, 3 Bt; *b* 27 Mar 1954; *m* 1978, Mrs Harriet M Thomson, yr da of late Dr Henry Miller; 1 s (Stephen b 1981), 1 da (Amanda b 1983); *Career* dir: Walter Wilson Ltd, De Lancey hands Ltd, NISA Ltd; *Style*— Edward Aitchison, Esq; Cuilfail, Apperley Rd, Stockfield, Northumberland

AITCHISON, Thomas Milne; MBE (1977); s of William and Jean Aitchison, of 5 Manse Rd, Whitburn, W Lothian; *b* 28 May 1930; *Educ* Bathgate Acad, Edinburgh Univ (BL 1953); *m* 18 Aug 1962, Flora Jane Stewart, da of Robert Paris (d 1965); 3 s (David William Millar b 1964, Iain Robert Paris b 1965, Andrew Thomas Macmillan b 1971); *Career* apprenticeship with MacPherson & Mackay WS Edinburgh 1950-53 (asst 1953-54); legal asst: Motherwell and Wishaw Town Cncl 1954-55, W Lothian CC 1955-61; first legal asst Lanark CC 1962-67; deputy county clerk (sr) Ross & Cromarty CC 1967-75, chief exec Ross & Cromarty DC 1974-78, ptnr P H Young & Co Slrs 1979-83, owner Aitchison & Co SSC Whitburn 1984-; county tres W Lothian Boy Scouts Assoc 1958-68 (co sec 1960-62); *Recreations* yachting, photography, skiing; *Style*— Thomas M Aitchison, Esq, MBE; 12 Merlin Park, Dollar, Clackmannanshire (☎ 025 94 3156); 17 East Main St, Whitburn, W Lothian (☎ 0501 43393)

AITHRIE, Viscount; Andrew Victor Arthur Charles Hope; s and h of Earl of Hopetoun and gs of 3 Marquess of Linlithgow; *b* 22 May 1969; *Heir* bro, Hon Alexander Hope; *Career* a page of honour to HM Queen Elizabeth the Queen Mother 1985-; *Style*— Viscount Aithrie

AITKEN, Hon Mrs; (Joan) Elizabeth; *née* Rees-Williams; da of 1 Baron Ogmore, TD, PC (d 1976); *b* 1 May 1936; *Educ* Croham Hurst Sch, Mont Olivet Lausanne; *m* 1, 1957 (m dis 1969), Richard St John Harris, actor; 3 s; m 2, 1971 (m dis 1975), Rex Carey Harrison, actor; m 3, 1980, Peter Michael Aitken, gs of 1 Lord Beaverbrook; *Style*— The Hon Mrs Aitken; 14 Lowndes Sq, Kensington, London SW1

AITKEN, James; s of James Aitken (d 1952); *b* 6 April 1917; *Educ* Rutherglen Acad, Glasgow Univ; *m* 1955, Sheila Elizabeth, da of Albert Gibson Deans (d 1964); *Career* served as Lt-Col SE Asia; slr; conslt with Wright Johnston & Mackenzie (slrs); chm F J C Lilley (civil engrg gp) 1974-; *Clubs* Royal Scottish Automobile (Glasgow); *Style*— James Aitken, Esq; 20 Tynwald Ave, High Burside, Rutherglen, Scotland (☎ 041 634 4500); Wright, Johnston & Mackenzie, 12 St Vincent Place, Glasgow G1 2EQ (☎ 041 221 6606)

AITKEN, Jonathan William Patrick; MP (C) S Thanet 1983-; s of Sir William Aitken, KBE, MP (d 1964), and Hon Lady Aitken, MBE, JP, *qv*; is gn of 1 Baron Beaverbrook and gs of 1 Baron Rugby; bro of Maria Aitken, *qv*, the actress; *b* 30 August 1942; *Educ* Eton, Christ Church Oxford; *m* 1979, Lolicia Olivera (economist), da of O A Azucki, of Zürich; 1 s (William, b 7 Sept 1982), twin da (Victoria, Alexandra b 14 June 1980); *Career* private sec to Selwyn Lloyd 1964-66; foreign corr Evening Standard 1966-71; md Slater Walker (M East) 1973-75; MP (C) Thanet E 1974-1983; fndr and chm Aitken Hume Int 1979-; temp chief exec TV-AM Mar-Apr 1983; *Books* A Short Walk on the Campus (1966), The Young Meteors (1967), Land of Fortune: A Study of the New Australia (1971), Officially Secret (1971); *Clubs* Beefsteak, Turf, Pratt's; *Style*— Jonathan Aitken, Esq, MP; 8 Lord North St, London SW1

AITKEN, Maria Penelope Katharine; da of Sir William Aitken, KBE, MP Bury St Edmunds 1950-64 (d 1964, s of Joseph Aitken, 2 s of Rev William Aitken and eld bro of 1 Baron Beaverbrook; Sir William's yr sis Margaret Annie was a Canadian MP in the early 1970s), and Hon Lady Aitken, *qv*, sis of Jonathan Aitken, MP, *qv*; *b* 12 Sept 1945; *Educ* privately, Riddlesworth Hall Norfolk, Sherborne Girls' Sch, St Anne's Coll Oxford; *m* 1, 1968 (m dis), Mark Durden-Smith, yst s of A J Durden-Smith, FRCS, of Kensington; m 2, 1972 (m dis 1980), Nigel Davenport, the actor, *qv*; 1 s (Jack); *Career* actress in (amongst others) Bedroom Farce, Blithe Spirit (both National Theatre), Travesties (RSC), The Happiest Days of Your Life (RSC 1984), Waste (RSC 1985), role of Amanda in 1979/80 London prodn of Noel Coward's Private Lives, of Filda in Coward's Design for Living 1982-83; Sister Mary Ignatius (Ambassadors Theatre 1983); directed Happy Family by Giles Cooper (Duke of York's Theatre, London 1983), Private Lives by Noel Coward at Oxford Playhouse 1984, After the Ball by William Douglas Home at The Old Vic 1985, The Rivals by Sheridan at the Court Theatre Chicago USA 1985; own chat show (Private Lives) on BBC2; own prodn co Dramatis Personae (produced Happy Family and Sister Mary Ignatius 1983); part-time journalist, 1985 Documentary (made going up the Amazon) for the BBC; *Style*— Miss

Maria Aitken; c/o Leading Artists, 60 St James's St, London SW1 (☎ 01 491 4400)

AITKEN, (Thomas) Patrick Howie; s of James Howie Aitken (d 1962); *b* 2 July 1925; *Educ* Munro Coll Jamaica; *m* 1953, Rosemary, da of Michael Decosmo (d 1974); 1 s (Michael), 2 da (Cassandra, Pamela); *Career* served RAF 1943-46; Gill & Duffus Gp: dir 1965-76, md 1976-78, dep chm 1978-79, chm 1980, resigned 1982; Gill & Duffus Inc USA; dir 1959-80, vice-pres 1954-62, pres 1963-80; pres Gill & Duffus Hldgs Inc 1980; dir: New York Cocoa Exchange 1971-78 (vice chm 1972-74, chm 1974-76), Futures Industry Assoc Inc 1972-77 (vice-chm 1974-75); *Recreations* usual country pastimes; *Clubs* India House (New York), Nat Golf Links of America (Southampton NY); *Style—* Patrick Aitken, Esq; 9 Southway, Bronxville, New York, NY 10708, USA (☎ (914) 779 1909/779 6626)

AITKEN, Hon Lady; Penelope; *née* Maffey; MBE (1955), JP, WRVS Long Service Medal; da of 1 Baron Rugby, GCMG, KCB, KCVO, CSI, CIE (d 1969); *b* 2 Dec 1910; *m* 1939, Sir William Aitken, KBE, MP (d 1964), s of Joseph Aitken, bro to first Lord Beaverbrook; 1 s (Jonathan, *qv*), 1 da (Maria, *qv*); *Career* JP; *Style—* The Hon Lady Aitken, MBE, JP; 2 North Court, Gt Peter St, London SW1

AITKEN, Robert Nicholas Reid; s of Bruce Ramsey Tweedie Aitken, of Wilmington, Kent, and Anne Constance, *née* Rolfe; *b* 25 Dec 1955; *Educ* Tonbridge; *m* 14 Sep 1985, Katherine Ann, da of William Edward Hampson, of Stamford, Lincs; *Career* articled clerk later mangr Touche Ross and Co 1976-83, CA 1980, mangr later ptnr Henderson Crosthwaite and Co 1983-86, dir Henderson Crosthwaite Ltd (subsidiary of Guinness Peat Gp) 1987-88; dr Guinness Mahon and Co Ltd (banking subsidiary Guinness Mahon Hldgs plc) 1986-; ACA 1980, IOD 1979, memb Int Stock Exchange of the UK and Ireland 1986; *Recreations* rugby, golf, tropical fish; *Clubs* Blackheath (Rugby) Football, Chislehurst Golf; *Style—* Robert Aitken, Esq; 104 Coleraine Rd, Blackheath, London SE3 7NZ (☎ 01 858 3477); Guinness Mahon and Co Ltd, 32 St Mary at Hill, London EC3P 3AJ (☎ 01 623 9333, fax 01 929 3398, telex 884035 GUIMAN G)

AITKEN, Ronald William; s of Brig William Henry Hutton Aitken (d 1978), of Woking, Surrey, and Mary Dorothea, *née* Davidson (d 1982); *b* 20 Sept 1933; *Educ* Cheltenham; *m* 3 Nov 1962, Frances Barbara, da of Edward John Wharton Farmer (d 1980), of 36 Buckingham Gate, London SW1; 6 da (Fiona b 1963, Sarah b 1964, Lucinda b 1968, Alexandra b 1970, Penelope b 1975, Georgiana b 1980); *Career* chm: Ford Stellar Morris Properties plc; Ecobric Hldgs plc, Health Screening Fndn, Ronnie Aitken & Associates, Stanley Gibbons Hldgs plc; dir: Kells Minerals Ltd, Charles Letts (Hldgs) Ltd, N Brown Group plc, Wankel Int SA; FCA; *Recreations* golf, tennis, backgammon; *Clubs* Brooks's; *Style—* Ronald Aitken, Esq; 212 Ashley Gdns, London SW1 (☎ 01 834 3110); business: 36 Ebury St, London SW1W 0AU (☎ 01 730 9277, fax 01 730 0242, telex 925812); car ☎ 0860 320414

AITKEN, Gp Capt Russell Faulkner (Digger); CBE (1958, OBE 1943), AFC (1941); s of Robert Aitken, of Lower Hutt (d 1965), and Christina Aitken (d 1978); *b* 15 Sept 1913; *Educ* Gore and Timaru HSs, London Univ, and Mil Staff Colls; *m* 1939, Rhoda Ruth (d 1984), da of Edward St John Bransome (d 1950), of London; 1 da; m 2, 1985, Barbara Thomas, da of Hedley Ernest Windeatt (d 1968) of Humberston, Lincs; *Career* RAF Gp Capt serv WWII: Europe, Burma, Cyprus, Palestine 1937-61; dir: Nat Safety Assoc of NZ 1962-75, Accident Copensation Cmmn 1975-78, ret; *Recreations* music, reading; *Style—* Gp Capt Russell Aitken, CBE, AFC; Rixlade, 64 Seaview Rd, Paremata, NZ (☎ 010 64 4 338 487)

AITKEN, Timothy Maxwell; er s of Hon Peter Rudyard Aitken (d 1947, yr s of 1 Baron Beaverbrook), by his 2 wife, Marie Patricia, da of Michael Joseph Maguire, of Melbourne, Australia; *b* 28 Oct 1944; *Educ* Repton, Sorbonne, McGill Univ Canada; *m* 1, 10 May 1966, Annette, da of Claus Hansen, of Denmark; m 2, Julie Ruth, da of Charles Filstead; 2 s (Theodore b 1976, Charles b 1979); *Career* chief exec Aitken Hume Int plc; chm: TV-AM Ltd, National Securities & Research Corp Inc; *Clubs* Royal Thames Yacht; *Style—* Timothy Aitken, Esq; c/o Tv - AM, Hawlpy Cres, London NW1 8EF

AITKEN, Lady; Ursula; da of Dr Herbert Wales; *m* 1937, Sir Peter (Arthur Percival Hay) Aitken (d 1984), s of late Canon R Aitken; 1 s, 1 da; *Style—* Lady Aitken; The Lodge, Alde House Drive, Aldeburgh, Suffolk IP15 5EE

AITKEN, Lady; Violet; *née* de Trafford; da of Sir Humphrey Edmund de Trafford, 4 Bt, MC (d 1971), and Hon Cynthia Cadogan who was 3 da of Viscount Chelsea (d 1908); *b* 1926; *m* 1951, as his 3 w, Sir Max Aitken, 2 Bt, DSO, DFC (d 1985; 2 Baron Beaverbrook who disclaimed peerage for life 1964); 1 s (3 Baron Beaverbrook, *qv*), 1 da; *Career* chllr Univ of New Brunswick Canada (1981-); *Recreations* racing, powerboat racing, hot air ballooning; *Style—* Lady Aitken; Mickleham Downs House, Dorking, Surrey RH5 6DP

AKABUSI, Kriss Kezie Uche-Chukwu Daru;; s of Daniel Kambi Duru Akabusi, and Clara, *née* Adams; *b* 28 Nov 1958; *Educ* Edmonton Co Comprehensive; *m* 2 April 1982, Monika, da of Heinrich Bernard Udhöfer; 2 da (Ashanti b 19 June 1984, Shakira b 20 Oct 1987); *Career* Army; jr signalman 1975, signalman 1976 (da telegraphist), Lance Corpl (AIPT) 1978, Corpl (AITP) 1980, Sgt SI APTC 1981, Staff Sgt SSI APTC 1985, WOII (QMSI) APTC 1988; Bronze Medalist 4 x 400m relay World Champs 1983, Olympic Silver Medallist 4 x 400m relay 1984, UK Champ 400m 1984, Capt English Athletics Team Engngland vs USA 1985, Euro and Cwlth 4 x 400m Gold Medallist and record holder 1986, finalist 400m hurdles and Silver Medallist 4 x 400m relay World Champs 1987, UK 400m hurdles Champ 1987, Olympic finalist 400m hurdles 1988, AAA Champ 400m 1988; involved with: Cwlth Games Appeal 1985-86, Olympic Games Appeal 1986-88; *Clubs* Army AAA, Team Solent AC; *Style—* Kriss Akabusi, Esq

AKEHURST, Gen Sir John Bryan; KCB (1984), CBE (1976); s of Geoffrey Akehurst and Doris Akehurst; *b* 12 Feb 1930; *Educ* Cranbrook Sch, RMA Sandhurst; *m* 1955, Shirley Ann, er da of Maj W G Webb, MBE; 1 s, 1 da (both decd); *Career* formerly with Northants Regt & Malay Regt; cmd 2 Royal Anglian Regt 1968-70, directing staff IDC 1970-72, Cdr Dhofar Bde Sultan of Oman's Armed Forces 1974-76, Dep Mil Sec (A) MOD 1976-79, GOC Armd Div BAOR 1979-82, Cmdt Staff Coll Camberley Jan 1982-83 (previously instr 1966-68), cmd UK Field Army and Inspr Gen TA 1984-87; dep Supreme Allied Commander Europe 1987-; govr Harrow Sch 1982-; Order of Oman (Third Class Mil); *Books* We Won a War (1982); *Recreations* golf, fly fishing; *Clubs* Army and Navy; *Style—* Gen Sir John Akehurst, KCB, CBE; SHAPE, BFPO26

AKERS, Colin Arthur; s of Lt Arthur William Akers JP RNVR (d 1985), of the Bryn, Yewlands, Hoddesdon, Herts, and Nora Edith, *née* Archer (d 1983); *b* 29 Sept 1931; *Educ* Canford, Univ Coll Oxford; *m* 8 April 1978, Jean, da of Albert Mills (d 1983), of Carisbrooke, Beech Rd, Hartford, Cheshire;; *Career* Nat Serv 1950-52, Gunner tech asst RA Korean War 1951-52; md: EJ Woollard Ltd (horticultural suppliers) 1968-81 (joined 1953), Selfridges Ltd (wine & spirits dept) 1984-; dir Cheshunt Bldg Soc 1975-; former chm Cheshunt & Waltham Cross C of C, vice pres Herts Lawn Tennis Assoc, hon life memb Broxbourne Sports Club (formerly chm), memb Herts CCC, 105 Caps Herts Co Hockey XI Capt 1958-61; *Recreations* hockey, wine-tasting, classical music,; *Clubs* Les Compagnons du Beaujolais, Wine and Spirit Trade C, Br Epicure Soc; *Style—* Colin Akers, Esq; The Fernery, 110 Bengeo St, Bengeo, Hertford, Herts SG14 3EX (☎ 0992 587300); Selfridges Ltd, 400 Oxford St, London W1 (☎ 01 629 1234)

AKERS, Robert; s of Kenneth W Akers (d 1977); *b* 25 Oct 1925; *Educ* Princeton Univ (BA), Harvard Business Sch (MBA); *m* 1952, Elizabeth Ann, *née* Hart; 3 children; *Career* former seaman US Navy; Burroughs Machines Ltd: regnl mangr N Europe 1972-76, md 1976-; *Recreations* golf, jogging; *Clubs* Moor Park Golf; *Style—* Robert Akers, Esq; 7 Astons Rd, Moor Park, Northwood, Middx (☎ 65 21554)

AKERS-JONES, Sir David; KBE (1985), CMG (1977); s of Walter George Jones, and the late Dorothy, *née* Akers; *b* 14 April 1927; *Educ* Worthing HS, Brasenose Coll Oxford (MA); *m* 8 Sept 1951, Jane, MBE, da of Capt Sir Frank Todd Spickernell CVO, KBE, CB, DSO (d 1959); 1 s (Simon b 1957, d 1981), 1 da;; *Career* with Br India Steam Navigation Co 1945-49, Malayan Civil Serv 1954- 57, Hong Kong Civil Serv: sec for New Territories 1973-83, sec for City and New Territories admin 1973-83, sec for dist admin 1983-85, chief sec 1985-86, actg govr 1986-87, advr to govr 1987; chm: Hong Kong Housing Authy, Nat Mutual Insur Hong Kong, Global Asset Mgmnt Hong Kong; dir Sime Darby Hong Kong, chm WWF Hong Kong and HK Artists Guild, pres Outward Bound Tst, hon pres HK Mountaineering Union, HK Girl Guide Assoc, Scout Assoc of HK; vice patron HK Football Assoc; Hon: DCL Univ of Kent 1987, LLD Chinese Univ of Hong Kong 1988; *Recreations* painting, gardening, walking, music; *Clubs* Athenaeum, Royal Overseas League, Hong Kong, Kowloon; *Style—* Sir David Akers-Jones, KBE, CMG; Dragon View, Tsing Lung Tau, NT, Hong Kong (☎ 04919319)

AKHTAR, Prof Muhammad; s of Muhammad Azeem Chaudhry; *b* 23 Feb 1933; *Educ* Punjab Univ Pakistan (MSc), Imperial Coll London (PhD, DIC); *m* 3 Aug 1963, Monika E, *née* Schurmann; 2 s (Marcus, Daniel); *Career* res scientist Res Inst for Med and Chem Cambridge USA 1959-63; prof and head of biochemistry Univ of Southampton 1987- (formerly lectr 1963-, reader sr lectr); chm Sch of Biochemical and Physiological Scis 1983-87; funding fell Third World Acad of Science 1984; FRS (memb cncl 1983-85), Royal Soc of Chemistry, American Chem Soc, Biochemical Soc award of Sitara-I-Imtiaz by Govt of Pakistan 1981; *Books* articles in learned jls; *Style—* Prof Muhammad Akhtar; School of Biochemical and Physiological Sciences, The University, Bassett Crescent East, Southampton SO9 3TU (☎ 0703 595000 ext 4338)

AL AZEIB, His Excellency Ahmad Dhaifellah; *Career* Yemen Arab Republic ambass to UK 1981-; *Style—* H E Mr Ahmad Dhaifellah Al Azeib; Embassy of the Yemen Arab Republic, 41 South St, London W1Y 5PD (☎ 01 499 5246/629 2085)

AL-SHAWI, His Excellency Hisham Ibrahim; s of Ibrahim Al-Shawi, and Najia Al-Shawi; *b* 16 Mar 1931; *Educ* Baghdad, American Univ Beirut; *m* 1966, Hadia Al-Atia; 1 s, 1 da; *Career* dean Coll of Law and Politics Mustansyria Univ 1970-72; Iraqi ambass to UK 1978-; *Style—* H E Hisham Ibrahim Al-Shawi; Embassy of the Republic of Iraq, 21 Queen's Gate, London SW7 (☎ 01 584 7141); 15 Kensington Palace Gdns, London W8

AL-TAJIR, His Excellency Mohamed Mahdi; *b* 26 Dec 1931; *Educ* Al Tajir Sch Bahrain, Preston GS Lancs; *m* 1956, Zohra Al-Tajir; 5 s, 1 da; *Career* dir: National Bank of Dubai 1963-, Dubai Petroleum Co 1963-, Dubai National Air Travel Agency 1966-, United Arab Emirates Currency Bd 1973-, Dubai Dry Dock Co 1973-; chm S E Dubai Drilling Co 1968-; United Arab Emirates ambass to UK 1972-86, and France 1972-77; *Style—* H E Mohamed Mahdi Al-Tajir; c/o Embassy of the United Arab Emirates, 30 Prince's Gate, London SW7

ALANBROOKE, 3 Viscount (UK 1946); Alan Victor Harold Brooke; s of 1 Viscount Alanbrooke, KG, GCB, OM, GCVO, DSO (d 1963), and his 2 w, Benita Blanche (d 1968), da of Sir Harold Pelly, 4 Bt, JP, and wid of Sir Thomas Lees, 2 Bt; suc half-bro, 2 Viscount, 1972; *b* 24 Nov 1932; *Educ* Harrow, Bristol Univ (BEd); *Career* serv army 1952-72, Germany, Korea, Malaya, UK, Capt RA ret; qualified teacher 1975; lectr for MOD Princess Marina Coll Arborfield 1978-; hon pres Salisbury and dist branch The 1940 Dunkirk Veterans 1970 (patron 1977-87 and hon pres 1987-); The UK Veterans of King Leopold III; *Recreations* private flying, radio control model aircraft, fencing, walking round the edge of Cornwall, restoring property ravaged by tenants; *Style—* The Rt Hon The Viscount Alanbrooke; Ferney Close, Hartley Wintney, Hants RG27 8JG

ALBEMARLE, Countess of; Dame Diana Cicely; DBE (1956); da of Maj John Grove; *b* 6 August 1909; *Educ* Sherborne Sch for Girls; *m* 1931, as his 2 w, 9 Earl of Albemarle, MC (d 1979); 1 da (Lady Anne-Louise Hamilton-Dalrymple, *qv*); *Career* chm: Devpt Cmmn 1948-74, Drama Bd 1964-78, Carnegie UK Tst 1977-82; chm: departmental ctee on Youth Service 1958-60, Nat Youth Employment Cncl 1962-68; vice-chm Br Cncl 1959-74; tstee: The Carnegie UK Tst, The Observer to 1977, Glyndebourne Arts Tst 1968-80; *Style—* The Rt Hon the Countess of Albemarle, DBE; Seymours, Melton, Woodbridge, Suffolk (☎ 039 43 2151)

ALBEMARLE, 10 Earl of (E 1696); Rufus Arnold Alexis Keppel; s of Viscount Bury (d 1968, eld s of 9 E of Albemarle, MC) by his 2 w, Marina, da of late Lt Cdr Count Serge Orloff-Davidoff, RNVR, and late Hon Elisabeth, *née* Scott-Ellis (2 da of 8 Baron Howard de Walden); *b* 16 July 1965; *Heir* cous, Crispian Walter John Keppel; *Style—* The Rt Hon The Earl of Albemarle; Piazza di Bellosguardo 10, Florence 50124, Italy; 20A Pembroke Sq, London W8 6PA

ALBERT, Sir Alexis François; CMG (1967), VRD (1942); s of Michel François Albert (d 1962), of Sydney, and Minnie Eliza Albert (d 1949); *b* 15 Oct 1904; *Educ* Knox Coll Sydney, Sydney Univ (BEc); *m* 1934, Elsa Karin Rigmor (decd), da of Capt Albert Edwin Lundgren (d 1942); 3 s; *Career* Lt-Cdr RANR Pacific WWII; chm Albert Investmts Property Ltd 1933-, underwriting memb Lloyd's of London 1944-74, dir Australasian Performing Right Assoc Ltd Sydney 1946-76, chm Australian B'dcasting Co Property Ltd 1955-, dir Amalgamated Television Servs Property Ltd Sydney 1955-79; memb cncl NSW Div Nat Heart Fndn of Australia 1959-, pres Royal Blind Soc of NSW 1972-78, fell cncl of St Paul's Coll Sydney Univ 1965-; KStJ 1984; kt

1972; *Recreations* swimming, yachting (yacht 'Norn'); *Clubs* Australian, Union, Royal Sydney Yacht Sqdn (Cdre 1971-75) Naval and Military (London), New York YC; *Style*— Sir Alexis Albert, CMG, VRD; 25 Coolong Rd, Vaucluse, NSW 2030, Australia (☎ 337 2464); Office: 175 Macquarie Street, Sydney, NSW 2000, Australia (☎ 232 2144)

ALBERY, Ian Bronson; s of Sir Donald Arthur Rolleston Albery (d 1988), and Ruby Gilchrist, *née* Macgilchrist (d 1956); Ian Albery is the fifth generation in the theatre and both father (Sir Donald Albery) and grandfather (Sir Bronson Albery) as well as step great-grandfather (Sir Charles Wyndham) all knighted for services to the theatre; *b* 21 Sept 1936; *Educ* Stowe, Lycée de Briançon France; *m* 1, 1966 (m dis 1985), Barbara Yuling, *née* Lee (m dis 1985); 2 s (Wyndham b 1968, Bronson b 1971); 1 da (Caitlin b 1985), by Jenny Beavan; *Career* Society of West End Theatre: exec 1965-, pres 1977-79, vice-pres 1979-82; tstee Theatres Tst 1977-, memb drama and dance panel Br Cncl 1978-88, dep chm London Festival Ballet Ltd 1984-, dir Ticketmaster Ltd 1985-, chm and md Donmar Ltd 1986-; prodr or co-prodr of over 50 West End prodns; prodr and md Theatre of Comedy Co Ltd 1987-; *Clubs* Garrick; *Style*— Ian B Albery, Esq; Raspit Hill, Ivy Hatch, Sevenoaks, Kent TN15 0PE; Donmar Ltd, 39 Earlham Street, Covent Garden, London WC2H 9LB (☎ 01 836 1371, telex: 264892 DONMAR G, fax 01 240 0961)

ALBROW, Desmond; er s of Frederick Albraw, and Agnes Albrow; *b* 22 Jan 1925; *Educ* St Bede's GS Bradford, Keble Coll Oxford; *m* 1950, Aileen Margaret Jennings; 1 s, 3 da; *Career* asst editor *Sunday Telegraph* 1976-; *Style*— Desmond Albrow, Esq; Totyngton Cottage, Victoria Rd, Teddington, Middx (☎ 01 979 4220)

ALBU, Sir George; 3 Bt (UK 1912), of Grosvenor Place, City of Westminster, and Richmond, Province of Natal, Repub of S Africa; s of Sir George Werner Albu, 2 Bt (d 1963); *b* 5 June 1944; *Educ* Michael House S Africa, Cedara Agric Coll; *m* 1969, Joan Valerie, da of late Malcolm Millar, and Joan Millar, of Weybridge, Surrey; 2 da (Camilla Jane b 22 Aug 1972, Victoria Mary b 14 Jan 1976); *Career* Rifleman Commandos SADF 1963; gen investor; *Recreations* horse racing (flat), motor racing; *Clubs* Victoria, Richmond Country (both S Africa), Pietermaritzburg Natal; *Style*— Sir George Albu, Bt; Glen Hamish, PO Box 62, Richmond 3780, Natal, S Africa

ALBUM, Edward Jonathan Corcos; s of Harry Album (d 1988), of 15 Willow Way, London N3, and Matilda, *née* Corcos; *b* 8 Sept 1936; *Educ* Emanuel Sch, Christ Church Oxford (MA); *m* 14 July 1970, Elizabeth Ann, da of Lancelot Ezra, of Belsize Road, London NW6; 1 s (Richard b 1974), 1 da (Victoria b 1977); *Career* Capt Reserve TA 1962-70; slr; dir: Leopold Lazarus Ltd, The London Metal & Ore Co SLtd, AMI Healthcare Gp plc, Harley Street Clinic Ltd, Atra Hldgs plc, Hartons Gp plc, Int House Assoc Ltd; chm: The Princess Margaret Hosp Windsor, The Chiltern Hosp, The Priory Hosp; *Recreations* military history, ornithology, railway preservation; *Clubs* Sir Walter Scott (Edinburgh), Naval & Military, AC Owners; *Style*— Edward Album, Esq; Sanderling House, High St, Cley, Norfolk (☎ 0263 740810); 47 Lyndale Ave, London NW2 2QB (☎ 01 431 2942)

ALBURY, Arthur James; s of Joseph Arthur Albury (d 1983), and Mildred Winifred, *née* Albury (d 1983); *b* 10 Oct 1926; *Educ* Central Sch Glos; *m* 4 Oct 1952, Gladys, da of William Arthur Stanley Rogers (d 1960); 4 da (Gillian b 1953, Judith b 1953, Susan b 1963, Sarah b 1963); *Career* chartered accountant; sr ptnr McCabe & Ford; *Recreations* golf; *Clubs* RAC, Farmers'; *Style*— Arthur J Albury, Esq; Bryanack, Sandyhurst Lane, Ashford, Kent (☎ 0233 22981); 4/6 Queen Street, Ashford, Kent (☎ 0233 25952); car telephone 0836 232838

ALBUTT, Dr Kenneth John; s of Leonard John Samuel Albutt, and Doris Rose, *née* Knight; *b* 8 Mar 1939; *Educ* Handsworth Tech Sch Birmingham, Univ of Aston Birmingham (BSc), Univ of Birmingham (PhD); *m* 14 Sept 1963, Jane Andree, da of Frederick Blick, of 33 Margaret Grove, Harborne, Birmingham; 1 s (Andrew Scott b 6 June 1968), 1 da (Nicola Jayne b 4 Dec 1966); *Career* sr res metallurgist BSA Gp Res Centre 1962-64, chief metallurgist BSA Motor Cycles Ltd 1967-69; md: Altrincham Labs Ltd (now Amtac Labs Ltd) 1976-82 (gen mangr 1969-71, dir 1971-76), PI Castings Ltd 1982- (tech dir 1974-77), Aical Ltd 1981-; chief exec: PI Castings Gp 1982-85, ATR Gp 1985-; vice pres Union Int des Labs Independants, memb Cncl of Assoc of Consulting Scientists, past pres Br Invesmt Casting Trade Assoc; past chm Holmes Chapel Round Table; CEng, FIM 1975; *Recreations* shooting, sailing, gardening; *Clubs* 41, Rotary; *Style*— Dr Kenneth Albutt; A T R Group Ltd, Davenport Lane, Broadheath, Altrincham, Cheshire (☎ 061 928 5811, fax 061 927 7023, telex 668606)

ALCE, Henry Thomas; AM (1980); s of John T Alce, master mariner (d 1918), and Eva Hunter (d 1962); *b* 8 Sept 1915; *Educ* Canterbury HS Sydney; *m* 1940, Johnann Rae, da of William Bannatyne (d 1942); 1 s, 3 da; *Career* Staff Sgt AIF Pacific (MID 1946); gen mangr and dir Millers Brewery Pty Ltd 1957-67, gen mangr Tooheys Ltd 1967-75, md Tooth & Co Ltd 1975-80; dir: Penfolds Wines, Wright Heaton Ltd, Royal N Shore Hosp 1979-; memb Sydney Cricket Ground Tst 1979-; Queen's Silver Jubilee Medal 1977; *Recreations* riding, tennis, reading; *Clubs* Union, American, Tattersall's (all Sydney); *Style*— Henry Alce, Esq, AM; Banool, Nangus, NSW 2722, Australia (☎ 069 447 292); 18 Dalmeny Rd, Northbridge, NSW 2063, Australia (☎ 95 6495)

ALCHIN, Hon Mrs (Juliet Alers); da of 2 Baron Hankey, KCMG, KCVO; *b* 15 Oct 1931; *m* 1957, Peter John Wrensted Alchin, only s of His Hon Judge Gordon Alchin, AFC (d 1947), of Duffields, Medmenham, Bucks; 1 s (Gordon David b 1961), 2 da (Vanessa Frances b 1962, Chloe Sylvia b 1965); *Style*— The Hon Mrs Alchin; Parkstone, Clenches Farm Rd, Sevenoaks, Kent (☎ 57 188)

ALCHIN, Peter John Wrensted; s of His Hon Judge Gordon Alchin, (d 1947), of Medmenham, nr Marlow, Bucks, and Sylvia, *née* Wrensted (d 1939); *b* 25 July 1947; *Educ* Tonbridge, Hertford Coll Oxford (MA); *m* 23 Feb 1957, Hon Juliet da of Lord Hankey, KCMG, CMG, KCVD, *qv*, of Hethe House, Courden, Kent; 1 s (Gordon b 1960), 2 da (Vanessa b 1961, Chloe b 1963); *Career* Nat Serv cmmnd 2 Lt York and Lancaster Regt 1947-49; barr Middle Temple 1951, practising South Eastern circuit until 1960, legal advsr and co sec in indust (incl 3 years with Turner & Newals Ltd) 1960-70; slr 1970, currently ptnr Stephenson Harwood; memb Footpaths ctee Sevenoaks Soc, elected Kent Jt Consultative Ctee 1988; Freeman Worshipful Co of Skinners 1947-; memb City of London Slr's Co; *Recreations* painting, music, walking, sailing; *Clubs* Little Ship; *Style*— Peter Alchin, Esq; 1 St Paul's Churchyard, London EC4 (☎ 01 329 4422, fax 01 606 0822, telex 886789)

ALCOCK, Jonathan Guest; s of Capt Ivor William Guest Alcock, of 80 Biddulph Way, Ledbury, Herefordshire, and Ada Violet, *née* Pike (d 1959); *b* 10 August 1955; *Educ* Ellitts Green GS, Harrow Coll of Art; *m* 5 Aug 1978, Nicole Elaine, da of Raimund Frederick Herincx, of Larkbarrow, E Compton, Somerset; *Career* creative dir Grange Advertising 1981-; *Recreations* tennis; *Style*— Jonathan Alcock, Esq; Grange Advertising Ltd, 113 High St, Berkhamstead, Hertfordshire HP4 2DJ (☎ 04428 74321, fax 0442 874102)

ALCOCK, Prof Leslie; s of Philip John Alcock, and Mary Ethel, *née* Bagley; *b* 24 April 1925; *Educ* Manchester GS, Brasenose Coll Oxford (BA, MA); *m* 29 July 1950, Elizabeth Annie, da of Robert Blair; 1 s (John b 1960) 1 da Penelope b 1957); *Career* WWII 1943-47, served Gurkha Rifles; 1950-52 supt of exploration and excavation Dept of Archaeology Govt of Pakistan 1950-52, curator Leeds City Museums 1952-53, prof of archaeology Univ Coll Cardiff (lectr, reader) 1953-73, prof of archaeology, Univ of Glasgow 1973-; pres: Cambrian Archaeological Assoc 1982, Soc of Antiquaries of Scot 1984-87; tstee nat Museum of Antiquities of Scot 1973-85, Ancient Monuments bd Scot 1974-; cmmr RC Ancient Monuments: Scot 1977-, Wales 1986-; FSA 1957, FRHists 1969; *Books* Dinas Powys (1963), Arthur's Britain (1971), By South Cadbury is that Camelot (1972), Economy Society and Warfare (1987); *Recreations* music, landscape; *Style*— Prof Leslie Alcock; The University, Glasgow, G12 8QQ, (☎ 041 330 4422)

ALCOCK, Peter John Osborne; s of John Frederick Alcock, OBE (d 1982), of Knaresborough, and Gwendoline Osborne, *née* Sampson; *b* 25 Sept 1936; *Educ* Oundle, McGill Univ (BEng); *m* 2 June 1962, Yvonne, da of Eric Dawson (d 1985); 2 s (John b 1968 Nicholas b 1972), 1 da (Amanda b 1965); *Career* dir: Hunslet 1965-, Greenbat Engrg Ltd 1980-88, Andrew Barclay & Sons Ltd 1982-88; chm: Hunslet Engine Co Ltd 1985-, Railway Indust Assoc 1988-; govr Leeds Poly 1988-; *Recreations* skiing, shooting; *Style*— Peter Alcock, Esq; Hunslet Engineering Co, Leeds LS10 1BT (☎ 0532 432261; telex: 55237; fax: 0532 420820)

ALDENHAM (AND HUNSDON OF HUNSDON), Mary, Lady; Mary Elizabeth; *née* Tyser; o da of late Walter Parkyns Tyser, of Gordonbush, Brora, Sutherland; *m* 16 July 1947, 5 Baron Aldenham and 3 Baron Hunsdon of Hunsdon (d 1986); 3 s (6 Lord Aldenham, *qv*, Hon George Henry Paul, Hon William Humphrey Durant d 1972), 1 da (Hon Antonia Mary); *Style*— The Rt Hon Mary, Lady Aldenham; Rimpton Manor, Yeovil, Somerset (☎ 0935 850223)

ALDENHAM (AND HUNSDON OF HUNSDON), 6 (and 4) Baron (UK 1896 and 1923) respectively; Vicary Tyser Gibbs; s of 5 Baron Aldenham and 3 Baron Hunsdon of Hunsdon (d 1986); *b* 9 June 1948; *Educ* Eton, Oriel Coll Oxford; *m* 16 May 1980, Josephine Nicola, er da of John Richmond Fell, of Lower Bourne, Farnham, Surrey; 1 s (Hon Humphrey William Fell b 31 Jan 1989), 1 da (Hon Jessica Juliet Mary b 1984); *Heir* s, Hon Humphrey William Fell Gibbs b 31 Jan 1989; *Style*— The Rt Hon Lord Aldenham; Aldenham Wood Lodge, Elstree, Herts WD6 3AA

ALDER, Elisabeth Mary; *née* Artus; da of Rev Hugh Neville More Artus (d 1978), and Phyllis, *née* Row; *b* 1 Nov 1942; *Educ* St Albert's Convent Hinckley, Nuneaton HS for Girls; *m* 1, 18 June 1966 (m dis), David Michael North, s of Douglas Edward North (d 1986), of Penn, Bucks; 1 s (Richard James b 1972), 1 da (Sarah Anne b 1968); m 2, 5 April 1980, Christopher John Adler, s of Rev William Alder, of Silchester, Berks; *Career* WRNS 1960-67, cmmnd 1963, WRNR 1980-, first offr 1984, now sr WRNR offr and ops trg offr Southwick RNR; *Recreations* sailing, music (church), bellringing (campanology); *Clubs* Thorney Island Sailing, Ensworth Slipper Sailing, Ladies' Naval Luncheon; *Style*— Mrs Christopher Alder; 56 Ellesmere Orchard, Westbourne, Emsworth, Hampshire (☎ 0243 375 311)

ALDER, Keith Frederick; s of Frederick Alder (d 1959), of Melbourne; *b* 4 Sept 1921; *Educ* Scotch Coll, Melbourne Univ, Ormond Coll (BSc, MSc); *m* 1947, Pauline Mary, da of Rev J Gray Robertson, OBE, of Sydney Univ (d 1974); 3s; *Career* metallurgist; dir AAEC Res Estab Lucas Heights 1962-76, cmmr (1968) and gen mangr Australian Atomic Energy Cmmn, ret 1982; AM, FTS, FIM, FIREE (Aust), FAIM; *Recreations* tennis, sailing (yacht Spellbound III); *Clubs* Royal Prince Alfred Yacht; *Style*— Keith Alder, Esq; 2 Eulbertie Avenue, Warrawee, NSW 2074, Australia

ALDER, Michael; s of Thomas Alder (d 1945), and Winifred Miller (d 1987); *b* 3 Nov 1928; *Educ* Ranelagh Sch Bracknell, Rutherford Coll Newcastle; *m* 1955, Freda, da of John Hall (d 1956); 2 da (Ann, Alison); *Career* with Newcastle Evening Chronicle 1947-59; BBC North East chief news asst and area news editor Newcastle rep 1959-69; head of regnl TV devpt BBC 1969-77, controller English Regnl TV BBC 1977-86; memb: Exec Relate Nat Marriage Guidance; chm Relate, S Warwicks MG; *Recreations* gardening, photography, walking, country pursuits; *Style*— Michael Alder, Esq; Red Roofs, Bates Lane, Tanworth in Arden, Warwicks B94 5AR

ALDER, (Samuel George) Sam; s of George Parker Alder (d 1981), of Douglas, IOM, and Brenda Margaret, *née* Moore (d 1980); *b* 28 Jan 1944; *Educ* King William Coll IOM, Grey Coll Durham Univ (BA); *m* 3 Sept 1983, Helen Mary, da of Dr Algernon Ivor Boyd OBE, of St Johns, Antigua; 1 da (Alison Margaret b 16 Feb 1989); *Career* Whinney Murray & Co CAs 1966-71, fin dir EG Mgmnt Ltd 1971-77, md EG Music Ltd 1977-88; chm: EG Gp Ltd 1980-, The Villiers Hotel Ltd 1981-, Yeoman Security Gp plc 1986-; sr ptnr Alder Dodsworth & Co (CAs) 1985-, md Old Chelsea Gp plc 1986-, ptnr Athol & Co 1989-; hon tres: Music Therapy Charity Jr Fund Raising Ctee 1975-81. Duke of Edinburgh's Award Int Project 1987, Duke of Edinburgh's Award Special Projects Gp 1988-; tstee: Bishop Barrow's Charity (govr King Williams Coll IOM) 1985-, LSO Tst 1988-; sec and tres The Nordoff-Robins Music Therapy centre 1981-, memb appeals ctee Royal Acad of Music Fndn 1989-; FCA 1977; *Recreations* music, farming, history; *Clubs* RAC; *Style*— Sam Alder, Esq; The Grange, Onchan, Isle of Man; Old Chelsea Group plc, 63A Kings Rd, London SW3 4NT, (☎ 01 730 2162, fax 01 730 1330)

ALDERSON, (John) Antony; s of Henry William Alderson (d 1960), of Sutton Coldfield, Warwicks, and Fanny, *née* Woolley (d 1969); *b* 11 July 1924; *Educ* King Edwards Sch Birmingham, Birmingham Univ (LLB); *m* 19 June 1948, Patricia Joyce, da of Lt Cdr William Leslie Jennings, RNVR (d 1980) of Walmley, Sutton Coldfield; 1 s (Richard b 1951), 2 da (Ann b 1953, Susan b 1956); *Career* Sub Lt RNVR 1943-46; slr, jt sr ptnr Edge and Ellison Hatwell Pritchett & Co; chm Wesleyan and General Assur Soc, dir Aston Villa FC plc; memb Birmingham Law Soc (past pres 1975); *Recreations* gardening, walking; *Clubs* The Birmingham; *Style*— J Antony Alderson, Esq; 9 Hartopp Rd, Sutton Coldfield, West Midlands, The Shieling, Helford, Cornwall (☎ 021 308 0517); Rutland House, 148 Edmund Street, Birmingham B3 2JR (☎ 021 200 2001), fax 021 200 1991), telex 336370 EDGECO G

ALDERSON, John Cottingham; CBE (1981), QPM (1974); s of late Ernest

Cottingham Alderson, and Elsie Lavinia Rose; *b* 28 May 1922; *Educ* Barnsley; *m* 1948, Irené Macmillan Stirling; 1 s; *Career* served WWII Warrant Offr Army Physical Training Corps N Africa and Italy; barr Middle Temple; Police Coll 1954, inspr 1955, dep chief constable Dorset 1964-66, dep asst cmmr (training) 1968, cmdt Police Coll 1970, asst cmmr (personnel and training) 1973, chief constable Devon and Cornwall 1973-83; advsr Centre for Police Studies Strathclyde Univ 1983-; conslt on human rights to Cncl of Europe 1981-, dir of Human Rights Strasbourg; Hon LLD Exeter 1979, Hon BLitt Bradford 1981; *Books* Policing Freedom (1979), Law and Disorder (1984), Human Rights and Police (1984); *Clubs* Royal Overseas League; *Style*— John Alderson, Esq, CBE, QPM; Centre for Police Studies, University of Strathclyde, 16 Richmond St, Glasgow

ALDERSON, Maggie Hanne; da of Douglas Arthur Alderson (d 1984), and Margaret Dura, *née* Mackay; *b* 31 July 1959; *Educ* Alleyne's Sch Staffs, Univ of St Andrews (MA); *Career* features ed Look Now, sr writer Woman's World, features ed Honey, commissioning ed You magazine, met features ed Evening Standard, assoc ed ES magazine; memb Br Soc Magazine Eds; *Clubs* Groucho; *Style*— Miss Maggie Alderson; Northcliffe Ho, 2 Derry St, London W8 5EE (☎ 01 938 6000)

ALDERSON, (Arthur) Stanley; s of James Richard Alderson, CBE (d 1970), of Sussex, and Daisy Cawley (d 1965); *b* 27 April 1927; *Educ* Rutlish Sch Merton, (BSc); *m* 4 April 1950, Pauline Olive, da of Clarence Henry Willott (d 1962), of Cornwall; 2 s (Andrew b 1958, Guy b 1960, d 1967); *Career* offr Cadet Royal Fusiliers invalided out after catching polio in India 1945-47; writer and author; *Books* Britain in the Sixties - Housing (1972), Yea or Nay? Referenda in the United Kingdom (1975); *Recreations* literature, theatre, music, walking; *Style*— Stanley Alderson, Esq; St Anthony's Cottage, West Downs, Delabole, Cornwall PL33 9DJ (☎ 0840 213 301)

ALDINGTON, 1 Baron (UK 1962); Toby Austin Richard William Low; KCMG (1957), CBE (1945, MBE 1944), DSO (1941), TD (and Clasp 1950), PC (1954), DL (Kent 1973); s of Col Stuart Low, DSO (d on active serv 1942; s of Sir Austin Low, CIE, JP), and Hon Gwen Atkin, da of Baron Atkin, PC (Life Peer, d 1944); *b* 25 May 1914; *Educ* Winchester, New Coll Oxford (BA, hon fell 1976); *m* 10 April 1947, (Felicité Anne) Araminta, er da of Sir Harold Alfred MacMichael, GCMG, DSO (d 1969), and former w of Capt Paul Humphrey Armytage Bowman; 1 s, 2 da; *Heir* s, Hon Charles Low; *Career* barr Middle Temple 1939; served WW II KRRC 1939-45, Brig BGS5 Corps 1944-45; MP (C) Blackpool N 1945-62, parl sec: Mining & Supply 1951-54; Min of State BOT 1954-57; dep chm Cons Pty Orgn 1959-63; chm: ctee of mgmnt Inst of Neurology 1962-80, Grindlays Bank 1964-76, Port of London Authy 1971-77, BBC Gen Advsy Cncl 1971-78, Nat Nuclear Corpn 1973-80, Sun Alliance & London Insur 1971-85, Westland plc 1978-85, Leeds Castle Fndn 1984-; dep chm GEC 1968-84 (chm 1963-68); dir: Citicorp (USA) 1969-83, Lloyds Bank 1967-85; warden Winchester Coll 1979-87; tstee Migraine Tst 1988-; *Recreations* gardening, golf; *Clubs* Carlton, Beefsteak, Royal St George's Golf, Royal and Ancient Golf; *Style*— The Rt Hon The Lord Aldington, KCMG, CBE, DSO, TD, PC, DL; Knoll Farm, Aldington, Ashford, Kent (☎ 023 372 292; office 0622 65400)

ALDIS, Basil Carlyle; JP (1973); s of Dr Carlyle Aldis, (d 1954), and Constance Smyth (d 1973); *b* 13 Sept 1917; *Educ* Eton, Jesus Coll Cambridge (MA); *m* 1 Jan 1946, Audrey Winifred, da of Capt J W Parker; 1 da (Gabrielle Carlyle); *Career* publisher; FPRI; *Clubs* Pathfinders, Royal Solent Yacht; *Style*— Basil C Aldis, Esq; Elm Cottage, Yarmouth, Isle of Wight (☎ (0983) 760475)

ALDISS, Brian Wilson; s of Stanley Aldiss, and May, *née* Wilson; *b* 18 August 1925; *Educ* Framlingham Coll, West Buckland Sch; *m* 1, 1949 (m dis 1965); 1 s (Clive b 1955), 1 da (Wendy b 1959); m 2, 11 Dec 1965, Margaret Christie, da of John Manson; 1 s (Clive b 1955), 1 da (Wendy b 1959); m 2, 11 Dec 1965, Margaret Christie, da of John Manson; 1 s (Tim b 1967), 1 da (Charlotte b 1969); *Career* RCS 1943-47; served India, Assam, Burma, Sumatra, Singapore, Hong Kong; bookseller Oxford 1948-56, literary ed Oxford Mail 1957-69; author & critic; prolific lectr and contrib to newspapers and jls; chm mgmnt ctee Soc of Authors 1975-78, memb Arts Council (lt panel) 1978-80, pres World SF 1982-84 (fndr memb), vice pres Soc for Anglo-Chinese Understanding;; *Books* novels incl: The Brightfount Diaries (1955), Non-Stop (1958), Greybeard (1964), Barefoot in the Head (1969), The Hand-Reared-Boy (1970), Soldier Erect (1971), Frankenstein Unbound (1973), The Malacia Tapestry (1976), A Rude Awakening (1978), Life in the West (1980), The Helliconia Trilogy (1982-1985), Forgotten Life (1988); short stories collections incl: Space, Time & Nathaniel (1957), The Canopy of Time (1959), The Saliva Tree (1966), Intangibles Inc (1969), The Moment of Eclipse (1970), Last Orders (1977), Seasons in Flight (1984); non-fiction incl: Cities and Stones (travel) (1966), The Shape of Further Things (1970), Billion Year Spree (1973) & Trillion Year Spree (update, 1986); *Recreations* amateur theatricals; *Style*— Brian Aldiss, Esq; Woodlands, Foxcombe Rd, Boars Hill, Oxford OX1 5DL (☎ 0865 735 744)

ALDISS, Thomas Edward; s of Noel Alfred Aldiss, of Caversham, Reading, Berkshire, and Ina Florence, *née* Wyllie (d 1947); *b* 8 August 1943; *Educ* Henley GS, Reading Coll of Tech, Univ of Bath; *m* 26 July 1969, Barbara Helen, da of Malcolm Frederick Mitchell, of Lancing, W Sussex; 1 s (David b 1974), 1 da (Suzanne b 1972); *Career* chartered accountant in private practice, princ Aldiss and Co; Freeman City of London; FCA 1972; *Clubs* Worthing Steyne Rotary; *Style*— Thomas Aldiss, Esq; 19 Broadwater Street East, Broadwater, Worthing, W Sussex (☎ 0903 205 819)

ALDOUS, Charles; QC (1985); s of Guy Travers Aldous (d 1981), of Suffolk, and Elizabeth Angela, *née* Paul; *b* 3 June 1943; *Educ* Harrow, Univ Coll London (LLB); *m* 17 May 1969, Hermione Sara, da of Montague George de Courcy-Ireland (d 1987), of Abington Pigotts Hall, Royston, Herts; 1 s (Alastair b 1979), 3 da (Hermione b 1971, d 1972, Charlotte b 1973, Antonia b 1975); *Career* called to the Bar (Inner Temple) 1967; *Recreations* fox hunting; *Style*— Charles Aldous, Esq, QC; 7 Stone Buildings, Lincolns Inn, London WC2 (☎ 01 405 3886)

ALDOUS, Hugh Graham Cazalet; s mf Maj Hugh Francis Travers Aldous (d 1979), and Emily, *née* Watkinson; *b* 1 June 1944; *Educ* Cheam Sch, Scarborough HS, Leeds Univ (BCom); *m* 25 Aug 1967, Christabel, da of Alan Marshall (d 1974); *Career* accountant; Robson Rhodes: ptnr 1976, head corp fin consultancy 1983-85, dep managing ptnr 1985-87, managing ptnr 1987-; seconded to Dept of Tport 1976-79; dir: Freightliner Ltd 1979-84, Sealink UK Ltd 1981-84; memb Br Waterways Bd 1983-86, DTI inspr into affairs of House of Fraser Hldgs plc 1987-88; ACA 1970, FCA 1979; *Recreations* walking, tennis, music; *Clubs* RAC; *Style*— Hugh Aldous, Esq; Robson Rhodes, 186 City Road, London EC1V 2NU (☎ 01 251 1644, fax 01 250 0801, telex 885734)

ALDOUS, Lucette; da of Charles Fellows Aldous, and Marie, *née* Rutherford; *b* 26 Sept 1938; *Educ* Toronto Pub Sch NSW, Brisbane Pub Sch Qld, Randwick Girls' HS NSW; *m* 1972, Alan Alder; 1 da; *Career* prima ballerina Australian Ballet 1971- (formerly with Ballet Rambert); has danced with: London Festival Ballet, Royal Ballet, Kirov Ballet; *Style*— Miss Lucette Aldous; 66 Grange Rd, Toorak, Vic 3142, Australia (☎ 269 2198)

ALDOUS, Sir William; Hon Mr Justice; s of Guy Travers Aldous, QC (d 1981), and Elizabeth Angela, *née* Paul; *b* 17 Mar 1936; *Educ* Harrow, Trinity Coll Cambridge (MA); *m* 1960, Gillian Frances, da of John Gordon Henson, CBE; 1 s, 2 da; *Career* barr Inner Temple 1960, QC 1976, memb jr counsel Dept of Trade and Industry 1972-76, chm Performing Right Tbnl 1987-88, High Court judge (chancery div) 1988-; kt 1988; *Recreations* horses; *Style*— Hon Mr Justice Aldous; Royal Courts of Justice, Strand, London

ALDRICH, Michael John; s of Charles Albert Aldrich (d 1978), and Kathleen Alice Aldrich; *b* 22 August 1941; *Educ* Clapham Coll, Hull Univ (BA); *m* 1962, Sandra Kay, *née* Hutchings; 2 s, 2 da; *Career* md: Rediffusion Computers Ltd 1980-84, Rediffusion Business Electronics Ltd 1983-84, ROCC Corpn 1984-; chm ROCC Computers Ltd 1984-; advsr to HM Govt for info technol 1981-86; pres Inst of Info Scientists 1984-85; chm: Brighton Poly Cncl 1987-89, Brighton Poly Bd 1988-, Videotex Industry Assoc 1986-88; *Publications* Videotex - Key to the Wired City (1982), Cable Systems (jtly 1982), Making a Business of Info (jtly 1983), Learning to Live with It (co-author, 1985), UK Videotex Market (1986); *Recreations* gardening, reading, riding; *Clubs* Gravetye; *Style*— Michael Aldrich, Esq; ROCC Computers Ltd, Kelvin Way, Crawley, Sussex RH10 2LY (☎ 0293 31211, telex 877369)

ALDRIDGE, (Harold Edward) James; s of William Thomas Aldridge, and Edith, *née* Quayle; *b* 10 July 1918; *Educ* Swan Hill HS Australia, Bradshaw Coll, The War; *m* 16 Oct 1942, Dina Mitchnik, *née* Shenoudah; 2 s (William Daoud, Thomas Hilal); *Career* reporter: Herald and Sun Melbourne 1937-38, Daily Sketch and Sunday Dispatch London 1939; Euro and Middle East war correspondent Australian Newspaper Serv and N American Newspaper Alliance 1939- 44, Teheran correspondent Time and Life 1944; recipient: Rys meml Proze 1945, World Peace Cncl Gold Medal, Int Orgn of Journalists Prize 1967, Lenin Meml Peace Prize 1972, Australian Children's Book Cncl Book of year Award 1985; *Books* novels incl: Signed With their Honous (1942), Of Many Men (1946), The Thinker (1961), Heroes of the Empty View (1954), I Wish He Would Not Die (1958), The Statesmen's Game (1966), A Sporting Proposition (1973), Mockery In Arms (1974), The Untouchable Juli (1976), Goodbye Un-America (1979); short stories: Gold and Sand (1960); plays: The 49th State (produced 1947), One Last Glimpse (produced 1981); children's books: The Flying 19 (1966), The Marvellous Mongolian (1974), The Broken Saddle (1983); TV scripts for Robin Hood; *Recreations* trout and salmon fishing; *Style*— James Aldridge, Esq; 21 Kersley St, London SW11 4PR (☎ 01 228 2681)

ALDRIDGE, Simon Anthony; s of Maj Anthony Harvey Aldridge, TD, of Manor Farm House, Seale, nr Farnham, Surrey, and Betty Angela, *née* Harbold; *b* 12 April 1942; *Educ* Marlborough, Grenoble Univ France; *m* 23 Feb 1968, Jennifer Roberta Anne, da of Maj Denzil Robert Noble Clarke (d 1986), of Puffins, South Drive, Wokingham; 1 da (Victoria Helmore Elizabeth b 1 May 1969); *Career* md Savory Milln 1986 (ptnr 1969-86); co-chm: Northgate Pacific Fund Jersey 1982, SBCI Savory Milln 1987, Stockbroking Swiss Bank Corpn; dir: French Prestige Fund Paris 1985, Croissance Imobilier Paris 1987; dep chm Croissance Britannia Paris 1987, dir Ducatel Duval Paris 1988; *Recreations* golf, shooting, tennis; *Clubs* Cercle de PUnion Interalliee (Paris), City of London; *Style*— Simon Aldridge, Esq; 31 Cadogan St, London SW3 (☎ 01 589 3895); SBC Stockborking, 1 High Timber St, London EC4 3SB (☎ 01 329 0329, telex 884287 SBCO G, fax 01 329 8700)

ALDRIDGE, Trevor Martin; s of Dr Sidney Aldridge (d 1972), and Isabel Rebecca, *née* Seelig (d 1960); *b* 22 Dec 1933; *Educ* Frensham Heights Sch, Sorbonne, St John's Coll Cambridge (MA); *m* 1966, Joanna Van Dedem, da of Cyril Van Dedem Edwards, of Isle of Man; 1 s (Neil b 1969), 1 da (Deborah b 1968); *Career* slr 1960; ptnr Bower Cotton & Bower 1962-84; chm of govrs Frensham Heights Sch 1976-; law cmmr 1984-; gen ed Property Law Bulletin 1980-84; *Books* Rent Control and Leasehold Enfranchisement, Letting Business Premises, Leasehold Law, Practical Conveyancing Precedents, Practical Lease Precedents; *Clubs* United Oxford and Cambridge; *Style*— Trevor M Aldridge, Esq; Conquest House, 37/38 John Street, Theobald's Road, London WC1N 2BQ

ALEKSANDER, Prof Igor; s of Branimir Aleksander (d 1972), and Maja, *née* Unger; *b* 26 Jan 1937; *Educ* Marist Bros Coll Johannesburg SA, Univ of Witwatersrand (BSc), Univ of London (PhD); *m* 23 Mar 1963 (m dis 1977), Myra Jeanette, *née* Kurland;; *Career* section head Standard Telephone & Cable Co 1958-61, reader Univ of Kent 1968-74; prof and head: electrical engrg dept Brunel Univ 1974-84, Kobler unit mgmnt IT Imperial Coll 1984-88, head electrical engrg dept Imperial Coll 1988-; FRSA 1983, FIEE 1988, CEng; *Books* Introduction To Logic Circuit Theory (1971), Microcircuit Learning Computers (1971), Automata Theory: An Engineering Approach (with FK Hanna, 1978), The Human Machine (1978), Reinventing Man (with Piers Burnett, 1984), Designing Intelligent Systems (1985), Decision And Intelligence (with Forraney and Ghalab, 1986), Thinking Machines (with Piers Burnett 1987), An Introduction To Neural Computing (with H Morton, 1989); *Style*— Prof Igor Aleksander; Dept of Electrical Engineering, Imperial Coll of Science and Technol, 180 Queen's Gate, London SW7 2BZ

ALEN-BUCKLEY, Hon Mrs (Giancarla); *née* Forte; 4 da of Baron Forte (Life Peer); *b* 1959,; *m* 1981, Michael Ulic Anthony Alen-Buckley; 1 s (Luke Charles Ulic Locke b 6 March 1987); *Style*— The Hon Mrs Alen-Buckley; 4 Lansdowne Road, Holland Park, London W11

ALESBURY, Alun; s of George Alesbury, of Weybridge, Surrey, and Eveline, *née* Richards; *b* 14 May 1949; *Educ* Tiffin Sch, Cambridge Univ, Seville Univ; *m* 26 June 1976, Julia Rosemary, 6 da of Herbert Archibald Graham Butt (d 1971), of Sibford Gower, Oxon; 1 s (Rupert b 1980), 1 da (Lucy b 1982); *Career* barr Inner Temple 1974; legal correspondent The Architect 1976-80; memb panel of jr Treasy Counsel (Lands Tbnl) 1978-; fndr memb Local Govt and Planning Bar Assoc 1986 (hon sec 1986-88); publications incl: Highways (part) Halsburys Laws of Eng (fourth edn), articles on planning law; *Recreations* walking, travel, old buildings, learning latin languages; *Style*— Alun Alesbury, Esq; Echo Pit House, 26 Fort Road, Guildford,

Surrey (☎ (0483) 573 557); 2 Mitre Court Buildings, The Temple, London EC4 (☎ 01 583 1380)

ALEXANDER; *see*: Hagart-Alexander

ALEXANDER, Hon Mrs (Ada Kate); *née* Bellew; yr da of Richard Bellew (4 s of 2 Baron Bellew and bro of 3 and 4 Barons) by his 1 w, Ada Kate, *née* Gilbey (2 da of Henry Gilbey, who was er bro of Sir Walter Gilbey, 1 Bt); sis of 5 Baron Bellew and was accordingly raised to rank, style and precedence of a Baron's da 1935; *b* 5 Mar 1893; *m* 1, 1917 (m dis 1936), Charles Domvile (d 1936); 1 s (Maj Denys Barry Herbert Domvile); m 2, 1937, Lt-Col Herbrand Charles Alexander, DSO (d 1965, 2 s of 4 Earl of Caledon); *Style*— The Hon Mrs Alexander; Jenkinstown House, Portarlington, Co Offaly, Ireland (☎ (0502) 2 34 59)

ALEXANDER, Sir Alex(ander Sandor); *b* 21 Nov 1916,Berehovo, Czechoslovakia; *Educ* Charles Univ Prague; *m* 1946, Margaret Irma (Maria), *née* Vogel; 2 s, 2 da; *Career* chm J Lyons & Co 1979-, dep chm Allied-Lyons plc 1982- (dir 1979-), dir Ross Gp Ltd 1954-69 (md and chief exec 1967-69, chm 1969), Imperial Gp 1969-79 (chm Imperial Foods 1969-79, dep chm Br Utd Trawlers 1969-81), Ransomes Sims & Jefferies 1974-83, Bain Dawes plc 1984-86, Inchcape Insur Hldgs 1978-86, Alfred McAlpine plc 1978-, Tate & Lyle 1978-, Unigate Ltd 1978-, London Wall Hldgs plc 1986-, Nat West Bank (SE Region Bd) 1973-84; chm: Theatre Royal (Norwich) Tst 1969-84, appeals ctee BRC (Norfolk Branch) 1958-74, Royal Opera House Tst 1987-; tstee: Glyndebourne Arts Tst 1975- (vice-chm 1978-), Charities Aid Fndn 1979-86; govr The Royal Ballet, former pres: Br Food Export Cncl 1973-76, Processors & Growers Research Orgn 1978-83; memb: Eastern Gas Bd 1963-72, ct Univ of E Anglia; High Sheriff Norfolk 1974; FBIM, FRSA; kt 1974; *Recreations* tennis, shooting, painting, opera, ballet; *Style*— Sir Alex Alexander; Westwick Hall, Westwick, Norwich (☎ 069 269 664); Allied-Lyons plc, Allied House, 156 St John St, London EC1P 1AR (☎ 01 253 9911)

ALEXANDER, Andrew Robin (Alex); s of Alan Geoffrey Alexander, of 1 Kenneth Ave, Erin, nr Toronto, Ontario, Canada, and Eileen Joan, *née* Daly; *b* 17 April 1949; *Educ* Colchester Royal GS; *m* 22 June 1970, Jane Walden, da of Howard Alfred Armstrong (d 1984), of 46 West Ave, Clacton-on-Sea, Essex; 2 da (Eve b 1974, Alexandra b 1979); *Career* ptnr Jameson Alexander Law & Co Clacton-on-Sea Essex 1973-; parent govr Colbayns HS, hon memb St John's Ambulance, memb Essex County Small Bore Rifle Team 1975-, hon tres Clacton-Valence Town Twining Assoc; FCA 1979; *Recreations* rifleman; *Clubs* The Clacton, The Fellows Soc; *Style*— Alex Alexander, Esq; 26 Arnold Rd, Clacton-on-Sea, Essex CO15 1DE (☎ 0255 429442); Mayfield Chambers, 93 Station Road, Clacton-on-Sea, Essex CO15 1TN (☎ 0255 220044, fax 0255 220999)

ALEXANDER, Anthony Ernest; s of Henry Gustav Alexander (d 1986), and Alice, *née* Polackova; *b* 7 Oct 1945; *Educ* St Paul's, Downing Coll Cambridge (MA); *m* 6 July 1969, Ilana, da of Maurice Raphael Setton, of Jerusalem, Israel; 1 s (Daniel b 17 Sept 1974), 1 da (Sharon b 10 May 1973); *Career* ptnr: Herbert Oppenheimer Nathan & Vandyk 1973-88 (sr ptnr 1988), Denton Hall Burgin and Warrens 1988-; Freeman Worshipful Co of Slrs 1988; memb: Law Soc 1971, The Pilgrims; *Books* England-Legal Aspects of Alien Acquisition of Real Property (contrib); *Recreations* music and classical studies; *Style*— Anthony Alexander, Esq; Colebrook, Merlewood Drive, Chislehurst, Kent BR7 5LQ (☎ 01 467 1669); Denton Hall Burgin & Warrens, Five Chancery Lane, London WC2A 1LF (☎ 01 242 1212, fax 01 404 0087, car tel 0860 375 698, telex 263567/262738 BURGIN G)

ALEXANDER, Anthony George Laurence; s of G W Alexander, of Beaconsfield; *b* 4 April 1938; *Educ* St Edward's Sch Oxford; *m* Frances, *née* Burdett; 1 s, 2 da; *Career* dir Hanson plc; FCA; *Recreations* tennis, golf; *Style*— Anthony Alexander, Esq; Crafnant, Gregories Farm Lane, Beaconsfield, Bucks

ALEXANDER, Anthony Victor; CBE (1987); s of Aaron Alexander (d 1945); *b* 17 Sept 1928; *Educ* Dragon Sch, Harrow, St John's Coll Cambridge (BA, LLB); *m* 1958, Hélène Esther, da of late Victor Adda; 1 da (Susannah); *Career* insur broker; md Sedgwick Collins (non marine div) 1968-73, chm Sedgwick Forbes UK and dir Sedgwick Forbes Hldgs 1973-78, dir Securicor Gp and Securicor Servs 1977-, dep chm Sedgwick Forbes Ltd 1978-79, dir Sedgwick Gp 1980-; chm: Sedgwick Gp Special Servs 1980-83, Sedgwick Gp Underwriting Servs 1982-85, Br Insur Brokers Assoc (BIBA) 1982-87 (dep chm to 1982); dir ARV Aviation Ltd 1985-88; memb: Mktg of Investmts Bd Organising Ctee 1985-85, Securities and Investmts Board 1986-; FCIB, FINE; *Recreations* home and garden, sailing, fishing, antique collecting, woodlands; *Style*— Anthony Alexander, Esq, CBE; 1 St Germans Place, Blackheath, London SE3 (☎ 01 858 5509); c/o Sedgwick Group plc, Sedgwick House, 33 Aldgate High St, London EC3N 1AJ (☎ 01 377 3456)

ALEXANDER, Hon Brian James; s of 1 Earl Alexander of Tunis, KG, GCB, OM, GCMG, CSI, DSO, MC, PC (d 1969; 3 s of 4 Earl of Caledon); hp of bro, 2 Earl; *b* 31 July 1939; *Educ* Harrow; *Career* Lt Irish Gds (Reserve); *Clubs* White's; *Style*— The Hon Brian Alexander; 11 The Little Boltons, London SW10 9LJ

ALEXANDER, Hon (Thomas) Bruce; only s of Baron Alexander of Potterhill (Life Peer) *qv*; *b* 31 Dec 1951; *Educ* Oundle, Clare Coll Cambridge (MA Cantab); *m* 2, 1984, Susan Joyce Allard; 1 s (Thomas b 1985), 2 step da; *Career* chartered patent agent, European patent attorney, ptnr in Boult, Wade and Tennant; *Recreations* golf, running; *Clubs* Woking Golf; *Style*— The Hon Bruce Alexander; 49 Northchurch Road, London N1 4EE (☎ 01 254 1409); office: 27 Furnival Street, London EC4A 1PQ (☎ 01 404 5921, telex 267 271)

ALEXANDER, Byron John; s of Capt Dimitrius Alexander (d 1975), of Athens, and June Doreen, *née* Eddy; *b* 18 May 1942; *Educ* Monkton House Sch; *m* 4 June 1969, Eileen May, da of Eric Leslie Page, of Eastcote, Middx; 2 s (Marc Byron b 4 Oct 1972, James Philip b 25 Dec 1976), 1 da (Nicola Jane b 10 March 1970); *Career* md: Alexander Advertising Int Ltd 1969-, Illustra Graphics Ltd 1984-, Illustra Print Ltd 1987-; memb HM Coastguard (Auxiliary Afloat Section), 1973-; MIPR 1973, MBIM 1975; *Books* Buying a Boat (1972); *Recreations* motor yachting, computers; *Clubs* Royal Corinthian, Oxford Ditch; *Style*— Byron Alexander, Esq; Alexander Advertising International, Alexander House, Wallingford, Oxon, OX10 0XF (☎ 0491 34966, fax 0491 33475, car tel 0860 511 589)

ALEXANDER, Sir Charles Gundry; 2 Bt (UK 1945), of Sundridge Park, Co Kent; s of Sir Frank Alexander, 1 Bt, JP (d 1959), and Elsa, da of Sir Charles Collett, 1 Bt; *b* 5 May 1923; *Educ* Bishop's Stortford Coll, St John's Coll Cambridge (MA); *m* 1, 1944, Mary Neale, o da of late Stanley R Richardson, of Maple Lawn, Lyndhurst, Hants; 1 s, 1 da; m 2, 1979, Eileen Ann, da of Gordon Stewart, of Inveresk, Finchampstead; *Heir* s, Richard Alexander, *qv*; *Career* served WWII Lt RN N Atlantic and Far East; chm Alexander Shipping Co, govr Care Ltd, dir Furness-Houlder Insurance Ltd and Reinsurance Service Ltd, Master Taylors' Co 1981-82, prime warden Shipwrights' Co 1983-84; *Clubs* RAC; *Style*— Sir Charles Alexander, Bt; Bells Farm, East Sutton, Maidstone, Kent ME17 3EB (☎ Sutton Valence 2410)

ALEXANDER, Sir Darnley Arthur Raymond; CBE (1963); s of late Pamphile Joseph Alexander, MBE, and late Lucy Alexander; *b* 28 Jan 1920, Castries, St Lucia; *Educ* St Mary's Coll St Lucia, UCL; *m* 1943, Mildred Margaret, *née* King (d 1980); 1 s, 1 da; *Career* barr Middle Temple 1942, chief justice Nigeria 1975-79; chm Nigerian Law Reform Cmmn 1979-88; CFR 1979; Grand Cdr of the Order of the Niger 1983; kt 1974; *Style*— Sir Darnley Alexander, CBE; Supreme Court of Nigeria, Lagos, Nigeria

ALEXANDER, Maj-Gen David Crichton; CB (1976); s of James Alexander (d 1978), and Margaret, *née* Craig; *b* 28 Nov 1926; *Educ* Edinburgh Acad, Staff Coll Camberley, Royal Coll of Def Studies; *m* 1957, Diana Joyce (Jane), da of Sydney Fisher, CVO (d 1980); 1 s, 2 da, 1 step s; *Career* served RM 1944-57, equerry and acting tres to Duke of Edinburgh 1957-60, staff Chief of Def Staff 1966-69, Col GS to CGRM 1970-73, ADC to HM The Queen 1973-75, MGRM Trg 1975-77; dir-gen English Speaking Union 1977-79; cmdt Scottish Police Coll 1979-87; *Recreations* gardening, fishing, golf; *Clubs* Army and Navy; *Style*— Maj-Gen David Alexander, CB

ALEXANDER, Sir Douglas; 3 Bt (UK 1921), of Edgehill, Stamford, Connecticut, USA; s of Lt-Cdr Archibald Gillespie Alexander, US Coast Guard (d 1978), and Margery Isabel, *née* Griffith; n of Sir Douglas Hamilton Alexander, 2 Bt (d 1983); *b* 9 Sept 1936; *Educ* Rice Univ, Houston Texas (MA, PhD), Univ of N Carolina; *m* 1958, Marylon, da of Leonidas Collins Scatterday, of Worthington, Ohio, USA; 2 s (Douglas Gillespie, *qv*, Andrew Llewellyn b 1967); *Heir* s, Douglas Gillespie; *Career* pres Edgehill Investment Co; *Style*— Sir Douglas Alexander II, Bt; 145 Main Street, Wickford, Rhode Island 02852, USA

ALEXANDER, Douglas Gillespie; s and h of Sir Douglas Alexander II, 3 Bt; *b* 24 July 1962; *Educ* Reed Coll Portland Oregon (BA); *Style*— Douglas G Alexander, Esq

ALEXANDER, Elsie Winifred May; da of late George Albert Barker, and late Lilian May, *née* Tomlin; *b* 13 Feb 1912; *Educ* Ware GS; *m* 1, 1936 (m dis 1946); 1 da; m 2, 1953 the late Herbert John Alexander; *Career* dir Alexander - H J Alexander Ltd 1953; started painting art and studied art Montelair State Coll USA 1958; work exhibited Christie's and art galleries; sec Wine Trade Art Sec; Freeman: City of London, Worshipful Co of Painter Stainers; *Recreations* painting in oils, gardening, reading; *Style*— Mrs Elsie Alexander; 20 Parkside Drive, Middlesex HA8 8JX (☎ 01 958 4440)

ALEXANDER, Franklyn William; s of Murray Lyn Alexander (d 1988), of Thrapston, Northants, and Emily Florence, *née* Tucker (d 1976); *b* 16 June 1937; *Educ* Dauntsey's Sch; *m* 3 Oct 1964, Brenda May, da of Henry Clarence George Henty, of Swindon, Wilts; 2 da (Helen Elizabeth b 1967, Judith b 1969); *Career* insurance broker, dir D & H Henty Ltd Swindon; *Recreations* art, theatre, hunting, shooting; *Style*— Franklyn Alexander, Esq; 1 St Helens View, Okus, Swindon SN1 4JN (☎ 0793 481317); D & H Henty Ltd, 54 Commercial Rd, Swindon SN1 5NZ (☎ 0793 35258)

ALEXANDER, Lady (Elizabeth) Jane; *née* Alexander; da of 6 Earl of Caledon (d 1980), and his 2 w, Baroness Anne (d 1963), da of late Baron Nicolai de Graevenitz; resumed the name of Alexander by Deed Poll; *b* 1962; *m* 1981 (m dis 1987), Rory F A Peck, er s of Julian Peck, of Prehen House, Co Londonderry; 2 s (James Julian b 1982, Alexander Nicolas de Graevenitz b 1984); *Style*— Lady Jane Alexander; 30 Onslow Gardens, London SW7

ALEXANDER, John Bernard Alexei; s of B G Alexander, of Gt Haseley, Oxford, and Mrs T Alexander, *née* Benckendorf; *b* 23 August 1941; *Educ* Westminster, Balliol Coll Oxford; *m* 1 July 1969, Jacquely, da of John Bray, of Sydney, Australia; 2 s (Nicolas b 1971, Christopher b 1974); m 2, 14 April 1981, Judy, da of Maj Patrick Chilton, of West Ashline, Sussex; 1 da (Tania b 1982); *Career* merchant banker; dir Hill Samuel & Co Ltd 1983, md Edward de Rothschild Securities 1984-; *Recreations* skiing, tennis, gardening; *Clubs* Brooks's; *Style*— John B A Alexander, Esq; Old Rectory, Gt Haseley, Oxford; 84 Fenchurch Street, London EC3M 4BY (☎ 01 481 0591)

ALEXANDER, Kenneth Alston; s of Brig-Gen Sir William Alexander, KBE, CB, CMG, DSO, MP (d 1954), and his 1 wife Beatrice Evelyn, *née* Ritchie (d 1928); *b* 21 Nov 1928; *Educ* Winchester, Trinity Coll Cambridge (BA); *m* 1957, Linda Mary, da of Edward Lefevre, of Cochin and Gargrave, Yorks; 1 s, 3 da; *Career* Royal Tank Regt; chem merchant and manufacturer; chm and chief exec Tennants Consolidated Ltd 1972- (previously holding various directorships within the Tennant Group); *Recreations* shooting, music; *Clubs* RAC; *Style*— Kenneth Alexander, Esq; 69 Grosvenor St, London W1 (☎ 01 493 5451)

ALEXANDER, Prof Sir Kenneth John Wilson; only s of late William Wilson Alexander; *b* 14 Mar 1922; *Educ* George Heriot's Sch Edinburgh, Dundee Sch of Economics; *m* 1949, Angela-May, da of late Capt G H Lane, RN; 1 s, 4 da; *Career* prof of economics Strathclyde Univ 1963-80 (on leave 1976-80), dean of Scottish Business Sch 1973-75, princ and vice-chllr Stirling Univ 1981-86; Univ of Aberdeen 1987; dir: Scottish Television plc, Stakis plc; chm Highlands and Islands Devpt Bd 1976-81; Hon LLD Cncl for Nat Academic Awards 1976, DUniv Stirling 1977; LLD Aberdeen, LLD Dundee 1985, DUniv Open Univ 1985; LLD Strathclyde 1986, DLit Aberdeen 1987; CBIM, FRSE, FEIS; kt 1978; *Recreations* sea fishing; *Clubs* Caledonian, Scottish Arts; *Style*— Prof Sir Kenneth Alexander, FRSE; 9 West Shore, Pittenweem, Fife KY10 2NV

ALEXANDER, Leslie William MacBryde; s of Thomas MacKelvie Alexander (d 1964), of Craigie, Moorcroft Rd, Liverpool, and Jane Muir, *née* MacBryde (d 1962); *b* 8 August 1917; *Educ* Liverpool Coll, Liverpool Univ (BArch 1939); *m* 25 March 1950, Margaret, da of Walter Haydn Ellwood (d 1958), of 33 Park View, Cheadle Heath, Cheshire; 1 d (Jane Margaret b 1956); *Career* Capt RE 1940-46 serv India; RIBA 1939; Pres Liverpool Architectural Soc 1956-58, Inst of Arbitrators 1973-74; memb: cncl RIBA 1956-58, cncl CIArb 1966-80, Architects Registration Council UK 1963-64, Jt Contracts Tbnl 1959-64; visiting lecturer on arbitration, contract admin and professional practice at Liverpool and York Univs; life govr Liverpool Coll 1962, JP (Liverpool CB 1971-81); FRIBA 1960, FRICS 1960, FCIArb 1964; *Books* The Architect as Arbitrator (second edn, 1978), contrib chapter on Construction Industry Arbitrations (R Bernstein's Handbook of Arbitration Practice); *Clubs* Royal Overseas League; *Style*— Leslie Alexander, Esq; Monreith, 47 Menlove Avenue, Liverpool L18

2EH (☎ 051 722 2491); T M Alexander & Son, 47 Menlove Ave, Liverpool L18 2EH (☎ 051 722 9669)

ALEXANDER, Sir (John) Lindsay; s of Ernest Daniel Alexander, MC (d 1975), and Florence Mary, *née* Mainsmith; *b* 12 Sept 1920; *Educ* Alleyn's Sch, BNC Oxford (MA, hon fell 1977); *m* 1944, Maud Lilian, 2 da of Oliver Ernest Collard; 2 s, 1 da; *Career* chm: Ocean Tport & Trading 1971-80, Overseas Container Hldgs 1976-82, Lloyds Bank Int 1980-85; dep chm Lloyds Bank 1980-88 (dir 1970-); dir: BP 1975-, Jebsens Drilling 1980-86, Hawker Siddeley 1981-, Abbey Life 1988-, Britoil 1988-; chm Ctee of Euro Shipowners' Assoc 1972-73; pres Chamber of Shipping 1974-75; Cdr Royal Order of St Olav Norway 1980; FCIT, CBIM; kt 1975; *Recreations* gardening, music, photography; *Clubs* Brooks's; *Style*— Sir Lindsay Alexander; Lloyds Bank plc, 71 Lombard St, London EC3P 3BS (☎ 01 626 1500)

ALEXANDER, Maurice Lionel; s of Abraham Alexander (d 1951); *b* 23 August 1916; *Educ* Manchester Central HS, Manchester Univ (LLB); *m* 1947, Irene, da of Robert Cohen, JP (d 1961); 2 s, 1 da; *Career* Major NW Europe; slr; sr ptnr for Alexander Tatham & Co Manchester; *Clubs* Manchester Football, Dunham Forest Golf; *Style*— Maurice Alexander, Esq

ALEXANDER, Prof (Robert) McNeill; s of Robert Priestley Alexander (d 1973), of Lisburn, Co Antrim, and Janet, *née* McNeill; *b* 7 July 1934; *Educ* Tonbridge Sch, Trinity Hall Cambridge (MA, PhD); *m* 29 July 1961, Ann Elizabeth, da of Gordon Francis Coulton (d 1946), of Pentney, Norfolk; 1 s (Gordon b 1964), 1 da (Jane b 1962); *Career* sr lectr Univ Coll of N Wales 1968-69 (lectr 1961-68, asst lectr 1958-61); prof of zoology Univ of Leeds 1969-; DSc (Wales) 1969; FRS, FIBiol; *Books* Functional Design in Fishes (1967), Animal Mechanics (1968), Size and Shape (1971), The Chordates (1975), The Invertebrates (1979), Optima for Animals (1982), Elastic Mechanisms in Animal Movement (1988) and other books and papers; *Recreations* local history, history of natural history; *Style*— Prof McNeill Alexander; 14 Moor Park Mount, Leeds LS6 4BU (☎ 0532 759218); Dept of Pure and Applied Biology, Univ of Leeds, Leeds LS2 9JT (☎ 0532 332911, fax 0532 336017, telex 556473 UNILDS G)

ALEXANDER, Michael Charles; s of late Rear Adm Charles Otway Alexander (whose gggf was er bro of 1 E of Caledon, and whose paternal gm was Julia, *née* Fane, herself ggda of 8 Earl of Westmorland, while the half-sister of the Admiral's paternal gf married, as his 2 w, Stratford Canning, who was later cr Viscount Stratford de Redcliffe; *see* Lord Garvagh). Michael's mother was Antonia, da of Adrianus Geermans, of The Hague; *b* 20 Nov 1920; *Educ* Stowe, Sandhurst; *m* 1963 (m dis), Sarah, 2 da of Lt-Col Frederick Wignall and Susan, da of late Brig-Gen Algernon Ferguson (Sarah's aunt, Doris Wignall, m Robert Arthur Grosvenor and their s Hugh (k 1947) would have become Duke of Westminster had he lived to succeed; Brig-Gen Algernon Ferguson's ggd is HRH The Duchess of York); 1 da; *Career* writer, traveller, dir Adastra Prodns Ltd; FZS, FRGS; *Books* The Privileged Nightmare (Hostages at Colditz), The True Blue, The Reluctant Legionnaire, Offbeat in Asia, Omai; Noble Savage, Mrs Fraser on the Fatal Shore, Queen Victoria's Maharajah, Delhi and Agra; A Traveller's Companion; *Style*— Michael Alexander, Esq; Skelbo House, Dornoch, Sutherland, (☎ 040 83 3180); 48 Eaton Place, London SW1 (☎ 01 235 2724)

ALEXANDER, Michael O'Donel Bjarne; CMG (1982); s of late Col Hugh O'Donel Alexander, CMG, CBE, and Enid Constance Crichton Neate; *b* 19 June 1936; *Educ* Foyle Coll Londonderry, St Paul's, King's Coll Cambridge, Yale and Berkeley Univs USA (Harkness Fell); *m* 1960, Traute Krohn; 2 s, 1 da; *Career* served RN 1955-57; joined FO 1962, asst private sec to Sir Alec Douglas-Home then James Callaghan as successive Foreign Secs 1972-74, cnsllr (Conference on Security and Co-operation in Europe) and subsequently head chancery UK Mission to the UN Geneva 1974-77, head POD FCO 1978-79 (dep head 1977-78), private sec (Overseas Affairs) to PM 1979-81, UK Ambass to Vienna 1982-86, UK Permanent Rep on N Atlantic Cncl, Brussels 1986-; *Style*— Michael Alexander, Esq, CMG; c/o Foreign and Commonwealth Office, King Charles St, London SW1; UK Delegation, OTAN/NATO, 1110 Brussels, Belgium

ALEXANDER, Sir Norman Stanley; CBE (1959); s of Charles Monrath Alexander, of NZ (d 1941), and Flora Elizabeth, *née* Reid (d 1944); *b* 25 Oct 1906; *Educ* Hamilton HS NZ, Univ Coll Auckland (MSc), Trinity Coll Cambridge (PhD); *m* 1, 1935, Frances Elizabeth Somerville, da of Kenneth Caldwell (d 1950); 1 s, 2 da; m 2, 1959, Constance Lilian Helen, da of Henry Geary (d 1950); *Career* prof physics: Malaya Univ 1936-52, Univ Coll Ibadan Nigeria 1952-59; vice-chllr Ahmadu Bello Univ Nigeria 1961-66, advsr on Higher Educn Miny Overseas Devpt; hon memb Order of the Niger (Nigeria) 1966; kt 1966; *Recreations* gardening; *Style*— Sir Norman Alexander, CBE; Yew Tree Cottage, Redisham, Beccles, Suffolk (☎ 050 279 256)

ALEXANDER, Major Paul Donald; MBE (1968); s of Donald Alexander, of Dudley, Worcs, and Alice Louisa, *née* Dunn (d 1988); *b* 30 Nov 1934; *Educ* Dudley GS, RMA Sandhurst, RSC Camberley, Nat Def Coll, RCDS; *m* 15 Nov 1958, Christine Winifred Marjorie, da of Fred Coakley, Dudley, Worcs (d 1966); 3 s (Stephen Nigel b 1959, Richard Neil b 1961, James Robert b 1966); *Career* 2 Lt 1955, Capt 1964, serv Hong Kong, seconded KAR in EAfrica, army staff duties MOD 1966-67, GSOR Sqdn Cdr in UK 1968-69 (NI 1969), DAAG Adj Gens Dept MOD 1970-71; asst dir of def policy (Col) Central Staff MOD 1977-79 (GSOI in cmd 1 Div HQ and Signal Regt 1974-76), Cdr RSC HQ 1 Br Corps 1979-81, dep mil sec MOD 1982-85, signal offr in chief (army); MOD 1985-; govr Welbeck Coll 1987-; *Recreations* gardening; *Clubs* Army and Navy; *Style*— Maj Gen Paul Alexander, MBE; c/o Army and Navy Club, St James Square, London SW1; Ministry of Defence, Main Building, Whiteham, London SW1 (☎ 01 218 7204)

ALEXANDER, Peter Charles; CMG (1980), OBE (1970); s of Charles Alexander, of London (ka 1915); *b* 9 Jan 1915; *Educ* Sydney Univ; *m* 1953, Rita, da of Frank Williams (d 1960), of Chesterfield; 3 da; *Career* Pilot Offr RAAF, served with Bomber Cmd and RAF N Africa; accountant; nat sec RAAF A 1960-, dir Dept of Productivity Mgmnt Advsy Branch 1968-80, chm: Aust Branch Assoc Certified Accountants 1974-81, Kenya-Australia Soc 1971-; vice-pres World Veterans Fedn 1979-; chm: Cncl for Scottish Gaelic 1981-83, Aust Tartan Ltd 1985-; vice-chm: Scottish Aust Heritage Cncl 1985-; convenor Celtic Cncl of Aust 1981-; nat pres Ryder-Ches Fndns 1977-79; Order of Polonia Restituta 1975; FC CA, FICS; *Publications* We Find and Destroy (1959 and 1979); *Recreations* cricket, journalism; *Clubs* Air Force (Sydney), Pitt; *Style*— Peter Alexander, Esq, CMG, OBE; 46 Hawthorn Avenue, Chatswood, NSW 2067, Australia (☎ 419 5024)

ALEXANDER, Richard; s and h of Sir Charles G Alexander, 2 Bt, and his 1 w, Mary, da of Stanley Richardson; *b* 1 Sept 1947; *Educ* Bishop's Stortford Coll; *m* 1971, Lesley Jane, da of Frederick William Jordan, of Orpington; 2 s (Edward b 1974, James b 1977); *Career* pub rels offr and ed house magazine Furness Withy Gp; Freeman City of London, Liveryman Worshipful Co of Merchant Taylors'; MIPR; *Style*— Richard Alexander, Esq; Squirrel Court, 262 Chislehurst Rd, Petts Wood, Kent BR5 1NT; Furness Withy Group, Furness House, 53 Brighton Road, Redhill, Surrey RH1 6YL

ALEXANDER, Richard Thain; MP (C) Newark 1979-; s of Richard Rennie Alexander, of Cockerham, Lancaster, and Gladys Alexander; *b* 29 June 1934; *Educ* Dewsbury GS, UCL, Inst of Advanced Legal Studies London; *m* 1, 1966 (m dis 1984), Valerie Ann, da of Harold Winn (d 1959); 1 s (Nicholas), 1 da (Emma); m 2, 1987, Patricia Diane Hanson; *Career* slr; cmmr for Oaths, former chm Doncaster Nat Insur Appeal Tribunal; sr ptnr Jones Alexander & Co Retford 1964-85, conslt Jones Alexander & Co Retford 1985-; *Recreations* tennis, riding; *Clubs* Newark Cons, Carlton, Retford Conservative; *Style*— Richard Alexander, Esq, MP; 409 Howard House, Dolphin Sq, London SW1

ALEXANDER, Rear Adm Robert Love; CB (1964), DSO (1943, DSC 1944); s of Capt Robert Love Alexander, DSO, RD, RNR, of Edinburgh; *b* 29 April 1913; *Educ* Merchiston, RNC Dartmouth; *m* 1936, Margaret Elizabeth, only da of late George Conrad Spring; 1 s, 4 da; *Career* Vice Naval Dep to Supreme Allied Cdr Europe 1962-65; *Style*— Rear Adm Robert Alexander, CB, DSO, DSC; Tythe Barn, South Harting, Hants

ALEXANDER, Simon Mayne; s of Bryan James Mildmay Alexander (d 1984), and Evelyn Edith; *b* 12 Mar 1950; *Educ* Worksop, Sheffield Univ (LLB); *m* 23 Dec 1975, Valerie Patricia, da of Leonard Williams; 2 da (Ruth Elizabeth b 1986, Kate Rosalinde b 1986 twins); *Career* solicitor; *Recreations* music, musical instrument making; *Style*— Simon M Alexander, Esq; 6 Foxholes Lane, Calverley, Leeds LS28 (☎ 0532 455366); 71 Great George Street, Leeds LS1 3BR

ALEXANDER, William (Bill); s of William Paterson, of Cragside, Coach Road, Warton, Lanc, and Rosemary, *née* McCormack; *b* 23 Feb 1948; *Educ* St Lawrence Coll Ramsgate, Keele Univ (BA); *m* 1 June 1979, Juliet Linda, da of Michael Hedley Harmer, of Perrot Wood, Fraffham, Petworth, West Sussex; 2 da (Jessie b 1974, Lola b 1979); *Career* assoc dir RSC 1978-, prodns incl: Richard III 1984, The Merry Wives of Windsor 1985, A Midsummer Night's Dream 1986, Twelfth Night, The Merchant of Venice, Cymbeline 1987;; *Style*— Bill Alexander, Esq; Rose Cottage, Tunley, Nr Cirencester, Glos (☎ 028 576 555); Barbican Theatre, London (☎ 01 628 3351)

ALEXANDER OF POTTERHILL, Baron (Life Peer UK 1974); William Picken Alexander; s of Thomas Alexander, of Paisley; *b* 13 Dec 1905; *Educ* Paisley GS, Glasgow Univ; *m* 1949, Joan, da of Robert Williamson, of Sheffield; 1 s (Hon Bruce b 1951); *Career* sits as independent peer in House of Lords; gen sec Assoc Educn Ctees England and Wales 1944-; kt 1960; *Style*— Rt Hon Lord Alexander of Potterhill; 3 Moor Park Gdns, Pembroke Rd, Moor Park, Northwood, Middx (☎ Northwood 21003)

ALEXANDER OF TUNIS, Countess; Hon Davina Mary; *née* Woodhouse; da of 4 Baron Terrington; *b* 12 April 1955; *m* 1981, as his 2 w, 2 Earl Alexander of Tunis; 2 da (b 1982 and 1984); *Career* lady in waiting to HRH The Princess Margaret, Countess of Snowdon 1975-79; extra lady in waiting 1979-; *Style*— The Rt Hon Countess Alexander of Tunis; 59 Wandsworth Common West Side, London SW18 2ED

ALEXANDER OF TUNIS, 2 Earl (UK 1952); Shane William Desmond Alexander; also Viscount Alexander of Tunis (UK 1946) and Baron Rideau (UK 1952); s of Field Marshal 1 Earl Alexander of Tunis, KG, GCB, OM, GCMG, CSI, DSO, MC, PC (3 s of 4 Earl Caledon, through whom the present Earl is hp to Earldom of Caledon), and Lady Margaret Bingham, GBE, JP (d 1977), da of 5 Earl of Lucan (gs of the Crimean War commander); *b* 30 June 1935; *Educ* Harrow, Ashbury Coll Ottawa; *m* 1, 1971 (m dis 1976), Hilary, da of John van Geest, of Lincs; m 2, 1981, Hon Davina Woodhouse, Extra Lady-in-Waiting to HRH Princess Margaret and da of 4 Baron Terrington; 2 da (Lady Rose Margaret b 23 April 1982, Lady Lucy Caroline b 20 Sept 1984); *Heir* bro, Hon Brian Alexander, *qv*; *Career* chm Capital & Commercial Devpts plc 1988-, pres Br-American Assocs 1988-; sits as Conservative peer in House of Lords; patron Br-Tunisian Soc; Lt Irish Gds (reserve); Lord in Waiting to HM The Queen 1974; chm Int Construction Gp; dir Int Hospitals Gp; Liveryman Worshipful Co of Mercers' ; *Clubs* MCC; *Style*— The Rt Hon Earl Alexander of Tunis; 59 Wandsworth Common West Side, London SW18 2ED

ALEXANDER OF WEEDON, Baron (Life Peer UK 1988) Robert Scott Alexander; QC (1973); s of late Samuel James and Hannah May Alexander; *b* 5 Sept 1936; *Educ* Brighton Coll, King's Coll Camb (BA 1959, MA 1963); *m* 1, 1963 (m dis 1973), Frances Rosemary Heveningham Pughe; 2s, 1 da; m 2, 1978 (m dis), Elizabeth, da of Col C R W Norman; 1 s (decd); m 3, 1985, Marie Sugrue; *Career* barr Middle Temple 1961, bencher 1979; pres King's Coll Assoc 1980- 81; chm of the Bar Cncl 1985-86 (vice-chm 1984-85); a judge of the Courts of Appeal of Jersey and Guernsey 1985-88; govr Wycombe Abbey Sch 1986-, chm Panel on Take-overs and Mergers 1987-; *Style*— The Rt Hon Lord Alexander of Weedon

ALEXANDER-SINCLAIR OF FRESWICK, Maj-Gen David Boyd; CB (1980); s of Cdr Mervyn Boyd Alexander-Sinclair of Freswick, RN (d 1979), and Avril Nora, *née* Fergusson-Buchanan (d 1980); *b* 2 May 1927; *Educ* Eton; *m* 1958, Ann Ruth, da of late Lt-Col Graeme Daglish; 2 s, 1 da; *Career* cmdg 3 Bn Royal Green Jackets 1967-69, Cdr 6 Armd Bde 1971-73, GOC 1 Div 1975-77, Chief of Staff UKLF 1978-79, Cmndt Staff Coll 1980-82, ret; *Style*— Maj-Gen David Alexander-Sinclair of Freswick, CB

ALFORD, Lady; Eileen; *née* Riddell; *m* 1967, as his 2 w, Sir Robert Edmund Alford, KBE, CMG (d 1979), sometime govr and c-in-c St Helena; *Style*— Lady Alford; The Barn, Staple Cross, Sussex

ALFORD, George Francis Onslow; s of Cdr Ian Francis Onslow Alford, RN (ret), of Magnolia House, St Mary Abbots Terrace, London, and Jacqueline Louise, *née* Herbert; *b* 10 Oct 1948; *Educ* Winchester, UCL (BSc); *m* 12 Jan 1974, Adronie Elizabeth, da of late Douglas Crisp Gall, of Chantersell, Nutley, Sussex; *Career* Kleinwort Benson GP 1970-: rep off Tokyo 1976-80 1976-80, mangr M East dept 1980-83, gp personnel dir 1987-; md Fendrake Ltd 1982-87; memb: Langbourne Wards Club, United World Club; cncl memb Br Export Houses Assoc 1984-87; Freeman City of London, Liveryman Worshipful Co of Basketmakers; FIPM; *Recreations* sailing, skiing, riding; *Clubs* Royal Solent YC, City Livery; *Style*— George

Alford, Esq; Claudian House, 58 Oxberry Ave, London SW6 5SS (☎ 01 736 2298); Kleinwort Benson Group, 20 Fenchurch St, London EC3P 3DB (☎ 01 623 8000, telex 888531)

ALFRED, (Arnold) Montague; s of Reuben Alfred, and Bessie, *née* Arbesfield; *b* 21 Mar 1925; *Educ* Central Fndn Boys' Sch, Imperial Coll London, LSE; *m* 1947, Sheila Jacqueline Gold; 3 s; *Career* dir CELON Div of Courtaulds 1964-69 (head economics dept 1953-69); chm BPC Publishing Ltd 1971-81 (dir BPC 1969), chm Caxton Publishing Hldgs 1971-81; chief exec PSA 1982-, 2 perm sec Dept Environment 1982-84; dep-chm Ling Kee (UK) 1985-; *Books* Business Economics; Discounted Cash Flow; *Recreations* active in Jewish community affairs; *Style*— Montague Alfred, Esq

ALGRANTI, Arabella Rosalind Hungerford; *née* Pollen; da of Peregrine Michael Hungerford Pollen, of Norton Hall, Mickleton, Gloucestershire and Patricia Helen, *née* Barry; *b* 22 June 1961; *Educ* St Swithuns Winchestwer, Queens Coll London; *m* 5 Aug 1985, Giacomo Dante Algranti, s of Gilberto Algranti, of Milan, Italy; 1 s (Jesse Gilberto b 4 Jan 1986); *Career* fashion designer; chm and head of design Arabella Pollen Ltd (exporting to 20 countries world wide); *Recreations* piano, literarature, travelling, art; *Style*— Ms Arabella Pollen; Block 20, Avon Trading Estate, Avonmore Rd, London W14 8TS (fax 602 8772, telex 8952022)

ALISON, Barley; da of James Stuart Irvine Alison (d 1932), and Marguerita, *née* Rose (d 1973); *b* 18 Jan 1920; *Educ* North Foreland Lodge; *Career* FANY 1942-45, Algiers and France, Capt; third sec British Embassy Paris 1945-49, second sec FO Whitehall 1949-53; dir Weidenfeld & Nicolson 1954-67, fndr Alison Press 1967; dir Secker & Warburg 1972; *Recreations* snorkelling, embroidery; *Clubs* Groucho; *Style*— Miss Barley Alison; 5 Harley Gdns, London SW10 9SW (☎ 01 373 1924); Michelin Rd, London SW3 6RB (☎ 01 581 9393, telex 920191, fax 01 589 8419)

ALISON, Rt Hon Michael James Hugh; PC (1981), MP (C) Selby 1983-; s of J S I Alison, of London and Sydney Australia; *b* 27 June 1926; *Educ* Eton, Wadham Coll Oxford, Ridley Hall Cambridge; *m* 1958, Sylvia Mary, da of Anthony Haigh, CMG; 2 s, 1 da; *Career* served Coldstream Gds 1944-48 as Lt; clerk with Lazard Bros (merchant bankers) 1951-53; memb Kensingon Cncl 1956-59, research offr London Municipal Soc 1954-58, CRD 1958-64, MP (C) Barkston Ash 1964-83, jt parly under sec DHSS 1970-74, Min of State NI Office 1979-81, Min State Dept Employment 1981-; pps to the Prime Minister 1983-; *Style*— The Rt Hon Michael Alison, MP; House of Commons, London SW1A 0AA (☎ 01 219 3000)

ALLAIRE, Paul Arthur; s of Arthur E Allaire (d 1960), of Worcester, Mass, USA, and Mrs G P Murphy; *b* 21 July 1938; *Educ* Worcester Polytechnic Inst (BS), Carnegie Mellon Univ (MS); *m* 1963, Kathleen, da of Thomas Buckley (d 1959), of New York; 1 s (Brian b 1964), 1 da (Christiana b 1967); *Career* vice-pres Xerox Corpn 1983-, md Rank Xerox 1980-83; bd memb American Chamber of Commerce 1980-; *Recreations* riding, tennis; *Style*— Paul Allaire, Esq; 727 Smith Ridge Road, New Canaan, Conn 06840, USA

ALLAN; *see*: Havelock-Allan

ALLAN, Hon Alexander Claud Stuart; only s of Baron Allan of Kilmahew, DSO, OBE (Life Baron) (d 1979); *b* 1951; *Style*— The Hon Alexander Allan; Copse Hill Farm, Lower Froyle, Alton, Hants

ALLAN, Sir Colin Hamilton; KCMG (1977), CMG (1968, OBE 1959); yr s of John Calder Allan (d 1963), of Cambridge, NZ, and Mabel, *née* Eastwood (d 1974); *b* 23 Oct 1921; *Educ* Hamilton HS NZ, Canterbury Univ (MA), Magdalene Coll Cambridge (Dip Anthropology); *m* 1955, Betty Dorothy, eldest da of Aubrey C Evans (d 1965), of Brisbane, Aust; 3 s; *Career* Colonial Admin Serv; served 1945-66: Fiji, Br Solomon Islands, New Hebrides Condominium, Br resident cmmr New Hebrides 1966-73, govr and C-in-C Seychelles and cmmr Br Indian Ocean Territory 1973-76, govr Solomon Islands and high cmmr W Pacific 1976-78; visiting fell Australian Nat Univ 1979, visiting lectr Auckland Univ 1981-, visiting lectr Univ NSW 1988; memb NZ Advsy Cncl Province of Melanesia 1982-; Leprosy Tst B NZ 1980-; chm and tstee Ranfurly Library Serv NZ 1983-; Commandeur de L'Ordre National du Mérite (France); *Recreations* collecting, reading The Times; *Clubs* Royal Cwlth Soc; *Style*— Sir Colin Allan, KCMG, CMG, OBE; Glen Rowan, 17 Sale St, Howick, Auckland, New Zealand (☎ 010 649 535 6462)

ALLAN, (Andrew) Garth; s of Andrew Allan, of Middx; *b* 9 Sept 1936; *Educ* King's Coll London (BSc); *m* 1959, Ann Mary, da of Patrick O'Callaghan; 3 s (incl twins); *Career* md: James Burn Bindings Ltd 1971-80, James Burn Overseas 1971-85, James Burn Eynsham 1974-85, James Burn International Ltd (div of Standex Int Corpn) 1980-85, AGA Associates Ltd; dir Rilecart SPA, co sec Bodley Knose Ltd; *Recreations* water colour painting, apiarist; *Style*— A Garth Allan, Esq; 2 Gateways, Epsom Rd, Guildford, Surrey (☎ 0483 67088)

ALLAN, George Alexander; s of William Allan (d 1976), of 13 Comely Bank Street, Edinburgh, and Janet Peters, *née* Watt (d 1976); *b* 3 Feb 1936; *Educ* Daniel Stewart's Coll Edinburgh, Edin Univ (MA); *m* 1 Sept 1962, Anne Violet, da of Vibert Ambrose George Veevers, of Kelso; 2 s (Victor Julian Douglas b 1964, Timothy Edward Douglas b 1966); *Career* Edin Univ Air Sqdn 1953-56, CCF RAF VR 1958-66; classics master Glasgow Acad 1958-60; Daniel Stewart's Coll Edinburgh: classics masters 1960-63, head of classics 1963-73, housemaster 1966-73; Robert Gordon's Coll Aberdeen: dep headmaster 1973-77, headmaster 1978-; schoolmaster fell commoner Corpus Christi Coll Cambridge 1972-; played rugby for Edinburgh XV 1960-62, Scottish trial 1963; Scottish Div HMC, sec 1980-87, rep on nat ctee 1982-83, chm 1988-; ctee memb Scottish Cncl of Ind Schs 1988; govr Welbeck Coll 1980, burgess of guild City of Aberdeen 1981-; HMC 1978; *Recreations* golf, gardening, music, travel; *Clubs* East India & Public Schools, Royal Northern & Univ (Aberdeen); *Style*— George Allan, Esq; 24 Woodend Rd, Aberdeen AB2 6YH (☎ 0224 321733); Robert Gordon's Coll, Schoolhill, Aberdeen AB9 1FR (☎ 0224 646346)

ALLAN, Ian; s of George A T Allan, OBE (d 1952), of Horsham, and Mary Louise, *née* Barnes; *b* 29 June 1922; *Educ* St Paul's; *m* 11 Oct 1947, Mollie Eileen, da of Edwin Franklin; 2 s (David Ian b 1954, Edwin Paul b 1957); *Career* chm Ian Allan Gp (publishers, printers and travel agents) 1962-; govr Christ's Hosp 1944- (Almoner 1980-), tres Bridewell Royal Hosp, chm Governors King Edward's Sch, Witley, Dart Valley Light Railway plc (chm 1976-86), vice-pres Tport Tst; *Books* many books on railways and associated subjects; *Recreations* miniature railways, swimming; *Style*— Ian Allan, Esq; The Jetty, Middleton-on-Sea, Bognor Regis, W Sussex (☎ 024 369 3378)

ALLAN, James Nicholas; CMG (1989), CBE (1976); s of late Morris Edward Allan, and Joan, *née* Bach; *b* 22 May 1932; *Educ* Gresham's, LSE; *m* 1961, Helena Susara Crouse; 1 s, 1 da; *Career* ambass Mozambique 1986-; *Style*— James Allan, Esq, CMG, CBE; c/o Foreign and Cwlth Off, London SW1

ALLAN, Hon Jane Maureen; only da of Baron Allan of Kilmahew, DSO, OBE (d 1979) (Life Peer); *b* 1952; *Style*— The Hon Jane Allan; Copse Hill Farm, Lower Froyle, Alton, Hants

ALLAN, John Clifford; s of James Arthur Allan (d 1955), of Liverpool, and Mary Alice, *née* Hill (d 1950); *b* 3 Feb 1920; *Educ* RNC Greenwich; *m* 1947, Dorothy Mary, da of Percival Dossett (d 1942); 2 da (Mary, Valerie); *Career* dir Manpower Dockyards (MOD) 1975-79, Royal Corps of Naval Constructors; ret; *Recreations* tennis, squash, painting, bridge; *Clubs* Lansdown Lawn Tennis, Squash Racquets (Bath) (pres); *Style*— J Allan, Esq; 21, Henrietta St, Bath, Avon BA2 6LP (☎ Bath 315237)

ALLAN, Sheriff John Douglas; s of Robert Taylor Allan, ARCM, of Edinburgh, and Christina Helen Blythe Allan (d 1970); *b* 2 Oct 1941; *Educ* George Watson's Coll Edinburgh, Univ of Edinburgh (LLB, Dip Mgmnt Studies); *m* 1966, Helen Elizabeth Jean, da of William Aiton (d 1959); 1 s (Graeme b 1967), 1 da (Anne b 1970); *Career* slr and notary public; slr 1963-67; dep procurator fiscal 1967-71, sr legal asst Crown Office 1971-76, asst procurator fiscal Glasgow 1976-77, sr asst procurator Fiscal Glasgow 1978-79, asst slr Crown Office 1979-83; now Regional Procurator Fiscal for Lothians & Borders 1983-88; now Sheriff of South Strathclyde, Dumfries and Galloway at Lanark 1988-; FBIM; *Recreations* youth work, church work, walking; *Style*— Sheriff J Douglas Allan; Minard, 80 Greenbank Crescent, Edinburgh EH10 5SW (☎ 031 447 2593); Sheriff Court, Hope St, Lanark, ML11 7NQ (☎ Lanark 61531)

ALLAN, Nicholas John; s of Colin Douglas Fitzgerald Allan, of Taunton, Somerset, and Barbara Mary Valentine, *née* Godfrey; *b* 8 August 1943; *Educ* Sherborne, Leeds Univ (LLB); *m* 6 April 1968, Isabel Rosemary Kinahan, da of Capt Lionel Blake Fisher (d 1983); 1 s (Jeremy Hugh b 1974), 1 da (Juliet Louise b 1972); *Career* slr, memb Law Soc and Somerset Law Soc, memb Somerton Parish Cncl 1983-, chm Somerton Twinning Assoc 1987-; *Recreations* tennis, cricket, choral singing, music, France; *Style*— Nicholas J Allan, Esq; The Old Rectory, Kingsdon, Somerton, Somerset TA11 7LD (☎ 0935 840878); Market Place, Somerton, Somerset TA11 7NA (☎ 0458 72347, fax 0458 73262)

ALLAN, Robert William; s of William Bennett Allan (d 1986), of NY, NY, USA and Mona Theresa Allen; *b* 4 May 1945; *Educ* Zaverian Coll Brighton; *m* 15 Jul 1979, Elizabeth, da of John Jackson, of Newcastle; 2 da (Charlotte b 1979, Kirsty b 1982); *Career* slr 1967; ptnr: Roney & Co 1971-73, Simons Muirhead & Allan 1973-86, Denton Hall Burgin & Warrens 1986-; memb Law Soc; *Recreations* skiing, clay pigeon shooting, horse riding; *Clubs* Grouchos; *Style*— Robert Allan, Esq; 5 Chancery Lane, London WC2A 1LF (☎ 01 242 1212, fax 01 404 0087)

ALLAN, William Roderick Buchanan; s of James Buchanan Allan and Mildred Pattenden; *b* 11 Sept 1945; *Educ* Stowe, Trin Coll Cambridge (MA); *m* 1973, Gillian Gail Colgan; 2 s (Alexander, Robert); *Career* editor *The Connoisseur* 1976-80 (joined staff 1972); arts consultant United Technologies Corporation; latest involvement: Franz Xaver Winterhalter and the Courts of Europe, National Portrait Gallery, London, Petit Palais, Paris; *Recreations* military history, cooking; *Clubs* Chelsea Arts; *Style*— William Allan, Esq; 54 South Western Rd, St Margaret's, Twickenham, Middx (☎ 01 891 0974)

ALLAN OF KILMAHEW, Baroness; Maureen; da of late Harold Stuart-Clark, of Singapore; *m* 1947, Baron Allan of Kilmahew, DSO, OBE (Life Peer) (d 1979); *Style*— The Rt Hon the Lady Allan of Kilmahew

ALLANBRIDGE, Hon Lord; William Ian Stewart; s of John Stewart, FRIBA (d 1954), and Mrs Maysie Shepherd Service or Stewart (d 1968), of Drimfearn, Bridge of Allan; *b* 8 Nov 1925; *Educ* Loretto, Edinburgh Univ, Glasgow Univ (MA, LLB); *m* 1955, Naomi Joan, da of Sir James Boyd Douglas, CBE (d 1964), of Barstibly, Castle Douglas; 1 s (John), 1 da (Angela); *Career* served WW II Sub-Lt RNVR, escort gp Western Approaches; advocate 1951, advocate depute 1959-64, memb Criminal Injuries Compensation Bd 1969-70, home adv dep 1970-71, solicitor gen for Scotland 1972-74, sen of Coll of Justice in Scotland (Scottish Ld of Session) 1977-; QC (Scot) 1965, sheriff principal of Dumfries and Galloway 1974; *Recreations* hill walking; *Clubs* New (Edinburgh), RNVR (Glasgow); *Style*— The Hon Lord Allanbridge; 60 Northumberland St, Edinburgh EH3 6JE, Scotland (☎ 031 556 2823)

ALLANBY, Lady Anne Sarah Elizabeth; *née* Savile; da of 7 Earl of Mexborough (d 1980); *b* 10 Sept 1938; *m* 1964, Charles Hynman Allanby, only s of late Maj Ronald Hynman Allanby, of Balblair, Nairn; 1 s (Henry Hynman b 1965); *Style*— Lady Anne Allanby; Balblair, Nairn

ALLANSON-BAILEY, (Thomas) Noel; s of Arthur Cecil Allanson-Bailey (d 1949), and Evelyn Lydia Margaret, *née* Northmore (d 1923); *b* 5 Jan 1909; *Educ* Newton Abbot; *m* 1, 1934, Monica Melhuish (d 1958), da of Preb John Peter Benson (d 1946); 2 s (Christopher John b 1935, Peter b 1941); m 2, 1959, Keren Elinor Bryan, da of E Bryan Wood (1952); *Career* JP County of Devon 1944; *Recreations* hunting, fishing, shooting; *Style*— T Noel Allanson-Bailey, Esq; Oare Manor, Oare, nr Lynton, Devon EX35 6NX (☎ 05987 240)

ALLANSON-WINN, Hon John Rowland; s and h of 7 Baron Headley; *b* 14 Oct 1934; *Educ* Canford Sch; *Style*— The Hon John Allanson-Winn; 59 West St, Bere Regis, Dorset

ALLANSON-WINN, Hon Owain Gwynedd; 5 and yst s of 5 Baron Headley (d 1935), and his 1 w, Teresa St Josephine, *née* Johnson (d 1919); *b* 15 Feb 1906; *Educ* Bedford Sch; *m* 29 Oct 1938, Ruth, 2 da of late Cecil Orpin, of Strand House, Youghal, Co Cork, and formerly wife of Harry Stuart Pearson; *Style*— The Hon Owain Allanson-Winn; 8 Genevafontein, P.O. Box 4340, George East, 6539, S Africa

ALLANSON-WINN, Hon Susan Ethel; da of 7 Baron Headley; *b* 26 May 1936; *Style*— The Hon Susan Allanson-Winn

ALLARD, Sir Gordon Laidlaw; s of late G Allard; *b* 7 August 1909; *Educ* Scotch Coll Melbourne; *m* 1935, Cherry, da of S R E Singleton; 1 s; *Career* sr ptnr Price Waterhouse until 1974, chm Grindlays Australia Ltd until 1982, AMI Toyoto Ltd until 1986-; pres Royal Victorian Eye and Ear Hosp 1964-80; kt 1981; *Recreations* golf, bowls, gardening; *Clubs* Melbourne, Australian, Royal Melbourne GC, MCC; *Style*— Sir Gordon Allard; 4 St Martins Close, Kooyong, Vic 3144, Australia

ALLARD, Gen Jean Victor; CC (1968), CBE (1946, DSO and 2 bars 1943, 1944, 1945, ED 1946, CD 1958); s of late Ernest Allard, of Nicolet, Quebec, and Victorine Trudel; *b* 12 June 1913; *Educ* St Laurent Coll Montreal, St Jerome Coll Kitchener Ont; *m* 1939, Simone, da of Gustave Clodomir Piché, OBE, DSc, of Montreal; 2 da;

Career joined Three Rivers Regt 1933, Capt 1938, Maj 1939, served WW II, Maj-Gen 1958, Lt-Gen 1964, General 1966, chief Canadian Def Staff 1966-69; representative for Province of Québec in New York 1969-70; business conslt in industl promotion 1970-; *Style*— General Jean Allard, CC, CBE, DSO, ED, CD; 3265 boulevard du Carmel, Trois Rivières, Québec, Canada

ALLARDICE, His Hon Judge; William Arthur Llewellyn Allardice; DL (Staffs 1980); s of late W C Allardice, MD, FRCSEd, JP, and late Constance Winifred Allardice; *b* 18 Dec 1924; *Educ* Stonyhurst, Univ Coll Oxford (MA); *m* 1956, Jennifer, Ann, da of late G H Jackson; 1 s, 1 da; *Career* barrister Lincoln's Inn 1950; circuit judge (Midland and Oxford) 1972-; *Style*— His Hon Judge Allardice, DL; c/o Courts Administrator, Stafford (☎ 55219)

ALLARDYCE, Hugh Winyett; s of Alexander Allardyce (d 1987), of Tunbridge Wells, Kent, and Phyllis Vandella, *née* de Kantzow; *b* 8 May 1951; *Educ* Bedford Sch, Leeds Univ; *Career* barr 1972; *Style*— Hugh Allardyce, Esq; 1 Middle Temple Lane, Temple, London EC4 (☎ 01 583 0659, fax 01 353 0652)

ALLASON, Lt-Col James Harry; OBE (1953); s of late Brig-Gen Walter Allason, DSO (d 1960), and Katharine Hamilton, *née* Poland; *b* 6 Sept 1912; *Educ* Haileybury, RMA Woolwich; *m* 1946 (m dis 1974), Nuala Elveen, da of late John A McArevey, of Foxrock, Co Dublin; 2 s; *Career* cmmnd RA 1932, transfd 3rd Carabiniers 1937, served WW II, ret 1953; MP (C) Hemel Hempstead 1959-74, pps to Sec of State for War 1960-64; *Clubs* White's, Royal Yacht Sqdn; *Style*— Lt-Col James Allason, OBE; 82 Ebury Mews, London SW1 (☎ 01 730 1576)

ALLASON, Julian Edward Thomas; s of Lt-Col James Harry Allason, OBE, FRSA, *qv*; *b* 14 May 1948; *Educ* Downside; *m* 1976, Jessica Marland, da of Richard Thomas Wingert, of Westport Connecticut, USA; 2 s (James b 1980, Benjamin b 1984), 1 da (Chloe b 1982); *Career* dir: Apricot Computers plc 1979-86, Sharp Technol Fund plc 1984-, Markham & Markham Ltd 1971-, chm Personal Robots Ltd 1985-; dir Megasat Satellite Communications Ltd 1986-, Elgie Stewart Smith plc 1987-, author, publisher Microcomputer Printout Magazine 1979-83, columnist The Observer 1981-83, Daily Telegraph 1983-86; JP (Inner London) 1973-78; memb information technol NEDC 1984-86; FRSA 1984; kt of Sov Mil Order of Malta 1985, vice-chllr Sov Mil Order of Malta 1986-, Offr of Merit Sov Mil Order of Malta 1987, kt Constantinian Order of St George 1986 (chllr British Delegation 1987-); *Books* The Pet Companion (1981), English Legal Heritage (co-ed 1979); *Recreations* photography, litigation, fullbore pistol shooting; *Clubs* Whites; *Style*— Julian Allason, Esq; 82 Ebury Mews, London SW1W 9NX (☎ 01-824-8241)

ALLASON, Rupert William Simon; MP (C), Torbay 1987-; s of Lt-Col James Allason, OBE, of London, and Nuala, *née* McArevey; *b* 8 Nov 1951; *Educ* Downside Sch, University Hall Buckland, Univ of Lille, Univ of Grenoble; *m* 1979, Nicole Jane da of M L Van Moppes, Bermuda (d 1963); 1 s (Thomas E b 1980), 1 da (Alexandra b 1987); *Career* author; Euro ed Intelligence Quarterly; *Books* SPY! (with Richard Deacon 1980), MI5 (1981), A Matter of Trust (1982), MI6 (1983), The Branch (1983), Unreliable Witness (1984), GARBO (with Juan Pujol 1985), GCHQ (1986), Molehunt (1987), The friends (1988); *Recreations* skiing, sailing; *Clubs* White's, Special Forces, RYS; *Style*— Rupert W S Allason, Esq; 310 Fulham Road, London SW10 (☎ 01 352 1110); House of Commons, London SW1A 0AA (☎ 01 219 4142)

ALLAUN, Frank J; s of Harry and Hannah Allaun; *b* 27 Feb 1913; *Educ* Manchester GS; *m* 1941, Lilian, da of J Ball, of Manchester; 1 s, 1 da; *Career* MP (Lab) E Salford 1955-83; pres Labour Action for Peace 1963-; chm: Labour Party 1979, Labour Press and Publicity Ctee to 1982, Labour NEC 1979 (memb 1967-83); memb: Labour Home Policy Ctee to 1982, life memb Nat Union of Journalists; ed Labour's Northern Voice 1953-67 Ctee 1967-83; *Style*— Frank Allaun, Esq; Manchester M21 2DX (☎ 061 881 7681)

ALLAWAY, Percy Albert; CBE (1973); s of Albert Edward Allaway, and Frances Beatrice, *née* Rogers; *b* 22 August 1915; *Educ* Southall Tech Coll; *m* 1959, Margaret Lilian Petyt; *Career* joined EMI 1930: dir: Nuclear Enterprises Ltd 1961-81, EMI 1965-81, SE Labs (EMI) 1967-81; chm: Electronics 1968-81, EMIMEC 1968-81, chm EMI Varian 1969-81; memb exec mgmnt bd Thorn EMI 1980-81, conslt Thorn EMI 1981-82; chm CEI 1980-81; pres Electronic Engrg Assoc 1970; Freeman City of London, Liveryman Worshipful Co of Scientific Instrument Makers; Hon DTech (Brunel) 1973; FRSA, FEng 1980, FIProdE, FIEE pres IERE 1976, FIQA; *Style*— Percy Allaway, Esq, CBE; Kroller, 54 Howards Wood Drive, Gerrards Cross, Bucks SL9 7HW (☎ 0753 885028)

ALLCARD, James Stanley; TD; s of Henry Allcard (d 1932); *b* 9 April 1911; *Educ* Framlingham Coll; *m* 1940, Shelagh Audrey; 3 children; *Career* served WW II Capt East Africa and Germany; Easterbrook Allcard & Co (mfr of engineers' cutting tools) 1930-; *Recreations* gardening; *Style*— James Allcard, Esq, TD; 3 Taptonville Rd, Broomhill, Sheffield S10 5BQ (☎ Sheffield 0742 661865); Easterbrook Allcard & Co, Penistone Rd, Sheffield 8 (☎ 0742 349361)

ALLCROFT; *see*: Magnus-Allcroft

ALLDAY, Coningsby; CBE (1971); s of late Esca and Margaret Allday, of Birmingham; *b* 21 Nov 1920; *Educ* Solihull Sch, London Univ (BSc); *m* 1945, Iris Helena, da of Frank Spencer Adams, of Birmingham; 1 s, 1 da; *Career* UK Atomic Energy Authy 1959-71 (chief chemist, tech dir, commercial dir, dep md), memb UKAEA 1976-85, md Br Nuclear Fuels Ltd 1971-86 (chief exec 1975-86, chm 1983-86), chm Allday Nuclear Consultants Ltd 1986-, non exec dir Nat West Bank Northern Region 1985-, chm Mintech NW 1986-; CEng, FI Chem E, Hon SDc (Salford); Chevalier de la Legion d'Honneur; *Recreations* gardening, music; *Style*— Coningsby Allday, Esq, CBE; Bredon, 54 Goughs Lane, Knutsford, Cheshire;

ALLDAY, Michael William; DL (Hereford and Worcester); s of Percy William Allday (d 1937), of Solihull, and Eleanor Julia Walker (d 1930), of Metchley Abbey, Harbourne; *b* 30 April 1919; *Educ* Clifton; *m* 1940, Mary Audrey, da of Robert David Roberts, JP (d 1968, High Sheriff Merioneth 1923), of Bryndedwydd, N Wales; 2 da; *Career* served WW II Capt RE, with 1 Assault Bde RE NW Europe; ret chm William Allday & Co (fans, forges, furnaces) 1959-; gen cmmr of Income Tax; chm: Utile Engineering Co Ltd; *Recreations* shooting, fishing; *Clubs* Naval & Military; *Style*— Michael Allday, Esq, DL; Bryndedwydd, Corwen, Clwyd (☎ Maerdy 308); Norchard Grange, Stourport-on-Severn, Worcs DY13 9SN (☎ (0299) 250304)

ALLDIS, Air Cdre Cecil Anderson; CBE (1962), DFC (1941, AFC 1953); 2 s of John Henry Alldis (d 1943), of Birkenhead, Cheshire, and Margaret Wright Alldis (d 1953); *b* 28 Sept 1918; *Educ* Birkenhead Inst, Emmanuel Coll Cambridge (MA); *m* 1942, Jeanette Claire, da of Albert Edward Collingwood Tarrant (d 1924), of Johannesburg, S Africa; *Career* served WWII (despatches), Pilot RAF, Asst Air Attaché Moscow 1947-49, Air Attaché Bonn 1963-66, ret 1966; entered Home Civil Serv 1966, MOD 1966-69, seconded to HM Dip Serv 1969, cnsllr (Defence Supply) Bonn 1969-80, ret 1980; sec-gen The Air League 1982-; *Recreations* golf, fishing; *Clubs* Naval & Military; *Style*— Air Cdre Cecil Alldis, CBE, DFC, AFC; Tudor Cottage, Oxshott Way, Cobham, Surrey (☎ 0932 66092); The Air League, Grey Tiles, Kingston Hill, Kingston-Upon-Thames (☎ 01 546 9325)

ALLDIS, Christopher John; s of Flt-Lt John Henry Alldis, RAF (d 1981), and Isabel Marjorie, *née* Carter; *b* 16 May 1947; *Educ* Birkenhead LSch, Emmanuel Coll Cambridge (MA, LLB); *m* 14 Sept 1985, Marcia Elizabeth, Kidman; 1 da (Amy Elizabeth b 1987); *Career* barr Gray's Inn 1970, practising Northern circuit; *Recreations* gliding, light aviation, skiing, fishing; *Clubs* Naval & Military; *Style*— Christopher Alldis, Esq; Romsdal, 3 Prenton Lane, Birkenhead, Merseyside (☎ 051 608 1828); Peel House, Harrington St, Liverpool (☎ 051 236 4321, fax 051 236 3332)

ALLDIS, John; s of William James and Nell Alldis; *b* 10 August 1929; *Educ* Felsted, King's Cambridge (MA); *m* 1960, Ursula Margaret, da of William Mason (d 1974); 2 s; *Career* conductor: John Alldis Choir 1962-, fndr conductor London Symphony Chorus 1963-66; conductor: London Philharmonic Choir 1969-82, Groupe Vocale de France 1979-83; memb Vaughan William Tst, RARCO, FGSM; Fellow Westminster Choir Coll, Princeton NJ 1978; Chevalier Des Arts et des Lettres 1984; *Style*— John Alldis, Esq; 3 Wool Rd, Wimbledon, London SW20 0HN (☎ 01 946 4168)

ALLEN, Anthony John Rowlatt; s of Stanley Rowlatt Allen, MBE, of 3 Mill Hill, Shoreham By Sea, W Sussex, and Peggy Marion, *née* Wing; *b* 23 Dec 1943; *Educ* Brighton Coll, Selwyn Coll Cambridge (MA); *m* 15 Oct 1971, Torill, da of Ludwig Berg-Nilsen, of Sarpsborg, Norway; 1 s (Henrik b 9 April 1981), 3 da (Kim b 23 April 1973, Emma b 1 June 1974, Rachel b 7 April 1977); *Career* admitted slr 1971, ptnr Donne Mileham & Haddock 1975-; memb Lewes Town Lab Pty; memb: Law Soc, UK Environmental Law Assoc, Slrs' Family Law Assoc, RTPI 1974; *Recreations* walking, sailing; *Style*— Anthony Allen, Esq; 33 Houndean Rise, Lewes, E Sussex BN7 1EQ (☎ 0273 475 014); Donne Mileham & Haddock, Albion House, Lewes, E Sussex (☎ 0273 480 205, fax 0273 480 507)

ALLEN, His Hon Judge; Hon Anthony Kenway Allen; OBE (1946); s of Charles Valentine Allen (d 1956), of Ashtead, Surrey, and Edith Kenway Allen (d 1974); *b* 31 Oct 1917; *Educ* St George's Coll Weybridge, St John's Coll Cambridge (BA), Freiburg Univ, Grenoble Univ; *m* 1975, Maureen Margot Murtough, da of Dr Peter Moran (d 1914); *Career* serv WWII RAF, Intelligence Wing Cmdr; barr Inner Temple 1947; circuit judge 1978-; *Recreations* tennis, music, walking, gardening; *Style*— His Hon Judge Allen, OBE; 73 Downswood, Epsom Downs, Surrey (☎ 073 73 50017)

ALLEN, Arnold Millman; CBE (1977); s of Wilfrid Millman and Edith Muriel Allen; *b* 30 Dec 1924; *Educ* Hackney Downs Secondary Sch, Peterhouse Coll Cambridge; *m* 1947, Beatrice Mary Whitaker; 3 s, 1 da; *Career* served Treasy 1945-55; UKAEA: memb for fin and admin 1976-81, dep chm 1981-84, chief exec 1982-84, chm 1984-; *Style*— Arnold Allen, Esq, CBE; Duntish Cottage, Duntish, Dorchester, Dorset (☎ 030 05 258); United Kingdon Atomic Energy Authority, 11 Charles II St, London SW1Y 4QP (☎ 01 930 5454)

ALLEN, Brian Luscombe; s of Thomas Edward Allen (d 1959), of Harrow, Middx, and Marion Catherine, *née* Luscombe; *b* 29 August 1930; *Educ* Merchants Taylors; *m* 4 Aug 1954, Dorothy Ann, da of Arthur Cecil Nicholls Ford, of Wembley, Middx; 1 s (David b 1960); *Career* CA; dir gen Far Eastern Freight Conference, formerly chm and or dir of a number of public cos; FICA; *Recreations* rifle shooting, gardening, history; *Style*— Brian L Allen, Esq; Bay House, Mile Path, Woking, Surrey GU22 0JX (☎ 61687); Bridge House, 4 Borough High Street, London SE1 9QZ (☎ 403 1700, telex 915073 MYRIOG G, fax 378 6691)

ALLEN, (Michael) Christopher Kinkead; s of Col Robert Langley Kinkead Allen, OBE (d 1976), and Phyllis Mary, *née* Serjeant; *b* 7 Jan 1940; *Educ* Haileybury, Jesus Coll Oxford (MA); *m* 10 April 1976, Jennifer Anne, da of Sir John Rogers Ellis, MBE, of Little Monkhams, Monkhams Lane, Woodford Gn, Essex; 1 s (Robert b 1978), 1 da (Kate b 1980); *Career* ptnr Penningtons slrs 1966-; chm Friends of St Peters Slinfold; govr St Andrews Sch Woking; *Recreations* squash, tennis, sailing, gardening; *Clubs* Lansdowne; *Style*— Christopher Allen, Esq; Phoenix House, 9 London Rd, Newbury, Berks RG13 1JL (☎ 0635 523344, fax 0635 523444)

ALLEN, Colin Mervyn Gordon; CBE (1978); s of Cecil Gordon Allen (d 1980), of 1 Roundmoor Close, Saltford, Bristol and Gwendoline Louise Allen, *née* Hutchinson (d 1974); *b* 17 April 1929; *Educ* King Edwards' Sch Bath, Open Univ (BA) London Univ (MA); *m* 1953 Patricia Mary, da of William Thomas Seddon (d 1943); 2 s (Timothy, Mark), 1 da (Claire); *Career* gen mangr Covent Garden Market Authority 1967-; pres Assoc of Wholesale Markets within Int Union of Local Authorities 1972-78; pres Inst of Purchasing and Supply 1982-83; *Style*— Colin Allen, Esq; 10 Whitecroft Way, Beckenham, Kent BR3 3AG; Covent House, Covent Garden Market, London SW8 5NX (☎ 01 720 2211)

ALLEN, David Robyn; s of Allen Richard David, of The Reach, Smugglers lane, Bosham, Chichester, W Sussex, and Allen Anne, *née* Douthwaite; *b* 24 Jan 1955; *Educ* Wellington Coll and Charing Cross Hosp Med Sch (MBBS, MS); *m* 30 July 1977, (Allen Anne) Judith, da of Hutcheson William (d 1983); 1 s (Robin William b 14 Sept 1983), 1 da (Kate Victoria b 26 Jan 1985); *Career* house surgn St Richards Hosp Chichester, sr house offr Kingston Hosp 1980; registar: Basingstoke Dist Hosp 1981, Royal Sussex Co Hosp Brighton 1983, St Thomas' Hosp 1984; lectr St Thomas' Hosp 1985; sr registrar: Royal Adelaide Hosp Australia 1987, Southampton and Bath 1989; FRCS 1982; *Style*— David Allen, Esq; 12 Queens Rd, Mortlake, London SW14 8PJ, (☎ 01 876 2276); Dept Surgery, St Thomas' Hospital, London SE1 7EH, (☎ 01 928 9292)

ALLEN, The Rev Canon Derek William; s of Rupert William Allen (d 1959), of Croydon, Surrey, and Ellen Gertrude Bailey (d 1962); *b* 2 Nov 1925; *Educ* Eastbourne Coll, Oriel Coll Oxford (BA); *Career* lectr in theology Kings Coll London, subwarden at Kings Coll Theological Hostel 1960-62, princ St Stephen's Ho Oxford 1962-74; warden of community of St Mary The Virgin Wantage 1966-80; vicar St Saviour and St Peter's Eastbourne 1976-; prebendary of Heathfield, canon of Chichester 1984-; member General Synod of the Church of England 1985-; *Recreations* music, poetry, bridge; *Style*— The Rev Canon Derek Allen; The Vicarage, Spencer Road, Eastbourne, East Sussex BN21 4PA (☎ Eastbourne 22317)

ALLEN, Donald George; CMG (1981); s of Sydney George Allen (d 1971), and Doris Elsie, *née* Abercrombie (d 1969); *b* 26 June 1930; *Educ* Southall GS; *m* 1955, Sheila Isobel, da of Wilfred Bebbington (d 1976); 3 s (Stephen, David, Mark); *Career* HM forces 1949-51; FO 1951-54; The Hague 1954-57; second sec (commercial) La Paz 1957-60, FO 1961-65, first sec 1962, asst private sec to Lord Privy Seal 1961-63 and to Min without Portfolio 1963-64, first sec head of Chancery, consul Panama 1966-69; FCO 1969-72; cnsllr on secondment to NI Off Belfast 1972-74, cnsllr and head of Chancery UK Perm Delgn to OECD Paris 1974-78, insp 1978-80, dir Off of Parly Cmmr 1980-82, dep Parly cmmr for admin (ombudsman) 1982-; *Recreations* squash, golf, tennis; *Clubs* RAC, West Surrey Squash; *Style*— Mr Donald Allen, CMG; 99 Parkland Grove, Ashford, Middlesex TW15 2JF (☎ 0784 255617); Church Ho, Great Smith Street, London SW1P 3BW (☎ 01 276 2119)

ALLEN, Fergus Hamilton; CB (1969); s of Charles Winckworth Allen (d 1971), of Dublin, and Marjorie Helen, *née* Budge (d 1986); *b* 3 Sept 1921; *Educ* Newtown Sch Waterford, Trin Coll Dublin (MA, MAI, ScD); *m* 1947, Margaret Joan, da of Prof Michael J Gorman (d 1982), of Dublin; 2 da (Mary m 1980 Robin Woodhead, Elizabeth); *Career* dir Hydraulics Res Station 1958-65, chief scientific offr Cabinet Off 1965-69, first civil serv cmmr Civil Serv Dept 1974-81, sr conslt Boyden Int 1982-86; *Recreations* reading, writing, painting; *Clubs* Athenaeum; *Style*— Fergus Allen, Esq, CB; Dundrum, Wantage Rd, Streatley, Berks RG8 9LB (☎ 0491 873 234)

ALLEN, Hon Mrs; Hon Fiona Mary; da of 17 Lord Lovat, DSO, MC, TD; *b* 6 July 1941; *m* 1982, Robin Richard Allen; *Style*— The Hon Mrs Allen; PO Box 7260, Dubai, United Arab Emirate

ALLEN, Hon Judge; Francis Andrew; His Hon Judge; s of Andrew Eric Allen and Joan Elizabeth Allen; *b* 7 Dec 1933; *Educ* Solihull Sch, Merton Coll Oxford (MA); *m* 1961, Marjorie Pearce; 1 s, 3 da; *Career* barr 1958; circuit judge 1979-; *Style*— His Hon Judge Allen; 116 Oxford Road, Moseley, Birmingham B13 9SQ (☎ 021 449 1270)

ALLEN, Gary James; s of Alfred Allen, of 59 George Frederick Rd, Sutton Coldfiels, W Midlands, and Alice Jane *née* Herworth; *b* 30 Sept 1944; *Educ* King Edward V11 GS Birmingham, Liverpool Univ (B Com); *m* 10/09/1966, Judith Anne, da of William Nattrass (d 1961); 3 s (Andrew, b 1969, Anthony, b 1971, James, b 1979); *Career* md IMI Range Ltd 1973-77, dir IMI plc 1978-(asst md 1985-86, md 1986-); chm: IMI Components Ltd 1981-85, Eley Ltd 1981-85, Optilen Ltd 1979-84; dir NV Bekaert SA Belguim 1987-; memb of cncl: CBI 1986 (W Midlands Regnl Cncl 1983-); Birmingham Chamber of Indust and Commerce 1983 (chm Indust Affrs Ctee 1985-88), Univ of Birmingham 1985 (hon life memb Ct 1984), W Midlands Region Lord Taverners 1985 (chm 1987), Midlands Indust Cncl 1986-; FICMA 1985, CBIM 1986, FRSA 1988; *Recreations* sport, reading, gardening; *Style*— Gary Allen, Esq; IMI plc, PO Box 216, Birmingham B6 OBT (☎ 021 356 4848, telex 336771 IMI KYN G)

ALLEN, Prof Sir Geoffrey; s of John James and Marjorie Allen, of Wingerworth, Derbyshire; *b* 29 Oct 1928; *Educ* Clay Cross Tupton Hall GS, Leeds Univ (BSc, PhD); *m* 1973, Valerie Frances, da of Arthur Duckworth (d 1979); 1 da (Naomi); *Career* scientist; prof of chemical physics Manchester Univ 1965-75, prof of chemical technol Imperial Coll 1976-81, chm Sci Res Cncl 1977-81 (memb 1976), visiting fell Robinson Coll Cambridge 1980-, head resh and engrg Unilever 1981-; Hon MSc Manchester; FPRI, FRS, 1976, FInstP; kt 1979; *Recreations* walking, talking, eating; *Style*— Professor Sir Geoffrey Allen

ALLEN, Sir George Oswald Browning; CBE (1962), TD (1945); s of Sir Walter McArthur Allen, KBE (d 1942), and Pearl, *née* Lamb; *b* 31 July 1902; *Educ* Eton, Trin Coll Cambridge; *Career* cricketer, Capt England XI: *v* India 1936, *v* Australia 1936-37, *v* W Indies 1948; pres MCC 1963-64 (tres 1964-76, tstee 1970-85; Offr Legion of Merit (USA) 1945; kt 1986; *Clubs* White's; *Style*— Sir George Allen, CBE, TD; 4 Grove End Rd, London NW8 (☎ 01 286 4601)

ALLEN, MP Graham W; MP (C) Nottingham N 1987-; s of William Allen, and Edna, *née* Holt; *b* 11 Jan 1953; *Educ* Robert Shaw Primary, Forest Fields GS; *Career* local govt sen offr, Nat Co-ordinator T U Political Fund Campaign, TU Offcr GMB; *Recreations* cricket, walking; *Clubs* Strelley Social, Dunkirk Cricket, Beechdale Community Assoc; *Style*— Graham W Allen, MP; House of Commons SW1A 0AA (☎ 01 219 4347)

ALLEN, Hamish McEwan; CB (1984); s of late Ernest Frank Allen, and Ada Florence, *née* Weeks; *b* 7 Sept 1920; *Educ* City of Bath Sch, Portsmouth Southern Secondary Sch; *m* 1951, Peggy Joan Fifoot; 1 s; *Career* served WW II RAF 1941-46; Air Miny: clerical offr 1938, exec offr 1948; House of Commons: asst accountant 1959, dep accountant 1962, head of Establishments Office 1968, head of Admin Dept 1981-85, ret 1985; *Style*— Hamish Allen Esq, CB; 124 Ridge Langley, South Croydon, Surrey CR2 0AS

ALLEN, Prof Harry Cranbrook; MC; s of Christopher Albert Allen (d 1960), of London, and Margaret Enid, *née* Hebb (d 1965); *b* 23 Mar 1917; *Educ* Bedford Sch, Pembroke Coll Oxford (MA), Harvard (Cwlth Fund Fellowship); *m* 23 Aug 1947, Mary Kathleen, da of Frank Andrews (d 1951), of Oxford; 1 s (Franklin), 2 da (Julia, Georgiana); *Career* WWII Sandhurst (OCTU) 1939, The Hertfordshire Regt 1940-44, The Dorset Regt 1944-45, cmdt 43 divn educnl coll 1945, Maj; history fell Lincoln Coll Oxford 1946-55, prof of american history Univ Coll London 1955-71, fndr dir Inst of US Studies Univ of London 1966-71, prof american studies Univ of E Anglia 1971-80; fndr ctee memb Br Assoc for American Studies 1955- (chm 1974-77), ctee memb Euro Assoc for American Studies 1972-80 (pres 1976-80); Dartmouth RN Review Ctee 1958, RN Educn Advsy Ctee 1960-66, academic planning bd Univ of Essex 1962; fell Royal Hist Soc 1955-80; *Books* Great Britain and the United States (1955), British Essays in American History (ed 1957), Bush and Backwoods (1959), The Anglo-American Relationship Since 1783 (1960), The Anglo-American Predicament (1960), The United States of America (1964), Contrast and Connection (ed 1976); *Recreations* travel; *Clubs* Athanaeum; *Style*— Prof HC Allen, MC; 1 Shepard Way, Chipping Norton, Oxfordshire OX7 5BE (☎ 0608 44381)

ALLEN, Janet Rosemary; da of John Algernon Allen (d 1972), of Leicester, and Edna Mary, *née* Orton; *b* 11 April 1936; *Educ* Cheltenham Ladies' Coll, Univ Coll Leicester (BA), Hughes Hall Cambridge (CertEd); *Career* schoolmistress Howell's Sch Denbigh 1959-75, head of history dept 1961-75, head of sixth form 1965-75, housemistress 1968-75, headmistress Benenden Sch 1976-85; memb: Boarding Schs Assoc Ctee 1980-83, GSA Educnl Sub-ctee 1983-85; vice-pres Women's Careers Fndn 1982-; sch govr St Catherine's Bramley Church Sch ; *Recreations* music, drama, walking, swimming; *Clubs* Royal Overseas League; *Style*— Miss Janet Allen; 1 The Broadway, Alfriston, E Sussex BN26 5XL (☎ 0323 870619)

ALLEN, Dr (Walter) John (Gardener); s of John Gardiner Allen (d 1971), of Deal, Kent, and Lucy Hester, *née* Bailey (d 1968); *b* 8 Dec 1916; *Educ* Manwoods Sandwich Kent, London (LLB); *m* 1944, Irene (d 1983), da of John Joseph Henderson (d 1920), of Lisburn, NI; 1 s (David), 1 da (Irene); *Career* RAF 1940-46, Flying Offr served in Europe and India; Inland Revenue 1934-78, last controller of death duties and first of capital taxes 1974-78; *Recreations* amateur geologist FGS; *Style*— John Allen, Esq; 43 The Chase, Eastcote, Pinner, Middx HA5 1SH

ALLEN, Prof John Anthony; s of George Leonard John Allen (d 1968), and Dorothy Mary, *née* Willoughby (d 1964); *b* 27 May 1926; *Educ* High Pavement Sch Nothingham, Univ of London (PhD, DSc); *m* 1, 10 Sept 1952 (m dis 1983), Marion Ferguson, da of John Crow (d 1960); 1 s (Hamish John Allen b 1955), 1 da (Elspeth Ferguson Allen b 1959); m 2, 12 Aug 1983, Margaret Porteous, da of James Aitken, of Motherwell; 1 step s adopted (Andrew Alexander Murdoch b 1972); *Career* Sherwood Foresters 1945-46, RAMC 1946-48; asst lectr Univ of Glasgow 1951-54, John Murray student Royal Soc 1952-54, lectr, sr lectr and reader in zoology and marine biol Univ Newcastle Upon Tyne 1954-76, prof marine biol Univ of London 1976-, dir Univ Marine Biol Station 1976-, visiting prof Univ of Washington 1968, 1970, 1971 and Univ of W Indies 1976, post doctoral fell and guest investigator Woods Hole Oceanographic Inst 1965-; memb: Natural Environment Res Cncl 1977-83 (chm univ affrs ctee 1975-83), Nature Conservancy Cncl 1982-, (chm advsy ctee on sci 1984-); pres Malacological Soc of London 1982-84; FIBiol 1969, FRSE 1968; *Books* many scientific pubns and articles etc on deapsea organisms, shellfish etc; *Recreations* travel, admiring gardens, pub lunching, squash; *Style*— Prof J A Allen; Bellevue, Isle of Cumbrae, Scotland, KA28 0ED (☎ 0475 530 260); Univ Marine & Biological Station, Millport, Isle of Cumbrae, Scotland KA28 0EG (☎ 0475 530 581)

ALLEN, John Derek; CBE (1987); s of William Henry Allen (d 1956), of Cardiff, and Lalla Dorothy, *née* Bowen (d 1987); *b* 6 Nov 1928; *Educ* Cardiff HS, Cardiff Coll of Tech (HND in Bldg); *m* 14 July 1951, Thelma Jean, da of John Henry Hooper (d 1971), of Cardiff; 1 s (Nicholas John b 1961); *Career* joined as civil engr and then chm and md John Morgan Gp of Cardiff 1947-79; chm Housing for Wales 1987-, dep chm Land Authy for Wales 1976-; tres Nat Fed of Bldg Trade Employers 1980-83 (pres 1979); Freeman City of London 1980; FCIOB 1980, FRSA 1988; *Recreations* fly fishing; *Clubs* Cardiff and County; *Style*— John D Allen, Esq, CBE; 6 Egremount Rd, Penylan, Cardiff CF2 5LN (☎ 0222 499 461); Housing for Wales, Custom House, Custom St, Cardiff CF1 5AP (☎ 0222 221 946)

ALLEN, Hon John Douglas; s of Baron Croham (Life Peer), *qv*; *b* 1945; *Educ* BSc, MPhil; *m* 1969, Sheila Ward; 2 s, 1 da; *Style*— The Hon John Allen; 3 Victoria Ave, Sanderstead, Surrey

ALLEN, Very Rev John Edward; s of Rev Canon Ronald Edward Taylor Allen, MC, MA (d 1984), and Isabel Edith, *née* Otter-Barry; *b* 9 June 1932; *Educ* Rugby, Univ Coll Oxford (MA), Fitzwilliam Coll Cambridge (MA), Westcott House Cambridge; *m* 1957, Eleanor, *née* Prynne; 1 s (Christopher), 3 da (Rebecca, Madeleine, Isabel); *Career* chaplain Bristol Univ 1971-79, vicar Chippenham 1979-82, provost Wakefield West Yorks 1982-; *Recreations* walking, fishing, people; *Style*— The Very Rev John Allen; The Cathedral Vicarage, Margaret Street, Wakefield, W Yorks WF1 2DQ (☎ 0924 372402)

ALLEN, Maj-Gen John Geoffrey Robyn; CB (1976); s of R A Allen, of Leatherhead, Surrey and Mrs R A Allen, *née* Youngman; *b* 19 August 1923; *Educ* Haileybury; *m* 1959, Ann Monica, da of Kenneth Morford, CBE; 1 s (Christopher b 1962), 1 da (Julia b 1965); *Career* cmmnd KRRC 1942, transfd RTR 1947, Dir-Gen Fighting Vehicles and Engr Equipment MOD 1973-74, dir RAC 1974-76, Sr Army Directing Staff RCDS 1976-78, ret 1979; Col Cmdt RTR 1976-80 (Rep 1978-80); lay observer attached to Lord Chllr's Dept 1979-85; memb: Lord Chllr's Advsy Ctee on Legal Aid 1979-85, Booth Ctee on Matrimonial Procedure 1982-85; Hon Col Royal Yeo (TA) and Hon Col HQ (Westminster Dragoons) Sqn 1982-87; *Recreations* dinghy sailing, gardening; *Clubs* Army and Navy, Bosham Sailing; *Style*— Maj-Gen John Allen, CB; Meadowleys, Charlton, Chichester, West Sussex PO18 0HU (☎ 024363 638)

ALLEN, Prof John Piers; OBE (1979); s of Percy Allen and Marjorie Isabel Agnes Nash; ggm on the paternal side was Fanny Stirling (1815-1895) whose life has been well documented by historians of the 19 Century theatre; *b* 30 Mar 1912; *Educ* Aldenham Sch, St John's Coll Cambridge; *m* 1, 1937 (m dis 1944), Modwena Sedgwick; 2 s (Jeremy, Toby); m 2, 1945, Anne Preston (d 1968); 2 s (Simon, Benjamin), 2 da (Charlotte, Harriet); m 3, 1981, Margaret Wootton; *Career* various engagements in profession of Theatre Inc 1931-, Gp Theatre 1933-36, memb of Old Vic Co 1937-38, organizer Left Book Club Theatre Guild; 1938 Staff of London Theatre Studio; directed Handel's Belshazzar Scala Theatre 1938, Pageant of Music of the People Albert Hall 1939; admin and prodr Glyndebourne Children's Theatre 1945-51; close assoc with UNESCO over children's theatre and educnl drama 1950-60, visit to Aust as UNESCO specialist 1959 and 1961; script-writer and prodr BBC Schools Broadcasting Dept 1951-61; HM Inspr of Schs with nat responsibility for drama 1961-72; princ Central Sch of Speech and Drama 1972-78; visiting prof of drama Westfield Coll 1979-82; chm Cncl for Dance Educn and Training 1980-; and various times during 1960s and 1970s chm Conference of Drama Sch Nat Cncl for Drama Training, vice-chm Br Theatre Assoc, lectr City Univ, memb dance and drama panels of Cncl for Nat Acad Awards; *Books* Producing Plays for Children (1950), Going to the Theatre (1951), Great Moments in the Theatre (1953), Masters of British Drama (1957), Masters of European Drama (1962), An Elizabethan Actor (1966), Three Medieval Plays (1953), Education Survey No2 - Drama (1968), Drama in Schools: theory and practice (1979), Theatre in Europe, a study of the European Theatre commissioned by the Cncl of Europe (1981), A History of the Theatre in Europe (1983); *Style*— John Allen, Esq, OBE; The Old Orchard, Lastingham, York YO6 6TQ (☎ 075 15 334)

ALLEN, Sir (William) Kenneth (Gwynne); DL (Beds 1978); er s of Harold Gwynne Allen, JP (d 1960), of Bedford, and Hilda Margaret, *née* Langley (d 1969); bro of (Harold) Norman Gwynne Allen, *qv*; *b* 23 May 1907; *Educ* Westminster, Univ of Neuchatel Switzerland; *m* 1931, Eleanor Mary, o da of late Henry Eeles, of Newcastle-upon-Tyne; 1 s, 1 da; *Career* chm: W H Allen Sons & Co 1955-70 (dir 1937-70, md 1946-70), Br Internal Combustion Engine Mfrs Assoc 1955-57; BEAMA 1959-61; dir: Whessoe Ltd 1954-65, Electrolux 1970-78; pres Engrg Employers' Fedn 1962-64; Freeman City of London, Liveryman Worshipful Co of Shipwrights; High Sheriff Beds 1958-59; FIMarE, MRINA; kt 1961; *Style*— Sir Kenneth Allen, DL;

Manor Close, Aspley Guise, Milton Keynes, Beds MK17 8HZ (☎ 0908 583161)

ALLEN, Leonard; s of Joseph Allen (d 1956), of 50 Fenton Rd, Southbourne, Bournemouth, and Henrietta Emily, *née* Fowle; *b* 30 Nov 1930; *m* 1, 1955 (m dis 1969), Diana *née* Love; m 2 27 April 1970, Theodora Jane, da of John Russell (d 1984), of 27 Derby Rd, Caversham, Reading; 1 da (Henrietta Sophie b 1972); *Career* Nat Serv RTR 1949-50; Cons Central Off: agent Reading 1959-64, political educn offr Eastern area 1964-67 (dep area agent 1967-74), dep dir and head of local govt dept Cons Central Off 1974-77, dir Fedn of Recruitment and Employment Servs 1977-; vice-chm Southern Region UNs Assoc 1955-57, chm Recruitment Soc 1982-84, memb governing body SPCK 1977-80, vice chm Bow Gp 1959-64, memb DoE advsy ctee on women's employment; Freeman: City of London 1978, Worshipful Co of Woolmen; *Recreations* conversation, music, reading, art galleries, dining (formally and informally); *Clubs* Athenaeum, Arts, City Livery; *Style*— Leonard Allen, Esq; 8 Carmel Court, Highfield, Marlow, Bucks (☎ 06284 72325); 36-38 Mortimer St, London W1N 7RB (☎ 01 323 4300, car telephone 0836 740 874)

ALLEN, Leslie Leonard; OBE (1975); s of Richard Allen (d 1952), of London, and Edith Elizabeth, *née* Miller (d 1951); *b* 8 Mar 1909; *Educ* Woolwich Poly, King's Coll London (BSc, AKC); *m* 19 Dec 1936, Doris May, da of John Thomas Bruce (d 1925), of Plumstead, London; 1 da (Sandra Kay (Mrs Russell) b 1943); *Career* sr asst designer Hackbridge Transformers 1934-36, lectr SE London Tech Coll 1936-47; head of engrg dept: Shrewsbury Tech Coll 1947-51, Hendon Coll of Technol 1951-60; princ Willesden Coll of Tech 1960-74, conslt and assessor City and Guilds Inst 1974-82, memb of cncl Inst of Mechanical Engrs 1980-82; memb Indust Tbnl 1971-75, chm Local Employment Ctee 1967-74, gen cmmr Income Tax 1974-84; hon memb City and Guilds Insts 1978; Liveryman Worshipful Co of Wheelwrights 1977; FIEE 1951, FIMechE 1958, FIProdE 1950, C Eng; *Recreations* now-walking and gardening; *Style*— Leslie Allen, Esq; Partingdale, 6 Burlington Close, Farnborough, Orpington, Kent BR6 8PP (☎ 0689 50159)

ALLEN, Hon Lionel Paul; s of Baron Allen of Fallowfield, CBE (Life Peer; d 1985); *b* 1943; *m* 1981, Irene Lynwen, *née* Morris; *Style*— The Hon Lionel Allen; Ivy House, Taddington, Buxton, Derbyshire SK17 9UF

ALLEN, Dr (Walter) Michael Critten; s of Walter Allen (d 1978), of Southport, and Contance, *née* Critten (d 1982); *b* 12 April 1928; *Educ* Manchester GS, Univ and Med Sch (MB, ChB, DMRD); *m* 14 Dec 1955, Dorothy Elizabeth, da of Herbert Norris Crowther (d 1980); 1 s (Patrick Allen b 16 Sept 1961), 1 da (Penelope (Mrs Minto) b 16 Oct 1958); *Career* RAMC Capt 1953-55, Maj TA AER 1955-83, conslt in radiology RARO; consult radiologist NHS 1955-82, conslt surgn Jockey Club 1981- (hon conslt surgn 1977-81); chm PSM/18 ctee of Br Standards Inst (riding headwear and body protectors ctee), tstee Stable lads Welfare Tst; *Recreations* golf; *Clubs* Royal & Ancient GC, Royal St Georges GC, TURF, Royal Lytham GC; *Style*— Dr Michael Allen; 18 Dorin Court, Warlingham, Surrey CR3 9JT (☎ 08832 2056); Jockey Club, 42 Portman Sq, London W1H OEN (☎ 01 486 4921, fax 01 935 8703, telex 21393)

ALLEN, Michael John; s of Edward Thomas Allen, of Bedford, and Dorothy May, *née* Leigh; *b* 22 July 1941; *Educ* Bedford Sch, St Catharine's Coll Cambridge (MA); *m* 11 Oct 1977, Marjolein Christina, da of De Heer Hendrik Casper Wytzes, of Bloemendaal, Netherlands; 2 da (Elizabeth b 1981, Caroline b 1983); *Career* dir of Extra Mural Studies Univ of Cambridge 1980-, fell of Churchill Coll Cambridge 1985-, memb of E Anglia Regl Ctee Nat Tst; *Recreations* natural history, gardening, squash; *Clubs* Royal Soc Arts; *Style*— Michael Allen, Esq; Madingley Hall, Madingley, Cambridge CB3 8AQ (☎ 0954 210636)

ALLEN, (Harold) Norman Gwynne; CBE (1965); yr s of Harold Gwynne Allen (d 1960), of Bedford, and Hilda Margaret, *née* Langley (d 1969); brother of Sir (William) Kenneth (Gwynne) Allen, *qv*; *b* 30 April 1912; *Educ* Westminster Sch, Trinity Coll Cambridge (MA); *m* 1938, Marjorie Ellen, da of William Henry Brown (d 1925), of Devizes, Wilts; 1 s (David), 3 da (Wendy, Corrine, Trisha); *Career* prof civil and mech engr; chm W H Allen Sons & Co 1970-77 (joined Co 1937, dir 1943-77, jt md 1952-70, dep chm 1962-70); dep chm Amalgamated Power Engrg Ltd 1970-77 (dir 1968-70); dir Bellis and Morcom Ltd 1968-77; memb Bedfordshire CC 1947-50; v-chm cncl Mander Coll of Further Educn 1958-74; govr Coll of Aeronautics Cranfield 1955-69; charter pro-chllr Cranfield Inst of Technology 1969-75; pres Instn of Mech Engrs 1965; Hon DSc: Bath Univ 1967, Cranfield 1977; FEng, FICE, FIMechE, FRINA, FIMarE, FIProdE; *Recreations* gardening, sailing, countryside; *Style*— H Norman G Allen, Esq, CBE; Long Mynd, 45 Berry Hill Cres, Cirencester GL7 2HF

ALLEN, Sir Peter Austin Phillip Jermyn; s of Donavan Jermyn Allen (d 1960), and Edith Jane, *née* Bates; *b* 20 Jan 1929; *Educ* Headlands Sch Swindon, London Univ (LLB); *Career* RA 1947-55, served Hong Kong 1949-51 and 1952-54 (Lt 1952-55); Colonial Police Serv Uganda 1955, asst supt, ADC to Govr of Uganda 1957; princ in law Uganda Law Sch 1964-70 (lectr 1962-64), chief magistrate Uganda 1970-73, judge Uganda High Ct 1973-85, chief justice of Uganda 1985-86, judge Lesotho High Ct 1987-89; dir Mbarara branch Uganda YMCA 1970-73; memb fndn ctee Uganda YMCA 1959; memb: Uganda Law Soc 1964-70, Uganda Law Reform Cmmn 1964-68; Uganda Independance Medal 1962; *Books* An Introduction to the Law of Uganda (jty, 1968), Days of Judgment (1987); *Clubs* Royal Commonwealth Society; *Style*— Sir Peter Allen; Fallons, Poplar Lane, Bransgore, Christhchurch, Dorset BH23 8JE (☎ 0425 72473)

ALLEN, Sir Peter Christopher; s of Sir Ernest King Allen, CBE (d 1937), and Florence Mary, *née* Gellathy; *b* 8 Sept 1905; *Educ* Harrow, Trinity Coll Oxford (BSc, MA); *m* 1, 1931, Violet Sylvester (d 1951), da of Sir Ernest Wingate-Saul; 2 da; m 2, 1952, Consuelo Maria Linares Rivas; *Career* chm ICI 1968-71 (joined ICI 1928); pres Canadian Indust Ltd 1959-62, chm ICI of Canada 1959-68; dir: Bank of Montreal 1968-75, BICC 1971-; chm Br Nat Export Cncl 1970-72; advsy dir New Perspective Fund of Los Angeles 1973; Gov Harrow Sch; FBIM. FInstD; kt 1967; *Recreations* writing, golf, tport history; *Clubs* Carlton, Royal & Ancient St Andrews, Augusta Nat; *Style*— Sir Peter Allen; Telham Hill House, nr Battle, E Sussex (☎ 042 46 3150)

ALLEN, Peter Dobson; s of Frederick Allen (d 1957), of Dewsbury, and Ethel, *née* Dobson; *b* 4 Jan 1931; *Educ* Wheelwright GS Dewsbury, Univ of Birmingham (Hons 2.1. Chem BSc CEng MIM); *m* 15 Sept 1956, Janet, da of Cyril Thurman (d 1983), of Dewsbury; 3 s (Timothy b 1958, Christopher b 1959, Nicholas b 1963); *Career* Lt RA 1957, dir Port Talbot Works BSC 1972-76, md Welsh Division, BSC 1976-80, md Operations, Strip Products Group, BSC 1980-, high sheriff Mid Glamorgan 1987-88, dir BSC (Overseas Services) Ltd 1977-, Benzole Producers Ltd 1982-, Benzene Marketing Co Ltd 1982-, Staveley Chemicals Ltd 1982-, GR Stein Refractories Ltd 1985-, A S W Hldgs plc 1987-; *Recreations* rugby football, cricket, the turf, music; *Style*— Peter D Allen, Esq; Furzebrook, Merthyr Mawr Road, Bridgend, Mid Glam CF31 3NS (☎ 0656 55803); P.O. Box 10, Newport, Gwent (☎ 0633 290022, telex 497601, car 0860 511119)

ALLEN, Peter John; s of William George (d 1974), and Florence Rose, *née* Betambeau; *b* 3 July 1949; *Educ* Wallington; *m* 23 June 1973, Jennifer, da of Cyril Robert Groves, of East Sussex; *Career* Kenneth Anderson and Co 1967-68, Centre File 1968-69, Rowe Swann and Co 1969-75, Sheppards and Chase Discretionary Fund Mgmnt 1975-77; Kleinwort Benson Inv Mgmnt 1977-: asst dir 1985-87, dir 1986-; MBIM; memb: Inst of dirs, Int Stock Exchange; *Recreations* riding, ballet, circus; *Clubs* RAF Honorary; *Style*— Peter Allen, Esq; Hestia, Woodland Way, Kingswood, Surrey KT20 6PA; 1 Churchill Villas, Churchill Rd, The Bourne, Brimscombe, Glos GL5 2UB; Kleinwort Benson Investmt Mgmnt Ltd, 10 Fenchurch St, London EC3M 3LB (☎ 01 623 8000, fax 01 42466, telex 9413545)

ALLEN, Peter William; s of Alfred William Allen (d 1987), of Sittingbourne, Kent, and Myra Nora, *née* Rogers (d 1982); *b* 22 July 1938; *Educ* Borden GS, Sidney Sussex Coll Cambridge Univ (MA); *m* 1965, Patricia Mary, da of Joseph Frederick Dunk, of Sheffield; 3 da (Samantha, Joanna, Annabel); *Career* RAF 1957-59; joined Coopers & Lybrand 1963: qualified CA 1966, ptnr 1973, chm int personnel ctee 1975-78, ptnr i/c London Off 1983, managing ptnr 1984-, memb UK mgt ctee 1984-, memb int exec ctee 1988-; Freeman Worshipful Co of Glaziers and Painters of Glass; FICA 1969; *Recreations* golf; *Clubs* Reform; *Style*— Peter W Allen, Esq; John O'Gaddesden's House, Little Gaddesden, Berkhamsted, Herts HP4 1Pf (☎ 044284 2710); Coopers & Lybrand, Plumtree Ct, London EC4A 4HT (☎ 01 583 5000, fax 01 822 4652)

ALLEN, Hon Polly - Joan Colette Clifford; only child of Baron Allen of Hurtwood (Life Baron) (d 1939); *b* 1922; *Style*— The Hon Polly Allen; 10 Selwood Terrace, London SW7

ALLEN, Dr (Kenneth) Radway; s of Alexander Radway Allen (d 1955); *b* 12 Feb 1911; *Educ* Manchester GS, Cambridge (BA, MA, DSc); *m* 1938, Rosa Mary, da of Harry Grimsdell Bullen (d 1945); *Career* Lt New Zealand; biologist; dir Fisheries Research NZ Marine Dept Wellington 1961-64, dir Pacific Biological Station Fisheries Research Board of Canada, Nanaimo, Br Columbia 1967-72; chief Div of Fisheries and Oceanography CSIRO Cronulla, NSW, Australia 1972-77; *Style*— Dr K Radway Allen; 192 Ewos Pde, Cronulla, NSW 2230, Australia

ALLEN, Hon Richard Anthony; yr s of Baron Croham, GCB (Life Peer), *qv*; *b* 1950; *Educ* Whitgift Sch Croydon, Southampton Univ (BSc); *m* 1, 1980 (m dis 1986), Karen, o da of F Hughes, of Whetstone, London; m 2, 1988, Gillian, o da of R Harroway, of Huddersfield; *Career* Official, Bank of England; *Recreations* music, squash racquets, shooting; *Style*— The Hon Richard Allen; 11 Worcester Close, Shirley, Surrey

ALLEN, Dr Thomas Boaz; CBE 1989; s of Thomas Boaz Allen (d 1987), of Seaham, Co Durham, and Florence, *née* Hemmings; *b* 10 Sept 1944; *Educ* Robert Richardson GS Ryhope Co Durham, RCM London (ARCM); *m* 1, 30 March 1968 (m dis 1986), Margaret, da of George Holley; (d 1980), of Seaham, Co Durham; 1 s (Stephen Boaz b 31 Jan 1970); m 2, 12 March 1988, Jeannie Gordon Lascelles, da of Norman Gordon Farquharson, of Southbroom, Natal, SA; *Career* singer; princ baritone: Welsh Nat Opera 1969-72, Royal Opera House Covent Garden 1972-77; guest appearances: Metropolitan Opera NY (debut) 1981, Bayerische Staatsoper München 1985, Wiener Staatsoper, Paris Opera, La Scala Milan (opened 1987/88 season as Don Giovanni), ENO, San Francisco Opera, Glyndebourne, Aldeburgh, Salzburg Festivals; memb The Arts for the Earth, bd Memb London Int Opera Fesival; Hon MA Newcastle 1984, Hon D Mus Durham 1988, Hon RAM 1988; FRCM 1988; *Recreations* golf, drawing, ornithology; *Clubs* Effingham GC; *Style*— Dr Thomas Allen, CBE; c/o John Coast, Manfield House, 376/9 Strand, London WC2 0LR (☎ 01 379 0022)

ALLEN, Prof Walter; s of Charles Henry Allen (d 1950), and Annie Maria Allen (d 1950); *b* 23 Feb 1911; *m* 8 April 1944, Peggy Yorke, da of Guy Lionel Joy; 2 s (John b 1947, Robert 1951), 2 da (Charlotte b 1949, Harriet b 1959); *Career* features ed Cater's News Agency Birmingham 1935-37, literary ed New Statesman 1960-61; visiting Prof of English: Coe Coll Iowa USA 1955-56, Vasser Coll NY 1963-64, Univ of Kansas 1967; prof English New Univ of Ulster 1967-73, Berg prof English NY Univ 1970-71, visiting prof Dalhousie Univ Canada 1973-74, prof English Virginia Poly Instit 1975-76; FRSL; *Books* Innocence is Drowned (1938), Blind Man's Ditch (1939), Dead Man Over All (1950), All in a Lifetime (1959), Get Out Early (1986); literary criticism: Arnold Bennett (1948), The English Novel (1954), Tradition and Dream (1964), The Short Story in English (1981); memoirs: As I Walked Down New Grub Street (1981); *Style*— Prof Walter Allen; 4B Alwyne Rd, London N1 2HH (☎ 01 226 7085)

ALLEN, Dr William Alexander; CBE (1980); s of Frank Allen (d 1965), of Winnipeg, Canada, and Sarah Estelle, *née* Harper (d 1915); *b* 29 June 1914; *Educ* Univ of Manitoba (BArch); *m* 10 Sept 1938, (Beatrice Mary Theresa) Tessa, da of Clarence Henry Pearson (d 1930), of Cheriton Fitzpaine, Devon; 2 s (Christopher b 1942, Nicholas b 1944), 1 da (Deborah b 1948); *Career* chief architect Bldg Res Estab 1953-61 (joined 1938), princ Architectural Assoc Sch of Architecture 1961-66, jt fndr ptnr Bickerdike Allen Ptnrs 1962-89; memb cncl RIBA 1954-72 and 1962-89; pres: Inst of Acoustics 1975-76, Ecclesiastic Architects & Surveryors Assoc 1980-81; former vice-chm govrs Sir Frederic Osborn Sch; Hon LLD Univ Manitoba 1977; FRIBA 1937; memb: Inst Acoustics 1946, hon assoc NZ Inst Architects 1965 memb Ecclesiastic Architects & Surveyors 1975, hon fell American Inst of Architects 1983; Ordem do Merito Portugal 1970; *Books* Sound Transmission in Buildings (with R Fitzmaurice, 1940), Professionalism and Architecture Encyclopedia of Architecture, (1989); *Recreations* walking, gardening, drawing, writing; *Clubs* Athenaeum; *Style*— Dr William Allen, CBE; 4 Ashley Close, Welwyn Garden City, Herts AL8 7LH (☎ 0707 324 178); Bickerdike Allen Ptnrs, 121 Salusbury Rd, London NW6 6RG (☎ 01 625 4411, fax 01 625 0250, telex 263889)

ALLEN, Sir William Guilford; s of Sir William Guilford Allen, CBE (d 1977), and his 1 wife Mona Maree, *née* Nolan (d 1956); *b* 22 April 1932; *Career* director (of companies incl Qantas); grazier and cattle breeder; honoured for serv to bdcasting and pastoral indust; kt 1981; *Style*— Sir William Allen; Toorak House, Hamilton, Qld 4007, Australia

ALLEN, Maj-Gen William Maurice; CB (1983); s of William James Allen and Elizabeth Jane Henrietta Allen; *b* 29 May 1931; *m* 1956, Patricia Mary Fletcher; 1 da (decd); *Career* joined Army 1949, Dir-Gen Transport and Movements (Army) 1981-83, ret; dir of trg and educn Burroughs Machines Ltd 1983-85; conslt SDC/UNISYS 1985-, dir Fortis Aviation SA 1988-, dir European Mgmnt Information 1988-; *Recreations* rough shooting, economics, gardening, ocean cruising, squash, keeping fit; *Clubs* Overseas, City Livery, Bristol Channel YC; *Style—* Maj-Gen William Allen, CB; c/o Williams & Glyn's Bank Ltd, Holts Farnborough Branch, Lawrie House, 31-37 Victoria Rd, Farnborough, Hants

ALLEN OF ABBEYDALE, Baron (Life Peer UK 1976); Philip; GCB (1970), KCB (1964, CB 1954); yr s of Arthur Allen (d 1962), of Sheffield, and Louie, *née* Tipper; *b* 8 July 1912; *Educ* King Edward VII Sch Sheffield, Queens' Coll Cambridge (MA); *m* 1938, Marjorie Brenda, da of Thomas John Colton Coe (d 1944); *Career* sits as independent in House of Lords, second sec Treasy 1963-66, PUS Home Off 1966-72; memb Security Cmmn 1973-, chm Gaming Bd for GB 1977-85, memb Tbnl of Inquiry into Crown Agents 1978-82, Hon fell Cambridge; *Style—* Rt Hon Lord Allen of Abbeydale, GCB, KCB, CB; Holly Lodge, Englefield Green, Surrey TW20 0JP (☎ 0784 32291)

ALLEN-JONES, Charles Martin; s of Air Vice Marshall John Ernest Allen-Jones, CBE, of Dunmow, Essex, and Margaret Ena, *née* Rix (d 1974); *b* 7 August 1939; *Educ* Clifton Coll Bristol; *m* 25 June 1966, Caroline, da of Keith Beale, OBE (d 1979), of Woodchurch, Kent; 1 s (Christof b 1968), 2 da (Nichola b 1970, Anna b 1972); *Career* articled to Clerk to the Justices Uxbridge Magistrates Ct 1958-60, articled to Vizard Oldham Crowder and Cash 1960-63, slr Supreme Ct 1963, ptnr Linklaters and Paines 1968- (joined 1964, opened Hong Kong Off 1976-81), memb City Taxation Ctee 1973-75, Hong Kong Banking Advsy Ctee 1978-80; *Recreations* gardening, tennis, travel, reading; *Style—* Charles Allen-Jones, Esq; Barrington House, 59-67 Gresham St, London EC2V 7JA (☎ 01 606 7080, fax 01 606 5113, telex 884349)

ALLENBY, Hon Mrs (Claude) Bill; Barbara Marion; da of late John Hall, of Felpham, Sussex; *b* 12 June 1917; *m* 1951, as his 2 w, the Hon Claude William Hynman Allenby (d 1975), Lt-Col 11 Hussars (R of O), elected to Cavalry Club Ctee, TV commentator, dir and prodr 1948-75, Guild of TV Prodrs and Dirs Merit Award for prodn of current events 1961; bro of 2 Viscount Allenby; *Career* served WW II 4 MT WAAF; *Style—* The Hon Mrs C W H Allenby; 29 Hovedene, Cromwell Rd, Hove, Sussex

ALLENBY, 3 Viscount (UK 1919); Michael Jaffray Hynman Allenby; s of 2 Viscount Allenby (d 1984, s of Capt Frederick Allenby, CBE, JP, RN; n of 1 Viscount Allenby, GCB, GCMG, GCVO), and his 1 w (Gertrude) Mary Lethbridge, *née* Champneys (d 1988); *b* 20 April 1931; *Educ* Eton; *m* 29 July 1965, Sara Margaret, o da of Lt-Col Peter Milner Wiggin; 1 s; *Heir* s, Hon Henry Jaffray Hynman Allenby, b 29 July 1968; *Career* Lt-Col Royal Hussars; CO Royal Yeo 1974-77; *Clubs* Cavalry and Guards; *Style—* The Rt Hon the Viscount Allenby of Meggido; The House of Lords, Westminster, London SW1

ALLENBY, Rt Rev (David Howard) Nicholas; s of William Allenby (d 1944), of London, and Irene Lambert, *née* Spratly (d 1962); *b* 28 Jan 1909; *Educ* House of Sacred Mission, Kelham Theological Coll (MA Lambeth); *Career* deacon 1934, priest 1935, curate St Jude W Derby Liverpool 1934-36, tutor Kelham Theological Coll and public preacher Diocese of Southwell 1936-44, rector Averham with Kelham 1944-57, proctor in convocation Southwell 1950-57, editor Diocesan News and Southwell Review 1950-55, hon canon Southwell 1953-57, canon emeritus 1957-62, personal chaplain to bishop of Southwell 1954-57, rural dean Newark 1955-57, provincial of Soc of Sacred Mission in Australia 1957-62, bishop of Kuching (Sarawak Malaysia) 1962-68, asst bishop Diocese of Worcester 1968-; *Books* Pray with the Church (jtly 1937); *Recreations* reading, painting; *Clubs* Roy Cwlth Soc; *Style—* The Rt Rev Nicholas Allenby; 16 Woodbine Rd, Barbourne, Worcester WR1 3JB (☎ 0905 27980)

ALLENBY, Lt Cdr Roy Massingberd Pentreath Norfolk; s of Capt John Norfolk Allenby, OBE, RN (d 1941), of Lincs and Suffolk; *b* 6 July 1916; *Educ* Haileybury Coll 1930-33; *m* 28 Aug 1940, Mary Agnes Heamans 3rd offr WRNS, da of Lt Cdr Ernest Charles Heamans Johns, RN (d 1946); 3 s (Adrian b 1944, Rupert b 1946, Jonathan b 1953); *Career* Naval Cadet RN 1935, serv Mediterranean, Home Fleet Destroyers; sec to Admirals Sir Philip Vian and Sir William Tennant; WWII serv: Atlantic, USA, Africa, on staff of C in C Portsmouth D Day, HMS Illustrious, RN Coll Greenwich (ret 1950); *Recreations* golf, flyfishing, tennis, shooting, swimming, birdwatching, geneaological research; *Style—* Commander Allenby; Camerons, Castle Fraser, Sauchen, Inverurie, Aberdeenshire AB3 7JR

ALLENDALE, Viscountess; Hon Sarah Field; da of 1 Baron Ismay (d 1965); *b* 16 May 1928; *m* 1948, 3 Viscount Allendale; *Style—* The Rt Hon the Viscountess Allendale; Bywell Hall, Stocksfield-on-Tyne, Northumberland; Allenheads Hall, Allenheads, Northumberland

ALLENDALE, 3 Viscount (UK 1911); Wentworth Hubert Charles Beaumont; DL (Northumberland 1961); also Baron Allendale (UK 1906); s of 2 Viscount Allendale, KG, CB, CBE, MC (d 1956), and Violet (d 1979), da of Sir Charles Seely, 2 Bt; *b* 12 Sept 1922; *Educ* Eton; *m* 1948, Hon Sarah Ismay, da of Gen 1 Baron Ismay, KG, GCB, CH, DSO, PC; 3 s; *Heir* s, Hon Wentworth Beaumont; *Career* served WW II Fl-Lt RAFVR (POW); ADC to Viceroy of India 1946-47; Hon Air Cdre 3508 Northumberland; pres Northumberland & Durham Assoc Bldg Socs; OStJ; steward Jockey Club 1963-65; *Style—* The Rt Hon the Viscount Allendale, DL; Allenheads Hall, Allenheads, Hexham, Northumberland (☎ Allenheads 205); Bywell Hall, Stocksfield-on-Tyne, Northumberland

ALLERTON, 3 Baron (UK 1902); George William Lawies Jackson; s of 2 Baron (d 1925); *b* 23 July 1903; *Educ* Eton, RMC; *m* 1, 1926 (m dis 1934), Joyce (d 1953), da of John Hatfeild, of Thorp Arch Hall, Yorks; 1 s; m 2, 1934 (m dis 1947), Hope (d 1987), da of Allan Havelock-Allan sis of Sir Anthony Allan, 4 Bt, the film producer; m 3, 1947, Anne, da of James Montagu; 1 da (decd); *Career* Sqdn Ldr AAF ret; late Lt Coldstream Gds; *Recreations* golf, shooting; *Clubs* Politics, Turf, Pratt's; *Style—* The Rt Hon Lord Allerton; Loddington House, Leics

ALLERTON, Reginald John; CBE (1964); s of Robert Sterry Allerton (d 1924), of Lowestoft, and Mary Maria, *née* Bailey (d 1945); *b* 20 June 1898; *Educ* Municipal Secondary Sch of Higher Educn Lowestoft (passed Cambridge Univ Sch leaving exam); *m* 1924, Dorothy Rose, da of Arthur William Saunders (d 1949), boot and shoe retailer from Lowestoft; *Career* joined RNVR 1917, trained as wireless operator, served in mine sweeping vessels in Scottish waters, demobilised 1919, telegraphist; chartered surveyor; estates surveyor City of Norwich 1930-39; housing mangr: to City of Bristol 1939-51, City of Birmingham 1951-54; dir Housing to LCC 1954-63, ret; vice-pres Surrey and Sussex Rent Assessment Panel 1966-72; fndr memb Hanover Housing Assoc; memb Govt Ctee on Housing in London 1965; *Recreations* gardening; *Style—* R J Allerton, Esq, CBE; 10 Mill Mead, Wendover, Aylesbury, Bucks HP22 6BY (☎ (0296) 622691)

ALLETZHAUSER, Albert Joseph; s of Albert Joseph Alletzhauser, of Madison Connecticut, and Sydney Louise, *née* Best; *b* 5 Jan 1960; *Educ* Colgate Univ (BA); *m* 8 Aug 1988, Anne, da of Louis Wellington Cabot; *Career* head int dept Chintung Investmt Hong Kong 1984-85, ptnr James Capel & Co Tokyo 1986-88, pncpl investor & stockholder of Bloomsbury Publishing Ltd 1988-; memb Singapore Int Monetary Exchange 1987-, Milton Roy Award by American Mgt 1982; *Books* The House of Nomura (1989); *Style—* Albert Alletzhauser, Esq; 6 Holland Pk Rd, Kensington, London W14 8LZ

ALLEYNE, Rev Sir John Olpherts Campbell; 5 Bt (GB 1769), of Four Hills, Barbados; s of Capt Sir John Alleyne, 4 Bt, DSO, DSC, RN (d 1983), and Alice Violet Emily, *née* Campbell (d 1984); *b* 18 Jan 1928; *Educ* Eton, Jesus Cambridge (BA, MA); *m* 1968, Honor Emily Margaret, da of late William Albert Irwin, of Belfast; 1 s, 1 da; *Heir* s, Richard Meynell Alleyne b 23 June 1972; *Career* deacon 1955, priest 1956; rector of Weeke Winchester; *Recreations* sailing, mountain walking, astronomy; *Style—* The Rev Sir John Alleyne, Bt; The Rectory, Cheriton Rd, Winchester, Hants (☎ 0962 54849)

ALLFREY, Maj Henry John; s of Maj Henry Sydney Allfrey, JP, DL (d 1975), of The Grange, How Caple, Hereford, and Vera, *née* Hazlehurst (d 1965); *b* 30 Dec 1924; *Educ* Winchester; *m* 1, 18 May 1957 (m dis 1980), Jocelyne, da of Cdr The Hon Maurice Fitzroy-Newdegate (d 1974, of Arbury Hall, Nuneaton, Warwicks; 2 s (David, Charles), 1 da (Lucia); m 2, 18 Oct 1980, Sonia Elisabeth, da of Col Juan Beresford Hobbs (d 1978, of Easthorpe Hall, Kelvedon, Colchester, Essex; *Career* cmmnd RHA 1944, WWII 1945-46 India Malaya and Java, Staff Capt SE Asia Land Forces HQ 1946-48; regtl serv: airborne RHA, jr ldrs regt and Berks Yeo 1948-59, staff coll 1956, GSO II HQ 4 Infantry Divn 1957-59, GSO II Brig Author MOD 1959-61; dir Harp Lager (Southern) 1965-70, dir Courage (Central) 1967-69, dir Courage (Eastern) 1969-70, md Courage (Central) 1971-79, dir Courage (Brewing) 1973-80, dir Regd Charity in Age Res 1980-89 (res into ageing 1988-); vice chm and chm Wokingham Cons Assoc 1966-72, govr Elstree Sch 1975-88, fndr and patron Berks Retirement Assoc 1976-89, memb exec cncls Assoc of Med Res Charities, and Br Soc for Res into Ageing; FInstD, MInst Mktg, MInst Fund Raising Mangrs; *Books* from 1959-61: The Nuclear Land Battle, Keeping The Peace, Training For War; *Recreations* fishing, shooting, gardening; *Clubs* Boodles; *Style—* Maj John Allfrey; The Dower House Castle, Hedingham, nr Halstead, Essex CO9 3DG (☎ 0787 61108); 25B Wilton Row, London SW1; Research Into Ageing, 49 Queen Victoria St, London EC4N 4SA (☎ 01 236 4365)

ALLFREY, Hon Mrs (Jocelyne); *née* FitzRoy Newdegate; yr da of Cdr Hon John Maurice FitzRoy Newdegate, RN (d 1976), and sis of 3 Viscount Daventry, *qv*; raised to the rank of a Viscount's da 1988; *b* 13 July 1929; *m* 1, 26 July 1952 (annulled 1953), Richard John Barton, o s of Col John Seddon Barton, OBE, MC, TD, DL, of Glan-y-Wern Hall, Denbigh; m 2, 18 May 1957, Maj Henry John Allfrey, RA (ret), er s of Maj Henry Sydney Allfrey, JP, DL, of Bishop's Acre, Upton Bishop, Ross- on-Wye, Herefordshire; 2 s, 1 da; Four Acre House, West Green, Hartley Wintney, Hants

ALLGOOD, Joseph William Edwin; s of Joseph Philip Allgood (d 1938), and Blanche, *née* Strutt (d 1966); *b* 6 Jan 1922; *Educ* Spring Grove GS; *m* 24 Sept 1949, Ann Elizabeth, da of Richard Halsey, Richmond, Surrey (d 1955); 1 da (Suzanne b 1964), 1 steps (Geoffrey b 1945); *Career* WW II RA 1943-47; served: N Africa, Italy, Greece, Trieste, Germany; (despatches); jeweller, joined Cartier 1938, non exec dir and conslt Cartier Ltd 1986- (vice chm UK 1983-86, md 1976-); has held Royal Warrants for HM The Queen and HM Queen Elizabeth the Queen Mother on behalf of Cartier for last 10 years; chm Bond St Assoc 1981-83; FGA; *Recreations* golf; *Clubs* Royal Overseas League, Royal IOD; *Style—* Joseph W E Allgood, Esq; Cartier Ltd, 175/176 New Bond Street, London W1Y 0QA (☎ 01 493 6962)

ALLHUSEN, Hon Mrs (Claudia Violet); *née* Betterton; da of 1 Baron Rushcliffe, GBE, PC (d 1949) by his 1 w; *b* 11 Oct 1917; *m* 1937, Maj Derek Allhusen, CVO, DL, *qv*, s of Lt-Col Frederick Allhusen, CMG, DSO (d 1957); 1 s (Timothy Frederick m 1965 Annabel Morris) also 1 s decd, 1 da (Rosemary Claudia m 1973 Maj Jeremy Groves, 17/21 Lancers); *Recreations* riding; *Clubs* Army and Navy, Cavalry and Guards; *Style—* The Hon Mrs Allhusen; The Manor House, Claxton, Norwich (☎ 050843 228)

ALLHUSEN, Maj Derek Swithin; CVO (1984), DL (Norfolk 1969); s of Lt-Col Fredrick Allhusen, CMG, DSO (d 1957), of Fulmer House, Fulmer, Bucks, and Enid, *née* Swithinbank (d 1948); *b* 9 Jan 1914; *Educ* Eton, Chillon Coll Switzerland, Trinity Coll Cambridge (MA); *m* 28 April 1937, Hon Claudia Violet, *qv*, da of 1 and last Baron Rushcliffe, GBE, PC (d 1949); 1 s (Timothy b 1942), 1 da (Mrs Rosemary Groves b 1944) and 1 s decd (Michael d 1960); *Career* served WW II 9 Queen's Royal Lancers France 1940, (wounded) N Africa and Italy (wounded); farmer, High Sheriff Norfolk 1958, standard bearer Hon Corps of Gentlemen-at-Arms 1981-84 (one of HM's Body Guard of Hon Corps of Gentlemen at Arms 1963-84; chm Riding for the Disabled Norwich and Dist Gp 1968- (vice-pres Eastern Region); pres: Royal Norfolk Agric Assoc 1974, National Pony Soc 1982, British Horse Soc 1986-; Freeman City of London, Hon Freeman Worshipful Co of Farriers 1969, Yeoman Worshipful Co of Saddlers; represented Great Britain: Winter Pentathlon Olympic Games 1948, equestrian team Mexico Olympics 1968 (individual silver, team gold), Br Olympic Equestrian Team Munich 1972, Equestrianism European Championships Three-Day Event 1957, 1959, 1965, 1967, 1969; Silver Star Medal (USA); *Recreations* riding, shooting, skiing; *Clubs* Cavalry and Guards', Army and Navy; *Style—* Maj Derek Allhusen, CVO, DL; Manor House, Claxton, Norwich, Norfolk (☎ 050843 228)

ALLHUSEN, Lt-Col Richard Christian; s of Lt Col F H Allhusen, CMG, DSO (d 1957), of Bucks, and Enid, *née* Swithinbank (d 1948); *b* 16 Mar 1910; *Educ* Eton Coll, Trinity Coll Cambridge; *m* 25 June 1950, Evelyn Jane, da of Lt Col Sir Richard Chenevix Trench, CIE, OBE (d 1954); 2 s (Christian Henry b 1956, Richard Frederick b 1960), 2 da (Elizabeth Mary b 1952, Rosalind Jane b 1954); *Career* served WW II, adj Lovat Scouts, gen staff offr 2 Scottish Cmd Staff Coll Camberley, Lt Col Admg 21 Army Gp; landowner, farmer; *Recreations* skiing, shooting, arboriculture; *Clubs* Bucks, Army & Navy, MCC; *Style—* Lt-Col Richard C Allhusen; Bradenham Hall, Thetford, Norfolk IP25 7QP (☎ 036 287 279)

ALLIBONE, Professor Thomas Edward; CBE (1960); s of Henry J Allibone (d

1936), of Sheffield, and Eliza, *née* Kidger (d 1941), of Kedleston; *b* 11 Nov 1903; *Educ* Sheffield Univ (Birley and Linley scholar, BSc, MSc, DSc, PhD), Gonville and Caius Coll Cambridge (PhD); *m* 1931, Dorothy Margery Ward, da of Frederick Boulden (d 1955) 2 da (Daphne, Noreen); *Career* i/c High-voltage Res Laboratory Metropolitan Vickers Elec Co Manchester 1930-46, Br team in USA developing the atomic bomb 1944-45; dir: Assoc Electrical Industs Ltd Res Lab 1946-63, Res and Educn Assoc Electrical Industs Ltd Woolwich 1955-63; chief scientist CEGB 1963-70, external prof Elec Engrg Dept Leeds 1961-79 (emeritus ext prof), visiting prof physics City Univ 1971-, Robert Kitchin Sadlers res prof City; Lord of the Manor Aldermaston 1953-85; tstee Br Museum, govr Down House, chm govrs Reading Tech Coll; pres Elec Indust Benevolent Assoc 1959; Freeman City of London, memb Ct Worshipful Co of Broderers; FRS 1948, FEng 1976 (Hon FIEE 1988),; *Publications* numerous scientific papers, books, Atomic Energy, Rutherford the Father of Atomic Energy, The Electric Spark (contrib), Cockcroft and the Atom, The Royal Society and its Dining Clubs, Cambridge Physics in the Thirties, Gabor and Holography; *Recreations* writing, history, gardening, philately; *Clubs* Royal Soc Dining; *Style*— Prof Thomas Edward Allibone, FRS; York Cottage, Winkfield, Windsor SL4 2ES (☎ 0344 884501)

ALLINSON, Sir (Walter) Leonard; KCVO (1979), MVO (1961, CMG 1976); s of Walter Allinson (d 1965), and Alice Frances, *née* Cassidy; *b* 1 May 1926; *Educ* Friern Barnet GS, Merton Coll Oxford (MA), Royal Coll of Defence Studies; *m* 1951, Margaret Patricia, *née* Watts; 3 da (incl twins); *Career* dep high cmmr Kenya 1972-73, RCDS 1974, dep high cmmr and min New Delhi 1975-78, high cmmr Lusaka 1978-80, asst under sec (Africa) FCO 1980-82, Br high cmmr Kenya 1982-86 (ret); vice-pres Royal African Soc 1982-; memb Cncl Br Inst for E Africa 1988-; *Recreations* reading, collecting driftwood, rough gardening; *Clubs* Oriental; *Style*— Sir Leonard Allinson, KCVO, MVO, CMG; c/o National Westminster Bank, 6 Tothill St, London SW1H 9ND

ALLIOTT, George Beckles; s of Hon Sir John Downes Alliott, and Lady Patsy Jennifer, *née* Beckles-Willson; *b* 10 Dec 1958; *Educ* Charterhouse, Warwick Univ (LLB); *m* 4 Feb 1989, Catherine Margaret, da of Anthony Coles;; *Career* Lt Coldstream Gds 1981-84; called to the Bar Inner Temple 1981, practising barrister 1985-; *Recreations* hunting, shooting, apiculture; *Style*— George Alliott, Esq; 82 Margravine Gardens, London W6 8RJ (☎ 01 741 0007); 2 Harcourt Bdgs, Temple, London EC4 (☎ 01 583 9020)

ALLIOTT, Hon Mr Justice; Hon Sir John Downes Alliott; s of Alexander Clifford Alliott (d 1967) and Ena Kathleen, *née* Downes (now Ellson); *b* 9 Jan 1932; *Educ* Charterhouse, Peterhouse Cambridge (BA); *m* 1957, Patsy Jennifer, da of late Gordon Beckles Willson; 2 s (George b 1958, Julian b 1968), 1 da (Katharine b 1967); *Career* cmmnd Coldstream Gds 1950-51; barr Inner Temple 1955; dep chm E Sussex QS 1970-71; recorder of Crown Ct 1972-86; QC 1973; bencher Inner Temple 1980; ldr South Eastern Circuit 1983-86; memb Home Off Advsy Bd on Restricted Patients 1983-86; judge of the High Court of Justice Queen's Bench Division 1986; presiding judge South Eastern Circuit 1989-; *Recreations* rural pursuits, France, Italy, mil history; *Style*— The Hon Mr Justice Alliott; Royal Courts of Justice, Strand, London WC1

ALLISON, (Samuel) Austin; s of Dr Samuel Allison, of Stedham, W Sussex, and Helen Burns Brighton, *née* Wilson; *b* 30 June 1947; *Educ* Liverpool Coll, Wadham Coll Oxford (BA, BCL); *m* 5 June 1971, June, da of the late Henry Edward Brassington, of Crofton, Kent; 2 s (Giles b 1973, Jonathan b 1975); *Career* barr Middle Temple 1969, private practice at the Bar 1970-87, gp compliance offr Standard Chartered Bank 1987-; memb: Ctee of London and Scottish Bankers (legal ctee, investmt regulation ctee), The Securities Assocs Panel of Arbitrators; *Recreations* the turf; *Style*— Austin Allison, Esq; 47 Elmfield Ave, Teddington, Middx TW11 8BX; 38 Bishopsgate, London EC2N 4DE (☎ 01 280 7165)

ALLISON, Air Vice-Marshal Dennis; CB (1987); s of George Richardson Allison (d 1951), and Joan Anne Sarah, *née* Little (d 1949); *b* 15 Oct 1932; *Educ* RAF Halton, RAF Coll Cranwell; *m* 16 June 1964, Rachel Anne, da of Air Vice-Marshal John Gerald Franks, CB, CBE, of Schull, Co Cork, Ireland; 1 s (Peter b 1970), 4 da (Jennifer b 1965, Susan b 1965, Rosemary b 1967, Rachel b 1970); *Career* No 87 Sqdn RAF 1955-58; flying instr and coll adjt Cranwell 1959-61; Sqdn Ldr 1961; OC RAF Sharjah 1961-62; OC Standards Sqdn RAF Strubby 1962-64; Indian Defence Services Staff Coll 1964-65; Wing Cdr 1965; staff HQ 224 Gp Singapore 1965-68; MOD Central Staffs 1968-70; OC Flying Wing RAF Bruggen 1970-72; Nat Defence Coll 1972-73; MOD Central Staffs 1973-74; Gp Capt 1974; OC RAF Coningsby 1974-76; Canadian Nat Defence Coll 1976-77; MOD Central Staffs 1977-79; Air Cdre 1979; cmdt Central Flying School 1979-83; dir flying trg MOD 1983-85; Air Vice-Marshal 1985; dir of Management and Support of Intelligence 1985-86; regnl gen mangr N Western RHA 1987-; govr Salford Coll of Technology; memb Nat Health Service Training Athy, standing ctee on Post-graduate Educn; Queen's Commendation for Valuable Services in the Air 1959; *Recreations* golf, bridge; *Clubs* RAF; *Style*— Air Vice-Marshal Dennis Allison, CB; The Old Forge, Castle Bytham, Grantham, Lincs NG33 4RV (☎ 078 081 372); Gateway House, Piccadilly South, Manchester M60 7LP (☎ 061 237 6324)

ALLISON, Rt Rev Doctor (Sherard) Falkner; s of William Sherard Allison (d 1931), and Emily Beatrice Allison, *née* Wheeler (d 1970); *b* 19 Jan 1907; *Educ* Dean Close Sch Cheltenham, Jesus Coll Cambridge (MA, DD, LLD); *m* 1936, Ruth, da of Henry Hills (d 1950); 2 s (Sherard, Anthony (decd)), 2 da (Rosamund, Philippa); *Career* princ Ridley Hall Cambridge 1945-50; bishop of Chelmsford 1951-61, bishop of Winchester and prelate of the Most Noble Order of the Garter 1961-74; hon fellow Jesus Coll Cambridge 1963; *Recreations* sailing, water colour sketching, bird watching; *Clubs* Utd Oxford and Cambridge Univ; *Style*— Rt Rev Dr Falkner Allison; Winton Lodge, Aldeburgh, Suffolk (☎ 072885 2485)

ALLISON, John; CBE (1975), DL (1975, JP 1966); s of Thomas William Allison (d 1974), and Margaret Allison, *née* Grey (d 1978); *b* 4 Oct 1919; *Educ* Glanmor Sec Sch, Swansea Tech Coll; *m* 12 April 1948, Elvira Gwendoline, da of William Evan Lewis (d 1945); 1 s (Richard Thomas William b 12 Aug 1956), 2 da (Susan Margaret b 12 May 1949, Jillian b 15 May 1955); *Career* dir: Picton Music Ltd 1969-, Swansea Sound 1974-, Municipal and Mutual Insur Ltd 1982-, Swansea Cork Ferry Co Ltd; memb Swansea County BC Cncl 1957-73, ldr City Authy 1967-73, dep Mayor 1966-67 and 1972-73; memb West Glamorgan Co Cncl 1973- (chm 1975-76, ldr 1979-), memb Assoc of Co Cncls 1973-, chm Assoc of Co Cncls 1986-87 and 1987-88; chm South Wales Police Authy 1987-89; contested Barry Constituency (L) 1970; *Recreations* gardening, fishing, golf; *Clubs* The Royal Overseas League (London), Morriston Golf (local); *Style*— John Allison, CBE, DL, JP; 155 Vicarage Rd, Morriston, Swansea SA6 6DT (☎ 0792 71331)

ALLISON, Ronald William Paul; CVO (1978); only s of Percy Allison, and Dorothy, *née* Doyle; *b* 26 Jan 1932; *Educ* Weymouth GS, Taunton's Sch Southampton; *m* 1956, Maureen Angela Macdonald; 2 da; *Career* BBC reporter/corr 1957-73; press sec to HM The Queen 1973-78; md Ronald Allison & Assocs 1978-80; presenter Thames TV 1978-, controller of Sport and Outside Broadcasts Thames TV 1980-85; dir, corporate affrs, Thames TV 1986-; *Books* Look Back in Wonder (1968), The Queen (1973), Charles, Prince of our Time (1978), Britain in the Seventies (1980); *Clubs* RAC; *Style*— Ronald Allison, Esq, CVO; c/o Thames TV, 306 Euston Rd, London NW1 3BB

ALLISON, Shaun Michael; s of Lt Cdr Jorgen Leslie William Michael Allison, of White Cottage, Beenham, Berks (d 1983); and Honoria Brenda, *née* Magill; *b* 12 Jan 1944; *Educ* Rugby Sch; *m* 14 Sept 1968, Lucy Howard Douglas, *née* Gray, da of Lt Col Charles Robert Douglas Gray, of Chilcombe, Greywell, Basingstoke, Hants; 2 s (Michael Douglas b 1971, Charles Howard b 1977); 1 da (Sophie Louise b 1976); *Career* stockbroker memb 1967; ptnr Hoare Govett Ltd 1978-85; *Recreations* skiing, shooting, sailing; *Clubs* City of London; *Style*— Shaun M Allison, Esq; Three Oaks, Bramshill, Basingstoke, Hants (☎ 0734 326 270); Hoare Govett Ltd, 4 Broadgate, London EC2 (☎ 01 601 0101)

ALLISON, Dr Wade William Magill; s of Jorgen Lt Cdr (Lesley William) Michael Allison, RN (d 1983), and Honoria Brenda, *née* Magill; *b* 23 April 1941; *Educ* Rugby, Trinity Coll Cambridge (MA), Christchurch Oxford (MA, DPhil); *m* 1, 9 Sept 1967 (m dis 1988), Sarah Jane, *née* Pallin; 1 s (Thomas b 1977), 3 da (Emma b and d 1968, Harriet b 1972, Rachel b 1974); m 2, 6 Dec 1988, Marilyn Frances (Kate), *née* Easterbrook; *Career* Oxford Univ: res offr Nuclear Physics Laboratory 1970-75, lectr Christchurch Coll 1973-75 (res lectr 1966-71), Univ lectr 1976-, sr tutor Keble Coll 1985-89 (tutorial fell 1976-); numerous papers and articles on elementary particle physics and experimental methods; fell Royal Cmmn for the Exhibition of 1851 1966-68; *Recreations* sailing, motoring; *Style*— Dr Wade Allison; Southfields, Ludgershall, Aylesbury, Bucks HP18 9PB (☎ 0844 237 602); Keble Coll, Oxford; Nuclear Physics Laboratory, Oxford (☎ 0865 272 734, fax 0865 273 418)

ALLMAN, Bryan; s of Leslie Allman (d 1976), and Ann, *née* Perkin (d 1978); *b* 12 Sept 1929; *Educ* Roundhay Sch Leeds; *m* 14 Sept 1957, Audrey, da of Arther Pollitt (d 1936); 1 s (Christopher John b 7 Aug 1961); *Career* Nat Serv in H M RM 1947-49; clerk Burton Gp 1945-51, semi sr audit clerk Blackburn Robson Coates & Co CAs 1952-55, chief accountant Darley Mills Gp Ltd 1955-62, fin dir Yorks Hut Co Ltd 1963-64, gp accountant Arthur Johnson (Paper) Ltd 1965-71, chief exec Gower Hldgs plc 1972-; FCCA; *Recreations* golf, walking; *Clubs* Scarcroft (Leeds); *Style*— Bryan Allman, Esq; Grey Gables, Ash Hill La, Shadwell, Leeds (☎ 0532 737 137); Gower Hldgs plc, Holmfield Industrial Estate, Halifax, HX2 9TN (☎ 0422 246 201, fax 0422 249 932, telex 517396)

ALLOM, Maurice (James Carrick); s of Gilbert Fox Allom (d 1953), ggs Thomas Allom 19th artist and architect who assisted Sir Charles Barry particularly on Houses of Parliament, and his wife Mary Constance, *née* Billin; *b* 23 Mar 1906; *Educ* Wellington Coll, Trinity Coll Cambridge (BA); *m* 1, 1934, Elizabeth Pamela, da of Oswald Thomas Norris, CBE (d 1973); 2 s (Anthony b 1938, Thomas b 1946), 1 da (Elizabeth b 1942); m 2, 1983, Audrey Estelle Liufling, da of Henry John Hydé-Johnson (d 1945); *Career* served WW II Wing-Cdr RAF 1939-45; dir: Allom Lighting Ltd 1928-82, Debenham Coe & Co Ltd 1946-75; played cricket for Surrey CC and England; memb MCC touring side: NZ 1929-30, SA 1930-31; notable performance of 4 wickets in 5 balls (inc hat-trick) in 1st Test against NZ 1930; pres: MCC 1969-70, Surrey CC 1970-77; *Books* (with Maurice Turnbull) The Book of the Two Maurices, The Two Maurices Again; *Clubs* cricket, golf

ALLOTT, Air Cdre Molly Greenwood; CB (1975); da of late Gerald William Allott; *b* 28 Dec 1918; *Educ* Sheffield HS for Girls; *Career* joined WAAF 1941, served WW II Fighter and Coastal Cmmd Supply branch 1944; appts: Egypt 1945-47, Singapore 1948-50; staff: of AOC in C RAF Germany 1960-63, AOC Fighter Cmmd 1963-66, Trg Cmmd 1971-73, dir WRAF 1973-76, ADC 1973-76; nat chm Girls Venture Corps 1977-83; cncl memb: Union Jack Club 1976, Main Grants Ctee and Educn Ctee RAF Benevolent Fund 1976-84; FBIM; *Recreations* foreign travel, decorative fine arts; *Clubs* RAF, Royal Lymington Yacht; *Style*— Air Cdre Molly Allott, CB; 15 Camden Hurst, Milford-on-sea, Lymington, Hants SO41 0WL

ALLPORT, Denis Ivor; s of late A Allport and E M, *née* Mashman; *b* 20 Nov 1922; *Educ* Highgate Sch; *m* 1949, Diana, *née* Marler; 2 s, 1 da; *Career* served WW II Indian Army; Metal Box plc: dir 1973, md 1977-79, chief exec 1977-, dep chm 1979, chm 1979-; memb Nat Enterprise Bd 1980-; dir Beecham Gp 1981-; FBIM; *Style*— Denis Allport, Esq; Elm Place, Mumbery Hill, Wargrave, Reading, Berks RG10 8EE (☎ (073 522) 3007)

ALLSEBROOK, Peter Winder; CBE (1987), DL (1986); s of Wilton Allsebrook, JP (d 1950), of Skegby Hall, Notts, and Charlotte, *née* Cole (d 1960); *b* 4 Nov 1917; *Educ* Fettes, Caen Univ France, BNC Oxford; *m* 10 Jan 1940, Elizabeth, da of Ulrich Rissik; 3 s (Antony b 1948, Christopher b 1950 (d 1981), Simon b 1962), 2 da (Charlotte b 1953, Katharine b 1957); *Career* enlisted RN 1939, transferred Army, captured Western Desert, POW escaped (despatches), demobbed Lt-Col; TNT Gp: chm TNT (UK) Ltd, dir TNT Ltd, chm TNT Express (UK) Ltd, chm TNT Sealion Ltd, dir numberous subsids; chm: Truckline Ferries Poole Ltd (former dep chm and dir), Dorset Enterprise Agency Ltd, Handling Conslts (Pty) Ltd, Imprefed (Pty) Ltd, Trans Channel Ferries Ltd, West of England Crafts Ltd; dir: A H Moody & Son Ltd, Collins Motor Corpn Ltd; md Seeatic Marine Ltd; chm: Dorset Employers' Network (LENS), Dorset Enterprise Agency; dir and former pres The Dorset C of C and Indust, vice pres Red Cross Soc (Dorset branch), memb Television SW Indust Advsy Bd; govr: Clayesmore Sch, Poole GS; FRSA 1967, CBIM, FCIT; Médaille d'Honneur, Queen's Award for Industry; *Recreations* sailing; *Clubs* Carlton, Oriental, Achilles, RNSA, Yacht Club de France, Royal Motor Yacht; *Style*— Peter Allsebrook, Esq, CBE, DL; Milton Mill, West Milton, Bridport, Dorset (☎ 030 885391); West Milton, Bridport, Dorset (☎ 030 885432/453, telex 418370 TNT UK G, fax 030 885 280)

ALLSOP, Peter Henry Bruce; CBE (1984); s of late Herbert Henry Allsop, and Elsie Hilpern, *née* Whitaker; *b* 22 August 1924; *Educ* Haileybury, Caius Coll Cambridge (MA); *m* 1950, Patricia Elizabeth Kingwell Bown; 2 s, 1 da; *Career* barr Lincoln's Inn 1948; chm Sweet & Maxwell 1974- (ed 1950-59, dir 1960-64, md 1965-73); md Associated Book Publishers 1968-76, chm 1976-87 (dir 1963, asst mangr 1965-67, chief exec to 1982); memb cncl Publishers' Assoc (tres 1973-75, 1979-81; pres 1975-77, vice pres 1977-78), chm Teleordering Ltd 1978-; dir: J Whitaker & Son Ltd 1987-; publishing conslt PUMA 1983-; tstee Yale UP 1981-, vice chm 1984-; chm Book Trade Ben Soc 1986-; chm King's Coll Taunton 1986-, dir Woodard Schs (Western Divn) Ltd 1985-; FRSA, FBIM; *Style—* Peter Allsop, Esq; Manor Farm, Charlton Mackrell, Somerton, Somerset (☎ 045 822 3650)

ALLSOPP, (Harold) Bruce; s of Henry Allsopp (d 1953), and Elizabeth May, *née* Robertson; *b* 4 July 1912; *Educ* Manchester GS, Liverpool Univ Sch of Architecture (BArch); *m* 1935, (Florence) Cyrilla Woodroffe; 2 s; *Career* served WW II RE, N Africa and Italy, Capt RE; author, artist, historian; chm: Oriel Press Ltd 1962-87, Independent Publishers Guild 1971-72; dir Routledge & Kegan Paul Books 1974-86; fndr-memb and chm Soc of Architectural Historians of GB 1959-65, reader history of architecture Newcastle Univ 1973-77, occasional TV presenter; master Artworkers Guild 1970; ARIBA, AMTPI, FRIBA, FSA; *Books* include: Decoration and Furniture (Vol 1 1952, Vol 2 1953), A General History of Architecture (1955), The Future of the Arts (1959), A History of Renaissance Architecture (1959), Architecture of France (1963), Architecture (1964), Architecture of Italy (1964), Architecture of England (1964), A history of Classical Architecture (1965), The Great Tradition of Western Architecture (1965), The Great Tradition of Western Architecture (1966), Civilization, The Next Stage (1969), Historic Architecture of Northumberland (1969), Modern Architecture of Northern England (1970), Romanesque Architecture (1971), Ecological Morality (1972), Towards a Humane Architecture (1974), Return of the Pagan (1974), Cecilia (1975), Inigo Jones and the Lords A'Leaping (1975), Historic Architecture of Northumberland and Newcastle 91977), English Architecture (with U Clark and H W Booton 1979), Appeal to the Gods (1980), The Country Life Companion to British and European Architecture (1985), Social Responsibility and the Responsible Society (1985), Guide de l'Arechitechere (1985), Larousse Guide to European Architecture (with Ursula Clark 1985), articles in Encyclopedia Americana, Encyclopaedia Britannica; *Recreations* music, gardening; *Clubs* Athenaeum; *Style—* Bruce Allsopp, Esq; Woodburn, 3 Batt House Rd, Stocksfield, Northumberland NE43 7QZ (☎ 0661 842323, studio: 0661 843065)

ALLSOPP, Hon Charles Henry; s and h of 5 Baron Hindlip, *qv*; *b* 5 August 1940; *Educ* Eton; *m* 18 April 1968, Fiona Victoria Jean Atherley, da of late Hon William Johnston McGowan, 2 s of 1 Baron McGowan; 1 s, 2 da; *Career* late Lt Coldstream Gds; chm Christles UK; dir Christles plc; *Recreations* painting, shooting; *Clubs* White's, Pratt's; *Style—* The Hon Charles Allsopp; The Cedar House, Inkpen, Berks; 63 Victoria Rd London W8.

ALLSOPP, Hon Elizabeth Tulla; da of 4 Baron Hindlip (d 1966); *b* 20 June 1942; *Style—* The Hon Elizabeth Allsopp

ALLSOPP, Hon John Peter; s of 5 Baron Hindlip; *b* 16 Nov 1942; *Educ* Eton; *m* 1976, Daryl, da of Leonard Shawzin, of Huisinbois, Constantia, CP, S Africa; 1 s, 1 da; *Style—* The Hon John Allsopp

ALLSOPP, Michael Edward Ranulph; s of Samuel Ranulph Allsopp, CBE (d 1975) of Stansted, Essex and Hon Norah Hyacinthe, *née* Littleton; *b* 9 Oct 1930; *Educ* Eton; *m* 1953, Patricia Ann, da of Geoffrey H Berners (d 1972) of Faringdon, Oxon; 4 da (Frances Jane Berners (Mrs David Woodd) b 1956, Carolyn Ann Berners b 1957, Davina Hyacinth Berners (m, 1987, Sir Nicholas Powell, 4 Bt, *qv*) b 1960, Jessica Elizabeth Berners, twin, (Mrs Edward Leigh Pemberton) b 1960); *Career* Subaltern 7 QOH Capt Royal Wilts Yeo (TA); chm: Allen Harvey & Ross Ltd 1968-79, Allied Dunbar & Co Ltd 1979-86, Granville Tst, Granville & Co Ltd, Baronsmead Venture Capital, Strata Investmts, Berners Allsopp Estate Mgmnt Co, Condon Discount Mkt Assoc 1974-76; *Recreations* foxhunting, Master of Old Berks Hounds 1960-81; *Clubs* White's, Pratt's, Cavalry & Guards; *Style—* Michael Allsopp, Esq; Little Coxwell Grove, Faringdon, Oxon SN7 7LW (☎ 0367 20 580, office 0367 20 138, car tel 0836 275 164)

ALLSOPP, Hon Mrs - Hon Norah Hyacinthe; *née* Littleton; da of 4 Baron Hatherton (d 1944); *b* 19 July 1899; *m* 1923, Samuel Ranulph Allsopp, CBE (d 1975); *Style—* The Hon Mrs Allsopp; Alsa Lodge, Stansted, Essex

ALLUM, Geoffrey Michael; s of Donald James Allum, and Brenda Mary, *née* Morgan; *b* 12 Oct 1957; *Educ* Hampton Sch, Univ of Aston (BSc), Manchester Business Sch (Dip Business Admin); *m* 31 May 1986, Amanda Jane, da of John Grierson Fleming; *Career* investmt analyst Fielding, Newson-Smith & Co 1982-86, assoc dir County Natwest 1986-; *Recreations* golf, skiing, reading; *Style—* Geoffrey Allum, Esq; County Natwest, Drapers Gardens, 12 Throgmorton Ave, London EC2P 2ES (☎ 01 382 1576, fax 01 382 1001, telex 916041)

ALLWARD, Lt-Col (Denis Raymond) Stewart; owner and restorer of Castle Stalker in Argyllshire. The Castle, which derives its name from the Gaelic 'Eilean na Stalcaire' (Island of the Deer Hunter), was last used as a residence, by Campbell of Airds, in the early eighteenth century and became a garrison for Hanoverian soldiers during the last Jacobite Rising; s of Frank Leonard Allward and Daisy Ellen Allward; *b* 18 Nov 1915; *Educ* Friends Sch Saffron Walden, London Univ (LLB); *m* 1946, Marion, da of John Dunlop; 2 s, 2 da; *Career* HAC 1933-39, served 1939-45, Europe, Gordon Highlanders, London Scottish; slr; *Clubs* HAC, London Scottish; *Style—* Lt-Col Stewart Allward; Allward & Son, 65 Westhall Road, Warlingham, Surrey CR3 9YE (☎ 08832 2768); Castle Stalker, Loch Laich, Appin, Argyllshire (☎ Appin 063 173 234)

ALMENT, Sir (Edward) Anthony (John); s of Edward and Alice Alment; *b* 3 Feb 1922; *Educ* Marlborough, St Bart's Hosp; *m* 1946, Elizabeth Innes Bacon; *Career* (MRCS, LRCP, FRCOG MRCOG 1951, memb Cncl RCOG 1961-67, hon sec 1968-73, pres 1978-81, FRCPI 1979, FRCP Ed 1981, FRCGP 1982; FRACOG 1985) conslt obstetrician and gynaecologist Northampton 1960-85, prev with Bart's, Norfolk and Norwich, Queen Charlotte's and Chelsea Hosp for Women, and London Hospitals; former memb Oxford Regnl Hosp Bd and chm Medical Advsy Ctee; memb: Oxford RHA 1973-75, UK Central Cncl for Nursing Midwifery and Health Visiting 1980-83; Hon DSc (Leicester) 1982; kt 1980; *Books* Competance to Practice (jty 1976), various articles on medical and wine subjects; *Recreations* engineering, fishing, wine; *Style—* Sir Anthony Alment; Winston House, Boughton, Northampton NN2 8RR

ALMOND, (Thomas) Clive; OBE (1989); s of Thomas Almond (d 1976), and Eveline, *née* Moss (d 1986); *b* 30 Nov 1939; *Educ* Bristol GS; *m* 4 Sept 1965, Auriol Gala Elizabeth Annette, da of Dr H C Hendry; *Career* joined Dip Serv 1967: FO 1967-68 and 1975-78, high comm Accra 1968-71, Paris Embassy 1971-75, Brussels Embassy 1978-80, Jakarta Embassy 1980-83, HM ambass Brazzaville Embassy 1983-88 (chargé d'affaires 1983-87), asst marshal of the Dip Corps FO 1988-; *Recreations* travel, golf; *Style—* Clive Almond, Esq, OBE; c/o FCO, King Charles St, London SW1A 2AH (☎ 01 210 6402)

ALMOND, David William; s of George Sydney Almond, of Lymington, Hants, and Madge Lilian, *née* Skegg; *b* 24 Oct 1945; *Educ* Purley GS Surrey; *m* 6 June 1970, Elizabeth (Liz), da of Percy Thomas Bisby (d 1978), of Aldwick, Sussex; 2 da (Amanda Jane b 25 Feb 1974, Juliette b 7 March 1977); *Career* CA; articles City of London 1962-67, ptnr Alliott Bullimore (formerly Evans Peirson) 1969-; chm: Alliot Peirson Assocs 1974-86, Alliott Peirson Int 1979-; dir Accounting Firms Assoc Inc 1982-; chm: Croydon Soc CA 1979-80 (sec 1975-79), Storrington Rural Preservation Soc; tres Pulborough and W Chiltington Scout and Guide Gp; Freeman City of London 1976, memb ct of Assts Worshipful Co Coachmakers and Coach Harness Makers 1977, Liveryman Worshipful Co of CA's 1980; FCA 1967, ATII 1967, FBIM 1978; *Recreations* sailing, Gardening; *Clubs* City Livery; *Style—* David Almond, Esq; Fryern Place, Storrington, West Sussex RH20 4HG (☎ 09066 3030); Alliot Bullimore, Canterbury House, Sydenham Rd, Croydon, Surrey CR9 2DG (☎ 01 681 6926, fax 01 680 3650)

ALMOND, Martin John; s of Stanley Wilton Almond, and Helen Prescott, *née* Baron (d 1979); *b* 8 May 1946; *Educ* Brookby Coll of Agric; *m* 12 Dec 1970, Elizabeth Enid; 2 da (Jennifer b 1977, Susan b 1979); *Career* CA; ptnr: H.R Davison & Co 1978-, Robert Parkinson & Co 1981-, Abbey Nursing Homes 1986-; dir Comparative Business Info Ltd 1983-; FCA 1973; *Recreations* walking, gardening; *Clubs* Royal Overseas; *Style—* Martin Almond, Esq; Kingswood House, Buckfastleigh, Devon TQ11 0BL; 100 Queen St, Newton Abbot, Devon TQ12 2E9 (☎ 0626 52 433)

ALPORT, Baron (Life Peer UK 1961); Cuthbert James McCall Alport; TD (1949), PC (1960), DL (Essex 1974); s of Prof Arthur Cecil Alport, (d 1958); *b* 22 Mar 1912; *Educ* Haileybury, Pembroke Cambridge; *m* 1945, Rachel (d 1983), da of Lt-Col Ralph Bingham, CVO, DSO (s of Maj-Gen Sir Cecil Bingham GVCO, KCMG, himself 2 s of 4 Earl of Lucan, KP, JP); 1 s, 2 da; *Career* served WW II Lt-Col (GSO 1 E Africa 1944-45); barr; MP (C) Colchester 1950-61, Min of State CRO 1959-61, high cmmr Fedn of Rhodesia and Nyasaland 1961-63; sits as ind Cons in Lords, dep speaker House of Lords 1971-; advsr to Home Sec 1974-83; high steward Colchester 1967-; *Clubs* Pratt's, Farmers; *Style—* The Rt Hon the Lord Alport, PC, TD, DL; The Cross House, Layer de la Haye, Colchester, Essex (☎ 0206 34 217)

ALPORT, Hon (Arthur) Edward Bingham; only s of Baron Alport, TD, PC (Life Peer), *qv*; *b* 22 May 1954; *Educ* Haileybury, Exeter Univ (BSc); *m* 1979, Anne Vivian, er da of Patrick Alexander Grove-White, of Crown Piece, Wormingford, Colchester; 1 s (Robert Michael Bingham b 1983); 1 da (Catherine Rachel b 1985); *Career* deputy Lloyd's underwriter; ACII 1979; *Recreations* music, writing; *Style—* The Hon Edward Alport; Huckleberry, Church Street, Boxted, Colchester, Essex CO4 5SX

ALSTEAD, Prof Stanley; CBE (1960); s of Robert Alstead, OBE, JP (d 1946), and (Sarah) Ann, *née* Deakin, JP (d 1960); *b* 6 June 1905; *Educ* Wigan GS, Univ of Liverpool (MB, ChB, MD), Univ of Glasgow; *m* 1, 27 July 1932, Nora (d 1980), da of Matthew William Sowden (d 1961), of Cambria, Whitchurch, Shropshire; 1 s (Allan b 1935); m 2, 15 Sept 1982 (Jessie) Janet McAlpine, da of Louis Pope (d 1924), of Bethshean, Cleland, Lanarkshire; *Career* emergency cmmn RAMC 1942-46, Maj med specialist casualty clearing station UK, N Africa, Italy (despatches), Lt Col offr i/c med div Gen Hosp Italy and Egypt; Hon Lt-Col RAMC 1946; jnr clinical appts English Midlands 1929-32, Pollok lectr in pharmacology Univ of Glasgow 1932, physician Highlands and Islands Scotland 1947-48, regius prof of materia medica Univ of Glasgow 1948-70, sr physician Stobhill Gen Hosp Glasgow 1948-70, hon prof and physician Kenyatta Nat Hosp Univ of E Africa 1965-66; memb: bd of mgmnt Glasgow Northern Hosps 1948-52, Br Pharmacopoeia Cmmn 1953-57, Standin Ctee on Classification of Proprietary Preparations; jt pres Soc of Friends of Dunblane Cathedral; FRCPS 1979, FRS Ed, FRCP Lond, FRCP Ed, FRCPS; *Books* jt ed 3 textbooks on pharmacology and therapeutics (1936-70); *Recreations* classical music, English literature; *Clubs* Coll (Glasgow), RSAC; *Style—* Prof Stanley Alstead, CBE; Glenholme, Glen Rd, Dunblane, Perthshire FK15 0DJ (☎ 0786 822 466)

ALSTON, Albert Edward Constable; TD (1947), DL (Essex 1958); s of Edward Constable Alston, of Wingfield Hall, Suffolk; *b* 22 Jan 1912; *Educ* St Paul's; *m* 1955, Betty Elaine, da of Charles Muggridge, of Thornton Heath; 1 s (Antony), 1 da (Amanda); *Career* served WWII in W Desert; pension conslt; *Recreations* gardening; *Style—* Col A E C Alton, TD, DL; Foxgloves, The Ridge, Little Baddow, Essex (☎ 0245 41 3205)

ALSTON, James Douglas; CBE (1967), JP (1960, DL (Norfolk 1981)); s of James Alston (d 1958), of Uphall, Norfolk; *b* 6 May 1913; *Educ* Thetford GS, Midland Agric Coll; *m* 1943, Gale Violet May, da of Edward Tyrrell Lewis (d 1934), of Manitoba, Canada; 2 s, 2 da; *Career* served WW II RAF; farmer, chm Eastern Counties Farmers Ltd 1954-68 (pres 1973-83); memb Agric Res Cncl 1957-67, vice-chm Roy Norfolk Agric Assoc 1963-83 (pres 1981), chm Plant Breeding Inst Cambridge 1971-83, vice-chm Norfolk Agric Station 1973-84, pres Br Fr Cattle Soc 1983; tstee TSB of Eastern England 1960-80 (vice-chm 1979-80); Norfolk CC 1969-73; memb Ct and Cncl UEA; *Recreations* shooting; *Clubs* Farmers, Norfolk; *Style—* James D Alston, Esq, CBE, JP, DL; South Lopham Hall, Diss, Norfolk IP22 2LW (☎ 037 977 286)

ALSTON, John Alistair; CBE; s of David Alston, of Lavenham, Suffolk, and Bathia Mary Davidson (d 1987); *b* 24 May 1937; *Educ* Orwell Park, Sherbourne RAC; *Career* farmer; elected Norfolk CC 1973 (ldr 1981-87, chm 1988), chm Broads Bill Steering Ctee, memb Cncl of Univs of E Anglia; *Recreations* shooting, gardening; *Style—* J A Alston, Esq, CBE; Besthorpe Hall, Norfolk NR17 2LJ (☎ 0953 452138)

ALSTON, John Denys; TD; s of Rev Alfred Edward Alston, of Framingham Earl, Norfolk (d 1927), and Audrey Alston, *née* Ffolkes (d 1966); *b* 8 April 1914; *Educ* Lancing, RAM; *Career* musician, dir of music Denstone Coll Staffs 1939-46, dir of music Lancing Coll 1948-74, examiner Assoc Bd Royal Schs of Music 1948-84; FRAM, FRCO; *Recreations* skiing, motoring; *Clubs* E India; *Style—* John Alston, Esq, TD; Walnut Tree Cottage, Clapham, Worthing, W Sussex BN1 13 3UU (☎ 090 674 335)

ALSTON, (Arthur) Rex; s of Rt Rev Arthur Fawsett Alston (d 1954), Suffragan Bishop of Middleton (Lanc), and of St Leonards-on-Sea, Sussex, and Mary Isabel Tebbutt (d 1957); *b* 2 July 1901; *Educ* Trent Coll, Clare Cambridge (MA, Athletics Blue); *m* 1, 1932, Elspeth (d 1985), da of Sir Stewart Stockman (d 1926); 1 s (Graham), 1 da (Gay); m 2, 1986, Joan Manthorp Wilson; *Career* BBC commentator on cricket (tests), rugby football (Internationales), athletics (5 Olympics), tennis (Wimbledon); cricket and rugby corr Daily Telegraph 1966-88; capt: Bedfordshire Cricket Club, County Rugby E Midlands; *Clubs* East India, MCC; *Style—* Rex Alston, Esq; (☎ 0483 277315)

ALSTON, Richard John William; s of Gordon Walter Alston, and Margaret Isabel, *née* Whitworth; *b* 30 Oct 1948; *Educ* Eton, Croydon Coll of Art; *Career* resident choreographer Ballet Rambert 1980-86, artistic dis Rambert Dance Co 1986-; *Style—* Richard Alston, Esq; Rambert Dance Co, 94 Chiswick High Rd, London W4 (☎ 01 995 4246)

ALSTON, Robert John; CMG (1987); s of Arthur William Alston, and Rita Alston; *b* 10 Feb 1938; *Educ* Ardingly Coll, New Coll Oxford (BA); *m* 1969, Patricia Claire Essex; 1 s (Jeremy b 1972), 1 da (Nadine b 1970); *Career* Dip Serv: third sec Kabul 1963, Eastern Dept FO 1966, head Computer Study Team FCO 1969, first sec (Econ) Paris 1971, first sec and head of chancery Tehran 1974, asst head Energy Sci and Space Dept FCO 1977, head Jt Nuclear Unit FCO 1978, political cnsllr UK delgn to NATO 1981, head Def Dept FCO 1984, ambass Oman 1986-; *Recreations* gardening, travel, music; *Style—* Robert J Alston, Esq, CMG; c/o Foreign and Commonwealth Office, King Charles St, London SW1A 2AH

ALSTON, Robin Carfrae; s of Wilfred Louis Alston, and Margaret Louise, *née* Mackenzie (d 1975); *b* 29 Jan 1933; *Educ* Queen's Royal Coll Trinidad, Lodge Sch Barbados, Rugby, Univ of Br Columbia (BA), Oxford Univ (MA), Univ of Toronto (MA), London Univ (PhD); *m* 1957, Joanna Dorothy, da of Harry Ormiston; 2 s (Brent (d 1987), Mark), 1 da (Jane); *Career* bibliographer, teaching fell Univ Coll Toronto 1956-58, lectr New Brunswick Univ 1958-60, lectr in Eng lit Leeds Univ 1964-76, David Murray lectr Glasgow Univ 1983; fndr chm and md Scolar Press 1965-73, fndr and md Janus Press 1973-80, conslt bibliographer to Br Library 1977-, ed-in-chief Eighteenth Century Short Title Catalogue 1978-, ed dir The Ninteenth Century 1985-; pres Bibliographical Soc 1988- (vice pres 1975-88, cncl memb 1968-74, pubns ctee 1970-, ed Occasional Papers 1984-); memb advsy ctee Modern Language Assoc of America for the Wing Project 1978-; external examiner Inst of Bibliography Leeds Univ 1983-, Cecil Oldman lectr Leeds Univ 1988-89, hon res fell UCL 1987-; FSA 1988; *Publications* Anglo-Saxon Composition for Beginners (1959), Materials for a History of the English Language (2 vols, 1960), An Introduction to Old English (1961, 1962), A Concise Introduction to Old English (1966), Alexander Gil's Logonomia Anglica 1619 (ed with B Danielsson, 1979), Cataloguing Rules for the Eighteenth Century Short Title Catalogue (1977), Bibliography, Machine Readable Cataloguing and the ESTC (with M J Jannetta, 1978), Eighteenth Century Subscription Lists (with F J G Robinson and C Wadham, 1983), The Eighteenth Century Short Title Catalogue: the Br Library Collection (ed 1983); The Nineteenth Century Subject Surge & Principles of Selection (1986), The Nineteenth Century - Cataloguing Rules (1986), Bibliography of the English Language 1500-1800 (22 vols) vols 1-12 pub to date, The British Library: Past Present Future (1989); *Style—* Robin Alston, Esq; 16 Medburn St, London; The British Library, Great Russell St, London WC1B 3DG (☎ 01 323 7609)

ALSTON-ROBERTS-WEST, Lt-Col George Arthur; CVO (1988), DL (Warwickshire 1988); yr s of Maj William Reginald James Alston-Roberts-West (ka 1940; the Major's gf James added Alston to his patronymic of Roberts-West 1918. James's ggf, another James, added the name Roberts to his patronymic of West 1808. This second James had as mother one Sarah, da of Christopher Wren, of Wroxall Abbey, Staffs, and a descendant of Sir Christopher Wren the architect), and Constance Isolde, er da of Lord Arthur Grosvenor, JP, DL, 2 s of 1 Duke of Westminster; *b* 23 Nov 1937; *Educ* Eton, RMA Sandhurst; *m* 20 May 1970, Hazel Elizabeth Margaret, yst da of Lt-Col Sir Thomas Russell Albert Mason Cook, JP (ggs of Thomas Cook, fndr of the eponymous tourist agency); extra lady-in-waiting to HRH The Princess of Wales 1981-; *Career* served Gren Gds 1957-80; comptroller Ld Chamberlain's Office 1987- (asst comptroller 1981-87), extra equerry to HM The Queen 1982-; *Style—* Lt-Col George Alston-Roberts-West; The Stable House, St James's Palace, London SW1

ALTAMONT, Earl of; Jeremy Ulick Browne; s and h of 10 Marquess of Sligo; *b* 4 June 1939; *Educ* St Columba's Coll Eire, RAC Cirencester; *m* 1961, Jennifer June, da of Maj Derek Cooper, of Dunlewey, Co Donegal, and Mrs C Heber Percy; 5 da; *Style—* Earl of Altamont; Westport House, Co Mayo, Republic of Ireland

ALTHAM, Hon Mrs (Elizabeth Oona); *née* McNair; da of 1 Baron McNair, CBE, QC, LLD (d 1975); *b* 7 Feb 1913; *m* 1939, Group Capt John Barrett Altham, CBE; 2 s, 2 da; *Style—* The Hon Mrs Altham; Ivy Cottage, Little Shelford, Cambridge

ALTHAM, Gp Capt John Barrett; CBE (1955); s of Capt Edward Altham, CB, RN (d 1951), and his 1 wife Fiorella Cecil, *née* Willis; gs of Lt-Gen Sir Edward Altham, KCB, KCIE, CMG; *b* 17 Mar 1909; *Educ* Eton, Trinity Coll Cambridge (MA); *m* 17 June 1939, Hon Elizabeth Oona, eldest da of 1 Baron McNair, CBE (d 1975); 2 s, 2 da; *Career* RAF 1932-62; pilot No 9 (B) Sqdn, CFS course, flying instr Digby, specialist Signals 1937, served WWII Wittering (Fighter Cmd), Empire Air Trg Australia, cmd 80 Wing NW Europe (despatches), CSE Wotton, RAF Seletar (Singapore) 1948, Signals staff appointments No 90 Gp, Flying Trg Cmd, Tech Trg Cmd, cmd Communications Gp Allied Air Forces Fontainbleau 1959-62; *Recreations* sailing, golf, landscape gardening, owns foxcub cruiser: 'Flying Fox'; *Clubs* Aldeburgh Yacht, Pitt (Cambridge), Gog Magog Golf; *Style—* Gp Capt John Altham, CBE; Ivy Cottage, Little Shelford, Cambridge (☎ 0223 842182)

ALTHAM, Richard James Livingstone; s of Harry Surtees Altham, CBE, DSO (d 1965), and Alison, *née* Livingstone Learmonth (d 1979); *b* 19 Jan 1924; *Educ* Marlborough, Trinity Coll Oxford (MA); *m* 28 Sept 1957, (Rowena) Jeanne, da of Sir Francis Spencer Portal, 5 Bt (d 1984); 3 s (David b 1959, Robert b 1960, Alastair b 1963); *Career* pilot RAFVR 1941-46 Fl Lt; ICI Ltd 1949-62, jt md Borax Hldgs 1968-82; dir: RTZ plc 1968-87, Boustead plc 1987; mem cncl: Radley Coll, United World Coll of Atlantic, Ranfurly Library; chm Fairbridge Drake Soc; *Recreations* reading, gardening, golf, cricket; *Clubs* MCC, RAF; *Style—* Richard J L Altham, Esq; Crunnells Green House, Preston, Hitchin, Hertfordshire (☎ 0462 32163)

ALTHAUS, Nigel Frederick; s of Frederick Rudolph Althaus, CBE (d 1975), and Margaret Frances, *née* Twist; *b* 28 Sept 1929; *m* 1958, Anne, da of P G Cardew; 3 s, 1 da; *Career* memb Stock Exchange 1955-; sr ptnr Pember & Boyle (stockbrokers) 1975-82; sr ptnr Mullens & Co (Stockbrokers to the Government and the Bank of England) 1982-86; sr govt broker (formally known as sr broker to the National Debt Commissioner) 11 Oct 1982-; *Style—* Nigel Althaus, Esq; Bank of England, Threadneedle St, London EC2R 8AH

ALTHORP, Viscount; Charles Edward Maurice Spencer; s (by 1 m) and h of 8 Earl Spencer, MVO, JP, DL, *qv*; bro of HRH The Princess of Wales (*see* Royal Family); *b* 20 May 1964; *Educ* Maidwell Hall, Eton, Magdalen Coll Oxford; *Career* page of honour to HM The Queen 1977-79; television correspondent NBC news 1987-; *Style—* Viscount Althorp

ALTMAN, Lionel Phillips; CBE (1979); s of Arnold Altman (d 1955), and Catherine, *née* Phillips (d 1982); *b* 21 Sept 1922; *m* 1; 1 s; m 2, 1977, Jan Mary Borrodell; 2 da; *Career* served HM Forces 1942-46; dir: Carmo Hldgs Ltd 1947-63, Sears Hldgs Motor Gp 1963-72, C & W Hldgs Ltd 1974-77; chm and ch exec: Pre-Divisional Investmts Ltd 1972-; dir: H P Information 1985-, Equity & General plc Gp of Companies 1978- (this gp includes: Equity & General Finance Ltd, Equity & General Finance Estates Ltd, Equity & General Finance (Investmts) Ltd, Equity & General Finance (Rentals) Ltd, Equity & General Finance (Leasing) Ltd, Lease Exchange Ltd, Bluebell Garages (Middlesborough) Ltd, Mountvale Ltd, Western General Trading Ltd, Reid & Lee Ltd, Technology Transfer Assocs Ltd, United Technologists Est, Murie Mines (Pvt) Ltd); pres Motor Agents Assoc 1975-77 (nat cncl 1965-); vice-pres and cncl Inst of Motor Industry 1970-78; chm Industry Taxation Panel; memb: cncl CBI 1977-, CBI Idustl Policy Ctee 1979-, Dun & Bradstreet Industry Panel 1982-; Liveryman Coachmakers and Coach Harness Makers Co, Freeman City of London, City of Glasgow; *Style—* Lionel Altman, Esq, CBE; The Cottage, Amersham Way, Little Chalfont, Bucks HP6 6SF; 66 Grosvenor St, Mayfair, London W1X 9DB (☎ 01 493 3371)

ALTON, David Patrick; MP (Lib) Liverpool, Mossley Hill 1983-; s of Frederick Alton, and Bridget, *née* Mulroe; *b* 15 Mar 1951; *Educ* Campion Sch, Christ's Coll of Educn Liverpool; *m* 23 July 1988, Lizzie, *née* Bell; *Career* city cncllr Liverpool 1972-80 (dep ldr cncl 1978-79, housing chm 1978-79), nat pres Nat League of Young Liberals 1979, MP (Lib) Liverpool Edge Hill March 1979-83, chm Lib Party Standing Ctee (policy) 1980-81, Lib chief whip 1985-87, Liberal and Alliance Spokesman on NI 1986-87; vice pres Life, tstee Crisis at Christmas, Parly Sponsor The Jubilee Campaign, pres Liverpool Old People's Hostels Assoc; memb Inst of Journalists; *Books* What Kind of Country (1987), Whose Choice Anyway (1988); *Style—* David Alton, Esq, MP; 25 North Mossley Hill Road, Liverpool 18 (☎ 051 724 6106)

ALTON, Euan Beresford Seaton; MBE (1945), MC (1943); s of William Lester St John Alton (d 1954), of Putney, London, and Ellen Sharpey, *née* Seaton (d 1963); *b* 22 April 1919; *Educ* St Paul's, Magdalen Coll Oxford (MA); *m* 22 Aug 1953, Diana Margaret, da of Dr Colin Ede, MD (d 1967), 1 s (Robert b 1958), 1 da (Sally b 1960); *Career* RA 1939-45 served in Egypt, N Africa Sicily, Italy, Maj 1945, Colonial Serv HM Oversea Civil Serv 1946-58, Gold Coast Ghana, Dist Cmmr, Admin Offr Class I 1957, Miny of Health, Dept of Health & Social Security 1958-76, asst sec 1961, under sec 1968-76; capt Oxford Univ Rifle Club Blue 1946; chm of area ctee Cruising Assoc 1984-88 (hon local rep 1988-); *Recreations* sailing; *Clubs* Stour SC, Cruising Assoc; *Style—* Euan Alton, Esq, MBE, MC; Spindlehurst, Sch Lane, Brantham, Nr Manningtree, Essex CO11 1QE (☎ 0206 393419)

ALTRINCHAM, Barony of; *see*: Grigg, John Edward Poynder

ALUN-JONES, Sir (John) Derek; s of Thomas Alun-Jones (d 1951), and Madge Beatrice, *née* Edwards (d 1968); *b* 6 June 1933; *Educ* Lancing, St Edmund Hall Oxford; *m* 1960, Gillian, da of Ian Palmer; 2 s (Jeremy b 1961, Nicholas b 1968), 3 da (Carella b 1963, Sophie b 1968, Emma b 1968); *Career* dir: Burmah Oil Trading Co 1974-70, Royal Insur 1981-, Reed Int 1984-, GKN 1986-88; chm exec and md Ferranti 1975-; kt 1987; *Recreations* shooting, fishing, riding; *Style—* Sir Derek Alun-Jones; The Willows, Effingham Common, Surrey KT24 5JE (☎ 0372 58158); Ferranti International Signal plc, Millbank Tower, Millbank, London SW1P 4QS (☎ 01 834 6611)

ALVAREZ, Alfred; s of Bertie Alvarez (d 1965), of London, and Katie Alvarez, *née* Levy (d 1982); *b* 5 August 1929; *Educ* Oundle, Corpus Christi Coll Oxford (BA, MA); *m* 1, 1956 (m dis 1961), Ursula Barr; 1 s (Adam); m 2, 1966, Anne, da of Jack Gilmore Adams, of Toronto, Canada; 1 s (Luke b 1968), 1 da (Kate b 1971); *Career* poet and author; *Books* The Shaping Spirit (1958), The School of Donne (1961), The New Poetry (ed and introd, 1962), Under Pressure (1965), Beyond All This Fiddle (1968), Lost (Poems, 1968), Penguin Modern Poets No18 (1970), Apparition (poems, 1971), The Savage God (1971), Beckett (1973), Hers (1974), Hunt (1978), Autumn to Autumn and Selected Poems (1978), Life After Marriage (1982), The Biggest Game in Town (1983), Offshore (1986), Feeding the Rat (1988); *Recreations* rock climbing, poker, music; *Clubs* Climbers'; *Style—* A Alvarez, Esq; c/o Aitken & Stone, 29 Fernshaw Rd, London SW10 OTG

ALVES, Colin; s of Donald Alexander Alves, of Somerset (d 1979), and Marjorie Alice, *née* Marsh (d 1968); *b* 19 April 1930; *Educ* Christ's Hosp, Oxford Univ (MA); *m* 31 Jan 1953, Peggy, da of Capt Ernest Henry Kember (RAOC) (d 1941); 2 s (William b 1956, Thomas b 1963), 1 da (Rachel b 1954); *Career* lectr King Alfred's Coll, Winchester 1959-68, head Dept Brighton Coll of Educn 1968-74, dir Religious Educn Centre, St Gabriel's Coll 1974-77, Sec Church Colls of Higher Educn 1977-84, Gen Sec General Synod Bd of Educn and Nat Soc 1984-; memb: Durham Commn on Religious Educn 1967-70, Voluntary Sector Consultative Cncl 1984-88, Nat Advsy Body on Public Sector High Educn (NAB) 1983-88, Advisory Ctee on the Supply and Educn of Teachers (ACSET) 1980-85; chm Schs Cncl Religious Educn Ctee 1971-77, Sec Assoc of Voluntary Colls 1978-84; *publications* Religion and The Secondary School (1968), The Christian in Education (1972), The Question of Jesus (1987); *Recreations* music, walking, gardens; *Clubs* Royal Commonwealth Soc; *Style—* Colin Alves, Esq; 9 Park Rd, Haywards Heath, W Sussex (☎ 0444 454496); Board of Education, Church House, Great Smith St, Westminster (☎ 01 222 9011); National Society (☎ 01 222 1672)

ALVEY, John; CB (1980); s of George Clarence Vincent Alvey (d 1929), and Hilda Eveline, *née* Pellat (d 1955); *b* 19 June 1925; *Educ* Reeds Sch, London U (BSc); *m* 1955, Celia Edmed, da of Dr Cecil Brittain Marson (d 1932); 3 s (David, Peter, Stephen); *Career* chief scientist RAF 1977-80; sr dir technol Br Telecom 1980-83, engr-in-chief Br Telecom 1983-86; chm SIRA Ltd 1987-; Hon DSc City Univ, Hon Fell QMC London; FIEE, FEng; *Recreations* skiing, walking, reading, travel; *Style—* John Alvey, Esq, CB

ALVINGHAM, 2 Baron (UK 1929); Robert Guy Eardley; CBE (1977, OBE 1972); s of 1 Baron Alvingham (d 1955) and Dorothea Gertrude Yerburgh (d 1927); *b* 16 Dec 1926; *Educ* Eton; *m* 1952, Beryl Elliot, da of William D Williams, of Hindhead; 1 s (Robert), 1 da (Susannah); *Heir* s, Capt Hon Robert Yerburgh; *Career* formerly Coldstream Gds (joined 1945, cmmnd 1946), served Palestine, Tripoli, FARELF, South America, Tripoli; Head Staff CDS 1972-74, RCDS 1975, dep dir Army Staff

Duties 1975-78, Maj-Gen 1978, dir Army Quartering MOD 1978-81; *Style*— Maj-Gen The Rt Hon Lord Alvingham, CBE; Bix Hall, Henley-on-Thames, Oxon

AMAN, Anthony John; s of John Godfrey Aman (d 1950), of Isle of Wight, and Ursula Mary Simmons (d 1982); *b* 31 Mar 1932; *Educ* Charterhouse, Pembroke Coll Oxford (MA); *Career* serv RA 1954-56; articled clerk 1954-60, Forestal Land Timber & Railways 1960-64, Mgmnt Selection 1964-66, Nat West Bankgroup 1966-78, dir County Bank 1969-78, Grovewood Securities 1978-80, dir Falcon Resources plc; Freeman City of London, Liveryman Worshipful Co of Makers of Playing Cards; *Clubs* Beefsteak, Carlton, Royal Solent Yacht, Berks Golf, Royal Cinque Ports Golf; *Style*— Anthony Aman, Esq; 133 The Colonnades, Porchester Square, London W2 6AP

AMBLER, Eric; OBE (1981); s of Alfred Percy Ambler (d 1929), and Amy Madeleine Ambler; *b* 28 June 1909; *Educ* Colfe's GS, London Univ; *m* 1, 1939, Louise Crombie; m 2, 1958, Joan Harrison; *Career* served WW II Lt-Col Europe, Bronze Star (USA) 1945; novelist and screenwriter; screenplays incl: The Way Ahead (1944), The October Man (1947), The Passionate Friends (1948), Highly Dangerous (1950), The Magic Box (1951), Gigolo and Gigolette in Encore (1952), The Card (1952), Rough Shoot (1953), The Cruel Sea (1953), Lease of Life (1954), The Purple Plain (1954), Yaugste Incident (1957), A Night to Remember (1958), Wreck of the Mary Deave (1959), Love Hate Love (1970); *Books* incl: The Dark Frontier (1936), Uncommon Danger (1937), Epitaph for a Spy (1938), Cause for Alarm (19380, The Mask of Dimitrios (1939), Journey into Fear (1940), Judgement of Deltchev (1951), The Schirmer Inheritence (1953), The Night Comers (1956), Passage of Arms (1959), The Light of Day (1962), The Ability to Kill (essays, 1963), To Catch a Spy (ed and intro, 1964), A King of Anger (Edgar Allen Poe Award, 1964), Dirty Story (1967), The Intercom Conspiracy (1969), The Levauter (1972, Golden Dagger Award, 1973), Dr Frigo (1974, MWA Grand Master Award 1975), Send No More Roses (1977), The Care of Time (1981), Here Lies (autobiography) 1985; *Clubs* Garrick, Savile; *Style*— Eric Ambler, Esq, OBE; c/o Campbell Thomson & McLaughin Ltd, 31 Newington Green, London N16 9PV

AMBRASEYS, Prof Nicholas; s of Neocles Amvrasis, of Athens, Greece, and Cleopatra, *née* Yambani (d 1986); *b* 19 Jan 1929; *Educ* Nat Tech Univ of Athens (Dipl Ing), Imperial Coll of Sci (DIC), Univ of London (PhD, DSc); *m* 25 Aug 1955, Xeni, da of Alexander Stavrou; *Career* lectr Imperial Coll of Sci 1958-61; prof: Univ of Illinois 1962-63, Nat Tech Univ of Athens 1963-64; reader Univ of London 1964-74, prof Imperial Coll of Sci and Tech 1974-; FRGS, FGS, FICE, FEng; *Recreations* historical geography, archaeology; *Style*— Prof Nicholas Ambraseys; 19 Bede House, Manor Fields, London SW15 3LT (☎ 01 788 4219); Dept Civil Engrg, Imperial Coll of Sci & Technol, London SW7 2AZ (☎ 01 589 5111, telex 261503)

AMBROSE, Hon Angela Francesca Hayward; da of Baron Blanch, *qv*; *b* 1950; *m* 1974, Timothy Ambrose; 2 da (Bethany b 1978, Emily b 1981); *Style*— The Hon Mrs Ambrose; 7 Plewlands Ave, Edinburgh

AMBROSE, Prof (Edmund) Jack; s of Hary Edmund Ambrose (d 1940), of Cambridgeshire, and Kate, *née* Stanley (d 1926); *b* 2 Mar 1914; *Educ* Perse Sch Cambridge, Emmanuel Coll Cambridge (BA, MA), Univ of London (DSc); *m* 31 July 1943, Andrée, da of Alphonse Huck, of Seine, France; 1 s (Edmund David b 1945), 1 da (Philippa Jane b 1948); *Career* WWII secret res Admty 1940-45; res offr (protein structure) Courtauld Basic Res Inst Maidenhead 1948-53, Chester Beatty Res Inst (cancer) 1953-73 (res on cell surfaces in normal and cancer cells), prof and head of dept cell biology Univ of London 1966-75 (emeritus prof 1976-); chm Sci Advsy Ctee and advsr in cancer to Govt of India Tate Meml Hosp and Res Inst Bombay 1965-73, advsr Regnl Cancer Centre Kerala India 1978-, co fndr and advsr fndn for Med Res (leprosy) Bombay 1975-; rec Zoology Section Br Assoc for Advancement of Sci 1968-73, fndr and convener Br Soc Cell Biology, emeritus memb Int Soc Biological Differentiation, pres Cell Tissue and Organ Culture Gp; diocesian reader Chichester Diocese 1981; Queen Elizabeth of Hungary Medal Ordre de St Jean de Matte Paris 1981 (for leprosy work in India); *Books* Cell Electrophonesis (1962), The Cancer Cell in Vitro (jtly 1968), Biology of Cancer (ed 1968, secnd edn 1975), Cell Biology (jtly 1970, secnd edn 1975), Nature and Origin of the Biological World (1981); *Recreations* sailing, pastal sketching; *Clubs* Royal Bombay YC, Chelsea Arts; *Style*— Prof Jack Ambrose; The Mill House, Westfield, Nr Hastings, E Sussex TN35 4RU (☎ 0424 753933)

AMBROSE, Marie Kosloff; da of Lewis Kosloff (d 1932), of London, and Vera, *née* Wolfson (d 1962); *b* 22 Nov 1916; *Educ* North London Collegiate Sch Mddx, Univ Coll Hosp London Univ (LDS, DOrth), Royal Dental Hosp London, Eastman Dept Univ of Rome; *m* 3 Sept 1940, Elwyn Ambrose (d 1971), s of Thomas Ambrose (d 1943), of Shrewsbury; 1 da (Anna (Mrs Whyte) b 1944, d 1985); *Career* dental surg community gen practice and hosp clinical assistantships 1941-74, specialist orthodontist communtiy serv and Kings Coll (teaching) 1974-79; music critic: Musical Opinion (monthly), Hampstead and Highgate Express 1977-; memb local dental ctee 1951-63; BDA: pres met branch 1977-78, chm br cncl 1978-80, memb rep bd 1980-88; Women In Dentistry: fndr memb, memb exec ctee, archivist, speaker; speaker and memb exec ctee 300 Gp (for trg women for Parl), chaired symposium on politics of health with extra mural dept Univ of London 1983; candidate (Lab) Hampstead local elections 1983; memb bd govrs FDR Sch for physically handicapped children; memb: Fawcett Soc, NUJ, Women Returners Network; hon memb: BDA 1986, Women In Dentistry 1988; *Recreations* sailing, music, theatre, travel; *Style*— Ms Marie Ambrose; 32 Belsize Park, London NW3 4DX (☎ 01 794 1255)

AMERY, Lady Catherine; *née* Macmillan; da of 1 Earl of Stockton, *qv*; *b* 1926; *m* 1950, Rt Hon Julian Amery, *qv*; 1 s, 3 da; *Style*— Lady Catherine Amery; 112 Eaton Sq, London SW1 (☎ 01 235 1543/7409); Forest Farm House, Chelwood Gate, Sussex

AMERY, Rt Hon Julian; PC (1960), MP (C) Brighton Pavilion 1969-; s of Rt Hon Leopold Stennett Amery, CH, PC (d 1955), and Florence, *née* Greenwood, sister of 1 Viscount Greenwood; *b* 27 Mar 1919; *Educ* Eton, Balliol Oxford; *m* 1950, Lady Catherine, *qv*, da of 1 Earl of Stockton; 1 s (Leopold b 1956), 3 da (Caroline b 1951, Theresa b 1954, Elizabeth b 1956); *Career* MP (C) Preston N 1950-66; parly under-sec of state and fin sec WO 1957-58, parly under-sec of state Colonial Off 1958-60, sec of state for Air 1960-62; min of: Aviation 1962-64, Public Bldg and Works 1970, for Housing and Construction DOE 1970-72; min of state FCO 1972-74; *Clubs* White's, Beefsteak, Carlton, Buck's; *Style*— The Rt Hon Julian Amery, MP; 112 Eaton Sq, London SW1 (☎ 01 235 1543/7409); Forest Farm House, Chelwood Gate, Sussex

AMES, Gerald George Singleton; s of George Singleton Ames (d 1956), and Florence Christian, *née* Hart (d 1982); *b* 15 April 1927; *Educ* Wade Deacon GS, Manchester Sch of Architecture, (DA Manc., RIBA (1949)); *m* 4 Feb 1950, Margaret, da of Frederick Atherton (d 1983) of Hillcrest, Cheshire; 2 s (Stephen b 1956, Mark b 1960); *Career* dir John Finlan Ltd 1956-70, md and deputy chm Finlan Group plc 1970-85, dir Finlan Group plc, company concerned in property design and development, export of building services and components, materials handling and merchanting 1985-87; *Recreations* sailing, music; *Clubs* Liverpool Artists; *Style*— Gerald Ames, Esq; Glan-Yr-Afon Hall, Llanferres, Mold, Clwyd; Sefton House, Exchange Street East, Liverpool L2 3RD (☎ 051 227 1553, fax: 051 236 1046)

AMES, Ruth Winifreda (Mrs Ameresekere); *née* Munasinha; da of Ronald Jackson Cyril Munasinha, of Colombo, Sri Lanka, and Mary Winifreda, *née* Dalpadado; *b* 24 June 1938; *Educ* Ave Maria Convent Negombo Sri Lanka, Good Shepherd Convent Colombo Sri Lanka, City of London Coll, Coll for Distributive Trades London (Dip Advertising); *m* 6 Jan 1960, Ranjit William Ebenezer Ameresekere, s of John William Ebenezer Ameresekere (d 1967); 1 s (Edward Ames); *Career* advertising exec Garland Compton Ltd (now Saatchi and Saatchi) 1964-73, i/c new business and accounts Lloyds Advertising 1974-75, md Ames Advertising 1975-, ptnr Ames Personnel 1987- (proprietor 1975-87); MCAM; *Recreations* badminton, reading, music; *Clubs* Inst of Dirs; *Style*— Mrs Ruth Ames; Benting Mead, Lonesome Lane, Reigate, Surrey RH2 7QT; Ames House, Kings Cross Lane, South Nutfield, Surrey RH1 5NG (☎ 0737 822122, fax 0737 822133)

AMESS, David Anthony Andrew; MP (C Basildon 1983-); s of James Henry Valentine Amess (d 1986), and Maud Ethel, *née* Martin; *b* 26 Mar 1952; *Educ* St Bonaventures GS, Bournemouth Coll of Technol; *m* 1983, Julia Margaret Monica, da of Graham Harry Arnold, of 55 Wansfell Gardens, Thorpe Bay, Essex; 1 s (David b 1984), 2 da (Katherine b 1985, Sarah Elizabeth b 1988); *Career* teacher St John Baptist Junior Mixed Sch Bethnall Green 1970-71, trainee underwriter Leslie & Godwin Agency 1974-76, sr conslt Accountancy Personnal 1976-80, ptnr Accountancy Aids Employment Agency 1981-87, chm Accountancy Solutions 1987; contested (c) Newham North West 1979; PPs 1987 to: Edwina Currie, Michael Portillo, Lord Skelmersdale; pps 1988 to: Michael Portillo Minister at Dept of Transport, Peter Bottomley Parly under Sec Dept of Transport; *Recreations* reading, writing, tennis, cricket, gardening, popular music; *Clubs* Carlton, Kingswood Squash; *Style*— David Amess, Esq, MP; House of Commons, London SW1A 0AA (☎ 01 219 6387); Accountancy Solutions, 18 Maddox Street, London W1

AMEY, Nicholas John; s of John William Thomas Amey, MBE, AFC, JP, of Tickford Abbey, Newport Pagnell, Bucks, and Margory Anne, *née* Willis (d 1986); *b* 15 Mar 1947; *Educ* Wellington; *m* 26 July 1984, Wendy Marion Cecile, da of Gerald Edward Atkinson (d 1964); 1 s (Robert b 1985); *Career* dir Moffatt & Co Ltd insur brokers 1974 (chm and md 1989), md life assur brokers 1976, memb Lloyds 1987, md Stronghold Tst Ltd; memb Cons Assoc; Freeman City of London 1978, memb Worshipful Co of Gold and Silver Wyre Drawers; ACII 1976; *Recreations* historic sports-racing car driver, skiing; *Clubs* Ferrari Owners, Historic Sports Car; *Style*— Nicholas Amey, Esq; The Manor House, Old Knebworth, Herts SG3 6QD (☎ 0438 812 713); Percy House, 796 High Rd, London N17 0DJ (☎ 01 808 3020, fax 01 801 4249, car tel 0836 201300)

AMHERST, 5 Earl (UK 1926); Jeffrey John Archer Amherst; MC (1918); also Baron Amherst (GB 1788) and Viscount Holmesdale (UK 1826); s of 4 Earl Amherst (d 1927, gs of 1 Earb, ambass to China 1816 and govr-gen of Bengal 1822-28, whose first w gave her name to the ornamental bird known as Amherst's pheasant) and Hon Eleanor St Aubyn, da of 1 Baron St Levan; *b* 13 Dec 1896; *Educ* Eton, Sandhurst; *Career* served WW I and II, Maj Coldstream Gds (ret) and Hon Wing Cdr RAF; journalist New York Morning World; former air advsr BR and memb staff BEA; commercial air pilot; *Books* Wandering Far Abroad (autobiography); *Clubs* Travellers', Cavalry and Guards, Pratt's, Garrick; *Style*— The Rt Hon the Earl Amherst, MC; c/o Royal Bank of Scotland, Drummonds Branch, 49 Charing Cross, London SW1

AMHERST OF HACKNEY, 4 Baron (UK 1892); (William) Hugh Amherst Cecil; s of 3 Baron Amherst, of Hackney, CBE (d 1980), and Margaret, Baroness Amherst, of Hackney, *qv*; *b* 28 Dec 1940; *Educ* Eton; *m* 1965, Elisabeth, da of Hugh Humphery Merriman, DSO, MC, TD, DL (d 1983), of Hazel Hall, Peaslake, Surrey; 1 s (Hon (Hugh) William Amherst), 1 da (Hon Aurelia Margaret Amherst b 1966); *Heir* s, Hon (Hugh) William Amherst Cecil b 17 July 1968; *Career* dir E A Gibson Shipbrokers Ltd; *Recreations* sailing (yacht Hal); *Clubs* Royal Yacht Sqdn, Royal Ocean Racing; *Style*— The Rt Hon the Lord Amherst of Hackney

AMHERST OF HACKNEY, Margaret, Baroness; Margaret Eirene Clifton; da of Brig-Gen Howard Brown, sometime MP Newbury, JP, DL (gs of Sir William Brown, 1 Bt, sometime MP S Lancs, JP, DL); *b* 23 Feb 1921; *m* 1939, 3 Baron Amherst of Hackney, CBE (d 1980); 2 s (4 Baron and Hon Anthony Cecil), 1 da (Hon Mrs Reid); *Style*— The Rt Hon Margaret, Lady Amherst of Hackney; 138 Cranmer Court, London SW3

AMIES, Colin MacDonald; s of Maj George Amies (d 1977), of Drumdevan Hse, Inverness, and Elizabeth Mary Phillips, *née* MacDonald; *b* 14 May 1940; *Educ* Oundle, Christs Church Coll Cambridge (MA); *m* 18 Sept 1965, Catherine Anne (Kate), da of Roland Haddon Lovett (d 1985), of Chatton, Alnwick, Northumberland; 4 s (James b 1968, Simon b 1969, William b 1974, Alexander b 1980); *Career* md Exacta Circuits Ltd 1970-77, mangr mfrg ops STC plc 1977-79, corporate fin dir Midland Bank plc 1981-85 (electronics indust advsr 1980-81); md Advert Ltd 1989- (dir 1985-); chm: Computer Security Int Ltd 1986- Scheduling Technol Gp Ltd 1986-, Anamartic Ltd 1987-; memb Scottish Regnl Cncl CBI 1971-74, teaching co mgmnt ctee SERC 1987-; MICE, CEng; *Recreations* skiing, gardening, tennis; *Clubs* Lansdowne; *Style*— Colin Amies, Esq; Advent Lrd, 25 Buckingham Gate, London SW1E 6LD (☎ 01 630 9811, fax 01 828 9958, car tel 0896 388 496, telex 296923)

AMIES, (Edwin) Hardy; CVO (1977); s of late Herbert William Amies; *b* 17 July 1909; *Career* dressmaker by appt to HM The Queen, dir Hardy Amies Ltd 1946-, design conslt to J Hepworth & Son 1960-; FRSA; *Style*— Hardy Amies, Esq, CVO; 29 Cornwall Gdns, London SW7; Hardy Amies Ltd, 14 Savile Row, London W1 (☎ 01 734 2436)

AMIES, Timothy (Tim) John; s of Maj George Amies (d 1976), of Drumdevan, Inverness, and Elizabeth Mary Phillips, *née* MacDonald; *b* 1 July 1938; *Educ* Oundle Sch; *m* 6 Nov 1969, Clare Rosemary, da of John Robert Payne, Crawfurd, of Surrey; 3 s (Tom b 1971, Edward b 1973, Harry b 1979), 2 da (Sarah b 1974, Alice b 1985);

Career 2 Lt Queen's Own Cameron Highlanders 1956-58; chartered accountant Casselton Elliott and Co 1959-64, merchant banker Morgan Grenfell and Co 1964-68, stockbroker and ptnr Laurie Milbank and Co 1968-86; Chase Manhattan Bank London 1986-89, dir Chase Investment Bank Ltd 1987-; memb London Stock Exchange; FCA, FSIA; *Recreations* children, reading, walking, golf, gardening; *Clubs* City of London, Inst of Directors, Woburn Country; *Style*— Tim Amies, Esq; The Old Farm, Great Brickhill, Buckinghamshire (☎ 052 526 243); Ballachar, Loch Ruthven, Inverness (☎ 08083 258); Chase Investmt Bank Ltd, Woolgate House, Coleman Street, London EC2 (☎ 01 726 5000, private line 01 726 5327, fax 01 726 7156)

AMIS, Kingsley; CBE (1981); s of William Robert and Rosa Amis; *b* 16 April 1922; *Educ* City of London Sch, St John's Oxford; *m* 1, 1948, Hilary Ann, da of Leonard Sidney Bardwell; 2 s, 1 da; m 2, 1965 (m dis 1983), Elizabeth Jane Howard, *qv*; *Career* novelist; *books include* Lucky Jim (1954), That Uncertain Feeling (1955; filmed as Only Two Can Play 1962), One Fat Englishman (1963), The Green Man (1969), Jake's Thing (1978), The New Oxford Book of Light Verse (1978), Collected Poems 1944-1979 (1979), Russian Hide-and-Seek (1980), Collected Short Stories (1980), The Golden Age of Science Fiction (1981), Every Day Drinking (1983), Stanley and the Woman (1984), Hows Your Glass? (1984), The Old Devils (1986); *Recreations* music, thrillers, television; *Style*— Kingsley Amis, Esq, CBE; c/o Jonathan Clowes, 22 Prince Allied Road, London NW1 7ST

AMIS, Richard Henry Allen; CBE (1983), JP (1984); s of Maj Ivan Roll Amis (d 1970), of the Georgian House, Ripley, Surrey, and Sylvia Emily, *née* Booth (d 1978); *b* 4 May 1932; *Educ* Eton (King's Scholar); *Career* Capt (TA) 1955; chm Alfred Booth & Co plc 1974-; dir Michelin Tyre Co 1982-; chm CBI Health & Safety Ctee 1978-83, cncllr Guildford Borough Cncl 1972-83; *Recreations* gardening, walking, hist reading; *Clubs* Carlton; *Style*— Richard Amis, Esq, CBE, JP; The Georgian House, Ripley, Woking, Surrey GU23 6AF (☎ 0483 224353); Alfred Booth & Co plc, 34 St James's St, London SW1A 1JA (☎ 01 930 8383)

AMLOT, Roy Douglas; s of Air Cdre Douglas Lloyd Amlot, CBE, DFC, AFC (d 1979), of Casa Jacaranda, Praia da Luz, Algarve, Portugal, and Ruby Luise, *née* Lawrence; *b* 22 Sept 1942; *Educ* Dulwich Coll; *m* 26 July 1969, Susan Margaret, da of Sir Henry McLorinan McDowell, KBE, of Dulwich; 2 s (Thomas b 1971, Richard b 1978); *Career* barr Lincoln's Inn 1963, bencher 1987, second prosecuting counsel to Inland Revenue (Central Criminal Ct and London Crown Ct) 1974, first prosecuting counsel to the Crown (Inner London Ct) 1975, jr prosecuting counsel to the Crown (Central Criminal Ct) 1977, sr prosecuting counsel to the Crown (Central Criminal Ct) 1981; *Publications* Phipson on Evidence (ed 11 edn); *Recreations* skiing, windsurfing, music, squash; *Clubs* St James's; *Style*— Roy Amlot, Esq; 6 King's Bench Walk, Temple, London EC4

AMORY; *see*: Heathcoat-Amory

AMOS, Alan Thomas; MP (C) Hexham 1987-; s of William Edmond Amos, of Harpenden, Hertfordshire, and Cynthia Florence Kathleen, *née* Hurford; *b* 10 Nov 1952; *Educ* St Albans Sch, St John's Coll Oxford (MA, PPE); *Career* dir of studies, head of Economics & Politics Dept, head of sixth form Dame Alice Owen's Sch, Hertfordshire 1976-84, head of agric & environment section Cons Res Dept 1984-86, asst princ Coll of Further Educn 1986-87, pres Oxford Univ Cons Assoc 1974-75, cncllr London Borough of Enfield 1978-, (dep ldr cncl); chm: Educn Ctee, London Borough Assoc Educn Ctee 1986-87,Backbench Forestry Ctee; sec Backbench Tport Ctee; memb: SPUC, ASH, Inter Parly Union, Br American Parly Gp; *Recreations* badminton, travel, USA Politics, bibliophilia; *Clubs* English-Speaking Union; *Style*— Alan T Amos, Esq, MP; House of Commons, London SW1A 0AA (☎01 219 6251; 0432 603777)

AMOS, Francis John Clarke; CBE (1973); s of Frank Amos (d 1970), and Alice Mary, *née* Clarke (d 1974); *b* 10 Sept 1924; *Educ* Dulwich Coll, Univ of London (BSc), London Poly (Dip Architecture), Sch of Planning London (Dip Planning); *m* Geraldine Mercy, MBE, JP, da of Capt Egbert Spear Sutton (d 1977); 1 s (Gideon), 2 da (Zephyr, Felicity); *Career* RIASC, Capt 1942-47; Liverpool city planning offr 1966-73, chief exec Birmingham City 1973-77, sr fell Univ of Birmingham 1977-, special prof of planning and mgmnt Univ of Nottingham 1980-, conslt UN Centre of Human Settlements 1974-, tstee Community Project Fndn 1977-, dir Action Resource Centre 1976-87; conslt: Bangladesh 1983-, Hong Kong 1983, India 1979-, Iraq 1985-, Kenya 1981-, Pakistan 1981-, Tanzania 1978-80, Turkey 1979-80, Uganda 1987-, Venezuela 1978, Zimbabwe 1981-; memb various govt sponsored bodies; memb: Community Work and Area Research Centres Gp 1970-; Int Soc of City and Regnl Planners 1973-, exec ctee Pub Serv Announcements 1978-, Nat Exec Ctee and Cncl Nat Assoc of Citizens Advice Bureaux 1982-46, St George's House Windsor 1981-, jt Land Requirements Ctee 1982-; hon sec Roy Town Planning Inst 1979- (pres 1971-72); lectr: Workers' Educnl Assoc, Univ extension serv, USA, India, Utrecht, Belgrade, Barcelona; int seminars organized by: UN, Orgn for Econ Co-op and Dvpt, Int Fedn of Housing and Planning, Int Soc of City and Regnl Planners; visiting prof Tech Coll Univ of Munich 1981; FRSA; *Books* Education for Planning and Urban Governance (1973), City Centre Redevelopment (1973), Planning and the Future (1977), Low Income Housing in the Developing World (1984), and various articles, conference papers and government papers; *Recreations* voluntary social work; *Style*— Francis Amos, Esq, CBE; Grindstones, 20 Westfield Rd, Edgbaston, Birmingham B15 3QG; Coach Ho, Ashton Gifford, Codford St Peter, Warminster, Wilts; Inst of Local Govt Studies, Univ of Birmingham, PO Box 363, Birmingham B15 2TT (☎ 021 472 1301 ext 2472, telex Birmingham 338938 SPAPHY G)

AMOS, Roy; s of Leonard Alfred Amos, of Birmingham; *b* 8 Sept 1934; *Educ* King Edward's Sch Birmingham, Birmingham Coll of Commerce; *m* 1956, Marjorie Ann, da of Arnold Hall, of Birmingham; *Career* chm and md Lightning Int Ltd 1969-74, exec gp dir IMI plc 1974-; chm: Manders Hldgs plc, Central Devpt Capital Ltd; FCMA; *Recreations* tennis, golf; *Clubs* Four Oaks, Sutton Coldfield GC; *Style*— Roy Amos, Esq; The Lodge, Roman Rd, Little Aston Park, Sutton Coldfield, W Midlands B74 3AA (☎ 021 353 5373)

AMPHLETT, Philip Nicholas; s of Colin Bernard Amphlett, of Farm Field, Wootton Village, Oxford, and Hilda, *née* Price (d 1972); *b* 20 Oct 1948; *Educ* Winchester, Balliol Coll Oxford (BA); *m* 4 Aug 1969, Marjolein Grantha, da of Jan Cornelius de Vries (d 1952), of Eindhoven, Holland; 1 s (Jan b 17 Aug 1972), 2 da (Jessica b 9 Jan 1970, Catherine b 14 Nov 1974); *Career* trainee mangr W H Brandts Sons and Co Ltd 1971-73, Henry Ansbacher and Co Ltd 1973-85 (dir 1981-85), sr vp Bank Julius Baer and Co Ltd 1985-; *Recreations* sailing, swimming, tennis; *Style*— Philip Amphlett, Esq; Howletts, Gt Hallingbury, Bishops Stortford, Herts (☎ 0279 54563); Balaminces Cottage, Little Pethcrick, nr Wadebridge, N Cornwall; Bank Julius Baer and Co Ltd, Bevis Marks House, Bevis Marks, London EC3A 7NE (☎ 01 623 4211, fax 01 283 6146, telex 887272)

AMPTHILL, 4 Baron (UK 1881); Geoffrey Denis Erskine Russell; CBE (1986); s of 3 Baron Ampthill, CBE, by his 1 w, Christabel, da of Lt-Col John Hart, by his w, Blanche, 4 da of Capt David Erskine (2 s of Sir David Erskine, 1 Bt); suc 1973 and petitioned HM The Queen for a Writ of Summons as Baron Ampthill on death of 3 Baron, the House of Lords Ctee on Privileges deciding in his favour 1976; *b* 15 Oct 1921; *Educ* Stowe; *m* 1, 1946 (m dis 1971), Susan Mary Sheila, da of Hon Charles Winn (2 s of 2 Baron St Oswald, JP, DL) by his 1 w, Hon Olive Paget (da of 1 and last Baron Queenborough, GBE, JP); 2 s (and 1 s decd), 1 da; m 2 (m dis 1987), 1972, Elisabeth Anne-Marie, da of late Claude Mallon, of Paris, and of Mme Chavane; *Heir* s, Hon David Russell; *Career* serv WWII as Capt Irish Gds; gen mangr Fortnum & Mason 1947-51, chm: New Providence Hotel Co Ltd 1952-58, Theatre Producing Cos 1958-71; md Theatre Owning Cos 1958-69; dir: Dualvest 1980-87, United Newspapers 1981-, Express Newspapers plc 1985-; dep chm of Ctees House of Lords 1981-, dep speaker 1983-, chm of Select Ctee on Channel Tunnel Bill 1987; *Style*— The Rt Hon The Lord Ampthill, CBE; 51 Sutherland St, London SW1 4JX

ANASTASI, George; s of Michael Anastasi, and Paraskevou, *née* Mattheou; *b* 20 Oct 1941; *Educ* The Quintin Sch London, Goldsmiths Coll London; *m* 19 Dec 1964, Maureen Gillian Gloria, da of Alfred Charles Adams (d 1959); 1 s (Robert Matthew b 23 Nov 1979); *Career* asst vice pres Deltec Trading Co Ltd London 1969-73; mangr: First Boston Corp London 1973-74, Williams & Glyn's Bank Ltd London 1974-78; dir Donaldson Lufkin & Jenrette London 1978-80, exec mangr Arab Int Fin Ltd London 1980-83, dir Svenska Int plc London 1983-; *Style*— George Anastasi, Esq; 7 Clarendon Way, Chislehurst, Kent (☎ 0689 20112); Svenska House, 3-5 Newgate St, London EC1A 7DA (☎ 01 329 4467, fax 01 329 0036/7, telex 894716)

ANCASTER, Earl of; *see*: Willoughby de Eresby, Baroness

ANCRAM, Earl of; Michael Andrew Foster Jude Kerr; MP (C) Edinburgh S 1979-; s and h of 12 Marquess of Lothian; *b* 7 July 1945; *Educ* Ampleforth, Ch Ch Oxford (MA), Edinburgh Univ (LLB); *m* 1975, Lady Jane Fitzalan-Howard, da of 16 Duke of Norfolk, KG, GCVO, GBE, TD, PC (d 1975), and Lavinia, Duchess of Norfolk; 2 da (Lady Clare b 1979, Lady Mary b 1981); *Heir* bro, Lord Ralph Kerr; *Career* advocate (Scot) 1970; MP (C) Berwickshire and E Lothian Feb-Sept 1974, chm Cons Party in Scotland 1980-83 (vice-chm 1975-80), memb Select Ctee on Energy 1979-83, parly under-sec Scottish Office (Home Affairs and Environment) 1983-87; *Recreations* photography, folksinging; *Clubs* New (Edinburgh); *Style*— Earl of Ancram; 6 Ainslie Place, Edinburgh, Scotland (☎ 031 226 3147); Monteviot, Jedburgh, Scotland

ANDERSON, Alastair William; TD (1966); s of Cecil Brown Anderson 5, Dorchester Court, Glasgow (d 1965), and Janet Davidson, *née* Bell (d 1966); *b* 9 August 1931; *Educ* The High Sch of Glasgow, Glasgow Univ (BSc); *m* 6 Sept 1957, Jennifer Mary, da of Maj Charles W Markham (d 1942), of Clarkston, Glasgow; 1 s (Keith Charles b 30 July 1962); *Career* Nat Serv cmmnd 2 Lt RE 1954, serv Britcom Engr Regt Br Cwlth Forces Korea 1954-56; Crouch and Hogg Conslt engrs 1956-: assoc 1966-, ptnr 1971, sr ptnr 1981; church elder Broom Parish Church Newton Mearns Glasgow 1972-; Freeman Citizen of Glasgow 1950, memb Incorp of Masons Glasgow 1950; CEng 1969, FICE 1967, FIHT 1968, FRSA 1989, MCons E 1979; *Recreations* golf, gardening, reading, walking; *Clubs* Royal Scottish Automobile; *Style*— Alastair William, Esq; Storrs, 7 Greenback Ave, Whitecraigs, Giffnock, Glasgow G46 6SG (☎ 041 639 2343); Crouch & Hogg, Consulting Civil and Structural Engineers, 18 Woodside Cres, Glasgow G3 7UU (☎ 041 332 9755, fax 041 332 3446, telex 779860)

ANDERSON, Albert Alfred James; OBE (1980); s of Frank Alfred Anderson (d 1963), of Oare, Faversham, Kent, and Alice Morley, *née* Cock (d 1978); *b* 15 April 1909; *m* 26 Dec 1931, Alice Rhoda, da of Hermanus Bertram Rupert Alphonso de Leur (ka 1915), of Strood, Kent; 2 s (John Malcolm b 1939, d 1961, Roger Frank b 1942), 1 da (Margaret (Mrs MacInnes) b 1933); *Career* Cdr V Co 13 Bn, Royal West Kent HG, Maj 1941-46; chm and fndr The Kent Art Printers Ltd, chm World Sporting Pubns Ltd; cncllr Rochester City Cncl 1936-58 (alderman 1952), chm: Kent Mayors' Assoc 1975-76, 1980-81 and 1988-89 (fndr memb), Kent Rating Vauation Panel 1976-81, Rochester and Chatham Cons Assoc 1973-76, tstees Baynards Charity 1980-; pres: Medway Mentally Handicapped Soc 1963-, Rochester and Chatham Parly Constituency 1976-83, Medway Parly Constituency 1983-; Medway F of C 1964-68; hon life pres Medway & Gillingham C of C; govr Sir Joseph Williamson Mathematical Sch Rochester; Home Off ind memb: Canterbury Prison Parole Review Ctee 1973-82, Ladies Cookham Wood Borstal Prison Parole Review Ctee 1977-83; Mayor of Rochester, Constable of the Castle, Adm of the River Medway, JP 1951-53; Freeman: City of London 1953, City of Rochester Minnesota USA 1952; Liveryman Worshipful Co of Stationers and Newspaper Makers 1953; *Recreations* golf, voluntary charitable and public work; *Clubs* City Livery, St Stephens, Castle (Rochester); *Style*— Albert Anderson, Esq, OBE; Satis Ct, Esplanade, Rochester, Kent ME1 1QE (☎ 0634 429 33); Kent Art Printers Ltd, 344 High St, Rochester, Kent ME1 1DT (☎ 0634 44 352, fax 0634 421 14)

ANDERSON, Alexander George; s of William J Anderson (d 1962), of Aberdeen; *b* 29 July 1924; *Educ* Aberdeen GS, Aberdeen Univ (BSc); *m* 1947, Daphne Patricia Hilary, *née* Pidwell, of Camborne; 1 s, 1 da; *Career* civil engr; chm: William Tawse Ltd 1972-87, Aberdeen Construction Gp 1981-87; *Recreations* amateur radio, philately; *Clubs* Caledonian, Royal Northern; *Style*— Alexander Anderson, Esq; West Balfour House, Durris, Banchory, Kincardineshire (☎ 033 08 483)

ANDERSON, (Pamela) Ann; *née* Bates; da of Kenneth Lindley Bates, of Grantham, and Winifred Ethel Little (d 1987); *b* 9 Feb 1941; *Educ* Kesteven & Grantham Girl's Sch, Neville's Cross Coll Durham, Nottingham Univ (BEd, Advanced Diploma in Educn); *m* 30 July 1966, Colin Peter Odell, s of John William Anderson (d 1968), of Grantham; 1 s (Marcus b 1977), 1 da (Caroline b 1979); *Career* head Geography Dept St Hugh's Sch Grantham 1964-73, second dep head William Robertson Comprehensive Sch 1973-80, headmistress and fndr owner of Heathlands Prep Sch 1981-; *Recreations* portrait & porcelain painting, dress design; *Clubs* UK Fedn of Business and Professional Women; *Style*— Mrs Ann Anderson; Endahna House, Somerby Hill, Grantham, Lincs (☎ 0476 62050); Heathlands Preparatory School, Gorse Lane, Grantham (☎ 0476 64444)

ANDERSON, Anthony John; QC; s of A Fraser Anderson (d 1982), and Margaret Gray, *née* Spence (d 1986); *b* 12 Sept 1938; *Educ* Harrow, Magdalen Coll Oxford (MA); *m* 1970, Fenja Ragnhild, da of Havard Gunn, OBE; *Career* 2 Lt Gordon Highlanders 1957-59; barr Inner Temple 1964; *Recreations* golf; *Clubs* Garrick; *Style*— Anthony Anderson, Esq, QC; 33 Abinger Rd, Bedford Pk, London W4 (☎ 01 994 2857); 2 Mitre Ct Bldgs, Temple, London EC4 (☎ 01 583 1380)

ANDERSON, Dr Arthur John Ritchie (Iain); CBE (1984); s of Dr John Anderson (d 1966), of Pontrhydygroes, and Dorothy Mary Anderson (d 1966); *b* 19 July 1933; *Educ* Bromsgrove Sch, Downing Coll Cambridge (MA, MB, BChir), St Mary's Hosp Medical Sch; *m* 1959, Janet Edith, *née* Norrish; 2 s (John b 1963, Alan b 1971), 1 da (Margaret b 1965); *Career* gen medical and hosp practitioner; memb Regional Planning Cncl for SE 1977-79; memb NW Thames Regional Health Authority 1978-85; vice-chm Herts CC 1985-87; (ldr 1977-83); MRCGP, MRCS, LRCP, DCH, DRCOG, FRSM; *Clubs* Herts 100 (exec chm); *Style*— Dr Iain Anderson, CBE; Leaside, Rucklers Lane, King's Langley, Herts WD4 9NQ (☎ K's L 62884); office: The Nap, King's Langley, Herts (☎ K's L 63214)

ANDERSON, Lt-Col Charles Groves Wright; VC (1942), MC (1914-18 War); s of A G W Anderson, of Kenya; *b* 12 Feb 1897; *m* 1931, Edith Marian, da of late S.T. Tout, of Young, NSW, Australia; 2 s, 2 da; *Career* memb House of Representatives Hume NSW 1949-51 and 1956-61; grazier; *Style*— Lt-Col Charles Anderson, VC, MC; 119 Mugga Way, Red Hill, Canberra, Australia

ANDERSON, (Richard James) Colin; s of Richard Henry Anderson (d 1979), and Roseina, *née* Blaney; *b* 11 May 1954; *Educ* Regent House GS, Univ of Ulster; *m* 18 May 1978, Hilary Ann, da of Wilson Somerville Smyth; 1 s (Kyle), 1 da (Kelly); *Career* trainee Thomson Newspapers Orgn, fndr md and princ shareholder Anderson Advertising Ltd; memb NI Tourist Bd (Govt appt); cncl memb: NI C of C and Indust, former cncl memb NI Branch Inst of Mktg; rugby rep for: Ulster, Ards Rugby Club, CIYMS Rugby Club; Duke of Edinburgh's Gold Award (ctee memb NI); MInstM, memb IOD; *Recreations* yachting, skiing, golf, rugby; *Clubs* Ulster Reform, Royal Ulster YC; *Style*— Colin Anderson, Esq; Anderson House, Holywood Rd, Belfast BT4 2GU (☎ 0232 760 901, fax 0232 761 678)

ANDERSON, Rear Adm (Charles) Courtney; CB (1971); s of Lt-Col Charles Anderson (d 1919), Australian Light Horse, and Mrs Constance Powell-Anderson, OBE, JP; *b* 8 Nov 1916; *Educ* RNC Dartmouth; *m* 1940, Pamela Ruth, da of Lt-Col William Miles, RM (d 1947); 3 s; *Career* RN 1930, served WWII, naval attaché Bonn 1962-64, dir Naval Recruiting 1965-68, ADC to HM The Queen 1968, flag offr Admty Interview Bd 1969-71, ed The Board Bulletin 1971-78; *Recreations* gardening, Sea Cadets; *Style*— Rear Adm Courtney Anderson, CB; Bybrook Cottage, Bustlers Hill, Sherston, Malmesbury, Wilts SN16 0ND (☎ 0666 840323)

ANDERSON, David Colville; VRD and Clasp (1947, 1958), QC (Scot 1957); s of late John Lindsay Anderson, of Pittormie, Fife (d 1943), and Etta Colville (d 1949); *b* 8 Sept 1916; *Educ* Trinity Coll Glenalmond (Ashburton Shield winner 1933), Pembroke Coll Oxford (BA), Edinburgh Univ (LLB); *m* 1948, Juliet, yr da of Hon Lord Hill Watson, MC, LLD, of Barlanark, Edinburgh (d 1957); 2 s (Laurence and Gavin), 1 da (Lorraine); *Career* served WWII Lt RNVR N Sea destroyers and in Norway (despatches); Admiralty Egerton Prize for 1943 in Naval Gunnery; advocate 1946, MP (C) Dumfries Dec 1963-Sept 1964, slr-gen Scotland 1960-64; chief reporter for pub inquiries SO 1972-74, under-sec Civil Serv 1972-74; King Haakon VII Freedom Medal (Norway) 1945; subject of the play *The Case of David Anderson, QC* by John Hale (Manchester 1980, Edinburgh 1980, Lyric Hammersmith 1981); *Clubs* New (Edinburgh); *Style*— David Anderson, Esq, VRD, QC; Barlanark, 8 Arboretum Rd, Edinburgh EH3 5PD, Scotland (☎ 031 552 3003)

ANDERSON, David Munro; s of Alexander Anderson, St Clements, Jersey, CI, and Jessica Hope, *née* Vincent-Innes; *b* 15 Dec 1937; *Educ* Strathallan, Perthshire Scotland; *m* 3 April 1965, Veronica Jane, da of Reginald Eric Stevens; 2 s (Angus b 1 Oct 1967, Duncan b 10 Nov 1968), 1 da (Lucy b 29 Sept 1973); *Career* cmmnd The Black Watch 1956-59, The London Scottish 1963-68; dir: Anderson Man Ltd, Anderson Man Investmt Serv Ltd (Hong Kong), Bishopsgate Commodity Serv Ltd, ARMAC Mangrs Ltd (Bermuda), E D and F Man Fin Mkts Ltd, Commodities and Equities Tst Mangrs Ltd (IOM), Mint Ltd (Bermuda), E D and F Man Ltd, Mint Guaranteed (Aust) Ltd; chm Assoc for Futures Investmts; churchwarden Holy Innocents Lamarsh, memb Lamarsh PCC; *Recreations* shooting, skiing, gundog training, the arts; *Clubs* Caledonian; *Style*— David Anderson, Esq; The Old Rectory, Lamarsh, Bures, Suffolk; E D and F Man International, Sugar Quay, Lower Thames Street, London EC3R 6DU (☎ 01 626 8788, fax 01 621 0149)

ANDERSON, David St Kevin; s of Frederick St Kevin Anderson (d 1982), of Worthing, Sussex, and Eileen Celia, *née* Warwick; *b* 4 Oct 1927; *Educ* Clayesmore Sch Dorset; *m* 26 June 1959, Mary Isabella, da of William Garnett Ivory (d 1972), of East Grinstead; 1 s (Nigel b 1960), 1 da (Rosanagh b 1962); *Career* RM 1945-46, Lt Royal Fus 1946-48, serv 1 Bn BAOR; with Calico Printers Assoc Manchester 1948-50, WA Beardsell & Co Ltd Madras India 1950-56, Dexion Ltd 1956-70, Gravity Randall Ltd Horsham 1970-75, WC Youngman Ltd 1975-84, Gravity Randall Ltd 1984-87, dir Frank Odell Ltd Teddington 1987-88, conslt N-R Assocs 1989-; chm Cowden Parish Cncl, churchwarden St Mary Magdalene Cowden, memb Royal Br Legion; Liveryman Worshipful Co of Vintners 1956; *Recreations* photography, gardening, walking; *Style*— David Anderson, Esq; Medway House, Cowden, Kent TN8 7JQ (☎ 034 286 578)

ANDERSON, Denis Richard; s of Maj Thomas Richard Anderson, of Cloch-Na-Larty, 42 Shore Rd, Greenisland, Co Antrim, and Florence Anderson, *née* Johnston; *b* 8 Feb 1933; *Educ* Grosvenor HS Belfast, Coll of Art Belfast, Univ of Sheffield (Dip Arch); *m* 24 July 1959 (m dis 1972), Jennifer Mary, da of Alan Basset Ward (d 1978), of Gorse Hill, Baslow, Derbyshire; 1 s (Michael James b 29 Dec 1964), 2 da (Clare Sharon b 15 Nov 1961, Louise Jane b 8 June 1963); *Career* private practice Dublin 1964, jt practice Diamond Redfern Anderson 1966 (Diamond Partnership in UK 1987-); Castlepark Village Co Cork: RIAI commendation 1974, Irish Concrete Soc 1975, Concours cembureau Commendation 1975, Euro Architectural Heritage Year Silver Medal 1975; Martello Mews Dublin: Europa Nostra Dip Merit 1979, RIAI Silver Medal 1983; RIBA Commendation Dervock Village Co Anrtim 1979, RICS/Times Conservation Commendation Massereene Hosp Co Antrim 1980; memb RIBA 1962, fell RIAI 1980; *Recreations* skiing, swimming, cars, birdwatching, painting, cricket; *Clubs* Kildare St, and Univ (Dublin), East India, Devonshire, MCC, United Artists (Dublin); *Style*— Denis Anderson, Esq; 66 Bolosover St, London W1 (☎ 01 387 9781, fax 01 387 2480)

ANDERSON, Donald; MP (Lab) Swansea E 1974-; s of David Robert Anderson (d 1954), of Swansea, and Eva, *née* Mathias; *b* 17 June 1939; *Educ* Swansea GS, Univ Coll Swansea (BA); *m* 1963, Dorothy, BSc, PhD, da of Rev Frank Trotman (d 1970), missionary in Bolivia; 3 s (Robert b 1964, Hugh b 1967, Geraint b 1972); *Career* barr Inner Temple 1969; memb of FCO 1960-64 (HM Embassy Budapest); lectr in politics Univ Coll Swansea 1964-66; MP (Lab) Monmouth 1966-70; pps: Min of Defence 1969-70, Attorney Gen 1974-79; chm Select Ctee Welsh Affairs 1981-83, Oppn Spokesman Foreign Affairs 1983-; chm Welsh Lab Gp 1977-78; Methodist local preacher; hon fell Univ Coll Swansea; Awarded from Fed Rep for contribution to Br German Relations 1986; *Style*— Donald Anderson, Esq, MP; c/o House of Commons, London SW1A 0AA (☎ 01 219 3425) Lamb Building, Temple, London EC4;

ANDERSON, Lady; Doris Norah; er da of Lt-Col John Henry Wybergh (d 1962), of Ewshott, Hants, and Norah Selina, *née* Perceval-Maxwell; *b* 5 August 1916; *m* 23 Dec 1942, Lt-Gen Sir Richard Neville Anderson KCB, CBE, DSO (d 1979), s of Lt-Col Sir Neville Anderson, CBE (d 1963); 2 s; *Recreations* horse breeding, whippet breeding and coursing, judging show ponies and dogs; *Style*— Lady Anderson; Tarrant Keynston House, Blandford, Dorset (☎ 0258 52138)

ANDERSON, Douglas Kinloch; OBE (1983); s of William James Kinloch Anderson, of 12 Abbotsford Ct, Edinburgh 10, and Margaret, *née* Margaret Gowenlock Harper; *b* 19 Feb 1939; *Educ* George Watsons Coll, Edinburgh, Univ of St Andrews (MA), Univ of Edinburgh; *m* 16 June 1962, Deirdre Anne Kinloch, da of Leonard Walter Loryman (d 1985); 2 s (Peter Douglas b 1964, John William b 1972), 1 da Claire Deirdre b 1964); *Career* chm Kinloch Anderson Ltd 1980- (dir 1962-72, md 1972-); dir: Edinburgh Capital Ltd, Chamber Devpts Ltd; bd memb Scottish Tourist Bd 1986-; pres Edinburgh Assoc of Royal Tradesmen 1986-88, Edinburgh C of C 1988-; tres Edinburgh Merchant Co 1988-, memb Edinburgh Festival C of C 1988-; *Recreations* fishing, golf, skiing, travel, reading; *Clubs* New (Edinburgh), Brunsfield Golfing Soc, Caledonian (Edinburgh); *Style*— Douglas Kinloch Anderson, OBE; Dalveen, 7 Barnton Park, Edinburgh EH4 6JF (☎ 031 336 3214); Kinloch Anderson Ltd, 2/4 Restalrig Dr, Edinburgh EH7 6JZ (☎ 031 661 7241, telex 727654 LOCHAN)

ANDERSON, Hon Mrs (Emily Mary); da of 3 Viscount Astor (d 1966), and his 2 w, Philippa, da of Lt-Col Henry Hunloke (o s of Maj Sir Philip Hunloke, GCVO) and Lady Anne Cavendish, MBE, JP, 5 da of 9 Duke of Devonshire, KG, GCMG, GCVO, PC, JP, DL; *b* 9 June 1956; *Educ* Francis Holland Sch; *m* 1, 1984, Alan McL Gregory, er s of Donald Gregory, of San Francisco, California, USA; m 2, 7 April 1988, as his 2 w, James Ian Anderson, o s of Capt John Murray Anderson, MC, and Lady Gillian Mary, *née* Drummond, da of 18 Earl of Perth; *Career* photographer; *Style*— The Hon Emily Astor; 14 Shalcomb St, London SW10 0HY (☎ 01 351 6554)

ANDERSON, (William) Eric Kinloch; s of William James Kinloch Anderson, of Edinburgh; *b* 27 May 1936; *Educ* George Watson's Coll, St Andrews Univ (MA), Balliol Coll Oxford (BLitt); *m* 1960, Anne Elizabeth (Poppy), da of William Mattock Mason (d 1988), of Yorks; 1 s (David b 1961), 1 da (Catherine b 1963); *Career* asst master: Fettes 1960-64 and 1966-70, Gordonstoun 1964-66; headmaster: Abingdon Sch 1970-75, Shrewsbury 1975-80, Eton 1980-; Hon DLitt St Andrews 1981; FRSE 1985; *Books* Journal of Sir Walter Scott (ed 1972), Percy Letter, Vol IX (ed 1989); *Recreations* golf, fishing; *Style*— Eric Anderson, Esq; The Cloisters, Eton College, Windsor, Berks

ANDERSON, Prof Sir (William) Ferguson; OBE (1961); s of Capt James Kirkwood Anderson, 7th Scottish Rifles (ka Gaza 1917), and late Sarah Barr Anderson; *b* 8 April 1914; *Educ* Merchiston, Glasgow Acad, Glasgow Univ (MB, ChB, MD); *m* 1940, Margaret Gebbie; 1 s, 2 da; *Career* physician in geriatric med Stobhill Gen Hosp and advsr in diseases of old age and chronic sickness; W Regn Hosp Bd Scotland 1952-74, David Cargill prof of geriatric med Glasgow Univ 1965-79; hon pres Crossroads (Scotland) Care Attendant Scheme; hon chm Euro Clinical Section Int Assoc Gerontology; KStJ 1974; co-author Practical Mgmnt of the Elderly 1989; awarded Brookdale Prize - The Gerontological Soc of America 1984; FRCPG, FRCPE, FRCP, FRCP (C), FRCPI, FACP; kt 1974; *Recreations* golf; *Clubs* Roy Scottish Automobile; *Style*— Prof Sir Ferguson Anderson, OBE; Rodel, Moor Rd, Strathblane, Glasgow G63 9EX (☎ 0360 70862)

ANDERSON, Lady Flavia Joan Lucy; *née* Giffard; da of 2 Earl of Halsbury, KC (d 1943), and Esmé Stewart Wallace; *b* 20 Sept 1910; *Educ* Queen's Gate Sch; *m* 1933, James Alasdair Anderson (d 1982), of Tullichewan; 1 s (Douglas Hardinge, portraitist and wild-life artist; m 1, 1962, Mary Jenkins; m 2, 1974, Veronica Markes), 1 da (Margaret Minette Rohais, m, 1961, Sir Ilay Campbell, 7 Bt, *qv*) *see* Halsbury, Earl of; *Career* author of six books; Medaille de Vermeil de la Reconaissance Française 1946; *Style*— Lady Flavia Anderson; 13 Carlton Terrace, Edinburgh EH7 5DD

ANDERSON, Lady Gillian Mary; *née* Drummond; yst da of 16 Earl of Perth, GCMG, CB, PC (d 1951); *b* 17 Feb 1920; *m* 1946, Capt John Murray Anderson, MC and bar, late Seaforth Highers; 1 s, 3 da; *Style*— Lady Gillian Anderson; Wilderwick House, E Grinstead, W Sussex RH19 3NS (☎ 034 287 242)

ANDERSON, Gordon Alexander; s of Cecil Brown Anderson (d 1965), of Glasgow, and Janet Davidson, *née* Bell (d 1966); *b* 9 August 1931; *Educ* Glasgow HS; *m* 12 Mar 1958, Eirene Cochrane Howie, da of Richmond Douglas (d 1980), of Troon; 2 s (David b 1958, Colin b 1961, Carolyn b 1967); *Career* Nat Serv Sub Lieut RN 1955-57; with Moores Carson & Watson Glasgow 1945-55; CA 1955; sr asst Moores Carson & Watson 1957-58; ptnr Moores Carson & Watson (and subsequent firms, McClelland Moores & Co, Arthur Young McClelland Moores & Co) now Arthur Young 1958- (memb exec ctee 1972-84, office managing ptnr Glasgow 1976-79, chm 1987-), dir High Sch of Glasgow Ltd 1975-81, pres Glasgow High Sch Club 1978-79, pres inst Chartered Accountants of Scotland 1986-87 (memb cncl 1980-84, vice pres 1984-86), memb Scottish Milk Marketing Bd 1979-85; FCMA (1984); *Recreations* golf, gardening, opera; *Clubs* Caledonian, Western (Glasgow), Glasgow Golf, Buchanan Castle Golf; *Style*— Gordon Anderson Esq; Ardwell, 41 Manse Road, Bearsden, Glasgow G61 3PN (☎ 041 942 2803); Arthur Young, Chartered Accountants, Rolls House, 7 Rolls Buildings, Fetter Lane, London EC4A 1NH (☎ 01 831 7130, fax 01 405 2147, telex 888604)

ANDERSON, Rev Hector David; LVO (1949); s of Rev David Anderson, LLD, (d 1922), Clerk in Holy Orders, of Leinster Square, Dublin, and Edith Pope (d 1940); *b* 16 August 1906; *Educ* The Abbey Tipperary, Trinity Coll Dublin; *m* 1931, Muriel Louise, da of Edwin Cecil Peters (d 1954), of The Ridgeway, Purleybury Avenue, Purley, Surrey; 1 s (Christopher); *Career* ordained priest Canterbury Cathedral 1931;

rector of: Sandringham 1942-55, Swanage, Dorset 1960-69; domestic chaplain to: HM King George VI 1942-55, HM The Queen 1955-70; ret; *Style—* The Rev H D Anderson; Adare, The Hyde, Langton Matravers, Dorset (☎ 423206)

ANDERSON, Prof John Allan Dalrymple; TD (1967), DL (Richmond); s of Lt Col John Allan Anderson, RAMC (d 1942), and Mary Winifred, *née* Lawson (d 1973); *b* 16 June 1926; *Educ* Loretto, Oxford Univ (BA, MA), Edinburgh Univ (MB, ChB, MD), London Univ (DPH); *m* 3 April 1965, Mairead Mary, da of Dr P D Maclaren (d 1967), of Edinburgh; 3 da (Sheena b 1966, Mary b 1968, Anne b 1972); *Career* Nat Serv Capt RAMC 1950-52, Maj RMO 7/9 Royal Scots (TA) 1953-63, Maj 51 Highland Vols OC G Co 1967-70, Lt Col CO 221 Field Ambulance RAMC (TA), Col London Dist TA 1981-83, Regtl and Dep Hon Col 51 Highland Vols 1983-; lectr dep of gen practice Univ of Edinburgh 1954-59, physician and res fell industrial survey unit dept of rheumatology Univ of Edinburgh 1960-63, sr lectr preventive med London Sch of Hygiene and Tropical Med 1963-68, dir of dept of community med Guys Hosp Med Sch (subsequently merged with St Thomas's to form Utd Med and Dental Schs) 1969-, hon conslt Guys Hosp 1969-, med dir Occupational Health Serv Lewisham & N Southwark Health Dist 1984-; hon physician Royal Scottish Corpn, academic registrar Faculty of Community Med; Freeman City of London; Liveryman Worshipful Co of Apothecaries (hon sec); FRCP 1987, FFCM 1974, FRCGP 1985, MFOM 1985; *Books* A New Look at Community Medicine (1966), Self-Medication (1970), Bibliography of Back Pain (1978), Epidemiological, Sociological and Enviromental Aspects of Rheumatic Diseases (1987); *Recreations* hill-climbing, golf, bridge; *Clubs* New Edinburgh; *Style—* Prof John Anderson, TD, DL; 24 Lytton Grove, Putney, London SW15 2HB (☎ 01 788 9420); Guy's Hospital, London SE1 (☎ 01 407 7600 ext 2157)

ANDERSON, Hon John Desmond Forbes; s and h of 2 Viscount Waverley; *b* 31 Oct 1949; *Educ* Malvern; *Style—* The Hon John Anderson

ANDERSON, Maj-Gen Sir John Evelyn; KBE (1971), CBE (1963); s of Lt-Col John Gibson Anderson, of Christchurch, NZ, and Margaret, *née* Scott; *b* 28 June 1916; *Educ* King's Sch Rochester, RMA Woolwich; *m* 1944, Jean Isobel, 2 da of Charles Tait, of Tarves, Aberdeenshire; 1 s, 1 da; *Career* cmmnd Royal Signals 1936, Lt-Col 1956, Col 1960, Brig 1964, Maj-Gen 1967, Signal Offr in Chief (Army) MOD 1967-69, ACDS (Signals) 1969-72; Hon Col: 71 (Yeo) Signal Regt TAVR 1969-76, Women's Tport Corps (FANY) 1970-76; dir-gen NATO Integrated Communication System Mgmnt Agency 1977-81, conslt (electronics and communications) 1981-; exec dir AFCEA Europe Group 1981-88, dir Space & Maritime Applications Inc 1988-; *Recreations* fishing, gardening; *Clubs* Army and Navy, Flyfishers; *Style—* Maj-Gen Sir John Anderson, KBE; The Beeches, Amport, nr Andover, Hants

ANDERSON, Sir John Muir; CMG (1957); s of John Weir Anderson, of 39 Drake St, Brighton, Victoria, Australia; *b* 14 Sept 1914; *Educ* Brighton GS, Melbourne Univ; *m* 1949, Audrey Drayton Jamieson; 1 s, 1 da; *Career* 2nd AIF with 2/6th Commando Co an d 1 Australian Parachute Bn, active serv in SE Asia, Papua and New Guinea; tres Lib Party 1956-61 and 1978-79, tstee Melbourne Exhibition 1960-67 (chm 1967), cmmr Melbourne Harbour Tst 1972-82, cmmr State Savings Bank Victoria 1962-, ch cmmr 1967; fndr John M Anderson & Co Pty Ltd 1951, md King Oscar Fine Foods Pty Ltd, dir Victorian Insurance Co Ltd 1968, New Zealand Insurance Co Ltd 1972, pres Liberal and Country Pty Victoria 1952-56; Coronation Medal 1953, Jubilee Medal 1977; kt 1969; *Clubs* Melbourne, VRC; *Style—* Sir John Anderson, CMG; 25 Cosham St, Brighton, Vic 3186, Australia (☎ 592 4790)

ANDERSON, John Stewart; TD and Bar; s of Percy Stewart Anderson (d 1960), and Mabel France, *née* Jones (d 1962); *b* 3 August 1935; *Educ* Shrewsbury Sch, Manchester Univ (BA), Salford Univ (MSc) ; *m* 28 Sept 1963, Alice Beatrice, da of Arthur Shelmerdine, of Holmes Chapel, Cheshire; 1 s (Guy Stewart b 1964); *Career* 2 Lieut RE, Lieut Suez Rerserve 1956, Major RE TA and RCT 1956-76; architect and planner private and publics offs 1962-74, dir planning and architecture Lincoln City Cncl 1974-85, conslt architect and town planner 1985-; cncl memb Royal Town Planning Inst (pres 1984); chm Int Affrs Bd; ARIBA, FRTPI, FRSA; *Style—* John Anderson, Esq, TD; The Old Stables, Harston, Grantham (☎ 0476 870 424, fax 0476 870 816)

ANDERSON, Mrs Ande; Josephine Clare; *see*: Barstow, Josephine Clare

ANDERSON, Dame Judith Frances Margaret; DBE (1960); da of James Anderson and Jessie Saltmarsh; *b* 10 Feb 1898; *Educ* Norwood HS S Australia; *m* 1, 1937 (m dis 1939) Prof B H Lehman; m 2, 1946 (m dis 1950), Luther Greene; *Career* stage and screen actress; *Films include* Rebecca (as Mrs Danvers), Spectre of the Rose, Cat on a Hot Tin Roof, A Man Called Horse, Star Trek III (1984); *Stage appearances include* Mourning Becomes Electra (1931), Macbeth (opposite Laurence Olivier, Old Vic 1937), Medea (1947-49, New York and on tour); The Oresteia (1966), Hamlet (1970); *Style—* Dame Judith Anderson, DBE; 808 San Ysidro Lane, Santa Barbara, Calif 93103, USA

ANDERSON, Julian Anthony; s of Sir Kenneth Anderson, of London, and Helen Veronica, *née* Grose (d 1986); *b* 12 June 1938; *Educ* King Alfred Sch, Wadham Coll Oxford (MA); *m* 1983, Penelope Ann, da of Arthur Stanley Slocombe (d 1969); *Career* entered civil service as asst principal 1961, asst private sec to Minister 1964-66, principal 1966; seconded FCO as memb UK EEC accession negotiating team 1970-73, asst sec 1973; seconded to FCO as Minister (Food and Agric), UK perm rep to EEC 1982-85, presently under sec Lands and Environmental Affairs Min of Agriculture, Fisheries and Food; *Recreations* music, sport, travel, photography, gardening, DIY; *Clubs* Civic Service; *Style—* Julian A Anderson, Esq; c/o Ministry of Agriculture, Fisheries & Food, Whitehall Place, London SW1

ANDERSON, Sir Kenneth; KBE (1962), CBE (1946, CB 1955); s of Walter Anderson (d 1953), of Exmouth, Devon, and Susannah, *née* Chirgwin; *b* 5 June 1906; *Educ* Swindon Sec Sch, Wadham Coll Oxford (MA); *m* 1932, Helen Veronica (d 1986), da of John Gilbert Grose (d 1965), of Bickington, Devon; 1 s (Julian), 1 da (Shirley); *Career* India Off 1928-47, Military Govt Germany 1947-48, HM Treasy 1949-52, dep dir-gen and comptroller & accountant-gen GPO 1952-66; Offr Order of Orange-Nassau 1947; *Recreations* music, art; *Clubs* United Oxford and Cambridge Univs; *Style—* Sir Kenneth Anderson, KBE, CBE, CB; 7 Milton Close, London N2 0QH (☎ 01 455 8701)

ANDERSON, Hon Sir Kenneth McColl; KBE (1972); s of late D M Anderson; *b* 11 Oct 1909; *m* 1936, Madge M; 1 da; *Career* sen NSW 1953-75, govt ldr in Senate 1968-72, cwlth min for Health 1971-72; kt 1970; *Style—* The Hon Sir Kenneth Anderson, KBE; 80 E Parade, Eastwood, NSW, Australia

ANDERSON, Hon Sir Kevin Victor; s of Robert Victor Anderson (d 1951), and Margaret Mary, *née* Collins (d 1961); *b* 4 Sept 1912; *Educ* Xavier Coll Kew, Melbourne Univ; *m* 1942, Claire Margaret, da of Laurence James Murphy (d 1943), 6 da (Jillian b 1943, Carol b 1945, Barbara b 1947, Frances b 1949, Judith b 1951, Suzanne b 1953); *Career* Lt RANVR Pacific 1942-46; Victorian Crown Law Dept 1929-42, barr 1946-69; QC (Vic) 1962, Supreme Ct Judge 1969-84; chm Vict Bar Cncl 1966-67, tres Law Cncl of Australia 1966-68; chm Scientology B of Inquiry 1963-65; Kt SMO Malta (Aust) 1979; kt 1980; *Books* Stamp Duties in Victoria (second edn 1968), Price Control (jtly 1947), Landlord and Tenant (third edn 1958), Victorian Licensing Law (1952), Victorian Police Manual (second edn 1969), Workers Compensation (second edn 1966), Fossil in the Sandstone, The Recollecting Judge (1986), Ed Victorian Law Reports 1956-69; *Recreations* yachting, woodworking; *Clubs* Royal Automobile of Vict, Victoria Racing, Celtic, Essoign; *Style—* The Hon Sir Kevin Anderson; 12 Power Ave, Toorak, Vic 3142, Australia (☎ 202901)

ANDERSON, Lindsay Gordon; s of late Maj-Gen A V Anderson and late Estelle Bell Sleigh; *b* 17 April 1923; *Educ* Cheltenham Coll, Wadham Coll Oxford (MA); *Career* Lt KRRC; film and theatre director; assoc artistic dir Roy Court Theatre 1969-75; *film documentaries include*: Thursday's Children (Hollywood Academy Award 1953), Every Day Except Christmas (Venice Grand Prix 1957), Raz, Dwa, Trzy (The Singing Lesson) 1967; If you were there.... (1985); feature films include: This Sporting Life (1963), If....(1968, Grand Prix Cannes 1969), O Lucky Man! (1973), In Celebration (1975), Britannia Hospital (1982), The Whales of August (1987); *Theatre productions include*: The Long and The Short and The Tall, Serjeant Musgrave's Dance, Billy Liar, In Celebration, The Contractor, Home, The Changing Room, The Farm, Life Class, The Sea Gull, The Bed Before Yesterday, Early Days, Hamlet, The Cherry Orchard, The Playboy of the Western World, In Celebration (New York), Hamlet (Washington DC), Holiday; *for Television*: The Old Crowd (Alan Bennett), Free Cinema (film Essay, 1986); *Books* Making a Film (1952), About John Ford (1980); *Style—* Lindsay Anderson, Esq; 9 Stirling Mansions, Canfield Gdns, London NW6

ANDERSON, Lady; Lorna Ticehurst; *m* 1974, as his 2 w, Sir David Anderson Stirling (d 1981); *Style—* Lady Anderson; Flat 10, Queen's Court, Helensburgh, Dunbartonshire G84 7PA (☎ Helensburgh 2227)

ANDERSON, Brig Hon Dame Mary McKenzie; *see*: Pihl, Brig Hon Dame M M

ANDERSON, Michael Arthur; JP (Chester 1979); s of Alexander William Anderson (d 1971), and Winifred Ann, *née* Pusill (d 1978); matriculation of Arms granted in 1980 by Lord Lyon, King of Arms, based on Arms granted in 1780 but in use prior to 1665; *b* 23 Mar 1928; *Educ* LSE (BSc); *m* 1954, Anne, da of Joseph Beynon (d 1965); 2 s (Michael, Richard), 2 da (Sarah, Deborah); *Career* fin dir Caribbean Printers Ltd Trinidad 1960-61, sr fin appts Ford Motor Co and Ford of Europe 1962-67, fin dir Manchester Guardian and Evening News Ltd 1968-69, gp fin dir Tillotson & Son Ltd 1970-71, sr fin appts BL 1972-75, fin dir Mersey Docks & Harbour Co 1975-84; dir: Liverpool Grain Storage & Transit Co Ltd 1979-, Anderson & Co (chartered accountants) 1984-, bus cnsllr to Govt Small Firms Service 1985-; FCA, FCMA; *Books* Anderson Families (Phillimore 1984); *Recreations* genealogy, walking, opera, classical music; *Style—* Michael Anderson, Esq, JP; Kintrave, Wood Lane, Burton, Cheshire, S Wirral L64 5TB (051 336 4349)

ANDERSON, Nigel James Moffatt; MC (1940), DL (1974 Wilts); s of Col John Hubback Anderson, CMG, CBE, MD, of Woodend, Victoria, Australia & Ruthin, Clwyd, N Wales (d 1951), and Ruby Claire, *née* Moffatt (d 1937); *b* 9 Mar 1920; *Educ* Marlborough Coll, Trinity Coll Oxford (MA); *m* 1 Jan 1942, Phyllis Daphne, da of George McKim Siggins, of Portrush, Co Antrim (d 1963); *Career* cmmnd TA, Lieut Royal Welch Fusiliers N W Europe invalided out 1943; forester; Wiltshire Country Cmd 1955-85 (chm 1979-84); pres Wiltshire CLA-, chm Wilts Scout Cncl, pres Wilts Youth Concert Orchestra; *Recreations* fishing, gardening; *Clubs* Leander; *Style—* Nigel Anderson, Esq, MC, DL; Hamptworth Lodge, Landford, Salisbury, Wiltshire SP5 2EA (☎ Romsey 390215)

ANDERSON, Prof Sir (James) Norman Dalrymple; OBE (mil 1945, MBE mil 1943), QC (1974); s of William Dalrymple Anderson (d 1946); *b* 29 Sept 1908; *Educ* St Lawrence Coll Ramsgate, Trinity Coll Cambridge (MA, LLB, LLD); *m* 1933, Patricia Hope, da of A Stock Givan; 1 s and 2 da (decd); *Career* served WWII in Army as arab liaison offr Libyan Arab Force 1940, Civil Affrs GHQ MEF 1941-46, ret as chief sec (Col); barrister; prof oriental laws London Univ 1954-75, dir Inst Advanced Legal Studies London Univ 1959-76, dean Faculty of Law London Univ 1965-69; pres Soc of Public Teachers of Law 1968-69, chm House of Laity General Synod C of E 1970-79; Hon DD (St Andrews) 1974; FBA 1970; Libyan Order of Independence 1959; kt 1975; *Recreations* reading, writing (has published 19 books); *Clubs* Athenaeum; *Style—* Prof Sir Norman Anderson, OBE, QC; 9 Larchfield, Gough Way, Cambridge (☎ 0223 358778)

ANDERSON, Hon (Patricia Mairead Janet); *née* Anderson; da of 2 Viscount Waverley *qv*; *b* 2 Mar 1955; *m* 1 June 1979 (m dis), Charles R Roberts, o s of Alan Roberts, of Eastwood Farm, Graffham, Petworth, Sussex; resumed her maiden name; *Recreations* 3 day eventing, dressage; *Clubs* Lansdowne; *Style—* The Hon Patricia Anderson

ANDERSON, Hon Mrs (Paulette Anne); *née* Sainsbury; only da of Baron Sainsbury by his 2 w; *b* 2 Mar 1946; *m* 1970, James Anderson; *Style—* The Hon Mrs Anderson; J Sainsbury plc, Stamford House, Stamford St, London SE1 9LL

ANDERSON, Dr Robert David; s of Robert David Anderson (d 1956), of 54 Hornton St, London W8 4NT, and Gladys, *née* Clayton (d 1973); *b* 20 August 1927; *Educ* Harrow, Gonville and Caius Coll Cambridge (MA); *Career* dir music Gordonstoun Sch 1958-62, extra mural lectr Egyptology Univ of London 1966-77, assoc ed The Musical Times 1967-85, conductor St Barts Hosp Choral Soc 1967-, visiting lectr in music City Univ 1983-, admin dir Egypt Exploration Soc (dig at Qasr Ibrim) 1977-80 (hon sec soc 1971-82), music critic for The Times, radio and TV for BBC; Freeman: City of London 1977, Worshipful Co of Musicians 1977; Hon DMus City Univ 1985; FSA 1983; *Books* Catalogue of Egyptian Antiquities in the British Museum III, Musical Instruments (1976), Wagner (1980), Egypt in 1800 (jt ed 1988); *Recreations* modulating from music to Egyptology; *Style—* Dr Robert Anderson; 54 Hornton St, London W8 4NT (☎ 01 937 5146); The Manor House, Burravoe, Yell, Shetland

ANDERSON, Dr Robert Geoffrey William; er s of Herbert Patrick Anderson, and Kathleen Diana, *née* Burns; *b* 2 May 1944; *Educ* Oxford (BSc, MA, DPhil); *m* 1973, Margaret Elizabeth Callis, da of John Austin Lea; 2 s (William b 1979, Edward b 1984); *Career* keeper of Chemistry Sci Museum 1980-84; dir: Royal Scottish Museum 1984-

85, Nat Museums of Scotland 1985-; *Clubs* Athenaeum; *Style—* Dr Robert Anderson; 11 Dryden Place, Edinburgh (☎ 031 667 8211); Royal Museum of Scotland, Chambers St, Edinburgh (☎ 031 225 7534)

ANDERSON, Prof Robert Henry; s of Henry Anderson (d 1981), and Doris Amy, *née* Callear (d 1977); *b* 4 April 1942; *Educ* Wellington, Manchester Univ (BSc, MB, ChB, MD); *m* 9 July 1966, Christine, da of Keith Ibbotson, of Grantham, Lincs; 1 s (John b 1972), 1 da (Elizabeth b 1970); *Career* travelling fell MRC Univ of Amsterdam 1973, sr res fell Br Heart Fndn Brompton Hosp 1974, Joseph Levy reader in paediatric cardiac morphology Cardiothoracic Inst 1977 (prof 1979), visiting prof Univ of Pittsburgh 1984-89, hon prof Univ of North Carolina 1984-89, visiting prof Univ of Liverpool 1988-89; Excerpta Medica Travel Award 1977, Br Heart Fndn Prize for Cardiovasular Res 1984; FRC Path 1979; publications: 300 articles, 200 chapters in books, 19 books incl: Cardiac Anatomy (1978), Cardiac Pathology (1983), Surgical Anatomy of the Heart (1985), Paediatric Cardiology (2 volumes, 1987); *Recreations* music, golf, wine; *Clubs* Roehampton; *Style—* Prof Robert Anderson; 60 Earlsfield Rd, Wandsworth, London SW18 3DN (☎ 01 870 4368); Department of Paediatrics, National Heart & Lung Institute, Dovehouse St, London SW3 6LY (☎ 01 352 8121, fax 01 376 3442)

ANDERSON, Robert O; *Career* dep chm Observer Newspaper Gp 1983- (chm to 1983); chm Atlantic Richfield 1983-; *Style—* Robert Anderson, Esq; Observer Ltd, 8 St Andrews Hill, London EC4V 5JA

ANDERSON, Robert Orville; s of Hugo August Anderson (d 1984), and Hilda Nelson (d 1974); *b* 13 April 1917; *Educ* Univ of Chicago (BA), Univ of Pennsylvania, Dr of Amherst Coll; *m* 1939, Barbara Phelps; 2 s (William, Robert), 5 da (Katherine, Maria, Barbara, Julia, Beverley); *Career* former chm of bd Atlantic Richfield Co LA California, chm The Diamond A Cattle Co Roswell New Mexico, chm Utd New Mexico Fin Corpn Albuquerque New Mexico; dir Weverhaeuser Co Co Tacoma Washington, Carter Hawley Hale Stores LA California; Swedish-American of the Year (Vasa Order) New York 1978, Cdrs Cross of the Order of Merit DRG 1978, Asia Soc Award 1984, Grand Cross North Star of the Royal Order of the Polar Star 1984, Herbert Hoover Humanitarian Award 1982; *Recreations* fishing, hunting; *Clubs* Athenaeum, California (LA), Capitol Hill (Washington DC), Links (NY), Metropolitan (Washington DC), Pacific Union (San Francisco); *Style—* Robert Anderson, Esq; PO Box 1000, Roswell, New Mexico 88201 (☎ 010 1 505 625 8700)

ANDERSON, Roger James; s of Eric Alfred Anderson, of Ringwood, Hants, and Joyce Eleanor Anderson (d 1987); *b* 27 Sept 1948; *Educ* Brockenhurst GS, UCL (BSc); *Career* reporter: Textile Trade Pubns 1968-70, Essex Chronicle Series 1970-75; ed Insurance Week 1979-85, dir Centaur Professional Publishing 1987-, publisher Money Marketing 1988-(ed 1985-88); *Books* Insurers Buyers Guide (1985), Directors Guide to Company Insurance (1986), Marketing Insurance (1986), Facing the Challenge of The Financial Services Act (1987); *Recreations* photography; *Style—* Roger Anderson, Esq; The Lodge, Troston, nr Bury St Edmunds, Suffolk (☎ 035 96 8337); Centaur Communications, 49-50 Poland St, London W1V 4AX (☎ 01 439 4222)

ANDERSON, Brig (James) Roy; CBE (1971, OBE 1964); s of George Anderson (d 1964), of Kirn, Argyllshire, and Elizabeth Cecily, *née* Findlater (d 1965); *b* 9 Dec 1919; *Educ* Graduate Army Staff Coll; *m* 1, 1948 (m dis 1978), Mollie Agatha, *née* Drake-Brockman; 1 s (Hamish b 1952), 1 da (Sheena b 1954); m 2, 1978, Patricia Mary Philomena Ramsay, da of Dr J J Morrin (d 1952), of 1 Walton Pl, London SW3; *Career* Roy Sussex Regt 1939-71, CO (Lt Col) 3 Bn KAR 1962-64, Asst Mil Sec MOD 1965-66, Regtl Col The Queen's Regt 1966, Chief of Staff (Brig) Kenyan Armed Forces 1966-70, Divnl Brig The Queen's Divn 1970-71; sales dir Brooke Marine (Warship Divn) 1972-84, chm E Anglian Rod Co (wholesale game fishing tackle co) 1984-88, non-exec dir Braunston Canal Marina 1989-; chm Shadingfield Beccles PCC 1983-88; MBIM 1969; *Recreations* game fishing, swimming, gardening; *Clubs* United Service, Naval & Military; *Style—* Brig Roy Anderson, CBE, OBE; Cherwell Cottage, Aston-Le-Walls, Northants NN11 6HF (☎ 029 586 737)

ANDERTON, John Bury; s of Lt-Cmdr Geoffrey Bury Anderton, DSC, RNVR (d 1954), of London, and Laura Maud Plumb (d 1968, stage name Ruby Lester), of London; originally strong RC family which went underground during reign of Henry VIII, Roger Anderton (priest) set up Clandestine Printing Press to publish RC tracts throughout England; *Educ* Corringe Memorial Sch Kent; *m* 28 March 1952, Audrey Gloria, da of John Westwood (d 1975), of Devon; 1 da (Lesley Jacqueline Bury b 1953); *Career* Lt 7 Rajput Regt (Indian Army) and Br Parachute Regt 1944-48; chm: Andy Hampers Ltd 1963-87, Pilgrims Progress Tours 1972-; md Turner & Price Ltd 1976-87; vice-chm Spreyton PCC, Spreyton rep on the Okehampton Deanry Synod, Okehampton Deanery Synod rep on Exeter Diocesan Synod; *Recreations* organ, philately, walking; *Style—* John Anderton, Esq; The Jolleys, Spreyton, Crediton, Devon EX17 5AN (☎ 064723 551); Westwood House, Spreyton, Crediton, Devon EX17 5AN (☎ 064723 552, telex 42628)

ANDERTON, John Woolven; OBE (1978), VRD (1958); s of Edward Cooke Anderton (d 1947), of Southport, Lancs, and Anne Nell Amelia, *née* Woolven (d 1965); *b* 8 August 1923; *Educ* Terra Nova PS Birkdale, Worksop Coll; *m* 1, 1951 (m dis 1964), Patricia Thompson-Smith; 2 s (Nigel b 1954, Mark b 1958), 1 da (Sally b 1955); m 2, 1966 (m dis 1974), Pamela Jane Astley-Cooper; m 3, 5 June 1975, Constance Mary, da of Dr Oswald Richardson (d 1966), of Milford-on-Sea, Hants; *Career* entered RN 1941, served Fleet Air Arm, Cmmnd 1943 served Atlantic and Russian convoys, comb ops Med and Normandy landing, Arctic and Far East, cmd major landing craft, MTBs, SDBs; past war attached Mersey Divn RNVR (later RNR) 1946-61; ret (own request) Lt-Cdr 1961; md E C Anderton Ltd (Textiles) 1947-52, dir 15 real estate cos on Merseyside 1952-64; hon sec and later dir Br Assoc for Shooting and Conservation (formerly WAGBI) 1957-88; fndr Standing Conf on countryside sports; memb: Nature Conservancy Wildfowl Conservation Ctee 1957-73 (chm 1967-69), Home Sec's Advsy Ctee for Protection of Birds 1961-77 (became DOE Ctee 1977-82, then Nature Conservancy Cncl Ctee 1982-84), Medway Panel of Inquiry into Shooting and Angling 1976-79; fndr memb UK Fedn of Hunting Assocs of the EEC 1977-87; past memb: Int Waterfowl Res Bureau, Game Conservation int chm int Advsy ctte (1981-82); contrib numerous articles to sporting and shooting press; *Recreations* all countryside activities, gerdening, shooting, sailing, photography, dogs, bridge, reading; *Clubs* Naval and Military, 94 Piccadilly; *Style—* John Anderton, Esq, OBE, VRD; Mill Burn Cottage, Bridge of Dee, By Castle Douglas, Galloway 055 76 255)

ANDOVER, Viscount; Alexander Charles Michael Winston Robsahm Howard; s and h of 21 Earl of Suffolk and Berkshire; *b* 17 Sept 1974; *Style—* Viscount Andover

ANDREAE-JONES, William Pearce; QC (1984); s of Willie Andreae-Jones (d 1975), and Minnie Charlotte, *née* Andreae; *b* 21 July 1942; *Educ* Canford, Corpus Christi Coll Cambridge (BA); *m* 1978, Anne-Marie, da of Michael Cox; 1 s (William b 1979); *Career* barr Inner Temple 1965; recorder Crown Court 1982-; *Recreations* yachting, shooting; *Clubs* Roy Thames Yacht, Leander, Frewen (Oxford), South West Shingles Yacht, Ocean Cruising; *Style—* William Andreae-Jones, Esq, QC; 6 Kings Bench Walk, Temple, London EC4 (☎ 01 353 9901)

ANDRESKI, Prof Stanislav Leonard; s of Teofil Andrzejewski (d 1967), and Zofia, *née* Karaszewicz-Tokarzewska (d 1939); *b* 8 May 1919; *Educ* Secondary Sch in Poznan, Univ of Poznan, LSE (BSc, MSc, PhD); *m* 1974, Ruth, da of Maurice Ash (d 1976); 2 s (Adam, Lucas), 2 da (Wanda, Sophia); *Career* mil serv Polish Army 1937-47, cmmnd 1944; lectr in sociology Rhodes USA 1947-53; sr res fell in anthropology Manchester Univ 1954-56; lectr in econs Acton Tech Coll London 1956-57, mgmnt studies Brunel Coll of Technol London 1957-60; prof of sociology Sch of Social Sciences Santiago Chile 1960-61; sr res fell Nigerian Inst of Social and Econ Res Ibadan Nigeria 1962-64; prof and head of dept of sociology Univ of Reading 1964-84 (prof emeritus 1984-); hon prof Polish Univ London 1978-; visiting prof: dept of sociology and anthropology City Coll, City Univ of NY, dept of sociology Simon Fraser Univ Canada; chm Divorce Law Reform Assoc 1988-; memb Inst of Patentees and Inventors; *Books* Military Organization and Society (1970), Elements of Comparative Sociology (1964), The Uses of Comparative Sociology (1969, Spanish ed 1972), Parasitism and Subversion: The Case of Latin America (1970, Spanish ed 1968), The African Predicament: a Study in Pathology of Modernisation (1968), Social Sciences as Sorcery (1972, ed: Spanish 1973, German 1974, French 1975, Italian 1977, Japanese 1981), The Prospects of a Revolution in the USA (1973), Max Weber's Insights and Errors (1984); Syphilis, Puritanism and Witch hunts: Historical Explanations in the Light of Medicine and Psychoanalysis with a Forecast about Aids (Macmillan 1989); *Recreations* sailing, (yacht Metamorfoza); *Clubs* Cruising Assoc, Berkshire Riding; *Style—* Prof Stanislav Andreski; Farriers, Village Green, Upper Basildon, Reading, Berks RG8 8LS (☎ Upper Basildon 671318)

ANDREW, Edward Duxbury; s of Roger Duxbury Andrew (d 1978), of Bury, Lancs, and Winifred Marjorie, *née* Hill; *b* 17 Sept 1936; *Educ* Arnold Sch, Leeds Univ (BSc); *m* 11 Nov 1959, Patricia, da of Douglas Gaskell (d 1979), of Briercliffe, Nelson, Lancs; 2 s (Mark b 1961, Simon b 1963), 1 da (Kathryn b 1966); *Career* chm Gaskell Broadloom plc 1971- (and subsidiaries); chm: Lancashire East Euro Industrialists 1984-, chm and md Edward W Andrew Ltd 1969- and subsidiaries, memb Worshipful Co of Feltmakers of London; *Recreations* yachting, golf, fell walking, swimming, shooting; *Clubs* Royal Yachting Association, Pleasington Golf, RAC, Livery; *Style—* Edward D Andrew, Esq; Greystones, Dinckley, Blackburn, Lancs BB6 8AN (☎ 0254 40098); Edward W Andrew Ltd, Walshaw Road, Bury, Lancs BL8 1NG (☎ 061 7611411, telex: 669809)

ANDREW, Elizabeth Honora; *née* Thomas; da of Dilwyn Thomas, of Pontypridd, S Wales, and Morfydd, *née* Horton; *b* 6 Mar 1946; *Educ* Pontypridd Girls GS, (LLB London); *m* 21 July 1967, Kenneth Andrew, s of Arthur James Andrew, of Benfleet, Essex; 2 s (Darius Pleydell b 1974, Giles Sheridan b 1976); *Career* trainee retail and personnel mgmnt Marks & Spencer 1963-65, res asst Welsh Hosp Bd 1965-66, fashion buyer 1966-68, mangr wholesale and retail fashion trade 1968-70; called to Bar Middle Temple 1974, pt/t legal advsr N London Law Centre 1975-78, tenancy 1981- (specialising commercial law, employment law and general common law); formerly parish cncllr Three River Parish Cncl; memb: Bar Assoc for Commerce Fin and Indust, Soc of Eng and American Lawyers, Admin Law Bar Assoc; *Recreations* writing, travel, antiques; *Style—* Mrs Elizabeth Andrew; 3 Cassiobury Park Avenue, Watford, Herts WD1 7LA (☎ 0923 220 956); 15 Old Square, Lincoln's Inn, London WC2 (☎ 01 831 0801, fax 01 405 1387, telex 291543)

ANDREW, Geoffrey Harry Langdon; s of Henry James Andrew (d 1961); *b* 1 Oct 1923; *Educ* Merton Coll Oxford (BA, BSc); *m* 1, 1946 (m dis 1976), Prudence Hastings; 2 da; m 2, 1976, Lilias Jean; *Career* chm Colloids Ltd; *Recreations* golf, squash, industl archaeology; *Style—* Geoffrey Andrew, Esq; 85 Woodlands Rd, Liverpool 17 (☎ 051 727 1545); Colloids Ltd: (051 424 7424); 733 Springdale, West Palm Beach, Fla, USA

ANDREW, Hon Mrs; Hon (Gwyneth Margaret); *née* Bruce; yr da of 3 Baron Aberdare, GBE (d 1957); *b* 3 July 1928; *m* 1952, Robert McCheyne Andrew; 1 s, 1 da (1 da decd); *Style—* The Hon Mrs Andrew; Hams Barton, Chudleigh, Newton Abbot, Devon TQ13 0DL (☎ 0626 853133)

ANDREW, Capt John Herbert; s of George Thomas Andrew (d 1947), and Martha Elizabeth, *née* Thompson (d 1957); *b* 18 Feb 1913; *Educ* Lord Taunton's; Southampton; *m* 6 June 1948, Barbara Mary, da of William Daniel Price (d 1954), of Plas Newydd, Cefncoed, Breconshire; 2 s (Michael b 1952, Jeremy b 1955); *Career* London Rifle Brigade (TA) 1932, cmmnd Essex Regt 1939; A/Maj Middle East, Egypt 1 RAQ (wounded 1943, despatches 1944), also served with Iraq Levies, later Para Regt, (de-mobilised Aug 1945); chm: Brecon Hunt 1957, Brecon branch Br Legion 1960-64; gp sec Brecon Branch 1957-78; *Recreations* fishing, shooting, horses (ex-MFH Royal Exodus Hunt, 1 RAQ); *Style—* Capt John Andrew; Farthings, Llanfrynach, Powys (☎ Llanfrynach 230)

ANDREW, Kenneth; s of Arthur James Andrew, of Benfleet, Essex, and Emily Sarah, *née* Elderkin; *b* 21 Dec 1944; *Educ* Enfield Coll & Technol (ONC), Imperial Coll London (MSc, DIC), Univ of Wales (BEng); *m* 21 July 1967, Elizabeth Honora, da of Dilwyn Thomas, of Pontypridd, S Wales; 2 s (Darius Pleydel b 16 Nov 1974, Giles Sheridan b 11 May) 1976); *Career* apprentice draughtsman 1961-64; NatWest Bank plc 1969-84: various posts including head of operational res, branch mgmnt City and West End London, head of mktg; gp mktg dir Good Relations Gp plc 1984-85, dir consumer mktg Europe The Chase Manhattan Bank NA 1985-87, commercial dir Nat & Provincial Bldg Soc 1987-; Hon MPhil IMCB 1984; MBIM, AIB, MBBA, MInstScB; *Books* The Bank Marketing Handbook (1986); *Recreations* swimming, reading, writing, travel; *Style—* Kenneth Andrew, Esq; 3 Cassiobury Park Ave, Watford, Herts WD1 7LA (☎ 0923 220 956); Nat & Provincial Building Soc, 2nd Floor, 77-79 High St, Watford, Herts WD1 2DJ (☎ 0923 246 450, fax 0923 244 482, car tel 0836 608 322)

ANDREW, Nicholas Anthony Samuel; s of Samuel Ogden Lees Andrew (d 1966), of Winchester, and Rosalind Molly Carlyon, *née* Evans (d 1984); *b* 20 Dec 1946; *Educ* Winchester, Queens' Coll Cambridge (MA); *m* 28 Nov 1981, Jeryl Christine, da of Col John George Harrison, OBE, TD, DL, of Devon; *Career* CA; ptnr Robson Rhodes

1986, md Robson Rhodes Financial Services Ltd 1986-; FIMBRA membership ctee 1986-; FCA, FCCA; *Books* Yuppies and their Money (1987), Robson Rhodes Personal Financial Planning Manual (jt author 2, 3 edns); *Recreations* golf, music, travel; *Clubs* RAC; *Style*— Nicholas A S Andrew, Esq; Robson Rhodes, 186 City Road, London EC1V 2NU (☎ 01 251 1644, telex 885734, fax 01 250 0801)

ANDREW, Patrick John Ramsay; s of John Ramsay Andrew, of Guernsey, and Betty, *née* Arnold (now Mrs Reginald MacLeod); *b* 25 June 1937; *Educ* Canford; *m* 11 Sept 1976, Philippa Rachel (d 1983), da of Cdr Felix Johnstone (d 1964) (see Peerage and Baronetage, B Derwent); 2 da (Edwina Elizabeth b 1981, Emily Katharine b 1983); *Career* former md MSJ Int (Guiness Gp) bd and exec appts with GD Searle, Assoc Industl Devpt, Rank Xerox, EMI, Cortaulds; dir and conslt, chm Strategy Resources Gp, dir Marlar Int Ltd; fndr Connaught Gallery; memb RIIA *Papers* Utilisation of Approopriate Tecnol in Educn, Healthcare and Rural Devpt in Asia and Africa; *Recreations* sculpturem design, sailing; *Clubs* Naval and Military; *Style*— Patrick R Andrew, Esq; Hill House, Dummer, Hampshire RG25

ANDREW, Sir Robert John; KCB (1986, CB 1979); s of Robert Young Andrew (d 1980), of Walton-on-the-Hill, Surrey; *b* 25 Oct 1928; *Educ* King's Coll Sch Wimbledon, Merton Coll Oxford (MA); *m* 1963, Elizabeth, da of Walter de Courcy Bayley (d 1951), of Barbados; 2 s (Christopher b 1967, John b 1968); *Career* served Intelligence Corps 1947-49; joined Civil Service 1952, served in MOD, Diplomatic Service and Civil Service Dept, dep under-sec of State in Home Office 1976-83, perm under-sec of state NI Office;dir Esmée Fairbairn Charitable Tst 1989-; conservater of Wimbledon and Putney Commons 1973-; govr King's Coll Sch Wimbledon 1976-; *Recreations* carpentry, growing vegetables; *Clubs* United Oxford and Cambridge Univ; *Style*— Sir Robert Andrew, KCB

ANDREW, Lady Serena Mary; *née* Bridgeman; da of 6 Earl of Bradford, TD, JP, DL (d 1981), and Mary, Countess of Bradford (d 1986); *b* 1 July 1949; *Educ* Benenden; *m* 1978 (m dis 1989), (m dis 1989), Richard Arnold Andrew, s of John Ramsay Andrew, of St Saviours, Guernsey, CI,and of Mrs R G MacLeod, of Painswick, Glos; *Style*— Lady Serena Andrew; 35 Hereford Sq, London SW7 (☎ 01 373 9345); Dell House, Whitebridge, Inverness-shire IV1 2UP (☎ 045 63 278)

ANDREWES, Edward David Eden; s of Edward Andrewes (d 1954), and Norah Andrewes; *b* 4 Oct 1909,, Portmadoc; *Educ* Repton, Oriel Coll Oxford (BA); *m* 1935, Katherine Sheila (d 1984), da of Brig Wlliam Bradley Gossett Barne, CBE, DSO (d 1952); 1 s, 2 da; *Career* serv WWII Lt-Col Europe and Far East; slr 1935; dep chm and md Tube Investmts Ltd 1972-75 (joined 1935); tstee Cheshire Fndn 1976-81; *Recreations* gardening, riding, fishing; *Clubs* Boodle's; *Style*— Edward Andrewes, Esq; Stockton House, Stockton, Worcester (☎ 058 470 272)

ANDREWS, Christopher Henry; s of Henry Thomas Gordon, of Beltinge, Kent, and Lorna Beatrix Alexandra, *née* Notton; *b* 24 Jan 1940; *Educ* Chislehurst GS, Sidcup GS; *m* 27 June 1964, Moira Kathlyn Frances, da of John Alfred Dunn (d 1978), of Truro, Cornwall; 2 da (Carey b 1968, Laura b 1970); *Career* dir Ladbroke Gp plc 1986- (sec 1974-); FCIS; *Recreations* walking, reading, family; *Style*— Christopher Andrews, Esq; Ladbroke Gp plc, Chancel House, Neasden Lane, London NW10 2XE (☎ 01 459 8031, fax 01 459 6744, telex 22274)

ANDREWS, David Roger Griffith; CBE (1980); s of C H R Andrews, and G M Andrews; *b* 27 Mar 1933; *Educ* Abingdon, Pembroke Coll Oxford (MA); *m* 1963, (Dorothy) Ann, da of B A Campbell, CBE (d 1962); 2 s, 1 da; *Career* exec vice-chm BL 1977-81; chm (1981-86) and chief exec Land Rover-Leyland Gp 1982-86; dir: Gwion Ltd, Glaxo Ltd Trustees Ltd, Clarges Pharmaceutical Trustees Ltd; ACMA, CBIM; *Recreations* sailing, photography; *Style*— David Andrews, Esq, CBE; Gainford, Mill Lane, Gerrards Cross, Bucks

ANDREWS, Derek Henry; CB (1984), CBE (1970); s of late Henry Andrews and Emma Jane Andrews (decd); *b* 17 Feb 1933; *Educ* LSE (BA); *m* 1956, Catharine May, *née* Childe (d 1982); 2 s, 1 da; *Career* MAFF: asst princ 1957, asst private sec to min of Agric, Fisheries & Food 1960-61, princ 1961, asst sec 1968, private sec to PM 1966-70, under-sec 1973, dep sec 1981-87 (perm sec 1987); Harvard U USA 1970-71; *Style*— Derek H Andrews, Esq, CB, CBE; c/o Miny of Agric, Fisheries & Food, Whitehall Place, London SW1

ANDREWS, Prof Edgar Harold; s of Richard Thomas Andrews (d 1968); *b* 16 Dec 1932; *Educ* Dartford GS, London Univ (BSc, PhD, DSc); *m* 1961, Thelma Doris, da of Selby John Walker, of Watford; 1 s (Martyn b 1964), 1 da (Rachel b 1966); *Career* prof of materials QMC London 1968- (dean of the faculty of engrg 1971-74); dir: QMC Industl Research Ltd 1970-88, Denbyware Ltd 1971-81, Evangelical Press 1975-, Fire and Materials Ltd 1985-88, Materials Technol Conslts Ltd 1974-; recipient A A Griffith Silver Medal 1977; FIP, FIM, CEng, CPhys; *Books* Fracture in Polymers (1968) From Nothing to Nature (1978), God, Science and Evolution (1980),The Promise of the Spirit (1982), Christ and the Cosmos (1986); *Recreations* writing, music, Church work; *Style*— Prof Edgar Andrews; Redcroft, 87 Harmer Green Lane, Welwyn, Herts (☎ 043 879 376); Queen Mary College, Mile End Rd, London E1 4NS (☎ 01 975 5152)

ANDREWS, Ernest Somers; s of Charles Andrews (d 1961), of Manchester, and Dorothy, *née* Tonks; *b* 10 June 1928; *Educ* Chorlton GS Manchester, Wigan Mining Coll, Salford Tech Coll, UMIST; *m* 22 Sept 1973, Norma, da of William Wilkinson (d 1974), of Manchester; 3 da (Elizabeth Sarah b 1974, Alexandra Dorothy b 1976, Victoria Mary Jane b 1983); *Career* WWII REME 1946-49; ptnr Charles Andrews & Sons Consulting Engrs 1956-, dir Northern Res & Devpt Co Ltd 1973-; former pres: Manchester Assoc of Engineers, Rotary Club of Manchester South; vice-chm Manchester Branch Inst Plant Engrg, memb UMIST Assoc Bd (also NW section); CEng, FIMechE, FIPlantE, FFB, MConsE; *Recreations* military history, industrial archeology, gardening; *Style*— Ernest Andrews, Esq; 65 South Drive, Chorltonville, Chorlton-cum-Hardy, Manchester M21 2DZ (☎ 061 881 1265); Charles Andrews & Sons, Ardenlee House, 66 Brooklands Rd, Sale, Manchester M33 3GJ (☎ 061 973 6782, fax 061 962 0617, telex 669757)

ANDREWS, Brig George Lewis Williams; CBE (1960), DSO (1944); s of Capt Charles George Williams Andrews (ka 1914), of The Border Regt, and Diana Gambier-Parry, *née* Norrington (d 1968); *b* 1 July 1910; *Educ* Haileybury, RMC Sandhurst; *m* 1938, Marianne, da of Carl Strindberg (d 1915), of Stockholm Sweden; 1 s (Charles); *Career* cmmnd Seaforth Highlanders 1930, active serv Palestine 1936, WWII Regt Serv and Staff: Western Desert, Sicily, NW Europe, cmd 2 Bn Seaforth Highlanders 1943-44, 1 Bn 1953-54, cmd 152 Infantry Bde (TA) 1954-57, Asst Cmdt RMA Sandhurst 1957-60; Chevalier Order of Leopold (Belgium) 1946; *Style*— Brig George Andrews, CBE, DSO; West Kingsteps, Nairn (☎ 0667 53231)

ANDREWS, Air Vice-Marshal John Oliver; CB (1942), DSO (1917), MC and bar; s of John Andrews, of Waterloo, Lancs; *b* 20 July 1896; *m* 1923, Bertha, da of Wilfred Bisdée, of Hambrook, Glos; 2 s; *Career* serv WWI RFC (despatches thrice), transfd to RAF 1919, ret 1945; *Style*— Air Vice-Marshal John Andrews, CB, DSO, MC

ANDREWS, Hon Katharine Ann; da of 1 and last Baron Douglas, of Kirtleside; *b* 26 July 1957; *m* 1984, Geoffrey Andrews; *Career* SRN, HV (Cert), NDN (Cert), SCM; *Style*— The Hon Mrs Andrews

ANDREWS, Lady Patricia Ann; *née* Le Poer Trench; da of late 6 Earl of Clancarty; *b* 20 Jan 1928; *m* 1, 1946, Eugene Nicodemus de Szpiganowicz (d 1965) , s of late Baron Klemens de Szpiganowicz, of Dobrynic, Poland; 2, 1977, Alan Sidney Andrews (d 1980); *Style*— Lady Patricia Andrews; Flat 2, Sunray House, Moory Meadow, Combe Martin, North Devon

ANDREWS, Raymond Denzil Anthony; MBE (1953), VRD (1959); s of Michael Joseph Andrews (d 1975), and Phylis Marie Andrews, *née* Crowley (d 1972); *b* 5 June 1925; *Educ* Highgate Sch, Christ Coll Cambridge, London Univ, Univ of Michigan; *m* 1958, (Anne) Gillian Whitlaw, da of David Small (d 1936); 1 s (Michael b 1965), 1 da (Emily b 1968); *Career* Lt RM 1946, Maj RMR 1960; sr ptnr Andrew Downie and Ptnrs Architects, pres Architectural Assoc 1977-78, Royal Mint Square Housing Competition (first prize), Order of El Rafidan of Iraz 1956; RIBA (vice pres 1984); *Recreations* sailing (sloop 'Blanche'); *Clubs* RIBA Sailing, Bosham Sailing; *Style*— Raymond Andrews, Esq, MBE, VRD; 34 Clarendon Road, London W11 (☎ 01 727 4129); Andrews Downie and Partners, 6 Addison Avenue, London W11 (☎ 01 602 7701)

ANDREWS, Richard Edward; s of William Reginald Andrews (d 1983), and Agnes Ruby Whiffen; *b* 15 August 1936; *Educ* Cambridge HS, St Catharine's Coll Cambridge (MA); *m* 18 Aug 1981, Stephanie Elizabeth, da of Percy Craig, CA, of Motueka, New Zealand; 1 s, 1 da; *Career* Flt-Offr RAF Fighter Cmd 1955-57; sr conslt PA 1965-72, personnel mangr BLMC 1972-74, personnel dir Franklin Mint USA 1974-78, business mangr Cassells 1979, gp personnel dir Dixons Gp plc 1980-, dir Barnet Enterprise Tst 1986-; FIPM; *Style*— Richard Andrews, Esq; Dixon House, 18 High St, Edgware, Middlesex (☎ 01 952 2345)

ANDREWS, Stuart Morrison; s of William Hannaford Andrews (d 1975), and Eileen Elizabeth, *née* Morrison (d 1987); *b* 23 June 1932; *Educ* Newton Abbot GS, St Dunstan's Coll, Sidney Sussex Coll Cambridge (MA); *m* 1962, Marie Elizabeth, da of Jacobus Petrus van Wyk, of SA; 2 s (Jeremy b 1963, Christopher b 1966); *Career* headmaster: Norwich Sch 1967-75, Clifton Coll 1975-; ed Conference 1971-82; dep chm Assisted Places Ctee; Nat Rep HMC Ctees 1986-87; *Books* Eighteenth Century Europe (1965), Enlightened Despotism (1967), Methodism and Society (1970); *Recreations* walking, writing; *Clubs* East India Sports Devonshire and Public Schs, Clifton; *Style*— Stuart Andrews, Esq; Headmaster's House, Clifton College, Bristol BS8 3HT (☎ 0272 735613); Auburn House, Clifton Down, Bristol BS8 3HT (☎ 0272 735613)

ANDRUS, (Francis) Sedley; LVO (1982); s of late Brig-Gen Thomas Alchin Andrus, CMG, JP (d 1959), and Alice Loveday, *née* Parr (d 1984); born on first anniversary of death of gf Adm Alfred Arthur Chase Parr, FRGS, sometime naval ADC to Queen Victoria; *b* 26 Feb 1915; *Educ* Wellington, St Peter's Coll Oxford (MA); *Career* Bluemantle Pursuivant of Arms 1970-72, Lancaster Herald of Arms 1972-82; Beaumont Herald of Arms Extraordinary 1982-; landowner; *Style*— Sedley Andrus, Esq, LVO; College of Arms, Queen Victoria St, London EC4V 4BT (☎ 01 248 2762); 8 Oakwood Rise, Longfield, nr Dartford, Kent DA3 7PA (☎ 047 47 5424)

ANDRY, Peter Edward; s of Dr Harold John Andry (d 1963), and Frances Elizabeth, *née* Scheerbarth; *b* 10 Mar 1927; *Educ* Melbourne COE GS, Melbourne Univ MusB, RCM (ARCM); *m* 1, 11 April 1956 (m dis 1964), Rosemary Jane, da of Lt Hilary Macklin, OBE (d 1965), of 14 Bedford Square; 2s (Miles, Christopher) m 2, Christine Ann, *née* Sunderland 1 da (Jennifer); *Career* prodr and freelance musician Australian Broadcasting Cmmn 1949-52, conductor Br Cncl Bursary 1953, prodr Decca Record Co 1954-56; EMI Music: asst mangr HMV 1954-56, asst mangr int artists dept 1962-69, pres int classical div 1972-1989; many recordings with: Inter Alia, Britten, Beecham, Karajan, Klemperer, Menuhin, Callas, De Los Angeles, Dieskau, Richter, Pollini, Rostropovich, Perlman; sr vp classical repertoire Wa Int Inc 1989; chm and vice-pres Barnet Soc MENCAP, chm music ctee and memb cncl RSA, tres Royal Philharmonic Soc, tstee and sec Australian Musical Fndn in London, chm of govrs Music Therapy Charity, hon memb RCM, memb Royal Soc of Musicians of GB; Freeman: City of London 1988, Worshipful Co of Musicians 1989; FRSA; *Recreations* reading, photography, tennis, running, gardening; *Clubs* Garrick; *Style*— Peter Andry, Esq; 95 Hampstead Way, London NW11 7LR (☎ 01 455 8787)

ANFIELD, Elizabeth Margaret; da of Michael Walter Fitton Brown (d 1975), of Mill Hill, London, and Beatrice (Lena) Elizabeth, *née* Moore; *b* 20 Mar 1949; *Educ* North London Collegiate Sch, Univ of Kent Canterbury (BSc); *m* 19 July 1969, Alan, s of Frederic Ernest Anfield, of Nethy Bridge, Inverness-shire; *Career* chartered accountant; Reading and Centl Berkshire C of C Exec 1985-88 (chm business womans section 1985), Newbury and W Berks C of C Exec 1985- (chm small business section 1986); tres Newbury Dist Churches Housing Tst 1984-, Inst of Taxation Thames Valley Branch Exec 1980- (tres 1984-88, sec 1988-); md Thames Valley Residential Properties plc 1988-; sec Newbury Twin Town Assoc 1986-; FCA, ATTI; *Recreations* skiing, theatre, foreign travel; *Style*— Mrs Elizabeth Anfield

ANGEL, Donald; CBE; *Educ* LSE (BSc Econ 1951); *m* ; 1 s, 1 da; *Career* chm Birds Eye Walls Ltd, Lipton Ltd 1972-74, Walls Meat Co Ltd 1974-78; pres UK Assocn of Frozen Food Producers 1984-86; cncl memb Food and Drinks Fedn 1986-; *Recreations* opera, antique furniture, gardening; *Style*— Donald Angel, Esq, CBE; Birds Eye Walls Ltd, Station Ave, Walton-on-Thames, Surrey KT12 1NT (☎ (0932) 228888; telex 261255)

ANGEL, Gerald Bernard Nathaniel Aylmer; s of Bernard Francis Angel (d 1963), and Ethel Angel (d 1988); *b* 4 Nov 1937; *Educ* St Mary's Sch Nairobi Kenya; *m* 1968, Lesley Susan, da of Rev Preb Cyril Kenneth Alfred Kemp (d 1987), 4 s (Matthew b 1971, Thomas b 1975, Benedict b and d 1978, Christopher b 1979), 1 da (Katharine b 1969); *Career* served Kenya Regt 1956-57; barr Inner Temple 1959; advocate Kenya 1960-62; practiced at Bar 1962-80; Registrar Family Divn High Ct 1980-; memb Civil and Family Sub Ctee Judicial Studies Bd 1985-; *Books* ed Industrial Tribunal Reports 1966-78, advsy ed and contributor Atkin's Court Forms (1988); *Style*— Gerald B N A

Angel, Esq; 9 Lancaster Avenue, London SE27 9EL; Principal Registry of the Family Division, Somerset House, Strand, London WC2

ANGEL, Richard Reeve; s of Edward Reeve Angel (d 1988), of Cranford, Northants, and Hope Aldrich Cleaveland Angel (d 1981); *b* 4 August 1928; *Educ* Oundle, Edinburgh Univ; *m* 1951, Margaret Vivien, da of William Warren (d 1956), of Taunton, Somerset; 2 da; *Career* dir: Whatman Reeve Angel plc 1974-, Reeve Angel Int Ltd 1959-74; pres Br Laboratory Ware Assoc 1970-72; *Recreations* reading, golf; *Style—* Richard Angel, Esq; Spring Walk, Nevill Court, Tunbridge Wells, Kent (☎ 0892 20592); Whatman Reeve Angel plc, Springfield Mill, Maidstone, Kent ME14 2LE (☎ 0622 692022)

ANGELL, Gordon Locksley; s of Harold Angell, of Granby House, Victoria St, Chatteris, Cambs (d 1962), and Ellen Locksley, *née* Hancock (d 1970); *b* 29 July 1927; *Educ* Cromwell Sch Chatteris; *m* 1, 19 April 1946, Norma; 1 s (Roger Gordon b 9 April 1948), 1 da (Glynis Roma (decd); m 2, 27 April 1965, Margaret Ruth, da of James Norris, of Merrilocks Green, Blundellsands, Liverpool 23; 1 s (Benjamin James b 10 May 1975), 1 da (Emma Kate b 22 March 1973); *Career* dir: BASF UK LTd, Knoll Pharmaceuticals; govr Long Ashton Res Station, memb agric mgmnt cmmn Univ of Bristol, chm Br Agrochemicals Assoc 1973-74 and 1981-83, fell Royal Entomological Soc; *Recreations* golf, gardening, swimming; *Clubs* Farmers; *Style—* Gordon Angell, Esq; Rendlesham, Sch Lane, Langham, Colchester, Essex CO4 5PB (☎ 0206 272398); BASF UK Ltd, Lady Lane, Hadleigh, Ipswich, Suffolk IP7 6BQ (☎ 0473 822531, telex 987752, fax 0473 827450)

ANGELL-JAMES, John; CBE (1967); s of late Dr John Angell-James, MRCS, LRCP, of Bristol, and Emily Cormell, *née* Ashwin; *b* 23 August 1901; *Educ* Bristol GS, Bristol Univ (MD, BS, MBChB); *m* 1930, Evelyn Miriam, da of Francis Over Everard (d 1951), of Devon; 1 s, 2 da; *Career* serv WWII Lt-Col RAMC; otolaryngologist; head Dept of Otolargngology Bristol Univ 1956-66; hon consulting surgn Utd Bristol Hosps 1966-; pres: Br Assoc of Otolaryngologists 1966, Otological Research Soc 1977-; farmer 1950-; FRCP, FRCS, Hon FRCS Edin; *Recreations* shooting, sailing, gardening; *Style—* John Angell-James, Esq, CBE; Sundayshill House, Falfield, Wotton-under-Edge, Glos (☎ 0454 260 351)

ANGERS, Brian Mason; s of Ernest Angers (d 1953), and Eunice Mason; *b* 18 Nov 1936; *Educ* Lancaster Roy GS, Oxford Univ (certificate in Mgmnt Studies); *Career* fin dir Cunard Steam-ship Co plc; Nat Serv Sgt RAFC Singapore; dir: Cunard Line Ltd, Cunard Ellerman Ltd, Ritz Hotel (London) Ltd; FCA; *Recreations* tennis, golf; *Clubs* Wentworth; *Style—* Brian M Angers, Esq; KU-Ring-Gai, Broomfield Park, Sunningdale, Ascot, Berkshire SL5 0JT (☎ Ascot 20296); 1 Berkeley St, London W1A 1BY (☎ 01 499 9020)

ANGEST, Henry; s of Walter Angst, and Ella, *née* Graf; *b* 6 July 1940; *Educ* Univ of Basle Switzerland; *Career* chm: Secure Homes Ltd 1982, Secure Tst Gp plc 1985; *Recreations* farming; *Style—* Henry Angest, Esq; 67 Cadogan Gardens, London SW3 2RA (☎ 01 589 8874); 23-27 Heathfield Rd, Kings Heath, Birmingham B14 7BY (☎ 021 443 1188, fax 021 444 8551, car tel 0860 303 153)

ANGGRD, Hon Mrs; Hon Adele Bevyl Alers; da of 2 Baron Hankey, KCMG, KCVO; *b* 31 July 1933; *m* 1964 (m dis 1987), Dr Erik Emil Anggård; 1 s (Jon), 2 da (Eola, Irene); *Career* International Stage Designer; *Recreations* tennis, skiing; *Style—* The Hon Mrs Anggård; Strandvagen 67, Stockholm, Sweden

ANGLES, James Walker; s of Andrew Angles, of Perth (d 1961), and Barbara Louden, *née* Walker; *b* 27 Dec 1935; *Educ* Perth Acad; *m* 30 Nov 1963, Katherine Gillian, da of Tom Bickerstaff, of Ipswich; 3 da (Alison b 1965, Helen b 1967, Lorna b 1969); *Career* md Britvic Corona Ltd; *Style—* James W Angles, Esq; Bloomfield Road, Chelmsford, Essex (☎ 0245 261871)

ANGLESEY, 7 Marquess of (UK 1815); Sir George Charles Henry Victor Paget; 10 Bt (I 1730); also Lord Paget of Beaudesert (E 1552) and Earl of Uxbridge (GB 1784); s of 6 Marquess of Anglesey (d 1947), and Lady Marjorie Manners, da of 8 Duke of Rutland; *b* 8 Oct 1922; *Educ* Eton; *m* 16 Oct 1948, Elizabeth Shirley Vaughan, DBE, LLD, da of Charles Langbridge Morgan, the writer (*see* Anglesey, Marchioness of); 2 s, 3 da; *Heir* s, Earl of Uxbridge; *Career* Maj RHG 1946; JP 1959-68, 1983- Vice-Lieutenant of Anglesey 1960-; dir for Wales Nationwide Bldg Soc 1973-; Pres Anglesey Con Assoc 1949-83; chm Historic Bldgs cncl for Wales 1977-; tstee National Portrait Gallery 1979-; memb: National Heritage Memorial Fund 1980-, Roy Cmmn on Historical Manuscripts 1984-; DL Anglesey 1960, Lord-Lieut for Gwynedd 1983-; author; FSA, FRHistS, FRSL, Hon FRIBA, Hon DLitt; *Books* The Capel Letters (1955), One-Leg (1961), Sergeant Pearman's Memoirs (1968), Little Hodge (1971), A History of the British Cavalry 1816-1919, Vol I (1973), Vol II (1975), Vol III (1982), Vol IV (1986); *Recreations* music, gardening; *Style—* The Most Hon the Marquess of Anglesey; Plâs Newydd, Llanfairpwll, Anglesey, Gwynedd (☎ Llanfairpwll 714330); 5 Walpole St, London SW3 (☎ 01 730 4140)

ANGLESEY, Marchioness of; (Elizabeth) Shirley Vaughan Paget; DBE (1982, CBE 1977); da of late Charles Morgan (the novelist); *b* 4 Dec 1924; *Educ* Francis Holland Sch, St James' Sch W Malvern, Kent Place Sch USA; *m* 1948, 7 Marquess of Anglesey; 2 s, 3 da; *Career* chm Nat Fedn of Women's Institutes 1966-69; vice-chm Govt Working Pty on Methods of Sewage Disposal 1969-70; dep chm Prince of Wales Ctee 1970-80; chm Welsh Arts Cncl 1975-81; memb IBA 1976-81; chm Br Cncl Drama and Dance Advsy Ctee 1981-; chm Broadcasting Complaints Cmmn 1987-; memb Museums and Galleries Cmmn 1981-; tstee Pilgrims Tst 1982-; Hon LLD Univ of Wales 1977; *Style—* The Most Hon the Marchioness of Anglesey, DBE; Plâs Newydd, Llanfairpwll, Gwynedd (☎ 0248 714330)

ANGUS, (William) Jestyn; s of Col Edmund Graham Angus, CBE, MC, TD, DL (d 1983), of Corbridge, Northumberland, and Bridget Ellen Isobel, *née* Spencer (d 1973); *b* 12 Dec 1930; *Educ* Gordonstoun, Harvard Business Sch; *m* 18 Sept 1965, Eleanor Gillian (Mimie), da of Cdr George Frederick Attwood (d 1979); 1 s (Henry b 1966), 1 da (Sarah b 1968); *Career* 2 Lt RA 1949-50, Lt RA (TA) 1950-56; export mangr/market research mangr George Angus & Co Ltd Newcastle-upon-Tyne and London 1952-59, dir Fire Armour Ltd 1959-65, gp personnel mangr 1965-70; sales mangr Matthew Hall & Co Ltd 1971-72; sr conslt MSL Management Selection 1973-82; dir (Scotland) Knight Wendling Ltd 1982-; dir: Glasgow Chamber of Commerce 1975-, The Merchants House of Glasgow; vice-pres Dumbarton Scottish Conservative Assoc; FIPM 1985, MIMC 1986; *Recreations* skiing, tennis, hillwalking, horticulture; *Clubs* Western (Glasgow), Northern Counties (Newcastle-upon-Tyne); *Style—* Jestyn Angus, Esq; Braeriach, Helensburgh, Dunbartonshire G84 9AH (☎ 0436 72393); Knight Wendling Ltd, 95 Bothwell St, Glasgow G2 7JZ (☎ 041 221 8676, telex 779688 WILLIS G)

ANGUS, Rev (James Alexander) Keith; TD; s of Rev Walter Chalmers Smith Angus (d 1956), and Isabella Margaret Stephen (d 1979); *b* 16 April 1929; *Educ* HS of Dundee, Univ of St Andrews (MA); *m* 1956, Alison Jane, da of Donald Cargill Daly (d 1951), of Kirkcubrightshire; 1 s (Hugh), 1 da (Alison); *Career* Nat Serv Army TA, RA Capt, TA Royal Chaplains Dept; minister: Hoddam Parish Church 1956-67, Gourock Old Parish Church 1967-79, Braemar and Crathie Parish Churches 1979-; domestic chaplain to HM The Queen 1979-; *Recreations* fishing, hillwalking, golf; *Clubs* New (Edinburgh); *Style—* The Rev Keith Angus, TD; The Manse of Crathie, Crathie, nr Ballater, Aberdeenshire AB3 5UL (☎ 033 84 208)

ANGUS, Michael Richardson; s of William Richardson Angus, and Doris Margaret Breach; *b* 5 May 1930; *Educ* Marling Sch, Stroud Glos, Bristol Univ (BSc); *m* Eileen Isabel May; 2 s, 1 da; *Career* chm Unilever PLC; vice chm Unilever NV; non exec dir: Whitbread & Co plc, Thorn EMI plc, British Airways Plc; jt chm Netherlands-British C of C; tstee Leverhulme Tst, tstee Conference Board (New York); CBIM; *Recreations* countryside, wine and puzzles; *Clubs* University, Knickerbocker (New York); *Style—* Michael Angus, Esq; c/o Unilever PLC, Unilever House, Blackfriars, London EC4P 4BQ (☎ 01 822 5252)

ANGUS, Col William Turnbull Calderhead; s of William Angus (d 1954), of Glasgow, and Elizabeth Galloway, *née* Calderhead (d 1952); *b* 20 July 1923; *Educ* Govan HS, Glasgow Univ, RMC of Sci; *m* 5 April 1947, Nola Leonie, da of William Alexander Campbell-Gillies (d 1965), of Nairobi; 2 s (Bruce b 1948, Roderigh b 1959), 2 da (Carolyn b 1950, Fiona b 1955); *Career* cmmnd Royal Regt of Artillery 1944, cmmd King's African Rifles (also Maj GSO2 HQ E Africa), 1945-47, tech staff course RMC of Sci 1949-51, Maj TSO2 Inspectorate of Armaments 1951-54, BAOR & Cyprus 1954-57, GSO2 G Tech HQ BAOR 1957-60, TSO2 Ordnance Bd 1960-63, TSO 2 Trials Estab Guided Weapons RA 1963-65, post-grad Guided Weapons Course RMC of Sci 1965-66, Lt-Col TSO1 Royal Armament Res & Dvpt Estab 1966-69, Col asst dir Guided Weapons Trials MOD Procurement Exec 1970-73, memb Ordnance Bd 1973-74, ret 1974; Scottish mangr Blakes Holidays, pres Campbeltown Rotary Club 1985-86; Hon Sheriff in Sheriffdom of N Strathclyde 1986; CEng 1970, MRAeS 1970, FIQA 1972, FBIM 1980; *Recreations* wood-turning, manufacture of spinning wheels; *Style—* Col William T C Angus; Kilchrist Castle, Campbeltown, Argyll PA28 6PH (☎ 0586 53210)

ANKARCRONA, Jan Gustaf Theodor Stensson; s of Stensson Ankarcrona RVO (d 1981), of Stockholm, Sweden, and Ebba, *née* Countess Mörner; *b* 18 April 1940; *Educ* Ostra Real Stockholm, Stockholm Sch of Econ (MBA), Univ of California Berkeley (MBA); *m* 1, 16 June 1968 (m dis 1978), E Margaretha Antonie, da of Erik von Eckermann, of Ripsa, Sweden; 2 s (Johan b 1969, Edward b 1972); m 2, 6 March 1981, Sandra G, da of E B Coxe, of New York, USA; 2 da (Aurore b 1983, Ariane b 1988); *Career* Royal Swedish Navy 1958-61, Lt Cdr Royal Swedish Navy Reserve 1974; Stockholms Enskilda Bank Stockholm 1964-65, Granges AB Stockholm 1966-69, American Express Securities SA Paris 1969-70, dep md Nordic Bank Ltd London 1971-83, md and chief exec FennoScandia Bank Ltd London 1983-; OStJ Sweden; *Recreations* shooting, sailing, tennis, music, history; *Clubs* Brooks's, Hurlingham, Nya Sällskapet Stockholm; *Style—* Jan Ankarcrona, Esq; 29 Argyll Rd, London W8 7DA (☎ 01 937 9438); The Old Deanery, Dean's Ct, London EC4V 5AA (☎ 01 236 4060, fax 01 248 4712, telex 892458 FENSCA G)

ANLEY, Nicholas Needham Fergus Philip Gore; s of Lt-Col Philip Maitland Gore Anley (d 1968), of Fakenham, Norfolk, and Lady Eleanor Noreen Patricia Needham (d 1965), da of 4 Earl of Kilmorey; *b* 30 Mar 1943; *Educ* HMS Conway Anglesey; *m* 11 Dec 1965, Julie Ann, da of James Nicholas Wilson (d 1982), of Winsford, Cheshire; 1 s (Philip James Needham b 1976), 2 da (Debonaire Norah Needham b 1967, Marion Scarlett Needham b 1969); *Career* ship broker and int freight consult; chm: Anley Maritime Agencies Ltd, Anley Shipping Ltd; *Recreations* workaholic; *Clubs* IOD, Pall Mall (Fell); *Style—* Nicholas Anley, Esq; Mourne Park, Kilkeel, Co Down, N Ireland (☎ 06937 62533); Anley Maritime Agencies Ltd, Port Offices, Warren Point, Co Down, N Ireland (☎ 06937 73731, fax 72821, telex 747558 AMAWPT G)

ANNALY, 5 Baron (UK 1863); Luke Robert White; s of 4 Baron Annaly, MC (d 1970), and Lady Lavinia Spencer, da of 6 Earl Spencer, KG, GCVO, VD, PC; is 1 cous once removed of HRH Princess of Wales; *b* 15 Mar 1927; *Educ* Eton, Trinity Coll Cambridge; *m* 1, 1953 (m dis 1957), Lady Marye Pepys (d 1958), da of 7 Earl of Cottenham; 1 s; m 2, 1960 (m dis 1967), Jennifer, da of Rupert Sausmarez Carey, OBE, of East Hoe Manor, Hambledon, Hants; 2 da; m 3, 1984, Mrs Beverley Healy, da of William Maxwell; 1 step-da; *Heir* s, Hon Luke White; *Career* served RAF 1944-48, RAuxAF 1948-53; ptnr W Greenwell & Co (stockbrokers); Freeman City of London 1953; *Clubs* Turf, RAF, Hawks, MCC; *Style—* The Rt Hon The Lord Annaly; Welches, Bentley, Farnham, Surrey (☎ Bentley 0420 22107); 45 Cadogan Sq, London SW1X 0HX

ANNAN, John Christopher; s of Alexander Annan and Christina, *née* Herbertson; *b* 4 Sept 1926; *Educ* Gordonstoun; *m* 1952, Margaret, da of Albert Marlow (d 1943); 1 s, 1 da; *Career* chm A & J C Annan Ltd; underwriting memb Lloyd's; *Recreations* golf, shooting, fishing, sailing (yacht 'Raku'); *Clubs* Lloyd's Yacht; *Style—* John Annan, Esq; Lower Snowdon Cottage, Burnhill Green, Staffordshire WV6 7HT (☎ 074 65 224); A & J C Annan Ltd, 53 Waterloo Rd, Wolverhampton, W Midlands WV1 4QJ (☎ 0902 22399)

ANNAN, Baron (Life Peer UK 1965); Noel Gilroy Annan; OBE (1946); s of James Gilroy Annan (d 1965), and Fannie Mildred, *née* Quinn (d 1970); *b* 25 Dec 1916; *Educ* Stowe, King's Coll Cambridge (MA); *m* 1950, Gabriele, da of Louis Ferdinand Ullstein, of Berlin; 2 da (Lucy, Juliet); *Career* provost: King's Cambridge 1956-66, UCL 1966-78; vice-chllr London Univ 1978-81 (Prof Sir Randolph Quirk succeeded); chm: Ctee on Future of Bdcasting 1974-77, tstees Nat Gallery 1978-85, Br Museum 1963-78; FRHistS; *Clubs* Brooks's; *Style—* The Rt Hon The Lord Annan, OBE; 16 St John's Wood Rd, London NW8 (☎ 01 289 2555)

ANNAND, Richard Wallace; VC (1940), DL (Co Durham 1956); s of Lt Cdr Wallace Moir Annand (k Gallipoli 1915), and Dora Elizabeth Chapman; *b* 5 Nov 1914; *Educ* Pocklington, E Yorks; *m* 1940, Shirley Osborne, JP; *Career* cmmnd RNVR 1933, transfd Durham LI 1938, Capt RARO 1948; personnel offr Finchale Abbey Tning Centre for the Disabled 1948-79; *Style—* Richard Annand, Esq, VC, DL; Springwell House, Whitesmocks, Durham

ANNANDALE AND HARTFELL, Dowager Countess of; Margaret Jane; *née* Hunter-Arundell; da of Herbert William Francis Hunter-Arundell, of Barjarg, Auldgirth, Dumfries-shire (who assumed the surname of Hunter-Arundell in lieu of Wadd 1913, on suc to Barjarg estate; s of T H Wadd, of St Leonards-on-Sea, by his w, Mary, da of William A Woodcock, by his w, Marianne, 2 da of William Francis Hunter-Arundell, of Barjarg); *b* 18 Nov 1910; *m* 1940, as his 2 w, Maj Percy Wentworth Hope Johnstone, TD, JP, Lanarkshire Yeomanry RA (TA), *de jure* 10 Earl of Annandale and Hartfell (d 1983); 1 s, 1 da; *Style*— The Rt Hon the Dowager Countess of Annandale and Hartfell; Blackburn House, Johnstonebridge, Dumfriesshire

ANNANDALE AND HARTFELL, 11 Earl of (S, by Charter, 1662) Patrick Andrew Wentworth Hope Johnstone of Annandale and of that Ilk; DL (Dumfriesshire 1987); also Lord of Johnstone (S 1662), Hereditary Steward of Stewartry of Annandale, Hereditary Keeper of Castle of Lochmaben, and Chief of Clan Johnstone; s of Maj Percy Wentworth Hope Johnstone, TD, JP, RA (TA), *de jure* 10 Earl (d 1983), by his 2 w, Margaret Jane Hunter-Arundell (*qv* Dowager Countess of Annandale and Hartfell); claim to Earldom (which had been dormant since 1792) admitted by Ctee for Privileges of House of Lords, and a writ issued summoning him to Parl in the Upper House 1986; *b* 19 April 1941; *Educ* Stowe, RAC Cirencester; *m* 1969, Susan, o da of Col Walter John Macdonald Ross, CB, OBE, TD, JP, Lord Lieut of the Stewardry of Netherhall, Castle Douglas, Kirkcudbrightshire; 1 s (Hon David Patrick Wentworth, Lord Johnstone and Master of Annandale & Hartfell b 13 Oct 1971); 1 da (Lady Julia Clare b 1974); *Heir* s, Lord Johnstone; *Career* underwriting memb Lloyds 1976-, memb: Solway River Purification Bd 1970-86, Scottish Valuation Advsy Cncl to sec of State for Scotland 1984-86, Annan Fishery Bd 1983-, standing cncl of Scottish Chiefs, various ctees, Dumfries CC; Dumfries and Galloway Regnl Cncl 1974-86, chm Royal Jubilee and Prince's Tst for Dumfries and Galloway 1985-88, Royal Scottish Forestry Soc 1981-84; dir Bowerings Members Agency; dir Murray Law revue memb Agency 1988-; *Recreations* golf; *Clubs* Puffin's (Edinburgh), Brooks's; *Style*— The Rt Hon the Earl of Annandale and Hartfell, DL; Raehills, St Anns, Lockerbie, Dumfriesshire

ANNEAR, John Frank; s of Frank Foster Annear (d 1977), of Watermouth House, Berrynarbor, Devon, and Alice Hilda, *née* Kelly (d 1962); *b* 3 June 1928; *Educ* St Edward's Oxford; *m* 26 July 1963, Catherine Blunson, da of Fred Blunson Hall (d 1987), of Worthing, Sussex; 1 s (Richard b 1968); *Career* admitted slr 1958, in private practise; *Recreations* sailing, shooting, gardening; *Clubs* Naval; *Style*— John Annear, Esq; Kes Tor, Langley, Ilfracombe, Devon EX34 8BE (☎ 0271 63538); Northfield Chambers, 3 Northfield Rd, Ilfracombe, Devon EX34 8AJ (☎ 0271 62411)

ANNESLEY, Lady Frances Elizabeth; yst da of 10 Earl Annesley; *b* 27 July 1957; *Style*— Lady Frances Annesley; 35 Spring Rise, Egham, Surrey

ANNESLEY, Hon Francis William Dighton; s and h of 15 Viscount Valentia; *b* 29 Dec 1959; *Style*— The Hon Francis Annesley

ANNESLEY, Gerald Francis; s of Cdr Gerald Sowerby, RN, and Lady Mabel Annesley (da of 5 Earl Annesley); assumed name of Annesley when mother inherited Castlewellan estates on death of her bro, 6 Earl Annesley; *b* 5 Nov 1904; *Educ* Wellington; *m* 1, 1927 (m dis 1940), as her 1 husb, Lady Elizabeth Jocelyn, da of 8 Earl of Roden; 2 da; m 2, 1941 (m dis 1954, she m 1976, as his 3 w, Hon Bernard Bruce, s of 9 Earl of Elgin and Kincardine), Mary, da of Maj Donald Ramsey MacDonald, DSO, MC, RA; 2 s (Rory b 1942, m 1, 1964, Anthea Urquhart; 2, 1981 Fiona, da of Maj James Ford; Richard b 1944, m 1968 Hon Haidée Rawlinson, da of Baron Rawlinson, of Ewell, *qv*); m 3, Mary Elizabeth Cromwell; 2 s (twin); *Style*— Gerald Annesley, Esq; Shimnah, 78 Bryansford Rd, Newcastle, Co Down BT33 0LD, N Ireland (☎ (039 67) 24686)

ANNESLEY, Hon Michael Robert; yst s of 9 Earl Annesley (d 1979); *b* 4 Dec 1933; *Educ* Strode's GS Egham; *m* 1956, Audrey Mary, o da of Ernest Goodwright, of Dartford, Kent; 2 s (Michael Stephen b 1957, Robert Francis b 1962), 1 da (Sheila Marie b 1961); *Career* Warrant Offr RAF; assoc memb Soc of Licenced Aircraft Engrs and Technols, flt simulator engr; dir S & D Leisure Ltd 1984; *Style*— The Hon Michael Annesley; 16 Coltash Rd, Furnace Green, Crawley, W Sussex RH10 6JY

ANNESLEY, Nora, Countess; Nora; da of Walter Harrison, of Sapperton, Glos; *b* 5 Nov 1900; *Educ* Sapperton C of E Sch; *m* 1922, 9 Earl Annesley (d 1979); 3 s; *Career* teacher; *Recreations* gardening, knitting, embroidery; *Style*— The Rt Hon Nora, Countess Annesley; 67 Vegal Crescent, Englefield Green, Surrey (☎ Egham 32162)

ANNESLEY, 10 Earl (I 1789); Patrick; also Baron Annesley (I 1758) and Viscount Glerawly (I 1766); s of 9 Earl Annesley (d 1979); *b* 12 August 1924; *Educ* Strode's GS Egham; *m* 1947, Catherine, da of John Forrest Burgess; 4 da; *Heir* bro, Hon Philip Annesley, *qv*; *Career* formerly in RN; *Style*— The Rt Hon The Earl Annesley; 35 Spring Rise, Egham, Surrey

ANNESLEY, Hon Peter John; 3 s of 15 Viscount Valentia; *b* 18 Dec 1967; *Style*— The Hon Peter Annesley

ANNESLEY, Hon Philip Harrison; s of 9 Earl Annesley (d 1979), and hp of bro, 10 Earl, *qv*; *b* 29 Mar 1927; *Educ* Strode's GS Egham; *m* 1951, Florence Eileen, da of late John Arthur Johnston, of Gillingham, Kent; *Career* late REME; *Style*— The Hon Philip Annesley; 48 Shackleton Rd, Tilgate, Crawley, Sussex

ANNESLEY, Hon Richard Dighton; 2 s of 15 Viscount Valentia; *b* 1 April 1962; *Style*— The Hon Richard Annesley

ANNESLEY, Hon Sarah Joy; da of 15 Viscount Valentia; *b* 3 August 1958; *Style*— The Hon Sarah Annesley

ANNETT, David Maurice; s of Maurice Walter Annett (d 1935), and Marguerite, *née* Hobson (d 1976); *b* 27 April 1917; *Educ* Haileybury, Queens' Coll Cambridge (MA); *m* 1953, Evelyn Rosemary, da of late Walter Maxwell Gordon, Headmaster of Wrekin Coll, and widow of R E Upcott; 1 step s, 1 da (Rosamund), 2 step da; *Career* war service in India and Burma with 27 Field Regt RA 1940-45; head of Classics Dept and housemaster Oundle Sch, 1939-53; headmaster: Marling Sch Stroud 1953-59, King's Sch Worcester 1959-79; ret; *Style*— David Annett, Esq; The Old Shop, Whitbourne, Worcester WR6 5SR (☎ 0886 21727)

ANNING, Cmmr Raymon Harry; CBE (1982), QPM (1975); 1949, Beryl Joan; 1 s (Nicholas b 17 April 1959), 1 da (Julie b 22 July 1955); *b* 22 July 1930; *Educ* E Surrey Regt and Royal Military Police 1948-50; Met Police 1952- 79, HM Inspr of Constabulary for England and Wales 1979-83, cmmr of Police Royal Hong Kong Police Force 1985- (dep cmmr 1983-85); CBIM 1980; *m* 1949, Beryl Joan; 1 s (Nicholas b 17 April 1959), 1 da (Julie b 22 July 1955); *Career* E Surrey Regt and Royal Military Police 1948-50; Met Police 1952- 79, HM Inspr of Constabulary for England and Wales 1979-83, cmmr of Police Royal Hong Kong Police Force 1985 - (dep cmmr 1983-85); CBIM 1980; *Style*— Cmmr Raymon Anning, CBE, QPM

ANNIS, Philip Geoffrey Walter; s of Walter Annis, of Bleak House, Windermere, Cumbria, and Lilian Alice, *née* Norris; *b* 7 Feb 1936; *Educ* Sale Co GS Sale Ches, Kelsick GS Ambleside Westmorland, Manchester Univ (BA); *m* 15 June 1967, Olive Winifred, da of Edward Walter Scarlett, OBE, of Ilford, Essex; 1 s (Edward Philip b 20 April 1970); *Career* Nat Serv 1957-59 2 Lt RA, Actg Flt Lt RAFVR (T) 1960-62, TA 1961-67, RA (TA); inspr grade 3 Bd of Inland Revenue 1959-62, Nat Maritime Museum: joined 1962, co-ordinator of museum servs 1971-79, dep dir 1979-86; mangr regtl history project RA Inst 1986-; FSA 1973, FRHistS 1975; Cdr of the Order of the Lion of Finland 1987; *Books* Naval Swords (1970), Swords for Sea Service (with Cdr W E May, 1970); *Recreations* gardening, walking, reading; *Style*— Philip Annis, Esq; Royal Artillery Institution, Old Royal Military Acad, Woolwich, London SE18 4DN (☎ 01 854 2242, ext 5613)

ANSDELL, Peter Murray Agnew; s of Thomas Agnew Ansdell (d 1966), and Beatrice Frances Clara, *née* St John (d 1957); *b* 8 August 1929; *Educ* Winchester, Lausanne Univ; *m* 25 Oct 1958, Susan Theodora, da of Lt-Col Guy Alexander Ingram Dury, MC (d 1976), of Essex; 1 s (Paul b 1965), 2 da (Alexandra b 1960, Belinda b 1963); *Career* 2 Lt Coldstream Gds Malaya 1947-49; Bowater Paper Corpn 1957-61, Eburite Packaging 1950-57, export mangr William Collins (publishers) 1961-70 (personnel exec 1966-70), md Heart of England Cottages 1970-; *Recreations* travel, music, tennis, reading, gardening, antiques; *Clubs* Tidapa; *Style*— Peter M A Ansdell, Esq; Iveson House, Ampney St Peter, Cirencester, Gloucestershire GL7 5SH (☎ 0285 87217)

ANSELL, Mark John; s of John Frederick Ansell, of Birmingham, and Irene Francis, *née* Spiers (d 1982); *b* 2 Jan 1952; *Educ* Waverley GS Birmingham; *m* 2 March 1974, Sheila Mary, da of Victor William Marston, of Sutton Coldfield; *Career* CA 1973, ptnr Joslyne Layton Bennett & Co Birmingham 1977, (later merging with Binder Hamlyn), managing ptnr Binder Hamlyn 1988; former chm City of Birmingham Round Table, Birmingham Rotary Club; ACA 1973, FCA 1977, BMA 1987; *Recreations* golf, football, (spectating Aston Villa); *Clubs* City of Birmingham Round Table, Birmingham Rotary; *Style*— Mark Ansell, Esq; Binder Hamlyn, The Rotunda, Isonfust, Birmingham, B2 4PD, (☎ 021 643 5544, fax 021 643 4665, car tel 0860 538524, telex 336015 BINDERG)

ANSELL, Col Sir Michael Picton; CBE (1951), DSO (1944), DL (Devon 1966); s of late Lt-Col George Kirkpatrick Ansell, and K Cross; *b* 26 Mar 1905; *Educ* Wellington, Sandhurst; *m* 1, 1936, Victoria Jacintha Fleetwood (d 1969), da of Sir John Michael Fleetwood Fuller, 1 Bt, KCMG; 2 s, 1 da; m 2, 1970, Eileen, (d 1971), da of late Col E A Stanton, of Brownshill Court, Stroud, Glos, and widow of Maj-Gen Roger Evans, CB, MC; *Career* gazetted 5 Roy Inniskilling Dragoon Gds 1924, served WW II (wounded, POW, discharged disabled 1944), Col 1957-62; chm Br Show Jumping Assoc 1945-64 and 1970-71 (pres 1964-66); hon dir: Horse of the Year Show 1949-75, Roy Int Horse Show 1950-75, Br Horse Soc 1952-73; pres Br Equestrian Fedn 1972-76; Bureau of Fédn Equestre Int 1955-70; pres St Dunstan's 1977-86; (memb 1958-86); High Sheriff Devon 1967; Freeman of Worshipful Co Farriers 1962, Worshipful Co Loriners 1962; Yeoman Worshipful Co of Saddlers 1963; Chevalier Order of Leopold (Belgium) 1932, Cdr's Cross Order of Merit (FDR) 1975, Olympic Order Silver 1977; kt 1968; *Books* Riding High, Soldier On, Leopold, the Story of my horse; *Recreations* polo and show jumping (international 1931-39); *Clubs* Guards and Cavalry; *Style*— Col Sir Michael Ansell, CBE, DSO, DL; Pillhead House, Bideford, N Devon (☎ (023 72) 72574)

ANSELL, Maj-Gen Nicholas George Picton; OBE (1980); s of Col Sir Mike Ansell, CBE, DSO, DL, of Pillhead, Bideford, Devon, and Victoria Jacintha Fleetwood, *née* Fuller (d 1969); *b* 17 August 1937; *Educ* Wellington, Magdalene Coll Cambridge (MA); *m* 17 June 1961, Vivien, da of Col Anthony Donnithorne Taylor, DSO, MC (d 1986), of N Aston, Oxon; 2 s (Mark b 1963, Julian b 1964), 1 da (Clare b 1968); *Career* cmmnd 5 Royal Inniskilling Dragoon Guards 1956 (served BAOR, Libya, Cyprus, NI), Staff Coll Camberley 1970, Bde Maj RAC HQ 1 (BR) Corps 1971-72, instr staff Coll Camberley 1976-77, CO 5 Royal Inniskilling Dragoon Guards 1977-80, Col GS Staff Coll Camberley 1980-81, OC 20 Armd Bde 1982-83, RCDS 1984, dep chief of staff HQ BAOR 1985-86, dir RAC 1987-89; *Recreations* country pursuits - riding, fishing, birdwatching; *Clubs* Cavalry and Guards; *Style*— Maj-Gen Nicholas Ansell, OBE; c/o Lloyds Bank plc, Bideford, N Devon

ANSON, Cdr (Norman) Alastair Bourne; OBE (1983); s of Sir (George) Wilfrid Anson, MBE, MC (d 1974), of West Hay, Wrington, Bristol, and Dinah Maud Lilian, *née* Bourne; *b* 14 Oct 1929; *Educ* Winchester; *m* 23 Feb 1952 (m dis 1965), Collette Lavinia, da of Lt-Col Richard Eldred Hindson (d 1964), of Hill Brow, Liss, Hants; 1 s (Richard b 11 Nov 1952), 1 da (Crispin b 5 Sept 1955); m 2, 27 Nov 1968, Lavinia Maude, da of Rear Adm Ion Tower, DSC (1917); *Career* RNC Dartmouth 1947, Midshipman HMS Triumph and HMS Newcastle Med 1948-49, Sub Lt 1949-51, Lt HMS Bermuda SA 1951-52, HMS Chequers and HMS Chivalrous Med 1952-54, HMS Drake Plymouth 1954-56, CO HMS Carhampton Med 1956-58, Lt Cdr 2 i/c HMS Loch Lomond Persian Gulf 1959-61, naval rep RMA Sandhurst 1961-63, CO HMS Keppel Arctic Fishery Sqdn 1963-65, CO HMS Londonderry Far East 1965-66, asst sec Chiefs of Staff Ctee 1967-69, 2 i/c HMS Fearless 1969-71, Cabinet Off 1972-75, NATO HQ Naples 1975-78, trg dir Sea Cadet Corps 1979-82, ret 1982; memb panel of Lord Chllr's Independent Inquiry Inspectors responsible for inquiries on maj trunk road and motorway schemes; sidesman St Martin-in-the-Fields; Freeman City of London 1982, Liveryman Worshipful Co of Tin Plate Workers 1982; FIL 1959, FRGS 1983; *Recreations* music (organist), tennis, skiing, photography; *Clubs* City Livery, Royal Geographical Soc; *Style*— Cdr Alastair Anson, OBE; 38 Catherine Place, London SW1E 6HL (☎ 01 834 5991)

ANSON, Colin Shane; s of Anthony John Anson (d 1981), of Highdown, Horam, Sussex, and Rosalind Désirée, *née* Arbuthnot (d 1985); *b* 29 July 1931; *Educ* Dragon Sch, Stowe, Slade Sch of Fine Art (Dip Fine Art); *Career* art dept Arts Cncl of GB 1956-66, picture dept Christie's 1967-70; Artemis Gp 1971-: dir David Carritt Ltd art dealers 1981- (res asst 1971-81), dir Artemis Fine Arts Ltd 1981-; *Clubs* Brooks's; *Style*— Colin Anson, Esq; 18 Ripplevale Grove, London N1 1HU (☎ 01 607 2995); David Carritt Ltd, 15 Duke St, St James's, London SW1Y 6DB (☎ 01 930 8733)

ANSON, Vice Adm Sir Edward Rosebery; KCB (1984); s of Ross Rosebery Anson (d 1959), and Ethel Jane, *née* Green; *b* 11 May 1929; *Educ* Prince of Wales Sch Nairobi, RNC Dartmouth; *m* 1960, Rosemary Anne Radcliffe; 1 s (Jonathan b 1965), 1 da (Mea); *Career* served Naval Air Sqdns 1952-64; graduated Empire Test Pilots Sch 1957; cmd: HMS Eskimo 1964-66, HMS Juno and Capt 4 Frigate Sqdn 1974-76; Captain 1971, cmd HMS Ark Royal 1976-78 (last CO of the last traditional Br aircraft carrier), Flag Offr Naval Air Cmd 1979-82, Rear Adm 1980, Vice Adm 1982, COS to C-in-C Fleet 1982-84; *Recreations* golf, photography, walking; *Style*— Vice-Adm Sir Edward Anson, KCB; c/o Lloyds Bank, 9 High Street, Yeovil, Somerset BA20 1RN

ANSON, Lady Elizabeth; *see*: Shakerley, Lady Elizabeth Georgiana

ANSON, James William; CBE (1969); s of Lt-Col George Frank Wemyss Anson, OBE (d 1942); *b* 9 Jan 1915; *Educ* Fettes Coll Edinburgh, Gonville and Caius Coll Cambridge (BA); *m* 1940, Barbara Mary, da of late Gordon Peace, OBE, FIC, FRAS; 1 s, 1 da; *Career* serv WWII as Maj 2 Royal Sikhs in Iraq, Persia, Syria, Palestine, Egypt, Western Desert, Italy, Greece and at GHQ MEF Cairo; chm and md Mackinnon Mackenzie & Co (agents for P&O Steam Navigation Co in India) 1964-69 (joined 1937), tstee Port of Bombay 1965-69; pres Bombay C of C and Industry 1967-68; dep pres Associated Chambers of Commerce of India 1967-68, gen mangr Overseas Containers Ltd London 1970-77; hon sec Br Italian Soc 1977; Cavaliere of the Order Al Merito della Republica Italiana 1982; *Recreations* golf, gardening, formerly cricket and rugby football; *Clubs* MCC, Royal St George's (Sandwich), Hawks Cambridge; *Style*— James Anson, Esq, CBE; Courtlands, Pilgrim's Way, Wrotham, Kent (☎ 0732 822400)

ANSON, John; CB (1980); s of Sir Edward Anson, 6 Bt (d 1951), and Frances, da of Hugh Pollock (gs of Sir George Pollock, 1 Bt, GCB, GCSI); bro of Rear Adm Sir Peter Anson, Bt, *qv*; *b* 3 August 1930; *Educ* Winchester, Magdalene Coll Cambridge (MA); *m* 1957, Myrica, da of Dr Harold Fergie-Woods, MD (d 1961); 2 s, 2 da; *Career* HM Treasury 1954-68, financial cnsllr Br Embassy Paris 1968-70, Cabinet Office 1971-74, under-sec HM Treasury 1974-77, dep sec HM Treasury 1977-, economic min Br Embassy Washington and UK exec dir IMF and World Bank 1980-83; *Style*— John Anson, Esq, CB; c/o HM Treasury, Parliament St, London SW1P 3AG (☎ 01 270 3000)

ANSON, Malcolm Allinson; s of Sir (George) Wilfrid Anson, MBE, MC (d 1974), of West Hay, Wrington, nr Bristol, and Dinah, *née* Bourne; *b* 23 April 1924; *Educ* Winchester, Trinity Coll Oxford (MA); *m* 1950, (Isabel) Alison Valerie, da of Sir Arthur Cunningham Lothian, KCIE, CSI (d 1962); 3 s, 1 da; *Career* Capt RHA N W Europe and India; chm: Imperial Gp Ltd 1980-81 (formerly dep chm), Wessex Water Authy 1982-87; memb int advsy cncl INSEAD; chm: careers advsy bd Bristol Univ, cncl Clifton Coll, Cancer Help Centre, Avon Enterprise Fund; High Sheriff Avon 1977-78, Master Soc of Merchant Vertures Bristol 1979-80; *Recreations* shooting, sailing, skiing, golf; *Clubs* Cavalry and Guards; *Style*— Malcolm Anson, Esq; Hill Court, Congresbury, Bristol (☎ 0934 832117)

ANSON, Rear Adm Sir Peter; 7 Bt (1831), CB (1974); s of Sir Edward Reynell Anson, 6 Bt (d 1951), and Alison, da of Hugh Pollock (gs of Sir George Pollock, 1 Bt, GCB, GCSI); bro of John Anson, CB, *qv*; *b* 31 July 1924; *Educ* RNC Dartmouth; *m* 1955, Elizabeth Audrey, da of Rear Adm Sir (Charles) Philip Clarke, KBE, CB, DSO (d 1966); 2 s, 2 da; *Heir* s, Philip Anson, *qv*; *Career* RN: Cdr Naval Forces, Gulf 1970-72 (Cdre), asst chief of Def Staff (Signals) 1972-74 (Rear Adm), ret from RN 1975; div mangr satellites Marconi Space and Def Systems Ltd 1977- (asst mktg dir 1975); md Marconi Space Systems Ltd 1984-85, (chm 1985-); CEng, FIEE; *Recreations* shooting, sailing, gardening, golf; *Clubs* Pratt's; *Style*— Rear Adm Sir Peter Anson, Bt, CB; Rosefield, 81 Boundstone Rd, Rowledge, Farnham, Surrey GU10 4AT (☎ Frensham (025 125) 2724); Marconi Space Systems Ltd; Anchorage Road, Portsmouth, Hants PO3 5PU (☎ 0705 674126)

ANSON, Philip Roland; s and h of Rear Adm Sir Peter Anson, 7 Bt, CB, *qv*; *b* 4 Oct 1957; *Educ* Charterhouse, Chelsea Coll London (BPharm); *Career* pharmacist; with Boots 1979-84, Waremoss Chemists Ltd 1984-; MPS 1980, MIPharmM 1980; *Style*— Philip Anson, Esq; 34 Martello Rd, Eastbourne, East Sussex BN22 7SS (☎ 0323 25990); Guy's Pharmacy, 26 Eastbourne Rd, Pevensey Bay, East Sussex BN24 6ET (☎ 0323 761321)

ANSON, Viscount; Thomas William Robert Hugh Anson; s and h of 5 Earl of Lichfield; *b* 19 July 1978; *Style*— Viscount Anson

ANSTEE, Margaret Joan; da of Edward Curtis Anstee (d 1971), and Anne Adaliza, *née* Mills (d 1972); *b* 25 June 1926; *Educ* Chelmsford Co HS for Girls, Newnham Coll Cambridge (MA), London (BSc); *Career* lectr in spanish Queen's Univ Belfast 1947-48, 3 sec FO 1948-52, admin offr UN Tech Assistance Bd Manila Philippines 1952-54, spanish supervisor Cambridge Univ 1955-56; UN Tech Assistance Bd: i/c Bogota Columbia 1956-57, Resident Rep Uruguay 1957-59, Dir Special Fund progs and UN Info Centre 1960-65; Resident Rep, UNDP Ethopia and liaison offr with UN Econ Cmmn for Africa 1965-67, sr econ advsr PM's off 1967-68, sr asst to Cmmr i/c of Study of Capacity of UN Devpt System 1968-69; Resident Rep UNDP: Morocco 1969-72, Chile and liaison offr with UN Econ Cmmn for Latin America 1972-74; dep to UN Under-Sec-Gen i/c of UN relief Op to Bangladesh and dep co-ordinator of UN emergency assistance to Zambia 1973; UNDP NY: dep asst admin and dep regnl dir for Latin America 1974-76, dir admins unit for special assignments 1976, asst dep admin 1976, asst admin and dir bureau for prog policy and evaluation 1977-78, asst sec-gen of UN dept of tech Co-Operation for devpt 1978-87, special rep of the sec-gen for co-ordination of int assistance following Mexico earthquake 1985-87, chm advsy gp on review of UN World Food Cncl 1985-86, special co-ordinator of UN sec-gen to ensure implementation of Gen Assembly resolution on fin and admin reform of the UN 1986-87; special rep of UN Sec Gen for Bolivia 1982, rep UN Sec Gen at Conf for the Adoption of a Convention Against Illicit Traffic in Narcotic Drugs and Psychotropic Substances 1988, dir gen UN off Vienna, Under Sec Gen UN, head of centre for Social Devpt and Humanitarian Affrs, co-ordinator of all UN drug control related activities 1987; *Books* The Administration of International Development Aid (USA 1969), Gate of the Sun: a prospect of Bolivia (ed with R K A Gardiner and C Patterson,1970, USA 1971); Africa and the World (1970); *Style*— Miss Margaret J Anstee; United Nations Office at Vienna, PO Box 500, Room E-1436, A-1400 Vienna, Austria (☎ 2631/5001, 5002, fax 232156, telex 135612 Unations Vienna)

ANSTEY, Edgar; s of Percy Lewis Anstey (d 1920), of Bombay, India, and Dr Vera, *née* Powell (d 1976); *b* 5 Mar 1917; *Educ* Winchester, King's Coll Cambridge (MA), UCL (PhD); *m* 3 June 1939, Zoë Lilian, da of John Thomson Robertson (d 1922), of Rangoon; 1 s (David John b 1947); *Career* 2 Lt Dorset Regt 1940-41, Maj directorate for selection of personnel WO 1941-45; asst princ Dominions Off 1938-39, private sec to Duke of Devonshire 1939-40; Home Off 1951-58, sr princ psychologist MOD 1958-64, chief psychologist Civil Serv Cmmn 1964-69 (princ 1945-51), dep chief scientific offr and head res div Civil Serv Dept 1969-77; pres: N Cornwall Lib Assoc 1984-88 (chm 1982-84), N Cornwall SLD Assoc 1988-; cncllr Esher DC 1972-74; FBPsS 1949; *Books* Interviewing For The Selection of Staff (with Dr EO Mercer 1956), Staff Reporting And Staff Development (1961), Committees - How They Work And How to Work Them (1962), Psychological Tests (1966), The Techniques of Interviewing (1968), Staff Appraisal and Development (with Dr CA Fletcher and Dr J Walker 1976), An Introduction to Selection Interviewing (1978); *Recreations* fell-walking, surfing, golf, bridge; *Clubs* Royal Cwlth Soc; *Style*— Dr Edgar Anstey; Sandrock, 3 Higher Tristram, Polzeath, Wadebridge, Cornwall PL27 6TF (☎ 020 886 3324)

ANSTICE, Michael John Christian; MC (1952), TD; s of Vice Adm Sir Edmund Walter Anstice (d 1979), of Inverdunning House, Dunning, Perth, and Leslie Doudney, *née* Ritchie; *b* 5 Oct 1929; *Educ* Wellington, RMA Sandhurst; *m* 11 July 1959, Carolyn May, da of Gerald Richard Powlett Wilson (d 1986), of Cliffe Hall, Piercebridge, Co Durham; 3 s (William b 1960, Mark b 1967, Richard b 1969), 1 da (Penelope b 1962); *Career* Capt 5 Royal Inniskilling Dragoon Gds 1956, Lt Col (cmdg) Highland Yeomanry 1968, Col Cmdt Angus/Dundee ACF 1968-75; serv: Germany, Korea, Egypt; ptnr Milldens partnership Letham, Angus; Late of Jute Indust Ltd Dundee and chm Jute Importers Assoc Dundee 1976-78; *Recreations* shooting, fishing, woodwork; *Clubs* Royal Perth; *Style*— Michael J C Anstice, Esq, MC, TD; Melgam House, Lintrathen, Kirriemuir, Angus DD8 5JH (☎ Lintrathen 269)

ANSTRUTHER, Ian Fife Campbell; s of Douglas Tollemache Anstruther (d 1956, gs of Sir Robert Anstruther, 5 Bt), and his 1 w Enid (d 1964), 2 da of Lord George Granville Campbell; *b* 11 May 1922; *Educ* Eton, New Coll Oxford; *m* 1, 1951 (m dis 1963), (Geraldine) Honor, elder da of late Capt Gerald Stuart Blake, MC; 1 da; m 2, 1963, Susan Margaret Walker, da of Henry St John Paten; 2 s, 3 da; *Career* Capt Royal Corps of Signals, former attaché Br Embassy Washington; author; memb Roy Co of Archers (Queen's Body Guard for Scotland); FSA; *Books* I Presume, The Knight and the Umbrella, The Scandal of the Andover Workhouse, Oscar Browning; *Clubs* Brooks's; *Style*— Ian Anstruther, Esq; Estate Office, Barlavington, Petworth, Sussex GU28 0LG (☎ 079 87 260)

ANSTRUTHER OF THAT ILK, Sir Ralph Hugo; 7 Bt (NS 1694) and 12 Bt (NS 1700), KCVO (1976, CVO 1967), MC (1943), DL (Fife 1960, Caithness 1965); s of late Capt Robert Anstruther, MC, and Marguerite (da of Hugo de Burgh, 3 s of Thomas de Burgh, of Oldtown, Co Kildare); suc gf, Sir Ralph Anstruther, 6 Bt, JP, Lord-Lt of Fife, 1934 and cous Sir Windham Carmichael-Anstruther 11 Bt 1980; *b* 13 June 1921; *Educ* Eton, Magdalene Coll Cambridge (BA); *Heir* cous, Ian Anstruther, *qv*; *Career* Maj (ret) Coldstream Gds; equerry to HM Queen Elizabeth The Queen Mother 1959- (tres 1961-, asst private sec 1959-64); memb Royal Co of Archers (Queen's Body Guard for Scotland); hereditary carver to HM The Queen; *Style*— Sir Ralph Anstruther, Bt, KCVO, MC, DL; Balcaskie, Pittenweem, Fife (☎ 0333 311202); Watten Mains, Caithness (☎ 095 582 228)

ANSTRUTHER-GOUGH-CALTHORPE, Sir Euan Hamilton; 3 Bt (UK 1929), of Elvetham Hall, Elvetham, Co Southampton; s of Niall Hamilton Anstruther-Gough-Calthorpe (d 1970), and Martha (who m 2, 1975, Charles Nicholson), da of Stuart Warren Don; suc gf, Brig Sir Richard Anstruther-Gough-Calthorpe, 2 Bt, CBE (d 1985); *b* 22 June 1966; *Educ* Harrow, Royal Agric Coll Cirencester; *Style*— Sir Euan Anstruther-Gough-Calthorpe, Bt; Turner's Green Farm, Elvetham, Hartley Wintney, Hants RG27 8BE

ANTHONY; *see*: Bank-Anthony

ANTHONY, David Gwilym; s of Ernest Anthony, and Megan Euron *née* Davies; *b* 10 Feb 1947; *Educ* Hull GS, St Catherine's Coll Oxford (MA); *m* 8 Oct 1974, (Ellen) Brigid, da of Air Vice-Marshal W J Crisham (d 1987); 1 s (Peter b 1979), 1 da (Jane b 1980); *Career* Barton Mayhew (now Ernst & Whinney) 1969-73, Dymo Business Systems Ltd 1973-75, Slater, Walker Finance Ltd 1975-77, Forward Trust (Ireland) Ltd 1977-82; dir and gen mangr Hitachi Credit (UK) Ltd 1982-; FCA 1973; *Recreations* walking, table tennis; *Style*— David G Anthony, Esq; Retreat, Church Lane, Stoke Pages, Bucks, SL2 4NZ (☎ (0753) 30895); Hitachi Credit (UK) Ltd, Hitachi Credit House, Stable Courtyard, Church Road, Hayes, Middx, UB3 2UH (☎ 01 561 8486), fax 01 561 1206

ANTHONY, Rt Hon (John) Doug(las); CH (1982), PC (1971); s of late Hon H L Anthony, former MHR for Richmond (for 20 years) and former Postmaster-General; *b* 31 Dec 1929; *Educ* King's Sch Parramatta, Qld Agric Coll (Dip Agric); *m* 1957, Margot MacDonald (pianist and Patron of Canberra Symphony Orchestra), da of J Alton Budd; 2 s, 1 da; *Career* MHR (Country Party) Richmond NSW Aust 1957-84; memb Exec Cncl 1963-72, min for The Interior 1964-67, dep leader Country Party 1966-71, min for Primary Industry 1967-71, leader Nat Country Party of Australia 1971-84, dep pm and min for Trade and Industry 1971-72, dep pm, min for National Resources and min for Overseas Trade 1975-77, dep pm and min for Trade and Resources 1977-1983; co dir; farmer; hon LLD Wellington Univ (1983), Queensland Agric Coll Gold Medal (1984); *Recreations* golf, tennis, swimming, fishing; *Clubs* Royal Sydney Golf, Union, Queensland; *Style*— The Rt Hon Doug Anthony, CH; Sunnymeadows, Murwillumbah, NSW 2484, Australia

ANTHONY, Evelyn Bridgett Patricia; da of Lt Cdr Henry Christian Stephens, RNVR (d 1953), of Cholderton, Wilts and Elizabeth, *née* Sharkey (d 1968), of Lower Leeson St, Dublin; ggf Henry Stephens invented writing ink, F H C Stephens invented Dome anti-aircraft trainer 1939-45 war; *b* 3 July 1928; *Educ* Convent of Sacred Heart Roehampton; *m* 1955, Michael Ward-Thomas, s of Richard Ward-Thomas (d 1954), of Hunsdon, Herts and Margery Bowles, *née* Madge (d 1981); 4 s (Anthony, Ewan, Christian, Luke), 2 da (Susan, Katharine); *Career* author; has produced 28 novels which have been translated into 14 languages and have sold over 10 million copies; *Books Incl:* The Occupying Power (won Yorkshire Post fiction prize 1973), The Tamarind Seed (made into a major film); *Recreations* nat hunt racing, music, gardening, salerooms; *Style*— Miss Evelyn Anthony; Horham Hall, Thaxted, Essex (☎ (0371) 830 389)

ANTHONY, Ronald Desmond; s of William Arthur Anthony (d 1987), and Olive Francis *née* Buck (d 1986); *b* 21 Nov 1925; *Educ* Sidcup & Chistlehurst GS, Imperial Coll of Sci & Technol (BSc,ACGI); *m* Betty Margaret da of Walter Frederick Newton

Croft (d 1971); 4 da (Frances b 1951, Jennifer b 1953, Rebecca b 1957, Sarah b 1958); *Career* served RCS 1943-48; Vickers Armstrongs (Supermarine) 1950-57, Nuclear Power Plant Co 1957-60, Inspectorate of Nuclear Installations 1960-85, HSE 1974-85 (hd of Safety Policy Div 1977-80 bd memb 1977-85), chief inspr of nuclear installations 1980-85, engrg conslt 1985-; FIMech E, FINUCE, MRAES, BNES 1987-89 (pres); *Recreations* golf; *Style—* Ronald Anthony Esq,; 3 Mereside, Orpington, Kent, BR6 8ET

ANTHONY, Vivian Stanley; Capt Arthur Stanley Anthony (d 1983), of Llandaff, Cardiff, and Ceinwen, *née* Thomas (d 1965); *b* 5 May 1938; *Educ* Cardiff HS, Univ of London, LSE (BSc), Fitzwilliam Coll Cambridge (DipEd); *m* 1969, Rosamund Anne, da of Colonel Frank McDermot Byrn, of Wicklow, Eire; 1 s (Thomas b 1971), 1 da (Jennifer b 1970); *Career* headmaster Colfe's Sch 1976-, asst master Leeds GS 1960-64, asst master and housemaster Tonbridge 1964-69, lectr in educn Univ of Leeds 1969-71, dep headmaster The King's Sch Macclesfield 1971-76, chm Econs Assoc 1974-77; external examiner: Univ of Manchester Postgrad Cert in Educn 1972-75, Univ of Birmingham Cert of Educn at Dudley Coll 1975-78, Lancaster Univ 1977-79; chief examiner in A and S Level econs for Oxford and Cambridge Bd 1975- (examiner 1970-75); memb: Ctee of Chief Examiners to examine Common Core in A level economics 1980-81, HMC Academic Policy ctee (chm 1989-), Professional devpt ctee 1983-88, Teacher Shortage Working Pty 1987-88, CBI/Schools Panel; area 1 chm govr Independent Schs 1988-89; rep on London U Examination Bd, scrutineer Oxford and NI Bds, sch master fellowship Merton Coll Oxford; *Books* Monopoly (1968), Overseas Trade (4 edn 1981), Tour of American Independent Schools (1984); articles include: The Economics Association and the Training of Teachers (Economics 1972), The Report of the Working Party on Economics and Economic History (Economics 1973), Report on Records of Achievement (HMC 1989); *Recreations* music (choral singing), rugby football, squash, tennis; *Clubs* East India, Old Colfeians; *Style—* Vivian Anthony, Esq; Lincoln Lodge, Pines Road, Bickley, Kent (☎ 01 467 7176); Colfe's School, London SE12 8AW (☎ 01 852 2283)

ANTICO, Sir Tristan; AC (1983); s of Terribile Giovanni Antico (d 1965), and Erminia Bertin (d 1979); *b* 25 Mar 1923; *Educ* Sydney HS; *m* 1950, Dorothy Brigid, da of William Shields; 3 s (William, Damien, Stephen), 4 da (Virginia, Helen, Elizabeth, Veronica); *Career* chm and md Pioneer Concrete Servs Ltd; dir Qantas Airways Ltd 1979-; former chm St Vincent's Hosp Bd; former tstee the Art Gallery of New South Wales; Commendatore dell'Ordine della Stella Solidarieta Italiana 1967; kt 1973; *Recreations* horseracing and breeding, swimming, cruising, tennis; *Clubs* Royal Sydney Yacht Squadron, Manly Golf, Tattersall's Australian Jockey, Sydney Turf, American National, Balmoral Beach; *Style—* Sir Tristan Antico, AC; 161 Raglan St, Mosman, NSW 2088, Australia (☎ 969 4070); 11th Floor, 55 Macquarie Street, Sydney 2000 (telex AA21445, fax 251 1595)

ANTONELLI, Count Pietro Hector Paolo Maria; Commendatore Ordine al Merito della Republica Italiana (2 June 1983); s of Count Giacomo Antonelli (d 1963; Cavalry Gen, Italian Army), and Countess Luisa Antonelli, *née* Piva (d 1954); descendant of Cardinal Giacomo Antonelli, sec of State to Pope Pius IX, and of Count Pietro Antonelli, African explorer and diplomat; *b* 14 Mar 1924; *Educ* Univ of Rome (Degree in Philosophy); *m* (m dis 1976), Countess Maria Benedetta Bossi Pucci; 3 da (Sibilla b 27 April 1947, Santa b 12 Nov 1950, Serena b 18 Jan 1953); *Career* mangr and subsequently dir Hambros Bank Ltd 1981; official Banca Commerciale 1948-62; md: Caboto Spa 1962-72, Banca Provinciale di Depositi e Sconti 1971; dir Banco Lariano 1986; *Recreations* yachting; *Clubs* Circolo della Caccia, Rome; *Style—* Count Pietro Antonelli; 12 Eaton Place, London SW1 (☎ 01 235 5923); Hambros Bank Ltd, 41 Bishopsgate, London EC2P 2AA (☎ 01 588 2851, telex 883851, fax 01 638 0480)

ANTRIM, 9 Earl of (I 1785); Alexander Randal Mark McDonnell; also Viscount Dunluce, by which title he continues to be known; s of 8 Earl of Antrim, KBE (d 1977), and Angela Christina, da of Col Sir Mark Sykes; *b* 3 Feb 1935; *Educ* Downside, Christ Church Oxford, Ruskin Sch of Art; *m* 1, 1963 (m dis 1974), Sarah Elizabeth Anne, 2 da of Sir John Bernard Vyvyan Harmsworth; 1 s, 2 da (Lady Flora Mary b 1963, Lady Alice Angela Jane b 1964); m 2, 1977, Elizabeth, da of Michael Moses Sacher; 1 da (Lady Rachel Frances b 1978); *Heir* s, Hon Randal Alexander St John McDonnell b 2 July 1967; *Career* keeper of conservation Tate Gallery 1975-; memb exec ctee City and Guilds of London Art Sch and of Court of Royal Coll of Art; dir Ulster TV; FRSA; *Style—* Viscount Dunluce; Glenarm Castle, Glenarm, Co Antrim, Northern Ireland

ANTROBUS, Edward Philip; s and h of Sir Philip Coutts Antrobus, 7 Bt, and Dorothy Margaret Mary, *née* Davis (d 1973); *b* 28 Sept 1938; *Educ* Witwatersrand Univ (BSc), Magdalene Coll Cambridge (MA); *m* 7 Oct 1966, Janet Sarah Elizabeth, da of Philip Walter Sceales, of Johannesburg; 1 s (Francis b 1972), 2 da (Barbara b 1968, Sarah b 1970); *Career* mangr Marley Johannesburg; landowner; *Recreations* golf, tennis; *Clubs* Johannesburg Country, Roy Johannesburg Golf; *Style—* Edward Antrobus, Esq; 70 Harry Street, Robertsham, Johannesburg, S Africa (☎ 011 680 3560)

ANTROBUS, Sir Philip Coutts; 7 Bt (UK 1815), of Antrobus, Cheshire; s of Geoffrey Edward Antrobus (gn of Sir Edmund Antrobus, 2 Bt, and gn through his m, Mary, *née* Shakerley, of Sir Charles Shakerley, 1 Bt); suc cous, Sir Philip Antrobus, 6 Bt, MC, 1968; *b* 10 April 1908; *m* 1, 1937, Dorothy Margaret Mary (d 1973), da of Rev William G Davis, of Grahamstown S Africa; 2 s, 1 da; m 2, 1975, Doris (d 1986), da of late Harry George Watts, and widow of Thomas Ralph Dawkins; *Heir* s, Edward Antrobus; *Career* serv WWII (POW); Lord of the Manor of Amesbury; *Recreations* golf; *Clubs* Old Andrean; *Style—* Sir Philip Antrobus, Bt; West Amesbury House, Amesbury, Wilts (☎ 0980 23860)

ANWAR, Tariq Rafiq; s of Rafiq Anwar (d 1976), of Chiswick, and Edith Fordham, *née* Reich; *b* 21 Sept 1945; *Educ* Walpole GS, Sir John Cass Coll London; *m* 29 Sept 1966, Shirley Natalie, da of John Richard Hills, of Hainault, Essex; 1 s (Dominic b 29 June 1967), 1 da (Gabrielle b 4 Feb 1970); *Career* asst film ed; films inc: Mackenna's Gold, Cromwell, Loot; film ed with BBC; Best Editor BAFTA Award: Caught on a Train, Oppenheimer; BAFTA Nominations: Monocled Mutineer, Fortunes of War; ACE Nomination for Tender is the Night; memb ACTT; *Recreations* music, tennis, bricklaying; *Style—* Tariq Anwar, Esq; BBC TV Film Studios, Ealing Green, London W5 (☎ 01 567 6655, ext 772/773)

ANWYL-DAVIES, His Hon Judge; Marcus John Anwyl-Davies; QC (1967); s of Thomas Anwyl-Davies, MD, FRCP (d 1971), and Kathleen Beryl, *née* Oakshott; *b* 11 July 1923; *Educ* Harrow, Christ Church Oxford (MA); *m* 1, 1954 (m dis 1974), Eva Hilda Elisabeth, *née* Paulson; 1 s, 1 da; m 2, 1983, Myrna Dashoff, attorney, of Westwood, California; *Career* serv WWII Capt RA (despatches), Hong Kong and Singapore RA; barr Inner Temple 1949, legal assessor GMC and GDC 1969-71, circuit judge 1972-, liaison judge Hertford Magistrates 1972-82; vice-pres Herts Magistrates Assoc 1975; *Recreations* farming, photography; *Clubs* Reform; *Style—* His Hon Judge Anwyl-Davies, QC

AP ROBERT, His Hon Judge; Hywel Wyn Jones; s of Rev Robert John Jones (d 1973), and Mrs Jones, *née* Evans; *b* 19 Nov 1923; *Educ* Cardiff HS, Corpus Christi Coll Oxford (MA); *m* 1956, Elizabeth, da of J Gareth Davies, of Penarth; 2 da; *Career* WWII FO and Intelligence Corps; barr Middle Temple 1950, contested Cardiganshire (Plaid Cymru) 1970, chm Industl Tbnls 1970-72, rec of the Crown Ct 1972-75, stipendiary magistrate Cardiff (now South Glamorgan) 1972-75, circuit judge 1975-; hon memb of the Gorsedd of Bards 1972; co ct judge in Mid and West Glamorgan 1985-; *Recreations* Welsh and classical literature, modern languages; *Clubs* Cardiff & County; *Style—* His Hon Judge ap Robert; Law Courts, Cardiff

APLETREE, John Anthony; s of Reginald Arthur Apletree, Guldud, Westley Rd, Langdon Hills, Essex, and Audrie, *née* Brooker; *b* 13 Oct 1944; *Educ* Kings Sch Canterbury; *m* 2 Oct 1971, Susan, da of Neville Dale, of 74 Croft Road, Yardley, Birmingham; 3 s (Christopher b 1972, Richard b 1974, Paul b 1977); *Career* dir: Medens Tst Ltd, Brown Shipley Pension Tstees Ltd, Medens Ltd (inc Jersey and Guernsey), Southern Finance Co Ltd, Tunedeck Systems Ltd; FICA; *Recreations* rugby, cricket, photography; *Style—* John Apletree, Esq; 51 Marshall Ave, Bognor Regis, West Sussex (☎ 0243 829 889); Southern House, 80 Shirley Rd, Southampton, Hants SO1 3EY (☎ 0703 226 745)

APPLEBY, His Hon Judge Brian John; QC (1971); s of Ernest Joel Appleby; *b* 25 Feb 1930; *Educ* Uppingham, St John's Coll Cambridge; *m* 1958, Rosa Helena, *née* Flitterman; 1 s, 1 da; *Career* barr Middle Temple 1953, rec Crown Ct 1972-88, judge of The Crown C 1988-; dep chm Notts QS 1970-71, bencher Middle Temple 1980; dist referee Notts Wages Conciliation Bd NCB 1980-88; memb Nottingham City Cncl 1955-58 and 1960-63; *Style—* His Hon Judge Brian Appleby, QC; The Poplars, Edwalton Village, Edwalton, Notts (☎ Nottingham 232814)

APPLEBY, Maj-Gen David Stanley; CB (1979), MC (1943), TD (1950); s of Stanley Appleby, and Mabel Dorothy Mary, *née* Dickson; *b* 4 Dec 1918; *Educ* St Peter's Sch; *m* 1942, Prudence Marianne, *née* Chilsholm; 1 s, 1 da (and 1 s decd); *Career* 2 Lt Royal Fusiliers (TA) 1939, served WWII, Capt 1950, dir Army Legal Servs 1976-78; called to the Bar Middle Temple 1951; *Style—* Maj-Gen David Appleby, CB, MC, TD; Two Acres, Beechwood Lane, Burley, Ringwood, Hants

APPLEBY, Douglas Edward Marrison; s of late Robert Appleby, MSc, and Muriel, *née* Surtees; *b* 17 May 1929; *Educ* Durham Johnston Sch, Nottingham U; *m* 1952, June Marrison; 1 s, 1 da; *Career* Corn Products Co (USA) 1958-63; fin dir Wilkinson Sword Co 1963-68; The Boots Co: fin dir 1968-72, md 1973-81, ret; memb Cncl Inst of CA 1971-75 and CBI 1977-81; farmer and stockbreeder; FCA; *Style—* Douglas Appleby, Esq; Pond Farm, Upper Broughton, Melton Mowbray, Leics

APPLEBY, (Lesley) Elizabeth; QC (1979); (Mrs Michael Collins); o da of Arthur Leslie Appleby, and Dorothy Evelyn, *née* Edwards; *b* 12 August 1942; *Educ* Wolverhampton Girls' HS, Manchester Univ (LLB); *m* 1978, Michael Kenneth Collins, OBE, BSc, MICE; 1 s, 1 da; *Career* barr Gray's Inn 1965, in practice Chancery Bar 1966-; memb of Senate of Inns of Court and Bar 1977-80 and 1981-82; bencher Lincolns Inn 1986; *Recreations* gardening, railway, tennis; *Clubs* Royal Lymington Yacht; *Style—* Miss Elizabeth Appleby, QC; 32 Pembroke Rd, London W8 (☎ 01 602 4141); 4/5 Gray's Inn Sq, Gray's Inn, London WC1R 5AY (☎ 01 404 5252)

APPLEBY, George; s of William Appleby (d 1942),of Felling, Gateshead, and Constance, *née* Forrest (d 1979); *b* 2 June 1919; *Educ* private schs, Sch of Mil Engrg and Radar, Newcastle upon Tyne Univ ; *m* 19 Aug 1955, Doreen, da of James Kidd Reed (d 1969), of Jesmond, Newcastle upon Tyne; 2 s (Stephen Mark b 1956, Jonathan Paul b 1963), 1 da (Carole Anne b 1958); *Career* WWII 1939-46 RE served: 50 Div France (Dunkirk), 8 Army, India; clerk G Raillard 1933-34, accountant Bolton & Wawn (now Thornton Baker) 1934-39, sr asst Peat Marwick Mitchell 1946-50, fin exec Armstrong Whitworth Thor Stewart Warner (USA and Italy) 1951-67, conslt advsr 1968-71, fin exec Blyth Harbour Cmmn 1971-78, advsr and instr Seaport Corpn Port Sudan (World Bank and Kuwaiti aid project) 1978-80, port cost accounting expert UN (USA and Turkey) 1980-81, professional accountant Port of London in team at Saudi Arabia (Yanbu project), conslt advsr secial devpt area 1982-; FCA, ATII, ABCS; *Recreations* singing, experiments, occasional golf, badminton, bathing; *Style—* George Appleby Esq; 67 Millview Dr, Tynemouth, Tyne and Wear NE30 2QD (☎ 091 2577 516)

APPLEBY, Malcolm Arthur; s of James William Appleby (d 1976), of West Wickham, Kent, and Marjory, *née* Stokes; *b* 6 Jan 1946; *Educ* Hawesdown Co Secdy Modern Sch for Boys, Beckenham Sch of Art, Ravensbourn Coll of Art and Design, Central Sch of Art and Design, Sir John Cass Sch of Art, Royal Coll of Art; *Career* started career as engraver 1968, now designer for silver and specialist gun engraver; developed gold fusing on to steel and created new silver engraving techniques; work incl: engraving Orb on Prince of Wales Coronet, King George VI Diamond Stakes trophy 1978, 500th Universary Silver Cup for London Assay Office, V & A Museum seal, condiment set destined for 10 Downing St; work in collections: Aberdeen Art Gallery, Royal Armouries, V & A crafts cncl, Contemporary Arts Soc, Goldsmiths Co, Br Cncl crafts exhibition to Japan, Sotheby's contemporary arts exhibition to Japan; memb Crathes Drumoak and Durris Community cncl (chm 1981), Br Art Medal Soc; Freeman Worshipful Co of Goldsmiths London 1976; *Recreations* work, standing in the garden, cups of tea with friends and neighbours, stilton cheese, darning my very old but colourful pullover; *Style—* Malcolm Appleby, Esq; Crathes Station, by Banchory, Kincardineshire, Scotland (☎ 033 044 642)

APPLETON, Lt-Col George Fortnam; OBE (1946), TD (1947), JP (1954), DL (Lancs 1971); s of James Arthur Appleton, JP (d 1961), of Ainsdale, Lancs and Wetwood, Staffs, and Ethel Maude, *née* Fortnam; *b* 23 July 1913; *Educ* Warwick Sch; *m* 1940, Patricia Margaret, da of Henry J L Dunlop, memb 1907/09 Shackleton Antarctic Expedition (d 1931), of Lancs; 1 s (John), 1 da (Jayne); *Career* 2 Lt 5 Bn The King's Regt 1933, Staff Capt 165 Inf Bde 1938, serv WWII, Staff Coll 1940, Gen Staff A & Q Branch appts HQ II Corps and HQ Eastern Cmd, Beach Co Cmd 'D' Day Invasion 1944 (despatches 2), DAQMG HQ 12 Corps, 2 Army and Port of Antwerp, AA & QMG HQ 20 L of C Sub-Area BAOR; ret co dir and farmer; cmdt Special

Constabulary 1950-54, chm Southport and N Sefton PSD 1971-83; former chm N Lancs and Merseyside Branches Magistrates' Assoc; County Borough Cnclr 1949-61; High Sheriff Merseyside 1977-78; hon county dir W Lancs BRCS 1964-74, pres Merseyside Co BRCS 1974-79; former chm Merseycare Charitable Tst; Lancs pres Forces Help Soc and Lord Roberts Workshops; pres: Southport and West Lancashire Branch Normandy Veterans Assoc, Southport and Dist Youth Band; patron Southport and Dist Branch: Burma Star Assoc, Dunkirk Veterans Assoc; govr School for Partially Hearing Birkdale; OStJ 1974; *Style*— Lt-Col George Appleton, OBE, TD, JP, DL; Shore House, Shore Rd, Ainsdale, Southport, Lancs PR8 2PU (☎ 0704 78211)

APPLETON, John Fortnam; s of Lt-Col George Fortnam Appleton, OBE, TD, JP, DL (*qv*), of Ainside, Merseyside, and Patricia Margaret, da of Henry J L Dunlop, (d 1931), memb Br Antarctic Expdn of 1907/9; *b* 8 April 1946; *Educ* Harrow, Bristol Univ (LLB); *m* 1983 Maureen Sellers, JP, *née* Williams and widow of John Sellers of Formby; 1 s (George); *Career* barr Middle Temple 1969; Rec Crown Ct 1985; sometime Lune correspondent for Trout and Salmon magazine; *Recreations* shooting, fishing; *Style*— John Appleton, Esq; The Old Vicarage, Abbeystead, Lancaster LA2 9BG; 14 Winckley Sq, Preston, Lancs

APPLETON, Michael John; s of Lt Cdr Maurice Appleton, RN (d 1962), of Bedford, and Helen Eugene, *née* Hailstone (d 1982); *b* 25 July 1932; *Educ* Bedford Sch, Mons (OCS) Chatham; *m* 2 June 1962, Damaris, da of Donald Ronald Armstrong Hoblyn (d 1974), of Tunbridge Wells; 1 s (Guy b 1972), 2 da (Tania b 1964, Alice b 1966); *Career* 2 Lt RE, Suez Canal Zone, MELF 1951-53; Capt RE (TA) 1953-56; ptnr Godfrey-Payton, Chartered Surveyors 1967-87; FRICS; *Recreations* skiing, sailing, gardening; *Style*— Michael J Appleton, Esq; Home Farm House, Avon Dassett, Leamington Spa CV33 0AR (☎ 0252 227); 25 High Street, Warwick (☎ 0926 492511)

APPLETON, Robert Michael Laurence; s of Laurence Charles Appleton (d 1973), of Wallington, Surrey, and Margaret Mary, *née* Yates (d 1960); *b* 2 April 1931; *Educ* John Fisher Sch Purley; *m* 23 April 1955, Mary Burdett, da of Reginald William Woodford, CBE (d 1980); 1 s (Dominic Robert Gerard), 2da (Claire Marguerite, Lucy Mary); *Career* Nat Serv RAF 1949-51; Burke Covington & Nash (CA's) 1946-48, Barclays Bank (Dcro) Ltd 1948-49; Vanpoulles Ltd (church furnishers): joined 1951, dir 1969, chm and md 1972-; chm and md Insignia Ltd 1981-, chm and dir Lodge Lane Property Ltd 1986-; dir: Slabbinck NV Belgium 1988-, Gill Vanpoulles Ltd Dublin; tres League of Friends West Park Hosp 1962-72 (memb 1957-); memb: Purley Tennis Club 1947-55, Downswood Tennis Club 1956-76, Cheam Sports Tennis Club 1979-82, Limpsfield Tennis Club 1982-, Surrey Tennis and Country Club 1985-, St Vincent De Paul Soc 1956-76; FInstD 1969 ; *Recreations* lawn tennis, golf, bridge; *Style*— Robert Appleton, Esq; 1 Old Westhall Close, Warlingham, Surrey CR3 (☎ 08832 5646); Vanpoulles Ltd, 1-6 Chalice Close, Lavender Vale, Wallington, Surrey SM6 9QS (☎ 01 669 3121, fax 01 669 7192, telex 918022 INSVAN G)

APPLEYARD, HE Leonard Vincent; CMG; s of Thomas William Appleyard, of Cawood, W Yorks (d 1979), and Beatrix, *née* Golton (d 1982); *b* 2 Sept 1938; *Educ* Read Sch, Drax, W Yorks, Queens' Coll Cambridge (MA); *m* 3 May 1964, Elizabeth Margaret, da of John Lees West, Grasmere, Cumbria; 2 da (Caroline b 1965, Rebecca b 1967); *Career* FO 1962, third sec Hong Kong 1964, second sec Peking 1966, second (later first) sec FO 1969, first sec Delhi 1971, Moscow 1975, HM Treas 1978, fin cnsllr Paris 1979-82, Head of Econ Relations Dept FCO 1982-84, princ private sec 1984-86; *Recreations* music, reading, tennis; *Clubs* Brooks's; *Style*— H E Leonard Appleyard, CMG; British Embassy, Budapest 1051, Harmincad u.6. (Telex: 22-4527)

APPLEYARD-LIST, Hon Mrs (Caroline Elizabeth); *née* Arbuthnot; da of Baroness Wharton (*see* Hon Mrs Robertson) and David Arbuthnot; *b* 28 August 1935; *m* 1970, Capt Jonathan Cecil Appleyard-List, CBE, RN; 1 da (Zoë b 1973); *Recreations* riding, painting; *Clubs* Soc of Equestrian Artists; *Style*— The Hon Mrs Appleyard-List; Birches, Stanford Common, Pirbright, Surrey

APSION, Robert Neville Peto; s of Cynddylan Apsion (d 1930), and Dorothy Neville Hesse, *née* Peto; *b* 16 May 1920; *Educ* Tonbridge, King's Coll Cambridge; *m* 1, 3 Dec 1942, Josephine, da of Sir Lennox O'Reilly, KC (d 1949), of Trinidad; 1 s (Gordon b 1943); m 2, 18 June 1955, Kathleen Isabelle, da of John Hudson (d 1961), of Christchurch, NZ; 2 da (Annabelle b 1960, Georgia b 1966); *Career* served as Lt RNVR in Atlantic and Indian Ocean (coastal forces, destroyers); civil servant (ret), HM Customs and Excise; *Recreations* bibliophily; *Style*— Robert N P Apsion, Esq; 17 Ganghill, Guildford, Surrey GU1 1XE (☎ 0483 31714)

APSION, Hon Mrs; Hon (Victoria Marion Ann); *née* Lever; 2 da of 3 Viscount Leverhulme, TD; *b* 23 Sept 1945; *m* 1, 1966 (m dis 1973), (John) Richard Walter Reginald Carew Pole, o s of Sir John Gawen Carew Pole, 12 Bt, DSO, TD; m 2, 1975 (m dis 1987), (Robert) Gordon Lennox Apsion; 2 s, 1 da; *Style*— The Hon Mrs Apsion; 77 Hillgate Place, London W8 7SS

APSLEY, Lord; Allen Christopher Bertram Bathurst; s and h of 8 Earl Bathurst; *b* 11 Mar 1961; *m* 31 May 1986, Hilary Jane, da of John F George, of Weston Lodge, Albury Surrey; *Style*— Lord Apsley

APTHORP, John Dorrington; s of Eric and Mildred Apthorp; *b* 28 April 1935; *Educ* Aldenham; *m* 1959, Jane Frances Arnold; 3 s, 1 da; *Career* exec chm Bejam Group plc (frozen food); chm: Chandos Press Ltd, Deer Publishers Ltd, Garland Credit Ltd, Rarefine Properties Ltd, Wolverton Transport Services Ltd; dir: John Apthorp Aviation & Leasing, Aberdeen Beef Packers (Scotland) Ltd, Exact Dental Laboratories Ltd, Lodge Residential Homes Ltd, Sterling Grade Ltd; *Style*— John Apthorp, Esq; Bejam Group plc, 1 Garland Rd, Honeypot Lane, Stanmore, Middx HA7 1LE (☎ 01 952 8311)

AQUILECCHIA, Prof Giovanni; s of Gen Vincenzo Aquilecchia d 1959, and Maria Letizia, *née* Filibeck; *b* 28 Nov 1923; *Educ* Lycee T Tasso Rome, Univ of Rome, Univ of Paris, Univ of London; *m* 7 May 1951 (m dis 1973), Costantina Maria, da of Adolfo Bacchetta (d 1940), Suez Canal Company; 2 s (Adolf b 1952, Vincent b 1956), 1 da (Maria Letizia b 1960); *Career* lectr in italian UCL 1955-59, Libero Docente di Le Hertura Italiana Univ of Rome 1958-, reader italian UCL 1959-61, prof of italian: Univ of Manchester 1961-70, Univ of London 1970-, visiting prof Univ of Melbourne 1983; chm Manchester Dante soc 1961-70, memb Byron Soc 1979-; hon MA Univ of Manchester 1965, hon res fell UCL 1964-; memb: AUT 1953-, Soc Italien Studies 1954 -, Soc Renaissance Studies 1981-; fell Arcadia Accademia Letteraria Italiana 1961-; *Books* Collected Essays on Italian Language and Literature (1971), numerous academic publications in Italian; *Recreations* walking, swimming; *Style*— Prof Giovanni Aquilecchia; 49 Hanover Gate Mansions, Park Road, London NW1 (☎ 01 723 8337); Dept of Italian, University College, Gower St, London WC1E 6BT (☎ 01 387 7050 ext. 3023)

ARANYOS, Alexander S; *b* 4 Sept 1909; *Educ* Technical Univ (Prague, Czechoslovakia); *m* 2 s (Alexander Paul, Vivian Aranyos Garcia); *Career* hon chm of the bd Fruehauf Int Ltd; French Legion of Honor; *Clubs* R Tary (New York); *Style*— Alexander Aranyos, Esq; Crane Fruehauf Ltd, Hayes Gate House, Uxbridge Rd, Hayes, Middx; 2 Bridle Lane, Sands Point, NY 11050, USA

ARBEID, Murray; s of Jack Arbeid (d 1968), of London, and Ida, *née* Davis (d 1972); *b* 30 May 1935; *Educ* Quintin Sch London; *Career* design asst to Michael Sherard 1952-54, opened own couture business 1955, started ready to wear div 1960, opened Sloane St boutique 1982, artistic dir and first collection for Hartnell Bruton St 1988; fndr memb: Fashion Indust Action Gp 1981, Br Fashion Cncl 1985; *Style*— Murray Arbeid, Esq; Castle House, 75-76 Wells St, London W1P 3RE (☎ 01 580 0911)

ARBIB, Martyn; s of Richard Arbib (d 1975), and Denise Margot, *née* Kelsey; *b* 27 June 1939; *Educ* Felsted; *m* 2 Aug 1969, Anne Hermione (Sally), da of Hugh Parton (d 1973); 2 s (James b 1971, Benjamin b 1980), 2 da (Annabel b 1970, Melanie b 1973); *Career* chm and fndr Perpetual plc 1974-; non exec dir Kelsey Industs plc 1975-; memb ICAEW 1961; *Recreations* golf, tennis; *Clubs* Huntercombe Golf; *Style*— Martyn Arbib, Esq; 48 Hart Street, Henley on Thames, Oxon RG9 2AZ (☎ 0491 576868)

ARBUTHNOT, Rev Andrew Robert Coghill; s of Capt Robert Wemyss Muir Arbuthnot, MC (d 1962, ggs of Sir William Arbuthnot, 1 Bt, of Edinburgh), and Mary, *née* Coghill; *b* 14 Jan 1926; *Educ* Eton; *m* 1952, Mrs Audrey Dutton-Barker, o da of Denys Billinghurst Johnson, MC, of Midhurst, West Sussex; 1 s (Charles b 1956), 1 da (Caroline b 1954); *Career* served WW II, Capt Scots Gds (wounded); contested (C) Houghton-le-Spring 1959; chm and chief exec Arbuthnot Latham Hldgs 1974-81; dir Sun Alliance and London Insur 1970-; ordained deacon 1974, priest 1975; missioner London Healing Mission 1983-; *Books* Love that Heals (jtly with his wife); *Recreations* painting, walking; *Style*— The Rev Andrew Arbuthnot; Monksfield House, Tilford, Farnham, Surrey GU10 2AL (☎ 025 18 2233); London Healing Mission, 20 Dawson Place, London W2 4TL (☎ 01 229 3641)

ARBUTHNOT, David William Patrick; s of Sir Hugh Fitzgerald Arbuthnot, 7 Bt (d 1983), and his 1 w, Elizabeth Kathleen (d 1972); hp of bro, Sir Keith Arbuthnot, 8 Bt; *b* 7 Mar 1953; *Educ* Wellington; *m* 12 March 1988, Diane, *née* Yeomans; 1 da (Phoebe Elizabeth b 18 Nov 1988) ; *Career* racehorse trainer; *Recreations* rugby, shooting; *Clubs* Turf; *Style*— David Arbuthnot, Esq; Uplands Stables, Lower Farm, Compton, Nr Newbury, Berks (☎ (0635 22) 427)

ARBUTHNOT, James Norwich; MP (C); yr s of Sir John Sinclair-Wemyss Arbuthnot, 1 Bt, MBE, TD, *qv*, and (Margaret) Jean, *née* Duff; *b* 4 August 1952; *Educ* Eton, Trinity Coll Cambridge (MA); *m* 6 Sept 1984, Emma Louise, da of John Michael Broadbent, of Avon; 1 s (Alexander b 1986); *Career* barr 1975, practising 1977-; cncllr Royal Borough of Kensington and Chelsea 1978-87; contested (C) Cynon Valley 1983, 1984; pres Cynon Valley Cons Assoc 1983-; *Recreations* skiing, guitar, theatre; *Style*— James N Arbuthnot, Esq, MP; 58 Ifield Rd, SW10 (☎ 01 352 3974); House of Commons SW1A 0AA (☎ 01 219 4541); 10 Old Square, Lincoln's Inn WC2 (☎ 01 405 0758)

ARBUTHNOT, Sir John Sinclair-Wemyss; 1 Bt (UK 1964), of Kittybrewster, Aberdeen, MBE (1944), TD (1951); s of Maj Kenneth Wyndham Arbuthnot, the Seaforth Highlanders (ka Second Battle of Ypres 1915; ggs of George Arbuthnot, JP, first of Elderslie, himself a yr bro of Sir William Arbuthnot, 1 Bt, of Edinburgh; *see* Arbuthnot, Bt, Sir Keith Robert Charles); *b* 11 Feb 1912; *Educ* Eton, Trin Coll Cambridge (MA); *m* 1943, (Margaret) Jean, yr da of (Alexander) Gordon Duff (d 1978); 2 s (William Reierson, *qv*, James Norwich, *qv*), 3 da (Elizabeth Mary b 27 May 1947, Louise Victoria b 26 Oct 1954, Alison Jane b 9 April 1957); *Heir* s, William Reierson Arbuthnot; *Career* dir and chm of Tea Companies 1934-75; MP (C) Dover 1950-64, PPS to: Min of Pensions 1952-55, to Min of Health 1956-57, chm of ctees and temp chm of House of Commons 1958-64; jt hon sec of Assoc of Br C of C 1953-59; vice-pres Tstee Savings Banks Assoc 1962-75, chm Folkestone and Dist Water Co, 1971-87; memb Church Assembly 1955-75 and Gen Synod of C of E 1955-75, Second Church Estates cmmr 1962-64, Church cmmr for E 1962-77, former tstee Lambeth Palace Library; KASG; *Recreations* gardening; *Clubs* Carlton; *Style*— Sir John Arbuthnot, Bt, MBE, TD; Poulton Manor, Ash, Canterbury, Kent CT3 2HW (☎ 0304 812516)

ARBUTHNOT, Julia, Lady; Julia Grace; *née* Peake; da of late Col Fredrick Gerard Peake Pasha, CMG, CBE (d 1970), and Elspeth Maclean, *née* Ritchie (d 1967); f campaigned with Lawrence of Arabia after serv in India and Sudan expedition; fndr and cmmdr of the Arab Legion Jordan; *b* 6 June 1941; *Educ* Oxonford Castle and Minto; *m* 1977, as his 2 w, Sir Hugh Fitzgerald Arbuthnot, 7 Bt (d 1983); *Career* farmer, landowner; *Recreations* hunting, racing, yachting (Cool Cucumber); *Clubs* Roy Northumberland Yacht; *Style*— Julia, Lady Arbuthnot; Brundeanlaws, Jedburgh, Roxburghshire; Carsaig, Route de Mons, Callian, Var, France

ARBUTHNOT, Sir Keith Robert Charles; 8 Bt (UK 1823), of Edinburgh; s of Sir Hugh Arbuthnot, 7 Bt (d 1983), by his 1 w, Elizabeth Kathleen (d 1972), da of Sqdn Ldr George Algernon Williams; *b* 23 Sept 1951; *Educ* Wellington, Edinburgh Univ; *m* 22 May 1982, Anne, yr da of Brig Peter Moore, of the Old Farmhouse, Hazeley Bottom, Hartley Wintney, Hants; 2 s (Robert Hugh Peter, Patrick William Martin b 13 July 1987); *Heir* s, Robert Hugh Peter Arbuthnot, b 2 March 1986; *Style*— Sir Keith Arbuthnot, Bt; Whitebridge, Peebles, Peebles-shire

ARBUTHNOT, William Reierson; s and h of Sir John Arbuthnot, 1 Bt, MBE, TD; *b* 2 Sept 1950; *Educ* Eton; *Career* employed Arbuthnot Latham Hldgs Ltd 1970-76, Joynson-Hicks & Co, (slrs) 1978-81; memb Lloyd's; Liveryman Worshipful Co of Grocers; *Recreations* genealogy, computer programming; *Style*— William Arbuthnot, Esq; 14 Ashburn Gdns, London SW7 4DG (☎ 01 370 4907)

ARBUTHNOTT, Col the Hon (William) David; MBE (1964); 2 s of 15 Viscount of Arbuthnott, CB, CBE, DSO, MC; *b* 5 Nov 1927; *Educ* Fettes, RMA Sandhurst; *m* 1955, Sonja Mary, er da of late Col Charles Thomson, CBE, DSO, TD, DL, of Carnoustie; 1 s (Charles b 1956), 2 da (Georgina b 1964, Elizabeth b 1967); *Career* Col (ret) The Black Watch; serv Korea 1952-53, Kenya 1953-55, N Ireland 1974 (despatches); Regimental Sec The Black Watch; *Style*— Col the Hon David Arbuthnott, MBE; Old Manse of Strathbraan, Dunkeld, Perthshire PH8 0DY (☎ 035 03 205)

ARBUTHNOTT, Dorothy, Viscountess of; Dorothy; OBE (1951); da of late Adm

Charles Lister Oxley, of The Hall, Ripon, Yorks; *b* 26 Mar 1890; *m* 1914, 14 Viscount of Arbuthnott (d 1960); *Style*— The Rt Hon Dorothy, Viscountess of Arbuthnott, OBE; The Lodge, Edzell, Angus

ARBUTHNOTT, Hugh James; CMG (1984); 2 s of Cdr James Gordon Arbuthnott (ggs of 8 Viscount of Arbuthnott); *b* 27 Dec 1936; *Educ* Ampleforth, New Coll Oxford; *m* 1964, Vanessa Rose, sole da of Edward Dyer, of Tunbridge Wells; 3 s (Dominic b 1965, Justin b 1967, Giles b 1970); *Career* late 2 Lt Black Watch; joined FO (subsequently FCO) 1960, third sec Tehran 1961-64, FO 1964-68 (private sec to min of State 1966-68), first sec Chancery Tehran 1971-74, head of Euro Integration Dept (External) FCO 1974-77, cnsllr (Agric and Econ) Paris 1978-80, head of Chancery Paris 1980-83, under sec Int Div ODA 1983-; *Style*— Hugh Arbuthnott, Esq, CMG; c/o Foreign and Commonwealth Office, London SW1A 2AH

ARBUTHNOTT, Hon Hugh Sinclair; 3 and yst s of 15 Viscount of Arbuthnott, CB, CBE, DSO, MC (d 1966), and Ursula, Dowager Viscountess of Arbuthnott, *qv*; *b* 14 Nov 1929; *Educ* Fettes, Gonville and Caius Coll Cambridge (MA), Edinburgh Univ (LLB); *m* 21 Sept 1963, Anne Rosamond, o da of late Charles Bentley Terdre, of Appledore, Cherry Walk, High Salvington, Worthing, Sussex; 1 s (Hugh James Hamilton b 1967), 1 da (Katherine Anne b 1970); *Career* late 2 Lt The Black Watch; with Shell Int Petroleum Co 1953-83; FCIS; *Style*— The Hon Hugh Arbuthnott; 7 Birch Close, Boundstone Road, Farnham, Surrey GU10 4TJ; Cairnhill, Forfar, Angus DD8 3TQ

ARBUTHNOTT, Maj James Francis; s of Hugh Forbes Arbuthnott (d 1982, s of late Donald Stuart Arbuthnott, CE, s of 8 Viscount of Arbuthnott) and Janet, da of late Vice Adm Herbert Marshall, of Gayton Hall, Ross, Herefs; *b* 27 April 1940; *Educ* Downside, RMA Sandhurst; *m* 1974, Hon Louisa, *qv*; 2 s, 2 da; *Career* Maj Black Watch; Kt of Honour and Devotion, Sov Mil Order of Malta; *Style*— Maj James Arbuthnott; Stone House Cottage, Stone, Kidderminster, Worcs (☎ 0562 69902)

ARBUTHNOTT, 16 Viscount of (S 1641); John Campbell Arbuthnott; DSC (1945), CBE (1986); also Lord Inverbervie (S 1641); s of 15 Viscount of Arbuthnott (d 1966), and Ursula, Viscountess of Arbuthnott, *qv*; Lord Arbuthnott is the thirty-third Laird of Arbuthnott and the twenty-seventh in descent from Hugh de Swinton, who acquired the estate of Aberbothenoth, of which he is recorded as having been styled *thanus* and *dominus*, towards the end of the twelfth century, and who was gggggggggggs of Edulf Edulfing, 1 Lord of Bamburgh (d 912); *b* 26 Oct 1924; *Educ* Fettes, Gonville and Caius Coll Cambridge; *m* 1949, Mary Elizabeth Darley, er da of Cdr Christopher Oxley, DSC, RN (himself 2 s of Adm Charles Oxley, JP, and whose yst sis m 14 Viscount of Arbuthnott); 1 s, 1 da (*see* Hon Mrs Smith); *Heir* s, Master of Arbuthnott, *qv*; *Career* serv WW II Fleet Air Arm Far East & Pacific; chm: Aberdeen & N Marts 1986- (dir 1973-), Scottish Widows and Life Assoc 1984-87 (dir 1978-); dir: Britoil 1988-, Clydesdale Bank 1985-, Scottish N Investmt Tst 1979-85; Lord-Lt Grampian Region (Kincardineshire) 1977-, Britoil plc 1988-; pres: Br Assoc for Shooting and Conservation (formerly WAGBI) 1973-, RZS Scotland 1976-, Royal Scottish Geographical Soc 1982-87; dep chm Nature Conservancy Cncl 1980-85 (chm Scottish advsy ctee); memb Royal Cmmmn Historical MSS 1987-; Lord High Cmmnr to Gen Assembly of Church of Scotland 1986 and 1987; Prior of the Order of St John of Jerusalem in Scotland 1983; FRSE; FRSA, FRICS; KStJ 1982; *Style*— The Rt Hon the Viscount of Arbuthnott, CBE, DSC; Arbuthnott House, by Laurencekirk, Kincardineshire AB3 1PA (☎ home: Inverbervie (0561) 61226; office: Auchenblae (056 12) 417)

ARBUTHNOTT, Master of; Hon (John) Keith Oxley; s and h of 16 Viscount of Arbuthnott, CBE, DSC, FRSE, *qv*; *b* 18 July 1950; *Educ* Fettes, N Scotland Coll of Agric Aberdeen (Higher Nat Dip, Dip in Farm Business, Organisation and Management); *m* 1974, Jill Mary, eldest da of Capt Colin Farquharson, of Whitehouse, Alford, Aberdeenshire; 1 s (Christopher Keith b 20 July 1977), 2 da (Clare Anne b 1974, Rachel Sarah b 1979); *Style*— The Master of Arbuthnott; Kilternan, Arbuthnott, Laurencekirk, Kincardineshire AB3 1NA

ARBUTHNOTT, Hon Mrs; (Louisa Nina); *née* Hughes-Young; 3 da of 1 Baron St Helens, MC, and sis of 2 Baron; *b* 31 August 1949; *m* 1974, Maj James F Arbuthnott, *qv*; 2 s (John Patrick b 1977, a son b 1988), 2 da (Elizabeth b 1980, Florence b 1981); *Style*— The Hon Mrs Arbuthnott; Stone House Cottage, Stone, Kidderminster, Worcs (☎ 0562 69902)

ARBUTHNOTT, Robert; s of Archibald Arbuthnott, MBE, ED (d 1977), and Barbara Joan, *née* Worteras (d 1988); *b* 28 Sept 1936; *Educ* Sedbergh Sch, Emmanuel Coll Cambridge (BA, MA); *m* 19 May 1962, (Sophie) Robina, da of Robin Alan Axford; 1 s (Robert Keith b 1968), 2 da (Alison b 1963, Catherine b 1965); *Career* Nat Serv 1955-57, 2 Lt The Black Watch RHR; The Br Cncl 1960-; Karachi 1960: Lahore 1962, London 1964, rep Nepal 1967, rep Malaysia 1973, dir Educational Contracts Dept 1976, controller Personnel Div 1978, rep Germany 1981, Royal Coll of Defence Studies 1986, minster (cultural affairs) New Delhi 1988-; *Recreations* music - making and listening, sport, travel, history; *Clubs* Utd Oxford and Cambridge, Royal Selangor Golf, Liphook Golf; *Style*— Robert Arbuthnott, Esq; Foundry Cottage, Foundry Lane, Haslemere, Surrey GU27 2QF (☎ 0428 54528); The British Council, 10 Spring Gardens, London SW1A 2BN)

ARBUTHNOTT, The Dowager Viscountess of; Ursula; da of Sir William Collingwood, KBE (d 1928), of Dedham Grove, Colchester; *m* 10 Jan 1924, Maj-Gen 15 Viscount of Arbuthnott, CB, CBE, DSO, MC, DL, sometime Lord-Lt of Kincardineshire (d 1966); 3 s (16 Viscount, Hon David Arbuthnott, Hon Hugh S Arbuthnott, *qqv*), 1 da (Hon Mrs Bing, *qv*); *Style*— The Rt Hon Dowager Viscountess of Arbuthnott; The Cottage, Main Rd, Hillside, Montrose, Angus

ARCHDALE, Sir Edward Folmer; DSC (1943),; 3 Bt (UK 1928), of Riversdale, Co Fermanagh; s of Vice-Adm Sir Edward Archdale, 2 Bt, CBE (d 1955), and Gerda, da of Frederik Sievers, of Copenhagen; *b* 8 Sept 1921; *Educ* Copthorne Sch, RNC Dartmouth; *m* 1954 (m dis 1978), Elizabeth Ann Stewart, da of Maj-Gen Wilfrid Boyd Fellowes Lukis, CBE, RM (d 1969); 1 s (Nicholas), 2 da (Annabel b 1956, Lucinda b 1958); *Heir* s, Nicholas Edward Archdale b 2 Dec 1965; *Career* Capt RN (ret), serv WWII (despatches); defence conslt, political economist; *Recreations* civilisation; *Style*— Sir Edward Archdale, Bt; 19 Dermott Rd, Comber, Co Down, NI BT23 5LG (☎ 0247 873195)

ARCHDEACON, Antony; s of Maurice Ignatius Archdeacon (d 1973), of Ruislip, Middx, and Nora Margery May, *née* Ball; *b* 25 Jan 1925; *Educ* Oxford House Sch, Buckingham Univ (LLB); *m* 3 Dec 1956 (m dis 1964), Elizabeth, da of Samuel Percy Ball, of The Cottage, Great Horwood, Bucks; 1 s (Timothy b 1957); *Career* admitted slr 1950, dir Skin Nick Supplies Ltd 1967-, Business Mortgages Tst plc 1969-86, chm Forum of St Albans plc 1985-; pres: Rotary Club Buckingham 1968, Northampton Anglo-German Club 1988-; town clerk Buckingham 1951-71; Freeman: City of London 1972, Worshipful Co of Feltmakers 1972; *Recreations* walking, languages; *Clubs* St Stephen's Constitutional, City Livery; *Style*— Antony Archdeacon, Esq; Trolly Hall, Buckingham MK18 1PT (☎ 0280 812 126, fax 0280 822 105, car tel 0860 355 748, telex 837204)

ARCHER, Bryan Russell; s of Donald Charles Archer, of Leverstock Green, Herts, and Lillian May, *née* Smith; *b* 18 April 1928; *Educ* Watford GS, Architectural Assoc Sch of Architecture (Dip Arch); *m* 31 March 1955, Nancy Sheila, da of Stanley James Dean, of Welwyn Garden City, Herts; 2 s (Richard b 1959, Andrew b 1960), 1 da (Susan b 1963); *Career* registered architect 1956; fndr ptnr Archer Boxer Ptnrs 1963; dir Archer Boxer Gp Ltd 1978; pres Hatfield C of C 1969-71, dir Herts Chamber of Commerce 1972-80; govr Sherrardswood Sch 1974-85; dist govr Rotary Int 1985-86; memb Worshipful Co of Constructors 1978 FRIBA 1954, FFB 1978; *Recreations* boating, watching cricket; *Clubs* Company of Constructors; *Style*— Bryan Archer, Esq; Pennyfathers, Pennyfathers Lane, Harmer Green, Welwyn, Herts (☎ 043 871 4627); Archer, Boxer Partners Ltd, ABP House, Salisbury Square, Hatfield, Herts (☎ 07072 69001, fax: 07072 75343)

ARCHER, Sir Clyde Vernon Harcourt; *b* 12 Nov 1904; *Educ* Harrison Coll Barbados, Cambridge; *Career* barr Gray's Inn; judge Petty Debt Ct (Bridgetown Barbados) 1938, legal draughtsman Trinidad and Tobago 1944, slr-gen Trinidad and Tobago 1953, puisne judge 1954, chief justice Windward and Leeward Islands 1958, fed justice WI 1958-62, judge Ct of Appeal Bahamas 1971-75; kt 1962; *Publications* Revised Edition of the Laws of Barbados (jointly, 1944); *Style*— Sir Clyde Archer; 40 Graeme Hall Terrace, Christchurch, Barbados

ARCHER, Jeffrey Howard; s of William Archer, and Lola, *née* Cook; *b* 15 April 1940; *Educ* Wellington Sch Somerset, Brasenose Coll Oxford (Athletics Blues 1963-65, Gymnastics Blue 1965, Oxford 100 yds record 1966); *m* 1966, Mary Weeden; 2 s; *Career* politician; memb GLC Havering 1966-70, MP (C) Louth 1969-74; dep chm Cons Pty 1985-86 pres: Somerset AAA, Somerset Wyverns; author; FRSA; *Books* Not a Penny More Not a Penny Less (1975), Shall We Tell The President? (1977), Kane and Abel (1979), A Quiver Full of Arrows (1980), The Prodigal Daughter (1982), First Among Equals (1984), A Matter of Honour (1986), Beyond Reasonable Doubt (1987, play); *Recreations* theatre, cinema, watching Somerset play cricket; *Clubs* MCC, Louth Working Mens; *Style*— Jeffrey Archer, Esq; Alembic House, 93 Albert Embankment, London SE1 (☎ 01 735 0077)

ARCHER, Gen Sir (Arthur) John; KCB (1976), OBE (1964, MBE 1960); s of Alfred Arthur Archer, of Fakenham, Norfolk, and Mildred Archer; *b* 12 Feb 1924; *Educ* King's Sch Peterborough, St Catharine's Coll Cambridge; *m* 1950, (Cynthia) Marie, da of Col Alexander Allan, DSO, MC (d 1967), of Swallowcliffe, Wilts; 2 s; *Career* entered Army 1943, Lt-Gen Bde of Gurkhas 1977-78, C-in-C UKLF 1978-79; Col Devonshire & Dorset Regt 1977-79; chief exec Roy Hong Kong Jockey Club 1980-; dir The Hong Kong & Shanghai Banking Corpn; CBIM; *Recreations* light aviation, gliding; *Clubs* Army and Navy (London), Hong Kong; *Style*— Gen Sir John Archer, KCB, OBE; 23 Rozel Manor, 48 Western Rd, Poole, Dorset BH13 6EX; Lynx Hill, 3 Deep Water Bay Rd, Hong Kong (☎ 5 921930); Roy Hong Kong Jockey Club, Sports Rd, Happy Valley, Hong Kong

ARCHER, John Francis Ashweek; QC (1975); s of late George Eric Archer, FRCSE, and Frances, *née* Ashweek; *b* 9 July 1925; *Educ* Winchester, New Coll Oxford (BA); *m* 1960, Doris Mary Hennessey; *Career* served WW II; barr Inner Temple 1950, rec Crown Ct 1974-; *Style*— John Archer, Esq, QC; 22a Connaught Sq, London W2 (☎ 01 262 9406); 2 Crown Office Row, Temple, London EC4 (☎ 01 353 9337)

ARCHER, John Norman; s of Clifford Banks Archer (d 1973), and Gracer, *née* King (d 1984); *b* 27 Feb 1921; *Educ* Wandsworth Sch; *m* 1, 1952, Gladys Joy (d 1985), da of Oliver John Barnes (d 1953), of Kent; m 2, 1986, Anne Lesley Margaret, da of Maj Nicholas Edward Padwick (d 1980), of Berks; stepdaughters; *Career* RA 1939-46 (Maj) Burma 1945; entered Civil Service Bd of Educn 1937, asst princ 1947, princ 1949, Miny of Educn 1960, asst sec architects and bldgs (Bramel) Miny of Educ 1962; techn branch assistance assignments educn: Nigeria, Yugoslavia, Tunisia 1961-63; asst sec Treasy O & M div 1964, asst sec mgmnt services devpt div 1968, under sec: Mgmntd Servs, Civil Serv Dept 1970, marine div Dept of Trade 1972-79; md The Int Tanker Owners Pollution Fedn 1979-86; competed Wimbledon Lawn Tennis Championships 1947; *Recreations* lawn tennis, bridge, watching cricket; *Clubs* All England Lawn Tennis and Croquet Wimbledon, Hurlingham, MCC; *Style*— John N Archer, Esq; 17 Sovereign House, Draxmont, Wimbledon Hill Rd, London SW19 (☎ 01 946 6429)

ARCHER, (Audrey Barbara) Nikki; *née* Greenall; da of Frank Greenall (d 1951), and late Margaret Ellen, *née* Holiday; *b* 13 Nov 1921; *Educ* Univ of Bristol (BA, Ed Cert), Guildhall Sch of Music and Drama, London Univ (Dip Ed); *m* 1, 13 Sept 1947 (m dis 1963), Cecil Watts Paul-Jones, s of Dr Walter Paul-Jones; 1 s (Richard b 3 Sept 1953), 1 da (Miranda (Mrs Scholefield) b 22 Feb 1951); m 2, 8 Oct 1964, Maj John Stafford Archer; *Career* teaching appts 1943-46, asst sec to assoc of teachers in colls and depts of educn and trg colls clearing house 1946-49, teaching appts 1949-59, head King Alfred Sch 1960-83 (dep head 1959-60), schoolmistress fell commoner Churchill Coll Cambridge Univ 1972, educnl conslt 1983-; JP Barnet Herts Bench 1971-84; ctee memb: Barnet branch Nat Marriage Guidance Cncl 1980-82, Secdy Heads Assoc; *Clubs* Bath & County, Army & Navy; *Style*— Mrs Nikki Archer; 15 Manor Rd, Alcombe, Minehead, Somerset TA24 6EH (☎ 0643 6785)

ARCHER, Rt Hon Peter Kingsley; PC (1977), QC (1971), MP (Lab) Warley W 1974-; s of Cyril Kinglsey Archer, MM (d 1974), and May, *née* Baker (d 1976); *b* 20 Nov 1926; *Educ* Wednesbury Boys' HS, UCL (LLB external), BA, LSE (LLM); *m* 6 Aug 1954, Margaret Irene, da of Sidney Smith (d 1936), of London, Ontario, Canada; 1 s (John Kingsley b 1962); *Career* barr Gray's Inn 1952, bencher 1974, rec SE Circuit 1982-; MP (Lab) Rowley Regis and Tipton 1966-74, slr-gen 1974-79, oppn front bench spokesman Legal Affrs 1981-82, Trade 1982-83, shadow sec NI 1983-87; fell UCL 1978; *Books* The Queen's Courts (1956), Social Welfare and the Citizen (ed, 1957), Communism and the Law (1963), Freedom at Stake (with Lord Reay, 1966), Human Rights (1969), Purpose in Socialism (jtly, 1973), The Role of the Law Officers (1978), More Law Reform Now (co-ed, 1984); *Recreations* music, writing, talking; *Style*— The

Rt Hon Peter Archer, QC, MP; House of Commons, London SW1A 0AA (☎ 01 219 4029); 7 Old School Court, Wraysbury, Staines, Middx (☎ 078 481 3136)

ARCHER, Peter Monahan; s of Thomas Wilson Archer, and Dorothy Maud, *née* Monahan; *b* 14 Mar 1942; *Educ* Univ Coll Sch, Coll of Estate Mgmnt; *m* 17 Sept 1966, Gina Susan Constance; 1 da (Francesca b 1972); *Career* dir Lazard Bros & Co Ltd 1986-; FRICS 1966; *Style—* Peter Archer, Esq; 21 Moorfields, London EC2 P2HT

ARCHER, Ronald Walter; s of Norman Ernest Archer, CMG, OBE (d 1970) and Hon Ruth Evelyn, *née* Pease (d 1983), da of 1 Baron Daryngton, PC; *b* 12 Dec 1929; *Educ* Winchester, Magdalene Coll Cambridge (MA); *m* 14 Nov 1959, Catherine Mary, da of Marcus RC Overton (d 1940); 3 s (James b 1960, Michael b 1962, Edward b 1964), 1 da (Mary b 1966); *Career* joined Unilever Ltd (now plc) as economist 1953, fin dir and vice-chm Hinduston Lever (Unilever subsidiary in India) 1966-70, comm dir Unilever plc & NV 1978, personal dir Unilever plc & NV 1983, dir Halifax Bldg Soc 1983, dep chm 1987; *Style—* Ronald Archer, Esq; Unilever plc, Blackfriars, London EC4 (☎ 01 822 6668)

ARCHER, Hon Mrs (Sonia Gina Ogilvie); *née* Birdwood; only da of 2 Baron Birdwood, MVO (d 1962), by his 1 w; *m* 21 July 1956, Geoffrey Thynne Valentine Archer, yst s of Maj Gerald Valentine Archer (d 1958), of High Salvington, Sussex; 1 s (David b 1959), 1 da (Sarah-Jane b 1957); *Career* mangr Hong Kong Arts Festival Soc Ltd 1972-75; Hong Kong Arts Centre, various mgmnt posts 1975-; additional appointment as Exhibition Conslt for 1988 ISCM-ACL (Int Soc for Contemporary Music/Asian Composers League) Conference; dir Archer Gp of Cos, Hong Kong; artist, exhibits in Hong Kong; *Recreations* music, choral singing; *Clubs* English Chamber Orch Soc; (life memb) Hong Kong Arts Centre, BACSA (British Assoc of Cemeteries in S Asia); *Style—* The Hon Mrs Archer; 18A Pine Crest, 65 Repulse Bay, Hong Kong (☎ 5 8121988)

ARCHER, William Frederick (Jock); s of Richard Henry Archer (d 1912), and Alice, *née* Aylett (d 1962); *b* 30 August 1906; *Educ* Windsor GS; *m* 30 Aug 1930, Dulcie Mary, da of Frederick Bates (d 1938); 2 s (Dudley Ian b 1933, Paul Richard Hedley b 1938), 1 da (Mary Sherrard (Mrs Gummer) b 1943); *Career* dir Br Celanese Ltd 1962-75 (sec 1955-62); Freeman City of London, memb Worshipful Co of Scriveners; FCIS (pres 1967); *Books* In Retrospect (autobiography); *Recreations* golf; *Style—* Jock Archer, Esq; Heronswood, Rockshaw Rd, Merstham, Surrey (☎ 073 74 3167)

ARCHIBALD, Barony of (UK 1949); *see*: Archibald, George Christopher

ARCHIBALD, Brig Brian Mortimer; CBE (1945), DSO (1944); s of Thomas Dickson Archibald, MD (d 1951), of Toronto, Canada; *b* 19 August 1906; *Educ* Trinity Coll Sch Port Hope Ontario, RMC Canada, Cambridge Univ (BA); *m* 1 1934 (m dis 1948), Margaret Olivia, da of Charles Illingworth (d 1961), of Bramley, Hants; 1 da; m 2, 1950, Daphne Frances (d 1983), 2 da of Capt Sir Claude Morrison-Bell, 2 Bt (d 1944); 1 da; m 3, 7 Dec 1988, Nancy Elizabeth, da of Gilbert Wenham (d 1972) of Croydon,; *Career* RA 1927-48, serv WWII N Africa and Italy, Lt-Col 1941, Col 1942, Brig 1944, ret 1948; Br Hydrocarbon Chemicals/BP Chemicals Ltd 1948-69 (co sec and admin dir); *Recreations* country life, travel; *Clubs* Naval and Military; *Style—* Brig Brian Archibald, CBE, DSO; Holly Cottage, Humshaugh, Hexham, Northumberland (☎ 043 481298)

ARCHIBALD, Baroness; Catherine Edith Mary; da of Rt Hon Andrew Bonar Law, MP, PM, and Annie Pitcairn, *née* Robley; sister of 1 Baron Coleraine; *m* 1, 1926 (m dis 1941), Kent Colwell; 1 s, 1 da; m 2, 1961, as his 2 w, 1 Baron Archibald (d 1975); *Style—* The Rt Hon the Lady Archibald; 29 Hampstead Hill Gdns, London NW3 2PG (☎ 01 435 8453)

ARCHIBALD, Prof George Christopher; s of 1 Baron Archibald, CBE (d 1975), and Dorothy Holroyd Edwards (d 1960); disclaimed peerage for life 1975; *b* 30 Dec 1926; *Educ* Phillips Exeter Acad USA, King's Coll Cambridge (MA), LSE (BSc); *m* 1, 1951 (m dis 1965), Liliana Barou (*see* Archibald, Liliana); m 2, 1971, Daphne May Vincent; *Career* served Army 1945-48; prof of Economics UBC 1970-; formerly: lectr in Economics Otago U NZ and LSE, prof of Ecomonics Essex U; fell: Econometric Soc 1976, R Soc of Canada; FRSC; *Books* Theory of the Firm (ed 1971), Introduction to a Mathematical treatment of Economics (1973); *Style—* Prof G C Archibald; c/o Dept of Economics, Univ of British Columbia, Vancouver, BC, Canada

ARCHIBALD, Liliana; da of late Noah Barou; *b* 25 May 1928; *Educ* Kingsley Sch, Geneva U; *m* 1951 (m dis 1965), George Christopher Archibald, *qv*; *Career* dir Adam Brothers Contingency Ltd 1970-85; Fenchurch Gp Int Ltd 1985-; memb Lloyd's 1973-; head of div Credit Insur and Export Credit EEC 1973-77; EEC advsr Lloyd's 1978-85; conslt BELMONT Europ Community Law Off Brussels 1985-; *Style—* Mrs Liliana Archibald; 21 Langland Gdns, London NW3 6QE

ARCHIBALD, Dr (Harry) Munro; CB (1976), MBE (1945); s of James Archibald (d 1952), and Isabella Archibald; *b* 17 June 1915; *Educ* Hillhead HS Glasgow, Glasgow Univ (MB, ChB, DPH); *Career* served WW II Lt-Col Italy (despatches); Colonial Medical Service (malariologist) Nigeria 1946-62; principal medical offr DHSS 1970-72, Sr Principal Medical Offr DHSS 1972-73, dep chief medical offr (dep sec) DHSS 1973-77, ret; *Recreations* travel; *Clubs* Caledonian; *Style—* Dr Munro Archibald, CB, MBE; 1 Camborne House, Camborne Rd, Sutton, Surrey SM2 6RL (☎ 01 643 1076)

ARCHIBALD, Wilfred William; s of Cyril Nadalie Archibald (d 1966), of London, and Ethele, *née* Polonski; *b* 13 July 1922; *Educ* Victoria Coll Alexandria Egypt; *m* 28 June 1947, Jean Pauline Scott, da of Alexander William Gibson (d 1961), of Ferring, W Sussex; 1 s (Duncan Archibald b 1948), 2 da (Juliet (Mrs Billingham) b 1949, Christine (Mrs Brewster) b 1959); *Career* WWII Navigator RAF 1940-44; Guardian Royal Exchange Assur Co 1947-56, inspr for Middle East; 1957-67 mangr: Singapore, Malaysia, Thailand, Borneo; md Union Ins Soc of Canton 1968-77, overseas mangr GRE gp head off London 1977-86, asst gen mangr (overseas), ret 1986; pres bd of govrs Alexandria Schs Tst; govr: City of London Freeman's Sch Ashstead, Mitchell City of London Charity and Educnl Fndn, Lady Eleanor Holles Sch (Cripplegate Schs Fndn); tstee St Margaret's Tst Bethnal Green, memb St Michaels Cornhill PCC; memb ct Common Cncl City of London (representing Cornhill) 1986-; memb: Cripplegate Ward Club, Lime St Ward Club, Utd Ward Club, Broadstreet Ward Club; Freeman City of London 1980, memb Worshipful Co of Insurers 1980; *Recreations* farming; *Style—* Wilfred Archibald, Esq; Deakes Manor, Deakes Lane, Cuckfield, West Sussex RH17 5JA (☎0444 454151); 184, Andrewes House, Barbican, London EC2

ARCULUS, Sir Ronald; KCMG (1979, CMG 1968), KCVO (1980); s of Cecil Arculus, MC (d 1968), and Ethel L Arculus (d 1982); *b* 11 Feb 1923; *Educ* Solihull Sch, Exeter Coll Oxford (MA); *m* 1953, Sheila Mary, da of Arthur Faux (d 1982); 1 s (Gerald), 1 da (Juliet); *Career* WWII, 4 Queen's Own Hussars Capt; entered HM Dip Serv 1947, min (Economic) Paris 1973-77, ambass and perm ldr UK Delegation UN Law of the Sea Conference 1977-79, ambass to Italy 1979-83, ret; dir Glaxo Hldgs 1983-; conslt: Trusthouse Forte 1983-86; London and Continental Bankers 1984-88; govr Brit Inst of Florence 1984-; dir King's Med res Tst 1984-88; Special Adviser to Min of Tport on Channel Tunnel Trains 1987-88; Freeman City of london 1981; Grand Cross Italian Order of Merit 1980; *Recreations* travel, opera, ballet, fine arts; *Clubs* Army and Navy, Hurlingham; *Style—* Sir Ronald Arculus, KCMG, KCVO; 20 Kensington Court Gdns, London W8 5QF

ARDEE, Lord; John Anthony Brabazon; s and h of 14 Earl of Meath; *b* 11 May 1941; *Educ* Harrow; *m* 1973, Xenia Goudime; 1 s, 2 da (Hon Corinna Lettice b 9 Nov 1974, Hon Serena Alexandra b 23 Feb 1979); *Heir* s, Hon Anthony Jaques Brabazon b 30 Jan 1977; *Career* page of honour to HM The Queen 1956-57, Gren Gds 1960-63; *Style—* Lord Ardee; Ballinacor, Rathdrum, Co Wicklow, Ireland (☎ 0404 46186)

ARDEN, Rt Rev Donald Seymour; CBE (1981); s of Stanley Arden, FLS (d 1942), of Sitiawan (Lower Perak) and Worthing, and Winifred, *née* Morland (d 1968); family a collateral branch of Arden of Harden Hall, Stockport who descend from Eustace de Arden, of Watford, Northants; *b* 12 April 1916; *Educ* St Peter's Coll Adelaide S Aust, Leeds Univ (BA), Coll of Resurrection Mirfield; *m* 1962, Jane Grace, da of Gerald Riddle (d 1967), of East Ogwell, Devon; 2 s (Bazil, Christopher); *Career* ordained: deacon 1939, priest 1940; curate: St Catherine's Hatcham 1939-40, Nettleden with Potten End 1941-43; asst priest Pretoria African Mission 1944-51; dir Usuthu Swaziland 1951-61 (canon of Zululand and Swaziland); bishop of: Nyasaland 1961, Malawi 1964-71, Southern Malawi 1971-81; archbishop of Central Africa 1971-80, p-in-c St Margaret Uxbridge 1981-86, asst bishop Willesden 1981-,vol asst priest St Alban's N Harrow 1986-; *Books* Youth's Job in the Parish (1938), Out of Africa Something New (1976); *Recreations* photography; *Style—* The Rt Rev Donald Arden CBE; 6 Frobisher Close, Pinner, Middx HA5 1NN (☎ 01 866 6009)

ARDEN, George Philip; s of William Arden (d 1954), and 3 cous twelve times removed of William Shakespeare (whose mother was an Arden); the family of Arden, one of the three oldest survg English families, is of Saxon origin and descends from Guy de Warwick (d 927) whose gggs Thurkill, last Saxon Earl of Warwick, was one of the first in England to adopt the Norman custom of surnames, calling himself, and his family, 'of Arden' (*see* Burke's Landed Gentry, 18th Edn, vol ii); *b* 4 June 1913; *Educ* Roy GS High Wycombe, UCL (MB, BS); *m* 1944, Kathleen, da of Edward McCaffrey, of Virginia Water; 4 da; *Career* served WW II Middle East, Wing Cdr RAF Medical Services; orthopaedic surgeon: King Edward VII Hosp Windsor 1947-78, Heatherwood Hosp Ascot 1948-78, Wexham Pk Hosp Slough 1966-78, FRCS, MRCS, LRCP; ret; *Recreations* golf, sailing, travel; *Clubs* Berks Golf, Swinley Golf; *Style—* George Arden, Esq; 24 Monks Rd, Virginia Water, Surrey (☎ Wentworth (099 04) 2525); Consulting Rooms, 1 Dorset Road, Windsor, Berks SL4 3BA (☎ Windsor 61111)

ARDEN, John; s of C A Arden, and A E Layland; *b* 26 Oct 1930; *Educ* Sedbergh Sch, King's Coll Cambridge, Edinburgh Coll of Art; *m* 1957, Margaretta Ruth D'Arcy; 4 s (and 1 decd); *Career* playwright; works include *Sergeant Musgrave's Dance* (1959), *The Non-Stop Connolly Show* (in collaboration with M D'Arcy), To Present The Pretence (Essays on Theatre) (1978), Silence Among The Weapons (Novel) (1982); *Style—* John Arden, Esq; c/o Margaret Ramsay Ltd, 14A Goodwin's Court, London WC2 (☎ 01 240 0691)

ARDEN, Yves Ralph; s of Charles Henry Arden, MBE (d 1955), of 59 Avenue Hoche, Paris 8, and Annette Lucie Arden, *née* Collignon (d 1982); *b* 15 Dec 1921; *Educ* Ste Croix De Neuilly, Paris-Sorbonne Univ Paris; *m* 23 June 1945, Moira Rosemary, da of James Rouse (d 1942), of Sheffield; 1 s (Philip b 1953), 1 da (Denise b 1946); *Career* served WW II 1941-47: W Africa, Italy, Austria, Maj TA 1950-61; dir: Tap & Die Corpn Ltd London 1966-69, Tadco Sales Ltd London 1967-69; mktg conslt Yves R Arden & Assocs; hon consul: Tunisia in Sheffield 1958-65, Dominican Repub in Sheffield 1959-65; memb Cncl of London C of C 1964-71 (chm French Section); *Recreations* writing, travel, numismatics??? *Books* Military Medals and Decorations - A Price Guide for Collectors (1976), Supplement to Kettridge's Dictionary of Technical Terms and Phrases (French/English and English/French) (1980); *Style—* Yves Arden, Esq; Hallam Grange, Hallam Grange Rise, Fulwood, Sheffield S10 4BE (☎ 0742 305827)

ARDRON, Peter Stuart; s of Wilfred Ardron, MBE (d 1982), of 16 Carrmyers, Hare Law, Annfield Plain, Co Durham, and Lucy Muriel, *née* Hawkins; *b* 11 June 1927; *Educ* Stanley GS, Stanley Co Durham, INSEAD Fontainebleau, Oxford Centre for Mgmnt Studies; *m* 1956, Marion McWilliams, da of William Ross (d 1972), of Dunoon; 1 s (David), 2 da (Carol, Lesley); *Career* vice-chm Barclays Int Ltd 1986-; dir and sr gen mangr: Barclays Bank plc 1985, Barclays Bank Int Ltd 1983-84; gen mangr Barclays Bank Int Ltd 1977-83; dir: Banque de la Société Financière Européenne Paris 1980-, Société Financière Européenne Luxembourg 1980-, Euro-Latinamerican Bank Ltd London 1983-, Barclays Int Hldgs 1985-, Barclays plc 1985-, Barclays Int Ltd 1985-; Int Bank plc 1987-; vice-chm: AK International Ltd 1987-, BAII Ltd 1987; chm Anglo-Romanian Ltd 1987; fell Inst of Bankers; *Recreations* cricket, tennis, gardening; *Clubs* Overseas Bankers, MCC; *Style—* P S Ardron, Esq; Oriel Cottage, Rookery Close, Fetcham, Leatherhead, Surrey (☎ (0372) 372958); Barclays International Ltd, 54 Lombard St, London EC3P 3AH (☎ 01 283 8989, telex 887591)

ARDWICK, Baron (Life Peer 1970 UK); John Cowburn Beavan; s of late Silas Beavan, and Alderman Emily Beavan, JP; *b* 19 April 1910; *Educ* Manchester GS; *m* 1934, Gladys, *née* Jones; 1 da; *Career* London editor Manchester Guardian 1946, editor Daily Herald 1960-62; MEP (Lab) 1975-79; sits as Labour Peer; *Style—* The Rt Hon The Lord Ardwick; 10 Chester Close, London SW13 (☎ 01 789 3490)

ARENGO-JONES, Brig Anthony James Arengo; OBE (1960); s of Cyril Edward Arengo-Jones (d 1955), of S Wales, and Eveline Alice Drummond (d 1961); *b* 17 August 1915; *Educ* Cheltenham Coll, RMC Sandhurst; *m* 31 Aug 1940, Gillian, da of Hugh Bertram Weston (d 1966), of Bristol; 1 s (Paul b 1944); *Career* Reg Army Brig 1964, Comdt School of Infantry 1964, dep Fortress Cdr 1967 (ret 1970); Col Gloucestershire Regt 1970-78; *Recreations* ceramics, rural pursuits, sport; *Style—* Brig Anthony J A Arango-James, OBE

ARENSON, Archy; *b* 5 July 1926; *Educ* Enfield Tech Coll; *m* 1949, Vicky; *Career* non exec dir and conslt Arenson Group plc 1989-; AMIMechE, AMIEE; *Style—* Archy Arenson, Esq; c/o Arenson Group plc, Lincoln House, Colney St, St Albans, Herts AL2 2DX (☎ 0923 85 7200, telex 922171)

ARGENT, Denis John; s of Robert Argent (d 1983), and Ellen, *née* Newman; *b* 28 August 1943; *Educ* Cardinal Vaughan Sch; *m* 30 July 1966, Marie Rose, da of John Barnard (d 1980); 3 s (Nicholas b 1968, Phillip b 1970, Christopher b 1973), 1 da (Marianne b 1981); *Career* dir fin Royal Pharmaceutical Soc of GB 1987-, chief accountant Cancer Research Fnd 1975-87, mgmnt conslt Coopers & Lybrand 1972-79; FCCA; *Recreations* rugby, squash, golf; *Clubs* MCC, E India, Challoner; *Style—* Denis Argent, Esq; 112 Waxwell Lane, Pinner, Middx (☎ 01 866 1526); 1 Lambeth High St, London SE1 7JN (☎ 01 735 9141)

ARGENT, Eric William; s of Eric George Argent, and Florence Mary Argent; *b* 5 Sept 1923; *Educ* Chiswick GS; *m* 1949, Pauline Grant; 2 da; *Career* served WW II; dir Anglia Building Soc 1978- (formerly dir and gen mangr Hastings & Thanet Bldg Soc); FCA, FCBSI; *Style—* Eric Argent, Esq; Fairmount, Carmel Close, Bexhill-on-Sea, Sussex (☎ (042 43) 2333)

ARGENT, (Bernard) Godfrey; s of Godfrey Stanley Albert ARgent (d 1972), and Helena, *née* Smith; *b* 06 Feb 1937; *Educ* Bexhill GS for Boys Sussex; *m* 1, 11 Nov 1956, Janet Rosemary, *née* Boniface (d 1970); 3 da (Lisa b 1957, Gina b 1958, Susan b 1960); m 2, Anne Yvonne, *née* Coxon (m dis 1973); m 3, 25 April 1975, Sally Dorothy, *née* McAlpine; 1 da (Jenna b 1980); *Career* Household Cavalry (The Life Gds) 1954-63; freelance photographer 1963, chm Godfrey Argent Ltd 1964-; owner mangr: Walter Bird Photographic Studios (London) 1968, Baron Studios (London) 1974; one man shows incl: Nat Portrait Gallery (London) 1971, Los Angeles 1978, Camera Club (London) 1988; photographer Royal Family 1964-, official photographer Nat Portrait Gallery (London) 1967-70, Royal Soc of Great Britain 1967-; chm: Aux-air gp of cos 1988, Skyrover Ltd 1988-; *Books* The Royal Mews (1965), The Household Brigade (1966), The Queen's Guards (1966), The Queen Rides (1966), Horses in the Sun (1966), Charles 21st Prince of Wales (1969), World of Horses (1969), Roaylty on Horseback (1974); *Clubs* Inanda (SA), Wellington; *Style—* Godfrey Argent, Esq; 12 Holland St, London W8 4LT (☎ 01 937 4008/0441, fax 01 376 1098, car tel 0863 621 657)

ARGENT, Malcolm; CBE (1985); s of Leonard James Argent, of 91 Marcus Ave, Thorpe Bay, Southend-on-Sea, Essex, and Winifred Hilda Argent (d 1980); *b* 14 August 1935; *Educ* Palmer's Sch Grays Essex; *m* 1, 4 March 1961, Mary Patricia Addis, da of Geoffrey Vivian Stimson, of Bickley, Kent; m 2, 5 Dec 1986, Thelma Hazel, da of Leonard Eddleston, of Eastry, Kent; 1 s, 1 da; *Career* sec of Br Telecommunications plc 1984; GPO, London Telecommunications Region: exec offr 1953-62, higher exec offr 1962-66, princ PO HQ 1966-70, private sec to md telecommunications 1970-74, personnel controller external telecommunications exec 1974-75; dir: chm's off PO Central HQ 1975-77, eastern telecommunications region 1977; sec: The PO 1978-81, Br Telecommunications Corpn 1981-; tstee Br Telecom Staff Superannuation Fund 1981-; tstee Br Telecom New Pension Scheme 1986-; Freeman City of London 1987; FBIM 1980; *Recreations* tennis; *Style—* Malcolm Argent, Esq, CBE; 4 Huskards, Fryerning, Ingatestone, Essex CM4 0HR; British Telecom Centre, 81 Newgate St, London EC1A 7AJ (☎ 01 356 5330, telex 883051, fax 01 356 5520) (car ☎ (0860) 371776)

ARGUE, (Arnold) Noel; s of William Henry Argue (d 1936), of Sligo, and Bertha Madeline, *née* McMunn (d 1948); *b* 12 Dec 1922; *Educ* St Columba's Coll Rathfarnham, Trinity Coll Dublin (BA, MSc), Univ of Cambridge (MA); *m* 9 Sept 1954, Margaret Mary, da of Robert Anson Francis (d 1917), of Ipswich; 1 s (Christopher); *Career* served RAF: AC2 wireless operator and mechanic 1941, (LAC 1944); sr observer The Observatories Univ of Cambridge 1960 (jr observer 1953-60); chm: Int Astromonical Union Working Gp on Extragalactic Radio/Optical Reference Frame 1979, Euro Space Agency Hipparcos Input Catalogue Consortium Working Gp for Radio/ Optical Reference Frame 1982; written approximately 60 papers in astronomical journals; FRAS 1957; *Recreations* music, reading, especially history and biography; *Clubs* Univ of Cambridge Sr Combination Room; *Style—* Noel Argue, Esq; 21 Pierce Lane, Fulbourn, Cambridge (☎ 0223 880279); Univ of Cambridge, The Observatories, Madingley Rd, Cambridge (☎ 0223 337530/48, fax 0223 337523, telex 817297 ASTRON G)

ARGYLE, His Hon; Maj Michael Victor; MC (1945), QC (1961); s of Harold Victor Argyle (d 1965), of Highways, Repton, Derbys, and Elsie Marion, *née* Richards; *b* 31 August 1915; *Educ* Westminster, Trinity Coll Cambridge (MA); *m* 1951, Ann Norah, da of late C A Newton, of Derby; 3 da; *Career* served WW II with 7 QOH; barr Lincoln's Inn 1938, rec of Northampton 1962-65 and Birmingham 1965-70, dep chm Holland Quarter Sessions 1965-71, lay judge Ct of Arches Canterbury 1968-, circuit judge 1970-88 (formerly additional judge of the Central Criminal Ct); pre: Nat Campaign for Restoration of Capital Punishment 1988-, Midland Counties Canine Soc 1988-; jr warden Worshipful Co of Playing Cards Makers 1982-83, sr warden 1983-84, Master 1984-85; tres Lincoln's Inn 1984-85; *Books* Phipson on Evidence (10th Edition); *Recreations* chess, boxing; *Clubs* Cavalry and Guards, Carlton, Kennel; *Style—* His Hon Michael Argyle, MC, QC; The Red House, Fiskerton, nr Southwell, Notts NG25 0UL; 30, Ives St, London SW3 2ND (☎ 01 225 258415)

ARGYLL, 12 Duke of (S 1701 and UK 1892); Sir Ian Campbell; 14 Bt (NS 1627); also Lord Campbell (S 1445), Earl of Argyll (S 1457), Lord Lorne (S 1470), Marquess of Kintyre and Lorne, Earl of Campbell and Cowal, Viscount Lochow and Glenilla, and Lord Inveraray, Mull, Morvern and Tiry (all S 1701), Baron Sundridge (GB 1766), Baron Hamilton (GB 1776), hereditary master of HM's Household in Scotland, keeper of the Great Seal of Scotland, keeper of Dunoon, Carrick, Dunstaffnage and Tarbert Castles, Admiral of the Western Isles, hereditary sheriff of Argyll; s of 11 Duke of Argyll (d 1973), by his 2 w Louise, da of Henry Clews; *b* 28 August 1937; *Educ* Le Rosey, Trinity Coll Glenalmond, McGill U Canada; *m* 1964, Iona, da of Capt Sir Ivar Iain Colquhoun of Luss, 8 Bt; 1 s, 1 da (Lady Louise Iona b 26 Oct 1972); *Heir* s, Marquess of Lorne; *Career* late Capt Argyll & Sutherland Highlanders; memb Roy Co of Archers (Queen's Body Guard for Scotland); KStJ 1975; *Clubs* White's, New (Edinburgh); *Style—* His Grace The Duke of Argyll; Inveraray Castle, Inveraray, Argyll (☎ (0499) 2275)

ARGYLL, Margaret, Duchess of; Margaret; da of George Hay Whigham (d 1960, fndr and chm of Br and Canadian and American Celanese Corpns) and Helen Mann (d 1955), da of Douglas Mann Hannay (Scottish cotton magnate); George Whigham's gf, Robert Whigham, m Jane, da of Sir Robert Dundas, 1 Bt, of cadet branch of Dundas family who became Viscounts Melville; George was bro of: Gen Sir Robert Whigham (Dep CIGS), James (editor Town and Country American magazine), Charles (dir Morgan Grenfell), Gilbert (md Burmah Oil), Walter (dir Bank of England and md London and NE Rlwy)); *Educ* Miss Hewitt's Classes (New York), Miss Wolff's (London), Heathfield (Ascot), Mlle Ozanne (Paris); *m* 1, 1933 (m dis 1947), Charles Sweeny; 1 s (Brian), 1 da (Frances: *see* Rutland, 10 Duke of); m 2, 1951 (m dis 1963), as his 3 w, 11 Duke of Argyll (d 1973); *Career* pres Bleakholt Animal Sanctuary Lancs 1968-; helped organise campaign to save Argyll & Sutherland Highlanders 1968; contributor Tatler social diary 1979-81; *Books* Forget Not (autobiography, 1975); *Recreations* animal and child welfare, photography, travel, writing; *Style—* Margaret, Duchess of Argyll; Grosvenor House, London W1 (☎ 01 499 6363)

ARIAS, Roberto Emilio; s of Dr Harmodio Arias (d 1962), pres of the Republic of Panama, and Rosario Guardia de Arias; *b* 26 Oct 1918; *Educ* Peddie Sch NJ USA, St John's Coll Cambridge (BA), Univ of Paris at La Sorbonne (Doctorat d'Etat), Columbia Univ; *m* 1, 1946, Querube Solis; 1 s, 2 da; m 2, 1955, Dame Margot Fonteyn, DBE, *qv*; *Career* barr (Panama) 1939, ed El Panama-America 1942-46, cncllr Embassy of Panama in Chile 1947, La Hora 1948-68, delegate to UN Assembly 1953, Panamanian ambass to UK 1955-58 and 1960-62, dep Panamanian Nat Assembly 1964-68; paralyzed in assassination attempt 1964; engaged in raising pedigree cattle 1980-; *Style—* Dr Roberto Arias; PO Box 6-1140, El Dorado, Panama, Republic of Panama

ARIE, Thomas Harry David; s of Dr OM Arie (d 1983), of Reading, and Hedy, *née* Glaser; *b* 9 August 1933; *Educ* Reading Sch, Balliol Coll Oxford (MA, BM, BCh); *m* 5 July 1963, Dr Eleanor, da of Sir Robert Aitken of Birmingham; 1 s (Samuel b 1974), 2 da (Laura b 1968, Sophie b 1971); *Career* conslt psychiatrist Goodmayes Hosp 1969-77, sr lectr in social med London Hosp 1967-77, hon sr lectr in psychiatry UCH London 1975-77; 1977-: Foundn prof of health care of the elderly Univ of Nottingham and hon conslt psychiatrist Nottingham Health Authy; Fotheringham lectr Univ of Toronto 1979, vis prof NZ Geriatrics Soc 1980, hon sec geriatric psychiatry section World Psychiatric Assoc 1983-; memb; standing med advsy ctee DHSS 1980-84, Ctee on Review Medicines, advsy and Centre for Policy on Ageing, res ctee Nat Inst Social Work, Central Cncl for Educn and Trg in Social Work 1975-81; RC Psych: vice pres 1983-85, chm specialist section on old age 1981-86, memb cncl and ct of electors; FRC Pysch, FRCP, FFCM ; *Books* Health Care of the Elderly (ed 1981), Recent Advances in Psychogeriatrics (ed 1985); *Style—* Prof Thomas Arie; Dept of Health Care of the Elderly, Medical Sch, Queen's Medical Centre, Nottingham N97 2UH (☎ 0602 421 421, 0602 780 608, fax 0602 588 138, telex UNINOT G)

ARIS, John Bernard Benedict; TD (1967); s of John Woodbridge Aris (d 1977), of Sedlescombe, Sussex, and Joyce Mary *née* Williams (d 1986); *b* 6 June 1934; *Educ* Eton, Magdalen Coll Oxford (BA, MA); *Career* Nat Serv RA 2 Lt Korea, Hong Kong 1952-54, Territorial Serv RA RHA served in 44 Para Bde ret Maj 1954-72; LEO Computers Ltd 1958-63, English Electric Computers Ltd 1963-69, ICL 1969-75 (directeur technique Europe de l'Ouest 1972-75), Imperial Gp plc 1975-85 (mangr Gp Mgmnt Serv 1982-85), chief exec Nat Computing Centre Ltd 1985- (non-exec dir 1981-85); chm FOCUS Private Sector Users Ctee 1984-85, Alvey User Panel 1985-88; Freeman City of London 1988, fndr Freeman Worshipful Co of Information Technologists 1987; FBCS, FInstD, FRSA; *Recreations* travel, music, art, scuba diving, gastronomy; *Style—* John Aris, Esq, TD; NCC Ltd, Oxford Rd, Manchester M1 7ED (☎ 061 228 6333, fax 061 228 2579, telex 668962)

ARKELL, Major James Rixon; s of Peter Arkell, and Anne, *née* Falcon; *b* 28 May 1951; *Educ* Milton Abbey; *m* 7 Sept 1974, Carolyn Jane, da of Charles Ralph Woosnam; 3 s (George b 9 Dec 1978, John b 17 Apr 1983, Alexander b 15 Aug 1985), 1 da (Emma 6 Feb 1976); *Career* cmmnd Royal Wiltshire (Yeo) TA 1976 (joined 1974), Sqdn-Ldr 1983, 2 i/c (V) 1989; md J Arkell & Sons Swindon Wilts, dir Edmont Joinery Ltd Swindon Wilts; *Recreations* shooting, fishing; *Clubs* Special Forces; *Style—* Maj James Arkell; Sterts House, Hannington-Wick, Highworth, Wilts (☎ 0285 810393); J Arkell & Sons Ltd, Kingsdown Brewery, Swindon, Wilts (☎ 0793 823 026)

ARKELL, John Heward; CBE (1961), TD; s of Rev H H Arkell, Vicar of Chipping Norton, Oxon, and Gertrude Mary Arkell, *née* Heward; *b* 20 May 1909; *Educ* Radley, Christ Church Oxford (MA); *m* 1, 1940, Helen Birgit, da of HE Emil Huitfeldt, sometime Norwegian ambass to Denmark; 2 s, 1 da; m 2, 1956 (m dis), Meta, da of Otto Bäche Grundtvig, of Trondheim, Norway; 1 s; *Career* served WWII KRRC, TA; sec Sir Max Michaelis Investmt Tst 1931-37, asst sec Cncl for Protection of Rural England 1937-39 (vice-pres 1984); personnel mangr J Lyons & Co 1945-49; with BBC 1949-70 (controller staff 1949-58, dir staff 1958-60, dir admin 1960-70); mgmnt conslt; chm Air Transport and Travel Industry Training Bd 1970-80; dir: The Boots Co 1970-79, The Coates Gp of Cos 1970-76, UK Provident Inst 1971-80; lay memb Nat Indust Relations Court 1972-74; memb cncl Nat Tst 1971-84 (chm NT advsy ctee on communications 1983), visiting fell Henley Mgmnt Coll 1971-, cncl CBI 1973-75, final selection bd Civil Service Cmmn 1978-82; vice pres BIM Fndn 1974- (chm cncl BIM 1972-74, dir BIM 1976-81); sr assoc Leo Kramer Int 1981-; govr Radley Coll 1965-70; gen hon sec and fndr Christ Church (Oxford) Utd Clubs SE London 1932, later chmn and now jt pres 1986, composer light music; CBIM, FRSA, FIPM; *Recreations* music, walking, swimming; *Clubs* Savile, Leander, Lansdowne; *Style—* John Arkell, Esq, CBE, TD; Pinnocks, Fawley, Nr Henley-on-Thames, Oxon RG9 6JH (☎ 0491 573017); Glen Cottage, Ringstead Bay, Nr Dorchester, Dorset DT2 8NG (☎ 0305 852686); Leo Kramer International Ltd, 4 New Burlington St, London W1X 1FE (☎ 01 439 6584)

ARKELL, Peter; s of Sir Noel Arkell, DL (d 1981), and Olive Arscott, *née* Quick (d 1988); *b* 24 Jan 1923; *m* 12 Aug 1949, Anne, da of Michael Falcon, Burlingham House, Norwich, Norfolk (d 1976); 1 s (James b 1951), 3 da (Jane b 1950, Alison b 1952, Rosalind b 1954); *Career* Mil Serv RAFVR 1941-45 Flt Lt 26 Sqdn Mustangs, 161 Sqdn (Special Duty) Lysander, Tempsford 357 Sqdn (Special Duty) Lysanders BURMA; chm: J Arkell and Sons Ltd, Kingsdown Brewery; *Recreations* riding, fishing, shooting, gardening; *Clubs* Special Forces, RAF, Leander; *Style—* Peter Arkell, Esq; Whelford Mill, Fairford, Gloucestershire

ARKWRIGHT, (Anthony) Mark (Garle); s of Maj Anthony Richard Frank Arkwright, and Diana Evelyn Mary, *née* Garle; *b* 15 July 1954; *Educ* Eton, Leeds Sch of Business and Accountancy, RMA Sandhurst; *Career* 9/12 Royal Lancers (PWO) 1975-79 (Capt 1976), Queens Own Yeomanry 1980-; dir Wise Speke Ltd Stockbrokers 1986; *Recreations* fishing, cresta; *Clubs* Cavalry, Northern Counties; *Style—* Mark Arkwright, Esq; Wise Speke Ltd, Provincial House, Albion St, Leeds LS1 6HX (☎ 0532 459341)

ARKWRIGHT, Thomas James; s of Thomas Joseph Arkwright (d 1963), of Holmlea,

Wigan Lane, Wigan, Lancs, and Mary Edna, *née* Ashurst; *b* 22 Mar 1932; *Educ* Mount St. Mary's Coll Sheffield, Univ of Liverpool (LLB); *m* 27 Aug 1958, (Margaret) Muriel, da of Wilfred Hague (d 1973), of Trafalgar Rd, Wigan, Lancs; 1 s (Paul b 1962), 5 da (Louise b 1960, Julie b 1963, Clare b 1966, Lucy b 1968, Helen b 1971); *Career* slr; articled to Sir John B McKaig Liverpool 1950-55, currently sr ptnr Cyril Morris Arkwright Bolton, notary public; pres: Bolton C of C and Indust 1971-73, Bolton Law Soc 1972; chm North West Area Cons Party 1972-73, dep pres Bolton NW Cons Assoc 1981-84 (pres 1973-76, chm 1966-71, sec 1961-66 Hon Life Vice-Pres); pres Bolton Catholic Musical and Choral Soc 1968-, dep pres Bolton Coronary Care 1970-, tres and mangr North West Catholic History Soc 1987-; memb: Law Soc 1955, Notaries Soc 1960; *Recreations* historical studies, genealogy, walking, gardening; *Clubs* Bolton; *Style*— Thomas Arkwright, Esq; Ivy Cottage, Limbrick, Chorley, Lancs PR6 9EE (☎ 025 72 68646); Churchgate House, 30 Churchgate, Bolton, Lancs BL1 1HS (☎ 0204 35261, fax 0204 363354)

ARLOTT, (Leslie Thomas) John; OBE (1970); s of late William John Arlott and Nellie Jenvey; *b* 25 Feb 1914; *Educ* Queen Mary's Sch Basingstoke; *m* 1, Dawn Rees; 1 s (and 1 s decd); m 2, Valerie France (d 1976); 1 s (and 1 da decd); m 3, 1977, Patricia Hoare; *Career* broadcaster (BBC cricket commentator for 36 years), author, wine writer, topographer worked as clerk in mental hosp; detective, BBC producer, contested (Lib) Epping 1955 and 1959; pres Cricketers' Assoc 1968-; *Style*— John Arlott, Esq, OBE; c/o The Guardian, 119 Farringdon Rd, London EC1

ARMAGH, Dean of; *see*: Crooks, John Robert Megaw

ARMAGH, Archbishop of 1986-; Most Rev Robert Henry Alexander Eames; s of William Edward Eames, and Mary Eleanor Thompson, *née* Alexander; *b* 27 April 1937; *Educ* Belfast Royal Acad, Methodist Coll Belfast, Queen's Univ Belfast, Trinity Coll Dublin (LLB, LLD, PhD); *m* 1966, (Ann) Christine, da of Capt W M Adrian Reynolds Daly (d 1943); 2 s (Niall b 1967, Michael b 1969); *Career* curate of Bangor Down Diocese 1963-66; incumbent of: Gilnahirk Down 1966-74, Dundela Down 1974-75; bishop of Derry and Raphoe 1975-80, bishop of Down and Dromore 1980-86; archbishop of Armagh and primate of all Ireland 1986; chm Archbishop of Canterbury's Int Cmmn on Communion and Women in the Episcopate 1988; *Recreations* sailing, reading; *Clubs* Strangford Yacht, Ringhaddy Yacht, Kildare St and Univ (Dublin); *Style*— Most Rev the Archbishop of Armagh, Primate of All Ireland; The See House, Cathedral Close, Armagh BT61 7EE (☎ 0861 522851)

ARMAGH, Archbishop of (RC), and Primate of All Ireland 1977-; His Eminence Cardinal Tomás Séamus O Fiaich; s of Patrick Fee (d 1964), of Anamar, Crossmaglen, Co Armagh, Ireland, and Annie, *née* Caraher; *b* 3 Nov 1923; *Educ* St Patrick's Coll Armagh, St Patrick's Coll Maynooth, St Peter's Coll Wexford, Univ Coll Dublin, Catholic Univ of Louvain Belgium; *Career* ordained priest 1948, curate parish of Clonfeacle Co Armagh 1952-53, lectr of modern hist Maynooth Univ Coll 1953-59 (prof in modern hist 1959-74), pres St Patrick's Coll Maynooth 1974-77, Cardinal of Holy Roman Church 1979; patron: GAA, Armagh Diocesan Historical Soc; pres Irish Episcopal Conf 1977-; Freedom of: Drogheda, Wexford; Hon DPh Nat Univ of Ireland; Hon Dr: St Mary's Notre Dame, Boston Coll, Thiel Coll, Seton Coll, St Thomas Coll (St Paul), Incarnate Word Coll (San Antonio); *Style*— His Eminence the Cardinal Archbishop of Armagh; Ara Coeli, Armagh, Ireland (☎ 0861 522 045)

ARMIT, Robin Marshall; s of Robert Lobley Armit (d 1963), and Enid Emily, *née* Nicholson; *b* 6 July 1943; *Educ* Hymers Coll Kingston upon Hull, Hull Univ (LLB); *m* 26 Apr 1969, Wendy, da of Stanley Smith (d 1987); 1 da (Claire b 1976); *Career* slr; *Style*— Robin M Armit, Esq; Beech Cottage, Northgate, Cottingham, E Yorks (☎ 0482 845843); Myre Wolff & Manley, 15 Bowlalley Lane, Hull

ARMIT, Hon Mrs; Hon Serena Helen Christian; *née* Inskip; da of 2 Viscount Caldecote, DSC; *b* 12 June 1943; *m* 1965, John Andrew Brodie Armit, s of late Maj Cecil Brodie Armit, RAMC; 1 s, 1 da; *Style*— The Hon Mrs Armit; 98 St Paul's Rd, London N1

ARMITAGE, Alexander James (Alex); s of Richard Noel Marshall Armitage (d 1986), of Stebbing Park, Essex, and Lady Caroline Tyrrell, *née* Hay; *b* 17 May 1958; *Educ* Eton; *m* 4 Nov 1987, Carolyn Margery, da of Peter Allen, of Portermouth; 1 da (Sophie Claire b 25 Dec 1987); *Career* dir Farworlds Ltd 1985, chm Noel Gay Artists Ltd 1987 (dir 1980), md Noel Gay Orgn 1987 (dir 1984), dir Billy Marsh Assocs 1988; prodr: Me and My Girl West End 1987 (Broadway 1987), High Society 1987, The Rink 1988; memb Soc West End Theatre 1987; *Recreations* snow skiing, photography, wine and food; *Clubs* Groucho, Lords Taveners; *Style*— Alex Armitage, Esq; 81 Lonsdale Rd, London SW13 (☎ 01 748 9722); Le Moulin Clos de Clauzel, Donnat, Bagnols-Sur-Ceze, France; The Noel Gay Orgn, 24 Denmark St, London WCZH 8NS (☎ 01 836 3941, fax 379 7027, telex 21760)

ARMITAGE, Edward; CB (1974); s of Harry Armitage (d 1979), and Florence Armitage; *b* 16 July 1917; *Educ* Huddersfield Coll, St Catharine's Coll Cambridge (MA); *m* 1940, Marjorie, da of William Henry Pope (d 1974); 1 s, 2 da; *Career* Patent Office Examiner Bd of Trade 1939, asst comptroller Patent Office 1966, comptroller gen Patent Office & Industrial Property & Copyright Dept Dept of Trade 1969-77, ret; *Recreations* tennis, bridge, gardening; *Style*— Edward Armitage, Esq, CB; Lynwood, Lascot Hill, Wedmore, Somerset BS28 4AE (☎ 0934 712079)

ARMITAGE, Maj-Gen Geoffrey Thomas Alexander; CBE (1968, MBE 1945); s of Lt-Col Harold Godfrey Parry Armitage (d 1958), of King's Co, Ireland, and Mary Madeline, *née* Drought (d 1933); *b* 5 July 1917; *Educ* Haileybury, RMA Woolwich; *m* 22 Oct 1949, Monica Wall, da of Frank Wall Poat (d 1972), of Guernsey; 1 s, 1 step da; *Career* cmmnd RA 1937, served WWII (despatches), transferred to Royal Dragoons (1st Dragoons) 1951, cmd 1956-59, instr (GSO1) IDC 1959-60, Col Gen Staff WO 1960-62, Cmdt RAC Centre 1962-65, COS HQ1 BR Corps 1966-68, dir Royal Armd Corps 1968-70, GOC Northumbrian Dist 1970-72, ret 1973; dir CLA Game Fair 1973-80; hon sec Countryside Fndn 1985-; *Recreations* some field sports, writing; *Clubs* Army and Navy, Kennel; *Style*— Maj-Gen Geoffrey Armitage, CBE; Clyffe, Tincleton, nr Dorchester, Dorset DT2 8QR (☎ 030 584227)

ARMITAGE, John Patrick; s of Rev Cyril Moxom Armitage, MVO (d 1966), of St Bride's Rectory, Fleet St, London, and Eva, *née* Brimsmead; *b* 17 Mar 1935; *Educ* Marlborough; *m* 1, 28 August 1965 (m dis 1973), Marian Helen, *née* Douglas; 1 s (Edward b 8 Dec 1967); m 2, 14 Oct 1984, Nicola Caroline, da of Larry Gaines, of Crosstrees, Saltwood, Kent; *Career* Nat Serv cmmnd 2 Lt E Yorks Regt UK, Malaya, Germany 1954-56; sales exec Noel Gay Music Co Ltd 1956-59, dir Ogilvy & Mather Ltd 1971-85 (account exec 1959-71); chm: Primary Contact Ltd 1985-, Ogilvy & Mather Focus Ltd 1988-; memb Mark Soc; *Recreations* golf; *Clubs* Littlestone Rye, Royal & Ancient; *Style*— John Armitage, Esq; Ludwell House, Chasing, Kent (☎ 023 371 2469)

ARMITAGE, Dr John Vernon; s of Horace Armitage, and Evelyn, *née* Hauton; through his mother, Dr Armitage is 2 cous of Baron Richardson, of Duntisbourne, *qv*; *b* 21 May 1932; *Educ* Rothwell GS, UCL (BSc, PhD), Cuddesdon Coll Oxford; *m* 1963, Sarah Catherine Clay; 2 s; *Career* mathematician; asst master Shrewsbury Sch 1958-59, lectr Durham Univ 1959-67, sr lectr King's Coll London 1967-70, prof Nottingham Univ 1970-75, princ Coll of St Hild and St Bede Durham 1975-; *Books* A Companion to Advanced Mathematics (with H B Griffiths); *Recreations* railways, cricket and most games; *Clubs* Athenaeum; *Style*— Prof John Armitage; The Principal's House, Pelaw, Leazes Lane, Durham DH1 1TB (☎ 091 374 3050)

ARMITAGE, Joshua Charles; s of Joshua Armitage (d 1944), of Hoylake, and Kate Louise, *née* Cooke (d 1953); *b* 26 Sept 1913; *Educ* private & public, Liverpool Sch of Art; *m* 27 May 1939, late Catherine Mary, *née* Buckle; 2 da (Judith Penelope b 19 Aug 1944, Lesley Elizabeth b 3 July 1946); *Career* WWII leading seaman RNVR 1940-45; free lance artist working under nom de plume Ionicus, associated with Punch for over forty years, illustrator of over 350 books for leading publishers, twelve watercolours for United Oxford and Cambridge Univ Club in London, closely associated with PG Wodehouse through Penguin Books, a watercolourist responsible for many pictures with golfing themes; fund raising for any worthwhile charity; *Recreations* golf, gardening, music; *Clubs* Royal Liverpool GC; *Style*— Joshua Armitage, Esq; 34 Avondale Rd, Hoylake Wirral, Cheshire (☎ 051 632 1298)

ARMITAGE, Kenneth Edward; s of William Henry Armitage (d 1964), of 54 Rufford Rd, Wallasey, Cheshire, and Edith Josephine Armitage, *née* Gaudie; *b* 30 March 1944; *Educ* Wallasey GS, Coll of Law London; *m* 28 Sept 1964, Elizabeth Anne, da of Thomas William Hansard (d 1977), of 45 Burrell Drive, Moreton, Wirrall, Cheshire; 3 s (Matthew b 1972, Daniel b 1974, James b 1977); *Career* slr to: Southery and Dist Int Drainage Bd; Feltwell & Dist Int Drainage Bd, sr ptnr Walton Jeffrey & Armitage 1976, slr to Downham Mkt Town Cncl; past pres Rotary Club of Downham Market and Dist 1985-86, chm Downham Mkt and Dist Round Table 1978-79; *Recreations* reading, music, wine, petanque; *Style*— Kenneth Armitage, Esq; The Hill House, Ryston Rd, Denver, Norfolk (☎ 0366 383869); 29 London Rd, Downham Market, Norfolk PE38 9AS (☎ 0366 383171)

ARMITAGE, Air Chief Marshal Sir Michael John; KCB (1983), CBE (1975); *b* 25 August 1930; *Educ* Newport GS, Aircraft Apprentice Halton, RAF Cranwell; *m* 1955 (m dis 1969), Mary Mannion; 3 s; m 2, 1970, Gretl Renate Steinig; *Career* commissioned 1953, various flying cmd staff and academic appointments, OC 17 Sqn 1967-69, OC RAF Luqa Malta 1972-74, RAF Dir of Forward Policy 1976-78, Dep Cdr RAF Germany 1978-80, Sr RAF Dir Staff Royal Coll of Defence Studies 1980-82, Dir of Service Intelligence 1982-83, Dep Chief Defence Staff (Intelligence) 1983, Chief of Defence Intelligence MOD 1984-85; Air Memb for Supply and Organisation Air Force Board 1985-87; Cmdt Royal College of Defence Studies 1988-; *Books* Air Power in the Nuclear Age 1982 & 1985 (jtly); articles in professional journals; *Recreations* field shooting, mil history; *Clubs* RAF, Eccentric; *Style*— Air Chief Marshal Sir Michael Armitage, KCB, CBE; c/o Lloyds Bank, 6 Pall Mall, London SW1; Commandant, Royal College of Defence Studies, Seaford House, 37 Belgrave Square, London SW1X 8NS (☎ 01 235 1091)

ARMITAGE, Peter Lockhart; s of Dennis Lockhart Armitage, of Rushton Temple Lane, East Meon, Hants, and Dorothy Margaret, *née* Lamb; *b* 13 Jan 1949; *Educ* Malvern, Manchester Univ (BA); *m* 7 Aug 1976, Fiona Christine Lilli, da of John Kingsley Hill, of Hen Ysgol, Llanfaethly, Holyhead, Anglesey, 2 s (Michael b 1980, Jonathan b 1985), 1 da (Melanie b 1982); *Career* CA and dir: OCS Gp Ltd 1987, Smarts Gp Ltd 1981, Collie Carpets Ltd 1980, Vitopan Ltd 1986; jt md Smarts Gp Ltd 1985-87 (all cos owned by OCS Gp); jt md J Mason & Son Leek Ltd 1977-78; *Recreations* tennis, squash, sailing, gardening; *Style*— Peter L Armitage, Esq; Longmead, Highfields, E Horsley, Leatherhead, Surrey KT24 5AA (☎ 04865 3327); OCS Gp Ltd, 79 Limpsfield Rd, Sanderstead, Surrey CR2 9LB (☎ 01 651 3211, fax 01 651 4832)

ARMITAGE, Sir Robert Perceval; KCMG (1954, CMG 1951), MBE (1944); s of Frank Armitage, CIE (d 1955), and Muriel, *née* Byrde-Grigg; *b* 21 Dec 1906; *Educ* Winchester, New Coll Oxford (MA); *m* 1930, Gwladys Lyona, da of Lt-Col Hugh Mowbray Meyler, CBE, DSO, MC (d 1929); 2 s (Robert, Richard); *Career* joined Colonial Civil Serv Kenya 1929, under sec Gold Coast 1948, min for fin Gold Coast 1951-53, govr and C-in-C Cyprus 1954-55, govr Nyasaland 1956-61; KStJ 1954; *Style*— Sir Robert Armitage, KCMG, MBE,; Amesbury Abbey Nursing Home, Amesbury, Wilts SP4 7EX (☎ 0980 23635)

ARMITAGE, Simon Michael; s of Peter William Armitage (d 1983), and Margaret Constance, *née* Hall; *b* 23 Nov 1949; *Educ* Burnham GS Bucks, Marling Sch Stroud, Univ of Exeter (LLB); *m* 3 June 1972, Kathryn, da of Leslie Alfred Basil Becker; 2 da (Helen Margaret b 1976, Caroline Victoria b 1979); *Career* legal asst (then asst slr, then princ asst slr) Tiverton (later Mid Devon) Dist Cncl 1974-79; princ Armitage & Co slrs Exeter 1979-87; *Recreations* sport, particularly squash, tennis, swimming; *Clubs* Exeter Golf, Country; *Style*— Simon M Armitage, Esq; Pearl Assurance House, 236 High Street, Exeter, Devon (☎ 0392 51364)

ARMITAGE, (Henry) St John Basil; CBE (1978, OBE 1968); s of (Henry) John Armitage (d 1978), of Co Tipperary and Lincoln, and Amelia Eleanor, *née* Hall (d 1967); *b* 5 May 1924; *Educ* Christs Hosp Lincoln, Trinity Coll Cambridge; *m* 1956, Jennifer Gerda, da of Prof Walter Horace Bruford; 1 s (Richard), 1 da (Elizabeth); *Career* served Army 1943-45; Arab Legion 1946, Br Mil Mission to Saudi Arabia 1946-49, mil advsr to Saudi Arabian MOD 1946-51, Desert Locust Control Kenya and Aden Protectorates 1952; mil serv Sultan of Muscat and Oman 1952-59; resident mangr Gen Geophysical Co (Houston) Libya 1959-60; oil conslt Astor Assocs Libya 1960-61, business conslt ME 1962; joined HM Dip Serv 1962; first sec (commercial): Baghdad 1963-67, Beirut 1967-68, Jedda 1968-74; chargé d'a1ffaires Jedda 1968, 1969, 1973; HM cncllr and consul gen Dubai 1974-78, Chargé d'Affaires 1975, 1976, 1977, ret 1978; conslt ME Affairs; dir: SCF Hldgs London, Socofi Geneva; hon sec All Party British Saudi Arabian Parly Gp; *Recreations* cricket, reading, travel; *Clubs* Travellers'; *Style*— St John Armitage, Esq, CBE; The Old Vicarage, East Horrington, Wells, Somerset

ARMITAGE, Stephen Robert; s of Sir Stephen Cecil Armitage, CBE (d 1962), of

Nottinghamshire, and Irene, *née* Bowen Smith (d 1984); *b* 19 Jan 1924; *Educ* Harrow; *m* 1, 1951, Jane Elizabeth, da of Dennis Charles Mackie (d 1954); 1 s (Stephen David b 1952), 3 da (Fiona Jane b 1956, Emma Louise b 1958); m 2, 1972, Diana Mary Alethea, da of Dr Patrick Joseph Henry (d 1944); 1 da (Charlotte Diana b 1976); *Career* serv Welsh Gds home and abroad 1942-47, ret as Capt; joined Armitage Bros plc 1945 as dir (chm 1962-); *Recreations* shooting, fishing, sailing, skiing; *Style*— Robert Armitage, Esq; Hawksworth Manor, Hawksworth, Nottinghamshire NG13 9DB (☎ 0949 50243); Armitage Bros plc, Armitage House, Colwick, Nottingham NG4 2BA (☎ 0602 614984, telex 377921, fax 0602 617496)

ARMSTRONG; *see*: Burnett Armstrong

ARMSTRONG, Andrew Charles; s of Terence George Armstrong, of Elsenham, nr Bishop's Stortford, Herts, and Marion, *née* Rigg; *b* 15 Mar 1959; *Educ* Newport GS Essex; *m* 4 July 1981, Jacqueline Mary, da of Maj Anthony Rokeby Roberts, of Sheering, nr Bishop's Stortford, Herts; 1 s (Robert Charles Armstrog b 1985); *Career* dir Robert Fleming & Co Ltd 1986-; *Recreations* golf; *Style*— A C Armstrong, Esq; Robert Fleming & Co Ltd, 25 Copthall Ave, London EC2R 7DR (☎ 01 382 9991, fax 01 256 5036)

ARMSTRONG, Sir Andrew Clarence Francis; 6 Bt (UK 1841), of Gallen Priory, King's Co; CMG (1959); er s of Edmund Clarence Richard Armstrong (d 1923), Bluemantle Pursuivant of Arms, and Mary Frances, *née* Cruise, 2 da of Sir Francis Cruise (d 1953); suc his cousin Sir Andrew St Clare Armstrong, 5 Bt (d 1987); *b* 1 May 1907; *Educ* St Edmund's Coll Old Hall Ware, Christ's Coll Cambridge; *m* 1, 8 Jan 1930, Phyllis Marguerite (d 18 Jan 1930), da of Lt-Col Roland Henry Waithman, DSO; m 2, 17 June 1932, Laurel May (d 1988), er da of late Alfred Wellington Stuart, of New Zealand; 1 s (and 1 s decd); *Heir* s, Lt Col Christopher John Edmund Stuart Armstrong, MBE *qv*; *Career* Colonial Admin Serv: W Pacific 1929, Nigeria 1941, Perm Sec Federal Miny of Mines and Power Nigeria; ret 1961; *Style*— Sir Andrew Armstrong, Bt, CMG; 15 Ravenscroft Rd, Henley-on-Thames, Oxon (☎ 0491 577635)

ARMSTRONG, Lt-Col Christopher John Edmund Stuart; MBE (1979); s and h of Sir Andrew Clarence Francis Armstrong, 6 Bt, CMG, *qv*; *b* 15 Jan 1940; *Educ* Ampleforth, RMA; *m* 1972, Georgina Elizabeth Carey, 2 da of Lt-Col W G Lewis, of Hayling Island; 3 s (Charles Andrew b 1973, James Hugo b 1974, Sam Edward b 1986), 1 da (Victoria Jane b 1980); *Career* Lt-Col RCT

ARMSTRONG, Colin Robert; s of Arthur Armstrong (d 1957), and Sylvia Ann, *née* Williamson (d 1945); *b* 4 July 1934; *Educ* Haileybury; *m* 10 Oct 1959, Stella Margaret, da of Harold Bracht (d 1985), of Bogota, Colombia; 1 s (Arthur Guthrie b 9 April 1962), 1 da (Annabel Clare b 16 Sept 1966); *Career* Nat Serv 1952-54: cmmnd Mddx Regt 1953, seconded to KAR (active serv E Africa and Malaya); 7 Middx Regt TA 1955-57; dir Tracey & Co (subsidiary of Bank of London and S America) 1963-71, mangr head off Bank of London and S America 1971-74, regnl mangr Lloyds Bank Int 1974-77, gen mangr Banco Anglo Colombiano 1977-81, dir and chief exec (Latin America & Caribbean) Inchcape Overseas Ltd 1981-86, exec dir Inchcape plc 1986-; chm Latin American Trade Advsy Gp 1984-86; memb: exec ctee Canning House 1986, Lloyds 1983-; *Recreations* fly fishing, cricket, ornithology; *Clubs* MCC, East India; *Style*— Colin Armstrong, Esq; The Old House, The Folly, Lightwater, Surrey (☎ 0276 73 258); Inchcape plc, St James House, 23 King Street, London SW1Y 6QY (☎ 01 321 0110, fax 01 321 0604, telex 885 395)

ARMSTRONG, Edmund Charles Mark; 2 s of Edmund Clarence Richard Armstrong (d 1923) Bluemantle Pursuivant of Arms, and Mary Frances (d 1953), da of the late Sir Francis Cruise, DL; *b* 17 Feb 1914; *Educ* France, St Edmund's Coll Ware, St John's Coll Cambridge (BA); *m* 1, 17 Oct 1939 (m dis 1949), Patricia Phyllis, da of Edward Robert Vassall-Adams (d 1943), of Horns Cross, N Devon; m 2, 16 Aug 1951, Dorice (d 1983), da of William Harold Austin (d 1949); 3 s (Mark Simon Warneford b 1954, Sean Andrew (triplet) b 1954, Patric Austin (triplet) b 1954); *Career* WWII 1939-45 Lt (S) RNR, HMS Ranchi E Indies Stn 1940, HMS Saker 1942-43, HMS Pursuer 1943-45, N patrol ops (escort duties Atlantic, Normandy and S France invasions); Schwab and Snelling (Stock Exchange) 1935-39; civil servant Admty/MOD 1945-77; *Recreations* music, designing and cutting wooden jigsaw puzzles; *Style*— Mark Armstrong, Esq; Free Hill House, Westbury-sub-Mendip, Wells, Somerset BA5 1HJ (☎ 0749 870 404)

ARMSTRONG, Rt Hon Ernest; PC (1979), MP (Lab) NW Durham 1964-; s of late John Armstrong, of Crook, Co Durham, and late Elizabeth, *née* Walker; *b* 12 Jan 1915; *Educ* Wolsingham GS, City of Leeds Teacher Training Coll; *m* 1941, Hannah P, da of Thomas Lamb, of Sunderland; 1 s (John), 1 da (Hilary, *qv*); *Career* Flying Offr RAF 1942-46 (Middle East); schoolmaster 1937-52, headmaster 1952-64, chm Sunderland Education Ctee 1960-65; asst govt whip 1967-69, Lord Cmmr HM Treasury 1969-70, oppn whip 1970-73, parly under-sec DES 1974-75, DOE 1975-79, dep chm Ways and Means Ctee and first dep chm of House of Commons 1981-; dep chm Municipal Mutual Insurance Ltd; vice-pres Methodist Conference 1974-75; *Recreations* walking; *Style*— The Rt Hon Ernest Armstrong, MP; Penny Well, Witton-le-Wear, Bishop Auckland, Co Durham (☎ 038 888 397); House of Commons, London SW1A 0AA (☎ 01 219 5551)

ARMSTRONG, Col Geoffrey Russell; DSO (1945), MC (1942), TD (1950); s of William Robinson Armstrong (d 1955), of Banstead, Surrey, and Beatrice, *née* Russell (d 1965); *b* 16 June 1910; *Educ* Sutton Valence; *m* 16 Nov 1945, Elizabeth Peace, da of George William Cole-Hamilton (d 1946), of Hertfordshire; 1 s (Johny b 1946), 1 da (Ruth Margaret b 1949); *Career* joined HAC 1930, cmmnd 1935, Capt 1939, 8 Army Western Desert 1941-42, Maj 1942, Iraq and India 1943, Lt-Col 1944, Burma 1943-45 (despatches), Col 1953; publisher 1953-58, chm and md Manufacturing Gp 1958-68, antiquarian bookseller 1968-85; memb Rural Preservation, served TA Assocs; *Books* various contributions to military histories; *Recreations* shooting, fishing, deerstalking; *Clubs* Army and Navy, Honourable Artillery Co; *Style*— Col Geoffrey Armstrong, DSO, MC, TD; Axmas Cottage, Rusper, West Sussex

ARMSTRONG, Hilary Jane; da of Rt Hon Ernest Armstrong (*qv*); *b* 30 Nov 1945; *Educ* Monkwearmouth Comp Sch Sunderland (BSc), West Ham Coll of Tech (Dip Social Work) Univ of Birmingham; *Career* social worker Newcastle City Council 1970-73; neighbourhood community work: Sunderland 1973; lecturer community and youth work Sunderland Polytechnic 1975-86; *Recreations* reading, theatre, knitting; *Style*— Ms Hilary Armstrong; Deneholme, Plantation Tce, Howden-le-Wear, Nr Crook, Co Durham (☎ 0388 767065); House of Commons, Westminster, London SW1A 0AA (☎ 01 219 5076)

ARMSTRONG, Dr Ian David; s of David Armstrong (d 1986), and Mary *née* Wardle; *b* 7 April 1943; *Educ* Peebles HS, Heriot-Watt Univ Edinburgh (BSc, PhD); *m* 17 Sept 1965, (Eileen) Carol, da of Fl Lt William Milne; 2 da (Kim b 26 Nov 1967, Sharon b 16 June 1969); *Career* lectr Heriot-Watt Univ 1967-69; Roughton & Ptnrs: sr engr 1969-75, ptnr 1975-85, md 1985; FICE 1972, FIStruct 1972, M Cons E 1984; *Recreations* horticulture, vinery, equine residue culture; *Clubs* Southampton YC; *Style*— Dr Ian Armstrong; Droxford, Hants; Fulham, London; Grenada, Spain; Roughton & Partners, 321 Millbrook Rd West, Southampton SO1 0HW (☎ 0703 705 533, fax 0703 701 060, telex 477 416 RAPCON G)

ARMSTRONG, James Hodgson; s of John James Armstrong (d 1958), of Carlisle, Cumbria, and Margaret Eleanor, *née* Hodgson (d 1959); *b* 11 May 1926; *Educ* Carlisle GS, Glasgow Univ (BSc); *m* 18 March 1950, Marjorie, da of Victor Allen Cartner (d 1960); 1 s (Hugh b 1954), 1 da (Jane b 1951); *Career* Duff and Geddes consulting engrs Edinburgh 1946-49, Rendel Palmer and Tritton Scotland Tyneside London 1948-54, specialist geotechnical engrg Soil Mechanics Ltd London 1954-60, Harris and Sutherland conslts 1960-63, design of Cwlth Inst; Building Design Ptnrship London 1966-(joined 1963); visiting prof: Cooper Union Coll NY, Kingston Poly, Queen's Univ Belfast, Leed's Univ; vice pres IStructE; chm tstees Euro Christian Industl Movement, memb Exec Ctee Higher Educn Fndn, Forum Memb Foundation for Study Christianity and Soc; govr St James's Schools Kensington, dir Task Undertakings, memb several professional and educnl ctees; FICE 1951, FIStructE 1951, MACE, MASCE, FGS, FID, FFB, FRSA, FCollP; *Recreations* philosophy, reading, walking, photography; *Clubs* Reform; *Style*— James Armstrong, Esq; 32 Longford Green, London SE5 8BX (☎ 01 733 8608); Building Design Partnership, 16 Gresse St, London W1A 4WD (☎ 01 631 4733, telex 25322)

ARMSTRONG, Lt-Col John Anderson; CB (1980), OBE (1945, TD 1945); s of William Anderson Armstrong, JP (d 1943), of Westoe House, South Shields, Co Durham, and Helen Marianne, *née* Clarke (d 1962); *b* 5 May 1910; *Educ* Wellington, Trinity Coll Cambridge (MA); *m* 1938, Barbara, da of Rev (William) Lewis Gantz (d 1940), of Abbots House, Stanstead Abbots, Hertfordshire, and Nina Margaret, *née* Thompson (d 1978); 1 s (William d 1976), 2 da (Susan, Jane); *Career* Lt Col cmdg 73 Light AA Regt 1940-45 (Normandy 1944-, cmdg N AA Assault Gp D day), City of London Yeo RHA (TA) 1931-40; barr Lincoln's Inn 1936, practice at Chancery Bar 1946-70, bencher Lincoln's Inn 1969, master of the Ct of Protection 1970-82; *Recreations* gardening, walking, fishing, golf; *Clubs* Brooks's; *Style*— Lt-Col John Armstrong, CB, OBE, TD; Dacre Cottage, Dacre, Penrith, Cumbria (☎ 08536 224)

ARMSTRONG, Lady; Millicent; *née* Ortlepp; da of late Adolph Leopold Ortlepp, of Graaff Reinert, Cape Province, S Africa; *m* 1925, as his 2 wife, Sir George Elliot Armstrong, 2 Bt, CMG (d 1940; btcy became ext on d of 3 Bt 1944); *Style*— Lady Armstrong

ARMSTRONG, Hon Peter William; only s of Baron Armstrong of Sanderstead, GCB, MVO, PC (Life Peer; d 1980); *b* 1943; *m* 1967, Kathleen Frances Widdicombe; *Style*— The Hon Peter Armstrong; 20 Ravensbourne Gardens, London W13

ARMSTRONG, Sir Robert Temple; GCB (1983, KCB 1978, CB 1974), CVO (1975); s of Sir Thomas (Henry Wait) Armstrong, *qv*, and Hester Muriel, *née* Draper (d 1982); *b* 30 Mar 1927; *Educ* Eton, Ch Ch Oxford; *m* 1953 (m dis 1985), Serena, da of Sir Roger Chance, 3 Bt; 2 da (June b 1954, Teresa b 1957); m 2, 1985, Patricia, da of Charles Cyril Carlow (d 1957); *Career* asst sec: Cabinet Office 1964-66, Treasury 1967-68; under sec Treasury 1968-70, PPS to PM 1970-75, dep under-sec Home Office 1975-77, PUS 1977-79, sec of the Cabinet 1979-87, head Home Civil Service 1981-87; sec Bd of Dirs Royal Opera House Covent Garden 1968-; Liveryman Salters 1983; fellow of Eton 1979, hon student Ch Ch Oxford 1985, Rhodes tstee 1975, hon fellow Royal Acad of Music 1985, hon bencher Inner Temper 1986, hon master Middle Temple 1988; *cr* a Life Peer 1988; *Recreations* music; *Clubs* Athenaeum, Brooks's; *Style*— Sir Robert Armstrong, GCB, CVO; Holt's, Kirkland House, 22 Whitehall, London SW1A 2EB

ARMSTRONG, Sir Thomas Henry Wait; s of Amos E Armstrong, of Peterborough, Northants; *b* 15 June 1898; *Educ* Choir Sch Chapel Royal, King's Sch Peterborough, Keble Coll Oxford, RCM; *m* 1926, Hester (d 1982), da of Rev William Henry Draper (d 1933); 1 s (*see* Baron Armstrongof Ilminster), 1 da; *Career* served WW I; organist Exeter Cathedral 1928-33, organist of Ch Ch Oxford 1933-55, univ lectr in music 1937-54, princ RAM 1955-69; student Ch Ch Oxford 1939-55, student emeritus 1955, hon student 1981-; tstee Countes of Munster Musical Tst; FRCM; kt 1958; *Clubs* Garrick; *Style*— Sir Thomas Armstrong; The Old Rectory, Newton Blossomville, nr Turvey, Beds

ARMSTRONG OF SANDERSTEAD, Baroness; Gwendoline Enid; da of John Bennett, of Putney; *m* 1942, Baron Armstrong of Sanderstead, GCB, MVO, PC (Life Peer, d 1980); 1 s, 1 da; *Style*— The Rt Hon the Lady Armstrong of Sanderstead; Pinewood House, Pleasure Pit Rd, Ashtead, Surrey

ARMSTRONG-JONES, Lady Sarah; *see*: HRH Princess Margaret, Countess of Snowdon in *Royal Family Section*

ARMYTAGE, Capt David George; CBE (1981); s of Rear Adm Reginald William Armytage, GC, CBE (d 1984), and Sylvia Beatrice, *née* Staveley-Staveley; cous and hp of Sir Martin Armytage, 9 Bt; *b* 4 Sept 1929; *m* 3 April 1954, Countess Antonia Cosima, er da of Count Cosimo Diodono de Bosdari, and his w Enid, o da of Lt-Col Sir Peter Carlaw Walker, 2 Bt; 2 s (Hugh b 1955, Charles b 1962), 1 da (Davina b 1956); *Career* Capt RN; cmd HMS Minerva 1968-70, Defence Policy Staff 1970-72, Naval Asst to 1 Sea Lord 1972-74, cmd 7 Frigate Sqdn 1976-77, dep dir Naval Warfare 1977-79, Cdre cmd Standing Naval Force Atlantic 1980-81; sec gen BDA 1981-, ADC 1981; *Recreations* sailing, shooting; *Clubs* Oriental; *Style*— Capt David Armytage, CBE, RN; Sharcott Manor, Pewsey, Wilts

ARMYTAGE, Lady; Maria Margarete; da of Paul Hugo Tenhaeff, of Bruenen, Niederhein; *m* 1949, as his 2 w, Capt Sir John Lionel Armytage, 8 Bt (d 1983); 1 da; *Style*— Lady Armytage; Kirklees Park, Brighouse, York

ARMYTAGE, Sir (John) Martin; 9 Bt (GB 1738), of Kirklees, Yorkshire; s of Capt Sir John Lionel Armytage, 8 Bt (d 1983), and Evelyn Mary Jessamine, *née* Fox; *b* 26 Feb 1933; *Educ* Eton; *Heir* cousin, Capt David George Armytage, CBE, RN, *qv*; *Style*— Sir Martin Armytage, Bt; Halewell, Withington, Cheltenham, Glos

ARNANDER, Christopher James Folke; s of Per Erik Arnander (d 1933), and Cynthia Anne, *née* Lindsay; *b* 22 Dec 1932; *Educ* Harrow, Oriel Coll Oxford (MA); *m* 7 April 1961, Pamela Primrose, da of David McKenna, CBE; 3 s (Conrad b 1963, Michael b 1964, Magnus b 1970), 1 da (Katharine b 1967); *Career* lectr Univ of

Minnesota USA 1956-57, Hill Samuel Merchant Bankers 1958-65, Williams & Glyn's Bank 1965-73 (dir 1970), financial exec in Kuwait 1973-79, chief advsr Riyad Bank Saudi Arabia 1979-85, dir Barclays de Zoete Wedd 1985-; memb Glyndebourne Arts Tst 1964-73 (cncl 1973-), cncllr RCM 1987-, tres Nat Assoc for Care & Resettlement of Offenders 1967-73; *Recreations* music, sports, reading, travel; *Style*— Christopher Arnander, Esq; Barclays de Zoete Wedd, Ebbgate House, 2 Swan Lane, London, EC4R 3TS, (☎ 01 623 2323 fax 8951518)

ARNELL, Richard Anthony Sayer; s of Richard Sayer Arnell (d 1952), and Hélène Marie Ray Scherf (d 1942); *b* 15 Sept 1917; *Educ* Hall Sch, Univ Coll Sch, Royal Coll of Music; *m* 1981, Audrey Millar Paul; 3 da (Jessie, Claudine, Jennifer); *Career* composer, conductor, film maker; princ lectr Trinity Coll of Music 1981- (teacher of composition 1949-81); music conslt BBC N American Serv 1943-46; lectr Royal Ballet Sch 1958-59; ed The Composer 1961-64; chm: Composers' Guild of GB 1965 and 1974-75, jt Ctee Songwriters' and Composers' Guilds 1977-, Young Musicians' Symph Orch Soc 1973-75; visiting lectr (Fullbright Exchange) Bowdoin Coll Maine 1967-68, visiting prof Hofstra Univ New York 1968-70; music dir and bd memb London Int Film Sch 1975- (chm Film Sch Tst 1981-); music dir Ram Filming Ltd 1980-, dir Organic Sounds Ltd 1982-; Composer of the Year 1966 (Music Teachers Assoc Award); compositions include: 5 symphonies, 2 concertos for violin, concerto for harpsichord, concerto for piano, 5 string quartets, 2 quintets, piano trio, piano work, songs, cantatas, organ work, music for string orchestra, wind ensembles, brass ensembles, song cycles, electronic music; opera: Love in Transit, Moonflowers; ballet scores: Punch and the Child for Ballet Soc NY 1947, Harlequin in April for Arts Cncl 1951, The Great Detective for Sadler's Wells Theatre Ballet 1953, The Angels for Royal Ballet 1957, Giselle (Adam) reorchestrated for Ballet Rambert 1965; film scores: The Land 1941, The Third Secret 1963, The Visit 1964, The Man Outside 1966, Topsail Schooner 1966, Bequest for a Village 1969, Second Best 1972, Stained Glass 1973, Wires over the Border 1974, Black Panther 1977, Antagonist 1980, Dilemma 1981; other works: Symphonic Portrait Lord Byron for Sir Thomas Beecham 1953, Landscapes and Figures for Sir Thomas Beecham 1956, Petrified Princess puppet operetta for BBC 1959, Robert Flaherty Impression for Radio Eireann 1960, Musica Pacifica for Edward Benjamin 1963, Festival Flourish for Salvation Army 1965, 2nd piano concerto for RPO 1967, Overture Food of Love for Portland Symph Orch 1968, My Ladye Green Sleeves for Hofstra Univ 1968, Nocturne Prague 1968, I Think of all Soft Limbs for Canadian Broadcasting Corpn 1971, Astronaut One 1973, Life Boat Voluntary for RNLI 1974, Call for LPO 1982, Ode to Beecham for RPO 1986: hon fellow Trinity Coll of Music London (FTCL); *Clubs* Savage; *Style*— Richard Arnell; 149 Shenley Rd, Borehamwood, Herts WD6 1AH (☎ 01 953 7572); London Int Film Sch, 24 Shelton St, London WC2 (☎ 01 240 0168)

ARNEY, David Barrie; s of Frank Douglas Arney, CBE (d 1983), of Bristol, and Mildred Winifred, *née* Dallin (d 1982); *b* 21 Oct 1933; *Educ* Bristol GS; *m* 25 Aug 1956, Patricia Esme da of James Edwin Webb (d 1977), of Bristol; 2 da (Louise b 1961, Alison b 1966); *Career* dir: Warwickshire Oil Storage Ltd 1982-, Bristol Oil Storage Ltd 1988, Texaco (UK) Ltd 1984-, mangr gp operations Texaco Ltd 1987-; *Recreations* shooting, fishing, golf; *Style*— David B Arney, Esq; 6 Oldbury Grove, Knotty Green, Beaconsfield, Bucks HP9 2AJ (☎ 04946 6847); Texaco Ltd, 195 Knightsbridge, London SW1X 7QJ (telex: 8956681)

ARNISON, Val (Mrs Arthur Brittenden); da of Thomas Arnison, of Wargrave, Berkshire, and Vera, *née* Christian; *b* 30 August 1940; *Educ* Lowther Coll Abergele N Wales; *m* 24 Oct 1975, (Charles) Arthur Brittenden, s of Tom Edwin Brittenden (d 1926); *Career* press and PR offr ICI Ltd 1970-79, asst vice pres and dir PR AMI Health Care Ltd 1982-87, account dir Countrywide Communications 1988-; memb Assoc of Women in PR 1975- (pres 1978-79); memb ctee Women of the Year Luncheon (exec chm 1987-89); MIPR, memb Foreign Press Assoc 1982-; *Recreations* gardening, reading, music, needlepoint; *Clubs* New Cavendish, RSM; *Style*— Miss Val Arnison; 22 Park St, Woodstock, Oxfordshire OX7 1SP Countrywide Communications, Countrywide House, West Bar, Banbury, Oxfordshire (☎ 0295 272 288, fax 0295 270 659, telex 837521 C WIDE G)

ARNOLD, Adrian Dawson Bernard; s of Adrian Joseph Arnold (d 1963), and Susan, *née* Dawson Miller; *b* 4 August 1947; *Educ* Winchester, Univ Coll Oxford (MA); *Career* Lancing Coll: head of classics 1986, sr tutor 1982-; chm Sussex Classics Assoc; Liveryman Worshipful Co of Skinners 1983; *Style*— Adrian Arnold, Esq; The Common Room, Lancing Coll, Sussex

ARNOLD, David Philip James; s of Philip Arthur Arnold (d 1988), and Christine May, *née* Rowe; *b* 13 August 1955; *Educ* Merchant Taylors, Univ of Exeter; *m* 19 Aug 1978, Carol Alice, da of Arthur George Edward Williams (d 1973); 1 da (Kirsten b 7 Feb 1986); *Career* CA, ptnr Ernst & Whinney 1988; Freeman City of London 1976, Liveryman Worshipful Co of Fishmongers 1982; ICAEW 1979; *Recreations* hockey; *Clubs* City Livery; *Style*— David Arnold, Esq; Ernst & Whinney, Becket House, 1 Lambeth Palace Rd, London SE1 7EU (☎ 01 928 2000, fax 01 928 1345, telex 885234)

ARNOLD, Jacques Arnold; MP ((C) Gravesham 1987-); s of Samuel Arnold (d 1985), and Eugenie, *née* Patentine; *b* 27 August 1947; *Educ* sch in Brazil, LSE; *m* 22 May 1976, Patricia Anne, da of Dennis Maunder, of Windsor, Berks; 1 s (David Samuel b 1984), 2 da (Hazel Jane b 1979, Philippa Rachel b 1981); *Career* asst gp rep Midland Bank Brazil 1976-78, regnl dir Thomas Cook Gp 1978-84, asst trade fin dir Midland Bank 1984-85, dir American Express Europe Ltd 1985-87; Cllr Oundle 1981-85; *Style*— Jacques A Arnold, Esq, MP; Fairlawn, 243 London Rd, West Malling, Kent ME19 5AD (☎ 0732 848573); House of Commons, London SW1A 0AA (☎ 01 219 4150)

ARNOLD, James Ronald Matthew; s of Capt Ronald M Arnold (d 1981), of Abington, Northampton, and K Sheila, *née* Chamberlain; *b* 15 Jan 1938; *Educ* Eaglehurst Sch Northampton, Northampton GS; *Career* slr 1960; articled clerk to Mr (now Lord) Boardman, fndr memb Agric Law Assoc, memb conseil de direction comité Europeen de Droit Rural, head agric dept Shoosmiths & Harrison, lectr on agric taxation and tenancy law; notary public 1971; memb Law Soc 1960; *Recreations* travel, gardening; *Clubs* Northampton and County; *Style*— James Arnold, Esq; Park House, Towcester Northamptons; Shoesmiths & Harrison, 205 Watling St West, Towcester, Northamptons (☎ 0327 50266, fax 0327 53567)

ARNOLD, Prof John André; s of Capt André Eugene Arnold (d 1974), and May, *née* Vickers (d 1977); *b* 30 April 1944; *Educ* Haberdashers Askes Hatcham, LSE (MSc); *m* 11 Jan 1975, Lynne Mary, da of Frederic Reaney Burgess, of Prestbury, Cheshire; 2 da (Kate Lynne b 1976, Mandy Louise b 1978); *Career* teaching fell mgmnt studies LSE 1967-69; lectr in accounting: Univ of Kent 1969-71, Univ of Manchester 1971-75; prof of accounting Univ of Manchester 1977-86 (sr lctr 1975-77), visiting prof Univ of Washington USA 1981-82, Peat Marwick McLintock prof of accounting Univ of Manchester 1986-, dean faculty of econ and social studies Univ of Manchester 1987-89, dir of res ICAEW 1987-; Hon MA (Econ) Manchester Univ; FCA 1967; *Books* Pricing and Output Decisions (1973), Topics in Management Accounting (1980), Accounting for Management Decisions (1983), Management Accounting Research and Practice (1983), Financial Accounting (1985); *Recreations* squash, opera; *Clubs* Marple Cricket & Squash; *Style*— Prof John Arnold; Department of Accounting & Finance, University of Manchester, Manchester M13 9PL (☎ 061 275 4010, fax 061 275 4023)

ARNOLD, Rt Hon Mr Justice; Rt Hon Sir John Lewis; PC (1979); s of Alfred Lewis Arnold (d 1917), of London, and E K Arnold; *b* 6 May 1915; *Educ* Wellington; *m* 1, 1940 (m dis 1963), Alice Margaret Dorothea, da of George Cookson (d 1949), of Thursley, Surrey; 1 s, 1 da; m 2, 1963, Florence Elizabeth, da of H M Hague, of Montreal; 1 s, 2 da; *Career* served WW II (despatches); barr Middle Temple 1937, QC 1958, chm Bar Cncl 1970-72, High Court judge (Family Div) 1972-, pres Family Div 1979-, tres of Middle Temple for 1982; Hon DLitt Reading 1982; kt 1972; *Style*— The Rt Hon Mr Justice Arnold; Little Horse Leas, Bradfield, Berks (☎ 0734 744 442); 6 Pump Court, London EC4 (☎ 01 583 0573); Roy Courts of Justice, London WC2 (☎ 01 936 6189)

ARNOLD, Very Rev John Robert; s of John Stanley Arnold (d 1977), of Rowan Cottage, Laleham, Middx, and Ivy, *née* Ireland; *b* 1 Nov 1933; *Educ* Christ's Hosp, Sidney Sussex Coll Cambridge (MA), Westcott House; *m* 29 Sept 1963, (Livia) Anneliese, da of Ernst Konrad Franke (Capt d 1944); 1 s (Matthew b 1965), 2 da (Frances b 1964, Miriam b 1972); *Career* Nat Serv Intelligence Corps 1952-54, 2 Lt, Civil Serv Cmmn Serv Interpreter Cert 1954; ordained: deacon 1960, priest 1961; curate Holy Trinity Millhouses Sheffield 1960-63, Sir Henry Stephenson fell Sheffield Univ 1962-72, sec Bd for Mission and Unity 1972-78, dean of Rochester 1978-89, dean of Durham 1989-; pres and vice chm Conf of Euro Churches 1986-, dir First Conference Estate plc 1978-; chm Govrs of King's Sch Rochester 1978-89, pres: St Bartholomew's Hosp Rochester 1978-89, United Nations Assoc 1978-89, City of Rochester Soc 1978-89, Rochester Choral Soc 1978-89; Order of Saint Vladimir (Russian Orthodox Church) 1974; *Books* The Eucharistic Liturgy of Taize (trans 1962), Strategist for the Spirit (contrib 1985), Rochester Cathedral (1987); *Recreations* music, languages, literature; *Clubs* Royal Commonwealth Soc, Christ's Hosp, Nicadean; *Style*— The Very Rev the Dean of Durham; The Deanery, Durham DH1 3EQ (☎ 091 384 7500)

ARNOLD, Malcolm; CBE (1970); s of William and Annie Arnold, of Northampton; *b* 21 Oct 1921; *Educ* RCM; *m* 1963, Isobel Katherine, da of David Inglis Wood Gray; 2 s, 1 da; *Career* composer; princ trumpet LPO 1941-44 and 1945-48; awarded Oscar for music for film Bridge on the River Kwai 1957, bard of Cornish Gorsedd 1969; Hon DMus: Exeter 1970, Durham 1982, Leicester 1984; FRCM; *Style*— Malcolm Arnold, Esq, CBE; c/o Faber Music, 3 Queen Sq, London WC1N 3AU

ARNOLD, Michael John; s of Thomas Henry Arnold and Cecily May Arnold; *b* 1 April 1935; *Career* Nat Serv, Lt RA 1958-59; Hilton Sharpe & Clark 1951-57; qualified CA 1957, ptnr Arthur Young 1966-(joined 1960); hon tres Youth Clubs;; *Recreations* horse racing, hunting, country; *Clubs* Turf; *Style*— Michael Arnold, Esq; Rolls House, 7 Rolls buildings, Fetter Lane, London ECHA 1NH, (☎ 01 831 7130, fax 01 405 2147, telex 888604 AYLO)

ARNOLD, (James) Olav; s of Edmund Arnold (d 1954), of Leeds, and (Gjertrude) Marie Mathilde Ravn *née* Bredal; *b* 18 Oct 1928; *Educ* Stowe, Clare Coll Cambridge (MA); *m* 1, 10 July 1956, Jacqueline Anne Nina (d 1977), da of Harry Wingate (d 1982), of London; 1 s (Christopher b 1960), 2 da (Karen b 1958, Rachel b 1962); m 2, 1 April 1978, Elizabeth Lenwood, da of Prof Roger Wilson, of Yealand Conyers, Carnforth, Lancashire; *Career* Rifle Bde, 2 Lt Green Howards 1947-49; dep md and dep chm E J Arnold & Son Ltd Educational Publishers and Suppliers 1952-84, pres Leeds & Holbeck Building Soc 1983-85 (dir 1978-), chm Leeds Western Dist Health Authy 1986-88; pres: Br Printing Industs Fedn 1977-78, Leeds Chamber of Commerce and Indust 1982-86; govr Leeds Poly 1978-87, chm Leeds Civic Tst 1983-; chm Scarcroft PC 1974-84; *Recreations* golf, tennis, fishing, painting, music, gardening; *Clubs* Lansdowne (Leeds); *Style*— Olav Arnold, Esq; Manor Close, Thorner Lane, Scarcroft, Leeds LS14 3AL (☎ 0532 892 314)

ARNOLD, (Clifford) Roy; s of Sydney Howard Arnold, and Edna May, *née* Davis; *b* 15 Nov 1932; *m* 22 June 1957, Doreen Margaret, da of William James Davies (d 1976), of Birmingham; 2 s (Stephen b 1962, James b 1964), 2 da (Sally b 1961, Alison b 1970); *Career* Bombadier RA 1957-1958; chief accountant Fulton (TI) Ltd 1970-74, dir Fletcher Homes 1979-, company sec Fletcher Estates 1979-; memb: Exec Ctee Shifnal Town FC, Shifnal Cons Assoc, Shifnal Town Cncl (chm fin ctee 1987-88); FCA; *Recreations* skiing (Alpine), walking, squash; *Clubs* Shifnal Squash, Midlands Ski; *Style*— Roy Arnold, Esq; 18 Vicarage Drive, Shifnal, Shropshire TF11 9AF (☎ 0952 460 635); 95 Mount Pleasant Rd, Shrewsbury SY1 3EL (☎ 0743 236 622)

ARNOLD, Simon Rory; s of Rory Watkin Williams Arnold (d 1950), and Rosemary Arnold (d 1948); *b* 10 Sept 1933; *Educ* Diocesan Coll S Africa; *m* 1960, Janet Linda, da of Peter J May (d 1980); 1 s (Guy Rory b 1964), 1 da (Clare Louise b 1963); *Career* Lt Duke of Wellington's Regiment 1957-59; various directorships with Minet Hldgs 1952-84 (deputy chm and gp md 1982); chief exec Bain Dawes plc 1984, chm and chief exec Bain Dawed plc 1986, chm and chief exec Bain Clarkson Ltd 1987; *Recreations* tennis, golf, walking; *Clubs* Royal Ashdown Golf; *Style*— Simon R Arnold, Esq; Meadows, Common Lane, Ditchling Common, Hassocks, Sussex (☎ 079 18 4246); 15 Minories, London EC3N 1NJ (☎ 01 481 3232, telex 8813411, fax 480 6137)

ARNOLD, Thomas Richard; MP (C) Hazel Grove 1974-; s of Thomas Charles Arnold, and Helen Breen; *b* 25 Jan 1947; *Educ* Bedales, Le Rosey, Pembroke Coll Oxford (MA); *m* 1984, Elizabeth Jane, widow of Robin Smithers; *Career* theatre prod*r and publisher; contested (C) Manchester Cheetham 1970, Hazel Grove Feb 1974; PPS to: Sec of State for NI 1979-81, Lord Privy Seal/FCO 1981-82; vice-chm of the Conservative Party Organisation 1983; *Style*— Thomas Arnold, Esq, MP; House of Commons, London SW1A 0AA (☎ 01 219 4096)

ARNOLD, Vere Arbuthnot; CBE (1970), MC (1945), TD (1953), JP (Co of Chester 1949), DL (Cheshire 1969); s of Rev Henry Abel Arnold (d 1934), of Wolsingham

Rectory, Co Durham; *b* 23 May 1902; *Educ* Haileybury, Jesus Coll Cambridge; *m* 1928, Joan Kathleen, da of Charles James Tully, of Wairarapa, NZ; 1 s, 1 da; *Career* served WWII Maj; chm: Ross T Smyth & Co 1957-75, Runcorn Devpt Corpn 1964-74, Liverpool Grain Storage and Transit Co 1958-84; High Sheriff Cheshire 1955; *Style*— Vere Arnold, Esq, CBE, MC, TD, JP, DL; Ardmore, Great Barrow, nr Chester (☎ 0829 40257)

ARNOLD-BAKER, Prof Charles; OBE (1966); s of Baron Albrecht von Blumenthal, and Alice Wilhelmine, *née* Hainsworth; *b* 25 June 1918; *Educ* Winchester, Magdalen Coll Oxford; *m* 1943, Edith, *née* Woods; 1 s, 1 da; *Career* served WW II Army Inf and War Off 1940-46; barr 1948; sec Nat Assoc of Local Cncls 1953-78, memb Royal Cmmn on Common Lands 1955-58; dep chm: Eastern Traffic Cmmrs 1978-, E Midlands Traffic Cmmrs 1981-; conslt lectr City Univ 1978-83 (visiting prof 1983-); author and occasional broadcaster; King Haakon VII Freedom Medal (Norway) 1946; *Books* The Local Government Act (1972), The Local Government, Planning and Land Act (1980), Local Council Administration (fifth edn 1981), The Five Thousand: The Living Constitution (1986); *Recreations* travel; *Clubs* Oxford Union; *Style*— Prof Charles Arnold-Baker, Esq, OBE; Top Floor, 2 Paper Bldgs, Inner Temple, London EC4 (☎ 01 353 3490)

ARNOLD-FORSTER, Hon Mrs (Valentine Harriet Isobel Dione); *née* Mitchison; da of Baron Mitchison, CBE, QC (Life Peer; d 1970), and Naomi Mitchison, the author; *Educ* Somerville Coll Oxford (BA); *m* 1955, Mark Arnold-Forster (b 16 Apr 1920, o s of William Edward Arnold-Forster; he is 15 in descent from Robert Maskelynge who was presented, as a freeholder of the manor of Lydiard Milisent, at a court of Henry VI held 5 Apr 1457); 3 s, 2 da; *Style*— The Hon Mrs Arnold-Forster; 50 Clarendon Rd, London W11

ARNOTT, Sir Alexander John Maxwell; 6 Bt (UK) 1896, of Woodlands, St Anne, Shandon, Co Cork; s of Sir John Arnott, 5 Bt (d 1981); *b* 18 Sept 1975; *Heir* bro, Andrew John Eric Arnott b 20 June 1978; *Style*— Sir Alexander Arnott, Bt; 11 Palmerston Road, Dublin

ARNOTT, Lady; Ann Margaret; da of Terence Alphonsus Farrelly, of Kilcar, Co Cavan; *b* 21 Dec 1924; *Educ* Bridlington High Sch, Cheltenham Ladies Coll, Somerville Coll Oxford; *m* 1974, Sir John Arnott, 5 Bt (d 1981); 2 s; *Clubs* Univ Womens'; *Style*— Lady Arnott; 11 Palmerston Road, Dublin

ARNOTT, Eric John; s of Capt Sir Robert Arnott, 4 Bt (d 1967), of Ounavarra, Lucan, Co Dublin, Ireland, and Cynthia Anita Amelia, *née* James (d 1948); *b* 12 June 1929; *Educ* Harrow, Trinity Coll Dublin (BA, MB, BCh, BAO), Univ of London (DO); *m* 19 Nov 1960, Veronica Mary, da of Capt Arvid Langue Querfeld Van Der Seedeck (d 1986), of Hazel Bank, Sandy Lane, Hartley, Wintney, Hants; 2 s (Stephen John b 1962, Robert Lariston John b 1971), 1 da (Tatiana Amelia b 1963); *Career* house offr Adelaide Hosp Dublin 1954-55, registrar Royal Victoria Eye and Ear Hosp Dublin 1956-57, resident offr (later sr resident offr) Moorfields Eye Hosp London 1959-61, sr registrar UCH 1962-65; conslt ophthalmologist: Royal Eye Hosp 1966-72, Charing Cross Hosp and Charing Cross Gp of Hosps 1967-; hon conslt opthalmologist Royal Masonic Hosp 1970-, reader Univ of London 1972-; pres and fndr Euro Soc for Phaco and Laser Surgery, former examiner Br Orhtopic Cncl; designer intra-oculor lens implants 1976-, pioineer of phaceimulsification in Europe 1968-75; FCophth 1988, FRCS 1963; *Books* Emergency Surgery (jtly, 1977), Cataract Extraction and Lens Implantation (jtly, 1983), Phacoemulsification (contrib 1988); *Recreations* swimming, golf; *Clubs* Kildare St Club (Dublin) Garrick; *Style*— Eric Arnott, Esq; Trottsford Farm, Headley, nr Bordon, Hampshire GU35 8TF (☎ 04203 2136); 11 Milford House, 7 Queen Anne St, London W1M 9FD (☎ 01 580 1074, fax 01 255 1524)

ARNOTT, Ian Emslie; s of Henry Arnott (d 1967), of Galashiels, and Margaret Hume Paton Emslie (d 1961); *b* 7 May 1929; *Educ* Galashiels Academy, Edinburgh Coll of Art (DA, Dip TP); *m* 17 Sept 1955, Mildred Stella; 1 da (Gillian Elisabeth b 1958); *Career* flying offr RAF 1955-57; architect; snr ptnr Campbell & Arnott 1963-; awards: gold medal for architecture, Royal Scottish Acad Civic Tst five times, Edinburgh Architectural Assoc twice; recent projects: Western Isles Arts Centre Stornoway, Lammermuir House Dunbar, Engrg Museum AEU London, Edinburgh Slrs' Property Centre, Scottish Fin Centre Castle Terrace Edinburgh, Maybury Business Technol Park Edinburgh, AEU HQ London; ARSA, RIBA, ARIAS; *Recreations* walking, travel, music, reading, photography; *Clubs* New (Edinburgh); *Style*— Ian Arnott, Esq; The Rink, Gifford, East Lothian (☎ 062 081 278); Campbell & Arnott, Albany Lane, Edinburgh EH1 3QP (☎ 031 557 1725, fax: 031 556 1199)

ARNOTT, John Michael Stewart; s of George Arnott (d 1970), of Kirriemuir, and Winifred Douglas, *née* Livingstone; *b* 12 June 1933; *Educ* King Edward's Sch Birmingham, Peterhouse Cambridge (BA); *m* 2 Jan 1965, (Hazel) Lynne, da of Rev W E Gladstone-Millar, MC (d 1982), of Arbroath; 1 s (Martin b 1967), 1 da (Hilary b 1970); *Career* Flying Offr RAF 1952-54; BBC: studio mangr 1960, announcer 1961-67, producer 1967-85, ed and mangr Edinburgh 1985-; vice-chm Countryside Cmmn Scotland 1986- (memb 1982-); chm: Isle of May Bird Observatory 1980-85, Fair Isle Bird Observatory Tst 1983-84; pres Scottish Ornithologists' Club 1984-87; *Recreations* ornithology, hill walking, Arctic travel; *Style*— John Arnott, Esq; East Redford House, Redford Rd, Edinburgh EH13 0AS (☎ 031 441 3567)

ARNOTT, Sir (William) Melville; TD (and clasps 1944); s of Rev Henry Arnott (d 1952), of Edinburgh, and Jeanette Main Arnott; *b* 14 Jan 1909; *Educ* George Watson's Coll, Edinburgh Univ (MB, ChB, BSc, MD); *m* 1938, Dorothy Eleanor, er da of George Frederick Seymour Hill, of Edinburgh; 1 s; *Career* served WW II siege of Tobruk (despatches 1945); William Withering prof of med Birmingham Univ 1946-71, Br Heart Fndn prof cardiology Birmingham Univ 1971-74 (emeritus 1974-); Hon Lt-Col RAMC; MD Birmingham; Hon DSc: Edinburgh 1975, Chinese Univ of Hong Kong 1983; Hon LLD: Rhodesia 1976, Dundee 1976; FRCP, FRCPE, FRCP(C), FRCPath, FACP, FRSE; pres Br Lung Fndn 1984-87; kt 1971; *Clubs* Naval and Military; *Style*— Sir Melville Arnott, TD; 40 Carpenter Rd, Edgbaston, Birmingham B15 2JJ (☎ 021 440 2195)

ARNOTT, Prof Struther; s of Charles McCann, and Christina, *née* Struthers; *b* 25 Sept 1934; *Educ* Hamilton Acad, Glasgow Univ (BSc, PhD); *m* 11 June 1970, Greta Maureen, da of James Reginald Edwards, of Dudley; 1 s (Euan b 1973); *Career* res scientist MRC Biophysic Units King's Coll London 1960-70 (physics demonstrator 1960-67, dir postgrad studies in biophysics 1967-70); Purdue Univ Indiana USA 1970-86 (prof of biology 1970-, head of biological sciences 1980-86, vice-pres for res and dean of Graduate Sch 1980-86); Oxford Univ, sr visiting fell Jesus Coll Oxford 1980-81, Nuffield res fell Green Coll 1985-86; princ and vice-chllr St Andrews Univ 1986-; Guggenheim Memorial fell 1985; govr: Sedbergh Sch, Glenalmond Coll Perthshire; FRS, FRSE, FRSC, FIBiol; *Recreations* birdwatching, botanizing; *Clubs* Athenaeum, Caledonian, Royal and Ancient (St Andrews); *Style*— Prof Struther Arnott; University House, The Scores, St Andrews KY16 9AR (☎ 0334 72492); University of St Andrews, College Gate, St Andrews KY16 9AJ (☎ 0334 76161, fax (0334) 75851

ARONSON, Sheriff Hazel Josephine; da of Moses Aron Aronson, of Glasgow, and Julia Tobias; *b* 12 Jan 1946; *Educ* Glasgow HS for Girls, Glasgow Univ (LLB); *m* 17 Dec 1967, John Allan, s of Rev Dr Isaac Kenneth Cosgrove, DL, JP (d 1973), 1 s (Nicholas Joseph b 1972), 1 da (Jillian Abigail b 1970); *Career* advocate Scottish Bar 1968-79; sheriff of Lothian and Borders at Edinburgh 1983- (formerly sheriff of Glasgow and Strathkelvin 1979-83); *Recreations* walking, langlauf, opera; *Style*— Sheriff Hazel J Aronson; 14 Gordon Terrace, Edinburgh EH16 5OR (☎ 031 667 8955); The Sheriff Ct, Lawnmarket, Edinburgh (☎ 031 226 7181)

ARRAN, 9 Earl of; Sir Arthur Desmond Colquhoun Gore; 11 Bt (I 1662); also Viscount Sudley, Baron Saunders (both I 1758), and Baron Sudley (UK 1884); s of 8 Earl of Arran (d 1983), and Fiona, Countess of Arran, *qv*; *b* 14 July 1938; *Educ* Eton, Balliol Coll Oxford; *m* 1974, Eleanor, da of Bernard van Cutsem and Lady Margaret Fortescue, *qv*, da of 5 Earl Fortescue; 2 da (Lady Laura b 1975, Lady Lucy b 1976); *Heir* kinsman, Paul Annesley Gore, CMG, CVO, JP, *qv*; *Career* Nat Serv Gren Gds, commissioned; asst mangr Daily Mail 1972-73, md Clark Nelson 1973-74, asst gen mangr Daily and Sunday Express 1974, co-fndr Gore Publishing 1980; dir Waterstone & Co Ltd 1984-87; a lord-in-waiting (government whip) 1987; co-chm Children's Country Holidays Fund; *Recreations* tennis, golf, gardening; *Clubs* Turf, Beefsteak, Pratt's; *Style*— The Rt Hon the Earl of Arran; Crocker End House, Nettlebed, Henley-on-Thames, Oxon (☎ 0491 641659)

ARRAN, Fiona, Countess of; Fiona Bryde; da of Sir Ian Colquhoun, 7 Bt, KT, DSO, and Geraldine, da of Francis Tennant (2 s of Sir Charles Tennant, 1 Bt; bro of 1 Baron Glenconner); *m* 1937, 8 Earl of Arran (d 1983), journalist and broadcaster; 1 s (9 Earl of Arran, *qv*) and 1 s decd; *Career* first person to average 100 mph in offshore boat (Lake Windermere 1980), awarded Segrave Trophy for outstanding courage on water, land or in the air 1981; *Style*— The Rt Hon Fiona, Countess of Arran; Pimlico House, Hemel Hempstead, Herts

ARRINDELL, HE Sir Clement Athelston; GCMG (1984), GCVO (1985), QC (1984); s of George Ernest Arrindell, and Hilda Iona Arrindell (d 1975); *b* 16 April 1931; *Educ* Bradley Private Sch, Basseterre Boy's Elementary, St Kitts-Nevis GS; *m* 1967, Evelyn Eugenia, da of Michael Cornelius O'Loughlin (d 1934), of Basseterre, St Kitts, and his w Dulcie (d 1972); *Career* tres clerk Tres Dept St Kitts 1951-54; barr Lincoln's Inn 1958, practising 1958-66, dist magistrate 1966-72, chief magistrate 1972-78, puisne judge W Indies Assoc States Supreme Court 1978-81; govr St Kitts-Nevis 1981-83, govr-gen St Kitts-Nevis 1983-; kt 1982; *Recreations* gardening, piano playing, classical music; *Style*— HE Sir Clement Arrindell, GCMG, GCVO, QC; Government House, St Kitts, West Indies (☎ 2315, 2260)

ARROW, Kenneth Joseph; s of Harry I Arrow (d 1955), of NY, and Lillian, *née* Greenberg (d 1973); *b* 23 August 1921; *Educ* Townsend Harris HS, City Coll NY (BSc), Columbia Univ (MA, PhD); *m* 31 Aug 1947, Selma, da of Albert Schweitzer (d 1945); 2 s (David b 1962, Andrew b 1965); *Career* WWII serv Capt US Army Air Force 1942-46; res asst Cowles Cmmn for Econ Res 1947-49, asst prof Univ of Chicago 1948-49, prof Stanford Univ 1953-68 (assoc prof 1950-53, acting asst prof 1949-50), prof of econs Harvard 1968-74, James Bryan Conant Univ prof Harvard 1974-79, Joan Kenney prof of econs and prof of ops res Stanford Univ 1979-; courtesy fell Hoover Inst 1981-, fell Churchill Coll Cambridge (1963-64, 1970, 1973 and 1986); guest prof Inst for Advanced Study (Vienna) 1964 and 1970, pt/t prof Euro Univ Inst 1986, visiting prof MIT 1966; memb and chm: Advsy Bd Acad Cncl Stanford Univ, Faculty Senate Stanford Univ; staff Cncl of Econ Advsrs Exec Off of the President USA 1962-63; hon LLD: Chicago 1967, City Univ Ny 1972, Hebrew Univ Jerusalem 1975, Univ of Pennsylvania 1976; Dr Soc and Econ Scis Vienna 1971, DS Columbia 1973, Dr Soc Sci Yale 1974; Dr (hon): Univ Rene Descartes 1974, Univ d'Aix-Marseille III; Dr Pol Sci Helsinki 1976; DLitt Cambridge 1986; Order of the Rising Sun (2 class) Japan 1984, Nobel Meml Prize in Econ Sci 1972; *Books* Social Choice and Individual Values (1951, 1963), Aspects of the Theory of Risk-Bearing (1965), Essays in the Theory of Risk-Bearing (1971), The Limits of Organization (1974), Collected Papers, 6 Vol (1983-85), Books in collaboration: Studies in the Mathematical Theory of Inventory and Production (1958), Studies in Linear and Nonlinear Programming (1959), A Time Series Analysis of Interindustry Demands (1959), Public Investment, the Rate of Return, and Optimal Fiscal Policy (1970), Studies in Resource Allocation Processes (1977), Social Choice and Multicriterion Decision-Making (1986); *Recreations* hiking, reading, listening to music; *Style*— Kenneth Arrow, Esq; 580 Constanzo St, Stanford, CA 94305, USA (☎ 415 327 3957); Dept of Economics, Stanford Univ, Stanford, CA 94305, USA (☎ 415 723 9165, fax 415 725 5702)

ARROWSMITH, Anthony; s of Arthur Arrowsmith and Winifred, *née* McDonough; *b* 11 May 1945; *Educ* St Chad's Coll Wolverhampton (Dip CAM); *m* 4 May 1968, Yvonne Mary, da of George Brannon; 1 s (Aidan b 1970), 2 da (Alexa b 1973, Sian b 1982); *Career* dir & chief exec: Charles Barker Black & Gross Ltd 1976; chm Charles Barker Scotland Ltd 1986; dir: Charles Barker plc 1987, Charles Barker Manchester Ltd 1986, Charles Barker PR Manchester Ltd 1986; chm regional operations Charles Barker Group 1986- (dir 1983-); MIPA; *Style*— Anthony Arrowsmith, Esq; The Hollies, Histons Hill, Codsall, West Midlands, WV8 2ER (☎ 09074 3987, office ☎ 021 236 9501)

ARROWSMITH, Sir Edwin Porter; KCMG (1959, CMG 1950); s of Edwin Arrowsmith (d 1924), of Cheltenham, and Kathleen Eggleston, *née* Porter (d 1971); *b* 23 May 1909; *Educ* Cheltenham, Trinity Coll Oxford (MA); *m* 1936, Clondagh, da of Dr William G Connor (d 1931), of Cheltenham; 2 da; *Career* Colonial Serv: joined 1932, various dist posts in Bechuanaland Protectorate 1932-38, cmmr Turks and Caicos Islands BWI 1940-46, admin Dominica BWI 1946-52, resident cmmr Basutoland 1952-56, govr and C-in-C Falkland Islands 1957-64, high cmmr Br Antarctic Territory 1962-64; pres: Royal Cwlth Soc for Blind 1985 (vice pres 1970-85), Freshwater Biological Assoc 1977-83; memb cncl St Dunstan's 1965-; *Recreations* flyfishing; *Clubs* Flyfishers', Hurlingham, Royal Commonwealth Soc; *Style*— Sir Edwin Arrowsmith, KCMG; 25 Rivermead Ct, London SW6 3RU (☎ 01 736 4757)

ARROWSMITH, John Anthony (Tony); s of Robert Edmund Arrowsmith (d 1983), of North Shields, and Kathleen Mitchel, *née* Cooper (d 1964); *b* 16 Jan 1940; *Educ* Tynemouth GS; *m* 1962, Rosamond Catherine Cecilia (Ros), da of Patrick Eardley (d 1953), of Stoke on Trent; 3 s (Anthony Edmund, John Patrick, Ian Dominic), 1 da (Jacqueline Rose); *Career* md: Ellis Maintenance & Sons Ltd 1976-86, Ellis Manpower Ltd 1976- 86, Tylin CAE Ltd 1979-86; md and chief exec Ellis Mechanical Servs Ltd 1987-88, dir Corrall Montenay Ltd 1988, md Ellis Tylin Ltd 1988 (chief exec 1986-88); chm Exec Assoc of GB 1986-87 (dir 1985-88); memb Nat Sporting Club; MCIOB, MIPM, MIOD; *Recreations* golf; *Style—* Tony Arrowsmith, Esq; 86 Sandy Lane, Cheam, Surrey SM2 7EP (☎ 01 642 3460); Ellis Tylin Ltd, Tolworth Tower, Ewell Rd, Surbiton, Surrey (☎ 01 390 8911, fax 01 399 8914)

ARTHINGTON-DAVY, Humphrey Augustine; LVO (1977), OBE (1965); *b* 1920; *Educ* Eastbourne Coll, Trinity Coll Cambridge; *Career* Br high cmmr: Western Samoa 1973-77, Tonga 1973-80; ret from HM Dip Serv 1980; *Clubs* Naval and Military; *Style—* Humphrey Arthington-Davy, Esq, LVO, OBE; c/o Grindlays Bank, 13 St James's Sq, London SW1; c/o P O Box 56, Nuku'Alofa, Tonga, South Pacific

ARTHUR, Alan David; s of David Edward John Arthur, of 3 Newport Rd, Bedwas, Gwent, and Elizabeth Ann, *née* Howell; *b* 3 July 1949; *Educ* Bedwellty GS, Univ Coll of Wales, Aberystwyth (BSc); *Career* CA, joined Deloitte Haskins & Sells direct from Univ and worked in S Wales W Yorks and Zambia; ptnr in their int practice 1983-84; fndr and first md Bradford Enterprise Agency 1984-86; corporate fin dir Booth & Co CAs 1986-; FCA 1974, FCIArb 1987; *Recreations* work; *Clubs* Bradford; *Style—* Alan Arthur, Esq; 76 Hallowes Park Rd, Cullingworth BD13 5AR (☎ 0535 273074); Booth & Co, Prince William House, Clifton Villas, Bradford BD8 7BY (☎ 0274 497124, fax 0274 488074, telex CHACOM G 30C0)

ARTHUR, Allan James Vincent; MBE (1948), DL (Essex 1974); s of Col Sir Charles Gordon Arthur, MC, VD (d 1953), and Dorothy Grace (d 1981), da of Sir William Hoare Vincent, GCIE, KCSI; *b* 16 Sept 1915; *Educ* Rugby, Magdalene Coll Cambridge; *m* 1, 1940 (m dis 1948), Joan Deirdre, da of Charles Heape; m 2, 1949, Dawn Rosemary Everil, da of Col Francis C Drake, OBE, MC, DL (d 1976), of Harlow, Essex; 2 s, 2 da; *Career* Indian CS 1938-47, Sudan Political Serv 1949-54, J V Drake and Co Ltd Sugar Brokers 1954-60, Woodhouse Drake and Carey Ltd 1960-75 (chm 1972-75); High Sheriff Essex 1971-72, Mayor Chelmsford 1977-78, Vice-Lord-Lieut of Essex 1978-85; memb Cncl of Univ of Essex 1980-87; pres Old Rugbeian Soc 1982-84; *Recreations* swimming, shooting, gardening; *Clubs* Oriental, Hawks (Cambridge); *Style—* Allan Arthur, Esq, MBE, DL; Mount Maskall, Boreham, Chelmsford, Essex CM3 3HW (☎ 0245 467 776)

ARTHUR, Dowager Lady; Doris Fay; da of Joseph Wooding, JP, of Woodbury, Geraldine, NZ; *m* 24 March 1928, Sir George Malcolm Arthur, 4 Bt (d 1949); 1 s (Hon Sir Basil Arthur, Bt d 1985); 4 da; *Style—* Dowager Lady Arthur; 421 Waimea Rd, Wakatu, Nelson, New Zealand

ARTHUR, Hon Edward Alexander; s and h of 4 Baron Glenarthur; *b* 9 April 1973; *Style—* The Hon Edward Arthur

ARTHUR, Hon Emily Victoria; da of 4 Baron Glenarthur; *b* 1975; *Style—* The Hon Emily Arthur

ARTHUR, Prof Geoffrey Herbert; s of William Gwyn Arthur, of Cefn Llech, Llangibby, Gwent (d 1945), and Ethel Jessie Parry (d 1967); *b* 6 Mar 1916; *Educ* Abersychan Secdy Sch, Liverpool Univ (BVSc, MVSc), London Univ (FRCVS); *m* 22 Feb 1948, Lorna Isabel, da of Isaac Alec Simpson (d 1969), of Ranworth, Heswall, Ches; 4 s (Richard b 1950, Hugh b 1954, Charles b 1960, James b 1963), 1 da (Angela (Mrs Sheard) b 1948); *Career* lectr in veterinary med Liverpool Univ 1945-49, prof of veterinary obstetrics London Univ 1964-73, head of dept of surgery RVC 1972-73, prof of veterinary surgery Univ of Bristol 1974-79, clinical veterinary prof King Faisal Saudi Arabia 1980-83, regnl postgrad veterinary dean RCVS 1985; cncl memb Soc for the Protection of Animals in N Africa; former pres: Br Cattle Veterinary Assoc, Soc for the Study of Animal Breeding; former cncl memb: RCVS, Br Veterinary Assoc; *Books* Veterinary Reproduction and Obstetrics (fifth edn 1981); *Recreations* observing natural phenomena and experimenting, North African travel; *Style—* Prof Geoffrey Herbert; Fallodene, Stone Allerton, Axbridge, Somerset, BS26 2NH (☎ 0934 712 077)

ARTHUR, James Stanley; CMG (1977); s of Laurence Arthur (d 1970), and Catherine Jane, *née* Charleson, of Lerwick, Shetland Islands; *b* 3 Feb 1923; *Educ* Trinity Academy Edinburgh, Liverpool Univ (BSc); *m* 1950, Marion North; 2 s (Stephen, Charles), 2 da (Judith, Shelley); *Career* Scottish Educn Dept 1946-47, Dept of Educn and Sci 1947-66 (princ private sec to Min 1960-62); Foreign Office 1966-; Br high cmmr: Suva (Fiji) 1974-78 (res), Republic of Nauru 1977-78 (non-res), Bridgetown Barbados 1978-82 (res), Dominica 1978-82, St Lucia and St Vincent 1979-82, Grenada 1980-82, Antigua and Barbuda 1981-82 (all non-res); Br govt rep to WI Assoc States 1978-1982, ret 1983; Memb of Ct of Univ of Liverpool; *Recreations* music, golf; *Clubs* Royal Cwlth Soc (memb central cncl); *Style—* James Arthur, Esq, CMG; Moreton House, Longborough, Moreton-in-Marsh, Glos GL56 0QQ (☎ 0451 30774)

ARTHUR, Lt-Col John Reginald; OBE (1985); s of Col Lionel Francis Arthur, DSO, OBE (d 1952), of Yockley House, Camberley, Surrey, and Muriel Irene, *née* Tilley; *b* 25 June 1935; *Educ* Winchester; *m* 21 Dec 1965, Princess Valerie Isolde Mary de Mahe, da of Prince John Bryant Digby de Mahe, MBE; 2 s (Malcolm Ian Charles b 5 Sept 1969, John Benjamin George b 25 Nov 1971), 1 da (Miss Anneliese Mary Arthur b 8 March 1967); *Career* joined Scots Gds 1953, RMA Sandhurst 1954-55, cmmnd 1 Bn Scots Gds 1955, Adj Gds Depot Pirbright 1961-63, Staff Coll Camberley 1966, DAQMG HQ London District 1968-70, DAAG Regtl Adj Scots Gds 1971-73, 2 i/c 2 Bn Scots Gds 1973-74, GSO2 Mil Asst Off MOD 1974-75, Lt-Col 1976, GS01 directing staff Nigerian Staff Coll 1976-78, GS01 foreign liaison staff MOD 1978-81, project offr Br Army Equipment Exhibition 82 1981-82, S01 PS 12 (Army) MOD 1982-84, ret 1984; co sec Laurence Prust & Co Ltd 1986- (joined 1984); pres Berks and Bucks branch Scots Gds Assoc; *Recreations* golf, gardening, music, watching cricket; *Clubs* Cavalry and Guards, MCC, Izingari, Free Foresters, Berkshire GC, Royal St Georges GC, Hon Co of Edinburgh Golfers; *Style—* Lt-Col John Arthur, OBE; 27 Finsbury Sq, London EC2A 1LP (☎ 01 628 1111)

ARTHUR, His Hon Judge; John Rhys Arthur; DFC (1944); s of John Morgan Arthur, JP (d 1973), and Eleanor Arthur; *b* 29 April 1923; *Educ* Mill Hill Sch, Christ's Coll Cambridge (MA); *m* 1951, Joan Tremearne, da of Richard Pickering (d 1961); 2 s, 1 da; *Career* serv WWII Fl-Lt RAF; barr Inner Temple 1949, asst recorder Blackburn 1970, dep chm Lancs County QS 1970-71, recorder 1972-75, circuit judge 1975-; JP (Lancs) 1970; *Clubs* MCC, Old Millhillians, Athenaeum (Liverpool); *Style—* His Hon Judge Arthur, DFC; Orovales, Caldy, Wirral, Merseyside L48 1LP (☎ 051 625 8624)

ARTHUR, Lady; Margaret; da of late Thomas Arnold Woodcock, OBE, of Ashby de la Zouch; *b* 21 Dec 1924; *Educ* Cheltenham Ladies' Coll, Somerville Coll Oxford; *m* 1946, Sir Geoffrey George Arthur, KCMG (d 1984, dep under-sec of state FCO 1973-75, master of Pembroke Coll Oxford 1975-84); *Clubs* Univ Women's; *Style—* Lady Arthur; 26 Cunliffe Close, Oxford, OX2 7BL

ARTHUR, Hon Matthew Richard; 2 s of 3 Baron Glenarthur, OBE, DL, *qv*; *b* 6 Mar 1948; *Educ* Eton; *m* 1974, Veronica, yr da of Michael Hall, of Kilternan, Co Dublin; 1 s (Matthew Frederick Michael b 1981), 1 da (Jessica Mary b 1979); *Career* chiropractor; *Style—* The Hon Matthew Arthur; Bingfield East Quarter, Hallington, Newcastle upon Tyne NE19 2LH (☎ 043 472 219)

ARTHUR, Lt-Gen Sir (John) Norman (Stewart); KCB (1985); s of Col Evelyn Stewart Arthur (d 1963), of Montgomerie, Mauchline, Ayrshire, and Elizabeth Burnett-Stuart (d 1976); *b* 6 Mar 1931; *Educ* Eton, RMA Sandhurst; *m* 1960, Theresa Mary, da of Francis Archibald Hopkinson, of Dundas Farm, Elmsted, Kent; 1 s (Simon b 1967), 1 da (Camilla b 1962), 1 s decd; *Career* cmmnd Royal Scots Greys 1951, CO Royal Scots Dragoon Gds 1972-74 (despatches 1974), 7 Armd Bde 1976-77, GOC 3 Armd Division 1980-82, dir Personal Servs (Army) MOD 1983-85, GOC Scotland and Govr Edinburgh Castle 1985-88, Col Cmdt Mil Provost Staff Corps 1983-88, Col The Royal Scots Dragoon Guards (Carabiniers and Greys) 1985-, Col 205 (Scottish) Gen Hosp RAMC (V) 1988-; offr Royal Co of Archers (Queen's Body Guard for Scotland); memb Br Olympic Team (equestrian three-day event) 1960; vice-pres Riding for the Disabled Edinburgh and Lowlands 1988-, chm Army Benevolent Fund Scotland 1988-, pres Scottish Conservation Projects 1989-; *Recreations* country pursuits, reading, field sports; *Clubs* Cavalry and Guards', Caledonian Hunt; *Style—* Lt-Gen Sir Norman Arthur, KCB; (☎ 055-663-227)

ARTHUR, Robin Anthony; s of Ronald Arthur, of Folkestone, Kent, and Flore Alzire, *née* Parmentier; *b* 15 August 1947; *Educ* Cambridge GS, London Univ (External); *m* Oct 1968 (sep 1986), Elizabeth Mary; 1 s (Richard b 1980), 1 da (Lucy b 1982); *Career* barrister; md: Parmentier-Arthur Financial & Valuation Services Ltd 1975-, Cambridge Estates Ltd 1982-; *Recreations* rugby, walking, the arts; *Style—* Robin A Arthur, Esq; The Manor House, The Green, Hilton, Huntingdon, Cambridgeshire; 7 The Waits, St Ives, Huntingdon, Cambs (☎ 0480 65522)

ARTHUR, Roland William; s of William Arthur (d 1976), and Olive, *née* Hayward; *b* 21 Dec 1938; *Educ* Monmouth Sch, St Catharines Coll Cambridge (MA); *m* 1 May 1965, Margot Frances, da of Ernest William Anstey (d 1988); 1 s (Robin b 1968), 1 da (Justine b 1967, Sarah b 1962); *Career* admitted slr 1964; St David's Investmt Tst plc: sec 1986, dir 1988; memb Law Soc; *Recreations* squash, golf; *Style—* Roland Arthur, Esq; Llandevaud Ctd, Llandevaud, Newport, Gwent; Queens Chambers, 2 North St, Newport, Gwent (☎ 0633 244233, fax 0633 246453)

ARTHUR, Sandra, Lady; Sandra Colleen Arthur; da of William Boaz, of Whangarei, New Zealand; *m* 1983, as his 2 w, Hon Sir Basil Arthur, 5 Bt (d 1985, MP (Lab) Timaru, New Zealand 1962-85); *Style—* Sandra, Lady Arthur; Grene Gables, No 3 Rd, Seadown, Timaru, New Zealand

ARTHUR, Sir Stephen John; 6 Bt (UK 1841), of Upper Canada; s of Hon Sir Basil Arthur, 5 Bt, MP (d 1985); *b* 1 July 1953; *Educ* Timaru Boys' HS, Seadown Primary Sch; *m* (m dis), Carolyn Margaret, da of Burnie Lawrence Diamond, of Cairns, Qld, Australia; 1 s , 2 da (Amanda b 1975, Melanie b 1976); *Heir* s, Benjamin Nathan Arthur b 27 March 1979; *Style—* Sir Stephen Arthur, Bt; Grene Gables, Seadown, No 3 Rd, Timaru, New Zealand

ARTHUR, Terence; s of William Gordon Arthur (d 1971), of West Hartlepool, and Dorothy, *née* Baker; *b* 5 Sept 1940; *Educ* West Hartlepool GS, Univ of Manchester (BSc), Univ of Cambridge (Dip Statistics); *m* 1, 15 May 1965 (m dis 1983), Valerie Ann Marie, da of Stephen Daniels, of Suffolk; 1 s (Richard b 1970), 2 da (Louise b 1966, Frances b 1968); m 2, 25 Nov 1983, Mary Clare,*née* Austick;; *Career* asst sec Equity & Law Life Assur Soc 1967 (joined 1963), ptnr Duncan C Fraser & Co Actuaries 1969-76 (joined 1967), T G Arthur Hargrave Actuaries 1976- (fndr 1976); memb: cncl Inst Actuaries 1977-87 (tres 1985-86), Co Actuaries; int Capt rugby football 1966; Freeman City of London; FIA 1966, FIS 1975, Fell Inst Pensions Mgmnt 1977; *Books* 95 per cent is Crap-A Plain Man's Guide to British Politics (1975); *Clubs* Birmingham Area Sports Internationalists, Wig and Pen; *Style—* Terence Arthur, Esq; 41 Calthorpe Rd, Edgebaston, Birmingham B15 1ST

ARTHURTON, Hon Mrs (Phillipa Susan); *née* Mills; yr da of 2 Viscount Mills (d 1988); *b* 25 Feb 1950; *m* 1970, Russell Scott Arthurton; *Style—* The Hon Mrs Arthurton; 96 Pannal Ash Rd, Harrogate, N Yorks

ARTUS, Ronald Edward; s of Ernest Edward Artus (d 1980), and Doris Isobel Goddard; *b* 8 Oct 1931; *Educ* Sir Thomas Rich's Sch Gloucester, Magdalen Coll Oxford (MA); *m* 1, 1956 (m dis 1987), Brenda Margaret, *née* Touche; 3 s (Colin, Alan, Philip), 1 da (Lucy); m 2, 1987, Dr Joan Mullaney; *Career* Prudential 1954-: head econ intelligence 1958-71, sr asst mangr 1973-75, jt sec and chief investmt mangr 1975-82; dir and dep chm: Prudential Assur Co Ltd, dir and chm: Prudential Portfolio Mangrs Ltd, Prudential Property Services Ltd, Prutec Ltd; dir Celltech Ltd; gp chief investmt mangr Prudential Corpn 1982- (exec dir 1984-); hon fell Soc of Investmt Analysts; memb: Accounting Standards Ctee 1982-86, City Capital Markets Ctee 1982, CBI City Indust Task Force; *Recreations* music, English watercolours; *Clubs* MCC; *Style—* Ronald E Artus, Esq; 142 Holborn Bars, London EC1N 2NH (☎ 01 405 9222)

ARUNDEL AND BRIGHTON, Bishop (RC) of 1977-; Rt Rev Cormac Murphy-O'Connor; s of George Patrick Murphy-O'Connor (d 1960), of 17 Parkside Rd, Reading, Berks, and Ellen Theresa, *née* Cuddigan (d 1971); *b* 24 Aug 1932; *Educ* Prior Park Coll Bath, The Ven English Coll Rome, Gregorian Univ Rome (PhL, STL); *Career* ordained to RC Priesthood 1956; parish priest Portswood Southampton 1970-71, rector Venerable Eng Coll Rome 1971-77; first chm Bishops' Ctee for Europe 1979-82, RC co-chm of Anglo-Roman Catholic Int Cmmn (ARCIC-II) 1983-; chm TVS Religious Advsrs Panel 1985-; *Recreations* walking, music (pianist), reading; *Style—* The Rt Rev the Bishop of Arundel; St Joseph's Hall, Storrington, Pulborough, W Sussex RH20 4HE (☎ 090 66 2172)

ARUNDEL AND SURREY, Earl of; Edward William Fitzalan-Howard; s and h of 17 Duke of Norfolk, KG, CB, CBE, MC, DL; *b* 2 Dec 1956; *Educ* Ampleforth, Lincoln Coll Oxford; *m* 27 June 1987, Georgina Susan, yr da of John Temple Gore; 1 s (Henry

Miles, Lord Maltravers b 3 Dec 1987); *Career* chm Sigas Ltd; *Recreations* motor racing, skiing, shooting; *Style*— Earl of Arundel and Surrey; Arundel Castle, Arundel, Sussex (☎ 0903 882173); 29 Montpelier Place, London SW7 (☎ 01 581 1686); Scar House, Arkengarthdale, N Yorks (☎ 0748 84726)

ARUNDELL, Hon Richard John Tennant; s and h of 10 Baron Talbot of Malahide, *qv*; *b* 28 Mar 1957; *Style*— The Hon Richard Tennant??? *Style*— The Hon Richard Tennant; Park Gate Farm, Donhead, Shaftesbury, Dorset (☎ 074 788 423)

ARWYN, Hon Arwyn Hugh Davies; only s of Baron Arwyn, Life Peer (d 1978), by his 2 w, Baroness Arwyn, *qv*; *b* 9 April 1949; *Educ* King Edward VI Sch Bath, Truro Sch, Univ of Wales, Sheffield Univ; *Career* barr Gray's Inn 1972, int lawyer, co dir; *Recreations* sailing, golf; *Clubs* Reform, Royal Fowey Yacht, House of Lords Yacht; *Style*— The Hon Arwyn H D Arwyn; Ewart, Ashley Rd, Bathford, Avon

ARWYN, Baroness; Beatrix Emily Bassett; da of Capt Francis Henry Organ, of St Austell, Cornwall; *m* 1946, as his 2 w, Baron Arwyn (Life Peer, d 1978); 1 s, 2 step da; *Style*— The Rt Hon the Lady Arwyn; Ormonde, Lostwithiel, Cornwall

ASAI, Kotaro; s of Mitsue Asai, and Nakayo, *née* Takayama; *b* 2 Jan 1942; *Educ* Tokyo Univ; *m* 4 May 1973, Kyko, da of Toshio Hirohata; 1 s (Ryuichi b 18 Dec 1976) 1 da (Safo b 18 March 1974); *Career* joined Yasuda Tst & Banking Co Tokyo 1965 (chief fund mangr for overseas investment 1979-86, dep gen mangr capital markets dept 1986); md Yasuda Trust Europe 1986-; memb Japanese Securities Analyst Assoc; *Recreations* go game; *Style*— K Asai, Esq; 10 Pilgrims Lane, Hampstead, London NW3 (☎ 01 433 1279); 1 Liverpool St, London EC2 (☎ 01 256 6188, fax 01 374 0831, telex 915 192 Yield G)

ASBURY, Capt John; CBE (1977); s of John Edwards Asbury (d 1979), of Bristol, and Hilda Mary Asbury, *née* Brotherston; *b* 22 Mar 1921; *Educ* Bristol GS; *m* 9 Aug 1948, Iona Margaret Amelia, da of Lt W G C Stokes, DSC, RN (d 1975); 3 da (Judith b 1951, Sarah b 1954, Jessica b 1960); *Career* RN AB 1940, cmmnd Pay/Sub Lt RNVR 1941, staff of Vice-Adm Cmd N Atlantic 1941-42, staff Naval Cmdr Expeditianary Force (Algiers) 1942-44, MID 1943, HMS Erebus at Normandy 1944-45, mine clearance Home Waters and Far East with 11 m/s flotilla 1945-46; cmmnd Permanent List RN 1947, Capt 1966, Cdre Sec to Int Mil Staff of NATO 1973-75; bursar Marlborough Coll 1976-85, govr Wellington Coll Berks 1985-; chm United Services RFC 1968-73; *Recreations* gardening; *Style*— Capt John Asbury; Beechcroft, Cross Lane, Marlborough, Wilts SN8 1LA (☎ 0672 54271)

ASCOTT, Robert Henry Charles; s of James Robert Ascott, of London, and Joan Daisy, *née* Le Feuvre; *b* 7 Mar 1943; *Educ* St Paul's, Trinity Coll Cambridge (MA), Admin Staff Coll Henley; *m* 15 May 1976, Madeleine Olivia, da of Ronald Oliver Blench (d 1975); *Career* pres EMI-Capitol de Mexico, SA de CV 1975-79, md Emidata 1979-82, gp sr exec Intermed 1982-84; bursar Univ of Reading 1984; *Recreations* coaching rowing, choral conducting, singing, organ playing, foreign languages; *Clubs* Leander; *Style*— Robert H C Ascott, Esq; 114 High St, Burbage, Marlborough, Wilts; Univ of Reading, Whiteknights, Reading, Berks

ASFA WOSSEN HAILE SELLASSIE, HIH Meredazmatch; GCMG (Hon 1965), GCVO (Hon 1930), GBE (Hon 1932); Crown Prince of Ethiopia 1930-; eldest s and h of HIM the late Emperor Haile Sellassie of Ethiopia, KG (d 1975), and HIM the late Empress Menen (d 1962); *b* 27 July 1916; *Educ* private, Liverpool Univ; *m* 1, 9 May 1932 (m dis 1944), Walatta Israel, da of HH Prince Ras Seyum Mangasha, and widow of Dejazmatch Gabre Sellassie; 1 da (decd); m 2, 8 April 1945, Medfariach Worq, da of Maj-Gen Abebe Damtew; 1 s, 3 da; *Heir* s, HIH Prince Zara Yaqob, b 15 Aug 1953; *Career* fought in Italo-Ethiopian War 1935-36; Grand Cross, Légion d'Honneur (France), Order of Leopold (Belgium), Order of the Netherlands, Order of Rising Sun (Japan), Order of White Elephant (Siam); *Style*— HIH Asfa Wossen Haile Sellassie, GCMG, GCVO, GBE; 82 Portland Place, London W1

ASH, Douglas Terence; s of Sydney Alexander Ash and Doreen Victoria, *née* Gornall; *b* 19 Dec 1947; *Educ* Wallington GS, Nottingham Univ (BA), Harvard Business Sch (MBA); *m* 19 Aug 1972, Rhona Helen, da of Harold James Bennett (d 1978), former vice-pres Rotary Internat; 1 s (Laurence b 1981), 3 da (Belinda 1975, Isobel b 1976, Amelia b 1981); *Career* chm and chief exec European Home Product plc, dir of various EHP subsidiaries throughout Europe; *Recreations* rugby football; *Style*— Douglas Ash, Esq; Cherry Croft, Kingwood Common, Henley on Thames, Oxon R69 5NA (☎ 04917 234); European Home Products plc, John Scott House, Bracknell, Berks RG12 1JB (☎ 0344 412512)

ASH, Prof Eric Albert; CBE (1982); s of Walter J Ash (d 1970), and Dorothea Cecily, *née* Schwarz (d 1974); *b* 31 Jan 1928; *Educ* Univ Coll Sch, Imperial Coll of Science & Technol (BSc, DIC, PhD, DSc); *m* 30 May 1954, Clare Mosher, *née* Babb; 5 da (Gillian Carol (Mrs Gillian Barr) b 1958, Carolyn Dian b 1960, Lucy Amanda b 1962, Emily Jane b 1966, Jennifer Dian (twin) b 1966); *Career* res fell Stanford Univ California 1952-54, res engr Standard Telecommunication Laboratories 1954-63, Pender prof and head of dept electronic and electrical engrg UCL 1980-85 (previously sr lectr, reader, prof) Rector Imperial Coll of Science & Technol 1985-; bd memb Br Telecom 1987-; tstee: Sci Museum 1988-, Wolfson Fndn 1988-; hon degrees from: Leicester Univ 1988, Edinburgh Univ 1988, INPG Grenoble 1987, Aston Univ 1987, Poly Univ New York 1988; FEng 1978, FRS 1977; memb: IOD, ABRC; *Recreations* reading, music, swimming, skiing; *Style*— Prof Eric Ash, CBE; 170 Queen's Gate, London SW7 5HF; Imperial Coll, London SW7 2AZ (☎ 01 589 5111 ext 3000, fax 01 584 7596)

ASH, Peter Edward; s of Albert Edward Ash (d 1945), and Mary Ellen Hadley; *b* 26 Dec 1924; *Educ* Henry Thornton Sch; *m* 16 Sept 1950, Audrey Edna, da of Bernard Joseph Betts (d 1957); 1 s (Nicolas b 1954), 1 da (Judith b 1952); *Career* Sub-Lt (A) RNVR 1943-46; admitted slr 1949; sr ptnr Wright Webb Syrett 1982-; legal advsr Music Publishers Assoc 1962-; *Recreations* reading, badminton, crosswords; *Style*— Peter E Ash, Esq; 38 Sutton Lane, Banstead, Surrey (☎ 0737 358105); 10 Soho Square, London W1 (☎ 01 439 3111, fax 01 434 1520, telex 22276)

ASH, Rear Adm Walter William Hector; CB (1962); s of late Hector Sidney Ash (d 1953), of Portsmouth, Hants, and Mabel Jessy Ash; *b* 2 May 1906; *Educ* City and Guilds Engrg Coll Kensington, RNC Greenwich; *m* 1932, Louisa Adelaide, da of late William Salt, of Jarrow-upon-Tyne; 3 da; *Career* chartered electrical engr; asst electrical engr Admiralty 1932-37, electrical engr Admiralty 1937-39, Fleet electrical engr staff CIC Mediterranean 1939-40, supt electrical engr Admiralty 1940-45 and HM Dockyard Hong Kong 1945-48, Cdr RN HMS Montclare 1950-51, Capt RN Admiralty 1951-54, electrical engr mangr HM Dockyard Devonport 1954-58, chm IEE S W Sub-Centre 1957-58, Rear-Adm 1960, Ship Design Directorate Admty 1959-63; ADC to HM The Queen 1958-60; CEng, FIEE; *Recreations* music (piano and organ); *Style*— Rear Adm Walter Ash, CB; 4 Vavasour House, North Embankment, Dartmouth, Devon TQ6 9PW (☎: 08043 4630)

ASH, Rear Adm William Noel; CB (1977), MVO (1959); s of H Arnold Ash, (d 1955), of Chorleywood, Herts; *b* 6 Mar 1921; *Educ* Merchant Taylors'; *m* 1951, Pamela, da of Harry Cornwall Davies (d 1973), of Hawkes Bay, New Zealand; 1 s, 1 da; *Career* RN 1938, HM Yacht Britannia 1955-58, Capt 1965, Canadian Nat Defence Coll 1965-66, Staff of SACLANT (NATO) 1966-69, Cabinet Office 1969-71, Cmd HMS Ganges 1971-73, Rear-Adm 1974, Dir of Service Intelligence 1974-77, ret 1977; sec to Defence Press and Broadcasting Ctee 1980-; *Clubs* Roy Cwlth Soc; *Style*— Rear Adm William Ash, CB, MVO; 7 Wonford Rd, Exeter, Devon EX2 4LF (☎ 58751)

ASHBOURNE, 4 Baron (UK 1885); (Edward) Barry (Greynville) Gibson; s of Vice Adm 3 Baron Ashbourne, CB, DSO, JP, of Liphook, Hants (d 1983), and Reta, Baroness Ashbourne, *qv*; *b* 28 Jan 1933; *Educ* Rugby; *m* 25 March 1967, Yvonne Georgina, da of Mrs Flora Ham; 3 s (Hon Charles b 1967, Hon Rodney b 1970, Hon Patrick b 1977); *Heir* s, Hon Edward Charles d'Olier Gibson b 31 Dec 1967; *Career* RN 1951-72, Lt-Cdr, cmd HMS Crofton 1963-64, RN Staff Coll 1965; stockbroker 1972-79, investmt mktg 1979-88; *Recreations* tennis, sailing, creative gardening; *Style*— The Rt Hon the Lord Ashbourne; 107 Sussex Rd, Petersfield, Hants GU31 4LB (☎ 0703 64636)

ASHBOURNE, Reta, Baroness; Reta Frances Manning; er da of Ernest Manning Hazeland, of Hong Kong; *b* 2 Mar 1903; *m* 1929, Vice Adm 3 Baron Ashbourne, CB, DSO (d 1983); 1 s (4 Baron, *qv*), 1 da; *Style*— The Rt Hon Reta, Lady Ashbourne; 56 Chiltley Way, Midhurst Rd, Liphook, Hants

ASHBROOD, Kate Jessie; da of John Benjamin Ashbrook, of Denham Village, Bucks, and Margaret, *née* Balfour; *b* 1 Feb 1955; *Educ* High March Sch, Benenden, Exeter Univ (BSc); *Career* sec Dartmoor Preservation Assoc 1981-84, gen sec Open Spaces Soc 1984-; memb: exec ctee Cncl for Nat Parks, gen cncl Cncl for Protection of Rural England, nat exec ctee Ramblers' Assoc (footpath sec Bucks and W Middx Area); *Books* Severnside A Guide to Family Walks (The Southern Quantocks 1977), The Walks of SE England (contrib 'A Walk round Denham 1975), Common Place No More, Common Land in the 1980s (1983), Make for the Hills (1983), Our Common Right (1987), Open Space (ed 1984-); *Recreations* walking, campaigning for access to countryside, music; *Style*— Miss Kate Ashbrook; Telfer's Cottage, Turville, Henley-on-Thames RG9 6QL (☎ 0491 63396); Open Spaces Society, 25A Bell St, Henley-on-Thames RG9 2BA (☎ 0491 573 535)

ASHBROOK, 10 Viscount (I 1751); Desmond Llowarch Edward Flower; KCVO (1977), MBE (1945), DL (Cheshire 1949); also Baron Castle Durrow (I 1733); s of 9 Viscount Ashbrook, DL (d 1936), and Gladys, da of Gen Sir George Higginson, GCB, GCVO; *b* 9 July 1905; *Educ* Eton, Balliol Coll Oxford; *m* 8 Nov 1934, Elizabeth, sis of Lady Newton (w of 4 Baron Newton) and da of Capt John Egerton-Warburton (whose f, Piers, was gn of Sir John and Sir Philip Egerton, 8 and 9 Bts, and whose m was Hon Antoinette Saumarez, da of 3 Baron de Saumarez; Piers was ggn of Sir Peter Warburton, 5 and last of the Warburton Baronetcy, and last male Warburton to own the Arley estate) by his w Hon Lettice Legh, JP, eld da of 2 Baron Newton); 2 s, 1 da; *Heir* s, Hon Michael Flower; *Career* Maj RA WW II; JP Cheshire 1946-67, Vice-Lieut 1961-67; memb Cncl Duchy of Lancaster 1957-77; former chartered accountant; chm Country Gentlemen's Assoc 1955-62; *Style*— The Rt Hon the Viscount Ashbrook, KCVO, MBE, DL

ASHBROOKE, (Philip) Biden Derwent; s of Philip Ashbrooke (d 1941), of Doveray Place, Porlock, Somerset, and Gladys Derwent, *née* Moger (d 1948); *b* 23 August 1925; *Educ* Westminster, St John's Coll Cambridge (MA) ; *m* 23 Oct 1954, Veronica Philippa, da of Eudo Philip Joseph Stourton (d 1975; ggs of 19 Baron Stourton), of La Grande Maison, St John, Jersey, CI; 1 s (Auberon b 1956), 1 da (Sophia b 1959, Viscountess Stormont, see Earl of Mansfield and Mansfield); *Career* joined Army 1943, Capt 8 Kings Royal Irish Hussars 1946-47, Capt City of London Yeomanry (Rough Riders) 1950-56, ADC to H E The Govr of Kenya 1946-47; barr Gray's Inn 1950; *Clubs* Boodle's; *Style*— Biden Ashbrooke, Esq; La Grande Maison, St John, Jersey, CI

ASHBURNHAM, Capt Sir Denny Reginald; 12 Bt (E 1661), of Broomham, Sussex; s of Sir Fleetwood Ashburnham, 11 Bt (d 1953); co-heir to Barony of Grandison (abeyant since 1328); *b* 24 Mar 1916; *m* 1946, Mary Frances, da of Maj Robert Pascoe Mair, of Wick, Udimore, Sussex; 1 s, 2 da; *Heir* gs, James Fleetwood Ashburnham b 17 Dec 1979 (s of John Anchitel Fleetwood Ashburnham (b 1951, d 1981) by his w Corinne, da of D W J O'Brien, of Chelwood Farm, Nutley, E Sussex); *Career* Capt S Staffs Regt; *Style*— Capt Sir Denny Ashburnham, Bt; Little Broomham, Guestling, Hastings, E Sussex

ASHBURTON, 6 Baron (UK 1835); Alexander Francis St Vincent Baring; KG (1969), KCVO (1961), JP (Hants 1951), DL (1973); s of 5 Baron Ashburton (d 1938), by 1 w Hon Mabel Hood (da of 4 Viscount Hood); *b* 7 April 1898; *Educ* Eton, Sandhurst; *m* 17 Nov 1924, Hon Doris Mary Thérèse Harcourt (d 1981), da of 1 Viscount Harcourt; 2 s; *Heir* s, Hon Sir John Baring, *qv*; *Career* Lt Scots Greys 1917-23, AAF 1939, Gp Capt 1944, ret; CC Hants 1945, CA 1955; md Baring Bros 1928-62 (dir to 1968), former dir Pressed Steel Co and Alliance Assurance; tstee: King George's Jubilee Tst 1949-68, Chantrey Bequest 1963-86; chm: Hants & IOW Police Authy 1967-71, Hampshire Police Authy 1967-71; pres E Wessex TA 1968-70, govr King Edward VII Hosp Fund for London 1971-5 (former tres), receiver-gen to Duchy of Cornwall 1961-74; Vice-Lieut Hants and IOW 1951-60, Lord Lieut and Custos Rotulorum 1960-73; High Steward of Winchester 1967-78; KStJ 1960; *Style*— The Rt Hon Lord Ashburton, KG, KCVO, JP, DL; Itchen Stoke House, Alresford, Hants SO24 0QU (☎ 096 273 732479)

ASHBY, Anne Mary; *née* Griffiths; da of George Griffiths (d 1942), and Mary Griffiths (d 1965); *b* 2 May 1938; *Educ* Priory Sch Shrewsbury; *m* 26 May 1956, John Ashby; 2 s (Mark b 1961, Edward b 1968), 1 da (Louise b 1971); *Career* SRN Royal Postgrad Hosp 1961, state registered midwife Hammersmith Hosp; co-fndr Womens Aid Ltd 1971 (dir 1971-83); chm Westminster Womens Aid 1987-, fieldworker Family Housing Assoc; named a Woman of the Year 1987; *Recreations* swimming, walking; *Clubs* Women of the Year Assoc, Network; *Style*— Mrs Anne Ashby; 12 Reynolds Place, Queens Rd, Richmond, Surrey (☎ 01 940 3683)

ASHBY, David Glynn; MP (C) North-West Leicestershire 1983-; s of Robert M Ashby and Isobel A, *née* Davidson; *b* 14 May 1940; *Educ* Royal GS High Wycombe,

Bristol Univ (LLB); *m* 1965, Silvana Morena; 1 da; *Career* barr Gray's Inn 1963; in practice SE Circuit; memb Hammersmith Borough Cncl 1968-71; memb GLC for W Woolwich 1977-81, ILEA 1977-81; *Recreations* gardening, skiing, music; *Clubs* Hurlingham; *Style—* David Ashby, Esq, MP; 29 Church Street, Appleby Magna, Leics; 132 West Hill, London SW15 2UE

ASHBY, Eric; s of Albert Ashby (d 1932), of Southsea, and (Dorothy) May, *née* Stoner (d 1975); *b* 19 Jan 1918; *Educ* St Judes Church Sch Southsea Hants; *m* 25 Sept 1975, Eileen, da of Hubert Charles Batchelor (d 1982), of Salisbury, Wilts; *Career* pioneer in filming of shy British animals, started Wildlife photography 1930; TV programmes incl: The Unknown Forest (1961), The Silent Watcher (1961), A Hares Life (1963), A Forest Diary (1963), Ponies of the New Forest (1964), Badgers (1966), The Best Of Eric Ashby (1967), At Home With Foxes (1968), The Living Forest (1970), Cranborne Chase (1973), The Private Life of the Fox (1975), At Home With Badgers (1978), The Year of the Deer (1977), Roadside View (1980), Eye on the Forest (1984), Through Two Cameras (1989), Badger Cottage (1989); memb: New Forest Badger Gp, New Forest Assoc, Hants and IOW Naturalists Tst, CPRE; vice pres Conservative Ant; Hunt Cncl; *Books* The Secret Life of the New Forest (1989); *Recreations* conservation of the precarious New Forest wildlife, caring for rescued foxes; *Style—* Eric Ashby, Esq; Badger Cottage, Linwood, Ringwood, Hampshire BH24 3QT

ASHBY, Baron (Life Peer UK 1973), of Brandon, Suffolk; Eric Ashby; s of Herbert Charles Ashby (d 1933), of Shortlands, Kent, and Helena Chater; *b* 24 August 1904; *Educ* City of London Sch, Imperial Coll of Science London U (DSc); *m* 1931, Elizabeth Helen Margaret, da of Francis Farries (d 1953), of Castle Douglas, Scotland; 2 s; *Career* prof of Botany Sydney Univ Australia 1938-46, chm Aust Nat Research Cncl 1940-42, chm Professorial Bd Sydney U 1942-44, tstee Aust Museum 1942-46, cnsllr and chargé d'affaires at Aust Legation Moscow USSR 1945-46; Harrison prof of botany and dir of Botanical Labs Manchester Univ 1946-50; memb: advsy cncl scientific policy 1950-53, advsy cncl scientific and industl research 1954-60; chm Scientific Grants Ctee DSIR 1955-56; vice-chllr Queen's Univ Belfast 1950-59, master Clare Coll Cambridge 1959-75 (fellow 1958, life fell 1975-), vice-chm Assoc of Univs of Br Cwlth 1959-61, v-chllr Cambridge U 1967-69, chllr Queen's U Belfast 1970-83; sits as memb of SDP in House of Lords; Hon LLD, Hon ScD, Hon DSc, Hon DLitt, HonDPhil, Hon DCL, Hon DHL; OStJ 1956, Order of Andrés Bello, Venezuela 1971(1 Class); hon fell Imp Coll of Science, hon foreign memb American Acad of Arts and Sciences; FRS, Hon FRSE, Hon FRIC; *Books* author of books on biology, environmental politics, and higher education; *Recreations* music; *Style—* The Rt Hon the Lord Ashby; 22 Eltisley Ave, Cambridge (☎ 0223 356216)

ASHBY, Prof the Hon Michael Farries; er s of Baron Ashby (Life Peer); *b* 20 Nov 1935; *Educ* Campbell Coll Belfast, Queens' Coll Cambridge (MA, PhD); *m* 1962, Maureen, da of James Stewart, of White House, Montgomery, Powys; 2 s, 1 da; *Career* asst prof Harvard Univ 1965-69, prof: Metallurgy Harvard Univ 1969-73, Engineering Materials Cambridge Univ 1973-, ed *Acta Metallurgica* 1974-; FRS; *Books* Engineering Materials (parts 1 and 2), Deformation-Mechanism Maps, The Structure and Properties of Cecllular Solids; *Recreations* music, design; *Style—* Prof the Hon Michael Ashby; 51 Maids Causeway, Cambridge CB5 8DE

ASHBY, Hon Peter; yr s of Baron Ashby, FRS (Life Peer), *qv*; *b* 1937; *Educ* Queen's Univ Belfast (MB, BCh, MD); *m* 1967, Moya, da of Surgn Rear Adm Maurice Henry Adams, CB, of Canberra, Rock, Cornwall; *Career* prof at Toronto Univ; *Style—* The Hon Peter Ashby; 42 Bennington Hts Drive, Toronto, Ontario M4G 1A6, Canada

ASHBY, (Alfred) Walter; s of Thomas Ashby (d 1965), and Edith, *née* Nicholes (d 1961); *b* 14 Oct 1909; *Educ* Berkhamsted Sch; *m* 16 Sept 1944, Doreen, da of William Thomas Hiscock Jones (d 1941); 2 s (Michael b 1946, James b 1951), 1 da (Penny b 1949); *Career* served HG WWII; dir Ivinghoe Lime Co 1961, AW Ashby & Sons; farmer 860 acres, former rural dist cncllr, parish cncllr, church warden Ivinghoe Church; memb: Country Landowners Assoc, Country Gentlemen's Assoc, Bucks Water Bd; tstee Ivinghoe Poors Land Charity, govr RAS; *Recreations* hunting, shooting; *Style—* Waller Ashby, Esq; Ivinghoe Aston Farm, nr Leighton Buzzard, Beds (☎ Eaton Bray 220247)

ASHCOMBE, 4 Baron (UK 1892); Henry Edward Cubitt; s of 3 Baron Ashcombe (d 1962) by his 1 w, Sonia, da of Lt-Col Hon George Keppel, MVO, (3 s of 7 Earl of Albemarle); *b* 31 Mar 1924; *Educ* Eton; *m* 1, 12 Sept 1955 (m dis 1968), Ghislaine, da of Cornelius Dresselhuys, of Long Island and formerly w of late Maj Denis Alexander (afterwards 6 Earl of Caledon); m 2, 1973 (m dis 1979), Hon Virginia Carrington, yr da of 6 Baron Carrington; m 3, 1979, Elizabeth, da of Dr Henry Chipps, of Lexington, Kentucky, and widow of Mark Dent-Brocklehurst, of Sudeley Castle, Glos; *Heir* kinsman, Mark Cubitt, *qv*; *Career* served WW II RAF; consul-gen for Monaco in London 1961-68, chm Cubitt Estates Ltd; *Clubs* White's; *Style—* The Rt Hon the Lord Ashcombe; Sudeley Castle, Winchcombe, Cheltenham, Glos GL54 5JD; Flat 6, 53 Drayton Gardens, London SW10 9RX

ASHCOMBE, Virginia, Baroness; Hon Virginia; *née* Carington; da of 6 Baron Carrington; *b* 23 June 1946; *m* 1973 (m dis 1979), 4 Baron Ashcombe; *Style—* Virginia, Lady Ashcombe; 5 Rutland Gate Mews, London SW7 (☎ 01 584 3678); The Manor House, Bledlow, nr Aylesbury, Bucks (☎ 084 44 3499)

ASHCROFT, George Denman; s of Frederick Ashcroft (d 1941), of Manchester, and Ethel Louise Gertrude, *née* Morgan-Sudlow; *b* 22 Oct 1909; *Educ* Manchester HS of Commerce, Manchester Univ; *m* 24 June 1944, (Clarice) Dorothy, da of William Alexander Park; 2 da (Jane b 1948, Judith b 1952); *Career* civil serv London; professional accountant branch MOD 1942-46, HG 1940-45; accountant 1927-38, Industl Fin 1938-42 and 1946-50, md Percy Brothers Ltd 1950-, dir Int Printers Ltd (IPC Gp) 1960-65, chm Hotspur Press Gp of Co's 1965-; memb cncl Br Fedn of Printing Industries (fin ctee, labour ctee) 1955-81, pres Lancs & Ches Alliance of Master Printers 1958-60, lay chm Manchester Diocesan Synod (C of E) 1960, chm Diocesan Bd of Fin 1966-; pres: Lancs and Ches Printers Pension Corpn 1965-66, Manchester Soc of CAs; former Tribunal memb Miny of Nat INCE, govr St Elphins Sch for Girls Derbys; FCA; *Recreations* golf, walking in Derbyshire hills; *Clubs* Manchester, Naval & Military, Withington GC; *Style—* George Ashcroft, Esq; Brantwood, Ballbrook Ave, Didsbury, Manchester M20 0AB; Hotspur House, Whitworth St, W Manchester M1 5QB (☎ 061 236 0374)

ASHCROFT, Kenneth; s of James Martland Ashcroft (d 1969), of Preston, and Mary Winifred, *née* Walker; *b* 22 Mar 1935; *Educ* Preston GS; *m* 1957, Patricia Maria, da of Henry Hothersall (d 1946), of Preston; 2 da (Jill b 1961, Jayne b 1963); *Career* CA and chartered mgmnt accountant; formerly with Philips Holland and Ford of Europe; dir: Ideal Standard 1970-73, Comet 1973-75, Hepworth-Next 1975-82, Dixons Ltd 1983-85, Amstrad plc 1985-; *Recreations* music, gardening; *Style—* Kenneth Ashcroft, Esq; Fendley Corner, Sauncey Wood, Harpenden, Herts AL5 5DW (☎ 05827 5549); Amstrad plc, Brentwood House, Kings Rd, Brentwood, Essex (☎ 0277 228 888)

ASHCROFT, Dame Peggy - Edith Margaret Emily; DBE (1956, CBE 1951); da of William Worsley Ashcroft and Violet Maud Bernheim; *b* 22 Dec 1907; *Educ* Woodford Sch Croydon and Central Sch of Speech Training and Dramatic Art; *m* 1, 1929 (m dis), Rupert (later Sir Rupert) Hart-Davis; m 2, 1934, Theodore Komisarjevsky; m 3, 1940 (m dis 1966), Jeremy Nicholas Hutchinson, QC (later Lord Hutchinson of Lullington); 1 s, 1 da; *Career* actress; dir Royal Shakespeare Co 1968-; Best Actress Award 1981 Monte Carlo TV Festival; *Style—* Dame Peggy Ashcroft, DBE; Manor Lodge, Frognal Lane, London NW3

ASHDOWN, David William; s of William Curtis Thomas, and Jean Vida Ashdown; *b* 11 Dec 1950; *Educ* Wandsworth Comprehensive; *m* 12 Aug 1978, Carol, da of Andrew Allan Smith (d 1963); 2 s (Michael b 1974, Peter b 1979); *Career* photographer; Keystone Press 1968-78, Daily Star 1978-86; chief sports photographer The Independent 1986-; Ilford Press Photographer of the Year 1974, runner-up Br Press Picture Awards 1979, Ilford Sports Picture of the Year 1985, Nikon Press Sports Photographer of the Year 1987, Adidas Euro Sports Picture of the Year 1987, Sports Photographer of the Year 1987; fell Royal Photographic Soc; *Recreations* golf; *Style—* David Ashdown, Esq; The Independent, 40 City Rd, London EC1 (☎ 01 253 1222, fax 01 608 1552, car tel 0836 251 672, telex 9419611)

ASHDOWN, Right Hon Jeremy John Durham (Paddy); PC (1989), MP (Lib) Yeovil 1983-; John W R D Ashdown and Lois A Ashdown; *b* 27 Feb 1941; *Educ* Bedford Sch, Language School Hong Kong; *m* 1961, Jane Courtenay; 1 s, 1 da; *Career* sometime Chinese interpreter, joined FCO 1972, 1 sec to Br Mission to UN Geneva 1974-76, contested (Lib) Yeovil 1979; *Style—* Paddy Ashdown, Esq, MP; House of Commons, London SW1A 0AA

ASHDOWN, Baroness; Lillian Nell; *née* King; CBE (1971); da of Ralph King (d 1966), of Rhodesia (now Zimbabwe) and London, and Mabel Kathleen King (d 1969); *b* 19 May 1915; *Educ* St Margaret's Harrow, Paris, King's Coll London; *m* 1937, Arnold Silverstone, kt 1964, cr Baron Ashdown (Life Peer) 1974 and d 1977; *Career* served WW II with Mechanised Transport Corps; Westminster City cllr 1955-65; memb Nat Union Cons Pty 1963-79, vice-chm NWAC 1967, chm SE Area Cons Pty 1971-75 (previously chm of women), served Cons Pty Policy Ctee 1973-79; fndr memb Women's Nat Cancer Campaign 1964- (vice-chm 1967-70); govr St George's Hosp 1971-75, pres E Sussex DGAA 1974-78, chm Friends of Moorfield Hosp 1979 and govr Moorfields Special Health Authy; conservator Ashdown Forest 1973-78; Westminster SSAFA 1988- (hon sec 1982-88); *Recreations* politics, reading; *Clubs* Carlton; *Style—* The Rt Hon the Lady Ashdown, CBE; c/o Barclays Bank, 8 West Halkin St, London SW1X 8JE

ASHE, Sir Derick Rosslyn; KCMG (1978, CMG 1966); s of Frederick Charles Allen Angelo Patrick Donnelly Ashe (d 1930), and Rosalind, *née* Mitchell; *b* 20 Jan 1919; *Educ* Bradfield, Trinity Coll Oxford (MA); *m* 1957, Mrs Rissa Guinness, da of late Capt Hon Trevor Tempest Parker, DSC, RN (s of Baron Parker of Waddington of the first creation); 1 s (Dominick), 1 da (Victoria); *Career* served WW II Capt (despatches); entered HM Diplomatic Service 1947, cnsllr: Br Embassy Addis Ababa 1962-64, Havana 1964-66; head Security Dept FO 1966-69; min Br Embassy Toyko 1969-71; HM ambass: Romania 1972-75, Argentina 1975-77; ambass and perm del to First UN Special Session on Disarmament NY 1977-78 and to Disarmament Conference Geneva 1977-79, ret 1979; Kt of the Order of Orange Nassau with Swords (Netherlands) 1945; *Recreations* gardening, fine arts; *Clubs* Travellers', Beefsteak, White's; *Style—* Sir Derick Ashe, KCMG; Dalton House, Hurstbourne Tarrant, Andover, Hants (☎ 026 476276)

ASHER, Alistair Hugh; s of Robert Alexander Asher, of Nairn and Norwich, and Jane, *née* Fraser; *b* 30 Dec 1955; *Educ* Norwich Sch, Southampton Univ (LLB), Amsterdam Univ (Dip Euro Law); *m* 25 May 1985, Patricia Margaret, da of Derrick Robinson (d 1979), of Lincoln and Maidenhaead; 1 da (Jenny b 29 Sept 1987); *Career* slr 1981, ptnr Allen & Overy 1987-(joined 1979); memb Law Soc; *Recreations* cycling, swimming, squash; *Clubs* Cannons; *Style—* Alistair Asher, Esq; 9 Cheapside, London EC2V 6AD (☎ 01 248 9898, fax 01 236 2192, telex 8812801)

ASHFIELD, Gerald William; s of Maj Percy Ashfield (d 1964) of Seaford, Sussex and Isabella von Herwarth (d 1976); *b* 7 Dec 1910; *Educ* Wellington; *m* 1, 5 March 1935, Lilian (d 1973), da of Maj H Grayson (d 1935), of London; 2 s (Michael b 1938, Philip b 1940); m 2, 28 Sept 1974, Gladys, da of William Miller (d 1965) of London; *Career* Maj Indian Army; memb Stock Exchange 1946-; chm & dir: Practical Investmt Co plc, London & St Lawrence Investmt Co plc; Lord of the manor Gt Ashfield Suffolk; vice pres Toc H; *Recreations* golf, walking; *Clubs* Piltdown Golf; *Style—* Gerald Ashfield, Esq; Wilmshurst-Fletching, Nr Uckfield, East Sussex (☎ 082 571 2523); Citicorp Scrimgeour Vickers, Cottons Centre, Hays Lane, London SE1 2QT (☎ 01 234 5678)

ASHFORD, Lady (Winifred) Anne Grizel; *née* Cochrane; only da of Hon Douglas Robert Hesketh Roger Cochrane (d 1942) and sis of 14 Earl of Dundonald; raised to the rank of an Earl's da 1960; *b* 1 Oct 1923; *m* 1967, Alfred Ashford, o son of late Alfred Ashford, of Bromley, Kent; 1 da (Alexis b 1969); *Style—* Lady Anne Ashford

ASHLEY, Lord; Anthony Nils Christian Ashley-Cooper; s and h of 10 Earl of Shaftesbury; *b* 24 June 1977; *Style—* Lord Ashley

ASHLEY, Sir Bernard Albert; s of Albert Ashley, of Rhayader, Powys, Wales, and Hilda Maud *née* Woodward; *b* 11 August 1926; *Educ* Whitgift Middle Sch, Wales Univ (DSc Econ); *m* 1949, Laura (d 1985), da of Stanley Mountney (d 1960); 2 s (David, Nicholas) 2 da (Jane, Emma); *Career* cmmnd Lt Royal Fus 1944-46, seconded 1 Gurkha Rifles 1944-45; chm Laura Ashley Hldgs plc; memb Army Sailing Assoc; FSIA; kt 1987; *Recreations* sailing (yacht 'Quaeso'), swimming, walking; *Clubs* Royal Thames Yacht, Lyford Cay Club (Nassau); *Style—* Sir Bernard Ashley; 43 Rue Ducale, Brussels, 1000

ASHLEY, Cedric; CBE (1984); s of Ronald Bednall Ashley (d 1980), and Gladys Vera, *née* Fincher; *b* 11 Nov 1936; *Educ* King Edwards Sch Birmingham, Univ of Birmingham (BSc, PhD); *m* 1, 1960, Pamela Jane (decd), da of William Turner; 1 s (Paul); m 2, 1965 (Marjorie) Vivien, da of Arnold Joseph Gooch (d 1960); 1 s (William b 1971), 1 da (Juliet b 1967); *Career* lectr Birmingham Univ 1965-73, int tech dir Bostrom Div UOP Ltd 1973-77; dir Motor Indust Res Assoc 1977-87, md Lotus Engrg

Ltd 1987-, princ Cedric Ashley and Assocs 1988-; FIME (vice chm Automobile Div), FRSA; *Recreations* gardening, walking, motoring; *Clubs* RAC, Anglo Belgian; *Style—* Cedric Ashley, Esq, CBE; Wilton Manor House, Wilton, Norwich NR9 5BZ

ASHLEY, Rt Hon Jack; CH (1975), PC (1979), MP (Lab) Stoke-on-Trent 1966-; s of John Ashley (d 1927), and Isabella, *née* Bridge; *b* 6 Dec 1922; *Educ* Ruskin Coll Oxford, Gonville and Caius Cambridge; *m* 1951, Pauline Kay Crispin; 3 da; *Career* former labourer, shop steward convenor Chem Workers' Union, BBC prodr; PPS to Sec of State Econ Affairs 1966-67, PPS to Sec of State DHSS 1974-76; *Style—* The Rt Hon Jack Ashley, Esq, CH, MP; House of Commons, London SW1A 0AA

ASHLEY, Maurice Percy; CBE (1978); s of Sir Percy Walter Llewellyn Ashley, KBE, CB (d 1945), and Doris, *née* Hayman (d 1941); *b* 4 Sept 1907; *Educ* St Paul's, New Coll Oxford; *m* 1935, Phyllis Mary Griffiths; 1 s, 1 da; *Career* historian and author; research asst to Sir Winston Churchill 1929-33, journalist with Guardian and The Times 1933-39, ed Britain Today 1939-40, dep ed The Listener 1946-58 (ed 1958-67); res fell Loughborough Univ of Technol 1968-70; *Books Incl:* Oliver Cromwell (1937), Marlborough (1939), John Wildman: Plotter and Postman (1947), England in the Seventeenth Century (1952, rev 1978), Cromwell's Generals (1954), The Greatness of Oliver Cromwell (1957, rev 1967), Oliver Cromwell and the Puritan Revolution (1958), The Stuarts in Love (1963), Life in Stuart England (1964), Churchill as Historian (1968), A Golden Century 1598-1715 (1969), Charles II: the man and the statesman (1971), Oliver Cromwell and His World (1972), The Life and Times of King John (1982), The Life and Times of King William I (1973), The Age of Absolutism 1648-1775 (1974), A Concise History fo the English Civil War (1975), Rupert of the Rhine (1976), General Monck (1977), James II (1978), The House of Stuart (1980); *Style—* Maurice Ashley, Esq, CBE; 34 Wood Lane, Ruislip, Middx (☎ Ruislip 35993)

ASHLEY, Nick Bernard; s of Sir Bernard Albert Ashley, and Laura Ashley, *née* Mountney (d 1985); *b* 15 Jan 1957; *Educ* Caersws Sch Powys Wales, Holland Park Comprehensive Kensington London, St Martins Sch of Art London, Academie Julien Paris, Central Sch of Art and Design London; *m* 7 July 1984, Arabella Jane Campbell, da of Patrick McNair-Wilson, MP ; *Career* design dir Laura Ashley Ltd 1980-; *Recreations* motorcycle, racing; *Clubs* Hafren Dirt Bike; *Style—* Nick Ashley, Esq; 27 Bagley's Lane, London SW6 2AR

ASHLEY MILLER, Lt Cdr Peter; s of Cyril Ashley Miller, of Seafield, Overstrand, Norfolk (d 23 Nov 1963), and Marjorie, *née* George (d 1974); *b* 26 Dec 1925; *Educ* RNC Dartmouth; *m* 11 Feb 1956, Catherine Jill, da of Maj John MacNaughton MC, of Upavon Wilts (d 1959), 1 s (Mark b 1962), 2 da (Bridget b 1957, Catherine b 1959); *Career* RN 1939-59 in: Home, Med and Far East Fleets and Admty; dir: Ionian Bank Ltd 1973-77, Arbuthnot Latham Bank Ltd 1978-; chm: Norland Nursery Trg Coll 1983-, Burlingham House Home for Mentally Handicapped 1984-; FCA; *Recreations* skiing, sailing, shooting; *Clubs* Travellers, Ski (GB), Overseas Bankers, Norfolk Punt; *Style—* Lt Cdr Peter Ashley Miller; Reedham Old Hall, Norwich, Norfolk NR13 3TZ

ASHLEY-BROWN, Michael Ashley; s of Lt Col Arthur Basil Brown, TD (d 1987), of Farnham, Surrey, and Myra Anne, *née* Walsh (d 1964); *b* 28 June 1948; *Educ* Cranleigh, Millbrook Sch New York, Coll of Law; *m* 3 June 1972, Rita Julia; 1 s (Miles b 1973), 1 da (Tabitha b 1975); *Career* slr Supreme Ct 1973-; dir: Brown Bros & Taylor Ltd 1985-, Kensington Corpn Ltd 1987-; cncllr York City Cncl 1977-80, co cncllr N Yorks 1977-81; regnl spokesman Br Atlantic Ctee 1982-86, memb Hunter Improvement Soc; Cons candidate Leeds Central 1983; memb Ct and Cncl York Univ 1978-82; govr Archbishop Holgate GS 1977-82; Freeman City of York; *Recreations* show hunters, skiing, long distance running; *Clubs* Oriental, Yorkshire; *Style—* Michael A Ashley-Brown, Esq; Kepwick Hall, Thirsk, North Yorks (☎ 0845 537286); 106 Micklegate, York YO1 1JX (☎ 0904 55834, fax 0904 30321; car tel 0836 594908 or 0836 612167)

ASHLEY-COOPER, Lady Frances Mary Elizabeth; da of late Lord Ashley (s of 9 Earl of Shaftesbury); sis of 10 Earl, *qv*; raised to the rank of an Earl's da 1962; *b* 9 April 1940; *Style—* Lady Frances Ashley-Cooper; La Combe, 30126 Tavel, Gard, France

ASHLEY-COOPER, Lady Lettice Mildred Mary; da of late 9 Earl of Shaftesbury and aunt of 10 Earl, *qv*; *b* 12 Feb 1911; *Career* served WW II Flight Officer WAAF (despatches); OStJ; *Style—* Lady Lettice Ashley-Cooper; Butts Close, Wimborne St Giles, Dorset

ASHLEY-MILLER, Dr Michael; Dr; s of Cyril Ashley-Miller (d 1964), and George Marjorie Ashley-Miller (d 1976); *b* 1 Dec 1930; *Educ* Charterhouse, Hertford Coll Oxford (BA, BM, BCh, MA), Kings Coll Hosp 1952-55, London Sch of Hygiene (DPH); *m* 31 May 1958, Yvonne Marcell, da of Cyril Marcell Townend; 3 da (Amanda b 1959, Tessa b 1961, Penny b 1964); *Career* house surgn and physician Kings Coll Hosp 1956, SMO Dulwich Hosp 1957, Nat Serv Flt Lt RAF : MO Oakington 1958-60, SMO Colerne 1960; SMO IOW CC 1961-64, MO and SMO MRC HQ 1964-74, SPMO SHHD 1983-86, sec Nuffield Prov Hosp Tst 1986-; FFCM FRCPEd MRCP (London); memb Soc Med, memb RSM; *Books* Screening for Risk of Coronary Heart Disease (jtly, 1986); *Recreations* walking, reading, visiting cathedrals; *Clubs* RSM; *Style—* Dr Michael Ashley-Miller; 3 Prince Albert Rd, London NW1 (☎ 01 485 6632)

ASHLEY-SMITH, Dr Jonathan; s of Ewart Trist Ashley-Smith (d 1972), of Sutton Valence, Kent, and Marian Tanfield, *née* Smith; *b* 25 August 1946; *Educ* Sutton Valence Sch, Univ of Bristol (Phd), Univ of Cambridge; *m* 19 Aug 1967, Diane Louise; 1 s (Joseph Daniel b 1975), 1 da (Zoë Elizabeth b 1985); *Career* V & A: scientific offr 1973-77, keeper conservation dept; memb crafts cncl, cncl for care of churches; chm UK Inst for Conservation 1983-84; FIIC 1985, FRCS C Chem 1987, FMA 1988; *Books* Scientific Ed Science for Conservators vols 1 - 3 (1984); *Recreations* legal combinations of driving fast, getting drunk, and heavy rock music; *Clubs* Anglesea; *Style—* Dr Jonathan Ashley-Smith, Esq; Conservation Dept, Victoria & Albert Museum, London SW7 2RL (☎ 01 938 8568, fax 01 938 8477)

ASHMALL, Harry A; *b* 22 Feb 1939; *Educ* Kilsyth Acad, Univ of Glasgow (MA, MLitt), Jordanhill Coll of Educn; *m* 2 da; *Career* asst HS of Glasgow 1961-66 (princ teacher of history 1968-71); rector: Forfar Acad 1971-79, Morrison's Acad 1979-; lectr various colls of educn, univs, scottish and ecumenical centres; BBC religious presenter, full series incl: In Opposite Corners, The Church and ..., The Apostles' Creed, Sunday Worship; individual presentations incl: Crossfire, Does God Exist After 1984?, Thought for the Day, A Personal View, Voyager Sixth Sense; chm Scottish Educnl Research Assoc 1980-83, vice chm The Educnl Bdcasting Cncl for Scotland; memb: UNICEF Exec Ctee (UK), bd of mgmnt Scottish Cncl for Research in Educn, Educn Ctee of the SSTA; FBIM, MMIM; *Books* The High School of Glasgow: a history (1976); also various pamphlets and articles; *Recreations* reading, writing, keep fit; *Clubs* New (Edinburgh), East India; *Style—* H A Ashmall, Esq; Fernbank, Ferntower Rd, Crieff PH7 3DH (☎ 0764 2844)

ASHMOLE, Michael Achille; s of Harold J Ashmole (d 1979); *b* 10 Feb 1939; *Educ* Bemrose GS Derby; *m* 1961, Jean, da of Samuel Higginbottom (d 1943); 2 s (Christopher b 1964, Alexander b 1968), 2 da (Susan b 1962, Brigid b 1966); *Career* RAF 1958-60; dir: Fountain Forestry Holdings Ltd, Fountain Forestry Inc, Highland Venison Ltd; chm Elite Trees Ltd, md Fountain Int Ltd; exec dir Int Union of Societies of Foresters; MIFor (memb cncl 1973-78); *Recreations* field sports, flying (sea plane pilot), philately; *Clubs* Catenian Assoc; *Style—* Michael Ashmole, Esq; 111 Burghmuir Rd, Perth, Scotland (☎ (0738) 27622)

ASHMORE, Adm of the Fleet Sir Edward Beckwith; GCB (1974, KCB 1971, CB 1966), DSC (1942); s of Vice Adm Leslie Haliburton Ashmore, CB, DSO (d 1974), and late Tamara Vasilievna, *née* Shutt, bro of Vice A William Beckwith Ashmore, *qv*; *b* 11 Dec 1919; *Educ* RNC Dartmouth; *m* 1942, Elizabeth, da of late Rear Adm Sir Lionel Sturdee, 2 Bt, CBE; 1 s, 1 da (and 1 da decd); *Career* joined RN 1938, asst naval attaché Moscow 1946-47, Capt 1955, Rear Adm 1965, Vice Adm 1968, Vice-Chief Naval Staff 1969-71, Adm 1970, CIC Western Fleet 1971, CIC Fleet 1971-74, First and Princ Naval ADC to HM The Queen 1974-77, Chief Naval Staff & First Sea Lord 1974-77, Chief Def Staff 1977; govr Sutton's Hosp 1976-; *Clubs* Naval and Military; *Style—* Adm of the Fleet Sir Edward Ashmore, GCB, DSC; c/o Nat Westminster Bank plc, 26 Haymarket, London SW17 4ER

ASHMORE, Vice Adm Sir Peter William Beckwith; KCB (1972, CB 1968), KCVO (1980, MVO (4 Class) 1948), DSC (1942); s of late Vice Adm Leslie Haliburton Ashmore, CB, DSO (d 1974), and late Tamara Vasilievna Shutt, of Petrograd; yr bro of Admiral of the Fleet Sir Edward Ashmore, *qv*; *b* 4 Feb 1921; *Educ* Yardley Court, RNC Dartmouth; *m* 1952, Patricia Moray, da of late Adm Sir Henry Tritton Buller, GCVO, CB (d 1960), and Lady Hermione, *née* Stuart, da of 17 Earl of Moray; 1 s, 3 da; *Career* midshipman RN 1939, served WW II (despatches), Lt 1941, Equerry to HM The King 1946-1948, Cdr 1951, Capt 1957, Rear Adm 1966, Chief Staff to CIC Western Fleet & NATO CIC E Atlantic 1967-69, Vice Adm 1969, Chief Allied Staff NATO Naval HQ S Europe 1970-72, ret; extra equerry to HM The Queen 1952-, master of HM's Household 1973-; *Recreations* golf, tennis, fishing; *Style—* Vice-Admiral Sir Peter Ashmore, KCB

ASHTON, Anthony Southcliffe; s of Prof Thomas Southcliffe Ashton (d 1968), and Marion Hague, *née* Slater (d 1979); *b* 5 July 1916; *Educ* Manchester GS, Hertford Coll Oxford (MA); *m* 28 Oct 1939, Katharine Marion Louise, da of Evelyn Charles Vivian (d 1947); 2 da (Theresa b 1943, Vivien b 1948); *Career* served with 55 Light AA Regt France and Norway 1940, cmmnd RASC, OCTU instr, Staff Maj AFHQ N Africa and Italy, 'Q' Staff Offr SHAEF, France and Germany 1942, ret as Maj; economist export credits dept Board of Trade 1837, asst dir of Marketing Nat Coal Bd 1947; Vacuum (later Mobil) Oil Co 1949-61: head off mangr in various depts (marketing, supply, corporate planning), advanced mgmnt programme Harvard Business Sch 1961, tres Esso Petroleum Co 1961 (finance dir 1967), cncl memb Manchester Business Sch 1961-81, bd memb fin and corporate planning PO Corpn 1969-73, dir Provincial Insur Co 1974-86, tstee PO Pension Fund 1974-83, dir Tyzack & Ptnrs 1974-84, course dir Oxford Univ Business Summer Sch 1974 memb steering ctee 1978-81; vice-pres Hertford Coll Soc 1977, dir Exeter Tst 1980 (chm 1982-86), ret 1986; *Recreations* moutains, philosophy; *Clubs* Army and Navy (RAG); *Style—* Anthony S Ashton, Esq; Quarry Field, Stonewall Hill, Presteigne, Dowys LD8 2HB

ASHTON, Donald Frederick; s of Rev Frederick Charles Ashton (d 1959), and Bertha Ann Ashton (d 1972), da of Thomas Moss, largest private cotton mfr (ret 1919), of Lowstock Hall, Lancs; *b* 1 June 1918; *Educ* Harrow, and Trinity Coll Camb (MA); *m* 5 May 1952, Ysobel Elma, da of Charles McCarthy, Somerville (d 1936); 1 da (Elaine b 9 Feb 1953); *Career* stockbroker with Gordon L Jacobs & Co, London (ret); churchwarden Parish Church of St Helier 1979-; *Recreations* golf; *Clubs* Royal and Ancient Golf, Royal Lytham St Annes, Royal Jersey; *Style—* Donald Ashton, Esq; The Riddings, Grouville, Jersey, CI (☎ 534 54109 (exd)); Hambros Bank (Jersey) Ltd, 13 Broad St, St Helier, Jersey, CI

ASHTON, George Arthur; s of Lewis Arthur Ashton (d 1952), and Mary Annie Ashton (d 1964); *b* 27 Nov 1921; *Educ* Llanidloes GS, Birmingham Central Tech Coll; *m* 1, 1948, Joan Rutter (decd); 1 s (Stephen); m 2, 1978, Pauline Jennifer, da of Albert Margett, of 89 Swanmore Road, Little Over, Derby; *Career* HM Forces (wartime) Maj Far East; engrg and mgmnt conslt; chm Seamless Tubes Ltd 1984-86, dep chm Wintech WDA 1984-; dir: TI Gp plc 1969-84, Arthur Lee & Sons plc 1978-; tech dir and business area chm TI Gp plc 1978-84, vice-pres Advanced Manufacturing Technology Research Inst (AMTRI) 1986-; *Recreations* walking, cycling, gardening, DIY; *Clubs* Naval and Military; *Style—* George Ashton, Esq; Barn Cottage, Longford, Derby DE6 3DT (☎ Great Cubley (033 523) 561)

ASHTON, Gordon Rayment; s of Gilbert Austin Ashton (d 1985), of Barrow-in-Furness, and Mabel Grace, *née* Rayment; *b* 31 Mar 1944; *Educ* Ashville Coll, Manchester Univ (LLB); *m* 20 March 1971, Marion, da of Joseph Turner (d 1972), of Windermere; 1 s (Paul b 1975), 2 da (Deborah b 1973, Clare b 1980); *Career* slr 1967, pt/t chm Social Security Appeal Tbnl 1983-, dep registrar High Ct of Justice 1985-; pres Furness and Dist Law Soc 1984-86, pres Grange Rotary Club 1977-78; memb Law Soc 1967; *Recreations* old cars, DIY, computers; *Style—* Gordon Ashton, Esq; Honeypotts, Grange-over-Sands, Cumbria LA11 7EN (☎ 05395 33124); Gedye & Sons, Grange-over-Sands, Cumbria LA11 6DR (☎ 05395 32313, fax 05395 32474)

ASHTON, Hon (Thomas) Henry; s and h of 3 Baron Ashton of Hyde; *b* 18 July 1958; *Educ* Eton, Trinity Coll Oxford; *m* 31 October 1987, Emma Louise, da of Colin Allinson, of Bath; *Career* short service cmmn with Royal Hussars (PWO), Lt Royal Wessex Yeomanry; reinsur broker C T Bowring Ltd; *Clubs* Boodle's; *Style—* The Hon Henry Ashton; 4 Poplar Grove, London W6 7RE

ASHTON, Hubert (Hugh) Gaitskell; DL (Essex 1983); s of Sir Hubert Ashton, KBE, MC, of Brentwood (d 1979), and Dorothy Margaret, *née* Gaitskell (d 1983); *b* 27 Jan 1930; *Educ* Winchester, Trinity Coll Cambridge (MA); *m* 1956, Anna-Brita, da of Gustav Bertil Rylander, of Sweden (d 1976); 3 s (Hubert, Peter, Charles), 1 da (Katherine b 1965); *Career* 2 Lt Irish Gds 1948-50; Peat Marwick Mitchell 1953-61, J Henry Schroder Wagg & Co (merchant bankers) 1961-85; dir: The Housing Corpn 1979-85, Brixton Estate 1983-85, Hanson plc 1985-, BAA plc 1986-; High Sheriff

Essex 1983-84; pres: Essex County Football Assoc 1984-, Essex Friends of YMCA 1985-; vice-chm of govrs Brentwood Sch 1983; master of the Skinners Co 1986-87; FCA; *Recreations* shooting, eating, drinking; *Clubs* MCC, City of London; *Style*— Hugh Ashton, Esq, DL; Wealdside, S Weald, Brentwood, Essex (☎ 0277 73406); 32 Garrick House, Carrington St, London W1 (☎ 01 499 3989); 1 Grosvenor Place, London SW1X 8JH (☎ 01 245 1245, telex 91 76 98)

ASHTON, Joe (Joseph William); MP (Lab) Bassetlaw 1968-; s of Arthur and Nellie Ashton, of Sheffield; *b* 9 Oct 1933; *Educ* High Storrs GS, Rotherham Tech Coll; *m* 1957, Margaret Patricia, da of George Lee, of Andover St, Sheffield; 1 da; *Career* journalist, columnist *Daily Star* 1979-; PPS to Sec of State Energy 1975-76, asst govt whip 1976-77, front bench spokesman on Energy 1979-81; author of: novel *Grassroots*, play *A Majority of One*; *What The Papers Say*; Granada TV Award *Columnist of the Year* 1984; *Style*— Joe Ashton, Esq, MP; 16 Ranmoor Park Rd, Sheffield (☎ (0742) 301763)

ASHTON, Hon John Edward; s of 3 Baron Ashton of Hyde; *b* 8 Jan 1966; *Style*— The Hon John Ashton

ASHTON, Hon Katharine Judith; da of 3 Baron Ashton of Hyde; *b* 30 Jan 1962; *Style*— The Hon Katharine Ashton

ASHTON, Kenneth Bruce (Ken); s of Harry Anstice Ashton (d 1926), and Olive May, *née* Hawkins; *b* 9 Nov 1925; *Educ* Latymer Upper Sch, Glasgow Univ; *m* 1955, Anne, *née* Sidebotham; 4 s (Paul, Mark, John, Richard); *Career* RA WW II, Egypt, Italy, Austria, Palestine 1942-47; former sub-editor Daily Express and Daily Mail; gen sec NUJ 1977-85 (pres 1975); memb: TUC Printing Industry Ctee 1975-85, TUC Media Working Gp 1977-85, printing and publishing industry training bd 1977-83, communications advsy ctee, UK Nat Cmmn for UNESCO 1981-85, Br Ctee Journalists in Europe 1981-86; pres Int Federation of Journalists 1982-86; *Style*— Ken Ashton, Esq; High Blean, Raydaleside, Askrigg, Leyburn, North Yorkshire DL8 3DJ

ASHTON, Rt Rev Leonard James; CB (1970); s of late Henry Ashton, of Chesham, Bucks, and late Sarah, *née* Ing; *b* 27 June 1915; *Educ* Tyndale Hall Trinity Coll Bristol; *Career* ordained 1942, chaplain RAF 1945-74, served: Far East (including Br Cwlth Occupation Forces in Japan) 1945-48, Middle East 1954-55 and 1960-61; RAF Coll Cranwell 1956-60, resident chaplain St Clement Danes 1965-69; chaplain-in-chief and archdeacon RAF (rank of Air Vice-Marshal) 1969-73; canon and prebendary of Lincoln Cathedral 1969-73 (canon emeritus 1973-), asst bishop in Jerusalem 1974-76, episcopal canon St George's Cathedral Jerusalem 1976-, bishop in Cyprus and The Gulf 1976-83, hon asst bishop of Oxford 1983, commissary for bishops in Jerusalem and Iran 1983-, episcopal canon St Pauls Cath Cyprus 1989-; hon chaplain to HM The Queen 1967-73; ChStJ 1976; *Recreations* photography, gardening; *Clubs* RAF; *Style*— The Rt Rev Leonard Ashton, CB; 60 Lowndes Ave, Chesham, Bucks (☎ 0494 782952);

ASHTON, Prof Norman Henry; CBE (1976); 2 s of late Henry James Ashton, of Herts, and late Margaret Ann, *née* Tuck; *b* 11 Sept 1913; *Educ* West Kensington Sch, Kings Coll London and Westminster Hosp Med Sch, Univ of London; *Career* Lt-Col RAMC, asst dir pathology and offr i/c Central Pathological Laboratory Middle East 1946; dir pathology Kent and Canterbury Hosp 1941; blood transfusion offr East Kent 1941, dir dept of pathology Inst of Ophthalmology Univ of London 1948-78; reader in pathology 1953, prof of pathology 1957-78, emeritus prof 1978-; FRS 1971; KStJ 1971; *Recreations* painting, gardening; *Clubs* Athenaeum, Garrick; *Style*— Prof Norman Ashton, CBE; 4 Blomfield Rd, Little Venice, London W9 1AH; Institute of Ophthalmology, Judd St, London WC1H 9QS (☎ 01 387 9621)

ASHTON, Prof Robert; s of Joseph Ashton (d 1979), of Chester, and Edith Frances, *née* Davies (d 1954) ; *b* 21 July 1924; *Educ* Magdalen Coll Sch Oxford, Univ Coll Southampton, LSE (BA,PhD); *m* 30 Aug 1946, Margaret Alice, da of T W Sedgwick (d 1948), of Dover; 2 da (Rosalind Helen b 1954, Celia Elizabeth b 1961); *Career* WWII served RAF 1943-46; sr lectr econ hist Univ of Nottingham 1961-63 (lectr 1954-61, asst lectr 1952-54), visiting assoc prof in history Univ of Calif 1962-63; prof english history Univ of E Anglia 1963-89 (dean Sch of Eng Studies 1964-47); visiting fell All Souls Coll Oxford 1973-74 and 1987; FRHistS (1961); *Books* The Crown and The Money Market 1603-42 (1960), James I By His Contemporaries (1969), The English Civil War 1603-49 (1978), The City and the Court 1603-43 (1979), Reformation and Revolution 1558-1660 (1984); *Recreations* wine, food, old buildings; *Style*— Prof Robert Ashton; The Manor House, Brundall, Norwich NR13 5JY (☎ 0603 713 368); School of English & American Studies, Univ of East Anglia, Norwich (☎ 0603 56161)

ASHTON, William Michael Allingham; MBE (1978); s of Eric Sandiford Ashton (d 1983), of Lytham, St Annes, and Zilla Dorothea, *née* Miles (d 1944); *b* 6 Dec 1936; *Educ* Rossall Sch, St Peter's Coll Oxford (BA, Dip Ed); *m* 22 Oct 1966, Kay Carol, da of John Stallard Watkins, of New Quay, Dyfed; 2 s (Grant b 1967, Miles b 1968), 1 da (Helen b 1983); *Career* Nat Serv RAF 1955-57; musical dir Nat Youth Jazz Orchestra 1965- (fndr 1965): numerous appearances before royalty incl Royal Variety Performance 1978, toured many countries on behalf of Br Cncl (USA, USSR, Australia, Turkey); memb: Musicians' Union, Br Assoc Jazz Musicians; *Recreations* reading, song writing; *Style*— William Ashton, Esq, MBE; 11 Victor Rd, Harrow, Middx HA2 6PT (☎ 01 863 2717)

ASHTON OF HYDE, Marjorie, Baroness; Marjorie Nell; *née* Brooks; JP; da of Hon Marshall Brooks (2 s of 1 Baron Crawshaw) and Florence,; *b* 1901; *Educ* Private; *m* 1925, 2 Baron Ashton of Hyde, JP, DL (d 1983); 1 s (3 Baron, *qv*), 2 da decd; *Clubs* Parrot; *Style*— The Rt Hon Marjorie, Lady Ashton of Hyde, JP; The Martins, Broadwell, Moreton-in-Marsh, Glos (☎ 045130105)

ASHTON OF HYDE, 3 Baron (UK 1911); Thomas John Ashton; TD, JP (Oxon); s of 2 Baron Ashton of Hyde, JP, DL (d 1983), and Marjorie, Baroness Ashton of Hyde, *qv*; *b* 19 Nov 1926; *Educ* Eton, New Coll Oxford; *m* 18 May 1957, Pauline Trewlove, er da of Lt-Col Robert Henry Langton Brackenbury, OBE, of Yerdley House, Long Compton, Shipston on Stour; 2 s, 2 da; *Heir* s, Hon Thomas Henry Ashton b 18 July 1958; *Career* formerly Lt 11 Hussars, Maj Royal Gloucestershire Hussars (TA); dir Barclays Bank plc and subsidiary cos 1969-87; *Clubs* Boodle's; *Style*— The Rt Hon the Lord Ashton of Hyde, TD, JP; Fir Farm, Upper Slaughter, Bourton on the Water, Glos (☎ 0451 30652)

ASHTON-BOSTOCK, David Ashton; s of Cdr John Bostock, DSC, RN; additional surname and arms assumed by Royal Licence 1953, at the wish of his great-uncle Samuel Ashton-Yates; *b* 17 Feb 1933; *Educ* Wellington Coll, Maidstone Coll of Art, Byam Shaw Art Sch; *m* 1965 (m dis 1983), Victoria Rosamond, da of Capt Richard White, DSO, RN; 1 da (1 s decd); *Career* interior designer; vice-pres Alexandra Rose Day, chm Ridley Art Soc, memb of cncl Interior Decorators and Designers Assoc; memb of Lloyd's; *Recreations* painting, gardening, genealogy; *Style*— David Ashton-Bostock, Esq; Danes Bottom Place, Wormshill, Sittingbourne, Kent (☎ 062 784 476); 28 Sutherland St, London SW1 (☎ 01 834 1696); Ashton-Bostock Interior Decorations, 21 Charlwood St, London SW1 (☎ 01 828 3656)

ASHTOWN, 6 Baron (I 1800); Christopher Oliver Trench; s of Algernon Oliver Trench (himself s of Hon William Trench, yr bro of 3 Baron); through his paternal grandmother, Frances, Lord Ashtown is gn to Desmond Shawe-Taylor, CBE, *qv*; suc 5 Baron (1 cous once removed) 1979; *b* 23 Mar 1931; *Educ* Owen Sound HS; *Heir* kinsman, Sir Nigel Clive Cosby Trench, KCMG, *qv*; *Career* worked with Canadian Imperial Bank of Commerce Toronto 1950-57; *Recreations* reading; *Style*— The Rt Hon the Lord Ashtown; c/o Main Branch Canadian Bank of Commerce, Ontario, Canada

ASHWORTH, Prof Graham William; CBE 1980; s of Frederick William Ashworth (d 1978), and Ivy Alice, *née* Courtiour (d 1982); *b* 14 July 1935; *Educ* Devonport HS, Univ of Liverpool (BArch); *m* 2 April 1960, Gwyneth Mai, da of John Morgan Jones (d 1959); 3 da (Clare, Alyson, Kate); *Career* architect/planner: London CC 1959-62, Graeme Shankland Assoc 1962-64; architect Civic Tst 1964-65, dir Northwest Civic Tst 1965-73, Prof of Urban Environmental Studies 1973-87, res prof Urban Environmental Studies 1987-, dir-gen Tidy Britain Gp; assoc pastor Carey Baptist Church Preston 1977-86; dir: Merseyside Devpt Corpn 1981-, Northwest Electricity Bd 1985-88; chm Ravenhead Renaissance Ltd 1988-; memb Baptist Union Cncl 1975-; RIBA 1962, FRTPI 1969, FRSA 1968, FBIM 1986; *Books* An Encyclopaedia of Planning (1973); *Clubs* National Liberal, Athenaeum; *Style*— Prof Graham Ashworth, CBE; Manor Court Farm, Preston New Road, Samlesbury, Preston, Lancs PR5 OUP (☎ 025481 2011); Tidy Britain Gp, The Pier, Wigan WN3 4EX (☎ 0942 824 620)

ASHWORTH, Sir Herbert; s of Joseph Hartley Ashworth (d 1954), of Burnley, Lancs; *b* 30 Jan 1910; *Educ* Burnley GS, London Univ (BSc, LLB); *m* 1936, Barbara Helen Mary, da of Douglas D Henderson (d 1932), of London; 2 s, 1 da; *Career* chm: Housing Corpn 1968-73, Nationwide Bldg Soc 1970-82; dir The Builder Ltd 1975-80; chm: Surrey and W Sussex Agricultural Wages Ctee 1974-88, Nationwide Housing Tst 1983-87; kt 1972; *Style*— Sir Herbert Ashworth; 8 Tracery, Park Rd, Banstead, Surrey (☎ 0737 352608)

ASHWORTH, Brig John Blackwood; CBE (1962), DSO (1944); s of Lt-Col Hugh Stirling Ashworth, Royal Sussex Regt (ka 1917), and Mrs E M Ashworth; *b* 7 Dec 1910; *Educ* Wellington, Sandhurst; *m* 1944, Eileen Patricia, da of late Maj Herbert Llewellyn Gifford, OBE, Royal Ulster Rifles, and Lady Gooch; 1 da; *Career* cmmnd 1930, served WW II (wounded, despatches twice), Cdt Jt Sch Chemical Warfare 1954, Cdr 133 Inf Bde (TA) 1957, dir Mil Training War Office 1962-65, ADC to the Queen 1961-65, Col The Royal Sussex Regt 1963-66, Dep Col The Queens Regt 1967-68; DL Sussex 1972-83; OStJ 1950; GO Order of the House of Orange; *Style*— Brig John Ashworth, CBE, DSO; 16 Castlegate, New Brook St, Ilkley, W Yorks LS29 8DF (☎ 0943 602404)

ASHWORTH, Prof John Michael; s of Jack Ashworth (d 1975), and Mary Constance, *née* Ousman (d 1971); *b* 27 Nov 1938; *Educ* West Buckland Sch, Exeter Coll Oxford (BA, BSc, MA), Univ of Leicester (PhD), Univ of Oxford (DSc); *m* 13 July 1963, Ann (d 1985), da of Peter Knight (d 1977); 1 s (Matthew b 24 Sept 1971), 3 da (Harriet b 23 Oct 1964, Sophia b 2 Dec 1968, Emily b 3 Aug 1970); m 2, 23 July 1988, Auriol Hazel Dawn, da of Capt E B K Stevens, DSO (d 1971); *Career* vice Chllr Univ of Salford 1981-, prof Univ of Essex 1974-79, secondment to central policy review staff 1976-79, under sec Cabinet Off 1979-81, chief scientist CPRS 1979-81, chm Salford Univ Business Servs Ltd and Business Enterprises Ltd 1981-; chm bd of Nat Computing Centre Ltd 1983-, chm Nat Accreditation Cncl for Certification Bodies 1984-88, memb bd Granada TV 1986-, memb BR (London Mainland) Bd 1987-; Business in the Community 1988, chm bd Salford ITEC 1982-, memb Manchester Literary and Philosophical Soc, tstee Granada Fndn; pres Res and Devpt Soc, chm Info Tech Economic Devpt Cncl, memb Electronic Indust EDC (NEDO), memb Library and Info Servs Cncl 1980-84: Colworth Medal of Biochemical Soc 1972; FIBiol 1973, companion BIM 1984; *Books* Cell Differentiation (1972), The Slime Moulds (with J Dee, 1970); *Recreations* fell walking, windsurfing; *Style*— Prof John Ashworth; 34 Hawthorn Lane, Wilmslow, Cheshire SK9 6DG (☎ 0625 530559); Univ of Salford, Salford M5 4WT (☎ 061 736 5843, fax 061 745 7808, telex 668680 SULIB)

ASHWORTH, Leonard; CBE (1981); s of James Walter Ashworth (d 1973); *b* 12 Jan 1921; *Educ* Stretford Tech Coll; *m* 1947, Edna, da of Arthur Bromfield (d 1956); 2 children; *Career* Warrant Offr RE SEAC; chief exec Davy McKee Int Ltd; main bd dir Davy Corpn, consulting exec Davy Corpn 1983; memb Process Plant EDC NEDO 1979; chm Br Metallurgical Plant Constructors' Assoc Sept 1981; pres Process Plant Assoc from Aug 1982; chm Mech & Elec Construction Indust Trg Bd 1982; memb EITB 1982; *Recreations* boating; *Clubs* Oriental, Poole Yacht; *Style*— Leonard Ashworth, Esq, CBE; 1 Burnage Court, Canford Cliffs, Poole, Dorset (☎ 0202 700853); Davy Corporation Ltd, 15 Portland Place, London W1A 4DD (☎ 01 637 2821)

ASHWORTH, Piers; QC (1973); s of Tom and Mollie Ashworth; *b* 27 May 1931; *Educ* Christ's Hosp, Pembroke Cambridge; *m* 1, 1959 (m dis 1978), Iolene Jennifer, yr da of W G Foxley; 3 s, 1 da; m 2, 1980, Elizabeth, elder da of A J S Aston; *Career* barr Middle Temple 1956, bencher 1984; rec Crown Ct 1974-; Midland and Oxford Circuit; *Style*— Piers Ashworth, Esq, QC; 2 Harcourt Bldgs, Temple, London EC4 (☎ 01 583 9020)

ASKE, Rev Sir Conan; 2 Bt (UK 1922), of Aughton, East Riding of Yorkshire; s of Sir Robert William Aske, 1 Bt, TD, QC, JP (d 1954), by his 2 w Edith; *b* 22 April 1912; *Educ* Rugby, Balliol Coll Oxford (MA); *m* 1, 13 Dec 1948, Vera (d 1960), yst da of late George Rowbotham, of Iffley, Oxford, and former w of Roland Faulkner; m 2, 23 Aug 1965, Rebecca, da of Hugh Fraser Grant (d 1967), of Wick, Caithness; *Heir* bro, Robert Aske, *qv*; *Career* served WW II Dunkirk 1940, Maj E Yorks Regt, ME 1941-51, Sudan Defence Force; schoolmaster Hillstone Malvern 1952-69; asst curate: Hagley 1970-72, St John's Worcester 1972-80; chaplain to Mayor of Worcester 1979-80; hon padre 1940 Dunkirk Veteran's Assoc Works branch; *Style*— The Rev Sir Conan Aske, Bt; 167 Malvern Rd, Worcester WR2 4NN (☎ 0905 422817)

ASKE, Robert Edward; 2 s of Sir Robert Aske, 1 Bt, TD, QC, JP, LLD, sometime MP Newcastle E; hp to bro, Rev Sir Conan Aske, 2 Bt, *qv*; *b* 21 Mar 1915; *m* 1940, Joan Bingham, o da of Capt Bingham Ackerley, of White Lodge, Cobham; 1 s; *Style*—

Robert Aske, Esq; 45 Holland Rd, London W14

ASKEW, Barry Reginald William; s of Reginald Ewart Askew (d 1969), and Jane Elisabeth Askew (d 1979); *b* 13 Dec 1936; *Educ* Lady Manners GS Bakewell; *m* 1, 1958 (m dis 1978), June, da of Vernon Roberts; 1 s, 1 da; m 2, 1980, Deborah, da of Harold Parker; *Career* journalist, broadcaster, public relations conslt; trainee reporter upwards Derbyshire Times 1952-57, reporter and sub-ed Sheffield Telegraph 1957-59, reporter, feature writer and broadcaster Raymonds News Agency Derby 1959-61, ed Matlock Mercury 1961-63, indust correspondent, asst ed, dep ed Sheffield Telegraphy (later Morning Telegraph) 1964-68, assoc ed The Star Sheffield 1968; ed: Lancashire Evening Post 1968-81 (dir 1978-81), News of the World 1981; presenter and anchor man: ITV 1970-81, BBC Radio 4 1971-72, BBC 1 1972, BBC 2 1972-76; memb Davies Ctee to reform hosp complaints procedures in UK 1971-73; Campaigning Journalist of 1971 IPC Nat Press Awards, Journalist of 1977 Br Press Awards, Crime Reporter of 1977 Witness Box Awards; *Recreations* rugby union, chess, golf, reading; *Clubs* Preston Grasshoppers RFC, Appleby Golf; *Style*— Barry Askew, Esq; School House, Orton, Nr Penrith, Cumbria (☎ (05874) 434)

ASKEW, Bryan; s of John Pinkney Askew (d 1940), and Matilda Brown; *b* 18 August 1930; *Educ* Wellfield GS Wingate Co Durham, Fitzwilliam Coll Cambridge (MA); *m* 10 Aug 1955, Millicent Rose, da of Thomas Henry Holder (d 1966); 2 da (Penelope Jane b 1957, Melissa Clare b 1966); *Career* ICI Ltd 1952-59, Consett Iron Co Ltd (later part of Br Steel Corp) 1959-71, own consultancy 1971-74, Samuel Smith Old Brewery (Tadcaster) 1974-, personnel dir 1982; chm Yorks Regnl Health Authy 1983; memb: Working Gp on Young People and Alcohol, Home Off Standing Conference on Crime Prevention 1987-; FRSA 1986; FRSM 1988; *Style*— Bryan Askew, Esq; The Old Brewery, Tadcaster, N Yorks LS24 9SB (☎ Tadcaster 832225, fax Tadcaster 834673)

ASKEW, Henry John; s of Maj John Marjoribanks Eskdale Askew, CBE, *qv*, of Ladykirk, Berwick-upon-Tweed, and Lady Susan Alice, *née* Egerton, *qv*; *b* 5 April 1940; *Educ* Eton; *m* 27 Jan 1978, Rosemary Eileen, da of Dr Charles Edmunds Darby Taylor, of Alnwick House, Little Shelford, Cambridge; 2 s (Jack b 1984, George b 1986); *Career* cmmnd Grenadier Guards 1959-62; dir then md Gerrar & Nat Hldgs plc (formerly Gerrard & Nat Ltd) 1967-; *Recreations* reading, music, opera, ballet; *Clubs* Pratts; *Style*— Henry Askew, Esq; The Factor's House, Ladykirk, Berwick-upon-Tweed (☎ 0289 309); 77 Chester Row, London SW1W 8JI (☎ 01 730 6151); Gerrard & National Holdings plc, 33 Lombard St, 2nd Floor, London EC3V 9BQ (☎ 01 623 9981, fax 01 623 6173, car telephone 883589)

ASKEW, Ian Voase; MC (1945), DL (E Sussex 1975); s of Sidney Bruce Askew (d 1955), of Buxshalls, Lindfield, Sussex; *b* 9 May 1921; *Educ* Charterhouse, Christ's Coll Cambridge; *Career* served WW II Italy Capt KRRC; jt master of foxhounds Southdown 1956-66; High Sheriff of Sussex 1969; *Clubs* Army and Navy; *Style*— Ian Askew, Esq, MC, DL; Wellingham Folly, Lewes, E Sussex (☎ 0273 812357)

ASKEW, John Marjoribanks; CBE (1974), JP (Berwicks); s of William Haggerston Askew, JP, of Ladykirk, Berwicks, and Castle Hills, Berwick on Tweed (d 1942), by his w Katherine (herself da of Hon John Gordon, sometime MP for Elgin & Nairn and for Brighton, who was in his turn eld s of Baron Gordon, PC, Lord Advocate for Scotland, a Lord of Appeal in Ordinary and a Life Peer); *b* 22 Sept 1908; *Educ* Eton, Magdalene Coll Cambridge; *m* 1, 1933 (m dis 1966), Lady Susan Alice Egerton, 4 da of 4 Earl of Ellesmere, MVO; 1 s (Henry John), 1 da (*see* Baron Faringdon); m 2, 1976, Priscilla Anne, da of Algernon Ross Farrow (d 1973); *Career* Lt 2 Bn Gren Gds 1932, Capt 1940, Maj 1943, served WW II France & Germany; Vice-Lt for Berwickshire 1955-65 (DL 1946-55); Brigadier Royal Co of Archers (Queen's Bodyguard for Scotland); convener: Berwicks CC 1961, Borders Regnl Cncl 1974-82; *Clubs* New (Edinburgh), Boodle's, Pratt's; *Style*— John Askew, Esq, CBE, JP; Ladykirk, Berwicks (☎ Berwick 0289 82229); Castle Hills, Berwick upon Tweed

ASKEW, Rev Canon Reginald James Albert; s of Paul Askew (d 1953), pioneer of Br Broadcasting, and Amy, *née* Wainwright (d 1976); *b* 16 May 1928; *Educ* Harrow Sch, CCC Cambridge (BA, MA); *m* 1953, Kate, yr da of Rev Henry Townsend Wigley (d 1970), gen sec Free Church Federal Cncl; 1 s (Paul), 2 da (Catherine, Rachel); *Career* curate Highgate 1957-61, lectr and vice-princ Wells Theological Coll 1961-69, vicar of Christ Church Lancaster Gate London 1969-73, canon of Salisbury and prebendary of Grantham Borealis 1975; chm The Southern Dioceses Ministerial Trg Scheme 1973-, princ Salisbury and Wells Theological Coll 1973-1987; Dean of King's Coll London 1988-; *Books* The Tree of Noah (1971); *Recreations* music, gardening, making lino-cuts, cricket; *Style*— Rev Canon Reginald Askew; Carters Cottage, North Wootton, Somerset BA4 4AF; King's College, Strand, London WC2R 2LS (☎ 01 836 5454)

ASKEW, Lady Susan Alice; *née* Egerton; da of late 4 Earl of Ellesmere, MVO and Lady Violet, *née* Lambton, da of 4 Earl of Durham; sis of 6 Duke of Sutherland; *b* 1913; *m* 1933 (m dis 1966), Maj John Marjoribanks Askew, Gren Gds; 1 s, 1 da (m 3 Baron Faringdon, *qv*); *Style*— Lady Susan Askew; Stone House, Sprouston, Kelso, Roxburghshire (☎ 0573 24338)

ASKEY WOOD, John Humphrey; s of Lt Col Edward Askey Wood, Leics Regt, and Irene Jeanne, *née* Parry; *b* 26 Nov 1932; *Educ* Winchester, CCC Cambridge (MA); *m* 1981, Katherine Ruth Stewart, da of Capt Horace Alan Peverley (d 1952), Canadian Gren Gds, of Wildwood, St Andrews East, Quebec, Canada; 1 s (Jason b 1966), 1 step s (Alexander b 1965), 1 step da (Kate b 1968); *Career* md Consolidated Gold Fields plc 1979-; chm: ARC Ltd 1979-86, De Havilland Aircraft Co Ltd 1956, Hawker Siddeley Aviation Ltd 1964; dir and gen mangr Manchester 1969-75; md industl and marine div Rolls-Royce Ltd 1976-79; cncl memb CBI 1983; vice-pres Nat Cncl of Bldg Products 1985; *Recreations* fly fishing, sailing, painting; *Style*— Humphrey Askey Wood, Esq; Consolidated Gold Fields Plc, 31 Charles II St, St James's Square, London SW1Y 4AG (☎ 01 930 6200; telex: 883071 Giovan G; fax: 01 930 9677)

ASPDEN, Hon Mrs (Judith Anne); *née* Nicholls; da of Baron Harmar-Nicholls, JP (Life Peer and 1 Bt); *b* 1941; *m* 1973, Alan Aspden; *Style*— The Hon Mrs Aspden

ASPEL, Michael Terence; s of Edward and Violet Aspel; *b* 12 Jan 1933; *Educ* Emanuel Sch; *m* 1 1957 (m dis), Dian; 2 s (Gregory, Richard); m 2 1962 (m dis), Ann; 1 s (Edward), 1 da (Jane) (twins); m 3 1977, Elizabeth Power, the actress; 2 s (Patrick, Daniel) (and 1 s decd); *Career* serv Nat Serv KRRC; writer and broadcaster; radio actor 1954-57, BBC TV news reader 1957-68, freelance 1968, Capital Radio disc jockey 1974-84, presenter: LWT The Six O'Clock Show from Jan 1982, Thames TV Give Us A Clue, This is Your Life, LWT Aspel & Company, LWT Child's Play; memb: Lord's Taverners, RYA; pres Stackpole Tst, vice-pres Baby Life Support Systems, hon vice-pres Assoc for Spina Bifida and Hydrocephalus; ord fellow Zoological Soc of London; *Books* Polly wants a Zebra, Hang on!; *Style*— Michael Aspel, Esq; c/o Bagenal Harvey Organisation, 141-143 Drury Lane, London WC2B 5TB (☎ 01 379 4625)

ASPELL, Col Gerald Laycock; TD (1948), DL (Leicestershire 1952); s of Samuel Frederick Aspell (d 1949), of Queniborough Grange, Leics, and Agnes Maude, *née* Laycock (1962); *b* 10 April 1915; *Educ* Uppingham; *m* 1939, Mary Leeson, da of Rev Ion Carroll of Edmondsham, Dorset; 1 s (Timothy), 2 da (Caroline, Penelope); *Career* Col TA 1933-1984 UK and Burma; CA 1938, ptnr Coopers & Lybrand 1952-78; dir Leicester Bldg Soc 1964-85 (chm 1978-85); tstee Uppingham Sch 1964-87 (chm 1977-87); vice-Lord Lt (Leicestershire) 1984-; *Recreations* tennis; *Clubs* Leicestershire; *Style*— Col Gerald Aspell, Esq, TD, DL; Laburnum Ho, Great Dalby, Melton Mowbray, Leics LE14 2HA (☎ 0664 63604)

ASPIN, Peter; s of Thomas Aspin (d 1955); *b* 3 Jan 1933; *Educ* Quarry Bank Sch Liverpool, King's Coll Cambridge (MA); *m* Maureen; 2 children; *Career* professional engr; chm (fomer MD) Allbook & Hashfield Ltd (formerly Giltspur Precision Industries Ltd); *Recreations* shooting; *Style*— Peter Aspin, Esq; Scylla House, Whatton-in-the-Vale, Notts; Allbook & Hashfield Ltd, 153 Huntingdon St, Nottingham (☎ 0602 582721)

ASPIN, William George; s of George Francis Aspin, of The Elms, Willow Ave, Constable Lee, Rawtenstall, Rossendale, Lancs, and Margaret, *née* Joyce; *b* 16 August 1954; *Educ* Cardinal Langley GS; *Career* CA, formed W G Aspin & Co 1980, ptnr Dymond Ashworth & Co, Accountants; chm and dir Spiralfair Properties Ltd 1987-; memb Rossendale Round Table; FICA (1983); *Recreations* golf, jogging, reading; *Clubs* Rossendale Golf; *Style*— William George Aspin Esq; The Elms, Willow Avenue, Constable Lee, Rawtenstall, Rossendale, Lancs (☎ 0706 216 442); Dymond Ashworth & Co, Accountants, 19 Ormerod Road, Burnley, Lancs (☎ 0282 37215)

ASPINALL, John Victor; s of late Col Robert Aspinall, and Mary Grace, *née* Horn later Lady Osborne (d 1987); *b* 11 June 1926; *Educ* Rugby (expelled), Jesus Coll Oxford (sent down); *m* 1, 1956 (m dis 1966), Jane Gordon Hastings; 1 s 1 da; m 2, 1966 (m dis 1972), Belinda Musker; m 3, 1972, Lady Sarah Marguerite Curzon; 1 s; *Career* WW II, Royal Marine 1943-45; fndr: Howletts Zoo Park 1958, Clermont Club 1962, Port Lympne Zoo Park 1973, Aspinall Club 1978, Aspinall's Curzon Club 1984; *Books* Best of Friends (1976); *Style*— John Aspinall, Esq; Howletts, Canterbury, Kent; Port Lympne, Lympne, Kent; 1 Lyall St London SW1; Noordhoek Manor, Cape Town 7985, SA; 64 Sloane St, London SW1 (☎ 235 2768, fax 235 4701)

ASPINALL, Martin Mark Charles; s of Charles Nicholas Bernard Aspinall, of family home, Standen Hall, Clitheroe, and Margaret Mary, *née* Worsley-Worswick; *b* 28 April 1951; *Educ* Redrice, RAC Cirencester; *Career* land agent, surveyor, with Miny of Agric and in private practice, chm and md Cotswold Sheepskins & Woollens Ltd 1985; dir Glenisla Property Co Ltd 1987; ARICS; *Recreations* shooting, fishing; *Style*— Martin Aspinall, Esq; c/o Barclays Bank, 128 High St, Cheltenham, Glos; Cotswold Sheepskins & Woollens Ltd, 2A Queens Circus, Montpellier, Cheltenham, Glos (☎ 0242 222377)

ASPINALL, Lady Sarah Marguerite; *née* Curzon; da of 5 Earl Howe, CBE, VD, PC (d 1964); *b* 25 Jan 1945; *m* 1, 1966, Piers Raymond Courage (d 1970); 2 s (Jason b 1967, Amos b 1969); m 2, 1972, John Victor Aspinall, s of late Col Robert Aspinall; 1 s (Bassa Wulfhere b 1972); *Style*— Lady Sarah Aspinall; 1 Lyall St, London SW1

ASPINALL, Wilfred; s of Charles Aspinall (d 1972), and Elizabeth, *née* Cadmen (d 1984); *b* 14 Sept 1942; *Educ* Poynton Secondary Modern Sch, Stockport Coll for Further Education; *m* 1973, Judith Mary, da of Leonard James Pimlott (d 1979); 1 da (Isabel b 1980); *Career* asst gen sec Nat Westminster Staff Assoc 1969-75, gen sec Confedn of Bank Staff Assoc 1975-79, memb Banking Staff Cncl 1970-77, tres and conslt: Managerial Professional and Staff Liaison Gp 1978-79, Nat Unilever Mangrs Assoc 1979-81, Royal Insur Branch Mangrs Assoc 1980-83; exec dir Fedn of Managerial Professional and General Assocs (MPG) 1979-, vice-pres Confédération Internationale des Cadres 1979- (observer 1978-79); memb: Hammersmith Special Health Authy 1982-, North Herts Health Authy 1982-6, North West Thames Reg Health Authy 1986-; memb Econ and Social Consultative Assembly Brussels 1986-; *Clubs* The Lighthouse, European; *Style*— Wilfred Aspinall, Esq; The Croft, 19 Shillington Rd, Pirton, Hitchin, Herts (☎ 0462 712316); Tavistock House, Tavistock Sq, London WC1 (☎ 01 380 0472)

ASPINWALL, Jack Heywood; MP (C) Wansdyke 1983-; *b* 1933,Feb; *Educ* Prescot GS Lancs, Marconi Coll Chelmsford; *m* Brenda Jean Aspinwall; *Career* RAF 1949-56, contested (Lib) Kingswood Feb and Oct 1974, Kingswood (C) 1979-1983; co dir; *Books* Kindly Sit Down, Tell me Another, Hit me Again, After Dinner Stories; *Style*— Jack Aspinwall, Esq, MP; House of Commons, London SW1A 0AA

ASPREY, Algernon; s of George Kenneth Asprey (d 1946), and Charlotte Esta Asprey; *b* 2 June 1912; *Educ* Charterhouse, Sch of Art; *m* 1939, Beatrice, da of Francis Bryant (d 1960); 1 s, 1 da (and 1 da decd); *Career* Capt Scots Gds 1940-46; artist and designer; Asprey Bond St 1933-71 (md); chm: Purchase Tax Ctee (post war years to its disbandment), Algernon Asprey Ltd 1971-80, Guards Club 1960-65; pres Bond St Assoc 1968-81 (chm 1965-68); ctee memb Friends of Royal Acad; Prime Warden Worshipful Co of Goldsmiths 1977-78; *Recreations* painting, sailing, golf; *Clubs* Buck's, Cavalry and Guards (Hon member); *Style*— Algernon Asprey, Esq; Magnolia Cottage, Shamley Green, Surrey GU5 0SX (☎ 0483 27 1502)

ASQUITH, Lady (Mary) Annunziata; da of 2 Earl of Oxford and Asquith, KCMG; *b* 28 July 1948; *Educ* Mayfield Sussex, Somerville Coll Oxford; *Career* formerly with Daily Telegraph Magazine; writer; art dealer; *Books* Marie Antoninette (1974); *Style*— Lady Annunziata Asquith; c/o The Manor House, Mells, Frome, Somerset

ASQUITH, Hon Mrs Paul; Caroline Anne; *née* Pole; yr da of Sir John Gawen Carew Pole, 12 Bt, DSO, TD, *qv*; *b* 11 Jan 1933; *m* 16 July 1963, as his 2 w, Hon Paul Asquith (d 1984), yr s of Baron Asquith of Bishopstone (Life Peer) (d 1954); 1 s, 1 da; *Style*— Hon Mrs Paul Asquith; 41 Quarrendon St, London SW6 (☎ 01 731 3955)

ASQUITH, Lady Clare Perpetua Frances; da of 2 Earl of Oxford and Asquith, KCMG; *b* 28 Mar 1955; *Style*— Lady Clare Asquith; c/o The Manor House, Mells, Frome

ASQUITH, Hon Dominic Anthony Gerard; s of 2 Earl of Oxford and Asquith, KCMG; *b* 7 Feb 1957; *m* 12 May 1988, Louise E, only da of John E Cotton, of Wollaton, Nottingham; *Style*— The Hon Dominic Asquith; c/o The Manor House, Mells, Frome

ASQUITH, Lady Helen Frances; OBE (1965); da of late Raymond Asquith (ka 1916, Battle of the Somme, s of 1 Earl of Oxford and Asquith); sis of 2 Earl; *b* 1908; *Educ* St Paul's Girls' Sch, Somerville Coll Oxford (BA); *Career* HM inspector of schools; *Style*— Lady Helen Asquith, OBE; Tynts Hill, Mells, Frome, Somerset

ASQUITH, Hon Luke; er s of Baron Asquith of Bishopstone, PC (Life Peer) (d 1954); *b* 18 Nov 1919; *Educ* Winchester; *m* 2 July 1954, (Ethel) Meriel, da of Maurice Cann Evans, of Arrow Lawn, Eardisland, Herefordshire; 2 da; *Career* served 1939-45 War in N Africa; Italy as GOC (3) Liaison Offr 8 Army Tai HQ; *Style*— The Hon Luke Asquith; The Paddock, Broad St, Alresford, Hants SO24 9AN

ASQUITH, Viscount; Raymond Benedict Bartholomew Michael Asquith; s and h of 2 Earl of Oxford and Asquith, KCMG; *b* 24 August 1952; *Educ* Ampleforth, Balliol Oxford; *m* 1978, Clare, da of Francis Pollen (d 1987), and Thérèse (da of His Hon Sir Joseph Sheridan) and gda of late Arthur Pollen (gn of Sir Richard Pollen, 3 Bt) by his w Hon Daphne Baring, da of 3 Baron Revelstoke; 1 s (Mark), 2 da (Magdalen and Frances); *Heir* s Hon Mark Julian Asquith b 13 May 1979; *Style*— Viscount Asquith; Little Claveys, Mells, Frome, Somerset

ASSCHER, (Adolf) William; s of William Benjamin Asscher (d 1982), and Roosje, *née* van der Molen; *b* 20 Mar 1931; *Educ* Maerlant Lyceum The Hague Netherlands, London Hosp Med Coll Univ (BSc, MB, BS, MD); *m* 1, 1960, Corrie, *née* van Welt (d 1961); m 2, 3 Nov 1961, Jennifer, da of Wynne Lloyd, CB (d 1973), of Cardiff; 2 da (Jane b 1963, Sophie b 1965); *Career* Nat Serv 1949-51 cmmnd Lt RE; jr med appts London Hosp 1957-64; WNSM Cardiff: conslt physician and sr lectr in medicine 1964-70, reader in medicine 1970-76, prof of medicine 1976-80; prof and hd of dept of renal medicine Univ of Wales Coll of Medicine 1980-87; St George's Hosp Med Sch London Univ 1988-: hon conslt physician, dean, prof of medicine; RCP: regnl advsr 1973-77, cncllr 1977-80; memb Welsh Arts Cncl 1985-88; Liveryman Soc of Apothecaries of London 1960; MRCP 1959, FRCP 1970; memb: Renal Assoc 1962 (pres 1986-89), Assoc of Physicians 1970, Med Res Soc 1957; *Books* The Challenge of Urinary Tract Infections (1981), Nephrology Ilustrated (1982), Nephro-Urology (1983); *Recreations* visual arts, golf; *Clubs* Reform, Radyr Lawn Tennis (chm 1972-78); *Style*— Prof William Asscher; Dean's Office, St George's Hospital Medical School, Cranmer Terrace, Tooting, London SW17 ORE (☎ 01 672 3122, fax 01 672 6940)

ASSERSON, Ronald Henry; s of David Asserson (d 1937), of London, and Charlotte Shire (d 1983); *b* 4 Jan 1923; *Educ* St Pauls, London Univ (BSc Hons in Chem Eng); *m* 1954, Denise Alice, da of Hugo Falk (d 1964) of London; 2 s (Trevor Richard b 1956, Stephen Charles b 1959), 1 da (Janine Karen b 1955); *Career* chm Boosey and Hawkes plc 1985-; dir Delta Gp plc 1972-85, BRE Ltd 1980-82, Benjamin Priest Gp plc 1985-, Yale and Valor plc 1981-; *Recreations* music, literature; *Clubs* Royal Automobile, City Livery; *Style*— Ronald H Asserson, Esq; 50 Wildwood Road, London NW11 6UP (☎ 01 458 1881); N Chailey Sussex; Boosey and Hawkes plc, Deansbrook Road, Edgeware, Middx HA8 9BB

ASSHETON, Hon Elizabeth Jane; da of 2 Baron Clitheroe; *b* 6 Oct 1968; *Style*— The Hon Elizabeth Assheton

ASSHETON, Hon John Hotham; yr s of 2 Baron Clitheroe; *b* 12 July 1964; *Educ* Harrow; *Style*— The Hon John Assheton

ASSHETON, Hon Nicholas; Lord of the Manor and Liberty of Slaidburn, Grindleton and Bradford; s of 1 Baron Clitheroe, KCVO, PC (d 1984), and Sylvia, Lady Clitheroe, da of 6 Baron Hotham; *b* 23 May 1934; *Educ* Eton, Ch Ch Oxford (MA); *m* 29 Feb 1960, Jacqueline Jill, da of Marshal of the RAF Sir Arthur Harris, 1 Bt, GCB, OBE, AFC (d 1984), of Goring-on-Thames, by his 2 w; 1 s (Thomas b 1963), 2 da (Caroline b 1961, Marie Thérèse b 1967); *Career* formerly 2 Lt Life Gds, Lt Inns of Court Regt; memb Stock Exchange (and cncl 1969); dir: Coutts & Co, Nat Mutual Life Assoc of Australasia; Liveryman of Vintners' Co; *Clubs* Pratt's, White's; *Style*— The Hon Nicholas Assheton; 15 Hammersmith Terrace, London W6 9TS (☎ 01 748 3464); Coutts & Co, 440 Strand, London WC1R 0QS (☎ 01 379 6262)

ASSHETON, Hon Ralph Christopher; Lord of the Manors of Downham and Cuervale; s and h of 2 Baron Clitheroe, *qv*; *b* 1962; *Educ* Eton; *Style*— The Hon Ralph Assheton

ASTAIRE, Edgar; s of Max Astaire; *b* 23 Jan 1930; *Educ* Harrow; *m* 1958 (m dis 1975); 3 s (Mark b 1959, Simon b 1961, Peter b 1963); *Career* stockbroker; chm Cl-Astaire & Co Ltd; Master Pattenmakers' Co 1982; *Clubs* MCC, Queens; *Style*— Edgar Astaire, Esq; 11 Lowndes Close, Lowndes Place, London SW1X 8BZ (☎ 01 235 5757); Cold Comfort Farm, Wendover, Bucks (☎ 0296 623172); Cl-Astaire & Co Ltd, 117 Bishopsgate, London EC2M 3TD (☎ 01 283 2081)

ASTBURY, Michael Henry Richardson; s of John Astbury, OBE (d 1968), and Joyce Elsie, *née* Richardson (d 1978); *b* 3 May 1929; *Educ* Edinburgh Acad, Perse Sch Cambridge, St Catharines Coll Cambridge (MA); *m* 31 March 1959, Margaret, da of Leslie Arthur Hammond (d 1981); 2 s (Peter John Hammond b 5 June 1960, Jonathan Robert Hammond b 27 June 1962); *Career* Nat Serv RAEC 1947-49 (Greece, Egypt); barr Middle Temple 1953, asst sec Manchester Ship Canal Co 1954-57, sec Employers Fedn of Ceylon 1961-63 (dep sec 1957-61), prosecuting slr DTI 1963-67, dep sec Gen Cncl of the Senate of the Inns of Ct and the Bar 1967-77, sec Inc Soc of Valuers and Auctioneers 1977-; memb Kent Family Practitioner Ctee, chm Kent Med Servs Ctee, memb St Peters PCC Ightham Kent; Freeman: City of London, Worshipful Co of Glovers; *Books* Halsburys' Laws of England (contrib fourth edn), Butterworths Encyclopaedia of Forms and Precedents (advsy ed fifth edn); *Recreations* sailing, gardening, reading; *Clubs* MCC, Caledonian; *Style*— Michael Astbury, Esq; The Coach House, Oldbury, Ightham, nr Sevenoaks, Kent (☎ 0732 884 163); 3 Cadogan Gate, London SW1 (☎ 01 235 2282)

ASTELL HOHLER, Thomas Sidney; MC (1944); s of Col Arthur Preston Hohler, DSO (d 1919), of Long Crendon Manor, Bucks, and Laline, *née* Astell (later Mrs Stanley Barry); granted the name and arms of Astell Hohler on inheriting the Woodbury and Great Houghton Estate from his maternal uncle Richard Astell 1978; *b* 30 Nov 1919; *Educ* Eton; *m* 1952, (Julie) Jacqueline, da of late Marquis de Jouffroy d'Abbans, of Chateau d'Abbans, Doubs, France; 1 da (Isabelle Jacqueline Laline, m 24 Earl of Erroll, *qv*); *Career* Maj Gren Gds, served in WWII in France, N Africa and Italy; ptnr King & Shaxson plc 1946- (chm 1965-84); chm London Discount Market Assoc 1972; Liveryman of Worshipful Co of Grocers 1956 ; *Recreations* shooting, farming; *Clubs* Brooks's, City of London; *Style*— Thomas Astell Hohler, Esq, MC; Wolverton Park, Basingstoke, Hants RG26 5RU (☎ 0635 298200)

ASTILL, His Hon Judge Michael John; s of Cyril Norman Astill; slr, of Thurnby, Leics, and Winifred Tuckley; *b* 31 Jan 1938; *Educ* Blackfriars Sch, Laxton, Northants; *m* 1 June 1968, Jean Elizabeth, da of late Dr John Chrisholm Hamilton Mackenzie; 3 s (Matthew b 28 Dec 1972, James b 28 Dec 28 Dec 1972, Mark b 11 Nov 1975), 1 da (Katherine b 11 July 1971); *Career* CJ Midland and Oxford Circuit 1984; *Recreations* reading, music, gardening, sport; *Style*— His Honour Judge Michael J Astill

ASTLEY, Hon Delaval Thomas Harold; s and h of 22 Baron Hastings; *b* 25 April 1960; *Educ* Radley & Durham; *m* 26 July 1987, Veronica, er da of Richard Smart, of Chester; *Style*— The Hon Delaval Astley

ASTLEY, Sir Francis Jacob Dugdale; 6 Bt (UK 1821), of Everleigh, Wilts; s of late Rev Anthony Aylmer Astley, 6 s of 2 Bt; suc kinsman, Capt Sir Francis Henry Rivers Astley-Corbett, 5 Bt, 1943; *b* 26 Oct 1908; *Educ* Marlborough, Trin Oxford; *m* 1934, Brita Margareta Josefina, da of Karl Nyström, of Stockholm; 1 da; *Career* sr lectr Univ Coll Ghana 1948-62, head of classics dept Atlantic Coll St Donat's Castle 1962-69; *Style*— Sir Francis Astley, Bt; 16 Doulton Mews, Lymington Road, London NW6 1XY (☎ 01 435 9945)

ASTLEY, Hon Harriet Marguerite; da of 22 Baron Hastings; *b* 15 Mar 1958; *Educ* Bedales; *Recreations* Riding, Foreign Travel; *Style*— The Hon Harriet Astley

ASTLEY, Hon Justin Edward; s of 22 Baron Hastings; *b* 22 April 1968; *Style*— The Hon Justin Astley

ASTLEY COOPER, Alexander Paston; s and h of Sir Patrick Graham Astley Cooper, 6 Bt; *b* 1 Feb 1943; *Educ* Kelly Coll Tavistock; *m* 1974, Minnie Margeret, da of Charles Harrison (d 1959); *Career* gp buyer, paper merchanting; *Recreations* cricket, badminton, rugby union, theatre, travel; *Style*— Alexander Astley Cooper, Esq; Gadebridge, 18A Station Rd, Rayleigh, Essex SS6 7HL (☎ Rayleigh (0268) 777506)

ASTLEY COOPER, Sir Patrick Graham; 6 Bt (UK 1821) of Gadebridge, Herts; s of late Col Clifton Graham Astley Cooper, DSO, RA (gs of 2 Bt); suc kinsman Sir Henry Lovick Cooper, 5 Bt (d 1959); *b* 4 August 1918; *Educ* Marlborough; *m* 7 April 1942, Audrey Ann Jervoise, yr da of late Major Douglas Philip Jervoise Collas, Military Knight of Windsor; 1 s, 2 da; *Heir* s, Alexander Paston Astley Cooper; *Career* former sr asst land cmmr MAFF, dir Crendon Concrete Ltd Long Crendon 1973-; *Style*— Sir Patrick Astley Cooper, Bt; Monkton Cottage, Monks Risborough, Aylesbury, Bucks HP17 9JF (☎ 084 44 4210)

ASTON, Archdeacon of; *see*: Cooper, Ven John Leslie

ASTON, Bishop Suffragan of, 1985-; Rt Rev Colin Ogilvie Buchanan; s of Prof Robert Ogilvie Buchanan (sometime prof of Economic Geography LSE), and Kathleen Mary, *née* Parnell; *b* 9 August 1934; *Educ* Whitgift Sch S Croydon, Lincoln Coll Oxford; *m* 1963, Diana Stephenie Gregory; 2 da; *Career* ordained 1961; princ London Coll of Divinity 1979-85 (became St John's Coll Nottingham 1970, joined staff 1964); pres Movement for the Reform of Infant Baptism 1988-; *Books* author of several specialised religious works; *Recreations* vice-pres Electoral Reform Soc; *Style*— The Rt Rev the Bishop of Aston; 60 Handsworth Wood Road, Birmingham B20 2DT (☎ 021 554 5129)

ASTON, Lady; Eileen Fitzgerald; da of John Bell McNair; *m* 1949, Sir Christopher (Kit) Aston, KCVO (d 1982), sometime chm Powell Duffryn; 1 s (James), 2 da (Mrs Sergio Martinuzzi, Harriet); *Style*— Lady Aston; 32 Bowerdean St, London SW6 (☎ 01 736 5133)

ASTON, Sir Harold George; CBE (1976); s of Harold John Aston (d 1958), and Annie Dorothea, *née* McKeown; bro of Hon Sir William John Aston, *qv*; *b* 13 Mar 1923; *Educ* Crown St Boys' Sch; *m* 1947, Joyce Thelma, da of H Smith; 1 s, 1 da; *Career* chm Nat Trades and Indust Cncl 1978-80, pres Confed of Aust Industry, chm and chief exec Bonds Coats Patons Ltd 1980-; kt 1983; *see Debrett's Handbook of Australia and New Zealand* for further details; *Style*— Sir Harold Aston, CBE; 44 Greenway Drive, Pymble, NSW 2073, Australia

ASTON, Capt John Anthony, RN; s of Ernest Gustav Aston (d 1971), and Haley Muriel Grutchfield (d 1988); *b* 8 June 1939; *Educ* Whitgift Sch, Britannia RNC Dartmouth, London Univ (BSc); *m* 19 Dec 1970, Elizabeth Constance Mark, da of Rear Adm William Penrose Mark-Wardlaw, DSO (d 1952); 2 da (Katie b 1972, Susie b 1975); *Career* Cdr: naval asst to Dir Gen of Weapons (Navy) 1974-76, Admty Surface Weapons Estab 1976-78, HMS Sheffield 1978-79, staff of C-in-C Fleet 1979-82, exec offr HMS Mercury 1982, Capt 1982, naval attache Brazil 1983-86, staff of Cdr Br Forces Falklands 1986; MOD Whitehall 1987-; memb Anglo Brazilian Soc; *Recreations* skiing, scottish dancing; *Clubs* The Goat; *Style*— Capt John Aston, RN; 43 Christchurch Rd, St Cross, Winchester, Hants (☎ 0962 62919)

ASTON, Peter George; s of Dr George William Aston (d 1980), and Dr Elizabeth Oliver, *née* Smith (d 1979); *b* 5 Oct 1938; *Educ* Tettenhall Coll, Birmingham Sch of Music (GBSM), Univ of York (D Phil); *m* 13 Aug 1960, Elaine Veronica, da of Harold Neale (d 1942); 1 s (David b 1963); *Career* sr lectr in music Univ of York 1972-74 (lectr 1964-72); prof and head of music Univ of East Anglia 1974- (dean Sch of Fine Arts and Music 1981-84); music dir: Tudor Consort 1959-65, Eng Baroque Ensemble 1967-70; conductor Aldeburgh Festival Singers 1975-88, gen ed UEA Recordings 1979-, jt artistic dir Norwich Festival of Contemporary Church Music 1981-; published compositions inc: chamber music, church music, opera, choral and orchestral works; ed complete works of George Jeffreys and music by var Baroque composers; numerous recordings and contribs to int journals; hon patron: Gt Yarmouth Musical Soc, Lowestoft Choral Soc; chm Eastern Arts Assoc Music Panel 1975-81, chorus master Norfolk & Norwich Triennial Festival 1982-85, hon pres Trianon Music Gp 1984-; FTCL, FCI, ARCM, FRSA 1980; *Books* The Music of York Minster (1972), Sound and Silence (jtly 1970, Germ edn 1972, Italian edn 1980, Japanese edn 1981); *Recreations* bridge, chess, cricket; *Clubs* Athenaeum, Norfolk ; *Style*— Prof Peter Aston; Univ of East Anglia, Music Centre, Sch of Fine Arts and Music, Norwich NR4 7TJ (☎ 0603 56161, fax 0603 58553, telex 975197)

ASTON, Stanley Collin; OBE (1973), TD and Clasps, DL (Cambs 1960); s of Alfred Ernest Aston (d 1961), of Lincoln; *b* 4 Sept 1915; *Educ* City Sch Lincoln, St Catharine's Coll Cambridge (BA, MA, PhD); Doct de l'Univ de Clermont; *m* 1940, Rosalind Molly, da of Rev Frank Fairfax (d 1964), of Bebington, Cheshire; 1 s, 2 da; *Career* serv WWII Suffolk Regt, RM Division, Int Corps; 1946-80 Cambs Regt and Royal Anglian Regt (TA); dep hon Col (TA) Roy Anglian Regt 1972-80, chm: Cambs ACF 1947-77 and TA 1967-77; Bye-fell Magdalene Coll Cambridge 1938-43; fell St Catharine's Coll Cambridge 1943, dean 1946-57, tutor 1957-59, bursar 1961-79, pres 1980; univ lectr Cambridge 1946-82, visiting prof Ohio State Univ 1955-56 and 1961-62; pres Modern Humanities Research Assoc 1970 (sec 1945-50, chm 1950-68); sec-gen International Fedn for Modern Languages and Literatures 1954-78, pres 1984-87; pres International Cncl for Philosophy and Hunanistic Sciences UNESCO 1979-84 (memb 1952-75, vice-pres 1975-79); *Books* Peirol, Troubadour of Auvergne (1953); numerous articles on medieval Romance literatures; editor of journals and bibliographies; *Recreations* sports, music, philately; *Clubs* Cambridge U Assoc Football (pres), National Liberal; *Style—* Colonel Stanley Aston, OBE, TD and; c/o St Catharine's College, Cambridge (☎ 0223 338300); 4 Manor Walk, Fulbourn, Cambridge CB1 5BN (☎ 0223 881323); 108 Rasen Lane, Lincoln, LN1 3HD 108 Rasen Lane, Lincoln 0223 47414)

ASTON, Hon Sir William John; KCMG (1970), JP (NSW 1954); s of Harold John Aston (d 1958), and Annie Dorothea, *née* McKeown; bro of Sir Harold George Aston, *qv*; *b* 19 Sept 1916; *m* 1941, Beatrice Delaney Burrett; 1 s, 2 da; *Career* MHR (Lib) for Phillip NSW 1955-61 and 1963-72, chief govt whip (Fed Lib) 1962-64, speaker House of Representatives Australia 1967-73; chm Kolotex Glo Hldgs 1973-77; dir: Neilson McCarthy & Ptnrs 1973-, Astyle Pty Ltd 1973-; Korean Order of Distinguished Service Merit (First Class) 1969; *Recreations* golf, bowls, fishing; *Style—* The Hon Sir William Aston, KCMG, JP; 55 Olola Ave, Vaucluse, NSW 2030, Australia (☎ 337 5992); *see Debrett's Handbook of Australia and New Zealand* for further details

ASTOR, (Janet) Bronwen Alun; yst da of His Hon Judge Sir (John) Alun Pugh (d 1971), and Kathleen Mary, *née* Goodyear (d 1970); *b* 6 June 1930; *Educ* Dr William's Sch Dolgellau, Central Sch of Speech and Drama (Dip); *m* 1960, as his 3 w, 3 Viscount Astor (d 1966); 2 da; has not used title Viscountess Astor since 1976; *Career* teacher, TV announcer, model girl, psychotherapist; runs a retreat house; *Recreations* fishing, tennis, windsurfing; *Clubs* Univ Women's; *Style—* Mrs Bronwen Astor; Tuesley Manor, Tuesley, Godalming, Surrey GU7 1UD (☎ 04868 7281)

ASTOR, Hon (Francis) David Langhorne; s of 2 Viscount Astor (d 1952), and Nancy, Viscountess Astor, CH, MP (d 1964); *b* 5 Mar 1912; *Educ* Eton, Balliol Coll Oxford; *m* 1, 1945, Melanie Hauser; 1 da; m 2, 1952, Bridget Aphra Wreford; 2 s, 3 da; *Career* serv WWII; The Observer: foreign ed 1946-48, ed 1948-75, dir 1976-81; *Style—* The Hon David Astor; 9 Cavendish Ave, St John's Wood, London NW8 (☎ 01 286 0223); Manor House, Sutton Courtenay, Oxon (☎ (023 848) 221)

ASTOR, David Waldorf; s of Hon Michael Langhorne Astor (MP for Surrey East 1945-51, d 1980, 3 s of 2 Viscount Astor), and his 1 w, Barbara Mary (d 1980), da of Capt Ronald McNeill; n of Hon Sir John Astor, *qv*; *b* 9 August 1943; *Educ* Eton, Harvard Univ; *m* 19 Sept 1968, Clare Pamela, er da of Cdr Michael Beauchamp St John, DSC, RN; 2 s (Henry b 17 April 1969, Tom b 24 July 1972), 2 da (Joanna b 23 June 1970, Rose b 9 June 1979); *Career* short service cmmn in Royal Scots Greys 1962-65; farmer 1973-; chm Cncl for the Protection of Rural England 1983-; contested (SDP) Plymouth Drake 1987; FRSA 1988; *Recreations* walking, reading, skiing, cricket; *Clubs* Brooks's, MCC; *Style—* David Astor, Esq; CPRE, 4 Hobart Place, London SW1 (☎ 01 351 7507); Bruern Grange, Milton-under-Wychwood, Oxford OX7 6HA (☎ 0993 830413)

ASTOR, Hon Hugh Waldorf; JP (Berks 1953); s of 1 Baron Astor of Hever (d 1971) and Violet Mary Elliot, da of Earl of Minto; *b* 20 Nov 1920; *Educ* Eton, New Coll Oxford; *m* 1950, Emily Lucy, da of Sir Alexander Kinloch, 12 Bt; 2 s (Robert, James), 3 da (Virginia, Rachel, Jean); *Career* serv WWII Lt-Col Intelligence Corps; dep chm The Times 1959-67; dir: Hambros plc 1960-; Winterbottom Tst 1961-86, Phoenix Assur 1962-85; memb cncl of Trusthouse Forte 1962 chm 1971-; chm: Times Tst 1967-82, Peabody Donation Fund 1981- (dep chm 1979), mgmnt ctee King Edward's Hosp Fund for London 1983-88 (dep chm 1981); High Sherrif Berks 1963; *Recreations* shooting, sailing (Motor Yacht: 'Nautacuintli'), flying; *Clubs* Brooks's, Buck's, Pratt's, Royal Yacht Sqdn, Royal Ocean Racing; *Style—* The Hon Hugh Astor, JP; 14 Culross St, London W1Y 3HN (☎ 01 629 4601); Folly Farm, Sulhamstead, Berks RG7 4DF (☎ 0734 302326)

ASTOR, Hon Janet Elizabeth; 2 da of 3 Viscount Astor (d 1966); *b* 1 Dec 1961; *Educ* Charterhouse, New Coll Oxford; *Style—* The Hon Janet Astor; 58A Berwick St, London W1

ASTOR, Hon Sir John Jacob; MBE (1945), DL (Cambs 1962); s of 2 Viscount Astor; u of David W Astor, *qv*; *b* 29 August 1918; *Educ* Eton, New Coll Oxford; *m* 1, 1944 (m dis 1972), Ana Inez, da of Señor Dr Don Miguel Carcano, (Hon) KCMG, (Hon) KBE, sometime Argentine ambass to UK; 1 s (Michael Ramon Langhorne m 1979 Daphne Warburg), 1 da (Stella m 1974 Martin Wilkinson); m 2, 1976 (m dis 1985), Susan, da of Maj Michael Eveleigh; m 3, 16 March 1988, Mrs Marcia de Savary; *Career* serv WWII as Maj, French Croix de Guerre and Legion d'Honneur 1945; former JP Cambs; MP (C) 1951-59 Plymouth Sutton, PPS to Fin Sec Treas 1951-52; chm: Governing Body of Nat Inst of Agric Engrg 1963-68, Agric Res Cncl 1968-78, NEDC for Agric Ind 1978-83; steward Jockey Club 1968-71 and 1983-85, memb Horserace Betting Levy Bd 1976-80; kt 1978; *Clubs* White's; *Style—* The Hon Sir John Astor, MBE, DL; The Dower House, Hatley Park, Hatley St George, Sandy, Beds (☎ 0767 50266)

ASTOR, Hon Mrs Michael; Judith Caroline Traill; da of Paul Innes; *m* 1970, as his 3 w, Hon Michael Langhorne Astor (d 1980), 3 s of 2 Viscount Astor; 1 s (Joshua b 1966), 1 da (Polly b 1971); *Style—* The Hon Mrs Michael Astor; Red Brick House, Bruern, Churchill, Oxon

ASTOR, Hon Pauline Marian; yr da of 3 Viscount Astor (d 1966) by his 3 w; *b* 26 Mar 1964; *Educ* Downside, Sarah Lawrence Coll; *Clubs* Women's Univ; *Style—* The Hon Pauline Astor; 34 Talbot Rd, London W2

ASTOR, Hon Philip Douglas Paul; yr s of 2 Baron Astor of Hever (d 1984); *b* 4 April 1959; *Educ* Eton, Ch Ch Oxford (BA); *Style—* The Hon Philip Astor; Flat 3, 6 Embankment Gdns, London SW3 4LJ (☎ 01 351 0018); Tillypronie, Tarland, Aboyne, Aberdeenshire AB3 4XX (☎ 033 981 238)

ASTOR, 4 Viscount (UK 1917); William Waldorf Astor; also Baron Astor (UK 1916); only child of 3 Viscount Astor (d 1966), by his 1 w, Hon Sarah, *née* Norton, da of 6 Baron Grantley; the recurrent forename Waldorf commemorates a village near Heidelberg from which John Jacob Astor (ggf of 1 Viscount) emigrated to the New World in the end of the eighteenth century and later bought lands in the area now covered by New York; *b* 27 Dec 1951; *Educ* Eton; *m* 1976, Annabel Lucy Veronica, da of Timothy Jones (himself s of Sir Roderick Jones, KBE, sometime chm of Reuters, and his w, better known as the writer Enid Bagnold). Annabel's mother was Pandora, *née* Clifford (niece of 11 and 12 Barons Clifford of Chudleigh and sis of Lady Norwich - *see* 2 Viscount Norwich); 2 s (Hon William Waldorf, Hon James Jacob b 18 Jan 1979), 1 da (Hon Flora Katherine b 7 June 1976); *Heir* s, Hon William Waldorf Astor b 18 Jan 1979; *Career* Company Director; *Recreations* fishing, shooting; *Clubs* White's, Turf; *Style—* The Rt Hon The Viscount Astor; Ginge Manor, Wantage, Oxon (☎ 0235 833228)

ASTOR OF HEVER, Irene, Lady Irene Violet Freesia Janet Augusta; da of Field Marshal 1 Earl Haig, KT, GCB, DM, GCVO, KCIE (d 1928); *b* 7 Oct 1919; *m* 4 Oct 1945, 2 Baron Astor of Hever (d 1984); 2 s, 3 da; *Career* hon life memb BRCS (holder of Queen's Badge of Honour); chm/pres: Kent Branch Br Red Cross Soc 1976-82; patron Kent Co Royal Br Legion Women's Section, nat pres Royal British Legion Scotland Women's Section; pres Kent Agric Soc 1981 and 1982; vice-pres RNIB, chm appeals ctee Sunshine Fund for Blind Babies and Young People, patron The Asthma Soc and Friends of Asthma Soc, memb asthma res cncl; CStJ; *Style—* The Rt Hon the Lady Astor of Hever; French Street Farm House, Westerham, Kent TN16 1PW (☎ 0959 62141); 11 Llyall St, Eaton Sq, London SW1X 8DH (☎ 01 235 4755)

ASTOR OF HEVER, 3 Baron (UK 1956); John Jacob Astor; s of 2 Baron Astor of Hever by his w, Lady Irene Haig, da of 1 Earl Haig, KT, GCB, OM, GCVO, KCIE; *b* 16 June 1946; *Educ* Eton; *m* 1970, Fiona Diana Lennox, da of Capt Roger Harvey, JP, DL, Scots Gds, and Diana (da of Sir Harry Mainwaring, 5 and last Bt, by his w Generis, eld da of Sir Richard Williams-Bulkeley, 12 Bt, KCB, VD, JP, and Lady Magdalen Yorke, da of 5 Earl of Hardwicke); 3 da (Hon Camilla Fiona b 1974, Hon Tania Jentie b 1978, Hon Violet Magdalene b 1980); *Heir* bro Hon Philip Douglas Paul Astor; *Career* formerly Lt Life Gds; serv: Malaysia, Hong Kong, N Ireland; dir: Terres Blanches Services Sarl 1975-, Valberg Plaza Sarl 1977-82; Electro-Nucleonics Inc 1984-, md Honon et Cie 1982-; *Clubs* White's, Cavalry and Guards'; *Style—* The Rt Hon the Lord Astor of Hever; High Quarry, Froghole Lane, Crockham Hill, Edenbridge, Kent TN8 6TD

ASTROM, Hon Mrs (Brenda); *née* Cooper; eld da of Baron Cooper of Stockton Heath (Life Peer, d 1988); *b* 31 Mar 1937; *m* 1, 1958 (m dis 1967), John Abbott; m 2, 1968, Pereric Astrom; *Style—* The Hon Mrs Astrom; 9 Rathen Rd, Withington, Manchester M20 9QJ

ASTWOOD, Hon Mr Justice; Hon Sir James Rufus Astwood; JP; s of late James Rufus Astwood, and Mabel Winifred Astwood; *b* 4 Oct 1923; *Educ* Berkeley Inst Bermuda, Toronto Univ; *m* 1952, Gloria Preston Norton; 1 s, 2 da; *Career* barr Gray's Inn 1956, started practice at Jamaican Bar 1956, dep clerk of courts Jamaica 1957-58, stipendiary magistrate & Judge of Grand Court Cayman Islands 1958-59, clerk of courts Jamaica 1958-63, resident magistrate Jamaica 1963-74, puisne judge Jamaica 1971-73, sr magistrate Bermuda 1974-76, slr gen Bermuda 1976-77, actg attorney gen Bermuda 1976 and 1977, temp actg dep govr Bermuda during 1977, chief justice Bermuda 1977-; hon MA Gray's Inn 1985; kt 1982; *Style—* The Hon Sir James Astwood, CJ, Bermuda; Clifton, 8 Middle Rd, Devonshire, DV03 Bermuda (☎ 8092920263); Chief Justice's Chambers, Supreme Court, Hamilton HM12, Bermuda (☎ 8092921350)

ASTWOOD, Lt-Col Sir Jeffrey Carlton; CBE (1966), OBE (mil 1946, ED 1942); s of late Jeffrey Burgess Astwood, of Neston, Bermuda, and Lilian Maude, *née* Searles; *b* 5 Oct 1907; *Educ* Saltus GS Bermuda; *m* 1928, Hilda Elizabeth Kay, da of Henry George Longhurst Onions, of Aberfeldy, Somerset, Bermuda; 1 s, 1 da; *Career* memb House of Assembly Bermuda 1948-72, memb exec cncl and dep speaker 1957-68, speaker 1968-72, min Agric, Immigration and Labour, Health; pres: Atlantic Investmt and Devpt Ltd, Aberfeldy Nurseries Ltd, J B Astwood & Son Ltd, Astwood Cycles Ltd; kt 1972; *Recreations* horticulture, theatre; *Clubs* Royal Bermuda Yacht, Directors, RHS Vincent SQ ; *Style—* Lt-Col Sir Jeffrey Astwood, CBE, OBE, ED; Greenfield, Somerset, Bermuda (☎ 234 1729 or 234 2765)

ATCHERLEY, Sir Harold Winter; s of L W Atcherley, and Maude Lester, *née* Nash; *b* 30 August 1918; *Educ* Gresham's, Heidelberg Univ, Geneva Univ; *m* 1946 (legally separated 1978), Anita Helen, *née* Leslie, and wid of Sub-Lt W D H Eves, RN; 1 s, 2 da; *Career* serv WWII 18 Inf Div Singapore (POW); with Royal Dutch Shell Gp 1937-39 and 1946-70 (personnel coordinator 1964-70), recruitment advsr to MOD 1970-71, chm Armed Forces Pay Review Body 1971-82, memb Top Salaries Review Body 1971-87; memb: Halsbury ctee of enquiry into Pay and Conditions of Service of Nurses and Midwives 1974, ctee of inquiry into Remuneration of Members of Local Authorities 1977-; dir Br Home Stores Ltd 1973-87, chm Tyzack & Ptnrs 1979-85; memb management ctee Toynbee Hall 1979-; chm: Toynbee Hall 1985-, Police Negotiating Bd 1983-85 (dep chm 1982-83); vice chm Suffolk Tst for Nature Conservation 1987-, dep chm Aldeburgh Fndn 1988-; Empress Leopoldina Medal Brazil; kt 1977; *Style—* Sir Harold Atcherley; Conduit House, The Green, Long Melford, Suffolk (☎ 0787 310 897)

ATHA, Bernard Peter; s of Horace Michael Atha, of Leeds (d 1984), and Mary, *née* Quinlan (d 1951); *b* 27 August 1928; *Educ* Leeds Modern GS, Leeds Univ (LLB), RAF Sch of Educn (Dip Ed); *Career* Nat Serv FO RAF 1950-52; called to Bar Gray's Inn 1950; actor and variety artist films and tv incl: Kes, Coronation St; princ lectr business studies Huddersfield Tech Coll 1973-; elected Leeds City Cncl 1957, contested (Lab): Penrith and Border 1959, Pudsey 1964; vice-chm Sports Cncl 1976-80, memb Arts Cncl 1979-82; chm: Nat Watersports Centre 1978-84, Educn Social Servs and Watch Ctees; current chm: Leisure Servs ctee, Leeds Co-op Soc, Grand Theatre, City of Varieties, Red Ladder Theatre Co, Yorkshire Dance Cente, Leeds Playhouse, UK Sports Assoc for People with Mental Handicap; memb: Sports Aid Fndn, Sports Aid Tst; vice-chm Leeds West Health Authy, govr Further Educn Staff Coll; FRSA; *Recreations* the arts, sport, politics; *Style—* Bernard Atha, Esq; 25 Moseley Wood Croft, Leeds LS16 7JJ (☎ 0532 6672 485, 0532 463 000)

ATHERTON, David; s of Robert Atherton, and Lavinia, *née* Burton; *b* 3 Jan 1944; *Educ* Cambridge Univ (MA); *m* 5 Sept 1970, Ann Gianetta, da of Cdr JF Drake (d 1978), of Ware, Herts; 1 s (John b 14 May 1979), 2 da (Elizabeth b 13 Feb 1974, Susan b 10 June 1977); *Career* conductor, fndr and musical dir London Sinfonietta 1967-73; Royal Opera House: repetiteur 1967-68, res conductor 1968-79; Royal Liverpool Philharmonic Orchestra: princ conductor and artistic advsr 1980-83, princ guest conductor 1983-86; musical dir and princ conductor San Diego Symphony Orchestra 1980-87, musical dir and princ conductor Hong Kong Philharmonic Orchestra 1989-; artistic dir and conductor: London Stravinsky Festival 1979-82, Ravel/Varese Festival 1983-84, musical dir and princ conductor Californian Mainly Mozart Festival 1989-; youngest conductor: Henry Wood Promenade Concerts Royal Albert Hall and Royal Opera House 1968, Royal Festival Hall debut 1969; performances abroad incl:

Europe, M East, F East, Australasia, N America; awards incl: Composers' Guild of GB Conductor of the Year 1971, Edison award 1973, Grand Prix du Disque 1977, Koussevitzky Award 1981, Internat Record Critics Award 1982, Prix Caecilia 1982; adapted and arranged Pandora by Robert Gerhard for Royal Ballet 1975; fell Royal Soc of Musicians 1976; *Books* The Complete Instrumental and Chamber Music of Arnold Schoenberg and Roberto Gerhard (ed 1973), Pandora and Don Quixote Suites by Roberto Gerhard (ed 1973), The Musical Companion (contrib 1978), The New Grove Dictionary (1981); *Recreations* travel, squash, theatre; *Style—* David Atherton, Esq; c/o Harold Holt Ltd, 31 Sinclair Rd, London W14 0NS (☎ 01 603 4600, fax 01 603 0019, telex 22339 HUNTER G)

ATHERTON, John Bryan; s of John James Atherton (d 1983), and Mona, *née* Hollings; *b* 17 Feb 1938; *Educ* Arnold Sch Blackpool, Sheffield Univ (BMet); *m* 1964, Valerie Anthea, da of Guy Easton, of Swindon, Kingswinford; *Career* md and chief exec Br Bright Bar Ltd; dir: Flather Bright Steels Ltd, Nationwide Steel Stock Ltd, Jaldon Ltd; *Recreations* golf, music; *Clubs* Enville; *Style—* John Bryan Atherton, Esq; Loneacre, Feiashill Rd, Trysull, nr Wolverhampton, W Midlands WV5 7HT (☎ 0902 896 500); British Bright Bar Ltd, Bloomfield Rd, Tipton, W Midlands DY4 9EP (☎ 021 520 8141, fax 021 520 8929, telex BBBTPT 336214)

ATHERTON, Maurice Alan; CBE (1981), JP (Kent 1982), DL (Kent 1984); s of Rev Harold Atherton (d 1975), of Sheffield, and Beatrice, *née* Shaw (d 1958); *b* 9 Oct 1926; *Educ* St John's Sch Leatherhead; *m* 28 Aug 1954, Guendolene Mary (Wendi), da of Col James Bryan Upton, MBE, TD, JP, DL (d 1976), of Hotham, York; 1 s (James b 1966), 1 da (Christine b 1965); *Career* E Yorks Regt 1944-58 serv: Egypt, Sudan, Malaysia, Austria, Germany, N Ireland; Staff Coll Camberley 1958, mil asst Hong Kong 1959-62, coll chief instr Sandhurst 1964-67, cmd 1 Green Howards 1967-69, def advsr Ghana 1971-73, cdr Dover/Shorncliffe Garrison and dep constable Dover Castle 1976-81; co pres (Kent): Royal Br Legion 1982-, Men of the Trees, co chm Army Benevolent Fund, govr Dover Coll, High Sheriff of Kent 1983-84; *Recreations* shooting, gardening, skiing; *Clubs* Army and Navy, Lansdowne; *Style—* A Atherton, Esq CBE, JP, DL; Digges Place, Barham, Canterbury, Kent CT4 6PJ (☎ 0227 831420)

ATHERTON, Peter; s of Joseph Ignatius Atherton (d 1984), of Wrightington, and Winifred, *née* Marsh; *b* 8 Nov 1952; *Educ* Mount St Mary's Coll Derby, Univ of Birmingham (LLB), Coll of Law; *m* 17 Oct 1981, Jennifer Marie, da of Charles Birch, of Ontrio Canada; 1 s (Timothy Peter b 4 Sept 1985), 1 da (Hilary Anne b 4 Jan 1984); *Career* called to the Bar Gray's Inn 1975, jnr Northern circuit 1978-79; chm young barr's ctee Senate of Inns of Ct and Bar Cncl for England and Wales 1982-83; memb Bar Cncl; *Recreations* tennis, golf, theatre; *Style—* Peter Atherton, Esq; Deans Court Chambers, Crown Squ, Manchester (☎ 061 834 4097)

ATHOLL, 10 Duke of (S 1703); George Iain Murray; also Lord Murray of Tullibardine (S 1604), Earl of Tullibardine (S 1606), Earl of Atholl (S 1629), Marquess of Atholl (S 1676), Marquess of Tullibardine (S 1703), Earl of Strathtay and Strathardle (S 1703), Viscount of Balwhidder, Glenalmond and Glenlyon (S 1703), and Lord Murray, Balvenie, and Gask (S 1703; s of Lt-Col George Murray, OBE, RA (ka 1945, s of Sir Evelyn Murray, KCB, himself gggs of Rt Rev Lord George Murray, DD, sometime Bishop of St David's and 2 s of 3 Duke of Atholl, KT), by his w, Hon Angela Pearson (later Hon Mrs Campbell-Preston, d 1981), da of 2 Viscount Cowdray; suc kinsman, 9 Duke of Atholl, 1957; *b* 19 June 1931; *Educ* Eton, Christ Church Coll Oxford; *Heir* kinsman, John Murray b 1929; *Career* proprietor of the Atholl Highlanders (sole legal private army in UK); Representative Peer for Scotland 1958-63; chm: Westminster Press 1974- (dir 1963-), RNLI 1979-89; dir: Pearson Longman 1975-83; vice-pres Nat Tst for Scotland 1977-; memb Red Deer Cmmn; pres Int Sheepdog Soc 1982-83 and 1987-88; Capt House of Lords Bridge Team in matches against the Commons 1979-; *Recreations* golf, bridge, shooting, stalking; *Clubs* Turf, White's, New (Edinburgh); *Style—* His Grace The Duke of Atholl; Blair Castle, Blair Atholl, Perthshire (☎ 079 681 212); 31 Marlborough Hill, London NW8 (☎ 01 586 2291); Westminster Press, 8-16 Great New St, London EC4P 4ER (☎ 01 353 1030)

ATIYAH, Prof Sir Michael Francis; s of Edward Selim Atiyah (d 1964), and Jean, *née* Levens (d 1964); *b* 22 May 1929; *Educ* Victoria Coll Egypt, Manchester GS, Cambridge Univ (MA, PhD); *m* 1955, Lily Jane Myles, da of John Cameron Brown (d 1970); 3 children; *Career* fell Trinity Coll Cambridge 1954-58, Savilian prof of geometry Oxford 1963-69, prof of mathematics Inst for Advanced Study Princeton USA 1969-72, Royal Soc Research prof Mathematical Inst Oxford Univ; hon ScD Cambridge Univ; FRS; kt 1983; *Recreations* gardening; *Style—* Prof Sir Michael Atiyah; Shotover Mound, Headington, Oxford (☎ 0865 62359); Mathematical Institute, 24 St Giles, Oxford OX1 3LB (☎ 0865 273 555)

ATIYAH, Prof Patrick Selim; s of Edward Selim Atiyah (d 1964), and D Jean C Atiyah, *née* Levens (d 1964); bro of Sir Michael Ariyah, *qv*; *b* 5 Mar 1931; *Educ* Woking County GS for Boys, Magdalen Coll Oxford (BA, BCL, MA, DCL); *m* 1951, Christine Ann, da of Reginald William Best (d 1978); 4 s (Julian, Andrew, Simon, Jeremy); *Career* asst lectr LSE 1954-55, lectr Univ of Khartown 1955-59; crown counsel Ghana 1959-61; legal asst Bd of Trade 1961-64; fell New Coll Oxford 1964-70; prof of Law ANU (Aust) 1970-73; prof Univ of Warwick 1973-77; prof of English Law Oxford 1977-; *Style—* Prof Patrick Atiyah; 9 Sheepway Court, Iffley, Oxford OX4 4JL (☎ (0865) 717637); St John's Coll, Oxford OX4 3JP (☎ (0865) 277372)

ATKIN, Alec Field; CBE (1978); s of Alec and Grace Atkin; *b* 26 April 1925; *Educ* Riley HS, Hull Tech Coll, Hull Univ (BSc, Dip Aero); *m* 1, 1948 (m dis 1982), Nora Helen Darby; 2 s (and 1 s adopted), 1 da; m 2, 1982, Wendy Atkin; *Career* asst md BAC (Military Aircraft Div) 1976-77; md (Military) Aircraft Gp Br Aerospace 1978-81, chm Warton, Kingston-Brough and Manchester Div 1978-81; md (Marketing) Aircraft Gp Br Aerospace 1981-82; aviation conslt 1982-; FEng, FIMechE, FRAes, FRSA; *Style—* Alec Atkin, Esq, CBE; Les Fougères d'Icart, Icart Rd, St Martin, Guernsey, Channel Islands

ATKIN, David John; s of Prof William Rearden Atkin (d 1950, of Heckmondwike, and Katharine Maud, *née* Senior (d 1981); *b* 15 Nov 1924; *Educ* Heckmondwike GS, Leeds Univ (BSc); *m* 4 Sept 1950, Phyllis Mary (Pat), da of Arthur Booth Wood (d 1956), of Heckmondwike; 1 s (Roger b 1956), 3 da (Catherine b 1954, Jane b 1958, Lucy b 1961); *Career* Stewarts and Lloyds Ltd 1951-67, BSC Tubes Div 1967-85; div dir Stanton and Staveley Gp 1969-85, non-exec dir Stanton plc 1985-; pres: Metcon 1981-83, Inst of Br Foundrymen 1986-87 BCIRA 1988; memb of Foundaries EDC 1976-84; vice pres cncl of Nottingham 1986-; *Recreations* gardening, walking, cycling, choral singing; *Style—* David J Atkin, Esq; Porlock House, Withybed Lane, Inkberrow, Worcester WR7 4JL (☎ 0386 792560)

ATKIN, Roger Dean; s of (Arthur) James Atkin, of Herne Bay, Kent, and Acie, *née* Dean; *b* 02 April 1939; *Educ* Herne Bay Sch; *m* 21 May 1969, Wendy Anne, da of Sqdn Ldr Thomas Alexander Stewart, DFC, AFC; 2 s (Stewart Dean b 15 April 1972, Alister Graham b 22 August 1973); *Career* signals RAF served UK and W Germany 1959-61; entered Lloyds Insurance Mkt specialising in marine insurance 1961, elected underwriting memb Lloyd's 1980, fndr Atkin Raggett Ltd (Lloyd's broker), dir Seascope Reinsurance Brokers Ltd; memb Herne Bay UDC 1967-69, chm SE Area Young Cons 1969-70; Freeman City of London 1969; Liveryman Worshipful Co of Cooks 1972, Worshipful Co of Insurers 1986; MIEx 1975; *Clubs* Royal Overseas League, City Liver; *Style—* Roger D Atkin, Esq; Herne Brow, Pigeon Lane, Herne Bay, Kent CT6 7ES (☎ 0227 374423); Seascope Reinsurance Brokers Ltd, Lloyd's of London, London EC3)

ATKIN, Ron; s of Oscar Ridgeway, of 6 Gray's Ct, Barrow-on-Soar, Leics, and Agatha Victoria, *née* Hull; *b* 3 Feb 1938; *Educ* Loughborough Coll of Art, Cert Royal Acad Schs; *m* 23 July 1960, Ann, da of Capt Arthur Charles Fawssett, DSO, RN (d 1961); 2 s (Francis Charles Edward b 1961, Richard Bernard b 1963); *Career* artist; first exhibition Royal Soc of Portrait Painters 1959, others incl: RA (summer) 1970 and 1975, Zurich 1988; paintings in private collections in GB, Australia, USA, Canada, Germany, Switzerland; public collections: Dartington Hall, Devon Schs Museum Serv, Lincoln Coll Oxford, The Wimbledon Lawn Tennis Museum, Plymouth City Museum and Art Gallery; recent portraits incl: Max Bygraves, Eileen Atkins, Sir Brian Rix, Ronnie Barker, Victoria Wood, HRF Keating, Alan Aykbourn, Richard Briers, Ernie Wise, Glenda Jackson, Paul Tortelier, Gerald R Ford, Bob Hope, Charlton Heston; memb London gp RCA 1984, FRSA; *Recreations* walking; *Style—* Ron Atkin, Esq; Studio 7, West Putford, Devon EX22 7XE (☎ 040 924 435)

ATKINS, Lady; Gladwys Gwendolen; da of Frank Harding Jones (d 1954), of Harlow, Essex; *m* 1933, Prof Sir Hedley John Barnard Atkins, KBE (surgn, former chm cncl Queen Elizabeth Coll London Univ; d 1983), s of late Col Sir John Atkins, KCMG, KCVO; 2 s; *Style—* Lady Atkins; Down House, Downe, nr Orpington, Kent BR6 7JT (☎ 66 51744)

ATKINS, Dr Peter William; s of William Henry Atkins (d 1988), and Ellen Louise, *née* Edwards (d 1978); *b* 10 August 1940; *Educ* Dr Challoner's Amersham, Univ of Leicester (BSc, PhD), Univ of Oxford (MA), UCLA; *m* 20 Aug 1964 (m dis 1983), Judith Ann Kearton; 1 da (Juliet b 1970); *Career* Oxford Univ: Harkness fell 1964-65, lectr physical chemistry 1965, fell and tutor Lincoln Coll 1965-; vsiting prof China France Israel and Japan, lectr California 1980, Firth visiting prof Sheffield Univ 1984; Meldola medal 1969; *Books* The Structure of Inorganic Radicals (1967), Quanta: A Handbook of Concepts (1974), The Creation (1981), Principles of Physical Chemistry (1982), Solutions Manual for MQM (1983), Molecular Quantum Mechanics (2 edn 1983), The Second Law (1984), Physical Chemistry (3 edn 1986), Solutions Manual for Physical Chemistry (3 edn 1986), Molecules (1987), Chemistry: Principles and Applications (1988), Gen Chemistry (1989); *Recreations* art; *Style—* Dr P W Atkins; Lincoln Coll, Oxford OX1 3DR (☎ 0865 279 797, fax 0865 279 802)

ATKINS, Robert James; MP (C) South Ribble 1983-; s of Reginald Alfred Atkins, of Chequers Cottage, S Heath, Gt Missenden, and Winifred Margaret Atkins; *b* 5 Feb 1946; *Educ* Highgate; *m* 1969, Dulcie Mary, da of Frederick Moon Chaplin, of Bexley; 1 s (James b 1979), 1 da (Victoria b 1976); *Career* MP (C) Preston N 1979-1983, jt sec Cons Parly Defence and Aviation Ctees, nat vice-pres Cons Trade Unionists, PPS to Norman Lamont as Min of State Indust 1982-; *Recreations* wine, cricket, old churches; *Style—* Robert Atkins, Esq, MP; 29c Haringey Park, Hornsey, London N8 (☎ 01 348 5316); 15 St Andrew's Rd, Preston, Lancs PR1 6NE (☎ (0772) 55477); House of Commons, London SW1

ATKINS, Sir William Sydney Albert; CBE (1966); 2 s of Robert Edward and Martha Atkins; *b* 6 Feb 1902; *Educ* Coopers Sch, UCL (BSc fell 1955); *m* 1928, Elsie Jessie, da of Edward Barrow, of Hockley, Essex; 2 da; *Career* chief engr Smith Walker Ltd 1928, fndr and The London Ferro-Concrete Co Ltd 1935-80, fndr and chm RE Eagan Ltd 1946-50, chm WS ATkins & Ptnrs 1950-82 (fndr and sr ptnr 1938-50), chm WS Atkins Gp Ltd and assoc cos 1970-84; pres: WS Atkins Ltd, WS Atkins Conslts and Atkins Holdings Ltd 1986-; fndr and ptnr Round Pond Nurseries 1965-; Hon Freeman Borough of Epsom and Ewell 1980; FEng, FICE, FIStructE, Hon FWeldI, CInstMechE, MInstM&C, PEng (Ont), FHS; Sir William Larke Medallist, Tellprd Premium Prize Winner; Kt 1976 ; *Books* numerous tech papers; *Recreations* gardening, hort res, swimming; *Style—* Sir William Atkins, CBE; Chobham Place, Chobham, nr Woking, Surrey GU24 8HN (☎ 099 05 8867)

ATKINSON, Sir Alec (John Alexander); KCB (1978), CB (1976), DFC (1943); yr s of Rev Robert F Atkinson (d 1943), and Harriet Harrold, *née* Lowdon; *b* 9 June 1919; *Educ* Kingswood Sch Bath, Queen's Coll Oxford (MA); *m* 1945, Marguerite Louise, da of George Pearson (d 1974); 1 da (Charlotte); *Career* serv WWII Flt Lt; entered Civil Serv 1946, dep sec DHSS 1973-76, 2 perm sec DHSS 1977-79, memb panel of chm Civil Serv Selection Bd 1979-88, memb Occupational Pensions Bd 1981-88;; *Recreations* walking, reading, theatre; *Clubs* Utd Oxford and Cambridge; *Style—* Sir Alec Atkinson, KCB, CB, DFC;; Bleak House, The Drive, Belmont, Sutton, Surrey SM2 7DH (☎ 01 642 6479)

ATKINSON, Prof Anthony Barnes (Tony); s of Norman Joseph Atkinson (d 1988), and Esther Muriel, *née* Stonehouse; *b* 4 Sept 1944; *Educ* Cranbrook Sch Kent, Churchill Coll Cambridge (MA); *m* 11 Dec 1965, Judith Mary, da of Alexander Mandeville, of Swansea; 2 s (Richard b 1972, Charles b 1976), 1 da (Sarah b 1974); *Career* fell St John's Coll Cambridge 1967-71, prof of economics Essex Univ 1971-76, prof Univ of London 1976- (Thomas Tooke prof of econ science and statistics 1987-), ed Journal of Public Economics 1971-; UAP Scientific Prize 1986; pres Econometric Soc 1988, pres Euro Econ Assoc 1989; memb: Roy Comm on Distribution of Income and Wealth 1978-79, Retail Prices Advsy Ctee 1984-; Freeman City of London 1983, memb Worshipful Co of Barbers (Livery 1985); Hon DR, RER, POL Univ of Frankfurt 1987; Hon Dr Sci Econ Univ of Lausanne 1988; vice-pres Br Acad 1988-; FBA 1984, hon memb American Econ Assoc 1985; *Books* Poverty in Britain (1969), Unequal Shares (1972), Economics of Inequality (1975), Distribution of Personal Wealth in Britain (1978), Lectures on Public Econ (1980), Social Justice and Public Policy (1982), Parents and Children (1983), Unemployment Benefits and Unemployment Duration (1986), Poverty and Social Security (1989); *Recreations* sailing; *Style—* Prof Tony

Atkinson; 33 Hurst Green, Brightlingsea, Colchester, Essex CO7 0HA; London Sch of Economics, Houghton St, Aldwych, London WC2A 2AE (☎ 01 405 7686, fax 01 242 2357)

ATKINSON, Colin Ronald Michael; s of R E Atkinson; *b* 23 July 1931; *Educ* Durham Univ and others; *m* 1957, Shirley Angus; 2 s, 1 da; *Career* headmaster Millfield 1971- (acting headmaster 1969-70); dir HTV Ltd; chm Edington Sch; pres Somerset County Cricket Club (former capt and chm); memb Cricket Cncl, Test and County Cricket Bd; *Style—* Colin Atkinson, Esq; Millfield School, Street, Somerset (☎ 0458 42291; home: 0458 33712)

ATKINSON, Daniel Elston; s of Frank Atkinson, of 15 Heene Tce, Worthing, Sussex, and Elsteen Ann, *née* Curnow (d 1986); *b* 19 Mar 1961; *Educ* Christ's Hosp; *Career* business corr Reading Evening Post 1983-85, ed Executive magazine 1983-85, dep City ed Press Assoc 1985-, publisher The Extremist 1987-; ctee memb Br Anti Common Market Campaign; *Clubs* Wig and Pen; *Style—* Daniel Atkinson, Esq; Flat Four, Four Crane Court, Fleet St, London EC4 (☎ 01 353 3580); Press Assoc, 85 Fleet St, London EC4 (☎ 01 353 7440, fax 01 353 5191)

ATKINSON, David Anthony; MP (C) Bournemouth E 1977-; s of late Arthur Joseph Atkinson, and Joan Margaret, *née* Zink, of Southbourne, Bournemouth; *b* 24 Mar 1940; *Educ* St George's Coll Weybridge, Coll of Automobile and Aeronautical Engrg Chelsea; *m* 1968, Susan Nicola, da of Dr Roy Pilsworth, of Benfleet, Essex; 1 s (Anthony b 1977), 1 da (Katherine b 1973); *Career* dir Chalkwell Motor Co Westcliff-on-Sea 1963-72; md David Graham Ltd 1972-78; pps to Rt Hon Paul Channon as: Min for Civil Service 1979-81, Min for Arts 1981-83, Min for Trade 1983-86, secretary of State for Trade & Industry 1986-87; UK rep on Cncl of Europe and Western European Union 1979-; UK pres: Christian Solidarity Int (CSI), Int Soc for Human Rights (ISHR); *Recreations* mountaineering, rock-climbing, art, architecture, travel; *Style—* David Atkinson, Esq, MP; House of Commons, London SW1A 0AA

ATKINSON, Air Marshal Sir David William; KBE (1982); s of late David william Atkinson, and Margaret Atkinson; *b* 29 Sept 1924; *Educ* Edinburgh Univ (MB, ChB); *m* 1948, Mary Sowerby; 1 s; *Career* joined RAF 1949, dir Health and Research RAF 1974-78, princ medical offr RAF Strike Cmd 1978-81, dir-gen RAF Medical Services 1981-84; dir gen: The Chest, Heart and Stroke Association 1985-; DPH, DIH; QHP 1978-84; FFCM, MFOM, FFOM, FRCP (Edin); *Style—* Air Marshal Sir David Atkinson, KBE; 39 Brim Hill, London N2; Tavistock House North, Tavistock Sq, London WC1H 9JE

ATKINSON, Col Francis Cuthbert; DL (Norfolk 1968); s of Lt-Col John Clayton Atkinson, and Elizabeth Gwendolen Atkinson, of Morland Hall Westmorland and Sheringham Norfolk; *b* 25 Nov 1912; *Educ* Bradfield, Sandhurst; *m* 1941, Susan Joanna de Burgh, da of Lt Cdr John de Burgh Jessop, DSO, RN, of Overton Hall, Derbys; 2 da (and 2 da decd); *Career* served NW Frontier; WWII: NW Europe (wounded), Palestine, Iraq; cmmd Depot Royal Norfolk Regt 1948-50, Malaya 1950-52, NATO Germany 1955-57; County Cmdt Norfolk Army Cadet Force 1965-69; memb: Norfolk CC 1963-74, Broadland DC 1963-76, N Norfolk DC 1979-84; chm Norfolk Branch SSAFA 1971-78; dep county cmmr St John Ambulance Bde 1963-73, CStJ 1973; *Recreations* looking back on memories of pig-sticking, polo, shooting, hunting, winter sports and athletics; *Clubs* Naval and Military, Norfolk; *Style—* Col Francis Atkinson, DL; Kettleby Lodge, Sheringham, Norfolk NR26 8JH (☎ 0263 822652)

ATKINSON, Sir Fred (Frederick John); KCB (1979, CB 1971); s of George Edward Atkinson, and Elizabeth Sabina Cooper; *b* 7 Dec 1919; *Educ* Dulwich, Jesus Coll Oxford; *m* 1947, Margaret Grace, da of Sidney Jeffrey Gibson; 2 da; *Career* HM tres 1955-62 and 1963-69, chief economic advsr Dept of Trade and Indust 1970-73, asst sec-gen OECD Paris 1973-75, dep sec and chief econ advsr Dept of Energy 1975-77, chief econ advsr to Tres 1977-79, head Govt Economic Serv 1977-79; hon fell Jesus Coll Oxford; *Books* Oil and the Br Economy (with S Hall, 1983); *Style—* Sir Fred Atkinson, KCB; 26 Lee Terrace, Blackheath, London SE3 (☎ 01 852 1040); Tickner Cottage, Aldington, Kent (☎ (023 372) 514)

ATKINSON, Dr Harry Hindmarsh; s of Harry Temple Atkinson (d 1961), late Commissioner of Patents etc for NZ (Wellington NZ) and Constance Hindmarsh, *née* Shields (d 1973); gf, Sir Harry Atkinson (b 1831 d 1892), PM of NZ five times between 1873 and 1890; *b* 5 August 1929; *Educ* Nelson Coll Nelson NZ, Canterbury Univ Coll NZ (BSc MSc), Cornell Univ, Univ of Camb, Corpus Christi Coll & Cavendish Lab (PhD); *m* 25 March 1958, Anne Judith, da of Thomas Kenneth Barrett (d 1964); 2 s ((Harry) David b 1960, (John) Benedict b 1966), 1 da (Katherine Hindmarsh b 1959); *Career* asst lectr physics Canterbury Univ Coll NZ 1952-53, res asst Cornell Univ USA 1954-55, sr res fell AERE Harwell UK 1958-61, head Gen Physics Gp Rutherford Lab UK 1961-69, staff chief scientific advsr to UK Gov Cabinet Off UK 1969-72, head of astronomy Space & Radio Div UK Science Res Cncl 1972-78, under sec dir astronomy Space & Nuclear Physics UK Sci Res Cncl 1979-83, under sec dir science UK Science & Engrg Res Cncl (incl responsibility for Internat Affairs) 1983-88; under sec (special responsibilities) 1988; assessor Univ Grants Ctee 1986-, UK memb EISCAT Cncl 1976-86; vice chm of cncl European Space Agency 1981-84, chm of cncl European Space Agency 1984-87; UK memb of Anglo-Australian Telescope Bd 1979-88; chm Anglo-Dutch Astronomy Ctee 1981-88; UK Delegate Summit Gp on High Energy Physics 1982-; chm and memb steering ctee of Institut Laue Langevin (ILL) Grenoble France 1984-88; UK delegate to Cncl Synchrotron Radiation Facility 1986-88; *Recreations* cycling, walking; *Clubs* Athenaeum, Royal Astronomical Society (fell); *Style—* Harry Atkinson, Esq; Science & Engineering Research Council, Polaris House, North Star Avenue, Swindon SN2 1ET (☎ 0793 26222, telex: 449466, fax: 0793 511181)

ATKINSON, Jack; DL (E Sussex 1975); s of Reginald James Atkinson, MBE (d 1966), of Broadway, Worcs; *b* 1 Jan 1917; *Educ* Prince Henry's GS Evesham, Bristol Univ (LLB); *m* 1944, Elizabeth Hewitt, da of Capt John Henry Trye, CBE, RN (d 1959), of Cheltenham; 1 s (Edward), 2 da (Elizabeth, Mary); *Career* WWII served RM; asst slr Cheltenham Cncl 1946-48, sr slr Hants CC 1948-53, dep clerk Oxon CC 1953-59, Clerk of the Peace and clerk of E Sussex CC 1959-74; memb: cncl Law Soc 1969-73, Nat Tst Kent and E Sussex Regnl Ctee 1974-85 (chm 1978-85); *Recreations* gardening, travel; *Style—* Jack Atkinson, Esq, DL; Ardsley, 78 Lewes Rd, Ditchling, E Sussex BN6 8TY (☎ 079 18 3657)

ATKINSON, Rev Canon Prof James; s of Nicholas Ridley Atkinson (d 1942), and Margaret Patience Bradford, *née* Hindhaugh (d 1970); *b* 27 April 1914; *Educ* Tynemouth HS, Univ of Durham (MA, MLitt), Univ of Muenster (DTh); *m* 1 Aug 1939, Laura Jean, da of George Nutley (d 1964); 1 s (Nicholas b 1949), 1 da (Mary b 1945); *Career* curate, Newcastle-on-Tyne 1937-41, precentor of Sheffield Cathedral 1941-44, vicar St Jas and Christopher Sheffield 1944-51, res fell Univ of Sheffield 1951-54, canon theologian Leicester Cathedral 1954-56, reader in theology Univ of Hull 1956-66, visiting prof Chicago 1966-67, prof of biblical studies Univ of Sheffield 1967-79, univ memb of Gen Synod 1975-80, examining chaplain to several dioceses; memb: Prep Ctee on Anglican/Roman Catholic Relations, several Ctee on Lutheran/Anglican relations, L'Acadamie Internationale des Sciences Religieuses Brussels; pres Soc for the Study of Theology; *Books* Luther's Early Theological Works (1962), Rome and Reformation (1966), Luther's Works, Vol 44 (1967), Luther and the Birth of Protestantism (1968, 1982), Luther: Prophet to the Church Catholic (1983), The Darkness of Faith (1987); *Recreations* music, gardening; *Style—* The Rev Canon Prof James Atkinson; Leach House, Hathersage, Via Sheffield S30 1BA (☎ 0433 50570)

ATKINSON, Sir (John) Kenneth; 2 s of James Oswald Atkinson (d 1949), of Liverpool, and Jane Parry; *b* 21 May 1905; *Educ* The Leys Sch Cambridge; *m* 17 Sept 1930, Ellen Elsie Godwin (d 1975), da of late Frederic Hastings Dod, of Manila and Liverpool; 1 da; *Career* Valuation Office: joined 1928, dep chief valuer 1950, chief valuer Valuation Office Inland Revenue 1951-66; kt 1953; *Style—* Sir Kenneth Atkinson; 38 Clarence Rd South, Weston-super-Mare, Avon BS23 4BW (☎ 0934 623205)

ATKINSON, Kenneth Neil; s of William Atkinson (d 1972), and Alice, *née* Reid; *b* 4 April 1931; *Educ* Kingussie HS; *Career* dir Designate Assoc of Br Travel Agents Nat Training Bd, dir Youth Training Manpower Servs Cmmn/Training Agency 1983-88; dir Scotland 1979-82; dir Industry Training Bd Relations 1975-78; dep chief conciliation offr Dept of Employment 1968-72; ARCM 1961, FIPM 1986; *Recreations* tennis, choral singing, conducting; *Clubs* Roy Scottish Automobile; *Style—* Kenneth N Atkinson, Esq; 17 Graham Court, Sheffield S10 3DX

ATKINSON, Maj-Gen Sir Leonard Henry; KBE (1966, OBE 1945); s of Arnold Henry Atkinson (d 1945), of Hale, Cheshire, and Manchester; *b* 4 Dec 1910; *Educ* Wellington, UCL (BSc); *m* 1939, Jean Eileen, da of Charles Atherton Atchley, OBE (d 1966), of ALLOA and Bristol; 1 s, 3 da; *Career* cmmd RAOC 1933, transfd to REME 1942, serv WWII Lt-Col, Cmdt REME Trg Centre and Cdr Berks Dist 1958-63, Dir (Maj-Gen) Electrical and Mechanical Engineering Army 1963-66, Col Cmdt REME 1967-72; chm cncl Engrg Institutions 1974; dir: Harland Engrg Co Alloa Scotland 1966-70, Weir Engrg Industs 1970-74, United Gas Industs 1972-76, C & W Walker 1974-77, Bespoke Securities 1974-79, Equity & General 1978-; chm: Christopher Gold Assocs 1976-87, Technology Transfer Assocs 1980-88, chm md Harland-Simon 1970-72; vice-chm S Regnl Cncl for FE 1978-85 chm Central Berks Trg (YTS) (1984-88) Liveryman Worshipful Co of Turners' Co 1966- (Master 1987); CEng, FIMechE, FIEE, FIGasE, FIERE (pres 1968-69); FRSA; *Recreations* philately (fellow Royal Philatelic Soc London), photography; *Clubs* Naval and Military; *Style—* Maj-Gen Sir Leonard Atkinson, KBE; Fair Oak, Ashford Hill, Nr Newbury RG15 8BJ (☎ 07356 4845)

ATKINSON, Michael William; CMG (1985), MBE (1970); *b* 11 April 1932; *Educ* Purley County GS, Queens Coll Oxford (BA); *m* 5 March 1963, Veronica Bobrovsky; 2 s (Nicholas b 1963, Paul b 1972), 1 da (Carina b 1967); *Career* HM Dip Serv 1957-, HM Embassy Vientiane 1957-59, FO News Dept 1959-60, HM Embassy Buenos Aires 1960-66, seconded to govt of Br Honduras 1969-71, HM Embassy Madrid 1971-75, NATO Def Coll Rome 1976, HM Embassy Budapest 1977-80, HM Embassy Peking 1980-83, head consular dept FCO 1983-85, HM Ambassador Quito 1985-; *Style—* Michael Atkinson, Esq, CMG, MBE; c/o FCO (Quito), King Charles St, London SW1A 2AH

ATKINSON, Norman; s of George Atkinson, of Manchester; *b* 25 Mar 1923; *m* 1948, Irene , da of E Parry, of Manchester; *Career* design engineer; contested (Lab) Wythenshawe 1955, MP (Lab): Tottenham 1964-74, Haringey 1974-1983, Tottenham 1983-87; tres Lab Party 1976-81, memb Tribune Gp of Lab MPs; govr: Imperial College of Science and Technology 1979-; *Style—* Norman Atkinson, Esq,

ATKINSON, Peter Graham; s of William Graham Atkinson (d 1984), of York, and Margaret, *née* Turnbull; *b* 12 Jan 1952; *Educ* Nunthorpe GS York; *m* 14 Sept 1977, Jane Maria, da of Eric Kaiser, of York; 1 s (Christopher Paul b 1984), 1 da (Helen Elizabeth b 1981); *Career* with Barron and Barron 1970-75, ACA 1975, Ernst and Whinney (W Africa) 1975-78, chief accountant Claxton and Garland 1978-82, fin dir Yorks Post Newspapers Ltd 1982-; tres: local sch parents assoc, Leeds Chamber of Trade; FCA 1975; *Recreations* my family, reading, gardening, swimming; *Style—* Peter Atkinson, Esq; 22 Usher Park Rd, Usher Lane, Haxby, York YO3 8RY (☎ 762854); PO Box 168, Wellington St, Leeds LS1 1RF (☎ 0532 432701, fax 0632 443430, telex 55425)

ATKINSON, Sir Robert; DSC (1941, 2 Bars 1943 and 1944), RD (1947); s of late Nicholas Atkinson (d 1944), and Margaret Bradford; *b* 7 Mar 1916; *Educ* London Univ (BSc), McGill Mathematics; *m* 1, 1941, Joyce, *née* Forster (d 1972); 1 s (Robert), 1 da (Gillian); m 2, 1977, Margaret Hazel Walker; *Career* serv WWII (despatches 1943); md: Wm Doxford 1957-61, Tube Investmts (Eng) 1961-67, Unicorn Industs 1967-72; chm: Aurora Hldgs Sheffield 1972-84, Br Shipbuilders 1980-84; non-exec dir Stag Furniture Hldgs 1971-; CEng, FEng, FIMechE, FIMarE; kt 1982; *Recreations* salmon fishing, walking; *Clubs* Royal Thames Yacht; *Style—* Sir Robert Atkinson, DSC, RD; Southwood House, Itchen Abbas, Winchester, Hants SO21 1AT (☎ 096 278 610)

ATKINSON, Rowan Sebastian; s of Eric Atkinson (d 1984); *b* 6 Jan 1955; *Educ* Durham Cathedral Choristers' Sch, St Bees Cumbria, Newcastle Univ (BSc), Oxford Univ (MSc); *Career* actor and writer; for BBC TV: Not The Nine O'Clock News 1979-82, The Black Adder, Blackadder II, Blackadder the Third, 1983-87. BBC TV Personality of the Year 1980, British Academy Award 1980. Theatre in London's West End: One Man Show 1981 (Soc of West end theatre award for Comedy Performance of the Year), The Nerd 1984 One Man Show 1986. One Man show tours to Australia, Canada, USA, and Far East.; *Style—* Rowan Atkinson, Esq; c/o CCC Ltd., 21 D'Arblay St, London W1V 3FN

ATKINSON, Prof Thomas; s of Thomas Bell Atkinson (d 1968), of Sacriston, Durham, and Elizabeth Dawson (d 1967); descendant of J J Atkinson, the pioneer of the science of mine ventilation; *b* 23 Jan 1924; *Educ* Sacriston Sch, Royal Sch of Mines London (PhD, DIC, DSc); *m* 1948, Dorothy, da of Harold Price (d 1967), of Tyne and Wear; 1 da (Dorothy b 1951); *Career* RN 1942-46, W/O North Atlantic & SEAC; prof and head of dept of mining engrg, Univ of Nottingham 1977-88, emeritus prof 1988-; chm

Consolidated Coalfields Ltd; dir West Seals Ltd; FEng; *Recreations* oil painting; *Clubs* Chaps, Snobs; *Style*— Professor Thomas Atkinson; 27 Kirk Lane, Ruddington, Nottingham NG11 6NN (☎ 0602 842400); University of Nottingham, Dept of Mining Engineering, Nottingham NG7 2RD (☎ 0602 506101, telex 37346)

ATKINSON, William Silver; s of Arthur George Atkinson (d 1971), and Kathleen Evelyn May, *née* Fitzgerald (d 1986); *b* 14 Sept 1937; *m* 1963 (m dis 1974), Mary, da of Mark Breadmore, of Bracknell, Berks; *Career* CA; dir: Continental Oil Co Ltd 1979-82, Conoco (UK) Ltd 1982-, Conoco Ltd 1982-, The Arts Club (London) Ltd 1984-; sec UK Oil Industry Taxation Ctee 1976-85; hon Tres The Arts Club 1985-; tstee The Arts Club 1987-; writer and speaker on taxation; FCA, FTII; *Recreations* opera, walking; *Clubs* Arts, Oriental; *Style*— William Atkinson, Esq; 1 Eton College Rd, London NW3 2BS; Conoco (UK) Ltd, 105 Wigmore St, London W1H 0EL (☎ 01 408 6000)

ATTALLAH, Naim Ibrahim; s of Ibrahim Attallah (decd), and Genevieve, *née* Geadah; *b* 1 May 1931; *m* 1957, Maria, da of Joseph Nykolyn; 1 s (Ramsay b 1965); *Career* book publisher: Quartet Books, Robin Clark, The Women's Press; magazine proprieter: Literary Review, Apollo, The Wire; film producer: The Slipper amd the Rose (co-producer with David Frost 1974-75), Brimstone and Treacle (exec Prod 1982); theatrical producer: Happy End (co-presenter Lyric Theatre 1975), The Beastly Beatitudes of Balthazar B (presenter and producer Duke of York's Theartre 1982); fin dir and jt md Asprey of Bond Street; parfumier (launched Parfums Namara 1985 with Avant L'Amour and Apr'es L'Amour, Nâdor in 1986).; *Books* "Women" Quartet books 1987; *Clubs* Arts; *Style*— Naim Attallah, Esq; Namara House, 45-46 Poland Street, London W1V 4AU (☎ 01 4396750, telex 919034 NAMARA) fax 01 439 6489

ATTENBOROUGH, Sir David Frederick; CBE (1974); s of late Frederick Levi Attenborough; bro of Sir Richard Attenborough, *qv*; *b* 8 May 1926; *Educ* Wyggeston GS for Boys Leicester, Clare Coll Cambridge (hon fell 1980); *m* 1950, Jane Elizabeth Ebsworth Oriel; 1 s, 1 da; *Career* traveller, broadcaster and writer; joined BBC 1952, controller BBC-2 TV 1965-68, dir of Programmes TV and memb Bd of Management 1969-72; writer and presenter BBC series: Tribal Eye 1976, Life on Earth 1979; tstee: World Wildlife Fund Int 1979-, Br Museum 1980-; Hon DLitt: Leicester, City, London, Birmingham; Hon LLD: Bristol, Glasgow; Hon DSc: Liverpool, Heriot-Watt, Sussex, Bath, Ulster, Durham; DUniv Open Univ; FRS; kt 1985; *Publications include* Zoo Quest to Guiana (1956), Quest in Paradise (1960), Quest under Capricorn (1963), The Tribal Eye (1976), Life on Earth (1979); *Recreations* tribal art, natural history; *Style*— Sir David Attenborough, CBE; 5 Park Rd, Richmond, Surrey

ATTENBOROUGH, John Philip; CMG (1958), CBE (1953, OBE 1946); s of Frederick Samuel Attenborough (d 1949), of Manchester, and Edith Attenborough; *b* 6 Nov 1901; *Educ* Manchester GS, Corpus Christi Coll Oxford (MA); *m* 1947, Lucie Blanche Woods, da of Rev Joseph Robert Prenter (d 1946), and wid of Dr P P Murphy; 1 step s; *Career* supt of educn N Nigeria 1924-30, lectr and sr inspr Educn Dept Palestine 1930-37, dir Educn Aden 1937-46, dep dir Educn Palestine 1946-48, dir Education Tanganyika 1948-55, min for Social Services Tanganyika 1955-58, consult UNICEF 1963-65, UNESCO 1967; memb: Devon CC 1961-68, SW Regnl Hosp Bd 1965-71; pres Torbay Cons Assoc 1967-79; *Style*— John Attenborough, Esq, CMG, CBE; 21 Thorncliff Close, Wellswood, Torquay, Devon (☎ 0803 27291)

ATTENBOROUGH, (Ralph) John; CBE (1972, MBE mil 1944); s of Ralph Ernest Attenborough (d 1965), of Bromley Common, Kent; *b* 30 Dec 1908; *Educ* Rugby, Trinity Coll Oxford (MA); *m* 1935, Edith Barbara, da of Henry Sandle (d 1960); 2 s (*see* Attenborough, Philip John), 1 da (*see* Bourne, Richard); *Career* serv WWII Maj RA (despatches 2); publisher; jt chief exec Hodder & Stoughton 1960-73; pres Publishers Assoc 1965-67; ldr Book Dvpt Cncl Mission: Sri Lanka and India 1969, Pakistan and Bangledesh 1971; author; *Books* A Living Memory (1975), One Man's Inheritance (1979), The Priest's Story (1984), Destiny our Choice (1987); *Recreations* golf, writing, watching cricket and professional football; *Clubs* Athenaeum, Roy St George's Golf, Society of Bookmen; *Style*— John Attenborough, Esq, CBE; Ashway, 7 Roehampton Drive, Chislehurst, Kent (☎ 01 467 1141)

ATTENBOROUGH, Michael Francis; s of Ralph John Attenborough, CBE, MBE, of Chislehurst, Kent, and Edith Barbara Attenborough (d 1988); *b* 21 Oct 1939; *Educ* Rugby, Trinity Coll Oxford (MA); *m* 7 March 1970, Carol Finlay, da of Dr George Alexander Sharp, of Bishops Stortford; 1 s (Thomas b 1972), 1 da (Sophie b 1975); *Career* Hodder & Stoughton Ltd: joined 1962, publishing dir 1972-; memb Worshipful Co of Haberdashers 1962; *Recreations* golf; *Clubs* Garrick, Royal St George's Golf, Royal and Ancient Golf (St Andrews), Band of Brothers; *Style*— Michael Attenborough, Esq; 17 Parkgate, London SE3 9XF (☎ 01 318 1914); 47 Bedford Square, London WC1B 3DP (☎ 01 636 9851, fax 01 631 5248, telex 885887)

ATTENBOROUGH, Peter John; s of John Frederick Attenborough (d 1967), and Eileen Mabel Attenborough, *née* Reavell; *b* 4 April 1938; *Educ* Christ's Hosp, Peterhouse Cambridge; *m* 1967, Alexandra Deidre, da of Alexander Henderson Campbell (d 1982), of Derby; 1 s (James b 1969), 1 da (Charlotte b 1971); *Career* asst master Uppingham Sch 1960-75 (head of classics dept and housemaster); headmaster: Sedbergh Sch 1975-81, Charterhouse 1982-; Liveryman Worshipful Co of Skinners; chm Ind Sch Cmmn Entrance Ctee; *Clubs* East India; *Style*— Peter Attenborough, Esq; The Headmaster's Ho, Charterhouse, Surrey (☎ Godalming 21171); Charterhouse (☎ Godalming 22589)

ATTENBOROUGH, Philip John; s of (Ralph) John Attenborough, CBE, *qv*; *b* 3 June 1936; *Educ* Rugby, Trinity Coll Oxford; *m* 1963, Rosemary, da of Dr William Brian Littler, CB; 1 s, 1 da; *Career* publisher; chm: Hodder & Stoughton Ltd (joined 1957), Hodder & Stoughton Hldgs 1975-, Lancet Ltd 1977-; memb Cncl Publishers Assoc 1976- (pres 1983-85); chm: Book Devpt Cncl 1977-79, Br Cncl Publishers Advsy Ctee 1989-;; *Style*— Philip Attenborough, Esq; Coldhanger, Seal Chart, Sevenoaks, Kent TN15 0EJ (☎ 0732 61516); Hodder & Stoughton, Mill Rd, Dunton Green, Sevenoaks, Kent TN13 2YA (☎ 0732 450111)

ATTENBOROUGH, Sir Richard Samuel; CBE (1967); s of late Frederick Levi Attenborough; bro of David Attenborough, *qv*; *b* 29 August 1923; *Educ* Wyggeston GS for Boys Leicester, RADA; *m* 1945, Sheila Beryl Grant, JP (actress), da of S G Sim, of Hove, Sussex; 1 s, 2 da; *Career* actor, film prodr and director; starred in over 50 films between 1942 and 1979 incl: Brighton Rock (1948), The Ship that Died of Shame, Privates Progress, Dunkirk (1958), I'm All Right Jack (1959), The Angry Silence, The Great Escape, Doctor Doolittle (1967), Only When I Larf (1968), David Copperfield, Loot, 10 Rillington Place, Ten Litte Indians (1974); produced: Whistle Down the Wind (1961), The L-Shaped Room (1982); produced and directed Oh! What a Lovely War (16 Int Awards incl Hollywood Golden Globe and BAFTA UN award 1968); directed: Young Winston (Hollywood Golden Globe 1972), A Bridge Too Far (Evening News Best Drama Award 1976), Magic 1978, A Chorus Line (1985); produced and directed Gandhi (8 Oscars, 5 BAFTA Awards, 5 Hollywood Golden Globes, Dirs' Guild of America Award for Outstanding Directorial Achievement 1980-81), Cry Freedom (Berlinale Kamera 1987); Chm: The Actor's Charitable Trust 1956-88, Combined Theatrical Charities Appeals Cncl 1964-8, BAFTA (vice-pres 1971-) 1969-70, RADA (Mem cncl 1963-, 1970-, Capital Radio 1972-, UK Trustees Waterford-Kamhlaba Sch Swaziland (govr 1987-) 1976-, Duke of York's Theatre 1979-, Br Film Inst 1981-, Goldcrest Film & Television 1982-87, ctte of Inquiry into the Atrs and Disabled People 1983-85, European Script Fund 1988-; pres: Muscular Dystrophy Gp of GB (vice-pres 1962-71) 1971-, The Gandhi Fndn 1983-, Brighton Festival 1984-, British Film Year 1984-86; govr Nat Film Sch 1970-81; dir Young Vic 1974-84; tstee: Help a London Child 1975-, patron Kingsley Hall Community Centre 1982-, pro-cncllr Sussex Univ 1970-; Hon DLitt: Leicester 1970, Kent 1981, Sussex 1987; Hon DCL Newcastle 1974 Hon LLD Dickinson Penn 1983; Evening Standard Film Award 40 Years serv to Br Cinema 1983; Martin Luther King Jr Peace Prize 1983; Padma Bhushan India 1983; Fellowship BAFTA 1983; Commandeur Ordre des Arts et des Lettres France 1985, Chevalier Ordre de la Legion d'Honneur France 1988; Kt 1976; *Books* In Search of Gandhi (1982), Richard Attenborough's Chorus Line (with Diana Carter 1986); Cry Freedom, A Pictorial Record 1987; *Style*— Sir Richard Attenborough, CBE; Old Friars, Richmond Green, Surrey

ATTERBURY, J Michael David; s of Jack Eric Atterbury (d 1977), and Joanne Atterbury, of Teignmouth; *b* 14 June 1935; *Educ* Whitgift Sch; *m* 1959, Margaret Rose, da of William Thomas Evans (d 1971); 1 s, 2 da; *Career* banker; gp sec Barclays Bank plc 1983-; *Recreations* music, chess, photography, natural history; *Style*— J Michael Atterbury, Esq; New Lodge, Woodham Rise, Horsell, Woking, Surrey GU21 4EE (☎ 0493 62418); Barclays Bank plc, 54 Lombard St, London EC3P 3AH (☎ 01 626 1567; telex 884970)

ATTERTO, Dr David Valentine; CBE (1981); s of Maj Frank Arthur Shepherd Atterton, MBE (d 1950), and Ella Constance, *née* Collins; *b* 13 Feb 1927; *Educ* King's Sch Rochester Kent, Bishop Wordsworth's Sch Salsbury, Peterhouse Cambridge (MA, PhD); *m* 1948, Sheila Ann, da of John McMahon (d 1960); 2 s (Charles, Edward), 1 da (Victoria); *Career* chm Foseco Minsep 1979-87; dep chm Assoc Engrg 1979-86; dir: Investors in Indust Gp plc (formerly Finance for Indust) 1974-, IMI Ltd 1976-, Barclays Bank plc 1982-; Marks & Spencer plc 1987-, The Rank Orgn plc 1987-, Bank of England 1984-, British Coal 1986-, memb bd of govrs Utd World Coll of the Atlantic 1968-85 (chm 1973-79); chm NEDO Iron and Steel Sector Working Pty 1977-82; memb Advsy Cncl for Applied Research and Dvpt 1982-85; FEng, FRSA; *Recreations* cartography, notaphilia, Japanese language; *Style*— Dr David Atterton, CBE; The Doctors House, Tanworth in Arden, Solihull, W Midlands B94 5AW; 14 Chesterfield House, South Audley St, London W1Y 5TB (☎ 01 499 8191); Marks & Spencer plc, Michael House, 57 Baker Street, London W1A 1DN (☎ 01 935 4422)

ATTLEE, Air Vice-Marshal Donald Laurence; CB (1977), LVO (1964); s of Maj Laurence Gillespie Attlee (d 1968; bro of 1 Earl Attlee, PM of GB 1945-51), of Groombridge, Sussex, and Letitia, *née* Rotton (d 1973); *b* 2 Sept 1922; *Educ* Haileybury; *m* 2 Feb 1952, Jane Hamilton, da of Capt Robert Murray Hamilton Young, RFC (d 1975), of Tichborne Grange, Hants; 1 s (Charles b 1955), 2 da (Carolyn b 1957, Jenny b 1963); *Career* joined RAF 1942, CO The Queen's Flight 1960-63, CO RAF Brize Norton 1968-70, MOD 1970-75, Air Vice-Marshal 1975, AOA Training Cmd Brampton 1975-77, ret 1977; dir Mid Devon Enterprise Agency; vice- chm mid-Devon district cncl 1987-89, chm 1989-; fruit farmer 1977; *Recreations* genealogy; *Clubs* RAF; *Style*— Air Vice-Marshal Donald Attlee, CB, LVO; Jerwoods, Culmstock, Cullompton, Devon (☎ 0823 680317)

ATTLEE, Lady Jane Elizabeth; only da of 2 Earl Attlee; *b* 29 Mar 1959; *Style*— Lady Jane Attlee; 125 Hendon Lane, London N3 3PR

ATTLEE, 2 Earl (UK 1955); Martin Richard Attlee; also Viscount Prestwood (UK 1955); s of 1 Earl Attlee, KG, OM, CH, PC, PM (Lab) 1945-51 (d 1967), and Violet (yst da of Henry Millar and 2 cous of 1 Baron Inchyra); *b* 10 August 1927; *Educ* Millfield, Southampton Univ; *m* 1, 1955 (m dis 1988), Anne Barbara, eldest da of late James Henderson, CBE, of Bath; 1 s, 1 da; m 2, 1988, Margaret (Gretta) Deane, o da of late Geoffrey Gouriet, CBE, of Paper House, Hampton Court, Middx; *Heir* s, Viscount Prestwood; *Career* served Merchant Navy 1945-50; MIPR 1964; asst PRO BR (S Regn) 1970-76, fndr memb of the SDP, memb: All Party Disablement, House of Lords Defence Study Gp; spokesman on Transport and Maritime Affairs for the SDP; pres NAIBO; patron of ASPIRE; tstee: Countrywide workshops; dir: WVB Advertising Ltd, Thames Help Tst 1985, Countrywide Workshops Charitable Tst Ltd 1985, Keith Wilden Public Relations Ltd, Conquest Ltd; contested (SDP) Hampshire European Constituency 1988; *Books* Bluff Your Way in PR (1968); *Recreations* Do-it-yourself, writing, inventing; *Clubs* Press, Pathfinders; *Style*— The Rt Hon Earl Attlee; 1 Cadet Way, Church Crookham, Aldershot, Hants GU13 0UG (☎ 0252 628007)

ATTLEE, Hon Mrs; Hon Rosemary; 2 da of late 1 Baron Elton; *b* 22 Jan 1925; *m* 1, 1946 (m dis 1955), William Yates, elder s of William Yates, of Appleby, Westmorland; 1 s (decd), 2 da; m 2, 1955, David Charles Attlee, s of Wilfrid Henry Walter Attlee, MD (d 1962); 1 s, 1 da; *Style*— The Hon Mrs Attlee; Great Woodland Farm, Lyminge, Folkestone, Kent

ATTRIDGE, Elizabeth Ann Johnston; da of Rev John Wothington Johnston (d 1952), and Mary Isobel Giraud, *née* McFadden (d 1957); *b* 26 Jan 1934; *Educ* Richmond Lodge Sch Belfast, St Andrew Univ (MA); *m* 1 Sept 1956, John Attridge, s of William Christopher Attridge, (d 1958), of Worthing; 1 s (John Worthington b 1959); *Career* civil servant; Miny of Educn NI 1955-56; MAFF 1956-: asst princ Land Div, princ Plant Health, asst sec Animal Health, chm Int Coffee Orgn, undersec EC Gp emergencies, food quality, pesticide safety; *Clubs* Royal Overseas League; *Style*— Mrs John Attridge; Ministry of Agriculture Fisheries & Food, Whitehall Place, London SW1

ATTRILL, Kenneth William; s of William James Attrill (d 1980), of Southgate, and Lilian Florence, *née* Dugan (d 1983); *b* 22 June 1917; *Educ* Dame Owen's Sch Islington, Regent St Poly; *m* 22 Dec 1961, da of Lord Gilbert Pope, of 46 Camlet Way, Hadley Wood, Herts; 1 s (Robin b 1968); *Career* Capt Middx Regt 1940-46, attached Princess Louise Kensington Regt Iceland 1942-43 winter warfare instr attached US Forces, rejoined Regt for D-Day landings 1944; ptnr Healey Baker 1952-77 (conslt 1977-87), dir Town Centre Securities plc 1981-; *Recreations* cricket, hockey, golf, sailing, skiing; *Clubs* Carlton, MCC, Royal Burnham Yacht, Hadley Wood Golf, Middx Regt Offrs; *Style—* Kenneth Attrill, Esq; Greyfriars, 393 Cockfosters Rd, Hadley Wood, Herts EN4 0JS (☎ 01 440 2474); Healey Baker, 29 St George St, London W1 (☎ 01 629 9292, fax 01 629 3375, telex 21800 HEABAK G)

ATTWELL, Rt Rev Arthur Henry; *see*: Sodor and Man, Bishop of

ATTWOOD, Frank Albert; s of Eric George Attwood, of Broadstairs, Kent, and Dorothy May, *née* Gifford; *b* 19 Jan 1943; *Educ* Leighton Park Sch Reading, Univ of Hull (BSc); *m* 10 Aug 1985, Pamela Ann Paget, da of Samuel Kennedy Pickavor Hunter, of Wareham, Dorset; 1 da (Rebecca b 1980); *Career* articled 1965-68 Sir Lawrence Robson; CA 1968, Chartered Sec 1969; ptnr Robson Rhodes 1974-; memb: Auditing Practices Ctee 1980-86, ICAEW Res Bd/Insur Sub-Ctee; chm: APC Lloyds Waking Pty,ASC Materiality Waking Pty; jt auditor ICEAW 1988; hon tres Schoolmistresses and Governesses Benevolent Inst; Freeman Worshipful Co of Scriveners 1989; FCA, FCIS; *Books* De Paula's Auditing (jtly 1976, 1982, 1986), Auditing Standards From Discussion Drafts to Practice (jtly 1978); *Recreations* rambling, gardening, travel, modern novel, weight training, watching cricket; *Style—* Frank Attwood, Esq; New Malden, Surrey; Robson Rhodes, 186 City Rd, London EC1 (☎ 01 251 1644, 01 251 0256, fax 01 250 0801, car tel 0836 701 668, telex 885 734)

ATTWOOD, Isobel Margaret; *née* Smith; da of Sydney Smith (d 1963), and Ann Eliza, *née* Attwood (d 1952); *b* 12 June 1933; *Educ* St Paul's Private Sch for Girls Stourbridge; *m* 1, 26 March 1951, late John S Bishop; 1 s (John b 1952); m 2, 15 May 1970, Brian Attwood; *Career* owner: residential home Reflex Zone Therapy Clinic and Buckleigh Grange; served on local cncl Trentishoe; breeder of Alsatian Dogs and Chihuahuas; *Recreations* horse riding, swimming, golf, horse breeding, dog breeding; *Clubs* CGA, Ladies Side Saddle Assoc; *Style—* Mrs Isobel M Attwood; Buckleigh Grange, Westward Ho, N Devon (☎ 02372 74468)

ATTWOOD, Thomas Jaymril; s of George Frederick Attwood (d 1969), and Avril Sandys, *née* Cargill (d 1963), of New Zealand, who was ggda of Capt William Cargill (b 1784) who founded Otago province in NZ; *b* 30 Mar 1931; *Educ* Haileybury, Sandhurst, Harvard and INSEAD (at Fontainebleau) Business Schs; *m* 1963, Lynette, da of late C Lewis; 1 s (Alistair b 1964), 1 da (Caroline b 1966); *Career* chm Cargill Attwood & Thomas (mgmnt consultancy gp) 1965-; pt/t chm POUNC 1982-83; pres Int Conslts Fndn 1978-81; former GLC borough cncllr; memb exec ctee Br Mgmnt Trg Export Cncl 1978-85; memb Ct Worshipful Co of Marketors 1985-; FIMC, FBIM, FID; *Recreations* cricket, travel, music; *Clubs* City Livery, MCC, Lord's Taverners; *Style—* Thomas Attwood, Esq; 8 Teddington Park, Teddington, Middx TW11 8DA (☎ 01 977 8091)

ATTWOOLL, Peter Henry; s of John Galpin Attwooll (d 1955), and Eliza Ellen Attwooll, *née* Built (d 1955); *b* 7 Mar 1927; *Educ* Sir Thomas Riches Sch Gloucester; *m* 8 Sept 1954, Sylvia Grace, da of Henry George Ractliffe (d 1965); 2 s (John b 1956, Nigel b 1958), 2 da (Heather b 1959, Ruth b 1965); *Career* dir: John Attwooll & Co (Tents) Ltd 1964, Western Facilities Ltd 1966, Emlyn Canvas & Cordage 1980, Attwoolls (Whitminster) Ltd 1982; *Recreations* golf, sailing; *Style—* Peter H Attwooll, Esq; Whitminster Lodge, Whitminster, Glos GL2 7PN; John Attwooll & Co (Tents) Ltd, Whitminster, Glos GL2 7LX

ATWILL, Sir (Milton) John (Napier); s of Milton Spencer Atwill (d 1965), and Isabella Caroline, *née* Cavaye (d 1973); *b* 16 Jan 1926; *Educ* Cranbrook Sch Sydney, Geelong GS, Jesus Coll Cambridge (MA); *m* 21 Feb 1955, Susan Campbell, da of E Strathmore Playfair, of Sydney; 2 da (Caroline b 19 Jan 1959, Fiona b 9 Oct 1962); *Career* served RAAF 1944-45; barr Gray's Inn and NSW 1953, in practice 1953-74; dep chm David Jones Ltd 1975-, dir: D J's Properties Ltd 1976-, Waugh & Josephson & Subsidiaries 1965-; chm: Waugh & Josephson & Subsidiaries 1983-; dir: MEPC Aust Ltd, Austore Ltd; Waugh & Josephson Hldgs 1965-; fed pres Lib Pty 1975-82 (pres NSW Div Lib Pty 1970-75); chm: Pacific Democrat Union 1982-84; vice-chm: Int Democrat Union 1983-84; Australian chm United World Colleges 1985-; kt 1979; *Recreations* cricket, tennis; *Clubs* Australian, Union; *Style—* Sir John Atwill; 5 Fullerton St, Woollahra, NSW 2025, Australia (☎ 010 61 241 1498); 139 Macquarie St, Sydney, NSW 2000, Australia

AUBREY-FLETCHER, Lt-Col Edward Henry Lancelot; DL (Northants 1983); 4 s of Maj Sir Henry Lancelot Aubrey-Fletcher, 6 Bt, CVO, DSO, Lord-Lieut for Bucks; *b* 6 May 1930; *Educ* Eton, New Coll Oxford; *m* 1, 1953, Bridget (d 1977), da of Brig Sir Henry Floyd, 5 Bt, CB, CBE, Lord-Lieut for Bucks, and Hon Kathleen, da of 1 Baron Gretton, CBE, VD, TD, PC; 2 s, 1 da; m 2, 1981, Baroness Braye, *qv*, da of 7 Baron Braye, DL(d 1985); *Career* served with Gren Gds until 1980, ret; *Style—* Lt-Col Edward Aubrey-Fletcher, DL; Stanford Hall, Lutterworth, Leics LE17 6DH (☎ 0788 860250)

AUBREY-FLETCHER, Henry Egerton; s and h of Sir John Aubrey-Fletcher, 7 Bt; *b* 27 Nov 1945; *Educ* Eton; *m* 1976, (Sara) Roberta, da of Maj Robert Buchanan, of Evanton, Rosshire; 3 s (John Robert b 1977, Thomas Egerton b 1980, Harry Buchanan b 1982); *Style—* Henry Aubrey-Fletcher, Esq; Town Hill Farm, Chilton, Aylesbury, Bucks (☎ 0844 208196)

AUBREY-FLETCHER, Sir John Henry Lancelot; 7 Bt (GB 1782), of Clea Hall, Cumberland, JP (Bucks); e s of Maj Sir Henry Lancelot Aubrey-Fletcher, 6 Bt, CVO, DSO (d 1969), and his 1 wife Mary Augusta, *née* Chilton (d 1963); *b* 22 August 1912; *Educ* Eton, New Coll Oxford (BA); *m* 25 April 1939, Diana Fynvola, o da of late Lt-Col Arthur George Edward Egerton, Coldstream Gds; 1 s (and 1 da decd); *Heir* s, Henry Egerton Aubrey-Fletcher; *Career* Grenadier Gds 1939-45, Lt Col, left as Hon Maj; barr 1937, dep chm Quarter Sessions 1959-71, a met magistrate 1959-71, rec Crown Ct 1972-74; High Sheriff of Bucks 1961; *Style—* Sir John Aubrey-Fletcher, Bt, JP; The Gate House, Chilton, Aylesbury, Bucks (☎ 0844-208-347)

AUBURY, Philip Norman; s of Norman Frederick Charles Aubury, of Yardley, Birmingham, and Hilary Winifred, *née* Brockman; *b* 9 August 1947; *Educ* Saltley GS, Pershore Coll of Hort (NDH); *m* 2 Jan 1967, Elisabeth Ann, da of Clide Thomas Riley, JP; 1 s (Matthew Philip b 16 Aug 1973), 2 da (Sally-Ann Elisabeth b 15 Feb 1968, Lucy Dawn b 1 Jan 1969); *Career* mangr Roseacre Gdn Centre 1974; City of Birmingham: lectr Hort Trg Sch 1974-79, parks mangr Recreation Dept 1979-87; dir Birmingham Botanical Gdns and Glassgouses 1987-; tres Arrow Canoe Club, lectr and judge local hort socs; *Recreations* garden design and construction, conservation; *Style—* Philip Aubury, Esq; Hill Cottage, Scarfield Hill, Alvechurch, Birmingham B48 7SF (☎ 021 445 3895); Birmingham Botanical Gdns and Glasshouses, Westbourne Rd, Edgbaston, Birmingham B15 3TR (☎ 021 454 1860)

AUCKLAND, 9 Baron (I 1789 & GB 1793); Ian George Eden; s of 8 Baron Auckland, MC (d 1957), and Evelyn, 3 da of Col Arthur Hay-Drummond of Cromlix (nephew of 12 Earl of Kinnoull), the latter's mother Arabella being maternal gda of the 1 Duke of Cleveland. The Duke's paternal gm Grace was gda of Barbara, cr Duchess of Cleveland, by whom Lord Auckland is ninth in descent from Charles II; *b* 23 June 1926; *Educ* Blundell's; *m* 1954, Dorothy, JP (Surrey), da of Henry Joseph Manser, of Eastbourne; 1 s, 2 da; *Heir* s, Hon Robert Eden; *Career* served Royal Signals 1945-48 & London Yeo Sharpshooters TA 1948-53; insur conslt; non-exec dir C J Sims & Co; Lloyd's Underwriter 1956-64; vice-pres Royal Soc Prevention Accidents; takes Cons Whip in House of Lords, Award: White Rose of Finland, Knight First-Class 1984; *Clubs* City Livery, St Stephen's Constitutional; *Style—* The Rt Hon the Lord Auckland; Tudor Rose House, 30 Links Rd, Ashtead, Surrey (☎ 03722 74393)

AUDAER, Wing Cdr Clifford Harold; s of Harold Audaer (d 1973), of York, and Frances Mary, *née* Whittaker (d 1973); *b* 3 Feb 1928; *Educ* St Michael's Coll, Univ of Leeds (BA, DipEd); *m* 11 Aug 1951, Janet Monro, da of Charles William Hoggard (d 1962); 1 s (Philip Neil b 1959), 1 da (Helen Jane b 1962); *Career* RAF 1950-78: appts incl ADC COS HQ AFCENT Fontainebleau 1956-59 and Chief Linguistic Servs HQ AF South Naples 1966-69; sec Inst Orthopaedics Univ of London 1978-; chm Arise the Scoliosis Res Tst; FAA 1978, FBIM 1978; *Recreations* golf, music, theatre; *Clubs* MCC, RAF; *Style—* Wing Cdr Clifford Audaer; Inst of Orthopaedics, Royal Nat Orthopaedic Hosp, Brockley Hill, Stanmore, Middx (☎ 01 954 2300 ext 494)

AUDLAND, Sir Christopher John; KCMG (1987, CMG 1973); s of Brig Edward Gordon Audland, CB, CBE, MC (d 1976), and Violet Mary, *née* Shepherd-Cross (d 1981); *b* 7 July 1926; *Educ* Winchester; *m* 1955, Maura Daphne, da of Gp Capt John Sullivan, CBE (d 1953); 2 s (Rupert b 1960, William b 1966), 1 da (Claire b 1963); *Career* serv Br Army 1944-48 RA Temp Capt; entered Diplomatic Serv 1948, serv in FO, Bonn, Strasbourg, Washington, Brussels; memb UK Delegation to the negotiations with Member States of the EEC 1961-63, head of chancery Buenos Aires 1963-67, ldr UK Delgn to UN Ctee on the Seabed and Ocean Floor at Rio de Janeiro 1968, head Science and Technology Dept FO 1968-70, cnsllr and hd of Chancery Bonn 1970-73 also dep ldr of the UK Delgn to the Four Power negotiations on Berlin; dep sec-gen Commission of the European Communities 1973-81, dir-gen for Energy CEC 1981-86 Ret 1986; hon fellow Faculty of Law & Visiting lecturer on European Institutions Edinburgh Univ 1986-; memb: cncl of Lancaster Univ 1988-, European Strategy bd of ICL 1988-, NW reg ctee Nat Tst 1987-; dep chm Nat Tst Lake District Appeal 1987-; memb exec ctee of Europa Nostra 1987-, vice-pres Int Castles Inst 1988-; *Recreations* gliding, skiing, walking; *Clubs* Utd Oxford and Cambridge; *Style—* Sir Christopher Audland, KCMG; The Old House, Ackenthwaite, Milnthorpe, Cumbria; LA7 7DH (☎ 04482 2202)

AUDLEY, 25 Baron (E 1312-13); Richard Michael Thomas Souter; s of Sir Charles Alexander Souter, KCIE, CSI, and Charlotte Dorothy Jesson (sis of Thomas Tuchet-Jesson, f of 23 Baron and the 23 Baron's sis who as Baroness Audley was 24 holder of that title; Charlotte and Thomas were children of Charlotte, da of John Thicknesse-Tuchet, bro of 21 Baron Audley, by her husb Thomas Jesson); suc cous 1973; *b* 31 May 1914; *Educ* Uppingham; *m* 1941, Pauline, da of Dallas Louis Eskell; 3 da; *Heir* all 3 da as coheiresses presumptive: Hon Mrs Carey Mackinnon, Hon Mrs Michael Carrington, Hon Amanda Souter, *qqv*; *Career* Capt RA WWII; fell Chartered Inst of Loss Adjusters; dir Graham Miller & Co, ret 1982; *Recreations* shooting, gardening; *Style—* The Rt Hon The Lord Audley; Friendly Green, Cowden, nr Edenbridge, Kent (☎ 034 286 682)

AUERBACH, Col Ernest; s of Dr Frank L Auerbach (d 1964), of USA, and Gertrude, *née* Rindskopf; *b* 22 Dec 1936; *Educ* George Washington Univ (BA, JD), US Army General Staff Coll; *m* 1 s (Hans Kevin b 1961); *Career* US Army 1962-70 (active serv), 1970-85 (Reserves); served through rank of Col; in European Theatre, Germany; South Vietnam, and the Pentagon; published legal, business and defence articles in: Wall Street Journal, The Officer, American Bar Association Journal, Neue Juristische Wochenschrift, Versicherungsrecht; chm Crusader Life Insurance plc 1986- (md 1984-86); pres Int Life & Gp Operations CIGNA Corporation 1984-; vice-pres and Assoc Gen Counsel CIGNA Corp 1978-79; managing attorney NL Inds 1975-77; Div Counsel Xerox Corp 1970-75; memb Computer Systems Tech Advsy Ctee US Dept of Commerce 1974, 1976; memb American Cncl on Germany 1979-; Legion of Merit w/ Oak Leaf Cluster 1986, Legion of Merit, 1970; Bronze Star Medal, Meritorious Service Medal, Army Commendation Medal; *Recreations* writing, running; *Clubs* Nat Arts (New York), Univ (New York), IOD; *Style—* Colonel Ernest Auerbach; CIGNA Corp., 1600 Arch Street/JFK 14, Philadelphia, Pennsylvania 19103, USA (☎ 215 523 1223)

AUERBACH, Frank Helmuth; s of Max Auerbach (d 1942), of Berlin, and Charlotte Norah, *née* Borchardt (d 1942); *b* 29 April 1931; *Educ* Bunce Ct Sch Kent, Borough Poly Sch of Art, St Martin's Sch of Art, RCA (ARCA 1955); *m* 10 March 1958, Julia, da of James Wolstenholme (d 1981); 1 s (Jacob b 1958); *Career* artist (painter); exhibited: Tate Gallery, Arts Cncl, Br Cncl, Museum of Modern Art New York, Metropolitan Museum NY, Nat Gallery of Australia, GB XLII Venice Biennale; Silver Medal RCA 1955; awarded Golden Lion Prize Venice Biennale 1986; *Style—* Frank Auerbach, Esq; c/o Marlborough Fine Art (London) Ltd, 6 Albemarle St, London W1X 4BY

AUGER, George Albert; s of Thomas Albert Auger (d 1977), and Lillian Daisy, *née* McDermott; *b* 21 Feb 1938; *Educ* Finchley Co GS; *m* 8 Sept 1962, Pauline June; 2 da (Jacqueline Susan (Mrs Bell) b 1965, Deborah Anne b 1969); *Career* Nat Serv RAF 1957-59; sr insolvency ptnr Stoy Hayward 1978-; memb cncl Chartered Assoc Certified Accountants 1980-86, pres Insolvency Practitioners Assoc 1981-82; chm govrs Channing Sch London; FCCA 1962, MIPA 1967; *Books* Hooper's Voluntary Liquidation (1978); *Recreations* cricket, tennis, opera, porcelain; *Style—* George Auger, Esq; Stoy Hayward, 8 Baker St, London W1M 1DA (☎ 01 486 5888, fax 01 487 3686, telex 367716 HORWAT)

AUGHTERSON, William Herbert; s of William Vencent aughterson, of Melbourne, Aust, and Mary Diana, *née* Wembridge; *b* 21 Dec 1937; *Educ* Zavier Coll Melbourne, Univ of Melbourne, Univ of Essex (MA); *m* 11 June 1960, Patricia Mary, da of Alfred Rowton Giblett; 4 s (Peter b 1963, James b 1965, Paul b 1967, Anthony b 1973), 1 da

(Kathleen b 1961); *Career* barr: Supreme Ct of Victoria 1964-, High Ct of Aust 1964-; slr Supreme Ct of England and Wales 1978-; chm Frating Parish Cncl 1977-78, clerk Stanway Parish Cncl 1979-81; memb: Law Inst Victoria 1964, Law Soc 1978; *Books* The Diseases of Bees (1956); *Recreations* golf, watching cricket; *Clubs* North Countrymans (Colchester), Birch Grove GC; *Style—* William Aughterson; 53 Victoria Rd, Colchester Essex (☎ 0206 56 270); 13 Gildan St, North Balwyn, Victoria, Australia; 58 North Hill, Colchester, Essex (☎ 0206 574 076, fax 0206 560 569)

AUKIN, David; s of Charles Aukin (d 1981), and Regina, *née* Unger; *b* 12 Feb 1942; *Educ* St Paul's, St Edmund Hall Oxford (BA); *m* 20 June 1979, Nancy Jane, da of Herman Meckler, of London and New York; 2 s (Daniel b 1970, Jethro b 1976); *Career* slr 1976-79; dir: Hampstead Theatre 1978-83, Leicester Haymarket Theatre 1983-86; exec dir Royal Nat Theatre 1986-; *Clubs* Garrick, RAC; *Style—* David Aukin, Esq; 27 Manor House Ct, Warrington Gdns, London W9 2PZ; National Theatre, South Bank, London (☎ 01 928 2033, fax 01 620 1197)

AULD, Margaret Gibson; da of Alexander John Sutton Auld (d 1988), of 9 Rhydypenau Close, Llanishen Cardiff, and Eleanor Margaret, *née* Ingram (d 1980); *b* 11 July 1932; *Educ* Cardiff HS for Girls, Univ of Edinburgh (Cert Nursing, MPhil); *Career* departmental sister Cardiff Maternity Hosp 1957-59 and 1961-66, ward sister Queen Mary Hosp Dunedin NZ 1960, matron Simpson Meml Maternity Pavilion Edinburgh 1968-73 (asst matron 1967), actg chief regnl nursing offr SE Region Scotland 1973, chief area nursing offr Borders Health Bd 1973-77, chief nursing offr Scottish Home and Health Dept 1977-88; memb: Ctee on Nursing 1970-72, Gen Nursing Cncl Scotland 1973-76, Central Midwives Bd Scotland 1972-76, Scottish Bd BIM 1983-; conslt WHO; memb: Scottish ctee of gen cncl Cancer Relief Macmillan Fund, Scottish ctee Action Smoking and Health; chm advsy ctee for Cancer Relief Macmillan Fund Scotland; Hon DSc Queen Margaret Coll Edinburgh 1987 (govr 1989); vice-pres Royal Coll of Midwives 1988; FRCN 1980, CBIM 1981; *Books* How Many Nurses? (1977); *Recreations* reading, music, entertaining; *Style—* Miss Margaret Auld; Staddlestones, Neidpath Rd, Peebles, Scotland EH45 8NN (☎ 0721 29594)

AULD, Sir Robin Ernest; QC (1975); s of late Ernest Auld; *b* 19 July 1937; *Educ* Brooklands Coll, King's Coll London (LLB, PhD); *m* 1963, Catherine Elenaor Mary, elder da of late David Henry Pritchard; 1 s, 1 da; *Career* barr Gray's Inn 1959; Bencher 1984; (NI bar 1973; New York State Bar 1984), rec Crown Ct 1977-; legal assessor to Gen Medical and Dental Cncls 1981-; justice High Ct of Justice 1988-; kt 1988; chm, Home Office ctee of Inquiry into Sunday and Late-Night Trading; *Style—* Robin Auld, Esq, QC; Lamb Bldg, Temple, London EC4Y 7AS (☎ 01 353 6701); 12 East 41st St, New York, New York, 10017 USA (☎ 212 685 0535)

AUSTEN, David James; s of Albert Richard Austen (d 1933); *b* 19 July 1925; *Educ* Margate Coll; *m* 1951, late Margaret Jane, da of Hewel Morgan Owen (d 1972); 1 s; *Career* serv WWII Flt Lt; dep md Charles Colston Gp, dir Tallent Engrg; FCA; *Recreations* photography, painting, ornithology, music, reading; *Style—* David Austen, Esq; Netherbury, Burtons Lane, Chalfont St Giles, Bucks (☎ 024 04 2269); Charles Colston Gp Ltd, PO Box 15, Henley-on-Thames, Oxon

AUSTEN, Derek; s of Alan Ewart Walter Austen, OBE (d 1978), of Sunbury on Thames, and Doreen Gladys Nowell, *née* Parr; *b* 7 August 1945; *Educ* St Paul's, St John's Coll Cambridge (MA); *Career* trainee accountant Coopers & Lybrand (1968-72), accountant Int Rectifier GB Ltd (1972-75), various positions with Reed Int incl Chief Accountant Walker Crosweller Ltd 1975-80; dir: Prudential Portfolio Mangrs Ltd, Prudential Financial Servs Ltd; FCA 1975; *Recreations* squash, sailing, opera; *Clubs* Little Ship, Colets; *Style—* Derek Austen, Esq; 41 Strand on the Green, London W4 3PB; Prudential Financial Services Ltd, 142 Holborn Bars, London EC1N 2NH (☎ 01 936 8473, telex 265082)

AUSTEN, Mark Edward; s of Capt George Ernest Austen (d 1987), of Ashtead, Surrey, and Eileen Gladys, *née* Thirkettle; *b* 25 August 1949; *Educ* City of London Freemen's Sch; *m* 28 May 1977, Priscilla, da of Reginald Cyril Hart (d 1986), of Chiddingfold, Surrey; 1 s (Timothy b 1980), 1 da (Rachel b 1982); *Career* corp accounts trainee Reecl Int 1967-72, asst fin controller Henry Ansbacher 1972-75, conslt Price Waterhouse 1975-82, ptnr in charge fin servs consulting UK and Europe Price Waterhouse Mgmnt Conslts 1985- (ptnr 1982-85); Freeman City of London; FCMA 1976; *Recreations* music, squash, food; *Clubs* Carlton; *Style—* Mark Austen, Esq; 18 Imber Park Rd, Esher, Surrey KT10 8JB (☎ 01 398 3144); Price Waterhouse Management Consultants, No 1 London Bridge, London SE1 9QL (☎ 01 378 7200, fax 01 403 5265, telex 931709)

AUSTEN, Richard William; s of William George Austen (d 1987), and Barbara Florence Mary, *née* Birch; *b* 18 July 1945; *m* 4 Nov 1973, Geraldine Margaret, William Edward Fallon, of Bath; 1 s (Robert b 1986), 1 da (Julia b 1984); *Career* chartered surveyor, ptnr Humberts; ARICA; *Recreations* tennis, squash, rugby football; *Clubs* Rotary; *Style—* Richard W Austen, Esq; Grove House, Redlynch, nr Salisbury (☎ 0725 21350); Humberts, 49 Castle Street, Salisbury (☎ 0722 24422)

AUSTEN-SMITH, Air Marshal Sir Roy David; KBE (1979), CB (1975), DFC (1953); s of D Austen Smith, of Kingsdown, Kent; *b* 28 June 1924; *Educ* Hurstpierpoint; *m* 1951, Patricia Ann, *née* Alderson, da of Mrs Molly Glover, of Bawtry, Yorkshire; 2 s; *Career* RAF, serv WWII, Cdr Br Forces Cyprus, AOC Air HQ Cyprus and Administrator Sovereign Base Areas Cyprus 1976-78; Head Br Defence Staff Washington and Defence Attaché 1978-81, ret; a gentleman usher to HM the Queen 1982-; *Style—* Air Marshal Sir Roy Austen-Smith; c/o Nat West Bank, Swanley, Kent

AUSTICK, David; s of Bertie Lister Austick (d 1938), and Hilda, *née* Spink (d 1968); *b* 8 Mar 1920; *Educ* City of Leeds Sch; *m* 1944, Florence Elizabeth Lomath; *Career* master bookseller Austicks Bookshops; memb Leeds City Cncl 1969-77 MP (Lib) Ripon 1973-74, memb W Yorks CC 1974-79; contested (Lib): Ripon 1974, Cheadle 1979, Leeds Euro Parl 1979; exec chmn: Electoral Reform Soc Ltd 1984-86; tres and co sec ERS Ltd 1987; co and fin sec ER (Ballot Services) Ltd 1969-; *Recreations* antiquarian books, illustrated books, limited editions, owner of yacht 'Frontispiece' - nat 12 foot class; *Clubs* Nat Lib, Fellowship of Reconcilliation; *Style—* David Austick, Esq; 29 Cookridge St, Leeds LS1 3AN (☎ 0532 455879); Clarence Place, Burley-in-Wharfedale (☎ 0943 863305); Cross Green, Otley, W Yorks (☎ 0943 466566); 6 Chancel St, Blackfriars SE1 0UU

AUSTIN, Brian; s of Harold Austin, and Florence, *née* Elliot; *b* 25 Dec 1929; *Educ* Kettering GS, Leicester Poly Sch of Architecture (Dip Arch); *m* 8 Oct 1955, Gwendoline, da of John Johnson (d 1979); 3 s (Jonathan b 1959, Nigel b 1961, Matthew b 1964); *Career* Nat Serv RE 2 Lt 1953-55; chartered architect, sr ptnr Featherstone Austin Woodward, architects, Northampton ARIBA; *Recreations* campanology, golf; *Clubs* Northampton Town & County; *Style—* Brian Austin, Esq; 24 Gipsy Lane, Kettering (☎ 0536 514910); 30A Billing Rd, Northampton (☎ 0604 34216)

AUSTIN, Dr Colin François Lloyd; s of Prof Lloyd James Austin, of Cambridge, and Jeanne Françoise, *née* Guérin; *b* 26 July 1941; *Educ* Lycée Lakanal Paris, Manchester GS, Jesus Coll Cambridge (MA), Christ Church Oxford (D Phil), Freie Univ W Berlin; *m* 28 June 1967, Mishtu, da of Sreepada Mojumder (d 1963), of Calcutta; 1 s (Topun b 1 Aug 1971), 1 da (Teesta b 21 Oct 1968); *Career* Cambridge Univ: dir of studies in classics and fell Trinity Hall 1965-, asst lectr 1969-72, lectr 1973-88, reader 1988-; tres: Cambridge Philological Soc 1971-, jt ctee Greek and Roman Socs 1983-; FBA 1983; *Books* Nova Fragmenta Euripidea (1968), Menandri Aspis et Samia (1969-70), Comicorum Graecorum Fragmenta in Papyris Reperta (1973), Poetae Comici Graeci (1983); *Recreations* cycling, philately, wine tasting; *Style—* Dr Colin Austin; 7 Park Terrace, Cambridge CB1 1JH (☎ 0223 62732); Trinity Hall, Cambridge CB2 1TJ (☎ 0223 332520)

AUSTIN, Ven George Bernard; s of Oswald Hulton Austin (d 1975), of Bury, Lancs, and Evelyn, *née* Twigg (d 1955); *b* 16 Jul 1931; *Educ* Bury HS, St David's Coll Lampeter (BA), Chichester Theol Coll; *m* 21 July 1962, Roberta (Bobbie) Anise, da of George Edward Thompson (d 1988), of Luton, Beds; 1 s (Jeremy Paul b 1969); *Career* ordained: deacon 1955, priest 1956, asst chaplain Univ of London 1960; vicar: St Mary's Eaton Bray 1964-70, St Peter's Bushey Heath 1970-88; archdeacon of York 1988-; proctor in convocation 1970-, church cmmr 1978-; *Books* Life of Our Lord (1960), When Will Ye Be Wise? (contrib 1983); *Recreations* cooking, theatre, photography; *Clubs* Athenaeum; *Style—* The Ven the Archdeacon of York; 7 Lang Rd, Bishopthorpe, York, N Yorks YO2 1QJ (☎ 0904 709541); 45 Kemp Place, Bushey, Watford, Herts WD2 1DW

AUSTIN, (William) James; s of John William Austin (d 1953), of Chelmsford; *b* 8 Feb 1913; *Educ* UCL (BSc); *m* 1943, Ann Penelope Maude, da of Sir Ronald Matthews (d 1959), of Doncaster; 1 s, 4 da; *Career* Lt RAOC (Ordnance Mech Engineer) 1936, serv WWII (despatches), Maj 1940, Lt-Col 1943 (RAOC 1936-42, REME 1942-53), ret 1953; dir of private companies; *Recreations* sailing, winter sports; *Clubs* Army & Navy; *Style—* Lt-Col James Austin; Hatfield Place, Hatfield Peverel, Chelmsford, Essex (☎ 0245 380363)

AUSTIN, John; TD; s of John Austin (d 1972), of Chesterfield; *b* 13 April 1927; *Educ* St George's Sch Harpenden, Glasgow Univ; *m* 1959, Shirley Frances Bonner, da of Maj G Proctor (d 1979), of Tullydoey, Co Tyrone; 1 s (James b 1960), 1 da (Frances b 1964); *Career* formerly Capt RASC; dir and chief exec J Mann & Son; dir: Claas (UK) Ltd, Howard Machinery plc; memb: Ipswich Port Authy, Eastern Electricity Bd; Ipswich Port Authy; MIProdE, CEng; *Recreations* walking, gardening; *Clubs* RAC; *Style—* John Austin, Esq, TD; The White Cottage, Woodbridge, Suffolk IP12 4BT (☎ 039 43 3044)

AUSTIN, Michael Trescawen; s and h of Sir William Austin, 4 Bt, by his 1 w; *b* 27 August 1927; *Educ* Downside; *m* 1951, Bridget Dorothea Patricia, da of late Francis Farrell, of Miltown, Clonmellon, Co Meath; 3 da (Mary b 1951, Jane b 1954, Susan b 1956); *Career* served WW II with RNVR; sometime Master of Braes of Derwent; *Style—* Michael Austin, Esq; Idestone Barton, Dunchideock, Exeter, Devon EX2 9UE (☎ (0392) 832282)

AUSTIN, Vice Adm Sir Peter Murray; KCB (1976); s of Vice Adm Sir Francis Murray Austin, KBE, CB (d 1953), and Marjorie Jane, *née* Barker (d 1968); *b* 16 April 1921; *Educ* RNC Dartmouth; *m* 1959, Josephine Rhoda Ann Shutte-Smith; 3 s, 1 da; *Career* naval cadet 1935, serv WWII at sea, qualified as pilot FAA 1946, Capt 1961, Rear Adm 1971, Flag Offr Naval Air Cmd 1973-76, Vice Adm 1974, ret 1976; CBIM; ops dir Mersey Docks and Harbour Co 1976-80; dir Avanova Int 1980-; chm: Special Trg Servs 1984-; dir Mastiff Electronic Systems 1987-; *Recreations* skiing, sailing, golf, HGV driving; *Clubs* Army and Navy, Royal Yacht Sqdn; *Style—* Vice Adm Sir Peter Austin, KCB; Dolphin Cottage, 93 The Parade, West Kirby, Wirral L48 0RR

AUSTIN, Air Vice-Marshal Roger Mark; AFC (1973); s of Mark Austin (d 1982), and Sylvia Joan, *née* Reed; *b* 9 Mar 1940; *Educ* King's Alfred GS Wantage; *m* 1, 1963 (m dis 1981), Carolyn de Recourt, *née* Martyn; 2 s (Stuart b 1965, Patrick b 1971), 1 da (Rachel b 1964); m2, 26 July 1986, Glenys Amy Beckley, da of Hugh Glyn Roberts, of Holyhead; 2 step da (Sarah b 1969, Emma b 1972); *Career* RAF: cmmnd 1957, Flying Instr 1960; flying appt: 20 Sqdn 1964, 54 Sqdn 1966, cmd 54 Sqdn 1969, flying appt 4 Sqdn 1970, Staff Coll Camberley 1973, cmd 233 OCU 1974, PSO to AOC in C Strike Cmd 1977, cmd RAF Chivenor; ADC to Queen 1980, Staff HQ Strike Cmd 1982, DOR 2 MOD 1984, RCDS 1986, AOIC Central Tactics and Trials Orgn 1987, Dir Gen Aircraft 1 MOD (Procurement Exec) 1987-; *Recreations* walking, transport systems; *Clubs* RAF; *Style—* Air Vice Marshal Roger Austin, AFC; St Giles Court, St Giles High St, London WC2H 8LD

AUSTIN, Sir William Ronald; 4 Bt (UK 1894), of Red Hill, Castleford, West Riding of York; yr s of Sir William Austin, 2 Bt (d 1940), by his w Violet, herself da of Alexander Fraser, JP (of a branch of the Frasers, Lords Lovat), and 1 cous of 1 Baron Fraser of Lonsdale; suc bro, Sir John Austin, 3 Bt, 1981; *b* 20 July 1900; *m* 1, 1926, Dorothy Mary (d 1957), da of late L A Bidwell, FRCS; 2 s (Michael, Anthony b 1930); m 2, 1958, Mary Helen, da of Francis Henry Arthur Joseph Farrell, of Miltown Ho, Co Meath; *Heir* s, Michael Austin, *qv*; *Style—* Sir William Austin, Bt; Creagan Park, Appin, Argyll (☎ 063 173 213)

AUSTIN, William Thomas Frederick; s of Percy Thomas Austin (d 1968), of Stratford upon Avon, and Winifred, *née* Farr (d 1954); *b* 1 Feb 1920; *Educ* Wolverhampton GS, King Edward VI HS Birmingham, Univ of Birmingham (BSc), Cornell Univ; *m* 1, 9 April 1955, Agnes Scott da of John Mitchell, of Biggar, Lanarkshire; 2 da (Carol Ann b 24 Aug 1957, Morag Elspeth b 21 May 1961); m 2, 12 Sept 1964, Muriel Eileen, da of John Redgrove Taylor (d 1968), of London Colney, Herts; *Career* serv WWII: offr cadet RE 1940-41, 2 Lt (later Lt) 5 FD Co RE 1941-44; Maj (later Lt-Col) Engr and Ry Staff corps TAVR (now Engr and Tport Staff Corps) 1981; site engr Sir Robert McAlpine & sons 1940, asst engr R Travers Morgan & Ptnrs 1944-45; Freeman Fox and Ptnrs (1945-(ptnr 1966-85, conslt 1985-): work incl Auckland Harbour Bridge, Forth Road Bridge, M2 and M5 motorways; work in USA on various long span bridges and turnpikes 1950-51; pres: Concrete Soc 1978-79, Inst of Highways and Tport 1984-85; memb Bld Div cncl and various ctees BSI

1977-86; Univ of Birmingham: pres Guild of Graduates (London branch) 1983-86, memb ct 1975-85; memb Glyndebourne Festival Soc 1977-; Freeman City of London, Liveryman Worshipful Co of Paviors 1979; CEng, FICE 1946, FIStruct E 1945, FIHT 1959, MASCE 1950 ; *Recreations* travel, photography, art, opera, literature; *Clubs* RAC; *Style—* William Austin, Esq; 3 Kingfisher Drive, Ham, Richmond, Surrey TW10 7UF (☎ 01 940 7957)

AUSTIN-COOPER, Richard Arthur; o s of Capt Adolphus Richard Cooper, of Ditton Kent, and Doris Rosina, *née* Wallen; see Burke's Irish Family Records under Cooper (co Tipperary.; *b* 21 Feb 1932; *Educ* Wellingborough GS; Diploma Inst of Bankers; *m* 1, 28 March 1953 (m dis 1963), Sylvia Anne Shirley Berringer; m 2, 28 Sept 1963 (m dis 1974), Valerie Georgina, da of Henry Drage, of Tottenham, London; 1 s (Matthew b 1969), 1 da (Samantha b 1967); m 3, 1986, Rosemary Swasland, *née* Gillespie; *Career* served RA Intelligence Corps 21 SAS Regt, Hon Artillery Co; dep head Stocks & Shares Dept Banque de Paris et des Pays Bas 1969-74; mangr Banking Div Brook St Bureau of Mayfair Ltd 1974-77; chief custodian and London registrar of Canadian Imp Bank of Commerce 1975-78; personnel offr Deutsche Bank AG London Branch 1978-85, snr mangr and head of personnel Deutsche Bank Capital Markets ltd; fndr Fell Inst of Heraldic and Genealogical Studies, memb bd of Mgmnt Barbican YMCA, City of London Central Markets Coal Corn and Rates, Leadenhall Market, Billingsgate Market, music mgmnt ctees 1978-81, Ct of Common Cncl for Cripplegate Ward 1978-81, City of London TAVR Assoc, Mgmnt Ctee Barbican Sch of Music and Drama and mature student, Irish Peers Assoc; govr: City of London Sch for Girls 1979-80, City of London Freemens Sch 1980-81, Lansbury Adult Educn Inst 1979-82, Sheriffs and Recorders Fund at the Old Bailey 1979-; represented the City of London Corpn on the Gtr London Arts Cncl 1979-80, Freedom of the City of London 1964, last tstee City of London Imp Vols 1980-81; prizes for athletics, operatic singing (tenor), painting; FCIB, FRSA, FRSAIre, MBIM, FSA (Scot); *Recreations* genealogical res, tenor concerts, sketching; *Clubs* Special Forces, SAS Old Comrades, Intelligence Corps Old Comrades; *Style—* Richard Austin-Cooper, Esq; Forge Cottage, Dunn Street, Road, Bredhurst, Kent ME7 3LX; (☎ 0634-378024); Deutsche Bank Capital Markets Ltd, 150 Leadenhall St, London EC3V 4RJ (☎ 01-2830933)

AUSTWICK, Prof Kenneth; s of Harry Austwick (d 1984), of Morecambe, Lancs, and Beatrice, *née* Lee (d 1954); *b* 26 May 1927; *Educ* Morecambe GS, Sheffield Univ (BSc, MSc, PhD); *m* 18 Aug 1956, Gillian, da of Frank Griffin (d 1983), of Bromsgrove, Worcs; 1 s (Malcolm b 1959), 1 da (Dawn b 1960); *Career* schoolmaster 1950-59, lectr (later sr lectr) Sheffield Univ 1959-65, reader Reading Univ 1965-66, prof Bath Univ 1966- (pro-vice chllr 1972-75); advsr HO; conslt: OECD, UTA, Br Rail; govr Bath Coll; FSS 1962, FSA 1970; *Books* Teaching Machnines (1962), Aspects of Educational Technology Vol Six (1972), Trigonometry (1967), Maths at Work (1985), Mathematics Connections (1985); *Recreations* gardening, wine-making; *Clubs* Royal Cwlth; *Style—* Prof Kenneth Austwick; Brook House, Combe Hay, Bath, Avon (☎ 0225 832541); Sch of Education, University of Bath, Bath, Avon (☎ 0225 826352, fax 0225 62508, telex 449097)

AUTY, Capt Richard Ian; s of Keith Ian Auty (Flt Lt RAF WWII), of Nyali, Huntersfield Close, Reigate, Surrey, and Marjorie, *née* Gwinnell; *b* 9 April 1946; *Educ* Trinity Sch of John Whitgift, RAF Coll Cranwell, Coll of Air Trg Hamble; *m* 4 June 1971 (m dis 1984), Carole Marie Brenda Hazel, da of Albert Bacuez (d 1951), French Army Off; 1 s (Charles b 1974), 1 da (Natalie b 1976); *Career* joined Br Euro Airways 1967, overseas div 1976, sr capt Br Airways; memb: BALPA, RHS; *Recreations* reading, water sports, tennis, golf, theatre; *Clubs* Naval; *Style—* Capt R I Auty; 24 Beechcrest View, Hook, Hampshire

AVEBURY, 4 Baron (UK 1900); Sir Eric Reginald Lubbock; 7 Bt (UK 1806); s of Hon Maurice Fox Pitt Lubbock (yst s of 1 Baron Avebury) and Hon Mary Stanley (eldest da of 5 Baron Stanley of Alderley and sis of the actress Pamela Stanley); suc cousin, 3 Baron 1971; *b* 29 Sept 1928; *Educ* Upper Canada Coll, Harrow, Balliol Coll Oxford; *m* 1, 1953 (m dis 1983), Kina Maria, da of Count Joseph O'Kelly de Gallagh (a yr s of the family whose head is a Count of the Holy Roman Empire by Imperial Letters Patent of 1767); 2 s (Hon Lyulph Ambrose Jonathan, Hon Maurice Patrick Guy, *qqv*), 1 da (Hon Mrs Binney, *qv*); 2, 1985, Lindsay Jean, da of Gordon Neil Stewart and of late Pamela Hansford Johnson (Lady Snow), writer; 1 s (Hon John William Stewart, b 8 Aug 1985); *Heir* s, Hon Lyulph Ambrose Jonathan Lubbock, *qv*; *Career* 2 Lt Welsh Gds 1949-51; engineer with Rolls Royce 1951-56; mgmnt conslt Charterhouse Gp 1960; sits as Lib in House of Lords; MP (Lib) Orpington 1962-70, Lib Chief Whip 1963-70; conslt Morgan-Grampian 1970-; dir C L Projects; pres Fluoridation Soc 1972-85, Conservation Soc 1973-82; memb Cncl Institute Race Relations 1972-74, Royal Cmmn on Standards of Conduct in Public Life 1974-76; MIMechE; *Style—* The Rt Hon the Lord Avebury; 53 Gloucester Street, London SW1V 4DY

AVERY, (Marshall) Angus; s of Maj Norman Bates Avery, MC (d 1957), of Redhill, Surrey, and Grace Avery; bro of Gillian Elise Avery, *qv*; *b* 6 May 1933; *Educ* Loretto, Sandhurst; *m* 1975, Penelope Maxwell, da of Alan Berners-Price; 2 s (Archie, Alexander); *Career* Capt Gordon Highlanders 1953-62; md Irish Vintners 1968-70, commercial mangr John Harvey & Sons (España) Ltd 1972-73, dir Waverley Vintners 1974-84, mangr Woodhouse Wines 1987-; *Recreations* sailing, skiing, shooting, squash; *Clubs* Naval and Military; *Style—* Angus Avery, Esq; Iwerne Hill Farmhouse, Iwerne Minster, Blandford Forum, Dorset DT11 8LE (☎ 0747 811867); Hall and Woodhouse Ltd, Blandford Forum, Dorset DT11 9LS

AVERY, Gillian Elise - (Mrs A O J Cockshut); da of Maj Norman Bates Avery, MC (d 1957), of Redhill, Surrey, and Grace Avery; sister of (Marshall) Angus Avery, *qv*; *b* 30 Sept 1926; *Educ* Dunottar Sch Reigate; *m* 1952, Anthony Oliver John Cockshut, s of Dr Rowland William Cockshut (d 1977), of Hendon; 1 da; *Career* writer of novels, children's books and non-fiction, *A Likely Lad* (Guardian Award 1972); chm Children's Books History Soc; *Style—* Miss Gillian Avery; 32 Charlbury Rd, Oxford (☎ 0865 56291)

AVERY, Graham; s of Walter Avery, of Shifnal, Shropshire, and Kathleen, *née* Hawkins; *b* 17 Feb 1945; *Educ* Shrewsbury Coll (HNC); *m* 25 July 1970, Susan Elizabeth, da of Walter Sidney Townes, of Westerfield, nr Ipswich, Suffolk; 1 s (Mark Nigel b 15 Dec 1965), 1 da (Michelle Louise b 28 July 1971); *Career* proprietor and chm Breckland Gp Hldgs 1964-, chm S Wales Devpt Inc plc 1987-; fndr memb and hon patron Appeal Theatre Gp Ipswich; qualified pilot ; *Recreations* tennis, flying, skiing, theatre; *Clubs* IOD; *Style—* Graham Avery, Esq; 25 Dover St, Mayfair, London W1 (☎ 01 499 0056, fax 01 408 1998); 43a Woodbridge Road East, Ipswich IP4 5QN (☎ 0473 715 751, fax 0473 719 500)

AVERY JONES, John Francis; CBE (1987); s of Sir Francis Avery Jones, CBE, of Nutbourne, West Sussex, and Dorothea Bessie, *née* Pfirter (d 1983); *b* 5 April 1940; *Educ* Rugby, Trinity Coll Cambridge (MA, LLM); *Career* admitted slr 1966, ptnr Bircham & Co 1970-85, sr ptnr Speechly Bircham 1985-, jt ed Br Tax Review 1974-, memb ed bd Simon's Taxes 1977-, visiting prof LSE 1986-; pres Inst Taxation 1980-82; memb: Keith ctee 1980-84, cncl Inst of Fiscal Studies 1988-; memb bd govrs Voluntary Hosp of St Bartholemew; Master Worshipful Co Barbers 1985-86; memb Law Soc (cncl 1986-); *Books* Tax Havens and Measures Against Tax Avoidance and Evasion in the EEC (ed 1974), Encyclopedia of VAT (1972); *Recreations* music (particulary opera); *Clubs* Athenaeum; *Style—* John Avery Jones, Esq, CBE; 7 Cleveland Gdns, London W2 6HA (☎ 01 258 1960); Bouverie Ho, 154 Fleet St, London EC4A 2HX (☎ 01 353 3290 , fax 01 353 4825, telex 22655)

AVNER, Ambass Yehuda; *b* 30 Dec 1928; *Educ* Manchester HS, London Sch of Journalism; *m* Miriam Avner; 1 s (Danny), 3 da (Deborah, Esther, Yael); *Career* ed of publications Jewish Agency Jerusalem 1956-64; Min of Foreign Affairs; ed of Political Publications, asst to PM Levi Eshkol 1964-67, consul of Israel New York 1967-68, first sec (later cnsllr) Embassy of Israel Washington DC 1968-72; dir of Foreign Press Bureau Foreign Miny Jerusalem, asst to PM Golda Meir 1972-74, seconded from Foreign Miny to PM's Bureau, advsr to: PM Yitzhak Rabin 1974-77, PM Begin 1977-83; ambass to Court of St James's 1983-; *Style—* Ambassador Yehuda Avner; 2 Palace Green, W8

AVON, Countess of; Clarissa; only da of late Maj John Strange Spencer-Churchill, DSO (himself bro of Rt Hon Sir Winston Churchill, KG, OM, CH, TD, PC); *see also* Churchill, John GS; *b* 28 June 1920; *m* 1952, as his 2 w, 1 Earl of Avon (d 1977); *Style—* The Rt Hon the Countess of Avon; 32 Bryanston Square, London W1

AVONSIDE, Rt Hon Lord; Ian Hamilton Shearer; PC (1962); s of Andrew Shearer, OBE, JP, of Dunfermline, and Jessie Macdonald; *b* 6 Nov 1914; *Educ* Dunfermline HS, Glasgow Univ (MA), Edinburgh Univ (LLB); *m* 1, 1942; 1 s, 1 da; m 2, 1954, Janet Sutherland Murray (*see Avonside, Lady*); *Career* serv WWII, Maj RA; advocate 1938, QC (Scotland) 1952, sheriff Renfrew and Argyll 1960-62, Lord Advocate 1962-64, Scottish Lord of Session (Senator of the Coll of Justice in Scotland) 1964-; memb Scottish Univs Ctee of the Privy Cncl 1971-; pres Stair Soc 1975-; *Clubs* Garrick; *Style—* The Rt Hon Lord Avonside; The Mill House, Samuelston, E Lothian (☎ 062 082 2396)

AVONSIDE, Lady; Janet Sutherland Shearer; OBE (1956); da of William Murray(d 1932), of Paisley, and Janet Harley Watson; *b* 31 May 1917; *Educ* St Columba's Sch Kilmacolm, Erlenhaus Baden Baden, Edinburgh Univ; *m* 1953, as his 2 w, Rt Hon Lord Avonside, *qv*; *Career* contested (C): Glasgow Maryhill 1950, Dundee E 1951, Leith 1955; lectr dept of Educnl Studies Edinburgh Univ 1957-69; Scottish govr BBC 1971-76; *Style—* Lady Avonside, OBE; The Mill Ho, Samuelston, E Lothian (☎ Haddington (062 082) 2396)

AWAK, His Excellency Alhaji Shehu; 'Alhaji' signifies that HE has made the pilgrimage to Mecca; s of Kuge Awak, village head (d 1942); *b* 14 May 1932; *Educ* Nigerian Coll, Manchester Univ, LSE; *m* 1953, A'ishatu; 4 s, 7 da; *Career* Nigerian Foreign Service: admin offr 1961-70, actg perm sec 1970-73, perm sec 1973-78, sec to mil govt 1978-79, head Nigerian Civil Service 1979-81; Nigerian high cmmr to UK 1981-; *Recreations* table tennis, gaming; *Style—* HE Alhaji Shehu Awak; The Nigerian High Commission, Nigeria Ho, 9 Northumberland Avenue, London WC2 (☎ 01 839 1244); 15A Kensington Palace Gardens, London W8 (☎ 01 221 3734)

AWDRY, Daniel Edmund; TD, DL (Wilts 1979); s of late Col Edmund Portman Awdry, MC, TD, DL, of Coters, Chippenham, Wilts, and Evelyn Daphne Alexandra Awdry, JP, *née* French; *b* 10 Sept 1924; *Educ* Winchester, Sandhurst; *m* 1950, Elizabeth, da of Mrs Joan Cattley, of London; 3 da; *Career* serv WWII; slr 1950; MP (C) Chippenham 1962-79, PPS to Slr Gen 1973-74; dir: BET Omnibus Servs 1966-80, Sheepbridge Engineering 1968-79, Rediffusion 1973-, Colonial Mutual Life Assur Soc 1974-; *Style—* Daniel Awdry, Esq, TD, DL; Old Manor, Beanacre, nr Melksham, Wilts (☎ Melksham 2315)

AWDRY, Henry Goodwin; s of Charles Selwyn Awdry, DSO (ka 1918), and Constance Lilias, *née* Bateson (d 1946); *b* 14 Feb 1911; *Educ* Winchester, New Coll Oxford (BA); *m* 5 May 1947, Philippa Joyce, da of Sgn Cdr Clifford Evans Holman (d 1954); 2 s (Godwin Antony b 1948, Robert Henry b 1951); *Career* 2 Lt Royal Wilts Yeomany TA 1934, ret 1947 with rank of Maj; admitted slr 1936; ptnr Awdry Bailey & Douglas; govr Dauntsy Sch Fndn 1972-82 (clerk to govrs 1952-72), cncllr Calne and Chippenham RDC 1948-53; memb Law Soc; *Style—* Henry Awdry, Esq; Bottle Farm, Bottlesford, Pewsey, Wilts (☎ 067 285 374); 33 St John St, Devises, Wilts (☎ 0380 2311)

AXFORD, Dr David Norman; s of Norman Axford (d 1961), and Joy Alicia (d 1970); *b* 14 June 1934; *Educ* Merchant Taylors, Plymouth Coll, St John's Coll Cambridge (BA, MA, PhD), Southampton Univ (MSc); *m* 1, 26 May 1962 (m dis 1979), Elizabeth Anne Moynihan, da of Ralph J Stiles (d 1973); 1 s (John b 1968), 2 da (Katy b 1964, Sophie b 1966); m 2, 8 March 1980, Diana Rosemary Joan, da of Leslie George Bufton (d 1970); 3 step s (Simon b 1959, Timothy b 1961, Jeremy b 1963), 1 step da (Nicola b 1968); *Career* Nat Serv RAF 1958-60, PO 1958, flying Offr 1959; Meteorological off: forecasting and res 1960-68, met res flight and radiosondes 1968-76, asst dir operational instrumentation 1976-80, asst dir telecommunications 1980-82, dep dir observational servs (grade 5) 1982-84, dir of servs (under-sec grade 3) 1984-; memb cncl and hon gen sec Royal Meteorological Soc 1983-88, pres N Atlantic observing stations Bd 1983-86, chm ctee of operational WWW systems evaluation 1986-; LG Groves Memorial Prize for Meteorology 1970; CEng 1975, FIEE 1982; *Recreations* swimming, reading, good food and wine, garden, music; *Style—* Dr David Axford; Meterological Office, London Rd, Bracknell, Berks (☎ 0344 420 242)

AXTELL, Stanley; s of Edwin Thomas Axtell (d as a result of active service 1917), of Surrey, and Mary, *née* Belbin (d 1951); *b* 8 June 1913; *Educ* Woking Ring GS; *m* 21 Aug 1937, Charlotte Wilhelmina, da of Charles William Hopley (d 1957), of Surrey; *Career* chartered quantity surveyer: fndr ptnr Axtell, Yates Hallet (London) 1946-80; RICS; ret; *Recreations* golf, tennis, dancing, theatre, food & wine, politics; *Style—* Stanley Axtell, Esq; Orchard Cottage, Willow Lane, Boxgrove Road, Guildford, Surrey GU1 2NH (☎ 0483 33954)

AXTON, Henry (Harry) Stuart; s of Wilfrid George Axton, and Mary Louise Laver; *b*

6 May 1923; *Educ* Rock Ferry, Sandhurst; *m* 1947, Constance Mary, da of Lycurgus Godefroy; 1 da; *Career* serv WWII N Africa & N W Europe, Royal Tank Regt and Fife & Forfar Yeomanry (wounded 3 times); chm Brixton Estate plc 1983- (md 1963-83, dep chm 1971-83); chm Invstmt Cos in Australia and Switzerland chm: Nuffield Hosps 1976-, St George's Hosp Med Sch 1977-; pres Br Property Fedn 1984-86; dep chm Audit Cmmn 1986-; dir Cathedral Works Orgn (Chichester) Ltd 1985-; FCA ; *Recreations* music, sailing (yacht 'Alpha IV'); *Clubs* Royal Thames Yacht, Royal Ocean Racing; *Style*— Harry Axton, Esq; Hook Place, Aldingbourne, nr Chichester (☎ 0243 542 291); Brixton Estate plc, 22-24 Ely Place, London EC1N 6TQ (☎ 01 242 6898)

AXWORTHY, Geoffrey John; s of William Henry Axworthy (d 1980), and Gladys Elizabeth, *née* Kingcombe (d 1953); *b* 10 August 1923; *Educ* Sutton HS Plymouth, Exeter Coll Oxford (MA); *m* 1, 21 Aug 1951, Irene, *née* Dickinson (d 1975); 2 s (Timothy John b 1958, Nigel Peter b 1961), 1 da (Carole Alison b 1954); m 2, Caroline Ann, da of Dr Theodore Griffiths, of Risca, Gwent; 1 s (Christopher Henry b 1986), 1 da (Eliza Jane b 1984); *Career* WWII RAFVR 1942-47; tutor Oxford Delegacy for Extra-Mural Studies 1950-51; lectr: Coll Arts and Sci Baghdad 1951-56, Univ Coll Ibadan Nigeria 1956-60; (dir of drama 1960-67, fndr-dir Univ Sch of Drama and Travelling Theatre) princ Central Sch Speech and Drama London 1970-88, dir drama Univ Coll Cardiff 1970-88, artistic dir Univ Sherman Theatre 1970-88, dir Sherman Theatre Ltd 1988-; *Recreations* travel; *Style*— Geoffrey Axworthy, Esq; 22 The Walk, West Grove, Cardiff CF2 3AF (☎ 0222 490 696)

AYCKBOURN, Alan; CBE (1987); s of Horace Ayckbourn, and Irene Maude, *née* Worley; *b* 12 April 1939; *Educ* Haileybury; *m* 1959, Christine Helen, *née* Roland; 2 s (Steven, Philip); *Career* playwright, theatre dir; artistic dir Stephen Joseph Theatre in the Round Scarborough *plays incl*: Relatively Speaking 1965, How the Other Half Loves 1969, Time and Time Again 1971, Absurd Person Singular 1972, The Norman Conquests 1973, Absent Friends 1974, Bedroom Farce 1975, Just Between Ourselves 1976, Taking Steps 1979, Seasons Greetings 1980, Intimate Exchanges 1982, Way Upstream 1981, A Chorus of Disapproval 1984, Woman in Mind 1985, A Small Family Business 1987, Henceforward 1987, Man of The Moment 1988;; *Clubs* Garrick; *Style*— Alan Ayckbourn, Esq, CBE; c/o Margaret Ramsay Ltd, 14a Goodwin's Court, St Martin's Lane, London WC2N 4LL (☎ 01 240 0691)

AYER, Prof Sir Alfred Jules; s of late Jules Louis Cyprien Ayer; *b* 29 Oct 1910; *Educ* Eton, Christ Church Oxford (MA); *m* 1, 1932, Grace Isabel Renée, da of late Col T H Lees; 1 s, 1 da; m 2, 1960 (m dis 1983), Alberta Constance Chapman (Dee Wells), da of late John Chapman, of Providence, RI, USA; 1 s; m 3, 1983, Mrs Vanessa Mary Addison Lawson, *née* Salmon (d 1985); *Career* philosopher; Grote prof of the philosophy of mind and logic London Univ 1946-59, Wykeham prof of logic Oxford Univ 1959-78; sponsor STOPP (Soc of Teachers Opposed to Physical Punishment) 1982- (memb from the start); Chevalier de la Légion d'Honneur 1977; FBA; kt 1970; *Clubs* Athenaeum, Beefsteak, Garrick; *Style*— Professor Sir Alfred Ayer; 51 York St, London W1 (☎ 01 402 0235)

AYKROYD, Sir Cecil William; 2 Bt (UK 1929), of Birstwith Hall, Harrogate, Co York; s of Sir Frederic Alfred Aykroyd, 1 Bt (d 1949), and Lily May (d 1964), da of Sir James Roberts, 1 Bt (d 1935); *b* 23 April 1905; *Educ* Charterhouse, Jesus Coll Cambridge (BA); *Heir* nephew, James Alexander Frederic Aykroyd, *qv*; *Career* dir National Provincial Bank 1958-69; *Style*— Sir Cecil Aykroyd, Bt; Birstwith Hall, nr Harrogate, N Yorks (☎ 0423 770250)

AYKROYD, David Peter; s of Lt-Col George Hammond Aykroyd (d 1972), of The Priory, Nun Monkton, York, and Margaret Roberts Aykroyd (d 1981); *b* 06 Jun 1937; *Educ* Eton; *m* 30 Oct 1958, (Lucia) Huldine, da of Richard Piggott Beamish, of Castle Lyons, Co Cork, Ireland; 1 s (Nicholas William b 1962), 3 da (Amanda Huldine b 1960, Emily Sorrell b 1970, Matilda Rose b 1978); *Career* Nat Serv 2 Lt Coldstream Gds; *Recreations* racing, shooting; *Style*— David Aykroyd, Esq; The Priory, Nun Monkton, York YO5 8ES (☎ 0423 330 334, office 0423 330 131, fax 0423 331 124, car tel 0836 612 199, telex 57445 YEW G); 6 William Mews, London SW1

AYKROYD, James Alexander Frederic; s of Bertram Aykroyd (d 1983), and his 1 w Margot, *née* Brown; nephew and hp of Sir Cecil William Aykroyd, 2 Bt; *b* 6 Sept 1943; *Educ* Eton, Aix en Provence Univ, Madrid Univ; *m* 1973, Jennifer, da of late Frederick William Marshall, MB, BS, DA (Eng), of 3 Penylan Ave, Porthcawl, Glam; 2 da (Gemma Jane b 1976, Victoria Louise b 1977); *Style*— James Aykroyd, Esq; 5 Highbury Terrace, London N5 1UP

AYKROYD, Michael David; s of late George Hammond Aykroyd, TD, s of Sir William Henry Aykroyd, 1 Bt; hp of cous, Sir William Aykroyd, 3 Bt, MC; *b* 14 June 1928; *m* 1952, Oenone Gillian Diana, da of Donald George Cowling, MBE, of Leeds; 1 s, 3 da; *Style*— Michael Aykroyd, Esq; The Homestead, Killinghall, Harrogate, Yorks

AYKROYD, Lady; Sylvia; *née* Walker; da of late Francis Walker, of Huddersfield; *m* 1, Lt-Col Foster Newton Thorne; m 2, 1919, Sir Alfred Hammond Aykroyd, 2 Bt (d 1965); 1 s (and 1 da decd); *Style*— Lady Aykroyd; Priests Ho, Stockeld Park, Wetherby, Yorks

AYKROYD, Sir William Miles; 3 Bt (UK 1920), of Lightcliffe, W Riding, Co of York, MC (1944); s of Sir Alfred Hammond Aykroyd, 2 Bt (d 1965); *b* 24 August 1923; *Career* Lt 5 Roy Inniskilling Dragoon Gds 1943-47; dir Hardy Amies 1950-69; *Style*— Sir William Aykroyd, Bt, MC; Buckland Newton Place, Dorchester, Dorset (☎ Buckland Newton 259)

AYLEN, Rear Adm Ian Gerald; CB (1962), OBE (1946), DSC (1942); s of Paymaster Cmdr Alfred Ernest Aylen, RN (d 1946), of Northam, N Devon, and S C M Aylen; *b* 12 Oct 1910; *Educ* Blundells Tiverton, RNEC Keyham, RNC Greenwich; *m* 1937, Alice Brough, da of Brough Maltby (d 1952), of Westward House, N Devon; 1 s, 2 da; *Career* HMS Galatea 1939-41, HMS Kelvin 1942-43, 30 Assault Unit 1944-45, CO RN Engrg Coll 1958-60, Rear Adm 1960, Adm Supt HM Dockyard Rosyth 1960-63, ret; dep sec Inst of Mech Engrs 1963-65, asst sec Cncl of Engrg Insts 1965-70, ret 1971; *Style*— Rear Adm Ian Aylen, CB, OBE, DSC; Tracey Mill Barn, Honiton, Devon EX14 8SL

AYLESFORD, 11 Earl of (GB 1714); Charles Ian Finch-Knightley; JP (Warwicks 1948); also Baron Guernsey (GB 1702); s of 10 Earl of Aylesford (d 1958); *b* 2 Nov 1918; *Educ* Oundle; *m* 1946, Margaret Rosemary, da of Maj Austin Tyer, MVO, TD; 1 s, 2 da; *Heir* s, Lord Guernsey; *Career* serv WWII Capt Black Watch; Vice-Lt Warwicks 1964-74, Lord-Lt W Midlands 1974-; regnl dir Lloyds Bank Birmingham & W Midlands Board; memb Water Space Amenity Commission 1973-; patron Warwicks Boy Scouts Assoc 1974-; pres: Warwicks CC 1980-, TAVRA 1982; KStJ 1974; *Recreations* shooting, fishing, archery, nature conservation, preservation of wildlife; *Clubs* Fly Fishers; *Style*— The Rt the Hon Earl of Aylesford, JP; Packington Old Hall, Coventry, W Midlands CV7 7HG (☎ 0676 232 273, office 22585)

AYLESFORD, Pamela, Countess of; Pamela Elizabeth; er da of Col Hon Charles Coventry, CB, JP, DL (d 1929, 2 s of 9 Earl of Coventry by Lady Blanche Craven, da of 2 Earl of Craven), and Lily, *née* Whitehouse; *b* 16 Oct 1901; *m* 1, 24 April 1928 (m dis 1940), as his 1 w, Lt Cdr James George Greville Dugdale, RN (ret) (d 1969), of Wroxall Abbey, Warwickshire; 1 da (Judy b 1929, m 1964, Sir Guy Millard, *qv*); m 2, 18 April 1940, 9 Earl of Aylesford (ka 28 May 1940); *Style*— The Rt Hon Pamela, Countess of Aylesford; 105 Dorset House, Gloucester Place, London NW1 (☎ 01 935 6490)

AYLESTONE, Baron (Life Peer UK 1967); Herbert William Bowden; CH (1975), CBE (1953), PC (1962); s of Herbert Henwood Bowden, of Cardiff, by Henrietta, *née* Gould; *b* 20 Jan 1905; *m* 1928, Louisa Grace, da of William Brown, of Cardiff; 1 da; *Career* served 1940-45 with RAF; MP (Lab) Leicester S 1945-50, MP (Lab) SW Div of Leics 1950-67, chief oppn whip 1955-64, lord pres of the cncl ldr of the House of Commons 1964-66, sec of state for Cwlth Affairs 1966-67; chm IBA 1967-75; SDP ldr in House of Lords 1981-82; dep speaker Ho of Lords 1983-; 1975-Gold Medal of Royal Television Soc; *Style*— The Rt Hon The Lord Aylestone CH, CBE, PC; Ho of Lords, London SW1

AYLING, Air Vice-Marshal Richard Cecil; CB (1965), CBE (1961, OBE 1948); s of Albert Cecil Ayling, LDS (d 1939), of Norwood, London; *b* 7 June 1916; *Educ* Dulwich; *m* 1, 1941, Patricia Doreen (d 1966), da of Karl Wright, of Norbury, Surrey; 1 s, 1 da; m 2, 1971, Virginia, 2 da of Col Frank Davis, of Northwood, Middx; 2 da; *Career* served RNZAF 1940-43, Bomber Cmd RAF 1943-45, Staff Coll 1945, Air Miny (dep dir Policy Air Staff) 1951-54, Station Cdr, Bomber Cmd, 1954-58, ACDS MOD 1958-59, dir of Organisation Air Miny 1960-61, SASO Flying Training Cmd 1962-65, MOD 1965-66, AOA RAF Air Support Cmd 1966-69, ret; adjudicator Immigration Appeals 1970-; *Recreations* skiing, gardening, sailing; *Clubs* Royal Lymington Yacht; *Style*— Air Vice-Marshal Richard Ayling, CB, CBE; Buckler's Spring, Buckler's Hard, Beaulieu, Brockenhurst, Hants SO42 7XA (☎ 059 063 204)

AYLMER, Althea, Baroness; Althea; da of late Lt-Col John Talbot, Indian Army; *m* 1939, 12 Baron Aylmer (d 1982); 1 da; *Style*— The Rt Hon Althea, Lady Aylmer; 601-1159 Beach Drive, Victoria, BC, Canada

AYLMER, Dr Gerald Edward; s of late Capt E A Aylmer, RN, and Mrs G P Aylmer, *née* Evans; *b* 30 April 1926; *Educ* Winchester, Balliol Coll Oxford (MA, DPhil); *m* 1955, Ursula Nixon; 1 s, 1 da; *Career* historian; prof of history and head of dept York Univ 1963-78, master St Peter's Coll Oxford 1978-; pres Royal Historical Soc 1984-88 (hon vice pres 1988-); memb: Royal Commission on Historical Manuscripts, ed bd History of Parliament Tst; FBA; *Style*— Dr Gerald Aylmer; Canal Ho, St Peter's College, Oxford (☎ 0865 278 862/278 856/240 554)

AYLMER, Hon Gioia Francesca; only da of 13 Baron Aylmer; *b* 14 Sept 1953; *Style*— The Hon Gioia Aylmer; 28 Napier Court, Ranelagh Gardens, London SW6 3UU (☎ 01 736 2622)

AYLMER, Helen, Baroness; Helen Cooper; da of late Thomas Hogg, of Toronto; *m* 1960, as his 2 w, 11 Baron (d 1977); *Style*— The Rt Hon Helen, Lady Aylmer

AYLMER, Hon (Anthony) Julian; only s and h of 13 Baron Aylmer; *b* 10 Dec 1951; *Educ* Westminster, Trinity Hall Cambridge; *Career* slr 1976-; *Style*— The Hon Julian Aylmer; c/o 42 Brampton Grove, London NW4

AYLMER, 13 Baron (I 1718); Sir Michael Anthony Aylmer; 16 Bt (I 1662); s of Christopher Aylmer (d 1955), and his 1 w, Marjorie Marianne Ellison, *née* Barber; suc 2 cous, 12 Baron Aylmer, 1982; *b* 27 Mar 1923; *Educ* privately, Trinity Hall Cambridge (MA, LLM); *m* 1950, Contessa Maddalena Sofia Maria Gabriella Cecilia Stefania Francesca, da of Count Arbeno Maria Attems di Santa Croce (d 1968), of Aiello del Friuli, and Sofie, eldest da of Prince Maximilian Karl Friedrich zu Löwenstein-Wertheim-Freudenberg; 1 s, 1 da; *Heir* s, Hon Julian Aylmer; *Career* slr 1948; in legal dept of Equity & Law Life Assur Soc 1951-1983; *Recreations* reading, music; *Style*— The Rt Hon The Lord Aylmer; 42 Brampton Grove, London NW4 4AQ (☎ 01 202 8300)

AYLMER, Sir Richard John; 16 Bt (I 1622), of Donadea, Co Kildare; s and h of Sir Fenton Aylmer, 15 Bt (d 1987); *b* 23 April 1937; *m* 1962, Lise, da of Paul Demers, of Montreal, Canada; 1 s (Fenton Paul), 1 da (Geneviève b 16 March 1963); *Heir* s, Fenton Paul Aylmer b 31 Oct 1965; *Style*— Sir Richard Aylmer, Bt; 3573 Lorne Ave, Montreal, Quebec H2X 2A4, Canada

AYLOTT, David Howard Frederick; s of David Henry Aylott (d 1969), and Anita Maria Celeste, *née* Marchetti (d 1985); *b* 28 May 1914; *Educ* Private; *m* 17 April 1948, Zena Margarita Aylott; 1 s (Stuart b 15 Sept 1944), 1 da (Susan b 17 Oct 1949); *Career* RAF 1940-46 (fndr member of a light entertainment unit producing shows for the service personnel); various trainee postions in film business 1930-35, make up artist various film studios incl Korda 1935-40, joined MGM Studios Elstree 1946, co fndr Eylure Ltd (with Brother Eric) 1947, freelance make up artist INT Films 1949-60, left film indust to run Eylure Ltd full-time in 1960 (developed internationally successful cosmetic concept which won Quenns Award for Indust in first year), chm Eylure Ltd 1960-; FInstD 1964, FInst MSM 1965; *Recreations* flying light aircraft, motor cruisers; *Clubs* Oriental; *Style*— David Aylott, Esq; Old Hundred Barn, Tormarton, Avon GL9 1JA (☎ 045421211); Eylure Ltd, Cwmbran, Gwent (☎ 0633838611, fax 0633838925, telex 498424)

AYLOTT, Eric Victor; s of David Aylott (d 1969), of 89 Harmer Green Lane, Welwyn, Herts, and Anita, *née* Marchetti (d 1968); *b* 20 Oct 1917; *Educ* private ; *m* 30 May 1953, Kathleen, da of Edgar Obbott (d 1953), of Palmers Green; 2 da (Elizabeth, Geraldine); *Career* RAF 1940-1960 (WWII serv: M East and Greece 1940-44; film indust make-up artist 1937-59, vice-chm Eylure Ltd 1959-; TV appearances with b David UK, NZ and Australia incl: Film Stars of Yesterday, The Movie Greats, M Inst D 1960, MInstM; *Books* The Eyelure Way of Make-Up (jt author, 1980); *Recreations* football, horse riding, flying (PPL), motor yachting; *Clubs* Oriental, St Pierre Country; *Style*— Eric Aylott, Esq; The Homestead, Raffin Green, Datchworth, Knebworth, Herts (☎ 0438 812297); Eyelure Ltd, Grange Est, Cwmbran, Gwent (☎ 0633 838 611)

AYLWIN, Capt RN (Charles) Kenneth Seymour; s of Claude Beresford Graham Aylwin (d 1962), and Evelyn, *née* Brocklebank (d 1971); *b* 5 Nov 1911; *Educ* RNC: Dartmouth, Greenwich; *m* 15 July 1939, Islay Campbell, da of Maj Ernest Charles

Holland (d 1947); 3 s (David b 1940, Nicholas b 1944, Andrew b 1947); *Career* Midshipman HMS Revenge Med 1929, HMS Achates (escort duties for TRH Prince of Wales and Prince George in Argentina, Uruguay and Brazil) 1931, cmmnd Sub Lt HMS Hood Home Fleet 1933-34, Lt HMS Colombo East Indies 1934-35, HMS Walpole Gibraltar 1936, HMS Iron Duke Portsmouth 1936-37, qualified gunnery specialist 1938, HMS Royal Sovereign Home and Med 1939, flotilla staff offr HMS Codrington Dover 1939-40; Lt Cdr Euryalus 1940-43: 15 Cruiser Sqdn Med, Malta Convoys, Battle of Sirte, N Africa Ops, Sicily Invasion; exec offr Radar Trg Sch HMS Valkrie 1943-44, staff offr to Flag Offr Western Germany 1944-45, Trg offr HMS Home 1946-47, Cdr intelligence div Admty 1948-49, RAF Staff Coll Bracknell 1949, Admty Air and Tactical Divs 1950-51, exec offr C-in-c Med HMS Liverpool 1952, CO HMS Loch Tralaig 1952, CO HMS Tenacious Coronation Review 1952-53, exec offr RN Air Station Brawdy 1954-55, Capt 1955, naval equipment div Admty 1956, ret 1958; BAT Co Ltd: asst to personnel dir 1958, personnel advsr to BAT cos Middle East and Med area 1960, mgmnt devpt and planning advsr 1968, ret 1973; memb: Wimbledon CAB 1974, branch sec Royal Br Legion Chulmleigh 1975-76, ward ctee Wimbledon Cons Pty 1978-81 (Cons cncllr Wimbledon Borough Cncl 1960-63), SE area ctee George Cross Island Assoc (Malta) 1988; memb Assoc of Hon Stewards of Wimbledon Lawn Tennis Championships 1979-87; RN Club 1965-85; *Recreations* golf, bridge, gardening; *Clubs* Royal Wimbledon Golf, RN, Wimbledon Bridge, Wimbledon Probus; *Style*— Capt Kenneth Aylwin, RN; 12 Barham Rd, Wimbledon, London SW20 OET (☎ 01 946 6805)

AYLWIN, Nicholas Claude; s of Capt Charles Kenneth Seymour Aylwin, RN, and Islay Campbell, *née* Holland; *b* 24 June 1944; *Educ* Haileybury and Imperial Serv Coll; *m* 27 July 1968, Nicola, da of Sir Peter Coleman Boon, KBE; 1 s (Andrew b 1970), 1 da (Kate b 1971); *Career* Allen Charlesworth & Co 1963-67, Arthur Young & Co 1967-68, Hoover Ltd 1968-70, Hill Samuel & Co Ltd 1970-76 and 1978-86, Chemical Bank (Paris) 1977-78, dir Hill Samuel 1981-86, md Paine Webber Inc 1986-; memb Worshipful Co of Armourers & Braziers; FCA; *Clubs* Royal Wimbledon Golf; *Style*— Nicholas Aylwin, Esq; Paine Webber International (UK) Ltd, 1 Finsbury Avenue, London EC2M 2PA (☎ 01 377 0055)

AYOUB, John Edward Moussa; s of Moussa Ayoub (d 1956; portrait painter) and Maria Katherine, *née* André (d 1926), mother's family included Maj John André, hanged for his country in 1778, by George Washington; *b* 7 Sept 1908; *Educ* St Paul's, Lincoln Coll Oxford (BA, BM, BCh), St Thomas's Hosp; *m* 1939, Madeleine Marion Coniston, da of William H Martin (d 1943), of Tiverton Devon; 1 s (Richard), 1 da (Ann); *Career* served RNVR 1938-46, Surg Lt Cdr, ophthalmic specialist Alexandria and Plymouth, Surgeon Moorfield Eye Hosp 1950-73, conslt Ophthalmic surgeon: The London 1947-73, Royal Masonic Hosp 1968-73; chm Br Ctee Alderney RNLI (1984-86); FRCS (Eng); Liveryman Soc Apothecaries; Freeman City of London; *Recreations* bell ringing, gardening; *Clubs* Leander, Roy Cruising; *Style*— John Ayoub, Esq; 2 Clarendon Rd, Boston Spa, W Yorks LS23 6NG (☎ 0937 842996)

AYRE, Lady Margaret Isabel; *née* Lane; da of Charles Lane, CSI (gs of Lady Frances Erskine, sis of 27 Earl of Mar) and sis of 30 Earl of Mar; raised to rank of Earl's da 1967; *b* 28 Mar 1921; *m* 1943, John Bulley Bray Ayre, TD, late Maj RA; 1 s (Michael), 1 da (Rosemary); *Style*— Lady Margaret Ayre; 1 Penhurst Park, Pointe Claire, PQ H9S 3Y6, Canada

AYRES, Andrew Charles; s of Harry Ayres, of Chinthurst Park, Shalford, Surrey, and Dorothy *née* Boxall; *b* 13 Dec 1944; *Educ* Reed's Sch Cobham; *m* 28 Sept 1968, Philippa Jill, da of Dr Martin Bristow; 3 s (Christian Andrew Martin b 31 March 1973, Alexander Charles Harry b 25 Sept 1977, Douglas William Robert b 25 Sept 1977); *Career* articled clerk: Candler Stannard & Co 1962-67, Blake Cassels and Graydon Toronto Canada 1967-68; slr Norton Rose Botterell & Roche 1968-71, ptnr Norton Rose Slrs 1971-; hon legal advsr Surrey Archaeological Soc, hon sec Mr Goschen's hound's point to point; Freeman City of London, Liveryman Worshipful Co of Slrs; memb: Law Soc, Baltic Exchange; *Recreations* hunting, steeplechasing, golf, vintage cars; *Clubs* City Univ, W Surrey Golf; *Style*— Andrew Ayres, Esq; Oakhill, Enton Green, Godalming, Surrey; Kempson House, Camomile St, London EC3 (☎ 01 283 2434, fax 01 588 1181, telex 883652)

AYRES, Gillian; OBE (1986); da of Stephen Ayres (d 1969), of Barnes, London, and Florence Olive Brown (d 1968); *b* 3 Feb 1930; *Educ* St Paul's Girls' Sch, Camberwell Sch of Art; *m* (m dis); 2 s (James, Sam); *Career* artist; taught painting: Corham 1959-65, St Martin's 1966-78; head BA painting dept Winchester Sch of Art 1978-81; memb fine art panel Arts Cncl 1981-85; one-woman exhibitions 1956-, Knoedler Gallery London 1966-; retrospective Serpentine Gallery 1983; exhibited Knoedler Gallery NY 1985; works included in public collections: Tate Gallery, Museum of Modern Art NY; ARA; *Style*— Miss Gillian Ayres; Old Rectory, Llaniestyn, Pwllheli, N Wales (☎ (075 883) 262)

AYRES, Rosalind Mary (Mrs Martin Jarvis); da of Sam Johnson (d1986), of Westbury, Wilts, and Daisy, *née* Hydon (d 1987); *b* 7 Dec 1946; *Educ* George Dixon GS for Girls Birmingham, Loughborough Coll of Educn (Dip Educn); *m* 23 Nov 1974, Martin John Jarvis, s of Denys Jarvis, of Sanderstead, Surrey; *Career* actor; TV: The Mill, The House of Bernarda Alba, Juliet Bravo, The Bounder, Hindle Wakes; Radio: A Room With A View, The Circle, Alphabetical Order; Theatre: Hamlet, The Three Sisters, Uncle Vanya, The Perfect Party Greenwich Theatre, Dracula Shaftesbury Theatre, I Claudius Queens's Theatre; Film: That'll be the Day, Stardust, The Slipper and the Rose; memb: RSC, Stars Organisation for Spastics; *Recreations* interior design, illustration; *Style*— Ms Rosalind Ayres; c/o Michael Whitehall Ltd, 125 GLoucester Rd, London SW7 (☎ 01 244 8466)

AYTON, Sylvia; da of Donald Ayton, of 49 Brockham Drive, Ilford, Essex, and Florence Mabel, *née* Sabine; *b* 27 Nov 1937; *Educ* Walthamstow Sch of Art (NDD), RCA Fashion Sch (Des RCA); *Career* freelance designer 1959-64; work incl: BEA Air Hostess Uniform autumn ranges for NY USA, collaboration with Doris Langley Moore at Costume Museum Bath, ptnr with Zandra Rhodes (opened Fulham Rd boutique backed by Vanessa Redgrave 1964), outerwear designer Wallis Fashion Gp 1969; lectr fashion design: Kingston Poly, Ravenstone Coll, Middlesex Poly, Newcastle Poly 1961-; external assessor Fashion and Textile course (BA Hons) 1976-, memb jury RSA Bursary Comp 1982; memb CNAA 1979, FRSA 1987; *Style*— Ms Sylvia Ayton; 28 Eburne Road, London N7 6AU (☎ 01 263 6806); Wallis Fashion Gp Ltd, Garrick Int Centre Garrick Road, Hendon, London NW9 6AQ (☎ 01 202 8252, telex 924895)

AZIZ, Khalid; s of Ahmad Aziz (d 1978), of London, and Sheila Frances, *née* Light; *b* 9 August 1953; *Educ* Westminster City Sch, Aitcheson Coll Lahore; *m* 27 March 1974, Barbara Elizabeth, da of Harry Etchells, of Sherburn-in-Elmet, Yorks; 2 da (Nadira b 1977, Fleur b 1981); *Career* broadcaster, journalist and dir; prodr presenter: BBC Radio and TV 1970-81, TV South 1981-; presenter On Course Channel 4 1988; TV Journalist of the Year 1987-88; author: 9 books principally on indian cooking; chm Royal Jubilee and Prince's Tst (Hants), S Counties Bd Prince Youth Business Tst; vice pres Pestalozzi Int Children's Village; cncl memb VSO; *Books* So you think your Business needs a Computer (1986); *Recreations* aviation, fishing, shooting, computers; *Style*— Khalid Aziz, Esq; West Stratton, Winchester, Hampshire (☎ 0962 89 673)

AZIZ, Suhail Ibne; s of Azizur Rahnan (d 1971), of Bangladesh, and Lutfunnessa Khatoon; *b* 3 Oct 1937; *Educ* RNC Dartmouth, London Univ (MSc); *m* 1960, Elizabeth Ann, da of Alfred Pyne, of Dartmouth; 2 da (Lisa, Rebecca); *Career* served Pakistan Navy 1954-61; personnel mangr Lever Bros Pakistan Ltd 1963-66, served as RAF offr in Br CS 1966-70, indust rels offr London 1970-73, labour rels exec Ford Motor Co UK 1973-74, personnel offr Pedigree Pet Foods 1974-78, dir of gen servs divs Cmmn for Racial Equality 1978-81, PA Int Mgmnt Conslts 1981-83; head econ and employment divn and dep dir London Borough of Lewisham 1982-88, mgmt conslt Fullemploy Consultancy 1988-, exec memb Nottingham Community Relations Cncl 1975-78; memb: Raee Rels Bd 1971-74, Gulbenkian Fndn Advsy Ctee 1976-82, Home Secretary's Standing Advsy Cncl 1977-78, Dept of Employment Min's employment advys Gp 1977-78, advsy ctee BBC 1977-82, employers panel Industl Tribunals 1978-, Bd of Tstees Brixton Neighbourhood Community Assoc 1979-82; chm Third World Specialist Gp Inst of Mgmnt Conslts 1984-, fndr chm E London Bangladeshi Enterprise Agency 1985, advsr Minority Business Devpt Unit City of London Poly 1986; CRE Bursary to USA to study minority econ devpt initiatives 1986, led preparation of Bangladeshi community response to House of Commons Select Ctee report "Bangladeshi in Britain and assisted organisations in the preparation of implementation plans" 1986-, memb QMC London res advsy ctee 1988-; FBIM, MIMC; *Recreations* travel, reading political economy; *Clubs* Sudan (Khartoum), RAF; *Style*— Suhail Aziz, Esq; 126 St Julian's Farm Rd, West Norwood, London SE27 0RR

B

BAART, Leonard William; s of Lein Wilhelmus Baart (d 1973), of S Africa, and Florence Emily, *née* Gilchrist (d 1967); *b* 5 April 1927; *Educ* Kimberley Boys HS, Witwatersrand Univ (BArch); *m* 21 March 1953, Diana Ingrid, da of Richard John Southwell Crowe (d 1980), of Avon; 1 s (John b 1960), 3 da (Veronica b 1954, Fiona b 1956, Angela b 1958); *Career* chartered architect in private practice, cmmnd architect to English Heritage 1986-89, consit architect to English Heritage for Re-Survey of Listed Buildings 1984-87; FRIA, FCIArb, Fellow Worshipful Co of Arbitrators (1985), Freeman City of London (1984); *Recreations* painting (water-colour), golf, squash, tennis, choir singing; *Clubs* Salop (Shrewsbury), Royal Cwlth London, Bulawayo Zimbabwe; *Style—* Leonard W Baart, Esq; Cobden House, Hanwood, nr Shrewsbury (☎ (0743) 860322); Bowdler's House, Town Walls, Shrewsbury (☎ (0743) 61261/2)

BABBER, (Rajindar) Paul; s of Arjan Das (d 1933), and Harbhajan Arora; *b* 13 Jan 1930,Amritsar, India; *Educ* (MA, MA, LLB); *m* 4 Nov 1956, Kamini, da of Gurdit Singh (d 1983); 1 s (Hemant b 1958), 3 da (Jyotsna b 1961, Monica b 1972, Renuka b (twin) 1972); *Career* practising as Paul Babbar & Co CAs; vice-chm Hillingdon Community Relations Cncl 1978-81; tres Ruislip Residents Assoc 1979-82; exec memb: Hillingdon Community Relations Cncl 1976-78 and 1982-, Ealing Community Relations Cncl 1984-86; fndr memb (sometime sec now tres) Hillingdon-Amritsar Town Twinning Assoc 1981-; exec memb Hillingdon Town Twinning Assoc 1978-83; tres Southall Chamber of Commerce 1983-85 (exec memb 1985-); FICA; *Recreations* travelling, reading, music, community work; *Clubs* Ruislip-Northwood Rotary; *Style—* Rajindar Babbar, Esq; The Manor House, The Green, Southall, Middlesex UB2 4BJ (☎ 01 843 1180)

BABER, Hon Mr Justice; Hon Ernest George; CBE (1987); s of late Walter Avertte Baber, and Kate Marion, *née* Pratt; *b* 18 July 1924; *Educ* Brentwood, Emmanuel Coll Cambridge; *m* 1960, Dr Flora Marion, da of late Dr Raymond Bisset Smith; 1 s, 2 da; *Career* serv WWII RN; barr Lincoln's Inn 1951, district judge Hong Kong 1967-73, judge of Supreme Court Hong Kong 1973-; *Style—* The Hon Mr Justice Baber, CBE; Supreme Court, Hong Kong

BABINGTON, His Honour Judge; Anthony Patrick; s of Oscar John Gilmore Babington (d 1930), of Monkstown, Co Cork; *b* 4 April 1920; *Educ* Reading Sch; *Career* serv WWII Maj; barr 1948, met stipendiary magistrate 1964-72, circuit judge 1972-87; Croix de Guerre with Gold Star France 1944; *Books* No Memorial (1954), The Power To Silence (1968), A House In Bow Street (1969), The English Bastille (1971), The Rule of Law In Britain (1978), For The Sake of Example (1983); *Clubs* Garrick, Special Forces; *Style—* His Hon Judge Babington; 3 Gledhow Gdns, Kensington, London SW5 0BL (☎ 01 373 4014); Thydon Cottage, Chilham, nr Canterbury, Kent CT4 8BX (☎ 0227 730 300)

BABOULÈNE (né PHILIE), Bernard Léon; s of Fernand Louis Philie (né Baboulène) (d 1975), and Matilda Philie, *née* Evans (d 1964); noted French painting family; identity changed to Philie 1914, changed back to Baboulene 1957; *b* 1 Sept 1922, ; *Educ* Ardingly Coll Sussex; Magdalen Coll Oxford (BA, MA); *m* 1, 16 June 1952, Doreen Ethel, da of Martin Rabey, of La Mielle du Parcq, Jersey, Channel Is (d 1974); 3 da (Margaret Elizabeth b 1953, Barbara Jean b 1955, Kathryn Hazel b 1963), 1 s (David Louis b 1960); m 2, 5 Oct 1977, Audrey Anne Frances, da of Albert George Conrad Tapster, of London (d 1980); Coronation Medals 1937 and 1953; *Career* RAF, 217 Squad (Far East), Flt Lt (air navigator) 1941-46; Admty Med Dr General's Dept 1939-41; mgmnt appt in aircraft indust and computers ICT (now ICL) 1950-64; mgmnt conslt 1964-, currently exec search consultant; professional tenor taking broadcast recordings and various solo engagements; currently takes exclusive musical tours of Westminster Abbey 10 times a year; FID, MIMC 1972, FIMC 1985; *Recreations* music (singing); *Clubs* Royal Over Seas League, IOD; *Style—* Bernard L Baboulene, Esq; BLB Consultants Ltd, 10 Richmond Ave, London SW20 8LA (☎ 01 542 8878)

BACCHUS, James; s of Cecil Bacchus, of Billericay; *b* 11 July 1941; *Educ* St Clement Danes London; *m* 1964, Marion, da of Thomas Victor Stratton (d 1970); 3 children; *Career* accountant, fin dir Jessups Hldgs and subsids 1973-; *Recreations* golf; *Clubs* Anglo-American Sporting; *Style—* James Bacchus Esq; 147 Western Rd, Billericay, Essex

BACH, John Theodore; s of late Dr Francis Bach, and Matine, *née* Thompson; *b* 18 Feb 1936; *Educ* Rugby, New Coll Oxford (MA); *m* 15 April 1967, Hilary Rose, da of late Gp Capt T E H Birley, OBE; 1 s (Alexander b 1969), 2 da (Emily b 1968, Susannah b 1973); *Career* slr; ptnr Stephenson Harwood 1966-; govr Moorfields Eye Hosp; *Clubs* City Univ; *Style—* John Bach, Esq; 1 St Paul's Churchyard, London EC4M 8SH (☎ 01 329 4422, fax 01 606 0822)

BACHE, Andrew Philip Foley; s of (Robert) Philip Sydney Bache, OBE (d 1984), of Himbleton, Worcs, and Jessie, *née* Pearman-Smith; *b* 29 Dec 1939; *Educ* Shrewsbury, Emmanuel Coll Cambridge (MA); *m* 20 Jul 1963, Shân, da of Rev L V Headley, OBE, of E Tisted, Hants; 2 s (Richard b 1964, Alexander b 1966), 1 da (Samantha b 1974); *Career* Dip Serv; FCO 1963-64, 1968-71, 1974-78; third sec Nicosia, second sec Sofia, first sec Lagos, first sec Vienna (commercial); cnsllr: Tokyo 1981-85, Ankara 1985-87; head Personnel Servs Dept FCO 1988; *Recreations* sport, fine arts, travel, ornithology; *Clubs* Jesters, MCC, RCS; *Style—* Andrew Bache, Esq

BACK, Frederick Charles Douglas; s of Herbert Back (d 1931); *b* 12 Feb 1919; *Educ* Queen's Coll Oxford; *m* 1953, Bernadette, da of Michael Anthony (d 1965); 2 s; *Career* dir Glaxo Hldgs and various subsids including Glaxo Inc (USA) and Nippon Glaxo Japan (jt pres); *Recreations* music, reading; *Style—* Frederick Back Esq; Orrong, Oval Way, Gerrards Cross, Bucks

BACK, Kenneth John Campbell; s of J L Back; *b* 13 August 1925; *Educ* Sydney HS, Sydney Univ; *m* 1950, Patricia, da of R O Cummings; 2 da; *Career* vice-chllr James Cook Univ of N Qld 1970-; *Style—* Kenneth Back Esq; 15 Yarrawonga Dve, Townsville, Qld 4810, Australia

BACK, Patrick; QC (1970); s of late Ivor Back, and Barbara, *née* Nash; *b* 23 August 1917; *Educ* Marlborough, Trinity Hall Cambridge; *Career* barr 1940, dep chm Devon QS 1968, Western circuit 1984-; *Style—* Patrick Back, Esq, QC; Flat 3, Marquess House, 74 Marquess Rd, London N1 (☎ 01 226 0991)

BACKHOUSE, David John; s of Joseph Helme Backhouse, of Devizes, Wilts, and Jessie, *née* Chivers; *b* 5 May 1941; *Educ* Lord Weymouth Sch Warminster, W of England Coll of Art (NDD), Univ of Bristol (ATD); *m* 19 July 1975, Sarah Patricia, da of Philip Gerald Barber, CBE (d 1988); 1 s (Theodore b 1980), 2 da (Katharine b 1977, Rosalind b 1984); *Career* sculptor in bronze; work incl: The Three Graces for BSC Warwicks 1973 (first sculpture cast in stainless steel in UK), Man with Hawk for Morgan Crucible Co Ltd Swansea 1974, Caring for Mercantile & Gen Reinsurance Co Ltd Cheltenham 1978, Aspiration for Haslemere Estates London 1983, Cloaked Horseman for Haslemere Estates Bristol 1984, The Stream of Life for Telford Devpt Corpn 1985, Shepherd With Ewe and Lamb for Southern & City Property Gp Abergavenny 1987, Dolphin Family for Tesco plc Londons Docklands 1988, Flying Figurehead for J Sainsbury plc Swansea 1989; portrait heads incl: Dame Alicia Marcova, Sir Colin Davis, late Prince Charles of Luxembourg; one man exhibitons incl: London 1979, 1981, 1982, 1983, 1986, 1989, Luxembourg 1980, NY and Washington 1982, Dublin 1985; ARBS, RWA; *Recreations* gardening, walking, cycling; *Style—* David Backhouse, Esq; Old Post Office, Lullington, Frome, Somerset BA11 2PW (☎ 0373 830319); La Chapelle Pommier, 24340 Mareuil, Dordogne, France; Studio, Old Baptist Chapel, Lower Westwood, Bradford on Avon, Wilts (☎ 02216 6606)

BACKHOUSE, David Miles; s of Jonathan Backhouse, *qv*, and Alice Joan (d 1984), *née* Woodroffe; *b* 30 Jan 1939; *Educ* Eton; *m* 1969, Sophia Ann, da of Col Clarence Henry Southgate Townsend (d 1953); 2 children; *Career* banker; chm: Authy Investmts plc, TSB Tst Co Ltd; dir: TSB GP plc, Witan Investmt Co plc; govr Royal Agric Coll Cirencester; *Clubs* Boodles; *Style—* David Backhouse, Esq; South Farm, Fairford, Glos GL7 3PN (☎ 0285 712225)

BACKHOUSE, Oliver Richard; s of late Maj Sir John Backhouse, 3 Bt, MC; hp of bro, Sir Jonathan Backhouse, 4 Bt; *b* 18 July 1941; *Educ* Ampleforth, RMA Sandhurst; *m* 1970, Gillian Irene, da of L W Lincoln, of Northwood, Middx; 1 adopted s, 1 adopted da; *Career* memb The Stock Exchange; FCA; *Style—* Oliver Backhouse Esq; 50 Moor Lane, Rickmansworth, Herts WD3 1LG

BACKHOUSE, William; s of Jonathan Backhouse, of Essex, and Alice Joan, *née* Woodroffe (d 1984); *b* 29 May 1942; *Educ* Eton; *m* 1971, Deborah Jane, da of Hon David Edward Hely-Hutchinson (d 1984), of Wilts; 1 s (Timothy b 1981), 2 da (Harriet b 1975, Tessa b 1977); *Career* chm: Baring Houston & Saunders Ltd 1984, Baring Bros & Co Ltd 1984-85, Baring Investmt Mgmnt Hldgs Ltd 1985-; md Baring Fund Mangrs Ltd 1985-; FCA; *Recreations* travel, photography, shooting; *Style—* William Backhouse, Esq; Layer Marney Wick, Colchester, Essex CO5 9UT (☎ 0206 330 267, work ☎ 01 283 8833, telex 883622)

BACON, Baroness (Life Peeress UK 1970); Alice Martha Bacon; CBE (1953), PC (1966), DL (W Yorks 1974); da of Benjamin Bacon (d 1958), of Normanton, Yorkshire; *Educ* Normanton Girls' HS, Stockwell T C, London & London Univ (external); *Career* schoolmistress; MP (Lab): NE Leeds 1945-55, SE Leeds 1955-70; Min of State: Home Off 1964-67, DES 1967-70; memb Nat Exec Lab Pty 1941-70 (chm of Lab Pty 1950-51); hon degree Leeds Univ 1972; Min of State DES 1967-70, chm Labour Pty Conference 1951; *Style—* The Rt Hon Lady Bacon, CBE, PC, DL; 53 Snydale Rd, Normanton, W Yorks WF6 1NY (☎ 0924 893229)

BACON, Anthony Gordon (Tony); TD (1973); s of Frederick Gordon Bacon, of Ingatestone, Essex, and Dorothy Winifred, *née* Ramsay; *b* 12 May 1938; *Educ* Highgate Sch, Hertford Coll Oxford (BA, MA); *m* 18 Aug 1962, Margaret Jocelyn, da of George Ronald Percival Ross, of Blackmore End, Herts; 3 s (Richard b 1965, Michael b 1967, Timothy b 1970); *Career* Nat Serv RA UK and Hong Kong 1956-58; TA Essex Yeo RHA 1959-74: Signal Sqdn, 71 Signal Regt (V); banker Barclays Bank Gp 1961- (UK, Australia, Cote d'Ivoire, Hong Kong), currently corporate mangr; churchwarden Kimpton Parish Church; ACIB 1966, FCIS 1985; *Recreations* real tennis, golf, music, country pursuits; *Clubs* Australian, Naval and Military, Melbourne (Australia), Overseas Bankers; *Style—* Tony Bacon, Esq, TD; 11 Blackmore Way, Wheathampstead, Herts AL4 8LJ (☎ 0438 832 757); Barclays Bank plc, 33 Old Broad St, London EC (☎ 01 638 1234)

BACON, Francis; *b* 1909,Dublin; *Career* artist, represented in major museums throughout the world; *Style—* Francis Bacon, Esq; c/o Marlborough Fine Art, 6 Albemarle St, London W1X 4BY

BACON, Francis Thomas; OBE (1967); s of Thomas Walter Bacon (d 1950), of Ramsden Hall, Billericay, Essex, and Edith Mary, *née* Leslie-Melville (d 1950); descendant of Sir Nicholas Bacon, Lord Keeper of the Great Seal *temp* Elizabeth I, and f of Sir Francis Bacon who was also Lord Keeper; *b* 21 Dec 1904; *Educ* Eton, Trinity Coll Cambridge (MA); *m* 1934, Barbara Winifred, da of Godfrey Keppel Papillon (d 1942); 1 s (and 1 s decd), 1 da; *Career* with C A Parsons & Co Ltd Newcastle upon Tyne 1925-40, experimental work on fuel cells King's Coll London 1940-41, temp experiment offr HM Anti-Submarine Experimental Estab 1941-46, experimental work on hydrogen-oxygen fuel cells Cambridge Univ 1946-56; conslt on fuel cells: NRDC

1956-62, Energy Conversion Ltd 1962-71, Fuel Cells Ltd 1971-72, Johnson-Matthey 1984-; S G Brown Award and Medal (Royal Soc) 1965, Br Silver Medal (RAeS) 1969, Melchett Medal (Inst of Fuel) 1972, Churchill Gold Medal (Soc of Engrs) 1972, Bruno Breyer Mem Lecture and Medal (Royal Aust Chemical Inst) 1976; Hon DSc Newcastle upon Tyne 1980; FRS, FEng, CEng, MIMechE, Hon FSE; *Publications* chapter 5 in Fuel Cells (ed G J Young, 1960), chapter 4 in Fuel Cells (ed W Mitchell, 1963); many papers on fuel cells; *Recreations* walking in the hills, gardening; *Clubs* Athenaeum; *Style—* Francis Bacon, Esq, OBE; Trees, 34 High St, Little Shelford, Cambridge CB2 5ES (☎ 0223 843 116)

BACON, Maj Keith Ashley; TD (1962); s of Alan Wood Bacon (d 1980), and Margaret, *née* Sherwen; *b* 13 April 1928; *Educ* St Bees Cumbria, Solihull Warwicks; *m* 11 Feb 1954, Elizabeth Margaret, da of John Gibson Nicholson; 1 s (Nicholas b 28 Feb 1955), 3 da (Amanda (Mrs Peet) b 23 Aug 1957, Sarah b 7 May 1961, Joanna b 12 Nov 1965); *Career* admitted slr 1967, sr ptnr Paisleys; chm DHSs Appeal Tbnl; clerk to various charitable tsts; memb Law Soc 1967; *Style—* Maj Keith Bacon, TD; Dearham Mill, Maryport, Cumbria (☎ 0900 812 040); El Pinar 9, Moraira, Spain; Paisleys, 31 Jane St, Workington, Cumbria (☎ 0900 602 235)

BACON, Kenneth Frank; s of Frank Bacon (d 1985), of Brighton, and Ethel Grace, *née* Bishop; *b* 15 Feb 1934; *Educ* Varndean GS, Brighton Tech Coll; *m* 7 July 1956, Cynthia Mary, da of Harry George Green (d 1976); 2 da (Helena b 1963, Blanche b 1967); *Career* md: Magnetic Components Ltd 1972-76, Southern Instrument Hldgs 1976-78; gp chief exec Fairey Hldgs Ltd 1978-81, md Mel Equipment Ltd 1981-83, div md Plessey Communications Div 1983-85, md STC Telecomunications Ltd 1985-87, chm STC-ICL Defence Systems 1987, exec dir Focon Int Ltd; Freeman City of London, Liveryman Worshipful Co of Glass Sellers; CEng, FIEE, CBIM; *Recreations* reading, history; *Clubs* RAC; *Style—* Kenneth Bacon, Esq; ffowlers Bucke, South Harting, Petersfield GU31 5QB (☎ 0730 825 592); Focon International Ltd, Bridge House, Bridge St, Walton-on-Thames KT12 1AL, Surrey (☎ 0932 253 311, fax 0932 253 473, car tel 0836 709 197, telex 934051 BSB G)

BACON, Sir Nicholas Hickman Ponsonby; 14 and 15 Bt (E 1611 and 1627), of Redgrave, Suffolk, and of Mildenhall, Suffolk, respectively; Premier Baronet of England; s of Sir Edmund Bacon, 13 and 14 Bt, KG, KBE, TD, JP, by his w Priscilla, da of Col Sir Charles Ponsonby, 1 Bt, TD, and Hon Winifred Gibbs (da of 1 Baron Hunsdon), Sir Nicholas is 12 in descent from Rt Hon Sir Nicholas Bacon, Lord Keeper of the Great Seal under Elizabeth I 1558-78 (in which latter year he d), his eld s was cr a Bt 1611 and this eld son's 3 s cr a Bt in 1627. Lord Keeper Bacon's 5 s by a second m (but yr s by this w, Anne, da of Sir Anthony Cooke, sometime tutor to Edward VI) was Lord High Chllr and was cr Viscount St Albans 1621; *b* 17 May 1953; *Educ* Eton, Dundee Univ; *m* 1981, Susan Henrietta, da of Raymond Dinnis, of Delaware Farm, Edenbridge; 2 s (Hicky b 1984, Edmund b 1986); *Heir* s, Henry Hickman Bacon b 23 April 1984; *Career* barr Gray's Inn 1978; page of honour to HM The Queen 1966-69; *Style—* Sir Nicholas Bacon, Bt; Raveningham Hall, Norwich (☎ (050 846) 206)

BACON, Priscilla, Lady; Priscilla Dora; *née* Ponsonby; DL (Norfolk); eld da of Sir Charles Edward Ponsonby, 1 Bt, TD, DL (d 1976), sometime MP for Sevenoaks (gs of 1 Baron De Mauley), and Hon Winifred Gibbs, JP, eld da of 1 Baron Hunsdon; *b* 3 June 1913; *m* 15 Jan 1936, Sir Edmund Castell Bacon, 13 and 14 Bt, KG, KBE, TD, JP (d 1982); 1 s (14 and 15 Bt), 4 da (Mrs John Bruce, Mrs Stephen Gibbs, Mrs Ronald Hoare, Mrs Paul Nicholson); *Career* Queen Elizabeth II Coronation Medal; *Books* contributed article on Raveningham Hall gardens to 23 edn of New Englishwoman Gardener (1987); *Style—* Priscilla, Lady Bacon, DL; Orchards Raveningham, Norfolk NR14 6NS

BACON, Sir Sidney Charles; CB (1971); s of Charles Bacon; *b* 11 Feb 1919; *Educ* Woolwich Poly, London Univ (BSc Eng); *Career* md Royal Ordnance Factories and dep chm bd 1972-79, ret; memb cncl City and Guilds of London Inst 1983-; FEng 1979, FIMechE, FIProd E; kt 1977; *Style—* Sir Sidney Bacon, CB; 228 Erith Rd, Bexley Heath, Kent DA7 6HP

BADCOCK, Maj-Gen John Michael Watson; CB (1976), MBE (1969); s of late R D Badcock, MC, JP; *b* 10 Nov 1922; *Educ* Sherborne, Worcester Coll Oxford; *m* 1948, Gillian Pauline, *née* Attfield; 1 s, 2 da; *Career* enlisted in ranks (Army) 1941, cmmnd Royal Signals 1942, war serv 1945-47: UK, BAOR, Ceylon, 1947-68 serv: UK, Persian Gulf, BAOR, Cyprus, cdr 2 Inf Bde and dep constable Dover Castle 1968-71, dep mil sec 1971-72, dir of manning (Army) 1972-74, def advsr and head Br Def Liaison Staff Canberra 1974-77, ret; Col Cmdt Royal Signals 1974-80 and 1982-, Master of Signals 1982-, Hon Sol 31 (London) Signal Regt (Vol) 1978-83, chm South East TA & VRA 1979-85, DL Kent 1980; *Recreations* rugby, football, cricket, hockey; *Clubs* Army and Navy; *Style—* Maj-Gen John Badcock, CB, MBE, DL; Autrum Lodge, Stodmarsh Rd, Canterbury CT4 5RH (☎ 0227 470 340)

BADCOCK, Julian Knighton; MBE (1984), AE (1946); s of Paul Badcock (d 1975), of Cobham Surrey, and Torfrida Gertrude, *née* Oldfield (d 1981); *b* 24 Mar 1919; *Educ* St Paul's, King's Coll London (BA, BSc); *m* 2 Sept 1944, Sophie, da of Capt Sergius Peter Skidmore (d 1974), of Athens, Greece; 1 s (Ashley b 1948), 2 da (Jane (Mrs Robb) b 1951, Alice (Mrs Chandler) b 1955); *Career* Univ of London Air Sqdn and RAF Volunteer Res 1938-39 (cmmnd 1939); WWII: navigator and air gunner 44 and 83 Bomber Sqdns 1940-41, navigation instr (memb Aircrew Classification Bd) 1942-43, Empire Air Trg Scheme SA (and liaison offr to Greek Air Force) 1944-45, released Flt Lt 1946; called to the Bar Lincolns Inn 1949; Br Employers Confedn 1947-50, asst sec and legal advsr to Limestone Fedn and Federated Quarry Owners GB 1950-61, gen mangr and sec to London Port Employers Assoc 1961-84 and assoc Lighterage Tea and Tug Orgns (nat and internat), exec dir Trade Assoc Mgmnt Servs Ltd, ret 1984; Cobham ward cncllr on Esher UDC 1949-67, govr of local sch's; chm of Esher UDC and ex officio JP for Co of Surrey 1963-64; Freeman: City of London 1977, Worshipful Co of Watermen 1977 (ct memb 1984); *Recreations* voluntary work, historical res; *Clubs* RAF; *Style—* Julian Badcock, Esq, MBE; Abington Orchard, Leigh Place, Cobham, Surrey KT11 2HL (☎ 0932 62969)

BADDELEY, Sir John Wolsey Beresford; 4 Bt (UK 1922), of Lakefield, Parish of St Mary, Stoke Newington, Co London; s of Sir John Beresford Baddeley, 3 Bt (d 1979); *b* 27 Jan 1938; *Educ* Bradfield; *m* 1962, Sara Rosalind, da of late Colin Crofts, of Scarborough; 3 da; *Heir* kinsman, Mark Baddeley; *Career* Champagne Bollinger (Mentzendorff & Co Ltd); *Recreations* squash, inland waterways; *Style—* Sir John Baddeley, Bt; Springwood, Sandgate Lane, Storrington, Sussex (☎ 09066 3054)

BADDELEY, Mark David; s of late Mark Baddeley (d 1930), gs of Sir John Baddeley, 1 Bt, and hp of kinsman Sir John Wolsey Baddeley, 4 Bt; *b* 10 May 1921; *Educ* Cliftonville Coll; *Style—* Mark Baddeley, Esq; Woodberry, George V Ave, Margate, Kent

BADDELEY, Nancy, Lady; Nancy Winifred; da of late Thomas Wolsey, of Smallburgh Hall, Norfolk; *m* 1929, Sir John Baddeley, 3 Bt (d 1979); 1 s, 2 da; *Style—* Nancy, Lady Baddeley; Chequers Hotel, Church Place, Pulborough, West Sussex

BADDELEY, Brig Robert John; s of Lieut-Col Robert John Halkett Baddeley, MC (d 1954), and Hilda Wardle, *née* Maitland Dougall; *b* 2 July 1934; *Educ* Wellington, Sandhurst; *m* Susan Marian, da of Edwin Colin Neale Edwards, of Eton Coll, Windsor; 2 da (Charlotte b 1965, Emma b 1968); *Career* cmmnd 4/7 Royal Dragoon Gds, ADC Chief of Defence Staff Ghana/UN Congo 1960, HQ Malta and Libya 1966, CO 4/7 Royal Dragoon Gds, directing staff Staff Coll Camberley 1976, defence attache Tehran 1978, dep dir Army Recruiting 1980, cdr Br Military Advsy Team Bangladesh 1983, dir of army training 1987, ADC to HM The Queen 1987; Freeman City of London, Liveryman Worshipful Co of Coachmakers and Coach Harness Makers Co; *Clubs* Cavalry and Guards, Lansdowne; *Style—* Brigadier R J Baddeley; Hazeldon House, Tisbury, Wilts (☎ (0747) 870867); MOD, Holborn, London WC1V 6HE (☎ 01 430 5649)

BADDELEY, Very Rev William Pye; s of William Herman Clinton Baddeley (d 1918), and Louise, *née* Bourdin (d 1920); *b* 20 Mar 1914; *Educ* privately, Durham Univ, Cuddesdon Coll Oxford; *m* 1947, Mary Frances Shirley, da of Col Ernest Robert Caldwell Wyatt, CBE, DSO; 1 da (Frances b 1955); *Career* vicar St Pancras 1949-58, dean of Brisbane 1958-67 (diocesan chaplain 1962-67), rector St James's Piccadilly 1967-80, chaplain Royal Academy of Arts 1968-80, visiting chaplain Westminster Abbey 1980-, area dean of Westminster 1974-80; commissary to: Primate of Australia 1967-, Bishop of Wangaratta 1970, Archbishop of Papua New Guinea 1972, Bishop of Newcastle NSW 1976; dean emeritus of Brisbane 1980-; dir Elizabethan Theatre Tst 1963-67; pres: Queensland Ballet Co 1962-67, Qld Univ Dramatic Soc 1961-67; life govr Thomas Coram Fndn, chm Malcolm Sargent Cancer Fund for Children 1968-; govr: Burlington Sch 1967-80, Archbishop Tenison's Sch 1967-80; frequent broadcaster on TV and radio in Australia 1958-67; chaplain OStJ 1971; *Recreations* theatre, photography, music; *Clubs* Carlton, Arts, East India; *Style—* The Very Rev William Baddeley; Cumberland House, Woodbridge, Suffolk IP12 4AH (☎ 03943 4104)

BADDILEY, Prof Sir James; s of late James Baddiley, and Ivy Logan Cato; *b* 15 May 1918; *Educ* Manchester GS, Manchester Univ (PhD, DSc), Cambridge Univ (ScD); *m* 1944, Hazel, yr da of Wesley Wilfrid Townsend; 1 s; *Career* ICI fell Cambridge Univ 1945-49, Swedish MRC fell Wenner-Grens Inst for Cell Biology Stockholm 1947-49, memb of staff dept of biochemistry Lister Inst of Preventive Medicine London 1949-54, Rockefeller fellowship Harvard Med Sch 1954, prof organic chemistry King's Coll Durham Univ 1954-77, prof of chemical microbiology 1977-83 and dir microbiological chemical Res Lab Newcastle Univ 1975-83, SERC sr fell dept of biochemistry Cambridge Univ 1981-83, fell Pembroke Coll Cambridge 1981-85 (emeritus fellow); hon memb American Soc of Biochemistry and Molecular Biology; Meldola Medal Royal Inst of Chemistry 1947, Tilden lectr 1959, Corday-Morgan Medal Chem Soc 1952 (Pedler lectr 1980); Hon DSc Heriot-Watt; Hon DSc Bath; kt 1977; FRS (Leeuwenhoek lectr 1967, Davy Medal 1974), FRSE; *Style—* Prof Sir James Baddiley, FRS; Hill Top Cottage, Hildersham, Cambridge CB1 6DA (☎ 0223 893055); Dept of Biochemistry, Univ of Cambridge, Tennis Court Rd, Cambridge CB2 1QW (☎ 0223 333600)

BADEN, (Edwin) John; s of Percy Baden (d 1972), of Parkstone, Dorset, and Jacoba Geertruij, *née* de Blank; *b* 18 August 1928; *Educ* Winchester, Corpus Christi Coll Cambridge (BA, MA); *m* 6 Sept 1952, Christine Irene, da of Edward Miall Grose (d 1973), of Farm View, Laughton, Sussex; 2 s (Peter b 1954, David b 1959), 3 da (Ann b 1956, Susan b 1958, Zoë b 1962); *Career* RA and RHA 1947-48, cmmnd 2 Lt; served: Eng, Palestine, Tripolitania: audit clerk Deliotte Haskins & Sells London 1951-54; sec/dir H Parrot & Co Ltd London 1955-61, fin advsr C & A Modes Ltd London 1961-63, dir Samuel Montagu & Co Ltd London 1963-78, chm Midland Montagu Industl Fin 1975-78, md and chief exec Italian Int Bank plc 1978-, chm N American Property Unit Tst London; memb of mgmnt ctee Pan Euro Property Unit Tst London; tstee Int Centre for Res in Accounting - Univ of Lancaster; dir and memb of audit ctee Girobank plc; MICAS 1954 (cncl memb), memb Inst of Taxation 1954; Cavaliere Officiale (Order of Merit of the Italian Republic) 1986); *Recreations* sailing, reading; *Style—* John Baden, Esq; The Old Manor House, Chilworth, Surrey GU4 8NE (☎ 0483 61203); Italian International Bank, 122 Leadenhall St, London EC3V 4PT (☎ 01 623 8700, telex 885379, fax 623 9750/621 0387)

BADEN HELLARD, Ronald; s of Ernest Baden Hellard (d 1975), of Longfield, Kent, and Alice May, *née* Banks (d 1980); *b* 30 Jan 1927; *Educ* Liskeard GS, The Poly Sch of Architecture (DipArch), Loughborough Tech Coll (now Loughborough Univ); *m* 16 Dec 1950, Kay Peggy, *née* Fiddes; 2 da (Sally b 1953, Diana Jacqueline b 1956); *Career* WWII Duke of Cornwalls LI 1945-48, Capt GHQ MELF 1947-48; fndr ptnr: Polycon Gp 1952-, Polycon Bldg Industl Conslts 1955-; chm Polycon Endispute Mgmnt Servs 1984-, chief exec Coll of Estate Mgmnt 1988-; architect of various industl and commerical bldgs incl Oxford Air Trg Sch at Kidlington, first chm RIBA mgmnt ctee 1956-64, developed a number of mgmnt techniques which are now standard mgmnt practise in construction indust; pres S London Soc of Architects 1967-69, chm SE London Branch BIM 1969-72, chm SE regnl BIM 1972-76, memb Nat Cncl 1971-77; cncl memb CIArb 1970-84 (actg sec 1973); Freeman City of London 1981, Liveryman Worshipful Co of Arbitrators 1981; FCIArb 1952, FRIBA 1955, FBIM 1966; *Books* Management in Architectural Practice (1964), Metric Change a Management Action Plan (1971), Training for Change - A Company Action Plan (1972), Construction Quality Coordinators Guide (1987), Managing Construction Conflict (1988); *Recreations* tennis, travel; *Style—* Ronald Baden Hellard, Esq; 97 Vanbrugh Park, Blackheath, London SE3 (☎ 01 853 2006); Polycon Group, 70 Greenwich High Rd, London SE10 (☎ 01 691 7425)

BADEN-POWELL, Carine, Baroness; Carine; da of late Clement Hamilton Crause Boardman, of Johannesburg; *m* 1936, 2 Baron Baden-Powell (d 1962); 2 s, 1 da; *Style—* The Rt Hon Carine, Lady Baden-Powell

BADEN-POWELL, Hon (David) Michael; s of 2 Baron Baden-Powell (d 1962); hp of bro, 3 Baron Baden-Powell; *b* 11 Dec 1940; *Educ* Pierrepont House; *m* 1966, Joan, da of Horace Berryman, of Melbourne; 3 s; *Career* insurance consultant, agent with

Australian Mutual Provident Soc 1972-, Freeman City of London, Memb Worshipful Co of Mercers; *Style*— The Hon Michael Baden-Powell; 18 Kalang Rd, Camberwell, Vict 3124, Australia (☎(29 5009)

BADEN-POWELL, Baroness; Patience Hélène Mary; CBE (1986); da of Maj Douglas Batty (d 1982), of Zimbabwe; *b* 27 Oct 1936; *Educ* St Peter's Diocesan Sch Bulawayo; *m* 1963, 3 Baron Baden-Powell, *qv*; *Career* int cmmr Girl Guides Assoc 1975-79, chief cmmr 1980-85, pres Cwlth Youth Exchange Cncl 1982-85; patron: Surrey Antiques Fair, (pres), Nat Playbus Assoc, Woodlarks Campsite Tst for the Disabled; dir Laurentian Hldg Co Ltd; *Style*— The Rt Hon the Lady Baden-Powell, CBE; Grove Heath Farm, Ripley, Woking, Surrey GU23 6ES (☎ 0483 224262)

BADEN-POWELL, 3 Baron (UK 1929); Sir Robert Crause Baden-Powell; 3 Bt (UK 1922); s of 2 Baron Baden-Powell (d 1962); *b* 15 Oct 1936; *Educ* Bryanston; *m* 1963, Patience (*see* Baden-Powell, Baroness);; *Heir* bro, Hon David Baden-Powell; *Career* RN 1955-57, chief scouts commissioner: Scout Assoc 1963-82, World Scout Fndn 1978-; vice-pres Scout Assoc 1982-; dir: Bolton Building Soc 1985-; chm Quarter Horse Racing U.K.; *Recreations* breeding racing quarter horses.; *Style*— The Rt Hon the Lord Baden-Powell; Grove Heath Farm, Ripley, Woking, Surrey GU23 6ES (☎ Guildford 224262)

BADEN-POWELL, Hon Wendy Dorothy Lilian; da of 2 Baron Baden-Powell (d 1962); *b* 16 Sept 1944; *Educ* St Cyprian's Sch Cape Town, The Sorbonne; *Style*— The Hon Wendy Baden-Powell; Turnstones, Old Bursledon, Southampton, Hants

BADENI, Count Jan; s of Count Stefan Badeni (d 1961), of Castle of Koropiec, Poland, and Mary, *née* Jablonowska; gs of Count Stanislaus Badeni Head of the State of Galicia; *b* 15 Jan 1921; *Educ* private; *m* 7 July 1956, June, da of Maj Noel Wilson, JP, of Norton Manor, Malmesbury, Wilts; 1 s (Michael b 1958), 1 da (Mary b 1960); *Heir* s, Count Michael Badeni; *Career* WWII Sqdn Ldr RAF, served East and Coastal Cmd; also in Malaya Emergency Cmd helicopter sqdns in Malaya and UK on search and rescue duties (lifted 67 casualties) 1955-58; Queen's Commendation for Valuable Serv in the Air 1962; High Sheriff of Wiltshire 1978-79; kt of Honour and Devotion (Polish Assoc) SMO Malta (1971); *Style*— The Count Badeni; Norton Manor, Malmesbury, Wilts

BADENOCH, Sir John; s of William Minty Badenoch, MB, and Ann Dyer, *née* Coutts; *b* 8 Mar 1920; *Educ* Rugby, Oriel Coll Oxford (MA); *m* Anne Newnham, da of Prof Lancelot Forster; 2 s, 2 da; *Career* former research asst dept of clinical medicine Oxford, former dir clinical studies Oxford Univ, former conslt physician Oxfordshire Dist Health Authy, univ lectr in medicine Oxford Univ; fell Merton Coll; former sr censor and sr vice pres Royal Coll of Physicians; Liveryman Soc of Apothecaries; dir Overseas Liaison Office Royal Coll of Physician; kt 1984; DM, FRCP, FRCPE; *Recreations* walking, travel, natural history; *Clubs* Athenaeum; *Style*— Sir John Badenoch; 21 Hartley Court, 84 Woodstock Rd, Oxford OX2 7PF

BADGER, Geoffrey Malcolm; AO (1975); s of John McDougall Badger, and Laura Mary Brooker Badger; *b* 10 Oct 1916; *Educ* Geelong Coll, Gordon Inst of Technol, Univs of Melbourne, London, Glasgow; *m* 1941, Edith Maud, da of Henry Chevis; *Career* res prof Adelaide Univ 1977-79, (vice-chllr 1967-77, prof Organic Chemistry 1955-64), pres Australian Acad of Sci 1974-78, chm Australian Sci and Technol Cncl 1977-82, chm SA branch Australia Assoc 1986-88; FRSC, FRACI, FACE, FTS, FAA, KLJ (1985); kt 1979; *Books* Over two hundred scientific papers and six books; *Recreations* walking; *Clubs* Adelaide, Adelaide South Australia; *Style*— Sir Geoffrey Badger, AO; 1 Anna Court, Delfin Island, West Lakes, S A, 5021, Australia

BADHAM, Douglas George; CBE (1975), JP (Glam 1962); s of late David Badham, JP; *b* 1 Dec 1914; *Educ* Leys Sch; *m* 1939, Doreen Spencer Phillips; 2 da; *Career* chm: Economic Forestry Gp 1981-88 (dir 1978-88), Hamell (West), Forest Thinnings 1978-81, Economic Forestry (Wales) until 1981, Minton Treharne & Davies until 1984, Powell Duffryn Wagon Co until 1986, Worldwide Travel (Wales) to 1985, T T Pascoe 1983-; exec dir Powell Duffryn Gp 1938-69; dep chm Welsh Devpt Agency 1980-85 (memb 1978-85); memb: Br Gas Corpn 1974-84 (part-time), Welsh Cncl 1971-80, BR (Western) Bd 1977-82, Devpt Corpn for Wales 1965-83 (chm 1971-80); dir: Align-rite Ltd 1985-88, T H Couch 1985-88, Pascoe Holdings 1985-88, World Trade Centre Wales Ltd 1985-; High Sheriff Mid Glam 1976, HM Lieut for Mid-Glamorgan 1982-85, HM Lord-Lieut for Mid Glamorgan 1985- (DL 1975-82); *Style*— Douglas Badham, Esq, CBE, JP; Plas Watford, Caerphilly, Mid Glam (☎ 0222 882094)

BADHAM, John; s of John William Badham, of Rotherham, Yorks (d 1978), and Wilhemina Frances, *née* Ratcliffe (d 1969); *b* 9 Dec 1934; *Educ* Mexborough GS, Sheffield Univ 1953-58 (Dip Arch, ARIBA, Dip TP); *m* 11 Sept 1958, Penelope, da of Francis Henry Stokes, of Potters Bar, Herts; 2 da (Francesca b 1964, Imogen b 1964); *Career* architect; ptnr: The Fitzroy Robinson Ptnrship 1972-, Edwards Stepan Assocs 1964-72, Sir John Burnet Tait & Ptnrs 1961-64, T P Bennett & Son 1959-61; *Recreations* music, piano playing, skiing; *Clubs* Ski (GB); *Style*— John Badham, Esq; 23 Onslow Gardens, London N10 3JT (☎ 01 883 2500); The Fitzroy Robinson Partnership, 77 Portland Place, London W1 (☎ 01 636 8033)

BADHAM, Leonard; s of John Randall Badham, and Emily Louise Badham; *b* 10 June 1923; *Educ* Wandsworth GS; *m* 1944, Joyce Rose Lowrie; 2 da; *Career* md J Lyons & Co 1977-, dir Allied-Lyons plc 1978-; FHCIMA, CBIM; *Style*— Leonard Badham, Esq; 26 Vicarage Drive, E Sheen, London SW14 (☎ 01 876 4373); J Lyons & Co, Cadbury Hall, London W14 0PA (☎ 01 603 2040)

BADNELL, Gordon John; s of Philip John Badnell, and Olive Thurza, *née* Pragnell; *b* 18 August 1936; *Educ* Sir William Borlase Sch Marlow, Sch of Architecture Northern Polytechnic London; *m* 1, 9 Sept 1962 (m dis); 1 s (Piers Apsley John b 1964), 2 da (Imogen Ruth Christina b 1967, Olivia Grace Rebecca b 1973); m 2, 30 Sept 1977, Gillian Elizabeth, da of Kenneth Sydney Rawlins (d 1986), of Treyarnon Bay, Cornwall; *Career* 2 Lt Royal Engrs, troop cdr Fortress Sqdn Malta 1959-61; chartered architect, princ ptnr Elaine Denby and Gordon Badnell chartered architects 1986- (ptnr 1973-), chm Lahnsohn Arbor Ltd 1982-, dir Tanist Ltd 1985-; *Recreations* art, music, Rotary Club; *Style*— Gordon Badnell, Esq; The Old Bakery, School Lane, Lane End, High Wycombe, Bucks (☎ 0494 882279); 65 High St, Marlow Bucks (☎ 06284 72715)

BAELZ, Very Rev Peter Richard; s of Eberhard Baelz (d 1986), and Dora, *née* Focke (d 1970); *b* 27 July 1923; *Educ* Dulwich, Christ's Coll (BA), Cambridge (MA), Westcott House Cambridge (BD Cantab, DD Oxon); *m* 15 July 1950, Anne Thelma, da of Edward Cleall-Harding (d 1942); 3 s (Simon b 1951, Nicholas b 1955, Timothy b 1956); *Career* curate: Bournville Birmingham 1947-50, Sherborne Dorset 1950-52; asst chaplain Ripon Hall Oxford 1952-53, rector Wishaw Birmingham 1953-56, vicar Bournville Birmingham 1956-60, dean Jesus Coll Cambridge 1960-72, regius prof of moral and pastoral theology and canon of Christ Church Oxford 1972-79, dean of Durham 1980-88 (dean emeritus); OStJ; *Books* Prayer and Providence (1966), The Forgotten Dream (1974); *Recreations* walking, cycling; *Style*— The Very Rev Peter Baelz; 36 Brynteg, Llandrindod Wells, Powys LD1 5NB (☎ 0597 5404)

BAER, Derek Alfred Howard; s of Alfred Max Baer (d 1987), and Olga Maud, *née* Howard (d 1985); *b* 5 Nov 1921; *Educ* Eton, Magdalene Coll Cambridge; *m* 25 June 1948, Elizabeth Sheila, da of Rupert Williams-Ellis, of Glasryn, nr Pwllheli, Gwynedd; 1 s (Richard b 1949), 3 da (Caroline b 1950, Charlotte b 1953, Susanna b 1962); *Career* WWII: Leics Yeo 1942-45, staff offr ALFSEA 1945-46; princ Miny of Civil Aviation and Tport 1947-54, vice-chm John Govett & Co 1954-79, chm Foreign and Colonial Investmt Tst plc 1979-85; dir various public cos incl: Brookmount plc, The Colonial Mutual Life Assur Soc Ltd (London Bd), Connells Estate Agents plc, Portmeirion Potteries plc, Unilever Pension Investmts Ltd; *Recreations* gardening; *Style*— Derek Baer, Esq; Freshford Hall, Freshford, Bath BA3 6EJ (☎ 022 122 2522, fax 0225 777 388); 1 Laurence Pountney Hill, London EC4R OBA (☎ 01 623 4680)

BAER, Jack Mervyn Frank; yr s of late Frank Baer and Alix Baer; *b* 29 August 1924; *Educ* Bryanston, Slade Sch of Fine Art, UCL; *m* 1, 1952 (m dis 1969), Jean (d 1973), only child of late L F St Clair and Evelyn Synnott; 1 da; m 2, 1970, Diana Downes Baillieu, da of Aubrey Clare Robinson and Mollie Panter-Downes; 2 step da; *Career* dir Hazlitt Gallery 1948, md Hazlitt Gooden & Fox 1973-, chm Soc of London Art Dealers 1977-80; *Clubs* Brooks's, Buck's, Beefsteak; *Style*— Jack Baer Esq; 9 Phillimore Terrace, W8 (☎ 01 937 6899)

BAGGALEY, David Anthony; s of Geoffrey (d 1944), and Joan, *née* Shackleton (d 1969); *b* 9 Jan 1943; *Educ* Merchant Taylors, Portsmouth Poly (Dip Business Admin); *m* 1965, Betty; 1 s (Jason b 1969), 1 da (Sasha b 1970); *Career* fin dir Abbey Life Gp plc 1985-, dir fin and investmt Girobank plc 1979-85; FCMA, FCT; *Recreations* sailing, mountaineering; *Clubs* Parkstone YC, Fell and Rock Climbing, The Lanz; *Style*— David Baggaley, Esq; Broadwater, 37 Alyth Rd, Talbot Woods, Bournemouth, Dorset BH3 7DG; Abbey Life Gp, 80 Holdenhurst Rd, Bournemouth, BH8 8AL (☎ 0202 27612, fax 0202 27693)

BAGGE, (Alfred) James Stephen; 2 s of Sir John Bagge, 6 Bt, ED, DL; *b* 7 Dec 1952; *Educ* Eton; *m* 10 Oct 1981, Victoria I, er da of Michael A Lyndon Skeggs, of Oakhall, Cornhill-on-Tweed, Northumberland; 1 da (Edwina Rose b 1985); *Career* Capt Blues and Royals, ADC to Govr S Australia 1975-77; barr 1979, memb Hon Soc of Lincoln's Inn, practising barr of S Eastern Circuit; *Style*— James Bagge, Esq; 28 Luttrell Av, London SW15; Queen Elizabeth Buildings, Temple, London EC4

BAGGE, (John) Jeremy Picton; s and h of Sir John Bagge, 6 Bt, ED, DL, and Elizabeth Helena, *née* Davies; *b* 21 June 1945; *Educ* Eton; *m* 1979, Sarah Margaret Phipps, da of late Maj James Shelley Phipps Armstrong, Agent-Gen for Ontario; 2 s (Alfred b 1 July 1980, Albert b 1 April 1985), 1 da (Alexandra b 26 Dec 1982); *Career* farmer; fin advsr HRH The Crown Prince of Ethiopia 1969-70; chm West Norfolk Enterprise 1985; dir: West Norfolk Grain 1983, King's Lynn Conservancy Bd 1983-87, Fermoy Centre Fndn 1985-: concllr King's Lynn and West Norfolk Borough Cncl 1981, chm Devpt and Estates 1983-; memb: Norfolk Ctee CLA 1986-, Norfolk RCC, Norfolk RDC; Freeman City of London, memb Worshipful Co of Haberdashers; FCA; *Recreations* shooting, stalking, hunting, fishing, water skiing; *Clubs* Boodles; *Style*— Jeremy Bagge, Esq; Stradsett Hall, Stradsett, King's Lynn, Norfolk PE33 9HA (☎ 036 64 562); Stradsett Estate Office, Stradsett, King's Lynn PE33 9HA (☎ 036 64 642)

BAGGE, Sir John Alfred Picton; 6 Bt (UK 1867), of Stradsett Hall, Norfolk; ED (1946), DL (Norfolk 1978); s of Sir Picton Bagge, 5 Bt, CMG (d 1967), and Olive, da of late Samuel Mendel; *b* 27 Oct 1914; *Educ* Eton and abroad; *m* 1939, Elizabeth Helena, da of late Daniel James Davies, CBE, Commissioner for Newfoundland; 3 s, 3 da; *Heir* s, Jeremy Bagge FCA; *Career* served WW II with Cheshire Yeo: Palestine, Sudan, Ethiopia, Maj 1941; landowner and farmer; chm W Norfolk DC 1976-77 (vice chm 1973-76), high sheriff Norfolk 1977; chm Cncl of St John in Norfolk 1969-80; KStJ 1975; *Recreations* shooting; *Style*— Sir John Bagge, Bt, ED, DL; Stradsett Hall, King's Lynn, Norfolk (☎ (036 64) 215)

BAGGE, Richard Anthony; s of Gordon Roy Bagge (d 1980), and Barbara Joan, *née* Sympson; *b* 5 August 1949; *Educ* Broad Green GS, Croydon Tech Coll, London Poly; *m* 15 June 1974, Shirley Anne, da of Reginald Ephraim White; 2 s (Jonathan Richard, Jeremy Edward); *Career* with Barclays Bank 1966-70, fund mangr Northcote & Co 1970-75, dir MIM Britannia 1975-; memb C of C; FInstD, FInstSMM; *Recreations* sailing, classic cars, gardening, antiques, music, theatre; *Style*— Richard Bagge, Esq; Heathfield, Raglan Rd, Reigate, Surrey, RH2 0DY; MIM Britannia Unit Trust Managers Ltd, 11 Devonshire Sq, London EC2M 4YR (☎ 01 626 3434, 0737 224488, fax 0737 222815, car tel 0860 380394); Reigate Hill House, Reigate RH2 9NG

BAGGE, Thomas (Tom) Philip; 3 s of Sir John Bagge, 6 Bt, ED, *qv*; *b* 4 May 1955; *Educ* Eton, RMAS and RAC Cirencester; *Career* Capt Blues and Royals, ADC to Gen Cmdg 4 Armed Div 1977-78; land agent; ARICS; *Style*— Thomas Bagge Esq; Hall Farm, Irnham, Grantham, Lincolnshire NG33 4JD

BAGIER, Gordon Alexander Thomas; DL (Tyne and Wear 1988); s of Alexander Thomas Bagier, of Glasgow; *b* 1924,July; *Educ* Pendower Secdy Tech Sch Newcastle; *m* 1949, Violet, da of John R Sinclair, of Edinburgh; 2 s, 2 da; *Career* MP (Lab) Sunderland S 1964-87; PPS to Home Sec 1968-69; memb select ctee Tport 1980- (chm 1985-87); *Recreations* golf; *Clubs* Westerhope Golf (Newcastle-upon-Tyne.); *Style*— Gordon Bagier, Esq, DL, MP; Rahana, Whickham Highway, Dunston, Gateshead, Co Durham

BAGNALL, John Keith; s of Alfred Studley Bagnall, of Otley, West Yorks, and Margaret, *née* Kirkham (d 1983); *b* 30 Dec 1941; *Educ* Oundle; *m* 10 Oct 1964, Valerie, da of Leslie Moxon (d 1985); 1 s (Stephen b 1968), 1 da (Caroline b 1966); *Career* Alfred Bagnall & Sons Ltd: dir 1962, gp md 1972, dir 7 subsid cos; pres: Nat Fedn Painting and Decorating Contractors 1983-84; memb: nat cncl Building Employers Confedn 1978-85; memb Standing ctee: Safety Health and Welfare 1976-79, Finance 1976-, Econ and Pub Affs Gp 1983-; vice-pres Bldg Employers Confedn 1986-; tres Keighley and Dist Trg Assoc 1966-70, auditor BIM Central Yorks 1973-78; FCA 1965, FBIM 1972; *Recreations* tennis, chess; *Style*— John Bagnall, Esq; Dale Lodge, Gilstead Lane, Bingley, West Yorkshire BD16 3LN (☎ 0274 563 867); Alfred Bagnall & Sons Ltd, 6 Manor Lane, Shipley, West Yorks BD18 3RD (☎ 0274 587 227, fax 0274 531 260)

BAGNALL, Kenneth Reginald; QC (1973), QC (Hongkong, 1983); s of Reginald and Elizabeth Bagnall; *b* 26 Nov 1927; *Educ* King Edward VI Sch Birmingham, Birmingham Univ (LLB) ; *m* 1, 1955, Margaret Edith Wall; 1 s, 1 da; m 2, 1963, Rosemary Hearn; 1 s, 1 da; *Career* barr 1950, dep judge Crown Court 1975-79; chm Hurstwood Timber Co 1972-9; memb Crafts Cncl 1982-4, jt fndr (with HM Govt) of the Bagnall Gallery (operated by the Crafts Cncl) 1982-; co-fndr Anglo American Real Property Inst 1980-, chm Anglo American Real Property Inst 1980-82; co-fndr The New Law Publishing Co. Ltd, chm edit board New Property Coles 1987, Choplet Properties Ltd; Freeman City of London 1972, Liveryman Worshipful Co of Barber Surgeons 1972;; *Books* Guide to Business Tenancies (1956), Development Land Tax (1978), Judicial Review (1985); *Style*— Kenneth Bagnall Esq, QC

BAGNALL, Field Marshal Sir Nigel Thomas; GCB (1985, KCB 1980), CVO (1980, MC (1950, and Bar 1953); s of Lt-Col Harry Stephen Bagnall, and Marjory May Bagnall; *b* 10 Feb 1927; *Educ* Wellington, Balliol Coll Oxford ; *m* 1959, Anna Caroline Church; 2 da (Emma, Sarah); *Career* joined Army 1945, cmmnd Green Howards 1946, 6 Airborne Div Palestine 1946-48, Malaya 1949-52, CSO1 (Intelligence) Borneo 1966-67, cmd 4/7 Royal Dragoon Guards BAOR and NI 1967-69, cmd RAC BAOR 1970-72, fdf fell Balliol Coll Oxford 1972-73, sec COS ctee MOD 1973-75, GOC 4 Div BAOR 1975-77, asst chief of def staff (policy) MOD 1978-80, cmd 1 (Br) Corps BAOR 1980-83, C-in-C BAOR and cmd N Army Gp BAOR 1983-, chief gen staff 1985-88, Col Cmdt RAC 1985-88, Col Cmdt Army Physical Trg Corps 1981-88, ADC Gen to HM The Queen 1985; hon fell Balliol Coll Oxford 1986; *Recreations* reading, walking, gardening; *Clubs* Cavalry and Guards; *Style*— Field Marshal Sir Nigel Bagnall, GCB, CVO, MC; c/o Royal Bank of Scotland, Kirkland House, 22 Whitehall, London SW1

BAGNELL, Capt (William) David Armstrong; s of Capt Robert Armstrong Bagnell (d 1959), of Longdown Chase, Hindhead, Surrey, and Phyllis Evelyn (d 1969), da of Capt George William Taylor, and Lady Elizabeth Emma Geraldine, o da of 4 Earl of Wilton; *b* 21 August 1926; *Educ* Eton; *m* 16 May 1962, Caroline Mary, o da of Edward Richard Whittington-Moë (d 1965), of The Hollies, St Peter, Jersey, CI; 1 s (William Edward Henry b 1966), 1 da (Sophia Mary b 1963); *Career* Capt RHG (Blues, ret 1955), served in WWII Capt Allied Liaison HQ, Belgian Army 1947-48; Parly candidate Hammersmith N 1959; Hants County Cncl 1964-67, chm E Hants (Petersfield) Cons and Unionist Assoc 1968-73, dep chm Cons Cwlth and Overseas Cncl 1976-83; at talks with World Bank and US Govt agencies on insurance against political risk 1961; chm DB Investment Co; underwriting memb of Lloyd's; memb central exec ctee NSPCC 1973-; Chev Order of the Dannebrog Denmark 1951; *Recreations* shooting; *Clubs* White's, Buck's; *Style*— Capt David Bagnell; East Worldham House, Alton, Hampshire GU34 3AS (☎ 0420 83143)

BAGOT, 9 Baron (GB 1780); Sir Heneage Charles Bagot; 14 Bt (E 1627); s of late Charles Frederick Heneage Bagot, ggs of 1 Baron; suc half-bro 1979; *b* 11 June 1914; *Educ* Harrow; *m* 1939, Muriel Patricia, da of late Maxwell James Moore Boyle; 1 s, 1 da; *Heir* s, Hon Shaun Bagot; *Career* late Maj Indian Army; *Style*— The Rt Hon The Lord Bagot; 16 Barclay Road, London SW6; Tyn-y-Mynydd, nr Llithfaen, Gwynedd, N Wales

BAGOT, Hon (Charles Hugh) Shaun; s and h of 9 Baron Bagot, *qv*; *b* 23 Feb 1944; *Educ* Abbotsholme; *m* 16 July 1986, Mrs Sally A Stone, da of D G Blunden, of Farnham, Surrey; *Style*— The Hon Shaun Bagot; 16 Barclay Road, London SW6

BAGULEY, Maurice Grant; s of Capt William Albert Baguley (d 1947), of Hounslow, Middx, and Phylis Amy, *née* Laverne (d 1987); *b* 2 May 1926; *Educ* Spring Grove GS, Acton Tech Coll, Brighton Poly, City Univ (MSc); *m* 1, 20 Nov 1948, Ivy Ethel (d 1983), da of Reginald Arthur Coomber (d 1952), of Ashford, Middx; 1 da (Claire Susan b 1953); m 2, 19 Nov 1983, Julie Elizabeth, *née* Barker, wid of Alec John Shickle; *Career* sr design engr Woodall Ducklam Ltd 1948-53, ptnr Malcolm Glover and Ptnrs 1953-62, fndr Maurice Baguley and Ptnrs 1962 (ret 1973); bldg control conslt; FICE 1973, FIStructE 1953, MAmerSCE 1974, MConsE 1960; *Recreations* sailing, cruising, pianoforte; *Clubs* Naval; *Style*— Maurice Baguley, Esq

BAILEY, (Thomas) Alan; s of Thomas Dobson Bailey, of Ryde, IOW (d 1983), and Violet Vera, *née* Walker (d 1983); *b* 28 Oct 1928; *Educ* Maidstone; *m* 7 Aug 1950, Mary, da of Maj Percy Baldock, IA (d 1973); 1 s (Kimball b 1957); *Career* Nat Serv 1946-49; TA 1949-64 (Capt Intelligence Corps); various local govt appts (incl asst clerk Brentwood DC) 1950-62, under sec RICS 1962-69, chief exec World of Property Housing Tst (now Sanctuary Housing Assoc) 1969-79, chm Focus Gp of Cos 1969-79, md Andrews Gp of Cos 1979-84, chm and md ABS Gp of Cos 1979-; chm: Placemakers Luncheon Club 1971-, City Dialogue Ltd 1985-; former tstee Voluntary and Christian Serv and Phyllis Tst (consequent appts as dir: Help The Aged, Action Aid, and other charities); dir: Int Shakespeare Globe Centre 1981-, Social Devpts Ltd 1982-; tstee Cyril Wood Meml Tst 1980-; vis lectr Coll of Estate Mgmnt Univ of Reading; MCAM, MIPR, MInstM; *Books* How To Be A Property Developer (1988); *Recreations* drawing, painting, writing; *Clubs* Special Forces, Wig & Pen; *Style*— Alan Bailey, Esq; The Bridge House, Sible Hedingham, Essex; 7 Bradbrook House, Studio Place, London, SW1 (☎ 01 235 3397); 14 Kinnerton Place South, Kinnerton St, London, SW1X 8EH (☎ 01 245 6262, fax 01 235 3916)

BAILEY, Dr Alison George Selborne (Joe); s of George Frederick Selborne Bailey (d 1969), of Claytons, Bourne End, Bucks, and Mabel Yardley, *née* Guard (d 1950); *b* 19 July 1915; *Educ* Radley, Gonville and Caius Coll Cambridge (MA), St Bartholomews Hosp; *m* 15 May 1947, Christine Margeurite, da of Edward Joseph Law Delfosse, of Ashtons Road, Moor Park; 2 s (George Henry Selborne b 1953, William Edward Selborne b 1955), 2 da (Alison (Mrs Wilson) b 1949, Margaret (Mrs Jenkins) b 1950); *Career* house surgeon: St Bartholomew's Hosp 1942-43, Addenbrookes Hosp 1942; gen practice Bourne End 1943-86; consulting manipulative surgeon 1947-; memb: Bucks LMC 1946-86, Bucks FPC 1950-86, Windsor Med Soc 1943- (pres 1959-60), Wooburn PC 1946-69 (chm 1949-61); chm bd of govrs Wooburn Infants Primary and Secdy Schs 1946-74, pres Radleian Soc 1986-; coach: many coll boats Oxford and Cambridge, Oxford Univ Boat Race crew 1956 and 1964, Cambridge Univ for visit to Japan 1954, Brazil 1956; Freeman City of London, Liveryman Soc of Apothecaries 1943; LMSSA 1942, FRGCP 1981, FRCS (1988); *Recreations* riding, rowing; *Clubs* Hawks, Leander; *Style*— Dr AGS Bailey; Clayfield House, Wooburn, High Wycombe, Bucks HP10 0HR (☎ 06285 23203)

BAILEY, (Keith Cyril) Austin; s of J Austin Bailey (d 1944), of Swansea; *b* 8 July 1919; *Educ* Wycliffe Coll; *m* 1948, Joan, da of Capt John Thomas (d 1979), of Southampton; 1 s (Clive); *Career* served WWII Capt RACS (POW Singapore 1942; pres S Wales Far East POW Assoc); former chm Bailey Carpets, Bailey Carpets Int, Redlands Flooring Distributors (Bristol); former dep chm Tstee Savings Bank for Wales and Border Counties; High Sheriff W Glam 1979-80; chm Friends of the Welsh Cncl of Churches 1983-5; vice chm Swansea and Brecon Diocescan Bd of Fin; vice pres Wales Cncl for the Disabled; memb: Cncl Swansea Univ Coll, nat cncl Wholesale Floorcovering Distributors Assoc 1955-87, rep body and governing body of Church of Wales, IOD cncl for Wales, court of Univ of Wales; *Recreations* walking, countryside; *Clubs* City and County (Swansea); *Style*— K C Austin Bailey Esq; 20 Woodridge Court, Langland Bay, Swansea SA3 4TH (☎ (0792) 66836)

BAILEY, Sir Brian Harry; OBE (1976), JP (Somerset 1964), DL (Somerset 1988); s of Harry Bailey, and Lilian, *née* Pulfer; *b* 25 Mar 1923; *Educ* Lowestoft GS; *m* 1948, Nina Olive Sylvia Saunders; 2 da; *Career* WWII RAF; orgn offr SW District NALGO 1951-82, SW regnl sec TUC 1968-81; memb: Somerset CC 1966-84, SW Econ Planning Cncl 1969-79, MRC 1978-86, Business Educn Cncl 1980-84; chm SW RHA 1975-82, dir Western Orchestral Soc Ltd 1982-; chm: Health Educn Cncl 1983-87, TV South West 1980-; memb NHS Mgmnt Inquiry Team 1983-85, vice chm BBC Radio Br Advsy Cncl 1971-78, memb BBC West Regnl Advsy Cncl 1973-78, memb Advsy Ctee Severn DOE 1978-81, advsr Home Sec under Prevention of Terrorism (Temp Provisions) Act 1984, 1985-; tstee Euro Community Chamber Orch 1987-, regnl pres MENCAP 1984-; kt 1983; *Style*— Sir Brian Bailey, OBE, JP, DL; 32 Stonegallows, Taunton, Somerset (☎ 0823 461265)

BAILEY, The Hon Christopher Russell; TD; only s and h of 4 Baron Glanusk; *b* 18 Mar 1942; *Educ* Eton, Clare Coll Cambridge (BA); *m* 1974, Frances Elizabeth, da of Air Chief Marshal Sir Douglas Charles Lowe, GCB, DFC, AFC, *qv*; 1 s, 1 da; *Career* gen mangr Lumenition Ltd 1986-; *Style*— The Hon Christopher Bailey; 51 Chertsey Rd, Chobham, Surrey (☎ (099 05) 6380)

BAILEY, Lady Daphne Magdalene; *née* Cadogan; da of 7 Earl Cadogan by his 1 w Primrose; *b* 23 Oct 1939; *m* 1961, David Malcolm Graham Bailey (b 24 Feb 1934), s of Ronald Graham Bailey, of 7 Lansdowne Crescent, W11; 2 s, 1 da; *Style*— Lady Daphne Bailey; The Manor House, Dry Sandford, Abingdon, Oxford (☎ Frilford Heath 390 834)

BAILEY, David Royston; s of William Bailey and Agnes, *née* Green; *b* 2 Jan 1938; *m* 1, 1960, Rosemary Bramble; m 2, 1967, Catherine Deneuve, the film actress; m 3, 1975 (m dis 1985), Marie Helvin, *qv*; m 4, 1986, Catherine Dyer; 1 s, 1 da; *Career* photographer; dir of commercials 1966-, dir and prodr of TV documentaries 1968- (titles include Beaton, Warhol, Visconti); memb Arts Cncl 1983-; retrospectives of his work at: Nat Portrait Gallery 1971, V & A Museum 1983, Int Centre of Photography NY 1984; FRPS, FSIAD; *Books* Box of Pinups (1964), Goodbye Baby and Amen (1969), Warhol (1974), Beady Minces (1974), Papua New Guinea (1975), Mixed Moments (1976), Trouble and Strife (1980), NW1 (1982), Black and White Memories (1983), Nudes 1981-84 (1984), Imagine (1985); *Recreations* photography, aviculture, travel; *Style*— David Bailey, Esq

BAILEY, Sir Derrick Thomas Louis; 3 Bt (UK 1919), of Cradock, Province of Cape of Good Hope, Union of South Africa, DFC; s of late Sir Abe Bailey, 1 Bt, KCMG; suc half-bro, Sir John Milner Bailey, 2 Bt (d 1946); *b* 15 August 1918; *Educ* Winchester, Christ Church Oxford; *m* 1, 1946, Katharine Nancy, da of Robert Stormonth Darling, of Kelso, Scotland; 4 s, 1 da; m 2, 1980, Mrs Jean Roscoe; *Heir* s, John Richard Bailey; *Career* Capt S African Air Force, formerly 2 Lt S African Irish; farmer; *Style*— Sir Derrick Bailey, Bt, DFC; De Poort, Colesberg, Cape, S Africa; Bluestones, Alderney, CI

BAILEY, His Honour Judge; Desmond Patrick; 3 s of Alfred John Bailey (d 1940), of Bowdon, Cheshire, and Ethel Ellis Johnson; *b* 6 May 1907; *Educ* Brighton Coll, Queens' Coll Cambridge; *Career* barr 1931, circuit judge 1965-79; *Style*— His Hon Judge Bailey; Chaseley, Bowdon, Altrincham, Cheshire WA14 4QG (☎ (061 928) 0059)

BAILEY, Air Vice-Marshal Dudley Graham (Bill); CB (1979), CBE (1970); *b* 12 Sept 1924; *m* 15 May 1948, Dorothy Barbara; 2 da (Deborah b 1956, Caroline b 1957); *Career* served RAF 1943-80; trained as pilot in Canada 1943-45; intelligence duties in Middle East 1946-48, Berlin Airlift No 47 Squadron 1949; Adj 50 Squadron and Flt Cdr 61 Squadron (Lincolns) 1950-52, exchange duties with USAF 1952-54 (B36 Aircraft), Flt Cdr 58 Squadron and OC 82 Squadron (Canberras) 1955-56, dept of operational requirements Air Ministry 1957-58, Army Staff Coll Camberley 1959, OC 57 (Victors) Squadron 1960-62, Wing Cdr Operations HQ Middle East Aden 1963-65, staff of Chief of Defence Staff 1965-66, deputy dir Air Plans MOD 1966-68, OC RAF Wildenrath 1968-70, sr personnel staff offr HQ Strike Command 1970-71, RCDS 1972, dir of personnel (RAF) 1973-74, sr air staff offr RAF Germany 1974-75, deputy cdr RAF Germany 1975-76, dir general of personal serv (RAF) MOD 1976-80; dep md and co sec The Services Sound and Vision Corp; (thin Clubs etc); *Clubs* RAF; *Style*— Air Vice-Marshal Bill Bailey, CB, CBE; Services Sound and Vision Corp, Gerrards Cross SL9 8TN (☎ 024 07 4461, ext 226)

BAILEY, Geoffrey Thomas; s of Thomas Henry Bailey (d 1947), of Preston, Lancs, and Mary Malvina, *née* Harrison (d 1950); *b* 29 June 1912; *Educ* Rossall, Royal Agric Coll, RMC Sandhurst; *m* 30 Sept 1939, Elsie Margaret, da of Harry Ramsden Maj Cripps (d 1935), of Shotley, Suffolk; 1 s (William b 1943), 1 da (Janet b 1944); *Career* serv WWII 1940-46 RTR: Asst Adj D and M Wing B Bonnington Camp, staff Capt 30 Corps HQ Hanover; chartered surveyor land agent, land agent and valuer Holland (Lincs) CC 1948-74, ret; churchwarden: St Mary's Church Frampton, St Michaels Church Frampton W; FRICS, MRAC; *Recreations* rugby, tennis, golf; *Clubs* Fylde, Norwich, Bath Rugby, Woodhall Spa, Boston Golf; *Style*— Geoffrey Bailey, Esq; Hall Alne Cottage, Frampton by Boston, Lincs PE20 1AB (☎ 0205 722259)

BAILEY, Glenda Adrianne; da of John Ernest Bailey, and Constance, *née* Groome; *b* 16 Nov 1958; *Educ* Noel Baker Sch Derby, Kingston Poly (BA); *Career* fashion forecasting Design Direction 1983-84, prodr (with Neville Brody) dummy magazine for IPC 1985; ed: Honey magazine 1986, Folio magazine 1987, Br Marie Claire 1988; *Style*— Miss Glenda Bailey; 2 Hatfields, London, SE1 9PG (☎ 01 261 5240, fax 261 5277, telex 915748 MAGDIVG)

BAILEY, Harry; s of Joseph Henry Lewis Bailey (d 1955), of Yorks, and Lily Groves (d 1953); *b* 28 Mar 1928; *Educ* Thorne GS, Rotherham Coll of Technol; *m* 1961, Sheila Margaret, da of Stanley Dance (d 1987), of Berks; 3 s (Lewis, David, Howard); *Career* RAF 1946-48, fitter 2 Engines; tech asst Pilkington Bros Ltd 1944-46 (devpt engr 1948-52), mech engr Burmah Oil Co Ltd 1952-60, construction supt Gulf Oil (GB)

Ltd 1961-68, dir and gen mangr Motherwell Bridge Nigeria Ltd 1969-71, sales mangr, (later sales dir and chief exec Singapore) Matthew Hall plc 1971-85; dir: Matthew Hall Engrg Sdn Bhd Kuala Lumpur 1981-85, Matthew Hall Engrg SE Asia PTE Ltd 1980-85, Matthew Hall Int Devpt Ltd London 1977-85; *Recreations* swimming, theatre, music; *Clubs* Les Ambassadeurs (London), Tanglin (Singapore), British (Singapore); *Style*— Harry Bailey, Esq; 19 Cookes Lane, Cheam Village, Sutton, Surrey SM3 8QG (☎ 01 644 6262); Shaw and Hatton International Ltd, 1 Chester St, London SW1X 7JD (☎ 01 235 2486, telex 8812154 HATTON G)

BAILEY, Jack Arthur; s of Horace Arthur Bailey, and Elsie Winifred Bailey; *b* 22 June 1930; *Educ* Christ's Hosp, Univ of Oxford; *m* 1957, Julianne Mary Squier; 1 s, 2 da; *Career* rugby football corr Sunday Telegraph 1962-74; sec MCC 1974-, sec Int Cricket Conf 1974-; *Style*— Jack Bailey Esq; 20 Elm Tree Rd, London NW8 (☎ 01 228 6246)

BAILEY, John Richard; s (by 1 m) and h of Sir Derrick Bailey, 3 Bt, DFC; *b* 11 June 1947; *Educ* Winchester, Christ's Coll Cambridge; *m* 1977, Philippa Jane, da of John Sherwin Mervyn Pearson Gregory, of Monnington-on-Wye, Herefords; 1 s, 1 da; *Style*— John Bailey Esq

BAILEY, Ven Jonathan Sansbury; s of Walter Eric Bailey, of Port Erin IOM, and Audrey Sansbury, *née* Keenan; *b* 24 Feb 1940; *Educ* Quarry Bank HS Liverpool, Trinity Coll Cambridge (MA); *m* 1965, Susan Mary, da of Maurice James Bennett-Jones (d 1980); 3 s (Mark, Colin, Howard); *Career* curate: Sutton Lancs 1965-68, Warrington 1968-71; warden Marrick Priory 1971-76, vicar Wetherby Yorks 1976-82, archdeacon Southend 1982-; *Style*— The Ven the Archdeacon of Southend; 136 Broomfield Rd, Chelmsford, Essex CM1 1RN (☎ 0245 258257)

BAILEY, Hon Mrs (Lucy Jane); *née* Hamilton-Russell; da of 10 Viscount Boyne, JP, DL; *b* 13 Sept 1961; *m* 1983 (m dis 1986), Patrick James Bailey, yst s of Sir Derrick Thomas Louis Bailey, 3 Bt, *qv*; *Style*— The Hon Mrs Bailey

BAILEY, Capt (Oswald) Nigel; OBE (1953); s of Lt-Col Frederick George Glyn Bailey (d 1952), and Lady Janet Lyle Bailey, *née* Mackay (d 1972); *b* 19 June 1913; *Educ* RNCs Dartmouth and Greenwich; *Career* joined RN as cadet 1927, specialised in Naval Aviation, served as Chief of Staff to C-in-C Channel 1961-62, rank of Cdre, ret as Capt 1963; *Recreations* fishing, shooting; *Clubs* White's, Institute of Directors; *Style*— Captain Nigel Bailey, OBE, RN; Lake House, Lake, Salisbury, Wilts SP4 7BP (☎ (0980) 22138 and 22752)

BAILEY, Dr Norman Stanley; s of Stanley Bailey (d 1986), and Agnes, *née* Gale; *b* 23 Mar 1933; *Educ* East Barnet GS Herts, Rhodes Univ SA (BMus), Vienna State Acad (Dip in Opera, Lieder, Oratorio); *m* 1, 21 Dec 1957 (m dis 1983), Doreen, da of late Leonard Simpson, of Kenya; 2 s (Brian Emeric b 1960, Richard Alan b 1967), 1 da (Catherine Noorah (Mrs Osbourne) b 1961); m 2, 25 July 1985, Kristine, da of Roman Anthony Ciesinski, of USA; *Career* prof of music RCM; princ baritone Sadlers Wells Opera 1967-71; regular engagements at world major opera houses and festivals incl: La Scala Milan, Royal Opera House Covent Gdn, Bayreuth Wagner Festival, Vienna State Opera, Met Opera NY, Paris Opera Edinburgh Festival, Hamburg State Opera; BBC TV performances: Falstaff, La Traviata, The Flying Dutchman, Macbeth; memb Baha'I world community; Hon memb RAM 1981, Hon DMUS Rhodes Univ S Africa 1986; *Recreations* chess, notaphily, golf, microcomputing; *Style*— Dr Norman Bailey; 84 Warham Rd, S Croydon, Surrey CR2 6LB (☎ 01 688 9742); c/o Music International, 13 Ardilaun Rd, Highbury, London N5 2QR (☎ 01 359 5183)

BAILEY, Patricia Lucy; da of Capt Robert Bailey (d 1986), of Blackpool, and Patricia Isobel, *née* Percival; *b* 24 Sept 1940; *Educ* Arnold HS for Girls, Univ of Sheffield (LLB), Univ of Manchester (Adv Dip); *Career* called to the Bar Middle Temple 1969; memb Br Fedn Univ Women Vegetarian Soc; former memb Community Health Cncl; *Recreations* church, languages, playing musical instruments, singing, computers, vegetarian cooking, gardening; *Style*— Miss Patricia Bailey; Hollins Chambers, 64a Bridge St, Manchester (☎ 061 834 3451, fax 061 835 2955)

BAILEY, Sir Richard John; CBE (1977); s of Philip Bailey, and Doris Margaret, *née* Freebody; *b* 8 July 1923; *Educ* Newcastle and Shrewsbury; *m* Marcia Rachel Cureton Webb; 1 s, 3 da; *Career* served RN 1942-46, Lt (Destroyers); joined Doulton Fine China 1946- (tech dir 1955-, md 1963-); chm Royal Doulton 1980- (md 1972-), chm Royal Crown Derby, dir Central TV, chm Business Initiative, dir West Midlands Industrial Development Assoc; memb council Keele Univ, chm school council Newcastle Under Lyme Sch; pres Stoke-on-Trent Repertory Theatre; chm Br Ceramic Manufacturers Federation 1973-47, pres Br Ceramic Soc 1980-81; FICeram, FRSA; kt 1984-; *Recreations* golfing, walking, gardening; *Style*— Sir Richard Bailey, CBE; Roy Doulton Ltd, Minton House, London Rd, Stoke-on-Trent ST4 7QD (☎ (0782) 49171, telex MINTON G 36502)

BAILEY, Robin; s of George Henry Bailey (d 1925), of Hucknall, Nottingham, and Thirza Ann Mettam (d 1979); *b* 5 Oct 1919; *Educ* Henry Mellish Sch Nottingham; *m* 6 Sept 1941, Patricia Mary, da of William Oliver Weekes; 3 s (Nicholas, Simon, Justin); *Career* WWII 1940-44, Lieut RASC; actor; London appearances incl: Othello 1947, The Rivals 1948, Love in Albania 1949, The Cocktail Party 1950, Pygmalion 1951, A Severed Head 1964, Quartermaine's Terms 1981, Camelot 1982, Beethoven's Tenth 1983; NT 1978-88: Volpone, The Country Wife, The Cherry Orchard, Macbeth, For Services Rendered, When We Are Married, Rough Crossing, Mrs Warren's Profession, Six Characters in Search of an Author, Fathers and Sons, TV incl: Bleak House, Potter, Rumpole of the Bailey; *Clubs* Garrick, MCC; *Style*— Robin Bailey, Esq; 130 Merton Rd, London SW18 5SP (☎ 01 874 8571)

BAILEY, Ronald William; CMG (1961); s of William S Bailey, of Southampton (d 1956); *b* 14 June 1917; *Educ* King Edward VI Sch Southampton, Trinity Hall Cambridge; *m* 1946, Joan Hassall, da of Albert E Gray, JP (d 1959), of Stoke-on-Trent; 1 s, 1 da; *Career* foreign serv 1939-75; ambass: Bolivia 1967-71, Morocco 1971-75; pres Soc for the Protection of Animals in N Africa, vice-pres British-Moroccan Soc; *Books* Records of Oman 1867-1947 (8 vols 1988); *Recreations* gardening; *Clubs* Oriental; *Style*— Ronald Bailey, Esq, CMG; Redwood, Tennyson's Lane, Haslemere, Surrey GU27 3AF (☎ 0428 2800)

BAILEY, Dr (Theodore Robert) Simon; s of Herbert Wheatcroft Bailey, of Shepshed, Leics, and Norah Violet, *née* Roberts; *b* 20 Dec 1943; *Educ* King Edward VII GS Coalville Leics, UCL (BSc), UCH Med Sch (MB BS); *m* 26 July 1975, Elizabeth Frances, da of John Harper, OBE, of Oakfield, Salwick, Preston, Lancs; 2 s (Jonathan b 1978, Timothy b 1981); *Career* GP 1973-, sr MO Newmarket Races, clinical teacher faculty medicine Cambridge Univ, organiser W Suffolk GP Trg Scheme, chm Cambridge Med Answering Serv; MRCGP 1976; *Style*— Dr Simon Bailey; Lincoln Lodge, Newmarket, Suffolk CB8 7AB (☎ 0638 663 792); Orchard Surgery, Newmarket, Suffolk CB8 8NU (☎ 0638 663 322)

BAILEY, Sir Stanley Ernest; CBE (1980), QPM (1975), DL (1986); s of John William Bailey (d 1962), of London, and Florence Mary, *née* Hibberd (d 1945); *b* 30 Sept 1926; *Educ* Lyulph Stanley Sch Camden Town London; *m* 27 March 1954, Marguerita Dorothea (Rita), da of George Whitbread (d 1963), of London; *Career* Met Police 1947-66 supt, asst chief constable Staffs Police 1966-70 (dep chief ocnstable 1973-75), dir police res Home Off 1970-72, chief constable Northumbria Police 1965-; regnl police cdr (designate) no 2 Home Def Region, memb steering ctee of Standing Conf on Crime Prevention 1984-, vice pres Assoc Chief Police Offrs England Wales & NI 1984-85, pres ACPO 1985-86; IACP: memb exec ctee 1985-, chm advsy ctee on int policy; chm first Int Police Conf and Exhibition London 1987; memb: INTERPOL 1985-88, organising ctee IPEC 1988; vice-chm Crime Concern 1988-; author of various articles in police jls on specialist subjects incl: crime prevention, intruder alarms, mgmnt and research; lectr and advsr on crime prevention, community policing and modern police mgmnt in: USA, NZ, Italy, Denmark, France, Germany, Thailand, Taiwan, Switzerland; OStJ 1981; Freeman City of London 1988; CBIM 1987; kt 1986; *Books* Articles in various police journals on specialist subjects; *Recreations* gardening, travel; *Clubs* Reform; *Style*— Sir Stanley Bailey, CBE, QPM, DL; Northumbria Police HQ, Ponteland, Newcastle-upon-Tyne NE20 0BL (☎ 0661 72555)

BAILEY, Stella, Lady; Stella Mary; *née* Chiappini; da of late Charles Chiappini, of 2 Stephen Street, Cape Town, S Africa; *m* 1945, as his 2 wife, Sir John Milner Bailey, 2 Bt (d 1946); *Style*— Stella, Lady Bailey; 123 Kloof Nek Road, Cape Town, South Africa

BAILEY, Terence Michael; s of Thomas Sturman Bailey, and Margaret Hilda, *née* Wright; *b* 20 Oct 1946; *Educ* Kettering GS, Lanchester Poly Coventry (BA); *m* 1, 21 Oct 1972 (m dis), Penelope Ann, da of Geoffrey Lever Butler; 1 s (Tobin b 1976); m 2, 20 July 1985, Susan Jane, da of Frederick Peter Runacres; 2 s (Tim b 1986, Christopher b 1987); *Career* slr to Corby Devpt Corpn 1972-73; ptnr Toller Hales & Collcutt Northamptonshire 1973-; *Recreations* skiing, gardening, keep-fit, reading, music; *Clubs* Northants Law Soc, Kettering GC, RHS; *Style*— Terence M Bailey, Esq; Yew Tree Farm House, Little Oakley, Corby, Northants (☎ 0536 742233); 53-57 High Street, Corby, Northants (☎ 0536 67341, fax 0536 400058, telex 341861)

BAILIE, Rt Hon Robin John; PC (NI 1971); *b* 6 Mar 1937; *Educ* Queen's Univ Belfast; *m* 1961, Margaret Frances, da of Charles Boggs; 1 s, 3 da; *Career* slr Supreme Ct of Judicature NI 1961-, MP (NI) Newtownabbey 1969-72, min of commerce NI 1971-72; *Style*— The Rt Hon Robin Bailie, PC; 39a Malone Pk, Belfast (☎ 668085); 5 Thurloe Close, London SW7 (☎ 01 581 4898); Timbers Parkwall Lane, Lower Basildon, Berks

BAILLIE, Hon Alexander James; yr s of 3 Baron Burton (by his 1 w); *b* 1 July 1963; *Educ* Eton, Oxford; *Clubs* Landowne, BASC; *Style*— The Hon Alexander Baillie

BAILLIE, Hon Evan Michael Ronald; s and h of 3 Baron Burton by his 1 w Elizabeth; *b* 19 Mar 1949; *Educ* Harrow; *m* 1970, Lucinda, da of Robin Law, of Haverhill; 2 s, 1 da; *Clubs* Brooks's; *Style*— The Hon Evan Baillie; Greenhill House, Redcastle, Muir of Ord, Ross-shire (☎ 0463 870 420)

BAILLIE, Sir Gawaine George Hope; 7 Bt (UK 1823); s of Sir Adrian Baillie, 6 Bt (d 1947), and Hon Olive, *née* Paget, da of 1 and last Baron Queenborough, GBE, JP (gs of 1 Marq of Anglesey); *b* 8 Mar 1934; *Educ* Eton, Cambridge; *m* 1966, Lucile Margot, da of Hon Louis Beaubien (Senator), of Ottawa; 1 s, 1 da; *Heir* s, Adrian Louis Baillie b 26 March 1973; *Career* co dir; *Recreations* golf, tennis, skiing; *Clubs* St George's Golf, Berkshire Golf; *Style*— Sir Gawaine Baillie, Bt; Freechase, Warninglid, Sussex RH17 5SZ (☎ 044 485 296)

BAILLIE, Hon Georgina Frances; da of 3 Baron Burton by 1 w Elizabeth; *b* 11 May 1955; *Educ* West Heath Sevenoaks; *Recreations* fishing, skiing, tennis; *Style*— The Hon Georgina Baillie; Dochfour, Inverness

BAILLIE, Iain Cameron; s of David Brown Baillie (d 1976), and Agnes Wiseman, *née* Thomson; *b* 14 July 1931; *Educ* High Sch Glasgow, Univ of Glasgow (BSc), Fordham Law Sch NY (JD); *m* 1959, Joan Mary Christine, da of Dr Allan F Miller (d 1967), of Rickmansworth, Herts; 1 s; *Career* int lawyer, sr Euro ptnr Ladas & Parry (NY, Chicago, Los Angeles, London, Munich); admitted NY Bar and Fed Cts incl Supreme Ct (USA); chartered patent attorney, fell Inst of Trade Marks; *Books* Practical Management of Intellectual Property (1986), Licensing - A Practical Guide for the Businessman (1987); *Recreations* law, walking, model making; *Clubs* Caledonian; *Style*— Iain Baillie Esq; 20 Chester St, London SW1X 7BL (☎ 01 235 1975); Ladas and Parry, 52 High Holborn, London WC1V 6RR (☎ 01 242 5566, telex 264255 LAWLAN G)

BAILLIE, Prof John; s of Arthur Baillie (d 1979), of Glasgow, and Agnes (d 1981); *b* 7 Oct 1944; *Educ* Whitehill Sr Secdy Sch; *m* 3 June 1973, Annette, da of James Alexander; 1 s (Kenneth b 22 Feb 1979), 1 da (Nicola b 13 Oct 1975); *Career* CA; ptnr Peat Marwich McLintock (formerly Thomson McLintock) 1978; memb various ctees of ICA 1978-; Johnstone Smith chair of accountancy Glasgow Univ 1983-88, visiting prof of accountancy Heriot-Watt Univ 1988; Hon MA Glasgow Univ 1983; MICAS 1967; *Books* Systems of Profit Measurement (1985), Consolidated Accounts and The Seventh Directive (1985); ; *Recreations* keeping fit, reading, golf, music, hill walking; *Clubs* Western (Glasgow), RSAC; *Style*— Prof John Baillie; The Glen, Glencairn Rd, Kilmacolm, Renfrewshire, PA13 4PJ (☎ 050587 3254); 24 Blythswood Sq, Glasgow, G2 4QS (☎ 041 226 5511)

BAILLIE, Maj Hon Peter Charles; JP (Hants 1968); s of Brig Hon Evan Baillie, MC, TD (d 1941), of Ballindarroch, Scaniport, Inverness; bro of 3 Baron Burton; raised to the rank of a Baron's son 1964; *b* 26 June 1927; *Educ* Eton; *m* 15 Nov 1955, Jennifer Priscilla, yr da of Harold Newgass, GC (d 1984), of Winterbourn, Dorset; 4 da; *Career* served with Life Gds 1945-60, ret Maj; *Recreations* deer shooting; *Style*— Maj The Hon Peter Baillie, JP; Wootton Hall, New Milton, Hants (☎ 0425 613722)

BAILLIE, Hon Philippa Ursula Maud; da of 3 Baron Burton by 1 w Elizabeth; *b* 30 August 1951; *Educ* West Heath Sevenoaks; *Recreations* riding; *Style*— The Hon Philippa Baillie; 9 Foxmore St, SW11 (☎ 01 223 5277)

BAILLIEU, Hon David Clive Latham; yr s of 2 Baron Baillieu (d 1973); *b* 2 Nov 1952; *Educ* Radley, Cranfield S of Management (MBA 1984); *Career* slr 1979; *Recreations* hill-walking, opera and classical music, swimming, tennis; *Clubs* Lansdowne; *Style*— The Hon David Baillieu; 3a Redcliffe Rd, London SW10 9NR (☎ 01 352 1198)

BAILLIEU, Hon Edward Latham; 3 s of 1 Baron Baillieu, KBE, CMG (d 1967); *b* 17 Oct 1919; *Educ* Winchester, BNC Oxford (MA); *m* 1942, Betty Anne Jardine, da of Henry Taylor; 2 s, 1 da; *Career* served WWII Capt RHA (invalided out); ret stockbroker, ptnr Hoare Govett; chm: NM (UK) Ltd, Wogen Res RTZ 1967-77, ANZ Bank 1967-80, Royal Humane Soc; dep grand master of Utd Grand Lodge (Freemasons) 1982; *Recreations* shooting, golf; *Clubs* Boodle's, Leander, Melbourne, Swinley Forest GC, MCC; *Style—* The Hon Edward Baillieu; Tangle Copse, West Drive, Sunningdale, Berks (☎ 099 042301)

BAILLIEU, 3 Baron (UK 1953); James William Latham Baillieu; er s of 2 Baron Baillieu (d 1973), and his 1 w, Anne Bayliss, *née* Page; *b* 16 Nov 1950; *Educ* Radley, Monash Univ Melbourne (BEc); *m* 1, 1974 (m dis 1985), Cornelia, da of late William Ladd; 1 s; m 2, 1985, Clare, da of Peter Stephenson; *Heir* s, Hon Robert Latham Baillieu b 2 Feb 1979; *Career* 2 Lt Coldstream Gds 1970-73; Banque Nationale de Paris 1978-80, assoc dir Rothschild Australia Limited 1980; *Clubs* Boodle's, Australia (Melbourne); *Style—* The Rt Hon the Lord Baillieu; c/o Mutual Tst Pty Ltd, 360 Collins St, Melbourne, Victoria 3000, Australia

BAILLIEU, Maj the Hon Robert Latham; MBE (1945), TD; 2 s of 1 Baron Baillieu, KBE, CMG (d 1967); *b* 18 July 1917; *Educ* Winchester, Magdalen Coll Oxford (MA); *m* 1949, Delphine Mary, yr da of the late Edgar Hastings Dowler; 2 s, 2 da; *Career* Maj Middx Yeo WWII (despatches); slr 1954; vice chm Banque Belge Ltd and md Dawnay Day Ltd; md: Henry Ansbacher Co Ltd, Fraser Ansbacher Ltd; dir: C H Goldrei, Foucard & Son Ltd, View Forth Investmt Tst Ltd; ret; *Recreations* golf; *Clubs* Overseas Bankers Club; *Style—* Maj the Hon Robert Baillieu, MBE, TD; Abingdon Court, Abingdon Villas, London W8;

BAILWARD, Hon Mrs; Hon (Diana) Penelope Florence; *née* Sclater-Booth; eldest da of 3 Baron Basing (d 1969), and Mary Alice Erle, *née* Benson (d 1970); *b* 29 Jan 1925; *Educ* Downham Bishops Stortford; *m* 1946, James Tennant Bailward, s of Cdr Maurice William Bailward, RN (ret) (d 1958) of Penny's Hill Lodge, Ferndown, Dorset; 1 s (Christopher John b 1949), 1 da (Clare Penelope b 1947); *Career* served WWII Lance Corpl FANY; *Recreations* music (principally singing); *Style—* The Hon Mrs Bailward; Causeway House, Radipole, Weymouth, Dorset DT4 9RX (☎ 0305 783916)

BAILY, John Leslie; s of Leslie Baily (d 1976), and Margaret Baily, *née* Jesper; family have been Quakers for two centuries; *b* 1 August 1933; *Educ* Ackworth Sch, Northern Poly, Leeds Univ (Dip Arch, PhD); *m* 21 Nov 1959, Maureen May, da of Capt William Jenkins (d 1967); 2 s (Paul b 1963, Christopher b 1964); *Career* architect and historian; princ John Baily & Assocs; md In House Property Mgmnt Ltd, govr Ackworth Sch Pontefract, dir Bootham and The Mount Schs York; architect and clerk of works to Dean and Chapter Lincoln Cathedral; FFAS, ARIBA; FRSA; *Recreations* filling in forms; *Clubs* Yorkshire; *Style—* John Baily, Esq; 4 Minster Yard, Lincoln; Midland Bank, Parliament St, York; 8 Blake St, York YO1 2QG (☎ 0904 644021)

BAILY, Lady Sarah Dorothea; *née* Boyle; el da of Rear Adm 9 Earl of Glasgow, CB, DSC; *b* 3 June 1941; *m* 1962, John Edward Baily, elder s of late Brig Michael Henry Hamilton Baily, DSO; 2 s, 2 da; *Style—* Lady Sarah Baily; 27 Park Walk, London SW10

BAIN, Angus Hugh Uniacke; s of Dr George Alexander Bain (d 1981), of Sheffield, and Sheila Beatrice, *née* Uniacke (d 1988); *b* 31 July 1940; *Educ* Uppingham; *m* 1, 24 March 1965 (m dis 1972); m 2, 3 May 1973, Jane Verel, da of Wing Cdr Coleman AFC, of Malta; 1 s (Hugo Alastair Uniacke b 28 April 1974); *Career* memb Stock Exchange 1962, dir Strauss Turnbull 1967; *Recreations* golf, tennis, racing, cricket, football; *Clubs* City of London, Royal Wimbledon GC; *Style—* Angus Bain, Esq; 27 Titchwell Rd, London SW18 (☎ 01 874 9461); 3 Morgate Pl, London EC2R (☎ 01 638 5699, fax 01 588 1437/3372, telex 883201/883204)

BAIN, Prof George Sayers; s of George Alexander Bain, of 181 Leighton Ave, Winnipeg, Canada, and Margaret Ioleen, *née* Bamford (d 1988); *b* 24 Feb 1939; *Educ* Winnipeg State Sch System, Univ of Manitoba (BA, MA), Oxford Univ (DPhil); *m* 24 Aug 1962 (m dis 1987), Carol Lynne Ogden, da of Herbert Fyffe White (d 1986); 1 s (David Thomas b 1969), 1 da (Katharine Anne b 1967); *Career* Royal Canadian Reserve; Midshipman 1957-60, Sub-Lt 1960, Lt 1963, ret 1963; Soc Sci Res Cncl's industl rels res unit Warwick Univ: dep dir 1970-74, actg dir 1974, dir 1975-81; Warwick Univ: titular prof 1974-79, Pressed Steel Fisher prof of industl res 1979-, chm Sch of Industl and Business Studies 1983-; memb of res staff of Royal Cmmn on Trade Unions and Employers Assoc (the Donovan Cmmn) 1966-67, conslt to Nat Bd for Prices and Incomes 1967-69; memb mechanical engrg econ devpt ctee of the Nat Econ Devpt Off 1974-76, Ctee of Inquiry on Industl Democracy 1975-76, cncl econ and Social Res Cncl 1986-, Cncl for Mgmnt Educn and Devpt 1988-; chm Cncl of Univ Mgmnt Schs 1987-, frequent arbitrator/mediator for ACAS; *Books* Growth and Recognition (1967), The Growth of White Collar Unionism (1970), The Reform of Collective Bargaining at Plant and Company Union Growth and the Business Cycle (jtly, 1976), A Bibliography of British Industrial Relations (second edn 1985), Profiles of Union Growth (1980); Industrial Relations in Britian (ed 1983); *Style—* Prof George Bain; 6 Beauchamp Avenue, Leamington Spa, Warwicks CV32 5TA (☎ 0926 21678); School of Industrial and Business Studies, University of Warwick, Coventry CV4 7AL (☎ 0203 523923, fax 0203 461606, telex 317472)

BAIN, Neville Clifford; s of Charles Alexander Bain, of St Kilda, Dunedin, NZ, and Gertrude Mae, *née* Howe (d 1986); *b* 14 July 1940; *Educ* Kings High Sch, Dunedin NZ, Otago Univ Dunedin NZ, (MCom); *m* 18 Sept 1987, Anne Patricia; (1 s Peter John b 1965), 1 da (Susan Mary b 1963) from previous m, 1 step da (Kristina Knights b 1979); *Career* md gp confectionery Cadbury Schweppes plc; chm: Cadbury Ltd, Itnet Ltd, Cadbury Ireland plc, Cadbury Exports Int Ltd, Reading Scientific Servs Ltd; dir: Hindustan Cocoa Products, Cadbury Schweppes S Africa, Cadbury Schweppes Overseas Ltd; non-exec dir London Int Gp plc; CMA, FCA, ACIS, FBIM; *Recreations* squash, photography; *Style—* Neville C Bain, Esq; Inglewood House, 21 Ince Rd, Burwood Park, Walton on Thames, Surrey; Cadbury Schweppes plc, 1-4 Connaught Place, London W2 2EX (telex: 338011; car ☎ (0836) 210348)

BAIN, Sally Patricia; da of Hamish Mowat Bain, of 1249 Greenford Rd, Greenford, Middx, and Violet Joy, *née* Huxtable (d 1978); *Educ* St Catherine's Convent Middx, London Coll of Fashion; *Career* PR exec Barker Newlines 1977-78, journalist textile trade pubns 1978-80, Drapers Record 1980-83 (writer 1983-86, fashion ed 1986-88), ed DR The Fashion Business (formerly Drapers Record) 1988-; *Recreations* body style mgmnt, clay pigeon shooting, tennis; *Clubs* Club on the Park; *Style—* Miss Sally Bain; 100 Avenue Rd, London NW3 3TP (☎ 01 935 6611, fax 01 722 4920, telex 299973 ITPLNG)

BAIN, Lady Sophia Anne; *née* Crichton-Stuart; er da of 6 Marquess of Bute; *b* 27 Feb 1956; *m* 1979 (m dis 1988), Jimmy Bain, musician; 1 da (Samantha Isabella b 1981); *Style—* Lady Sophia Bain; Mount Stuart, Rothesay, Isle of Bute, Scotland

BAIN SMITH, Lady Corisande; da of 8 Earl of Tankerville (d 1971), of Chillingham, Northumberland, and Violet, Countess of Tankerville, JP, *née* Pallin; *b* 10 April 1938; *Educ* St James West Malvern, Oxford Univ; *m* 1963, Lt-Cdr Timothy Bain Smith, CPA, RN, s of Lt-Col George Stewart Bain Smith, GC (d 1972); 2 s (James b 1964, Charles b 1966); *Style—* Lady Corisande Bain Smith; Wickens Manor, Charing, Kent

BAINBRIDGE, Beryl; da of Richard Bainbridge, and Winifred, *née* Baines; *b* 21 Nov 1934; *Educ* Merchant Taylors' Sch Liverpool, Arts Educnl Schs Tring; *m* 1954 (m dis), Austin Davies; 1 s, 2 da; *Career* actress, writer, FRSL *Plays*: Tiptoe Through the Tulips (1976), The Warriors Return (1977), Its a Lovely Day Tomorrow (1977), Journal of Bridget Hitler (1981), Somewhere More Central (TV 1981), Evensong (TV 1986); *Books*: A Weekend with Claud (1967, revised edn 1981), Another Part of the Wood (1968, revised edn 1979), Harriet Said.... (1972), The Dressmaker (1973), The Bottle Factory Outing (1974, Guardian Fiction Award), Sweet William (1975, film 1980), A Quiet Life (1976), Injury Time (1977, Whitbread Award), Young Adolf (1978), Winter Garden (1980), English Journey (1984, TV series), Watson's Apology (1984), Mum and Mr Armitage (1985), Forever England (1986, TV series 1986), Filthy Lucre (1986); *Style—* Miss Beryl Bainbridge; 42 Albert St, London NW1 (☎ 01 387 3113)

BAINBRIDGE, Cyril; s of Arthur Herman Bainbridge (d 1966), and Edith, *née* Whitaker (d 1988); *b* 15 Nov 1928; *Educ* Negus Coll Bradford; *m* 20 Jan 1953, Barbara Hannah, da of Sydney Crook; 1 s (Christopher b 1958), 2 da (Susan b 1954, Amanda b 1958); *Career* Nat Serv Army 1947-49; author and journalist; reporter: provincial newspapers 1944-54, Press Association 1954-63; joined The Times 1963-; dep news ed 1967-69, regnl news ed 1969-77, managing news ed 1977-82, asst managing ed 1982-86, ed data mangr 1986-88, vice-pres 1977-78; pres Inst of Journalists 1978-79 (vice-pres 1977-78), Press Cncl 1980-, Nat Cncl for Trg Journalists 1983-87; (vice-president 1977-78, pres Inst of Journalists 1978-79; memb: Press Cncl 1980-, Nat Cncl for Trg Journalists 1983-87; *Books* The Brontes and Their Country (1978), Brass Triumphant (1980), North Yorkshire and North Humberside (1984) One Hundred Years of Journalism (ed 1984), Pavilions on the Sea (1986); *Recreations* reading, walking; *Style—* Cyril Bainbridge, Esq; 98 Mayfield Avenue, London NI2 (☎ 01 445 4178);

BAINES; *see*: Grenfell-Baines

BAINES, George Arthur; JP (Kent 1973); s of George Joseph Baines (d 1973), of Rockley Rd, Hammersmith, and Julia Ada, *née* Ryder; *b* 12 Sept 1926; *m* 25 June 1949, Maggie Rosemary, da of late William McDermid, of 1 Castle St, Swanscombe, Kent; 2 da (Margaret Anne (Dr Hellicar) b 17 Aug 1953, Brenda Alison (Mrs J Downes) b 25 May 1956); *Career* WWII RASC (serv France, Germany, Belguim, Holland, M East) 1944-48; construction engr 1948-51, insur indust 1952-77, life/marine claims conslt and casualty underwriter 1977-86; chm Gravesend Industl Life Offs Assoc 1968-70, hon tres N Kent Chartered Insur Inst 1972-76 (chm 1970-71); memb: Genealogical Soc, Heraldry Soc, Essex Family History Soc, Yorks Archaeological Soc; Freeman City of London, Liveryman Worshipful Co of Bowyers; memb Guild of Freemen of the City of London; fell Inst Public Loss Assessors, FLIA; memb: Life Underwriters Assoc of GB, Chartered Insur Inst; *Style—* George Baines, Esq, JP; Meadowside, Dover Castle Hill, nr Gravesend, Kent DA13 9EF

BAINES, Leslie Henry; OBE (1974); s of Henry Eaton Baines (d 1956), of Bedford; *b* 23 Sept 1909; *Educ* Bedford Sch, BNC Oxford (MA); *m* 1943, Irvina Addison Hope, da of Rev Frank Kent (d 1969), of Leeming, Yorks; 2 s (1 s decd), 1 da; *Career* slr 1934; clerk of the peace and memb IOW CC 1946-74; chm Health Educn Cncl 1979; *Style—* Leslie Baines, Esq, OBE; Blackthorn, Salisbury Rd, Shaftesbury, Dorset SP7 8NL (☎ 0747 4628)

BAINS, Lawrence Arthur; CBE (1983), DL (Gtr London 1978); s of late Arthur Bains, and Mabel, *née* Payn; *b* 11 May 1920; *Educ* Stationers' Co Sch; *m* 1954, Margaret, da of Sir William J Grimshaw (d 1958); 2 s, 1 da; *Career* chm: GLC 1977-78, Haringey Health Authority 1981-; dir: Bains Bros Ltd, Crowland Leasing Ltd; memb Lloyd's; *Clubs* City Livery; *Style—* Lawrence Bains, Esq, CBE, DL; Crowland Lodge, 100 Galley Lane, Arkley, Barnet, EN5 4AL (☎ 01 440 3499)

BAINS, Malcolm Arnold; JP (Norfolk Island), DL (Kent 1976); s of Herbert Bains, of Newcastle-upon-Tyne; *b* 12 Sept 1921; *Educ* Hymers Coll, Durham Univ (LLB); *m* 1, 1942 (m dis 1961), Winifred Agnes Davies; 3 s; m 2, 1968, Margaret Hunter; *Career* slr; clerk of Kent CC and clerk to Lieutenancy of Kent 1970-74; fell ANU and advsr to NSW govt Australia 1977-78; chm Local Govt Review Bd of Victoria 1978-79; head Norfolk Island Public Serv 1979-82; FRSA; *Books* The 'Bains' Report on Local Authority Mgmnt 1973; *Style—* Malcolm Bains Esq, JP, DL; Somers Cottage, Lamer Street, Meopham, Kent; PO Box 244, Norfolk Island, via Australia 2899

BAINTON, Lady Annabel Elizabeth Hélène; *née* Sutherland; da of Countess of Sutherland in her own right (who adopted the surname of Sutherland according to Scots law 1963) and her husb Charles Janson, DL; *b* 16 May 1952; *m* 29 Oct 1982, John Vernon Bainton, o s of late John Richard Bainton, of Point Piper, Sydney, Australia; 2 s (Edward b 1983, Nicholas John Vernon b 1988), 1 da (Alice b 1985); *Style—* Lady Annabel Bainton; 9 Eaton Sq, London SW1

BAINTON, Richard Leslie; s of Richard Bainton (d 1970); *b* 4 Mar 1923; *Educ* Christ Church Cathedral GS; *m* 1954, Ruth; 1 s, 3 da; *Career* md Portland Gp of Cos 1977- (exec dir 1969-); *Recreations* golf, youth and church work; *Clubs* Badgemore Golf; *Style—* Richard Bainton Esq; Apnagar, 139 Wilderness Rd, Earley, Berks (☎ Reading 0734 home: 873156; work: 866777)

BAIRD, Hon Alexander (David); s of 12 Earl of Kintore; *b* 21 April 1946; *Style—* The Hon Alexander Baird; 3 Osterley Crescent, Isleworth, Middx TW7 5LF (☎ 01 560 0274)

BAIRD, Sir David Charles; 5 Bt (UK 1809), of Newbyth, Haddingtonshire; s of William Arthur Baird, JP, DL (himself 2 s of Sir David Baird, 3 Bt, JP, DL, by his w Hon Ellen Stuart, 2 da and coheir of 12 Lord Blantyre). The present Bt's mother was Lady Hersey Conyngham, 3 da of 4 Marquess Conyngham; suc unc, Sir David Baird, 4 Bt, MVO, JP, DL, 1941. Sir David's ggg uncle, the Rt Hon Sir David Baird, 1 Bt, KCB, PC, was a distinguished soldier and himself gn of Sir James Baird, 2 Bt, of

Saughton; *b* 6 July 1912; *Educ* Eton, Cambridge; *Heir* bro, Robert Walter Stuart Baird b 5 March 1914; *m* 1, 1938 (m dis 1960), Maxine, sole child of Rupert Darrell, of NY; 1 s (Charles Suart Baird b 1939); m 2, 1960, Maria Florine Viscart; 1 da; *Style*— Sir David Baird, Bt; 52 High St, Kirkudbright, Scotland DG6

BAIRD, James Andrew Gardiner; s and h of Sir James Baird, 10 Bt, MC, of The Old Vicarage, Arreton, Isle of Wight and Mabel Annie Gill; *b* 2 May 1946; *Educ* Eton; *m* 1984, Jean Margaret, da of Brig Sir Ian Liddell Jardine, 4 Bt, OBE, MC (d 1982), of Coombe Place, Meonstoke, Southampton; *Recreations* shooting, fishing, photography; *Clubs* Boodles; *Style*— James Baird Esq; 68 Lessar Avenue, Clapham Common, London SW4 9HQ (☎ 01 673 2035)

BAIRD, Lt-Gen Sir James Parlane; KBE (1973); s of Rev David Baird, of Lochgoilhead, Argyllshire, and Sara Kathleen Black; *b* 12 May 1915; *Educ* Bathgate Acad, Edinburgh Univ (MD); *m* 1948, Anne Patricia, da of David Patrick Anderson, of Houghton, Arundel, Sussex; 1 s, 1 da; *Career* cmmnd RAMC 1939, cmdt and dir of studies Royal Army Med Coll 1971-73, dir-gen AMS 1973-77; med advsr Nat Advice Centre for Postgrad Educn 1977-84; QHP 1969; awarded Hilal-i-Quaid-i-Azam Pakistan; FRCP; FRCPEd; *Style*— Lt-Gen Sir James Baird, KBE; c/o Royal Bank of Scotland, Kirkland House, Whitehall, London SW1

BAIRD, Sir James Richard Gardiner; 10 Bt (NS 1695), MC; s of late Capt William Frank Gardiner Baird, 2 s of 8 Bt; suc unc, Maj Sir James Hozier Gardiner Baird, 9 Bt, MC, 1966; *b* 12 July 1913; *Educ* Eton, Univ Coll Oxford; *m* 1941, Mabel Ann Tempest, da of Algernon Gill, 2 s, 1 da; *Heir* s, James Andrew Gardiner Baird; *Career* formerly Capt Kent Yeo; hon tres: SSAFA Central London, The Ada Cole Meml Stables Ltd; *Style*— Sir James Baird, Bt, MC; The Old Vicarage, Arreton, Isle of Wight (☎ (0983) 525814)

BAIRD, (John) Stewart; s of John Baird (d 1971), and Louisa Jane Wright, *née* Stewart; *b* 8 June 1943; *Educ* Allan Glens Sch Glasgow, Glasgow Univ; *m* 22 March 1985, Lorna Jane, da of Andrew Bayne, of 7 James Place, Stanley, Perthshire; 1 s (Andrew b 14 Aug 1977), 3 da (Karen b 12 May 1969, Emma b 12 Nov 1972, Amanda b 1 Jan 1977); *Career* Pannell Kerr Forster: apprentice Glasgow 1962-67, audit sr Liberia 1967-68, ptnr Gambia 1968-72, ptnr Sierra Leone 1972-85, ptnr London 1985-87, managing ptnr London 1987-; memb: IOD, Walton Heath GC, Kingswood GC; Freeman City of London 1987, Liveryman Worshipful Co of Loriners 1987; MICAS 1967-, memb Inst of CAs of Ghana 1977-; Royal Order of the Polar Star Sweden, 1985; *Recreations* golf, reading; *Clubs* Caledonian; *Style*— Stewart Baird, Esq; Glenshee, 10 Warren Lodge Drive, Kingswood, Surrey, KT20 6QN (☎ 0737 832010); Pannell Kerr Forster, 78 Hatton Garden, London EC1N 8JA (☎ 01 831 7393, fax 01 405 6736, car tel 0836 210893, telex 295298)

BAIRD, Dr (Thomas) Terence; CB (1977); s of Ven Thomas Baird, Archdeacon of Derry (d 1967), of Strabane, Co Tyrone, and Hildegarde, *née*, Nolan (d 1919); *b* 31 May 1916; *Educ* Haileybury, Queen's Univ Belfast (MB BCh, BAO, DPH); *m* 1, 1940, Joan, da of Dr Douglas Edward Crosbie, MC (d 1952), of Londonderry; 2 da (Eileen, Sheelagh); m 2, 1982, Mary Wilson, da of Henry Claudius Powell (d 1966), of Manchester; *Career* RN 1940-46, Surgn Lt RNVR; served: N Atlantic, Indian Ocean, SW Pacific Ocean; med practitioner; dep co med offr Berks CC 1950-54, sr med offr Welsh Bd of Health 1956-62; chief surgn for Wales St John Ambulance Bde 1958-62, chief med offr Dept of Health and Social Servs NI 1972-78; landowner (30 acres); chm: NI Med Manpower Advsy Ctee, NI Advsy Ctee on Infant Mobility and Handicaps; CStJ 1988, FRCPI, FFCM, FFCMI, MRCPE; *Recreations* fishing, forestry; *Clubs* Carlton; *Style*— Dr Terence Baird, CB; 2 Kensington Rd, Belfast BT5 6NF (☎ 798020); Port-a-Chapel, Greencastle, Co Donegal (☎ 077 21038)

BAIRD, Vice Adm Sir Thomas Henry Eustace; KCB (1980), DL (Ayr and Arran 1982); s of Geoffrey Henry, and Helen Jane Baird; *b* 17 May 1924; *Educ* RNC Dartmouth; *m* 1953, Angela Florence Ann Paul, of Symington, Ayrshire; 1 s, 1 da; *Career* joined RN 1941, COS to C-in-C Naval Home Cmd 1976-77, Rear Adm 1976, dir-gen naval personal servs 1978-79, Vice Adm 1979, Flag Offr Scotland and NI, cdr N Sub Area E Atlantic and cdr Nore Sub Area Channel 1979-82, ret 1982; chm: Erskine Hosp Exec Ctee 1986,; Erskine Hospital Executive Committee 1986; *Recreations* shooting, fishing, golf, diy; *Clubs* Army & Navy, Prestwick Golf; *Style*— Vice Adm Sir Thomas Baird, KCB, DL; Craigrethill, Symington, Ayrshire (☎ 830339)

BAIRD, William Stanley; TD (1951); s of Brig-Gen Edward William David Baird, CBE (d 1956), of Kelloe, Duns, Berwicks, and Forse, Caithness, and his 1 wife Millicent Bessie (d 1936), 2 da of Maj-Gen Sir Stanley Clarke, GCVO, CMG; *b* 19 August 1903; *Educ* Eton, Edinburgh Acad, Christ Church Oxford (MA); *m* 1, 1944 (m dis 1964), Johanna Elizabeth, da of Barthold, Baron Mackay, of The Hague; m 2, 1968, Sigrid Wootton, da of John Jacob Egeland, of Durban; *Career* Lt Royal Hussars 1924-30, served with RA (TA) 1938-51 (Bt Col 1951); gen sec Victoria League in Scotland 1958-64; govr Gordonstoun Sch 1956-68; memb Royal Co of Archers (Queen's Bodyguard in Scotland); DL Caithness 1946-68; *Clubs* New (Edinburgh), Country (Durban); *Style*— William Baird Esq, TD; 11 Nuttall Gdns, Durban, S Africa (☎ 337357)

BAIRSTO, Air Marshal Sir Peter Edward; KBE (1981, CBE 1973), CB (1980), AFC (1957); s of late Arthur Bairsto, and Beatrice, *née* Lewis; *b* 3 August 1926; *Educ* Rhyl GS; *m* 1947, Kathleen, *née* Clarbour; 2 s, 1 da; *Career* RN 1944-46, RAF 1946-84; ret Air Marshal; mil aviation advsr Ferranti Scottish Gp 1984-, vice chm (Air) Highland TA & VRA 1984-, HM cmmr Queen Victoria Sch Dunblane 1984-; memb: Scottish Sports Cncl 1985-, cncl RAF Benevolent Fund 1985-, Scottish Air Cadet Cncl 1988-; CBIM; *Recreations* gardening, shooting, fishing, golf; *Clubs* RAF, New (Edinburgh), New (Golf) St Andrews, Royal and Ancient Golf,; *Style*— Air Marshal Sir Peter Bairsto, KBE, CB, AFC; Lucklaw House, Logie, by Cupar, Fife (☎ 0334 870546)

BAIRSTOW, Maria Elizabeth Jane; *née* Frank; da of Sir Robert John Frank (d 1987), of Ruscombe End, Waltham St Lawrence, Berks, and Angela Elizabeth, *née* Cayley; *b* 26 Jan 1952; *Educ* Hampden House Sch, Great Missenden Bucks; *m* 13 Sept 1975, Vivian Murray Bairstow, s of Alan Murray Bairstow, of 34 Manor Way, Egham, Surrey; 1 s (George b 1987), 1 da (Katharine b 1982); *Career* slr Rooks Rider Egham Surrey; involved with local C of C and Church govr Manorscroft Sch Egham; memb Law Soc 1981; *Recreations* family, dramatic society, squash; *Clubs* Wentworth GC; *Style*— Mrs Maria Bairstow; Englewick, Englefield Green, Surrey TW20 0NX (☎ 0784 436645); Milton House, 27 Station Rd, Egham, Surrey TW20 9LD (☎ 0784 436121/432277/431115, fax 0784 439659, telex 8814 225)

BAKER *see also*: Arnold-Baker, Sherston-Baker

BAKER, Andrew Joseph; s of Joseph Lawley Baker, FCA (d 1980), and Mary, *née* Haffner; *b* 4 August 1943; *Educ* Greenmore Coll; *m* 1970, Hilary Julia, da of John E Jones, of Coventry; 2 da (Joanne Emma b 1971, Caroline Julia b 1973); *Career* timber importing and sales dir Cox Long Ltd 1985; *Recreations* golf; *Style*— Andrew J Baker, Esq; Woodreeves, Wood Lane, Uttoxeter, Staffordshire ST14 8BE (☎ Uttoxeter 3533); Cox Long Ltd, Rickerscote Road, Stafford ST17 9EX (telex: 36430)

BAKER, Anthony Castelli; LVO (1980), MBE (1975); s of Alfred Guy Baker (d 1956), Wing Cdr RAFVR, and Luciana Maria Lorenzo Baker, *née* Castelli Spinola; *b* 27 Dec 1921; *Educ* Merchant Taylors's Sch; *Career* munitions worker 1940-41, RAFVR 1941-46; served: UK, ME, Italy; Flt Lt; Dip Serv 1946-81; served Rome and Paris 1946-50; third sec: Prague 1951, Hamburg 1953, Milan 1954; third (later second) sec Athens 1959, Beirut 1963, first sec: Cairo 1965, Naples 1968, Turin 1970, first sec (commercial) Calcutta 1972, consul Montreal 1975, first sec (commercial) Port of Spain 1976, consul Genoa 1979-81, ret 1981; Order of Merit Italy 1980; *Recreations* travelling, watching cricket, jazz music; *Clubs* MCC, RAF, Gloucestershire CCC; *Style*— Anthony Baker,Esq; Box 91, 17100 La Bisbal, Girona, Spain (☎ (72) 490438); c/o 2/44 Elsworthy Road, London NW3 3BU

BAKER, Anthony James Morton; s of Harris James Morton Baker (d 1960), of N Barningham, Norfolk, and Cicely Margaret, *née* Howgate (d 1986); *b* 30 Jan 1932; *Educ* Greshams Sch Holt, Emmanuel Coll Cambridge (MA, LLM); *m* 19 July 1958, Vivienne Marguerite, da of Alexander Barclay Loggie MBE (d 1967); 1 s (Malcolm b 1961) 1 da (Katherine (Mrs McGoldrick) b 1963); *Career* Nat Serv 2 Lt RA 1951-52; TA: Lt RA 1952-54, Lt Norfolk Yeo 1954-55, Lt RA 1955-58, Capt RA 1958-60; slr 1958; ptnr: Walters and Hart 1960-72, Walters Vandercom and Hart 1972-78, Walters Feadgate 1978-87; sr ptnr: Walters Feadgate 1988, Feadgate Fielder 1988-; pres: Old Greshamian Club 1985-87, Bucks Co Hockey Assoc 1981-84, memb cncl Hockey Assoc 1980-87; memb Law Soc; *Recreations* mens hockey, golf, reading; *Clubs* Beaconsfield GC, Sheringham GC; *Style*— Anthony Baker, Esq; 15 Cosway St, London NW1 5NR (☎ 01 723 9601); The Old Farm, West Runton, Cromer, Norfolk NR27 9QJ; 9 Queen Anne St, London W1M 0BQ (☎ 01 637 5181, fax 01 637 4098, telex 23578)

BAKER, Caroline Christian; da of Maj Hugh Armitage Baker, MC (d 1972), of Risence, Argentina, and Nettie Christian, *née* Cook; *b* 8 Jan 1943; *Educ* Northlands Buenos Aires; 1 da (Elodene Baker Murphy b 1984); *Career* asst to Shirley Conran at the Observer 1966-68, fashion ed Nova Magazine 1968-76, freelance fashion contributor Vogue Magazine 1976, fashion ed Cosmopolitan 1980-83, fashion ed Sunday Times 1987-; *Recreations* swimming, tennis, painting, writing; *Style*— Ms Caroline Baker; 111 Aylmer Rd, London; Sunday Times, New International, 1 Pennington St, Wapping, London (☎ 01 782 7183)

BAKER, Cecil John; s of Frederick William Baker (d 1944), and Mildred Beatrice, *née* Palmer (d 1965); *b* 2 Sept 1915; *Educ* Whitgift Sch, (LLB, BSc); *m* 1, 1942 (m dis 1965), Kathleen Cecilia Henning; 1 s (John Howard); m 2, 1971, Joan Beatrice, da of Henry Thomas Barnes (d 1950), of Farnborough, Kent; 1 da (Amanda Claire b 7 Nov 1971); *Career* actuary; chm: Alliance & Leicester Bldg Soc 1985- (chm Alliance Bldg Soc 1981-85, dir 1970-), Hunting Gate Gp Ltd 1980- (dir 1978-); dir Abbey Life Gp plc 1965-88; FIA, ACII; *Recreations* golf; *Clubs* Savile; *Style*— Cecil Baker, Esq; 73 Brook St, London W1Y 1YE (☎ 01 935 8632)

BAKER, Christopher James; s of James Alfred Baker, and Alice Marjorie Baker, *née* Yeomans; *b* 5 Nov 1951; *Educ* Dulwich, Christ's Coll Cambridge (MA); *m* 27 March 1978, Anne Elizabeth Sylvia, da of Francis George James Morris, of 172 Oxbridge Lane, Stockton-on-Tees; 2 s (James b 1981, Francis, b 1985), 2 da (Amy b 1983, Hannah b 1988); *Career* principal HM Treasy 1973-80; banker: Morgan Grenfell & Co Ltd 1981-83, Hill Samuel Bank Ltd 1983-; dir Hill Samuel Bank Ltd 1987-; *Recreations* walking, motoring, photography; *Style*— Christopher J Baker, Esq; 25 Kidbrooke Gardens, London SE3 0PD (☎ 01 305 1315); 100 Wood St, London EC2P 2AJ (☎ 01 628 8011)

BAKER, Christopher Paul; s of Roland Midelton Baker (d 1949), and Hilda May, *née* Paul (d 1968), of Clifton; *b* 31 Oct 1925; *Educ* Marlborough; *m* 1956, Jane, da of Maj-Gen Sir Charles Dunphie, CB, CBE, DSO, of Wincanton, *qv*; 2 s, 1 da; *Career* Capt Reconnaissance Corps 1944-47; insur broker (Lloyd's); dep chm Mid Southern Water Co; dep chm Cncl of the Water Co (Pension Fund) Tstee Co, former dir Glanvill Enthoven & Co Ltd and subsidiary cos; dep chm: Mid Southern Water Co ; *Recreations* gardening, steam trains, preservation of the Book of Common Prayer; *Clubs* City of London; *Style*— Christopher Baker, Esq; Broad Oak House, Odiham, Hants RG25 1AH (☎ 025 671 2482)

BAKER, Rev (Walter) Donald; s of Archibald Baker (d 1946), of Birkenhead, and Edith Alice, *née* Barber (d 1942); *b* 29 July 1906; *Educ* St Aidan's Coll; *m* 31 Aug 1934, Dorothea Frances, da of Harper Marrs (d 1944); 1 s (Ronald Duncan b 7 Sept 1935); *Career* officiating chaplain: RAF Hockering 1948, RAF Coltishall 1952, RAF Digby 1956; hon chaplain ATC 1965; organist and choirmaster: West Church Ballymena 1928, Portrush Parish Church 1932, Lanark Parish Church 1935; rector: Elsing with Bylangh and Little Hantsbois 1947, Lamas with Scottow 1950, vicar Old Ford London 1958, rector Hanwell London 1964, vicar St Stephen Upper Holloway 1969, conductor Wenfield Singers 1965, princ Victoria Coll of Music 1988; pres Lincoln Diocesan Guild of Bellringers 1956; cncllr Mitford and Lannditch RDC; life govr Royal Hosp and Home for Incurables Putney; Freeman City of London 1961, Liveryman Worshipful Co of Musicians 1968 (Almoner 1988); FRSA; *Books* Organ and Choral Aspects and Prospects (contrib 1958); *Clubs* City Livery; *Style*— The Rev Donald Baker; 8 Bishop St, London N1 (☎ 01 359 3498); St James Garlickythe, Garlick Hill, London EC4 (☎ 01 236 1719)

BAKER, His Honour Judge Geoffrey; QC (1970); er s of Sidney Baker (d 1960), of Bradford, and Cecilia Baker; *b* 5 April 1925; *Educ* Bradford GS, Leeds Univ; *m* 1948, Sheila, da of M Hill, of Leeds; 2 s, 1 da; *Career* barr 1947; rec: Pontefract 1967-71, Sunderland 1971-72, Crown Court 1972-78; circuit judge 1978-, pres Leeds Law Graduates Assoc, chm Leeds Univ convocation 1987; *Style*— His Honour Judge Geoffrey Baker, QC; c/o Courts Administrator, Bank House, Park Place, Leeds LS1 5QS

BAKER, George William; CBE (1977, OBE 1971), VRD (1952 and Clasp 1979); s of George William Baker (d 1956), and Lilian Turnbull, *née* Best (d 1976), of Priors Haven, Babbacombe, Devon; *b* 7 July 1917; *Educ* Chigwell Sch, Hertford Coll Oxford;

m 1942, Audrey Martha Elizabeth, da of Robert Day Barnes (d 1965); 2 da (Susan, Pamela m 5 Baron Coleridge, *qv*); *Career* Lt Cdr RNVE, London Div RNVR 1937-62, WWII RN 1939-45: N Atlantic, Norway, Med, S Atlantic, Indian Ocean, Persian Gulf, India, Ceylon, Singapore, Malaya, Java seas, American seaboard, Combined Ops 1942-45; colonial admin serv Tanganyika 1946-62; asst colonial attaché Washington 1957, def sec Tanganyika 1959, head of Tanganyika Govt Info Dept 1959-62, first sec and dir Br Info Servs Br High Cmmn Freetown 1962-65, served FCO 1965-69, first sec and head of chancery Br Embassy Kinshasa 1969-72, dep Br govt rep St Vincent and Grenada 1972-74, Br high cmmr to Papua New Guinea 1974-77; vice pres Royal African Soc 1970; chm: Heathfield Ctee Sussex Housing Assoc for the Aged 1979-84, Waldron Branch Wealden Cons Assoc 1983-84, E Sussex ctee VSO, Exeter Flotilla 1987-; ctee memb E Devon Luncheon Club, Devon branch Oxford Soc; memb Sidmouth Dramatic Soc, ed The Clockmakers' Times 1987-, conslt Operation Raleigh; chm E Devon Luncheon Club; Freeman: City of London 1980, Worshipful Co of Clockmakers 1981 (Liveryman 1984, Stewart 1987), memb Guild of Freeman; *Recreations* photography, cabinet making, fishing, sailing, cricket, flying, rugby union; *Clubs* MCC, SES, Exeter Flotilla, City of London; *Style*— George Baker Esq, CBE, VRD; Crosswinds, Coreway, Sidford, Sidmouth, Devon EX10 9SD (☎ 039 55 78845)

BAKER, Gordon Meldrum; s of Ralph Gordon Walter John Baker, of Burnham-on-Sea, Somerset, and Kathleen Margaret Henrietta, *née* Dawe; *b* 4 July 1941; *Educ* St Andrew's Sch Bridgwater, Univ of Bradford (MSc); *m* 8 April 1978, Sheila Mary, da of Edward Megson (d 1977); *Career* Lord Chllr's dept 1959-66; Dip Serv 1966: Cwlth Off 1966-68, FCO (formerly FO) 1968-69, Br High Cmm Lagos 1969-72, first sec W Africa dept FCO 1973-75, res clerk FCO 1974-75 and 1976-78, sabbatical Bradford Univ 1975-76, FCO 1976-78 (sci and technol, later maritime, aviation and environment depts), first sec head of chancery and HM consul Brasilia 1978-81, asst head Mexico and Central America dept FCO 1982-84, cnsllr FCO 1984, seconded to Br Aerospace plc 1984-86, cnsllr head of chancery and HM consul-gen Santiaigo 1986-; *Recreations* reading, walking, watching birds, amateur dramatics; *Style*— G M Baker, Esq; c/o FCO, King Charles St, London SW14 2AH

BAKER, Dr (John) Harry Edmund; s of late Joseph Elmer Grieff Baker, and Mary Irene Elizabeth, *née* Bolton; *b* 8 Jan 1949; *Educ* Epsom Coll, The Middx Hosp Med Sch, Univ of London (BSc, MB BS); *Career* Maj RAMC TA, specialist pool HQ AMS, Br Army Trauma Life Support Team, chief med advsr ACFA/CCFA, lately DADMS (TA) HQ W Mid Dist; lectr Univ of Nottingham Med Sch 1976-77, registrar Nat Hosp for Nervous Diseases 1977-80, sr registrar Nat Spinal Injuries Centre Stoke Manderville 1980-83, Midland Spinal Injury Centre Owestry 1983-85, conslt in rehabilitation med S Glamorgan Health Authy and Welsh Health Common Servs Authy 1985-; asst surgn in chief St John Ambulance Bde, chm professional panel St John Aero Med Servs, vice chm Wales and memb exec bd (UK) Br Assoc of Socs of Immediate Care, memb med bd of St John Ambulance (priory for Wales); memb cncl: Int Soc of Aeromedical Servs, Int Med Soc of Paraplegia, World Assoc of Emergency and Disaster Med; conslt advsr to Conjoint Ctee of the Voluntary Aid Socs on Cardiovascular Aspects and Long Term Complications of Paraplegia; advsr and lectr in mgmnt of spinal cord injury to: Fire Servs, NHS Trg Authy, Ambulance Serv, Med Equestrain Assoc, various equestrian bodies, RAC, MSA, various other motor sports orgns, mountain rescue team, RLSS; MRCP 1976, fell NY Acad Sci (USA) 1988; publications in med journals on immediate care and emergency handling of spinal cord injury, mangmnt of spinal injuries at accident sites, accident and disaster medicine, chapters in Management Of Mass Casualties (1980); *Style*— Dr Harry Baker; 5 Bridge Rd, Llandaff, Cardiff CF5 2PT (☎ 0222 731 908); Rookwood Hospital, Fairwater Rd, Llandaff, Cardiff CF5 2YN (☎ 0222 566 281, 0222 555 677, car tel 0836 586 445)

BAKER, Dr Harvey; s of Isaac Baker (d 1971), and Rose, *née* Rifkin (d 1982); *b* 19 August 1930; *Educ* Leeds Univ (MB ChB, MD); *m* 6 June 1960, Adrienne Dawn, da of Leonard Lever, of London; 1 s (Laurence b 1961), 2 da (Caroline b 1962, Marion b 1967); *Career* Capt RAMC served KAR Kenya 1955-57; conslt physician The London Hosp 1968-; pres St Johns Hosp Dermatological Soc 1973, conslt dermatologist 1968-; FRCP (London); *Books* Concise Text Book of Dermatology (1979), Clinical Dermatology (1989); *Recreations* music, literature; *Style*— Dr Harvey Baker; 16 Sheldon Ave, Highgate, London N6 4JT (☎ 01 340 5970); 152 Harley St, London W1 (☎ 01 935 8868, fax 01 224 2574)

BAKER, Maj-Gen Ian Helstrip; CBE (1977, MBE 1965); s of Henry Hubert Baker, and Mary Clare, *née* Coles; *b* 26 Nov 1927; *Educ* St Peter's Sch York, St Edmund Hall Oxford; *m* 1956, Susan Anne, da of Maj Henry Osmond Lock, of York House, Dorchester, Dorset; 2 s (1 decd), 1 da; *Career* cmmnd RA 1948, transfered to RTR 1955, Staff Coll 1959, DAAG HQ17 Gurkha Div Malaya 1960-62, OC Parachute Sqdn RAC 1963-65, instr Staff Coll and Brevet Lt-Col 1965, GSO1 Chiefs of Staff Ctee MOD 1966-67, CO 1 RTR 1967-69 and 1970, Col RTR 1970-71, Brig 1972, cdr 7 Armd Bde 1972-74, RCDS 1974, BGS HQ UKLF 1975-77, fell St Catharine's Coll Cambridge 1977, Maj-Gen 1978, asst chief of gen staff MOD 1978-80, GOC NE Dist 1980-82, Col Cmdt RTR 1981-86, sec UCL 1982-; *Recreations* skiing, sailing, outdoor pursuits; *Clubs* Athenaeum; *Style*— Maj-Gen Ian Baker, CBE; University College London (☎ 01 380 7000) Owen's Farm, Hook, Hants (☎ 025 6722524)

BAKER, Sir (Allan) Ivor; CBE (1944), JP (Cambridgeshire 1954), DL (Cambridgeshire 1973); s of late Allan Richard Baker (d 1942), of Easton-on-the-Hill, Stamford, Lincs; *b* 2 June 1908; *Educ* Bootham York, King's Coll Cambridge, Harvard; *m* 1935, Josephine, da of late A M Harley, KC, of Brantford, Ontario, Canada; 3 s, 1 da; *Career* chm Baker Perkins Hldgs 1944-75; kt 1972; *Style*— Sir Ivor Baker, CBE, JP, DL; 214 Thorpe Rd, Peterborough PE3 6LW (☎ 0733 262437)

BAKER, Dame Janet Abbott; DBE (1976, CBE 1970); da of Robert Abbott Baker and May, *née* Pollard; *b* 21 August 1933; *Educ* The Coll for Girls York; *m* 1957, James Keith Shelley; *Career* singer; memb Munster Tst; Hon DMus: Oxford, Cambridge, London, Birmingham, Hull, Lancaster, Leeds, Leicester, York; Hon fell St Anne's Coll Oxford, Hon DLitt Bradford, Hon LLD Aberdeen; holder of Hamburg Shakespeare Prize and Copenhagen Sonning Prize; FRSA; *Books* Full Circle (autobiography, 1982); *Style*— Dame Janet Baker, DBE; c/o Ibbs & Tillett Ltd, 18b Pindock Mews, London W9 2PY

BAKER, Jennifer Myrle; s of Colin Hamilton Macfie, (d 1981), and Beatrice Mary, *née* Hogg (d 1975); *b* 22 August 1949; *Educ* Whyteleafe Co GS for Girls, Mackie Acad Stonehaven, Inverness Royal Acad, Edinburgh Univ (BSc); *m* 4 Jan 1980, Martin John, s of (William) Stanley Baker, KBE (d 1976); 2 s (Liam b 1982, Alexander b 1986); *Career* asst gen mangr Hard Rock Cafe 1972-75; dir: Rock Biz Pix 1976-80, Martin Baker Enterprises Ltd 1984-, Hemisphere Prodns Ltd 1988-; freelance writer 1980- (several episodes for Storybook Int Hemisphere Prodns HTV Ltd); *Recreations* gardening, walking, reading; *Style*— Mrs Martin Baker; 61 Deacon Rd, Kingston, Surrey KT2 6LS; Hemisphere Prodns Ltd, 105 Mount St, London W1Y 5HE (☎ 01 493 5041, fax 01 499 3024)

BAKER, His Honour Judge; John Arnold Baker; DL (Surrey 1986); s of late William Sydney Baker, MC, and Hilda Dora, *née* Swiss; *b* 5 Nov 1925, Calcutta; *Educ* Plymouth Coll, Wellington Sch, Wadham Coll Oxford (MA, BCL); *m* 1954, (Edith Muriel) Joy Heward; 2 da; *Career* circuit judge 1973-, slr 1951, barr 1960; Parly candidate (Lib): Richmond 1959 and 1964, Dorking 1970, chm Lib Party exec 1969-70; pres Medico Legal Soc 1986-; *Recreations* music, boating; *Style*— His Honour Judge Baker, DL; 1 Rosemont Rd, Richmond, Surrey (☎ 01 940 6983)

BAKER, Rt Rev John Austin; *see*: Salisbury, Bishop of

BAKER, John Bellyse; s of Bellyse Baker (d 1947), of Highfields, Audlem, and Lilian, *née* Crosland (d 1971); *b* 29 Nov 1915; *Educ* Pownall Sch; *m* 4 Oct 1952, Josephine May, da of Maj Joseph Henry Hendersen (d 1958), of Rosemeath, Wilmslow; 1 s (John b 1956), 1 da (Charity b 1960); *Career* joined family business Parr Baker & Co Ltd (Manchester cotton mfrs) 1934 (dir 1944, chm 1947-); chm N Staffs Hunt Supporters Club; booklet: Highfields Audlem (1982); *Recreations* ornithology, painting, fox hunting; *Style*— John Baker, Esq; Highfields, Audlem, nr Market Drayton, Cheshire (☎ 0630 3825)

BAKER, His Honour Judge John Burkett; QC (1975); s of Philip Baker, and Grace Baker, of Finchley; *b* 17 Sept 1931; *Educ* Finchley Catholic GS, Univ Coll Exeter; *m* Margaret Mary Smeaton, of East Ham; 3 s, 7 da; *Career* barr 1957, circuit judge 1978-; *Recreations* marriage counselling; *Style*— His Hon Judge J. Burkett, QC; 43 The Ridgeway, Enfield, Middx

BAKER, John Derek; s of Bertie Baker (d 1972), of Walsall, and Edith Annie Doris Baker, *née* Sheldon; *b* 8 May 1982; *Educ* Queen Mary's GS Walsall ; *m* 1955, Mary Elizabeth, da of John Herbert Hancox (d 1970); 1 s (Richard b 1959), 2 da (Elizabeth b 1957, Catherine b 1966); *Career* chartered accountant, sr ptnr Baker & Co; fndr chm Walsall Gp CAs 1978; dir: West Bromwich Building Soc 1984-, Arbor Accounting Services Ltd, Arbor Estates Ltd, Walsall Unionist Hldgs Ltd, Unionist Buildings Ltd, WBBS (SRS) Ltd, Walsall Chamber of Commerce and Industry, Walsall Chamber of Commerce Engng Tning Centre Ltd, Arbor Financial Services Ltd; appointed magistrate Walsall Bench 1971 (chm 1987), chm Walsall Parish Church Restoration Appeal Ctee 1978-; memb of Worshipful Co of Chartered Accountants 1980, Freeman City of London; FCA; *Recreations* gardening & Bridge; *Style*— John D Baker, Esq; 16 Broadway, North Walsall, West Midlands WS1 2AN (☎ 21661)

BAKER, Prof John Hamilton; s of Kenneth Lee Vincent Baker, QPM, of Hintlesman, Suffolk, and Marjorie, *née* Bagshaw; *b* 10 April 1944; *Educ* King Edward VI GS Chelmsford, Univ Coll London (LLB, PhD), Cambridge Univ (MA, LLD); *m* 20 April 1968, Veronica Margaret, da of Rev William Stephen Lloyd, TD (d 1971), Vicar of Southsea and Berse Drelincourt, Denbighshire; 2 da (Alys b 1973, Anstice b 1978); *Career* barr Inner Temple 1966 (hon bencher 1988), lectr in Law Univ Coll London 1967-71 (asst lectr 1965-67), fell St Catharine's Coll Cambridge 1971-, lectr in legal history Inns of Ct Sch of Law 1973-78; Cambridge Univ: librarian Squire Law Library 1971-73, lectr 1973-83, jr proctor 1980-81, prof of eng legal history 1988- (reader 1983-88); visiting prof: Euro Univ Inst Florence 1979, Harvard Law Sch 1982, Yale Law Sch 1987, NY Univ Law Sch 1988-; jt literary dir Selden Soc 1981-; FRHistS 1980, FBA 1984; *Books* Introduction to English Legal History (1971, second edn 1979), The Reports of Sir John Spelman (1978), Manual of Law French (1979), The Order of Serjeants at Law (1984), English Legal Mss in the USA (1985), The Legal Profession and the Common Law (1987), Sources of English Legal History: Private Law to 1750 (with Milsom, 1987); *Style*— Prof John Baker; 75 Hurst Park Ave, Cambridge CB4 2AB (☎ 0223 622 51); St Catharine's Coll, Cambridge CB2 1RL (☎ 0223 338 317)

BAKER, Sir (Stanislaus) Joseph; CB (1947); s of Henry G Baker, of Liverpool; *b* 7 Mar 1898; *Educ* St Francis Xavier Sch, Liverpool Univ; *m* 1920, Eleonora (d 1981), da of S White; 1 da (and 1 da decd); *Career* receiver Met Police Dist and Courts 1952-60; kt 1958; *Style*— Sir Joseph Baker, CB; Camplehaye Hotel, Lamerton, Tavistock, Devon PL19 8QD

BAKER, Rt Hon Kenneth Wilfred; PC (1984), MP (C) Mole Valley 1983-; s of late Wilfred M Baker, OBE, of Twickenham, Middx, and Mrs Baker, *née* Harries; *b* 3 Nov 1934; *Educ* St Paul's, Magdalen Coll Oxford; *m* 1963, Mary Elizabeth, qv, da of William Gray Muir, of Edinburgh; 1 s, 2 da; *Career* industl conslt; MP (C): Acton 1968-70, St Marylebone 1970-1983; PPS to ldr of oppn 1974-75, min of state Indust (special responsibility info technol) 1981-84, min for Local Govt 1984-85, sec of DOE 1985-86, sec of State Educn and Science 1986-; memb exec 1922 Ctee 1975-81, chm Hansard Soc 1978-81; *Books* I Have No Gun But I Can Spit (1980), London Lines (1982), The Faber Book of English History in Verse (1988); *Style*— The Rt Hon Kenneth Baker, MP; House of Commons, London SW1A 0AA

BAKER, Mark Alexander Wyndham; s of Lt Cdr Alexander Arthur Wyndham Baker (d 1969), and Renée Gavrelle Stenson, *née* Macnaghten; *b* 19 June 1940; *Educ* Prince Edward Sch Salisbury Rhodesia, Univ Coll Of Rhodesia and Nyasaland (BA), Christ Church Oxford (BA, MA); *m* 30 July 1964, Meriel, da of Capt Edward Hugh Frederick Chetwynd-Talbot, MBE, of Milton Lilbourne, Pewsey, Wilts; 1 s (Alexander b 1968), 1 da (Miranda b 1970); *Career* UKAEA 1964-: various admin appts 1964-76, sec AERE Harwell 1976-78, gen sec AERE Harwell 1978-81, dir of personnel and admin Northern Div 1981-84, authy personnel offr 1984-86, authy sec 1986-; *Recreations* squash, bridge, walking, gardening, words; *Clubs* Utd Oxford and Cambridge, Antrobus Dining (Cheshire); *Style*— Mark Baker, Esq; The Old School, Fyfield, Abingdon OX13 5LR (☎ 0865 390724); UKAEA, 11 Charles II St, London SW1Y 4QP (☎ 01 930 5454 ext 495, telex 83135)

BAKER, Mary Elizabeth; da of William Gray Muir, WS (d 1959), of Edinburgh; *b* 5 Feb 1937; *Educ* St Mary's Wantage, St Andrew's Univ; *m* 1963, Kenneth Baker, MP, *qv*; 1 s, 2 da; *Career* teacher 1959-67, dir Thames TV 1975-, govr Bedford Coll 1980-85, chm London Tourist Bd 1980-83, dir: Avon Cosmetics Ltd 1981-, Barclays Bank UK Ltd 1983-88, Barclays Bank plc 1988-, Prudential Corpn plc 1988-, Freeman of the City of London 1980-; memb Womens' National Commission 1973-8; chm: Holiday Care Service 1986-, Thames/LWT Telethon Tst 1987-; fell Tourism Soc; govr

Westminster Sch 1982-; *Style*— Mrs Mary Baker; c/o The Secretary, Fifth Floor, 54 Lombard Street, EC3P 3AH

BAKER, Michael Glendrew; s of Wing Cdr A Stanley Baker, of Abbey Cottage, Turvey, Bedfordshire, and Audrey, *née* Laing; *b* 3 July 1947; *Educ* Bedford Modern Sch, Leicester Univ Manchester Business Sch (DipBA, PhD); *m* 1970 (m dis 1983); 2 s (Alexander b 1974, Thomas b 1978), 1 da (Lucinda b 1976); *Career* dir Kleinwort Benson Ltd 1985- (asst mangr, mangr, asst dir 1972-85); *Recreations* family, skiing, sailing; *Style*— Michael Baker; Kleinwort Benson Ltd, 20 Fenchurch St, London EC3P 3DB (☎ 01 956 5940)

BAKER, Prof Michael John; TD (1971); s of John Overend Baker (d 1960), of York, and Constance Dorothy Smith (d 1979); *b* 5 Nov 1935; *Educ* Worksop Coll, Gosforth and Harvey GS, Durham Univ (BA), London Univ (BSc) Harvard (Cert ITP, DBA); *m* 1959, Sheila, da of Miles Bell (d 1964), of Carlisle; 1 s (John), 2 da (Fiona, Anne); *Career* served in TA 1953-55, 2 Lt RA 1956-57, Lt 624 LAA Regt RA (TA) 1958-61, Capt City of London RF 1961-64, Capt PWO 1965-67; salesman Richard Thomas & Baldwins (Sales) Ltd 1958-64, lectr Hull & Medway COT's 1964-68, FME fell 1968-71, res assoc Harvard Business Sch 1969-71, prof Strathclyde Univ 1971-, dean Strathclyde Business Sch 1978-84 (dep princ 1984-); md: Baker Gordon (Business Res) Ltd 1973-, Westburn Publishers Ltd 1982-, Stoddard Sekers Int plc 1983-, Scottish Tport Gp 1987-; chm: Scottish Mktg Projects Ltd 1986, Inst of Mktg 1987; Secretary of State for Scotland's nominee Scottish Hosps Endowment Res Tst 1984-, memb Chief Scientist's Ctee SHHD 1985-; SCOTBEC 1973-85 (chm 1983-85), memb UGC business and mgmnt sub-ctee 1985-; FInstM, FCAM, FRSA, FScotVec; *Books* Marketing: An Introductory Text (1985, fourth edn), Marketing Mgmnt and Strategy (1985), Market Dvpt (1983), Marketing: Theory & Practice (second end 1983), Innovation: Technology, Policy & Diffusion (1979), Marketing New Industrial Products (1975), Organisational Buying Behaviour (1986) The Marketing Book (ed 1987); *Recreations* travel, gardening, DIY, sailing (Lurline III and Ornsay); *Clubs* Royal Overseas League; *Style*— Prof Michael Baker, TD; Westburn, Helensburgh, Scotland (☎ 0436 4686); Univ of Strathclyde, Glasgow G4 0RQ (☎ 041 5524400)

BAKER, His Hon Judge Michael John David; s of Ernest Bowden Baker (d 1979), and Dulcie, *née* Davies; *b* 17 April 1934; *Educ* Trinity Sch of John Whitgift, Bristol Univ (LLB); *m* 4 April 1958, Edna Harriet, da of John Herbert Lane (d 1950); 1 s (Matthew b 1963), 1 da (Amanda b 1961); *Career* Flying Offr RAF 1957-60; slr 1957, ptnr Glanvilles 1962-88, coroner S Hants 1973-88, rec Crown Ct 1980-88, circuit judge 1988; *Recreations* walking, swimming, tennis, theatre, photography; *Clubs* The Law Society, RAF; *Style*— His Hon Judge Michael Baker; The Drift, Park Crescent, Emsworth, Hampshire (☎ 0243 372 748)

BAKER, Michael Verdun; s of Albert Ernest Thomas Baker, of Rochford Way, Frinton-on-Sea, Essex, and Eva Louisa Florence, *née* Phillips; *b* 30 July 1942; *Educ* Caterham Sch; *m* 21 Sept 1963, Rita Ann, da of Walter James Marks, of 7 Kirkland Ave, Clayhall, Ilford, Essex; 2 da (Carolyn b 1967, Louise b 1970); *Career* insur official Alliance Assur Co Ltd 1959-63, O & M systems analyst Plessey Co 1963-66, sr conslt Coopers & Lybrand 1967-72; The Stock Exchange: talisman project dir 1972-78, settlement dir 1978-82, admin dir 1982-84, divnl dir settlement servs 1984-87, exec dir mkts 1987-(responsible for overall exec direction of the Int Stock Exchange's four mkts); memb: ISE Foreign Equity Mkt Ctee, ISE Domestic Equity Mkt Ctee, ISE Gilt Edged Mkt Ctee, ISE Traded Options Mkt Ctee, ISE Exec and Managing Bd, FIBV Settlement Task Force, Gp of Thirty Working Ctee; chm Securities Indust Exec Liaison Ctee; author of various booklets and brochures on O & M, clerical work mgmnt and Stock Exchange settlement; *Recreations* running, photography, travel, squash, record collecting; *Clubs* Bigbury GC; *Style*— Michael Baker, Esq; The International Stock Exchange, Old Broad St, London EC2N 1HP (☎ 01 588 2355)

BAKER, Nicholas Brian; MP (C) N Dorset 1979-; *b* 23 Nov 1938; *Educ* Clifton, Exeter Coll Oxford; *m* 1970, (Penelope) Carol, da of Maj Edward Nassau Nicolai d'Abo, of The Grange, Bexhill-on-Sea, Sussex; 1 s, 1 da; *Career* PPS to: Min State Armed Forces 1981 and Procurement 1983, Michael Heseltine sec of State for Def 1984-86, Lord Young of Graffham sec of State for Trade and Indust 1987-88; ptnr Frere Cholmeley Slrs 1973-; *Clubs* Blandford Constitutional, Wimborne Cons; *Style*— Nicholas Baker Esq, MP; House of Commons, London SW1A 0AA

BAKER, Paul Kenneth Hay; s of George Kenneth Baker (d 1976), of Beckenham, and Margaret Elizabeth Hay, *née* Greenaway; *b* 20 Feb 1948; *Educ* Eastbourne Coll; *Career* mangr Deloitte Haskins & Sells CAs 1967-78, dir accounting servs RAC 1978-83, fin dir Deinhard & Co Ltd Wine Shippers 1983-; memb Croydon Dist Soc of CAs; ctee memb London Philharmonic Soc, tres and chm designate Crystal Palace FC Vice President's club; ACA 1972, FCA 1979, FBIM 1980; *Clubs* RAC, Croydon Dining (pres), Kent CCC, Croydon Cons, Croham Hurst GC, RAC; *Style*— Paul Baker, Esq; Deinhard & Co Ltd, 29 Addington St, London SE1 TXT (☎ 01 261 1111, fax 01 261 9569, car telephone 0836 619 139, telex 918181)

BAKER, His Hon Judge Paul Vivian; QC (1972); er s of Vivian Cyril Baker, and Maud Lydia Baker; *b* 27 Mar 1923; *Educ* City of London Sch, Univ Coll Oxford; *m* 1957, Stella Paterson, da of late William Eadie; 1 s, 1 da; *Career* barr 1950, circuit judge (SE) 1983-; editor Law Quarterly Review 1971-87; Bencher Lincoln's Inn 1979-; *Clubs* Athenaeum, Authors; *Style*— His Hon Judge Paul Baker, QC; 9 Old Sq, Lincoln's Inn, London WC2A 3SR (☎ 01 242 2633); 27 Peaks Hill, Purley, Surrey CR2 3JG (☎ 01 660 5465)

BAKER, His Hon Judge; Peter Maxwell; QC (1974); s of Harold Baker (d 1971), and Rose Baker; *b* 26 Mar 1930; *Educ* King Edward VII Sch Sheffield, Exeter Coll Oxford; *m* 1954, Jacqueline Mary, da of William Marshall, of Sheffield; 3 da; *Career* barr 1956, Crown Court recorder 1972-83, circuit judge 1983-; *Recreations* owner yacht ('Susajo II', seamaster 30 TSDY); *Style*— His Hon Judge Baker, QC; 28 Snaithing Lane, Sheffield, S10 3LG; 2 Harcourt Buildings, Temple, London EC4Y 9DB (☎ 01 353 1394)

BAKER, Peter Portway; AFC (1957); s of Wing Cdr Alfred Guy Baker (d 1955), of Beaconsfield, Bucks, and Luciana Maria Lorenza, *née* Castelli; *b* 2 Sept 1925; *Educ* Merchant Taylors, St John's Coll Oxford; *Career* RAF: U/T Aircrew 1944, GD Offr (Pilot Offr) 1945, memb 201, 209 and 230 sqdns as pilot 1946-49, Central Flying Sch 1949, flying instr (Flt-Lt) 1949-52, Empire Test Pilots Sch 1953, testpilot A and AEE Boscombe Down 1954-56, tutor (Sqdn Ldr) Empire Test Pilots Sch 1957-59, voluntarily resigned 1959, test pilot Handley Page Ltd 1959 (test flying Dark Herald and Victor aircraft); joined BAC Weybridge 1962: test pilot for VC10 BAC 1-11 and Concorde aircraft, asst chief test pilot Concorde 1969, dep chief test pilot BA Filton Div 1980 (ret 1982); CAA Airworthiness Div 1982 (chief test pilot 1984-87, ret 1987), self employed aviation conslt and freelance commercial pilot 1987-; Queens commendation for Valuable Serv in the Air, RP Auston Meml Medal 1978; Liveryman Worshipful Co Air Pilots and Air Navigators 1971 (Freeman 1961-); memb; Royal Aeronautical Soc 1964, Soc of experimental Test Pilots 1965; *Recreations* walking, reading, aviation; *Clubs* RAF; *Style*— Peter Baker, Esq, AFC; 4 Cedar Ct, Grove Rd, Coombe Dingle, Bristol BS9 2RE (☎ 0272 685 950); Flat 2, 44 Elsworthy Rd, London NW3 3BU (☎ 01 722 4759)

BAKER, Richard Douglas James; OBE (1976), RD (1978); s of Albert Baker, and Jane Isobel Baker; *b* 15 June 1925; *Educ* Kilburn GS, Peterhouse Cambridge; *m* 1961, Margaret Celia Martin; 2 s; *Career* served WWII RN; broadcaster and author; BBC TV newsreader 1954-82; TV Newscaster of the Year (Radio Industs Club) 1972, 1974 and 1979; presenter: Omnibus (BBC 1) 1983, Start the Week (Radio 4) 1970-, Baker's Dozen (Radio 4) 1971-; Hon LLD Strathclyde 1979, Hon LLD Aberdeen 1982; FRSA, Hon FLCM; *Style*— Richard Baker, Esq, OBE; Hadley Lodge, 12 Watford Rd, Radlett, Herts (☎ 01 637 5541)

BAKER, Richard William Shelmerdine; s of Lt-col Charles Bradbeer Baker (d 1978), and Vera Margaret, *née* Shelmerdine; *b* 17 Dec 1933; *Educ* Buxton Coll; *m* 1 (m dis 1975), Teresa Mary Elizabeth, *née* Smith; 1 s (David b 22 Feb 1960), 1 da (Lisa b 31 July 1962); m 2, 30 May 1975, Vanda, da of Percy William Macey, of Redic House, Sutton Valence, Kent; *Career* Nat Serv 1952-54, cmmnd 2 Lt; transferred Army Emergencey Res 1955, Lt 1956, Actg Capt 1960; magmnt Marks and Spencer 1954060, rep Sun Life Assur Co of Canada 1960-72, sales dir and gp md Barbour Index Ltd 1972-79; sr vice-pres and gen mangr Sun Life Assur Co of Canada (memb sr advsy cncl for int ops), md Sun Life of Canada (UK) Ltd; chm: Sun Life of Canada Unit Mangrs Ltd, Sun Life of Canada Home Loans Ltd; govr Queen mary's Coll Basingstoke; dir Life Assur and Unit Tst Regulatory Orgn; pres: Canada-UK C of C, GB Wheelchair Basketball Assoc; MIOD; *Recreations* horse racing, golf, tennis, cricket, collecting antiques; *Clubs* Canada, East India, Devonshire Sports and Public Schools, MCC, Lord's Taverners; *Style*— Richard Baker, Esq; Wissenden Hse Oast, Bethersden, Kent TN26 3EL (☎ 023 382 352); 2 Fisher Hse, Hillside Park, Sunningdale, Berks SL5 9RP (☎ 0990 226 64); Sun Life of Canada, Basing View, Basingstoke, Hants RG21 2DZ (☎ 0256 841 414, fax 0256 460 067, car tel 0860 541 386, telex 858654)

BAKER, The Hon Mr Justice (Thomas) Scott Gillespie; QC (1978); s of Rt Hon Sir George Gillespie Baker, OBE (d 1984), and Jessie McCall, *née* Findlay (d 1983); *b* 10 Dec 1937; *Educ* Haileybury, Brasenose Coll Oxford; *m* 1973, Margaret Joy Strange; 2 s, 1 da; *Career* called to the Bar 1961, rec Crown Ct 1976-88, memb Warnock ctee 1982-84, bencher Middle Temple 1985, justice of the High Ct Family Div 1988-; *Recreations* golf, fishing; *Clubs* MCC; *Style*— The Hon Justice Mr Baker; Royal Courts of Justice, Strand, London WC2

BAKER, Stephen; OBE (1987); s of late Arthur Baker, and Nancy Baker; *b* 27 Mar 1926; *Educ* Epsom Coll, Clare Coll Cambridge; *m* 1950, Margaret Julia Wright; 1 s, 2 da; *Career* md Br Electricity Int 1978-, dir Davy Ashmore 1963, chm and chief exec Davy Utd Engrg, Ashmore Benson Pease Ltd and Loewy Robertson Engrg 1968, md Kearney & Trecker Ltd 1970; former chief indust advsr Dept of Trade; FIMechE; *Style*— Stephen Baker Esq, OBE; Beeley House, Beeley, Matlock, Derbys DE4 2NT

BAKER, Susan Mary; da of Lt Leo Kingsley Baker, DFC, RAF (d 1986), and Eileen Frida, *née* Brooks (d 1982); *b* 22 July 1930; *Educ* Stroud HS, Francis Holland Sch, RCM (ARCM); *m* 12 July 1958, William Bealby-Wright, s of George Edward Wright (d 1931; stage name George Bealby); 1 s (Edmund b 1962), 1 da (Sarah b 1960); *Career* violinist, mangr Barrow Poets 1960-; princ performances incl: UK festivals 1960s and 1970s, 4 tours in America 1969-71; one woman show Violins Fiddles and Follies 1976-princ performances incl: Edinburgh Int Festival, Brighton, Belfast; solo album Fiddles and Follies; memb Musicians Union; *Recreations* cooking, swimming; *Style*— Miss Susan Baker; 70 Parliament Hill, Hampstead, London NW3 2TJ (☎ 01 435 7817)

BAKER, Lady; Valerie Stirling Hamilton; da of late Maj Ian Lockhart; *m* 1946, Field Marshal Sir Geoffrey Harding Baker, GCB, CMG, CBE, MC (d 1980); 2 s, 1 da; *Style*— Lady Baker; Pond Hse, Wadhurst, Sussex (☎ 089 2883409)

BAKER, Wei Mei; *b* 2 May 1949; *Educ* Malaysian Schs; *m* 1975, Stephen Andrew Baker; *Career* fin dir Leopold Joseph & Sons Ltd 1985-, non-exec dir RLJ Fin Ltd 1986-, dir Leopold Joseph & Sons Ltd Guernsey 1988-; FCA; *Style*— Mrs Mei Baker; Hobbits Oast, Goodnestone, Faversham, Kent (☎ 0795 532 555); 31-45 Gresham Street, London Ec2V 7EA (☎ 01 588 2323, fax 01 726 0105, telex 886454-5)

BAKER, Willfred Harold Kerton; TD; s of late Walter H Baker, of Portland, Dorset; *b* 6 Jan 1920; *Educ* Hardye's Sch, Edinburgh Univ, Cornell; *m* 1945, Mrs Kathleen Helen Sloan, da of Lt-Col W T Murray Bisset, TD, JP, DL (d 1949), of Lessendrum, Drumblade, Aberdeenshire; 1 s, 2 da (and 1 step da); *Career* MP (C) Banffshire 1964-74; co dir; *Style*— Willfred Baker Esq, TD; 42 Southfield Avenue, Paignton, S Devon TQ3 1LH

BAKER CRESSWELL, Charles Addison Fitzherbert; OBE (1973), TD (1965, DL (Northumberland 1983)); s of Capt A J Baker Cresswell, DSO, RN, of Budle Hall, Bamburgh, Northumberland, and Mrs A J Baker Cresswell; *b* 20 Mar 1935; *Educ* Winchester, RAC; *m* 28 July 1964, Barbara, s of Ralph Henry Scrope (d 1981), of South Thorpe, Banard Castle, Co Durham; 3 s (John Addison b 18 May 1965, Edward Joe b 28 Feb 1967, Ralph Robert b 10 May 1969); *Career* Nat Serv 2 Lt 1 Bn The Rifle Bde (despatches); TA: Lt (later Maj) 7 Bn The Royal Northumberland Fusiliers 1955-70, Lt-Col raised and cmd The Northumbria Volunteers 1970-73, Col dep cdr NE Dist 1973-75; farmer; dir: London and Overseas Land plc (formerly British Photographic Industs) 1979-, Coastal Grains (former chm) 1982-; memb: local advsy ctee Nature Conservancy Cncl, North of England Territorial Assoc, Northumberland Co Ctee CLA, Northern Region Agric Panel; former memb: social servs ctee Northumberland CC, Northumberland Nat Parks Ctee; parly candidate (Cons) Berwick-on-Tweed 1975 and 1979; *Recreations* environmental studies; *Clubs* Farmers, London Business Sch Alumnae; *Style*— Charles Baker Cresswell, Esq, OBE, TD, DL; Bamburgh Hall, Bamburgh, Northumberland NE69 7AB (☎ 06684 230)

BAKER WILBRAHAM, Randle; s & h of Sir Richard Baker Wilbraham, 8 Bt; *b* 28 May 1963; *Educ* Harrow; *Career* London Fire Brigade, stationed at Hammersmith; *Style*— Randle Baker Wilbraham Esq; Rode Hall, Scholar Green, Cheshire (☎ 0270 873237)

BAKER WILBRAHAM, Sir Richard; 8 Bt (GB 1776); s of Sir Randle John Baker Wilbraham, 7 Bt, JP, DL (d 1980); *b* 5 Feb 1934; *Educ* Harrow; *m* 2 March 1962, Anne Christine Peto, da of late Charles Peto Bennett, OBE, of Jersey; 1 s, 3 da; *Heir* s, Randle Baker Wilbraham, *qv*; *Career* late Lt Welsh Gds; dir: J Henry Schroder Wagg & Co 1969-, Brixton Estate plc 1985-, Charles Barker plc 1986-, Really Useful Gp plc 1985-; tstee Grosvenor Estate 1981-, govr Harrow Sch 1982-; *Clubs* Brooks's, Pratts; *Style*— Sir Richard Baker Wilbraham, Bt; Rode Hall, Scholar Green, Ches (☎ 0270 873237)

BAKER-BATES, Merrick Stuart; s of Eric Tom Baker-Bates (d 1986) and Norah Stuart, *née* Kirk ham (d 1981); *b* 22 July 1939; *Educ* Shrewsbury, Hertford Coll Oxford (MA), Coll of Europe Bruges; *m* 6 April 1963, Chrystal Jacqueline Goodacre, of da of John Hugh Mackenzie Goodacre, Court Farm House, Frowlesworth Road, Ullesthorpe, Leics; 1 s (Jonathan b 1966) 1 da (Harriet b 1969); *Career* journalist Brussels 1962-3; Dip Serv 1963. third sec (later second sec) Tokyo 1963-68, FCO 1968-73, first sec: (info) Washington 1973-76, (comm) Tokyo 1976-82 (later cnsllr); dir Cornes & Co Ltd and rep dir Gestetner (Japan) Ltd Tokyo 1982-85; rejoined Dip Serv 1985, dep high cmmr and cnsllr (commercial and economic) Kuala Lumpur 1986-89, FCO 1989-;; *Recreations* photography, golf, things Japanese; *Clubs* Brooks's, Tokyo; *Style*— Merrick Baker-Bates, Esq; c/o Foreign & Commonwealth Office, London SW1A 2AH

BAKER-CARR, Air Marshal Sir John Darcy; KBE (1962, CBE 1951), CB (1957), AFC (1944); s of Brig-Gen Christopher Teesdale Baker-Carr, CMG, DSO (d 1949), and Sarah de Witt, *née* Quinan; *b* 13 Jan 1906; *Educ* Harrow, Phillips Acad USA, Massachusetts Inst of Technology; *m* 30 June 1934, Margery Alexandra Grant, da of Maj-Gen Alister Grant Dallas, CB, CMG (d 1931); *Career* entered RAF 1929, 2 Fighter Sqdn UK, served flying boats at home and abroad, specialist armament course HQ Bomber Command, 3 Bomber Gp 1939-45 (res and devpt air testing of aircraft rocket Central Fighter Estab), dir of armament devpt Miny of Supply, Imperial Def Coll 1952, cmdt RAF Station St Altau 1953, HQ Fighter Command 1956, AOC 4 Gp 1959, controller engrg and equipment Air Miny 1962, ret 1964; *Style*— Air Marshal Sir John Baker-Carr, KBE, CB, AFC; Thatchwell Cottage, King's Somborne, Hants

BAKER-CRESSWELL, Capt Addison Joe; DSO (1941), JP (1952); s of Maj Addison Francis Baker-Cresswell, JP, DL (d 1921), of Cresswell Hall and Harehope Hall Northumberland, and Idonea, *née* Widdrington; *b* 2 Feb 1901; *Educ* Gresham's; *m* 1926, Rona Eileen, da of late Hubert Earle Vaile, of Glade Hall, Auckland, NZ; 1 s, 2 da; *Career* joined RN 1919, Cdr 1937, Capt 1941, ret 1951; High Sheriff of Northumberland 1963-64; *Style*— Captain Addison Baker-Cresswell, DSO, JP; Budle Hall, Bamburgh, Northumberland (☎ 066 84 297)

BAKER-CRESSWELL, Maj Thomas Henry; JP (Northumberland 1959), DL (Northumberland 1971); s of Maj Henry Gilfrid Baker-Cresswell (d 1956), and Vera Mabel, *née* Ward (d 1962); *b* 13 Mar 1917; *Educ* Westminster; *m* 1946, Anne Sylvia (who m, 1938, his elder bro, Maj Gilfrid Edward Baker-Cresswell, RE, ka 1942, and had by him 1 s, 1 da), yr da of Sir John Charrington (d 1978), of High Quarry, Crockham Hill, Edenbridge, Kent ; 2 da; *Career* offr RM 1935-57; *Clubs* Army and Navy; *Style*— Maj Thomas Baker-Cresswell, R.M., JP, DL; Preston Tower, Chathill, Northumberland (☎ 066 589227)

BAKEWELL, Joan Dawson; da of John Rowlands, and Rose, *née* Bland; *b* 16 April 1933; *Educ* Stockport HS for Girls, Newnham Coll Cambridge; *m* 1, 1955 (m dis 1972), Michael Bakewell, 1 s, 1 da; m 2, 1975, Jack Emery (theatre prodr); *Career* broadcaster and writer; arts corr BBC TV 1981-87, presenter Heart of the Matter 1988-; columnist Sunday Times; pres Soc of Arts Publicists; *Books* The New Priesthood (with Nicholas Gauham), A Fine & Private Place (with John Drummond), The Complete Traveller; *Style*— Miss Joan Bakewell; BBC Television, Television Centre, Wood Lane, London W12

BALCHIN, Robert George Alexander; s of Leonard George Balchin (d 1968), and Elizabeth, *née* Skelton; the Balchin family settled in Surrey c1190, Sir Roger de Balchen owning lands in both Normandy and Surrey, Adm Sir John Balchin (1669-1744) was Governor of Greenwich RN Hosp; *b* 31 July 1942; *Educ* Bec Sch, Univ of London and Hull (MEd, Adv Dip Ed); *m* 1970, Jennifer, da of Bernard Kevin Kinlay (d 1975), of Cape Town; 2 s (Alexander b 1975, Thomas (twins) b 1975); *Career* asst master Chinthurst Sch 1964-68, head english dept Ewell Sch 1968-69, headmaster Hill Sch Westerham 1972-80 (dir 1980-), dir gen St John Ambulance 1984-; chm Campaign for a Gen Teaching Cncl 1981-; memb Surrey CC 1981-85, memb Centre for Policy Studies 1982-; tres E Surrey Cons Assoc 1982-85, Cons Pty dep area tres 1983-86, vice chm Cons Pty SE Area 1986-, conslt dir Cons Centl Off 1988-: Hon DPhil Northland Open Univ Canada (1985), Freeman Worshipful Co of Goldsmiths 1980 (Liveryman 1987), Commander's Cross Pro Merito Melitensi SMOM 1987; KStJ 1984; Hon FCP 1987, Hon FHS 1987; *Books* Emergency Aid in Schools (1984), New Money (1985); *Recreations* restoration of elderly houses; *Clubs* Athenaeum, Carlton, St Stephen's Constitutional; *Style*— Robert Balchin, Esq; New Place, Lingfield, Surrey RH7 6EF (☎ 0342 834543); 7 Ashley Ct, Westminster, SW1P 1EN; 1 Grosvenor Cres, London SW1 (☎ 01 235 5231)

BALCHIN, Prof William George Victor; s of Victor Balchin (d 1944), of Aldershot, Hants, and Ellen Winifred Gertrude, *née* Chapple (d 1988); *b* 20 June 1916; *Educ* Aldershot HS, St Catharine's Coll Cambridge (BA, MA), Kings Coll London (PhD); *m* 10 Dec 1939, Lily, da of Henry Gordon Kettlewood (d 1965), of Otley, Yorks; 1 s (Peter Malcolm b 6 Sept 1940), 2 da (Joan Margaret b 10 May 1942, d 1985, Ann Catharine b 10 Oct 1948); *Career* WWII, hydrographic offr hydrographic dept Admiralty 1939-45; jr demonstrator in geography Univ of Cambridge 1937-39 (geomorphologist Cambridge Spitsbergen Expedition 1938), lectr Univ of Bristol Regnl Ctee on Educn and WEA tutor 1939-45, lectr King's Coll London 1945-54 (geomorphologist on US Sonora-Mohave Desert Expedition 1952), prof of geography and head dept Univ Coll Swansea 1954-78 (dean of science 1959-61, vice-princ 1964-66 and 1970-73, emeritus prof 1978-), Leverhulme emeritus fell 1982; RGS: Open Essay Prize 1936-37, Gill Memorial Award 1954, memb cncl 1962-65 and 1975-88, chm educn ctee 1975-88, vice pres 1978-82, chm ordnance survey ctee 1983-; Geographical Assoc: conference organiser 1950-54, memb cncl 1950-81, tstee 1954-77; pres 1971, hon memb 1980; BAAS: pres (section on geography) 1972, tres 2 Land Utilisation Survey of Britain 1961-, chm Land Decade Educnl Cncl 1978-83; memb: meteorological ctee MOD 1963-69, Br Nat Ctee for Geography 1964-70 and 1976-78, (and cartography 1961-71), Nature Conservancy Ctee for Wales 1959-68, vice pres Glamorgan Co Naturalist Tst 1961-80, hydrology ctee ICE 1962-76, ct of govrs Nat Mus Wales 1966-74, Univ Coll Swansea 1980-, St Davids Coll Lampeter 1968-80; hon FKC 1984; FRGS 1937, FRMetS 1945, FRCSoc 1978; *Books* Geography and Man (3 vols, ed 1947), Climatic and Weather Exercises (with A W Richards, 1949), Practical and Experimental Geography (with A W Richards, 1952), Cornwall Making of the English Landscape (1954), Geography for the Intending Student (1970), Swansea and Its Region (ed, 1971), Living History of Britain (ed, 1981), Concern for Geography (1981), The Cornish Landscape (1983); *Recreations* travel, writing; *Clubs* Royal Cwlth Soc, Geographical; *Style*— Prof William Balchin; 10 Low Wood Rise, Ben Rhydding, Ilkley, W Yorks LS29 8AZ (☎ 0943 600 768)

BALCOMBE, Rt Hon Lord Justice; Rt Hon Sir (Alfred) John; PC (1985), QC (1969); er s of Edwin Kesteven Balcombe (d 1986), of London, and Jane Phyllis, *née* Abrahams (d 1982); *b* 29 Sept 1925; *Educ* Winchester, New Coll Oxford (BA, MA); *m* 24 May 1950, Jacqueline Rosemary, yr da of Julian Cowan (d 1957), of Harrow, Middx: 2 s (Peter b 1955, David b 1958), 1 da (Jennifer (Mrs Suthers) b 1952); *Career* barr Lincoln's Inn 1950, bencher 1977; High Court judge (Family Div) 1977, Lord Justice of Appeal 1985-; Liveryman Worshipful Co of Tin Plate Workers (alias Wire Workers; Master 1971); kt 1977; *Books* Exempt Private Companies (1953); *Clubs* Garrick; *Style*— The Rt Hon Lord Justice Balcombe; Royal Courts of Justice, Strand, London WC2A 2LL

BALCON, Jonathan Michael Henry; TD (1965); s of Sir Michael Balcon (d 1977, film prodr), and Aileen Freda, *née* Leatherman; *b* 7 Dec 1931; *Educ* Eton, Gonville and Caius Coll Cambridge; *m* 1 Oct 1955, Hon Sarah Patricia Mills, da of 5 Baron Hillingdon (d 1982); 3 da (Deborah b 1956, Sarah-Clair b 1957, Henrietta b 1960); *Career* TA 1951-67, City of London Yeo (Rough Riders) 1951-62 (cmmnd 1956), Inns of Ct and City Yeo 1962-67 (Maj 1966 cmdg B Sqdn); underwriting agent at Lloyds, dir C I de Rougemont & Co Ltd, chm Michael Balcon Prodns Ltd; Kent Special Constabulary 1967- (cmdt C Divn), pres Sevenoaks Combined Div St John Ambulance, memb Kent ctee SE TA & VRA (chm recruiting Kent 1983-87); Queen's Jubilee Medal, Special Constabulary Long Service Medal and bar; *Recreations* shooting; *Clubs* City of London; *Style*— Jonathan Balcon, Esq, TD; The Grey House, Seal, Kent (☎ (0732) 61592/61819); C I de Rougemont & Co Ltd, 52 Mark Lane, London EC3 (☎ 01 481 9277)

BALCON, Hon Mrs (Sarah Patricia); *née* Mills; da of 5 Baron Hillingdon, MC, TD; *b* 1933; *Educ* Westonbirt; *m* 1955, Jonathan Michael Henry Balcon, TD, o s of late Sir Michael Balcon, and of Lady Henry Balcon; 3 da (Deborah b 1956, Sarah Clair b 1957, Henrietta b 1960); *Recreations* travelling, paleontology, fine arts.; *Style*— The Hon Mrs Balcon; The Grey Hon, Seal, Sevenoaks, Kent (☎ 0732 61592)

BALDERSTONE, Sir James Schofield; s of James Schofield Balderstone (d 1953), and Mary Essendon, *née* Taylor (d 1960); *b* 2 May 1921; *Educ* Scotch Coll Melbourne; *m* 1946, Mary Henrietta, da of William James Tyree; 2 s (James, Richard), 2 da (Susan, Elizabeth); *Career* gen mangr (Aust) Thomas Borthwick & Sons 1953-67; chm: Australian Meat Exporters Fedn CI 1963-64, Squatting Investmt Co Ltd 1966-73, Cwlth Govt Working Gp on Agric Policy Issues and Options for the 1980's 1981-82, Stanbroke Pastoral Co 1982- (md 1964-81), Broken Hill Proprietary Co Ltd 1984- (dir 1971-, chm 1984-), Vic Br Bd AMP Soc 1984- (dir 1962-); dir: Commerical Bank of Australia 1979-81, Westpac Banking Corpn 1981-84, NW Shelf Devpt Party Ltd, Woodside Petroleum Ltd 1976-83; princ: Bd AMP Soc 1979-, ICI Aust Ltd 1981-84, Chase AMP Bank 1985-; pres Inst of Public Affairs 1981-84; memb: rep Meat Exporters on Australian Meat Bd 1964-67, Export Devpt Cncl 1968-71; kt 1983 *see Debrett's Handbook of Australia and New Zealand for further details*; *Recreations* farming, reading, watching sport; *Clubs* Australian, Melbourne, Union (Sydney), MCC, Queensland; *Style*— Sir James Balderstone; 115 Mont Albert Rd, Canterbury, Vic 3126, Australia (☎ (836) 3137); off: The Broken Hill Proprietary Co Ltd, 140 William Street, Melbourne, Australia 3000 (☎ (03) 609 3883, telex 30408)

BALDOCK, Brian Ford; s of Ernest John Baldock, of 12 Ferry Road, Teddington, Middx, and Florence Ford (d 1983); *b* 10 June 1934; *Educ* Clapham Coll London; *m* 1 (m dis 1966), Mary Lillian, *née* Bartolo; 2 s (Simon b 1958, Nicholas b 1961); m 2, 30 Nov 1968, Carole Anthea, da of F R Mason (d 1978); 1 s (Alexander b 1970); *Career* Lt 1952-55, Royal W Kent Regt 1952-53, Corps of Royal Mil Police 1953-55; mgmnt trainee Procter & Gamble Ltd 1956-61, assoc dir Ted Bates inc 1961-63, mktg mangr Rank Orgn 1963-66, dir Smith & Nephen 1966-75, vice pres Europe ME and Africa Revlon Inc 1975-78, md Imp Leisure & Retail 1978-86, chm and md Guiness Brewing Worldwide 1986-; cncl memb Lord's Taverners; memb Worshipful Co of Brewers 1988, Freeman City of London 1988; FInst 1976, Fell Mktg Soc 1988, FRSA 1987; *Recreations* theatre, music, travel; *Clubs* RAC; *Style*— Brian Baldock, Esq; The White House, Donnington, Newbury, Berkshire (☎ 0635 41200); Guinness plc, 39 Portman Sq, London W1 (☎ 01 965 7700, fax 01 961 8727, telex 23822)

BALDOCK, John Markham; VRD (1949); s of Capt William P Baldock (ka Gallipoli 1915), of Frinsted, Kent, and Mrs H Chalcraft ; *b* 19 Nov 1915; *Educ* Rugby, Balliol Coll Oxford (Dip Agric 1937), Freiburg Univ; *m* 1949, Pauline Ruth, da of O Gauntlett; 2 s; *Career* Lt Cdr RNVR; chm Lenscrete Ltd 1949, dir CIBA-GEIGY (UK) Ltd; MP (C) Harborough Leics 1950-59; fndr Hollycombe Steam Collection; *Style*— John Baldock, Esq, VRD; 17 Aylesford St, London SW1 (☎ 01 821 8759); Hollycombe Ho, Liphook, Hants (☎ 0428 723233)

BALDREY, Frank William; s of William Baldrey (d 1960), of London; *b* 7 Jan 1921; *Educ* City of London Sch, King's Coll London (BSc); *m* 1, 1946, Nancy (d 1969), da of William Mullins (d 1945), of Co Mayo; 2 s, 2 da; m 2, 1974, Patricia, da of Francis Clements (d 1974), of Droitwich; *Career* md Stanley Bridges Ltd to 1967, chm Garringtons Ltd to 1976, chief exec IP & SD BOC Ltd to 1984; dir: Technicare Int NOWSCO UK Gp, Thompson Engrg & Mgmnt, S Wales Forgemaster; CEng, FICE, FIMechE, FIEE; *Recreations* sports administration, horse racing; *Style*— Frank Baldrey Esq; Deancroft, Cookham Dean, Berks (☎ 062 84 6699)

BALDRY, Antony Brian; MP (C) Banbury 1983-; known as Tony; eldest s of Peter Edward Baldry and Oina, *née* Paterson; *b* 10 July 1950; *Educ* Leighton Park, Sussex Univ (BA, LLB), Lincoln's Inn; *m* 1979, Catherine Elizabeth, 2 da of Capt James Weir, RN (ret), of Chagford, Devon; 1 s; 1 da; *Career* barr and publisher; PA to Mrs Thatcher in Oct 1974 election, in ldr of oppn's off Mar-Oct 1975, awarded Robert Schumann Silver Medal (for contributions to Euro politics) 1978, memb Carlton Club political ctee, Parly candidate (C) Thurrock 1979, memb Parly Select Ctee on Employment 1983-85; PPS to Lynda Chalker 1955-87, PPS to John Wakeham 1987-; dir Newpoint Gp 1974-; *Recreations* walking, beagling; *Clubs* Carlton; *Style*— Antony

Baldry Esq, MP; Ho of Commons, London SW1

BALDWIN, Hon Mrs; Hon (Alison Mary); *née* Sandilands; da of 14 Lord Torphichen; *b* 18 July 1944; *m* 1966, David Maurice Baldwin, s of Maurice Balwin, of 43 Laxey, Rd, Rotton Pk, Birmingham 16; 2 da; *Style—* The Hon Mrs Baldwin; 30 Rochford Ave, Shenfield, Essex

BALDWIN, Christopher William Kennard; s of Peter Godfrey Kennard Baldwin (d 1979), of Lindsay Hill, Antigua, West Indies, and Joan Lillian, *née* Burgess-Driver; *b* 26 Dec 1945; *Educ* Skinners Sch; *m* 5 March 1984, Emma Margaret. da of Lt-Col Humphrey Crossman, of Cheswick House, Berwick upon Tweed, Northumberland; 1 s (John Lindsay Alexander b 23 Jan 1989); *Career* landowner Bedgebury Estate Kent; capt Br Bobsleigh Team and Br Bobsleigh Champion (Cervinia 1974, St Moritz 1976); chm Kent co ctee Game Conservancy Tst 1987-; *Recreations* shooting, skiing, fishing; *Style—* Christopher Baldwin, Esq; Twyssenden Manor, Bedgebury, Goudhurst, Kent

BALDWIN, Claude Rosemary; da of Archibald Walter Dickson Dove, of Kingston Hill, Surrey (d 1960); *b* 22 Sept 1917; *Educ* Eton Rectory Beverley, St John's Bexhill, Château d'Oex; *m* 1, 1938, Peter George Calvert, of Ockley Court, Dorking; 3 da (Amanda, Hon Mrs (Jinty) Money-Coutts, Mrs Blake (Victoria) Tyler); m 2, 1947, Hon 'Taffy' (Gustaf) Rodd (4 s of 1 Baron Rennell); m 3, 1962, Ken Baldwin, of Kusadasi, Turkey; *Career* tour guide; *Recreations* lying on a bed of thyme under an olive tree; *Clubs* Cotton Ho; *Style—* Mrs Ken Baldwin; c/o Coutts & Co, 440 The Strand, WC2

BALDWIN, David Arthur; s of Isaac Arthur Baldwin (d 1983), of Twickenham, and Edith Mary, *née* Collins; *b* 1 Sept 1936; *Educ* Twickenham Tech Coll, Wimbledon Tech Coll; *m* 1961, (Jacqueline) Anne, da of Frederick Edward Westcott (d 1947), of Twickenham; 1 s (Richard David b 1975), 1 da (Sarah b 1967); *Career* R & D engr EMI Ltd 1954-63, sales engr Solartron Ltd 1963-65, sales engr and mangr Hewlett Packard Ltd 1965-73, euro mktg mangr Hewlett Packard SA 1973-78, chm and md Hewlett Packard Ltd 1988- (md 1978-88); memb: electronics indust sector gp NEDO, ITSA & Butcher IT Skills Shortage Ctee, econ and fin planning ctee CBI, cncl for indust and higher educn, PITCOM, Berks Assoc of Boys Clubs, Thames Action Res Gp for Educn and Trg; Freeman City of London, memb of Guild of Information Technologists; FIEE, MIERE, MInstD, MInstM; *Recreations* golf, skiing, photography, painting; *Clubs* RAC; *Style—* David Baldwin, Esq; Hewlett Packard Ltd, Nine Mile Ride, Workingham, Berks RG11 3LL (☎ 0344 773100, fax 0344 763526)

BALDWIN, Maj-Gen Peter Alan Charles; s of Alec Baldwin, and Anne Dance; *b* 19 Feb 1927; *Educ* King Edward VI GS, Chelmsford; *m* 1, 1953, Judith Elizabeth Mace; m 2, 1982, Gail J Roberts; *Career* enlisted 1942, served WW II, Korean War, Borneo Ops (despatches 1967), ACOS Jt Exercises Div Allied Forces Centl Europe 1976-77, Chief Signal Offr HQ BAOR 1977-79; dep dir Radio IBA 1987- (dep dir 1979-87); *Recreations* cricket, theatre, golf; *Clubs* Army and Navy, MCC; *Style—* Maj-Gen Peter Baldwin; c/o Lloyds Bank Ltd, 6 Pall Mall, London SW1

BALDWIN, Sir Peter Robert; KCB (1977, CB 1973); s of Charles Baldwin (d 1962) and Katie Isobel, *née* Field (d 1957); *b* 10 Nov 1922; *Educ* City of London Sch, CCC Oxford; *m* 1951, Margaret Helen Moar; 2 s; *Career* served FO 1942-45, Gen Register Office 1948-54, Treasy 1954-62, Cabinet Off 1962-64; Treasy 1964-76: under-sec 1968-72, dep sec 1972-76; second perm sec DOE 1976, perm sec Dept of Tport 1976-82 (when ret); chm: S E Thames RHA 1983-, Royal Soc of Arts 1985-87, PHAB 1982-87; memb: Automobile Assoc Ctee 1983-, Public Fin Fndn 1984-, RSA 1987-, vice pres Royal Nat Inst for the Deaf 1983-; memb Civil Serv Sports Cncl 1982; *Style—* Sir Peter Baldwin, KCB; 123 Alderney St, London SW1V 4HE (☎ 01 821 7157)

BALDWIN, Roger James Maxwell; s of George Maxwell Baldwin (d 1984), of Brixham, Devon, and Norah Joan, *née* Smith; *b* 2 August 1939; *Educ* Orange Hill GS Mill Hill (DipArch Hons); *m* 7 Oct 1967 (m dis 1988) Heather, da of Andrew Douglas Kyd (d 1979); 2 s (Mark b 1973, Jonathan b 1980), 1 da (Lara b 1976); *Career* racing driver 1964-, chartered architect; ptnr: Baldwin Beaton Everton Isbell 1970, Baldwin Everton Ptnrship 1976-; Freeman: City of London 1975, Worshipful Co of Constructors 1975; RIBA; *Recreations* work, drawing, reading, antiques, driving, tennis, karate; *Style—* Roger Baldwin, Esq; Stepping Stones, Trout Rise, Loudwater, Rickmansworth, Herts WD3 4JR; Baldwin Everton Partnership, Coach House Yard, London NW3 1QD (☎ 01 435 0153, fax 01 431 2982)

BALDWIN OF BEWDLEY, 4 Earl (UK 1937); Edward Alfred Alexander Baldwin; also Viscount Corvedale (UK 1937); s of 3 Earl (d 1976, 2 s of 1 Earl, otherwise Stanley Baldwin, thrice PM and 1 cous of Rudyard Kipling); *b* 3 Jan 1938; *Educ* Eton, Trinity Coll Cambridge (MA); *m* 1970, Sarah MacMurray, da of Evan James, of Upwood Park, Abingdon, Oxon (and sis of Countess of Selborne); 3 s (Viscount Corvedale, Hon James Conrad b 1976, Hon Mark Thomas Maitland b 1980); *Heir* s, Viscount Corvedale, *qv*; *Style—* The Rt Hon The Earl Baldwin of Bewdley; Manor Farm House, Godstow Rd, Upper Wolvercote, Oxon

BALEAN, Sqdn Ldr Peter Bradford; yr but only surv s of Oswald Balean, JP (d 1928), and Millicent Nora, *née* Ames (d 1947); descended from Guillaume Baléan (d 1810), who is said to have fled to Germany from the French Revolution in 1793, and whose grandson Hermann (d 1900) settled in England at Brighton, Sussex, and was father of Oswald Balean (*see* Burke's Landed Gentry, 18 edn, vol I, 1965); *b* 25 August 1920; *Educ* The Beacon Sch Crowborough, Kelly Coll Tavistock, RAF Coll Cranwell; *m* 15 July 1955, Dorothy Anne, yr da of Frederick John Nettlefold (d 1949), of Chelwood Vachery, Nutley, Sussex; 1 s (Richard Etienne b 4 Jan 1957); *Career* cmmnd RAF 1939, ret Sqdn Ldr 1951; dir: Strettons Derby Brewery, Alton & Co and Pountain & Co 1956-61, Drake & Cubitt 1961-79; *Recreations* foxhunting, shooting, fishing, tennis, squash; *Clubs* RAF Piccadilly; *Style—* Sqdn-Ldr Peter Balean, RAF (ret); Crailing Hall, Jedburgh, Roxburghshire TD8 6LU (☎ 083 55 365)

BALFE, Richard Andrew; MEP (Lab) London S Inner 1979-; s of Dr Richard J Balfe, of Yorks, and Dorothy L, *née* de Cann; *b* 14 May 1944; *Educ* Brook Secdy Sch Sheffield, LSE; *m* 1, 1978, Vivienne, *née* Job; 1 s; m 2, 1986, Susan Jane, *née* Honeyford; *Career* Corpl London Irish Rifles TA 1961-67; FO 1965-67, res offr Finer Ctee on one Parent Families 1970-72, political sec Royal Arsenal Co-op 1973-79, dir CWS Ltd 1979-80; *Recreations* walking, reading, music; *Clubs* Peckham Labour, Lewisham Labour, Reform; *Style—* Richard Balfe Esq, MEP; 53 Chatsworth Way London SE27 9HN; 132 Powis St, London SE18 6NL (☎ 01 855 2128, telex 896484 RACS G); 2 Queen Anne's Gate, London SW1

BALFOUR; *see*: FitzGeorge-Balfour

BALFOUR, Alexander (Alastair) Norman; DL (Tweeddale 1954); s of Frederick Robert Stephen Balfour, CVO, DL (d 1945), and Gertrude, *née* Norman; *b* 20 Mar 1909; *Educ* Stowe, Oxford; *m* 1942, Elizabeth Eugenie, da of Horace W Cowell, of Abington Park, nr Cambridge; 1 s (Robert Roxburgh b 1947), 1 da (Belinda Louise b 1953); *Career* memb Royal Co of Archers (Queen's Bodyguard for Scotland) 1930-; *Recreations* gardening, shooting, travel; *Clubs* New (Edinburgh), Brooks's, Pratt's; *Style—* Alastair Balfour, Esq, DL; Dawyck House, Stobo, Peebles, Tweeddale, Scotland (☎ Stobo (072 16) 242)

BALFOUR, Charles George Yule; s of Eustace Arthur Goshen Balfour, of France, and Dorothy Melicent Anne, *née* Yule; *b* 23 April 1951; *Educ* Eton; *m* 1, 18 Sept 1978 (m dis 1985), Audrey Margaret, da of H P Hoare (d 1983), of Stourhead, Wilts; m 2, 1987, Svea Maria, da of Ernst-Friedrich Reichsgraf von Goess, of Carinthia, Austria; *Career* Hill Samuel 1973-76, Dillon Read 1976-79, exec dir Banque Paribas London 1979- ; *Recreations* shooting, fishing; *Clubs* Turf, City of London, Puffins; *Style—* Charles Balfour, Esq; 15 Oakley St, London SW3 (☎ 01 351 6527); 68 Lombard St, London EC3V 9EH (☎ 01 929 4545, fax 01 726 6761, car telephone 0836 200772, telex 945881)

BALFOUR, Christopher Roxburgh; s of Archibald Roxburgh Balfour (d 1958), and Lilian, *née* Cooper; strong links with S America 1850-1960 via Balfour Williamson & Co; *b* 24 August 1941; *Educ* Ampleforth, Queen's Coll Oxford (BA); *Career* merchant banker Hambros Bank Ltd 1968-87; (appointed dir 1984); *Recreations* horses, tennis, shooting, bridge, skiing; *Clubs* Pratts; *Style—* Christopher R Balfour, Esq; 35 Kelso Place W8 (☎ 937 7178); Hambros Bank Ltd, 41 Bishopsgate, London EC2 (☎ 588 2851, fax 374 8908)

BALFOUR, Cdr Colin James; DL (Hants 1973-); s of Maj Melville Balfour, MC (d 1962), of Wintershill Hall, Durley, Hants, and Margaret (Daisy) Mary, *née* Lascelles (d 1972); *b* 12 June 1924; *Educ* Eton; *m* 27 Aug 1949, Prudence Elisabeth, JP, da of Adm Sir Ragnar Colvin, KBE, CB (d 1954), of Curdridge House, Curdridge, Hants; 1 s (James b 1951), 1 da (Belinda (Mrs Hextall) b 1953); *Career* RN 1942, serv HMS Nelson Med 1943, D Day and N Russian Convoys 1944-45, HMS Cossack Korean War 1950-52, RN Staff Coll 1955, 1 Lt HM Yacht Britannia 1956-57, Cdr 1957, cmd HMS Finisterre 1960-62, resigned 1965; chm CLA legal and parly sub ctee and memb nat exec ctee 1982-87 (chm Hants branch 1980-81, pres 1987)), pres Hants Fedn of Young Farmers Clubs 1982; liaison offr Hampshire Duke of Edinburgh's Award Scheme 1966-76, memb Hampshire Local Valuation Panel 1971-81 (chm 1977-), govr and vice chm Lankhills Special Sch Winchester 1975-80, chm of govrs Durley C of E Primary Sch 1980-; High Sheriff of Hampshire 1972, Freeman City of London, Liveryman Worshipful Co of Farmers 1983; *Recreations* shooting, small woodland management; *Clubs* Brook's, Pratts; *Style—* Cdr Colin Balfour, DL, RN; Wintershill Hall, Durley, Hants SO3 2AL; Flat 4, Cygnet House, 188 Kings Rd, London SW3

BALFOUR, Hon David Rowland; s of 2 Baron Riverdale, DL, *qv*, and Christian Mary, *née* Hill; *b* 15 May 1938; *Educ* Harrow, Queens' Coll Cambridge (BA); *Style—* The Hon David Balfour

BALFOUR, Eustace Arthur Goschen; s of late Lt-Col Francis Cecil Campbell Balfour, CIE, CVO, CBE, MC, and gn of 1 E of Balfour, KG, OM, PC (d 1930), and Hon Phyllis Evelyn Goschen (d 1976), da of 2 Viscount Goschen; h to Earldom of Balfour; *b* 26 May 1921; *Educ* Eton; *m* 1, 1946 (m dis 1971), Anne, da of late Maj Victor Yule; 2 s (Roderick, Charles) (*see* Lady Tessa Balfour); m 2, 1971, Mrs Paula Susan Cuene-Grandidier, da of late John Maurice Davis, MBE; *Career* serv WWII, Capt Scots Guards, 1939-46, N Africa, Italy and Greece; wounded Anzio beach head; *Clubs* Naval & Military; *Style—* Eustace Balfour, Esq

BALFOUR, Lady Evelyn Barbara; 4 da of 2 Earl of Balfour, PC (d 1945); *b* 16 July 1898; *Educ* Reading Univ; *Career* farmer; fndr The Soil Assoc; *Books* The Living Soil (1943), The Living Soil and the Haughley Experiment (1975); *Recreations* gardening, music, riding, swimming; *Style—* Lady Evelyn Balfour; 4 Rattla Corner, Theberton, Leiston, Suffolk IP16 4SD

BALFOUR, Hon Francis Henry; TD; s of 1 Baron Riverdale, GBE, (d 1957); *b* 25 August 1905; *Educ* Oundle; *m* 1, 1932, Muriel Anne (d 1970), da of late Eng Rear Adm Ralph Berry; 2 s, 2 da; m 2, 1971, Daphne Cecelia Keefe, da of A C Moss, of Rochfort, Bathampton, Bath; *Career* Vice-Consul for Denmark 1946-50; kt of Order of Dannebrog (Denmark); *Style—* The Hon Francis Balfour, TD; Holcombe Cottage, Holcombe Lane, Bathampton, Bath BA2 6UN (☎ 0225 60811)

BALFOUR, 4 Earl of (UK 1922); Gerald Arthur James Balfour; JP (E Lothian 1970); also Viscount Traprain (UK 1922); s of 3 Earl (d 1968, nephew of 1 Earl, otherwise Arthur Balfour, PM (C) 1902-05), and Jean Lily (d 1981), da of late Rev John James Cooke-Yarborough (fourth in descent from George, 2 s of Sir George Cooke, 3 Bt); *b* 23 Dec 1925; *Educ* Eton, HMS Conway; *m* 14 Dec 1956, Mrs Natasha Georgina Lousada, da of late Capt George Anton, of Archangel, Russia; *Heir* kinsman, Eustace Balfour; *Career* master mariner; cncllr E Lothian till 1974; serv Merchant Navy WWII; *Clubs* Association of International Cape Horners, English Speaking Union; *Style—* The Rt Hon the Earl of Balfour, JP; Whittingehame Tower, Haddington, E Lothian (☎ 036 85 208)

BALFOUR, Hugh Crawford; s of Maj John Selby Balfour (d 1987), of West Wittering, and Elizabeth Barbara, *née* Crawford; *b* 21 Sept 1936; *Educ* Felsted, Sussex Univ (Dip Struct Engrg); *m* 3 Sept 1966, Ethne Gillian, da of Maurice James Bennett-Jones (d 1980), of Grange Hollies, Grange lane, Gatacre, Liverpool; 2 s (Robert David b 4 May 1972, Martin Hugh b 25 May 1976), 2 da (Sarah Elizabeth b 13 March 1968, Catherine Hilary b 24 Oct 1969); *Career* engr specialising in water supply, sewage in treatment pollution prevention in UK, Mali Senegal, ptnr Balfours Consltg Engrs 1966-88; regnl dir Sir M Macdonald 1988-; chm Friends City of Sheffield Youth Orch; FICE, Fell Soc French Engrs, Consulting Engrs; *Recreations* veteran cars; *Clubs* RAC; *Style—* Hugh Balfour, Esq; 78 Ivy Park Road, Ranmoor, Sheffield S10 3LD (☎ 0742 3074 562)

BALFOUR, Rear Adm (George) Ian Mackintosh; CB (1962), DSC (1943); s of Tom Stevenson Balfour (d 1912), and Ina Mary, *née* Tabuteau (d 1953); *b* 14 Jan 1912; *Educ* RNC Dartmouth; *m* 8 Aug 1939, (Gertrude) Pamela Carlyle, da of late Major Hugh Carlyle Forrester, DL, of Tullibody House, Cambus; 2 s (David b 1944 (ka HMS Sheffield, Falklands 1983), Patrick b 1950), 1 da (Jane b 1953); *Career* HMS Emperor of India 1929-30, HMS Cornwall and HMS Kent (China) 1930-32, Sub Lt's courses 1932-33, HMS Viceroy 1933-34, HMS Carlisle (SA), and on loan ad ADC to Govr Gen, Flag Lt to C in C 1935-37; HMS Caledonia 1937-39, Lt HMS Kelvin 1939-42 (despatches 1941), i/c: HMS Foxhound 1942, HMS Decoy 1942-43, HMS Tuscan 1943, HMS Scourge 1943-45, HMS Solebay 1945-46, HMS Onslow 1946; jt planning staff cabinet offs 1946-48, American Jt Staff Course 1948, exec offr HMS Triumph 1948-50, jt servs staff course 1950, asst dir of plans Admty 1951, Capt Plans Washington 1952-54, i/c HMS Osprey 1954-56, i/c and Actg Capt D2 DF HMS Daring 1956-58, dir of offrs appointmentS Admty 1958-60, sr directing staff (navy), IDC 1960-63, ret 1963; chief appeals offr and dep sec Cancer Res Campaign 1963-78 (cncl memb 1978-86); vice-pres RN Sch Haslemere (former govr),; *Recreations* fishing; *Style*— Rear Adm Ian Balfour, CB, DSC; Westover, Farnham Lane, Haslemere, Surrey GU27 1HD (☎ 0428 3876)

BALFOUR, Dr (Elizabeth) Jean; CBE (1981), JP (Fife 1963); da of late Maj-Gen Sir James Syme Drew, KBE, CB, DSO, MC (d 1955), and late Victoria Maxwell of Munches; *b* 4 Nov 1927; *Educ* Edinburgh Univ (BSc); *m* 1950, John Charles Balfour, *qv*; 3 s; *Career* dir A J Bowen & Co; ptnr Balbirnie Home Farms; dir: Chieftain Industries 1983-85, Scottish Dairy Trade Fedn 1983-6; pres Roy Scottish Forestry Soc 1969-71; chm Countryside Commission Scotland 1972-83; vice pres East of Scotland Coll of Agric 1982 (govr 1958-), dir Scottish Agric Colls 1987-; memb: Fife CC 1958-70, Nature Conservancy Cncl 1973-80, Scottish Economic Cncl 1978-83, Court St Andrew's Univ 1983-87; vice pres Scottish Youth Hostel Assoc, hon fellow Zoological Soc of Scotland; Hon DSc (St A) 1977; FRSE, FICF; *Clubs* farmers; *Style*— Dr Jean Balfour, CBE, JP; Kirkforthar House, Markinch, Glenrothes, Fife (☎0592 752233); Scourie, by Lairg, Sutherland

BALFOUR, John Charles; OBE (1978), MC (1943), JP (Fife 1957), DL (Fife 1958); s of late Brig Edward Balfour, CVO, DSO, OBE, MC, and Lady Ruth, CBE (d 1967), *née* Balfour, da of 2 Earl of Balfour (d 1945) and Lady Elizabeth Bulwer-Lytton, da of 1 Earl of Lytton; *b* 28 July 1919; *Educ* Eton, Trinity Cambridge; *m* 1950, Jean, *née* Drew, *qv*; 3 s; *Career* memb Royal Co of Archers (Queen's Bodyguard for Scotland) 1949-; chm Fife Area Health Bd 1983 (memb 1981-87); *Style*— John Balfour, Esq, OBE, MC, JP, DL; Kirkforthar House, Markinch, Glenrothes, Fife (☎ 0592 752233)

BALFOUR, John Manning; s of James Richard Balfour, and Eunice Barbara, *née* Manning; *b* 2 Oct 1952; *Educ* Fettes, Worcester Coll Oxford (MA); *Career* slr Frere Cholmeley 1979- (ptnr 1986-); *Books* Air Law (contrib ed 1988); *Recreations* swimming, reading; *Clubs* Lansdowne; *Style*— John Balfour, Esq; 52 Ingestre Court, Ingestre Place, London W1R 3LU (☎ 01 437 2420); Frere Cholmeley, 28 Lincoln's Inn Fields, London WC2A 3HH (☎ 01 405 7878, fax 01 405 9056, telex 27623)

BALFOUR, Lady; (Catharine) Marjorie; da of Sir Charles Rugge-Price, 7 Bt (d 1953); *b* 5 Jan 1904; *m* 1930, Lt-Gen Sir Philip Maxwell Balfour, KBE, CB, MC (d 1977); *Style*— Lady Balfour; Bridles, Donhead St Mary, Shaftesbury, Dorset

BALFOUR, Hon Mark Robin; s and h of 2 Baron Riverdale; *b* 16 July 1927; *Educ* Aysgarth Sch Yorks, Trinity Coll Sch Port Hope Canada; *m* 1959, Susan Ann, da of Robert Percival Phillips, of Sheffield; 1 s (Anthony Robert b 1960), 2 da (Nancy Ann b 1963, Kate Frances b 1967); *Career* chm: Sheffield Rolling Mills Ltd 1969-75, Balfour Darwins Ltd 1971-75, Light Trades House Ltd, Finglands Servs Ltd (property co); proprietor Multilog Logging Tools; non-exec dir: W M Ridgway & Sons 1964-72 (also dep chm), BSC Special Steels Bd 1970-73, Newton Chambers 1972; pres Nat Fedn of Engineer's Tool Mfrs 1974-76; memb: exec ctee BISPA 1967-75, Economic Dvpt Cncl for Machine Tools 1975-78, Aust Br Trade Assoc Cncl, Aust & NZ Trade Advsy Ctee (BOTB 1975-86), High Sheriff South Yorkshire 1986-87, memb (pres 1979) Sheffield C of C Sheffield, Ctee SSAFA, chm cncl of management Ashdell Schools Tst; memb Worshipful Co of Blacksmiths, memb Master Cutlers' Co 1969-70, Freeman City of London; guardian Sheffield Assay Office; vice-consul for Finland in Sheffield 1962-; *Clubs* Sheffield; *Style*— The Hon Mark Balfour; Fairways, Saltergate Lane, Bamford, nr Sheffield, Derbys S30 2BE (☎ 0433 51314)

BALFOUR, Michael John; s of Duncan Balfour (d 1952), of Englefield Green, Surrey, and Jeanne Germaine, *née* Picot (d 1974); *b* 17 Oct 1925; *Educ* Eton, Christ Church Oxford (MA); *m* 15 Sep 1951, Mary Campbell, da of Maj-Gen Sir William Ronald Campbell Penney, KBE, CB, DSO, MC (d 1964), of Stanford Dingley, Berks; 3 s (James b 1952, d 1974, William b 1955, Andrew b 1963), 1 da (Emma b 1953); *Career* WWII RAF 1944-47, Bank of Eng 1950- 85: sr advsr Euro affrs 1973, chief advsr 1976, asst dir overseas affrs 1980-83, alternate dir Bank for Int Settlements 1972-85; chm: Balgonie Estates 1975- (dir 1955-), IMI Capital Mkts (UK) Ltd 1987-, IMI Securities Ltd 1988-; dep chm IMI Bank (Int) 1987-; JP; *Recreations* fishing, boating, music; *Style*— M J Balfour, Esq; Harrietfield, Kelso, Roxburghshire TD5 7SY (☎ 0573 24825); 17 Shrewsbury Mews, London W2 5PN; IMI Capital Markets (UK) Ltd 8 Laurence Pountney Hill, London EC4R OBE (☎ 01 283 1751, telex 9419091 IMICAP)

BALFOUR, Nancy; OBE (1965); da of Alexander Balfour, and Ruth Macfarland Balfour; *b* 1911; *Educ* Wycombe Abbey, Lady Margaret Hall Oxford; *Career* asst ed The Economist 1948-72; chm Contemporary Art Soc 1976-82, vice chm Crafts Cncl 1983-5; chm Art Servs Grants 1982-89; *Style*— Miss Nancy Balfour, OBE; 36E Eaton Sq, London SW1 (☎ 01 235 7874)

BALFOUR, (George) Patrick; s of David Mathers Balfour, CBE, of Littlegarnstone Manor, Seal, Sevenoaks, Kent, and Mary Elisabeth, *née* Beddall (d 1988), gs of George Balfour, MP; *b* 17 Sept 1941; *Educ* Shrewsbury Sch, Pembroke Coll Cambridge (MA); *m* 18 March 1978, Lesley Ann, da of John Denis Johnston, of Glenfuir, Fidra Rd, N Berwick, Scotland; 2 s (James David Johnston b 1980, Matthew Alexander Patrick b 1982); *Career* slr, ptnr Slaughter and May 1973; dir Slrs Benevolent Assoc; memb Law Soc; *Recreations* theatre, opera, golf, country pursuits; *Style*— Patrick Balfour, Esq; 70 Lansdowne Rd, London W11 (☎ 01 221 7814); 35 Basinghall St, London EC2V 5DB (☎ 01 600 1200, fax 01 726 0038, telex 883486)

BALFOUR, Peter Edward Gerald; CBE (1984); s of Brig Edward William Sturgis Balfour, CVO, DSO, OBE, MC (d 1955), and Lady Ruth, CBE (d 1967), *née* Balfour, da of 2 Earl of Balfour (d 1945) and Lady Elizabeth Bulwer-Lytton, da of 1 Earl of Lytton; *b* 9 July 1921; *Educ* Eton; *m* 1, 1948 (m dis 1967), Lady Grizelda, *née* Ogilvy, da of 7 (12 but for attainder) Earl of Airlie, KT, GCVO, MC (d 1968); 2 s, 1 da; m 2, 1968, Diana Wainman; 1 s, 1 da; *Career* served Scots Guards 1940-54; chm and chief exec Scottish and Newcastle Breweries 1970-83; chm: Selective Assets Tst 1978- (dir 1962-), Charterhouse plc, First Charlotte Assets Tst; vice chm Roy Bank of Scotland plc (dir 1971-); dir: Roy Bank of Scotland Gp 1978-, Br Assets Tst plc; pres Scottish Cncl (Dvpt and Indust) 1986- (chm exec ctee 1978-85); *Style*— Peter Balfour, Esq, CBE; Scadlaw House, Humbie, E Lothian (☎ 087 533 252)

BALFOUR, Richard Creighton; MBE (1945); s of Donald Creighton Balfour and Muriel Fonçeca; *b* 3 Feb 1916; *Educ* St Edward's Sch Oxford; *m* 1943, Adela Rosemary Welch; 2 s; *Career* chief accountant Bank of England 1970-75; pres: Royal Nat Rose Soc 1973-74, World Fedn of Rose Societies 1983-85; int rose Judge, Gold Medal of World Fedn of Rose Societies 1985, DHM; Liveryman and memb Ct of Worshipful Co of Gardeners, Freeman City of London; *Books* photographs in many books inc Classic Roses by Peter Beales; *Style*— Richard Balfour, Esq, MBE; Albion House, Little Waltham, Chelmsford, Essex CM3 3LA (☎ Chelmsford 360410)

BALFOUR, Roderick Frances Arthur; s of Eustace Arthur Goschen Balfour, and Anne, *née* Yule; *b* 9 Dec 1948; *Educ* Eton, London Business Sch (sr exec program); *m* 14 July 1971, Lady Tessa Balfour, da of 17 Duke of Norfolk; 4 da (Willa b 1973, Kinvara b 1975, Maria b 1977, Candida b 1984); *Career* ptnr Grierson Grant and Co Stockbrokers 1972-81, investmt dir Tessel Toynbee and Co 1981-83, int and UK investmt dir Union Discount Co of London plc 1983-; Freeman City of London 1977, Liveryman Worshipful Co of Clothworkers 1986; *Recreations* tennis, skiing, water skiing; *Clubs* City of London; *Style*— Roderick Balfour, Esq; Burpuam Lodge, Arundel, West Sussex BN18 9RR; Union Discounts Co of London plc, 39 Cornwill, London EC3V 3NV (☎ 01 623 1020, fax 01 929 2110)

BALFOUR, Lady Tessa Mary Isobel; *née* Fitzalan Howard; da of 17 Duke of Norfolk, CB, CBE, MC, DL, *qv*; *b* 30 Sept 1950; *m* 1971, Roderick Francis Arthur Balfour, s of Eustace Arthur Goschen Balfour, *qv*; 4 da (Willa Anne b 1973, Kinvara Clare b 1975, Maria Alice Jubilee b 1977, Candida Rose b 1984); *Style*— Lady Tessa Balfour

BALFOUR, William Harold St Clair; s of Francis Edmund Balfour (d 1974), and Isobel MacIntosh Shaw Balfour, *née* Ingram (d 1980), originally of Balgonie, Fife: then of Westray Orkney; *b* 29 August 1934; *Educ* Edinburgh Acad, Edinburgh Univ; *m* 1961, (m dis 1980), Patricia, *née* Waite; 1 s (Michael), 2 da (Sonia, Jillian); *Career* slr, clerk to Admission of Notaries Public in Scotland; *Recreations* walking, sailing, yacht "Tekoa"; *Clubs* New (Edinburgh), Royal Forth Yacht ; *Style*— William Balfour, Esq; 31 India St, Edinburgh (☎ 031 226 2708); office: 58 Frederick St, Edinburgh (☎ 031 226 8291, telex 72175, fax 031 225 5687)

BALFOUR OF BURLEIGH, 8 (*de facto* and 12 but for the Attainder) Lord (S 1607); **Robert Bruce**; s of 7 Lord Balfour of Burleigh (11 but for the Attainder, d 1967); *b* 6 Jan 1927; *Educ* Westminster; *m* 1971, Jennifer, da of late E S Manasseh; 2 da (Hon Victoria, Hon Ishbel b 1976); *Heir* (hp) da, Hon Victoria Bruce b 5 April 1973; *Career* foreman supt English Electric Co Ltd Stafford & Liverpool 1952-57, gen mangr: Eng Electric Co India Ltd 1957-64, Eng Electric Netherton Works 1964-66, D Napier & Son Ltd 1966-68; dir: Bank of Scotland 1968-, Wm. Lawson Distillers Ltd. 1984-, Tarmac plc 1981-, Scottish Investment Tst plc 1971-; chm: Scottish Arts Cncl 1971-80, Edinburgh Book Festival 1982-87, National Book League Scotland 1981-86, Cablevision (Scotland) plc, 1983- The Turing Institute 1983-, Viking Oil Ltd 1971-80, Fedn of Scottish Bank Employers 1977-86; tres Royal Scottish Corpn; chllr Univ of Stirling 1988-; CEng, FIEE, Hon FRIAS, FRSE; *Style*— The Rt Hon the Lord Balfour of Burleigh; Brucefield, Clackmannan FK10 3QF (☎ 0259 30228)

BALFOUR OF INCHRYE, 2 Baron (UK 1945); Ian Balfour; s of 1 Baron Balfour of Inchrye, MC, PC (d 1988), and his 1 w Diana Blanche (d 1982), da of Sir Robert Grenville Harvey, 2 Bt; *b* 21 Dec 1924; *Educ* Eton, Magdalen Coll Oxford; *m* 28 Nov 1953, Josephine Maria Jane, o da of Morogh Wyndham Percy Bernard; 1 da (Roxane, *see* Hon Mrs Laird Craig); *Heir* none; *Career* author and composer.; *Books* Famous Diamonds (1987); *Recreations* reading, walking, watching cricket and association football.; *Style*— The Hon Ian Balfour; 10 Limerston Street, London SW10 0HH

BALFOUR OF INCHRYE, Mary Ainslie; Baroness; yr da of Baron Albert Peter Anthony Profumo, KC (d 1940), and Martha Thom, *née* Walker; sis of John Profumo, *qv*; *b* 7 May 1911; *m* 2 Jan 1947, as his 2 w, 1 Baron Balfour of Inchrye, PC, MC (d 1988); 1 da (Mary Ann, *see* Hon Mrs Sutherland Janson); *Style*— The Rt Hon Mary, Lady Balfour of Inchrye; End House, St Mary Abbots Place, London W8 6LS

BALFOUR PAUL, Maj Lyon; TD; s of Lt-Col John William Balfour Paul, DSO, DL (d 1957) (sometime Marchmont Herald and s of Sir James Balfour Paul, KCVO, Lord Lyon King of Arms (d 1931)), and Muriel Cassels, *née* Monteith (d 1964); *b* 21 April 1914; *Educ* Sedbergh, Edinburgh Coll of Art (Architect); *m* 28 May 1954, Carola Mary Eve, da of Lt Col A H Marlowe, QC, MP; 1 s (Hugh b 1955), 4 da (Fiona b 1956, Veronica b 1957, Philippa b 1959, Mary b 1964); *Career* joined Lovat Scouts (TA) 1935, Major WW II served Faroe Islands, Italy; architect; ptnr winemaking firm Inverness, farmer on Isle of Mull; memb of Queens Bodyguard for Scotland, ARIBA; *Recreations* fishing, shooting, skiing, piping; *Clubs* New Club (Edinburgh); *Style*— Major Lyon Balfour Paul, TD; Eskadale Cottage, Kiltarlity, Invernessshire (☎ 0463 550); Moniack Castle, Kirkhill, Inverness (☎ 046 383 283)

BALGONIE, Lord; David Alexander Leslie Melville; s and h of 14 Earl of Leven and (13 of) Melville, DL; *b* 26 Jan 1954; *Educ* Eton; *m* 1981, Julia Clare, yr da of Col I R Critchley, of Lindores, Muthill, Perths; 1 s (Hon Alexander b 1984), 1 da (Hon Louisa Clare b 1987); *Heir* s Hon Alexander Leslie Melville; *Career* Lt Queen's Own Highlanders, RARO 1979-81, relinquished commission 1981, reappointed to RARO July 1981; dir: Wood Conversion Ltd Slough 1984-, Treske Shop Ltd London 1988-; *Style*— Lord Balgonie; The Old Farmhouse, West Street, Burghclere, Newbury, Berks RG15 9LB (☎ 0635 27241)

BALL, Alan Hugh; s of late Sir (George) Joseph Ball, KBE (d 1961), and his wife, Mary Caroline, *née* Penhorwood (d 1957); *b* 8 June 1924; *Educ* Eton; *m* 1948, Eleanor Katharine Turner; 2 s, 1 da; *Career* dir Lonrho Ltd and associated cos (chm and joint md 1961-72); *Style*— Alan Ball Esq; The Old Mill, Ramsbury, Wilts (☎ Ramsbury 266)

BALL, Air Marshal Sir Alfred Henry Wynne; KCB (1976, CB 1967), DSO (1943), DFC (1942); s of Capt J A E Ball, MC (d 1957), and Josephine Hilda Wynne, *née* Rowland-Thomas, of Rostrevor, Co Down and BNR India; *b* 18 Jan 1921, Rawalpindi, Br India,; *Educ* Campbell Coll Belfast, RAF Coll Cranwell, RAF Staff Coll, Jt Servs Staff Coll, IDC; *m* 1942, Nan, da of late A G McDonald, of Tipperary; 3 s, 1 da; *Career* serv WWII RAF (despatches twice), Air Medal (USA) 1943, asst COS SHAPE 1968-71, dir Gen of RAF Orgn 1971-75; UK Mil Rep CENTO Ankara 1975-77, Dep C-in-C RAF Strike Cmd 1977-78, ret 1979; mil advsr ICL 1979-83; vice chm: (Air) TAVRA Cncl 1979-84, Hon Air Cdre RAuxAF 1984-; Hon FBCS 1984; *Recreations* golf, bridge; *Clubs* RAF, Phyllis Court, Huntercombe; *Style*— Air Marshal Sir Alfred Ball, KCB, DSO, DFC, FBCS; Tarshyne, Lambridge Wood Rd, Henley-on-Thames, Oxon RG9 3BP

BALL, Dr the Hon Ann Marguerite; *née* Gordon-Walker; da of Baron Gordon-Walker, CH, PC,; *b* 1944; *Educ* N London Collegiate Sch, Queen's Coll Dundee, St Andrews Univ, Oxford; *m* 1968 (m dis 1983), Laurence Andrew Ball; 2 da (Jennifer b 1974, Katherine b 1976); *Style*— Dr the Hon Ann Ball; 1230 University Bay Drive,

Madison, Wisconsin 53705, USA

BALL, Anthony George; MBE (1986); s of Harry and Mary Irene Ball, of Bridgwater; *b* 14 Nov 1934; *Educ* Bridgwater GS; *m* 1957, Ruth Parry, *née* Davies; 2 s, 1 da; *Career* indentured engrg apprentice Austin Motor Co 1950, responsible for launch of Mini 1959, sales mangr Austin Motor Co 1962-66, sales and marketing exec BMC 1966-67, chm Barlow Rand UK Motor Gp 1967-78 (md: Barlow Rand Ford S Africa 1971-73, Barlow Rand Euro Ops 1973-78), md Br Leyland Overseas Trading Ops 1978; dir BL Cars, BL Int, Rover Triumph, Austin Morris, Jaguar Cars, Jaguar Rover Triumph Inc (USA) 1978-82; chm Nuffield Press 1978-80; chm BL Europe and Overseas 1979-82; BL Cars World Sales Ch 1979-82, responsible for BL's Buy British campaign and launch of Austin Metro 1980; ch exec Henlys plc 1982-83; chm: Tony Ball Assocs, plc; (Marketing, Product Launch and Sales Promotion Agency); Tony Ball Conslts, Geoff Howe Assocs; dep chm: Lumley Ins, LI Mgmnt; dir: Customer Concern Ltd, freeman City of London 1980; Liveryman: Worshipful Co of Coach Makers and Coach Harness Makers 1980, Worshipful Co of Carmen 1983; awarded: FInstM 1981 for launch of Metro and services to Br motor industry, Hon memb City & Guilds of London for Educational & vocational services 1982, the 1984 Prince Philip Medal for Marketing Achievement and Services to Br Motor Industry; marketing advsr to Sec of State for Energy 1983-; responsible for UK dealer launch of Vauxhall Astra for General Motors 1984; launches for other car manufacturers - importers; spl advsy to sec of State for Wales 1987; marketing exec, broadcaster, writer, lectr and after dinner speaker; FIMI, ACIArb; *Recreations* military history, theatre, golf, gliding, sharing good humour; *Clubs* Oriental; *Style*— Tony Ball, Esq, MBE; Blythe House, Bidford-on-Avon, Warwicks B50 4BY (☎ 0789 778 015)

BALL, Arthur Beresford; OBE (1971); s of Charles Henry Ball (d 1943) and Lilian Houlden Ball, *née* Hinde (d 1945); *b* 15 August 1923; *Educ* Bede Collegiate Boys Sch, Univ of East Anglia (BA); *m* 1961, June Stella, da of Edward John Luckett (d 1977); 1 s (Jonathan), 2 da (Abigail, Johanna); *Career* HM Dipl Serv 1949-80: Bahrain, Tripoli, MECAS, Ramullah, Damascus, Kuwait, New Orleans, Saô Paulo, Lisbon, Jedda, Ankara; Br Consul-Gen Perth WA 1978-80; ret 1980; *Recreations* ice skating, historical studies; *Style*— Arthur Ball, Esq, OBE; 15 Eccles Rd, Holt, Norfolk NR25 6HT

BALL, Sir Charles Irwin; 4 Bt (UK 1911), of Merrion Sq, City of Dublin, and Killybegs, Co Donegal; s of Sir Nigel Gresley Ball, 3 Bt (d 1978), and Florine Isabel, *née* Irwin; *b* 12 Jan 1924; *Educ* Sherborne; *m* 2 Sept 1950 (m dis 1983), Alison Mary, o da of Lt-Col Percy Holman Bentley, MBE, MC, of Farnham, Surrey; 1 s, 1 da (Diana Margaret b 1955); *Heir* s, Richard Bentley Ball, *qv*; *Career* serv WWII and to 1947 in RA (Capt 1946); chartered accountant (FCA 1960), with Peat, Marwick, Mitchell 1950-54; former dir: Kleinwort Benson (vice-chm 1974-76), memb Br Tport Docks Bd 1971-82, dep chm Associated Br Ports Hldgs 1982-; dir: Sun Alliance & London Insurance 1971-83, Tunnel Hldgs 1976-82, Rockware Gp 1978-84, Peachey Property Corpn 1978-88 (chm 1981-88); chm: Barclays Merchant Bank 1976-77 (dir Barclays Bank 1976-77), Telephone Rentals 1981-89 (vice-chm 1978-81, dir 1971-89); Master Worshipful Co of Clockmakers 1985; *Style*— Sir Charles Ball, Bt; Appletree Cottage, Heath Lane, Ewshot, Farnham, Surrey (☎ 0252 850208)

BALL, Christopher Charles; s of Reginald Charles Ball, of Essex and Amelia Ellen *née* Garner; *b* 25 Dec 1945; *Educ* Harold Hill GS; *m* 17 July 1971, Frances Jean, da of Philip Elliott, Barry Island, Wales; 1 s (Ian b 1987); *Career* dir: Capel-Cure Myers 1986, Linton Nominees Ltd 1986, Richardson Glover and Case Nominees Ltd 1986, CCM Nominees Ltd 1986; memb Stock Exchange (individual membership); *Recreations* golf, reading, shooting; *Style*— Christopher Ball, Esq; 147 Western Rd, Leigh-on-Sea, Essex (☎ 0702 711032); 65 Holborn Viaduct, London (☎ 01 236 5080, telex: 9419251, fax: 248 1103)

BALL, Sir Christopher John Elinger; er s of late Laurence Elinger Ball, OBE, and Christine Florence Mary, *née* Howe; *b* 22 April 1935; *Educ* St George's Sch Harpenden, Merton Coll Oxford (MA); *m* 1958, Wendy Ruth, da of Cecil Frederick Colyer; 3 s (David, Peter, Richard), 3 da (Helen, Diana, Yasmin); *Career* 2 Lt Para Regt 1955-56; lectr english language Merton Coll Oxford 1960-61, lectr in comparative linguistics SOAS London 1961-64; Lincoln Coll Oxford: fell and tutor in english language 1964-79, sr tutor and tutor for admission 1971-72, bursar 1972-79, hon fell 1981; Keble Coll Oxford: warden 1980-88, hon fell 1989; chm Bd of Nat Advsy Body for Public Sector Higher Educn in England 1982-88, sec Lingustics Assoc of GB 1964-67, pres Oxford Assoc of Univ Teachers 1968-71, publications sec Philological Soc 1969-75, chm Oxford Univ English Bd 1977-79, founding fell Kellogg Forum for Continuing Educn Oxford Univ 1988-89, chm Educn-Indust (Indust Matters, RSA) 1988-; Jt Standing Ctee for Linguistics 1979-82, Conf of Colls Fees Ctee, 1979-85; memb: Gen Bd of the Faculties 1979-82, Hebdomadal Cncl 1985-, CNAA 1982-88, (chm English Studies Bd 1973-80, Linguistics Bd 1977-82), BTEC 1984-, IT Skills Shortages Ctee (Butcher Ctee) 1984-85, CBI IT Skills Agency 1985-88, cncl and exec Templeton Coll Oxford 1981-; govr St George's Sch Harpenden 1985-, Centre for Medieval and Renaissance Studies Oxford 1987-, Brathay Hall Tst 1988-, Manchester Poly 1989- (hon fell 1988), chm Higher Educn Info Servs Tst 1987-, Jt Founding Ed (with late Angus Cameron) Toronto Dictionary of Old English 1970, memb editorial bd Oxford rev of Educn 1984-; FRSA 1987; kt 1988;; *Books* Fitness for Purpose (1985); *Clubs* United Oxford and Cambridge Univs; *Style*— Christopher Ball, Esq; Keble Coll, Oxford OX1 3PG (☎ 0865 59201)

BALL, Denis William; MBE (1971); s of William Charles Thomas Ball, of 17 Warburton Close, Park Lane, Eastbourne, Sussex, and Dora Adelaide, *née* Smith; *b* 20 Oct 1928; *Educ* Tonbridge, Brasenoze Coll Oxford (MA); *m* 5 Aug 1972, Marja Tellervo (d 1987), da of Osmo Lumijarvi, of Sontula 42, Toijala, Finland; 2 s (Christian b 1975, Robin b 1976), 1 da (Sasha b 1981); *Career* served RN 1947-49, RNR 1953-85, (Lt Cdr 1958-); asst master King's Sch Canterbury 1953-72 (housemaster 1954-72), headmaster Kelly Coll Tavistock 1972-85; dir: Western Bloodstock Ltd 1986-, James Wilkes Plc 1987, Perkins Foods Plc 1987-; conslt Throgmorton Investmt Mgmnt Ltd 1987-88; Squash Rackets for Oxford Univ and Kent, Real Tennis for Jesters and MCC; tstee Tavistock Sch 1972-85, vice-chm of Govrs St Michael's Sch Tawstock 1974-; memb: Johnson Club 1987-, Ickham PCC 1986-; HMC 1972-85, HMA 1972-85; *Recreations* Elizabethan history, cryptography, literary and mathematical puzzles, cricket, golf; *Clubs* East India, Devonshire, Sports and Public Schools, MCC; *Style*— Denis Ball, Esq, MBE; Ickham Hall, Ickham, Nr Canterbury, Kent

BALL, (Wilfred) Dennis; s of Frederick Thomas Ball, of Hammerwich Hall, 105 Burntwood Rd, Hammerwich, nr Lichfield, Staffs, and Ethel, *née* Cope (d 1973); *b* 27 Sept 1922; *Educ* Queen Elizabeth's GS Tamworth, Wednesbury Commercial Coll, Br Tutorial Inst; *m* 1, 19 Oct 1946 (m dis 1974), Jean Mildred, da of late Albert Bates; 1 s (David John Wilfred Lumley b 9 Dec 1952), 1 da (Elaine Patricia (Mrs Bates) b 29 Nov 1947); m 2, 10 Aug 1974, Marian Ball, JP, da of William Merrifield (d 1985), 2 da (Anne Margaret b 1 May 1977, Helen Patricia b 10 July 1979); *Career* Corpl RAF 1942-46 (despatches); accountant Brockhouse Trading Facilities Ltd 1952-57, co sec and accountant subsidaries of FMC Ltd 1957-65, orgn and methods offr (later chief exec) J Brockhouse & Co Ltd 1965-68; dir Brockhouse Ltd (parent co) 1968-; Brockhouse Gp: asst md 1968-84, fin dir 1970-84, conslt 1984-; hon tres Birmingham Rathbone Soc; hon auditor: St John Ambulance W Midland Co, Cannon St Baptist Church Handsworth; memb: local branch assoc of corporate tres, Birmingham and Midlands Soc of Fin, W Midlands Regnl Bd BIM; patron Sandwell Dist Spastics Soc; FAIA 1982, FCT 1979, CBIM 1982; *Recreations* gardening, reading, travel; *Style*— Dennis Ball, Esq; 54 Hinstock Rd, Handsworth Wood, Birmingham B20 2EU (☎ 021 554 5957)

BALL, Florine, Lady - Florine Isabel; da of late Col Herbert Edwardes Irwin; *m* 1922, Sir Nigel Gresley Ball, 3 Bt (d 1978); *Style*— Florine, Lady Ball; Flat 30, Homesearle House, Goring Rd, Worthing, W Sussex

BALL, Geoffrey Arthur; s of Henry Arthur Ball, of Bristol, and Phyllis Edna, *née* Webber; *b* 4 August 1943; *Educ* Cotham GS Bristol; *m* 1968, Mary Elizabeth, da of late S George Richards, of Bristol; 3 s (Nicholas b 1971, Nathan b 1972, Thomas b 1975), 1 da (Esther b 1977); *Career* chm & chief exec of CALA plc; dir: Abaco Investmts plc, The Scottish Mortgage & Tst plc, Stenhouse Western Ltd, The Standard Life Assur Co; memb: Scottish Arts Cncl, ISCO (Scotland); asst to the Master's Ct of The Co of Merchants of the City of Edinburgh; Clydesdale Bank Young Business Personality of the Year 1983; FCA; *Recreations* golf, birdwatching, music; *Clubs* New (Edinburgh), MCC, The Lord's Taverners; *Style*— Geoffrey Arthur Ball, Esq, FCA; 34 Colinton Rd, Edinburgh EH10 5DG (☎ 031 337 1528); CALA plc, 42 Colinton Rd, Edinburgh EH10 5BT (☎ 031 346 0194, fax 031 346 4190)

BALL, Prof Sir (Robert) James; s of Arnold James Hector Ball; *b* 15 July 1933; *Educ* St Marylebone GS, Queen's Coll Oxford (BA 1957, MA 1960), Univ of Pennsylvania (PhD); *m* 1, 1954 (m dis 1970), Patricia Mary Hart Davies; 1 s (Charles), 3 da (Stephanie, Deborah, Joanne) (and 1 s decd); m 2, 1970, Mrs Lindsay Jackson, *née* Wonnacott; 1 step s (Nigel); *Career* Flying Offr RAF (Navigator) 1952-54; research offr Oxford Univ Inst of Statistics 1957-58; IBM Fell Univ of Pennsylvania 1958-60; lecturer, subsequently sr lecturer Univ of Manchester 1960-65; prof Economics London Business Sch 1965- (govr 1968-84, dep princ 1971-72, princ 1972-84); dir: Ogilvy & Mather Ltd 1969-71, Economic Models Ltd 1971-72, Barclays Bank Tst Co 1973-86, Tuke Investments 1974-84; memb ctee to review Nat Savings (Page Ctee) 1971-73; chm Legal & General Gp plc 1980-; dir: IBM (UK) Hldgs 1979-, London & Scottish Marine Oil (LASMO) 1988-; tstee: Foulkes Foundations 1984-, The Civic Tst 1986-, The Economist Newspaper 1987-; memb British-N American Ctee 1985-, Marshall Aid Commemoration cmmr 1987-; Fell Econometric Soc 1973, CBIM 1974, FIAM 1985; Freeman of City of London 1987; Hon DSc Aston 1987, Hon DSocSc Manchester 1988; kt 1984; *Books* An Econometric Model of the United Kingdom (1961), Inflation and the Theory of Money (1964), (ed): Inflation (1969), The International Linkage of National Economic Models (1972); Money and Employment (1982), (with M Albert) Toward European Economic Recovery in the 1980's (1984) and numerous articles in professional journals; *Recreations* fishing, chess; *Clubs* RAC; *Style*— Prof Sir James Ball; London Business School, Sussex Place, Regent's Park London NW1 4SA (☎ 01 262 5050, fax 01 724 7875, telex 27461)

BALL, Jonathan Macartney; s of Christopher Edward Ball (d 1978), and Dorothy Ethel Macartney; *b* 4 June 1947; *Educ* Truro Sch, The Arch Assoc (AA Dip); *m* 2[illegible] June 1974, Victoria Mary Ogilvie, da of Dr A M O Blood, of Bude; 2 da (Jemima b 1976, Morwenna b 1979); *Career* chartered architect, principal The Jonathan Ball Practice 1974-; Concrete Soc Award (mention) 1971 and 1986, RIBA Award (commendation) 1983, CPRE/CLA Henley Award 1981, occasional lectr, conference speaker, contrib to architectural periodicals, assessor for RIBA architecture awards, memb Architectural Advsy Bd Plymouth Poly; memb RIBA Cncl 1981-, chm RIBA Parly Liaison Ctee 1981-87; vice-pres RIBA 1983-85, hon sec RIBA 1988-; memb Worshipful Co of Chartered Architects 1986, Freeman City of London 1987; RNLI sn Helmsman-Bude Lifeboat; chm Bude Surf Life Saving Club, Service Award-Surf Life Saving Assoc GB; ACIArb 1978, FRSA 1985; *Recreations* enjoying Cornwall; *Clubs* Athenaeum; *Style*— Jonathan Ball, Esq; Tregarthens, Diddies Road, Stratton, Bude Cornwall EX23 9DW (☎ 0288 2198); 5 Belle Vue, Bude, Cornwall EX23 8JJ (☎ 028[illegible] 3898)

BALL, Rt Rev Michael Thomas; *see*: Jarrow, Bishop of

BALL, Rt Rev Pater John; *see*: Lewes, Bishop of

BALL, Rev Canon Peter William; s of Leonard Wevell Ball (d 1976), of St Albans and Dorothy Mary, *née* Burrows; *b* 17 Jan 1930; *Educ* Aldenham Sch, Worcester Coll Oxford (MA), Cuddesdon Coll; *m* 11 Sept 1956, Angela Jane, *née* Dunlop; 1 s (Michael b 1961), 2 da (Lucy b 1957, Katharine b 1959); *Career* 2 Lt RA 1948; curate All Saints Poplar 1955-61, vicar The Ascension Wembley 1961-68, rector St Nicholas Shepperton 1968-84, area dean Spelthorne 1972-84, prebendary St Paul's Cathedral 1976-84 canon residentiary and chllr St Paul's Cathedral 1984-, chapter treas 1985-, dir Post Ordination Trg and Continuing Ministerial Educn Kensington Area 1984-87; chaplain Associated Rediffusion TV 1961-68, Thames Television 1970-; fndr and chr Catechumenate Network 1984-, dir Samaritans Brent and NW Surrey 1965-75 Freeman of the City of London 1986; *Books* Journey into Faith (1984), Adult Believin (1988); *Style*— The Rev Canon Peter Ball; 1 Amen Ct, London EC4M 7BU (☎ 01 24 1817)

BALL, Richard Bentley; s and h of Sir Charles Irwin Ball, 4 Bt; *b* 29 Jan 1953; *Educ* Dragon Sch, Sherborne, Leicester Univ; *Career* chartered accountant with: Peat Marwick Mitchell 1975-82, Int Computers Ltd 1982-; ACA; *Recreations* tennis hockey, squash; *Clubs* Roehampton, Hampstead Hockey; *Style*— Richard Ball, Esq; 1 Rotherwood Rd, London SW15 1LA (☎ 01 785 9887)

BALL, Robert Edward; CB (1977), MBE (1946); s of James Ball (d 1965), of Hythe Kent, and Mabel Louise, *née* Laver (d 1973); *b* 8 Mar 1911; *Educ* Westminster London Univ (LLB); *m* 1935, (Edith) Margaret Barbara, da of Dr Patrick Edward Campbell (d 1927), of Caterham, Surrey; 1 s (Robert), 1 s (decd), 2 da (Sylvia

Felicity); *Career* slr 1933, Army serv 1939-45, served France and India (attached to IA, Lt-Col); slr in Chester and London 1946-54, many local appts in Chester, master of the Supreme Ct of Judicature (Chancery Divn) 1954-79, chief chancery master 1969-79, associated with the Inst of Moralogy, Chiba-Ken Japan 1980-, chm Friends of Friendless Churches 1988-; part landowner (232 acres); *Books* The Law and the Cloud of Unknowing (1976), The Crown, The Sages and Supreme Morality (1983); *Recreations* gardening, history, oriental studies, forestry; *Clubs* Athenaeum; *Style—* Robert Ball Esq, CB, MBE; 62 Stanstead Rd, Caterham, Surrey CR3 6AB (☎ 0883 43675)

BALL, Tony; *see*: Ball, Anthony George

BALLANTINE, Dr Brian Neil; *b* 27 Jan 1936; *Educ* Queen Elizabeth Sch, Univ of London (BSc), St Bart's London (MB BS); *m* 18 Dec 1982, Annette; *Career* occupational physician; chm to UK Offshore Ops Assoc Med Advsy Cte; MFOM 1988 (RCP), DIH 1985 (London Univ); *Style—* Dr Brian Ballantine; Red Lion House, The Lee, Gt Missenden, Bucks HP16 9NH (☎ 024 020 339); British Gas plc, 59 Bryanston St, London W1A 2AZ (☎ 01 723 7030)

BALLANTINE, (Matthew) Dumfries; s of Arthur Ballantine (d 1959), of Ayrshire, and Gladys Ballantine, *née* Brown (d 1965); *b* 21 Mar 1911; *Educ* Merchiston Castle Edinburgh; *m* 24 Feb 1940, Joan Aline, s of late William Russell; 2 da (Catherine Aline b 1946, Gillian Anne b 1953); *Career* serv RN 1940-46, Lt Cmdr, took part in evacuation at Dunkirk and D-Day; ophthalmic optician (ret); chm: J Lizars Ltd, and J Lizars (NI) Ltd; *Recreations* sailing, shooting, fishing; *Clubs* Western Glasgow, Ulster Reform Belfast; *Style—* Dumfries Ballantine, Esq; Kilewnan Cottage, Fintry, Stirlingshire G63 0YH (☎ 036 086 243); 101 & 107 Buchanan St, Glasgow G1 3HF (☎ 041 221 8062)

BALLANTINE, Dr Robert Ian Waverley; s of Richard Waverley Head Ballantine, CBE (d 1965), and Olive Norma, *née* Law (d 1973); *b* 15 May 1922; *Educ* Wellington, London Univ (St Bart's Hosp, DA); *m* 13 April 1946, Jill Muriel, da of Col Cyril Helm DSO, OBE, MC (d 1972); 2 s (Alistair b 1948, Giles (twin) b 1948), 1 da (Alison b 1952); *Career* resident anaesthetist Addenbrookes Hosp Cambridge 1947), chief asst anaesthetist Hillingdon and Harefield Hosps 1947-52, asst prof of anaesthesia Johnson Willis Hosp Richmond Virginia USA 1956; St Bart's Hosp: house surgn 1946, resident anaesthetist 1947-, conslt anaesthetist 1952-86, sr anaesthetist 1978-86; teacher in anaesthetics Univ of London; MRCS, LRCP, FFARCS; memb BMA 1946-, Assoc of Anaesthetist 1946-; The Most Distinguished Order of Paduka Seri Laila Jasa (SLJ) of Brunei; *Books* General Anaesthesia For Neurosurgery 91960); *Recreations* golf, gardening, jazz music, reading; *Style—* Dr Robert Ballantine

BALLANTINE, Capt Ronald George; LVO (1952); s of William Henry Ballantine (d 1961), of Dublin, and Catherine Dalgairns, *née* Roberts (d 1982); *b* 2 August 1913; *Educ* Plymouth Coll, Plymouth Sch of Art; *m* 4 April 1942, Cherrie Julian Maybeth, da of George Whitby (d 1966), of Yeovil and Colombo; 2 s (Nicholas Whitby b 1942, Alistair Nigel Stuart b 1946), 1 da (Clare Catherine b 1954); *Career* Capt Imperial Airways 1937, chief pilot Hong Kong Airways 1947-49, flight mangr BOAC 1957-59, dir flight ops Malaysia Singapore Airline 1969-71; Newbury CAB 1972-83; King's Commendation for valuable service in the air 1943; Freeman City of London, Liveryman Worshipful Co Air Pilots and Air Navigators; *Recreations* tennis, gardening, travelling; *Clubs* Naval & Military; *Style—* Capt Ronald Ballantine, LVO; Hitchens, Woolton Hill, Newbury, Berkshire RG15 9TX (☎ 0635 253 565)

BALLARD, Maj Anthony William (Tony); s of Maj John Francis Ballard, of Over Worton Heath Farm, Oxon OX5 4EH, and Jean Carolina, *née* Rawle; *b* 27 May 1957; *Educ* Eton, RMA Sandhurst; *m* 25 Oct 1986, Petronella Johanna Antonia Maria, da of Sjoerd Wiegersma, of Amsterdam; *Career* Sandhurst 1976, cmmnd 1 Bn Welsh Guards 1977, Guards Depot 1979, 1 Bn Welsh Guards 1980 (Falklands 1982), SO3 G2/G3 HQ Logistic Support Gp 1987, SO3 G3 (Log/Trg) HQ UK Mobile Force 1988, Maj 1 Bn Welsh Guards 1989-; *Recreations* polo, hunting; *Clubs* Cavalry and Guards, Guards Polo; *Style—* Maj A.W. Ballard; Over Worton Heath Farm, Oxon OX5 4EH (☎ 060 883 237)

BALLARD, Geoffrey Horace; CBE (1978), JP (Worcs 1967); s of Horace and Mary Catherine Ballard; *b* 21 May 1927; *Educ* Hanley Castle GS; *m* 1, 1948, Dorothy Sheila Bache (d 1979); 2 s, 1 da; m 2, 1983, Anne, *née* Ballard; *Career* chm MSF Ltd (former vice-chm); md: GH Ballard (Farms), GH Ballard (Leasing); vice chm: NFU Mutual Insur Soc, chm: MSF Ltd, Woodbury Growers; *Style—* Geoffrey Ballard Esq, CBE, JP; Orchard House, Stud Farm, Abberley, Worcester WR6 6AT (☎ 029 921 307)

BALLARD, (Richard) Graham John; s of Alfred John Ballard (d 1979), of Worcs, and Ada Mary (d 1981); *b* 17 Jan 1927; *Educ* Prince Henrys GS Evesham, Wadham Coll Oxford (MA), Cambridge Univ (MA); *m* 10 July 1954, Domini Gabrielle, da of Dr Alfred Johannes Wright (d 1941), of Bucks; 2 s (Sebastian John b 1961, Toby Graham Dominic b 1963); *Career* chm and md Liebigs Rhodesia Ltd 1973-78, md Brooke Bond Kenya 1978-83, dir Tea Bd of Kenya 1978-83, bursar and fell Christs' Coll Cambridge 1983-; tstee Wesley House Cambridge 1986-, sr tres Cambridge Univ Opera Soc 1985-, memb overseas ctee Save The Children Fund 1984-, chm: Br Business Assoc Kenya 1982-83, Cambridge Univ Lodging House Syndicate 1986-, Cambridge Univ Stewards Ctee 1986-; *Recreations* opera, chamber music, reading, french culture; *Style—* Graham Ballard, Esq; 23 Bentley Road, Cambridge CB2 2AW (☎ 0223 323547); Christ's Coll, Cambridge CB2 3BU (☎ 0223 334949)

BALLARD, Kenneth Alfred; MC (1944); s of Charles John Ballard, of Cromer Lodge, Glengall Rd, Woodford Green, Essex (d 1930), and Elizabeth Anne Ballard (d 1950); *b* 17 Sept 1915; *m* 30 March 1940, Ann, da of Frederick Joseph Anthony, of Warley Road, Woodford Green, Essex, and Peaches Close, Cheam, Surrey; 3 da (Lesley Ann b 1947, Gillian Elizabeth b 1949, Patricia Katherine b b 1951); *Career* RA 1940-, cmmnd 1941, serv W Desert, Italy (MC), France, Germany, Holland; dir: Murray Pipework Ltd 1964-78, Patent Lightning Crusher Ltd 1965-85; chm: K A Ballard Ltd, Ballard Fired Heaters Ltd, Medium Trading Co Ltd, Prematechnik (UK) Ltd, Baynard Engrg Co Ltd; elected memb Ct of Common Cncl Corpn of London; chm City of London Police 1973-77; Sheriff of London 1978-79; chm New Victoria Hosp Kingston 1965-73, tstee Castle Baynard Educnl Tst; govr: Christ's Hosp, Bridewell Hosp, City of London Freemens Sch; *Recreations* music, photography; *Style—* Kenneth Ballard, Esq, MC; Giles Barn Cottage, Church Lane, Horsted Keynes, Danehill, Sussex (☎ 0825 790 795)

BALLARD, Richard Michael; s of Michael Agar Ballard, and Junella, *née* Ashton (d 1960); *b* 3 August 1953; *Educ* St Edmunds Coll Ware, Queens' Coll Cambridge (MA); *m* 28 Feb 1981, Penelope Ann, da of Dilwyn John Davies, DFC (d 1988), of Glamorgan; 2 s (Hayden b 1984, Thomas b 1985), 1 da (Sophie b 1987); *Career* admitted slr 1978, ptnr Freshfields 1984-; memb Law Soc; *Recreations* sport, wine, country pursuits; *Style—* Richard Ballard, Esq; Nether Hall, Pakenham, Suffolk; 25 Newgate St, London EC1A 7LH (☎ 01 606 6677, fax 01 248 3487, telex 889292)

BALLARD, (Geoffrey) William; s of Geoffrey Horace Ballard, CBE, JP, of Orchard House, Abberley, Worcestershire, and Dorothy Sheila (d 1979); *b* 30 May 1954; *Educ* Malvern Coll, Bristol Univ (BSc), Scholar of Federation of Civil Engineering Contractors; *m* 12 April 1980, Louisa Alden, da of David Chavasse Alden Quinney, of Reins Farm, Sambourne, Redditch, Worcestershire; 2 s (George b 1984, William b 1987), 1 da (Ceila b 1986); *Career* chartered acct, fndr G William Ballard 1985-; tres Br Caspian Soc; scholar FCEC; fndr memb Tolzey Debating Soc; ACA (1978); *Recreations* farming, sailing; *Style—* G W Ballard, Esq; Broc House, Purshull Green, Rushock, Nr Droitwich, Worcs, WR9 0NL (☎ 056283 520); 14 Victoria Square, Droitwich, Worcs, WR9 8DS (☎ 0905 772 749), car tel 0860 525 738, fax 0905 778 999

BALLENTYNE, Donald Francis; CMG (1985); s of Henry Quiney Ballentyne (d 1971), of London, and Frances Rose, *née* McLaren (d 1985); *b* 5 May 1929; *Educ* Haberdashers Aske's Sch; *m* 10 June 1950, Elizabeth, da of Leslie Alfred Heywood, of Benson, Oxon; 1 s (Christoher John b 1950), 1 da (Sarah Leslie (Mrs Pringle) b 1957); *Career* serv HM Forces 1948-50; HM For Serv: joined 1948, jr attaché Berne and Ankara; consul: Munich 1957-59, Stanleyville 1961-62, Cape Town 1962-65; first sec and dep head of mission: Luxembourg 1965-69, Havana 1969-72; cnsllr (commercial): The Hague 1974-78, Bonn 1978-82; dep head of mission E Berlin 1982-84, consul gen Los Angeles 1984-; *Recreations* sailing, riding, tennis, music; *Clubs* St James's; *Style—* Donald Ballentyne, Esq, CMG; c/o Foreign and Commonwealth Office, Whitehall, London SW1A 2AH

BALLIN, Robert Andrew; s of Harold Ballin (d 1976), E Dean, E Sussex, and Mollie Ballin, *née* Dunn; *b* 8 July 1943; *Educ* Highgate Sch, City of London Coll; *m* 27 Nov 1975, Serena Mary Ann, da of Richard Goode, OBE, (d 1966) of Chelsea, London SW3; 1 s (Edward b 1980), 2 da (Annabel b 1981, Chloe b 1985); *Career* int account dir and dep to md Impact-FCB Belgium 1975-77, dir Foote Cone and Belding (Advertising) Ltd 1977 (dep chm 1988-); *Recreations* music, theatre, sport; *Clubs* Naval and Military, RAC, MCC, Annabel's; *Style—* Robert Ballin, Esq; The Old Vicarage, Froxfield, Marlborough, Wilts (☎ 0488 82736); Foote, Cone and Belding Ltd, 82 Baker St, London W1 (☎ 01 935 4426, telex 263526)

BALLS, Alastair Gordon; s of Rev Ernest George Balls, of Stevenson, Ayrshire, Scotland, and Elspeth Russell *née* McMillan; *b* 18 Mar 1944; *Educ* Hamilton Acad Lanarkshire, St Andrews Univ (MA), Manchester Univ (MA); *m* 26 Nov 1977, Beryl May da of John Nichol, of Harlow, Essex; 1 s (Thomas b 1979), 1 da (Helen b 1982); *Career* asst sec treasy Govt of Tanzania 1966-68, economist Dept of Tport UK govt 1969-73, sec Cairncross Ctee on Channel Tunnel 1974-75, sr econ advsr HM Treasy 1976-79, under sec DOE 1983-87, chief exec Tyne & Wear Urban Devpt Corpn 1987-; CBIM 1988; *Recreations* fishing, camping; *Clubs* Wylam Angling; *Style—* Alastair Balls, Esq; Tyne & Wear Development Corporation, Hadrian House, Higham Place, Newcastle upon Tyne NE1 8AF, (☎ 091 222 1222, fax 091 232 8760)

BALLS, (Henry) Derek; s of Maj Henry Burgess Balls, TD (d 1960), and Gladys Jane, *née* Harris (d 1948); *b* 31 July 1923; *Educ* City of London Sch; *m* 24 July 1950, Sheila Muriel, da of Harold Chiesman (d 1985), of Beckenham, Kent; 1 s (Richard b 12 May 1953), 3 da (Christine b 11 March 1952, Catharine b 25 May 1959, Rosemary b 28 Sept 1961); *Career* joined Army 1941-46, Capt 7 Light Cavalry (Indian Army), served India, Burma, Japan; memb Common Cncl City London 1970-, dep Cripplegate ward 1977; chm: Bd of London Sch 1983-86, City of London Health Ctee 1977-80; Liveryman Worshipful Co of Innholders (Master 1977-78); JP Essex 1975-86; one of the conservators of Epping Forest; FHCIMA 1980; *Recreations* skiing, shooting, sailing, fishing; *Clubs* City Livery, Royal Burnham YC; *Style—* Derek Balls, Esq; Greengates, Albion Hill, Loughton, Essex; Balls Bros Ltd, 311 Cambridge Heath Rd, London E2 9LQ (☎ 01 739 6466, telex 298610)

BALLS, Vincent Alfred (Vin); s of Vincent Alfred Balls (d 1957), and Louisa Ethel, *née* Pyefinch (d 1968); *b* 5 Jan 1901; *Educ* Grove House Sch S Tottenham; *m* 19 July 1941, Mary Kathleen (d 1984), da of George Allen (d 1940), of Whitelead, N Ireland; *Career* civil engr; experience in building wharves and concrete ships, area mangr Sir William Prescott & Sons Huntingdon 1923-35, mangr own business 1935-77 work incl: by-pass roads, sewage disposal works, housing estate devpts; Freeman: City of London 1923, Worshipful Co of Farriers 1946, Worshipful Co of Loriners 1946; memb Fedn Bldg Trades Employers; *Recreations* swimming, yachting; *Clubs* City Livery, United Wards; *Style—* Vin Balls, Esq

BALMER, Sir Joseph Reginald; JP; s of Joseph Balmer, of Birmingham; *b* 22 Sept 1899; *Educ* King Edward's GS Birmingham; *m* 1927, Dora, da of A Johnson; *Career* Nat Chm Guild of Insurance Officials 1943-47; kt 1965; *Style—* Sir Joseph Balmer, JP; 26 Stechford Lane, Ward End, Birmingham (☎ (021 783) 3198)

BALMFORTH, Ven Anthony James; s of Rev Joseph Henry Balmforth (d 1943), and Daisy Florence, *née* Mawby (d 1973); *b* 3 Sept 1926; *Educ* Sebright Sch Wolverley Worcs, BNC Oxford (MA), Lincoln Theol Coll; *m* 16 April 1952, Eileen Julia, da of James Raymond Evans (d 1939); 1 s (Timothy b 19 Feb 1954), 2 da (Theresa b 7 Aug 1958, Anne b 5 Dec 1964); *Career* served Army 1944-48; ordained 1952, curate Mansfield 1952-55; vicar: Skegby Notts 1955-61, St Johns Kidderminster 1961-65; rector Kings Norton Birmingham 1965-79 (rural dean 1973-79), canon of Birmingham Diocese 1976-79, archdeacon of Bristol and canon Bristol Cathedral 1979-; memb Gen Synod of C of E 1982-; *Recreations* gardening; *Style—* The Ven the Archdeacon of Bristol; 10 Great Brockeridge, Westbury-on-Trym, Bristol BS9 3TY (☎ 0272 622 438)

BALNIEL, Lord; Anthony Robert Lindsay; s and h of 29 Earl of Crawford and (12 of) Balcarres, PC, *qv*; *b* 24 Nov 1958; *Educ* Eton, Edinburgh Univ; dir J O Hambro Investment Management Ltd.; *Clubs* New (Edinburgh); *Style—* Lord Balniel; 82 Onslow Gardens, London SW7

BALOGH, Baroness; Catherine; da of Arthur Cole (d 1968) ; *Educ* Cambridge Univ, W London Hosp (MRCS Eng, LRCP Lond 1944); *m* 1, Dr Storr; 3 da, m 2, 1970, as his 2 w, Baron Balogh (d 1985; Life Peer UK 1968), of Hampstead; *Career* psychiatrist; writer; *Books* Growing Up (1975), Freud and The Concept of Parental

Guilt (chapter in The World of Freud (1972), chapter in Discipline in Schools (1973); *Style—* The Rt Hon the Lady Balogh; Flat 9, 12 Frognal Gardens, London NW3; Fongives, Campagne, Dordogne, France

BALOGH, Hon Christopher Thomas; yr s of Baron Balogh (d 1985), and his 1 wife, Penelope Noel Mary Ingram, *née* Tower (d 1975); *b* 16 Nov 1948; *Educ* Westminster, King's Cambridge; *Style—* The Hon Christopher Balogh; 30 Daleham Gardens, London, NW3

BALOGH, Hon Penelope Kathryn Teresa; da of Baron Balogh (d 1985), and his 1 wife, Penelope Noel Mary Ingram, *née* Tower (d 1975); *b* 17 Oct 1957; *Style—* The Hon Penelope Balogh; 10 St George's Terrace, Regents Park, London, NW1

BALOGH, Hon Stephen Bernard; er s of Baron Balogh (d 1985), and his 1 wife, Penelope Noel Mary Ingram, *née* Tower (d 1975); *b* 18 Jan 1946; *Educ* Westminster, Balliol Coll Oxford; *Style—* The Hon Stephen Balogh; Loweswater Hall, Cockesmouth, Cumbria

BALSTON, His Honour Judge Antony Francis; s of Cdr Edward Francis Balston, DSO, RN, of Oast Ho, Crowhurst, Battle, E Sussex, and Diana Beatrice Louise, *née* Ferrers; *b* 18 Jan 1939; *Educ* Downside, Christs Coll Cambridge (MA); *m* 1966, Anne Marie Judith, da of Gerald Ball (d 1971); 2 s (James b 1967, Andrew b 1969), 1 da (Alexandra b 1972); *Career* RN 1957-59; ptnr Herington Willings & Penry Davey Slrs 1966-85; recorder 1980, hon recorder of Hastings 1984; circuit judge 1985; *Recreations* gardening; *Style—* His Honour Judge Antony Balston; Elmside, Northam, Rye, E Sussex (☎ 079 74 2270)

BALY, Dr Monica Eileen; da of Albert Frank Baly (d 1953), of Shirley, Surrey, and Annie Elizabeth, *née* Marlow (d 1961); *b* 24 May 1914; *Educ* St Hilda's Sch for Girls London, Open Univ (BA), London Univ (PhD); *Career* WWII: sister Princess Mary RAF Nursing Serv 1942-46 ME and Italian campaigns (despatches 1944); chief nursing offr Displaced Persons Div Germany (Br Zone) FO 1949-51, regnl nursing offr W Area Royal Coll of Nursing 1951-74, lectr and examiner in nursing London Univ, official historian Nightingale Fund Cncl, fndr and chm Royal Coll of Nursing History of Nursing Gp, vice chm Arthritis Res Cncl Bath, lectr history of nursing England and N America; FRCN 1986, centenary fell Queen's Inst Nursing; *Books* History of the Queen's Nursing Institute (1987), Nursing and Social Change (second edn 1980), Professional Responsibility (second edn 1984), District Nursing (second edn 1987), Florence Nightingale and the Nursing Legacy; *Recreations* music, particularly opera, theatre; *Style—* Dr Monica Baly; 19 Royal Cres, Bath BA1 2LT (☎ 0225 24 736)

BALY, Patrick Thomas; s of Albert Frank Baly (d 1956), and Annie Elizabeth, *née* Marlow (d 1967); *b* 22 Feb 1921; *Educ* Whitgift Middle Sch Croydon; *m* 5 Nov 1949, Margaret Elizabeth, da of Percival Allen Butland (d 1965); 1 s (Nigel b 1957) 1 da (Gillian b 1962); *Career* RAF 1941-46; ptnr: Hatfield Dixon Roberts Wright & Co 1956-84, Rowley Pemberton Roberts & Co 1967- (sr ptnr 1976-80), Pannell Kerr Forster (vice chm Nat Exec 1980-82); official liquidator De Lorean Motor Cars Ltd 1982-; memb bd of mgmnt Royal Masonic Hosp 1985- (hon tres and tstee 1987-) Freeman Worshipful Co of Gold and Silver Wyre Drawers; FCA 1951; *Recreations* cricket, tennis, fly-fishing; *Clubs* MCC, City Livery Club; *Style—* Patrick Baly, Esq

BAMBERG, Harold Rolf; CBE (1968); s of Ernest Bamberg; *b* 17 Nov 1923; *Educ* Fleet Sch and William Ellis Sch Hampstead; *m* 1957, June Winifred, da of John Clarke; 1 s, 2 da (and 1 s, 1 da of a former m); *Career* chm Bamberg Gp Ltd, Eagle Aircraft Servs Ltd; *Style—* Harold Bamberg Esq, CBE; Harewood Park, Sunninghill, Berks

BAMBOROUGH, John Bernard; s of John George Bamborough (d 1931), and Elsie Louise, *née* Brogden; *b* 3 Jan 1921; *Educ* Haberdasher's Aske's Hampstead Sch, New Coll Oxford; *m* 1947, Anne, da of Olav Indrehus (d.1984),of Indrehus, Norway; 1 s (Paul), 2 da (Karin, Cecilia); *Career* RN 1941-46, Lt Instr Europe; fell and tutor Wadham Coll Oxford 1947-62 (lectr in english 1951-62), princ Linacre Coll Oxford 1962-68, pro vice chancellor Oxford 1966-68; *Style—* John Bamborough, Esq; 18 Winchester Rd, Oxford (☎ 0865 59886); Linacre Coll, St Cross Rd, Oxford (☎ 0865 271650)

BAMFIELD, Clifford; CB (1980); s of G H Bamfield; *b* 21 Mar 1922; *Educ* Wintringham GS; *Career* cmmr HM Customs & Excise 1973-74; under sec CSD 1974-80; *Style—* Clifford Bamfield Esq, CB; 15 The Linkway, Sutton, Surrey (☎ 01 642 5377)

BAMFORD, Alan George; CBE (1985), JP (1977); s of James Ross Bamford (d 1976), of Liverpool, and Margaret Emily, *née* Ramsay; *b* 12 July 1930; *Educ* Prescot GS, Borough Road Coll (Cert Ed), Liverpool Univ (Dip Ed, MEd), Cambridge (MA); *m* 7 Aug 1954, Joan Margaret, da of Arthur William Vint (d 1985), of Hastings; 4 s (Stephen Mark b 1955, Timothy David b 1959, Simon John b 1960, Peter Andrew b 1967); *Career* Corpl RAF 1948-50; teacher then dep headmaster Lancs Primary Schs 1952-62, lectr in educn Liverpool Univ 1962-63, sr lectr Chester Coll 1963-66, princ lectr and head of dept St Katherine's Coll Liverpool 1966-71; princ: Westhill Coll Birmingham 1971-85, Homerton Coll Cambridge 1985-; memb: advsy ctee on religious broadcasts BBC Radio Birmingham 1972-80, cncl Br and For Sch Soc 1972-85; chm Birmingham Assoc of Youth Clubs 1972-85; memb: Br Cncl of Churches Standing Ctee on Theological Educn 1979-82, cncl of mgmnt Central Register and Clearing House, exec ctee Assoc of Voluntary Colls 1979-86; Birmingham Cmmn 1977-85; govr London Bible Coll 1981-89; memb: cncl Nat Youth Bureau 1974-80, exec ctee Standing Conf on Studies in Educn 1978-87 (sec 1982-84), educn ctee Free Church Fed Cncl 1978-, ctee Standing Conf on Principals of Colls and Insts of Higher Educn 1986-, Cambridge Health Authy (and tstee) 1987, Voluntary Sector Consultative Cncl 1987-88, Standing Ctee on Educn and Trg of Teachers (vice chm 1988, chm 1989); Hon MA Birmingham Univ 1981; FRSA 1975; *Recreations* travel, photography; *Clubs* Royal Cwlth Soc, United Oxford and Cambridge; *Style—* Alan Bamford, Esq, CBE, JP; Principal's Ho, Homerton Coll, Cambridge CB2 2PH (☎ 0223 411 141)

BAMFORD, Anthony Paul; s of Joseph Cyril Bamford, *qv*; *b* 23 Oct 1945; *Educ* Ampleforth,; *m* 1974, Carole Gray Whitt; 2 s, 1 da; *Career* chm and md J C Bamford Group 1976; Young Exporter of the Year 1972, Young Businessman of the Year 1979; High Sheriff of Staffordshire 1985-86; memb: Design Council, Presidents Committee C.B.I.; Pres Staffordshire Agric Soc 1988.; *Clubs* BRDC, Pratts; *Style—* Anthony Bamford, Esq; J C Bamford Excavators, Rocester, Uttoxeter, Staffs (☎ Rocester 590312)

BAMFORD, Brig (Percy) Geoffrey; CBE (1959, OBE 1951), DSO (1944); s of Lt-Col Percy Bamford, OBE, TD, JP (d 1951), of Cottage Field, Ightham, Kent; *b* 23 May 1907; *Educ* Cranleigh Sch, RMA Sandhurst; *m* 1930, Betty Fallding (d 1981), da of Lt-Col Henry Joseph Crossley, CIE, RAMC (d 1939); 1 s (and 1 da decd); *Career* Brig, Cdr 150 Inf Bde 1954-56; Col The Lancs Fusiliers 1955-64; *Recreations* hunting; *Clubs* Army and Navy; *Style—* Brig Geoffrey Bamford, CBE, DSO; The Square, Swalcliffe, Banbury, Oxon (☎ 029 578 240)

BAMFORD, John William; s of William Harry Bamford (d 1961), of Thrapston, and Harriet Ethel, *née* Fogell (d 1969); *b* 27 August 1918; *Educ* Kimbolton, Open Univ (BA); *m* 11 Oct 1941, Denise Mary, da of Hubert Morris; 3 da (Penelope b 1950, Ann b 1957, Sarah b 1959); *Career* WWII 1940-46; local govt offr 1935-78, city tres Westminster 1974-78, public fin conslt; St John Ambulance; memb Chapter Gen, chm cncl, dep pres, cdr, dir London dist; OStJ; Freeman City of London 1978, Liveryman Worshipful Co of Gardeners 1983; memb: IPFA 1949, FRVA 1964; KStJ 1985; *Recreations* reading, crosswords, fell walking, watching cricket, gardening; *Clubs* MCC; *Style—* John Bamford, Esq; 21 West Way, Pinner, Middx HA5 3NX (☎ 01 866 4869)

BAMFORD, Joseph Cyril; CBE (1969); Cyril Joseph Bamford (d 1953), of the Parks, Uttoxeter, Staffs; *b* 21 June 1916; *Educ* St John's Alton Staffs, Stonyhurst; *m* 1941, Marjorie, da of William Griffin, of Uttoxeter, Staffs; 2 s (including Anthony Paul, *qv*); *Career* chm and md J C Bamford Excavators 1945-76; Hon DTech (Loughborough) 1983; *Style—* Joseph Bamford, Esq, CBE; 16 Rue de Bourg, CH 1003 Lausanne, Switzerland

BAMFORD, Richard Brian; DL (1987); s of Dr James Brian Bamford, DL (d 1979), and Eileen Mary, *née* Leeming; *b* 24 April 1938; *Educ* Wellington, Selwyn Coll Cambridge (MA); *m* 8 April 1978, Elizabeth Ann, da of Lt-Col H W Faure Walker; 1 s (John b 1981), 1 da (Peggy b 1979); *Career* Nat Serv 2 Lt 1 Bn XX Lancashire Fusiliers Cyprus; slr; Slrs Disciplinary Tribunal 1984-; *Recreations* shooting, golf; *Clubs* Royal Worlington (Capt 1986/87), Royal West Norfolk; *Style—* Richard Bamford, Esq; Vineyard Lodge, Market Place, Ely, Cambs CB7 4NP (☎ 0353 662203)

BAMPFYLDE, Hon David Cecil Warwick; s of 6 Baron Poltimore (d 1978), and Margret Mary (d 1981), da of 4 Marquis de la Pasture (cr France 1768); *b* 3 Mar 1924; *Educ* Eton; *m* 1950, Jean Margaret, da of Lt-Col Patrick Kinloch Campbell; 3 s; *Style—* The Hon David Bampfylde; Coombe Lea, Malmesbury, Wilts

BANBURY, Nigel Graham Cedric (Peregrine); s of Ralph Cecil Banbury (d 1951), of Ebury St, London SW1, and Florence Leslie St Clair Keith; *b* 23 May 1948; *Educ* Gordonstoun; *m* 1, 17 Nov 1973, Rosemary Henrietta Dorothy, da of Capt Anthony Henry Heber Villiers, of The Old Priory, Woodchester, Glos; m 2, 28 Sept 1978, Susan Margaret, da of Lt-Col Joseph Patrick Feeny, of Estoril, Portugal (d 1970); 2 s (Alexander b 1981, Ralph b 1987); *Career* Coutts & Co 1967-70, stockbroker 1971-81, Robert Fleming 1981-86, dir EBC Amro Asset Mgmnt Ltd 1986-87; Head Investmt Dept Coutts & Co 1987-; Freeman City of London; *Recreations* shooting, skiing, gardening, golf; *Style—* Peregrine Banbury, Esq; Coutts & Co, 440 Strand, London WC2R 0QS (☎ 01 379 6262)

BANBURY OF SOUTHAM, 3 Baron (UK 1924); Sir Charles William Banbury; 3 Bt (UK 1902); s of 2 Baron Banbury, DL (d 1981), and Hilda, *née* Carr (m dis 1958; she m 2, Maj R Gardner, MC); *b* 29 July 1953; *m* 1984 (m dis 1986), Lucinda Trehearne; *Style—* The Rt Hon The Lord Banbury of Southam; The Mill, Fossebridge, nr Cheltenham, Glos

BANCROFT, Hon Adam David Powell; yr s of Baron Bancroft, GCB (Life Peer); *b* 1955; *Educ* King's Coll Sch Wimbledon, LSE (BSc); *m* 1985, Amanda C, da of late A J McCance, of SW19; *Career* wine supplier; *Style—* The Hon Adam Bancroft; 12c Severus Rd, London SW11 (☎ 01 223 2058)

BANCROFT, Brig Donald Royle Jackson; OBE (1961); s of Maj Peter Henson Bancroft (d 1969), and Florence Adolphine, *née* Jackson (d 1962); *b* 18 July 1916; *Educ* Ilminster, RMA Sandhurst; *m* 1, (m dis), Phyllis Catherine, *née* Anghs (d 1977); m 2, 8 May 1948, Elizabeth Ann Rosetta, da of Maj Lawrence Lee Bazeley Angas, MC (d 1972), of S Aust, London and New York; 1 s (Richard Lee b 23 Nov 1950), 1 da (Catherine Clase Elizabeth b 3 March 1949); *Career* cmmnd KSLI 1936, WWII: France and Burma (depatches), Korea (despatches), E Africa (despatches), cmd KSLI 1953-56, cmd 149 Inf Bde 1962-65, def attaché and cdr Cwlth Mission Korea 1966-68, ret 1968; farmer 1968-, breeder of Sussex Cattle and Blonde d'Acquitaire; pres Kilndown Br Logian, vice pres Bewl Flyfishers; *Recreations* shooting, fishing; *Clubs* Naval and Military; *Style—* Brig Donald Bancroft, OBE; Chicks Farm, Kilndown, Cranbrook, Kent (☎ 0892 890 396); Flat 19, 34 Sloane Ct West, London SW3 (☎ 01 730 1058)

BANCROFT, Baron (Life Peer UK 1981); Ian Powell Bancroft; GCB (1979, KCB 1975, CB 1971); s of Alfred Ernest Bancroft (d 1954) and L Bancroft; *b* 23 Dec 1922; *Educ* Coatham Sch, Balliol Coll Oxford (scholar, hon fellow); *m* 1950, Jean Hilda Patricia, da of David Richard Swaine; 2 s, 1 da; *Career* served Rifle Bde WW II; joined Treasury 1947, with Cabinet Office 1957-59, PPS to Chllrs of Exchequer 1964-66, under-sec Treasury 1966-68, under-sec CSD 1968-70, dep-sec Dir Gen Orgn & Estabmnts (DOE) 1970-72, cmmr of Customs & Excise and dep chm Bd 1972-73, 2 perm sec CSD 1973-75, perm sec Environment 1975-77, head Home Civil Service and perm sec CSD 1978-81, ret; dir: Bass 1982-, The Rugby Gp 1982-, Grindlays Bank 1983-, Sun Life Assurance 1983-, Bass Leisure Ltd 1984-, ANZ Merchant Bank 1987-; vice-pres Building Societies Assoc 1983-; visiting fellow Nuffield Coll Oxford 1973-81, chm cncl Mansfield Coll Oxford 1981-; chm: Royal Hosp and Home, Putney 1984-; memb Advsy Cncl on Public Records 1983-; govr Cranleigh Sch 1983-; pres Bldg Centre Tst 1987-; *Style—* The Rt Hon Lord Bancroft, GCB; 13 Putney Heath Lane, London SW15 (☎ 01 789 6971)

BANCROFT, Hon Simon Powell; er s of Baron Bancroft, GCB (Life Peer); *b* 3 Sept 1953; *Educ* KCS Wimbledon, LSE (BSc); *m* 1985, Vicki Lynn, da of Glenn Rosenqvist, of Dallas, Texas; *Career* asst vice pres Swett & Crawford (wholesale insurance brokers) Dallas USA; *Recreations* squash, racquetball; *Style—* The Hon Simon Bancroft; 2001 Bryan Tower, Suite 3970, Dallas, Texas 75229, USA (☎ (214 742) 8131)

BAND, His Honour Judge; Robert Murray Niven Band; MC (1944), QC (1974); s of Robert Niven Band and Agnes Jane Band; *b* 23 Nov 1919; *Educ* Trinity Coll Glenalmond, Hertford Coll Oxford; *m* 1948, Nancy Margery Redhead; 2 da; *Career* barr 1947, circuit judge 1978-; *Style—* His Honour Judge Band, MC, QC

BAND, Thomas Mollison (Tom); s of late Robert Boyce Band, and Elizabeth, *née* Mollison; *b* 28 Mar 1934; *Educ* Perth Acad; *m* 9 May 1959, Jean McKenzie, da of Robert Brien, JP; 1 s (Ewan b 1960), 2 da (Susan b 1962, Margaret b 1966); *Career* Nat Serv RAF 1952-54; joined CS 1954, princ BOT 1966-73, dir location of Indust

DOI Scotland 1973-76, asst sec SO 1976-84, dir Historic Bldgs & Monuments 1984-87, chief exec Scottish Tourist Bd 1987-; FSA (Scot) 1984, FIT 1988; *Recreations* skiing, gardening, beating; *Style*— Tom Band, Esq; Heathfield, Pitcairngreen, Perth (☎ 073 883 403); Scottish Torist Board, 23 Ravelstone Torr, Edinburgh (☎ 031 332 0350)

BANDET, Frederick; s of Henry Bandet (d 1944); entered UK 1939, naturalised 1947; *b* 3 Oct 1913; *Educ* German State Gymnasium Czechoslovakia, Prague Univ (LLD); *m* 1958, Dorothy-Rose, da of Clifford Harper; 1 s, 2 da; *Career* fndg chm and md: Banton Manufacturing Co Ltd, Erecta Gp of Cos, Hunting Gate Gp Ltd; pres Hunting Gate Gp Ltd (Hitchin, London and USA), and Hunting Gate Management Co Inc (Menlo Park, California); dir: Erecta Properties Ltd, Hitchin Industrial Estates Ltd, Erecta Hitchin Ltd, Hunting Gate Pacific Ltd, Erecta Properties Inc (N America); *Clubs* Gresham, Menlo Circus (California); *Style*— Frederick Bandet Esq; 147 Atherton Ave, Atherton, California, USA (☎ (415 327) 4444)

BANDEY, Derek Charles; s of Percy William Bandey (d 1942), of Bedford, and Beatrice Ellen, *née* Lawrence (d 1965); *b* 9 Nov 1924; *Educ* Bedford Modern Sch; *m* 2 Aug 1949, Mary, da of John Henderson Hutcheson (d 1954); 2 da (Pamela Ann b 15 March 1944 d 1971, Jill Mary b 18 Feb 1951); *Career* MN: cadet 1941-45, 3 Offr 1945-47, 2 Offr 1947-49, 1 Offr 1949-51, Master Mariner (foreign going) 1951; William M Mercer Fraser Ltd (formerly Met Pensions Assoc Ltd) 1951-: office mangr 1956-59, area mangr 1959-65, dir 1965-71, dep md 1971-75, md 1975-82 (ret), conslt 1982-; pres: Pensions Mgmnt Inst 1976-78, Soc of Pension Consits 1978-82; chm Occupational Pension Schemes Jt Working Gp 1980-81, memb cncl Nat Assoc of Pension Funds (chm educn ctee and parly ctee) 1981-88 (previously 1970-77); FPMI; *Recreations* sailing, voluntary work; *Style*— Derek Bandey, Esq; 4 Hunters Way, Chichester, W Sussex, PO19 4RB (☎ 0243 527 831)

BANDON, Countess of; Lois; da of Francis Russell, of Victoria, Australia; *m* 1, Sqdn Ldr Frederick Arthur White, RAF; m 2, 1946, as his 2 w, Air Chief Marshal 5 Earl of Bandon, GBE, CB, CVO, DSO, (d 1979, when the title became extinct); *Style*— The Rt Hon the Countess of Bandon

BANG, Christian Francis Lanyon; s of Christian Lucien Bang of White House, Old Bosham, nr Chichester W Sussex, and Agnes Elizabeth Lanyon, *née* Penno; *b* 12 August 1948; *Educ* Forres and Crookham Court; *Career* HAC 1967-75; CA Blease Lloyd and Co 1967-72, Thomson McLintock and Co 1973-76, Robson Rhodes 1977-78, Norton Warburg Ltd 1979-80, sr ptnr Christian Bang and Co 1981-; dir numerous cos: memb Bow Gp 1975-84; FCA; *Recreations* riding, sailing; *Style*— Christian Bang, Esq; 44 Cathcart Rd, London SW10 9JA; Francis House, Francis St, London SW1P 1DE (☎ 01 834 6262)

BANGOR, 7 Viscount (I 1781); Edward Henry Harold Ward; also Baron Bangor (I 1770); s of 6 Viscount Bangor, PC, OBE; *b* 5 Nov 1905; *Educ* Harrow, RMA Woolwich; *m* 1, 1933 (m dis 1937), Elizabeth, da of Thomas Balfour, JP, of Wrockwardine Hall, Wellington, Salop; m 2, 1937, May Kathleen (d 1969), da of W Middleton, of Shanghai; m 3, 1947 (m dis 1951), Leila Mary (d 1959) da of David Rimington Heaton, DSO; 1 s; m 4, 1951, Mrs Marjorie Alice Simpson, da of late Peter Banks; 1 s (Hon Edward Ward), 1 da (Hon Mrs (Sarah) Baker - the actress Lalla Ward); *Heir* s, Hon William Ward; *Career* broadcaster and journalist, sometime Reuter's correspondent in China and Far East; BBC news observer: Finland 1939-40, Libya 1941, Germany 1945, worldwide 1947-65; *Clubs* Savile, Garrick; *Style*— The Rt Hon The Viscount Bangor; 59 Cadogan Sq, London SW1 (☎ 01 235 3202)

BANGOR, Bishop of 1983-; Rt Rev John Cledan Mears; s of Joseph Mears (d 1972), of Aberystwyth, and Anna LLoyd (d 1968) ; *b* 8 Sept 1922; *Educ* Ardwyn GS Aberystwyth, Univ Coll of Wales Aberystwyth, (BA, MA), Wycliffe Hall Oxford; *m* 1949, Enid Margaret, da of James Tudor Williams (d 1952), of Glam; 1 s (Wyn b 1950), 1 da (Eleri b 1955); *Career* curate: Mostyn 1947-49, Rhosllannerchrugog 1949-55 (vicar 1955-58); lectr (chaplain) St Michael's Coll Llandaff and UC of Wales Cardiff 1959-67 (sub warden 1967-73), vicar of Gabalfa 1973-82, clerical sec Governing Body 1977-82, hon canon of Llandaff Cathedral 1981; author of articles on: Eucharistic Sacrifice, Prayers For the Dead, Comparative Religion, Marriage and Divorce ; *Recreations* hill walking, long distance paths; *Style*— The Rt Rev the Bishop of Bangor; Ty'r Esqob, Bangor, Gwynedd LL57 2SS (☎ 0248 362895)

BANHAM, Belinda Joan; CBE (1977), JP; da of Col Charles Henry Unwin (d 1939), of Chelsea and Winifred Woodman, *née* Wilson (d 1922); *b* 5 Oct 1919; *Educ* privately, West Bank Sch, London Univ (BSc); *m* 1939, Terence Middlecott Banham, MD, s of Rev Vivian Greaves Banham, MC (d 1973); 2 s (John, Simon), 2 da (Susan, Joanna); *Career* chm: Cornwall & Isles of Scilly Health Authy 1967-77, Kensington Chelsea & Westminster FPC 1979-85, Paddington & N Kensington Health Authy 1981-86; memb: SW Regional Hosp Bd 1965-74, Medical Research Cncl 1979-; vice chm Disabled Living Fndn 1983-; memb Lambeth Southwark & Lewisham FPC 1987-; *Style*— Mrs Terence Banham, CBE, JP; Ponsmaen, St Feock, Truro, Cornwall TR3 6QG (☎ (0872) 862275); 81 Vandon Court, Petty France, London SW1; Chairman's Office, Paddington and North Kensington Health Authy, South Wharf Rd, London W1

BANHAM, Dr John Michael Middlecott; s of Terence Middlecott Banham, and Belinda Joan Broadbent, CBE, JP; *b* 22 August 1940; *Educ* Charterhouse, Queens' Coll Cambridge (MA); *m* 30 Oct 1965, Frances Barbara Molyneux, da of Cdr R M Favell, DSC, RN, of St Buryan, Cornwall; 1 s (Mark Richard Middlecot b 1968), 2 da (Serena Frances Tasmin b 1970, Morwenna Bridget Favell b 1972); *Career* temp asst princ Dip Serv 1962-64, mktg exec J Walker Thompson 1964-65, mktg dir mktg div Reed Int 1965-69; McKinsey & Co Inc 1969-83: assoc 1969-75, princ 1975-80, dir 1980-83, controller Audit Cmmn 1983-87, dir gen CBI 1987-; Hon LLD Bath; *Books* numerous reports on mgmnt health and local authy servs; *Recreations* gardening, cliff walking, sailing, ground clearing; *Clubs* Travellers, Oriental; *Style*— Dr John Banham; St Buryan, Cornwall; Centre Point, 103 Oxford St, London WC1A (☎ 01 379 7400)

BANISTER, John Michael; s of Frederick Banister (d 1963); *b* 30 Nov 1924; *Educ* St Peter's Sch York, BNC Oxford (MA); *m* 1960, Thelma, da of William Smart, of Solihull; 1 s, 1 da; *Career* chm Toon & Heath 1972-84 (md 1961-72); dir Royds, Toon & Heath Ltd 1984-85; ret 1986; MCAM, FIPA; *Recreations* philately, bridge, genealogy; *Clubs* Rotary; *Style*— John Banister, Esq; 102 Ladbrook Rd, Solihull, W Mids B91 3RW (☎ 021 705 3332);

BANISTER, (Halcyone) Judith; da of Charles John Banister (d 1953), of Torquay, and May, *née* Fowler (d 1972); *b* 8 May 1925; *Educ* Richmond Co Sch for Girls, King's Coll Univ of London (BA); *Career* asst ed Watchmaker Jeweller & Silversmith 1948-60, PRO Smiths Clocks & Watches Ltd 1961-63, ed Proceedings of the Silver Soc 1961-87, curator pt/t James Walker Goldsmith & Silversmith Ltd Co Museum 1964-84, ed The Goldsmith's Review 1985-87; ed Right Ahead Putney Cons Assoc 1948-60; Freeman City of London 1977, Liveryman Worshipful Co of Goldsmiths 1984; hon memb Silver Soc 1961-, FGA 1959; *Books* Old English Silver (1965), English Silver (1965), Gli Argent: Ingles; (in English 1969), Late Georgian and Regency Silver (1971), Mid-Georgian Silver (1972), Collecting Antique Silver (1972), Country Life Pocket Book of Silver (1982); *Style*— Miss Judith Banister; 20 Marlborough Gdns, Lovelace Rd, Surbiton, Surrey KT6 6NF (☎ 01 399 1707)

BANISTER, (Stephen) Michael (Alvin); s of Dr Harry Banister (d 1963), of Grantchester Cambridge, and Idwen, *née* Thomas (d 1980); *b* 7 Oct 1918; *Educ* Eton, King's Coll Cambridge (MA); *m* 1944, Rachel Joan, da of Claude Vivian Rawlence (d 1967), of Weybridge, Surrey; 4 s (Peter, Christopher and David (twins) and Huw); *Career* Maj HG 1944, Min of Civil Aviation 1946, private sec to 6 successive Mins of Tport & Civil Aviation 1950-56, asst sec Miny of Tport and Bd of Trade 1956-70, UK Shipping Delg UNCTAD 1964, under sec DOE and Dept of Tport 1970-78, UK dep in Euro Conf of Mins of Tport 1976-78, sec Br and For Sch Soc 1978-, dir Taylor & Francis Ltd 1978-, fndr ed Tport reviews 1981-, memb Nat Insur Appeals Tribunal 1978-85; FO 1939-45; *Recreations* country, walking, singing, formerly cricket (played Cambridge Univ vs Austs 1938); *Style*— Michael Banister, Esq; Bramshaw, Lower Farm Rd, Effingham, Surrey (☎ 0372 52778); BFSS, Richard Mayo Hall, Eden St, Kingston-on-Thames (☎ 01 546 2379); T & F, 4 John St, London (☎ 01 405 2237)

BANISTER, William Bisset; MBE (Mil 1958); s of Capt Gerald Courtney Banister, RN, CBE (d 1979), and Constance Cecilia, *née* Bisset; *b* 1 Oct 1919; *Educ* West Downs, Stowe Sch, RMA Woolwich; *m* 8 July 1954, Nancy Openshaw, da of Rev Preb Thomas Openshaw Coupe; 1 s (Ivan b 1955); *Career* cmmnd 1939 RA; served ME 1941, India, Burma (despatches 1945), Palestine 1947; ret 1958; chm Northants NFU 1971; *Recreations* field trials, shooting, fishing; *Clubs* United Service, IOD, Farmers; *Style*— William B Banister, MBE; Warden Hill, Chipping Warden, Banbury, Oxon OX17 1AJ (☎ (0295) 86219)

BANKES, Hon Mrs (Juliet Anne); *née* Williamson; da of 3 Baron Forres (d 1978), and Gillian Ann Maclean, *née* Grant (who *m* 2, 1968, Miles Herman de Zoete, who d 1987); *b* 29 August 1949; *m* 1972, Nigel John Eldon Bankes; 1 s, 2 da; *Style*— The Hon Mrs Bankes

BANKS, Hon Alistair Richard Harvie; s of Baron Banks, CBE, *qv*; *b* 1950; *m* 1977, Loretta Ann Owen; *Style*— The Hon Alistair Banks

BANKS, Brian; s of Albert Edward Banks (d 1981), of London, and Evylyn Lilian, *née* Bilyard (d 1981); *b* 02 July 1938; *Educ* Henry Thornton GS; *m* 6 Oct 1962, Barbara Eileen, da of Edward Townsend (d 1972), of London; 2 s (Andrew Nicholas b 1964, Alexander James b 1973), 1 da (Joanne b 1967); *Career* res analyst L Messel & Co 1964-66, investmnt mangr Nat Provident Inst 1966-68, md Britannia Arrow Hldgs 1975-78 (investmt dir 1968078), dir Dunbar Gp and md Dunbar Fund Mangrs 1978-83, chm Guildhall Investmt Mgmnt 1983-86, md Asset Tst plc 1986-; memb Lloyds; Freeman City of London, memb Worshipful Co of Carmen; *Recreations* Golf; *Clubs* RAC, MCC, City Livery; *Style*— Brian Banks, Esq; Asset Tst plc, Shackleton Hse, 4 Battle Bridge Lane, London SE1 2QE (☎ 01 378 1850, fax 01 407 4843, car tel 0836 234 949, telex 9419723)

BANKS, Hon Mrs; Hon (Caroline Veronica); *née* Hamilton-Russell; da of 10 Viscount Boyne, JP, DL; *b* 15 Feb 1957; *m* 1975, David George Fothergill Banks, FRICS; 1 s, 1 da; *Style*— The Hon Mrs Banks; Upper Norton, Bromyard, Herefordshire; Banks and Silvers (Chartered Surveyor), 66 Foregate St, Worcester (☎ (0905) 23456)

BANKS, Colin; s of William James Banks, and Ida Jenny, *née* Hood; *b* 16 Jan 1932; *m* 1961, Caroline Grigson, PhD; 1 s, 1 da (decd); *Career* fndr ptnr Banks and Miles (graphic designers) 1958-; design conslt: Zool Soc 1962-82, Br Cncl 1968-83, E Midlands Arts Assoc 1974-77, ENO 1975-76; design advsr: Natural Environment Research Cncl, Cmmn for Racial Equality, London Tport, British Telecom, Property Services Agency, art editor Which? 1964-; mangr Blackheath Sch of Art 1981-; FRSA; *Recreations* India; *Clubs* Arts, Wynkyn de Worde, Double Crown; *Style*— Colin Banks, Esq; 1 Tranquil Vale, Blackheath, London SE3 0BU; Little Town Farmhouse, Wilts

BANKS, Baron (Life Peer UK 1974); Desmond Anderson Harvie Banks; CBE (1972); s of James Banks, OBE; *b* 23 Oct 1918; *Educ* UCS Hampstead; *m* 1948, Barbara, da of Richard Taylor Wells; 2 s; *Career* served WW II M East & Italy KRRC & RA as Maj (Ch PRO Allied Mil Govt Trieste 1946); sits as Liberal Peer in Lords; life assur broker, dir Tweddle French & Co (Life & Pensions) Ltd 1973-; chm Lib Pty Exec 1961-63 & 1969-70, pres: Lib Pty 1968-69, Nat Liberal Club; memb For Affrs & Soc Securities Panel 1961-, Lib ppokesman soc servs 1977-, dep Lib whip Ho Lds 1977-, pres Lib Euro Action Gp 1971-; parly candidate (Lib): Harrow E 1950, St Ives 1955, SW Herts 1959; vice chm Euro Atlantic Gp 1979-, Br Cncl Euro Movement 1979-; elder of the Utd Reformed Church; *Style*— The Rt Hon Lord Banks CBE; 58 The Ridgeway, Kenton, Middx (☎ 01 907 7369)

BANKS, Frank David; s of Samuel and Elizabeth Banks; *b* 11 April 1933; *Educ* Liverpool Collegiate Sch, Carnegie Mellon Univ; *m* 1, 1955, Catherine Jacob; 1 s, 2 da; m 2, 1967, Sonia Gay Coleman; 1 da; *Career* chm H Berkeley (Hldgs) Ltd, dir Constructors John Brown Ltd 1974-; FCA; *Style*— Frank Banks Esq; Town House, Ightham, Sevenoaks, Kent TN15 9HH

BANKS, Hon Graham Thorton Harvie; s of Baron Banks, CBE, *qv*; *b* 1953; *Style*— The Hon Graham Banks

BANKS, James Alastair Crawford; s of Maj Alastair Arthur Banks, MC, of Thursley, Surrey, and Ann Paton, *née* Crichton; *b* 11 Mar 1947; *Educ* Dover Coll, Greenwich HS USA, Grenoble Univ France; *m* 15 May 1976, Sally Christable, da of Richard Geoffrey Hugh Coles, of Sandleheath, Fordingbridge, Hants; 2 s (Alastair b 1979, Stuart b 1981); *Career* works mangr H Taylor (Drums) Ltd 1972-78, dir and gen mangr Victor Blagden Ltd 1978-88, gp business devpt exec Blagden Industs plc 1988-; chm E London area ctee CBI 1987, (memb London regnl cncl 1987), pres Barking & Dagenham COC 1987, chm Barking & Dagenham Trg Initiative Ltd 1987, govr Meadgate Primary Sch Gt Baddow 1988; *Recreations* sailing, squash, bridge, skiing, badminton, theatre; *Style*— James Banks, Esq; Brickwalls, High St, Great Baddow, Essex, CM2 7HQ (☎ 0245 72053); Blagden Industries plc, Claire Hse, Bridge St, Leatherhead, Surrey, KT22 8HY (☎ 0372 378 080, fax 0372 378 580)

BANKS, John; s of John Banks (d 1982), of Rainhill, Lancs, and Jane, *née* Dewhurst (d

1987); *b* 2 Dec 1920; *Educ* Univ of Liverpool (BEng 1941, MEng 1944); *m* 18 Aug 1943, Nancy Olive, da of William James Yates (d 1947), of St Helens, Lancs; 2 s (John Rodney b 30 Oct 1944, Roger Howard b 20 July 1947); *Career* exec chm BICC Research & Engrg Ltd 1975-84; exec dir BICC plc bd memb St James Venture Capital Fund Ltd 1985-89; visiting prof Univ of Liverpool; Freeman of City of London, Liveryman of Worshipful Co of Engineers; FEng 1983, FIEE (pres 1982-83); *Recreations* golf, music, bridge; *Clubs* Seaford Golf; *Style—* John Banks, Esq; Flat B1, Marine Gate, Marine Drive, Brighton BN2 5TQ (☎ 0273 690756)

BANKS, (Ernest) John; s of Ernest Frederick Banks, and Marian Blanche, *née* Nuttall; *b* 2 July 1945; 1 da (Charlotte Marianne Blanche b 5 May 1983); *Career* chm and chief exec offr Young and Rubicam Gp Advertising Agency; memb: The Prince's Youth Business Trust, The Prince's Trust, Business in the Community; M Inst M, memb Market Res Soc GB, FIPA; *Clubs* Carlton, RAC; *Style—* John Banks, Esq; Young & Rubicam Ltd, Greater London House, Hampstead Rd, London NW1 7QP (☎ 01 380 6555, fax 01 380 6570, telex 25 197)

BANKS, (William) Lawrence; s of Richard Alford Banks, CBE, of Herefords, and Lilian Jean, *née* Walker (d 1973); *b* 7 June 1938; *Educ* Rugby, ChCh Oxford (MA); *m* 1963, Elizabeth Christina, da of Capt Leslie Swain Saunders, DSO, RN, of Northants; 2 s (Richard b 1965, Edward b 1967); *Career* merchant banker; dep chm Robert Fleming & Co Ltd; hon tres Royal Postgrad Med Sch Hammersmith, hon tres RHS, tstee Chevening Estate; *Recreations* gardening, fishing, shooting & theatre; *Clubs* MCC, Pratts; *Style—* Lawrence Banks, Esq; 13 Abercorn Place, London NW8 9EA (☎ 01 624 5740); Robert Fleming & Co Ltd, 25 Copthall Ave, London EC2R 7DR (☎ 01 638 5858)

BANKS, Lynne Reid; da of Dr James Reid-Banks GP (d 1953), and Muriel Alexandra Marsh (d 1982, actress stage name Muriel Alexander); *b* 31 July 1929; *Educ* various schs in Canada, attended Italia Conti Stage Sch and RADA 1946-49; *m* 1965, Chaim Stephenson; 3 s (Adiel b 1965, Gillon b 1967, Omri b 1968); *Career* actress 1949-54, reporter ITN 1955-62, teacher of english in Israel 1963-71; full time writer and lectr 1971-; visiting teacher Tanzania Int Sch 1988; *Books* The L-Shaped Room (1960), An End to Running (1962), Children at the Gate (1968), The Backward Shadow (1970), Two is Lonely (1974), Defy the Wilderness (1981), The Warning Bell (1984), Casualties (1987), biographical novels: Dark Quartet, The Story of the Brontes (1976), Path to the Silent Country (sequel 1977); books for young adults: One More River (1973), Sarah and After (1975), My Darling Villain (1977), The Writing on the Wall (1981), Melusine, a Mystery (1988): childrens' books: The Adventures of King Midas (1977), The Farthest-Away Mountain (1977), Houdini (1978), The Indian in the Cupboard (1980), Maura's Angel (1984), The Fairy Rebel (1985), Return of the Indian (1986); history: Letters to My Israeli Sons (1979), Torn Country, An Oral History of Israel's War of Independence (1982); *Recreations* theatre, gardening, talking; *Style—* Ms Lynne Reid Banks; c/o Sheila Watson, Watson, Little Ltd, Suite 8, 26 Charing Cross Rd, London WC2H 0DG (☎ 01 836 5880)

BANKS, Sir Maurice Alfred Lister; s of Alfred Banks, and Elizabeth, *née* Davey; *b* 11 August 1901; *Educ* Westminster, Manchester U (BSc); *m* 1933, Ruth, da of Perry D Hall, of Philadelphia; 1 s, 2 da; *Career* joined Anglo Persian Oil Co 1924; Br Petroleum: md 1960, dep chm 1965, ret 1967; chm Bd of Trade Dept Ctee to enquire into patent law and procedure 1967-70; chm Laird Gp 1970-75; FRIC, MIChemE; kt 1971; *Style—* Sir Maurice Banks; Beech Copice, Kingswood, Surrey (☎ Mogador (0737) 2270)

BANKS, Norman Dinsdale; s of William Dinsdale Banks, MBE (d 1963), and Rose Mary, *née* Sculpher (d 1983); *b* 18 May 1929; *Educ* St Dunstan's Coll Catford London, London Univ (LLB); *m* 3 Jan 1970, Gwendoline Georgina, da of FlLt George Frederick Stubbings (d 1974); *Career* barr Lincoln's Inn 1952, conslt ed Rating and Valuation Reporter 1978; chm W Lewisham Cons Assoc 1966-68; memb: LLC (Cons) 1961-65, Lewisham Borough Cncl (Cons) 1959-71 ldr cncl (1968-71); *Recreations* gardening, walking, one bull terrier; *Style—* Norman Banks, Esq; 1 Essex Court, Temple, London EC4Y 9AR (☎ 01 583 7759, fax 01 353 8620)

BANKS, Philip Francis; *b* 27 August 1933; *Educ* London Univ (BSc); *m* 1957, Judith Monica; 1 da (Jessica); *Career* served Nat Service Lt Army; md A T Kearney Ltd 1978-85; chm Management Consultants Assoc 1983; head Int AT Kearney Inc 1986-; *Recreations* politics; *Clubs* Lansdown; *Style—* Philip Banks, Esq; Ferndale, Pool Hayes Lane, Willenhall, Staffs (☎ (0902) 65834); Kearneys, Lon Ednyfed, Criccieth, Gwynedd (☎ (076 671) 2926); c/o A T Kearney Ltd, (☎ 01 834 6886)

BANKS, Robert George; MP (C) Harrogate 1974-; s of late George Walmsley Banks, MBE, and Olive Beryl, *née* Tyler; *b* 18 Jan 1937; *Educ* Haileybury; *m* 1967, Diana Margaret Payne Crawfurd; 4 s, 1 da; *Career* Lt Cdr RNR; memb Paddington Borough Cncl 1959-65; jt fndr dir Antocks Lairn Ltd 1963-67; jt sec Cons Parly Def Ctee 1976-79, memb Cncl of Europe and W Euro Union 1977-81, sec Anglo-Sudan Gp 1978-83 and chm 1983-, vice chm All-Pty Tourism Gp 1979- (sec 1974-79), pps to: Min of State FO 1979-82, Min of State for Overseas Dvpt FO 1981-82; memb Select Ctee on Foreign Affairs 1982-83 (memb of overseas dvpt sub-ctee 1982-); memb: N Atlantic Assembly, Alcohol Educn & Research Cncl 1982-; *Books* Britain's Home Defence Gamble (1979, co-author); *Recreations* travel, architecture; *Style—* Robert Banks Esq, MP; Bretteston Hall, Stanstead, Sudbury, Suffolk; Cow Myers, Galphay, Ripon, Yorks

BANKS, Robert James; s of Maj Kenneth Banks (d 1986), of Yalding, Kent and Nona Banks; *b* 26 Feb 1951; *Educ* Dover Coll, Univ of Wales (BSc); *Career* barr Inner Temple 1978; co fndr Yalding and Nettlestead Protection Soc; *Recreations* antiques, country pursuits; *Style—* Robert J Banks, Esq; 8 Kings Bench Walk, Temple, London, EC4 (☎ 01 353 7851, fax 01 353 2146)

BANKS, Roderick Charles I'Anson; s of Charles I'Anson Banks of Kingston upon Thames, and Suzanne Mary Gwendoline *née* Hall; *b* 5 Dec 1951; *Educ* Westminster, UCL (LLB); *m* 11 Aug 1979, Susan Elizabeth Lavington, da of His Hon Judge Albert William Clark, *qv*, of Worthing, Sussex; 2 s (Oliver b 1982, Frederick b 1986); *Career* barr Lincoln's Inn, 1974, legal author; memb Country Landowners Assoc; *Books* co-ed: Lindley on Partnership (14 edn 1979, 15 edn 1984), Encyclopaedia of Professional Partnerships (1987); *Recreations* reluctant gardener, TV/video addict; *Style—* Roderick Banks, Esq; 3 Stone Buildings, Lincolns Inn, London WC2A 3XL (☎ 01 242 4937, fax 01 405 3896, telex 892300 ADVICE G REF TW)

BANKS, Tony; MP (Lab) Newham North West 1983-; *b* 1943,April; *Educ* Archibishop Tensors GS Kennington, York Univ, London Sch of Economics; *Career* sponsored by TGWU, contested (Lab): East Grinstead 1970, Newcastle North Oct 1974, Watford 1979; sometime political advsr to Dame Judith Hart and AUEW head of research; asst gen sec Assoc of Broadcasting and Allied Staffs 1976-83; memb: Co-operative Pty, GLC 1970-77 and 1981-86; chm: Gen Purposes Ctee 1975-77, Arts Ctee 1981-83; last chm GLC 1985-86; former Bd Memb: Nat Theatre, English Nat Opera, London Festival Ballet, London Orchestral Concert Bd, Treasury Select Ctee; *Style—* Tony Banks, Esq, MP; House of Commons, London SW1

BANNATYNE, Dugald Swanwick; s of Lt-Col Frederic Cooke Bannatyne (d 1963), of Sandhurst, Camberley, and Emma Margaret, *née* Swanwick (d 1966); *b* 31 Jan 1919; *Educ* Wellington Coll Berks, Pembroke Coll Cambridge (BA); *m* 15 June 1946, Vera Pauline, da of Dr Charles Henry Nash, of Sandhurst, Berks (d 1952); 2 da (Penelope b 1947, Melinda b 1949); *Career* Lt Queens Own Cameron Highlanders 1939-46 (POW 1941-45); CA 1948, asst co sec Knapp Drewett & Sons Ltd Kingston-on-Thames 1948-53, chief accountant Abbott Laboratories Ltd Queenborough Kent 1953-56 (co sec 1961-74, fin dir and co sec 1977-81), fin dir Abbott Europe 1974-77, chief accountant Royal Stafford China Ltd Borslem Stoke-on-Trent 1981-83, fin dir and co sec Spartan Luggage Co Ltd 1983-85, pt/t mgmnt accountant COSIRA 1985-86, pt/t practice 1986-; chm and tres local Cons Pty; FCA; *Recreations* horse racing and eventing, squash, tennis; *Style—* Dugald Bannatyne, Esq; Pool Cottage, Bouldon, Nr Craven Arms, Shropshire SY7 9DT (☎ 058476 372)

BANNEN, Ian; s of John James Bannen (d 1958), of Coatbridge, Scotland, and Agnes Clare, *née* Galloway (d 1976); *b* 29 June 1928; *Educ* St Aloyious Jesuit Sch Glasgow, Ratcliffe Coll Leics; *m* 16 Nov 1978, Marilyn, da of John Salisbury (d 1984), of Wrexham; *Career* Nat Serv RE; actor; RSC 1951-54, first West End appearance as Marco in a View from the Bridge Comedy Theatre 1956-57, title role in Sergeant Musgrave's Dance Royal Ct Theatre 1958, Julian in Toys in the Attic Piccadilly Theatre 1960; RSC 1961-62: title role in Hamlet, Orlando to Vanessa Redgrave's Rosalind in As You Like It, Mercutio in Romeo and Juliet, Iago to Sir John Gielgud's Othello; Yvonne Arnaud Theatre: Dick Dudgeon in The Devils Disciple 1965, The Brass Hat 1972; Hickey in The Iceman Cometh Royal Lyceum Theatre Edinburgh 1974, Judge Brack to Janet Suzmann's Hedda Gabler Duke of York's Theatre and Edinburgh Festival 1977, Hugh in Translations Hampstead Theatre and Nat Theatre 1981-82 (Critics Award Actor of the Year), Tyrone in Moon for the Misbegotten Riverside Theatre and Mermaid Theatre (also American Rep Harvard and Broadway) 1983-84; recent films and tv incl: Hope and Glory (Best Supporting Actor Nomination BAFTA), Flight of the Phoenix (Oscar nomination), Gandhi, Gorky Park, Eye of the Needle, Defence of the Realm, Tinker Tailor Soldier Spy, Dr Jekyll and Mr Hyde; memb St Vincent de Paul Soc; vice pres Catholic Stage Guild, memb American Acad (AMPAS) 1966-; BAFTA; *Recreations* walking, swimming, reading, photography; *Style—* Ian Bannen, Esq; c/o London Management, 235-241 Regent St, London W1 (☎ 01 493 1610)

BANNER; *see*: Harmood-Banner

BANNER, Christopher Victor; s of Samuel Victor Banner, (d 1981), of Whinhurst, Birkenhead, and Nora Dorothy, *née* Stott (d 1968); *b* 4 Mar 1936; *Educ* Stowe; *m* 1, (m dis 1974), Elizabeth Anne, da of Col R C Blair; 2 da (Juliette Christine b 11 Oct 1964, Fiona Jane b 23 June 1966); m 2, 12 May 1977, Alison Hilary, da of Stanley Gardner; 1 da (Charlotte Sarah b 29 March 1979); *Career* Nat Serv 1 Lt 21 Field Regt RA, TA Capt 359 Medium Regt RA; lab tech Shell Mex BP 1956-57, plant asst J Bibby and Sons 1957-58; Samuel Banner Ltd: sales rep, dir mktg, md; *Recreations* golf, tennis; *Clubs* Racquetts (Liverpool), Artists (Liverpool); *Style—* Christopher Banner, Esq; Samuel Banner and Co Ltd, 59 Sandhills Lane, Liverpool L5 9XL (☎ 051 922 7871, fax 051 922 0407, telex 627025)

BANNER, David Ian; s of John David Banner, of Uddingston, Glasgow, and Georgina Stewart, *née* Johnston; *b* 14 April 1936; *Educ* Uddingston GS, Glasgow Univ (BL 1956); *m* 18 June 1975, Mary Elizabeth, da of John Rourke, of Greenock (d 1974); 2 da (Peta b 1978, Clare b 1981); *Career* cmmnd RAF during Nat Serv, Flying Offr; slr, sr ptnr Neill Clerk of Greenock and Glasgow; chm Sir Gabriel Wood's Mariner's Home Greenock 1982-, dep chm Greenock Dist Scout Cncl 1976-; *Recreations* tennis, curling, bridge, scouting; *Style—* D I Banner, Esq; 33 The Esplanade, Greenock (☎ 0475 20621); 3 Ardgowan Sq, Greenock (☎ 0475 24522, telex 777471, fax 0475 84339)

BANNERMAN, Alexander Patrick; s and h of Sir Donald Arthur Gordon Bannerman, 13 Bt, *qv*; *b* 5 May 1933; *Educ* Gordonstoun, Salem, Edinburgh Univ, RAC Cirencester; *m* 1977, Joan Mary, da of late John Henry Wilcox of Tadcaster, Yorks; *Career* formerly with Queen's Own Cameron Highlanders and at Queen Elizabeth's Training Coll for The Disabled, Leatherhead; E Surrey Water Co.; *Style—* Alexander Bannerman, Esq; 73 New Causeway, Reigate, Surrey RH2 7PP (☎ (073 72) 21560)

BANNERMAN, Hon Calum Ruairi Mundell; yr s of Baron Bannerman of Kildonan (Life Peer, d 1969); *b* 9 May 1936; *Educ* Kelvinside Acad Glasgow, Merchiston Castle and St Catharine's Coll Cambridge (BA); *m* 1962, Mary, *née* Parker; 1 s, 2 da; *Style—* The Hon Calum Bannerman

BANNERMAN, Lt-Col Sir Donald Arthur Gordon; 13 Bt (NS 1682); s of Lt-Col Sir Arthur Bannerman, 12 Bt, KCVO, CIE (d 1955), and Virginia Emilie Bedford (d 1913); *b* 2 July 1899; *Educ* Harrow, Sandhurst; *m* 1932, Barbara Charlotte, da of Lt-Col Alec Cameron, OBE, IMS (d 1932); 2 s (Patrick and David), 2 da (Ruth and Janet); *Heir* s, Alexander Bannerman; *Career* Regular Army offr Cameron Highlanders 1918-47; ret as Lt-Col; served in N Russia 1915, Aldershot, Germany, Inverness, India (Ahmednagar, Poona, Jyzabad), Mil Govt Germany 1945-48 as PRO and SCO; housemaster: Gordonstoun 1948-52, Fettes 1952-69; *Style—* Lt-Col Sir Donald Bannerman, Bt

BANNERMAN, (George) Gordon; s of George Bannerman (d 1961), of Glasgow; *b* 25 Feb 1932; *Educ* Glasgow HS, Glasgow Acad, Sidney Sussex Coll Cambridge; *m* 1959, Ann, da of James Gemmell, of Milngavie (d 1977); 1 s, 1 da; *Career* actuary; dir and actuary C T Bowring & Layborn Ltd 1972, dir and chief actuary Fenchurch Fin Services Ltd 1987; FFA, AIA, ASA, FPMI, ACII; *Style—* Gordon Bannerman Esq; 37 Westbury Rd, London N12 (☎ 01 445 1795)

BANNERMAN, James Charles Christopher; s of Prof Lloyd Charles Bannerman, of Ontario, Canada, and Ethel Leah, *née* Dakin; *b* 23 Feb 1949; *Educ* Univ of Kent (BA); *m* 2 Sept 1988, Sara Elizabeth, da of Thomas Haig; *Career* dancer Nat Ballet of Canada 1968-72, dancer and choreographer London Comtemporary Dance Theatre 1975-; choreographed: Treading, The Singing, Sandsteps, Shadows in the Sun, Unfolding Field; *Recreations* gardening, travel, wilderness canoe trips in Canada; *Style—* James Bannerman, Esq; 20 Tetherdown, Muswell Hill, London N10 1NB (☎ 01 883 7399); c/o LCDT 16 Flaxman Terrace, London WC1 (☎ 01 387 0324)

BANNERMAN, Hon John Walter MacDonald; er s of Baron Bannerman of Kildonan (Life Peer, d 1969); *b* 13 August 1932; *Educ* Glasgow Univ (MA), Emmanuel Coll Cambridge (BA, PhD); *Style*— The Hon John Bannerman

BANNERMAN OF KILDONAN, Baroness; Ray; *née* Mundell; da of late Walter Mundell, of Swordale, Evanton, Ross-shire; *m* 1931, Baron Bannerman of Kildonan (Life Peer, d 1969); 2 s, 2 da; *Style*— The Rt Hon Lady Bannerman of Kildonan; The Old Manse, Balmaha, Stirlingshire

BANNINGTON, Adrian John (Barney); s of Donald Bertram Bannington, of Tollesbury, Essex, and Sylvia Ada, *née* Mann; *b* 4 April 1956; *Educ* Lucton Boys Secondary Sch Loughton, W Hatch Tech High Chigwell, NE London Poly; *m* 19 Sept 1981, Elizabeth Jennifer Jane, da of Capt Peter Richardson, JP, of Loughton, Essex; 1 da (Amy Louise b 16 Apr 1985); *Career* Saffery Champness (formerly Saffery Sons & Co) 1975-1988: articled 1979, qualified CA 1980, mangr 1985-88; fin dir Planning Res & Systems plc 1988-; memb ICAEW; *Recreations* sailing, golf, chess; *Style*— Barney Bannington, Esq; 9 Chapel Rd, Epping, Essex (☎ 0378 72625); Planning Research & Systems plc, Premier House, 44-48 Dover St, London W1X 3RF (☎ 01 409 1635)

BANNISTER, Brian; s of Norman Bannister, and Sarah Ann, *née* Jolly;; *b* 31 Dec 1933; *Educ* King Edward VII Sch Lytham St Annes, Birmingham Sch of Architecture (Dip Arch); *m* 1, 5 April 1961 (m dis 1973), Pauline Mary, da of Jack Miller (d 1987) of Preston Lancs; 1 s (Dominic b 3 Feb 1964, d 1981), 1 da (Karen b 23 July 1962); m 2, 25 May 1973, Avril, da of James Wigley Allen (d 1987); 1 s (Richard b 8 July 1975), 1 da (Katie 10 Feb 1979); *Career* Nat Serv 1958-59; architect Lancs CC 1956-58 and 1969; John H D Martin and Ptnrs: sr architect 1959-64, assoc 1964-68; assoc ic Watkins Grey Woodgate Int Birmingham Off 1968-70; ptnr: Burman Goodhal and Ptnrs 1970-72, Brian Bannister and Assocs 1972-85, Brian Bannister partnership 1985-; dir Co-ordinated Project Mgmnt 1971-, dir and co sec BMW Properties Ltd 1986-; sub ed Architecture West Midlands 1970-75, memb ctee Birmingham Architechtural Assoc 1972-82, vice pres Birmingham Architectural Assoc 1980-82 (ctee memb 1972-82, pres 1982-84); ARIBA 1958, FBIM 1980; *Recreations* golf, squash, sailing; *Clubs* Edgbaston GC, Edgbaston Priory; *Style*— Brian Bannister, Esq; 180 Lordswood Rd, Harborne, Birmingham B17 8QH (☎ 021 426 3671); Brian Bannister Partnership, Belmont House, 40 Vicarage Rd, Edgbaston, Birmingham B15 3EZ (☎ 021 454 7373, fax 021 454 7109)

BANNISTER, Col Desmond John Howard; MBE (1942), MC (1942); s of Alfred Charles Bannister (d 1959), of Devon, and Alice Maud, *née* Guppy (d 1959); *b* 3 Feb 1915; *Educ* Downside, RMC Sandhurst; *m* 2 March 1946, Pamela Marian (d 1976), da of Capt Brian Pratt (d 1955), of Watford, Herts; 1 step s (Andre Petre b 1944); *Career* cmmnd The Devonshire Regt 1935, Kings African Rifles 1938-42, Middle East 1940-42, Burma 1944, NW Europe b 1948, Malaya b 1949-51, NATO (Turkey) Staff 1954-57, dep cdr Tropical Oman Scouts 1955-60, MOD 1958-70, Col 1963, ret 1970; *Recreations* painting (watercolours), bridge, fell walking; *Clubs* Army and Navy, Pall Mall; *Style*— Col Desmond J H Bannister, MBE, MC; Wisteria Cottage, North Cheriton, Temple Combe, Somerset (☎ (0963) 33415)

BANNISTER, Sir Roger Gilbert; CBE (1955); s of late Ralph and Alice Bannister, of Harrow; *b* 23 Mar 1929; *Educ* Univ Coll Sch, Exeter and Merton Coll Oxford (MA, MSc), Harvard Univ USA; *m* 1955, Moyra, da of Per Jacobsson, of Sweden,(chm IMF); 2 s, 2 da; *Career* first man to run the four minute mile 1954; conslt neurologist: Nat Hosp Nervous Diseases, hon conslt neurologist Oxford Regnl and Dist Health Authy; master Pembroke Coll Oxford 1985-; hon fell Merton Coll Oxford; Hon Doctorate: Jyvaskyla Univ (Finland) 1983, Univ Bath 1984, Univ Rochester NY USA 1985, Univ Pavia Italy 1986, Williams Coll USA 1987; FRCP; kt 1975; *Style*— Sir Roger Bannister, CBE; The Master's Lodgings, Pembroke College, Oxford OX1 1DW (☎ 0865 276 444)

BANNOCK, Graham Bertram; s of Eric Burton Bannock (d 1977), and Winifred, *née* Sargent (d 1972); *b* 10 July 1932; *Educ* Crewkerne Sch, LSE (Bsc Econ); *m* 26 Feb 1971, Françoise Marcelle, *née* Vrancky; 1 s Laurent Graham b 1972); *Career* Sgt RASC 1950-52; market analyst Ford Motor Co 1955-56; asst mangr: market res Richard Thomas & Baldwins Ltd 1957-58, Rover Co 1958-60; sr admin OECD Paris 1960-62; chief econ & market research Rover Company 1962-67; mangr advanced progs Ford of Europe Inc 1968-69, dir res ctee of Inquiry on Small Firms 1970-71; md: Econ Advsy Gp Ltd 1971-81, Economist Intelligence Unit Ltd 1981-84; chm Graham Bannock & Ptnrs Ltd 1985-; *Books* Business Economics and Statistics (with A J Merrett, 1962); The Penguin Dictionary of Economics (with R E Baxter and Evan Davis, 1972); The Juggernauts (1971); How to Survive the Slump (1975); Smaller Business in Britain and Germany (1976); The Economics of Small Firms (1981); Going Public (1987); *Recreations* badminton, gymnastics, karate, the arts; *Clubs* Royal Automobile, London World Traders; *Style*— Graham Bannock, Esq; Graham Bannock & Partners Ltd, 53 Clarewood Court, Crawford St, London W1H 5DF (☎ 01 723 1845)

BANSKI, Norman Alexander Fyfe Ritchie; s of Richard Carol Stanislaw Bański, Lieut 9 Polish Lancers, of Kincardineshire, and Marion Alexandra Watt Fyfe later (d 1970, as Mrs George A Ritchie); *b* 3 August 1955; *Educ* Laurencekirk Secdy Sch, Mackie Acad Stonehaven, Aberdeen Univ (LLB); *Career* slr: ptnr W J C Reed & Sons, registrar births deaths and marriages, cemetery clerk, census offr (S Kincardine) 1981, sec Milltown Community (maladjusted children), tstee various local charitable tsts, dir of Milltown Community, Howe O'The Mearns Devpts Ltd, dir Laurencekirk and Dist Angling Assoc, RWM Lodge St Laurence 136; past princ: Chapter Haran 8, Off Bearer Provincial Grand Lodge Kincardineshire; memb: Grand Lodge of Scotland, Law Soc of Scotland, Scottish Law Agents Soc, Assoc of Registrars for Scotland, WWF; *Recreations* golf, angling, clay pigeon shooting, sailing, philately, rugby; *Clubs* Laurencekirk and Dist Angling Assoc, Caledonian Golf, Montrose, MacKie Acad F P Rugby, Lodge St Laurence 136, Chapter Haran 8; *Style*— Norman Bański, Esq; W J C Reed & Sons, Royal Banks Buildings, Laurencekirk

BANSZKY von AMBROZ, Baron (Hungary) Nicholas Laszlo; s of Baron Dr Laszlo Banszky von Ambroz (d 1965), of London, and Veronica, *née* Racz (now Lady Wyatt of Weeford); *b* 18 July 1952; *Educ* Westminster, Worcester Coll Oxford (MA); *m* 31 March 1984, Caroline Janet, da of Harold Arthur Armstrong While, of London; 2 da (Genevra b 1985, Antonella b 1987); *Career* merchant banker; N M Rothschild & Sons Ltd 1974-84, Charterhouse J Rothschild Gp 1984-86, Smith NewCourt plc 1986- (head corp fin, dir 1988); *Recreations* skiing, riding, cooking, gardening; *Style*— Baron Nicholas Banszky von Ambroz; 6 Rylett Crescent, Stamford Brook, London W12 (☎ 01 749 3700); Chetwynd House, 24 St Swithin's Lane, London EC4 (☎ 01 628 4433)

BANTON, Prof Michael Parker; JP (Bristol) 1966; s of Francis Clive Banton (d 1985), of Maids, Morton, Buckingham, and Kathleen Blanche, *née* Parkes (d 1945); *b* 8 Sept 1926; *Educ* King Edwards Sch, Univ of London (LSE, BSc), Univ of Edingburgh (PhD, DSc); *m* 23 July 1952,(Rut) Marianne, da of Lars Robert Jacobson (d 1954), of Lulea, Sweden; 2 s (Sven Christopher b 1953, Nicholas b 1956), 2 da (Ragnhild b 1955, Dagmar b 1959); *Career* Sub-Lt RNVR 1946-47; lectr in Social Anthropology Univ of Edinburgh 1955-62, reader 1962-65, prof Sociology Univ of Bristol 1965- (pro-vice chllr 1985-88), memb Roy Cmmn on: Criminal Procedure 1978-81, Civil Disorders in Bermuda 1978; memb UN Ctee for Elimination of Racial Discrimination 1986-; pres Royal Anthropological Inst 1987-89; *Books* The Coloured Quarter (1955), West African City 91957), White and Coloured (1959), The Policeman in the Community (1964), Roles (1965), Race Relations (1967), Racial Minorities (1972), Police-Community Relations (1973), The Idea of Race (1977), Racial and Ethnic Competition (1983), Promoting Racial Harmony (1985), Investigating Robbery (1985), Racial Theories (1987), Racial Consciousness (1988); *Style*— Prof Michael Banton, JP; The Court Hse, Llanvair Discoed, Gwent NP6 6LX (☎ 0633 400 208); Univ Dept of Sociology, 12 Woodland Rd, Bristol BS8 1UQ (☎ 0272 30 30 30, ext 3141)

BAR, Geoffrey; s of Frank Gordon Henry Bar (d 1979); *b* 19 Mar 1929; *Educ* Aldenham; *m* 1954, Jeannie Campbell Penton, da of Arthur Wellington Blackwood (d 1964); 3 s; *Career* asst md Dickinson Robinson Gp, div chief exec DRG Packaging; chief exec: Milk Mktg Bd 1981-85, Dairy Crest Ltd 1985-, CTT Ltd: FCA; *Recreations* tennis, sailing, music, squash, skiing; *Clubs* Royal Lymington Yacht, Milford Country; *Style*— Geoffrey Bar, Esq; 6 Leicester House, Ditton Close, Thames Ditton, Surrey (☎ 01 398 4101); Dairy Crest House, Portsmouth Road, Surbiton, Surrey KT6 5QL (☎ 01 398 4155, telex 8956671)

BARBARY, Lady Pamela Joan; *née* Nugent; o da of 12 Earl of Westmeath (d 1971), and Doris, *née* Imlach (d 1968); *b* 31 Jan 1921; *m* 23 Sept 1950, Lt-Col Peter John Barbary, OBE, GM, TD, DL (d 1969), eldest s of late Brig John Ewart Trounce Barbary, CBE, TD, ADC, DL, of Trevarth House, Gwennap, Cornwall; 1 s, 1 da; *Career* sometime section officer WAAF; *Style*— Lady Pamela Barbary; Briar Rose Cottage, 17 Landeryon Gdns, Penzance, Cornwall

BARBER, Baron (Life Peer UK 1974), of Wentbridge, W Yorks; Anthony Perrinott Lysberg Barber; TD, PC (1963); s of late John Barber, CBE, of Doncaster, and Musse, *née* Lysberg; *b* 4 July 1920; *Educ* Retford GS, Oriel Coll Oxford (MA, LLB); *m* 1950, Jean Patricia (d 1983), da of Milton Asquith, of Wentbridge; 2 da (Hon Louise, Hon Josephine); *Career* barr 1948; MP (C): Doncaster 1951-64, Altrincham and Sale 1965-74; chllr of exchequer 1970-74; chm Cons Pty Orgn 1967-70; chm Standard Chartered Bank 1974-87; memb: Franks Ctee on Falklands 1982; Cwlth Eminent Persons Gp on S Africa 1985-86; *Style*— The Rt Hon The Lord Barber, TD, PC; House of Lords, London SW1

BARBER, Colin Thomas; s of Frank Barber, OBE, of Folkestone, Kent, and Lilian Barber, MBE; *b* 8 Feb 1948; *Educ* Haileybury, Kingston Coll of Advanced Technology, London Univ (BSc); *m* 9 June 1973, Diana Elizabeth, da of Peter Parkyn (d 1987), of S Africa; *Career* dir Scac UK Ltd; memb ICA 1972; FICA 1979; *Recreations* tennis, bridge, watching rugby union and American football; *Clubs* Old Haileyburian RFC, Bidborough Tennis, Leigh Tennis, The Club, The Danish; *Style*— Colin T Barber, Esq; Bidborough Close, Frank's Hollow Road, Bidborough, Kent TN3 0UD; Unit 6, Colnestate, Old Bath Road, Colnbrook, Bucks SU3 0NJ (☎ (0753) 683530)

BARBER, David Stewart; s of Jack Barber (d 1961), of Manchester, and Margaret, *née* Hall (d 1960); *b* 21 Sept 1931; *Educ* Rossendale GS; *m* 25 Jan 1965, Hazel Valerie, da of Francis Smith (d 1968), of Whitstable, Kent; 1 s (Nicholas b 1968), 1 da (Suzanna b 1971); *Career* 2 Lt Lancs Fus 1950-52; trainee and subsequently mangr Imperial Tobacco Co (John Player & Sons) 1952-57; PA management conslts (various appointments) 1958-69; divnl ch exec Bovis Ltd 1969-71; chm and ch exec Halma plc 1972-; *Recreations* tennis, golf, squash; *Style*— David Barber, Esq; Ballinger House, Ballinger Common, Bucks HP16 9LQ (☎ 024 06 2345); Halma plc, Misbourne Court, Rectory Way, Amersham, Bucks HP7 0DE (☎ 0494 721111)

BARBER, (Thomas) David; s and h of Sir William Barber, 2 Bt, TD; *b* 18 Nov 1937; *Educ* Eton, Trin Coll Cambridge (MA); *m* 1, 1972 (m dis 1975), Amanda Mary, da of Frank Rabone, and widow of Maj Michael Healing, Gren Guards; 1 s (Thomas b 14 March 1973); m 2, 1978, Jeannine Mary, former w of John Richard Boyle (gs of Col Lionel Boyle, CMG, MVO, himself ggs of 7 Earl of Cork and Orrery), by whom she had 3 s, and da of Capt Timothy John Gurney by his w Bridget, half sister of Sir Christopher de Bathe, 6 and last Bt; 1 s (W Samuel T b 23 Sept 1982), 1 da (Sarah b 19 June 1981); *Career* 2nd Lt RA 1957-58; *Style*— David Barber, Esq; Windrush House, Inkpen, nr Newbury, Berks RG15 0QY (☎ (048 84) 419)

BARBER, Sir Derek Coates; s of Thomas Smith-Barber (d 1967), of The Thatched House, nr Stradbroke, Suffolk and Elsie Agnes, *née* Coates (d 1967); descendant of John Coates, whose three sons, due to a disagreement, swore not to bear his name, 1870; instead they adopted Coates, Cotts and Coutts; *b* 17 June 1918; *Educ* RAC Cirencester; *m* 1 (m dis 1981); m 2, 1983, Rosemary Jennifer Brougham, da of Lt-Cdr Randolph Brougham Pearson RN (d 1946 on active service); *Career* farmer and land conslt; ed, chm: BBC's Central Agric Advsy Ctee 1974-80, cncl Royal Soc for Protection of Birds 1976-81, Countryside Cmmn 1981-; environment conslt Humberts Charterted Surveyors 1972-, conslt Humberts Landplan 1974-; dep chm The Groundwork Fndn 1985-; fndr memb Farming & Wildlife Advsy Gp 1969-, bd memb Centre for Econ and Environmental Devpt 1983-, memb advsy ctee Centre for Agric Strategy 1985-; tstee Farming and Wildlife Tst 1984-; pres Glos Naturalists' Soc 1982-; John Haygarth Gold Medal in Agric 1939, Bledisloe Gold Medal for Distinguished Servs to UK Agric 1969, RSPB Gold Medal for Servs to Wildlife Conservation 1983; Queen's Silver Jubilee Medal 1977; kt 1984; *Books* Farming for Profits (with Keith Dexter 1961), Farming in Britain Today (with Frances and J G S Donaldson 1969), Farming and Wildlife: a Study in Compromise (1971); *Recreations* birds, farming; *Clubs* Farmers; *Style*— Sir Derek Barber; The Manor Farm, Stanley Pontlarge, Winchcombe, Glos GL54 5HD (☎ (0242) 602394); The Countryside Commission, John Dower House, Crescent Place, Cheltenham, Glos GL50 3RA (☎ (0242) 521381)

BARBER, Edmund Patrick Harty; s of Maj Leslie Bernard Michael Barber (d 1983), of Marley House, Marley Commom, Haselmere, and Ellen, *née* Harty; *b* 25 August

1946; *Educ* Glenstal Abbey Sch Co Limerick, Univ Coll Dublin; *m* 20 Dec 1969, Elizabeth Marguerite, da of Eric Fowler Sherrif, of Tewin, Welwyn, Herts; 1 s (Samuel), 2 da (Catherine, Lucy); *Career* CA 1973-, specialising in int tax work; Freeman of City of London, memb Worshipfull CO Chartered Accountants; FCA 1973; *Recreations* squash, golf; *Clubs* Naval & Military; *Style—* Edmund Barber, Esq; 1 Harmer Green Lane, Digswell, Welwyn, Herts (☎ 043 871 6088); Flat 2, 25 Marden Lane, Covent Garden, London WC2E 7NA (☎ 01 379 0422); 17-18 Henrietta St, Covent Garden, London WC2E 8QX (☎ 01 379 7711, fax 01 240 2618, car tel 0860 339559, telex 266489)

BARBER, Hon Sir (Edward Hamilton) Esler; s of late Rev John Andrew Barber and Maggie Rorke; *b* 26 July 1905; *Educ* Hamilton Coll Vict, Scots Coll Sydney, Scotch Coll Melbourne, Melbourne Univ; *m* 1954, Constance, da of Capt C W Palmer; 1 s, 1 da; *Career* barr 1929, Puisne Judge Vict Supreme Court Australia 1965-77, QC (Vict) 1955; kt 1976; *Style—* Hon Sir Esler Barber; 1 St George's Court, Toorak, Vict 3142, Australia (☎ 24 5104)

BARBER, Frank; s of Sidney Barber, and Florence, *née* Seath; *b* 5 July 1923; *Educ* W Norwood Central Sch; *m* Dec 1945, Gertrude Kathleen, *née* Carson; 2 s (John b 1951, Alan b 1947, decd), 1 da (Ann b 1948); *Career* WWII Fl Lt RAFVR 1942-46; Lloyd's 1939-, underwriter Frank Barber & Others 1962-81, ptnr Morgan Fentiman & Barber 1968-; memb: Ctee of Lloyds (1977-80, 1981-85, 1987), Cncl of Lloyds (1983-85, 1987); chm Lloyd's Underwriters Non Marine Assoc 1972; dep chm: Br Insurers Euro Ctee 1983, Lloyd's 1983-84; *Recreations* music, walking, sailing; *Clubs* Royal Dart YC, Lloyd's YC; *Style—* Frank Barber, Esq; Godden House, Godden Green, Sevenoaks, Kent, TN15 0HP (☎ 0732 61170); Morgan Fentiman & Barber, Lloyd's, London (☎ 01 623 7100, fax 01 623 8233)

BARBER, Glynis Sharon; da of Frederick Werndly Barry van der Riet, of Durban, SA, and Heather Maureen, *née* Robb (d 1973); *b* 25 Oct 1955; *Educ* Mountview Theatre Sch; *Career* actress; TV: Blake's 7 1981, Jane 1982, Harriet Makepeace in Dempsey and Makepeace 1984-86, Visitors 1986; Films: Jekyll and Hyde - The Edge of Sanity 1988, The Wicked Lady 1982, Tangier, Terror, The Hound of the Baskervilles; *Recreations* tennis, yoga, reading; *Style—* Miss Glynis Barber; c/o James Sharkey, 15 Golden Square, London W11 (☎ 01 434 3801)

BARBER, Graham Lister; s of William Lister Barber, JP (d 1976), of Wimbledon, and Marjorie Gertrude, *née* Grose (d 1978); *b* 20 August 1930; *Educ* Uppingham; *m* 19 April 1935, Carol Valentine, da of Douglas Colinson Brown, of Wimbledon; 2 s (Miles b 1958, Mark b 1960), 1 da (Emma Rose b 1963); *Career* Nat Serv Lt RASC 1949-51; chm and md F H Barber & Co Ltd Fulham 1976- (dir 1956, md 1965); chm: Assoc Dept Stores 1965, Drapers Chambers of Trade 1986-88; first chm Assoc Ind Stores 1976-78, vice chm Sunday Special Campaign 1988-; chm Winnowing Club 1966-67, pres Twenty Club 1975-76; memb Glovers Co; *Recreations* golf, bridge; *Clubs* Royal Wimbledon GC; *Style—* Graham Barber, Esq; Flat 2, 36 Lingfield Rd, Wimbledon, London SW19 7DN (☎ 01 946 4654); F H Barber & Co Ltd, 427-429 North End Rd, Fulham, London SW6 (☎ 01 385 6666)

BARBER, Dr James Peden; s of John Barber (d 1973), and Carrie Barber (d 1967); *b* 6 Nov 1931; *Educ* Liverpool Inst HS, Pembroke Coll Cambridge, Queens Coll Oxford (MA, PhD); *m* 3 Sept 1955, (Margaret) June Barber, da of Henry James McCormac, of Beetham, Cumbria; 3 s (Michael James b 1958, Andrew John b 1959, Mark Henry b 1965), 1 da (Anne Elizabeth b 1965); *Career* Nat Serv PO RAF 1950-52; dist offr 1956-61, HM CS Overseas Uganda 1956-63, asst sec to PM and clerk to cabinet 1961-63, lectr Univ of NSW Australia 1963-65, lectr in Govte Univ of Exeter 1965-69 (seconded to Univ Coll Rhodesia 1965-67), prof of political sci Open Univ 1969-80, master Hatfield Coll Univ of Durham 1980-, pro vice chllr Univ of Durham 1987-; pres Soc of Fells 1985-88; RIIA 1968; Uganda Independence Medal; *Books* Rhodesia: The Road to Rebellion (1967), Imperial Frontier (1968), South Africa's Foreign Policy (1973), European Community: vision and reality (1974), The Nature of Foreign Policy (1975), Who Makes British Foreign Policy? (1977), The West and South Africa (1982), The Uneasy Relationship: Britain and South Africa (1983); *Recreations* hockey, walking, choral singing; *Clubs* Royal Cwlth Soc; *Style—* Dr James Barber; Kingsgate House, Bow Lane, Durham City DH1 3ER (☎ 091 384 8651); Hatfield Coll, Univ of Durham, North Bailey, Durham City DH1 3RQ (☎ 091 374 3160, fax 091 374 3740, telex 537351 DURLIB G)

BARBER, John Norman Romney; s of George Ernest, and Gladys Eleanor Barber; *b* 22 April 1919; *Educ* Westcliff; *m* 1941, Babette, da of Louis Chalu (d 1975); 1 s; *Career* dir: Ford Motor Co Ltd 1955-65, AEI 1966-67, BL Motor Corpn 1968-75 (dep chm 1973-75); chm: Aberhurst Ltd 1976-, A C Edwards Engrg 1977-81, C & K Consulting Gp 1981-88, UK Investmts 1985-; dep chm John E Wiltshier Gp plc 1980-88, Cox's & Kings 1980-81; dir: Acrow plc 1977-1984, Good Relations Gp plc 1979-84, Amalgamated Metal Corpn 1980-81, Spear & Jackson Int plc 1980-85, Economists Advsy Gp 1981-; chm Advsy Ctee to BOT on Investmt Grants 1967-68; memb: Royal Cmmn on Med Educn 1965-68, Advsy Cncl for Energy Conservation 1974-75; vice pres Soc of Motor Mfrs and Trades 1974-76; CBIM; *Style—* John Barber, Esq; Balcary, Earleswood, Cobham, Surrey KT11 2BZ; 35 Albemarle St, London W1X 3FB (☎ 01 629 7209)

BARBER, Hon Josephine Julia Asquith; yr da of Baron Barber, PC, TD (Life Peer), *qv*; *b* 1952; *Style—* The Hon Josephine Barber; 43 Basuto Rd, London SW6 4BL

BARBER, Gp Capt Leslie Thomas Godard; OBE (1951), AFC (1941); s of Thomas Robert Barber, DSM (d 1932), of Daintrees, Chaldon, Surrey, and Eleanor Mary, *née* Michell (d 1976); *b* 18 Jan 1910; *Educ* Caterham Sch; *m* 2 Dec 1932, Evelyn Jessie Lilian Ruth, da of Frederick Thomas Williams (d 1954), of Caterham, Surrey; 2 da (Dinah (Mrs Streeter) b 31 March 1936, Peta (Mrs Martin) b 28 April 1937); *Career* RAF Pilot Branch 1930-35, 4(AC) 201 (FB) Sqdns, Instr Sch of Air Pilotage; Flying Instr 6 ERFS 1935-40, Fl-Lt RAFO 1937, Sqdn Ldr Chief Flying Instr 6 EFTS 1940-42, Empire Central Flying Sch, Air Staff HQ Rhodesian Air Trg Gp 1942-44, Wing-Cdr 1943, sr tutor & instrument weather flying specialist Empire Central Flying Sch 1944-46, jt fndr Instrument Rating Scheme RAF pilots, 1947 appt permanent cmmn, Wing-Cdr Admin RAF Grantham, Air Staff HQ 23 Gp 1948-50, Offr Cdg Flying Wing 203 AFS 1950-52, (208 AFS 1952-53), PS2 Dept of Air Memb for Personnel Air Miny 1953-54, Gp-Capt 1954, Cdr offr 4 FTS, ret 1957; Fl-Capt East African Airways Corpn Nairobi and Dar-es-Salaam 1946-47, Brooklands Aviation Ltd: asst md and chief test pilot 1957, md 1969-73, chm 1976-83; Freeman City of London 1957, Master Air Pilot Guild of Air Pilots 1963 (Liveryman 1957, Freeman 1934); MRAeS 1964; *Recreations* gardening, motoring; *Clubs* RAF; *Style—* Gp Capt Leslie T G Barber, OBE, AFC; 8 Goldrings Rd, Oxshott, Leatherhead, Surrey KT22 0QR (☎ 0372 842914)

BARBER, Hon Louise Patricia Lysberg; er da of Baron Barber, PC, TD (Life Peer), *qv*; *b* 1951; *Style—* The Hon Louise Barber

BARBER, Lynn (Mrs David Cardiff); da of Richard Barber, of Ebbesborne Wake, Wilts, and Beryl Barber; *b* 22 May 1944; *Educ* The Lady Eleanor Holles Sch for Girls, St Anne's Coll Oxford (BA); *m* 1 Sept 1971, David Maurice Cloudesley Cardiff, s of Maj Maurice Cardiff, CBE, of Little Haseley, Oxford; 2 da (Rose b 1975, Theodora b 1978); *Career* asst ed Penhouse magazine 1967-72, staff writer Sunday Express Magazine 1984-, winner of British Press Awards Magazine Writer of the Year 1986 and 87; *Books* How to Improve Your Man in Bed (1973), The Single Woman's Sex Book (1975), The Heyday of Natural History (1980); *Recreations* gossip; *Style—* Ms Lyn Barber; Sunday Express Magazine, 245 Blackfriars Road, London SE1 (☎ 01 353 8000)

BARBER, Dr Morgan James; s of William Brian Barber (d 1968), and Kate, *née* Morgan (d 1982); *b* 18 June 1927; *Educ* Luton GS, RCS, Imperial Coll, Univ of London (BSc, ARCS, PhD, DIC, CEng); *m* 14 June 1951, Audrey Mary, da of Alfred Horley Derbyshire (d 1980), of Sydney, Aust; 1 s (James b 1968), 3 da (Katie b 1958, Philippa b 1962, Sara b 1963); *Career* dir Powell Duffryn Tech Servs 1969-74, md PD-NCB Conslts 1974-80; chm: Br Mining Conslts Ltd 1988- (md 1980-88), Assoc Mining Conslts Ltd Canada 1987- (dir 1978-86); dir: Br Mining Contractors (1987) Ltd 1988-, Br Mining Contractors (Ghusick) Ltd 1988-, Int Mining Conslts Ltd 1988-, Br Coal Int, Sedgman/BMC Aust 1988-; pres Paul Weir Ltd USA 1988-; *Recreations* tennis, squash, reading, bridge; *Clubs* IOD; *Style—* Dr Morgan Barber; Higham Cliffe, Higham, Derbys DE5 6EA (☎ 0773 835 336); BMC Ltd, Huthwaite, Notts NG17 2NS (☎ 0623 441444, telex 37419, fax 0623 440333)

BARBER, Nicholas Charles Faithorn; s of Bertram Harold Barber (d 1982), and Nancy Lorraine, *née* Belsham (d 1984); *b* 7 Sept 1940; *Educ* Ludgrove Sch, Shrewsbury Sch, Wadham Coll Oxford (MA), Columbia Univ, NY (MBA); *m* 8 Jan 1966, Sheena Macrae, da of Donald Graham (d 1984); 2 s (James Henry b 1969, George Belsham b 1974), 1 da (Fenella Macrae b 1972); *Career* gp chief exec Ocean Tport & Trading plc 1987- (dir 1980-, joined 1964); tstee Nat Museums & Galleries Merseyside 1986-, vice pres Liverpool Sch of Tropical Medicine; memb: advsy ctee Tate Gallery Liverpool, govr Shrewsbury Sch; CBIM; *Recreations* mountain walking, destructive gardening; *Clubs* Oxford and Cambridge, MCC; *Style—* Nicholas Barber Esq; Ocean Transport & Trading plc, 47 Russell Sq, London WC1B 4JP (☎ 01 636 6844, fax 01 636 0289, telex 291689)

BARBER, Paul Jason; s of Victor William Barber, of Peterborough, Cambs, and Phyllis May, *née* Lamb; *b* 21 May 1955; *Educ* The Kings Sch Peterborough; *m* 30 Aug 1980, Jennifer, da of John Douglas Redford, of Peterborough, Cambs; 2 s (Michael James b 1 Oct 1984, Stephen Daniel b 23 April 1987); *Career* hockey player; Bronze Medal: Euro Cup 1979, Olympic Games 1984; Silver Medal: World Cup 1986, Euro Cup 1987; Gold Medal Olympic Games 1988; Hockey Player of the Year 1983; MCIB (memb Chartered Inst of Bldg); *Recreations* travel, golf, most sports generally; *Style—* Paul Barber, Esq; 48 Glendale Avenue, Wash Common, Newbury, Berks (☎ 0635 832267); c/o G Percy Thentham Ltd, Pangbourne, Berks (☎ 07357 3333, fax 07357 2392)

BARBER, Philip Petley; s of Ernest Walter Barber (d 1953), of Moseley B'ham & Stratford Upon Avon, and Hilda (d 1933), *née* McMichael; *b* 22 Sept 1917; *Educ* Hallfield Prep Sch Edgbaston, Sebright Sch Wolverley; *m* 18 December 1947, Magdalene Emma, da of George Silcock (d 1931), of Smethwick; 1 s (John Petley b 1953); *Career* TA (Royal Warwicks) RE 1939, Cmmnd RA 1941, served BAOR (wounded Rhine crossing 1944), staff Capt 50th AA Brigade 1945-46; articled to Clement Geoffrey Keys (Clement Keys & Co Chartered Accountants Birmingham) 1936, qual FCA 1947, ptnr Clement Keys & Co (Birmingham) 1951 and ret a sr ptnr 1983, appointed Approved Auditor (Industrial Provident Soc Act) 1954, conslt 1983-; tstee Hallfield Prep Sch Edgbaston 1979; FCA; *Recreations* golf; *Clubs* Edgbaston GC; *Style—* Philip Barber Esq; Marborne, Edgbaston, Birmingham; 7 Westbourne Gardens, Edgbaston, Birmingham B15 3TJ (☎ (021) 454 5042)

BARBER, Stephen David; s of Dr Frederick Barber, of 38 Brookfield Park, London, NW5 1ET, and Edith Renate Wolfenstein (d 1987); *b* 15 Mar 1952; *Educ* Univ Coll Sch, LSE (BSc); *m* 1 April 1978, Suzanne Jane, da of Graham Hugh Presland (d 1986); 1 s (Andrew Charles b 1985), 1 da (Claire Louise b 1982); *Career* CA Price Waterhouse 1973-, (ptnr 1985); *Recreations* family, skiing, running, films; *Style—* Steve Barber, Esq; Southwark Towers, 32 London Bridge Str, London, SE1 9SY (☎ 01 407 8989, fax 01 378 0647, telex 884 657)

BARBER, Stephen Douglas; s of Frank Douglas Barber, of London, and Joan Elizabeth, *née* Nolan; *b* 18 Jan 1955; *Educ* Dulwich, St John's Coll Oxford (MA); *m* 9 Apr 1983, Kimiko, of Kobe; *Career* Samuel Montagu & Co Ltd 1977-, dir Montagu Investmt Mgmnt (MIM) 1985-; md MIM Tokyo KK 1987-; memb: Liszt Soc (UK), Guild of Rahere, Asiatic Soc of Japan; *Recreations* book collecting, Kyudo, drawing; *Style—* Stephen Barber, Esq; 3-20-2 Ebisu, Shibuya-Ku, Tokyo, Japan (☎ 03 432 6451); MIM Ltd, 11 Devonshire Square, London EC2M 4YR (☎ 01 626 3434)

BARBIERI, Margaret Elizabeth; da of Ettore and Lea Barbieri; *b* 2 Mar 1947; *Educ* Durban, Royal Ballet Sr Sch; *m* 1982, Iain Webb; 1 s (Jason Alexander b July 1987); *Career* sr princ Sadler's Wells Royal Ballet 1974-; *Style—* Miss Margaret Barbieri; Chiswick, London W4

BARBOR, Dr Peter Ronald Hubback; JP; s of Dr Ronald Charles Blair Barbor, and Yvonne, *née* Hubback; *b* 7 May 1936; *Educ* Haileybury, Clare Coll Cambridge (BA, MB), St Thomas's Hosp; *m* 4 Sept 1965, Patricia, da of Dr N J P Hewlings, of Banbury; 2 s, 1 da; *Career* physician; worked in West Indies 1967, Vietnam 1970, Libya 1985; conslt paediatrician Univ Hospital Nottingham 1973-; memb of NSPCC Central Exec and professional advsy ctees; JP City of Nottingham 1980; FRCP; *Books* jt author of books and articles on child abuse and childhood cancers; *Style—* Dr Peter R H Barbor, JP; The Old Vicarage, Ab Kettleby, Melton Mowbray LE14 3JA (☎ 0664 822912); office: (☎ 0602 421421)

BARBOUR, Alec Walter; CBE (1989); s of George Freeland Barbour (d 1948), of Fincastle House, Pitlochry Perthshire, and Hon Helen Victoria, *née* Hepburne-Scott (d 1982); *b* 15 Jan 1925; *Educ* Rugby, Edinburgh Univ (BSc); *m* 6 Sept 1950, Hazel

Thomson, da of William Byers Brown, of Peebles (d 1960); 3 s (John b 1951, Alastair b 1953, Walter b 1956), 2 da (Jean b 1958, Kirstie (twin) b 1958); *Career* agric advsr E Scot coll of Agric 1948-52; Renton Finhayson Land Agents and Surveyors Aberfeldy Perthshire: ptnr 1960-75, conslt 1975-79; factor Duke of Atholl Atholl Estates Blair Atholl Perthshire 1975-89; pres bd govrs E Scot Coll of Agric 1981-89, vice chm Sco Agric Colls 1985-89; memb cncl NFU Scot 1960-70 (memb and chm local ctees 1954-89), chm Killiecrankie Community Co, session clerk Tenandry Parish Church Pitlochry, quartermaster Atholl Highlanders, area memb ctee Timber Growers UK; FRICS 1960; *Style—* Alec Barbour, Esq, CBE; Mains of Bonskeid, Pitlochry, Perthshire PH16 5RN (☎ 0796 3 234) Atholl Estates Office, Blair Atholl, Perthshire PH18 5TH (☎ 0796 81 355, fax 0796 487)

BARBOUR, Brig David Charles; OBE (1956), DL (Berks 1972); 2 s of Maj Robert Barbour, TD, JP, DL (d 1928), of Bolesworth Castle, Tattenhall, Cheshire; *b* 1 Oct 1912; *Educ* Harrow, Trinity Coll Cambridge; *m* 1940, Antoinette Mary Daphne, da of Brig-Gen Francis George Alston, CMG, DSO, Scots Gds (d 1961); 1 s, 2 da; *Career* 2 Lt 17/21 Lancers 1934, served WW II N Africa and Italy, cdr Sherwood Rangers Yeo 1951-53 and 17/21 Lancers 1953-56, Col (temp Brig) 22 Armoured Bde (TA) 1958, ret (Hon Brig) 1960; sec Berks T&AF Assoc 1960-68; dep sec E Wessex T & AF Assoc 1968-71; county cmmr and cdr St John Ambulance Bde 1971-81; KStJ 1982; *Style—* Brig David Barbour, OBE, DL; Shortheath House, Sulhamstead Abbots, Reading, Berks RG7 4EF (☎ 073 529 2057)

BARBOUR, (John) Roy; s of Alexander Ewan Barbour (d 1964), of Lanarkshire, and Mary Hart, *née* Cornwall (d 1970); *b* 25 Nov 1929; *Educ* Uddingston GS, Royal Tech Coll Glasgow (now Strathclyde Univ); *m* 4 July 1953, Jean Livingstone Trotter, da of Flt Lt Alexander Thompson (d 1981), of Ashgill, Lanarkshire; 1 s (Ewan b 1961), 1 da (Jane b 1957); *Career* nat serv 1953-55, cmmnd 2 Lt 1954, cmmnd Lt TA 1957, Maj 1964 (cmd 128 Corps FD PK SQM RE, 105 Plant SQM RE), posted R of O 1970; sr civil engr 1962-67 and 1967-68; assoc ptnr 1968-70, Cooper MacDonald & Ptnrs 1970-(assoc ptnr 1968-70); Lanarkshire County Youth Half Mile Champ 1947; Freeman City of London, memb Worshipful Co of Constructors; MConsE, FICE, FIHT, FFB, FIArb; *Recreations* overseas travel, walking, gardening; *Clubs* RAC; *Style—* Roy Barbour, Esq; Anavryta, Grove Rd, Camberley, Surrey (☎ 0276 22590); Cooper, McDonald & Partners, Consulting Engs, Loxford House, East St, Epsom, Surrey, KT17 1HG (☎ 03727 28511, fax 03727 42129, car tel 0836 779136, telex 928439 COMACE G)

BARBOUR OF BONSKEID, Very Rev Prof Robert (Robin) Alexander Stewart; MC (1945); s of Dr George Freeland Barbour of Bonskeid and Fincastle, Pitlochry (d 1946; s of Rev Robert Barbour and his w Charlotte, 2 da of Sir Robert Fowler, 1 Bt (Btcy cr 1885, extinct 1902)), and Hon Helen Victoria, *née* Hepburne-Scott (d 1982), eldest da of 9 Lord Polwarth, CBE, DL; *b* 11 May 1921; *Educ* Rugby, Balliol Coll Oxford (MA), St Mary's Coll St Andrews (BD), Yale Univ (STM); *m* 18 March 1950, Margaret Isobel, da of Lt-Col Harold Pigot (d 1982), of Beccles; 3 s (Freeland b 1951, David b 1954, Andrew b 1959), 1 da (Alison b 1956); *Career* late Maj Scottish Horse; Dean of Chapel Royal in Scotland 1981- and Chaplain in Ordinary to HM The Queen in Scotland 1976-; Prelate of Priory of Scotland of Order of St John 1977-; Moderator of Gen Assembly of Church of Scotland 1979-80; prof New Testament Exegesis Aberdeen Univ 1971-85 (lecturer then sr lecturer New Testament Language, Literature and Theology Edinburgh Univ 1955-71); Master Christ's Coll Aberdeen 1977-82; chm govrs Rannoch Sch 1971-77; chm Scottish Churches' Cncl 1982-86; Hon DD St Andrews 1979; *Books* The Scottish Horse 1939-45 (1950), Traditio-Historical Criticism of the Gospels (1972), What is the Church for? (1973); *Recreations* music, rural pursuits; *Clubs* New (Edinburgh); *Style—* The Very Reverend Professor Robert Bar; Fincastle, Pitlochry, Perthshire PH16 5RJ (☎ 0796 3209)

BARBY, Hon Mrs (Rosemary Gail); *née* Pritchard; da of Baron Pritchard (Life Peer); *b* 1946; *m* 1, 1967 (m dis 1977), Ernest Raymond Anthony Travis, *qv*; m 2, 1979, Ian Barby; 1 s, 1 da; *Style—* The Hon Mrs Barby

BARCHARD, John Harley; s of William Stanley Barchard (d 1981), of Silvergates, Tranby Park, Hessle, N Humberside, and Gladys Evelyn, *née* Bright (d 1956); *b* 22 August 1927; *Educ* Hymers Coll, Pocklington Sch; *m* 7 June 1975, Marguerite Claire, da of Oscar Ernest Warburton, of 10 Westella Way, Kirkella, Hull, N Humberside; *Career* md: Barchards Ltd (family business founded 1873), Barchards Hldgs Ltd, Barchards (Timber) Ltd; *Recreations* shooting; *Style—* John Barchard, Esq; The Mount, N Ferriby, N Humberside (☎ 0482 631628); Barchards Ltd, Gibson Lane, Melton, N Ferriby, N Humberside (☎ 0482 633388, telex 592528), car ☎ 0860 818838, fax 0482 633751)

BARCLAY, Capt Charles Geoffrey Edward; s of Maj Maurice Edward Barclay (d 1962), of Brent, Pelham Hall, Buntingford, Herts, and Margaret Eleanor, *née* Pryor; *b* 13 August 1919; *Educ* Eton, Magdalene Coll Cambridge (MA); *m* 1, 14 June 1947, Laura May (d 1972), da of Lt-Col Thomas Slingsby, MC, of Danceys, Clavering, Saffron Walden, Essex; 3 s (Thomas Patrick Edward b 16 Jan 1951, Robert Charles William b 26 Dec 1957, Maurice James b 19 Aug 1959), 1 da (Diana Margaret (Mrs Pyper) b 10 March 1949); m 2, 10 May 1985, Kathleen Anne, da of Sir Edward Foster, of Newton, Bridgnorth, Shrops; *Career* serv N Somerset Yeo 1939-46, Palestine, Syria, Western Desert, Sicily, Italy, France, Belguim, Holland and Germany (despatches, wounded twice); farmer; cncl memb Royal Agric Soc of England 1959-, chm Hatfield Forest Nat Tst Mgmnt Ctee 1964; master of fox hounds Puckeridge 1947-; High Sheriff elect (1990); Freeman: City of London, Worshipful Co of Farriers; memb: NFU, Country Landowners Assoc; *Recreations* all fields sports, travel, british countryside; *Clubs* Cavalry & Guards, Farmers; *Style—* Capt Charles Barclay; Brent Pelham Hall, Buntingford, Herts (☎ 027 978 220); Estate Office, Brent Pelham, Buntingford, Herts (☎ 027 978 223)

BARCLAY, Christopher Francis Robert; CMG (1967); s of Capt Robert Barclay (d 1941), of Toddington, Beds, and Annie Douglas Dowdeswell, *née* Davidson (d 1958); *b* 8 June 1919; *Educ* Summer Fields, Eton, Magdalen Coll Oxford (MA); *m* 1, 29 Sept 1950 (m dis 1962), Clare Justice, da of Sir John Monro Troutbeck, GBE, KCMG (d 1970), of Horsham; 2 s (Christopher b 1951, John b 1954), 1 da (Jane b 1955); m 2, 14 June 1962, Diana Elizabeth, da of Cdr (John) Michael Goodman (ka 1940); 1 s (Charles b 1963), 1 da (Henrietta b 1966); *Career* Army Offr Cadet 1939, 2 Lt RB 1940, Capt 1942, Maj 1943, serv Middle East (Egypt, Palestine, Iraq), demobbed 1946; Diplomatic Serv, FO 1946, Br Embassy Cairo 1947, FO 1950, Br Embassy Bonn 1953, FO 1956, Br Embassy Beirut 1959, FO 1960, cnsllr and head info res dept 1962, head personnel dept (trg and gen) FCO 1967, asst sec Civil Serv Dept 1969, DOE 1973, sec Govt Hospitality 1976-80; memb cncl City Univ 1976-84, chm Jt Nat Horse Educn and Trg Cncl 1988-; Freeman City of London 1942, Liveryman Worshipful Co Saddlers 1942 (Master 1983-84); FRSA 1984; cdr of the Order of the Infante DOM Henrique Portugal 1979; *Recreations* fishing, gardening; *Clubs* Army & Navy; *Style—* Christopher Barclay, Esq, CMG; Croft Edge, Hollyhock Lane, Painswick, Glos GL6 6XH (☎ 0452 812 332)

BARCLAY, Sir Colville Herbert Sanford; 14 Bt (NS 1668); s of late Rt Hon Sir Colville Adrian de Rune Barclay, KCMG, 3 s of 11 Bt; suc unc, Sir Robert Cecil de Belzim Barclay, 13 Bt, 1930; *b* 7 May 1913; *Educ* Eton, Trin Oxford; *m* 1949, Rosamond Grant Renton, da of late Dr W Armstrong Elliott, of Chandler's Ford, Hants; 3 s; *Heir* s, Robert Colraine Barclay; *Career* 3 Sec Diplomatic Service 1938-41; Lt-Cdr RNVR WW II; *Books* Crete, Checklist of Vascular Plants; *Clubs* Naval; *Style—* Sir Colville Barclay, Bt; Pitshill, Petworth, W Sussex (☎ 079 85 341)

BARCLAY, David William; s of Theodore Barclay, of Desnage Lodge, Bury St Edmunds; *b* 29 Nov 1942; *Educ* Harrow, Trinity Coll Cambridge; *m* 1967, Celia, da of Maj Hugh Cairns, MC, of St Boswell's, Roxburghshire; 1 s, 1 da; *Career* local dir Barclays Bank Pall Mall 1973-79, Ipswich 1979-85, London Northern 1985-; *Recreations* shooting, fishing,; *Clubs* Boodle's, Pratt's; *Style—* David Barclay Esq; Desnage Lodge, Higham, Bury St Edmunds, Suffolk (☎ (0638) 750254)

BARCLAY, Hugh Maben; s of William Barclay (d 1972), and Mary Frances, *née* Laird (d 1983); *b* 20 Feb 1927; *Educ* Fettes, Gonville and Caius Coll Cambridge (MA); *m* 8 Sept 1956, Margaret Hilda Hope, da of George Gilbert Hope Johnston (d 1973), of Beith, Ayrshire and latterly of Sevenoaks, Kent; 1 s (David b 1961), 1 da (Alison b 1957); *Career* RA Egypt 1948-50; entered Dept of the Clerk of the House of Commons May 1950; sr clerk 1955; dep princ clerk 1967; Clerk of Standing Ctees 1976; Clerk of Private Bills 1982, Clerk of Public Bills 1988-; *Style—* Hugh Barclay, Esq; 37 Stockwell Green, London SW9 9HZ (☎ 01 274 7375); House of Commons, London SW1 A0AA (☎ 01 219 3255)

BARCLAY, James Christopher; s of Theodore David Barclay (d 1981), and Anne Mallard, *née* Bennett; *b* 7 July 1945; *Educ* Harrow; *m* 1975, Rolleen Anne, da of Lt-Col Walter Arthur Hastings Forbes, (d 1987); 2 children; *Career* bill broker; chm and jt md Cater Allen Ltd (bankers) 1981-; chm Cater Allen Hldgs plc 1985-; *Recreations* fishing, shooting; *Style—* James Barclay Esq; Cater Allen Holdings plc, 1 King William St, London EC4N 7AU, (☎ 01 623 2070; telex 888553/4)

BARCLAY, Joseph Gurney; s of Sir Roderick Edward Barclay, GCVO, KCMG, *qv*; *b* 17 Jan 1946; *Educ* Harrow, St Edmund Hall Oxford; *m* 1978, Joanna, da of Brig Anthony Douglas Brindley, CBE; 1 s, 2 da; *Career* local dir Barclays Bank Birmingham 1978-85, res dir Barclays Bank Paris 1986-; *Recreations* shooting, travel; *Clubs* Cercle de L'Union Interalliée, Paris; *Style—* Joseph Barclay, Esq; c/o Barclays Bank, 54 Lombard St, London EC3

BARCLAY, Brig Neil; DL (Shropshire 1986); s of Eric Lionel Barclay (1974), of Chelmsford, Essex, and Muriel Clare, *née* Copeland (d 1975); *b* 18 April 1917; *Educ* Private; *m* 27 Sept 1941, Mary Emma (Mollie), da of David Scott-Shurmer (d 1964), of Bicknacre, Essex; 1 s (John Allardice b 7 Aug 1944), 3 da (Jane Allardice b 13 Jan 1947, Mary Allardice b 23 Sept 1954, Emma Allardice b 4 Nov 1957); *Career* RHA TA 1933-38, RA 1939-51, serv Gibraltar, Malta, Cyprus, at sea with the RN, W Africa, NW Europe (Airborne Forces), India, transferred RAOC 1951, served Libya, Persia, Egypt, Germany, East Africa, South Arabia and Persian Gulf; Lt-Col 1958, Col 1964, Brig 1968; sr princ (sr planning inspr) DOE 1972-; cdr St John Ambulance Shropshire; memb County ctee SSAFA, vice chm ABF Shropshire; pres: ACF League Branch, RA Assoc Branch; FASMC 1962, FBIM 1968, FCIArb 1973; *Recreations* talking, gardening; *Clubs* Army & Navy Muthaiga (Nairobi); *Style—* Brig Neil Barclay, DL; Strinebrook House, The Hincks, Lilleshall, Newport, Shropshire (☎ 0952 604204)

BARCLAY, Norman Veitch Lothian; s of James Barclay, JP (d 1963), and Florence, *née* Lothian (d 1976); *Educ* Trinity Coll Glenalmond, St John's Coll Cambridge (MA); *m* 1, 20 Jan 1954, Joan, da of George Ogg; 3 s (James b 1955, Rupert b 1957, Jeremy b 1958); m 2, 20 Sept 1969, Thérèse Ann, da of Lt-Cdr O M De Las Casas, LVO, OBE, RN; 2 s (Maxwell b 1970, Alexander b 1974); *Career* dir (former chief exec) Aberdeen Combworks Ltd (now MacFarlane Gp plc); GB bobsleigh champion 1958-60, Gold Medallist 4 man bob Cwlth Winter Games 1958, GB luge champion 1960-63, memb luge team 1964-68, winner of many class 1 and 2 powerboat races, boat round Britain 1969, Trans-Irish waterskier, winter Trans-Alpine balloon crossing 1972; *Recreations* all winter sports, speedsports, golf, diving, ballooning; *Clubs* Turf, Lyford Cay, RSAC, St Moritz Sporting, St M Tobogganing (Cresta), UKOBA Dracula etc; *Style—* Norman Barclay, Esq; c/o Royal Bank of Scotland, Douglas, Isle of Man; British Bobsleigh Association (☎ 01 736 9795)

BARCLAY, Peter Maurice; CBE (1984); s of George Ronald Barclay, OBE (d 1975), and Josephine Stephanie, *née* Lambert (d 1968); *b* 6 Mar 1926; *Educ* Bryanston, Magdalene Coll Cambridge (MA); *m* 1953, Elizabeth Mary, da of Herbert H S Wright, of Wellington Coll; 1 s (Simon), 2 da (Alison, Nicola); *Career* RNVR 1944-46 Sub-Lt; slr 1952; sr ptnr Beachcroft & Co 1964-74, ptnr Beachcrofts 1974-88; chm Nat Inst for Social Work 1973-85 (pres 1988); govr Bryanston Sch 1972-88; chm: Ctee on Role and Tasks of Social Workers 1981-82, St Pancreas Housing Assoc 1983-, Social Security Advsy Ctee 1985-; *Recreations* gardening, walking, painting; *Style—* Peter Barclay, Esq; Ferry Hill, E Portlemouth, nr Kingsbridge, S Devon (☎ 054 884 3443); Flat 4, 43 Ladbrooke Grove, London W11 3AR

BARCLAY, Richard Fenton; s of Rev Gilbert Arthur Barclay (d 1972), of Holly Cottage, Lamer Lane, Wheathampstead, Herts, and Dorothy Catherine Topsy, *née* Studd (d 1980); *b* 3 Dec 1926; *Educ* Greshams Sch, Trinity Coll Cambridge (MA); *m* 27 April 1957, Alison Mary, da of Stanley Richard Cummings, of East Culme, Cullompton, Devon; 3 s (Charles b 1962, Angus b 1964, Michael b 1967), 1 da (Juliet b 1959); *Career* WWII 1944-46 Sub Lt RNVR; from clerk to sr local dir Barclays Bank plc 1948-86; dep chm Nat Provident Inst 1987-(dir 1967), dir Portsmouth Bldg Soc 1987-; memb: Ctee of Mgmnt RNLI, Ct of the Mary Rose; tstee Hampshire and the Islands Historic Churches Tst, memb fund raising ctee Southampton Univ; Freeman City of London; FCIB, FIOD; *Recreations* history, travel; *Clubs* Army & Navy; *Style—* Richard Barclay, Esq; Solent House, 28 Cliff Road, Hill Head, Fareham, Hants PO14 3JT (☎ 0329 662 128)

BARCLAY, Robert Colraine; s and h of Sir Colville Herbert Sanford Barclay, 14 Bt, *qv*; *b* 12 Feb 1950; *m* 1980, Lucilia Saboia, da of Carlos Saboia de Albuquerque, of

Ipanema, Rio de Janeiro; 1 s, 1 da; *Career* chartered accountant; *Style*— Robert Barclay, Esq; Pitshill, Petworth, W Sussex

BARCLAY, Sir Roderick Edward; GCVO (1966, KCVO 1957, CVO 1953), KCMG (1955, CMG 1948); s of late J Gurney Barclay, and Gillian, *née* Birkbeck; *b* 22 Feb 1909; *Educ* Harrow, Trinity Cambridge; *m* 1934, Jean, da of late Sir Hugh Gladstone, of Capenoch, Dumfries; 1 s, 3 da; *Career* Diplomatic Service 1932-69, priv sec to Sec of State for Foreign Affairs 1949-51, ambass Denmark 1956-60, dep under-sec of State 1960-63, ambass Belgium 1963-69; dir: Barclays Bank SA (France) 1969-79 (chm 1970-74), Barclays Bank Int 1971-77, Banque de Bruxelles 1971-77, Slough Estates 1969-84; *Books* Ernest Bevin and the Foreign Office 1932-69 (1975); *Style*— Sir Roderick Barclay, GCVO, KCMG; Great White End, Latimer, Bucks (☎ (024 04) 2050)

BARCLAY, Timothy Humphrey; s of Rev Humphrey Gordon Barclay, CVO, MC (d 1955), of Thurgarton Lodge, Norwich, and Evermar Beatrice, *née* Bond Cabbell (d 1975); *b* 18 June 1923; *Educ* Stowe; *m* 23 June 1947, June, da of Thomas Ramsden (d 1960), of Middleton Tower, King's Lynn; 1 s (Thomas Julian b 12 June 1950); *Career* RN 1941-46; Rootes Gp 1946-50, farmer and agent 1950-, rep Bonhams Auctioneers E Anglia 1965-85, dealer fine arts 1960-; High Sheriff of Norfolk 1983-84; master and huntsman: W Norfolk Foxhounds 1958-68 (sec 1953-68), Sennow Park Harries 1970-75; Liveryman Worshipful Co of Farriers 1976, hon life memb BHS; *Recreations* hunting, fishing, shooting, coursing; *Clubs* MCC; *Style*— Timothy Barclay, Esq; Middleton Tower, King's Lynn, Norfolk PE32 1EE (☎ 0553 840 203)

BARCLAY-BROWN, Cdr Kenneth; s of Maj Robert Barclay-Brown, OBE, and Margaret Nancy, *née* Frizelle; *b* 3 August 1929; *Educ* Britannia RNC Dartmouth, RNC Greenwich; *m* 12 Sept 1959, Susan, da of Richard (Dick) Gillard; 2 s (Simon b 4 Feb 1962, James b 7 Jan 1967), 1 da (Kerry b 6 July 1960); *Career* cmmnd Sub Lt RN 1949, seconded Royal Aust Navy 1950-53, qualified TAS course 1956, staff BRNC Dartmouth 1959-60, CO HMS Brocklesby 1961-63, Cdr 1964, naval offr i/c Takoradi Ghana 1964-66, SO dir of naval equipment (DNE) 1966-68, ret 1969; joined Grieveson Grant & Co (now Kleinwort Benson) 1969: ptnr 1977, dir Kleinwort Grieveson Investmt Mgmnt 1986-88; memb Stock Exchange 1974, AMSIA; *Recreations* golf, fishing, sailing, windsurfing, squash, tennis, photography, skiing; *Clubs* Hankley Common GC, Rye GC SCGB; *Style*— Kenneth Barclay-Brown, Esq; Priory Lodge, Tilford, Surrey GU10 2EJ (☎ 025 125 2037)

BARCLAY-TIMMIS, Dr Kenneth Frank John; TD; s of Brig William Frank De-Chaunce Timmis, and Elizabeth Sara *née* Archer; desc of Capt Gabriel Archer who landed (1607) in N America and named Cape COD and was a fndr of Jamestown; *b* 18 Oct 1939; *Educ* UCS, UCL (BSc/Eng), Canada (MSc), Aston Univ (PhD); *m* 1, 1962, Marie Barclay; 2 s (Pazul b 1965, Jonathan b 1966), 1 da (Sarah b 1963), m 2, 1981, Janet Christine, da of Capt Joseph Philip Howe; 1 da (Victoria b 1982); *Career* Inns of Ct Regt 1976-, Maj RGJ (TAVR); pres chm: European Dvpt Gp Ltd 1986-, DPK Ltd, Hosp Computer System (UK) Ltd, Computer Int Hosp Equipment Ltd (Cdn), Int Supplies Ltd 1975-; *Recreations* golf, Hazelmere and Buckingham clubs; *Clubs* Army and Navy, RAC; *Style*— Dr Kenneth Barclay-Timmis, TD; Springhill House, Hethe, Oxfordshire (☎ (08697) 8350), car (☎ (0860) 527112)

BARD, Dr Basil Joseph Asher; CBE (1968); s of late Abram Isaac Bard, of Finchley, and Anita Bard; *b* 20 August 1914; *Educ* Owen's Sch, RCS (Imperial Coll); *m* 1942, Ena Dora, da of late B Birk, of Newcastle-upon-Tyne and London; 3 s; *Career* barr Gray's Inn 1938; chm: New Product Management (NPM) Gp 1977-83, Birmingham Mint Ltd 1977-82, Transcan Video Ltd 1978-82, Xtec 1983-6; dir The Technology and Innovations Exchange (TIE) 1982-83; dir: Interflex Structural Coatings Ltd 1984-; dir: Scanning Technology Ltd 1984-86; Chm Promicro Ltd, 1986- former md Nat Research Devpt Corpn; pres: Anglo-Jewish Assoc 1977-83, Jewish Memorial Cncl 1982-; *Recreations* Athenaeum; *Style*— Dr Basil Bard, CBE; 23 Mourne House, Maresfield Gdns, London NW3 5SL (☎ 01 435 5340; business 01 328) 8138)

BARDSLEY, Andrew Tromlow; JP (Essex 1975); s of Andrew Bardsley (d 1950), of Ashton-under-Lyne, Lancs, and Gladys Ada, *née* Tromlow; *b* 7 Dec 1927; *Educ* Ashton-under-Lyne GS, Manchester Regnl Coll of Art, UMIST; *m* 27 Nov 1954 (June) Patricia, da of Patrick Ford (d 1968), of Ashton-under-Lyne; 1 s (Dr Philip Andrew b 6 Apr 1958), 1 da (Catherine Patricia b 17 March 1962); *Career* served RN, communications branch 1946-49; Borough engr and surveyor Worksop BC 1963-69, dir tech servs: Corby New Town 1969-71, Luton Co BC 1971-73; gen mangr Harlow Devpt Corp 1973-80; princ Westgate Devpt Consultancy 1981-; govr Harlow Tertiary Coll 1986-, Gen Cmmnr of Taxes for England and Wales 1957; CEng, FICE; *Recreations* golf, tennis, music appreciation, most spectator sports; *Clubs* Ferndown Golf (Dorset); *Style*— Andrew Bardsley, Esq, JP; Grenville Lodge, 30 Barton Rd, Luton Beds; 19 Copper Court, Sawbridgeworth, Herts CM21 9ER (☎ 0279 723 210)

BAREAU, Paul Louis Jean; OBE (1971); s of Louis Bareau (d 1925), and Elisa van Caneghem (d 1909); *b* 27 April 1901; *Educ* Athénée Antwerp, Dulwich Coll, LSE (BCom); *m* 15 Sept 1934, Katharine Dorothy, da of Basil Gibson, ICS (d 1950); 2 s (Michael b 1936, Peter b 1942), 2 da (Juliet b 1935, Suzanne b 1939); *Career* econ journalist and conslt: Statist 1926-29, Financial News 1929-33, News Chronicle 1933-44; UK Treasy (Washington) 1944-47; News Chronicle 1947-58 (City ed 1953-58); ed The Statist 1961-67; lectr on Comparative Banking LSE 1947-51; econ advsr: Publishing Corpn, Mirror Gp Newspaper 1968-, Barclays Bank Gp 1967-80; dir: M & G Investmt Mgmnt 1973-, Halifax Bldg Soc (London Bd) 1974-76, UK Provident Inst 1959-73, dir Broadstone Investmt Tst 1973-81; hon fell LSE; *Recreations* music; *Clubs* Reform, Political Economy; *Style*— Paul Bareau, Esq, OBE; Glebe Lodge, Crondall, Farnham, Surrey (☎ Aldershot 850294); Mirror Group, City Office, Holborn Circus EC1P 1DQ (☎ 01 822 3885)

BAREFOOT, Peter Thomas; s of Herbert John Leslie Barefoot, GC, ARIBA (d 1958), and Amy Gladys, *née* Goddard; *b* 20 Jan 1924; *Educ* Ipswich Sch, Architectural Assoc Sch of Architecture (AA Dip); *m* 3 July 1948, Patience Heaslop, da of John Francis Cunningham, OBE, FRCS (d 1932), of London W1; 1 s (Guy b 1957), 3 da (Ann b 1949, Julia b 1951, Sara b 1953); *Career* Royal Navy (hostilities only) 1943-46; Petty Offr Mediterranean Combined Operations; chartered architect priv practice 1954-; chartered designer 1976-; formerly architect: County Hall, LCC 1951-54 and Stevenage Development Corp 1949-50; Hospital, awarded Bronze Medal of the RIBA for Suffolk buildings Elizabeth Court, sheltered housing for old people at Aldeburgh (Ministry of Housing Award and Civic Trust Award) 1962-63; Club House for Royal Harwich Yacht Club 1966-68; Dept of Environment Award for WRVS Housing Assoc 1969-70; Peter Runge House, Conference Centre in Westminster for The Industrial Soc (The Times/RICS Conservation Award) 1970-71; 273 dwellings in Central Lancashire New Town 1975-76; Sheltered Housing and Hostel in Brixton for Church Housing Assn 1980-83; Laboratory for the Prof of Surgery, St Bartholomew's Hosp London 1986; drawings and models have been exhibited at: Royal Academy Summer Exhibition, RIBA and the AA, London, Le Grand Palais, Paris; *Recreations* sailing, travel; *Clubs* Royal Harwich Yacht, Little Ship, Waldringfield Sailing; *Style*— Peter T Barefoot, Esq; 1 Gaston Street, East Bergholt, Colchester CO7 6SD (☎ (0206 298) 422); 9 Heneage Street, Spitalfields, London E1 5LJ (☎ 01 377 9262, fax 01 247 7854)

BARENBOIM, Daniel; s of Enrique Barenboim and Aida, *née* Schuster; *b* 15 Nov 1942, Buenos Aires; *Educ* Santa Cecilia Acad Rome, coached by Edwin Fischer, Nadia Boulanger and Igor Markevitch; *m* 1967, Jacqueline, OBE (1976), violoncellist (d 1987), da of Derek du Pré, by his w Iris Maud, *née* Greep (d 1985), m 2, Nov 1988, Elena Bashkirova; *Career* pianist and conductor; musical dir Orchestre de Paris 1975-89; debut with Israel Philharmonic Orch 1953, Royal Philharmonic Orch 1956, Berlin Philharmonic Orch 1963, NY Philharmonic 1964; reg tours to Australia, North and South America, Far East; regular appearances at Bayreuth, Edinburgh, Lucerne Prague and Salzburg Festivals; Beethoven Medal 1958; Paderewski Medal 1963; *Style*— Daniel Barenboim, Esq; c/o Harold Holt Ltd, 31 Sinclair Rd, London W14 (☎ 01 603 4600)

BARFETT, Ven Thomas; s of Rev Thomas Clarence Fairchild Barfett (d 1968), and Mary Deborah, *née* Hancock (d 1961); *b* 2 Oct 1916; *Educ* St John's Leatherhead, Keble Coll Oxford (BA, MA); *m* 1945, Edna, da of Robert Toy (d 1924); 1 s (Paul), 1 da (Susan); *Career* asst curate: Christ Church Gosport 1939-43, St Francis Gladstone Park NW10 1944-47, St Andrew Undershaft London 1947-49; asst sec London Diocesan Cncl for Youth 1944-49; vicar St Paul Penzance diocese of Truro 1949-55; rector Falmouth diocese of Truro 1955-77; sec Truro Diocesan Conf 1952-67; proctor in Convocation 1958-77; Archidiaconal memb of Gen Synod of C of E 1977-82; memb of Central Bd of Finance C of E 1969-77; church commr 1975-82; memb of C of E Pension Bd 1973-85 (chm Invstmts Finance Ctee 1985); archdeacon of Hereford and residentiary canon of Hereford Cathedral 1977-82 (canon tres of Cathedral); chaplain to HM The Queen 1975-86; archdeacon emeritus 1982; freeman City of London 1973; freeman liveryman Scriveners' Co 1976; asst chaplain; Order of St John of Jerusalem 1963; sub chaplain 1971; Jubilee Medal 1977; *Books* Trebarfoote - A Cornish Family (1975); *Recreations* genealogy, heraldry; *Clubs* Oxford and Cambridge; *Style*— The Ven Thomas Barfett; Treberveth, 57 Falmouth Rd, Truro, Cornwall TR1 2HL (☎ (0872) 73726)

BARFORD, Clive Julian Stanley; s of Maj Edward James Barford, MC (d 1979), late Royal Horse Guards (Special Reserve), and Hon Grace Lowrey Stanley (now Hon Mrs Buckmaster, *qv*), da of 1 and last Baron Ashfield; *b* 11 May 1933; *Educ* Eton; *m* 1961, Helen Gay Woodroffe, da of Hon Mr Justice (Sir Peter Harry Batson Woodroffe) Foster, MBE, TD; 1 s (James Edward Clive b 1972), 3 da (Emma Jane b 1962, Amanda Helen b 1964, Charlotte Gay b 1967); *Career* chm and md Aldworth Investments Ltd and Abex Ltd, memb Lloyd's; *Recreations* shooting, golf, gardening; *Clubs* Buck's; *Style*— Clive Barford, Esq; Pibworth House, Aldworth, Berks (☎ Compton 578495)

BARFORD, Sir Leonard; s of William Barford, of Harley House, Sutton Road, Seaford, Sussex, and Ada Barford; *b* 1 August 1908; *Educ* Dame Alice Owen's Sch, St Catharine's Coll Cambridge; *m* 1939, Betty Edna, da of Thomas Crichton, of Plymouth; 2 s; *Career* dep chm Horserace Totalisator Bd 1974-77, chief inspector Taxes Bd of Inland Revenue 1964-73; kt 1967; *Style*— Sir Leonard Barford; Harley House, 79 Sutton Rd, Seaford, E Sussex (☎ 893364)

BARFORD, Hon Mrs (Marian Woodruff); *née* Stanley; da of 1 and last Baron Ashfield (d 1948), and Grace Lowrey, *née* Woodruff (d 1962); *b* 1906; *m* 1, 1927 (m dis 1934), James Hart Rutland, s of Archibald Hart Rutland; 1 s; m 2, 1934 (m dis 1940), James Henry Royds, eldest s of Col Albert Henry Royds, OBE; 1 da; m 3, 1940 (m dis 1954), Ralph Arthur Hubbard, eldest s of Capt Gerald Hubbard; 2 da; m 4, 1964 (m dis 1971), Edward James Barford, MC (d 1979), s of James Golby Barford, JP, of Gayhurst, Peterborough; *Style*— The Hon Mrs Barford; Lowood House, Sunninghill, Ascot, Berks

BARGE, Ronald Mansfield; DSC (1942), VRD (1950), DL (Dunbartonshire 1972); s of Lt-Col Kenneth Barge, DSO, MC, DL, JP, IA (d 1971), and Debonair Eva Ruth, *née* Mansfield (d 1959); *b* 10 Nov 1920; *Educ* Trinity Coll Glenalmond, Glasgow Art Sch, Munich Univ, Durham Univ, RCA; *m* 1950, Elizabeth Ann, da of Col John Robertson Lamberton, DSO, MC (d 1974), of Helensburgh; 3 s (Nigel, Alastair, Henry), 3 da (Rosanna, Veronica, Lisa); *Career* salmon farmer; chm: Otter Ferry Salmon Ltd, Onshore Aquaculture, Bitmac Tport Ltd, dir: Bitmac Lamberton Ltd, Hldgs; *Recreations* art, gardening, fishing; *Clubs* Roy Northern & Clyde YC, Mudhook YC; *Style*— Ronald Barge, Esq, DSC, VRD, DL; Whistlers' Hill, Rhu, Dunbartonshire (☎ 0436 820285); Evanachan, Otterferry, Argyll (☎ 070 082284)

BARHAM, David George Wilfrid; JP; s of Harold Arthur Barham (d 1978), of Rolvenden, Kent, and Edith Dulcie Brown, *née* Taylor; *b* 6 Oct 1926; *Educ* Malvern Coll, RAC Cirencester (Dip Estate Mgmnt); *m* 28 Oct 1955, Catherine Margaret, da of Col Rixon Bucknall, MBE (d 1975), of Rotherfield, Sussex; 3 s (William b 1958, Edward b 1962, Robert b 1965), 1 da (Jennifer b 1957); *Career* Lieut RHG 1944-48; farmer, land agent in private practice; general cmmr Taxation 1985-; chm: Kent Ctee COSIRA (now Rural Devpt Cmmn) 1982-, Kent TAVRA Assoc 1975-81; former chm Kent branch County Landowners Assoc, memb Kent CC for Tenterden 1959-69; High Sheriff of Kent 1974-75; FRIS; *Recreations* gardening, country persuits; *Clubs* Army & Navy, RAC; *Style*— D G W Barham, Esq, JP

BARHAM, (Geoffrey) Simon; s of Denis Patrick Barham (d 1978), of Cavendish, Suffolk, and Pleasance, *née* Brooke; *b* 23 Dec 1945; *Educ* Malvern Coll, Christs Coll Cambridge (BA, MA); *m* 18 Sept 1976, Sarah, da of Rev Godfrey Seebold; 1 s (Thomas b 1980), 1 da (Lucy b 1979); *Career* bar, recorder 1987; *Clubs* Norfolk; *Style*— Simon Barham, Esq; Wensum Chambers, Wensum Street, Norwich, Norfolk (☎ (0603) 617 351)

BARING, Hon Anne; da of 4 Baron Northbrook (d 1947); *b* 13 Feb 1917; *Style*— The Hon Anne Baring; Westwood, Wet Meon, Petersfield, Hants

BARING, Hon Catherine Margaret; da of 5 Baron Northbrook; *b* 12 May 1965; *Style*— The Hon Catherine Baring

BARING, Sir Charles Christian; 2 Bt (UK 1911), JP (IOW 1956), DL (Hants later IOW 1962); s of Sir Godfrey Baring, 1 Bt, KBE, DL (d 1957, himself gs of Henry Baring, whose two yr half-bros were cr Baron Revelstoke and Earl of Cromer) by his 1 w, Eva, MBE, JP, only child of Alexander Mackintosh of Mackintosh, JP, DL; *b* 16 Dec 1898; *Educ* Eton; *m* 1948, Jeanette (d 1985), da of Henry Charles Daykin (d 3 April 1985); *Heir* n, John Francis Baring b 21 May 1947; *Career* served WW I (Lt Coldsream Gds, wounded), WW II (Maj Coldstream Gds, PWE, also Staff and in Italy); attaché Warsaw 1922-23, with Cunard White Star Ltd 1933-36, Prison Service 1936-38 (subsequently probation offr W London Magistrates' Court 1938-40 & Centl Criminal Court 1945-46, Probation Branch Inspector for Home Office 1946-49, Warder of Prisons Bermuda (under Colonial Office) 1949-53, Chm Justices IOW Petty Sessional Div 1962-70, memb Ctee Mgmnt Board of Visitors Parkhurst Prison 1956-70); *Style*— Sir Charles Baring, Bt, JP, DL; Springvale Hotel, Seaview, IOW (☎ (0983) 612533)

BARING, Desmond Charles Nigel; s of Godfrey Nigel Everard Baring (d 1934), and Hon Ada Sybil Roche (d 1944), da of 2 Baron Fermoy; *b* 5 Jan 1914; *Educ* Eton, Sandhurst; *m* 12 Sept 1938, Mary Eileen, da of B W Warner (d 1974); 2 s (Peter b 1939, Nigel b 1940), 1 da (Anne b 1944); *Career* FHCIMA 1954-; dir Queen's Moat Houses plc; *Style*— Desmond C N Baring, Esq; Ardington House, Wantage, Oxon (☎ 0235 833244)

BARING, Hon Francis Thomas; s and h of 5 Baron Northbrook, *qv*; *b* 21 Feb 1954; *Educ* Winchester, Bristol Univ; *m* 27 June 1987, Amelia S E, er da of Dr Reginald David Taylor, of Hursley, Hants; *Style*— The Hon Francis Baring; Baring Bros & Co Ltd, 8 Bishopsgate, London EC3

BARING, Hon James Cecil; s of 4 Baron Revelstoke, *qv*; *b* 16 August 1938; *Educ* Eton; *m* 1, 1968, Aneta Laline Dennis, da of late Erskine Arthur Hamilton Fisher, of Mickleham, Surrey; 2 s; m 2, 1983, Sarah, da of William Edward Stubbs, MBE; 1 da; *Style*— The Hon James Baring; 105 Elgin Cres, London W11

BARING, Hon John; s and h of 4 Baron Revelstoke, *qv*; *b* 2 Dec 1934; *Educ* Eton; *Style*— The Hon John Baring

BARING, Hon Sir John Francis Harcourt; CVO (1980); s and h of 6 Baron Ashburton, *qv*; *b* 2 Nov 1928; *Educ* Eton (Fellow 1982), Trinity Coll Oxford (MA); *m* 1, 1955 (m dis 1984), Hon Susan Mary Renwick, da of 1 Baron Renwick, KBE; 2 s, 2 da; m 2, 27 Oct 1987, Mrs Sarah Crewe; *Career* chm: Baring Bros & Co 1974- (md) 1955-74), Stratton Investment Tst plc 1986-, Br Petroleum Co plc 1982-, Bank of England 1983-; dir: Outwich Investment Tst 1965-1986, Royal Insur Co 1964-82 (dep chm 1975-82), Trafford Park Estates Ltd 1964-77, Pye Hldgs 1966-79, Outwich Ltd (Johannesburg) 1967-77 ; non-exec dir Dunlop Hldgs 1981-84 (resigned); receiver-gen Duchy of Cornwall 1974-; chm Accepting Houses Ctee 1977-81; tstee Nat Gallery 1981-87; hon fell Hertford Coll Oxford 1976, fell Eton 1982; kt 1983; *Style*— The Hon Sir John Baring, CVO; Lake House, Northington, Alresford, Hants SO24 9TG (☎ 0962 734293); Baring Brothers & Co, 8 Bishopsgate, London EC2N 4AE (☎ 01 283 8833)

BARING, Lady Rose Gwendolen Louisa; *née* McDonnell; DCVO (1972, CVO 1964); er da of 7 Earl of Antrim (d 1932), and Margaret Isabel (d 1974), da of Rt Hon John Gilbert Talbot; *b* 23 May 1909; *m* 22 April 1933, Francis Anthony Baring (ka 1940), s of Hon Hugo Baring (s of 1 Baron Revelstoke, OBE), and Lady Evelyn, *née* Ashley-Cooper, da of 8 Earl of Shaftesbury; 2 s, 1 da; *Career* woman of the bedchamber to HM The Queen 1953-73, extra woman of the bedchamber 1973-; *Style*— Lady Rose Baring, DCVO; 43 Pembroke Square, London W8

BARING, Hon Mrs (Sarah Katherine Elinor); *née* Norton; o da of 6 Baron Grantley (d 1954); *b* 20 Jan 1920; *Educ* private; *m* 1, 14 June 1945 (m dis 1953), 3 Viscount Astor (d 1966); 1 s; m 2, 17 April 1953 (m dis 1965), Thomas Michael Baring, eldest s of Maj Edward Baring, of Heronry House, Beckley, Sussex; 1 s; *Style*— The Hon Mrs Baring; 23 Scarsdale Villas, London W8

BARING, Hon Lady; Susan Mary; *née* Renwick; da of 1 Baron Renwick, KBE; *b* 5 June 1930; *m* 1955 (m dis 1984), Hon Sir John Francis Harcourt Baring, *qv*; 2 s, 2 da; *Style*— The Hon Lady Baring; 4 Onslow Gdns, London SW7; 13 Alexander St, London W2 5NT

BARING, Hon Vivian John Rowland; 2 s of 3 Earl of Cromer, KG, GCMG, MBE, PC, *qv*; *b* 12 June 1950; *Educ* Stanbridge Earls Sch Romsey, Royal Farms Windsor, RAC Cirencester; *m* 1974, his 2 cous, Lavinia Gweneth (extra lady-in-waiting to HRH The Princess of Wales), er da of Sir Mark Baring, KCVO (d 1988); 2 s (Rowley b 1977, Thomas b 1979), 1 da (Camilla b 1985); *Career* dir: Gen Tours Ltd 1981-, Gen & Executive Travel Ltd 1981-, Courier Printing & Publishing Co Ltd 1985-, Essex Chronicle Series Ltd 1985-, Gloucestershire Newspapers Ltd 1988-, The Cheltenham Newspaper Co Ltd 1988-; dep pres Kent County St John Ambulance; memb cncl of St John: Kent 1978-88 (chm 1985-87), Glos 1988-; *Clubs* White's; *Style*— The Hon Vivian Baring; The Stone House, Lower Swell, Stow on the Wold, Glos GL54 1LQ (☎ 0451 30622)

BARKER, Hon Adam Campbell; s of Baroness Trumpington of Sandwich (Jean, *née* Campbell-Harris) (Life Baroness), *qv*, and William Alan Barker, of Sandwich, Kent (d 1988); *b* 31 August 1955; *Educ* The Kings Sch Canterbury, Queens' Coll Cambridge (MA); *m* 1985, Elizabeth Mary, da of Eric Marsden, OBE, and Mary Julia, *née* Pryor; 1 da (Virginia Giverny b 1987); *Career* lawyer, assoc Webster & Sheffield, NY 1980-; door tenant 12 King's Bench Walk London 1980-; *Recreations* golf, tennis, bridge; *Clubs* Oxford and Cambridge, Royal St George's Sandwich, Hurlingham, Pilgrims; *Style*— The Hon Adam Barker; Rose Cottage, 54 King St, Sandwich, Kent CT13 9BL (☎ 0304 617256); 169 East 90th Street 9, NY 10128, USA; 19th Floor, 237 Park Avenue, NY, NY 10017 (☎ 212 808 6128)

BARKER, Sir Alwyn Bowman; CMG (1962); s of late Alfred James Barker, of Mt Barker, S Australia; *b* 5 August 1900; *Educ* St Peter's Coll Adelaide, Geelong GS, Adelaide Univ (BSc); *m* 1926, Isabel Barron, da of Sir Edward Lucas (d 1950); 1 s (Donald, decd), 1 da (Shirley); *Career* chm: Kelvinator Australia Ltd 1967-80, Adelaide Electrolysis Ctee 1935-78, Industl Devpt Advsy Cncl 1968-70; chmn of bd Municipal Tramways Tst 1953-68; dep chm Australian Mineral Fndn 1969-83; pres: Australian Inst of Mgmnt SA Div 1952-54 (fed pres 1952-53 and 1959-61), Instn of Prodn Engrs (Australian Cncl) 1970-72; memb: Faculty of Engrg Univ of Adelaide 1937-66, Mfrg Industs Advsy Cncl 1958-72, Research and Devpt Advsy Ctee 1967-72; John Storey Meml Medal 1965, Jack Finlay Nat Award 1965; *see Debrett's Handbook of Australia and New Zealand for further details*; landowner (5250 acres); BSc, BE, FIEAust; kt 1969; *Publications* Three Presidential Addresses (1954), William Queale Memorial Lecture (1965); *Clubs* Adelaide; *Style*— Sir Alwyn Barker, CMG; 51 Hackney rd, Hackney, SA 5069, Australia (☎ 42 2838)

BARKER, Hon Mrs (Angela Margaret); o da of 10 Baron Dufferin and Clandeboye, *qv*; *Educ* Sydney Univ (BSc); *m* 1965, Clifton Elliott Barker, BSc; 1 s (Stephen Michael b 1969), 3 da (Zoë Frances b 1971, Lucinda Alice b 1975, Karina Emily b 1980); *Style*— The Hon Mrs Barker; 141 Campbell Drive, Wahroonga, NSW 2076, Australia

BARKER, Anthony; QC (1985); s of Robert Herbert Barker, of Barlaston, Stoke-on-Trent, Staffs, and Ellen Doreen, *née* Maskery; *b* 10 Jan 1944; *Educ* Newcastle-under-Lyme HS, Clare Coll Cambridge (BA); *m* 12 Feb 1983, Valerie Ann, da of Dr William Chatterley Baird, of Caterham, Surrey; 2 da (Sarah Louise b 1971, Vanessa Ann b 1973), 1 step s (Scott William Kenneth Ellis b 1975); *Career* barr 1966; rec of the Crown Ct 1985; *Style*— Anthony Barker, Esq, QC; Hilderstone House, Hilderstone, Nr Stone, Staffs (☎ 088 924 331); 5 Fountain Ct, Steelhouse Lane, Birmingham 4 (☎ 021 236 5771)

BARKER, Anthony Arnold; s of Kenneth Walter Barker, of Toys Hill Westerham, Kent, and Dorothy Vere, *née* Arnold (d 1981); *b* 28 June 1934; *Educ* Gordonstoun Sch; *m* 1, Patricia Anne Butler (d 1972); m 2, 1974, Valerie Jean, da of Cdr Henry James Norman William Taylor RN (ret) (d 1981); 3 s (Timothy, James, Matthew), 2 da (Caroline, Lucy); *Career* Nat serv RA 1952-54; sales mangr: 1940 Gp of Cos 1957-59, Marlowe Cleaners 1959-60; fndg dir Harlequin Cleaners Ltd 1960-72 (md 1967-72), dir Harlequin Engrg 1964-68, md Commodore Cleaners Ltd 1967-72, sales and marketing conslt Tony Steven Assoc 1962-67, conslt Clissold Stevens Admin Services 1962-75; chm and md: Anthony A Barker Ltd 1972-, Anthony A Barker (The Argyle Laundry) Ltd 1973-, Anthony A Barker (The Dry Cleaner) Ltd 1973-; memb Nat Cncl Assoc Br Launderers & Cleaners 1985-87; Freeman City of London, Liveryman Worshipful Co of Launderers 1984; FIOD; *Recreations* reading, collecting, antiques, washing other peoples linen; *Clubs* Naval & Military, RMYC; *Style*— Anthony Barker, Esq; The Old Rectory, Durweston, Blandford Forum, Dorset (☎ 0258 563 46); Anthony A Barker Ltd, 29 Latimer Rd, Winton, Bournemouth (☎ Bournemouth 526 431/2, car tel 0860 828 360)

BARKER, Audrey Lilian; da of Harry Barker (d 1963), and Elsie Annie Dutton (d 1976); *b* 13 April 1918; *Educ* Co Secdy Schs of Co Kent and Surrey; *Career* writer; exec ctee Eng Centre Int PEN 1981-85; memb panel of judges for: Katherine Mansfield Prize 1984, Judge Macmillan Silver Pen Award for Fiction 1986; *Awards*: Atlantic Award in Literature 1946, Somerset Maugham Award 1947, Cheltenham Festival of Lit Award 1963, Arts Cncl Award 1970, SE Arts Creative Book Award 1981, Macmillan Silver Pen Award 1987; FRSL; *Books* Innocents (1947), Apology for a Hero (1950), Novelette (1951), The Joy Ride (1963), Lost Upon the Roundabouts (1964), A Case Examined (1965), The Middling (1967), John Brown's Body (1969), Femina Real (1971), A Source of Embarrassment (1974), A Heavy Feather (1979), Life Stories (1981), Relative Successes (1984), No Word of Love (1985), The Gooseboy (1987); *Style*— Ms Audrey Barker; 103 Harrow Rd, Carshalton, Surrey SM5 3QF

BARKER, Barry; MBE (1960); s of Francis Walter Barker (d 1974),and Amy Barker, *née* Rumsey; *b* 28 Dec 1929; *Educ* Ipswich Sch, Trinity Coll Oxford (MA); *m* 1954, Vira, da of Jehangir Dubash, of Bombay, India; 2 s (Christopher, David); *Career* sec: Bombay Chamber of Commerce Indust 1956-62, The Metal Box Co of India Ltd 1962-67; dir Shipbuilding Indust Bds 1967-71; conslt DOI 1972; sec Pye Hldgs Ltd 1972-76; sec and chief exec Inst of Chartered Secs and Administrators (formerly Chartered Inst of Secs) 1976-; *Recreations* theatre, arts; *Clubs* Oriental; *Style*— Barry Barker, Esq, MBE; 82 Darwin Court, Gloucester Ave, London NW1 7BQ; The Institute of Chartered Secretaries and Adminstrators, 16 Park Cres, London W1N 4AH

BARKER, Bridget Caroline; da of Michael John Barker, of 14 Bollinwood Chase, Wilmslow Park, Wilmslow, Ches, and Brenda, *née* Sawdon (d 1987); *b* 7 Mar 1958; *Educ* Monmouth Sch for Girls, Southampton Univ (LLB); *Career* slr 1983; Macfarlanes slrs 1983-, Skadden Arps Slate Meagher & Flom, NY USA 1986-1987; memb Law Soc; *Recreations* tennis, swimming, theatre; *Style*— Ms Bridget Barker; 11a Highbury Terrace Mews, London N5 1UT (☎ 01 354 3278); 10 Norwich Street, London EC4 (☎ 01 831 9222, fax 01 831 9607)

BARKER, Charles Richard; s of Brian Barker (d 1982), of Halifax, and Sybil Mabel, *née* Busfield; *b* 24 Mar 1951; *Educ* Hipperholme GS Halifax, Imperial Coll of Sci and Technol Univ of London (BSc); *Career* CA, trained Spicer and Pegler, Robson Rhodes, dir and sec Low Moor Properties Ltd 1974, sole practioner 1979-; FCA; *Style*— Charles Barker, Esq; Hill Top House, Main Street, Burley-in-Wharfedale, Ilkley, West Yorkshire (☎ 0943 862 912)

BARKER, Christopher Shelley; DL (1984); s of Ernest Anthony Barker, CBE (d 1979), of Lindrick, nr Worksop, and Barbara Mary, *née* Bishop; *b* 13 Nov 1932; *Educ* Rugby, New College Oxford (BA); *m* 11 June 1960, Jennifer Mary, da of Harold Sydney Biggs (d 1981), of Hornsea; 3 da (Caroline, Victoria, Belinda); *Career* Nat Serv RE 1950-52 (cmmnd 1951), TA RE 1952-62; admitted slr 1959; ptnr: H Shelley Barker & Son 1960-68, Neals & Shelley Barkers 1969-77, Broomheads 1978-87 (sr ptnr from 1981); sr ptnr Dibb Lupton Broomhead 1988-; directorships incl: Dengel & Barker (Hldgs) Ltd and subsidiaries (chm 1983-), Circuitt & Hinchcliffe Ltd and subsidiaries, Rittal Holdings Ltd and subsidiaries; tstee The Sheffield Town Tst 1984-, The Talbot Tsts 1962-; gen cmmr of taxes 1967-72, memb cncl Univ of Sheffield 1964- (tres 1971-79, pro chllr 1979-87, chm 1981-87); DL S Yorks 1984-, Freeman Co of Culters in Hallamshire, hon LLD Univ of Sheffield 1988; memb Law Soc; *Recreations* golf; *Clubs* R & A GC, Lindrick GC, Hunstanton Golf, Royal Worlington & Newmarket GC; *Style*— Christopher Barker, Esq, DL; Lion Cottage, Firbeck, nr Worksop, Notts S81 8JT (☎ 0709 817 011); The Old School House, Brancaster, West Norfolk PE31 8AP (☎0485 210689); Dibb Lupton Broomhead, Fountain Precinct, Balm Green, Sheffield S1 1RZ (☎ 0742 760 351, fax 0742 700 568, car tel 0837 273 094, telex 547566)

BARKER, Clifford Conder; *see*: Selby, Bishop of

BARKER, David; QC (1976); s of Frederick Barker (d 1987), of The Old Cottage, Woodhouse, Leics, and Amy Evelyn, *née* Lundie; *b* 13 April 1932; *Educ* Sir John Deane's GS, Univ Coll London (LLM), Univ of Michigan (USA); *m* 1957, Diana Mary Vinson, da of Alan Duckworth (d 1981), of Hill House, Rochdale, Lancs; 1 s (Jonathan), 3 da (Jane, Rachel, Caroline); *Career* RAF Flt Lt 1956-58; recorder of the

Crown Court 1974; bencher Inner Temple 1985; *Style*— David Barker, Esq, QC; Nanhill, Woodhouse, Eaves, Leics (☎ 0509 890224); 7 King's Bench Walk, EC4; Francis Taylor Bldg, Temple, EC4 (☎ 01 353 7768)

BARKER, David; s of Samuel Barker, of 162 Rochdale Rd, Royton, Oldham, Lancs, and Alice, *née* Bailey; *b* 31 March 1943; *Educ* N Chadderton Sch, Royal Coll Advanced Technol Salford (HNC); *m* 20 Feb 1965 (separated 1988), June; 2 s (Simon David b 23 Sept 1965, Timothy Jason b 5 Nov 1968); *Career* md Styles & Wood Ltd 1966-, chm Meridian Hldgs Gp 1981-; memb bd of dirs: Wembley Stadium 1984, Young Presidents' Orgn Inc USA 1986-; exec chm Crown Store Equipment Inc USA 1987; JP Oldham Bench 1976-78; chm: Oldham Round Table 1976-77, Manchester Chapter Young Presidents Orgn Inc; nat cncllr Round Tale Br & Ireland 1979-82, vice-pres Euro Middle-East & N Africa Young Presidents Orgn Inc; FInstD, memb IOD; *Recreations* skiing, walking, flying; *Style*— David Barker, Esq; 31 Culvercliff Walk, St John's Gardens, Manchester M3 4FL (☎ 061 832 6616); Meridian Hldgs Ltd, Brook House, 77 Fountain St, Manchester M2 2EE (☎ 061 236 7030, fax 061 834 6124)

BARKER, David Edward; s of Edward Reginald Barker, of Radlett, Herts, and Frances Barker, *née* Solly; *b* 28 May 1946; *Educ* Bushey Sch, Watford Art Coll; *m* 9 Oct 1971, Jennifer Ann, da of Ernest Farnham (d 1960), of Morden, Surrey; 1 s (Leo Farnham b 1979), 1 da (Cassia Eve b 1978); *Career* art dir Leo Burnet London 1966-68, creative gp head J Walter Thompson London New York 1970-75 (art dir 1968-70); creative dir: Rupert Chetwynd 1975-79, Benton & Bowles London 1979-80, Geers & Gross 1980-84; fndr and creative dir Humpheys Bull & Barker 1984-87, fndr and exec creative dir KHBB 1987-89; *Recreations* motor racing, photography, music; *Clubs* BARC, BRSCC; *Style*— David Barker, Esq; 82 Charing Cross Rd, London WC2H 0BA (☎ 01 379 5656, 01 836 3283, fax 01 836 3716, telex 22635

BARKER, Prof David Faubert; s of Faubert Barker (d 1980), and Doreen Maude, *née* Hitchcock (d 1955); *b* 18 Feb 1922; *Educ* Bryanston Sch, Magdalen Coll Oxford (BA, DPhil, MA, DSc); *m* 1, 16 June 1945 (m dis 1977), Kathleen Mary Frances, da of William Pocock (d 1951); 3 s (Ian b 1947, Jolyon b 1952, Guy b 1954), 2 da (Susan b 1948, Jillian b 1955); m 2, 29 Jan 1978, Patricia Margaret, *née* Drake; 1 step s (John b 1970), 1 step da (Annabel b 1974); *Career* demonstrator dept of zoology Oxford Univ 1947-50, prof of zoology Univ of Hong Kong 1950-62 (dean faculty of sci 1959-60), prof of zoology Univ of Durham 1962-87, Sir Dermon Christopherson fell Durham Univ Res Fndn 1985-86, emeritus prof 1987-); memb Physiological Soc, sr memb Anatomical Soc; *Recreations* gardening; *Style*— Prof David Barker; Dept of Biological Sciences, Univ of Durham, South Rd, Durham DH1 3LE (☎ 091 374 3341)

BARKER, Dennis Albert; QC (1968); s of John William Barker, of Lowdham, Notts, and R E Barker; *b* 9 June 1926; *Educ* Nottingham HS, Queen's Coll Oxford; *m* 1, 1949 (m dis 1984), Daphne, da of Percy Ruffle, of Lowdham, Notts; 1 s, 1 da (and 1 da decd); m 2, 1984, Deirdre, *née* Rendall-Day; *Career* barr 1950, Crown Court Recorder 1972-79, Justice of Appeal, Hong Kong 1981-; *Style*— The Hon Mr Justice Barker; Supreme Court, Hong Kong

BARKER, George Granville; s of George Barker (d 1961), and Marion Frances, *née* Taaffe (d 1955); *b* 26 Feb 1913; *Educ* Marlborough Rd Sch London; *m* 1964, Elspeth Roberta Cameron, da of Robert Langlands, of Butterstone, Scotland; 3 s, 2 da; *Career* writer; prof of eng lit Imperial Tohoku Univ Japan 1939-40, visiting prof NY State Univ, Arts fellowship York Univ; author of various collected poems, essays and two plays; *Style*— George Barker, Esq; Bintry House, Itteringham, Aylsham, Norfolk (☎ 0263 87240); c/o Faber & Faber Ltd, 3 Queen's Sq, London WC1

BARKER, Graham Harold; TD (1985); s of Harold George Barker (d 1962), of Cambridge, and Dorothy, *née* Speechley (d 1986); *b* 11 Jan 1949; *Educ* Cambridge GS, Kings Coll London, St George's Hosp Med Sch London (MB, BS, AKC); *m* 23 Sept 1978, Esther Louise, da of John Owen Farrow, of Norwich; 1 s (Douglas Graham b 23 June 1982), 1 da (Louise Elizabeth b 9 Jan 1987); *Career* Surgn 217 (L) Gen Hosp RAMC (V) 1973-, Capt 1974, Maj 1980; lectr Inst of Cancer Res London 1977-79, registrar Queen Charlotte's and Chelsea Hosps London 1980, sr registrar in gynaecology and obstetrics The Middx and Univ Coll Hosp London 1981-87, gynaecologist St Georges Hosp London and Portland Hosp for Women and Children London; memb: Br Soc for Colposcopy and Cervical Pathology, Br Gynaecologicial Cancer Soc, Gynaecological Res Soc, Chelsea Clinical Soc; Freeman City of London, Liveryman Worshipful Co of Apothecaries 1980; MRCOG 1978, FRCS(Ed) 1979, Astor fell Harvard Univ Hosps 1984; *Books* Family Health And Medicine Guide (1979), Your Search For Fertility (1981), Chemotherapy of Gynaecological Malignancies (1983), The New Fertility (1986), Your Smear Test - A Guide To Screening, Colposcopy And The Prevention Of Cervical Cancer (1987); *Recreations* writing, the organ/piano; *Style*— Graham Barker, Esq, TD; 12 Wolsey Close, Kingston Upon Thames, Surrey KT2 7ER (☎ 01 942 2614); 8 Denham Way, Cambersands, Rye, East Sussex; St George's Hosp, Blackshaw Rd, London SW17 (☎ 01 672 1255)

BARKER, Sir Harry Heaton; KBE (1978, CBE 1972, OBE 1964), JP; s of John Heaton Barker; *b* 18 July 1898; *Educ* Wellington and Auckland, New Plymouth Boys' HS; *m* 1926, Anita Pearl, MBE, da of Hubert Greaves; *Career* journalist, ed Gisborne Herald 1935-43, Mayor of Gisborne 1950, 1953, 1956, 1959, 1962, 1965, 1968, 1971, 1974; *Style*— Sir Harry Barker, KBE, JP; 218 Harris St, Gisborne, N Zealand (☎ 6405)

BARKER, John Francis Holroyd; CB (1984); s of Rev C H Barker, and B A Barker, *née* Bullivant; *b* 3 Feb 1925; *m* 1954, Felicity Ann Martindale; 3 da; *Career* princ dir MOD; *Style*— John Barker Esq, CB; c/o Coutts & Co, 440 Strand, London WC2

BARKER, Air Vice-Marshal John Lindsay; CB (1963), CBE (1946), DFC (1945); s of Dr Abraham Cockroft Barker (d 1971), and Lilian Alice, *née* Woods (d 1969); *b* 12 Nov 1910; *Educ* Trent Coll, BNC Oxford; *m* 1948, Eleanor Margaret Hannah, da of E B Williams, of Co Cork; 1 s; *Career* RAFO 1930, RAF 1933, served WW II, Air Attaché Rome 1955-58, Cdr Royal Ceylon Air Force 1958-63, ret; barr Middle Temple 1947; Order of Merit (Italy) 1958; *Recreations* sailing, golf, photography; *Clubs* RAF; *Style*— Air Vice-Marshal John Barker, CB, CBE, DFC; The Old Cider Press, Mill Court, Frogmore, Kingsbridge, South Devon TQ7 2PB (☎ 054853 746)

BARKER, Rear Adm John Perronet; CB (1985); s of Gilbert Barker (d 1969, gs of Thomas Perronet Barker, constructional engr, who built all the waterless gasholders in Britain in the 1930s), and Dorothy Gwendoline, *née* Moore (d 1972), of Edgbaston, Birmingham; *Educ* Nautical Coll Pangbourne; *m* 1955, (Evelyn) Priscilla Summerson, da of Sir William Christie, KCIE, CSI, MC (d 1983), of Gerrards Cross, Bucks; 2 s (b 1957 and 1959); *Career* joined RN 1948, supply offr HMS Lagos 1957-58, Britannia RN Coll Dartmouth 1958-61, sec to Br Naval Attaché Washington 1961-64, sec to ACNS (Warfare) 1964-67, supply offr HMS Hampshire 1967-68, sec to Controller of the Navy 1972-76, Cdre HMS Centurion 1980-83, Rear Adm 1983, COS to C-in-C Naval Home Cmd 1983-85, ret RN 1986; Administrator Mission to Seamen 1987-; chm Assoc of RN offrs; Liveryman of Worshipful Company of Shipwrights 1983; *Recreations* dinghy sailing in 14 foot dinghies, gardening, DIY; *Clubs* RN Sailing, Midland Sailing, Royal Yacht Sqdn; *Style*— Rear-Adm John Barker; c/o Lloyds Bank plc, Colmore Row, Birmingham B3 3AD

BARKER, Maj John Sowerby Gartside; RA; s of Lt-Col Robert Hewitt Barker, JP (d 1961), of Todmorden and Rochdale (MP IND Sowerby 1919-22), and Violet Kathleen, *née* Gartside (d 1982); *b* 27 June 1921; *Educ* King Edward VII Sch Lytham St Annes; *m* 15 Sept 1951, Judith Mary, da of Herbert Wilson Collier, JP, (d 1977), of Gloucester; 2s (Robert, Richard), 2 da (Hazel, Sara); *Career* WWII served RA 1941-46 (despatches 1946); articled F Hunter Gregory & Lord 1938, qualified CA 1949, commercial appt 1948-53, ptnr F Hunter Gregory & Lord (merged with Binder Hamlyn 1974) 1953-87, conslt 1987-; past pres NW Soc CAS 1983-84; memb Bacup Rotary Club; tres: Rochdale Music Soc, Rochdale Chamber of Trade; MICA; *Recreations* music, pianoforte, rugby, tennis, golf; *Style*— Maj John S G Barker; BDO Binder Hamlyn, 7-9 Irwell Terr, Bacup, Lancs OL13 9AJ, (☎ 0706 873 213, fax 0706 874 211)

BARKER, Kenneth; s of Raymond Charles Barker, of Leics, and Ivy, *née* Blackburn; *b* 15 August 1947; *Educ* Gateway Sch Leics; *m* 1, 30 Oct 1970 (m dis 1983), (Elizabeth) Peris, da of Thomas Stephens (d 1985); 1 s (Michael b 1974); m 2, 8 July 1987, Julie, da of Joseph Casling (d 1984); 1 s (Edward b 1984); *Career* CA; F W Clarke & Co (later Touche Ross & Co) 1964-78, Barker Crowfoot & Co 1978-; tres & memb: Leicester CC 1962-82, Old Lancastrians Football Club 1963-85; tres Leics Badminton Assoc 1981-84; FCA 1979; *Recreations* golf, badminton; *Clubs* Glen Gorce GC, Coalville Badminton; *Style*— Kenneth Barker, Esq; The Old Coach House, Church Lane, Dunton Bassett, Lutterworth, Leics (☎ 0455 202140); Barker Crowfoot & Co, Lonsdale High St, Lutterworth, Leics (☎ 0455 5 57322, fax 045 55 4144)

BARKER, Nicolas John; s of Sir Ernest Barker (d 1960), and Olivia Stuart, *née* Horner (d 1976); *b* 6 Dec 1932; *Educ* Westminster Sch, New Coll Oxford (MA); *m* 11 Aug 1962, Joanna Mary Nyda Sophia, da of Col Henry Edward Mariano Cotton, OBE (d 1988); 2 s (Christian b 1964, Cosmo b 1973), 3 da (Emma b 1963, Olivia b 1963, Cecilia b 1969); *Career* with Rupert Hart-Davis Ltd 1959, asst keeper Nat Portrait Gallery 1964; with: Macmillan and Co 1965, OUP 1971; dep keeper Br Library 1976, ed The Book Collector 1965; *Books* The Publications of the Roxburghe Club (1967), The Printer and the Poet (1970), Stanley Morison (1972), The Early Life of James McBey (1977), Bibliotheca Lindesiana (1977), The Oxford University Press and the Spread of Learning (1978), A Sequel to an Enquiry (with J Collins 1983), Aldus Manutius and the Development of Greek Script and Type (1985), The Butterfly Books (1987); *Clubs* Garrick, Beefsteak; *Style*— Nicolas John Barker, Esq; 22 Clarendon Road, London W11 3AB (☎ 727 4340); British Library, Great Russell Street, London WC1B 3DG (☎ 323 7550, telex 21462)

BARKER, Hon Mrs; Hon Olwen Gwynne; *née* Philipps; JP; da of 1 and last Baron Kylsant (d 1937); *b* 1905; *m* 1, 1925 (m dis 1937), 7 Baron Suffield; m 2, 1937, Lt-Col Frank Richard Peter Barker, TD, RA (d 1974), s of late Christopher Barker, of Oakhyrst Grange, Caterham, Surrey; 1 s (Timothy Gwynne, *qv*); *Style*— The Hon Mrs Barker, JP; Lund Court, Nawton, York

BARKER, Paul; s of Donald Barker (d 1981), and Marion, *née* Ashworth; *b* 24 August 1935; *Educ* Hebden Bridge GS, Calder HS, Brasenoze Coll Oxford (MA); *m* 1960, Sally, da of James Huddleston (d 1965); 3 s (Nicholas, Tom, Daniel), 1 da (Kate); *Career* writer and broadcaster; lectr Ecole Normale Superieure Paris 1958-59; ed staff: The Times 1959-63, Economist 1964-65; ed New Society 1968-86 (staff writer 1964, asst ed 1965-68), social policy ed Sunday Telegraph 1986-88, columnist London Evening Standard 1987-, assoc ed The Independent magazine 1988-; visiting fell Centre for the Analysis of Social Policy Univ of Bath 1986-; dir: The Fiction Magazine 1981-89, Pennine Heritage 1978-86; *Books* A Sociological Portrait (ed 1972), One for Sorrow, Two for Joy (ed and contrib 1972), The Social Sciences Today (ed 1975), Arts in Society (ed and contrib 1977), The Other Britain (ed and contrib 1982), Founders of the Welfare State (ed 1985); *Style*— Paul Barker, Esq; 15 Dartmouth Park Ave, London NW5 (☎ 01 485 8861)

BARKER, Peter Denis; *b* 16 Sept 1925; *m* 1950, Sylvia Edna; 1 s; *Career* chm: Palmer Research 1982-, Rare Earth Products 1982-, Johnson Matthey Hong Kong 1983-; divisional dir Chemicals and Refining Div Johnson Matthey 1981-; dir: Johnson Matthey Chemicals 1968- (md 1973-82; Queen's Award for Export 1982), Roques Chimie SA France 1982-, Johnson Matthey Chimie France 1982-, Johnson Matthey Investments 1982-, Johnson Matthey Services 1983-, ret; *Recreations* gardening, cricket, music; *Clubs* MCC; *Style*— Peter Barker Esq; Johnson Matthey plc, Chemicals and Refining Division, 100 High St, Southgate, London N14 6ET (☎ 01 882 6111)

BARKER, Peter William; CBE (1988); *Career* chm J H Fenner (Hldgs) plc (power transmission engrs) 1982-; chm: J H Fenner & Co, Fenner Int; dir: Mastabar Mining Equipment, James Dawson & Son, Neepsend plc, Fenner America, Fenner (India), Fenner (Australia), Fenner (S Africa), Fenner Industl Controls, Fenner SA, Fenner GmbH; memb: CBI Nat Cncl, Yorks and Humberside Regnl Industl Devpt Bd; CBIM, FIIM, FInstD, MInstM; *Clubs* Hurlingham, Oriental; *Style*— Peter W Barker, Esq; J H Fenner (Holdings) plc, Marfleet, Hull, Yorks HU9 5RA (☎ 0482 781234)

BARKER, Richard Philip; JP; s of Philip Watson Barker (d 1971), and Helen May, *née* Latham; *b* 17 July 1939; *Educ* Repton, Trinity Coll Cambridge (MA), Bristol Univ (Cert Ed); *m* 1966, Imogen Margaret, da of Sir Ronald Montague Joseph Harris, KCVO, CB, of Slyfield Farmhouse, Stoke D'Abernon, Surrey; 2 s (Jolyon b 1967, Thorold b 1971), 1 da (Rosalind b 1969); *Career* asst master Bedales Sch 1963-65, Marlborough 1967-81, dir A Level Business Studies Project 1966-75; lectr Inst of Educn London 1974-75; headmaster Sevenoaks Sch 1981-; series ed Understanding Business (Longmans) 1975-; *Recreations* fishing, sailing, educational matters; *Clubs* RSA; *Style*— Richard Barker, Esq, JP; The Headmaster's Ho, Sevenoaks Sch, Kent TN13 1HU (☎ 0732 455133)

BARKER, Ronnie (Ronald William George Barker); OBE (1978); s of Leonard and Edith Barker; *b* 25 Sept 1929; *Educ* Oxford HS; *m* 1957, Joy Tubb; 2 s, 1 da; *Career* actor; winner of eighteen awards for performances, including three Br Acad

Awards; *Style*— Ronnie Barker, Esq, OBE; High Tawcarisks, Loudwater, Bucks SL4 38L

BARKER, Thomas Christopher; s of Col Rowland Barker, OBE, MC (d 1965), of Brighton, and Kathleen Maude, *née* Welch (d 1956); *b* 28 June 1928; *Educ* Uppingham, New Coll Oxford (MA); *m* 3 Sept 1960, Griselda Helen, da of Robert Cormack (d 1982), of Ayr; 2 s (Christopher b 1964, Robert b 1966), 1 da (Rosanna b 1961); *Career* 2 Lt Worcs Regt 1945; HM Dip Serv: third sec Paris 1953-55, second sec Baghdad 1955-58, first sec Mexico City 1962-67 (also head of chancery and consul), cnsllr and head of chancery Caracas 1969-71, under sec Belfast 1975-76; curator Scottish Nat War Meml 1978-88 (sec to tstees 1988-); FSAS 1988; *Style*— Thomas Barker, Esq; Carmurie, South St, Elie, Fife KY9 1DN; Scottish National War Memorial, The Castle, Edinburgh EH1 2YT

BARKER, Thomas Lloyd; s of Edmund Cadwaladyr Barker, of Loughton, Essex, and Patricia Josephine May, *née* Yates (d 1982); *b* 11 Jan 1939; *Educ* Bancroft's Sch, Univ of Brimingham (LLB); *m* 2 Oct 1971, Edwina Ethel, da of Albert Edward Wright, of Chelmondiston, Suffolk; 1 s (Oliver b 1972), 1 da (Charlotte b 1974); *Career* slr 1967, currently ptnr Vanderpump and Sykes; Notary Public 1977; memb ctee Buckhurst Hill & Loughton Green Belt Preservation Soc, tstee Barts-Oxford Family Study of Childhood Diabetes, chm Hon Artillary Co's Saddle Club, special constable; Freeman City of London 1981, Liveryman Worshipful Co Farriers 1981 (asst ct 1988); memb: Law Soc, Soc Provincial Notaries; *Recreations* horse riding, walking, historical res; *Clubs* City Livery, HAC; *Style*— Thomas Barker, Esq; Clovelly, 45 Hillcrest Rd, Loughton, Essex (☎ 01 508 1199); Vanderpump and Sykes, 58-60 Silver St, Enfield, Middx (☎ 01 366 4101/01 807 5871, fax 01 807 5347)

BARKER, Timothy Gwynne; s of Lt-Col (Frank Richard) Peter Barker (d 1974), of Lund Ct, Nawton, York, and Hon Olwen Gwynne, *née* Philipps, *qv*; *b* 8 April 1940; *Educ* Eton, Jesus Coll Cambridge (MA), McGill Univ Montreal; *m* 14 July 1964, Philippa Rachel Mary, da of Brig Mervyn Christopher Thursby-Pelham, OBE, of Ridgeland House, Finchampstead, Berks; 1 s (Christopher b 1970), 1 da (Camilla b 1968); *Career* dir: Kleinwort Benson Ltd 1973-, Kleinwort Benson Gp plc 1988-; dir-gen Panel on Take-overs and Mergers, Cncl for the Securities Indust 1984-85; *Style*— Timothy Barker, Esq; Kleinwort Benson Ltd, PO Box 560, 20 Fenchurch St, London EC3P 3DB

BARKER, Trevor; s of Samuel Lawrence Barker (d 1987), of Middlesbrough, and Lilian, *née* Dawson (d 1970); *b* 24 Mar 1935; *Educ* GS; *m* 7 Sept 1957, Joan Elizabeth, da of Frederick Cross (d 1972), of Stockton-on-Tees; 1 s (Roy b 21 Feb 1961), 1 da (Karen (Mrs Dent) b 17 July 1958); *Career* articled to Leonard C Bye FCA Middlesbrough, Price Waterhouse & Co 1957-58, Cooper Bros 1958-62, practised in Leyburn Yorks 1962-70, chm and chief exec Gold Case Travel Ltd 1964-77, dir Ellerman Wilson Lines Ltd 1977-80; chm and chief exec John Crowther Gp plc 1981-88, William Morris Fine Arts plc 1982-88, Alpha Consolidated Hldgs Ltd 1988-; memb bd of Peterlee and Aycliffe Devpt Corpn 1986-88; Freeman City of London, Liveryman Worshipful Co of Woolmen; FCA 1957; *Recreations* racing thoroughbreds, opera, books; *Style*— Trevor Barker, Esq; Windways, 323 Coniscliffe Rd, Darlington, Co Durham, DL3 8AH (☎ 0325 50436); Dickens House, 15 Tooks Ct, Cursitor Str, London EC4A 1LB (☎ 01 831 1256, car tel 0860 311 194)

BARKER, Sir William; KCMG (1967, CMG 1958), OBE (1949); s of Alfred Barker (d 1961), of Leigh, Lancs; *b* 19 July 1909; *Educ* Liverpool and Prague Univs; *m* 1939, Margaret, da of Thomas P Beirne, of Leigh, Lancs; 1 s, 1 da; *Career* Br Ambass to Czechoslovakia 1966-68, Bowes prof of Russian Liverpool Univ 1969-76; *Style*— Sir William Barker, KCMG, OBE; 19 Moors Way, Woodbridge, Suffolk IP12 4HQ (☎ 03943 3673)

BARKER-WYATT, Brig Desmond Alfred; CBE (1973), MBE (1958); s of John Harold G Barker Wyatt (d 1981), and Florence Pearl Lloyd Channer (d 1977); *b* 13 Feb 1924; *Educ* Worcester RGS, Army and Jt Servs Staff Coll (1955 and 1965); *m* 15 Sept 1951, Jancis, da of Brig R W Andrews, DSO, MC (d 1978); 2 s (Charles b 1952, William b 1959), 1 da (Amanda b 1954); *Career* cmmnd RE 1945, served Bombay and Bengal Sappers Miners (Indian Airborne Div) - 1948; cmdg Maj Ind Fd Sqdn Cyprus (despatches 1959), cmdg Lt Col Para Engr Regt TA 1966-68, chief of logistics UN Forces Cyprus 1969-70, chief of personnel and logistics NI 1971-72 (Col), cdr Engr Brigade 1974-76, ret 1978; Hon Col Commando Sqdn RE (V) 1980-85; Inspr for Highways Public Enquiries (Lord Chancellor's Panel); FRGS; *Recreations* sailing, shooting; *Clubs* Royal Ocean Racing; *Style*— Brig Desmond Barker-Wyatt, CBE; North Close, Littleton Panell, Devizes, Wilts SN10 4ES (☎ 0380 813387)

BARKES, Neville Rogerson; TD; s of W Barkes, MD, of Northumberland, and Kathleen Herbert Ranken; *b* 11 July 1924; *Educ* Sedbergh, Edinburgh Univ (short course); *m* 1952, Gillian, da of Col J C B Cookson, DSO, DL, of Meldon Park, Morpeth, Northumberland; 2 s (Richard, George), 1 da (Caroline); *Career* Capt 6 RHA 1946-47, Lt-Col 272 (N) Field Regt RA (TA) 1965-67; dir: Br Electrical & Mfrg Co, TSB Hldgs 1980-82; TSB Gp Computer Servs 1981-1984; chm: TSB Computer Servs 1973-84, TSB NE 1980-83; memb TSB Central Bd 1980-86, dir Central Tstee Savings Bank 1982-86; memb TSB England and Wales 1983-86; dir TSB Group plc 1985-, TSB England and Wales plc 1986-; *Recreations* shooting, gardening; *Clubs* Northern Counties; *Style*— Neville Barkes Esq, TD; West Muckleridge, Matfen, Northumberland NE20 0SQ (☎ 066 16 230)

BARKING, Bishop Suffragan of, 1983-; Rt Rev James William Roxburgh; s of James Thomas and Margaret Roxburgh; *b* 5 July 1921; *Educ* Whitgift, St Catharine's Coll Cambridge; *m* 1949, Marjorie Winifred, *née* Hipkiss; 1 s, 1 da; *Career* ordained priest 1945, vicar of Barking 1965-77, archdeacon of Colchester 1977-83, pro-prolocutor Convocation of Canterbury 1977-83; *Recreations* travel, philately; *Clubs* Rotary, Essex.; *Style*— The Rt Rev The Bishop of Barking; Barking Lodge, 28A Connaught Ave, Loughton, Essex 1G10 4DS (Tel: 01 508 6680)

BARKSHIRE, (Robert Renny St John) John; TD (1970), JP (Lewes 1980), DL (1986); s of Robert Hugh Barkshire, CBE, *qv*; *b* 31 August 1935; *Educ* Bedford Sch; *m* 1960, Margaret Elizabeth, da of Leslie Robinson (d 1986), of Great Dunmow, Essex; 2 s (Charles b 1963, William b 1965), 1 da (Sarah b 1969); *Career* 2 Lt Duke of Wellington's Regt 1953-55, TA Hon Artillery Co 1955-74, CO 1970-72, (Regt Col 1972-74); banker; Cater Ryder & Co 1955-72 (jt md 1963-72), chm Mercantile House Hldgs 1972-8, chm Alexanders Laing & Cruickshank Hldgs Ltd 1984-, non-exec dir Extel Gp 1979-87 (dep chm 1986-87), advsy bd IMM Div of Chicago Mercantile Exchange 1981-84; dir LIFE 1982- (chm: FFWP 1980, LIFFE St.Ct 1981 (LIFFE 1982-85); chm: Ctee on Market in Single Properties 1985-, Int Commodities Clearing Exchange 1986-; gen cmmr for income tax City of London 1981-; govr: Eastbourne Coll, Roedean Sch, Duke of York's Royal Military Sch Dover (dep chm) Bedford Sch Ctee (chm); memb Chiddingly Parish Cncl 1979-87, tres Chiddingly PCC 1976-86; chm: Chiddingly and Dist Br Legion 1982-87, Reserve Forces Assoc 1983-87, Sussex TA Ctee 1983-85, SE TAVR Assoc 1985-, vice-chm TA Sport Bd 1983- (memb 1979-); fin advsr Victory Services Club 1981-; dir Offrs' Pensions Soc Investment Co 1982-; freeman City of London, liveryman Worshipful Co of Farmers; 300 acre farm in Sussex; ACIB; *Recreations* sailing, shooting; *Clubs* City of London, Cavalry and Guards, MCC, Royal Fowey Yacht; *Style*— John Barkshire, Esq, TD, JP, DL; Flat 4, 115 Alderney Street, London SW1V 4HF (☎ 01 828 5055); 66 Cannon St, London EC4N 6AE (☎ 01 236 0233)

BARKSHIRE, Robert Hugh; CBE (1968); yr s of Lt-Col Charles Robert Barkshire, OBE (d 1951), and Clara Gunston (d 1958); *b* 24 Oct 1909; *Educ* King's Sch Bruton; *m* 1934, Emily May, da of Albert Sidney Blunt (d 1970), of Bedford; 1 s (John, *qv*); *Career* Bank of England 1927-55; priv sec to Govr C F Cobbold (later Lord Cobbold) 1949-53; sec: Ctee of London Clearing Bankers, Br Bankers Assoc, Bankers Clearing House; memb various Inter-Bank Ctees 1955-70; hon sec meetings of Offrs of Euro Bankers Assocs 1959-72; gen cmmr of Income Tax for City of London 1969-78; govr NIESR 1970-78; FIB, Freeman City of London; *Clubs* Royal Thames Yacht, Royal Fowey Yacht; *Style*— R H Barkshire, Esq, CBE; The Boat House, Fowey, Cornwall (☎ Fowey 3389)

BARKWORTH, Paul Raymond Braithwaite; JP; s of Frederic Basil Stileman Barkworth, of Eastbourne, E Sussex, and Beryl Nellie, *née* Wright; *b* 26 Jan 1947; *Educ* Monkton Combe Sch; *m* 18 June 1970, Janet Elizabeth, da of Charles Arthur Crees, of Plymouth; *Career* CA public practice, dir Baptist Insur Co Plc 1985, chm Baptist Housing Assoc 1988, memb of cncl Baptist Union of GB, parish cncllr; freeman City of London; FCA; *Recreations* motor cycling, music, travel, photography; *Clubs* Bristol Commercial Rooms; *Style*— P R B Barkworth, Esq, JP; Tranby House, Norton Lane, Whitchurch, Nr Bristol BS14 0BT (☎ 0272 837101); Bristol Chambers, 6/10 St Nicholas St, Bristol BS1 1UQ (☎ 0272 294 833, fax 0272 221 493)

BARKWORTH, Peter Wynn; s of Walter Wynn Barkworth (d 1974), of Bramhall, Cheshire, and Irene May, *née* Brown (d 1972); *b* 14 Jan 1929; *Educ* Stockport Sch, Royal Acad of Dramatic Art; *Career* actor; theatre: Crown Matrimonial 1972 (BAFTA award best actor 1974), Donkey's Years 1976, Can You Hear Me At The Back? 1979, A Coat of Varnish 1982, Siegfried Sassoon 1986; television: Professional Foul (BAFTA best actor award 1977), The Power Game, Manhunt, Telford's Change, The Price, Late Starter, The Gospel According to St Matthew, dir: Sisterly Feelings, Night and Day; producer and dir independent prodn co Astramead Ltd; *Books* About Acting (1980), First Houses (1983), More About Acting (1984); *Recreations* walking, looking at paintings, gardening; *Style*— P Barkworth, Esq; 47 Flask Walk, London NW3 1HH (☎ 01 794 4591); c/o Duncan Heath Associates Ltd, Paramount House, 162 Wardour St, W1V 3AT (☎ 01 439 1471)

BARLOW, Sir Christopher Hilaro; 7 Bt (UK 1803), of Fort William, Bengal; s of Sir Richard Barlow, 6 Bt, AFC (d 1946), and Rosamund Sylvia, *née* Anderton; *b* 1 Dec 1929; *Educ* Eton, McGill Univ (BArch); *m* 1952, Jacqueline Claire de Marigny, da of John Edmund Audley (d 1980); 1 s (and 1 s decd), 2 da; *Heir* s, Crispian John Edmund Audley Barlow; *Career* architect; *Recreations* dressage (horse Camboldt), sailing (owner of ketch 'Phoebe'); *Clubs* Royal Cwlth Soc; *Style*— Sir Christopher Barlow, Bt; 18 Winter Ave, St John's, Newfoundland A1A 1T3, Canada (☎ (709) 726 5913)

BARLOW, Crispian John Edmund Audley; s and h of Sir Christopher Hilaro Barlow, 7 Bt, *qv*; *b* 20 April 1958; *Educ* Marine Electronics, Coll of Fisheries, St John's, Newfoundland; *m* 1981, Anne Waiching Siu; *Career* Inspector of Police, Royal Hong Kong Police Force 1978-; memb Int Assoc of Bomb Technicians and Investigators; *Recreations* shooting, sailing; *Clubs* OCH, 100 club; *Style*— Crispian Barlow, Esq; c/o Royal Hong Kong Police Headquarters, Arsenal Street, Hong Kong

BARLOW, David John; s of F Ralph Barlow, of Birmingham, and Joan M, *née* Barber; *b* 20 Oct 1937; *Educ* Leighton Park Sch, The Queen's Coll Oxford, Leeds Univ (MA, DipEd, DipESL); *m* 1; 3 s (John, Andrew, Simon); m 2, 1981, Sanchia Beatrice, da of Marcel Oppenheimer; 2 s (Luke, Nathan), 1 da (Imogen); *Career* gen sec ITCA 1980-81; BBC: sec 1981-83; controller public affairs and int relations 1983-85, controller public affairs 1985-87, controller regnl broadcasting 1987-; *Clubs* English Speaking Union, BAFTA, Royal TV Soc; *Style*— David Barlow, Esq; 1 St Joseph's Close, Olney, Bucks; c/o BBC Broadcasting Ho, London W1A 1AA

BARLOW, Erasmus Darwin; s of Sir Alan Barlow, 2 Bt, GCB, KBE (d 1968); *b* 15 April 1915; *Educ* Marlborough, Trin Coll Cambridge, UCH Medical Sch, MA, MB, BChir, FRC Psych; *m* 1938, Brigit, da of Ladbroke Black, of Wendover; 1 s, 2 da; *Career* research fell and consultant psychiatrist St Thomas's Hosp 1951-66; chm Bath Inst of Medical Engineering 1976-88; master Worshipful Co of Scientific Instrument Makers 1976-77; sec Zoological Soc of London 1980-82; chm and dep chm Cambridge Instrument Co 1964-79; *Recreations* home, garden, music, travel; *Clubs* Savile; *Style*— Erasmus Barlow, Esq; Elbrook House, Ashwell, Baldock, Herts SG7 5NE

BARLOW, James Alan; s and h of Sir Thomas Barlow, 3 Bt, DSC, DL, *qv*; *b* 10 July 1956; *Educ* Highgate, Manchester Univ (BSc); *Career* metallurgist; res engr The Welding Inst Cambridge 1978-82; mangr: Harland & Wolff Belfast 1982-84, Glassdrumman House Annalong 1984-; *Style*— James Barlow, Esq; The Beatings, Glassdrumman Road, Annalong, Co Down; Glasdrumman House, Annalong,Newry, Co Down BT34 6QN (☎ 039 67 68585)

BARLOW, James Mellodew; s of Capt Cecil Barlow (d 1988), of Oldham, and Florence Patricia, *née* Mellodew; *b* 23 Dec 1943; *Educ* Mill Hill Sch, Nottingham Univ (LLB); *Career* admitted slr 1967, ptnr Clifford Chance (formerly Coward Chance), 1980-; hon sec Cumberland LTC 1976-82; memb Worshipful Co of Slrs 1980; memb Law Soc 1967, ATII 1968; *Recreations* squash, tennis, skiing, fell walking, bridge; *Clubs* Old Mill Hillians; *Style*— James Barlow, Esq; 11 Edmunds Walk, London N2 0NH (☎ 01 883 6972); Clifford Chance, Royex House, Aldermanbury Sq, London EC2V 7LD (☎ 01 600 0808, fax 01 726 8561, telex 8959991)

BARLOW, Sir John Kemp; 3 Bt (UK 1907), of Bradwall Hall, Cheshire; s of Sir John Denman Barlow, 2 Bt (d 1986), and Hon Diana Helen Kemp, yr da of 1 Baron Rochdale; *b* 22 April 1934; *Educ* Winchester, Trinity Coll Cambridge; *m* 1962, Susan, da of Col Sir Andrew Horsbrugh Porter, 3 Bt, DSO; 4 s; *Heir* s, John William Marshall b 12 March 1964; *Career* farmer; chm Majedie Investmts plc; chm Rubber Growers

Assoc 1974-75; *Clubs* Brooks's, Jockey (steward 1988-), City of London; *Style*— Sir John Barlow, Bt; Bulkeley Grange, Malpas, Cheshire (☎ 082 922 316)

BARLOW, (Alan) Keith; MC; s of Keith Barlow (d 1930), former chm Wiggins Teape & Co; *b* 3 Nov 1921; *Educ* Eton, Sandhurst; *m* ; 1 s, 1 da; *Career* served Coldstream Gds 1940-54; memb Stock Exchange 1954; sr ptnr Henderson Crosthwaite & Co (Stockbrokers), ret 1986; *Recreations* golf, racing (horse Pegwell Bay); *Clubs* White's, Royal St George's Golf, Swinley Forest Golf; *Style*— Major Keith Barlow, MC; Sunning Cottage, Sunningdale, Berks

BARLOW, Nora, Lady; (Emma) Nora; da of late Sir Horace Darwin, KBE; *m* 1911, Sir (James) Alan (Noel) Barlow, 2 Bt, GCB, KBE (d 1968); *Style*— Nora, Lady Barlow; Sellenger, Sylvester Rd, Cambridge

BARLOW, Roy Oxspring; s of George and Clarice Barlow; *b* 13 Feb 1927; *Educ* King Edward VII Sch Sheffield, Queen's Coll Oxford, Sheffield Univ; *m* 1957, Kathleen Mary Roberts; 2 s, 1 da; *Career* slr, crown court recorder 1975; *Style*— Roy Barlow, Esq; The Cottage, Oxton Rakes, Barlow, Sheffield (☎ 0742 890652)

BARLOW, Sir Thomas Erasmus; 3 Bt (UK 1902), DSC (1945), DL (Bucks 1976); s of Sir Alan Barlow, 2 Bt, GCB, KBE (d 1968); *b* 23 Jan 1914; *Educ* Winchester; *m* 1955, Isabel, da of late Thomas Munn Body, MRCS, LRCP, of Middlesbrough; 2 s, 2 da; *Heir* s, James Barlow; *Career* RN 1932, Capt, ret 1964; *Recreations* birdwatching, wildlife conservation; *Clubs* Athenaeum, Savile; *Style*— Sir Thomas Barlow, Bt, DSC, DL; 45 Shepherds Hill, Highgate, London N6 5QJ (☎ 01 340 9653)

BARLOW, Sir (George) William; s of Albert Edward and Annice Barlow; *b* 8 June 1924; *Educ* Manchester GS, Manchester Univ (BSc); *m* 1948, Elaine Mary Atherton, da of William Adamson; 1 s, 1 da; *Career* chm Ransome Hoffman Pollard 1971-77, PO 1977-80 (organised sep of PO and Br Telecom), Design Cncl 1980-86; dir Thorn EMI plc 1980, Racal Telecom plc 1988; chm BICC plc 1985-, Ericsson Ltd 1988-, Bain & Co Inc UK 1988-, Engrg Cncl 1988-; pres BEAMA 1986-87; Hon DSc: Cranfield 1979, Bath 1986, Aston 1988; Hon Dtech Liverpool Poly 1988; FEng, FIMechE, FIEE, CBM; Int 1977; *Style*— Sir William Barlow; 2 Neville Drive, London N2 0QR; BICC Devonshire House, Mayfair Place, London W1X 5FH

BARLOW, (John) William Marshall; s and h of Sir John Kemp Barlow, 3 Bt; *b* 12 Mar 1964; *Style*— William Barlow, Esq; Bulkeley Grange, Malpas, Cheshire

BARLTROP, Prof Donald; s of Albert Edward Barltrop (d 1976), and Mabel, *née* Redding (d 1984); *b* 26 June 1933; *Educ* Southall GS, Univ of London (BSc, MB BS, MD); *m* 1 Aug 1959, Mair Angharad, da of Rev Richard Evan Edwards (d 1971), of Swansea; 2 s (Andrew b 1965, Richard b 1968), 1 da (Elen b 1970); *Career* Capt RAMC 1959-61; Fulbright Scholar Harvard Univ 1963-64, Wellcome sr res fell in clinical sci 1968-74, prof of child health Westminster London Univ 1982- (reader in paediatrics St Mary's 1975-82), adjunct prof of community health Tufts Univ Boston Mass 1984-; examiner: RCP, Univs of London, Capetown, Hong Kong, Al-Fateh Tripoli; memb: lead and health ctee DHSS Working Pty (composition of infant foods ctee), steering ctee on food policy and surveillance MAFF; chm Westminster Children Res Tst; medical advsr: Bliss, Buttle Tst; Freeman City of London 1977, Liveryman Worshipful Co of Barbers 1978; FRCP; *Books* Mineral Metabolism in Paediatrics (jtly 1969), Children in Health and Disease (jtly 1977); *Recreations* offshore sailing; *Clubs* Naval, RNVR YC; *Style*— Prof Donald Barltrop; 7 Grove Rd, Northwood, Middx (☎ 09274 26461); Westminster Childrens Hosp, Vincent Sq, London (☎ 01 828 9811, fax 834 4200, telex 919263 RIVHAG)

BARLTROP, Roger Arnold Rowlandson; CMG (1987), CVO (1982); s of Ernest William Barltrop, CMG, CBE, DSO (d 1957), and Ethel Alice Lucy, *née* Baker (d 1966); *b* 19 Jan 1930; *Educ* Solihull Sch, Leeds GS, Exeter Coll Oxford (MA); *m* 1962, Penelope Pierrepont, da of Denys Neale Dalton (d 1986); 2 s (Paul, Richard), 2 da (Fiona, Mary); *Career* RN 1949-50, RNVR, RNR 1950-64 (Lt-Cdr); HM Diplomatic Serv, served in India, Nigeria, Rhodesia, Turkey, Eastern Caribbean and Ethiopia; ambassador (formerly high cmmnr) to Fiji and currently high cmmnr to Nauru and Tuvalu 1982-; *Recreations* sailing (sloop Dove), opera, genealogy; *Clubs* Royal Cwlth Soc, Royal Suva Yacht, Fiji; *Style*— R A R Barltrop Esq, CMG, CVO; c/o FCO, King Charles St, London SW1A 2AH

BARNARD, Baroness; Lady Davina Mary; *née* Cecil; da of 6 Marquess of Exeter, KCMG (d 1981), and 1 w, Lady Mary Montagu Douglas Scott, da of 7 Duke of Buccleuch; *b* 1931; *m* 1952, 11 Baron Barnard, *qv*; *Career* DStJ; *Style*— The Rt Hon the Lady Barnard; Selaby Hall, Gainford, Darlington, Co Durham DL2 3HF (☎ 0325 730 206)

BARNARD, Capt Sir George Edward; 2 s of Michael and Alice Louise Barnard; *b* 11 August 1907; *m* 1940, Barbara Emma (d 1976), da of Percy Vann Hughes; 1 s; *Career* elder brother of Trinity House 1958, dep master 1961-72; tres Int Assoc of Lighthouse Authorities 1961-72, tstee Nat Maritime Museum 1967-74, pres Nautical Inst 1972-75; FRSA; kt 1968; *Style*— Capt Sir George Barnard; Warden, Station Rd, Much Hadham, Herts (☎ 3133)

BARNARD, 11 Baron (E 1698); Harry John Neville Vane; TD (1960), JP (Durham 1961), DL (Durham 1956); patron of ten livings; s of 10 Baron Barnard, CMG, OBE, MC, TD, JP (d 1964), and Dowager Baroness Barnard, *qv*; *b* 21 Sept 1923; *Educ* Eton, Durham Univ Business Sch (MSc); *m* 8 Oct 1952, Lady Davina Mary Cecil, DStJ, *qv*, da of 6 Marquess of Exeter (d 1981); 1 s, 4 da; *Heir* s, Hon Henry Vane; *Career* flying offr RAFVR 1942-42, Northumberland Hussars 1948-66, Lt Col Cmdg 1964-66, Hon Col 7 Bn LI 1979, pres North of England TAVRA 1974-77; landowner, farmer; ccllr Durham 1952-61, Durham Co Agricultural Exec Ctee 1953-72 (chm 1970-72), pres Durham Co Branch CLA 1965-88, vice-lt Durham 1969-70, pres Durham Co St John Convent 1971-88, pres Durham Co Seat Assoc 1972-88, Pres Durham and Cleveland Co Bn Royal Br Legion 1973, pres Durham Wildlife Tst 1984, vice chm Br Red Cross Soc 1987-; Lord Lt and Custos Rotolorum Co Durham 1970-88; *Clubs* Brooks's, Durham County, Northern Counties (Newcastle); *Style*— The Rt Hon the Lord Barnard, TD, JP; Selaby Hall, Gainford, Darlington, Co Durham DL2 3HF (☎ 0325 730206); Raby Castle, Staindrop, PO Box 50, Darlington, Co Durham DL2 3DY (☎ 0833 60751)

BARNARD, Jennifer Sarah; da of Prof Thomas Theodore Barnard (d 1983), of Furzebrook Cottage, Wareham, Dorset BH20 5AT, and Gillian Sarah, *née* Byng (d 1961); *b* 10 Jan 1929; *Educ* Long Stowe Hall, Cambridgeshire; *Career* dir Barbrook (Blue Pool) Ltd since 1961; *Recreations* historical res; *Style*— Miss Jennifer Barnard; Furzebrook Cottage, Wareham, Dorset BH20 5AT (☎ 09295 51403); Barbook (Blue Pool) Ltd, Furzebrook, Wareham, Dorset (☎ 09295 51408)

BARNARD, Sir Joseph Brian; JP (1973), DL (N Yorks 1988); s of Joseph Ernest Barnard (d 1942), and Elizabeth Loudon Barnard (d 1980); *b* 22 Jan 1928; *Educ* Sedbergh; *m* 21 Jan 1959, Suzanne Hamilton, da of Clifford Bray, of Ilkley, W Yorks; 3 s (Nicholas b 1960, Simon b 1966, Marcus (twin) b 1966;; *Career* cmmnd KRRC 1946-48; dir: Joseph Constantine Steamship Line Ltd 1952-66, Teesside Warehousing Co Ltd 1966-, NE Electricity Bd 1987-; chm: NE Electricity Consultative Cncl 1987, Alletonshire Petty Sessional Div 1981-, govrs Ingleby Arncliffe C of E Primary Sch 1981-, Nat Union of Cons and Unionist Assocs Yorks Area 1983-88 (vice chm 1988-), pres Yorks area Cons Trade Unionists; Yorks Magistrates Ct Ctee 1981-; patron and church warden St Oswalds E Harsley, chm E Harsley Parish Cncl 1973-; kt 1986; *Recreations* walking, shooting, gardening; *Clubs* Carlton; *Style*— Sir Joseph Barnard, JP, DL; Harlsey Hall, Northallerton, N Yorks DL6 2BL (☎ 0609 82 203)

BARNARD, Hon Lance Herbert; AO; s of Hon H Barnard; *b* 1 May 1919; *Educ* Launceston Tech Coll; *m* 1; 1 da; *m* 2, 1962, Jill, da of Senator H Cant; 1 s, 2 da (and 1 da decd); *Career* state pres Tasmanian Branch Australian Lab Party, Min for Defence 1972-75, Dep PM 1972-74; Australian ambass to Sweden, Norway and Finland 1975-78; *Style*— Hon Lance Barnard AO; 6 Bertland Court, Launceston, Tasmania 7250, Australia

BARNARD, Surgn Rear Adm (Ernest Edward) Peter; s of Lionel Edward Barnard (d 1965), of Milford on Sea, and Ernestine, *née* Lethbridge (d 1986); *b* 22 Feb 1927; *Educ* schs in UK and S Aust, St Johns Coll Oxford (DPhil); *m* 1955, Joan Marion, da of Arthur William Gunn (d 1984), of Grays, Essex; 1 s (Christopher), 1 da (Penelope); *Career* exec dir Med Cncl on Alcoholism; formerly Surgn Rear Adm (Operational Med Support) 1982-84, dep med dir gen (Naval) 1980-82; publications on underwater medicine and physiology 1962-85; FFCM; *Recreations* gardening, photography; *Clubs* Royal Soc of Med; *Style*— Surgn Rear Adm Peter Barnard; Chesilcote, Chapel Rd, Swanmore, Southampton SO3 2QA (☎ 04893 2373); 1 St Andrews Place, London NW1 4LB (☎ 01 487 4445)

BARNARD, Stephen Geoffrey; s of Geoffrey Thomas Barnard, of Beech Cottage, Sudbourne, Suffolk, and Diana Pixle, *née* Rivron; *b* 4 May 1950; *Educ* Gresham's Sch, Southampton Univ (LLB); *m* 4 Oct 1980, Jane Elizabeth Lisa, da of Dr Oliver Vivian Maxim, of the Windhovers, Gretton, Northants; *Career* slr 1974; Herbert Smith: joined 1976, NY 1980-82, ptnr 1983; *Recreations* golf, bridge, skiing, reading; *Style*— Stephen Barnard, Esq; Herbert Smith, Watling House, 35 Cannon Street, London EC4M 55D (☎ 01 489 8000, fax 01 236 5733, telex 886633)

BARNARD, Dowager Baroness; Sylvia Mary; o da of Herbert Straker (d 1929), of Hartforth Grange, Richmond, Yorks, and Gwendolin Georgiana, née Cradock (d 1932); *b* 26 August 1898; *m* 14 Oct 1920, 10 Baron Barnard, CMG, OBE, MC (d 1964); 2 s, 1 da; *Career* late Chief Cmdt ATS; *Style*— The Rt Hon the Dowager Lady Barnard; The White House, Gainford, Darlington DL2 3DN (☎ 0325 730 389)

BARNE, Lady Elizabeth Beatrice; *née* Montgomerie; da of 17 Earl of Eglinton and Winton (d 1966), and Ursula Joan, da of Hon Ronald Bannatyne Watson (d 1987); *b* 29 August 1945; *m* 1976, Maj Christopher Miles Barne; 1 s; *Style*— Lady Elizabeth Barne; Culeaze Farm, Wareham, Dorset

BARNE, Hon Mrs; Hon (Janet Elizabeth); *née* Maclean; da of Baron Maclean, KT, GCVO, KBE, PC (Life Peer and 11 Bt); *b* 27 Dec 1944; *m* 1974, Maj Nicholas M L Barne, Scots Guards; 2 s; *Style*— The Hon Mrs Barne; Blofield House, Blofield, Norwich

BARNEBY, Lt-Col Henry Habington; TD (1946), DL (Herefordshire 1958); er s of Richard Hicks Barneby, JP, DL (d 1923), of Longworth Hall, Hereford, and Margaret Elizabeth, *née* Howard; *b* 19 June 1909; *Educ* Radley, Sandhurst; *m* 1, 1935 (m dis 1942), Evelyn Georgina, da of late Lt-Col George Basil Heywood, TD, of Caradoc Court, Ross; 1 s ; m 2, 1944, Angela Margaret (d 1979), da of late Capt W Campbell, of Harewood Park, Ross-on-Wye; 4 s (1 decd), 1 da; *Career* 2 Lieut KSLI 1929 (Resigned 1935), cmmnd 1 Hereford Reg TA 1936, regranted regular cmmn KSLI 1947; cmd: Hereford Regt (TA) 1946, Hereford LI (TA) 1947-51, Jamaica Bn 1951-54, ret 1955; memb Hereford County PSD 1957-79 (chm 1976-79); memb: Hereford RDC 1955-67 (chm 1964-72), Dore and Bredwardine RDC 1966-73, S Hereford RDC 1973-76; JP Herefs 1960-79, High Sheriff Herefs 1972, Vice Lieut 1973-74, Vice Lord Lieut 1974-76; *Style*— Lt-Col Henry Barneby, TD, DL; Llanerch-y-Coed, Dorstone, Herefordshire (☎ 04973 215)

BARNEBY, John Henry; s of Lt Col Henry Habington Barneby, TD, DL, of Llanerc-Y-Coed, Dorstone, Herefordshire, and Angela Margaret, *née* Campbell (d 1979); *b* 29 July 1949; *Educ* Radley Coll, Christ Church Oxford (MA); *m* 2 Dec 1978, Alison (Sophie), da of Alan David Donger, of Winchester; 1 s (Thomas Henry b 1985), 2 da (Emily Henrietta b 1981, Laura Katherine b 1982); *Career* dir C Czarnikow Ltd 1984-; *Style*— John Barneby Esq; Cleveland Farm House, Longcot, Faringdon, Oxfordshire (☎ 0793 783 220), 66 Mark Lane, London EC3 (☎ 01 480 9333, fax 01 480 9500)

BARNEBY, Colonel Michael Paul; s of Capt Richard Paul Barneby (d 1944), of Longworth, Hereford, and Vera Margery Freedman, *née* Bromilow; *b* 29 Mar 1939; *Educ* Radley Coll; *m* 13 April 1973, Bridget Mary, da of Col Arthur Gordon Roberts, DSO, of Crickhowell, Powys, S Wales; 3 da (Camilla b 1974, Vanessa b 1976, Georgina b 1980); *Career* cmmnd 1958 into 15/19 The King's Royal Hussars and served principally in Germany, N Ireland, Hong Kong where cmd Royal Hong Kong Regt (Volunteers) 1981-83, ret Army 1988; dir planning and admin Clark Whitehill, London; *Recreations* hunting, shooting; *Clubs* Cavalry and Guards; *Style*— Col Michael P Barneby; The Old Vicarage, Preston Candover, Hants RG25 2EJ (☎ 025 687 248)

BARNES; *see*: Gorell Barnes

BARNES, (Charles) Antony; s of Charles Herbert Barnes (d 1965), of Hampstead, London, and Nellie Gertrude, *née* Croxton (d 1963); *b* 5 July 1925; *Educ* Westminster; *m* 8 Sept 1951, Margaret Helen, da of Frank Cuthbert Jones, of Montgomeryshire; 1 s (David b 1954); *Career* memb cncl of Inst of CA's in England and Wales; dir City Merchants Bank Ltd, dir ACA Ltd, CA Tstees Ltd, FCA Ltd, Manor Fields Est Ltd, Soc of Inc Acct Ltd; ex dir Samuel Montagu & Co Ltd and subsidiaries 1986, and various other companies; *Recreations* theatre, classical music, opera; *Clubs* Hurlingham; *Style*— Antony Barnes, Esq; 3 Selwyn House, Manor Fields, Putney Hill, London SW15 3LR

BARNES, Clive Leslie; s of Harry Leslie Barnes (d 1981), of Warwick, and Mabel Caroline, *née* Reed (d 1963); *b* 14 Sept 1940; *Educ* Cheltenham; *m* 27 Nov 1965 (m dis 1987), Miriam Rosalind, da of Francis Vincent Everard, of Bucks; 2 s (Luke b 1968, Thomas b 1969); *Career* CA; Midland Counties & Olympic Trialist Hockey;

Recreations real Tennis, lawn tennis, skiing; *Clubs* Farmers; *Style—* Clive L Barnes, Esq; Ettington Hall, Ettington, Stratford-on-Avon (☎ 0789 740515); 22 Queens Rd, Coventry (☎ 0203 56331)

BARNES, Daniel Sennett; CBE (1977); s of John Daniel and Paula Sennett Barnes; *b* 13 Sept 1924; *Educ* Dulwich, London Univ (BSc); *m* 1955, Jean A Steadman; 1 s; *Career* md Sperry Gyroscope 1971-82; Electronic Systems and Equipment Div, Br Aerospace (formerly Sperry Gyroscope) 1982-86 dir: Sperry Ltd 1971-82, Sperry AG Switzerland 1979-83; pres Electronic Engrg Assoc 1981-82; bd memb Bracknell Devpt Cncl 1976-82; chm: Berks and Oxon Area Manpower Bd, Manpower Servs Cmmn 1983-88; CEng, FIEE; *Style—* Daniel Barnes, Esq, CBE; Zenda, 9 Eastwick Rd, Burwood Pk, Walton-on-Thames, Surrey (☎ 0932 28042);

BARNES, (James) David Francis; CBE (1987); s of Eric Cecil Barnes, CMG (d 1987), and Jean Margaret Procter, *née* Dickens; *b* 21 Feb 1914; *Educ* Shrewsbury Sch, Univ of Liverpool; *m* 1 May 1963, (Wendy) Fiona Mary, da of John Leighton Riddell, of Limetree Ho, Gawsworth, Macclesfield, Cheshire; 1 s (Jonathan Mark b 8 July 1967), 1 da (Alison Jane b 9 Nov 1964); *Career* Nat Serv 1958-60, cmmnd N Battery (The Eagle Troop) 2 Regt RA; ICI Pharmaceuticals Div: euro mangr 1968, overseas dir 1971, dep chm 1977; chm ICI Paints Div 1983, exec dir ICI plc 1986, non exec dir Thorn EMI plc 1987; Thames Valley Hospice: vice pres 1987, chm of Capital Appeal 1984-88; chm pharmaceuticals econ devpt ctee NEDO, chm industl materials advsy ctee DTI 1988; FInstD 1983, CBIM 1987, FRSA 1988; *Recreations* fishing, shooting, gardening; *Style—* David Barnes, Esq, CBE; ICI plc, 9 Millbank, London SW1P 2JF (☎ 01 834 4444, fax 01 834 2042, car tel 0836 599 960, 0836 233 329, telex 21324 ICIHQG)

BARNES, Sir Denis Charles; KCB (1967, CB 1964); s of Frederick Charles Barnes (d 1944); *b* 15 Dec 1914; *Educ* Hulme GS Manchester, Merton Coll Oxford; *m* 1938, Patricia, da of Col Charles Murray Abercrombie, CMG, CBE (d 1933), of Prestbury, Cheshire; *Career* entered Home Civil Service 1938, dep sec Miny of Labour 1964-66, perm sec 1966-73, chm Manpower Services Cmmn 1973-75; dir Glynwed Ltd, Gen Accident Fire & Life Assur Corpn 1976-, pres Manpower Soc 1976-, perm sec Dept of Emp 1968-73, FIPM; *Clubs* Savile; *Style—* Sir Denis Barnes, KCB; The Old Inn, 30 The Street, Wittersham, Kent (☎ 528)

BARNES, Donald Tom; *b* 2 June 1926; *m* ; 2 da (Elizabeth, Helen); *Career* chm Fine Art Developments plc 1983-; *Recreations* cricket, golf; *Style—* Donald Barnes, Esq; Fine Art Developments plc, Fine Art House, Queen St, Burton on Trent, Staffs

BARNES, Edward Campbell; s of Hubert Turnbull Barnes and (Annie) Mabel, *née* Latham; *b* 8 Oct 1928; *Educ* Wigan Coll; *m* 1950, Dorothy Smith; 1 s, 2 da; *Career* head Children's Programmes BBC TV 1978-86; prodr/dir: Treasure Houses 1986, Childhood 1987-; silver medal Royal TV Soc 1986, Pye Award for services on childrens' TV 1986; *Books* 23 Blue Peter Books and Blue Peter Special Assignment Book; *Recreations* cricket; *Clubs* Bafra; *Style—* Edward Barnes, Esq

BARNES, Francis Walter Ibbetson; s of Rev Walter W Barnes (d 1959), and Alice Mary, *née* Ibbetson; bro of Dame Josephine Barnes, *qv*; *b* 10 May 1914; *Educ* Mill Hill, Balliol Coll Oxford; *m* 1, 1943 (m dis 1953), Heather Kathleen, da of late Frank Tamplin, of Warlingham, Surrey; 2 s; m 2, 1955, Sonia Nina (Nina Walker, the pianist), o da of late Harold Higginbottom, of Hyde, Cheshire; 2 s, 1 da; *Career* barr 1938, Bar Cncl representative at various meetings of the Advsy Ctee of Lawyers of the EEC 1962-71, recorder (Smethwick and Warley) 1964-71, dep chm Quarter Sessions (Oxon) 1965-71, crown court recorder 1972-76, chm Industl Tribunals 1976-87; *Recreations* music, gardening, motoring; *Style—* Francis Barnes, Esq; c/o Office of industrial Tribunals, Renslade House, Bonhay Rd, Exeter EX4 3BX

BARNES, Frederick Brian; s of Frederick George James Barnes (d 1984), of Berks, and Agnes Ethel, *née* Colgate; *b* 1 Sept 1937; *Educ* Slough GS, LSE (BSc); *m* 1962, Susan Felicity, da of James Michael Pattemore (d 1986); 1 s (Christopher James b 1968), 2 da (Katherine Helen b 1965, Victoria Jane b 1970); *Career* flying offr RAF 1958-61; First Nat Finance Corpn 1970-76, assoc dir Assocs Capital Corpn (chm and md 1976-), Assocs Int Mgmnt Co, pres 1984; *Recreations* golf, ballet, horse racing; *Clubs* Stoke Poges GC; *Style—* Brian Barnes, Esq; Associates House, PO Box 200, Windsor, Berks (☎ 0753 857100)

BARNES, Gerald William; s of George William Barnes (d 1977), and Violet *née* Stevens, (d 1975); *b* 4 Sept 1928; *Educ* Southend HS, Brentwood Sch; *m* 4 Dec 1954, Jean Dorothy, da of James Robert Hills, of Holland-on-Sea; 1 s (Robin Richard b 1963); *Career* nat ser 13/18 Royal Hussars; CA 1956, budget offr, Int Computers Ltd 1957-1959, fin dir Pembroke Carton and Printing Co Ltd 1959-64, fin dir W S Cowell Ltd and Cowells plc 1964-87; corporate consultant 1988-; formerly chm Parish Council, Rotarian; involvement in number of local charities and clubs; various offices held in Br printing indust fedn (pres East Anglian Alliance memb of fin ctee, educ ctee, Eastern regn bd, chm book production section, etc), memb various DTI ctees; FCA 1956; *Recreations* cricket, theatre, travel; *Clubs* Ipswich and Suffolk; *Style—* Gerald W Barnes Esq; Sweynes, 1 Church Crescent, Sproughton, Ipswich, Suffolk IP8 3BJ

BARNES, Harold (Harry); s of Joseph Barnes, of Easington Colliery, Co Durham, and Betsy, *née* Gray; *b* 22 July 1936; *Educ* Ruskin Coll Oxford, Hull Univ; *m* 14 Sept 1963, Elizabeth Ann, da of Richard Stephenson (d 1983); 1 s (Stephen b 1968), 1 da (Joanne b 1972); *Career* RAF 1954-56; lectr Sheffield Univ 1966-87, (dir mature matriculation courses 1984-87); variety of positions NE Derbys Constituency Lab Pty 1970-87; memb cncl of Nat Admin Cncl of Independent Lab Pubns 1977-80 and 1982-85, memb ctee stage Local Govt Fin Act 1988 ; *Style—* H Barnes, Esq; 16 Gosforth Lane, Dronfield, Sheffield S18 6PR (☎ 0246 412 588); House of Commons, London SW1A 0AA (☎ 01 219 4521)

BARNES, Capt James David Kentish; s of Arthur James Kentish Barnes (d 1976), of Caldecot, Caldy, Wirral, Cheshire, and Hester Beatrice, *née* Cromwell-Jones; *b* 18 April 1930; *Educ* Eton, Sandhurst; *m* 1, 1955, Julie Ann; 1 s (Timothy James Kentish b 1961), 1 da (Nicola Jane Kentish b 1963); m 2, 1975, Susan Mary, da of Maj Gen James Francis Harter DSO, MC, DL (d 1965), of Whalebone House, Langham, Colchester; *Career* Capt 5 Royal Inniskilling Dragoon Gds 1950-57, served Korea, M East, Germany; joined John Waterer Sons & Crisp (md 1967-84), presently md and chm Dobbies of Edinburgh, dir Scotstock Nurseries Ltd; fell RHS; *Recreations* cricket, golf, gardening, shooting, fishing; *Clubs* MCC, The Honourable Co of Edinburgh Golfers, Cavalry and Guards; *Style—* Capt James Barnes; Biggar Park, Biggar, Lanarks (☎ 0899 29185); Dobbie & Co Ltd, Melville Nurseries, Lasswade, nr Dalkeith, Midlothian

BARNES, James Frederick; CB (1982); s of Wilfred Barnes (d 1984), and Doris Martha, *née* Deighton (d 1985); *b* 8 Mar 1932; *Educ* Taunton's Sch Southampton, The Queen's Coll Oxford (BA, MA); *m* 1957, Dorothy Jean, da of William Jeffrey Drew (d 1980); 1 s (Richard), 2 da (Amanda, Elizabeth); *Career* chartered engr, dep chief scientific advsr MOD 1987-89, church warden All Saint's Farringdon 1984-89; lay memb Winchester Diocesan Synod 1985-89, stewardship advsr Diocese of Monmouth 1989-; chm of govrs Yateley Manor 1981-88; *Recreations* garden, local history; *Clubs* Athenaeum; *Style—* James Barnes, Esq, CB; Monmouth Diocesan Offices, 64 Caerau Rd, Newport, Gwent NP9 4HV

BARNES, Sir James George; MBE (1946), JP; s of Richard R Barnes; *b* 1908, of Dunedin, NZ; *Educ* King Edward Tech HS; *m* 1938, Elsie, da of James D Clark; 1 da; *Career* Mayor of Dunedin NZ 1968-77, sharebroker; kt 1967; *Style—* Sir James Barnes, MBE, JP; 11 Cavell St, Dunedin, New Zealand

BARNES, Lady; Joan Alice Katherine; *née* Schwabe; da of Prof Randolph Schwabe, Slade Prof at London Univ and memb Royal Soc Painters in Watercolours; *m* 1941, Sir Harry Jefferson Barnes, CBE (d 1982), sometime dir Glasgow Sch of Art; 2 da (and 1 s decd); *Style—* Lady Barnes; 11 Whittingehame Drive, Glasgow (☎ 041 339 1019)

BARNES, John Alfred; s of John Joseph Barnes (d 1951), of Sunderland, and Margaret Carr (d 1984), *née* Glenwright; *b* 29 April 1930; *Educ* Bede Boys GS Sunderland, Univ of Durham (BSc, MA, MEd); *m* 7 Aug 1954, Ivy May, da of Robert Rowntree Walker (d 1981), of Sunderland; 2 da (Shirley May b 1957, Jennifer Ann b 1960); *Career* Nat Serv RAF 1948-49; dept head Grangefield GS Stockton-on-Tees 1953-57, asst educn offr Barnsley Co Borough 1957-61, dir of educn (previously dep dir 1961-63) 1963-68, chief educn offr (previously dir of educn 1968-73) 1973-84; dir-gen City & Guilds of London Inst 1984-; chm: Assoc Colls of Further Educn 1980-81, Northern Examining Assoc 1979-82, Assoc Lancs Sch Examining Bd 1972-84; hon sec Assoc Educn Offrs 1977-84; tres NFER 1979-84, pres Educn Devpt Assocn 1980-85; FRSA, FITD; *Recreations* cultural activities, foreign travel; *Clubs* Athenaeum; Two Oaks, 37 Woodfield Park, Amersham, Bucks HP6 5QH (☎ 0494 726120); City and Guilds of London Inst, 76 Portland Place, London W1N 4AA (☎ 01 580 3050, fax 01 436 7630, telex 266586)

BARNES, Sir (Ernest) John Ward; KCMG (1974), MBE (Mil 1946); s of Rt Rev Ernest William Barnes, Bp of Birmingham (d 1953), and Adelaide, da of Sir Adolphus Ward, Master of Peterhouse Cambridge; *b* 22 June 1917; *Educ* Winchester, Trinity Coll Cambridge (MA); *m* 1948, Cynthia Margaret Ray, JP (E Sussex), OStJ (1981), da of Sir Herbert Stewart, CIE, *qv*; 2 s, 3 da; *Career* Lt-Col RA WW II (US Bronze Star 1946); HM Diplomatic Service 1946-77: ambass to Israel 1969-72, to The Netherlands 1972-77; dir: Alliance Investment Co 1977-87, Whiteaway Laidlaw & Co 1979-88; chm Sussex Rural Community Cncl 1982-87; memb of cncl Sussex Univ 1981-85 (vice chm 1982-84); chm of govrs Hurstpierpoint Coll 1983-87; *Books* Ahead of his Age (1979); *Clubs* Athenaeum, Beefsteak, Brooks's, MCC; *Style—* Sir John Barnes, KCMG, MBE; Hampton Lodge, Hurstpierpoint, E Sussex BN6 9QN (☎ 0273 833247); 20 Thurloe Place Mews, London SW7 2HL (☎ 01 584 9652)

BARNES, Jonathan; s of Albert Leonard Barnes, and Kathleen Mabel, *née* Scoltock; *b* 26 Dec 1942; *Educ* City of London Sch, Balliol Coll Oxford; *m* Jennifer Mary, da of Ormond Postgate; 2 da (Catherine, Camilla); *Career* fell Oriel Coll Oxford 1968-78, (Balliol Coll 1978-), lectr in Philosophy Oxford Univ 1968-; visiting appointments at: Univ of Chicago, Inst for Advanced Study Princeton, Univ of Massachusetts Amherst, Univ of Texas Austin, Wissenschaftskolleg Zu Berlin, Univ of Edmonton, Univ of Zurich, Istituto Italiano per gli Studi Filosfici Naples; memb: FBA (1987); *Books* The Ontological Argument (1972), Aristotle's Posterior Analytics (1975), The Presocratic Philosophers (1979), Aristotle (1982), Early Greek Philosophy (1987); *Recreations* rowing, tennis, tapestry, crosswords; *Style—* Jonathan Barnes, Esq; Balliol College, Oxford OX1 3BJ (☎ 0865 277754, fax 0865 270708 ATTN BALLIOL)

BARNES, Dame (Alice) Josephine Mary Taylor; DBE (1974); Dame Josephine Warren; da of late Rev Walter W Barnes, MA (Oxon) (d 1959), and Alice Mary Ibbetson, FRCO, ARCM; sis of Francis Walter Ibbetson Barnes, *qv*; *b* 18 August 1912; *Educ* Oxford HS, LMH Oxford, Univ Coll Hosp Med Sch; *m* 1942 (m dis 1964), Sir Brian Warren, *qv*; 1 s, 2 da; *Career* consulting obstetrician and gynaecologist Charing Cross Hosp and Elizabeth Garrett Anderson Hosp; pres: Women's Nat Cancer Control Campaign 1974-, BMA 1979-80; memb Cncl Advertising Standards Authority 1980-; FRCP, FRCS, FRCOG; *Books* Lecture Notes on Gynaecology (5th ed 1983), Scientific Formulators of Obstetrics and Gynaecology (editor, 3rd ed 1986); *Recreations* music, gastronomy, motoring, foreign travel; *Style—* Dame Josephine Barnes, DBE; 8 Aubrey Walk, London W8 (☎ 01 727 9832)

BARNES, Keith Miles; s of Ernest Victor Barnes, of Hadley Wood, Herts, and Jessie Mabel, *née* Hildrwo (d 1968); *b* 31 Jul 1945; *Educ* Berkhamsted Sch; *m* 20 May 1967, Brenda Joyce, da of Arthur Banks, of Burnham Market, Norfolk; 2 s (Dominic b 1969, Robin b 1971); *Career* Branta Gp Ltd (Hldg Co): joined 1965, dir 1968, md 1972; FIOD, FZSL; *Recreations* opera, music generally, rugby, swimming, golf; *Clubs* RAC, Hadley Wood GC; *Style—* Keith Barnes, Esq; Branta House, Homecroft Rd, Wood Green, London N22 5EN (☎ 01 881 2000, fax 01 889 2255)

BARNES, Sir Kenneth; KCB (1977), CB (1970); s of Arthur and Doris Barnes, of Accrington, Lancs; *b* 26 August 1922; *Educ* Accrington GS, Balliol Coll Oxford; *m* 1948, Barbara Ainsworth; 1 s, 2 da; *Career* permanent sec Dept of Employment 1976-82; *Style—* Sir Kenneth Barnes, KCB; South Sandhills, Sandy Lane, Betchworth, Surrey, RH3 7AA (☎ 073784 2445); Glebe Rise, Glebelands, Studland, Dorset

BARNES, (Nicholas) Martin Limer; s of Geoffrey Lambe Barnes, MA, FCA, of Craven Arms, Shropshire and Birmingham (d 1984) and Emily *née* Dicken (d 1976); *b* 18 Jan 1939; *Educ* King Edwards Sch Birmingham, Imperial Coll, Univ of London (BSc), Univ of Manchester Inst of Sci and Technol (PhD); *m* 23 Feb 1963, Diana Marion, da of Barrie Campbell (d 1968); 1 s (Matthew b 1966) 1 da (Kate b 1964); *Career* res fell Univ of Manchester 1968-71, ptnr Martin Barnes and Partners 1971-85; ptnr Deloitte Haskins and Sells mgmnt cnslt (Martin Barnes Project Mgmnt); Churchill Fellowship 1971, FEng, FICE, FCIOB, FAPM, (chm 1986-), FInstCES (pres 1978-86), FRSA, MBCS, ACIArb, ACGI; *Books* Measurement in Contract Control (1977), The CESMM2 Handbook (1986); *Recreations* railway and canal history, victorian paintings; *Style—* Dr Martin Barnes; 322 Shakespeare Tower, Barbican, London EC2Y 8DR (☎ 01 628 3961) Hill Top Farm, Cheadle Hulme, Cheshire SK8 7HN; Deloitte Haskins and Sells, Hillgate House, 26 Old Bailey, London EC4M 7PL (☎ 01 248 3913, fax 01 236 2367, telex 8955899 DHSHH G)

BARNES, Michael Cecil John; s of Maj Cecil Horace Reginald Barnes, OBE (d 1969), and Katherine Louise, *née* Kennedy; *b* 22 Sept 1932; *Educ* Malvern Coll, CCC Oxford (MA); *m* 21 Apr 1962, Anne, da of Basil Mason (d 1974), of London W2; 1 s (Hugh b 1963), 1 da (Katy b 1966); *Career* nat serv, 2 Lt The Wilts Regt served Hong Kong 1952-53; MP (Lab) for Brentford and Chiswick 1966-74, chm Electricity Consumers Cncl 1977-83; dir UK Immigrants Advsy Serv 1984-; chm: Hounslow Arts Tst 1974-82, Notting Hill Social Cncl 1976-79, Housing Action Centre N Kensington 1980-87; memb: Nat Consumer Cnsl 1975-80, Advertising Standards Authy 1979-85; Burgess City of Bristol 1953; *Recreations* walking, swimming, dogs; *Style—* Michael Barnes, Esq; 45 Ladbroke Grove, London W11 3AR (☎ 01 727 2533); 84 Monkton Deverill, nr Warminster, Wilts BA12 7EX; UKIAS, 190 Gt Dover St, London SE1 4YB (☎ 01 357 7511)

BARNES, (David) Michael William; QC (1981); s of David Charles Barnes (d 1954), and Florence Maud, *née* Matthews (d 1967); *b* 16 July 1943; *Educ* Monmouth Sch, Wadham Coll Oxford (BA); *m* 10 Sept 1970, Susan Dorothy, da of William Turner; 3 s (Andrew b 1972, Edmund b 1974, Peter b 1979); *Career* barr Middle Temple 1965; hon res fell Lady Margaret Hall Oxford 1979; recorder of Crown Court 1984; ed 15, 16 and 17 edns of Hill & Redmans Law of Landlord and Tenant; *Style—* Michael Barnes, Esq, QC; 2 Paper Bldgs, Temple, London EC4

BARNES, Neil Richard; s of Maj Harold William Barnes (d 1981), of W Wickham, Kent, and Mary Mabel, *née* Butchart (d 1980); *b* 14 Jan 1947; *Educ* Sutton Valence Sch, Univ of Reading (BSc); *m* 18 Sept 1971, Susan Jane, da of Douglas Norman Smith, of Beckenham, Kent; 1 s (Stephen b 24 May 1979), 1 da (Nicola b 20 Nov 1975); *Career* md IDC Property Investmts 1979-; chm Round Table W Wickham 1986-87; Freeman City of London, Liveryman Worshipful Co Masons; FRICS 1983; *Recreations* golf, badminton; *Style—* Neil Barnes, Esq; IDC Property Investments Ltd, IDC House, 23 St James's Sq, London SW1Y 4JH (☎ 01 839 6241, fax 01 839 6248)

BARNES, Peter; s of Frederick Barnes (d 1955), and Martha (d 1981); *b* 10 Jan 1931; *Educ* Stroud GS; *m* 18 Oct 1961, Charlotte Beck; *Career* playwright and dir; plays: The Ruling Class (1968), Leonardo's Last Supper and Noonday Demons (1969), Lulu (1970), The Devil is an Ass (1973), The Bewitched (1974), The Frontiers of Farce (1976), Laughter! (1978), Antonio (1979), Red Noses (1985); Radio plays include: Barnes People I, II, III (1981-86), No End to Dreaming (1987); films include: Leonardo's last Supper (1971), The Ruling Class (1972); directed: Lulu (1970), Bartholomew Fair (1977), Frontiers of Farce (1976), Antonio (1979), The Devil Himself (1980), Somersaults (1981), Bartholomew Fair (1987); awards: Winner of the John Whiting Award (1969), Evening Standard Award (1969), Best Radio Play Award (1981), Olivier Award (1985); FRSL 1984; *Style—* Peter Barnes, Esq; 7 Archery Close, Connaught St, London W2; Margaret Ramsay Ltd, 14A Goodwins Ct, St Martins Lane, London WC1 (☎ 01 240 0691)

BARNES, Peter Robert; CB (1981); s of Robert Stanley Barnes and Marguerite, *née* Dunkels; *b* 1 Feb 1921; *Educ* Eton, Trinity Coll Cambridge; *m* 1955, Pauline Belinda Hannen; 2 s, 1 da; *Career* barr Inner Temple 1947, legal asst to DPP 1951, sr Legal asst 1958, asst slr 1970, asst dir 1974, principal asst dir 1977, dep dir Public Prosecutions 1977-82; pres Video Appeals Ctee 1985-; *Style—* Peter Barnes, Esq, CB; The Old Vicarage, Church Lane, Witley, Surrey (☎ 042879 4509)

BARNES, Dr Robert Sandford; s of William Edward Barnes (d 1981), and Ada Elsie, *née* Sutherst (d 1983); *b* 8 July 1924; *Educ* Manchester Univ (BSc, MSc, DSc); *m* 1952, Julia Frances Marriott Grant; 1 s, 3 da; *Career* dir: Robert S Barnes Conslt Ltd 1978-; princ Queen Elizabeth Coll London Univ 1978-85; dir: Res and Devpt chief scientist Br Steel Corp 1970-78, BISRA 1968-70; head of Metallurgy Div Harwell 1966-68; *Recreations* sailing (yacht 'Cassis of St Helier'); *Clubs* Athenaeum, Cruising Assoc; *Style—* Dr Robert S. Barnes; Pigeon Forge, Daneshill, The Hockering, Woking, Surrey (☎ 048 62 61529)

BARNES, Dr Robert Sandford; s of William Edward Barnes (d 1981), of Maghull, Lancs, and Ada Elsie, *née* Suthurst (d 1983); *b* 08 Jul 1924; *Educ* Ormskirk GS, Manchester Unvi (BSc, MSc, DSc); *m* 16 Aug 1952, Jullia Frances marriott, da of Roger Douglas Marriott Grant (d 1978), of IOW; 1 s (Richard b 1963), 3 da (Philippa b 1956, Alison b 1958, Penelope b 1959); *Career* radar res Admty Res Estab Witley 1944-47, head irradiation branch AERE Harwell 1962-65 (scientist 1948-62), visiting scientist N American Aviation California 1965, head metallurgy div Harwell 1966-68, dir BISRA 1969-70 (dep dir 1969), chief scientist Br Steel Corpn 1975-78 (dir & D 1979-75), chm Ruthner Continuous Crop Ltd 1976-78, chm Robert S Barnes Conslts Ltd 1978-, tech advsr to the bd BOC Ltd 1978-79 and BOC Int 1979-81, princ Queen Elizabeth Coll London 1978-85; Hadfield Meml Lecture 1972, Joan Player Lecture 1976; pres Inst of Metnurists 1982-85, cncl memb Backpain Assoc 1979-; Rosenhain Medal 1964; Freeman City of London 1984, Liveryman Worshipful Co of Engrs 1984; FInstP 1961, FIM 1965, FRSA 1976, CEng 1977; *Clubs* Athenaeum, Cruising Assoc; *Style—* Dr Robert Barnes; Pigeon Forge, Daneshill, The Hockering, Woking, Surrey GU22 7HQ (☎ 048 62 615 79)

BARNES, Hon Ronald Alexander Henry; yr s of 3 Baron Gorell, CBE, MC (d 1963); hp of 4 Baron; *b* 28 June 1931; *Educ* Harrow, New Coll Oxford; *m* 1957, Gillian Picton, yst da of late Picton Hughes-Jones, of Henstridge, Somerset; 1 s, 1 da; *Career* late Lt Royal Fusiliers, seconded King's African Rifles, Capt Royal Northumberland Fusiliers (TA); formerly Public Relations Offr P&O Orient Lines; sr ptnr Stockton & Barnes (estate agents); *Style—* The Hon Ronald Barnes; Fernbank, Mingoose, Mount Hawke, Truro, Cornwall (☎ 0209 890310)

BARNES, Timothy Paul; QC (1986); s of the late Arthur Morley Barnes, of The Homestead, Seal, Nr Sevenoaks, Kent (decd), and Valerie Enid Mary *née* Willis; *b* 23 April 1944; *Educ* Bradfield Coll, Christs Coll Cambridge (MA); *m* Aug 1969, Patricia Margaret, da of Leslie Ralph G (d 1974); 1 s (Christopher b 1973), 3 da (Olivia b 1975, Jessica b 1978, Natasha b 1986); *Career* barr Gray's Inn 1968, asst rec 1983, rec 1987, memb of Midland and Oxford Circuit; memb ctee Greenwich soc; *Recreations* hockey, gardening, music; *Clubs* MCC; *Style—* Timothy P Barnes, Esq, QC; The White House, Crooms Hill, London, SE10 8HH (☎ 01 858 1185); 2 Crown Office Row, Temple, London, EC4 (☎ 01 353 1365)

BARNETSON, Hon (William) Denholm; s of Baron Barnetson Life Peer, (d 1981), and Joan Fairley, *née* Davidson; *b* 30 May 1955; *Educ* Cranleigh Sch, Sorbonne Univ Paris; *Career* journalist; Utd Press Int Washington DC 1983- (in Paris 1980-81, NY 1981-83); *Style—* The Hon William Barnetson; c/o Broom, Chillies Lane, Crowborough, E Sussex TN6 3TB; UPI, Eye Street, Washington DC, USA

BARNETSON, Baroness; Joan Fairley; da of William Fairley Davidson (d 1958), and Augustina, *née* Bjarnadottir (d 1969); *b* 22 July 1918; *m* 1940, William Denholm, Baron Barnetson (Life Peer 1975, kt 1972, d 1981); 1 s (Denholm), 3 da (Astraea, Louise, Julia); *Recreations* sculpture, tapestry; *Style—* The Rt Hon the Lady Barnetson; Broom, Chillies Lane, Crowborough, East Sussex TN6 3TB (☎ 0892 655748)

BARNETSON, Hon Julia Claire Denholm; da of Baron Barnetson (Life Peer, d 1981), and Joan Fairley, *née* Davidson; *b* 23 Oct 1963; *Educ* Benenden, Queen's Secretarial Coll London, Pru Leith's Sch of Wine & Cookery; *Career* theatrical agent; *Style—* The Hon Julia Barnetson; c/o Broom, Chillies Lane, Crowborough, E Sussex

BARNETT, Maj Benjamin George; MBE (1946), TD; s of Col George Henry Barnett, CMG, DSO (d 1942), of Glympton Park, Oxon, and Mary Dorothea, *née* Lowbridge-Baker; *b* 5 Dec 1912; *Educ* Malvern; *m* 1943, Delia Barnett JP (1953, Oxon), da of Maj Sir Algernon Peyton, 7 Bt (d 1962); 2 s, 1 da; *Career* served with Oxfordshire Yeomanry, Maj, ret 1947; retired memb of Stock Exchange; high sheriff Oxfordshire 1969; *Recreations* shooting, fishing; *Style—* Maj Benjamin Barnett, MBE, TD; Woodbine Cottage, Swifts House, nr Bicester, Oxon (☎ (086 96 6819)

BARNETT, His Honour Judge Christopher John Anthony; QC (1983); s of Richard Adrian Barnett, of Battle, Sussex, and Phyllis, *née* Cartwright (d 1947); *b* 18 May 1936; *Educ* Repton, Coll of Law London; *m* 31 Oct 1959, (Sylvia) Marieliese (Marlies), da of George Lyn Ashby Pritt (d 1983); 2 s (Peter b 1962, Marcus b 1970), 1 da (Susannah b 1965); *Career* nat serv with Kenya Regt and Kenya Govt, Dist Offr (Kikuyu Gd 1954- 56; Kenya Govt Service 1956-60; Dist Offr HM Overseas Civil Service in Kenya 1960-62; barr Gray's Inn 1965, recorder of the Crown Court 1982, Circuit Judge 1988; chm SE Circuit Area Liaison Ctee 1985-88; memb: Court of Essex Univ 1983-, Wine Ctee of SE Circuit 1984-88; *Recreations* cricket, tennis, walking; *Clubs* Kenya Kongonis Cricket; *Style—* Christopher Barnett, Esq, QC; 4 Paper Buildings, Temple, London EC4Y 7EX (☎ 01 583 7765, fax 01 353 4674)

BARNETT, Correlli Douglas; s of D A Barnett; *b* 28 June 1927; *Educ* Trinity Sch Croydon, Exeter Coll Oxford; *m* 1950, Ruth Murby; 2 da; *Career* keeper of the Churchill Archives Centre and fell Churchill Coll Cambridge 1977-, writer and historian; FRHistS, FRSL; *Style—* Correlli Barnett, Esq; Catbridge House, E Carleton, Norwich (☎ 0508 410)

BARNETT, Air Chief Marshal Sir Denis Hensley Fulton; GCB (1964, KCB 1957, CB 1956), CBE (1945), DFC (1940); yst s of late Sir Louis Edward Barnett, CMG, MB, CM, FRCS (d 1946), and Mabel Violet, *née* Fulton; *b* 11 Feb 1906; *Educ* Christ's Coll NZ, Clare Coll Cambridge (MA); *m* 1939, Pamela, yst da of Sir Allan John Grant (d 1955); 1 s, 2 da; *Career* cmmnd RAF 1929, served WW II Bomber Cmd, AOC-in-C RAF Tport Cmd 1959-62, RAF Near East, Cdr Br Forces Cyprus and Admin Sovereign Base Area 1962-64, ret; memb Weapons R & D AEA 1965-72; *Style—* Air Chief Marshal Sir Denis Barnett, GCB, CBE, DFC; River House, Rushall, Pewsey, Wilts SN9 6EN

BARNETT, Eric Oliver; s of Eric Everard Barnett, of Johannesburg, S Africa, and Maud Emily Louise, *née* Oliver (d 1948); *b* 13 Feb 1929; *Educ* St Johns Coll Johannesburg, Witwatersrand Coll of Art, Univ of Cape Town, Univ of South Africa, Univ of Natal, UCL; *m* 1, 13 Feb 1950, Louise Francesca (d 1984), da of Nicholas Peter Lindenberg (d 1978), of Durban; m 2, 13 March 1986, Vivienne, da of Samuel Arthur Goodwin, of Northwood, London; *Career* lectr psychology Univ of Natal 1957; Arthur Barnett Fndn: res dir 1963-71, vice-chm 1969-71, chm 1971-; chm Rural Ecology & Resources Ctee Southern Africa 1978-88; *Recreations* music, painting, history of science, salmon fishing, shooting; *Style—* Eric Barnett, Esq; Baldarroch House, Murthly, Perthshire; St Huberts, St Huberts Lane, Gerrards Cross, Bucks (☎ 073 871 309)

BARNETT, Hon Erica Hazel; da of Baron Barnett; *b* 1951; *Style—* The Hon Erica Barnett; 7 Hillingdon Rd, Whitefield, Lancs M25 7QQ

BARNETT, Baron (Life Peer UK 1983), of Heywood and Royton, in Greater Manchester; Joel Barnett; PC (1975), JP (Lancs 1960); s of Louis Barnett, of Manchester (d 1964), and Ettie Barnett; *b* 14 Oct 1923; *Educ* Derby Street Jewish Sch, Manchester Centl HS; *m* 1949, Lillian Stella, da of Abraham Goldstone; 1 da; *Career* served WW II, RASC; sr ptnr J C Allen & Co Manchester 1954-74; fought Runcorn 1959 (gen election), MP (Lab) Lancs Heywood and Royton 1964-83; chm Lab Party Econ and Financial Gp 1967-70; memb: Public Accounts Ctee 1966-71, Public Expenditure Ctee 1971-74, Select Ctee on Tax Credits 1973; chief sec Treasury 1974-79 (oppn spokesman Treasury 1970-74, Cabinet memb 1977-79), chm Commons Select Ctee Public Accounts 1979-83; oppn spokesman (Lords) Treasury 1983-86; memb Hallé Soc of Manchester 1982-; hon visiting fell Strathclyde Univ 1980-, tstee V & A 1983-, vice-pres Assoc of Metropolitan Authorities 1983-; vice-chm BBC 1986-; chm Hansard Soc for Parly Govt 1984-; Hon LLD (Strathclyde) 1983; gov Birkbeck Coll Univ of London; pres RIPA 1988-; dir various public and private cos; FCCA; *Books* Inside the Treasury (1982); *Style—* The Rt Hon the Lord Barnett, PC, JP; Flat 92, 24 John Islip St, London SW1; 7 Hillingdon Rd, Whitefield, Manchester M25 7QQ

BARNETT, Joseph Anthony; CBE (1983); s of Joseph Edward Barnett (d 1962), and Helen Yanocatis (d 1976); *b* 19 Dec 1931; *Educ* St Albans Sch, Pembroke Coll Cambridge (MA); *m* 1960, Carolina Johnson, da of Baldwin Rice (d 1974), of USA; 1 s (Lindsay b 1965), 1 da (Sujata b 1970); *Career* Unilever Ltd 1954-58; Br Council 1958 overseas serv: E Pakistan 1958-63, India 1967-71, Ethiopia 1971-75, Brazil 1978-83, rep Japan 1983-; *Style—* Joseph Barnett, Esq, CBE; The Thatch, Stebbing Green, Gt Dunmow, Essex (☎ 037 186 352); Br Cncl, 2 Kagura Zaka-1 Chome, Shinjuku-Ku, Tokyo 162, Japan

BARNETT, Hon Mrs; Hon (Kathleen Irene Mary); *née* Hennessy; da of 1 Baron Windlesham, OBE (d 1953); *b* 1914; *Educ* private; *m* 1947 (m dis), Wilfred Ernest Barnett, 3 s of Ernest Barnett, of Chesterfield, Derbyshire; 2 s (Robin George, Nicholas James); *Style—* The Hon Mrs Barnett; Pullington Cottage, Benenden, Cranbrook, Kent (☎ 0580 240435)

BARNETT, Kenneth Thomas; CB (1979); yr s of Frederick Charles Barnett (d 1975), and Ethel, *née* Powell (d 1965); *b* 12 Jan 1921; *Educ* Howard Gdns HS Cardiff; *m* 1943, Emily May, da of Edward Lovering (d 1962); 1 da; *Career* served RAF 1941-46 as radar mechanic (NCO); entered Miny of Tport 1937, exec offr Sea Tport 1946-51, accountant offr and sec to divnl sea tport offr ME, Port Said 1951-54, higher exec and sr exec posts Roads Divns 1954-61, princ Finance Div 1961-65, asst sec then under-sec Ports 1965-71, under-sec: Cabinet Office (on secondment) 1971-73, Housing Dept of Environment 1973-76; dep sec Housing 1976-80, ret 1980; dir Abbey Data Systems

Ltd 1984-; *Style—* Kenneth Barnett, Esq, CB; The Stone House, Frith End, Nr Bordon, Hants (☎ 04203 2856)

BARNETT, Hon Mrs; Hon Laura Miriam Elizabeth; da of Baron Weidenfeld (Life Peer), by his 1 w; *b* 1953; *m* 1976, Christopher Andrew Barnett; 3 s (Benjamin b 1979, Rowan b 1981, Nathaniel b 1984), 1 da (Clara b 1986); *Style—* The Hon Mrs Barnett; Awdry House, Sunnyside, West Lavington, nr Devizes, Wilts SN10 4HU

BARNETT, Sir Oliver Charles; CBE (1954, OBE 1946), QC (1956); s of Charles Frederick Robert Barnett (TA) (ka 1915); *b* 7 Feb 1907; *Educ* Eton; *m* 1945, Joan, da of W H Eve (Capt 13 Hurrars, ka 1917), and gda of Rt Hon Sir Harry Eve (d 1940, High Court Judge); *Career* barr 1928, Judge Advocate Gen of the Forces 1963-68, bencher Middle Temple 1964, dep chm Somerset Quarter Sessions 1967-71; kt 1968; *Clubs* Brooks's, Pratt's; *Style—* Sir Oliver Barnett, CBE, QC; The Almonry, Stogumber, nr Taunton, Somerset (☎ 0984 56291)

BARNETT, Ulric David; s of Peter Cedric Barnett (d 1980), and Sylvia Irina, *née* Kenny; *b* 29 Sept 1942; *Educ* Eton, Magdalen Coll Oxford; *m* 5 Jan 1969, Marie-Jane Hélène, da of Capitaine de Fregate Jean Levasseur (d 1947); 2 s (Rory b 1971, Oliver b 1979), 1 da (Natalie b 1974); *Career* joined Cazenove & Co Stockbrokers 1965 (ptnr since 1971); dir Br Kidney Patient Assoc Investmt Tst; *Clubs* MCC, City Univ; *Style—* Ulric Barnett, Esq; 12 Token House Yard, London EC2R 7AN

BARNETT, William Evans; QC (1984); s of Alec Barnett (d 1981), of Penarth, S Glam, and Esmé Georgiana, *née* Leon; *b* 10 Mar 1937; *Educ* Repton, Keble Coll Oxford (BA, MA); *m* 24 July 1976, Lucinda Jane Gilbert, JP, da of Richard William Gilbert (d 1980), of Addington, Surrey; 2 s (Nicholas b 1978, James b 1980); *Career* Nat Serv RCS 1956-58; barr 1962, practicing Midland and Oxford Circuit 1963; memb Personal Injuries Litigation Procedure Working Pty 1976-78, rec Crown Ct 1981; memb Croydon Medico-Legal Soc; *Recreations* golf, photography, gardening, DIY; *Clubs* Addington Golf; *Style—* William Barnett, Esq, QC; Carleon, 6 Castlemaine Avenue, S Croydon, Surrey CR2 7HQ (☎ 01 688 9559); 12 King's Bench Walk, Temple, London EC4Y 7EL (☎ 01 583 0811, fax 01 583 7228)

BARNEWALL, Hon Anthony Edward; s and h of 19 Baron Trimlestown; *b* 2 Feb 1928; *Educ* Ampleforth; *m* 1, 1963 (m dis), Lorna Margaret Marion (d 1988), da of late Charles Douglas Ramsay; m 2, 1977, Mary Wonderly, da of late Judge Thomas F McAllister, of Grand Rapids, Michigan; *Career* late Irish Gds; *Style—* The Hon Anthony Barnewall; Ada, Michigan 49301, USA

BARNEWALL, Peter Joseph; s and h of Sir Reginald Robert Barnewall, 13 Bt, *qv*; *b* 26 Oct 1963; *Educ* Univ of Queensland (BAgrSc); *Career* agricultural economist; Lt served with Australian Army Reserve, Queensland Univ Regt 1981-86; 2/14 Light Horse (Queensland Mounted Inf) 1987-; *Recreations* game shooting, water skiing, tennis; *Clubs* United Service, Tamborine Mountain RSC; *Style—* Peter Barnewall, Esq

BARNEWALL, Hon Raymond Charles; s of 19 Baron Trimlestown; *b* 29 Dec 1930; *Educ* Ampleforth; *Style—* The Hon Raymond Barnewall; Autumn Cottage, Chiddingfold, Surrey

BARNEWALL, Sir Reginald Robert; 13 Bt (I 1623); s of Sir Reginald John Barnewall, 12 Bt (d 1961); *b* 1 Oct 1924; *Educ* Xavier Coll Melbourne; *m* 1, 1946, Elsie Muriel (d 1962), da of Thomas Matthews Frederick, of Brisbane, Queensland; 3 da; m 2, 1962, Maureen Ellen, da of William Daly, of S Caulfield, Victoria; 1 s; *Heir* s, Peter Joseph Barnewall b 26 Oct 1963; *Career* wool grower, cattle breeder, orchardist; former dir Island Airways Pty Ltd (Pialba, Qld), operator and owner Coastal-Air Co (Qld) 1971-76, former dir and vice chm J Roy Stevens Pty Ltd; *Style—* Sir Reginald Barnewall, Bt; Mount Tamborine, Queensland 4272, Australia

BARNICOAT, Wing Cdr David Ross; s of Frank Ross Barnicoat (d 1977), and Olive Mary, *née* Collins (d 1982); *b* 21 July 1925; *Educ* Cranbrook Sch, Wadham Coll Oxford, RAF Coll Cranwell; *m* 1, 25 March 1944, Audrey Margaret, da of Harold Wilson (d 1981); 1 s (Ian b 1946), 2 da (Jacqueline b 1944, Jennifer b 1950); m 2, 1960, Elizabeth Christine, da of Maurice Cecil Johnes Lloyd (d 1950); 1 s (Oliver b 1963), 1 da (Katherine b 1965); *Career* RAF Offr 1944-75 Wing Cdr Air Attache Cairo; chm B&B Servs Conslts Ltd 1977-, sr ptnr D R Barnicoat Assoc 1975-87; FBIM, FInstD; *Recreations* travel, skiing, swimming, boating; *Clubs* RAF; *Style—* Wing Cdr David R Barnicoat; Garden House, Wyke Hall. Gillingham, Dorset SP8 5NS (☎ 07476 3409); Villa Pasqualino, Porto Cervo, Costa Smeralda, Sardinia

BARNS-GRAHAM, Patrick Allan; TD; s of Allan Barns-Graham (d 1957), of Lymekilns, and Wilhelmina Menzies, *née* Bayne-Meldrum; *b* 19 Feb 1915; *Educ* Sedbergh; *m* 31 Dec 1944, Daphne Blanche Rosemary, da of Lt William Henry Braisty Skaife-d'Ingerthorpe, RNVR; 2 s (Allan b 1948, Peter b 1951), 2 da (Rosemary b 1946, Christina b 1959); *Career* RA (TA): 2Lt 1938, Capt 1940, Maj 1942, serv M East 1935-45, demobilised as Maj; CA Thomson McLintock & Co Glasgow 1938; Brownlee & Co plc: account sec 1946, sec 1948, dir 1958, md 1968, chm 1973-80; dir: Alliance Alders and assoc cos 1973-80, Diversion Insur Timber Trade UK Ltd; Lord Dean Guild of City of Glasgow 1977-87, dir Glasgow C of C 1969-77, chm Glasgow Humane Soc 1977-87 (dir 1976-), preceptor Royal Incorpn of Hutcheson's Hosp 1987-; MICAS; *Recreations* formerly shooting and fishing; *Style—* Patrick Barns-Graham, Esq, TD; Carbeth Guthrie, Blanefield, Stirlingshire G63 9AT (☎ 0360 70249)

BARNSLEY, Thomas Edward; OBE (1975); s of Alfred E Barnsley and Ada F Nightingale; *b* 10 Sept 1919; *Educ* Wednesbury Boys' HS; *m* 1947, Margaret Gwyneth Llewellin; 1 s, 1 da; *Career* md Tube Investments 1974-82; dir H P Bulmer Hldgs 1982-; FCA; *Style—* Thomas Barnsley Esq; Old Rectory, Cossington, nr Leicester (☎ (050 981 2623)

BARNWELL, Hon Mrs; Hon (Elizabeth Mary); *née* Shore; da of 6 Baron Teignmouth (d 1964); *b* 1916; *m* 1942, Maj Charles John Patrick Barnwell, yr s of late Frederick Arthur Lowry Barnwell, Hinton St George, Somerset; 1 s (and 1 s decd); *Style—* The Hon Mrs Barnwell; Standerwick, Fivehead, Taunton, Somerset TA3 6PT (☎ (04608 228)

BARON, Alexander; s of Barnet Baron (d 1977), and Fanny, *née* Levinson (d 1974); *b* 4 Dec 1917; *Educ* Hackney Downs Sch; *m* 4 Aug 1960, Delores Lopez, da of Sidney Loper Salzedo (d 1987); 1 s (Nicholas b 1969); *Career* WWII 1940-46 served Army in Sicily and NW Europe; novelist and scriptwriter; many film scripts, TV plays and classic serials for the BBC incl Vanity Fair (1987); *Books* From the City, From the Plough (1948), There's No Home (1950), The Human Kind (1953), France is Dying (1977); *Clubs* Pen; *Style—* Alexander Baron, Esq; 30 Cranbourne Gardens, London, NW11, (☎ 01 455 8352)

BARON, Anthony; s of John Baron, and Doreen, *née* Eastman; *b* 26 Sept 1950; *Educ* LSE (BSc), QMC London (MSc); *m* 13 Nov 1970(m dis 1984) Ruzena Eliska Michaela, da of Dr Ctibor Haluza; 2 da (Andrea b 9 July 1975, Georgina b 4 April 1978); m 2, Jane Edith Mary, da of John Patrick Lynch; *Career* sr info offr Centl Off of Info 1973-77, UK economist Hoare Govett 1977-81, chief economist Savory Milln & Co 1981-83, ptnr Laurie Milbank & Co 1983-87, md Chase Investmt Bank 1987-; memb Int Stock Exchange; *Recreations* swimming, squash; *Style—* Anthony Baron, Esq; Prior House, Cleeve Prior, Nr Evesham, Worcs; 5 Westwood Park, London SE25; Chase Investment Bank, Woolgate House, Coleman St London EC2P 2HD (☎ 01 726 3183, fax 01 726 5952, telex 8958831)

BARON, (Henry William) Anthony; s of Alfred Edward Baron (d 1981), of Brackens Pinhoe, Exeter, Devon and Constance Evelyn, *née* Palmer (d 1972); *b* 31 Dec 1917; *Educ* Oundle, Trinity Coll Cambridge (MA, MB, MChir), St Barth Hosp; *m* 2 July 1952, (Margaret) Ann, da of Maj Geoffrey Thomas Floyd, of Birkenhead, Bombay; 1 s (Andy (Anthony) John Prescot b 4 Jan 1955), 1 da (Elizabeth Ann b 24 April 1957); *Career* RAMC Capt served in Far east 1943-46; res fell St Georges Hosp 1950- 54 (surgical first asst 1947-50); conslt surgn 1950-80: St Margarets Hosp Epping, Princess Alexandra Hosp Harlow, Ongar War Meml Hosp, Waltham Abbey Meml Hosp; Freeman City of London 1955, Liveryman Worshipful Soc of Apothecaries 1952; memb BMA 1942, RSM 1947, FRCS 1946; *Recreations* reading, shooting; *Clubs* United Oxford and Cambridge, MCC; *Style—* Anthony Baron, Esq; 3 Lansdowne Place, Hove, E Sussex; 66 Shepherds Hill N 6; 103 Los Pinos, El Rosario, Marbella, Spain (☎ 0273 735 853); 17 Harley St, London W1N 1DA (☎ 01 935 1928)

BARON, Cecil Saul; s of Henry (Harry) Donald Baron (d 1973), of Brondesbury Park, and Henrietta (Hetty) Ethel, *née* Solomons (d 1973); *b* 18 Feb 1925; *Educ* Haberdasher's Askes, Cambridge Univ, LSE (B Com); *m* 31 March 1962, Caroline Ann, da of Stanley Victor Blackman (d 1982); 1 da (Lyn Harriet Ruth b 29 Sept 1963); *Career* WWII Capt RCS served India and Burma; fin offr chain store fin tst 1955-56, mangr Lloyds and Scottish Gp subsidiary 1957-59, dir S Essex Motors 1960-64, pa to chm and gp co sec Oxley Indus 1965-78; dir Sm Bus Computers and Microcomputer Conslt Computech Systems Ltd 1979-; hon audit Thos Martyn Fdn; FCA 1962; *Recreations* overseas travel, swimming; *Style—* Cecil Baron, Esq; 6 Stradbrook, Bratton, nr Westbury, Wilts; Computech, 168 Finchley Rd, London NW3 6HP (☎ 01 794 0202)

BARON, Prof Denis Neville; s of Dr Edward Baron (d 1964), of London, and Lilian Dolly, *née* Silman (d 1985); *b* 3 Oct 1924; *Educ* Univ Coll Sch London, Middx Hosp Med Sch Univ of London (MB BS, MD, DSc); *m* 6 Dec 1951, Yvonne Elsa, da of Hugo Stern (d 1963), of London; 1 s (Justin b 1963), 3 da (Leonora b 1954, Jessica b 1956, Olivia b 1958); *Career* Flt Lt RAF (med branch) 1946-49; Royal Free Hosp and Sch of Meds London: conslt chemical pathologist, reader in chemical pathology 1954-63, prof chemical pathology 1963-88; senator Univ of London 1985-88; ed in chief Clinical Science 1966-68, chm Assoc of Profs of Chemical Pathology 1980-81; memb: Medicines Cmmn 1982-, standing med advsy ctee DHSS 1966-74, med ctee Chemical Def Advsy Bd 1969-76, Camden & Islington AHA 1978-81, Barnet Health Authy 1982-85; govr Henrietta Barnet Sch 1987-; Freeman Worshipful Soc of Apothecaries 1951, memb BMA 1945, FRSA 1952, FRCPath 1963 (vice pres 1972-75), FRCP 1971; *Books* Short Textbook of Chemical Pathology (fourth edn 1982), Units, Symbols, and Abbreviations (ed, fourth edn 1988); *Recreations* opera, gardening, sight-seeing; *Clubs* RSM; *Style—* Prof D N Baron; 47 Holne Chase, London N2 0QG (☎ 01 458 2340)

BARON COHEN, Gerald; s of Morris Baron Cohen (d 1972), of Cardiff, S Glam, and Miriam, *née* Nicholsby (d 1987); *b* 13 July 1932; *Educ* Univ of Wales (BA); *m* 12 June 1962, Daniella Naomi, da of Hans Isidore Weiser, of Telaviv, Israel; 3 s (Jonathon Ammon b 1964, Erran Boaz b 1968, Sacha Noam b 1971); *Career* CA, co dir, ed Mosaic 1960-62, dep ed New Middle East 1967-68; past pres Bnai Brith First Lodge 1979-80 (nat tres 1984) vice chm Hillel fndn 1970-, past vice chm Union Jewish Students, chm Forum for Jewish Dialogue; FCA 1954; *Style—* Gerald Baron Cohen, Esq; 70 Wildwood Road, London NW11 6UJ (☎ 01 458 1552); 760 Finchley Rd, London NW11 7TH (☎ 01 455 0994)

BARR, David; s of Walter Barr (d 1981), latterly of Glasgow, and Betty, *née* Shulman; *b* 15 Oct 1925; *Educ* Haberdashers Askes, Brookline HS Boston USA, Edinburgh Univ, UCL (LLB); *m* 8 June 1960, Ruth, da of David Weitzman, QC, MP (d 1987); 1 s (Andrew b 9 April 1961), 1 da (Frances b 14 March 1964); *Career* RN 1943-47; slr 1953, met stipendiary magistrate 1976; JP Inner London Area 1963-76, dep chm N Westminster PSD 1968-76, chm Inner London Juvenile Panel 1969; mangr Finnant House Sch 1955-81 (chm & tstee 1973-); Freeman City of London 1959; *Recreations* book collecting, bridge; *Clubs* Garrick, MCC; *Style—* David Barr, Esq; Highbury Corner Magistrates Ct, London N7 (☎ 01 607 6757)

BARR, Derek Julian; s of Peter Joachim Barr, of 1 Woodspring Rd, London SW19, and Ingrid Gerda, *née* Dannenbaum; *b* 16 Sept 1945; *Educ* St Paul's Imperial Coll (BSc, ACGI); *m* 19 Dec 1970, Zoe Maxine, da of Wing Cdr Jack Leon Elson-Rees (d 1962); 2 s (James b 1976, Nicholas b 1981), 2 da (Katrina b 1972, Annabelle b 1974); *Career* chemical engr (expert in industl drying and process technol); md Barr & Murphy 1974 - (founded firm with father 1962); awarded Queen's Award for Export Achievement 1976; FIChE 1987; *Recreations* skiing, sailing, tennis, music; *Clubs* IOD, Roehampton; *Style—* Derek Barr, Esq; Wifflescombe, 1 Vineyard Hill Rd, London SW1 7JL (☎ 01 946 1044); B & M House, 48 Bell St, Maidenhead, Berks SL6 1BR (☎ 0628 776177, fax 0628 776118, telex 849165)

BARR, Graham Robert; s of Robert Barr (d 1986), of Roundhay, Leeds, and Barbara Moyra Mary, *née* Keene; *b* 25 Jan 1926; *Educ* Rounday GS, Kitson Coll; *m* 16 March 1985, Diane, da of Raymond Thomas Mastin; 1 da (Emma Victoria b 16 Jan 1975); *Career* investmt mangr Stockbrokers, sales and mktg mangr Wardley Investmt Servs Ltd 1986-; *Recreations* shooting, gun dog; *Clubs* Sloane; *Style—* Graham Barr, Esq; 165 Oakwood Lane, Oakwood, Leeds LS8 2PB (☎ 0532 402 068), Cloth Hall Ct, Infirmary St, Leeds LS1 2HR (☎ 0532 459 494, fax 01 374 0861, car phone 0860 612 567)

BARR, Ian; s of Peter McAlpine Barr (d 1961), of Dalserf, Lanarkshire, and Isobel Baillie (d 1979); *b* 6 April 1927; *Educ* Boroughmuir HS Edinburgh; *m* 1, 1951 (m dis 1988), Gertrud Karla, da of August Otto Odefey (d 1976), of Schleswig-Holstein; 2 da (Karen, Kirsten); m 2, 1988, his cousin Margaret Annie, da of Andrew McAlpine Barr; *Career* Post Off; asst postal controller NW region 1955, inspr of postal servs Post Off HQ 1962, princ regnl dir Eastern Postal regn 1976, dir buildings mechanisation and planning Post Off HQ 1978-81, dir Post Off estates exec 1981-84, chm Scottish Post

Off Bd 1984-88; chm Post Off Nat Arts Ctee 1976-87, pres Conference Européenne des Postes et des Telecommunications (Batiments) 1982-86; memb: Br Materials Handling Bd 1978-81, bd Girobank Scotland 1984-88, Scottish cncl CBI 1984-88; chm: Saltire Soc 1986-87, Scottish ctee Assoc for Business Sponsorship of the Arts 1986-88; dir: St Mary's Music Sch 1986- (chm mgmnt exec ctee 1988), SNO 1988, Cameratu of St Andrew 1988 (chamber music gp); tstee: Endocrine Res Tst 1987-, Lamp of Lothian Collegiate Tst 1988; memb Edinburgh Festival 1988; *Recreations* practicing solipsism, constructing a metaphysical system, composing serial music; *Style—* Ian Barr, Esq; 9 Ravelston Heights, Edinburgh EH4 3LX

BARR, Kenneth Glen; o s of Rev Gavin Barr, and Catherine McLellan, *née* McGhie; *b* 20 Jan 1941; *Educ* Ardrossan Acad, Royal HS, Edinburgh Univ; *m* 1970, Susanne Crichton Keir; *Career* Sheriff S Strathclyde Dumfries and Galloway 1976-; *Style—* Sheriff Kenneth Barr; Sheriff Court House, Dumfries

BARR, (John) Malcolm; CBE; *b* 23 Dec 1926; *Educ* Shrewsbury, Clare Coll Cambridge; *m* Elaine Mary Rhodes; 2 da (Margaret Clare, Janine Ruth); *Career* Sub Lt RNVR 1944-48; Barr and Wallace Arnold Tst plc 1952-: chm and gp md 1962-88, gp exec chm 1988-; dir Leeds Permanent Bldg Soc 1970, non-exec dir Hickson Int plc 1971; pres City of Leeds YMCA, chm fin ctee Br Show Jumping Assoc, memb fin ctee Fedn Equestre Internationale, dir Br Equestrian Promotion Ltd; High Sheriff West Yorkshire; *Recreations* drama, literature, music, show jumping; *Clubs* Royal Ocean Racing, Climbers'; *Style—* Malcolm Barr Esq, CBE; 3 Killingbeck Dr, Killingbeck, Leeds LS14 6UF (☎ 0532 499 3622, fax 0532 491 192, car tel 0836 505 150, telex 557 734 BWAT G)

BARR, Prof Murray Llewellyn; OC (1968); s of William Llewellyn Barr (d 1911), and Margaret (McLellan) Barr (d 1953) ; *b* 20 June 1908; *Educ* Univ of W Ontario London Canada (BA, MD, MSc); *m* 1934, Ruth Vivian, da of Wallace Edward King, of Ashtabula, Ohio (d 1956); 3 s (Hugh, Robert, David), 1 da (Carolyn); *Career* prof of anatomy Univ of W Ontario 1949-73, MO RCAF 1939-45, Canada and Wing Cdr, author of The Human Nervous System, Harper & Row 1972 (1 ed) J B Lippincott (5 edn with J A Kiernan 1988); A Century of Medicine at Western UWO 1977; 110 scientific papers most of them on human cytogenetics; FRS; *Recreations* philately, short-wave radio; *Style—* Prof Murray Barr, OC; 452 Old Wonderland Rd, London, Ontario N6K 3R2, Canada (☎ 519 471 5618)

BARR, Hon Mrs (Penelope Carol); yst da of Baron Crowther-Hunt (Life Peer d 1987); *b* 1955; *m* 23 July 1988, Andrew A Barr, er s of W G Barr, of Oxford; *Style—* The Hon Mrs Barr; 30 Upland Park Road, Oxford

BARR, His Honour Judge; Reginald Alfred Barr; s of Alfred Charles Barr (d 1950); *b* 21 Nov 1920; *Educ* Christ's Hosp, Trin Coll Oxford; *m* 1946, Elaine, 2 da of James William Charles O'Bala Morris, of Llanstephan, Carmarthenshire; *Career* barr 1954, circuit judge 1970; *Style—* His Hon Judge Barr; 42 Bathurst Mews, Hyde Pk, W2 (☎ 01 262 5731)

BARR, Robert Zbigniew; MBE (1944); s of Stanislaw Bachurzewski; *b* 2 Nov 1920; *Educ* Stefan Bathory Univ Vilno (Poland); *m* 1947, Ewa, da of Capt Evgraf Cutjev (d 1979); 1 s; *Career* Capt Polish Army WW II, engineer, export dir Head Wrightson & Co 1971-76, md Head Wrightson Process Engrg 1976-80; VM (Polish) 1944; *Recreations* sailing (yacht 'Punia'); *Style—* Robert Barr Esq; 37 Ladbroke Sq, W11 (☎ 01 727 4616)

BARR, Stuart Alan; DL (W Yorks 1987); s of Robert Barr (d 1960), and Edith, *née* Midgley (d 1963) of Shadwell, Leeds; *b* 18 Nov 1930; *Educ* Shrewsbury; *m* 1 (m dis 1964); 2 s (Nicholas, Robert); m 2, 1969, Karin Johanne, da of Col Donald Blake Smiley, DFC, RCAF (d 1985), of Florida, USA; 2 da (Lucinda b 1971, Camilla b 1976); *Career* Maj Queen's Own Yorks Dragoons (TA), Lt 9 Queen's Royal Lancers; dep chm and md Barr & Wallace Arnold Tst; dir: Wallace Arnold, Tst Motors, Wass Ltd, BCB Motor Factors, Euroways (Eurolines) Ltd, Oswalds Hotel, Robert Sibbald Travel Agents, Wayahead Fuel Services, Wilks & Meade; vice-pres: Leeds Tradesmen's Inst, Yorks Area Boy Scouts Assoc; pres: Knaresborough Div St John Ambulance, W Yorks Youth Assoc; memb: high steward's cncl and tstee York Minster, W Yorks Industrialists' Cncl; High Sheriff W Yorks 1984; *Recreations* racing, shooting; *Clubs* Cavalry and Guards; *Style—* Stuart Barr, Esq, DL; Barr & Wallace Arnold plc, 21 The Calls, Leeds LS2 7ER (☎ 0532 436041)

BARRACK, William Sample; s of William Sample Barrack, and Edna Mae Henderson; *b* 26 July 1929; *Educ* Univ of Pittsburgh, RNC Dartmouth; *m* 1953, Evelyn Irene Ball; 1 s, 1 da; *Career* offr in USN; joined Texaco's US Marketing Orgn 1953, dist mangr: Portland Me 1962, Providence RI 1963; asst mangr Distribution Devpt Marketing-US, NY, 1965; asst mangr Market Research and Project Devpt 1966; asst div mangr Norfolk VA; mangr distribution devpt Texaco Brussels 1967, Area div 1969; vice pres Texaco Services (Europe) Ltd 1969-, gen mangr 1970, exec asst to chm Exec Ctee and ch exec offr Texaco Inc NY 1971, vice-pres Texaco Inc 1971, chm of bd and ch exec offr Texaco Ltd 1980-, pres Texaco Oil Trading and Supply Co NY 1982-, sr vice-pres Texaco Inc 1983-; dir: Arabian American Oil Co, Texaco Canada Inc, Texaco Ltd, Texaco Philanthropic Fndn Inc, Deutsche Texaco AG, Caltex Petroleum Corpn; bd of govrs For Policy Assoc; fell of Inst of Petroleum; vice-chm bd of Tstees Manhattanville 611, Purchase NY; *Recreations* golf, fishing, shooting, sailing; *Clubs* Ox Ridge (Connecticut), Woodway Country (Connecticut); *Style—* William Barrack, Esq; Texaco Inc, 2000 Westchester Avenue, White Plains, NY 10650

BARRACLOUGH, Air Chief Marshal Sir John; KCB (1970, CB 1969), CBE (1961), DFC (1942), AFC (1941); s of late Horatio Leonard Barraclough, of London, and Marguerite Maude Barraclough; *b* 2 May 1918; *Educ* Cranbrook Sch; *m* 1946, Maureen, da of Dr William John McCormack, of Wicklow, and niece of George, Noble Count Plunkett; 1 da (Moy, m 1981 David Scott); *Career* Air Vice-Marshal 1964; dir Public Relations Air Ministry 1961-64, vice-chm Def Staff 1970-72, Air Sec 1972-74; Cmdt Royal Coll Def Studies 1974-76; Cmdt RCDS 1974-76, Air-Sec 1972-74; vice-chm Commonwealth War Graves Cmmn 1981-; FIPM, MBIM, MIPR; *Style—* Air Chief Marshal Sir John Barraclough, KCB, CBE, DFC, AFC; Crapstone House, Buckland Monachorum, Devon (☎ (082 285 3639); c/o Barclays Bank, 11 Newgate st, EC1

BARRACLOUGH, Lt-Col Michael Charles; OBE (1986); s of Maj Ernest Barraclough (d 1942), of Kenya, and Margery, *née* Goulden (d 1962); *b* 1 July 1923; *Educ* Haileybury; *m* 22 Jan 1949, Anne Marie, da of Capt Henry D'Olier Vigne (d 1982), of Essex; 1 s (Charles Henry Thomas b 1950), 1 da (Jane b 1953); *Career* cmmnd 22 Dragoons 1942-45, 4/7 Royal Dragoon Gds 1945-71, cmd 4/7 RDG 1966-66, Staff Coll 1957, DAAG & QMG HQ RAC 1 Br Corps 1958-60, GSO 2 HQ Land Forces Persian Gulf 1962-64, GSO (OPS) Allied Forces AFCENT 1967-69, GSO Royal Armament R & D Estab 1969-71; gen sec Homoeopathic Tst for Res & Educn & Faculty of Homoeopathy 1972-; *Recreations* fishing, shooting; *Clubs* Cavalry and Guards'; *Style—* Lt-Col M C Barraclough, OBE; Ivy Cottage, Mill Green, Ingatestone, Essex CM4 0HY (☎ 0277 352769)

BARRAN, Dowager Lady; Esther Frances Eveleigh; da of late Hon F M B Fisher, of Rotorua, New Zealand; *m* 1946, as his 2 w, Sir John Nicholson Barran, 2 Bt (d 1952); *Style—* Dowager Lady Barran; 2 Phillimore Place, London W8 7BU (☎ 01 937 1907)

BARRAN, Sir John Napoleon Ruthven; 4 Bt (UK 1895); s of Sir John Leighton Barran, 3 Bt (d 1974), and Hon Alison (d 1973), da of 9 Lord Ruthven of Freeland, CB, CMG, DSO; n of Sir David Barran, chm of the Midland Bank and ex-chm Shell; *b* 14 Feb 1934; *Educ* Heatherdown Ascot, Winchester; *m* 1965, Jane Margaret, da of Sir Stanley George Hooker, CBE (d 1984), and his 1 w Hon Margaret Bradbury, da of 1 Baron Bradbury; 1 s, 1 da (Susannah Margaret b 1981); *Heir* s, John Ruthven Barran b 10 Nov 1971; *Career* Lt 5 Royal Inniskillen Dragoon Gds 1952-54; in advertising 1956-63, served Br High Cmmn Ottawa 1964-67; head Viewdata Unit COI 1978-85; head of Info Technol Unit 1985-87; *Recreations* Shooting, Fishing, Gardening, Entertaining; *Clubs* RAC; *Style—* Sir John Barran, Bt; 17 St Leonard's Terrace, London SW3 (☎ 01 730 2801); The Hermitage, East Bergholt, Suffolk (☎ (020 028 8236); Middle Rigg Farm, Sawley, Yorkshire (☎ 076 586 207)

BARRASS, Christopher Patrick; s of Maj Patrick Rae Barrass, of Chobham, Surrey, and Ann Delory, *née* Bertram; *b* 12 Nov 1953; *Educ* Dauntsey Sch Wiltshire; *Career* chief reporter: Westminster Press Surrey Herald 1976-78, Sutton Seibert Publishing 1980-82; md Sovereign Servs 1979-82, conslt Granard Communications 1982-85, dir Edelman Pub Rels 1987- (assoc dir 1985-87); memb: Clandon Soc, Clandon Horticultural Soc; *Recreations* classic cars, literature, arts, water and snow skiing; *Style—* Christopher Barrass, Esq; Edelman Public Relations, Kingsgate House, 536 Kings Road, London SW10 OTE (☎ 01 835 1222, fax 01 351 7676)

BARRATT, Eric George; s of Frank Barratt, of Stokenchurch, Bucks; *b* 15 April 1938; *Educ* Oriel Coll Oxford (MA); *Career* ptnr MacIntyre Hudson; dir cmmn for: the Newtowns, Esthwaite Estate Ltd, Ely Place Investmts, Heath field Sch Ltd, Grangehouse Investmnts Ltd, SC Brannan & Sons Ltd; tres and fell Oriel Coll; FCA; *Clubs* Athenaeum, Carlton, City of London, Bucks CC; *Style—* Eric Barratt, Esq; Stockfield, Stokenchurch, Bucks (☎ 024 026 2284); work: MacIntyre Hudson, 28 Ely Place, London EC1N 6LR (☎ 01 242 0242)

BARRATT, Francis Russell; CB (1975); s of Frederick Russell Barratt (d 1957); *b* 16 Nov 1924; *Educ* Durban HS, Clifton, Univ Coll Oxford; *m* 1, 1949 (m dis 1978), Janet Mary, *née* Sherborne; 3 s; m 2, 1979, Josephine Norah Harrison, da of Brig D McCririck (d 1947); *Career* dep sec HM Treasury; *Recreations* reading, music, golf; *Style—* Francis Barratt, Esq, CB; 8 Arlington Ave, London N1 (☎ 01 359 1747)

BARRATT, Jeffery Vernon Courtney Lewis; s of Arnold Douglas Courtney Lewis, and Edith Joyce, *née* Terry; *b* 31 Oct 1950; *Educ* Scots Coll Wellington NZ, Adelaide Univ (LLB), Sydney Univ (LLB,LLM); *Career* articled clerk Giovanell and Burges 1971-73, slr Stephen Jaques and Stephen 1973-75; trg ptnr Norton Rose 1987-(ptnr since 1979; estab Bahrain Off 1972-82) memb ed bd Butterworths Jl of Int Banking and Fin Law; author of num articles on selling Loan Assets and Sterling Commercial Paper in learned jnls; memb London Legal Educn Ctee, Law Soc, IBA, QMC (summer sch Faculty); *Recreations* cricket, squash, skiing, tennis, opera; *Clubs* Hampstead Cricket (Capt 1987), RAC, MCC; *Style—* Jeffrey Barratt, Esq; Norton Rose, Kempson House, Camomile Street, London, EC3A 7AN (☎ 01 283 2434, fax 588 1181, telex 883652)

BARRATT, Sir Lawrence Arthur (Lawrie); *b* 14 Nov 1927; *m* 1, 1951 (m dis 1984); 2 s; m 2, 1984, Mary Sheila Brierley; *Career* fndr 1958, now chm and md Barratt Devpts plc (UK's largest private house bldg co); FCIS; kt 1982; *Recreations* golf, shooting, sailing; *Style—* Sir Lawrie Barratt; Wingrove House, Ponteland Rd, Newcastle-upon-Tyne NE5 3DP (☎ (091 2866811)

BARRATT, Michael Fieldhouse; s of Wallace Milner Barratt (d 1980), and Doris, *née* Fieldhouse (d 1934); *b* 3 Jan 1928; *Educ* Rossall and Paisley GS, Aberdeen Univ; *m* 1, 1952 (m dis), Joan Francesca Warner; 3 s (Mark, Andrew, Paul), 3 da (Eve, Rachel, Jane); m 2, 1977, Dilys Jane, da of David Morgan (d 1985); 2 s (Oliver, Barnaby), 1 da (Jessica); *Career* entered journalism Kemsley Newspapers 1945, ed Nigerian Citizen 1956, reporter Panorama 1963; presenter: 24 Hours 1965-69, Nationwide 1969-77, Songs of Praise 1977-82, Reporting London 1983-88; radio: question master Gardeners', Question Time 1973-79; Hon LLD Aberdeen Univ; FRHS; *Books* Michael Barratt (1973), Down to Earth Gardening Book (1974), Michael Barratt's Complete Gardening Guide (1977), Golf with Tony Jacklin (1978); *Recreations* cricket, listening; *Clubs* Lord's Taverners; *Style—* Michael Barratt, Esq; 5/7 Forlease Rd, Maidenhead, Berks SL6 1RP (☎ 0628 770 800)

BARRATT BROWN, Dr Michael; s of Alfred Barratt Brown, of Ruskin Coll Oxford (d 1947), and Doris Eileen, *née* Cockshott (d 1984); f imprisoned as a conscientious objector for two and a half years in WW 1, princ of Ruskin Coll, Oxford 1921-44; *b* 15 Mar 1918; *Educ* Dragon Sch Oxford, Bootham Sch York, Corpus Christi Coll Oxford (MA); *m* 1, 12 Aug 1940, Frances Mary, da of Edward Mayo Hastings Lloyd (d 1963), of Hemel Hempstead Herts; 2 s (Christopher John b 1945, Richard Rollo b 1947); m 2, 17 July 1948, Eleanor Mary, da of David Jacob Singer, of Penn Bucks (d 1933); 1 s (Daniel b 1949), 1 da (Deborah b 1950); *Career* lectr and writer; sr lectr industl studies Univ of Sheffield 1959-77; princ Northern Coll Barnsley 1977-83, chm Third World Info Network Ltd and Twin Trading Ltd 1984-; dir Bertrand Russell Peace Fndn; hon fell Sheffield City Poly 1984, Hon Doctorate Open Univ 1985; pres Soc of Industl Tutors 1983; *Books* (most important works): After Imperialism (1963) (Spanish, Portuguese and Italian edns), What Economics is About (1970), The Economics of Imperialism (1974) (Spanish, Portuguese and Italian editions), From Labourism to Socialism (1972), Information at Work (1978), Models in Political Economy (1984), Editorial Bds: New Reasoner, Universities and Left Review, New Left Review, Spokesman, Institute for Workers Control, Conference of Socialist Economists, New Socialist; *Recreations* gardening, boating; *Style—* Dr Michael Barratt Brown; Robin Hood Farm, Baslow, Nr Bakewell, Derbyshire (☎ 0246 88 2281); 345 Goswell Rd, London EC1 (☎ 01 837 8222)

BARRATT-BOYES, Sir Brian Gerald; KBE (1971, CBE 1966); s of Gerald Cave

Boyes and Edna Myrtle, *née* Barratt; *b* 13 Jan 1924; *Educ* Johnsonville Sch, Wellington Coll & Sch of Medicine, Otago Univ, Dunedin, NZ (MB, ChM); *m* 1, 1949 (m dis 1986), Norma Margaret, da of late John Norman Thompson; 5 s (David, John, Mark, Stephen, Simon); m 2, 1986, Sara Rose Monester, da of Wolf Kanat; *Career* fellowship Cardiothoracic Surgery Mayo Clinic 1953-55, NZ Nuffield Travelling Fell Bristol Univ UK 1956-, sr thoracic surgn Green Lane Hosp Auckland NZ 1957-65, surgn in charge Cardio-Thoracic Surgical Unit Green Lane Hosp 1965-89, private practice Mater Misericordiae Hosp Auckland NZ 1966-; Professor of Surgery (Hon) Univ of Auckland; FRACS, FACS, FRSNZ; *Books* Heart Disease in Infancy: Diagnosis and Surgical Treatment (1973, Textbook of Cardiac Surgery (1973), co-author Dr J W Kirklin); *Recreations* farming, fishing, golf; *Clubs* Northern; *Style—* Sir Brian Barratt-Boyes, KBE; Greenhills, Box 51, Waiwera, Hibiscus Coast, New Zealand (☎0942 65 737); 1/102 Remuera Road, Remuera, Auckland 5, New Zealand (☎ 500 176)

BARRAUD, Hon Mrs; Hon Jane; *née* King-Hall; da of Baron King-Hall (Life Peer, d 1966); *b* 1930; *m* 1951, Yves Barraud, s of Dr J Barraud (d 1941), of Lausanne, Switzerland; 3 s; *Style—* The Hon Mrs Barraud; Les Saules, Les Cullayes, Vaud, Switzerland

BARRELL, Alan Walter; s of Leslie Walter Barrell, of Waltham Forest, Essex, and Margaret Louise Emily Barrell; *b* 21 July 1940; *Educ* Willesden GS, Cambridge Coll of Arts and Technol (DipM); *m* 3 March 1963, Pamela Mollie, da of Marcel Herbert Whitley, of Southend, Essex; 2 s (James, Julian), 2 da (Helene, Louise); *Career* gp mangr Domino Printing Scis plc 1984-; chm: Domino Am Jet Ltd (UK), Domino Am Jet Inc (USA), Domino GmBMC (Germany), Domino Am Jet BVC; dir QCA Ltd; govr Thetford GS, tstee Cambs Work Relations Gp; FIOD, FBIM, AIMLS, MRSH; *Style—* Alan Barrell, Esq; 6 Hills Ave, Cambridge CB1 4XA (☎ 0223 249597); Domino plc, Barr Hill, Cambridge (☎ 0954 81888)

BARRELL, Anthony Charles; s of William Frederick Barrell (d 1973), and Ruth Eleanor, *née* Painter; *b* 4 June 1933; *Educ* Friars Sch Bangor, Kingston GS, Birmingham Univ, Imperial Coll London (BSc); *m* 26 Jan 1963, Jean, da of Francis Henry Hawkes, and Clarice Jean Sithe, of Halberton, Devon; 1s (Andrew Mark b 1966), 1 da (Samantha Ruth b 1968); *Career* chemist Miny of Supply (later War Dept) 1959-64, commissioning engr African Explosives and Chem Industs 1964-65, shift mangr MOD 1965-66; HM Factory Inspectorate 1966-78: chem inspr, supt specialist inspr; dir of technol Health and Safety Exec 1985- (head of maj hazards assessment unit 1978-85); CEng 1974, FIChemE 1984, Eur Ing 1988; *Recreations* offshore sailing, fell walking, reading; *Clubs* West Kirby Sailing ; *Style—* Anthony Barrell, Esq; Sanderling, Baskervyle Rd, Gayton, Wirral L60 8NJ (☎ 051 342 8255); Health and Safety Executive, Bootle, Merseyside L20 3MF (☎ 051 951 4574, fax 051 951 4232, telex 628235 HSEG)

BARRER, Prof Richard Maling; s of Thomas Robert Barrer (d 1952), of Masterton, New Zealand and Nina Agatha Rosamund *née* Greensill, MBE (d 1966); *b* 16 June 1910; *Educ* Wairarapa HS NZ, Canterbury Univ NZ (DSc), Cambridge Univ (PhD, ScD); *m* 15 Aug 1939 Helen Frances da of Garnet Jeffrey Yule (d 1947) of Invercargill NZ, 1 s (Peter b 1942), 3 da (Margaret b 1944, Hilary b 1950, Christine b 1952); *Career* research fell Clare Coll Cambridge 1937-39, head of chem Dept Bradford Tech Coll 1939-46, reading in chem London Univ at Bedford Coll 1946-48; Aberdeen Univ 1948-54; chair of chem 1954-77, hd chem Dept 1956-77; dean Royal Coll of Sci 1963-66, prof emeritus London Univ and sr res fell Imperial Coll London 1977-; memb Faraday soc 1952-55, memb Royal soc of Chem 1956-59 & 1974-77, Royal Inst of chem 1961-64, memb soc of chem Industry 1965-68; govr Chelsea Coll of Sci & Tech London Univ 1960-72, chm Zeolite Nomendature ctee of Int Union of Pure & Applied chem 1967-72, Assoc memb of the colloid & surface chem, cmm of the union, 1970-72; FRS (1956), Hon ARCS (1959), Hon FRS (NZ) (1965); Hon DSc Bradford Univ, (1967), Hon DSc Aberdeen Univ, Hon Fellow Soc of chem Ind, NZ (1987); *Books* Diffusion in & through solids (1941 & 1950), Zeolites and Clay minerals as sobents & molecular sieves (1978), Hydrothermal chemistry of Zeolites (1982); *Recreations* tennis, gardening; *Clubs* Hawks, Achilles; *Style—* Prof Richard Barrer, Esq; Flossmoor, Orpington Road, Chistlehurst, BR7 6RA

BARRETT; *see*: Scott-Barrett

BARRETT, Edwin Radford (Ted); s of William barrett, and Florence Adeline, *née* Kohlar (d 1985); *b* 26 Mar 1929; *Educ* Itchen Sch Southampton, Burnley GS Lancs, London Univ (BSc); *m* 26 Sept 1957, Patricia, da of Egbert Shuttleworth; 1 s (Nicholas Radford b 1960), 1 da (Juliet Jane b 1964); *Career* pa to non-conformist Champlain RAF 1950-52; reporter and sub-ed Evening Telegraph Blackburn 1952-56, sub-ed Press Assoc London 1956-59; Daily Telegraph: joined 1959, seconded to Sports Room 1959, dep sports ed 1962, sports ed 1979-88, sports mngrg ed 1988-; sports broadcaster: Sports Report, Overseas Serv BBC 1960-80's; Inst of Journalists; *Books* contributions ot Oxford Companion to Sports and Games (1975); *Recreations* golf; *Clubs* Press Golfing Soc, Upminster Golf; *Style—* Ted Barrett, Esq; 12 Ock Ave, Upminster, Essex (☎ 04022 24709); 181 Marsh Wall, London E14 9SR (☎ 01 538 5000, fax 01 538 1332, telex 22874)

BARRETT, Ernest; s of Ernest Barrett and Marion Conyers; *b* 8 April 1917; *Educ* Charterhouse; *m* 1940, Eileen Maria Peel; 1 da; *Career* jt md Henry Barrett & Sons 1968-, chm Steel Stockholding Dvn Henry Barrett & Sons 1967-, John France & Co 1969-, Henry Lindsay Ltd 1974-; *Style—* Ernest Barrett, Esq; West Ghyll, Victoria ave, Ilkley, W Yorks (☎ 609294)

BARRETT, Air Cdre Frederick (Onslow Barrington) Oliver (Barry); CBE (1968), DFC (1945); s of Edwin Victor George Oliver Barrett (d 1930), of London, and Edith, *née* Haines (d 1971); *b* 21 Dec 1918; *Educ* City of London Sch, RAF; *m* 11 June 1976, (Penelope) Gay Rowland, da of Ralph Rowland Absalom, of Brechfa, Carmarthen, Wales; *Career* RAF 1938-72: operational serv Europe and Africa 1939-45, SASO HQ No 38 Gp 1968-71, dir Flight Safety RAF and Army Air Corps 1972-73, graduate RAF Staff Coll, JSSC, RAF Flying Coll; md Air Gregory Ltd, Surrey and Kent Flying Sch; Exec Air Birmingham, dir Air Gregory Petroleum Servs 1973-75, gen mangr aviation dept GKN 1976-81, conslt GKN 1982-84, aviation conslt and aircraft broker 1982-; vice pres SSAFA for Warwicks; Freeman City of London 1984, Liveryman Worshipful Co Air Pilots and Navigators 1984; *Recreations* golf, fishing; *Clubs* RAF; *Style—* Air Cdre Barry Barrett, CBE, DFC; Ct Farm House, Lower Fulbrook, Warwick CV35 8AS (☎ 0926 624 379)

BARRETT, Guy Crossland; OBE (1986); s of John Catton Barrett (d 1982), and Marian Braithwaite (d 1980); *b* 17 Mar 1925; *Educ* Giggleswick, Bradford Tech Coll; ; *m* 1950, Mavis, da of Nathaniel James Yeadon (d 1968), of Leeds; 2 s (James b 1955, Richard b 1957), 1 da (Elizabeth b 1951); *Career* structural engr; exec chm Henry Barrett Gp plc 1987- (md 1965-87); pres Bradford C of C 1977-79, Br Constructional Steelwork Assoc 1983-86, La Féderation Colombophile Internationale 1983-87, Royal Pigeon Racing Assoc 1976-79, ECCS; CEng, FIStructE; *Recreations* shooting, pigeon racing; *Clubs* Bradford; *Style—* Guy Barrett, Esq, OBE; Fence End, Calverley Lane, Horsforth, Leeds LS18 4ED (☎ 0532 582655); Henry Barrett Gp plc, Barrett House, Dudley Hill, Bradford, BD4 9HU (☎ 0274 682281)

BARRETT, Jack Wheeler; CBE (1971); s of John Samuel Barrett, of Cheltenham; *b* 13 June 1912; *Educ* Cheltenham GS, Imperial Coll London (BSc, PhD); *m* 1935, Muriel Audley, da of late Sydney Henry Read, of Coventry; 2 s, 2 da; *Career* dir Monsanto Chemicals 1955-78; chm: Info-Line 1976-80, Cole Gp 1978-87; CChem, FEng, FRSC, FIChemE; *Style—* Dr Jack Barrett, CBE; 195 Latymer Ct, Hammersmith Rd, London W6 (☎ 01 748 7080); West Manor House, Bourton-on-the-Water, Glos GL54 2AP (☎ 0451 20296)

BARRETT, John Barbenson; s of George William Barrett, of Jersey, and Vera, *née* Simon; *b* 19 July 1950; *Educ* De La Salle Coll Jersey; *m* 1 June 1974, Joan Madelene, da of Francis John Le Corre; 1 s (Simon), 2 da (Caroline, Louise); *Career* CA; ptnr BDO Binder, sr ptnr Carnaby Barrett; FICA 1975; *Recreations* flying, reading; *Style—* John Barrett, Esq; La Platiere, Le Hocq, St Clement, Jersey; Carnaby Barrett, Seaton House, Seaton Place, St Helier, Jersey (☎ 0534 21565, fax 0534 21987, telex 4912337)

BARRETT, Rev Prof (Charles) Kingsley; s of Rev Fred Barrett (d 1957), and Clara, *née* Seed (d 1941); *b* 4 May 1917; *Educ* Shebbear, Pembroke Coll Cambridge (BA, MA, BD, DD); *m* 1944, Margaret E, da of Percy Leathley Heap (d 1952), of Calverley, Yorkshire; 1 s (Martin), 1 da (Penelope); *Career* lectr in theology Durham Univ 1945-58, prof of divinity Durham Univ 1958-82; visiting lectureships and professorships in Europe, Aust, NZ and USA; Burkitt Medal for Biblical Study; Forschungs Preis of the Von Humboldt-Stiftung 1988; pres Studiorum Novi Testamenti Societas 1973-74; FBA 1961; *Books include* The Holy Spirit and The Gospel Tradition (1947), Gospel According to St John (1955, 2nd edn 1978), The Gospel of John and Judaism (1975), Essays on Paul (1982), Essays on John (1982) Freedom and Obligation (1985); many contributions to learned journals and symposia; *Style—* The Rev Prof C K Barrett; 8 Prince's St, Durham DH1 4RP (☎ 091 386 1340)

BARRETT, Michael Joseph; s of Michael Joseph Barrett, MBE (d 1983), of Acklam, Middlesbrough, Cleveland, and Hilda Patricia, *née* Davy; *b* 15 Oct 1943; *Educ* Ratcliffe Coll Leics, Advanced Mgmnt Programme Harvard Business Sch (AMP); *m* 7 Sept 1967, Sheila Katherine, da of Arnold Willis Little, of 49 Tunstall Ave, Billingham, Cleveland; 1 s (Peter b 1982), 1 da (Louise b 1973); *Career* underwriter and insurance broker; chief exec offr Alexander Stenhouse Europe Ltd and subsidiaries; cncl memb Soc Gen de Courtage d'Assurances Paris; dir Bekouw Mendes BV Amsterdam; *Recreations* fishing, shooting; *Clubs* Annabel's; *Style—* Michael Barrett, Esq; Birch House, Duncombe Rd, Bengeo, Herts SG14 3BU (☎ 0992 553485); Alexander Stenhouse Europe Ltd, 10 Devonshire Sq, London EC2M 4LE (☎ 01 621 9990, telex 920368, fax 01 621 9950)

BARRETT, Rodney James; s of Sidney Wilson Barrett (d 1977), and Dorothy Lucy Barrett (d 1960); *b* 7 April 1947; *Educ* Paston Sch N Walsham Norfolk, Univ of Essex (BA); *m* 23 Sept 1968, Janet Ann, da of Albert Edward Sealey (d 1957); 1 s (Daniel b 1975), 1 da (Anna b 1978); *Career* res asst Univ of Essex 1968-70, res assoc Univ of Manchester 1970-71, fin res dir Hoare Govett 1983- (bank analyst 1971); ASIA; *Recreations* entertaining family and friends, following horse-racing from a safe distance; *Style—* Rod Barrett, Esq; Hoare Govett, 4 Broadgate, London EC2M 7LE (☎ 01 601 0101)

BARRETT, Stephen Jeremy; CMG (1982); s of Wilfred Phillips Barrett (d 1978), of Keene Valley, NY, and Dorothy, *née* Sommers (d 1987); *b* 4 Dec 1931; *Educ* Westminster, Christ Church Oxford (BA, MA); *m* 1958, Alison Mary, da of Col Leonard George Irvine (d 1972); 3 s (Timothy b 1959, Nicholas b 1960, Matthew b 1962); *Career* Dip Serv 1955-, head of chancery Helsinki embasy 1965-68, cnsllr and head chancery Prague embassy 1972-74, head of SW Euro Dept FCO 1974, princ private sec to Foreign and Cwlth Sec 1975, head of sci and technol dept FCO 1976-77, fell Centre for Int Affrs Harvard Univ 1977-78, cnsllr Ankara 1978-81, head Br interests section Tehran 1981, dir of communications and tech servs FCO 1981-84, ambassador Prague 1985, ambassador Warsaw 1988-; *Recreations* climbing small mountains, reading; *Clubs* Travellers; *Style—* Stephen Barrett, Esq, CMG; c/o Foreign & Cwlth Off, King Charles St, London SW1

BARRETT-LENNARD, Rev Sir Hugh Dacre; 6 Bt (UK 1801); s of Sir Fiennes Cecil Arthur Barrett-Lennard (d 1963), gggs of 1 Bt; suc kinsman, Sir (Thomas) Richard Fiennes Barrett-Lennard, 5 Bt, OBE, 1977; *b* 27 June 1917; *Educ* Radley, Pontifical Beda Coll Rome; *Heir* cous, Richard Barrett-Lennard; *Career* serv WWII Capt Essex Regt (despatches); ordained in Roman Catholic Church 1950; priest London Oratory 1950-; *Recreations* in Scotland; *Style—* Rev Sir Hugh Barrett-Lennard, Bt; The Oratory, South Kensington, London SW7 (☎ 01 589 4811)

BARRETT-LENNARD, Richard Fynes; s of Roy Barrett-Lennard (d 1979); hp of kinsman, Rev Sir Hugh Barrett-Lennard, 6 Bt; *b* 6 April 1942; *Style—* Richard Barrett-Lennard, Esq

BARRIE, Dr Herbert; *b* 9 Oct 1927; *Educ* Wallington County GS, Univ Coll and Med Sch London (MB BS, MD); *m* 1963, Dinah Castle, MB, BS, FRCPath; 1 s (Michael), 1 da (Caroline); *Career* hon conslt paediatrician Charing Cross Hosp 1966-; sr physician 1984-86; hon conslt paediatrician Parkside Hosp Wimbledon; examiner London Univ and RCP; FRCP; *Recreations* tennis, writing; *Style—* Dr Herbert Barrie; 3 Burghley Ave, Coombe Hill, New Malden, Surrey KT3 4SW (☎ 01 942 2836); Parkside Hospital, London SW19 5NX

BARRIE, Jane Elizabeth; *née* Pearson; da of William Pearson, of Somerset, and Bessie, *née* Knowles; *b* 11 Sept 1946; *Educ* Bishop Fox GS for Girls, Imperial Coll of Sc & Technol (BSc, ARCS); *m* 12 Dec 1970, Dr William Robert Ian, s of Dr Robert Barrie, of Somerset; *Career* stockbroker; memb of The Int Stock Exchange 1973-; dir CL Laing & Cruickshank Investmt Mgmnt Services 1985-; vice-pres Soroptimist Int of GB and Ireland 1987-, chm of govrs Bishop Fox's Sch Taunton 1984-, chm Somerset & Avon Constabulary Taunton Deane & W Somerset Div Crime Prevention Panel 1987-; *Recreations* sailing, bridge; *Clubs* Royal Dart Yacht; *Style—* Mrs Jane E Barrie; Hollydene, Kingston St Mary, Taunton, Somerset TA2 8HW (☎ 0823 45388); Cl-

Alexanders Laing & Cruickshank, 4 Mendip House, High Street, Taunton, Somerset TA1 3SX (☎ 0823 254351, fax 0823 334225)

BARRINGTON, Lady; Constance Doris; da of Ernest James J Elkington, of London; *m* 1930, Sir Charles Barrington, 6 Bt (d 1980); 2 da; *Style—* Lady Barrington

BARRINGTON, John William; s of late Col John Barrington, DSO, and gggs of Sir Joseph Barrington, 1 Bt; hp to Baronetcy of cous, Sir Alexander Barrington, 7 Bt; *b* 28 Oct 1917; *Educ* Stowe, RMC Sandhurst; *m* 1, 1948, Annie (d 1985), da of late Florian Wetten, of Chur, Switzerland; 2 s, 1 da; m 2, 27 Dec 1986, Evelyn Carol Paterson, da of late Oscar Bernard Broten, of Oslo, Norway; *Career* serv WWII, Maj Royal Irish Fusiliers, served Middle E 1937-39, France 1939 and at Dunkirk, captured Leros Nov 1943, (POW Germany), GHQ Mid E Jerusalem to 1948; professional real estate appraiser (private practice Alberta and Br Columbia); AACI, FRI; *Recreations* skiing, hunting, fishing; *Clubs* Calgary Petroleum; *Style—* John Barrington, Esq; Ste 204, 119 Muskrat St, Bariff, Alberta, Canada; Barrington & Co, PO Box 894, Invermere, BC, V0A 1K0, Canada (☎ 604 342 3591); 300 Kipling Sq, 611 - 10th Ave S W, Calgary, Alberta, T2R 0B2, Canada (☎ 403 266 1370)

BARRINGTON, Nicholas John; CMG (1982), CVO (1975); s of Eric Alan Barrington (d 1974), of Trumpington, Cambridge, and Agnes Mildred, *née* Bill; *b* 23 July 1934; *Educ* Repton, Clare Coll Cambridge (MA); *Career* 2 Lt RA 1952-54; FO (Persian language trg) 1957-58, language student Tehran 1958-59, oriental sec Kabul 1959-61, FO 1961-63; UK Delgn to Euro Communities 1963-65, first sec Pakistan 1965-67; euro econ dept FO 1967-72 (later private sec Cwlth Rets Off and FCO); head of chancery and counsellor Japan 1972-75, FO 1975-78 counsellor Cairo 1978-81, head of Br interests section Tehran 1981-83, UK Mission to UN (NYC), econ summit coordinator 1984, asst under sec of state (public depts) 1984-87, ambass to Pakistan 1987-; Order of Sacred Treasure third class Japan 1975; FRSA, Fell Royal Soc of Asian Studies, Fell Egypt Exploration Soc; *Recreations* tennis, drawing, theatre; *Clubs* Athenaeum, Royal Cwlth Soc; *Style—* Nicholas Barrington, Esq, CMG, CVO; c/o Foreign and Commonwealth Office, King Charles St, London SW1; 33 Gilmerton Ct, Trumpington, Cambridge

BARRINGTON, 11 Viscount (I 1720); Patrick William Daines Barrington; also Baron Barrington (I 1720), Baron Shute (UK 1880); sits as Baron Shute; s of Hon Bernard Barrington (d 1959, 2 s of 9th Viscount Barrington, JP, DL), and Eleanor, da of Sir Thomas Snagge, KCMG, JP, DL, sometime a Co Ct judge; suc unc 1960; *b* 29 Oct 1908; *Educ* Eton, Magdalen Coll Oxford; *Heir* none; *Career* barr 1940, formerly hon attaché Berlin; *Style—* The Rt Hon the Viscount Barrington; c/o House of Lords, SW1

BARRINGTON, Raymond Lewis; s of Walter Lewis Barrington, of Redland, Bristol, and Muriel, *née* Adams (d 1980); *b* 25 July 1928; *Educ* St Brendans Coll Bristol; *m* 14 March 1953, Shirley, George William Yarwood (d 1981), of Hilperton, Wilts; 1 da (Katharine b 1958); *Career* Glos Regt 1946-48; mgmnt conslt Peat Marwick Mitchell & Co 1957 (consultancy ptnr 1963, ret 1981), chm Fairford Electronics Ltd 1982 (chm and md 1985); hon tres Kingsbridge Cons Club 1982-; town cncllr Kingsbridge 1982-87, dist cncllr South Hams 1983- (chm Housing 1988-); Freeman City of London 1977, Liveryman Worshipful Co of Wheelwrights 1977; FCA 1963, FCMA 1966, Hon FBCS (pres 1973-74); *Recreations* golf, crossword solving; *Clubs* Thurlestone Golf ; *Style—* Raymond Barrington, Esq; Lukes Farm, Kingsbridge, Devon (☎ 0548 3933); Fairford Electronics Ltd, Coombe Works, Derby Rd, Kingsbridge, Devon (☎ 0548 7494, fax 0548 3118)

BARRINGTON-WARD, Dr Edward James; s of Sir Lancelot Barrington Ward, KCVO, FRCS (d 1953), of St Edmunds, and Catherine (Mamie), *née* Reuter (d 1984); *b* 19 July 1942; *Educ* Eton, Gonville and Caius Coll Cambridge, St Bartholomews Hosp (MA, MBChir); *m* 24 July 1969, Brigid, da of William J Concannon Tuam, of Co Galway; 2 da (Elaine b 1971, Catherine b 1973); *Career* GP Bury St Edmunds 1970-87, med dir: St Nicholas Hospice Bury St Edmunds 1986-87, Highland Hospice Inverness 1987; cncl memb BASC 1935-82, fndr chm research/conservation ctee BASC, memb disciplinary ctee BASC 1977; tstee Youth & The Countryside Educn Tst, vice pres Fenland Wildfowlers Assoc; MRCS, LRCP; *Recreations* shooting, fly fishing; *Style—* Dr Edward J Barrington-Ward; c/o Natwest Bank, 7 Cornhill, Bury St Edmunds; Highland Hospice, Ness House, 1 Bishops Road, Inverness (☎ 0463 243132)

BARRINGTON-WARD, Frank; s of Frank Ward (d 1940), and Florence Bertha, *née* Thompson (d 1936); *b* 8 April 1928; *Educ* Kind Edward VI Sch Aston Birmingham, St Catherine's Coll Oxford (MA); *m* 11 Aug 1951, Heather Beatrice, da of Reginald Walter William Warmington (d 1947); 3 s (Miles b 1956, Simon b 1957, d 1985, Piers b 1963); *Career* Army 1946-48, RAEC HQ Berlin 1947; overseas magistrate Fiji 1971-74, high ct dist registrar Birmingham 1974-80 co ct registrar Oxford 1980-; memb: Rotary Club Oxford, Oxfordshire cc 1958-67; memb The Law Soc 1956; *Recreations* rowing, skiing; *Clubs* Leander, Henley, Oxon, Ski Club of GB; *Style—* Frank Barrington-Ward, Esq; Crown Ct Co Ct, Oxford Combined Ct Centre, St. Aldate's, Oxford OX1 1TL (☎ 0865 248448)

BARRINGTON-WARD, Simon; *see*: Coventry, Bishop of

BARRITT, Sir David Thurlow; s of late David Webster Barritt (d 1945), and Rachel Barritt; *b* 17 Oct 1903; *Educ* Newcastle-under-Lyme HS, N Staffs Poly (BSc Eng); *m* 1931, Hilda Marshall, da of Ernest Carbert Creyke; 1 s; *Career* chm Cammell Laird 1971-79; FEng, FInstE, FIChemE; kt 1969; *Style—* Sir David Barritt; 7 Prestbury Court, Castle Rise, Prestbury, Cheshire SK10 4UR (☎ 0625 829716)

BARRON, Derek Donald; s of Donald Frederick James Baron (d 1967), of Beckenham, Kent, and Hettie Barbara, *née* McGregor; *b* 7 June 1929; *Educ* Beckenham GS, Univ Coll London; *m* 16 June 1963, Rosemary Ingrid, da of Lionel George Brian (d 1984); 2 s (Andrew b 1965, Adam b 1968); *Career* served intelligence Corps 1947-49; cncl memb: Prince's Youth Business Tst, Business in the Community; chm and Chief Exec Ford Motor Co Ltd 1986-; chm Ford Motor Credit Co Ltd 1986-, dir and vice-pres ops Ford Brazil 1985-86, vice pres Ford Motor de Venezuela 1982-85, sales and mktg dir Ford Brazil 1979-82, gp dir southern Euro sales Ford Europe 1977-79, MD Ford Italy 1973-77, gen sales mgr overseas mkts, Ford US 1971-73 Mktg Assoc Ford US 1970-71, tractor mangr, Ford Italiana 1963-70, Ford 1951 and Tractor Gp 1961; CBIM 1987, FIM 1987, FIMI 1987; *Clubs* RAC; *Style—* Derek Barron, Esq; Ford Motor Co Ltd, Warley, Essex (☎ 0277 253000, fax 0277 262066, telex 995311 FORDCO G)

BARRON, Sir Donald James; DL (N Yorks 1971); s of Albert Gibson Barron, of Edinburgh, and Elizabeth, *née* Macdonald; *b* 17 Mar 1921; *Educ* George Heriot's Sch Edinburgh, Edinburgh Univ; *m* 1956, Gillian Mary, da of John Saville, of York; 3 s, 2 da; *Career* CA; chm: Rowntree Mackintosh 1966-81, Midland Bank plc 1982-87 (dir 1972-, vice-chm 1981-82), ctee of London & Scottish Bankers 1986-1987 (memb 1985-) ; memb Bd of Banking Supervision 1987-; tstee Joseph Rowntree Meml Tst 1966-73 and 1975- (chm 1981-); dir Investors in Indust Gp plc 1980-; dep chm: Canada Life Assur Co of GB Ltd 1980-, Canada Life Unit Tst Mngrs Ltd 1980-; dir: Canada Life Assur Co Toronto 1980-, BIM Fndn 1977-80 (memb cncl BIM 1978-80); memb: cncl CBI 1966-81 (chm CBI Educn Fndn 1981-84), NEDC 1983-85; kt 1972; *Recreations* golf, tennis, gardening; *Clubs* Athenaeum, Yorkshire (York); *Style—* Sir Donald Barron, DL; Greenfield, Sim Balk Lane, Bishopthorpe, York (☎ 0904 705 675); Joseph Rowntree Memorial Trust, Beverley House, Shipton Road, York YO3 6RB (☎ 0904 29241)

BARRON, Iann Marchant; s of William A Barron (d 1974), and Lilian E Barron (d 1969); *b* 16 June 1936; *Educ* UC Sch, Christ's Coll Cambridge (exhibitioner, MA); *m* 1961, Jacqueline Rosemary, da of Arthur W Almond (d 1978); 2 s (Marc b 1965, Simon b 1967), 2 da (Clare b 1963, Sian b 1969); *Career* chief strategic offr Inmos Ltd 1984- (dir 1978-); md: Inmos Ltd 1981-88, Computer Technol Ltd 1965-72, Microcomputer Analysis 1973-78; industl prof Bristol Univ 1985-, visiting prof Westfield Coll London Univ 1976-78, visiting fell Sci Policy Res Unit Univ of Sussex 1977-1978, visitng fell QMC London 1976, JJ Thompson medal IEE 1986, distinguished fell Br Computer Soc 1986, memb cncl Univ Coll Sch 1983-;p Hon DSc Bristol Poly 1988; *Publications* The Future with Microelectronics (with Ray Curnow) (1977), technical papers; *Style—* Iann M Barron, Esq; Barrow Ct, Barrow Gurney, Bristol; Inmos International plc, 1000 Aztec West Almondsbury, Bristol (☎ 0454 616616)

BARRON, Kevin John; MP (Lab) Rother Valley 1983-; s of Richard Barron; *b* 26 Oct 1946; *m* 1969; 1 s, 2 da; *Career* coal miner, NUM exec for Maltby colliery, pres Rotherham and District TUC; *Style—* Kevin Barron, Esq, MP; House of Commons, London SW1

BARRON, Brig Richard Alexander; s of Claud Alexander Barron, CSI, CIE, CVO (d 1948), of Newbury, and Ida Mary, *née* Ewart (d 1953); *b* 19 Mar 1913; *Educ* Wellington, RMA Woolwich, Clare Coll Cambridge (BA); *m* 11 Jan 1938, Katherine Helen, da of William Arthur Butterfield, OBE (d 1943); 2 s (Peter b 1941, Richard b 1943), 1 da (Elizabeth b 1938); *Career* cmmnd 2 Lt RE 1933, regtl duty Hong Kong and Chatham 1936-39, intelligence offr HQ 1 Corps BEF France 1939-40, instr Sch of Mil Engrg 1940-41, cmdg RE field sqdn Gds Armd Div UK 1941-42, student Staff Coll Camberley 1943, GSO2 79 Armd Div 1943-44, sr liaison offr Assault Trg and Devpt Centre 1944-45; missions to: Normandy, Italy, India, Burma, Aust, New Guinea, Germany; Lt-Col chief instr combined ops Estab India 1946-47, tech staff offr Miny of Supply UK 1948-51; missions to: USA, Canada, Germany (ex gratia award for invention of anti-tank mine), Jt Servs Staff Coll 1951, Lt Col cmdg 32 Assault Engr Regt UK 1951-55, Asst Adj Gen PS3 WO 1955-57, Col chief exec offr Atomic Test Range Aust 1957-59, sr offrs war course RN Coll Greenwich 1959-60, Col gen staff Allied Forces Central Europe France 1960-62, cmdg Engr Gp TA UK 1962-64, Brig cmdg Engr Bde TA UK 1964-67, chief engr Northern Cmd 1967-68, ret Brig 1968; dir Br Red Cross Dumfrieshire 1968-75, SSAFA rep Dumfrieshire 1968-75; memb RE team Modern Pentathlon Champs 1935; *Recreations* fishing, genealogy; *Clubs* MCC; *Style—* Brig Richard Barron; Auchenstane, Townhead St, Thornhill, Dumfriesshire DG3 5NW (☎ 0848 30556)

BARRON, Dr Thomas Hugh Kenneth; s of Thomas Bertrum Barron (d 1963), of Worthing, and Florence Nightingale Kingston; *b* 27 July 1926; *Educ* Epsom Coll, New Coll Oxford (MA, DPhil); *m* 11 July 1956, Gillian Mary, da of Owen Aubrey Sherrard (d 1962), of Lyme Regis; 3 s (Thomas b 1957, William b 1960, James b 1963), 1 da (Ruth b 1969); *Career* Petty Offr (Radar) UK 1944-47; post-doctorate fell Div of Pure Physics, Nat Research Cncl Ottawa 1955-57 (asst res offr 1957-58); lectr Sch of Chem, Univ of Bristol (reader in Theoretical Chem 1968-77); principal res scientist CSIRO Sydney 1975-76, hd of Hons Sch of Chemical Physics, Univ of Bristol (ret 1988), reader in Chemical Physics 1977 Univ of Bristol 1977-; papers and review articles on Thermal Expansion and other thermodynamic properties of solids; *Style—* Dr T H K Barron; 3 Carnarvon Rd, Redland, Bristol (☎ 0272 43956); School of Chemistry, Univ of Bristol, Bristol 8 (☎ 0272 303682)

BARROW, Anthony John Grenfell; s and h of Capt Sir Richard John Uniacke Barrow, 6 Bt; *b* 24 May 1962; *Style—* Anthony Barrow, Esq

BARROW, Brian Morris; s of Geoffrey Barrow (d 1963), of Torquay, and Winifred Horbury Gaston, *née* Morris (d 1965); *b* 16 Jan 1924; *Educ* HMS Worcester, Stanford Univ (BSc); *m* 1, 1948, Jane Vandervort; 1 s (Andrew), 3 da (Pamela, Victoria, Melanie); m 2, 1963, Joan Barnes; m 3, 1975, Kari Elizabeth, da of Per Aasen (d 1985), of Hamar, Norway; 2 s (Nicolai b 1976, Jonathan b 1981); *Career* Naval Offr 1941-46, N and S Atlantic, Indian Ocean, Pacific; petroleum geologist: Peru 1951-54, Colombia 1954-58, Bolivia 1958, Ecuador 1958-60, Nigeria 1960-63, USA 1963-64, UK 1964-68, Argentina 1968-71, Sweden 1971-74, Norway 1974-84; md A J Drilling Ltd, dir Jebsens Travel; dir Pacnorse Drilling Corp; *Recreations* sailing (yacht 'Our Boys'), fishing, shooting; *Clubs* Royal Norwegian Yacht (Oslo); *Style—* Brian M Barrow, Esq; 4 Primrosebank Ave, Cults, Aberdeen AB1 9PD (☎ 0224 861994); A J Drilling Ltd, Jebsen House, Crawpeel Rd, Aberdeen AB1 4LG (☎ 0224 878218, telex 739527)

BARROW, Charles Murray MacFarlane; s of Dr Richard Murray Barrow (d 1962), of Wokingham, and Eleanor Mary, *née* Vincent (d 1962); *b* 4 Jan 1917; *Educ* Harrow; *m* 28 April 1953, Stella Huguette, da of Paul Burnell Binnie (d 1971), of France; 1 da (Priscilla b 1954); *Career* civil servant; served Maj KSLI 1940-46 and No20 Mil Mission Madagascar, Col serv 1949, princ immigration offr Tanganyika 1960; Tanganyika Foreign Serv 1961, ret 1963; *Recreations* genealogy, walking, travel, visiting antiquities; *Style—* Charles M M Barrow, Esq; Mornewood Cottage, Piddlehinton, Dorchester, Dorset DT2 7TE (☎03004 446)

BARROW, Hon Mrs Hilary Ann; *née* Evans; o da of Baron Evans of Hungershall (Life Peer); *b* 22 July 1931; *m* 1954 (m dis 1963), William John Barrow, s of Hugh P Barrow, of Ockley, Surrey; 2 s (Sebastian b 1955, Ashley b 1958), 1 da (Melanie b 1961); *Style—* The Hon Mrs Barrow; Duck Cottage, Puncknowle, Dorchester, Dorset DT2 9BW

BARROW, Dr Jack; s of Stanley Barrow (d 1963), of Surrey, and Winifred Evelyn, *née* Fox; *b* 14 Dec 1916; *Educ* City of London Sch, St Thomas's Hosp Med Sch (MB BS, MRCS, LRCP); *m* 10 March 1942, Mariane Wynne, da of Robert Noel Anderson (d

1966), of Glos; 1 s (Peter b 1947), 1 da (Ann b 1949); *Career* Capt RAMC, ME and Burma 1942-46; conslt to Home Office in Genito-Urinary Med, physician i/c dept of genito-urinary med St Thomas's Hosp, ret 1981; past pres Med Soc for Study of Veneral Diseases 1980-81; author of works on genito-urinary medicine and contributor to medical textbooks; FRSM; *Recreations* walking, gardening; *Style—* Dr Jack Barrow; 1 Lauriston Rd, Wimbledon, London SW19 4TJ; Carters Cottage, Sherrington, Warminster, Wilts BA12 0SN; Albert Embarkment Conslting Rooms, 199 Westminster Bridge Rd, London (☎ 01 928 5485)

BARROW, Julian Gurney; s of G Erskine Barrow (d 1979), and Margaret Armine Macinnes (d 1977); bro of Simon Hoare Barrow, *qv*; *b* 28 August 1939; *Educ* Harrow; *m* 1971, Serena Catherine Lucy, *née* Harington; 2 da; *Career* landscape and portrait painter; *Recreations* painting, travel; *Style—* Julian Barrow, Esq; 33 Tite St, London SW3 4JP (☎ 01 352 4337)

BARROW, Kate, Lady; (Alison) Kate; da of Capt Russell Grenfell, RN (d 1954, writer and naval historian; Naval Correspondent for The Times during WWII; attended Nuremberg Trials to defend a German Admiral; descendant of Pascoe Grenfell (1729-1810), of Marazion), of Wick House, Downton, Salisbury, and Helen Sidney Lindsay-Young, yst da of Col George Sidney Sheppard, CMG, JP, of Malton House, Shanklin, Isle of Wight; *b* 24 June 1940; *Educ* Hatherop Castle Glos; *m* 1961 (m dis 1976), Capt Sir Richard John Uniacke Barrow, 6 Bt; 1 s (Anthony b 1962), 2 da (Nony b 1963, Frances b 1971); *Career* Seccombe Marshall & Campion plc; *Recreations* opera, ballet, music, theatre, gardening; *Style—* Kate, Lady Barrow; 36 South Vale, London SE19; Seccombe Marshall & Campion plc, 7 Birchin Lane, London EC3V 9DE (☎ 01 283 5031)

BARROW, Maj (Samuel) Peter; MC (1940); of Hugh Palliser Barrow (d 1978), and Claire Sinclair, *née* Styles (d 1974); *b* 29 June 1916; *Educ* Wellington, RMA Woolwich; *m* 1, 1 Jan 1944 (m dis 1950), Peggy Hester Pauline Gibbes, da of Lord Victor Paget; 1 s (Bryan b 6 Aug 1946); m 2, 20 May 1950, Mary Constance Astley-Cooper, da of Capt Basil Hamilton Piercy RN (d 1957); 4 s (Charles b 16 March 1951, Antony b 6 April 1953, Christopher (triplet) b 6 April 1953, James (triplet) b 6 April 1953); *Career* cmmnd RA 1936, serv WWII France, Belgium, Holland, Germany (despatches 1940), captured 1940, escaped 1940, ret with rank of Maj 1947; dir: Samuel Barrow and Co Ltd 1948-68, Barrow Hepburn and Gale Ltd 1961-68; mangr Abbey Life Assur Co 1968-81, ret 1981; chm Laughton Cons Assoc, hon tres Laughton PCC, hon tres E Sussex Army Benevolent Fund; Liveryman Worshipful Co of Leathersellers 1948, (Master 1981-82); *Recreations* shooting, fishing, gardening, painting; *Clubs* Army and Navy; *Style—* Maj Peter Barrow, MC; Prospect House, Laughton, Lewes, Sussex (☎ 032 183 249)

BARROW, Capt Sir Richard John Uniacke; 6 Bt (UK 1835); s of Maj Sir Wilfrid Barrow, 5 Bt (d 1960); *b* 2 August 1933; *Educ* Beaumont; *m* 1961 (m dis 1976), (Alison) Kate, da of late Capt Russell Grenfell, RN; 1 s; 2 da; *Heir* s, Anthony John Grenfell Barrow b 24 May 1962; *Career* served Irish Gds 1952-60; Int Computers and Tabulators Ltd 1973; *Style—* Capt Sir Richard Barrow, Bt

BARROW, Simon Hoare; s of G Erskine Barrow (d 1979), of IOM, and Margaret Armine MacInnes (d 1977), bro of Julian Gurney Barrow, *qv*; *b* 4 Nov 1937; *Educ* Harrow, Christ Church Oxford, Hill Sch Pennsylvania ESU Exchange; *m* 1, 1964 (m dis 1977), Caroline Peto Bennett; 1 s (Thomas), 3 da (Sasha, Emmeline, Rebecca); m 2, 1983, Sheena Margaret, da of Maj Gen Sir John Anderson KBE; 1 da (Kate); *Career* 2 Lt Scots Gds 1956-58; dir Charles Barker Gp 1978; Ayer Barker 1978, chief exec Charles Barker Human Resources 1987; *Recreations* sailing; *Clubs* Brooks's; *Style—* Simon Barrow, Esq; 16 Chelsea Embankment, London SW3 (☎ 01 352 7531); Charles Barker plc, 30 Farringdon St, EC4 (☎ 01 634 1180)

BARROW, Simon Richard; s of Brig Richard Barrow, CBE (d 1977), of Liphook, Hants, and Jean, *née* McKay; *b* 11 Jan 1936; *Educ* Charterhouse; *m* 17 Aug 1962, Kirsten Ingrid Louise, da of Niels-Christian Stenerup, of Lugano, Switzerland; 3 da (Louise Ingrid Jean b 9 Nov 1964, Pernille Margaretha b 10 Oct 1966, Nicola Kirsten b 31 March 1972); *Career* Binder Hamlyn 1954-60, Darling & Co (Sydney Aust) 1961-65, Schroder Wagg & Co Ltd 1965-67, Kleinwart Benson Ltd 1967-84 (dir 1979-84), ptnr Ernst & Whinney 1984-87, dir Henry Ansbacher & Co Ltd 1987-; memb Worshipful Co of Skinners 1957; memb ICAEW; *Recreations* golf, tennis, skiing, opera; *Clubs* City of London, Liphook GC; *Style—* Simon Barrow, Esq; Fiddlers Copse, Richmond Lane, Plaistow, Nr Billinghurst, West Sussex RH14 0NT (☎ 040 388 250); Henry Pinsbacher & Co Ltd, One Mitre Square, London EC3A 5AN (☎ 01 283 2500, fax 01 626 9707)

BARROWCLOUGH, Sir Anthony Richard; QC (1974); s of Sidney Barrowclough, of 28 Albion St, W2; *b* 24 June 1924; *Educ* Stowe, New Coll Oxford; *m* 1949, Mary Agnes, yr da of Brig Arthur Francis Gore Pery-Knox-Gore, CB, DSO (d 1954); 1 s (Richard b 1953), 1 da (Claire b 1956); *Career* barr Inner Temple 1949, rec of the Crown Ct 1972-; Parly cmmr for Admin 1985-, Health Serv cmms 1985-; kt 1988; *Style—* Sir Anthony Barrowclough, QC; 60 Ladbroke Grove, London W11; The Old Vicarage, Winsford, nr Minehead, Somerset

BARRY; *see*: Milner-Barry

BARRY, Anthony James; s of late Edmund Barry, of Douglas, IOM; *b* 31 July 1931; *Educ* Old Swan Inst, Liverpool Coll of Bldg; *m* 1958, Margaret, da of William Foulkes; 1 s, 1 da; *Career* md R Mansell (Westminster), dir Englemere Services Ltd; past pres Chartered Inst of Building, chm Business and Technician Educn Cncl; memb Cncl of Nat Academic Awards: tres Chartered Inst of Building ; *Recreations* swimming, reading, shooting, flying; *Clubs* Sonning Working Men's, RAC, The Livery; *Style—* Anthony Barry, Esq

BARRY, Sir (Lawrence) Edward Anthony Tress; 5 Bt (UK 1899), of St Leonard's Hill, Clewer, Berks, and Keiss Castle, Wick, Caithness-shire; Baron de Barry of Portugal, Lord of the Manors of Ockwells and Lillibrooke, Berks; s of Maj Sir Rupert Barry, 4 Bt, MBE (d 1977); *b* 1 Nov 1939; *Educ* Haileybury; *m* 1968, Fenella, da of Mrs Hilda Hoult, of Knutsford, Cheshire; 1 s, 1 da; *Heir* s, William Rupert Philip Tress Barry b 13 Dec 1973; *Career* former Capt Gren Gds; *Style—* Sir Edward Barry, Bt; 3 Sunnyside Cottages, Warehorne Rd, Ham Street, Kent (☎ 023 373 2454)

BARRY, James Edward; s of James Douglas Barry (d 1971), of Southgate, Glamorgan, and Margaret Agnes, *née* Thornton; *b* 27 May 1938; *Educ* Merchant Taylors' Crosby, Brasenose Coll Oxford (MA); *m* 11 June 1963, (Ann) Pauline; 3 s (Matthew b 28 Sept 1967, David b 23 Jan 1972, William b 23 Dec 1976); *Career* Nat Serv RASC and Intelligence Corps 1957-59; called to the Bar Inner Temple 1963, practiced NE circuit 1963-85, stipendiary magistrate South Yorks 1985-; rec of Crown Ct 1985-; *Recreations* reading, home life; *Style—* James Barry, Esq; Law Courts, College Rd, Doncaster, South Yorkshire DN1 3HS

BARRY, Lady Margaret; *née* Pleydell-Bouverie; da of 6 Earl of Radnor, CIE, CBE (d 1930); *b* 26 June 1903; *m* 1923, Lt-Col Gerald Barry, MC (d 1977), late Coldstream Guards, elder s of William James Barry, JP (d 1952), 4 s of Sir Francis Tress Barry, 1 Bt; 1 s, 5 da; *Style—* Lady Margaret Barry

BARRY, (John) Michael; s of Thomas Ernest Barry, MBE (d 1942), and Mary Josephine, *née* Furlong (d 1964); *b* 20 April 1924; *Educ* Dulwich, Queen's Coll Oxford (BA, MA, DPhil); *m* 8 Sept 1956, Elaine Mary, da of Ryle Edward Charles Morris (d 1972), of Carmarthen; 2 s (Thomas b 1958, Alexander b 1960), 1 da (Veronica b 1965); *Career* res fell Univ of Chicago 1948-51, univ lectr in agric sci Oxford Univ 1951-, fell St John's Coll Oxford 1960-, estates bursar St John's 1977-87; author of numerous scientific books and pubns; tres Oxford Univ Boat Club 1967- (memb Oxford crew 1946 boat race); *Recreations* hunting; *Clubs* Vincent's, Leander; *Style—* Michael Barry, Esq; Shilton House, Shilton, Oxon OX8 4AG (☎ 0993 842369); St John's Coll, Oxford OX1 3JP (☎ 0865 277300)

BARRY, Patrick Hayden; OBE (1989); s of Eric Hayden Barry (d 1969), of Storrington, Sussex, and Nancy Muriel, *née* Farror (d 1979); *b* 30 Jan 1924; *Educ* Clifton, Royal West of England Acad, Sch of Architecture Bristol; *m* 8 May 1954, Elizabeth Selina (Bess), da of Sir Thomas Symonds Tomlinson (d 1965); 1 s (William Hayden b 1957); *Career* architect 1947; asst Easton & Robertson 1948-56, conslt Fairhursts 1989- (ptnr 1957-81, sr ptnr 1981-89); chm Jt Contracts Tbnl for Standard Form of Bldg Contract 1984-88 (memb 1974-79 and 1981-83), pres Manchester Soc of Architects 1977, chm The Selcare (Gtr Manchester) Trust 1984-89, memb ct Univ of Manchester; RIBA 1947, ACIArb 1976; *Recreations* astronomy and sailing; *Clubs* Arts, St James's (Manchester), Itchenor Sailing, Royal Anglesey YC, Royal Northern and Clyde YC; *Style—* Patrick Barry, Esq, OBE; Fairhursts, PO Box 24, Bank Chambers, Faulkner St, Manchester M60 1EH (☎ 061 236 7722, fax 061 236 2226, telex 668 682)

BARRY, Rt Rev (Noel) Patrick; 2 s of Dr T St J Barry (d 1962), of Wallasey, Cheshire and Helen Agnes, *née* Walsh (d 1977); *b* 6 Dec 1917; *Educ* Ampleforth, St Benet's Hall Oxford (MA); *Career* headmaster Ampleforth 1964-79 (housemaster 1954-64); chm Headmasters' Conf 1975, Conf of Catholic Colls 1973-75; Abbot of Ampleforth 1984-; *Style—* The Rt Rev Patrick Barry, OSB; Ampleforth Abbey, York (☎ 043 93 421)

BARRY, (Donald Angus) Philip; CBE (1980, OBE 1969); s of John Angus Barry (d 1946), and Dorothy Ellen Averill; *b* 16 Sept 1920; *Educ* Fort Augustus Abbey Sch; *m* 1942, Margaret Ethel Balfour, da of David Orr, MD (d 1941); 5 s (Michael, Hugh, Gavin, Nigel, Richard), 1 da (Philippa); *Career* dir: John Barry Ltd 1946-81 (md 1965-81), Swanfield Mill Ltd 1963-; memb: visiting ctees HM Borstal Instns Edinburgh, Dumfries, Polmont 1946-58 (chm 1965-81), SACTO 1953-58, Parole Bd for Scotland 1968-80 (chm 1974-80); chief inspr of Prisons for Scotland 1981-85; ret; *Clubs* Univ of Edinburgh Staff; *Style—* Philip Barry Esq, CBE; c/o Bank of Scotland, 28 Bernard St, Edinburgh EH6 6OD

BARRY, Lady Sarah Sue; *née* Stanhope; da of 11 Earl of Harrington; *b* 12 Dec 1951; *Educ* Lawnside; *m* 1970, Robert John Barry; 3 s (Mark b 1972, Guy b 1975, Tristan (twin); *Career* involved in bloodstock business with husband; *Recreations* art, gardening; *Style—* Lady Sarah Barry; Mellon Stud, Kildimo, Co Limerick, Eire (☎ 061 393329, fax: 061 393541)

BARRY, Sheila, Lady; Sheila Georgina Veronica; da of Maj George Joseph Francis White, MBE, of Longacre, Andover Rd, Winchester; *m* 12 May 1951, as his 2 w, Maj Sir Rupert Barry, 4 Bt, MBE (d 1977); 3 s (Timothy b 1952, Nicholas b 1957, Jonathan b 1960) 2 da (Tara b 1954, Xandra b 1962); *Style—* Sheila, Lady Barry; Brisley Rise, Willesborough Lees, Ashford, Kent

BARSTOW, Josephine Clare (Mrs A Anderson); CBE (1985); da of Harold Barstow, of Sussex, and Clara Edith, *née* Shaw; *b* 27 Sept 1940; *Educ* Birmingham Univ (BA), London Opera Centre; *m* 1, 1964 (m dis) Terry Hands; m 2, 1969, Ande Anderson; *Career* opera singer, freelance 1971-; most important roles: Violetta in Traviata, Elisabeth de Valois, Lady Macbeth, Leonora in Forza del Destino, Salome, Arabella, The Marschallin, Jenufa, Emilia Marty in The Makropoulos Case, Katya Kabanova, Leonore in Fidelio, Sieglinde, Mimi, Tosca, Lady Macbeth of Mtseusk; Hon DMus Birmingham; *Recreations* breeding Arabian horses (stud farm in Sussex); *Style—* Miss Josephine Barstow; c/o John Coast, Manfield House, 376/9 Strand, Covent Garden, London WC2R OLR

BARSTOW, Stan; s of Wilfred Barstow (d 1958), and Elsie, *née* Gosnay; *b* 28 June 1928; *Educ* Ossett GS; *m* 1951, Constance Mary, da of Arnold Kershaw (d 1935); 1 s (Neil), 1 da (Gillian); *Career* novelist, short story-writer, script writer for TV; dramatisations incl: Joby, A Raging Calm, South Riding (Royal Television Socs Writer's Award 1975), A Kind of Loving, Travellers and A Brother's Tale; also written for radio and theatre; hon fell Bretton Coll, Hon MA Open Univ.; *Publications* A Kind of Loving (1960), The Desperadoes (1961), Ask Me Tomorrow (1962), Joby (1964), The Watchers on the Shore (1966), A Raging Calm (1968), A Season with Eros (1971), The Right True End (1975), A Brother's Tale (1980), The Glad Eye (1984), Just You Wait and See (1986), B- Movie (1987); *Style—* Stan Barstow, Esq; 56 Millfields, Wesley St, Ossett, W Yorks WF5 8HE (☎ 0924 273362)

BART, Lionel; *b* 1 August 1930; *Career* songwriter and playwright; *Style—* Lionel Bart, Esq; c/o 8-10 Bulstrode St, London W1M 6AH

BARTELL, Lt-Col (Hon) Kenneth George William; CBE (1977); s of William Richard Aust Bartell, and Daisy Florence, *née* Kendall; *b* 5 Dec 1914; *Educ* Coopers' Co's Sch; *m* 1955, Lucie Adèle George; *Career* pres Cncl Br Chambers of Commerce in Europe 1977-; dir: ICL (France), Wimpey France; FIB; *Style—* Lt-Col Kenneth Bartell, CBE; 5 Ave St Honore d'Eylau, Paris 75116, France (☎ 553 69 48)

BARTER, Rosemary Joy; *née* Wingfield; da of Charles Ralph Borlase Wingfield (d 1923), of Shrewsbury, and Mary Nesta Harriet, *née* Williams (d 1947); *b* 20 April 1923; *Educ* St James's Sch West Malvern; *m* 22 April 1944, Kenneth Wood Barter, s of Herbert Wood Barter (d 1944), of Sussex; 2 s (Andrew George b 1950, Peter David b 1955), 1 da (Mary Nesta b 1952); *Career* WRNS 1942-44; fruit grower, dir Revells Fruit Farm Ltd 1975; *Recreations* gardening, archaeology, music, art; *Style—* Mrs Kenneth W Barter; Little Revells, Linton, Ross-on-Wye, Herefordshire HR9 7SD (☎ 098 982 486); Revells Farm, Linton, Ross-on-Wye, Herefordshire HR9 7SD (☎

098 982 270)

BARTHOLOMEW, Col Hugh James; OBE (1953); s of Lt William George Bartholomew (The Border Regiment, ka Gallipoli 1915), and Hetty Octavia, *née* Jenkin (d 1942); *b* 26 August 1914; *Educ* Plymouth Coll, Sandhurst Staff Coll, RNC Greenwich; *m* 19 Aug 1943, Yvonne, da of J L Bartlett, CBE (d 1969); 2 da (Julia b 1945, Joanna b 1952); *Career* cmmnd Border Regt 1934, served N Ireland, India, NW Europe (wounded, despatches), Canal Zone, Germany; cmd 1 Queen's Own Nigeria Regt 1957-60, Cdr Trucial Oman Scouts 1961-64, Defence Attaché Cairo 1965; *Recreations* game fishing, watching sport particularly rugby, roulette, bridge; *Style*— Col H J Bartholomew, OBE; The Hive, 50 North St, Ashburton, S Devon TQ13 7QG (☎ 0364 53619)

BARTHOLOMEW, Hon Mrs; Hon Noreen; da of 3 Viscount Long, TD, DL (1967); *b* 21 Jan 1921; *m* 1947, Capt John Cairns Bartholomew, TD, o son of late John Bartholomew, of Rowde Court, Devizes; 2 s, 1 da; *Style*— The Hon Mrs Bartholomew; Poulshot House, Poulshot, Devizes, Wilts

BARTHROPP, Wing-Cdr Patrick Peter Colum; DFC (1941, AFC 1953); s of Capt Elton Peter Maxwell D'Arley Barthropp, and Winifred Mary, *née* Maxwell (d 1920); *b* 9 Nov 1920; *Educ* Ampleforth; *m* 1, Barbara Pal (m dis); m 2, 29 Aug 1962, Elizabeth Lady Rendlesham, da of Col Robin Cowper Rome, MC, of Monks Hall, Glemsford, Suffolk; *Career* RAF joined 1938, 602 Sqdn 1940 (Battle of Br), 91 Sqdn 1941 (298 operational flights), 122 Sqdn 1942 (POW 1942-45, escaped twice), Empire Test Pilots Sch 1945, Boscombe Down test pilot 1945-49, Fighter Wing Ldr 1950-52, OC admin Hong Kong 1952-54, OC RAF Honiley 1954-56, Wing-Cdr RAF Cottishall 1956-58, ret 1958; fndr Patrick Barthropp Ltd (luxury chauffeur drive private hire co) 1958, sold co to Savoy Hotel plc 1986; tstee Douglas Bader Fndn, pres 613 Sqdn Assoc; Freeman City of Hull 1941; ARAES, Cross of Lorraine, Order of King Haakon VII second class; *Books* Paddy (auto biog, second edn 1987); *Recreations* shooting, fishing; *Clubs* RAF, Aspinalls, Marks, Harry Bal; *Style*— Wing-Cdr Patrick Barthropp, DFC, AFC; The Cottage, Berwick St James, Salisbury, (☎ 0722 790476); Camelot Barthropp Ltd, Headfort Place, London SW1X 7DE, (☎ 01 235 0234, telex 8952647 CAMBAR)

BARTLAM, Thomas Hugh; s of Howard Bennett Bartlam (d 1970), and Mary Isobel Bartlam, *née* Lambert, of D'Oyley House, Ascott-under-Wychwood, Oxford; *b* 4 Dec 1947; *Educ* Repton, Cambridge Univ (MA); *m* 4 June 1977, Elizabeth Gabriel, da of Andrew David Arthur Balfour, Beech House, Shalford, Surrey; 2 s (Edward b 1979, Henry b 1985), 1 da (Harriet b 1981); *Career* merchant banker; dir: Charterhouse Bank 1984-, Charterhouse Venture Capital Fund, Charterhouse Buy-Out Fund, Charterhouse Business Expansion Fund; *Recreations* opera, gardening; *Clubs* MCC; *Style*— Thomas H Bartlam, Esq; 9 St. Ann's Villas, London W11 (☎ 01 603 6781); Southwold, Guiting Power, Glos; 1 Paternoster Row, St Pauls, London EC4 (☎ 01 248 4000)

BARTLE, Ronald David; s of Rev George Clement Bartle, of Surrey, and Winifred Marie Bartle; *b* 14 April 1929; *Educ* St John's Sch Leatherhead, Jesus Coll Cambridge (MA); *m* 1981, Hisako, da of Shigeo Yagi (d 1983), of Japan; 1 s (Nicholas b 1967), 1 da (Elizabeth b 1965) (both by former m); *Career* Nat Service 1947-49, RAEC 1948, army athletic colours 1954; barr Lincoln's Inn; practised in leading criminal chambers 1956-72; parly candidate 1958, 1959; appt Met stipendary magistrate 1972, dep circuit judge 1974-78; chm Inner London Juvenile Courts 1973-79; memb of HO Advsy Cncl on Drug Abuse 1987; Freeman City of London 1976; elected Steward of Worshipful Co of Basket Makers 1987; memb Royal Soc of St George; *Books* Introduction to Shipping Law (1958), The Police Officer in Court (1984), Crime and the New Magistrate (1985), The Law and the Lawless (1987); *Recreations* reading, walking, travel, relaxing at home; *Clubs* Lansdowne, Garrick; *Style*— Ronald D Bartle, Esq; c/o Bow Street Magistrates Court, London WC2 (☎ 01 434 5270)

BARTLES-SMITH, Ven Douglas Leslie; s of Leslie Charles Bartles-Smith (d 1975), of Salop, and Muriel Rose Bartles-Smith; *b* 3 June 1937; *Educ* Shrewsbury, St Edmund Hall Oxford (MA), Wells Theol Coll; *m* 1967, Patricia Ann, da of James Garlick Coburn (d 1971), of Derbyshire; 2 s (Andrew James b 1969, Peter Nathaniel b 1976), 1 da (Sarah Elizabeth b 1971); *Career* Nat Serv 1956-58, 2 Lt RASC 1957, Lt 1958; curate St Stephens Westminster 1963-68, priest i/c St Michael and All Angels and All Souls 1968-72 (vicar 1972-75), vicar St Lukes Battersea 1975-85 (rural dean 1981-85), archdeacon of Southwark 1985-; *Books* Urban Ghetto (jtly 1976); *Recreations* Shrewsbury Town football, travel, reading; *Style*— The Ven the Archdeacon of Southwark; 1A Dog Kennel Hill, East Dulwich, London SE22 8AA (☎ 01 274 6767)

BARTLETT, Anthony David (Tony); s of Clifford Sydney McDonald Bartlett, of Ash, Surrey, and Sylvia Patricia, *née* Samson; *b* 21 Feb 1951; *Educ* Stamford Sch Lincs; *m* 19 April 1980, Cathy Voon Pow, da of Hiu Hon Leung, of Malaysia; 1 s (Joshua b 1984), 1 da (Melissa b 1982); *Career* chartered accountant; Neville Russell & Co 1971-74, ptnr Coopers & Lybrand 1984- (joined 1975); fell Singapore Inst of Accountants, FICA; *Recreations* swimming, theatre, gardening; *Clubs* Surrey Tennis and Country; *Style*— Tony Bartlett, Esq; 39 Brambledown Rd, Wallington, Surrey SM6 OTF (☎ 01 647 8164); Coopers & Lybrand, Plumtree Court, London EC4A 4HT (☎ 01 583 5000, 01 822 4507, fax 01 822 4652, telex 887470)

BARTLETT, (Harold) Charles; s of Charles Henry Bartlett, and Frances Kate; *b* 23 Sept 1921; *Educ* Eastbourne GS, Eastbourne Sch of Art, RCA (ARCA); *m* 1, 1950, (m dis), Elizabeth, *née* Robertson; 1 s (Dr Charles Bartlett b 1956); m 2, 1970, Olwen Elizabeth Jones; *Career* WWII servd RCS 1942-45; professional artist; many one man exhibitions in London, exhibited widely in UK and abroad, work in private & public collections; official purchases inc: V & A, Arts Cncl of GB, Nat Gallery of S Australia, Albertina Collection Vienna; pres Royal Soc of Painters in Watercolours, fell Royal Soc of Painters Etchers and Engravers; RWS, RE; *Recreations* music, sailing; *Style*— Charles Bartlett, Esq; St Andrews House, Fingringhoe, Colchester, Essex CO5 7BG (☎ 0206 28 406)

BARTLETT, Hon Charlotte Trewlove; da of 3 Baron Ashton of Hyde; *b* 22 Feb 1960; *Style*— The Hon Mrs A D Bartlett

BARTLETT, Sir (Henry) David Hardington; MBE (1944); 3 Bt (UK 1913), of Hardington-Mandeville, Somerset; s of late Hardington Bartlett and gs of Sir Herbert Bartlett, 1 Bt (d 1921); suc bro, Sir Basil Bartlett, 2 Bt (d 2 Jan 1985); *b* 18 Mar 1912; *Educ* Stowe, CCC Cambridge; *m* 1, 1936 (m dis 1974), Kathlene Rosamund, 2 da of Lt-Col W H Stanbury, of Putney; 3 s; m 2, 1974, Joyce Lillian (d 1982), da of Malcolm Odell, of Surbiton, Surrey; m 3, 1982, Jeanne Margaret Esther, da of Charles William Brewer, of St John's Wood, London; *Heir* s, John Hardington, *qv*; *Career* Lt-Col RA (TA); dir Bartlett Tst; Mens Amateur Foil Champion 1934-35, Br Olympic Fencing Team Berlin 1936; *Recreations* gardening; *Style*— Sir David Bartlett, Bt, MBE; Brockley Place, Brockley, Bury St Edmunds, Suffolk IP29 4AG

BARTLETT, George Robert; QC (1986); s of Cdr Howard Volins Bartlett, RN (d 1988), of Putney, and Angela Margaret, *née* Webster; *b* 22 Oct 1944; *Educ* Tonbridge, Trinity Coll Oxford (MA); *m* 6 May 1972, Dr Clare Virginia, da of Gordon Chalmers Fortin, of Castle Hedingham; 3 s (William b 1973, Frederick b 1979, Charles b 1982); *Career* barr Middle Temple 1966; *Recreations* cricket and other games; *Style*— George R Bartlett, Esq, QC; 9 Bowerdean Str, London, SW6 3TN; New Barn Cottage, Bepton, Midhurst Sussex, GU29 0HY; 2 Mitre Court Buildings, Temple, London, EC4Y 7BX (☎ 01 583 1380, telex 28916)

BARTLETT, James Michael Gilbert; s of Maj Michael George Bartlett, TD, and Elizabeth Marjorie, *née* Grieve; *b* 21 Mar 1947; *Educ* Bromsgrove; *m* 20 Sept 1975, (Patricia) Anne, da of Ronald Dean Cranfield (d 1976); 1 s ((James) Michael Ronald b 1981), 1 da (Catherine Anne b 1978); *Career* princ Bartlett & Co CAs 1983, chm Drive Communications Ltd 1988; dir several private cos; chm Winchcombe Deanery Synod 1980, memb Gloucs Diocesan Synod 1980; dir Gloucester Diocesan Bd of Finance 1982; tres Gloucs Branch Cncl for Preservation of Rural England 1987; Freeman City of London 1979, Liveryman Worshipful Co of Builders Merchants; FCA 1971, FBIM 1988; *Recreations* sailing, riding; *Clubs* Royal Ocean Racing, Royal Northumberland YC; *Style*— James Bartlett, Esq; Cleeve House, West Approach Drive, Cheltenham, Gloucestershire (☎ 0242 575000); Bartlett & Co, 80a Eastgate St, Gloucester, GL1 1QN (☎ 0452 501635, fax 0452 304585)

BARTLETT, John Hardington David; s and h of Sir Henry David Hardington Bartlett, 3 Bt, and Kathlene Rosamund, da of late Lt-Col W H Stanbury; *b* 11 March 1938; *Educ* St Peter's Guildford; *m* 1971, Elizabeth Joyce, da of George Thomas Raine, of Kingston; 2 s, (Andrew b 1973, Stephen b 1975); *Career* electrical and gen engrg; MInstSE, FGMC; *Recreations* construction design, model making, woodwork; *Style*— John Bartlett, Esq; Hardington House, Ermyn Way, Leatherhead, Surrey KT22 8TW

BARTLETT, John Vernon; CBE (1976); s of late Vernon F Bartlett and Olga, *née* Testrup; *b* 18 June 1927; *Educ* Stowe, Trinity Coll Cambridge (MA); *m* 1951, Gillian, da of late Philip Hoffmann, of Sturmer Hall, Essex; 4 s; *Career* consulting engr; sr ptnr and jt chm Mott Hay & Anderson; pres Inst of Civil Engrs 1982-83; FEng, FICE, FASCE, FIEAust; *Recreations* sailing; *Clubs* REYC; *Style*— John Bartlett, Esq, CBE; Mott Hay & Anderson, 20/26 Wellesley Rd, Croydon, Surrey CR9 2UL (☎ 01 686 5041)

BARTLETT, Maj-Gen (John) Leonard; CB (1985); s of Frederick Bartlett (d 1941), of Liverpool, and Eva, *née* Woods (d 1984); *b* 17 Aug 1926; *Educ* Holt GS; *m* 1952, Pauline, da of James Waite (d 1979); 2 s (Nigel, David); *Career* cmmnd RAPC 1946, served Hong Kong, Singapore, BAOR, War Off, Washington, Malta, Libya, HQ MELF 1966-67 (despatches), staff pmr and offr i/c FBPO Berlin 1968-69, GS01 (Sec) NATO Military Agency for Standardisation 1969-71, pmr Hong Kong 1972-74, Col GS MOD 1974-76, chief pmr ADP and Station Cdr Worthy Down 1976-79, chief pmr BAOR 1980-82, pmr-in-chief and inspr of Army Pay Servs 1983-86, ret; mgmnt conslt; Col cmdt RAPC 1987; Freeman City of London 1984; MBCS, FBIM; *Recreations* golf; *Clubs* Lansdowne, Royal Winchester GC, Meon Valley GC; *Style*— Maj-Gen Leonard Bartlett, CB; Lloyds Bank Ltd, The Sq, Wickham, Hants PO17 5JQ;

BARTLEY, Joseph Haydn; s of Joseph Henry (d 1968), of Cardiff, and Gertrude Lucy, *née* Wilde (d 1983); *b* 13 April 1929; *Educ* Whitchurch GS Cardiff; *m* 15 June 1957, Dianne Evine, da of Harry Rupert Marjoram, of Cardiff; 1 s (Richard b 1961), 1 da (Deborah b 1959); *Career* trg instr RAPC Nat Serv 1950-52; CA, sr ptnr Hopkin Bartley Jones & Co (until 1986), admin Merrils Ede slrs Cardiff 1987-; vice chm Welsh Assoc of Youth Clubs 1984-, scout ldr 1947-65, youth ldr 1967-85, deacon local church 1972-87, chm local festival ctee 1988; memb: Soc Incorporated Accountants 1956, FCA 1964; *Clubs* Cardiff Athletic, Glamorgan Wanderers RFC; *Style*— Haydn Bartley, Esq; 112 Rhiwbina Hill, Rhiwbina, Cardiff (☎ 0222 371111)

BARTMAN, Barry David; s of John Bartman, of London, and Lillian, *née* Mitchell; *b* 3 July 1941; *Educ* City of London Sch, LSE (BEcon); *m* 8 Oct 1966, Ennis, da of Maj Edward Guy Patrick Jessiman (d 1977), of Shoreham-by-Sea, Sussex; 1 s (Nicholas b 1972), 1 da (Carolyn b 1969); *Career* chartered accountant and fin advsr; dir: The Beckenham Gp Ltd, Meatpak Hampshire Gp Ltd, Polyfield Services Ltd, Capital Wholesale Ltd; FCA; *Recreations* tennis, skiing, astronomy, classical music, antique clocks; *Style*— Barry D Bartman, Esq; Orford, 11 Park Avenue South, Harpenden, Herts AL5 2DZ (☎ 05827 69731); 17 Albemarle St, London W1 (☎ 01 495 3909, fax 01 495 3141)

BARTMAN, Capt Roy; VRD; s of Nico Hofmeyr Bartman (d 1977), and Ruth Garner Wood (d 1986); *b* 31 Oct 1925; *Educ* Heath Mount Hertford, Aldenham; *m* 1950, Lynda Lucie, da of Frederick Louis Croxon, of Northolt, Middx; 1 s (Nicholas b 1954), 2 da (Louise b 1951, Rylla b 1958); *Career* Lt RNVR 1943-47, RNVR and RNR 1950-57; pilot BOAC 1952-64, independent airlines incl Britannia Airways, Iran Air, Nigeria Airways 1965-85 rank Capt; took part in the three Long Distance Air Races since 1945 (completed London to Sydney in record 49 hrs 44 mins 1969); *Recreations* air racing, swimming, sailing, golf; *Clubs* Navy, RAC; *Style*— Capt Roy Bartman, VRD; Belmore Hotel, Store Mandeville, Aylesbury, Bucks HP22 5UT (☎ 0296 61 2022)

BARTOLOME; *see*: de Bartolome

BARTON, Prof (Barbara) Anne; *née* Roesen; da of Oscar Charles Roesen (d 1955), of New York, NY, USA, and Blanche Godfrey Williams (d 1968); *b* 9 May 1933; *Educ* Bryn Mawr Coll Pennsylvania USA (BA), Cambridge Univ (PhD); *m* 1, 1957 (m dis 1968), William Harvey Righter; m 2, Aug 1969, John Bernard Adie Barton, *qv*, s of the late Sir Harold Montagu Barton of London; *Career* Cambridge Univ 1962-72, fell Girton Coll 1962-72, Hildred Carlile prof Bedford Coll Univ of London 1972-74, fell and tutor New Coll Oxford 1974-84, Grace II Prof of English Cambridge Univ 1984-, fell Trinity Coll Cambridge 1986-; *Books* Shakespeare and the Idea of the Play (1962), Introductions to the Comedies, The Riverside Shakespeare (1974), Ben Jonson, Dramatist (1984); *Recreations* travel, opera, fine arts; *Style*— Prof Anne Barton; Leverington Hall, Wisbech, Cambridgeshire PE13 5DE; Trinity College, Cambridge CB2 1TQ (☎ 0223 338 466)

BARTON, Sir Charles Newton; OBE, ED; s of J Barton, of Maryborough, Queensland; *b* 5 July 1907; *Educ* Maryborough Boys' GS, Qld Univ; *m* 1935, Enid, da of W Wetherell; *Career* chm Brisbane Port Authority, Qld Local Govt Grants

Commission; kt 1974; *see Debrett's Handbook of Australia and New Zealand for further details*; *Recreations* gardening; *Style*— Sir Charles Barton, OBE, ED; 78 Jilba St, Indooroopilly, Qld 4068, Australia

BARTON, David Garbutt; s of James Richard Barton (d 1983), of York, and Marion Joyce, *née* Garbutt; *b* 29 Jan 1937; *Educ* St Peters Sch York, Emmanuel Coll Cambridge, Univ Coll Hosp Med Sch, London Univ (MA, MB, BChir, MRCS, LRCS, DCH); *m* 2 April 1961, Bernice Ann, da of George Birnie Banton, of Wallasey; 2 s (Sebastian b 1963, Hugo b 1968); *Career* 2 Lt 5 W Yorks Regt (TA) 1958, Lt 1960, resigned 1962; GP Herne Bay Kent 1968-; asst med offr Univ of Kent at Canterbury 1970-; co surgn St John Ambulance Kent; Freeman City of London 1977, Liveryman Worshipful Co of Apothecaries 1977; FRCS (Ed) 1969, FRCGP 1976; *Books* author of chapter on Urinary Tract Infections in Childhood in Child Care in General Practice (second edn 1982); *Recreations* theatre, ballet, opera, member of Glyndbourne; *Clubs* BMA ; *Style*— Dr David Barton; 64 Western Esplanade, Herne Bay, Kent CT6 8DN; Lower Chitty Farm, Chislet, Near Canterbury, Kent; St Annes Surgery, Herne Bay, Kent (☎ 0227 366 945)

BARTON, Derek; s of Ronald Pascoe Barton (ka 1944), and Hetty Iris Barton; *b* 16 Oct 1934; *Educ* Henry Thornton GS; *m* 24 Aug 1957, Angela Mary, da of Patrick John O'Connell, of Oxford; 2 da (Julie Ann b Sept 3 1958, Deborah b 19 March 1963); *Career* RAF Police 1952-55; advertisement rep TV Times 1957-60, advertising mangr IPC 1960-67; Farming Press: advertisement mangr 1967-70, advertisement dir 1970-74, jt md 1974-76, chm and md 1976-; *Recreations* travel, golf, DIY; *Style*— Derek Barton, Esq; 9 Mayfield Road, Ipswich, Suffolk (☎ 0473 724 942); Farming Press Ltd, Wharfedale Rd, Ipswich (☎ 0473 43011)

BARTON, Sir Derek Harold Richard; s of William Thomas and Maude Henrietta Barton; *b* 8 Sept 1918; *Educ* Tonbridge, Imperial Coll London; *m* 1, 1944, Jeanne Kate Wilkins; 1 s; m 2, 1969, Christiane Cognet; *Career* organic chemist; directeur Inst de Chimie des Substances Naturelles Gif-sur-Yvette 1978-; FRS, FRSE; kt 1972; *Style*— Sir Derek Barton; Texas A&M University Chemistry Department College Station, TX 77843-3255 U.S.A.

BARTON, Hon Mrs Elizabeth Joan Boyd (Judy); *née* Orr; da of 1 and last Baron Boyd-Orr of Brechin, CH, DSO, MC (d 1971), and Elizabeth Pearson, *née* Callum (d 1979); *b* 8 Jan 1916; *Educ* Aberdeen Univ (MB, ChB); *m* 1943, Lt-Col Kenneth Alfred John Hale Barton, s of Robert Arthur Barton, of Grove Farm, Rogerstone, Mon; 2 s (Robert John and Kenneth Callum), 1 da (Elizabeth Anne Marie); *Career* Capt RAMC UK and India; clinical asst Stracathro Hosp until Dec 1982; *Recreations* reading, gardening; *Clubs* Oriental; *Style*— The Hon Mrs Barton; Rose Hill, North Latch, Brechin, Angus DD9 6LF (☎ 035 62 3732)

BARTON, Eric James; s of James Barton (d 1957), and Robina Edith, *née* Beveridge; *b* 2 Nov 1953; *Educ* Cumberland HS, Glasgow Univ (MA), Strathclyde Univ (LLB); *m* 13 July 1978, Heather, da of George Kennedy, of Cumbernauld; 2 s (Iain b 1980, Stuart b 1982); *Career* solicitor; tstee and co sec Cumbernauld and Kilsyth Enterprise Tst Ltd 1985-, sr ptnr Barton & Hendry slrs; *Recreations* literature, historical reading; *Style*— Eric J Barton, Esq; 14 Birkenburn Road, Cumbernauld; Barton & Hendry slrs, 8 Ettrick Walk, Cumbernauld (☎ (0236) 731816, fax 0236 730038)

BARTON, Maj-Gen Eric Walter; CB (1983), MBE (1966); s of Reginald John Barton (d 1968), and Dorothy, *née* Bradfield (d 1965); *b* 27 April 1928; *Educ* St Clement Danes Sch, Royal Mil Coll of Science (BSc), Univ Coll London (Dip Photogrammetry); *m* 1, 1963 (m dis 1983), Margaret Ann, *née* Jenkins; 2 s; m 2, 1984, Mrs Pamela Clare Frimann, da of late Reginald D Mason, of Winchelsea; *Career* RE 1948, served Mid E 1948-52, E Africa 1957-59, Mid E 1965-67; asst dir Survey MOD 1967-70, dep dir Ordnance Survey 1972-74, geographic advsr HQ AFCENT 1974-76, dir Surveys and Production, Ordnance Survey 1977-80, Maj-Gen 1980, dir of Military Survey 1980-84; Col Cmdt RE 1982-87, Hon Col TA 1984-; dir Caravan Club 1984-; *Recreations* water sports, numismatics; *Clubs* Army and Navy, Geographical; *Style*— Maj-Gen Eric Barton, CB, MBE; Aquarius, Jesters, Rectory Lane, Haywards Heath, Sussex RH16 4RQ

BARTON, (Alan) John; s of Alan Luke Barton (d 1971), of Corthorne Rd, Rickmansworth, Herts, and Helen, *née* Pullen; *b* 9 Nov 1927; *Educ* Watford GS; *m* 1, 19 July 1953 (m dis 1970), Pamela Elizabeth, da of John Errington Gibb (d 1955); 1 s (Richard b 4 Jan 1962), 1 da (Anne-Marie b 15 Nov 1964); m 2, 8 April 1982, Angela, da of Leslie Maddock Brew (d 1972), of Mettingham Castle, nr Bungay, Suffolk; *Career* Fleet Air Arm 1945-47; md (formerly gen mangr) Brew Bros Ltd 1972-83, chm and md Pennington Cross Garage Ltd 1983-; vice-pres Kensington and Chelsea C of C 1987- (chm and pres 1979-87); Freeman City of London 1981, Liveryman Worshipful Co of Coachmakers and Harness Makers 1981; FInst D 1980; *Recreations* sailing, photography; *Clubs* RAC, Royal Lymington YC; *Style*— John Barton, Esq; 24 Stanford Rd, London W8 5PZ (☎ 01 937 6855); 33 Milford Rd, Lymington, Hants SO41 8DH (☎ 0590 73 227, car tel 0836 511 197)

BARTON, John Bernard Adie; CBE (1981); s of Sir Harold Montagu Barton (d 1963), and Joyce, *née* Wale (d 1988); *b* 26 Nov 1928; *Educ* Eton, King's Coll Cambridge (BA, MA); *m* 1968 (Barbara) Anne Righter (*qv* Prof B A Barton), da of Oscar Charles Roesen; *Career* drama dir and adaptor; assoc dir RSC 1964-; dir or co-dir numerous plays incl: Othello 1972, Richard II 1973, Dr Faustus, King John and Cymbeline 1974-75, Much Ado about Nothing, Winter's Tale, Troilus & Cressida and King Lear 1976, Midsummer Night's Dream, Pillars of the Community and The Way of the World 1977, The Merchant of Venice and Love's Labour Lost 1978, The Greeks and Hamlet 1980, Titus Andronicus and Two Gentlemen of Verona 1981, La Ronde 1982, Life's a Dream 1983, The Devils 1984, Dream Play 1985, The Rover 1986, The Three Sisters 1988; dir: School for Scandal Haymarket Theatre 1983, own adaptation of The Vikings Den National Scene Bergen, Norway 1983; fell King's Coll Cambridge 1954-60; *Books* The Hollow Crown (1962, 1971), The War of The Roses (1970), The Greeks (1981), La Ronde (1981); *Recreations* travel, chess, work; *Style*— John Barton, Esq, CBE; 14 De Walden Court, 85 New Cavendish St, London W1 (☎ 01 580 6196/ 01 636 7031)

BARTON, Martin; s of Walter Barton, of 215 Cyncoed Rd, Cardiff, and Sadie, *née* Shipman; *b* 7 May 1944; *Educ* Quakers Yard GS nr Cardiff, Co GS Merthyr Tydfil S Wales; *m* 6 May 1969, Jeanette, da of Arran Lermon (d 1988), of Cardiff; 1 s (David b 1970), 1 da (Susannah b 1972); *Career* articled clerk Leyshon & Lewis CAs Merthyr Tydfil 1963-68, ptnr Curitz Berg & Co 1971 (joined 1970), formed own practice Barton Felman & Co 1979 (Barton Felman & Cotsen 1981, Barton Cotsen & Co 1983); memb: Cardiff United Synagogue, South Glamorgan Bridge Club; ACA 1968, FCA 1976; *Recreations* bridge, badminton; *Style*— Martin Barton, Esq; 15 Ty Gwyn Crescent, Cyncoed, Cardiff (☎ 0222 481471); Dominions House North, Dominions Arcade, Cardiff (☎ 0222 372641)

BARTON, (Malcolm) Peter Speight; s of Michael Hugh Barton, of Brockenhurst, Hants, and Diana Blanche, *née* Taylor; *b* 26 Mar 1937; *Educ* St Edward's Sch Oxford, Magdalen Coll Oxford (BA); *m* 7 Sept 1963, Julia Margaret, da of Hon James Louis Lindsay, *qv*; 2 s (Henry (Harry) b 1967, Christopher b 1970), 1 da (Fenella b 1965); *Career* Nat Serv 2 Lt Oxford and Bucks LI (later 1 Greenjackets) 1955-56, Capt London Rifle Bde Rangers TA 1960-63; admitted slr 1964; ptnr Travers Smith Braithwaite 1967-86; memb Stock Exchange 1986; exec dir Shearson Lehman Hutton Int Inc and Shearson Lehman Hutton Securities (formerly L Messel & Co) 1986-; memb: gen ctee house ctee and finance ctee City of London Club, Law Soc, Int Bar Assoc, City Law Club; *Recreations* walking, shooting, skiing; *Clubs* City of London; Primrose Hill, Hawkhurst (Kent) (☎ 05805 2132); 29 Campden Street, London W8 (☎ 01 229 4006); Shearson Lehman Hutton Int Inc, 1 Broadgate, London EC2M 7HA (☎ 01 260 2931 & 01 601 0011)

BARTON, Sheila Elizabeth; s of George Richard Andrews (d 1979), and Marjorie Anne Andrews; *b* 4 Jan 1929; *Educ* Beverley HS, Hull Tech Coll; *m* 1 Jan 1950, Gerald Douglas Barton, s of Douglas Stanley Barton (d 1957); 3 da (Sally b 1953, Jane b 1955, Lucy b 1958); *Career* co dir and housewife; dir: Humbrol Ltd 1957-76, Saluja Hldgs Ltd 1987-; Name at Lloyd's No 183018 1978-; tstee Charity of William Turner Beverley 1965-; *Recreations* swimming, tennis; *Clubs* Beverley Decorative and Fine Arts Soc; *Style*— Mrs Gerald D Barton; Cherry Burton, Beverley, E Yorks HU17 7RF (☎ 0964 550242)

BARTON, Stephen James; s of Thomas James Barton, of Birkenhead, Merseyside, and Vera Margaret, *née* Francis (d 1983); *b* 4 May 1947; *Educ* Birkenhead Sch, Jesus Coll Cambridge (MA), Coll of Law; *m* 20 April 1974, Catherine Monica Lloyd, da of Arthur Frederick Buttery (d 1986); 2 da (Tamsin b 1975, Claire b 1977); *Career* ptnr Herbert Smith (slrs) 1978-(asst slr 1971-78, articled 1969), memb: UK Oil Lawyers Gp, Soc for Computers and Law; Freeman Worshipful Co of Slrs; memb: Law Soc, IBA; *Books* contributing ed Butterworths Co Law Service 1985-; *Recreations* photography, gardening, walking, reading; *Clubs* Barbican Health and Fitness Centre; *Style*— Stephen Barton, Esq; Herbert Smith, Watling House, 35 Cannon Street, London EC4M 5SD (☎ 01 489 8000, fax 01 329 0426, telex 886633)

BARTOSIK, Rear Adm Josef C; CB (1968), DSC (1943); s of Tomasz Bartosik (d 1983), of Warsaw; *b* 20 July 1917,Poland; *Educ* in Poland; *m* 1, 1943 (m dis 1969), (Cynthia) Pamela (Mary), da of Humphrey Ernest Bowman, CMG, CBE (d 1965); 3 s, 1 da; m 2, 1969, Jeannine Patricia, da of Cdr Paul Orlando Bridgeman RN (d 1930), and formerly w of Alan Forde Scott (d 1986); *Career* joined Polish Navy 1935, served in Polish destroyers under Br Naval Cmd 1939-46; transfered to RN 1948; served in Admty (Ops) as Cdr 1953-54 (dep dir 1958-59); cmd: HMS Comus 1955-56, HMS Scarborough, and the 5 Frigate Sqdn 1960-61, RN Air Station Culdrose 1962-63, HMS London 1964-65; Rear Adm 1966, asst Chief of Naval Staff (Ops) MOD 1966-68; co-ord dir Aust NZ Europe Container Service ANZECS 1969-81; ret 1981; *Style*— Rear Adm Josef Bartosik, CB, DSC; 33 Cheval Place, London SW7 1EW

BARTRAM, (George) Christopher; TD (1958); s of Lt-Col Robert Appleby Bartram (d 1981), of Co Durham, and Winifred Hannah, *née* Murray (d 1985); *b* 23 August 1927; *Educ* Rugby, St Catharines Coll Cambridge (MA); *m* 9 Aug 1969, Josephine Anne Ker, da of Edward William Staveley (d 1973), of Northumberland; 2 s (Robert b 1972, Edward b 1973); *Career* second in cmd 6 Bn Durham LI 1960-63; dir Endeavour Housing Assoc 1975-; High Sheriff Co Durham 1982; *Recreations* competing with sons; *Style*— G C Bartram, Esq, TD; Eldon House, Heighington, Co Durham (☎ 0325 312 270); Endeavour Housing Assoc, 1 Grange Rd, Middlesbrough

BARTRAM, Dr Clive Issell; s of Henry George Bartram, of 42 Blenheim Drive, Oxford, and Muriel Barbara, *née* Partridge; *b* 30 June 1943; *Educ* Dragon Sch, St Edward Sch Oxford, Westminster Hosp Med Sch (MB, BS); *m* 29 Oct 1966, Michele Juliette Francois, da of John Anthony Beeston Clark (d 1988), of 11 Northanger Ct, Grove St, Bath; 2 s (Damian b 1970, Guy b 1974); *Career* conslt radiologist St Bart's Hosp 1974; St Mark's Hosp: conslt radiologist 1974, dean of postgraduate studies 1985-88 (subdean 1976), chm radiology div 1987; radiologist King Edward VII Hosp 1978; FRCR 1972, FRCP 1985; *Books* Clinical Radiology in Gastroenterolgoy (1981), Radiology in Inflammatory Bowel Disease (1983); *Recreations* walking, theatre, music; *Style*— Dr Clive Bartram; 89 Normandy Ave, Barnet, Herts EN5 2NJ (☎ 01 449 9751); St Mark's Hosp, City Rd, London EC1V 2PS (☎ 01 253 1050 ext 4055)

BARTRAM, Wing-Cdr Lionel Cecil (Bill); s of Cecil Bartram (d 1960), of Woodstock Rd, Oxford, and Lilian Maud Bartram (d 1972); *b* 20 Jan 1915; *Educ* Dragon Sch Oxford, Cheltenham; *m* 29 June 1940, Ida Mollie, da of Thomas Souness, MBE (d 1960), of Orchard Ave, Finchley, London; 2 s (Jeremy Bill b 1943, Robin Rex b 1946); *Career* joined BAF 1937, held staff and sqdn appointments, Substantive Wing Cdr 1947, served in Middle East 1937-41, UK and N Africa 1941-49, BAFO 1949, UK 1949 until ret 1958; Oxfordshire County Cncl 1958-74; transferred to Oxfordshire Area Health Authy 1974, took voluntary ret 1974 but continued to work for AHA until 1978; *Recreations* rugby, squash, tennis, caravanning; *Style*— Wing-Cdr Lionel Bartram; Hoopers, East Row, South Somercotes, Louth, Lincs LN11 7BL (☎ N Somercotes 418)

BARTRUM, Patrick Hugo; s of Stanley Hugo Bartrum (d 1939), of Kent, and Kathleen Joan, *née* Ellis (d 1987); *b* 12 Jan 1926; *Educ* Charterhouse, New Coll Oxford (BA); *m* 1950, Jacqueline Luigia, da of Albert Alfred Jucker (d 1980), of Cheshire; 2 s (Hugo b 1951, Oliver b 1957), 1 da (Giulia b 1954); *Career* served Grenadier Gds (Lt) 1944-47; dir and gen mangr Sun Alliance Insurance Gp 1978; dir Nat Supervisory Cncl for Intruder Alarms (chm 1972-80); dir Motor Insurance Repair Res Centre 1977-82; memb of HO Standing Ctee for Crime Prevention 1976-80; pres: Insurance Inst of London 1980-81, Chartered Insurance Inst 1985-86; *Recreations* skiing, hill walking, tennis, bridge, opera; *Clubs* RAC; *Style*— Patrick Bartrum, Esq; Prospect House, Whitchurch-on-Thames, Pangbourne, Berkshire (☎ Pangbourne 2158); Sun Alliance Insurance Gp, 1 Bartholomew Lane, London EC2N 2AB (☎ 01 588 2345, telex 888310-G)

BARTTELOT, Col Sir Brian Walter de Stopham; 5 Bt (UK 1875), OBE (1983), DL; s of Lt-Col Sir Walter Barttelot, 4 Bt (d 1944), and Sara, da of late Lt-Col Herbert Ravenscroft, JP, of The Abbey, Storrington, Sussex; *b* 17 July 1941; *Educ*

Eton, Sandhurst, Staff Coll Camberley; *m* 1969, Hon Fiona, *née* Weld-Forester, *qv*; 4 da; *Heir* bro, Robin Barttelot; *Career* equerry to HM The Queen 1970-71; mil sec to Maj-Gen cmdg London Dist and Household Div 1978-80, CO 1 Bn Coldstream Gds 1983-85, gen staff HQ BAOR 1985-86, Regt Lt-Col cmdg Coldstream Gds 1987-, Col 1989-; Liveryman Worshipful Co Gunmakers 1980; *Clubs* Buck's, Cavalry and Guards', Pratt's, Farmers'; *Style*— Col Sir Brian Barttelot, Bt, OBE, DL; Stopham Park, Pulborough, W Sussex RH20 1EB

BARTTELOT, Hon Lady; (Mary Angela) Fiona; *née* Weld-Forester; da of late 7 Baron Forester and Marie, da of Sir Herbert Perrott, 6 Bt, CH, CB; *b* 26 Feb 1944; *m* 1969, Lt-Col Sir Brian Walter de Stopham Barttelot, 5 Bt, *qv*; 4 da; *Career* memb Inst of King Edward VII Hosp Midhurst 1981-, pres Western Area Sussex St John Ambulance Bde 1983-; *Style*— The Hon Lady Barttelot; Keepers, Stopham, Pulborough, W Sussex

BARTTELOT, Robin Ravenscroft; s of Lt-Col Sir Walter Barttelot, 4 Bt (d 1944), and Sara, *née* Ravenscroft; bro and h of Lt-Col Sir Brian Barttelot, 5 Bt; *b* 15 Dec 1943; *Educ* Seaford Coll, Perth Univ W Australia; *m* 1987, Teresa, er da of late Kenneth Greenlees; 1 da (Emily Rose b 1 May 1988); *Career* stockbroker; *Style*— Robin Barttelot, Esq

BARWELL, David John Frank; s of James Howard Barwell, of Abbey Road, Harborne, Birmingham, and Helen Mary, *née* Phillips (d 1986); *b* 12 Oct 1938; *Educ* Lancing, Trinity Coll Oxford (MA), Institut des Hautes Etudes Internationales Geneva; *m* 1968, Christine Sarah, da of Joseph Henry Carter (d 1969) of Manor Farm, Bow Brickhill, Bucks; 1 s (Thomas b 1976); *Career* FCO 1965, Aden 1967, Baghdad 1968, Bahrain 1971, Cairo 1973, FCO 1976, Nicosia 1982, Paris 1985; *Recreations* Gregorian chant, singing Bach, wandering round the Mediterranean; *Clubs* Cercle de L'Union Interalliée Paris; *Style*— David Barwell, Esq; c/o Foreign & Commonwealth Office, King Charles Street, London SW1; British Embassy, Paris

BARWELL, Hon Mrs; Hon Sheila Margaret Ramsay; *née* McNair; 2 da of 1 Baron McNair, CBE, QC; *b* 19 Feb 1918; *m* 1946, John Harold Barwell (d 1983), s of Reginald Barwell (d 1959), of Swavesey, Cambs; 1 s (Hugh John b 1949), 3 da (Alice Marjorie Sheila b 1947, Lucy Elizabeth b 1951, Claire Bridget b 1953); *Style*— The Hon Mrs Barwell; 33 Fulbrooke Rd, Cambridge CB3 9EE

BARWICK, David John; JP; s of Richard Robert Oliver Barwick, OBE (d 1982), and Phylis Mary Goodban; *b* 10 Sept 1932; *Educ* St Lawrence Coll Ramsgate; *m* 4 Oct 1958, Gillian Cowell, da of Gerald Cowell Williams (d 1985); 3 s (Richard b 1960, Jonathan b 1961, Jeremy b 1963), 1 da (Susan); *Career* builder; pres Southern Region Building Employers Confederation 1984; dir R J Barwick & Sons Ltd 1960-87 (md 1975-87 chm 1982-87), md RJB (Plant) Ltd 1974-87; FCIOB; *Recreations* golf, gardening; *Clubs* Royal Cinque Ports Golf, IOD; *Style*— David J Barwick, Esq, JP; Overglen, St Clare Road, Walmen, Deal, Kent CT14 7QB (☎ 374897); Coombe Valley Road, Dover, Kent CT17 0UJ (☎ 203716, fax 240293)

BARWICK, Rt Hon Sir Garfield Edward John; AK (1981), GCMG (1965), PC (1964), QC (Australia 1958); s of late Jabez Edward Barwick (d 1948) and Lilian Grace Ellicott; *b* 22 June 1903; *Educ* Fort St Boys' HS Sydney, Sydney Univ (BA, LLB, LLD); *m* 1929, Norma Mountier Symons; 1 s, 1 da; *Career* barr NSW 1927, KC 1941, barr Vict 1945 (KC 1945), QC Qld 1958, pres NSW Bar Assoc 1950-52 and 1955-56, pres Law Cncl of Australia 1952-54; MHR (Lib) Parramatta NSW 1958-64, Cwlth attorney-gen 1958-64; min for External Affrs 1961-64, ldr Australia Delgn to UN 1960-64, chllr Macquarie Univ Sydney 1967-78, Chief Justice Australia 1964-81, pres Aust Inst for International Affairs 1972-; former pres Aust Nat Cncl for the Blind; kt 1953; *Recreations* sailing, gardening; *Clubs* Australian, Melbourne, Commonwealth, Royal Yacht Sqdn, Royal Sydney Yacht Sqdn; *Style*— The Rt Hon Sir Garfield Barwick, AK, GCMG; Mundroola, 133 George st, Careel Bay, Sydney, Australia

BARWICK, Neville; s of Fred Wilkinson Barwick (d 1966), of Cheshire, and Mary Neville (d 1978); *b* 19 June 1916; *Educ* Shrewsbury, Cambridge Univ (MA); *m* 3 Jan 1953, Penelope Agnes Coverdale, da of Major Roland Hampden Wall (d 1977), of Devon; 2 s (Julian b 1953, Hugo b 1957); *Career* served RA 1940-46, air defence of GB, Bde Major RA Malta, sr district offr Colonial Service Nigeria 1948-59, asst gen sec The Missions to Seamen 1967-81, hon sec annual nat service for seafarers in St Paul's Cathedral 1971-81, Church Army 1981-88 (hon tres and bd memb); *Recreations* music, theatre, film; *Clubs* Bath and County, Royal Cwlth Soc; *Style*— Neville Barwick, Esq; 6 George Street, Bathwick Hill, Bath BA2 6BW (☎ 0225 4464907)

BARWICK, Norman; s of John Barwick (d 1963), of Bristol, and Gertrude, *née* Liddell (d 1927); *b* 12 June 1917; *Educ* Sexey's Sch Bruton Somerset; *m* 21 Sept 1940, Esme Maud Sophia, da of Edward Peters (d 1942), of Bristol; 1 s (John b 1946), 1 da (Susan b 1944); *Career* mil serv RA 1939-46, Adjutant 181(M) HAA Regt 1943-44, Major, legal advsr welfare Army & RAF Middle East Forces; admitted slr 1939; Law Society Divorce Dept Newcastle-upon-Tyne 1947-57; private practice: Sunderland 1957-66, Havant 1966-; *Style*— Norman Barwick, Esq; 28 Wade Court Road, Havant, Hants (☎ 0705 484242); Longcroft Barwick & McEldowney, 13 The Pallant, Havant, Hants (☎ 0705 492295)

BASING, 5 Baron (UK 1887); Neil Lutley Sclater-Booth; s of 4 Baron Basing (d 1983), and 1 w Jeanette (d 1957), da of late Neil Bruce MacKelvie, of New York; *b* 16 Jan 1939; *Educ* Eton, Harvard (BA); *m* 1967, Patricia Ann, da of George Bryan Whitfield (d 1967), of New Haven, Conn, USA; 2 s (Hon Stuart, Hon Andrew b 1973); *Heir* s, Hon Stuart Whitfield Sclater-Booth b 18 Dec 1969; *Clubs* Harvard, Meadow Brook; *Style*— The Rt Hon the Lord Basing; 112 East 74 St, New York, NY 10021, USA (☎ 212 535 1945); 60 Broad Street, New York, NY, USA (☎ 212 269 0049)

BASINGSTOKE, Archdeacon of; see: Nash, The Ven Trevor

BASINGSTOKE, Bishop Suffragan of, 1977-; Rt Rev Michael Richard John Manktelow; s of Sir (Arthur) Richard Manktelow, KBE, CB (d 1977), of Dorking, and (Edith) Helen Saxby (d 1965); *b* 23 Sept 1927; *Educ* Whitgift Sch Croydon, Cambridge Univ (BA, MA), Chichester Theol Coll; *m* 1966, Rosamund, da of Alfred Mann, of Penrith; 3 da (Helen b 1967, Elizabeth b 1969, Katharine b 1971); *Career* ordained deacon 1953, priest 1954; curate Boston Lincs 1953-57; chaplain Christ's Coll Cambridge 1957-61; chaplain and sub-warden Lincoln Theol Coll 1961-66; vicar: Knaresborough 1966-73, St Wilfrid's Harrogate 1972-77; rural dean Harrogate 1972-77; bishop of Basingstoke and canon residentiary of Winchester Cathedral 1977-; pres: Anglican and Eastern Churches Assoc 1980-, Assoc for Promoting Retreats 1982-; *Books* Forbes Robinson: Disciple of Love (ed 1961); *Recreations* walking, reading, music; *Clubs* Nat Liberal; *Style*— The Rt Rev the Bishop of Basingstoke; 1 The Close, Winchester, Hants SO23 9LS (☎ 0962 69374)

BASS, Harry Godfrey Mitchell; CMG (1972); s of Rev Arthur Edward Bass (d 1965), of Rainford, Lancs; *b* 26 August 1914; *Educ* Marlborough, Gonville and Caius Coll Cambridge, St John's Coll Oxford; *m* 1948, Monica Mary, da of Rev Henry Frederick Burroughs (d 1957), of Hammerwood; 2 s, 1 da; *Career* high cmmr Lesotho 1970-73; *Recreations* birdwatching; *Style*— H G M Bass Esq, CMG; Tyler's Mead, Dereham Rd, Reepham, Norfolk NR10 4LA (☎ 0603 870252)

BASS, Neville M; s of Arthur Bass, of Manchester; *b* 8 June 1938; *Educ* Manchester GS, Univ of Manchester, Turner Dental Sch (LDS, BDS, VU), Eastman Dental Inst (Dip Orth); *m* 6 Jan 1968, Mona; 2 s (Alexander b 1970, Anthony b 1973); *Career* house surgn Manchester Dental Hosp 1960-61, Eastmans Dental Hosp London 1961-62 (registrar orthodontic and paedodontic depts 1962-63), gen dental practice 1964-65, conslt orthodontist USAF London 1965-69, private practice 1969-, hon clinical lectr postgrad teaching staff Royal Dental Hosp London 1972-76; Angle Soc of Europe: memb 1974-, sec 1978-81, memb scientific ctee 1988-; certification Br Orthodontic Cert Bd 1984 (memb mgmnt ctee 1985-) memb Tweed Orthodontic Fndn USA; hon lectr postgrad orthodontic teaching staff London Hosp Dental Sch 1989-; FOS, FRCS (Eng); *Recreations* listening to jazz & classical music, jogging, weight training, swimming, skiing, reading, wind surfing, sailing; *Style*— Neville M Bass, Esq; 4 Queen Anne St, London W1 (☎ 01 580 8780)

BASSET, Lady Carey Elizabeth; *née* Coke; da of 5 Earl of Leicester; *b* 5 May 1934; *m* 1960, Bryan Ronald Basset, o surviving s of Ronald Lambart Basset (d 1972), and Lady Elizabeth Basset, *qv*. He is the sr rep of the ancient family of Basset of Tehidy, Cornwall, whose ancestor, Thurstan Basset, is said to have come to England with William the Conqueror; 3 s (David b 1961, Michael b 1963, James b 1968 a Page of Honour to HM The Queen); *Style*— Lady Carey Basset; 10 Stack House, Cundy St, SW1 (☎ 01 730 2785)); Quarles, Wells-next-Sea, Norfolk

BASSET, Lady Elizabeth; *née* Legge; CVO; 2 da of 7 Earl of Dartmouth, GCVO (d 1958); *b* 5 Mar 1908; *Educ* at home; *m* 1931, Ronald Lambart Basset (d 1972, whose mother Rebecca was da of Sir William Salusbury-Trelawny, 10 Bt); 1 s (*see* Lady Carey Basset) and 1 s decd; *Career* extra woman of the bedchamber to HM Queen Elizabeth the Queen Mother 1958-82, full time woman of the bedchamber 1982-; *Recreations* reading, writing (three anthologies published); *Style*— Lady Elizabeth Basset, CVO; 67 Cottesmore Court, Stanford Road, London W8 (☎ 01 937 1803)

BASSETT, Prof Douglas Anthony; s of Hugh Bassett and Annie Jane, *née* Bassett; *b* 11 August 1927; *Educ* Llanelli GS for Boys, Univ Coll of Wales Aberystwyth (BSc, PhD); *m* 1954, Elizabeth Menna, da of Gwylim Roberts; 3 da (Sarah, Sian, Rhian); *Career* lectr Univ of Glasgow 1954-59; keeper of geology Nat Museum of Wales 1959-77 (dir 1977-85); chm: ctee for Wales of the Water Resources Bd 1968-73, advsy ctee for Wales Nature Conservancy Cncl 1973-85; Assoc of Teachers of Geology: fndr chm 1967, pres 1969, ed 1969-74; fndr memb and dir Nat Welsh-American Fndn 1980-87, memb Ordinance Survey Review Ctee 1978-80, hon professorial fell Univ of Wales Cardiff Coll 1977-; Officier de l'Ordre des Art et des Lettres 1984, Silver Medal of the Czechoslovak Soc for Int Relations 1985, Aberconway Medal of the Instn of Geologists 1985; *Style*— Dr Douglas Bassett; 4 Romilly Rd, Canton, Cardiff CF5 1FH (☎ 0222 227823); Nat Museum of Wales, Cardiff CF1 3NP (☎ 0222 397951)

BASSETT, John Cecil; s of Cecil John Bassett, of 6 Mallard Crescent, Lagoon Estate, Pagham, Sussex, and his wife Elizabeth (d 1977); descendant of J T Bassett, sometime mason contractor involved in Royal Albert Hall and Alexandra Palace; *b* 13 Jan 1928; *Educ* Cheshunt GS; *m* 20 Mar 1953, Josephine, da of Ernest Saunders White (d 1964; descendant of Thomas White, of Stonehouse Manor, Gloucester); 2 s (Peter John b 1955, Robert Edward b 1965); *Career* served RE 1946-49; chartered surveyor, incorporated rating valuer, arbitrator; erstwhile Surveyor of Works Egypt 1949; three times examination prizewinner RICS; pres: Rating & Valuation Assoc 1974, Surveyors Assoc 1982; serving memb and Father of Cncl R & VA; memb cncl London Chamber of Commerce and Industry; advsr many city insts incl: Bank of England, Corpn of Lloyd's, Stock Exchange, Olympia & York; FRICS, PPRVA, ACIArb, FInstD; *Publications* author numerous technical articles; Bean & Lockwood's Rating Valuation Practice (co-author sixth & seventh editions); *Recreations* sailing, rugby football; *Clubs* Gresham, American, Little Ship; *Style*— John C Bassett, Esq; 19 Solent Ave, Lymington, Hants SO41 9SD (☎ 0590 76388); 22 Sandstone, 5 Kent Rd, Kew, Richmond (☎ 01 948 5618); 71 Queen Victoria St, London, EC4V 4DE (☎ 01 236 4040)

BASSNETT, Peter; s of Herbert Bassnett, and Emma, *née* Bacon; *b* 6 Dec 1940; *Educ* Stand GS Manchester; *m* 12 March 1965, Gabrielle Charlotte, *née* Hall; 2 da (Samantha Jane b 1970, Annabelle b 1972); *Career* dir field ops Abbey Life 1982-86 (agency mangr 1971-82), sales dir Aetna Life Insur Co Ltd 1986-; memb judging panel Br Quality Assoc; FLIA; *Recreations* sailing; *Clubs* Royal Motor YC; *Style*— Peter Bassnett, Esq; 21 Branksome Towers, Westminster Rd, Poole, Dorset BH13 6JT

BASTABLE, Arthur Cyprian; OBE (1984); s of Herbert Arthur Bastable (d 1943), and Edith Ellen, *née* Allen (d 1954); *b* 9 May 1923; *Educ* St Georges Sch Harpenden, Manchester Univ (BSc); *m* 3 April 1946, Joan, da of David Cardwell, of 59 Pastoral Way, Swansea; 1 s (Roger b 1952), 1 da (Susan b 1955); *Career* served WW II RNVR; chartered electrical engr; Fielden Electronics Ltd 1947-50, Ferranti plc 1950-88, sales mangr Vac Physics Dept Scottish Gp Ferranti 1957-71, gen mangr Ferranti Dundee 1971-86, dir Ferranti Astron Ltd 1983-86, dir Ferranti Indust/Electronics Ltd 1984-86; memb: Dundee Port Authy, CBI in Scotland, Dundee and Tayside Chamber of Commerce (pres 1970-71); CEng, FIEE, FBIM; *Recreations* sailing, skiing, hill-walking; *Clubs* Danish, R Tay YC, Scottish Ornithologists; *Style*— Arthur Bastable, Esq, OBE; Hunters Moon, 14 Lorne Street, Monifieth, Dundee DD5 4DU (☎ 0382 532043); Ferranti Industrial Electronics Ltd, Thornybank, Dalkeith, Midlothian EH22 2NG (☎ 031 663 2821)

BASTIN, Prof John Andrew; s of Authur Edward Bastin (d 1930), of London, and Emma Lucy Price, *née* Dunk (d 1955), of Essex; *b* 3 Jan 1929; *Educ* Sir George Monoux GS, CCC Oxford (BA), London Univ (PhD); *m* 1, 1959 (m dis 1982); 1 s (Richard Edward b 28 Feb 1964), 1 da (Claire Damaris b 2 Jan 1962); m 2, Oct 1985, Aida Baterina, da of Felicano Delfino (d 1985), of Sala Cabuyao, Laguna, Luzon; *Career* Nat Serv Leading Seaman RN 1948-49; lectr Univ of Nigeria Ibadan 1952-56, res fell Univ of Reading 1956-59; Queen Mary Coll London Univ 1959-84: lectr, reader-in-astrophysics, prof, head of dept, now emeritus prof; initiated res gp in far infrared astronomy 1960- 75 (discovered solar enhancements at these wavelengths assoc with sunspots, lunar dumbbell formation and seismic propagation, the liquification model and limitations of earths atmosphere for astronomy); princ investigator NASA US Lunar Samples prog (far infrared and thermal measurements made with lunar rock) 1969-76, Leverhulme emeritus fell (light scattering applied to landscape) 1985-88; landscape painting currently exhibited in several London and provincial galleries; hon MA Oxon 1956; FRAS (former cncl memb); *Recreations* architecture, music, tennis; *Style*— Prof John Bastin; 27 Endwell Road, Brockley London SE4 2NE (☎ 01 635 8501)

BASTYAN, Lady - Victoria Eugénie Helen; *née* Bett; da of William Bett, of St Leonard's-on-Sea, Sussex; *b* 24 Jan 1907; *Educ* governess schs in: Russia, England, Switzerland; *m* 1944, Lt-Gen Sir Edric Montague Bastyan, KCMG, KCVO, KBE, CB (d 1980); 1 s (David Ion Gordon b 1945); *Career* Secretarial MD 1945, DStJ 1969; *Clubs* Special Forces; *Style*— Lady Bastyan; Flat 42, 52 Brougham Place, N Adelaide, 5006, S Australia

BASUALDO, Hon Mrs (Lucy); *née* Pearson; da of 3 Viscount Cowdray; first cous of Duke of Atholl and third cous of Duke of Marlborough, through her paternal gm, Agnes, da of Lord Edward Spencer Churchill, 5 s of 6 Duke of Marlborough; *b* 11 April 1954; *Educ* Daneshill Basingstoke; *m* 1972 (m dis 1978), Capt (Hector) Luis Juan Sosa-Basualdo, s of Lt-Col Hector Sosa-Basualdo, of Inocencio Sosa, Argentina; 1 s (Rupert Peregrine b 1976), 1 da (Charlotte Pearson b 1974); *Career* landowner, farmer; *Recreations* skiing, tennis, polo; *Clubs* Piping Rock (Long Island NY), Wellington (Palm Beach); *Style*— The Hon Mrs Lucy Basualdo; 370 Park Avenue, Box 48, New York, NY 10022, USA; Cowdray Park, Midhurst, Sussex; Dunecht, Aberdeenshire

BASUALDO, Capt (Hector) Luis Juan Sosa de Sosa; s of Lt-Col Don Hector de Sosa-Basualdo, of Inocencio Sosa, Argentina, and Countess Amanda Theresa Bissone-Facio de Arias; *b* 5 Sept 1945; *Educ* Catholic Univ Buenos Aires (DL), Yale, RAC Cirencester; *m* 1972 (m dis 1978), Hon Lucy Pearson, da of 3 Viscount Cowdray (*qv*); 1 s (Rupert Peregrine Pearson b 1976), 1 da (Charlotte Pearson b 1974); *Career* Capt Argentine Mounted Grenadiers 1964-69; emigrated to USA 1969, drafted by US Army, fought in Vietnam (wounded in action 1971; Purple Heart 1971), discharged with honours; dir Onassis Inc; Knight of Malta, Order of St George (Argentina) 1969; *Recreations* polo, hunting, shooting, flying helicopters, fishing; *Clubs* Racquet & Tennis (New York), Beaufort Hunt; *Style*— Capt Luis Basualdo; 370 Park Av, New York, NY 10022, USA(☎ 212 735 9700); c/o Onassis, 104 Rue de l'Universite, Paris 7 (☎ 010 331 4550 4975); Junin 1339, Buenos Aires, Argentina (☎ 010 541 83 2068)

BATCHELOR, Geoffrey Maurice; s of Col Maurice Batchelor, CBE (d 1973), and Ella, *née* Turner (d 1960); *b* 24 Feb 1928; *Educ* Repton, Pembroke Coll Oxford (MA); *m* 3 Sept 1955, Yvonne, da of Denis G Flather, of Sheffield; 4 s (Stephen b 1958, Nigel b 1959, Martin b 1962, Roger b 1964); *Career* cmmnd RA 1947-48; barr Gray's Inn; Unilever plc 1952-87 (head of external affairs 1980-87), Elida-Gibbs Mktg 1952-60, head of external affairs Lever Bros 1970-80 (formerly advtsg mangr 1960-69), sr conslt Sanders and Sidney plc 1987-, dir gen Mktg Soc 1988; memb Worshipful Co of Glaziers 1956; *Recreations* travel, golf, family; *Clubs* Oxford and Cambridge, St Georges Hill GC; *Style*— Geoffrey Batchelor, Esq; The Marketing Society, 206 Worple Rd, London SW20 8PN (☎ 01 879 3464, fax 01 879 0362)

BATCHELOR, Prof Sir Ivor Ralph Campbell; CBE (1976); s of Ralph C L Batchelor, and Muriel, *née* Shaw; *b* 29 Nov 1916; *Educ* Edinburgh Academy, Edinburgh Univ; *m* 1941, Honor Wallace Williamson; 1 s, 3 da; *Career* emeritus prof of psychiatry Univ of Dundee (ret 1982); memb: Med Res Cncl 1972-76, Royal Cmmn on the NHS 1976-79, Scottish Hosp Endowments Res Tst 1984-; FRSE 1960-; hon fell Royal Coll Psychiatrists 1984-; kt 1981; *Clubs* Athenaeum; Royal and Ancient Golf; *Style*— Prof Sir Ivor Batchelor, CBE

BATCHELOR, Prof (John) Richard; s of Basil William Batchelor CBE (d 1956), of Pembury, Kent, and Esme Clare, *née* Cornwall; *b* 4 Oct 1931; *Educ* Marlborough, Emmanuel Coll Cambridge (MA, MD) , Guy's Hosp Med Sch; *m* 23 Jul 1955, Dr Moira Ann, da of William McLellan (d 1987), of Tadworth, Surrey; 2 s (Andrew b 1957, Simon b 1962), 2 da (Annabel b 1959, Lucinda b 1964); *Career* Nat Serv MO RAMC 1957-59; lectr & sr lectr Dept of Pathology, Guy's Hosp Med Sch 1962-67; dir Blond McIndoe Res Centre Queen Victoria Hosp East Grinstead, prof of transplantation res RCS 1967-79, prof of tissue immunology Royal Postgrad Med Sch 1979-82, prof of immunology Royal Postgrad Med Sch 1982-; memb MRC Grants Ctees and Cell Bd 1972-78; chm: Arthritis & Rheumatism Cncl Grants Ctee 1986-88, Scientific Coordinating Ctee 1988-; pres Int Transplantation Soc 1988-; memb Court Worshipful Co of Skinners (master skinner 1984-85); FI Biol; *Recreations* tennis, skiing; *Clubs* Brooks Queen's; *Style*— Prof JR Batchelor; Little Ambrook, Nursery Rd, Walton-on-the-Hill, Tadworth, Surrey KT20 7TU (☎ 0737 812028); Dept of Immunology, Royal Postgraduate Medical School, Hammersmith Hospital, Du Cane Rd, London W12 0NN (☎ 01 740 3225)

BATCHELOR, Stephen James; s of Frank Ralph Batchelor, of The Spinney Mynthurst, Leigh, Reigate Surrey, and Doreen Majorie Batchelor; *b* 22 June 1961; *Educ* Millfield; *Career* hockey player; Silver Medallist Champions Trophy, Bronze Medallist Los Angeles Olympic Games 1984, Silver Medallist World Cup London 1986, Silver Medallist European Cup Moscow 1987, Gold Medallist Olympic Games Seoul 1988; *Style*— Stephen Batchelor, Esq; The Spinney, Mynthurst, Leigh, Nr Reigate, Surrey (☎ 0293 862 849)

BATE, Anthony; s of Hubert George Cookson Bate (d 1986), and Cecile Marjorie, *née* Canadine (d 1973); *b* 31 August 1927; *Educ* King Edward VI Sch Stourbridge Worcs; *m* 22 May 1954, Diana Fay, da of Kenneth Alfred Charles Caws Watson (d 1939), of Seaview, IOW; 2 s (Gavin Watson b 25 Feb 1961, Mark Hewitt b 23 Sept 1963); *Career* Nat Serv RNVR 1945-47; actor; entered professional theatre 1953, numerous performances since; first West End appearance Inherit the Wind (St Martins 1960), Treasure Island (Mermaid Theatre 1960), Happy Family (Hampstead Theatre Club 1966), Much Ado About Nothing, and Silence (RSC Aldwych 1969), Find Your Way Home (Open Space Theatre 1970), Eden End (tour 1972), Economic Necessity (Haymarket Leicester 1973), Getting Away with Murder (Comedy Theatre 1976), Shadow Box (Cambridge Theatre Co 1979), The Old Jest (tour 1980), A Flea in her Ear (Plymouth Theatre Co 1980), Little Lies (Wyndhams Theatre 1983), Master Class (tour 1984), The Deep Blue Sea (Theatre Royal Haymarket 1988), first TV appearance 1955, numerous appearances since incl: Philby Burgess and Maclean (1976), The Dutch Train Hijack (1976), The Seagull (1977), An Englishmans Castle (1978), The Trial of dUri Urlov (1978), Tinker Tailor Soldier Spy (1978), Crime and Punishment (1979), T'is Pity She's A Whore (1979), The Human Crocodile (1980), Smiley's People (1981), A Woman Called Golda (1981), Game Set and Match (1987); films incl: The Set Up (1961), Stopover Forever (1963), Act of Murder (1964), Davey Jones Locker (1964), Ghost Story (1973), Bismark (1975), Give My Ragards to Broad Street (1982), Exploits at West Poley (1985); memb BAFTA; *Recreations* listening to music; *Style*— Anthony Bate, Esq; c/o Al Parker Ltd, 55 Park Lane, London W1Y 3LB, (☎ 01 499 4232)

BATE, Sir David Lindsay; KBE (1977, CBE 1968); s of Brig-Gen Thomas Reginald Fraser Bate, CMG (d 1964), of Glanmonnow House, Garway, Herefs and Mary Ulrica Alicia, *née* Fitzwilliams (d 1974); *b* 3 March 1916; *Educ* Marlborough, Trinity Coll Cambridge (BA); *m* 1948, Thadeen June, da of Robert F O'Donnell Peet (d 1977); 2 s (David and Thomas); *Career* Maj RA 1939-46; barr, slr-gen N Nigeria 1956, high court judge N Nigeria 1957-73 (chief judge Plateau State N Nigeria 1973-77); *Recreations* fishing, gardening; *Style*— Sir David Bate, KBE; 4029 Lanchaster Rd, RR2 Duncan, BC, Canada (☎ 748 4400)

BATE, Sir (Walter) Edwin; OBE (1955); s of Peter Bate (d 1967), of Wellington, NZ, and Florence Eleanor Bate; *b* 12 Mar 1901; *Educ* Napier Boys' HS, Victoria Univ Wellington; *m* 1925, Louise, da of James Jordan; 2 s, 1 da; *Career* barr and slr 1922, pres Hosp Bds Assoc of NZ 1953-74, tstee Savings Banks Assoc of NZ 1967-69; OStJ 1957; kt 1969; *Recreations* gardening; *Style*— Sir Edwin Bate, OBE; 38 Busby Hill, Havelock North, New Zealand (☎ 777448); 53 Rainbow Drive, Taupo

BATE, Rex; OBE (1980); s of Ferdinand Bate (d 1958), of Solihull, and Kate Emeline, *née* Batchelor (d 1975); *b* 18 June 1911; *Educ* West Bridgford Sch, Loughborough Univ; *m* 1937, Peggie, da of James Heron Watt (d 1955), of Ealing; 1 s (Richard), 2 da (Penelope, Sara); *Career* RE attached Indian Army 1940-45, served Burma Army and XIVth Army in Burma Lt Col; chartered electrical and mechanical engr; dir: Brush Electrical Engrg Co Ltd 1946-54, Enfield Cables Ltd 1954-58; md Renold Ltd 1959-73 (dir 1973-80); chm London Assoc for the Blind 1975-; *Recreations* music, rowing, fishing, bridge; *Clubs* East India and Sports, Leander; *Style*— Rex Bate, Esq, OBE; The Dial House, Chobham, Surrey (☎ 099 05 8176)

BATE, Terence Charles; s of Harry James Bate (d 1975), of Preston, Lancs, and Annie Evelyn, *née* Gore (later Graffy); *b* 3 Oct 1930; *Educ* Hele's Sch Exeter, Liverpool Univ (BVSc), Lancashire Poly (LLB), Inns of Court Sch of Law; *m* 24 Feb 1961, Mary Evelyn, da of Capt Herbert Edgar Newth (d 1964); 2 s (Anthony John b 1961, Christopher David b 1962), 2 da (Carolyn Mary b 1964, Nicola Anne b 1967 d 1969); *Career* vet surgn, ptnr practice 1955-85; head clinical vet services RSPCA 1987-; memb: cncl BVA 1978-, cncl Vet Pub Health Assoc (past pres); former vet advsr Assoc of Dist Cncls, vet surgn W Lancs DC 1979-85; former part time lectr: Manchester Poly, Lancs Coll of Agric; called to the Bar Lincoln's Inn 1986; MRCVS; *Recreations* cycling, running, walking; *Clubs* Cyclists' Touring; *Style*— Terence C Bate, Esq; Lowden Lodge, Lowden Hill, Chippenham, Wilts SN15 2BT (☎ 0249 651385); RSPCA Headquarters, Causeway, Horsham, West Sussex RH12 1HG (☎ 0403 64181, fax 0403 41048)

BATE, Maj-Gen William; CB (1974), OBE (1963), DL (Surrey 1980); s of S Bate, of Warrington; *b* 6 June 1920; *m* 1946, Veronica Mary Josephine, *née* Quinn; 2 s, 2 da; *Career* cmmnd 1941, served WW II Burma (despatches three times), Co Cdr 7 and 11 Armd Divs 1951-53, DQ (Ops and Plans) 1955-57, Admin Staff Coll Henley 1958, directing staff at Staff Coll Camberley 1958-60, AQ (Ops and Plans) BAOR 1961-63, Col GS Staff Coll 1965-67, ADC to HM The Queen 1969-71, Dir Admin Planning (Army) 1970-71, Dir Movements (Army) MOD 1971-73, ret; Col Cmdt RCT 1974-1986, Rep Col Cmdt RCT (1975, 1977, 1982, 1986); sec TAVR Assocs 1975-86 (dep sec 1973-75); FCIT 1967; *Recreations* cricket, tennis; *Clubs* East India, Devonshire Sports and Public Schools, MCC; *Style*— Maj-Gen William Bate, CB, OBE, DL; Netherbury, 14 Belton Road, Camberley, Surrey (☎ 0276 63529)

BATE, Dame Zara Kate; *née* Dickens; DBE (1968); da of Sidney Herbert Dickens, of Melbourne; *Educ* Ruyton and Toorak Coll; *m* 1, 1935, Capt James Fell; 3 s; m 2, 1946, Rt Hon Harold Edward Holt, PC, CH (d 1967), Prime Minister of Australia; m 3, 1969, Hon Henry Jefferson Percival Bate, MHR; *Career* chm bd St Laurent Melbourne; dir: John Stafford & Co, Colebrook Estates; Coronation Medal 1953; *Style*— Dame Zara Bate, DBE

BATE-WILLIAMS, John Robert Alexander; yr s of Maj Michael Thomas Jerome Bate-Williams, RA (ret), of Goldmead, Bindoon, Western Australia, and Rosemary Suzanne, *née* Bate (d 1979); *b* 25 Sept 1951; *Educ* private tuition, Whitefriars Sch, Stoke on Trent Coll of Building and Comerce, Univ of Wales (LLB), Inns of Court Sch of Law; *m* 4 Aug 1984, Elizabeth Anne, da of Richard Lippiatt; 1 s (Rory b 1987); *Career* called to the Bar Inner Temple 1976; memb Hon Soc of Inner Temple 1976; *Recreations* travel, rowing, tennis; *Clubs* Jokers; *Style*— John Bate-Williams, Esq; 4 Swan Studios, 69 Deodar Road, London, SW15 (☎ 01 874 5739); 24 Dollar St, Cirencester, Gloucestershire (☎ 0285 650567); 1 Temple Gardens, Temple, London EC4Y 9BB (☎ 01 583 1315, fax 01 353 3969)

BATEMAN, Barry Richard James; *b* 21 June 1945; *Educ* Univ of Exeter (BA); *m* Christine; 1 s (James b 1980); *Career* res dir Hoare Govett 1972-75 (investmt analyst 1967-72), mktg dir Datastream 1975-81, sr mktg dir Fidelity Int Mgmnt Ltd 1981-86, md Fidelity Investmt Servs Ltd 1986-; memb Soc of Investmt Analysts; *Recreations* photography, music, E Type Jaguars, writing; *Clubs* Jaguar Drivers; *Style*— Barry Bateman, Esq; High Trees, Pine Coombe, Shirley Hills, Croydon, Surrey CR0 5HS (☎ 01 656 8638); Fidelity Investment Services Ltd, Oakhill House, 130 Tonbridge Rd, Hildenborough, Tonbridge, Kent TN11 9DZ (☎ 0732 361144, fax 0732 832792, telex 957344 FIMLO)

BATEMAN, Sir Cecil Joseph; KBE (1967, MBE 1944); s of Samuel Bateman, of Belfast, and Annie Jane, *née* Mills; *b* 6 Jan 1910; *Educ* Queen's Univ Belfast; *m* 7 June 1938, Doris Mitchell, da of late William Linklater Simpson, of Belfast and Thurso; 1 s, 1 da; *Career* WWII Maj RA; entered NICS 1927, dir of estab Min of Fin 1958-63, sec to Cabinet and clerk of Privy Cncl of NI 1963-65, perm sec Min of Finance and head NICS 1965-70; chm G Heyn & Sons Ltd 1971-88; dir: Nationwide Bldg Soc 1970-85, Allied Irish Banks 1970-80, Allied Irish Investmt Bank 1971-80; *Style*— Sir Cecil Bateman, KBE; 26 Schomberg Pk, Belfast BT4 2HH (☎ 0232 63484)

BATEMAN, Dr Christopher John Turner; s of Sir Geoffrey Hirst Bateman, of Thorney, Graffham, W Sussex, and Lady Margaret Bateman; *b* 3 June 1937; *Educ* Marlborough, Univ Coll Oxford (MA, BM, BCh), St Thomas's Hosp Med Sch; *m* 1,

1961, Hilary (d 1984), da of James Stirk, of Worcester; 1 s (Alastair b 1963), 2 da (Jennifer b 1964, Caroline b 1966); m 2, 1986, Joan Valerie, da of Dr J Cann, of Southampton; *Career* conslt haematologist: Chichester Health Authy 1973, King Edward VII Hosp Midhurst; vice chm St Wilfrids Hospice Chichester; Freeman City of London 1961, memb of Ct Worshipful Co Haberdashers 1987; FRC Path 1982; *Recreations* fishing, tennis, golf, shooting; *Style—* Dr Christopher Bateman; The Barn, Fordwater Lane, Chichester PO19 4PT (☎ 0243 528 638); St Richards Hospital, Chichester PO19 4SE (☎ 0243 788 122, extn 706)

BATEMAN, Derek; s of Thomas Bateman, of Ellesmere Port, and Millicent,*née* Blackburn; *b* 8 Feb 1949; *Educ* Stanney Secdy Modern Tech Sch; *m* 5 Aug 1978, Jenny, da of Samuel Howarth (d 1986), of Gateshead, Tyne and Wear; 4 step s (Hilton b 1960, Sean b 1965, Wayne b 1967, Craig b 1971), 1 step da (Jaqualine b 1962); *Career* engr Vauxhall Motors 1965-70, machinest and fitter Vauxhall 1970-82; elected: borough cncllr Ellesmere Port and Neston 1974-78, cncllr 1977- (dep ldr Cncl and chm Strategic Planning and Transportation ctee); chm: Mancester Ship Canal Steering Ctee, Nat Public Tport Forum; vice chm: Assoc of CCs Planning and Tport Ctee and Sub Ctee 1987-88; *Recreations* Labour Party; *Style—* Derek Bateman, Esq; 168 Cambridge Road, Ellesmere Port, Cheshire (☎ 051)355 6575; County Hall, Chester (☎ 0244 602 194, fax 0244 603 800)

BATEMAN, Geoffrey Campion; s of George Campion Bateman (d 1969), of Guildford, and Jessie, *née* Grantham (d 1962); *b* 5 Nov 1901; *Educ* Cranleigh; *m* 31 Dec 1925, Margery Prudence, da of Edgar Tremellen (d 1920), of London ; 1 s (Peter Tremellen Campion b 1928), 1 da (Wendy April Campion b 1933); *Career* WWII Maj RASC 1939-45, serv France, W Desert (POW despatches 1945); ophthalmic optician; chm: G C Bateman Ltd, Guildford Round Table No3 1929-30, Soc of Opticians 1946-47; dir Yvonne Arnaud Theatre Guildford 1956-76;; *Books* Diary of a Temporary Soldier (1986); *Recreations* fly fishing, gardening, reading; *Style—* Geoffrey Bateman, Esq; Midland Bank Guildford, Ladymead, 13 Flower Walk, Guildford GU2 5EP (☎ 0483 504571); The Hallams, Littleford Lane, Shamley Green, Surrey GU5 0RH (☎ 893933)

BATEMAN, Sir Geoffrey Hirst; s of Dr William Hirst Bateman, JP (d 1959), of Rochdale, Lancs, and Ethel Jane, *née* Scrimgeour (d 1964); bro of Sir Ralph Melton Bateman, *qv*; *b* 24 Oct 1906; *Educ* Epsom Coll, Univ Coll Oxford; *m* 1931, Margaret, da of Sir Samuel Turner (d 1955); 3 s, 1 da; *Career* surgn St Thomas's 1938-71; memb cncl Royal Coll of Surgeons 1963-67; kt 1972; *Recreations* golf, fishing; *Style—* Sir Geoffrey Bateman; Thorney, Graffham, Petworth, W Sussex GU28 0QA (☎ 079 86314)

BATEMAN, Lt Col Giles Barthrop; OBE (1982); s of Sqn-Ldr Anthony Edward Barthrop Bateman (d 1970), and Dorothea May Pryce, Aspinalli (d 1973); *b* 10 Jan 1939; *Educ* Sutton Valence Sch, Staff Coll, Nat Defence Coll; *m* 31 Dec 1966, Susan Jennifer (Sue), da of Robert Ben Chalcraft, of Greenford, Middlesex; 2 s (Noel Christopher Barthrop b 1969, Alexander (Alex) James Barthrop b 1972); *Career* cmmnd Queen's Own Royal W Kent Regt 1958, regtl and staff posts incl: England and Cyprus 1958, Kenya 1961, Br Guiana 1964, Singapore 1965-67, Bahrain 1968, N Ireland 1969 and 1975, Australia 1976-78; Sch of Service Intelligence 1982-85; MOD; Defence Intelligence and Gen Staff posts 1985-89 ; *Recreations* gardening, music, books; *Clubs* Royal Cwlth Soc; *Style—* Lt Col Giles Bateman, OBE; c/o Lloyds Bank, Hawkhurst, Kent; MOD, Metropole Building, Northumberland Ave, London WC2N 5BL (☎ 01 218 5788)

BATEMAN, Maryrose Christine; da of Cdr G A Bateman, RN, and M R Bateman, *née* Carruthers; *b* 16 Mar 1935; *Educ* The Abbey Malvern Wells Worcs, St Anne's Coll Oxford (MA); *Career* asst English mistress: Westonbirt Sch 1957-60, Ashford Sch Kent 1960-61, Lady Eleanor Holles Sch Middlesex 1961-64; head of English dept: Westonbirt Sch 1964-69, Brighton and Hove HS 1969-71; headmistress: Berkhamsted Sch for Girls 1971-80, Perse Sch for Girls 1980-; *Recreations* theatre, opera, crosswords; *Style—* Miss Maryrose Bateman; 27 Leys Rd, Cambridge CB4 2AR (☎ 0223 315 373); Perse Sch for Girls, Union Rd, Cambridge (☎ 0223 359 589)

BATEMAN, Paul Terence; s of Nelson John Bateman (d 1984), and Frances Ellen, *née* Johnston; *b* 28 April 1946; *Educ* Westcliff HS, Univ of Leicester (BSc); *m* 18 Jan 1970, Moira; 2 s (Michael b 1973, Timothy b 1977); *Career* Save and Prosper Gp Ltd 1967-: graduate in secretarial dept 1967-68, asst to gp actuary 1968-73, mktg mangr 1973-75, gp mktg mangr 1975-80, gp mktg and devpt mangr 1980-81, exec dir mktg and devpt 1981-88, chief exec 1988-; exec dir Robert Fleming Holdings Ltd 1988-; chm bd of govrs Westcliff HS for boys; *Recreations* yachting, squash; *Clubs* Royal Burnham YC; *Style—* Paul Bateman, Esq; 25 Plymtree, Thorpe Bay, Essex SS1 3RA (☎ 0702 587152); Save and Prosper Group Ltd, 1 Finsbury Ave, London EC2M 2QY (☎ 01 588 1717, fax 01 247 5006, telex 883838 SAVPRO G)

BATEMAN, Peter Tremellen Campion; s of Capt Geoffrey Campion Bateman, of Ladymead, Flower Walk, Guildford, and Margery Prudence, *née* Tremellen (d 1985); *b* 12 June 1928; *Educ* Clifton, Hertford Coll Oxford (MA); *m* 1 May 1954, Janet Katherine, da of Capt Ernest Hyatt Box (d 1953), of Guildford; 2 s (Nicholas Peter b 1955, Dominic Charles b 1960), 1 da (Anna Katherine b 1958); *Career* Nat Serv RASC 1947-49, 2 Lt 1948; md GC Bateman Ltd (family co of ophthalmic opticians) 1975- (dir 1954); chm Soc of Opticians 1968-70, Optical Info Cncl 1987-88; Capt Hertford Coll RUFC 1951, memb Guildford Round Table 1952-64; Freeman City of London, Liveryman Worshipful Co of Spectacle Makers 1971; *Recreations* skiing, swimming, photography, oil painting; *Style—* Peter Bateman, Esq; Holly House, Goose Rye Rd, Worplesdon, Surrey (☎ 0483 232 636); The Hallams, Littleford Lane, Shamley Green, Guildford, Surrey GU5 0RH (☎ 0483 893933)

BATEMAN, Sir Ralph (Melton); KBE (1975); 3 s of Dr William Hirst Bateman, JP (d 1959), of Rochdale, Lancs, and Ethel Jane, *née* Scrimgeour (d 1964); bro of Sir Geoffrey Hirst Bateman, *qv*; *b* 15 May 1910; *Educ* Epsom Coll, Univ Coll Oxford (MA); *m* 1935, Barbara Yvonne, 2 da of Herbert Percy Litton (d 1939), of Heywood, Lancs, and Grace Vera Litton (d 1968); 2 s, 2 da; *Career* chm Stothert and Pitt 1977-85; dep chm Rea Bros 1979-85 (dir 1977-), Furness Withy 1979-84 (dir 1977-84); pres Confedn of Br Indust 1974-1976, former chm Turner and Newall plc; former dep chm Crosby Woodfield; vice pres and former chm of governors of Ashridge Coll of Mgmnt, former chm Cncl of Buckingham Univ; Hon DSc Univ Salford, hon fell Univ of Manchester Inst of Science and Technol; FCIS, CBIM, FRSA, FInstD ; *Style—* Sir Ralph Bateman, KBE; 2 Bollin Court, Macclesfield Rd, Wilmslow, Cheshire SK9 2AP

BATEMAN, Richard Harrison; s of Herbert F A Bateman, of Southborough, Kent, and Minnie, *née* Harrison (d 1986); *b* 21 April 1945; *Educ* Hampton Sch; *m* 1 April 1967, Maureen Winifred, da of Michael Devaney; 1 s (Stephen Harrison b 7 April 1968), 1 da (Kate Mary b 12 May 1970); *Career* Coutts & Co 1963-67, Charles Fulton & Co (int money brokers) 1967-70, Kirkland Whittaker Gp Ltd 1970- (dir 1978-); chm London Subsidiaries: KW (Foreign Exchange) Ltd, KW (Sterling) Ltd, KW (Currency Deposits) Ltd 1986-; England rugby football trials 1966; *Recreations* sports, metaphysical poetry; *Clubs* Richmond RFC; *Style—* Richard Bateman, Esq; Kirkland Whittaker Group Ltd, 76-80 Great Eastern Street, London EC2A 3JL (☎ 01 739 0099, fax 01 739 7629, telex 894710)

BATES, Alan Arthur; s of Harold Arthur Bates (d 1976), of Bank House, Bradbourne, Derbyshire, and Florence Mary, *née* Wheatcroft; *b* 17 Feb 1934; *Educ* Herbert Strutt GS, Belper Derbys, RADA; *m* 1970, Victoria Valerie, da of Roland Ward (d 1980); 2 s (Tristan b Nov 1970, Benedick (twin) b Nov 1970); *Career* RAF 1952-54; actor; *Theatre* English Stage Co (Royal Court Theatre, London): The Mulberry Bush, Cards of Identity, Look Back in Anger, The Country Wife, In Celebration; London (West End): Long Day's Journey into Night, The Caretaker, The Four Seasons, Hamlet; Butley London and NY (Evening Standard Best Actor award 1972, Antoinette Perry Best Actor award 1973), Poor Richard NY, Richard III and The Merry Wives of Windsor Stratford Ontario, Venice Preserved Bristol Old Vic, Taming of the Shrew Stratford-on-Avon 1973, Life Class 1974, Otherwise Engaged Queen's 1975 (Variety Club of GB Best Stage award 1975), The Seagull Duke of York's 1976, Stage Struck Vaudeville 1979, A Patriot for Me Chichester Haymarket 1983, Victoria Station and One for the Road Lyric Studio 1984, The Dance of Death Riverside Studios Hammersmith 1985, Yonadab NT 1985, Melon Haymarket 1987; *Films* The Entertainer, Whistle Down the Wind, A Kind of Loving, The Running Man, The Caretaker, Zorba the Greek, Nothing but the Best, Georgie Girl, King of Hearts, Far from the Madding Crowd, The Fixer (Oscar Nomination), Women in Love, The Three Sisters, A Day in the Death of Joe Egg, The Go-Between, Second Best (prodr), Impossible Object, Butley, In Celebration, Royal Flash, An Unmarried Woman, The Shout, The Rose, Nijinsky, Quarter, THe Return of the Soldier, The Wicked Lady, Duet for One, Prayer for the Dying, Pack of Lies; *Television* various plays: Plaintiff and Defendant, Two Sundays, The Collection 1977; The Mayor of Casterbridge 1978, Very Like a Whale, The Trespasser 1980, A Voyage Round My Father, Separate Tables, An Englishman Abroad 1983 (BAFTA Best TV Actor award 1984), Dr Fisher of Geneva 1984; *Recreations* driving, swimming, riding; *Style—* Alan Bates, Esq; c/o Chatto & Linnit, Prince of Wales Theatre, Coventry St, London W1 (☎ 01 930 6677)

BATES, Allan Frederick; CMG (1958); s of John Frederick Lawes Bates (d 1953), of Plumstead, London, and Ethel Hannah, *née* Potter (d 1958); *b* 15 July 1911; *Educ* Woolwich Central Sch, London Univ, Open Univ (BA 1982); *m* 1937, Ena Edith, da of John Richard Boxall (d 1944), of Charlton, London; 3 s; *Career* fin sec: Cyprus 1952-60, Mauritius 1960-64; CA 1959-; md Devpt Bank Mauritius 1964-70; IMF fin advsr: Bahama Govt 1971-74, Lesotho 1975-76; accounts advsr Belize 1982-; *Recreations* painting, carving; *Clubs* Royal Cwlth Soc, IOD; *Style—* Allan Bates, Esq, CMG; 5 Redford Ave, Coulsdon, Surrey (☎ 01 660 7421)

BATES, Sir (Julian) Darrell; CMG (1956), CVO (1954); s of E Stuart Bates, author (d 1944); *b* 10 Nov 1913; *Educ* Sevenoaks Sch, Keble Coll Oxford; *m* 1944, Susan Evelyn June, da of late Frank Sinclair; 2 s, 1 da; *Career* Colonial Service 1936-68, perm sec Gibraltar 1964-68; kt 1966; *Books* A Fly Switch from the Sultan (1961), The Shell at thy Ear (1961), The Mango and the Palm (1962), A Longing for Quails (1964), Susie (1964), A Gust of Plumes (1972), The Companion Guide to Devon and Cornwall (1976), The Abyssinian Difficulty (1979), The Fashoda Incident of 1898 (1984); *Style—* Sir Darrell Bates, CMG, CVO; 21 Carrallack, Terrace St Just, Penzance, Cornwall (☎ 073 787 640)

BATES, Air Vice-Marshal David Frank; CB (1983); s of S F Bates (d 1977), and N A Bates, *née* Story; *b* 10 April 1928; *Educ* RAF Coll Cranwell; *m* 1954, Margaret Winifred, *née* Biles; 1 s, 1 da; *Career* RAF: Station Cdr Uxbridge 1974-75, Dir of Personnel Ground 1975-76, Dir Personnel Mgmnt (ADP) 1976-79, air offr admin HQ RAF Support Cmd 1979-82; bursar of Warwick Sch 1983-85; *Recreations* cricket, most sports, gardening, model railways; *Clubs* RAF, MCC; *Style—* Air Vice-Marshal David Bates, CB; c/o Lloyds Bank Ltd, 73 Parade, Leamington Spa, Warwicks CV32 4BB

BATES, Sir David Robert; s of Walter Vivian Bates (d 1937), of Co Tyrone, and Mary Olive Bates; *b* 18 Nov 1916; *Educ* Royal Belfast Academical Inst, Queen's Univ Belfast, UCL; *m* 1956, Barbara, da of Joseph Bailey, DSO, of Qld; 1 s, 1 da; *Career* prof theoretical physics Queen's Univ Belfast 1968-73, research prof 1973-83, prof emeritus 1983-; Smithsonian Regent's fellow Harvard-Smithsonian Center for Astrophysics 1983-84; FRS; kt 1978; *Recreations* reading (history, biography); *Style—* Sir David Bates; 1 Newforge Grange, Belfast BT9 5QB (☎ 0232 665640)

BATES, Sir (John) Dawson; 2 Bt (UK 1937), MC (1943); s of Rt Hon Sir Dawson Bates, 1 Bt, OBE (d 1949), and Muriel (d 1972), da of Sir Charles Cleland, KBE, MVO, LLD; *b* 21 Sept 1921; *Educ* Winchester, Balliol Coll Oxford; *m* 30 April 1953, Mary Murray, da of late Lt- Col Joseph Murray Hoult, RA, of Norton Place, Lincoln; 2 s, 1 da; *Heir* s, Richard Dawson Hoult Bates b 12 May 1956; *Career* WWII Maj Rifle Brigade WWII; regional dir Nat Tst, ret; FRICS; *Style—* Sir Dawson Bates, Bt, MC; Butleigh House, Butleigh, Glastonbury, Somerset

BATES, Edward Robert; s and h of Sir Geoffrey Bates, 5 Bt, MC; *b* 4 July 1946; *Educ* Gordonstoun; *Style—* Edward Bates, Esq; Gyrn Castle, Llanasa, Holywell, Clwyd (☎ Prestatyn 3500)

BATES, Sir Geoffrey Voltelin; 5 Bt (UK 1880), MC (1942); o s of Maj Cecil Robert Bates, DSO, MC (d 1935), and Hylda Madeleine (d 1960), da of Sir James Heath, 1 Bt; suc (1946) unc, Sir Percy Bates, 4 Bt, GBE; *b* 2 Oct 1921; *Educ* Radley; *m* 1, 12 July 1945, Kitty (d 1956), da of Ernest Kendall-Lane, of Saskatchewan; 2 s; m 2, 31 July 1957, Hon Olivia Gwyneth Zoë FitzRoy (d 1969), da of 2 Visc Daventry; 1 da (and 1 da decd); m 3, 1971, Mrs Juliet Eleanor Hugolyn Whitelocke-Winter, da of late Cdr G Whitelocke, RN, and wid of Edward Winter; *Heir* s, Edward Bates; *Career* High Sheriff Flintshire 1969, Maj (ret) Cheshire Yeomanry; *Recreations* hunting, shooting, fishing; *Style—* Sir Geoffrey Bates, Bt, MC; Gyrn Castle, Llanasa, Holywell, Clwyd (☎ Prestatyn 3500)

BATES, Maj-Gen Sir (Edward) John (Hunter); KBE (1969, OBE 1952), CB (1965), MC (1944); s of Ernest Bates, (d 1954), of Bournemouth; *b* 5 Dec 1911; *Educ* Wellington, CCC Cambridge (MA); *m* 1947, Sheila Ann, da of Maj Herbert Norman (d 1962), of Victoria, BC, Canada; 2 s, 2 da; *Career* dir RA WO 1961-64, Cmdt RMCS

1964-67, dir Royal Def Acad 1967-69, Col Cmdt RA 1966-76, Special Cmmr Duke of York's Royal Mil Sch 1972-; personnel dir Thomson Regnl Newspapers 1969-78; master Worshipful Co of Haberdashers 1978-79; *Recreations* fishing, shooting; *Clubs* Army and Navy, Rye Golf; *Style—* Maj-Gen Sir John Bates, KBE, CB, MC; Chaffenden, Frensham Rd, Rolvenden Layne, Cranbrook, Kent TN17 4NP (☎ 0580 241 536)

BATES, John Fielding; s of Arnold Fielding Bates, OBE (d 1961), of Sheffield, and Winifred Margaret, *née* Crosland (d 1965); *b* 11 May 1925; *Educ* Trent Coll, Kings Coll Cambridge, Rotherham Tech Coll, City Polytechnic London (BSc); *m* 31 July 1954, Joan, da of John Elliott (d 1976), of Sheffield; 3 s (Martin b 1957, James b 1960, Timothy b 1964); *Career* RAF 1943-47, PO 1 Offr Air Sea Rescue 1945-46, FO Personel Offr HQ Med Cairo, AHQ Malta, HQ 90 Gp Medmenham 1946-47, released 1947; asst engr Charles Brand and Son 1952-57; res engr E Middlesex Main Drainage for J D and D M Watson later Watson Hawksley 1957-64 (ptnr 1969-85, sr conslt 1985-); FICE 1971, M Cons E 1973; *Recreations* sailing, boating; *Style—* John F Bates, Esq; 17 Marlow Mill, Mill Road, Marlow, Bucks, SL7 1QD (☎ 06284 6780); Watson Hawksley, Terriers House, Amersham Road, High Wycombe, Bucks, HP13 5AS (☎ 0494 26240, fax 0494 22074, telex 83439 WATSON G)

BATES, Lilian Marie-Adrienne; *née* Loir; da of Dr Adrien-Charles Loir (d 1941), of Paris, and Helene Catherine, *née* de Montes (d 1946); *b* 7 Nov 1908; *Educ* Cours du Parc Monceau Paris, Faculte de Medecine Paris (MD, DPH); *m* 7 March 1934, Ralph Marshall Bates, OBE, s of William Bates (d 1945), of Saltash, Cornwall; 1 s (Ralph b 1940), 2 da (Liliane b 1934, Elisabeth b 1936); *Career* med asst Miny of Health Paris 1933-34, sr med offr (mental health) Essex CC 1948-60; conslt psychiatrist: NE Essex Health Authy 1960- 81 NE Met Regnl Hosp Bd 1952-68; life memb Assoc Francaise pour l'Avancement des Sciences 1930-; MRC Psych 1971, memb BMA 1948; *Books* Notion de Droit Administratif a l'Usage du Medecin, fonctionnaire d'hygiene (1933); *Recreations* playing the harp, gardening (especially growing vegetables); *Clubs* English Speaking Union; *Style—* Dr Lilian Bates; 66 North Road, Highgate Village, London N6 4AA (☎ 01 348 1376)

BATES, Malcolm Rowland; s of Rowland Bates, of Waterlooville, Hants; *b* 23 Sept 1934; *Educ* Portsmouth GS, Univ of Warwick, Harvard Graduate Sch of Business Admin; *m* 1960, Lynda, da of Maurice Price, of Bristol; 3 da; *Career* chm Picker Int Inc, dir GEC Inc; jt md: Wm Brandt's and Sons 1974-, A B Dick Inc, Associated Electrical Industries Ltd, The English Electric Co Ltd, dep md GEC plc 1980-; *Recreations* classical music, reading, tennis; *Style—* Malcolm Bates, Esq; Mulberry Close, Croft Rd, Goring-on-Thames, Oxon RG8 9ES (☎ 0491 872214)

BATES, Hon Mrs (Margaret Eleanor); *née* Shepherd; o da of 1 Baron Shepherd, PC; *b* 14 Feb 1922; *m* 1949, Theodore Leonard Bates, s of late Theodore Leonard Bates, of 95 North Street, London; 1 s (Andrew Michael b 1952), 1 da (Suzanne Katherine Michèle b 1960); *Style—* The Hon Mrs Bates; 3 Victoria Cottages, Lydiate Lane, Lynton, N Devon

BATES, Peter Edward Gascoigne; CBE (1987); s of James Edward Bates (d 1952), and Esme Grace Gascoigne, *née* Roy (d 1960); *b* 6 August 1924; *Educ* Kingston GS, SOAS London, Lincoln Coll Oxford; *m* 15 Dec 1947, Jean Irene Hearne, da of Brig W. Campbell Grant, MC, RA (d 1966); 2 s (Jeremy b 3 March 1949, Nigel b 23 Feb 1953), 1 da (Deborah b 13 Feb 1957); *Career* cmmnd Intelligence Corps 1944, serv India, Burma, Malaya, Japan 1944-46, released 1946 with rank of Capt; Malayan Civil Serv 1947-55, Rolls-Royce Ltd 1955-57, Bristol Aircraft Ltd (later British Aircraft Corpn) 1957-64; Plessey Co plc (formerly Ltd) : gen mangr Plessey Radar 1967-71, md radar div 1971-76, dep chm Plessey Electronic Systems Ltd 1976-86; dir Gen Technol Systems Ltd 1986-, chm BOMI Ltd 1986-; memb: Electronic Engrg Assoc 1973-85 (pres 1976), cncl SBAC 1978-86 (pres 1983-86), Br Overseas Trade Bd 1984-87; FRSA 1988; *Recreations* golf, theatre, gardening; *Clubs* Army and Navy, Royal Wimbledon Golf; *Style—* Peter Bates, Esq, CBE; 12 Lindisfarne Rd, Wimbledon, London SW20 0NW (☎ 01 946 0345); General Technology Systems, Brunel Science Park, Kingston Lane, Uxbridge UB8 3PQ (☎ 0895 56767, fax 0895 32078, telex 295 607 GENTEL G)

BATES, Peter Francis; s of Lt-Col Charles Donald bates (d 1979), and Gladys Elizabeth, *née* Wilson; *b* 12 August 1934; *Educ* Friends Sch Lisburn NI, Royal GS Lancaster, Gonville and Catus Coll Cambridge (MB, BA, MB BChir), St Mary's Hosp London; *m* 1, Aug 1964 (m dis 1970), Cynthia Joan, da of Leslie Herbert Trace, of Twickenham, Middx; m 2, June 1971 (m dis 1980), Maggie, da of Bernard Wright; *Career* W Middx Hosp 1961-64, surgical registrar Wellington Hosp 1965-68; hon tutor: Royal Coll of Surgeons 1974-83, Guy's Hosp 1981; conslt gen surgn Dartford and Gravesham Health Dist 1974-; memb: Hosp Conslt Specialsts Assoc, Br Assoc of Surgical Oncology, Euro Soc of Oncology, Br Soc of Gastroenterology, Br Assoc of Surgns of GB and Ireland, Br Compter Assoc, World Medical Assoc; Freeman: Guild of the City of London 1988-, City of London 1983; Member Worshipful Co of Apothecaries 1983; FRCSI 1967, FRCSEng 1969, FICS, FRSM; *Recreations* theatre, skiing, books, collecting pictures, sculpture; *Clubs* Oxford and Cambridge, Arts, Wig and Pen, Rugby; *Style—* Peter Bates, Esq; 1 River Court, 82 St George's Sq, London SW1V 3QX (☎ 01 821 0768); 144 Harley Street London W1 (☎ 01 935 0023, fax Voice Bank 01 400 0403)

BATES, Stewart Taverner; QC (1970); s of John Bates (d 1946), of Greenock; *b* 17 Dec 1926; *Educ* St Andrews Univ, CCC Oxford; *m* 1950, Anne Patricia, da of David West, of Pinner; 2 s, 4 da; *Career* barr 1954, memb Bar Cncl 1962-66, recorder 1981-; *Style—* Stewart Bates, Esq, QC; The Grange, Horsington, Templecombe, Somerset (☎ 0963 0521)

BATES, William Paul Norman; s of Maj-Gen Sir John Bates KBE, CB, MC, of Rolvenden, Kent, and Sheila Ann, *née* Norman; *b* 29 Oct 1953; *Educ* Stonyhurst, Univ Coll London (BSC, DipArch); *m* 29 Sept 1979, Carolyn Anne Lothian, da of William Patrick Lothian Nicholson (d 1972); 1 s (Robert b 1988), 2 da (Fenella b 1982, Annabel b 1985); *Career* architect RIBA 1980, formed own practice 1984; dir Scorpio Estates Ltd 1986-; Liveryman Worshipful Co Haberdashers ; *Recreations* skiing, golf, family; *Clubs* MCC; *Style—* William Bates, Esq; 18 Kings Rd, Wimbledon, London SW19 8QN (☎ 01 540 4307)

BATESON, Alec John; s of Rear Adm Stuart Latham Bateson, CB, CBE, DL (d 1980), Pine's Nook, Ridlington, nr Uppingham, Rutland, and Marie Elphinstone Fleming, *née* Cullen (d 1985); *b* 23 Jan 1925; *Educ* Rugby, Trinity Coll Oxford; *m* 3 June 1950, (Alice) Barbara (d 1985), da of Capt (Alexander) Comrie Cowan, MC (d 1937), of 5 St Petersburg Place, London; 2 s (David Stuart b 1955, Hugh Comrie b 1957), 1 da (Julia Mary (Mrs Langton) b 1951); *Career* The Rifle Bde 1943-1947, Capt 1946, HQ 6 Airlanding Bde, 1 Para Bde in Palestine 1945-47; slr Lincolns Inn 1950; ptnr: Trowers & Hamlins (formerly Trower Still & Keeling) 1955-, Hamlins Grammer & Hamlins 1970-86 (sr ptnr); ctee memb Holborn Law Soc 1969-82 (pres 1978-79), tstee Herts Nursing Tst 1985-; memb: appeal ctee N Herts Hospice Care Assoc 1988, memb Slrs Disciplinary Tbnl 1975-, cncl Queen's Nursing Inst 1986-, The Law Soc 1950, The Lowtonian Soc 1973; *Recreations* reading, travel; *Clubs* Law Soc, Inst of Dirs; *Style—* Alec J Bateson, Esq; Bradley Springs, Codicote, Nr Hitchin, Herts; Trowers & Hamlins, 6 New Sq, Lincolns Inn, London, WC2A 3RP (☎ 01 831 6292, fax 01 831 8700)

BATESON, John Swinburne; s of William Swinburne Bateson (d 1970) and Kathryn Urquart, *née* Lyttle; *b* 11 Jan 1942; *Educ* Appleby GS, Lancaster Royal GS; *m* 30 Jan 1964, Jean Vivien, da of Robert Forsyth (d 1977); 1 s (John William Swinburne b 1972), 2 da (Kathryn Ann b 1967, Janet Mary b 1969); *Career* dir: AMEC plc 1982-, Fairclough Construction Gp plc 1980-82, Fairclough Homes Ltd, Wentworth Club Ltd, Batesons Hotels 1958 Ltd; *Recreations* gardening, chess, light aviation, golf; *Clubs* Blackpool and Fylde Aero, Wentworth Golf; *Style—* John Bateson, Esq; Clayton Croft, Ribchester Road, Clayton-le-Dale, Blackburn, Lancashire (☎ 0254 40748); AMEC plc, Sandiway House, Northwich, Cheshire, CW8 2YA (☎ 0606 883885, telex 669708)

BATESON, Prof Paul Patrick Gordon; s of Capt Richard Gordon Bateson (d 1956), and Solvi Helene, *née* Berg (d 1987); *b* 31 Mar 1938; *Educ* Westminster, King's Coll Cambridge (BA, PhD, ScD); *m* 20 Jul 1963, Dusha, da of Kenneth Matthews, of Halesworth, Suffolk; 2 da (Melissa 1968, Anna 1972); *Career* Stanford Univ Calif 1963-65; Cambridge Univ: Harkness fell, sr asst res 1965-69, lectr in zoology 1969-78, reader in animal behaviour 1978-84, dir sub dept animal behaviour 1976-88, prof of ethology 1984-; provost King's Coll Cambridge 1988- (fell 1984-88); FRS 1983; *Books* Defended to Death (with G Prins & others, 1984), Measuring Behaviour (with P Martin 1986), Growing Points of Ethology (ed with R A Hinde, 1976), Perspectives in Ethology vols 1-8 (ed with P Klopper, 1972-89), Mate Choice (ed 1983), The Domestic Cat (ed with D Turner, 1988); *Clubs* United Oxford and Cambridge; *Style—* Prof Patrick Bateson; Provost's Lodge, Kings College, Cambridge CB2 1ST (☎ 0223 350411)

BATEUP, John Brian; s of John Maynard Bateup (d 1971), of Horsmonden, Kent, and Dorothy Nellie, *née* Rose; *b* 22 August 1949; *Educ* The Judd Sch Tonbridge Kent; *m* 5 Jan 1974, Christine Anne, da of Rev William Preston, of Horsmonden, Kent; 2 s (Matthew b 1983, Timothy b 1986), 2 da (Helen b 1975, Anne b 1977); *Career* actuary; md: Reliance Mutual Insur Soc Ltd 1982-, The British Life Office Ltd, Reliance Fire and Accident Insur Corpn Ltd, Reliance Unit Mangrs Ltd, Reliance Pension Scheme Tstee Ltd; FIA; *Recreations* sport, especially table-tennis; *Clubs* IOD, Actuarial Dining; *Style—* John B Bateup, Esq; Reliance House, Tunbridge Wells, Kent TN4 8BL (☎ 0892 510033, fax 0892 510676)

BATH, 6 Marquess (GB 1789); Sir Henry Frederick Thynne; 9 Bt (GB 1641), ED, JP (Wilts 1938); also Viscount Weymouth and Baron Thynne of Warminster (GB 1682); s of 5 Marquess, KG, CB, PC (d 1946), and Violet, da of Sir Charles Mordaunt, 10 Bt; *b* 26 Jan 1905; *Educ* Harrow, Christ Church Oxford; *m* 1, 1927 (m dis 1953), Hon Daphne, da of 4 Baron Vivian, DSO; 2 s, 1 da; m 2, 1953, Virginia Penelope, da of late Alan Parsons and formerly w of Hon David Francis Tennant; 1 da; *Heir* s, Viscount Weymouth; *Career* formerly Maj Royal Wilts Yeo, memb of Cncl of HRH The Prince of Wales 1933-36, sat as MP for Frome Div of Somerset (C) Oct 1931-Oct 1935; chm Football Pools Panel 1966-87; *Style—* The Most Hon The Marquess of Bath, ED, JP; Job's Mill, Crockerton, Warminster, Wilts (☎ 0985 212279); Longleat, Warminster, Wilts

BATH AND WELLS, Bishop of 1987-; Rt Rev Dr George Leonard Carey; s of George Thomas Carey, and Ruby Catherine, *née* Gurney; *b* 13 Nov 1935; *Educ* Bifrons Secdy Modern Sch, London Coll of Divinity, Kings Coll London (ALCD, BD, MTh, PhD); *m* 25 June 1960, Eileen Harmsworth, da of Douglas Cunningham Hood; 2 s (Mark Jonathan b 28 Feb 1965, Andrew Stephen b 18 Feb 1966), 2 da (Rachel Helen b 30 May 1963, Elizabeth Ruth b 26 Oct 1971); *Career* Nat Serv 1954-56, served Egypt, Shaibah Iraq; curate St Mary's Islington 1962-66; lectr: Oakhill Theol Coll London 1966-70, St John's Theol Coll Nottingham 1970-75; vicar St Nicholas' Church Durham 1975-82, princ Trinity Coll Bristol 1982-87; memb cncl Bath Int Art Festival, patron and pres of many organizations; *Books* I Believe in Man (1976), God Incarnate (1977), The Church in The Market Place (1982), The Great Acquittal (1983), The Gate of Glory (1985), The Meeting of The Waters (1986); *Recreations* walking, reading, music, family life; *Style—* The Rt Rev the Bishop of Bath and Wells; The Palace, Wells, Somerset BA5 2PD (☎ 0749 72341, fax 0749 79355)

BATHAM, Cryil Ernest Kila Northwood; s of Ernest Northwood Batham (d 1941), and Susan Penelope, *née* Herridge (d 1940); *b* 29 June 1909; *Educ* Bishop Veseys GS Sutton Coldfield; *m* 8 August 1931, Alys Gillian, da of Ernest Drinkwater (d 1962), of Ross-on-Wye, Herefordshire; 1 da (Ruth Penelope (Mrs Bell) b 28 Feb 1948); *Career* Yorks Insur Co Ltd (now Gen Accident Fire & Life Assur Corpn plc): mangr Bristol branch 1946-57, mangr Manchester branch 1957-63, liason offr Paris 1963-67, head offr underwriter 1967-72; insur, broker Mann Rutler & Collins (Life & Pensions) Ltd 1972-76, company dir QC Correspondence Circle Ltd 1976-; lectr on Freemasonry, insur theatre; chm Bristol Old Vic Theatre Club 1955, asst Summer Sch for Teachers of Eng Stratford-upon-Avon 1948-71; ed Hrs Quatuor Coronatorum 1975-85; Freeman: City of London 1972, Worshipful Co of Gold and Silver Wyre Drawers 1972; OStJ 1980, ACII 1928; *Recreations* theatre, classical music; *Style—* Cyril Batham, Esq; 17 Romeland, Waltham Abbey, Essex EN9 1QZ (☎ 0992 713527); QC Correspondence Circle Ltd, 60 Great Queen Street, London WC2A 5BA (☎ 01 405 7340 or 01 831 2493)

BATHO, Sir Maurice Benjamin; 2 Bt (UK 1928); s of Sir Charles Batho, 1 Bt (d 1938); *b* 14 Jan 1910; *Educ* Uppingham and in Belgium; *m* 1934, Antoinette Marie, da of Baron d'Udekem d'Acoz, of Ghent; 2 s, 2 da; *Heir* s, Peter Batho; *Career* chm and md Ridgley (Huntingdon) Ltd and assoc cos, md Reed Paper 1959-65; *Style—* Sir Maurice Batho, Bt; Carlton Hall, Saxmundham, Suffolk (☎ 0728 2505)

BATHO, Peter Ghislain; s and h of Sir Maurice Batho, 2 Bt, by his w, Antoinette, da of Baron d'Udekem d'Acoz, of Ghent; *b* 9 Dec 1939; *Educ* Ampleforth; *m* 1966, Lucille Mary, da of late Wilfrid Williamson, of Saxmundham; 3 s; *Style—* Peter Batho, Esq; Park Farm, Saxmundham, Suffolk

BATHURST, Hon Alexander Edward Seymour; s of 8 Earl Bathurst, DL; *b* 8 August 1965; *Style—* The Hon Alexander Bathurst

BATHURST, Lady (Elizabeth) Ann; da of Capt Hon Chandos Graham Temple-Gore-Langton (d 1921), and Ethel Frances, da of the Rev A L Gore; sis of 7 Earl Temple of Stowe; raised to rank of Earl's da 1941; *b* 3 April 1908; *m* 1927, Gp-Capt Peter Bathurst (d 1970), o son of late Lt-Col Hon Allen Benjamin Bathurst, 3 s of 6 Earl Bathurst; 2 s; *Style—* Lady Ann Bathurst; 12A Northanger Court, Grove St, Bath, Avon BA2 6PE

BATHURST, Hon David Charles Lopes; s of 2 Viscount Bledisloe, QC (d 1979); *b* 15 Dec 1937; *Educ* Eton, Magdalen Coll Oxford; *m* 1967, Mary Cornelia, da of Andrew Kirkwood McCosh, of Coulter, Lanarks; 3 da; *Career* 2 Lt 12 Royal Lancers 1956-58; pres Christie Manson & Woods 1978-84 (New York); *Clubs* Boodle's, White's; *Style—* The Hon David Bathurst; South Lodge, E Heath Rd, London NW3 (☎ 01 794 6999)

BATHURST, Hon George Bertram; TD; s of Lt-Col Lord Apsley, DSO, MC, TD, MP (k on active serv 1942); bro of 8 Earl Bathurst, DL; *b* 12 March 1929; *Educ* Eton, Trinity Coll Oxford; *m* 1973, Susan, da of Malcolm Messer, of Manor Farm House, Tarlton, Glos; *Career* late Capt Royal Wilts Yeomanry, late Lt 10 Hussars; *Style—* The Hon George Bathurst, TD; Hullasey House, Tarlton, Cirencester, Glos

BATHURST, Lady Henrietta Mary Lilias; da of 8 Earl Bathurst, DL; *b* 17 Oct 1962; *Style—* Lady Henrietta Bathurst; Cirencester Park, Cirencester, Glos (☎ (0285) 3412)

BATHURST, 8 Earl (GB 1772); Henry Allen John Bathurst; DL (Glos 1960); also Baron Bathurst (GB 1711) and Baron Apsley (GB 1771); s of Lt-Col Lord Apsley, DSO, MC, TD, MP (k on active serv 1942) and late Lady Apsley, CBE; suc gf (7 Earl) 1943; *b* 1 May 1927; *Educ* Eton, Christ Church Oxford, Ridley Coll Canada; *m* 1, 1959 (m dis 1976), Judith Mary, da of late Amos Christopher Nelson, of Fosse Corner, Cirencester; 2 s, 1 da; m 2, 1978, Gloria, da of Harold Edward Clarry, of Vancouver, and wid of David Rutherston; *Heir* s, Lord Apsley; *Career* Lt 10 Royal Hussars 1946-48, Royal Glos Hussars 1948-59, Capt TA; master VWH Hounds 1950-64, jt master VWH Hounds 1964-66; Lord in Waiting 1957-61; chllr Primrose League 1959-61; jt parly under-sec Home Off 1961-62; govr Royal Agric Coll; pres: Royal Forestry Soc 1976-78, Inst of Sales & Mktg Mgmnt 1981-, Assoc of Professional Foresters 1983-86, cncl memb CLA & TGO; dir Forestor Ltd; *Clubs* White's, Cavalry; *Style—* The Rt Hon the Earl Bathurst, DL; Manor Farm, Sapperton, Nr Cirencester, Glos office (☎ 0285 653135)

BATHURST, Lady (Joan) Caroline; da of James Alexander Petrie (d 1977), of London, and Adrienne Johanna, *née* van den Bergh; *b* 02 Nov 1920; *Educ* Wycombe Abbey Sch, Newnham Coll, Cambridge (BA, MA); *m* 8 Aug 1968, Sir Maurice Edward Bathurst, CMB, CBE, QC, *qv*, s of Edward John James Bathurst (d 1978), of East Horsley, Surrey; 1 step s (Adrian Edward b 1948); *Career* Dip Serv 1947-72; FO 1947-48, second sec The Hague 1948-50, FO 1950-54, fist sec 1953, UK High Cmmn and Embassy Bonn 1954-58, FO (later FCO) 1958-71, cnsllr 1969, head Euro Communities Info Unit FCO 1969-71; memb UK del to Colombo Plan Consultative Ctee Jogjakarta 1959, advsr Br gp Inter-Parly Union 1962-68; Offr Order of Leopold Belgium 1966; *Recreations* genealogy, gardening, music; *Clubs* Utd Oxford and Cambridge; *Style—* Lady Bathurst; Airlie, The Highlands, East Horsley, Surrey KT24 5BG (☎ 048 65 3269)

BATHURST, Sir Maurice Edward; CMG (1953), CBE (1947), QC (1964); o s of Edward John James Bathurst, of E Horsley, Surrey, and Annie Mary Bathurst; *b* 2 Dec 1913; *Educ* Haberdashers' Aske's Hatcham, King's Coll London (LLB, LLD), Columbia Univ New York (LLM), Gonville and Caius Coll Cambridge (PhD); *m* 1, 1941 (m dis 1963), Dorothy Eunice, da of late W S Stevens, of Gravesend, Kent; 1 s; m 2, 1968, Joan Caroline, da of James Alexander Petrie, barr; *Career* slr 1938-56, barr Gray's Inn and Inner Temple 1957, bencher Gray's Inn 1970; legal advsr Br Info Services 1941-43, legal advsr Br Embassy Washington 1943-46, legal memb UK Delgn to UN 1946-48, dep legal advsr Control Cmmn Germany 1949-51; legal advsr to UK High Cmmn for Germany 1951-55, judge Supreme Court, Br Zone 1953-55, legal advsr to Br Embassy Bonn 1955-57, Br judge Arbitral Cmmn Germany 1968-69; memb Panel of Presidents Arbitral Tbnls Int Telecommunications Satellite Orgn 1974-78; memb UK delgns: UNRRA, WHO, UN Gen Assembly, NATO Status of Forces Conf; memb: Panel of Arbitrators Int Centre for Settlement of Investmt Disputes 1968-87, UK Ctee UNICEF 1959-84; hon visiting prof int law King's Coll London 1967-77 (hon fell); judge Arbitral Tbnl and Mixed Cmmn for the Agreement on German External Debts 1977-88; memb: Senate of Inns of Court 1971-73, Senate of Inns of Court and the Bar 1974-77; chm govrs Haberdashers' Aske's Hatcham Schs 1972-80;; - Master Worshipful Co of Haberdashers 1980-81; Freeman: City of London, City of Bathurst NB; Hon DCL Sacred Heart NB; kt 1984; *Style—* Sir Maurice Bathurst, CMG, CBE, QC; Airlie, The Highlands, East Horsley, Leatherhead, Surrey KT24 5BG (☎ 04865 3269)

BATISTE, Spencer Lee; MP (C) Elmet 1983-; s of Samuel and Lottie Batiste; *b* 5 June 1945; *Educ* Carmel Coll, Sorbonne, Cambridge Univ; *m* 1969, Susan Elizabeth, da of late Ronald William Atkin; 1 s, 1 da; *Career* slr; contested (C) Sheffield, Chesterfield and NE Derbyshire Euro election 1979; vice chm nat bd Small Business Bureau; memb cncl: Sheffield C of C, Sheffield Univ; law clerk Sheffield Assay Office; vice-pres Cons Trade Unionists, former memb Energy Select Ctee; PPS to min of State for Indust and Info Technol, PPS to Min of State for Defence Procurement; *Recreations* gardening, reading, photography; *Style—* Spencer Batiste, Esq, MP; House of Commons, London SW1A 0AA (☎ 01 219 6054)

BATLEY, John Geoffrey; OBE (1987); s of John William Batley (d 1971), of Keighley, W Yorks, and Doris, *née* Midgeley (d 1985); *b* 21 May 1930; *Educ* Keighley GS; *m* 1953, Cicely Anne, da of William Bean Pindar, of Bradford; 1 s (John), 1 da (Janet); *Career* BR: trained and qualified as chartered engr NE Region 1947-53, asst divnl engr Leeds 1962, mgmnt services offr BR HQ London 1965, dep princ Br Tport Staff Coll Woking 1970, divnl mangr Leeds 1976, dep chief sec BRB London 1982, sec BR Bd 1984-87; CEng, MICE, MCIT; *Recreations* walking, golf, gardening; *Clubs* Savile; *Style—* John Batley, Esq, OBE; c/o Savile Club, 69 Brook st, London W1Y 2ER (☎ 01 629 5462)

BATLEY, Lawrence; s of John Arthur Batley (d 1947), of Huddersfield; *b* 15 Feb 1914; *Educ* Hillhouse Central Sch Huddersfield; *m* 1937, Dorothie, da of Wilfred Hepworth (d 1918), of Huddersfield; 1 da; *Career* cash and carry wholesaler; inventor and pioneer of cash and carry in Great Britain May 1958; fndr and chm Batleys of Yorkshire; originator and sole sponsor of Lawrence Batley Int Golf Tournament 1981; dir: Yorkshire General Unit Trust, Lawrence Batley Art Archives, Bretton Hall Wakefield; *Recreations* golf, swimming; *Clubs* Huddersfield Borough; *Style—* Lawrence Batley, Esq; Heaton Park House, Heaton Rd, Huddersfield; 10 Pier Court, St Annes on Sea, Lancs; Batleys plc, Leeds Rd, Huddersfield HD2 1UN (☎ 0484 44211)

BATSFORD, Sir Brian Caldwell Cook; s of late Arthur Caldwell Cook, of Gerrards Cross, Bucks; assumed mother's maiden name by deed poll 1946; *b* 18 Dec 1910; *Educ* Repton; *m* 1945, Joan (Wendy), da of Norman Cunliffe (d 1964), of Oxford; 2 da; *Career* serv WWII, Fl Lt RAF; chm B T Batsford (publishers) 1952-74 (pres 1974-76); contested Chelmsford for Nat Govt 1945, MP (C) Ealing S 1958-74, asst govt whip 1962-64, oppn dep chief whip 1964-67, chm House of Commons Library Ctee 1970-74; Alderman GLC, pres Old Reptonian Soc 1973, govr Repton Sch 1973; vice pres RSA 1975- (chm 1973-75); fell Chartered Soc Designers 1971, exhibited Arts Cncl exhibition: British Landscape Painting 1850-1950 Hayward Gallery 1983; one-man exhibition Parker Gallery 1987; Hon RI 1985; hon memb Soc of Graphic Art 1987; kt 1974; *Books* The Britain of Brian Cook (1987); *Recreations* painting, gardening; *Clubs* Pratt's, RAF; *Style—* Sir Brian Batsford; Buckland House, Mill Road, Winchelsea, E Sussex TN36 4HJ (☎ 0797 226131)

BATT, Reginald Joseph Alexander; s of Benjamin and Alice Harriett Batt; *b* 22 July 1920; *m* 1951, Mary Margaret Canning; 1 da; *Career* barr Inner Temple 1952, rec SE Circuit 1982-, bencher 1986.; *Style—* Reginald Batt, Esq; 6 King's Bench Walk, Temple, London EC4Y 7DR (☎ 01 583 0410)

BATT, William Frederic; MBE (Mil 1945), JP, DL; s of Lt-Col Reginald Cossley Batt, CBE, MVO, of Gresham Hall, Norwich (d 1952), by his 1 w Violet, *née* Knowles (d 1910); *b* 4 April 1904; *Educ* Winchester, Sandhurst; *m* 1928, Hon Elisabeth (d 1988), 1 s, 2 da (and 1 s decd); *Career* Maj Coldstream Gds 1924-29 and 1939-45 (served NW Europe); High Sheriff Norfolk 1963, ret landowner and farmer; memb Gen Synod C of E; *Clubs* Cavalry and Guards; *Style—* William Batt Esq, MBE, JP, DL; Chaucer's Farm, Gresham, Norwich (☎ 026 377 223)

BATTEN, (William) Henry; TD (1963), JP (Dorset 1960-); s of Col Herbert Copeland Cary Batten, DSO (d 1963), of Aldon House, Yeovil, Somerset, and Dorothy Lilian Hyde, *née* Milne (d 1951); *b* 29 Jan 1926; *Educ* Marlborough; *m* 2 Sept 1950, Susan Helen Frances, da of Sir Philip Colfox, 1 Bt, MC, of Symondsbury Manor, Bridport, Dorset; 2 s (David Henry Cary b 3 March 1952, Michael John b 29 Jan 1960), 2 da (Tessa Mary b 22 Oct 1953, Caroline Bridget b 13 July 1955); *Career* cmmnd Lt RM 1944-48;, cmmnd 294 Field Regt TA (Queens Own Dorset Yeomanry) 1948-64, ret Maj; admitted slr 1954, sr ptnr Batten & Co (slrs and land agents) 1963-87; chm Wessex Water Bd, clerk Yeovil Gen Cmmrs for Income Tax 1964-, vice pres Royal Bath and West and Southern Counties Soc, vice chm Sherborne RDC; *Recreations* foxhunting, sailing; *Clubs* Royal Cruising; *Style—* Henry Batten, Esq, TD, JP; Church Farm, Ryme Intrinseca, Sherborne, Dorset (☎ 0935 872 482); Church Ho, Yeovil, Somerset (☎ 0835 236 85, fax 0935 706 054, telex 46124)

BATTEN, Sir John Charles; KCVO (1987); s of Raymond Wallis Batten, JP (d 1979), of Worthing, Sussex, and Kathleen Gladys, *née* Charles (d 1982); *b* 11 Mar 1924; *Educ* Mill Hill Sch, St Bartholomews Med Coll Univ of London (MB, BS, MD); *m* 14 Oct 1950, Anne Mary Margaret, da of John Augustus Oriel, CBE, MC; 1 s (Mark b 1957), 3 da (Elizabeth b 1951, Sarah b 1953 (d 1955), Clare b 1957); *Career* Surgn Capt RHG 1947-49; jr hosp appts St Georges and Brompton Hosps 1946-57; physician: St Georges Hosp 1958-79 (now hon physician), Brompton Hosp 1959-87 (now hon physician), King Edward VII Hosp for Offrs 1968-; hd HM Med Household 1981, physician to HM the Queen 1974-, censor 1977 and sr censor 1981 RCP, pres Med Protection Soc, pres Br Lung Fndn, pres Cystic Fibrosis Res Tst; Freeman Worshipful Co of Apothecaries; FRSM, memb Assoc of Physicians, memb Br Thoraic Soc; *Recreations* music, sailing, plants; *Clubs* Oriental; *Style—* Sir John Batten, KCVO; 7 Lion Gate Gdns, Richmond, Surrey TW9 2DF

BATTEN, Mark Wilfrid; s of late Edward Batten, and late Elizabeth, *née* Denne; *Educ* Chelsea Sch of Art; *m* 1933, Elsie May Owston Thorneloe (d 1961); 1 da (Griselda); *Career* sculptor, direct carver in stone; sculptures on: Old Bodleian Library, Trinity Coll Oxford, Goldershill Park N London, USA, Aust, Pakistan; pres Royal Soc of Br Sculptors 1956-61; memb Art Socs: RBA, RBS, RSA; hon memb Nat Sculpture Soc of USA; *Books* Direct Carving in Stone; *Clubs* Chelsea Arts; *Style—* Mark Batten, Esq; Christian's River Studio, Dallington, Heathfield, Sussex TN21 9NX

BATTERSBY, Prof Alan Rushton; s of William Battersby (d 1967), and Hilda, *née* Rushton (d 1972); *b* 4 Mar 1925; *Educ* Leigh GS, Univ of Manchester (BSc, MSc), Univ of St Andrews (PhD), Bristol (DSc), Cambridge Univ (ScD); *m* 18 June 1949, Margaret Ruth, da of Thomas Hart (d 1965); 2 s (Martin b 29 July 1953, Stephen b 24 April 1956); *Career* lectr in chemistry: Univ of St Andrews 1948-53, Univ of Bristol 1954-62, second chair organic chem Univ of Liverpool 1962; elected to chair of organic chemistry Univ of Cambridge 1969 (elected to 1702 chair 1988); non-exec dir Schering Agrochemicals Ltd, chm exec cncl CIBA Fndn; hon: DSc Rockerfeller Univ NY 1977, LLD Univ of St Andrews 1977, DSc Univ of Sheffield 1986, DSc Heriot-Watt Univ 1987; FRS 1966; Deutsche Akademie der Naturforscher Leopolding (Germany) 1967, Soc Royal de Chimie (Belgium) 1987, hon memb American Acad of Arts and Sci (USA) 1988; *Recreations* music, camping, sailing, gardening and fly fishing; *Style—* Prof Alan Battersby; 20 Barrow Road, Cambridge CB2 2AS (☎ 0223 63799); University Chemical Labrotary, Lensfield Road, Cambridge CB2 1EW (☎ 0223 336400, fax 0223 336362)

BATTERSBY, Betty Kathleen Ada; da of James Allan Battersby OBE, Barr at Law (d 1931), and Loie Allen, *née* Beale (d 1955); *b* 13 July 1908; *Educ* Nottingham HS for Girls, Nottingham Sch of Art; *Career* joined Br Colour Cncl 1931; asst to dir Robert F Wilson, assisted in compilation of BBC Dictionary of Colour Standards 1934; research and prods of colour charts; studio dir 1937-, ret 1968; UK delegate and advsr to Mode Europe and Int Cmmn on Colours 1959-68 (pres 1966-68); colour research and application conslt Battersby Colour-design Conslts; memb Colour Gp of GB; RHS, FRSA; *Books* jointly ed with Robert F Wilson: The 3 vol Dictionary of Colours for Interior Decoration (1949), Colour and Lighting in Factories and Offices (1946, 2 ed 1956, 3 ed 1964); *Recreations* reading; *Clubs* Naval and Military; *Style—* Miss Betty Battersby, BKA, FRSA; Rosebay, Sissinghurst Rd, Biddenden, Ashford, Kent TN27 8EQ (☎ Biddenden 291 498); Battersby Colour-design Consultants, Sissinghurst Rd, Biddenden, Ashford, Kent

BATTERSBY, Eric Worsley; OBE (1965, MBE mil 1946); s of Charles Worsley Battersby (d 1952), of Pountney Copse, Alton, Hants, and Susie Agnes Shelly, *née* Kennard-Davies (d 1964); *b* 18 April 1916; *Educ* Marlborough Coll; *m* 13 July 1946, Edna Iris Prudence, da of Col John Norman Gwynne (d 1969), of Toronto; 3 s (Nicholas b 1947, Timothy b 1949, Simon b 1953), 1 da (Tessa b 1956, d 1959); *Career* joined Indian Police Burma 1935-40, ADC to Govr of Burma Hon Sir Archibald Cochrane (successor Rt Hon Sir Reginald Dorman-Smith) 1940-42, staff duties Eastern Army India Cmd 1942-44, Maj Force 136 SOE Far East 1944-46, demob 1946; civil servant; civil asst WO 1946-: Malaya 1946-48, Jamaica 1955-57; seconded to FO 1960-65, MOD 1965-76, ret 1976; chm: Warsash and Dist Art Gp, Botley Soc (regd with Civic Tst); Freeman City of London 1944, Liveryman Worshipful Co of Fishmongers; *Recreations* painting, golf; *Style*— Eric Battersby, Esq, OBE, MBE

BATTERSBY, Rita; da of John Baybutt, and Zena May *née* Cowell; *b* 29 Sept 1942; *Educ* Wigan Mining & Techn Coll; *m* 21 March 1964, Albert Battersby OBE , s of Albert Battersby (d 1952); 2 da (Zena b 26 Jan 1965, Debra b 9 March 1967); *Career* fndr VDU Installations Ltd 1977; awards: First award winner Industrial Achievement Award 1981, Business Woman of the Year 1986 Runner-up, Inst of sales and Marketing mgmt award 1988; memb local PCC 1986; *Recreations* swimming, sailing; *Style*— Mrs Rita Battersby; VDU Installations Ltd, 43 Western Rd, Bracknell, Berks, RG12 1RW, (☎ 0344 424000, fax 0344 424063, telex 846545 VDUINS G)

BATTERSBY, Robert Christopher; MBE (1971), MEP (C) Humberside 1979-; s of late Maj Robert Luther Battersby, MM, RFA, late IA, and Dorothea Gladys, *née* Middleton; *b* 14 Dec 1924; *Educ* Edinburgh Univ, Cambridge Univ (BA, MA), Sorbonne, Toulouse Univ; *m* 1, 1949 (m dis), June Scriven; 1 da; m 2, 1955, Marjorie Bispham; 2 s, 1 da; *Career* RA and Intelligence Corps 1942-47, Lt RARO; mangr Dowsett Gp; dir Associated Engineering and Guest-Keen and Nettlefolds Gps; principal administrator European Cmmn 1973-79; dep chief whip (EDG) 1983-86, chief whip 1987-; chm Fisheries sub-ctee European Parliament 1979-84, vice-chm 1984-87; vice-chm Ep-China Interparly Delgn 1981-87; vice-chm EP-USSR Delegation 1987-; *Clubs* Carlton; *Style*— Robert Battersby, Esq, MBE, MEP; West Cross, Rockshaw Road, Merstham, Surrey

BATTISCOMBE, Christopher Charles Richard; s of Lt-Col Christopher Robert Battiscombe (d 1989), and Karin Sigrid, *née* Timberg (d 1983) ; *b* 27 April 1940; *Educ* Wellington Coll, New Coll Oxford (BA); *m* 1972, Brigid Melita Theresa, da of Peter Northcote Lunn; 1 s (Max b 1977), 1 da (Antonia b 1975); *Career* cncllr Foreign Office 1986-; *Recreations* golf, tennis, ski-ing; *Clubs* Moorpark GC; *Style*— Christopher Battiscombe, Esq; 8 Gayton Rd, London NW3 (☎ 01 794 8778);

BATTLE, John; s of John Battle, and Audrey, *née* Rathbone (d 1984); *b* 26 April 1951; *Educ* Upholland Coll, Univ of Leeds (BA); *m* 12 April 1977, Mary Geraldine, da of Jerry Meenan; 1 s (Joseph b 1978), 2 da (Anna b 1981, Clare b 1982); *Career* trg for RC priesthood 1969-73, res offr to Derek Enright MEP 1979-83 nat co-ordinator Church Action on Poverty 1983-87; cncllr Leeds 1980-87, chm housing ctee Leeds CC 1983-; *Style*— John Battle, Esq; 26 Victoria Park Ave, Leeds LS5 3DG

BATTY, John Christopher Ralph; s of Ralph Frank Batty of London and Georgina, *née* Chambers; *b* 13 Sept 1941; *Educ* Brighton Coll, Manchester Univ (BSc), Cranfield Inst of Tech (MBA), Coll of Law; *m* Sept 1986, Hannah-May Eugenia, da of Eugene Stuart Lyddane, MD (d 1986), of Washington DC, USA; *Career* admitted slr 1968, articled Slaughter and May (asst slr 1968-74), counsel Lloyds Bank Int Ltd 1978-81, ptnr Berwin Leighton 1983-; dir: Science Business Interface plc 1988-, Beta Sigma Ltd and Subsidiaries 1988-; memb: London Mathematical 1964, Int Bar Assoc; *Recreations* music, history of mathematics, Dr Samuel Johnson, Samuel Pepys; *Style*— John Batty, Esq; c/o Adelaide House, London Bridge, London EC4R 9HA (☎ 01 623 3144, fax 01 623 4416)

BATTY, Peter Wright; s of Ernest Faulkner Batty (d 1986), of Surrey, and Gladys Victoria, *née* Wright (d 1979); *b* 18 June 1931; *Educ* Bede GS Sunderland, Queen's Coll Oxford (MA); *m* 1959, Anne Elizabeth, da of Edmund Stringer, of Devon; 2 s (David, Richard), 1 da (Charlotte); *Career* feature writer Financial Times 1954-56, freelance journalist 1956-58, prodr BBC TV 1958-64, memb original Tonight team (ed 1963-64); other BBC prodns incl: The Quiet Revolution, The Big Freeze, The Katanga Affair, Sons of the Navvy Man; exec prodr and assoc head of Factual Programming ATV 1964-68; prodns include: The Fall and Rise of the House of Krupp (Grand Prix for Documentary Venice Film Festival 1965, Silver Dove Leipzig Film Festival 1965), The Road to Suez, The Suez Affair, Vietnam Fly-in, Battle for the Desert; chief exec Peter Batty Prodns 1970-; recent programmes directed, produced and scripted for BBC-TV, ITV and Channel 4 incl: The Plutocrats, The Aristocrats, Battle for Cassino, Battle for the Bulge, Birth of the Bomb, Farouk: Last of the Pharaohs, Operation Barbarossa, Superspy, Spy Extraordinary, Sunderland's Pride and Passion, A Rothschild and his Red Gold, Search for the Super, The World of Television, Battle for Warsaw, The Story of Wine, The Rise and Rise of Laura Ashley, The Gospel According to St Michael, Battle for Dien Bien Phu, Nuclear Nightmares, A Turn Up In a Million, Il Poverello, Swindle!, The Algerian War, Fonteyn and Nureyev, The Perfect Partnership, The Divided Union; contributed 6 episodes to The World at War series; *Books* The House of Krupp (1966), The Divided Union (1987); *Recreations* walking, reading, listening to music; *Clubs* White Elephant; *Style*— Peter Batty, Esq; Claremont Ho, Renfrew Rd, Kingston, Surrey KT2 7NT (☎ 01 942 6304, telex 261507 MONREF 2685, fax 01 336 1661)

BATTY, Sir William Bradshaw; TD (1946); s of Rowland Batty and Nellie; *b* 15 May 1913; *Educ* Hulme GS Manchester; *m* 1946, Jean Ella Brice; 1 s, 1 da (and 1 s decd); *Career* chm Ford Motor Co 1972-75, ret; pres SMMT 1975-76; FBIM; kt 1973; *Recreations* golf, sailing, gardening; *Clubs* Roy Western YC; *Style*— Sir William Batty, TD; Glenhaven Cottage, Riverside Rd West, Newton Ferrers, S Devon

BATTY SHAW, Patricia Dorothy Mary; CBE (1982), JP (Norfolk 1968); da of Dr Graham Heckels, MB, BS, of Norwich, and Dorothy Clark (d 1980); *b* 18 Nov 1928; *Educ* Wimbledon HS for Girls, Southampton Univ; *m* 1954, Anthony Batty Shaw, s of Harold Batty Shaw (d 1936); 1 da; *Career* tax cmmr Wymondham 1975- (chm 1987-), nat chm Nat Fedn of Women's Inst 1977-81, dep chm Norfolk Magistrates Ctee 1985-88 (chm 1987); memb: VEA Cncl 1978-85, Devpt Cmmn 1981-, AG Wages Bd England and Wales 1984-, Eng Advsy Ctee on Telecommunciations 1985-, Archbishop's Cmmn of Rural Affrs; tstee: Theatre Royal Norwich 1982-88, Charities Aid Fndn 1983-, govr Norwich HS for Girls 1981-; AMIA; *Style*— Mrs Anthony Batty Shaw, CBE, JP; Appleacre, Barford, Norwich NR9 4BD (☎ 060 545 268)

BATY, Clifford John; s of Herbert Thomas Baty (d 1937), and Ethel Beatrice, *née* Garrod; *b* 6 Nov 1934; *Educ* Haberdashers' Aske's, Hampstead Sch, North Western Poly; *m* 19 March 1960, Brenda Anne, da of Edward Laurie Fonceca (d 1955); 1 da (Helen Jane b 1967); *Career* ATV Network Ltd: accountant 1963-74, fin controller 1974-77, fin dir 1977-81; Central Independent Television plc: dir of fin 1982-88, commercial dir 1988-; *Recreations* golf, bridge; *Style*— Clifford Baty, Esq; Central Independent Television plc, Central House, Broad Street, Birmingham

BAUCH, (Friedrich) Wilhelm Otto; s of Wilhelm Otto Bauch (d 1936), of Berlin, and Elise Margarethe, *née* Brömer (d 1948); *b* 15 Nov 1903; *Educ* Andreas Real-Gymnasium Berlin, Techn Univ and Friedrich-Wilhelm Univ Berlin; *m* 7 Aug 1937, Helen Irene Alexandra, da of Bertie John Ball (d 1935), of London; 2 s (John b 1941, Michael Roger b 1945); *Career* scientific memb Heinrich Hertz Inst Berlin 1930-34, dir Philips-Electro-Special GmbH Berlin 1935-42, techn dir American Broadcast RIAS Berlin 1946-47, dir Loewe Radio Co Ltd London 1948-64, personal advsr to the late Sir Allen Clark, chm Plessey Co Ltd, formed own Comp 1950 and 1950-62, chm F W O Bauch Ltd 1960-; hon memb Audio Engineering Soc (NY) 1986; *Style*— F W O Bauch, Esq; 6 Roedean Cres, Brighton, Sussex BN2 5RH (☎ 0273 607893); F W O Bauch Ltd, 49 Theobald St, Boreham Wood, Herts WD6 4RZ (☎ 01 953 0091, telex 27502, fax 01 207 5970)

BAUDINO, Dr Catherine Anne; da of Jean Rene Baudino, and Anne-Marie, *née* Camus; *b* 26 Oct 1952; *Educ* Lycee Francais De Londres, University Coll London (BA, PhD); *Career* dir Institutional Investor 1980-87, chief exec Maxwell Satellite Communications Ltd 1988-; *Recreations* opera, theatre, wine and food; *Style*— Dr Catherine A Baudino; Maxwell Satellite Communications, 3 Thavies Inn, London EC1P 1DR (☎ 01 822 3681 fax, 01 583 3135 car telephone 0836 376 672, telex 929791 CABSAT G)

BAUER, Baron (Life Peer UK 1983), of Market Ward in the City of Cambridge; Prof Peter Thomas Bauer; s of Baladar Auer (d 1944), of Budapest; *b* 6 Nov 1915; *Educ* Scholae Piae Budapest, Gonville and Caius Cambridge (MA); *Career* reader Agric Economics London Univ 1947-48, economics lectr Cambridge Univ 1948-56, Smuts reader Cwlth Studies Cambridge Univ 1956-60, prof of economics LSE 1960-83; fell Gonville and Caius 1946-60 and 1968-; FBA; *Publications* The Rubber Industry (1948), West African Trade (1954), The Economics of Under-Developed Countries (with B S Yamey, 1957), Economic Analysis and Policy in Under-developed Countries (1958), Indian Economic Policy and Development (1961), Markets, Market Control and Marketing Reform (with B S Yamey, 1968), Dissent on Development (1972), Aspects of Nigerian Development (1974), Equality, the Third World and Economic Delusion (1981), *Reality and Rhetoric: Studies in the Economics of Development* (1984); *Clubs* Garrick; *Style*— The Rt Hon the Lord Bauer; London School of Economics, Houghton St, London WC2

BAUGHAN, Michael Christopher; s of Prof Edward Baughan, CBE; *b* 25 April 1942; *Educ* Westminster; *m* 1975, Moira, da of Percy Levy; 2 s; *Career* md Lazard Bros & Co; dir Goode Durrant plc; memb bd of govrs Westminster School; *Style*— Michael Baughan, Esq; 21 Moorfields, EC2

BAUGHEN, Rt Rev Michael Alfred; *see*: Chester, Bishop of

BAUM, Prof Harold; s of Isidor(e) Baum (d 1980), and Mary, *née* Rosenberg (d 1974); *b* 14 Nov 1930; *Educ* Halesowen GS Worcs, Birmingham Univ (BSc, PhD); *m* 30 Oct 1962, Patricia Glenda, da of Maj George Magrill, OBE, JP, of Roehampton, London; a direct desc of The Marahil, Jacob Moelln, a great 14 C Rabbi; 1 s (David b 1965), 2 da (Mandy b 1967, Alison b 1969); *Career* prof of biochemistry 1968-; head of dept of biochemistry and dean of faculty of life sciences Kings Coll London 1987-; dir Taylor and Francis Gp Ltd; chm professional and educnl ctee Biochemical Soc 1981-, chm of govrs S Thames Coll 1983-87, memb of cncl Glynn Research Fndn, tstee Nuffield Chelsea Curriculum Tst; memb prog advsy ctee on continuing educ BBC, tres Internal Fedn of Scientists for Soviet Refuseniks, radio and TV broadcaster; FRSC, CChem, FIBiol, CBiol; *Recreations* squash, skiing, songwriting, bridge; *Clubs* Roehampton; *Style*— Prof Harold Baum; Yew Trees, 356 Dover House Rd, London SW15 5BL (☎ 01 789 9352, 788 2471); King's College London, Strand, London WC2 (☎ 01 836 5454) and Campden Hill Rd, London W8 (☎ 01 937 5411)

BAVIN, Timothy John; *see*: Portsmouth, Bishop of

BAVISTER, Edward John; CBE (1988); s of Aubrey John Bavister (d 1974), of Herts, and Ethel, *née* Dennis; *b* 19 April 1933; *Educ* Berkhamsted Sch, St John's Coll Cambridge (MA); *m* 1958, Barbara Jean, da of Harold Foster (d 1973), of Cumbria; 3 da (Heather Jane b 1960, Anne Kirsten b 1963, Gillian Fiona b 1965); *Career* chartered engr; dep md John Brown plc 1987-, dir John Brown plc 1982-; FIChemE, CBIM; *Recreations* sailing, walking, opera; *Clubs* Oriental; *Style*— Edward Bavister, Esq, CBE; Marsham Cottage, Marsham Way, Gerrards Cross, Bucks (☎ 0753 882415); John Brown plc, 20 Eastbourne Terrace, London W2 6LE (☎ 01 262 8080, telex 263521)

BAWDEN, Nina Mary (Mrs Austen Kark); *née* MABEY; da of Cdr Charles Mabey (d 1976), and Ellaline Ursula May, *née* Cushing (d 1986); *b* 19 Jan 1925; *Educ* Ilford County HS for Girls, Somerville Coll Oxford, (MA); *m* 1 Oct 1946 (m dis 1954), Henry Walton Bawden, s of Victor Bawden; 2 s (Robert Humphrey Felix b 1951, Nicholas Charles b 1948 (d 1982); m 2, 5 Aug 1954, Austen Steven Kark, s of Maj Norman Benjamin Kark, of East India Club, St James's Square, London; 1 da (Perdita Emily Helena b 1957); *Career* novelist: Devil by the Sea (1955), Just Like a Lady (1960), In Honour Bound (1961), Tortoise by Candlelight (1963), Under the Skin (1964), A Little Love, A Little Learning (1965), A Woman of My Age (1967), The Grain of Truth (1969), The Birds on the Trees (1970), Anna Apparent (1972), George Beneath a Paper Moon (1974), Afternoon of a Good Woman (1976), Familiar Passions (1979), Walking Naked (1981), The Ice House (1983), Circles of Deceit (1987); *for children*: The Secret Passage, On The Run, The White Horse Gang, A Handful of Thieves, Squib, Carrie's War, The Peppermint Pig, The Finding, Keeping Henry, The Outside Child; Prizes: Yorkshire Post Novel of the Year Award (1976), Guardian Award for Children's Fiction (1976), Booker Short List for Circles of Deceit (1987); JP Surrey 1969-76; memb Video Appeals Ctee; FRSL; *Recreations* food, films, theatre, travel, politics, garden croquet; *Clubs* Groucho, Oriental; *Style*— Miss Nina Bawden; 22 Noel Road, London N1 8HA (☎ 01 226 2839); 19 Kapadistriov, Nauplism, Greece

BAXENDALE, Lady Elizabeth Joan; *née* Fortescue; da of 5 Earl Fortescue, KG, PC, CB, OBE, MC, (d 1958); *b* 1 Oct 1926; *m* 1946, Maj William Lloyd (John) Baxendale, JP, DL (d 1982), s of Capt Guy Vernon Baxendale (d 1969), of Framfield

Place, Uckfield, Sussex ; 2 s, 1 da; *Style—* Lady Elizabeth Baxendale; Hailwell House, Framfield, Uckfield, E Sussex (☎ 082 582 256)

BAXENDALE, Lily; s of Herbert Baxendale (d 1959), and Rebecca Baxendale (d 1983); *b* 7 August 1924; *Educ* Accrington GS, Bedford Coll London (BSc, BSc); *Career* md Biorex Laboratories Ltd 1983- (sec and dir 1950-83); Queens Award for Technical Innovation 1950-83; CChem; *Style—* Miss Lily Baxendale; Biorex Laboratories Ltd, Biorex Hse, Canonbury Villas, London N1 2HB (☎ 01 359 0011, telex 268076 BIOREX G)

BAXENDELL, Sir Peter Brian; CBE (1972); s of Lesley Wilfred Edward Baxendell (d 1968), and Evelyn Mary, *née* Gaskin; *b* 28 Feb 1925; *Educ* St Francis Xavier's Liverpool, Royal Sch of Mines (ARSM, BSc); *m* 1949, Rosemary, da of Herbert Leo Lacey; 2 s, 2 da; *Career* dir Shell Transport and Trading 1973- (chm 1979-85); chm ctee of mds Royal Dutch Shell Gp of Cos 1982-85; dir: Hawker Siddeley Gp plc 1984- (chm 1986-), Inchcape plc 1986-, Sun Life Assurance Co of Canada 1986-; memb Univ Grants Ctee 1983-; Cdr of the Order of Orange-Nassau 1985; fell Fellowship of Eng 1978; fell Imperial Coll London 1983-; Hon DSc: Heriot-Watt Univ 1982-, Queen's Belfast 1986-, Univ London 1986-, Univ of Technology Loughborough 1987; *Recreations* tennis, fishing; *Clubs* Hurlingham; *Style—* Sir Peter Baxendell, CBE; Shell Centre, London SE1 7NA (☎ 01 934 2772)

BAXI, Vibhaker Kishore; s of Kishore Jayantilad Baxi (d 1967), and Indira Kishore Baxi; *b* 25 Dec 1947; *Educ* Brooklands Co Tech Coll Surrey, Surrey Univ Guildford (BSc), Brunel Univ Uxbridge (PGCE), Manchester Business Sch (MBA); *m* 12 Nov 1978, Hina, da of Indulal Vaikunthrai Vaidya, of India; 1 da (Mamta b 1982); *Career* financial inst account offr Citibank Dubai 1975-76, asst tres Citibank NA Dubai 1976-78, tres Citibank NA Bahrain 1979-80, tres Chem Bank Hong Kong 1981-85, hd and md Money Mkt and Securities Trading Chem Bank London 1985, or risk mangr (interest rates) Hong Kong and Shanghai Banking Corpn London 1989; *Style—* Vibhaker Baxi, Esq; 22 Sherwood Rd, London NW1AD (☎ 01 203 1503); Hong Kong Bank, 99 Bishopsgate, London EC2P 2LA (☎ 01 588 4591, fax 628 5450, telex 886340)

BAXTER, Dr (William) Gordon; OBE (1964), DL (Morayshire 1985); s of William Alexander Baxter (d 1973), of Fochabers, Moray, and Ethelreda, *née* Adam (d 1963); *b* 8 Feb 1918; *Educ* Ashville Coll Harrogate, Univ of Aberdeen (BSc); *m* 26 Sept 1952, Euphemia Ellen (Ena), da of Thomas William Robertson (d 1955), of Castlepark, Huntly; 2 s (Andrew b 1958, Michael b 1962), 1 da (Audrey b 1961); *Career* research and devpt mangr ICI Explosives Ltd 1940-45; returned to family business WA Baxter & Sons Ltd as prodn dir 1946 (md 1947, chm and md 1973); chm: Baxters of Speyside Ltd, Gordon & Ena Baxter Ltd; dir Grampian Regnl Bd of Bank of Scotland; memb: Scottish cncl devpt and industry, cncl Royal Warrant Holders Assoc, Aberdeen Assoc Royal Warrant Holders, Scottish Cons Party's Business Gp, cncl Food Mfrs Fedn, N American Advsy Gp to the BOTB; Hon LLD Strathclyde 1987; FIGD 1983, MIOD 1970; *Recreations* fishing; *Clubs* Caledonian; *Style—* Dr Gordon Baxter, OBE, DL; Speybank House, Fochabers, Morayshire IV32 7HH (☎ 0343 821234); W A Baxter & Sons Ltd, Fochabers, Moryashire IV32 7LD (☎ 0343 820393, fax 0343 820286, telex 73327; car ☎ 73327)

BAXTER, Hon Mrs (Helen Margaretta); *née* Maude; da of 7 Viscount Hawarden, of Bossington, Adisham, Canterbury, Kent (d 1958); *b* 23 August 1921; *Educ* Bedgebury Park Goudhurst Kent; *m* 10 May 1947, (Walter) Peter Baxter (d 1977), eld s of Col Donald Baxter MC, of Longburton House, Sherborne, Dorset (d 1969); 1 s (Charles), 3 da (Joanna, Margaretta and Victoria); *Style—* The Hon Mrs Baxter; Stourbridge House, Milton-on-Stour, Gillingham, Dorset (☎ 07476 3222)

BAXTER, Maj-Gen Ian Stuart; CBE (1982) (MBE 1973); s of Charles Henry Baxter of Pendle, nr Nelson, Lancs (d 1972), and Edith May, *née* Trindler; *b* 20 July 1937; *Educ* Ottershaw Sch; *m* 19 Aug 1961, Meg Lillian, da of Ronald Bullock, of Pensnett, Brierly Hill, Staffs; 3 da (Deborah b 1962, Louise b 1964, Marianna b 1971); *Career* cmmnd RASC 1958, regtl duty in UK, Kenya, India, NI (2Lt- Capt) 1958-69, student Staff Coll Camberley (Maj) 1970, DAA and QMG 8 Inf Bde Londonderry 1971-73, OC 60 Sqn RCT 1973-74, student NDC 1974-75, GSO 1 DS Staff Coll Camberley (Lt-Col) 1975-78, CO 2 Armd Div Tport Regt RCT 1978-80, Col AQ Commando Forces RM and Col station cdr Plymouth (incl Falklands campaign) 1980-84, student RCDS 1984, Brig dir army recruiting MOD 1985-87; Ma-Gen ACDS (L) MOD 1987-; Col Cmdt RCT 1989; *Recreations* antique restoration, gardening; *Style—* Maj-Gen Ian S Baxter, CBE; c/o Barclays Bank, 17-21 High Street, East Grinstead, West Sussex

BAXTER, Sir (John) Philip; KBE (1965, OBE 1945), CMG (1959); s of late John and Mary Netta Baxter, of Hereford; *b* 7 May 1905; *Educ* Birmingham Univ (BSc, PhD); *m* 1931, Lilian May, da of Arthur John Thatcher; 2 s, 1 da; *Career* res dir ICI Gen Chemical to 1950, vice-chllr NSW Univ 1953-69 (former prof of Chemical Engrg), chm Aust Atomic Energy Cmmn 1957-72, chm Sydney Opera House Tst 1968-75; Hon LLD Montreal, Hon DSc Newcastle Qld NSW, Hon DTech Loughborough, FRACI, MIE (Aust); *Style—* Sir Philip Baxter, KBE, CMG; 1 Kelso St, Enfield, NSW 2136, Australia (☎ 747 4261)

BAXTER, Reginald de St Clair; s of Henry George Charles Baxter (d 1971), of Smithenwood House, Offordcluny, Huntingdon, Cambridgeshire, and Edith *née* Palmer (d 1972); *b* 3 August 1918; *Educ* Kimbolton Sch Huntingdon, Cambridge Sch, Guildhall Sch of Music and Drama; *Career* serv WWII RA 1939-45 star, France & Germany star, Defence Medal, End of War Medal; marine broker Sedgwick Collins & Co Ltd 1936-60, chief hull broker Pitman & Dean 1960-70 (later dir and md), md J H Minet & co 1970- (new broking house Reginald Baxter 7 Co Ltd formed 1977); memb Lloyds's 1963; close friend of Ivor Novello, established his memorial in crypt of St Paul's Cathedral; Freeman City of London 1964, memb Worshipful Co of Carmen 1965; *Style—* Reginald Baxter, Esq; Cityside House, 40 Adler Street, London E1 1EE (☎ 01 247 3203 fax 01 377 1995)

BAXTER, Dr Roger George; s of Rev Benjamin George Baxter and Gweneth Muriel, *née* Causer; *b* 21 April 1940; *Educ* Handsworth GS Birmingham, Univ of Sheffield (BSc, PhD); *m* 1967, Dorothy Ann, da of Albert Leslie Cook (d 1949); 1 s (Philip b 1968), 1 da (Fiona b 1972); *Career* jr res fell Univ of Sheffield 1965-66, lectr dept of applied mathematics Univ of Sheffield 1966-70; asst mathematics master Winchester Coll 1970-81, under master Winchester Coll 1976-81; headmaster Sedbergh Sch 1982-; govr: Bramcote Sch Scarborough, Hurworth House Sch Darlington, Mowden Hall Sch Northumberland, The Cathedral Choir Sch Ripon, Cundall Manor Sch York; memb: HMC Academic Policy Ctee Common Entrance Ctee; FRAS, FRSA; *Books* author of various papers on numerical studies in magnetoplasm diffusion with applications to the F-2 layer of the ionosphere including contribution to Proceedings of the Royal Society; *Recreations* prodn of opera, opera, music, cooking; *Clubs* E India; *Style—* Dr Roger Baxter; Birksholme, Sedbergh, Cumbria LA10 5HQ (☎ 05396 20491); Sedbergh Sch, Sedbergh, Cumbria LA10 5HG (☎ 05396 20535)

BAXTER, William Gordon; OBE (1967) DL Morayshire (1985); s of William Alexander Baxter (d 1973), of Fochabers, and Etheldreda Adam, of Burghead; *b* 8 Feb 1918; *Educ* Ashville Coll Harrogate, Aberdeen Univ (BSc); *m* 1952, Ena Ellen, da of Thomas Robertson, of Huntly; 2 s, 1 da; *Career* research and devpt mangr various mil projects for ICI (explosives) 1940-46; W A Baxter & Sons: joined 1946, md 1947-, chm 1973- (holder of 3 Royal Warrants; Queen's Award for Export 1979); chm subsidiary cos Baxters of Speyside, Gordon & Ena Baxter; dir Bank of Scotland (Grampian Regnl Bd); memb: cncl CBI in Scotland 1964-69, Scottish Export Ctee 1964-69, cncl Food Manufacturers' Fedn (London), N American Advsy Gp to Br Overseas Trade Bd; pres Royal Warrant Holders Assoc (Aberdeen branch) 1978-79; and 1987-88; appeal ctees: Duke of Edinburgh's Award Scheme, Aberdeen Univ Devpt Tst, Cancer Relief (Scottish Appeal), LLD Univ of Strathclyde 1987; *Recreations* salmon fishing, tennis, cricket; *Clubs* Caledonian; *Style—* Gordon Baxter, Esq, OBE, DL; Speybank House, Fochabers, Morayshire IV32 7HH; telex 73327

BAYFIELD, Stephen Peter; s of Stanley William Henry Bayfield, of Harlow, and Eileen Lilian, *née* Sears; *b* 21 May 1954; *Educ* Brays Grove Harlow; *m* 20 July 1974, Margaret Anne, da of Edwin Stanley Barrett, of Brockholes, nr Huddesfield; 2 s (Richard b 1981, Mark b 1986), 1 da (Sarah b 1983); *Career* Inland Revenue 1976-78, Frazer Whiting & Co CA 1978-81, princ Robson Rhodes 1985- (joined 1981); memb Inst Taxation 1979; *Recreations* athletics, swimming; *Style—* Stephen Bayfield, Esq; Robson Rhodes, 186 City Rd, London EC1V 2NU (☎ 01 251 1644/ 251 0316 (after 6 pm), 0245 468123, fax 250 0801, telex 885734)

BAYLEY, Michael Hugh Headington; s of Lt Frederic Hugh Bayley (d 1938), and Elsa Dorothy Bayley (d 1987); *b* 13 Oct 1922; *Educ* Imperial Serv Coll Windsor, Sch of Arch Oxford (DipArch); *m* 7 Aug 1948, Pauline Denys, da of Gustav Oppenheimer (d 1945), of Raymead, Maidenhead, Berks; 2 s (Hugh b 1952, Antony b 1964), 2 da (Justine b 1950, Annabel b 1961); *Career* cmmnd Cheshire Regt 1944, Keninsgton Regt France Germany 1944-45, OBLI 6 Airborne 1945, 6 Palestine RASC Greece 1946, Lt; chartered architect in private practice 1959-, asst to Diocesan Architect for Bucks 1956-59; memb: Maidenhead Civic Soc, Maidenhead C of C, Berks Local Hist Assoc; ARIBA; *Recreations* drawing, local history and legends, celtic place names; *Style—* Michael Bayley, Esq; New Britwell, Westmorland Rd, Maidenhead, Berks SL6 4HD (☎ 0628 20576)

BAYLEY, Prof Peter James; s of John Henry Bayley, of Portreath, Cornwall and Margaret *née* Burness; *b* 20 Nov 1944; *Educ* Redruth GS, Emmanuel Coll Cambridge, (MA, PhD), Ecole Normale Superieure Paris; *Career* fell: Emmanuel Coll Cambridge 1969-71, Gonville and Caius Coll 1971-, lectr in french Cambridge Univ 1978-85; Drapers prof of french Cambridge Univ 1985-; *Books* French Pulpit Oratory 1598-1650 (1980) Selected Sermans of the French Baroque (1983); *Recreations* Spain, wine and food, gardening; *Clubs* Reform; *Style—* Prof Peter Bayley; Department of French, Sidgwick Ave, Cambridge, CB3 9DA, (☎ 0223 335009)

BAYLIS, Clifford Henry; CB (1973); s of Arthur Charles Baylis (d 1953), and Caroline Jane Baylis (d 1975), of Alcester, Warwicks; *b* 20 Mar 1915; *Educ* Alcester GS, Keble Coll Oxford; *m* 1, 1939, Phyllis Mary Clark; 2 s; m 2, 1979, Margaret A Hawkins; *Career* serv WWII; Civil Serv 1947-74, controller HMSO 1969-74; dir: Shipbuilders and Repairers Nat Assoc 1974-77, Harland and Wolff 1978-82; clerk Worshipful Co of Shipwrights 1977-86; *Style—* Clifford H Baylis, Esq, CB; 38 Cleaver St, London SE11 4DP (☎ 01 587 0817)

BAYLIS, Rear Adm Robert Goodwin (Bob); CB (1984), OBE (1964); s of Harold Goodwin Baylis (d 1963), and Evelyn May, *née* Whitworth (d 1961); *b* 29 Nov 1925; *Educ* Highgate Sch, Cambridge Univ (MA); *m* 1949, Joyce Rosemary, da of Lawrence Dyer Churchill (d 1952); 2 s (Mark, Nicholas), 1 da (Rachel); *Career* joined RN 1943; Fleet Weapons Engr Offr 1973-75, Capt RNEC 1975-78, Staff of Vice-Chief of Def Staff 1979-80; chief exec R G Baylis & Assocs (mgmnt and engrg conslt), conslt GEC Avionics, dir Reliability Conslts Ltd, pres Ordnance Bd 1980-84; memb Nuffield Theatre Tst, assoc memb (emeritus) Aust Ordnance Cncl, memb Southampton Univ Devpt Tst; *Recreations* windsurfing, theatre, tennis; *Clubs* Owls; *Style—* Rear Adm Robert Baylis, CB, OBE; Broadwaters, 4 Cliff Rd, Hill Head, Fareham, Hants PO14 3JS (☎ 0329 663392); Fearnside, Segensworth West, Fareham, Hants PO15 5SU (☎ 0489 885252)

BAYLISS, John Leslie; s of Leslie William Bayliss (d 1987), of Birmingham, and Ellen, *née* Rose; *b* 29 Nov 1940; *Educ* Handsworth GS Birmingham, Univ of Leeds (BSc), Univ of Aston; *m* 19 March 1966, Fiona Lennox, da of Frederick Charles Hicks, of Wootton Bassett, Wilts; 3 s (Richard b 1969, Jonathan b 1971, David b 1973); *Career* distribution mangr Lucas Batteries Ltd 1973-78, dir Flockvale Ltd 1982- (divnl mangr 1978-81), chm Flockvale Distribution Ltd 1982-; memb: Solihull Indust Liaison Gp, Solihull Careers Assoc; govr Lyndon Sch Solihull, ctee memb 1 Solihull Scout Gp; author of numerous papers and articles in professional jls; fell Br Interplanetary Soc 1984, fell Inst of Logistics and Distribution Mgmnt 1984, FBIM 1985, FIOD 1987, fell Inst of Admin Accountants; *Recreations* badminton, family history, industrial archeaology; *Style—* John Bayliss, Esq; 44 Links Drive, Solihull, W Midlands B91 2DL; Flockvale Distribution Ltd, Minworth Industrial Pk, Sutton Coldfield, W Mids B76 8AH (☎ 021 351 6111, fax 021 351 4895, car 0836 720477)

BAYLISS, Hon Mrs; (Mary Selina); *née* Bridgeman; da of 2 Viscount Bridgeman, KBE, CB, DSO, MC (d 1982); *b* 14 Jan 1940; *m* 1962, Jeremy David Bagot Bayliss, s of Edmund Bayliss; 3 s; memb Court of Reading Univ 1982; govr Chiltern Nursery Training Coll; *Recreations* music, gardening; *Style—* The Hon Mrs Bayliss, JP; Sheepbridge Court, Swallowfield, nr Reading, Berks RG1 1PT

BAYLISS, Sir Noel Stanley; CBE (1960); s of Henry Bayliss (d 1948), of NSW, and Nelly Stothers; *b* 19 Dec 1906; *Educ* Melbourne HS, Queen's Coll Melbourne Univ, Lincoln Coll Oxford, Univ of California Berkeley; *m* 1933, Nellie Elise, da of Arthur Banks, of Los Angeles; 2 s; *Career* prof chem W Australia Univ 1938-71 (emeritus 1972), memb Aust Univs Cmmn 1959-70, memb Hong Kong Univs and Pol6ys Grants cmmn 1966-73, chm Murdoch Univ Planning Bd 1970-73; kt 1979; *see Debrett's Handbook of Australia and New Zealand for further details*; *Recreations* music, golf; *Clubs* Royal Perth Yacht, Nedlands Golf (WA); *Style—* Sir Noel Bayliss, CBE; 104

Thomas St, Nedlands, W Australia 6009 (☎ 09 386 1453)

BAYLISS, Sir Richard (Ian Samuel); KCVO (1978); s of late Frederick William Bayliss, of Tettenhall, and late Muryel Anne Bayliss; *b* 2 Jan 1917; *Educ* Rugby, Clare Coll Cambridge, St Thomas' Hosp London (MD); *m* 1, 1941 (m dis 1956), Margaret Joan Lawson; 1 s, 1 da; m 2, 1957, Constance Ellen, da of Wilbur J Frey, of Connecticut; 2 da; m 3, 1979, Marina, wid of Charles Rankin; *Career* conslt physician: Westminster Hosp 1954-81, King Edward VII's Hosp for Offrs 1964-86, Med dir Swiss Reinsurance Co 1969-85, physician to HM the Queen 1970-82, head of HM's Med Household 1973-82, dir and vice-chm Private Patients Plan plc 1979-, dir J S Pathology Servs, hon med advsr Nuffield Hosps 1981-88, asst dir RCP Res Unit 1982-88; second vice-pres RCP 1983-84; hon fell Clare Coll Cambridge; FRCP; *Recreations* skiing, photography, music; *Clubs* Garrick; *Style—* Sir Richard Bayliss, KCVO; 6 Harley Street, London W1N 1AA (☎ 01 935 2071)

BAYLY, Vice Adm Sir Patrick Uniacke; KBE (1968), CB (1965), DSC (1944) and two bars (1944, 1951); s of Lancelot F S Bayly (d 1951), and Eileen M Bayly, of Nenagh, Co Tipperary; *b* 4 August 1914; *Educ* Aravon Bray Co Wicklow, RNC Dartmouth; *m* 1945, Moy Gourlay, da of Robert Gourlay Jardine, of Newtonmearns, Scotland; 2 da (Caroline, Jennifer); *Career* Midshipman 1932, combined ops 1941-44, Lt Cdr 1944, HMS Mauritius 1946, Cdr 1948, Korean War 1952-53, Capt 1954, IDC 1957, Capt (D) 6 Destroyer Sqdn 1958, staff SACLANT Norfolk Va 1960, C of S Mediterranean 1962, Rear Adm 1963, Flag Offr Sea Training 1963, Adm Pres RNC Greenwich 1965, Vice Adm 1967, C of S COMNAVSOUTH Malta 1967, ret 1970; dir The Maritime Tst 1971-88; chm Falklands Appeal 1983-; *Style—* Vice Adm Sir Patrick Bayly, KBE, CB, DSC and two bars; Dunning House, Liphook, Hants (☎ 0428 723116)

BAYMAN, Margaret Elizabeth; *née* WALSH; da of George William Walsh, of 22 South Park, Lytham, Lytham St Annes, Lancs, and Janet Featherstone, *née* Firth; *b* 2 August 1943; *Educ* Fylde Lodge HS for Girls Stockport, Arnold HS for Girls Lancs; *m* 9 Sept 1967, Paul Aubrey Robert, s of Capt Aubrey Fredrick James Bayman, of 14 Romney Road, New Malden, Surrey; 2 s (David b 1973, Matthew b 1974), 2 da (Catherine b 1969, Sarah b 1970); *Career* accountant Br Health-Care Export Cncl Ltd 1981-88; tres 1st Claygate Scout Gp 1982-; memb PTA Claremont Fan Court Sch 1987-; FCA (1968); *Recreations* reading, theatre, history; *Style—* Mrs Margaret Bayman; 45 Oaken Lane, Claygate, Esher, Sussex

BAYNE, Nicholas Peter; CMG (1984); s of Capt Ronald Bayne, RN (d 1978), and Elisabeth Margaret, *née* Ashcroft; *b* 15 Feb 1937; *Educ* Eton, Christ Church Oxford (MA, DPhil); *m* 1961, Diana, da of Thomas Wilde, of Bideford, N Devon; 3 s; *Career* HM Dip Ser; ambass: Zaire 1983-85, (non resident) Congo, Rwanda and Burundi 1984-85; UK perm rep OECD Paris 1985-88; Dep Under-Sen of State FCO 1988-; ; *Style—* Nicholas Bayne, Esq, CMG; c/o Foreign and Commonwealth Office, King Charles St, London SW1

BAYNE-JARDINE, Colin Charles; s of Brig Christian West Bayne-Jardine, CBE, DSO, MC (d 1959), and Isobel Anna, *née* Forman; *b* 08 Jan 1932; *Educ* Marlborough, Univ Coll Oxford (MA), Bristol Univ (MEd); *m* 7 Sept 1957, (Helen) Elizabeth, da of Arthur Douglas Roberts, OBE (d 1979); 4 s (John b 1958, Charles b 1960, Thomas b 1962, Andrew b 1963); *Career* 2 Lt RA BAOR; Capt RA TA; teacher: St Paul's Sch Concord New Hampshire USA 1956-57, Upper Canada Coll Toronto Canada 1957-58, Glasgow Acad 1958-61, Blundell's Sch 1961-65, Henbury Sch Bristol 1976-85; sr inspr (secdy) Staffs 1985-88, princ co inspr Hereford and Worcester 1988-; chm of govrs Downs Sch Wrascall; memb local review ctee Bristol Prison, cncl memb Cheltenham Coll; *Books* Mussolini and Italy (1966), World War Two (1968), World War Two and Its Aftermath (1986); *Recreations* walking, skiing, travel, music, shooting; *Style—* Colin Bayne-Jardine, Esq; The Half Timbered Barn, Church Lane, Eldersfield, Glos GL19 4NP; Education Office, Castle St, Worcester WA1 3AG (☎ 0905 353 366)

BAYNES, Christopher Rory; s and h of Sir John Baynes, 7 Bt, *qv*; *b* 11 May 1956; *Career* ACA 1982; *Style—* Christopher Baynes, Esq

BAYNES, Sir John Christopher Malcolm; 7 Bt (UK 1801); s of Lt-Col Sir Rory Malcolm Stuart Baynes, 6 Bt (d 1979), and Ethel Audrey, *née* Giles (d 1947); *b* 24 April 1928; *Educ* Sedbergh Sch, RMA Sandhurst, Edinburgh Univ (MSc); *m* 1955, Shirley Maxwell, da of Robert A Dodds, of Foxbury House, Lesbury, Alnwick, Northumberland (d 1952); 4 s (Christopher, Timothy b 1957, Simon b 1960, William b 1966); *Heir* s, Christopher Rory, b 11 May 1956; *Career* Ranks and Sandhurst 1946-48; offr 1948-72; Lt-Col (ret) Cameronians (Scot Rifles) 1948-68, Malaya 1952 (despatches), Aden 1966, cmd 52 (L) vols 1969-72; Queen's Own Highlanders 1968-72; writer Order of the Sword 1 Class (Sweden) 1965; *Publications* Morale: A Study of Men and Courage (1967 and 1987), The Jacobite Rising of 1715 (1970), The Soldier in Modern Society (1971), Vol IV of The History of The Cameronians (Scot Rifles) (1971), Soldiers of Scotland (1988), The Forgotten Victor: The Life of General Sir Richard O'Connor (1989); *Recreations* shooting, fishing, golf, reading; *Clubs* Army and Navy; *Style—* Lt Col Sir John Baynes, Bt; Talwrn Bach, Llanfyllin, Powys SY22 5LQ (☎ 069 184 576)

BAYNES, Pauline Diana; da of Frederick William Wilberforce Baynes, CIE, and Jessie Harriet Maud Cunningham; *b* 9 Sept 1922; *Educ* Beaufront Sch Camberley, Farnham Sch of Art, Slade Sch of Art; *m* 1961, Fritz Otto Gasch; *Career* designer and book illustrator; *Style—* Miss Pauline Baynes; Rock Barn Cottage, Dockenfield, Farnham, Surrey (☎ (0428) 713306)

BAYNHAM, (Alexander) Christopher; s of Alexander Baynham (d 1965), of Stroud, Glos, and Dulcie Rowena, *née* Rees (d 1959); *b* 22 Dec 1935; *Educ* Marling Sch, Reading Univ (BSc), Warwick Univ (PhD), RCDS; *m* 5 Aug 1961, Eileen May, da of George Wilson, of Tadcaster, Yorks; 2 s (Andrew b 27 April 1965, Peter b 13 Oct 1966), 1 da (Sharon b 8 March 1968); *Career* Civil Serv 1955-: dir Royal Signals and Radar Estab 1984-86, dir Royal Armament R & D Estab 1986-; involved in local church activities; *Style—* Dr Christopher Baynham; Rarde, Fort Halstead, Sevenoaks, Kent TN14 7BP (☎ 0959 32222 ext 2008 and fax ext 2533, telex 95267)

BAYNTUN-COWARD, Hylton Henry; s of Leslie Lancelot Coward (d 1982), of Combe Royal, Bath, and Constance Louise Muriel, *née* Bayntun; *b* 17 Nov 1932; *Educ* Cheltenham; *m* 1 June 1963, Charlotte Anne Wentworth, da of Sir John Gibbons, Bt (d 1982), of Preston, Dorset; 2 s (Edward b 1966, Jo b 1972), 2 da (Emma b 1964, Polly b 1970); *Career* antiquarian bookseller, md George Bayntun incorporating Robert Riviere 1954-, proprietor, George Gregory Gallery 1963-, fndr Museum of Bookbinding 1977, pres Antiquarian Booksellers' Assoc (Int) 1980-82 (hon tres 1977-80), 1985-; *Recreations* farming, conservation; *Style—* Hylton Bayntun-Coward, Esq; Dunkerton Grange, nr Bath BA2 8BL (☎ 0761 32366); Manvers St, Bath BA1 1JW (☎ 0225 66000)

BAZALGETTE, Rear Adm Derek Willoughby; CB (1976); yr s of Harry L Bazalgette (d 1953); *b* 22 July 1924; *Educ* RNC Dartmouth; *m* 1947, Angela Hilda Vera, da of Sir Henry Hinchcliffe (d 1980); 4 da; *Career* RN 1938-76, Adm Pres Royal Naval Coll Greenwich 1974-76, ADC 1974; princ Netley Waterside House 1977-83 (Local Govt); HQ cmmr Scout Assoc 1977-1987; Independent Inquiry insp 1983-; memb General Synod 1985, tres Corp of the Sons of the Clergy 1988; *Clubs* Lansdowne; *Style—* Rear Adm Derek Bazalgette, CB; The Glebe House, Newtown, Fareham, Hants (☎ 0329 833138)

BAZLEY, Thomas John Sebastian; s and h of Sir Thomas Bazley, 3 Bt, *qv*; *b* 31 August 1948; *Style—* Thomas Bazley, Esq

BAZLEY, Sir Thomas Stafford; 3 Bt (UK 1869); s of late Gardner Sebastian Bazley, o s of 2 Bt; suc gf, Sir Thomas Sebastian Bazley, 2 Bt, 1919; *b* 5 Oct 1907; *Educ* Harrow, Magdalen Coll Oxford; *m* 1945, Carmen, da of J Tulla; 3 s, 2 da; *Heir* s, Thomas John Sebastian Bazley; *Style—* Sir Thomas Bazley, Bt; Eastleach Downs Farm, New Eastleach, Cirencester, Gloucester.

BEACH, Gen Sir (William Gerald) Hugh; GBE (1980, OBE 1966), KCB (1976), MC (1944); s of Maj-Gen William Henry Beach, CB, CMG, DSO (d 1952), and Constance Maude, *née* Cammell; *b* 20 May 1923; *Educ* Winchester, Peterhouse Cambridge (MA), Edinburgh Univ (MSc); *m* 1951, Estelle Mary, da of Gordon Henry, of Epsom, Surrey; 3 s, 1 da; *Career* serv WWII RE, NW Europe and Far East, Lt-Col 1963, Brig 1968, Cdr 12 Inf Bde BAOR 1968-71, dir Army Staff Duties MOD 1971-74, Maj-Gen 1971, Cmdt Staff Coll Camberley 1974-75, dep C-in-C UK Land Forces 1976-77, master-gen of the Ordnance 1977-81; Col Cmdt RE 1977-81, Hon Col Cambridge Univ OTC 1987-; Vice-Lord-Lt Gter London 1981-87 (DL 1981); warden St George's House Windsor 1981-86; pres CCF Assoc 1981; memb Security Commission 1982-; Chief Royal Engr 1982-87; chm study gp on censorship to protect mil info 1983, dir The Council for Arms Control; *Recreations* sailing, skiing; *Clubs* Farmers', Royal Lymington Yacht; *Style—* Gen Sir Hugh Beach, GBE, KCB, MC; The Ropeway, Beaulieu, Hants (☎ 0590 612269)

BEACH, Surgn Rear Adm William Vincent; CB (1961), OBE (1949), QHS (1960); yr s of William Henry Beach (d 1918), of Belvedere Estate, St Vincent, W Indies; *b* 22 Nov 1903; *Educ* Seaford Coll, Guy's Hosp; *m* 1931, Daphne Muriel, yr da of Eustace Acworth Joseph (d 1952), late ICS; 2 da; *Career* RN Med Serv 1928-62, ser WWII: Atlantic, Pacific and Mediterranean Fleets, sr specialist in surgery to RN, ret; sr surgn Shaw Savill Line 1966-75; MRCS, LRCP, FRCS; *Recreations* shooting, gardening; *Clubs* Naval and Military; *Style—* Surgn Rear Adm William Beach, CB, OBE, QHS; Cherry Tree Cottage, Easton, Winchester, Hants SO21 1EG (☎ 096 278 222)

BEADON, Wing Cdr Clive Vernon; DFC; s of Lt-Col Vernon Beadon, MC (d 1967), of Dublin, and Beryl Edith, *née* Martin (d 1947); descended paternally from Rt Rev Richard Beadon, Bishop of Bath and Wells; *b* 15 April 1919; *Educ* Imperial Serv Coll Windsor, RAF Cranwell, Staff Coll Haifa; *m* 1, 29 March 1952, Violet Mary Oliver (d 1964); 1 step s; m 2, 11 Feb 1965, Mrs (Vera) Jane Whigham, da of John Siddons Corby (d 1956); *Career* cmmnd RAF 1939; WWII, Coastal Cmd on Western approaches, Flying Instr, SE Asia Cmd 1942, psc 1944, ACSEA HQ Ceylon; Air Attaché to seven Latin American Countries 1953-57; cmdg RAF Butzweilerhof, Germany 1960-63; Asst Air Attaché Paris 1964; vice-pres Br Soc of Dowsers; Venezuelan Air Force Cross; *Recreations* sailing, scuba diving; *Clubs* RAF, RAF Yacht; *Style—* Wing Cdr Clive Beadon, DFC; 15 Sylvan Lane, The Copse, Hamble, Hants SO3 5RG (☎ (0703) 456266)

BEAKBANE, (Henry) Renault; s of Henry Beakbane, of Stourport-on-Severn (d 1953); *b* 28 April 1923; *Educ* Leighton Pk, Leeds Univ, LSE (BSc); *m* 1951, Joan, da of Henry Epton Hornby, OBE, FRCVS, DVSM, of Zimbabwe (d 1976); 2 s, 1 da; *Career* Colonial Serv Tanganyika 1946-50, chm Beakbane Ltd; Master Worshipful Co of Glovers 1979; Quaker; CBIM, FRSA; *Recreations* riding (horses Figeac, Myricaria); *Clubs* City Livery; *Style—* Renault Beakbane, Esq; Jacob's Ladder, Low Habberley, Kidderminster, Worcs (☎ 0562 745125/820561)

BEAL, Anthony Ridley; s of Harold Beal, and Nesta Beal; *b* 28 Feb 1925; *Educ* Haberdashers' Aske's, Downing Coll Cambridge; *m* 1958, Rosemary Jean Howarth; 3 da; *Career* chm Heinemann Educational Books 1979-85; md Heinemann Educational Books (Int) 1979-85; chm Educational Publishers Cncl 1980-83; memb Cncl of the Publishers Assoc 1982-86;; *Books* D H Lawrence, D H Lawrence: selected literary criticism; *Style—* Anthony Beal, Esq; 19 Homefield Rd, Radlett, Herts (☎ 09276 4567)

BEALE, (Thomas) Edward; CBE (1966), JP (Inner London 1950); s of Thomas Henderson Beale (d 1956), of London; *b* 5 Mar 1904; *Educ* City of London Sch; *m* 6 Sept 1932, Beatrice May (d 1986), da of William Steele McLaughlin, JP (d 1936), of Enniskillen; 1 s (Trevor Howard b 1934); *Career* chm Beale's Ltd; chm Caterers' Assoc of GB 1949-52, pres Int Ho-Re-Ca 1954-64; memb bd Br Travel Assoc 1950-70 (dep chm 1965-70); chm Treasy Ctee of Enquiry House of Commons Refreshment Dept 1951; Master Worshipful Co of Bakers 1955; Médaille d'Argent de Paris 1960; FRSH 1957, FRSA 1968; *Recreations* arboriculture; *Clubs* Carlton; *Style—* T Edward Beale, Esq, CBE, JP; West Lodge Park, Hadley Wood, Herts EN4 0PY (☎ 01 440 8311)

BEALE, Nicholas Clive Lansdowne; s of Prof Evelyn Martin Lansdowne Beale, FRS (d 1985), and Violette Elizabeth Anne, *née* Lewis; *b* 22 Feb 1955; *Educ* Winchester, Trinity Coll Cambridge (MA); *m* 16 July 1977, Christine Ann, da of Peter Macpoland, of Bedford; 1 s (Rupert Christopher Lansdowne b 1977), 1 da (Rebecca Merryn Elizabeth b 1980); *Career* md Beale Electronic Systems Ltd 1977-85; exec vice-chm Beale Int Technology Ltd 1985-; *Recreations* piano, sulkido; *Clubs* IOD; *Style—* Nicholas C L Beale, Esq; c/o Whitehall, Whitehall Lane, Wraysbury, Middx TW19 5NJ (☎ 0784 813115, fax 0784 813874)

BEALE, Trevor Howard; s of Thomas Edward Beale, CBE, JP, of West Lodge Park, Hadley Wood, Herts, and Beatrice May, *née* MacLaughlin (d 1986); *b* 28 Nov 1934; *Educ* Westminster, Trinity Coll Cambridge (MA); *m* 5 May 1962, Susan Jane, da of Philip Reginald Brierley, of Maple Cottage, Chalfont St, Peter, Bucks; 3 s (Andrew b 30 Nov 1963, Christopher b 20 Nov 1967, Nicholas b 30 Dec 1969), 1 da (Philippa b 5 Nov 1965); *Career* barr Gray's Inn 1960; md Beales Ltd 1970; churchwarden St Michael's Highgate 1979-82; Liveryman Worshipful Co of Bakers 1955; MHCIMA

1969; *Recreations* music; *Style*— Trevor Beale, Esq; Bunkers Ho, Gaddesden Row, nr Hemel Hempstead, Herts; West Lodge Park, Hadley Wood, Herts (☎ 01 440 8311)

BEALE, Sir William Francis; OBE (1945); s of late George Beale, of Potterspury Lodge, Towcester, Northants, and Elizabeth, *née* Potts; *b* 27 Jan 1908; *Educ* Downside, Pembroke Coll Cambridge; *m* 1934, Dèva, da of Hynek Zaloudek, of Llandudno; 1 s, 1 da; *Career* chm NAAFI 1953-61, dep chm Randall Group Br West Africa Corpn 1964-78, chm Staple Green, dir Radio Rentals NCR 1964-78, MFH Tedworth Foxhounds 1972-81; kt 1956; *Recreations* hunting, shooting; *Clubs* Army and Navy, Hawks; *Style*— Sir William Beale, OBE; The Old Rectory, Woodborough, Pewsey, Wilts SN9 5PH (☎ 0672 85595)

BEALES, Prof Derek Edward Dawson; s of Edward Beales (d 1984), and Dorothy Kathleen, *née* Dawson; *b* 12 June 1931; *Educ* Bishop's Stortford Coll, Sidney Sussex Coll Cambridge (BA, MA, PhD, LittD ; *m* 14 Aug 1964, Sara (Sally) Jean, da of Francis Harris Ledbury (d 1971); 1 s (Richard Derek b 1967), 1 da (Christina (Kitty) Margaret b 1965); *Career* nat serv Sgt RA 1949-50; res fell Sidney Sussex Coll Cambridge 1955-58, fell 1958-; vice-master 1973-75, univ asst lect 1962-65, lect 1965-80, prof Mod Hist 1980-, chm Bd of Hist 1979-81; visiting lect Harvard Univ 1965; ed Hist Journal 1971-75, Univ Library Syndicate Cambridge 1981-, General Bd of the Faculties 1987-; fell of Roy Hist Soc (memb of cncl 1984-88); *Books* England & Italy 1859-60 (1961), From Castlereagh to Gladstone (1969), The Risorgiments and Unification of Italy (1971), Hist & Biography (1981), (ed with Geoffrey Best) History Society & the Churches (1985), Joseph II: the Shadow of Maria Theresa 1741-80 (1987), many articles in learned jls; *Recreations* music, walking, bridge; *Style*— Prof Derek Beales; Sidney Sussex Coll, Cambridge, CB2 3HU (☎ 0223 738800)

BEALEY, Prof Frank William; s of Ernest Bealey (d 1951), of Netherton, Dudley, and Nora, *née* Hampton (d 1982); *b* 31 August 1922; *Educ* King Edward VI GS Stourbridge 1933-41, LSE 1946-48; *m* 2 Jul 1960, Sheila, da of James Hurst (d 1955); 1 s (William b 1968), 2 da (Rachel b 1963, Rosalind b 1967); *Career* Finnish Govt Scholar 1948-49, res fell LSE 1950-51, extra mural lectr Univ of Manchester 1951-52, asst lectr, lectr, sr lectr Univ of Keele 1952-64; prof of politics Univ of Aberdeen 1964-; FRHS 1974; *Books* Labour and Politics (with Henry Pelling, 1958), Constituency Politics (with J Blondel and W P McCann, 1965), The Social and Political Thought of the British Labour Party (1970), The Post Office Engineering Union (1976), The Politics of Independence (with John Sewel, 1981), Democracy in the Contemporary State (1988); *Recreations* watching football and cricket, swimming, darts; *Clubs* Economicals Assoc Football and Cricket Club; *Style*— Prof Frank Bealey; 355 Clifton Rd, Aberdeen AB2 2DT (☎ 0224 484689); Dept of Politics, Univ of Aberdeen AB9 2UB (☎ 0224 272715)

BEAMENT, Sir James William Longman; o s of Tom Beament (d 1958), of Crewkerne, Somerset; *b* 17 Nov 1921; *Educ* Crewkerne GS, Queens' Coll Cambridge (MA), London Sch of Tropical Med (PhD), Cambridge Univ (ScD); *m* 1962, (Sara) Juliet, yst da of Prof Sir Ernest Barker (d 1959); 2 s; *Career* princ scientific offr Agricultural Res Cncl to 1961; fell and tutor Queens' Coll Cambridge 1962-67, reader Cambridge Univ 1967-69, Drapers prof of agriculture and head of dept of applied biology Cambridge 1969-; vice-pres Queens' Coll Cambridge 1982-; chm Natural Environment Research Cncl 1978-81; FRS; kt 1980; *Recreations* composing music, playing music, DIY; *Clubs* Farmers', Amateur Dramatic (Cambridge); *Style*— Sir James Beament; 19 Sedley Taylor Rd, Cambridge CB2 2PW (☎ 0223 246045)

BEAMISH, Adrian John; CMG; s of Thomas Charles Constantine Bernard Beamish (d 1948), and Josephine Mary, *née* Lee (d 1968); *b* 21 Jan 1939; *Educ* Prior Park Coll Bath, Cambridge Univ (BA); *m* 1965, Caroline, da of Dr John Lipscomb, of Chilham, Kent; 2 da (Catherine b 1966, Antonia b 1968); *Career* HM Dip Serv; third sec Tehran, second sec FO, first sec Paris; dir Br Info Servs New Delhi, dep head Personnel Operations FCO, cnsllr Bonn 1981-85, head Falklands Islands Dept FCO 1985-87, ambass Lima 1987-; *Recreations* books, plants; *Style*— Adrian Beamish, Esq, CME; British Embassy, Lima, Peru

BEAMISH, Hon Andrea Tufton; yr da of Baron Chelwood, MC, DL, by his 1 w; *b* 7 Mar 1955; *Style*— The Hon Andrea Beamish

BEAMISH, Hon Claudia Hamilton; er da of Baron Chelwood, MC, DL, by his 1 w; *b* 1952; *Style*— The Hon Claudia Beamish

BEAMISH, Michael John; s of lewis Stanley Beamish (d 1983), and Beatrice Ivy, *née* Beazley; *b* 9 May 1916; *Educ* Keys Coll Sussex (no longer in existence), Worthing Art Coll; *m* 21 Sept 1963 (m dis 1979) Christine Ann, da of Frank Alfred Nichols; *Career* designer John Michael Gp 1969-72, Freelance interior design conslt UK and abroad 1972-82, fndr Prizelake Ltd and Prizelake Southern Ltd interior design conslts 1982-(Prizelake USA 1988-); clients incl: Glyndebourne Festival Opera, Br Maritime Museum; memb: Master Builders Fedn, Fedn Master Craftsmen; *Recreations* boating, keep fit and weight training, swimming, art, architecture; *Style*— Michael Beamish, Esq; "Bearlands", Dyke Rd Ave, Brighton, Sussex BN1 5NU; "Singing Waters" 501 Solar Isle Drive, Fort Lauderdale, Florida USA; P O Box 995, BN1 5NU (☎ 0273 559 630, fax 0273 564 436)

BEAMONT, Wing Cdr Roland Prosper; CBE (1969, OBE 1953), DSO (1943) and bar (1944), DFC (1941) and bar (1942), DFC (USA 1945), DL (1977); s of Lt-Col E C Beamont, of Summersdale Chichester (d 1955), and Dorothy Mary, *née* Haynes (d 1951); *b* 10 August 1920; *Educ* Eastbourne Coll; *m* 1, 1942, Shirley, (d 1945), da of Bernard Adams, Artist, of Chelsea; 1 da (Carol); m 2, 1946, Patricia, da of Capt Richard Galpine Raworth, of Harrogate; 1 step s (Richard), 2 da (Patricia, Elizabeth); *Career* RAF Fighter Cmd 1939-46 (despatches 1940); chief test pilot: English Electric 1947-60, dep chief test pilot Br Aircraft Corpn Weybridge 1960-65; dir flight ops: Br Aircraft Corpn, Br Aerospace Warton 1965-78, Panavia Gmbh Munich (Tornado programme) 1971-79; Master Pilot and Liveryman Guild of Air Pilots; hon fell Soc of Experimental Test Pilots of USA, memb Battle of Britain Fighter Assoc; FRAcS; *Books* Phoenix into Ashes (1968), Typhoon and Tempest at War (1979), Testing Years (1980), English Electric Canberra (1982), Fighter Test Pilot (1986), English Electric Lightning (1984), My Part of the Sky (1988); *Recreations* fishing, aviation; *Clubs* RAF, Sweatford Flyfishers, Bustard Frying (hon memb); *Style*— Wing Cdr Roland Beamont, CBE, DSO, DFC, DL; Cross Cottage, Pentridge, Salisbury SP5 5QX

BEAN, Basil; CBE (1985); s of Walter Bean (d 1976), of York, and Alice Louise Chambers (d 1978); *b* 2 July 1931; *Educ* Archbishop Holgate Sch York; *m* 1956, Janet Mary, da of Frederick Cecil Rex Brown (d 1961), of West Bromwich; 1 da (Rachel); *Career* dir gen Nat House Bldg Cncl 1985-; chief exec Merseyside Devpt Corpn 1980-85; gen mangr Northampton Devpt Corpn 1977-80; memb Chartered Inst of Public Finances and Accountancy; hon fell Incorp Assoc of Architects and Surveyors; memb Br Waterways Bd 1985-88; *Recreations* travel, walking, bridge; *Clubs* Royal Cwlth, Northampton and Co; *Style*— Basil Bean, Esq, CBE; The Forge, Manor Farm, Church Lane, Princes Risborough, Bucks (☎ 08444 6133); Nat House Bldg Cncl, Chilton Avenue, Amersham, Bucks HP6 5AP (☎ 0494 434477)

BEAN, Christopher Robin; *b* 25 August 1934; *Educ* Bungay GS, Suffolk; *m* 31 March 1956, Mavis Kathleen; 2 da (Susan b 5 April 1958, Judith Marie b 27 Feb 1960); *Career* dep chm and chief exec Dubilier Int plc; *Recreations* interested in all sporting activities; *Style*— Christopher R Bean, Esq; Dubilier International plc, Dubilier House, Radley Rd, Abingdon, Oxon OX14 3XA (☎ 0235 28271)

BEAN, Lady; Constance Mary; da of William James Greenlees, of Adelaide; *m* 1927, Sir Edgar Layton Bean, CMG (d 1977); 2 s; *Clubs* Ormskirk GS; *Style*— Lady Bean; 51 Godfrey Terrace, Leabrook, S Australia

BEAN, Hugh Cecil; CBE (1970); s of Cecil Walter Claude Bean, MBE (d 1975), and Gertrude Alice, *née* Chapman (d 1982); *b* 22 Sept 1929; *Educ* Beckenham GS, RCM; *m* 16 April 1963, Mary Dorothy, da of Henry Unwin Harrow (d 1981); 1 da (Fiona b 8 May 1969); *Career* Grenadier Gds 1949-51; prof of violin RCM 1954, ldr Philharmonia Orch 1956-67, assoc ldr BBC Symphony Orch 1967-69, ldr LSO 1969-71; memb Music Gp of London 1951-; recordings: Elgar Violin Concerto (EMI), Vivaldi's Seasons (Decca), numerous works of chamber music for various companies; memb Royal Philharmonic Soc; FRCM 1968; *Recreations* model aircraft, steam railways, record collecting; *Style*— Hugh Bean, Esq, CBE; 30 Stone Park Ave, Beckenham, Kent BR3 3LX (☎ 01 650 8774)

BEAN, Rev Canon John Victor; s of Albert Victor Bean (d 1961), and Eleanor Ethel Bean (d 1975); *b* 1 Dec 1925; *Educ* Gt Yarmouth GS, Cambridge Univ (MA), Salisbury Theological Coll; *m* 1955, Nancy Evelyn, da of Capt Thomas Allen Evans, MC (d 1964); 2 s (Simon, Martin), 2 da (Judith d 1961, Rosalind); *Career* war serv RNVR; ordained: deacon 1950, priest 1951; various appts in diocese of Portsmouth, hon canon Portsmouth Cathedral 1970-, vicar St Mary Cowes 1966-, priest i-c All Saints Gurnard 1978-; chaplain to HM The Queen 1980-; *Recreations* boatwatching, photography; *Clubs* Island Sailing, Gurnard Sailing, Cowes Rotary, Cowes Golf; *Style*— Canon John Bean; The Vicarage, Church Rd, Cowes, Isle of Wight PO31 8HA (☎ 0983 292509)

BEANLAND, John Hoare; s of John Beanland (d 1953), of Hill Top Hall, Pannal, Harrogate, North Yorks, and Harriet Henrietta Hoare (d 1983); *b* 30 Mar 1930; *Educ* Shrewsbury; *m* 1, 6 April 1959 (m dis), 1 da (Susan b 1960); m 2, 9 July 1967; 1 s (Simon b 1968), 1 da Hannah b 1970); *Career* Lt Royal Corps of Signals (cipher Kingston-on-Thames) 1948; English amateur Golf Championship quarter finals 1950; md Hookstone Securities Ltd 1968; *Recreations* golf, gardening, walking; *Clubs* Pannal Golf Harrogate; *Style*— John H Beanland, Esq; Old Winery, Reynard Crag Lane, High Birstwith, North Yorks HG3 2JQ (☎ 0423 771456); National Industrial Sales Manager, Rakusen House, Clayton Wood Rise, Leeds (☎ 0532 784821, telex 556349)

BEARCROFT, (Joseph) Peter; s of Arthur William Blearcroft (d 1975), of 17 Filey Rd, Scarborough, and Elizabeth Jane, *née* McKinley (d 1982); *b* 15 July 1923; *Educ* St Mary's GS, Hammersknott nr Darlington, Queensland Univ Brisbane Aust, Balliol Coll Oxford (MA); *m* 14 June 1952, Dr Rosalind Irene, da of Albert Victor Chamberlain, MBE (d 1978); 1 s (Philip b 13 March 1964), 2 da (Charlotte b 5 June 1962, Emma b 19 May 1968); *Career* Flying cadet Fleet Air Arm 1942, flying trg with US Navy 1943-44, Sub Lt RNVR, Flying control offr Fleet Air Arm HQ for the Normandy Landings 1944, TAMY I and MONAB 5 Aust SE Asia Cmd 1945, demob Lt RNVR 1946; jr commercial asst Distribution Centre Ltd Billingham, trainee Manchester Assur Co Ltd 1949, trainee tech asst Howards & Sons (Ilford) Ltd; Horlicks Ltd 1950-63: mgmnt trainee, mkt res offr, asst to co sec, head of mktg div, dir Pristine Products Ltd and Airwick Ltd; Br Railways Bd 1963-83: dir of mktg (HQ) 1963-65, mktg and sales mangr (freight), chief freight mangr Western Region (Paddington) HQ, mktg advsr freight (HQ) 1978-83, ret 1983; business cnsllr DTI and Dept of Employment 1983-86, currently private industl mktg consl̇t and business advsr; underwriting memb Lloyds 1981; fndr chm: Railway Mktg Soc 1971-83, Tport and Distribution Gp Inst of Mktg (memb nat cncl); memb Ctee for Terotechnology with DTI 1973-78; Fndr memb SDP 1981; Freeman City of London, Liveryman Worshipful Co of Marketors 1976; fell: Chartered Inst of Tport, Chartered Inst of Mktg, Inst of Logistics and Physical Distribution Mgmnt; *Recreations* swimming, golf, reading, travelling; *Style*— Peter Bearcroft, Esq; Barming Place, Maidstone, Kent ME16 9ED (☎ 0622 28844)

BEARD, Allan Geoffrey; CB (1979); s of Maj Henry Thomas Beard (d 1969), and Florence Mercy Beard; *b* 18 Oct 1919; *Educ* Ormskirk GS; *m* 1945, Helen Matthews, da of Michael James McDonagh (d 1956); 1 da; *Career* Capt RE UK; under-sec DHSS until 1979; hon tres Motability 1985; *Recreations* gardening; *Clubs* RAC; *Style*— Allan Beard, Esq, CB; 51 Rectory Park, Sanderstead, Surrey CR2 9JR (☎ 01 657 4197)

BEARD, Malcolm Douglas; s of Harold William Poynter Beard (d 1982), and Doris Helena, *née* Cuthbert; *b* 26 April 1930; *Educ* Buckhurst Hill Co HS; *m* 11 Sept 1954, (Edith) Jeanne, da of Charles Edward May; 2 s (Graham Michael b 28 March 1958, David Christopher b 8 April 1960), 1 da (Gillian Margaret b 30 June 1955); *Career* RN 1949-51; Fred Olsen Lines Oslo Norway 1947-49, H Maclaine & Co Ltd London 1951-52, Galbraith Pembrove & Co Ltd 1952-68 (dir 1963-68)own co MD Beard & Co Ltd 1968-; vice-chm Old Buckwellian Assoc, tres Chigwell Lawn Tennis Club, capt St John's Badminton Club Buckhurst Hill; Freeman City of London 1978, Liveryman Worshipful Co of Shipwrights 1978; memb The Baltic Exchange, London; *Recreations* tennis, badminton; *Clubs* City Livery Club; *Style*— Malcolm D Beard, Esq; 17 Luctons Ave, Buckhurst Hill, Essex (☎ 01 504 7850); Pine Lodge, Grove Ave, West Mersea, Essex(☎ 0206 382034); M D Beard & Co Ltd, 25 Phipp Street, London EC2A 4NP (☎ 01 490 3361, fax 01 739 8093)

BEARD, (Christopher) Nigel; s of Albert Leonard Beard (d 1958) of, Castleford, Yorks, and Irene, *née* Bowes (d 1968); *b* 10 Oct 1936; *Educ* Castleford GS Yorks, UCL (BSc); *m* 1969, Jennifer Anne, da of Thomas Beckerleg Cotton, of 35 Mountside, Guildford, Surrey; 1 s (Daniel b 1971), 1 da (Jessica b 1973); *Career* supt land ops and reinforcement policy studies Def Operational Analysis Establishment 1968-73, chief planner strategy GLC 1973-74; dir London Docklands Devpt Orgn 1974-79, sr mangr New Business Devpt ICI Millbank 1979-, memb SW Thames Regnl Health Authy 1978-86; memb bd Royal Marsden Cancer Hosp and Inst of Cancer Res 1981-; FRSA; *Recreations* reading, sailing, talking; *Clubs* Atheneum, Royal Instn; *Style*— Nigel Beard, Esq; Lanquhart, The Ridgway, Pyrford, Woking, Surrey (☎ 093 23 48630);

ICI plc, 9 Millbank, London SW1P 3JF (☎ 01 834 4444)

BEARD, Paul Michael; s of Harold Beard (d 1971), of Sheffield, and Phyllis Mary, *née* Bailey; *b* 21 May 1930; *Educ* City GS Sheffield, King's Coll London (LLB); *m* 1 April 1959, (Rhoda) Margaret, da of James Henry Asquith (d 1970), of Morley, Yorks; 1 s (Julian Asquith b 1961), 1 da (Katherine Margaret b 1963); *Career* Nat Serv, cmmnd RASC, serv BAOR (Berlin) 1949-50; barr Gray's Inn 1955, practised NE circuit; chm Med Appeal Trib Nottingham 1984-; rec Crown Cts 1972-; memb East Markham Parish cncl 1986-; Cons candidate gen elections: Huddersfield E 1959, Oldham E 1966, Wigan 1974 (Feb and Oct), Docaster 1979; *Recreations* reading, walking; *Clubs* Sheffield, Naval; *Style—* P M Beard, Esq; Flowerdale, Church St, East Markham, Newark, Notts NG22 0SA (☎ 0777 870074); 42 Bank St, Sheffield S1 1EE (☎ 0742 751223, fax 0742 768439, telex MDX 10522)

BEARD, Prof Richard William; s of Brig William Horace Gladstone Beard, of Ash Lodge, and Irene, *née* Foote; *b* 4 May 1931; *Educ* Westminster, Christ's Coll Cambridge (MA, MB BChir) St Bartholomew's Hosp Cambridge (MD); *m* 1, 28 Aug 1957 (m dis 1979), Jane Elizabeth, *née* Copsey; 2 s (Charles b 3 Sept 1959, Nicholas b 10 March 1962); m 2, 24 Feb 1979, Irene Victore da of Comte de Marotte de Montigny (d 1973), of Versailles, France; 1 s (Thomas b 14 Dec 1979); *Career* obstetrician and gynaecologist RAF Changi Singapore 1957-60; house surgn Chelsea Hosp for Women 1961-62, asst obstetrician Univ Coll Hosp 1962-69; sr lectr/honorary conslt: Queen Charlotte's and Chelsea Hosps 1964-68, King's Coll Hosp 1968-72; prof of obstetrics and gynaecology St Marys's Hosp Med Sch 1972-; civilian conslt advsr in obstetrics and gynaecology RAF 1983-, advsr social servs select ctee House of Commons 1978-, conslt advsr in obstetrics and gynaecology Chief Med Offr DHSS; RCOG: chm scientific advsy and pathology ctee 1983-86, chm birthright res ctee 1987-, memb cncl 1988; FRCOG 1972; *Books* Fetal Medicine (1974), Fetal Physiology and Medicine (second edn 1983); *Recreations* tennis, sailing, chinese history; *Clubs* Garrick; *Style—* Prof Richard Beard; 64 Elgin Crescent, London, W11 2JJ (☎ 01 221 1930); Department of Obstetrics and Gynaecology, St Mary's Hospital Medical School, Paddington, London W2 1PG (☎ 0 725 1461, fax 724 7349)

BEARD, Robert Ian (Rob); s of Reginald Oliver Beard (d 1968), of Rottingdean, Sussex, and May F (d 1970); *b* 14 Sept 1932; *Educ* Epsom Co GS, Bristol Univ (BA); *m* 8 Oct 1961, Diane Betty, da of Jack R Sanders, of Cheam, Surrey; 2 s (Duncan Richard, Alex Neil), 1 da (Joanna Louise); *Career* chief exec Spicer and Pegler Assoc (formerly Spicer and Pegler & Co) 1968-79; ptnr Spicer and Oppenheim (formerly Spicer and Pegler) 1966-; memb: FCA, FIMC, FID; *Recreations* swimming, gardening, photography, theatre, reading; *Style—* Rob Beard, Esq; Frenchlands, Ockham Road South, E Horseley, Surrey KT24 6SN; Spicer and Oppenheim, Friary Court, 65 Crutched Friars, London EC3 (☎ 01 480 7766); Domaine de St Pierre, Plan de la Tour, Var, France

BEARDMORE, Prof John Alec; s of George Edward Beardmore, of Sheffield, and Anne Jean, *née* Warrington; *b* 1 May 1930; *Educ* Burton on Trent GS, Birmingham Central Tech Coll, Univ of Sheffield (BSc, PhD); *m* 26 Dec 1956, Anne Patricia, da of Frederick William Wallace (d 1951); 3 s (James b 1960, Hugo b 1963, Charles b 1965), 1 da (Virginia b 1957); *Career* Radar Operator RAF 1948-49; res demonstrator Univ of Sheffield 1954-56, Cwlth Fund Fell (Harkness) Columbia Univ NY 1956-58, visiting asst prof Plant Breeding Cornell Univ 1958, lectr in genetics Univ of Sheffield 1958-61, prof genetics and dir genetics Inst Univ of Groningen The Netherlands 1961-66, sr fell Nat Sci Fndn Pennsylvania State Univ 1966, prof of genetics 1966- and head of dept Univ Coll of Swansea 1966-87, dean of sci UCS 1974-76 (vice-princ 1977-80, dir Inst of Marine Studies 1983-87, head Sch of Bio Sci 1988-); hon sec Inst of Biology 1980-85 (vice pres 1985-87); memb: NERC Aquatic Life Sci Ctee 1982-87 (chm 1984-87), Br Nat Ctee for Biology 1983-87; chm CSTI Bd 1984-85; FIBiol, FRSA, FLS; Univ of Helsinki Medal (1980); *Books* Marine Organisms: Genetics Ecology and Evolution (co ed with B Battaglia, 1977); *Recreations* bridge, hill walking; *Clubs* Athenaeum; *Style—* Prof John A Beardmore; 153 Derwen Fawr Road, Swansea SA2 8ED (☎ 0792 206 232); School of Biological Sciences, Univ Coll of Swansea, Swansea SA2 8PP (☎ 0792 295 382, fax 0792 295 447, telex 48358 ULSWAN G)

BEARDSWORTH, Maj-Gen Simon John; CB (1984); s of Paymaster Capt Stanley Thomas Beardsworth, RN (ka 1941), and Pearl Sylvia Emma (Biddy), *née* Blake; *b* 18 April 1929; *Educ* St Edmund's Coll, RMA Sandhurst, Royal Mil Coll of Sci (BSc); *m* 1954, Barbara Bingham, da of Brig James Bingham Turner, RA (d 1963); 3 s; *Career* cmd 1 Royal Tank Regt 1970-71, Project Mangr 1973-77 (Col), Dir of Projects 1977-80 (Brig), Dep Cmdt Royal Mil Coll of Sci 1980-81, Maj-Gen 1981, vice-master Gen of the Ordnance 1981-84; FBIM; ret; *Recreations* game shooting, pony club tetrathlon, amateur dramatics, contemplating authorship, garden; *Clubs* Army & Navy; *Style—* Maj-Gen S J Beardsworth, CB; VMGO, Ministry of Defence, Main Building, Whitehall, London SW1A 2HB (☎ 01 218 6341)

BEARMAN, Garth Russell; s of Russell Legerton Bearman (d 1986), and Barbara Maye Fester, *née* Limb (d 1971); *b* 3 Oct 1946; *Educ* Harrow; *m* 26 Jan 1972, Diana Jane, da of Clair Morrel Waterbury, of Virginia, Water, Surrey; 1 s (Christian), 1 da (Katherine); *Career* chm and md Robet Fraser Insur Brokers Ltd, dir of the Robert Fraser Gp; *Recreations* polo, tennis, squash; *Clubs* Turf, Naval and Military, City, Cowdray Park Polo, Lloyds Saddle; *Style—* Garth Bearman, Esq; Harcombe House, Ropley, nr Alresford, Hampshire; Robert Fraser Insurance Brokers Ltd, 32/38 Leman Street, London E1 (☎ 01 481 0111, telex 894460, fax 01 481 9377

BEARNE, Air Vice-Marshal Guy; CB (1956); s of Lt-Col Lewis Collingwood Bearne, DSO, AM (d 1940), and Violet Hetty Rogers, *née* Gibbs (d 1970); *b* 5 Nov 1908; *Educ* Newton Coll; *m* 1933, Aileen Cartwright, da of Henry James Randall (d 1951), of Hove, Sussex; 1 s (Richard), 2 da (Jill, Anne); *Career* cmmnd RAF 1929, various bomber sqdns 1930-33, armament duties 1933-36, RAF Iraq 1937-39, bomber cmd Air Miny 1939-45, Air HQ Malaya 1946, Jt Serv Staff Coll 1947, Air Miny 1948-49, Cmdt Central Gunnery Sch 1950-51, SASO Rhodesian Air Trg Gp 1951-52, Air Offr cmdg Rhodesian Air Trg Gp 1953, Dir of Orgn Air Miny 1954-56, Air Offr i/c Admin HQ Tech Trg cmd 1956-61; ret; *Recreations* golf; *Style—* Air Vice-Marshal Guy Bearne, CB; 2 Mill Close, Hill Deverill, Warminster, Wilts BA12 7EE (☎ Warminster 40533)

BEARSTED, 4 Viscount (UK 1925); Sir Peter Montefiore Samuel; 4 Bt (UK 1903), MC (1942), TD (1951); 2 s of 2 Viscount Bearsted, MC (d 1948), and Dorothea (d 1949), da of late E Montefiore Micholls; *b* 9 Dec 1911; *Educ* Eton, New Coll Oxford; *m* 1, 11 Oct 1939 (m dis 1942), Deirdre du Barry; m 2, 20 March 1946, Hon Elizabeth Adelaide (d 1983), da of Baron Cohen, PC (Life Peer, d 1973), and widow of Capt Arthur John Pearce-Serocold, Welsh Gds; 2 s, 1 da; m 3, 2 Feb 1984, Nina Alice Hilary, da of Reginald John Hearn, of London, and widow of Michael Pocock, CBE; *Heir* s, Nicholas Alan b 22 Jan 1950; *Career* Maj Warwicks Yeomanry; dep chm Hill Samuel Gp 1935-82 (dir 1935-87); chm: Mayborn Group plc 1946-, Dylon Int 1958-84, Hill Samuel & Co (Ireland) 1964-84, Samuel Properties 1982-86 (dir 1961-86); dir: Shell Transport and Trading 1938-82, Trades Union Unit Tst Managers 1961-82, Gen Consolidated Investmt Tst 1975-82; chm cncl Royal Free Hosp Sch of Medicine 1973-82 (memb 1948-87); *Recreations* golf, shooting; *Clubs* White's; *Style—* The Rt Hon the Viscount Bearsted, MC, TD; Farley Hall, Farley Hill, nr Reading, Berks (☎ 0734 733242); 9 Campden Hill Court, London W8 7HX (☎ 01 937 6204)

BEASLEY, Alan Walter; s of Frederick Hancock Beasley (d 1980); *b* 10 Feb 1935; *Educ* King Edward VI GS Nuneaton; *m* 1960, Margaret, da of Frederick Payne; 3 s; *Career* dir Charrington Industl Hldgs 1974 to takeover by Coalite Gp 1977, dir Coalite Gp Bd 1979-; vice-chm: Bolsover Enterprise Agency Ptnrship 1988-, E Midlands region CBI 1988- (cncl memb 1981-87) ; *Recreations* sport, reading, theatre, home and garden, family, travelling, rotary; *Style—* Alan Beasley, Esq; 694 Chatsworth Rd, Brookside, Chesterfield, Derbys S40 3PB (☎ 0246 568785)

BEASLEY, Lady Alexandra Mariota Flora; *née* Egerton; da of 6 Earl of Wilton (d 1927); *b* 9 Nov 1919; *m* 1939 (m dis 1962), Patrick Beasley, s of Henry Herbert Beasley, of Eyrefield House, Curragh, Co Kildare; 1 da; *Style—* Lady Alexandra Beasley; Chimney Cottage, Gressenhall, East Dereham, Norfolk

BEASTALL, John Sale; s of Howard Bestall, and Marjorie Betty, *née* Sale, of Milford-On-Sea, Hants; *b* 2 July 1941; *Educ* St Paul's, Balliol Coll Oxford (BA); *Career* HM Treasy: asst princ 1963-66, asst private sec to Chllr of Exchequer 1966-67, princ 1967-68 and 1971-74, (CS Dept 1968-71), private sec to Paymaster Gen 1974-75, asst sec 1975-79 and 1981-85, (CS Dept 1979-81); asst sec DES 1985-87, treasy offr of accounts 1987-; *Recreations* Christian youth work, rugby football refereeing; *Clubs* Utd Oxford and Cambridge; *Style—* John Beastall, Esq; HM Treasury, Parliment St, London SW1

BEATON, Ian Gordon; s of Gordon Beaton, of 4 Spencer Park, London SW18 (d 1968), and Elsie Mary, *née* Allen (d 1963); *b* 27 August 1924; *Educ* Dulwich; *m* 4 April 1953, Joan Elizabeth, da of Robert Charles Ridgwell, of Southgate, London (d 1974); 1 s (Alastair b 1954), 1 da (Jane b 1959); *Career* RNVR Sub Lt (E) gun mounting engineer; dept md The 600 Gp plc; FCA, FCMA; *Recreations* books, glass, gardening, occasional golf; *Style—* Ian G Beaton, Esq; The White Cottage, Bulstrode Way, Gerrards Cross, Bucks (☎ 0753 882897); Hytheend House, Chertsey Lane, Staines, Middx (☎ 0784 61545, telex 23997, fax 0784 63405)

BEATON, Chief Superintendent James Wallace; GC (1974); s of J A Beaton, and B McDonald; *b* 16 Feb 1943; *Educ* Peterhead Acad, Aberdeenshire; *m* 1965, Anne C Ballantyne; 2 da; *Career* chief inspr Metropolitan Police 1979-83, chief superintendent 1983-; *Style—* Chief Superintendent James Beaton, GC; 12 Embry Way, Stanmore, Middx (☎ 01 954 5054)

BEATTIE, Hon Mr Justice; Hon Sir Alexander Craig; s of Edmund Douglas Beattie and Amie Louisa Beattie; *b* 24 Jan 1912; *Educ* Fort St HS, Sydney Univ (BA, LLB), LLE (Hon) Sydney; *m* 1, 1944, Joyce Pearl Alder (d 1977); 2 s; m 2, 1978, Joyce Elizabeth de Groot; *Career* Capt 2 AIF New Guinea and Borneo 1939-45; pres Industl Cmmn of NSW 1966-81 (Justice 1955); chm: The Eryldene Tst 1983-, Royal Botanic Gdns & Domain Tst 1980-82; kt 1973; *Style—* The Hon Sir Alexander Beattie; 10A Cherry St, Turramurra, NSW 2074, Australia

BEATTIE, Charles Noel; s of Michael William Beattie (d 1956), of Sussex, and Edith, *née* Lickfold (d 1964); *b* 4 Nov 1912; *Educ* Lewes GS, London Univ (LLB); *m* 2 Aug 1972, Wendy, da of John Lawrenson, of Norfolk; 3 da (Elizabeth b 1947, Patricia b 1947, Lucy b 1976); *Career* WWII Capt RASC (despatches); serv: Egypt, Libya, Tunisia, Yugoslavia, Italy; barr; *Style—* Charles N Beattie, Esq; 27 Old Buildings, Lincoln's Inn, London WC2; 24 Old Buildings, Lincoln's Inn, London WC2 (fax 01 831 8095)

BEATTIE, David; CMG (1989); s of George William David Beattie, and Norna Alice, *née* Nicolson; *b* 5 Mar 1938; *Educ* Merchant Taylors', Lincoln Coll Oxford (BA, MA); *m* 1966, Ulla Marita, da of Allan Alha (d 1987), of Helsinki, Finland; 2 da; *Career* Nat Serv RN 1957-59; RNR Sub Lt 1959-62, Lt 1962-67; Dip Serv 1963-: FO 1963-64, Moscow 1964-66, FO 1966-70, Nicosia 1970-74, FCO 1974-78, dep head (former cnsllr) UK delgn to negotiations on mutual reduction of forces and armaments and assoc measures in Central Europe Vienna 1978-82, cnsllr (commercial) Moscow 1982-85, head energy sci space dept FCO 1985-87, min and dep UK permanent rep to NATO Brussels 1987-; *Recreations* walking, bridge, history of the House of Stuart; *Clubs* Travellers'; *Style—* David Beattie, Esq, CMG; Ukdel Nato, Brussels; c/o Foreign & Commonwealth Office, King Charles St, London SW1A 2AH

BEATTIE, Hon Sir David Stuart; GCMG (1980), GCVO (1981, QSO 1985); s of Joseph Nesbitt Beattie; *b* 29 Feb 1924,Sydney, Australia; *m* 1950, Norma, da of John Macdonald; 3 s, 4 da; *Career* barr, slr; QC (1965); judge Supreme (now High) Ct of New Zealand 1969-80, govr-gen of New Zealand 1980-85; chm: Royal Cmmn on the Cts 1978-79, Ministerial Ctee on Sci and Technol 1986; patron: NZ Rugby Football Union, NZ Squash Raquets; chm NZ Int Festival of the Arts; Hon LLD; *Style—* The Hon Sir David Beattie, GCMG, GCVO; 18 Golf Rd, Heretaunga, Upper Hutt, New Zealand

BEATTIE, Capt George Kenneth; CBE (1984), RD (1968, bar 1978) DL (Greater London 1982); s of Harold Beattie, JP (d 1956), of Manchester, and Isobel Kerr-Muir, *née* Gallaher; *b* 5 Oct 1931; *Educ* Harrow, Trinity Coll Oxford; *m* 5 Sept 1964, Jane Katherine, *née* Herbert, da of Baron Tangley, KBE, (Life Peer d 1973), of Tangley Way, Blackheath, Guildford, Surrey; 3 da (Sarah b 1965, Joanna b 1966, Alison b 1968); *Career* RNVR 1952, Nat Serv RN 1954-56, cmd patrol craft Cyprus, joined London Div RNVR 1957, Capt RNR 1978, cmd London Div (HMS President) 1979-83; called to Bar Gray's Inn 1958, practiced at Admty Bar, ADC to the Queen 1981-83; memb HM Lieutenancy City of London 1983, vice chm (Navy) Greater London TAVR Assoc 1984-; panel memb Lloyds Salvage Arbitrators 1983-; Freeman: City of London, Worshipful Co of Watermen and Lightermen of the River Thames; Liveryman Worshipful Co of Shipwrights; *Recreations* sailing, music; *Clubs* Naval, Royal Cruising, Royal Naval Sailing Assoc; *Style—* Capt George Beattie, CBE, RD, DL RNR; Big Oak, Churt, Surrey (☎ 0428 713163); Queen Elizabeth Building, Temple, London EC4Y 9BS (☎ 01 353 9153, telex 262762 INREM G)

BEATTIE, James; OBE, TD, DL (Stafford 1952-), JP (Wolverhampton 1949-); s of

Arthur Beattie, and Christine Brown; *b* 30 Sept 1914; *Educ* Repton; *m* 22 Sept 1939, Joan, da of Arthur Avent; 1 s (David b 1942), 1 da (Victoria b 1944); *Career* md James Beattie plc 1948-79 (chm 1979-); Mayor of Wolverhampton 1951-52 (memb borough cncl 1935-56); chm Wolverhampton Borough Justices 1959-64, cmmnr of Income Tax 1958-84; TA 1932-48, chm Wolverhampton Savings Ctee 1958-66; FRSA 1972; *Recreations* golf, bridge; *Clubs* Royal and Ancient Golf, Staffordshire CCC; *Style—* James Beattie, Esq, OBE, TD, DL, JP; Perton Orchard, Pattingham Rd, Perton, Wolverhampton WV6 7HD (☎ 0902 700266)

BEATTIE, Hon Mrs (Jane Katherine); *née* Herbert; 2 da of Baron Tangley, KBE (Life Peer, d 1973); *b* 4 Oct 1938; *m* 5 Sept 1964, Capt George Kenneth Beattie, CBE, RD, RNR, DL, *qv*; 3 da; *Style—* The Hon Mrs Beattie; Big Oak, Churt, Surrey (☎ 0428 713163)

BEATTIE, Jennifer Jane Belissa; da of Maj Ian Dunbar Beattie (d 1987), of Brighton, Sussex, and Belissa Mary Hunter Graves, *née* Stanley; *b* 20 July 1947; *Educ* Queen Anne's Sch Caversham; *Career* slr; ptnr: Blacket Gill & Langhams 1973-77 (joined 1972), Blacket Gill & Swain 1977-85, Beattie & Co 1985-; dep chm Womens Nat Cancer Control Campaign 1983-86; memb Law Soc 1972; *Recreations* skiing, tennis, reading, dog walking; *Clubs* Naval & Military; *Style—* Miss Jennifer Beattie; 41 Great Percy St, London WC1 (☎ 01 278 5203); St Martins, East Bergholt, Suffolk; 1 Raymond Bldgs, Gray's Inn, London WC1R 5BH (☎ 01 831 1011, fax 01 831 8913)

BEATTIE, Mary Frances Pamela Aufrere; JP (1963), DL (Essex 1979); da of Col Henry Haslett Beattie, of Heath Lodge, Lexden, Colchester, Essex (d 1960), and Gwendolin Edith, *née* Morton (d 1958); *b* 15 July 1922; *Educ* Princess Helena Coll, Hitchin Herts; *Career* chm bd of govs, Princess Helena Coll Hitchin Herts 1970; JP 1963; dep lieut of Essex 1979; *Recreations* bridge, tennis; *Style—* Miss Mary F P A Beattie, JP, DL; Heath Lodge, Lexden, Colchester, Essex, (☎ (0206) 572493)

BEATTIE, Noel Cunningham; s of Samuel Beattie (d 1984), and Annie Adair, *née* Heslip; *b* 30 Dec 1941; *Educ* Belfast Royal Acad; *m* 7 Sept 1967, (Margaret) Annette, da of Thomas John Malcomson; 1 s (Alistair Samuel Noel b 1970), 1 da (Andrea Margaret b 1972); *Career* co sec Northern Bank Ltd; dir Northern Bank: Fin Servs Ltd, Leasing Ltd, Nominees Ltd, Pension Tst Ltd, Equipment Leasing Ltd, Commercial Leasing Ltd, Industrial Leasing Ltd; dir Causeway Credit Ltd; *Recreations* photography, hill walking, music; *Style—* Noel Beattie, Esq; Northern Bank Limited, Donegall Square West, Belfast BT1 6JT (☎ 0232 245277 ext 3521)

BEATTY, 3 Earl (UK 1919); David Beatty; also Viscount Borodale and Baron Beatty (UK 1919); s of 2 Earl Beatty, DSC (d 1972); *b* 21 Nov 1946; *Educ* Eton; *m* 1, 23 June 1971 (m dis 1983), Anne, da of A Please, of Wokingham; 2 s (Viscount Borodale, Hon Peter Wystan b 28 May 1975); m 2, 18 June 1984, Anoma Corinne Wijewardene; *Heir* s, Viscount Borodale, *qv*; *Career* photographer and writer; *Style—* The Rt Hon The Earl Beatty; 2 Larkhall Place, Larkhall, Bath, Avon (☎ 0225 310523)

BEATTY, Col Michael Philip Kenneth; TD (1971) and Bar (1977), DL (Staffs 1980); s of Col George Kenneth Beatty, MC, MRCS, LRCP, of Upland Grange, Kidderminster (d 1962); *b* 9 June 1941; *Educ* St Edward's Sch Oxford; *m* 13 Dec 1969, Frances Elizabeth, JP, o da of Richard Nathaniel Twisleton-Wykeham-Fiennes (ggs of 16 Baron Saye and Sele by his 1 w, Hon Emily Wingfield, da of 4 Visc Powerscourt; also gs of Rev Hon Wingfield Twisleton-Wykeham-Fiennes by his w, Alice, da of Very Rev Hon Grantham Munton Yorke, bro of 4 Earl of Hardwicke, PC); 4 da (Geraldine, Zasie, Katie, Caroline); *Career* Glynwed Int 1965-84; chm and md BGS Ltd; cmmnd Queen's own Mercian Yeomanry 1978-80; TA Col Western District 1985; hon Col 35 Midland Signal Regt (Vols) 1986; ADC to HM The Queen 1987; *Recreations* restoring ruined old houses, gardening; *Style—* Col Michael Beatty, TD, DL; Tixall Farmhouse, Tixall, Stafford

BEATTY, Lady Miranda Katherine; da of 2 Earl Beatty, DSC (1972); *b* 18 Feb 1963; *Style—* Lady Miranda Beatty

BEATTY, Hon Nicholas Duncan; s of 2 Earl Beatty, DSC (d 1972); *b* 1 April 1961; *Style—* The Hon Nicholas Beatty

BEAUCHAMP; *see*: Proctor-Beauchamp

BEAUCHAMP, Countess; Else; MBE; da of late Viggo Schiwe and Fru J Birkerod-Schiwe; *m* 1, dir C P Dornonville de la Cour, of Copenhagen (d 1924); m 2, 1936, 8 and last Earl Beauchamp, JP, DL (d 1979); *Career* DstJ; Grand Cdr Order of Dannebroy of Denmark; *Style—* The Rt Hon The Countess Beauchamp, MBE; Madresfield Court, Malvern, Worcs (☎ 068 45 3024)

BEAUCLERK, Lady Emma Caroline de Vere; o da of 14 Duke of St Albans; *b* 22 July 1963; *Educ* Roedean, St John's Coll Cambridge; *Style—* Lady Emma Beauclerk; Canonteign, Exeter, Devon EX6 7RH

BEAUCLERK, James Charles Fesq de Vere; s of 13 Duke of St Albans, OBE (d 1988); *b* 6 Feb 1949; *Educ* Eton; *Style—* Lord James Beauclerk; Barn House, Midgham, Reading, Berks RG7 5UG

BEAUCLERK, Lord John William Aubrey de Vere; s of 13 Duke of St Albans, OBE (d 1988); *b* 10 Feb 1950; *Educ* Eton; *Style—* Lord John Beauclerk; c/o Lady Caroline Ffrench-Blake, Barn House, Reading, Berks, RG7 5UG

BEAUCLERK, Lord Peter Charles de Vere; s of 13 Duke of St Albans, OBE (d 1988); *b* 13 Jan 1948; *Educ* Eton; *m* 1972 (m dis), Beverley June, *née* Bailey, of California; 1 s (Robin decd), 1 da (Angela b 1974); *Career* served RNR 1966-69; property investmt and devpt; *Recreations* skiing, sail boarding; *Style—* Lord Peter Beauclerk; 2726 Shelter Island Drive 332, San Diego, California 92106, USA

BEAUCLERK-DEWAR, Peter de Vere; RD (1980), JP (Inner London 1983); s of James Dewar, MBE, GM, AE (d 1983), and Hermione de Vere (d 1969), yr da and co-heir of Maj Aubrey Nelthorpe Beauclerk, of Little Grimsby Hall, Lincs (d 1916, heir-in-line to Dukedom of St Albans); recognised by Lord Lyon King of Arms 1965 in additional surname and arms of Beauclerk; *b* 19 Feb 1943; *Educ* Ampleforth; *m* 1967, Sarah Ann Sweet Verge, da of Maj Lionel John Verge Rudder, DCLI of Bibury, Glos; 1 s (James William Aubrey de Vere b 1970), 3 da (Alexandra Hermione Sarah b 1972, Emma Diana Reta b 1973, Philippa Caroline Frances b 1982); *Career* Lt Cdr RNR; genealogist: Falkland Pursuivant Extraordinary 1975, 1982, 1984, 1986 and 1987; usher: (Silver Stick) Silver Jubilee Thanksgiving Service 1977, (Liaison) HM Queen Elizabeth The Queen Mother's 80th Birthday Thanksgiving Service 1980; hon tres: Inst of Heraldic and Genealogical Studies 1979- (Hon FHG), Royal Stuart Soc 1985-; heraldry conslt to Christie's Fine Art Auctioneers 1979-; chm Assoc of Genealogists and Record Agents 1982-83, chief accountant Archdiocese of Westminster 1982-85; dir: Mgmnt Search Int Ltd 1985-87, Five Arrows Ltd 1986-87, Clifton Nurseries (hldgs) Ltd 1986-88, Room Twelve Ltd 1987-88; govr More House Sch SW1 1986-; memb Queen's Body Gd for Scotland (Royal Co of Archers) 1981; kt of Honour and Devotion SMO Malta 1971, kt Sacred Mil Order of Constantine St George 1981; OStJ 1987; Liveryman Haberdashers' Co; FBIM, FFA, FInstSMM, FSA Scot, SAT; *Books* The House of Nell Gwyn 1670-1974 (co-author) and contributor to many pubns; *Clubs* Puffin's, New (Edinburgh); *Style—* Peter Beauclerk-Dewar, Esq, RD, JP; 45 Airedale Ave, Chiswick, London W4 2NW (☎ 01 995 6770); Holm of Hulp by Stronsay, Orkney Islands

BEAUFORT, Duchess of; Lady Caroline Jane Somerset; *née* Thynne; da (by 1 w) of 6 Marquess of Bath; *b* 28 August 1928; *m* 1950, 11 Duke of Beaufort, *qv*; 3 s, 1 da; *Style—* Her Grace the Duchess of Beaufort; Badminton House, Avon; 90 Eaton Terrace, London SW1

BEAUFORT, 11 Duke of (E 1682); David Robert Somerset; also Baron Herbert of Raglan, Chepstow and Gower (E 1506), Earl of Worcester (E 1513), Marquess of Worcester (E 1642) and hereditary keeper of Raglan Castle; s of Henry Somerset, DSO (d 1965; s of Henry Somerset, OBE, JP, DL, by his 1 w, Lady Katherine Beauclerk, da of 10 Duke of St Albans), and Bettine (d 1978), yr da of Maj Charles Malcolm (bro of Sir James Malcolm, 9 Bt) by his w, Hon Beatrix Hore-Ruthven (only da of 8 Lord Ruthven); suc cous, 10 Duke of Beaufort, KG, GCVO, PC, 1984; *b* 23 Feb 1928; *Educ* Eton; *m* 1950, Lady Caroline Jane Thynne, *qv*, da of 6 Marquess of Bath; 3 s, 1 da; *Career* late Lt Coldstream Gds; chm Marlborough Fine Art 1977-; *Clubs* White's; *Style—* His Grace the Duke of Beaufort; Badminton House, Glos GL9 1DB; 90 Eaton Terrace, London SW1

BEAUMAN, Wing Cdr (Eric) Bentley; s of Bentley Martin Beauman (d 1945), of London, and Estelle, *née* Beddington; *b* 7 Feb 1891; *Educ* Windlesham House Portslade, Malvern Coll, Geneva Univ; *m* 22 June 1940, Katharine Burgoyne Miller, da of Frank Wolstonecroft Jones (d 1945), of Leeds; 1 s (Christopher Burgoyne Bentley b 1944); *Career* WWI 1914-18; cmmnd RNAS 1914 served anti-submarine patrols UK and Aegean, home def, flying instr, cmd Seaplane stations Dundee and Newhaven, Maj RAF 1918; PSA, RAF Staff Coll 1922-23, PSC 1929-30, Wing Cdr RAF 1931, instr: RAF Staff Coll 1932-33, ret 1938; ret Offr Air Miny 1938-51, WWII RAF liason Offr BBC 1939-45; expeditions incl: Mount Kamet Himalaya 1931, Coast Range BC 1934 (climbed Matterhorn 5 times); memb Alpine Club 1920, pres Alpine Ski Club 1933-35 (hon librarian 1947-58, hon memb 1978-), vice-pres RAF Mountaineering Assoc 1951-, chm touring and mountaineering ctee Ski Club GB 1952-54, librarian Royal United Serv Inst 1952-57; contribs to incl: The Times, The Guardian, The Listener, The Geographical Magazine, Alpine Journal, British Ski Year Book, Encyclopaedia Britannica; *Books* Winged Words (compiled 1941), The Airmen Speak (with Cecil Day Lewis 1941), We Speak From the Air (compiled 1942), Over to You (1943), Travellers Tales (1945), The Boys Country Book (1955); *Recreations* writing, reading, gardening; *Clubs* Alpine, RAF; *Style—* Wing Cdr Bentley Beauman; 59 Chester Row, London SW1W 8JL (☎ 01 730 9038)

BEAUMAN, Christopher Bentley; s of Wing Cdr Eric Bentley Beauman, of Chester Row, SW1, and Katharine Burgoyne, *née* Jones; *b* 12 Oct 1944; *Educ* Winchester, Trinity Coll Cambridge, Harkness fell at Johns Hopkins Sch of Advanced Int Studies and Columbia Univ; *m* 1, 1966 (m dis 1976), Sally, *née* Kinsey-Miles; m 2, 1976, Nicola, da of Dr Francis Mann, of Manchester Sq, W1; 1 s, 1 da, 3 step children; *Career* corporate fin exec Hill Samuel 1968-72; dir: Guinness Mahon 1973-76, FMC Ltd 1975-81; advsr to chm BSC 1976-81, Central Policy Review Staff 1981-83, Morgan Grenfell Gp 1983- (dir 1989-); dir FMC Ltd 1975-81; memb Channel 4 Current Affairs Advsy Bd 1986-; *Recreations* reading, family, London; *Style—* Christopher Beauman, Esq; 35 Christchurch Hill, London NW3 (☎ 01 435 1975)

BEAUMONT, Hon Ariadne Grace; da of Baron Beaumont of Whitley (Life Peer), *qv*; *b* 22 April 1963; *Educ* Chrish Church, Oxford; *Career* investmt banking; *Style—* The Hon Ariadne Beaumont

BEAUMONT, Bryan Kenneth; s of Cyril Beaumont (d 1918); *b* 16 July 1918; *Educ* Firth Park Sch Sheffield; *m* 1940, Kathleen (d 1987), da of Henry Greaves (d 1948); 1 da; *Career* chm Luncheon Vouchers Ltd 1970-82; fin dir: Express Dairy Foods 1975, Express Dairy 1980-83; FCA; *Recreations* listening to music, reading, gardening, golf; *Style—* Bryan Beaumont, Esq; 20 York Ave, East Sheen, London SW14 (☎ 01 876 4270)

BEAUMONT, Hon Charles Richard; s of 3 Viscount Allendale; *b* 8 Mar 1954; *Educ* Eton, RAC Cirencester; *m* 27 Oct 1979, Charlotte Sybil, da of Lt-Col Richard Ian Griffith Taylor, DSO, MC, JP, DL; 2 s (Edward b 1983, Harry b 1987), 1 da (Laura b 1985); *Career* farmer; co dir; *Recreations* skiing, cricket, tennis; *Clubs* Turf, Northern Counties, Borderers Cricket, Cloth Cap; *Style—* The Hon Charles Beaumont; Swallowship House, Hexham, Northumberland NE46 1RJ (☎ 0434 603891)

BEAUMONT, Christopher; s and h of Michael Beaumont, Seigneur of Sark, *qv*; *b* 4 Feb 1957; m 20 Sept 1980, Sarah Vivienne, *née* Rees; *Career* Capt RE; *Style—* Christopher Beaumont, Esq; La Seigneurie, Sark, Channel Islands

BEAUMONT, His Hon (Herbert) Christopher Beaumont; MBE (1948); s of Maj Gerald Beaumont, MC (d 1933), of Woolley Moor House, Wakefield, and Gwendolene, *née* Haworth; *b* 3 June 1912; *Educ* Uppingham, Worcester Coll Oxford; *m* 1940, Helen Magaret Gordon, da of William Mitchell Smail, of Edinburgh; 1 s, 2 da; *Career* formerly ICS and FO; barr 1951-72, circuit judge 1972-89; *Recreations* Euro travel; *Clubs* Brooks's, Yorkshire (York); *Style—* His Hon Christopher Beaumont, MBE; Minskip Lodge, Boroughbridge, N Yorks (☎ 0437 32 2365)

BEAUMONT, Christopher Hubert; s of Hubert Beaumont, MP (d 1948), and Beatrix Beaumont (d 1982); *b* 10 Feb 1926; *Educ* West Monmouth Sch Pontypool, Balliol Coll Oxford (MA); *m* 1, 31 Aug 1959, Catherine (d 1971), da of Eric Clark (d 1982); 2 s (Simon b 1962, Guy b 1964); m 2, 28 June 1972, Sara Patricia, da of Cdr William Magee, RN (d 1976); 1 da (Justine b 1973); *Career* served RN 1944-47 (Sub Lt, RNVR); called to the Bar Middle Temple 1950, rec Crown Ct 1981-; chm Agric Land Tribunal Eastern Area 1985- (dept chm 1979-85); asst deputy Coroner Inner W London 1963-81; *Books* Law Relating to Sheriffs (1968), Town and Country Planning Act, 1968 (1969), Town and Country Planning Acts 1971 and 1972 (1972), Land Compensation Act 1973 (with W G Nutley, 1973), Community Land Act, 1975 (with W G Nutley, 1976), Planning Appeal Decisions (jt ed with W G Nutley, in series from 1986-); *Style—* Christopher H Beaumont, Esq; Rose Cottage, Lower Eashing, Godalming, Surrey GU7 2QG (☎ 048 68 6316); 2 Harcourt Buildings, Temple, London EC4Y 9DB (☎ 01 353 8415)

BEAUMONT, Ernest George; s of George Bunzl (d 1976); *b* 9 August 1921; *Educ* Austria, Manchester Univ, London Univ; *m* 1947, Eva Marie, da of Walter Dux, of London; 3 children; *Career* interned on the Isle of Man 1940 before being allowed to serve in REME; chm Bunzl plc 1981- (previously md and dep chm); *Recreations* golf, filming, travel, theatre; *Clubs* RAC; *Style*— Ernest Beaumont, Esq; Wych Elm, Fitzgeorge Ave, New Malden, Surrey KT3 4SH (☎ 01 949 6500); Bunzl plc, Friendly House, 21-24 Chiswell St, London EC1 (☎ 01 606 9966)

BEAUMONT, Sir George Howland Francis; 12 Bt (E 1661); s of Sir George Arthur Hamilton Beaumont, 11 Bt (d 1933); *b* 24 Sept 1924; *Educ* Stowe; *m* 1, 1949 (m annulled 1951), Barbara, da of William Singleton; m 2, 1963 (m dis 1985), Henrietta Anne, da of late Dr Arthur Weymouth; 2 da (twins); *Heir* none; *Career* formerly warrant offr Australian Army; Coldstream Gds, Lt 60 Rifles WW II; *Clubs* Lansdowne; *Style*— Sir George Beaumont, Bt; The Corner House, Manor Court, Stretton-on-Fosse, nr Moreton-in-Marsh, Glos GL56 9SB

BEAUMONT, Hon Hubert Wentworth; s of Baron Beaumont of Whitley (Life Peer); *b* 12 April 1956; *Educ* Gordonstoun, S Bank Poly; *m* 1980, Katherine Emma, da of Richard Abel Smith, *qv*; 1 s (George b 1985), 1 da (Amelia b 1983); *Career* chartered surveyor; *Recreations* shooting; *Style*— The Hon Hubert Beaumont; Harristown House, Brannockstown, Kildare, Eire

BEAUMONT, Janet Elizabeth; da of Cdr Surg Robert Holden Tincker, RNVR, DSO (d 1982), of Painswick, Gloucestershire, and Kathleen Aldrich (d 1973), *née* Bates; *b* 5 Jan 1937; *Educ* St Mary's & St Anne's Sec Sch Uttoxeter, 1953; Surrey Univ (MPhil) ; *m* 19 Jul 1958, Stephen Francis Beaumont, s of Hugh Beaumont (d 1936), of Ipswich; 2 s (Robert Stephen b 1959, James Hugh b 1961), 1 da (Elizabeth Frances b 1964); *Career* CA 1973; lectr Oxford Poly 1973-82; fin dir OSS Scaffolding Ltd 1983-; FCA; *Style*— Mrs Janet Beaumont; Rye Farm, Culham, Abingdon, OX14 3NN (☎ 0235 20484); Red Barn Farm Woodstock Rd, Oxford, OX2R 8JR (☎ 0865 510230, 0865 510 238)

BEAUMONT, John Richard; s of Stanley Beaumont, of Denmead, Hampshire, and Winifred Louise, *née* Williams (d 1984); *b* 22 June 1947; *Educ* Wolverhampton GS, Merton Coll Oxford (BA, MA); *m* 18 Oct 1986, Susan Margaret, da of Ivan Stanley Blowers, of Oulton Broad, Suffolk; 1 da (Anna Jane b 1988), 1 step s (Christopher Jones b 1983); *Career* schoolmaster Buckingham Coll Harrow 1969-71; Shelter Nat Campaign for the Homeless Ltd: regnl organiser W Mids 1971-73, nat projects dir 1973-74; legal offr: Alnwick DC Northumberland 1974, Thurrock Borough cncl 1974-75; called to the Bar Inner Temple 1976, memb Northern Circuit, pt/t legal advsr Assoc Newspapers plc; former memb: mgmnt ctees of Bradford Housing and Renewal Experiment (SHARE), North Islington Housing Rights Project; *Recreations* walking, reading history and Victorian literature; *Style*— John Beaumont, Esq; 9 Valley Way, Knutsford, Cheshire (☎ 0565 3419); Queens Chambers, 5 John Dalton St, Manchester (previously at 43 King St, Manchester); 5 Essex Ct, Temple, London (☎ 061 834 6875/4738, fax 061 834 8557)

BEAUMONT, Maj Keith John Lancelot; TD (1976); s of Frank Charles Beaumont (d 1987), of Worthing Sussex, and Dorothy Kate, *née* Turner (d 1971); *b* 7 May 1937; *Educ* Alleyns & Dulwich Colls; *Career* RAVR 1959-63 Flying offr, Middx Yeomanry (TA) 1963-79; Royal Signals: Lt 1963, Capt 1970, Actg Maj 1976; dir Dominion Assoc Leasing Ltd, Dominion Corp Fin Ltd; chief exec Dominion Credit & Fin Ltd 1983-, underwriter Lloyds 1989; vice-chm Execs Assoc of GB; Freeman City of London 1978, Liveryman Worshipful Cos of: Joiners and Ceilers 1973 and Carmen 1983; FICM; *Recreations* golf, shooting, arts, racehorse owner; *Clubs* Cavalry & Guards, St Georges Hill GC; *Style*— Maj Keith Beaumont, TD; Elbury, Oxshott Way, Cobham, Surrey, KT11 2RO (☎ 0932 65914); Dominion Credit & Finance Ltd, Dominion House, 49 Parkside, Wimbledon SW19 5RB (☎ 01 947 1150)

BEAUMONT, Hon Mark Henry; 2 s of 3 Viscount Allendale; *b* 21 July 1950; *Educ* Eton; *m* 1982, Diana Elizabeth, yst da of Lt-Col J E Benson, of Chesters, Humshaugh, Northumberland; 1 s (George Richard Benson b 1987); *Style*— The Hon Mark Beaumont; Dilston House, Corbridge, Northumberland (☎ 043 471 3137)

BEAUMONT, Martin Dudley; s of Patrick Beaumont, JP, DL, of Donadea Lodge, Clwyd, N Wales, and (Doreen Elizabeth) Lindesay, *née* Howard; *b* 6 August 1949; *Educ* Stowe, Magdalene Coll Cambridge (MA); *m* 12 June 1976, Andrea Evelyn, da of John Wilberforce, of The Red House, Corbridge; 2 da (Alice b 11 July 1980, Jessica 22 Dec 1981); *Career* ptnr Peat Marwick McLintock (formerly Thomson McLintock) 1983-87 dir 1980-87), gp fin dir Egmont Publishing Gp 1987-; dir: World Int Publishing Ltd 1987, Ward Lock Ltd 1987; chief exec Children's Books of Stafford Ltd 1988-; memb Parochial Church Cncl; FCA 1977, MIMC 1981; *Recreations* shooting, fishing, tennis; *Style*— M D Beaumont, Esq; Beech Cottage, Hand Green, Tarporley, Cheshire (☎ 08293 2994); Egmont House, 61 Great Ducie St, Manchester M14 HS (☎ 061 834 3110)

BEAUMONT, Hon Matthew Henry; s of 2 Viscount Allendale, KG, CB, CBE, MC (d 1956); *b* 10 April 1933; *Educ* Bradfield; *m* 1, 1959 (m dis 1972), Anne Christina Margaret, da of Gerald Hamilton; 1 s, 1 da; m 2, 1973, Belinda Jane Elizabeth, da of late Harold David Cuthbert, of Beaufront Castle, Hexham, Northumberland; *Career* underwriting memb of Lloyd's 1960; *Clubs* Boodle's; *Style*— The Hon Matthew Beaumont

BEAUMONT, (John) Michael; Seigneur of Sark (cr 1565) 1974-; s of late Lionel (Buster) Beaumont, and Enid, *née* Ripley; gs of Dame Sibyl Mary Hathaway, DBE, Dame of Sark, whom he suc on her death; *b* 20 Dec 1927; *Educ* Loughborough Coll; *m* 1956, Diana, *née* La Trobe-Bateman; 2 s; *Heir* s, Christopher Beaumont, *qv*; *Career* aircraft design engineer to 1975; *Style*— Michael Beaumont, Esq; La Seigneurie, Sark, Channel Islands (☎ Sark 2017)

BEAUMONT, Hon (Edward) Nicholas Canning; CVO (1986, MVO 1976), DL (Berks 1982); 3 s of 2 Viscount Allendale; *b* 14 Dec 1929; *Educ* Eton; *m* 1953, Jane Caroline Falconer, da of Alexander Lewis Paget Falconer Wallace, JP, of Candacraig, Strathdon, Aberdeen; 2 s (Thomas b 1962, Henry b 1966, a page of hon to HM Queen Elizabeth The Queen Mother 1979-82); *Career* joined Life Gds 1948, Capt 1956, ret 1960; asst to clerk of the course Ascot 1964-69, clerk of the course and sec to the Ascot Authority 1969; SBStJ 1982 (pres Berkshire St John 1988) ; *Style*— Capt The Hon Nicholas Beaumont, CVO, DL; Secretary's Office, Ascot Racecourse, Ascot, Berks (☎ 0990 22211)

BEAUMONT, Sir Richard Ashton; KCMG (1965, CMG 1955), OBE (1949); s of A R Beaumont (d 1962), of Uppingham, Rutland, and Evelyn Frances, *née* Rendle; *b* 29 Dec 1912; *Educ* Repton, Oriel Coll Oxford; *m* 1, 1942, Alou (d 1985), da of M Camran, of Istanbul; 1 da; m 2, 24 Feb 1989, Mrs Melanie E M Anns; *Career* served WWII; joined HM Consular Serv 1936, served Beirut and Damascus; FO 1945-72: head of Arabian Dept 1959, ambass Morocco 1961-65, ambass Iraq 1965-67: dep under-sec of state 1967-69, ambass Egypt 1969-72; chm: Arab-Br C of C 1980-, Anglo-Arab Assoc 1979-; tstee Thomson Fndn 1974-; *Style*— Sir Richard Beaumont, KCMG, OBE; 14 Cadogan Sq, London SW1

BEAUMONT, Hon Richard Blackett; 2 s of 2 Viscount Allendale, KG, CB, CBE, MC (d 1956); *b* 13 August 1926; *Educ* Eton; *m* 1971, Lavinia Mary (sometime Governess to HRH The Prince Edward), da of late Lt-Col Arnold Keppel (gggs of Rt Rev Hon Frederick Keppel, sometime Bp of Exeter and 4 s of 2 Earl of Albemarle); *Career* joined RNVR 1944, Sub Lt 1946; PA to Sir Walter Monckton Hyderabad 1947-48, joined James Purdey and Sons 1949 (dir 1952), ADC to Sir Donald MacGillivray Malaya 1954-55, chm James Purdey and Sons 1971-; Worshipful Co of Master Gunmakers 1969 and 1985; *Books* Purdey's, The Guns and the Family (1984); *Recreations* shooting, travel; *Clubs* White's, Turf, Beefsteak, Pratt's; *Style*— The Hon Richard Beaumont; Flat 1, 58 South Audley St, London W1 (☎ 01 499 5845)

BEAUMONT, Rupert Roger Seymour; s of Robert Beaumont of London, and Peggy Marie Stubbs *née* Bassett (d 1938); *b* 24 Feb 1944; *Educ* Wellington, Grenoble Univ France; *m* 24/02/1968, Susie Diane, da of Noel Sampson James Wishart, 1 s (James, b 1971) 1 da (Juliet, b 1972); *Career* articled Beaumont & Son 1962-68, asmitted solr 1968, with Appleton Rice and Perrin NY USA, 1968-69; ptnr Slaughter and May 1974 (joined 1969, Hong Kong office 1976-81; Law Soc 1973; *Books* author varous articles for learned jls; *Recreations* tennis, fishing, carpentry; *Style*— Rupert Beaumont, Esq; 35 Basinghall Street, London EC2V 5DB (☎ 01 600 1200, fax 01 726 0038/01 600 0289, telex 883486/888926)

BEAUMONT, Hon Wentworth Peter Ismay; s and h of 3 Viscount Allendale; *b* 13 Nov 1948; *Educ* Harrow; *m* 1975, Theresa Mary Magdalene, da of Frank More O'Ferrall (d 1977); 1 s, 3 da; *Career* farmer; chm of Northumberland Association of Boys' Clubs; *Recreations* shooting, skiing, horseracing; *Clubs* Jockey, Northern Counties, Whites; *Style*— The Hon Wentworth Beaumont; Bywell Castle, Stocksfield-on-Tyne, Northumberland (☎ 0661 842450; office: 0661 843296)

BEAUMONT, William Anderson; CB (1986), OBE (1961), AE (1958); s of William Lionel Beaumont of Nesbit Hall, Pudsey, W Yorks (d 1956), and Ivy Mima Taverner, *née* Anderson; *b* 30 Oct 1924; *Educ* Moorlands Sch Leeds, Terrington Hall Yorks, Cranleigh, Christ Church Oxford (BA, DipEd); *m* 24 August 1946, Kythé, da of Maj Kenneth Gordon Mackenzie, Canadian Army (d 1988); 1 da (Kythé Victoria b 1958); *Career* md Beaumont and Smith Ltd Pudsey Yorks textile manufacturers 1954-66, md Henry Mason (Shipley) Ltd Textile Manufacturers 1966-76; assist sec Welsh Office, Cardiff 1976-82 speaker's sec House of Commons 1982-86; ret; active in various official and semi-official bodies; *Recreations* Public Service, aviation, walking; *Clubs* RAF, United Services (Cardiff), Maison des Ailes (Brussels); *Style*— William Beaumont, Esq, CB, OBE, AE; Kelowna, St Hilary, Cowbridge, S Glamorgan CF7 7DP (☎ 04463 3251)

BEAUMONT, William Blackledge; OBE (1982); s of Ronald Walton Beaumont, of Croston, Lancs, and Joyce, *née* Blackledge; *b* 9 Mar 1952; *Educ* Ellesmere Coll; *m* 1977, Hilary Jane, da of Kenneth Seed, of Iken House, Freckleton, Preston, Lancs; 2 s (Daniel b 1982, Samuel b 1985); *Career* co dir J Blackledge and Son Ltd 1981; dir: Red Rose Radio 1981, Chorley and District Bldg Soc 1983; England Rugby Capt 1977-82, Br Lions Capt SA 1980, Barbarians Capt, Lancashire Capt, Capt England to Grand Slam 1980; BBC sports presenter: Grandstand, Question of Sport and Rugby Special; *Books* Thanks to Rugby (autobiography 1982); *Recreations* golf, boating; *Clubs* E India, Royal Lytham Golf, Fydle RUFC; *Style*— William Beaumont Esq, OBE; Alderley, 113 Liverpool Rd, Longton, Preston, Lancs (☎ 0772 617435); J Blackledge and Son Ltd, Park Mills, Chorley, Lancs (☎ 02572 63065)

BEAUMONT OF WHITLEY, Baron (Life Peer UK 1967); Timothy Wentworth Beaumont; o s of late Maj Michael Wentworth Beaumont, TD (d 1958, gs of 1 Baron Allendale) by 1 w, Hon Faith Muriel, *née* Pease (d 1935), da of 1 Baron Gainford; *b* 22 Nov 1928; *Educ* Eton, Gordonstoun, Christ Church Oxford; *m* 13 June 1955, Mary Rose, yr da of Lt-Col Charles Edward Wauchope, MC; 2 s (1 decd), 2 da; *Career* vicar of Christ Church Kowloon Hong Kong 1957-59 (resigned Holy Orders 1979, resumed 1984); prop various periodicals incl Time and Tide, New Christian 1960-70; pres Lib Pty 1969-70 (Head of Orgn 1965-66), del to Parly Assembly Cncl of Europe and Western Euro Union 1974-77; chm Studio Vista Books 1963-68; dir Green Alliance 1977-9; Lib spokesman House of Lords on Educ, Arts and the Environment 1967-85; vicar of St Luke's and St Philip's (The Barn Church) Kew 1986-; *Books* Where Shall I Place My Cross? (1987); *Style*— The Rev The Rt Hon Lord Beaumont of Whitley; 70 Marksbury Avenue, Richmond, Surrey

BEAUMONT-DARK, Anthony Michael; MP (C) Birmingham Selly Oak 1979-; s of Leonard Cecil Dark; *b* 11 Oct 1932; *Educ* Birmingham Coll of Arts and Crafts, Birmingham Univ; *m* 1959, Sheelagh Irene, da of R Cassey; 1 s, 1 da; *Career* fndr fund for dependents of Br servicemen k in Falkland Islands 1982; investmt analyst and co dir; chm Birmingham Executive Airways 1983-; *Style*— Anthony Beaumont-Dark, Esq, MP; House of Commons, SW1

BEAUREPAIRE, Dame Beryl Edith; DBE (1981, OBE 1975); da of E L Bedggood; *b* 24 Sept 1923; *Educ* Fintona GS Vic, Univ of Melbourne; *m* 1946, Ian Francis Beaurepaire, CMG, former Lord Mayor of Melbourne; 2 s; *Career* WAAAF 1942-45; memb Nat Exec YWCA of Australia 1969-77, chm Vic Women's Ctee Section Lib Party 1973-76, chm bd of mgmnt Fintona Girls' Sch 1973-87, chm Fed Women's Ctee Lib Party 1974-6, vice-pres Vic Div Lib Party 1976-86, convener Nat Women's Advsy Cncl 1978-1982; memb: cncl Aust War Meml 1982- (chm 1985-), bd Victoria's 150 Authority 1982-86; Queen's Silver Jubilee Medal 1977-; chm: Cncl Australian War Meml 1985-; *Style*— Dame Beryl Beaurepaire, DBE; 18 Barton Drive, Mt Eliza, Victoria, 3930, Australia

BEAVEN, John Lewis; CMG (1986), CVO (1983, MVO 1974); s of Charles Beaven (d 1967), and Margaret Beaven (d 1973); *b* 30 July 1930; *Educ* Newport HS Gwent; *m* 1, 1960 (m dis), Jane Beeson; 1 s, 1 da; m 2, 1975, Jean McComb Campbell; *Career* Board of Trade 1947; Flying Offr RAF Reserve 1948-50; HM Dip Serv 1956-, dep consul-gen New York and dir Br Trade Devpt Office NY 1978-82, consul-gen San Francisco 1982-86, ambass Khartoum 1986-; *Recreations* music, walking, needlepoint; *Clubs* Brook (New York); *Style*— John Beaven, Esq, CMG, CVO; c/o Foreign and

Commonwealth Office, King Charles St, London SW1; Scannell Rd, Bhent, NY 12075, USA

BEAVERBROOK, 3 Baron (UK 1917); Sir Maxwell William Humphrey (Aitken); 3 Bt (UK 1916); s of Sir Max Aitken, 2 Bt, DSO, DFC (d 1985; suc as 2 Baron Beaverbrook 1964, which he disclaimed for life 1964) by his 3 w, Violet (*see* Lady Aitken); *b* 29 Dec 1951; *Educ* Charterhouse, Pembroke Coll Cambridge; *m* 1974, Susan (Susie) Angela, da of Francis More O'Ferrall and Angela (niece of Sir George Mather-Jackson, 5 Bt, and da of Sir Anthony Mather-Jackson 6 Bt, JP, DL, by his w, Evelyn, da of Lt-Col Sir Henry Stephenson, 1 Bt, DSO); 2 s (Maxwell b 1977, Alexander b 1978), 2 da (Charlotte 1982, Sophia b 1985); *Heir* s, Hon Maxwell Francis Aitken, b 17 March 1977; *Career* tstee Beaverbrook Fndn 1974- (chm 1985-); dir Ventech Ltd 1983-86, chm Ventech Healthcare Inc 1986; Govt Whip House of Lords 1986-88; 1988-: dep tres Cons Party, chm and pres Ventech Healthcare Inc, ememb cncl Homeopathic Tst; *Clubs* White's, Royal Yacht Squadron; *Style—* The Rt Hon the Lord Beaverbrook; House of Lords, London SW1

BEAVIS, Air Chief Marshal Sir Michael Gordon; KCB (1981), CBE (1977, OBE 1969), AFC (1962); s of Walter Erle Beavis (d 1972), of Haverhill, and Mary Ann, *née* Sarjantson; *b* 13 August 1929; *Educ* Kilburn GS; *m* 9 Dec 1949, Joy Marion, da of Arthur Olwen Jones (d 1974); 1 s (Simon Anthony b 1 Jan 1960), 1 da (Lynn Alison Deborah b 16 April 1956); *Career* joined RAF 1947, Air Marshal 1981, AOC-in-C RAF Support Cmd 1981-84, Air Chief Marshal 1984, Dep C-in-C Allied Forces Central Europe 1984-86, ret 1987; dir: Fine Features Ltd (chm 1987-), Tubular Exhibition Group 1987-; Liveryman Guild of Air Pilots and Navigators 1982; CBIM; *Recreations* golf, travel; *Clubs* RAF; *Style—* Air Chief Marshal Sir Michael Beavis KCB, CBE, AFC; c/o Lloyds Bank plc, 202 High Street, Lincoln LN5 7AP

BEAZLEY, (Hugh) John Sherard; DFC (1944); s of His Hon Sir Hugh Loveday Beazley, KB (d 1964), of Mill Lane Broxbourne, Herts, and Beatrice Constance, *née* Veasey (d 1979); *b* 18 July 1916; *Educ* Cheltenham, Pembroke Coll Oxford (MA); *m* 19 April 1947, Mary Loveday, da of Admiral Sir Bernard Rawlings, GCB (d 1982), of Clerkenwater House, Cornwall; 2 s (Richard b 1949, Charles b 1959), 1 da (Anne b 1951); *Career* serv WWII Wing Cdr RAF, fighter cmd UK 1940-41, Malta 1941-42, Mid East 1942-44, Colonial Admin Serv Nigeria 1947-57; qualified CA 1961, dir BET subsid cos; ret 1981; FCA; *Recreations* golf, fishing, sailing; *Clubs* RAF, Piccadilly; *Style—* John Beazley, Esq; Glebe House, Church Lane, Wormley, Herts; Clerkenwater Lodge, Clerkenwater, Nr Bodmin, Cornwall

BEAZLEY, Peter George; MEP (EDG) Beds 1979-; s of late Thomas Alfred and Agnes Alice Mary Beazley; *b* 9 June 1922; *Educ* Highgate Sch, St John's Coll Oxford; *m* 1945, Joyce Marion, *née* Sulman; 1 s (Christopher John Pridham, MEP Cornwall and Plymouth 1984-, b 1952), 2 da (and 1 da decd); *Career* with ICI 1947-78: dir ICI Italia 1965-73; vice-chm and md South African Nylon Spinners and Pan Textiles 1973-76; res fell Royal Inst of Int Affairs 1977-78; *Clubs* Oriental, Royal Institution, Willingdon Golf; *Style—* Peter Beazley, Esq, MEP; Rest Harrow, 14 The Combe, Ratton, Eastbourne (☎ 0323 54460); 4 Bridgewater Court, Little Gaddesden, Herts (☎ 044 284 3548)

BEBBINGTON, Andrew John Price; s of Jack Price Bebbington (d 1987), of Hazel Gr nr Stockport, Cheshire and Elizabeth *née* Riding; *b* 10 Mar 1952; *Educ* Stockport GS; *m* 8 March 1975, Heather Winifred, da of Benjamin Harold Linton (d 1954); *Career* CA: Neville Russell 1969-75, Dearden Farrow 1977-82, own practice 1982-; fixtures sec Cheshire Cricket League; FCA 1976; *Recreations* sport, military modelling; *Clubs* MENSA; *Style—* Andrew J P Bebbington, Esq; 13 Rushside Road, Cheadle Hume, Cheadle, Cheshire, SK8 6NW (☎ 061 485 7136)

BECHER; *see*: Wrixon-Becher

BECHMANN, Hon Mrs (Elizabeth Suzanne); *née* Duke; o da of 2 Baron Merrivale, OBE (d 1951); *b* 27 August 1921; *m* 1, 1942 (m dis 1953), Capt Jean Pompei, French Air Force, s of Louis Pompei; 1 s, 1 da; m 2, 1955, Jacques Bechmann s of René Bechmann; 1 s; *Clubs* Chantilly Golf Club; *Style—* The Hon Mrs Bechmann; La Charité, 60 500 Vineuil-St Firmin, Chantilly, France (☎ 4 457 0169)

BECK, Charles Theodore Heathfield; s of Richard Theodore Beck, of Blundens House, Upper Froyle, Alton, Hants, and Margaret Beryl, *née* Page; *b* 3 April 1954; *Educ* Winchester, Jesus Coll Cambridge (MA); *Career* Bank of England 1975-79; JM Finn & Co stockbrokers: joined 1979, ptnr 1984, fin ptnr 1988; co-developer Genesis Securities Computer Software; Freeman City of London 1980, Liveryman Worshipful Co of Broderers 1981; memb AMSIA 1980; *Recreations* fencing, japanese fencing, archaelogy; *Style—* Charles Beck, Esq; Blundens House, Upper Froyle, Alton, Hants GU34 4LB (☎ 0420 23 147); J M Finn & Co, Salisbury House, London Wall, London EC2N 5TA (☎ 01 628 9688, fax 01 628 7314, telex 887 281)

BECK, Clive; s of Sir Edgar Charles Beck, CBE, and his 1 wife, Mary Agnes, *née* Sorapure; *b* 12 April 1937; *Educ* Ampleforth; *m* 1960, Philippa, da of Dr Philip Flood (d 1968); 6 children; *Career* dep chm and jt md John Mowlem; chm and Company plc and various other UK and overseas subsidiaries; SGB plc.; *Recreations* fishing, shooting, golf; *Clubs* Swinley Forest Golf, Bucks; *Style—* Clive Beck, Esq; Westgate House, Ealing Road, Brentford, Middx

BECK, Prof John Swanson; s of John Beck (d 1976), of Glasgow, and Mary, *née* Barbour (d 1976); *b* 22 August 1928; *Educ* Glasgow Acad, Univ of Glasgow (BSc, MB, MD); *m* 10 June 1960, Marion Tudhope, da of Lt Cdr John Clendinning Paterson, DSO, RNVR (d 1970), of Glasgow; 1 s (John b 1962), 1 da (Patricia Mary Swanson b 1965); *Career* lectr Glasgow Univ 1958-63, sr lectr Aberdeen Univ 1963-71, prof of pathology Dundee Univ 1971-; MRC: memb cell bd 1978-82, chm breast tumour panel 1979-; chm biomed res ctee Scottish Home and Health Dept 1983-; memb: cncl RSE 1986-, med advsy bd LEPRA 1987-, Nat Biol Standards Bd 1988-, Tayside Health Bd 1983-, Incorpn of Masons Glasgow 1960; bonnetmaker craftsman Incorporated Trades Dundee 1973; FRCPG 1965, FRCPE 1966, FRCPath 1975, FRSE 1984, FIBiol 1987; *Recreations* DIY, work; *Clubs* Clyde Canoe, Royal Cwlth Soc; *Style—* Prof John Beck; 598 Perth Road, Dundee, Tayside DD2 1QA (☎ 0382 562298); Pathology Department, Ninewells Hospital and Medical School, Dundee (☎ 0382 60111 ext 3120)

BECK, (Edgar) Philip; s of Sir Edgar Charles Beck, CBE, of 13 Eaton Place, London SW1 and his 1 wife Mary Agnes, *née* Sorapure; *b* 9 August 1934; *Educ* Ampleforth, Jesus Coll Cambridge (MA); *m* 2 s (Adam and Thomas); *Career* chm John Mowlem and Co (construction, mechanical engineering, property devpt and invstmt gp); dir var associated cos; chm Federation of Civil Eng Contractors 1982-83; *Recreations* flying (fixed wing, land and sea and helicopters), sailing; *Clubs* Buck's; *Style—* Philip Beck, Esq; Westgate House, Ealing Rd, Brentford, Middx TW8 0QZ (☎ 01 568 9111, telex 24414)

BECK, Baron Rolf (Rudolph); s of Baron Dr Otto Beck, and Baroness Margaret Beck; *b* 25 Mar 1914; *Educ* Theresanianum Mil Acad, Geneva Univ, Lausanne Univ, Vienna Univ; *m* 1, 1944 (m dis), Elizabeth Lesley Brenchley, da of Capt Fletcher, RN; 1 s (Stephen b 1948); m 2, 1979, Countess (Signe) Mariana, da of Count Carl Göran Axel Mörner of Morlanda, of Sweden, and formerly w of Count von Rosen; *Career* petrochem engr and researcher, fndr various companies, chm and md Slip and Molyslip Gp of Cos 1939-; fndr memb: IoD, Scientific Exploration Soc; corporate memb Euro Atlantic Gp, vice-pres Small Business Bureau; sustaining member American C of C; *Clubs* RAC, Royal Scottish Automobile, Royal Harwich Yacht, W Mersey Yacht, Hurlingham, Union Interalliée (Paris), Princeton (New York); *Style—* Baron Rolf Beck; 62 Bishops Mansion, Bishops Park Rd., London, SW6 6DZ (☎ 01 731 3021) Cap Davia, Marine De Davia, Ile Rousse, Corsica (☎ 95 600625); Molyslip Holdings Ltd, Reform Road, Maidenhead, Berkshire SL6 8BY (☎ 0628 74991, telex 849850, fax 0628 773199)

BECK-MACKAY, Colin; s of Capt John Mackay (d 1957), of Sutherland, and Patricia Kate, *née* Beck (d 1972); *b* 31 August 1947; *Educ* Loughborough Univ, RMA Sandhurst; *Career* Home Civil Service 1972, hon sec Br Field Sports Soc 1980; *Recreations* fishing, shooting, military history; *Clubs* Naval; *Style—* Colin Beck-Mackay, Esq; Thornhill Cottage, by Earlston, Ayrshire KA2 9AD

BECKER, Basil George Christie; VRD (1964); s of Leslie Becker (d 1976), of Frinton, and Elizabeth Webster, *née* White (d 1966); *b* 17 May 1928; *Educ* Shrewsbury; *m* 1952, Gillian, da of Henry Paul Dawson (d 1984); 1 s, 1 da; *Career* served RM 1944-47, RMR 1948-65; chm: Beatson Gp Ltd, Contract Cleaning and Maintenance Assoc 1972-74r, G S Chemicals Ltd; dir: RJ Barwick and Son, The Kent Chemical Co Ltd; Master Worshipful Co of Horners 1987; *Recreations* golf, gardening, sailing; *Clubs* City Livery, RAC; *Style—* Basil Becker, Esq, VRD; National Westminster Bank plc, 96 Fenchurch St, London EC3M 4EN

BECKER, Lady (Gladys Sarah); da of Percival John and Mary Elizabeth, *née* Duggan, of Adelaide, S Australia; *m* 1928, Sir (Jack) Ellerton Becker (d 1980); *Style—* Lady Becker; Palomera, Fairylands, Pembroke, Bermuda

BECKER, (Edward) Lionel; s of Isaac (Jack) Becker (d 1956), and Sarah, *née* Reiss; *b* 5 Jan 1926; *Educ* King George V Sch Southport, Manchester Univ (BA); *m* 1979, Deborah Ann, da of Dr Sydney Hepworth (d 1980); 1 s (Jon), 4 da (Karen, Jacqueline, Nicola, Rachel); *Career* CA; chm Euro Corporate Servs Gp 1982-; dep chm and chief exec Apollo Leisure Gp Ltd 1977-86. dep chm Triumph Apollo Prodns Ltd 1982-86; FCA; *Recreations* golf,; *Style—* Edward Becker, Esq; 19 Calle de Felipe II, Sotogrande, Cadiz, Spain (☎ (010 34) 56 792356); Suite 23/5 Don House, 30/38 Main Street, Gibraltar (☎ (010 350) 76513, telex 2368 FACTOR GK, fax 010 350 79523)

BECKETT, Allan Harry; MBE; s of Sgt George William Harry Beckett (d 1949), of Belvedere, Kent, and Emma Louise, *née* Stokes (d 1983); *b* 4 Mar 1914; *Educ* Eastham Secdy Sch, London Univ (BSc); *m* 25 June 1949, Ida Gwladys, da of Kenbryd Morris James, DCM (d 1983), of Keston Kent; 2 s (Michael b 1950, Timothy b 1953), 1 da (Sian b 1957); *Career* RE 1940, 142 OCTU 1940, cmmnd 2 Ltd 1941, capt 1942, Staff Maj 1942, tech advsr in field 21 Army RE 1944, seconded to BAOR 1945; engrg asst: A J Bridle 1934-35, HM Office of Works 1935-37; bridge designer Br Steelwork Assoc 1937-38, asst site engr Chief Architects Dept 1938-39, sr engr Sir Bruce White, Wolfe Barry and Ptnrs Conslting Engrs 1946 (ptnr 1957-, sr ptnr 1983-); FICE, MIConsE; *Books* numerous tech papers on engrg; *Recreations* sailing; *Clubs* St Stephens and Erith Yacht; *Style—* Allan Beckett, Esq, MBE; Thistledown, Wood Way, Franborough Park, Kent; 83 Abbey St, Faversham, Kent (☎ 0689 52193); Douglas House, Douglas St, London SW1 (☎ 01 821 6171, telex 28679)

BECKETT, (John) Angus; CB (1965), CMG (1956); s of John Beckett, BA (d 1960), of Purley, Surrey, and Helen Isobella Caithness, *née* Hart (d 1919); *b* 6 July 1909; *Educ* Sidney Sussex Coll Cambridge, (MA); *m* 1935, Una Joan, yr da of late George Henry Wright, of Wilby, Northants; 1 s (John), 2 da (Philippa, Tessa); *Career* schoolmaster 1933-40; entered Civil Service 1940, PPS to Min of Fuel and Power 1946-7 (asst sec 1947-59), chm Petroleum Ctee of OEEC 1948-50 (1955-59 and 1965-72), petroleum attaché Br Embassy Washington DC 1950-53, under sec Miny of Power and Technology 1959 (Gas Div 1959-64, Petroleum Div 1964-72), ret; Davy Offshore Modules Ltd, William Press Prodn Systems Ltd 1972-83 (chm 1981-83); dir Total Oil Marine Ltd 1979-; memb Cambridge Iceland Expedition 1932; *Books* Iceland Adventure (1934); *Recreations* following rugby football, rowing, enjoying French wines; *Clubs* St Stephen's Constitutional, Arctic, Union (Cambridge); *Style—* Angus Beckett, Esq, CB, CMG; Tyle Cottage, Needles Bank, Godstone, Surrey (☎ 0883 842295)

BECKETT, Bruce Probart; s of Capt James Donald Lancaster Beckett (d 1969), and Florence Theresa, *née* Probart (d 1983); *b* 7 June 1924; *Educ* Rondebosch Boys HS Capetown, Capetown Univ (B Arch), UCL (Dip TP); *m* 9 May 1957, Jean, da of William Low McDonald (d 1949); 2 s (John, Malcolm), 3 da (Elizabeth, Janet, Margaret); *Career* Sea Cadet RNVR SA Div 1938-42, later Cadet Petty Offr; WWII SANF seconded RN 1942, Midshipman 1943, Sub Lt 1944, active serv S Atlantic, W Africa, Med, Western Approaches; Indian Ocean Lt 1946, Antartic Expdn SANR 1948, Lt Cdre 1950, resigned cmmn 1960; architect: Lightfoot Twentyman-Jones & Kent 1951-59, Arthur Kenyon & Ptnrs 1960-61; civil serv 1961-84: sr architect WO 1961-64, supt architect DGRED, MPBW 1964-67, chief architect and under sec Scottish Off 1967-84; ptnr Hutchison Locke & Monk 1984-86, private practice as chartered architect, town and country planner, building cnslt; hon sec Cape Town Architectural Assoc, Sr vice pres Edinburgh Architectural Assoc, cncllr Royal Incorpn of Architects (Scotland), vice pres RIBA; ARCUK Councillor 1968-; FRIBA, FRIAS, FRTPI, FCIOB, MISA Architects; 39/45 star, Atlantic star, Africa star, Italy star, Defence Medal, 39/45 War Medal, Coronation Medal 57 Africa Serv Medal 1944; *Recreations* gardening, drawing, water colours, DIY; *Clubs* New (Edinburgh) Arts; *Style—* Bruce Beckett, Esq; Summerfield, Vines Cross Road, Horam, Near Heathfield, East Sussex, TN21 OHE (☎ 04353 2042)

BECKETT, Maj-Gen Denis Arthur; CB (1971), DSO (1944), OBE (1960); s of Archibald Edward Beckett (d 1976), of Radlett, Herts, and Margery Mildred, *née* Robinson (d 1954); *b* 19 May 1917; *Educ* Forest Sch Essex, Chard Sch Somerset; *m* 1, 1946, Elizabeth, da of Col Guy Edwards, DSO, MC (d 1962), of Rockcliff House, Upper Slaughter, Glos; 1 s (Nigel); m 2, 1978, Nancy Ann, da of Charles Bradford Hitt (d 1957), of Gross Pointe, Michigan, USA; *Career* Maj-Gen (late Parachute Regt), Chief of Staff Far East Land Forces 1966-68, Dir Personal Servs (Army) 1968-71;

Clubs Army and Navy, Lansdowne; *Style—* Maj-Gen Denis Beckett, CB, DSO, OBE; 12 Wellington House, Eton Rd, London NW3 4SY

BECKETT, Hon Edward John; s and h of 4 Baron Grimthorpe, OBE; *b* 20 Nov 1954; *Educ* Hawtreys, Harrow; *Style—* The Hon Edward Beckett

BECKETT, Maj-Gen Edwin Horace Alexander; CB (1988), MBE (1974); s of William Alexander Beckett (d 1986), of Sheffield, and Doris, *née* Whitham; *b* 16 May 1937; *Educ* Henry Fanshawe Sch, RMA Sandhurst; *m* 1963, Micaela Elizabeth Benedicta, yr da of Col Sir Edward Malet; 3 s (Simon b 1965, Alexander b 1979, Thomas b 1980), 1 da (Diana b 1964); *Career* cmmnd West Yorks Regt 1957, regtl serv: Aden (despatches 1968), Gibraltar, Germany, NI; DAA and QMG 11 Armd Bde 1972-74, CO 1 PWO 1976-78 (despatches 1977), GSO1 (DS) Staff Coll 1979, Cmdt Jr Div Staff Coll 1980, Cdr UKMF and 6 Field Force 1981, Cdr UKMF 1 Inf Brigade and Tidworth Garrison 1982; dir Concepts MOD 1983-84, dir Army Plans and Programmes MOD 1984-85, chief of staff HQ BAOR 1985-88, head of Br Def Stff and def attaché Washington DC; *Recreations* fishing, golf; *Clubs* Naval and Military; *Style—* Maj-Gen Edwin Beckett, CB, MBE

BECKETT, John Michael; yr s of Horace Norman Beckett, MBE, and Clarice Lillian, *née* Allsop; bro of Sir Terence Norman Beckett, *qv*; *b* 22 June 1929; *Educ* Wolverhampton GS, Magdalen Coll Oxford; *m* 1955, Joan Mary, o da of Percy Rogerson; 5 da; *Career* barr; former chief exec Br Sugar; chm Woolworth Hldgs; *Style—* John Beckett, Esq; Belton House, Rutland, Leics (☎ 057 286 682)

BECKETT, Margaret Mary; MP ((Lab) Derby S 1983-); da of Cyril Jackson, and Winifred Jackson; *b* Jan 1943; *Educ* Notre Dame HS, Manchester Coll of Sci and Technol; *m* 1979, Lionel A Beckett; *Career* sometime metallurgist, sponsored by TGWU, as Miss Margaret Jackson, MP (Lab) Lincoln Oct 1974-1979 (contested same Feb 1974), asst govt whip 1975-76, under sec for Educn and Science 1976-79, princ researcher Granada TV 1979-83; memb: Lab Pty NEC 1980-81, 1985-86 and 1988-, Tribune Gp, Fabian Soc, CND; *Style—* Mrs Lionel Beckett, MP; House of Commons, London SW1

BECKETT, Sir Martyn Gervase; 2 Bt (UK 1921), MC (1945); s of Hon Sir William Gervase Beckett, 1 Bt (d 1937), bro of 2 Baron Grimthorpe, and Lady Marjorie (d 1964), da of 5 Earl of Warwick and wid of 2 Earl of Feversham; *b* 6 Nov 1918; *Educ* Eton, Trinity Coll Cambridge (BA); *m* 1941, Hon Priscilla Léonie Helen Brett, da of 3 Viscount Esher, GBE (d 1964); 2 s, 1 da; *Heir* s, Richard Gervase Beckett; *Career* Capt Welsh Gds 1944-45; architect; tstee: Wallace Collection 1972- (chm 1976), Br Museum 1978-; chm Yorkshire Regional Ctee Nat Tst 1980-85; cncl of mgmnt Chatsworth House Tst 1981, tstee CPRE Tst 1983; memb cncl RSPB 1985-87; ARIBA 1952; FRSA 1982; *Recreations* painting, piano; *Clubs* Brooks's, MCC; *Style—* Sir Martyn Beckett, Bt, MC; 3 St Alban's Grove, London W8 (☎ 01 937 7834); Kirkdale Farm, Nawton, Yorks (☎ 0751 31301)

BECKETT, Hon Oliver Ralph; 2 s of 2 Baron Grimthorpe (d 1963); *b* 21 August 1918; *Educ* Eton, Trinity Coll Cambridge; *m* 6 April 1944, Hélène Agnes, da of Constantine Fessas, and formerely w of Richard Tasker Evans; 2 da; *Career* author and lecturer; FRSA; *Books* J F Herring and Sons, Horses and Movement; *Style—* The Hon Oliver Beckett; 55 Carlisle Avenue, St Albans, Herts AL3 5LX (☎ 0727 62389)

BECKETT, Hon Lady; Hon Priscilla Léonie Helen; *née* Brett; da of 3 Viscount Esher, GBE (d 1963); *b* 31 May 1921; *m* 1941, Sir Martyn Beckett, 2 Bt, MC, *qv*; 2 s, 1 da; *Style—* The Hon Lady Beckett; 3 St Alban's Grove, London W8 (☎ 01 937 7834)

BECKETT, Hon Ralph Daniel; s of 4 Baron Grimthorpe, OBE; *b* 11 April 1957; *m* 22 Jan 1987, Susaa w, er da of Colin Townsend-Rose; *Style—* The Hon Ralph Beckett

BECKETT, Richard Gervase; s and h of Sir Martyn Beckett, 2 Bt, MC, *qv*; *b* 27 Mar 1944; *Educ* Eton; *m* 1976, Elizabeth Ann, da of Maj (Charles) Hugo Waterhouse; 1 s (Walter Gervase b 16 Jan 1987), 3 da; *Career* barr, QC 1988; *Recreations* walking; *Clubs* Pratt's, Portland; *Style—* Richard Beckett, Esq; 33 Groveway, London SW9 (☎ 01 735 3350)

BECKETT, Samuel; *b* 1906; *Educ* Portora Royal Sch, Trinity Coll Dublin; *Career* author and playwright; *Style—* Samuel Beckett, Esq; c/o Faber and Faber Ltd, 24 Russell Sq, WC1

BECKETT, Sir Terence Norman; KBE (1987, CBE 1974); s of Horace Norman Beckett, MBE, and Clarice Lillian, *née* Allsop; bro of John Michael Beckett, *qv*; *b* 13 Dec 1923; *Educ* engrg cadet 1943-45, LSE (BSc); *m* 1950, Sylvia Gladys Asprey; 1 da; *Career* serv WWII Capt REME, UK, India, Malaysia; RARO 1949-62; co trainee Ford Motor Co Ltd 1950, mangr product planning staff 1955-63 (responsible for Cortina, Transit Van and D series truck), exec dir 1966, md and chief exec 1974-80, chm 1976-80; dir ICI 1976-80; dir-gen CBI 1980-87 (memb cncl 1976-80); pt/t memb CEGB 1987-; conslt Milk Mktg Bd and Dairy Trade Fedn, pres IVCA 1987-; memb: Top Salaries Review Body 1987-, Engrg Industs Cncl 1975-80, BIM Cncl 1976-80 (Gold Medal 1980), cncl Automotive Div IMechE 1979-80, NEDC 1980-87; chm governing body London Business Sch 1979-86 (hon fell 1987-); memb ct Cranfield Inst of Technol 1977-82; govr Nat Inst Econ and Soc Res 1978-; govr and memb ct LSE 1978-; memb ct and cncl Essex Univ 1986-; (chm Cncl and Pro-Chllr 1989-); memb Cncl BTO 1986-; vice-pres Conference on Schs Science and Technol 1979-80; govr Chigwell Sch 1986-; Hon DSc: Cranfield 1977, Heriot-Watt 1981, London 1982; Hambro Businessman of the Year 1978, hon fell Sidney Sussex Coll Cambridge 1981-, Stamp lectr London Univ 1982, Pfizer lectr Univ of Kent 1983; FEng, FIMechE, CBIM, FIMI (vice-pres 1974-80); *Recreations* ornithology, music; *Clubs* Athenaeum; *Style—* Sir Terence Beckett, KBE

BECKETT, William Alan; s of William Alexander Beckett (d 1986), of Sheffield, and Doris, *née* Whitham); *b* 5 Jan 1946; *Educ* High Stores GS; *m* 30 Sept 1965, Linda, da of George Frederick Sanders, of Walsall; 1 s (Marcus b 1966), 3 da (Sarah b 1967, d 1985, Rachel b 1971, Clare b 1971); *Career* md: William Beckett & Co Ltd 1972-, Roder Beckett Fine Art Ltd 1975-83, Polyplas Ltd 1987-; co chm SCI Safe; *Recreations* cricket, tennis, occasional skier, potential golfer; *Style—* William Beckett, Esq; 274 Ecclesall Rd South, Sheffield S11 9PS (☎ 0742 351 405); William Beckett & Co (Plastics) Ltd, Tinsley Indust Park, Shepcote Way, Sheffield S9 1TH (☎ 0742 434 399, fax 0742 560 196, telex 547241)

BECKETT, Hon William Ernest; yst s of 3 Baron Grimthorpe (d 1963); *b* 30 June 1945; *Educ* Eton; *m* 15 June 1968, Virginia Helen Clark, o da of Michael Clark Hutchison, sometime MP for Edinburgh; 1 s, 1 da; *Career* Lt 9/12 Royal Lancers (POW) 1964-68;gen mangr electronic publishing Co; *Recreations* sailing, shooting, skiing, windsurfing, hunting, tennis; *Clubs* Annabel's; *Style—* The Hon William Beckett; The Estate House, Serlby, nr Bawtry, S Yorks (☎ 0777 818282)

BECKINGHAM, Dr David Clive; s of Capt Clive Walter Beckingham (d 1954), of Inverness-shire, and Alice, *née* Hatcher; *b* 8 August 1928; *Educ* St Andrews Sch Eastbourne, Harrow, New Coll Oxford (MA, BM, BCh); *m* 12 Aug 1972, Mary Chaldecot, da of Thomas Preston Everett, of Gwent; 1 da (Sarah Jane b 1975); *Career* RN 1956-75: PMO HMS Albion, SMO and conslt gynaecologist RN Hosp Gibraltar, PMO HMS Hermes, ret Surgn Cdr; conslt physician Cardiff Royal Infirmary and Royal Gwent Hosp Newport 1976-; former chm Gwent div BMA; memb: Welsh Cncl BMS, Welsh Ctee for Hosp Medical Services, (former) Welsh Medical Cttee, Gwent Medical Ctee (chm 1980-82, Gwent Dist Health Authy Mgmnt Team 1979-; chm S Gwent Medical Exec Cttee; MRCOG; *Recreations* sailing, swimming, cooking, military history, Spain; *Clubs* Army and Navy, Pall Mall, United Services (Cardiff); *Style—* Dr David C Beckingham; The Gables, Llandevaud, Gwent NP6 2AF (☎ 0633 400921); Dept Gu Medicine, Royal Gwent Hospital, Newport (☎ 0633 52244)

BECKMAN, Hon Mrs; (Angela Clare); o da of Baron Mais, GBE, ERD, TD, JP, DL (Life Peer); *b* 4 Nov 1946; *Educ* St Margaret's Bushey, House of Citizenship; *m* 1976, Robert Beckman, of Washington DC; *Style—* The Hon Mrs Beckman; 11100 River Rd, Potomac, Maryland 20854, USA

BECKMAN, Michael; QC; s of Nathan Beckman, and Esther, *née* Sonabend; *b* 6 April 1932; *Educ* King's Coll London (LLB); *m* 1966, (m dis) Sheryl Robin, *née* Kyle; 2 da (Amanda, Natasha); *Career* nat serv; called to Bar Lincoln's Inn 1954; head of chambers; *Recreations* tennis, food, wine, cinema, theatre, travel, people, animals; *Style—* Michael Beckman, Esq, QC; Ballards, Widford, Herts; St Germaine de Talloires, 74290 Veyrier du Lac, France; 19 Old Buildings, Lincoln's Inn, London WC2 (☎ 01 831 63811)

BECKWITH, Lady Antonia Pamela Mary; *née* Crichton; da of 5 Earl of Erne (d 1940), and Lady Davidema, da of 2 Earl of Lytton; *b* 18 April 1934; *Educ* privately; *m* 1, 1953, Timothy William Wardell, Sub Lt (ret) RN, gs of Sir Kenneth Crossley, 2 Bt; 3 s, 2 da; m 2, 1981, Charles William Beckwith; *Recreations* hunting, fishing; *Clubs* Meath Hunt; *Style—* Lady Antonia Beckwith; Highfield, Dunsany, Co Meath, Eire

BECKWITH, Rev Canon John Douglas; o s of William Albert Beckwith (d 1977), of Leeds, and Gladys Ruberry, *née* Barley; *b* 6 July 1933; *Educ* Leeds Modern, King's Coll London (AKC); *Career* Nat Serv WO 1951-53; ordained: deacon 1958, priest 1965; curate Streatham St Leon Southwark 1958-59, licence to officiate Ripon 1959-60, tutor Ijebu-Igo GS and lectr Nolusi Coll W Nigeria 1960-62, tutor Eltham Coll 1964-69, chaplain Gothenburg 1969-70, chaplain to Bishop of Edmonton 1970-77 (hon Chaplain 1977-84), dir of ordinands 1970-77, vicar St Anne Highgate 1977-88, canon Gibraltar Cath and commissary Diocese in Europe 1984-, rector Bladon-cum-Woodstock 1988-; memb Br Factory Gothenbury 1979, tstee Highgate Cemetery 1979-87, chm Church Needlework News 1979; Freeman City of London 1979, Liveryman Worshipful Co of Broderers 1979; Order of Thyateira and GB (First Class) 1974; *Recreations* graphic and applied arts, writing, pilgrimages; *Clubs* City Livery, Nikaean; *Style—* The Rev Canon John Beckwith; Woodstock Rectory, Oxford OX7 1UQ (☎ 0993 811 415); Olicana, Brompton-by-Sawdon, N Yorks

BECKWITH, Peter Michael; s of Col Harold Andrew Beckwith (d 1966), of Hong Kong, and Agnes Camilla McMichael, *née* Duncan (d 1980); *b* 20 Jan 1945; *Educ* Harrow, Emmanuel Coll Cambridge (BA); *m* 19 Oct 1968, Paula, da of late Robin Stuart Bateman, of Cliftonville, Kent; 2 da (Tamara Jane b 1970, Clare Tamsin b 1972); *Career* slr Supreme Court of Judicature 1970-, dep chm London and Edinburgh Tst plc 1983-; *Recreations* association football, tennis, skiing, opera, gardening, dogs; *Clubs* Riverside Racquets, OHAFC, Downhill Only, Covent Garden Friends; *Style—* Peter Beckwith, Esq; 243 Knightsbridge, London SW7

BECTIVE, Earl of; Thomas Michael Ronald Christopher Taylour; s and h of 6 Marquess of Headfort; *b* 10 Feb 1959; *Educ* Harrow, RAC Cirencester; *m* 17 Oct 1987, Susan Jane, da of Charles Anthony Vandervell (d 1987), of Burnham, Bucks; *Career* Estate Agency John D Wood and Co; *Style—* Earl of Bective; Cusby Farm, Bride, Ramsey, Isle of Man

BEDBROOK, Sir George Montario; OBE (1963); s of Arthur Bedbrook, and Ethel, *née* Prince; *b* 8 Nov 1921; *Educ* Univ HS Melbourne, Med Sch Melbourne Univ; *m* 1946, Jessie Violet, *née* Page; 2 s, 3 da; *Career* emeritus orthopaedic surgeon 1986; Royal Perth Rehabilitation Hosp MB, BS, MS, FRCS, FRACS, DPRM, OStJ, Hon MD, Hon FRCS (Edin), Hon D Tech; kt 1978; *see Debrett's Handbook of Australia and New Zealand for further details*; *Recreations* reading, music, travel, walking; *Style—* Sir George Bedbrook, OBE; 29 Ulster Road, Floreat Park, W Australia 6014 (☎ 01 387 3582)

BEDDALL, Hugh Richard Muir; s of Herbert Muir Beddall (d 1952), and Jennie, *née* Fowler (d 1973); *b* 20 May 1922; *Educ* Stowe, Ecole de Commerce Neuchatel Switzerland; *m* 22 June 1946, Monique Henriette, da of Herman Haefliger (d 1953), of Neuchatel, Switzerland; 3 s (Richard Grant Muir b 1949, Keith Ian Muir b 1954, Alastair Clive Hugh b 1962), 1 da (Angela Claire Muir b 1951); *Career* 2 Lt RM 1941, Lt 1941, Capt 1944, troop cdr A Troop 45 RM Commando and 1 Commando Bde HQ; chm: Muir Beddall and Co Ltd 1962-, C T Bowring & Co Ltd 1963-83; memb of Lloyd's 1943-; *Recreations* shooting, racing; *Clubs* Buck's, East India, Pilgrims'; *Style—* Hugh Muir Beddall, Esq; 53 Cadogan Square, London SW1X OHY (☎ 01 235 9461)

BEDDARD, Dominic Anthony Hamilton; s of Terence Elliot Beddard (d 1966), and Ursula Mary Howard, *née* Gurney Richards, BEM; *b* 14 May 1937; *Educ* Cheam Sch, Eton; *m* 17 Sept 1966, Susan Claire, da of Leslie Leo Stevens, of E Sussex; 1 s (Matthew b 1968), 2 da (Emma b 1969, Henrietta b 1971); *Career* KRRC (60 Rifles) 1955-57, cmmnd 1956 served Libya and Cyprus, TA (Queen Victoria's Rifles, Queens Royal Rifles, 4 Bn Royal Green Jackets) 1958-69, Capt 1961, Major 1964; NSU (GB) Ltd 1957-62, ptnr Wilson Smithett and Co 1968- (joined 1962); chm Tea Brokers Assoc of London 1988 (chm 1986, vice chm 1987); church warden St Thomas A Becket Brightling 1979-84, sec Brightling Village Tst 1985-88; *Recreations* golf, gardening; *Clubs* Lansdowne, Royal Greenjackets London; *Style—* Dominic Beddard, Esq; Wyland Wood, Robertsbridge, E Sussex; Wilson Smithett & Co, Sir John Lyon House, Upper Thames Street, London EC4V 3LS (☎ 01 236 0611, fax 01 236 4976, telex 888627)

BEDDARD, Lt-Col Jonathan Patrick Owen; MBE (1981); s of Terence Elliot Beddard (d 1964), and Ursula Mary Howard, *née* Richards (d 1985); *b* 17 Mar 1944;

Educ Eton; *m* 4 Dec 1979, Felicity Victoria, da of Lt-Col Granville Reginald Arthur Brooking, of Sussex; 1 s (Henry Terence b 1981), 1 da (Genevieve Daisy b 1984); *Career* served Far East, Ops in Borneo 1963-64, Instructor Jungle Warfare Sch 1967-69, Loan Service Fiji 1972-74, Staff Coll Camberley 1977, Ops N Ireland 1969/71/81, BAOR 1970-72 and 1982-85, CO 2 Bn Royal Green Jackets 1983-85, MOD 1985-87; dir London Portfolio Services Ltd; Freeman City of London, Liveryman Worshipful Co of Skinners; *Recreations* fencing, subaqua, diving; *Clubs* Epee, British Sub Aqua (instructor), Landsdowne; *Style*— Jonathan Beddard, Esq, MBE; Barnfield House, Hawkhurst, Kent TN18 4PX (☎ 05805 2388); C Hare and Co, 37 Fleet St, London EC4; London Portfolio Services, 52 Grosvenor Gardens, London W1A 0AU

BEDDARD, His Hon Judge Nicholas Elliot; s of Terence Elliot Beddard (d 1966), of Kensington, London, and Ursula Mary Hamilton Howard, *née* Gurney-Richards, BEM (d 1985); *b* 26 April 1934; *Educ* Eton; *m* 25 Apr 1964, Gillian Elisabeth Vaughan, da of Llewelyn Vaughan Bevan (d 1987), of Cambridge; 2 s (James b 1966, Benedict b 1968), 1 da (Emily b 1974); *Career* Royal Sussex Regt 1952-54, cmmnd 1953, TA 1955-64; mgmnt trainee United Africa Co, asst public policy exec RAC 1958-68, called to the Bar Inner Temple 1967, practiced SE Circuit 1968-86, rec Crown Ct 1986, circuit judge 1986; fndr memb Barnsbury Singers; Liveryman Worshipful Co of Skinners 1957, Freeman City of London; memb cncl HM Circuit Judges 1986; *Recreations* choral singing, squash, golf; *Clubs* Lansdowne, Orford Sailing; *Style*— His Hon Judge Beddard; Farrar's Building, Temple, London EC4Y 7BD (☎ 01 583 9241)

BEDDINGTON, Nadine Dagmar Antionette Sarah; MBE (1982); da of Maj Frank Maurice Beddington (d 1930), and Mathilde, *née* Kohle (d 1978); *Educ* New Hall Chelmsford, Regent Poly (Dip Arch); *Career* London C C Ambulance Serv 1939-42; architect, asst in local and centl govt 1940-45, private practice 1945-55, chief architect to (pt) British Shoe Corp 1957-67, princ in private practice 1967-; chm Camberwell Soc 1970-77 (pres 1977-81), govr Grove Vale Sch Dulwich 1985-, vice chm Brixton and Dist Dog Training Club; vice chm Architects in Indust Gp 1963-67, vice pres RIBA 1972-73 (memb of cncl 1969-73, 1975-79), memb: Arcuk Cncl 1969-87, Cncl Assoc Conslt Architects; ARIBA 1940, FRIBA, FCSO, FRSA, FAMS; *Books* Design for Shopping Centres (1982), plus numerous articles on architectural subjects; *Recreations* dogs, travel, music, reading; *Clubs* Reform; *Style*— Miss Nadine Beddington, Esq, MBE; 17 Champion Grove, London SE5 8BN (☎ 01 274 3372)

BEDDINGTON, (Charles) Richard; s of Charles Beddington (d 1947), and Stella, *née* de Goldschmidt (d 1942); *b* 22 August 1911; *Educ* Eton, Balliol Coll Oxford (BA); *m* 30 March 1939, Joan Appleby, da of Frederick Appleby Holt (d 1984), of Brede Place, Sussex; 2 s (John b 1942, Charles b 1960), 1 da (Charlotte b 1940); *Career* TA 1939-45, Maj RA; barr Inner Temple 1934, met stipendiary magistrate 1963-80; *Clubs* MCC, Royal Ashdown Golf ; *Style*— Richard Beddington, Esq; Rosehill, Cuckfield, W Sussex RH17 5EU (☎ 0444 454063)

BEDDINGTON, (Julian) Roy; s of Reginald Beddington, CBE (d 1961), of Old Basing, and Sybil Elizabeth, *née* Henriques (d 1939); *b* 16 June 1910; *Educ* Rugby, Corpus Christi Coll Oxford, Slade Sch of Art, Florence Sch of Art; *m* 1 (m dis), Anna, *née* Griffith; 2 da (Phillipa (Mrs Foulkes), Rosa (Dr Denniston)); m 2, 1961, Diana Mary, da of W Dobson, of Marnhull, Dorset; 1 da (Sarah Anne); *Career* London Electrical Engrs, RA Lt Intelligence Offr 38 AA Bde, invalided out; fisheries off MAFF; artist, illustrator, author and poet; rep GB Olympic Games (Art) London, cmmnd to paint Winston Churchill in Silver Jubilee Procession; seven one man exhibitions incl Bond Street, Grafton Gallery, Ackermann, Walker's Gallery; other exhibitions incl: Whitechapel Art Gallery, NEAC Royal Cambrian & Acad; fishing corr Country Life; vice pres Salmon & Trout Assoc; chm fisheries' ctee Hampshire River Bd; FRSA; *Books* The adventures of Thomas Trout (1939), To be a Fisherman (1955), The Pigeon and the Boy (1957), Pindar a dog to remember (1979), A Countryman's Verse (1981); illustrator: The Happy Fisherman, River to River, Alexander and Angling, Riverside Reflections, Beyond the Caspian; *Recreations* fishing, gardening; *Clubs* Arts; *Style*— Roy Beddington, Esq; Home Farm, Chute Cadley, Nr Andover, Hants (☎ 026 470 282)

BEDDOES, Air Vice-Marshal John Geoffrey Genior; CB (1980); s of Algernon Geoffrey Beddoes (d 1967), and Lucy Isobel, *née* Collier (d 1935); *b* 21 May 1925; *Educ* Wirral GS; *m* 1947, Betty Morris, *née* Kendrick; 3 s; *Career* pilot trg in Rhodesia and Egypt 1943-45, served 114 Sqdn Italy and Aden 1945-46, No 30 Sqdn Abingdon and Berlin Airlift, 1947-49, flying instr RAF Coll Cranwell and Central Flying Sch 1950-55, Fl Cdr No 57 Sqdn Canberra 1955, Air Miny 1956-57, Flying Coll 1958, Fl Cdr No 57 Sqdn 1959-61, sc Bracknell 1962, OC 139 (Jamaica) Sqdn 1963-65, Wing Cdr Ops HQ No 3 Gp 1965-67, directing Staff Coll of Air Warfare 1968-69, OC RAF Laarbruch 1969-71, MOD dep dir Operational Requirements 1971-73, HQ 2 ATAF Asst COS Offensive Operations 1974-75, MOD Dir Operational Requirements 1975-78, Dir Gen Aircraft (2) MOD Procurement Exec 1978-81, ret; chm St Gregory's Tst Norwich; FRACS; *Recreations* gardening, DIY, cricket, golf; *Clubs* RAF, MCC; *Style*— Air Vice-Marshal John Beddoes, CB; White Stables, Stow Bedon, Norfolk (☎ 095 383 524)

BEDDOW, Cecil Miles; s of late Leslie Towne Beddow, of Southwold; *b* 18 Sept 1920; *Educ* King's Sch Bruton Somerset; *m* 1947, Modwena Keyna, da of late Thomas Austin Rafferty, of Paris, France; 2 s (1 decd), 1 da; *Career* Jardine Matheson and Co Hong Kong 1949-53; Carreras/Rothmans Ltd to 1960, dir Aspro-Nicholas to 1969; fin dir F W Woolworth and Co 1969-73; advsr Morgan Grenfell 1973-86; chm and chief exec London and Midland Industls plc; chm: Aspro-Nicholas (Tstees) Ltd; dir: Yule Catto and Co plc, Amersham International plc, McPhersons (UK) Ltd, Harold Holt Ltd, Oriflame Int SA, Gordon and Gotch Hldgs plc; fell and memb cncl of Royal Soc of Arts Manufacturers and Commerce; FCA; *Recreations* swimming, skiing; *Clubs* Carlton, Garrick; *Style*— Bill Beddow, Esq; Flat 7, Seven Princes Gate, London SW7 (☎ 01 584 8391; work: 01 723 5123); Robbers Wood, Lymore, Lymington, Hants

BEDELIAN, Haro Moushegh; OBE (1986); s of Moushegh Haroutune Bedelian (d 1974), and Annig, *née* Nigogosian; *b* 6 Mar 1943; *Educ* English Sch Nicosia Cyprus, St Catharine's Coll Cambridge (MA); *m* 1970, Yvonne Mildred, da of Stephen Gregory Arratoon, of London; 1 s (Stepan b 1973), 2 da (Lisa 1975, Claire b 1978); *Career* dir Balfour Beatty Ltd 1988, md Balfour Beatty Construction Ltd 1988- (dir 1985-); memb cncl Inst of Civil Engs 1987-; *Recreations* squash; *Clubs* RAC; *Style*— Haro M Bedelian, Esq, OBE; Bryn Stoke, 30 Downs Way, Tadworth, Surrey (☎ 073 781 3261); Balfour Beatty Construction, 7 Mayday Rd, Thornton Heath, Surrey CR4 7XA (☎ 01 684 6922)

BEDELL-PEARCE, Keith Leonard; s of Leonard Bedell-Pearce, of Purley, Surrey, and Irene, *née* Debell; *b* 11 Mar 1946; *Educ* Trinity Sch of John Whitgift, Univ of Exeter(LLB), Univ of Warwick, Graduate Business Sch (MSc); *m* 2 October 1971, Gaynor Mary, da of Frederick Charles Pemberthy, of Exeter, Devon; 1 s (Jack b 1980), 2 da (Olivia b 1976, Harriet b 1988); *Career* systems analyst: Plessey 1969-70, Wiggins Teape 1970-72; joined Prudential Assurance 1972 (computer projects mangr 1972-75, legal dept 1975, solr 1978); dir: Prudential Portfolio Mangr Ltd 1985, Prudential Unit Trust Mangrs Ltd 1986; gen mangr Field Operations Prudential Assurance 1986 (additional responsability for mktg 1987); dir Prudential Assurance 1988-; memb: Law Soc, Mktg Soc; *Books* Checklists for Data Processing Contracts (1978), Computers & Information Technology (1979, 2nd ed 1982); *Recreations* shooting, squash, tennis; *Style*— Keith Bedell-Pearce Esq; 142 Holborn Bars, London EC1N 2NH (☎ 01 405 9222, fax 01 831 1625, car tel 0860 368 751, 0836 286 830, telex 266431)

BEDFORD, Alfred William (Bill); OBE, AFC; s of Lewis Alfred Bedford (d 1926), of Delamore House, Boyer St, Loughborough, Leics, and Edith, *née* Lawrence; *b* 18 Nov 1920; *Educ* Loughborough Coll; *m* 30 Nov 1941, Mary, da of Frederick Bryer Averill (d 1975); 1 s (Peter b 28 May 1946), 1 da (Janet b 1 Nov 1948, d 1976); *Career* joined RAF 1940, fighter pilot 1941-45 (flying Hurricanes, Thunderbolts and Mustangs in the Far East and Europe), graduate Air Fighting Trg Unit 1944, qualified flying instr 1945, graduate Empire Flying Sch 1947, graduate Empire Test Pilots' Sch 1949 (later tutor), research test pilot experimental flying dept Royal Aircraft Estab Farnborough (also detached to Nat Gas Turbine Estab on Jet Engine Res, resigned RAF 1951; experimental test pilot Hawker Aircraft Ltd 1951-67 on fighter aircraft (chief test pilot 1956), made first flights and involved with the devpt of the Harrier VSTOL aircraft; Hawker Siddeley Aviation/British Aerospace appts: int mktg mangr, regnl exec SE Asia (latterly dedicated to Indonesia); aviation conslt 1986-; first chm and fndr memb test pilots' gp Royal Aeronautical Soc; pres: Godalming and Farncombe branch RAF Assoc, Godalming sqdn ATC; held various aircraft and glider altitude records, frequent lectr and writer on aircraft-related topics; FRAeS, memb Soc of Experimental Test Pilots; award First Class Wings of the Indonesian Air Force; varous air awards incl: King's commendations, Britannia and Seagrove trophies; FRAeS; *Recreations* walking, swimming, squash, tennis, nature; *Clubs* RAF, Esher and British Aerospace Squash; *Style*— A W (Bill) Bedford, Esq, OBE, AFC; The Chequers, West End Lane, Esher, Surrey KT10 8LF (☎ 0372 62285)

BEDFORD, Anthony Peter; s of Philip Derek Bedford, MP, MRCP (d 1962), and Jean Rachel, *née* Whyman; *b* 30 Sept 1951; *Educ* Kings Sch Canterbury, St Catherine's Coll Oxford (MA), Univ of London (MPhil); *m* 14 March 1974, Anita Susan, da of Charles Hamilton-Matthews, of Cornwall; 1 s (Tobias b 1974), 1 da (Anouska b 1977); *Career* conslt clinical psychologist; head of psychology dept St Andrews Hosp Northampton 1974-84; dir: Psychiatric and Psychological Conslt Servs Ltd 1981-, Centre for Occupational Res 1984-; *Recreations* riding; *Style*— Anthony P Bedford, Esq; The Old Rectory, East Martin, Nr Fordingbridge, Hants; 14 Devonshire Place, London W1 (☎ 01 935 0640)

BEDFORD, Bishop of 1981-; Rt Rev David John Farmbrough; 2 s of late Charles Septimus and Ida Mabel Farmbrough; *b* 4 May 1929; *Educ* Bedford, Lincoln Coll Oxford; *m* 1955, Angela Priscilla, da of Walter Adam Hill; 1 s, 3 da; *Career* ordained: deacon 1953, priest 1954; priest-in-charge St John's Hatfield 1957-63, vicar of Bishop's Stortford 1963-74, archdeacon of St Albans 1974-81; *Recreations* sailing, gardening; *Style*— The Rt Rev The Bishop of Bedford; 168 Kimbolton Rd, Bedford MK41 8DN (☎ 0234 57551)

BEDFORD, David Vickerman; s of Leslie Herbert Bedford, CBE, and Lesley Florence Keitley (d 1987); *b* 4 August 1937; *Educ* Lancing, RAM; *m* 1, 4 Sept 1958, (m dis 1968), Maureen, *née* Parsonage; 2 da (Tamara b 1960, Chloe b 1962); m 2, 27 Sept 1970 (m dis 1986), Susan, da of Gorgon Pilgrim; 2 da (Sarah b 1969, Emily b 1971); *Career* composer of over eighty published musical pieces to date, assoc visiting composer Gordonstown Sch 1984, youth music dir eng Sinfonia 1986; pres Br Music Info Centre 1988; *Recreations* cricket, squash, film; *Style*— David Bedford, Esq; 39 Shakespeare Rd, London NW7 4BA (☎ 01 959 3165)

BEDFORD, (Charlotte) Gaby; *née* Martin-Langley; da of Charles Harold Martin-Langley (d 1977), and Ruby, *née* Middleton Rowe; *b* 14 June 1943; *Educ* St Monicas Sch for Girls, Falmouth County HS for Girls; *m* 1, 1965 (m dis 1966), Raymond Argent; m 2, 18 May 1974, Piers Errol James Bedford, s of Errol Bedford, of 23 Farmer St, London W8; 2 s (James Simon b 12 May 1966, Timothy Piers James b 15 Sept 1975); *Career* film prodr Eyeline Films Ltd 1970-74, dir and prodr Piers Bedford Prodns Ltd 1974-; fndr and dir: Component Editing Ltd 1984-, Component TV Prodns Ltd 1987-(client work incl: IBA, Memorex Computers, Telstar Records, Royco Varia Investmt among others); area collection oraniser Greenpeace, memb Cons Pty; *Recreations* skiing, gardening; *Style*— Mrs Piers Bedford; 77 Barrowgate Rd, Chiswick, London W4 4QS (☎ 01 747 0069); Saltings, Park Rd, Aldeburgh, Suffolk; The Component Gp, 1 Newman Passage, London W1P 3PF (☎ 01 631 4400, fax 01 995 0137)

BEDFORD, 13 Duke of (E 1694); John Robert Russell; also Baron Russell (E 1539), Earl of Bedford (E 1550), Baron Russell of Thornhaugh (E 1603), Marquess of Tavistock (E 1694), Baron Howland (E 1695); s of 12 Duke (d 1953); *b* 24 May 1917; *m* 1, 1939, Mrs Clare Gwendolen Hollway, da of late John Bridgman; 2 s; m 2, 1947 (m dis 1960), Hon Lydia Yarde-Buller, da of 3 Baron Churston and late Duchess of Leinster, and wid of Capt Ian Archibald de Hoghton Lyle, Black Watch; 1 s; m 3, 1960, Mme Nicole Milinaire, da of Paul Schneider, of Paris; *Heir* s, Marquess of Tavistock; *Career* Coldstream Gds WWII (invalided out); *Style*— His Grace The Duke of Bedford; Les Ligures, 2 Rue Honoré Labande, MC98000 Monaco

BEDFORD, Lydia, Duchess of - Hon Lydia; *née* Yarde-Buller; 3 da of 3 Baron Churston, MVO, OBE (d 1930); *b* 17 Oct 1917; *m* 1, 1938, Capt Ian Archibald de Hoghton Lyle, Black Watch (d 1942); 1 s (Sir Gavin Lyle, 3 Bt, *qv*), 1 da; m 2 (m dis 1960) 13 Duke of Bedford, *qv*; *Style*— Lydia, Duchess of Bedford

BEDFORD, Peter Wyatt; s of David Edwin Wyatt Bedford (d 1979), of Hampshire, and Ruth Lakin, *née* Jackson; *b* 9 Mar 1935; *Educ* Spyway Sch Langton Matravers Dorset, Marlborough, Wilts; *m* 1959, Valerie Clare, da of John Walton Collins, of IOW; 4 s (Rupert b 1960, Julian b 1962, Mark b 1963, Hugo b 1970); *Career* dir Fenchurch Insur Hldgs Ltd, chm Fenchurch Insur Brokers Ltd; *Recreations* golf, shooting, horseracing; *Clubs* MCC, Sunningdale, Swinley Forest; *Style—* Peter Bedford, Esq; Elderfield House, Herriard, Basingstoke, Hampshire (☎ Herriard 339); 89 High Road, South Woodford, London E18 2RH (☎ 01 505 3333)

BEDFORD, Hon Mrs (Sarah); *née* Lyttelton; twin da of 10 Visc Cobham, KG, GCMG, GCVO, TD, PC (d 1977); *b* 10 June 1954; *Educ* The Abbey Sch Malvern Wells; *m* 1976, C Nicholas Bedford; 1 da; *Style—* The Hon Mrs Bedford; Armsworth Hill Cottage, Old Alresford, Hants

BEDFORD RUSSELL, Anthony; s of Harold George Bedford Russell (d 1958), of London, and Lilian May, *née* Longmore-Mavius; *b* 20 April 1930; *Educ* Eton, RMA Sandhurst; *m* 26 April 1955, Jane March, da of Lt John Hughes, RNVR (ka 1943), of London; 3 s (Mark b 1957, James b 1959, Christopher b 1962); *Career* Regular Army 1948-83, Coldstream Gds UK, Cyprus, Egypt, Br Guiana, BAOR, Malay Regt 1958-61;, Asst Mil Attache Saigon 1966-68, Intelligence Corps 1968: SHAPE, Australia; Maj; apptd entomologist (butterflies) to Indonesian phase of Op DRAKE 1980, lectr, entomologist, furniture restorer; FRES, FRGS; *Recreations* philately, bridge, tennis, lapidary, natural history, photography, fly-fishing, languags, travelling, ; *Style—* Anthony Bedford Russell; The Post House, Porton, Salisbury, Wilts SP4 0LF (☎ 0980 610796)

BEDINGFELD, Sir Edmund George Felix Paston-; 9 Bt (E 1660); co-heir to Barony of Grandison (abeyant since *temp* Edward III); s of Sir Henry Edward (Paston-)Bedingfeld, 8 Bt (d 1941), and Sybil, *née* Lyne-Stephens (d 1985 aged 101); *b* 2 June 1915; *Educ* The Oratory, New Coll Oxford; *m* 1, 1942 (m dis 1953), Joan Lynette (d 1965), da of Edgar G Rees, of Llwyneithin, Llanelly; 1 s, 1 da; m 2, 1957, Agnes Danos (d 1974), da of late Miklos Gluck, of Budapest, Hungary; m 3, 1975, Peggy Hannaford-Hill, of Fort Victoria, Rhodesia (now Zimbabwe); *Heir* s, Henry Edgar (Paston-)Bedingfeld, *qv*; Freeman City of London 1988, Liveryman Worshipful Co of Bowyers; *Career* Maj Welsh Gds; md Handley Walker (Europe) Ltd 1969-80; *Recreations* ornithology, heraldry, fly fishing; *Clubs* Naval and Military; *Style—* Sir Edmund Bedingfeld, Bt; 153 Southgate St Bury St Edmunds Suffolk (☎ 0284 754764) Oxburgh Hall, Kings Lynn, Norfolk

BEDINGFELD, Henry Edgar Paston-; s and h of Maj Sir Edmund George Felix (Paston) Bedingfeld, 9 Bt, *qv*, and his 1 w, Joan Lynette, *née* Rees (d 1965); *b* 7 Dec 1943; *Educ* Ampleforth; *m* 7 Sept 1968, Mary Kathleen, da of Brig Robert Denis Ambrose, CIE, OBE, MC (d 1974); 2 s (Richard Edmund Ambrose b 8 Feb 1975, Thomas Henry b 6 Sept 1976), 2 da (Katherine Mary b 4 Oct 1969, Charlotte Alexandra b 6 May 1971); *Career* chartered surveyor 1968; fndr chm Norfolk Heraldry Soc 1975-80, vice-pres 1980-; Rouge Croix Pursuivant of Arms 1983-; sec Standing Cncl of the Baronetage 1984-88; memb cncl: Norfolk & Norwich Genealogical Soc, Norfolk Record Soc; vice-pres Camb Univ Heraldic and Genealogical Soc; Freeman City of London 1985, Liveryman Worshipful Co of Scriveners; Kt of Sov Mil Order of Malta 1975; *Books* Oxburgh Hall - The first 500 years (1982); *Recreations* redecorating; *Clubs* Norfolk (Norwich); *Style—* Henry Bedingfeld, Esq; Oxburgh Hall, King's Lynn, Norfolk PE33 9PS (☎ 036 621 269); The College of Arms, Queen Victoria St, London EC4V 4BT (☎ 01 236 6420)

BEDSER, Alec Victor; CBE (1982, OBE 1964); s of Arthur Bedser (d 1979), and Florence Beatrice, *née* Badcock; *b* 4 July 1918; *Career* WWII RAF 1939-, served in France with BEF 1939-40, evacuated S of Dunkirk 1940, Flt Sgt; serv N Africa, Sicily, Greece, Italy, Austria 1942-46; cricket player: Surrey professional staff 1946-60 (pt of Surrey winning team when championship won 7 consecutive years 1952-59), played for England in First Test after war at Lords v India 1946, record Test debut taking 22 wickets in first two Test matches, played 51 Test Matches for England, 21 times for England against Aust; memb: England cricket team to Aust and NZ 1946-47, SA 1948-49, Aust and NZ 1950-51, Aust and NZ 1954-55; asst mangr Aust and NZ 1962-63; mangr England team: to Aust and NZ 1974-75, to Aust and India 1979-80; journalist and tv commentator England Tour of Aust 1958-59; memb: England Test Team Selection Panel 1962-85 (chm 1969-82), Surrey CCC Ctee 1961-, vice-pres Surrey CCC (pres Surrey CCC 1987-88), MCC Cricket Ctee; *Recreations* golf, gardening, cricket, charities; *Clubs* MCC, Surrey CCC, E India and Sports, W Hill Golf; *Style—* Alec Bedser, Esq, CBE; c/o Initial Contract Services Ltd, 1/5 Bermondsey St, London SE1 2ER (☎ 01 403 3566)

BEEBEE, Meyrick Frederick Legge; JP (Radnorshire 1966), DL (1962); s of Meyrick John Legge Beebee (d 1956), of Womastron, Radnorshire; *b* 16 July 1910; *Educ* RNC Dartmouth; *m* 1, 1935 (m dis 1960), Jean Mary Joy, da of Cdr K Walker, RNVR; 1 s; 2 da 1962, Angela Inez Green, da of Santos Diego (d 1924); 2 s, 3 da; *Career* served RN 1924-49; memb FO 1949-58; md Woodcemair Ltd 1959-72; vice-chm Welsh Cons 1975-80; memb: Powys Magistrates' Ctee and Probation After-Care Ctee 1974-80, Dyfed-Powys Police Authority; *Clubs* Army and Navy; *Style—* Meyrick Beebee, Esq, JP, DL; 26 Lower Sloane St, London SW3

BEECH, (Thomas) Hugh; s of Capt John Beech, RE (ka 1918), of Kuala Lumpur, and Anna Nellie, *née* Scott; *b* 21 June 1917; *Educ* Sir Roger Manwood's Sch, Gonvill and Caius Coll Cambridge (BA, MA); *m* 7 Sept 1949 (Ethel) Nancy Beech, da of Arthur Horace Papworth (d 1955), of 77 The Avenue, Muswell Hill; 1 s (John Greatrex b 24 Oct 1947); *Career* actuarial conslt 1956, asst actuary Leslie & Godwin 1961, co actuary and statistician Int Computers and Tabulators (dir of pension tst fund) 1962, co dir (later dir) Antony Gibbs Pensions 1964, dir Martin Paterson Assocs 1972, sole proprietor Micro Consul (software consulting agency) 1982; vice-pres Bedhampton Cricket Club; Freeman City of London 1979, memb Worshipful Co of Actuaries 1979; AIA 1956, FIA 1958, FSS 1961, FPMI 1976; *Recreations* pianist, dance band leader, steam train enthusiast; *Clubs* Chelsea Arts, Argonauts, Coda; *Style—* Hugh Beech, Esq; Downing Cottage, 11 Havant Rd, Bedhampton, Hants (☎ 0705 475149)

BEECH, Sydney John; s of Sydney Beech, of Stoke-on-Trent, Staffs, and Ruth, *née* Baskeyfield; *b* 6 Feb 1945; *Educ* Hanley HS, Sheffield Univ (BA); *m* 6 Sept 1969, Jean Ann, da of Bertram Gibson, of Gillow Heath, Biddulph, Staffs; *Career* graduate trainee Peat Marwick Mitchell & Co 1966-69, lectr in accounting taxation and quantitative techniques 1969-72, ptnr's pa Lyon Griffiths and Co 1972-74 (ptnr 1974-86, sr ptnr 1986-); memb of Clark Whitehill Assocs 1986-88 (memb exec ctee); FCA, ATII; *Recreations* golf, weightlifting, music; *Clubs* Hill Valley Golf and Country, Dabbers Golf Soc; *Style—* S J Beech, Esq; 8 Woodland Ave, Nantwich, Cheshire (☎ 0270 629 586); Lyon Griffiths & Co, 63/67 Welsh Row, Nantwich, Cheshire (☎ 0270 624 445, fax 0270 623 916)

BEECHAM, Alan; *b* 12 June 1935; *Educ* Boston GS, Open Univ (BA); *m* (m dis); 2 s (Jonathan b 1967, Christopher b 1969); *Career* journalist 1951-62, newspapers: Lincs Standard Series, Southern Times, Southern Jl, Surrey Comet, News Chronicle, Daily Express; external news services BBC 1961-62; radio news and current affrs BBC 1962-: chief sub-ed 1967-69, duty ed 1969-70, sr duty ed 1970-78, asst ed radio news 1978-87, news output ed 1987-; responsible for radio: general election, european election, referenda, budget, local and by election news programmes, Falklands War coverage, Royal Weddings 1964-; created modern BBC Internal News Agency and news service (between London and local radio); FRSA (silver medal, advanced English); *Recreations* media, theatre, cinema, writing; *Style—* Alan Beecham, Esq; 7 Thalia Close, Greenwich, London SE10 (☎ 858 7887); BBC, Broadcasting House, London W1

BEECHAM, Jeremy Hugh; s of Laurence Beecham (d 1975), of Newcastle upon Tyne, and Florence, *née* Fishkin (d 1986); *b* 17 Nov 1944; *Educ* Royal GS Newcastle upon Tyne, Univ Coll Oxford (MA); *m* 7 Jul 1968, Brenda Elizabeth, da of Dr Sidney Woolf; 1 s (Richard b 1973), 1 da (Sara b 1972); *Career* admitted slr 1968; ptnr Allan Henderson Beecham & Peacock 1968-; memb: Local & Regnl Govt sub Ctee Lab Pty NEC 1971-83, pres ctee Business in the Community 1988-, cncl Neighbourhood Energy Assoc 1987, Theatre Royal Tst 1985-; dir N Devpt Co Ltd 1986; cncllr Newcastle upon Tyne 1967- (chm: Social Serv Ctee 1973-77, Policy Resources Ctee 1977-, Fin Ctee 1979-85, ldr 1977-); vice chm AMA 1986- (dep chm 1984-86), cmmr English Heritage 1983-87; party candidate (Lab) Tynemouth 1970; *Recreations* reading (esp Novels and History), music; *Clubs* Mans Social Newcastle upon Tyne; 39 The Drive, Gosforth, Newcastle upon Tyne (☎ 0912 851 888); 7 Collingwood Street, Newcastle upon Tyne (☎ 0912 325 048); Civic Centre, Newcastle upon Tyne (☎ 0912 610 352)

BEECHAM, (Sir) John Stratford Roland; 4 Bt (UK 1914), of Ewanville, Huyton, Co Palatine of Lancaster; s of Sir Adrian Beecham, 3 Bt (d 1982), and gs of Sir Thomas Beecham, 2 Bt, the conductor; does not use title; *b* 21 April 1940; *Educ* Winchester, Queen's Coll Oxford; *Heir* bro, Robert Beecham; *Recreations* walking, gardening; *Style—* John Beecham, Esq; Shalom, Station Rd, Shipston-on-Stour, Warwicks CV36 4BT (☎ 0608 61608)

BEECHAM, Joyce, Lady; (Barbara) Joyce; da of late Edward Cairn; *m* 1939, Sir Adrian Beecham, 3 Bt (d 1982); 2 s, 1 da; *Style—* Joyce, Lady Beecham; Compton Scorpion Manor, Shipston-on-Stour, Warwicks (☎ 0608 61482)

BEECHAM, Robert Adrian; 2 s of Sir Adrian Welles Beecham, 3 Bt (d 1982), and hp to er bro, Sir John Beecham, 4 Bt; *b* 6 Jan 1942; *Educ* Winchester, Clare Coll Cambridge (MA); *m* 1969, Daphne, da of Edmund Mattinson (d 1968); 1 s (Michael John b 1972), 1 da (Judith Mary b 1970); *Career* computers; *Style—* Robert Beecham, Esq; 30 Church Rd, Barnes, London SW13 9HN (☎ 01 748 5813)

BEECHAM, Shirley, Lady; Shirley Jean; da of Albert George Hudson; *m* 1959, as his 3 w, Sir Thomas Beecham, 2 Bt, CH (d 1961); internationally renowned conductor, composer, author and wit; *Career* dir and tstee Sir Thomas Beecham Tst Ltd, formerly administrator Royal Philharmonic Orchestra; *Style—* Shirley, Lady Beecham; The West Wing, Denton House, Denton, Harleston, Norfolk IP20 OAA (☎ 098 686780)

BEECHING, Baroness; Ella Margaret Beeching; da of William John Tiley, of Maidstone, Kent; *m* 1938, Baron Beeching (d 1985, Life Peer UK 1965); *Style—* The Rt Hon the Lady Beeching; Little Manor, East Grinstead, West Sussex

BEEDHAM, Brian James; CBE (1989); s of James Victor Beedham (d 1973), of Nottingham, and Nina Florence Grace, *née* Zambra (d 1964); *b* 12 Jan 1928; *Educ* Leeds GS, Queen's Coll Oxford (MA); *m* 1960, (Ruth) Barbara, da of Werner Zollikofer (d 1975), of Zurich; *Career* Capt RA 1950-52; journalist: foreign ed The Economist 1964-89 (assoc dir 1989-); *Recreations* music, walking; *Clubs* Traveller's; *Style—* Brian Beedham, Esq, CBE; 9 Hillside, London SW19 (☎ 01 946 4454); The Economist, 25 St James's St, London SW1 (☎ 01 839 7000)

BEEKE, Peter James; s of Leonard James Beeke (d 1966), of London, and Violet Ruth Beeke (d 1985); *b* 2 May 1942; *Educ* Erith GS, UCL; *m* 14 Aug 1970 (m dis 1987), Gillian Mary, da of John Patterson Irvine, of London; 1 s (James b 1977), 1 da (Eleanor b 1975); *Career* programmer W H Smith & Son 1962, chief programmer Br Euro Airways 1964, mgmnt conslt Peat Marwick Mitchell 1967, gen mangr Woolwich Bldg Soc 1984 (formerly data processing mangr and asst gen mangr), gen mangr Pearl Assur plc 1989; govr Bexley Tech Sch; memb ctee: London Soc Rugby Football Referees, Kent Co Rugby Football; cnsllr Relate-MG; memb Br Computer Soc 1970; MBCS 1970, FCBSI 1987; *Recreations* rugby football, golf, music, personal counselling; *Style—* Peter Beeke, Esq; Pearl Assur plc, Thorpewood, Peterborough PE3 6SA (☎ 0733 632 12, fax 0733 312 743)

BEELEY, Sir Harold; KCMG (1961, CMG 1953), CBE (1946); s of Frank Arthur Beeley (d 1966), of Southport, Lancs, and Ada, *née* Marsh; *b* 15 Feb 1909; *Educ* Highgate Sch, Queen's Coll Oxford; *m* 1, 1933 (m dis 1953), Millicent Marv, da of late W G Chinn, of Newton Abbot, Devon; 2 da; m 2, 1958, Mrs Patricia Karen Brett-Smith, da of William Cecil Shields, OBE; 1 da, 1 step s, 2 step da; *Career* lectr: Queen's Coll Oxford 1935-38, UC Leicester 1938-39, QMC 1969-75; memb RIIA 1939-45; entered Foreign Serv 1946, ambass Saudi Arabia 1955, asst under sec FO 1956-58, dep UK rep to UN 1958-61, ambass UAR 1961-64 and 1967-69, UK rep Disarmament Conf Geneva 1964-67; pres Egypt Exploration Soc 1969-88; chm: World of Islam Festival Tst 1973-, Egyptian-Br C of C 1981-; *Style—* Sir Harold Beeley, KCMG, CBE; 38 Slaidburn St, London SW10 (☎ 01 351 0997)

BEER, Fritz Bedrich Frederick; OBE (1979); s of Capt Berthold Beer (d 1942), and Jeanette, *née* Glasner (d 1941); *b* 25 August 1911; *Educ* Realgymnasium Brno, Charles Univ Prague, Univ of Dijon, LSE; *m* 30 June 1940, Ursula Rosemary, da of Dr Franz Davidson (d 1942); 1 da (Maria Pauline (Mrs Lacheze) b 11 April 1943); *Career* 5 Cavalry Regt Czechoslavak Army 1936-38, Czechoslavak Armoured Bde with Br Forces 1940-45; journalist and writer: dep ed Peoples Illustrated Weekly Prague 1934-36, script writer and political commentator BBC German Serv 1945-72, London correspondent German Newspapers 1956-79, radio and tv feature writer for West German Stations 1948-79; Literary Peace Prize Moscow 1934, Franz Brunner Journalism Prize Essen 1968; pres Foreign Press Assoc 1978-80, pres PEN Centre of German Speaking Authors Abroad 1988-; Czechoslavac Military Medal 1944; *Books* Shots at Dawn (1931), Black Coffres (1934), The House on the Bridge (1949), Intervention in CSSR (1968), The Future Does Not Yet Work (1969); *Recreations* reading, music, gardening, DIY; *Style—* Fritz Beer, Esq, OBE; Hill Ho, 31B

Arterberry Rd, London SW20 8AG (☎ 01 946 0178)

BEER, Ian David Stafford; JP (Middlesex 1981-); s of William John Beer (d 1976), of Surrey, and Doris Ethel, *née* Rose; *b* 28 April 1931; *Educ* St Catharine's Coll Cambridge (MA, PGCE); *m* 1960, Angela Felce, da of Eric Spencer Gravely Howard, MC, RA (d 1977); 2 s (Martin b 1962, Philip b 1965), 1 da (Caroline b 1967); *Career* 1 Bn Royal Fusiliers Berlin 1949-51; asst master Marlborough Coll 1955-57; house master Marlborough Coll 1957-61; head master: Ellesmere Coll Shropshire 1961-69, Lancing Coll Sussex 1969-81, Harrow Sch 1981-; chm HMC 1980, advsy ctee ISJC 1988-; govr Whitgift Fndn, exec ctee RFU 1985-; JP: Shropshire 1962-69, West Sussex 1969-81; tstee Welfare Tst, RMC; *Recreations* rugby football, gardening, natural history; *Clubs* Hawks (Cambridge), East India and Sport; *Style*— Ian D S Beer, Esq; Peel House, Football Lane, Harrow on the Hill, Middlesex HA1 3EA (☎ 01 423 2366); Harrow School, Harrow on the Hill, Middlesex HA1 3HW (☎ 01 423 2366)

BEER, James Edmund; s of Edmund Huxtable Beer (d 1965), and Gwendoline Kate Beer; *b* 17 Mar 1931; *Educ* Torquay Boys GS; *m* 1953, Barbara Mollie, da of Francis Tunley (d 1960); 2 s, 1 da; *Career* dir of fin Leeds CC until 1978; fin advsr AMA until 1978; rate support grant negotiator until 1978; dir: Short Loan and Mortgage Co 1978-87, Shortloan (Leasing) Co 1978-87, London and Univ Fin Futures Ltd 1983-87; fin advsr London and Cambridge Investmts Ltd 1987-88; public sector conslt: Citicorps Insur Brokers Ltd, Scrimgeous Citicorp (Investmt Mgmnt) Ltd; memb: Leeds exec ctee, Leeds Music Festival 1987, London Ctee YHDA; Liveryman, Worshipful Co of Basketmakers 1981-; *Recreations* walking, theatre, swimming; *Clubs* City Livery, Gresham; *Style*— James Beer, Esq; 48 High Ash Ave, Alwoodley, Leeds LS17 8RG (☎ 0532 683907)

BEER, (Ernest) Trevor; CBE (1946, OBE 1945); s of (Alfred) Ernest Beer (d 1952), of Cockfosters; *b* 12 Jan 1906; *Educ* Highgate Sch, Neuchatel Univ Switzerland; *m* 1939, Countess Eleonore Klara Sophia, da of Count Paul Szubinski, of Poland; 2 s, 2 da; *Career* chm I Beer and Sons to 1965; dep chm Fitch Lovell to 1971; ret; *Clubs* RAF; *Style*— Trevor Beer, Esq, CBE; Langbrae, Moorlands Rd, Budleigh Salterton, Devon EX9 6AG (☎ 03954 2604)

BEERLING, John (Johnny) William; s of Raymond Starr Beerling, and May Elizabeth Julia, *née* Holden; *b* 12 April 1937; *Educ* Sir Roger Manwood's GS Sandwich Kent; *m* 1959, Carol Ann, *née* Reynolds; 1 s (David John b 1965), 1 da (Julie Margaret b 1963); *Career* Nat Serv wireless fitter RAF 1955-57; joined BBC 1957, studio mangr 1958, prodr 1962, head Radio 1 Programmes 1983, controller Radio 1 1985-; *Publications* Emperor Rosko's DJ Handbook (1976); *Recreations* photography, angling; *Style*— Johnny Beerling, Esq; Egton House, Langham Street, London W1A 1AA (☎ 01 927 4561, fax 01 323 4726)

BEESLEY, Mark Christopher; s of George Carter Beesley, and Agnes Winifred Ross; *b* 22 Sept 1945; *Educ* St Joseph's Acad London; *m* 1968, Margaret Clare, da of Sean Byrne, of Ireland; 3 s (Stephen b 1972, Christopher b 1974, David b 1978), 1 da (Clare b 1982); *Career* chartered accountant, accountant at Royal London Mutual Insur Soc Ltd 1974-; dir: Royal London Unit Tst Managers Ltd 1980-, Triton Fund Managers Ltd 1986-, Atrium Mgmnt Ltd 1982-; FCA; *Style*— Mark Beesley, Esq; Rodings, 65 Mill Road, Great Totham, Maldon, Essex CM9 8DH (☎ 0621 891946); Royal London House, Middleborough, Colchester, Essex CO1 1RA (☎ 0206 761761)

BEESON, Andrew Nigel Wendover; s of Capt Nigel Wendover Beeson (d 1944), and Ann Margaret, *née* Sutherland; *b* 30 Mar 1944; *Educ* Eton; *m* 1, 1971, Susan Roberta Caroline, da of Guy Standish Gerard (d 1981); 1 s (James b 1976), 1 da (Susanna b 1973); m 2, Carrie Joy, da of Norman Joseph Martin; *Career* stockbroker; dir: Capel Cure Myers Ltd 1984, ANZ Merchant Bank Ltd 1984, ANZ Securities Asia 1984, ANZ Securites Inc 1985; *Recreations* tennis, rackets; *Clubs* Whites, Pratts, MCC; *Style*— Andrew N W Beeson, Esq; 21 Warwick Square, London SW1V 2AB; 65 Horburn Viaduct, London EC1A 2EV

BEESON, Headley Thomas; s of Thomas Benjamin Beeson (d 1942), of Headley Park, Headley, nr Epsom, Surrey, and Elizabeth, *née* Brezovits; *b* 20 August 1942; *Educ* Clark's GS Surbiton; *m* 7 Sept 1968, Lesley Ann, da of Roland Conrad Wontner, of Heathlands, Woodside Rd, Cobham, Surrey; 1 s (Miles b 1973), 1 da (Caroline b 1975); *Career* Fenn & Crosthwaite (stockbrokers) 1962-67, investmt mgmnt and mktg Barclays Bank Gp 1967-81, dir N M Schroder Unit Tst Mangrs Ltd 1981-88, Schroder Investmt Mgmnt Ltd 1988-; AMSIA 1972; *Recreations* rowing, motor sports; *Style*— Headley Beeson, Esq; Courtlands, 14 The Ridings, Cobham, Surrey KT11 2PU (☎ 0372 843230); Schroder Investmt Mgmnt Ltd, 36 Old Jewry, London EC2R 8BS (☎ 01 382 6000, 01 382 6498, fax 01 382 6965, telex 885029)

BEESON, Prof Paul Bruce; Hon KBE (1973); s of John Bradley Beeson, of Livingston, Montana; *b* 18 Oct 1908; *Educ* Washington Univ, McGill Univ Med Sch; *m* 1942, Barbara, da of Ray C Neal, of Buffalo, NY; 2 s, 1 da; *Career* prof Medicine Washington Univ 1974-; FRCP; *Style*— Prof Paul Beeson, Hon KBE; US Veterans' Admin Hospital, Seattle, Washington, USA

BEESON, Very Rev Trevor Randall; s of Arthur William Beeson (d 1979), and Matilda Beeson (d 1980); *b* 2 Mar 1926; *Educ* King's Coll London, St Boniface Coll Warminster (MA); *m* 1950, Josephine Grace, da of Ernest Joseph Cope (d 1974); 2 da (Jean, Catherine); *Career* dean of Winchester 1987-; FKC; *Books* The Church of England in Crisis (1973); Discretion and Valour (1974), A Vision of Hope (1984); *Recreations* gardening, cricket; *Style*— The Very Rev the Dean of Winchester; The Deanery, Winchester SO23 9LS; Grove House, Church St, St Clements, Sandwich, Kent

BEETHAM, Lady; (Eileen Joy); da of Arthur Leslie Parkinson (d 1968), of Polegate, and Adeline, *née* Wood; *b* 1910,March; *Educ* Godolphin Salisbury; *m* 1933, Sir Edward Beetham, KCMG, CVO, OBE (d 1979), s of Dr Fredrick Beetham (d 1943); 1 da; *Career* worked for the Navy in Freetown, W Africa 1941-45; *Clubs* Phyllis Court, Anglo-Belgian; *Style*— Lady Beetham; 26 Adam Court, Henley-on-Thames, Oxon RG9 2BJ (☎ 0491 574865)

BEETHAM, Marshal of the RAF Sir Michael James; GCB (1978, KCB 1976), CBE (1967), DFC (1944), AFC (1960); s of Maj George C Beetham, MC (d 1953), of Broadstairs, Kent; *b* 17 May 1923; *Educ* St Marylebone GS; *m* 1956, Patricia Elizabeth, da of Henry Lane, of Christchurch, NZ; 1 s, 1 da; *Career* joined RAF 1941, Bomber Cmd 1943-46 (flying 30 combat missions in Lancaster bombers of 50 Sqdn), psa 1952, idc 1967, Dir Ops (RAF) MOD 1968-70, Cmdt RAF Staff Coll 1970-72, ACOS (plans and policy) SHAPE 1972-75, Dep C-in-C Strike Cmd 1975-76, C-in-C RAF Germany & Cdr 2 Allied Tactical Air Force 1976-77, Chief of the Air Staff 1977-82, Air ADC to HM the Queen 1977-82, Marshal of the RAF 1982; dir Brixton Estate 1983-, Hon Air Cdre RAUX AF. 1983-; dir GEC Avionics Ltd 1984- (chm 1986-); chm Tstees RAF Museum 1983-; govr Cheltenham College 1983-; FRSA, FRAES; *Clubs* RAF; *Style*— Marshal of the RAF Sir Michael Beetham, GCB, CBE, DFC, AFC; c/o Lloyds Bank Ltd, 6 Pall Mall, London SW1

BEETHAM, Roger Campbell; LVO (1976); s of Henry Campbell Beetham (d 1986), of Budleighsalterton, Devon, and Mary Beetham, *née* Baldwin (d 1978); *b* 22 Nov 1937; *Educ* Peter Symonds Sch Winchester, Brasenose Coll Oxford (MA); *m* 1, 1965, (m dis 1986), Judith, *née* Rees; m2, 19 Dec 1986, Christine Marguerite, da of Adrien Malerme, of Callas, S France; *Career* HM Dip serv 1960-: UKDIS Geneva 1962-65, Washington 1965-68, FCO 1969-72, Helsinki 1972-76, EC cmmn 1977-81, cnsllr (econ & commercial) New Delhi 1981-85, head maritime, aviation & environment dept FCO 1985-; order of the White Rose of Finland 1976; *Recreations* travel, cooking, wine; *Clubs* Travellers; *Style*— Roger Beetham, Esq, LVO; FCO, King Charles St, London SW1A 2AH (☎ 01 270 2621)

BEEVOR, Antony Romer; s of Miles Beevor, of Welwyn; *b* 18 May 1940; *Educ* Winchester, New Coll Oxford; *m* 1970, Cecilia, da of John Hopton (d 1969); 1 s, 1 da; *Career* dir Hambros Bank 1974-87 (on secondment dir gen Panel on Takeovers and Mergers); *Style*— Antony Beevor, Esq; 20 Radipole Rd, London SW6 (☎ 01 731 8015)

BEEVOR, Carola, Lady; Carola; da of His Hon Judge Jesse Basil Herbert, MC, QC (d 1971), and Hon Isabella Russell, *née* Rea, *qv*; *b* 17 July 1930; *Educ* St Paul's Girls' Sch, St Hugh's Coll Oxford (MA); *m* 1966 (m dis 1975), as his 2 w, Sir Thomas Agnew Beevor, 7 Bt; *Career* economist US Embassy London 1958-67; *Books* Debrett's Register of Yachts (ed 1983); *Recreations* sailing (owner of 'Isla'), beagling; *Clubs* Pin Mill Sailing; *Style*— Carola, Lady Beevor; Lark Cottage, Pin Mill, Ipswich, Suffolk (☎ 047 384 579)

BEEVOR, Sir Thomas Agnew; 7 Bt (GB 1784); s of Cdr Sir Thomas Beevor, 6 Bt (d 1943), and Edith Margaret, *née* Agnew (d 1985, having m 2, 1944, Rear Adm Robert Alexander Currie, CB, DSC); *b* 6 Jan 1929; *Educ* Eton, Magdalene Coll Cambridge; *m* 1, 1957 (m dis 1965), Barbara Clare, yst da of Capt Robert Lionel Brooke Cunliffe, CBE, RN (ret); 1 s, 2 da; m 2, 1966 (m dis 1975), Carola, da of His Hon Judge Jesse Basil Herbert, MC, QC; m 3, 1976, Mrs Sally Elisabeth Bouwens, da of Edward Madoc, of White Hall, Thetford; *Heir* s, Thomas Beevor; *Style*— Sir Thomas Beevor, Bt; Hargham Hall, Norwich

BEEVOR, Thomas Hugh Cunliffe; s and h of Sir Thomas Beevor, 7 Bt; *b* 1 Oct 1962; *Style*— Thomas Beevor, Esq; Hargham Hall, Norwich

BEGG, Alastair Currie; s of Henry Currie Begg (d 1983), of Edinburgh, and Rosemary Anne, *née* Kemp; *b* 6 Feb 1954; *Educ* King's Sch, Sidney Sussex Coll Cambridge (MA); *m* 12 June 1982, Patricia Barbara Wigham, da of Sir George Wigham Richardson Bt (d 1981), of Benendon, Kent; 1 s (Andrew b 1986), 1 da (Camilla b 1984); *Career* admin trainee Home Civil Ser 1976-78, Bank of America Int Ltd 1978-81, Kleinwort Benson Investment Mgmnt Ltd 1981- (dir 1987); memb Int Stock Exchange; *Style*— A C Begg, Esq; Monks Manor, Fir Toll Lane, Mayfield, E Sussex TN20 6NE (☎ 0435 872429); 10 Fenchurch St, London EC3M 3LB (☎ 01 956 5005, fax 01 623 5519, telex 9415345)

BEGG, Alexander Hugh; s of Norman Fraser Buchanan Begg (d 1952), and Olive Jane, *née* Wood (d 1982); *b* 23 Jan 1931; *Educ* St Paul's, Nautical Coll Pangbourne, RNC Dartmouth; *m* 18 April 1958, Robin, da of Horace Victor Gundry, of Sydney, Australia; 3 da (Nicola b 1959, Alexandra b 1960, Louisa b 1962); *Career* Lt RN (ret 1958); served in HM Submarines in Mediterranean and Far East; md Thomson Television Int Ltd 1961-63; chief exec Overseas Operations Thomson Orgn 1963-65; md Thomson Yellow Pages Ltd 1965-71; chm and md London Editions Ltd 1971-78; md Siemssen Hunter Ltd 1979-84; deputy chm and chief exec Seymour Int Press Distributors Ltd 1984-; dir: Atlas Publishing Ltd, K James and Son Ltd, London Office Facilities Ltd; *Recreations* golf; *Clubs* Carlton, Royal Wimbledon GC, Rye GC; *Style*— A H Begg, Esq; 29 Holmead Rd, London SW6 2JD (☎ 01 731 8346); (☎ 01 679 1899, fax 679 8919, car ☎ 0836 224042)

BEGG, Robert William; CBE (1977); s of David Begg (d 1968), and Elizabeth Young Thomson; *b* 19 Feb 1922; *Educ* Greenock Aca, Glasgow Univ (MA); *m* 1948, Sheena Margaret, da of Archibald Boyd, slr (d 1958), of Largs; 2 s; *Career* CA; chm Nat Galleries of Scotland; pres Royal Glasgow Inst of Fine Arts 1987-, memb Ct Univ of Glasgow 1986, exec memb Nat Tst for Scotland 1986; *Recreations* painting; *Clubs* Glasgow Art, New (Edinburgh); *Style*— Robert Begg Esq, CBE; 3 Colquhoun Dr, Bearsden, Glasgow G61 4NQ (☎ 041 942 2436); Moores and Rowland, Allan House, 25 Bothwell St, Glasgow G2 6NL (☎ 041 221 6991, telex 777036)

BEGG, Adm of the Fleet Sir Varyl (Cargill); GCB (1965, KCB 1962, CB 1959), DSO (1952), DSC (1941); s of Francis Cargill Begg (d 1952), of Henley-on-Thames, and Muriel Clare Robinson; *b* 1 Oct 1908; *Educ* St Andrews Sch Eastbourne, Malvern Coll; *m* 1943, Rosemary, CStJ, da of Francis Edward Cowan (d 1961), of Helens Bay, N Ireland; 2 s (Timothy, Peter); *Career* entered RN 1926, Gunnery Offr 1933, Cmdr 1942, Capt 1947, idc 1954, Rear Adm 1957, Vice Adm 1960, Adm 1963, PMN 1966, Chief of Naval Staff and First Sea Lord 1966-68, ret; Govr and C-in-C Gibralter 1969-73; KStJ 1969; *Style*— Adm of the Fleet Sir Varyl Begg, GCB, DSO, DSC; Copyhold Cottage, Chilbolton, Stockbridge, Hants (☎ (026 474) 320)

BEGGS, Roy; MP (UU) East Antrim 1983-; *b* 20 Feb 1936,Belfast,; *Educ* Ballyclare HS, Stranmillis Training Coll; *m* ; 2 s, 2 da; *Career* teacher Larne HS 1957; memb Larne Borough Cncl 1973-, mayor of Larne 1978-83; elected NI Assembly for Stormont 1982, chm Economic Devpt Ctee 1982-84; vice-chm NE Educn and Library Bd 1981-85, chm 1985-; pres Assoc Educn and Library Bds NI 1984-85; vice-pres Gleno Valley Young Farmers Club; memb: Ulster Farmers Union, Nat Assoc School Masters and Union of Women Teachers; ptnr Central Coachworks Larne; *Style*— Roy Beggs, Esq, MP; House of Commons, London SW1

BEGLEY, (Percival) Percy; s of Percival John Begley (d 1960), of Dublin, and Alicia, *née* Keogh, the Irish Contralto (d 1960); *b* 6 Dec 1908; *Educ* The HS Dublin, Rosse Coll Dublin; *m* 1934, Gertrude Agnes, da of Frederick W Crossley (d 1945), 2 s (Colum Patrick b 1935, Dermot David b 1939), 1 da (Noreen Florence b 1937); *Career* clerk in family firm of Coach Builders; sales rep Spratts and later Brown and Polson; joined A Guinness Son and Co Ltd; eventually promotions and visits mangr Dublin; played Rugby for Munster; *Recreations* rugby, shooting, fishing, golf, tennis; *Clubs* Lansdowne Rugby, Killarney and Carlow Golf, Guinness Athletic, NY Athletic; *Style*—

Percy Begley, Esq; Disgwylfa, New Moat, Clarbeston Road, Dyfed, Wales SA63 4RY (☎ 09913 496)

BEHARRELL, Steven Roderic; s of late Douglas Wells Beharrell, TD, and Pamela, *née* Pearman Smith; *b* 22 Dec 1944; *Educ* Uppingham; *m* 10 June 1967, Julia Elizabeth, da of William Wilson Powell, DL; 2 da (Victoria Jane b 5 Aug 1971, Rebecca Clare b 9 Oct 1973); *Career* slr 1969, ptnr Denton Hail Burgin & Warrens 1973-; Freeman Worshipful Co of Drapers; memb: Law Soc, Int Bar Assoc; *Style*— Steven Beharrell, Esq; Five Chancery Lane, London WC2A 1LF (☎ 01 242 1212. fax 01 404 0087, telex 263 567)

BEHRENS, John Stephen; JP (1970); s of Edgar Charles Behrens, CBE, JP (d 1975), of Norwood House, Ilkley, Yorks, and Winifred Wrigley, *née* Luckhurst (d 1976); *b* 9 July 1927; *Educ* Rugby; *m* 1964, Kathleen Shirley, da of Richard Alfred Leicester Billson, JP (d 1949); 2 s (Charles, James), 1 da (Philippa); *Career* dir: Sir Jacob Behrens and Sons Ltd and subsidiary cos; chm: Francis Willey (British Wools 1935) Ltd and subsidiary cos, John Smith and Sons (Shrewsbury) Ltd, Craig Home for Children, Bradford Tradesmen's Homes; pres Country Wool Merchants Assoc; *Style*— John Behrens, Esq, JP; Park Green, Littlethorpe, Ripon, N Yorks (☎ 0765 87262); Ravenscliffe Mills, Calverley, Pudsey, W Yorks (☎ 0274 612541)

BEILL, Air Vice-Marshal Alfred; CB (1986); s of Gp Capt Robert Beill, CBE, DFC (d 1970), and Sophie, *née* Kulczycka; *b* 14 Feb 1931; *Educ* Rossall Sch, RAF Coll Cranwell; *m* 1953, Vyvian Mary, da of Dr Basil Crowhurst-Archer (d 1981); 4 da (Francesca b 1956, Jacqueline b 1957, Anna-Louise b 1961, Miranda b 1962); *Career* cmmnd RAF 1952; serv UK, Aden, Singapore, Cyprus; student RAF Staff Coll 1964; Jt Servs Staff Coll 1968 and on staff 1970-73; ADC to HM The Queen 1974-75; Air Vice Marshal 1984; dir gen of Supply (RAF) 1984-87, ret 1987; appeals sec King Edward VII's Hospital for Offrs; pres RAF Swimming Assoc 1982-87; life vice-pres 1987-; *Clubs* RAF; *Style*— Air Vice-Marshal Alfred Beill, CB; Old Leigh Court, 25 The Avenue, Datchet, Berks GL3 9DQ; Appeals Office, King Edward VII's Hospital for Officers, 6 Buckingham Place, London SW1E 6HR (☎ 01 828 4454)

BEISHON, Dr (Ronald) John; s of Arthur Robson Beishon, of Brighton, and Irene, *née* Westerman; *b* 10 Nov 1930; *Educ* Battersea Poly, Birkbeck Coll London (BSc), Oxford Univ (D Phil); *m* 25 March 1955, Gwenda Jean; 2 s (Marc, Daniel), 2 da (Jessica, Judith); *Career* Nat Serv marine engr RASC 1951-53; tech offr ICI 1954-58, section ldr BICC 1958-61; sr res offr Oxford Univ 1961-64, lectr Bristol Univ 1964-68, reader Sussex Univ 1968-71, prof Open Univ 1971-80; dir: South Bank Poly 1980-85, North London Poly 1985-87; cheif exec Consumers' Assoc 1987-; govr Brighton Poly; CEng, FRSA, MIM, MWeldI; *Recreations* squash; *Clubs* Wig and Pen; *Style*— Dr John Beishon; 421 Ditchling Rd, Brighton BN1 6XB (☎ 0273 552 100); 2 Marylebone Rd, London NW1 4DX (☎ 01 486 5544)

BEIT, Sir Alfred Lane; 2 Bt (UK 1924); s of Sir Otto (John) Beit, KCMG (d 1930); *b* 19 Jan 1903; *Educ* Eton, Christ Church Oxford (MA); *m* 1939, Clementine Mabell Kitty, da of late Maj Hon Clement Bertram Ogilvy Freeman-Mitford, DSO (k 1915), s of 1 Baron Redesdale; *Heir* none; *Career* Sqdn RAFVR (ret); contested (C) S E Div of St Pancras May 1929, MP Oct 1931 to June 1945; PPS (unpaid) to Fin Sec to WO 1935-38, sec of state for Colonies 1944-45; former memb Advsy Ctee of Tanganyika Concessions Ltd; tstee Beit Tst; Hon LLD Nat Univ of Ireland; *Clubs* Brooks's, Carlton, Kildare St and University (Dublin); *Style*— Sir Alfred Beit, Bt; Russborough, Blessington, Co Wicklow, Eire; Beach Rd, Gordon's Bay, S Africa

BEITH, Alan James; MP (Lib) Berwick-upon-Tweed, by-election 1973-; o s of James Beith (d 1962) of Poynton, Cheshire, and Joan Beith; *b* 20 April 1943,Poynton,; *Educ* King's Sch Macclesfield, Balliol and Nuffield Colls Oxford; *m* 1965, Barbara Jean Ward; *Career* lectr Dept of Politics, Newcastle upon Tyne Univ 1966-73; contested (Lib) Berwick-upon-Tweed 1970, Lib chief whip March 1976-85, Lib dep ldr and For Affrs Spokesman 1985- Treasy Spokesman SLD 1988-, memb House of Commons Cmmn; *Recreations* walking, music; *Clubs* Nat Lib; *Style*— Alan Beith, Esq, MP; West End Cottage, Whittingham, Alnwick, Northumberland

BEITH, Sir John Greville Stanley; KCMG (1969, CMG 1959); s of William Beith (d 1922), of Toowoomba, Qld, and Margaret, *née* Stanley; *b* 4 April 1914; *Educ* Eton, King's Coll Cambridge; *m* 1949, Diana (d 1987), da of Sir John Little Gilmour, 2 Bt, and former w of Maj Alexander Gregory-Hood, MC, Gren Guards; 1 s (Ian Mark b 1950), 1 da (Emma b 1956) (and 1 da decd), 1 step s, 1 step da; *Career* HM Dip Serv; ambass to Belgium 1969-74; *Recreations* music, racing, books; *Clubs* White's; *Style*— Sir John Beith, KCMG; Dean Farm House, Sparsholt, Hants (☎ 096 272 326)

BEKER, Prof Henry Joseph; s of Jozef Beker (d 1960), and Mary, *née* Gewaid; *b* 22 Dec 1951; *Educ* Kilburn GS, Univ of London (BSc), Open Univ (PhD); *m* 30 Oct 1976, Mary Louise, *née* Keilthy; 1 da (Hannah Louise b 1979); *Career* visiting prof of info technol Royal Holloway and Bedford New Coll, London, sr res asst dept of statistics Univ Coll Swansea 1976-77, princ mathematician Racal Comsec Ltd 1977-80 (chief mathematician 1980-83), dir of res, Racal Res Ltd 1983-85, dir of systems Racal-Chubb Security Systems Ltd 1985-86, md Racal-Guardata Ltd 1986-88, md Zergo Ltd 1988-; visiting prof IT Westfield Coll Univ of London 1983-84, visiting prof of info technol Royal Holloway and Bedford New Coll London; MIS, AFIMA, MIEE, CEng; *Books* Cipher Systems (with Prof F C Piper, 1982), Secure Speech Communications (with Prof F C Piper, 1985); *Recreations* music, reading, travel; *Style*— Prof Henry Beker; Richmond Ct, 309 Fleet Rd, Fleet, Hampshire (☎ 0252 622144)

BELCHAMBER, Peter John; s of John Belchamber (d 1983), of Derbyshire, and Sheila, *née* Warwick; *b* 5 Sept 1943; *Educ* Monkton Combe Sch, Nottingham Peoples Coll, Alexander Hamilton Inst (Dip Business Admin); *m* 2 Sept 1972, Margaret Anne Elizabeth, da of George William Bowes (d 1968), of Hutton Mount, Essex; 1 s (James), 2 da (Emma, Fiona); *Career* journalist Nottingham Evening Post 1962-66, ed Nottingham Observer 1965-67, account mangr Ogilvy and Mather 1967-71, account dir J Walter Thompson 1971-74, dir Charles Baker Lyons 1976-86, md Charles Barker Traverse-Healy 1986-; church reader; fndr memb exec ctee Br Assoc of Cancer United Patients 1986-, Hon PR Advsr Nat Assoc for Welfare of Children in Hosp; Wishing Well Appeal Gt Ormond St Hosp for Children; Open College of the Arts; *Books* East Midlands Airport (1965); *Recreations* opera, ballet, reading, music, cricket; *Clubs* Scribes; *Style*— Peter Belchamber, Esq; Oakwood, High St, Whittlesford, Cambridge (☎ 0223 833 729); 20 Lincolns Inn Field, London WC2 (☎ 01 242 4875)

BELCHAMBERS, Anthony Murray; s of Lyonal Eustace Belchambers (d 1981), of Ashamton, Devon, and Dorothy Joan, *née* Wylie; *b* 14 April 1947; *Educ* Christ Coll Brecon, Coll of Law; *m* 14 Jan 1980, Penelope Brabazon, *née* Howard; *Career* barr Inner Temple, W Circuit 1972-75, lawyer: DTI 1975-82, Dir of Public Prosectutions 1982-84, Treasy Slr 1984-86, co sec and gen counsel Assoc of Futures Brokers and Dealers 1986-; *Recreations* tennis, riding, bridge; *Clubs* HAC; *Style*— Anthony Belchambers, Esq; Kensington, London W8; Association of Futures Brokers and Dealers, Plantation House, Mincing Lane (☎ 01 626 9763)

BELCHER, John Leonard; s of Leonard Charles Belcher, and Hannah Joan, *née* Collins; *b* 27 Oct 1949; *Educ* Kesteven Coll, Univ of Nottingham, Univ of London; *Career* educationalist; lectr Open Univ 1974-75, asst prof Sociology American Coll of Switzerland 1975-80, various academic appts in US 1980-83, dir external relations Queen Mary Coll London 1983; chm Assoc of Univ Int Liaison Offrs, exec memb Br Univs Transatlantic Exchange Ctee; memb: Br Cncl ECS Steering Ctee, Cwlth Secretarial Ctee of Legal Educn and Cwlth Students, preparatory ctee Euro Consultation on Advising and Counselling Foreign Students (EEC); govr William Palmer Sixth Form Coll, tstee William Palmer Tst; *Recreations* running, skiing, reading, travel; *Style*— John Belcher, Esq; 10 Green Lane Cottages, Green Lane, Stanmore, Middx H47 3AA; Queen Mary Coll, Univ of London, Mile End Rd, London E1 4NS (☎ 01 975 5071, telex 893750, fax 01 981 5497)

BELDAM, Robert Geoffrey; CBE (1975); s of late Ernest Asplan Beldam; *b* 3 Jan 1914; *Educ* Repton, Corpus Christi Coll Cambridge (MA); *Career* chm and md Beldam Asbestos Co Ltd and Auto-Klean Strainers Ltd; memb CBI Cncl 1965-86, CBI Smaller Firms Cncl 1965-79 (chm until 1974), CBI London Regional Cncl 1952-80, 1981-87; SE Economic Planning Cncl 1966-73 (acting chm 1971), Woking UDC 1947-70 (chm 1954-55); FCA, CEng, FIMarE; *Recreations* travel, gardening, historic buildings; *Clubs* MCC, Carlton; *Style*— Robert Beldam, Esq, CBE; Rocombe, Grange Rd, Horsell, Woking Surrey GU 214DA (☎ 04862 61400)

BELDAM, Hon Mr Justice; Hon Sir (Alexander) Roy Asplin; QC (1969); s of George William Beldam (d 1937), of Brentford and Shiness Lodge, Lairg, and Margaret Frew Shettle, formerly Beldam, *née* Underwood; *b* 29 Mar 1925; *Educ* Oundle, Brasenose Coll Oxford; *m* 1953, Elisabeth Bryant, da of Frank James Farr, MB, CLB, LDS, DMRE (d 1969), of Hong Kong; 2 s (Rufus, Royston), 1 da (Alexandra); *Career* serv WWII Sub Lt RNVR Air Branch 1943-46; barr 1950, bencher 1977; rec Crown Court 1972-81, High Court judge (Queen's Bench) 1981-; presiding judge Wales and Chester Circuit 1985; chm: The Law Cmmn 1985-; kt 1981; *Style*— The Hon Mr Justice Beldam; Royal Courts of Justice, Strand, London WC2 2LL

BELFAST, Earl of; (Arthur) Patrick Chichester; s and h of 7 Marquess of Donegall; *b* 9 May 1952; *Educ* Harrow, RAC Cirencester; *Career* Lt Coldstream Gds, ret 1977; entered Cater Allen (Bill Brokers), res 1986; *Recreations* shooting, racing (horses); *Style*— Earl of Belfast

BELGEONNE, Capt Peter Edward; s of Capt Oscar Victor Belgeonne (Kt Order of Crown of Belgium), of Antwerp (d 1936), and Gabriele, *née* Gysels (d 1974); *b* 7 Dec 1915; *Educ* Antwerp, Louvain Univ; *m* 1, (m dis 1947), Terry Verellen; 2 s (Philip b 1938, Rudy b 1939), 2 da (Vivian b 1940, Nicolette b 1943); m 2, 24 July 1948, Berenice (decd), da of Charles Fletcher Lumb (d 1969); 1 s (Clive b 1958), 1 da (Alexandra b 1959); *Career* OCTU Staff Coll, Int Corps SOE, Capt 1944; serv England, Belgium, Germany, France (ret 1946); chm and md English subsidiary of French Gp (Chemicals) 1951-85 (ret); formerly chm Bourbon Products Ltd, PE Belgeonne Ltd; Kt Order of Crown of Belgium 1945, Kt Order of Agric Merit France 1982; *Recreations* painting, reading, riding, travel; *Clubs* Arts London; *Style*— Capt Peter E Belgeonne; Ballycronigan, Kilrane, Co Wexford, Ireland (☎ 33185)

BELHAVEN, Master of; Hon Frederick Carmichael Arthur Hamilton; s and h of 13 Lord Belhaven and Stenton; *b* 27 Sept 1953; *Educ* Eton; *m* 1981, Elizabeth Anne, da of S V Tredinnick, of Naldretts Court, Wisborough Green, W Sussex; 2 s (William Richard b 30 Dec 1982, James Frederick b 25 Dec 1984); *Style*— The Master of Belhaven

BELHAVEN AND STENTON, Ann, Lady; (Elizabeth) Ann; da of late Col Arthur H Moseley, DSO, of Hastings Rd, Warrawee, NSW; *m* 1952 (m dis 1973), 13 Lord Belhaven and Stenton; 1 s, 1 da; *Style*— Ann, Lady Belhaven and Stenton; 15 Duke St, Sydney, NSW, Australia

BELHAVEN AND STENTON, 13 Lord (S 1647); Robert Anthony Carmichael Hamilton; s of 12 Lord Belhaven and Stenton (d 1961); *b* 27 Feb 1927; *Educ* Eton; *m* 1, 1952 (m dis 1973), (Elizabeth) Ann, da of late Col Arthur Moseley, DSO, of NSW; 1 s, 1 da; m 2, 1973 (m dis 1986), Rosemary, da of Sir Herbert Williams, 1 Bt, MP (d 1954), sis of Sir Robin Williams, Bt *qv*, and formerly w of Sir Ian Mactaggart, 3 Bt; 1 adopted da; m 3, 1986, Malgorzata Maria, da of Tadeusz Pobog Hruzik-Mazurkiewicz of Krakow, Poland; 1 da (Alexandra Maria b 1987); *Heir* s, Master of Belhaven; *Career* Army 1945-48 cmmnd Cameronians 1947; farmer 1950-72, cook 1972-80; sits as Conservative in House of Lords; *Recreations* writing children's stories, growing vegetables; *Clubs* Army and Navy; *Style*— The Rt Hon The Lord Belhaven and Stenton; 16 Broadwater Down, Tunbridge Wells, Kent

BELL, Alan Scott; s of late Stanley Bell, of Sunderland, and late Iris *née* Scott; *b* 8 May 1942; *Educ* Ashville Coll, Selwyn Coll Cambridge (MA), Oxford (MA); *m* 1966, Olivia da of Prof J E Butt, FBA; 1 s (Nicolas), 1 da (Julia); *Career* asst registrar royal Cmmn on Historical Manuscripts 1963-66, asst keeper Nat Lib of Scotland 1966-81, visiting fell All Souls Coll Oxford 1980, librarian Rhodes House Library Oxford Univ 1981-; FR Hist S; *Books* Sydney Smith (1980), Leslie Stephen's Mausoleum Book (ed 1976), Lord Cockburn (1979); *Clubs* Beefsteak, Brooks's; *Style*— Alan Bell, Esq; Rhodes House Library, South Parks Rd, Oxford OX2 3RG (☎ 0865 270907)

BELL, Maj Alexander Fulton; s of Harry Bell, OBE (d 1984), of Viewpark, St Andrews, Fife, and Sophia McDonald, *née* Fulton; *b* 20 Jan 1937; *Educ* Shrewsbury, RMA Sandhurst, Dundee Coll of Tech and Commerce; *m* 4 Jan 1969, Sophia, Lilian Elizabeth Morgan (d 1971), da of Cdr Donald Hugh Elles, RN, of N Tullich, Inveraray, Argyll; 2 s (Harry b 7 Dec 1969, Thomas b 25 Feb 1971); m 2, 23 April 1984, Alison Mary, da of John Cole Compton, MBE, of Ward of Turin, Forfar, Angus; *Career* cmmnd Argyll and Sutherland Highlanders 1957, Capt HM The Queen's Gd Balmoral 1963, Adj 1 Bn Singapore/Borneo 1964-65, serv Cyprus, BAOR, Malaya, Borneo, Berlin; ADC to GOC 51 Highland Div 1966 ret 1969; Maj 1/51 Highland Vols TAVR 1972-74, Home Serv Force 1982-83; sales exec Assoc Br Maltsters 1969, ABM (parent Dalgety plc): sales mangr 1971, dir of sales 1973-87 dir of mktg Pauls Malt (parent Harrisons and Crossfield plc) 1987; chm and pres Inst of Mktg (Tayside branch) 1975-77, advsy cncl Dundee Coll of Commerce 1976-78, govr Ardvreck Sch

Crieff 1982-86; MIBrew 1970, MInstM 1972, MBIM 1975; *Recreations* golf, fishing, shooting, skiing, walking; *Clubs* Royal & Ancient (St Andrews), The Honourable Co of Edinburgh Golfers, Highland Bde; *Style*— Maj Alexander Bell; Drumclune, By Forfar, Angus DD8 3TS (☎ 0575 72074); Pauls Malt Ltd, Victoria St, Carnoustie, Angus (☎ 0241 52641, fax 0241 55267, car 0860 413685)

BELL, Andrew Richard; s of Richard Erskine Bell, of Little Bookham, Surrey, and Sandra Hayhurst *née* Smith; *b* 23 July 1960; *Educ* Glyn Sch Epsom, Mansfield Coll Oxford (MA); *Career* asst dir E B Savory, Milln and Co 1981-86, assoc dir Wood MacKenzie and Co 1986-88, dir Kleinwort Benson Securities 1988-; memb: Int Stock Exchange, Soc Investment Analysts; *Recreations* skiing, horse-riding, running, tennis, football; *Clubs* RAC, United Oxford and Cambridge; *Style*— Andrew R Bell, Esq; Kleinwort Benson Securities Ltd, 20 Fenchurch St, London, EC3P 3DB (01 623 8000, fax 01 623 4572, telex 922241)

BELL, Anthony Holbrook (Tony); s of late Alan Brewis Bell, of Abergele, Clwyd, and Kathleen Burton, *née* Holbrook, of Waco, Texas, USA; *b* 7 Nov 1930; *Educ* Haberdashers' Askes'; *m* 15 Sept 1956, Lorraine Every, da of Leslie Charles Wood (d 1956), of Stanmore, Middx; 1 s (Ian Charles b 1958), 1 da (Susan Nicola (Mrs Auden) b 1960); *Career* Nat Serv cmmnd 2Lt RA 1949, Lt 1950; chm: A H Bell and Co, (Insur Brokers) Ltd, AH Bell and Co (Fin Planning) Ltd, Bell Eteson and Co Ltd and Pennine (Derby) Insur Servs; dir The Derbyshire Bldg Soc; former pres Insur Inst of Derby 1976, former capt Chevin Golf 1984, pres Derby RFC 1987-89; ACII 1961, ACIArb 1971, FBIIBA 1974; *Recreations* golf, rugby football; *Clubs* Chevin GC, Derby Rugby Football; *Style*— A H Bell, Esq; Hob Hill Cottage, Hazelwood, Derby DE6 4AL (☎ 0332 840747); AH Bell and Co (Insurance Brokers) Ltd, Avenue House, 3 Charnwood Street, Derby DE1 2GT (☎ 0332 372111, fax 0332 290786, car tel 0836 717782)

BELL, Christopher John; TD; s of Alfred Bell (d 1979), and Dorothy Craven, *née* Fletcher; *b* 11 Jan 1929; *Educ* Worksop Coll; *m* 1951, Margaret, da of Thomas Beaumont (d 1938); 1 s (Richard), 1 da (Susan); *Career* chm M M Bell and Sons Ltd (cardboard box mfrs); pres Br Paper Box Assoc 1978-80; pres Packaging Employers Confedn 1980-82, regnl cncl CBI 1979-82; nat tres Br Box and Packaging Assoc and Nat Packaging Confedn; dir Richard Bell Design (Leeds) Ltd; *Recreations* gardening, scouting; *Style*— Christopher Bell, Esq, TD; 529 Fulwood Rd, Sheffield (☎ 0742 305272); M M Bell & Sons Ltd, 102 Arundel St, Sheffield S1 3BA (☎ 0742 24740/ 29839)

BELL, Colin Murray; s of Vernon Robert Bell, of Lymington, Hants, and Nell Yates (d 1979); *b* 11 Jan 1927; *Educ* Southgate C Sch; *m* 9 Dec 1949, Elizabeth Fryns, da of Francois Joseph Fryns (d 1963), of La Calamine, Belgium; 3 s (Godfrey b 1951, Colin b 1951, Michael b 1959), 1 da (Teresa b 1953); *Career* RHA Sgt Europe, Middle E 1943-48; Newspaper dir and Building Co chm dir: Bennett Bros (Journal Newspapers) Ltd 1959-65 (mangr 1962-65), Weekly Newspaper Advertising Bureau 1970-80 (chm 1974-75), Audit Bureau of Circulations 1973-81 (chm 1979-81), Verified Free Distribution Ltd 1982-85 (chm 1983-5), Regional Newspaper Advertising Bureau Ltd 1980- (vice-chm 1985-), Colchester Business Enterprise Agency Ltd 1982- (chm 1983-5); *Recreations* walking, golf; *Clubs* IOD; *Style*— Colin Bell, Esq; Essex County Newspapers, Doriec House, North Hill, Colchester, Essex CO1 1TZ

BELL, David Charles Maurice; s of R M Bell, of London, and M F Bell (d 1973); *b* 30 Sept 1946; *Educ* Worth Sch, Trinity Hall Cambridge (BA), Univ of Pennsylvania (MA) ; *m* 30 Dec 1972, Primrose Frances, da of E S Moran (d 1973); 2 s (Charles Alexander b 1978, Thomas George b 1981), 1 da (Emma Theodora b 1975); *Career* Oxford Mail and Times 1970-72, managing ed FT 1985-: ed, int ed 1978-80, asst ed features 1980-85; chm Islington SDP 1981-86, dir Ambache Chamber Orchestra 1987-; *Recreations* theatre, cycling, family, Victorian Social history; *Style*— David Bell, Esq; 35 Belitha Villas, London N1 1PE (☎ 01 609 4000); Financial Times, No 1 Southwark Bridge, London SE

BELL, David Hugh; s of Sir Hugh Bell, 4 Bt (d 1970); bro and hp of Sir John Lowthian Bell, 5 Bt; *b* 8 Oct 1961; *Style*— David Bell, Esq; Arncliffe Hall, Ingleby Cross, Northallerton, N Yorks (☎ (060 982) 202)

BELL, Dr Donald Atkinson; s of Robert Hamilton Bell, and Gladys Mildred, *née* Russell (d 1979); *b* 28 May 1941; *Educ* Royal Belfast Acad Inst, Queen's Univ Belfast (BSc), Southampton Univ (PhD); *m* 25 March 1967, Joyce Louisa, da of James Conroy Godber; 2 s (Alistair b 1971, Richard b 1973); *Career* res asst King's Coll London 1962-66, princ sci offr 1966-77, dep chief sci offr DTI 1978-82, dir Nat Engng Laboratory 1983-, visiting prof Strathclyde Univ; memb: FIMechE 1987, MIEE 1978; *Style*— Dr Donald Bell; National Engineering Lab, East Kilbride, Glasgow G75 OQU (☎ 03552 20222, fax 03552 36930, telex 77888)

BELL, Dr (George) Douglas Hutton; CBE (1965); s of late George Henry Bell, of Swansea, and Lilian Mary Matilda, *née* Hutton; *b* 18 Oct 1905; *Educ* Bishop Gore's GS Swansea, Univ Coll Bangor (BSc), Cambridge (PhD); *m* 1934, Eileen Gertrude, da of late A W Wright, of Hamilton, Ontario; 2 da; *Career* demonstrator and univ lectr Cambridge 1932-47, dir Plant Breeding Inst Cambridge 1947-71, memb cncl and vice-pres Royal Soc 1976-78 (Mullard Award 1967); RASE Research Medal 1956, Massey Ferguson Nat Award 1973; hon fell Selwyn Coll Cambridge; Hon DSc: Wales 1968, Reading 1968, Liverpool 1970; Hon ScD Cambridge 1978; FRS 1965; *Books* Cultivated Plants of the Farm; *Recreations* walking, gardening, natural history; *Style*— Dr Douglas Bell, CBE, FRS; 6 Worts Causeway, Cambridge CB1 4RL (☎ 0223 247449)

BELL, Douglas Maurice; CBE (1972); s of Alexander Dunlop Bell of Shanghai, China (d 1938) and Nora Sunderland (d 1966); gn of Dr Joseph Bell of Edinburgh, the original of Sherlock Holmes; *b* 15 April 1914; *Educ* Cathedral Sch Shanghai, The Edinburgh Acad, St Andrews Univ (BSc); *m* 7 Nov 1947, Elizabeth Mary, da of Charles William Edelsten, Exmouth (d 1955); 1 s (Benjamin b 1952), 2 da (Janet b 1950, Margaret b 1951); *Career* md: ICI Ltd Billingham Div 1955-57, ICI Ltd Petrochemical Div 1958-61; chm: ICI Europa Ltd 1961-73, Tioxide Ltd and assoc companies 1973-8; dir Bekaert NV (Belgium) 1973-; chm: TWIL Gp (Tinsley Wire Industries Ltd) 1978-; pres Soc of Chem Industry 1976-8; hon Fell BIM, Inst of Chem Engineering; hon LLD St Andrews Univ; Kt Commander of Order of Civil Merit (Spain) 1971; Commander Order of Leopold II (Belgium) 1973; *Recreations* sports, gardens; *Clubs* Edinburgh Academicals, Wasps Rugby Football, St Andrews Alumis, Waterloo Golf (Brussels), Anglo Belgian, West Sussex Golf; *Style*— Douglas Bell, Esq, CBE; Stocks Cottage, West Chiltington, Sussex RH20 2JW (☎ Chiltington 2284)

BELL, Sir Gawain Westray; KCMG (1957), CBE (1955, MBE Mil 1942); s of William Westray Bell (d 1947); *b* 21 Jan 1909; *Educ* Winchester, Oxford Univ (BA); *m* 1945, Silvia, da of Maj Adrian Cornwell-Clyne, MBE (d 1969); 3 da; *Career* 2 Lt TA 1929-32, served WWII M East, Kaimakam Col Arab Legion; Sudan Political Serv 1931, seconded to Palestine Govt 1938-41, dist cmmr Sudan Political Serv 1945-49, dep Sudan agent Cairo 1949-51, dep civil sec Sudan Govt 1953-54, perm sec Miny of Interior Sudan 1954-55; HM Political Agent Kuwait 1955-57, govr Northern Nigeria 1957-62; sec gen: Cncl Middle East Trade 1963-64, S Pacific Cmmn 1967-70; vice-pres: exec ctee LEPRA 84-; Anglo-Jordanian Soc 1985-; pt/t chm CS Selection Bds 1972-77; memb govt body SOAS London Univ 1971-81; Order of Independence 3 Class (Jordan) 1944; KStJ 1959 (memb chapter gen 1964-); *Books* Shadows on the Sand (1983), An Imperial Twilight (1989); *Recreations* walking, riding, gardening, swimming; *Clubs* Army and Navy; *Style*— Sir Gawain Bell, KCMG, CBE; Hidcote Bartrim Manor, Chipping Camden, Glos GL55 6LP (☎ 0386 438 305)

BELL, Hon Mrs (Heather Doreen); *née* Parnell; yst da of 6 Baron Congleton (d 1932), and Hon Edith Mary Palmer Howard, MBE (d 1980), da of Baroness Strathcona and Mount Royal in her own right; *b* 11 Jan 1929; *m* 23 April 1960, (Robert) Peter Mangin Bell, *qv*; 2 s, 1 da; *Style*— The Hon Mrs Bell; Sarsen House, 5 Mead Rd, St Cross, Winchester, Hants (☎ 0962 65320)

BELL, Ian; s of John Robert Bell (d 1967); *b* 29 May 1942; *Educ* Hymers Coll Hull; *m* 1965, Kate; 3 children; *Career* asst gen mangr Leeds Permanent Bldg Soc 1977-81, gen mangr (devpt) Provincial Bldg Soc 1981-82, gen mangr (ops) Nat and Prov Bldg Soc 1983-87, md Town and Country Bldg Soc 1987; FCII, FCBSI, MBIM; *Recreations* shooting, ski-ing, sailing; *Style*— Ian Bell, Esq; 52 Hurlingham Rd, Fulham, London SW6 1XX; Town and Country Bldg Soc, 12 Devereux Ct, London WC2R 3JJ (☎ 01 353 2438, fax 01 353 2933)

BELL, Rear Adm John Anthony; CB (1977); s of Mathew Bell (d 1948), of Dundee, and Mary Ann Ellen, *née* Goss (d 1979); *b* 25 Nov 1924; *Educ* St Ignatius Coll, Univ Coll of S Wales (BA, BSc, LLB); *m* 1946, (Eileen) Joan, da of Daniel Woodman (d 1934); 3 da; *Career* RM 1943-45, RAN 1948-52, SACLANT USA 1961-64, dir Naval MET 1973-75, Rear Adm 1975, dir Naval Educn 1975-79; barr Gray's Inn 1970; educn sec BBC 1979-83; vice-pres Utd Servs Catholic Assoc 1979-; chm Kent Ecumenical Cmmn 1982-; pres Kent Area RN Assoc 1982-; vice-pres RN Assoc 1983-; dep chm Police Complaints Bd 1983-; KSG 1983; *Recreations* swimming, travel, France; *Style*— Rear Adm John Bell, CB; The Beild, Conifer Ave, Hartley, Kent DA3 8BX (☎ 047 47 2485)

BELL, Sir John Lowthian; 5 Bt (UK 1885); s of Sir Hugh Francis Bell, 4 Bt (d 1970); *b* 14 June 1960; *Educ* Glenalmond, RAC Cirencester; *m* 22 June 1985, Venetia Mary Frances, 2 da of J A Perry, of Taunton, Som; 1 s (John Hugh b 1988); *Heir* bro, David Hugh Bell; *Career* farmer; *Recreations* fishing, shooting; *Style*— Sir John Bell, Bt; Hollins House, East Rounton, Northallerton, N Yorks; Arncliffe Hall, Ingleby Cross, Northallerton, N Yorks (☎ 060 982 202)

BELL, John Sydney; s of Percy Bell (d 1970),of Northampton, and Florence Annie, *née* Jones; *b* 5 Oct 1930; *Educ* Northampton GS, St Catharine's Coll Cambridge, (MA); *m* 5 March 1966, Margot Diana, da of Wing Cdr Cedric Alfred Wright, of Worlebury, Weston-Super-Mare; 2 s (Stuart b 1967, Edward b 1971), 1 da (Caroline b 1969); *Career* Nat Serv RAF 1949-50 Pilot Offr; qualified slr 1957, ptnr Aplin Stockton Slrs 1968- (sr ptnr 1987-), Notary Public, Clerk to Cmmrs of Income Tax; chm N Oxfordshire Cons Assoc 1980-85 (vice pres 1986-), pres Banbury Chamber of Commerce 1986-87; memb Law Soc 1957; *Recreations* horticulture, politics, model engineering; *Style*— John Bell, Esq; The Manor House, Overthorpe, Banbury, Oxon (☎ 0295 710005); Aplin Stockton, 36 West Bar, Banbury, Oxon (☎ 0295 51234)

BELL, Joseph; CBE (1953); s of Joseph Bell (d 1941), and Elizabeth Bell, *née* Phillips (d 1926); *b* 15 July 1899; *Educ* Alderman Wood Sch Co Durham; *m* 1926, Edith (d 1980), da of Matthew Adamson (d 1909); 1 s (Joseph Arthur), 1 da (Constance, d 1953); *Career* RNVR 1917-19; Newcastle upon Tyne City Police 1919-33; chief constable Hastings 1933-41; asst chief constable City of Manchester 1941-43 (chief constable 1943-58); ret 1958; *Style*— Joseph Bell, Esq, CBE; Norwood, 246 Windlehurst Rd, Marple, Cheshire SK6 7EN (☎ 01 427 3129)

BELL, Col (Francis Cecil) Leonard; DSO (1945), MC (1943), TD (1949); s of Cecil Walker Bell (d 1947), of Lincolnshire, and Frances Ethel, *née* Heath (d 1967); *b* 25 Sept 1912; *Educ* St Christopher's Eastbourne, Greshams Sch Holt; *m* 16 Dec 1942, Mary Wynne, da of Lt-Col A L B Jacob (d 1958), DSO, of Surrey; 1 s (Simon b 1949), 1 da (Elizabeth b 1943); *Career* Lt Col cmd 6 Bn Lincolnshire Regt 1944-45 (despatches 1940, 1943, 1945); serv: Dunkirk, N Africa, Italy, Greece; Hon Col 4/6 Bn Royal Lincolnshire Reg 1962-67, Hon Col Royal Lincolnshire Regt TA 1967; slr 1936, legal advsr Lloyds Bank plc 1965-76, chm legal ctee Banking Fedn of EEC 1974-75; *Recreations* fishing, shooting; *Style*— Col Leonard Bell, DSO, MC, TD; Cross Glades, Chiddingfold, Godalming, Surrey (☎ 042 879 3430)

BELL, Martin George Henry; s of Leonard George Bell (d 1968), of Loughton, and Phyllis, *née* Green; *b* 16 Jan 1935; *Educ* Charterhouse; *m* 2 Jan 1965, Shirley, da of William Henry Wrightson (d 1960), of Bournemouth; 2 s (Thomas b 1966, Jeremy b 1969); *Career* Nat Serv RAF 1953-55; admitted slr 1961, sr ptnr Ashurst Morris Crisp (ptnr 1963-); Freeman City of London, memb Worshipful Co of Slrs; memb: Law Soc, Int Bar Assoc; assoc memb American Bar Assoc; *Recreations* walking, photography; *Style*— Martin Bell, Esq; Mulberry, Woodbury Hill, Loughton, Essex IG10 1JB (☎ 01 508 1188); Broadgate House, 7 Eldon Street, London EC2M 7HD (☎ 01 247 7666, fax 01 377 5659, telex 887067 ASHLAW)

BELL, Martin Irvine; MBE (1985); s of George Alfred Bell (d 1975), and Margaret Martin, *née* Young; *b* 9 Dec 1938; *Educ* King's Park Sr Secdy Sch, Glasgow Univ (BSc); *m* 5 Sept 1962, Joyce Hislop, da of John Shearer (d 1972); 1 s (Adrian b 1971), 1 da (Fiona b 1965); *Career* engr dir Barr and Stroud Ltd 1984-85 (asst md operations 1985), chm and non-exec dir A and S Engrg Designs 1985-; *Recreations* sailing, skiing, squash, music, reading; *Clubs* Royal Northern and Clyde Yacht, Helensburgh Sailing; *Style*— Martin Bell, Esq; 7 Lower Sutherland Crescent, Helensburgh, Dunbartonshire G84 9PG (☎ 0436 2606); Barr and Stroud Ltd, Caxton St, Anniesland, Glasgow G13 1HZ (☎ 041 954 9601, telex 778114 BS GLWG, fax 041 954 2380)

BELL, Martin Neil; s of Flt Lt Arthur Rodney Bell, of Harrogate, and Dorothy Jean Bell; *b* 6 Dec 1964; *Educ* George Watson's Coll Edinburgh, Internatsschule Für Schisportler Stams Austria; *Career* skier; Br champion: jr 1978-80, slalom 1987 (1981), giant slalom 1986 (1980), downhill 1986 (1981); Australia & NZ cup winner 1981, Australian slalom champion 1981, FIS downhill winner Italy 1985, 5th World Cup downhill Sweden 1986, FIS Super G winner Canada 1986, 8th Olympic downhill Canada (best British men's Olympic skiing result); columnist Ski Survey Magazine, pt/t coach Harrogate Ski Centre, conslt ICI Tactel and Skizi Ski fitness aids; *Books* The British Ski Federation Guide to Better Skiing (contributor 1986); *Recreations* football, tennis, squash, volleyball, windsurfing, waterskiing, grass skiing; *Clubs* Kandahar, Harrogate Ski; *Style*— Martin Bell, Esq; 32 Wildcroft Manor, London SW15 3TT (☎ 01 785 6589); IMG, The Pier House, Strand-on-the-Green, London W4 3NN (☎ 01 994 1444, fax 01 935 5820)

BELL, Lady; Mary; JP (Yorks 1972); da of George Howson, MC (d 1936), of Hambledon Bucks; *b* 2 Nov 1923; *Educ* Edinburgh Univ (MB, ChB); *m* 1959, as his 2 w, Sir Hugh Francis Bell, 4 Bt (d 1970); 4 s (*see* Sir John Bell, 5 Bt); *Career* ret doctor; farmer; DObst, RCOG; *Recreations* travel, reading history; *Clubs* Farmers'; *Style*— Lady Bell, JP; Arncliffe Hall, Ingleby Cross, Northallerton, N Yorks DL6 3PA (☎ 060 982 202 or 214)

BELL, Michael Jaffray de Hauteville; s of Capt CL de Hauteville Bell, DSC, RD, RNR (d 1972); *b* 7 April 1941; *Educ* Charterhouse; *m* 1965, Christine Mary, *née* Morgan; 1 s, 4 da; *Career* ptnr R Watson and Sons 1967-, actuary to various life assurance co's in UK and overseas; FIA 1964, ASA, FPMI; *Style*— Michael Bell, Esq; R Watson & Sons, Watson Ho, London Rd, Reigate, Surrey RH2 9PQ

BELL, Michael John Vincent; s of Christopher Richard Vincent, OBE, and Jane Violet Irene Edith Lorna Bell MBE of Ditchling, Sussex; *b* 9 Sept 1941; *Educ* Winchester Coll, Magdalen Coll Oxford; *m* 3 Sept 1983, Mary, da of John William Shippen (d 1957), of Shiremoor, Northumberland; 1 s (John b 1985), 1 da (Julia b 1987); *Career* res assoc Inst for Strategic Studies 1964-65, asst princ MOD 1965, asst private sec to Sec of State for Def 1968-69, princ MOD 1969, private sec to Perm Under Sec MOD 1973-75, asst sec MOD 1975, on loan to HM Treasy 1977-79, asst under sec MOD 1982, asst sec gen def planning and policy NATO 1986-88, Dep Under Sec of State (Fin) MOD; *Recreations* motor cycling, military history; *Style*— Michael Bell, Esq; MOD, London SW1A 2HB ((☎ 01 218 6182)

BELL, (William) Michael; s of William Bell, and Hilda, *née* Taylor (d 1984); *b* 16 Sept 1944; *Educ* Berwick upon Tweed GS; *m* 4 Oct 1969, Helen Robina, da of William John Brown (d 1978), of Langleeford, Wooler, Northumberland; 3 da (Alison b 1971, Sarah b 1974, Lesley b 1977); *Career* CA; Thornton Baker & Co 1967-70, G A Wheeler & Co Wisbech 1970 (ptnr 1972-); memb Wisbech Rotary 1982- (hon asst sec 1985-87, hon sec 1987-), clerk to and Govr St Peter's Junior Sch Wisbech 1971-, memb St Peter and St Paul PCC 1972-85 (hon tres 1972-85); FCA; *Recreations* golf; *Clubs* Sutton Bridge GC Thetford GC; *Style*— Michael Bell, Esq; Apple Acre, Park Lane, Leverington, Wisbech, Cambs PE13 5EH (☎ 0945 870 736); G A Wheeler & Co, 30 Old Market, Wisbech, Cambs PE13 1NE (☎ 0945 582 547)

BELL, Patricia Ann; *née* O'Callaghan; o da of Maj Cornelius Edward Alexander O'Callaghan, The Green Howards (d 1978), and his 1 w, Dorothy Edith, JP (d 1961), o da and heiress of Col D'Arcy Brownlow Preston, CMG (d 1932), of Askham Bryan Hall, N Yorkshire; descended from D'Arcy Preston (d 1749), who purchased Askham Bryan 1725 (*see* Burke's Landed Gentry, 18 edn, vol II, 1969); *b* 3 June 1929; *Educ* Queen Margaret's Woodard Sch; *m* 1 Jan 1955, Lt Cdr (Harold) Peter George Bell, RN, 3 s of Harold Robert Bell (d 1950), of Carr Hall, Sleights, N Yorkshire; 3 s (Charles D'Arcy b 24 Dec 1957, Nigel Edward Hugh b 12 March 1960, Michael Richard John b 17 July 1964); *Style*— Mrs Patricia Bell; Yeabridge Close, South Petherton, Somerset (☎ 0460 40571); Blacksmith's Cottage, Askham Bryan, N Yorks

BELL, Prof Peter Frank; s of Frank Bell, Quatermaster, of Sheffield, and Ruby, *née* Corks; *b* 12 June 1938; *Educ* Univ of Sheffield (MB, ChB Hon 1961); *m* 26 Aug 1961, Anne, da of Oliver Jennings (d 1981), of Dewsbury, Yorks; 1 s (Mark b 1967), 2 da (Jane Marie b 1962, Louise b 1963); *Career* registrar in surgery, Sheffield Health Bd, Sheffield Yorks 1963-65, lectr in surgery Univ of Glasgow 1965-68, Sir Henry Wellcome Travelling Fellow, Wellcome Fndn, Denver Coll, USA 1968-69; sr lectr in surgery Univ of Glasgow 1969-74; Fndn Prof of surgery Univ of Leicester 1974-; memb LOROS (Leics Orgn for Relief of Suffering), chm organising ctee Transplant Games; former pres, Surgical Res Soc, former sec Int Transplantation Soc; FRCS London 1965, FRCSG Glasgow 1969, MD Sheffield 1970; *Books* Operative Arterial Surgery (1983), Surgical Aspects of Haemodialysts (1985), ed and contributor Vascular Surgery (1985), author many articles in learned journals; *Recreations* painting, gardening, woodwork; *Clubs* Leics; *Style*— Prof Peter Bell; 22 Powys Avenue, Oadby, Leicester (☎ 0533 709579); Dept of Surgery, Clinical Sciences Bldg, Leicester Royal Infirmary, Leicester LE2 7LX (☎ 0533 523142)

BELL, (Robert) Peter Mangin; 2 s of Rev Robert William Bell (d 1940), of Stamfordham Vicarage, Northumberland; *b* 11 Sept 1918; *Educ* Durham Sch, Jesus Coll Cambridge; *m* 23 April 1960, Hon Heather, *née* Parnell, da of 6 Baron Congleton (d 1932); 2 s (Robert Simon Parnell b 1961, Aidan William George b 1967), 1 da (Penelope Edith b 1963); *Career* slr; *Clubs* United Oxford and Cambridge Univ, Royal Lymington Yacht, Leander; *Style*— Peter Bell, Esq; Sarsen House, 5 Mead Rd, St Cross, Winchester, Hants (☎ 0962 65320)

BELL, Prof Quentin (Claudian Stephen); 2 s of Clive Bell (d 1964), the author and art critic, and Vanessa, *née* Stephen (d 1961), the artist; nephew of Virginia Woolf; *b* 19 August 1910; *m* 1952, Anne Olivier Popham; 1 s, 2 da; *Career* painter, potter, author; emeritus prof of history and theory of art Sussex; DLitt Newcastle 1983; FRSA, FRSL; *Books* Ruskin (1963), Bloomsbury (1968), Virginia Woolf, a biography (1972), A New and Noble School (1982); *Clubs* Reform; *Style*— Prof Quentin Bell; 8 Heighton Street, Firle, Sussex

BELL, Sir (George) Raymond; KCMG (1973), CB (1967); eldest s of William Bell (d 1954), of Bradford, and Christabel, *née* Appleton; *b* 13 Mar 1916; *Educ* Bradford GS, St John's Coll Cambridge; *m* 1944, Joan Elizabeth, o da of William George (d 1951), of London, and Christina Coltham; 2 s, 2 da; *Career* WWII Lt RNVR; entered Civil Service 1938, sec (Fin) Off of UK High Cmmr (Canada) 1945-48, dep sec HM Treasury 1966-72 (asst sec 1951, under sec 1960), memb UK delgn to Brussels Conf 1961-62 and 1970-72; *Style*— Sir Raymond Bell, KCMG, CB; Quartier des Bories, Aouste-sur-Sye, 26400 Crest, Drôme, France (☎ 75 25 26 94)

BELL, Rodger; QC (1982); s of John Thornton Bell (d 1974), and Edith, *née* Rodger; *b* 13 Sept 1939; *Educ* Brentwood Sch, Brasenose Coll Oxford; *m* 27 Sept 1969, (Sylvia) Claire, only surv da of William Eden Tatton Brown, CB, of Berkhamsted, Herts, by his w Aileen Hope Johnston, da of late Joseph Knox Sparrow, MC; 1 s (Benjamin b 1970), 3 da (Natasha b 1972, Lucinda b 1975, Sophie b 1982); barr 1963, rec Crown Ct 1980, legal memb Mental Health Review Tribunal 1983; *Recreations* running, rowing; *Clubs* Thames Hare and Hounds, Dacre Boat; *Style*— Rodger Bell, Esq, QC; 14 Castello Avenue, London SW15 6EA (☎ 01 788 3857); 1 Crown Office Row, Temple, London EC4Y 7HH)

BELL, Roger Wallace; s of Frederick Nelson Bell, and Kathleen Joyce, *née* Slater ; *b* 23 June 1941; *Educ* Primary Sch Trinidad W Indies, Gosfield's Boy's Sch Essex; *m* 1, Sally Warick (m diss); 2 da (Deborah Jane b 1964, Joanne Louise b 1966); 2 m, June 1988, Pamela Annette, *née* Nolan; *Career* articled Edmond D White 1958-67; sit acct Br Oxygen Co Ltd 1967-69, fin controller Hoke Int Ltd 1969-73, co acct John Brown Earl & Wright Ltd 1973-80, accounting mangr John Brown Engrg Ltd 1980-83, fin controller Earl and Wright Ltd 1983-86; computer conslt 1986- (practice suspended since heart transplant in 1988); tres Br Heart Fndn (Reading Branch) 1988-; FCA; *Recreations* computer programming, walking, reading, travel, fund raising; *Style*— Roger Bell, Esq; 25 Purfield Drive, Wargrave, Berkshire, RG10 8AP (☎ 075322 2720)

BELL, (Alexander) Scott; s of William Scott Bell (d 1978), of Falkirk, Scotland, and Catherine Irene, *née* Traill; *b* 4 Dec 1941; *Educ* Daniel Stewart's Coll Edinburgh; *m* 12 Oct 1965, Veronica Jane, da of James Simpson (d 1985), of Edinburgh; 2 s (Scott b 1968, David b 1970), 1 da (Victoria b 1974); *Career* Standard Life Assur Co 1958- (md and actuary 1988-); dir: Bank of Scotland 1988-, The Hammerson Property Investmt and Devpt Corpn plc 1988-; FFA 1966, FPMI 1978; *Recreations* golf, travel, reading; *Clubs* New (Edinburgh), Bruntsfield Links Golfing Soc; *Style*— Scott Bell, Esq; 28 East Barnton Ave, Edinburgh EH4 6AQ (☎ 031 312 7591); Standard Life Assurance Co, 3 George St, Edinburgh EH2 2XZ (☎ 031 245 6011, fax 031 245 6010, car tel 08 606 11928, telex 72530)

BELL, Hon Mrs; Hon Serena Frances; *née* Fairfax; da of 13 Lord Fairfax of Cameron (d 1964); *b* 12 Dec 1952; *m* 1976, W Robert G Bell; 1 s (b 1986), 2 da; *Style*— The Hon Mrs Bell

BELL, Sheriff Principal Stewart Edward; QC (1982); s of Charles Edward Bell (d 1947), of 9 Botanic Cres, Glasgow, and Rosalind Bell, *née* Stewart (d 1964); *b* 4 August 1919; *Educ* Kelvinside Acad Glasgow, Trinity Hall Cambridge (BA, MA), Glasgow Univ (LLB); *m* 1, 1948, Isla Janet Malcolm (d 1983), da of James Spencer (d 1978), of Jersey; 3 da (Adelin, Fiona, Linda); m 2, 1985, Margaret Virginia, da of Andrew St Clair Jameson (d 1978), of Edinburgh; 2 step da (Virginia, Jane); *Career* cmmnd Loyal Regt 1939, serv Singapore, Malaya Lt (POW); advocate 1948-61, Sheriff Glasgow 1961-82, Sheriff Princ of Grampian Highland and Islands 1983-88; *Recreations* highland bagpipe; *Clubs* New (Edinburgh), Royal Northern Aberdeen; *Style*— Sheriff Principal Stewart Bell, QC; The Little House, Thurlow Rd, Nairn IV12 4HJ (☎ 0667 52131); 43 Braid Rd, Edinburgh EH10 (☎ 031 447 3754)

BELL, Stuart; MP (Lab) Middlesbrough 1983-; s of Ernest and Margaret Rose Bell; *b* 16 May 1938; *Educ* Hookergate GS Durham; *m* 1, 1960, Margaret, da of Mary Bruce; 1 s, 1 da; m 2, Margaret, da of Mary Allan; 1 s; *Career* barr Gray's Inn; sometime journalist; joined Lab Pty 1964, contested (Lab) Hexham 1979, memb Newcastle City Cncl 1980-83; legal advsr Trade Unions for Lab Victory N Region; PPS to dep ldr Lab Pty (Rt Hon Roy Hattersley); memb: Police and Criminal Evidence Bill Ctee, Soc of Labour Lawyers, Fabian Soc, Co-operative Soc, Gen and Municipal Boilermakers and Allied Trade Union; Front Bench spokesman for the Oppn on NI 1984-87; *Publications* Paris 69, Days That Used To Be, When Salem Came to the Boro, How to Abolish the Lords (Fabian tract), The Principles of US Customs Valuation (legal pubn); *Recreations* short story and novel writing; *Style*— Stuart Bell, Esq, MP; House of Commons, London SW1A 0AA

BELL, William Archibald Ottley Juxon; s of William Archibald Juxon Bell (d 1970), (late of Pendell Court), of Bletchingley Sy, and Mary Isabel Maude (d 1969), *née* Ottley; *b* 7 July 1919; *Educ* Eton, Trinity Coll Oxford (MA); *m* 19 July 1947, Belinda Mary, da of Geoffrey Dawson (d 1944), of Langcliffe Hall, Settle; 2 s (Robert b 1950, Nicholas b 1952), 3 da (Georgiana b 1948, Caroline b 1955, Joanna b 1958); m 2, Margaret Cecilia (d 1969), da of 6 Baron Wenlock; *Career* WW11 Temp Capt Welsh Guards 1940-45 served N Africa, Italy, Austria; Entered F O 1945, Egyptian dept 1945-46, political private sec to High Commr India 1946-47; private sec to exec dirs Br s Africa Co 1947-50; dir King & Shaxson plc (Bill-brokers) 1950- (md 1950-70); memb for Chelsea GLC & ILEA 1970-86; chm: GLC Historic Blydgs Ctee 1977-81, and fndr Heritage of London Tst 1980-, Oxon Bildgs Tst 1987-, Diocesan Bd of fin Oxon 1974-75; memb: London Adusy Ctee English Heritage 1986-, Ctee of Oxon Historic Churches Tst; High Sheriff Oxon 1978-79; *Recreations* shooting, golf tennis, painting; *Clubs* White's, Pratt's; *Style*— William Bell Esq; 165 Cranmer Ct, London SW3 3HF (☎ 01 589 1033); Cottisford Hse, Nr Brackley, Northamptonshire NN13 5SW (☎ 02804 247); c/o English Heritage, Chesham Hse, 30 Warwick St, London W1R 6AB (☎ 01 734 8144)

BELL, William Edwin; CBE (1980); s of Cuthbert Edwin Bell (d 1961), and Winifred Mary, *née* Simpson; *b* 4 August 1926; *Educ* Birmingham Univ, Royal Sch of Mines; *m* 1952, Angela Josephine, da of Fl-Lt E Vaughan, MC (d 1931); 2 s, 2 da; *Career* exec Royal Dutch/Shell Gp; dir Shell Int 1980-84; non-exec dir Costain Gp plc; chm Enterprise Oil plc 1984-; CBIM, FInstPet; *Recreations* golf, sailing (yacht 'Bel Esprit'); *Clubs* Chichester Yacht, Nevill Golf; *Style*— William Bell, Esq, CBE; Fordcombe Manor, nr Tunbridge Wells, Kent

BELL, William Lewis; CMG (1970), MBE (1945); s of Frederick Robinson Bell (d 1957), of Cheltenham, and Kate Harper, *née* Lewis (d 1984); *b* 31 Dec 1919; *Educ* Hymers Coll Hull, Oriel Coll Oxford; *m* 1 Sept 1943, Margaret, da of William Giles (d 1957), of Carmarthen; 1 s (Richard Jeremy Giles), 1 da (Rosalind Margaret (Mrs Bowlby)); *Career* Glos-Regt 1940-46; Capt and Adj 2 Bn 1942; Maj and DAAG 49 (WR) Inf Div 1943-46; HM Colonial Admin Serv Uganda: dist offr 1946-54, asst fin sec 1954, dep sec to tres 1956, perm sec miny of educn 1958-62; dir Cox & Danks Ltd MI Gp 1963-64, sec Westfield Coll Univ of London 1964-65, founding head Br Devpt Div Caribbean Miny of Overseas Devpt 1966-72, UK dir Caribbean Devpt Bank 1970-72, founding dir-gen Tech Educn & Trg Orgn Miny of Overseas Devpt 1972-77, inf offr Univ of Oxford 1977-84; chm Uganda Nat Parks 1962, pres Uganda Sports Union 1961-62; fell Econ Devpt Inst World Bank 1958; *Recreations* collecting, Caribbeana, gardening; *Clubs* MCC, Vincent's; *Style*— William Bell, Esq, CMG, MBE; Greystones, Stanton St John, Oxford OX9 1HF (☎ 086 735 477)

BELL DAVIES, Vice Adm Sir Lancelot Richard; KBE (1977); s of Vice Adm Richard Bell Davies, VC, CB, DSO, AFC (d 1966), and Mary Pipon Bell Davies, *née*

Montgomery (d 1975); f VC Gallipoli Campaign one of the first RNAS pilots; *b* 18 Feb 1926; *Educ* Boxgrove Sch Guildford, RNC Dartmouth (13 year old entry); *m* 1949, Emmeline Joan, da of Prof G J H Molengraaff (d 1961), of Holland; 1 s (Richard William b 1955), 2 da (Emmeline Anne b 1950, Daphane Alexandra b 1956); *Career* Midshipman HMS Norfolk 1943 Battle of North Cape, joined submarines 1944, cmd HMS Subtle 1953, HMS Explorer 1955, HMS Leander 1962, HMS Forth 1967, dir naval warfare 1969, Capt HMS Bulwark 1972-73, naval attaché Washington DC 1973-75, supreme allied cdr Atlantic Rep Europe 1975-78, cmdt NATO Def Coll Rome 1978-81; chm Sea Cadet Cncl 1983; CBIM; *Recreations* sailing, gardening; *Clubs* Royal Yacht Squadron, Naval and Military, RNSA; *Style—* Vice Adm Sir Lancelot Bell Davies, KBE; Holly Hill Lodge, 123 Barnes Lane, Sarisbury Green SO3 6BH (☎ 04895 3131)

BELLAIGUE; *see*: de Bellaigue

BELLAIRS, Prof Angus d'Albini; s of Nigel Bellairs (d 1979), of King's Rd, St Peter Port, Guerney, and Kathleen, *née* Niblett (d 1946); *b* 11 Jan 1918; *Educ* Stowe, Queens' Coll Cambridge (MA), UCH London (DSc); *m* 5 July 1949, Madeline Ruth, da of Trevor Morgan (d 1973), of Bell Croft Hse, Southowram, Halifax, Yorks; 1 da (Vivien St Joseph b 1959); *Career* WWII RAMC 1942-46, Med Offr 4 Div Engrs, Maj Operational Res Section 14 Army; served: N Africa, Middle East, Italy, India, Burma, Washington; lectr Cambridge 1951-53, reader in anatomy and embryology St Mary's Hosp Med Sch Univ of London 1953-70, prof of vertebrate morphology 1970-82 (emeritus prof 1982-); pres First World Congress of Herpetology 1989; MRCS, LRCP; fell: Inst of Biology, Linnean and Zoological Socs; *Books* The World of Reptiles (with R Carrington 1966), The Life of Reptiles 2 Vols (1969), Reptiles (with J Attridge fourth edn 1975), The Isle of Sea Lizards (novel), First World Congress of Herpetology (1989); *Recreations* natural history (especially reptiles and cats), antiques, modern novels; *Style—* Prof Angus Bellairs; 7 Champion Grove, London SE5 8BN (☎ 01 274 1834)

BELLAK, John George; *b* 19 Nov 1930; *Educ* Uppingham, Haute Ecole Commerciale Lausanne Switzerland, Clare Coll Cambridge (MA); *m* Mary Prudence (Pru); 3 s (Max b 1962, Leo b 1966, Benjy b 1968, Maria b 1964); *Career* J Whittingham & Sons Ltd 1952-58, A Hoffmann & Co Ltd 1958-68; Doulton & Co Ltd 1968-83: sales dir (Fine China), commercial dir (Tableware), mktg dir 1972, dep md, Euro distributive NV Royal Doulton (Belgium) SA, md Royal Doulton Tablewear Ltd 1980; chm: Royal Crown Derby Porcelain Co Ltd, Lawleys Ltd; memb: cncl CBI Ct Univ of Keele, Cncl of Newcastle under Lyme Schs; contested (cons): Kingston upon Hull West 1964, Keighley 1966, tres Ripon Div Cons Assoc 1967; chm Severn Trent Water Authy 1983; FRSA; *Recreations* politics, shooting, ornithology, wild life, conservation, ancient Chinese artefacts; *Clubs* Carlton; *Style—* John Bellak, Esq; Severn-Trent Water, Abelson House, 2297 Coventry Rd, Birmingham, W Mids B26 3PU (☎ 021 722 4000, fax 021 722 4477, car tel 0836 507295, telex 339333)

BELLAMY, Alan Nicholas Fothergill; s of Gilbert Bernard Bellamy (d 1965), and Nina, *née* Fothergill; *b* 2 Nov 1939; *Educ* Nottingham HS, Birmingham Univ (BSc); *m* 10 Jan 1970, Dorothy Jane, da of Leslie Stuart Hooley (d 1984); 1 s (Jonathan b 1972), 2 da (Vanessa b 1970, Amanda b 1973); *Career* dir Hestair plc; md Hestair Hope Ltd; *Style—* Alan N F Bellamy, Esq; 50 Hawthorn Lane, Wilmslow, Cheshire (☎ 0625 532 651); 17 Buckingham Gate, London SW1

BELLAMY, Rear Adm (Albert) John; CB (1968), OBE (1956); s of Albert Edward Bellamy (d 1951), of Upton-on-Severn, Worcester, and Marian, *née* Price (d 1968); *b* 26 Feb 1915; *Educ* Hanley Castle GS, Downing Coll Cambridge; *m* 1942, Dorothy Joan, da of Cdr Noel John Cecil Lawson, RNR (d 1964), of Orchard Cottage, Horsham; 1 s (Michael), 1 da (Rosemary); *Career* RN 1939-70, Instr Rear Adm 1965-70, dean RNEC 1956-60, Head of Instr Branch and Dir Naval Educn Serv 1965-70; dep dir Poly of the South Bank London 1970-80; *Recreations* gardening, show jumping administration and judging, work with charities; *Style—* Rear Adm John Bellamy, CB, OBE; The Cottage, Kington Magna, Gillingham, Dorset (☎ 074 785 668)

BELLAMY, Richard Anthony; s of Maj Roland Cecil Bellamy, OBE, TD, JP, DL, *qv*, and Kathleen Alice, *née* Beacock; *b* 21 Mar 1939; *Educ* Shrewsbury; *m* 1965, Wendy, *née* Hopwood; 2 s, 1 da; *Career* fndr chm Avia Fuels (UK) Ltd; memb Cncl of Hull Univ 1981-87; Liveryman Worshipful Co of Coach and Harness Makers; High Sheriff Humberside 1980-81; FInstPet; *Recreations* shooting; *Clubs* Army and Navy, Rotary; *Style—* Richard A Bellamy, Esq; Parklands, Barnoldby-Le-Beck, Great Grimsby, S Humberside (☎ 0472 823680)

BELLAMY, Maj Roland Cecil; OBE (1974), TD (1950), JP (1943), DL (Humberside 1974, Lincs 1964); s of William Henry Bellamy (d 1945), of Grimsby, Lincs; *b* 17 May 1902; *Educ* Rossall; *m* 1927, Kathleen Alice, da of Edwin Beacock; 1 s (*see* Richard A Bellamy), 2 da; *Career* chm Bell Petroleum; high sheriff Lincs 1971; CEng, MIMechE; *Recreations* country pursuits; *Clubs* Army and Navy; *Style—* Maj Roland Bellamy, OBE, TD, JP, DL; West Park, Barnoldby-Le-Beck, nr Grimsby, S Humberside (☎ 0472 823150)

BELLANY, Prof Ian; s of James Bellany (d 1984), of Sheffield and Bristol, and Jemima, *née* Emlay; *b* 21 Feb 1941; *Educ* Preston Lodge, Prestonpans, Firth Park Sheffield, Balliol Coll Oxford (BA, MA, D Phil); *m* 7 Aug 1965, Wendy Ivey, da of Glyndwr Thomas (d 1978) of Gilwern, Abergavenny; 1 s (Alastair b 1968), 1 da (Alison b 1971); *Career* asst princ FCO 1965-68, res fell Aust Nat Univ Canberra 1968-70; Lancaster Univ: lectr in politics (sr lectr 1974-79), prof of politics and dir of the Centre for the Study of Arms Control and Int Security 1979-; founding ed Arms Control, memb advsy panel on disarmament FCO, external examiner, intl rels LSE; *Books* Australia in the Nuclear Age, Anti-Ballistic Missile Defence in the 1980s (ed), The Verification of Arms Control Agreements (ed), The Nuclear Non Proliferation Treaty (ed), New Conventional Weapons and Western Defence (ed); *Recreations* carpentry and computing; *Style—* Prof Ian Bellany; University of Lancaster, Bailrigg, Lancaster, LA1 4YL (☎ 0524 65 201)

BELLANY, John; s of Richard Weatherhead Bellany (d 1985), of Port Seton, E Lothian, Scotland, and Agnes Craig Maltman Bellany; *b* 18 June 1942; *Educ* Cockenzie Sch E Lothian, Preston Lodge Prestonpans, Edinbrugh Coll of Art (DA), RCA (MA); *m* 1, 19 Sept 1964 (m dis 1974), Helen Margaret, da of late Harold Percy of Golspie, Sutherland, Scotland; 2 s (Jonathan b 22 Dec 1965, Tristan b 20 Aug 1968), 1 da (Anya b 30 Sept 1970); m 2, 1980, Juliet Gray, *née* Lister (d 1985); m 3, his first wife Helen Margaret; *Career* lectr in fine art Winchester Sch of Art 1969-73, head of faculty of painting Croydon Coll of Art 1973-78, visiting lectr in painting RCA 1975-85, lectr in fine art Goldsmiths Coll London 1978-84, artist in residence The Victorian Coll of the Arts Melbourne Aust 1985; Maj Arts Cncl Award 1981, jt first prize Athena Int Award 1985; maj one man exhibitions: Drian Gallery London 1970 (1971, 1972, 1973, 1974), Aberdeen City Art Gallery 1975, Acme Gallery London 1977 (1980), Scottish Arts Cncl Gallery 1978 3rd Eye Centre Glasgow 1979, Southampton Art Gallery, Rosa Esman Gallery NY 1982 (1983, 1984); arts cncl touring exhibition 1983: Iron Gallery Birmingham, Walker Art Gallery Liverpool, Graves Art Gallery Sheffield; arts cncl touring exhibition 1984: Christine Abrahams Gallery Melbourne, Dusseldorf Gallery Perth Aust, Roslyn Oxley Gallery Sydney Aust; Nat Portrait Gallery 1986, Fischer Fine Art Ltd London, Galerie Kirkhaar Amsterdam; retrospective exhibitions: Scottish Nat Gallery of Modern Art, Serpentine Gallery London, RCA Gallery 1987, Roslyn Oxley Gallery Aust, Butler Gallery Kilkenny Castle, Hendrix Gallery Dublin, 3rd Eye Centre Glasgow (prints) 1988, Ruth Siegel Gallery NY, Kunshalle Hamburg, Gaux Arts Gallery Bristol; public collections: Aberdeen Art Gallery, Arts Cncl of GB, Br Cncl, Br Govt Collection Whitehall, Contemporary Arts Soc, Hatton Art Gallery, Kelving Grove Art Gallery, Leeds Art Gallery, Leicester Art Gallery, Middlesborough Art Gallery, Nat Gallery of Poland Warsaw, Nat Library of Congress Washington USA, Museum of Modern Art NY, Met Museum NY, Nat Portrait Gallery, Nat Portrait Gallery of Poland, Nat Gallery of Modern Art Scotland, Gulbenkian Museum Lisbon, J F Kennedy Library Boston USA, V and A, Br Museum, Tate; fell commoner Trinity Hall Cambridge 1988; Hon RSA 1987; elected ARA 1986; *Clubs* Chelsea Arts, Scottish Arts (Edinburgh); *Style—* John Bellany, Esq; 59 Northside, Clapham Common, London SW4 9SA; 19 Great Stuart St, Edinburgh, Scotland; c/o Fischer Fine Art, 30 King St, St James's, London SW1 (☎ 01 839 3942)

BELLEW; *see*: Grattan-Bellew

BELLEW, Hon Bryan Edward; s and h of 7 Baron Bellew; *b* 19 Mar 1943; *Educ* Eton, RMA Sandhurst; *m* 1968, Rosemary Sarah, er da of Maj Reginald Kilner Brasier Hitchcock, of Meers Court, Mayfield, Sussex; 2 s (Patrick Edward b 1969, Anthony Richard Brooke b 1972); *Career* Maj (ret) Irish Gds; *Style—* Maj the Hon Bryan Bellew; Barmeath Castle, Togher, Drogheda, Co Louth, Eire

BELLEW, Hon Christopher James; 2 s of 7 Baron Bellew; *b* 3 April 1954; *Educ* Eton; *m* 1984, Hon Rose Griselda, *née* Eden, yst da of 7 Baron Henley, and former w of Stuart Ballin; *Style—* The Hon Christopher Bellew; Barmeath Castle, Dunleer, Co Louth, Eire

BELLEW, Hon Sir George (Rothe); KCB (1961), KCVO (1953, CVO 1950, MVO 1935); s of Hon Richard Bellew, by his w Gwendoline, da of William R J Fitzherbert Herbert-Huddleston, of Clytha; *b* 13 Dec 1899; *Educ* Wellington Coll, Ch Ch Oxford; *m* 1935, Ursula Kennard, da of Anders Eric Knös Cull; 1 s; *Career* serv WWII RAFVR (despatches); registrar Coll of Arms 1935-46; genealogist Order of the Bath 1950-61, OStJ 1951-61; Knight Principal of Imperial Soc of Knights Bachelor 1957-62 (Dep Knight Princ 1962-71); Garter Principal King of Arms 1950-61; Inspector of Regimental Colours 1957-61; Sec of the Order of the Garter 1961-74; FSA; kt 1950; *Style—* Hon Sir George Bellew, KCB, KCVO; The Grange, Farnham, Surrey (☎ 0252 715146)

BELLEW, 7 Baron (I 1848); Sir James Bryan Bellew; 13 Bt (I 1688); s of 6 Baron Bellew, MC; suc f 1981; *b* 5 Jan 1920; *m* 1, 1942, Mary Elizabeth (d 1978), er da of Rev Edward Hill, of West Malling; 2 s, 1 da; m 2, 1978, Gwendoline, da of Charles Redmond Clayton-Daubeny, of Bridgwater, Somerset, and Bihar, India, and formerly w of Maj P Hall; *Heir* s, Hon Bryan Bellew; *Career* late Capt Irish Gds, served WW II; *Style—* The Rt Hon The Lord Bellew; Barmeath Castle, Togher, Drogheda, Co Louth, Eire (☎ 041 5 12 05)

BELLEW, Hon Patrick Herbert; s of Richard Eustace Bellew (d 1933, 4 s of 2 Baron Bellew) by his 2 w Gwendoline (herself da of William Reginald Joseph Fitzherbert Herbert-Huddleston, JP, DL, of Clytha Park, Monmouthshire, and Sawston Hall, Cambs, by his first w, Charlotte Giffard, one of the Giffards of Chillington; *see* Giffard, Peter); half-bro of 5 Baron Bellew, MBE (d 1975); granted, rank, title and precedence of a Baron's s 1935; *b* 2 April 1905; *Educ* privately, Cambridge Univ; *m* 1, 1936, Hon Catherine Moya de la Poer Beresford (m dis 1946 and who d 1967), da of 5 Baron Decies, DSO, PC (d 1944); 1 s (John); m 2, 1954, Helen Carol, da of late Walter Clinton Louchheim, of New York; *Career* Lt RNVR 1938; *Style—* The Hon Patrick Bellew; Litchfield, Connecticut, USA

BELLEW, Hon Mrs (Rose Griselda); *née* Eden; da of 7 Baron Henley (d 1977); *b* 17 Nov 1957; *m* 1976 (m dis 1979), Stuart Ballin; m 2, 1984, Hon Christopher Bellew, *qv*, yr s of 7 Baron Bellew; *Style—* The Hon Mrs Bellew; 56 Margravine Gardens, London W6

BELLINGER, Sir Robert Ian; GBE (1967); s of David Morgan Bellinger, of Cardiganshire, by his w Jane Ballantine Deans; *b* 10 Mar 1910; *Educ* Church of England Sch; *m* 1962, Christiane Marie Louise, da of Maurice Clement Janssens, of Brussels; 1 s, 1 da; *Career* chm: Kinloch (PM) Ltd 1964-75, Nat Savings Ctee 1970-75 (pres 1972-75), Danish Trade Advsy Bd 1977-82; dir Rank Orgn 1971-83; Lord Mayor of London 1966-67; one of HM Lts City of London 1976-; chm fin ctee BBC, govr BBC 1968-71; Gentleman Usher of the Purple Rod, Order of the Br Empire 1969-85; KStJ 1966; kt 1964; *Style—* Sir Robert Bellinger, GBE; Penn Wood, Fulmer, Bucks (☎ 02816 395 2029)

BELLINGHAM, Anthony Edward Norman; s of Sir Roger Bellingham, 6 Bt (d 1973); bro and hp of Sir Noel Bellingham, 7 Bt; *b* 24 Mar 1947; *Educ* Rossall; *Style—* Anthony Bellingham, Esq

BELLINGHAM, Henry Campbell; MP (C) Norfolk NW 1983-; s of (Arthur) Henry Bellingham (d 1959), and June Marion Cloudesley, *née* Smith; *b* 29 Mar 1955; *Educ* Eton, Magdalene Coll Cambridge, Cncl of Legal Educn; *Career* called to Bar Middle Temple 1978; elected MP for NW Norfolk in 1983, 1983-87 jt sec Cons Backbench Smaller Businesses Ctee, 1987- vice-chm Cons Backbench Smaller Businesses Ctee, 1983- jt sec, Cons NI Ctee, 1987- memb of All Pty Environment Select Ctee; *Clubs* White's, Pratt's; *Style—* Henry Bellingham, Esq, MP; House of Commons, London SW1

BELLINGHAM, Lynda (Mrs Nunzio Peluso); da of Capt D J Bellingham, and Ruth Bellingham; *b* 31 May 1948; *Educ* Convent GS, Central Sch of Speech and Drama; *m* 22 July 1981, Nunzio Peluso; 2 s (Michael b 1983, Robert Ciro b 3 April 1988); *Career* actress; W End appearances: Noises Off, Look no Hans, Double Double; TV appearances incl: Mackenzie, Dr Who, Funny Man, All Creatures Great and Small; *Style—* Ms Lynda Bellingham; c/o Saraband Associates, 265 Liverpool Rd, London N1

(☎ 01 609 5313)

BELLINGHAM, Sir Noel Peter Roger; 7 Bt (GB 1796); s of Sir Roger Bellingham, 6 Bt, MB, ChB, DA (d 1973); *b* 4 Sept 1943; *Educ* Lindisfarne Coll; *m* 1977, Jane, da of Edwin William Taylor, of Sale, Cheshire; *Heir* bro, Anthony Bellingham, *qv*; *Career* accountant; *Style—* Sir Noel Bellingham, Bt; 20 Davenport Park Rd, Davenport, Stockport, Cheshire (☎ 061 483 7168)

BELLIS, John Herbert; s of Thomas Bellis (d 1953), of Wernto, Llanfairfechan, Gwynedd, and Jane Blodwen, *née* Roberts (d 1980); *b* 11 April 1930; *Educ* Friars GS Bangor, Liverpool Univ (LLB); *m* 4 Mar 1961, Sheila (Helen), da of Alastair McNeil Ford (d 1979), of Rhos on Sea, Clwyd; 2 s (Nicholas, Mark), 1 da (Linda); *Career* Nat Serv 2 Lt The Welch Regt 1953-55; admitted solr 1953; princ John Bellis & Co, solrs, Penmaenmawr, Gwynedd 1958-84; chm Industl Tribunals, Manchester 1984-; parly candidate (L) Conway Gaernarvonshire 1959-64; *Recreations* golf, gardening, horse racing, walking; *Style—* John Bellis Esq; Heron Watch, 148 Grovelane, Cheadle Hulme, Cheadle, Cheshire SK8 7NH (☎ 061 439 7582); Alexandra House, Parsonage Gardens, Manchester (☎ 061 833 0581)

BELLIS, Michael John; s of Herbert Henry Bellis (d 1976) of Sherborne, Dorset, and Majorie Dudley, *née* Charlton; *b* 28 April 1937; *Educ* Bancrofts Sch Woodford Green; *Career* Nat Serv RCS 1956-58; admitted slr 1968, cmmr for oaths 1973, sr ptnr Edward Oliver of Bellis 1975-; chm med serv ctee FPC London Boroughs of Redbridge and Waltham Forest 1978-, former vice-pres W Essex Law Soc, former pres Rotary Club Ilford; Freeman City of London, Liveryman Worshipful Co Bakers; memb Law Soc 1968; *Recreations* collecting rare books, travel in the USA, growing and eating asparagus; *Style—* Michael John Bellis, Esq; Beck Farm Coach House, The St, Kelling, Holt, Norfolk NR25 7EL (☎ 026 370 435); Edward Oliver & Bellis, City House, 9 Cranbrook Rd, Ilford, Essex (☎ 01 553 1214, fax 01 478 7762)

BELLOW, Hon Stephen Jeremy; o s of Baron Bellwin, JP (Life Peer); *b* 1953; *Educ* Leeds GS, Leeds Polytechnic; *m* 1974, Marilyn Stern; 1 da (Milena b 1986); *Style—* The Hon Stephen Bellow; 10 Shadwell Park Ct, Leeds LS17 8TS (☎ 0532 665208, work 0532 438994) F

BELLVILLE, Lady Lucinda Ruth; *née* Wallop; da of Viscount Lymington (d 1984), and sis of 10 Earl of Portsmouth; *b* 9 Feb 1956; *m* 1984, Patrick Anthony Ewen Bellville, s of late Anthony Seymour Bellville, late Lt Gren Guards, of Bembridge, Isle of Wight; 2 s (Blaise b 1985, Oscar b 1986); *Style—* Lady Lucinda Bellville; The White House, Bembridge, Isle of Wight

BELLWIN, Baron (Life Peer UK 1979); Irwin Norman Bellow; JP (Leeds 1969); s of Abraham and Leah Bellow; *b* 7 Feb 1923; *Educ* Leeds GS, Leeds Univ (LLB); *m* 1948, Doreen Barbara Saperia; 1 s, 2 da; *Career* alderman Leeds CC 1968-, ldr Leeds City Cncl 1975-79; Parly under-sec state DOE 1979-83, min of state for Local Govt 1983-84; bd memb: New Towns Cmmn 1985-; vice-pres: Int New Towns Assoc 1985-; non-exec dir: Taylor Woodrow plc 1985-; Sinclair Goldsmith plc 1987-, Mountleigh Bp plc 1987-; *Recreations* golf; *Clubs* Moor Allerton (Hon Pres); *Style—* The Rt Hon The Lord Bellwin, JP; Woodside Lodge, Ling Lane, Scarcroft, Leeds LS14 3HX (☎ 0532 892908)

BELLWOOD, Raymond Lee; TD (1950), DL (Tyne and Wear 1980); s of Norman Arthur Bellwood (d 1953); *b* 19 Dec 1913; *Educ* privately, Durham Univ; *m* 1939, Moyra Lindores, *née* Reid; 1 s, 2 da (and 1 decd); *Career* Maj RA (TA) ret, slr, ret; KStJ 1969, memb Chapter General Order of St John 1969-, chm St John Cncl for Northumbria 1963-85, cdr St John Ambulance Northumbria 1970-81; *Clubs* Northern Counties (Newcastle on Tyne); *Style—* Raymond Bellwood, Esq, TD, DL; Hawkwell, Stamfordham, Northumberland NE18 0QT (☎ 066 16 254)

BELMONT, Michael Jeremy Kindersley; s of Algernon Spencer Belmont (ka 1944), and Hon Margaret Marion, *née* Kindersley; er da of 1 Baron Kindersley, GBE; *b* 26 Feb 1930; *Educ* Eton; *m* 1953, Virginia Ann, da of Vernon George Tate, MC (d 1956); 2 s (Piers b 1954, Antony b 1956), 1 da (Lisa b 1959); *Career* 10 Royal Hussars (POW); ptnr Cazenove and Co, dir: LASMO, Ivory & Sime; *Recreations* shooting, golf, gardening; *Clubs* City of London, Pratt's, Bohemian, San Francisco; *Style—* M J K Belmont, Esq; 52 Warwick Square, London SW1; 12 Tokenhouse Yard, London EC2R 7AN (telex 886758/886798, fax 01 606 9205)

BELMORE, 8 Earl (I 1797); John Armar Lowry-Corry; also Baron Belmore (I 1781) and Viscount Belmore (I 1789); s of 7 Earl Belmore, JP, DL (d 1960) and Gloria Anthea Harker; *b* 4 Sept 1951; *Educ* Lancing; *m* 1984, Lady Mary Jane Meade, 2 da of 6 Earl of Clanwilliam; 1 s (Viscount Corry b 1985); *Heir* s, Viscount Corry, *qv*; *Career* farmer; *Recreations* art; *Clubs* Kildare Street Dublin; *Style—* The Rt Hon the Earl Belmore; Castle Coole, Enniskillen, N Ireland (☎ 0365 22463)

BELOFF, Hon Jeremy Benjamin; yr s of Baron Beloff (Life Peer), *qv*; *b* 1943; *m* 1973, Carol Macdonald; 2 s (Nicholas b 1975, Jonathan Max b 1986), 1 da (Catherine b 1978); *Style—* The Hon Jeremy Beloff; Glenwood, Templewood Lane, Farnham Common, Bucks SL2 3HW

BELOFF, Baron (Life Peer UK 1981), of Wolvercote, Co Oxfordshire; Sir Max Beloff; er s of Simon and Mary Beloff; *b* 2 July 1913; *Educ* St Paul's, Corpus Christi Coll Oxford (MA, DLitt); *m* 1938, Helen, da of Samuel Dobrin; 2 s; *Career* sits as Cons in House of Lords; Nuffield reader in comparative study of instns Oxford Univ 1946-56, Nuffield fell 1947-57; Gladstone prof of govt and public admin Oxford Univ 1957-74, fell All Souls Coll Oxford 1957-74 (emeritus fell 1980-), princ UC Buckingham 1974-79, supernumerary fell St Antony's Coll Oxford 1975-84; pres Conf for Ind Further Educn 1983-, memb Wilton Park Academic Cncl to 1983; Hon LLD: (Pittsburgh) USA, Manchester; Hon DCL (Bishop's) Canada, Hon DLitt: (Bowdoin) USA, Buckingham; Hon DrUniv Aix-Marseille II; FBA, FRHistS, FRSA; kt 1980; *Style—* The Rt Hon Lord Beloff; Flat 9, 22 Lewes Crescent, Brighton BN2 1GB (☎ 0273 688622)

BELOFF, Hon Michael Jacob; QC (1981); er s of Baron Beloff (Life Peer), *qv*; *b* 19 April 1942; *Educ* Eton, Oxford Univ (MA); *m* 1969, Judith Mary Arkinstall; 1 s, 1 da; *Career* barr Gray's Inn 1967, bencher 1988; former lectr Trinity Coll Oxford; legal corr: New Society, The Observer; rec Crown Ct 1985-; *Style—* The Hon Michael Beloff, QC; 11 Holland Park Mews, London W11

BELOFF, Nora (Mrs Clifford Makins); da of Simon Beloff (d 1964), and Marie Katzin Beloff; *b* 24 Jan 1919; *Educ* King Alfred Sch London, Lady Margaret Hall Oxford (BA); *m* 10 March 1977, Clifford George Makins; *Career* political intelligence dept FO (UK and Paris) 1940-46; Reuters News Agency (Paris Off) 1945-46, Paris corr The Economist 1946-50; editorial staff The Observer 1948-77: chief political corr 1964-76, corr (Paris, Washington, Moscow, Brussels, roving); *Books* The General Says No (1963, French Trans 1964), Transit of Britain (1973), Freedom Under Foot (1976), No Travel Like Russian (1979, USA edn Inside the Soviet Empire 1980), Tito's Flawed Legacy (1985, USA 1986, Italien trans 1987); *Recreations* walking, conversation; *Clubs* Chatham House, London Library; *Style—* Miss Nora Beloff; 11 Belsige Rd, London NW6 4RX (☎ 01 586 0378)

BELPER, 4 Baron (UK 1856); (Alexander) Ronald George Strutt; s of 3 Baron (d 1956) by 1 w, Hon Dame Eva Bruce, DBE, JP, da of 2 Baron Aberdare; bro of Lavinia, Duchess of Norfolk; *b* 23 April 1912; *Educ* Harrow; *m* 1940 (m dis 1949), Zara Sophie Kathleen Mary, da of Sir Harry Mainwaring, 5 Bt; 1 s; *Heir* s, Hon Richard Strutt; *Career* formerly Maj Coldstream Gds; *Style—* The Rt Hon The Lord Belper; Kingston Hall, Nottingham

BELSHAW, Kenneth John Thomas; s of John Everton Belshaw, and Lilian Elizabeth, *née* Stewart; *b* 14 May 1952; *Educ* Orangefield Sch for Boys Belfast; *m* 24 Nov 1979, Iris Elizabeth, da of Sydney Miller McKeown, of Shanliss, Stewartstown, co Tynone, N Ireland; 1 s (Stephen John Doran b 1987), 1 da (Maeve Elizabeth b 1983); *Career* recruitment consult; md: Grafton Recruitment Ltd (Ireland's largest employment agency), Grafton Recruitment UK Ltd 1982-; *Recreations* fine wines, reading; *Clubs* Kildare St and Univ (Dublin); Cranmore, 27 Eaton Sq, Dublin 6, Ireland (☎ Dublin 900323), Grafton Recruitment, 37-40 Upper Mound St, Dublin 2 (☎ Dublin 684388, fax 614897)

BELSKY, Franta; s of Josef Belsky (d 1963, economist), and Martha Grunbaum (d 1973); *b* 6 April 1921; *Educ* Acad of Fine Arts Prague, RCAL; *m* 1944, Margaret, da of Albert Edward Owen, DSO (d 1959); *Career* gunner France 1940, Normandy 1944; sculptor taught in art schs 1950-55; pres Soc of Portrait Sculptors 1963-68; govr St Martin's Sch of Art 1967-; work in Nat Portrait Gallery and collections in USA, Europe for numerous CC's, industl shipping and private cos and educn authorities; Paratroop Meml Prague 1947, statue of Cecil Rhodes Bulawayo 1953, Triga Knightsbridge 1958, Astronomer Herschel Meml Slough 1969; fountains: Euro Shell Centre; Jean Masson Davidson Award for distinction in Portrait Sculpture; portraits include: Queen Mother 1962, HM The Queen 1981, Prince Andrew 1963 and 1984, Prince Philip 1979, Prince William 1985; statue of Sir Winston Churchill for Churchill Meml and Library in US and bust in Churchill Archives Cambridge 1971, Harry S Truman, Lord Cottesloe, Queen Mother 80 Birthday Crown Coin; FRBS; *Books* illustrations and contributions to various books and journals; *Recreations* ski-ing, gardening, amateur archaeology; *Style—* Franta Belsky; 12 Pembroke Studios, London W8 6HX

BELSON, Dorrien Berkeley Euan; s of Frederic Charles Belson (d 1952); *b* 10 Feb 1917; *Educ* St Edmund's Sch Canterbury; *m* 1948, Mary, da of Charles Deane Cowper (d 1956); 3 s, 1 da; *Career* chm: IDV (Export) Ltd 1969-78, Justerini and Brooks 1971-78, chm Spastics Soc 1973-80; High Sheriff Bucks 1981; kt of Honour and Devotion SMOM 1977; *Recreations* fly fishing, wine, gardening, photography; *Clubs* Leander (chm 1981-83), Army and Navy; *Style—* Dorrien Belson, Esq; Rosehill, Henley-on-Thames, Oxon RG9 3EB (☎ 062 882 5404)

BELSON, Col Philip Charles Euan; TD (1947); s of Fredrick Charles Belson (d 1952), and Hilda Carlyon, *née* Euan-Smith (d 1954); blessed Thomas Belson - beatified in Rome 1987; 1815 Lt-Gen Sir C P Belson commanded the Gloucestershsire Regt at the Battle of Waterloo; *b* 15 Dec 1915; *Educ* Westminster, Staff Coll (psc); *m* 21 Dec 1945, Sheila Agnes, da of Edwin Chappel Keliher (d 1968); 1 s (Euan Charles b 1962), 3 da (Anne Julie b 1947, Adelle Carolyn b 1949, Nicola Mary b 1954); *Career* Col, RA 1939-44 and 1946-64, seconded Parachute Regt 1944-45; served BEF France 1939-40, UK instr in gunnery (Maj) 1941-43, Capt Parachute Regt Ardennes 1944-45, Maj Rhine Crossing 1945, Maj RA Egypt 1948-49, BAOR 1952-53, M East Bahrain 1953-55, Lt-Col Liaison Offr to US Army 1957-60, Lt-Col (Hon Col) War Office 1962-64 (ret); dir R and M Management Conslts Ltd 1965-80, mangr Bd Servs W H Smith (Hldgs) Ltd 1965-80; *Recreations* sailing, skiing; *Clubs* Royal Lymington YC, Royal Artillery YC; *Style—* Col Philip Belson, TD; Old Bank House, Beaulieu, Hampshire SO42 7YA (☎ 0590 612141)

BELSTEAD, 2 Baron (UK 1938); Sir John Julian Ganzoni; 2 Bt (UK 1929), PC (1982), JP (Ipswich), DL (Suffolk 1979); s of 1 Baron Belstead, JP, DL (d 1958), sometime MP Ipswich and PPS to postmaster-gen 1924; *b* 30 Sept 1932; *Educ* Eton, Christ Church Coll Oxford; *Career* parly sec: DES 1970-73, NI 1973-74, Home Off 1979-82 (responsibility for broadcasting); min of state: FCO 1982-83, MAFF 1983-87; Environment Countryside and Water DOE 1987-; Lord Privy Seal and Ldr of House of Lords 1988-; chm Governing Bodies Assoc 1974-79; *Clubs* MCC, All England Lawn Tennis and Croquet (Wimbledon); *Style—* The Rt Hon The Lord Belstead, PC, JP, DL; House of Lords, London SW1A 0PW 01 219 3000

BELTON, Leslie Frederick; DFC (1944); s of Ernest Joseph George Belton (d 1943) of Streetly, Sutton Coldfield, and Gertrude Ann *née* Allsopp (d 1970); *b* 14 Sept 1912; *Educ* King Edward VI Sch Birmingham, Coll of Art and Crafts Birmingham (ATD); *m* 28 Dec 1939, Helen Grace, da of Charles Rodgers, OBE (d 1946), of Watford; 1 s (John), 1 da (Sally); *Career* RAF U/T pilot RAFVR 1940, cmmnd 1941; Flying Instr: RAF Coll Cranwell 1941, RAF Brize Norton heavy gliders 1942; Bomber Cmd 1943, 149 East India Sqdn 1944, completed tour of ops 1944; p/t instr Coll of Art Birmingham 1934-37; teacher of arts and craft: the GS Rye Sussex 1937-39, The GS Adwick-le-Street 1939-40; asst Sch of Art Winchester 1946-51, teacher trg dept Coll of Art Bournemouth 1951-54, head Sch of Art Swindon 1954; one man annual exhibition of pastels and water colours Bembridge and Henley 1977-82fndr Basingstoke Art Club 1948 (past pres, vice pres, hon fndr memb, fell of the club), memb Reading Guild of Artists;; *Recreations* caravanning, swimming, gardening; *Style—* Leslie Belton, Esq, DFC; 132 Westwood Rd, Tilehurst, Reading, Berks RG3 6LL (☎ 0734 425867)

BELTRAMI, Joseph; s of Egidio Beltrami (d 1971), and Isabel *née* Battison; *b* 15 May 1932; *Educ* St Aloysius Coll Glasgow, Glasgow Univ (BL); *m* 18 Jan 1958, Brigid D, da of Edward Fallon; 3 s (Edwin Joseph b 23 Sept 1962, Adrian Joseph b 8 Nov 1964, Jason Joseph b 23 Sept 1967); *Career* Intelligence Corps 1954-56: attached to Br Mil Delegation to European Defence Community at Br Embassy Paris, detatchment Cdr Field Security SW Dist Taunton; admitted slr 1956, ptnr Beltrami & Co (slr in cases of only two Royal pardons in Scotland this century: Maurice Swanson 1975, Patrick Meehan 1976); formerly: pres Bothwell Bowling Club, mangr and coach Bothwell AFC; memb Scottish Law Soc; *Books* The Defender (1980), Glasgow - A Celebration (contrib 1984), Tales of the Suspected (1988), The Importance of Being Innocent (1989); *Style—* Joseph Beltrami, Esq; Blenid, Bothwell, Scotland (☎ 0698 852374); 54

West Nile St, Glasgow (☎ 041 221 0981)

BEMROSE, Esmond Clive; OBE (1971), DL (Derbyshire); s of late Dr Henry Howe Bemrose, ScD, JP, of Derby; *b* 6 July 1902; *Educ* Abbotsholme Sch Derbyshire, Clare Coll Cambridge; *m* 1946, Enid Marjorie, da of Maj Ian Ainslie, of Edinburgh; 1 s, 3 da (1 da decd); *Career* intelligence offr RAF 1940-45; dir Bemrose and Sons Ltd, ret 1967; chm: St Christophers Railway Orphanage 1947-65, Abbotsholme Sch Exec 1947-74; past pres Derby and Derbyshire C of C, Co Cmmr Scouts 1950-69, pres Duke of Edinburgh Award Scheme 1969-79; High Sheriff Derbyshire 1967; *Recreations* walking, music, freemasonry, literature; *Style—* E Clive Bemrose, Esq, OBE; Wychelm, 27 Broadway, Duffield, Derby DE6 4BT

BEMROSE, William Alan Wright (Alan); s of Col William Lloyd Bemrose, OBE (1980), of Umtali, Zimbabwe, and Lucy Mabel Lewis (d 1982); *b* 13 June 1929; *Educ* Repton; *m* 1, 21 July 1952 (m dis 1984), (Elizabeth) Anne, da of John William Rose (d 1955), of Duffield; 1 da (Sarah b 15 July 1959); m 2, 31 Aug 1985, Elizabeth (Nibby), da of Reginald William Melling, of Downderry, Cornwall; *Career* Sherwood Foresters (Notts & Derby), RCS, Selous Scouts Rhodesia; chief exec Br Historic Bldgs Tst 1983-, Historic Bldgs & Monuments Cmmn (HBMC): princ conslt bldgs at risk 1986-, memb advsy ctees Bldgs and Areas 1984-; Derbyshire CC: memb 1964-77, alderman 1967, chm fin 1967-74, ldr CC 1968-74, vice-chm 1977-79; tstee: Chatsworth House Tst 1982-, Barlarton Hall Tst 1980-; govr Sir John Port's Charity (Repton Sch) 1965-, fndr chm Derbyshire Historic Tst 1974-, memb Historic Bldgs Cncl for England 1979-84; Freeman and Liveryman Worshipful Co of Stationers and Newspaper Makers 1952, memb Ct of Assts 1979-87; FRSA 1985; *Recreations* hunting, equestrian sports; *Style—* Alan Bemrose, Esq; Tinkersley Farm, Great Rowsley, Derbyshire DE4 2NJ (☎ 0629 824 905, fax 0629 825385)

BENCE, John Douglas; *b* 18 June 1932; *Educ* King Edward Sch Birmingham; *m* Jennifer Patricia; 5 children; *Career* md and chief exec offr MacMillan Smurfit SCA Ltd 1983-; dir: Scotpack Ltd, Pakfast Ltd, Touring Club of GB and I Ltd, Hygrade Corrugated Cases Ltd, Inst of Packaging Ltd, The Caravan Club, MacMillan Bathurst Inc, MacMillan Bloedel Containers Hldgs Ltd, UK Corrugated Ltd, UK Corrugated (North West) Ltd, UK Corrugated (Southern) Ltd, UK Corrugated (Sheet Sales) Ltd, UK Corrugated (Preprint) Ltd, UK Corrugated (Properties) Ltd, UK Corrugated (1983) Ltd, UK Corrugated (1984) Ltd, Smurfit Corrugated Hldgs Ltd, UKC Lairds Ltd, The Central Box Co Ltd; hon tres The Caravan Club; *Recreations* sailing, caravanning; *Clubs* Royal Thames Yacht, Royal Lymington Yacht; *Style—* John Bence, Esq; The Old Vicarage, Cholesbury, nr Tring, Herts (☎ 024 029 695); MacMillan Smurfit SCA Ltd, 24-30 King St, Watford, Herts WD1 8BP (☎ 0923 42306, telex 922375)

BENCE, Hon Mrs (Patricia Mary); *née* Dent; da of Baroness Furnivall (d 1968, herself da of 14 Baron Petre and co-heir with Lord Mowbray, Segrave and Stourton to the Baronies of Strange de Blackmere, Talbot, Howard, and others; the Barony of Furnivall, abeyant since the d in 1777 of the 9 Duke of Norfolk who was also 18 Baron Furnivall, was called out in her favour by Letters Patent 1913) and co-heiress to that Barony of Furnivall, abeyant since 1968; *b* 4 April 1935; *Educ* Mayfield Sussex; *m* 1, 1956 (m dis 1963), Capt Thomas Hornsby (d 1967); 1 s (Francis Walton Petre b 1958), 1 da (Clare Mary Petre b 1957); m 2, 1970, Roger Thomas John Bence; 1 s (Richard William Petre b 1976), 1 da (Katharine Rosamond Petre b 1971); *Style—* The Hon Mrs Bence; Trotwood, 11 Gresham Rd, Limpsfield, Oxted, Surrey (☎ 088 33 714062)

BENCE-TROWER, Nicholas Alexander; s of Capt Peter Alexander Bence-Trower, DL, RN, of West Meon, Hants, and Sheena Margaret, *née* Grant; *b* 21 Feb 1957; *Educ* Winchester; *Career* J Henry Schroder Wagg & Co Ltd 1977-; Freeman City of London 1978, Liveryman Worshipful Co of Drapers 1982; *Recreations* golf, skiing, flying, cinema and theatre; *Style—* Nicholas Bence-Trower, Esq; 47 Sloane Gardens, London SW1W 8ED (☎ 01 730 7277); J Henry Schroder Wagg & Co Ltd, 120 Cheapside, London EC2V 6DS (☎ 01 382 6000, fax 01 382 3950, telex 8850529)

BENCE-TROWER, Capt Peter Alexander; DL (Hants 1985); s of Richard Alexander Bence-Trower, of Medmenham, Bucks, and Violet Elizabeth Mabel, *née* Weatherall; *b* 10 Jan 1925; *Educ* Winchester; *m* 9 June 1951, Sheena Margaret, da of Lewis Russell Harley Grant (d 1945), of Langside, Peebles; 2 s (Nicholas Alexander b 21 Feb 1957, Mark Grant b 16 May 1960), 2 da (Anna Marguerite b 22 Sept 1961, Caroline Jane b 30 April 1965); *Career* Midshipman HMS Glasgow and HMS Malaya 1944, HMS King George V 1945, Sub Lt i/c HMS Tahay, minesweepers Iceland and Butt of Lewis 1945-47, Lt HMS Liverpool 1947, Flag Lt to 1 Sea Lord (Lord Fraser of N Cape) 1950-51, qualified as navigation specialist HMS Actaeon (S Africa and S America) 1952-54, HMS Vanguard 1954, Lt Cdr 1955, HMS Battleaxe 1956, Army Staff Coll Camberley 1957, HMS Newfoundland 1958-60, HMY Britannia 1960, i/c HMS Carron 1961, Cdr i/c HMS Surprise 1962-64, SO ops to C in C Portsmouth 1964-66, i/c HMS Ghurkha 1966, Capt i/c HMS Protector 1967, naval attaché HM Embassy Paris 1969-71, RCDS 1971, Capt of the Fleet 1972, ret 1973; dir: The Glenlivet Whiskey Co 1958-64, JCS Computor Bureau 1976-80; govr Queen Mary's Coll 1980-87, tstee Wessex Med Sch Tst 1982-88, pres Hants branch Nat Deaf Child Soc; High Sheriff of Hampshire 1983; Freeman City of London 1946, Past Master Worshipful Co of Drapers 1984; *Recreations* fishing, golf, travel, sea; *Clubs* Whites, Royal Yacht Sqdn, Army and Navy; *Style—* Capt Peter Bence-Trower, DL, RN; West Meon House, West Meon, Hampshire GU32 1JG; Glendalloch, Glenlivet, Banffshire (☎ 073 086 278)

BENDALL, David Vere; CMG (1946), MBE (1945); s of John Manley Bendall (d 1970); *b* 27 Feb 1920; *Educ* Winchester, King's Coll Cambridge (BA); *m* 1941, Eve Stephanie Merrilees, da of Charles Galpin (d 1928), of Colombo; 1 da; *Career* Grenadier Guards 1941-46; HM Dip Serv 1946-71, asst undersec of state 1969-71; merchant banker 1971-85; chm: Morgan Grenfell Int 1982-86, Morgan Grenfell Italy, Banque Morgan Grenfell en Suisse, Banca Nazionale de Lavoro Investment Bank plc 1986-, Br Red Cross Soc 1981-85; *Recreations* tennis, shooting; *Clubs* Boodle's; *Style—* David Bendall, Esq, CMG, MBE; 3 Eaton Terrace Mews, London SW1 (☎ 01 730 4229); Ashbocking Hall, Ipswich, Suffolk (☎ 047 339 262)

BENDALL, Vivian Walter Hough; MP (Cons Ilford North 1978-); s of Cecil Aubrey Bendall (d 1963), and Olive Alvina, *née* Hough (d 1980); *b* 14 Dec 1938; *Educ* Broad Green Coll Croydon; *m* 1969, Ann Rosalind, da of Henry Jarvis; *Career* surveyor and valuer; MP (C) Redbridge 1978-1983, Cons backbench Ctee positions held: former vice-chm Employment, former sec Foreign and Cwlth Affairs, former vice-chm Transport; *Recreations* cricket, golf; *Clubs* Carlton, Essex CC; *Style—* Vivian Bendall, Esq, MP; 25 Brighton Rd, Croydon, Surrey

BENDIX, Michael; OBE (1982), DL (Essex 1977); s of Carl Bendix (d 1944), and Daisy, da of late Charles Hancox, who m 2, Col Lionel Neame and m 3, (as his 2 w), 2 Viscount Allenby; *b* 9 Feb 1925; *Educ* Eton, Magdalene Coll Cambridge; *m* 1951, Ingrid, da of Ivan de Rehren (d 1966), of Brussels; 1 s, 1 da; *Career* served Coldstream Gds 1942-47, Capt NW Europe; dir Barclays Bank UK 1973-82, sr dir Barclays Bank Chelmsford dist 1968-82; JP 1964-80; chm Norfolk Agric Wages Ctee 1986-, pres N Norfolk Area St John Ambulance 1986-; memb: regnl ctee Nat Tst E Anglia 1986-, ctee Norfolk Army Benevolent Fund 1988-; FIOB, Fell Linnaean Soc; OStJ 1966, CStJ 1989; *Recreations* shooting, botany, ornithology, music; *Style—* Michael Bendix, Esq, OBE, DL; Swan Lodge Cottage, Cley Road, Holt, Norfolk NR25 7EA (☎ 0263 740637)

BENEY, Cedric Ivor; s of Frederick William Beney, CBE, QC (d 1986), and Irene Constance, *née* Ward-Meyer, the concert pianist; *b* 12 July 1917; *Educ* Mill Hill Sch, Reading Univ;; *m* 1, 1968, Mercia Silverthorne (d 1976); m 2, 1977, Suzanne Joselyn Frances Neville; 1 step da (Christine b 1953); *Career* WW II Lance Corpl RASC BEF 1929-41 (invalided out); worked in book publishing 1937-39, farmer 1948-50, estate mangr 1950-68, private proprietor 1968-77; *Recreations* gardening, music, reading, opera; *Style—* Cedric I Beney, Esq; Mandalay, 3 Horns Park, Bishopsteignton, Teignmouth, S Devon TQ14 9RP

BENGER, Patrick; s of Harold Albert Benger (d 1978), of Worcester, and Mildred Nancy, *née* Freeman (d 1988); *b* 29 Sept 1939; *Educ* Farnborough GS, Royal Aircraft Establishment Tech Coll; *m* 20 Oct 1966, Frances Ann, da of Owen Alfred Francis Finch (d 1982); 1 da (Georgina Anne b 1968); *Career* asst experimental offr RAE Farnborough, seconded as tech offr E African Meteorological Dept Tanganyika 1962-64, conslt meteorologist to offshore indust: M East 1965-71, N Sea and Europe 1972-; meteorologist during installation of approx 20 major UK offshore structures; dir Seaplace Ltd 1985-; scientific advsr Hampshire County Emergency Planning Organisation; FRMets author of technical papers and articles on meteorological aspects of offshore installation techniques; *Recreations* shooting, antique collecting; *Style—* Patrick Benger, Esq; c/o National Westminster Bank plc, 39 The Borough, Farnham GU9 7NR

BENHAM, David Hamilton; s of George Frederick Augustus Benham (d 1980), and Pamela Ruth, *née* Kellond; *b* 7 Jan 1942; *Educ* Public Sch Univ (BA); *m* 14 Oct 1968, Ann Pyta, da of Sqdn Ldr L L Thomas (d 1975); 1 s (Nicholas Hamilton b 18 March 1971), 1 da (Fiona-Jane Teresa b 1 Oct 1973); *Career* admitted slr 1970, sr litigation ptnr Bischoff and Co; Freeman City of Lonodn 1980, Liveryman City Livery Co 1980; memb Law Soc; *Recreations* serious squash, serious father, collecting antiques; *Clubs* Lambs, Colets; *Style—* David Benham, Esq; Bischoff and Co, Epworth House, 25 City Rd, London EC1 (☎ 01 628 4222, fax 01 638 3345, telex 885062)

BENHAM, Keith Peter; s of Peter Gray Benham, of Wrays, Hookwood, Horley, SY, and Susan Phoebe, *née* Brown; *b* 10 Mar 1943; *Educ* Eagle House, Sandhurst, Marlborough Sch; *m* 26 Nov 1969, Memlyn Anne, da of Maj Philip Norman Holbrook, of Pond House, Well, Long Sutton, Herts; 3 da (Samantha b 1972, Lucy b 1974, Henrietta b 1978); *Career* slr; ptnr Linklater & Paines 1973- (asst slr 1968-73, articled 1963); memb: City of London Law Soc 1963-, The law Soc 1963-; Freeman City of London 1968, memb City of London Slrs (memb law sub ctee 1976-85); *Recreations* gardening, sailing, skiing, tennis; *Clubs* City Law, Sea View Yacht; *Style—* Keith Benham, Esq; Linklater & Paines, Barrington House, 59/67 Gresham St, London EC2V 7JA (☎ 01 606 7080, fax 01 606 5113, telex 884349, 888167)

BENHAM, Peter Carr; MBE (Mil 1945), TD (1946); s of Gerald Carr Benham, MC, TD (d 1962); *b* 17 June 1917; *Educ* Uppingham; *m* 1940, Eileen Mary, *née* Adams; 1 s; *Career* Maj N Africa Field Artillery Normandy; slr 1947, coroner for Borough of Colchester 1958-74, chm Colchester Permanent Building Soc 1977-80; *Recreations* golf (represented Essex at golf, hockey and squash rackets); *Clubs* Colchester Garrison Officers, Frinton GC; *Style—* Peter Benham, Esq; 21 Queens Rd, Colchester, Essex (☎ 0206 72019)

BENJAMIN, George; s of William Benjamin, and Susan Benjamin, *née* Bendon; *b* 31 Jan 1960; *Educ* Westminster, Paris Conservatoire, King's Coll Cambridge (MA, MusB); *Career* composer, conductor, pianist; princ works incl: Ringed by the Flat Horizon 1980 (performed BBC Proms then over 50 times worldwide), A Mind of Winter for soprano and orch (Aldeburgh Festival) 1981, At First Light (cmmnd by London Sinfonietta) 1982, Three Studies for Solo piano 1982-85, Jubilation (written for London Schs Symphony Orch) 1985, Antara, (cmmnd by Pierre Boulez for 10th anniversary of Pompidou Centre Paris) 1987 (subject of BBC TV documentary); conductor of orchs in: UK, France, Italy, Germany, USA, Switzerland; awards incl: Lili Boulanger Award Boston 1985, Koussevitsky Int Record Award 1987, Grand Prix du disque Paris 1987; visiting prof composition RCM 1985-; *Style—* George Benjamin, Esq; C/o Faber Music, 3 Queen Square, London WC1N 3AU (☎ 01 278 2654)

BENJAMIN, John Circus; s of Bernard Benjamin, of 12a The Mount, Wembley Park, Middx, and Doris, *née* Mindel; *b* 15 Jan 1955; *Educ* John Lyon Sch Middx; *m* 27 June 1986, Patricia Adele Ruane, da of Sqdn-Ldr Michael Joseph Francis Burgess, of 193 Hale, Hale, Cheshire; *Career* Phillips Auctioneers: catalogues, sr cataloguer, mamgr 1976-, dir jewellery dept 1986-; memb Harrow Hill Tst Planning Sub-Ctee, regular lectr or history of jewellery; FGA 1976,; *Clubs* Lansdowne; *Style—* John Benjamin, Esq; 7 Blenheim St, London W1Y 0AS (☎ 01 499 1827, fax 01 629 8879, telex 298855 BLEN G)

BENJAMIN, (Isaac) Louis; s of Benjamin Benjamin, and Harriet, *née* Boekbinder; *b* 17 Oct 1922; *Educ* Highbury County Secondary Sch; *m* 23 May 1954, Vera Doreen, da of Thomas Frederick Ketteman; 2 da (Reica (Mrs Gray) b 19 June 1955, Diane b 28 March 1960); *Career* serv WWII with RAC in India, Burma and Singapore; joined Moss Empires Ltd 1937; 2 asst mangr London Palladium 1945; asst mangr/box office mangr Victoria Palace 1948; gen mangr Winter Gardens, Morecmbe; sales controller Pye Records 1959, gen mangr 1962, md 1963, chm 1975-80; jt md ATV Corpn 1975-80; md Stoll Moss Theatres Ltd 1980-81, chief exec 1982-85, pres 1985-; pres British Music Hall Soc; vice-pres Entertainment Artistes Benevolent Fund 1971-82, life govr 1982-; presenter of Royal Variety Performance 1979-85; memb exec ctee Variety Club of Great Britain; Companion of Grand Order of Water Rats; hon memb NSPCC; *Style—* Louis Benjamin Esq; Cranbourn Mansions, Cranbourn Street, London WC2 (☎ 01 437 2274, fax 01 434 1217)

BENJAMIN, Sidney; *b* 6 June 1928; *Educ* Bancroft Sch Essex, Cambridge Univ (MA); *m* 1951, Golda Julia, *née* Blinder; 1 s, 1 da; *Career* Serv RAF 1946-49; Prudential Assurance Co 1952-59, Ferranti Computers 1959-62, ptnr Bacon & Woodrow 1964- (joined 1962), Inst of Actuaries: memb Cncl 1961-85, chm res ctee 1964-87; visiting prof actuarial science The City Univ; memb Cncl Royal Statistical Soc 1982-84; awarded Inst of Actuaries Gold Medal 1985; FIA, FIS, FBCS, ASA; *Recreations* painting, sketching; *Clubs* Actuaries, Gallio (past chm); *Style—* Mr Sidney Benjamin; Bacon & Woodrow, Empire House, St Martin's-le-Grand, London EC1A 4ED (☎ 01 600 2747, fax 01 726 6519, telex 8953206 BWLON G)

BENN, Hon David Julian Wedgwood; s of 1 Viscount Stansgate, DSO, DFC, PC (d 1960); bro of Rt Hon Tony Benn; *b* 28 Dec 1928; *Educ* Balliol Oxford; *m* 1959, June Mary, da of late Ernest Charles Barraclough; 1 s, 1 da; *Style—* The Hon David Benn; 4 Liskeard Gdns, Blackheath, SE3 (☎ 01 858 0912); Stansgate Cottage, nr Steeple, Southminster, Essex

BENN, (Edward) Glanvill; s of Sir Ernest Benn, CBE, (d 1954), and Gwendolen Dorothy, *née* Andrews, JP; *b* 31 Dec 1905; *Educ* Harrow, Clare Coll Cambridge; *m* 4 Jun 1931, (Beatrice) Catherine, MBE, da of Claude Newbald (d 1943) of Wallington, Surrey; 1 s (James b 1944, 1 da (Elizabeth b 1936); *Career* MOI 1939, 2 Lt E Surrey Regt 1940, Adj 11 Bn E Surrey Regt 1941-42, Staff Coll Camberley 1943, Bde Maj 138 Brigade Italy 1944, GSO2 Land Forces Adriatic 1945 (despatches); office boy NY Times 1925; dir: Ernest Benn Ltd publishers 1928-75, Benn Bros Ltd publishers 1928-75 (chm 1945-75), Exchange Telegraph Co Ltd 1961-72 (chm 1969-72); pres Periodical Publishers Assoc 1976-77, Appeals chm Newspaper Press Fund 1971, hon tres Cwlth Press Union 1967-77 (hon life memb 1975), cncl memb Nat Advertising Benevolent Soc 1937-61, (chm Fin Ctee 1950-60, tstee 1951-71), chm Advertising Advsy Ctee ITA 1959-63; Liveryman Worshipful Co of Stationers ans Newspaper Makers 1935 (Master 1977-78); *Clubs* Reform, Aldeburgh Golf; *Style—* Glanvill Benn, Esq; Crescent Cottage, Aldeburgh, Suffolk IP15 5HW; Benn Bros plc, Sovereign Way, Tonbridge, Kent

BENN, Hilary James Wedgwood; s of Rt Hon Tony Benn, PC (disclaimed Viscountcy of Stansgate for life 1963); *b* 26 Nov 1953; *Educ* Holland Park Sch; *m* Rosalind (d 1979); *Career* Labour memb Ealing Cncl, researcher with ASTMS, chm Acton Labour Party; *Style—* Hilary Benn, Esq; 19 Rothchild Rd, Acton Green, London W4

BENN, Dr John Meriton; CB (1969); s of Ernest Benn (d 1935), of Burnley, and Emily Louise, *née* Hey (d 1957); *b* 16 July 1908; *Educ* Burnley GS, Christ's Coll Cambridge (BA, MA); *m* 1933, Valentine Rosemary, da of William Seward (d 1932), of Hanwell, Middlesex; 2 da (Susan, Diana); *Career* inspr of schs Miny of Educn for NI 1935-44 (princ 1944-51, asst sec 1951-64, permanent sec 1964-69), cmmr for complaints for NI 1969-73; parly cmmnr for admin for NI 1972-73, ret; chm: NI Civil Serv Appeals Bd 1974-78, NI Schs Examinations Cncl 1974-81; memb Senate Queen's Univ of Belfast 1973-86 (pro-chllr 1979-86); *Style—* Dr John Benn, CB; 7 Tudor Oaks, Holywood, Co Down BT18 0PA (☎ 02317 2817)

BENN, Sir (James) Jonathan; 4 Bt (UK 1914), of The Old Knoll, Metropolitan Borough of Lewisham; s of Sir John Andrews Benn, 3 Bt (d 1984), and Hon Ursula Lady Benn, da of 1 Baron Hankey, *qv*; *b* 27 July 1933; *Educ* Harrow, Clare Coll Cambridge; *m* 2 July 1960, Jennifer Mary, eld da of Dr Wilfred Vivian Howells, OBE (d 1987), of The Ferns, Clun, Shropshire; 1 s, 1 da (Juliet b 1966); *Heir* s, Robert Ernest Benn, *qv*; *Career* dir Reedpack Ltd, chm and chief exec Reed Paper and Bd (UK) Ltd, chm J & J Maybank Ltd; pres Br Paper and Bd Industries Federation 1985-87; *Style—* Sir Jonathan Benn, Bt; Fielden Lodge, Tonbridge Road, Ightham, nr Sevenoaks, Kent TN15 9AN

BENN, Joshua William Wedgwood; s of Rt Hon Tony Benn, PC (disclaimed Viscountcy of Stansgate for life 1963); *b* 9 May 1958; *Educ* Holland Park Sch; *Style—* Joshua Benn, Esq

BENN, Melissa Anne Wedgwood; da of Rt Hon Tony Benn, PC (disclaimed Viscountcy of Stansgate for life 1963); *b* 20 Feb 1957; *Educ* Holland Pk Sch; *Style—* Miss Melissa Benn

BENN, Capt Sir Patrick Ion Hamilton; 2 Bt (UK 1920); s of late Col Ion Bridges Hamilton Benn, s of 1 Bt; suc gf, Capt Sir (Ion) Hamilton Benn, 1 Bt, CB, DSO, TD, RNVR, 1961; *b* 26 Feb 1922; *Educ* Rugby; *m* 1959, Edel J/orgine, da of late Col W S J/obach, formerly Roy Norwegian Army; *Heir* none; *Career* Capt Reserve of Offrs late Duke of Cornwall's LI, Maj Norfolk Army Cadet Force; tstee and govr E Anglian Tstee Savings Bank, cmmr Gt Yarmouth Port and Haven; *Style—* Capt Sir Patrick Benn, Bt; Rollesby Hall, nr Gt Yarmouth, Norfolk

BENN, Robert Ernest; s and h of Sir Jonathan Benn, 4 Bt, and Jennifer Mary, da of Dr Wilfred Vivian Howells, OBE; *b* 17 Oct 1963; *Educ* Judd Sch, Tonbridge, Corpus Christi Coll Cambridge (MA); *m* 1985, Sheila Margaret, 2 da of Dr Alastair Macleod Blain, of Braco Lodge, Elgin, Moray; *Recreations* music, walking, photography; *Style—* Robert Benn, Esq; 6, Rangers Square, Hyde Vale, Greenwich SE10 8HR (☎ 01 691 0120)

BENN, Stephen Michael Wedgwood; s of Rt Hon Tony Benn PC, MP and h to Viscountcy of Stansgate, which was disclaimed by his f for life 1963; *b* 21 August 1951; *Educ* Holland Park Sch, Keele Univ; *Career* memb: Inner London Educn Authority, General Purposes Ctee 1986-; *Books* The White House Staff (1984), Politics and International Relations (1979); *Style—* Stephen Benn, Esq

BENN, Rt Hon Tony (Anthony) Neil Wedgwood; PC (1964), MP (Lab) Chesterfield 1984-; s of 1 Viscount Stansgate, DSO, DFC, PC (d 1960); suc as 2 Viscount 1960, but made it known that he did not wish to claim the Viscountcy; disclaimed his peerage for life 31 July 1963, having unsuccessfully attempted to renounce his right of succession 1955 and 1960; *b* 3 April 1925; *Educ* Westminster, New Coll Oxford; *m* 1949, Caroline Middleton, da of late James Milton De Camp, of Cincinnati, USA; 3 s, 1 da; *Career* WWII RAFVR 1943-45, RNVR 1945-46; joined Lab Pty 1943, MP (Lab) Bristol SE 1950-60 and 1963-83; memb nat exec ctee Lab Pty 1959-60 and 1962 (chm 1971-72), candidate for leadership Lab Pty 1976 and for dep leadership 1971 and 1981; Postmaster-Gen 1964-66, min of Technol 1966-70 (also temporarily held portfolios Aviation 1967 and Power 1969), oppn spokesman Trade and Indust 1970-74, sec of state for Indust and min Posts and Telecommunications 1974-75, sec of State for Energy 1975-79; pres EEC Cncl of Energy Mins 1977, chm Campaign Gp 1987-; chm Lab Home Policy Ctee until 1982; memb until 1982: Labour-TUC Liaison Ctee, Women's Ctee, Tribune Gp; *Books* The Privy Cncl as a Second Chamber (1957), The Regeneration of Britain (1964), The New Policies (1970), Speeches (1974), Arguments for Socialism (1979), Arguments for Democracy (1981), Writings on the Wall: a radical and socialist anthology 1215-1984 (ed 1984), Out of the Wilderness Diaries 1963-67 (1987), Fighting Back: speaking out for Socialism in the Eighties (1988); *Style—* The Rt Hon Tony Benn; House of Commons, London SW1A 0AA

BENN, Hon Lady - Hon Ursula Helen Alers; *née* Hankey; o da of 1 Baron Hankey, GCB, GCMG, GCVO, PC (d 1963); *b* 5 Feb 1909; *Educ* Priors Field Godalming; *m* 1929, Sir John Benn, 3 Bt (d 1984); 2 s (Sir Jonathan Benn, Bt, Timothy John Benn, *qqv*), 3 da; *Career* teacher of The Alexander Technique; *Style—* The Hon Lady Benn; High Field, Limpsfield, Oxted, Surrey

BENNARD, Hon Mrs (Edith Ellen); *née* Quibell; JP (Parts of Lindsay Lincs); da of 1 and last Baron Quibell (d 1962); *b* 1904; *m* 1954, Eric Bennard Cuthbert, who took name of Bennard by deed poll 1962, s of G E Cuthbert (d 1960), of Scawby, Lincs; *Career* dir Quibell and Hardy Ltd; pres RSPCA, Scunthorpe; Mayoress of Scunthorpe 1953-54; *Style—* The Hon Mrs Bennard, JP; Sweeting Thorns, Holme Lane, Raventhorpe, Scunthorpe, S Humberside

BENNELL, Capt Alan Charles; RD (1969) and clasp (1979); s of Harold Charles Bennell (d 1972), and Ruby Mary, *née* White (d 1954); *b* 26 Sept 1931; *Educ* Wallington Co GS, HMS Conway Nautical Coll Bangor N Wales; *m* 20 Sept 1958, Sheila Margaret, da of Arthur Thomas Hill (d 1970); 1 s (Vaughn b 1967, k 1979), 1 da (Carin b 1964); *Career* Cadet HMS Conway 1946-48, sub Lt RNR 1955 (Lt 1957, Lt-Cdr 1965, Cdr 1969, Capt 1977); apprentice 4 offr Shell tankers 1948-51 (2 mates certificate 1951), 3 to chief offr Cayzer Irvine and Co 1951-57 (mates certificate 1954, masters foreign going certificate 1957); navigation offr to staff capt 1957-82: Scythia, Carinthia, Queen Elizabeth, Queen Mary, Mauretania, Caronia, Carmania, Franconia, Cunard Adventurer, Queen Elizabeth 2, Cunard Conquest, Cunard Princess, Cunard Countess; capt Cunard Princess 1982 (General Mangr 1982-87), master and asst general mangr Queen Elizabeth 2 1987; FBIM 1982; *Recreations* yachting, sport, fishing, walking; *Style—* Capt Alan Bennell, RD; 766842); Cunard Line Ltd, South Western House, Canute Rd, Southampton SO9 1ZA (☎ 0703 229933, fax 0703 225843, telex 477577)

BENNER, Patrick; CB (1975); s of Henry Grey Benner (d 1971), of Ipswich, and Gwendolen May, *née* Freeman (d 1974); *b* 26 May 1923; *Educ* Ipswich Sch, Univ Coll Oxford (BA); *m* 1952, Joan Christabel, da of John Godfrey Beresford Draper (d 1972); 2 da (Lucy, Mary); *Career* admin civil servant 1949-84; dep sec: Cabinet Off 1972-76, DHSS 1976-84; *Style—* Patrick Benner, Esq, CB; 44 Ormond Cres, Hampton, Middlesex TW12 2TH (☎ 01 979 1099)

BENNER, Peter Charles (Priddis); s of Charles William Benner (d 1978), of Balcombe, Sussex, and Joyce, *née* Oldroyd (d 1976); *b* 1 June 1937; *Educ* Ardingly Coll Sussex, Downing Coll Cambridge (BA, MA); *m* 16 Jan 1965, Elizabeth Anne, da of Ronald Wilkinson Kenyon, of Horsham, W Sussex; 2 da (Tracy Caroline Alice b 10 Dec 1965, Lucinda Diana Kate b 17 May 1969); *Career* slr, Notary Public, sr ptnr Charles Benner & Son 1976-86, ptnr Houseman Rohan & Benner 1986-; NP 1979, chm Sussex Co Young Cons 1964-65, tres SE Area Young Cons 1965-66, parish cllr Slaugham W Sussex, chm Mid Sussex Gp of Slrs 1983-84, memb Law Soc 1963; *Recreations* Sussex local History, old cars, dog walking; *Clubs* Utd Oxford and Cambridge Univ; *Style—* Peter Benner, Esq; Pear Trees, Warninglid, Haywards Heath, W Sussex RH17 5TY (☎ 0444 85 251); Aberdeen Ho, Haywards Heath, W Sussex RH16 4NG (☎ 0444 414 081, fax 0444 457 384, telex 877555 LAWYER G)

BENNET, Lady Alexandra Katherine; da of 9 Earl of Tankerville (d 1980); *b* 5 May 1955; *Style—* Lady Alexandra Bennet

BENNET, Rev the Hon George Arthur Grey; s of 8 Earl of Tankerville (d 1971), and hp of n, 10 Earl of Tankerville; *b* 12 Mar 1925; *Educ* Radley, Corpus Christi Coll Cambridge, Clifton Theol Coll; *m* 1957, Hazel (Jane) Glyddon, da of late Ernest W G Judson, of Bishopswood, Chard, Somerset; 2 s, 1 da; *Career* sr physics master Clifton Coll; ordained 1969, vicar Shaston Team Ministry 1973-80, rector Redenhall Harleston Wortwell and Needham 1980-; *Books* Electricity and Modern Physics (1965); with T B Akrill and C J Millar: Physics (1979), Practice in Physics (1979); *Style—* Rev the Hon George Bennet; The Rectory, Harleston, Norfolk (☎ 0379 852068)

BENNET, Hon Ian; s of 8 Earl of Tankerville (d 1971), and his 2 w, Violet, *qv*; *b* 16 April 1935; *Educ* Radley, CCC Cambridge (MA Agric); *Career* Lt RNR; farmer and landagent; mangr Chillingham Estates 1961-83; chm Northumbria Region Historic Houses Assoc 1982-85, vice-chm Duke's Sch Alnwick (govr 1983-), memb: (Cons) Berwick-upon-Tweed Borough Cncl 1983-, River Tweed Cmmn 1983-, Governing Cncl, Chillingham Wild Cattle Assoc 1967-; *Recreations* shooting, forestry; *Style—* The Hon Ian Bennet; Estate House, Chillingham, Alnwick, Northumberland NE66 5NJ (☎ 066 85 213)

BENNETT, (Frederick Onslow) Alexander Godwyn; TD; s of Alfred Bennett, of Sulhamstead, Berks, and Marjorie Muir Bremner; *b* 21 Dec 1913; *Educ* Winchester, Trinity Coll Cambridge; *m* 18 Nov 1942, Rosemary, er da of Sir Malcolm Perks, 2 Bt; 1 s, 4 da; *Career* serv WWII (despatches); joined Whitbread and Co 1935; chm: Whitbread and Co Ltd 1972-77, Whitbread Investmt Co Ltd 1977-88; master Brewers Co 1965, chm Brewers Soc 1970-72; pres Kent CCC 1983; *Clubs* MCC; *Style—* Alexander Bennett, Esq, TD; Grove House, Selling, Faversham, Kent (☎ 0227 752250)

BENNETT, Andrew Francis; MP (Lab) Denton and Reddish 1983-; *b* 9 Mar 1939; *Educ* Birmingham Univ; *m* 2 s, 1 da; *Career* teacher, NUT, cllr Oldham Boro 1964-74, contested (Lab) Knutsford 1970, MP (Lab) Stockport North Feb 1974-1983, memb Select Ctees: (Jt S Ctee) Statutory Instruments, (former S Ctee) Violence in the Family, Members' Interests 1979-, Social Services 1979-; chm PLP Health and Social Services Gp, sec PLP Civil Liberties Gp, oppn front bench spokesman Educ Nov 1983-; *Style—* Andrew Bennett, Esq, MP; House of Commons, London SW1

BENNETT, Andrew John; s of Leonard Charles Bennett, and Edna Mary, *née* Harding (d 1984); *b* 25 April 1942; *Educ* St Edwards Sch Oxford, Univ Coll N Wales - Bangor (BSc), Univ of W Indies Trinidad, (Dip), Univ of Reading (MSc); *Career* Lt 6/7 Bn Royal Welch Fus TA 1961-66; voluntary serv overseas Kenya 1965-66, agric res offr Govt of St Vincent W Indies 1967-69, maize agromist govt Republic of Malawi 1971-74, chief res offr (agric) regnl Miny of Agric Southern Sudan 1976-70; Overseas Devpt Admin FCO London: agric admin advsr 1980-83, nat resources advsr SE Asia devpt dir Bangkpk 1983-85, head Br devpt div in the pacific Fiji 1985-87, chief nat res advsr; memb: RASE (cncl), TAA; *Recreations* walking, boating; *Style—* Andrew Bennett, Esq; Overseas Development Administration, Eland House, Stag Place, London SW1E

5DH (☎ 01 273 0513)

BENNETT, Arthur James; s of Harry Bennett (d 1973); *b* 28 August 1922; *Educ* Perse Sch Malvern, Queens' Coll Cambridge (MA); *m* 1945, Jean, da of Ernest Baynham (d 1967); 2 da; *Career* dir Transmission Engrg 1977-84; ret; FIEF; *Recreations* sailing (boat 'White Rose'); *Style*— Arthur Bennett, Esq; 44 Thornton Close, Girton, Cambridge (☎ 0223 276175)

BENNETT, Chris John Arthur; s of Arthur Stanley Bennett (d 1973), and Beatrice Ross, *née* Helsdon; *b* 22 August 1947; *Educ* Ewell Castle Sch; *m* 1, 25 Jan 1975 (m dis 1985), Barbara Lois, da of Michael Burn, of Somerset; 1 s (Benjamin James b July 1980); m 2, 2 April 1988, Jennifer Margaret, da of Herbert Edward Dabuor, of Macclesfield, Cheshire; *Career* sales dir Autochem Instruments Ltd 1978-79, sr ptnr Bennett & Co 1979-81, md C B Scientific Ltd 1981-, md Bennett & Co Ltd 1985-; *Recreations* sailing; *Style*— Chris Bennett, Esq; Field House, Newton Tony, Salisbury, Wilt (☎ 0980 643 21); Bennett & Co Ltd, Field House, Newton Tony, Salisbury, Wilt SP4 OHF (☎ 0980 644 8819, fax 0980 64 327)

BENNETT, Christopher Heal; s of Philip Hugh Pemberthy Bennett, CBE, and Jeanne Reynolds, *née* Heal; *b* 15 Mar 1945; *Educ* Harrow, London Univ, Open Univ (BA); *m* 29 May 1971 (m dis), Mary Ruth, da of Ernest Samuel Stock; 1 s (Jeremy b 1977), 1 da (Georgina b 1973); *Career* ptnr Richard Ellis 1985, chm Nat Ctee Industl Agents Soc 1988 (memb 1982, tres 1984, vice-chm 1986); tres North Colchester Constituency Cons Assoc 1983-85; Freeman City of London 1971, Liveryman Worshipful Co of Painter Stainers; FRICS; *Recreations* reading, walking; *Clubs* RAC; *Style*— Christopher Bennett, Esq; Lynwood House, North Entrance, Saxmundham, Suffolk (☎ 0728 3557); Richard Ellis, Berkeley Sq House, London W1X 6AN (☎ 01 629 6290, car 0836 208802)

BENNETT, (George) Colin; s of Rowland Bennett, OBE (d 1973), and Mary, *née* Hutchinson (d 1972); *b* 10 May 1924; *Educ* Rydal Sch, Trinity Hall Cambridge; *m* 1953, Mary Christina Barron, *née* Jones; 2 s (Mark, Michael), 1 da (Georgina); *Career* slr, notary public; *Recreations* sport, jazz, photography; *Clubs* MCC; *Style*— Colin Bennett, Esq; Colwyn, Woodlands Lane, Gt Oakley, Corby, Northants (☎ 0536 743475); office: West St, Kettering, Northants (☎ 0536 513195)

BENNETT, Dudley Paul; s of Patrick James Bennett, of Bognor Regis, and Mary, *née* Edmondson; *b* 4 August 1948; *Educ* Bradfield Coll Berks, London Univ (LLB); *m* 24 May 1986, Patricia Ann, da of James Kinngar Martin, of Notts; 1 da (Olivia Mary b 4 Feb 1988); *Career* barr Inner Temple 1972, rec Crown Ct 1988-; *Recreations* gardening, travel; *Style*— Dudley Bennett, Esq; 50 High Pavement, Nottingham (☎ 0602 503 503)

BENNETT, Air Vice-Marshal Erik Peter; CB (1984); s of Robert Francis and Anne Myra Bennett; *b* 3 Sept 1928; *Educ* The King's Hosp Dublin; *Career* air advsr to King Hussein 1961-62, RAF Staff Coll 1963, Jt Services Staff Coll 1971, Cdr Sultan of Oman's Air Force 1974-; Order of Istiqlal (Jordan) 1960, Order of Oman 1980; *Style*— Air Vice-Marshal Erik Bennett, CB; PO Box 6803, Muscat

BENNETT, Francis Ernest Herman; CBE (1963); s of Sir Ernest Nathaniel Bennett (d 1947), of Cwmllecoediog, Aberangell, Machynlleth, and Marguerite, *née* Kleinwort; bro of Rt Hon Sir Frederic Mackarness Bennett, *qv*; *b* 5 Nov 1916; *Educ* Westminster, New Coll Oxford; *m* 1947, Hon Ruth Gordon, *qv*, da of 1 Baron Catto, CBE (d 1959); 2 s; 1 da (Olivia); *Career* WWII Capt RA 1939-46; 3 sec to HM Legation Bucharest 1947-49; sec-gen Lib Int 1951-52; barr 1953; chief whip Cons LCC 1959, ald and chief whip Cons GLC 1965-79 (dep chm 1975-76); chm W J Cox Ltd 1959-74; chm and cmmr advsy ctee on gen cmmrs of income tax 1978-; memb ct and cncl Brunel Univ; former govr London Festival Ballet; Hon doctorate Brunel Univ 1987; *Recreations* skiing, shooting, travelling, entomolgy; *Clubs* Reform, Carlton; *Style*— Francis Bennett, Esq, CBE; C Hoare and Co, 37 Fleet St, London EC4

BENNETT, Rt Hon Sir Frederic (Mackarness); PC (1985); 2 s of Sir Ernest Nathaniel Bennett (d 1947), of Cwmllecoediog, Aberangell, Machynlleth, and Marguerite, *née* Kleinwort; bro of Francis Ernest Herman Bennett, *qv*; *b* 2 Dec 1918; *Educ* Westminster; *m* 1945, Marion Patricia, da of late Maj Cecil Burnham, OBE, FRCSE, of Manor Farm, Rustington, Sussex; *Career* serv WWII RA: barr Lincoln's Inn 1946; contested (C) Burslem 1945, MP Reading North (C) 1951-55, Torquay 1955-87; ldr Br Delegation to Cncl of Europe and WEU 1979-87 (vice-pres 1979-87); chm and dir of various cos; Lord of the Manor of Mawddwy; Cdr Order of Phoenix (Greece) 1963, Star of Pakistan (Sithari) (Pakistan) 1964, Cdr Polonia Restituta (Poland) 1977, (Grand Cdr's Cross 1984), Order of Al-Istiqlal (Jordan) 1980, Cdr Isabel la Catolica (Spain) 1982, Hilal-i-Quaid-i-Azam (Pakistan) 1983; Hon DLit Instanbul Univ (1984); Freeman City of London 1984; kt 1964; *Books* Reds under the Bed? Or the Enemy at Our Gates - Or Within (1982); *Recreations* shooting, skiing, sailing; *Clubs* Carlton, Beefsteak; *Style*— The Rt Hon Sir Frederic Bennett, MP; Cwmllecoediog, Aberangell, nr Machynlleth, Powys (☎ (065 02) 430); Oswego Island, St Davids, Bermuda; 2 Stone Bldgs, Lincoln's Inn, London WC2 (☎ 01 242 3900)

BENNETT, Capt Gordon Beresford; s of Ernest Bennett (d 1977), of Abbotts Way, Newcastle, Staffs, and Annie, *née* Beresford (d 1978); *b* 14 May 1922; *Educ* The HS Newcastle under Lyme Staffs; *m* 10 Jan 1948, Iris McFarlane (Mac), da of Harold Mayhew, (d 1970), of 7 The Chine, Saltburn, Yorks; 2 da (Rosemary Elizabeth (Mrs Smeaton) b 1951), Catherine Rosamund (Mrs McIlroy) b 1954); *Career* S Staff Regt 1941-42, OCTU Lanark and Sandhurst 1942-43, cmmnd 6 Bn Royal Northumberland Fus 1943, 3 Div Reconnaissance Regt Reconnaissance Corps 1943, served in Italy with 44 Recon Regt, 56 Div and GHQ, CMF, demob 1946; sr ptnr Donald H Bates and Co, Stoke on Trent 1981-88 (ptnr 1953-88), ret 1988, (conslt to practise); pres: N Staffs Soc of CAs 1971-72, Staffs Salop and Wolverhampton Soc of CAs 1982-83; memb: ICAEW 1952, FCA; *Recreations* walking, photography, gardening; *Clubs* Br Pottery Mfrs Fedn; *Style*— Gordon Bennett Esq; Glen How, Park Wood Drive, Baldwins Gate, Newcastle, Staffs (☎ 0782 680711); Donald H Bates & Co, 110 Lichfield St, Hanley, Stoke on Trent ST1 3DS (☎ 0782 262121, fax 0782 287246)

BENNETT, Guy Patrick de Courcy; s of Patrick John de Courcy Bennett, of Thames Ditton, and Pamela Mary Ray, *née* Kirchner; *b* 27 Oct 1958; *Educ* Wimbledon Coll, Manchester Univ (BSc); *m* 5 Nov 1988, Monica Beatrice, da of Alfred Cecil Francis Brodermann (d 1974); *Career* investmt analyst Equity & Law Life 1980-83, dir marketable securities div CIN Mgmnt 1984-; *Recreations* rugby, tennis, squash; *Style*— Guy Bennett, Esq; 10 Jedburgh St, Clapham Common, London SW11 5QB (☎ 01 350 1200); P.O. Box 10, Hobart House, Grosvenor Place, London Sw1X 7AD (☎ 01 389 7014)

BENNETT, Sir Hubert; s of Arthur Bennett, JP, and Eleanor, *née* Peel; *b* 4 Sept 1909; *Educ* Victoria Univ, Manchester Sch of Architecture; *m* 1938, Louise F C Aldred; 3 da (Louise, Elizabeth, Helen); *Career* architect in private practice; chief architect to LCC and GLC 1956-71, exec dir English Property Corpn 1971-79; assessor: Vauxhall Cross Competition, City Polytechnic Hong Kong 1982; conslt architect for guest palace for HM Sultan of Oman 1982, architect to UNESCO Paris 1982, memb RIBA Cncl (1952-55, 1957-62, 1965-66, 1967-69); recipient of various architectural and design awards; FRIBA; kt 1970; *Recreations* golf; *Style*— Sir Hubert Bennett; Shepherds Close, Munstead Park, Godalming, Surrey GU8 4AR (☎ 048 68 28828)

BENNETT, James Douglas Scott; s of Andrew Carmichael Bennett, (d 1983) of Edinburgh, and Margaret Catherine, *née* Nelson; *b* 1 Mar 1942; *Educ* Fettes Coll, Edinburgh Univ (MA); *m* 14 June 1969, Lorna Elizabeth Margaret, da of John Trevor William Peat (d 1974); 2 s (Hamish b 1974, Fraser b 1977); *Career* dir: Anglo Continental Trust 1972-5; Chloride Alcad Ltd 1978-81, East of Scotland Indust Investments Ltd 1984-, John Menzies plc 1981-; Accounts Commission for Local Authority in Scotland 1983-; CA; FBIM; FRSA; *Recreations* golf, reading; *Clubs* New (Edinburgh), Denham Golf, IOD, Luffness New, Murrayfield; *Style*— James Bennett, Esq; John Menzies plc, 108 Princes Street, Edinburgh (☎ 031 225 8555)

BENNETT, Jeremy James Balfe; s of Arthur Henry Bennett (d 1968), and Anne Gladys Bennett (d 1976); *b* 20 Jan 1934; *Educ* Repton; *m* 24 April 1965, Shelagh Winifred, da of Robert Jones (d 1968); 3 da (Sarah b 1962, Charlotte b 1967, Jane b 1967); *Career* cmmnd Sherwood Foresters, Cheshire Yeomanry (TA); dir Grants of St James's Ltd 1975; md Grants Wine & Spirit Merchants 1978; chm: London Wine Importers 1981, Wine & Spirit Educn Tst 1988, Acad of Wine Service 1988; corporate affairs dir European Cellars Ltd 1987; *Recreations* photography, music, reading, walking; *Clubs* Cavalry and Guards'; *Style*— Jeremy Bennett, Esq; The Vine House, Rooks Lane, Broughton, nr Stockbridge, Hants SO20 8AZ (☎ 0794 301219); c/o European Cellars, Moorfield Road, Guildford, Surrey (☎ 0483 64861)

BENNETT, Jill; da of James Randle Bennett (d 1969), of Sidmouth, S Devon, and Nora Adeline, *née* Becket (d 1982); *b* 24 Dec 1932; *Educ* Penang, Tortington Park, Priors Field, RADA; *m* 1, 1962, Willis Hall (m dis 1965); m 2, 1969, John Osborne; *Career* actress; London debut in Captain Corvallo 1950; London appearances include: Iris in Anthony and Cleopatra (with Olivier and Vivien Leigh) 1951, The Countess in A Patriot For Me 1965, West of Suez 1971, Hedda Gabler 1972, Amanda in Private Lives 1973, Loot 1975, Watch It Come Down 1976, Separate Tables 1977, Hamlet 1980, The Little Foxes 1981, Mary Stuart 1987, Infidelities 1986, The Letter; films include: The Nanny, The Charge of the Light Brigade, Inadmissible Evidence, Julius Ceasar, Quilp, Britannia Hospital, Lady Jane; numerous TV appearances include: The Old Crowd, Paradise Postponed; *Recreations* collecting paintings, riding, tennis, water-skiing, swimming, sun; *Style*— Miss Jill Bennett; c/o James Sharkey, 3rd Floor Suite, 15 Golden Square, London W1

BENNETT, John Martyn; s of Dr John Garner Bennett JP, and Dorothy, *née* Batty,; *b* 14 Feb 1946; *Educ* Rydal Sch, Liverpool Univ; *m* 6 Sept 1980, Catherine Elizabeth, da of Cornelius Raphael O'Leary (d 1988); 2 s (Henry b 1985, Edwin b 1987); *Career* lect in Law 1967-68, barr Gray's Inn 1969, Northern circuit 1969-, dir Bennett Safety Wear Ltd and assoc cos 1984-, memb Area Legal aid ctee 1986; asst rec 1988, various contributions to legal jls; represented N Wales at rugby 1967-69, chm Rydal Bankhall Youth Centre 1980-83, govr local Primary Schools 1986-88; memb Family Law Bar Assoc; *Recreations* watching rugby, fell walking; *Clubs* Liverpool Racquet, Waterloo ; *Style*— Martyn Bennett, Esq; Peel House, 5/7 Harrington St, Liverpool, L2 9QA; 5 Essex Court, Temple, London EC4Y 9AH, (☎ 051 236 4321)

BENNETT, Leon Samuel; s of Solomon Bennett, of Caesarea, Israel, and Freda, *née* Canter; *b* 14 June 1935; *Educ* Liverpool Coll, Liverpool Univ (LLB); *m* 6 Feb 1966, Beverley Elaine, da of Solomon (Sid) Levene (d 1980); *Career* slr; chm fund raising ctee Stapely Home and Hosp 1972-89; Freeman of Hale 1986; *Recreations* golf, squash, tennis, snooker, bridge; *Clubs* Racquet Liverpool, Lee Park Golf Liverpool; *Style*— Leon S Bennett, Esq; Thimble Cottage, 16 Hale Road, Hale Cheshire L24 5RE (☎ 051 425 2184); 46 Castle Street, Liverpool L2 7LA (☎ 051 277 1126)

BENNETT, Dowager Lady; Leopoldine; da of Leopold Armata, of Vienna; *m* 1938, as his 2 w, Sir Albert Bennett, 1 Bt (d 1945); *Style*— Dowager Lady Bennett; c/o 46 High Point, Weybridge, Surrey

BENNETT, Lilian Margery; *née* Barnett; da of Maurice Sydney Barnett, of London (d 1981), and Sophia Levy (d 1975); *b* 22 August 1922; *Educ* West Ham Secondary Sch; *m* 2 Nov 1952, Ronald, s of Alec Bennett, of London (d 1974); 1 s (Jonathan b 1954); *Career* dir: Thermo-Plastics Ltd 1957-68, Manpower plc 1968-, Girlpower Ltd 1968-, Overdrive plc 1968-; memb of The Parole Board & Community Service Volunteers Employment Panel; FRSA; *Recreations* reading, music, community work; *Style*— Mrs Lilian Bennett; 67 Porchester Terrace, London W2 3TT (☎ 01 262 4001); Manpower plc, 1 Harewood Place, Oxford Street, London W1 (☎ 01 493 7776, fax 01 629 1029)

BENNETT, Linda Margaret; da of Norman James Turner (d 1981), of Swanage, Dorset, and Margaret Doris, *née* Kneller; *b* 28 August 1950; *Educ* Sutton HS GPDST, Univ Coll of Wales Aberystwyth (BSc); *m* 28 Aug 1982, Thomas John Paterson, s of Thomas Bennett, Amesbury, Wilts; *Career* regnl mangr Angus Fire Armour 1972-78, dir Rayner Advertising 1978-81; Eros Mailing: client servs dir 1982-87, md 1987-; dir Cresta Corporate Servs 1987-; MInstM, FIOD; *Recreations* water skiing, snow skiing, sailing; *Style*— Mrs Linda Bennett; Eros Mailing, Central Way, Feltham, Middx TW14 0TG (☎ 01 751 6373, fax 01 751 6562, telex 24346)

BENNETT, Mrs John; Mary Letitia Somerville; da of Rt Hon Herbert Albert Laurens Fisher, OM, FRS (d 1940), and Lettice, *née* Ilbert; *b* 9 Jan 1913; *Educ* Oxford HS, Somerville Coll Oxford; *m* 1955, John Sloman Bennett, CMG, s of late Ralph Bennett, FRCVS; *Career* principal St Hilda's Coll Oxford 1965-80; *Style*— Mrs John Bennett; 25a Alma Place, Oxford

BENNETT, Michael; s of late Frank Carlton Bennett (d 1973); h to Btcy of cousin, Sir Ronald Bennett, Bt, *qv*; *b* 15 Feb 1924; *m* 1952, Janet Hazel Margaret, da of Brig Edward Joseph Todhunter, TD; 1 s, 2 da; *Style*— Michael Bennett, Esq; Flat 70, Albert Hall Mansions, London SW7

BENNETT, Dr Michael Camm; s of Francis Camm Bennett (d 1971), of Bath, Somerset, and Lilian Mabel, *née* Pegler (d 1951); *b* 29 Sept 1929; *Educ* King Edward VI School Bath, King's Coll London (BSc, PhD); *m* 9 Jan 1954, Mollie, da of Alan Charles Riches (d 1962), of Beetley, Norfolk; 1 s (Richard b 1957), 2 da (Jane b 1955,

Suzanne b 1962); *Career* sr physical chemist Imperial Coll of Tropical Agric Trinidad 1954-59; Tate & Lyle: head of physical chemistry dept res London 1960-68, dir tech servs 1969-75, dir engrg 1975-85; chm Br Charcoals & Macdonalds, Process Tech, Farrow Irrigation, Smith-Mirrlees 1975-85, md Int Div 1985-87, dir Industs Ltd 1986-, gp tech dir 1987-; chm Int Soc Sugar Cane Technologists 1974-80; pres: Sugar Processing Res Inc USA 1978-82, Br Soc of Sugar Cane Technologists 1981-87, Sugar Indust Technologists Inc USA 1982-83; CChem, FRSC 1976, memb Soc Chem Indust 1968; George & Eleanor Meade Award 1970 USA, SASTA Golden Jubilee Award 1975 South Africa, The Crystal Award 1978 USA; *Recreations* gardening, walking, shooting, sailing; *Style—* Dr Michael Bennett; Arden, Pastens Rd, Limpsfield Chart, Surrey RH8 0RE (☎ 0883 722 171); Tate & Lyle plc, Sugar Quay, Lower Thames St, London EC3R 6DQ (☎ 01 626 6525, fax 01 623 5213, telex 884084)

BENNETT, Nicholas Jerome; MP (C Pembroke 1987-; s of Peter Ramsden Bennett, and Antonia Mary Bennett (d 1984); *b* 7 May 1949; *Educ* Univ of London (BA), Univ of Sussex (MA); *Career* former: teacher, lectr and educn offr; cncllr London Borough of Lewisham 1974-82 (ldr of the oppn 1979-81), memb ILEA 1978-81, contested Hackney Central Gen Election 1979; memb: Select Ctee on Procedure, Select Ctee on Welsh Affrs; *Recreations* swimming, history, transport, browsing in second hand bookshops; *Style—* Nicholas Bennett, MP; c/o House of Commons, London SW1 (☎ 01 219 4415)

BENNETT, HE Gen Sir Phillip Harvey; AC, KBE, DSO; *b* 27 Dec 1928; *Educ* Perth Modern Sch, Roy Mil Coll, Dunstroon, Aust Staff Coll, Joint Service Staff; *m* 1955, Margaret Heywood; 2 s, 1 da; *Career* (despatches 1951); chief of the General Staff Australia 1982-84, chief of the Defence Force Australia 1984-87, Govr Tasmania Australia 1987-; *Recreations* golf, sailing, reading; *Clubs* Australian (Sydney), Cwlth, Utd Ser, Univ House; *Style—* HE Gen Sir Phillip Bennett, AC, KBE, DSO; Governor of Tasmania, Government House, Hobart, Tasmania 7000 Australia

BENNETT, Raymond Clayton Watson; s of Harold Watson (Church Army Capt, d 1941), and Doris Helena, *née* Edwards (later Bennett d 1988); *b* 20 June 1939; *Educ* Glasgow Acad, Bury GS, Manchester Univ (LLB); *m* 24 April 1965, Elaine Margaret, da of William Haworth, of Clitheroe; 1 s (John b 1966), 1 da (Jane b 1969); *Career* slr Blackburn 1964-72, called to the Bar Middle Temple 1972, Northern circuit 1972-, rec of Crown Ct; memb Hon Soc of the Middle Temple; *Recreations* tennis, squash, sailing, cycling; *Clubs* Cricket Bowling and Tennis (Clitheroe), Squash (Clitheroe); *Style—* Raymond C W Bennett, Esq; St James's Chambers, 68 Quay St, Manchester (☎ 061 834 7000)

BENNETT, Sir Reginald Frederick Brittain; VRD (1944); s of Samuel Robert Bennett (d 1964), and Gertrude, *née* Brittain (d 1946); *b* 22 July 1911; *Educ* Winchester, New Coll Oxford (MA, BM, BCh), LMSSA, Inst of Psychiatry London (DPM) ; *m* 1947, Henrietta, da of Capt Henry Berwick Crane, CBE, RN (d 1987); 1 s (Timothy), 3 da (Antonia, Medina, Belinda); *Career* Surgn Lt-Cdr RNVR and Fleet Air Arm Pilot 1939-46; MP (C) Gosport and Fareh 1950-79; PPS Iain Macleod 1954-63; chm: Parly and Scientific Ctee 1959-61, Parly Anglo-Italian Ctee 1969-79; vice pres Parly Franco-Br Ctee 1972-79, memb Services Ctee, chm Catering Sub Ctee 1970-79; wine conslt and co dir, chm Nadder Wine Co Ltd 1985-, dir Italian General Shipping Co Ltd 1977-; chm: Amateur Yacht Research Soc 1972-, World Sailing Speed Record Cnl (formerly Ctee) (IYRU) 1980-, Portland Speed Sailing Ctee (RYA) 1980-; Grande Ufficiale Italian Order of Merit 1977; kt 1979; *Recreations* yacht racing, foreign travel, basking in the sun; *Clubs* White's, Imperial Poona Yacht (cdre); *Style—* Sir Reginald Bennett, VRD; 30 Strand-on-the-Green, London W4 3PH (☎ 01 995 1777)

BENNETT, Richard Rodney; CBE (1977); s of H Rodney and Joan Esther Bennett; *b* 29 Mar 1936; *Educ* Leighton Park, Royal Acad of Music; *Career* composer; memb gen cncl Performing Right Soc 1975-, vice-pres London Coll of Music 1983-; *Style—* Richard Bennett, Esq, CBE; c/o Mrs Keys, London Management, Regent House, 235 Regent St, London W1

BENNETT, Robert; s of late Robert Bennett, and Emily, *née* Clegg; *b* 16 June 1940; *Educ* Rossall; *m* 5 Oct 1963, Alice Mary, da of late George William Ormerod; 1 s (Robin b 1964, d 1966), 2 da (Georgina b 1967, Jill b 1968); *Career* chm Lancs CCC 1987- (cricketer 1962-66); *Style—* Robert Bennett, Esq; Pippin Bank, Braaid Rd, Marown Douglas, Isle of Man

BENNETT, Ronald Alistair; CBE (1986), QC (1959); s of Arthur George Bennett, MC (d 1946), of Edinburgh, and Edythe, *née* Sutherland (d 1970); *b* 11 Dec 1922; *Educ* Edinburgh Acad, Edinburgh Univ, Balliol Coll Oxford (MA, LLB); *m* 1950, Margret, da of Sigursteinn Magnusson (d 1985), Consul Gen for Iceland; 3 s (Mark, Sigurdur, Magnus), 3 da (Ingibjorg, Vivien, Fleur); *Career* 79 (Scottish Horse) Medium Regt RA 1943-45, Capt RAOC, India and Japan 1945-46; advocate Scotland 1947; Vans Dunlop Sch in Scots Law and Conveyancing 1948; standing cnsl to Miny of Labour and Nat Serv 1957-59; sheriff princ: Roxburgh, Berwick, Selkirk 1971-74; S Strathclyde, Dumfries and Galloway 1981-82; N Strathclyde 1982-83; lectr in mercantile law: Edinburgh Univ 1956-68, Heriot-Watt Univ 1968-75; chm: Medical Appeal Tribunals (Scotland) 1971-, Agric Wages Bd for Scotland 1973-, Local Govt Boundaries Cmmn for Scotland 1974-, Northern Lighthouse Bd 1974, Industl Tribunals (Scotland) 1977-; War Pensions Tribunal 1983-; Arbiter Motor Insurers' Bureau Appeals 1975-; memb Scottish Medical Practices Ctee 1976-88; *Books* Bennett's Company Law (2 edn 1950), Fraser's Rent Acts in Scotland (2 edn 1952), Scottish Current Law and Scots Law Times Sheriff Ct Reports (1948-74, ed), Ct of Session Reports (1976-88, ed); *Recreations* gardening, music, reading; *Clubs* New (Edinburgh); *Style—* Ronald Bennett, Esq, CBE, QC; Laxamyri, 46 Cammo Rd, Edinburgh EH4 8AP (☎ 031 339 6111)

BENNETT, Sir Ronald Wilfred Murdoch; 3 Bt (UK 1929); o s of Sir Wilfred Bennett, 2 Bt (d 1952), and Marion Agnes, OBE (d 1985), da of James Somervell, of Sorn Castle, Ayrshire; *b* 25 Mar 1930; *Educ* Wellington, Trinity Coll Oxford; *m* 1, 1953, Rose-Marie Audrey Patricia, o d of Maj A L J H Aubépin; 2 da; m 2, 1968, Anne, da of late Leslie George Tooker; m 3, Princess Victoria Komukyeya of Toro (d 1988); *Heir* kinsman, Mark Edward Francis Bennett b 5 April 1960

BENNETT, Roy Grissell; CMG (1971), TD (1946); s of Charles Ernest Bennett (d 1962), and Lilian, *née* Bluff (d 1972); *b* 21 Nov 1917; *Educ* privately, RMC Sandhurst; *Career* served WW II 17/21 Lancers, 24 Lancers D Day, 2 Lothian Border Horse 2 in Cmd; dir: Vavasseur and Co Penang 1948-52, Maclaine Watson and Co Singapore 1956-72 (chm 1968-72); chm: Singapore Anti Tuberculosis Assoc 1958-62, Singapore Int Chamber of Commerce 1968-70; ctee memb and chm: Rubber Assoc Singapore 1960-72, Singapore Chamber of Commerce Rubber Assoc 1960-72; chm: Pilkington SEA Pte Ltd 1972-, Fibre Glass Pilkington Sdn Brd 1972-, Racehorse Spelling Station (Malaya) 1976-, Beder Int Singapore; fndr chm Utd World College SEA 1970-78 (now bd memb), patron Singapore Polo Club (chm 1968-70), dep chm Singapore Turf 1966-; IOD; *Recreations* polo (5 handicap 1967-78), racing, swimming, shooting, travelling, gardening, photography, people of all races, building projects; *Clubs* Cavalry and Guards', Tanglin (Singapore), Turf, Polo, Polo (Penang), Swimming (Penang); *Style—* Roy Bennett, Esq, CMG, TD; Oak Tree House, S Holmwood, Surrey RH5 4NF (☎ 0306 889414); Taman Indera, 22 Jalan Perdana, Johore Bharu, 80300, Malaysia (☎ 010 60 7224 505)

BENNETT, Hon Ruth Gordon; *née* Catto; yst da of 1 Baron Catto, CBE, PC (d 1959); *b* 1919; *m* 1947, Francis Ernest Herman Bennett, CBE, *qv*; 2 s, 1 da; *Career* serv WWII LACW RAF 11 Gp HQ 1942-45, Pilot Offr 1945-46; *Style—* The Hon Mrs Bennett; C Hoare and Co, 37 Fleet St, London EC4

BENNETT, Stephen Scott; s of Montague Bennett (d 1976), and Rachel, *née* Lopez-Dias, of Sutton; *b* 6 Dec 1946; *Educ* Rutlish Sch Merton; *m* 22 June 1969, Bobbi, da of Leon Hanover; *Career* qualified ca 1968, tax specialist Fuller Jenks Beecroft 1968-70, ptnr Accountancy Tuition Centre 1970-78; Deloitte Haskins & Sells: dir of educn 1978-82 ptnr 1982-, head of Mergers and Acquisitions in Corporate Finance Div; ctee memb Merton RFC; FCA 1968, FCCA 1973, ATII 1970; *Recreations* squash, rugby, drama; *Clubs* RAC; *Style—* Stephen Bennett, Esq; Foxcote, 50 West Hill, Sanderstead, Surrey (☎ 01 657 4228); 26 Old Bailey, London EC4 (☎ 01 248 3913, fax 01 236 2367, car tel 0836 242 581)

BENNETT, Todd Anthony; s of Anthony Henry Jack Bennett, of Southampton, and Jean Patricia, *née* Marshall; *b* 6 July 1962; *Educ* Romsey Sch, Barton Peveril VI Form ; *m* 19 Sept 1987, Vanessa Lorraine, da of Peter Frank Drodge, of Romsey, Hants; *Career* sprinter; Euro Jr Championships 1981 Gold 400m and Silver 4 x 400m, Euro Championships 1982 Silver 4 x 400m, Cwlth Games 1982 Gold 4 x 400m, World Championships 1983 Bronze 4 x 400m, Olympics 1984 Silver 4 x 400m, Euro Indoor 1985 Gold 400m (world record), World Indoor 1985 Silver 400m, Cwlth Games 1986 Silver 200m and Gold 4 x 400m, Euro Indoor 1987 Gold 400m, Euro Championships Gold 4 x 400m, World Championships 1987 Silver 4 x 400, Olympics 1988 fifth 4 x 400m; *Recreations* golf, basketball, gardening; *Style—* Todd Bennett, Esq; Sandmartins, 8 The Street, Binsted, Nr Alton, Hants GU34 4PB (☎ 0420 23235); Hampshire Family Practitioner Committee, Friarsgate, Winchester (☎ 0420 23235)

BENNETT, Trevor Tyrer; s of Tom Bennett (d 1950), of Preston, Lancs, and Isabella, *née* Tyrer; *b* 8 July 1932; *Educ* Preston GS; *m* 1, 7 June 1951, (m dis 1983), Barbara Alice, da of Walter Bateman, of Barton; 1 s (Richard b 1964), 2 da (Susan (Mrs Cox) b 1952, Nicola b 1969); m 2, 11 Aug 1984, Judith Anne, da of Anthony Morris, of Wellington; 1 s (Charles b 1986); *Career* admitted slr 1955; sr ptnr Russell & Russell 1984- (ptnr 1960-); dir Nat Assoc Investment Clubs Ltd; former pres: Bolton Jr Chamber of Commerce, Bolton Investment Club; memb Law Society 1955; *Books* Guide to Buying Property in Portugal, Guide to Buying Property in Spain, Guide to Buying Property in France; *Recreations* cinema, books, travel, spectator sports; *Clubs* 41; *Style—* Trevor Bennett, Esq; White Oaks, Brook Lane, Alderley Edge, Cheshire SK9 7RU; (☎ 0625 583 596); Casa Das Castanhas, Foia, Monchique, Algarve, Portugal; Russell & Russell, Solicitors, 9-13 Wood St, Bolton, Lancs BL1 1EE (☎ 0204 340 51, fax 0204 389 223, car tel 0836 733 522, telex 635454 RUSSEL)

BENNETT, Dr William Arthur; s of Thomas Arthur Bennett (d 1964) of Kensington, London, and Alice Maud, *née* Cressey, (d 1947); *b* 10 Nov 1930; *Educ* Latymer Upper Sch, Gonville and Caius Coll Cambridge (BA), Univ of London (Academic DipEd), Univ of Cambridge (PhD); *m* 7 Aug 1954, Doreen May, da of Leonard Albert Humphreys (d 1978), of East Barnet, Herts; 1 s (Geoffrey William Michael b 1959), 1 da (Joanne b 1960); *Career* Nat Serv RAF 1949-51; sr lectr modern languages Ealing Tech Coll 1962-65, asst dir of res in applied linguistics Univ of Cambridge 1965-74, reader in French linguistics King's Coll London 1974-; memb Philological Soc, Linguistics Assoc of GB, Soc for French Studies, Henry Sweet Soc; *Books* Aspects of Language and Language Teaching (1968 and 1969), Applied Linguistics and Language Learning (1974); *Recreations* walking, talking; *Style—* Dr William Bennett; Arncliffe, 20 Haslingfield Rd, Harlton, Cambridge CB3 7ER (☎ 0223 262586) King's College London, The Strand, London WC2R 2LS (01 836 5454)

BENNEY, (Adrian) Gerald (Sallis); s of Ernest Alfred Sallis Benney, and Aileen Mary *née* Ward; *b* 21 April 1930; *Educ* Brighton GS, Brighton Coll of Art (Nat Dip), Royal Coll of Art (Des RCA); *m* 4 May 1957, Janet, da of Harold Neville Edwards of Rawlins Farm, Ramsdell nr Basingstoke, Hants; 3 s (Paul b 1959, Jonathan b 1961, Simon b 1966), 1 da (Genevieve b 1962); *Career* REME 1949-51; conslt designer to Viners Ltd 1957-59; holder of Royal Warrants to: HM The Queen 1974-, HRH The Duke of Edinburgh 1975-, HM Queen Elizabeth The Queen Mother 1975-, HRH The Prince of Wales 1980-; memb: Govts Craft Advsy Ctee 1972-77, advsy ctee UK Atomic Energy Ceramics Centre 1979-83; metalwork design advsr to Indian Govt 1977-78, chm Govt of India Hallmarking Survey 1981, memb Br Hallmarking Cncl 1983-88, export advsr and conslt designer to Royal Selangor Pewter Co Kuala Lumpar 1986-, designer and maker of domestic and liturgical silver started workshops London 1955, commenced Reading Civic Plate 1960; Freedom Borough of Reading 1984, Freeman City of London 1957, Liveryman Worshipful Co of Goldsmiths 1964; Hon MA Leicester Univ 1963; RDI (Royal Designer to Industry) 1971, FRSA 1971; *Recreations* walking, landscape gardening, painting; *Style—* Gerald Benney, Esq; Beenham House, Beenham, Nr Reading, Berks (☎ 0734 744 370)

BENNION, Francis Alan Roscoe; s of Thomas Roscoe Bennion (d 1968), of Hove, Sussex, and Ellen Norah, *née* Robinson (d 1986); *b* 2 Jan 1923; *Educ* John Lyon's Sch Harrow, Univ of St Andrews, Balliol Coll Oxford (MA); *m* 28 July 1951 (m dis 1975), Barbara Elizabeth, da of Harry Arnold Braendle (d 1964), of Little Hadham, Herts; 3 da (Sarah, Carola, Venetia); m 2, 2 Nov 1977, Mary Anne, widow of William Field, da of Patrick Lynch (d 1962), of Limerick; *Career* WWII Flt-Lt Pilot RAFVR 1941-46; barr Middle Temple 1951-53 and 1985-88, lectr and tutor law St Edmund Hall Oxford 1951-53, memb Parly Cnsl 1953-65 and 1973-75, sec-gen RICS 1965-68; constitutional advsr: Pakistan 1956, Ghana 1959-61, Jamaica 1969-71; govr Coll Estate Mgmnt 1965-68, co-fndr and 1 chm Professional Assoc Teachers 1968-72, fndr and 1 chm World of Property Housing Tst (now Sanctuary Housing Assoc) 1968-72 (vice pres 1986-); fndr: Statute Law Soc 1968 (chm 1978-79), Freedom Under Law 1971, Dicey Tst 1973, Towards One World 1979; co-fndr Areopagitica Educnl Tst 1979; chm

Oxford City FC 1988-; *Books* Constitutional Law of Ghana (1962), Professional Ethics (1969), Tangling With The Law (1970), Consumer Credit Control (1976-), Consumer Credit Act Manual (1978, third edn 1986), Statute Law (1980, 2 edn 1983), Statutory Interpretation (1984), Victorian Railway Days (1989); *Recreations* cricket, Victoriana, old railways; *Clubs* MCC; *Style—* Francis Bennion, Esq; Bodleian Law Library, Oxford

BENNISON, Dr (Robert) John; s of John Jennings Bennison (d 1966), and Agnes, *née* Hinchley; *b* 4 Feb 1928; *Educ* Sedbergh, Corpus Christi Coll Cambridge, London Hosp Med Coll Univ of London (MA, MB BChir, D(Obst)RCOG); *m* 19 July 1952, Kathleen Mary, da of Frank Underwood, (d 1955), of Nottingham; 2 s (Peter b 1953, Timothy b 1961), 3 da (Sarah b 1955, Nicola b 1958, Jennifer b 1964); *Career* Flt Lt med branch RAF 1952-54; GP 1957-88; princ Hatfield Broad Oak Essex 1959-88; memb Cncl RCGP 1975-84 (chm educn ctee 1978-81; vice chm Cncl 1982-83), assoc advsr in gen practice NE Thames regn 1975-79, med ed TV Channel 4 Well Being 1982-85, memb English Nat Bd for Nursing Midwifery and Health Visiting 1983-88; author and contrib to numerous med textbooks and learned jls (especially on health educn and alcohol); FRSM, FRCGP; *Recreations* music, drama, wine, making things; *Style—* Dr John Bennison; The Old Parsonage, Hampsthwaite, Harrogate, North Yorks HG3 2HA, (☎ 0423 771168)

BENNITT, (Mortimer) Wilmot; s of Rev F W Bennitt (d 1950), of The Rectory, Bletchley, Bucks, and Honoria, *née* Booth (d 1960); *b* 28 August 1910; *Educ* Charterhouse, Trinity Coll Oxford (MA); *m* (m dis 1951), Cecilia Bowman; *Career* RAF Motor Boat Crew 1940-43 LAC, IO FO 1943-44; under sec Miny of Works 1951-63 (1935-51), Land Cmmn 1966-71; hon sec Islington Soc 1985- (1961-63), chm Islington Archaeology and History Soc 1988-; *Books* Guide to Canonbury Tower (1962); *Recreations* theatre, looking at pictures; *Clubs* United Oxford and Cambridge Univ, Tavisteck Rep; *Style—* Wilmot Bennitt, Esq; 5 Highbury Grove, Islington, London N5 (☎ 01 226 5937); British Theatre Assoc, Regent Coll, London NW1

BENSON, Sir Arthur Edward Trevor; GCMG (1959, KCMG 1954, CMG 1952); s of Rev Arthur Hill Trevor Benson (d 1926), Vicar of Ilam, Staffs, and Emily Maud Malcomson (d 1960), of Woodlock, Co Waterford; *b* 21 Dec 1907; *Educ* Wolverhampton Sch, Exeter Coll Oxford (MA); *m* 1933, Daphne Mary Joyce, da of late E Hugh Macdonald Fynn, of Serui, Hartley, S Rhodesia; 2 da; *Career* joined Colonial Admin Serv 1932 Dist Offr Colonial Office 1939 N Rhodesia, Prime Minister's Office London 1940-43, War Cabinet Office 1943-44, dist cmmr N Rhodesia 1944-46, admin sec Uganda 1946-49, chief sec Central African Cncl 1949-51, chief sec to Govt of Nigeria 1951-54, govr of Northern Rhodesia 1954-59; JP Devon 1962-66; hon fell Exeter Coll Oxford; KStJ 1954; *Style—* Sir Arthur Benson, GCMG; Otter Hill, Tipton St John, Sidmouth EX10 0AJ??? **Sir**

BENSON, Christopher John; s of late Charles Woodburn Benson and Catherine Clara, *née* Bishton; *b* 20 July 1933; *Educ* Worcester Cathedral Kings Sch, The Incorporated Thames Nautical Training Coll HMS Worcester; *m* 1960, Margaret Josephine, OBE, JP, da of Ernest Jefferies Bundy; 2 s; *Career* Sub-Lt RN; dir Arndale Devpts Ltd 1965-69; fndr chm: Dolphin Devpts, Dolphin Property Ltd 1969-72; asst md The Law Land Co Ltd 1972-74, md MEPC plc 1976-88 (dir 1974-), dir House of Fraser plc 1982-86, md MEPC plc 1976-88 (chm 1988-), dir Sun Alliance and London Insur plc 1988-; chm: property advsy gp to the Dept of the Environment 1988-, Reedpack Ltd 1989-, pres Br Property Fedn 1981-83; memb: investment ctee BP Pension Fund 1979-84, cncl Marlborough Coll 1982-; underwriting memb Lloyds 1979-; dir Royal Opera House Covent Gdn Ltd 1984-; chm: Civic Tst 1985-, London Docklands Devpt Corpn 1984-88; Worshipful Co of Watermen and Lightermen; tstee Metropolitan Police Museum; Freeman Guild of Air Pilots and Air Navigators 1980-; Hon bencher Middle Temple 1984-; FRICS; *Recreations* farming, aviation, opera, swimming; *Clubs* City Livery, Naval, RAC, MCC; *Style—* Sir Christopher Benson; Pauls Dene House, Castle Road, Salisbury, Wilts (☎ 0722 22187); Flat 2, 50 South Audley Street, London W1 (☎ 01 499 3570); MEPC plc, Brook House, 113 Park Lane, London W1Y 4AY (☎ 01 491 5303)

BENSON, David Holford; s of Lt-Col Sir Reginald (Rex) Lindsay Benson, DSO, MVO, MC (d 1968), of Cucumber Farm, Singleton, nr Chichester, Sussex, and Leslie, *née* Foster (d 1981); half-bro (through his mother's former marriage to Condé Nast) of Lady Bonham -Carter (*see* Lord Bonham-Carter); *b* 26 Feb 1938; *Educ* Eton, Madrid Univ; *m* 1964, Lady Elizabeth Mary, *née* Charteris, da of 12 Earl of Wemyss and (8 of) March, KT, JP; 1 s, 2 da; *Career* merchant banker; vice chm: Kleinwort Benson Gp plc, Br Gas plc, Wemyss and March Estate Co, Campbell Soups, The Rouse Co; tstee: Charities Official Investmt Fund; *Recreations* painting; *Clubs* White's, ESU; *Style—* David Benson, Esq; 11 Brunswick Gdns, London W8 (☎ 01 727 4949); Cucumber Farm, Singleton, Sussex (☎ 024 363 222)

BENSON, Lady Elizabeth Mary; *née* Charteris; o surv da of 12 Earl of Wemyss, KT, *qv*; *b* 2 July 1941; *m* 17 Oct 1964, David Holford Benson, yr son of late Lt-Col Sir Reginald Lindsay (Rex) Benson, DSO, MVO, MC (d 1968), by his wife, Leslie, formerly wife of late Condé Nast, and da of late Volney Foster, of Ill, USA; 1s, 2 da; *Style—* Lady Elizabeth Benson; 11 Brunswick Gdns, W8 (☎ 01 727 4949)

BENSON, Prof Frank Atkinson; OBE (1988), DL (South Yorks 1979); s of late John Benson and Selina Benson; *b* 21 Nov 1921; *Educ* Ulverston GS, Univ of Liverpool (BEng, MEng), Univ of Sheffield (DEng, PhD); *m* 1950, Kathleen May Paskell; 2 s; *Career* prof and head of dept of electronic and electrical engrg Univ of Sheffield 1967-87 (emeritus prof 1987-); FIEE, FIEEE; *Style—* Prof Frank Benson, OBE, DL; 64 Grove Rd, Sheffield S7 2GZ (☎ 0742 363493); Dept of Electronic and Electrical Engrg, Univ of Sheffield, Mappin St, Sheffield S1 3JD (☎ 0742 768555)

BENSON, Baron (Life Peer UK 1980); Henry Alexander Benson; GBE (1971, CBE 1946); s of Alexander Stanley Benson and Florence Mary, *née* Cooper; *b* 2 August 1909; *Educ* Johannesburg; *m* 1939, Anne Virginia, da of Charles Macleod; 2 s, 1 da; *Career* former ptnr Coopers and Lybrand; pres ICAEW 1966; chm Royal Cmmn on Legal Servs 1976-79; tstee Times Tst 1967-81; advsr to Govr of Bank of England 1975-83; hon master of Bench of Inner Temple 1983; sits as Independent in House of Lords; FCA; kt 1964; *Recreations* shooting, sailing (sloop 'Drover'); *Clubs* Brooks's, Royal Yacht Sqdn, Jockey; *Style—* The Rt Hon Lord Benson, GBE; 9 Durward House, 31 Kensington Court, London W8 5BH (☎ 01 937 4850)

BENSON, James; s of Henry Herbert Benson and Olive, *née* Hutchinson; *b* 17 July 1925; *Educ* Bromley GS, Emmanuel Coll Cambridge (MA); *m* 1950, Honoria Margaret, da of Patrick Hurley (d 1952), of Dublin; 1 da; *Career* served WW II RNVR, N Atlantic and East Indies; advertising exec: Kemsley 1948-58, Mather and Crowther Ltd (subsequently Ogilvy and Mather Ltd) 1959-78, dir 1960, md 1967, chm 1970); Ogilvy and Mather International (parent co) dir 1966, (vice-chm 1970-); govr Brasilinvest SA 1977-, memb advsy bd 1984; chm international ctee American Assoc of Advertising Agencies 18183; chm of tstees American Assocs of the Royal Acad 1983-; *Recreations* travelling, fishing, music, reading, writing; *Style—* James Benson Esq; 550 Park Avenue, New York, NY 10021, USA (☎ (212) 355 0291); Kelsey Road, Box 271, Sheffield, Mass 01257, USA

BENSON, Lady Jane Helen Harbord; *née* Lowther; da of 7 Earl of Lonsdale, *qv*; *b* 13 Nov 1947; *m* 1, 19 Dec 1968 (m dis 1970), Gary Hunter Wooton, of California, USA; m 2, 6 Dec 1978, Robert Charles Benson, eldest son of Lt Cdr Nicholas Robin Benson, RN (eldest son of Guy Holford Benson by his wife, Lady Violet Catherine, widow of Hugo Francis, Lord Elcho, and da of 8 Duke of Rutland); 2 da (Laura Jane b 1980, Sophie Camilla b 1984); *Career* master of Ullswater Fox Hounds; ctee memb: Red Cross, Lifeboat Assoc; *Recreations* diving, swimming, gun dogs, tennis, sailing; *Style—* Lady Jane Benson; Glebe House, Lowther, Penrith, Cumbria (☎ 09312 577)

BENSON, Sir (William) Jeffrey; s of Herbert Benson (d 1950), of Bramley, Leeds, and Lilian Benson, *née* Goodson (d 1950); *b* 15 July 1922; *Educ* West Leeds HS; *m* 8 Sept 1947, Audrey Winifred, da of Ebineezer Parsons (d 1962), of Canterbury; 2 s (Martin Jeffrey b 22 March 1954, Stephen Nigel b 10 Feb 1957); *Career* RAF 1941-46 (despatches); joined Nat Prov bank 1939; sr appointment Nat West Bank: regnl exec dir 1968-73, gen mangr 1973-75, dep gp chief exec 1975-77, gp chief exec 1978-82, dep chm 1987; chm Export Advsy Cncl 1982-87, chm 600 Gp plc 1987-; FCIB, pres Inst of Bankers 1983-85; kt 1987; *Recreations* golf; *Clubs* Clifton Phyllis Court; *Style—* Sir Jeffrey Benson; Auben, 24 Spencer Walk, Rickmansworth, Herts WD3 4EZ (☎ 0927 778 260); Hythe End House, Chertsey Lane, Staines, Middx TW18 3EL (☎ 0784 61 545)

BENSON, John Blair; s of Robert Spence Thom Benson, of Ascot Ct, Glasgow, and Anna Margaret, *née* Blair; *b* 6 Sept 1945; *Educ* Clydebank HS, Strathclyde Univ (BA); *m* 9 Aug 1969, Anne, da of Albert Carter (d 1978); 3 da (Joanne b 28 Sept 1971, Victoria b 2 Dec 1974, Sarah b 8 Oct 1976); *Career* dir gp personnel servs Scottish & Newcastle Breweries 1978-84; gp personnel dir: Nabisco Gp Ltd 1984-87, Reed Int Manuf Gp 1987-88; dir personnel and corp servs Reedpack Ltd 1988-; govr Westgate Sch; FIPM; *Recreations* golf, hill walking, art literature

BENSON, Lt-Col John Elliott; JP (Northumberland 1954); 3 s of Walter John Benson (d 1923), of Newbrough Hall, Fourstones, Hexham, Northumberland; bro of William Arthur Benson, *qv*; *b* 15 Jan 1915; *Educ* Eton, Sandhurst; *m* 1948, Alice Elisabeth Kalmia, eldest da of Capt Alexander Milne Keith, of Chesters, Humshaugh, Northumberland; 1 s, 3 da; *Career* 2 Lt Black Watch 1935, cmd 2 Bn 1945-47, High Sheriff Northumberland 1973-74; *Recreations* shooting, fishing, golf; *Style—* Lt-Col John Benson, JP; Chesters, Humshaugh, Hexham, Northumberland (☎ 043 481 203)

BENSON, Julian Riou; s of Maj-Gen Edward Riou Benson, CB, CMG, CBE (d 1985), of Well House, Aldermaston, Berkshire, and Isolda Mary Stuart, *née* Shea; *b* 17 May 1933; *Educ* Winchester, New Coll Oxford (BA); *m* 1 Oct 1960, Lilias Jane, da of Lt-Col Gerald Alan Hill-Walker (d 1980), of Maunby Hall, Thirsk, Yorkshire; 2 s (John b 1961, Charles b 1966), 2 da (Camilla b 1963, Fiona b 1970); *Career* Nat Serv 2 Lt 11 Hussars (Prince Albert's Own) 1952-53; bank clerk Barclays Bank 1956-59; Cl-Alexanders Laing & Cruickshank (formerly Laing & Cruickshank Stockbrokers) 1959-: ptnr 1959-71, dir 1971-84, currently dir corporate fin div; *Recreations* stalking, skiing, gardening; *Clubs* White's, City University, MCC; *Style—* Julian Benson, Esq; The Old Rectory, Abbott's Ann, Andover, Hampshire SP11 7NR (☎ 0264 710 389); Cl-Alexanders Laing & Cruickshank, Piercy House, 7 Copthall Ave, London EC2R 7BE (☎ 01 588 2800)

BENSON, Hon Michael D'Arcy; yr s of Baron Benson, GBE (Life Peer), *qv*; *b* 1943; *m* 1969, Rachel Candia Woods; 1 s (Charles D'Arcy b 1976), 2 da (Catherine Rachel b 1971, Harriet Anne b 1974); *Style—* The Hon Michael Benson; 34 St John's Ave, London SW15 6AN (☎ 01 788 3828)

BENSON, Michael Stewart; s of (Seymour) Stewart Benson, AFC (Air Cdre RAF ret), of Haughley, Suffolk, and Eva Margaret, *née* Sully; *b* 23 July 1929; *Educ* Rugby; *m* 20 June 1953, Mary Scott, da of Lt-Col James Kenneth Matheson, MC (d 1956), of Sotik, Kenya; 1 s (Peter b 13 Feb 1956), 1 da (Sarah b 30 April 1958); *Career* Army 1947-49, cmmnd 2 Lt RA 1948; Br-American Tobacco Co Ltd: mgmnt pupil UK 1949, purchasing mangr E Africa 1951, area mktg mangr E Africa 1957, sales mangr Tripoli 1958; Givaudan and Co Ltd (subsid of Hoffmann La-Roche): asst to md 1962, sales dir 1970, md 1977, non-exec chm (ret) 1989-; chm Br Fragance Assoc 1987-89; memb PCC Parish of All Saints Dane Hill Sussex 1985-(church warden 1982-88); *Recreations* fly fishing, sailing; *Clubs* Caledonian, Lansdowne; *Style—* Michael Benson, Esq; High Pines, Church Lane, Dane Hill, Haywards Heath, Sussex RH17 7EU (☎ 0825 790 583); Givaudan & Co Ltd, Whyteleafe, Surrey CR3 7EU (☎ 08832 3377, fax 08832 6414, car tel 0836 296 920; telex 28558)

BENSON, Peter Charles; s of Robert Benson, of Baildon, Yorks (d 1970), and Dorothy *née* Cartman; *b* 16 June 1949; *Educ* Bradford GS, Birmingham Univ (BSocSc); *Career* Called to the Bar (Middle Temple) 1975, memb NE Circuit 1975; junior NE Circuit 1980; tstee the Henry Scott Fund; tres Bradford Cricket Club, Pres The Hon Soc of Gentleman Troughers; *Recreations* golf, reading, conversation; *Clubs* Ilkley Golf, various Cricket, Ilkley RFU; *Style—* Peter Benson, Esq; Bygrew Cottage, Parish Ghyll Drive, Ilkley, Yorkshire (☎ 0943 601 245); Fifth Floor, St Paul's Hse, Park Sq, Leeds, LS1 2ND; (☎ 0532 455 866, fax 0532 455 807)

BENSON, Hon Peter Macleod; er s of Baron Benson, GBE (Life Peer), *qv*; *b* 1940; *Educ* Eton, Edinburgh Univ (MA); *m* 1970 (m dis 1987), Hermione Jane Boulton; 1 s (Edward Henry b 1975), 2 da (Candida Jane b 1972, Hermione Emily b 1980); *Career* CA; ptnr Coopers and Lybrand; *Recreations* shooting, golf; *Clubs* Brooks's, Hurlingham, MCC, Tandridge Golf; *Style—* The Hon Peter Benson; 22 Larpent Ave, London SW15 (☎ 01 788 3758); Coopers and Lybrand, Plumtree Court, Farrington St, London EC4 (☎ 01 583 5000)

BENSON, (Harry) Peter Neville; CBE (1982), MC (1945); s of Harry Leedham Benson, and Iolanthe Benson; *b* 10 Feb 1917; *Educ* Cheltenham; *m* 1948, Margaret Young; 2s, 1 da; *Career* dir and chm Davy Corpn plc 1982-85; FCA; *Style—* Peter Benson, Esq, CBE, MC; Davy Corporation Ltd, 15 Portland Place, London W1A 4DD (☎ 01 637 2821)

BENSON, Robert Charles; s of Lt-Cdr Nicholas Robin Benson, of Barn Court, Coln St Dennis, Cheltenham, and Barbara, *née* Kitchiner; *b* 17 Nov 1952; *Educ* Eton,

Southampton Univ (BSc); *m* 6 Dec 1978, Lady Jane, da of 7 Earl of Lonsdale, Askham Hall, Penrith, Cumbria; 2 da (Laura Jane b 1980, Sophie Camilla b 1984); *Career* land agent and sporting mangr Lowther Estates 1976, dir Lakeland Investmt Co 1980, chm: North West Br Field Sports Soc, Lowther Driving Trials and Country Fair; ctee memb: Timber Growers UK, Country Land Owners Assoc, Br Deer Soc; sch govr; *Recreations* shooting, fishing, hunting, tennis, golf, cricket; *Clubs* MCC; *Style—* Robert Benson, Esq; Glebe House, Lowther, Penrith, Cumbria (☎ 09312 270); Lakeland Investments, Estate Office, Lowther, Penrith, Cumbria (☎ 09312 577)

BENSON, Robin Stephen; s of Lt Col Sir Rex Benson, DSO, MVO, MC (d 1968), of 30 Cadogan Place, London SW1, and Leslie, *née* Foster (d 1981); *b* 11 August 1934; *Educ* Eton, Balliol Coll Oxford; *m* 23 July 1964, Jane Elliott, LVO, da of Col F E (Bill) Allday, OBE, TD, DL; 2 da (Lucinda b 1965, Camilla b 1968); *Career* Lt 9 Lancers 1952-54; marketing mangr Holt Products Ltd 1965-71, dir Bensonic Ltd 1971-84, chm and md Herbert Johnson Ltd 1984-; MInstM 1969; *Recreations* shooting, tennis, music, motor racing; *Clubs* Whites, Queens, Vanderbilt Racquet; *Style—* Robin Benson, Esq; 11 Kensington Gate, London W8; Herbert Johnson Ltd, 30 New Bond St, London W1Y 9HD (☎ 01 434 4330)

BENSON, Roger Scholes; s of Thomas Scholes Benson, of Radcliffe-on-Trent, Nottingham, and Jane Benson, *née* Bridge (d 1955); *b* 20 Oct 1932; *Educ* Roundhay Sch Leeds; *m* 15 Oct 1955, Hilary Margaret, da of late George Morris Brown, of Nottingham; 3 da (Jane b 1957, (d 1983), Jo b 1959, Nicky b 1962); *Career* qual chartered accountant 1954; taxation mangr Peat Marwick Mitchell and Co 1954-59, own practice (Benson Brooks) West Bridgford Nottingham 1959-79; fin dir Speedograph-Richfield 1980-, hotelier Burleigh Court Hotel Minchinhampton Glos 1980-; parish cllr 1967-76, rural district cllr 1972-76; rotarian 1963-81, past pres Rotary Club of W Bridgford; FCA 1959 (memb ctee 1973-81); *Recreations* golf, cricket, travel; *Clubs* Minchinhampton Golf, Bramcote (Notts) Cricket; *Style—* Roger Benson, Esq; Cornerstones, Burleigh, Stroud, Glos (☎ 0453 883804); Burleigh Court, Stroud, Glos (☎ 0453 883804, fax 0453 88687)

BENSON, Ross; s of Stanley Ross Benson, of St John's Wood, London, and Marbella, Spain, and Mabel, *née* Greaves; *b* 29 Sept 1948; *Educ* Sydney GS, Gordonstown; *m* 1, 1968 (m dis 1974), Beverly Jane, da of K A Rose; 1 s (Dorian Ross b 1974); m 2, 1975 (m dis 1986), Zoé, da of G D Bennett; 1 da (Anouchka b 1975); m 3, 27 Nov 1987, Ingrid, da of Dr Eric Canton Seward; *Career* journalist; dep diary ed: Daily Mail 1968-71, Sunday Express 1971-72; Daily Express 1973-: foreign news ed 1975-76, specialist writer 1976-78, US W Coast corr 1978-82, chief foreign corr 1982-87, chief feature writer 1987-88, diary ed 1988-; Int Reporter of the Year Br Press Awards 1983; *Recreations* skiing, motor racing, fishing; *Style—* Ross Benson, Esq; c/o Daily Express, Blackfriars Rd, London SE1 (☎ 01 922 1148)

BENSON, Stephen; s of A Benson; *b* 7 June 1943; *Educ* Highgate, Magdalen Coll Oxford; *m* 1966, Jacqueline, *née* Russell; 3 da; *Career* dir Davidson Pearce (ad agency) 1974-; *Recreations* music, running; *Style—* Stephen Benson, Esq; 8 Laurier Rd, London NW5 (☎ 01 485 0287; office: 01 589 4595)

BENSON, Air Cdre (Seymour) Stewart; AFC (1919); s of Robert Seymour (d 1938), and Lilian Dora, *née* Crewdson; *b* 4 Dec 1896; *Educ* Rugby, Cambridge (MA); *m* Aug 1923 (m dis), Eva Margaret, da of Robert Sully; 1 s (Michael b 1929); m 2, Jan 1989 Elizabeth Mary *née* Barker; *Career* cmmnd RNAS as Flight Sub-Lt 1915 and ret with rank of Air Cdre 1945; serv Malta and Otranto 1916-17; Maj RAF 1918, Flying Offr 1919; most of early flying done on flying boats like the twin 80hp Anzani engined Curtiss or the H and F class with RR engines and included submarine patrol duties in S Adriatic; staff duties Iraq 1936-39, Sr Air Staff 20 Gp cmdg RAF Weeton 1939-41, joined Air Staff India, Sr Engr responsible for maintenance SEAC 1941-45; *Style—* Air Cdre Stewart Benson, AFC

BENSON, Maj William Arthur; TD, DL (Northumberland 1953); 2 s of Walter John Benson (d 1923), of Newbrough Hall, Hexham, Northumberland; bro of John Elliott Benson, *qv*; *b* 27 June 1905; *Educ* Eton; *m* 1948, Adela Clare Thomasine (d 1980), 3 da of Maj William Percy Standish (d 1922), of Marwell Hall, Hants, and former w of Cdr John Samuel Hervey Lawrence, RN; *Career* Maj with Northumberland Hussars, served WW II Greece, W Desert, Normandy; memb Cncl Royal Agric Soc of England 1949, hon show dir 1955-62, dep pres 1963; High Sheriff Northumberland 1951; *Clubs* Cavalry; *Style—* Maj William Benson, TD, DL; Newbrough Hall, Hexham, Northumberland (☎ 0434 74202)

BENTALL, (Leonard Edward) Rowan; DL (Greater London 1977); s of Leonard H Bentall, JP (d 1942), of Oakwood Court, Leatherhead, Surrey; *b* 27 Nov 1911; *Educ* Eastbourne Coll; *m* 1, 1937, Adelia Elizabeth (d 1986), yr da of David Hawes (d 1946), of Holly Hill, Meopham, Kent; 3 s, 2 da; m 2, 1987, Katherine Christina Allan, of Hants; *Career* served WWII, cmmnd Royal Welch Fusiliers 1941; pres Bentalls plc 1978- (dir 1936-78, md 1963-78, chm 1968-78); pres Steadfast Sea Cadet Corps, govr and vice pres The Horse Rangers Assoc; Freeman City of London; Cavaliere Order Al Merito della Republica Italiana 1971-; *Books* My Store of Memories (1974); *Recreations* ornithology, gardening; *Clubs* RAC, IOD; *Style—* Rowan Bentall, Esq, DL

BENTATA, (Morris) David Albert; s of Robert Victor Bentata (d 1961), of Didsbury, Manchester, and Joyce Ethel, *née* Weinberg; *b* 22 Oct 1913; *Educ* Blundell's, Christ Church Oxford (BA, MA); *m* 20 Feb 1964, Alison Jessica, da of Christopher Henley Boyle Gilroy, of Boundstone, nr Farnham, Surrey; 1 s (Robert b 5 Nov 1968), 1 da (Victoria b 10 Feb 1966); *Career* Nat Serv: enlisted N Staffs Regt 1957, OCS Eaton Hall and Mons 1957-58, cmmnd 2 Lt Intelligence Corps 1958, serv BAOR 1958-59, cmmnd Lt Intelligence Corps (TA) 1959, reg army reserve of offrs 1963; md M Bentata & Son Ltd 1962-67, fndr int mangr Hill Samuel & Co Ltd 1969-72 (investmt analyst 1968-69), int investmt mangr Charterhouse Japhet Ltd 1972-79, md Charterhouse Investmt Mgmnt Ltd 1979-88 (int dir 1979-86), dir bd Charterhouse Portfolio Mangrs Ltd 1986-88, chm and fndr Bentata Assocs Ltd 1988-; elected Lloyd's underwriter 1976; vice chm and chm Stoke d'Abernon Residents Assoc 1969-77, memb ctee Oxshott Cons Assoc 1969-72, memb The Sherlock Holmes Soc of London; Liveryman Worshipful Co of Feltmakers 1983, Freeman City of London 1984; AMSIA 1969, FInstD 1988, FRGS 1988; *Recreations* full-bore rifle shooting, travel; *Clubs* Special Forces; *Style—* David Bentata, Esq; Normandy, Blundel Lane, Cobham, Surrey KT11 2SP (☎ 0372 84 3000)

BENTHALL, Jonathan Charles Mackenzie; s of Sir (Arthur) Paul Benthall, KBE, of Benthall Hall, Broseley, Salop, and Mary Lucy, *née* Pringle (d 1988); *b* 12 Sept 1941; *Educ* Eton, King's Coll Cambridge (MA); *m* 23 Oct 1975, Zamira, da of Sir Yehudi Menuhin OM, KBE, of London; 2 s (Dominic b 1976, William b 1981); *Career* sec ICA 1971-73, dir RAI 1974-, ed Anthropology Today 1985- (RAIN 1974-84); author: Science and Technology in Art Today (1972), The Body Electric Patterns of Western Industrial Culture (1976), memb cncl Save the Children Fund 1987-(former memb UK Child Care and Overseas Ctees); memb Assoc of Social Anthropologists 1983-; Chevalier de l'Ordere des Arts et des Lettres France 1973, FRSA; *Recreations* listening to music, swimming, skiing; *Clubs* Athenaeum; *Style—* Jonathan Benthall, Esq; 212 Hammersmith Grove, London W6 7HG; 50 Fitzroy Street, London W1P 5HS

BENTHALL, Maxim Trevor; s of Leslie Norman Benthall, of Northants, and Gwendoline Alice Benthall; *b* 25 Mar 1947; *Educ* Royal GS High Wycombe, Architectural Assoc Sch of Architecture (AA Dipl, RIBA); *m* (m dis); 2 da (Karen b 1975, Sarah b 1979); *Career* architect; fndg ptnr Benthall Potter Assocs; *Recreations* boating, fishing, painting; *Style—* Maxim Benthall, Esq; 21 Earlsfield Rd, London SW18

BENTHALL, Sir (Arthur) Paul; KBE (1950); s of Rev Charles Francis Benthall (d 1936), of Teignmouth, and Annie Theodosia Benthall; *b* 25 Jan 1902; *Educ* Eton, Ch Ch Oxford; *m* 1932, Mary Lucy (d 1988), da of John Archibald Pringle (d 1952), of Horam, Sussex; 4 s (including Jonathan Charles Mackenzie, *qv*); *Career* chm Amalgamated Metal Corpn 1959-73; dir: Chartered Bank 1953-72, Royal Insur Co and assoc cos 1953-73; pres Assoc Chambers of Commerce of India 1950 and 1948; FLS; *Clubs* Oriental, Lansdowne; *Style—* Sir Paul Benthall, KBE; Benthall Hall, Broseley, Salop (☎ Telford 882254)

BENTHAM, Prof Richard Walker; s of Richard Hardy Bentham (d 1980), of Woodbridge, Suffolk, and Ellen Walker *née* Fisher (d 1983); *b* 26 June 1930; *Educ* Campbell Coll Belfast, Trinity Coll Dublin, (BA, LLB); *m* 16 May 1956, Stella Winifred, da of Henry George Matthews (d 1969), of Hobart, Tasmania; 1 da (Stella); *Career* barr Middle Temple 1955; lectr in law: Univ of Tasmania Hobart 1955-57, Univ of Sydney NSW 1957-61; visiting scholar UCL 1961-62, BP legal dept 1961-83, (dep legal advsr 1979-83); Dundee Univ: prof of petroleum and mineral law, dir centre for petroleum and mineral law studies; pubns in learned journals in the UK and overseas; govr Heatherton House Sch Amersham 1969-83, memb: Int Law Assoc (cncl memb 1980-), Int Bar Assoc 1978, FRSA 1986;; *Books* State Petroleum Corporations (with WGR Smith 1987), Precedents in Petroleum Law (with WGR Smith, 1988),; *Recreations* cricket, military history; *Clubs* Dundee Univ; *Style—* Prof Richard Bentham; Centre for Petroleum and Mineral Law Studies, The University of Dundee, Park Place, Dundee, Scotland, (☎ 0382 23181 ext 4298 fax 0382 201604)

BENTINCK; *see*: Cavendish-Bentinck

BENTINCK, Count (HRE 1732 by Charles VI); Henry Noel Bentinck; mediatised Count of the Holy Roman Empire (decree of German Diet 1945); Queen Victoria permitted 4 Count's descendants to bear title of Count/Countess in England 1888; this was rescinded in respect of all such foreign titles by George V in 1932, starting with Count Henry's heirs; s of Capt 6 Count Bentinck (Robert Charles) d 1932, ggggs of 1 Count (who was in turn half-bro of 1 Duke of Portland and s (by his 2 w) of 1 Earl of Portland), by the Count's w, Lady Norah Noel (da of 3 Earl of Gainsborough); hp to Earldom of Portland, Viscountcy of Woodstock, and Barony of Cirencester, at present held by kinsman, 9 Duke of Portland, *qv*; *b* 2 Oct 1919; *Educ* Harrow; *m* 1, 1940, Pauline (d 1967), da of late Frederick William Mellowes; 1 s (Timothy Robert Charles Noel b 1953, actor, m 1979, Judith Ann Emerson), 2 da (Sorrel m Sir John Lister-Kaye, 8 Bt, *qv*; and Anna); m 2, 1974, Jenifer, only da of late Reginald Hopkins and Mrs McLaren, of Ferring, Sussex; *Career* Lt Coldstream Gds WWII Italian Campaign (wounded 2), BBC producer, TV producer J Walter Thompson; author; *Books* Anyone Can Understand The Atom, The Avenue Of Flutes, Isoworg.; *Style—* Count Bentinck; Little Cudworthy, Dolton, N Devon EX19 8PU

BENTINCK (VON SCHOONHETEN), Baron Steven - Carel Johannes; s of Baron Adolph Willem Carel Bentinck von Schoonheten (former Dutch Ambass to London) and Baroness Thyssen-Bornemisza von Kaszony (sister of Baron Heini Thyssen); male heir of the Barons Bentinck, founded by Johan Bentinck (recorded in Heerde 1361-86) from whom the Dukes of Portland also descend; *b* 1 Mar 1957; *Educ* Sunningdale, Valley Forge Mil Acad USA, Brunel Sch of Econ UK; *m* Nora, da of Fernand Piciotto, and formerly w of Prince Adam Czartoryski; *Career* chm: Renewable Resource Systems Inc USA, Applied Power Technology USA, Applied Power Technology Int; *Clubs* Turf; *Style—* Baron Steven Bentinck; 20 The Vale, London SW3

BENTLEY, His Hon Judge David Ronald; QC (1984); s of Edgar Norman Bentley (d 1982), and Hilda, *née* Thirlwall (d 1959); *b* 24 Feb 1942; *Educ* King Edward VII Sch Sheffield, Univ Coll London (LLB, LLM); *m* 1978, Christine Elizabeth, da of Alec Stewart (d 1978); 1 s (Thomas b 1985); *Career* barr, recorder 1985; Circuit Judge North Eastern Circuit 1988-; *Recreations* legal history, literature, cinema, dogs; *Style—* His Hon Judge David Bentley, QC

BENTLEY, The Ven Frank William Henry; s of Nowell James Bentley (d 1945), and May Sophia Bentley, *née* Gribble; *b* 4 Mar 1934; *Educ* Yeovil Boys GS, Kings Coll London (AKC); *m* 1, 28 Sept 1957, Murial (d 1958), da of Maj Lionel Stewart Bland (d 1983); 1 s (Michael b 1958); m 2, 29 Oct 1960, Yvonne Mary, da of Bernard Henry Wilson; 2 s (Stephen b 1962, Richard b 1971), 1 da (Frances b 1964); *Career* curate Shepton Mallet 1958-62; vector Kingsdon with Podymore Milton 1962-66; curate in charge: Yeovilton 1962-66, Babcary 1964-66; vicar Wiveliscombe 1966-76, rural dean Tone 1973-76, vicar St John in Bednerdine 1976-84, rural dean Martley and Worcester West 1979-84, hon canon Worcester Cathedral 1981-, archdeacon Worcester (and residentiary Cathedral canon) 1984-; memb General Synod 1986-; *Recreations* gardening, motoring; *Style—* The Ven Frank Bentley; 7 College Yard, Worcester WR1 2LA (☎ 0905 25046); Dioceson Office, The Old Palace, Deonsway, Worcester WR1 2JE (☎ 0905 20537)

BENTLEY, Prof George; s of George Bentley (d 1964), and Doris, *née* Blagden; *b* 19 Jan 1936; *Educ* Rotherham GS, Univ of Sheffield (MB, ChB, ChM); *m* 4 June 1960, Ann Gillian, da of Herbert Hutchings (d 1953); 2 s (Paul b 4 March 1964, Stephen b 2 March 1966), 1 da (Sarah b 2 Dec 1962); *Career* lectr in anatomy Birmingham Univ 1961-62, surgical registrar Sheffield Royal Infirmary 1963-65, orthopaedic registrar orthopaedic Hosp Oswestry 1965-67, sr orthopaedic registrar Nuffield Orthopaedic Centre Oxford 1967-69, instr in orthopaedics Univ of Pittsburgh USA 1969-70; Oxford Univ 1970-76: lectr, sr lectr, clinical reader in orthopaedics; prof of orthopaedics: Univ of Liverpool 1976-82, Univ of London 1982-;hon conslt orthopaedic surgeon Royal Nat Orthopaedic Hosp 1982-;FRCS 1968; *Books* Rob and Smith Operative Surgery - Orthopaedics Vols I and II (conslt ed 1979), Mercer's Orthopaedic Surgery (jt ed

1983); *Recreations* music, tennis, horology; *Style*— Prof George Bentley; 120 Fishpool Street, St Albans, Herts AL3 4RX (☎ 0727 51600); University Department of Orthopaedics, Royal National Orthopaedic Hospital, Stanmore, Middlesex HA7 1LP (☎ 01 954 2300 ext 531/532)

BENTLEY, Henry Brian; s of John Clarence Hayes Bentley (d 1972), and Emily Mary, *née* Church; *b* 9 August 1933; *Educ* castleford GS, Open Univ (BA), CNAA (MPhil), Leeds Univ (M ed); *m* 30 Nov 1957, Sylvia Mary, da of William Drabble (d 1984), of Thrybergh, Rotherham; 1 s (Phillip John Henry b 1971), 2 da (Alison Deborah (Mrs Clark) b 1960), Susan Lesley (Mrs Jackson) b 1965); *Career* Nat Serv RAF served war RAF hosps 1955-57; trained nurse Rotherham Hosp 1951-55, RGN 1954; princ Sch of Radiography Gen Infirmary at Leeds 1968- (radiographor 1957-68); memb: Leeds Univ Gp for Study of Ageing, Leeds Univ Bone and Mineral res Gp, ctee Yorks branch Soc of Radiographers (chm 1972-74 and 1978-80), memb cncl Coll of Radiographers 1974-84 (pres 1981-82); co ordinating sec Leeds Med Gp; external examiner Univ of Dublin, examiner Coll of Radiographers (chm var ctees), memb Garforth St Mary's PCC; FCR (1966), FRIPHE (1985); *Books* A Textbook of Radiographic Science (editor 1986); contrib many paper to learned jnls; *Recreations* traction engine rally, church choir; *Style*— Henry Bentley, Esq; Fairfield, Aberford Rd, Garforth, Leeds LS25 1PZ (☎ 0532 862 276); The General Infirmary At Leeds (☎ 0532 432 799)

BENTLEY, John Philip; s of Roland Cunard Bentley (d 1917), of Bexleyheath, Kent, and Margaret, *née* Budd (d 1951); *b* 5 Jan 1916; *Educ* Christ's Hosp Horsham, Charing Cross Hosp, London Univ (MB BS); *m* 31 Oct 1945, Daphne Kathleen, da of Col Charles Burridge Rennick, OBE (d 1968), of Bournemouth; 1 s (Christopher b 1940); *Career* WWII Flying Offr RAF 1940; jr surgn: RAF Halton 1940, RAF Hosp Ely 1940-42; sqdn ldr CO 1 Mobile Surgical Unit RAF (India) 1943-45, Wing Cdr CO GC Mobile Field Hosp (India) 1945-46; surgical registrar Charing Cross Hosp 1946-49, Moynihan Fellowship Assoc of Surgns 1947, Cwlth fell Harkness Fndn 1947-48, lectr surgery Columbia Univ NY 1948; conslt surgn: Connaught Hosp London 1948, Harrow Hosp 1949, Wansted Hosp 1950, Italian Hosp 1959, ret 1981; private conslt practice Harley St 1949-82; Freeman City of London, Liveryman Worshipful Co of Apothecaries; FRSM 1938, MBMA 1938, FRCS 1942, FACS 1955; *Recreations* music, gardening, sailing; *Clubs* RAC, Hurlingham, West Mersea YC; *Style*— John Bentley, Esq; 1 Victoria Esplanade, West Mersea, Colchester, Essex CO5 8AT (☎ 0206 382 452)

BENTLEY, Michael John; s of Leopold John Bentley, (d 1987), and Ann Margaret, *née* Macgillivray (d 1968); *b* 23 Nov 1933; *Educ* Morrisons Acad Crieff Perth; *m* 24 June 1961, Sally Jacqueline, da of Stanley Bertram James Hogan; 4 s (Jeremy b 26 March 1963, Rupert b 29 April 1966, Andrew b 4 March 1968, David b 27 Aug 1970); *Career* joined S G Warburg & Co Ltd 1962, (dir 1968-76), dir Mercury Securities Ltd 1974-76, dir and exec vice-pres Korea Merchant Banking Corpn Seoul 1977-79, dir Lazard Bros & Co Ltd 1977-80, jt vice-chm J Henry Schroder Wagg & Co Ltd 1980-85; dir Schroders plc 1980-85, gp md (corporate fin) 1984-85, chm Electra Mgmnt Services Ltd 1986-, dep chm and chief exec Electra Investmt Tst plc 1986-; chm: fin ctee London Borough of Islington 1968-71, Islington Nat Savings Ctee 1968-71; FCA 1963; *Recreations* music, sailing, gardening, opera; *Clubs* Links (New York); *Style*— Michael Bentley, Esq; 65 Kingsway, London WC2B 6QT (☎ 01 831 6464, telex 265525, fax 01 404 5388)

BENTLEY, Susan Jane; da of Dennis Herbert Bentley, of Caterham, Surrey, and Shirley Constantine, *née* Nineham; *b* 19 July 1955; *Educ* Notre Dame Convent, Univ of Dundee (BSc); *Career* Ernst & Whinney 1977-87, gp acquisitions exec Abaco Investmts plc (now part of Br & Cwlth Hldgs plc) 1987-; ACA 1980; *Recreations* skiing, tennis, entertaining, music; *Style*— Ms Susan Bentley; Kings Hse, 36-37 King St, London EC2V 8BE (☎ 01 600 0840)

BENTLEY, Hon Mrs (Victoria Elizabeth); *née* Mansfield; da of 5 Baron Sandhurst, DFC; *b* 30 Jan 1957; *Educ* Benenden, Bordeaux Univ; *m* 1978, (Charles) James Sharp Bentley, s of Kenneth Bentley, of Balmuir, Angus: 1 s (James b 1982), 1 da (Sophie b 1985); *Recreations* skiing, riding, tennis; *Style*— The Hon Mrs Bentley

BENTLEY, Sir William; KCMG (1985, CMG 1977); s of Lawrence Bentley, and Elsie Jane Bentley; *b* 15 Feb 1927; *Educ* Bury HS, Manchester Univ, Wadham Coll Oxford, Coll of Europe Bruges; *m* 1950, Karen Ellen, *née* Christensen; *Career* joined FO 1952, head Far Eastern dept FCO 1974-76, ambassador The Philippines 1976-81, fifth cmmr to Malaysia 1981-83, ambassador Norway 1983-87; chm Coflexip (UK) Ltd, Soc of Pension Conslts, Roehampton Inst; dep chm Protech Int (UK) Ltd; bd memb: Vienmore Refrigeration Equipment, Dyno Industs (UK); *Style*— Sir William Bentley, KCMG; 48 Bathgate Rd, London, SW19; Oak Cottage, Great Oak Lane, Crickhavell, Powys

BENTON, Kenneth Carter; CMG (1966); s of William Alfred Benton (d 1944), and Amy Adeline, *née* Kirton; *b* 4 Mar 1909; *Educ* Wolverhampton GS, London Univ; *m* 1938, Winifred (Peggie), da of Maj-Gen Charles Pollock, CB, CBE, DSO (d 1929); 1 s, 2 step s (1 decd); *Career* cncllr Rio 1966-68, HM Foreign Serv; Vienna, Riga, Madrid (twice), Rome (twice) Lima, Rio (ret); *Books* Eleven thrillers, publ: Collins, Macmillan, Hale; two historical novels Chatto and Hale; *Recreations* enamelling, writing; *Clubs* Detection; *Style*— Kenneth Benton, Esq, CMG; 2 Jubilee Terrace, Chichester, W Sussex PO19 1XL (☎ 0243 787148)

BENTON, Peter Faulkner; s of Shirley Faulkner Benton (d 1985), of India and Haslemere Surrey, and Hilda Dorothy Benton; *b* 6 Oct 1934; *Educ* Oundle, Queens' Coll Cambridge (MA); *m* 1959, Ruth Stansfeld, da of Robert Stanley Cobb, MC, of Nairobi and Kidlington, Oxon; 2 s (Robert, Thomas), 3 da (Sarah, Juliet, Katherine); *Career* co dir and business conslt specialising in information technology; chm Euro Practice Nolan Norton and Co 1984-87; dir: Turing Inst 1985-, Singer and Friedlander Ltd 1983-, Tandata Hldgs 1983-; formerly md then dep chm Br Telecom; memb: PO Bd 1978-81, gp Bd Gallaher Ltd 1973-77, dir gen Br Institute of Mgmnt 1987-; *Recreations* reading, conversation; *Clubs* United Oxford and Cambridge Univ, The Pilgrims, Highgate Literary and Scientific; *Style*— Peter Benton, Esq; Northgate House, Highgate Hill, London N6 5HD (☎ 01 341 1133);

BENYON, Thomas Yates; s of Capt Thomas Yates Benyon (d 1958, s of Capt Thomas Yates Benyon d 1893) and Hon Christina Philippa Agnes, OBE (da of 11 Baron North, JP, and his 2 wife, Joan Ida Walters d 1982); *b* 13 August 1942; *Educ* Wellington Sch Somerset, RMA Sandhurst; *m* 1968, (Olivia) Jane, da of Humphrey Scott Plummer by his w, Hon Pamela, *née* Balfour, da of 2 Baron Kinross, KC; 2 s, 2 da; *Career* former Lt Scots Gds, served Kenya, Muscat; MP (C) Abingdon 1979-83; chm Assoc of Lloyd's Membs 1982-86, chm Homecare Residential Servs plc, dir Intelligence Technol Hldgs plc; *Recreations* hunting; music; *Clubs* RAC, Pratt's; *Style*— Thomas Benyon, Esq; The Old Rectory, Adstock, Buckingham, Bucks MK18 2HY (☎ 029671 4255); 17 Marshall St, London W1

BENYON, William Richard; DL (1970), MP (C) Milton Keynes 1983-; s of Vice Adm Richard Benyon, CB, CBE (d 1968, 2 s of Sir John Shelley, 9 Bt, JP, DL, a distant cous of the Shelley Bts who produced the poet, and Marion, da of Richard Benyon), and Eve, twin da of Rt Rev Lord William Cecil, sometime Bishop of Exeter (2 s of 3 Marquess of Salisbury); the Adm changed his name to Benyon by Deed Poll on inheriting the Benyon estates of his cous Sir Henry Benyon, Bt; William Benyon is ggs of the Conservative PM, Lord Salisbury; *b* 17 Jan 1930; *Educ* RNC Dartmouth; *m* 1957, Elizabeth Ann, da of Vice Adm Ronald Hallifax, CB, CBE (d 1943), of The Red House, Shenfield, Hants; 2 s (Richard, Edward); 3 da (Catherine Rose Ingrid, Mary, Susannah); *Career* RN 1947-56; MP (C) Buckingham 1970-83, PPS to Paul Channon as Min of Housing 1972-74, oppn whip 1974-77, memb exec 1922 Ctee 1982-; JP Berks 1962-77; *Clubs* Boodle's, Pratt's; *Style*— William Benyon, Esq, DL, MP; Englefield House, Englefield, Reading, Berks (☎ 0734 302221); House of Commons, London SW1 (☎ 01 219 4047)

BERE, Rennie Montague; CMG (1957); s of Rev Montague Acland Bere (d 1947), and Sarah Lucy Troyte, *née* Griffith (d 1942); *b* 28 Nov 1907; *Educ* Marlborough, Selwyn Coll Cambridge (MA); *m* 13 April 1936, (Anne) Maree, da of Cecil Charles Barber (d 1962), of Ceylon; *Career* HM Overseas Serv 1930-55, provincial cmmr Uganda 1951-55; dir and chief warden Uganda Nat Parks 1955-60, pres Cornwall Tst for Nature Conservation 1967-70; author of books on wildlife in Africa and Cornwall; *Books* The Wild Mammals of Uganda (1962), The Way to the Mountains of the Moon (1966), The African Elephant (1966), Birds in an African National Park (1969), Antelopes (1970), Crocodile's Eggs for Supper (folk tales, 1973), Wildlife in Cornwall (1970), The Book of Bude and Stratton (with B D Stamp, 1980), The Nature of Cornwall (1982), has contributed articles to alpine and other journals; *Recreations* mountaineering, cricket, walking, watching wildlife; *Clubs* Alpine, Climbers', Royal Cwlth Soc; *Style*— Rennie Bere, Esq, CMG; West Cottage, Bude Haven, Bude, N Cornwall (☎ 0288 2082)

BERENDT, Lady Frances Virginia Susan; *née* Ryder; da of 6 Earl of Harrowby and Helena Blanche Coventry; *b* 20 June 1926; *Educ* St Hugh's Oxford; *m* 1949, Frank Ernest Berendt, s of Siegfried Berendt (d 1947), of London; 1 s (Anthony), 1 da (Susan); *Career* dir and permissions ed Calibre (Cassette Library for the Blind and Handicapped); *Style*— Lady Frances Berendt; 34 The Marlowes, Boundary Road, NW8

BERENDT, Richard Arthur; s of Harold Berendt (d 1971), of Roydon, Essex, and Winifred, *née* Chipperfield; *b* 14 June 1926; *Educ* The Coll Bishops Stortford, Univ of Reading (BSc Agric); *m* 7 June 1952, Jean Marr, da of Lt-Col Arthur Cyril Robert Croom-Johnson (d 1964), of Sloane Square, London; 1 s (Peter b 1956), 1 da (Julia b 1963); *Career* served HAC 1948-59, Capt; gen mangr Shell Chemical Co E Africa and Central Africa 1966-71, dir Berendt Bros Ltd 1972-81; fin advsr 1976-; *Recreations* golf, beekeeping; *Clubs* Farmers; *Style*— Richard A Berendt, Esq; Kelsale Place, Kelsale, Saxmundham, Suffolk IP17 2RD (☎ 0728 2410; Hill Samuel Investment Services Ltd, Mount Pleasant House, Huntingdon Road, Cambridge CB3 0BL (☎ 0223 462233)

BERENS, David John Cecil; s of Herbert Cecil Berens, MC (d 1981), of Bentworth Hall, Alton, Hants, and Moyra Nancy Mellard, niece and adopted da of 1 and last Baron Greene, PC, OBE, MC, KC; descendant of Joseph Berens, of Kevington, Kent (d 1853), whose ancestors accompanied William of Orange from Holland in 1688; 6 generations have matric at Christ Church Oxford; *b* 7 Oct 1939; *Educ* Eton, Ch Ch Oxford (MA); *m* 3 Oct 1963, Janet Roxburgh, yst da of Archibald Roxburgh Balfour, MC (d 1958), of Dawyck, Peeblesshire; sister of Christopher and Neil Balfour (*qqv*); 2 s (Archie b 1965, Jasper b 1970), 2 da (Emily b 1967, Henrietta b 1981); *Career* merchant banker: Lazard Bros 1962-72, invest mangr Trafalgar House 1972-82, md London Trust 1982-85; exec dir Tyndall Holdings 1985-; *Recreations* arts, literature, sport, wine, shooting; *Clubs* White's; *Style*— Henry Berens, Esq; 71 Church Rd, Wimbledon Village, SW19; Tyndall Holdings plc, 25 Bucklesbury, London EC4 8TH (car ☎ 0836 272 583)

BERESFORD, Lord Charles Richard de la Poer; 2 s of 8 Marquess of Waterford; *b* 18 Jan 1960; *Style*— Lord Charles Beresford; Curraghmore, Portlaw, Co Waterford

BERESFORD, Christopher Charles Howard; s of (Richard) Marcus Beresford (d 1968), of Oundle, and Diana Katharine, *née* Howard; *b* 9 July 1946; *Educ* Dragon Sch, Rugby, Trinity Coll Cambridge (MA); *m* 5 May 1973, (Phillipa) Susan, da of Dennis Yates (d 1968); 1 s (Nicholas b 1979), 2 da (Antonia b 1975, Fiona b 1977); *Career* CA, ptnr Peat Marwick McLintock 1981; vice chm Br Ski Club for the Disabled; Liveryman Worshipful Co of Grocers; FCA; *Recreations* skiing, tennis, shooting, badminton, bridge; *Clubs* City Livery, Ski Club of GB; *Style*— Christopher Beresford, Esq; Peat Marwick McLintock, 1 Puddle Dock, Blackfriars, London EC4V 3PD; (☎ 01 236 8000, fax 01 583 1938, telex 8811541 PMM LON G)

BERESFORD, Hon Clare Antoinette Gabrielle de la Poer; yr da of 6 Baron Decies (by 2 w); *b* 31 Dec 1956; *m* Jorge J Koechlin; 1 s (Michael Joseph Tristram b 1986); *Style*— Hon Clare Beresford; c/o Coutts and Co, 1 Old Park Lane, London W1Y 4BS

BERESFORD, Lord James Patrick de la Poer; 3 s of 8 Marquess of Waterford; *b* 10 Dec 1965; *Style*— Lord James Beresford; Curraghmore, Portlaw, Co Waterford

BERESFORD, Marcus de la Poer; s of Anthony de la Poer Beresford, TD, of Harrow-on-the-hill, Middx and Emmala Mary Alwina Beresford; *b* 15 May 1942; *Educ* Harrow, St John's Coll Cambridge (MA); *m* 25 Sept 1965, Jean Helen, da of H T Kitchener, of Shepreth, Cambs; 2 s (Thomas, William); *Career* Smiths Industs 1960-83 (operating gp md 1979-83), dir and gen mangr Lucas Electronics & Systems 1983-85, md Plessey Controls Ltd 1985-; dir Dorset C of C and Indust; chm: bd of govrs Dorset Inst of Higher Educn, CBI; Freeman City of London 1963, Liveryman Worshipful Co of Skinners; FIEE, MIMechE; *Recreations* golf; *Style*— Marcus Beresford, Esq; Plessey Controls Ltd, Sopers Lane, Poole, Dorset BH17 7ER (☎ 0202 782294, telex 41272)

BERESFORD, Hon Marcus Hugh Tristam de la Poer; only s and heir of 6 Baron Decies (by 2 w); *b* 5 August 1948; *Educ* St Columba's Coll, Dublin Univ; *m* 1, 1970 (m dis 1974), Sarah Jane, only da of Col Basil Gunnell; m 2, 1981, Edel Jeanette, da of late Vincent Ambrose Hendron of Dublin; 1 da (Louisa b 1984); *Style*— Hon Marcus Beresford; c/o Coutts and Co, 1 Old Park Lane, W1Y 4BS

BERESFORD, Lord Patrick Tristram de la Poer; s of 7 Marquis of Waterford (d 1934); *b* 16 June 1934; *Educ* Eton, Sandhurst; *m* 1964 (m dis 1971), Mrs Julia Carey, da of Col Thomas Cromwell Williamson, DSO; 1 s, 1 da; *Career* Capt RHG (ret); bloodstock agent; chef d'Équipe Br 3 day event team 1985; *Clubs* White's; *Style*— Lord Patrick Beresford; Fairview Cottage, Wicks Green, Binfield, Berks RG12 5PF (☎ 0344 860976)

BERESFORD, Lady William Rachel Wyborn; *née* Page; yr da of late George Kennett Page, JP, of Upton Lodge, Bursledon, Hants, and Edith Mary, *née* Hill; *b* 5 July 1908; *Educ* Godolphin Sch Wilts; *m* 1945, Maj Lord William Mostyn de la Poer Beresford (d 1973), 2 s of 7 Marquess of Waterford ; 2 da (Meriel, Nicola); *Style*— Lady William Beresford; The Thatched Cottage, Church Lane, Stradbally, Co Waterford (☎ 24275)

BERESFORD, Hon Sarah Ann Vivien de la Poer; el da of 6 Baron Decies (by 2 w); *b* 23 June 1949; *m* 1975, Joerg Schnapka; 1 s (Roland b 1976); *Style*— Hon Sarah Beresford; c/o Coutts and Co, 1 Old Park Lane, London W1Y 4BS

BERESFORD JONES, David; s of Capt Sidney Albert Jones, RD, RNR (d 1975), of Bournemouth (former Capt Queen Mary and Queen Elizabeth) and Bertha Mary Moldram, *née* Barnes; *b* 19 August 1936; *Educ* King's Sch Bruton; *m* 1, 12 Sept 1959 (m dis 1972), Sheila, *née* Lewis; 2 da (Nicola b 1963, Sarah b 1965); m 2, 19 Aug 1972, Lynda Caroline, da of Kenneth Roy Dolleymore (d 1976); 1 s (Edward b 1976), 1 da (Caroline b 1979); *Career* pilot offr RAF 1954-56; dir: Bland Welch (Reinsurance Brokers) Ltd 1971-74, Bland Payne Reinsurance Brokers Ltd 1974-76, Steel Burrill Jones Gp plc (co-fndr 1977); chm Steel Burrill Jones Ltd 1985-; *Recreations* cricket, real tennis, hockey, tennis; *Clubs* MCC, HAC, RTC (Hampton Court), Tulse Hill and Honor Oak, Roehampton, Institute of Directors; *Style*— David Beresford Jones, Esq; Bankside House, 107-112 Leadenhall Street, London EC3A 4AP (☎ 01 623 4411, telex 887830 SBJG, fax: 01 621 1848)

BERESFORD-ASH, John Randal; s of Maj Douglas Beresford-Ash, DSO, DL (d 1976), of Co Londonderry, N Ireland, and Lady Helena Betty Joanna Rous (d 1969); *b* 21 Jan 1938; *Educ* Eton; *m* 27 March 1968, Agnes Marie Colette, da of Comte Jules Marie Guy de Lamberterie, L'Ensouleiada Av de Bénéfiat, of Cannes, Frances; 3 da (Melanie b 1968, Louisa-Jane b 1971, Angelique b 1978); *Career* Londonderry Grand Jury 1959-68, High Sheriff County Londonderry 1976, pres Afghan Aid (Ireland) 1986-, farmer; *Recreations* golf; *Style*— John R Beresfod-Ash, Esq; Ashbrook, Drumahoe, Co Londonderry, N Ireland (☎ 0504 49223)

BERESFORD-PEIRSE, Sir Henry Grant de la Poer; 6 Bt (UK 1814), of Bagnall, Waterford; s of Sir Henry Beresford-Peirse, 5 Bt, CB (d 1972), and Margaret, Lady Beresford-Peirse, *qv*; *b* 7 Feb 1933; *Educ* Eton, Ontario Agric Coll; *m* 1966, Jadranka, da of Ivan Njerš, of Zagreb; 2 s; *Heir* s, Henry Beresford-Peirse; *Career* investment mgmnt; *Recreations* tennis, golf, country homes in Yorkshire and Portugal; *Clubs* Cavalry and Guards; *Style*— Sir Henry Beresford-Peirse, Bt; Bedall Manor, Bedale, N Yorks (☎ 0677 22811); 34 Cadogan Sq, London SW1 (☎ 01 589 1134)

BERESFORD-PEIRSE, Henry Njerš de la Poer; s and h of Sir Henry Grant de la Poer Beresford-Peirse, 6 Bt; *b* 25 Mar 1969; *Educ* Harrow; *Recreations* cricket, golf, tennis; *Style*— Henry Beresford-Peirse, Esq; c/o Bedall Manor, Bedale, N Yorks

BERESFORD-PEIRSE, Margaret, Lady; Margaret; da of Frank Morrison Seafield Grant, of Knockie Whitebridge Inverness-shire and Caroline Frances Grant, *née* Philips; *b* 15 Oct 1907; *Educ* Cheltenham Ladies Coll; *m* 1932, Sir Henry Campell de la Poer Beresford-Peirse, 5 Bt, CB (d 1972); 2 s (Sir Henry Grant de la Poer Beresford-Peirse, 6 Bt, John David de la Poer 1 adopted da (Mary, m Andrew, yr s of Sir John Gilmour, Bt, *qv*, of Montrave Fife Scotland; 2 s (Robert, David); *Clubs* Lansdowne; *Style*— Margaret, Lady Beresford-Peirse; Bedall Manor, Bedale, N Yorks (☎ 0677 22811); Monte Elvas, S Bras de Alportel, Algarve, Portugal (☎ 089 42843)

BERESFORD-STOOKE, Lady; Creenagh; da of Sir Henry George Richards, KBE, KC (d 1928), sometime Chief Justice of Allahabad, and Frances Maud Lyster, OBE, *née* Smythe; *m* 1931, Sir George Beresford-Stooke, KCMG (d 1983), Gentleman Usher of the Blue Rod 1959-71; 1 s, 1; *Career* CStJ; *Style*— Lady Beresford-Stooke; Little Rydon, Hillfarrance, Taunton, Somerset TA4 1AW (☎ 0823 461640)

BERESFORD-WEST, Michael Charles; QC (1975); s of Arthur Charles and Ida Dagmar West; *b* 3 June 1928; *Educ* St Peters, Portsmouth GS, BNC Oxford (MA); *m* 1956 (m dis), Patricia Eileen, *née* Beresford; 2 s, 1 da; m 2, 1986, Sheilagh Elizabeth Davies; *Career* Serv Intelligence Middle East, barr 1952, Western Circuit 1953-65, South Eastern Circuit 1965, chm Independent Schs Tribunal 1974-80, recorder of the Crown Court 1975-83; *Recreations* tennis, music, swimming; *Clubs* Oxford and Cambridge, MCC, Hampshire Hogs, Aldeburgh Golf and Aldeburgh Yacht, Bar Yacht; *Style*— Michael Beresford-West, Esq, QC; 1 Grays Inn Square, London WC1R 5AG

BERGEL, Hon Mrs; (Alexandra Mary Swinford); *née* Shackleton; only da of Baron Shackleton, KG, OBE, PC (Life Peer); *b* 15 July 1940; *Educ* Raven's Croft, Eastbourne, Trinity Coll Dublin; *m* 1969, Richard Charles Bergel, MB, BS, yr s of Hugh Charles Bergel, of Stamford Brook House, W6; 2 s; *Style*— The Hon Mrs Bergel; Dolphin House, Cricket Hill, Yateley, Hants

BERGENDAHL, (Carl) Anders; s of Carl Johan Bergendahl, of Djursholms, Sweden, and Ingrid Bergendahl (d 1964); *b* 20 Mar 1952; *Educ* Djursholm Samskola Sweden, Stockholm Sch of Econs; *m* 18 March 1984, Maria, da of Stephen Heineman (d 1967); 2 s (David b 11 Sept 1985, Alexander b 18 June 1987); *Career* assoc Merrill Lynch 1977-, md Merrill Lynch Capital Markets 1985-; *Recreations* sailing, tennis, squash, skiing; *Clubs* Sallskapet, RAC; *Style*— Anders Bergendahl, Esq; 25 Ropemaker St, Ropemaker Place, London EC2Y 9LY (☎ 01 867 2800, fax 01 867 2040)

BERGER, Vice Adm Sir Peter Egerton Capel; KCB (1979), LVO (1960), DSC (1949); s of Capel Colquhoun Berger (d 1941), and Winifred Violet, *née* Levett-Scrivener (d 1981); *b* 11 Feb 1925; *Educ* Harrow; *m* 1956, June Kathleen, da of Cdr Frederick Arthur Pigou, RN (d 1979); 3 da (Sarah b 1959, Louisa b 1961, Katy b 1964); *Career* joined RN 1943, Normandy and S of France landings in HMS Ajax 1944, Lt 1946, Yangtse Incident served in HMS Amethyst 1948, Lt-Cdr 1953, Cdr 1956, Fleet Navigating Offr, Home Fleet 1956-58, Navigating Offr, HM Yacht Britannia 1958-60, i/c HMS Torquay 1962-64, Capt 1964, i/c HMS Phoebe 1966-68; Cdre, Clyde 1971-73; Rear Adm 1973; Asst Chief of Naval Staff (Policy) 1973-75; Chief of Staff to C-in-C Fleet 1976-78; Flag Offr Plymouth, Port Adm Devonport, Cdr Centl Sub Area E Atlantic and Cdr Plymouth Sub Area Channel 1979-81; bursar and fell Selwyn Coll Cambridge 1981-; Hon MA Cantab 1984; *Recreations* reading history, shooting, fishing; *Style*— Vice Adm Sir Peter Berger, KCB, LVO, DSC; Linton End House, Linton Road, Balsham, Cambs CB1 6HA; Selwyn College, Cambridge CB3 9DQ (☎ 0223 335891)

BERGNE, Hon Mrs; (Phyllis) Dorothy; *née* Borwick; yr da of 3 Baron Borwick (d 1961) by his 1 w; *b* 24 August 1916; *m* 1963, as his 2 wife, John A'Court Bergne, ARSM, MIMM (d 1978), s of Hervey A'Court Bergne (d 1941), of Budleigh Salterton, Devon; *Career* late Fl Offr WAAF; *Style*— The Hon Mrs Bergne; 16 Woodlane, Falmouth, Cornwall (☎ 0326 312430)

BERHAM, Richard Andrew; s of Laurence S Berman, CB, of 10 Carlton Close, Edgeware, Middx, and Kathleen, *née* Lewis; *b* 3 April 1956; *Educ* Haberdashers' Askes, Churchill Coll Cambridge (BA, MA); *m* 31 Aug 1985, Susan, *née* Charles; *Career* tres Andrea Merzarion Spa 1981-83, gp tres, Heron Corpn plc 1984; dir: IFM Term Investments Ltd 1985-, Pine St Investments Ltd 1987, Ashbourne Fin plc 1988-, Crosby Hldgs Ltd 1988-, Ellastone plc 1988-, Law Dempsey & Co Ltd 1988-, Fin Ventures Ltd 1988-; memb Assoc of Corporate Treasurers

BERKELEY, Andrew Wilson Atkins; s of Andrew Berkeley, JP (d 1952), of Cookstown, Co Tyrone, NI, and Mabel Berkeley; *b* 15 July 1936; *Educ* Rainey Sch Co Derry, Queen's Univ Belfast (BSc), Harvard Business Sch (AMP); *m* 30 Nov 1968, Carolyn Blyth Hinshaw Ross, of Milngavie, Glasgow, Scotland; 2 da (Kirsten b 16 Nov 1972, Iona b 27 April 1978); *Career* HAC Inf Bn TA 1966-67; barr Grays Inn 1965, memb legal dept ICI Ltd 1966-78, dir ICI Petroleum Ltd 1978-81, slr 1980, sec Br Nat Oil Corpn 1981-84, dir legal corporate affrs STC plc 1984-87, gp gen counsel Laporte plc 1987-; vice chm section for energy and nat resources Law Int Bar Assoc 1979-83; Law Soc: memb standing ctee on revenue Law, chm ctee on petroleum taxation 1980-84; memb cncl: Inst of Industl and Commercial Law and Practice, Int C of C Paris; ACIArb 1986; *Recreations* riding; *Clubs* Athenaeum; *Style*— Andrew Berkeley, Esq; 49 Arden Rd, London N3 3AD(☎ 01 346 4114); Laporte House, Kingsway, Luton, Beds LU4 8EW (☎ 0582 21212)

BERKELEY, David James; s of Aubrey William Grandidier Berkeley, of Reigate, Surrey, and Sheena Elsie, *née* Turner; *b* 7 August 1944; *Educ* Rugby; *m* 28 Sept 1968, Gay Veronica, da of Robert Geoffrey William Hudson, MBE, of Naivasha Kenya; 2 da (Georgina b 1972, Louisa b 1975); *Career* chm and md Brown Shipley (Jersey) Ltd, non-exec dir Brown Shipley and Co Ltd London; FCA; *Recreations* lawn tennis, hockey; *Clubs* Public Schools Old Boys Lawn Tennis Assoc; *Style*— David J Berkeley, Esq; La Grange, St Mary, Jersey, CI (☎ 0534 81760); Brown Shipley (Jersey) Ltd, Channel House, Green St, St Helier, Jersey, Channel Islands

BERKELEY, Frederic George; s of Dr Augustus Frederic Millard Berkeley, (d 1952), of Kennington, and the late Anna Louisa Berkeley *née* Inniss (d 1954); bro of Maurice Berkeley, CB, *qv*; *b* 21 Dec 1919; *Educ* Elstree Sch, Aldenham Sch, Pembroke Coll Cambridge (MA); *m* 1964 (m dis), Mrs Gillian Eugenie Louise Depreux, da of E Willis 1 s, 1 da (and 1 decd), 1 step da; *Career* served WW II, Maj Normandy (wounded); slr, ptnr Lewis and Lewis 1951-70, vice-chm and chm Legal Aid Area Ctee 1964-70, master of the Supreme Ct 1971-; gen ed Butterworths Costs Service; *Recreations* reading, gardening, travel, writing; *Style*— Frederic Berkeley, Esq; The Royal Courts of Justice, Strand, London WC2A 2LL (☎ 01 136 6343)

BERKELEY, Humphry John; s of Capt Reginald Cheyne Berkeley, MC (d 1935), sometime Liberal MP, and his 2 wife Hildegarde (Mrs Hildegarde Tinne); *b* 21 Feb 1926; *Educ* Malvern, Pembroke Coll Cambridge (pres Cambridge Union 1948); *Career* served at Cons Political Centre 1949-56, chm Coningsby Club 1952-55, dir-gen UK Cncl Euro Movement 1956-57; MP (C) Lancaster 1959-66; joined Labour Party 1970, fought North Fylde (Lab) Oct 1974, joined SDP 1981, contested (SDP) Homefields Ward of Hounslow for borough cncl election of May 1982, fought Southend East (SDP Liberal Alliance) 1987; dir: Caspair Ltd, Island Devpts; dir Sharon Allen Leukaemia Tst 1984-; contested Southend East (SDP/Liberal Alliance) 1987; *Books* The Power of the Prime Minister (1968), Crossing the Floor (1972), The Life and Death of Rochester Sneath (1974), The Odyssey of Enoch - A Political Memoir (1976), The Myth that will not Die - The Formation of the National Government (1978), Faces of The Eightes (with Jeffrey Archer) 1987; *Clubs* Savile; *Style*— Humphry Berkeley, Esq; 3 Pages Yard, Church St, Chiswick, W4 (☎ 01 994 5575)

BERKELEY, (Robert) John Grantley; TD (1967), JP (Glos 1960), DL (Glos 1982, Hereford and Worcester 1983); s of Capt Robert George Wilmot Berkeley (d 1969, himself 13 in descent from Hon Thomas Berkeley (4 s of 1 Baron Berkeley cr 1421, gs of 4 Baron Berkeley cr 1295, and descended in direct male line from Eadnoth the Staller, pre-Conquest Anglo-Saxon nobleman at Court of King Edward the Confessor) by his 2 w Isabel, da and co-heir of Thomas Mowbray, 1 Duke of Norfolk and Hon Myrtle, da of 14 Baron Dormer); *b* 24 July 1931; *Educ* Oratory Sch, Magdalen Coll Oxford; *m* 25 Jan 1967, Georgina Bridget, eldest da of Maj Andrew Charles Stirling Home Drummond Moray (d 1971), of Easter Ross, Comrie, Perthshire; 2 s (Robert Charles b 1968, Henry John Mowbray b 1969); *Career* Maj Queen's Own Warwicks Yeo 1963; jt master Berkeley Hunt 1960-84; High Sheriff: Worcs 1967, Glos 1982-83; *Clubs* Cavalry and Guards; *Style*— Major John Berkeley, TD, JP, DL; Berkeley Castle, Glos (☎ 0453 810 202); Spetchley Park, nr Worcester (☎ 090 565 224)

BERKELEY, Sir Lennox Randal; CBE (1957); s of Capt Hastings George Fitzhardinge Berkeley, RN (d 1934), and Aline Carla, *née* Harris; *b* 12 May 1903; *Educ* Gresham's, Merton Coll Oxford; *m* 1946, (Elizabeth) Freda, da of Isaac Bernstein (d 1926), of London; 3 s; *Career* composer, pres Performing Rights Soc 1975-; kt 1974; *Recreations* reading; *Style*— Sir Lennox Berkeley, CBE; 8 Warwick Ave, W2 (☎ 01 262 3922)

BERKELEY, Baroness (E 1421); Mary Lalle Foley Berkeley; da of Col Frank Wigram Foley, CBE, DSO (d 1949), and Eva Mary Fitz-Hardinge, Baroness Berkeley (d 1964); *b* 9 Oct 1905; *Heir* sister, Hon Mrs Gueterbock; *Style*— The Rt Hon the Lady Berkeley; Pickade Cottage, Gt Kimble, Aylesbury, Bucks (☎ (084 44) 3051)

BERKELEY, (Augustus Fitzhardinge) Maurice; CB (1975); s of Dr Augustus Frederic Millard Berkeley (d 1952), of Kennington, and Anne Louisa, *née* Inniss (d 1954); bro of Frederic George Berkeley, *qv*; *b* 26 Feb 1903; *Educ* Aldenham, Pembroke Coll Cambridge; *m* 1, 1931, Elaine Emily (d 1985), da of Aden Simmonds; m 2, 1985, Margaret Mary Thérèse, da of late Edward Cyril Arthur Crookes; *Career* barr 1927, chief registrar High Court Bankruptcy 1966-75; *Recreations* watching cricket, travel, reading; *Clubs* Garrick, MCC; *Style*— Maurice Berkeley, Esq, CB; 3 Dr Johnson's Bldgs, Temple, London EC4 (☎ 01 353 2448); 11 Boyes Croft, White

Street, Great Dunmow, Essex (☎ (0371) 3079)

BERKELEY, Michael Fitzhardinge; s of Sir Lennox Randolph Francis Berkeley, CBE, of 8 Warwick Avenue, London, and Elizabeth Freda, *née* Bernstein; *b* 29 May 1948; *Educ* Westminster Cathedral Choir Sch, The Oratory Royal Acad of Music (ARAM), post grad work with Richard Rodney Bennett *qv*; *m* 19 Nov 1979, Deborah Jane Coltman, da of Guy Coltman Rogers(d 1976), of Stanage Park, Knighton, Powys; 1 da (Jessica Rose b 28 Jun 1986); *Career* composer and broadcaster; phlebotonist St Bartholomew's Hosp 1969-71, announcer BBC Radio 1974-79, regular broadcaster on music and the arts BBC radio and tv 1974-; music panel advsr Arts Cncl of GB, memb central music advsy ctee BBC; assoc composer Scottish Chamber Orch 1979; pres Presteigne Festival; compositons incl: Meditation (Guiness prize for composition) 1977, Primavera 1979, Uprising 1980, Wessex Graves 1981, Oratorio Or Shall We Die 1982, Music from Chaucer 1983, Fierce Tears 1984, Pas de Deux 1985, Songs of Awakening Love 1986, Organ Concerto 1987, The red Macula 1989; memb Composer's Guild of GB, APC; *Recreations* contemporary printing, walking, hill farming; *Style*— Michael Berkeley, Esq; 49 Blenheim Cresc, London W11 2EF (☎ 01 229 6945)

BERKLEY-MATTHEWS, John; s of John Matthews Berkley-Matthews (ka 1954), and Elizabeth Joan Harcourt, *née* Wheeler later Barlow; *b* 20 Nov 1940; *Educ* Wellington, Sandhurst; *m* 1 April 1967, Susan Margaret, da of Lt-Col Richard John Gyde Heaven (ret), of Dinton, Salisbury; 1 s (Richard John b 1968), 3 da (Mara Elizabeth b 1970, Hellen Loring b 1972, Charlotte Margaret b 1974); *Career* cmmnd RE; responsible for construction of a harbour at Akrotiri Cyprus 1965; diving team Germany 1964; ret as Capt 1970; pioneer trout farmer UK 1970-; *Recreations* family, shooting; *Clubs* Army and Navy; *Style*— John Berkley-Matthews, Esq; The Old Manse, Tisbury, Wiltshire (☎ 0747 870791)

BERLIAND, David Michael; s of Jasha Berliand (d 1976), and Phyllis, *née* Doresa; *b* 17 Dec 1935; *Educ* Charterhouse; *m* 1961, Diana Jill, da of Antony Maynard Puckle, of Hants; 1 s (Richard b 1962), 2 da (Louise b 1964, Penelope b 1967); *Career* Nat Serv Lt RA 1955, Germany; dir Bain Clarkson Ltd (insurance brokers) 1987-; chm and md Int Div, dir Inchcape Insur Hldgs Ltd;; *Recreations* tennis, golf; *Clubs* Boodle's, MCC; *Style*— David Berliand, Esq; Bridgefoot Farm, Ripley, Surrey (0483 224354); 15 Minories, London EC3N 1NJ (☎ 01 481 3232, telex 8813411, fax 01 480 6137)

BERLIN, Sir Isaiah; OM (1971), CBE (1946); s of Mendel and Marie Berlin, of London; *b* 6 June 1909; *Educ* St Paul's Sch, CCC Oxford; *m* 1956, Aline, da of Baron Pierre de Gunzbourg, of Paris and formerly w of Dr Hans Halban; *Career* serv WWII with Miny of Info and FO; Chichele prof of social and political theory Oxford Univ 1957-67, visiting prof of humanities City Univ NY 1966-71, pres Wolfson Coll Oxford 1966-75; pres Br Acad 1974-78, fell: New Coll Oxford 1938-50, All Souls Coll Oxford; memb bd of dirs Roya;l Opera House Covent Garden 1954-65 and 1974-87; tstee Nat Gallery 1975-85; awarded Erasmus Prize 1983 for promoting Euro culture; recipient of hon doctorates from Br, Israeli and American Univs; FBA; kt 1957; *Books* Karl Marx (1939, 1978), First Love by I A Turgenev (translation 1950), The Age of Enlightenment (1956), Four Essays on Liberty (1969), Vico and Herder (1976), Concepts and Categories (1978), Russian Thinkers (1978), Against the Current (1979), Personal Impressions (1980); *Style*— Sir Isaiah Berlin, OM, CBE; All Souls College, Oxford

BERMAN, Franklin Delou; CMG (1987); s of Joshua Zelic Berman, of Cape Town, and Gertrude Levin; *b* 23 Dec 1939; *Educ* Rondebosch Boys HS, Univ of Cape Town (BA, BSc), Wadham and Nuffield Coll Oxford (MA); *m* 24 July 1964, Christine Mary, da of Edward Francis Lawler (d 1978); 2 s (Jonathan b 1966, Stefan b 1968), 3 da (Katharine b 1972, Judith b 1972, Victoria b 1972); *Career* HM Dip Serv 1965, asst legal advsr FCO 1965-71, legal advsr Br Mil Govt Berlin 1971-72, legal advsr Br Embassy Bonn 1972-74; legal cnsllr FCO 1974-82, cnsllr UK Mission UN 1982-85, dep legal advsr FCO 1988-; chm: Dip Serv Assoc 1979-82, Staff Tbnl Int Oil Pollution Compensation Fund 1985-; *Recreations* reading, walking, choral singing, gardening; *Style*— Franklin Berman, Esq; Foreign and Commonwealth Office, King Charles St, London SW1A 2AH (☎ 01 270 3000)

BERMAN, Lawrence Sam; CB (1975); s of Jack Berman, and Violet Berman (d 1980); *b* 15 May 1928; *Educ* St Clement Danes GS, LSE (BSc, MSc); *m* 1954, Kathleen D Lewis; 1 s (Richard), 1 da (Caroline); *Career* central statistical Off 1952-72, dir of statistics Dept of Trade and Industry 1972-83; statistical advsr Caribbean Tourism Research and Dept Centre Bardados 1984-85; *Recreations* travel, theatre, collecting bow ties; *Style*— Lawrence Berman, Esq, CB; 10 Carlton Close, Edgware, Middx HA8 7PY (☎ 01 958 6938)

BERMAN, Richard Andrew; s of Laurence S Berman CB, of 10 Carlton Close, Edgware, Middx, and Kathleen, *née* Lewis; *b* 3 April 1956; *Educ* Haberdashers' Aske's, Churchill Coll. Cambridge (BA, MA); *m* 31 Aug 1985, Susan, *née* Charles; *Career* tres Andrea Merzario Spa 1982-83, gp tres Heron Corpn plc 1984; dir: IFM Term Investments Ltd 1985-, Pine St Investmts Ltd 1987-, Ashbourne Fin plc 1988-, Crosby Securities Hldgs Ltd 1988-, Ellastone plc 1988-, Law Dempsey & Co Ltd 1988-, Fin Ventures Ltd 1988-; memb Assoc of Corporate Treasurers; *Recreations* eclectic collecting, walking, reading; *Style*— Richard Berman, Esq; Pine St Investments Ltd, Bowater House West, 68 Knightsbridge, London SW1X 7LT (☎ 01 225 3911, fax 01 581 0131)

BERMANT, Chaim Icyk; s of Azriel Bermant (d 1962), of Glasgow, and Feiga, *née* Daets (d 1971); *b* 26 Feb 1929; *Educ* Queens Park Sch, Glasgow, Glasgow Univ (MA MLitt), LSE (MSc); *m* 16 Dec 1962, Judy, da of Fred Weil, of Jerusalem; 2 s (Azriel b 1968, Daniel b 1972), 2 da (Alisa b 1963, Evie b 1966); *Career* staff writer: Scot TV 1957-59, Granada TV 1959-61, journalist Jewish Chronicle,; *Style*— Chaim Bermant, Esq; c/o Aitken and Stone, 29 Fernshaw Rd, London SW10 OTG

BERMINGHAM, Gerald Edward; MP (Lab) St Helens S 1983-; s of late Patrick Xavier Bermingham and Eva Terescena Bermingham; *b* 20 August 1940; *Educ* Cotton Coll, Wellingborough GS, Sheffield Univ; *m* 1, 1964 (m dis), Joan; 2 s; m 2, 1978, Judith; *Career* barrister formerly slr, memb Sheffield City Cncl 1975-79, contested (Lab) Derbyshire S E 1979; *Style*— Gerald Bermingham, Esq, MP; House of Commons, London SW1

BERNARD, Sir Dallas Edmund; 2 Bt (UK 1954), of Snakemoor, Co Southampton; s of Sir Dallas Gerald Mercer Bernard, 1 Bt (d 1975); *b* 14 Dec 1926; *Educ* Eton, Corpus Christi Coll Oxford (MA); *m* 1, 1959 (m dis 1978); 3 da (Juliet Mary b 1961, Alicia Elizabeth b 1964, Sarah Jane b 1968); m 2, 1979, Mrs Monica J Montford, da of late James Edward Hudson; 1 da (Olivia Louise b 1981); *Heir* none; *Career* dir: Morgan Grenfell and Co Ltd 1964-77, Morgan Grenfell Hldgs Ltd 1970-79, Italian Int Bank plc 1978-; memb Monopolies and Mergers Cmmn 1973-79; chm: Nat and Foreign Securities Tst Ltd 1981-86, Thames Tst Ltd 1983-86; dir Dreyfus Intercontinental Investmt Fund NY 1970-; cncl memb Girls Public Day Sch Tst 1978-; *Clubs* Brooks's, Lansdowne; *Style*— Sir Dallas Bernard, Bt; 8 Eaton Place, London SW1X 8AD

BERNARD, Jeffrey Joseph; s of Maj Oliver Bernard, OBE, MC, FRIBA (d 1939); *b* 27 May 1932; *Educ* Pangbourne; *m* 1978, Susan; 1 da (by previous mar); *Career* journalist Spectator and Private Eye, columnist formerly with New Statesman, Daily Mirror, Pacemaker; feature writer Sunday Times Mag, reviewer Punch, racing columnist Harpers and Queen; *Recreations* cooking, music, racing, drinking with friends; *Clubs* Colony Room, Chelsea Arts, Gerry's; *Style*— Jeffrey Bernard, Esq

BERNARD, Lady Jennifer Jane; er da of Air Chief Marshal 5 and last Earl of Bandon, GBE, CB, CVO, DSO (d 1979), and his 1 w, (Maybel) Elizabeth (*see* Holcroft, Elizabeth, Lady); *b* 30 April 1935; *Style*— Lady Jennifer Bernard; Padworth House, Reading, Berks

BERNARD, (Francis) William (Wigan); s of Brig Ronald Playfair St Vincent Bernard, DSO, MC, IA (d 1943), and Katharine Etheldreda Bernard, *née* Wigan (d 1978); *b* 5 June 1924; *Educ* Bedford Sch, Brasenose Coll Oxford (MA); *m* 7 Feb 1958, Margaret Renee, da of Capt Wilfrid Harry Dowman RNVR (d 1936), of Weymouth; 1 s (James b 1959), 4 da (Catherine b 1960, Antonia b 1961, Frances (twin) b 1961, Sarah b 1964); *Career* Capt RA 1942-47; ADC to govr gen of Fedn of Rhodesia and Nyasaland (Lord Llewellin) 1953-57; Maj Rhodesia and Nyasaland Def Staff 1954-58; politics in Rhodesia, cncllr Salisbury 9 yrs; dir Central African Bldg Soc; cdr for Jersey 1987, St John Ambulance Brigade (see also Who's Who of Central Africa 1968); OStJ 1988 ; *Recreations* ornithology, tennis; *Clubs* Boodle's; *Style*— William Bernard, Esq; Herupe House, St John, Jersey, CI (☎ 0534 62356)

BERNAYS, Richard Oliver; s of Robert Hamilton Bernarys (MP for Bristol North 1931-45) (ka 1945), and Nancy *née* Britton (d 1987); *b* 22 Feb 1943; *Educ* Eton, Trinity Coll Oxford (MA); *m* 12 Feb 1972, Karen, da of Russell Henry Forney of New Castle, PA, USA (d 1979); 3 da (Lucy b 1975, Mary b 1977, Amy b 1979); *Career* dir: Mercury Asset Mgmnt plc, Lautro; chm Mercury Fund Managers; *Recreations* golf, fishing; *Clubs* Brooks's, Rye Golf; *Style*— Richard Bernays, Esq; 82 Elgin Crescent, London W11 2JL; 33 King William St, London EC4R 9AS

BERNERS, Baroness (15 in line, E 1455); Vera Ruby Williams; *née* Tyrwhitt; da of Maj the Hon Rupert Tyrwhitt, 5 s of Emma Harriet, Baroness Berners (12 holder of title *de jure* and seventeenth in descent from Edward III); *b* 25 Dec 1901; *Educ* Ladies Coll Eastbourne, St Agnes E Grinstead; *m* 1927, Harold Williams, JP; 2 da; *Heir* (co-heiresses) daughters, Hon Mrs P V Kirkham and Hon Mrs R T Pollock, *qqv*; *Career* nursing, Guy's Hosp; *Recreations* gardening; *Style*— The Rt Hon the Lady Berners; Ashwellthorpe, Charlton Lane, Cheltenham, Glos (☎ 0242 519595)

BERNEY, John Verel; JP (Norfolk 1957); s of George Augustus Berney (d 1952), of Morton Hall, Norfolk, and Marjory Scott, *née* Verel (d 1966); *b* 17 Feb 1924; *Educ* Radley, Clare Coll Cambridge (BA); *m* 1, 3 Jan 1950 (m dis 1984), Jill, da of Capt Gilbert Philip Makinson (d 1935), of Sydney, Aust; 1 s (Ralph), 3 da (Philipps (Mrs Moll), Sylvia, Rosalind); m 2, 23 March 1984, Pauline Jenkins, da of Ernest George Emms, of South Cottage, Pulham Market, Norfolk; *Career* serv WWII 1942-47: Capt Royal Norfolk and Hants Regts (wounded); landowner, farmer; memb: CLA Norfolk Ctee 1957-, Agric Land Tbnl (also Land Drainage Section); High Sheriff Norfolk 1978; *Recreations* shooting, fishing, beagling, walking, travel; *Clubs* Norfolk (Norwich); *Style*— John Berney, Esq, JP; Hockering House, E Dereham, Norfolk (☎ 0603 880339)

BERNEY, Sir Julian Reedham Stuart; 11 Bt (E 1620), of Parkehall in Redham, Norfolk; s of Lt John Berney (k on active serv Korea 1952) and Hon Jean (who m 2, P Jesson), da of 1 Viscount Stuart of Findhorn, CH, MVO, MC, PC; (m 3, M Ritchie); suc gf 1975;; *b* 26 Sept 1952; *Educ* Wellington, N E London Poly; *m* 1976, Sheena, da of Ralph Day, of Danbury, Essex; 2 s (William b 1980, Hugo Ralph b 1987), 1 da (Jessica Mary b 1982); *Heir* s, William Reedham John Berney b 29 June 1980; *Career* chartered surveyor, ARICS; *Recreations* sailing, hill walking; *Clubs* Royal Ocean Racing; *Style*— Sir Julian Berney, Bt; Reeds House, 40 London Rd, Maldon, Essex CM9 6HE (☎ 0621 53420)

BERNS, Richard Michael; s of Leonard Berns (d 1978), of Cobham, Surrey, and Elizabeth Grace, *née* Turner; *b* 16 August 1947; *Educ* Dulwich; *m* 16 Dec 1968, Roberta, da of Robert Dunlop Fleming (d 1978), of Perth, Scotland; 1 s (Ashley b 1969), 1 da (Antonia b 1974); *Career* slr; jt sr ptnr Piper Smith and Basham; dir: Ansad Properties (Manchester) Ltd 1979-87, Dist and Central Fin Ltd 1979-87, Grange Park Securities Ltd 1981-87, Naughton Centre Ltd 1988; life govr Imperial Cancer Res Fund; memb Law Soc; *Recreations* sailing, skiing, tennis; *Style*— Richard M Berns, Esq; Leigh Hill House, Leigh Hill Rd, Cobham, Surrey (☎ 0932 62284); 31 Warwick Sq, London SW1 (☎ 01 828 8685, telex 916604 PSBG, fax 01 630 6976, car ☎ 0836 227 653)

BERNSEN, Svend Aage; s of Hans Henrik Bernsen (d 1966), and Johanne, *née* Loenborg; *b* 23 April 1934; *Educ* commercial training in Denmark, Germany and the UK; *m* 28 Feb 1959, Vivienne, da of Edwin Brace (d 1973); 2 da (Karen b 1959, Elizabeth b 1966); *Career* Ess-Food, Denmark (Danish bacon factories' export assoc) 1959- (hd clerk 1961, hd department 1968, sales dir 1973, md Ess-Food (UK) Ltd 1977, group md 1986-); dir Danish Bacon Company plc; chm: Ess-Food Danepak Ltd, Anglo-Danish Food Transport Ltd, Bacon Distribution Centre Ltd, Ess-Food Fresh Meat Ltd; *Recreations* golf; *Style*— Svend Bernsen, Esq; White Lodge, 24 Astons Rd, Moor Park, Northwood, Middlesex HA6 2LD (☎ 09274 25076); Ess-Food (UK) Group Ltd, Howardsgate, Welwyn Garden City, AL8 6NN (☎ 0707 323421, car ☎ 0836 200421)

BERNSTEIN, Baron Anthony Webber; s of Cyril Philip (d 1952), of Manchester, and Dorothy, *née* Webber (d 1985); *b* 22 Sept 1938; *Educ* Clifton; *m* 16 Aug 1961, (Sara) Frances, da of Lazarus Rayman (d 1948), of Singapore and Manchester; 3 s (Simon Laurence b 20 Aug 1963, Jeremy Paul b 16 Oct 1965, Robin Daniel b 27 Feb 1970); *Career* Cyril Bernstein Ltd (now Bernstein Gp plc): dir 1964-72, md 1972-85, chm 1985-; chm: Honmark Int Ltd, Century Locks Ltd; tres Br Furniture Mfrs Assoc 1984-88, memb Funiture EDC 1985-88, pres NW Furniture Trades Fedn 1983-87 (offr 1966-86, tres 1979-83); *Recreations* football, swimming, water-skiing, tennis; *Style*—

Baron Bernstein, Esq; Richmond House, Norman's Place, Altrincham, Cheshire WA14 2AB (☎ 061 941 2404); Bernstein Gp plc, PO Box 33, Middleton, Manchester M24 1AR (☎ 061 653 9191, fax 061 653 5392, telex 668111 OODAIR)

BERNSTEIN, Baron (Life Peer UK 1969), of Leigh; Sidney Lewis Bernstein; s of Alexander and Jane Bernstein; bro of late Cecil Bernstein (jt fndr with him of Granada) and unc of Alex Bernstein, chm Granada Gp; *b* 30 Jan 1899; *Educ* LLD; *m* 1954, Sandra, da of Charles and Charlotte Malone, of Toronto; 1 s, 2 da; *Career* fndr Film Soc 1924, memb Middlesex CC 1925-31, chm Granada Gp Ltd 1934-79; pres 1979-: Granada Gp plc, Granada Television, Granada Leisure Ltd, Granada TV Rental, Granada Motorway Services; films advsr Miny of Information 1940-45, liaison Br Embassy Washington 1942, chief Film Section AFHQ N Africa 1942-43, chief Film section SHAEF 1943-45; lectr on film and int affrs New York Univ and Yale; memb Resources for Learning Constitutional Ctee of Nuffield Fndn 1965-72, govr Sevenoaks Sch 1964-74; *Clubs* Garrick; *Style*— The Rt Hon the Lord Bernstein; 36 Golden Square, London W1R 4AH (☎ 01 734 8080)

BERRAGAN, Maj Gen Gerald Brian; CB (1988); s of William James Berragan (d 1982), of York, and Marion Beatrice Berragan; *b* 2 May 1933; *Educ* various schs in India and UK; *m* Anne Helen, da of David Boyd Kelly (d 1971), of York; 3 s (Howard Neil b 1959, Nigel Boyd b 1962, Nicholas Jeremy b 1967); *Career* cmmnd REME 1954, Lt attached 7 Hussars, trans RAOC 1956, Capt UK Belgium and Germany, Staff Coll 1966, served Maj York & BAOR, Lt-Col 1972; cmd: RAOC 3 Div 1976-78, AQMG HQ N I 1978-80; Col 1978, HQ DGOS 1978-80, Brig 1980, cmd COD Chilwell 1980-82, Cmd COD Bicester 1982-83, Dir Supply Ops Army 1983-85, Maj Gen Ord Serv 1985-88; chief exec Inst of Packaging 1988-; FBIM, FInstPS; *Recreations* sailing, skiing, tennis; *Clubs* Athenaeum, Army and Navy; *Style*— Maj Gen Gerald Berragan, CB

BERRIDGE, David; s of William Berridge, of Hull, and Phyllis, *née* Langley; *b* 12 Nov 1947; *Educ* Hull GS, Univ of Hull (MA); *m* 19 July 1969, Barbara May, da of James Sutherland, of Willerby, nr Hull; 1 s (Christopher b 1970), 4 da (Lisa b 1971, Emma b 1975, Kathryn b 1978, Amy b 1987); *Career* CA; fndr and princ D Berridge, sr lectr Humberside Coll, dir Hull Collectors Centre 1976-77, accountant Rediffusion Ltd 1972-73, hon tres Anlaby Community Care Assoc, involved in local charity work; FCA, ACIS; *Recreations* reading, jogging, watching rugby league; *Style*— David Berridge, Esq; 31 Westella Way, Kirkella, Hull HU10 7LN (☎ 0482 650747)

BERRIDGE, Dr Michael John; s of George Kirton Berridge, and Stella Elaine, *née* Hards; *b* 22 Oct 1938; *Educ* Univ Coll of Rhodesia & Nyasaland, Salisbury, Rhodesia (BSc), Univ of Cambridge (PhD); *m* 5 March 1965, Susan Graham *née* Winter; 1 s (Paul b 19 March 1969), 1 da (Rozanne b 4 June 1967); *Career* post doctors fell: Univ of Virginia 1965-66, Case Western Res Univ 1966-69 (res assoc 1967-69); Univ of Cambridge: sr scientific offr Unit of Invertebrate Chemistry and Physiology 1969, chief sci offr Unit of Insect Neurophysiology and Pharmacology 1987-; Prizes and Awards: Feldberg Prize (1984), The King Faisal Internat Prize in Science (1986), Louis Jeantet Prize in Med (1986), William Bate Hardy Prize (Cambridge Philosophical Soc (1987), Abraham White Scientific Achievement Award (George Washington Univ Sch of Med, 1987), Gairdner Foundation Internat Award (1988), Baly Medal (RCP, 1989); fell Trinity Coll Cambridge 1972, FRS 1984; *Recreations* golf, gardening; *Style*— Dr Michael Berridge; 13 Home Close, Histon, Cambridge CB4 43L (☎ 0223 232416); Dept of Zoology, Downing St, Cambridge CB2 3EJ (☎ 0223 336600 ext 6603, fax 0223 461954)

BERRIDGE, (Donald) Roy; CBE (1980); s of (Alfred) Leonard Berridge (d 1966), of Peterborough, and Pattie Annie Elizabeth, *née* Holloway; *b* 24 Mar 1922; *Educ* King's Sch Peterborough; *m* 1945, Marie, da of Harold Kinder (d 1958), of Leicester; 1 da; *Career* chm South of Scotland Electricity Bd 1977-82; dir Howden Gp plc 1982-88; FEng, FIMechE; *Style*— Roy Berridge, Esq, CBE; East Gate, Chapel Square, Deddington, Oxford OX5 4SG (☎ 0869 38400)

BERRIEDALE, Lord; Alexander James Richard Sinclair; s and h of 20 Earl of Caithness, *qv*; *b* 26 Mar 1981; *Style*— Lord Berriedale

BERRILL, Geoffrey William; s of William George Berrill (d 1969), of Cheam, Surrey, and Ada Alice, *née* Martin; *b* 4 June 1948; *Educ* Uppingham; *m* 10 June 1972, Karen Peta Berrill, da of Peter Frank (d 1974), of Tadworth, Surrey; 2 da (Victoria b 6 April 1977, Charlotte b 3 Oct 1979); *Career* dir: Alexander Howden Insur Brokers Ltd 1980-83, Alexander Howden Ltd 1983-85, Halford Shead and Co Ltd 1984-86, Hartley Cooper Assoc Ltd 1986-; Freeman City of London 1969, Liveryman Worshipful Co of Glass Sellers 1969 (Apprentice 1962); *Recreations* walking, gardening; *Style*— Geoffrey Berrill, Esq; Rook Hall, Kelvedon, Essex CO5 9DB; Bishops Court, 27-33 Artillery Lane, London E1 7LP (☎ 01 247 5433, fax 01 377 2139, telex 8950791)

BERRILL, Sir Kenneth; GBE (1988), KCB (1971); s of Stanley Berrill, of London; *b* 28 August 1920; *Educ* LSE, Trinity Coll Cambridge; *m* 1, 1941 (m dis), Brenda West; 1 s; m 2, 1950 (m dis), June, da of Arthur Phillips, of London; 1 s, 1 da; m 3, 1977, Jane Marris; *Career* serv WWII REME; economist; former fell and bursar St Catharine's Coll Cambridge, King's Coll Cambridge; prof MIT 1962; special advsr Tresy 1967-69, chief econ advsr 1973-74, head CPRS Cabinet Off 1974-80; chm Vickers da Costa 1981-85 (joined 1980); memb of The Stock Exchange London 1981-85; dep chm: Univs Superannuation Scheme 1980-85, General Funds Invstmt Tst 1982-85, govt nominee on Review Bd for Govt Contracts 1981-85; nominated memb Cncl of Lloyds 1983-88; chm: Securities & Investmt Bd 1985-88; chm Robert Horne Gp 1987-; pro-chllr Open Univ (chm governing body) 1983-; *Style*— Sir Kenneth Berrill, GBE, KCB; 207 Queen's Quay, 58 Upper Thames Street, London EC4V 3EH

BERRILL, Simon Philip; s of Sir Kenneth Berrill, GBE, KCB, of Salt Hill, Bridle Way, Grantcheiter, Cambs, and June Myrtle Berrill; *b* 17 August 1953; *Educ* Westminster, Magdalen Coll Oxford (BA); *m* 6 Feb 1988, Anneke, da of Alan John Waple, OBE (d 1986); 1 s (Daniel Philip b 1988); *Career* called to the Bar Middle Temple 1975, GEC Ltd 1978, dir Michael Laurie and Ptnrs Inc 1981, dir Morgan Grenfell Laurie Ltd 1988, chm and chief exec Benlox Hldgs plc 1988; *Style*— Simon Berrill, Esq; 53 Gloucester Ave, Primrose Hill, London NW1 7BA (☎ 01 267 9804); Benlox Hldgs plc, Prince Rupert House, 9-10 College Hill, London EC4 (☎ 01 248 8678, fax 01 286 0373)

BERRIMAN, David; s of late Algernon Edward Berriman, OBE and late Enid Kathleen, *née* Sutcliffe; *b* 20 May 1928; *Educ* Winchester, New Coll Oxford (MA), Harvard Business Sch (PMD course); *m* 1, 1954 (m dis 1969), Margaret Lloyd, *née* Owen; 2 s; m 2, 1971, Shirley Elizabeth, *née* Wright; *Career* Citibank 1952-56, Ford Motor Co UK 1956-60, AEI Hotpoint 1960-63, United Leasing Corp 1963-; dir: Morgan Grenfell, later Morgan Grenfell Hldgs 1963-73, Guinness Mahon 1973-87; chm Bunzl Textile Hldgs Ltd, dir: Satellite Television plc (chm 1981-85), Britannia Building Soc, Alban Communications Ltd, Bahrein Telecommunications Co, Cable and Wireless plc, The Nat Film and Television Sch; chm North East Thames Regional Health Authy 1984-; memb Br Screen Advisory Council (formerly Interim Action Ctee on Future of Br Film Indust), former memb govt ctee on Harland and Wolff Diversification; chm of govrs MacIntyre Schs (for the Mentally Handicapped); govr United Medical and Dental Schs of St Thomas' and Guy's Hosps 1982-84; FCIB, CBIM; *Books* XYZ Case; *Recreations* golf, tennis; *Clubs* RAC, Royal St George's Golf; *Style*— David Berriman, Esq; c/o North East Thames Regional Health Authority, 40 Eastbourne Terrace, London W1 3QR (☎ 01 262 8011)

BERRINGTON, Richard Norman; *b* 25 July 1930; *Educ* Loughborough Endowed Sch; *m* -Freda Mary; 1 s (Richard), 1 da (Rachel); *Career* md Manesty Machines Ltd, winner Queen's Award for Export Achievement; *Recreations* music, golf, gardening; *Style*— R N Berrington, Esq; c/o Manesty Machines Ltd, Speke, Liverpool

BERRY, Hon Adrian Michael; s of Baron Hartwell, MBE, TD (Life Peer); *b* 15 June 1937; *Educ* Eton and Ch Ch Oxford; *m* 1967, Marina Beatrice, da of Cyrus Sulzberger, of Paris; 1 s, 1 da; *Style*— The Hon Adrian Berry; 11 Cottesmore Gdns, London W8

BERRY, Anthony Arthur; s of Francis Berry (d 1936), of London, and Amy Marie Freeman (d 1966); family have been wine merchants in Exeter and 3 St James's St London since 1700's; *b* 16 Mar 1915; *Educ* Charterhouse, Trinity Hall Cambridge (BA); *m* 1953, Sonia Alice, da of Sir Harold Graham-Hodgson, KCVO (d 1960); 1 s (Simon), 1 da (Victoria); *Career* wine merchant, dir Berry Bros and Rudd Ltd 1946- (chm 1965-85); master Vintners' Co 1980-81; chm Wine Trade Benevolent Soc 1968; cellarer Saintsbury Club 1978-; *Recreations* golf, walking; *Clubs* Boodle's, Royal St George Golf, Royal Wimbledon Golf, Saintsbury, Bath and County; *Style*— Anthony Berry, Esq; 4 Cavendish Crescent, Bath BA1 2UG (☎ 0225 22669); Windy Peak, St Margaret's Bay, Kent (☎ 0304 952413)

BERRY, Hon Mrs; Hon Bride Faith Louisa; *née* Fremantle; 3 da of 3 Baron Cottesloe, CB, VD, TD (d 1956), and Florence, *née* Tapling (d 1956); *b* 1 July 1910; *Educ* PNEU Sch Burgess Hill, Girton Coll Cambridge; *m* 20 Aug 1936, John Berry, CBE, DL, *qv*; 2 s, 1 da; *Style*— The Hon Mrs Berry; Tayfield, Newport-on-Tay, Fife DD6 8HA (☎ 0382 543118)

BERRY, Prof Francis; s of James Berry (d 1952), of Malay States and Cheltenham, and Jane, *née* Ivens (d 1915); *b* 23 Mar 1915; *Educ* Hereford Cathedral Sch, Dean Close Sch, Univ of London (BA), Univ of Exeter (MA); *m* 4 Sept 1947 (d 1967), Nancy Melloney, da of Cecil Newton Graham (d 1929); 1 s (Scyld), 1 da (Melloney Poole); m 2, 1969 (m dis 1971), Patricia Tyler, da of John Gordon Thomson; m 3, 9 April 1979, Eileen Marjorie, da of Charles Eric Lear; *Career* 4 Bn Devonshire Regt 1939-46, Malta 1940-43; Univ of Sheffield 1947-70: asst lectr, lectr, sr lectr, reader, prof of english; prof of english Royal Holloway Coll Univ of London 1970-80, (prof emeritus 1980); visiting appts: Carleton Coll Minnesota 1951-52, Jamaica 1957, India 1966-67; visiting fell Aust Nat Univ Canberra 1979; visiting prof: Malawi 1980-81, Japan 1983, NZ 1988; FRSL 1969; *Books* The Iron Christ (1938), Murdock and Other Poems (1947), The Galloping Centaur (1952), Herbert Read 1953, Poets Grammar (1958), Poetry and the Physical Voice (1958), Morant Bay (1961), The Shakespeare Inset (1965), Ghosts of Greenland (1967), I Tell of Greenland (1977), From the Red Fort (1984); *Recreations* following first class cricket; *Clubs* Hampshire (Winchester); *Style*— Prof Francis Berry; 4 Eastgate St, Winchester, Hants SO23 8EB (☎ 0962 54439)

BERRY, Frank Alfred John; s of Frank Walter Berry (d 1966), and Elsie Mary, *née* Gibbs; *b* 3 Feb 1930; *Educ* Edmonton Latymer; *m* 17 Sept 1955, Cicely Edith, da of Arthur Ernest Stockhausen (d 1971); 1 s (John b 1961), 2 da (Janet b 1959, Elizabeth b 1965); *Career* dir: Sun Life Assur plc, Sun Life Unit Servs Ltd, Sun Life Direct Mktg Ltd, Sun Life Pensions Mgmnt Ltd, Sun Life Portfolio Counselling Servs Ltd, Sun Life Promotions Ltd, Sun Life Trust Mgmnt Ltd; *Recreations* bowls, philately; *Style*— Frank Berry, Esq; Broadwater, Woodlands Rd, Portishead, Bristol BS20 9HE; Sun Life Assurance Society plc, Sun Life Court, St James Barton, Bristol BS1 3TH

BERRY, Dr Hedley; s of Edward Basil Berry, and Mathilde Josephine Berry (d 1982); *b* 18 Feb 1943; *Educ* Reading Sch, Wadham Coll Oxford (MA, DM); *m* 27 June 1974, Sonia, da of Joseph Tchoudy; 1 s (Michael b 1976); *Career* conslt physician and rheumatologist Kings Coll Hosp 1976-; FRCP; *Books* Rheumatology and Rehabilitation (1985); *Recreations* music, travelling, eating, theatre; *Clubs* RSM, Br Soc of Rheumatology; *Style*— Dr Hedley Berry, Esq; 21 Dorset Drive, Edgware, Middx HA8 7NT; 96 Harley St, London (☎ 01 486 0967); Kings Coll Hosp, London SE5

BERRY, Ian Andrew; s of W S Berry, and Shirley, *née* Mackay; *b* 10 Jan 1953; *Educ* Univ of Toronto (BA); *m* 30 April 1983, Helen; *Career* trg Canadian Imperial Bank of Commerce 1976-80; fixed income dept: Eliott and Page Fin Conslts 1980-82, Canada Permanent Tst 1982-84, dir Scotia McCleod (formerly McCleod Young & Weir) 1987- (trader 1984-87); *Style*— Ian Berry, Esq; Scotia McCleod, 3 Finsbury Sq, London, EC2 (☎ 01 256 5656)

BERRY, Ian Robert; s of Lt-Col Frank Berry, IA (d 1982), and Mary Margaret Ann Berry, *née* Chater (d 1973); *b* 29 Nov 1933; *Educ* Charterhouse, Open Univ (BA), Southampton Univ (MSc); *m* 19 Sept 1959, Elizabeth Douglas, da of James Smurthwaite (d 1975); 2 s (Robert James b 1962, Michael John b 1966), 2 da (Elizabeth Jane b 1960, Jennifer Ann b 1965); *Career* Nat Serv; 2 Lt RAPC 1954-56, Army Emergency Reserve: Lt and Paymaster RAPC 1956-60, Capt RE (144 Bomb Disposal Regt) 1961-71; co sec: Sealectro Ltd 1968-69, Savage and Parsons 1970-74, fin dir Savage Indus Ltd 1975-77; sr lectr Portsmouth Poly 1978-; pres Bushey and Oxhey Rotary Club 1977-78, vice pres Int Commn Paritaire (Euro Dip in Business and Mgmnt); FCA 1972 (ACA 1962), FCMA 1971 (ACMA 1966); *Recreations* auxilliary coastguard, sailing, photography; *Style*— Ian Berry, Esq; 51 Park Rd, Hayling Island, Hants PO11 0HT (☎ 0705 466693; Portsmouth Poly Business School, Locksway Rd, Milton, Portsmouth, Hants (☎ 0705 827681)

BERRY, Jamie Alistair Jagoe; s of Raymond Berry, of Dower House, Stonor, Oxon, and Phyllis, *née* Pegg; *b* 22 Dec 1955; *Educ* Harrow; *m* 15 Dec 1979, Veronica (Charlotte Herbert), da of Col F H Scobie; *Career* GT Mgmnt plc 1973-81, md Berry Asset Mgmnt plc 1981-, dir Berry Starquest plc (investmt tst); FIMBRA (memb cncl 1984-87); *Recreations* sailing, shooting; *Clubs* City of London, Annabel's; *Style*— Jamie

Berry, Esq; Gowan House, 71 Gowan Avenue, London SW6; The Chambers, Chelsea Harbour, London SW10 (☎ 01 376 3476, car tel 0836 226 079)

BERRY, John; CBE (1968), DL (Fife 1969); s of William Berry, OBE, DL (d 1954), of Tayfield Fife; *b* 5 August 1907; *Educ* Eton, Trinity Coll Cambridge (BA, MA), St Andrews Univ (PhD); *m* 1936, Hon Bride Faith Louisa Fremantle *qv*, da of 3 Baron Cottesloe, CB, VD, TD (d 1956); 2 s (William, Peter), 1 da (Margaret); *Career* research offr Biological Res Station Univ Coll Southampton 1932-36 (dir 1936-39); chief pres censor Scotland 1940-44; biologist and info offr for N of Scotland Hydro-electric Bd 1944-49; dir of Nature Conservation in Scotland 1949-67; fndr memb Int Union for Conservation of Natural Resources, first pres of its Cmmn on Ecology; Environmental Conservation and Fisheries Advsr N Scotland Hydro Bd 1968-80; dir Br Pavillion, EXPO 71, Budapest 1971; advsr S of Scotland Electricity Bd, ind advsr to other authorities 1973-89; memb of Court Univ of Dundee and of various Ct Appt Bds and Ctees, notably the Tay Estuary Research Centre (Int); Br official rep Int Symposium on Hydropower and the Environment, Guyana 1976; invited prof 'Cursurile de VaraInternationale' held in Al I Cuza Univ, Moldavia 1980; conslt on environmental conservation and freshwater fisheries, specialist on environmental and wildlife conservation and in Water Use Projects and their environmental and sociolgical impacts; Hon LLD Dundee Univ 1970; FRSE 1936; *Studies* Future Power Generation having regard to environmental conservation (financed by New Zealand conservation Cncl 1970 and 1975), Hydropower and the Environment, the Upper Mazarumi Devpt project (UK Miny of Overseas Dvpt, Nat Sci Research Cncl Guyana, 1976), Nature Reserves and Conservation in Iran (Iranian Miny for the Environment and the Br Cncl, 1975); *Recreations* natural history (especially wild geese), music; *Clubs* New (Edinburgh); *Style*— John Berry Esq, CBE, DL; Tayfield, Newport-on-Tay, Fife DD6 8HA (☎ 0382 543118)

BERRY, John Arthur; CBE (1980, OBE 1969), JP (1963), DL (1968); s of Arthur James Berry (d 1968), and Ethel Georgina, *née* May (d 1975); *b* 10 Dec 1910; *Educ* Dr Morgan's GS; Taunton Sch; *m* 23 April 1932, Winifred Josephine, da of W Bagot (d 1928), of St Helens; 1 s (Derek b 1937), 2 da (Sheilagh b 1933 (decd), Jacqueline b 1941); *Career* former md Aluminium Corpn Ltd; chm CBI NWales 1972 (cncl memb 1963-72); dir Devpt Corpn for Wales; memb: Civil Tst for Wales, Economic Cncl 1964-67 (chm Tport Panel, dep chm Employment and Indus Panel), Hosp Bd for Wales 1968-73 (chm Gwynedd Area Health Authy 1973), Lord Chllrs Advsy Ctee (rep for Gwynedd on Magistrates Cncl for UK 1975-80), Cncl and Ct Univ Coll of N Wales; memb Bangor Finance and General Purposes Ctee; FID (former pres); *Recreations* shooting, fishing; *Clubs* East India, Cardiff and County (res 1982), City, Chester; *Style*— John A Berry, Esq, CBE, JP, DL; Bryn Glas, Warren Drive, Deganwy, Gwynedd (☎ 0492 83544)

BERRY, Hon (William) Neville; s of 1 Viscount Kemsley, GBE (d 1968); *b* 16 June 1914; *Educ* Harrow, Magdalen Coll Oxford; *m* 1951, Mrs Christobel (Ruby) Norrie, da of late John Wallis More Molyneux; whose family has been seated at Loseley Park, Guildford, for over 500 years (*see* Burke's Landed Gentry 18th Edn, vol 3); *Career* Capt Grenadier Gds 1939-46; md Daily Record and Sunday Mail Glasgow 1938-39, ed News Guardian (Guards Div) 1945-46; dir: Kemslay Newspapers 1938-59, London Assur 1950-59; *Books* Dunkirk (1940); *Clubs* Turf, Pratt's; *Style*— The Hon Neville Berry; Bermuda 49, Av Hector Otto, Monaco 98000 (☎ 93 30 82 70)

BERRY, Hon Nicholas William; s of Baron Hartwell, MBE, TD (Life Peer); *b* 3 July 1942; *Educ* Eton, Christ Church Oxford; *m* 1977, Evelyn, *née* Prouvost; 2 s (William b 1978, Alexander b 1981); *Style*— The Hon Nicholas Berry; 22 Rutland Gate, London SW7

BERRY, Norman Stevenson McLean; s of James Stevenson Berry, of Glasgow, and Mary Jane, *née* Oliver; *b* 23 Jan 1933; *Educ* Shawlands Acad Glasgow, Univ of Glasgow (BSc), Univ of Strathclyde (BSc); *m* 20 Oct 1965, Sheila Margaret, da of John Allan McMillan, DSO (d 1967), of Glasgow; 2 s (David John b 1969, Andrew James b 1970), 1 da (Ruth Margaret b 1966); *Career* student then asst engr Hugh Fraser & Ptnrs 1952-57, Public Works Dept Eastern Nigeria 1957-61 (exec engr roads dept 1957, zone engr for rural water supplies programme 1958-61), water and sewerage engr Public Works Dept Solomon Islands 1967-71; Babtie Shaw & Morton: asst engr water supply 1961-67, projects engr 1967, assoc 1975, ptnr 1977 (responsible for the Kielder Transfer Works incl 30km of hard rock tunnelling); awards: Telford Medal for paper on Kielder Transfer Works ICE 1983, Telford Premium for paper on Kielder Experimental Tunnel Final Results ICE 1984, Inst Medal for paper on Large Diameter Flexible Steel Pipes for the Transfer Works of the Kielder Water Scheme IWES 1986; renovation convener and tres Findlay Memorial Church Glasgow; FICE, fell Inst of Water and Environmental Mgmnt (FIWEM); memb American Soc of Civil Engrs; *Clubs* Royal Scottish Automobile; *Style*— Norman Berry, Esq; 2 Fintry Gdns, Bearsden, Glasgow G61 4RJ (☎ 041 942 0637); Babtie Shaw & Morton, 95 Bothwell St, Glasgow G2 7HX (☎ 041 204 2511, fax 041 226 3109, telex 77202)

BERRY, The Very Rev Peter Austin; s of Austin James Berry, of Worcestershire; of Phyllis Evelyn Brettell; *b* 27 April 1935; *Educ* Solihull Sch, Keble Coll Oxford (BA) (MA); *Career* Capt Intelligence Corps (TA); bishop's chaplain, Coventry Cathedral 1963-70; Midlands Regnl Off Community Relations Cmmn 1970-73; vice-provost of Coventry 1977-86; canon residentiary Coventry Cathedral 1973-86; fell Lanchester Coll Coventry 1985-; Provost of Birmingham of 1986; *Recreations* theatre, architecture; *Clubs* St Paul's Club Birmingham; *Style*— The Very Reverend Peter A Berry; Provost's House, 16 Pebble Mill Road, Birmingham B5 7SA (☎ 021 471 0709); The Round House, Ilmington, Warwickshire (☎ 060 882 518); Birmingham Cathedral, Colmore Row, Birmingham B3 2QB (☎ 021 236 6323)

BERRY, Peter Fremantle; s of John Berry, CBE, DL, of Newport-on-Tay, Fife, and Hon Bride Faith Louisa, *née* Fremantle (*see* Burke's Landed Gentry for Berry, Debrett for Fremantle); *b* 17 May 1944; *Educ* Eton, Lincoln Coll Oxford (MA); *m* 1972, Paola, da of Giovanni Padovani (d 1951); 1 s (Richard b 1979), 2 da (Sara b 1974, Anna b 1977); *Career* mgmnt appts Harrisons & Crosfield plc SE Asia 1967-73, dir Anglo-Indonesian Corpn plc 1974-82; dir assocs and subsids notably: Anglo-Asian Investmts Ltd, Ampat Rubber Estate Ltd Sumatra, Central Province Ceylon Tea Hldgs Ltd, Colman & Co (Agric) Ltd, Walker Sons & Co Ltd; Crown Agents For Oversea Govts and Admins: dir Asia and Pacific (res Singapore) 1982-84, dir M East Asia and Pacific 1984, md and Crown Agent 1988; dir: Thomas Tapling & Co Ltd, Caphco Ltd and various subsids and assocs of Crown Agents; chm Br Arabian Tech Co-op, Indonesian subsids and assocs of Crown Agnets; chm Br Arabian Tech Co-op, Indonesian Assoc; *Recreations* travel, wildlife, country pursuits; *Clubs* RAC; *Style*— Peter Berry, Esq; 58 Pyrland Rd, N5 (☎ 01 226 3908); office: St Nicholas House, Sutton, Surrey (☎ 643 3311, telex 267103)

BERRY, Richard Gomer; s of late Hon Denis Gomer Berry, TD; n and hp of 2 Viscount Kemsley; *b* 17 April 1951; *Educ* Eton; *m* 9 May 1981, Tana-Marie, er da of Clive Lester, of Beufre, Beaulieu, Hants; *Style*— Richard Berry, Esq; Brockenhurst Park, Brockenhurst, Hants SD42 7QP

BERRY, Prof Robert James; s of Albert Edward James Berry (d 1952), of Preston, Lancs, and Nellie, *née* Hodgson (d 1956); *b* 26 Oct 1934; *Educ* Shrewsbury, Gonville and Caius Coll Cambridge (BA, MA), Univ Coll London (PhD, DSc); *m* 13 Jun 1958, Anne Caroline, da of Charles Rushton Elliott; 1 s (Andrew b 11 July 1963), 2 da (Alison b 11 July 1963, Susan b 26 June 1965); *Career* lectr Royal Free Hosp of Med 1962-78 (reader, prof), prof of Genetics Univ Coll London 1978-; author: Teach Yourself Genetics (1965, 3 ed 1977), Adam and the Ape (1975), Natural History of Shetland, jtly 1980), Neo Darwinison (1982), Free to be Different (jtly 1984), Natural History of Orkney (1985), God and Evolution (1988); ed: Biol of the House Mouse (1981), Evolution in the Galapagos (1984), Encyclopaedia of Animal Evolution (1986), Nature, Natural History and Ecology (1987); govr Monkton Coombe Sch 1979-; memb: Gen Synod of C of E 1970-, Cncl of Natural Environmental Res Cncl 1981-87; pres Linnean Soc 1982-85, tres Mammal Soc 1981-87, pres British Ecological Soc 1987-89, Vice-pres Zoological Soc 1981-88, tstee Nat Museums and Galleries on Merseyside; F I Biol 1974, FRSE 1981; *Recreations* walking, resting; *Style*— Prof Robert Berry; Quarfseter, Sackville Close, Sevenoaks, Kent TN13 3QD; Department of Biology, Medawar Building, University College London, Gower St, London WC1E 6BT (☎ 01 380 7170, fax 01 380 7026)

BERRY, Hon Lady; Sarah Anne; *née* Clifford-Turner; da of Raymond Clifford-Turner, and Zöe *née* Vachell; *b* 9 Mar 1939; *m* 5 April 1966, as his 2 w, Hon Sir Anthony George Berry (k in the IRA bomb explosion at the Grand Hotel, Brighton, 1984); yst s of 1 Viscount Kemsley (d 1968); 1 s, 1 da; *Style*— Hon Lady Berry; 1 Graham Terr, London SW1W 8JE

BERRY, William; WS; s of John Berry, CBE, DL, *qv* of Tayfield; *b* 26 Sept 1939; *Educ* Eton, St Andrews Univ, Edinburgh Univ (MA, LLB); *m* 1973, Elizabeth, da of Sir Edward Warner, KCMG, OBE, of Blockley Glos; 2 s (John b 1976, Robert b 1978); *Career* ptnr Murray Beith and Murray WS Edinburgh 1967-; dir: Scottish Life Assur Co, Scottish American Investmt Co, Fleming Universal Investmt Tst, Dawnfresh Seafoods Ltd; memb Royal Co of Archers (Queen's Bodyguard for Scotland); dep chm Edinburgh Int Festival 1985-; *Recreations* music, shooting, forestry.; *Clubs* New (Edinburgh); *Style*— William Berry, Esq, WS; 27 Saxe Coburg Place, Edinburgh; Tayfield, Newport-on-Tay, Fife

BERRY OTTAWAY, Peter; s of Cecil Berry Ottaway (d 1986), of Sutton St Nicholas, Hereford, and Myfanwy, *née* Thomas; *b* 17 Feb 1942; *Educ* Steyning GS, Univ of London (BSc), Univ Coll of Rhodesia and Nyasaland; *m* 21 Dec 1963, Andrea, da of Richard Sampson, ED, of Illinois, USA; 2 s (Gareth b 10 July 1965, d 7 Jan 1979, Charles b 9 Oct 1986), 2 da (Samantha b 20 April 1969, Georgina b 17 Jan 1981); *Career* cmnd trg branch RAFVR 1968- (currently sqdn ldr); res scientist Zambian Govt/WHO 1963-65; res mgmnt: Unilever Ltd 1965-67, General Foods Ltd 1967-74; int consultancy in food technol, Food Sci and nutrition 1974-81, dir sci and technol (Europe) Shaklee Corpn California USA 1981-87, md Berry Ottaway & Assoc Ltd Consulting Scientist 1987-; memb Duke of Edinburgh's Award Ctee Herefordshire (sec 1977-82); C Biol, FRSH 1974, MIBioL 1978, FIFST 1981, MRIPHH; *Books* Food for Sport (1985), Nutrition In Sport (ed with Dr D H Shrimpton 1986); *Recreations* light aviation, hill walking, art; *Clubs* RAF; *Style*— Peter Berry Ottaway, Esq; The Cedars, St Margaret's Rd, Hereford HR1 1TS (☎ 0432 276 368); Berry Ottaway & Assocs Ltd, Plough Lane, Hereford HR4 0EL (☎ 0432 270 886, fax 0432 270 808, telex 35302)

BERRYMAN, John Dennis; s of William Roberts Berryman, and Dorothy, *née* Morcom; *b* 3 Jan 1927; *Educ* Plymouth Coll, Brasenose Coll Oxford; *m* 4 April 1955, Barbara, da of Joseph Brooks; 1 s (Peter Jonn b 27 Sept 1959), 1 da (Lesley b 1 Jan 1956); *Career* Nat Serv RN, writer; called to the Bar Middle Temple 1951, barr W Circuit 1952-54, dep chief clerk Met Magistrates Cts 1954-58, clerk to Nuneaton and Atherstone Justices Warwickshire 1958-62, clerk to Havering Justices in Outer London and Brentwood Justice in Essex 1962-70, clerk to Croydon Justices 1970-88; *Books* Anthony and Berryman's Magistrates' Court Guide (jt author 1966), Anthony and Berryman's Legal Guide to Domestic Proceedings (jt author 1968), Anthony and Berryman's Guide ot Licensing Law (jt author, 1967); *Recreations* reading, golf, bridge; *Clubs* Tavistock Golf, Yelverton Golf; *Style*— John Berryman, Esq; 30 Widewell Rd, Roborough, Plymouth PL6 7DW (☎ 0752 791757)

BERRYMAN, Lady; Muriel Alice Ann; *née* Whipp; CBE (1972); da of James Henry Whipp, of Sydney, NSW; *m* 1925, Lt-Gen Sir Frank Horton Berryman, KCVO, CB, CBE, DSO (d 1981); 1 s, 1 da; *Style*— Lady Berryman, CBE; 17 Wentworth St, Point Piper, Sydney, NSW 2027, Australia

BERTELSEN, Aage; s of Jens Bertelsen (d 1947), of Denmark; *b* 2 Sept 1921; *Educ* Engineering Sch Denmark; *m* 1958, Dorthe, da of August Hald, of Denmark (d 1960); 1 s, 1 da; *Career* md Celcon Ltd 1956-, chm 1979-; *Recreations* bridge, gardening; *Clubs* Danish, Norwegian; *Style*— Aage Bertelsen Esq; Chalford, Traps Hill, Loughton, Essex (☎ 01 508 1778)

BERTHON, Vice Adm Sir Stephen Ferrier; KCB (1979); s of Rear Adm Charles Pierre Berthon, CBE (d 1965), of Deddington, Oxon, and Ruth, *née* Ferrier; *b* 24 August 1922; *Educ* RNC Dartmouth; *m* 1948, Elizabeth, da of Henry Leigh-Bennett; 2 s, 2 da; *Career* serv WWII RN, Dep Chief Def Staff (Operational Requirements) 1978-80, ret 1981; *Recreations* riding, hunting, gardening, walking; *Clubs* Army and Navy; *Style*— Vice Adm Sir Stephen Berthon, KCB; Garden House, Stert, Devizes, Wilts (☎ 0380 3713)

BERTHOUD, Sir Eric Alfred; KCMG (1954, CMG 1945), DL (1969); 2 s of Alfred E Berthoud (d 1918), of London, and Helene Berthoud; *b* 10 Dec 1900; *Educ* Gresham's Sch Holt, Magdalen Coll Oxford (MA); *m* 1927, Ruth Tilston, da of Sir Charles Bright (d 1937), and Isabella Gosling; 2 s (and 1 s decd), 2 da; *Career* Anglo-Austrian Bank 1922-26; Anglo-Persian Oil Co (BP) 1926-39, wartime mandate 1939-44 denial of oil to Axis; asst under-sec FO 1948-52, ambass to: Denmark 1952-56, Poland 1956-60; ret 1960; govr Atlantic Coll 1962-; memb: cncl SSEES London Univ 1964-76, ct Essex Univ (memb cncl 1962-73); pres Colchester Constituency Liberal Assoc 1974-76; Kt

Cdr Polonia Restituta 1962-83; Commanders Order of Merit with Star (Poland); *Recreations* country pursuits, formerly cricket (MCC), riding; *Clubs* Brooks's; *Style*— Sir Eric Berthoud, KCMG, DL; Gosfield Hall, Halstead, Essex CO9 1SF (☎ 0787 473844)

BERTIE, HMEH Prince and Grand Master of the Sovereign Military Hospitaller Order of St John of Jerusalem, of Rhodes and of Malta; Frà Andrew Willoughby Ninian; er s of Lt Cdr the Hon James Willoughby Bertie, RN (d 1966; yst s of 7 Earl of Abingdon), and Lady Jean Crichton-Stuart *qv*, yr da of 4 Marquess of Bute, kt; *b* 15 May 1929; *Educ* Ampleforth, Christ Church Oxford (MA), SAOS London; *Career* Lt Scots Guards 1948-50; with City Press 1954-57, Ethicon 1957-59, Worth Sch 1960-83; elected Prince and Grand Master of the Sovereign Military Hospitaller OStJ of Jerusalem, of Rhodes and of Malta 1988; Collars of the Order of the Annunziata (House of Savoy), of Orden del Libertador (Venezuela), and Constantinian Order of St George, Grand Cross Légion d'Honneur (France); Gd Offr: Order of Merit of Italian Republic; St Agatha (Republic of San Merino); medal Pro Hungaria (SMOM); *Recreations* reading, gardening, judo, fencing; *Clubs* Turf, RAC, Caccia (Rome), Scacchi (Rome), Casino (Malta); *Style*— His Most Eminent Highness the Prince and Grand Master of the Sovereign Military Hospitaller Order of St John of Jerusalem, of Rhodes and of Malta; Via Condotti 68, 00187 Rome, Italy (☎ 679-8851; fax (Rome) 679- 7202; telex, 612622 SMOM)

BERTIE, Lady Jean; Crichton-Stuart; da of 4 Marquess of Bute, KT (d 1947); *b* 28 Oct 1908; *m* 1928, Hon James Willoughby Bertie (d 1966), yst s of 7 Earl of Abingdon; 2 s (Andrew Willoughby Ninian, *qv*, (Charles) Peregrine Albelmarle, *qv*); *Style*— Lady Jean Bertie; Casa De Piro, Attard, Malta, GC

BERTIE, Hon Mrs Arthur; Lillian Isabel; da of late Charles-Elwes, KM (ie Knight of Malta), and Edythe Isabel, *née* Roper-Parkington, da of Sir John Roper-Parkington JP, DL, consul gen for Montenegro, fndr memb of Entente Cordial; *b* 23 June 1902; *Educ* Sacred Heart Convent Roehampton; *m* 1 1949, Lt-Cdr Francis Crackanthorpe, RN (decd), 1 s (David), 1 da (Elizabeth); m 2, 1949, as his 2 wife, Lt-Col Hon Arthur Michael Cosmo Bertie, DSO, MC, 2 s of 7 Earl of Abingdon (d 1957); *Style*— The Hon Mrs Arthur Bertie; Hunters Lodge, Bergh Apton, Norfolk NR15 1BJ

BERTIE, (Charles) Peregrine Albemarle; s of Lt Cdr the HonJames Willoughby Bertie, RN (d 1966, yst s of 7 Earl of Abingdon), and Lady Kean Crichton-Stuart, *qv*, yr da of 4 Marquess of Bute, KT; bro of the Prince and Grand Master SMOM, *qv*; *Educ* Ampleforth; *m* 20 April 1960, Susan Griselda Ann Lyon, da of Maj John Lycett Wills, of Allanbay Park, Binfield, Berks; 1 s (David Montagu Albemarle b 12 Feb 1963), 1 da (Caroline Georgina Rose b 16 March 1965); *Career* Capt Scots Gds 1959-54; memb Stock Exchange; Hign Sherriff of Berkshire 1986-87; kt of Honour and Devotion SMOM; memb Queen's Bodyguard for Scotland (Royal Co of Archers), Liveryman Worshipful Co of Armourers and Brasiers; OStJ; Kt Cdr Order of St Gregory the Great 1983, Cdr of Merit with Swords Order Pro Merito Melitensai; *Clubs* Turf, Whites, Pratts; *Style*— Peregrine Bertie, Esq; Frilsham Manor, Hermitage, Newbury, Berkshire RG16 9UZ (☎ 0635 201 291)

BERTLIN, Dennis Percy; s of Percy Walter Bertlin (d 1952); *b* 18 May 1911; *Educ* Manchester GS, Liverpool Univ (BEng, MEng); *m* 1954, Patricia, da of Dr Ashley Daly (d 1977); 2 s, 3 da; *Career* WWII Lt-Col RE BEF France, 1 Army N Africa, 21 Army Gp; consulting engr; sr ptnr Bertlin and Ptnrs 1960-81, (conslt 1981-), offr Order of Orange Nassau (Netherlands) 1946; FICE, FCIArb; *Recreations* chess, gardening, painting; *Clubs* Savile, Royal Thames Yacht, Royal Cruising, Royal Ocean Racing; *Style*— Dennis Bertlin, Esq; Castlefield, Bletchingley, Surrey RH1 4LB (☎ 0883 843 186)

BERTRAM, John Alexander; s of Major David Craig Bertram, GM, TD, of 19 Eastgate Rd, Tenterden, Kent, and Phyllis Mary Bertram (d 1986); *b* 2 Mar 1934; *Educ* Forest Sch, Dover Coll, London Univ (LLB); *m* 4 April 1959 (m dis 1985), Elizabeth Sarah, da of Hugh Gwylym Hughes; 1 s (Mark b 1966), 1 da (Jane b 1963); *Career* RASC 1957-59 2 Lt 1958; admitted slr 1957, ptnr Thomson Snell & Passmore Slrs 1964-; pres Tunbridge Wells Tonbridge and District Law Soc 1984; memb The Law Soc 1957; *Clubs* Army and Navy; *Style*— John Bertram, Esq; The Coach Hse, Cabbage Stalk Lane, Tunbridge Wells, Kent (☎ 0892 356 99); Thomson Snell & Passmore, Lyons East St, Tonbridge, Kent (☎ 0732 771 411, telex 57263 ESPTON G)

BERTRAM, Dr (Cicely) Kate; da of Harry Ralph Ricardo (d 1974), and Beatrice Bertha, *née* Hale (d 1975); *b* 8 July 1912; *Educ* Hayes Ct, Kent, and Newnham Coll, Cambridge (MA, PhD); *m* 28 Sept 1939, George Colin Lawder Bertram, s of Francis George Lawder Bertram, CBE (d 1938); 4 s (Mark b 1942, Brian b 1944, Roger b 1946, William b 1950); *Career* zoological research in Africa 1935-36, memb Col Off Nutrition Survey in Nyasa Land 1939, adviser on Freshwater Fisheries to Palestine Govt 1940-43, joint research with husband on Sea-Cows (Sirenia) 1962-79; tutor Lucy Cavendish Collegiate Soc Camb 1965-70, (pres 1970-79); JP Cambs and Isle of Ely 1959-79; *Recreations* travel, sylviculture, bell ringing; *Clubs* English Speaking Union; *Style*— Dr Cicely Bertram

BERTRAM, Peter John Andrew; s of Capt George Robert Bertram (d 1936), and Ann Mary, *née* Regan (d 1985); *b* 26 April 1930; *Educ* Henry Mellish Sch Nottingham, Gottingen Univ Germany; *m* 14 Sept 1957, Winifred Rita, da of Wilfred Henry Parr (d 1974); 2 s (Christopher b 1958, Timothy b 1964), 1 da (Nicola b 1961); *Career* chartered accountant in own practice P J A Bertram; md Old Market Square Securities Ltd 1984-; dir: Ryland Vehicle Gp Ltd, Longcliffe Golf Co Ltd, Premier Portfolio Ltd, Denham Grange Ltd, NXD Assocs Ltd; tstee The Shand Tst; FCA, FCMA, FCT;; *Recreations* golf, bridge, music, literature, travel; *Clubs* RAC, Royal Overseas League, Longcliffe Golf; *Style*— Peter Bertram, Esq; Cedar House, Nanpantan, Loughborough, Leics (☎ 0509 239 253); 89 Thomas More House, Barbican, London EC2 (☎ 01 588 8431)

BERTRAM, Robert David Darney; WS (1969); s of David Noble Stewart Bertram (d 1981), of Edinburgh, and Angela Jean Weston, *née* Devlin; *b* 6 Oct 1941; *Educ* Edinburgh Acad, Oriel Coll Oxford (MA), Edinburgh Univ (LLB); *m* 23 Sept 1967, Patricia John, da of John Laithwaite, formerly of Prescot, Lancashire; 2 s (Andrew b 1972, Nicholas b 1975); *Career* ptnr Dundas and Wilson CS Edinburgh 1969-, non-exec dir The Weir Gp plc 1983; memb: VAT tbnl, Tech Ctee Inst Taxation 1986, Scottish Law Cmmn 1978-86; examiner Law Soc Scotland, memb Scottish review panel on Reform of Law on Security over Moveables 1986; ATII; *Recreations* books; *Clubs* Scottish Arts, Edinburgh Univ Staff; *Style*— R D Bertram, Esq, WS; 4 Arboretum Rd, Edinburgh; (☎ 031 225 1234, fax 031 556 5594, telex 72404)

BERTRAM, Dr Roger Charles Richard; s of George Colin Lawder Bertram, of Ricardo's Graffham, Petworth, Sussex, and Cicely Kate Ricardo Bertram, JP, *née* Ricardo; *b* 23 Feb 1946; *Educ* Friends Sch Saffron Walden, St John's Coll Cambridge (MA), Inst of Educn of London Univ, Sch of Clinical Med Univ of Cambridge; *m* 29 June 1968, Julia Ruth, da of Prof Richard Stanley Peters of Inst of Educn London Univ; 1 s (Aldous b 22 Sept 1984), 3 da (Rebecca b 16 June 1971, Esther b 16 May 1974, Beatrice b 9 May 1983); *Career* head biology dept Nethall Sch Cambridge 1974-76, ptnr in general practise Linton; sec Cambridge Med Soc, memb locla Med Ctee; *Recreations* riding, gardening, reading; *Style*— Dr Roger Bertram; Linton House, Linton, Cambridgeshire (☎ 0223 891 368); The Health Centre, Linton, Cambs (☎ 0223 891 456)

BERTRAM, (Anthony Allan) Tony; s of Gp Capt Ian Anstruther Bertram (d 1962), and Dorothy Cecil, *née* Eliott-Lockhart; gggs of John Bateman, fndr of Melbourne, Australia and ggggs of Dr Arnaud de Lapeyre, Physician to Napoleon; *b* 6 June 1926; *Educ* Stowe Sch, Univ Coll Oxford (MA); *m* 8 Aug 1968, Carin, da of Christian Langöe-Conradsen (d 1984), of Stockholm, Sweden; 1 da (Grizel Louisa Christine b 1972); *Career* subaltern: QVO Corps of Guides India 1946-47 15/19 KRH Palestine and Sudan 1947-48; Gp Offr ROC Edinburgh 1958-71; steamer agent Gladstone Lyall, Calcutta (India) and Khulna (E Pakistan now Bangladesh) 1951-52, commodity broker Hale and Son (London) 1954-55, translator Indonesian Legation Stockholm 1955-56; now farming; made 1 Br guideless traverse Higuille de Grépon to Aiguille de Roc (Alps) 1950, 1 traverse Äpartizkko Group (Lapland) 1959, first ascents of peaks and ridges and major traverse of Pärte group and Byggäsberget (Lapland) 1961, pte expedition in Langrtand Himal (Nepal) with minor 1 ascent on Tibetan Frontier 1962; *Recreations* travel; *Clubs* Alpine, Himalayan; *Style*— Tony Bertram, Esq; Nisbet, Culter, Biggar, Lanarkshire (☎ 0899 20530)

BERWICK, Lt-Col Edward Walter Hall; s of Walter Mark Berwick (d 1929), of Toronto; *b* 2 August 1908; *Educ* Ridley Coll, St Catherine's Ontario; *m* 1944, as her 2 husb, Lady Elizabeth, *née* Harris (d 1983), da of 5 Earl of Malmesbury (d 1950); 1 da (Dorothea); *Career* 2 Lt Canadian Regular Army (Royal Canadian Dragoons) 1930, serv WWII: UK, Burma, NW Europe; Lt-Col 1944, psc, GSO (1) HQ Australian Mil Forces (Melbourne) 1949-51, Col (Chief of Staff) UN Mil Org India/Pakistan (Kashmir) 1957-58, ret 1960; *Clubs* Cavalry and Guards; *Style*— Lt-Col Edward Berwick; 17 Montpelier Villas, Brighton, Sussex BN1 3DG (☎ 0273 29645)

BESLY, Lt-Col John Richard Seymour; s of Ernest Withers Francis Besly, CMG (d 1964), and Helen Judith Besly (d 1974); *b* 28 Sept 1931; *Educ* Winchester; *m* 21 Jan 1958, Dinah Priscilla (d 1987), da of Brig Adrian Clements Gore, DSO, of Ashford, Kent; 2 s (Adrian Thomas Francis b 1963, Michael John b 1966), 3 da (Emma Belinda b 1958, Lucinda Mary b 1960, Sarah Jane Beatrice b 1964); *Career* mil serv 1950-78, joined 3 Bn Gren Guards, Adjt (12 Bn) 1955-57, Staff Coll 1963, BLI ST CYR 1962-69, 2 i/c 1 Bn 1970-72, offr leading 2 Bn 1972-74, AGMG London Dist 1974-77; location of Offices Bureau 1978-80; development offr King's Coll London 1980-82; regional dir Br Heart Fndn 1983-; *Recreations* sailing, shooting, tennis swimming; *Clubs* Aldeburgh Yacht; *Style*— Lt-Col John R S Besly; 33 High Street, Ticehurst, Wadhurst, E Sussex (☎ 0580 200443)

BESSBOROUGH, 10 Earl of (I 1739, UK 1937); Frederick Edward Neuflize Ponsonby; DL (W Sussex 1977); also Baron Bessborough (I 1721), Viscount Duncannon (I 1723), Baron Ponsonby of Sysonby (GB 1749); s of 9 Earl of Bessborough, GCMG, PC (d 1956) and Roberte, JP (GCStJ), da of Baron Neuflize, of Paris; *b* 29 Mar 1913; *Educ* Eton, Trinity Coll Cambridge; *m* 1948, Mary, da of Charles A Munn, of New York and Paris; 1 da; *Heir* (to Irish Earldom and UK Barony only) cous, Arthur Ponsonby; *Career* sits as Cons House of Lords; Co-pres Euro-Atlantic Gp; first sec Br Embassy Paris 1944-48 (formerly 2 sec), merchant banker Robert Benson, Lonsdale and Co Ltd 1950-56, dir ATV Ltd 1955-63 and other cos; Parly sec for Science 1963-64, jt parly under-sec of State for Educn and Science 1964, dep chm Metrication Bd 1969-70, min of state Miny of Technol 1970, chm cttee of Enquiry into Research Assocs 1971-73; MEP 1972-79, vice-pres and dep ldr Cons Gp 1973-77; chm Stansted Park Fndn 1984-; pres: Men of the Trees, UK memb of Bentinck Prize Jury; Chichester Festival Theatre Tst, Br Theatre Assoc; author of plays and other publications; OStJ, FRGS, Chevalier of Legion of Honour; memb American Philosophical Soc; *Clubs* Turf, Garrick, Beefsteak, Roxburghe; *Style*— The Rt Hon Earl of Bessborough DL; Stansted Park, Rowlands Castle, Hants (☎ 0705 412223; 4 Westminster Gdns, London SW1 (☎ 01 828 5959)

BESSER, Aubrey Derek; s of Hymen Besser (d 1982), and Leah Geller; *b* 27 Nov 1929; *Educ* Rutlish GS, Hove County GS; *m* 6 May 1962, Susan Elisabeth, da of Leslie Edward Hutchinson (d 1967), of Hove Sussex; 3 da (Julia b 1964, Sarah b 1967, Abigail b 1970); *Career* md Steel and Oil Import/Export, Metal Enterprises and Co (London) Ltd 1952-87; *Recreations* tennis, bridge, swimming; *Clubs* Tramp, Les Ambassadeurs; *Style*— Aubrey Besser, Esq; Metal Enterprises and Co (London) Ltd, 2 Grosvenor Gardens, London SW1W 0DH (☎ 01 730 6134, telex 916475, fax 01 730 0740)

BESSEY, Gordon Scott; CBE (1967); s of Edward Emerson Bessey (d 1952), and Mabel Kate Bessey (d 1976); *b* 20 Oct 1910; *Educ* Heath Sch Halifax, St Edmund Hall Oxford (MA, DipEd); *m* 18 Dec 1937, Cynthia Mary Mabel, da of William Henry Bird; 1 s (Nicholas Edward b 1948), 3 da (Catherine Clare (Mrs Julien) b 1944, Amanda Gillian (Mrs Ward) b 1946, Charlotte Ann (Mrs Rowland) b 1946); *Career* teacher Keighley and Cheltenham 1933-37, admin asst Surrey 1937-45, dep educn offr Somerset 1945-49; dir of educn: Cumberland 1949-73, Cumbria 1973-75; memb Youth Serv Devpt Cncl 1960-67, chm working pty on pt/t trg of youth leaders 1961-62, pres Assoc of Chief Educn Offrs 1969-70; former chm: Voluntary Action Cumbria, Community Health Cncls; Hon DCL Newcastle 1970; *Recreations* fishing, golf, fell walking, ornithology; *Clubs* Border and County (Carlisle); *Style*— Gordon Bessey, Esq, CBE; 8 St George's Cres, Carlisle, Cumbria (☎ 0228 22253)

BEST, Anthony Arthur; s of late Arthur Best, and Dorothy Rose Amelia Best; *b* 11 Oct 1935; *Educ* Fell Chartered Institute of Bankers; *m* 31 March 1962, Mary Ann; 2 s (Mark b 1963, Nigel b 1965), 1 da (Natalie b 1968); *Career* exec dir: Rothschild Intercontinental Bank (London) 1968-74, Amex Bank London (dir subsdiary Bds) 1974-75; gen mangr Pierson, Heldring and Pierson, Amsterdam (dir, Pierson, Heldring and Pierson London) 1975-78, gen mangr Pierson, Heldring and Pierson; dir Polcreate 1980-; sr exec Amsterdam-Rotterdam Bank NV, Amsterdam 1980-82; md The Royal

Tst Co of Canada, London; dir: Royal Tst Bank (Jersey) Ltd, Royal Tst Bank (Isle of Man) 1982-86; vice-chm Charterhouse (Suisse) SA, Geneva 1987-; md Charterhouse Bank Ltd 1986-; *Recreations* gardening; *Clubs* Overseas Bankers, Walbrook Ward, European Atlantic; *Style—* Anthony A Best, Esq; Lodgefield, Newdigate Rd, Beare Green, Dorking, Surrey (☎ (0306) 711341); Charterhouse Bank Ltd, 1 Paternoster Row, London EC4M 7DH (☎ 01 248 8000, fax 01 248 6522, telex 884276)

BEST, Edward Wallace; CMG (1971), JP; s of Edward Lewis Best and Mary, *née* Wallace; *b* 11 Sept 1917; *Educ* Trinity GS, Wesley Coll Melbourne; *m* 1940, Joan Winifred, da of Harold Doughty Ramsay; 3 da; *Career* former Lord Mayor of Melbourne, dep chm Melbourne and Metropolitan Board of Works 1975-; *Style—* Edward Best, Esq, CMG, JP; 670 Orrong Road, Toorak, Victoria, Australia

BEST, Gary Martin; s of Charles William Best, of South Shields, and Doreen, *née* Wright; *b* 6 Oct 1951; *Educ* South Shields Grammar Tech Sch, Exeter Coll Oxford (MA), Oxford Dept of Educn (PGCE); *m* 9 Aug 1975, Frances Elizabeth, da of Edward Albert Rolling, of Redruth; 1 da (Claire Frances b 1981); *Career* asst history teacher King Edward's Sch Bath 1974-80; head of sixth form Newcastle-under-Lyme Sch 1983-87 (head of history 1980-83), headmaster Kingswood Sch 1987-; Methodist local preacher; *Books* Seventeenth-century Europe (1980), Wesley and Kingswood (1988); *Recreations* painting, music, reading, walking; *Style—* Gary Best, Esq; Summerfield, Coll Rd, Bath BA1 5SD (☎ 0225 317907); Kingswood Sch, Bath BA1 5RG (☎ 0225 311627)

BEST, Prof Geoffrey Francis Andrew; s of Frederick Ebenezer Best (d 1940), and Catherine Sarah Vanderbrook, *née* Bultz; *Educ* St Paul's, Trinity Coll Cambridge (BA, PhD), Harvard Univ (As Joseph Hodges Choate fell); *m* 9 Jul 1955, (Gwenllyan) Marigold, da of Reginald Davies, CMG; 2 s (Simon Geoffrey b 1956, Edward Hugh b 1958), 1 da (Rosamund Margaret b 1961); *Career* 2 Lt RAEC 1956-47; asst lectr Cambridge Univ 1956-61; Edinburgh Univ: lectr 1961-66, Sir Richard Lodge prof of history 1966-73; Sussex Univ: prof of history 1974-82, dean Sch of eur studies 1980-82; visitor and res fell LSE 1982-89; visiting fell; All Souls Coll Oxford 1969-70, Woodrow Wilson Center Washington DC 1978-79, Aust Nat Univ 1984; BRCS: chm priniciples and law ctee 1980-84, hon conslt on humanitarian law 1985-; *Books* incl: Temporal Pillars (1964), Mid-Victorian Britain (1971), Humanity in Warfare (1980), Honour among Men & Nations (1982), War & Society in Revolutionary Europe (1982), The Permanent Revolution (1988); *Style—* Prof Geoffrey Best; 19 Buckingham St, Oxford OX1 4LH

BEST, Capt George Frederic Matthew; OBE (1985), RN; s of Adm Sir Matthew Robert Best, KCB, DSO, MVO (d 1940), of Crockway, Maiden Newton, nr Dorchester, Dorset, and Annis Elizabeth, *née* Wood (d 1971); *b* 14 Dec 1908; *Educ* Britannia RNC, Dartmouth, RN Staff Coll; *m* 26 July 1940, Rosemary Elizabeth, da of John Chadwick Brooks, OBE (d 1964); 1 s (John b 1948), 1 da (Georgina (Mrs Connaughton) b 1944); *Career* serv WWII: Atlantic, W Africa, E Indies, Rangoon (despatches); Mil Staff Ctee UN 1946-48, CO HMS Loch Quoich Persian Gulf 1948-50, exec offr RN Air Station Ford 1950-52, liaison offr Staff of Br Naval C-in-C Med (at HQ Allied Forces S Europe) 1952-55, dep dir Naval Intelligence Admty 1956-58, cde Arabian Seas and Persian Gulf and Naval cdr S Arabian Cmd 1958-60; cncllr Dorset 1962-85, dep chm Wessex Regnl Water Authy 1973-85, chm Dorset Rural Devpt Area Jt Ctee 1984-; *Recreations* sailing, shooting, fishing, gardening; *Clubs* Army and Navy; *Style—* Capt George Best, OBE, RN; Wallhayes, Nettlecombe, Bridport, Dorset (☎ 030 885 358)

BEST, His Hon Judge Giles Bernard; s of Hon James William Best, OBE (d 1960), of Hincknowle, Melplash, Bridport, Dorset, and Florence Mary Bernarda, *née* Lees (d 1961); *b* 19 Oct 1925; *Educ* Wellington, Jesus Coll Oxford; *Career* Lt RM 1944-50; called to the Bar Inner Temple 1951, dep chm Dorset QS 1967-72, rec 1972-75, circuit judge 1975-; *Recreations* gardening, fishing; *Style—* His Hon Judge Best

BEST, Henry Nicholas; yst s of Hon James William Best, OBE, VD (d 1960, yst s of 5 Baron Wynford), and Florence Mary Bernarda (d 1961), da of Sir Elliott Lees, 1 Bt, DSO; *b* 3 May 1930; *Educ* Wellington; *m* 30 July 1963, Elisabeth Rose Ursula, da of Hans Joachim Druckenbrodt (d 1977), of Marburg, Germany; 2 s, 1 da; *Career* md: Anglo Blackwells Ltd (Queen's Award for Export Achievement 1979 and 1985), SKW Metals UK Ltd; FBIM, FIOD; *Recreations* hill walking, gardening, reading, local affrs; *Style—* Henry Nicholas Best, Esq; Bank House, Goldford Lane, Bickerton, Malpas, Cheshire SY14 8LL (☎ 082 925 287); Anglo Blackwells Ltd, Ditton Road, Widnes, Cheshire WA8 ONT (☎ 051 495 1400, telex 627653); SKW Metals UK Ltd, Ferry Lane, Rainham, Essex RM13 9DP (☎ 04027 53322, telex 896296/7)

BEST, Hon John Philip Robert; only s and heir, of 8 Baron Wynford, MBE; *b* 23 Nov 1950; *Educ* Radley, Keele Univ (BA), RAC Cirencester; *m* 10 Oct 1981, Fenella Christian Mary, o da of Capt Arthur Danks, MBE, TD, and Hon Serena Mary, da of 4 Baron Gifford; 1 s (Harry Robert Francis b 1987), 1 da (Sophie Hannah Elizabeth b 1985); *Career* ARICS land agency div 1979; *Style—* The Hon John Best; The Manor, Wynford Eagle, Dorchester, Dorset DT2 0ER (☎ 0300 20763)

BEST, John Robert Hall; s of Robert Dudley Best; *b* 11 Feb 1929; *Educ* Leighton Pk, Christ's Coll Cambridge; *m* 1961, Avril; 2 s; *Career* md Best & Lloyd 1970-, chm 1975-; Tstee of William Dudley's Tst; *Clubs* Savile, Thames Hare and Hounds; *Style—* John Best, Esq; 16 Oak Hill Drive, Edgbaston, Birmingham B15 (☎ 021 454 8702); Best & Lloyd Ltd, William St West, Smethwick, Warley, W Midlands B66 2NX (☎ 021 558 1191)

BEST, Keith Howard; OBE (1983); s of Herbert Henry Best (d 1958), of Sheffield, and Margeret Appleyard (d 1925); *b* 16 Jan 1923; *Educ* High Storrs GS, Sheffield Univ (BEng); *m* 5 Apr 1947, Maire Raymonde, da of George Ernest Lissenden (d 1965); 2 s (Jonathan b 1948, Clive b 1952), 1 da (Sarah b 1947); *Career* serv WWII 1942-46, parachute sqdns RE France and Germany, Lt 1944, Palestine, 1945 Capt; Husband and Co: asst engr Sheffield 1947-54, princ engr Ceylon 1954-57, ptnr London 1957-70; Bullen and Ptnrs: ptnr Croydon 1970-81, ptnr Durham 1981-88, sr ptnr 1988-; cncl memb I Struct E 1968-71, pres Br sec Societe des Ingenieurs et Scientifiques de France 1976, chm Maritime Eng Gp ICE 1981-84, EDC (Civil Eng) 1978-84, chm Assoc Consulting Engrs 1987-88; chm N Regn Engrg Cncl 1988-; Freeman City of London, Liveryman Worshipful Company of Engineers 1985, FICE 1958, FIStructE 1957; *Recreations* sailing; *Clubs* Army and Navy, Royal Engr Yacht; *Style—* Keith Best, Esq, OBE; The Forge, Castle Eden, Co Durham (☎ 0429 836340); Neville Ct, Nevilles Cross, Durham DH1 4ET (☎ 091 384 8594, fax 091 384 6082, telex 53543)

BEST, Norman Alexander; CBE (1980); s of Harold Ernest Best (d 1954), and Emily, *née* Webster; *b* 5 May 1924; *Educ* St Gregorys Luton, Eggars GS Alton; *m* 11 Sept 1948, (Valerie) Mary, JP, da of Frank Archibald Apleton (d 1968); 1 s (Nicholas b 1964), 3 da (Julia b 1949, Hilary b 1953, Vivienne b 1954); *Career* WWII Dorset Regt and Queen's Own Royal W Kent Regt serv with 8th Army N Africa and Italy 1943-47; Legal profession 35 years (ret); cnsllr Southampton City Cncl 1967- (ldr Cons Gp 1972-88, ldr Cncl 1972 and 1976-84; memb: policy and resources ctee, Econ Devpt and other ctees); memb Hants CC 1973- (vice chm Cons Gp 1973-; memb: policy resources ctee, pub protection ctee, econ strategic panel, coastal conservation panel etc); memb: exec ACC 1974-, consumer serv ctee 1974-, fire and emergency planning ctee 1974-, nat Jt Cncl for Local Authy Fire Bdes 1974-, Advsy Ctee on control of pollution of the sea 1974-, LACOTS (fndr chm 1979); 2 yrs rep Southampton City Cncl; memb: Southampton Univ Ct and cncl Nuffield theatre Tst, Mayflower Theatre Tst; dir: Southampton City Leisure Ltd, Southampton Econ Devpt Corp Ltd; sheriff and dep mayor of Southampton 1988-89; pres Southampton Test Cons Assoc 1981-, memb Wessex Area cons local Govt Advsy ctee; pres Age Concern Southampton 1987-, memb mgmnt ctee Hants CCC; FInstLEx; *Recreations* cricket, photography; *Style—* Norman Best, Esq, CBE; 1 Bassett Ct, Bassett Ave, Bassett, Southampton, Hants SO1 7DR (☎ 0703 769 320)

BEST, Hon Patrick George Mathew; yst s of 7 Baron Wynford (d 1943), and Evelyn Mary Aylmer, *née* May (d 1929); *b* 5 Oct 1923; *Educ* Wellington; *m* 29 March 1947, Heather Elizabeth, yr da of Hamilton Alexander Gardner (d 1952), of London and Assam; 4 s (Christopher b 1948, Michael b 1951 d 1952, David b 1953, Philip b 1960), 1 da (Clare b 1945); *Career* Lt RNVR, Channel, Atlantic, Mediterranean 1941-46; chm Wiggins Teape Gp 1979-84; dir: BAT Industs 1979-84, BAT US Inc 1980-84; non exec dir Rank Hovis MacDougal 1984; Master Worshipful Co of Ironmongers 1985-; FRSA, CBIM; offr Ordre de la Couronne (Belgium) 1982, Offr Order of the Crown of Belgium; CBIM, FRSA; *Recreations* skiing, theatre, the arts, golf; *Clubs* Boodle's; *Style—* The Hon Patrick Best; c/o Child & Co, 1 Fleet Street, London EC4Y 1BD

BEST, Richard Radford; CBE (1989, MBE 1977); s of Charles Ronald Best (d 1960), and Frances Mary, *née* Raymond; *b* 28 July 1933; *Educ* Worthing HS, Univ Coll London (BA); *m* 1, 1957, Elizabeth Vera, *née* Wait (d 1968); 2, 18 Jan 1969, Mary Kathleen Susan, da of Ernest Harry Wait (d 1977); 1 s (John Radford b 1973), 2 da (Anne Elizabeth Mary b 1961, Clare Caroline Frances b 1964); *Career* Home Off 1957-66; Dip Serv 1966-: second sec (info) Lusaka 1969, first sec (econ) Stockholm 1972, first sec (commercial) New Delhi 1979, actg dep high cmmr Calcutta 1982, asst head personnel ops dept FCO 1983, dep high cmmr Kaduna 1984; ambassador Iceland 1989-; BBC 'Brain of Britain' 1966; *Clubs* Royal Overseas League, Nigeria Britain Assoc (life memb); *Style—* Richard R Best, Esq, CBE; c/o FCO, King Charles St, London SW1 2AH

BEST-SHAW, Sir John Michael Robert; 10 Bt (E 1665), of Eltham, Kent; s of Cdr Sir John Best-Shaw, 9 Bt, RN (d 1984), and Elizabeth Mary Theodora, eld da of late Sir Robert Heywood Hughes, 12 Bt of East Bergholt; *b* 28 Sept 1924; *Educ* Lancing, Hertford Coll Oxford (MA), London Univ (Cert Ed); *m* 1960, Jane, da of Alexander Guthrie; 2 s (Thomas, Samuel b 1971), 1 da (Lucy b 1961), (& 1 child decd); *Heir* s, Thomas Joshua *qv*; *Career* late Capt Queen's Own Royal W Kent Regt, serv WWII NW Europe; with Fedn Malaya Police 1950-58, church work 1959-71, teaching 1972-82, social work 1982-; *Recreations* gardening, writing; *Clubs* Royal Cwlth Soc; *Style—* Sir John Best-Shaw, Bt; The Stone Ho, Boxley, Maidstone, Kent ME14 3DJ (☎ 0622 57524)

BEST-SHAW, Thomas Joshua; s and h of Sir John Michael Robert Best-Shaw, 10 Bt, *qv*; *b* 7 Mar 1965; *Style—* Thomas Best-Shaw, Esq; c/o The Stone Ho, Boxley, Maidstone, Kent

BESTERMAN, Prof Edwin Melville Mack; s of Theodore Besterman (d 1976), of Thorpe Mandeville, and Evelyn, *née* Mack (d 1964); *b* 4 May 1924; *Educ* Stowe, Trinity Coll Cambridge (BA, MA), Guy's Hosp (MB), MD (Cambridge, Raymond Horton Smith prize 1955); *m* 23 Sept 1944 (m dis) 1955, Audrey, *née* Heald; m 2, 9 Jul 1955 (m dis) 1978, Eleanor, *née* Till; 4 s (Harvey, Tristram, Adam, Gregory) from foregoing marriages; m 3, 7 Jul 1987, Perri Marjorie, da of Roy Burrowes of Kingston Jamaica; *Career* MO Outpatient dept Guys Hosp 1947, house physician Br Post-graduate Med Sch Hammersmith 1948, registrar rheumatic unit Canadian Red Cross Memorial Hosp 1949-52, lectr Inst of Cardiology and Nat Heart Hosp 1953-55, sr registrar Middlesex Hosp 1956-62; conslt cardiologist: St Marys Hosp, Paddington Green Children's Hosp 1962-85; vis cardiologist Malta Govt 1966-85, head cnslt Roy Post-graduate Med Sch Hammersmith 1981-85; hon cnslt cardiologist Univ of WI, Jamaica 1986-; FRCP, FACC; *Books* contribution to Paul Woods Diseases of Heart and Circulation (1968), num articles on Cardiological topics in learned journals; *Recreations* photography, breeding German Shepherd dogs, gardening; *Clubs* Liguanea (Jamica); *Style—* Prof Edwin Besterman; Airy View, Stockfarm Road, Golden Spring, St Andrew, Jamaica, W I (☎ (Jamaica) 942 2308); P O Box 340, Stony Hill, Kingston 9, Jamaica; Dept of Medicine, Univ of West Indies, Mona, Kingston 7, Jamaica, W I (☎ (Jamaica) 9271707

BESWICK, Hon Frank Jesse; s of Baron Beswick, PC (Life Peer), (d 1987); *b* 12 May 1949; *Educ* Latymer Upper Sch; *Style—* The Hon Frank Beswick; 28 Skeena Hill, SW18

BETHEL, David Percival; CBE (1983); s of William George Bethell (d 1982), of Lydney, Glos, and Elsie Evelyn Gladys, *née* Cossins (d 1984); *b* 7 Dec 1923; *Educ* King Edward VI Sch Bath & Crypt GS, West of England Coll of Art, Bristol Univ (NDD, ATD); *m* 1943, Margaret Elizabeth, da of Alexander John Dent-Wrigglesworth (d 1957); 1 s (Paul), 1 da (Ruth); *Career* designer and educator; lectr Stafford Sch of Art 1951-54, vice-princ Coventry Coll of Art 1955-56 (princ 1965-69), dep dir Leics Poly 1969-73 (dir 1973-87), pres Nat Soc for Art Educn 1965-66; memb: Cncl Int Soc for Educn through Art 1970-77, cncl for Educnl Technology 1974-80, CNAA ctee for Art and Design 1975-81, Hong Kong Univ and Poly Grants Ctee 1982-, Nat Advsy Body for Pub Sector Higher Educn 1982-; directing gp OECD Institutional Mgmnt of HE, Nat Advsy Bd for Public Sector HE, chm Study Team Primary Health Care Servs (Leics); chm: Chartered Soc of Designers' Educn Ctee 1987-, Planning Ctee for Academic Awards, Hong Kong 1986-87, East Midlands Regnl Advsy Cncl for Further Educn Academic Bd 1977-81, Ctee of dirs of Polys 1975-81, Cwlth of Aust Visiting Fellowship 1979-, educn advsy ctee Design Cncl 1980-88, Cyril Wood Trust, Jt NAB/UGC/SED Gp for Town & Country Planning 1985-, study team Primary Health Care Servs (Leics) 1987-88; vice-chm Inter-Univ cncl for Higher Educn Overseas 1981-83;

Freeman: City of London, Worshipful Co of Frame Work Knitters 1976; hon LLD Leics 1979; hon D Litt, Loughborough 1987; ARWA, FSAE, FSTC, FRSA, FCSD; *Recreations* travel, genealogy; *Clubs* Athenaeum; *Style—* Dr David Bethel, CBE; Stoke Lodge, 48 Holmfield Road, Stoneygate, Leics LE2 1SA (☎ 0533 704921)

BETHEL, Martin; QC (1983); s of Rev Ralph Arnold Bethel (d 1946), and Enid Ambery, *née* Smith; *b* 12 Mar 1943; *Educ* Kingswood Sch, Fitzwilliam House Cambridge (MA, LLM); *m* 14 Sept 1974, Kathryn Jane, da of Isaac Allan Denby, of Riddlesden, Keighley, Yorkshire; 2 s (Thomas b 1980, William b 1981), 1 da (Sarah b 1976); *Career* barr Inner Temple 1965; rec Crown Ct 1979-; *Recreations* sailing, skiing; *Style—* Martin Bethel Esq, QC; Pearl Chambers, 22 East Parade, Leeds LS1 5BU (☎ 0532 452702, fax 0532 420683)

BETHEL, Robert George Hankin; s of Horace Hankin Bethel (d 1961), of London & Eastbourne, and Eileen Maude (Mollie) *née* Motyer; *b* 7 June 1948; *Educ* Eastbourne GS, Pembroke Coll Cambridge (BA, MA, MB, BChir), St Mary's Hosp Med Sch; *Career* med practitioner: house physician Queen Elizabeth Hosp London 1972, house surgeon Nottingham Gen Hosp 1973, sr house offr Northwick Park Hosp and Clinical Res Centre Harrow 1974, registrar W Middx Univ Hosp 1974-76, gen med practitioner Englefield Green and Old Windsor 1976; course tutor The Open University 1979-80, hospital practitioner (geriatrics) 1980-, trainer for GP (Oxford Regn) 1984, advsy ed Horizons 1988; chm The Cambridge Soc (Surrey branch) 1988- (sec 1982-85); wardsman St Paul's Cathedral 1988; Freeman City of London 1977, memb Guild of Freemen City of London 1979, Liveryman Worshipful Co of Apothecaries 1981 (Freeman 1977); FRSM 1975, MRCGP 1979; *Books* Scientific papers in medical journals, particularly on rheumatological and general practice topics; *Recreations* genealogy, books, gardening; *Clubs* Utd Oxford and Cambridge Univ; *Style—* Dr Robert Bethel; Newton Court Med Centre, Burfield Road, Old Windsor, Berkshire SL4 2QF (☎ 0753 863 642)

BETHELL, Dr Hugh James Newton; s of Brig Richard Brian Wyndham Bethell, DSO, of Pilton House Barn, Pilton nr Shepton Mallet, Somerset, and Jackomina Alice, *née* Barton (d 1979); *b* 31 Mar 1942; *Educ* Tonbridge, St John's Coll Cambridge (BA), Guy's Hosp (MB BChir, D Obst RCOG); *m* 1, 1968, Astrid Jill, née Short (d 1979); 2 da (Katharine Emma b 25 Dec 1969, Christina Louise b 12 April 1973); m 2, 1984, Lesley *née* Harris;; *Career* cardiac registrar Charing Cross Hosp 1969-72, dermatology registrar Guy's Hosp 1972-74; princ in gen practice 1974-; dir Alton Coronary Rehabilitation Unit 1976-, chm Advsy Ctee on Coronary Rehabilitation to the Coronary Prevention Gp 1987-, dir Cardiac Rehabilitation Unit London Bridge Hosp 1987-, MO Sunday Times Nat Fun Run 1985-, fndr chm Alton Joggers; MRCP 1970, MRCGP 1974; *Recreations* running, cinema; *Style—* Dr Hugh Bethell; Farringdon Hurst, Nr Alton, Hants GU34 3DH (☎ 0420 58 592) The Health Centre, Alton, Hants (☎ 0420 84676)

BETHELL, Hon James David William; s of 5 Baron Westbury, MC; *b* 22 Feb 1952; *Educ* Harrow; *m* 1, 1974, Emma Hermione, da of Malise Nicolson, of Frog Hall, Tilston, Malpas, Cheshire; 2 da; m 2, 21 Nov 1987, Mrs Sally Le Gallais; 1 da (b 31 May 1988); *Career* racehorse trainer; *Recreations* shooting; *Style—* The Hon James Bethell; Downs Ho, Chilton, Didcot, Oxon OX11 0RR (☎ Abingdon 834333)

BETHELL, Lady Jane; *née* Pleydell-Bouverie; eldest da of 7 Earl of Radnor, KG, KCVO (d 1968), and his 1 w, Helen Olivia, *neé* Adeane; *b* 14 Sept 1923; *Educ* Godolphin Sch Salisbury; *m* 27 Sept 1945, Richard Anthony Bethell, *qv*; 2 s (Hugh, William), 2 da (Camilla, Sarah); *Style—* Lady Jane Bethell; Rise Park, Hull, Humberside HU11 5BL (☎ 0964 562241)

BETHELL, 4 Baron (UK 1922) Nicholas William Bethell; 4 Bt (UK 1911), MEP (EDG) London NW 1979-; s of Hon William Gladstone Bethell (d 1964), 3 s of 1 Baron Bethell; suc cous 1967; *b* 19 July 1938; *Educ* Harrow, Pembroke Coll Cambridge (PhD); *m* 1964 (m dis 1971), Cecilia Mary Lothian (d 1977), da of Prof Alexander Mackie Honeyman, of Oldtown, Ardgay, Ross-shire; 2 s (Hon James Nicholas, Hon William Alexander b 18 March 1969, ed Harrow); *Heir* s, Hon James Nicholas Bethell b 1 Oct 1967, ed Harrow, Edinburgh Univ; *Career* takes Cons Whip in House of Lords; chm Freedom of the Skies Campaign (lobby gp against Europe airline fares cartel); sub-editor TLS 1962-64; script editor BBC Radio Drama 1964-67; a govt whip 1970-71, nominated MEP 1975-79; *Books* Gomulka, The War Hitler Won, The Last Secret, Russia Besieged, The Palestine Triangle, The Great Betrayal, (translator) Cancer Ward by Alexander Solzhenitsyn, Elegy to John Donne by Joseph Brodsky; *Recreations* poker, cricket; *Clubs* Pratt's, Garrick, Carlton, MCC; *Style—* The Rt Hon the Lord Bethell, MEP; 73 Sussex Sq, London W2 2SS (☎ 01 402 6877)

BETHELL, Richard Anthony; JP (Humberside 1950); eldest s of Lt-Col (William) Adrian Vincent Bethell (d 1941), of Rise Park, Hull, and Watton Abbey, nr Driffield, and Cicely, da of Sir John Richard Geers Cotterell, 4 Bt, by his w, Lady Evelyn Gordon-Lennox, da of 7 Duke of Richmond, KG; *b* 22 Mar 1922; *Educ* Eton; *m* 27 Sept 1945, Lady Jane, *qv*, da of 7 Earl of Radnor, KG, KCVO (d 1968); 2 s, 2 da; *Career* landowner and farmer; 2 Lt Life Gds 1941, served UK and overseas 1941-45; DL Humberside 1975; Lord-Lieut 1983-; High Sheriff Humberside 1976-77; *Recreations* hunting, shooting, racing, farming; *Style—* Richard Bethell, Esq, JP; Rise Park, Hull, Humberside HU11 5BL (☎ 0964 56 224)

BETHELL, Hon Richard Nicholas; MBE (1979); s and h of 5 Baron Westbury, MC; *b* 29 May 1950; *Educ* Harrow, RMA Sandhurst; *m* 1975, Caroline, da of Richard Palmer, JP, of Swallowfield, Berks; 1 s, 2 da; *Career* Maj Scots Gds 1982; Off Brother Order of St John; *Style—* Major the Hon Richard Bethell, MBE

BETHELL-JONES, Richard James Stephen; s of Geoffrey Bethell-Jones (d 1977), and Nancy Hartland, *née* Martin; *b* 16 Sept 1945; *Educ* St Johns Leatherhead, Cambridge Univ; *m* 15 Sept 1973, Sarah Landells, da of Lt Col Felix Hodson; 2 da (Jessica b 1977, Harriet b 1979); *Career* admitted slr 1970, ptnr Wilde Sapte 1975-; memb City of London Slrs Co 1984; *Recreations* tennis; *Style—* Richard Bethell-Jones, Esq; Queensbridge House, 60 Upper Thames St, London EC4V 3BD (☎ 01 236 3050, fax 01 236 9624, telex 887793)

BETHENOD, Gilles Marie Nicolas; s of Maurice Bethenod (d 1980), of Paris, and Solange Salteur De La Serraz; *b* 28 Sept 1948; *Educ* Ecole Des Roches Verneuil France, Paris Univ; *m* 26 Oct 1974, Sylvie Paule Jeanne, da of Yvon Colin (d 1988); 2 s (Alexis b 18 Oct 1975, Nicolas b 20 Jan 1977), 1 da (Marie Astrid b 18 Oct 1979); *Career* Offr French Navy (reserve); Banque Nationale de Paris 1975-86, exec dir Yamaichi Int Europe Ltd 1986-; *Recreations* tennis, skiing; *Clubs* Riverside; *Style—* Gilles Bethenod, Esq; 26 Dorville Cres, London W6 0HJ (☎ 01 846 9204); 21 Quai Le Gallo, 92 000 Boulogne, France; Baratoire Marray, 37320 Neuvy LeRoi, France; Yamaichi International (Europe) Ltd, Finsbury Ct, 111/117 Finsbury Pavement, London EC2A 1EQ (☎ 01 638 5599, fax 01 588 4602, telex 887414)

BETHUNE, Sir Alexander Maitland Sharp; 10 Bt (NS 1683); s of Sir Alexander Sharp Bethune, 9 Bt, JP (d 1917), by Elisabeth (d 1935), da of Frederick Maitland-Heriot; *b* 28 Mar 1909; *Educ* Eton, Magdalene Coll Cambridge; *m* 11 Jan 1955, (Ruth) Mary, da of James Hurst Hayes, of Marden House, East Harting, Sussex; 1 da (Lucy b 1959); *Heir* none; *Career* formerly Capt Intelligence Corps; dir Contoura Photocopying Ltd, Copytec Services Ltd; *Recreations* golf, nature; *Style—* Sir Alexander Sharp Bethune, Bt; 21 Victoria Grove, London W8

BETHUNE, Hon Sir (Walter) Angus; s of Frank Pogson and Laura Eileen Bethune; *b* 10 Sept 1908; *m* 1936, Alexandra, da of P A Pritchard; 1 s, 1 da; *Career* premier and tres of Tasmania 1969-72; pastoralist; kt 1979; *see Debrett's Handbook of Australia and New Zealand for further details0*; *Style—* The Hon Sir Angus Bethune; 553 Churchill Avenue, Sandy Bay, Tasania 7005

BETHWAITE, Cyril Forrester; s of Albert Henry Bethwaite (d 1954), and Anne, *née* Forrester (d 1979); *b* 23 July 1920; *Educ* Whitehaven GS, Leeds Univ (BSc); *m* 1944, Hylda Mollie (d 1987), da of Leslie Bexon (d 1946); 2 s (Malcolm, David); *Career* exec dir Hawker Siddeley Aviation Ltd 1970-78, divnl dir Br Aerospace (Aircraft Gp) 1978-82, ret July 1982; FRAES, CEng; *Recreations* music; *Style—* Cyril Bethwaite, Esq; 4 Glendene Ave, Bramhall, Stockport, Cheshire SK7 1BH (☎ 061 439 3711)

BETT, Michael; s of Arthur Bett, OBE, and Nina, *née* Daniells; *b* 18 Jan 1935; *Educ* Aldenham Sch, Pembroke Coll Cambridge (MA); *m* 3 Oct 1959, Christine Angela, da of Major Horace Reid, JP; 1 s (Timothy Mark b 1961), 2 da (Sally Maria b 1963, Lucy Ann b 1965); *Career* 2 Lt Essex Regt 1953-55; dir Industl Relations Engrg Employers Fedn 1970-72; personnel dir: General Electric Co 1972-77, BBC 1977-81; Br Telecom: personnel dir 1981-85, md LCS Div, UK Div and corporate dir Br Telecom plc 1985-; former memb: Pay Bd, May Ctee of Inquiry into UK Prison Serv, Ctee of Inquiry into Water Dispute 1983, Griffiths Inquiry into NHS Mgmnt, Armed Forces Pay Review, Manpower Servs Cmmn; memb cncl: Cranfield Inst of Technol, Inst of Manpower Studies, Int Mgmnt Centre Buckingham; vice pres Royal TV Soc, chm mgmnt ctee Bromley CAB; CBIM, FIPM, FRSA; *Style—* Michael Bett, Esq; Colets Well, The Green, Otford, Sevenoaks, Kent

BETTINSON, John Richard; s of Harold Richard Bettinson, MC (d 1986), of Edgbaston, and Barbara, *née* Keene (d 1984); *b* 27 June 1932; *Educ* Haileybury, Birmingham Univ (LLB); *m* 1 Nov 1958, (Margaret) Angela, da of Richard Good (d 1955), of Edgbaston; 1 s (Richard b 1961), 1 da (Hayley b 1963); *Career* Lt 3 Carabiniers 1955-57; slr 1955; sr ptnr Bettinsons, Birmingham; chm: Victoria Carpets Hldgs plc, Assay Office Birmingham, Birmingham Repertory Theatre Ltd, Birmingham Research Park Ltd; dep chm Concentric plc; pres W Midland Rent Assessment Panel 1985-; memb: Cncl of Birmingham Univ 1984-, exec ctee Age Concern England 1984-; chm: Birmingham Area Health Authority 1973-82, Nat Assoc of Health Authorities 1976-79; gen cmmr for Income Tax 1970-; memb Glaziers Co; memb Law Soc; *Recreations* theatre, bricklaying, reading; *Clubs* Cavalry and Guards'; *Style—* John Bettinson, Esq; Storey House, 4 Pritchatts Rd, Edgbaston, Birmingham B15 2QT (☎ 021 455 7588); 83 Newhall St, Birmingham B3 1LP (☎ 021 236 8282, fax 021 236 0598, telex 335961)

BETTISON, Paul David; s of Capt Kenneth Henry David Bettison, of Worcester Park, Surrey, and Ona Patricia, *née* Ratcliffe; *b* 18 April 1953; *Educ* Tiffin Boys Sch Kingston-Upon-Thames; *m* 15 May 1976, Jean Margaret, da of Flt Lt Kenneth Charles Bradshaw, of Ewell, Epsom, Surrey; 2 da (Clare Louise b 1983, Emily Margaret b 1985); *Career* memb mgmnt Rockwell Graphic Systems Ltd 1978-87, md Graphic Systems Int Ltd 1987-; F Inst SMM 1979; *Recreations* travel, cars, wine; *Style—* Paul Bettison, Esq; Longdown House, Mickle Hill, Little Sandhurst, Camberley, Surrey GU17 8QL; Graphic Systems International Ltd, Unit 2 Hook Hse Farm Estate, London Rd, Hook, Hampshire RG27 9EQ (☎ 025 672 8353, fax 025 672 8355, car tel 0836 287050, telex 858902 BARON G)

BETTLEY, Dr Francis Ray; TD (1942); yr s of Francis James Bettley (d 1961), of Bournemouth, and Charlotte, *née* Wood (d 1970); *b* 18 August 1909; *Educ* Whitgift Sch, UCL (MD); *m* 1951, Jean Rogers, da of Archibald Barnet McIntyre (d 1935), of Bexley, Kent; 1 s (Francis), 2 da (Katherine, Virginia (adopted)); *Career* TA RAMC 1933-50, Lt-Col WWII 1939-45; serv UK, ME, E Africa; emeritus physician to: Middx Hosp London, St John's Hosp for Diseases of the Skin, King Edward VII Hosp Midhurst, ret; FRCP; *Books* many contributions to medical journals; *Clubs* Athenaeum; *Style—* Dr Francis Bettley, TP; 4 Edgar Villas, Edgar Rd, Winchester, Hants SO23 9TD (☎ 0962 67595)

BETTON, David John William; s of John Clifford Betton, of Milverton, Taunton, Somerset, and Evelyn Naomi, *née* Byatt; *b* 30 Dec 1947; *Educ* Dulwich, Emmanuel Coll Cambridge (BA, MA); *m* 6 Jan 1968 (m dis 1975), Christine Judith Patey, da of Very Rev Edward Patey, Dean of Liverpool, Merseyside; m 2, 5 Sept 1980, Nicola Mary Mallen, da of John McGregor Carter (d 1983); 1 s (Jack David McGregor), 3 da (Victoria Christine Naomi, Polly Nicola, Nancy Evelyn Mary); *Career* barr 1972, sr legal advsr HM Customs and Excise 1976-86, nat dir of VAT Clark Whitehill, CAs 1976-; *Recreations* cricket, theatre, walking; *Clubs* MCC; *Style—* David Betton, Esq; 32 Thaxted Rd, Saffron Walden, Essex CB11 3AA (☎ 0799 27958); 25 New Street Square, London EC4A 3LN (☎ 01 353 1577, fax 01 583 1720, telex 887422)

BETTS, Rt Rev Stanley Woodley; CBE (1967); s of Hubert Woodley Betts (d 1950), of Cambridge, and Lilian Esther, *née* Cranfield (d 1962); *b* 23 Mar 1912; *Educ* The Perse Sch Cambridge, Jesus Coll Cambridge (MA); *Career* curate St Paul's Cheltenham 1935-38, chaplain RAF 1938-47, sr chaplain BAFO Germany 1946-47, Cmdt RAF Chaplain's Sch 1947, chaplain Clare Coll Cambridge 1947-49, vicar Holy Trinity Cambridge 1949-56; bishop: of Maidstone, to HM Forces 1956-66, dean of Rochester 1966-77, chm bd of the Church Army 1970-80, vice-pres Lee Abbey Wadhurst Coll (chm of cncl 1976-84); *Clubs* The National; *Style—* The Rt Rev Stanley Betts, CBE; 2 Kings Houses, Old Pevensey, E Sussex BH24 5JR (☎ 0323 62421)

BETTS, Air Vice-Marshal (Charles) Stephen; CBE (1962); s of Herbert Charles Betts (d 1971), of Nuneaton, Warwicks, and Edith Whiting, *née* French (d 1979); *b* 8 April 1919; *Educ* King Edward VI Sch Nuneaton, Sidney Sussex Coll Cambridge (MA); *m* 1, 1943 (m dis 1964), Pauline Mary (d 1965) da of Lt-Col P Heath, IA; 2 da (Susan, Stephanie); m 2, 1964, Margaret Doreen, da of Col Walter Herbert Young, DSO (d 1941), of Farnham, Surrey; *Career* RAF 1941-74 (Engr Offr), Asst Cmdt RAF Coll

Cranwell 1971, Air Offr cmdg No24 Gp Rudloe Manor 1972-74, head of inspection and control div The Armaments Control Agency Western Euro Union Paris 1974-84; ret; *Recreations* travel, music; *Clubs* RAF; *Style—* Air Vice-Marshal Stephen Betts, CBE; Cranford, Weston Rd, Bath BA1 2XX (☎ 0225 310995); Le Moulin de Bourgeade, Bourg du Bost, 24600 Riberac, France (☎ 53 90 96 93)

BETTS, William Reuben; s of William Louis Betts (d 1961), and Doris Pumfrey (d 1977); *b* 27 June 1924; *Educ* St John's Sch Leatherhead Surrey; *m* 24 May 1950, Barbara Nellie, da of James George Wilkin (d 1941); 1 da (Rosemary Frances); *Career* chartered surveyer: snr ptnr Burrows & Day, Chartered Surveyors 1977-85; Kent County Agric Soc, vice-chm 1971-84 (hon life gov 1984-); chartered memb Weald of Kent Round Table 1957- (fndr memb Lagos, Nigeria 1963); pres Central Assoc Agricultural Valuers (Kent) 1977-79; fell RICS (chm Kent branch 1980); assoc Chartered Auctioneers & Estate Agents Inst 1948-; *Recreations* beekeeping, DIY; *Clubs* Elwick Ashford; *Style—* William R Betts, Esq; Ilex Cottage, Bramble Lane, Wye, Ashford, Kent TN25 5EH (☎ 0233 812693)

BEUTHIN, Allan John Elrick; *née* Burnett; s of Prof R C Beuthin, Johannesburg, S Africa, and Beryl Ada *née* Bray; *b* 19 Jan 1944; *Educ* St Stithians Coll, Parktown Boys High S Africa; *m* 15 April 1968, Sharon Alice, da of Lawrence John Landey; 1 s (Charles Lawrence b 1975), 1 da (Teresa b 1971); *Career* dir Menell Jack Hyman & Co 1962-68, memb Johannesburg Stock Exchange 1969-78, memb The Stock Exchange - London 1980-, dir Merrill Lynch Ltd 1985-88; *Recreations* golf, cycling, theatre; *Clubs* Hadley Wood Golf; *Style—* Allan Beuthin, Esq; 26 Beech Hill Avenue, Hadley Wood, Herts (☎ 01 440 1304)

BEVAN; *see*: Evans-Bevan

BEVAN, Rear Adm Christopher Martin; CB (1978); s of Humphrey Charles Bevan (d 1982) and Mary F, *née* Mackenzie; *b* 22 Jan 1923; *Educ* Stowe, Victoria Univ Wellington NZ; *m* 1948, Patricia Constance, da of Rev Arthur William Bedford (d 1950); 1 s, 3 da; *Career* joined RN 1942, ADC to HM The Queen 1976, flag offr Medway and Port Adm Chatham 1976-78; under-tres Gray's Inn 1980-; *Recreations* theatre, music, photography; *Style—* Rear Adm Christopher Bevan, CB; c/o C Hoare & Co, 37 Fleet St, London EC4P 4DQ (☎ 01 405 8164)

BEVAN, (Andrew) David Gilroy; MP (C) Birmingham, Yardley 1979-; s of Rev Thomas John Bevan (d 1944), and Norah *née* Gilroy (d 1974); bro of Prof Peter Gilroy Bevan, CBE, *qv*; *b* 10 April 1928; *Educ* King Edward VI Sch Birmingham; *m* 1967, Cynthia Ann Villiers, da of T J Boulstridge; 1 s, 3 da; *Career* FIAA&S 1962 (past chm W Midlands br), FRVA 1971, FSVA 1968 (past chm W Midlands br), FFB 1972, FCIA 1954, MRSH 1957; served on Birmingham CC and later W Midlands CC 1959-80; princ A Gilroy Bevan Incorporated Valuers and Surveyors; chm: Conservative Backbench Tourism Ctee, Parly Road Passenger Transport Co, vic chm Urban Affairs Ctee; *Recreations* gardening, walking; *Clubs* Carlton; *Style—* David Bevan, Esq, MP; The Cottage, 12 Wentworth Rd, Four Oaks Park, Sutton Coldfield, W Midlands (☎ 021 308 3292; business 021 308 6319); 16 Courtenay Sq, London SE11 (☎ 01 735 5548)

BEVAN, Hon Mrs; Hon Hilary Evelyn Spicer; *née* Pakington; da of 5 Baron Hampton, OBE; *b* 24 May 1914; *m* 1938, David John Vaughan Bevan, TD, 2 s of late Penry Vaughan Bevan, fell of Trinity Coll Cambridge, and bro of Dr Edward Vaughan Bevan, *qv*; 3 s, 2 da; *Style—* The Hon Mrs Bevan; Kingsland, Bledington, Oxford

BEVAN, Dr James Stuart; s of Peter James Stuart Bevan (d 1968), of London, and Phyllis Marjorie, *née* Enthoven (d 1978); *b* 28 Sept 1930; *Educ* Bryanston, Trinity Coll Cambridge (MA, MB, BChir); *m* 21 April 1962, Rosemary, da of John Mendus (d 1988), of Pembroke; 1 s (Richard Stuart b 1964), 1 da (Katherine b 1966); *Career* Capt and jr specialist in medicine RAMC, active serv Malaya and Singapore 1958-59; princ GP 1960-, sr med conslt AA, med advsr London Coll of Music and other orgns; chm Fndn of Nursing Studies, sec of Ethics ctee Humana-Wellington Hosp; memb BMA 1955, MRCGP 1962, D(Obst)RCOG; *Books* Your Family Doctor, Anatomy and Physiology, Pocket Medical and First Aid Guide; *Style—* Dr James Bevan; 9 Hill Rd, London NW8 9QE (☎ 01 286 8340); 6A Palace Gate, London W8 5NF (☎ 01 589 2478)

BEVAN, John Penry Vaughan; s of Llewelyn Vaughan Bevan (d 1987), and Hilda molly, *née* Yates; *b* 7 Sept 1947; *Educ* Radley, Magdalene Coll Cambridge (BA); *m* 1 1971(m dis 1976), Dinah, *née* Nicholson; 2 da (Amelia b 1972, Lucinda b 1975); m 2 12 June 1978, Veronica *née* Aliaga-Kelly; 1 s (Henry b 1981), 1 da (Charlotte b 1985); *Career* barr, jr prosecuting counsel to the Crown at Central Criminal Ct, rec 1987-; *Recreations* sailing, tennis; *Clubs* Leander, Aldeburgh Yacht, Orford Sailing; *Style—* John Bevan, Esq; 2 Harcourt Buildings, Temple, London EC4 (☎ 01 353 2112)

BEVAN, John Stuart; s of Frank Oakland Bevan, of East Stour, and Ruth Mary, *née* Sadler; *b* 19 Nov 1935; *Educ* Eggar's GS, Jesus Coll Oxford (MA), St Bartholomew's Hosp (MSc) Med Coll; *m* 30 Jul 1960, Pat(ricia) Vera Beatrice, da of Alfred Charles William Joyce, of Shillingstone; 2 s (David b 1961, Robin b 1966), 2 da (Elizabeth b 1962, Sally b 1965); *Career* Harefield Hosp (Pathology Lab) 1954-56; physicist UKAEA 1960-62, lectr and sr lectr Poly of the S Bank (Prev Boro Poly) 1962-73, dir educn ILEA 1979-82 (dep educn offr 1977-79, asst then sr asst educn offr 1973-76); sec NAB 1982-; Scout Assoc (Dep Co Cmmr, Kent); memb exec ctees: ATTI 1968-73 (Presi 1972-73), NUT 1970-73, AEO 1977-82 (chm 1981-82); hon fell Poly of the South Bank (1988); F Inst P 1972; *Books* Jt The Space Environment (1969); *Recreations* classical music, mountaineering; *Style—* John Bevan Esq; 4 Woodland Way, Bidborough, Tunbridge Wells, Kent TN4 0UX (☎ 0892 27461); Metropolis House, 22 Percy Street, London W1P 9FF (☎ 01 637 1132, fax 01 436 4320)

BEVAN, Jonathan Stuart Vaughan; s of Dr Edward Vaughan Bevan, TD, DL (d 1988), and Joan Margot, *née* Goddard; *b* 15 June 1940; *Educ* St Faiths Cambridge, Bedford Sch; *m* 17 Sept 1960 (m dis 1986), Victoria Judith Helen, da of Hugh Leycester (d 1952), of Hilton, Hunts; 3 da (Charlotte Victoria b 1961, Francesca b 1963, Tiffany Alice b 1965); *Career* dep export dir and PA to chm Pye of Cambridge 1959-66, Grievson Grant and Co 1966-85 (assoc memb 1968, ptnr 1970), dir Kleinwort Benson Securities 1985-88; chm and memb of exec local cons orgn 1963-72, memb Cambridge Rowing Soc, dist cmmr pony club 1981-85; 1984-: life pres St Moriz Sporting Club, chm and chief exec SMOMC; FRGS, London Stock Exchange 1970, Stock Exchange 1987; *Books* Very Large Numbers (1984); *Recreations* tobogganinng, shooting, walking; *Clubs* St Moritz Tobagganning, SMOMC; *Style—* Jonathan Bevan, Esq; 17 Eaton Terrace, London SW1; (☎ 01 730 3344); La Forge, Les Houches, Mont Blanc, France; Chesa Cattanio, Via Maistra, 46 St Moritz, Switzerland

BEVAN, Prof Peter Gilroy; CBE (1983); s of Rev Thomas John Bevan (d 1944), and Norah Gilroy (d 1974); bro of (Andrew) David Gilroy Bevan, MP, *qv*; *b* 13 Dec 1922; *Educ* King Edwards HS Birmingham, Univ of Birmingham Med Sch (MB, ChB, ChM), Univ of London (LRCP, MRCS); *m* 1949, Patricia Joan (d 1985), da of Maj Gen Rufus Henry Laurie (d 1960); 1 s (Jonathan), 1 da (Deirdre); *Career* RAMC (Capt) BAOR 1947-49; conslt surgn Dudley Rd Hosp Birmingham 1958-87; postgraduate dir Univ of Birmingham Med Sch 1978-87; memb cncl Royal Coll of Surgns of England 1971-83 (vice-pres 1980-81); advsr in general surgery to the RN 1983-88; dir Overseas Dr's Trg Scheme (RCS England) 1987-, medical memb Parsions Appeal Tbnls 1987-; pres: Assoc of Surgns of Great Br and Ireland 1985, Br Inst of Surgical Technologists 1983-; *Books* Reconstructive Procedures in Surgery (1981), various papers on surgery and surgical training; *Recreations* inland waterways (narrow boat Petricia), golf, photography; *Clubs* Edgbaston Golf Birmingham; *Style—* Prof Peter G Bevan, CBE; 10 Russell Rd, Moseley, Birmingham B13 8RD (☎ 021 449 3055)

BEVAN, Rev Canon Richard Justin William; s of Rev Richard Bevan (vicar of St Harmon Radnorshire, d 1928), and Margaret Mabel, *née* Pugh; *b* 21 April 1922; *Educ* St Edmund's Sch Canterbury, St Augustine's Coll Canterbury, St Chad's Coll, Univ of Durham (BA, LTh), Lichfield Theol Coll; *m* 4 Sept 1949, Sheila Rosemary, da of Thomas Barrow (d 1963), of Fazakerley, Liverpool; 4 s (Roderick, Nicholas, Timothy, Christopher b 1967, d 1968), 1 da (Rosemary); *Career* ordained Lichfield Cathedral: deacon 1945, priest 1946; asst curate Stoke-on-Trent 1945-49, chaplain Aberlour Orphanage Scotland 1949-51, asst master Towneley Tech HS Burnley 1951-60, licence to officiate Diocese of Blackburn 1951; hon asst curate: Church Kirk 1951-56, Whalley 1956-60; rector St Mary-le-Bow Durham 1964-74, vicar United Benefice St Oswaid with St Mary-le-Bow Durham 1964-74; chaplain: Durham Univ 1961-74 (convenor of chaplains 1966-74), Durham Girls' HS 1966-74, St Cuthbert's Soc Durham Univ 1966-72, St Aidan's Soc 1960-64, Trevelyan Coll Durham Univ 1966-72; examining chaplain to Bishop of Carlisle 1970-, govr St Chad's Coll Durham 1969-, rector Grasmere 1974-82, canon residentiary Carlisle Cathedral 1982- (tres and librarian 1982-, vice dean 1986-), Chaplain to HM the Queen 1986-; first pres and fndr memb Grasmere Village Soc; theol conslt Churchman Publishing Ltd 1986-; Hon ThD Geneva Theol Coll 1972, Hon PhD Columbia Pacific Univ 1980; *Books* Steps to Christian Understanding (ed 1959), The Churches and Christian Unity (ed 1964), Durham Sermons (ed 1964), Unfurl the Flame (poetry, 1980), A Twig of Evidence: Does Belief in God Make Sense? (1986); *Recreations* poetry, reading, musical appreciation, train travel; *Style—* The Rev Canon Richard Bevan; 3 The Abbey, Carlisle, Cumbria CA3 8TZ (☎ 0228 21834); The Cathedral, Carlisle, Cumbria

BEVAN, Sir Timothy Hugh; s of late Hugh Bevan, and Pleasance, *née* Scrutton; *b* 24 May 1927; *Educ* Eton; *m* 1952, Pamela, da of late Norman Smith; 2 s, 2 da; *Career* called to the Bar Middle Temple 1950, joined Barclays Bank 1950, chm 1981-87, (dep chm 1973-81), chm BET plc 1988-; kt 1984; *Style—* Sir Timothy Bevan; c/o BET plc, Stratton House, Piccadilly, London W1X 6AS (☎ 01 629 8886)

BEVAN, Rear Adm Timothy Michael; CB (1986); s of Thomas Richard Bevan (d 1967), and Margaret Richmond Bevan, *née* Turnure (d 1974); *b* 7 April 1931; *Educ* Eton; *m* 1970, Sarah, Maj Claude Thorburn Knight, of Sussex; 3 s (Thomas b 1973, Michael b 1975, Richard b 1977); *Career* RN 1949; cmd: HMS Decoy 1966, HMS Caprice 1967-68, HMS Minerva 1971-72, HMS Ariadne 1976-78; Capt of 8 Frigate Sqdn 1980-82; Britannia RNC 1982-84; Asst CDS (Intelligence) 1984-; ret 1987; *Clubs* Brook's; *Style—* Rear Adm Timothy Bevan

BEVAN-THOMAS, Philip Morgan; s of William Ewart Thomas (d 1970), of 67 Grand Ave, Worthing, and Doris Winifred *née* Morgan (d 1966); *b* 2 Dec 1934; *Educ* Cheltenham, St Edmund Hall Oxford (MA); *m* 18 Jun 1962, Janet Mary, da of Eric Walter Ward (d 1979) of 13 Manor Close, Havant; 2 s (Giles b 1965, Oliver b 1967); *Career* Nat Serv: 2 Lt RA 1953-55, TA Capt RHA (Para) 1958-63; slr; ptnr: Francis and Parkes 1964-86, Field Seymour Parkes 1987-; pres: Berks, Bucks and Oxford Law Soc 1982-83; chm Shiplake Parish Council 1985; memb Law Soc 1963-;; *Recreations* sailing, golf; *Clubs* Huntercombe Golf, Leander Sea View Yacht; *Style—* Philip Bevan-Thomas, Esq; The Moorings, Wharfe Lane, Henley-on-Thames, Oxford RG9 2LL (☎ 0491 572143); The Old Coroners Ct, 1 London Street, Reading, RG1 4QW (☎ 0734 391011, fax 0734 502704)

BEVERIDGE, Dr Gordon Smith Grieve; s of Victor Beattie Beveridge (d 1983), and Elizabeth Fairbairn, *née* Grieve (d 1971); *b* 28 Nov 1933; *Educ* Inverness Royal Acad, Univ of Glasgow (BSc), Royal Coll of Science and Technol Glasgow (ARCST), Univ of Edinburgh (PhD); *m* 1963, Geertruida Hillegonda Johanna, da of Gerrit Hendrik Bruijn (d 1944); 2 s, 1 da; *Career* lectr chem engrg Univ of Edinburgh 1962-67, sr lectr and reader chem engrg Heriot-Watt Univ 1967-71, prof chem engrg Univ of Strathclyde 1971-86 (head dept of chem and process engrg), vice-chllr Queen's Univ Belfast 1986-; memb: cncl Soc of Chemical Ind 1978-88 (vice-pres 1985-88); Engrg Cncl 1981-, engrg bd of SERC 1983-86, chem econ dvpt ctee NEDO 1983-; Harkness fell the Cwlth Fund (NY), resident at Univ of Minnesota 1960-62, chm Cremer & Warner Gp of Cos; CEng, FEng, FIChemE (pres 1984-85), FRSE, FRSA 1988; *Recreations* Scottish and Dutch history; *Clubs* Caledonian; *Style—* Dr Gordon Beveridge; 10 Eglinton Crescent, Edinburgh EH12 5DD; The Vice-Chancellors Lodge, 16 Lennoxvale, Belfast BT9 5BY

BEVERIDGE, John Caldwell; QC (1979); s of Prof William Ian Beardmore Beveridge, of Canberra, and Patricia, *née* Thomson; *b* 26 Sept 1937; *Educ* privately, Jesus Coll Cambridge; *m* 1973, (m dis 1988), Frances Anne Clunes Grant Martineau, da of Dr John Sutherland, of Edinburgh; *Career* barr, rec Crown Ct 1975-, bencher Inner Temple 1985; Freeman City of London 1965; *Recreations* hunting, shooting; *Clubs* Turf, Brooks's, The Beefsteak; *Style—* John Beveridge Esq, QC; 5 St James's Chamber, Ryder Street, London SW17 6QA (☎ 01 839 2660); 4 Pump Ct, Temple, London EC4 (☎ 01 353 2656)

BEVERTON, Prof Raymond John Heaphy; CBE (1968); s of Edgar John Beverton (d 1968), of London, and Dorothy Sybil Mary, *née* Heaphy; *b* 29 August 1922; *Educ* Forest Sch Snaresbrook, Downing Coll Cambridge (BA, MA); *m* June 10 1947, Kathleen Edith, da of Frederick Henry Marner (d 1956), of London; 3 da (Susan Lorinda b 1950, Julia Rosemary b 1953, Valerie Louise b 1955); *Career* operational researcher 1942-45; fisheries laboratory MAAF Lowestoft Suffolk: res scientist 1947-65, dep dir 1959-65; sec Natural Environment Res Cncl 1965-80, prof dept applied biology UWIST 1983- 87, prof and head sch of pure and applied biology Univ of Wales and Coll of Cardiff 1987-; Hon DSc Univ of Wales 1989; FIBiol 1973, FRS 1975; *Books* On The Dynamics of Exploited Fish Populations (with S J Holt 1957); *Recreations* gardening, music, DIY, golf; *Style*— Prof Raymond Beverton; Montana, Old Roman Rd, Langstone, Gwent, South Wales NP6 2JU (☎ 0633 412 392); Sch of Pure & Applied Biology, Univ of Wales, P.O. Box 915, Cardiff CF1 3TL (☎ 0222 874 305, fax 0222 371 921)

BEVES, Brian Montague; s of Montague Hebb Beves (d 1943), of Hove, and Dorothy Hamlyn, *née* Lawrence-Smith (d 1960); *b* 8 Jan 1924; *Educ* Haileybury, King's Coll Cambridge (MA); *m* 28 Sept 1957, Carolyn Langworthy, da of Rear-Adm Cecil Ramsden Langworthy Parry (d 1977), of Coachmans, Westbourne, Sussex; 2 da (Lucy b 1959, Frances b 1963); *Career* temp admin appt FO 1945-47; special corr Times on Antarctic Expedition 1948; served in Sudan Political Serv 1951-54; broker and underwriter Lloyds (Sedgwick Collins) 1955-73, ret 1973; vice-chm Hereford Diocesan Bd of Fin 1979-80 (chm 1980-); *Recreations* gardening, music; *Style*— Brian Beves, Esq; Abbey House, Ledbury, Herefords HR8 1BP (☎ 0531 2762)

BEVINGTON, Eric Raymond; CMG (1961); s of Reginald Bevington (d 1954), of Bournemouth, and Netta Ethel, *née* Sutton (d 1938); the surname of Bevington arises from a grant of land by Lord Berkeley to one Maurice at Bevington, Glos ca 1156; *b* 23 Jan 1914; *Educ* Monkton Combe Sch, Loughborough Coll (DipMech), Queens' Coll Cambridge ; *m* 1939, Enid Mary Selina, da of Lionel Victor Homer, slr (d 1955), of Bournemouth; 1 s (David), 1 da (Jean); *Career* admin offr Gilbert and Ellice Islands Colony 1937, dist off Fiji 1941, asst col sec Fiji 1951, devpt cmmnr Brunei 1954, fin sec Fiji 1958; Appeals inspr DoE 1967, sr inspr DoE 1974; MIMechE; *Recreations* golf, sailing; *Style*— Eric Bevington Esq, CMG; Holmans Cottage, Bisterne Close, Burley, Hants BH24 4AZ

BEVINS, Anthony John; s of Rt Hon John Reginald Bevins, *qv*; *b* 16 August 1942; *Educ* Liverpool Collegiate GS, LSE (BSc); *m* 1965, Ruchira Mistuni, da of Kshitis Roy, of Santiniketan, West Bengal, India; 1 s (Robert b 1968), 1 da (Nandini b 1972); *Career* political corr; Liverpool Daily Post 1967-73, Sunday Express 1973, The Sun 1973-76, Daily Mail 1976-81, The Times 1981-86, political ed The Independent 1986-; *Style*— Anthony Bevins, Esq; Press Gallery, House of Commons, London SW1 (☎ 01 833 7262)

BEVINS, Rt Hon John Reginald; PC (1959); s of John Milton and Grace Eveline Bevins, of Liverpool; bro of Kenneth Milton Bevins, *qv*; *b* 20 August 1908; *Educ* Liverpool Collegiate Sch; *m* 1933, Mary Leonora, da of J O Jones, of Liverpool; 3 s (including Anthony John *qv*); *Career* postmaster-gen 1959-64, Parly sec: Miny Housing and Local Govt 1957-59 (pps to Min 1951-53), Miny Works 1953-57; MP (C) Toxteth 1950-64, fought Toxteth West and Edgehill 1945 and 1947; serv WWII RASC MEF and Europe; *Style*— The Rt Hon John Bevins; 37 Queen's Dve, Liverpool L18 2DT (☎ 051 722 8484)

BEVINS, Kenneth Milton; CBE (1973), TD (1951); s of John Milton Bevins (d 1928), of Liverpool, and Grace Eveline Bevins, bro of Rt Hon John Reginald Bevins; *b* 2 Nov 1918; *Educ* Liverpool Collegiate Sch; *m* 1, 1940, Joan Harding (d 1969); 2 da; m 2, 1971, Diana B, da of the late Godfrey J Sellers, of Keighley; *Career* dir: Royal Insur 1970-89, Br Aerospace 1980-87; chief exec Royal Insur 1970-80, chm Br Insur Assoc 1971-73; *Recreations* travel, gardening, reading, photography, handiwork; *Clubs* Army and Navy, Oriental; *Style*— Kenneth Bevins, Esq, CBE, TD; Linton, The Drive, Sevenoaks, Kent (☎ 0732 456909)

BEWES, Rev Prebendary Richard Thomas; s of Rev Canon Thomas Francis Cecil Bewes, and Nellie Sylvia Cohu, *née* De Berry; *b* 1 Dec 1934; *Educ* Marlborough, Emmanuel Coll Cambridge (MA), Ridley Hall Theol Coll Cambridge; *m* 18 April 1964, Elisabeth Ingrid, da of Lionel Jaques; 2 s (Timothy b 1966, Stephen b 1971), 1 da (Wendy b 1968); *Career* vicar: St Peter's Harold Wood Essex 1965-74, Emmanuel Northwood Middx 1974-83; rector All Souls Langham Place London 1983-, prebendary St Paul's Cathedral 1988; Freedom of The City of Charlotte N Carolina USA 1984; memb Guild of Br Songwriters 1975; *Books* God in Ward 12 (1973), Advantage Mr Christian (1975), Talking About Prayer (1979), The Pocket Handbook of Christian Truth (1981), John Wesley's England (1981), The Church Reaches Out (1981), The Church Overcomes (1983), On The Way (1984), Quest For Life (1985), Quest For Truth (1985), The Church Marches On (1986), When God Surprises (1986); *Recreations* tennis, photography, reading, writing; *Style*— The Rev Prebendary Richard Bewes; 12 Weymouth St, London W1N 3FB (☎ 01 580 6029); All Souls Church 2 All Souls Place, London W1N 3DB (☎ 01 580 6029, fax 01 436 3019)

BEWICKE-COPLEY, Hon Davina Mary; da of 6 Baron Cromwell (d 1982); *b* 19 June 1958; *Style*— The Hon Davina Bewicke-Copley

BEWICKE-COPLEY, Hon Thomas David (Percy); yr s of 6 Baron Cromwell and hp to er bro, 7 Baron; *b* 6 August 1964; *Educ* summerfields Oxford, Eton, Webber-Douglas Acad of Dramatic Art London (Dip); *Career* actor (as Percy Copley), season at Brunton Theatre Scotland Sept-Nov 1985, Augustus Gloop in Charlie and the Chocolate Factory 1985-86, Gala performance for Save The Wells Royal Opera House 1986, Giant Gormless and Lagopus Scoticus in "The Old man of Lochnagar" based on the book by HRH Prince of Wales 1986-87, Frederick Willow in "Bless The Bride" Sadlers Wells 1987; *Recreations* jazz music, ukulele, bagpipes, banjo, collects 78 rpm records; *Style*— The Hon Thomas Bewicke-Copley; Flat 1, 52 Braxted Park, London SW16 3AU (☎ 01 764 4273)

BEWLEY, Dr Beulah Rosemary; da of John B Knox (d 1975), of Coulsdon, Surrey, and Ina E Knox, *née* Eagleson; *b* 2 Sept 1929; *Educ* Trinity Coll Dublin (MB, BCh, MA, MD), Univ of London (MSc); *m* 20 April 1955, Thomas Henry Bewley@ s of Dr A G Bewley (d 1980), of Dublin; 1 s (Henry John b 1963), 4 da (Susan Jane b 1958, Sarah Elizabeth b 1959, Louisa Mary b 1961, Emma Caroline b 1966); *Career* conslt sr lectr Community Medicine St Georges Hosp Medicine Sch (London); SWTRA reg post grad tutor in Community Medicine; memb: The General Medical Cncl, Central Ctee for Educ of Social Workers; past pres Medical Women's Fedn; *Recreations* music, travel, food; *Clubs* RSM (London); *Style*— Dr (Mrs) Beulah R Bewley; 11 Garrads Road, London SW16 1JU (☎ 01 769 1703); Dept of Clinical Epidemology and Social Medicine, St Georges Hosp Medical Sch SW17 0RE (☎ 01 672 9944)

BEWLEY, Dr Thomas Henry; Hon CBE (1988); s of Dr Geoffrey Bewley (d 1981), and Victoria Jane, *née* Wilson (d 1953); *b* 8 July 1926; *Educ* Rugby, St Columbus Coll Dublin, Trinity Coll Dublin (BA, MB, MA, MD); *m* 20 Apr 1955, Beulah da of John Knox (d 1975); 1 s (Henry b 1963), 4 da (Susan b 1958, Sarah b 1959, Louisa b 1961, Emma b 1966); *Career* conslt psychiatrist: St Thomas Hosp, St George's Hosp, Tooting Bec Hosp 1961-88, hon sr lectr St George's Hosp Med Sch 1988-, WHO Expert advsy panel on drug dependence and alcohol problems 1988-; pres Royal Coll Psychiatrists 1984-87 (dean 1977-82), physician memb Social Security and Med Appeal Tbnls 1987-, memb Parole Bd 1988; Hon MD Dublin Univ 1987; FRCPI 1963, FRC Psych 1972, FRCP (London) 1988; *Style*— Dr Thomas Bewley; 11 Garrads Rd, London SW16 1JU, (☎ 01 769 1703)

BEWSHER, (John) Gowen; s of Edmund Gordon Bewsher (d 1952), and Decima Mary, *née* Cross (d 1978); *b* 11 Jan 1935; *Educ* Mill Hill; *m* 1, 29 July 1959 (m dis 1977), Moiya Ann, *née* Kelly; 3 s (Guy b 1962, James b 1965, Charles b 1971), 2 da (Elizabeth b 1964, Charlotte b 1971); m 2, 21 July 1979, Angela Margaret, da of Gerald Austin Reed, of Maidenhead, Berks; *Career* Nat Serv RAF 1953-55; md Group Four Advertising 1976- (chm 1986-); govr Mill Hill Sch 1974-; Freeman City of London 1982, Liveryman Worshipful Co of Needlemakers 1984; FInstD, MInstM; *Books* Nobis - The Story of a Club (1979); *Recreations* cruising, politics, genealogy; *Clubs* United and Cecil, Phyllis Court, Old Millhillians, Int Churchill Soc; *Style*— Gowen Bewsher, Esq; The Bridge House, High St, Eton, Windsor, Berks (☎ 0753 868000, fax 0753 840952, car tel 0836 293255)

BEXON, Michael Laurence; MC (1945); s of MacAlister Bexon, CBE (d 1976), of High Wycombe and Nora Hope, *née* Jenner (d 1976); bro of Roger Bexon, *qv*; *b* 28 June 1923; *Educ* Denstone Coll, St John's Coll Oxford, (MA); *m* 1949, Joan Agnes Mary, da of Joseph Austin (d 1938), of Wadhurst; 2 s (Julian, Dominic); *Career* WWII Capt North Irish Horse 1941-46, serv Italy and Palestine; Capt Westminster Dragoons TA 1957-62; joined Dunlop Rubber Co Ltd 1948, Denmark 1950-54, Lebanon 1954-6, India 1960-5; dir: Dunlop Hldgs (formerly Dunlop Rubber) 1967-83, Sumitomo Rubber Industs Ltd 1970-84; mgmnt conslt 1983-; *Style*— Michael Bexon, Esq, MC; 14a Ashley Gdns, London SW1P 1QD (☎ 01 834 7362)

BEXON, Roger; CBE (1985); s of MacAlister Bexon, CBE (d 1976), of High Wycombe, and Nora Hope, *née* Jenner (d 1976); bro of Michael Laurence Bexon, *qv*; *b* 11 April 1926; *Educ* St John's Coll Oxford, Univ of Tulsa Oklahoma (MA); *m* 1952 Lois Loughran Walling; 1 s, 1 da; *Career* dep chm The Br Petroleum Co plc 1983-; chm BP Exploration Ltd, BP Gas Int Ltd, non-exec dir BICC 1985-; *Style*— Roger Bexon, Esq; c/o Br Petroleum Co Ltd, Britannic Ho, Moor Lane, London EC2Y 9BU (☎ 01 920 6021, telex 888811)

BEXSON, Peter James; s of Thomas William Bexson (d 1984), of East Molesey, Surrey, and Elsie Constance, *née* Cox (d 1986); *b* 2 May 1926; *Educ* Glasgow Acad, Gonville and Caius Coll Cambridge, Coll of Estate Mgmnt London Univ; *m* 7 Feb 1953, Edna May, da of Harold Glover, of Hartley, Dartford, Kent; 2 s (Robert b 9 July 1956, William b 18 May 1961); *Career* WWII cadet pilot Canada and USA 1944-45, instr PT branch Germany 1946-47; chief surveyor Greencoat Properties 1956-63; ptnr: Gravesson & Pilcher 1963-86, Stiles Harold Williams 1986-; memb gen cncl RICS (chm conduct investigation ctee), pres Int Real Estate Fedn Paris; memb London Rent Assessment Panel DOE, valuation conslt Mid-Sussex DC; former pres soc of London Ragamuffins; Freeman: City of London, Worshipful Co of Tallow Chandlers, Worshipful Co of Painter Stainers; FRICS 1961; *Recreations* walking, travel; *Clubs* RAC, London Scottish FC, RSAC; *Style*— Peter J Bexson, Esq; 1 Paxton Terrace, London SW1V 3DA (☎ 01 834 4565); 43 Old Queen St, London SW1H 9JA (☎ 01 222 4477)

BEYFUS, Drusilla Norman (Mrs M Shulman); da of Norman Beyfus (decd) and Florence Noël Barker (decd); *Educ* RN Sch, Channing Sch; *m* 1956, Milton Shulman; 1 s (Jason), 2 da (Alexandra, Nicola); *Career* assoc ed Queen Magazine 1958-63, home ed The Observer 1963-64, assoc ed Daily Telegraph Colour Supplement 1964-70, ed Brides Magazine 1971-79, assoc ed Br Vogue Magazine Condé Nast 1979-86 (contributing ed 1986-), ed Harrods Magazine 1987-88; author and broadcaster; *Style*— Miss Drusilla Beyfus; 51G Eaton Square, London SW1 (☎ 01 235 7162)

BEYNON, David William Stephen; s of William Henry Beynon (d 1983), and Eileen Beynon; *b* 14 Mar 1934; *Educ* King Edward VII Sch Sheffield, Trinity Hall Cambridge (MA); *m* 23 Sept 1961, Joyce Noreen, da of George Trevor Richards, of Wallasey, Ches; 2 s (Stephen b 1965, Daniel b 1971), 1 da (Jane b 1962); *Career* Nat Serv RA 1952-54; ICI: joined 1954, commercial appts petrochemicals div 1954-77, head of policy gps dept London 1977-79, dep chm plastics div 1979-81, gp dir petrochemicals & plastics div 1981-87, dir ICI Chemicals and Polymers Ltd 1987-, dir ICI Resources Ltd 1987-; dir Euro Vinyls Corpn 1987-, pres Br Plastics Fedn 1987-88 (cncl memb 1980-); cncl memb: Assoc of Euro Plastics MPrs (APME) 1987-, Assoc of Euro Petrochem Mfrs (APPE) 1986-; ctee memb Euro Petrochem Assoc 1987-; Capt: Gt Ayton CC 1971-76, Welwyn Garden City CC 1980-86; Freeman: City of London 1984, Liveryman Worshipful Co of Horners 1984 (memb 1983); *Recreations* family, cricket; *Clubs* Forty, MCC; *Style*— David Beynon, Esq; ICI Chemicals and Polymers Ltd, The Heath, Runcorn, Cheshire (☎ 0928 513339, car 0836 628796, telex 629655)

BEYNON, (Ernest) Geoffrey; s of late Frank William George Beynon, and Frances Alice Pretoria, *née* Kirkpatrick; *b* 4 Oct 1926; *Educ* Borden GS Sittingbourne, Univ of Bristol (BSc, CertEd); *m* 2 Aug 1956, Denise Gwendoline, da of late Frederick Charles Rees; 2 s (David Michael b 25 July 1957, Peter b 16 Nov 1961), 1 da (Dina b 16 June 1959); *Career* RA 1947-49; mathematics master Thornbury GS Glos 1950-56, sr mathematics master and sixth form master St George GS Bristol 1956-64, asst sec Asst Masters Assoc 1964-78, jt gen sec Asst Masters and Mistresses Assoc 1979-87; former chm teachers' panel Burnham Primary and Secdy Ctee 1985-87; memb ct Univ of Bristol; ctee memb: Welwyn Garden City Soc, St Albans dist Hertford County Assoc of Change-Ringers; Charter Fell The Coll of Preceptors (Hon FCP) 1985; memb RIPA; *Recreations* campanology, canal boating, walking, books; *Style*— Geoffrey Beynon, Esq; 3 Templewood, Welwyn Garden City, Herts AL8 7HT (☎ 0707 321 380)

BEYNON, Prof Sir (William John) Granville; CBE (1959); s of late William and Mary Beynon, of Dunvant, Swansea; *b* 24 May 1914; *Educ* Gowerton GS, Univ Coll Swansea; *m* 1942, Megan Medi, da of Arthur Morgan James; 2 s, 1 da; *Career* scientific offr Nat Physical Laboratory 1938-46; lectr Univ Coll Swansea 1946-58; prof and head of Dept of Physics Univ Coll of Wales Aberystwyth 1958-; memb SRC 1976-; numerous publications in scientific journals; FRS; kt 1976; *Style*— Prof Sir Granville Baynon, CBE; Bryn Eithin, 103 Dunvant Rd, Swansea, Wales (☎ 0792 23585); Caebryn, Caergôg, Aberystwyth, Wales (☎ 0970 3947)

BEYNON, Prof John David Emrys; s of John Emrys Beynon (d 1973), and Elvira, *née* Williams; *b* 11 Mar 1939; *Educ* Pontywaun GS Risca Gwent, Univ of Wales (BSc), Univ of Southampton (MSc); *m* 28 March 1964, Hazel Janet, da of Albert Hurley (d 1983); 2 s (Graham b 1968, Nigel b 1968), 1 da (Sarah b 1966); *Career* scientific offr DSIR Radio and Space Res Station Slough 1962-64, reader dept of electronics Univ of

Southampton (lectr, sr lectr) 1964-77, prof of electronics Univ of Wales Inst of Sci and Technol Cardiff 1977-79; Univ of Surrey: prof of electrical enrg 1979-, hd of dept of electronic and electrical engr 1979-83, pro vice-chllr 1983-87; MIEE 1968, FIEE 1979, FIERE 1979, FRSA 1982, FEng 1988; *Books* Charge-Coupled Devices and Their Applications (1980); *Recreations* music, photography, travel; *Style—* Prof John D E Beynon; Chalkdene, Great Quarry, Guildford, Surrey (☎ 04083 503 458); University of Surrey, Stag Hill, Guildford, Surrey, GU2 5XH (☎ 0438 509 106, fax 0483 300 803, telex 859331)

BEYNON, Timothy George (Tim); s of George Beynon (d 1976), of Mumbles, Swansea, and Fona Inanda, *née* Smith; *b* 13 Jan 1939; *Educ* Swansea GS, King's Coll Cambridge (MA); *m* 1 March 1979, Sally Jane, da of John Wilson, of Foresters Lodge, Ashridge Park, Little Gadesden, Berkhamsted, Herts; 2 da (Sorrel b 1974, Polly b 1976); *Career* asst master City of London Sch 1962-63, Merchant Taylors' Sch 1963- (housemaster 1970-78, sr master 1977-78); headmaster: Denstone Coll 1978-86, The Leys Sch 1986-; expdns: Petra (overland) 1961, Spain, Hungary, Austria, Romania (ornithological); Denstone Expdn to Inaccessible Is 1982/83, sci advsr on Wetland reserves to Glamorgan Co Naturalists Tst; memb: Eng Cncl 1986-, Oxford and Cambridge Sch Examination Syndicate Appts Ctee; FRGS 1973, HMC 1978; *Recreations* ornithology, fishing, shooting, sport, music, expeditions; *Style—* Tim Beynon, Esq; Headmaster's House, The Leys School, Cambridge CB2 2AD (☎ 0223 355 540, bus 0223 355 327); The Croft, College Rd, Denstone, Uttoxeter, Staffs

BHAURA, Kulbir Singh; s of Harkishan Singh Bhaura, of Southall and Kirpal, *née* Kaur; *b* 15 Oct 1955; *Educ* Julundur India, Featherstone Sch Southall Middx; 1 s (Nicholas Banns b 25 Sept 1981); *Career* systems analyst with Kyle Stewart Wembley; hockey player, 147 int caps for England and GB, Olympic Games 1984 Bronze Medallist, World Cup 1986 Silver Medallist, Olympic Games 1988 Gold Medallist; capt: Indian Gymkhana Hockey Club, Middx Co Hockey team (nat champions 1987); *Recreations* hockey, music, badminton, family; *Style—* Kulbir Bhaura, Esq; 64 Alexandra Rd, Kew, Richmond, Surrey (☎ 01 940 5135); Ardshell House, Empire Way, Wembley, Middlesex (☎ 01 902 5321)

BIBBY, Sir Derek James; 2 Bt (UK 1959), of Tarporley, Co Palatine of Chester; MC (1945), DL (1987); s and h of Sir (Arthur) Harold Bibby, 1 Bt, DSO, DL, LLD; *b* 29 June 1922; *Educ* Rugby, Trinity Coll Oxford (MA); *m* 1961, Christine Maud, da of Rt Rev Frank Jackson Okell, Bishop of Stockport (d 1950); 4 s (Michael James, Geoffrey Frank Harold b 1965, Peter John b 1969, David Richard b 1970), 1 da (Jennifer Margaret b 1962); *Heir* s, Michael James Bibby b 2 Aug 1963; *Career* serv WWII Capt RA (wounded, MC); chm: Bibby Bros and Co (Mgmnt) Ltd, Bibby Line Ltd 1969- (shipowning co; Queen's Award for Export 1972, 1976, 1982); pres Indefatigable and Nat Sea Trg Sch for Boys; *Recreations* gardening, shooting; *Clubs* Royal Cwlth Soc; *Style—* Sir Derek Bibby, Bt, MC, DL; Willaston Grange, Hadlow Rd, Willaston, S Wirral, Cheshire L64 2UN (☎ 051 327 4913); Bibby Line Ltd, 401 Norwich House, Water St, Liverpool L2 8UW (☎ 051 236 0492)

BIBBY, John Roland; s of William Henry Bibby (d 1947), of Morpeth, and Margaret Jane, *née* Davison (d 1963); *b* 17 May 1917; *Educ* King Edward VI GS Morpeth, Durham Univ (BA); *m* 12 Aug 1948, Winifred Maude, da of Robert Tweedie (d 1971), of Morpeth; 1 s (John Trevor b 1949), 1 da (Katherine Marie b 1953); *Career* teacher, historian, writer; The Border Regt 1940-44, The Royal Warwickshire Regt 1944-46; India Burma (Capt, Adj); sec Gateshead Cncl of Soc Serv 1947-52; teacher 1952-82; hd of history Blyth Ridley HS; local historian researcher, writer Northumbrian history, lore, language and conservation 1946-, ed of Northumbriana magazine, specialising in Northumbrian language research, survival, literature 1975-, lectr on Northumbria history 1947, on language 1955-; hon degree of MA by Univ of Newcastel for services to Northumberland 1987; pres Northumbrian Pipers' Soc 1980-; Fellow of the Northumbrian Language Soc 1986-; *Recreations* Northumbrian history, law, language, conservation; *Style—* Roland Bibby, Esq; Westgate House, Dogger Bank, Morpeth, Northumberland NE61 1RF (☎ 0670 513308)

BIBICA ROSETTI, Princess Raoul; Dorothy; *née* Acton; da of Henry Acton (ggs of Lt-Gen Joseph Acton, bro of Sir John Acton, 6 Bt, by his w, Eleanora Countess Berghe von Trips) and Elly, da of Prince Cleon Rizo Rangabe, of Greece; *b* 20 April 1893; *m* 1921, Prince Raoul Bibica Rosetti (d 1967), sometime Greek ambass to Canada and s of Prince Salvator Bibica Rosetti; 1 da: Princess Lobanov-Rostovsky, *qv*; *Style—* Princess Raoul Bibica Rosetti; Swallowdale, 67 Woodruff Ave, Hove, Sussex BN3 6PJ

BICESTER, 3 Baron (UK 1938); Angus Edward Vivian Smith; s of late Lt-Col the Hon Stephen Edward Vivian Smith, 2 s of 1 Baron by Lady Sybil McDonnell (da of 6 Earl of Antrim); 4 cous once removed to Lord Carrington, the For Sec; suc unc 1968; *b* 20 Feb 1932; *Educ* Eton; *Heir* bro, Hugh Charles Vivian Smith; *Style—* The Rt Hon The Lord Bicester; House of Lords, SW1

BICHAN, Dr Herbert Roy; *b* 5 Nov 1941; *Educ* Univ of Aberdeen (BSc), Univ of Leeds (PhD); *m* Fiona Keay; 1 s (Michael Roy b 8 May 1969), 2 da (Inga Jane b 16 Feb 1967, Susan Elizabeth b 1 Aug 1971); *Career* chief exec The Robertson Gp plc, pres Inst of Mining and Metallurgy; Adrian fell Leicester Univ 1988; FIMM, MIGeol; *Recreations* golf; *Style—* Dr Roy Bichan; The Robertson Group plc, Ty'n-y-Coed, Llandudno, Gwynedd LL30 1SA (☎ 0492 81811, fax 0492 83416, telex 61216 ROBRES G)

BICK, David Robert; s of Roy Leslie Samuel Bick, and Vera Grace, *née* Collis; *b* 9 April 1957; *Educ* Glyn GS Epsom, Univ of Essex; *m* 21 July 1984, Susan Christine, da of Joseph Esmond Stobbs (d 1979); 2 da (Antonia b 1987, Harriet b 1989); *Career* PA to David Atkinson MP 1979-80, exec: KH Publicity Ltd 1981-81, and Shandwick Conslts Ltd 1981-83; account dir Good Relations City Ltd 1984-85 (account mangr 1983-84), dir and jnt fndr Lombard Communications plc 1985-; cncllr London Borough of Lambeth 1980-86, (chm Amenity Servs 1982), memb Assoc for Free Russia; *Recreations* theatre, reading, cricket, cinema; *Style—* David R Bick, Esq; Farthings, Pilgrim Hill, Elmdon, Nr Saffron Waldren, Essex, CB11 4NL (☎ 0763 838 733); 22 Cardigan Street, Kennington, London, SE11 127 Cheapside, London, EC2V 6BT (☎ 01 600 0064, fax 01 600 7406, mobile tel 0836 202 676

BICKER, Edwina Carole; da of Eric Millward, and Frances Morris, *née* Norton; *b* 20 Sept 1943; *Educ* Thornes House Sch Wakefield, Ilkley Coll of Housecraft, London Univ (LLB); *m* 11 Nov 1972, David Charles, s of Arthur Charles Bicker; *Career* teacher 1965-67, slr 1972-; nat pres UK Fedn of Business and Professional Women 1985-87, active memb various ctees, memb Kent Law Soc 1980-, co sec Maidstone Hospice Appeal 1987, memb Womens National Cmmn 1985-87; *Recreations* acting swimming, needlework; *Style—* Edwina C Bicker; Loanhead, Simmonds Lane, Otham Maidstone, Kent ME14 8RH; Gill Turner and Tucker, Colman House, King Street Maidstone, Kent (☎ 0622 59051, fax 0622)

BICKERSTAFF, Hon Mrs (Sara Gillian Mary); *née* Bramall; o da of Baron Bramall GCB, OBE, MC (Life Peer), *qv*; *b* 16 April 1951; *m* 12 June 1987, Dr Edwin F Bickerstaff; *Style—* The Hon Mrs Bickerstaff; St Helens, The Close, Trevone Padstow, Cornwall

BICKERSTETH, Edward; s of Rev Canon Edward Monier Bickersteth, OBE (d 1976 of Worton, nr Devizes, Wilts, and Katharine, *née* Jelf (d 1936); *b* 27 April 1915; *Edu* Haileybury, Christ Church Oxford (MA); *m* Elspeth, da of Dr Hector Charles Camero (d 1959), of Witley, Surrey; 3 s (Michael b 1948, Anthony b 1951, Peter b 1956) *Career* asst private sec to the higher cmmr in Palestine 1937-38; Sudan Political Ser 1938-55; overseas dir and asst dir personnel Reckitt & Colman plc 1955-75; cnc memb: Royal Cwlth Soc, Missions to Seamen; *Recreations* fishing, walking; *Club* Travellers; *Style—* Edward Bickersteth, Esq; 29 The Close, Salisbury, Wilts SP1 2E (☎ 0722 22 449)

BICKERSTETH, Rt Rev John Monier; yr s of Rev Canon Edward Monie Bickersteth, OBE (d 1976); *b* 6 Sept 1921; *Educ* Rugby, Christ Church Oxford (MA) *m* 1955, Rosemary, yr da of Edward Cleveland-Stevens (d 1962), of Gaines, Oxted; s, 1 da; *Career* Capt RA 1941-46; ordained 1951; curate Moorfields Bristol 1950-54 curate i/c Hurst Green Southwark 1054-62, vicar St Stephen Chatham Rochdale 1962 70, hon canon Rochdale Cath 1968-70, bishop of Warrington 1970-75, bishop of Bat and Wells 1975-87; chaplain and sub-prelate Order of St John 1977-, Clerk of th Closet to HM The Queen 1979-; took seat in House of Lords 1981; memb Cn Marlborough Coll 1981; Freeman City of London 1978; *Recreations* country pursuits *Clubs* Royal Cwlth Soc; *Style—* The Rt Rev John Bickersteth; Beckfords, Newtow Tisbury, Wilts SP3 6NY (☎ 0747 870479)

BICKERTON, Peter W; *b* 4 July 1940; *Educ* Abbotsholme School, Derbyshire Durham Univ (BSc), INSEAD, Univ of Grenoble; *m* 1967 Anne da of John Mitchell, o Cheltenham; *Career* dep chm and Ltd md Sime Darby (London) to 1983; assoc di Mfrs Hanover 1983-84, exec dir 1984-; prev dep chm: Sime-Darby London Ltd; g tres Sime-Darby Hldgs Ltd; gp fin mangr Fisons plc; *Recreations* classical music *Style—* Peter Bickerton, Esq; Manufacturers Hanover Ltd, 7 Princes St, Londo EC2P 2EN (☎ 01 600 4585, telex 884901)

BICKET, Henry Brussel; JP (Liverpool 1960), DL (Merseyside 1977); s of Alexande Bicket (d 1981), of Oxton, Merseyside, and Amelia, *née* Brussel (d 1967); *b* 1 Jun 1922; *Educ* Radley, Brasenose Coll Oxford; *m* 21 April 1956, Katharine Morris, da o Clarence Hascy Young (d 1957), of Greenwich, Conn USA; 2 s (Henry Alexande Clarence (Harry) b 1961, Robert Morris b 1963), 2 da (Margreta Elizabeth Simpson 1957, Jennie Hascy b 1958); *Career* Ordinary Seaman RN 1940-41; RNV (Midshipman 1941-42, Sub Lt 1942-43, Lt 1943-50), Lt Cdr RNR 1950; md Th Alexandra Towing Co Ltd 1972-83 (chm 1972-88), chm Euro Tug Owners Asso 1983-84, pres Br Tug Owners Assoc 1986-(chm 1972-74), chm Liverpool Shipowner Assoc 1980-88, regnl asvsy dir Barclays Bank plc; chm: Spirit of Merseyside Tst Fairbridge Drake Soc Merseyside; memb: Liverpool Shipwreck and Humane Soc Merseyside Assoc for Alcoholism High Sheriff 1983-84; *Recreations* boating, gardening *Clubs* Royal Yacht Sqdn, Royal Ocean Racing, Naval and Military, Liverpool Racquet *Style—* Henry Bicket, Esq, JP, DL; 3 The Orchard, N Sudley Rd, Liverpool L17 6BT Achahoish Lodge, By Lochgilphead, Argyll; 43 Castle St, Liverpool 2 (☎ 051 22 2151)

BICKFORD SMITH, John Roger; CB (1988), TD (1950); er s of late Leonard W Bickford Smith, of Camborne, Cornwall, and Anny Grete, *née* Huth (d 1986); *b* 31 Oc 1915; *Educ* Eton, Hertford Coll Oxford; *m* 1, 1939 (m dis), Cecilia Judge, er da of W W Heath, of Leicester; 2 s; m 2, 1972, Baronin Miranda von Kirchberg-Hohenheim *Career* barr Inner Temple 1942, master of the Supreme Ct Queen's Bench Div 1967 88, bencher 1984; sr master and Queen's Remembrancer 1983-88; Master Worshipfu Co of Bowyers 1986-88; *Clubs* Garrick; *Style—* John Bickford Smith, Esq, CB, TD; 6 Gibson Sq, London NQ ORA

BICKFORD-SMITH, Hon Mrs (Joan Angel Allsebrook); da (by 1 m) of 1 Viscoun Simon, GCSI, GCVO, OBE, PC, QC (d 1954); *b* 8 August 1901; *m* 1924, Capt Joh Allan Bickford-Smith, RN (ret), who d 1970; 1 s, 2 da; *Style—* The Hon Mr Bickford-Smith; Younghouse, Liss, Hants

BICKMORE, Laurence Hyde Neild; OBE (Mil 1945); o s of Harry C Bickmore, MA JP (d 1948), of 44 Edwardes Sq, W8; *b* 29 Mar 1905; *Educ* City of London Sch; *m* 1 1932 (m dis 1937), Audrey Fairless (d 1970), da of Vivian Trestrail Dampier-Palmer OBE, JP; m 2, 1941, (m dis 1947) Anne, da of Vice Adm Hon (Edmund) Ruper Drummond, CB, CVO (s of 16 Earl of Perth and 10 Viscount Strathallan, GCMG, CB PC, by his w, Hon Angela, *née* Constable-Maxwell, da of 11 Lord Herries o Terregles), and Lady Evelyn, *née* Butler, da of 4 Marquess of Ormonde; 1 s; m 3 1949, Elizabeth, da of Frederick H Smith (d 1963), of Palo Alto, Calif; 1 s, 1 da *Career* chm Hobbs Savill and Bradford Ltd Pension Consultants, ret 1970; Liveryma Worshipful Co pf Skinners 1946-; *Recreations* golf, bridge; *Clubs* American, Royal S Georges Golf (Sandwich); *Style—* Laurence Bickmore Esq, OBE

BICKNELL, Claud; OBE (1946); s of Raymond Bicknell (d 1927), of Newcastle upo Tyne, and Phillis Ellen, *née* Lovibond (d 1957); *b* 15 June 1910; *Educ* Oundle, Queens Coll Cambridge (MA); *m* 1, 15 Dec 1934, Esther Irene (d 1958), da of Rev Kenneth Norman Bell (d 1951), of Oxford; 1 s (Mark b 1936), 3 da (Meriel (Mr Mastroyannopoulou) b 1939, d 1977, Clare (wife of Dr (Sir) John Richard Shelley, 1 Bt) b 1943, Phillis (Mrs Jones) b 1949); m 2, 7 May 1960, Christine Betty, CBE, da o Walter Edward Reynolds (d 1940), of Dulwich; *Career* WWII Auxiliary Fire Ser Newcastle upon Tyne 1939-41, Nat Fire Serv 1941-45, sr fire staff offr HO 1943-45 admitted slr 1934, Stanton Atkinson & Bird Newcastle upon Tyne 1934-70, law cmm 1970-75, chm of industl tbnls 1975-83; dir Northern Corpn Ltd 1939-53, mem planning bd Lake Dist Nat Park 1951-70 (chm devpt control ctee 1957-70), memb Lor Jelicoe's Ctee on Water Resources in the NW 1963, pres Newcastle upon Tyn Incorporated Law Soc 1969, chm Newcastle upon Tyne Housing Improvement Tst Lt 1966-70; *Clubs* Garrick, Alpine; *Style—* Claud Bicknell, Esq, OBE; End Cottage, 11 Burneside Rd, Kendal, Cumbria LA9 6DZ

BICKNELL, Eric Arthur; s of Frederick Arthur Bicknell (d 1974), and May, *né* Downes (d 1943); *b* 11 Dec 1919; *Educ* Beaufort House Sch, Hammersmith Sch

Building Arts and Crafts; *m* 16 Feb 1941, Patricia Marie, da of Augustus Markland (d 1936); 2 s (Brian b 1946, Stephen b 1950); *Career* served Royal Marines 1940-46, Capt; mangr and dir A Stone & Sons Ltd 1946, md H C Wakefield & Sons Ltd 1951, dir and gen mangr Troy Gp of Cos 1954, founded EA Bicknell & Sons Ltd 1955, chm Bicknell Hldgs plc; FCIOB 1955, FFB 1975, MJMA 1962; *Recreations* golf, soccer, tennis, racing; *Clubs* Clifton, University & Literary, Long Ashton Golf, Bristol Central Tennis; *Style*— Eric Bicknell, Esq; Penthouse A, Marklands, Julian Rd, Sneyd Park, Bristol, Avon BS9 1NP; Bicknell Holdings plc, Merstham Rd, Bristol BS2 9TQ

BICKNELL, Julian; s of Wing Cdr Nigel Bicknell, DSO, DFC, of Butlers Cottages, Semley, Wilts, and Sarah Greenaway *née* Leith; *b* 23 Feb 1945; *Educ* Winchester, King's Coll Cambridge (MA, DipArch); *m* 18 Nov 1967, Treld, da of Arthur Pelkey (d 1979), of New Hertford Connecticut USA; 1 s (Titus b 1971), 1 da (Poppaea b 1982); *Career* asst (later ptnr) Edward Cullinan 1966-72; tutor and dir of project off Royal Coll of Art 1973-80: The Old Gaol, Abingdon (RIBA Award 1976), The Garden Hall and Library, Castle Howard (Carpenters Award 1984); staff architect Arup Assocs 1981-84: reconstruction of Bedford Sch; private practice 1984-: Henbury Rotonda, HM Ambassador's Residence Moscow; RIBA 1971, FFB 1985, AA 1987, FRSA 1988; *Books* The Design for Need Papers (1979); *Recreations* architecture, music, the countryside; *Style*— Julian Bicknell, Esq; 29 Lancaster Park, Richmond, Surrey (☎ 01 940 3929); The White Cottage, Fontmell Magna, Dorset; office, 20 Bedford St, London WC2 (☎ 01 836 5875)

BICKNELL, Mark; s of Claud Bicknell, OBE, MA, of Aikrigg End Cottage, Burneside Rd, Kendal, Westmoreland, and Esther Irene *née* Bell (d 1958); *b* 21 April 1936; *Educ* Winchester, Corpus Christi Coll Cambridge (MA); *m* 1,28 Apr 1962, Jennifer Claire, *née* Fairley (1977); 2 s (William b 13 June 1966, Tristran Samuel (Sam) b 12 Jan 1969), 1 da (Georgia (twin) b 13 Jun 1966); m 2, 19 Aug 1978, Countess Ilona Esterhazy; 1 s (Charles Esterhazy b 3 Jan 1979); *Career* Nat Serv, 2 Lt RTR; engrg appts: UKAEA 1961-62 (apprentice 1959-61), Charrington & Co Ltd 1963-64, J D & D M Watson (1964-66), Morganite Carbon Ltd 1967, Pencol Cnslts 1967-70; ptnr J D & D M Watson 1976-77 (chief mech engr 1973, rejoined 1970); ptnr Watson Hawksley 1978-; memb cncl ACE 1979-82, 1983-86, 1988-; FIMech 1975, FICE 1982, MConsE 1978; *Books* various tech papers in learned jnls; *Clubs* Alpine, Leander; *Style*— Mark Bicknell, Esq; 11 High Street, Nettlebed, Henley on Thames, Oxon RG9 5DA (☎ 0491 641 619); Watson Hawksley, Terriers House, Amersham Road, High Wycombe, Buckinghamshire HP13 5AJ (☎ 0494 26240, fax 0494 22074, telex 83439)

BIDDLE, Donald Frank; s of Kenneth Barrington Biddle, of Poole, Dorset, and Judy Hill, *née* Downie (d 1964); *b* 6 Mar 1933; *Educ* Uppingham; *m* 3 Oct 1963, Anne Muriel, da of Maj Charles Deane Cowper; 2 s (Justin b 1968, Mark b 1971), 2 da (Georgina b 1973, Anne-Marie b 1973); *Career* 2 Lt RA Germany 1956-57, HAC 1957-63; Price Waterhouse 1957-62, sr audit ptnr Smith and Williamson 1962-, dir Smith and Williamson Securities 1970-; gen cmmr of Taxation 1970-87; tstee: English Language Servs Internat 1963-, Ada Lewis Housing Tst 1967-82 (chm 1978-80), Samuel Lewis Housing Tst 1978-; CA Cons Party at local and area levels, sec Int Dragon Assoc 1982-; memb Olympic Yachting Ctee 1964-74; FCA; *Recreations* yachting, skiing, wine; *Clubs* Carlton, Boodle's, Royal Yacht Sqdn; *Style*— Donald F Biddle, Esq,; The Old House, Milton-on-Stour, Gillingham, Dorset (☎ 074 76 3487); 23 Eaton Place, London SW1 (☎ 01 235 8950); 1 Riding House St, London W1A 3AS (☎ 01 637 5377, telex 25187, fax 01 631 0741)

BIDDLE, Martin; s of Reginald Samuel Biddle (d 1971), and Gwladys Florence, *née* Baker (d 1986); *b* 4 June 1937; *Educ* Merchant Taylors', Pembroke Coll Cambridge (BA, MA), Oxford (MA by incorporation); *m* 1 9 Sept 1961 (m dis 1966), Hannelore Bäker; 2 da (Joanna b 1962, Barbara b 1965); m 2, 19 Nov 1966, Birthe Kjølbye, da of Landsretssagfører Axel Th Kjølbye (d 1972), of Sønderborg Denmark; 2 da (Signe b 1969, Solvej b 1971); *Career* Officer Cadet Mons OCS RAC 1956; 2 Lt 4 RTR 1956, Indep Sqdn RTR Berlin 1956-57; asst inspr ancient monuments Miny of Public Bldg and Works 1961-63, lectr medieval archaeology Univ of Exeter 1963-67, visiting fell All Souls Coll Oxford 1967-68, dir Winchester res unit 1968-, dir Univ Museum and prof of anthropology and history of art Univ of Pennsylvania 1977-81, lectr of the house Christ Church Oxford 1983-86; excavations with Sir Mortimer Wheeler St Albans and Stanwick 1949 and 1952, with Dame Kathleen Kenyon Jericho 1957-58; dir excavations: Nonsuch Palace 1959-60, Winchester 1961-71, St Albans 1978 and 1982-84, Repton 1974-88; archaeological conslt: Canterbury Cathedral, St Albans Abbey and Cathedral Church, Eurotunnel; chm Rescue The Trust for Br Archaeology 1971-75, cmmr Royal Cmmn on the Historical Monuments of England 1984-; Hon kt of the Hon Soc of Kts of the Round Table 1971; Freeman Worshipful Co of Merchant Taylor's 1963, Freeman City of London 1963; chm Winchester in Europe (nat referendum 1975), served Cons pty ctees Winchester 1973-77 (and currently Oxford 1982-); Univ Pennsylvania: MA 1977, Phi Beta Kappa 1978; FSA 1964, FRHistS 1970, FBA 1985; *Books* Future of London's Past (1973), Winchester in the Early Middle Ages (ed 1976), numerous articles; *Recreations* travel, especially hellenic and middle east, reading; *Clubs* Athenaeum; *Style*— Martin Biddle, Esq; 19 Hamilton Rd, Oxford OX2 7PY (☎ 0865 513 056); The Winchester Res Unit, 75 Hyde St, Winchester (☎ 0962 65 183, 0865 59 017 (Research Asst))

BIDDULPH *see also*: Maitland Biddulph

BIDDULPH, Hon Edward Sidney; s of 3 Baron Biddulph (d 1972); *b* 16 Nov 1934; *Educ* Eton; *Career* Lt RHG 1955; ret fruit farmer; *Recreations* racing, hunting, shooting, gardening; *Clubs* White's; *Style*— The Hon Edward Biddulph; Ribston Lawn, Much Marcle, Ledbury, Herefordshire HR8 2ND (☎ 053 184 204

BIDDULPH, Sir Ian D'Olier; 11 Bt (E 1664); s of Sir Stuart Royden Biddulph, 10 Bt (d 1986), and Muriel Margaret, *née* Harkness; *b* 28 Feb 1940; *Educ* Slade Sch Warwick Queensland; *m* 1967, Margaret Eleanor, o da of late John Gablonski, of Oxley, Brisbane; 1 s, 2 da; *Heir* s, Paul William Biddulph b 30 Oct 1967; *Career* grazier; *Style*— Sir Ian Biddulph, Bt; 18 Hume St, Pittsworth, Queensland 4356, Australia

BIDDULPH, Baroness; Lady Mary Helena; *née* Maitland; eldest da of Viscount Maitland (ka 1943; s and h of 15 Earl of Lauderdale), and Helena Ruth, *née* Perrott; *b* 23 Oct 1938; *m* 9 April 1958, 4 Baron Biddulph (d 1988); 2 s (5 Baron, Hon William Ian Robert Maitland Biddulph, *qv*), 1 da (Hon Fiona Maitland Biddulph, *qv*); *Style*— Lady Biddulph; Makerstoun, Kelso, Roxburghshire TD5 7PA

BIDDULPH, 5 Baron (UK 1903); (Anthony) Nicholas Colin Maitland Biddulph; er s of 4 Baron Biddulph (d 1988), and Lady Mary Maitland, da of Viscount Maitland, s of 15 Earl of Lauderdale; *b* 8 April 1959; *Educ* Cheltenham, RAC Cirencester; *Heir* bro, Hon William Ian Robert Maitland Biddulp, *qv*; *Career* interior designer; *Recreations* shooting; *Clubs* Raffles; *Style*— The Rt Hon Lord Biddulph; Makerstoun, Kelso, Roxburghshire TD5 7PA

BIDDULPH, Hon Susan Louise; yr da of 3 Baron Biddulph (d 1972); *b* 24 August 1929; *Educ* Lawnside Sch Malvern; *Style*— The Hon Susan Biddulph; Ribston Lawn, Much Marcle, Ledbury, Herefordshire H48 2ND (☎ 053 184 204

BIDE, Sir Austin Ernest; o s of Ernest Arthur Bide (d 1918) and Eliza, *née* Young (d 1976); *b* 11 Sept 1915; *Educ* Acton Co Sch, London Univ;; *m* 1941, Irene, da of Ernest Auckland Ward (d 1953); 3 da; *Career* Maj 21 Army GP Germany; Dept of Govt Chemist until 1940; joined Glaxo Labs Ltd (research dept) 1940, consecutively head of chem investigation and devpt dept, pa to dep md Glaxo Labs Ltd, head of patents and trademarks; first factory mangr Montrose 1951, dep sec Glaxo Labs Ltd 1954, sec 1959-65, dir Glaxo Gp 1963, dep chm Glaxo Hldgs 1971-73, chm and chief exec 1973-85, hon pres 1985-; non exec dir J Lyons & Co Ltd 1977-78; non-exec chm BL 1982- (non exec dir 1977-82); CBIM (memb: cncl 1976-, companions' ctee; chm Finance Ctee 1977-79 and dir BIM Fndn; BIM Gold Medal for outstanding achievements in mgmnt of Glaxo Gp 1982); chm CBI Res and Technological Ctee 1977- (memb cncl CBI 1974-, memb cos ctee 1974-80); memb: CBI President's Ctee 1983-, CBI Us, Polys and Ind Ctee 1984-, CBI Industl Performance Steering Gp 1985-, Ct of Br Shippers' Cncl 1984-, Advsy Ctee on Ind to the vice-chllrs and princs of the affairs of the Univ grants Ctee 1984-; cncl of the Inst of Manpower Studies 1985-, body to review the affairs of the U Grants Ctee 1985-; chm visiting ctee Open Univ 1982-, tstee Br Motor Ind Heritage Tst 1983-; FRSC, Hon FICE 1983, hon fell and vice-pres Imperial Soc of Knights Bachelor 1980-, hon fell of Inst for Biotechnological Studies and memb of its advsy cncl 1984-; kt 1984; *Recreations* fishing, handicrafts; *Clubs* Hurlingham; *Style*— Sir Austin Bide; Glaxo Hldgs plc, Clarges House, 6-12 Clarges St, London W1Y 8DH (☎ 01 493 4060, telex 25456)

BIDE, Margaret Helen; da of Herbert William Bide (d 1957), of Hillcrest, Runfolk, Farnham, Surrey, and Helen Maud, *née* Edmunds (d 1984); gggf Richard Bide (1802-70), founded in 1854 Alma Nurseries of Farnham Surrey, ggf Samuel Bide (1842-1915), developed and expanded the business, known this century as S Bide & Sons Ltd, horticulturalists, farmers and hop growers; business remained in the family until closing nursery 1971 and farm 1982; *b* 15 Mar 1937; *Educ* Farnham Sch of Art (now W Surrey Coll of Art and Design), (Nat Dip in Design), Univ of Leeds (post grad study); *Career* head dept of textiles W Surrey Coll of Art and Design Farnham 1973-85 (lectr 1965-67, sr lectr 1967-73); developing own textile mill in Wales 1987-; *Style*— Miss Margaret Bide; 44 Beavers Rd, Farnham, Surrey GU9 7BD (☎ 0252 722367); Glanffrwd Mill, Cellan, Lampeter, Dyfed SA48 8HY (☎ 057 045 489)

BIDGOOD, John Claude; s of Edward Charles Bidgood (d 1967), of Leeds; *b* 12 May 1914; *Educ* London Choir Sch, Woodhouse Tech Sch; *m* 1945, Sheila Nancy, da of Dr James Walker-Wood (d 1968), of Harrogate; 1 s, 2 da; *Career* MP (C) Bury and Radcliffe 1955-64; chm: Anglo-Dominion Finance Co, A-D Construction, A-D Trading; dir: Bidgood Hldgs, Edward Bidgood & Co, Bidgood Larsson Ltd, Wright & Summerhill, R Horsfield & Co; Freeman City of London, Liveryman Horners Co, memb Hon Soc of Knights of the Round Table; *Recreations* music, travel; *Clubs* Naval and Military, City Livery, Leeds; *Style*— John Bidgood, Esq; The Old Joinery, Walton, Wetherby, W Yorks (☎ home 0937 844028, work 0532 459068)

BIDWELL, Sydney James; MP (Lab) Ealing - Southall 1974-; s of late Herbert Emmett Bidwell, of Southall; *b* 14 Jan 1917; *Educ* elementary sch, (evening classes) Nat Cncl of Lab Colls; *m* 1941, Daphne, da of late Robert Peart, of Southall; 1 s, 1 da; *Career* former: railwayman, memb NUR, offr Southall Trades Cncl; lectr, memb Southall Boro Cncl 1951-55, contested (Lab): Herts E 1959, Herts SW 1964; TUC London regnl offr up to election 1966, sponsored by TGWU, MP (Lab) Southall 1966-74, chm Tribune Gp 1975-, vice-chm PLP Tport Grp 1977, former memb select ctee on Race Relations and Immigration, memb select ctee on Tport 1979-; *Books* Red White & Black, Turban Victory; *Recreations* artist, soccer enthusiast; *Style*— Sydney Bidwell, Esq, MP; House of Commons, London SW1

BIELCKUS, Colin David; s of Louis Reginald Bielckus, Thornhill, Southampton, and Lorna Elizabeth Mary; *b* 17 June 1956; *Educ* King Edward VI Sch Southampton, Univ of E Anglia (BSc); *m* 11 Oct 1981, Lorraine, da of Reginald Alexander, of Southampton; *Career* CA; audit mangr Alliott Millar, Fareham, 1985-; *Recreations* railways, collecting books, collecting beermats, collecting cacti and other succulent plants; *Style*— Colin Bielckus, Esq; 2 Lilydale Cottages, Portsmouth Rd, Lowford, Southampton SO5 8EQ (☎ Bursledon 4681); Alliott Millar, Kintyre House, 70 High St, Fareham, Hants (☎ 0329 822232, fax 822402)

BIENKOWSKI, Jan Stanislaw; s of Zygmunt Witymir Bienkowski (d 1978) Polish Air Force Col, and Halina Wita Bienkowska, *née* Grzybowska; *b* 7 Nov 1948; *Educ* Salesian Coll, Univ of Surrey & AA Sch of Architecture (BSc Eng, AAdip); *m* 21 Sept 1974, Zofia Joanna, da of Leszek Josef Rybicki, Maj 15th Lancers (Polish Cavalry); 1 s (Andrzej b 1984), 2 da (Lidia b 1977, Monika b 1978); *Career* chartered architect; asst architect John R Harris (London & ME) 1975-77; architect The Fitzroy Robinson Partnership London 1977-79; founding ptnr Spiromega Partnership (architects & designers) 1980-; jt md Blythe Projects plc 1985-; dir Myviad Ltd 1986-; RIBA; memb Chartered Society of Designers; *Recreations* landscape painting, sailing, squash; *Style*— Jan S Bienbkowski, Esq; 86 Ranelagh Rd, London W5 5RP (☎ 01 579 1623); 259 King St, London W6 9LW (☎ 01 748 8525, fax 01 748 5094, car tel 0836 521967

BIFFA, Richard Charles; s of Richard Frank Biffa, and Alice Ethel Amiens, *née* Berryman; *b* 23 Dec 1939; *Educ* Berkhamsted Sch; *m* 19 Feb 1983, Gillian, da of William L Poole-Warren (d 1978); 2 s (Matthew b 1969, Antony b 1972), 1 da (Harriet b 1984); *Career* chm and md Biffa Ltd 1977-85, chm Rechem Int Ltd 1985-; tres Nat Assoc of Waste Disposal Contractors 1985- (vice-pres 1975-77); *Recreations* tennis, squash, sailing; *Clubs* Phyllis Court, Henley; *Style*— Richard C Biffa, Esq; Chalkpit House, Burchetts Green, Maidenhead, Berks SL6 6RR; Rechem International Ltd, Madeley House, 8 Packhorse Rd, Gerrards Cross, Bucks

BIFFEN, Rt Hon (William) John; PC (1979), MP (C) N Shropshire 1983-; s of Victor W Biffen, of Otterhampton, Somerset; *b* 3 Nov 1930; *Educ* Dr Morgan's GS Bridgwater, Jesus Coll Cambridge; *m* 1979, Mrs Sarah Wood, *née* Drew; 1 step s, 1 step da; *Career* with Tube Investmts 1953-60, Economist Intelligence Unit 1960-61, MP (C) Oswestry 1961-83; chief sec to Treasy 1979-81, trade sec 1981-82, lord pres of the Cncl 1982-83, ldr House of Commons 1982-, lord privy seal 1983-; *Style*— The

Rt Hon John Biffen, MP; c/o House of Commons, London SW1

BIGGAR, (Walter) Andrew; CBE (1979, OBE 1967), MC (1945); s of Walter Biggar (d 1949), of Grange, Castle Douglas, and Margaret, *née* Sproat (d 1965); *b* 6 Mar 1915; *Educ* Sedburgh, Edinburgh Univ (BSc); *m* 11 June 1945, Patricia Mary Irving, da of William Elliot (d 1949), of Middletown, Stow, Midlothian; 1 s (Michael b 1949), 1 da (Susan b 1947); *Career* WWII 1939-46, cmmnd Royal Signals (POW Germany 1940-45); dir Caledonian Investment & Fin Co 1986-, Rowett Res Inst 1935-54; farmer 1956-89; memb: Agric Res Cncl 1969-79, Scottish Agric Devpt Cncl 1971-81; govr Grassland Res Inst 1961-80; dir and tstee: Scottish Soc for Crop Res 1958-88, Animal Diseases Res Inst 1960-; chm: Moredoun Animal Health Tst 1988-, Animals Bd Jt Consultative Orgn for Res in Ag 1973-80; govr St Margaret's Sch Edinburgh 1959-79; hon fell Animal & Grassland Res Inst 1980; FRAgs 1969; *Recreations* photography, rugby football; *Style*— W Andrew Biggar, Esq, CBE, MC; Magdalene Hall, St Boswells, Roxburghshire, Scotland (☎ 0835 23741)

BIGGART, (Thomas) Norman; CBE (1984), WS; o s of Andrew Stevenson Biggart, JP, and his w Marjorie Scott; *b* 24 Jan 1930; *Educ* Morrisons Acad Crieff, Glasgow Univ (MA, LLB); *m* 1956, Eileen Jean Anne Gemmell; 1 s, 1 da; *Career* RN 1954-56, Sub-Lt RNVR; slr; ptnr Biggart Baillie & Gifford WS, Glasgow & Edinburgh 1959-; pres Law Soc of Scotland 1982-83 (memb cncl 1977-86, vice-pres 1981-82); pres Business Archives Cncl Scotland 1977-86; memb: Scottish Tertiary Educn Advsy Cncl 1984-87; memb exec Scottish Cncl Devpt and Indust 1984-; dir Clydesdale Bank plc 1985-, New Scotland Insur Gp 1986-; Hon Memb American Bar Assoc 1982; OStJ 1968; *Recreations* golf, hill-walking; *Clubs* Royal Scottish Automobile, Western (Glasgow); *Style*— Norman Biggart, Esq, CBE, WS; Gailes, Kilmacolm, Renfrewshire PA13 4LZ (☎ 050 587 2645)

BIGGIN, Alan Keith; s of Herbert Biggin, of Bradford, W Yorks, and Ada *née* Richardson; *b* 19 Dec 1949; *Educ* Hanson GS, Bradford, W Yorks; *m* 27 May 1978, Angela (Susan), da of Clifford Crompton (d 1966); *Career* CA; fin controller PLC 1978-79; sr ptnr: A K Biggin & Co 1980-81, Bostock & Co 1987-88; memb C of C in: Bradford, Halifax, Kirkless and Wakefield, Borough Club in Huddesfield, Executive Club at Bradford City AFC, Bradford Civic Soc; FCA, MBIM; *Recreations* golf, squash, fishing, shooting; *Clubs* West Bradford GC; *Style*— Alan Biggin, Esq; The Counting House, Wade House Rd, Shelf, Nr Bradford HX3 7PB (☎ 0274 673 642); St Georges House, 7 St Georges Square, Huddersfield HD1 1LA (☎ 0484 530 647); La Plata House, 147 Sunbridge Rd, Bradford BD1 2NA

BIGGINS, Christopher; s of William Biggins, of Salisbury, Wilts, and Pamela Parsons; *b* 16 Dec 1948; *Educ* St Probus Salisbury, Bristol Old Vic Theatre Sch; *Career* actor, dir and personality; *Recreations* eating, swimming, enjoying life; *Style*— Christopher Biggins, Esq; IMG The Pier House, Strand on the Green, Chiswick W4 3NN (☎ 01 994 1444)

BIGGLESTONE, John George; s of John Bigglestone, and Lillian Bigglestone (d 1978); *b* 10 August 1934; *Educ* Bablake Sch, Coventry; *m* 22 Dec 1984, Annette Vivian, da of Kenneth Bull, of Devizes; *Career* professional photographer, journalist, broadcaster and lectr 1951-; photographic clients inc many leading indust cos; sr tutor in photography country courses Devizes; sr lectr in photography Salisbury Coll of Art 1966-; ABIPP; memb IOJ; *Recreations* learning; *Style*— John Bigglestone, Esq; The Gables, Potterne Park, Devizes (☎ 0380 5709); Salisbury College of Art, Southampton Rd, Salisbury (☎ 0722 26122)

BIGGS, Brig Michael Worthington; CBE (1962, OBE 1944); s of Lt-Col Charles William Biggs, OBE (d 1965), of Montpellier Grove, Cheltenham, Glos, and Winifred Jesse Bell Biggs, *née* Dickinson (d 1932); *Educ* Cheltenham, RMA Woolwich, Pembroke Coll Cambridge (MA); *m* 1940, Katharine Mary, da of Sir Walter Harragin, CMG, KC (d 1966); 2 da (Patricia, Hilary); *Career* military serv RE (cmmnd 1931) and King's African Rifles, including active serv in Abyssinia (BM) and Burma (GSO1 & CRE) COS E Africa Cmd 1960-63, Dir of Quartering (Army) 1963-66; gp bldg exec Forte's Hldgs 1966-67; mangr Hatfield & Welwyn Garden City Cmmn for the New Towns 1967-78, pres KAR & EAF Offrs Dinner Club 1972-, chm Herts Building Preservation Tst 1978-86, cncl memb Town & Country Planning Assoc 1978-84, memb exec ctee Herts Soc 1978-; CEng, MICE, Freeman City of London; *Recreations* tennis, golf; *Clubs* Army and Navy; *Style*— Brig Michael Biggs, CBE; Strawyards, Kimpton, Hitchin, Herts SG4 8PT (☎ Kimpton 832498)

BIGGS, Neil William; s of Sir Lionel Biggs (d 1985), of 151 Richmond Park Rd, Bournemouth, and Doris Rose, *née* Davies; *b* 29 Mar 1939; *Educ* Shrewsbury; *m* 1 Sept 1969, Shirley Evelyn, da of Albert Harfield Simpson (d 1957); *Career* slr; ptnr: Withington Petty & Co (Manchester) 1962-73, Masons (London) 1973-; Notary Public; involved in CAB and numerous artistic socs; memb Law Soc; *Recreations* swimming, theatre, literature; *Clubs* RAC; *Style*— Neil Biggs, Esq; 40 South Hill Park, London NW3 2SJ; 10 Fleet St, London EC4G 1BA (☎ 01 583 9990, fax 01 353 8810, telex 8811117)

BIGGS, Sir Norman Parris; s of John Gordon Biggs, and Mary Sharpe Dickson; *b* 23 Dec 1907; *Educ* John Watson's Sch Edinburgh; *m* 1936, Peggy Helena Stammwitz; 2 s, 1 da; *Career* Bank of England 1927-46; dir: Kleinwort, Sons & Co 1946-52, ESSO Petroleum 1952-66 (chm 1968-72), Gillet Bros Discount 1963-71; chm: Williams & Glyns Bank 1972-76, United Int Bank 1970-79; dep chm Privatbanker Ltd 1980-83, div Banco de Bilbao 1981-87; memb Bullock Ctee Industl Democracy 1976; kt 1977; *Style*— Sir Norman Biggs; Northbrooks, Danworth lane, Hurstpierpoint, Sussex (☎ 832022)

BIGGS, Prof Peter Martin; CBE (1987); s of (George) Ronald Biggs (d 1985), and Cécile Agnes, *née* Player (d 1981); *b* 13 August 1926; *Educ* Bedales Sch, Cambridge Sch Mass USA, RVC (BSc), Univ of Bristol (PhD), Univ of London (DSc); *m* 9 Sept 1950, Alison Janet, da of late Malcolm Christian Molteno; 2 s (Andrew b 20 May 1957, John b 15 Nov 1963), 1 da (Alison (Mrs Stanley) b 28 May 1955); *Career* RAF: univ short course Queens Univ Oct 1944-March 1945, air crew undertraining, remustered Corpl, demobed April 1948; lectr in veterinary clinical pathology Univ of Bristol 1955-59 (res asst 1953-55); Houghton Poultry Res Station: head leukosis experimental unit 1959-73, dep dir 1971-73, dir 1974-86; visiting prof RVC Univ of London 1982-, dir AFRC Inst for Animal Health 1986-88, Andrew D White prof-at-large Cornell Univ USA 1988-, chm scientific advsy ctee Animal Health Tst; memb: Vet Prods Ctee, Meds Commn 1973-, Individual Merit Promos Panel, Mgmnt and Person Off, Advsy Ctee on Dangerous Pathogens 1988-; hon doc vet med Maximillian Univ Munich W Germany; MRCVS, FRCVS, FRCPath, FIBiol, CBiol, FRS; *Recreations* music, boating; *Clubs* Farmers; *Style*— Prof Peter Biggs, CBE; Willows, London Rd, St Ives, Huntingdon, Cambs PE17 4ES (☎ 0480 63471)

BIGHAM, (Derek) Alastair; s of Capt Robert Alexander Bigham (d 1968), and Dorothy May, *née* Bowyer (d 1963); *b* 7 Mar 1926; *Educ* Whitgift Sch, Trinity Hall Cambridge, Univ Coll Oxford (MA); *m* 1, 22 Aug 1952 (m dis 1983), June Diana, da of Lt Col John Grenville Fortescue (d 1964), of Stowford Grange, Lewdown, N Devon; 2 da (Diana Susan (Mrs W Grundy) b 1954, Julia Rosemary b 1959); m 2, 3 April 1984, Mary Elizabeth, *née* Gregory; *Career* war serv RM subsequently Lt Seaforth Highlanders 1944-48; barr 1952, legal advsr/pa to Lloyds Brokers; pa to sec RIBA; chartered land agent (estate mgmnt) and chartered surveyor (planning and devpt div) ptnrship in practice Bath 1959-69, specialised bar practice enviromental and real property Middle Temple 1969-82; chm: Rent Assessment, Panel 1971-82, Industrial Tribunals (full-time) 1982- UK Ministerial Delegation at Conf on the Environment Bern 1976, Ctee of Agric Law Assoc (UK) 1978-82; conslt to: Euro Cmmn 1979-, Cmmn Permanente Droit et Technique of Int Union of Advocates 1979-; memb Cmmn on Enviromental Policy Law and Admin of Int Union for Conservation of Nature and Natural Resources (IUCN) 1980-; memb International Council of Environmental Law 1984-, visiting Fell Sheffield Univ 1986; memb Windsor Borough Cncl 1954-58, Som CC 1967-77 (chm Co Planning Ctee 1969-70), short listed for four Party seats (C) prior to 1969; FCIArb 1965, FRICS 1972, MI Env Sc 1974, FRSA 1980; *Books* The Law and Administration Relating to Protection of the Environment (1973), The Impact of Marine Pollution (with others 1980); *Recreations* natural history, history, visual arts, fly fishing, shooting; *Style*— Alastair Bigham, Esq; 1 Simon Ct, Graham Rd, Ranmoor, Sheffield S10 3GR, South Yorkshire (☎ 0742 307392); Office of the Industrial Tribunals, 14 East Parade, Sheffield S1 2ET (☎ 0742 760348)

BIGHAM, Hon Andrew Charles; yst s of 3 Viscount Mersey, and Lady Nairne (12 holder of that title), *qqv*; *b* 26 June 1941; *Educ* Eton, Worcester Coll Oxford; *Career* short serv cmmn Ir Gds 1964-66; asst master (and sr French master) Aysgarth Sch, Bedale, N Yorks 1968-; *Style*— The Hon Andrew Bigham; Bignor Park, Pulborough, Sussex (☎ Sutton, Sussex 214); Aysgarth School, Bedale, N Yorks (☎ Bedale 50359)

BIGHAM, Hon David Edward Hugh; s of 3 Viscount Mersey and Lady Nairne; *b* 14 April 1938; *Educ* Eton; *m* 1965, Anthea Rosemary, da of Leo Seymour, of Easterknowe Farm, Stobo, Peebles, Border District; 3 s, 1 da; *Style*— The Hon David Bigham; Hurston Place, Pulborough, West Sussex RH20 2EW (☎ 090 66 2428)

BIGHAM, Hon Edward John Hallam; s and h of 4 Viscount Mersey; *b* 23 May 1966; *Educ* Eton, Balliol Coll Oxford; *Style*— The Hon Edward Bigham; 1 Rosmead Rd, London W11 2JG

BIGHAM, Hon (Ralph) John; s of 2 Viscount Mersey, PC (d 1956); *b* 3 August 1913; *Educ* Eton; *m* 1954, Cicely Ruth (d 1986), yst da of Percy Johnson, of Douglas, IOM; *Career* OStJ; *Style*— The Hon John Bigham

BILBY, David; s of Walter Bilby (d 1983), and Violet Florence, *née* Trinder; *b* 19 Jan 1943; *Educ* Archbishop Temple Sch; *m* 25 Sept 1965, Ann Kathleen, da of Harold Poulter (d 1983); 2 s (Jonathan b 1971, Andrew b 1980), 1 da (Laura b 1969); *Career* sales/showroom dir Garrard Crown Jewellers 1985-88, formed David Bilby & Ptnrs Ltd 1988, chm and md Bilby & Holloway (Fine Jewels Silver & Objets D'Art) 1988-; FGA 1963; *Style*— David Bilby, Esq; 13A Grafton St, Mayfair, London W1X 3LA (☎ 01 495 4636, fax 495 5946)

BILES, Michael James; s of Walter James Biles, of Little Chalfont, Bucks, and Olive Irene, *née* Dawson; *b* 23 June 1946; *Educ* St Nicholas GS Northwood, Nottingham Univ (BA); *m* 18 Sept 1971, Angela Rosemary, da of Geoffrey Walter Griffin (d 1979), of Newport Pagnell, Bucks; 1 s (Alexander James Walter b 10 June 1981), 1 da (Louise Elizabeth b 21 Feb 1979); *Career* qualified CA 1970, ptnr Robson Rhodes 1977- (mangr 1972-77); tres Hornsey Housing Tst Ltd; FCA 1970; *Recreations* all sports, walking, family; *Style*— Michael Biles, Esq; Robson Rhodes, 186 City Road, London EC21V 2NU (☎ 01 251 1644, fax 01 250 0801)

BILLETER, Alex (Pierre); s of Maurice Billeter, of Switzerland, and Beate *née* Oesterle (d 1985); *b* 10 April 1944; *Educ* Gymnase cantonal de Neuchatel, Swiss Inst of Technol (ETH) Zurich, Switzerland (Dip in Architecture); *Career* ptnr: Billeter & Thompson chartered architects, Dupuis and Billeter architects SIA Geneva; pt/t teacher in architecture N London Poly; works in UK, Switzerland and Africa, RIBA, SIA; *Recreations* friends, saxophone, music, books, travels (Africa); *Style*— Alex Billeter, Esq; Billeter & Thompson, 39 Marylebone High St, London W1M 3AB (☎ 01 486 7434)

BILLETT, Cncllr John Anthony; s of Ernest Edward Billett (d 1981), of Middlesex, and Angelina Christina Billett, *née* Martinelli; *b* 22 June 1945; *Educ* Hordenden Junior, Ealing County GS, RNC Dartmouth; *m* 3 July 1971, Carole Elizabeth, da of Harold Edwad Jarvis; 1 s (Christian b 1976), 1 da (Elizabeth b 1986); *Career* RN pilot RN 1962-71; insurance broker principal 1971-72; with American Int Gp (UK production mangr, dep regnl dir East Africa, dep regnl dir Mid East, gen mangr Netherlands, dir of Ops Caribbean) 1972-81; vice pres The Continential Corpn (regnl dir Euro, Mid East) 1981-85; chm Continental Hellas; dir: Continental Life, Continental Pensions; dir and conslt Tillinghast Nelson and Warren Ltd 1985-87; chm and CEO: Barkers Fin Services Ltd; *Recreations* squash, shooting, sailing, golf; *Clubs* Chiltern Squash, Glyfada Golf; *Style*— Cncllr John A Billett; Barkers Farmhouse, Little Chalfont, Buckingham HP7 9JY (☎ (02404) 2026); Barkers Financial Services Ltd, Barkers Farmhouse, Little Chalfont, Bucks HP7 9JY

BILLINGHAM, Hon Mrs - Hon Brenda Dolores Bowden; da of Baron Aylestone, CBE, PC (Life Peer); *b* 17 Feb 1929; *m* 1951, John Leonard Billingham; 1 s, 1 da; *Style*— The Hon Mrs Billingham; 67 Kingsmead Av, Worcester Park, Surrey

BILLINGTON, Guy; s of Reginald Arthur Billington (d 1960), of 1 Arterberry Rd, London SW20, and Constance May, *née* Riches; *b* 12 Nov 1946; *Educ* King's Col Sch Wimbledon, St John's Coll Cambridge (MA); *m* 5 July 1966, Christine Ellen, da of Rev Frederick Charles Bonner, of 4 Ham View, Upton-upon-Severn, Worcs; 2 da (Nicole b 13 Dec 1966, Suzanne b 21 Jan 1971); *Career* articled clerk Lovell White and King 1969-72, ptnr McKenna and Co 1972- (asst slr); City of London Slr's Co; memb Law Soc; *Recreations* rugby, music, scuba diving; *Clubs* The Gresham, Rosslyn Park FC, BSAC; *Style*— Guy Billington, Esq; 16 Belvedere Grove, London SW19 7RL (☎ 01 946 4889); McKenna and Co, 71 Queen Victoria Street, London EC4V 4EB (☎ 01 236 4340, fax 01 236 4485, telex 264826)

BILLINGTON, (Edward) John; RD; s of Edward Billington and Nesta, *née* Boxwell; *b* 21 Dec 1934; *Educ* Uppingham; *m* 5 Dec 1964, Fenella, da of Dr Hamilton-Turner; 2 s

(Edward b 1966, Richard b 1970), 1 da (Suzetta b 1968); *Career* RNR 1953-86; commodity broker; chm Edward Billington & Son Ltd; memb cncl of Liverpool Univ; CBIM; *Style—* John Billington Esq, RD; Cunard Building, Liverpool L3 1EL

BILLINGTON, Lady Rachel Mary; *née* Pakenham; da of 7 Earl of Longford, KG, PC, and sis of Lady Antonia Pinter (*see* Lady Antonia Fraser); *b* 11 May 1942; *Educ* London Univ; *m* 1967, Kevin Billington (b 12 June 1934, film, theatre and tv dir), s of Richard Billington, of Warrington, Lancs; 2 s, 2 da; *Career* author; *Books Incl:* A Woman's Age, Occasion of Sin, The Garish Day; *Style—* Lady Rachel Billington; 30 Addison Ave, London W11 4QR; The Court House, Poyntington, nr Sherborne, Dorset

BINDER, Alan Naismith; OBE (1974); s of Frederick John Binder (d 1961), of Hampshire, and Kathleen Mary, *née* Darker (d 1967); *b* 4 August 1931; *Educ* Bedford Sch, Magdalen Coll Oxford (MA); *m* 1958, Gillian Patricia, da of George Francis Wilson, of Sussex; 1 s (Jonathan b 1962), 2 da (Jennifer b 1958, Stephanie b 1959); *Career* dir Shell Int Petroleum Co Ltd 1984, pres Shell Int Trading Co 1987; *Recreations* tennis, skiing, reading, music; *Clubs* Carlton, Leander, MCC; *Style—* Alan Binder, Esq, OBE; Old Place, Speldhurst, Kent TN3 0PA (☎ 089 286 3227); Shell Centre, London SE1 7NA (☎ 01 934 5878)

BINDMAN, Geoffrey Lionel; s of Dr Gerald Bindman (d 1974); *b* 3 Jan 1933; *Educ* Royal GS Newcastle-on-Tyne, Oriel Oxford; *m* 1961, Lynn Janice; 3 children; *Career* slr; Bindman & Partners London NW1, legal advsr Cmmn for Racial Equality 1977-83, chm Legal Action Gp 1976-78, cncllr London Borough of Camden 1971-74, dep ldr London Borough of Camden 1973-74; *Recreations* book collecting, music, walking; *Clubs* Law Society; *Style—* Geoffrey Bindman Esq; 26 Hillway, Highgate, London N6 (☎ 348 0941)

BING, Hon Mrs (Christian Keith); da of 15 Viscount of Arbuthnott, CB, CBE, DSO, MC (d 1966); *b* 1 Oct 1933; *Educ* Edinburgh Univ; *m* 1954, Cdr Peter John Bing, OBE, RN, s of William Leslie Bing, of High Hedges, Crowborough, Sussex; 3 s, 1 da; *Style—* The Hon Mrs Bing; The Cottage, Hillside, Montrose, Angus

BING, Peter John; OBE (1974); s of William Leslie Bing, of High Hedges, Crowborough, Sussex; *b* 30 August 1925; *Educ* Felsted, RN Eng Coll Plymouth; *m* 1954, Hon Christian Keith, da of 15 Viscount of Arbuthnott, CB, CBE, DSO, MC; 3 s, 1 da; *Career* Cdr RN (ret 1974), bd sec OPITB, Offshore Tning Centre Montrose Angus 1983-; dir Montrose C of C, memb Cncl Humberside Offshore Trg Assoc Hull; CEng, FIMechE, FCIS, FBIM, FInstPet; *Recreations* restoring houses; *Clubs* Army and Navy; *Style—* Peter Bing Esq; Hillside, Montrose, Angus (☎ 0674 83 267)

BINGHAM, Charlotte; *see*: Brady, Hon Mrs (C M T)

BINGHAM, Lord; George Charles Bingham; s and h of 7 Earl of Lucan; *b* 21 Sept 1967; *Style—* Lord Bingham

BINGHAM, Hon Hugh; s of 6 Earl of Lucan, MC (d 1964); *b* 24 April 1939; *Educ* Charterhouse, Hertford Coll Oxford; *Style—* The Hon Hugh Bingham; 6 Gledhow Gdns, London SW5 (☎ 01 373 4489)

BINGHAM, Hon John Edward; TD; s of 5 Earl of Lucan, GCVO, KBE, CB, TD, PC (d 1949); *b* 29 Feb 1904; *Educ* Eton, Trinity Coll Cambridge (MA); *m* 1942, Dorothea, da of late Rev John Kyrle Chatfield; 3 s (Nicholas Charles b 1943, Peter John b 1945, David Julian b 1951); *Career* late Derbyshire Yeo and 2 SAS Regt; 1939-45 War in N Africa; *Clubs* Pratt's, ESU; *Style—* The Hon John Bingham; Nicholls, Udimore, Rye, East Sussex (☎ 0797 223120)

BINGHAM, John Temple; o s of Rear Adm Edward Barry Stewart Bingham, VC, OBE (d 1939), and Vera Maud Temple, *née* Patterson; kinsman and h p of 8 Baron Clanmorris, *qv* ; *b* 22 Feb 1923; *m* 28 April 1949, Joan Muriel Bown (d 1955); *Style—* John Bingham, Esq; Flat 1, 48 Holland Road, London W14

BINGHAM, Stephen Denis; OBE; s of Cdr Francis Bingham, RN (d 1986); *b* 28 June 1934; *Educ* Ampleforth, St Catharine's Coll Cambridge (BA); *m* 1962, Elizabeth, da of Cdr G Paine, RN (d 1980); 3 s (Benedict, Thomas, Patrick), 2 da (Emma, Catherine); *Career* Lt Irish Gds; md Sodastream Ltd 1974-78, gp md Servotomic Ltd 1986-88; memb bd Peterborough Devpt Corpn, nat dir World Family Foster Parents Plan; *Recreations* sailing, golf, painting; *Style—* Stephen Bingham, OBE; Geeston, Ketton, Stamford, Lincs (☎ 0780 720135)

BINGHAM, Thomas Bruce Bennet; s of James Bennet Bingham, (d 1942), of Holmfield, Kirkcaldy, Fife, and Elizabeth Fisken, *née* Begg, (d 1962); *b* 4 July 1910; *Educ* Merchiston Castle Sch; *m* 3 April 1937, Janet Mary Douglas (Jean), da of Robert Douglas, (d 1929), of Kirkcaldy; 1 s (Elliott Robert James Bennet b 1946), 1 da (Susan Elizabeth Mary Bennet b 1940); *Career* 2 Lt 51 Highland Div Signals (TA) 1929-32, Lt 1932-39, Capt 1939-42, Maj NCO Trg Bn Royal Signals 1942-44, Maj 12 Air Formation Signals 1944-45, demobilised with hon rank of Maj 1945; Nat Bank of Scotland: inspr 1946-51, chief inspr 1951-53, superintendent of branches 1953-59; superintendent of branches: Nat Commercial Bank of Scotland 1959-69, Royal Bank of Scotland 1969-70; FIBScot; *Recreations* photography, golf, fishing, shooting; *Clubs* Elie Golfhouse, Newtonmore Golf; *Style—* Thomas Bingham, Esq; Kirk House, By Largo, Leven, Fife KY8 6JE (☎ 033 336 379)

BINGHAM, Hon Mr Justice; Hon Sir Thomas Henry Bingham; s of Dr Thomas Henry Bingham, of Reigate, Surrey, and Catherine, *née* Watterson; *b* 13 Oct 1933; *Educ* Sedbergh Sch, Balliol Oxford; *m* 1963, Elizabeth, o da of Peter Loxley (d 1945); 2 s, 1 da; *Career* barr 1959, jr counsel Dept of Employment 1968-72, QC (1972), ldr Investigation into Supply of Petroleum and Petroleum Prods to Rhodesia 1977-78, High Court judge (Queen's Bench Div) 1980-; kt 1980; *Style—* The Hon Mr Justice Bingham; 74 Lansdowne Rd, London W11 (☎ 01 727 8891)

BINGLEY, Clive Hamilton; s of Alexander Hamilton Bingley (d 1985), and Stella, *née* Hanscomb (d 1981); *b* 2 April 1936; *Educ* Highgate Sch, St Johns Coll Johannesburg, Oxford Univ (MA); *m* 16 March 1963, Anne Edith, da of Basil Henry Chichester-Constable (d 1968); 3 da (Miranda b 1964, Kate b 1966, Zillah b 1968); *Career* dir numerous publishing cos inc: Book Publishing Devpt plc, The Athloe Press Ltd, Library Assoc Publishing Ltd, Lund Humphries Publishers Ltd; hon fell of the Library Assoc 1986, hon tres The Nat Book League 1980-84; co-fndr The London Book Fair; *Books* Book Publishing Practice (1966), The Business of Book Publishing (1970); ed New Library World (1970-77); *Recreations* switching off; *Clubs* Savile, MCC; *Style—* Clive Bingley, Esq; 16 Pembridge Rd, London W11 3HL (☎ 01 229 1825)

BINGLEY, Lady Juliet Martin Bingley; *née* Vick; da of Reginald Martin Vick, OBE, FRCS, MChir (d 1970) and Mary Kate Neville; *b* 18 July 1925; *Educ* King Alfred's Sch Hampstead, LSE (Cert Soc Admin); *m* 8 Aug 1948, Alexander Noel Campbell; 1 s (William Neville b 1950), 2 da (Elizabeth Charlott b 1950, Penelope Juliet b 1954); *Career* med social worker: City Corp, St Marks Hospital London EC1; past chm MIND (Nat assoc of Mental Health); Commander O St J, Honour of the Rep of Malta 1976; *Recreations* music, collecting antiques; *Style—* Lady Juliet Bingley; Hoddesdonbury, Hoddesdon, Herts; St Marks Hosp, City Rd, London EC1

BINGLEY, May (Olivia); *née* Lenox-Conyngham; da of Col Hubert Maxwell Lenox-Conyngham, DSO, OBE (d 1916), and Eva Lenox-Conyngham, *née* Darley; *b* 10 April 1913; *m* 21 Dec 1941, Robert Albert Glanvile; 1 da (Alexandra Maeve b 1942); *Style—* Mrs Robert Bingley; office: (☎ 0992 444343)

BINGLEY, Lt-Col Robert Noel Charles; s of Col Robert Albert Glanville Bingley, DSO, OBE, MVO (d 1977), of Higher Eggbeer, Exeter, Devon, and Sybil Gladys Williamson, *née* Duff; *b* 28 Dec 1936; *Educ* Abberley Hall Malvern Worcs; *m* 23 Nov 1962, Elizabeth Anne, da of Col Thomas Charles Stanley Haywood, OBE, JP, DL, of Gunthorpe, Oakham, Rutland; 2 s (Piers b 1967, Alexander b 1971), 1 da (Claire b 1963); *Career* troop ldr 11 Hussars (PAO) 1957, Staff Capt HQ 17 div Malaya Dist 1965, Staff Coll Pakistan 1969, GSO 2 MOD 1970, 2 i/c Royal Hussars 1972, Nat Def Coll 1974, instr Australia Army Staff Coll 1976, CO Royal Yeo 1977; antique dealer 1978-; memb; Cancer Relief MacMillan Fund, TAVR; *Recreations* shooting, fishing, waterskiing; *Clubs* Kingswater Ski; *Style—* Lt-Col Robert Bingley; Wing House, Oakham, Rutland (☎ 057 285 314); Coul Cottage, Scatwell, Marybank by Muir-of-ord, Ross-Shire; Robert Bingley Antiques, Church St, Wing, Oakham, Rutland, LE15 8RS (☎ 057 285 725)

BINKS, William Richard; s of William Henry Binks (d 1961), of London, and Ellen French *née* Wintle (d 1943); *b* 29 Jan 1922; *Educ* Downshall Secy Sch, London Univ (LLB); *m* 21 May 1943, Kathleen Elsie, da of Frederick John Le May (d 1976), of Eastbourne; 1 s (Alan), 1 da (Karen); *Career* FH Lt RAF 1942-46, res 1946-52; slr 1965, ptnr Binks Stern and Ptnrs 1965- (sr ptnr 1982-); memb Law Soc; *Recreations* sailing; *Clubs* RAF, Royal Ocean Racing, Royal Burnham Yacht; *Style—* William R Binks, Esq; 91 Manor Road, Chigwell, Essex, IG7 5PN (☎ 01 500 8664); Queens House, 55/56 Lincolns Inn Fields, London, WC2A 3LT (☎ 01 404 4321), fax 01 405 5040, car tel 0836 202 519, telex 295408

BINNEY, Ivor Ronald; s of Ronald Frederick Binney (d 1979), and Ethel Alice, *née* Dredge; *b* 11 Oct 1929; *Educ* Haberdashers' Aske's Hampstead Sch; *m* 1957, Susan Mary Campbell, da of Capt John Calendar Ritchie (d 1939); 1 s (Hugo), 3 da (Emma, Lucy, Sara); *Career* dir: CT Bowring & Co Ltd 1970-87 (dep chm), Terra Nova Insur Co Ltd 1970-87, Marsh & McLennan Cos Inc 1980-97, A J Archer & Co Ltd 1987-; chm Additional Underwriting Agencies (No 4) Ltd 1987-, conslt Insur and Reinsur 1987-; Lloyds: ctee memb 1978-81 and 1984-87, cncl memb 1984-87; *Recreations* golf; *Clubs* MCC, Pilgrims; *Style—* Ivor Binney, Esq; Southease Place, Southease, nr Lewes, Sussex

BINNEY, Marcus Hugh Crofton; OBE (1983); s of late Lt Col Francis Crofton Simms, MC, and Sonia (d 1985), da of Rear Adm Sir William Marcus Charles Beresford-Whyte, KCB, CMG (she m 2, 1955, as his 2 wife, Sir George Binney, DSO, who d 1972); *b* 21 Sept 1944; *Educ* Eton, Magdalene Coll Cambridge (BA); *m* 1, 1966 (m dis 1976), Hon Sara Anne Vanneck (d 1979), da of 6 Baron Huntingfield; m 2 , 1981, Anne Carolyn, da of Dr T H Hills of Merstham, Surrey; 2 s (Francis Charles Thomas b 1982, Christopher Crofton b 1985); *Career* writer; ed Country Life 1984-86 (architectural writer 1968-77, architectural ed 1977-84), ed of Landscape 1987-; pres SAVE Britain's Heritage 1984- (chm 1975-84), sec UK Ctee Int Cncl on Monuments and Sites 1972-81, dir Railway Heritage Tst 1984-, co-organizer of: The Destruction of the Country House exhibition V and A 1974, Change and Decay: the Future of our Churches V and A 1977; *Books* Change and Decay: the future of our churches (with Peter Burman 1977), Chapels and Churches: who cares? (with Peter Burman 1977), Preservation Pays (with Max Hanna 1978), Railway Architecture (ed jtly 1979), Our Past Before Us (ed jtly 1981), The Country House: to be or not to be (with Kit Martin, 1982), Preserve and Prosper (with Max Hanna 1983), Sir Robert Taylor (1984), Our Vanishing Heritage (1984), contributor to: Satanic Mills (1979), Elysian Gardens (1979), Lost Houses of Scotland (1980), Taking the Plunge (1982), SAVE Gibraltar's Heritage 1982, Vanishing Houses of England (1983), Time Gentlemen Please (1983), Great Railway Stations of Europe (1984); *Style—* Marcus Binney, Esq, OBE; Domaine des Vaux, St Lawrence, Jersey, CI

BINNEY, (Harry Augustus) Roy; CB (1950); s of Harry Augustus Binney (d 1960), of Churston, Devon; *b* 18 May 1907; *Educ* Royal Dockyard Sch Devonport, London Univ (BSc); *m* 1944, Barbara (d 1975), da of Jeffrey Poole (d 1952), of Harborne, Birmingham; 3 s, 1 da (and 1 da decd); *Career* under-sec Bd of Trade 1947-50, dir-gen Br Standards Instn 1950-72 (memb Cncl Int Standards Orgn 1951-72 (vice pres 1964-69), UN advsr on standards Cyprus 1974-77; *Recreations* gardening; *Style—* Roy Binney, Esq, CB; Hambutts Orchard, Edge Rd, Painswick, Glos (☎ 0452 813718)

BINNEY, Hon Mrs (Victoria Sarah Maria); *née* Lubbock; da of 4 Baron Lubbock, *qv*, and his 1 w, Kina Maria, *née* O'Kelly de Gallagh; *b* 27 April 1959; *m* 1983, Alan Binney; 2 s (Archie b 1983, Alastair b 1985); *Style—* The Hon Mrs Binney; c/o The Rt Hon Lord Avebury, 53 Gloucester Street, London SW1V 4DY

BINNIE, Geoffrey Morse; s of William James Eames Binnie (d 1949), of 12 Stafford Terr, Kensington, London, and Ethel, *née* Morse (d 1947); *b* 13 Nov 1908; *Educ* Charterhouse, Trinity Hall Cambridge (MA), Zurich Univ (ETH); *m* 1, 1932, Yanka Parycako (d 1964); 1 s (Alexander Yanek b 1939), 1 da (Diana Yolande (m Dr Kenneth Wright CMG) b 1936); m 2, 15 July 1964, Elspeth Maud Cicely (d 1987), da of late Rev Tom Thompson; *Career* WWII 1939-45, cmmnd RE (Maj) served Sudan, Ethiopia, Iraq, Iran and Egypt (despatches); jr asst on construction Gorge dam Hong Kong 1933-37, chief asst res engr Eye Brook reservoir Northants 1937-39, ptnr Binnie, Deacon & Gourley (now Binnie & Ptnrs) responsible inter alia for design and construction supervision of Kalawata dam Columbo and many UK water supplies 1945-56, sr ptnr responsible des and constr supervision of Dokan Dam Iraq and Mangla project Pakistan 1956-72, chm Advsy Panel on Peace River Hydro-Electric project in Br Columbia 1962-68, conslt to Binnie & Ptnrs 1973-82; chm Mornos Dam for Athens water supply 1975-78, chief tech advsr Chiru Puria irragation project Puria irrigation project Peru 1975-78; memb Severn Barrage Ctee 1978-81; pres Kent branch Cambridge Soc; FRS (1975), FEng (1976), FICE (1937 2nd vice pres 1970-72), FGS (1959), FIWEM (1946); *Books* Early Victorian Water Engineers (1981), Early Dam Builders in Britain (1987); *Recreations* exercising a dog, gardening occasionally, reading; *Clubs* Athenaeum, Lansdowne; *Style—* Geoffrey Binnie, Esq; St Michael's

Lodge, Benenden, nr Cranbrook, Kent TN17 4EZ (☎ 0580 240 498)

BINNING, Kenneth George Henry; CMG (1976); s of Henry Binning (d 1976), of Wivenhoe, Essex, and Hilda, *née* Powell (d 1987); *b* 5 Jan 1928; *Educ* Bristol GS, Balliol Coll Oxford (MA); *m* 28 Feb 1953, Pamela Dorothy, da of Alfred Edward Pronger (d 1963), of Streatham, London; 3 s (Simon Kenneth b 1955, Julian Charles b 1957, Marcus Adam b 1963), 1 da (Susanna Clare b 1960); *Career* Nat Serv Capt RAEC 1950-52; HM Treasury 1952-59 (private sec to Fin Sec 1956), UK AEA 1959-65, seconded Miny of Technol 1965-67 (1969-), asst dir Progs Analysis Unit 1967-69, dir gen Concorde Prog (UK) 1973-76, set up Invest in Br Bureau 1976-80, govt dir BSC 1980-82, dir govt rels NEI plc 1983-; *Recreations* music, gardening; *Clubs* Reform; *Style—* Kenneth Binning, Esq, CMG; 12 Kemerton Road, Beckenham, Kent BR3 2NJ (☎ 01 650 0273); NEI plc, Tavistock House East, Woburn Walk, Burton St, London WC1 (☎ 01 387 9393)

BINNING, Lady Nora Kathleen; da of 10 Earl Annesley; *b* 27 Mar 1950; *m* 1969, John Binning; 2 s, 2 da; *Style—* Lady Nora Binning; 6 Baron's Way, Egham, Surrey

BINNINGTON, Bernard Thomas; s of Richard Binnington, (d 1963), of Jersey, and Florence Mary, *née* Quenault; *b* 23 Nov 1930; *Educ* Victoria Coll Jersey; *m* 28 Sept 1953, Elizabeth Rowley, da of James Davidson (d 1979), of Edinburgh; 1 s (Alan Richard), 1 da (Anne Elizabeth); *Career* exec dir: Chelsea Hotels Ltd 1955-, Pioneer Coaches Ltd 1965-; dir Samuel Montagu & Co (Jersey) Ltd 1979-87, chm Jersey Electricity Co Ltd 1982-88 (dir 1976-82), dir A Degruchy & Co Ltd 1987-; St Helier Jersey Parl: dep 1969 and 1972, Senator 1975 (1982 and 1987); pres Jersey Hotel and Guest House Assoc 1966-68, States of Jersey Harbours and Airport Ctee 1981-; chm Jersey Transport Authy 1981-; MHCIMA 1974; *Recreations* sailing, music; *Style—* Bernard Binnington, Esq; La Rochelle, St Aubin, Jersey (☎ 0534 43303); Chelsea Hotel, St Helier, Jersey (☎ 0534 30241)

BINNS, Surgn Rear Adm George Augustus; CB (1975); s of Cuthbert Charles Harber Binns (d 1971), of Leicester, and Julia Johanna Isobella, *née* Frommel (d 1974); *b* 23 Jan 1918; *Educ* Repton, St Bartholomews Hosp (MRCS, LRCP, DO); *m* 1949, Joan, da of Brian Harold Whitaker (d 1978), of Ewell, and Ifold, Sussex; 1 s (Jonathan), 2 da (Julia, Susan); *Career* registered med practitioner 1942, joined RNVR 1942, casualty house surgn Luton and Dunstable hosp; served UK, W Africa, Far East, Ceylon, Malta, Gibraltar; specialist in ophthalmology 196; med offr in charge RN Hosps Gibraltar and Plymouth; Surgn Rear-Adm 1972; ret RN 1975; ophthalmic med practitioner 1975-; CStJ 1972; memb: Coll of Ophthalmologists, Royal Soc of Medicine, Br Medical Assoc, Southern Oph Soc, Medical Eye Centre Assoc, London Medical Soc; pres: Farnham Branch Royal Naval Assoc, Grayshott Horticultural Soc; *Recreations* photography, house and garden maintenance, listening to music; *Clubs* Naval and Military; *Style—* Surg Rear-Adm George Binns, CB; Netherseal, Hindhead Rd, Haslemere, Surrey GU27 3PJ (☎ 0428 4281); Med Eye Centre, 37 Weyhill, Haslemere GU27 1BZ (☎ 0428 3975)

BINNS, Malcolm; s of Douglas Priestley Binns (d 1988), of Keighley, Yorkshire, and May, *née* Walker; *b* 29 Jan 1936; *Educ* Bradford GS, RCM (ARCM); *Career* prof RCM 1961-65; concert pianist: London Debut 1959, debut Promenade Concerts 1962, regular performances at Proms since 1962, Royal Fest Hall debut 1961, and has appeared in London Philharmonic seasons 1962-; soloist with all major Br orchs, over 30 recordings, first complete recording of Beethoven Piano Sonatas on original instruments, played Far East and toured with Scottish Nat Orch and Limbourg Orch 1987-88; ARCM; *Style—* Malcolm Binns, Esq; Ibbs and Tillett, 18B Pindock Mews, London W9 2PY (☎ 01 286 7526)

BINNS, Peter John Ellison; s of Edward Richard Brett Binns (d 1963), of Lincs, and Mary Jane, *née* Ellison; *b* 25 Oct 1916; *Educ* Uppingham, Coll of Estate Mgmnt, FRICS; *m* 25 May 1954, Irene Elizabeth, da of Herbert Davenport Sale (d 1967), of Cheshire; *Career* chartered surveyor; APM 3 Br Inf Div, Maj UK, BAOR and ME; US Bronze Star Medal 1945; *Recreations* motor racing (driver); *Style—* Peter J E Binns, Esq; The Paddocks, Potters Heath, Welwyn, Herts

BINNY, Brig Robert Angus Graham; CBE (1961), OBE (1946); s of Graham Binny, of Moray Place, Edinburgh (d 1929); *b* 26 Nov 1908; *Educ* Cheltenham, Trinity Hall Cambridge (BA); *m* 1934, Joanna Mary, da of Maj-Gen Sir Philip Grant, KCB, CMG (d 1943), of Hurstbourne Priors, Whitchurch, Hants; 1 s, 3 da; *Career* 2 Lt RE 1929, 1939-45 India and Burma, CRE Special Force (Chindits), CRE 20 Ind Div (OBE, despatches), Brig 1956, CE Eastern Cmd 1956-59, CE FARELF 1959-61, ret 1961; FICE 1956; London rep Christiani and Nielsen A/S of Copenhagen 1961-70, ret; *Style—* Brig Angus Binny, CBE, OBE; Pitt Farmhouse, Skilgate, Taunton, Somerset TA4 2DQ (☎ 0398 313 46)

BINSTED, John Wadkin; s of George Percy Binsted, and May Emma, *née* Wadkin; *b* 6 Oct 1923; *Educ* Worthing HS; *m* 17 June 1950, Gloria Patricia, da of Albert Harry Bringes; 2 s (Andrew John Bringes b 8 March 1953, David Christopher b 11 Aug 1954), 2 da (Julia Gloria (Mrs Doig) b 3 Jan 1957, Elizabeth Angela b 20 Oct 1966); *Career* 1 Br Airborne Corps RCS 1943-45, served Arnhem 1944, Lt RCS MELF 1946-47 served Cairo, Alexandria, Ismailia, Capt RCS E Africa 1947-48 served Nairobi; CA; Arthur Stubbs and Spofforth 1948-51, audit mangr Ogden Hibberd Bull and Langton 1951-54, fin dir and sec BSA Motor Cycles Ltd Birmingham 1954-70, gp controller Br Utd Shoe Machinery Gp Leicester 1971-73, dir fin and admin Whittaker Ellis Ltd Staffs 1973-77, accountancy servs MOD 1977-87, ind fin intermediary J W Binsted Fin Servs Co; chm civilian ctee 194 ATC Sqdn 1960-, tstee Solihull Sch Parent's Assoc Careers Fund 1975-, dir Solihull Masonic Temple 1978-, former pres Solihull Sch Parents' Assoc 1970; FCA 1954, FIMBRA 1987; *Recreations* golf, tennis; *Clubs* Olton GC, Solihull Cricket and Tennis; *Style—* John Binsted, Esq; Brueton House, 34 Brueton Ave, Solihull, W Mids B91 3EN; Southwinds Ct, 26 West Parade, West Worthing, W Sussex (☎ 021 705 2581)

BINTLEY, David Julian; s of David Bintley, of Honley, Huddersfield, and Glenys, *née* Ellinthorpe; *b* 17 Sept 1957; *Educ* Holme Valley GS, Royal Ballet Upper Sch; *m* 12 Dec 1981, Jennifer Catherine Ursula, da of Bernard Mills, of San Diego, California; 1 s (Michael b 21 March 1985); *Career* Sadlers Wells Royal Ballet 1976-: debut The Outsider 1978, res choreographer and princ dancer 1983, res choreographer and princ dancer 1983; res choreographer and princ dances Royal Ballet 1986-, Evening Standard Award Choros and Concert Lessons 1983, Lawrence Olivier Award Petrushka (title-role) 1984, Manchester Evening News Award Still Life at the Penguin Café 1988; other works incl: Galanteries, Allegri Diversi, The Sons of Horos; *Style—* David Bintley, Esq; c/o Royal Opera House, Covent Garden, London EC1 (☎ 01 240 1200)

BIRCH, Dennis Arthur; CBE (1977), DL (W Midlands 1979); s of George Howard Birch (d 1960), of Wolverhampton, and Leah, *née* Draycott; *b* 11 Feb 1925; *Educ* Wolverhampton Municipal GS; *m* 1948, Mary Therese, da of Bernard Lyons (d 1964); 1 da (Imelda); *Career* draughtsman and estimator John Thompson Ltd (Wolverhampton) 1942-64, PR exec George Wimpey and Co Ltd Birmingham 1966-77; marketing mangr: C Bryant and Son Birmingham 1978-83; E Manton Ltd Birmingham 1983-; *Style—* Dennis Birch, Esq, CBE, DL; 3 Tern Close, Wolverhampton Road East, Wolverhampton (☎ 090 73 3837); E Manton Ltd, 100 Saltley Road, Birmingham (☎ 021 359 5987)

BIRCH, Frank Stanley Heath; s of John Stanley Birch (d 1985), and Phyllis Edna, *née* Heath (d 1981); *b* 8 Feb 1939; *Educ* The Grammar Sch for Boys Weston-super-Mare, Univ Coll Cardiff (BA), Birmingham Univ; *m* 7 Sept 1963, Diana Jacqueline, da of William Walter Frederick Davies, of Chislehurst, Kent; 1 da (Jocelyn b 1968); *Career* various appts city tres dept Cardiff 1962-69, chief auditor Dudley CBC 1969-73, asst chief exec West Midlands CC 1974-76 (asst co tres 1974-76), chief exec Lewisham London Borough Cncl 1976-82, town clerk and chief exec Croydon 1982-; memb cncl Order St John for Gtr London (Prince of Wales dist) 1986-, vice-pres St John Ambulance Bde 1988-; OStJ (1988); Freeman City of London 1980; IPFA 1969, MBIM 1969, FRSA 1980; *Recreations* music, travel, the countryside; *Style—* Frank Birch, Esq; Town Clerk's Office, Taverner Ho, Park Lane, Croydon CR9 3JS (☎ 01 686 4433, fax 01 760 0871)

BIRCH, Henry Langton; MBE (1944), TD, JP (Chester 1955), DL (Cheshire 1966); s of Arthur Lyle Birch (d 1967), of Chester; *b* 7 Mar 1915; *Educ* Charterhouse, Oriel Coll Oxford; *m* 1948, Helen Margaret (d 1984), da of Capt Harvey Blease (ka 1915); 1 da; *Career* Lt-Col (Hon Col) TA; slr; *Style—* Henry Birch, Esq, MBE, TD, JP, DL; Lion House, Tattenhall, nr Chester (☎ 0829 70347)

BIRCH, James; s of Simon Birch, of London, and Bettine, *née* Coventry; *b* 24 July 1956; *Educ* Milton Abbey Sch, Aix-en-Provence Univ (Dip Histoire D'Art); *Career* Christies 1976-78 (old masters dept and 1950s rock and roll dept), opened own gallery Kings Rd 1983, opened Birch & Conran Gallery Soho 1987, organised A Salute to English Surrealism (Colchester, Hull City Art Gallery, Newcastle), instigated Francis Bacon exhibition in Moscow; Liveryman Worshipful Co of Fishmongers 1980; *Recreations* backgammon, collecting Messerschmidt bubble cars; *Clubs* Groucho's, Colony Room, Little House; *Style—* James Birch, Esq; 40 Dean St, Soho, London W1 (☎ 01 434 1246)

BIRCH, John Allan; CMG (1987); s of Dr C. Allan Birch (d 1983); *b* 24 May 1935; *Educ* Leighton Park Sch, Corpus Christi Coll Cambridge (MA); *m* 5 March 1960, Primula Haselden; 3 s (James b 1962, Alexander b 1963, Henry b 1969), 1 da (Melanie b 1967); *Career* Nat Serv Army 1954-56; joined HM Diplomatic Serv 1959, serv: Paris, Singapore, Bucharest, Geneva, Kabul, Budapest; Royal Coll Def Studies 1977; ambass and Br dep permanent rep to United Nations1986-89, ambass Hungary 1989-; *Recreations* skiing, tennis; *Clubs* Athenaeum; *Style—* John Birch, Esq; Foreign and Commonwealth Office, London SW1)

BIRCH, John Anthony; s of Charles Aylmer Birch (d 1966), of Leek, Staffs, and Mabel, *née* Greenwood (d 1971); *b* 9 July 1929; *Educ* Trent Coll Notts, RCM; *Career* Nat Serv RCS 1949-50; organist and choirmaster St Thomas's Church Regent St 1950-53, accompanist St Michael's singers 1952-58, organist and choirmaster All Saints Church Margaret St London 1953-58, sub-organist HM Chapels Royal 1957-58, organist and master of the choristers Chichester Cathedral 1958-80, prof RCM 1959-, re-established the Southern Cathedrals Festival with Cathedral Organists of Salibsbury and Winchester 1960, musical advsr Chichester Festival Theatre 1962-80, choirmaster Bishop Other Coll Chichester 1963-69, accompanist Royal Choral Soc 1965-70 (organist 1966-), md CA Birch Ltd Staffs 1966-73 (rep 1950-66), Univ organist Univ of Sussex 1967- (visiting lectr in music 1971-83), special cmmr Royal Sch of Church Music, organist and choir dir Temple Church 1982-, organist & Royal Philharmonic Orchestra 1983-, curator-organist royal Albert Hall 1984-; concert appearances: Frnace, Belgium, Germany, Switzerland, Netherlands, Spain, Portugal, Scandavnavia, Far E; recital Tours: Canada and US 1966 and 1967, Aust and NZ 1969, SA 1978; examiner assoc bd Royal Schs of Music 1958-77, fell Corpn of SS Mary and Nicolas (Woodard Schs) 1973-, govr Hurstpierpoint Coll 1974-, govr St Catherine's Bramley 1981-, pres RCO 1984-86 (memb cncl 1964-); hon MA Univ of Sussex 1971; ARCM, LRAM, FRCM 1981, FRCO (chm); *Recreations* collecting pictures; *Clubs* Garrick; *Style—* John Birch, Esq; 13 King's Bench Walk, Temple, London EC4Y 7EN (☎ 01 353 5115); Fielding House, The Close, Salisbury, Wilts SP1 2EB (☎ 0722 412 458)

BIRCH, John Richard; s of Cedric Ronald Birch, of 36 Gervase Drive, Dudley, W Mids, and Joan Mary, *née* Stafford; *b* 1 April 1945; *Educ* Dudley GS, Birmingham Univ; *m* 17 Aug 1968, Maureen May, da of John Thomas Sanders, of Netherton, W Mids; 1 da (Amanada Jayne b 3 April 1971); *Career* Br Fed Ltd: tech sales mangr 1976-81, electronics dir 1981-84, md 1984-; 1975: C ENG, MIEE, MIERE; *Recreations* golf; *Style—* John Birch, Esq; 9 St Johns Close, Swindon, Dudley, W Mids DY3 4PQ (☎ 0384 279592); British Federation Ltd, Castle Mill Works, Dudley, W Mid, DT1 4DA (☎ 0384 455400, 459400 night, fax 0384 455554, telex 337416)

BIRCH, Peter Gibbs; s of William Birch (d 1971), and Gladys Birch, *née* Gibbs (d 1971); *b* 4 Dec 1937; *Educ* Allhallows Sch; *m* 17 March 1962, Gillian Heather, da of Leonard Brade Sale Benge; 3 s (James b 1964, Simon b 1967, Alexander b 1970), 1 da (Sophie b 1972); *Career* Nat Serv 2 Lt, Royal West Kent Regiment 1956-58; Nestle UK, Switzerland, Singapore Malaysia 1958-65; marketing positions Gillette 1965-68, Gillette Australia (Melbourne) 1969-71; gen mangr: Gillette New Zealand 1971-73, Gillette South East Asia 1973-75; gp gen mangr Gillette Eastern Europe 1975-81, md Gillette (UK) 1981-84, chief exec Abbey National 1984-; *Recreations* swimming, wind surfing, cycling, skiing; *Style—* Peter Birch, Esq; Abbey National Building Soc, Baker St, London NW1 (☎ 01 486 5555)

BIRCH, Robin Arthur; s of Arthur Birch, and Olive Birch; *b* 12 Oct 1939; *Educ* King Henry VIII Sch Coventry, Christ Church Oxford (MA); *m* 15 Dec 1962, Jane Marion Irvine, da of Vivian Sturdy (d 1965); 2 s (David b 1965, Michael b 1967); *Career* Civil Serv: princ Miny of Health 1966-69 (asst princ 1961-66), seconded Interdepartmental Social Work Gp 1969-70, Home Office 1970-72, asst sec DHSS 1973, princ private sec to Leader of House of Commons 1980-81, under sec DHSS 1982, seconded NAO as asst auditor gen (under sec) 1984-86, dir regnl orgn DSS 1988-; hon sec: Friends of Christ Church Cathedral Oxford 1978-; *Recreations* family and friends, books, listening to music; *Clubs* Oxford Union; *Style*— Robin Birch, Esq; DSS, Room 1008A, Euston Tower, 286 Euston Rd, London NW1 3DN (☎ 01 388 1188, ext 3474)

BIRCH, Roger; CBE (1987), QPM (1980); s of John Edward Lawrence Birch (d 1981), and Ruby Birch; *b* 27 Sept 1930; *Educ* Teignmouth GS, Torquay GS, King's Coll Taunton; *m* Jeanne Margaret, da of Herbert Ernest Head (d 1976); 1 s (Steven); *Career* Pilot Offr RAF Canada 1950-52; under mangr family retail business 1952-54; joined Police 1954, chief supt CID and Uniform Branch 1954-72, asst chief constable Mid Anglia Constabulary 1972, dep ch constable of Kent 1974, chief constable: Warwickshire 1978, Sussex 1983; dir Police Extended Interviews; vice pres of ACPO 1986/87; UK vice-pres The Royal Life Saving Soc (chm SE Region); tstee: Police Dependants Tst, Gurney Fund for Police Orphans; memb: cncl of the Inst of Advanced Motorists, Guild of Experienced Motorists; lectr Cambridge Univ Bd of Extra-Mural Studies on Police Subjects; FBIM; *Recreations* swimming, music; *Clubs* RAF; *Style*— Roger Birch, Esq, CBE, QPM; Sussex Police HQ, Malling Hse, Lewes, E Sussex (☎ 0273 475432)

BIRCH REYNARDSON, Major Richard Francis; s of Lt Col Henry Thomas Birch Reynardson, CMG (d 1979), of Oxon, and late Diana Helen Ponsonby; Sir Jacob Reynardson, Lord Mayor of London during Civil War; *b* 26 Sept 1926; *Educ* Eton; *m* 18 June 1951, Mary, da of Major Sir John Crocker Bulteel, KCVO, DSO, MC (d 1955), of Berks; 1 s (Charles Crocker b 1963), 2 da (Sara b 1952, Marie-Therese b 1960); *Career* ADC to C in C Far East Land Forces 1948-49, PA to chm Combined Chiefs of Staff Pentagon 1949-51; dir Goddard Kay Rogers and Associates; *Recreations* shooting, fishing; *Clubs* Whites, The Turf, Pratts; *Style*— Major Richard F Birch Reynardson, Esq; The Stables, Brailes House, Brailes Banbury, Oxon; Old London House, 32 St James's Square, London SW1 (☎ 01 930 5100)

BIRCH REYNARDSON, William Robert Ashley; s of Lt-Col Henry Thomas Birch Reynardson, CMG (d 1972), and his 1 w Diana Helen, *née* Ponsonby (d 1962); *b* 7 Dec 1923; *Educ* Eton, Ch Ch Oxford; *m* 30 Nov 1950, (Pamela) Matnika, da of Lt-Gen Sir (Edward) Thomas Humphreys, KCB, CMG, DSO; 1 s (Thomas), 2 da (Juliet (Mrs Stewart- Brown), Clare (Mrs Hopkinson)); *Career* cmmnd 9 QR Lancers 1941, served in N Africa and Italy; barr Inner Temple 1950; sr ptnr and chm Thomas Miller, ret 1987; dir Graham Miller & Co; hon sec Br Maritime Law Assoc, vice-pres Comité Maritime Int; High Sheriff of Oxfordshire 1974-75; past memb Bullingdon RDC; *Recreations* hunting, shooting, painting, gardening; *Clubs* Cavalry and Guards', Pratt's, City of London; *Style*— William Birch Reynardson, Esq; Adwell House, Tetsworth, Oxfordshire OX9 7DQ (☎ 084 428 204); 111 Marsham Court, Marsham Street, London SW1 (☎ 01 630 1191)

BIRCHALL, Mark Dearman; s of Maj Peter Dearman Birchall, CBE, and Susan Auriol Charrington (d 1972); *b* 26 July 1933; *Educ* Eton, Trinity Coll Oxford; *m* 6 July 1962, Helen Iona, da of Capt Alexander Francis Matheson (d 1976), of Conon Bridge, Ross-Shire; 1 s (John b 1970), 2 da Clare (b 1965, Katharine b 1967); *Career* Nat Service 1951-53; stockbroker 1956-82 ptnr Mullens and Co 1966-82; memb Gen Synod 1980-, chm Mayflower Family Centre; dir: Careerplan 1973-, Christian Weekly Newspapers Ltd 1979-, Lella plc 1984-; *Books* The Gospel Community and its Leadership (with John Tiller 1987); *Recreations* wild flowers, walking; *Style*— Mark D Birchall, Esq; 3 Melrose Road, London SW18 1ND

BIRD; *see*: Martin Bird

BIRD, Rev Dr Anthony Peter; s of Rev Prebendary Albert Harry Bird (d 1986), and Noel Whitehouse, *née* Oakley (d 1940); *b* 2 Mar 1931; *Educ* St John's Sch Leatherhead, St John's Coll Oxford (BA, MA), Birmingham Univ (MB, ChB); *m* 29 Sept 1962 (m dis 1981), Sabine, *née* Boehmig; 2 s (Markus b 1963, Dominic b 1973), 1 da (Stephanie b 1965); *Career* Nat Serv 1949-50, cmmnd RASC; ordained Lichfield Cath: deacon 1957, priest 1958; asst curate St Mary's Stafford 1957-60, chaplain and vice princ Cuddesdon Theol Coll 1960-64; medical practitioner Hosp Appts 1970-71, gen practitioner Birmingham 1972-73; princ Queen's Theol Coll Birmingham 1974-79, recognized lectr Dept of Theol Birmingham Univ 1974-; gen practitioner Balsall Heath Birmingham 1979-; memb Advsy Ctee on Sexual Offences 1976-80, Parole Bd memb 1978-80; Freedom of Information Campaign Award 1987; *Books* The Search for Health: A Response from the Inner City (1981); *Recreations* swimming, walking, music, reading; *Style*— The Rev Dr Anthony Bird; 93 Bournbrook Rd, Birmingham B29 7BX; Edward Rd Health Centre, 43 Edward Rd, Birmingham B12 9JB (☎ 021 440 2574)

BIRD, Hon Mrs (Catherine Mary); da of 15 Baron Dormer (d 1975); *b* 2 April 1950; *m* 1973, Christopher J G Bird; *Style*— The Hon Mrs Bird; 45 Addison Ave, London W11

BIRD, (George) Eric; s of Capt George Albert Bird (d 1965), of Kenton, Middx, and Winifred Fanny, *née* Hood (d 1973); *b* 9 Nov 1913; *Educ* Harrow GS, RMC Sandhurst; *m* 11 May 1968, Adrienne Sandra, da of Haydn Alexander King, of Canons Park, Edgware, Middx; 1 s (Alexander Hamilton b 1969); *Career* RTR; dir Claudius Ash Sons and Co (USA) Inc 1947-52, dir Amalgamated Dental Co Ltd 1954-77, patent and trademark consit 1977-; tstee Morse-Boycott Bursary Fund, govr Felpham Community Coll, memb PROBUS, memb Arundel CC, memb Chichester Festival Theatre; Arun dist cncllr; *Recreations* theatre-going, ecclesiology, reading; *Style*— Eric Bird, Esq; 3 Glynde Cres, Felpham, Bognor Regis, West Sussex PO22 8T (☎ 0243 867171)

BIRD, Brig Garth Raymond Godrey; s of Herbert William Bird Norther (d 1945), of Surrey, and Nora Constance Shaw, *née* Vernon (d 1957); *b* 4 Sept 1909; *Educ* Stonyhurst Coll, RMC Sandhurst; *m* 19 Sept 1942, Elizabeth Mary Vavasour, da of the late Sir Leonard Vavasour Bart (Capt RN) 2 s (Christopher b 1946, Anthony b 1952), 1 da (Fiona b 1953), 1 step s (Simon De La Walters b 1941); *Career* regular army: The Sherwood Foresters 1929-52; WWII 1939-45 serv: N Africa, Italy; Army Interpretships: French, Italian; military attaché, Col, British Embassy Belgrade 1952-55, brig 1956, CO Bde 1956-59, dep CO Home Counties Dist 1959-62; ADC to HM The Queen 1959-62; exec Brit Nat Export Cncl 1962-72; *Recreations* hunting, shooting; *Clubs* Naval and Military; *Style*— Brig Garth R G Bird; Oast House, Gt Broadhurst Broad Oak, Heathfield, E Sussex TN21 8UX; Lloyds, Cox and Kings, 6 Pall Mall, London SW1

BIRD, Harold Dennis (Dickie); MBE (1986); s of James Harold Bird (d 1969), and Ethel Bird, *née* Smith (d 1978); *b* 19 April 1933; *Educ* Raley Sch Barnsley; *Career* Test and World Cup Final cricket umpire (the only man to umpire 3 World Cup finals: W Indies v Australia Lord's 1975, W Indies v England Lord's 1979, and W Indies v India Lord's 1983); has umpired 110 int cricket matches and 43 test matches and many other cricketing events (inc Gillett, Nat West and Benson and Hedges Cup Finals); Yorkshire Personality of the Year 1977; *Books* Not Out (1978), That's Out (1985); *Clubs* Lord's Taverners; *Style*— Dickie Bird Esq, MBE; White Rose Cottage, 40 Paddock Rd, Staincross, Barnsley, Yorks (☎ 0226 384491); Test and County Cricket Board, Lords Cricket Ground, London NW8 8QN (☎ 01 286 4405)

BIRD, James Gurth; MBE (1945), TD (1951); s of Charles Harold Bird (d 1923), of Harrogate, and Alice Jane, *née* Kirtland (d 1964); *b* 30 Jan 1909; *Educ* King William's Coll IOM, St Catharine's Coll Cambridge (MA); *m* 1940, Phyllis Ellis, da of Charles Llewelyn Pownall (d 1937); 1 s (Richard), 2 da (Pamela, Gillian); *Career* Maj, India, Paiforce, Sicily, Italy; sch master and head master William Hulme's GS 1947-74; *Recreations* golf, gardening; *Style*— James Bird, Esq, MBE, TD; Ty Deryn, Ravenspoint Road, Trearddur Bay, Holyhead, Gwynedd LL65 2AX (☎ 0407 860178)

BIRD, John Andrew; s and h of Sir Richard Bird, 4 Bt; *b* 19 Jan 1964; *Style*— John Bird Esq

BIRD, Capt Lionel Armitage; LVO (1972); s of George Armitage Bird (d 1976), and Noreen Phyllis Bird, *née* Bailey (d 1967); *b* 6 Oct 1928; *Educ* RNC Dartmouth; *m* 17 Aug 1957, Barbara Jane, da of Scott Henry (d 1963); 1 s (Simon b 1960), 1 da (Amanda b 1961); *Career* HM Yacht Britannia 1970-72; naval attaché Paris 1973-75; CO HMS Fearless 1974-77; lectr: Brit Atlantic Ctee, Peace through NATO; former chm: combined services FA, RN FA (life memb); first class Football referee; church warden; FBIM; *Recreations* fishing, cricket, golf, gardening, horse racing (syndicate owner); *Clubs* RN CC; *Style*— Capt Lionel A Bird, LVO; Manor Farmhouse, Trent, Sherborne, Dorset DT9 4SW (☎ (0935) 850 576)

BIRD, Sir Richard Geoffrey Chapman; 4 Bt (UK 1922); s of Sir Donald Geoffrey Bird, 3 Bt (d 1963); *b* 3 Nov 1935; *Educ* Beaumont; *m* 1, 1957, Gillian Frances (d 1966), da of Bernard Haggett; 2 s, 4 da; m 2, 1968, Helen Patricia, da of Frank Beaumont, of Pontefract; *Heir* s, John Andrew Bird b 19 Jan 1964; *Style*— Sir Richard Bird, Bt; 39 Ashleigh Road, Solihull, W Midlands B91 1AF

BIRD, Richard Herries; CB (1983); s of Edgar Clarence Frederick Bird and Armorel, *née* Dudley-Scott; *b* 8 June 1932; *Educ* Winchester Coll, Clare Coll Cambridge (BA); *m* 1963, (Margaret) Valerie, da of Edward Robson Sanderson: 2 da (Caroline b 1964, Julia b 1966); *Career* joined Civil Service 1955, private sec to perm sec Miny of Tport 1958-60, pps to min Tport 1966-67, under-sec Dept of Educn and Science 1975-80, dep sec (higher and further educn and science) DES 1980-; *Recreations* music, reading, gardening; *Clubs* Reform; *Style*— Richard Bird Esq, CB; Department of Education and Science, Elizabeth House, London SE1 7PH (☎ 01 934 9956, telex 23171)

BIRD, Thomas Arthur; DSO (1942), MC (and bar 1941); s of Arthur Wheen Bird (d 1953), of Crockmore, Fawley, Henley-on-Thames, and Eveline Mary, *née* Huggins (d 1950); *b* 11 August 1918; *Educ* Winchester, Architectural Assoc Sch of Architecture (Dip AA); *m* 9 March 1946, Alice Hunsaker, da of Prof Jerome Clarke Hunsaker (d 1984), of Louisburg Square, Boston, Mass, USA; 2 s (Antony b 1947, Nicholas b 1948), 1 da (Sarah (Mrs Squires) b 1956); *Career* WWII 2 Bn RB in ME (wounded 3 times) 1939-43, ADC to Field Marshal Lord Wavell in India (Maj) 1943, 2 i/c 8 Bn RB in NW Europe (wounded) 1944, ADC to Field Marshal Lord Wilson in Washington (Maj) 1945; fndr ptnr Bird and Tyler Assocs (architects) London and Cambridge 1952-85, practising from home at Turville Heath House Henley-On-Thames 1985-; High Sheriff of Bucks 1989; RIBA 1949; *Recreations* shooting, gardening, tennis, drawing; *Clubs* Boodles; *Style*— Thomas Bird, Esq, DSO, MC; Turville Heath House, Turville Heath, Henley-On-Thames (☎ 049163 331)

BIRD, Rt Hon Vere Cornwall; PC (1982); *b* 7 Dec 1910; *Educ* St John's Boys' Sch Antigua, Salvation Army Training Sch Trinidad; *Career* memb Executive Antigua Trades and Labour Union (ATL and U) 1939- and pres 1943-67, memb Antigua Legislative Cncl 1945 and memb Exec Cncl 1946, ctee chm Exec Cncl 1951-56 (in which capacity instituted Peasant Devpt Scheme, whereby land was redistributed and development loans were made possible), min Trade and Production 1956, first chief minister Antigua 1960, co-founder Caribbean Free Trade Assoc 1965, first premier Antigua 1967-71 (when lost seat in Parliament); MP (Antigua) 1976, first pm of Antigua and Barbuda 1981-; *Style*— The Rt Hon Vere Bird Snr.; Office of the Prime Minister, Antigua and Barbuda, West Indies

BIRD-WILSON, Air Vice-Marshal Harold Arthur Cooper (Birdy); CBE (1962), DSO (1944, DFC 1940, bar 1943, AFC 1946, bar 1955); s of Harold Bird-Wilson (d 1957), and Victoria Mabel, *née* Cooper; *b* 20 Nov 1919; *Educ* Liverpool Coll; *m* 21 March 1942, Audrey, da of Robert James Wallace, MVO, OBE (d 1963); 1 s (Robert Stuart b 30 Nov 1943), 1 da (Caryl b 22 June 1945); *Career* joined RAF 1937, 17 Fighter Sqdn Kenley 1938, WW II served France, Dunkirk and Battle of Britain, Flt Cdr 234 Spitfire Sqdn 1941 (despatches) Sqdn Ldr 152 Sqdn then 66 Sqdn 1942, Wing Ldr 83 Gp 1943, chm and gen Staff Sch Fort Leavenworth USA 1944, Wing Ldr Harrowbeer Spitfire Wing later Bradwell Bay and Mustang Fighter wing at Bentwaters 1944-45, CO first jet conversion unit 1945-46, CO air fighting devpt sqdn Central Fighter Estab 1946-47, Ops Staff HQ MEAF 1948, RAF Staff Col 1949, personal SO to C in C MEAF 1949-50, RAF Flying Coll Manby 1951, OC tactics (later AFDS), Central Fighter Estab 1952-54, staff BJSM Washington USA 1954-57, staff air sec dept Air Miny 1957-59, CO RAF Coltishall 1959-61, staff intelligence Air Miny 1961-63, AOC and Cmdt Central Flying Sch 1963-65, AOC Hong Kong 1965-67, dir of flying R & D Miny of Technol 1967-70, AOC 23 Gp 1970-73, cdr S Maritime Air Region Mount Batten 1973-74, ret 1974; dep chief exec Br Aircraft Corpn Riyad, Saudi Arabia 1974-76, mil liaison Br Aerospace, ret; 1984 Czechoslovak Medal of Merit first class 1945, Dutch DFC 1945; *Clubs* RAF; *Style*— Air Vice-Marshal Harold Bird-Wilson, CBE, DSO, DFC, AFC; Whytecroft, Gong Hill Drive, Lower Bourne, Farnham, Surrey GU10 3HQ

BIRDWOOD, Dowager Lady; Joan Pollock; *née* Graham; da of Christopher Norman Graham, of Ealing; *m* 22 Feb 1954, as his 2 w, 2 Baron Birdwood, MVO (d 1962); *Career* independent patriot candidate Bermondsey By-Election 1983; *Style*— The Rt Hon the Dowager Lady Birdwood; 114 Gunnersbury Ave, London W5

BIRDWOOD, 3 Baron (UK 1938), of Anzac and of Totnes, Devon; Sir Mark William Ogilvie Birdwood; 3 Bt (UK 1919); s of 2 Baron, MVO (d 1962), and Elizabeth) Vere Drummond, CVO, da of Lt-Col Sir George Drummond Ogilvie, KCIE, CSI; *b* 23 Nov 1938; *Educ* Radley, Trinity Coll Cambridge; *m* 27 April 1963, Judith Helen, er da of Reginald Gordon Seymour Roberts; 1 da (m 1987 Earl of Woolton, *qv*); *Career* former 2 Lt RHG; J Walter Thompson Cambridge Consits, vice-pres Boyden Int, Wrightson Wood (md 1984), chm: Martlet Ltd 1986-, MHG Advertising Ltd

1987-; dir: Du Pont Pixel Systems Ltd (formerly Benchmark Technol), Comac plc, Scientific Generics Ltd 1989; *Clubs* Brooks's; *Style*— The Rt Hon the Lord Birdwood; Russell House, Broadway, Worcs WR12 79V; 5 Holbein Mews, London SW1 W8NW

BIRDWOOD, Lt-Col Richard Douglas Davis; MC (1942), JP ((Devon 1964), DL (1964)); s of Lt-Col Gordon Birdwood (d 1945); *b* 5 Jan 1905; *Educ* Clifton, Peterhouse Cambridge (MA); *m* 1930, Phyllis, JP, da of Lt-Col Sir Thomas Bilbe-Robinson, GBE, KCMG (d 1939); 2 s, 1 da; *Career* High Sheriff Devon 1962, Mayor Bideford 1963; pres: Torrington Farmers' Hunt, Devon County Agric Assoc 1970, Royal North Devon Golf Club 1977, Appledore Branch RNLI; Hon Freeman Borough of Bideford 1972; *Recreations* fishing, golf; *Style*— Lt-Col Richard Birdwood, MC, JP, DL; Horwood House, Horwood, Bideford, Devon (☎ 0271 185 231)

BIRDWOOD, Vere, Baroness; (Elizabeth) Vere Drummond; CVO (1972, MVO 1958); da of Lt-Col Sir George Drummond Ogilvie, KCIE, CSI (d 1966); *b* 7 August 1909; *m* 7 March 1931 (m dis 1954), 2 Baron Birdwood, MVO (d 1962); 1 s, 1 da; *Career* administrator King Edward VII's Hosp for Offs 1950-72, ed Public Record Off 1972-; vice-chm Provident Assoc for Med Care 1977-82 (bd memb 1958-82); memb Area AHA: Westminster, Kensington, Chelsea 1973-76; memb Chelsea Borough cncl 1954-60; *Style*— Vere, Lady Birdwood, CVO, MVO; 11 Whitelands House, Cheltenham Terrace, London SW3

BIRK, Baroness (Life Peer UK 1967); Alma Lillian Birk; JP (Highgate 1952); da of late Barnett Wilson, of London, and Alice, *née* Tosh; *Educ* S Hampstead HS, LSE; *m* 1939, Ellis Samuel Birk, *qv*; 1 s, 1 da; *Career* sits as Lab Peer in House of Lords; memb Fabian Soc 1946-; contested (Lab) Ruislip-Northwood 1950 and Portsmouth West 1951 and 1955; former lectr and visitor Holloway Prison, assoc ed Nova 1965-69, memb London Pregnancy Advsy Service 1968-; a baroness-in-waiting to HM 1974, under-sec of state DOE 1974-79, min of state Privy Cncl Office 1979; govr and tstee Raymond Mander and Joe Mitchenson Theatre Collection, dir New Shakespeare Co 1979-; tstee: Balfour Diamond Jubilee 1982-, Jerusalem Fndn 1982-, Health Promotion Research 1983-, Stress Syndrome Fndn 1983-; vice-pres Family Planning Assoc 1983-; oppn spokesman (Lords) Environment 1983-86, Arts Heritage Broadcasting 1986-; govr Br Film Inst 1980-87; memb Cncl RSA 1983-87; FRSA; *Recreations* theatre, travelling, trying to relax; *Style*— The Rt Hon the Lady Birk, JP; 3 Wells Rise, Regents Park, London NW8 7LH (☎ 01 722 6226)

BIRK, Dr David Barry Wilson; o s of Baroness Birk (Life Peeress) and Ellis Samuel Birk; *b* 25 June 1943; *Educ* Clifton, Cambridge Univ, Univ of Hull, Univ Coll London, Australian Nat Univ; *m* 1969, Kate, da of Joseph Green, of London NW8; 3 da; *Style*— Dr David Birk; 28 Charlbury Road, Oxford OX2 6UU

BIRK, Ellis Samuel; s of Barnett Birk, of London and Newcastle; *b* 30 Oct 1915; *Educ* Clifton Coll, Jesus Coll Cambridge; *m* 1939, Baroness Birk (Life Peer), *qv*; 1 s, 1 da; *Career* slr 1945; conslt Nicholson, Graham and Jones; chm Jewish Chronicle 1987-, dir Bank Leumi (UK) 1982-; chm Cental Independent Television Pension Fund Tstees 1985-; *Clubs* Garrick, Royal Automobile; *Style*— Ellis Birk Esq; 3 Wells Rise, Regents Park, London NW8 7LH; c/o Nicholson Graham and Jones, 19-21 Moorgate, London EC2 (☎ 01 628 9151)

BIRKBECK, Capt Henry; DL; eldest s of Maj Henry Anthony Birkbeck, MC, JP, DL (d 1956), of Westacre High House; bro of William Birkbeck, *qv*; *b* 15 Nov 1915; *Educ* Eton, Magdalene Coll Cambridge; *m* 1939, Nadine Mary, da of Maj Francis Wilfred Gore-Langton (d 1931), of Tingewick, Buckingham; 1 s, 4 da; *Career* Capt Gren Gds, landowner and farmer; *Recreations* ornithology, shooting, fishing; *Clubs* Cavalry and Guards'; *Style*— Capt Henry Birkbeck, DL; Westacre High House, Castleacre, King's Lynn, Norfolk (☎ 076 05 203)

BIRKBECK, John Oliver Charles; yr s of Col Oliver Birkbeck (d 1952) and Lady Joan Cator, *qv*; *b* 22 June 1936; *Educ* Gordonstoun, Cirencester; *m* 2 May 1964, Hermione Anne, o da of Maj D'Arcy Dawes (d 1967), of Leacon Hall, Warehorne, Ashford, Kent; 1 s (Oliver b 1973), 2 da (Lucy b 1966, Roseanna b 1974); *Career* chm Breckland Dist Cncl 1987-88 (memb from 1969), memb Norfolk County Cncl 1970-; *Clubs* Norfolk, Whites; *Style*— John Birkbeck, Esq; Litcham Hall, Kings Lynn, Norfolk PE32 2QQ (☎ 0328 701 389)

BIRKBECK, Mark Nigel Thomas; s of Capt Maurice Birkbeck (d 1972), and Billie, *née* Hoyland,; *b* 02 July 1948; *Educ* Eshton Hall Yorks; *m* Linda Mary, da of William Hird, of Fern Croft, Casterton, Kirkby Lonsdale; 2 s (Patrick Mark b 14 Dec 1972, Tom Mackenzie b 19 March 1985), 2 da (Alexandra Robin b 18 June 1976, Georgina Amy b 27 Jan 1983); *Career* chm Mark Birkbeck & Co (Westmorland Wollens, estab 1971), Jumpers Ltd (retail div), Sheepskin Warehouse Shops Ltd (retail div); *Recreations* fishing, shooting, rugby; *Style*— Mark Birkbeck, Esq; Low Gale, Cowan Bridge, Carnforth, Lancs (☎ 0468 715 42); Strathulchan, Advie, nr Grantown on Spey, Morayshire; Bridge Mill, Cowan Bridge, Carnforth, Lancs (☎ 0468 710 71, fax 0468 720 58, car tel 0836 523 967, telex 65109 MB CO G)

BIRKBECK, Hon Mrs (Mary); *née* Crossley; JP (1966, Huntingdon and Peterborough); o da of 2 Baron Somerleyton, MC (d 1959), and Bridget, MBE, JP, *née* Hoare; *b* 3 Feb 1926; *m* 7 July 1950, Maj William Birkbeck, DL, Coldstream Guards (ret), yst s of late Maj Henry Anthony Birkbeck, MC, JP, DL, of Westacre, Norfolk; 1 s, 3 da; *Style*— The Hon Mrs Birkbeck, JP; Bainton House, Stamford, Lincs, (☎ 740227)

BIRKBECK, William; DL (Huntingdon and Peterborough 1965, subsequently Cambs); yst s of Maj Henry Anthony Birkbeck, MC, JP, DL (d 1956), of Westacre High House, Norfolk, and Sybil, *née* Harley (d 1948); bro of Capt Henry Birkbeck, *qv*; *b* 13 April 1922; *Educ* Eton; *m* 7 July 1950, Hon Mary Crossley, JP, *qv*, o da of 2 Baron Somerleyton, MC; 1 s, 3 da; *Career* Coldstream Gds 1941-57, Maj; banker: dir Barclays Bank 1970-86, Bank of Scotland 1971-85; *Recreations* country sports; *Clubs* Army and Navy; *Style*— Maj William Birkbeck, DL; Bainton House, Stamford, Lincs (☎ 740227)

BIRKENHEAD, Bishop of, 1974-; Rt Rev Ronald Brown; s of Fred Brown (d 1977), and Ellen, *née* Billington (d 1969); *b* 7 August 1926; *Educ* Kirkham GS, St John's Coll, Durham Univ (BA DipTheol); *m* 14 July 1951, Joyce (d 1987), da of William Hymers (d 1955); 1 s (Laurence Frederick Mark b 1953), 1 da (Janet Elizabeth b 1956); *Career* vicar: Whittle-le-Woods Lancs 1956-61, St Thomas' Halliwell Bolton 1961-70; rector and rural dean Ashton-under-Lyne Lancs 1970-74, bishop of Birkenhead 1974; *Recreations* DIY activities, antiques; *Style*— The Rt Rev the Bishop of Birkenhead; Trafford House, Victoria Crescent, Queen's Park, Chester CH4 7AX (☎ 0244 675895)

BIRKENHEAD, Countess of; Hon Sheila; *née* Berry; DL (Northants 1979); da of 1 Visc Camrose; *b* 3 May 1913; *m* 1935, 2 Earl of Birkenhead, TD (d 1985, extinct); 1 da; (1 s dec'd); *Career* authoress, lady-in-waiting to HRH Princess Marina Duchess of Kent 1949-53, chm Northants Branch CPRE 1975-, vice-pres RSL 1975-, chm Keats-Shelley Assoc 1977-; *Recreations* reading, gardening, watching tennis; *Style*— The Rt Hon The Countess of Birkenhead DL; 24 Wilton St, SW1 (☎ 01 235 4111); Charlton, Banbury, Oxon (☎ (0295) 811224)

BIRKETT, Brig John Brian; OBE (1958); s of John Guy Giberne Birkett (d 1967), of Cambrian House, Burgess Hill, Sussex; *b* 2 Oct 1916; *Educ* Marlborough, RMA Woolwich; *m* 1941, Emily Margaret, da of John Higginson; 1 da, 1 s (and 1 s decd); *Career* served in WW II, France, Belgium and Germany; Lt-Col 1958, Brig 1966; Brigadier General Staff Ministry of Defence 1966-69; dir Trade Association 1969-83; Master Worshipful Co of Ironmongers 1974; *Recreations* active outdoor occupations; *Clubs* Army and Navy, Boodle's, Harlequin FC, MCC; *Style*— Brig Brian Birkett, OBE; West Tillingham House, Upper Hartfield, Sussex

BIRKETT, 2 Baron (UK 1958); Michael Birkett; s of 1 Baron Birkett (d 1962); *b* 22 Oct 1929; *Educ* Stowe, Trinity Coll Cambridge; *m* 1, 10 Oct 1960, Mrs Junia Crawford (d 1973), da of Harold Elliott; m 2, 1978, Gloria, da of Thomas Taylor, of Queen's Gate, London SW; 1 s; *Heir* s, Hon Thomas Birkett b 25 July 1982; *Career* film prodr 1961-: productions incl: The Caretaker, Marat/Sade, A Midsummer Night's Dream, King Lear; dep dir Nat Theatre 1975-77, conslt to Nat Theatre on films, TV and sponsorship 1977-79, dir Recreation and the Arts GLC 1979-86; Master Worshipful Co of Curriers' 1975-76; *Recreations* the arts; *Style*— The Rt Hon The Lord Birkett; House of Lords, London SW1

BIRKIN, (John) Derek; TD (1965); s of Noah Birkin, and Rebecca, *née* Stranks; *b* 30 Sept 1929; *Educ* Hemsworth GS; *m* 1 April 1952, Sadie, da of Ernest Wade-Smith; 1 s (Michael b 16 April 1957), 1 da (Alison (Mrs Lear) b 16 July 1958); *Career* 2 Lt RA (nat serv) 1948-50; Maj TA; md: Velmar Ltd 1966-67, Nairn Williamson Ltd 1967-70, Tunnel Holdings Ltd 1971-75; chm and md Tunnel Holdings Ltd 1975-83; dir: The Rio Tinto-Zinc Corpn 1982- (dep ch exec 1983-85, ch exec and dep chm 1985-), Smiths Industries Ltd 1977-84, British Gas Corpn 1982-85, George Wimpey plc 1984-, CRA Ltd (Australia) 1985-, Rio Algom Ltd (Canada) 1985-, British Steel Corpn 1986-, The Merchants Trust plc 1986-; memb: Cncl of The Industrial Soc 1985-, Top Salaries Review Bd 1986-; CBIM 1980, FRSA 1988; *Recreations* opera, rugby, cricket; *Clubs* MCC, Harlequins; *Style*— Derek Birkin, Esq, TD; The RTZ Corporation plc, 6 St James's Sq, London SW1Y 4LD (☎ 01 930 2399, fax 01 930 3249, telex 24639 RTZLDN G)

BIRKIN, Sir John Christian William; 6 Bt (UK 1905), of Ruddington Grange, Notts; o s of Sir Charles Birkin, 5 Bt (d 1985), and Janet Ramsay, *née* Johnson; *b* 1 July 1953; *Educ* Eton; *Heir* Kinsman, James Francis Richard Birkin b 27 Feb 1957; *Career* BBC tv, dir Compound Eye Productions; *Style*— Sir John Birkin, Bt; 23 St Luke's St, London SW3 5RP (☎ 01 351 4810)

BIRKMYRE, Archibald; s and h of Sir Henry Birkmyre, 2 Bt; *b* 12 Feb 1923; *Educ* Radley; *m* 1953, Gillian Mary, o da of late Eric M Downes, OBE; 1 s, 2 da (*see* Hon John Fellowes); *Career* Capt RA Burma 1941-45; memb London Stock Exchange; *Recreations* golf, shooting, fishing; *Clubs* Boodle's, Swinley Forest, Geoff; *Style*— Archibald Birkmyre, Esq; The Old Presbytery, Buckland, Faringdon, Oxon, SN7 8QW, (☎ 036 787253)

BIRKMYRE, Sir Henry; 2 Bt (UK 1921), of Dalmunzie, Co Perth; s of Sir Archibald Birkmyre, 1 Bt, CBE (d 1935); *b* 24 Mar 1898; *Educ* Wellington; *m* 1922, Doris Gertrude, da of Col Herbert Austen Smith, CIE (d 1949); 1 s, 1 da; *Heir* s, Archibald Birkmyre; *Career* serv WW I with RFA in France; former co dir; *Recreations* golf; *Clubs* Rye Golf, Cooden Beach Golf; *Style*— Sir Henry Birkmyre, Bt; Tudor Rest, 2 Calvely Park Gardens, Tunbridge Wells, Kent TN1 2JW

BIRKS, George Teasdale; *b* 13 Sept 1932; *Career* sr dir Phillips and Drew (stockbrokers); memb Stock Exchange 1961 (ret); *Style*— George Birks, Esq; Bockmer House, Medmenham, nr Marlow, Bucks SL7 2HL

BIRKS, Dr Jack; CBE (1975); s of Herbert Horace Birks (d 1950), and Ann Birks; *b* 1 Jan 1920; *Educ* Ecclesfield GS, Leeds Univ (BSc, PhD); *m* 1948, Vere Elizabeth, da of Barnard Burrell-Davis (d 1960); 2 s, 2 da; *Career* engr; md BP 1978-82 (ret); chm: Charterhouse Petroleum plc 1982-86, NMI Ltd 1982-85, BMT 1985-, Mountain Petroleum 1988-; dir: Wimpey Gp 1982-, Jebsons Drilling 1982-, Petrofina (UK) 1986-, Bellwether Exploration Co 1988-, BP Minerals Int 1982-85, London American Energy NV 1982-88, Mountain Petroleum 1985-; memb: SRC 1976-80, Meteorological Ctee 1977-82, cncl Surrey Univ 1982-87, Maritime League 1982-86, Royal Instn 1982-85 and 1988-; pres Institute of Petroleum 1984-86; Hon LLD: Aberdeen 1981, Surrey 1981; CEng, FEng, FIMM, FInstPet, FIMechE; *Recreations* golf, tennis; *Clubs* Athenaeum; *Style*— Dr Jack Birks, CBE; British Maritime Technology Ltd, Orlando House, Waldegrave Rd, Teddington, Middlesex TW11 8LZ (☎ 01 943 5544); 1a Alwyne Rd, Canonbury, London N1 (☎ 01 226 4905); High Silver, High St, Holt, Norfolk (☎ 0263 712847); High Bank, Laceys Lane, Niton, Isle of Wight (☎ 0983 730282)

BIRKS, His Hon Judge Michael; s of Falconer Moffat Birks, CBE (d 1960) and Monica Katherine Lushington, *née* Mellor (d 1957); *b* 21 May 1920; *Educ* Oundle, Trinity Coll Cambridge (MA); *m* 1947, Ann Ethne, da of Capt Henry Stafford Morgan (d 1957); 1 da; *Career* Lt 22 Dragoons; slr 1946, asst registrar Chancery Div of High Ct 1953, asst county ct registrar 1960; registrar Birkenhead and Chester Gp of County Cts 1961-66, West London County Ct 1966-83, rec 1979, circuit judge S Eastern Circuit 1983-; advsy editor Atkins Ct Forms 1966-; *Books* Gentlemen of the Law (1960), contributor to fourth edn Halsbury's Laws of England; *Recreations* painting, sailing; *Style*— His Hon Judge Michael Birks

BIRLEY, Anthony Addison; CB (1979); s of Charles Fair Birley, of Rosemary Cottage, Rue Milbraie, Jersey, CI, and Eileen Mia Rouse; *b* 28 Nov 1920; *Educ* Winchester and Christ Church Oxford (MA); *m* 1951, Jane Mary, o da of Capt Evelyn Coope Ruggles-Brise, of 4 Cheyne Gardens, SW3; 2 da (Mary Eileen b 1957, Susanna Jane b 1958); *Career* clerk of Public Bills, House of Commons 1973-82; *Style*— Anthony Birley Esq, CB; Holtom House, Paxford, Chipping Campden, Glos (☎ Paxford 318)

BIRLEY, Lady; Elinor Margaret; da of Eustace Corrie Frere, FRIBA (d 1944), and Marion Edith Grant; *b* 15 Oct 1904; *Educ* Dragon, St Leonard's Sch St Andrews Fife, Lady Margaret Hall Oxford (MA); *m* 1930, Sir Robert Birley, KCMG (d 1982, sometime headmaster of Charterhouse and Eton), s of Leonard Birley, CSI, CIE; 1 da (Rachael) (1 da decd); *Recreations* reading, gardening, grandchildren; *Style*— Lady Birley; Lomans, West End, Somerton, Somerset (☎ 0458 72640)

BIRLEY, Marcus Oswald Hornby Lecky (Mark); s of Sir Oswald Birley (d 1952); *Educ* Eton, Univ Coll Oxford; *m* 1954 (m dis 1975), Lady Annabel Vane-Tempest-Stewart, d of 8 Marquess of Londonderry; 2 s, 1 da; *Clubs* White's, Travellers' (Paris), Jockey (Paris), The Brook (New York); *Style*— Mark Birley, Esq

BIRLEY, Richard Yvon; s of Stephen Harvey Yvon Birley, of Br Columbia (d 1941), and Erica Pressey (d 1971); *b* 16 Jan 1928; *Educ* RN Coll Dartmouth; *m* 1, April 1943 (m diss 1958), Constance da of Richard Rheem, of San Francisco (d 1975); m 2, August 1958, Maureen Ann, da of James McNicol, of Perth, Scotland; 4 s (Richard b 1954, Jeremy b 1959, Mark b 1962, Stephen b 1965), 1 da (Nicolette b 1956); *Career* RN Lieut Submarines 1944-55; Shell Internat (London, Hague, S Africa, Iran) 1947-66; dir: W M Brandts and Sons Ltd 1969-72, Edward Bates 1972-75; md KCA Drilling Ltd 1975-75; chm REA Bros Leasing 1976-; *Style*— Richard Birley, Esq; Alderman's House, Alderman's Walk, London EC2M 3XR (☎ 01 623 1155, telex 886503, telex 01 626 0310)

BIRMINGHAM, 8 Archbishop of (RC) 1982-; Most Rev Maurice Noël Léon Couve de Murville; s of Noël Couve de Murville, and Marie, da of Sir Louis Souchon; 4 cous once removed of Maurice Couve de Murville, French PM 1968-69; *b* 27 June 1929, in France; *Educ* Downside, Trinity Coll Cambridge (MA), Institut Catholique Paris (STL), Sch of Oriental and African Studies London Univ (MPhil); *Career* priest 1957, curate St Anselm's Dartford 1957-60, priest-in-charge St Francis Moulsecoomb 1961-64, Catholic chaplain Sussex Univ 1961-77, Cambridge Univ 1977-82; *Style*— The Most Rev Maurice Couve de Murville; Archbishop's House, St Chad's Queensway, Birmingham B4 6EX (☎ 021 236 5535)

BIRNBERG, Benedict Michael; s of Jonas Birnberg (d 1970), and Naomi Hilda, *née* Bentwich; *b* 8 Sept 1930; *Educ* Minehead GS, The King's Sch Canterbury, Cambridge Univ (BA Hons); *m* 29 April 1968, Triantafyllia (Felitsa), da of Kyriakos Matziorinis (d 1946); 1 da (Ariadne b 1971); *Career* slr admitted 1958; sr ptnr B M Birnberg and Co; chm Nat Cncl for Civil Liberties 1974; co sec War on Want 1979-, past chm Lewisham Citizens Advice Bureaux Serv 1979-84; govr Greenwich Theatre Ltd 1974-78; *Recreations* music, theatre, politics; *Style*— Benedict Birnberg, Esq; 4 Eliot Place, Blackheath, London SE3 (☎ 01 852 1937); 103 Borough High St, London Se1 (☎ 01 403 3166)

BIRNIE, John; s of John Birnie, of Ellon, Aberdeenshire, and Helen, *née* Russell (d 1982); *b* 31 Oct 1935; *Educ* Peterhead Academy; *m* 20 June 1962, Helen Summers, da of Andrew Taylor (d 1965), of Fraserburgh; 2 s (Russell b 1964, Owen b 1972), 1 da (Linzi b 1967); *Career* 1954-57: Gordon Highlanders, WO; cmmnd RAPC (TA) 1957-67, transferred to RARO 1967; scholarship SparBanken Stockholm 1975; mangr Aberdeen TSB: Stornoway 1975-79, Elgin 1979-86; sr fin advsr Hill Samuel; chm: Local Mutual Improvement Assoc, Business Studies Advsr Ctee, Cncl Moray Coll of FE; vice chm Local Cons Assoc, (formerly pres Junior Chamber, Speakers club, sec Rotary Club; memb local community cncl); ACIB 1962; *Recreations* salmon fishing, walking, gardening; *Style*— John Birnie, Esq; Druimchoille, Fochabers, Moray

BIRNIE, Lady (Marguerite) Kathleen; *née* Courtenay; 3 da of Rev 16 Earl of Devon (d 1935), and Marguerite, *née* Silva (d 1950); *b* 15 Feb 1911; *m* 22 Nov 1933, Col Eugene St John Birnie, OBE (d 1976), s of Cyril Montague Birnie (d 1958), of Melbourne, Australia; 2 da (Marguerite Susan b 1934, Angela Patricia Jane b 1936; *Style*— Lady Kathleen Birnie; The Cottage, Longparish, Hants (☎ 346)

BIRON, Lady; Margaret Henderson; *née* Colville; *m* 1958, Sir Philip Biron, sr puisne judge Tanzania 1965-82 (d 1982); kt 1980; *Style*— Lady Biron; The High Ct, PO Box 9004, Dar es Salaam, Tanzania

BIRRELL, James Gibson; WS (1979); s of James Adamson Birrell, of 5-6 Fettes Rise, Edinburgh, and Louisa Elizabeth *née* Silvester; *b* 10 June 1948; *Educ* Loretto Sch, Queen Mary Coll, Univ of London (BA); *m* 15 Aug 1970, Angela Hilary, da of Eric Robert Soame, of Radley Rd, Abingdon, Oxon; 2 s (Gordon, b 1976, David, 1978), 1 da (Jane, b 1982); *Career* slr 1972, ptnr: Brodies 1976-85, Dickson Minto 1985-; external examiner in Commercial Law Univ of Edinburgh, memb of Insolvency Practioners Adjudication Panel (Scot); memb Law Soc: Eng and Wales 1972, Scotland; *Books* contributor Stair Memorial Encylopaedia (1987); *Recreations* music, photography, squash, golf; *Clubs* Caledonian; *Style*— James Birrell, Esq, WS; 26 Kinnear Rd, Edinburgh, EN3 5PE (☎ 031 552 1077; 11 Walker Street, Edinburgh, EN3 7NE (☎ 031 225 4455, fax 031 225 2712); 6-7 Gough Square, London EC4A 3DE (☎ 01 353 5845, fax 01 353 0005)

BIRSAY, Lady; Robina Margaret; only da of J G Marwick, FSA (Scot), sometime Provost of Stromness, Orkney; *m* 1945, Sir Harald Robert Leslie, Hon Lord Birsay, KT, CBE, TD, QC, DL (d 1982), a Lord of Session; 1 s, 1 da; *Career* MB, ChB (Edinburgh); Capt RAMC (despatches); *Style*— Lady Birsay; Queenafjold, Birsay, Orkney KW17 2LZ (☎ 286); 27 Queensferry Rd, Edinburgh EH4 3HB (☎ 031 332 3315)

BIRSE, Peter Malcolm; s of Peter Alexander McCauley Birse, of 7 MacKenzie St, Carnoustie, Scotland, and Margaret Cumming, *née* Craib; *b* 24 Nov 1942; *Educ* Arbroath HS, Univ of St Andrews (BSc); *m* 25 Jan 1969, Helen, da of Paul Stanley Searle, of Bishopston, Bristol; 2 s (James Peter Alexander b 1971, Robert Archibald b 1975), 1 da Bridget b 1969); *Career* engr John Mowlem Ltd 1963-65, engr and project mangr Gammon Ghana Ltd 1965-67, contract mangr Gammon (UK) Ltd 1967-70, established Birse Gp Ltd (Construction Gp) 1970-; chm Peter Birse Charitable Tst; MICE 1971; *Recreations* sailing, skiing, tennis, golf, fishing; *Clubs* Royal Ocean Racing; *Style*— Peter Birse, Esq; 14 Marylebone St, London, W1; High Hall Etton, Beverley, Humberside, HU17 7PE (☎ 0430 810 230); c/o Birse Gp Ltd, Humber Rd, Barton-On-Humber, Humberside, DN18 5BN (☎ 0652 33222, fax 0652 33360, car tel 0836 724 463, telex 527442)

BIRT, Alan Beckett; CBE (1979); s of Guy Capper Birt, CVO (d 1972), and Roberta, *née* Ross (d 1976); *b* 24 June 1915; *Educ* Wellington Berks, St Thomas's Hosp Med Sch London Univ (MRCS, LRCP, MB, BS, FRCS); *m* 1, 15 Sept 1939 (m dis 1986), Joyce Staunton (d 1986), da of Capt Husband, IMS, DSO (d 1916), of India; 1 s (Christopher Alan b 1942); 3 da (Rosemary Alison (Mrs Zakrzewski) b 1946, Alix Mary (Mrs Barbabas) b 1948, Jennifer Anne (Mrs Garner) b 1950); m 2, 8 Oct 1986, Peggy Jean; *Career* RAMC 1941-46: Major N Africa, Sicily, Italy 1942-45, Lt-Col Italy and Greece 1945-46; St Thomas's Hosp London: casualty offr 1937, house surgn 1938, surgical registrar and tutor 1939-41; conslt surgn: Norfolk & Norwich Hosp, Jenny Lind Children's Hosp Norwich 1946-79; examiner in surgery Univ of Cambridge, Univ of Edinburgh 1975-80, memb and chm Specialist Advsy Ctee for Gen Surgery of the Four Royal Colls of Surgns, pres The Assoc of Surgns of GB and Ireland, cncl memb The Int Trauma Fndn 1984-, Univ of East Anglia ScD 1979; fell Assoc of Surgns of GB and Ireland, memb Soc of Thoraic Surgns of GB, fell Assoc of Surgns of Poland (elected 1972); *Books* chapters in British Practice - Surgical Progress (1961), numerous articles in scientific surgical jnls; *Recreations* gardening, mountain climbing, sailing; *Style*— Alan Birt, Esq, CBE; 246A Reepham Rd, Hellesdon, Norwich, Norfolk NR6 5SP (☎ 0603 787199)

BIRT, John; s of Leo Vincent Birt, of Richmond, Surrey, and Ida Birt; *b* 10 Dec 1944; *Educ* St Mary's Coll Liverpool, St Catherine's Coll Oxford (MA); *m* 14 Sept 1965, Jane Frances, da of James Harris Lake (d 1982, 2 Lt US Navy), of Chevy Chase, Maryland, USA; 1 s (Jonathan b 1968), 1 da (Eliza b 1971); *Career* prodr Nice Time 1968-69, jt ed World in Action 1969-70, prodr The Frost Programme 1971-72, exec prodr Weekend World 1972-74, head current affairs LWT 1974-77, co prodr The Nixon Interviews 1977, controller of features and current affairs LWT 1977-81, dir of programmes LWT 1982-87, dep dir gen BBC 1987-; memb: Wilton Park Academic Cncl 1980-83, Media Law Gp 1983-, working pty on the new technols Broadcasting Res Unit 1981-83 (memb exec ctee 1983-87) ; *Style*— John Birt Esq; BBC, Broadcasting House, London W1A 1AA (☎ 01 580 4468)

BIRTS, Peter William; s of John Claude Birts, solicitor (d 1969), and Audrey Lavinia, *née* McIntyre; *b* 9 Feb 1946; *Educ* Lancing Coll, St John's Cambridge (Choral Scholar) (MA); *m* 24 Apr 1971, Penelope Ann, da of Wing Cdr Anthony Eyre, DFC (d 1946); 1 s (William b 1979), 2 da (Melanie b 1972, Charlotte b 1975); *Career* barrister, called to Bar (Gray's Inn) 1986, Rec of the Crown Ct (South Eastern Circ) 1989; Freedom of City of London 1967; Liveryman Carpenters Co 1967; *Books* Trespass: Summary Procedure for Possession of Land (with Alan Willis 1987); *Recreations* music, shooting, tennis; *Clubs* Hurlingham; *Style*— P W Birts, Esq; Farrar's Building, Temple, EC4Y 7BD (☎ 01 583 9241)

BIRTWISTLE, Maj-Gen Archibald Cull; CB (1983), CBE (1976, OBE 1971); s of Walter Edwin Birtwistle, and Eila Louise, *née* Cull; *b* 19 August 1927; *Educ* St John's Coll Cambridge (MA); *m* 1956, Sylvia Elleray; 2 s, 1 da; *Career* cmmnd RCS 1949, served Korea (despatches), Dep Cmdt RMCS 1975-79, Chief Signal Offr BAOR 1979-80, Signal Offr-in-C (Army) 1980-83, ret; memb Def Spectrum Review Ctee; Col Cmdt RCS 1983-, Hon Col 34 (Northern) Signal Regt (Volunteers) 1988-; CEng, MIEE; *Recreations* gardening; *Style*— Maj-Gen Archibald Birtwistle, CB, CBE, OBE; c/o Nat Westminster Bank plc, 97 High St, Northallerton, N Yorks DL7 8PS

BIRTWISTLE, Hon Mrs; Hon Diana; *née* Barnewall; da of 19 Baron Trimlestown; *b* 13 Oct 1929; *m* 1954, Anthony Gerard Astley Birtwistle, yst s of James Astley Birtwistle, of Hoghton, nr Preston, Lancs, and Wroxton, Banbury, Oxon; 4 da; *Style*— The Hon Mrs Birtwistle; Hatch Hill House, Hindhead, Surrey (☎ 042 873 4388)

BIRTWISTLE, Harrison; *b* 1934; *Educ* Royal Manchester Coll of Music; RAM; *m* Sheila; 1 s; *Career* composer; associate dir National Theatre 1975-; *Style*— Harrison Birtwistle Esq; c/o Allied Artists Agency, 42 Montpelier Square, London SW7 1JZ

BIRTWISTLE, Sue Elizabeth; da of Frank Edgar Birtwistle (d 1987), of Northwich, Cheshire, and Brenda Mary, *née* Higham; *b* 12 Dec 1945; *m* 14 July 1973, Richard Charles Hastings Eyre, s of Cdr Richard Galfredus Hastings Giles Eyre; 1 da (Lucy b 25 Sept 1974); *Career* theatre dir: Royal Lyceum Theatre in Educn Co 1970-72, Nottingham Playhouse Roundabout Co 1973-78, freelance 1978-80; freelance TV prodr 1980-; films include: Hotel Du Lac (BAFTA award 1987, ACE award 1988), Scoop, V (Royal TV Soc award), Or Shall We Die, Dutch Girls; memb: Arts Cncl Drama Panel 1975-77, ACTT 1979; *Recreations* the countryside, books, theatre, music, croquet; *Style*— Miss Sue Birtwistle; c/o Peter Murphy, Curtis Brown, 162-168 Regent St, London W1 (☎ 01 872 0331)

BISCHOFF, Winfried Franz Wilhelm; s of Paul Helmut Bischoff, of Dunkeld, Johannesburg SA, and Hildegard, *née* Kühne; *b* 10 May 1941; *Educ* schs in Germany, Marist Bros Johannesburg SA, Univ of Witwatersrand Johannesburg (BCom); *m* 1972, Rosemary Elizabeth, da of Hon Leslie John Leathers, *qv*; 2 s (Christopher b 1973, Charles b 1976); *Career* merchant banker; formerly with Chase Manhattan in NY, md Schroders Asia Ltd (formerly Scroders & Chartered Ltd) Hong Kong 1971-82, chm J Henry Schroder Wagg and Co Ltd London 1983-, gp chief exec Schroders plc 1984-; *Recreations* golf, opera, music, the country; *Clubs* Hurlingham, Woking GC, Frilford Heath GC; *Style*— Winfried Bischoff, Esq; 28 Bloomfield Terr, London SW1W 8PQ; J Henry Schroder Wagg and Co Ltd, 120 Cheapside, London EC2V 6DS (☎ 01 382 6000, telex London 885029)

BISCOE, Michael; s of Guy Biscoe (d 1967), of London, and Sheila Mary, *née* Seymour Chalk; *b* 4 May 1938; *Educ* Westminster, Selwyn Coll Cambridge (MA, DipArch); *m* 28 Jan 1967, Kari Jetten, da of Edward Beresford Davies, of Cambridge; 1 s (Guy b 14 May 1970), 1 da (Henrietta b 5 Jan 1968); *Career* Nat Serv 2 Lt 43 LAA Regt RA 1956-58, serv Cyprus; sr ptnr Biscoe & Stanton 1977 (ptnr 1967-); Liveryman: Worshipful Co of Leathersellers 1972, Worshipful Co of Chartered Surveyors 1975; memb RIBA, FRICS; *Recreations* music, golf, rowing, shooting, fishing; *Clubs* Carlton, RAC, Chelsea Arts; *Style*— Michael Biscoe, Esq; Biscoe & Stanton Architects, 1 Snow Hill Court, London EC1A 2EJ (☎ 01 248 5258, fax 01 248 3768, car tel 0836 210 244)

BISHOP, Alan Henry; s of Robert Dick Bishop (d 1968), and May Douglas, *née* Watson (d 1968); *b* 12 Sept 1929; *Educ* George Heriots Sch Edinburgh, Edinburgh Univ (MA); *m* 30 Mar 1959, Marjorie Ann, da of Joseph Henry Conlan, of Edinburgh; 1 s (Keith b 1961) 1 da (Susan b 1960); *Career* asst princ Dept of Agric 1954-59, private sec to Lord John Hope and G Leburn (jr mins Scottish Off) 1958-59, prics Dept of Agric and Fisheries Scot 1960-63 and 1967-68, first sec Food and Agric Copenhagen and The Hague 1963-66; asst sec: Scot Devpt 1968-69, Royal Cmmn on the Constitution 1969-73, Scot Off 1973-80; asst under sec of state Scot Off 1980-84 (princ estab off 1984-); *Recreations* contract bridge; *Clubs* Murrayfield Golf, Melville Bridge; *Style*— Alan Bishop, Esq; 19/8 Wester Coates Gardens, Edinburgh EH12 5LT (☎ 031 346 4641); Scottish Office, Establishments Division, 16 Waterloo Place, Edinburgh EH1 (☎ 031 244 3938)

BISHOP, Christopher David; s of Joseph Charles Bishop, and Zephyr Ethel, *née* Breese; *b* 8 Sept 1938; *Educ* Eastbourne Coll; *m* 22 July 1961, Judith, da of Harry Leonard Wise (d 1986); 3 s (David Charles b 1962, Simon Christopher b 1965, Guy

Elliott b 1970), 1 da (Lucinda b 1968); *Career* articled clerk/mangr Baker Sutton and Co 1956-71, co sec GR Merton (Agencies) Ltd 1971-74, princ Christopher Bishop and Co 1974-85, ptnr Ernst and Whinney 1985-; FCA; *Recreations* hunting, equestrian sports, golf; *Clubs* City of London; *Style*— Christopher Bishop, Esq; Becket House, 1 Lambeth Palace Rd, London SE1 7EU (☎ 01 928 2000, fax 928 1345, telex 885234)

BISHOP, Dr (Arthur) Clive; s of Charles Henry Bishop (d 1966), of Newcastle, Staffs, and Hilda *née* Clowes; *b* 9 July 1930; *Educ* Wolstanton Co GS Newcastle, King's Coll London (BSc, PhD); *m* 8 Sept 1962, Helen, da of Joseph Benninson (d 1983), of Stoke-on-Trent; 1 da (Anne b 1965); *Career* Nat Serv Education Branch RAF 1955-57; geologist HM geological survey Edinburgh 1954-58, lectrer in geology Queen Mary Coll London 1958-69; Br Natural History Museum: princ sci off 1969-72, keeper of mineralogy 1975- (dep keeper 1972-74), dep dir 1982-; fell King's Coll London 1985, Membre d'Honneur La Societe Jersase 1983; pres: Geologists Assoc 1978-80, Mineralogical Soc 1978-80; FGS (London), memb Geologist Assoc, life memb Mineralogical Soc; *Books* An Outline of Crystal Morphology (1967), Countrt Life Guide to Minerals, Rocks and Fossils (with W R Hamilton and A R Woolley 1974); *Recreations* drawing and painting; *Style*— Dr Clive Bishop; British Museum (Natural History), Cromwell Road, SW7 5BD (☎ 01 589 6323)

BISHOP, David Broughton Gibson; s of Col A W G Bishop, MC (d 1979); *b* 1 Feb 1933; *Educ* Wellington, Jesus Coll Cambridge; *m* 1974, Judith, *née* Brown; 1 s, 1 da; *Career* slr, ptnr Baileys Shaw & Gillett 1961 (sr ptnr 1979-88), dir Syndicate Administration and other cos; *Recreations* cricket, skiing, shooting, gardening, antiques; *Clubs* Sunningdale Golf, United Oxford and Cambridge; *Style*— David Bishop, Esq; Old Rectory Easton Nr Winchester Hants (☎ 096 278 205); Baileys Shaw and Gillett, 17 Queen Sq, London WC1N 3RH (☎ 01 837 5455)

BISHOP, (Thomas) David; s of Thomas Challis Bishop (d 1981), of Conifer, Underhill Park Road, Reigate, Surrey, and Mary, *née* Simmons; *b* 22 August 1934; *Educ* Charterhouse; *m* 20 Sept 1966, Josephine Anne, da of Lionel Mitchell Robinson, of Rodney, Brockenhurst, Hants; 1 s (Jeremy b 1970), 1 da (Belinda b 1973); *Career* Nat Serv RA 1955-56; slr 1960, ptnr Hunters 1961-, clerk Worhsipful Co of Masons 1986-87; *Recreations* cricket, tennis, skiing, shooting, classical music, travelling; *Clubs* Boodle's, MCC; *Style*— David Bishop, Esq; Spur Point, Marley Heights, Haslemere, Surrey (☎ 0428 3050); 9 New Square, Lincoln's Inn, London WC2A 3QN (☎ 01 242 4931)

BISHOP, Errol Simon Owen; s of Dr Peter Maxwell Farrow Bishop (d 1979), and Winifred Phyllis, *née* Thurston (d 1981); *b* 1 August 1938; *Educ* Charterhouse, Southampton Univ (BSc Eng); *m* 1961, Sandra June, da of Maj Matthew Braithwaite (d 1986); 1 s (Max b 1970), 2 da (Charlotte b 1966, Katherine b 1970); *Career* exec dir Barclays Dvpt Capital Ltd and related Cos; currently dir: Carpet Express Hldgs plc, Mecro Gp Ltd, Barons of Farnborough Ltd, Bath Plant Holdings Ltd, NE Technology Ltd; previously dir and dep chm Systems Designers Int Ltd 1976-81, dir and gp md Dihurst Hldgs Ltd 1976-80; CEng, MIMechE, FBIM; *Recreations* motor racing, DIY; *Style*— Errol Bishop, Esq; Parnells, Witherenden Hill, Burwash Common, E Sussex; Barclays Dvpt Capital Ltd, Pickfords Wharf, Clink Street, London SE1 9DG (fax 01 407 3362)

BISHOP, Sir Frederick Arthur; CB (1960), CVO (1957); s of late A J Bishop, of Bristol, and Mary Shaw; *b* 4 Dec 1915; *Educ* Colston's Hosp, Bristol and London Univ (LLB); *m* 1940, Elizabeth Finlay, da of Samuel Stevenson, of Belfast; 2 s, 1 da; *Career* Miny of Food 1947, pps to Min of Food 1949-52, asst sec to Cabinet Office 1952-55, pps to PM 1956-59; dep sec: Cabinet 1959-61, Miny of Agric, Fish and Food 1961-64; perm sec Miny of Land and Natural Resources 1964-65; dir: S Pearson and Sons Ltd 1966-70, Pearson Longman Ltd 1970-77; dir-gen Nat Tst 1971-75; dir: English China Clays, Lloyds Bank Ltd (Devon and Cornwall) 1975-86; kt 1975; *Style*— Sir Frederick Bishop, CB, CVO; Manor Barn, Bramshott, Liphook, Hants

BISHOP, Sir George Sidney; CB (1958), OBE (1947); s of late Joseph Bishop, of Wigan, Lancs; *b* 15 Oct 1913; *Educ* Ashton-in-Makerfield GS, LSE; *m* 1, 1940 (m dis 1961), Marjorie, da of C H Woodruff, of Illingworth; 1 da; m 2, 1961, Una, da of late C F C Padel, of Inkpen, Berks; *Career* joined Civil Serv 1940, under-sec Miny of Agric, Fish and Food 1949, dep sec 1959-61, chm Bookers Int Hldgs Ltd 1964-70, v-chm Int Wheat Cncl 1959, dir Nigerian Sugar Co Ltd 1966-70, v-chm Booker McConnell Ltd 1970-71, chm 1972-79, dir 1961-, dir Ibec (agribusiness assoc of Booker McConnell) to 1983; chm West India Ctee 1969-71, memb Panel for Civil Serv Manpower Review 1968-70, dir Barclays Bank Int 1972-, Barclays Bank 1974-, Rank Hovis McDougall 1976-, Int Basic Economy Corpn USA; kt 1975; *Style*— Sir George Bishop CB, OBE; Brenva, Egham's Wood Rd, Beaconsfield, Bucks (☎ Beaconsfield 3096)

BISHOP, James Drew; s of Sir (Frank) Patrick Bishop, MBE, MP (d 1972), and his 1 wife Vera Sophie, *née* Drew (d 1953); *b* 18 June 1929; *Educ* Haileybury, CCC Cambridge; *m* 1959, Brenda, da of George Pearson; 2 s; *Career* for corr The Times 1957-64, (for news ed 1964-66, asst ed features 1966-70), ed Illustrated London News 1971-1987, ed-in-chief Illustrated London News Pbns 1987-, memb advsy bd Annual Register 1970-; dir: Int Thomson Publishing Ltd 1980-85, Illustrated London News and Sketch Ltd 1971-; *Books* A Social History of Edwardian Britain (1977), A Social History of the First World War (1982), The Story of the Times (1983; with Oliver Woods); ed of The Illustrated Counties of England (1985); *Recreations* reading, walking; *Clubs* Oxford and Cambridge, MCC; *Style*— James Bishop, Esq; 11 Willow Rd, London NW3 (☎ 01 435 4403); office: 91-93 Southwark St, London SE1 0HX (☎ 01 928 2111)

BISHOP, Dr John Edward; s of Reginald John Bishop, and Eva, *née* Lucas; *b* 23 Feb 1935; *Educ* Cotham Sch Bristol, St John's Coll Cambridge (MA, MusB), Univ of Reading, Univ of Edinburgh (DMus); *Career* asst dir then sr dir of Music Worksop Coll 1958-72; dir of studies, head of sch, head of admissions, head of organ studies, Birmingham Sch of Music 1972-86; free lance musician 1986-; conslt in organ studies Wells Cathedral Sch; former pres Birmingham, Sheffield and Bristol Organists' Assocns, former govr City of Birmingham Poly, dir of music Cotham Parish Church Bristol, dir Bristol Highbury Singers, chm Bristol Centre Inc Soc of Musicians; Hon fell Birmingham Sch of Music 1986; FRCO (chm), ADCM, ISM (chm Bristol Centre); *Recreations* walking, savouring the countryside, railways; *Style*— Dr John Bishop; 98 High Kingsdown, Bristol, BS2 8ER (☎ 0272 423373)

BISHOP, John Michael; s of Lt Wilfred Charles John Michael Bishop (d 1988), of Whitstable, Kent, and Margery Bains, *née* Emmerson; *b* 1 Mar 1947; *Educ* Kent Coll Canterbury, LSE (LLB); *m* 12 Aug 1982, Laurie Marie, da of Lyman Charles Harris (d 1980), of Virginia Beach, Virginia, USA; 2 da (Heather Virginia, Lucy Cecilia); *Career* Kent and Co of London Yeomanry (TA) 1965-67; hd barr of chambers at 7 Stone Buildings Lincolns Inn 1986, hd of chambers at Butchery Lane Canterbury Kent 1988-; memb hon soc Middle Temple Lincolns Inn; *Recreations* photography, antiquarian books; *Style*— John Bishop, Esq; 7 Stone Buildings, Lincolns Inn, London WC2A 3SZ (☎ 01 242 0961, fax 01 405 7028); Butchery Lane, Canterbury, Kent (☎ 0227 456 865)

BISHOP, Dame (Margaret) Joyce; DBE (1963), CBE (1953); 2 da of Charles Benjamin Bishop (d 1933), and Amy Stewart Tyndall (d 1965); *b* 28 July 1896; *Educ* Edgbaston HS Birmingham, Lady Margaret Hall Oxford (MA); *Career* english mistress Herfordshire and Essex High Sch 1918-24; head mistress: Holly Lodge High Sch Smethwick Staffs 1924-35, Godolphin and Latymer Sch London 1935-63; memb Working Pty set up by Min of Educn to enquire into Recruitment of Women to Teaching Profession 1947, pres Assoc of Head Mistresses 1950-52; memb: Secondary Sch Examinations Cncl 1950-62, Univ Grants Ctee 1961-63; Cncl for Professions Supplementary to Medicine 1961-70, TV Res Ctee 1963-69, chm Joint Ctee of the Four Secondary Assocs 1956-58; FKC 1973; *Recreations* listening to cassettes, theatre; *Style*— Dame Joyce Bishop, DBE, CBE; 22 Malbrook Rd, Putney, London SW15 6UF (☎ 01 788 5862)

BISHOP, Michael David; CBE (1986); s of Clive Leonard Bishop (d 1980), and Lilian, *née* Frost; *b* 10 Feb 1942; *Educ* Mill Hill; *Career* chm: Airlines of Britain Hldgs plc, Manx Airlines 1982-, Loganair 1983-, London City Airways 1986-; chm and md Br Midland Airways (joined co 1964), dir Airtours plc 1987-; memb: E Midlands Elec Bd 1980-83, E Midlands Bd Central Ind TV plc 1981-; *Recreations* music; *Clubs* St James's (Manchester), Union (Sydney); *Style*— Michael Bishop, Esq, CBE; Donington Hall, Castle Donington, nr Derby (☎ 0332 810741, telex 37172)

BISHOP, Prof Richard Evelyn Donohue; CBE (1979); s of Rev Dr Norman Richard Bishop (d 1968), and Dorothy Mary, *née* Wood (d 1971); *b* 1 Jan 1925; *Educ* Roan Sch Greenwich, UCL (BSc), Stanford Univ Calif (MS, PhD), London Univ (DSc), Cambridge Univ (MA, ScD); *m* 1 July 1949, Jean, da of Hector Cross Buchanan Paterson (d 1976), of London; 1 s (John b 1957), 1 da (Susan Julia (Mrs James) b 1954); *Career* RNVR 1943-46; Univ of Cambridge: fell Pembroke Coll and univ lectr 1952-57; Kennedy prof of mechanical engrg UCL 1957-81, vice-chllr and princ Brunel Univ Uxbridge 1981-; boards memb Def Scientific Advsy Cncl 1968-88; govr Portsmouth GS 1985-; Liveryman Worshipful Co of Shipwrights 1979-; hon fell Portsmouth Poly 1982; FEng 1977, FRS 1980; *Books* Vibration Analysis Tables (with D C Johnson, 1956), The Mechanics of Vibration (with D C Johnson, 1960 and 1979), The Matrix Analysis of Vibration (with G M L Gladwell and S Michaelson, 1965 and 1979), Vibration (1965 and 1979), Probabilistic Theory of Ship Dynamics (with W G Price, 1974), Hydroelasticity of Ships (with W G Price, 1979), Mechanics of Marine Vehicles (with B R Clayton, 1982); *Recreations* sailing, music; *Clubs* RN, Royal Albert YC; *Style*— Prof Richard Bishop, CBE; Brenton Cottage, Woodgason Lane, North Hayling, Hayling Island, Hants PO11 ORL (☎ 0705 463441); Brunel Univ, Uxbridge, Middx UB8 3PH (☎ 0895 37188, telex 261173 Brunel G)

BISHOP, Stanley Victor; MC (1944); s of George Stanley Bishop (d 1963), of SA, and Elsie Gordon, *née* Milne (d 1967); *b* 11 May 1916; *Educ* Leeds Sch; *m* 30 Apr 1946, Dorothy Primrose, da of Ralph Herbert Dodds, MC (d 1951), of Berwick-upon-Tweed; 2 s (John Stuart b 3 Apr 1947, Richard Anthony b 31 Mar 1949), 1 da (Victoria Jane b 23 Jan 1957); *Career* Corpl 1 London Scottish 1937-40, cmmnd W Yorks Regt 1940, 2 Lt 2 W Yorks Regt 1941-42 (ME), Capt ME Training Centre 1942-43, 2 W Yorks 1943-44 (ME, Burma, Maj 1944), W Yorks ITC 1944-45; chief cost accountant A E Reed & Co Ltd 1945-51, comptroller: Petters Ltd 1951-56, Costains 1956-59, Massey Ferguson Tractors 1959-60, plans coordinator UK 1960-61 (worldwide 1961-63), fin dir Perkins Ltd 1963-65 (gen mangr Madrid 1965-66), chief exec British Printing Corpn 1966-71, dir Massey Ferguson Europe 1973-78, mgmnt conslt/non exec dir with various co's 1971-73 (1978-); memb cncl Br Inst Mgmnt 1967-70; FCA, FICA 1937, FBIM (cncl 1967-70), FInstD; *Books* Business Planning and Control (1966); *Recreations* swimming, gardening; *Style*— Mr Stanley Bishop, Esq, MC; Halidon, Rogers Lane, Ettington, Stratford-upon-Avon

BISHOP, Thomas (Tim) Frederick; s of Frederick Stanley Bishop (d 1970), and Edith Gertrude, *née* Pore (d 1968); *b* 4 April 1937; *Educ* St Olaves and St Saviors GS London, Timaru Boys HS New Zealand, Canterbury Coll, Univ of New Zealand; *m* 13 march 1959, Jennifer Clare, da of Darcley Francis Hocking (d 1963); 1 s (Tristram b 1961), 1 da (Charlotte b 1959); *Career* nat dir Arthur Young McClelland Moores and Co 1977-82 (part 1975), chm of Spicer and Pegler Assoc 1987 (md 1983-87), chm Spicer and Oppenheim Conslts 1987 (chm of UK Consltg Operations 1988); *Recreations* tstee, rye art gallery; *Style*— Tim Bishop, Esq; Spicer and Oppenheim, 13 Bruton Street, London (☎ 01 480 7766)

BISHOP, Instr Rear Adm Sir William Alfred; KBE (1955), OBE (1941, CB 1950); s of Alfred Bishop (d 1954), of Purley, Surrey; *b* 29 May 1899; *Educ* Whitgift Sch, CCC Cambridge (MA); *m* 1929, Stella Margaret, MBE (1952), da of Robert Warner Macfarlane, of Hobart, Tasmania (d 1985); *Career* RN 1922, Instr Rear Adm 1951, Naval ADC to HM The King 1950, Dir of Naval Educ Serv 1948-56, ret; *Style*— Instr Rear-Adm Sir William Bishop, KBE, CB, OBE; Fore Dore, Trebetherick Wadebridge, Cornwall PL27 6SB (☎ 020 886 3471)

BISS, Godfrey Charles d'Arcy; s of Gerald Biss and Sarah Ann Coutts Allan; *b* 2 Sept 1909; *Educ* St Paul's Sch, Worcester Coll Oxford; *m* 1946, Margaret Jean Ellis; 2 s; *Career* chm Siebe Gorman and Co Ltd, dir other cos; *Style*— Godfrey Biss Esq; Spring Bank, Back Street, Thornborough, Bucks MK18 2DH

BISSIL, JP Eileen; *née* Grey; da of Sir John Foley Grey, 8 Bt (d 1938), and Jean Jessie Mary, *née* De Sales La Terriere; *b* 01 Feb 1922; *Educ* privately; *m* 1, 5 Feb 1942 (m dis 1946), 11 Earl of Harrington; 1 s, 2 da (1 decd); m 2, 23 Jan 1947, John Philip Bissill, da of William Norman Bisill; 1 da (Alexander Diana b 15 Feb 1950); *Recreations* fishing, shooting, gardening; *Style*— Mrs Eileen Bissill, JP; Evnille Hall, Stourbridge, Worc

BISSILL, Hon Mrs - Hon Charmiane Elizabeth Violet Cecilia; *née* Wilson; da of 3 Baron Nunburnholme; *b* 4 August 1930; *m* 19 Jan 1957, William Rippon Bissill (d 1973), er s of William Norman Bissill (d 1936), of Cranmer House, Aslockton; 1 s (and 1 s decd), 1 da; *Style*— The Hon Mrs Bissill; Cranmer House, Aslockton, Notts (☎ Whatton 50226)

BISSILL, Raymond Norman; s of Herbert Cyril Bissill (d 1973), of Chestfield, Whitstable, Kent, and Evelyn Violet, *née* Sydney; *b* 14 Oct 1938; *Educ* Chatham GS for Boys; Medway Coll of Tech (Dip Bdlg); *m* 7 Feb 1975, Sally Ann, da of Maj Roy Albert Smith MBE (ret), of Whitstable, Kent; 2 s (Adam b 1976, James b 1977), 1 da (Abigail b 1974); *Career* chm and md: Abbey Grove Securities Ltd, R Bailey and Co Ltd, Errill Securities Ltd, Bailey Builders Ltd; past pres The Canterbury and Dist Bldg Employees Confedn 1979-81, chm The E Kent Jt Consultative Ctee of Building; FID, FCIOB; *Recreations* squash, skiing, windsurfing; *Clubs* Kent and Cantab, Whitstable Yacht; *Style*— Raymond N Bissill, Esq; Penraevon, Chestfield Rd, Chestfield, Whitstable, Kent; R Bailey and Co Ltd, Malvern House, Broad St, Canterbury, Kent

BLACH, Rudolf Karl (Rolf); s of Paul Samuel Blach (d 1940), and Hedwig Jeanette Blach (d 1968); *b* 21 Jan 1930; *Educ* Berkhamsted Sch, Trinity Coll Cambridge, St Thomas's Hosp London (MA, MB BChir, MD); *m* 26 March 1960, Lynette (Lyn) Cecilia, da of Jaffray Andrew Conynghame Sceales; 2 s (Thomas b 1962, Richard b 1968), 1 da (Catherine b 1964); *Career* Lt RAMC 1956 (Capt 1957); conslt ophthalmic surgn St Mary's Hosp Paddington 1963-70, hon conslt ophthalmologist Royal Postgrad Med Sch Hammersmith 1967-74, conslt ophthalmologist St Dunstans 1967, conslt surgn Moorfields Eye Hosp 1969, Dean Inst of Ophthalmology Univ of London 1985-; Freeman City of London 1967, Liveryman Worshipful Soc of Apothecaries; FRCS, FCOphth, FRSM; *Style*— Rolf Blach, Esq; 88A College Rd, Dulwich, London SE21 7NA (☎ 01 693 1917); Lister House, 11/12 Wimpole St, London W1M 7AB (☎ 01 636 3407)

BLACK, Alastair Kenneth Lamond; DL (Greater London 1978); s of Kenneth Black (decd), and Althea Joan Black, *née* Hanks, (d 1984); *b* 14 Dec 1929; *Educ* Sherborne Sch, Law Soc Sch of Law; *m* 1955, Elizabeth Jane, da of Sir Henry Darlington, KCB, CMG, TD (d 1959); 1 s (Rupert), 2 da (Sarah, Susan); *Career* slr 1953, Nat Serv, Intelligence Corps, 1953-55, Lieut; ptnr Messrs Burchell and Ruston 1953-; dep sheriff County of London, then Gtr London, 1953-74, under sheriff of Gtr London, 1974-; clerk to the Gen Cmmrs of Income Tax for the Divs of Holborn, Finsbury and St Paul's Covent Garden 1966-, clerk to the Bowyers Co, 1985-; memb Ho of Laity Gen Synod 1982-, lay reader 1983-; pres Under Sheriffs Assoc 1987- (vice pres 1985-87); memb cncl Shrievalty Assoc, 1985-; *Books* Contributions to Halsbury's Laws of England, 4th edition, vol 25, (1978) vol 42 (1983), Atkins Court Forms, 3rd edition, vol 19 (1972 and revised edition 1985), vol 22 (1986), vol 36 (1977), Execution of a Judgment, Oyez Practice Notes, 6th edition (1979) 7th edition (1986); *Recreations* horse racing, gardening, travel; *Style*— Alastair Black, Esq, DL; South Lodge, Guildford Road, Effingham, Surrey, 2 Serjeants' Inn, Fleet Street, London EC4Y 1LL (☎ 01 353 5385)

BLACK, Barrington; s of Louis L. Black and Millicent *née* Brash; *b* 16 August 1932; *Educ* Roundhay Sch, Leeds Univ (LLB); *m* 19 June 1962, Diana, da of Simon Heller; 2 s (Matthew b 1965, Jonathan b 1968), 2 da (Harriette b 1963, Anna b 1971); *Career* slr 1956, asst recorder Inner London Crown Ct, chm Inner London Juvenille Ct 1986-, Metropolitan Stipendiary magistrate 1984; memb: Inner London Probation Ctee, Br Acad Forensic Sci 1976-; former pres Leeds Univ Union, memb Ct and Cncl Leeds Univ, vice pres NUS; *Recreations* music, opera, ski-bobbing; *Style*— Barrington Black, Esq; Marylebone Magistrates Ct, London (☎ 01 725 4379)

BLACK, Sir Cyril Wilson; JP (London 1942), DL (Surrey 1957, Gtr London 1966); s of Robert Wilson Black, JP (d 1951), and Annie Louise, *née* North; *b* 8 April 1902; *Educ* King's Coll Sch Wimbledon; *m* 1930, Dorothy Joyce, da of Thomas Birkett (d 1962), Wigston Hall, Leicester; 1 s, 2 da; *Career* chartered surveyor; MP (C) Wimbledon 1950-70; mayor: Wimbledon 1945-47 (memb borough cncl 1942-65), Merton 1966-67 (memb borough cncl 1965-78); chm Surrey CC 1956-59 (memb 1943-65, v-chm 1953-56); conslt to Knight and Co Estate Agents and Surveyors; chm: Temperance Permanent Building Soc 1939-73, Beaumont Properties 1947-80, M F North Hotels Gp 1948-81, London Shop Property Tst 1951-79; nat tres Girls' Bde 1939-69 (vice pres 1969-), tres Boys' Bde 1962-69 (hon vice pres 1970-), hon tres London Baptist Assoc 1942-76 (pres 1965-66, life memb 1976-); memb: Baptist Union Cncl (vice pres 1969-70, pres 1970-71), Free Church Federal Cncl, Cncl of Christians and Jews; pres: Christian Union for the Estate Profession, United Kingdom Alliance, 18F (Wimbledon) Sqdn Air Training Corps, Wimbledon and Merton Dist Scout Cncl 1974-; FRICS, FRSA; kt 1959; *Recreations* teetotaller and anti-drink campaigner, reading, music, public and Christian work; *Style*— Sir Cyril Black, JP, DL; Rosewall, Calonne Rd, London SW19 (☎ 01 946 2588); Windmill Cottage, Sea Way, Middleton-on-Sea, Sussex (☎ 024 369 2288)

BLACK, (William) David (Anthony); s of William Milnes Black, of Clwyd, and Dorothy Charlotte, *née* Harrison; *b* 19 June 1938; *Educ* Stonyhurst, Manchester Univ (BSc); *m* 2 April 1964, Charmain Jennifer, da of Sidney Stewart Downing (d 1986); 1 s (William Benjamin David b 1965), 2 da (Nicola Louise b 1967, Jane Ruth b 1979); *Career* chm and md: Harrison and Jones Gp Ltd 1976- (dir 1962-76), Bysingwood Gp Ltd 1973-; *Recreations* shooting, vintage motor racing, steamboating; *Clubs* RAC, Bugatti Owners; *Style*— David Black, Esq; Douglas Bank Farm, Appley Bridge, via Skelmersdale, Lancs (☎ 0257 52844); Harrison and Jones Gp Ltd, Swan Mill, Middleton Junction, Manchester (☎ 061 643 2468)

BLACK, Sir (Robert) David; 3 Bt (UK 1922), of Midgham, Co Berks; s of Sir Robert Andrew Stransham Black, 2 Bt, ED (d 1979); *b* 29 Mar 1929; *Educ* Eton; *m* 1, 1953 (m dis 1972), Rosemary Diana, da of Sir Rupert John Hardy, 4 Bt; 2 da (Diana Sarah b 1955, m 1979 Mark Newton, Joanna Rosemary b 1966 and 1 da decd); m 2, 1973, (Dorothy) Maureen, da of Maj Charles Robert Eustace Radclyffe, and wid of Alan Roger Douglas Pilkington; *Heir* none; *Career* formerly Maj Royal Horse Gds and Maj Berks and Westminster Dragoon Yeo 1964-67; Joint MFH Garth and S Berks Hunt 1964-72; vice chm Berks Eastern Wessex TAVR 1985-; *Clubs* Cavalry and Guards; *Style*— Sir David Black, Bt; Elvendon Priory, Goring, nr Reading, Berks (☎ 0491 872160); Shurrery Lodge, Shebster, Thurso, Caithness (☎ 084 781 252)

BLACK, Donald Sinclair; s of Frank Charles Briscoe Black (d 1988), of 26 Learmonth Terrace, Edinburgh, and Anne Betty Hirst, *née* Sinclair; *b* 4 July 1941; *Educ* Merchiston Castle Sch Edinburgh, Edinburgh Univ (LLB); *m* 30 Sept 1972, (Evelyn) Bronwen Louise, da of William Kennedy, of Sidmouth, Devon; 3 s (Roderick b 1975, Graeme b 1979, Alistair b 1982), 1 da (Tamara b 1973); *Career* articled CA Deloittes Edinburgh 1963-67, Royal Bank of Scotland Investmt Dept 1967-68, Edinburgh Fund Mangrs Fund 1968-70, dir Panmure Gordon & Co Ltd 1975-(joined 1970); MICAS 1966; *Recreations* skiing, tennis; *Style*— Donald Black, Esq; 244 Residence Mondzev, Verbiet, Switzerland; 19 Ennismore Ave, Guilford, Surrey GU1 1SP; Panmure Gordon & Co Ltd, 9 Moorfields Highwalk, London EC2 (☎ 01 628 4010, fax 01 920 9305, telex 883832)

BLACK, Sir Douglas Andrew Kilgour; s of Rev Walter Kilgour Black (d 1951), and Mary Jane Crichton; *b* 29 May 1913; *Educ* Forfar Acad, St Andrews Univ; *m* 1948, Mollie, da of Edward Thorn (d 1962); 1 s, 2 da; *Career* served WW II in RAMC as Maj (India); prof of medicine Manchester Univ 1959-78, chief scientist DHSS 1973-77; pres Royal Coll of Physicians 1977-83; chm working pty on inequalities in health (1977-80) and childhood leukaemia in W Cumbria (1983-84) pres BMA 1984-85; kt 1973; *Books* Invitation to Medicine, Blackwell (1987), Recollections and Reflections, BMJ Publications, (1987); *Recreations* reading, writing; *Clubs* Athenaeum; *Style*— Sir Douglas Black; The Old Forge, Duchess Close, Whitchurch-on:Thames, nr Reading RG8 7EN (☎ 073 57 4693)

BLACK, Geoffrey Howard; s of Robert Black, of Liverpool, and Renée Black; *b* 23 Dec 1948; *Educ* Quarry Bank HS Liverpool, private accountancy colls; *m* 26 May 1972, Linda Margaret, da of Joseph Dowsing (d 1959); 2 s (Andrew b 1980, Michael b 1989), 2 da (Rachel b 1976, Susannah b 1978); *Career* princ GH Black and Co 1976-83, hd of accountancy Cambridgeshire Coll of Arts and Technol 1984-88, ptnr The Guidelines Ptnrship ed conslts 1986-, chief examiner A level accountancy London Univ Exam Bd 1983-; lib parliamentary candidate Liverpool Garston Constituency 1974 gen elections, lib parliamentary agent Shrewsbury Constituency 1979 gen elections; FCA 1971; *Books* Financial Accounting (1986), Accounting Standards (1987), Applied Economics (contribution 1989); *Recreations* avoiding sporting activities; *Clubs* University Centre, Cambridge; *Style*— Geoff Black, Esq; 18 Pretoria Rd, Cambridge CB4 1HE (☎ 0223 314 668)

BLACK, Air Vice-Marshal George Philip; CB (1987), OBE (1967, AFC 1962, and bar 1971); s of William Black, and Elizabeth Edward, *née* Philip; *b* 10 July 1932; *Educ* Aberdeen Acad, Joint Services Staff Coll, Royal Coll of Defence Studies; *m* 1954, Ella Ruddiman, da of Edwin Stanley Walker (d 1961); 2 s (Stuart Douglas b 1955, Ian Craig b 1959); *Career* RAF, pilot/general duties branch, air defence; experience of Central European Theatre including Mediterranean; several appointments in NATO; ADC to HM The Queen 1981-83; co 111 Squadron 5 Squadron RAF Wildenrath; commander socl; commandant Royal Observer Corps; sr def advsr Ferranti plc; *Recreations* military aviation, philately, model railways; *Clubs* RAF; *Style*— Air Vice-Marshal George Black, CB, OBE, AFC; Lloyds Bank plc, 6 Pall Mall, London SW1Y 5NH; Ferranti plc, Millbank Tower, London (☎ 01 834 6611)

BLACK, Prof Gordon; s of Martin Black (d 1942), of Whitehaven, Cumbria, and Gladys Lee (d 1984); *b* 30 July 1923; *Educ* Workington GS, Durham Univ (BSc), London Univ (Phd, DIC), Manchester Univ (MSc); *m* 17 Oct 1953, Brenda Janette, da of Harry Josiah Balsom (d 1958), of London; 2 s (Jonathan David Gordon b 1961, Roger Duncan Martin b 1964), 2 da (Janette Claire b 1956, Susan Catherine b 1958); *Career* prof of computation faculty of tech Manchester Univ, physicist Br Scientific Instrument Res Assoc 1946-56; UKAEA 1956-66: princ sci offr 1956-58, sr princ sci offr 1958-60, dep chief sci offr 1960-64; dir Nat Computing Centre 1965-69, dir regnl computing centre Manchester Univ 1969-83, dir Int Computers Ltd 1976-84, chm computer policy ctee Vickers Ltd 1977-79, govr Huddersfield Poly 1974-80, UN conslt 1983; Hon MSc Manchester 1967; FInstP 1952, FBCS 1968, CPhys 1984, FBCS; *Books* scientific papers in learned jls (physics and computers); *Recreations* playing piano, old clocks; *Clubs* Athenaeum; *Style*— Professor Gordon Black; UMIST, Sackville St, Manchester (☎ 061 236 3311)

BLACK, Ian Roger Maclean; s of Lewis Worcester Maclean Black (d 1973), of Gillingham, and Norah, *née* Greenwood; *b* 30 July 1949; *Educ* Kings Sch Rochester, Univ of Warwick (BSc), IMCB (MBA); *m* 29 June 1974, Madeleine Alix, da of Howard Richard Clutterbuck, of Combe St Nicholas, Somerset; 2 da (Emma b 1977, Stephanie b 1980); *Career* chief scientist Forth River Purification Bd 1985-89, princ Dames & Moore Int 1989; CChem, MRSC, MBIM; *Recreations* cycling, squash, alpine gardening; *Style*— Ian Black, Esq; Booth House, 15-17 Church St, Twickenham TW1 3NJ 01 891 6161, fax 01 891 4457, telex 929861)

BLACK, Sir James Whyte; *b* 14 June 1924; *Educ* Beath HS, St Andrew's Univ (MB, ChB); *Career* prof and head of Dept of Pharmacology Univ Coll London 1973-77; dir of therapeutic research Wellcome Research Laboratories 1978-84; prof of Analytical Pharmacology 1984-; awarded Nobel Prize for medicine 1988; FRCP, FRS; kt 1981; *Style*— Sir James Black; Analytical Pharmacology Unit, Rayne Institute, 123 Coldharbour Lane, London SE5 9NU (☎ 01 274 7437)

BLACK, Adm Sir (John) Jeremy; KCB (1987), DSO (1982, MBE 1963); s of Alan Henry Black and Gwendoline, *née* Westcott; kinsman Capt George Blagdon Westcott k in cmd of HMS Majestic at the battle of the Nile 1798; *b* 17 Nov 1932; *Educ* RNC Dartmouth; *m* 1958, Alison Pamela, da of Col Philip Thomas Barber, MC (d 1965), Baluch Regt; 2 s (Simon b 1967, Julian b 1968), 1 da (Carolyn b 1965); *Career* served in HMS Belfast (Korean War, Malaysian Emergency) 1950, specialized in naval gunnery 1958; CO HMS Fiskerton (Borneo confrontation) 1962; CO HMS Decoy (Far East and Mediterranean) 1968; Naval Staff Appts 1970, 1975 and 1980: RCDS 1979, elected yr bro of Trinity Ho; CO HMS Invincible (Falklands War) 1982, Flag Offr First Flotilla 1983-, Asst Chief Naval Staff 1985-, Deputy Chief of Defence Staff (Systems) 1986-89; Cncl Royal United Services Inst; *Recreations* history, sailing; *Clubs* Royal Cwlth Soc; *Style*— Vice Adm Sir Jeremy Black, KCB, DSO, MBE; Ministry of Defence, Main Building, Whitehall, SW1A 2HB (☎ 01 218 3825)

BLACK, Lady; Joan Edna; da of George Fairbrother, of Birkenhead, and Gertrude Campbell Shanks; *m* 1955, Sir Misha Black, OBE (d 1977); 2 s, 1 da; *Style*— Lady Black; 78 Primrose Mansions, Prince of Wales Drive, SW11; Thistley Common, Boyton End, Halstead, Essex

BLACK, John Alexander; CBE (1983); s of Arthur Alexander Black (d 1958); *b* 8 July 1923; *Educ* Cheltenham, Univ of Birmingham; *m* 1950, Joan, da of Henry Knight (d 1954); 2 da; *Career* memb bd of mgmnt Birmingham Cncl of Social Serv 1964-67, S Birmingham Hospital Mgmnt Ctee 1972-74, Solihull Area Health Authy 1977-82, Birmingham Venture 1985-85; gen cmmnr for income tax 1966-72; dir AA Black Ltd 1948-63; chm Longleys & Huffman Ltd 1972 (dir !963-72, vice-chm and md 1970-72); chm: Charles Barker Black and Gross Ltd 1976-83, Charles Barker Cross Courtenay Ltd 1978-83, Charles Barker Scotland Ltd 1980-83, Solihull Health Authy 1982-88; dir: Charles Barker Gp Ltd 1976-83, Birmingham Convention and Visitor Bureau Ltd 1982-87, Task Undertakings Ltd 1988-; pres: Birmingham Jr C of C 1956-57,

Birmingham Publicity Assoc 1974-75, Commerce 1981-82 (tres 1974-78); *Recreations* gardening, woodturning, walking, photography; *Style*— John A Black, Esq, CBE; 36 Hampton Lane, Solihull, W Midlands B91 2PZ (☎ 021 705 4131)

BLACK, Lady; Margaret; da of John Milton Saxton (d 1951), of Belfast; *m* 1940, Sir Harold Black (sometime dep sec NI Office; d 1985), s of Alexander Black (d 1946), of Belfast; 1 s, 1 da; *Style*— Lady Black; 19 Rosepark, Belfast, N Ireland

BLACK, Lady Moorea; *née* Hastings; JP; da of 15 Earl of Huntingdon by his 1 w, Cristina, da of Marchese Casati; *b* 4 Mar 1928; *m* 1, 1957 (m dis 1966), Woodrow Wyatt (later Lord Wyatt of Weeford), *qv*; 1 s (Pericles Plantagenet James Casati b 1963); m 2, 1967, Brinsley Black; 1 s (Octavius Orlando Irvine Casati b 1968); *Career* JP; *Style*— Lady Moorea Black, JP; 17 Lansdowne Walk, London W11 3AH (☎ 01 727 3528)

BLACK, Peter; JP; s of Peter Blair Black of 3 Tudor Close, Ealing, London, and Cissie Crawford *née* Samuel; *b* 22 April 1917; *Educ* Sir Walter St John, Battersea, Bearsden Acad, London Sch of Building; *m* 1952, Mary Madeleine, da of Dr Joseph Hilly of Philadelphia, USA (d 1930); 1 s (Peter b 1957), 3 da (Susan b 1952, Ann b 1954, Margaret b 1955); *Career* memb GLC 1982-87, chm Thames Water Authy 1973-78, pres Pure Rivers Soc 1976-; leader GLC Group to Moscow and Leningrad 1971; sr ptnr P Blair and Ptnrs since 1984; former memb: Thames Conservancy Bd, Met Water Bd, Cncl Nat Fedn of Housing Socs; pres Abbey London Region; Freeman City of London; *Recreations* small boats, fishing; *Clubs* Middleton Sports, Sewers Synonymous; *Style*— Peter Black Esq, JP; The New House, 101A Limmer Lane, Felpham, Bognor Regis, Sussex PO22 7LP (☎ 0243 69 2054)

BLACK, (Francis) Peter; s of Francis Raymond Black (d 1985), and Rosina Mary, *née* De Burgh; *b* 20 August 1932; *Educ* Gunnersbsury GS, Hammersmith Coll of Art; *m* 15 March 1958, Jillian Elsie; 2 da (Susan b 1961, Caroline b 1964); *Career* architect with Norman and Dawbarn for 4 years designing Imperial Coll building; joined Scott Brownrigg and Turner 1961 (ptnr 1970-); bldgs include: Sport City Dubai, three airports in Iraq; RIBA, FSIAD, FCSD, FRSA, MBIM; *Recreations* runs a small farm at Englefield Green specialising in breeding and showing Dexters, short-legged rare breed of British cattle; *Style*— Peter Black, Esq; Sandylands Home Farm, Wick Road, Englefield Green, Surrey TW20 0HJ (☎ 0784 32782); Scott Brownrigg and Turner, 10-13 King Street, London WC2E 8HZ (☎ 01 240 2961, telex: 25897, fax: 01 831 1231)

BLACK, Prof Robert; QC (1987); s of James Little Black, of Lockerbie, Scotland, and Jeannie Findlay, *née* Lyon; *b* 12 June 1947; *Educ* Lockerbie Acad, Dumfries Acad, Univ of Edinburgh (LLB), McGill Univ Montreal (LLM); *Career* sr legal offr Scottish Law Sommn 1975-78, in practice Scottish Bar 1978-81, prof of scots law Univ of Edinburgh 1981- (lectr in Scots Law 1972-75); temp Sheriff 1981-; gen ed The Laws of Scotland: Stair Meml Encyclopaedia 1988- (dep, then jt, gen ed 1981-88); memb: exec cncl Scottish Nat Dictionary Assoc, legal ctee RSSPCC, bd of Scottish Cncl for Arbitration; Advocate of the British Bar 1972; *Books* An Introduction to Written Pleading (1982), Civil Jurisdiction: The New Rules (1983); *Recreations* beer, wine, tea (not always in that order); *Clubs* Sloane, London; Scottish Arts, Edinburgh; *Style*— Prof Robert Black, QC; 6/4 Glenogle Rd, Edinburgh EH3 5HW (☎ 031 557 3571); Dept of Scots Law, Old Coll, Sth Bridge, Edinburgh EH8 9YL (☎ 031 667 1011, fax 031 662 4902, telex 727442)

BLACK, Robert Anderson; s of Thomas Black (d 1960), of Tarriebank, Arbroath, and Agnes *née* Leggat; *b* 08 March 1923; *Educ* Giggleswick Sch, Glasgow Univ; *m* 20 Sept 1956, Mary Wallace, da of William Lees Weir (d 1948), of Carnoustie, Angus; 2 s (Tony b 1959, Robert b 1961), 2 da (Kaye b 1957, Susan b 1962); *Career* WWII Ferry Serv Admty 1943-46; md Tarriebank Estates (146-61, chm and md Border Oats Ltd 1979-; pres Br Oatmeal and Barley Millers Assoc 1986-88 (vice pres 1984-86), memb cereal ctee Agric Food Res Cncl 1987-88; fndr memb NSPPA, memb Carmyllie Community Fund, fndr Angus SC; LiBiol, MInstM; *Recreations* Golf, fishing, curling; *Clubs* Royal Overseas, CGA, RHAS, Chirnside Curling; *Style*— Robert Black, Esq; Edington Mill House, Chirnside, Duns, Berwickshire TD11 3LE (☎ 089 081 723); Border Oats Ltd, Edington Mill, Chirnside, Duns, Berwickshire TD11 3LE (☎ 089 081 252, telex 727176)

BLACK, Sir Robert Brown; GCMG (1962), KCMG (1955, CMG 1953, OBE 1949, MBE (Military) 1948); s of Robert Black (d 1929), of Blair Lodge, Stirlingshire, and Catherine Black; *b* 3 June 1906; *Educ* George Watson's Coll Edinburgh, Univ of Edinburgh (MA); *m* 1937, (Elsie) Anne, da of Allan Stevenson (d 1960), of Edinburgh; 2 da; *Career* Capt Intelligence Corps (Special Ops) Far East, 43 special mil missions; Colonial Admin Serv; govr and C-in-C: Singapore 1955-57, Hong Kong 1958-64; cmmr Cwlth War Graves Cmmn 1964-82; pres Int Social Serv (GB) 1973-82 (chm 1965-73), chm Clerical, Medical and General Life Assur Soc 1975-78; Hon LLD Hong Kong Univ, Chinese Univ of Hong Kong; KStJ 1955; Grand Cross Order of Merit (Peru) 1962; *Recreations* fishing, walking; *Clubs* E India Sports Devonshire and Public Schools; *Style*— Sir Robert Black, GCMG, KCMG, CMG, OBE, MBE; Mapletons House, Ashampstead Common, nr Reading, Berks RG8 8QN (☎ 0635 201 254)

BLACK, Dr Robert Monro; s of Thomas Henry Black (d 1944), and Ada, *née* Wright (d 1930); *b* 13 Jan 1925; *Educ* Eltham Coll Kent, Kings Coll London (BSc), Sir John Cass Coll London (MSc, PhD); *m* 29 Oct 1957, Beatrice Maud, da of Albert Ernest Higgs (d 1949); *Career* res chemist BICC plc 1945-87: (seconded to AERE Harwell 1953-55), Head Irradiation Dept 1955-61, head physical chemistry dept 1961-68, PA to Dir Res and Engrg 1968-72, special projects and info 1972-87; Freeman City of London, Freeman (by servitude) Worshipful Co of Merchant Taylors; FChem Soc 1945, memb Soc Chemical Ind 1945, ARIC 1950 memb Soc History of Alchemy and Early Chemistry; *Books* Electric Cables in Victorian Times (1972), The History of Electric Wires and Cables (1983) author or co-author numerous scientific and technical papers; *Recreations* music, reading, freemasonry; *Style*— Dr Robert M Black, Esq; 93 Roxborough Ave, Isleworth, Middlesex TW7 5HH (☎ 01 560 8519)

BLACK, Russell; s of Samuel Joseph Black, of Cardiff, and Muriel, *née* Lustig; *b* 12 Oct 1957; *Educ* Cardiff HS, Salford Univ (B Sc); *Career* CA, Gerald Edelman & Co 1979-83, Stoy Hayward 1983-86, Glazers 1987- (tax ptnr 1987-); ACA (1983), ATII (1987); *Recreations* squash, golf, soccer, music, bridge; *Clubs* Finchley Manor LT and SR; *Style*— Russell Black, Esq; Glazers, 843 Finchley Road, London NW11 8NA (☎ 01 458 7427, fax 01 455 2379, telex 268695)

BLACK, Prof Samuel (Sam); MBE (1969); s of Lionel Black (d 1960), of London, and Sophia, *née* Divinsky (d 1968); *b* 6 Jan 1915; *Educ* Owens Sch, Northampton Engrg Coll London Univ; *m* 24 June 1939, Muriel Cecilia Emily (d 1982), da of Cornelius George Snudden (d 1924), of Woodford, Essex; 1 s (Christopher), 1 da (Patricia); m 2, 27 Sept 1986, (Lucy) Gwendoline, da of George Bowles (d 1969), of Northampton; *Career* RAMC 1941-46; head of p/r: Assoc of Optical Practitioners 1946-55, Br Electrical and Allied Mfrs Assoc 1955-60; p/r advsr London C of C 1965-72, p/r cnsllr 1961- memb Miny of Health Ophthalmic Optical advsy ctee Optical Whitley Cncl; chm Inst Public Relations, pres Int Public Relations Assoc; sec Finchley Chess Club; visiting prof Coll of St Mark and St John Plymouth 1989; Freedman City of London 1956, Liveryman Worshipful Co of Spectacle Makers 1956; hon prof Relations Univ of Stirling 1988; FBIM, FIPR, FRSA, FBCO, FSMC, MJI; *Books* Practical Public Relations (1962), Exhibiting Overseas (1971), Role of Public Relations in Management (1972), Businessman's Guide to The Centrally Planned Economies (1972), Public Relations in the 1980's (1979), Exhibitions and Conferences from A-Z (1989), Introduction to Public Relations (1989); *Recreations* chess, travel; *Clubs* Reform; *Style*— Prof Sam Black, MBE; Keswick House, 3 Greenway, London N20 8EE (☎ 01 445 5256, fax 01 446 9108, telex 24224 ref 3237)

BLACK, Sheila Psyche; OBE (1986); da of Clement Johnston Black, and Mildred Beryl Black; *b* 6 May 1920; *Educ* Dorset, Switzerland and RADA; *m* 1 1939 (m dis 1951), Geoffrey Davien; 1 da (and 1 s decd); m 2, 1951 (m dis 1973), L A Lee Howard; *Career* woman's ed Financial Times 1959-72, specialist feature writer nat newspaper and magazines, author of several books; dir MAL plc 1976-; memb: Liquor Licensing Law Reform Ctee 1967-70, Price Cmmn 1973-77, cncl IOD 1975-, Nat Consumer Cncl 1981-; chm Gas Consumers Cncl 1980-; dir MAL plc 1976-; *Style*— Miss Sheila Black, OBE; 12A Earls Ct Gdns, London SW5 0TD (☎ 01 373 3620)

BLACK, Thomas Charteris; s of John Sutherland Charteris Black (d 1967), and Gertrude Margaret, *née* Stout (d 1976); *b* 12 Sept 1914; *Educ* Univ Coll Sch Frognal London, Sch of Pharmacy London; *m* 28 March 1942, (Violet) Lorna, da of Brig-Gen William Denman Croft, CB, CMG, DSO (d 1968), of Mawnan Smith, Cornwall; 1 s (Peter b 1952), 2 da (Jane b 1943, Susan b 1945); *Career* HG 1940-41: Cdr No 1 Platoon, No 3 Co, 1 Co of London Bn, Cdr Buckingham Palace Detachment of Kings Gd 1941; seaman RN Patrol Serv 1941-42, cmmnd Fighter Direction Offr 1942; RNVR Sub Lt HMS Victorious 1942-43, Lt HMS Ukussa 1944, Lt HMS Valiant 1944, Lt HMS Boxer 1945, Lt Cdr HMS Glory 1945-46; Menley & James Ltd: factory worker 1930-33, off mangr 1933-39, manufactured Stilboestrol 1938-39, mktg mangr 1939-41 and 1946-49, mktg dir 1949-56; mangr of commercial devpt Pfizers Ltd 1957-59, mktg mangr Miles Ltd 1959-67, vice-pres of int ops Miles Inc USA 1969-79 (mktg dir Ames div 1967-69); sec local PCC, tres local Cons branch; Freeman City of London 1952, Liveryman Worshipful Soc Apothecaries 1951; MPharmS 1938, FRSA 1951, FRPharmS 1977; *Recreations* sailing, bowls, walking; *Style*— Thomas Black, Esq; Michaelmas, Convent Close, St Margarets-at-Cliffe, Dover, Kent CT15 6JD (☎ 0304 853142)

BLACKABY, Frank Thomas; s of Rev Edgar Percival Blackaby (d 1977), and Muriel Ruth, *née* Hawkins (d 1977); *b* 25 Oct 1921; *Educ* Perse Sch Cambridge, Emmanuel Coll Cambridge (BA); *m* 1, 27 Oct 1961, Elizabeth; 1 s (Mark b 1962); m 2, 31 Dec 1975, Mary Mildred, da of Hon Arthur John Palmer Fuller-Acland-Hood (d 1964), of Somerset; 1 s (John b 1979), 1 da (Susan b 1977); *Career* dep dir Nat Inst of Economic and Social Research 1971-81, dir Stockholm Int Peace Research Inst 1981-86; ed: British Economic Policy 1960-74, Cambridge Univ Press 1978, World Armaments and Disarmament Yearbooks; *Recreations* tennis; *Style*— Frank T Blackaby, Esq; 9 Fentiman Road, London SW8 (☎ 01 735 3193)

BLACKADDER, Dr Eric Sutton; RD (1968, clasp 1978); s of John Williamson Blackadder (d 1946), of Falkirk, and Phoebe Euodia, *née* Sutton (d 1973); *b* 25 Nov 1927; *Educ* Falkirk HS, Edinburgh Univ (MB ChB); *m* 28 July 1955, Jean, da of William Law Gordon (d 1985), of Sunningdale; 2 s (Mark b 1956, John b 1957), 1 da (Averil b 1959); *Career* Nat Serv Surgn Lt RNVR 1953-55; RNR 1958-81: Surgn Lt Cdr 1960, Surgn Cdr 1965, ret 1981; jr hosp appts 1952-58, princ in gen practice 1958-68, fell in med admin Scottish Home and Health Dept 1968-70, med inspr of factories 1970-71, dep dir of med servs Health and Safety Exec 1977-80 (sr employment med advsr 1972-77), chief med offr Br Broadcasting Corpn 1980-84, gp med dir BUPA 1986-; govr BUPA Med Fndn Ltd 1986-, exec govr BUPA 1987-, dir: BUPA Health Insur 1987-, BUPA Int 1987-; hon lectr dept of gen practice Univ of Edinburgh 1963-68, hon clinical lectr in community med Univ of Glasgow 1975-77, guest lectr dept of social med Univ of Edinburgh and dept of occupational med Univ of Dundee 1968-77; cncl memb Rotary Club of London 1987-, vice pres Int Med Assoc for Radio and TV 1980-84, hon tres Int Assoc of Physicians for Overseas Servs 1986-, chm fin ctee Royal Inst of Public Health and Hygiene 1988- contrib numerous articles to medical and scientific jls; MRCP Glasgow 1980, FRCP Glasgow 1983, MRCP Edinburgh 1985, FRCP Edinburgh 1988, MFOM 1978, FFOM 1984, MRCGP 1961, MFCM 1974, FRSM; fell Royal Inst of Public Health and Hygiene, memb BMA; *Recreations* sailing, golf; *Clubs* Royal and Ancient GC, Royal Burgess Golfing Soc of Edinburgh, Royal Naval Sailing Assoc, Royal Yachting Assoc Phyllis Ct, Henley-upon-Thames, Oxfordshire; *Style*— Dr Eric Blackadder, RD; 2 Gloucester Gate Mews, Regents Park London NW1 4AD (☎ 01 486 7758) BUPA, Provident House, Essex St, London WC2R 3AX (☎ 01 353 5212, fax 01 353 0134, telex 883059)

BLACKBURN, Captain (David) Anthony (James); LVO (1978); s of late Lt J Blackburn, DSC, RN, and late Mrs M J G Pickering-Pick; *b* 18 Jan 1945; *Educ* Taunton Sch, RNC Dartmouth; *m* 1973, Elizabeth Barstow; 3 da; *Career* cmd HMS Kirkliston 1972-73; equerry-in-waiting to HRH The Duke of Edinburgh 1976-78; exec offr HMS Antrim 1978-81, Cdr HMS Birmingham 1983-84, HMS York 1987-88; *Style*— Capt Anthony Blackburn, LVO, RN

BLACKBURN, Archdeacon of; *see*: Robinson, The Ven (William) David

BLACKBURN, Barrie; s of Harold Blackburn, of Harlow, Essex, and Kathleen May (d 1984), *née* King; *b* 23 June 1948; *Educ* Marling Sch Stroud, Univ of Leeds (B Comm (hons)); *m* 9 Jan 1971, Julie Maureen, da of Phillip Ronald Baker, of Abingdon, Oxon; 2 s (David Charles b 1971, Luke b 1979), 1 da (Jane b 1984); *Career* articled clerk Touche Ross & Co 1970-78, taxation mangr Davy Corporation Plc 1975-84, gr taxation controller The Plessey Co Plc 1984-87, gp dir of taxation TI Group Plc 1987-; FCA, ATII; *Recreations* skiing, reading, watching sport, gardening; *Style*— Barrie Blackburn Esq; Woodbrook, 13 Stony Wood, Harlow, Essex CM18 6AU (☎ 0279 24495); TI Group Plc, 50 Curzon Street, London W1Y 7PN (☎ 01 499 9131, fax 01 493 6533, telex 263740 TIGROUP G)

BLACKBURN, David Michael; s of Rudolph Isaac Blackburn, of London, and Esther Sybil, *née* Levy; *b* 23 Dec 1937; *Educ* City of London Sch, St John's Coll Cambridge (MA, LLM); *m* 1, 11 Jan 1962 (m dis 1969), Louise Joy, da of Louis Courts, of London: 1 s (James b 1964), 1 da (Deborah b 1963); m 2, 30 April 1970, Janice, da of Louis Brown (d 1987); 2 s (Oliver b 1971, Joshua b 1973); *Career* slr, ptnr Courts & Co 1962-81; dir: Rosehaugh plc 1979-85, Rosehaugh Stanhope devpts plc 1983-, Blackburn Assoc Ltd 1986-; property project conslt 1985-; memb Law Soc 1962; *Style*— David Blackburn, Esq; 6 Rosslyn Mews, London NW3 1NN (☎ 01 431 3467, fax 01 435 0332, car tel 0836 229530)

BLACKBURN, George Alexander Peskett; OBE (1981); s of late G C Blackburn; *b* 26 Oct 1920; *Educ* Birkenhead Inst; *m* 1965, Betty Rigby, *née* Machell; 1 da; *Career* chartered marine engineer, presently tech dir Cammell Laird Shipbuilders, prev tech mangr 1971-74, chief marine engineer 1967-71; *Recreations* swimming, dancing, walking; *Clubs* White's; *Style*— George Blackburn, Esq, OBE; 67 Thingwall Rd, Irby, Merseyside

BLACKBURN, John Graham; MP (C) Dudley W 1979-; s of Charles Frederick Blackburn (d 1969), and Grace Blackburn; *b* 2 Sept 1934; *Educ* Liverpool Collegiate Sch, Liverpool U; *m* 1958, Marjorie, da of George Thompson (d 1974), of Wigan; 1 s, 2 da; *Career* formerly police offr Liverpool; sales dir Solway Engrg 1965-; memb POUNC 1972-; freeman Cities of London and Tel Aviv; *Recreations* yachting (yacht 'Tobermory'); *Clubs* Wolverhampton and Bilston Athletic, Traeth Coch Yacht (Anglesey); *Style*— John Blackburn, Esq, MP; 906 Howard House, Dolphin Square Westminster, London

BLACKBURN, Michael John; s of Francis Blackburn (d 1970), and Ann Elizabeth, *née* Thornley (d 1973); *b* 25 Oct 1930; *Educ* Kingston GS; *m* 19 March 1955, Maureen Beatrice, da of Arnold Dale; 1 s (Alastair b 1957), 2 da (Fiona b 1958, Anna b 1966); *Career* managing ptnr Touche Ross & Co 1984 (ptnr 1960-84); FCA 1953, CBIM 1986; *Recreations* horse racing, gardening; *Clubs* City of London; *Style*— Michael Blackburn, Esq; Touche Ross & Co, Hill Ho, 1 Little New St, London EC4 3TR (☎ 01 936 3000, fax 01 583 8517, telex 884739)

BLACKBURN, Ronald Henry Albert; s of Sydney James Blackburn (d 1954), of Prestbury, Knock, Belfast, and Ellen Margaret Selina, *née* German (d 1952); *b* 9 Feb 1924; *Educ* Royal Belfast Academical Inst, Univ of London (LLB); *m* 13 Sept 1950, Annabell, da of John Hunter (d 1941), of Whiteabbey, NI; 2 s (Alan b 1952, Paul b 1957); *Career* WWII FO 1943-45; NI Parly reporting staff 1946-52, second clerk asst Parliament 1952-62 (clerk asst 1962-71, clerk of the Parls 1971-73), clerk NI Assembly 1973-79, memb NI Planning Appeals Commn 1980-89, clerk NI Constitutional Convention 1976-76; memb Cwlth Parly Assoc 1952-79 (attended conferences in Malaysia, Gibraltar, CI, London and IOM); *Recreations* gardening, golf; *Style*— Ronald Blackburn, Esq; Trelawn, 9 Jordanstown Road, Newtownabbey, Co Antrim, NI BT37 OQD (☎ 0232 862035); Planning Appeals Commission (NI), Carlton House, Shaftesbury Sq, Belfast (☎ 0232 244710)

BLACKBURN, Thomas; s of Thomas Blackburn, of Preston; *b* 22 July 1932; *Educ* Oundle; *m* 1955, Diana Christine, da of William Ascough Lillico (d 1983), of Barnet; 1 s, 2 da; *Career* engr dir: C Seward & Co Hldgs 1960-, Shard Bridge Co 1980- (chm 1984); jt md C Seward & Co 1967-(chm 1987); *Recreations* shooting, fishing; *Style*— Thomas Blackburn, Esq; Hill Top Farm, Thornley with Wheatley, Longridge, Preston, Lancs PR3 2TY (☎ 0774 78 3353); C Seward and Co Ltd, West View, Ribbleton, Preston, Lancs PR1 5JA (☎ 0772 796424)

BLACKBURN, William Howard; s of Thomas Cather Johnston Blackburn (d 1960), and Elizabeth, *née* Thomas-Jones (d 1978); *b* 23 Dec 1932; *Educ* Holt Sch, Liverpool Univ (LLB); *m* 1, 23 July 1985 (m dis), Chloë Marya Tickell, da of Sir James Gunn (d 1964); 2 s (Alexander b 1963, James b 1965); m 2, 9 April 1960, Marie-Thérèse (d 1983), da of Gen Andre Dorange (d 1985); *Career* ptnr Theodore Goddard Paris (1957-62); IBM 1962-84: mangr legal dept, co sec, md (Euro Off SA); memb: Br Cncl Law Advsy Ctee, Inst of Actuaries Appeals Bd, UK Delgn to Cncl of Euro Bars and Law Socs (CCBE), cncl Law Soc; chm Int Ctee Law Soc; *Recreations* golf; *Clubs* RAC, Royal Mid-Surrey GC; *Style*— William Blackburn, Esq; 18 Alma Square, London NW8 9RA (☎ 01 286 5273); c/o Theodore Goddard, 16 St Martins-le-Grand, London EC1A 4EJ (☎ 01 606 8865, fax 01 606 4390)

BLACKBURNE, Lady; Bridget Senhouse Constant; *née* Wilson; da of James Mackay Wilson, JP, DL (d 1934), of Currygrane, Co Longford, and Amy Alice Goldie-Taubman (d 1944); *b* 28 Sept 1903; *Educ* Private; *m* 1935, Sir Kenneth William Blackburne, GCMG, GBE, (d 1980); 1 s (Martin d 1985), 1 da (Jean m Richard Hall; 3 da); *Style*— Lady Blackburne; Garvagh, Ballasalla, Isle of Man (☎ Castletown (0624) 823640)

BLACKBURNE, Rt Rev Hugh Charles; s of Very Rev Harry William Blackburne, DSO, MC, Dean of Bristol (d 1963), and Haidée Frances, *née* Creagh (d 1958); *b* 4 June 1912; *Educ* Marlborough, Clare Cambridge, Westcott House; *m* 1944, Doris Freda, wid of Pilot Offr H L N Davis; 2 s, 1 da; *Career* deacon 1937, priest 1938, curate Almondbury Yorks, chaplain to the Forces 1939-47, served with 1 Guards Bde, 11 Armd Div, HQ AA Cmd and as chaplain RMC Sandhurst, rector of New Milton Hants 1947-53, vicar of St Mary's Harrow 1953-61, rector of Hilborough Group 1961-72, vicar of Ranworth and chaplain for Norfolk Broads 1972-77, bishop of Thetford 1977-80; chaplain to HM The Queen 1962-77; *Recreations* sailing, birdwatching; *Style*— The Rt Rev Hugh Blackburne; 39 Northgate, Beccles, Suffolk (☎ Beccles (0502) 716374)

BLACKER, Hon Mrs (Caroline Susan Dean); da of Rev Lord Soper and Marie Gertrude Dean; *b* 11 August 1946; *Educ* Queenswood, Exeter U (BA); *m* 1975, Terence Blacker, s of Gen Sir Cecil Hugh Blacker, KCB, OBE, MC, *qv*; 1 s (Alexander b 1977), 1 da (Alice b 1979); *Style*— The Hon Mrs Blacker; 91 Wendell Road, W12 (☎ 01 743 8746)

BLACKER, Gen Sir Cecil Hugh; GCB (1975, KCB 1969, CB 1967), OBE (1960), MC (1944); s of Col Norman Valentine Blacker, DSO, MC (d 1958), and Olive Georgina, *née* Hope (d 1978); *b* 4 June 1916; *Educ* Wellington, RMC Sandhurst; *m* 26 Feb 1947, Felicity Mary, da of Maj Ivor Buxton, DSO, TD (d 1969), and widow of Maj John Rew (ka 1943); 2 s; *Career* 2 Lt Royal Inniskilling Dragoon Gds 1936, GOC-in-C Northern Cmd 1969-70, V-Ch of Gen Staff 1970-73, Adj-Gen 1973-76, ret 1976; ADC to HM The Queen 1962-64, ADC (Gen) to HM The Queen 1974-76; FBIM 1973; pres: Br Showjumping Assoc 1976-80, Br Equestrian Fedn 1980-84; chm Racecourse Security Servs Ltd 1980-83; memb Horserace Betting Levy Bd 1980-83; dep sr steward Jockey Club 1984-86; *Recreations* painting, hothouse gardening; *Clubs* Jockey; *Style*— Gen Sir Cecil Blacker, GCB, OBE, MC; Cowpasture Farm, Hook Norton, Banbury, Oxon (☎ Hook Norton 730344)

BLACKER, Hon Mrs (Mary Rose); er da of 2 Baron Rathcavan (o da by his 1 w); *b* 26 August 1935; *m* 1960, David Stewart Wellesley Blacker, JP, DL, er twin s of Lt-Col Latham Valentine Stewart Blacker, OBE, of Cold Hayes, Liss, Hants (whose maternal gm was Marie Leszczynska, ggda of last Elector of Posen and gt grand-niece of Stanislas Leszczynski, Count of Lesno and, as Stanislaw I, King of Poland, hence cous to all the descendants of Louis XV of France by his m with Marie Leszczynska, King Stanislaw I's da) by Col Blacker's w Lady Doris Peel, JP, o da of 1 E Peel; 3 s (Barnaby b 1961, William b 1962, Rohan b 1966); *Style*— The Hon Mrs Blacker; Molecomb, Goodwood, Chichester, Sussex

BLACKER, Norman; s of Cyril Norman Blacker, and Agnes Margaret Blacker; *b* 22 May 1938; *Educ* Wolverton GS; *m* 8 July 1961, Jenifer Mary Anderson; *Career* chm Br Gas N Eastern 1985-, dir of fin Br Gas Corpn 1980-84; IPFA, CIGasE, CBIM; *Style*— Norman Blacker, Esq; British Gas North Eastern, New York Rd, Leeds LS2 7PE (☎ 0532 436291)

BLACKETT, Francis Hugh; s of Sir Hugh Douglas Blackett, 8 Bt (d 1960); hp to btcy of bro, Sir George Blackett, 10 Bt; *b* 16 Oct 1907; *Educ* Eton; *m* 1, 1950, Mrs Elizabeth Eily Barrie (d 1982), da of late Howard Dennison, of Valparaiso, Chile; 2 s, 2 da; m 2, 1985, Mrs Catherine Joan Chowdry, da of late Edward Watson, of Bloxham, Oxfordshire; *Career* Maj The Royals (ret); served WWII; *Style*— Francis Blackett, Esq; Ramshope Lodge, Catcleugh, Otterburn, Newcastle upon Tyne NE19 1TZ

BLACKETT, Sir George William; 10 Bt (E 1673); s of late Sir Hugh Blackett, 8 Bt; suc bro, Sir Charles Douglas Blackett (d 1968); *b* 26 April 1906; *m* 1, 1933, Euphemia Cicely (d 1960), da of late Maj Nicholas Robinson, of Frankton Grange, Shropshire; m 2, 1964, Daphne Laing, da of late Maj Guy Laing Bradley, TD, of Bridge End House, Hexham; *Heir* bro, Maj Francis Hugh Blackett, *qv*; *Career* Shropshire Yeo and CMP WW II; *Style*— Sir George Blackett, Bt; Colwyn, Corbridge-on-Tyne, Northumberland (☎ Corbridge 2252)

BLACKETT, Hon Mrs (Geva Charlotte Caroline); *née* Winn; o da of 5 Baron St Oswald, *qv*; *b* 15 Sept 1955; *m* 12 June 1987, John Simon Blackett, er s of John Harold Booth Blackett, of Whalton, Northumberland; 1 da (Helena Charlotte Rose b 22 Sept 1988); *Style*— The Hon Mrs Blackett; The Corner House, Maveham Lane, Scredington, Sleaford, Lincolns NG34 0AW

BLACKETT, Hon Nicolas Maynard; s of Baron Blackett, OM, CH (Life Peer, d 1974); *b* 25 May 1928; *Educ* Univ Coll Sch London and Univ of Bristol; *m* 1951, Patricia Kathleen Tankins, of Bristol; 1 s (Peter b 1962); *Career* research scientist; Inst of Cancer Research London 1954-83, ret; *Style*— The Hon Nicolas Blackett; 18 Farquhar Road, London SW19

BLACKETT-ORD, His Honour (Andrew) James; CVO (1988); 2 s of John Reginald Blackett-Ord, JP (d 1967), of Whitfield Hall, Hexham, Northumberland, and Lena Mary, *née* Blackett-Ord (d 1961); yr bro of John Christopher Blackett-Ord, *qv*; *b* 21 August 1921; *Educ* Eton, New Coll Oxford (MA); *m* 9 June 1945, Rosemary, da of Edward William Bovill (d 1966), of Brook House, Moreton, Essex; 4 s (Christopher b and d 13 Feb 1946, Charles b 6 Feb 1948, Martin b 10 May 1950, Benjamin James b 12 Feb 1963), 1 da (Nicola Mary Lena (Mrs George St Leger Granville) b 25 Oct 1961); *Career* Lt Scots Guards, served in UK, N Africa and Italy 1941-46 (prisoner (Anzio) 1944-45); barr Inner Temple 1947, Lincoln's Inn 1948; County Court Judge 1971; Vice-Chllr Co Palatine of Lancaster, memb Cncl of Duchy of Lancaster and High Court Judge (Chancery Divn) in Northern Area 1973-87; chllr Diocese of Newcastle-upon-Tyne 1971-; Bencher Lincoln's Inn 1985; *Recreations* rural life, reading, travel; *Clubs* Garrick, Lansdowne; *Style*— His Honour A J Blackett-Ord, CVO; Helbeck Hall, Brough, Kirkby Stephen, Cumbria (☎ 09304 323)

BLACKETT-ORD, John Christopher; JP (1960); elder s of John Reginald Blackett-Ord, JP (d 1967), of Whitfield Hall, Hexham, Northumberland, and Lena Mary, *née* Blackett-Ord (d 1961); bro of Andrew James Blackett-Ord, *qv*; *b* 30 Sept 1918; *Educ* Eton, New Coll Oxford; *m* 1, 1941, Elisabeth Hamilton (d 1977), da of Maj Charles Mitchell, DSO, OBE (d 1958), of Pallinsburn, Cornhill on Tweed; 1 s, 2 da; m 2, 1985, Pamela Margaret, da of Frederic Blagden Malim, of Myddylton House, Saffron Walden (d 1964), and widow of John Humphrey Edmund Craster (d 1983); *Career* Maj served in Scots Guards 1939-45 (Italy 1943-45) FRICS 1949; farmer; *Recreations* shooting, fishing; *Clubs* Lansdowne; *Style*— John Blackett-Ord, Esq, JP; Whitfield Hall, Hexham, Northumberland (☎ Whitfield (049 85) home 272, office 273)

BLACKETT-ORD, Mark; s of His Hon Judge Andrew James Blackett-Ord, CVO, *qv*, and Rosemary, *née* Bovill; *b* 10 May 1950; *Educ* Eton, New Coll Oxford; *m* 2 Dec 1981, Carol Theresa Anne, da of Sir David Scott-Fox, KCMG (d 1984); 2 da (Katherine b 1983, Elinor b 1986); *Career* called to the Bar (Lincoln's Inn) 1974; *Books* Hell-Fire Duke (1981), ed Partnership Law in Halsbury's Laws of England (1981); *Recreations* restoration of ancient buildings; *Style*— M Blackett-Ord, Esq; Warcop Hall, Warcop, Appleby, Cumbria; 81 Church St, Stoke Newington, London N16; 2 New Square, Lincoln's Inn, London WC2A 3RU (☎ 01 242 6201, fax 01 831 8102)

BLACKFORD, Sqdn Ldr Peter Fitzgerald; s of Joseph Blackford (d 1959), and Sheila O'Halligan (d 1952); *b* 22 Nov 1920; *Educ* Tonbridge, RAF Coll Cranwell; *m* 23 July 1943, Sheila, da of Lt Col Henry Joseph Higgs (d 1936), of Notts; 4 s (Timothy b 1945, Christopher b 1948, Jeremy b 1952, Patrick b 1954); *Career* regular RAF offr 1938-57, wartime ops in UK and Europe, ret as Sqdn 1957; subsequently worked as personnel mangr in several cos incl Wellcome Fndn 1969-82; *Recreations* gardening; *Style*— Sqdn Ldr Peter F Blackford; Shode House, Dux Lane, Plaxtol, nr Sevenoaks, Kent

BLACKFORD HICKMAN, Rivers; s of late Leslie Blackford Hickman, LDS, and Rose Alice, *née* Begg; *b* 15 July 1936; *Educ* Cheltenham; *m* 1966, Patricia May, da of Richard Alfred Coombs (decd); 1 s (Gavin b 1966), 2 da (Susan b 1958, Amanda b 1962); *Career* nat serv (Lt) Army inc service in Malaya 1954-56; slr 1964; a Recorder of the Crown Court 1987-; *Recreations* hunting, watching son compete Motor Cross; *Style*— Rivers Blackford Hickman, Esq; Thoulds Barn House, Uckinghall, Tewkesbury, Glos GL20 6ES; 21 Brouch Street, Pershore, Worcs; 3 Foregate Street, Worcester

BLACKHAM, Rear Adm Joseph Leslie; CB (1965), DL (Hants & IOW 1970); s of Dr Walter Charles Blackham, of Birmingham (d 1969), and Margaret Eva, *née* Bavin (d 1983); *b* 29 Feb 1912; *Educ* W House Sch Birmingham, RNC Dartmouth; *m* 1938,

Coreen Shelford, da of Paymaster-Capt William Shelford Skinner, CBE, RN, of Blackheath; 1 s, 1 da; *Career* served RN 1925-66, Korea 1951-52 (despatches), Adm Supt Portsmouth Dockyard 1964-66; chm IOW CC 1975-77, v-chm IOW AHA 1974-81; chm: IOW Family Practitioners Ctee 1974-85, St John Ambulance Centre Ctee IOW 1982-, Bd of Visitors HM Prison Parkhurst 1974-77 (memb 1968-72), pres C of E Soldiers, Sailors and Airmen's Clubs 1979-; High Sheriff IOW 1975; *Style—* Rear-Adm Joseph Blackham, CB, DL; Trinity Cottage, Love Lane, Bembridge, IOW PO35 5NH (☎ 0983 874386)

BLACKIE, John Walter Graham; s of Walter Graham Blackie (d 1972); *b* 2 Oct 1946; *Educ* Uppingham, Cambridge Univ, Harvard, Merton Coll Oxford, Edinburgh Univ; *m* 1972, Jane; *Career* advocate 1974, lectr in Scots Law Univ of Edinburgh 1975, visiting lectr Univ of Göttingen 1981, dir Blackie & Son Ltd (Publishers) 1970; *Recreations* singing, playing wind instruments; *Style—* John Blackie, Esq; The Old Coach House, 23a Russell Place, Trinity, Edinburgh EH5 (☎ 031 552 3103)

BLACKLEE, Jillian Mary; *née* Clough; da of Dr John Henry Harper Clough, of London, NW11, and Margaret Vaughan, *née* Edwards; *b* 30 Mar 1955; *Educ* Wycombe Abbey Sch High Wycombe Bucks, The Middx Hosp London W1 (Dip Physiotherapy); *m* 1 June 1985, Andrew Gimson Blacklee, s of Frederick Phillips Blacklee, of Northampton, England; *Career* physiotherapist: Northwick Park Hosp 1976-79, Thermalbaeder Bd Ragaz Switzerland 1979-81; sr physiotherapist: Behring Krankenhaus W Berlin 1981-83, St Mary's Hosp London 1983-86, Paddington Community Hosp London 1986-; MCSP 1976; *Recreations* snow skiing; *Style—* Mrs Jillian Blacklee; 27 Leinster Mews, Hyde Park, London W2 3EY (☎ 01 402 7106); Paddington Community Hosp, 7A Woodfield Rd, London W9 (☎ 01 286 6669, ext 210)

BLACKLEY, John Lorimer; JP; s of John Blackley (d 1951); *b* 22 Nov 1915; *Educ* Sedbergh; *m* 1940, Christina Ferrier, da of Robert Stepford, of Dumfries; 1 s; *Career* farmer; chm W Cumberland Farmers' Ltd 1976-, EFG (New Lands) Ltd 1976-; *Recreations* angling, shooting, gardening; *Clubs* Farmers'; *Style—* John Blackley, Esq, JP; Berscar, Closeburn, Thornhill, Dumfriesshire (☎ Closeburn 246)

BLACKLEY, Neil Ramsay; s of (Samuel) Ramsay Blackley, OBE, of Hamdon House, New Galloway, Kirkcudbrightshire, and Deirdre, *née* Wilson; *b* 30 August 1955; *Educ* Malvern, Imperial Coll (BSc), London Business Sch (MBA); *m* 8 Nov 1986, Susan Valerie, da of Keith Lawrence Porter, of Plover, 1 Kenwyn Rd, Torquay; *Career* shipping analyst Lindsay Blee (chartering) Ltd 1979-82; investmt analyst: Esso Pension Fund 1982-83, James Capel 1983-; memb Business Graduates Assoc; ACGI 1977, MBIM; *Books* pubns incl: The Design Consultancy Marketplace, The Global Advertising Marketplace; *Recreations* squash; *Style—* Neil Blackley, Esq; 19 Gordon Rd, Grove Park, London W4; James Capel & Co, James Capel House, 6 Bevis Marks, London EC3 (☎ 01 621 0011)

BLACKMAN, Carol Anne; da of Herbert Owen Francis Smith, and Gladys, *née* Huggins; *b* 11 Mar 1947; *Educ* Southampton Univ (BA), Bradford Univ (MSc); *m* 28 March 1970 (m dis 1981), Robert Stephen Blackman, s of Jack Blackman; *Career* vice pres Industl Marketing Research Assoc 1985- (chm 1981-86, vice chm 1982-84), chm Conference and Educn Ctee; memb: Market Research Soc, Industl Marketing Research Assoc, Inst of Marketing, Marketing Educn Gp, Assoc for Mgmnt Educn Dvpt; *Recreations* sailing, golf; *Style—* Ms Carol Blackman; Polytechnic of Central London, Management Centre, 35 Marylebone Road, London NW2 5LS (☎ 01-486-5811); 42 High Rd, Essendon, Hatfield, Herts AL9 6AW (☎ 07072 61242); B & W Associates, Deni House, 11 The Warren, Chesham, Bucks HP5 2RX (☎ 0494 771325)

BLACKMORE, (Edward) Anthony; s of Hilary Blackmore (d 1986), of Midhurst, and Florence Olive, *née* Simpson (d 1982); *b* 9 April 1933; *Educ* Winchester, Emmanuel Coll Cambridge (BA); *m* 5 Sept 1959, Caroline Ann, da of Oliver Haworth Jones (d 1978); 2 s (James Blackmore b 1960, Simon Blackmore b 1964), 1 da (Emma Blackmore b 1962); *Career* admitted slr 1957, asst slr Slaughter & May 1957-59, sr ptnr Simpson Curtis 1988 (asst slr 1959-62, ptnr 1962-88); memb Leeds Law Soc: chm trg sub-ctee, technol sub-ctee; memb City of London Slrs Co, memb Law Soc; *Recreations* skiing, swimming; *Clubs* The Leeds; *Style—* Anthony Blackmore, Esq; 41 Park Square, Leeds LS1 2NS (☎ 0532 433 433, fax 0532 445 598, car tel 0860 227 373, telex 44376)

BLACKMORE, Antony John; s of John Wilfrid Blackmore, of Bridlington, E Yorks, and Marjorie, *née* Sims; *b* 3 Sept 1949; *Educ* The King's Sch Canterbury, Magdalene Coll Cambridge (MA), Hull Sch of Architecture (DipArch); *m* 28 Dec 1973, Helena Mary, da of Arthur Reynolds Carter; 3 s (John Robin b 30 Dec 1975, Edward Antony James b 23 July 1979, Timothy Andrew John b 26 Sept 1985), 2 da (Charlotte Sophie d 6 Aug 1977, Charlotte Mary b 6 Feb 1981); *Career* architect; Blackmore Son & Co Hull 1980-, architect Lincoln and York Dioceses 1984-, regnl panel architect Nat Assoc of Almshouses, Civil Tst Award for Hart Homes Hornsea, involved in the restoration of many churhces and almshouses; tstee Georgian Soc for E Yorks, memb Hunsley Beacon Beagles; gen cmmr Inland Revenue (Hull); memb: RIBA 1975, EASA 1982; *Books* Uniformity of Groundplan in Cistercian Abbeys (1973); *Recreations* athletics (Cambridge Blue), gardening, heraldry; *Clubs* Arts, Hawks (Cambridge); *Style—* Antony Blackmore, Esq; The Old Rectory, Brandesburton, Driffield, E Yorks (☎ 0964 542 904); Kilmun, Loch Avich, by Taynuilt, Argyll; Blackmore Son & Co, Blaydes House, High St, Hull HU1 1PZ (☎ 0482 26406)

BLACKMORE, Courtenay Thomas Gardner; 2 s of late Rev Canon Alfred T G Blackmore, of Apple Trees, Steeple Ashton, Wilts; *b* 16 Oct 1922; *Educ* Oakham Sch, Keble Coll Oxford; *m* 26 Oct 1957, as her 2 husb, Lady Pamela, *qv*, da of 1 and last Earl of Kilmuir (d 1967); 1 s, 2 da; *Career* formerly with ICI; head of admin Lloyd's 1975-83; memb Cncl Sail Tning Assoc 1978-; memb Exec Ctee Industl Soc 1976-84; ptnr Project Client Conslts 1984-; dir Lloyd's of London Press Ltd, Royal Institution; Freeman City of London; pres Oxford Union Soc 1943; FIPM, FRSA, Hon FRIBA; *Recreations* gardening, reading, photography, painting; *Clubs* Architecture, Carlton, MCC, 1900; *Style—* Courtenay Blackmore, Esq; 61 Riverview Gardens, Castelnau, London SW13 9QZ

BLACKMORE, Lady Pamela Maxwell; *née* Fyfe; JP (Inner London); da of 1 Earl and last Earl of Kilmuir, GCVO, PC (d 1967); *b* 14 Oct 1928; *Educ* Crofton Grange, LMH Oxford; *m* 1, 24 May 1950, Clive Wigram (d 1956), o son of late Nathan Graham Wigram, FRCS; 1 da; m 2, 26 Oct 1957, Courtenay Thomas Gardner Blackmore, *qv*; 1 s, 2 da; *Career* dep chm Greenwich & Woolwich Div Inner London Bench; memb exec ctee and appeals ctee Peckham Settlement; chm Greenwich and Woolwich Div Inner London Bench 1983-86; memb David Isaac Ctee 1980-; Freeman City of London; *Clubs* Roy Cwlth Soc; *Style—* Lady Pamela Blackmore, JP; 61 Riverview Gdns, Castelnau, London SW13 9QZ (☎ 01 741 1239)

BLACKSHAW, Alan; VRD (1970); s of Frederick William Blackshaw (d 1983), of Blundellsands, Liverpool, and Elsie, *née* MacDougall (d 1978); *b* 7 April 1933; *Educ* Merchant Taylors' Sch Crosby, Wadham Coll Oxford (MA); *m* 1, 1956 (m dis 1983), Jane Elizabeth Turner; 1 da (Sara); m 2, 1984, Dr Elspeth Paterson, da of late Rev Gavin C Martin; 1 s (Alasdair b 1985), 1 da (Elsie b 1987); *Career* RM 1954-56, Roy Marine Reserve 1954-74, Capt; business conslt and author; civil servant 1956-79; dir gen Offshore Supplies Off 1977-78; pres Br Mountaineering Cncl 1973-76; chm Br Ski Fedn 1984-86; chm Nat Centre for Mountain Activities, Plas y Brenin 1986-; *Books* Editor The Alpine Journal 1968-70; Mountaineering (3rd edn. 1975); *Recreations* mountaineering, skiing; *Clubs* Alpine, Ski Club of GB, Royal Scottish Automobile; *Style—* Alan Blackshaw, Esq, VRD; 4 St George's Sq, London SW1V 2HP (☎ 01 821 8720); Les Autannes, Le Tour, Chamonix Mt Blanc, Frnnce 74440 (☎50 54 12 20)

BLACKSTONE, Baroness (Life Peeress UK 1987), of Stoke Newington, Greater London; Tessa Ann Vosper Evans; *née* Blackstone; er da of Geoffrey Vaughan Blackstone, CBE, GM (d 1989), of Bures, Suffolk, and Joanna, *née* Vosper; *b* 27 Sept 1942; *Educ* Ware GS for Girls, London Sch of Economics and Political Science (BSc (Soc) 1964, PhD 1969); *m* 1963 (m dis), Thomas Charles Evans (d 1985); 1 s (Hon Benedict Evans, *qv*), 1 da (Hon Liesel, *qv*); *Career* Assoc lectr in sociology Enfield Coll of Technology 1965-66; asst lectr, then lectr, in social admin LSE 1966-75; fell Centre for Studies in Social Policy 1972-74; advsr Central Policy Review Staff, Cabinet Office 1975-78; prof of educational administration Univ of London Inst of Education 1978-83; dep education offr (Resources) ILEA 1983-86; Clerk to the Authority and Dir of Education, ILEA April-Nov 1986; Rowntree special res fell Policy Studies Inst 1986-87; master Birkbeck Coll, Univ of London 1987-; chm: Fabian Soc 1984-85, General Advisory Cncl BBC 1988-, Institute for Public Policy Res 1988-; memb Arts Cncl Planning Board 1986-, Board Royal Opera House 1987; *Books* Students in Conflict, LSE in 1967 (1970, co-author), A Fair Start: The Provision of the Pre-School Education (1971); The Academic Labour Market: Economic and Social Aspects of a Profession (1974 and 1982, co-author), Disadvantage and Education (1982, co-author); Testing Children: Standardised Testing in Local Education Authorities and Schools (1983, co-author), Response to Adversity (1983, co-author), Inside the Think Tank: Advising the Cabinet 1971-83 (1988, co-author); *Style—* The Rt Hon Baroness Blackstone; 2 Gower Street, London WC1 (☎ 01 636 0067); Birkbeck College, Malet Street, London WC1 (☎ 01 631 6274)

BLACKTOP, Rev Graham Leonard; s of Leonard Blacktop (d 1981), and Grace Ivy May, *née* Evans (d 1988); *b* 21 July 1933; *Educ* Christ's Coll, Finchley; *m* 9 May 1959, Alison Margaret, da of Kenneth Campbell; 3 da (Louise b 1960, Catherine b 1962, Ruth b 1965); *Career* cmmnd Royal Fusiliers City of London Regt and Royal West African Frontier Force 1951-54, TA Middx Regt (Duke of Cambridge's Own) and Herts Regt 1954-61; jr clerk Standard Bank of S Africa 1949-51, md Alexanders Discount plc 1983- (joined 1954); contrib articles to: Euromoney, American Banker, Journal of the Inst of Chartered Accountants in Scotland, Journal of the Cricket Soc; non-stipendiary Anglican priest (see Crockford's); Liveryman: Worshipful Co of Painter-Stainers 1969, Worshipful Co of Parish Clerks 1980; *Recreations* cricket; *Clubs* MCC, Army & Navy; *Style—* The Rev Graham Blacktop; 52 Shepherd's Way, Rickmansworth, Herts WD3 2NL (☎ 0923 772022); Alexanders Discount plc, 65 Cornhill, London EC3V 3PP (☎ 01 626 5467)

BLACKWELL, Sir Basil Davenport; s of late Alfred Blackwell, and late Hilda Kathleen Sophia Bretherick (later Mrs Lloyd); *b* 8 Feb 1922; *Educ* Leeds GS, St John's Coll Cambridge (MA), London Univ BSc Eng.; *m* 1948, Betty, da of Engr Capt Meggs, RN; 1 da (Susan); *Career* v-chm and chief exec Westland Gp of Cos 1974-, dep chm and chief exec 1984-85; chm: Westland Helicopters Ltd 1976-85, Br Hovercraft Corpn 1979-85, Normalair-Garrett Ltd 1979-85; FEng (1978), Hon DSc Bath (1984), FIMechE, FRAeS (Gold Medal 1982); kt 1983; *Recreations* gardens, gardening; *Clubs* United Oxford and Cambridge; *Style—* Sir Basil Blackwell; High Newland, Newland Garden, Sherborne, Dorset DT9 3AF (☎ (0935) 813516)

BLACKWELL, Colin Roy; s of John Harris (d 1931), of Witheridge, and Marjorie Grace Blackwell (d 1982); *b* 4 Sept 1927; *Educ* West Buckland, Univ of Bristol (BSc); *m* 1979, Susan Elizabeth, da of Brig Cecil Hunt, CBE (d 1985), of Chichester; *Career* consulting engr cmmnd 83 LAA Regt RA served ME 1946-48; Freeman Fox and Ptnrs Conslt Engrs: joined 1951, site engr Ghana (later Gold Coast) 1955-57, sr engr 1957-68, princ engr 1969-82; dir Freeman Fox Ltd 1983-87, int conslt on telescopes and observatories, Acer Freeman Fox 1987-; memb: CIRIA res ctee 1976-79, Br Cncl Mission to Saudi Arabia 1985, BSI CSB Ctee 1986-; FICE, FASCE, FRAS, FRSA; *Clubs* Athenaeum; *Style—* Colin Blackwell, Esq; 34 Drayton Gdns, London SW10 9SA (☎ 01 370 1145); Acer Freeman Fox Ltd, 25 Victoria St (S Block), Westminster, London SW1H 0EX (☎ 01 222 8050, fax 01 222 6818, telex 916018 ACERV G)

BLACKWOOD, Brian; s of George Blackwood, of Reigate, Surrey, and Eva Blackwood; *b* 4 Feb 1926; *Educ* Redhill Tech Coll, Inverness HS, Architectural Assoc, Northern Poly, Univ Coll London (Dip TP), Univ of York Inst Advanced Architectural Studies (Dip Con Studies); *m* 1950 (m dis 1974); 1 s, 2 da; *Career* artist, photographer, architect, conservationist, town planner and leading authy on lives and works of architects Smith and Brewer; local govt 1945-70; Tunbridge Wells Borough cncl 1951-62, Stevenage Devpt Corp 1962-66, hd of design Herts Co Planning Dept 1966-70; architectural advsr The Victorian Soc 1974-75; memb City of Cambridge Listed Bldgs Panel 1974-, memb Cncl Ancient Monuments Soc 1982-, memb cases ctee Herts Conservation Soc 1987-, memb N Herts Crime Prevention Panel 1977-87, vice chm Stevenage and Dist Crime Prevention Panel 1988-; Freeman City of London 1979, Liveryman Worshipful Co of Painter-Stainers 1984; FRSA 1947, ARIBA 1961, FRIBA 1968, AMTPI 1968, FRTPI 1974, FSAScot 1972, ARHist 1976, FSAI 1976, FRGS 1983, fell Cambridge Philosphical Soc 1986; *Recreations* archaeology, coffee, lichen, music, writing; *Clubs* Art Workers Guild; *Style—* Brian Blackwood, Esq; Ebony House, Whitney Drive, Stevenage SG1 4BL (☎ 0438 725111)

BLACKWOOD, Wing-Cdr (George) Douglas Morant; s of James Hugh Blackwood (d 1951), of London, and Sybil Mary, *née* Morant, da of Adm Sir Digby (d 1966); *b* 11 Oct 1909; *Educ* Eton, Clare Coll Cambridge; *m* 22 Feb 1936, Phyllis Marion, da of Sir John Caulcutt, KCMG, (d 1942); 1 s ((John) Michael Douglas b Dec 1942), 1 da (Maureen Lavinia b March 1940); *Career* cmmnd RAF 1932, sqdn-ldr formed 1 Czech Fighter Sqdn 1940, served Battle of Britain wing-cdr 1941, Czech wing 2nd TAF 1944 (despatches twice), ret 1945; ed Blackwoods' Magazine 1952-72 (gggs of William Blackwood fndr), ret 1976; Czech War Cross 1940, Czech first class 1944; *Recreations* countryside, sports; *Style—* Wing-Cdr Douglas Blackwood; Airhouse, Oxton, Lauder, Berwickshire (☎ 057 85 225)

BLACKWOOD, Hon John Francis; s and h of 10 Baron Dufferin and Clandeboye, *qv*; *b* 18 Oct 1944; *Educ* Barker Coll Hornsby, Univ of NSW (BArch); *m* 1971, (Annette) Kay, da of Harold Greenhill, of Seaforth, Sydney, NSW; 1 s (Francis Senden b 6 Jan 1979), 1 da (Freya Jodie b 1975); *Career* architect in private practice; ARAIA; *Style—* John Blackwood, Esq; 169 Anson Street, Orange, NSW 2800, Australia

BLACKWOOD, Lilian, Lady; Lilian Margaret; da of late Fulton J MacGougan, of Vancouver; *m* 1921, Sir Francis Elliot Temple Blackwood, 6 Bt (d 1979); *Style—* Lilian, Lady Blackwood; c/o Rivesdale Convalescent Hospital, 1090 Rio Lane, Sacramento, California 35822, USA

BLACKWOOD, Hon Peter Maurice; yr s of 10 Baron Dufferin and Clandeboye, *qv*; *Educ* Knox GS Wahroonga, Macquarie Univ (BA); *m* 1979, Kay Lynette, *née* Winkle; 1 da (Alice b 1982)

BLAGG, Dr Thomas Frederick Colston; s of Lt Col Thomas Colston Blagg (d 1983), of Brunsel Hall, Car-Colston, Notts, and Loys Willis, *née* Cope; *b* 10 August 1942; *Educ* Oakham, Keble Coll Oxford (BA, MA), Inst of Archaeology Univ of London (PhD); *Career* admitted slr 1967; in practice 1967-70, freelance archaeologist 1970-78, memb educn serv Br Museum 1978; lectr in archaeology Univ of Kent 1978-; FSA 1983; *Books* jointly: The Roman Riverside Wall and Monumental Arch in London (1980), Papers in Iberian Archaeology (1984), Military and Civilian in Roman Britain (1984); *Recreations* travel (wine and ruins), shooting, London; *Style—* Dr Thomas Blagg; 70 North Side, Clapham Common, London SW4 (☎ 01 228 1192); Rutherford Coll, The Univ, Canterbury, Kent CT2 7NX (☎ 0227 764000)

BLAHNIK, Manolo; s of E Blahnidík (d 1986), and Manuela, *née* Rodrigo-Acosta; *b* 28 Nov 1943; *Educ* Univ of Geneva, Louvre Art Sch Paris; *Career* designer of shoes and furniture; co proprietor 1973-; winner Fashion Cncl of America Award 1988; *Recreations* travel and painting; *Style—* Manolo Blahník, Esq; 49-51 Old Church St, London SW3 (☎ 01 352 8622, 01 352 3863)

BLAIR; *see*: Hunter Blair

BLAIR, Sir Alastair Campbell; KCVO (1969, CVO 1953), TD (1950), WS (1932), JP (Edinburgh 1954); 2 s of late William Blair, WS, of Edinburgh, and late Emelia Mylne Campbell; *b* 16 Jan 1908; *Educ* Charterhouse, Clare Coll Camb (BA), Edinburgh Univ (LLB); *m* 1933, Catriona Hatchard, o da of late Dr William Basil Orr, of Edinburgh; 4 s (incl Michael Campbell Blair, *qv*); *Career* former ptnr Dundas & Wilson, CS; sec Royal Co of Archers (Queen's Body Guard for Scotland) 1946-59, Capt 1982-84; purse bearer to The Lord High Cmmr to the General Assembly of the Church of Scotland 1961-69; *Style—* Sir Alastair Blair, KCVO, TD, WS, JP; 7 Abbotsford Court, Colinton Road, Edinburgh EH10 5EH (☎ 031 447 3095)

BLAIR, Anthony Charles Lynton; MP (Lab) Sedgefield 1983-; s of Leo Charles Lynton Blair and late Hazel Blair; *b* 6 May 1953; *Educ* Durham Choristers Sch, Fettes Coll, St John's Coll Oxford; *m* 1980, Cherie Booth, 2 s, 1 da; *Career* barr Lincoln's Inn 1976; *Style—* Anthony Blair, Esq, MP; House of Commons, London SW1A 0AA

BLAIR, Lt-Gen Sir Chandos; KCVO (1972), OBE (1962), MC (1941) and Bar (1944); s of Brig-Gen Arthur Blair, DSO, KOSB (d 1947), and Elizabeth Mary, *née* Hoskyns; *b* 25 Feb 1919; *Educ* Harrow and RMC Sandhurst; *m* 1947, Audrey Mary, da of F Guy Travers; 1 s, 1 da; *Career* 2 Lt Seaforth Highlanders 1939, served WW II 2 and 7 Seaforth Highlanders, Lt-Col 1957, Brig 1964, GOC 2 Div BAOR 1968-70, Maj-Gen 1968, Defence Servs Sec MOD 1970-72, GOC Scotland and Govr of Edinburgh Castle 1972-76, Lt-Gen 1972; *Style—* Lt-Gen Sir Chandos Blair, KCVO, OBE, MC; Applegarth, Audbury, Tring, Herts

BLAIR, Sir Edward Thomas Hunter; 8 Bt (GB 1786), of Dunskey; s of Sir James Hunter Blair, 7 Bt (d 1985); *b* 15 Dec 1920; *Educ* Eton, Univ of Paris (Dip French Lang and Lit), Balliol Coll Oxford (BA); *m* 1956, Norma (d 1972), da of Walter S Harris (d 1972); *Heir* bro, James b 18 March 1926; *Career* Civil Service 1941-43, asst foreign ed 1944-49, md of own company 1950-63; memb Kirkcudbright CC 1970-71, former pres Dumfries and Galloway Mountaineering Club 1939-45; *Books* Scotland Sings and A Story of Me (1981), A Future Time (With an Earlier Life) (1984), A Mission in Life (1987); *Recreations* gerdening, hill walking; *Style—* Sir Edward Hunter Blair, Bt; Parton House, Castle Douglas, Kirkcudbrightshire

BLAIR, Air Cdre Henry Gordon; CBE (1958), DL (Berks 1975); s of Henry Blair (d 1955), of Manchester; *b* 2 July 1909; *Educ* privately; *m* 1937, Margaret, da of late James Kelly, of Edinburgh; 1 s (ka Ulster 1979), 1 da; *Career* Air Cdre RAF, ret 1960; memb: Newbury RDC 1964-70, Berks CC 1970-85 (vice chm 1983-85); *Recreations* gardening, birds; *Clubs* RAF; *Style—* Air Cdre H G Blair, CBE, DL; Upover, Cold Ash, Newbury, Berks RG16 9HZ (☎ Thatcham (0635) 63122)

BLAIR, Michael Campbell; s of Sir Alastair Campbell Blair, KCVO, TD, WS, *qv*; *b* 26 August 1941; *Educ* Cargilfield Sch Edinburgh, Rugby, Clare Coll Cambridge (MA, LLM), Yale USA (MA); *m* 1966, Halldóra Isabel, da of Richard Anthony Conolly Tunnard, DL, of Lincs; 1 s (Alastair Magnus b 1974); *Career* barr Mid'le Temple 1965; circuit admin Midland and Oxford circuit 1982-86, under-sec Lord Chllrs Dept 1982-1987 (entered Lord Chllrs Dept 1966, private sec to Lord Chllr and dep Sgt at Arms House of Lords, 1968-71), Cabinet Off Top Mgmnt Programme 1986; dir legal servs, The Securities and Investments Bd 1987-, memb Gen Cncl of the Bar 1989-; *Books* Sale of Goods Act 1979 (Butterworths 1980); *Recreations* family life; *Clubs* Athenaeum; *Style—* Michael Blair, Esq; The Securities and Investments Board, 3 Royal Exchange Buildings, London EC3

BLAIR, Nicholas Peter; TD; s of Maj Peter Blair TD, and Ann De Quincey, *née* Walker; *b* 22 Feb 1949; *Educ* Wood Tutorial Coll; *Career* Collett Dickenson Pearce and Ptnrs Ltd 1967-71, vice chm BSB Dorland Ltd 1971-; Freeman: City of London 1970, Worshipful Company of Dyers 1970; MIPA, Minst M; *Recreations* eating, drinking, horseracing; *Clubs* Buck's; *Style—* Nicholas Blair, Esq, TD; 41 Southwood Park, Highgate, London N6 5SG (☎ 01 348 5730); BSB Dorland Ltd, 121-141 Westbourne Terrace, London W2 6JR (☎ 01 262 5077, fax 01 724 3845, car tel 0860 355 937, telex 27778)

BLAIR, Robin Orr; WS (1965); s of Sir Alastair Blair, KCVO, *qv*; *b* 1 Jan 1940; *Educ* Rugby, St Andrews Univ (MA), Edinburgh Univ (LLB); *m* 20 May 1972, Caroline, da of Ian McCallum Webster (d 1973), of Walberswick, Suffolk; 2 s (Matthew b 1974, Benjamin b 1976), 1 da (Alice b 1980); *Career* ptnr Davidson & Syme WS 1967-74, exec ptnr Dundas & Wilson CS 1988- (ptnr 1974-), managing ptnr 1976-83; non exec dir: Top Flight Leisure Gp 1977- (chm 1987-), Tullis Russell & Co Ltd 1978-; Purse Bearer to the Lord High Cmmr to the Gen Assembly of the Church of Scotland 1988-; sec Assoc of Edinburgh Royal Tradesmen 1966-, memb Queen's Body Guard for Scotland (Royal Co of Archers) 1970-; memb Law Soc of Scotland 1965; *Recreations* skiing, hill walking; *Clubs* New (Edinburgh), Hon Co of Edinburgh Golfers; *Style—* Robin Blair, Esq, WS; 2 Greenhill Pk, Edinburgh; 25 Charlotte Sq, Edinburgh (☎ 031 225 1234, fax 031 225 5594, telex 72404)

BLAIR OLIPHANT, Laurence Philip Kington; s of Maj Philip James Kington Blair Oliphant (d 1963), of Ardblair Castle, Blairgowrie, Perthshire, and Beatrice Mary Moore, *née* Carroll; *b* 26 Aug 1945; *Educ* Trinity Coll Glenalmond; *m* 11 Aug 1973, Jenny Caroline, da of Leonard Lockwood Anscombe, Taranaki, NZ; 1 s (Charles b 1976), 2 da (Amelia b 1977, Philippa b 1981); Laurence Blair Oliphant, Esq; *Books* Ardblair Castle, Blairgowrie, Perthshire (☎ 0250 3155)

BLAIR-CUNYNGHAME, Sir James Ogilvy; OBE (1945, MBE 1943); 2 s of late Edwin Blair-Cunynghame, of Edinburgh, and Anne Tod; *b* 28 Feb 1913; *Educ* Sedbergh, King's Coll Cambridge; *Career* served WW II RA & Intelligence, Lt Col, Mediterranean & Europe; FO 1946,47, chief personnel offr BOAC 1947-55, dir gen staff NCB 1955-57, chm: Royal Bank of Scotland 1971-76 (gp chm 1968-78), dir Williams & Glyn's Bank 1976-78; dir Scottish Mortgage & Tst, memb: Queen's Body Guard for Scotland (Royal Co of Archers), Exec Ctee Scottish Cncl Dvpt of Industry, Cncl of Industry for Management Educn, cncl Industl Soc; part time memb Pay Bd, govr Sedbergh Sch, tstee Int Centre for Research in Accountancy; Hon DSc Edinburgh, Hon LLD St Andrews, Hon FRCSE, FIB, FBIM, CIPM; kt 1978; *Style—* Sir James Blair-Cunynghame, OBE; Broomfield, Moniaive, Thornhill, Dumfriesshire (☎ 084 82 217)

BLAIR-KERR, Sir Alastair; christened William Alexander but changed name by Declaration of change of name 1973; s of William Alexander Milne Kerr (d 1941), of Dunblane, Perthshire, and Annie, *née* Blair (d 1968); *b* 1 Dec 1911; *Educ* McLaren HS Callander, Edinburgh Univ (MA, LLB); *m* 1942, Esther Margaret, da of Sydney Fowler Wright (d 1947); 1 s, 1 da; *Career* advocate (Scots Bar); judge of Supreme Ct Hong Kong 1959-73; pres Ct of Appeal: Bahamas 1978, Bermuda 1979, Belize 1979; memb Gibraltar Ct of Appeal 1982; kt 1973; *Recreations* music, walking; *Clubs* Royal Overseas League; *Style—* Sir Alastair Blair-Kerr; Gairn, Kinbuck, Dunblane, Perthshire FK15 0NQ (☎ 0786 823377)

BLAIR-OLIPHANT, Air Vice-Marshal (David) Nigel Kington; CB (1966), OBE (1945); s of Col Philip Laurence Kington Blair-Oliphant, DSO (d of wounds received in action 1918), of Ardblair Castle, Blairgowrie, Perthshire, and Laura Geraldine, *née* Bodenham (d 1941); *b* 22 Dec 1911; *Educ* Harrow, Trinity Hall Cambridge (BA); *m* 1942, Helen Nathalie (d 1983), da of Sir John Stewart Donald, KCIE, CSI (d 1948); 2 s (Nigel, Alastair (decd)), 1 da (Geraldine (decd)); *Career* joined RAF 1934, WWII Middle East and Euro campaigns 1939-45, RAF Staff Coll 1945-48, Gp Capt 1949, Air Cdre 1958, dir weapons engrg Air Miny 1958-60, Br Def Staff Washington 1960-63, acting Air Vice-Marshal 1963, pres Ordnance Bd 1965-66, Air Vice-Marshal 1966; *Clubs* RAF; *Style—* Air Vice-Marshal Nigel Blair-Oliphant, CB, OBE; 9 Northfield Rd, Sherfield-on-Loddon, Basingstoke, Hants (☎ 0256 882724)

BLAKE, Sir Alfred Lapthorn; KCVO (1979, CVO 1975), MC (1945); s of late Leonard Nicholson Blake and Nora Woodfall Blake, *née* Lapthorn; *b* 6 Oct 1915; *Educ* Dauntsey's Sch, London Univ (LLB); *m* 1, 1940, Beatrice Grace Nellthorp (d 1967); 2 s; m 2, 1969, Mrs Alison Kelsey Dick, of Boston, Mass, USA; *Career* slr and notary public; former ptnr Blake Lapthorn Slrs Portsmouth (conslt 1985-); Lord Mayor of Portsmouth 1958-59, dir The Duke of Edinburgh's Award Scheme 1967-78; lay canon Portsmouth Cathedral 1962-72, pres Portsmouth Youth Activities Ctee and other local community organisations; hon fell Portsmouth Poly; *Recreations* golf; *Clubs* Royal Naval, Royal Albert (Portsmouth); *Style—* Sir Alfred Blake, KCVO, MC; 1 Kitnocks Cottages, Wickham Rd, Curdridge, Southampton SO3 2HG

BLAKE, Andrew Nicholas Hubert; s of John Berchmans Blake, of Clitheroe, Lancs, and Beryl Mary, *née* Murphy; *b* 18 August 1946; *Educ* Ampleforth, Hertford Coll Oxford (MA); *m* 7 July 1978, Joy Ruth, da of Ronald Shevloff (d 1986), of Southport; 1 s (Ben b 4 June 1980); *Career* barr 1971 Inner Temple, rec Northern circuit 1988; *Recreations* skiing, the turf, fishing; *Style—* Andrew Blake, Esq; Brae House, 12 New Rd, Lymm, Cheshire; 18 St John St, Manchester (☎ 061 834 9843)

BLAKE, Anthony Teilo Bruce; s of Maj Charles Anthony Howell Bruce Blake (ka Korea 1951); h to baronetcy of kinsman, Sir Richard Valentine Blake, 17 Bt; *b* 5 May 1951; *Educ* Wellington, Lanchester Poly; *Career* engr; *Style—* Anthony Blake, Esq; 20 Lavender Gardens, Battersea, London SW11 1DL

BLAKE, Prof Christopher; s of George Blake (d 1961), of 75 Queen Margaret Drive, Glasgow, and Eliza Malcolm, *née* Lawson (d 1983); *b* 28 April 1926; *Educ* Dollar Acad, St Andrews Univ, (MA, PhD); *m* 25 July 1951, Elizabeth, da of John Easson McIntyre, of Embden House, Broughty Ferry (d 1947); 2 s (Duncan b 1952, Neil b 1954), 2 da (Catriona b 1959, Janet b 1960); *Career* Sub-L RNVR, served 1944-47 Mediterranean; Bonar Professor Applied Economics Dundee Univ 1974-88; dir Alliance Trust plc 1974-, chm: William Low & Company plc 1985-, Glenrothes Devpt Corpn 1987-; memb Royal Cmmn of Environmental Pollution 1980-85, tres Royal Soc of Edinburgh 1985-; *Recreations* golf, reading; *Clubs* New (Edinburgh), Royal and Ancient St Andrews; *Style—* Prof Christopher Blake; Westlea, Wardlaw Gdns, St Andrews, Fife KY16 9DW

BLAKE, Prof David Leonard; s of Leonard Arthur Blake (d 1979), and Dorothy Violet, *née* Bristow; *b* 2 Sept 1936; *Educ* Latymer Upper Sch Hammersmith, Gonville and Caius Coll Cambridge (BA, MA), Deutsche Akademie der Künste Berlin DDR; *m* 24 Sept 1960, Rita Mary, da of Frank Adolphus Muir (d 1975), 2 s (Andrew b 23 Aug 1961, Daniel b 11 July 1964), 1 da (Claire b 24 Nov 1962); *Career* Nat Serv RAF 1955-57; teacher; Prof of Music Univ of York 1976- (lectr 1964, sr lectr 1971, Head of Dept 1981-84); composer: Chamber Symphony 1966, Lumina (cantata) 1969, Violin Concerto 1976, Toussaint Opera 3 acts 1977, From the Mattress Grave song cycle 1978, Clarinet Quintet 1980, Rise Dove for bass and orchestra 1983, The Plumber's Gift opera in two acts 1988; *Recreations* squash, golf, water mill restoration; *Style—* Prof David Blake; Mill Gill, Askrigg, nr Leyburn, N Yorks DL8 3HR (☎ 0969 50364), Dept of Music, University of York (☎ 0904 430000)

BLAKE, Hon Deborah Cicelie; da of Baron Blake (Life Peer); *b* 1955; *Style—* The Hon Deborah Blake; 15 Rowsley Avenue, Hendon, London NW4

BLAKE, Dennis Arthur; MBE (1945) JP (1974); s of Lt-Col Terence Joseph Edward Blake, DSO (d 1921), of Hampstead, London, and Ethel Maud, *née* Moore (d 1986); *b* 13 April 1920; *Educ* The Hall Sch Hampstead, Douai Sch Woolhampton; *m* 10 July 1948, Helen Drake Milne, da of Capt Thomas Milne Swan (d 1977), of Kirkcaldy; 1 s (Terence b 1954), 1 da (Vanessa b 1949); *Career* WWII Army 1939-46; London Rifle Bde 1939, cmmnd Royal Fusiliers 1940, joined IRF and served 4 Indian Div Western Desert, Eritrean and Syrian Campaigns (awarded French Croix de Guerre and mentioned in despatches) 1940-41) GSO2 HQ 3 Corps and Force 140 1942-45 served: Iraq, Italy, Greece, demob Hon Maj 1946; CA 1948-88: auditor accounts of the Chamberlain and Bridge Masters of Corpn of London 1956-78, sr ptnr Baker Rooke 1970-78; chm Horsham Bench and gen commr income tax (chm Horsham Div) 1978-; Freeman City of London, memb Worshipful Co of Loriners 1956; FCA 1953; *Recreations* walking; *Clubs* Army and Navy, MCC; *Style—* Dennis Blake, Esq; 13 Causeway, Horsham, W Sussex RH12 1HE (☎ 0403 53638)

BLAKE, Sir Francis Michael; 3 Bt (UK 1907); s of Sir (Francis) Edward Colquhoun Blake, 2 Bt (d 1950); *b* 11 July 1943; *Educ* Rugby; *m* 1968, Joan Ashbridge, o da of Frederic Cecil Ashbridge Miller, of Ramsay Lodge, Kelso; 2 s; *Heir* s, Francis Julian Blake b 17 Feb 1971; *Career* Stockbroker; *Style—* Sir Francis Blake, Bt; The Dower House, Tillmouth Park, Cornhill-on-Tweed, Northumberland (☎ Coldstream (0890) 2443)

BLAKE, John; s of Frederick Blake; *b* 4 Jan 1936; *Educ* The Leiston Sch; *m* 1961, Beryl, da of Jack English; 1 child; *Career* chartered sec; dep md: Serif Cowells plc; dir: W S Cowell Ltd, Cowells Financial Printing Ltd, Cowells Bingo Ltd, Cowells Security Ltd, Cowells Book Colour Ltd, United Greeting Cards UK Ltd; *Recreations* photography, walking, travel, publishing; *Style—* John Blake, Esq; Brackendale, Bromeswell, Woodbridge, Suffolk

BLAKE, John Clifford; CB (1957); s of Alfred Harold Blake (d 1959), of 45 Hilton Lane, Prestwich, Lancs, and Ada, *née* Yates (d 1931); *b* 12 July 1901; *Educ* Manchester GS, Oxford (MA); *m* 1928, Mary Lilian, da of Thomas Rothwell (d 1939), of Salford, Lancs; 1 s (John), 2 da (Hebe, Rosemary); *Career* slr in govt legal serv Miny of Health and successor depts 1929-65, slr and legal advsr to Minys of Health and Housing and Local Govt 1957-65 (including Registrar Gen); *Recreations* music, especially organ, piano, and choral, bowls; *Style—* John Blake, Esq, CB; 3 Clifton Ct, 297 Clifton Drive South, St Annes on Sea, Lancs FY8 1HN (☎ 0253 728365)

BLAKE, John Michael; s of Maj Edwin Francis Blake, MBE (d 1972), of London, and (Evelyn) Joyce, *née* Meadows; *b* 6 Nov 1948; *Educ* Westminster City GS, NW London Poly; *m* 29 June 1968, Diane Sutherland, da of Peter John Campbell (d 1973), of London,; 1 s (Adam b 1985), 2 da (Emma b 1969, Charlotte b 1971); *Career* reporter: Hackney Gazette 1965-68, Evening Post Luton 1968-69, Fleet Street News Agency 1969-71; columnist: London Evening News 1971-80, London Evening Standard 1980-82, The Sun 1982-84; asst ed Daily Mirror 1984-88, ed The People 1988; *Books* Up And Down With The Rolling Stones (1979), All You Needed Was Love (1981); *Recreations* sailing, skiing, distance running, travel; *Style—* John Blake, Esq; The People, 1 New Fetter Lane, London EC4A 1AR (☎ 01 822 3400, fax 01 353, telex 266888)

BLAKE, Hon Letitia Lindley; da of Baron Blake (Life Peer); *b* 1960; *Style—* The Hon Letitia Blake

BLAKE, Philip Haslewood; s of Robert Frederick Blake, (d 1944), of Belfast, and Josephine Anne Isabella, *née* Sloss (d 1962); descended from all the sons of Edward III that left issue, all the like Magna Carta Barons, Sir Thomas More and William Haslewood, executor of Lord Nelson; Lordship of Barham Kent in family since 1597; *b* 3 May 1907; *Educ* Campbell Coll Belfast, Royal Coll of Music London; *Career* sub-editor Northern Whig Belfast 1927-30; info offr Br Pavilion NY World's Fair 1939-40; temp admin offr Br Info Services NY, and set up Govt Exhibition Serv in USA 1940-43; ed Br Topography, Encyc Brit 1943-44; conductor Belfast Concerts for Sch Children and ENSA Orch 1944-45; music advsr ENSA in BLA 1945; pro i/c visual publicity Min of Town and Country Planning 1946-48; Inland Revenue 1949-51; press offr: Fedn of Civil Engrg Contractors 1952-60, Royal Mint 1960-61; sec Soc of Genealogists, fndr res dept and first dir 1961-62; genealogist 1963-; memb: Cncl Br Record Soc 1949-, Kent Arch Soc 1982-; chm Records Ctee, cncl memb Irish Genealogical Res Soc 1986-87, fell and dir of res 1987); fndr Assoc of Genealogists and Record Agents (AGRA) 1968, and of Kent Record Collections 1985; author; many articles in learned journals; *Books* History of Federation of Civil Engineering Contractors (1960), Canterbury Cathedral, Christ Church Gate (1965); *Recreations* chess, vintage cars; *Style—* Philip Blake, Esq; 5 Watkin Rd, Folkestone, Kent CT19 5EP (☎ 0303 41739)

BLAKE, Quentin Saxby; OBE (1988); s of William Blake, and Evelyn Blake; *b* 16 Dec 1932; *Educ* Downing Coll Cambridge (MA); *Career* freelance artist and illustrator; head of dept of illustration RCA 1978-86; RDI, FCSD, sr fell RCA 1988; *Style—* Quentin Blake, Esq; 30 Bramham Gdns, London SW5

BLAKE, Sir (Thomas) Richard (Valentine); 17 Bt (I 1622); s of Sir Ulick Temple Blake, 16 Bt, Saltergill, Yarm-on-Tees, Yorkshire (d 1963), and Elizabeth Longley-Cook (d 1978); *b* 7 Jan 1942; *Educ* Bradfield Coll; *m* 1, 1976, Jacqueline, da of late Desmond E Daroux, and formerly w of Peter Alers Hankey; m 2, 1982 (m dis 1986) (as her 3 husb), the singer Bertice Reading formerly w of Eddie Meyer); *Heir* kinsman, Anthony Teilo Bruce Blake; *Career* motor trade 1959; former car sales mngr; Lavant Motor Centre; dir: Sir Richard Blake & Assocs 1967-, City Chase Ltd 1980-84 (specialist in Rolls-Royce, Bentley, Gordon-Keeble cars), proprietor Autobart 1988-, md Axtell of Haslemere; *Recreations* three day eventing, vintage cars; *Clubs* Gordon-Keeble Owners (hon life memb), Rolls-Royce Enthusiasts; *Style—* Sir Richard Blake, Bt; Axtell of Haslemere, Kings Rd, Haslemere, Surrey GU27 2QD (☎ 0428 53301, 0860 742766)

BLAKE, Baron (Life Peer UK 1971); Robert Norman William Blake; FBA (1967), JP (Oxford); er s of William Joseph Blake (d 1964), of Brundall, Norfolk, and Norah Lindley Daynes; *b* 23 Dec 1916; *Educ* King Edward VI Sch Norwich, Magdalen Coll Oxford (DLitt, MA); *m* 1953, Patricia Mary, eldest da of Thomas Richard Waters (d 1983), of Great Plumstead, Norfolk; 3 da; *Career* sits as Conservative in House of Lords; served WW II Capt RA (POW Italy 1942-44, escaped 1944; despatches); student and tutor in politics Christ Church Coll Oxford 1947-68 (lecturer 1946-47, censor 1950-55, sr proctor 1969-60, Ford's Lecturer in Eng History 1967-68); provost Queen's Coll Oxford 1968-87; pro-vice-chllr Oxford U 1971-87; tstee Br Museum 1978-88; ed Dictionary of Nat Biography 1980-; chm: Roy Cmmn Historical Manuscripts 1982-, Rhodes Tst 1983-87; dir Channel Four Television Co 1983-87; FBA; *Books* The Unknown Prime Minister, Bonar Law (1955), Disraeli (1966), The Conservative Party from Peel to Churchill (1970), The Off of Prime Minister (1975), A History of Rhodesia (1977); The English World (editor, 1982) Disraeli's Grand Tour (19k82), The Decline of Power 1915-1964 (1985); *Recreations* reading and writing; *Clubs* Beefsteak, Brooks's, United Oxford and Cambridge, Norfolk County, Pratt's; *Style—* The Rt Hon The Lord Blake, JP; Riverview House, Brundall, Norwich (☎ (0603) 712133);

BLAKE, (William) Seymour; TD (1965); s of William Harvey Blake, JP (d 1932), of Bridge, S Petherton, Som, and Gweneth Margaret, *née* Evans (d 1983); *b* 5 Feb 1919; *Educ* Uppingham Sch, Oxford Univ (MA); *m* 16 Sept 1950, (Ione) Daphne, da of Maj Charles Ion McKay, MC (d 1936), of Hythe, Kent; 4 s (John b 1951, Francis b 1953, Rodney b 1960, Andrew b 1963); *Career* RA 1940-46, Capt 1944, TA 1949-66, Maj 1959; slr Crewkerne Som 1949-88 Notary Public; memb Bath & Wells Diocesan Synod, chm S Petherton Village Hall mgmnt ctee 1968-88; memb Law Soc, Som Law Soc; *Recreations* family history, church architecture, walking, conjuring; *Clubs* English Speaking Union; *Style—* Seymour Blake, Esq, TD; Newbridge, 14 Palmer St, S Petherton, Somerset TA13 5DB (☎ 0460 40426)

BLAKE, Hon Victoria Mary; yst da of Baron Blake (Life Peer); *b* 1963; *Style—* The Hon Victoria Blake

BLAKEMORE, Michael Howell; s of Dr Conrad Howel Blakemore (d 1976), and Una Mary, *née* Litchfield (later Mrs Heyworth) (d 1982); related through American paternal gm Maud Howell to US presidents John Quincy Adams and John Adams; *b* 19 June 1928,Sydney, NSW; *Educ* Cranbrook Sch, The King's Sch, Univ of Sydney, RADA; *m* 1, 1960 (m dis 1986), Shirley Mary Bush; 1 s (Conrad); m 2, 1986, Tanya, da of Clement McCallin (d 1978 actor); 2 da (Beatrice b 1981, Clementine b 1984); *Career* stage and film dir (occasionally writer and actor); co-artistic dir Glasgow Citizen's Theatre 1966-68, assoc dir Nat Theatre 1971-76, resident dir Lyric Theatre Hammersmith 1980 freelance, dir of prize winning prodns: A Day in the Death of Joe Egg 1968, Arturo Ui 1969, Forget-Me-Not-Lane 1971; also dir of: The Nat Health 1969, Plunder 1975, Long Day's Journey Into Night 1971, The Front Page 1972 (Plays and Players Best Dir award for the latter two prodns), The Wild Duck, Make and Break, Noises Off, Design for Living, Knuckle, Candida, Separate Tables, Privates on Parade, Deathtrap, All My Sons, Benefactors, Made in Bangkok, Lettice and Lovage, Uncle Vanya; dir (abroad) of: Noises Off (on Broadway and in Australia, received Drama Desk Award 1984), A Personal History of the Australian Surf (also wrote and acted in the latter, Peter Seller's Award for Comedy in the Standard Film Awards); dir film Privates on Parade 1982; actor drama documentary for Channel 10 TV in Australia 1984; *Books* Next Season (1969); *Recreations* surfing, houses; *Clubs* RAC; *Style—* Michael Blakemore, Esq; 11A St Martin's Almshouses, Bayham St, London NW1 (☎ 01 267 3952)

BLAKENEY, Frederick Joseph; CBE (1968); s of Frederick Joseph Blakeney, of Sydney, NSW; *b* 2 July 1913; *Educ* Marist Darlinghurst & Mittagong, Sydney Univ (BA); *m* 1943, Marjorie Grosmont, da of John Martin, of Griffith, NSW; 1 da; *Career* AMF 1940-42, RAAF (navigator) 1942-45 (Euro theatre), joined Australian Diplomatic Serv 1946, Paris 1947-49, Moscow 1949-51 (Chargé d'affaires 1950-51), Canberra 1952-53; cnsllr Washington 1953-56; min Aust legation Phnom Penh 1957, Saigon & Vietnam 1957-59; asst sec Canberra 1959-62; Aust ambass to Fed Republic of Germany 1962-68; Aust ambass to USSR 1968-71; first ass sec Canberra 1972-74; Aust ambass to the Netherlands 1974-77; perm rep to UNO Geneva 1977-78; ret; *Style—* Frederick Blakeney, Esq, CBE; 19 Grey Street, Deakin, Canberra, ACT, Australia

BLAKENHAM, 2 Viscount (UK 1963); Michael John Hare; s of 1 Viscount Blakenham, OBE, PC (d 1982, 3 s of 4 E of Listowel), and Nancy, Viscountess Blakenham, *qv*; *b* 25 Jan 1938; *Educ* Eton, Harvard (AB Econ); *m* 12 Jan 1965, his 1 cous, Marcia Persephone, da of Maj Hon Alan Victor Hare; MC; 1 s, 2 da; *Career* 2nd Lt The Life Gds 1956-57, with English Electric 1958; Lazard Bros 1961-63; Standard Industl Gp 1963-71; Royal Doulton 1972-77; md Pearson plc 1978-83; chm S Pearson plc 1983-; chm Financial Times 1983-; ptnr of Lazard ptnrs 1984-; dir Sotheby's Hldgs Inc 1987-, dir Elsevier NV 1988-; memb: int advsy bd Lafarge Coppe 1979-, House of Lords Select Ctee on Science and Technol 1985-88, Nature Conservancy Cncl 1986-; pres Sussex Wildlife Tst 1983-; chm Royal Soc for the Protection of Birds 1981-86; *Style—* The Rt Hon Viscount Blakenham; 17th Floor, Millbank Tower, Millbank, London SW1P 4QZ (☎ 01 828 9020, telex 8953869)

BLAKENHAM, Nancy, Viscountess; Hon (Beryl) Nancy; *née* Pearson; da of 2nd Viscount Cowdray and Agnes, da of Lord Edward Spencer-Churchill; *b* 25 Feb 1908; *m* 1934, 1st Viscount Blakenham, OBE, PC (d 1982); 1 s (2nd Viscount), 2 da (Hon Mrs Sergison-Brooke, Hon Mrs Breyer); *Style—* Rt Hon Nancy, Viscountess Blakenham; 10 Holland Park, W11; Cottage Farm, Litle Blakenham, nr Ipswich

BLAKER, George; CMG (1963); s of Col William Frederick Blaker (d 1933), and Helen Elizabeth, *née* Blaker (d 1971); *b* 30 Sept 1912,Simla, India; *Educ* Eton, Trinity Coll Cambridge (BA); *m* 1938, Richenda Dorothy, da of Rev Arthur Buxton (d 1958; sometime Rector of All Souls', Langham Place); 1 da (Jennifer); *Career* under-sec HM Treasy 1955-63; tresy rep in India, Ceylon, Burma 1957-63; pres Surrey Tst for Nature Conservation 1969-80; hon sec Scientific and Medical Network 1973-86, pres 1987-; owner Vann Lake Nature Reserve (30 acres) 1963-87; *Style—* George Blaker, Esq, CMG; Lake House, Ockley, Dorking, Surrey RH5 5NS

BLAKER, Sir John; 3 Bt (UK 1919); s of Maj Sir Reginald Blaker, 2 Bt, TD (d 1975); *b* 22 Mar 1935; *m* 1, 1960 (m dis 1965), Catherine Ann, da of late Francis John Anselm Thorold; m 2, 1968, Elizabeth Katherine, da of Col John Tinsley Russell, DSO; *Style—* Sir John Blaker, Bt; Stantons Farm, E Chiltington, nr Lewes, Sussex

BLAKER, (Derek) John Renshaw; s of Col Cedric Blaker, CBE, MC (d 1965), of Town House, Scaynes Hill, Sussex, and Louise Douglas, *née* Chapple (d 1984); *b* 15 Oct 1924; *Educ* Haileybury, Ridley Coll Toronto Ontario, Univ of Toronto (BA), New Coll Oxford (Dip Econs); *m* 20 June 1956, Marie-Françoise Alice, da of Guy Quoniam de Schompre; 3 da (Marie-Louise b 1958, Alexandra b 1961, Bettina (Countess Bettina de Pontevés) b 1964); *Career* Canadian Offrs Trg Corps TA 1942-44, Intelligence Corps Br Army 1944-46, Hong Kong Regt TA 1950-58; Gilman & Co Ltd Hong Kong: joined 1946, dir 1958-70, md 1967-70; dir 1967-70: The Hong Kong and Shanghai Banking Corpn, Union Insur Soc of Canton Ltd, Hong Kong Television Broadcasts

Ltd, Nan Yang Cotton Mill Ltd; memb Urban Cncl Hong Kong 1967-71, JP Hong Kong 1967-71; Freeman City of London 1945, Liveryman Worshipful Co of Vintners 1945; *Clubs* The Royal Hong-Kong YC; *Style*— John Blaker, Esq; Manoir de la Houbarderie, 35400 St Malo, France

BLAKER, His Honour Judge; Nathaniel Robert Blaker; QC (1972); s of Maj Herbert Harry Blaker, of Anstye Place, Cuckfield, Sussex, and Annie Muriel, *née* Atkinson; *b* 31 Jan 1921; *Educ* Winchester, Univ Coll Oxford; *m* 1951, Celia Margaret, o da of Walter Hedley, DSO, KC, of Westminster; 2 da; *Career* barr 1948, circuit judge 1976-; DL 1985, *Recreations* photography; *Style*— His Hon Judge Blaker, QC; 2 Culver Road, Winchester (☎ 0962 69826)

BLAKER, Rt Hon Sir Peter Allan Renshaw; KCMG (1983), PC (1983), MP (C) Blackpool S 1964-; s of Cedric Blaker, CBE, MC, ED (d 1965), of Scaynes Hill, Sussex, and Louise Douglas, *née* Chapple; *b* 4 Oct 1922,Hong Kong; *Educ* Shrewsbury, Trinity Coll Toronto, New Coll Oxford; *m* 1953, Jennifer, er da of Sir Pierson John Dixon, GCMG, CB (d 1965); 1 s, 2 da; *Career* slr 1948, barr 1952; Foreign Serv 1953-64; parly under-sec Army 1972-74 and FCO 1974, min of state FCO 1979-81, min of state for Armed Forces 1981-83; chm Cons Pty Foreign and Cwlth Affairs Ctee 1983- (vice chm 1974-79); *Recreations* tennis, sailing, swimming, opera; *Clubs* Garrick; *Style*— The Rt Hon Sir Peter Blaker, KCMG, PC, MP; House of Commons, London SW1A 0AA

BLAKER, Lt-Col (Guy) Peter; s of Guy Stewart Blaker (d 1969), of Rotherfield Greys, Henley-on-Thames, and Dawn Laetitia Prudence, *née* Watson; *b* 10 Nov 1936; *Educ* Lancing, Jesus Coll Cambridge (MA, LLB); *m* 18 Jan 1969, Hiltegund Maria, da of Dr Hermann Bastian (d 1945), of Freiburg-im-Breisgau; 2 s (Dominic b 1971, Nicholas b 1975), 1 da (Alexandra b 1970); *Career* Nat Serv, cmmnd W Yorks Regt 1957; Royal Green Jackets 1961-84, served Malaya, Borneo, Singapore, Cyprus, UK, Germany, Belgium (SHAPE); Army Aviation Pilot 1964-67, Staff Coll 1968, cmd Cambridge Univ Offrs Trg Corps 1979-82; Queens Messenger 1984-85; gen mangr Newdata Publishing 1985-86; sec Gen Cncl and Register of Osteopaths 1987-; lay chm Rotherfield Greys PCC; *Recreations* classical music, history, languages, ornithology, fly-fishing, rowing; *Clubs* Naval and Military, MCC; *Style*— Lt-Col Peter Blaker; Greys Piece, Rotherfield Greys, Henley-on-Thames, Oxfordshire RG9 4QG (☎ 04917 308)

BLAKER, Sheila, Lady - Sheila Kellas; da of Alexander Cran, MB, of Little Court, Merrow, nr Guildford; *m* 1930, Maj Sir Reginald Blaker, 2 Bt, TD (d 1975); *Style*— Sheila, Lady Blaker; Knowles, Ardingly, Sussex

BLAKESLEY, Maj John Cadman; MBE (1958); s of Reginald Harry Blakesley (d 1978), of Ramsey, IOM, and Cassie Hilda, *née* Cadman (d 1978); *b* 28 July 1926; *Educ* Cheltenham Coll; *m* 1, 5 July 1956 (m dis 1981), Selina Margaret (Patricia) Wynne-Eyton (d 1984); m 2, 19 March 1988, Mary (Robin) Ruane, da of C E Lucas-Phillips, OBE, MC, Croix de Guerre (d 1984), of Oxshott, Surrey; *Career* joined LG 1944, cmmd Kings Company Grenadier Gds 1946-53, transferred Royal Mil Police 1953, cmd 5 Units (despatches 1958), ret 1966; barr Middle Temple 1966, md RHB Hldgs Ltd 1978-, dir Allen Power Equipment 1982-87; memb Cons Pty 1966-, memb NFU 1973, sec Vale of Aylesbury Hutn 1982-86, memb County Gentleman's Assoc 1987-; memb Hon Soc of the Middle Temple 1966; *Recreations* foxhunting, cricket, music, breeding Hereford cattle and sheep; *Clubs* Army & Navy; *Style*— Maj John Blakesley, MBE; Shepherd's Hill House, Pinnock, Nr Winchcombe, Glos (☎ 0242 602620)

BLAKESTON, Henry Taylor; VRD (1953); s of William Henry Blakeston, of Asen House, Beverley Rd, Driffield, E Yorks (d 1965), and Lillian Habbijam, *née* Taylor (d 1971); *b* 24 August 1910; *Educ* Woodhouse Grove Sch, Leeds Univ; *m* 1, 26 Aug 1936, Esmé Rose (d 1974); 1 da (Esme Sonja b 1937); m 2, 3 Oct 1974, Joyce Norma; *Career* Royal Naval Volunteer Reserve 1939-58 (cdr); slr Magistrate Clerk, Bainton Beacon Div 1965-79; dep coroner (E Yorks) 1951-68; coroner: Buckrose Div 1968-74; Ryedale Div 1974-80; deputy coroner North West Yorks 1980; Lions Clubs Int District Governor District 105 NE (NE England and all Scotland) 1983-84; chm Cncl of Governors Multiple District 105 (England, Scotland, Wales, Channel Island and all Ireland) 1984-85; *Recreations* sailing (royal Yorks yacht, flag offr 1965-66) walking, gliding; *Clubs* Royal Yorkshire Yacht; Yorkshire Gliding; *Style*— Henry T Blakeston, Esq, VRD; Church View, Kirby Wiske, Thirsk, North Yorkshire

BLAKEWAY, (Arthur) John; s of Francis Lett Blakeway (d 1949), of Staverton, Cheltenham, Glos, and Bernice Marinda, *née* Matthews (d 1949); *b* 5 July 1925; *Educ* The Crypt GS, Gloucester; *m* 1, 24 April 1946, Joyce Cynthia, da of Horace Forty; 3 s (Philip John b 1950, Francis Mark b 1952, Richard Clive b 1959), 1 da (Gillian Bridget b 1948); m 2, 8 April 1986, Rosemary Catherine de Courcy, da of Cdr Henry Leslie Spofforth Baker, RN, of Carrowduff House, Ballymacurley, Co Westmeath; *Career* served RN 1943-46; chm and md of family co, started by father in 1925, Francis Blakeway Ltd, Fruit Merchants, formerly farmer; chm BSJA 1976-83, now vice-pres; MFH Croome 1961-68, Belvoir (Duke of Rutland's Hounds) 1983-; show dir Horse of Year Show 1987-; *Recreations* hunting; *Style*— John Blakeway, Esq; Blacklains Farm, Birdlip, Gloucester (☎ (0452) 862355); 26 Eastbrooke Rd, Eastern Ave, Gloucester (☎ (0452) 303376)

BLAKEY, Ian Johnston; Walter James Blakey, BEM, of 252 Northgate, Cottingham, N Humberside, and Freda Blakey, *née* Johnston; *b* 25 August 1932; *Educ* Hull GS; *m* 9 June 1956, Pamela Mary, da of George Edward McMurran (decd); 1 s (Jeremy Sean b 1961), 1 da (Zelda Rebecca b 1965); *Career* Nat Serv RN 1950-52; dir Robertson Dale Transport Co Ltd 1952-62, chm IJ Blakey Haulage co Ltd 1962-; dir: Harlequin Fabrics 1976-, Northbridge Warehousing Co Ltd 1972-; chm Viking Radio Ltd 1983-, dep chm Yorkshire & Humberside Radio Ltd 1986-; dir: Pennine Radio Ltd 1986-, Humberside Cont Health Scheme 1987-; chm Video Filming Servs 1987-, conslt Nisa Ltd 1986-; govr Hull GS, chm: Humberside Wishing Well Appeal, Finance Gen Purpose Order of St John Humberside; FCIT 1981, fell Inst Traffic Admin 1976; *Recreations* golf, horse racing; *Style*— Ian Blakey, Esq; Beech house, Northgate, Cottingham, North Humberside HU 16SQL (☎ 0482 846 131); I J Blakey Haulage Co Ltd Fleet House, Woodhouse Street, Hedon Road, Hull HU 91AP North Humberside (☎ 0482 27359, telex 592649)

BLAKISTON, Ann, Lady; Ann Hope Percival; da of late Purcell Cooke Jeans, of Cortington Grange, Warminster, Wilts; *m* 1954, as his 2 w, Sir Arthur Frederick Blakiston, 7 Bt, MC (d 1974); *Style*— Ann, Lady Blakiston; Corton, Warminster, Wilts

BLAKISTON, Sir Ferguson Arthur James; 9 Bt (GB 1763); s of Sir (Arthur) Norman Hunter Blakiston, 8 Bt (d 1977); *b* 19 Feb 1963; *Educ* Lincoln Coll New Zealand (Dip Ag); *Heir* bro, Norman John Balfour Blakiston, *qv*; *Career* Farmer; *Style*— Sir Ferguson Blakiston, Bt; 28 McKenzie St, Geraldine, S Canterbury, New Zealand

BLAKISTON, Lt-Col John Alan Cubitt; s of John Francis Blakiston, CIE (d 1965), of Anelog, Aberdaron, Pwllheli, Gwynedd, and Margaret Dora, *née* Ward-Jackson; descended from Sir Matthew Blakiston, Lord Mayor of London 1760; *b* 15 July 1938; *Educ* Wellington, London Univ; *m* 30 May 1975, Sally Ann, da of Lt-Col J D L Dickson, MC (d 1958); 1 s (Matthew b 11 Nov 1982), 2 da (Caroline b 22 Nov 1979, Emma b 1 July 1981); *Career* RNVR 1956-60; cmmnd 13/18 Royal Hussars (QMO) 1961; seconded to 4 Royal Tank Regt in Borneo 1964; seconded to UN Forces, Cyprus 1966-67; staff coll RMCS and Camberley 1969-71; regtl duty in Northern Ireland 1972; cmd Demonstration Sqdn Sch of Infantry 1972-74; SO2 (W) Defence Intelligence Staff 1974-76; regtl duty in BAOR and Northern Ireland 1976-78; atttended German Staff Coll 1979-81; SO1 Defence Intelligence Staff 1981-85; SO1 Ops HQ AFLENT 1985-88; *Recreations* riding, hunting; *Clubs* Cavalry and Guards'; *Style*— Lt-Col John A C Blakiston; Grove House, Lydiard Millicent, Swindon, Wilts (☎ 0793 770450)

BLAKISTON, Norman John Balfour; s of Sir (Arthur) Norman Hunter Blakiston, 8 Bt (d 1977); hp to baronetcy of bro, Sir Ferguson Blakiston, 9 Bt, *qv*; *b* 7 April 1964; *Style*— Norman Blakiston, Esq

BLAKSTAD, Michael Björn; s of Gabriel Clifford Clark, and Alice Blakstad; *b* 18 April 1940; *Educ* Ampleforth, Oriel Coll Oxford (MA); *m* 1965, Patricia Marilyn, da of Robert Andrew Wotherspoon, DL (d 1977); 1 s, 2 da (twins); *Career* producer: Papa Doc, The Black Sheep ITV 1970, Children in Crossfire BBC 1974; editor BBC 1974-80 (Tomorrow's World, The Risk Business); prizes include: BAFTA/Shell 1975, John Player 1975, RTS best science programme 1975, 1977, 1979; Hon MSc (Salford) 1983-; chm and chief exec: Workhouse Prodns Ltd and Workhouse Ltd, jt chief exec: The Videodisc Co; chm: Friday Prodns Ltd; Workday Ltd; *Books* 'The Risk Business' 'Tomorrow's World Looks to the Eighties'; *Recreations* golf, squash, writing; *Clubs* Reform, RSA, Royal Inst; *Style*— Michael Blakstad, Esq; The Tudor Ho, Workhouse Lane, East Meon, Petersfield, Hants; work: Workhouse Prodns Ltd, Granville Ho, St Peter St, Winchester, Hants SO23 9AF and Flat 3, 31 Moreton St, London SW1

BLAKSTAD, Nigel Henry; s of Erick Blakstad (d 1978); *b* 8 April 1929; *Educ* Warwick Sch; *m* 1956, Patricia, *née* Hall; 1 s, 2 da; *Career* gp md Rendol Ltd 1979-86; *Style*— Nigel Blakstad, Esq; Greenmeadows, Withilee Road, Presbury, Cheshire

BLAMIRE-BROWN, John; DL (Staffs 1974); s of Rev Frederick J Blamire-Brown, MA; *b* 16 April 1915; *Educ* Cheam Sch, St Edmund's Canterbury; *m* 1945, Joyce Olivia, da of Harry Pearson, of Newcastle; 2 s; *Career* Capt RM 1941-45; slr 1937; chief exec Staffs CC 1973-78; clerk to Staffs Ltcy 1972-78; chm St Giles Home Ltd 1979-83; memb Beth Johnson Fndn Cncl 1978-83; dir Crypt Assoc Ltd 1983-86; dep chm Manpower Servs Comm Area Bd West Midlands (North) 1978-83; vice-pres Codrall Civic Soc 1983-; *Recreations* gardening, painting, local history; *Style*— John Blamire-Brown, Esq, DL; The Mount, Codsall Wood, Wolverhampton (☎ Codsall (090 74) 2044)

BLANCH, Hon Alison Sarah; da of Baron Blanch, *qv*; *b* 1955; *Style*— The Hon Alison Blanch; 37 Lucerne St, Liverpool

BLANCH, Hon Hilary Jane; da of Baron Blanch, *qv*; *b* 1948; *Style*— The Hon Hilary Blanch; 1 Chapel Cottages, Shutford, Oxon

BLANCH, John William; s of Lt-Col John Blanch, of Betchworth, Surrey; *b* 10 May 1933; *Educ* Dulwich; *m* 1959, Nikola, da of William Thompson, of Dorking; 1 s, 1 da; *Career* dir Wasey Campbell-Ewald 1978-; *Recreations* travel, theatre, photography; *Style*— John Blanch, Esq

BLANCH, Baron (Life Peer UK 1983), of Bishopthorpe in the Co of N Yorks; Stuart Yarworth Blanch; PC (1975); s of late William Edwin and Elizabeth Blanch; *b* 2 Feb 1918; *Educ* Alleyns Sch Dulwich, St Catherine's Coll and Wycliffe Hall Oxford; *m* 1943, Brenda Gertrude, da of William Arthur Coyte; 1 s, 4 da; *Career* served WW II navigator RAF, Tport Cmd India; DD; V of Eynsham Oxon 1952-57, tutor and vice-princ Wycliffe Hall 1957-60 (chm Cncl 1967-); Oriel Canon of Rochester and warden Rochester Theological Coll 1960-66, Bp of Liverpool 1966-75, 94 Archp of York 1975-83, ret 1983; pro-chllr Hull Univ 1975-83, York Univ 1977-83; Hon DD Toronto, Hon Dr York; *Books* The World Our Orphanage (1972), For All Mankind (1976), The Christian Militant (1978), The Burning Bush (1978), The Trumpet in the Morning (1979), The Ten Commandments (1981), Living by Faith (1983), Way of Blessedness (1985); *Recreations* squash, walking, music, meteorology; *Clubs* Royal Cwlth Soc; *Style*— The Rt Rev and Rt Hon the Lord Blanch, PC; Little Garth, Church Street, Bloxham, nr Banbury, Oxfordshire

BLANCH, Hon Susan Elizabeth; da of Baron Blanch, *qv*; *b* 1946; *Style*— The Hon Susan Blanch; 1 Chapel Cottages, Shutford, Oxon

BLANCH, Hon Timothy Julian Yarworth; s of Baron Blanch, *qv*; *b* 11 July 1953; *Educ* King's Sch Rochester, Keble Coll Oxford; *m* 1982, Monica Mary, da of late H M Keeble, of Cerne Abbas, Dorset; 1 da (Rosa Katherine b 1984); *Career* dir Housing Association; *Style*— The Hon Timothy Blanch

BLANCHARD, George Herbert; CBE (1972), JP (Derbys 1958); s of Edward Blanchard (d 1920), of Kimberley, Notts; *b* 17 Jan 1912; *Educ* privately, Nottingham Univ Coll; *m* 1940, Edith, da of George Housley (d 1966), of Nuthall, Notts; 1 s, 1 da; *Career* chm and md Blanchards Bakers 1956-73, chm Rod Blanchard Motors Ltd 1968; memb Cons E Midlands Area Executive 1964-73, area tres Cons E Midlands 1968-73; Freeman of City of London, Liveryman Worshipful Co of Bakers; *Style*— George Blanchard, Esq, CBE, JP; Spinney Lodge, Church Street, Kilburn, Derbyshire DE5 0LU (☎ Derby 880315)

BLANCO WHITE, Thomas Anthony; QC (1969); s of George Rivers Blanco White, QC (d 1966), of London, and Amber *née* Reeves, OBE (d 1981); *b* 19 Jan 1915; *Educ* Gresham's Sch Holt, Trinity Coll Cambridge; *m* 20 Aug 1950, Anne Katherine, da of James Ironside-Smith, ICS (d 1929) 2 s (James b 1952, Henry b 1956), 1 da (Susan b 1955); *Career* RAFVR 1940-1946; barr Lincolns Inn 1937 (bencher); *Books* Patents for Inventions (1950, 1955, 1962, 1974, 1983 etc); *Recreations* gardening, photography; *Style*— Thomas A Blanco White, Esq, QC; Francis Taylor Building, Temple, London, EC4Y 7BY (☎ 01 353 5657); 7 South Hill Park, London, NW3 2SN; Mants, Bedham, Fittleworth, Pulborough, Sussex, RH20 1JR (☎ Fittleworth 421)

BLAND, (Francis) Christopher Buchan; eldest s of James Franklin MacMahon Bland, of Co Down, and Jess Buchan, *née* Brodie; *b* 29 May 1938; *Educ* Sedbergh,

Queen's Coll Oxford; *m* 1981, Jennifer Mary Denise, elder da of late Rt Hon William Morrison May, MP, of Mertown Hall, Co Down, and formerly w of Viscount Enfield (now 8 Earl of Stafford); 1 s; *Career* chm: Sir Joseph Causton & Sons 1977-85, LWT Hldgs 1984-, Bow Gp 1970; dir Nat Provident Inst; *Recreations* fishing, skiing; *Clubs* Beefsteak, Flyfishers; *Style*— Christopher Bland, Esq; 10 Catherine Place, London SW1 (☎ 01 834 0021)

BLAND, Hamilton Edwin; s of Herbert Bland, and Alice Bland; *b* 4 June 1943; *Educ* Folds Rd Sch Bolton, Hayward Sch Bolton, Loughborough Coll (DLC); *m* 26 March 1967, Hazel, da of Leslie Gear; 1 da (Anna Danielle b 16 Aug 1978); *Career* master Rugby Sch 1965-67, nat tech offr Amateur Swimming Assoc 1967-72, dir of swimming Coventry 1972-81, chm/md Hamilton Bland (Prods) Ltd 1981-86, proprietor Hamilton Bland Consits 1987-, BBC TV swimming commentator 1975-; formerly: memb Coventry Round Table, chm Coventry Mentally Handicapped Soc; *Books* Waterpolo, Swimming To Win; *Recreations* swimming; *Style*— Hamilton Bland, Esq; Chadwick Barns, Sparrowcock Lane, Chadwick End, Knowle, Warwicks (☎ 021 708 1454, car tel 0836 520 981)

BLAND, Sir Henry Armand; CBE (1957); s of Emeritus Prof Francis Armand Bland, CMG (d 1967), and Elizabeth Bates Jacobs (d 1910); *b* 28 Dec 1909; *Educ* Sydney HS, Sydney Univ (LLB); *m* 1933, Rosamund, da of John Nickal; 2 da (and 1 decd); *Career* perm sec Dept of Lab and Nat Serv 1952-67 and Dept of Defence 1967-70; FRSA; kt 1965; *see Debrett's Handbook of Australia and New Zealand for further details*; *Recreations* gardening, golf; *Clubs* Athenaeum (Melbourne), Bowral Golf; *Style*— Sir Henry Bland, CBE; PO Box 326, 27 Charlton Close, Bowral, NSW 2576, Australia (☎ 048 613320)

BLAND, Lt-Col Sir Simon Claud Michael; KCVO (1982, CVO 1973, MVO 1967); s of Sir (George) Nevile Maltby Bland, KCMG, KCVO (d 1972), and Portia Christabel Irene, *née* Ottley (d 1968); *b* 4 Dec 1923; *Educ* Eton; *m* 1954, Olivia Beatrice, da of late Maj William Blackett, of Dumfries; 1 s, 3 da; *Career* WW II Scots Gds (served Italy), Br Jt Servs Mission Washington DC 1948-49, 2 Bn Scots Gds Malaya 1949-51, asst mil advr UK High Cmmn Karachi 1959-60, comptroller and asst private sec to HRH late Duke of Gloucester 1961-74, to HRH late Prince William 1968-72, comptroller, private sec and equerry to HRH Princess Alice, Duchess of Gloucester and to TRH Duke and Duchess of Gloucester 1972-; dir West End Branch Commercial Union; CStJ 1978; *Recreations* shooting; *Clubs* Buck's; *Style*— Lt-Col Sir Simon Bland, KCVO; Tower Flat, Kensington Palace, London W8 (☎ 01 937 6374); Gabriels Manor, Edenbridge, Kent (☎ 0732 2340)

BLANDFORD, Heinz Hermann; CBE (1981); s of Judge Richard Blumenfeld (d 1944), and Hedwig Blandford-Blumenfeld, *née* Kersten (d 1954); *b* 28 August 1908; *Educ* K & K Augusta Gymnasium, Berlin U, Hamburg U; *m* 1933, Hilde, da of M S Kleczewer; 1 s (Robin), 1 da (Jill); *Career* chm Ulvir Ltd 1936-76; pioneered synthesis, mfr and use of liquid fertilisers in the UK 1945-60; dep chm and fell Royal Postgrad Med Sch Hammersmith Hosp (memb cncl 1962-, hon tres 1964-82); vice chm Sch of Pharmacy (memb cncl 1975-); chm Br Postgrad Med Fedn 1977-86 (memb governing body, 1976-); memb: Mgmnt Ctee Inst of Ophthalmology 1974-86, Ct of Govrs London Sch of Hygiene and Tropical Medicine 1982-87; founded Blandford Tst for advancement of health and prevention and relief of sickness by medical research and teaching; govr London House for Overseas Graduates 1977-80; bd of govrs Hammersmith and St Mark's Hosps 1972-74; landowner (500 acres); *Recreations* gardening, walking; *Clubs* Farmer's; *Style*— H H Blandford, Esq, CBE; Holtsmere Manor, Holtsmere End, Redbourn, Herts (☎ Redbourn 2206)

BLANDFORD, Marquess of; (Charles) James (Jamie) Spencer-Churchill; s and h (by 1 w, *see* Mrs John Gough), of 11 Duke of Marlborough, JP, DL; *b* 24 Nov 1955; *Educ* Pinewood, Harrow, RAC Cirencester; *Career* insurance broker and helicopter pilot; *Recreations* skiing, flying, shooting; *Clubs* Turf, Annabel's; *Style*— Marquess of Blandford

BLANDY, Prof John Peter; s of Sir Edmond Nicolas Blandy, KCIE, CSI, ICS (d 1942), of Calcutta, and Dorothy Kathleen, *née* Marshall (d 1985); *b* 11 Sept 1927; *Educ* Clifton Coll, Balliol Coll Oxford (MA, DM, M, Ch), The London Hosp Med Coll; 6 Aug 1953, Anne, da of the late Henry Hugh Mathias, of Tenby; 4 da (Susan, Caroline, Nicola, Kitty); *Career* Nat Serv RAMC 1953-55 (Lt, Capt Actg Maj), Maj 22 London Gen Hosp (TA), Maj RARO; conslt surgn: London Hosp 1964, St Peters Hosp 1968; prof urology Univ of London 1969, vice pres urology section RSM 1973; pres: Br Assoc Urological Surgns 1985-86, Euro Assoc of Urology 1986-88, cncl memb RCS 1982; St Peters Medal 1982; FRCS 1956, FAC 1980; *Books* Tumours of the Testicles (1970), Transurethral Resection (1970), Lecture Notes on Urology (1976), The Prostate (1986), Operative Urology (1978); translations into Italian, Spanish, Portuguese; *Recreations* painting, sculpture; *Clubs* The Royal Society of Medicine; *Style*— Prof John Blandy; 61 Traps Hill, Loughton, Essex 1G10 1TD; The London Hospital, of London, Whitechapel E1 1BB (☎ 377 7000)

BLANE, Michael Lawrence; *b* 17 August 1938; *Educ* Washington & Lee Univ, Cape Western Reserve Univ (BA, LLB); *Career* vice pres and asst gen counsel Dean Witter Reynolds Inc 1973-81, sr counsel Merrill Lynch Europe Ltd 1981-, dir Int Securities Regulatory Orgn 1985-86; memb: rules ctee, enforcement ctee, authorisation ctee of the Securities Assoc Bd 1986-88, 1992 ctee Int Stock Exchange, Nat Assoc of Securities Dealers, American Arbitration Assoc, Commodity Futures Indust Assoc; *Style*— Michael Blane, Esq; Merrill Lynch Europe Ltd, Ropemaker Place, 25 Ropemaker St, London EC2Y 9LY (☎ 01 867 2067, fax 01 867 4818)

BLANK, Herbert; s of Alfred Blank; *b* 18 Dec 1923; *Educ* Dorking GS, Edinburgh Univ; *m* 1952, Joyce, da of Alfred Pulfer; 1 s, 1 da; *Career* md and dep chm Polymark Int Ltd (ret 1985); formed consultancy Co (Gate Lodge Int Cons Ltd); *Recreations* chess, bridge, tennis, squash, skiing; *Style*— Herbert Blank, Esq; Gate Lodge, 17 The Crescent, Hadley Common, Barnet, Herts EN5 5QQ

BLANK, (Maurice) Victor; s of Joseph Blank, and Ruth *née* Levey; *b* 9 Nov 1942; *Educ* Stockport GS, St Catherine's Coll Oxford (MA); *m* 29 June 1977, Sylvia Helen, *née* Richford; 2 s (Simon b 1 May 1978, Robert b 23 June 1984), 1 da (Anna b 16 Sept 1979); *Career* slr; ptnr Clifford Turner 1969-81, dir Pentos plc 1979-, chm and chief exec Charterhouse Bank Ltd 1985-, chm Charterhouse plc, dir The Royal Bank of Scotland Gp plc 1985-, dir Porter Chadburn plc 1988-; memb: Business in the Community Birthright, Childline, Campaign for Oxford, RSA, Great Ormond St Hosp Appeal; Freeman City of London, memb City of London slr Co; Memb: Law Soc, CBIM; *Books* Weinberg and Blank on takeovers and mergers; *Recreations* family, tennis, cricket, theatre; *Clubs* IOD; *Style*— Victor Blank, Esq; 1 Paternoster Row, St Paul's, London EC4M 7DH (☎ 01 248 8000, fax 01 248-6522)

BLANKENHORN, Herbert; GCVO (Hon 1965); s of Erich Blankenhorn; *b* 15 Dec 1904; *Educ* Gymnasiums in Strasbourg, Berlin and Karlsruhe and Munich, London, Heidelberg and Paris Univs; *m* 1944, Gisela Krug; 2 s, 2 da; *Career* German ambass to London 1965-70; conslt to Dir-Gen UNESCO 1977-; *Style*— Herbert Blankenhorn, Esq, GCVO; 7847 Badenweiler, Hintere Au 2, Germany

BLASHFORD-SNELL, Col John Nicholas; MBE (1969); s of Alderman The Rev Prebendary Leland John Blashford-Snell, MBE, TD (d 1978), of Angmering-on-Sea, Sussex, and Gwendolen Ives, *née* Sadler (d 1968); *b* 22 Oct 1936; *Educ* Victoria Coll Jersey, RMA Sandhurst, The Staff Coll Camberley; *m* 27 Aug 1960, Judith (Frances), da of Lt Col Beresford Thomas Sherman, OBE (d 1982), of Tivoli Court, Westbourne, Dorset; 2 d (Emma b 1964, Victoria b 1967); *Career* cmmnd RE 1957, Trg Adi 33 Ind Field Sqdn RE Cyprus 1959-62 (Tp Cdr 1958-59), Tp Cdr, Junior Leaders Regt RE 1962-63, Instr & Adventure Trg Offr RMA Sandhurst 1963-66, Adj 3 Divn Engrs 1966-67, leader Gt Abbai (Blue Nile) Expedn 1968, Staff Coll (RMCS and Camberley) 1968-69, GSO2 MOD 1970-72, leader Br Trans-American Expedn 1972, OC 48 Field Sqdn RE (Belize, Oman, N Ireland) 1972-74, leader Zaire River Expedn 1974-75, GSO1 MOD 1975-76, co junior Leader Regt RE 1976-78, Cdr Operation Drake 1978-81, ACPR MOD 1981-82, Cdr Fort George Volunteers 1983, Cdr Operation Raleigh 1984-; chm: The Scientific Exploration Soc, Br Chapter Explorers Club; pres: Galley Hill Gun Club, Hereford Branch RE Assoc; Freedom, The City of Hereford (1984); Hon DSC (Durham 1986); FRSGS 1976; *Books* Weapons and Tactics (with Tom Wintringham, 1973), Where the Trails Run Out (1974), In the Steps of Stanley (1975), A Taste for Adventure (1978), Expedition the Experts Way (with Alistair Ballantine, 1977), In the Wake of Drake (with Mike Cable, 1980), Operation Drake (with Mike Cable, 1981), Mysteries, Encounters with the Unexplained (1983), Operation Raleigh the Start of an Adventure (1987), Operation Raleigh, Adventure Challenge (with Anne Tweedy, 1988); *Recreations* shooting, diving, photography; *Clubs* RAC, Little Ship, Wig and Pen; *Style*— Col John Blashford-Snell; c/o CHQ, Operation Raleigh, Alpha Place, Flood Street, London SW3 (☎ 01 351 7541, fax 01 351 9372)

BLATCH, Baroness (Life Peer UK 1987), of Hinchingbrooke in the country of Cambridgeshire; Rt Hon Lady Emily May; CBE (1983); da of late Stephen Joseph Triggs, and late Sarah Ann, *née* Carpenter; *b* 24 Jul 1937; *Educ* Prenton Secdy Girls Sch, Huntingdonshire Coll; 7 Sept 1963, John Richard Blatch, AFC, s of George Henry Blatch (d 1963); 3 s (David b Nov 1964, d 1979, James b Feb 1967, Andrew b Dec 1968), 1 da (Elizabeth (twin) b Dec 1968); *Career* WRAF 1955-59; ccncllr Cambs 1977-89 (ldr of the cncl 1981-85); pres Nat Benevolent Inst; memb: Euro Economic and Social Ctee, Assoc of Co Cncls 1981-85, Sch's Cncl 1981-; bd memb Peterborough Devpt Corpn, chm Anglo American community relations ctee RAF Alconbury; govr: Kimbolton Independent Sch, St Peters and Hinchingbrooke Comprehensive Schs; FRSA 1983; *Recreations* reading, theatre, music; *Clubs* RAF; *Style*— The Rt Hon Lady Blatch, CBE; House of Lords, Westminster, London (☎ 01 219 3000)

BLATCHFORD, Brian Stephen; s of Brian Geoffrey Blatchford, MBE (1985), of Four Seasons, Cranes Road, Sherborne St John, Basingstoke, and May Joyce, *née* Faulkner; *b* 7 Dec 1959; *Educ* St Edwards Sch Oxford, St Catherine's Coll Oxford (BA, MSc); *m* 22 March 1986, Caroline Mary, da of Colin Greenwood, of Brooklyn, Jarman Road, Sutton, Macclesfield, Cheshire; *Career* IBM Laboratories Ltd Hursley 1979, tech offr in off automation 1983-85, md Chas A Blatchford and Sons Ltd 1986- (mgmnt trainee 1985-86); govr London Sch of Prosthetics 1986-, chm prosthetics section British Surgical Trades Assoc 1988-; memb: Basingstoke C of C, Basingstoke and Andover Enterprise Centre; memb: Biological Engrg Soc 1986-, Int Soc of Prosthetics and Orthotics 1986; *Recreations* badminton, computers, wine tasting, reading; *Clubs* Beechdown Badminton, IOD; *Style*— Brian Blatchford, Esq; Rondel, 1 Beaurepaire Close, Bramley, Basingstoke, Hampshire RG26 5DT (☎ 0256 881937); Chas A Blatchford and Sons Ltd, Lister Road, Basingstoke, Hampshire RG22 4AH (☎ 0256 465771, fax 0256 479705, car 0836 726992)

BLATCHLY, Dr John Marcus; s of Alfred Ernest Blatchly (d 1982), and Edith Selina, *née* Giddings; *b* 7 Oct 1932; *Educ* Sutton GS Surrey, Christs Coll Cambridge (MA, PhD); *m* 1955, Pamela Winifred, JP, da of Maj Lawrence James Smith (d 1942); 1 s (Mark), 1 da (Janet); *Career* asst master and head of Science Dept; King's Bruton 1957-62, Eastbourne Coll 1962-66, Charterhouse 1966-72; headmaster Ipswich Sch 1972; FSA 1975; *Books* Editor Conference & Common Room (The Journal of HMC), Eighty Ipswich Portraits (1980), Davy's Suffolk Journal 1983; *Recreations* Suffolk countryside and history, all forms of music and music making; *Clubs* E India; *Style*— Dr John Blatchly; Headmaster's House, Ipswich Sch, Suffolk IP1 3QY (☎ (0473) 59941); Ipswich Sch IP1 3SG (☎ (0473) 55313)

BLAU, Dr Joseph Norman; s of Abraham Moses Blau (d 1942), and Reisla, *née* Vogel (d 1942); *b* 5 Oct 1928; *Educ* Dame Alice Owens Sch, St Bart's Hosp and London Univ (MB BS, MD); *m* 19 Dec 1968, Jill Elise, da of Geoffrey C Seligman; 2 s (Justin b 15 Jan 1970, Adrian b 27 April 1972), 1 da (Rosie b 9 Sept 1975); *Career* Nat Serv Lt and Capt RAMC 1953-55; med offr: SW Dist HQ Taunton 1954, Army Neurological Unit Wheatley Oxon 1955; sr registrar The London and Maida Vale Hosp, Nuffied Med Res Fellowship Mass Gen Hosp Boston USA; conslt neurologist: Nat Hosps for Nervous Diseases Queen Square and Maida Vale 1962-, Royal Nat Throat Nose and Ear Hosp 1965-, Northwick Park Hosp Harrow Middx 1972-; hon sr lectr histopathology dept Guy's Hosp Med Sch 1970-, jt hon dir and conslt neurologist City of London Migraine Clinic 1980-, cncl memb Soc of Authors (med section) 1988-; former pres London Jewish Med Soc, hon med advsr Br Migraine Assoc 1980-, cncl memb neurological section Royal Soc of Med 1984-87; FRCP, FRCPath, memb Assoc of Br Neurologists; *Publications* Headache and Migraine Handbook (1986), Migraine - Clinical, Therapeutic, Conceptual and Research Aspects (ed and contrib 1987), author of chapters in books and original articles on Headache, migraine and other neurological topics; *Recreations* cello playing, philosophy; *Clubs* Royal Soc of Med; *Style*— Dr J N Blau; 5 Marlborough Hill, London NW8 0NN (☎ 01 586 3804; Nat Hosp for Nervous Diseases, Queen Square, London WC1N 3BG (☎ 01 829 8741)

BLAUHORN, Karl Max; s of Dr Josef Blauhorn; *b* 6 May 1912; *Educ* Real Gymnasium Vienna, Fed Inst of Technol Zurich (Dipl Ing); *m* 1938, Kate, da of Julius Steiner; 1 da; *Career* formerly md J B Jackson & Ptnrs; consulting engineer 1967-; chm Product Search & Dvpt Ltd 1968-; chm Inst of Int Licensing Practitioners 1980-; CEng, FIMechE, FInstE, FCIBSE, FWeldI; *Recreations* reading; *Clubs* RAC; *Style*— Karl

Blauhorn, Esq; 4 Wellington House, Eton Rd, London NW3 (☎ 01 586 1814)

BLAUSTEN, Cyril; JP; *b* 1916; *m* 1944, Norma Marion Cinnamon; 4 s (Richard, Douglas, Simon, Peter); *Career* Lloyd's underwriter; dir: New Islington and Hackney Housing Assoc, JBG Housing Soc; cmmr of taxes, vice-pres Jewish Welfare Bd and Maccabi Assoc; freeman City of London, liveryman of the Worshipful Co of Glaziers and Painters of Glass; FZS; *Clubs* City Livery, United Univ, MCC; *Style—* Cyril Blausten, Esq, JP; 5 Linnell Close, Meadway, London NW11; office: 25 Gilbert Street, Grosvenor Square, London W1

BLAUTH-MUSZKOWSKI, Peter Christopher; s of Dr Jan Muszkowski (d 1953); *b* 18 Sept 1919; *Educ* Grenoble Univ; *m* 1948, Izabella, da of Tadeusz Blauth (d 1951); 2 s; *Career* served WW II Lieut Polish AF, subst Flying Offr with RAF; Lloyd's broker Int Reinsur conslt; dir Bain Dawes (reinsur brokers) 1970-84, dep chm Gil Carvajal & Ptnrs 1980-84; 1987 memb of the Ctee Assoc of Polish Writers Abroad; awarded Polish Cross of Valour; *Recreations* writing, translating; *Clubs* City of London, Traveller's; *Style—* Peter Blauth-Muszkowski, Esq; 45 Meadvale Rd, London W5 (☎ 01 997 8970)

BLAXLAND, Dame Helen Frances; DBE (1975, OBE 1967); da of Brig-Gen Sir Robert Murray McCheyne Anderson, KCMG (d 1940), and Jean Cairns, *née* Amos (d 1928); *b* 21 June 1907; *Educ* Bedales Hants Eng, Frensham Mittagong NSW; *m* 1927, Geoffrey Blaxland; 1 da; *Career* work for Red Cross and other charitable organisations, fndn chm Women's Ctee of NSW Nat Tst, Lindesay Ctee, Parramatta Properties Ctee; *Clubs* Union (Sydney); *Style—* Dame Helen Blaxland, DBE; 4 Silchester, Trahlee Rd, Bellevue Hill, NSW 2023, Australia

BLAXTER, Prof John Harry Savage; s of Kenneth William Blaxter, CMG (d 1964), and Janet Hollis (d 1981); *b* 6 Jan 1929; *Educ* Berkhamsted Sch, Oxford Univ (BA Zoo, DSc); *m* 20 Dec 1952, Valerie Ann, da of Gerald McElligott; 1 s (Timothy b 1958), 1 da (Julia b 1955); *Career* scientific offr (then sr SO) Marine Lab Aberdeen 1952-64; lectr Zoology Dept Aberdeen Univ 1964-69; principal scientific offr Scottish Marine Biological Assoc Dunstaffnage Marine Research Lab, Oban, Argyll 1969-74 (sr PSO (special merit) 1974-85, dep chief SO (special merit) 1985-; hon prof dept of Biol Sciences & Inst of Aquaculture Stirling Univ 1986-; FRS Edin; *Books* Advances in Marine Biology (ed), Over 120 papers in learned journals on fish behaviour & physiology; *Recreations* sailing, gardening; *Style—* Prof John H S Blaxter; Letterwalton House, Ledaig, Oban, Argyll PA37 1RY (☎ Ledaig 206); Scottish Marine Biological Assoc, Dunstaffnage Marine Research Laboratory, Oban, Argyll PA34 4AD (☎ Oban 62244)

BLAXTER, Sir Kenneth Lyon; s of Gaspard Culling Blaxter and Charlotte Ellen, *née* Lyon; *b* 19 June 1919; *Educ* City of Norwich Sch, Reading and Illinois Univs; *m* 1957, Mildred Lillington Hall (memb Alcohol Educn & Research Cncl 1982-); 2 s (Mark, Piers), 1 da (Alison); *Career* dir Rowett Research Inst 1965-82, conslt dir Cwlth Bureau of Nutrition 1965-82; BSc (Ag), PhD, DSc, NDA; visiting prof Agric Biochemistry & Nutrition Newcastle Univ 1982-85; pres: Nutrition Soc 1974-7, Royal Soc of Edinburgh 1979-83, Inst of Biology 1986-; FRS 1967, FRSE 1965; fell Inst of Biology, Royal Soc of Arts, Royal Agric Socs; Hon Degrees: DSc Queen's Univ Belfast, DSc Leeds Univ, DSc Univ of Newcastle upon Tyne, LLD Aberdeen Univ, DAgr Univ of Oslo; Honorary Appts: memb Académie d'Agriculture de France, Lenin Acad of Agric Science USSR, Royal Dutch Acad; Hon assoc Royal Coll Veterinary Surgns; kt 1977; *Recreations* painting; *Clubs* Farmers; *Style—* Sir Kenneth Blaxter; Stradbroke Hall, Stradbroke, Suffolk IP21 5HH

BLAYNEY, Robert Hamilton; s of Lt-Col Owen Geoffrey Blayney, MC (d 1957), and Olive Agar, *née* Lazenby (d 1962); *b* 23 June 1934; *Educ* Uppingham; *m* 16 Jan 1965, Ann, da of James Francis Angus Turner; 2 s (Andrew Owen b 1966, David James b 1969); *Career* Lt Royal Northumberland Fusiliers TA; wine trade; dir: Blayney & Co Ltd 1956-68, Blayneys Park Hotels Ltd 1957-68, Leslie Rankin Ltd St Helier 1969-78; memb Cncl Wine and Spirit Assoc GB 1961-68; dir Lamare Vineyards Ltd Jersey; *Recreations* gardening, genealogy, wine with friends; *Clubs* Royal Overseas League London; *Style—* Robert H Blayney, Esq; Elms Farm, St Mary, Jersey, Channel Islands (☎ 0534 81491); La Marre Vineyards, Jersey (☎ 0534 81178)

BLEAKLEY, Rt Hon David Wylie; PC (1971), CBE (1984); s of John Wesley Bleakley, of Belfast, and Sarah, *née* Wylie; *b* 11 Jan 1925; *Educ* Ruskin Coll Oxford, Queen's Univ Belfast (MA); *m* 1949, Winifred, da of Alfred Wason (d 1931); 3 s; *Career* MP (Lab) Victoria (Belfast) NI Parl 1958-65; memb NI Assembly 1973-75, NI Convention 1975-76; min Community Rels NI Govt 1972; chm standing advsy ctee on Human Rights 1980-; ch exec Ir Cncl of Churches 1980-; pres Church Missionary Soc London 1983-; lectr in Industl Rels Kivukoni Coll (Dar es Salaam) 1967-69; Memb Ctee of Inquiry on UK Police 1979; Hon MA Open Univ; *Books* Irish Peacemaker (1981), In Place of Work (1981), Work-Shadow & Substance (1983), Beyond Work-Free to Be (1985), Peace Together (Symposium); *Recreations* reading, writing, travelling; *Style—* The Rt Hon David Bleakley, CBE; 8 Thornhill, Bangor, Co Down, N Ireland BT19 1RD (☎ (0247) 454898); Church Missionary Soc. 157 Waterloo Rd, London SE1 (☎ 01 928 8681)

BLEASDALE, Cyril; OBE (1988); s of Frederick Bleasdale, and Alice (d 1976); *b* 8 July 1934; *Educ* Stanford Business Sch (US); *m* 1970, Catherine Valerie; 2 da (Jane b 1970, Emma b 1972); *Career* md Freightliner 1975-82, dir BR Intercity 1982-86 (gen mangr 1986-) FBA, MBIM, FCIl; *Recreations* sqaush, jogging; *Style—* Cyril Bleasdale, Esq, OBE; 41 New Field Road, Hagley, Stourbridge, W Mids, (☎ 0562 885806)

BLEASDALE, Prof John Kenneth Anthony; CBE (1988); s of John Henry Bleasdale (d 1958), and Helen, *née* Rushworth (d 1960); *b* 17 May 1928; *Educ* Manchester GS, Univ of Manchester (BSc, PhD); *m* 24 Sept 1953, Zoë Patricia, da of Frederick Vivian Wallis (d 1962); 2 s (Richard b 1956, Robert b 1959); *Career* cmmnd Fighter Controller RAf 1952-54; dir Nat Vegetable Res Station Wellesbourne Warwicks 1977-88 (joined 1954, head of plant physiology section 1961-77), head of crop prodn Inst of Horticultural Res 1985-88; past nat pres: Assoc of Applied Biologists, agric section of Br Assoc for the Advancement of Sci, The Inst of Horticulture; cncl memb Inst of Hort (chm professional affrs standing ctee), govr Pershore Coll, memb NFU's Horticultural devpt & educn ctee; emeritus prof Univ of Birmingham 1988- (hon prof 1977-), special prof Univ of Nottingham 1977-; Res Medal RASE 1973, Veitch Gold Medal RHS 1989; FIBiol 1976, FIHort 1985; hon memb Assoc Applied Biologists 1988; *Books* Plant Physiology in Relation to Horticulture (1973), Know and Grow Vegetables vol 1 (co-ed and contrib 1979), vol 2 (1982); *Style—* Prof John Bleasdale, CBE

BLEASE, Hon Maurice Caldwell; 2 s of Baron Blease, JP (Life Peer), *qv*; *b* 1944; *m* 1967, Mary, da of Philip Carrol; issue; *Style—* The Hon Maurice Blease; The Warden's Residence, Stranmillis College, Belfast BT9, Northern Ireland

BLEASE, Hon Paul Charles; yst s of Baron Blease, JP (Life Peer), *qv*; *b* 1953; *m* 1979, Ann, da of Howard Jennings; 1 s; *Style—* The Hon Paul Blease; Four Winds, 4 Lochinver Avenue, Holywood, Co Down, Northern Ireland

BLEASE, Baron (Life Peer UK 1978), of Cromac, City of Belfast; William John Blease; JP (Belfast 1974); s of late William John and Sarah Blease; *b* 28 May 1914; *Educ* Belfast Tech, New U of Ulster; *m* 1939, Sarah Evelyn, da of William Caldwell; 3 s, 1 da; *Career* industl rels conslt, former union official; memb IBA 1974-79; Hon DLitt (U of Ulster) 1972, Hon LLD (Queen's) Belfast 1982; *Recreations* reading, DIY; *Clubs* Sloane; *Style—* The Rt Hon Lord Blease; House of Lords, Westminster, London SW1

BLEASE, Hon William Victor; eldest s of Baron Blease, JP (Life Peer), *qv*; *b* 1942; *m* 1969, Rose Mary, da of Alan Seaton; issue; *Style—* The Hon William Blease; 26 Ormiston Park, Belfast BT4, Northern Ireland

BLECH, Harry; CBE (1984), OBE (1962); *b* 2 Mar 1910; *Educ* Trinity Coll of Music, Manchester Coll of Music; *m* 1, 1935, Enid Marion Lessing (d 1977); 1 s, 2 da; m 2, 1957, Marion Manley, pianist; 1 s, 3 da; *Career* musical dir Haydn-Mozart Soc, fndr and conductor London Mozart Players 1949-84, ret 1984; conductor laureate; *Style—* Harry Blech, Esq CBE, OBE; The Owls, 70 Leopold Road, SW19 (☎ 01 946 8135)

BLEDISLOE, 3 Viscount (1935 UK); Christopher Hiley Ludlow Bathurst; QC (1978); s of 2 Viscount Bledisloe, QC (d 1979); *b* 24 June 1934; *Educ* Eton, Trinity Coll Oxford; *m* 1962 (m dis 1986), Elizabeth Mary, da of Sir Edward Thompson, *qv*; 2 s (Hon Rupert, Hon Otto Benjamin Charles b 16 June 1971), 1 da (Hon Matilda Blanche b 16 Feb 1967); *Heir* s, Hon Rupert Bathurst, *qv*; *Career* barr 1959-; *Clubs* Garrick; *Style—* The Rt Hon the Viscount Bledisloe, QC; Fountain Court, Temple, London EC4 (☎ 01 353 7356)

BLEDISLOE, Joan, Viscountess; Joan Isobel; da of late Otto Krishaber, of 113 Mount St, W1; *m* 1933, 2 Viscount Bledisloe, QC (d 1979); 2 s; *Style—* The Rt Hon Joan, Viscountess Bledisloe; East Wing, Lydney Park, Glos (☎ Dean 0594 43543); 14 Mulberry Walk, London SW3 (☎ 01 352 7533)

BLEEHEN, Prof Norman Montague; s of Soloman Bleehen (d 1972), of London, and Leana, *née* Shlosberg; *b* 24 Feb 1930; *Educ* Manchester GS, Haberdashers' Aske's Sch, Univ of Oxford (MA, BSc, MB, BCh), Middx Hosp Med Sch; *m* 14 Dec 1969, Tirza, da of Arnold Loebe, of Sydney, Aust; *Career* Nat Serv BAOR 1957-59: med specialist Br Military Hosp and Berlin MO to Spandau Military Goal 1958-59-; prof radiotherapy Middx Hosp Med Sch 1969-75, prof clinical oncology Univ of Cambridge 1975-, hon dir med res cncl Clinical Ocnology and Radiotherapeutics Unit 1975-, chm Br Assoc Cancer Res 1977-80, pres Int Soc Radiation Oncology 1985-89, vice-pres Int Assoc Study of Lung Cancer 1987-; hon fell American Coll Radiologist 1973; Liveryman Worshipful Co Apothecaries 1973; FRCR 1964, FRCP 1970; *Books* Tumours of the Brain (1986), Radiology in Radiotherapy (1988); *Recreations* reading, gardening; *Clubs* Athanaeum; *Style—* Prof Norman Bleehen; 21 Bentley Rd, Cambridge CB2 2AW (☎ 0223 354320); Univ of Cambridge Sch of Clinical Med, Dept of Clinical Oncology and Radiotherapeutics, Addenbrooke's Hosp, Hills Rd, Cambridge CB2 2QQ (☎ 0223 337733, fax 0223 213556, telex 81532)

BLEICHROEDER, Rudolf P J; s of Dr Fritz Bleichroeder, of Berlin (d 1938); *b* 9 Mar 1914; *Educ* Berlin and Holzminden (W Germany), Berlin and Madrid Univs; *m* 1940, Wera, da of Gustav Fuerstenberg, of Berlin (d 1931); 2 da; *Career* dir: Samuel Montagu & Co Ltd, City & Commercial Investmt plc, Drayton Consolidated plc, Drayton Premier Investmt plc, Dualvest Ltd, Fundinvest Ltd, Triplevest Ltd, G T Investmt Fund S A, Drayton Japan Tst plc (ret); *Recreations* bridge, swimming, walking; *Clubs* Brooks's; *Style—* Rudolf Bleichroeder, Esq; 58 Avenue Close, Avenue Rd, London NW8 (☎ 01 722 9933); 70 Les Oliviers, Beaulieu-sur-Mer, France (☎ 93 011342); Samuel Montagu & Co Ltd, 114 Old Broad St, London EC2P 2HY (☎ 01 588 6464)

BLENKINSOP, Henry Gerald; DL (1970 Warwickshire); s of late Henry Maxwell Blenkinsop, of Warwick; *b* 31 Jan 1925; *Educ* Marlborough; *m* 1957, Tessa Susan, da of Dr Eric Leonard Edmondson, of Leamington Spa; 1 s, 2 da; *Career* served WW II, RAF (pilot) 1943-47; slr 1951; undersheriff Warwickshire 1951, pt W Midlands 1972; conslt 1981; pres undersheriffs Assoc 1984-87; *Recreations* sailing (yacht 'Callooh'); *Clubs* Island Sailing, Bentley Drivers, R-REC; *Style—* Gerald Blenkinsop, Esq, DL; 45 Mill St, Warwick (☎ 0926 491000); office: 1 New St, Warwick (☎ 0926 492407)

BLENKINSOPP, Robert John; s of Capt John Leslie Blenkinsopp, JP, of Sheriff Hutton Hall, York, and Judith Carol, *née* Cooper; *b* 12 May 1948; *Educ* Ampleforth; *Career* md Owen & Robinson plc 1975-87, Henry Hardcastle Ltd 1975-87, Murgatroyd & Horsfall Ltd 1975-87 (goldsmiths, silversmiths, jewellers and diamond merchants); *Recreations* fishing, shooting; *Clubs* Yorkshire; *Style—* Robert Blenkinsopp, Esq; Valley House, Scackleton, Hovingham, York (☎ 065382 339)

BLENNERHASSETT, Sir (Marmaduke) Adrian Francis William; 7 Bt (UK 1809); s of Lt Sir Marmaduke Charles Henry Joseph Casimir Blennerhassett, 6 Bt, RNVR (d 1940), and Gwenfra Mary, *née* Harrington-Morgan; *b* 25 May 1940; *Educ* Michael Hall, McGill Univ Montreal Canada (BSc), Imperial Coll London (MSc), Cranfield Business Sch (MBA); *m* 1972, Carolyn Margaret, da of late Gilbert Brown; 1 s (Charles b 1975), 1 da (Celina b 1973); *Heir* s, Charles Henry Marmaduke Blennerhassett b 18 July 1975; *Clubs* Royal Ocean Racing; *Style—* Sir Adrian Blennerhassett, Bt; 54 Staveley Road, Chiswick, London W4 3ES (☎ 01 994 4908)

BLENNERHASSETT, His Honour Judge; Francis Alfred Blennerhassett; QC (1965); 2 s of John Blennerhassett, of Knowle, Warwicks, and Annie Elizabeth Blennerhassett; *b* 7 July 1916; *Educ* Solihull Sch; *m* 1946, Betty Muriel, da of Rex Bray, of Sheffield; 2 da; *Career* barr 1946, circuit judge 1978-; *Recreations* golf; *Clubs* Capt Heath Golf; *Style—* His Hon Judge Blennerhassett, QC; Manor Cottage, Hampton in Arden, Solihull, Warwicks

BLETSOE-BROWN, Maj Peter; TD (1949), DL (Northants 1983); s of James Harold Brown, DCM, MM (d 1965), and Mildred Alice Bletsoe (d 1958); *b* 11 Sept 1916; *Educ* Bilton Grange and Oakham; *m* 1950, Kathleen Cynthia Thelma, da of Col Murley, MC, of Devon; 3 s, 2 da; *Career* company dir and farmer; *Recreations* hunting; *Style—* Maj Peter Bletsoe-Brown, TD, DL; Sywell House, Sywell, Northants (☎ 0604 44156)

BLEWITT, Maj Shane Gabriel Basil; CVO (1987), LVO (1981); s of late Col Basil

Blewitt; *b* 25 Mar 1935; *Educ* Ampleforth and Ch Ch Oxford; *m* 1969, Julia, da of late Robert Henry Calvert, of Picts House, Horsham, Sussex, and wid of Maj John Morrogh-Bernard, Ir Gds; 1 s, 1 da (1 step s, 1 step da); *Career* Army Service Ir Gds 1956-74 (BAOR, Germany, Aden, Hong Kong); keeper of the privy purse and treasurer to HM The Queen 1988- (dep keeper 1985-87, asst keeper 1975-85); *Recreations* shooting, gardening; *Clubs* White's; *Style*— Maj Shane Blewitt, CVO, LVO; South Corner House, Duncton, nr Petworth, W Sussex (☎ Petworth 42143)

BLICKETT, Douglas Stanley; s of Walter Blickett (d 1958), of Hendon, and Ivy Beatrice, *née* Palmer (d 1971); *b* 24 Nov 1929; *Educ* Orange Hill GS Middx; *m* 6 March 1954, Ingeborg Hermine, da of Reginald George Gunton-Kendall of Dulwich; 1 s (Philip b 2 Sept 1959), 1 da (Denise b 25 Feb 1955); *Career* Nat Serv RAF 1948-50; res offr GEC Res Laboratories 1957-59, pubns writer Marconi Co Ltd 1959-61, fndr and dir J & B Engrg Co pubn conslts 1961-72, mgmnt trg GEC Marconi Coll 1972, chief author GEC Marconi Avionics 1972-85, tech pubns conslt Industl Artists Ltd 1985-; memb ctee EEA and BSI tech pubns ctee (standards, procedures, symbols) 1979-80; CEng 1967, MIEE, MISTC; *Recreations* walking, writing; *Style*— Douglas Blickett, Esq; Industrial Artists Ltd, Croft House, 11 Bancroft, Hitchin, Herts (☎ 0462 420024, fax 0462 420 394)

BLIGH, Lady Harriet Esme Ghislaine; da of 9 Earl of Darnley (d 1955); *b* 27 April 1949; *Educ* Cobham Hall, Somerville Oxford; *Style*— Lady Harriet Bligh; Meadow House, Cobham, nr Gravesend, Kent DA12 3BZ (☎ 0474 814 210)

BLIN-STOYLE, Prof Roger John; s of Cuthbert Basil St John Blin-Stoyle (d 1978), and Ada Mary, *née* Nash (d 1983); *b* 24 Dec 1924; *Educ* Alderman Newton's Boys' Sch Leicester, Wadham Coll Oxford (MA, D Phil); *m* 30 Aug 1949, Audrey Elizabeth, da of Joseph Clifford Balmford (d 1977); 1 s (Anthony b 1955), 1 da (Helena b 1952); *Career* Royal Corps of Signals 1943-46, commissioned 1944, served WWII 1943-46, RCS cmmnd 1944; res fell Pressed Steel Co Oxford Univ 1951- 53, lectr in mathematical physics Birmingham Univ 1953-54, snr res offr in theoretical physics Oxford Univ 1954-62, fell and lectrer in physics Wadham Coll Oxford 1956-62, (hon fell 1987), visiting asso prof of physics MIT 1959-60; Sussex Univ: prof of theoretical physics 1962-, founding Science Dean 1962-68, Pro-vice-chancellor 1965-67, deputy vice-chllr 1970-72, pro-vice-chllr (science) 1977-79; chm sch curriculum devpt ctee 1983-88 memb/chm of various ctees incl, serc, Royal Soc CVCP; FRS (1976), FRSA (1986), F Inst P (1962); *Books* Theories of Nuclear Moments (1957), Fundamental Interactions and the Nucleus (1973); *Recreations* making music; *Style*— Prof Roger Blin-Stoyle; 14 Hill Road, Lewes, E Sussex BN7 1DB (☎ 0273 473640); Physics Building, The University of Sussex, Brighton, E Sussex BN1 9QH (☎ 0273 678088, fax 0273 678335)

BLISS, Dr Christopher John Emile; s of John Llwelyn Bliss of London (d 1978), founder of the BBC TV service from 1936, working as a "boffin" designer, etc, and Patricia Paula, *née* Dubern; *b* 17 Feb 1940; *Educ* Finchley Catholic GS, King's Coll Cambridge (BA, PhD); *m* 1, 1964, Heather, da of Cyril Midmer, Dublin; 1 s (John Benet b 1966), 2 da (Anna Katharine b 1968, Madeline Frances b 1974); m 2, 1983, Ghada, da of Adel Saqf El Hait, of Kuwait; *Career* fellow Christ's College Cambridge 1965-71, asst lecturer 1965-67, lecturer 1967-71; prof economics Univ of Essex 1971-77, fell Econometric Soc 1978, ed Review of Economic Studies 1967-71, Nuffield reader in int economics and fell Nuffield Coll Oxford 1977-; *Books* Capital Theory of the Distribution of Income 1975, Palanpur: the Economy of an Indian Village (with N H Stern); *Recreations* music; *Style*— Dr Christopher Bliss; Tamarisk Cottage, South Street, Steeple Aston, Oxon OX5 3RT; Nuffield College, Oxford OX1 1NF (☎ 0865 278573)

BLISS, John Cordeux; QPM (1969); s of Herbert Bliss (d 1954), of Chipping Norton, Oxon, and Ida Muriel, *née* Hays (d 1969); *b* 16 Mar 1914; *Educ* Haileybury, Met Police Coll Hendon; *m* 18 Oct 1947, Elizabeth Mary, da of Charles Gordon Howard (d 1981), of Reigate; 1 s (Thomas John Cordeux b 1955), 2 da (Jane Katherine b 1949, Anne Elizabeth b 1951); *Career* WWII Flt Lt RAF 1942-45 served 227 Sqdn Coastal Cmd (Beaufighters), MEF; joined Met Police 1936, served CID in various divnl and HQ postings incl City & Met Company Fraud Squad 1954-57, dir criminal law Police Staff Coll Bramshill 1961-63 seconded Home Off to set up Regnl Crime Squads, dep asst cmmr and nat co-ordinator regnl Crime Squads England and Wales 1964-70; called to Bar Middle Temple 1954; Parole Bd 1973-76 and 1978-81; Freeman City of London, Liveryman Worshipful Co of Merchant Taylors (1947); fell Churchill Meml Tst 1967; Medico-Legal Soc 1948; *Recreations* Met Police RFC (vice pres), gardening; *Clubs* RAF; *Style*— John C Bliss, Esq, QPM; Foxhanger Down, Hurtmore, Godalming GU7 2RG

BLOCH, (Andrew Charles) Danby; s of late Prof Moishe Rudolf Bloch, and Mary Hall Bloch; *b* 19 Dec 1945; *Educ* Tonbridge, Wadham Coll Oxford (MA); *m* 1968, Sandra, da of late William Wilkinson; 1 s (Adam b 1972), 1 da (Hester b 1974); *Career* researcher Oxford Centre for Management Studies (now Templeton Coll) 1968-70; dir: Grosvenor Advisory Services Ltd 1971-74, Oxford Fine Arts Ltd 1975-85, Raymond Godfrey & Ptnrs Ltd 1974-, Taxbriefs Ltd 1975-; reg weekly column on taxation The Times 1979-82, and 1986-, reg financial column in Daily Telegraph 1982-86; *Style*— Danby Bloch, Esq; 17 Norham Road, Oxford (☎ Oxford 54971); 193 St John Street, London EC1 (☎ 01 251 4916)

BLOCK, Maj-Gen Adam Johnstone Cheyne; CB (1962), CBE (1959, OBE 1951, DSO 1945); s of Col Arthur Hugh Block, RA (d 1931), and Hilda Rose Nugent, *née* Johnstone (d 1970); twin bro of Brig Donald Block, CBE, DSO, MG *qv*; *b* 13 June 1908; *Educ* Blundell's, RMA Woolwich; *m* 1945, Pauline Bingham, da of Col Norman Kennedy, CBE, DSO, TD, DL (d 1960), of Doonholm, Ayr; 3 da (1 decd); *Career* served WW II 1939-45, France, UK, N Africa, Italy, Cmdt Sch of Artillery Larkhill 1956, GOC Troops Malta and Libya 1959-62, Col Cmdt Royal Regt of Artillery 1965-73, ret 1963; chief info offr Church of England 1965-73; chcllr Basingstoke Distris Council 1973-75; *Recreations* all country pursuits, golf; *Style*— Maj-Gen Adam Block, CB, CBE, OBE, DSO; St Cross House, Whitchurch, Hants RG28 7AS (☎ 025 689 2344)

BLOCK, Brigadier David Arthur Kennedy William; CBE (1961), DSO (1945), MC (1943); s of Col Arthur Hugh Block, RA (d 1931), and Hilda Rose Nugent, *née* Johnstone (d 1970); twin bro of Maj-Gen Adam Block *qv*; *b* 13 June 1908; *Educ* Blundell's Sch, RMA Woolwich; *m* 1949, Elizabeth Grace, da of Lt-Col Edward George Troyte-Bullock, CMG, TD (d 1942), and widow of Edmund Sebag-Montefiore; *Career* cmmnd 2 Lt RA 1928, served WW II, N Africa, Italy, Co 152 (Ayrshire Yeomanry) Fd Regt RA (despatches), Lt-Col CO 2 Regt RHA, Col 1953, Brig 1959, CRA 7 Armd Divn Cmd 18 Training Bde RA, ret 1961, ADC to HM The Queen 1959-61; *Recreations* all country pursuits; *Clubs* Army & Navy; *Style*— Brigadier David Block, CBE, DSO, MC; Benville Manor Lodge, Corscombe, Dorchester, Dorset DT2 0NW (☎ Corscombe 093 589 205)

BLOCK, Simon Anthony Allen; s of Gerald Allen Block (d 1969), of Little Park Farm, Battle, E Sussex, and Eileen Marjorie, *née* Handley (d 1982); *b* 19 July 1935; *Educ* Marlborough, Pembroke Coll Cambridge (MA); *m* 16 Aug 1958, Patricia Ann, da of Gen Sir Rodney Moore, GCVO, KCB, CBE, DSO (d 1985), Chief Steward of Hampton Court Palace; 3 s (Adam b 1960, Robert b 1962, Justin b 1964); *Career* 2 Lt 1Bn Queens Royal West Surrey Regt 1952-54; slr, sr ptnr Crossman Block and Keith 1977-88, ptnr Withers Crossman Block 1988-; memb Common Cncl City of London 1988-89; Liveryman: Broderers Co 1958 (Master 1979-80), Weavers Co, City of London Solicitors Co 1988; *Recreations* fine wines, field sports; *Clubs* Leander, City Livery; *Style*— Simon A A Block, Esq; c/o Withers, Crossman Block, 20 Essex Street, Strand, London, WC2R 3AL (☎ 01 836 8400, fax 01 240 2278, telex 24213)

BLOCKEY, Wing-Cdr Robert (Robin) Sandland; s of Air-Vice-Marshal Paul Sandland Blockey, CB, CBE (d 1963), and Ella, *née* Temple (d 1987); *b* 16 July 1933; *Educ* Cranleigh, RAF Coll Cranwick; *m* 27 April 1957, Susan Rae, da of Hubert Arnold Pallant, DSO, MC (d 1977); 1 s (Charles b 1960), 2 da (Caroline b 1958, Fae b 1962); *Career* served RAF 1951-78; Sword of Honour Cranwell 1954; cmmnd Univ of Birmingham Air Sqdn 1962-65, chief flying instructor No 1 FTS 1972-73, Nat Defence Coll 1974; prop Tiroran County House Hotel Isle of Mull 1977-; *Recreations* portrait paintings (pastel), game shooting, gardening; *Clubs* RAF; *Style*— Wing-Cdr Robin S Blockey; Tiroran House, Isle of Mull, Argyll, Scotland (☎ 068 15 232)

BLOFELD, His Hon Judge; John Christopher Calthorpe; QC (1975); s of late Thomas Robert Calthorpe Blofeld, CBE, JP, High Sheriff Norfolk 1953 & Chm CGA, of Hoveton House, Wroxham, Norfolk, and Grizel Blance, *née* Turner; *b* 11 July 1932; *Educ* Eton, King's Coll Cambridge; *m* 1961, Judith Anne, elder da of late Dr Alan Mohun, and Mrs James Mitchell; 2 s, 1 da; *Career* barr; rec 1975, chllr Dioc St Edmundbury 1973, chm CGA 1977; circuit judge (SE) 1982-; *Recreations* gardening, antiques, pottering; *Clubs* Boodle's, Norfolk County; *Style*— His Honour Judge Blofeld, QC

BLOIS, Lady (Elizabeth) Caroline Elinor Evelyn; *née* Giffard; da of 3 Earl of Halsbury; *b* 4 Mar 1939; *m* 1968, Rodney John Derek Blois, 2 s of Capt Sir Gervase Ralph Edmund Blois, 10 Bt, MC (d 1968); 2 da (Camilla b 1970, Susanna b 1972); *Style*— Lady Caroline Blois; Cockfield Hall, Yoxford, Suffolk

BLOIS, Sir Charles Nicholas Gervase; 11 Bt (E 1686), of Grundisburgh Hall Suffolk; elder s of Capt Sir Gervase Blois, 10 Bt, MC (d 1968); *b* 25 Dec 1939; *Educ* Harrow, Trinity Coll Dublin; *m* 8 July 1967, Celia Helen Mary, o da of Cyril George Francis Pritchett, CBE, of Aldburgh, Suffolk; 1 s, 1 da; *Heir* s, Andrew Charles David Blois b 7 Feb 1971; *Career* farmer and landowner; *Recreations* yacht cruising (yacht 'Caleta'), travel, shooting; *Clubs* Cruising Assoc, Ocean Cruising; *Style*— Sir Charles Blois, Bt; Red House, Westleton, Saxmundham, Suffolk (☎ 072 873 200)

BLOIS-BROOKE, Lieut Cdr RNR (ret) Michael Steuart; s of Major Eardley Steuart Blois-Brooke, TA, of Uford Place, Woodbridge, Suffolk (d 1956), and Violet Mary, *née* Sproat (d 1945); *b* 13 August 1919; *Educ* Orwell Park Prep Sch Suffolk, HMS 'Conway' naval training ship at Rock Ferry, Cheshire; *m* 20 Aug 1949, Mary, da of Cecil Harvey Mead, of Oak House, Crawley Down, Sussex (d 1950: bank official); 1 s (Mark Harvey b 1954), 2 da (Susan Penelope b 1950, Diana Mary b 1959); *Career* served in RN 1938-57 as Royal Naval Reserve officer; ranks: midshipman 1937, sub lieut 1941, lieut 1943, lieut cdr 1951; served: Home Fleet, Mediterranean Fleet, and Far East Fleet; took part in Normandy Landings; taught in schools in Norfolk 1951-; ret from Naval Reserve 1957; *Recreations* writing and gardening; *Clubs* Overseas; *Style*— Lieut Cdr Michael Steuart Blois-Brooke; St Austin's House, Curtis Lane, Sheringham, Norfolk NR26 8DE (☎ 0263 823157)

BLOM-COOPER, Louis Jacques; QC (1970); s of Alfred Blom-Cooper (d 1964), of Los Angeles, California, USA, and Ella, *née* Flesseman (d 1932); *b* 27 Mar 1926; *Educ* Seaford Coll, King's Coll London (LLB), Municipal Univ of Amsterdam (Dr Juris); *m* 1, 7 July 1952 (m dis 1970), Miriam Eve, da of Daniel Swift (d 1988); 2 s (Jeremy Rupert Louis b 25 Jan 1961, Keith Sebastian Daniel b (twin) 25 Jan 1961), 1 da (Alison Jeanette b 13 April 1958); m 2, 16 Oct 1970, Jane Elizabeth, da of Maurice Douglas Smither; 1 s ((Samuel) George Abbott b 8 July 1979), 2 da (Martha Clare Justine b 6 Jan 1971, Hannah Jane Notcutt b 13 Nov 1972); *Career* RCS 1944, cmmnd 2 Lt E Yorks Regt 1945, Capt 1946, demobbed 1947, barr Middle Temple 1952, bencher 1978, memb Home Sec's Advsy Cncl on the Penal System 1966-78; chm: Mental Health Act Cmmn 1988-, Press Cncl 1989-, Independent Ctee for the Supervision of Standards of Telephone Info Servs 1986-, BBC London Local Radio Advsy Cncl 1970-73; vice pres Howard League for Penal Reform 1984- (chm 197384), jt dir Legal Res Unit Bedford Coll Univ of London 1967-82, visiting prof QMC London Univ 1983-, tstee Scott Tst (The Guardian Newspaper) 1982-; jt ed Common Market Law Reports; JP Inner London 1966-79 (transferred City of London 1969); FRSA 1964; *Books* Bankruptcy in Private International Law (1954), The Law as Literature (1962), The A6 Murder (A Semblance of Truth) (1963), A Calender of Murder (with TP Morris 1964), Language of the Law (1965), Separated Spouses (with O R McGregor and Colin Gibson 1970), Final Appeal: a study of the House of Lords in its judicial capacity (with G Drewry 1972), Progress in Penal Reform (ed 1975), Law and Morality (ed with G Drewry 1976); *Recreations* watching and reporting on Association football, reading, music, writing, broadcasting; *Clubs* MCC, Athenaeum; *Style*— Louis Blom-Cooper, Esq, QC; 25 Richmond Crescent, London N1 OLY (☎ 01 607 8045); Press Council, 1 Salisbury Square, London EC4 (☎ 01 353 1248)

BLOMEFIELD, Sir (Thomas) Charles Peregrine; 6 Bt (UK 1807), of Attleborough Co Norfolk; s of Sir Thomas Edward Peregrine Blomefield, 5 Bt (d 1984); *b* 24 July 1948; *Educ* Wellington, Mansfield Coll Oxford; *m* 1975, Georgina Geraldine, da of Cdr Charles Over, RN, of Lugger End, Portscatho, Cornwall; 1 s (William), 2 da (Emma, Harriet); *Heir* s, Thomas William Peregrine Blomefield b 16 July 1983; *Career* fine art dealer; Christies 1970-75, Wildenstein and Co 1975-76; dir: Lidchi Art Gallery Johannesburg 1976-78, Thomas Heneage and Co 1981-87, Fleetwood-Hesketh Ltd 1982-; md Charles Blomefield and Co 1980-; *Recreations* travel; *Style*— Sir Charles Blomefield, Bt; Clapton Manor, Cheltenham GL54 2LG

BLOMEFIELD, Ginette, Lady; Ginette; *née* Massart; da of late Dr Raphael

Massart, of 15 Boulevard des Invalides, Paris; *m* 1, George Harting; m 2, 1947, Lt-Cdr Sir Thomas Edward Peregrine Blomefield, 5 Bt, RNVR (d 1984); 1 s (Sir Charles Blomefield, 6 Bt, *qv*); *Style*— Ginette, Lady Blomefield; 1 Great Lane, Shaftesbury, Dorset

BLOMEFIELD, His Honour; Peregrine Maitland; 2 s of Lt-Col Wilmot Blomefield, OBE (d 1926; s of Sir Thomas Blomefield, 4 Bt, CB, JP), and Jessie Leila Hodges (d 1976); *b* 25 Oct 1917; *Educ* Repton, Trinity Coll Oxford (MA); *m* 1941, Angela Catherine, da of Maj Geoffrey Hugh Shenley Crofton, of Heytesbury, Wilts; 1 s (Adam); *Career* served WW II Capt Royal Signals W Desert and Italy; barr 1947, bencher Middle Temple 1967, rec Burton-upon-Trent 1969, county court judge 1969, circuit judge 1972-1987; *Recreations* music, living in the country; *Style*— His Hon Judge Blomefield; The Coach House, Frilsham, Newbury, Berks RG16 9XA (☎ 0635 201421)

BLOMFIELD, Brig John Reginald; OBE (1957), MC (1945); s of late Douglas John Blomfield, CIE (1979), and Coralie, *née* Tucker (d 1967); *b* 10 Jan 1916; *Educ* Clifton, RMA Woolwich, Peterhouse Cambridge; *m* 1939, Patricia Mary, *née* McKim; 2 da; *Career* RE 1936-69, mangr Cmmn for New Towns Hemel Hempstead 1969-78; *Recreations* cruising, ocean racing (yacht: 'Trefoil'); *Clubs* Roy Ocean Racing, Roy Engrs Yacht, Roy Lymington Yacht; *Style*— Brig John Blomfield, OBE, MC; 9 Armstrong Close, Brockenhurst, Hants (☎ Brockenhurst 2164)

BLOMFIELD-SMITH, Brig Denis Cecil; MBE (1962); s of Cecil Herbert Blomfield-Smith (d 1959), of Westwefield, Suffolk and Lilian Bosley; *b* 6 May 1920; *Educ* Felsted; *m* 1, 1942, Mary Rosemary Smythe; 1 s (Clive b 1947), 1 da (Vivien b 1944); m 2, 5 July 1956, Moyra McLeod, da of Roderick McLeod Mitchell (d 1959), of London; *Career* British Army Offr; cmmnd Royal Regiment of Artillery 1940; 109 Field Regt (Cumberland Yeomanry): 11 Field Regt (4 Indian Div); 33 Airborne Light Regt (6 Airborne Div); 2 Regt Royal Horse Artillery; 14 Field Regt; 6 Field Regt; war service in Middle East, Europe; postwar service Egypt, Palestine, Germany, Hong Kong, Singapore, Turkey; instr Gunnery 1945-47; Staff Coll Camberley 1954; War Office 1955-56; Jt Services Staff Coll 1957; Military Asst Staff of Chief of Defence Staff 1960-62; HQ Far East Land Forces and C-in-C Far East 1962-64; Princ Staff Offr UK permanent Military Dep CENTO 1964-67; Chief Staff Offr to Cmmndr British Forces Hong Kong 1967-70; HQ BAOR 1970-72; cmmndt Royal Artillery Range, Hebrides 1972-73; Brig Author MOD 1973-74; (ret 1974); dir British Red Cross Soc Hertfordshire 1974-76; sec Royal Patriotic Fund Corpn 1979-; *Recreations* writing, gardening; *Clubs* Army and Navy; *Style*— Brig Denis C Blomfield-Smith, MBE; c/o Lloyds Bank plc, 6 Pall Mall, London SW1

BLOOD, Peter Bindon; o s of Brig William Edmund Robarts Blood, CBE, MC (d 1976), and Eva Gwendoline Olive Clarisse Mends, *née* Harrison (d 1981); collateral descendant of Col Thomas Blood who attempted to steal the Crown Jewels on 9 May 1671, later pardoned and pensioned by Charles II; *b* 24 Sept 1920; *Educ* Imperial Service Coll, Windsor; *m* 20 June 1953, Elizabeth Ann, da of Harold Drummond Hillier, MC, of Sudbury, Suffolk; 1 s (Anthony b 1956), 1 da (Jennifer b 1954); *Career* served RE 1941-46 (despatches), regular cmmn RE 1948, Staff Coll Camberley 1951, sec Army Bd NATO Mil Agency for Standardisation 1952-53, invalided from service 1953; Intelligence Co-ordination Staff FO 1953-58; fndr and md: Isora Integrated Ceilings Ltd, Clean Room Construction Ltd, Mitchel and King Sales Ltd 1959-71; dir-gen Inst of Marketing 1972-84, chm: Indust Market Research Ltd 1984-1987, vrs Berks Coll of Art and Design 1981-86; FRSA, FInstM; *Recreations* local community activities, photography, travel, music, furniture restoration; *Style*— Peter Blood, Esq; The Malt Cottage, School Lane, Cookham Village, Berks SL6 9QN (☎ 062 85 25319); Industrial Market Research Ltd, Kew Bridge House, Kew Bridge Road, Brentford, Middx TW8 0ED

BLOOM, Charles; QC (1987); s of Abraham Barnet Bloom (d 1973), of Manchester, and Freda, *née* Craft; *b* 6 Nov 1940; *Educ* Manchester Central GS, Manchester Univ (LLB); *m* 16 Aug 1967, Janice Rachelle, da of Reuben Goldberg, of Gwendor Ave, Crumpsal, Manchester; 1 s (David Benjamin b 31 Aug 1972), 1 da (Sarah Rebecca b 10 July 1969); *Career* barr Gray's Inn 1963; dep circuit judge 1979, rec Crown Ct 1983; chm Med Appeal Tribunals 1979; *Recreations* theatre, tennis; *Clubs* Friedland Postmusaf Tennis; *Style*— Charles Bloom, Esq, QC; 10 Barcheston Road, Cheadle, Cheshire SH8 1LL (☎ 061 428 3725); 28 St John Street, Manchester M2 4DJ (☎ 061 834 8418, fax 061 835 3929)

BLOOM, Claire; da of late Edward Bloom and Elizabeth Bloom; *b* 15 Feb 1931; *Educ* Badminton, USA and privately; *m* 1, 1959 (m dis 1969), Rod Steiger; 1 da; m 2, 1969 (m dis 1976), Hillard Elkins; *Career* actress; has appeared in theatre, film and television productions; *Style*— Miss Claire Bloom; c/o Michael Linnitt, Globe Theatre, W1

BLOOM, (George) Cromarty; CBE (1974); s of late George Highfield Bloom, and Jessie, *née* Cromarty; *b* 8 June 1910; *Educ* privately and Keble Coll Oxford; *m* 1, 1940, Patricia Suzanne Ramplin (d 1957); 2 s; m 2, 1961, Sheila Louise Curran; 1 s; *Career* dep chm LBC; *Style*— Cromarty Bloom, Esq, CBE; 1 Tivoli Court, Tivoli Rd, Cheltenham, Glos (☎ 39413)

BLOOM, Patricia; da of Leonard Bloom (d 1988), of 12A Clifton Court, St John's Wood Rd, London NW8, and Freda *née* Myers; *b* 20 July 1940; *Educ* Maida Vale HS; *Career* account exec Alexander Butterfield 1964-67, launch team Mary Quant Cosmetics 1968-69, promotions ed Queen Magazine 1970, nat fund raiser Nat Fund Raising Charity 1971-79, fndr Pet Plan Gp (providing comprehensive insur cover for cats, dogs and horses, underwritten by Lloyd's); finalist Veuve Clicquot Business Woman of the Year Award 1989; IBRC; *Recreations* bridge, tennis; *Style*— Miss Patsy Bloom; Pet Plan Ltd, 319/327 Chiswick High Rd, London W4 4HH (☎ 01 995 1414, fax 01 994 7585)

BLOOM, Dr Victor Roy; s of Froim Bloom (d 1961), of Westbourne, and Jesse Selina Tomson, *née* Parker; *b* 13 Mar 1932; *Educ* Bembridge Sch, Oxford Univ (MA, BM, BSch); *m* 4 April 1964 (m dis 1976), Chloe Ann, da of Frederick Jack Rich; 1 s (Marston), 1 da (Emma); *Career* UCH 1957-58, Bristol Royal Infirmary 1958-59, Hosp for Sick Children Gt Ormond St 1959-60, Nat Heart Hosp 1960, Hammersmith Hosp 1960-62, Central Middx Hosp 1962-64, physician Harley St and Harley House 1964-; ed journal of RSM 1976-88, chm Med Investmts Ltd; vice-pres Hornsby Educnl Tst; memb: Nichiren Shoshu of the UK, advsy panel pro-dogs, Dartmoor Preservation Soc, Torquay Pottery Collectors Soc, Med Soc London, Assurance Med Soc; Freeman City of London 1979, Liveryman Worshipful Co Apothecaries 1978; MRCP 1964, MFOM (RCP) 1982; *Recreations* opera, theatre, ceramics, cricket, association football; *Clubs* United Oxford & Cambridge; *Style*— Dr Victor Bloom; 40 Harley House, Marylebone Rd, London NW1 5HF (☎ 01 935 1411, fax 01 224 0178, car 0836 203783)

BLOOMER, Robin Howard; s of Arthur Hugh Bloomer (d 1972), of Mulberry House, The Avenue, Healing, Grimsby, Humberside, and Elizabeth Kathleen, *née* Watson (d 1964); *b* 6 May 1930; *Educ* Shrewsbury; *m* 24 May 1958, Edith Alice, da of Charles William Green (d 1954); 1 s (Charles b 1961), 1 da (Susan b 1966); *Career* slr, sr ptnr H K & H S Bloomer & Co Slrs, 1964-; pres Grimsby and Cleethorpes Law Soc 1978; *Style*— Robin Bloomer, Esq; 1 Bargate Avenue, Great Grimsby (☎ 0472 43251); 28 Hainton Avenue, Great Grimsby, S Humberside DN32 9BG (☎ 0472 350711)

BLOOMFIELD, Barry Cambray; s of Clifford Wilson Bloomfield (d 1981), and Eileen Elizabeth (d 1953); *b* 1 June 1931; *Educ* East ham GS, Univ Coll Exeter (BA), Birkbeck Coll London (MA); *m* 29 Dec 1958, Valerie Jean, da of George Philpot (d 1964); *Career* Nat Serv 1952-54; asst Nat centl Library 1955, Librarian Coll of St Mark & St John 1956-61, asst Librarian LSE 1961-63, dep librarian Sch of Oriental and African Studies 1963-72 (librarian 1972-78), dir India Off Library & Records FCO 1978-82, keeper Dept of Oriental Manuscrips and Printed Books 1983 (dir collection devpt), Br Library 1985; cncl Royal Asiatic soc 1980-84, cncl Britain - Burma Soc 1979-, VP Bibligraphical Soc 1979-, cncl Br Assoc for Cemetries in S Asia 1980-, exec ctee Friends of the Nat Libraries 1981-; memb: Fell Library Assoc 1965, Bibliography Soc, Oxford Bibliegraphy Soc, Cambridge Bibliography Soc; *Books* W H Auden: a bibliography (1972, 2 edn with E Mendelson), An author index to selected British little magazines (1976), Philip Larkin: a bibliography (1979), Middle East studies and Librarianship (1980); *Recreations* reading, music; *Clubs* Royal Cnwlth Soc; *Style*— Barry Bloomfield, Esq; British Library, 14 Stone Street, London, W4E 7DG, (☎ 01 323 7637)

BLOOMFIELD, Hon Sir John Stoughton; s of Arthur Stoughton Bloomfield, CA, of Melbourne and Ada Victoria Bloomfield; *b* 9 Oct 1901; *Educ* Geelong GS, Trinity Coll Melbourne U (LLB); *m* 1931, (Beatrice) Madge, da of William Henry Taylor, of Overnewton, Syndenham, Victoria; 1 s, 1 da; *Career* Lt-Col AIF 1940-45; barr Vic 1945, Vic MLA (Lib) for Malvern Vic 1953-70, min of Labour, Industry and Electrical Undertakings 1955-56, min of Educn 1956-67, ret; QC Vic 1965; kt 1967; *Style*— The Hon Sir John Bloomfield, QC; 1/22 Mercer Rd, Armadale, Vic 3143, Australia (☎ 20 2947)

BLOOR, Hon Mrs - Hon Giovanna; da of Baron Blackett, OM, CH (Life Peer); *b* 1926; *m* 1950, Kenneth Bloor; *Style*— The Hon Mrs Bloor; 9 Queenston Rd, West Didsbury, Manchester 20

BLOSSE; *see*: Lynch-Blosse

BLOUNT, Lt Col Anthony Hubert; s of Col Hubert Blount, MC, TD, DL (d 1979) and Marion Emily, *née* Barclay; *b* 13 Mar 1934; *Educ* Harrow, RMA Sandhurst; *m* 15 Jan 1966, Sarah Georgina da of Maj George Tunley Howard (d 1968); 3 da (Emma b 1967, Alice b 1968, Kitty b 1969); *Career* cmmd 13/18 Royal Hussars 1954, resigned as Maj 1974; landowner and farmer; hon sec Norfolk Ctee Army Benevolent Fund 1983, Cmdt Norfolk ACF 1988-; *Recreations* shooting, sailing; *Clubs* Norfolk; *Style*— Lt Col A H Blount; Cley Hall Farms, Holt, Norfolk, NR25 7TX

BLOUNT, Hon Mrs; Susan Victoria; da of 1 Baron Cobbold, GCVO, PC, DL (d 1987), and Lady Hermione, da of 2 Earl of Lytton; *b* 24 May 1933; *m* 1957, Sqdn Ldr Christopher Charles Blount, LVO, yr s of Air Vice-Marshal Charles Hubert Boulby Blount, CB, OBE, MC (d 1940); 2 s, 2 da; *Style*— The Hon Mrs Blount; Manor Farm, Barkway, nr Royston, Herts SG8 8EJ (☎ 076 384 550)

BLOUNT, Sir Walter Edward Alpin (Jasper); 12 Bt (E 1642), DSC (1943 and two bars 1945); s of Sir Edward Robert Blount, 11 Bt (d 1978), and Violet Ellen, *née* Fowler (d 1969); *b* 31 Oct 1917; *Educ* Beaumont Coll, Sidney Sussex Coll Cambridge; *m* 1954, Eileen Audrey, da of late Hugh Blasson Carritt; 1 da (Nicola Jane Eileen b 1955); *Heir* none; *Career* Lt RNVR; slr; farmer; Lloyds underwriter; *Recreations* sailing; *Clubs* Bembridge Sailing, Seaview YC, CUCC, RNVRYC, Law Soc YC; *Style*— Sir Walter Blount, Bt; 19 St Ann's Terrrace, St John's Wood, London NW8 (☎ 01 722 0802)

BLOW, Joyce (Mrs Anthony Darlington); da of Walter Blow (d 1962), and Phyllis, *née* Grainger (d 1961); *b* 4 May 1929; *Educ* Bell-Baxter Sch Cupar Fife, Univ of Edinburgh (MA); *m* 27 March 1974, (John) Anthony Basil Darlington (ret Lt-Col RE), s of Arthur James Darlington, DSO, JP (ret Lt-Col RE, d 1960); *Career* princ Bd of Trade 1965-67, M & MC 1967-70, asst sec DTI 1972-77, under sec OFT 1977-80, under sec DTI 1980-84; cncl memb Money Mgmnt Cncl 1985-, chm Mail Order Publishers Authy 1985-, vice pres Inst of Trading Standards Admin 1985-, bd memb Br Standards Inst (chm consumer policy ctee) 1986-, dir Arts Club 1987; vice chm Friends of the Elizabeth Garrett Anderson Hosp; Freedom City of London; FIPR 1964, FBIM 1977; *Recreations* music, the arts, travel, France; *Clubs* Arts, Reform; *Style*— Miss Joyce Blow; 9 Crouchfield Close, Seaford, E Sussex (☎ 01 735 4023); 17 Fentiman Rd, London SW8 1LD

BLOWER, Owen George; s of Frederick Blower (d 1967), and Clara (d 1980); *b* 3 June 1932; *Educ* Loughborough Coll; *m* 1 Dec 1956, Mollie Doreen, da of Francis Victor Forryan, of Leicester; 2 da (Jacqueline Claire Yvonne b 1962, Maria Tracey Michelle b 1964); *Career* md: Owen Blower Knitwear (Leicester) Ltd 1967-, Owen Blower Int Cycles Ltd 1976-, Veloce Ital Ltd 1983-; British Best All Rounder Cycling Champion 1958, nat record holder, Multi GB International; *Recreations* cycling, ornithology; *Style*— Owen G Blower, Esq; Heatherfields, Priory Lane, Ulverscroft, Leicestershire LE6 0PA; Owen Blower Knitwear (Leicester) Ltd, Town Green Street, Rothley, Leicestershire LE7 7NW (☎ 0533 302459, telex 265451 MONREF G, ATT MAILBOX; 83:MI0170)

BLOWERS, Dr Anthony John; CBE 1985, JP ((Surrey 1970), DL (Surrey 1986)); s of Geoffrey Hathaway Blowers (d 1973), of Sunnymead Weir Rd, Chertsey, Surrey, and Louise, *née* Jux; *b* 11 August 1926; *Educ* Sloane GS Chelsea, Sir John Cass Coll Univ of London, Univ of Surrey (PhD); *m* 4 Sep 1948, Yvonne, da of Capt Alan Victor Boiteux-Buchanan (d 1986); 2 s (Colin b 1953, Christopher b 1955), 1 da (Anne (Mrs Ricketts) b 1951); *Career* RCS 1944-45, RAMC 1945-46, RWAFF (serv Nigeria) 1946-48; experimental offr Miny of Agric 1953-59 (sr sci asst 1949-53), Sandoz Pharmaceuticals 1959-(sr res offr 1973-87, conslt psychopharmacology 1987-), sr conslt Market Access Int 1987-, conslt bacteriology Mansi Laboratories 1973-; NHS: vice chm Surrey Area Health Authy 1976-77 (memb 1973-80), memb SW Thames Regnl Health Authy 1980-81, chm W Surrey and NE Hants Health Authy 1981-86, cmmr Mental Health Act Cmmn 1987-, memb Mental Health Review Tbnl 1975-; govr: Fullbrook Sch 1967-85 (chm 1981-85), Ottershaw Sch 1975-81 (chm 1979-81); memb Cons Policy Gp on Mental Health 1978-81, pres Runnymede Scout Cncl 1970-84; chm: Runnymede & Elmbridge Police Community Liason Ctee 1983-, SW Surrey Crime Prevention Ctee 1986-; vice chm Farnham Police Community Liason Ctee 1985-; memb: Psychiatry Res Tst 1986-, Ct Surrey Univ 1986-, cncl Magistrates Assoc 1986-; chm Surrey Magistrates Soc 1988-, asst dir gen St John Ambulance 1985-(cdr Surrey branch 1987-), vice chm Woking Duke of Edinburgh Award Ctee 1987-; chm Surrey Ctee Police Convalescence and Rehabilitation Tst 1986-88, Runnymede & Elmbridge Ctee Wishing Well Appeal; Surrey cncllr 1970-85; chm: Chertsey Urban DC 1969-70 and 1973-74 (memb 1964-74), Runnymede Borough Cncl 1973-74 (memb 1973-84), Surrey Police Authy 1981-85 (memb 1973-); memb bd visitors Coldingley Prison 1978-, O St J 1986; Freeman: Borough of Runnymede 1985, City of London 1983; Liveryman Worshipful Soc of Apothecaries 1988 (Yeoman 1983-88); CBiol 1983, FIMLS 1983; *Books* numerous contributions to books and sci jls; *Recreations* fund raising, running, gardening; *Style*— Dr Anthony Blowers, CBE, JP, DL; Westward, 12 Birch Close, Boundstone, Farnham, Surrey GU10 4TJ (☎ 025 125 2769); Sandoz Pharmaceuticals, Frimley Business Park, Camberley, Surrey GU16 5SG (☎ 0276 692 255, fax 0276 692 508, telex 858685)

BLOXHAM, John; s of John Bloxham (d 1953), of Doncaster, Yorkshire, and Lillian Mary, *née* Sherriff (d 1936); *b* 20 Mar 1917; *Educ* Doncaster GS, Doncaster Tech Coll, Architectural Assoc Sch of Architecture (AA Dip); *m* 29 Dec 1945, Peggy Lovell, da of Captain J O N Wood, RN; 1 s (Jeffrey St John b 1953), 1 da (Christine Gillian (Mrs Blanks) b 1948); *Career* 61 HAA Regt RA 1940, Battle of Br Essex RAF, RE 1942, cmmnd 2 Lt 1942, served 15 Scottish Div RE North Africa 1943, joined 1 Br Inf Div Tunis, Italy 1943, Anzio 1944, Rome, Palestine, Egypt demobbed 1946; pupilage 1932-37, Architectural Assoc Sch of Architecture 1937-40, Miners' Welfare Cmmn 1947, Private Office 1947-48, design architect Iraq Petroleum Co 1948-57, Private Practice 1957-; chm City of London Round Table 1956, hon sec Sch Old Boys Club, and memb City Livery Club 1972 (chm: Aero Section, Music Section; hon sec Aero Section), pres Lewisham C of C and Indust, neighbourhood watch, ctee memb Catford Police Security Panel, cncl memb Utd Wards' Club of City of London Governing Body; Freeman City of London, Liveryman Worshipful Co of Basketmakers; memb: Architectural Assoc 1938-, RIBA; ARCUK, FSAI; *Recreations* walking, tennis, badminton, cricket; *Style*— John Bloxham, Esq; 36 Hall Drive, London SE26 6XB (☎ 01 778 8645)

BLUCK, Duncan Robert Yorke; OBE (1984); s of Thomas Edward Bluck and Ida Bluck; *b* 19 Mar 1927; *m* 1952, Stella Wardaw Murdoch; 1 s, 3 da; *Career* chm Swire Pacific plc, Cathay Pacific Airways, Hong Kong Aircraft Engrg Co; dir The Hongkong and Shanghai Banking Corpn, John Swire & Sons (HK) Ltd; chm British Tourist Authority 1984-, English Tourist Bd 1984-; *Style*— Duncan Bluck, Esq, OBE; c/o Swire Pacific plc, Swire House, Hong Kong (☎ 5-230011)

BLUETT, David Frederick; s of Frederick Dawson Bluett (d 1977), of 6 Fairleas Ct, Courtdown Rd, Beckenham, Kent, and Muriel Emma, *née* Fells (d 1982); *b* 5 Dec 1937; *Educ* Cranleigh; *m* (m dis), Gillian Lalage, da of Richard Travis Harris; 2 s (James Edward Nutcombe b 3 Oct 1974, Charles Piers b 28 June 1978); *Career* CCF Artillery Section Cranleigh Sch 1951-55, HAC 1955-56, Nat Serv RA 1956-58, cmmnd 1957, Kent Yeo 1958-63; Royal Insur Co 1955-56; chm: Bluett Smith & Co Ltd (and subsidaries of family co) 1972 (joined 1959, md 1968), Sunset Cleaning Gp 1975-89, subsidaries of TKM plc 1980-83, Saunders Abbott 1987; Old Cranleighan RFC: former Capt, sec, chm and vice-pres; former chm Old Cranleighan Soc, past Capt Old Cranleighans Golf Soc, involved with St Christopher's Hospice; Liveryman: Worshipful Co Skinners 1968 (Freeman 1961), Worshipful Co Carmen 1979 (memb ct); FInstD 1960; *Recreations* tennis, golf, previously squash and rugby; *Clubs* City Livery, E India, RAC, IOD, HAC, Royal Clinque Ports, Old Cranleighan, Tower Ward, Offrs Dining (Kent), County of London Yeo; *Style*— David Bluett, Esq; Fairfield, Furze Hill, Kingwood, Tadworth, Surrey KT20 6HB (☎ 07373 51867); Bluett House, 189-195 High St, Beckenham, Kent BR3 1BA (☎ 01 658 2222, 01 658 0915, fax 01 650 1017, car 0860 300748, telex 946254)

BLUETT, Dr Desmond; s of Montague Clarke Bluett (d 1942), and Elizabeth Stirling, *née* Gilliland (d 1957); *Educ* Guys Hosp and Univ of London (MB BS); *m* 12 Sept 1953, Elizabeth Jean Ward-Booth, da of Robert Christie, of Norfolk; 1 da (Anne Elizabeth b 22 Feb 1959); *Career* RN 1953-67, Surgn Cdr and sr conslt in obstetrics and gynaecology serv SA and Malta; gynaecologist Princess Margaret Hosp Nassau Bahamas, attending surgn Met and Fifth Ave Hosps NY, lectr in obstetrics and gynaecology Royal Postgrad Med Sch Hammersmith Hosp London; Freeman City of London, Liveryman Worshipful Soc of Apothecaries; Hon MD Univ of NY; FRCOG, LRCP, MRCS, LMSSA, DObst; fell Int Coll of Surgns, American Coll of Surgns; *Books* Resuscitation of The Neonate (1962), Update on Intrauterine Devices (1974); *Recreations* polo, sailing, travel; *Clubs* Royal Naval, RSM, Gds Polo Windsor; *Style*— Dr Desmond Bluett; 21 Devonshire Place, London W1 (☎ 01 935 5979)

BLUGLASS, Prof Robert Saul; s of Henry Bluglass (d 1973), and Fay, *née* Griew; *b* 22 Sept 1930; *Educ* Warwick Sch, Univ of St Andrews (MB, ChB, DPM, MD); *m* 24 Aug 1961, Dr Jean Margaret Kerry; 1 s (Charles Edward b 1963), 1 da (Amanda Clare b 1967); *Career* Nat Serv RAF 1948-49; house offr appts 1957-58, registrar in psychiatry Dundee 1958-61, sr registrar in psychiatry Royal Dundee Liff Hosp 1961-67, conslt in Forensic psychiatry W Midlands RHA and Ho 1967-, prof of forensic psychiatry Univ of Birmingham 1979-, regnl advsr (formerly dep regnl advsr) 1986-, clinical dir Reaside Clinic 1986-; memb: Mental Health Review Tribunal 1979-, Mental Health Act 1983-85; RCPsych: vice pres 1984-85, former chm forensic psychiatry special section, chm Midlands Div 1986-, cncl memb; MRCPsych 1971, FRCPsych 1976, FRSM, memb Br Acad of Forensic Sci, memb BHA; *Books* A Guide to the Mental Health Act 1983 (1983), Psychiatry, Human Rights and the Law (with Sir Martin Roth 1985); *Recreations* water colour painting, swimming, listening to music; *Clubs* RSM; *Style*— Prof Robert Bluglass; Reaside Clinic, Bristol Road South, Birmingham B45 9BE (☎ 021 453 6161)

BLUMSOM, John David; TD (1964); s of Thomas George Blumsom, of Bosham, Sussex, and Joan, *née* Dixon; *b* 7 Dec 1932; *Educ* Merchant Taylors, London Business Sch; *m* 23 Feb 1957, Gillian Mary, da of Russell Paul, of Berkhamsted; 3 s (Giles, David, William), 2 da (Alexandra, Elizabeth); *Career* Nat Serv cmmnd Queens Royal Regt 1951-53, TA: QRR 1953-59, Beds and Herts Regt (ret as Major) 1960-69; articled clerk Moore Stephens & Co, CAs, 1953-59, gen mangr Electolux Commerical Equipment Ltd 1969-71 (commercial mangr 1967-69, joined 1959); dir Hambros Bank Ltd 1986- (joined 1971), non exec dir Hemmington Scott Publishing Ltd 1986-; chm Herts ctee Army Benevolent Fund 1986-; ICA, FCA; *Recreations* golf, squash, walking; *Style*— John Blumsom, Esq; 25 Shrublands Rd, Berkhamstead, Herts HP4 3HX (☎ 0442 865 854); Hambros Bank Ltd, 41 Tower Hill, London EC3N 4HA (☎ 01 480 5000, telex 887465)

BLUNDELL, Sir Michael; KBE (1962), MBE (1943); s of Alfred Herbert Blundell, of Monks Hall, Appletreewick, Yorkshire, and Amelia Woodward, *née* Richardson; *b* 7 April 1907; *Educ* Wellington; *m* 1946, Geraldine Lötte (d 1983), da of Gerald Stanley Robarts; 1 da (Susan); *Career* 2nd Lt RE 1940, Maj 1940, Lt Col 1941, Col 1944, Hon Col 3rd Kings African Rifles 1955-61; farmer in Kenya 1925-75, cmmr for Euro Settlement 1946-47, MLC Rift Valley Constituency Kenya 1948-63, ldr: New Kenya Gp 1959-63, Euro membs 1952; min Emergency War Cncl 1954-55, min of Agric 1955-59 and 1961-62; chm: EA Breweries Ltd 1964-77, Egerton Agric Coll 1962-72, Kenya Soc for the Blind 1978-81; dir Barclays Bank Kenya 1968-82; judge Guernsey Cattle RASE Show 1977; Freeman Worshipful Co of Goldsmiths 1953; *Publications* So Rough a Wind (1964), The Wild Flowers of Kenya (1982), Collins Guide To the Wild Flowers of East Africa (1987); *Recreations* music, gardening; *Clubs* Muthaiga (Nairobi), Brooks'; *Style*— Sir Michael Blundell, KBE; Box 30181, Nairobi, Kenya (☎ Nairobi 512278)

BLUNDEN, Hubert Chisholm; er s and h of Sir Philip Overington Blunden, 7 Bt; *b* 9 August 1948; *Educ* Avoca Sch Blackrock; *Career* 1 Bn Irish Guards; *Style*— Hubert Blunden Esq

BLUNDEN, Pamela, Lady; Pamela Mary; *née* Purser; da of John Purser, of Merton House, Dublin 6; *m* 1945, Sir William Blunden, 6 Bt (d 1985); 6 da; *Career* formerly 2 Offr WRNS; *Style*— Pamela, Lady Blunden; Castle Blunden, Kilkenny

BLUNDEN, Sir Philip Overington; 7 Bt (I 1766), of Castle Blunden, Kilkenny; s of Sir John Blunden, 5 Bt (d 1923); suc bro Sir Wm Blunden, 6 Bt (d 1985); *b* 27 Jan 1922; *Educ* Repton; *m* 1945, Jeanette Francesca Alexandra (WRNS), da of Capt Duncan Macdonald, RNR, of Portree, Isle of Skye; 2 s, 1 da; *Heir* s, Hubert Chisholm, *qv*; *Career* WWII 1942-45 with RN; estate mangr Castle Blunden 1948-62, mrktg industl plastics 1962-83; now engaged in fine art restoration and painting; *Recreations* gardening, fishing, field sports, reading, painting; *Clubs* Royal Dublin Soc (Life Memb); *Style*— Sir Philip Blunden, Bt; 66 Lucan Heights, Lucan, Co Dublin

BLUNKETT, David; MP (Lab) Sheffield Brightside 1987-; s of Arthur Blunkett (d 1960), and Doris Matilda Flizabeth, *née* Williams (d 1983); *b* 6 June 1947; *Educ* Univ of Sheffield (BA); *m* 18 July 1970, Ruth Gwynneth, da of Albert Mitchell, of 19 Longley Lane, Sheffield, Vice Princ Coll of Technol; 3 s (Alastair Todd b 27 March 1977, Hugh Sanders b 13 July 1980, Andrew Keir b 31 Oct 1982); *Career* clerk typist 1967-69; lectr and tutor Industl Rels and Politics 1973-81 seconded 1981-87; ldr Sheffield City Cncl 1980-87 (memb 1970-88); *Books* Building from the Bottom (1983), Democracy in Crisis (1987); *Recreations* poetry, walking, music, sailing, being with friends; *Style*— David Blunkett, Esq, MP; Room 1, St Paul's Chambers, St Paul's Parade, Sheffield S1 1JL; House of Commons, London SW1A 0AA (☎ 01 219 3559)

BLUNT, Sir David Richard Reginald Harvey; 12 Bt (GB 1720); s of Sir Richard David Harvey Blunt, 11 Bt (d 1975); *b* 8 Nov 1938; *m* 1969, Sonia Tudor Rosemary, da of late Albert Edward Day; 1 da; *Heir* kinsman, Robin Anthony Blunt; *Style*— Sir David Blunt, Bt; 74 Kirkstall Rd, SW2 4HF

BLUNT, Margaret, Lady; Margaret Constance; *née* Dean; da of John H Dean, of Nutbeam, Cirencester, Glos; *b* 19 April 1912; *m* 1943, as his 2 w, Sir Richard David Harvey Blunt, 11 Bt (d 1975); 2 da (Georgina b 1945, m 1981 Martin Trotter; Caroline b 1947); *Style*— Margaret, Lady Blunt

BLUNT, Oliver Simon Peter; s of Maj Gen Peter John Blunt, CBE, GM, of Harefield House, Ramsbury, Wilts, and Adrienne, *née* Richardson; *b* 8 Mar 1951; *Educ* Bedford Sch, Univ of Southampton (LLB); *m* 29 Sept 1979, Joanna Margaret, da of Robert Dixon (d 1985); 2 da (Felicity b 1981, Emily b 1983); *Career* barr Middle Temple 1974; *Recreations* cricket, squash; *Clubs* Barnes Sports; *Style*— Oliver Blunt, Esq; 39 Crestway, Roehampton, London SW15 (☎ 01 788 5122); 2 Gdn Ct, Temple, London EC4 (☎ 01 583 0434, fax 01 353 3987)

BLUNT, Maj-Gen Peter; CB (1978), MBE (1955, GM 1959); s of Albert George Blunt (d 1942), and Claudia Wintle (d 1962); *b* 18 August 1923; *m* 5 March 1949, Adrienne, da of General T W Richardson; 3 s (Oliver, Robin, Crispin); *Career* joined army at 14 in 1937, cmmnd Royal Fus; served DCLI and Royal Scots Fus, 1946; Foreign Serv 1946-49, Staff Coll 1957, Jt Services Staff Coll 1963, RCDS 1972, cmd 26 Regt Bridging 1965, GSO 1 Def Plans FARELF 1968, Cdr RCT 1 Corps 1970; dep tport offr-in-chief (Army), later tport offr-in-chief 1973; Asst CPL (Army), MoD 1977-78; ACDS (Personnel and Logistics), MoD 1978-79; md Earls Court Ltd 1979-80, exec vice-chm Brompton and Kensington Special Catering Co Ltd 1979-80; jt md Angex-Watson 1980-83, chm and md Angex Ltd 1983-88 (non exec chm 1988-), dir Assoc Newspaper Hldgs plc 1984-; Col cmd RCT 1974-; specially apptd cmmr Royal Hosp Chelsea 1979; Liveryman Worshipful Co of Carmen 1973; *Recreations* sea fishing; *Style*— Maj-Gen Peter Blunt, CB, MBE, GM; Harefield House, Crowood Lane, Ramsbury, Marlborough, Wiltshire SN8 2PT; Angex Limited, Europa House, St Matthew St, London SW1P 2JT (fax 01 222 1248)

BLUNT, Robin Anthony; s of Capt Charles William Lockhart Blunt (d 1958, 3 s of 8 Bt) and Lilian (d 1958), da of late C Calcutt, of Goudhurst, Kent; hp of kinsman, Sir David Blunt, 12 Bt; *b* 2 Feb 1926; *Educ* Wellington, Derby Tech Coll; *m* 1, 1949 (m dis 1962), Sheila Stuart, da of C Stuart Brindley; 1 s; m 2, 1962, June Elizabeth, da of Charles Wigginton, of Heckington, Lincs; 1 s; *Career* engineer; exec dir Rolls Royce (France) Ltd Paris; CEng, MIMechE; *Recreations* golf, sailing; *Style*— Robin Blunt, Esq; 15 York House, Turk's Row, London SW3; 5 Bis Avenue Kléber, 78110 Le Vesinet, France; Office: 122 Avenue Charles de Gaulle, 92522 Neuilly-sur-Seine, France

BLYTH, Hon Adrian Ulrick Christopher David; yr s of 3 Baron Blyth (d 1977); *b* 23 Oct 1944; *Educ* Sebright Sch, Northants Coll of Agric; *m* 1966, Patricia Maureen, da of Desmond C Southey, of Northampton; 2 s (Mark Terence b 1969, Ian Christopher b 1975), 3 da (Sarah Ursula b 1967, Verena Rosemary b 1971, Natasha Rachael b 1973); *Career* engine reconditioner; *Recreations* sailing, flying, scuba diving; *Clubs* Galway Bay Sailing, Galway Flying, Galway Sub Aqua; *Style*— The Hon Adrian Blyth; Torwood Maree, Oranmore, Co Galway, Eire

BLYTH, Hon Alexandra; da of 4 Baron Blyth; *b* 1957; *Style*— The Hon Alexandra Blyth

BLYTH, Hon Anne Shelagh Jennifer; 20 Oct 1936; yst da (twin) of 3 Baron Blyth; *Style*— The Hon Anne Blyth; Athenry, Co Galway, Eire

BLYTH, 4 Baron (1907 UK); Sir Anthony Audley Rupert Blyth; 4 Bt (1895); s of 3 Baron Blyth (d 1977); *b* 3 June 1931; *Educ* St Columba's Coll, Dublin; *m* 1, 1954 (m dis 1962), Elizabeth Dorothea, da of Robert T Sparrow, of Vancouver, BC, Canada; 1 s, 2 da; m 2, 1963, Oonagh Elizabeth Ann, yr da of late William Henry Conway, of Dundrum, Dublin; 1 s (Hon James Audley Ian b 1970), 1 da (Hon Lucinda Audley Jane b 1966); *Heir* s, Hon Riley Blyth; *Style*— The Rt Hon the Lord Blyth; Blythwood Estate, Athenry, Co Galway, Eire

BLYTH, Hon Barbara Patricia Edna; 2 da (twin) of 3 Baron Blyth; *b* 20 Oct 1936; *Educ* Alexandra Sch Dublin, Moreton Hall Oswestry; *Style*— The Hon Barbara Blyth; Rockfield House, Athenry, Co Galway, Eire

BLYTH, Charles (Chay); CBE (1972), BEM (1967); s of Robert Blyth (d 1971), and Jessie Pat, *née* Patterson (d 1965); *b* 14 May 1940; *Educ* Hawick HS; *m* 1962, Maureen Margaret, da of Albert Morris (d 1956); 1 da (Samantha b 1967); *Career* Sgt HM Forces Para Regt 1958-67; Cadbury Schweppes 1968-69, md: Rainbow Charters Ltd 1974-, South West Properties Ltd 1978-, Br Clippers Ltd 1985-; chm Silk Cut Awards Ctee 1983-; conslt Hill & Knaulton Ltd 1983-; *Books* A Fighting Change (1966), Innocent Aboard (1968) The Impossible Voyage (1971) Theirs is the Glory (1974); *Sporting Achievements* rowed North Atlantic with Captain John Ridgway 1966, solo circumnavigated the world westwards in yacht British Steel 1970-71, competed in Whitbread Round the World yacht race with crew in Great Britain II 1973-74 (Winnina Elapsed Time Prize); won Round Britain Race in Great Britain IV 1978, won two handed trans-Atlantic Race and broke existing record 1981, number one to Blue Riband attempt in Virgin Atlantic Challenge I and II 1985 and 1986, chm The British Steel Challenge; *Recreations* horse riding, ski-ing; *Clubs* Royal Southern Yacht, Royal Western Yacht, Royal Ocean Racing, Caledonian, Special Forces; *Style*— Chay Blyth, Esq, CBE, BEM; Hill Farm Cottage, 18 Highlands Road, Fareham, Hampshire PO16 7BN (☎ 0579 46008)

BLYTH, Hon Marcia Edna Dorothea; da of 4 Baron Blyth; *b* 1956; *Style*— The Hon Marcia Blyth

BLYTH, Dr Nicola; da of Peter Eden Blyth, of Sheffield, and Rosemary, *née* Goodswen; *b* 6 Oct 1956; *Educ* Maltby GS, Univ of Newcastle-on-Tyne (BSc), Univ of Canterbury NZ (PhD); *Career* econ Agri Econ Res Unit Lincoln NZ 1980-83, ACM Trade Policy & Export Mktg AMLC Sydney Australia 1983-86, conslt Agripac Incorp USA 1986-, dir Blyth & Co Ltd 1987-; memb Inst of Mangrs; AFUW 1984, AES 1986, AAES 1983, memb LCOSA 1983; *Recreations* outdoor sports, farming, arts, cinema; *Style*— Dr Nicola Blyth; Stone Mill, Maltby, S Yorks S88 8NU (☎ 0709 812321); Blyth & Co Ltd, Industrial Estate, Carlton, Notts S81 9LB (☎ 0909 730807, fax 0909 731573)

BLYTH, Peter Eden; s of Edward Eden Blyth (d 1978), of Doncaster, S Yorks, and Irene Gertrude, *née* Foster (d 1985); *b* 14 April 1927; *Educ* King Edward VII Sheffield; *m* 6 Sept 1952, Rosemary, da of John Goodswen (d 1933), of Booton, Norfolk; 1 s (Eden John b 1954), 1 da (Nicola Ellen b 1956); *Career* served Army Inteligence Corps in India 1944-54, Capt; md/chm: E E Blyth & Co Ltd, Blyth Metals Ltd, Blyth Marble Ltd, Blyth USA Inc, Blyth Japan Ltd, Blyth Portugal Ltd 1962-87; chm Br Microlight Aircraft Assoc 1984-89; *Style*— Peter E Blyth, Esq; Stone Mill, Maltby, S Yorkshire; E E Blyth & Co Ltd, Industrial Estate, Callton in Lindrick, Worksop, Notts (fax 0409 731573, ☎ 0909 731666)

BLYTH, Hon Riley Audley John; s and h of 4 Baron Blyth; *b* 4 Mar 1955; *Style*— The Hon Riley Blyth

BLYTH, Hon Tanya Ormonde Audley; eldest da of 3 Baron Blyth; *b* 1 Sept 1929; *Educ* Alexandra Sch Dublin, Moreton Hall Oswestry, Univ Coll Galway (BA); *Career* SRN, SCM; *Style*— The Hon Tanya Blyth; Rockfield House, Athenry, Co Galway, Eire

BLYTHE, Hon Mrs - Hon Rachel Georgiana; yst da of 2 Baron Rennell; *b* 1 Nov 1935; *Educ* MA (Oxon); *m* 1964 (m dis 1983), Richard Douglas Gordon Blythe, er s of L Gordon Blythe, of 7 Karoo St, S Perth, W Australia; 2 s (Joseph b 1968, Matthew b 1970); *Style*— The Hon Mrs Blythe; 43 McMaster Street, Victoria Park, Perth, W Australia

BOAL, (John) Graham; s of Surgn-Capt Jackson Graham Boal (d 1958), and Dorothy Kenley, *née* Hall (d 1984); *b* 24 Oct 1943; *Educ* Eastbourne Coll, Kings Coll London Univ (LLB); *m* 28 June 1978, Elizabeth Mary, da of Col LC East, DSO, OBE; 1 s (Thomas Henry b 1980); *Career* barr Grays Inn 1966, sr prosecuting counsel to Crown at Centl Criminal Ct 1985-, rec Crown Ct 1985-; *Clubs* Garrick, Royal Wimbledon GC, MCC; *Style*— Graham Boal, Esq; Queen Elizabeth Building, Temple, London EC4 (☎ 583 5766, fax 353 0339)

BOAL, John Graham; s of Jackson Graham Boal (d 1958), and Dorothy Kenley, *née* Hall (d 1984); *b* 24 Oct 1943; *Educ* Eastbourne Coll, Kings Coll London (LLB); *m* 1978, Elizabeth Mary, da of Col L C East, DSO, OBE; 1 s (Thomas Henry b 1980); *Career* called to Bar Gray's Inn 1966, sr prosecuting counsel to the crown, central Criminal Ct 1985-, rec of the Crown Ct 1985-; *Clubs* Garrick, Royal Wimbledon Golf; *Style*— Graham Boal, Esq; Queen Elizabeth Building, Temple, London EC4 (☎ 01-583 5766)

BOAM, Maj Gen (Thomas) Anthony; CB (1987), CBE (1978, OBE 1973); s of Lt-Col T S Boam, OBE; *b* 1932; *m* 1961, Penelope Christine Mary, da of Cyril Alfred Roberts, CBE, DL, *qv*; 1 s, 2 da; *Career* cmmnd Scots Gds 1952, served NI, Canal Zone Egypt, Kenya, Malaysia, W Germany (BOAR); cmd Br Army Tning Team Nigeria 1976-78; Dep Cdr and COS Hong Kong 1979-81, head Br Defence Staff Washington and def attaché 1981-84; cmd Br Forces Hong Kong, Maj Gen Bde of Gurkhas; memb Hong Kong Exec Cncl 1985-87, dir Br Consultancy Bureau 1988-; *Recreations* fishing, shooting, gardening, sport, bridge; *Clubs* MCC; *Style*— Maj-Gen Anthony Boam, CB, CBE, OBE; 2 Charlwood Place, London SW1V 2LU (☎ 01 630 0418)

BOARD, (Clinton) Julian; s of Frederick E Board (d 1966), and Eve Board, *née* Howson; *b* 19 April 1937; *Educ* Oundle; *m* 23 Aug 1980, Elizabeth Jennifer, da of Lt Col F W Pywell; *Career* dir several UK and overseas cos; landowner, FICA; *Recreations* cresta run, bobsleigh, skiing, estate mgmnt; *Clubs* The Sheffield, St Moritz Tobogganing (Hon Tres 1973-); *Style*— Julian Board, Esq; Longwood Court, Darley Dale, Derbyshire DE4 2HE; 39 Cloth Fair, London Ec1A 7JQ (☎ 01-242-0942); Fountain House, Broomgrove Road, Sheffield S10 2LS (☎ 0742-664491); 4 York House, Turks Row, London SW3, (☎ 01 730 8941)

BOARDLEY, Hon Mrs; (Katherine Susan); *née* FitzRoy; da of 2 Viscount Daventry 9d 1986); *b* 24 August 1923; *Educ* private schs; *m* 1, 1945 (m dis 1958), Phil John Turner, eldest s of Phil Turner; m 2, 1958, Anthony Woodington Boardley (d 1967), yr s of late Bertie Welton Boardley; 1 s (Kevan Anthony FitzRoy, b 1961); *Career* late Cadet Ensign First Aid Nursing Yeo; served Ceylon/Singapore 1943-46; programme asst Gen Overseas Service BBC 1953-61; editor Who's Who of Southern Africa 1979-85; *Recreations* gardening, music; *Style*— The Hon Mrs Boardley; 17 Sandown Lodge, Rivonia Rd, Sandown 2196, Transvaal, S Africa (☎ 011 884 1678)

BOARDMAN, Hon Anthony Hubert Gray; s of Baron Boardman; *b* 6 May 1949; *Educ* Ampleforth; *m* 1977, Catherine, da of Thomas William Penn, of Manor Farm, Denton, Northampton; 3 da; *Style*— The Hon Anthony Boardman; Lodge Farm, Hall Lane, Welford, Northants NN6 7JB

BOARDMAN, Sir Kenneth Ormrod; s of Edgar Nicholas and Emily Boardman; *b* 18 May 1914; *Educ* St Peter's Sch Swinton; *m* 1939, Lucy, *née* Stafford; 1 s, 2 da; *Career* served RA WW II; Maj; chm: K O Boardman Int Ltd 1954-78, Planned Giving Ltd 1959-, Boardman Securities Ltd; memb: NW Industrial Cncl 1967-, Nat Union of Con & Unionist Assocs 1975-, hon tres NW Area of Con Pty 1977-; kt 1981; *Style*— Sir Kenneth Boardman; Clarendon House, Carrwood Road, Bramhall, Cheshire SK7 3LR

BOARDMAN, Hon Nigel Patrick Gray; s of Baron Boardman; *b* 1950; *Educ* Ampleforth, Univ of Bristol; *m* 1975, Sarah, da of T A Coslett, of Cambridge; 5 da (Tamsin, b 1980, Charlotte b 1981, Rebecca b 1984, Victoria d 1985, Cordelia b 1987); *Career* slr, ptnr Slaughter and May; *Style*— The Hon Nigel Boardman; London

BOARDMAN, Baron (Life Peer UK 1980); Thomas Gray Boardman; MC (1944), TD (1952, DL Northants 1977); s of John Clayton Boardman (d 1944), of Daventry, Northants, and Janet, *née* Houston; *b* 12 Jan 1919; *Educ* Bromsgrove Sch; *m* 1948, (Norah Mary) Deirdre, da of Hubert Vincent Gough, of Pangbourne, and wid of John Henry Chaworth-Musters, of Annesley Park, Nottingham; 2 s, 1 da; *Career* sits as Conservative in House of Lords; served WW II Northants Yeo, cmdg 1956; MP (C) Leicester SW 1967-74 & Leicester S Feb-Sept 1974; min for Indust 1972-74, chief sec Treasy 1974; jt tres Cons Pty to 1982; High Sheriff Northants 1979; chm Steetley Co 1978-83; former pres Assoc of Br Chambers of Commerce; dir: MEPC Ltd 1980-89, Nat West Bank 1979- (chm 1983-); *Style*— The Rt Hon Lord Boardman, MC, TD, DL; The Manor House, Welford, Northants NN6 7HX (☎ 085 881 235); House of Lords, Westminster, London SW1A 0PW (☎ 01 219 3000)

BOAS, (John) Robert Sotheby; s of Edgar Henry Boas, of Teddington, Middx, and Mary Katherine, *née* Beattie; *b* 28 Feb 1937; *Educ* Clifton, Corpus Christi Coll Cambridge; *m* 25 Sept 1965, (Karen) Elisabeth, da of Gunnar Gersted of Copenhagen; 2 s (Christopher b 1972, Nicholas b 1975), 1 da (Helena b 1970); *Career* 2 Lt Royal Signals 1955-57; merchant banker; with Price Waterhouse 1960-64, ICI 1964-65; joined S G Warburg & Co Ltd 1970, dir 1971-; non-exec dir Chesterfield Properties 1978-; bd memb The Securities Assoc 1988-; cncl memb The English Stage Co 1978-83; FCA; *Recreations* opera, theatre, reading; *Style*— Robert Boas, Esq; 5 Longwood Drive, London SW15 5DL (☎ 01 788 9667); 2 Finsbury Avenue, London EC4 (☎ 01 860 1090)

BOASE, Martin; s of late Prof Alan Boase, Inverleith Place, Edinburgh, and late Elizabeth Grizelle, *née* Forster; *b* 14 July 1932; *Educ* Rendcomb Coll, New Coll Oxford (MA); *m* 1960 (m dis 1971), Terry Anne, *née* Moir; m 2, 1974, Pauline Valerie, da of Philip Henry Akerman Brownrigg, of Wheelers, Checkendon, nr Reading, Berks; 1 s (Daniel b 1962, Luke b 1981), 2 da (Rachel b 1964, Hannah b 1976); *Career* chm Boase Massimi Pollitt plc; *Recreations* The Turf; *Style*— Martin Boase, Esq; Boase Massimi Pollitt plc, 12 Bishops Bridge Rd, London W2 (☎ 01 258 3979)

BOAST, Roy Stanley; CBE (1964), OBE (1960, DFC, AE); s of Henry Boast (d 1932); *b* 21 Dec 1920; *Educ* Southend HS for Boys; *m* 1943, Maureen, da of Albert Ratcliffe; 1 s, 1 da; *Career* Gp Capt Bomber Cmd serv Far E RAF; exec vice pres Br Scrap Metal Fedn 1968-83; *Recreations* bowls, reading; *Clubs* RAF; *Style*— Roy Boast, Esq, CBE, OBE, DFC, AE; 14 Hadley Road, Sheringham, Norfolk (☎ 0263 822869)

BOBROWSKI, Dr Jan Jozef; s of Aleksander Bobrowski (d 1987), of Poland and Antonina Bobrowska *née* Kandefer (d 1978); *b* 31 Mar 1925; *Educ* London Univ, Battersea Coll of Advanced Technol (BSc), ACT (Battersea), Surrey Univ (PhD); *m* 28 Aug 1954, Zofia Bobrowska, da of Boleslaw Kowalski (d 1972), of Poland; 1 da (Izabella Cecylia Antonina b 3 June 1957); *Career* Polish Corps 1942-47, 2 Lt 1945; practical design training with Twisteel Reinforcement Ltd 1952-53, pt/t lectr Battersea Coll of Advanced Technol 1952-58, eng asst CJ Pell & Ptnrs 1953-58 (asst); chief eng: Pierhead Engrg Div of Unit Construction Co 1958-59, Pierhead Ltd 1959-62, Unit Construction co 1961-62, Jan Bobrowski and Ptnrs 1962-; Medal for contributions to prestressed concrete 1978, currently holds record for longest span concrete shell constructed at the Olympic Saddledome Calgary; Visiting Prof Imperial Coll of Sci & Technol 1981; VP Univ of Surrey Soc; pres of the Concrete Soc 1986/7; VP: Inst of Structural Engs 1985/6, (UK) Fed Internationale Precontrainte; memb: comite Euro-Int Du Beton Econ Devpt ctee; Freedom of the City of London 1977, Liveryman Worshipful Company of Constructors - 1977; FEng 1983, FICE 1962, FIStructE 1973, MCSCE, HON FICT, MConsE, MSocIS (France), PEng (Alberta and BC); Sovereign Military Order of St John of Jerusalem Knights of Malta 1984, Polish Army Medal 1945, Cross of Monte Casino 1945, Polish Defence Medal 1945 ; *Books* author of numerous articles to tech jls; *Recreations* equestrianism, fishing; *Style*— Dr Jan Bobrowksi; Grosvenor House, Grosvenor Road, Twickenham, Middlesex TW1 4AA; 1004-8 Avenue SE, Calgary, Alberta, Canada T2G OM4, (☎ 01 892 7627, fax 01 891 3151, telex 8954665 VBSTLX G JBP)

BOCHMANN, Michael Paul Boulter; s of Martin Paul Bochmann (d 1983), and Mary Beatrice Consitt, *née* Boulter; *b* 30 Sept 1953,, Burford GS, Royal Acad of Music; *Career* violinist: finalist and winner of prize for Best British Entrant, Carl Flesch Prize 1972; prize winner Jacques Thibaud Prize Paris 1973; ldr of Bochmann Quartet 1976-87; frequent broadcaster on BBC Radio, also BBC 2 TV; in residence Southampton Univ 1983-87; ARAM; *Recreations* drawing, ornithology, calligraphy; *Style*— Michael P B Bochmann, Esq; Flat 2, The Lodge, The Avenue, Cheswick, London W4 1HX (☎ 01-995-9330)

BOCKETT, Herbert Leslie; CMG (1961); s of Charles Frederick Bockett and L M Bockett, *née* Bridger; *b* 29 June 1905; *Educ* Seddon Memorial Technical Coll; *m* 1932, Constance Olive, da of Arthur Ramsay; 2 da; *Career* accountant; memb Shipping Indust Tbnl 1972-; *Style*— Herbert Bockett, Esq, CMG; 189 The Parade, Island Bay, Wellington, New Zealand (☎ 838 549)

BOCKSTOCE, Lady Romayne Bryony; *née* Grimston; da of 6 Earl of Verulam; *b* 18 August 1946; *m* 1973, John Roberts Bockstoce; 1 s; *Style*— Lady Romayne Bockstoce; 1 Hill St, S Dartmouth, Mass 02748, USA

BODDEN, John; s of Harry Bodden (d 1954), of Oldham, Lancs, and Catherine, *née* Wood (d 1969); *b* 15 May 1923; *Educ* Felsted, Manchester Univ (BSc, BA), Wadham Coll Oxford; *m* 30 April 1988, Patricia Anne Bodden; *Career* Lt RNVR, anti-submarine electrical branch RN 1943-46; slr and notary public 1949; sr ptnr Platt Bodden & Co/ Butcher & Barlow; chm and dir Ernest Broadbelt Investments Ltd; tstee Oldham Foundation; memb Manchester City Cncl 1959-62; pres Bury and District Law Soc 1989; underwriting memb of Lloyds; FRSA; *Recreations* golf; *Clubs* St James's (Manchester), Manchester Tennis and Racquet, Hale Golf; *Style*— John Bodden, Esq; 10 Woodhead Drive, Park Rd, Hale, Altrincham, Cheshire WA15 9LG (☎ 061 980 6061); Kensham, Moat Hill, Totnes, S Devon TQ9 5ER (☎ 0803 863491); Butcher & Barlow, Bank Street, Bury, Lancs BL9 ODL (☎ 061 764 4062)

BODDINGTON, (Robert) Christopher Hance; s of Lt Robert Evelyn Boddington (KA 1942), of Peterchurch, Herefordshire, and Heather Elizabeth Bryant, *née* Hance; *b* 4 May 1941; *Educ* Rugby, The Queen's Coll Oxford (MA); *m* 21 Sept 1963 (m dis 1983), Mary Jane, da of John Baughn Wiggs (d 197 3), of Bournemouth; 2 da (Naomi b 1964, Lucia b 1965); *Career* admitted slr 1966, ptnr Zilman and Co 1973, ptnr Nabarro Nathanson 1977; memb: Law Soc 1966; *Recreations* travel, opera, food; *Clubs* Brooks.s; *Style*— Christopher Boddington, Esq; 53 Blenheim Cres, London W11; 50 Stratton St, London W1 (☎ 01 493 9933, fax 01 629 7900)

BODDINGTON, Ewart Agnew; JP; s of Charles Geoffrey Boddington (d 1982), and Edith Norah, *née* Agnew; *b* 7 April 1927; *Educ* Stowe, Trinity Cambridge (MA); *m* 1954, (Vine) Anne, da of Louis Arthur Hubert Clayton, (d 1969); 2 s, 1 da; *Career* exec chm Boddingtons' Breweries plc 1970-, chm Brewers Soc 1985-, pres Inst of Brewing 1972-74, dir Nat Westminster Bank (northern bd) 1977-; Hon MA Manchester Univ; *Recreations* shooting, fishing, golf; *Style*— Ewart A Boddington, Esq, JP; Boddingtons' Breweries plc, Strangeways Brewery, New Bridge St, Manchester, M60 3EL (☎ 061 831 7881)

BODEN, (John James) Jim; s of Dick Boden (d 1979), of Ashbourne, Derbyshire and Betty, *née* Bayliss; *b* 11 July 1947; *Educ* Denstone Coll, Liverpool Univ (LLB); *m* 21 July 1975, Patricia Jane, da of Dr Philip William Bowden, of Brailsford Derbyshire; 1 s (Andrew b 1978), 1 da (Nicola b 1980); *Career* slr of the Supreme Court; dir Nottingham Conveyancers Ltd; former Ashbourne UDC; *Recreations* country sports; *Clubs* Victoria (Nottingham); *Style*— Jim Boden, Esq; Brook Farm, Cubley, nr Ashbourne, Derbyshire DE6 2EZ (☎ 033 525 451); 158 High Rd, Beeston, Nottingham NG9 2LZ (☎ 0602 258277)

BODEN, Kenneth Henry Edmund; s of Henry James Randolph Boden (d 1982 formerly 4QOH and Inspr Palestine Police), and Ada Dorothy, *née* Hazle; *b* 15 Dec 1941; *Educ* Southend HS for Boys Southend on Sea; *m* 20 Sept 1969, June Irene, da of Harold Gibbs, of London; *Career* underwriter Gardner Mountain D'Ambrumenil and Rennie Lloyds Insur Brokers 1958, marine cargo surveyor Insur Co of N America 1966-68, dep marine underwriter at Lloyds for Laurence Philipps Agencies 1968-80 active underwriter 1980-; memb: Round Table until 1982, Assoc of Ex-Tablers Club (41 Club), Lloyds 1978; ACII 1968; *Recreations* skiing, travel, gardening, cage birds; *Style*— Kenneth Boden, Esq; Box 043, Lloyds, London (☎ 01 623 7100, ext 3765)

BODEN, Prof Margaret Ann; da of Leonard Forbes Boden, OBE, (d 1986), of London, and Violet Dorothy, *née* Dawson, (d 1967); *b* 26 Nov 1936; *Educ* City of London Sch for Girls, Newnham Coll Cambridge (MA), Harvard Graduate Sch for Arts and Sciences (AM, PhD); *m* 24 June 1967 (m dis 1981), John Raymond Spiers; 1 s (Ruskin b 1968), 1 da (Jehane b 1972); *Career* lectr Univ of Birmingham 1959-65, prof in philosophy and psychology Univ of Sussex 1980- (lectr and reader 1959-65), founding dean Sch of Cognitive and Computing Sci Univ of Sussex 1987, co-fndr Harvester Press Ltd 1969; memb: Cncl for Science and Society, Mind Assoc, Aristotelian Soc, Royal Inst of Philosophy (cncl memb 1988-), Br Psychological Soc, American Assoc for Artificial Intelligence, Br Soc for Philosophy of Science; memb advsy bd Res Cncls 1989-, chm Cncl Science and Society Working Pty on Benefits and Dangers of Knowledge-Based Systems 1987-88; FBA (1983-, cncl memb 1988-); *Books* Purposive Explanation in Psychology (1972), Artificial Intelligence and Natural Man (1977), Piaget (1979), Minds and Mechanisms (1981), Computer Models of Mind (1988), Artificial Intelligence in Psychology (1989), The Philosophy of Artificial Intelligence (1989); *Recreations* dress-making, travel; *Clubs* Reform; *Style*— Prof Margaret Boden; School of Cognitive and Computing Sciences, Univ of Sussex, Brighton (☎ 0273 606755)

BODEN, Peter Horrox; s of Albert Boden (d 1931), of Romiley, Cheshire, and Lucy Isabel, *née* Horrox; *b* 19 April 1926; *Educ* Cheadle Hulme Sch, Univ of London (BSc, LLB), Univ of Manchester (cert of educn); *Career* barr Gray's Inn; Miny of Labour 1943-57, lectr Coll of Commerce Birmingham Poly 1958-66, head of dept N Tyneside Coll 1966-88; publications inc: Revision Notes in English Law; Whitley Bay Pantomime Soc, Playhouse Players; *Style*— P H Boden, Esq; 14 Kingston Drive, Whitley Bay, Tyne and Wear NE26 1JH (☎ 091 252 4660)

BODILLY, Sir Jocelyn; VRD; s of Cdr Ralph Burland Bodilly RN, of Trenarren, Alverton, Penzance, Cornwall, and Mrs Sybil Bodilly; *b* 15 Sept 1913; *Educ* Munro Coll Jamaica; Schloss Schule, Salem, Baden, Germany; Wadham Coll Oxford; *m* 1, 1936, Phyllis Maureen (d 1963), da of Thomas Cooper Gotch, ARA; m 2, 1964, Marjorie, da of Walter Fogg, of St Helens, Lancs; *Career* RNVR 1937-56 (Lt- Cdr (S)), served WW II; barr Inner Temple 1937, judge High Court Sudan 1946-55, crown counsel Hong Kong 1955, princ crown counsel Hong Kong 1961, law draftsman Hong Kong 1964, chief justice Western Pacific 1965-75, chm Industrial Tribunals for London (South) 1976-; kt 1969; *Clubs* Royal Ocean Racing; *Style*— Sir Jocelyn Bodilly, VRD; Myrtle Cottage, St Peter's Hill, Newlyn, Penzance, Cornwall TR18 5EQ

BODMER, Sir Walter Fred; s of Dr Ernest Julius Bodmer (d 1968), and Sylvia Emily, *née* Bodmer; *b* 10 Jan 1936; *Educ* Manchester GS, Cambridge (BA, PhD); *m* 1956, Julia Gwynaeth, da of William Gwyn Pilkington (d 1976); 2 s (Mark, Charles), 1 da (Helen); *Career* Cambridge Univ: res fell Clare Coll 1958-60, official fell 1961, demonstrator dept genetics 1960-61; asst prof dept genetics Stanford Univ Sch of Med 1962-66 (assoc prof 1966-68, prof 1968-70); prof of genetics Oxford Univ 1970-79; dir of res Imperial Cancer Res Fund 1979-; chm Science Consultative Gp BBC 1981-87; memb Advsy Bd for the Res Cncls 1983-88; tstee: Br Museum (Nat History) 1983- (chm 1988-), Sir John Soane's Museum; for hon memb American Acad of Arts and Science's, FRS, for assoc US Nat Acad Science's, vice-pres Royal Instn 1982-82, hon fell Keble Coll Oxford, pres Royal Statistical Soc 1984-85, pres Br Assoc for the Advancement of Science 1987-88, pres Assoc for Science Educn 1989; The William Allan Meml Award 1980, The Conway Evans Prize 1982, The Rabbi Shai Shacknai Meml Prize Lectureship in Immunology and Cancer Res 1983, The John Alexander Meml Prize Lectureship 1984, The Rose Payne Distinguished Scientist Lectureship 1985; Laurea 'Honoris Causa' in Medicine and Surgery, Univ of Bologna 1987; Hon DSc Univ of Bath 1988, Hon DSc Univ of Oxford 1988; FRCPath, hon FRCP, hon FRCS, hon memb American Assoc of Immunologists, for memb Czechoslovak Acad of Sciences 1988-; kt 1986; *Books* The Genetics of Human Populations (with L Cavalli-Sforza 1971), Our Future Inheritance: Choice or Chance? (with A Jones 1974), Genetics, Evolution and Man (with L Cavalli-Sforza 1976); *Recreations* playing piano, riding, swimming; *Clubs* Athenaeum; *Style*— Sir Walter Bodmer; 44 Lincoln's Inn Fields, London WC2A 3PX (☎ 01 242 0200); Imperial Cancer Res Fund, PO Box 123, Lincoln's Inn Fields, London WC2A 3PX (☎ 01 242 0200, telex 265107 ICRF G)

BODY, Lady Julia Frances; *née* Montagu; da of Victor Montagu (10 Earl of Sandwich, who disclaimed his peerages for life 1964); *b* 12 April 1947; *Educ* Crantorne Chase; *m* 1, 1972 (m dis 1976), Martin Lee Oakley; m 2, 1976 (sep 1984), Peter Gerald Edward Body; 1 s (Timothy b 1982); *Style*— Lady Julia Body; Garden Cottage, Mapperton, Beaminster, Dorset

BODY, Sir Richard Bernard Frank Stewart; MP (C) Holland with Boston 1966-; s of Lt-Col Bernard Richard Body, of Donnington, Berkshire, and Daphne Mary Eleanor, *née* Corbett; *b* 18 May 1927; *Educ* Reading Sch; *m* 1959, (Doris) Marion, da of late Maj Harold John Graham, OBE, of Midhurst Sussex; 1 s, 1 da; *Career* barr 1949, MP (C) Billericay 1955-59, Lloyd's underwriter 1979-; kt 1986; *Books* Agriculture: The Triumph and the Shame (1982), Farming in the Clouds (1984), Red or Green for Farmers (and the Rest of Us) (1987); *Recreations* hunting with own pack of bloodhounds; *Clubs* Carlton, Reform, Farmers'; *Style*— Sir Richard Body, MP; Jewell's Farm, Stanford Dingley, Reading, Berks (☎ Reading 744295 295)

BOE, Norman Wallace; s of Alexander Thomson Boe, of Edinburgh, and Margaret Wallace, *née* Revans; *b* 30 August 1943; *Educ* George Heriot's Sch, Edinburgh Univ (LLB); *m* 9 Aug 1968, Margaret Irene, da of Alexander McKenzie; 1 s (Douglas), 1 da (Sheila); *Career* off of slr to Sec of State for Scotland: legal asst 1970-73, sr legal ast 1973-82, divnl slr 1982-87, dep slr 1987; *Recreations* golf, Badminton, dog walking; *Clubs* Edinburgh University Staff; *Style*— Norman Boe, Esq; Solicitor's Office, Scottish Office, New St Andrew's House, Edinburgh, Lothian (☎ 031 244 4884)

BOEVEY; see Crawley-Boevey

BOGDANOV, Michael; s of Francis Benzion Bogdin (d 1962), and Rhoda, *née* Rees; *b* 15 Dec 1938; *Educ* Lower Sch of John Lyon, Harrow, Trinity Coll Dublin (MA), Univ of Munich, Sorbonne; *m* 17 Dec 1966, Patricia Ann, da of Walter Stanley Warwick 1985; 2 s (Jethro Rhys Warwick b 1968, Malachi Taplin b 1969), 1 da (Ffion b 1971); *Career* artistic dir; Phoenix Theatre Leicester 1973-77, Young Vic 1978-80, assoc dir National Theatre 1980-, artistic dir and fndr English Shakespeare Co 1986-, intendant Deutsches Schauspielhaus Hamburg 1988-; Dir of the Year Swet Award 1979, outstanding achievement Drama Awards 1987, Melbourne Spoleto Golden Pegasus Award 1988; *Recreations* sport, music, celtic languages, wine; *Clubs* Lords Taverners; *Style*— Michael Bogdanov, Esq; The ESC, 9 Duke St, London W1 (☎ 01 224 2020)

BOGERT, Maj-Gen (Mortimer) Patrick; CBE (1953), DSO (1944), CD (1952); s of Mortimer Selwyn Bogert (d 1958), of Montreal, Canada; *b* 17 Mar 1908; *Educ* Ashbury Coll Ottawa, RMC Kingston Canada; *m* 1, 1946 (m dis 1955), Pauline Louise Brandt, da of Philip Martin, of Cowden, Dorset; 1 s; m 2, 1964, Mrs Gertrude Grace Poole-Warren, da of late Hugh MacPhee, of Ottawa; *Career* GOC E Command Canada 1958-62; *Recreations* shooting, bridge; *Clubs* Boodle's, Army and Navy; *Style*— Maj-Gen Patrick Bogert, CBE, DSO, CD; 11 Donnington Park, Donnington, Newbury, Berks RG13 2DZ (☎ 0635 40631)

BOGGIS-ROLFE, Hume; CB (1971), CBE (1962); s of Douglass Horace Boggis-Rolfe (d 1966), of The Grange, Wormingford, Colchester, and Maria Maud, *née* Bailey; *b* 20 Oct 1911; *Educ* Westminster, Freiburg Univ, Trinity Cambridge; *m* 1941, Anne Dorothea, da of Capt Eric Noble, of Park Place, Henley; Oxon; 2 s, 1 da; *Career* barr 1935, dep clerk of the Crown and dep perm sec Ld Chancellor's Office 1968-75; farmer; chm Friends of the Elderly 1977-84; Master Merchant Taylors' Co 1971-72; *Recreations* gardening, travel; *Clubs* Athenaeum; *Style*— Hume Boggis-Rolfe, Esq, CB, CBE; The Grange, Wormingford, Colchester, Essex (☎ 0787 227303)

BOGGIS-ROLFE, Richard; s of Paul Boggis-Rolfe (d 1988), of 54 Rue Du Faubourg St Honoré, 75008 Paris, France, and (Anne) Verena, *née* Collins; *b* 5 April 1950; *Educ* Eton, Trinity Coll Cambridge (MA), London Business Sch; *m* 7 March 1987, Lucy Elisabeth, da of Lt-Col Stephen Jenkins, MC, DL, of Ballingers House, Hampnett, Glos; 1 da (Elisabeth Verena b 1988); *Career* cmmnd Coldstream Gds 1970, ADC to Lt Gen Sir Richard Worsley (GOC 1 (Br) Corps) 1975-77, Co Cdr 1977-79, Staff Capt QMG MOD 1979-80, ret Hon Maj 1980; dir: Russell Reynolds Assocs 1983, Norman Broadbent Int Ltd 1984; md: Norman Broadbent (Hong Kong) 1986, NB Selection Ltd 1987-; Freeman City of London, Liveryman Worshipful Co of Pewterers; *Recreations* hunting, travel; *Clubs* Brooks's, Beefsteak, Pratts; *Style*— Richard Boggis-Rolfe, Esq; The Glebe House, Shipton Moyne, Tetbury, Glos (☎ 0666 88441); 15 Brechin Place, London SW7 (☎ 01 373 5910); 54 Jermyn St, London SW1 (☎ 01 493 6392, fax 01 409 1786, car tel 0836 225 769)

BOGIE, David Wilson; s of Robert T Bogie (d 1978), of Edinburgh, and Isobel, *née* Wilson; *b* 17 July 1946; *Educ* George Watson's Coll, Grenoble Univ, Edinburgh Univ (LLB), Balliol Coll Oxford (MA); *m* April 1983 (m dis 1987), Lady Lucinda Louise Mackay, da of 3 Earl of Inchcape; *Career* admitted memb of Faculty of Advocates 1972, temp Sheriff 1981; Sheriff of Grampian, Highland and Islands, at Aberdeen and Stonehaven 1985; FSA Scot; *Clubs* New (Edinburgh), Royal Northern and Univ (Aberdeen); 50 Whitehall Road, Aberdeen; 31 Mortonhall Rd, Edinburgh; Sheriff's Chambers, Aberdeen

BOILEAU, Lt-Col Sir Guy Francis; 8 Bt (UK 1838); s of Sir Edmond Charles Boileau, 7 Bt (d 1980); *b* 23 Feb 1935; *Educ* Xavier Coll Melbourne, RMC Duntroon

Australia; *m* 1962, Judith Frances, da of Senator George Conrad Hannan, of Glen Iris, Canberra; 2 s, 3 da; *Heir* s, Nicolas Boileau; *Career* Lt-Col Australian Army; co dir; *Style*— Lt-Col Sir Guy Boileau, Bt; 14 Faircroft Av, Glen Iris, Victoria 3146, Australia

BOILEAU, Mary, Lady - Mary Catherine; da of late Lawrence Riordan, of Cradock, S Australia; *m* 1941, as his 2 w, Maj Sir Gilbert Boileau, 6 Bt (d 1978); 3 da; *Style*— Mary, Lady Boileau; Minto Lodge, 1480 Heatherston Rd, Dandenong, Victoria, Australia

BOILEAU, Nicolas Edmond George; s and h of Lt-Col Sir Guy Boileau, 8 Bt; *b* 17 Nov 1964; *Style*— Nicolas Boileau, Esq

BOISSIER, Roger Humphrey; 3 and yst s of Ernest Gabriel Boissier, DFC (d 1976), of Derby, and Doris Mary, *née* Bingham (d 1958); descended from Gaspard Boissier (d 1705), of Geneva, whose grandson Jean- Daniel Boissier (d 1770), settled in England at Putney (*see* Burke's Landed Gentry, 18 edn, vol I, 1965); *b* 30 June 1930; *Educ* Harrow; *m* 30 Oct 1965, Elizabeth (Bridget) Rhoda, eldest da of Sir Gerald Gordon Ley, 3 Bt, TD (d 1980) (*see* Debrett's Peerage and Baronetage, 1980); 1 s (Rupert John b 25 May 1967), 1 da (Clare Louise b 16 Nov 1968); *Career* md Aiton & Co Ltd 1971-83; dir: Derbyshire Building Soc 1972-81, Ley's Foundaries and Engrg plc 1977-82; dir: Br Gas plc 1981, Pressac Holdings plc 1984-, T & N plc 1987-, Edward Lumley Overseas Ltd 1988-; conslt Allot & lomax 1984-; memb Severn-Trent Water Authy 1986-; vice-pres Br Jr Chambers of Commerce 1961-64; High Sheriff of Derbyshire 1987-88; Master Worshipful Co of Tin Plate Workers alias Wire Workers 1988-89; govr Harrow Sch 1976- (dep chm 1988); *Clubs* City Livery, MCC, County (Derby); Easton House, The Pastures, Repton, Derbyshire DE6 6GG (☎ 0283 702274)

BOL, Lt-Col George Philip; s of Paulus Willem Bol (d 1963), and Petronella Johanna Jacoba van der Graaf (d 1962); *b* 3 August 1922; *Educ* Hogere Burger Sch (Leiden, Nijmegen), Mons Aldershot; *m* 5 Oct 1963, Muriel Evelyn, da of Henry William Clarke (d 1954); *Career* Army Offr Royal Netherlands Army 1945-77; served UK 1945-46, Indonesia 1946-50, Netherlands 1950-62; SO HQN Army Gp Germany 1962-65, Netherlands 1965-70; SO HQ Chief GS 1970-77; *Style*— Lt-Col George P Bol; The Manor House, Worstead, Norfolk NR28 9SD (☎ 0692 60 6186)

BOLAND, John Anthony; s of Daniel Boland, MBE (d 1973), of Dublin, and Hannah, *née* Barton (d 1982); *b* 23 Jan 1931; *Educ* Castleknock Coll Co Dublin, Xavier Sch Dublin, Christian Brothers Dublin, Trinity Coll Dublin (MA, LLB); *m* 21 Oct 1972, Ann Mary, da of James C Doyle, of Mitchelstown, Co Cork; *Career* barr Middle Temple 1956; called to Irish Bar Kings Inns Dublin 1967; joined Public Tstee Off London 1956, chief admin offr 1974-79; asst public tstee 1979-80, public tstee 1980-87, public tstee and accountant gen 1987-; asst ed The Supreme Ct Practice; hon memb Coll Historical Soc Trinity Coll Dublin, tstee Trinity Coll Dublin Tst; chm London Ctee Irish Sch of Ecumenics of Dublin, tst section Holborn Law Soc; *Recreations* walking, foreign travel, study of history; *Clubs* Kildare Street and University (Dublin); *Style*— John Boland, Esq; Stewart House, Kingsway, London WC2B 6JX (☎ 01 269 7010, fax 01 831 0060)

BOLÉAT, Mark John; s of Paul John Boléat, and Edith Maud, *née* Still; *b* 21 Jan 1949; *Educ* Victoria Coll Jersey, Lanchester Poly (BA), Univ of Reading (MA); *Career* dir-gen The Bldg Socs Assoc, sec-gen Int Union of Bldg Socs Savings Assns, chm Tennant Housing Tst, vice-chm Circle 33 Housing Tst, md European Fedn of Bldg Socs; *Books* The Building Society Industry (2 edn 1986), National Housing Finance Systems (1985), The Mortgage Market (with Adrian Coles 1987); *Recreations* squash, golf, reading; *Clubs* Carlton; *Style*— Mark Boléat, Esq; 35 Girton Rd, London SE26 5DJ; BSA, 3 Savile Row, London W1X 1AF (☎ 01 437 0655, telex 24538 BSA G, fax 01 734 6416)

BOLES, Lady Anne Hermione; *née* Waldegrave; da of 12 Earl Waldegrave, KG; *b* 24 Dec 1937; *Educ* St Paul Girls Sch; *m* 1971, Sir Jack Boles, MBE, *qv*; *Style*— Lady Anne Boles; Rydon House, Talaton, nr Exeter, Devon

BOLES, Sir Jack (John Dennis); MBE (1960); s of Cdr Geoffrey Coleridge Boles (d 1976), and Hilda Frances, *née* Crofton; *b* 25 June 1925; *Educ* Winchester; *m* 1, Benita (d 1969), da of Maj Leslie Graham Wormald; 2 s, 3 da; m 2, 1971, Lady Anne Hermione, *qv*, da of 12 Earl Waldegrave; *Career* Colonial Serv N Borneo 1947-64; Nat Tst 1965-83 (dir-gen 1975-83); chm Duchy of Cornwall Advsy Gp on Wildlife and the Landscape 1983-; regional dir Lloyds Bank 1984; kt 1983; *Clubs* Army and Navy; *Style*— Sir Jack Boles, MBE; Rydon House, Talaton, nr Exeter, Devon (☎ 0404 850225)

BOLES, Sir Jeremy John Fortescue; 3 Bt (UK 1922); s of Capt Sir Gerald Fortescue Boles, 2 Bt (d 1945); *b* 9 Jan 1932; *Educ* Stowe; *m* 1, 1955 (m dis 1970), Dorothy Jane, da of James Alexander Worswick; 2 s, 1 da; m 2, 1970, Elisabeth Gildroy, da of Edward Phillip Shaw, of Englefield Green, Surrey, and wid of Oliver Simon Willis Fleming; 1 da; m 3, 1982, Marigold Aspey, *née* Seckington; *Heir* s, Richard Boles; *Style*— Sir Jeremy Boles, Bt; Brook House, Stogumber, Taunton, Somerset TA4 3FZ

BOLES, Richard Fortescue; s and h of Sir Jeremy Boles, 3 Bt; *b* 12 Dec 1958; *Style*— Richard Boles, Esq

BOLINGBROKE AND ST JOHN, 7 Viscount (GB 1712); Sir Kenneth Oliver Musgrave St John; 11 Bt (E 1611); also Baron St John of Lydiard Tregoze (GB 1712), Viscount St John and Baron St John of Battersea (GB 1716); s of Capt Geoffrey St John, MC (d 1972), gggs of 3 Viscount, by his 2 w, Isabella Charlotte Antoinette Sophia, Baroness Hompesch (d 1848); suc kinsman 1974; *b* 22 Mar 1927; *Educ* Eton; *m* 1, 1953 (m dis 1972), Patricia Mary, da of B J McKenna, of Christchurch, NZ; 1 s; m 2, 1972 (m dis 1987), Jainey Anne, da of late Alexander Duncan McRae, of Timaru, NZ; 2 s (Hon Oliver b 1972, Hon Nicholas b 1974); *Heir* s, Hon Henry St John; *Career* patron of one living; pres of Travel Agents Assoc of NZ 1966-68, dir of World Assoc of Travel Agencies 1967-75, chm: Atlantic & Pacific Travel Gp of Cos 1958-76, Australian Cncl of Tour Wholesalers 1972-75; dir Bolingbroke and Ptnrs Ltd 1976-; fell Aust Inst of Travel; *Recreations* tennis, history, cricket; *Clubs* Christchurch Club (Christchurch); *Style*— The Rt Hon The Viscount Bolingbroke and St John; 15 Tonbridge Mews, Shrewsbury Street, New Zealand

BOLITHO, Maj Simon Edward; MC (1945), JP ((Cornwall 1959), DL 1964); s of Col Sir Edward Hoblyn Warren Bolitho, KBE, CB, DSO (d 1969), and his 1 wife Agnes, *née* Johnson (d 1950); *b* 13 Mar 1916; *Educ* RNC Dartmouth, RMC Sandhurst; *m* 1953, Elizabeth Margaret, da of Rear Adm George Hector Creswell, CB, DSO, DSC (d 1967); 2 s (Edward, Alverne), 2 da (Mary, Loveday); *Career* Maj Gren Gds (N Africa and Italy), Lt-Col DCLI (TA), Hon Air Cdre 2625 Sqdn RAF 1984; dir Barclays Bank 1959-86, English China Clays 1966-86; High Sheriff of Cornwall 1956-57, Vice-Lieut for Cornwall 1970-; *Recreations* shooting, fishing, sailing; *Clubs* Army and Navy, Pratt's, MCC, Royal Yacht Sqdn; *Style*— Maj Simon Bolitho, MC, JP, DL; Trengwainton, Penzance, Cornwall (☎ 0736 63106)

BOLLAND, Sir Edwin; KCMG (1981), CMG (1971); s of George Bolland, of Moerly, Yorks; *b* 20 Oct 1922; *Educ* Morley GS, Univ Coll Oxford; *m* 1948, Winifred, da of William Mellor, of Moerly, Yorks; 1 s, 3 da; *Career* joined Foreign Office 1947, head Far Eastern Dept 1965-67, cnsllr Washington 1967-71, ambass Bulgaria 1973-76, head Br delgn to negotiate MBFR 1976-80, ambass Belgrade 1980-82; *Style*— Sir Edwin Bolland, KCMG, CMG; Lord's Spring Cottage, Godden Green, Sevenoaks, Kent

BOLLERS, Hon Sir Harold Brodie Smith; s of late John Bollers; *b* 5 Feb 1915; *Educ* Queen's Coll Guyana, London Univ; *m* 1, 1951, Irene Mahadeo (d 1965); 2 s, 1 da; m 2, 1968, Eileen Indrani, da of James Hanoman; 1 s; *Career* chief justice of Guyana 1966-81, chm Election's Cmmn 1982; kt 1969; *Style*— The Hon Sir Harold Bollers; c/o Chief Justice's Residence, 245 Vlissengen Rd, Georgetown, Guyana; 252 South Rd, Bavinda, Georgetown, Guyana

BOLLOM, Joseph; s of Ernest Bollom (d 1939), of Old St, London, and Sarah Myers, *née* Wilkins; *b* 7 Jan 1936; *Educ* Central Fndn London; *m* 6 Sept 1958, Sylvia Iris, da of John Green, of Virginia Water, Surrey; 1 s (Michael John b 10 Sept 1959), 2 da (Karen Sarah b 22 July 1963, Deborah Jane (twin) b 22 July 1963); *Career* chm Arlington Printers Ltd 1959, chm Steelchrome Furniture Ltd 1963, chm Kewlox Furniture Ltd 1972, chm Ingersoll Watch Co plc 1970-75, chm Ingersoll Gp 1975-80, chm Arlington Leisure 1982, chm Blue Chip (UK) Ltd 1983, dir First Leisure plc 1983; chm Lady Mayoress Charity (Lady Gardener Thorpe) 1982 on behalf of Gt Ormond St Hosp for Sick Children, former ctee memb Prince Charles Charity; Freeman City of London 1973, Liveryman Worshipful Co of Watchmakers 1973, Liveryman Worshipful Co of Painters and Stainers 1983; *Style*— Joseph Bollom, Esq; The White House, Totteridge Common, London N20 (☎ 01 959 7555); Arlington Leisure Ltd, The Hawthorne Centre, Elmgrove Rd, Harrow, Middx (☎ 01 863 8311, fax 01 427 0240, car 0836 501 408/0836 610 064)

BOLLOM, Philip; s of Ivor Bertie Bollom, and Ruth Elizabeth, *née* Gear; *b* 30 Mar 1926; *Educ* Wycliffe Coll; *m* 1, 9 April 1949 (m dis 1984), Patricia Elizabeth, da of Walter Vincent Carr Sweeting; 2 s (Ian b 8 March 1950, Peter b 11 Sept 1952), 2 da (Anne b 26 July 1956, Patricia b 25 July 1958); m 2, 1 June 1985, Sheila *née* Watkins; *Career* served RN 1944-47; chm: Johnson Gp of Cleaners plc 1985 (md 1977), Johnson Gp Cleaners Properties plc 1985, Johnson Bros (Cleaners Ltd) 1977, Bollom Ltd 1977, James Smith and Sons Ltd 1977, John Crockatt Ltd 1977, J Pullar & Sons Ltd 1977, Hartonclean Ltd 1977, Joseph Harris Ltd 1977, Zernys Ltd 1977, Kneels Ltd 1979, James Hayes & Sons 1981, Johnson Micronclean Ltd 1985, HF Witton (Shopfitters) Ltd 1977, Apparelmaster Design Ltd 1986, Johnson Gp Inc 1987, Apparelmaster Inc 1987, Tuchman Cleaners Inc 1987, Capitol Varsity Inc 1987, Garrett Drycleaning Inc 1987, Al Phillips Inc 1987, Coleman Young Enterprises Inc 1987, Dodge Cleaners Inc 1987, Pride Cleaners Inc 1987, Camelot Cleaners Inc 1987, Dryclean USA Inc 1988, Insty Prints of Nashville Inc 1988; Freeman Worshipful Co of Launderers;FID 1961; memb Cncl of Br Retailers Assoc 1985; *Recreations* riding, sailing, reading; *Style*— Philip Bollom, Esq; Steetly House, 20 Avon Park Drive, Avon Park, Ringwood, Hants BH24 2AT (☎ 0425 475935); Johnson Group Cleaners plc, Mildmay Road, Bootle, Merseyside L20 5EW (☎ 051 933 6161, fax 051 922 8089)

BOLONGARO, Michael Francis; s of Louis Harold Bolongaro (d 1969), of Tapley, Fleetwood Rd, Fleetwood, Lancs, and Millicent Dorcus, *née* Wrathall (d 1963); *b* 22 Feb 1930; *Educ* St Joseph's Coll Blackpool; *m* 30 Dec 1958, Anne June, da of John Frederick Dodding (d 1981), of The White Hart Hotel, Exeter; 3 s (Gregory John b 1966, Dominic Louis b 1972, Guy Francis b 1978), 4 da (Clare Celeste b 1962, Lucy Anne b 1965, Catherine Emma b 1968, Emma Louise b 1971); *Career* chartered surveyor; estates surveyor Shell-Mex and BP 1955-65, chief valuer of Dublin City & County 1970-73, Fine Art conslt and connoiseur of Old Master Paintings 1975-; FRICS; *Recreations* formerly cricket and rugby, now mountain walking, historical and art study; *Style*— Michael Bolongaro, Esq; 'Overbeck', 78 Greenside, Kendal, Cumbria LA9 5DT (☎ 0539 25435); 'Woodlands', Queens Rd, Kendal, Cumbria (☎ 0539 27934)

BOLSOVER, John Derrick; s of Dr G D Bolsover, MBE, of The Shrubbery, Eynsham, Oxford and Yoma Constance, *née* Stephens; *b* 21 June 1947; *Educ* Repton, McGill Univ Canada (BA); *m* 11 Sept 1971, Susan Elizabeth, da of Fletcher Peacock, of Gulfshore Boulevard, Naples, Florida; 2 s (Michael b 1976, Lincoln b 1978), 1 da (Jacqueline b 1974); *Career* chief exec & chief investmt offr Baring Int Investmt Mngmt Ltd 1985-; *Recreations* sport; *Clubs* Boodles, City; *Style*— John Bolsover, Esq; 15 Hereford Square, London SW7 4TS; 9 Bishopsgate, London EC2N 3AQ (☎ 01 588 6133, telex: 894989, fax: 01 588 2591)

BOLT, Roderick Langston; s of Lt Cdr Geoffrey Peter Langston Bolt, of 20 Barneby Close, Downton, Salisbury, Wilts, and Margaret Elmslie Ashley Hall, *née* Brebner; *b* 14 Oct 1943; *Educ* Sedbergh; *m* 20 July 1968, Gillian Rosamond, da of Lt-Col John Russell Palmer, MC, of Holly House, Carlton Hustwaite, Thirsk, Yorks; 1 s (Charles Henry Langston b 8 Jan 1971), 1 da (Amabel Margaret Langston b 27 May 1972); *Career* 13/18 Royal Hussars (Queen Mary's Own) 1962-67: 2 Lt troop ldr 1963, Lt RAC Trg Regt Catterick 1966, sec Army Horse Trials Tidworth 1967, medically discharged; asst agent for Earl of Harewood 1969-74, sr asst Cluttons 1974-77, resident agent for Lord St Oswald Wakefield 1977-79, resident sub agent Nat Tst 1977-79, princ land agent Hampshire CC 1979-82, factor for the Crown Estate Cmmrs Glenlivet and Auchindoun Estates with Smiths Gore 1983-86, def land agent Catterick 1986; FRICS 1986;; *Recreations* shooting, fishing; *Style*— Roderick Bolt, Esq; Graystone Lodge, Maunby, Thirsk, N Yorks (☎ 0845 587321); Defence Land Agent, Gough Rd, Catterick Garrison, N Yorks (☎ 0748 834208)

BOLTE, Hon Sir Henry Edward; GCMG (1972), KCMG (1966); s of James Henry Bolte; *b* 20 May 1908; *Educ* Skipton State Sch, Ballarat C of E GS; *m* 1934, Dame Edith, DBE, *qv*; *Career* premier and tres of Victoria 1955-73; *see Debrett's Handbook of Australia and New Zealand for further details*; *Style*— The Hon Sir Henry Bolte, GCMG; Kialla, Meredith, Vic 3333, Australia

BOLTON, Anthony Hale; s of Eric Hale Bolton (d 1986), and Betty Maude (d 1986), of New Barnet, Herts; *b* 8 August 1942; *Educ* St Albans Sch, Herts; *m* 12 May 1962, Olive Muriel, da of Thomas Brian O'Loughlin, Brookmans Park; 1 s (David b 1968), 1

da (Jenny b 1971); *Career* chm Bowring Aviation 1981-; chm Bowring Int Insurance Brokers 1988-, dep chm C T Bowring & Co (Insurance) 1984-, a md of Marsh & MacLennan Inc of USA 1985-; memb of Aviation ctee of Lloyds Insurance Brokers ctee; *Recreations* golf, music, ballet; *Clubs* RAC, Brookmans Park Golf Club; *Style—* Anthony Bolton Esq; Brookmans Park, Herts; Bowring Aviation, The Bowring Building, Tower Place, London, EC3

BOLTON, Archdeacon of; *see*: Brison, Ven William Stanley (Bill)

BOLTON, Bishop of 1984-; Rt Rev David George Galliford; s of Alfred Edward Bruce Galliford, of Warneford Gardens, Withycombe Raleigh, Exmouth, Devon, and Amy Doris, *née* Pawley; *b* 20 June 1925; *Educ* Bede Coll Sunderland, Clare Coll Cambridge (MA); *m* 1, 27 May 1954, Enid May (d 1983), da of late Arthur Drax, of 219 Sewerby Road, Bridlington; 1 da (Clare Frances Hope b 1956); m 2, 21 April 1987, Mrs Claire Margaret Phoenix, da of late Alfred Henry Smalley, of 95 Edge Lane, Stretford, Manchester; *Career* curate St John's Newland Hull 1951-54, minor canon Windsor 1954-56, vicar St Oswald's Middlesbrough 1956-61, rector Bolton Percy and diocesan training officer 1961-71, canon of York 1965-76, residentiary canon and treasurer of York Minster 1970-75, bishop of Hulme 1975-84; *Recreations* music, painting; *Clubs* Manchester; *Style—* The Rt Rev the Bishop of Bolton; Bishop's House, Sandfield Drive, Lostock, Bolton BL6 4DU (☎ 0204 43400)

BOLTON, Sir Frederic Bernard; MC (1945); s of Louis Hamilton Bolton (d 1953), of Woodford Halse, nr Rugby, and Beryl (d 1977), da of Dr Bernard Shirley Dyer (d 1948); *b* 9 Mar 1921; *Educ* Rugby; *m* 1, 1950, Valerie Margaret (d 1970), da of George Short Barwick (d 1937); 2 s; m 2, 1971, Vanessa Mary Anne, da of Lt-Col Anthony Vere Cyprian Robarts (d 1981); 2 s, 2 da; *Career* served WW II Maj N Africa, Italy; shipowner; chm F Bolton Gp 1953-; pres Chamber of Shipping 1966-67, Inst of Marine Engrs 1968-70, Br Shipping Fedn 1972-75, General Cncl of Br Shipping 1975-76, Int Shipping Fedn 1973-82; chm Dover Harbour Bd 1983-88, Br Ports Assoc 1985-88; pres British Maritime League 1985-; kt 1976; *Recreations* country sports; *Clubs* City of London, Cavalry & Guards; *Style—* Sir Frederic Bolton, MC; Pudlicote, nr Charlbury, Oxon (☎ 060 876 427);

BOLTON, James Douglas; TD (1962), DL (Herts 1968); s of Percy Bolton, MA (d 1981), and Florence Madeleine, *née* Scott (d 1 976), of Brabourne, Kimpton, nr Hitchin; *b* 4 Feb 1921; *Educ* Oundle, King's Coll Cambridge (BA); *m* 1959, Margaret Jean, da of James Forsyth (d 1959), of St Albans, Herts; 1 s, 1 da; *Career* slr: memb cncl Law Soc 1975-; coroner east Herts District of Herefordshire 1966-; chm Lee Valley Water Co 1986-; *Recreations* tennis, swimming; *Style—* James Bolton, Esq, TD, DL; Cox's, 23 Park Ave South, Harpenden, Herts AL5 2DZ (☎ 058 27 2222); business: 24 Castle St, Hertford, Herts (☎ 0992 586781, fax 0992 552662)

BOLTON, John Eveleigh; CBE (1972), DSC (1945, DL 1974); s of Ernest Bolton (d 1933), of Burley in Wharfedale, and Edith Mary *née* Duckhouse (d 1968); *b* 17 Oct 1920; *Educ* Ilkley Sch, Wolverhampton Sch, Trinity Coll Cambridge (MA), Harvard Business Sch (MBA); *m* 21 Aug 1948, Gabrielle Healey (Gay), da of Joseph Hall (d 1945), of Penn House, Penn, Wolverhampton, Staffs; 1 s (Nicholas b 1949), 1 da (Athalie b 1951); *Career* WWII ordinary seaman RN (later Lt RNVR); serv: Atlantic, Arctic, Mediterranean; chm solartron laboratory instruments Ltd 1953 (fin dir 1951-53), chm and md Solartron Electronic Gp Ltd 1954-63, chm and md Growth Capital Gp Ltd 1968- (dep chm 1963-65) chm Devpt Capital Gp Ltd 1984-88 (chm 1982-84); current non exec dir: AA Ltd, Alphameric plc, Black & Decker Corpn USA, Dawson Int plc, Johnson Was Ltd, NCR Ltd, Plasmec Ltd, Redland plc, Hoskyns Gp plc, Business advisers plc; chm cncl BIM 1964-66 (life vice pres), Advanced Mgmt Tst Int 1965- (fndr subscriber, chm tstees, chm emeritus), vice chm Royal Cmmn on Local Govt in England 1966-69, chm ctee of Inquiry on Small Firms 1969-71, pres Engrg Industs Assoc 1981-84, cncl memb IOD 1972-, former chm Business Graduates Assoc advisory ctee, former pres West End Br Legion, vice pres Cobham CC, former tres and chm cncl Surrey Univ, High Sheriff of Surrey 1980-81, Bowie Medal 1969; Hon D Surrey Univ, Hon DSc Bath Univ; FBIM 1966, CBIM 1976, Life Fell RSA 1967; *Recreations* shooting, swimming, the arts; *Clubs* IOD; *Style—* John Bolton, Esq, CBE, DCS, DL; Sunnymead, Tite Hill, Englefield Green, Surrey TW20 ONH (☎ 0784 35 172); (☎ 0784030 523)

BOLTON, Hon Mrs (Lavinia Valerie); *née* Woodhouse; da of 4 Baron Terrington; *b* 29 August 1943; *Educ* Downham Herts, Montesano Gstaad; *m* 1974 (m dis), Nicholas George Bolton, s of Sir George Lewis French Bolton, KCMG; 2 da (Carina b 1976, Sophie b 1979); *Recreations* antique collecting, gardening; *Style—* The Hon Mrs Bolton; 13 crail View, Nothleach, Glos GL54 3QH

BOLTON, Lucinda Carol; da of Gordon Gustav-Adolf Winter, TD, of Noble Tree End, Hildenborough, Kent, and Elspeth Kerr, *née* Bone; *b* 3 Dec 1952; *Educ* Benenden Sch, St Hugh's Coll Oxford (MA); *m* 12 June 1982, (Francis) Edward Kennaway Bolton, s of Martin Alfred Butts Bolton, DL, JP, of Croxden Abbey, Nr Uttoxeter, Staffordshire; 1 da (Camilla b 1985); *Career* dir: Guinness Mahon & Co Ltd 1987-, Lockton Superstores plc 1988-, Lockton Retail Stores plc 1988-; cncllr London Borough of Hammersmith and Fulham 1980-82; *Style—* Mrs Lucinda Bolton; Guinness Mahon & Co Ltd, 32 St Mary At Hill, London EC3 (☎ 01 623 9333)

BOLTON, Martin Alfred Butts; JP (Staffs 1959), DL (1969); o s of Francis Alfred Bolton, JP, CA (d 1951), of Moor Court, Oakmoor, Staffs; *b* 27 June 1923; *Educ* Shrewsbury, Magdalene Coll Cambridge; *m* 1946, Margaret Hazel, da of C G Kennaway, WS, of Kenwood Park, Auchterarder, Perthshire; 2 s, 3 da; *Career* farmer, memb CLA Cncl 1962-82, chm Cmmn of Income Tax Staffs 1972-, W Midlands Agric Land Tbnl 1974-, pres Staffs Agric Soc 1971; High Sheriff Staffs 1960-61; *Recreations* shooting, golf, tennis; *Clubs* Farmers'; *Style—* Martin Bolton, Esq, JP, DL; Croxden Abbey, Uttoxeter, Staffs (☎ 088 926 225)

BOLTON, Lady; May (Maisie); da of Charles Amelia Howcroft; *b* 3 Sept 1900; *m* 1928, Sir George Lewis French Bolton, KCMG (d 1982), sometime chm Bank London & S America; 1 s (Nicholas), 2 da (Sheila, Gillian); *Style—* Lady Bolton; 305 Frobisher House, Dolphin Sq, London SW1V 3LL (☎ 01 834 7278)

BOLTON, (Clifford) Nicholas; s of William Louis George Bolton (d 1942), of Sparrows Farm Way, Buckhurst Hill, and Beatrice Louise, *née* French (d 1972); *b* 22 Jan 1915; *Educ* Secdy Sch Leyton London; *m* 13 Nov 1944, Dorothy Pamela Marshall, da of Col Henry Marshall Fordham, OBE (d 1947), of Eastbourne; 1 s (Nicholas b 1960), 2 da (Jacaranda b 1952, Victoria b 1956); *Career* with Helbert Wagg Merchant Bank 1932-39; Maj Essex Regt, France Sierra Leone, Western Desert, Ethiopia, Kenya 1939-46; dir of Audit Colonial Audit Service: Uganda, Solomon Islanjds, Nigeria, Kenya 1946-66; inspector of statutory bds Kenya 1966-74, cwlth secretarial 1976-79, Int Monetary Fund 1980; *Recreations* gardening, reading, rough shooting; *Clubs* Muthaiga (Kenya), Royal Oversea, Cwlth, Victory Services; *Style—* Clifford Bolton, Esq; Gorse Farm, Blaxhall; No 9 London Rd, Harleston, Norfolk

BOLTON, 7 Baron (GB 1797); Richard William Algar Orde-Powlett; s of 6 Baron Bolton (d 1963) and Victoria, da of late Henry Montagu Villiers, MVO, gn of 4 Earl of Clarendon; *b* 11 July 1929; *Educ* Eton, Trinity Coll Cambridge; *m* 1, 1951 (m dis 1981), Hon Christine Helena Weld Forester, da of 7 Baron Forester and Marie, CStJ, da of Sir Herbert Perrott, 6 Bt, CH, CB; 2 s, 1 da; m 2, 1981, Masha Anne, da of Maj F E Hudson, of Winterfield House, Hornby, Bedale, Yorks; *Heir* s, Hon Harry Orde-Powlett; *Career* Gen Accident Life Assur Ltd; former chm: Wateners Gp, Yorks Soc of Agric, Yorks Branch Royal Forestry Soc 1963-64; JP N Riding of Yorks 1957-78; FRICS; *Style—* The Rt Hon The Lord Bolton; Park House, Wensley Leyburn, Yorks (☎ 0969 22464)

BOMFORD, Nicholas Raymond; s of Ernest Raymond Bomford (d 1962) and Patricia Clive, *née* Brooke; *b* 27 Jan 1939; *Educ* Kelly Coll, Trinity Coll Oxford (MA); *m* 1966, Gillian Mary, da of Maj Peter Beckingham Reynolds (ka 1943); 2 da (Kate b 1967, Rebecca b 1969); *Career* memb academic staff: RNC Dartmouth 1964-68, Wellington Coll 1968-77; headmaster: Monmouth Sch 1977-82, Uppingham Sch 1982-; *Books* Documents in World History, 1914-70 (1973); *Recreations* shooting, fishing, music, gardening; *Style—* Nicholas Bomford, Esq; Headmaster's House, Uppingham School, Rutland LE15 9TT (☎ 0572 822688)

BOMPAS, Donald George; CMG (1966), Hon JMN (Malaya) (1961); s of Rev Edward Anstie Bompas (d 1956), of London; *b* 20 Nov 1920; *Educ* Merchant Taylors', Oriel Coll Oxford; *m* 1946, Freda Vice, da of Fred Milner Smithyman (d 1969), of Malawi; 1 s, 1 da; *Career* formerly with Overseas Audit Service; auditor-gen: Malaya 1960-63, Malaysia 1963-66; sec: Guy's Hosp Med and Dental Schs 1969-82, United Med and Dental Schs of Guy's and St Thomas's Hosps 1984-86; managing exec: Philip & Pauline Harris Charitable Tst 1986-; Liveryman Merchant Taylors' Co 1951; *Clubs* Royal Cwlth Soc; *Style—* Donald Bompas, Esq, CMG; 8 Birchwood Rd, Petts Wood, Kent (☎ 0689 21661)

BONALLACK, Michael Francis; OBE (1971); s of Col Sir Richard Frank Bonallack, CBE, *qv*, and (Winifred) Evelyn Mary, *née* Esplen (d 1986); *b* 31 Dec 1934; *Educ* Chigwell Sch, Haileybury; *m* 8 Feb 1958, Angela, da of Harry Vivian Ward, of Birchington, Kent; 1 s (Robert Richard Ward b 1967), 3 da (Glenna (Mrs Beasley) b 1959, Jane (Mrs Baker) b 1961, Sara b 1965); *Career* Lt RASC (nat serv) 1953-55; joined Bonallack & Sons Ltd (later Freight Bonallack Ltd) 1955, dir 1962-74; dir Miller Buckley and Buckley Investments Ltd 1976-84; chm: Cotton (CK) Pennink & Ptnrs Ltd 1980-83, Miller Buckley Leisure Ltd 1980-83; sec Royal and Ancient Golf Club St Andrews 1983-; 5 times British Amateur Golf Champion, 5 times English Amateur Golf Champion, 4 times English Amateur Stroke Play Champion, twice Leading Amateur Open Golf Championship, played for England 1957-74 (Capt 1962-67), played for British Walker Cup Team 1957-73 (Capt 1969-71), awarded Bobby Jones Trophy by US Golf Assoc 1972; chm: Golf Fndn 1977-83, Professional Golfers Assoc 1976-82; pres English Golf Union 1982; Freeman of City of City of London, Liveryman of Worshipful Co of Coachmakers and Coach Harness Makers 1962; *Recreations* all sports, reading ; *Style—* Michael Bonallack, Esq, OBE; Clatto Lodge, Blebo Craigs, Cupar, Fife KY15 5UF (☎ 0334 85600); Royal and Ancient Golf Club, St Andrews, Fife KY16 9JD (☎ 0334 72112, fax 0334 77580, telex 76348)

BONALLACK, Sir Richard Frank; CBE (1955, OBE Mil 1945); s of Francis Bonallack (d 1955), of Loughton, Essex, and Ada Frances, *née* Bateman (d 1963); *b* 2 June 1904; *Educ* Haileybury; *m* 1930, (Winifred) Evelyn Mary (d 1986), da of James Johnstone Esplen, OBE (d 1934), of Buckhurst Hill, Essex; 2 s (*see* Michael Bonallack), 1 da; *Career* served WW II Col M East; md Bonallack Gp 1946-71 (chm 1955-77), pres Freight Bonallack Ltd 1977-87, dir Alcan Transport Products 1979-85; kt 1963; *Recreations* golf; *Style—* Sir Richard Bonallack, CBE, OBE; 4 The Willows, Thorpe Bay, Southend on Sea, Essex SS1 3SH (☎ 0702 588180)

BONAPARTE WYSE, William Lucien; o s of Andrew Reginald Nicholas Duncan Bonaparte Wyse, CB, CBE (d 1940, gs of Rt Hon Sir Thomas Wyse, KCB, PC, DL, of a family settled in Waterford since *temp* Richard Earl of Pembroke and which provided Waterford with 36 Mayors and High Sheriffs 1452-1690; Sir Thomas m HH Laetizia Cristina, Princess Bonaparte, da of HIH Lucien Bonaparte, the bro of the Emperor, who nonetheless played a vital role in the 19 Brumaire coup and who was the last to support Napoleon during the tail end of the Hundred Days in 1815); Andrew m Countess Marie (d 1960), da of Count Dmitri Chiriponov, of Orel province, Russia; *b* 13 Mar 1908; *Educ* Downside, Pembroke Cambridge; *m* 1, 1933 (m annulled 1946), Benedicta Madeleine Elizabeth Stephanie Marie Gabrielle (d 1969), o da of Charles Renfric Chichester, of Jersey; m 2, 1954, Olga Marie, da of Henry Clive Rollason, of Southsea, Hants; 1 s (Henry, b 11 July 1950), 1 da (Frances, b 28 Jan 1948); *Career* served WW II Lt Free Fr Navy, ADC to Adm Auboyneau (CIC 1942-45); *Style—* William Bonaparte Wyse, Esq; Beaumarchais, 22690 Pleudihen-sur-Rance, France

BONAR, Sir Herbert Vernon; CBE (1946); s of late George Bonar, of The Bughties, Broughty Ferry, Dundee, and Julia, *née* Seehusen; *b* 26 Feb 1907; *Educ* Fettes, Brasenose Coll Oxford (BA); *m* 1935, Marjory, da of late Albert East, of Hill Rice, Dundee; 2 s; *Career* chm Low and Bonar Gp 1949-74 (md 1938-73); Hon LLD: St Andrew's Univ; TOT Commandant of the Golden Ark (Netherlands), vice pres WWF (UK); kt 1967; *Style—* Sir Herbert Bonar, CBE; St Kitts, Albany Rd, Broughty Ferry, Dundee, Angus (☎ Dundee 79947)

BONAS, Lady Mary Gaye Georgiana Lorna; *née* Curzon; da of 6 Earl Howe, CBE; *b* 21 Feb 1947; *m* 1, 1971 (m dis 1976), (Kevin) Esmond Peter Cooper-Key (d 1985); 1 da (Pandora b 1973); m 2, 1977 (m dis 1987), John Austen Anstruther-Gough-Calthorpe, s of Brig Sir Richard Anstruther-Gough-Calthorpe, 2 Bt, CBE (d 1985); 1 s (Jacobi b 1983), 2 da (Georgiana b 1978, Isabella b 1980); m 3, 29 Jan 1988, Jeffrey Bonas, s of late Harry Bonas, of Grangewood Hall, Netherseale, Burton-on-Trent; 1 da (Cressida b 1989); *Style—* Lady Mary Gaye Bonas; The Old Rectory, Ovington, Alresford, Hants (☎ 0962 732821)

BOND, Alan; AO (1984); s of late Frank and late Kathleen Bond; *b* 22 April 1939; *Educ* UK and Fremantle Boys' Sch Australia; *m* 1955, Eileen Teresa, da of W Hughes; 2 s, 2 da; *Career* chm: Bond Corpn Hldgs Ltd 1982- (formerly chief exec), Swan Brewery Co Ltd; dir: North Kalgurli Mines Ltd, Metals Exploration Ltd, Bond Media UK Ltd, Airship Industries UK, Bond Univ Ltd, Hampton Gold Mining Areas plc; winner Americas Cup 1983 (with 'Australia II'); memb: Australian Sports Cmmn, WA Business Advisory Gp, WA Devpt Corporation, Royal Blind Soc, Opera Fnd of Australia; *Recreations* yachting, tennis, swimming; *Clubs* Young Presidents Organisation, Royal Perth Yacht, RORC (UK); *Style*— Alan Bond, Esq, AO; Watkins Close, Dalkeith, 6009, W Australia

BOND, Anthony Hugh; s of Lt-Col James Hugh Bond, MC (d 1983), of The Coach House, Burford, Shepton Mallet, Somerset, and Joan Winifred Dobman, *née* Turner; *b* 7 July 1951; *Educ* Radley; *m* 27 July 1974, Caroline Mary, s of Brig Frederick Manus De Butts, CMG, OBE, DL, of The Old Vicarage, Great Gaadesafn, Hemel Hempstead, Herts; 2 s (Jonathon James Hugh b 16 Aug 1977, Rupert Charles b 23 April 1980), 1 da (Victoria Jane b 3 Oct 1984); *Career* trainee CA Moore Stephens London, qualified CA 1977; Peat Marwick McLintock (formerly Peat Marwick Mitchell & Co): joined 1977, ptnr i/c Bahrain and Qatar, 1982-84, ptnr London, nat co-ordinator for business servs 1987-; ACA 1977, FAC 1983; *Recreations* golf, tennis, skiing; *Style*— Anthony Bond, Esq; The Granary, Reads Lane, Cublington, Leighton Buzzard, Beds LU7 OLE (☎ 0296 681 648); Peat Marwick McLintock, Norfolk House, 499 Silbury Boulevard, Central Milton Keynes MK9 2HA (☎ 0908 661 881, fax 0908 664 363)

BOND, (Charles) Derek; *see*: Bradwell, Bishop of

BOND, Edward; *b* 18 July 1934; *m* 1971, Elisabeth Pablé; *Career* playwright and dir; George Devine Award 1968, John Whiting Award 1968; *Style*— Edward Bond, Esq; c/o Margaret Ramsay, 14a Goodwins Court, St Martin's Lane, WC2

BOND, Maj Gen Henry Mark Garneys; JP 1972; DL 1977; Vice Lt of Dorset 1984; s of William Ralph Garneys Bond (d 1952), of Dorset, and Evelyn Isobel Blake (d 1954); *b* 1922; *Educ* Eton Coll; *Career* cmmnd in Rifle Bde 1941, served Middle East and Italy; Parachute Regt 1947-50; ADC to Field Marshal Viscount Montgomery 1950-52; cmd: Rifle Bde 1964-66, 12 Bde 1967-68; idc 1969; asst ch of Def Staff (ops) 1970-72; ret 1972; *Recreations* walking, forestry, reading; *Clubs* Boodles; *Style*— Major General Mark Bond, JP, DL; Moigne Combe, Dorchester, Dorset DT2 8JA; (☎ 0305 852265)

BOND, Ian Charles Winsor; s of Charles Walter Bond (d 1961), and Beryl Irene Bond (d 1961); *b* 15 June 1938; *Educ* King Edward VI Sch Camp Hill; *m* 28 July 1962, Audrey Kathleen, da of William Edward Robinson (d 1965), of Thornton Clevely, S Lancs; 2 s (Richard b 1965, Andrew b 1967), 2 da (Jane b 1963, Catherine b 1968); *Career* CA; managing ptnr Midlands Offs Baker Tilly 1988 (ptnr constituent firm 1964-), dir Bake-Tilly Mgmnt Consits Ltd 1988; farmer breeds Charolais Cattle; memb gen cncl Stonehouse Gang; FCA 1960; *Recreations* shooting, farming; *Style*— Ian Bond, Esq; Baker Tilly, Tricorn House, Hagley Rd, Edgbaston, Birmingham B16 8TP (☎ 021 456 1483, fax 021 456 1485, car 0860 531103)

BOND, John David; MVO (1988); s of Arthur Henry Bond (d 1968), and Agnes Mary, *née* Peters (d 1984); *b* 14 June 1932; *Educ* St Marys Welwyn; *m* 18 Jan 1958, Edna, da of William Samuel Reeves (d 1975); 1 s (Christopher John b 1962), 1 da (Susan Mary b 1959); *Career* keeper of the gdns The Great Park Windsor 1970-; (memb cncl 1985-), chm Rhododendron and Camelia ctee RHS 1987; Victoria Medal of Honour in Horticulture 1982; *Recreations* horticulture, natural history, travel, railways; *Style*— John Bond, MVO; Verderers, Wick Rd, Englefield Green, Egham, Surrey TW2 0HL (☎ 0784 32168); Crown Estate Office, The Great Park, Windsor, Berks (☎ 0753 860222)

BOND, Sir Kenneth Raymond Boyden; s of James Edwin Bond (d 1962), and Gertrude Deplidge, *née* Boyden (d 1980); *b* 1 Feb 1920; *Educ* Selhurst GS; *m* 1958, Jennifer Margaret, da of Sir Cecil Brooksby Crabbe (d 1971); 3 s, 3 da; *Career* ptnr Cooper & Cooper (chartered accountants) 1954-57, dir Radio & Allied Industs Ltd 1957-62, fin dir Gen Electric Co Ltd 1962-66, vice chm Gen Electric Co plc 1985- (dep md 1966-85); FCA; kt 1977; *Recreations* golf; *Style*— Sir Kenneth Bond; Woodstock, Wayside Gdns, Gerrards Cross, Bucks (☎ 0753 883513); The Gen Electric Co plc, 1 Stanhope Gate, London W1A 1EH (☎ 01 493 8484, telex 22451)

BOND, Prof Michael Richard; s of Frederick Richard Bond, of 10 Falstone Ave, Newark on Trent, Notts, and Dorothy, *née* Gardner (d 1988); *b* 15 April 1936; *Educ* Magnos GS Newark Notts, Univ of Sheffield (MB, ChB, MD, PhD); *m* 24 June 1961, Jane, da of Charles Issitt (d 1962); 1 s (Matthew b 9 Aug 1970), 1 da (Lucy b 2 June 1975); *Career* lectr psychiatry Univ of Sheffield 1964-67 (asst lectr and res registrar surgery 1961-64); Univ of Glasgow: sr house offr, registrar, sr registrar neurosurgery 1967-71, lectr and sr lectr neurosurgery 1971-73, prof psychological medicine 1973-, vice princ 1986-; govr Glasgow HS, chm Head Injury Tst Scotland; FRCSE 1969, FRCPsych 1981, FRCPS 1981; *Books* Pain: It's Nature Analysis Treatment (2 edns 1979, 1984); *Recreations* painting, forest walking, physical fitness, antique book collecting; *Clubs* Atheneum; *Style*— Prof Michael Bond; 33 Ralston Rd, Bearsden, Glasgow G61 3BA (☎ 041 942 4391); Dept Psychological Medicine, 6 Whittinghame Gdns, Great Western Rd, Glasgow (☎ 041 339 8826)

BOND GUNNING, Rufus Gordon; s of Lt-Col John Trehane Hamilton Gunning and Beatrice Ibea Burton, *née* Todd (d 1973); the Gunnings are an old county family, and were seated at Tregonning in Cornwall during the reign of Henry IV, AD 1400; *b* 24 Sept 1940; *Educ* Harrow, RMA Sandhurst; *m* 1967, Lilah Mary, da of Capt John Bowen McKay, OBE (d 1971), of Laguna, Brightwalton Holt, Nr Newbury, Berkshire; 1 s (Heyrick b 1971), 1 da (Anastasia b 1974); *Career* 9/12 Royal Lancers (POW) 1961, Capt, ret 1967; joined Chubb Alarms Ltd 1967, dir Chubb Alarms Hong Kong Ltd 1972, md Chubb Hong Kong Ltd 1974, chm: Chubb Alarms Ltd 1981, Chubb Wardens Ltd, dir Racial Chubb Ltd 1986, md Kalamazoo plc 1989 (joined 1988); *Clubs* Cavalry and Guards'; *Style*— R G Bond Gunning, Esq; Hopton Court, Alfrick, Worcestershire

BOND-WILLIAMS, Noel Ignace; CBE (1979); s of late W H Williams; *b* 7 Nov 1914; *Educ* Oundle, Birmingham Univ; *m* 1939, Mary Gwendoline Tomey; 1 s, 2 da; *Career* dir Nat Exhibition Centre Ltd 1970-, v-chm Lucas Ltd 1979-84, chm Remploy Ltd 1979-82, pro-chllr Univ of Aston in Birmingham 1970-82; *Style*— Noel Bond-Williams, Esq, CBE; Courtyard House, High Street, Lymington, Hampshire SO4 9AH (☎ 0590 72593)

BONDI, Prof Sir Hermann; KCB (1973); s of Samuel Bondi (d 1959), of NYC, and Helene Bondi (d 1960); *b* 1 Nov 1919,, Vienna; *Educ* Realgymnasium Vienna, Trinity Coll Cambridge; *m* 1947, Christine M, da of Henry Watson Stockman, CBE (d 1982); 2 s, 3 da; *Career* former lectr maths Cambridge, prof mathematics King's Coll London 1954-85 (leave of absence 1967-85); chm space ctee MOD 1964-65; dir-gen Euro Space Research Orgn 1967-71; chief scientific advsr MOD 1971-77; chief scientist DoE 1977-80; chm: advsy cncl Energy Conservation 1980-82, chm Natural Environment Research Cncl 1980-84; pres: Tst of Mathematics & its Applications 1974-75 Br Humanist Assoc 1982-, Assoc of Br Science Writers 1981-83, Soc Research into Higher Educn 1981-; master Churchill Coll Cambridge 1983-; memb: Rationalist Press Assoc, Science Policy Fndn; fell: Trinity Coll Cambridge 1943-49 and 1952-54, KCL 1968-; Hon DSc: York, Sussex, Bath, Surrey, Southampton, Salford, Birmingham, St Andrews; FRS 1959; *Books* Cosmology, The Universe at Large, Assumption & Myth in Physical Theory, Relativity and Common Sense; *Recreations* walking, talking, skiing; *Style*— Prof Sir Hermann Bondi, KCB; Master's Lodge, Churchill College, Cambridge CB3 0DS (☎ 0223 61200)

BONE, Charles William Henry; s of William Stanley Bone (d 1966), and Elizabeth, *née* Burfoot; *b* 15 Sept 1926; *Educ* Farnham Coll of Art, Royal Coll of Art; *m* 1950, Sheila Mary, da of Lionel Mitchell (d 1956); 2 s (Richard, Sebastian); *Career* lectr Brighton Coll of Art 1950-86, conslt COSIRA 1952-70; craft advsr Malta Industs Assoc 1952-78, designer Stourhead Ball 1959-69, dir RI Galleries Piccadilly 1965-70; govr Fedn of Br Artists 1976-81, 1983- and 1986-88 (memb exec cncl 1984-84), pres Royal Inst of Painters in Water Colours 1979- (vice-pres 1974-79); oils and water colours in exhibitions Medici Gallery 1950-: London Gp, NEAC, RBA 1950- (RA (1987-); 28 one-man exhibitions 1950-; works in private collections: France, Italy, Malta, America, Canada, Japan, Aust, Norway, Sweden, Germany; produced Ceramic Mural on the History of Aerial Photography; critic for Arts Review; memb cncl RI 1964- (vice-pres 1974); Hunting Gp Prize for the Most Outstanding Watercolour by a Br Artist 1984; memb hon Fedn of Canadian Artists, PRI, ARCA, FRSA, hon FCA; *Style*— Charles Bone, PRI, ARCA; Winters Farm, Puttenham, Guildford, Surrey (☎ Guildford 810226); 17 Carlton Ho Terrace, London

BONE, Ven John Frank Ewan; s of Jack Bone (d 1944), and Herberta Blanche, *née* Ewan (d 1984); *b* 28 August 1930; *Educ* Monkton Combe Sch, St Peter's Hall Oxford (MA), Ely Theological Coll, Whitelands Coll of Ed; *m* 26 June 1954, Ruth Margaret, da of Wilfrid John Crudgington (d 1968); 3 s (Nicholas b 1961, Stephen b 1964, Patrick (adptd) b 1972), 2 da (Sarah b 1955, Elizabeth b 1958); *Career* asst curate: St Gabriel's Pimlico 1956-60; St Mary's Henley-on-Thames 1960-63; vicar St Mary's Datchet 1963-76 rural dean Burnham 1974-77, rector St Mary's Slough 1976-78, archdeacon of Buckingham 1978-, memb General Synod 1980-85; *Style*— The Ven the Archdeacon of Buckingham; 60 Wendover Rd, Aylesbury, Bucks (☎ 0296 23269); 24 New St, Padstow, Cornwall

BONE, Michael John Stuart; s of Cyril Bone (d 1983) and Ethel Florence; *b* 5 Feb 1937; *Educ* Framlingham Coll; *m* 20 April 1963, Valanda Penelope, da of Phillip Henry Lane, of Banstead, Surrey; 2 s (Timothy b 1964, Jason b 1972); *Career* adm chartered accountant 1960; ptnrship practice 1960-86; md George Lines (Merchants) Ltd 1986-; Freeman Horner Co, Freeman City of London; FCA; *Recreations* fishing, windsurfing; *Clubs* City Livery; *Style*— Michael Bone, Esq; Stradbroke House, Valley Way, Gerrards Cross, Bucks (☎ 0753 886410); Coln Industrial Estate, Old Bath Road, Colnbrook (☎ 0753 685354, fax: 0753 686031)

BONE, Dr Quentin; JP; s of Stephen Bone (d 1958), and Sylvia Mary, *née* Adshead; *b* 17 August 1931; *Educ* Warwick Sch, St John's Coll and Magdalen Coll Oxford; *m* 1958, Susan Elizabeth, da of Sidney Smith (d 1963), of Merryfield House, Witney, Oxon; 4 s (Matthew, Oliver, Alexander, Daniel); *Career* zoologist Plymouth Lab of the Marine Biological Assoc UK, sr princ and dep chief scientific offr; FRS 1984; *Recreations* travel, botany; *Style*— Dr Q Bone, JP; Marchant Ho, Church Rd, Plymstock, Plymouth (☎ 0752 21761); The Marine Lab, Citadel Hill, Plymouth

BONES, Dr Roger Alec; s of Stanley Frederick Bones (d 1953), and Ethel Kate, *née* Coles (d 1978); *b* 8 Feb 1928; *Educ* BSc, PhD; *m* 10 March 1955, Elizabeth, da of late William Henry Taylor; *Career* sci offr Govt Communications HQ 1952-55, physics lectr Univ of Hong Kong 1955-58, econ advsr Nigerian Miny Commerce and Indust 1958-60, head trials assessment DeHavilland Propellors 1960, head govt contract labs Wayne Kerr Laboratories 1961-63; Standard Telephones and Cables Ltd (now STC plc) 1963-84: co tech ed 1963-64, mangr tech admin and coordination 1964-77, project asst to md STC plc 1977-79, mangr educnl liason 1979-84, project dir Faraday Lecture 1981-84; dir industl projects City and Guilds of London Inst 1984-86, (hon memb) sr ptnr RAB Assocs conslts 1987-,; govr Middx Poly; Freeman City of London, Liveryman Worshipful Co Horners; ACIS, FIEE, CEng, CPhys, MInst P; *Books* Dictionary of Telecommunications (1973); *Recreations* classical music, photography, DIY, gardening; *Clubs* IOD; *Style*— Dr Roger Bones; White Jade, 5 Derwent Close, Claygate, Surrey KT10 ORF (☎ 0372 66018); RAB Assocs, 5 Derwent Close, Claygate, Surrey (☎ 0372 66018)

BONFIELD, Dr Peter Leahy; CBE (1989); s of George Robert Bonfield (d 1975), of Baldock, Herts, and Dora Patricia, *née* Talbot; *b* 3 June 1944; *Educ* Hitchin Boys' GS, Loughborough Univ (BTech, DTech 1988); *m* 9 March 1968, Josephine, da of George Houghton, of Whitton, Humberside; *Career* divn mangr Texas Instruments Inc Dallas USA 1966-81; exec dir and gp marketing dir Int Computers Ltd London 1981-84; md STC Int Computers 1984-, chm 1986-, dep chief exec 1987-; memb: cncl Confederation of British Industry, court of Cranfield Inst of Technology, co of Technologists; CBIM; *Recreations* music, sailing, jogging; *Clubs* RAC; *Style*— Dr Peter Bonfield, CBE; STC International Computers Ltd, London SW6 3JX (☎ 01 788 7272, fax 01 788 3016)

BONHAM, Sir Antony Lionel Thomas; 4 Bt (UK 1852); DL (Glos 1983); s of Maj Sir Eric Bonham, 3 Bt, CVO, JP (d 1937), and Ethel, da of Lt-Col Leopold Seymour (s of Rt Hon Sir George Seymour, GCB, GCH, PC, and Hon Gertrude, da of 21 Baron Dacre; Sir George Seymour was s of Lord George Seymour, MP, s of 1 Marquess of Hertford); Sir Samuel George Bonham, 1 Bt, KCB, was govr and C-in-C Hong Kong and chief supt Br Trade in China 1847-53; *b* 21 Oct 1916; *Educ* Eton, Sandhurst; *m* 1944, Felicity, da of Col Frank Lionel Pardoe, DSO, of Bartonbury, Cirencester; 3 s; *Heir* s, (George) Martin Antony Bonham; *Career* serv Royal Scots Greys 1937-49, Maj; dir wine business to 1970, ret; *Style*— Sir Antony Bonham, Bt, DL; Ash House, Ampney Crucis, Cirencester, Glos (☎ 028 585 391)

BONHAM, Hon Mrs; Caroline; *née* Hamilton; da of 2 Baron Holm Patrick, DSO, MC (d 1942); *b* 21 Oct 1926; *Educ* Lawnside Malvern, Froebel Inst Roehampton; *m* 1951, Maj John Henry Hamilton Bonham, er s of Maj John Wroughton Bonham (d 1937), of Ballintaggart, Colbinstown, Co Kildare; 3 s; *Career* teacher Miss Ironside's Sch Elvaston Place SW7 1948-50; *Recreations* reading, craftwork, languages; *Style*— The

Hon Mrs Bonham; Trumroe, Castlepollard, Co Westmeath, Ireland (☎ Mullingar 61132)

BONHAM, (Arthur) Keith; s of George Bonham, of Plymouth, and Phyllis Ann, *née* Hammond; *b* 28 Mar 1939; *Educ* Plymouth Coll, Univ of Keele (BA); *m* 4 July 1964, Gillian Ann, da of William Ortelli Vokins (d 1981), of Bristol; 1 s, 2 da; *Career* CA 1966; ptnr Ernst & Whinney 1975 (managing ptnr Bristol off 1985); pres West of England Soc of CAs 1987-88; tres and vice pres Clifton RFC 1967-; *Style—* Keith Bonham, Esq; Erust & Whinney, Prince House, 43-51 Prince St, Bristol BS1 4QL

BONHAM, (Arthur) Keith; s of George Bonham, of Plymouth, and Phyllis, *née* Hammond; *b* 28 Mar 1939; *Educ* Plymouth Coll, Univ of Keele (BA); *m* 4 July 1964, Gillian Ann, da of William Ortelli Vokins (d 1981), of Bristol, 1 s (Adrian b 25 Sept 1970), 1 da (Tracy b 6 Aug 1968); *Career* CA; ptnr Ernst & Whinney 1975 (managing ptnr Bristol off 1985); pres West of England Soc of CAs 1987-88; tres and vice pres Clifton RFC 1967-; *Clubs* Keith Bonham, Esq; *Style—* Ernst & Whinney, Prince House, 43-51 Price St, Bristol BS1 4QL

BONHAM, (George) Martin Antony; s and h of Sir Antony Bonham, 4th Bt, *qv*; *b* 18 Feb 1945; *Educ* Eton, Aston Univ; *m* 1979, Nenon Baillieu (b 1948), da of Robert Ruttan Wilson, of Petersfield (whose gggf in the male line, the Rev George Wilson, was bro of 9th and 10th Barons Berners), and Hon Yvette Baillieu, da of 1st Baron Baillieu; 1 s (Michael b 1980), 3 da (Lucie b 1982, Camilla b 1984, Sarah b 1987); *Career* sales mangr Calor Gas Ltd; *Recreations* sailing, skiing, golf, tennis, squash; *Clubs* Hurlingham, Bembridge Sailing; *Style—* Martin Bonham, Esq; The Old Vicarage, Gosfield, Halstead, Essex; Appleton Park, Riding Court Rd, Datchet, Slough, Berks (☎ Slough 40000)

BONHAM, Nicholas; s of the late Leonard Charles Bonham and Diana Maureen, *née* Magwood; *b* 7 Sept 1948; *Educ* Trent Coll; *m* 7 April 1977, Kaye Eleanor, da of John Robert Ivett, of Brisbane, Australia; 2 da (Katie b 1981, Jessica b 1982); *Career* dir Montpelier Properties 1970, dep chm W & FC Bonham & Sons Ltd 1987 (md 1975-87, dir 1970); Freeman of City 1970, memb Worshipful Co of Pewterers; *Recreations* sailing, tobogganing, golf, skiing, elephant polo; *Clubs* South West Shingle Yacht, Acton Turville Bobsleigh, St Moritz Sporting; *Style—* Nicholas Bonham, Esq; Gavel House, Templar St, London SE5; W & FC Bonham & Sons Ltd, Montpelier St, London SW7 1HH (☎ 01 584 9161, fax 01 589 4079)

BONHAM CARTER, Baron (Life Peer UK 1986) Mark Raymond; s of Sir Maurice Bonham-Carter, KCB, KCVO (d 1960), and Helen Violet, Baroness Asquith of Yarnbury, DBE (d 1969); gs of H H Asquith (first Earl of Asquith of Oxford); *b* 11 Feb 1922; *Educ* Winchester, Balliol Coll Oxford, Univ of Chicago (MA); *m* 1955, Leslie, da of Condé Nast (d 1942), of New York, and formerly w of 2 Baron St Just; 3 da (Jane b 1957, Virginia b 1959, Elizabeth b 1961) and 1 step-da; *Career* Capt Gran Gds; served WWII in N Africa and NW Europe (despatches, POW 1943, escaped 1943); MP (Lib) Torrington 1958-59; chm: Race Rels Bd 1966-71, Community Rels Commn 1971-77; vice-chm and govr of BBC 1975-81; chm: Outer Circle Policy Unit 1976-81, Index on Censorship, Royal Ballet Govr 1985-; dir Royal Opera House 1958-82; vice-chm BBC 1975-81; *Clubs* Brooks's, MCC; *Style—* The Rt Hon Lord Bonham Carter; 13 Clarendon Rd, London W11 4JB (☎ 01 229 5200)

BONHAM CARTER, Richard Erskine; s of Capt Alfred Erskine Bonham Carter (d 1921), and Margaret Emily, *née* Malcolm (d 1952); *b* 27 August 1910; *Educ* Clifton Coll, Peterhouse Coll Cambridge, St Thomas' Hosp; *m* 1946, Margaret, o da of Robert Arthur Stace (d 1960), master printer; 3 da; *Career* served WW II Maj RAMC N Africa, Sicily, Holland, Germany; paediatrician: Hosp for Sick Children Gt Ormond St 1947-75, Univ Coll Hosp London 1948-65; *Recreations* gardening, fishing; *Style—* Richard Bonham Carter, Esq; 18 Doughty Mews, London WC1N 2PF (☎ 01 405 3062); Castle Sweyn Cottage, Achnamara, by Lochgilphead, Argyll (☎ (054 685) 249)

BONHAM-CARTER, Lady; Charlotte Helen; *née* Ogilvy; o da of Col William Lewis Kinloch Ogilvy, CB (gs of Rear Adm Sir William Ogilvy, 8 Bt), by his w Lucy, JP (d 1946), da of William Wickham, JP, DL, MP; *b* 22 August 1893; *m* 27 April 1926, Sir Edgar Bonham-Carter, KCMG, CIE (d 1956, 5 s of Henry Bonham Carter and unc of Lord Bonham Carter and Raymond Bonham Carter and Lady Grimond); *Career* served WW I as VAD, subsequently (1916-19) Mil Intelligence (War Office), on secretariat Paris Peace Conference 1919, WW II as instrument mechanic WAAF, offr special duties 1941-44, Miny Ec Warfare then FO 1944-49; memb Paddington Borough Cncl 1934, Alton RDC 1949; dir Ballet Rambert; *Style—* Lady Bonham-Carter; Wyck Place, Alton, Hants; 5 Connaught Sq, W2 (☎ 01 723 4980)

BONHAM-CARTER, Lady; Diane Anastasia; da of Mervyn Madden (d 1983); *m* 1973, as his 2 w, Sir (Arthur) Desmond Bonham-Carter, TD (former: dir Unilever, chm bd of govrs Univ Coll Hosp; d 1985), s of Gen Sir Charles Bonham-Carter, GCB, CMG, DSO (d 1955); *Career* memb hon sec The Nightingale Fund Cncl; assoc tstee Florence Nightingale Museum Tst, tstee W Sussex Nursing Benevolent Assoc, memb Chicester Community Health Cncl; *Style—* Lady Bonham-Carter; 15 Ashfield Close, Midhurst, Sussex GU29 9RP (☎ 073 081 2109)

BONHAM-CARTER, John Arkwright; CVO (1975), DSO (1942, OBE 1967, ERD 1952); s of Capt Guy Bonham-Carter, of 19 Hussars (ka 1915), and Kathleen Rebecca, *née* Arkwright (d 1943); *b* 27 Mar 1915; *Educ* Winchester, Kings Coll Cambridge (MA); *m* 1939, Anne Louisa, da of Col Nigel Keppel Charteris, CMG, DS0, OBE (d 1967); 2 s (Richard, Nigel); *Career* TA Engr and Tport Staff Corps RE, Col 1971; chief operating offr BR Bd 1966-68; chm and gen mangr BR: W Regn 1968-71, LM Regn 1971-75; cdr St John Ambulance Dorset 1984-87; KStJ 1984; FInstT; *Recreations* carpentry, cabinet making; *Clubs* Army & Navy; *Style—* John Bonham-Carter, Esq, CVO, DSO, OBE, ERD; 12 Redbridge Rd, Crossways, Dorchester DT2 8DY (☎0305 852669)

BONHAM-CARTER, Lord (Life Peer 1986) Mark Raymond; s of Sir Maurice Bonham Carter, KCB, KCVO, and Helen Violet, of Yarnbury; gs of H H Asquith (first Earl of Asquith of Oxford); *b* 11 Feb 1922; *Educ* Winchester, Balliol Coll Oxford, Univ of Chicago (MA); *m* 1955, Leslie, da of Conde Nast (d 1942), of New York; 3 da (Jane b 1957, Virginia b 1959, Eliza b 1961); *Career* Grenadier Gds 1941-45; MP Torrinston Div (L) 1958; chm: Race Relations Bd 1966-70, Community Relations Cmmns 1971-77; dir Royal Opera House 1958-82; vice-chm BBC 1975-81; *Clubs* Brooks's, MCC; *Style—* Lord Mark R Bonham-Carter; 13 Clarendon Road, London W4 4JB (☎ 01 229 5200)

BONHAM-CARTER, Victor; 3 s of Gen Sir Charles Bonham-Carter, GCB, CMG, DSO (d 1955), by his 2 w Gabrielle Madge Jeanette, *née* Fisher (d 1962); 1 cous of Lord Bonham Carter, *qv*; *b* 13 Dec 1913; *Educ* Winchester, Magdalene Coll Cambridge (MA); *m* 1, 1938 (m dis 1979), Audrey Edith, yr da of late Francis Rowe Stogdon, of Harrow, Middx; 2 s; m 2, 1979, Cynthia Claire Sanford, *née* Young; *Career* author; pubns offr Soc of Authors 1963-71 (joint-sec 1971-78, conslt 1978-82), sec Royal Literary Fund 1966-82; *Books* The English Village, (co-author 1952) Dartington Hall (1958), Exploring Parish Churches (1959), Farming the Land (1959), In a Liberal Tradition (1960), Soldier True (1965), Surgeon in the Crimea (1969), The Survival of the English Countryside (1971), Authors by Profession; (vol 1 1978, vol 2 1984), contribs to many journals; many radio broadcasts; *Recreations* listening to good music; *Clubs* Authors'; *Style—* Victor Bonham-Carter, Esq; The Mount, Milverton, Taunton TA4 1QZ (☎ 0823 400553)

BONINGTON, Christian John Storey; CBE (1976); s of Charles Bonington (d 1983), and Helen Anne, *née* Storey; *b* 6 August 1934; *Educ* Univ Coll Sch London, RMA Sandhurst; *m* 1962, (Muriel) Wendy, da of Leslie Marchant; 2 s (and 1 son decd); *Career* cmmnd RTR 1956, served in N Germany, Army Outward Bound Sch (mountaineering instr); mgmnt trainee Unilever 1961-62; freelance writer, photographer and mountaineer 1962-; climbing career, first ascent: Annapurna II (26,041 feet) Nepal with Dick Grant 1960, Nuptse (25,850 feet) third peak of Everest with Sherpa Ang Pemba 1961, Central Pillar of Freney Mont Blanc with Whillans, Clough and Djuclosz 1961; first Br ascent North Wall of the Eiger with Clough 1962, first ascent: Central Tower of Paine Patagonia with Whillans 1963, Old Man of Hoy with Patey and Bailey 1966; ascent Sangay in Ecuador (highest active volcano in the world) 1966; leader: Annapurna South Face Expedition 1970, Br Everest Expedition 1972; first ascent: Brammah (21,036 feet) Kashmir with Estcourt 1973, Changabang Garhwal Himalaya with Boysen, Haston, Scott and Sandhu 1974; ldr Br K2 Expedition 1978, climbing ldr Br Mount Kongur Expedition 1981 (first ascent with Boardman, Rouse and Tasker 1981), ldr Br Everest Expedition NE Ridge 1982, first ascent W Summit of Shivling (21,330 feet) Gangotri with Fotheringham 1983, first Br ascent (solo) Mount Vinson (highest in Antarctica) 1983, ascent of Mount Everest (29,028 feet) as a memb of 1985 Norwegian Everest Expedition; pres Lepra; dir Outward Bound Mountain Sch Eskdale; pres BNL 1988; vice-pres: Br Mountaineering Cncl, Army Mountaineering Assoc, Youth Hostels Assoc, Br Lung Fndn; tstee Calvert Tst Outdoor Activity Centre for the Disabled; hon DSc Sheffield, hon DSc Lancaster, hon MA Salford, Founder's Medal Royal Geographical Soc; *Books* I Chose to Climb, Annapurna South Face, The Next Horizon, Everest South West Face, Changabang (jt author), Everest the Hard Way, Quest for Adventure, Kongur: China's Elusive Summit, Everest: The Unclimbed Ridge (with Dr Charles Clarke); The Everest Years; *Clubs* Alpine, Climbers, Fell Rock, Climbing, Army & Navy; *Style—* Chris Bonington, Esq, CBE; Badger Hill, Hesket Newmarket, Wigton, Cumbria CA7 8LA (☎ 06998 286)

BONN, Michael Walter; s of Maj Walter Basil Louis Bonn, DSO, MC (d 1973), of Oaklands, St Peter, Jersey, CI, and Lena Theodora, *née* Davidson; *b* 12 Jan 1927; *Educ* Eton; *m* 16 June 1951, Elizabeth Mary, da of Maj Anthony Buxton, DSO (d 1970), of Horsey Hall, Gt Yarmouth, Norfolk; 1 s (Simon b 1953), 3 da (Sara b 1952, Mary b 1956, Theresa b 1959); *Career* Lt Welsh Gds 1944-48, cmmnd 1945; joined Willis Faber & Dumas Ltd 1949 (dir 1965-76, md (Agencies) 1967-76); dir: Anglo American Securities Ltd 1972-75, North Atlantic Securities Ltd 1972-75, Morgan Grenfell (Jersey) Ltd 1960-, Jersey Electricity Co Ltd 1980-, Fleming Ventures Ltd 1987-, Equity Capital for Indust Ltd 1987-; memb: Men of the Trees Ctee 1976-88, Jersey Assoc of Youth & Friendship (tres 1976-78, chm 1984-88), Soc Jersiaise Ctee 1985-88; dep of St Peter in States of Jersey 1978-84, Jurat of the Royal Jersey 1985-; Knight of Magistral Grace SMOM 1979; *Recreations* gardening; *Clubs* United; *Style—* Michael Bonn, Esq; Oaklands, St Peter, Jersey, CI (☎ 0534 814 81)

BONNAR, Douglas Kershaw; s of Thomas Bonnar; *b* 3 July 1931; *Educ* Edinburgh Acad, Melville Coll Edinburgh; *m* 1960, Suzanne, da of Charles Bettinson; 3 s, 1 da; *Career* memb ICA Scotland; md Chase Bank (Ireland) 1983-; *Recreations* bridge, snooker, golf; *Clubs* Caledonian, United (Jersey), Carrickmines GC (Dublin), Kildare Street and University (Dublin); *Style—* Douglas Bonnar, Esq; Belmont, Kerrymount Ave, Foxrock, Co Dublin, Ireland

BONNAR, Joseph Hugh; s of Robert Bonnar (d 1978), of Dunfermline, and Jane Cant, *née* Paterson; *b* 31 August 1948; *Educ* Queen Anne Sch; *Career* md Joseph Bonnar Inc (specialising in antique and period jewellery); ctee memb Edinburgh and E Scot Assoc of Goldsmiths and Watchmakers; memb: Nat Assoc of Goldsmiths, Soc of Jewellery Historians; *Recreations* foreign travel, the arts, good food; *Style—* Joseph Bonnar, Esq; 30 Raeburn Place, Edinburgh, Scotland; 72 Thistle St, Edinburgh (☎ 031 226 2811)

BONNELL, John Aubrey Luther; s of Thomas Luther Bonnell (d 1933), of Llanelli, and Ruth Griffiths (d 1982); *b* 2 Mar 1924; *Educ* Llanelli GS, King's Coll London, King's Coll Hosp (MB, BS); *m* 1, June 1954 (m dis 1964), Joan Perhum; 2 da (Sian Lesley b 2 April 1956, Armand Jane b 10 Oct 1957); m 2, 26 March 1966, Maureen Knowle da of Alfred Charles Warner (d 1985), of Ewell; *Career* asst physician Dept for Res in Industl Med MRC London Hosp 1950-58, chief med advsr CEGB 1978-86 (dep chief nuclear health and safety offr 1958-78), med advsr Electricity Cncl 1978-, specialist advsr occupational med SW Thames RHA 1979-85; bd memb int Cmmn Occupational Health 1980-86; past pres: Soc Occupational Med 1976-77, Soc Radiological Protection 1972-74, Section of Occupational Med RSM 1982; Freeman: City of London 1968, Worshipful Co Apothecaries 1971 (chm Livery ctee 1987-88); FFOM 1979, FRCP 1987, FSRP 1989; *Books* Chapters in: Recent Advances in Occpational Medicine 3 (1987), Current Approaches in Occupational Health 3 (1987), Fitness For Work (1988), author various scientific and med pubns on occupational med, radiological protection and toxicology; *Recreations* gardening, bridge; *Style—* Dr John Bonnell; 71 The Green, Ewell, Surrey KT17 3JX (☎ 01 393 1461); The Electricity Council, 30 Millbank, London SW1 (☎ 01 834 2333)

BONNER, Paul Max; s of Frank Max Bonner (d 1985), and Lily Elizabeth Marchant, *née* Jupp; *b* 30 Nov 1934; *Educ* Felsted; *m* 26 July 1956, (Nora) Jenifer, da of Dr George Raymond Hubbard; 2 s (Neil b 6 Jan 1957, Mark b 27 May 1959), 1 da (Alison b 27 June 1962); *Career* Nat Serv 1953-55, cmmnd 2 Lt RASC 1953, Acting Capt 1955, served in Egypt; radio studio mangr BBC 1955, asst producer 1957, BBC TV current affairs producer 1960, documentary producer 1965, head of science and features 1977, controller of programmes Channel Four 1980 and exec dir 1983, dir Programme Planning Secretariat ITV 1987; memb ctee for Public Understanding of Science; dir Broadcast Support Services; FRTS 1989; *Books* The Third Age of

Broadcasting (jtly); *Recreations* walking, photography, sailing; *Clubs* Reform; *Style*— Paul Bonner, Esq; Independent Television Association, Knighton House, 56 Mortimer St, London W1N 8AN (☎ 01 636 6866, telex 262988)

BONNET, Maj-Gen Peter Robert Frank; MBE (1975); s of James Robert Bonnet (d 1970), and Phyllis Elsie, *née* Lumsden (d 1985; *b* 12 Dec 1936; *Educ* RMA Sandhurst, London Univ (BSc); *m* 29 Dec 1961, Sylvia Mary, da of George William Coy (d 1964; 2 s (Gavin b 21 Oct 1962, Timothy b 6 June 1964); *Career* cmmnd 2 Lt Royal Reg of Artillery 1958, regtl duty Parachute Bde 1958-59, undergraduate London Univ 1959-62, Lt 3 Regt RHA 1962-64, Capt 17 Trg Regt RA 1964-66, 3 Regt RHA 1966-68, Maj Royal Mill Coll of Sci 1969, Staff Coll Camberley 1970, GS02 intelligence centre Ashford 1971-72, battery cdr 40 Field Regt RA 1973-75, Lt-Col HQ Dir RA 1975-78, CO 26 Regt RA 1978-81, Brig Cdr RA 2 Div 1982-84, Nat Def Coll New Delhi India 1984-85, Maj Gen dir RA 1986-89, GOC Western Dist 1989 ; *Recreations* painting and sculpture; *Clubs* Army & Navy; *Style*— Maj-Gen Peter Bonnet, MBE; The Old Rectory, East St, South Molton, Devon (☎ 076 95 2344)

BONNETT, Ralph; s of William Herbert Bonnett (d 1961), of Bedford, and Mary Elizabeth, *née* Orpin (d 1975); *b* 6 Jan 1928; *Educ* Bedford Sch, Pembroke Coll Cambridge (BA); *m* 2 April 1964, Jean Sloss, da of Bertie Reginald Pearn, OBE (d 1976), of Norfolk; 1 s (Andrew James William b 17 Oct 1966); *Career* cmmnd Lt Suffolk Regt RA 1946-49; articled clerk Speechly Mumford & Craig 1952-55, slr Long & Gardiner 1956-61, ptnr Linklaters & Paines 1967 (joined 1961); Liveryman of the Worshipful Co of Coachmakers & Coach Harness Makers (Clerk 1957-58); memb: Law Soc, City of London Law Soc; *Recreations* gardening, walking; *Style*— Ralph Bonnett, Esq; 42 Hazlewell Rd, Putney, London SW15 6LR (☎ 01 788 2832); Linklaters & Paines, Barrington Hse, 59/67 Gresham St, London EC2V 7JA (☎ 01 606 7080, fax 01 606 5113)

BONNETT, Prof Raymond; s of Harry Bonnett (d 1955), of Lakenheath, and Maud *née* Rolph; *b* 13 July 1931; *Educ* Bury St Edmunds Co GS, Imperial Coll (BSc), Cambridge Univ (PhD), London Univ (DSc); *m* 24 Aug 1956, Shirley, da of Samuel James Rowe (d 1959), of Bewdley; 2 s (Paul b 1962, Alastair b 1964), 1 da (Helen b 1960); *Career* served RAF 1949-51, cmmnd PO 1950, RAF Lyneham 1950, RAF Mauripur 1951 (air movements offr); Salters fell Cambridge 1957-58, res fell Harvard 1958-59, assoc prof chemistry UBC 1959-61; QMC: lectr organic chemistry 1961-66, reader 1966-74, prof 1974-76, chair of organic chemistry 1976-, hd of dept chemistry 1982-87; Friend of: Tate, William Morris Gallery and theatre; FRSC, CChem; *Clubs* Epping Soc; *Style*— Prof Raymond Bonnett; Chemistry Dept, Queen Mary College, Mile End Rd, London E1 4NS, (☎ 01 975 5024 fax 01 981 7517)

BONNEY, George Louis William; s of Dr Ernest Henry Bonney (d 1938), of 3 Vicarage Gdns, London W8, and Gertrude Mary, *née* Williams; *b* 10 Jan 1920; *Educ* Eton, St Mary's Hosp Med Sch (MB, BS, MS); *m* 26 Dec 1950, Margaret, da of Thomas William Morgan, of Nelson, Glamorgan; 2 da (Mary b 1952, Victoria b 1954); *Career* Surgn-Lt RNVR 1945-47, RN Res 1949-53; house surgn St Mary's Hosp and Park Prewett Hosp 1943-44, surgical registrar Royal Nat Orthopaedic Hosp 1947-50, travelling fellowship postgrad Medical Fedn 1950-51, clinical res asst Inst of Orthopaedics 1951-54; orthopaedic surgn: Southend-on-Sea Gp of Hosps 1953-55, St Mary's Hosp Paddington 1954-84; Watson-Jones lectr RCS 1976, Henry Floyd lectr Inst Orthopaedics 1977; assoc ed Journal of Bone and Joint Surgery 1960-68; chm: St Mary's Hosp Med Ctee 1972-74, Dist Hosp Med Ctee and Dist Med Ctee Paddington and N Kensington Health Dist 1978-80; memb: cncl Med Def union 1964-88 (hon fell), bd of govrs St Mary's Hosp 1972-74, mgmnt team Paddington and N Kensington Health Dist 1978-80, SICOT; FRSM, MRCS, FRCS, LRCP; *chapters in*: British Surgical Practice (1957), Clinical Surgery (1966), Operative Surgery (var ed), Clinical Orthopaedics (1983), Microreconstruction of Nerve Injuries (1987), Current Therapy in Neurologic Disease (1987); *Recreations* fishing, reading, photography, listening to music; *Clubs* Leander; *Style*— G L W Bonney, Esq; 71 Porchester Terrace, London W2 3TT (☎ 01 262 4236); Wyeside Cottage, Fawley, Hereford HR1 4SP (☎ 0432 70219)

BONNOR-MAURICE, Maj Edward Arthur Trevor; DL (Powys 1983); s of Trevor Bonnor-Maurice (d 1959); *b* 24 April 1928; *Educ* Winchester; *m* 1958, Lavinia, eldest da of Sir Richard Leighton, 10 Bt, TD (d 1957); 2 da (Emma Mary b 1959 (m 1987 Mark Fane), Frances Flavia b 1962); *Career* served Coldstream Gds 1946-61, Maj; MFH Tanatside Foxhounds 1971-; memb CC Montgomeryshire 1961-74; High Sheriff 1975-76; *Clubs* Guards & Cavalry, MCC; *Style*— Maj Edward Bonnor-Maurice, DL; Bodynfoel Hall, Llanfechain, Powys (☎ 069 184 486)

BONSALL, Sir Arthur Wilfred; KCMG (1977), CBE (1957); s of Wilfred Cook Bonsall (d 1963), of Beck House, Seathwaite, Broughton-in-Furness, and Sarah Bonsall; *b* 25 June 1917; *Educ* Bishop's Stortford Coll and St Catharine's Cambridge; *m* 1941, Joan Isabel, da of late G C Wingfield, of Bournemouth; 4 s, 3 da; *Career* joined Air Ministry 1940, dir Government Communications Headquarters 1973-78; *Style*— Sir Arthur Bonsall, KCMG, CBE; 176 Slad Rd, Stroud, Glos GL5 1RJ

BONSER, Ven David; s of George Frederick Bonser (d 1981), of 123 Newsome Rd South, Huddersfield, and Alice, *née* Roe; *b* 1 Feb 1934; *Educ* Hillhouse Secdy Sch Huddersfield, Huddersfield Tech Coll, Kings Coll London Univ (AKC), Manchester Univ (MA); *m* 21 Aug 1960, Shirley, da of Irving Wilkinson (d 1965), of 24 Trinity St, Huddersfield; 1 s (Simon b 8 March 1965), 2 da (Jane b 21 June 1963, Elizabeth b 26 April 1967); *Career* Nat Serv SAC (RAF) 1955-57; textile mangr 1958; curate St James Heckmondwike 1962-65, asst chaplain Univ of Sheffield and curate St George's Sheffield 1965-68, rector St Clements Chorlton-cum-Hardy Manchester 1968-82, canon of Manchester Cathedral 1980-, area dean of Hulme 1981-82, vicar and archdeacon of Rochdale 1982-86, archdeacon of Rochdale 1986-; *Recreations* golf, tennis, reading, theatre; *Clubs* Cwlth; *Style*— The Ven the Archdeacon of Rochdale; 21 Belmont Way, Rochdale, Lancs OL12 6HR (☎ 0706 486 40)

BONSER, Air Vice-Marshal Stanley Haslam; CB (1969), MBE (1941); s of late Sam and Phoebe Ellen Bonser, of Sheffield; *b* 17 May 1916; *Educ* High Storrs GS, Sheffield Univ (C Eng); *m* 1941, Margaret Betty, da of William Mason Howard, of Norton, Sheffield; 2 s; *Career* armaments offr RAF 1939-44, Br Air Cmmn Washington DC 1944-46, Coll of Aeronautics 1946-47, RAE 1947-51, chief instr RAF Tech Coll 1951-52, Staff Coll Brackwell 1953, psa 1953 Miny of Technol 1954-57, asst dir GW Engrg 1963-64; dir RAF Aircraft Devpt 1964-69, dep controller of equip Miny of Technol and MOD 1969-71, Aircraft C MOD 1971-72; dir Easams Ltd 1972-81; FRAcS; *Recreations* scout movement, gardening; *Style*— Air Vice-Marshal Stanley Bonser, CB, MBE; Chalfont, Waverley Ave, Fleet, Hants (☎ 0252 615835)

BONSOR, Elizabeth, Lady; Elizabeth; da of Capt Angus Valdimar Hambro, JP, DL (d 1957), of Milton Abbas, Dorset, and his 2 wife, Vanda Dorothy Julia, *née* Charlton (d 1981); *b* 22 Oct 1920; *m* 1942, Maj Sir Bryan Cosmo Bonsor, 3 Bt, MC, TD (d 1977); 2 s; *Style*— Elizabeth, Lady Bonsor; Ascot Lodge, London Road, Ascot, Berks

BONSOR, Hon Lady; Hon Nadine Marisa; *née* Lampson; JP (Beds); da of 2 Baron Killearn; *b* 23 August 1948; *Educ* Francis Holland Sch, Oxford Univ (MA); *m* 4 Sept 1969, Sir Nicholas Cosmo Bonsor, 4 Bt; 2 s (Alexander Cosmo, b 1976, James Charles b 1982), 3 da (Sacha Henrietta b 1974, Elizabeth Nadine, Mary Catherine (twins) b 1987); *Style*— The Hon Lady Bonsor, JP; Liscombe Park, Leighton Buzzard, Beds

BONSOR, Sir Nicholas Cosmo; 4 Bt (UK 1925), of Kingswood, Epsom, Surrey; MP (C) Upminster 1983-; s of Sir Bryan Bonsor, 3 Bt, MC, TD (d 1979), and Elizabeth, *née* Hambro, (*see* Bonsor, Elizabeth, Lady); *b* 9 Dec 1942; *Educ* Eton, Keble Oxford; *m* 4 Sept 1969, Hon Nadine Marisa Lampson, da of 2 Baron Killearn; 2 s, 3 da; *Heir* s, (Alexander) Cosmo Bonsor b 8 Sept 1976; *Career* served The Royal Bucks Yeo (RA TA) 1964-69; barr Inner Temple, in practice 1967-75; MP (C) Nantwich 1979-83; vice-chm: Tourism Sub-Ctee 1980-83, Cons Parly Foreign Affairs Ctee 1981-83, Cons Parly Defence Ctee 1987-; chm: Food Hygiene Bureau Ltd 1986-, The Cyclotron Tst for Cancer Treatment 1984-, The Br Field Sports Soc 1988-; memb Cncl of Lloyd's 1987-; vice chm Standing Cncl of the Baronetage 1987-; FRSA 1970; *Recreations* sailing, military history, shooting; *Clubs* White's, Royal Yacht Sqdn, House of Commons Yacht (commodore 1985-86) Pratt,s, Beefsteak; *Style*— Sir Nicholas Bonsor, Bt, MP; Liscombe Park, Leighton Buzzard, Beds

BONYNGE, Richard; AO (1983), CBE (1977); s of C A Bonynge, of Epping, NSW; *b* 29 Sept 1930; *Educ* Sydney Conservatorium; *m* 1954, Dame Joan Sutherland, *qv*; 1 s; *Career* artistic dir, Vancouver Opera Assoc 1975-; *Style*— Richard Bonynge, Esq, AO, CBE; c/o Australian Opera, PO Box J194, Brickfield Hill, NSW 2000, Australia

BOOBBYER, Hon Mrs (Juliet) Honor; *née* Rodd; da of 2 Baron Rennell, KBE, CB (d 1978), and Lady Rennell of Rodd-, Mary Constance Vivian Smith (d 1981); *b* 28 Oct 1930; *Educ* Westonbirt Sch; *m* 1957, Brian Boobbyer, s of Dr Philip Watson Boobbyer (d 1960), of Ealing, WS; 2 s (Philip, Mark); *Career* Moral Rearmament in Asia, U.S., Australia and Europe; *Books* 'Columba', a play with music (1982); *Recreations* writing, painting; *Style*— The Hon Mrs Boobbyer; 4 Victoria Rd, Oxford OX2 7GD (☎ 0865 58624); Little Rodd, Presteigne, Powys (☎ 0544 260 060)

BOODLE, John Victor; s of Rev John Boodle (d 1971); *b* 28 Oct 1926; *Educ* Wadham Coll Oxford (MA); *m* 1957, Lorna Eileen, da of James Vincent (d 1970); 1 da; *Career* md Br Germentation Products 1981- (dir 1957-), dir G R Spinks & Co Ltd 1986; memb: cncl CBI eastern region 1971-87, CBI Anglian Water & Environment ctee 1972 (chm 1987), industl rels bd Chemical Industs Assoc 1972, East Anglian Economic Devpt Cncl 1973-80, Anglian Water Authy 1977-; *Recreations* shooting, fishing, music, lit; *Style*— John Boodle, Esq; 26 Graham Rd, Ipswich, Suffolk (☎ 0473 54647)

BOOK, Anthony; JP (1987); s of Alec Book (d 1987), of Newcastle Upon Tyne, and Betty Book (d 1957); *b* 19 June 1946; *Educ* Newcastle Royal GS, Univ of Bristol (BSc); *m* 5 Aug 1969, Susan Lynn (d 1985), da of Irving Brand, of Long Beach, California; 1 s (Jeffrey Adam b 1971), 2 da (Jennifer Beth b 1973, Juliette Hiliary b 1977); *Career* brand mangr and mkt res Lever Brothers Ltd 1969-78, dir of Consumer Servs American Express Europe Ltd 1978-84, managing ptnr Compass Consultancy 1984-; Awards: winner Br Computer Soc Award (for Applications) 1982, winner Int Direct Mktg Symposium (for Tech Innovation in Mktg) 1984; speaker on direct mktg and electronic media at major confs in UK and Overseas; govr Stanley Deason Sch; FBIM 1986; *Books* Database Marketing (1989); *Recreations* flying, DIY, gardening, philatelly, travel; *Style*— Anthony Book, Esq; 57 Hill Dr, Hove BN3 6QL; Compass House, 13 Dover St, London W1X 3PH (☎ 01 491 9100)

BOOKER, Christopher John Penrice; s of the late John Mackarness Booker, of Shillingstone, Dorset, and Margaret Booker; *b* 7 Oct 1937; *Educ* Shrewsbury, Corpus Christi Cambridge; *m* 1, 1963 (m dis), Hon Mrs Emma C Tennant, *qv*; m 2, 1972, Christine Verity (m dis); m 3, 1979, Valerie, da of late Dr M S Patrick, OBE; 2 s; *Career* author, journalist and broadcaster; *Style*— Christopher Booker, Esq; The Old Rectory, Litton, Bath BA3 4PW (☎ 076 121 263)

BOON, Maj John McMillan; OBE (1982); s of Percy Edmund Boon, of London (d 1916), and Lily Ellen, *née* Payne (d 1965); *b* 5 Oct 1914; *Educ* Great Yarmouth GS; *m* 16 April 1938, Barbara Olive, da of Charles George Wilkerson, of Great Yarmouth, Norfolk (d 1941); 2 s (Michael b 1942, Peter b 1945), 1 da (Susan b 1944); *Career* served WW II, Maj Norfolk Yeo (TA) (ret 1956); Chartered Sec and Accountant; man dir: E Anglian Water Co 1961-84, dep chm 1985-; memb of Council of British Waterworks Assoc 1961-73 and Water Co's Assoc 1956- (chm 1979-84); memb of Council of Water Research Centre 1965-82, E Suffolk & Norfolk River Authority 1963-73, and Council of River Authorities' Assoc 1963-73 (dep chm 1970-73); Liveryman Co of Plumbers 1972, Freeman of City of London; Hon Fell Inst of Water and Environmental Mgmnt 1984; *Recreations* fishing, shooting, golf; *Clubs* Royal Norfolk & Suffolk Yacht; *Style*— Major John Boon; Lyndhurst, Burgh Road, Gorleston, Great Yarmouth, Norfolk (☎ Gt Yarmouth 662811)

BOON, John Trevor; CBE (1968); s of Charles Boon (d 1943), of 42 Aylmer Road, London N2, and Mary Alice, *née* Cowpe (d 1964); *b* 21 Dec 1916; *Educ* Felsted, Trinity Hall Cambridge (MA); *m* 9 Sept 1943, Felicity Ann, da of Stewart Logan (d 1933), of Kuala Lumpur, Malaysia; 4 s (Christopher John b 1946, Nicholas Stewart b 1949, Charles Logan b 1955, Humphrey Fullerton b 1958); *Career* served WW II NW Europe (despatches); chm: Mills and Boon Ltd 1972-, Harlequin Overseas 1978-, Marshall Editions 1977-; dir Torstar Corpn 1981-85; pres: Soc of Bookmen 1981-, Publishers' Assoc 1961-63, Int Publishers' Assoc 1972-76 (hon memb 1982); hon MA (Open Univ) 1983; *Recreations* family and social life, walking, swimming, wine; *Clubs* Beefsteak, Garrick, Savile, RAC; *Style*— John Boon, Esq, CBE; Mills & Boon Ltd, Eton House, 18-24 Paradise Road, Richmond, Surrey TW9 1SR (☎ 01 948 0444, fax 01 940 5899, telex 24420)

BOON, Sir Peter Coleman; s of Frank and Evelyn Clara Boon; *b* 2 Sept 1916; *Educ* Felsted; *m* 1940, Pamela; 1 s, 1 da; *Career* former chm and md Hoover (joined 1946, md (Australia) 1955-65, md 1965-75, chm 1975-78); chm: Highclere Investment Tst 1979-, Hoover Administrative Services Brussels 1978-; jt dep chm London Sound 1982-; Goodyear exec prof at Kent State Univ (USA); hon LLD (Strathclyde); Chevalier de l'Ordre de la Couronne (Belgium) 1976; FBIM, FRSA; kt 1979; *Clubs*

Hurlingham, Western Racing (Ayr), Australia Jockey, American National (Sydney), Royal Sydney Yacht Sqdn; *Style*— Sir Peter Boon; 2969 Harriett Road, Cuyahoga Falls, Ohio 44224, USA; Goodyear Executive Professor, c/o Kent State University, Dept of Business Administration, Room 450, Kent, Ohio 44240, USA; c/o Hoover Ltd, PO Box 22, Perivale, Greenford, Middx

BOORD, Antony Andrew; s of Sqdn-Ldr Sir Richard Boord, 3 Bt (d 1975), and bro and hp of Sir Nicolas Boord, 4 Bt; *b* 21 May 1938; *Educ* Charterhouse; *m* 1960, Anna Christina von Krogh; 1 s (Andrew Richard b 1962), 1 da (Tamsin Katrina b 1961); *Career* dir: Planned Packaging Ltd; *Clubs* Special Forces; *Style*— Antony Boord, Esq; Darch House, Stogursey, Bridgwater, Somerset

BOORD, Sir Nicolas John Charles; 4 Bt (UK 1896); s of Sqdn-Ldr Sir Richard William Boord, 3 Bt (d 1975); *b* 10 June 1936; *Educ* Eton, Sorbonne, Societa Dante Alighieri (Italy), U of Santander (Spain); *m* 1, 1960 (m dis 1965), Françoise, da of Giuseppe Tempra; m 2, 1965, Françoise Renée Louise, da of Marcel Clovis Mouret, of Marseilles; *Heir* bro, Antony Andrew Boord; *Career* scientific translator/English tning specialist; jt translator of *The History of Physics and The Philosophy of Science* 1972, and numerous scientific papers; *Style*— Sir Nicolas Boord, Bt; Résidence Les Aloadès, Bâtiment L, 94 Traverse Prat, 13008 Marseilles, France

BOORER, David Ian; s of Thomas Percy Broorer, of Sussex, and Edna Elsie, *née* Stakings; *b* 10 Sept 1948; *Educ* Worthing Tech HS, City of London Poly (BA); *m* 3 Nov 1973, Caroline Gail, da of John Graham Jackson, of France; 1 s (Nicholas b 1976), 3 da (Joanna b 1979, Emma b 1981, Louise b 1984); *Career* dep gen mangr Bann of Tokyo Int; *Recreations* rowing, music, fishing, plumbing; *Style*— David I Boorer, Esq; Byfleets Cottage, Warnham, Sussex RH12 3RB; 20/24 Moorgate, London EC2 (☎ 01 628 3000)

BOORMAN, Lt-Gen Derek; KCB (1986), CB (1982); s of late N R Boorman, MBE, and Mrs A L Boorman, *née* Patman; *b* 13 Sept 1930; *Educ* Wolstanton, Sandhurst; *m* 1956, Jennifer Jane Skinner; 1 s, 2 da; *Career* Public Rels Army 1978-79, Dir Military Ops 1980-82, Cdr Br Forces Hong Kong 1982-, Maj-Gen Bde of Gurkhas 1982-, Col 6 Gurkha Rifles 1982-; *Recreations* gardening, music, shooting; *Clubs* Naval and Military; *Style*— Lt-Gen Derek Boorman, KCB, CB; c/o Lloyds Bank Ltd, Cox's and King's Branch, Pall Mall, London SW1

BOORMAN, Edwin Roy Pratt; s of Henry Roy Pratt Boorman, *qv*; *b* 7 Nov 1935; *Educ* Rydal Sch, Queens' Cambridge (MA); *m* 1, (m dis 1982), Merrilyn Ruth Pettit; 4 da; m 2, 1983, Janine Mary, da of William Craske, of Penenden Heath, Maidstone; 1 s; *Career* md Kent Messenger Ltd 1965-, chm 1986-; *Recreations* sailing, yacht 'Messenger'; *Clubs* Ocean Cruising, Medway Yacht; *Style*— Edwin Boorman, Esq; Redhill Farm, 339 Redhill, Wateringbury, Kent; Kent Messenger, Messenger House, New Hythe Lane, Larkfield, Kent (☎ 77880)

BOORMAN, Henry Roy Pratt; CBE (1966), MBE (1945); s of Barham Pratt Boorman, JP, of Cedars, Maidstone (d 1928), and Elizabeth Rogers Boorman (d 1932); *b* 21 Sept 1900; *Educ* Leys Sch Cambridge, Queens' Cambridge (BA, MA); *m* 1, 1933, Enid, Margaret, da of Edgar E Starke; 1 s (Edwin Roy Pratt, *qv*; m 2, 1947, Evelyn Mary, da of Frederick G Clinch; 1 da Mary Elizabeth; *Career* Dep County Welfare Offr 1941, Major 1944 (served Europe); journalist Kent Messenger 1922-28, ed/proprietor 1928-52, chm 1952-82, pres 1982-; FJI 1936, pres Newspaper Soc 1960-61; Kent CC 1933-46, Mayor of Maidstone 1962-63, ald Maidstone 1964-70, JP 1962-63, DL Kent 1968-82; ed journal 'Kent' 1931-62 (for which awarded Sir Edward Hardy Gold Medal by Assoc of Men of Kent and Kentish Men 1964); tenor bell given to Canterbury Cathedral in H Boorman's name by Kent Messenger 1980; *Recreations* travel; *Clubs* Royal Cwlth Soc; *Style*— Henry Boorman, Esq, CBE, MBE; St Augustine's Priory, Bilsington, Ashford, Kent TN25 7AU (☎ Aldington 252)

BOOSEY, Georgina Caroline; da of Dr Donald Harden, CBE, LFBA, *qv*, and Cecil Ursula, *née* Harriss (d 1963); *b* 3 Jan 1936; *m* 1960, Anthony Leslie Marchant Boosey, hon ed The Hawk Tst, s of Leslie Boosey (d 1979), sometime chm of Boosey and Hawkes; *Career* managing ed Vogue Magazine, dir Friends of the Earth Tst, memb UK Ctee of Fndn Jules et Paul-Emile Léger of Quebec; *Style*— Mrs Anthony Boosey; Vogue, Vogue House, Hanover Sq, London W1R 0AD (☎ 01 499 9080)

BOOT, David Henry; s of Henry Matthews Boot (d 1974); *b* 15 Sept 1931; *Educ* Uppingham Sch, Loughborough Univ of Technology (DLC); *m* 1956, Gillian Mary, da of Reeves Charlesworth (d 1974); 4 s; *Career* chm Henry Boot & Sons; *Recreations* photography, golf, walking; *Style*— David Boot, Esq; Henry Boot & Sons plc, Banner Cross Hall, Sheffield S11 9PD (☎ 0742 555444, fax 585548)

BOOT, Edward James (Jamie); s of (Edward) Hamer Boot, OBE, MM (d 1987), and Joan Margaret, *née* Denniff; *b* 19 Nov 1951; *Educ* Rossall Sch; *m* Susan Philippa (Sue), da of John Humphrey Gowers (d 1988); 2 s (Hamer b 1981, William b 1987), 1 da (Georgina b 1984); *Career* md Henry Boot & Sons plc 1986-; *Recreations* shooting; *Style*— Jamie Boot, Esq; Henry Boot & Sons plc, Banner Cross Hall, Ecclesall Road South, Sheffield S11 9PD (☎ 0742 555 444)

BOOTE, Barbara Mary; da of Arthur Boote (d 1989), of Colehill, Wimborne, Dorset, and Joan C, *née* West (d 1980); *b* 8 June 1954; *Educ* Bromley GS; *Career* sec & ed asst: Coronet Books 1973-77, Magnum Books 1977-80; ed mngr: Sphere 1981-86; ed dir: Sphere April 1986; *Style*— Barbara Boote; Sphere Books Ltd, 27 Wrights Lane, London W8 5TZ (☎ 01 937 8070)

BOOTE, Charles Richard Michael; TD (1971) and two clasps (1978, 1983), DL Staffs 1988; s of Col (Charles Geoffrey) Michael Boote MBE, TD, JP, DL, *qv* and Elizabeth Gertrude Boote *née* Davies (d 1980); *b* 7 August 1939; *Educ* Cheltenham Coll; *m* 9 Oct 1965, Alison Brookes, da of Charles Kenneth Stott, JP (d 1979), of Tixall Lodge, Stafford; 1 s (James b 1974), 2 da (Vanessa b 1967, Emma b 1970); *Career* Maj TA cmd B (staffs Yeo) Sqn The Queens Own Mercian Yeo 1974-78; 2 i/c The Queens Own Mercian Yeo 1978-80; md Armitage Shanks Woodwork 1988-, corp devpt dir Home Products Divn Blue Circle Industs plc 1987-; chm Staffs Business Ctee Rural Devpt Cmmn 1984- (memb Econ Advsy Panel 1988-); vice-chm and tres Staffs Assoc of Boy's Clubs 1976-; Employers Rep W Midlands TAVR Assoc Ctee 1983-; FCA, FCMA, CMI; *Recreations* skiing, salmon fishing, stalking, tennis, squash, pedigree Suffolk sheep farming; *Clubs* Squash Raquets Assoc (life memb), Pointless (private dining); *Style*— Charles Boote, Esq, TD, DL; Enson Moor House, Sandon, Staffs (☎ 088 97 223); Armitage Shanks Woodwork, Alserflat Drive, Newstead Ind Est, Trentham, Stoke on Trent ST4 8HX (☎ 0782 642221)

BOOTE, Gervase William Alexander; Col Charles Geoffrey Michael Boote MBE, TD, JP, DL, of (Morile Mhor, Tomatin) Inverness-Shire, and Elizabeth Gertrude Boote, *née* Davies (d 1980); *b* 2 April 1944; *Educ* Cheltenham Coll; *m* 7 Oct 1967, Janet Mary Pierrette, da of Alan Edward Stott, JP, DL, of 8 Rupert Close, Henley-on-Thames, Oxon; 1 s (Richard b 1969), 1 da (Caroline b 1972); *Career* Peat Marwick Mitchell & Co -1972; Samuel Montagu & Co Ltd, merchant bankers 1972-, exec dir 1984-; FCA; *Recreations* tennis, golf, fishing; *Clubs* Worplesdon Golf; *Style*— Gervase W A Boote, Esq; 2A Hurlingham Court, Ranelagh Gardens, London SW6 3UL (☎ 01 736 6530); Samuel Montagu & Co Ltd, 10 Lower Thames Street, London EC3R 6AE (☎ 01 260 9000)

BOOTE, Col (Charles Geoffrey) Michael; MBE (1945), TD (1943, JP (Stoke-on-Trent 1955-65, Staffs 1959-76), DL (Staffs 1958)); s of Lt Col Charles Edmund Boote, TD (ka 1916), of Stoke-on-Trent, and Gertrude Ethel, *née* Laybourn (d 1954); *b* 29 Sept 1909; *Educ* Bedford Sch; *m* 1937, Elizabeth Gertrude (d 1980), er da of Evan Richard Davies (d 1933), of Market Drayton, Salop; 3 s (Charles (*qv*), Gervase, Nicholas); *Career* 2 Lt 5 Bn N Staffs Regt 1927, WWII served in UK and NW Europe (despatches), Lt-Col 1947, Hon Col 5/6 Bn N Staffs Regt 1963-67; dir: T & R Boote Ltd 1930-63, H Clarkson (Midlands) Ltd 1969-75, Br Pottery Mfrs Fedn (tstee) Ltd 1955-69 (pres 1957-58); vice chm Glazed & Floor Tile Mfrs Assoc 1953-57; chm Eccleshall PSD 1971-76; memb Ct of Govrs Keele Univ 1957; Staffs TAVR Ctee 1947-76; vice Lord Lt Staffs 1969-76, High Sheriff 1967-68; *Recreations* salmon fishing; *Clubs* Army & Navy, British Racing Drivers (life memb), N Staffs Hunt (hon sec 1948-59); *Style*— Col Michael Boote; Morile Mhor, Tomatin, Inverness-shire (☎ 080 82 319)

BOOTH *see also*: Gore-Booth

BOOTH, Alan James; s of His Hon James Booth, of Worsley, Manchester, and Joyce Doreen, *née* Mather; *b* 18 Jan 1955; *Educ* Bolton Sch, Selwyn Coll Cambridge (MA); *m* 4 April 1983, Anne Lesley, da of Eric Binns, of Bramhall, Stockport, Cheshire; 1 s (Charles b 13 Nov 1988), 1 da (Jane b 29 March 1987); *Career* barr Grays Inn 1978, practising Northern circuit; memb Sale Harriers; *Recreations* athletics; *Clubs* Hawks Cambridge, Last Drop Bolton; *Style*— Alan Booth, Esq; Wayoh View House, Chapeltown, Turton, Lancs; Deans Ct Chambers, Cumberland House, Crown Square, Manchester (☎ 061 834 4097, fax 061 834 4805)

BOOTH, His Honour Judge Alan Shore Booth; QC (1975); 4 s of Parkin Stanley Booth, and Ethel Mary, *née* Shore; *b* 20 August 1922; *Educ* Shrewsbury, Liverpool Univ; *m* 1954, Mary Gwendoline, da of John Hilton; 1 s, 1 da; *Career* barr 1949, circuit judge 1976-; *Recreations* golf; *Clubs* Royal Liverpool Golf, Royal and Ancient (St Andrews); *Style*— His Hon Judge Alan Booth, QC; 18 Abbey Rd, West Kirby, Wirral L48 7EW (☎ 051 625 5796)

BOOTH, Rt Hon Albert Edward; PC (1976); s of Albert Henry Booth, of Scarborough, and Janet, *née* Mathieson; *b* 28 May 1928; *Educ* St Thomas's Winchester, South Shields Marine Sch, Rutherford Coll of Technol; *m* 1957, Joan, da of Josiah Amis, of North Shields; 3 s; *Career* MP (Lab) Barrow-in-Furness 1966-83; election agent 1951, 1955; contested (Lab) Tynemouth 1964; min state employment 1974-76, employment sec 1976-79; oppn front bench spokesman Transport 1981; dir S Yorks Passenger Transport Exec 1983-; CIMechE; *Style*— The Rt Hon Albert Booth

BOOTH, Charles Leonard; CMG (1978), LVO (1961); s of Charles Leonard Booth (d 1987), and Marion, *née* Lawton (d 1981); *b* 7 Mar 1925; *Educ* Heywood GS, Pembroke Coll Oxford (MA); *m* 1 Aug 1958, Mary Gillian, da of Archibald George Emms (d 1978); 2 s (Charles b 1959, James b 1962), 2 da (Lydia b 1960, Rachel b 1964); *Career* WWII Capt RA 1943-47; Dip Serv; third sec (later second sec) 1950-55, FO 1955-60 (private sec to parly under-sec 1958-60), first sec Rome 1960-63; head of chancery: Rangoon 1963-64, Bangkok 1964-67, FO 1967-69; dep high cmmr Kampala 1969-71, cnsllr and consul-gen Washington 1971-73, cnsllt Belgrade 1973-77, ambassador Burma 1978-82, high cmmr Malta 1982-85, FCO 1985-; offr of the Order of Merit of the Italian Republic 1961; of Merit of the Italian Republic 1961; *Recreations* opera, gardening, walking; *Clubs* Travellers'; *Style*— Charles Booth, Esq, CMG, LVO; Foreign and Commonwealth Office, King Charles Street, London SW1A 2AH

BOOTH, Sir Christopher Charles; s of Lionel Barton Booth and Phyllis Petley, *née* Duncan; *b* 22 June 1924; *Educ* Sedbergh Sch, St Andrew's Univ (MB, MD); *m* 1, 1959, Lavinia Loughridge, of Belfast; 1 s, 1 da; m 2, 1970, Soad Tabaqchali; 1 da; *Career* former sr lectr London Postgrad Medical Sch, prof & dir Dept Medicine RPMS London Univ 1966-77, dir Clinical Research Centre MRC 1978-; FRCP, FRCPEd, Hon FACP; kt 1982; *Style*— Sir Christopher Booth; 33 Dukes Ave, W4 (☎ 01 994 4914)

BOOTH, Dr Clive; s of Henry Booth, of Poynton, Cheshire, and Freda Mary Booth; *b* 18 April 1943; *Educ* King's Sch Macclesfield, Trinity Coll Cambridge (MA), Univ of Calif Berkeley (PhD); *m* 28 June 1969, (Gwendolen) Margaret, da of George Sardeson (d 1967); *Career* Dept of Educn and Sci 1965 and 1975-81 (princ private sec to sec of State 1975-77), Harkness fell Univ of Calif 1973-75, dep dir Plymouth Poly 1981-84, HM inspr of schs 1984-86, dir Oxford Poly 1986-; involved with: Thames Action Resource Gp for Educn and Trg, Oxford Consortium, First Oxfordshire Radio; memb: computer bd for Univs and Res Cncls, Fulbright Fellowship Scheme, Polys and Colls Employers Forum, Soc for Res into Higher Educn; *Recreations* walking, bridge, opera; *Style*— Dr Clive Booth; Oxford Polytechnic, Oxford OX3 0BP (☎ 0865 819001, fax 0865 819073, telex 83147 VIA)

BOOTH, Rev Canon David Herbert; MBE (1944); s of Robert Booth (d 1941), of Milborne St Andrews, and Clara Annette, *née* Harvey; *b* 21 Jan 1907; *Educ* Bedford Sch, Pembroke Coll Cambridge (MA); *m* 2 May 1942, Diana Mary, da of Lt-Col William Wheaton Chard, MC (d 1953), of Brighton; 2 s (Peter b 1947, David b 1951), 1 da (Bridget b 1952); *Career* WW11 RNVR 1939-45, served Chaplain HMS Orion, HMS Collingwood, advanced party Western Desert, 30 AV RM; asst curate Hampton Parish Church 1932-34, chaplain Tonbridge Sch 1935-39, rector of Stepney 1945-53, vicar of Brighton 1953-59, archdeacon of Lewes 1959-71, provost Shoreham Coll 1977- (headmaster 1972-77); chaplain to HM the Queen 1975-77; memb local educn ctees; govr: Brighton Coll, Haileybury Coll; fndr and pres Nat Schools Jumping Championship 1963-; *Style*— The Rev Canon David Booth, MBE; Courtyard Cottage, School Road, Charing, Ashford, Kent TN27 (☎ 023371 3349)

BOOTH, Dr Derek Blake; s of Sir Philip Booth, 2 Bt (d 1960); h to Btcy of bro, Sir Douglas Booth, 3 Bt, *qv*; *b* 7 April 1953; *Educ* Hampshire Coll, Univ of California, Stanford Univ, Univ of Washington; *m* 1981, Elizabeth Dreisbach; 1 s (Colin b 1982), 1 da (Rachel b 1986); *Career* geologist; *Style*— Dr Derek Booth

BOOTH, Sir Douglas Allen; 3 Bt (UK 1916); s of Sir Philip Booth, 2 Bt (d 1960); *b* 2 Dec 1949; *Educ* Gaspar de Portolà Junior High Sch, Beverly Hills High Sch California,

Harvard Univ; *Heir* bro, Derek Blake Booth; *Career* television and film writer; *Style—* Sir Douglas Booth, Bt; 438 South Cochran, Apt 108, LA, Ca 90036, USA

BOOTH, Sqdn-Ldr Frank; s of late William Booth, of Cheshire, and late Jessie Irene, *née* Dedman; *b* 27 August 1931; *Educ* Sir John Deanes GS Northwich; *m* 19 March 1955, Janice Ann, da of late Jack Clayton, of Hartford, Cheshire; 1 s (Jonathan Frank b 1965), 1 da (Heather Ann b 1957); *Career* served in RAF Canada, Far East, Madagascar, Europe; flying appointments with 12 and 210 Sqdn (Flt Cdr) Navigation Inst Cambridge Univ Air Sqdn, instr/flying duties RAF Flying Coll Manby, ops duties Wildenrath, Gp Navigation/Weapons Staff Offr, HQ 18 Gps/HQ Northern Maritime Air Region, Staff Offr Underwater Weapons Operational Requirements MOD (Air), RAF Exercise Co-ordinator MOD (Air), RAF Cdr RAF Lakenheath, Staff Offr Establishments, HQ RAF Support Cmd Ret 1986; bursar Forres Sch Swanage Dorset 1986-; *Recreations* sailing, walking, painting; *Style—* Sqdn-Ldr Frank Booth; 24 Dacombe Close, Upton, Poole, Dorset (☎ 0202 623950); Forres Sch, Swanage, Dorset (☎ 0929 422760)

BOOTH, Sir Gordon; KCMG (1980, CMG 1969), CVO (1976); s of Walter and Grace Booth, of Bolton, Lancs; *b* 22 Nov 1921; *Educ* Canon Slade Sch, London Univ; *m* 1944, Jeanne Mary, da of James Herbert Kirkham, of Bolton; 1 s; *Career* served WWII Capt RAC and 13/18 Royal Hussars; memb HM Diplomatic Serv 1965-80; cnsllr Copenhagen 1965-69, consul-gen Sydney 1971-74, New York 1975-80; advsr on int trade and investmt and dir Hanson plc 1982-, vice-chm Bechtel Ltd 1986-, chm Simplification of Int Trade Procedures Bd 1980-86; memb British Overseas Trade Bd 1981-85; *Clubs* Brooks's, Walton Heath Golf; *Style—* Sir Gordon Booth, KCMG, CVO; Pilgrims Corner, Ebbisham Lane, Walton on the Hill, Surrey KT2O 5BT (☎ 073781 3788)

BOOTH, Dr (Vernon Edward) Hartley; s of Vernon William Hartley Booth, and Eilish, *née* Morrow; *b* 17 July 1946; *Educ* Queens Coll Taunton, Univ of Bristol (LLB), Downing Coll Cambridge (LLB, Dip Int Law, PhD); *m* 30 July 1977, Adrianne Claire Hartley, da of Knivett Gorton Cranefield, DFC; 2 s (Peter Toby Hartley b 1985, Thomas Edward Hartley b 1988), 1 da (Emily Claire Hartley b 1982); *Career* barr Inner Temple practising 1970-84, special advsr to PM and memb 10 Downing St Policy Unit 1984-88, chief exec and md Br Urban Devpt Ltd 1988-; contested (C) Hackney and Stoke Newington 1983, vice-pres Order of Christianity, advsr Royal Life Saving Soc; former govr schs, chm cncl reference Norwich Drug Abuse Centre; memb IOD; *Books* British Extradition Law and Procedure (volume I 1980, volume II 1981); *Clubs* Carlton, St Stevens, IOD; *Style—* Dr Hartley Booth; British Urban Devpt Ltd, 32 Queen Anne's Gate, London SW1H 9AB (☎ 01 222 5375, fax 01 222 1993)

BOOTH, John Aidan; s of Sidney Booth (d 1953), and Ruth, *née* Traylor (d 1977); *b* 7 Dec 1926; *Educ* Selby Abbey Sch, Selby Technic Inst, Univ of Goettingen, Univ of Bristol; *m* 21 Oct 1947, Pamela Jean, *née* Olivant; 3 da (Dorinda b 1949, Kathryn b 1954, Joanne b 1961); *Career* WWII RE 1944-48, dep chief clerk, chief engr 5 Div BAOR 1947; univ extra mural lectr in fine art, freelance author, publisher Cambridge House Books; fndr Univ of Bristol Bowman 1950, fndr Royal Leamington Spa Canoe Club 1954, fndr memb West Wilts Youth Sailing Assoc 1966; FRSA 1977; *Books* Antique Maps of Wales (1977), Looking at Old Maps (1979), Looking at Old Prints (1983), Day War Broke Out (St Dunstan's Charity Book (1984), Our Forgotton History (filmscript 1986); *Recreations* collecting, chess, brassband music, power boating; *Style—* John Booth, Esq; 30 Edenvale, Westbury, Wiltshire BA13 3NY (☎ 0373 823 271)

BOOTH, John Barton; s of Capt (Percy) Leonard Booth (d 1972), of Bournemouth, and Mildred Amy, *née* Wilson (d 1975); *b* 19 Nov 1937; *Educ* Canford, King's Coll London and King's Coll Hosp Med Sch (MB BS, AKC, MRCS, LRCP); *m* 18 June 1966, Carroll, da of Lt-Col James Ivor Griffiths (d 1983), of Peel, IOM; 1 s (James b 29 Aug 1972); *Career* conslt ENT Surgn London Hosp 1972-, conslt surgn Royal Nat Throat Nose and Ear Hosp 1973-78, conslt ENT surgn St Luke's Hosp for the Clergy 1983-, civil conslt (otology) RAF 1983; Hunterian prof RCS 1980-81; civil conslt laryngologist: Musicians Benevolent Fund 1974-, Royal Coll of Music 1974-, Newspaper Press Fund 1982-, Royal Opera House Covent Garden 1983, Royal Soc of Musicians of GB 1987-; chm Fedn of Univ Cons 1961-62 (vice-chm 1960-61, vice pres 1962-63), memb gen purposes and exec ctees Cons Pty 1961-62; ed Journal of Laryngology and Otology 1988- (asst ed 1979-88; memb cncl RSM 1980- 88 (memb Sci and exec ctee 1984-87); Freeman City of London 1972, Liveryman Worshipful Soc of Apothecaries of London 1969; assoc Zoological Soc of London; *Books* The Ear vol 3 (ed, fifth edn Scott Brown's Otolaryngology 1987); *Recreations* golf, the arts; *Clubs* MCC, RAC, Utd and Cecil; *Style—* John Booth, Esq; 18 Upper Wimpole St, London W1M 7TB (☎ 01 935 5631)

BOOTH, John Sebastian Macaulay; 2 s of George Macaulay Booth (d 1970), sometime dir Bank of England (1 cous, through his f, Rt Hon Charles Booth, of Sir Alfred Booth, 1 Bt), and Margaret, aunt of Daniel Meinertzhagen, *qv*; *b* 26 April 1913; *Educ* Harrow, Trinity Coll Cambridge (BA); *m* 1957, Juno (d 1968), 2 da of Guy Maynard Liddell, CB, CBE, MC (d 1958; 2 cous once removed through his f Augustus of Alice Liddell, the model for Lewis Carroll's Alice, and gs of Hon George Liddell, 5 s of 1 Baron Ravensworth); 2 da (Georgina b 1959, Theresa b 1961); *Career* served WWII Capt Dunkirk, 1 Army N Africa, 11 Armoured Division Normandy; tanner; dir Garnar Booth; *Recreations* skiing; *Clubs* Reform; *Style—* John Booth, Esq; Bramley Tree Cottage, Manor Lane, West Hendred, Oxon OX12 8RP (☎ 0235 832436)

BOOTH, Hon Mrs Justice; Hon Dame Margaret Myfanwy Wood; DBE (1979); da of late Alec Wood Booth and Lillian May Booth; *b* 1933; *Educ* Northwood Coll UC London (LLM, fell 1982); *m* 1982, Joseph Jackson, QC, s of Samuel Jackson (d 1987); *Career* govr Northwood Coll 1975-; barr Middle and Inner Temples 1956, QC 1976, chm Family Law Bar Assoc 1976-78, bencher Middle Temple 1979; memb Cncl UC London 1980-84; *Books* (co-ed) Rayden on Divorce, 10th-13th edns, (co-ed) Clarke Hall and Morrison on Children, 9th edn 1977; *Clubs* Reform; *Style—* Dame Margaret Booth, DBE; c/o Roy Courts of Justice, Strand, WC2A 2LL

BOOTH, Neil Douglas; s of Charles Douglas Booth, of Hartlepool, and Greta Lawrence, *née* Sylvester; *b* 11 Feb 1942; *Educ* Keighley Boys GS, St John's Coll Durham Univ; *m* 1, Barbara Ann, da of Edwin Cullerton, of Bradford; 2 da (Heidi Amanda b 1971, Christy Elizabeth b 1974); m 2, 22 July 1978, Yvonne Margaret, da of Peter Holdsworth Kennedy, of Bradford; *Career* CA; managing ptnr J Wm Thompson & Co Keighley 1969-73, ordinand in trg for Anglican Miny 1973-76, various accountancy posts 1976-81, ptnr Rawlinsons Bradford 1981-83, sr ptnr Booth & Co Bradford 1983-, dir Butterworth Tax Publishers Ltd; Inst of Taxation Thesis Prize 1985; chm nat insur ctee ICAEW; FCA 1964, FTII 1985; *Books* Social Security Contributions (1982), National Insurance Contributions (1984), DHSS Official Contribution Guides (1985), NIC Legislation and Cases (1986), Residence, Domicile and UK Taxation (1987); *Recreations* reading, water colour painting, video photography; *Style—* Neil Booth, Esq; Rivendell, 1114 Bolton Rd, Bradford, W Yorks BD2 4HS (☎ 0274 631154); Booth & Co, Chartered Accountants, Prince William House, Clifton Villas, Bradford, W Yorks BD8 7BY (☎ 0274 497124, fax 0274 488074)

BOOTH, Raymond Trygve; s of Douglas Edward Booth, of Brentwood, Essex, and Gerharda Jacoba, *née* Olsen (d 1965); *b* 14 July 1925; *Educ* Ilford Co HS, Middx Hosp London Univ (MB BS); *m* 8 Aug 1953, Enid, da of George Charles, *née* Everitt (d 1982); 3 s (John b 1954, Andrew b 1956, Christopher b 1963), 1 da (Elizabeth b 1960); *Career* WWII Sgt Navigator (air crew) RAF 1943-47; conslt obstetrician and gynaecologist SE Essex Gp of Hosps 1965-85; hon sec RCOG 1973-80; cncllr Brentwood DC; Freeman: City of London 1972, Worshipful Co of Apothecaries 1970; FRCOG 1974; *Recreations* aviation, music; *Style—* Dr Raymond Booth; Friars, 192 Brentwood Rd, Herongate, Brentwood, Essex CM13 3PN (☎ 0277 810527)

BOOTH, Richard George William Pitt; *b* 12 Sept 1938; *Educ* Rugby, Oxford; *Career* chm Richard Booth (Booksellers) Ltd 1961-; pres Welsh Booksellers Assoc; *Books* Country Life Book of Bookcolleting (ed); *Style—* Richard Booth, Esq; Hay Castle, Hay-on-Wye, Herefordshire

BOOTH, Sir Robert Camm; CBE (1967), TD; s of Robert Wainhouse Booth (d 1955), of Bowdon Cheshire, and Ann Gladys Taylor (d 1960); *b* 9 May 1916; *Educ* Altrincham GS, Manchester Univ; *m* 1939, Veronica Courtenay, da of late F C Lamb, of Bowdon, Cheshire; 1 s (Nigel), 3 da (Anthea, Sarah, Joanna); *Career* WWII 8 (A) Bn Manchester Regt, Maj, serv: France, Malta, ME, Italy; barr Gray's Inn; chm Nat Exhibition Centre 1975-82 (fndr dir 1970-82, chief exec 1977-78); pres Birmingham Chamber of Indust and Commerce 1978-79 (dir 1965-78, sec 1958-65), local non-exec dir Barclays Bank 1977-84; memb bd: Legal & Gen Assur Soc 1979-87, BR (Midlands and NW) Bd 1979-87, Inst of Occupational Health 1980-; tstee Nuffield Tst for the Forces of the Crown 1977-; memb: BOT Advsy Cncl 1975-82, W Midlands Econ Planning Cncl 1974-79; life memb Ct of Govrs Birmingham Univ (cncl memb 1973-78), govr Sixth Form Coll Solihull 1974-77; winner Midland Man of the Year Press Radio and TV Award 1970; travel with 20 Trade Missions and author of several mktg and econ pubns; Hon DSc Aston Univ 1975, Hon FInstM 1975, Hon FRSA 1975, Hon memb Br Exhibitions Promotions Cncl 1982; Officier de la Legion d'Honneur 1982; kt 1977; *Recreations* travel, writing, photography; *Style—* Sir Robert Booth, CBE, TD; White House, 7 Sandal Rise, Solihull, Warwickshire B19 3ET (☎ 021 705 5311)

BOOTH, Dr Victor Hubert Alexander; s of Alexander Booth (d 1949), of Glengormley, Co Antrim, and Laura Louisa Elizabeth Booth, *née* French (d 1985), descendant of William Booth of the London Drapers' Co, Architect of Draperstown, a model town in the Plantation of Ulster; *b* 18 April 1929; *Educ* Belfast HS, Trinity Coll (MA) Queen's Univ Belfast (MA) Univ of Southampton (PhD); *m* 17 July 1956, Lorna Jackaleen, da of Capt John Mann (d 1982), of Bangor, Co Down; 3 s (John b 1958, Christopher b 1962, Conor b 1965), 1 da (Karen b 1960); *Career* head of english Holywood Co Secdy Sch 1959, sr remedial teacher Co Antrim 1966, advr for special and remedial educn Worcestershire LEA 1972, county inspr for language, res and educnl devpt Hereford and Worcester LEA 1974-, specialist in learning disability; won scholarship Br Dyslexia Assoc to Texas 1972, visiting fell Queens Univ, Belfast 1970; *Recreations* travel, squash, country pursuits; *Style—* Dr Victor H A Booth; Kinnersley House, 269 Wells Rd, Malvern Wells, Worcs WR14 4HH (☎ 06845 572970); c/o Education Office, Castle St, Worcester WR1 3AG (☎ 0905 763763 ext 3440)

BOOTH-CLIBBORN, Rt Rev Stanley Eric Francis; *see*: Manchester, Bishop of

BOOTH-JONES, Charles Vernon Colville; s of Maj Thomas Vernon Booth-Jones JP, DL, of Hale Park, Fordingbridge, Hampshire (d 1966), and Margaret Wallace, *née* Colville (d 1984); *b* 5 Feb 1928; *Educ* Eton, Sandhurst; *m* 1, 2 Oct 1951 (m dis 1973), Louise Anne, 2 da of Col Guy Janion Edwards DSO; 1 s (Roderick Vernon b 1954), 1 da (Thalia Jane b 1951); m 2, 19 Jan 1974, Pauline Celia, 3 da of Sir James Gunn RA; *Career* RHG 1946, Sqdn Ldr 1957-64, (despatches 1959), 2 i/c 1965, Maj MOD HQ RAC 3 Div 1970; with Picture Gallery 1971, dealer in paintings 17-20 centuries, picture restorer; *Recreations* all country sports, painting; *Style—* Charles Booth-Jones; Hill Barn, Monkton Deverill, Wiltshire BA12 7EY; Fox Studio, Maiden Bradley (☎ 479)

BOOTHBY, Sir Brooke Charles; 16 Bt (1660), of Broadlow Ash; s of Sir Hugo Boothby, 15 Bt (d 1986); *b* 6 April 1949; *Educ* Eton, Trinity Coll Cambridge (BA); *m* 1976, Georgiana Alexandra, da of Sir John Wriothesley Russell, GCVO, CMG (d 1984), and Lady (Aliki) Russell, *qv*; 2 da; *Heir* kinsman, George William Boothby; *Career* High Sheriff S Glamorgan 1986-87; *Recreations* shooting; *Style—* Sir Brooke Boothby, Bt; Fonmon Castle, Barry, S Glam CF6 9ZN (☎ 0446 710206)

BOOTHBY, Baroness; Wanda; *née* Sanna; da of Giuseppe Sanna, of Sardinia; *m* 30 Aug 1967, Baron Boothby (Life Peer 1958; d 1986); *Style—* The Rt Hon Lady Boothby; 1 Eaton Square, London SW1

BOOTHMAN, Philip Comrie; s of John Comrie Boothman, of Hartford, Ches, and Audrey Johnson, *née* Leather; *b* 25 April 1953; *Educ* Manchester GS, New Coll Oxford (MA); *Career* barr Inner Temple 1977, dir Kleinwort Benson Ltd 1989-; *Style—* Philip Boothman, Esq; Kleinwort Benson Ltd, 20 Fenchurch St, London EC3P 3DB (☎ 01 623 8000, fax 01 623 5535, telex 888531)

BOOTHROYD, Betty; MP (Lab) West Bromwich West 1974-; da of Archibald Boothroyd (d 1948) of Dewsbury, Yorks, and Mary Boothroyd (d 1982); *b* 8 Oct 1929; *Educ* Dewsbury Tech Coll & Sch of Art; *Career* contested (Lab): Leicester South-East (by-election) 1957, Peterborough 1959, Nelson and Colne (by-election) June 1960, Rossendale 1970; memb Hammersmith Boro Cncl 1965-68, MP (Lab) West Bromwich May 1973-Feb 74, asst govt whip 1974-75, UK memb Euro Parl 1975-77, Speaker's Panel of Chairmen 1980-87, Lab Pty Nat Exec Ctee 1981-87, House of Commons Cmmn 1983-87, second dep chm Ways and Means, dep speaker 1987; *Style—* Miss Betty Boothroyd, MP; House of Commons, London SW1A 0AA (☎ 01 219 4136)

BOOTLE, Roger Paul; s of David Bootle, MBE (d 1972), and Florence Ethel, *née* Denman (d 1982); *b* 22 June 1952; *Educ* Downer GS, Merton Coll Oxford (BA, PPE MPhil); *Career* chief economist: Lloyds Merchant Bank 1986- (dir 1986-), Capel Cure Myres 1982-86 (exec dir) Greenwell Montague Gilt Edged 1989-; contrib Financial Times, Times, numerous pubns, various TU radio appearances as commentator on economic affairs; *Books* Theory of Money (jt author, 1978), Index-Linked Gilts (1986); *Recreations* bridge, squash, horseracing, classical music, theatre, reading; *Style—* Roger Bootle; 98F Richmond Hill, Richmond, Surrey TW10 6RJ (☎ 01 948 4605); Lloyds Merchant Bank, 40-66 Queen Victoria St EC4P 4EL (☎ 01 248 2244); Greenwell Montague Gilt-Edged, 10 Lower Thames St, London EC3R 6AE (☎ 01 260 9664)

BOOTYMAN, John Trevor; s of Walter Bootyman (d 1979), of Healing, and Gladys Mary, *née* Allenby (d 1980); *b* 14 Mar 1927; *Educ* Humberston Fndn Sch; *m* Helena Villette, da of John Thornton (d 1970), of London W14; 1 s (David b 1954), 1 da (Jane b 1958); *Career* RN 1945-48; CA 1954-, conslt Boyd 1989- (ptnr 1958-89); tstee: GF Sleight Settled Estates 1966-, May Watkinson Charity Tst 1971-; pres Grimsby and N Lincs Soc of CAs 1968-69, Humberside & Dist Soc of CAs 1973-74; pres Rotary Club of Grimsby 1986-87; RI Paul Harris Fell 1988; FCA; *Recreations* gardening, rotary activities; *Style—* J T Bootyman, Esq; Twigmoor, 51 Welholme Ave, Grimsby (☎ 0472 43588); 26 South St Mary's Gate, Grimsby DN31 1LW (☎ 0472 350601, fax 0472 241748)

BORDASS, Dorothy Trotman; da of Reginald Wilson Foster (d 1963), and the late Alice, *née* Skinner; *b* 19 Nov 1905; *Educ* South Hampstead HS, Northwood Coll, Harrow Sch of Art, Academie Julian Paris, Heatherley Sch of Art; *m* 22 April 1930, Brig William Harrison Bordass, CBE, MC, RA, s of William Bordass (d 1974); 1 s (William Trotman b 17 Nov 1943), 1 da (Jane (Mrs Shears) b 16 April 1931); *Career* painter, etcher and illuminator; 28 one man exhibitions since 1958 and many mixed exhibitions incl: RA, RBA, RSA, Redfern Gallery, Nelson Art Gallery Kansas City USA, Nat Gallery Kuala Lumpar, Contemporary Art Soc Sydney, Gallery on the Cam; purchasers inc ILEA, F W Woolworth Manhattan, Usher Gallery Lincoln, Darlington City Art Centre, Br Rail, Univ of E Anglia, Amstedamsche Beleggins Tst, Open Univ and many pte collectors; prizes incl: Reeves E of Eng Exhibition 1971 (for collage), Linton Prize Hesketh Hubbard London (for mixed media), silver medal Société des Artistés Francais Paris, Cambridge Drawing Soc Centenary prize; memb: ctee Penwith Soc St Ives Cornwall, Cambridge Drawing Soc; former chm Singapore Art Soc, former memb Royal Soc Painter Etchers, former fell Freepainters and Sculptors; *Recreations* gardening, embroidery; *Style—* Ms Dorothy Bordass; 30 Pretoria Rd, Cambridge CB4 1HE (☎ 0223 610 20)

BORDELL, Gerald Jacob; s of Gabriel Bordell, and Eve, *née* Gavelber (d 1980); *b* 3 April 1934; *Educ* Alleyn Ct PS Westcliff-on-Sea, City of London Sch; *m* 20 March 1960, Valerie Joyce, da of John Alick (d 1967); 2 s (Keith Stephen b 1963, Jonathan David b 1967); *Career* md Little Lady (London) Ltd 1967-1987, chm Mermaid Theatre Assoc 1977-81, fndr and hon organiser the Friends of the RSC 1982-87, memb of Cncl of Mgmnt Royal Shakespeare Theatre Tst 1984-87; md London Theatre Tours Ltd 1987; admin Friends of the Br Theatre 1987, chm Friends of the Br Theatre (Charitable Tst) Ltd 1988-; Freeman City of London (1973), Liveryman Worshipful Co of Basketmakers (1975); *Recreations* theatre, gardening; *Clubs* The City Livery, ESU; *Style—* Gerald Bordell, Esq; 5 Abbotswood Gdns, Clayhall, Ilford, Essex IG5 0BG (☎ 01 550 0576)

BOREEL, Jonkheer Sir Francis David; 13 Bt (E 1645); s of Jonkheer Sir Alfred Boreel, 12 Bt (d 1964), and Countess Reiniera Adriana (d 1957), da of Count Francis David Schimmelpennick; *b* 14 June 1926; *Educ* Univ of Utrecht; *m* 1964, Suzanne, da of Willy Campagne, of Paris; 3 da; *Heir* kinsman, Jonkheer Stephan Boreel; *Career* cncllr Netherlands Foreign Serv; *Style—* Jonkheer Sir Francis Boreel, Bt; Kapellestraat 25, 4351 AL Veere, Netherlands

BOREEL, Jonkheer Stephan Gerard; s of Jonkheer Gerard Lucas Cornelis Boreel (d 1970); h to Btcy of kinsman, Jonkheer Sir Francis Boreel, 13 Bt; *b* 9 Feb 1945; *m* Francien P Kooyman; 1 s; *Style—* Jonkheer Stephan Boreel; Elzenoord, 30, Vaassen, Holland

BOREHAM, Sir (Arthur) John; KCB (1980); 3 s of Ven Frederick Boreham (d 1966), Archdeacon of Cornwall and Chaplain to the Queen, and Caroline Mildred, *née* Slater (d 1943); *b* 30 July 1925; *Educ* Marlborough, Trinity Coll Oxford; *m* 1948, Heather, o da of Harold Edwin Horth, FRIBA (d 1952); 3 s, 1 da; *Career* served RAF Flt Lt 1943-46; dir Central Statistical Office and head Govt Statistics 1978-85; Visiting Fell Nuffield Coll Oxford 1979-87, pres Inst of Statisticians 1984-; *Recreations* music, golf; *Clubs* Knole Park Golf; *Style—* Sir John Boreham, KCB; Piperscroft, Brittains Lane, Sevenoaks, Kent TN13 2NG (☎ 0732 454678)

BOREHAM, Hon Mr Justice; (Hon) Sir Leslie Kenneth; *m* m; 1 s, 1 da; *Career* barr 1947, QC 1965, judge of the High Ct Queen's Bench Division 1972-, presiding judge North Eastern Circuit 1974-79; kt 1972; *Style—* The Hon Mr Justice Boreham; 1 Paper Buildings, Temple, London EC4

BOREHAM, Michael Bryant; s of Harold Leslie Boreham, of Beach Hotel, Worthing, Sussex (d 1971), and Irene Ethel Boreham, *née* Bryant (d 1967); *b* 7 June 1928; *Educ* Highgate Sch, London Univ (LLB); *m* 21 Jan 1956, Alison Jane, da of Douglas Archibald Clarke, of 7 Middle Field, St Johns Wood Park NW8, and Shardeloes, Old Amersham, Bucks; 2 da (Jane Caroline b 13 March 1959, Penelope Lucy b 18 Dec 1962); *Career* slr; Lt 16/15 Lancers 1947; sr ptnr Frere Cholmeley 1979-; dir: Harris Int Finance NV, Haverhill Meat Products Ltd, Knowles Electronics Co, Xomox Ltd, Polaroid (UK) Ltd (alternate), Canada Packers (UK) Ltd, Raychem Ltd, RCA Int Ltd, Warner Communications (UK) Hldgs; *Recreations* reading, theatre, shooting, fishing; *Clubs* Brooks's, Naval and Military; *Style—* Michael B Boreham, Esq; 26 Campden Hill Gate, Duchess of Bedford's Walk (☎ 937 4545); The Old Rectory, Sutton, nr Pulborough, W Sussex RH20 1PS (☎ 97987 258); 28 Lincoln's Inn Fields, London WC2A 3HH (☎ 405 7878, telex 27623, fax 405 9056, (01) 242 7724)

BORG, Dr Alan Charles Nelson; s of Charles John Nelson Borg (d 1986), and Frances Mary Olive, *née* Hughes (d 1985); *b* 21 Jan 1942; *Educ* Westminster, Brasenose Coll Oxford (BA, MA), Courtauld Inst, London Univ (MA, PhD); *m* 1, 1964; 1 s (Giles b 1965), 1 da (Emma b 1970); m 2, 1976, Caroline Sylvia, da of Lord Francis Hill; 2 da (Leonora b 1980, Helen b 1982); *Career* lectr: d'anglais Univ d'Aix-Marseille 1964-65, history of art Indiana Univ 1967-69; asst prof of history of art Princeton Univ 1969-70; asst keeper of the armouries HM Tower of London 1970-78, keeper Sainsbury Centre for visual arts Univ of East Anglia 1978-82; dir-gen Imperial War Museum 1982-; FSA; *Books* Architectural Sculpture in Romanesque Provence (1972), European Swords and Daggers in the Tower of London (1974), Torture and Punishment (1975), Heads and Horses (1976), Arms and Armour in Britain (1979); *Recreations* music, travel; *Style—* Dr A C N Borg; Telegraph House, 36 West Square, London SE11 4SP (☎ 01 582 8122); Imperial War Museum (☎ 01 735 8922)

BORG, Colin David Nelson; s of Charles John Nelson Borg (d 1986), and Frances Mary Olive, *née* Hughes (d 1985); *b* 11 Mar 1936; *Educ* Westminster, Trinity Coll Cambridge (MA); *m* 16 April 1971, Amanda Portman, da of Paul Charles Lindo (d 1969); 2 s (Christopher Paul Nelson b 1973, Guy Charles Nelson b 1975); *Career* Nat Serv RAF 1954-56; copywriter: Benton & Bowles 1959-60, BBDO 1960-62, Masius Wynne-Williams 1962-66; dir Butler & Gardner 1966-77, managing ptnr Butler Dennis Garland 1977-85, fndr chm Butler Borg 1985-; govr: Lanchester Poly 1975-80, King's Coll Sch; Coronation Medal 1953; MIPA 1974; *Recreations* transport history; *Clubs* Oriental; *Style—* Colin Borg, Esq; Butler Borg, 4 Gee's Ct, London W1 (☎01 408 2301, fax 01 408 0382, telex 267529)

BORGES, Thomas William Alfred; s of Arthur and Paula Borges, of Prague; *b* 1 April 1923; *Educ* Luton Tech Coll; *m* 1, (dis); m 2, 1966, Serena Katerhine Stewart, *née* Jamieson; 2 s; *Career* md Thomas Borges and Sons 1949-; chm Smith Whitworth Ltd 1974-; *Style—* Thomas Borges, Esq; 50 Aubrey Walk, W8 (☎ 01 221 4397)

BORINGDON, Viscount; Mark Lionel Parker; s and h of 6 Earl of Morley, *qv*; *b* 22 August 1956; *Educ* Eton; *m* 12 Nov 1983, Carolyn Jill, da of Donald McVicar, of Meols, Wirral, Cheshire; 2 da (Alexandra b 1985, Olivia b 1987); *Career* Lt 1982 Royal Green Jackets; *Style—* Viscount Boringdon; Pound House, Yelverton, South Devon

BORLAND, David Morton; s of David and Annie J Borland; *b* 17 Jan 1911; *Educ* Glasgow Acad, Brasenose Coll Oxford; *m* 1947, Nessa Claire Helwig; 1 s, 1 da; *Career* dir Cadbury Schweppes Ltd 1968-76 and UBM Gp Ltd 1976-81; pro-chllr Bristol Univ 1982-; *Style—* David Borland, Esq; Garden Cottage, 3 Hollymead lane, Stoke Bishop, Bristol (☎ 683978)

BORLEY, Lester; s of Edwin Richard Borley and Mary Dorena, *née* Davies; *b* 7 April 1931; *Educ* London Univ; *m* Mary Alison, eldest da of Edward John Pearce; 3 da; *Career* chief exec Eng Tourist Bd 1975-; *Style—* Lester Borley, Esq; 27 Blandy Rd, Henley-on-Thames, Oxon (☎ 6613)

BORODALE, Viscount; Sean David Beatty; s and h of 3 E Beatty; *b* 12 June 1973; *Style—* Viscount Borodale

BORRIE, Sir Gordon Johnson; s of Stanley Borrie, slr; *b* 13 Mar 1931; *Educ* John Bright GS Llandudno, Manchester Univ (LLB, LLM); *m* 1960, Dorene, da of Herbert Toland, of Toronto, Canada; *Career* called to the Bar Middle Temple 1952, bencher 1980, in practise 1954-57, lectr then sr lectr Coll of Law 1957-64; Birmingham Univ: sr lectr 1965-68, Prof Eng Law and dir Inst Judicial Admin 1969-76, dean Law Faculty 1974-76; dir-Gen of Fair Trading 1976-, memb Law Cmmn Advsy Panel Contract Law 1966-; former govr Birmingham Coll Commerce; former memb: Parole Bd, Consumers' Assoc Cncl, Equal Opportunities Cmmn; contested (Lab) Croydon NE 1955, Ilford South 1959 QC 1986; kt 1982; *Books* Commercial Law (6th ed. 1988), The Development of Consumer Law and Policy (1984) others in joint authorship; *Clubs* Reform, Garrick; *Style—* Sir Gordon Borrie, QC; Manor Farm, Abbots Morton, Worcestershire (☎ 0386 792330); 1 Plowden Buildings, Temple, London EC4 (☎ 01 353 4434)

BORRIE, Michael Anthony Frederick; s of Douglas Armitage Borrie (d 1964), of London, and Lucy Mary, *née* White (d 1981); *Educ* The Salesian Colls London and Oxford, King's Coll London (BA), Inst of Historical Res; *m* 24 March 1974, Gillian Elizabeth, da of Clifford John Pollard, of Ipswich; 2 s (George b 1980, Thomas b 1981); *Career* asst keeper dept of MSS Br Museum 1960, manuscripts librarian Br Library 1987; memb: cncl Br Records Assoc 1972, cncl Friends of the Nat Libraries 1973, Ctee for Establishing the Museum of London 1973-76, comité de sigillographie Conseil International Des Archives 1974-88, ctee Friends of the Geffye Museum 1985; tres Plainsong and Medieval Music Soc 1966-79; First Div Assoc: sec museums sub-ctee 1968-75, nat exec memb 1971-79; articles and reviews: The Spectator, Jl of the Br Archaeological Assoc, Jl of the Soc of ARchivists, Library History, Br Museum Quarterly; FRHistS 1969, FSA 1984; *Books* Magna Carta (1976), Vocabulaire International de Sigillographie (1984); *Recreations* gardening, reading, walking; *Style—* Michael Borrie, Esq; Department of Manuscripts, British Library, London WC1B 3DG (☎ 01 636 1544, fax 01 323 7745, telex 21462)

BORTHWICK, Antony Thomas; s and h of Sir John Borthwick, 3 Bt, MBE; *b* 12 Feb 1941; *Educ* Eton; *m* 1, 1966, Gillian Deirdre Broke, twin da of late Nigel Vere Broke Thurston, RN; 1 s, 2 da; m 2, 1985, Jenny, eldest da of George Lanning; *Style—* Antony Borthwick, Esq; 1 Arundel Gardens, London W11

BORTHWICK, (William) Jason (Maxwell); DSC (1942); s of Hon William Borthwick (d 1958), bro of 1 and last Baron Whitburgh (their f Thomas, chm and sr ptnr Thos Borthwick & Sons, was nominated a Peer 1912 but d before the patent passed the Great Seal); *b* 1 Nov 1910; *m* 1937, Elizabeth Cleveland, *née* Elworthy (d 1978); 1 s, 3 da; *Career* barr 1932, Thos Borthwick & Sons Ltd 1933 (dir 1946-76); International Commodity Clearing House 1952-83; Central Cncl of Physical Recreation 1950-; Cwlth Devpt Corpn 1971-77; *Recreations* shooting, sailing; *Clubs* United Oxford and Cambridge, Royal Thames Yacht; *Style—* Jason Borthwick, Esq, DSC; North House, Brancaster Staithe, King's Lynn, Norfolk PE31 8BY (☎ 0485 210475)

BORTHWICK, 23 Lord (S 1450) John Henry Stuart Borthwick of that Ilk; TD (1943), JP (Midlothian 1938), DL (Midlothian 1965); Baron (territorial) of Heriotmuir, Borthwick and Lockerwart, and as such was one of the four representative Scottish Barons at HM's post-coronation state visit to Edinburgh, carrying the crown canopy; Hereditary Falconer of Scotland to HM The Queen; o s of Henry Borthwick of Borthwick, *de jure* 22 Lord Borthwick (d 1937); claim as h male and 23 Lord Borthwick admitted by Lord Lyon 1986; *b* 13 Sept 1905; *Educ* Fettes, King's Coll Newcastle; *m* 8 Jan 1938, Margaret (d 1976), da of Alexander Campbell Cormack, of Leith; 2 s (twins); *Heir* s, John Borthwick, Master of Borthwick, *qv*; *Career* Lt-Col RATA, served WWII; chm Heriotmuir Properties Ltd 1965-, Heriotmuir Exporters 1972-; dir Ronald Morrison and Co 1972-; memb Lothians Area Ctee NFU Mutual Insur Soc 1969-87; chm Monitoring Ctee Scottish Tartans 1976; memb Standing Cncl Scottish Chiefs;patron Normandy Veterans' Assoc 1985; *Recreations* shooting, travel, history; *Clubs* New (Edinburgh), Puffin's (Edinburgh); *Style—* The Rt Hon Lord Borthwick, TD, JP, DL, NN. RL, GCLJ; Crookston, Heriot, Midlothian (☎ 087 535 232)

BORTHWICK, Master of; Hon John Hugh Borthwick; er (twin) s and h of 23 Lord Borthwick, TD, JP, DL, *qv*; *b* 14 Nov 1940; *Educ* Gordonstoun; *m* 1974, Adelaide, o da of Archy Birkmyre, of Lower Dalchonzie, Comrie, Perthshire; 2 da (Georgina b 1975, Alexandra b 1977); *Career* pres: North Country Cheviot Sheep Assoc 1988-89,

Scotch Half Breed Sheep Soc 1988-; memb local SE ctee Scottish Landowners Fedn, local ctee Wool Mktg Bd; *Recreations* trout fishing, stalking; *Clubs* New (Edinburgh); *Style*— The Master of Borthwick; The Neuk, Heriot, Midlothian EH38 5YS (☎ 087 535 236)

BORTHWICK, Sir John Thomas; 3 Bt (UK 1908), MBE (1945); s of late Hon James Alexander Borthwick, 2 s of 1 Bt; suc to Btcy of unc, 1 Baron Whitburgh, formerly Sir Thomas Banks Borthwick, 2 Bt, who d 1967, when Barony became ext; *b* 5 Dec 1917; *Educ* Eton, Trinity Coll Oxford; *m* 1, 1939 (m dis 1961), Irene (d 1978), o da of Joseph Heller; 3 s; m 2, 1962, Irene, da of late Leo Fink, of Paris XVI; 2 s; *Heir* s, Antony Borthwick; *Career* late Maj Rifle Bde (TA); dir Thomas Borthwick & Sons Ltd to 1981, vice-chm 1979-81; *Style*— Sir John Borthwick, Bt, MBE; Virginia House, Belmont, Warwick, Bermuda (☎ 296 0947)

BORTHWICK, Kenneth White; CBE (1979), JP (1966), DL (1980 Edinburgh); s of Andrew Graham Borthwick; *b* 4 Nov 1915; *Educ* George Heriot Sch Edinburgh; *m* 1942, Irene Margaret, da of John Graham Wilson, of Aberdeen; 2 s, 1 da; *Career* Rt Hon Lord Provost of City of Edinburgh and Lord-Lieut of City and Co of Edinburgh 1977-80; chm Commonwealth Games Scotland 1986; Hon Consul for Malawi in Scotland; *Recreations* golf, gardening; *Style*— Kenneth Borthwick, Esq, CBE, JP, DL; 62 Trinity Road, Edinburgh EH5 3HT (☎ 031 552 2519)

BORTHWICK OF GLENGELT, Hon James Henry Alexander; yr (twin) s of 23 Lord Borthwick, TD, JP, DL, *qv*; *b* 14 Nov 1940; *Educ* Gordonstoun, Heriot-Watt Univ; *m* 1972, Elspeth, da of Lt-Col Allan Dunn MacConachie, of Lauder, Berwickshire; 1 s (Malcolm Henry b 1973); *Style*— The Hon James Borthwick of Glengelt; Channelkirk Cottage, Oxton, Lauder, Berwickshire TD2 6PT

BORTON, Stephen James; s of John Charles Borton, of Porlock, Somerset, and Marion May, *née* Hadfield; *b* 21 April 1953; *Educ* All Saints' Choir Sch Margaret St London, Ellesmere Coll Shropshire, Royal Sch of Church Music; *Career* dir of music St Magnus London Bridge 1973-85, asst to dir of music All Saints Margaret St 1985-88, asst dir of music St Peter's Eaton Square 1988-; chief clerk and chief sealer Ct of Faculties of the Archbishop of Canterbury 1986-; Freeman City of London 1984-, Liveryman Worshipful Co of Musicians 1985 (Asst Clerk 1988-); *Recreations* cooking, wine, books, looking at churches, Victorian art; *Style*— Stephen Borton, Esq; 6 Saint Barnabas St, London SW1W 8PE (☎ 01 730 4983); 1 The Sanctuary, Westminster, London SW1P 3JT (☎ 01 222 5381, fax 01 222 7502)

BORWICK, Hon Diana; da of 4 Baron Borwick, MC; *b* 28 June 1959; *Style*— The Hon Diana Borwick; 109A Ingelow Rd, Battersea, London SW8 3PE (☎ 01 622 0150)

BORWICK, Geoffrey Robert Jamie; s of Hon Robin Sandbach Borwick, of Guernsey, and Hon Patricia Garnet Borwick, *née* McAlpine; *b* 7 Mar 1955; *Educ* Eton Coll; *m* 1981, Victoria Lorne Peta, da of R Dennis Poore (d 1987), of London; 2 s (Edwin b 1984, Thomas b 1987); *Career* md: Federated Tst Corp 1981-, Manganese Bronze Hldgs plc 1984-, Scottish and Mercantile Investment Tst plc 1985-, Stocklake Hldgs plc; chm London Taxis Int; *Recreations* travel; *Clubs* Caledonian; *Style*— Jamie Borwick, Esq; 22 Ilchester Place, London W14 8AA (☎ 01 603 0993); 1 Love Lane, London EC2V 7HJ (☎ 01 606 8744)

BORWICK, Hon George Sandbach; 2 s of 3 Baron Borwick (d 1961), but er s by his 2 w, Betty; half-bro and hp of 4 Baron Borwick, MC; *b* 18 Oct 1922; *Educ* Eton; *m* 1981, Esther (d 1985), wid of Sir John Ellerman, 2 and last Bt (d 1973, s of Sir John Ellerman, CH, 1 Bt), and yr da of Clarence de Sola, of Montreal, Canada; *Clubs* Garrick; *Style*— The Hon George Borwick; 7 Basil Mansions, London SW3 1PA

BORWICK, 4 Baron (UK 1922); Sir James Hugh Myles Borwick; 4 Bt (UK 1916), MC (1945); s of 3 Baron Borwick (d 1961), and his 1 w, Irene Phyllis, *née* Patterson; *b* 12 Dec 1917; *Educ* Eton, RMC Sandhurst; *m* 14 Sept 1954, Hyllarie Adalia Mary, yr da of late Lt-Col William Hamilton Hall Johnston, DSO, MC, DL, of Bryn-y-Groes, Bala, N Wales; 4 da; *Heir* half-bro, Hon George Borwick; *Career* Maj (ret) Highland Light Infantry; *Clubs* Royal Ocean Racing; *Style*— The Rt Hon The Lord Borwick, MC; Lower Minchingdown, Black Dog, Crediton, Devon EX17 4QX (☎ 0884 860735)

BORWICK, Hon Mary-Anne; da of 4 Baron Borwick, MC; *b* 11 July 1957; *Style*— The Hon Mary-Anne Borwick

BORWICK, Hon Mrs Robin; Patricia Garnett; *née* McAlpine; only da of Lord McAlpine of Moffat (Life Peer); *b* 5 Feb 1932; *m* 1950, Hon Robin Sandbach Borwick, *qv*; 2 s, 1 da; *Style*— The Hon Mrs Robin Borwick; Lihou Island, nr Guernsey, Channel Islands (☎ 0481 65656)

BORWICK, Hon Robin Sandbach; s of 3 Baron Borwick (d 1961); *b* 22 Mar 1927; *Educ* Eton; *m* 1950, Hon Patricia, *qv*; 2 s (James, Richard) 1 da (Judith); *Career* memb Lloyd's 1958-; Lt Life Gds 1946-52; founded Donkey Breed Soc 1967, former first chm, now vice-pres; pres Br Mule Soc 1978-; *Books* People With Long Ears (1965), Donkeys (1970), Esel, Freunde der Kinder (1970), The Book of the Donkey (1981), Esel Halten (1984), A Brief Guide to Lihou Island (1986); *Recreations* horses, donkeys, all equines; *Clubs* Cavalry; *Style*— The Hon Robin Borwick; Lihou Island, nr Guernsey, Channel Islands (☎ 0481 65656)

BOSANQUET, Dr Camilla; da of Sir Harry Ricardo (d 1974), of Woodside, Graffham, Nr Petworth, Sussex, and Beatrice, *née* Hale (d 1975); *b* 18 Jan 1921; *Educ* Benenden Sch, Newnham Coll Cambridge and Univ Coll Hosp (BA, MB, BChir, DCH, DPM, FRC Psych); *m* 23 Aug 1941, David Graham Bosanquet, s of Robert Carr Bosanquet (d 1935), of Rock Moor, Alnwick, Northumberland; 1 s (Robin b 1944) 2 da (Joanna b 1946, Annabel b 1950); *Career* house surgn and casuality offr Elizabeth Garret Anderson Hosp 1949, GP 1953-56, sr house offr Oakwood Mental Hosp 1956-58, clinical asst Bethlem Royal Maudsley Hosp 1959-60, Univ Coll Hosp 1964-86, conslt psychiatrist (student health serv) LSE 1969-87, trg analyst and former chm Soc of Analytical Psychology, fndr memb Guild of Psychotherapists 1973-; memb: BMA, Royal Coll of Psychiatrists; *Recreations* animals, gardening, music; *Style*— Dr Camilla Bosanquet; 18 Montagu Square, London W1H 1RD (☎ 01 935 0119)

BOSANQUET, David Graham; s of Prof Robert Carr Bosanquet (d 1935), of Alnwick, Northumberland, and Ellen Sophia, *née* Hodgkin (d 1965); *b* 8 Oct 1916; *Educ* Winchester, Trinity Coll Cambridge (MA, LLM); *m* 23 Aug 1941, Camilla, da of Sir Harry Ralph Ricardo (d 1974), of Woodside, Graffham, Sussex; 1 s (Robin b 1944), 2 da (Joanna b 1946, Annabel b 1950); *Career* Maj RA 1940-46 served NW Europe; slr Curry & Co (ptnr 1951-87, conslt 1987-); dir: Provincial Insur plc 1970-86, Provincial Gp plc 1986-, Fitzwilliam (Peterborough) Properties 1968-; *Recreations* gardening, painting, amateur dramatics; *Clubs* United Oxford and Cambridge; *Style*— David Bosanquet, Esq; Wyndside, Ryarsh, West Malling, Kent (☎ 0732 842351); 18 Montagu Square, London (☎ 01 935 0119); 21 Buckingham Gate, London SW1 (☎ 01 828 4091, fax 01 828 5049)

BOSANQUET, Nicholas Francis Gustavus; s of Lt Col Neville Richard Gustavus Bosanquet, of Wiltshire, and nancy Bosanquet, *née* Mason; *b* 17 Jan 1942; *Educ* Winchester, Clare Coll Cambridge, Yale Univ, LSE; *m* 31 Aug 1974, Connolly; 2 da (Kate b 1978, Helen b 1981); *Career* snr research fell Centre for Health Economics Univ of York; formerly lectr in Econs London Sch of Econs and the City Univ; econ advsr: Nat Bd for Prices and Incomes, Royal Cmmn on Distribution of Income and Wealth; conslt World Bank, the OECD and to health authys in Britain, arbitrator ACAS; contributor Econ Journal, Br Med Journal; *Books* After the New Right (1983), Industrial Relations in the NHS: The Search for a System (1980); *Recreations* collecting books on WW I, running; *Style*— Nicholas F G Bosanquet, Esq; Kelfield House, Flaxton, York YO6 7RP (☎ 0904 86389); Che, Univ of York YO1 5DD (☎ 0904 430000)

BOSANQUET, Samuel Anthony John Pierre; JP (1982); s of Samuel John Anson Bosanquet (ka 1944), and Muriel Daphne, *née* Griffith(; *b* 11 Jan 1944; *Educ* Eton, Keble Coll Oxford (MA); *m* 1975, Helen Margaret, da of William Hanbury Saumarez Smith, OBE; 2 s, 1 da; *Heir* Samuel David Saumarez Bosanquet (b 1977); *Career* landowner and sch master; music master Eton 1970-74; head of music King Henry VIII Sch Abergavenny 1974-79, asst music master Monmouth Sch 1979-; Welsh Rural Products Group (1987); chm Gwent Branch Coutry Landowners Assoc 1988; *Recreations* gardening, country pursuits, music; *Style*— Anthony Bosanquet Esq, JP; Dingestow Court, Monmouth, Gwent NP5 4YD (☎ Dingestow 060 083 238)

BOSCAWEN, Hon Charles Richard; s of 9 Viscount Falmouth; *b* 10 Oct 1958; *m* 1985, Frances Diana, yst da of late Maj Hon George Nathaniel Rous, of Dennington Hall, Woodbridge, Suffolk; 1 da (Rosanna Frances, b 3 Jan 1989); *Style*— The Hon Charles Boscawen

BOSCAWEN, Hon (Henry) Edward; s of 8 Viscount Falmouth (d 1962); *b* 4 Oct 1921; *Educ* Eton, Peterhouse Cambridge; *m* 1951, Anne Philippa, da of Sir Edward Warner, 2 Bt, DSO, MC; 1 s, 2 da; *Career* WWII Lt RE; chartered civil engr; High Sheriff W Sussex 1979-80; *Recreations* sailing, gardening; *Style*— The Hon Edward Boscawen; The High Beeches, Handcross, Sussex

BOSCAWEN, Hon Evelyn Arthur Hugh; s and h of 9 Viscount Falmouth; *b* 13 May 1955; *Educ* Eton, RAC Cirencester; *m* 1977, Lucia Caroline, da of Ralph Vivian-Neal, of Poundisford Park, Somerset; 1 s (b 1979), 1 da (b 1982); *Career* farmer; dir Goonvean & Rostowrack China Clay Co 1979-; local dir Sun Alliance; *Recreations* shooting, sailing; *Style*— The Hon Evelyn Boscawen; c/o Tregothnan Estate Office, Truro, Cornwall (☎ 087 252 310)

BOSCAWEN, Hon Nicholas John; 2 s of 9 Viscount Falmouth; *b* 14 Jan 1957; *Educ* Eton, RAC Cirencester; *m* 6 July 1985, Virginia M R, yr da of Robin Beare, MB, BS, FRCS, of Scraggs Farm, Cowden, Kent; *Career* land agent Cluttons 1980-85, institutional stockbroker Sheppards 1985-87, dir The Invisible Chef 1988-; ARICS; *Recreations* shooting, fishing, skiing, sailing, gardening; *Clubs* Annabel's; *Style*— Hon Nicholas Boscawen; Peckham Place, Peckham Bush, Towbridge, Kent TN12 5NA (☎ 0732 851 975, 0860 200 318)

BOSCAWEN, Hon Robert Thomas; MC (1944), MP ((C) Somerton and Frome 1983-); s of 8 Viscount Falmouth; *b* 17 Mar 1923; *Educ* Eton, Trinity Cambridge; *m* 1949, Mary Alice, JP (London), er da of Sir Geoffrey Codrington, KCVO, CB, CMG, DSO, OBE, TD; 1 s (Hugh), 2 da (Dozmary, Karenza); *Career* served NW Europe 1941-45, Capt Coldstream Gds 1945; Lloyd's underwriter 1952-, memb London exec cncl NHS 1954-65, contested (C) Falmouth and Camborne 1964 and 1966, MP (C) Wells 1970-83, memb Select Ctee on Expenditure 1974, memb Parly Delgn to Soviet Union 1978 and to Nepal 1981, vice-chm Cons Parly Health and Social Security Ctee 1974, asst govt whip 1979-81, lord cmmr of the Treasury (govt whip) 1981-83, vice-chamberlain of HM's Household 1983-86, comptroller HM Household 1986-88; *Clubs* Pratt's, Royal Yacht Sqdn; *Style*— The Hon Robert Boscawen, MC, MP; House of Commons, London SW1A 0AA

BOSCAWEN, Hon Vere George; s of 9 Viscount Falmouth; *b* 18 Sept 1964; *Style*— The Hon Vere Boscawen

BOSEL, Charles Henry; s of Douglas Henry Bosel (d 1985), of Brisbane, Australia, and Edith May, *née* Bouel (d 1987); *b* 4 July 1937; *Educ* Queensland Univ (BArch 1960), Liverpool Univ (Master of Civic Design 1964), Academica Britannica, Rome (Rome Scholar in Architecture 1961-62); *m* 6 Feb 1960, (Betty) Eunice, da of Cyril Allan Asplin (d 1977), of Tully, Australia; 2 s (Michael Charles b 1964, Stuart Allan b 1966), 2 da (Juliet Ann b 1971, Nicole Betty b 1975); *Career* architect and town planner; chm: Claverton House (Avon) Ltd 1984, St Georges Hill Ltd 1981, SSC Overseas Ltd 1986, Ecinue Hldgs Ltd 1987; dir: Al Marzouk and Abi Hanna 1980-; pres: Cor-Dor Gp NV 1986-; memb: Royal Town Planning Inst, RIBA, Royal Inst Australian Architects, Royal Australian Planning Inst, Soc of Rome Scholars, Soc of Kuwait Engrs; *Recreations* tennis, squash; *Style*— Charles Bosel, Esq; St Georges Hall, Easton-in-Gordano, Bristol BS20 0PX (☎ Pill 4881, telex: 449480 SSC G, fax: PILL 2392)

BOSOMWORTH, (Albert) John; s of John Bosomworth, of Beamsley, Skipton, and Agnes Mary, *née* Searle; *b* 28 Nov 1945; *m* 17 Sept 1977, Anne Caroline Mary, da of Charles Michael Pinnisson Roberts; *Career* farmer/landowner; dir: John Bosomworth (Holdings), J B Cara-Cars, CC Yacht Charter, Shooting Sch, Arms Dealing (JB); *Recreations* shooting (ex Br and English shooting teams), hunting, fishing, yachting, motor racing; *Clubs* RYA, CPSA; *Style*— John Bosomworth, Esq; Beamsley Estate, Beamsley, Skipton, N Yorkshire (☎ 0756 71344, car tel 0860 611924)

BOSSOM, Lady Barbara Joan; *née* North; da of Maj Lord North (d 1940), and sis of 9 Earl of Guilford, JP, DL; raised to rank of Earl's da 1950; *b* 28 Sept 1928; *m* 1951, Maj The Hon Sir Clive Bossom, 2 Bt, *qv*; 3 s, 1 da; *Career* memb bd of Habinteg (housing for handicapped) 1972-, dir exports and pub rels Vantona Viyella plc 1976-; OStJ; *Style*— Lady Barbara Bossom; 3 Eaton Mansions, Cliveden Place, London SW1 (☎ 01 730 1108)

BOSSOM, Bruce Charles; s and h of Hon Sir Clive Bossom 2 Bt, and Lady Barbara Bossom, *née* North of 3 Eaton Mansions, London SW1; *b* 22 August 1952; *Educ* Eton, Coll of Estate Mgmnt, Harvard Business Sch, FRICS; *m* 1985, Penelope Jane, da of Edward Holland-Martin (d 1981), of Overbury Court, Glos; 1 da (Amanda b 1988); *Heir* Rosanna Emily Bossom; *Career* chartered surveyor; dir: Phoenix Properties &

Finance plc, New Court Property Fund; Liveryman Worshipful Co of Grocers; FRSA; *Clubs* White's, Pilgrims; *Style*— Bruce Bossom Esq; Overbury Court, Nre. Tewkesbury, Gloucestershire, GL20 7NP (☎ 038 689 303). 34, Princedale Road, London W11 (☎ 01 727 5127) Phoenix Properties & Finance plc, 22, Gilbert Street, London W1Y 1RJ (☎ 01 408 0880)

BOSSOM, Hon Sir Clive; 2 Bt (UK 1953), of Maidstone, Kent; s of Baron Bossom (Life Peer and 1 Bt) by his 1 w Emily, *née* Bayne (d 1932); Sir Clive suc to Btcy 1965; *b* 4 Feb 1918; *Educ* Eton; *m* 1951, Lady Barbara Joan, *qv*, *née* North, da of late Lord North and sis of 9 Earl of Guilford; 3 s, 1 da; *Heir* s, Bruce Charles Bossom; *Career* Maj Europe and Far East (regular soldier The Buffs 1939-48); CC Kent 1949-51; MP (C) Leominster 1959-74, pps: jt parly secs of mins of Pensions 1960, sec of state for Air 1962-64, Home Sec 1970-72; chm Euro Assistance Ltd 1972-88, dir Vosper Ltd 1973-83; chm: Ex-Servs War Disabled Help Ctee 1973-88, Br Motor Sports Cncl 1975-82; vice-chm Br Road Fedn 1975-82; Int pres Int Social Serv for Refugees 1984-, IFPA 1969-81, Anglo-Netherlands Soc 1978-, Anglo-Belgian Soc 1983-85; vice-pres: (d'honneur) FIA, Iran Soc (past pres); cncl memb RGS 1971; Master Worshipful Co of Grocers 1979-80; vice-chm Jt Ctee Red Cross and St John 1987-; Almoner OStJ 1987-; FRSA; Cdr of Leopold II (Belgium), Cdr Order of Crown (Belgium), Kt Cdr Order of Orange Nassau (Netherlands), Order of Homayoun (Iran); KStJ (memb of Chapter Gen 1960-); *Recreations* travel; *Clubs* Carlton, RAC (chm 1975-78), BRDC, BARC (President 1984-); *Style*— The Hon Sir Clive Bossom, Bt; 97 Cadogan Lane, London SW1X 9DU (☎ 01 245 6531)

BOSSONS, William Raymond; s of William Henry Bossons (d 1951) and Maude Bowers (d 1948);; *b* 20 Oct 1918; *Educ* Wolstanton GS, Manchester Univ; *m* 22 Dec 1943, Ruth, da of William Alexander Fraser (d 1948); 2 s (Richard b 1952, John b 1953 d 1978), 1 da (Jane b 1955); *Career* WWII 1940-46, cmmnd RA Capt/Adjt served Germany; md WH Bossons Ltd 1951 (dir 1948-); chm and governing dir WH Bossons (Sales) Ltd 1952-; chm Congleton Chamber of Indust 1972 (designed Congleton Boro Indus Exhibn), fndr chm SE Cheshire Indust Liaison Gp 1974 ASIAD; *Recreations* sea sailing, photography, water colour painting; *Style*— WR Bossons, Esq; WH Bossons Ltd, Brook Mills, Mountbatten Way, Congleton Cheshire CW12 1DQ (☎ 0260 273693, fax 0260 270045)

BOSTELMANN, Michael John; s of Martin Horst Bostelmann; *b* 16 Nov 1947; *Educ* Bradfield; *m* 1973, Gillian, da of Allan Vickery; 1 s; *Career* CA, ptnr Arnold Hill; dir Quadrem Hope Ltd, Br Paper Co, Br Paper (Waste) Ltd, Frogmore Mill Ltd; *Recreations* long distance running, squash, tennis; *Clubs* Thames Hare and Hounds, Hurlingham; *Style*— Michael Bostelmann, Esq; 33 West Temple Sheen, East Sheen, London SW14 7AP

BOSTOCK; *see*: Ashton-Bostock

BOSTOCK, Edward; CBE (1975); s of Geoffrey Bostock (d 1961), of Hampstead; *b* 21 August 1908; *Educ* Charterhouse, Queen's Coll Oxford (MA); *m* 1934, Alice, da of George Smale; 3 s, 1 da; *Career* CA 1934, sr ptnr Annan Dexter & Co 1961-71, Dearden & Co 1972-75; FCA; *Recreations* gardening, opera, motoring; *Style*— Edward Bostock, Esq, CBE; 94 Richmond Hill, Richmond, Surrey TW10 6RJ (☎ 01 948 5834)

BOSTOCK, Godfrey Stafford; s of Henry John Bostock, CBE, JP (d 1956), of Shawms, Radford Bank, Stafford, and Eleanora, *née* Handley; *b* 23 June 1915; *Educ* Uppingham and Switzerland; *m* 1940, Diana, da of William Dickins Heywood (d 1922), of Little Onn Hall, Stafford; 2 s, 1 da; *Career* dir: The Claverley Co, Lichfield Cathedral Arts Ltd, Econ Estate Planning Co Ltd; High Sheriff Staffordshire 1958, Lord of the Manor of Kirkby Malzeard (and others); *Recreations* shooting, conservation, gardening; *Clubs* Boodle's; *Style*— Godfrey Bostock, Esq; Tixall, Stafford ST18 0XT (☎ 0785 661039); The Moor House, Dallowgill, Ripon, Yorks (☎ 076 583 371/491)

BOSTOCK, Nicholas Stephen Godfrey; DL (Staffordshire 1989); s of Godfrey Stafford Bostock, of Tixall House, Tixall, Stafford, and Diana, *née* Heywood; *b* 8 July 1942; *Educ* Eton; *m* 9 Aug 1968, Marise Cynthia, da of Rupert Thomas Bebb; 1 s (Richard b 1969), 1 da (Tania b 1972); *Career* CA and farmer; dir Econ Estate Planning Co Ltd 1978-; memb: CLA Co ctee 1980-, water sub ctee 1988-, current chm Ingestre with Tixall Parish Cncl (cncl memb 1983), High Sheriff of Staffordshire 1987-88; FCA 1979; *Recreations* shooting, inland waterways; *Style*— Nicholas Bostock, Esq, DL; Tixall Lodge, Tixall, Stafford ST18 0XS (☎ 0785 661713); Kennels Farm, Tixall, Stafford ST18 0XT (☎ 0785 662626, fax 0785 660780)

BOSTON, David Merrick; OBE (1976); s of Dr Hugh Merrick Boston (d 1980), of 86 Crane St, Salisbury, Wilts, and Jessie Mary, *née* Ingham (d 1979); *b* 15 May 1931; *Educ* Bishop Wordworth's Sch Salisbury Wilts, Selwyn Coll Cambridge (BA, MA), Univ of Cape Town; *m* 12 Aug 1961, Catharine Mary, da of Rev Prof E G S Parrinder, of Orpington, Kent; 1 s (Peter b 1966), 2 da (Janet b 1963, Andrea b 1969); *Career* Nat Serv 1950-51, Adj Marine Craft Trg Sch RAF Calshot, Flying Offr RAFRO 1951-55; Field Survey South African Inst of Race Relations 1955, keeper of ethnology (formerly special offr) Liverpool Museums 1956-62, asst keeper dept of ethrography Br Museum 1962-65, dir (formerly curator) Horniman Museum and Library 1965-; visiting scientist: Nat Museum of Man Ottawa 1970, Japan Fndn Tokyo 1986; chm Br Nat Ctee of the Int Cncl of Museums 1976-80, hon sec Royal Anthropological Inst 1985-88 (vice-pres 1972-75 and 1977-80); vice pres Dulwich Decorative and Fine Arts Soc, tstee Photographers' Gallery; FMA, FRAI, FRAS, FRGS; Ordenom Jugoslavenske Zastave sa zlatnom zvezdom na ogrlici (Yugoslavia) 1981; *Books* Pre-Columbian Pottery of the Americas (1980); *Recreations* travel; *Style*— David Boston, Esq, OBE; 10 Oakleigh Park Aven, Chislehurst, Kent (☎ 01 467 1049); Horniman Museum, London Road, Forest Hill, London SE23 (☎ 01 699 1872/2339)

BOSTON, Erica, Baroness; Erica Nelly; da of T H Hill; *m* 1936, as his 2 w, 9 Baron Boston (d 1978); 1 s (10 Baron Boston, *qv*); *Style*— The Rt Hon Erica, Lady Boston; Rosemary Court Esher Park Avenue Esher, Surrey.

BOSTON, Richard; s of Frank and Janet Boston; *b* 29 Dec 1938; *Educ* Stowe, King's Coll Cambridge (MA); *Career* writer, author of Anatomy of Laughter, The Admirable Urquhart, Beer and Skittles, Baldness Be My Friend, contributor to numerous newspapers and periodicals, especially The Guardian, fndr and ed The Vole and Quarto magazines; *Style*— Richard Boston, Esq; The Old Sch, Aldworth, Reading, Berks (☎ 0635 578 587

BOSTON, 10 Baron (GB 1761); Sir Timothy George Frank Boteler Irby; 11 Bt (E 1704); s of 9 Baron, MBE (d 1978), by his 2 w Erica; *b* 27 Mar 1939; *Educ* Clayesmore Sch Dorset, Southampton Univ (BSc); *m* 1967, Rhonda Anne, da of Ronald Albert Bate, of Balgowlah, NSW, Australia; 2 s (Hon George, Hon Jonathan b 1975), 1 da (Hon Rebecca b 1970); *Heir* s, Hon George William Eustace Boteler Irby b 1 Aug 1971; *Style*— The Rt Hon the Lord Boston; 135 Bishops Mansions, Stevenage Rd, Fulham SW6 6DX

BOSTON OF FAVERSHAM, Baron (Life Peer UK 1976); Terence George; QC (1981); s of George Thomas Boston (d 1986), and Kate, *née* Bellati; *b* 21 Mar 1930; *Educ* Woolwich Poly Sch, King's Coll London; *m* 1962, Margaret Joyce, da of Rowley Henry Jack Head (d 1932), of Toorak, Vic, Australia; *Career* sits as Lab Peer in Lords; Flt Lt RAF 1950-52; barr Inner Temple 1960, Gray's Inn 1973; former news sub-editor BBC External Services, sr prodr BBC (current affairs) 1960-64, chm TVS (now TVS Entertainment plc) 1981-; MP (Lab) Faversham Kent 1964-70, PPS to min of Public Bldg and Works 1964-66, to min of Power 1966-68, to min of Transport 1968-69, asst govt whip 1969-70, min of state Home Off 1979, oppn front bench spokesman on Home Off Affrs 1979-84; on Defence 1984-86; *Style*— The Rt Hon The Lord Boston of Faversham, QC; House of Lords, London SW1A 0AA;

BOSVILLE MACDONALD OF SLEAT, Sir Ian Godfrey; 17 Bt (NS 1625); also 25 Chief of Sleat; s of Sir Somerled Bosville Macdonald of Sleat, 16 Bt, MC (24 Chief of Sleat, d 1958), and Mary, Lady Bosville Macdonald of Sleat, *qv*; *b* 18 July 1947; *Educ* Pinewood Sch, Eton, RAC Cirencester; *m* 1970, Juliet Fleury, o da of Maj-Gen John Ward-Harrison, OBE, MC; 1 s, 2 da; *Heir* s, Somerled Alexander Bosville Macdonald, yr of Sleat, b 30 Jan 1976; *Career* chartered surveyor 1972; memb: Royal Soc of Health 1972, Economic Research Cncl 1979; ccncllr Bridlington S 1981-85; pres: Humberside br Br Red Cross 1988, Br Ford and Farming Humberside 1989, chm Rural Devpt Cmmn Humberside 1988, High Sheriff of Humberside 1988-89; *Recreations* ornithology; *Clubs* Brooks's, Puffin's; *Style*— Sir Ian Bosville Macdonald of Sleat, Bt; Thorpe Hall, Rudston, Driffield, N Humberside (☎ 026 282 239); Upper Duntulm, Kilmuir, Isle of Skye (☎ 047 052 206)

BOSVILLE MACDONALD OF SLEAT, Mary, Lady; Mary Elizabeth; da of Lt-Col Ralph Crawley-Boevy Gibbs (1 cous of 1 Baron Wraxall); *b* 5 June 1919; *m* 1946, Sir (Alexander) Somerled Angus Bosville Macdonald of Sleat, 16 Bt, MC (d 1958); *Style*— Mary, Lady Bosville Macdonald of Sleat; Westcroft Farm, Rudston, Driffield, N Humberside (☎ 026 282 614)

BOSWALL; *see*: Houstoun-Boswall

BOSWELL, Timothy Eric; MP (C) Daventry 1987; s of Eric New Boswell, of Lower Aynho Grounds, Banbury (d 1974), and Joan Winifred Caroline, *née* Jones; *b* 2 Dec 1942; *Educ* Marlborough, New Coll Oxford (Literae Humaniores, Post graduate Diploma in Agricultural Economics); *m* 2 Aug 1969, Helen Delahay, da of the Rev Arthur Delahay Rees of Pennard Vicarage, Swansea (d 1956); 3 da (Victoria b 1971, Emily b 1975, Caroline b 1978); *Career* agric & economical advsr Cons Research Dept 1966-73 (head of Economic Section 1970-73); managed family farm from father's death in 1974; chm Northants, Leics & Rutland Counties Branch of NFU 1983, tres (1976-9) and chm (1979-83) Daventry Constituency Cons Assoc, cncl memb Perry Fndn for Agric Research 1966- (pres 1984-), special advsr Min of Agriculture, Fisheries & Food 1984-86, sec Cons Backbench Agric Ctee 1987-, chm Parly Charity Law Reform Panel 1988-; memb: Agric Select Ctee 1987-, Agric and Food Res Cncl 1988-; *Recreations* countryside, shooting, snooker, poetry, travel; *Clubs* Farmers'; *Style*— Timothy Boswell, Esq, MP; Lower Aynho Grounds, Banbury, Oxon OX17 3BW (☎ 0869 810224); House of Commons, London SW1A 0AA (☎ 01 219 3000)

BOSWOOD, Anthony Richard; QC (1986); s of Noel Gordon Paul Boswood, of Radnage, Bucks, and Cicily Ann, *née* Watson; *b* 1 Oct 1947; *Educ* St Paul's, New Coll Oxford (BCL, MA); *m* 4 Jan 1973, Sarah Bridget, da of Sir John Lindsay Alexander, 3 da (Eleanor b 1976, Louise b 1978, Grace b 1983); *Career* called to the Bar Middle Temple 1970; *Recreations* opera, riding, tennis; *Clubs* Hurlingham; *Style*— Anthony Boswood, Esq, QC; Fountain Court, Temple, London EC4 (☎ 01 583 3335, fax 01 353 0329/1794, car tel 0860 419437, telex 8813408 FONLEG G); Podere Casanuova, Pieveasciata, Castelnuovo Berardenga (SI), Italy

BOSWORTH, Sir Neville Bruce Alfred; KBE (1987, CBE 1982); s of William Charles Neville Bosworth, of nr Birmingham (decd), and Nellie Ada Lawton *née* Wheeler (decd); *b* 18 April 1918; *Educ* King Edward's Sch Birmingham, Birmingham Univ (LLB); *m* 22 Aug 1945, Charlotte Marian, da of William Jacob Davis, of Birmingham (decd); 1 s (Simon b 1946), 2 da (Jane b 1949, Josephine b 1950); *Career* slr (adm 1941); sr ptnr Bosworth Bailey Cox & Co; dir: Nat Exhibition Centre and many pte companies; memb (C) Birmingham CC since 1950 and held numerous offices, Lord Mayor 1969-70, govr King Edward Sch (former tstee) chm and tstee Hook Memorial Homes, chm West Midlands Police Authy 1985-, vice chm Assoc of Municipal Authorities 1979-80, Freeman City of B'ham (1982), pres Edgbaston Supper Club 1974-; *Recreations* bridge, football; *Style*— Sir Neville Bosworth; "Hollington", 8 Luttrell Road, Four Oaks, Sutton Coldfield, Birmingham B74 2SR (☎021 308 0647); 54 Newhall Street, Birmingham B3 3QG (☎ 021 236 8091)

BOSWORTH, Simon Charles Neville; s of Sir Neville Bruce Alfred Bosworth, CBE, and Lady Charlotte Marian Bosworth, *née* Davis; *b* 6 August 1946; *Educ* Stouts Hill Gloucester, Bradfield; *m* 2 Feb 1979, Evelyn Fay, da of William Leslie Wallace (d 1984); 1 da (Claudia b 1984); *Career* dir: W H Cutler (Midlands) Ltd 1968-70, Sutton (wine bars) Ltd 1972-74, Hill Alveston & Co Ltd 1973-, Luttrell Park Investmts Ltd 1974, Berkswell Properties Ltd 1983-, Berkswell Investmts Ltd 1984-; *Recreations* football, gardening; *Style*— Simon C N Bosworth, Esq; The Thatched Cottage, Meriden Road, Berkswell, Coventry CV7 7BE; Hill Alveston Gp of Cos, Meriden Road, Berkswell, Coventry CV7 7BE (☎ 0676 33699)

BOTHAM, Brian William; s of William Botham (d 1979), of Staffordshire, and Ellen , *née* Burgess (d 1983); *b* 13 Feb 1932; *Educ* HS Newcastle under Lyme; *m* 14 Oct 1966, Christine, da of Wilfred Lord, of Bagnall Hall, Staffs; 1 s (Richard b 1968); *Career* slr; snr ptnr Clyde Chappell & Botham Slrs, (Tunstall, Meir and Biddulph Staffs); *Style*— Brian W Botham, Esq; The Retreat, Farley, nr Oakamoor, Staffs (☎ 0538 702230); 84 Weston Rd, Meir, Stoke-on-Trent (☎ 599577)

BOTT, Alan John; s of Albert John Henry Bott, and Eileen Mary, *née* Spiers; *b* 30 Mar 1935; *Educ* King's Coll Sch Wimbledon, Merton Coll Oxford (MA); *m* 10 Sept 1966, Caroline Gaenor, da of Frank Leslie Williams (d 1943) and Barbara Gwyneth Manby; 2 s (Jonathan b 3 April 1968, Simon b 26 June 1970), 1 da (Alison b 24 March 1972); *Career* dir The NZ Shipping Co 1971 (joined 1956), dir P & O Containers Ltd (formerly Overseas Containers Ltd) 1976-, chm The Aust and NZ Shipping Confces

1978-, dir CAACE and CENSA; churchwarden Godalming Parish Church 1979-, tstee Godalming Museum 1986-; FSA 1965; *Books* Monuments in Merton College Chapel (1964), Sailing Ships of the NZSCO (1973), Baptisms and Marriages at Merton College Oxford (1981), Godalming Parish Church (1988); *Recreations* tennis, gardening, writing & lecturing on the history of euro architecture; *Clubs* Travellers'; *Style*— Alan Bott, Esq; Rake Court, Milford, Godalming, Surrey GU8 5AD (☎ 048 68 654); P & O Containers Ltd, Beagle House, Braham St, London E1 8EP (☎ 01 488 1313)

BOTT, (Charles) Harry Arden; s of Richard Harry Bott (d 1976), of Benington Lordship, Stevenage, Herts, and Esme' Blanche, *née* Brierley; *b* 26 Feb 1935; *Educ* Eton, Trinity Coll Cambridge (MA); *m* 4 April 1959 (Sarah) Naylor da of late George Romney Fox, of Trewardreva, Constantine, Falmouth, Cornwall; 3 s (Richard b 6 Oct 1963, Andrew b 11 June 1965, Harry b 7 Dec 1966), 1 da (Susan b 12 April 1960); *Career* Nat Serv 2 Lt 4 QOH 1954; farmer 1959-, dir Lea Valley Water Co 1985-; chm Benington Parish Cncl, ctee memb CLA; pres: local Young Farmers Club, Herts Assoc for Care and Resettlement of Offenders; exec ctee memb Herts Conservation Soc, JP Hertford & Ware 1965-86, High Sheriff of Herts 1987-88, gen cmmr for income tax 1964-,; *Recreations* country sports, flying old light aircraft; *Style*— Harry Bott, Esq; Benington Lordship, Stevenage, Hertfordshire (☎ 043 885 668)

BOTT, Prof Martin Harold Phillips; s of Harold Bott (d 1958), and Dorothy, *née* Phillips (d 1970); *b* 12 July 1926; *Educ* Clayesmore Sch Dorset, Magdalene Coll Cambridge (BA, PhD); *m* 17 April 1961, Joyce Cynthia, da of Flying Offr John William Hughes (d 1969), of Lewes, Sussex; 2 s (Andrew Martin b 28 Aug 1962, Nicholas John b 6 Jan 1964), 1 da (Jacqueline Joyce Dorothy b 16 Jan 1966); *Career* Nat Serv RCS 1945-48 (Lt); Durham Univ: Turner and Newall Res fell dept of geology 1954-56, lectr in geophysics 1956-63, reader 1963-66, prof 1966-88, res prof pt/t 1988-; anglian reader St Nicholas Church Durham; FRS 1977, FRAS, FGS; *Books* The Interior of the Earth (1982), and ed for other pubns; *Recreations* mountain walking; *Style*— Prof Martin Bott; 11 St Mary's Close, Shincliffe, Durham DH1 2ND (☎ 091 386 4021), Department of Geological Sciences, Durham University, South Road, Durham DH1 3LE (☎ 091 374 2511)

BOTT, Rosemary Margaret; da of Brian Russell Thorpe, CBE, of 55 First Ave, Worthing, Sussex, and Ann Sinclair, *née* Raby; *b* 27 Nov 1956; *Educ* Convent of Our Lady of Sion, Worthing, Southampton Univ (LLB, upper second Maxwell Law Prize); *m* 1980, Adrian Bott; *Career* admitted slr 1980; marketing ptnr Frere Cholmeley 1988- (ptnr 1986, articled 1978); The Law Society, The Holborn Law Society; *Recreations* skiing, sailing, swimming, theatre (dance and opera); *Style*— Ms Rosemary Bott; 28 Lincoln's Inn Fields, London WC2A 3HH (☎ 01 405 7878, fax 01 405 9056, telex 27623 Freres G)

BOTTENHEIM, Michael Charles; s of Jack Charles Bottenheim (d 1972), and Caryl Rosemary Squires, *née* Baring-Gould (d 1978); *b* 1 Nov 1947; *Educ* Leiden Univ - Netherlands Doctoral in Law (1970); Michigan State Univ -(1971); *m* 1981, Yvonne Maria Josephina, da of Edwin Eugen Meile (ret); 2 children; *Career* Pierson Heldring & Pierson, Amsterdam NL 1972-76; asst mangr: Citicorp Int Bank Ltd, London UK 1976-79, Citicorp Int Finance SA, Zurich- CH 1979-80; exec dir Citicorp Int Bank Ltd, exec dir Lazard Bros & Co Ltd, (London UK); *Recreations* skiing, reading, opera; *Style*— Michael Bottenheim, Esq; Lazard Bros & Co Ltd, 21 Moorfields, London EC2P 2HT (☎ 01 588 2721, fax 01 628 2485)

BOTTERILL, Deryck; s of Cecil Botterill (d 1966), of St Austell, Cornwall, and Adela, *née* Salt (d 1978); *b* 31 May 1933; *Educ* St Austell GS; *m* 9 Aug 1958, Anne Fraser, da of Edward Fraser Treweek (d 1957), of St Austell, Cornwall; 1 s (Paul b 1964), 1 da (Hilary b 1961); *Career* CA; articles clerk Phillips Frith & Co St Austell, managing clerk Tribe Clerk & Co Bristol 1956-59; supervisor and sr mngr Cooper Bros & Co London 1959-64, mangr new issue dep Wm Brandt's Sons & Co Ltd London 1964-66, asst to fin controller/fin dir (corporate fin) Inchcape & Co Ltd 1966-71, dir Gray Dawes & Co Ltd 1966-77, ptnr Kidsons CA London 1971-, chm Kidsons Assocs Ltd 1982-, chm Kidsons Corporate Fin Ltd 1988-; Insp DTI 1987-; reader licensed to Anglican Parish of St Nicholas Great Bookham; memb Worshipful Co of Pattenmakers 1978; FCA 1956; *Books* The Creation and Protection of Capital (contrib 1974); *Recreations* flat green bowls, walking, cross country skiing, theology, family history; *Clubs* City Livery; *Style*— Deryck Botterill, Esq; Kidsons, Russell Square House, 10-12 Russell Square, London WC1B 5AE (☎ 01 436 3636, fax 01 436 6603, telex 263901)

BOTTOMLEY, Alan Ingham; TD; s of George R Bottomley (d 1980), and Olive, *née* Ingham; *b* 14 Nov 1931; *Educ* Shrewsbury; *m* 25 March 1961, Jane Susan, da of Robert Werner (d 1973), of Harrogate; 1 s (Simon b 1962), 1 da (Anabel b 1964); *Career* Maj RA (TA), ret 1965; slr; jt sr ptnr Hammond Suddards Bradford and Leeds; *Recreations* sailing, opera, theatre, travel; *Clubs* Army and Navy; *Style*— Alan I Bottomley, TD; Dormy Lodge, 40 Kent Rd, Harrogate, N Yorks; Empire House, 10 Piccadilly, Bradford, W Yorks BD1 3LR

BOTTOMLEY, Baron (Life Peer UK 1984), of Middlesbrough in the Co of Cleveland; Rt Hon Arthur George Bottomley; OBE (1941), PC (1951); s of late George Howard and Alice Bottomley, of Tottenham, Middx; *b* 7 Feb 1907; *Educ* Gamuel Rd Cncl Sch, Toynbee Hall (extension classes); *m* 1936, Dame Bessie Bottomley, DBE (*see* Bottomley, Baroness); *Career* delegate UN 1946, 1947, 1949; parly under-sec Dominions 1946-47, overseas trade soc BOT 1949-51, cwlth affairs soc 1964-66, min overseas devpt 1966-67; MP (Lab): Chatham 1945-50, Rochester and Chatham 1950-59, Middlesborough East 1962-74, Teeside Middlesborough 1974-83; former London organiser NUPE; chm: Select Commons Ctee Race Rels and Immigration 1969-71, House of Commons Cmmn 1980-83; tres Cwlth Parly Assoc 1974-78; chm Attlee Fndn 1978-; Freeman City of London, Chatham, Middlesborough; Burma Aung San Fagum; *Books* Commonwealth Comrades and Friends, The Use and Abuse of Trade Unions; *Style*— The Rt Hon the Lord Bottomley, OBE, PC; 19 Lichfield Rd, Woodford Green, Essex

BOTTOMLEY, Baroness; Dame Bessie (Ellen) Bottomley; *née* Wiles; DBE (1970); da of Edward Charles Wiles, of Walthamstow, and Ellen, *née* Estall; *b* 28 Nov 1906; *Educ* Maynard Rd Girls' Sch, N Walthamstow Central Sch; *m* 1936, Rt Hon Arthur George Bottomley, OBE, MP (now Baron Bottomley, *qv*); no children; *Career* on staff of NUT 1925-36; memb Walthamstow Borough Cncl 1945-48, Essex CC 1962-65, chm Lab Party Women's Section E Walthamstow 1946-71, Chingford 1973-; memb Forest Group Hosp Man Ctee 1949-73, memb W Roding Community Health Cncl 1973-76, chm Walthamstow Nat Savings Ctee 1949-65, vice-pres Waltham Forest Nat Savings Ctee 1965, chm 1975; Mayoress of Walthamstow 1945-46; memb WVS Regional Staff (SE England) 1941-45, former memb Home Off Advsy Ctee on Child Care, chm of govs of two Secdy Mod Schs 1948-68, also gp of Primary and Infant Schs, chm of govs of High Schs, memb Whitefield Tst; JP 1955-76, Juvenile Bench 1955-71, dep chm Waltham Forest Bench; *Recreations* theatre, gardening; *Style*— The Rt Hon the Lady Bottomley, DBE; 19 Lichfield Rd, Woodford Green, Essex

BOTTOMLEY, Brian Rogers; s of Harry Bottomley, (d 1958), of Sale Cheshire, and Ivy, *née* Wragg (d 1974); *b* 14 Dec 1927; *Educ* Sale Central Sch; *m* 1950,; *Heir* Kathleen, da of Thomas Neville, of Altrincham; 1 s (Nigel Rogers); *Career* chartered engr, fell of Inst of Mech Engrs, fell of Inst of Prod Engrs, tech dir Churchill Machine Tool Co Ltd 1968-73; md: TI Matrix Ltd 1973-81, Staveley Mach Tools 1981-84; chm, md and owner of Kearns-Richards Ltd and KRS Ltd 1984-;; *Recreations* sailing, shooting (Br short range pistol champion 1969); *Style*— Brian Bottomley, Esq; Kearns-Richards Ltd, Atlantic St, Broadheath, Altrincham, Cheshire (☎ 061 928 3284)

BOTTOMLEY, James Barry; s of Edgar Bottomley (d 1981), of 'The Towers', Lytham St Annes, freeman of the Borough of Mossley, and Elizabeth Pryce Bottomley *née* Thompson (d 1975); *b* 21 Feb 1940; *Educ* The Hulme GS for Boys, Oldham, Manchester Univ Degree LLB (Hons) (Vict); *Career* slr 1968: NP (1984), Paul Harris Fellow, appointed by the Rotary Club of Bredbury & Romiley 1975; *Recreations* ornithology, field studies; *Clubs* Manchester Literary and Philosophical Soc; *Style*— James Bottomley; 'The Gables', Stalybride, Cheshire SK15 2RT (☎ 061 303 0578); Castle's, 61 Mottram Rd, Stalybridge, Cheshire SK15 2QP (☎ 061 338 2135)

BOTTOMLEY, Sir James Reginald Alfred; KCMG (1973, CMG 1965); s of Sir (William) Cecil Bottomley, KCMG, CB, OBE (d 1954), and Alice Thistle, *née* Robinson, JP; *b* 12 Jan 1920; *Educ* King's Coll Sch Wimbledon, Trinity Cambridge; *m* 1941, Barbara Evelyn, da of Henry Vardon, of Market Drayton; 2 s (including Peter Bottomley, MP, *qv*) and 1s decd, 2 da; *Career* Inns of Court Regt NW Europe 1940-46; Commonwealth Relations Off 1946, S Africa 1948-50, Pakistan 1953-55, USA 1955-59, UN New York 1959, dep high cmmr Malaysia 1963-67, dep under-sec of state FCO 1970, ambass to S Africa 1973-76, perm UK rep to UN at Geneva 1976-78; dir Johnson Matthey plc 1979-85; *Recreations* golf; *Style*— Sir James Bottomley, KCMG; 22 Beaufort Place, Thompson's Lane, Cambridge CB5 8AG

BOTTOMLEY, Jeffrey; s of George Henry Bottomley (d 1981), of Audenshan, Manchester, Lancs, and Ada Lily, *née* Mathews (d 1985); *b* 29 Mar 1940; *Educ* St Margarets Sch Manchester, Manchester Art Sch; *m* 14 Feb 1974, Beverley Ann, da of Henry Arthur Mantle, of Weston-super-Mare; *Career* art dir Image Arts Ltd 1973-78, chm Kingsley Cards Ltd 1980-(md 1979-80); *Recreations* collector of classic cars, antiques and silver; *Clubs* White Elephant, Stringfellows, Jaguar Drivers, Fleet St; *Style*— Jeffrey Bottomley, Esq; Horseshoes, High St, Nash, Milton Keynes MK17 0ED (☎ 0908 502 943); La Alcazaba, Puerto Banus, Marbella, Spain; Kingsley Card Ltd, Catsbrain Farm, Oakley, Aylesbury, Bucks (☎ 08447 8874)

BOTTOMLEY, Peter James; MP (C) Eltham 1983; s of Sir James Bottomley, *qv*; *b* 30 July 1944; *Educ* Westminster, Trinity Coll Cambridge; *m* 1967, Virginia Hilda Brunette Maxwell, MP, *qv*, da of John Garnett, CBE, *qv*; 1 s, 2 da; *Career* MP (C) Greenwich Woolwich West 1975-83; sec Cons Parly Social Servs Ctee 1977-79, sec Cons Foreign Affairs Ctee 1979-81, PPS to min of state FCO 1982-83, PPS to sec of state Social Services 1983-84; parly undersec of state: Dept of Employment 1984-86, Dept of Transport (min for roads) 1986-; chm: Br Union of Family Orgns 1973-80, Family Forum 1980-82, C of E Children's Soc 1983-84; tstee Christian Aid 1978-84; *Recreations* children, sailing; *Clubs* TGWU; *Style*— Peter Bottomley, Esq, MP; House of Commons, London SW1 (☎ 01 219 5060)

BOTTOMLEY, Virginia Hilda Brunette Maxwell; JP, MP (C) Surrey South-West 1984-; da of John Garnett, CBE, *qv*; *b* 12 Mar 1948; *Educ* Putney HS, Essex Univ (BA), LSE (MSc); *m* 1967, Peter James Bottomley, MP, *qv*; 1 s, 2 da; *Style*— Virginia Bottomley, JP, MP; House of Commons, London SW1

BOUCHER, Arthur James Kinnear; s of Frederick Boucher, OBE (d 1982); *b* 3 Oct 1934; *Educ* Campbell Coll, Queen's Univ Belfast; *m* 1962, Karen, da of William Andrew Leitch, CB, of Belfast; 4 da; *Career* FCA Ireland; chm Francis Curley Ltd; *Style*— Arthur Boucher, Esq; 9 Tweskard Park, Belfast BT4 2JY (☎ 0232 63153)

BOUCHIER, Lady; (Isabella) Dorothy Guyver; da of Frank Guyver Britton, MIMechE, MInstMet (d 1934), of Elmdon, Essex, and Alice Hiller (d 1966), of San Francisco; ggda of Count Johann Friedrich von Hillerscheidt, of Berlin; *b* 14 Feb 1922; *Educ* Claremont Sch England, Mills Coll Calif, San Francisco Conservatory of Music; *m* 1968, as his 2 w, Air Vice-Marshal Sir Cecil Arthur Bouchier, KBE, CB, DFC (d 1979), s of Arthur Couch Bouchier, of Chichester (d 1904); 1 step s; *Career* composer, author, poet (under maiden name); own TV programme NHK, Tokyo 1960-70; music pubs include orchestral suites Tokyo Impressions, Yedo Fantasy (Los Angeles 1957); Cantata And Certain Women (New York 1957); 20 folksongs of Japan (Tokyo 1969); *Books* A Haiku Journey (Tokyo 1975), National Parks of Japan (Tokyo 1980), The Japanese Crane: Bird of Happiness Tokyo 1981), Totto-chan: the Little Girl at the Window (trans Tokyo 1982); The Spider's Thread and other stories (trans Tokyo 1987); *Recreations* chess, shell collecting, birdwatching, watercolour painting; *Clubs* RAF, International House of Japan; *Style*— Lady Bouchier; 2275 Isshiki, Hayama, Kanagawa-ken 240-01, Japan (☎ 0468 75 1217); c/o Barclays Bank plc, 208 Kensington High St, London W8 7RJ

BOUCHIER, Prof Ian Arthur Dennis; s of Edward Alfred Bouchier, of Cape Town, SA, and May, *née* Simons; *b* 7 Sept 1932; *Educ* Rondebosch Boys HS, Cape Town Univ, London Univ, Boston Univ Med Sch USA (MB, ChB, MD); *m* 5 Sept 1959, Patricia Norma, da of Thomas Henshilwood (d 1985), of Cape Town, SA; 2 s (Anthony James b 1962, David Ian b 1964); *Career* med registrar Groote Schuur Hosp 1958-61; various res posts 1961-65: Royal Free Hosp London, Boston Univ Med Sch; sr lectr in med London Univ 1965-70 (reader 1970-73); prof of medicine: Dundee Univ 1973-86, Edinburgh Univ 1986-; memb: Chief Scientist Ctee in Scotland, Tenovus-Scotland Advsy Ctee, Cncl of Mgmnt Inst of Occupational Med; chm Scot Aids Res Appeal; Sec-Gen World Orgn of Gastroenterology, former memb MRC, former dean Faculty of Med Dundee Univ; FRCP 1970, FRCPE 1973, FRSE 1985, FIBiol 1988; *Books* Gastroenterology (1973, 1977, 1982), Recent Advances in Gastroenterology (1976, 1980, 1983), Clinical Investigation of Gastrointestinal Function (1969, 1981, 1988), Textbook of Gastroenterology (1984); *Recreations* gardening, history of whaling, music; *Clubs* New (Edinburgh), Angus; *Style*— Prof Ian Bouchier; Department of Medicine, Royal Infirmary, Edinburgh EH3 9YW (☎ 031 229 2477, fax 031 229 2948, telex 727 442 (UNIVED G)

BOUCKLEY, Christopher Paul Michael; s of John Gordon Bouckley, and Shelagh Mary, *née* McCrea; *b* 21 Mar 1956; *Educ* Colchester Royal GS, Corpus Christi Coll Cambridge (MA); *m* 16 April 1979, Alison Forster, da of Wilfred Walker (d 1972); 1 s (Timothy b 22 April 1987), 1 da (Stephanie b 15 May 1985); *Career* Euro res analyst Quilter Goodison & Co 1978-80, sr Euro fund mangr Hill Samuel Investmt Mgmnt 1980-83, dir Carnegie Int Ltd 1983- (md 1985-); *Recreations* tennis, country pursuits; *Style*— Christopher Bouckley, Esq; Carnegie Int Ltd, Gate House, 1 Farringdon St, Ludgate Circus, London EC4 (☎ 01 489 1947, fax 01 236 2990, telex 892409)

BOUDARD, Robin; JP; s of Mark Victor Charles Boudard (d 1969), of Notts, and Isabel Helen, *née* Blurton (d 1979); *b* 29 Mar 1925; *Educ* Sedbergh Sch Yorks, Corpus Christi Coll Cambridge; *m* 1967, Elizabeth Isobel (d 1979), da of Noel William Radford (d 1977), of Notts; 1 s (Simon b 1970), 1 da (Lucinda b 1973); *Career* textile manufacturer, hon sec Roosevelt Scholarship; *Recreations* fishing; *Clubs* Brooks's, St James's Street; *Style*— Robin Boudard, Esq, JP; The Old Vicarage, Bleasby, Nottinghamshire (☎ 0636 830254); Christopher Day Ltd, Plumptre Place, Stoney Street, Nottingham (☎ 0602 505505)

BOUGHEY, Lady; Gillian Claire; da of Maj Robert Moubray, DL, late 16th Lancers (d 1961), of Kelso, Roxburghshire; *b* 15 Oct 1933; *m* 1976, as his 2 w, Sir Richard Boughey, 10 Bt, JP, DL (d 1978); *Style*— Lady Boughey; The Old Rectory, Quarley, Andover, Hants SP11 8PZ (☎ 026 488 245)

BOUGHEY, James Richard; s of Sir Richard Boughey, 10 Bt, JP, DL (d 1978); h to Btcy of bro, Sir John Boughey, 11 Bt; *b* 29 August 1960; *Educ* Eton, Royal Agricultural Coll Cirencester; *Career* agriculture; *Clubs* Cavalry and Guards'; *Style*— James Boughey, Esq

BOUGHEY, Sir John George Fletcher; 11 Bt (GB 1798); s of Sir Richard Boughey, 10 Bt, JP, DL (d 1978); *b* 12 August 1959; *Educ* Eton, Univ of Harare; *Heir* bro, James Richard Boughey; *Career* medical; *Clubs* Boodle's; *Style*— Sir John Boughey, Bt; Bratton House, Westbury, Wilts

BOUGHTON, John Henry; OBE (1967); s of Thomas Trafford Boughton (d 1959), of Bucks, and Fanny Boughton, *née* Smith (d 1958); *b* 2 Sept 1918; *Educ* Dr Challoners GS Amersham; *m* 1949, Elisabeth Anne, da of Harold Hawgood (d 1970); 1 s (John b 1968), 4 da (Gillian b 1949, Ruth b 1952, Margaret b 1956, Pamela b 1960); *Career* dir: T T Boughton & Sons Ltd 1942-, Reynolds Boughton Ltd 1946-; chm: Agricultural Enterprises Ltd 1957-, Ulrich Manufacturing Co (GB) Ltd 1965, Buckets Imports Ltd 1963-, TTB Fabrications Ltd 1966-; dir Anchorpac Ltd 1966-, Scottom Trailers Ltd 1970-, Hearncrest Boughton Engrg Ltd 1974, Boughton Transmissions Ltd 1974-, Reynolds Boughton Chassis Ltd 1977-; govr: Dr Challoners GS Amersham 1983, Coll of Further Educn Amersham 1985, Counsel of Order of St John Bucks Div 1985; *Recreations* sailing, travelling, winter sports, reading, writing, painting; *Style*— John Boughton, OBE; 69 Amersham Road, Little Chalfont, Bucks HP6 6SP (☎ 02404 2480); T T Boughton & Sons Ltd, Bell Lane, Amersham, Bucks HP6 6PE (☎ 02404 4411, telex 83132, fax 02404 5218)

BOUGHTON, Michael Linnell Gerald; s of Edward Morley Westwood Boughton (d 1951), and Iris Dorothy, *née* Linnell; *b* 14 May 1925; *Educ* King Edwards Sch Birmingham (HND); *m* 1953, Barbara Janette, da of Sir Ivan Arthur Rice Stedeford, GBE (d 1975); 3 children; *Career* serv WWII, Capt RE Middle East; co dir; dep gp md TI Gp 1982-84, dep chm 1984-86, md (operations) 1984-86; chm: TI Domestic Appliances 1974-83, Midland Aluminium 1975-, TI Raleigh Int 1981-85; dir: TI Gp 1964-86, Br Aluminium 1973-82, EIS Gp 1979-84 and 1986-; bd memb Port of London Authy; *Recreations* sailing, golf; *Clubs* Huntercombe Golf; *Style*— Michael Boughton, Esq; Little Heath, Crays Pond, Oxon (☎ 0491 872622)

BOUGHTON, Stephen David; s of Gerald Leslie Grantham Boughton, and Marjorie Hilda, *née* Johns (d 1986); *b* 29 Sept 1955; *Educ* George Abbot Boy's Sch Guildford, Trinity Hall Cambridge (MA); *Career* slr: assoc Sullivan & Cromwell NY 1982-83, ptnr Linklaters & Paines 1986- (slr 1980-82); memb: Law Soc, City of London Slr Co; *Recreations* sport, travel, theatre, cinema; *Style*— S D Boughton, Esq; Linklaters & Paines, Barrington House, 59/67 Gresham St, London EC2V 7JA (☎ 01 606 7080)

BOUGHTON, (Thomas) Trafford; s of T T Boughton (d 1959), of Amersham, and Fanny, *née* Smith (d 1958); *b* 25 Oct 1913; *m* 1, 25 Feb 1943, Barbara, *née* Langston; 3 s (Thomas b 1947, Richard b 1950, Stephen b 1952), 1 da (Bridget b 1944); m 2, 15 May 1968, Diana, da of William Southam Cox; 2 s (Robert b 1969, Edward b 1974); *Career* dir T T Boughton & Sons Ltd 1942 (chm 1959); *Style*— Trafford Boughton, Esq; Dodds Mill, Chenies, Bucks WD3 6EU (☎ 09278 2973); Boughton Gp, Bell Lane, Amersham, Bucks (☎ 02404 4411, telex 83132, fax 02404 5218)

BOULAY; *see*: Houssemayne du Boulay

BOULDEN, Daphne Fraser; da of William Stanley Richards (d 1955), of S Devon, and Janette Fraser Kalberer (d 1939); *b* 21 July 1919; *Educ* Roundham Sch Paignton, Triangle Secretarial Coll London; *m* 27 May 1947, Claud Peter Fabian (d 1982), s of The Rev Leonard Boulden (d 1945), of Middlesex; *Career* sec to General Practitioners, Lab Technician; main work at Victoria Memorial Hosp Deal (outpatients, path lab, wards 1944-55), with various Drs and Husband; ret fulltime 1971, pt/t work continues; *Recreations* swimming, writing, watercolours, English porcelain; *Style*— Mrs Daphne F Boulden

BOULT, David Luard; s of Maj Peter Boult, MC (d 1955), of Hoylake; *b* 6 Dec 1924; *Educ* Shrewsbury; *m* 1957, Elizabeth Anne, da of David Collett, of Rickmansworth, Herts; 2 s, 1 da; *Career* serv WWII, Capt RE; dir: BICC Cables 1980-83, Community of St Helens Tst Ltd 1983-87; chm Merseyside Playing Fields Assoc 1978-84; bd memb Merseyside and N Wales Electricity Bd 1983-; *Recreations* golf, gardening, Rugby Union admin; *Clubs* Delamere Forest Golf, Liverpool RUFC, Liverpool Racquets; *Style*— David Boult, Esq; Manor House, Norley, Cheshire (☎ 0928 88382); Community of St Helens Tst Lts, PO Box 36, St Helens, Merseyside (☎ 0744 696770)

BOULT, Lt-Col Peter Walter Swinton; TD; s of Maj Peter Swinton Boult, MC (d 1955), of New Bunnee, Hoylake, Cheshire, and Rose Cawston, *née* Pattisson (d 1948); *b* 13 Sept 1919; *Educ* Shrewsbury; *m* 11 June 1949, (Elizabeth) Jane, da of Sir Frank Samuel Alexander, 1 Bt (d 1959); 2 s (Nigel b 1952, d 1984, Geoffrey b 1955), 2 da (Rosanne b 1950, Alison b 1953); *Career* WWII cmmnd 2 Lt RA TA 1939, served 149 RHA Regt Western Desert, instr RA OCTU Cairo, served 102 Regt Northumberland Hussars, instr Gunnery Sch of Artillery Salisbury Plain 1944, demob 1946; cmd Lt Col 290 (City of London) FD Regt RA (TA) 1955-57; articled to CAs Liverpool 1937-39, produce merchant and dir of cos trading in London Commodity Exchange 1946-64; dir: Symbol Biscuits Ltd (subsid of J Lyons & Co Ltd) 1964-68, Metlex Industs (chm 1980-82); dir of other cos within IS plc, pres Hardware Mfrs Assoc 1977-79; cncl memb CBI 1973-82 (chm Surrey area) 1977-81, cncl chm Nat Artillery Assoc 1969-80, dep chm TA Sports Bd 1970-79; Liveryman: Worshipful Co of Distillers 1958, Worshipful Co of Tallow Chandler 1960 (Warden 1980); *Recreations* watching sport, bridge, golf, golf course design; *Clubs* MCC, Aldeburgh and Chislehurst GCs, Kent CCC; *Style*— Lt-Col Peter W S Boult, TD; Wellwood, Chislehurst, Kent BR7 5PJ (☎ 01 467 3216)

BOULTER, Brig Hereward Emanuel; CBE (1965), DSO (1945); s of Edward Emanuel Boulter, of Chelmsford; *b* 12 June 1911; *Educ* Brentwood Sch, RMC Sandhurst; *m* 1949, Rosemary, da of Robert Owen-Swaffield, of Dorset; 1 s, 2 da; *Career* 2 Lt IA 1931, serv WWII: India, Middle E, Italy; Lt-Col 1944, cmd First Frontier Force Regt 1944-46, cmd First West Yorks Regt 1954-57, Brig 1962, Dep Fortress Cdr Gibraltar 1962-64, ret; sec Royal Patriotic Fund Corpn 1965-79; *Recreations* racing, bird watching; *Clubs* Army and Navy; *Style*— Brig Hereward Boulter, CBE, DSO; Upper Herons, Fyfield, Ongar, Essex (☎ 0277 85362)

BOULTING, Roy A C; s of Walter Arthur Boulting (d 1957) and Rose Bennett (d 1980); twin bro of John Boulting, bro of Sydney Boulting, *qv*; *b* 21 Nov 1913; *Educ* HMS Worcester, Reading Sch; *m* 1, 1936 (m dis 1941), Angela, da of Rt Hon Edmond Warnock, KC, Home Sec NI (d 1971); m 2, 1942 (m dis 1951), Mrs Jean Capon, da of Eric Gamage, chm Gamages Ltd; 2 s (Jonathan Eric Shaw b 1944, Laurence Roy Oliver b 1945); m 3, 1951 (m dis 1964), Mrs Enid Munnick, da of Pieter Groenwald, of S Africa (she m 1970, 9 Earl of Hardwicke); 3 s (Fitzroy Linde b 1951, Rupert Alan Francis David b 1952, Edmund Charles Alexander b (twin) 1952); common-law-wife (until 1967), Victoria, da of James Vaughan; 1 s (Fitzroy William Humphrey Rufus b 1965); m 4, 1971 (m dis 1978), Hayley Mills, the actress, da of Sir John Mills, CBE (*qv*); 1 s (Crispian b 1973); m 5, 1978 (m dis 1984), Sandra, da of Gilbert Spencer Payne; *Career* cmmd Yorks Hussars RAC 1940, seconded Army Film Unit 1941; active serv: Norway, france, Belgium, Holland, Germany; formed charter film Prodns Ltd with late twin bro John 1937; for Army made Desert Victory (1942), Tunisian Victory (1943), Burma Victory (1945). After war films made by Brothers incl: Brighton Rock 1947, The Guinea Pig 1948, Privates Progress 1951, Carlton Browne of the FO 1958, I'm All Right Jack 1960, The Family Way 1967, There's A Girl In My Soup (1973); dir: British Lion Films 1958-72, Shepperton Studios 1964-70; memb: exec ctee Assoc of Cine Technicians 1946-47, cncl Dirs and Producers Rights Soc 1987, cncl local Radio Assoc 1965; *Recreations* film making; *Clubs* The Lord's Taverners; *Style*— Roy Boulting, Esq; Charter Film Productions Ltd, Twickenham Film Studios, St Margaret's, Twickenham, Middlesex

BOULTING, Sydney Arthur Rembrandt; *see*: Cotes, Peter

BOULTON, Sir (Harold Hugh) Christian; 4 Bt (UK 1905); s of Sir (Denis Duncan) Harold (Owen) Boulton, 3 Bt (d 1968); *b* 29 Oct 1918; *Educ* Ampleforth; *m* 1944, Patricia Mary, OBE (who re-assumed by deed poll 1951 her maiden name of Maxwell-Scott), da of late Maj-Gen Sir Walter Joseph Constable-Maxwell-Scott, 1 Bt, CB, DSO; *Career* late Capt Irish Gds (Sup Reserve); *Style*— Sir Christian Boulton, Bt; c/o Bank of Montreal, City View Branch, 1481 Merivale Rd, Ottawa, Ontario, Canada

BOULTON, Clifford John; CB (1985); s of Stanley Boulton and Evelyn, *née* Hey, of Cocknage, Staffs; *b* 25 July 1930; *Educ* Newcastle-under-Lyme HS, St John Coll Oxford (MA); *m* 1955, Anne, da of Rev E E Raven, of Cambridge; 1 adopted s, 1 adopted da; *Career* Nat Serv RAC 1949-50 Lt Staffs Yeomanry TA; clerk in Ho of Commons 1953-: clerk of Select Ctees on Procedure 1964-68 and 1976-77, Public Accounts 1968-70, Parly Questions 1971-72, Privileges 1972-77; clerk Overseas Off 1977-79, princ clerk Table Off 1979-83, clerk asst 1983-87, Clerk of the House of Commons 1987- sch govr then bd memb Church Schs 1965-79; *Publications* Erskine May's Parliamentary Practice (ed 21 edn), contrib to Halsbury's Laws of England (4 edn), parly jnls; *Style*— Clifford Boulton, Esq; The Elms, Lyddington, Oakham, Rutland, Leics LE15 9LT (☎ 0572 823487); House of Commons, London SW1A 0AA

BOULTON, (Joseph) Sidney; s of Harry Boulton (d 1981), and Sarah, *née* Bithell (d 1981); *b* 15 May 1930; *Educ* Hawarden GS Flintshire; *m* 28 Aug 1954, Winifred Eileen, da of William James Wilson (d 1983); 2 da (Linda Joan b 1955, Elizabeth Anne b 1961); *Career* asst Chester Magisterial Serv 1946-53, sr asst Flintshire Magistrates' Cts Ctee 1954-55, princ asst Salop Magistrates Cts Ctee 1956-64, dep clerk to the Justices Rochdale magistrates Cts Ctee 1965-71; clerk to the Justices for 5 Divns in Herefordshire 1972-85; chief Exec to the Hereford & Worcs Magistrates' Cts Ctee 1986-; *Recreations* ballroom dancing, model railways; *Style*— Sidney Boulton, Esq; 91 Lichfield Avenue, Hereford HR1 2RL (☎ 0432 50458); Shirehall, Hereford HR1 2HP (☎ 0432 279729)

BOULTON, Sir William Whytehead; 3 Bt (UK 1944), of Braxted Park, Co Essex, kt 1975, CBE (1958), TD (1949); 2 s of Sir William Boulton, 1 Bt, sometime MP (C) Sheffield Central and vice-Chamberlain of HM's Household, by his w Rosalind (d 1969), herself da of Sir John Milburn, 1 Bt; suc bro, Sir Edward (Teddy) Boulton, 2 Bt, 1982; *b* 21 June 1912; *Educ* Eton (Capt Oppidans 1931), Trinity Coll Cambridge; *m* 30 Sept 1944, Margaret Elizabeth, da of late Brig Henry Noel Alexander Hunter, DSO; 1 s (John), 2 da (Julia, Susan); *Heir* s, John Gibson Boulton, b 1946; *Career* serv WWII Middle E with 104 Regt RHA (Essex Yeo) and 14 Regt RHA 1940-44, Staff Coll Camberley 1944, Hon Lt-Col; barr Inner Temple 1936, practised 1937-39; Miny of Justice control branch, legal div Control Cmmn Germany 1945-50; sec: Gen Cncl of the Bar 1950-74, Senate of the Inns of Ct and the Bar 1974-75;; *Books* A Guide to Conduct and Etiquette at the Bar of England and Wales (sixth edn 1975); *Style*— Sir William Boulton, Bt, CBE, TD; The Quarters House, Alresford, nr Colchester, Essex CO7 8AY (☎ 020 622 2450); 37 Rutland Gate, London SW7 (☎ 01 581 2938)

BOULTON-LEA, Paul Anthony; s of Lt-Cdr John Francis Boulton-Lea, VRD, BSc, RN (d 1988), of Ashtead, Surrey, and Joan Doris Boulton-Lea, *née* Palmer; *b* 19 June 1955; *Educ* Sheepnatch Sch, Therfield Sch; *Career* asst housemaster Kingham Hill Sch 1974-75, housefather Nat Childrens Home 1976-77, welfare and recreation offr Queen Elizabeth's Fndn 1978, housefather Marchant Holiday Sch 1979; housemaster Royal Caledonian Sch 1983-; *Recreations* photography, sailing, cooking, travel, conservation; *Style*— Paul A Boulton-Lea, Esq; The Vicarage, Hersham, Walton-on-Thames, Surrey KT12 4AA (☎ 0932 227445); Royal Caledonian Sch, Bushey, Herts WD2 3TS (☎ 0923 226642)

BOURDEAUX, Rev Michael Alan; s of Richard Edward Bourdeaux, and Lillian Myra

Blair; *b* 19 Mar 1934; *Educ* Truro Sch, St Edmund Hall Oxford (MA, BD), Moscow State Univ; *m* 1, 1960, Gillian Mary Davies (d 1978); 1 s (Mark), 1 da (Karen); m 2, 1979, Lorna Elizabeth, da of John Waterton, of Birch Ho, Preston St Mary, Sudbury, Suffolk; 1 s (Adrian); 1 s (Adrian); *Career* ordained deacon 1960, priest 1961; Centre de Recherches Geneva Switzerland res assoc 1965-68, Univ of London, LSE, London res fellow 1968-70; visiting prof St Bernard's Seminary Rochester NY 1969, res fell Roy Inst of Int Affairs 1970-72, Kathryn C Davis Prof of Slavic Studies Wellesley Mass 1981; fndr and gen dir Keston Coll 1969-; memb: Br Tennis Umpires Assoc 1974-, Philharmonia Chorus 1961-; *Books* Opium of the People (1965, 2 edn 1977), Religious Ferment in Russia (1968), Patriarch and Prophets (1970, 2 edn 1975), Faith on Trial in Russia (1971), Land of Crosses (1979), Risen Indeed (1983), Ten Growing Soviet Churches (1987); *Clubs* Athenaeum; *Style*— The Rev Michael Bourdeaux; Bishopsdown, 34 Lubbock Rd, Chislehurst, Kent BR7 5JJ (☎ 01 467 3550); Keston Coll, Heathfield Rd, Keston, Kent BR2 6BA (☎ 0689 50116, telex KESCOL 897684)

BOURDILLON, Mervyn Leigh; JP (1970), DL (1962); s of Prebendary Gerard Leigh Bourdillon (d 1971), and Cara Phyllis Evan-Thomas (d 1971); *b* 9 August 1924; *Educ* Haileybury; *m* 1961, Penelope Anne, da of Peter Wellesbourne Kemp-Welch, OBE (d 1964); 1 s (Patrick), 3 da (Katherine, Sarah, Lucinda); *Career* servd RNVR 1943-46; High Sheriff Breconshire 1970; Vice Lord-Lt of Powys 1978-86; C.C. Breconshire 62-73; Forestry Commr 73-76; Lord-Lt Powys 1986-; *Clubs* Army and Navy; *Style*— Mervyn Bourdillon, Esq, JP

BOURKE, Christopher John; s of John Francis Bourke (d 1967), of Westwood House, Droitwich, and Eileen Winifred, *née* Beddoes (d 1976); *b* 31 Mar 1926; *Educ* Stonyhurst, Oriel Coll Oxford (MA); *m* 23 June 1956, Maureen, da of Gerald Antony Barron-Boshell (d 1935), of Trichinopoly, S India; 2 s (Rory b 20 May 1960, Toby b 7 Feb 1965), 1 da (Cressida b 31 July 1969); *Career* Nat Serv, cmmnd Gloucestershire Regt 1946, ADC to Govr Sir John Huggins served in BAOR and Jamaica; called to the Bar Gray's Inn 1953, Oxford Circuit dir Public Prosecutions 1955-74, Metropolitan Stipendary Magistrate 1974-; *Recreations* painting; *Style*— Christopher Bourke, Esq; 61 Kingsmead Rd, London SW2 3HY (☎ 01 671 3977); Clerkenwell Magistrates Ct

BOURKE, Hon Harry Richard; s of 10 E of Mayo; *b* 23 Sept 1960; *Style*— The Hon Harry Bourke; Doon House, Maam, Co Galway, Eire

BOURKE, John Oliver Paget; s of Sir Paget John Bourke (d 1983), and Susan Dorothy, *née* Killeen; *b* 19 Feb 1937; *Educ* Clongowes Wood Coll, Univ Coll Dublin, BL, BCL; *m* Margaret, da of Joseph Paffrath, of Dublin; 2 s, 2 da; *Career* chm Br Credit Tst Ltd; dir Bank of Ireland 1978-, Hibernian Insur, M D Power Securities Ltd; md UDT Bank Ltd; FCA; *Recreations* sailing (yacht 'Miss Fionnuala'), golf, music; *Clubs* Royal St George Yacht, Milltown Golf, Royal Yacht Sqdn; *Style*— John Bourke, Esq; Albert House, Victoria Road, Dalkey, Dublin, Eire (☎ 858355)

BOURKE, Hon Mrs Geoffrey; Nancy Lisette; da of Douglas Theodore Thring (d 1931), estates bursar of Merton Coll Oxford; *m* 1926, Hon Geoffrey John Bourke (d 1982), FRICS; 4 s of 8 Earl of Mayo; 1 da (Elizabeth b 1928, m 1954 John Auden, of Switzerland; 1 s, 1 da) & 1 da decd 1956; *Style*— The Hon Mrs Geoffrey Bourke; 167 Russell Court, Woburn Pl, London WC1

BOURKE, Hon Mrs Bryan; Patricia May; *née* Dickinson; er da of late Harold Bertie Dickinson, MD, FRCS, of Tannachie, W Malvern, Worcs; *b* 29 July 1912; *Educ* Wycombe Abbey, London Univ (BA); *m* 1952, as his 2 w, Capt the Hon Bryan Longley Bourke, RIF (d 1961, f (by his 1 w) of 10 E of Mayo, *qv*), 3 s of 8 E of Mayo; *Career* section offr WAAF, serv: S Africa, Egypt, England; JP Glos 1959-61, govr Dursley Grammar and Secdy Mod Schs, dist cncllr Wadebridge Cornwall, memb Truro Diocesan Synod and Diocesan Bd of Educn; *Recreations* art active and passive, musical appreciation; *Style*— The Hon Mrs Bryan L Bourke; Dashells, Dog Village, Broadclyst, Exeter, Devon EX5 3AB (☎ 0392 61334)

BOURKE, Hon Patrick Antony; s of 10 E of Mayo; *b* 16 Dec 1955; *Educ* St Aubyn's Rottingdean; *Style*— The Hon Patrick Bourke; Doon House, Maam, Co Galway, Eire

BOURN, Dr John Bryant; CB (1986); s of Henry Thomas Bryant Bourne, Esq, of 65 Dawlish Avenue, Palmers Green, London N13 and Beatrice Grace *née* Pope (d 1979); *b* 21 Feb 1934; *Educ* Southgate Co GS, LSE (BSc, PhD); *m* 21 March 1959, Ardita Ann, da of Maurice Wilfred Fleming (d 1940); 1 s (Jonathan b 1967), 1 da (Sherida b 1962); *Career* dep under sec of state (Defence Procurement) MOD 1985-; dep sec N Ireland Office 1982-85; visiting prof London Sch Economics 1983-; *Recreations* swimming; *Style*— Dr John Bourn; Ministry of Defence, Main Building, Whitehall, London SW1A 2HB

BOURNE, Baroness; Agnes Evelyn; o da of Sir (William) Ernest Thompson (d 1941), of Delverton House, Mottram St Andrew, Prestbury, Cheshire, and Elizabeth Alice, *née* Goodwin; *m* 1928, Maj-Gen Baron Bourne, GCB, KBE, CMG (Life Peer d 1982); 1 s, 1 da; *Style*— The Rt Hon The Lady Bourne

BOURNE, Cecil John; s of Ernest John Bourne (d 1965), and Lilian Emily, *née* Bishop (d 1961); *b* 26 Sept 1920; *Educ* Worcester Royal GS, Birmingham Sch of Architecture (DipArch); *m* 14 June 1952, Adeline Catherine, da of Thomas Reuben Leonard Gibson, MBE (d 1964); 3 s (Richard b 1953, Robert b 1957, Thomas b 1963), 3 da (Rachel b 1955, Josephine b 1965, Lydia b 1976); *Career* chartered architect; WWII Sgt serv: Egypt, Persia, Iraq, Palestine; private practice (founded 1956), Civic Tst Awards 1959, 1962; DOE Housing Medal 1980, King of Prussia's Gold Medal 1987, memb of Art Workers Guild 1971; fell Ancient Monuments Soc 1967; chm and vice-pres Cambridgshire Branch CPRE; chm Cambridge Assoc of Architects 1956-57 and 1967-68; memb Ecclesiastical Architects & Surveyors Assoc; fndr chm Cambridge Civic Soc; memb of Ely Diocesan Advisory Ctee for Care of Churches; chm Listed Buildings Panel Advising Cambridge City Cncl; chm Countryside Advisory Working Party for Cambs County Cncl 1985 and 1986; FRSA, FRSH, ARIBA, FRIBA; *Recreations* watercolour painting, garden landscape, archaeology; *Style*— Cecil J Bourne, Esq; The Abbey, Abbey Lane, Swaffham Bulbeck, Cambridge CB5 0NQ; Commercial End, Swaffham Bulbeck

BOURNE, Lady; Heather Frances; da of Lt-Col F W Burbury, Royal W Kent Regt of Barnsley; *m* 1918, Sir Frederick Chalmers Bourne, KCSI, CIE (d 1977); *Career* awarded (Kaisar-i-Hind gold medal); *Style*— Lady Bourne; Fern Cottage, East Hoathly, nr Lewes, E Sussex BN8 6DP (☎ 082 584 386)

BOURNE, Dr James Gerald; s of Walter William Bourne (d 1921), of Garston Manor, Hertfordshire, and Clara Louise, *née* Hollingworth (d 1941); *b* 6 Mar 1906; *Educ* Rugby, Cambridge Univ (BA, MA), St Thomas' Hosp (MB, BChir, MD, DA); *m* 1, Jenny Liddell (d 1967); 1 s (Michael b 18 Sept 1958); m 2, 18 May 1968, Susan Annette, da of Cdr William de Montiguy Clarke (d 1966), of Stoke Poges; 2 s (William b 9 July 1969, Giles b 22 June 1970); *Career* WWII RAMC 1939-45: France 6 Casualty Clearing Station 1939-40, serv Middle E (gen hosps 1 Mobile Surgical Team Western Desert) 1941-45, ret Maj 1945; casualty offr and house physician St Thoma Hosp 1937-38, ho physician London Chest Hosp 1939, conslt anaestetist: St Thomas Hosp 1946-66, Salisbury Hosp Gp 1950-71; *Books* Nitrous Oxide in Dentistry: Its Danger and Alternatives (1960), Studies In Anaesthitics (1967); *Recreations* fishing, walking, music; *Clubs* RAC; *Style*— Dr James Bourne; Melstock, Nunton, Salisbury, Wilts SP5 4HN (☎ 0722 29734)

BOURNE, Hon Michael Kemp; s of Baron Bourne, GCB, KBE, CMG (Life Peer, d 1982); *b* 9 June 1937; *Educ* Harrow; *m* 1, 1963 (m dis 1980), Penelope Jane, da of Capt H W Blyth, of Wyncombe Hill, Fittleworth, Sussex; 1 s, 2 da; m 2, 1985, Marian Lockhart, eldest da of Maj John Francis Leatherham Robinson, MC, of Bilbrough, Yorks; *Clubs* Cavalry and Guards', City of London; *Style*— The Hon Michael Bourne; 50 Bradbourne St, London SW6 3TE

BOURNE, (Rowland) Richard; s of Arthur Brittan and Edith Mary Bourne; *b* 27 July 1940; *Educ* Uppingham, Brasenose Coll Oxford; *m* 1966, Juliet Mary, da of John Attenborough, CBE, *qv*; 2 s, 1 da; *Career* journalist and author; educn corr The Guardian 1968-72, asst ed New Society 1972-77, dep ed and columnist London Evening Standard 1977-78, ed Learn Magazine 1979; freelance and conslt 1980-83; dep dir Cwlth Inst 1983-89; *Recreations* gardening, fishing, the theatre; *Clubs* RAC; *Style*— Richard Bourne, Esq; 36 Burney St, London SE10 8EX (☎ 01 853 0642)

BOURNE, Sir (John) Wilfrid; KCB (1979, CB 1975), QC (1981); s of Capt Rt Hon Robert Croft Bourne, PC, JP, sometime MP Oxford (d 1938, himself s of Gilbert Bourne, FRS, and Constance, da of Sir John Croft, 2 Bt), by his w Lady Hester, *née* Cairns, da of 4 Earl Cairns; *b* 27 Jan 1922; *Educ* Eton, New Coll Oxford (MA); *m* 1958, Elizabeth Juliet, da of George Romney Fox (d 1969), of Trewardreva, Constantine, Cornwall; 2 s; *Career* WWII Rifle Bde Actg Capt (W/S Lt): W Desert, Tunisia, Italy, NW Europe; barr Middle Temple 1948, bencher 1977, practised Oxford circuit 1969-56; joined Lord Chllr's Off 1956, dep clerk of Crown 1975-77, clerk of the Crown in Chancery and perm sec Lord Chllr's Dept 1977-82, ret 1982; *Recreations* gardening; *Clubs* Leander; *Style*— Sir Wilfrid Bourne, KCB, QC; Povey's Farm, Ramsdell, Basingstoke, Hants (☎ 0256 850158)

BOURNE-ARTON, Maj Anthony Temple; MBE (1944); s of (William) Ronald Temple Bourne, of Walker Hall, Winston, Co Durham (d 1945) and Evelyn Rose Wills (d 1934); a gda of H.O. Wills, co-founder of W D & H O Wills tobacco manufacturers; *b* 1 Mar 1913; *Educ* Clifton, Bristol Univ; *m* 16 July 1938, Margaret Elaine, da of William Denby Arton, JP of Sleningford Park , Ripon, Yorkshire (d 1949); 2 s (Christopher b 1941, Simon b 1949), 2 da (Caroline b 1940, Hilary b 1944); *Career* RA 1933-48 Palestine 1936, France 1939-40 (despatches), N Africa, Sicily, Italy 1944-45, Malaya 1947-48; ret as Maj 1948; CC York NR 1949-61 and CC York WR 1967-70; Bedale RDC 1950-52; JP York NR 1950; gen commr Inc Tax 1952-80; MP (C) Darlington 1959-64; PPS to Home Secretary 1962-64; memb Select Cttee of Estimates 1960-64; memb Yorkshire River Authy 1967-74, chm Yorkshire Regional Land Drainage Cttee and dep chm Yorkshire Water Authy 1974-80; *Recreations* fishing, shooting; *Clubs* (formerly)Carlton, Army and Navy; *Style*— Maj Anthony Bourne-Arton; The Old Rectory, West Tanfield, Ripon, N Yorkshire (☎ 0677 70333)

BOUTFLOWER, John Charles; s of Charles Henry Boutflower (d 1969), and Jacqueline Marie, *née* Culverwell; *b* 26 Jan 1933; *Educ* Cheltenham Coll, Univ of Bristol (BVSc, MRCVS); *m* 9 May 1964, Sheina Bridget, da of Lt Col Douglas Bostock Duff (d 1976); 1 s (Robert Charles b 1965), 1 da (Kirstin Bridget b 1966); *Career* Nat Serv Royal Veterinary Corps, Capt Cyprus 1959-61; veterinary surgeon; dir Wyevern Veterinary Co Ltd 1987-; *Recreations* fishing, hunting, ornithology, rose growing; *Style*— John Boutflower, Esq; Woodcroft House, Woodcroft, Chepstow (☎ 02912 3518); Veterinary Health Centre, 17a Moor Street, Chepstow (☎ 02912 5205)

BOVENIZER, John Gordon Fitzell; s of Vernon Gordon Fitzell Bovenizer, of 6 Cambanks, Union Lane, Cambridge, and Lilian Cherry *née* Rowe (d 1970); family descended from resettled Huguenots from the Palatinate given land near Limerick Ireland in 1706; *b* 26 Jan 1945; *Educ* Tonbridge, Fitzwilliam Coll Cambridge Univ (MA); *m* 1 April 1970, Helma, da of Jose Soares Limaverde of Fortaleza, Ceara, Brazil (d 1985); 3 s (George b 1971, John b 1974, Ernest b 1976); *Career* Banker; exec vice pres of Lloyds Bank plc in New York; dir Lloyds Bank Financial Futures Ltd; *Recreations* sports, chess; *Style*— John Bovenizer, Esq; 35 Swifts Lane, Darien, Conn., USA

BOVEY, Barry William Vincent; OBE (1979); s of William Vincent Bovey (d 1965), of Worcester, and Irene Ida, *née* Holderness (d 1982); *b* 29 Oct 1929; *Educ* Haileybury, Univ of London; *m* 1, 23 June 1954 (m dis 1978), Daphne Joan, da of Cdr Arthur Gordon Marshall RNR (d 1981), of Hampton Ct; 2 s (Michael b 1957, Nigel b 1961); m 2, 22 Dec 1979, Jean Christine, da of Ronald Yeardley Goddard, of Sheffield; *Career* Nat Serv cmmnd RA 1951-53, Capt RA (TA) 1953-57; gp sales dir Robert Jenkins Ltd 1967-72, md Orbit Valve Ltd 1972-, vice pres Energy Industries Cncl 1984 (chm 1980-84), Process Plant EDC: memb Nat Econ Devpt Off 1980-87, chm Int Mktg Gp 1981-87; Freeman: City of London, Worshipful Co of Glovers; FInstM 1980, FIEx 1987, FInstD 1979; *Recreations* yachting, golf; *Clubs* Royal Thames Yacht; *Style*— Barry Bovey, Esq, OBE; Chadmore House, Willersey, Broadway WR12 7PH (☎ 0386 858 922); Orbit Valve Ltd, Orbit House, Swallowfield Way, Hayes, Middx UB3 1DQ (☎ 01 561 8049, fax 01 561 2954, car tel 0860 746 630, telex 938171)

BOVEY, Dr Leonard; s of Alfred Bovey (d 1968, twice Mayor of Exeter), and Gladys, *née* Brereton; *b* 9 May 1924; *Educ* Hele's Sch Exeter, Emmanuel Coll Cambridge (BA, PhD); *m* Nov 1943, Constance, da of Thomas Hudson (d 1970); 1 s (Christopher b 1951), 1 da (Jennifer b 1955); *Career* post doctoral fell Nat Regnl Cncl Ottawa 1950-52; AERE Harwell 1952-65; dir: W Midlands Regnl Office, Miny of Technol 1966-70, Yorks & Humberside DTI 1970-73; cnsllr Scientific & Technol Affrs High Commn Ottawa 1974-77, head Technol Requirements Branch DTI 1977-84, ed Materials & Design 1985-; FInstP; *Recreations* theatre, music; *Clubs* Civil Service; *Style*— Dr Leonard Bovey; 32 Radnor Walk, London SW3 4BN (☎ 01 352 4142; Scientific & Technical Press, Reigate RH2 0NT (☎ 07372 43521, telex 8952387, fax 07372 49471)

BOVEY, Norman Henry; OBE (1957), DSC (1944), VRD (1960); s of Alfred Henry Bovry (d 1940), and Florence Emily, *née* Litle (d 1962); *b* 16 Sept 1922; *Educ* St Dunstans Coll; *m* 21 Dec 1946, Dorothy Yvonne, da of Henry Williams (d 1938); 3 s (Philip Henry b 1948, Andrew John b 1952, William Evan Norman b 1956), 1 da (Susan

Katherine b 1949); *Career* WWII Lt (A) RNVR 1940-46, Cdr (A) RNR and fndg CO Channel Air Div RNVR 1948-62; snr contracts mangr Bovis Ltd 1946-60, gen mangr J Parnell & Son Ltd 1960-68; regnl mngr Midland Construction Indust Trg Bd 1968-87; vice-pres Fleet Air Arm Offrs Assoc; MCIOB; *Recreations* gardening, house maintenance (listed building); *Clubs* Naval and Military; *Style—* Norman H Bovey, OBE, DSC, VRD; Killock House, Laughton, Lutterworth, Leicestershire LE17 6QD (☎ Leicester 402278)

BOVEY, Philip Henry; s of Cdr Norman Henry Bovey, OBE, DSC, VRD, of Killock House, Laughton, Lutterworth, Leics, and Dorothy Yvonne Kent, *née* Kent Williams; *b* 11 July 1948; *Educ* Rugby, Peterhouse Cambridge (BA, MA); *m* 14 Sept 1974, Jenet Alison, da of Canon James Mitchell McTear (d 1973); 1 s (Stephen b 1978), 1 da (Katherine b 1976); *Career* FCO 1970-71, slr 1974, Salughter & May 1972-75, DTI 1976-, under sec Cabinet Off 1985; Companies Act inspr 1984-88; *Recreations* photography; *Style—* Philip Bovey, Esq; 102 Cleveland Gdns, Barnes, London SW13 0AH (☎ 01 876 3710); 10-18 Victoria St, London SW1 (☎ 01 215 3452)

BOVILL, (William) Geoffrey; s of Edward William Bovill (d 1966), and Sylvia Mary Bovill, OBE, *née* Cheston; *b* 8 Oct 1926; *Educ* Eton; *m* 4 March 1957, Prudence Winifred Leonora, da of Maj Gen Clifford Thomason Beckett, CB, CBE, MC (d 1972); 3 s (Hugo b 1958, Desmond b 1960, Giles b 1965); *Career* Lt Grenadier Guards serv NW Europe 1945-48; md Henry W Peabody Grain Ltd 1966-86; chm R C Treatt & Co Ltd 1963-; *Recreations* shooting, gardening, travel; *Style—* Geoffrey Bovill, Esq; Woodham Mortimer Grange, Maldon, Essex (☎ 024 541 2605)

BOWACK, Michael Hamilton; s of Norman Hamilton Bowack (ka 1942), and Vera Marion Ives, *née* Franklin; *b* 26 July 1942; *Educ* Uppingham; *m* 6 Aug 1983, Ann Jennifer, da of Frank Charles Sherwill (d 1988); 1 da (Claire b 1985); *Career* Blease Lloyd & Co 1960-66, Touche Ross & Co 1966-67, various appointments: Imperial Gp plc 1967-74, The RTZ Corpn plc 1974-85, The Plessey Co plc 1985-88, co sec GEC Plessey Telecommunications Ltd 1988-; *Recreations* cricket, rugby football, gardening, music; *Clubs* MCC; *Style—* Michael Bowack, Esq; Pathways, 53 Fairmile Lane, Cobham, Surrey KT11 2DH (☎ 0932 65451); GEC Plessey Telecommunications Ltd, Maidenhead, Berkshire (☎ 0628 23351)

BOWATER, Sir John Vansittart; 4 Bt (UK 1914); s of Capt Victor Spencer Bowater (d 1967), 3 s of 1 Bt; suc unc, Sir (Thomas) Dudley (Blennerhassett) Bowater, 3 Bt, 1972; *b* 6 April 1918; *m* 1943, Joan Kathleen (d 1982), da of Wilfrid Ernest Henry Scullard (d 1963), of Boscombe; 1 s, 1 da; *Heir* s, Michael Patrick Bowater; *Career* dir Oswald Bailey Gp of Cos; town cllr Bournemouth 1983-; *Style—* Sir John Bowater, Bt; 214 Runnymede Ave, Bearwood, Bournemouth, Dorset (☎ 0202 571782)

BOWATER, Marina; da of Lt Alexandre Vassilievich Yakovleff (d 1975), of Imperial Russian Navy, and Nathalia Dmitrievna, *née* Paltova (d 1959); *b* 16 Dec 1920; *Educ* Normanhurst Ct Sch Catsfield Sussex; *m* Dec 1945, Cdr William Henry Irving Bowater; *Career* WAAF 1941-45, special duties (ops), Fighter Cmd; entered commercial world of art with galleries in Kensington and St James's London, specialised in Imperial Russian art (about which little was known at the time) 1959-78, presently a conslt in Russian Art; memb RSPCA; Royal Drawing Soc (full hons cert, 1935); former memb Br Antique Dealers Assoc; *Books* writer of numerous articles on Russian art; *Recreations* writing; *Style—* Mrs Marina Bowater

BOWATER, Hon Lady; Hon Ursula Margaret; *née* Dawson; da of 1 and last Viscount Dawson of Penn, GCVO, KCB, KCMG, PC (d 1945); *b* 1907; *m* 1927, Lt-Col Sir Ian Bowater, GBE, DSO, TD (d 1982), Lord-Mayor of London 1969-70; 1 s, 2 da; *Style—* The Hon Lady Bowater; 38 Burton Court, Franklins Row, London SW3 4SZ (☎ 01 730 2963)

BOWDEN, Andrew; MBE (1961), MP (C) Brighton Kemptown 1970-; s of William Victor Bowden, slr, of Brighton, Francesa Wilson; *b* 8 April 1930; *Educ* Ardingly; *m* 1970, Benita, da of B A Napier, of Brighton; 1 s, 1 da; *Career* worked in paint indust 1955-68; personnel conslt 1967-; contested (C): N Hammersmith 1955, N Kensington 1964, Kemp Town Brighton 1966; jt chm All-Party Parly Gp for Pensioners 1971-; memb select ctee: Expenditure 1973-74, Abortion 1975, Employment 1979-; int chm People to People 1981-; *Recreations* fishing, chess, golf; *Clubs* Carlton; *Style—* Andrew Bowden, Esq, MBE, MP; House of Commons, London SW1A 0AA; Flat 11, 19/20 Sussex Sq, Brighton, Sussex (☎ (01) 219 5047)

BOWDEN, Maj Aubrey Henry; DSO (1918); s of Henry White Bowden, MICE, OF Great Missenden; *Educ* Oundle; *m* 1, 1918, Helen (d 1939), o da of R G Modera, of Wilbury Lodge, Hove; 1 s, 1 da; m 2, 1941, Andrée Marguerite July; 1 s, 2 da; *Career* chm Bowden Bros Ltd; *Style—* Maj Aubrey Bowden; 28 Berkeley Court, Baker Street, London NW1

BOWDEN, Baron (Life Peer UK 1963); Bertram Vivian Bowden; s of Bertram Caleb Bowden (d 1961), and Sarah Elizabeth, *née* Moulton, of Chesterfield; *b* 18 Jan 1910; *Educ* Chesterfield GS, Emmanuel Coll Cambridge; *m* 1, 1937 (m dis 1954), Marjorie Browne (d 1956); 1 s, 2 da; m 2, 1967, Mary (d 1971), da of late Bernard Whitman Maltby, of Ilkeston, Derbyshire; m 3, 1974 (m dis 1982), Phyllis (former chm Manchester Marriage Guidance Cncl and asst under-sec in civil service, former pres Lucy Cavendish Coll Cambridge), da of Stanley Henry Lewis Myson and wid of John James; *Career* leader of gp of English scientists and engrs to Washington DC 1942-45; with Ferranti Ltd 1950-53; chm electronics res cncl Miny of Aviation 1960-64; min of state DES 1964-65; princ Inst of Sci and Technol Manchester Univ 1964-76; given Pioneer Award by American Inst of Electrical and Electronic Engrs 1973 for work which led to the universal use of secondary radar to control both civil and mil aircraft in the Western World; *Recreations* music; *Clubs* Athenaeum; *Style—* The Rt Hon The Lord Bowden; Pine Croft, Stanhope Rd, Bowdon, Cheshire (☎ 061 928 4005)

BOWDEN, Francis William; s of Stanley Bowden (d 1951), of Stockport, and Ruth Grant, *née* Jenson ; *b* 21 May 1944; *Educ* Manchester GS, Christ's Coll Cambridge (MA); *m* 2 May 1970, Bridget Elizabeth, da of Randle Leigh Smith (d 1982), of Solihull; 1 s (John b 1973), 1 da (Susanna b 1974); *Career* actuary Godwins Ltd 1970-73, actuary and dir Fenchurch Gp 1973-84; ptnr Hymans Robertson & Co 1985-; FIA 1968, FPMI 1978; *Recreations* gardening, philately; *Style—* Francis Bowden, Esq; 55 Somerset Rd, New Barnet, Herts (☎ 01 449 4268); Hymans Robertson & Co, 190 Fleet St, London EC4A 2AH (☎ 01 831 9561, fax 01 831 6800, telex 8813716)

BOWDEN, Sir Frank Houston; 3 Bt (UK 1915); s of Sir Harold Bowden, 2 Bt, GBE (d 1960), and his 1 w Vera, *née* Whitaker; *b* 10 August 1909; *Educ* Rugby, Merton Coll Oxford (MA); *m* 1, 28 April 1934 (m dis 1936), Marie-José, da of Charles Stiénon, of Paris, and Comtesse Laure de Messey; 1 s; m 2, 3 March 1937, Lydia Eveline (d 1981), da of Jean Manolovici, of Bucharest; 3 s (Adrian, Aubrey, Gregory); *Heir* s, Nicholas Bowden; *Career* served as Paymaster Lt RNVR 1939-44; industrialist and landowner; vice-chm Japan Soc, and memb Exec Ctee; hon vice-pres World Kendo Championships 1976, pres British Kendo Assoc 1969-; pres University Hall, Buckland 1967-71; vice-pres Oxfordshire County Scout Cncl; has written collected and lectured on Japanese swords and armour; *Recreations* Kendo, bird-watching; *Clubs* White's, Royal Thames Yacht; *Style—* Sir Frank Bowden, Bt; The Old Vicarage, Winkfield, Windsor, Berks SL4 4SE (☎ 0344 886310)

BOWDEN, Geoffrey Anthony; s of James Benjamin Phillip Bowden (d 1986); *b* 5 June 1939; *Educ* Farnborough, Wimbledon; *m* 1; m 2, 1973, Wendy, da of Alfred Powell, of Richmond Surrey; 1 s, 3 da; *Career* md Siebe Gorman & Co 1977-82; dep chm: Merryweather & Sons 1979-82, John Morris & Sons 1979-82; chm and md Glossmark Ltd 1982-; chm Mainstay Computer Cover Ltd 1983-85; chm and md RJT 40 Ltd 1985 (business conslt); to Mitel Telecommunications); chief exec Ministry Computer Cover NV and BV 1986; MinstM, FInstD, FBIM; *Recreations* golf, squash, theatre; *Clubs* St Pierre; *Style—* Geoffrey Bowden, Esq; Belair, Bryn Rhedyn, Llanfrechfa, Cwmbran, Gwent (☎ 063 33 60849)

BOWDEN, Gerald Francis; TD, MP (C) Dulwich 1983-; s of Frank Albert Bowden and Elsie, *née* Burrill; *b* 26 August 1935; *Educ* Battersea GS, Magdalen Coll Oxford, Coll of Estate Mgmnt; *m* 1967, Heather Elizabeth Hill, *née* Hall (d 1984); 2 da, 1 step s, 1 step da; *Career* Dulwich GLC memb 1977-81, barr Gray's Inn, chartered surveyor; princ lectr Dept of Estate Mgmnt, S Bank Poly; *Style—* Gerald Bowden Esq, TD, MP

BOWDEN, Col (John Wallace) Guy; CBE (1962); s of Thomas Lake Bowden (d 1945), of Ranby Hall, Lincolnshire, and Margery Harnet, *née* Stack (d 1963); *b* 25 Sept 1915; *Educ* Westminster, Clare Coll Cambridge (MA); *m* 1, Jan 1947, Jean (d 1951), da of Sir John Humphrey Wise, KCMG, CBE (d 1984); m 2, July 1954, Countess Ilona Horthy, da of Count Edelsheim Gulyi (d 1984), of Cannes, France; *Career* cmmnd 3 King's Own Hussars 1939, serv: Falkland Islands 1939, Germany, Egypt, Pakistan, Burma; Military Attaché: Br Embassy Lisbon 1952-54; Br Embassy Iraq 1958-63; Inspr Staff Coll Quetta 1952-54; owner of: Cicerone Properties, Real Estate Agents, Estoril, Portugal; pres Royal British Legion (Lisbon) 1967-89, life vice-pres 1989-; *Recreations* hunting, polo; *Clubs* Cavalry and Guards'; *Style—* Col Guy Bowden, CBE; Quinta de Janes, Malvera da Serra, 2750 Cascais, Portugal (☎ 010 351 2850 148); Cicerone Properties, 4 Av Bombieros Voluntarios, Estoril, Portugal (☎ 010 351 2860 387)

BOWDEN, Hon Mrs; Hon Mary; *née* Bowden; da of Baron Bowden (Life Peer 1963); *b* 6 May 1940; *Educ* McGill Univ Montreal (MEd), Concordia Univ Montreal (BA), Manchester Univ England (Cert teach Deaf); *m* 1964 (m dis), Dr Roger George Davey; 2 da (Lisa b 1969, Julie b 1971); has resumed her maiden name; *Career* teacher of hearing impaired children and prof assoc McGill Univ Montreal; *Clubs* Toastmasters Organization; *Style—* The Hon Mary Bowden; 4 Martin Avenue, Dorval, Québec H9S 3R3, Canada

BOWDEN, Nicholas Richard; s and h of Sir Frank Houston Bowden, 3 Bt; *b* 13 August 1935; *Educ* Millfield; *Career* Nat Serv former trooper Life Gds; farmer; *Recreations* riding; *Style—* Nicholas Bowden, Esq; 4 Hensting Farm Cottages, Hensting Lane, Fishers Pond, Eastleigh, Hants (☎ 096 274 260)

BOWDEN, Hon Robin Charles; only s of Baron Bowden (Life Peer) by his 1 w; *b* 22 Feb 1945; *Educ* Old Swinford Hosp Sch, Loughborough Univ; *m* 1, Jess (*née* MacPherson Duncan); 1 s (Alastair Robin b 1982), 1 da (Lindsay Catherine b 1979); *Career* cold store factory mangr; *Recreations* painting; *Style—* The Hon Robin Bowden; 12 Craigton Avenue, Mannofield, Aberdeen, Scotland

BOWDEN, Prof Ruth Elizabeth Mary; OBE (1980); s of Sqdn Ldr Frank Harold Bowden (d 1959), and Louise Ellen, *née* Flick (d 1976); *b* 21 Feb 1915; *Educ* St Paul's Girls' Sch, Univ of London (MB BS, DSc); *Career* graduate asst Nuffield dept of orthopaedic surgery Peripheral Nerve Inquiry Unit 1942-45; Royal Free Hosp Sch of Med Univ of London: reader 1949 (formerly lectr), prof of anatomy 1951-80, emeritus prof 1980-; hon res fell Inst of Neurology 1980-, Sir William Collins prof of anatomy RCS; WHO conslt in anatomy Sudan: 1970, 1972, 1974; former pres Anatomical Soc of GB and Ireland, vice pres (formerly chm) cncl Chartered Soc of Physiotherapy; N London Hospice Gp: cncl memb, exec ctee memb, chm professional sub ctee; memb exec ctee Women's Nat Cmmn, vice pres Riding For the Disabled; memb: Anatomical Soc GB and Ireland, Zoological Soc, Royal Institution, Med Women's Fedn; Freeman City of London, Liveryman Worshipful Soc of Apothecaries; Jubilee Medal 1977; *Recreations* photography, painting, carpentry, reading; *Clubs* RSM, Univ Women; *Style—* Prof Ruth Bowden, OBE; 6 Hartham Close, Hartham Rd, London N7 9JH (☎ 01 607 3464); Royal Coll of Surgeons of England, Lincoln's Inn Fields, London (☎ 01 607 3464/01 405 3474)

BOWDEN-SMITH, Patrick Duncan Hurdis; s of Duncan James Hurdis Bowden-Smith, and Isabella Mary, *née* Hadow; ggs of Sir Alexander Macrieff, KCP, inventor of the 'Moncrieff Disappearing Gun'; *b* 7 Jun 1959; *Educ* Rugby Sch, RAC Cirencester; *Career* farming and estate mgmnt; *Recreations* shooting, fishing, messing about in boats; *Style—* Patrick D H Bowden-Smith, Esq; Chestnub, Hacheston, Woodbridge, Suffolk (☎ 0728 746339); Hemley Estates Ltd, Eels Foot, Hemley, Woodbridge, Suffolk

BOWEN, Prof David Aubrey Llewellyn; s of Thomas Rufus Bowen, JP (d 1946), and Catherine, *née* LLewellyn (d 1973); *b* 31 Jan 1924; *Educ* Caterham Sch Surrey, Univ of Wales, Cambridge Univ (MA, MB); *m* 1, 1950 (d 1973), Joan Rosemary, *née* Davis; 2 s (Mark b 1952, Roderic b 1966), 1 da (Diana b 1953); m 2, 21 Jan 1975, Helen Rosamund, da of Ralph Landcastle, of Haddenham, Bucks; *Career* Capt RAMC 1947-49, served: ME, Kenya, Somaliland; house offr: W Middex Hosp 1947, London Chest Hosp 1949-50, Bristol Royal Infirmary 1950-51; registrar: London Chest Hosp (Pathology) 1951-52, Nat Hosp for Nervous Diseases 1952-55, Royal Marsden Hosp 1955-56; forensic med lectr St Georges Hosp 1956-66, sr lectr Charing Cross Hosp Med Sch 1966-73 (reader 1973-77, prof 1977-); lectr in Forensic Med Univ of Oxford 1974-; chm Med Ctees Charing Cross Hosp and Med Sch; memb: Med Legal Soc (vice-pres 1977-), Br Assoc Forensic Med (pres 1977-79), Int Academy Legal and Social Med 1976-, Br Academy Forensic Sci; vice pres Old Caterhamians Assoc 1987-88, pres W London Medico Chirurgical Soc 1987-88; Freeman City of London, Liveryman Worshipful Co of Apothecaries; FRCP, FRCP (Edinburgh), FRCPath, DPath, DMJ; *Recreations* hockey, running (jogging); *Clubs* West Herts Hockey;

Style— Prof D A L Bowen; 19 Letchmore Rd, Radlett, Herts WD7 8HU (☎ 09273 856936); Dept of Forensic Med & Toxicology, Charing Cross & Westminster Med Sch, London W6 (☎ 01 846 7014)

BOWEN, Prof David Quentin; s of William Esmond Bowen (d 1984), of Heddlys, Glasfryn, Llanelli, and Jane, *née* Wiliams; *b* 14 Feb 1938; *Educ* Llanelli GS, UCL (BSc, PhD); *m* 18 Sept 1965, Elizabeth, da of David Islwyn Williams, of 58 Maesceinion, Aberystwyth; 2 s (Huw b 1966, Wyn b 1969), 1 da (Wyn b 1969); *Career* prof: physical geography UCW Aberystwyth 1983, geography Univ of London Royal Holloway and Bedford New Coll 1985; prof and dir Inst Earth Studies UCW 1988; ed in chief Quaternary Science Review 1982-, pres Quaternary Res Assoc (UK) 1979-81; memb: Natural Environment Res Cncl Ctees 1978-88, Nature Conservancy Cncl 1986-; FRGS 1985, memb Geological America 1987, FGS 1988; *Books* Quaternary Geology (1978, Russian ed 1982, 1987), The Llanelli Landscape (1980), Glaciations in the Northern Hemisphere (1986); *Recreations* music, rugby, football, cricket; *Clubs* Llanelli RFC, Geographical; *Style—* Prof David Bowen; Castell Brychan, Aberystwyth, SY23 2JD (☎ 0970 625 563); Inst of Earth Studies, UCW, Aberystwyth SY23 3DB (☎ 0970 623 111, fax 0970 617 172)

BOWEN, Duncan; s of William Henry Bowen, of Derbyshire, and Ivy, *née* Sanderson; *b* 6 June 1940; *Educ* Tupton Hall GS Chesterfield, Open Univ (BA); *m* 24 Aug 1963, Susan Elizabeth, da of James Geoffrey Reynolds, of Derbyshire; *Career* admin Nat Tst, philosopher; *Recreations* strolling; *Style—* Duncan Bowen, Esq; Laundry Cottage, Belton House, Grantham, Lincs NG32 2LS; Belton House, Grantham, Lincs NG32 2LS

BOWEN, Sheriff Edward Farquharson; TD (1977); s of Stanley Bowen, CBE, *qv*; *b* 1 May 1945; *Educ* Melville Coll Edinburgh, Univ of Edinburgh (LLB); *m* 1975, Patricia Margaret, da of Rev Robert Russell Brown, of Gowanbank, Isla Rd, Perth; 2 s (James, David), 2 da (Helen, Alexandra).; *Career* slr 1968, advocate 1970, advocate depute 1979-83; Sheriff of Tayside Central and Fife at Dundee 1983; *Recreations* golf; *Clubs* New, Hon Co of Edinburgh Golfers, Panmure GC; *Style—* Sheriff Edward Bowen, TD; Westgate, 12 Glamis Drive, Dundee; Sheriff Ct, West Bell St, Dundee (☎ 0382 29961)

BOWEN, Rear Adm Frank; s of Alfred Bowen (d 1976), of St Helens Lancs, and Lily, *née* Jenkins; *b* 25 Jan 1930; *Educ* Cowley Sch St Helens, RNC Dartmouth, RNEC Manadon, RNC Greenwich, RCDS; *m* 1954, Elizabeth Lilian, da of Louis Charles Gibson Richards (d 1971) of Truro Cornwall; 1 s (Peter), 2 da (Sarah, Emily); *Career* CSO to Chief Polaris Exec MOD 1974-76, special project rep (Navy) Washington DC 1976-78, dep chief Strategic Systems Exec 1980-81, Capt HMS Collingwood 1981-82, special project exec MOD 1982-84; dep chm (non exec dir) Dowty-Cap Ltd (def industry conslt 1985-88), now indep def industry conslt 1988-; MIMechE, FBIM; *Recreations* golf, amateur theatre; *Clubs* IOD; *Style—* Rear Adm F Bowen, CEng, MIMechE, FBIM; c/o Midland Bank plc, 102 High St, Lymington, Hants SO41 9ZP

BOWEN, Sir Geoffrey Fraser; s of late Edward J Bowen, architect; *b* 23 June 1912; *m* 1, Ruth (decd), da of H E Horsburgh; 2 s, 1 da; m 2, Isabel, da of H T Underwood; *Career* gen mangr Commercial Banking Co of Sydney Ltd 1970-73 (md 1973-76), ret; kt 1977; *Clubs* Union (Sydney), Killara Golf, Warrawee Bowling; *Style—* Sir Geoffrey Bowen; Cavendish, 16/562 Pacific Highway, Killara, NSW 2071, Australia

BOWEN, Jill, Lady; Jill Claude Murray; *née* Evans; da of Cyril Lloyd Evans, of Prestea, Ghana; *m* 30 Aug 1947, Sir Thomas Frederic Charles Bowen, 4 Bt (d 1989); 1 s (Sir Mark, 5 Bt, *qv*), 2 da (Julia Rosemary b 10 July 1950, Margot Claire b 30 March 1952) and 1 da decd (b and d 13 Jan 1954); *Style—* Jill, Lady Bowen; 1 Barford Close, Fleet, Hants GU13 9HJ

BOWEN, Kenneth John; s of Hector John Bowen (d 1980), of Llanelli, Carmarthenshire, and Sarah Ann (Sally), *née* Davies (d 1939); *b* 3 August 1932; *Educ* Llanelli GS, Univ Coll of Wales Aberystwyth (BA), St John's Coll Cambridge (MA, MusB), Inst of Educn Univ of London; *m* 31 March 1959, Angela Mary, da of George Stanley Evenden, of Morecambe, Lancs; 2 s (Geraint, Meurig); *Career* Flying Offr Educn branch RAF 1958-60; opera singer; head of vocal studies Royal Acad of Music 1987-(prof singing 1967-); conductor: London Welsh Chorale 1983-, London Welsh Festival Chorus 1987-, former concert and operatic tenor (ret 1988) debut Tom Rakewell New Opera Co Sadlers Wells 1957; appeared: Promenade concerts, Three Choirs Festival, Aldeburgh, Bath, Swansea and Llandaff; performed at: Royal Opera House ENO, WNO Glyndebourne Touring Opera, English Opera Gp, English Music Theatre, Kent Opera, Handel Opera Soc; numerous recordings and int appearances, winner first prize Munich Int Competition and Queens Prize; memb: Gorsedd of Bards, Royal Nat Eisteddfod of Wales, cncl Br Youth Opera, Royal Soc of Musicians, Inc Soc of Musicians; vice pres Guild for Promotion of Welsh Music; hon memb RAM 1973; *Recreations* golf, fell-walking, cinema, wine; *Style—* Kenneth Bowen, Esq; 12 Steeles Rd, London NW3 4SE; Royal Academy of Music, Marylebone Rd, London NW1 5HT

BOWEN, Sir Mark Edward Mortimer; 5 Bt (UK 1921), of Colworth, Co Bedford; o s of Sir Thomas Frederic Charles Bowen, 4 Bt (d 1989), and Jill Claude Murray, *née* Evans; *b* 17 Oct 1958; *Educ* Wellington; *m* 1983, Kerry Tessa, da of Michael John Moriarty, of The Grey House, Links Road, Worthing, Sussex; *Career* Lloyd's broker 1978-; *Recreations* swimming, golf; *Style—* Sir Mark Bowen, Bt; 21 Tolverne Road, West Wimbledon, London SW20 8RA (☎ 01 947 5542); Minet House, 100 Leman Street, London E1 8HG

BOWEN, Dr (John) Myles; OBE (1977); s of Cdr Harold Townshend Bowen, OBE (d 1971), and Cicely Frances Anne, *née* Cooper; *b* 23 August 1928; *Educ* Sherborne, Lincoln Coll Oxford (BA), Edinburgh Univ (PhD); *m* 7 Jan 1961, Margaret Compton, da of James Guthrie (d 1938); 3 da (Frances Belinda b 1963, Joanna Marion b 1964, Jennifer Isabel b 1968); *Career* cmmnd RA 1946; worked as exploration geologist for Royal Dutch/Shell Gp 1954-84 (Far East, Africa, S America, Europe), exploration dir Enterprise Oil London 1984-88; dir N Sea exploration discovering 8 oil and 3 gas fields; FGS, AAPG; *Recreations* sailing, skiing, rough shooting; *Clubs* Little Ship; *Style—* Dr Myles Bowen, OBE; 5 The Strand, London WC2 (☎ 01 930 1212, telex 895011 EPRISE G)

BOWEN, Maj-Gen (William) Neville; Maj- Gen William Oswald Bowen, CB, CBE (d 1961), of Winchester, and Ethel Gwenllian, *née* Davies; *b* 16 Mar 1935; *Educ* Shrewsbury, New York Univ Grad Sch of Business Admin; *m* 1960, Rosemary Rowena, da of Trevlyn Acheson-Williams-Flanagan; 2 da (Suzanne b 1963, Joanna b 1966); *Career* investment banker and advsr NY and Toronto 1957-72, md Hill Samuel Unit Tst Mangrs Ltd 1973-76, chief exec Bank von Ernot & Cie AG Switzerland 1976-80, dep chm Hill Samuel Life Assur Co Ltd 1980-82; chm: Hill Samuel Investmt Mgmnt Ltd 1982- (dep chm 1980-82), Investmt Advsrs Inc (USA) 1986-, Hill Samuel Investmt Advsrs Ltd 1987-, Hill Samuel Fagan Investmt Mgmnt Ltd 1988-; chief exec Hill Samuel Investmt Mgmnt Gp Ltd 1986-; CBIM; *Recreations* skiing, swimming, gardening; *Clubs* Brooks's; *Style—* Neville Bowen, Esq; Hill Samuel Investment Management Group Ltd, 45 Beech Street, London EC2P 2LX (☎ 01 628 8011, ext 2702)

BOWEN, Hon Sir Nigel Hubert; AC, KBE (1976); s of Otway P Bowen, of Ludlow; *b* 26 May 1911; *Educ* King's Sch Parramatta NSW, St Paul's Coll, Sydney Univ; *m* 1, 1947, Eileen Cecily (d 1983), da of Francis J Mullens; 3 da; m 2, 1984, Ermyn Winifred Krippner; *Career* barr NSW 1936, Victoria 1954, QC (Australia) 1953; MHR (Lib) Parramatta 1964-73, attorney-gen Australia 1966-69 and 1971, min Educn & Science 1969-71, min Foreign Affrs 1971-72; chief justice Federal Court of Australia 1976-; *Recreations* swimming, music; *Clubs* Union (Sydney); *Style—* Hon Sir Nigel Bowen, AC, KBE; Union Club, Bent St, Sydney, NSW 2000, Australia (☎ 230 8438)

BOWEN, Stanley; CBE (1972); s of Edward Bowen (d 1967), of Carnoustie, Angus, and Ellen Esther Powles (d 1967); *b* 4 August 1910; *Educ* Barry Sch Angus, Grove Acad Dundee, Univ Coll Dundee; *m* 1943, Mary Shepherd, da of Alexander Greig (d 1955), of Carnoustie Angus; 2 s (Edward (*qv*), Douglas), 1 da (Mary); *Career* slr 1932, memb Procurator Fiscal Serv 1933-41, princ asst Crown Off Edinburgh 1945-67, crown agent for Scotland 1967-74; Hon Sheriff of Lothian and Borders 1975-; Coronation Medal 1953; *Clubs* New and Press (Edinburgh); *Style—* Stanley Bowen, Esq, CBE; Achray, 20 Dovecot Rd, Corstorphine, Edinburgh EH12 7LE (☎ 031 334 4096)

BOWEN, Col Thomas Jim; MC (1941); s of Thomas Oliver Bowen (d 1941); *b* 21 July 1917; *Educ* The Leys Sch, St John's Coll Cambridge; *m* 1950, Anne Bowen (cousin); 2 s, 1 da; *Career* Col Worcs Regt 1967-70, Col Worcs and Sherwood Foresters Regt 1972-77; steward to Dean and Chapter of Worcester 1970-82; High Sheriff Hereford and Worcester 1980; Cdr of Order of S Arabia 1967; *Style—* Col T.J. Bowen, MC; Little Blakes, Shelsley Beauchamp, Worcs WR6 6RH (☎ 088 65 261)

BOWEN, Timothy James Glyn; s of John Glyn Bowen, FRCS; *b* 15 Mar 1946; *Educ* Harrow; *m* 1979, Suzanne, da of Griffith Eaton Jeffreys, of Swansea; *Career* dir Chesterfield Properties Ltd; FCA; *Recreations* cricket; *Style—* Timothy Bowen, Esq; 4 Thornton Rd, Wimbledon Common, SW19 (☎ 01 947 9798)

BOWEN-SIMPKINS, Peter; s of Horace John Bowen-Simpkins (d 1969), and Christine Dulce, *née* Clarke; *b* 28 Oct 1941; *Educ* Malvern, Selwyn Coll Cambridge (MA, MB, BChir), Guys Hosp; *m* 19 Aug 1967, Kathrin, da of Karl Otto Ganguin (d 1987); 2 da (Emma Jane b 6 Nov 1969, Philippa b 28 Dec 1971); *Career* resident med offr Queen Charlottes Maternity Hosp London 1971, resident surgical offr Samaritan Hosp for Women London 1972, sr registrar and lectr in obstetrics and gynaecology Middx Hosp and Hosp for Women 1973-78, conslt gynaecologist and obstetrician Singleton Hosp Swansea 1979-, examiner Royal Coll of Obstetrics and Gynaeology Univ of Wales and Gen Med Cncl, former examiner Central Midwives Bd, lectr in family planning Margaret Pyke Centre London; bdcaster; Freeman City of London 1980, Liveryman Worshipful Soc of Apothecaries; Handcock Prize for Surgery RCS 1966, LRCP 1966, MRCS 1966, MRCOG 1973, FRCOG 1985; *Books* Pocket Examiner in Obstetrics & Gynaecology (1983), chapters in other books on obst and gynae and papers and publications in medical journals; BMJ, Br J of Obst & Gynae, Br J Anasthesia, Obstetrics & Gynecology, Fertility & Sterility); *Recreations* fly fishing, skiing, golf, sailing, tennis; *Clubs* Royal Porthcawl Golf, Royal Overseas League; *Style—* Peter Bowen-Simpkins, Esq; Bosco's Knoll, 73 Pennard Rd, Southgate, Swansea SA3 2AJ (☎ 044128 2252); 38 Walter Rd, Swansea SA1 5NW (☎ 0792 655 600); Singleton Hosp, Swansea (☎ 0792 205 666)

BOWER, Hon Lady; Catherine Muriel; da of Capt Henry Edward Hotham (d 1912), and aunt of 8 Baron Hotham; raised to rank of Baron's da 1924; *b* 1908; *m* 1939, Lt-Gen Sir Roger Herbert Bower, KCB, KBE, *qv*; 1 s (adopted), 1 da; *Style—* The Hon Lady Bower; Ash House, St Mary Bourne, Andover, Hants

BOWER, Air Marshal Sir Leslie William Clement; KCB (1962, CB 1954), DSO (1945), DFC (1943); s of William Clarke Bower (d 1950), of Co Cork; *b* 11 July 1909; *Educ* The Harvey GS, RAF Coll Cranwell, USAF Air Univ; *m* 1, 1947 (m dis 1955), Phyllis Maude, da of Rev B Roberts; m 2, 1963, Clare (d 1971), da of H W Etkins, OBE, of Curlews, Constantine Bay, Cornwall, and wid of Cde Jasper Abbott, RN; m 3, 1980, Patricia Winifred, da of William Beresford Mortimer (d 1962), and wid of W/Cdr D N Fearon; *Career* NE frontier, India 1931-33; instructor Cambridge Univ Air Squadron 1933-35; instructor Central Flying Sch 1935-37; 202 Flying Boat Sqdn 1937-39; AHQ Malta 1939-45; (despatches 1944) faculty memb USAF Air War Coll 1947-50 Air Univ 1948-50, AOC No 81 Gp Fighter Cmd 1952-54, SASO Fighter Cmd 1954-57, Dep C-in-C M East Air Force 1957-59, AOC 19 Gp and Cdr (Air) East Atlantic and Cdr (Air) Channel 1959-62, UK rep Perm Mil Deps Ctee (Ankara) CENTO 1962-65; *Recreations* formerly: cricket, squash, soccer, golf, tennis; *Clubs* RAF; *Style—* Air Marshal Sir Leslie Bower, KCB, DSO, DFC; c/o Lloyds Bank, Cox's & King's Branch, 6 Pall Mall, London SW1

BOWER, Michael James Eills Graham; s of James Graham Bower (d 1968), of Hants, and Sybil Galilee, *née* Eills (d 1971); *b* 14 June 1938; *Educ* Eton, Ch Ch Oxford (MA); *m* 23 June 1967, Carloyne Patricia Sherwell, da of Derek Frank Sherwell Clogg (d 1986), of London; 1 s (Michael b 3 Nov 1968); *Career* Rea Bros 1961- (dir 1974-), md Rea Bros Investmt Mgmnt 1988-; *Recreations* golf, bridge; *Clubs* Whites, The Brook, Royal and Ancient, Royal St Georges; *Style—* Michael Bower, Esq; 38 Chartfield Aave, London SW15; Aldermans House, Aldermans Walk, London EC2 (☎ 01 623 1155)

BOWER, Roger; s of Norman Franklin Bower, of Onchan, Isle of Man, and Dorothy Vera, *née* Lawson; *b* 30 Mar 1953; *Educ* Bootham Sch York, William Hulme's GS Manchester, Manchester Poly (BA); *m* 11 March 1979, Sonya Ruth, da of Dr Hyman Davies, of Prestwich, Manchester; 2 da (Anna Michelle b 1980, Jodie Samantha b 1982); *Career* slr; *Recreations* music appreciation, tennis, golf; *Style—* Roger Bower, Esq; West Winds, Hale Road, Hale Barn, Cheshire (☎ 061 980 7093); Bower Harrison & Co, Solicitors, 211 Deansgate, Manchester (☎ 061 832 9404)

BOWER, Lt-Gen Sir Roger Herbert; KCB (1959, CB 1950), KBE (1957, CBE 1944); s of Herbert Morris Bower, JP (d 1940), of Ripon, Yorks, and Eileen Francis Fitzgerald, *née* Thompson (d 1949); *b* 13 Feb 1903; *Educ* Repton, RMC Sandhurst; *m*

12 April 1939, Hon Catherine Muriel, *née* Hotham (*see Hon Lady Bower*); 1 adopted s (Michael b 1952)(and 1 s decd), 1 da (Anne b 1940); *Career* Lt-Col KOYLI 1941, Brig 1944, Maj-Gen 1948, Lt-Gen 1956, served N W Europe HQ Br Airborne Corps 1944, Palestine 1945-46 (despatches), Cdr Hamburg Dist 1948-49, Cdr E Anglian Dist 1953-55, Ch of Staff to C-in-C Allied Forces Northern Europe 1955-56, GOC Malaya Command and Dir of Ops Malaya 1956-57, C-in-C MELF 1958-60, ret 1960; tres to HRH Princess Margaret, Countess of Snowdon 1960-62, Lt of the Tower of London 1960-63, Col KOYLI 1960-66; chm Nat Fund for Res into Crippling Diseases 1974-75; chm Action Research for the Crippled Child 1974-75; Bronze Star Medal (USA) 1944, King Haakon VII Liberty Cross (Norway); *Recreations* formerly shooting, fishing, sailing; *Clubs* Army and Navy, Royal Cruising; *Style*— Lt-Gen Sir Roger Bower, KCB, KBE; Ash House, St Mary Bourne, Andover, Hants

BOWERING, Ven Michael Ernest; s of Hubert James Bowering (d 1961), of Barnstaple, and Mary Elizabeth, *née* Tucker (d 1982); *b* 25 June 1935; *Educ* Barnstaple GS, Kelham Theol Coll; *m* 18 Aug 1962, Aileen, da of James William Fox (d 1979), of Middlesbrough; 1 s (Paul b 1963), 2 da (Alice b 1965, Joanne b 1967); *Career* curate: St Oswald Middlesbrough 1959-62, All Saints Huntington 1962-64; vicar St Wilfrid Brayton with Barlow 1964-72, rural dean Selby 1971-72, vicar Emmanuel Saltburn By The Sea 1972-81, canon residentiary York Minster 1981-87, sec for Mission and Evangelism York Diocese 1981-87, archdeacon of Lindisfarne 1987-; *Recreations* photography, walking; *Style*— The Ven the Archdeacon of Lindisfarne; 12 Rectory Park, Morpeth, Northumberland NE61 2SZ (☎ 0670 513 207)

BOWERMAN, Ian Nicholas; s of Duncan Bowerman and Olivia Irene, *née* Osborne; *b* 21 June 1921; *Educ* privately; *Career* Qualified Army Staff Coll, Middle East 1944; dir: Louis Dreyfus & Co Ltd 1972-81, Int Trade Devpt Co 1969-81; fndn fell Assoc of Corporate Treasurers; liveryman Horner's Co, FRGS, FIOD, Freeman City of London, life memb Guild of Freemen of City of London; writer and lecturer in philosophy; *Recreations* collecting oriental ceramics specialising in Chinese, Japanese and Tibetan artefacts; *Clubs* City Livery, Royal Overseas League, Royal Cwlth Soc; *Style*— Ian Bowerman, Esq; 6 Phoenix Lodge Mansions, Brook Green, London W6 7BG (☎ 01 603 9326)

BOWERS, Frederick John; s of Frederick Bowers (d 1971); *b* 23 Sept 1941; *Educ* Pembroke GS; *m* 1964, Sheila May, da of Hector Macdonald (d 1963); 2 s; *Career* dir: Johnston Construction, Samuel Johnston Ltd (Sri Lanka), Johnston Int Ltd (W Indies), Hadsphaltic Int (W Indies) Ltd, quantity surveyor; *Recreations* sailing, walking, scouting; *Clubs* Commonwealth; *Style*— Frederick Bowers, Esq; Hawkshaw, Eastbourne Rd, Blindley Heath, Lingfield, Surrey RH7 6JN (☎ 0342 833201)

BOWERS, (John) Michael; s of FG Bowers, CB (d 1937), of Surrey, and Frances Bowers (d 1982); *b* 24 April 1927; *Educ* Dauntsey's Sch, Balliol Coll Oxford (BA); *m* 13 Sept 1958, (Rosalind) Mary, da of Percy Bourdon Smith, ME; 2 s (Philip b 1960, Robert b 1963), 2 da (Joanna b 1961, Valery b 1965); *Career* ptnr McKenna & Co 1958-; chm: Citizens Advice Bureaux, CARE Britain, Performing Right Tbnl; dir London Sinfonietta, memb Hyde Housing Assoc, founding dir Greenwich Theatre; sailed across Atlantic 1982; *Recreations* sailing, music; *Clubs* Garrick; *Style*— Michael Bowers, Esq; 39 Cloudesley Rd, London N1 OEL; Yew Tree Farm, Swessling, Saxmundham, Suffolk; McKenna & Co, 1 Aldwych, London WC2

BOWERS, Michael John; s of Arthur Patrick Bowers (d 1961), and Lena Frances, *née* Maher (d 1983); *b* 1 Oct 1933; *Educ* Cardinal Vaughan Sch Kensington; *m* 29 Aug 1959, Caroline, da of William Joseph Clifford (d 1985); 2 da (Karen b 1963, Samantha b 1966); *Career* vice-pres and dir BP N America Inc 1973-76, chief exec BP Gas Ltd 1976-81; regnl co-ordinator Western Hemisphere BP Co plc 1981-83, chief exec The Int Petroleum Exchange of London Ltd 1983-85, md Two (UK) Ltd 1985-; *Recreations* gardening, bridge, chess, music; *Clubs* RAC, St James's; *Style*— Michael J Bowers, Esq; Wood End, Warren Drive, Kingswood, Surrey KT20 6PZ (☎ 0737 832629); 3 St James's Square, London SW1Y 4JF (telex 917831/881303)

BOWERS, Ronald Courtney; MBE (1959); s of Maj Stanley Bowers, TD (d 1938), of Warlingham, Surrey, and Mary, *née* Gadsdon (d 1938); *b* 18 May 1922; *Educ* Whitgift, RAF Apprentice Sch Halton; *Career* RAF Engrg Wing Cdr, Staff Offr HQ Air Support Cmd, mangr RAF Motor Sports 'Cyprus Rally' Team 1972, cmd 103 MU Cyprus; family historian and author of 'Combs, Combmaking and The Combmakers Company' (1987); CEng, MRAeS; *Recreations* bird watching, photography, oil painting, genealogy; *Clubs* RAF, Royal Aeronautical Soc; *Style*— Ronald Bowers, Esq, MBE; Road End Cottage, Stockland, Honiton, Devon EX14 9LJ (☎ (040 488) 581)

BOWERY, Leigh; s of Thomas Bradley Bowery, of 147 Morris Street, Sunshine, Victoria 3020 Australia, and Evelyn Joyce, *née* Griffiths; *b* 26 Mar 1955; *Educ* Sunshine West HS Sunshine Australia, Melbourne Boys HS; *Career* collections shown: New York 1983 and 1984, London (ICA) 1983 and 1984, Tokyo 1985, Vienna 1985 and 1986; subject of LWT documentary 1985, starred in Hail the New Puritan (film) 1985; with Michael Clark & Co: two seasons (Sadlers Wells), 1987 and 1988 touring Britain, Spain, Italy, Germany, Australia, Yugoslavia, America, Holland; exhibit at Anthony D'Offay Art Gallery 1988; *Recreations* Kung-Fu; *Clubs* Heaven; *Style*— Leigh Bowery, Esq; 43 Farrell House, Ronald St, London E1; 9-23 Dering Street, New Bond Street, London W1 (☎ 01 499 4100)

BOWES LYON, Hon (Michael) Albemarle; s of late Hon Michael Claude Hamilton Bowes-Lyon, 5 s of 14 E of Strathmore and Kinghorne; bro of 17 E; raised to the rank of a E's s 1974; *b* 29 May 1940; *Educ* Eton, Magdalen Coll Oxford; *Career* dir Coutts & Co 1969-; *Style*— The Hon Albemarle Bowes Lyon; 138 'B' Whitehall Court, London SW1A 2EP

BOWES LYON, Lady Diana Evelyn; da of 17 E of Strathmore and Kinghorne; *b* 29 Dec 1966; *Style*— Lady Diana Bowes Lyon

BOWES LYON, Lady Elizabeth Mary Cecilia; da of 17 E of Strathmore and Kinghorne (d 1987); *b* 23 Dec 1959; *Style*— Lady Elizabeth Bowes Lyon

BOWES LYON, Hon Lady; Rachel Pauline; da of late Col the Rt Hon Herbert Spender-Clay, CMG, MC, PC, MP, and Pauline, JP, da of 1 Viscount Astor and sis of 1 Baron Astor of Hever; *m* 1929, Hon Sir David Bowes Lyon, KCVO (d 1961), s of 14 E of Strathmore and Kinghorne; 1 s (*see* S A Bowes-Lyon), 1 da (*see* 13 E of Stair, KCVO, MBE); *Style*— The Hon Lady Bowes Lyon; St Paul's Walden Bury, Hitchin, Herts (☎ (043 887) 218)

BOWES LYON, Simon Alexander; s of Hon Sir David Bowes Lyon, KCVO (d 1961), and Rachel Pauline, *née* Spender Clay (*see* Hon Lady Bowes Lyon); *b* 17 June 1932; *Educ* Eton, Magdalen Coll Oxford; *m* 1966, Caroline Mary Victoria, elder da of Rt Rev Victor Joseph Pike, CB, CBE, MA, DD, Bishop of Sherborne (1959-76); 3 s (Fergus b 1970, David b 1973, Andrew b 1979), 1 da (Rosie b 1968); *Career* dir: Financial Insurance Gp Ltd, Dominion Insurance Co Ltd, Balfour Maclaine Int Ltd, WRVS Tstees Ltd and other cos; Lord Lieut of Hertfordshire 1986-; FCA; *Recreations* shooting, music, gardening, botany; *Clubs* White's, Brooks's; *Style*— Simon Bowes Lyon, Esq; St Paul's Walden Bury, Hitchin, Herts (☎ 043 887 218)

BOWES-LYON, David James; s of Maj-Gen Sir James Bowes-Lyon, KCVO, CB, OBE, MC (d 1977), and Mary, *née* De Trafford; *b* 21 July 1947; *Educ* Ampleforth; *m* 1976, Elizabeth Harriet, da of Sir John Colville, CB, CVO, of Broughton, nr Stockbridge, Hants; 1 s (James b 1979), 2 da (Georgina b 1977, Alexandra b 1986); *Career* Capt 14/20 Kings Hussars 1970-78 NI, W Germany, Cyprus, Zaire; with The Union Discount Co of London 1979- (dir various subsid cos); dir: Scottish Business Achievement Tst 1981-, Aitken Campbell and Co Ltd 1987-, Lothian Racecourse Ltd (Edinburgh) 1987-; memb The Queen's Bodyguard for Scotland the Royal Company of Archers; *Recreations* shooting, fishing, racing; *Clubs* White's, Turf; *Style*— David Bowes-Lyon, Esq; Heriot Water, Heriot, Midlothian (☎ 087 535 281; work 031 226 3535)

BOWES-LYON, John Francis; s of Maj-Gen Sir James Bowes-Lyon, KCVO, CB, OBE, MC (d 1977), and Lady Bowes-Lyon, da of Sir Humphrey de Trafford (Bt); *b* 13 June 1942; *Educ* Ampleforth; *Career* dir Sotheby's 1970-80, conslt Garrard & Co; ed at large Condé Nast Publications Inc USA; *Clubs* Bucks, Pratts; *Style*— John Bowes-Lyon, Esq; D5 Albany, Piccadilly, London W1

BOWETT, Prof Derek William; CBE (1983), QC (1978); s of Arnold William Bowett (d 1960), of Sale, Cheshire, and Marion, *née* Wood (d 1948); *b* 20 April 1927; *Educ* William Hulme's GS, Downing Coll Cambridge (MA, LLB, PhD, LLD); *m* 29 Dec 1953, Betty, da of William Sidney Northall (d 1983), of Rhyl, N Wales; 2 s (Richard William b 1956, Adam Northall b 1958), 1 da (Louise Marion b 1961); *Career* AB RNVR 1945-47; barr Middle Temple 1953, bencher 1976; lectr in law Manchester Univ 1951-59; pres Queens' Coll Cambridge 1970-82 (fell 1960-70 and 1982-); Whewell Prof of Int Law Cambridge 1981- (lectr then reader law faculty Cambridge Univ 1960-81); former memb Royal Cmmn Environmental Pollution; PhD (Manchester); FBA 1984; *Books* Self-Defence in International Law (1957), Law of International Institutions (1964), United Nations Forces (1964), Search for Peace (1970), Legal Regime of Islands (1978); *Recreations* music, walking, gardening; *Style*— Professor Derek Bowett, CBE, QC; 228 Hills Road, Cambridge CB2 2QE (☎ 0453 210688); Queens' College, Cambridge CB3 9ET (☎ 0453 335555, fax 0223 335533, telex 81240 CAM SPL-G)

BOWIE, Rev (Alexander) Glen; CBE (1984); s of Alexander Bowie (d 1983), of Stevenston, Ayrshire, and Annie Robertson, *née* McGhie (d 1977); *b* 10 May 1928; *Educ* Stevenston HS, Irvine Royal Acad, Glasgow Univ (BSc), Glasgow Univ Trinity Coll (Dip Theol), Open Univ (BA); *m* 15 March 1952, Mary, da of John McKillop (d 1945); 2 da (Alexandra b 8 March 1955, Jenifer b 12 Sept 1960); *Career* ordained minister Church of Scotland 1954; chaplain RAF Henlow 1954, Padgate 1955-56, Akrotiri 1956-59, Stafford 1959-61, Butzweilerhof 1961-64, Halton 1964-67, Akrotiri 1967-70, RAF Coll Cranwell 1970-75, asst princ chaplain 1975, HQ Rheindahlen 1975-76, HQ RAFSC 1976-80, Princ Chaplain Church of Scotland and Free Churches 1980-84, hon chaplain to HM the Queen 1980-84, ret from RAF 1984; editor Scottish Forces Bullentin 1985-, moderator and presbytery of England 1988-89; hon chaplain Royal Scottish Corpn 1981-, pres Scottish Chaplains Assoc 1987-88; memb Calendonian Soc of London; *Recreations* painting, boating and leading holy land pilgrimages; *Clubs* RAF; *Style*— The Rev Glen Bowie, CBE; 16 Weir Road, Hemingford Grey, Huntingdon, Cambs (☎ 0480 632 69)

BOWIE, Kathleen Cecelia; da of John Augustus Hanningan (d 1965), of Highgate, and Emily Cecelia, *née* Mulligan (d 1926); *b* 3 May 1915; *Educ* St Aloysius Convent; *m* 23 June 1947, Norman Walter Bowie, s of Walter Stronach Bowie (d 1950), of Beckenham, Kent; *Career* Nat Fire Serv 1941-45; dir J A Hannigan & Sons Ltd 1965-85; life fell RSPB; *Recreations* needlework, writing, singing; *Style*— Mrs Kathleen C Bowie,; 1 Uplands Close, East Sheen, London SW14 7AS (☎ 01 876 1434); White Horses, Coastal Road, W Kingston, Littlehampton, W Sussex

BOWIE, Norman Walter; s of Walter Stronach Bowie (d 1950) and Marion Louise, *née* Thomson (d 1956), of Beckenham; *b* 10 Oct 1914; *Educ* Stationers' Co's Sch, Coll of Estate Mgmnt; *m* 1947, Kathleen Cecelia, da of John Augustus Hannigan (d 1965), of Highgate; *Career* serv WWII, Maj RE, 14 Army SE Asia Cmd; surveyor to Prudential Assur Co 1934-59; ptnr Jones Lang Wootton chartered surveyors 1959-74 (conslt 1975-); dir Town and City Properties 1962-73; memb of ctee of mgmnt The Pension Fund Property Unit Tst 1966-74; dir Es Court 1967-72; property conslt: Br Land plc 1974-84, Water Authorities Superannuation Fund 1974-, Crown Agents for Oversea Govts and Admins 1976-82; dir Imry Property Hldgs 1965-86; chm Euro Gp of Valuers of Fixed Assets 1977-82; sec Int Assets Valuation Standards Ctee 1981-84; dir London Small Businesses Property Tst 1987-; memb cncl Dr Barnardo's 1981- (chm 1984-87); property conslt to chief exec Property Services Agency DOE 1982-83 and London Borough of Bromley 1982-84; hon fell Coll of Estate Mgmnt 1981; chm admin bd Jones Lang Wootton Travelling Scholarship; pres Chiswick Amateur Regatta 1987: FRICS; *Recreations* rowing, writing on property invstmt and valuation; *Clubs* Ibis Rowing; *Style*— Norman Bowie Esq; 1 Uplands Close, London SW14 7AS (☎ 01 876 1434); White Horses, 30 Coastal Rd, West Kingston, Littlehampton, W Sussex; office: 22 Hanover Square, London W1A 2BN (☎ 01 493 6040, telex 23858, fax 01-408 0220)

BOWIE, Ronald Steward; s of Robert Hunter Bowie, of Greenock, and Jessie Dalziel, *née* Clark; *b* 23 Jan 1954; *Educ* Greenock Acad, Univ of St Andrews (BSc); *m* 23 June 1986, Stella Elizabeth Gordon, da of Dr John Goudie, of Greenock; 1 da (Audrey b 1988); *Career* ptnr Hymans Robertson & Co; FFA 1980; *Recreations* sport, family; *Clubs* RSAC; *Style*— Ronald Bowie, Esq; Hymans Robertson, 121 West George St, Glasgow (☎ 041 248 7007, fax 041 221 8426, telex 776 564)

BOWIER, Michael James Eills Graham; s of James Graham Bowier (d 1968), of Hants, and Sybil Gailee, *née* Eills (1971); *Educ* Eton, Christ Church Oxford (MA); *m* 23 June 1967, Carolyne Patricia Sherwell, da of Derek Frank Sherwell Clogg (d 1986), of London; 1 s (Michael b 3 Nov 1968); *Career* joined Rea Bros-, (dir 1974-), md Rea Bros Investmt Mgmnt 1988-; *Recreations* golf, bridge; *Clubs* Whites, The Brook, RA, Royal St Georges; *Style*— Michael Bowier, Esq

BOWIS, John Crocket; OBE (1981), MP (C) Battersea 1987-; s of Thomas Palin

Bowis (d 1957), of Brighton, and Georgiana Joyce Bowis, *née* Crocket; *b* 2 August 1945; *Educ* Tonbridge, Brasenose Coll Oxford (MA); *m* 1968, Caroline Taylor of Oxon; 2 s (Duncan b 1972, Alistair b 1978), 1 da (Imogen b 1970); *Career* Cons Central Office 1972-80; Public Affairs Dir British Insurance Brokers' Assocn 1981-86; cncllr Royal Borough of Kingston upon Thames 1982-86 (chief of educn 1985-85); *Recreations* theatre, music, art, sport; *Style*— John Bowis, OBE, MP; House of Commons, London SW1A 0AA (☎ 01-219-3535 or 6214 or 01-949-2555)

BOWKER, Alfred Johnstone (John); MC (1944); s of Alfred Bowker, of Winchester, and Isabel Florence, *née* Brett; *b* 9 April 1922; *Educ* Dragon Sch, Winchester, Christ Church Oxford (MA); *m* 1947, Ann, da of John Christopher Fairweather (d 1978); 1 s (Robert b 1952), 1 da (Judith b 1954; actress known as Judi Bowker); *Career* Coldstream Gds, Capt Italian Campaign 1941-46; slr in Winchester 1949-57; Master Meon Valley Beagles 1954-56; Winchester City Cncllr 1954-57; Resident Magistrate N Rhodesia 1957-65; slr in Salisbury Wilts 1965-72; joint Master Horsley Foxhounds 1968-69 and 1970-71; chm Industrial Tribunals Newcastle-on-Tyne 1972; ret 1978; Regional Chm Industrial Tribunals, Southampton 1987; Liveryman Worshipful Co of Skinners; *Recreations* hunting, reading history; *Style*— John Bowker, Esq

BOWLBY, Lady Ann Lavinia Maud Montagu Stuart-Wortley; da of 3 E of Wharncliffe (d 1953); *b* 25 Jan 1919; *m* 1939, as his 2 w, Cdr Vivian Russell Salvin Bowlby, RN (d 1972), s of Col Robert Russell Bowlby, of Tunbridge Wells; 1 s (Michael Robin Salvin b 1947); *Books* Maternal Care & Mental Health (1951), Attachment & Loss (3 vols, 1969-80); *Style*— Lady Ann Bowlby; Sutton Stables, Felixkirk Rd, Sutton-under-Whitestonecliffe, Thirsk, Yorks

BOWLBY, Sir Anthony Hugh Mostyn; 2 Bt (UK 1923); s of Sir Anthony Alfred Bowlby, 1 Bt, KCB, KCMG, KCVO, FRCS (d 1929); *b* 13 Jan 1906; *Educ* Wellington, New Coll Oxford; *m* 27 Jan 1930, Dora Evelyn, da of late John Charles Allen, of York; 2 da; *Heir* bro, (Edward) John Bowlby; *Style*— Sir Anthony Bowlby, Bt; The Old Rectory, Ozleworth, nr Wotton-under-Edge, Glos

BOWLBY, Hon Mrs (Dorothy Anne); da of Hon Dudley North, MC, JP (d 1936); sis and co-heiress of 13 Baron North (E 1554), ka 1941, since when the Barony has been in abeyance; *b* 4 May 1915; *m* 1, 1937 (m dis 1950), Clive Graham, Lt Sherwood Foresters; 1 da; m 2, 1950, Maj John Bowlby, 1 Royal Dragoons, s of Hon Mrs (Lettice) Bowlby, *qv*; 1 da; *Style*— The Hon Mrs Bowlby; 51 Shawfield St, London SW3 (☎ 01 352 0573)

BOWLBY, (Edward) John Mostyn; CBE (1972); s of Sir Anthony Alfred Bowlby, 1 Bt, KCB, KCMG, KCVO (d 1929); hp to Btcy of bro, Sir Anthony Bowlby, 2 Bt; *b* 26 Feb 1907; *Educ* RNC Dartmouth, Trinity Coll Cambridge (MA, MD); *m* 1938, Ursula, da of Tom G Longstaff, MD (d 1964); 2 s, 2 da; *Career* serv temp Lt-Col RAMC 1940-45; family psychiatrist; conslt: Tavistock Clinic 1946-72, WHO 1950-55; author; Hon ScD Cambridge Univ, Hon DLitt Leicester; FRCP, FRCPsych; *Recreations* natural history, field sports; *Style*— Dr John Bowlby, CBE; Wyldes Close Corner, Hampstead Way, London NW11 7JB (☎ 01 455 9380); Ullinish, Struan, Isle of Skye (☎ (047 072 237)

BOWLBY, Hon Mrs (Penelope Isobel); da of 7 Viscount Portman (d 1948); *b* 21 July 1913; *m* 1, 1934 (m dis 1949), Brig Archer Francis Lawrence Clive, DSO, MC, s of Lt-Gen Sir George Sidney Clive, GCVO, KCB, CMG, DSO, of Perryshire Court, Hereford; 1 s, 1 da; m 2, 1949, David Arthur Salvin Bowlby (d 1985), 2 s of late Arthur Salvin Bowlby, of Gilston Park, Harlow, Essex; *Career* breeding racehorses; *Style*— The Hon Mrs Bowlby; Inverinate, Kyle of Lochalsh, Ross-shire; The Manor, Healing, Grimsby

BOWLBY, Rt Rev Ronald Oliver; *see*: Southwark, Bishop of

BOWLER, Geoffrey; s of James Henry and Hilda May Bowler; *b* 11 July 1924; *Educ* Sloane Sch Chelsea; *Career* chief gen mangr Sun Alliance and London Insurance Gp 1977-87; FCIS; *Style*— Geoffrey Bowler, Esq; 13 Green Lane, Purley, Surrey CR2 3PP (☎ 01 660 0756)

BOWLER, Ian John; CBE (1971, OBE 1957); s of Maj John Arthur Bowler; *b* 1920; *Educ* King's Sch Worcester, Oxford Univ; *m* 1963, Hamideh, da of Prince Yadollah Azodi, GCMG; 2 da; 1 step s, 1 step d; *Career* pres Iranian Management and Engineering Gp Ltd 1965-; chm International Management and Engineering Gp Ltd 1973-; Kinhill/IMEG, Australia 1971-; *Style*— Ian Bowler Esq, CBE; 4 Kucheh, Bagh Bank, Golhak, Tehran, Iran; 28 Mallord st, SW3 (☎ 01 351 3322)

BOWLES, Rt Rev Cyril William Johnston; s of late William C A Bowles, of Scotstoun, Glasgow; *b* 9 May 1916; *Educ* Brentwood Sch, Emmanuel Coll Cambridge, Jesus Coll Cambridge, Ridley Hall Cambridge; *m* 1965, Florence Joan, da of late John Eastaugh, of Windlesham, Surrey; *Career* ordained deacon 1939, priest 1940; principal Ridley Hall 1951-63, archdeacon of Swindon dioc of Bristol 1963-69, hon canon of Ely Cathedral 1959-63, bishop of Derby 1969-87; memb House of Lords 1973-87; *Style*— The Rt Rev C W J Bowles; Rose Lodge, Tewkesbury Rd, Stow-on-the-Wold, Cheltenham, Glos GL54 1EN

BOWLES, Dr John Arthur; s of Thomas Holdsworth Bowles (d 1968), and Elizabeth, *née* Carr (d 1982); *b* 20 August 1920; *Educ* St Andrews Univ (MB, ChB, DRCOG); *m* 4 July 1944, Anne May, da of David Richard Price (d 1956); 1 s (David b 1956), 1 da (Bronwen b 1952); *Career* RN 1940-46; medical practitioner Swansea, medical offr Morgamite Carbon Co Swansea; *Recreations* sailing, walking, work; *Style*— Dr John Bowles; Mile End House, Landore, Swansea (☎ (0792) 55083); Brym Hyfryd Surgery, Brynhyrryd, Swansea

BOWLES, Sidney Theodore; s of Reginald Arthur Bowles (d 1988), of Norwich, and Elsie Maud Bowles, *née* Houseago (d 1964); *b* 11 May 1926; *Educ* Avenue Sch Norwich; *m* 7 Aug 1954, Ronalda Elizabeth, da of Cyril Joseph Coan (d 1979) of Hull, Yorks; 1 s (Andrew Theodore b 1961); *Career* FCA; FCCA; *Recreations* reading, music; *Style*— Sidney T Bowles, FCA, FCCA; 6 Grange Road, Christchurch Road, Norwich NR2 3NH

BOWMAN, Sir George; 2 Bt (UK 1961); s of Sir James Bowman, 1 Bt, KBE (d 1978); *b* 2 July 1923; *m* 1960, Olive, *née* Case; 3 da; *Heir* none; *Style*— Sir George Bowman, Bt; Parkside, Killingworth Drive, Killingworth Station, Newcastle-upon-Tyne NE12 0ES

BOWMAN, James Thomas; s of Benjamin and Cecilia Bowman; *b* 6 Nov 1941; *Educ* Ely Cathedral Choir Sch, King's Sch Ely, New Coll Oxford; *Career* counter-tenor; schoolmaster 1965-67; operatic performances with: Glyndebourne Festival Opera 1970-, Sydney Opera 1978, Opéra Comique Paris 1979, also Santa Fe, San Francisco, Dallas in USA; Theatre du Châtelet Paris 1983-, Badisches Staatstheater, Karlsruhe 1984-, Royal Opera House 1972-, English National Opera 1985-, La Scala Milan 1987-, Scottish Opera 1971-; prof of singing Guildhall Sch of music; pres Hinckley music club; *Style*— James Bowman, Esq; 19a Wetherby Gdns, London SW5

BOWMAN, Jean, Lady; Jean; da of Henry Brooks, of Ashington, Northumberland; *m* 1922, Sir James Bowman, 1 Bt, KBE (d 1978); 1 s, 1 da; *Style*— Jean, Lady Bowman; Woodlands, Killingworth Station, Forest Hall, Newcastle-upon-Tyne

BOWMAN, Jeffery Haverstock; s of Alfred Haverstock Bowman (d 1974), and Doris Gertrude, *née* Beck (d 1983); *b* 3 April 1935; *Educ* Winchester, Trinity Hall Cambridge (BA); *m* 15 June 1963, Susan Claudia, da of Dr Oliver Hays Bostock (d 1982), of Guernsey; 1 s (Mark b 1970), 2 da (Caroline b 1964, Victoria b 1967); *Career* 2 Lt RHG 1953-55; articled with Price Waterhouse 1958-61, mangr 1964, ptnr 1966, memb firm's policy ctee 1972-, dir technical services 1973-76, dir London office 1979-81, sr ptnr 1982-; personal auditor Duchy of Cornwall 1971-; memb ICAEW Accounting Standards Ctee 1982-87, ICAEW Cncl 1986-, Cncl of the Industrial Soc 1985-, Governing and Business in the Community 1985-; vice-pres union of Ind Companies; govr Brentwood Sch 1985-; FCA 1962; *Recreations* golf, opera, gardening, sailing; *Clubs* Garrick; *Style*— Jeffery Bowman, Esq; The Old Rectory, Boreham, Chelmsford, Essex CM3 3EP (☎ 0245 467233); Price Waterhouse, Southwark Towers, 32 London Bridge Street, London SE1 9SY (☎ 01 407 8989, fax 01 378 0647, telex 884657/8)

BOWMAN, Maj Gen John (Jack) Francis; CB (1986); s of Francis Bowman (d 1985), and Gladys Rose (d 1985); *b* 5 Feb 1927; *Educ* QEGS Penrith, Hertford Coll Oxford (MA); *m* 1956, Laura, da of John Moore (d 1952); 1 s (John b 1959), 1 da (Tessa b 1961); *Career* RN 1945-48; serv: Med, Atlantic and Antarctica; Army Maj-Gen; barr Gray's Inn; dir Army Legal Services 1983-86; served Africa, Far E, Near and Middle E, UK, BAOR; life vice pres Army Boxing Assoc, cncl memb Br Red Cross Soc; *Recreations* sailing, mountain walking, skiing; *Clubs* Royal Naval, Royal Albert Yacht; *Style*— Maj-Gen Jack Bowman; Browhead, Spark Bridge, Ulverston, Cumbria LA12 8BT (☎ 022986 343)

BOWMAN, Dr John Christopher; CBE (1986); s of Mark Christopher Bowman (d 1987), of Prestbury, and Clara Vera, *née* Simister; *b* 13 August 1933; *Educ* Manchester GS, Reading Univ (BSc), Edinburgh Univ (PhD), N Carolina State Univ; *m* 15 July 1961, Sheila Jean, da of James Lorimer (d 1953), of Bramhall; 3 da (Hilary b 1962, Jillian b 1964, Bernadette b 1968); *Career* geneticist (later chief geneticist) Thornber Bros Ltd 1958-66, prof of animal prodn (dir of Univ farms) Reading Univ 1966-81, dir Centre for Agric Strategy Reading Univ 1975-81, sec to cncl NERC 1981-; chm Sonning Lawn Tennis Club, memb Sonning Parish Cncl; FIBioL 1970, FRSA 1976; *Books* Introduction to Animal Breeding, Animals for Man, Future of Beef Production in the EEc (with P Susmel), Hammonds Farm Animals (with J Hammond Jr); *Recreations* gardening, tennis, golf; *Style*— Dr John Bowman, CBE; Farmhouse, Charvil Lane, Sonning, Reading RG4 0TH (☎ 0734 693224); Natural Environment Research Council, Polaris House, North Star Ave, Swindon (☎ 0793 411654, 0793 485567, fax 0793 641652, telex 444293 ENVRE G)

BOWMAN, Sir John Paget; 4 Bt (UK 1884); s of Rev Sir Paget Mervyn Bowman, 3 Bt (d 1955); *b* 12 Feb 1904; *Educ* Eton; *m* 1, 1931, Countess Cajetana Hoyos (d 1948), da of Count Edgar Hoyos, of Schloss Soos, Lower Austria; 1 da (1 s decd); m 2, 1948, Frances Edith Marian, da of late Sir (James) Beethom Whitehead, KCMG; *Heir* kinsman, Paul Humphrey Armytage Bowman, *qv*; *Career* late 2 Lt 98 Surrey and Sussex Yeomanry, Field Bde RA; asst to chief accountant Western Electric London 1928-30, fin mangr Central Europe (Vienna) 1930-31, chief auditor London 1931-33; co sec Decca Record Co Ltd 1933-36; gen mangr Brymbo Steel Co Ltd 1936-40, fin mangr BSA Co 1940-43, commercial mangr Rolls-Royce Ltd (gas turbine engines) 1943-45; own business in Stoke-on-Trent 1945-48; gen mangr and dir Carter & Co Ltd Poole 1948-51; owner and mangr Purbeck Decorative Tile Co 1951-84; *Style*— Sir John Bowman, Bt; Bishops Green House, Greenham Common South, nr Newbury, Berks (☎ 063 523 202)

BOWMAN, Paul Humphrey Armytage; s of Maj Humphrey Ernest Bowman, CMG, CBE (d 1965; gs of Sir William Bowman, 1 Bt) and Frances Guinevere (d 1923), da of late Lt-Col Arthur Henry Armytage; hp of kinsman, Sir John Paget Bowman, 4 Bt, *qv*; *see also* Vice-Adm Sir Roderick Douglas Macdonald, KBE, Rear-Adm Josef Bartosik, CB, DSC, RN; *b* 10 August 1921; *Educ* Eton; *m* 1, 1943 (m dis 1947), Felicité Anne Araminta, da of Sir Harold Alfred MacMichael, GCMG, DSO; m 2, 1947 (m dis 1974), Gabrielle May, formerly w of Lt-Col Walter Currie, US Army; 1 da; m 3, 1974, Elizabeth Deirdre, da of late Bruce Campbell and formerly w of Maj-Gen Thomas Bell Lindsay Churchill, CB, CBE, MC; *Career* former Maj Coldstream Guards; dir Hill Samuel and Co Ltd 1962-78; *Clubs* White's, Roy Corinthian Yacht, The Brook (New York); *Style*— Paul Bowman, Esq; 24 Cooper Street, Double Bay, Sydney 2028, Australia

BOWMAN, Stephen Lindsay; s of Robert Lindsay Bowman, of 18 Fryent Way, Kingsbury, London, and Violet Elizabeth, *née* Lovelock; *b* 14 Feb 1950; *Educ* Preston Manor GS; *m* 1 Oct 1980, Marion Grace, da of Stanley Edward Kisbee (d 1985); 1 s (Gavin Lindsay b 12 June 1983); *Career* ptnr Blackburn Mellstrom (CAs) 1983-; ACA 1975, FCA 1981; *Recreations* gold, cricket, charitable societies; *Clubs* IOD; *Style*— Stephen Bowman, Esq; Blackborn Mellstrom, Greencoat House, Francis St, London SW1P 1DH (☎ 1 834 9434, fax 1 834 1592, car tel 836 24222, telex SQQ153 265871)

BOWMAN, William Archibald; s of Archibald George Bowman (d 1978), of Auchtermuchty, and Eleanor Little, *née* Ratcliff; *b* 30 May 1950; *Educ* George Watson's Coll Edinburgh, Univ Edinburgh (BCom); *m* 10 April 1973, Helen Macaulay, da of Malcolm Macleod, of Strathkinness; *Career* CA, ptnr Peat Marwick McLintock; *Clubs* Royal Northern, Univ Aberdeen; *Style*— William A Bowman, Esq; c/o Peat Marwick McLintock, Royfold House, Hill of Rubislaw, Anderson Drive, Aberdeen AB9 1JE (☎ 0224 208888, telex 739972, fax 0224 208027)

BOWMAN, William Powell; OBE (1972); s of George Edward Bowman (d 1977), and Isobel Conyers Dix (d 1971); *b* 22 Oct 1932; *Educ* Uppingham; *m* 26 April 1956, Patricia Elizabeth, da of Wallace Normand McCoskrie, of Hemel Hempstead, Herts; 2 s (Jonathan b 1957, Edward b 1959); *Career* RAF 1951-53, Royal Auxiliary Air Force 1953-58, Flying Offr (UK); United Biscuits plc 1966-77, (md intl div 1977-84 gp personnel dir); chm: Trident tst 1985-, Occupational Counselling and Unemployment Serv Ltd 1986-89, Van der Haas BV Holland 1987-89, Covent Gdn Market Authy 1988-; dir: Twyna & Fishlock Advertising Ltd 1987-88, Harvey Bergenroth Ltd (mgmnt conslts) 1987-; chm Br Food & Farming (Buckinghamshire Ctee) 1987-; tstee London Zoological Soc Devpt Cncl 1986-; fell London Zoological Soc, FInstD, FInstM,

MInstM, FIPM; *Recreations* gardening, tennis, travel; *Clubs* RAF, White Elephant; *Style*— William P Bowman, Esq; The Coach House, Shardeloes, Old Amersham, Bucks HP7 0RL (☎ 0494 724 187); Covent House, New Covent Garden, London SW8 (☎ 01 720 2211)

BOWMAN-SHAW, Sir (George) Neville; s of George Bowman-Shaw; *b* 4 Oct 1930; *Educ* Caldicott Prep Sch and privately; *m* 1962, Georgina, da of G Blundell; 3 s, 1 da; *Career* chm: Lancer Boss Rentals 1971-, Lancer Boss France 1967-, Lancer Boss Austria 1966-, Lancer Boss Ireland 1966-, Lancer Boss Gp 1966-, Lancer Boss Ltd 1967-, Boss Trucks & Equipment 1959-, Lancer Boss Int SA Lausanne 1962-, Boss Engrs 1961-, Lancer Boss España, Boss Trucks España, Steinbock GmbH Moosburg 1984-; memb: Design Cncl 1979-, Br Overseas Trade Bd Sept 1982-; kt 1984; *Recreations* shooting, wildlife, rare breeds and vintage tractors collections; *Clubs* Cavalry and Guards', Carlton, Hurlingham Constitutional; *Style*— Sir Neville Bowman-Shaw; Toddington Manor, Toddington, Beds (☎ 052 55 2576); Lancer Boss Group Ltd, Grovebury Rd, Leighton Buzzard, Beds (☎ 0525 372031)

BOWMER, Christopher Kenneth John; s of Kenneth Claude Bowmer, of Farnham, Surrey, and Violet Audrey, *née* Appleton; *b* 13 Dec 1946; *Educ* Farnham GS, Leeds Univ (BSc); *m* 28 March 1970, Rosalind Elizabeth Georgina, da of Kenneth Prosser, of Chester; 1 s (Simon b 1973), 1 da (Clare b 1971); *Career* fin dir Bowater Consumer Packaging Ltd 1980-85 (fin controller 1978-80), tres Bowater Industs plc 1988-; memb: Round Table, London Treasurers Club; ACMA 1973; *Recreations* tennis, theatre, music; *Clubs* Surrey Tennis and Country; *Style*— Christopher Bowmer, Esq; 114 Burdon Lane, Cheam, Surrey SM2 7DA (☎ 01 643 7156); Bowater Industries plc, Bowater Ho, Knightsbridge, London SW1X 7NN (☎ 01 584 7070, fax 01 581 1149)

BOWMONT AND CESSFORD, Marquess of; Charles Robert George Innes-Ker; s and h of 10 Duke of Roxburghe by Lady Jane Grosvenor, da of 5 Duke of Westminster; *b* 18 Feb 1981; *Style*— Marquess of Bowmont and Cessford

BOWN, Michael John David; s of Gordon Burley Bown (d 1979), of Leicester, and Sybil Charlotte, *née* Ellis (d 1973); *b* 22 May 1932; *Educ* Wyggeston Sch Leicester, Univ of Tubingen Germany, Queens' Coll Cambridge (BA, MA); *m* 2 July 1955, Dora Winifred, da of Wilfrid (d 1980), of Freckleton, Lancs; 2 s (Christopher b 1956, Jeremy b 1962), 1 da (Stephanie b 1959); *Career* Nat Serv Ra 2 Lt 1954-56; euro mangr Unicam Instruments Ltd 1958-60, mgmnt conslt PA Mgmnt Conslts Ltd 1960-64, dir and gen mangr John Dale Ltd 1964-69, chief exec Sturtevant Engrg co Ltd and subsidiaries 1969-74, gp pres Peabody Int Corpn 1974-82, chm Contessa Yachts Ltd 1982-85, dir UK Centre for Econ and Environmental Devpt 1984-86, dep chief exec Darchem Ltd 1986-88, business conslt 1988-; FRSA; *Recreations* sailing, hill walking, theatre, opera; *Clubs* United Oxford and Cambridge, Royal Lymington Yacht; *Style*— Michael Bown, Esq; Crow Wood House, Little Broughton, Stokesley, N Yorks; 7 Kreisel Walk, Kew Green, Richmond, Surrey (☎ 01 940 6775)

BOWN, Philip Arnold; MBE (1987); s of Ernest Bown (d 1984), and Gladys Bown; *b* 1 Sept 1934; *Educ* King Edwards Bath, Newport HS; *m* 28 April 1962, Diana, *née* Richards; 1 s (Damian), 3 da (Olivia, Tiffany, Coralie); *Career* Lt RA 1957-59; CA: Peat Marwick 1951-56, United Tport plc and subsids 1959-85 (dir 1977-85), chm and chief exec Brushes Int 1979-; High Sheriff Co of Gwent 1989-90; navigator winning Br Admirals Cup Teams; *Recreations* sailing; *Clubs* Royal Thames Yacht, Royal Yacht Sqdn, Royal Soc Arts; *Style*— Philip A Bown, Esq; Uplands, Chepstow, Gwent NP6 6BQ (☎ 0291 622419); Brushes Int Ltd, Lower Church St, Chepstow, Gwent NP6 5XT (☎ 02912 79022, fax 0291 2356)

BOWNESS, Sir Alan; CBE (1976); er s of George Bowness (d 1951), and Kathleen, *née* Benton (d 1973); *b* 11 Jan 1928; *Educ* Univ Coll Sch Hampstead, Downing Coll Cambridge (MA), Courtauld Inst of Art London Univ; *m* 1957, Sarah, da of Ben Nicholson OM (d 1982), the painter, and Dame Barbara Hepworth, DBE (d 1975), the sculptor; 1 s (Paul), 1 da (Sophie); *Career* lectr, reader and finally prof & dep dir Courtauld Inst of Art (London Univ) 1957-79; dir Tate Gallery 1980-88; dir Henry Moore Fndn 1988-; kt 1988; *Clubs* Athenaeum; *Style*— Sir Alan Bowness, CBE; 91 Castelnau, London SW13 (☎ 01 748 9696)

BOWNESS, Sir Peter Spencer; CBE (1981), DL Greater London (1982); s of Hubert Spencer Bowness (d 1981) and Doreen (Peggy) Blundell *née* Davies; *b* 19 May 1943; *Educ* Whitgift Sch Croydon; *m* 1, 27 July 1969, Marianne Hall; 1 da (Caroline b 1978); m 2, 6 June 1984, Mrs Patricia Jane Cook; *Career* slr; chm London Boroughs Assoc 1978-; dep chm Assoc Metropolitan Authys 1978/80; ldr Croydon Cncl 1976-79 and 1980-; memb: Audit Cmmn England & Wales 1983-, London Residuary Body 1985-, govr Whitgift Fndn; ret 1986; Freeman City of London 1987; kt 1987; *Recreations* travel, theatre; *Clubs* Carlton; *Style*— Sir Peter Bowness, CBE, DL

BOWRING, Lt-Col (Henry) Christopher White; s of Henry Illingworth Bowring (d 1934), of Whelprigg, Barbon, Westmorland, and Margaret Hardcastle, *née* White (d 1973); *Educ* Marlborough, Univ Coll Oxford (BA); *m* 4 Sept 1939, Helen Lydia Victoria, da of Rev David Denholm Fraser (d 1948), of Kelso, Roxburghshire; 1 s (Henry Charles Fraser b 30 April 1949), 3 da (Victoria Ann b 25 July 1941, Priscilla Jane b 11 August 1943, Bridget Charlotte Helen b 21 Feb 1948); *Career* cmmnd 2 Bn Royal Fus 1932, 1 Bn Royal Fus Ahmednegar India 1933-35, sick leave due to typhoid fever 1935-37, rejoined 2 Bn 1937-39, BEF 1939-40 (evacuated Dunkirk), Staff Coll Camberley 1941, GSO 2 Corps Dist Newmarket, Staff Duties N Africa ret 1948; qualified land agent, ptnr Davis & Bowring, ret 1971; High Sheriff of Westmorland 1955, JP Westmorland, DL Westmorland (subsequently Cumbria), lay reader Carlisle Diocese, prison visitor (open prison Milnthrope), memb Carlisle Diocesan Dilapidation Bd; FLAS 1961, FRICS; *Recreations* shooting, fishing; *Clubs* Army & Navy; *Style*— Lt-Col Christopher Bowring; Willow Cottage, Arkholme, Carnforth, Lancs (☎ 0468 21 205)

BOWRING, Edgar Rennie Harvey; MC (1945); yst s of Arthur Bowring (d 1960), of Goudhurst, Kent, and Margaret Harvey, *née* Beakbane (d 1944); *b* 5 Nov 1915; *Educ* Eastbourne Coll, Clare Coll Cambridge (MA), Berkeley Coll Yale, Law Soc Sch of Law; *m* 6 April 1940, Margaret (Peggy) Grace, da of John Grant Brook (d 1938), of Goudhurst, Kent; 2 s (Anthony b 1941, Philip b 1942), 1 da (Clare b 1959); *Career* cmmnd Kent Yeo RA 1939, served in Iceland 1940-42, Capt 1941, served in UK 1942-44, Maj 1942, served in France and Germany 1944-45 (despatches 1944), demobilised 1946, acting Lt-Col; slr 1949; ptnr Cripps Harries Hall 1950-55; joined C T Bowring & Co (Insurance) Ltd 1956, dir 1960; dir C T Bowring & Co Ltd 1962; chm English and American Insurance Co Ltd 1965-71; dep chm C T Bowring (Insurance) Holdings Ltd 1966-73; chm and chief exec C T Bowring & Co Ltd 1973-78; chm C T Bowring Insurance Holdings, Bowmaker Ltd, Crusader Insurance Co Ltd and other cos 1973-77; dir Marsh & McLennan Cos Inc New York USA 1980-88, advsy dir 1988-; Cmdt W Kent Special Constabulary 1965-71; tstee Memorial Univ of Newfoundland, Harlow Campus 1977-; pres Insurance Inst of London 1971-72 (dep pres 1970-71); vice-pres Corporation of Insurance Brokers 1970-77; memb Insurance Brokers Registration Cncl 1979-81; chm City Ctee for Electoral Reform 1978-81; CBIM (FBIM 1970); *Recreations* golf, gardening; *Clubs* City Univ, Rye Golf, Piltdown Golf; *Style*— Edgar Bowring, Esq, MC; Leopards Mill, Horam, Heathfield, East Sussex TN21 OPD (☎ 043 53 2687); The Bowring Building, Tower Place, London EC3 (☎ 01 283 3100)

BOWRING, Maj-Gen John Humphrey Stephen; CB (1968), OBE (1958), MC (1941); s of Maj Francis Stephen Bowring (ka 1915), of Torquay, and Helen Jessie Stonor, *née* McNabb (d 1945); *b* 13 Feb 1913; *Educ* Downside, RMA Woolwich, Trinity Coll Camb (MA); *m* 1956, Iona Margaret, da of Lenox Biggar Murray, OBE, of Painswick, Gloucs; 2 s (Charles, (twin), Michael), 2 da (Caroline (twin), Camilla); *Career* 2 Lt RE 1933, serv WWII Middle E and Burma, Bt Lt-Col 1953, IRE 17 Gurkha Div Malaya 1955-58, Col GS WO 1959-61, Brig 1961, m engr FARELF 1961-62, GS MOD 1964-65, Maj-Gen 1965, Engr-in-Chief (Army) 1965-68, Col Gurkha Engrs 1966-71, Col Cmdt RE 1968-73; dir Consolidated Gold Fields 1969-82; High Sheriff Wilts 1984; FICE; kt Sov Mid Order of malta 1986; *Recreations* flying, sailing, riding; *Clubs* Army and Navy, Royal Ocean Racing; *Style*— Maj-Gen John Bowring, CB, OBE, MC; The Manor Coln, St Aldwyns Cirencester, Gloucs GL7 5AG (☎ 0285 75 492)

BOWRING, Rev Lyndon; s of Arthur Bowing, of Caerphilly, Mid Glam, and Ellen May, *née* Gardner; *b* 15 Feb 1948; *Educ* Caerphilly GS, London Bible Coll; *m* 25 May 1974, Celia Joan, da of Capt Edward Ernest Bartholomew (d 1980), of Shoreham-by-Sea; 1 s (Daniel Alexander), 1 da (Emma Charlotte); *Career* Elim Pentecostal minister Kensington Temple 1972-80 (assoc minister 1980-), chm NFOL 1981-83, exec chm Care 1983-; vice chm: Billy Graham's Mission 1989, Luis Palau's Mission 1984; chm Maranatha Christian Tst, memb Evangelical Alliance Cncl 1988-; dir Kingsway Pubns and Music, London and Nationwide Missions; public speaker christian events; *Recreations* family, reading, walking, exploring London; *Style*— The Rev Lyndon Bowring; 22 Thornton Ave, Chiswick, London W4 (☎ 01 747 3796); Care, 53 Romney St, London SW1 (☎ 01 233 0455, fax 01 233 0983)

BOWRING, Peter; eldest s of Frederick Clive Bowring (d 1965), and Agnes Walker, *née* Cairns (d 1961); *b* 22 April 1923; *Educ* Shrewsbury; *m* 1, 1946 (m dis) Barbara Ekaterina Brewis; 1 s (Antony), 1 da (Thérèsa); m 2, 1979 (m dis), Carol Hutchings; m 3, 1986, Carole M Dear; *Career* serv WWII 1939-46, cmmnd Rifle Brigade 1942; serv: Egypt, N Africa, Italy, Austria (despatches); chm: Help the Aged 1977-87, C T Bowring & Co 1978-82; vice-chm Marsh & McLennan 1982-84 (dir 1980- 84); memb of Lloyds; dir Centre for Policy Studies 1983-88; chm City Arts Tst 1987- (dep chm 1986-87); dir Ind Primary and Secdy Educn Tst; chm: Aldeburgh Fndn 1982-89, bd of govrs St Dunstan's Educnl Fndn; memb: bd of govrs Shrewsbury Sch, Guild of Freemen of City of London, Liveryman Worshipful Co of Insurers; Guild of World Traders (sr Warden 1988-89); FRSA; *Recreations* sailing, motoring, listening to music, cooking, photography; *Clubs* Royal Thames Yacht, Royal Green Jackets; *Style*— Peter Bowring, Esq; 79 New Concordia Wharf, Mill St, London SE1 2BA (☎ 01 237 0818)

BOWRON, John Lewis; CBE (1986); s of John Henry Bowron (d 1944) and Lavinia *née* Prosser (d 1967); *b* 1 Feb 1924; *Educ* Grangefield GS Stockton on Tees, King's Coll London (LLB, FKC); *m* 19 Aug 1950, Patricia, da of Arthur Cobby (d 1959) of Worthing; 2 da (Judith b 1952, Margaret b 1956); *Career* RAF 1943-46; slr 1950; ptnr Malcolm Wilson & Cobby, sls, Worthing 1952 and sr ptnr 1964-74); sec general of The Law Society 1974, ret 1987; legal assessor Insur Brokers Registration Cncl 1987-; memb Disciplinary Appeals Ctee of the Stock Exchange; pt/t chm Social Security Appeal Tbnl 1988-; *Recreations* golf, listening to music; *Style*— John Bowron, Esq; Wellington Cottage, Albourne, Hassocks, West Sussex BN6 9DE (☎ 0273 833345)

BOWSER OF ARGATY AND THE KING'S LUNDIES, David Stewart; JP (Perthshire 1956); s of Maj David Charles Bowser, CBE, (d 1979), and Maysie Murray, *née* Henderson (d 1974); in direct descent from William Bowser of Wharram le Street, Yorkshire, who lived in the mid 15 century; *b* 11 Mar 1926; *Educ* Harrow, Trinity Cambridge (BA Agric); *m* 1951, Judith, da of Col Sir John Gordon Crabbe, OBE, MC (d 1961), of Duncow, Dumfries; 1 s (Niall), 4 da (Emma, Susan, Fiona, Anna); *Career* Capt Scots guards 1944-47; forestry cmmnr 1974-82, tstee Scottish Forestry Tst 1983-, (chm 1987-88); memb Queen's Body Guard for Scotland (Royal Company of Archers); elder Killin and Ardeonaig Parish Church, Convener Property Ctee of the Presbytery of Stirling; *Recreations* shooting, fishing, stalking; *Style*— David Bowser, Esq, JP; Auchlyne, Killin, Perthshire FK21 8RG (☎ 056 72 506)

BOWSHER, His Hon Judge Peter Charles; QC (1978); s of Charles and Ellen Bowsher; *b* 9 Feb 1935; *Educ* Ardingly, Oriel Coll Oxford; *m* 1960, Deborah, da of Frederick Wilkins, of Vancouver; 2 s; *Career* barrister 1959, rec Crown Ct SE circuit 1983-87, bencher Middle Temple 1985-, official referee and circuit judge 1987-; *Clubs* Brooks's, RAC; *Style*— His Hon Judge Bowsher, QC; Royal Courts of Justice, Strand, London WC2A 2LL

BOWTELL, Ann Elizabeth; *née* Kewell; da of John Albert Kewell, of Hove, and Olive Rose, *née* Sims; *b* 25 April 1938; *Educ* Kendrick Girls Sch Reading, Girton Coll Cambridge (BA); *m* 11 Feb 1961, Michael John, s of Norman Bowtell; 2 s (Thomas, Samuel), 2 da (Sophie, Harriet); *Career* asst princ Nat Assistance Bd 1960-64; DHSS: princ 1964-73, asst sec 1973-80, under sec 1980-86, dep sec 1986-; *Style*— Mrs Michael Bowtell; DHSS, Richmond House, Whitehall (☎ 01 210 5459)

BOWYER, Barry Robert; s of Flt Lt Frederick George Bowyer (d 1955), of Purley, Surrey, and Norah Margaret, *née* Bonwick (d 1966); *b* 31 July 1936; *Educ* Glenwood Sch Surrey; *m* 1962, Gillian Margaret, da of Walter Henry Mann (d 1948), of Suffolk; 3 s (Christopher b 1964, Jonathan b 1967, Robert b 1969); *Career* RAF 1956-59; tech advsr to electronics indust 1959-63, publishing and advtg accounts mangr 1963-67, founded Bowyer Design Consultancy Ltd 1967 (added BD Advtg 1978, BD PR in 1980), memb (Cons) Ashford Borough Cncl (representing Beddenden Ward); govr John Mayne Sch; *Recreations* vintage cars, painting, sculpture, travel; *Clubs* Naval and Military, Bentley Drivers, Aston Martin Owners; *Style*— Barry Bowyer, Esq; Toll Gate House, Biddenden, Ashford, Kent (☎ 0580 291830/291 560, fax 0580 292 080)

BOWYER, (Arthur) David; s of Sir Eric Blacklock Bowyer, KCB, KBE, (d 1964), and Elizabeth Crane *née* Nicholls (now (m 1975) Lady Caine w of Sir Sidney Caine,

KCMG, *qv*); *b* 27 August 1988; *Educ* Tonbridge, Trinity Hall Cambridge (BA); *m* 6 Dec 1969, Ann Victoria, da of His Hon Judge Herbert Christopher Beaumont, MBE, of Minskip Lodge, Minskip, Boroughbridge, Yorks *qv*, 2 s (Edward Christopher b 1972, Andrew Mark b 1975), 1 da (Katharine Sarah b 1971); *Career* admitted slr 165; ptnr Clifford Chance (formerly Clifford-Turner) 1968-; Law Society 1976, Int Acad of Estate and Tst Law (USA); *Recreations* skiing, golf, tennis, shooting; *Clubs* Boodles; *Style—* A D Bowyer, Esq; Ashe Warren House, Ashe Warren, Overton, Basingstoke, Hants, RG25 3AW (☎ 0256 770 215); Clifford Chance, Blackfriars House, 19 New Bridge Street, London, EC4 (☎ 01 353 0211)

BOWYER, Hon George Philip Paul; 3 s of 2 Baron Denham; *b* 13 Dec 1964; *Style—* The Hon George Bowyer

BOWYER, Hon Henry Martin Mitford; 2 s of 2 Baron Denham; *b* 9 May 1963; *Style—* The Hon Henry Bowyer

BOWYER, Hon Jocelyn Jane; o da of 2 Baron Denham; *b* 18 Oct 1957; *Educ* Riddlesworth Hall, Sherborne Sch for Girls; *Career* chartered physiotherapist; *Style—* The Hon Jocelyn Bowyer; The Farmhouse, 23 Broadhinton Rd, London SW4

BOWYER, (Arthur) William; s of Arthur Bowyer (d 1979), of Leek, Staffs, and Emma Bowyer (d 1983); *b* 25 May 1926; *Educ* Burslem Sch of Art, Royal Coll of Art; *m* Vera Mary, da of William Norman Small (d 1986); 2 s (Francis David b 1951, Jason Richard b 1957), 1 da (Emma Jane b 1966); *Career* Bevin Boy Sneyd Colliery Burslem 1942-44; teacher Gravesend Sch of Art, Central Sch of Art, Walthamstow Sch of Art, Sir John Cass, head of fine art Maidstone Coll of Art 1971-81, ret to paint; work in collections: Royal Acad, Royal Soc of Painters in Watercolour, Nat Portrait Gallery, Graves Gallery Sheffield, Arts Cncl of GB; hon sec New English Art Club; ARA 1964; memb: Royal Soc of Painters in Watercolour 1969, Royal Acad 1973, Royal Soc of Portrait Painters; *Recreations* cricket, swimming; *Clubs* Arts; *Style—* William Bowyer, Esq; 12 Cleveland Avenue, Chiswick, London W4 (☎ 01 994 0346); Studio, 8 Gainsborough Rd, Chiswick, London W4

BOWYER-SMYTH, Sir Thomas Weyland; 15 Bt (E 1661); s of Capt Sir Philip Weyland Bowyer-Smyth, 14 Bt, RN (d 1978); *b* 25 June 1960; *Heir* kinsman, John Windham; *Style—* Sir Thomas Bowyer-Smyth, Bt

BOWYER-SMYTH, Lady - Veronica Mary; 2 da of Capt Cyril Whichelo Bower, DSC, RN (ret), of Rose Cottage, Fordwich, Kent; *m* 1951, as his 2 w, Capt Sir Philip Weyland Bowyer-Smyth, 14 Bt, RN (d 1978); 1 s, 1 da, (and 1 s decd); *Style—* Lady Bowyer-Smyth

BOX, Donald Stewart; s of late Stanley Carter Box (d 1957), of Penarth, Glam, and Elizabeth Mary Stewart Box; *b* 22 Nov 1917; *Educ* Llandaff Cathedral Sch, St John's Sch Pinner, Co Sch Harrow; *m* 1, 1940 (m dis 1947), Margaret Kennington, da of Charles Bates; m 2, 1948 (m dis 1973) Peggy Farr, *née* Gooding, of London; m 3, 1973, Margaret Rose Davies; 1 da; *Career* served RAF 1939-45, Egypt, Palestine, Transjordan, Flt Lt 1945; memb Stock Exchange 1945, former sr ptnr Lyddon (stockbrokers) Cardiff, Swansea and London; MP (C) Cardiff North 1959-66; *Clubs* Cardiff and Co; *Style—* Donald Box, Esq; Laburnum Cottage, Sully Rd, Penarth, S Glam CF6 2TX (☎ 0222 707966; Douglas Buildings, Royal Stuart Lane, Cardiff CF1 6EL (☎ 0222 494822, telex 497618 TPES G)

BOX, Stephen Thomas; s of Thomas George of Nungaton, and Edith Helen *née* Reid; *Educ* Queen Elizabeth GS Atherstone, Salford Univ (BSc), Physical Electronics City Business Sch (DipBA); *m* 8 Jan 1988, Sarah, da of Dennis Grimwood Roscow; 1 da (Daisy Philippa b 24 Aug 1988); *Career* sci offr AERE Harwell 1968-74, computer cnslt CSI Ltd 1974-76, systems analyst Chase Manhattan Bank 1976-78, head int systems dvpt Citicorp 1978-80, freelance mgmnt cnslt 1980-86; dir, debt Decuriti securities operations, Kleinwort Benson Ltd 1987-; *Recreations* shooting, tennis, golf, music, opera; *Style—* Stephen T Box, Esq; Woodmans Farm, Perrymans Lane, Burwash, East Sussex, TN19 7DN (☎ 0435 882 812); Kleinwort Benson Ltd, 20 Fenchurch Street, London, EC3P (☎ 01 623 8000, telex 888531)

BOX-GRAINGER, Christopher Charles Walter; s of Walter Thomas Reginald Box (d 1970), of Rainham, Essex, and Olive Maud, *née* Henley (d 1976); *b* 18 April 1921; *Educ* Hugh Myddleton Sch, City and Guilds Inst, Victoria Coll Alexandria, El Azhar Univ Cairo (BA), Brunel Coll Technol (DipTech); *m* 23 Nov 1951, Jane Avril, da of George Kenneth Hampshire (d 1964), of Hallam Court, Hallam St, London; 1 s (Paul b Aug 1954), 2 da (Eve b Jan 1953, Jill b April 1957); *Career* GPO Film Unit and Crown Film Unit 1937-39; serv WWII 1939-46; 1946-54: Features and outside broadcasting depts BBC, freelance radio and theatre work UK and N America; dir: Hampshire Tutorials Ltd 1969-, Cricket Soc Ltd 1969-81, L'Ecole Hampshire Sarl France 1977-, Telephone Rentals Gp 1979-88 (joined 1954); exec dir Telecommunications Engrg & Mfrg Assoc Ltd 1980-86 (joined 1967), dir Peter Nicholas & Co Ltd 1986-; chm working pty on telecommunications for disabled RNIB/TEMA, hon admin Hants Sch 50 Anniversary Educnl Tst; chm: Cricket Soc 1967-81 (joined 1953), MCCLI 1970-73, MCC sub-ctees 1973-85, Cricket Welfare Fund 1986-; Freeman City of London 1985, Liveryman Worshipful Co Marketors 1982; FRGS (1953), M/Prod E 1959, MBIM 1959, FInst BE 1981, FInst M 1981; Order of the Nile Egypt 1943 Silver Cross of Liberation Greece 1946; *Recreations* cricket, writing, reading, geographical survey, wine and food; *Clubs* MCC, The Cricket Soc, RAC, Jesters, Lord's Taverners, Eccentric; *Style—* Christopher Box-Grainger, Esq; 23 Melton Crt, Old Brompton Rd, London SW7 3JQ (☎ 01 584 0744); 42 Urbanización Doña Pillar, Mijas, Malaga, Spain; L'Eole Hampshire, SARL, Veyrines-de-Domme, 24250 DOMME, Dordogne France (☎ 01033 53 29 53 15)

BOXALL, Bernard; CBE 1963; s of Arthur Sidney Boxall (d 1960), of Banstead, Surrey, and Maude Mary, *née* Mills (d 1974); *b* 17 August 1906; *Educ* King's Coll Sch Wimbledon, Imperial Coll London (BSc); *m* 11 July 1931, Marjorie Lilian, da of William George Emery (d 1959), of Deal, Kent; 1 s (Gerald b 27 May 1936), 1 da (Caroline Jill b 17 March 1939); *Career* gen mangr J A King & Co Ltd 1934-41, mgmnt cnslt P E Int 1942-59; dir: Export Packing Service Ltd 1954-77, Booker Bros (Eng Hldgs) Ltd 1956-62; chm Scottish Aviation Ltd 1957-66, memb SBAC 1959-65, dep chm Lindustries Ltd 1960-70, mgmnt cnslt Bernard Boxall CBE 1960-, memb Highland Transport Bd 1963-66, dep chm Alvis Ltd 1963-67, memb Scot Advsy Ctee for Civil Aviation 1965-71, dir: Industl Reorganisation Corpn 1966-71, Chrysler (UK) Ltd 1967-71, chm Br United Trawlers Ltd 1969-71; dir: A J Mills (Hldgs) Ltd 1969-78, Erma Ltd 1972-85; dep chm Lancer Boss Gp Ltd 1974-; memb: Scottish Econ Planning Cncl 1967-71, Monopolies Commn 1969-74; Freeman City of London 1962, Master Worshipful Co of Coachmakers and Coach Harness Makers 1977; FCGI Imperial Coll London 1969, FIC Imperial Coll London 1971; FIMech E, FIProd E, FIMC; *Recreations* golf, gardening; *Clubs* Walton Heath GC; *Style—* Bernard Boxall, Esq, CBE

BOXALL, Richard George; s of Thomas Boxall, OBE, of Honiton, Devon; *b* 23 May 1936; *Educ* Bedford Sch, Christ's Coll Cambridge (MA); *m* 1960, Dorothy, da of Samuel Breeze, of Folkestone; 2 s, 1 da; *Career* mech engr, dir: Ibstock Johnson plc; pres: CEO Glen-Gery Corpn Reading PA USA; *Recreations* sailing, gardening; *Clubs* Naval; *Style—* Richard Boxall, Esq; Four Winds, S Tulpehocken Rd, Reading, PA, USA; Rue du Commandant Charcot, Jard sur Mer, France 85520

BOYCE, Graham Hugh; s of Cdr Hugh Boyce, DSC, RN, and Madeline Millicent, *née* Manley; *b* 6 Oct 1945; *Educ* Hurstpierpoint Coll, Jesus Coll Cambridge (MA); *m* 11 April 1970, Janet Elizabeth, da of Rev Gordon Charles Craig Spencer, of Bath; 1 s (James b 1971), 3 da (Rachel b 1974, Sara b 1980, Josephine b 1984); *Career* VSO Antigua 1967, HM Dip Serv 1968; 2 sec Ottawa 1971 (3 sec), MECAS Shemlan 1972-74, 1 sec Tripoli 1974-77, FCO 1977-81, 1 sec Kuwait 1981-85, asst head Middle E Dept FCO 1985-86, cnsllr and consul gen Stockholm 1987; *Recreations* squash, tennis, reading; *Clubs* Sällskapet, Cannons; *Style—* Graham Boyce, Esq; c/o FCO, King Charles St, London SW1A 2AH

BOYCE, John Leslie; s of late Sir (Harold) Leslie Boyce, 1 Bt, KBE; hp of nephew, Sir Robert Boyce, 3 Bt; *b* 16 Nov 1934; *m* 1, 1957 (m dis 1975), Finola Mary, da of late James Patrick Maxwell, of Bansha, Co Tipperary; 1 s, 3 da; m 2, 1980, Fusako, da of Yonesaku Ishibashi, of Shinagawa-ku, Tokyo, Japan; 2 da; *Style—* John Boyce, Esq,; 182 Huntingdon Rd, Mt Waverley, Victoria 3149, Australia

BOYCE, Joseph Frederick; JP 1975; s of Frederick Arthur Boyce (d 1976), and Rosalie Mary Pinck (d 1987); *b* 10 August 1926; *Educ* Roundhay Sch Leeds, Leeds Poly; *m* 1953, Nina Margaret, da of Arthur Frederick Tebb (d 1956), of Leeds; 2 s (Nicholas Joseph b 1954, Jeremy Frederick b 1957); *Career* chartered surveyor 1947-, gen mangr Telford Devpt Corpn 1979-86 (chief quantity surveyor 1964-71, technical dir 1971-75, dep gen mangr 1975-79); mgmnt conslt (UK and France) 1986-; pres Ironbridge Rowing Club 1974-; FRICS; *Recreations* reading, rugby, rowing, walking, water colour painting, travel; *Clubs* Ironbridge Rowing (pres); *Style—* Joseph Boyce, Esq, JP; The Uplands, Port Hill Gdns, Shrewsbury; Gpieres, 06620 Le Bar Sur Loup, France

BOYCE, Sir Robert (Charles) Leslie; 3 Bt (UK 1952); s of Sir Richard (Leslie) Boyce, 2 Bt (d 1968), and Jacqueline Anne Boyce-Dennis, *née* Hill; *b* 2 May 1962; *Educ* Cheltenham, Salford Univ; *m* 1985, Fiona Margaret, 2 da of John Savage, of Harborough Road, Coventry; *Heir* unc, John Leslie Boyce; *Career* electronics engr; *Clubs* IEE; *Style—* Sir Robert Boyce, Bt; 117 Derby Road, Northampton NN1 4JP; Plessy Research (Caswell) Ltd, Caswell, nr Towcester, Northants

BOYCE, Thomas Anthony John; s of John Boyce of Wellesley House, Broadstairs, Kent (d 1978) and Barbara Maude *née* Blackwell (d 1970); *b* 4 Dec 1942; *Educ* Eton, Christ Church Oxford; *m* 7 April 1973, Lucy Caroline Penelope, only da of Capt. Thomas Edward Harold Parsons, of Ampney House, Cirencester, Glos (d 1950); 1 s (Edward b 1975), 1 da (Caroline b 1978); *Career* banker; dir: Hambros Bank Ltd, Hambros Australia Ltd; Capt - Royal Yeo; *Recreations* hunting, stalking; *Clubs* Boodles, Pratts; *Style—* Thomas Boyce, Esq; Downs Lodge, Shipton-under-Wychwood, Oxfordshire, OX7 6HY (☎ Burford 2269); 41 Bishopsgate, London Ec2P 2AA (☎ 01 588 2851, telex: 886337, fax: 01 628 5131)

BOYCE, Walter Edwin; OBE (1970); s of Rev Joseph Edwin Boyce (d 1928), and Alice Elizabeth, *née* Gibbs (d 1968); *b* 30 July 1918; *Educ* HS for Boys Trowbridge; *m* 8 Oct 1942, Edna Lane, da of Harold James Gargett (d 1957); 2 da (Diana b 1944, Helen b 1948); *Career* served RA 1939-46, 52(L) Scottish Div 1940-43, Gunnery Staff Course 1943, Inst in Gunnery Sch of Artillery Larkhill and ME Sch of Artillery Cairo 1943-46, Maj, attached Mil Mission to Greece 1945-46; Social Services Director: dir Social Services Essex 1969-78, Co Welfare Offr Essex 1957-70, dep Co Welfare Offr Cheshire 1952-57, Shropshire Div 1949-52; hon appts, advisor to Assoc of Co Cncls 1965-78, pres Co Welfare Offrs Soc 1967-68, memb Sec of State's Advsy Personal Soc Servs Cncl 1973-80, (chm of Cncls Persons with Handicaps Gp); memb Nat Working Parties Reorganisation of Health Servs 1972-74; voluntary servs: memb nat exec ctee Royal Nat Inst for the Blind and Age Concern, govr and exec ctee memb Queen Elizabeth's Fndn for the Disabled Leatherhead; *Recreations* golf, sailing, travel; *Style—* Walter E Boyce, Esq, OBE; Highlanders Barn, Rodbridge Lane, Long Melford, Suffolk CO10 0AD (☎ 0787 73751)

BOYCOTT, Geoffrey; OBE (1981); s of late Thomas Wilfred Boycott, and Jane, *née* Speight; *b* 21 Oct 1940; *Educ* Kinsley Secdy Mod, Hemsworth GS; *Career* cricketer; played for: Yorks 1962-86 (Co Cap 1963, Capt 1971-78), England 1964-74, 1977-82; scored one hundredth first class century 1977 (England v Australia); one hundred and fiftieth century 1986, exceeded world record no of runs scored in Test Matches Delhi 1981; memb Yorks CCC (gen ctee 1984-); *Books* Geoff Boycott's Book for Young Cricketers (1976), Put to the Test: England in Australia 1978-79 (1979), Geoff Boycott's Cricket Quiz (1979), Boycott On Batting (1980), Opening Up (1980), In the Fast Lane: Eng in WI (1981), Master Class (1982), Boycott, The Autobiography (1987); *Recreations* golf, tennis; *Style—* Geoff Boycott, Esq, OBE; Pear Tree Farm, Water Lane, Woolley, Wafefield, W Yorks WF4 2JQ

BOYD, Sir Alexander Walter; 3 Bt (UK 1916); s of late Maj Cecil Anderson Boyd, MC, MD, late RAMC, 2 s of 1 Bt; suc unc, Sir Walter Herbert Boyd, 2 Bt, 1948; *b* 16 June 1934; *m* 1958, Molly Madeline, da of late Ernest Arthur Rendell, of Vernon, Br Columbia; 2 s, 3 da, m 1988, Lee Ann Dillon; 1 s (Kyle Robert Rendell b 1987); *Heir* s, Ian Walter Rendell Boyd; *Style—* Sir Alexander Boyd, Bt; RR3, Vernon, Br Columbia, Canada

BOYD, Hon Mrs (Catherine); *née* Jay; yr (twin) da of Baron Jay, PC (Life Peer), *qv*; *b* 1945; *Educ* (BA); *m* 197-, Stewart Boyd QC; 1 s (Matthew b 1976), 3 da (Rachel b 1972, Emily b 1973, Hannah b 1987); *Books* The Br Way of Birth (jtly 1982); *Style—* The Hon Mrs Boyd; 1 Gayton Crescent, Hampstead, London NW3; Wraxall Manor, Higher Wraxall, Dorchester, Dorset

BOYD, David Barclay; JP (Argyll and Bute); s of David Boyd, and Janet McLellan Barclay Boyd; *b* 23 July 1933; *Educ* Dunoon GS, Edinburgh Univ (BSc); *m* 8 Nov 1958, Emily Margaret, da of James Wilson, of Dunoon; 2 s (David James b 1960, Andrew Wilson b 1968), 2 da (Kirsty Allan b 1959, Bryony McFarlane b 1964); *Career* cmmnd 2 Lt RE 1957, active serv Cyprus 1957-58; dist offr Forestry Cmmn, asst regnl offr Argyll 1960-62, factor Glencruitten Estate Oban 1962-66, factor Islay Estate

Islay of Islay 1966-; dir and former chm Islay Farmers Ltd, cncl memb Scottish Landowners Fedn, memb BBC Scottish Rural Affrs Advsy Ctee; memb Argyl and Bute rating and valuation appeals ctee, crew memb Sceptre America's Cup Challenge at Newport Rhode Island 1958; fell Inst of Chartered Foresters; *Recreations* shooting, sailing; *Clubs* Royal Socttish Automobile; *Style*— David Boyd, Esq, JP; 105 Hyndland Rd, Glasgow (☎ 041 339 7641); Ceannloch Hse, Bridgend, Islay, Argyll (☎ 049 681 464); Islay Estate Off, Bridgend, Isle of Islay, Argyll (☎ 049 681 221)

BOYD, Dennis Galt; CBE (1988); s of Thomas Ayre Boyd (d 1968), and Minnie, *née* Galt (d 1962); *b* 3 Feb 1931; *Educ* S Shields Boys Sch; *m* 1953, Pamela Mary, da of John Moore McLean (d 1980); 1 s (Simon) 1 da (Angela); *Career* dir Corporate Servs Health and Safety Exec 1975-80, chief conciliation offr Advsy, Conciliation and Arbitration Serv 1980-; *Recreations* golf; *Clubs* Civil Serv; *Style*— Dennis Boyd, Esq, CBE; Dunelm, Silchester Rd, Little London, Nr Basingstoke, Hants; Advsy, Conciliation and Arbitration Serv, 11/12 St James's Sq, London SW1Y 4LA

BOYD, Sir (John) Francis; s of John Crichton Dick Boyd, of Ilkley, and Kate Boyd; *b* 11 July 1910; *Educ* Ilkley GS, Silcoates Sch Wakefield; *m* 1946, Margaret, da of George Dobson, of Scarborough; 1 s, 2 da; *Career* served WWII 1939-45; Parly correspondent Manchester Guardian 1937-39, political correspondent Manchester Guardian and Guardian 1945-72, political ed 1972-75; chm Lobby Journalists 1949-50; hon tres Commons Preservation Soc 1977-81, vice pres 1981-; hon LLD (Leeds) 1973; kt 1976; *Style*— Sir Francis Boyd; 7 Summerlee Avenue, London N2 9QP (☎ 01 444 8601)

BOYD, Ian Mair; s of John Telfer Boyd (d 1976), of Ayr, and Margaret Mair, *née* Murdoch; *b* 4 Sept 1944; *Educ* Ayr Acad, London Business Sch (MSc); *m* 20 Dec 1975, Theodora (Toody), da of Theodor Georgopoulos, of Athens; 2 s (Telfer, Fraser), 1 da (Amber); *Career* CA 1966, gp fin dir The Weir Gp plc 1981-, cncl memb Inst of CA's of Scotland 1987-; fell ICAS 1966; *Recreations* golf, hill-walking, skiing, bird watching, fishing; *Clubs* Prestwick Golf; *Style*— Ian Boyd, Esq; Bonnybrae, 5A Bruce Rd, Glasgow G41 5EL (☎ 041 429 1840); The Weir Group Plc, 149 Newlands Rd, Glasgow G44 4EX (☎ 041 637 7111, fax 041 637 2221, telex 77161 WPL CRT)

BOYD, Ian Walter Rendell; s and h of Sir Alexander Boyd, 3 Bt; *b* 14 Mar 1964; *Style*— Ian Boyd Esq

BOYD, James Edward; s of Robert Edward Boyd and Elizabeth Reid Sinclair; *b* 14 Sept 1928; *Educ* Kelvinside Acad, The Leys Sch Cambridge; *m* Judy Ann Christey Scott; 2 s, 2 da; *Career* CA Scot (dist) 1951; ptnr McClelland Ker & Co 1953-61; fin dir: Lithgows Ltd 1962-69, Scott Lithgow Ltd 1970-78; dir and fin advsr Denholm Gp of Cos 1968-; dir: Lithgows (Hldgs) Ltd 1962-, Ayrshire Metal Products plc 1965-, Invergordon Distillers (Hldgs) plc 1966-88 (md 1966-67), Nairn & Williamson (Hldgs) Ltd 1968-75, GB Papers plc 1977-87, Carlton Industries plc 1978-84, James Liver UK Hldgs Ltd 1987-, Jebsens Drilling plc 1978-85, Save & Prosper Gp ltd 1987-; Scottish Widows' Fund & Life Assurance Soc 1981-, (dep chm 1988-) Br Linen Bank Ltd 1983- (Gov 1986-), Shanks & McEwan Gp plc 1983-, Scottish Exhibition Centre 1983-,; Civil Aviation Authority 1984-85,; Bank of Scotland 1984-,; Bank of Wales 1986-88; dep chm: BAA plc (formerly British Airports Authy) 1985-; chm: Fairfield Shipbuilding & Engrg Co Ltd 1964-65, Gartmore European Investmt Tst plc 1978-, English & Caledonian Investment plc 1981-, Yarrow plc 1984-86; memb: Clyde Port Authority 1974-80, cncl Inst of Chartered Accountants of Scotland 1977-83 (vice pres 1980-82, pres 1982-83), exec ctee Accountants Jt Disciplinary Scheme 1979-81; *Recreations* tennis, golf, gardening; *Style*— James E Boyd, Esq; Dunard, Station Road, Rhu, Dunbartonshire G84 8LW (☎ 0436 820441); The Denholm Group, Inter-City House, 80 Oswald Street, Glasgow G1 4PX (☎ 041 204 1004)

BOYD, John; s of John Richardson Boyd, and Janet, *née* Anderson; *b* 5 April 1925; *Educ* Heriot Watts Edinburgh; *Career* WWII served RN 1942-45; Royal Milliner; *Style*— John Boyd, Esq; 93 Walton St, London SW3 2HP (☎ 01 589 7601); 91 Walton Street, London SW3 2HP (☎ 01 589 7601)

BOYD, (David) John; QC (1982); s of David Boyd (d 1964), and Ellen Jane, *née* Gruer (d 1953); *b* 11 Feb 1935; *Educ* Eastbourne Coll, St George's Sch Newport USA, Gonville and Caius Coll Cambridge (MA); *m* 1960, Raija Sinikka, da of Onni Lindholm (d 1952), of Finland, 1 s (Roderick b 1972), 1 da (Karin b 1969); *Career* barr Gray's Inn 1963, bencher 1988; sec asst ICI 1957-62, legal asst Pfizer 1962-66, legal offr Henry Wiggin and Co 1966-68; joined Inco Europe Ltd 1968, sec and chief legal offr Inco Europe Ltd 1972-86, dir 1984-86; in private practice at Bar 1986; dir legal services Digital Equipment Co 1986-; chm CBI competition panel 1988-; dir Impala Platinum 1972-78; gen cmmr of Income Tax 1978-81; memb Senate of Inns of Ct and Bar 1978-81; chm Bar Assoc for Commerce, Finance and Industry 1980-81; sec-gen Assoc des Juristes d'Enterprise Européens 1983-84; legal advsr Review Bd for Govt Contracts 1984-; FCIArb; *Style*— John Boyd Esq, QC; 3 St Katherine's Road, Henley-on-Thames, Oxon RG9 1PJ (☎ 0491 572095)

BOYD, John George; s of John Boyd (d 1980), of Corby, Northampton, and Christina Blair, *née* Wood; *b* 7 April 1940; *Educ* Mackie Acad Stonehaven Kincardineshire, Gray's Sch of Art Aberdeen (DA), Hospitalfield Coll of Art Arbroath, Jordanhill Coll of Educn Glasgow; *m* 1, 23 Oct 1965 (m dis 1975), Janet, *née* Binns; m 2, 10 June 1980 (m dis 1985), Marilyn E, *née* Apps; m 3, 11 Nov 1985, Estrild W, *née* Macdougal; *Career* teacher 1963-78; pt/t lectr: Glasgow Sch of Art 1967-88, further educn 1978-; artist exhibitions incl: New 57 Gallery Edinburgh 1967, Armstrong Gallery Glasgow 1970, Glasgow Art Club (1971, 1973, 1974, 1976, 1980, 1984), Present Gallery Lanark 1975 and 1980, Henderson's Gallery Edinburgh 1978, Corners Gallery Glasgow 1985, Barclay Lennie Fine Art Glasgow 1988; regular exhibitor at: RSA, RA, RGI, RP; works in private collections of Earl of Moray, Sir Norman McFarlane, Robert Fleming Hldgs; public collections: People's Palace Glasgow, Paisley Art Gallery, Lillie Art Gallery Milngavie; Latimer Award RSA 1972; elected RGI 1982 (memb cncl 1984-); *Recreations* reading, music, wine; *Clubs* Glasgow Art; *Style*— John Boyd, Esq; Hayston, 26 Cleveden Rd, Glasgow G12 OPX (☎ 041 357 2176)

BOYD, Sir John McFarlane; CBE (1974); s of late James Boyd and late Mary *née* Marshall; *b* 8 Oct 1917; *Educ* Hamilton St Public Sch, Glencairn Secdy Modern; *m* 1940, Elizabeth Inglis, da of late James McIntyre, of Motherwell; 2 da (Catherine, Mary); *Career* eng apprenticeship 1932-37; div offr AEU 1946-53; exec offr AUEW 1953-75; gen sec AUEW 1975-82; chm: nat exec Br Lab Pty 1967 (memb 1957-67); TUC gen cncl memb 1967-75 and 1978-82; memb ACAS 1979-82; dir: Industl Trg Servs 1982-86, UKAEA 1980-1985, ICL (UK) Ltd 1983-88; BSC 1981-86; govr BBC 1982-87; Pres. Hour-of Revival Association (Internat Radio Evangelism); awarded Order of the Founder by the Salvation Army 1981; kt 1979; *Clubs* Caledonian; *Style*— Sir John Boyd, CBE; 24 Pearl Court, Cornfield Terrace, Eastbourne, Sussex

BOYD, Hon Jonathan Aubrey Lewis; 3 s of 6 Baron Kilmarnock, MBE (d 1975); *b* 1 Oct 1956; *m* 20 March 1982, Annette Madeleine, er da of Joseph Constantine, FRICS, *qv*; 1 s (b 14 March 1989); *Style*— The Hon Jonathan Boyd

BOYD, Lawrence David; s of William Robert Boyd, of Bothwell, Glasgow, and Agnes Jane, *née* Armstrong; *b* 25 May 1949; *Educ* Hamilton Acad Lanarkshire, Glasgow Univ (BSc), Imperial Coll London (MPhil, DIC); *m* 23 July 1977, Nicola Judith Ann, da of Norman Mahy, of Derby; 1 s (Neil b 30 Nov 1984), 1 da (Joanna b 16 April 1983); *Career* Alliance & Leicester Bldg Soc: fin res offr 1976-80, corporate planning mangr 1980-82, chief accountant 1982-83, mgmnt servs controller 1983-85, asst gen mangr (mortgage admin) 1985-87, asst gen mangr (corporate devpt) 1987-; ACBSI 1979, ACIS 1979, FCCA 1981; *Books* Accounting - Principles and Practice (1983); *Recreations* walking, fencing; *Style*— Lawrence Boyd, Esq; 28 Mallory Rd, Hove, E Sussex BN3 6TD (☎ 0273 504253); Alliance & Leicester Bldg Soc, Hove Pk, Hove, E Sussex BN3 7AZ (☎ 0273 775454)

BOYD, Dr (John) Morton; CBE (1987); s of Thomas Pollock Boyd (d 1953), of Darvel, Ayrshire, and Jeanie Reid Morton (d 1955); *b* 31 Jan 1925; *Educ* Darvel Sch, Kilmarnock Acad, Glasgow Univ (BSc, PhD, DSc); *m* 1954, Winifred Isobel, da of John Rome (d 1971), of Kilmarnock; 4 s (Alan, Ian, Neil, Keith); *Career* air navigator Station Adj RAF 1943-47, Flt Lt; regnl offr West Scotland Nature Conservancy 1957-68, asst dir Nature Conservancy (Scotland) 1968-70, dir (Scotland) Nature Conservancy Cncl 1971-85; ecological conslt: Forestry Cmmn 1985-, N Scotland Hydro Electric 1985- Nat Tst for Scotland; vice-pres Scottish Conservation Projects Tst; Nuffield travel fellow (ME and E Africa) 1964-65; FRSE 1968 (Neill Prize 1983), CBiol, FIBiol, FRSA, Hon FRZSS, Hon FRSGS; *Books* St Kilda Summer (with K Williamson, 1960), Mosaic of Islands (with K Williamson, 1963), The Highlands and Islands (with F F Darling, 1964), Travels in the ME and E Africa (1966), Island Survivors (with P A Jewell and C Milner, 1974), The Natural Environment of the Outer Hebrides (ed 1979), The National Environment of the Inner Hebrides (ed with D R Bowes 1983), Fraser Darling's Islands (1986), ed Island Biology Series; *Recreations* travel, painting, photography; *Clubs* New (Edinburgh); *Style*— Dr J Morton Boyd, CBE; 57 Hailes Gardens, Edinburgh EH13 0JH (☎ 031 441 3220); Balephuil Tiree, Argyll PA77 6UE (☎ 08792 521)

BOYD, Prof Sir Robert Lewis Fullarton; CBE (1972); s of William John Boyd, PhD, BSc, of Sanderstead, Surrey; *b* 19 Oct 1922; *Educ* Whitgift Sch, London Univ; *m* 1949, Mary, da of late John Higgins; 2 s, 1 da; *Career* dir (Mullard) Space Science Lab UCL 1954-83; prof of astronomy Royal Instn 1961-67, prof of physics London Univ 1962-83; tstee National Maritime Museum 1980-89, memb SRC 1977-81; Fell UCL (1989), FRS 1969; kt 1983; *Recreations* elderly Rolls Royce motor cars; *Style*— Prof Sir Robert Boyd, CBE, FRS; Roseneath, 41 Church St, Littlehampton, W Sussex BN17 5PU (☎ 0903 714438)

BOYD, Robert Nathaniel; CBE (1971); s of Peter Ferguson Boyd, and Annie Jane Newton; *b* 17 Nov 1918; *Educ* Boys' GS Suva Fiji, Churchers' Coll Petersfield; *m* 1947, Carrie, da of Harry Squires; 2 s; *Career* Lt Col (ret) Br Somaliland 1940, Abyssinia, Madagascar, Burma, 30 years Territorial and Reserve service in Central Africa; practicing arbitrator, co dir; Auditor-Gen Zambia 1966-68; sec and fin controller Air Transport and Travel Industry Trg Bd 1969-77; memb Wokingham Borough Cncl (later DC) 1972-77 (chm dist fin ctee 1974-77); tres United Soc for Propagation of Gospel 1982-; Efficiency Decoration (Zambia) 1968, Order of the Epiphany (Anglican Church in Central Africa) 1968; FCIS, FCIArb, FBIM; *Recreations* bowls; *Clubs* Hurst Bowling, Royal Cwlth Soc; *Style*— Robert Boyd, Esq, CBE; 7 Acorn Drive, Glebelands Ct, Wokingham, Berks RG11 1EQ (☎ 0734 781122)

BOYD, Dr Hon Robin Jordan; 2 s of 6 Baron Kilmarnock, MBE (d 1975), and hp of bro, 7 Baron; *b* 6 June 1941; *Educ* Eton, Strasbourg Univ, Keble Coll Oxford; *Career* page to Lord High Constable of Scotland at Coronation of HM the Queen, 1953; MB BS, LRCP, MRCS, DCH, MRCP, MRCPEd; *Style*— Dr The Hon Robin Boyd

BOYD, (Thomas) Rodney; s of Thomas Guthrie Boyd (d 1983), of Dumfries, and Mary Isabella Dunlop, *née* Irvine (d 1987); *b* 18 August 1944; *Educ* Dumfries Acad, Heriot-Watt Univ Edinburgh (BArch); *m* 1, 5 Sept 1968, Josephine Mary; 1 s (Rodney Alexander Guthrie b 1983), 4 da (Kirsty Robyn b 1972, Philippa Harriet b 1974, Tara Dunlop b 1979, Mandy McLeod b 1981); m 2, 14 Dec 1984, Maureen, da of Alexander Aitken, of Aberdeen; *Career* CA; design architect Melbourne Aust 1968-73, princ architect (late ptnr) Ian G Lindsay & Ptnrs 1973-81, own practice The Boyd Reid Gp 1981-; dir: Strathedin Properties Ltd 1984-, Criton Estates Ltd 1984-; *Style*— Rodney Boyd, Esq; c/o Slateford House, Lanark Road, Edinburgh EH14 1TL (☎ 031 443 4467, fax 031 443 9442)

BOYD, Stewart Craufurd; QC (1981); s of Leslie Balfour Boyd, OBE, of 12 Burgh St, London N1, and Wendy Marie Boyd, *née* Blake; *b* 25 Oct 1943; *Educ* Winchester, Trinity Coll Cambridge (MA); *m* 1970, Catherine, da of The Rt Hon Lord Jay of Batterea; 1 s (Matthew b 1975), 3 da (Rachel b 1972, Emily b 1973, Hannah b 1987); *Career* barr; *Recreations* sailing, gardening, music; *Style*— Stewart Boyd Esq, QC; 1 Gayton Cres, London NW3 1TT (☎ 01 431 1581); Wraxall Manor, Higher Wraxall, Dorchester, Dorset (☎ Evershot 283); 4 Essex Ct, Temple, London EC4Y 9AJ (☎ 01 583 9191, telex COMCAS 888465)

BOYD, Hon Timothy Iain; s of 6 Baron Kilmarnock, MBE (d 1975); *b* 5 April 1959; *m* 1 July 1988, Lucy Teresa Emily, yr da of Michael Gray; *Style*— The Hon Timothy Boyd; Flat 2, 23 Ladbroke Crescent, London W11 1PS

BOYD, William Andrew Murray; s of Alexander Murray Boyd (d 1979), and Evelyn, *née* Smith; *b* 7 Mar 1952; *Educ* Gordonstoun, Univ of Nice (Dip), Glasgow Univ (MA), Jesus Coll Oxford; *m* Susan Anne, da of David Leslie Wilson, of Maxwell Park, Glasgow; *Career* lectr in english lit St Hilda's Coll Oxford 1980-83, TV critic New Statesman 1981-83, author, novels: A Good Man in Africa (1981), On the Yankee Station (1981), An Ice-Cream War (1982), Stars and Bars (1984), School Ties (1985), The New Confessions (1987); films: Good and Bad at Games (1983), Dutch Girls (1985), Scoop (1986), Stars and Bars (1988); FRSL 1982; *Clubs* Chelsea Arts, Two Brydges Place; *Style*— William Boyd, Esq; c/o Harvey Unna & Stephen Durbridge, 24 Pottery Lane, Holland Park, London W11

BOYD MAUNSELL, Nevill Francis Wray; s of Col Cecil Robert Wray Boyd Maunsell (d 1961), of Worcester, and Elizabeth Frances, *née* Boyd; *b* 22 Dec 1930; *Educ* Winchester, Univ Coll Oxford (BA); *m* 5 Oct 1957, Lyghia, da of Dr Mihai

Peterson (d 1954), of London; 1 s (Michael b 1958), 1 da (Indi b 1963); *Career* nat serv: 2 Lt Royal Warwick Regt 1949-50; schoolmaster in UK and USA 1953-55; journalist: Reuters 1955-57, Financial Times 1957-60, Time and Tide 1960-61, Daily Sketch 1961-65, Freelance 1965-73; city ed The Birmingham Post 1986- (dep citied 1973-88); *Recreations* gardening, reading, idle chatter; *Style*— Nevill Boyd Maunsell, Esq; 19/21 Tudor Street, London EC4 (☎ 01 353 0811, fax 01 353 1762)

BOYD OF MERTON, Patricia, Viscountess; Lady Patricia Florence Susan; *née* Guinness; da of 2 Earl of Iveagh (d 1967); aunt of 3 Earl; *b* 3 Mar 1918; *m* 1938, 1 Viscount Boyd of Merton, CH, PC, DL (d 1983, sometime MP (C) Mid-Bedfordshire, Sec of State for the Colonies, dir ICI and jt vice-chm Arthur Guinness Son & Co); 3 s; *Style*— The Rt Hon Patricia, Viscountess Boyd of Merton; Ince Castle, Saltash, Cornwall PL12 4RA (☎ 075 55 2274)

BOYD OF MERTON, 2 Viscount (UK 1960); Simon Donald Rupert Neville Lennox-Boyd; s of 1 Viscount Boyd of Merton, CH, PC, DL (d 1983), and Patricia, Viscountess Boyd of Merton, *qv*; *b* 7 Dec 1939; *Educ* Eton, Christ Church Oxford (MA); *m* 1962, Alice Mary JP (high sheriff of Cornwall 1987), da of Maj Meysey George Dallas Clive (ka 1943); 2 s (Hon Benjamin, Hon Edward b 30 March 1968), 2 da (Hon Charlotte b 1963, Hon Philippa b 1970); *Heir* s, Hon Benjamin Alan Lennox-Boyd; *Career* dir The Iveagh Tstees Ltd; chm Save the Children Fund; *Recreations* planting trees; *Clubs* White's, Royal Yacht Sqdn; *Style*— The Rt Hon the Viscount Boyd of Mert; 9 Warwick Sq, London SW1 (☎ 01 821 1618); Wivelscombe, Saltash, Cornwall (☎ Saltash (075 55) 2672); office: Iveagh House, 41 Harrington Gdns, London SW7 (☎ 01 373 7261, telex 917935, fax 01 244 8281)

BOYD-CARPENTER, Alan Michael Haydon; VRD (1965); s of Gilbert Denys Ewart Boyd-Carpenter (d 1966), and Lydia Mary, *née* Cowan; *b* 19 Feb 1932; *Educ* Dragon Sch, Malvern; *m* 2 June 1956, Jennifer Ann, da of Arthur Alfred Prestwich (d 1986), of Edenbridge, Kent; 1 s (Patrick b 1966), 4 da (Kate (Mrs Blacker) b 1957, Susan (Mrs Mangham) b 1959, Hester b 1960, Alexandra (Mrs Richardson) b 1962); *Career* Nat Serv RN Midshipman submarine serv RNVR 1950-52; List 1 RNR 1952-76, ret Lt Cdr 1976; Beecham Gp 1952-53, Union Discount Co of London Ltd 1953-56, chm Joseph Sebag & Co 1980 (joined 1956, ptnr 1959), jt sr ptnr Carr Sebag & co 1980-82; fin conslt and dir 1982-: Fitzgrade Ltd, Stapro Ltd; memb Stock Exchange 1956 (specialist in Portugese stocks); *Recreations* restoring old machinery and wooden boats; *Clubs* Athenaeum, MCC; *Style*— Michael Boyd-Carpenter, Esq, VRD; Wyddial Hall, Buntingford, Herts SG9 0EL (☎ 0763 71273, car tel 0836 251466, fax 0763 72068)

BOYD-CARPENTER, Hon Anne Mary; da of Baron Boyd-Carpenter, PC, DL (Life Peer); *b* 1942; *Style*— The Hon Anne Boyd-Carpenter; c/o 12 Eaton Terrace, London SW1

BOYD-CARPENTER, Baron (Life Peer UK 1972) (of Crux Easton, co Southampton); John Archibald Boyd-Carpenter; PC (1954), DL (Gtr London 1973); s of Maj Sir Archibald Boyd Boyd-Carpenter, MP (d 1937), of River House, Walton-on-Thames, and Annie, *née* Dugdale; gs of Rt Rev William Boyd-Carpenter, KCVO, DD, Bishop of Ripon (d 1918); *b* 2 June 1908; *Educ* Stowe, Balliol Coll Oxford (BA, pres Oxford Union Soc 1930),; *m* 1937, Margaret Mary, da of Lt-Col George Leslie Hall, OBE, by his w, Dorothy, *née* Coventry, ggggda of 6 Earl of Coventry; 1 s, 2 da; *Career* served Scots Gds 1939-45, Maj 1942; Harmsworth law scholar Middle Temple 1932, barr 1934, practiced London and SE Circuit 1934-39, jr SE circuit 1939; MP (C) Kingston-upon-Thames 1945-72; fin sec Treasury 1951-54; Min of Transport and Civil Aviation 1954-55, Min of Pensions and Nat Ins 1955-62, ch sec Treasury and Paymaster-Gen 1962-64, opposition front bench spokesman on housing & land 1964-66, chm Public Accounts Ctee 1964-70 (opposition front bench spokesman on Housing & Land 1964-66), sits as Conservative in Ho of Lords, chm Assoc of Cons Peers 1981-; chm: Orion Insur Co and CLRP Investmt Tst 1968-72, Civil Aviation Authority 1972-77, Rugby Portland Cement Co 1976-84; dir of other cos; high steward The Royal Borough of Kingston-upon-Thames 1976-; *Books* Way of Life; *Recreations* swimming, tennis, walking, gardening; *Clubs* Carlton (chm 1979-86); *Style*— The Rt Hon Lord Boyd-Carpenter, PC, DL; 12 Eaton Terrace, London SW1 (☎ 01 730 7765); Crux Easton House, Crux Easton, Highclere, Newbury, Berks (☎ 0635 253037)

BOYD-CARPENTER, Maj-Gen Hon Thomas Patrick John; MBE (1973); s of Baron Boyd-Carpenter, PC, DL (Life Peer); *b* 1938; *Educ* Stowe; *m* 1972, Mary Jean, da of John Elwes Duffield; 3 children; *Career* Scots Gds, Col GSAT3 MOD 1981, Cmd 24 Inf Bde 1983-84, D Def Pol MOD 1985-87; Cos HQ BAOR 1988-89; *Style*— Brig the Hon Thomas Boyd-Carpenter, MBE

BOYD-MOSS, Robin James; s of Michael Robin Peter Boyd-Moss, of Cyhohoa Estate, Rwanda, Central Africa, and Shelagh Boyd-Moss; gf shot maneater of Trincomalee (79 victims) in 1949; *b* 16 Dec 1958; *Educ* Bedford Sch, Cambridge Univ; *Career* professional cricketer, Northants CCC Capt 1984 man of the match Nat West Quarter Final 1984, century in each innings Varsity Match 1983, dismissed Gavaskar & Dev & Viswanath in same innings; *Recreations* fishing, windsurfing, golf, photography; *Style*— Robin Boyd-Moss

BOYD-ROCHFORT, Lady; (Elizabeth) Rohays Mary; da of Sir James Lauderdale Gilbert Burnett of Leys, 13 Bt, CB, CMG, DSO, DL (d 1953); *b* 30 August 1916; *m* 1, 1938, Hon Henry Kerr Auchmuty Cecil (ka 1942), yr s of late Capt Hon William Amherst Cecil, MC (who was s of Baroness Amherst of Hackney, who succeeded her father, 1 Baron Amherst of Hackney); 4 s; m 2, 1944, Sir Cecil Charles Boyd-Rochfort, KCVO (d 1983), s of Maj R H Boyd-Rochfort, 15 Hussars; 1 s; *Style*— Lady Boyd-Rochfort; The Clydesdale Bank of Scotland, Banchory, Kincardineshire AB3 3QE

BOYDELL, Chllr Peter Thomas Sherrington; QC (1965); s of late Frank Richard Boydell, JP and late Frances Barton Boydell; *b* 20 Sept 1920; *Educ* Arnold Sch Blackpool, Manchester Univ (LLB); *Career* Adj 17 Field Regt RA 1943, Bde Maj RA 1 Armoured Div 1944, Bde Maj RA 10 Indian Div 1945; solicitor 1947, barr Middle Temple 1948, bencher 1970; memb Legal Bd of Church Assembly 1958-71; contested (C) Carlisle 1964; chm Planning and Local Govt Ctee of the Bar 1973-86; (chm Local Govt and Planning Bar Assoc 1986-), leader Parly bar 1975-; chancellor: Diocese Truro 1957-, Worcester 1959-; Diocese Oxford 1958; assoc RICS 1982; *Recreations* mountaineering, travel, music; *Clubs* Garrick, Royal Automobile, Climbers; *Style*— The Worshipful Chllr Peter Boydell, QC; 45 Wilton Crescent, London SW1 (☎ 01 235 5505); 2 Harcourt Buildings, Temple, London EC4 (☎ 01 353 8415)

BOYER, Ernest Stanley; s of Walter Boyer (d 1981), of Holmstall, Quorn, Leics, and Evelyn, *née* Hudson (d 1976); *b* 30 Nov 1925; *Educ* Kingsbury GS, Regent St Sch of Architecture; *m* 27 March 1954, Patricia, da of Montegue Cecil Cuthbertson (d 1950), of Hampstead, London; 1 s (Guy b 1959); *Career* architect, assoc ptnr Monro & Sons 1949-57, fndr E S Boyer & Ptnrs 1957, Boyer Design Gp 1974; dir: Boyer Professional Servs, Count Croft Properties; cncl memb RIBA for Essex, Cambs and Herts 1961; memb: Worshipful Co of Bowyers, Worshipful Co of Constructors; FRIBA 1957, FFAS 1976; *Recreations* riding, painting, cricket; *Clubs* Les Ambassadeurs, Wig and Pen, MCC; *Style*— Ernest Boyer, Esq; Lone Pine, 100 Green Lane, Bovingdon, Herts HP3 OLA (☎ 0442 834 365); Boyer Design Group/E S Boyer & Ptnrs, Westminster House, High St, Egham, Surrey TW20 9HE (☎ 0784 39181, fax 0784 39242, car tel 0836 288149)

BOYER, John Leslie; OBE (1982); s of Albert and Gladys Boyer; *b* 13 Nov 1926; *Educ* Nantwich and Acton GS; *m* 1953, Joyce Enid, *née* Thomasson; 1 s, 2 da; *Career* served Army 1944-48; dep chm Hongkong and Shanghai Banking Corpn 1977-81 (joined 1948, gen mangr Hong Kong 1973); chm: Wardley Ltd to 1981, Antony Gibbs Hldgs 1981-83; South China Morning Post; dir Anglo and Overseas Securities 1981-; former chm South China Morning Post; former dir: Eastern Asia Navigation Ltd, Mercantile Bank Ltd, British Bank of the Middle East, Swire Pacific Ltd, Mass Transit Railway Corpn; *Recreations* bridge; *Style*— John Boyer, Esq, OBE; Friars Lawn, Norwood Green Rd, Norwood Green, Middx UB2 4LA (☎ 01 574 8489)

BOYES; *see*: Barratt-Boyes

BOYES, (Charles) Robin; s of Norman Frank Boyes, of Huntingdon, Cambs, and Rose Margaret, *née* Slingsby; *b* 16 Nov 1939; *Educ* Oundle Sch; *m* 20 April 1968, Carroll Anne, da of Raymond Elkerton (d 1972), of St Albans, Herts; 1 s (Christopher b 1969); *Career* slr; dir Argyle Building Soc 1966-85; ptnr: Grover Humphreys & Boyes 1965-75, Warrens 1976-85, Warrens Boyes & Archer 1985-; hon slr Royal Photographic Soc of GB, Fenton Medal 1980; *Recreations* cricket, golf, collecting old toy soldiers; *Clubs* East India; *Style*— Robin Boyes, Esq; Punch's Grove, Hilton, Huntingdon, Cambs (☎ 0480 830335); 20 Hartford Road, Huntingdon, Cambs (☎ 0480 411331, fax 0480 59012)

BOYES, Roland; MP (Lab Houghton and Washington 1983-), MEP (Lab) Durham 1979-84); *b* 12 Feb 1937; *m* ; 2 s; *Career* former teacher and former assist dir Social Servs; Memb GMB, chm Tribune Gp 1985-86; Front Bench: Environment Spokesman 1985-88, defence spokesman 1985-; chm All Pty Photography Gp 1987-; dir Hartlepool Utd AFC; *Recreations* photography, sports, brass bands; *Clubs* Peterlee CC (pres); *Style*— Roland Boyes, Esq, MP; 12 Spire Hollin, Peterlee, Co Durham (☎ 091 586 3917; office 091 385 7825)

BOYKO, Dr David Alexander; *b* 29 May 1954; *Educ* George Watsons Coll Edinburgh, Aberdeen Univ Med Sch (MB ChB, DipPharmMed, RCPUK); *m* 20 July 1979, Valerie Thomson, da of R Reid Jack, of E Lothian; *Career* physician, former sr med avsr Smith Kline and French Labs Ltd (Welwyn Garden City) 1984-87, head of med dept and dep md Stuart Pharmaceuticals Ltd (ICI Pharmaceuticals); memb exec ctee and tres Br Assoc of Pharmaceutical Physicians 1986-; memb Br Med Assoc; FRSM; *Books* Dyspepsia and Cimetidine (Lancet), Cimetidine and the Critically Ill Patient (Br Journal of Hosp Medicine), Atenold and Pregnancy (Int Pharmacy Journal); *Recreations* skiing, physical fitness, food and wine, current affairs; *Clubs* Royal Soc of Medicine (Fell), Br Medical Assoc (memb); *Style*— Dr David A Boyko; Glenmuir, Leicester Road, Hale, Cheshire WA14 9QA (☎ 061 927 7322); Stuart House, 50 Alderley Rd, Wilmslow, Cheshire (☎ 0625 535999, telex 668585)

BOYLE, Andrew Philip More; s of Andrew Boyle (d 1972), of Fenham, Newcastle upon Tyne, and Rose, *née* McCann (d 1964); *b* 27 May 1919; *Educ* Blairs Coll, Aberdeen, Sorbonne (escaped from France 1940); *m* 1, 20 Nov 1943, Christina (d 1984), da of Thomas Galvin (d 1922); 1 s (Edmund Campion), 1 da (Diana Rosemary); m 2, 4 April 1986, Eleanor; *Career* RAFVR 1941-43, Maj (later temp Col) Br Mil Inteligence; serv: Far East, India and Burma 1943-47; BBC: prodr and scriptwriter Radio Newsreel, fndr ed The World At One 1965-76, head of news and current affrs radio and TV BBC Scotland 1976, ret early to concentrate on writing; work published 1979 led to the exposure of Anthony Blunt as a spy, occasional contrib to newspapers including: Times, Spectator, Washington Post; memb Authors Soc; *Books* No Passing Glory: The Authorised Biography of Gp Capt Leonard Cheshire (1955), Trenchard: Man of Vision (1962), Montagu Norman: A Biography (1967), Only The Wind Will Listen: Reith of the BBC (1972), Poor, Dear Brendan (1974, Whitbread Award: Biography of the Year), Erkine Childers: A Biography (1977), The Climate of Treason (1979), The Fourth Man: Anthony Blunt (1986), co-author of three other books; *Style*— Andrew Boyle, Esq; 39 Lansdowne Rd, London W11 2LQ (☎ 01 727 5758)

BOYLE, Dr Archibald Cabbourn; s of Arthur Hislop Boyle (d 1935), of London, and Flora Ellen, *née* Sanders (d 1984); *b* 14 Mar 1918; *Educ* Dulwich Coll, Univ of London (DPhys Med); *m* 1, Patricia Evelyn, *née* Tallack (d 1944); 1 da (Patricia Anne b 1943); m 2 (m dis 1983), Dorothy Evelyn, *née* May; 1 s (Richard Anthony Cabbourn b 1949); m 3, 14 Feb 1983, June Rosmary, da of William George Pickett (d 1971), of London; *Career* Maj RAMC 1942-46, serv in Far East, later as cmd specialist S Cmd; conslt rheumatologist: Middx Hosp London 1949-83, Arthur Stanley Inst for Rheumatic Diseases 1950-65, Charterhouse Rheumatism Clinic 1969-80; pres Br Assoc Rheumatology and Rehabilitation 1970-72, Ernest Fletcher Meml lectr RSM 1971; hon conslt rheumatologist: King Edward VII Hosp for Offrs 1980-83, King Edward VII Hosp Midhurst 1984-87; hon memb Br Soc for Rheumatology; memb: (C) Ctee Stedham and Iping, Midhurst branch of Arthritis and Rheumatism Cncl; Liveryman Worshipful Co of Apothecaries 1950, Freeman City of London 1951; FRCP; *Books* A Colour Atlas of Rheumatology (1974); *Recreations* gardening; *Style*— Dr Archibald Boyle; Iping Barn, Iping, Midhurst, W Sussex (☎ 073 081 6467)

BOYLE, Brian; s of Peter Joseph Boyle; *b* 24 Nov 1952; *Educ* Winchmore Sch; *Career* AV photographer/jt ptnr photographic company; *Recreations* photography, music, sport, driving; *Style*— Brian Boyle, Esq; 2 Haslemere Rd, Winchmore Hill, N21 (☎ 886 2026)

BOYLE, Lady Caroline Mary Victoria; yr da of 9 Earl of Shannon; *b* 12 Oct 1965; *Style*— Lady Caroline Boyle; Brandfold Barn Cottage, Goudhurst, Kent TN17 1JJ

BOYLE, Marshal of the RAF Sir Dermot Alexander; GCB (1957, CB 1946), KCVO (1953), KBE (1953, CBE 1945), AFC (1939); s of Alexander Francis Boyle, JP, of Belmont House, Queen's Co Anna Maria, *née* Harpur; *b* 2 Oct 1904; *Educ* St Columba's Coll, RAF Coll Cranwell; *m* 1931, Una, da of Edward Valentine Carey, of Guernsey; 3 s (Timothy b and d 1933, Anthony Alexander b 1935, Christopher Patrick b 1937), 1 da (Penelope Susan b 1946); *Career* cmmnd RAF 1924, Air ADC to the King 1943, Air Cdre 1944, Dir-Gen of Personnel Air Miny 1948-49, Air Vice Marshal 1949, Dir-Gen of Manning 1949-51, AOC No 1 Gp Bomber Command 1951-53, AOCIC Fighter Command 1953-55, Air Marshal 1954, Air Chief Marshal 1956, Chief of Air Staff 1956-59, Marshal of the RAF 1958; vice-chm Br Aircraft Corpn 1962-71; *Style—* Marshal of RAF Sir Dermot Boyle, GCB; Fair Gallop, Brighton Rd, Sway, Hants (☎ 0590 682322)

BOYLE, George Hamilton; s of Capt E M G L Boyle (d 1982), and Maida Cecil, *née* Evans-Freke; *b* 15 Sept 1928; *Educ* Canford, London Univ (BSc); *m* 25 July 1953, Alathea Henriette Mary March Phillipps de Lisle; 3 s (Robert b 28 Sept 1954, Richard b 8 Jan 1959, Rupert b 19 Sept 1960); *Career* non-exec dir E Midland Electricity Bd 1980-; pres Friends of Rutland Co Museum and Record Soc; High Sheriff Co of Rutland 1964, (Leicestershire 1976), DL Leicestershire 1980; *Style—* George Boyle, Esq

BOYLE, Lady Georgina Susan; da of 9 Earl of Shannon; *b* 7 Feb 1961; *Career* artist, watercolourist; *Style—* Lady Georgina Boyle; Brandfold Barn Cottage, Goudhurst, Kent TN17 1JJ

BOYLE, (Samuel) Gerald; s of Samuel Joseph Boyle of Belfast (d 1972), and Mary Alice, *née* Edgar; *b* 23 May 1937; *Educ* Saintfield Primary Sch, St Patricks HS, Downpatrick, Co Down; *m* 5 Oct 1965, Kathleen Bernadette, da of Hugh Blaney Crossey (d 1983); 3 s (Gary b 1966, Jonathan b 1968, Nicholas b 1972); *Career* dir: Shield Ins Co Ltd Dublin 1984-, Europ Assistance Ltd Croydon 1987-; divsnl dir (gen mngr 1985-87) Eagle Star Ins Co Ltd 1987-; dir Indus and Agric Safety Conslts 1989-; ACII; *Recreations* golf; *Clubs* Effingham GC Surrey; *Style—* Gerald Boyle, Esq; Eaves Cottage, 42 Lowr Rd, Fetcham, Surrey KT22 9ER (☎ 0372 373025); Eagle Star Ins Co Ltd, Eagle Star House, 9 Aldgate High St, London EC3N 1LD (☎ 01 377 8000, fax 01 377 6180, telex 883018)

BOYLE, Lady Geraldine Lilian; da of Col Gerald Edmund Boyle (d 1927), and half sis of 12 Earl of Cork and Orrery, GCB, GCVO; *b* 1899; *Career* granted rank, title and precedence of an Earl's da which would have been hers had her father survived to succeed to the title; *Style—* Lady Geraldine Boyle; 38 Strand Court, Topsham, Exeter, Devon

BOYLE, John Godfrey (Geoff); OBE (1977); s of John Boyle (d 1980), of Edinburgh, and Maude Craven (d 1935); *b* 17 Nov 1928; *Educ* Daniel Stewart Coll Edinburgh; *m* 1955, Sarah, da of George Death Ward (d 1968), of Edinburgh; 1 s (Adrian), 1 da (Philippa); *Career* CA; former finance dir Burmah Oil Exploration Ltd 1980-; dir: Burmah Oil Somalia Ltd 1982-, Burmah Shell Oil Storage & Distribution Co of India Ltd 1978-, Bladite Hldgs Ltd 1978-, Burmah Oil Co Pakistan Trading Ltd 1978-, PS & S (Personnel) Ltd 1983-, Assam Oil Co Ltd 1978-, Burmah Oil Kenya Ltd 1982-; *Recreations* literature, music, yachting; *Clubs* Sind, Karachi, East Lothian Yacht, North Berwick; *Style—* John Godfrey Boyle, Esq, OBE,; Baltrenon, 22 Dirleton Ave, North Berwick, East Lothian EH39 4BQ; (☎ (0620) 2642)

BOYLE, Sheriff John Sebastian; s of Edward Joseph Boyle, of Glasgow (d 1960), and Constance Mary, *née* Hook (d 1983); *b* 29 Mar 1933; *Educ* St Aloysius Coll Glasgow, Glasgow Univ (BL); *m* 1, 1955, Catherine Denise, da of John Croall, of Glasgow (d 1975); 1 s (Stephen b 1958), 2 da (Susan b 1957, Cecilia b 1960); m 2, 1978, Isobel Margaret, da of James Ryan (d 1984), of Ballytrent, Co Wexford, Ireland; 1 s (Edward b 1981), 1 da (Elizabeth b 1979); *Career* slr Glasgow 1955-83; Sheriff of South Strathclyde Dumfries & Galloway at Airdrie 1983-; pres: Glasgow Bar Assoc 1963; memb: Scottish Arts Cncl 1966-72; memb: Cncl Law Soc of Scotland 1968-75; memb: Criminal Injuries Compensation Bd 1975-83; dir: Scottish Opera 1984-; *Style—* Sheriff John Boyle; 5 Great Western Terr, Glasgow G12 0UP (☎ 041 357 1459); Sheriff's Chambers, Airdrie Sheriff Ct, Graham St, Airdrie ML6 6EE (☎ 02364 51121)

BOYLE, Hon John William; DSC (1945); s of Hon Reginald Courtenay Boyle, MBE, MC (d 1946), and Violet *née* Flower (d 1974); bro of 13 Earl of Cork and Orrery; granted title, rank and precedence of an Earl's son 1967; *b* 12 May 1916; *Educ* Harrow, King's Coll London (BSc); *m* 16 Oct 1943, Mary Leslie, da of Gen Sir Robert Gordon-Finlayson, KCB, CMG, DSO (d 1956); 3 s (John Richard b 1945, Robert William b 1948, (Charles) Reginald b 1957); *Career* serv WWII (despatches 2), Lt Cdr RNVR, six years afloat with RN in most Western theatres; FICE (ret), some time MIMechE; *Recreations* country and family life, making and mending, reading; *Style—* The Hon John Boyle, DSC; Nether Craigantaggart, Dunkeld, Perthshire PH8 0HQ (☎ 073871 239)

BOYLE, Katie Catherine Irene Helen Mary; da of Marchese Demetrio Imperiali dei Principi di Francavilla and Dorothy Kate *née* Ramsden; *b* 29 May 1926; *Educ* Switzerland and Italy; *m* 1, 1947, Viscount Boyle, now Earl of Shannon (m dis 1955); m 2, 1955, Greville Baylis (d 1976); m 3, 1979, Sir Peter Saunders; *Career* author of "Dear Katie" column TV Times 1969-, occasional contributor to Evening Standard, The Sun, Sunday Mirror and for 8 years to Here's Health; numerous TV appearances (inc Quite Contrary 1954, Golden Girl, Eurovision Song Contest) and stage and film work; dir: Peter Saunders Ltd 1979-, Peter Saunders Co Ltd 1979-; ctee memb Battersea Dogs' Home; tstee: Peter Saunders Fndn, Katie Boyle Animal Welfare Fndn; *Recreations* animal welfare, embroidery, gardening, jigsaw puzzles; *Style—* Miss Katie Boyle; 10 Maiden Lane, London WC2E 7NA (☎ 01 240 3177)

BOYLE, Sir Lawrence; JP (Glasgow 1970), DL (1985); s of Hugh Boyle (d 1961), and Kate, *née* Callaghan; *b* 31 Jan 1920; *Educ* Holy Cross Acad Leith, Edinburgh Univ (BCom, PhD); *m* 1952, Mary, da of late Andrew McWilliam; 1 s, 3 da; *Career* ptnr Sir Lawrence Boyle Assoc (fin and mgmnt conslts); dir: Pension Fund Property Unit Tst, Scottish Mutual Assurance Soc; advsr Schroder Investmt Mgmnt Ltd; memb Widdicombe Ctee on the Conduct of Local Authy Business 1985-86; chief exec Strathclyde Regnl Cncl 1974-80; chm Scottish Nat Orchestra 1980-84; visiting prof Strathclyde Univ Business Sch 1979-85; kt 1979; *Recreations* music; *Clubs* Royal Cwlth Soc; *Style—* Sir Lawrence Boyle, JP, DL; 24 Broomburn Drive, Newton Mearns, Glasgow G77 5JF (☎ 041 639 3776)

BOYLE, Leonard Butler; CBE (1976); s of Harold and Edith Boyle; *b* 13 Jan 1913; *Educ* Roundhay Sch Leeds; *m* 1938, Alice Baldwin Yarborough; 2 s; *Career* dir and gen mangr Principality Bldg Soc 1956-78; chm Bldg Soc Assoc 1973-75 (vice-pres 1978-), vice-pres Chartered Bldg Socs Inst 1978-; conslt Manchester Exchange Tst 1978-; *Style—* Leonard Boyle, Esq, CBE; Northwick Cottage, Marlpit Lane, Seaton, Devon (☎ 0297 22194)

BOYLE, Hon Mrs John; Marie; *née* Gibb; da of John Gibb, of Chillesford, Orford, Suffolk; *m* 1 (m dis), George Chettle; m 2, 1934, as his 2 w, Air Cdre the Hon John David Boyle, CBE, DSC (d 1974), yst s of 7 Earl of Glasgow, GCMG; JP and CC for Wigtownshire; *Style—* The Hon Mrs John Boyle; Cushat Wood, Portpatrick, Stranraer, Wigtownshire

BOYLE, Capt Michael Patrick Radcliffe; DL (Hants 1982); s of Patrick Spencer Boyle (s of late Capt Hon E Spencer H Boyle, RN, 5 s of 5 Earl of Shannon, by his 2 w, Julia, da of Sir William Hartopp, 3 Bt); *b* 25 Jan 1934; *Educ* Eton; *m* 1962, Lady Nell Carleton Harris, da of 6 Earl of Malmesbury, TD, DL, and Hon Diana Carleton, da of 2 Baron Dorchester; 2 s, 1 da; *Career* cmmnd Irish Gds 1953, Capt 1961, ret 1966; High Sheriff Hants 1976-77, memb Hants CC 1970-, chm Hants Police Authority 1976-88; cmmnr St John Ambulance Bde Hants 1969-75; Freeman City of London, Liveryman Worshipful Co of Gunmakers; FBIM; CStJ; *Recreations* shooting, sailing; *Clubs* Boodle's, Pratt's Royal Yacht Sqdn; *Style—* Capt Michael Boyle, DL; Forest Lodge, Ashe Park, Basingstoke, Hants RG25 3AZ (☎ 0256 781611)

BOYLE, Ranald Hugh Montgomerie; DSC (1944); 2 s of David Hugh Montgomerie Boyle, CMG (d 1970), ggs of Rt Hon David Boyle, Lord Justice General and Pres of the Court of Session in Scotland, himself gs of 2 Earl of Glasgow, and of Laura Grant Tennant (d 1971), 3 da of James Tennant, of Fairlie, who was nephew of Sir Charles Tennant, 1 Bt, and 1 cous of 1 Baron Glenconner; *b* 19 August 1921; *Educ* Wellington, Exeter Coll Oxford (BA); *m* 1957, Norma, yst da of Alexander Gray (d 1932), merchant, of Calcutta and London; 5 s (Fergus, Alexander, Patrick, John, Hamish), 2 da (Laura, Beatrice); *Career* serv WWII Lt RNVR, Channel convoys, Dieppe Raid 1942 (wounded), Mediterranean, Far East (Br Pacific Fleet); Sudan Political Serv 1946-53; freelance journalist 1954; Iraq Petroleum Co 1955-56; HM Overseas Civil Serv Kenya 1956-64, first sec HM Diplomatic Serv 1964-70; Hambros Bank 1970-81 (dir 1975-81); sr rep (London) Arab Banking Corpn 1981-82; conslt Ranald Boyle 1982-; memb Royal Co of Archers (Queen's Body Guard for Scotland); *Recreations* fishing, shooting, tennis, squash, sailing, reading, writing; *Clubs* Utd Oxford and Cambridge, Vincent's (Oxford), Mombasa, Puffin's (Edinburgh); *Style—* Ranald Boyle, Esq, DSC; 906 Beatty House, Dolphin Sq, London SW1V 3PN (☎ 01 821 8028); Downcraig Ferry, Millport, Isle of Cumbrae, Scotland (☎ 0475 530550); The Wooden House, Fairlie, Ayrshire, Scotland (☎ 0475 568284)

BOYLE, Hon Mrs (Rebecca Juliet); *née* Noble; da of Baron Glenkinglas (Life Peer, d 1984), and Baroness Glenkinglas, *qv*; *b* 1950; *m* 1973, Lt-Cdr John Richard Boyle, RN, s of Hon John William Boyle, DSC, *qv*; 1 s (Rory Jonathan Courtenay b 10 Dec 1978), 2 da (Cara Mary Cecilia b 1976, Davina Claire Theresa b (twin) 1978); *Style—* The Hon Mrs Boyle; Lickfold House, Petworth, Sussex

BOYLE, Viscount; Richard Henry John Boyle; s (by 2 m) and h of 9 Earl of Shannon; *b* 19 Jan 1960; *Educ* Northease Manor Sch; *Career* in catering business; *Style—* Viscount Boyle; Old Loose Court, Maidstone, Kent

BOYLE, Sir Stephen Gurney; 5 Bt (UK 1904); el s of Sir Richard Gurney, 4 Bt (d 1983), s of Sir Edward Boyle, 2 Bt; suc to Btcy only of bro, Baron Boyle of Handsworth, (1981), and Elizabeth Anne, yr da of Norman Dennes; *b* 15 Jan 1962; *Style—* Sir Stephen Boyle, Bt; 28 The Lawn, Harlow, Essex

BOYLE, William Russell; s of Charles Harry Boyle, of Wimborne St Giles, Dorset, and Winifred Boyle (d 1967); *b* 15 Feb 1945; *m* 19 July 1969, Janet Elizabeth; 1 s (Matthew b 1974), 1 da (Joanne b 1971); *Career* insurance broker; dir CT Bowring & Co (Insurance) Ltd; exec div Bowring Marine & Energy Insurance Brokers Ltd; *Style—* William R Boyle, Esq; C T Bowring & Co (Ins) Ltd, The Bowring Building, Tower Place, London EC3 (☎ 01 283 3100)

BOYNE, 10 Viscount (I 1717); Gustavus Michael George Hamilton-Russell; JP (Salop 1961), DL (Salop 1965); also Baron Hamilton of Stackallen (I 1715) and Baron Brancepeth (UK 1866); sits as Baron Brancepeth; s of Hon Gustavus Hamilton-Russell (ka 1940, s and h of 9 Viscount Boyne, JP, DL, by his w, Lady Margaret Lascelles, CBE, da of 5 Earl of Harewood) and Joan, da of Sir Harry Lloyd Verney, GCVO (gs of Sir Harry Verney, 2 Bt), by his w, Lady Joan Cuffe (da of 5 and last Earl of Desart, KP); suc gf 1942; *b* 10 Dec 1931; *Educ* Eton, Sandhurst, RAC Cirencester; *m* 11 April 1956, Rosemary Ann, 2 da of Sir Denis Stucley, 5 Bt (d 1983); 1 s, 3 da; *Heir* s, Hon Gustavus Hamilton-Russell; *Career* formerly Lt Gren Gds (ret 1956); dir Nat West Bank 1976- (chm W Midland & Wales Regnl Bd); dep chm Telford Dvpt Corpn 1976-82; Lord- in-waiting to HM The Queen 1981-; CStJ; govr: Harper Adams Agric Coll; dir: Ludlow Race Club Ltd, Private Patients Plan Ltd; *Recreations* skiing, shooting, fishing, motoring; *Clubs* White's; *Style—* The Rt Hon The Viscount Boyne, JP, DL; Burwarton House, Bridgnorth, Shropshire (☎ 074 633 203, office 207)

BOYNE, Sir (Harry) Henry Brian; CBE (1969); 2 s of late Lockhart Alexander Boyne, of Inverness, and Elizabeth Jane Mactavish; *b* 29 July 1910; *Educ* HS, Royal Acad Inverness; *m* 1935, Margaret Little, da of John Templeton, of Dundee; 1 da; *Career* political correspondent Daily Telegraph 1956-76; dir communications Cons Central Office 1980-82; kt 1976; *Books* The Houses of Parliament (1981), Scotland Rediscovered (1986); *Recreations* reading, walking; *Clubs* Victory; *Style—* Sir Harry Boyne, CBE; 122 Harefield Rd, Uxbridge, Middx UB8 1PN (☎ 0895 55211)

BOYNTON, Sir John Keyworth; MC (1944), DL (Cheshire 1975); s of Ernest Boynton (d 1940), of Hull; *b* 14 Feb 1918; *Educ* Dulwich; *m* 1, 1947, Gabrielle (d 1978), da of G Stanglmaier, of Munich; 2 da; m 2, 1979, Edith Laane, of The Hague; *Career* slr; ch exec Cheshire CC 1974-79, election cmmr S Rhodesia 1979-80; kt 1979; *Books* Compulsory Puchase (5 edn, 1983), Job at the Top (1986); *Recreations* golf; *Clubs* Army and Navy; *Style—* Sir John Boynton, MC, DL; 1B Oakhill Avenue, London NW3 7RD (☎ 01 435 0012)

BOYNTON-WOOD; *see*: Wood

BOYS, John Philip; s of late Stephen Philip Boys, and late Constance Rhoda Towns; *Educ* Glasgow and Dundee Colleges of Art, DA; *m* 29 June 1963 (m dis 1988), Christine Bridget, da of late Jørgen Svend Jensen; 2 s (Adam b 1967, Jamie b 1970), 1 da (Amanda Jo b 1974); *Career* RAEC Egypt and Kenya 1946-48; joined Boys Jarvis Partnership 1960 (now John Boys Architects); Awards and commendations (with others) finalist Sydney Opera House competition, finalist Financial Times Indust Award, Assoc for the Protection of Rural Scotland Award, Civic Tst and Saltire Soc Commendations; memb Royal Fine Art Cmmn for Scotland; ARSA, FRIBA, FRIAS; *Recreations* painting, curling, sailing; *Clubs* Glasgow Art; *Style—* John Boys, Esq; Sai Makessan, Gartocharn, Dunbartonshire G83 9LX (☎ 038 983 228); 19 Woodside Place, Glasgow G3 7QL (☎ 041 332 2228)

BOYSON, Rt Hon Sir Rhodes; MP (C) Brent North Feb 1974-; s of Alderman William

Boyson, MBE, JP, of Haslingden, Lancs, and Bertha Boyson; *b* 11 May 1925; *Educ* Haslingden GS, Manchester Univ, Univ Coll Cardiff, LSE, Corpus Christi Coll Cambridge (BA, MA, PhD); *m* 1, 1946 (m dis), Violet Burletson; 2 da; m 2, 1971, Florette MacFarlane; *Career* headmaster: Lea Bank Secondary Modern (Rossendale) 1955-61, Robert Montefiore Secondary Sch (Stepney) 1961-66, Highbury G S 1966-67, Highbury Grove Sch 1967-74; chm Nat Cncl Educnl Standards 1974-79; contested (C) Eccles 1970; vice-chm Cons Parly Educn Ctee 1975-76, oppn spokesman Educn 1976-79, Parly under-sec DES 1979-83, min for social security DHSS 1983-4, dep sec for NI 1984-86; min for local govt 1986-87; *Recreations* gardening, sport, writing, talking; *Clubs* St Stephen's, Carlton; *Style*— Rt Hon Sir Rhodes Boyson, MP; 71 Paines Lane, Pinner, Middx (☎ 01 866 2071)

BOZMAN, Michale Steven; s of John Michael Bozman (d 1988), and Ann Elizabeth, *née* Capper; *b* 2 Feb 1957; *Educ* Lancing; *m* 5 June 1982, Sally Ann, da of John Kimberley, of Hinksey Hill, Oxford; *Career* buyer Harrods Ltd 1975-84, mktg dir Totes 1984-; memb Mktg Soc 1988; *Recreations* cricket, tennis; *Clubs* MCC, Sussex Martless; *Style*— Michael Bozman, Esq; 42 Gosberton Rd, London SW12 8LF (☎ 01 675 4991); Totes, Eastman House, Billericay, Essex (☎ 0860 345125)

BRABAZON, Hon David Geoffrey Normand; yr s of 14 Earl of Meath; *b* 9 Oct 1948; *Educ* Tabley House; *m* 1972, Gay Dorothea, da of late Cdr William (Jock) Whitworth, DSC, RN (d 1955, s of Adml Sir William Whitworth, KCB, DSO) by his w Dorothea (whose mother Sophia was sis of 8 Marquess of Ely's f, George); 1 s, 2 da; *Style*— The Hon David Brabazon; North Wing, Killruddery, Bray, Co Wicklow, Ireland

BRABAZON OF TARA, 3 Baron (UK 1942); Ivon Anthony Moore-Brabazon; s of 2 Baron Brabazon of Tara, CBE (d 1974, whose f, 1 Baron, was min of Aircraft Production after Beaverbrook; the Bristol-Brabazon airliner was named after him); *b* 20 Dec 1946; *Educ* Harrow; *m* 8 Sept 1979, Harriet, da of Mervyn de Courcy Hamilton, of Harare, Zimbabwe, by his w, Lovell Ann, da of Rowland Cullinan, of Olifantsfontein, Transvaal; 1 s (Benjamin Ralph b 1983), 1 da (Hon Anabel Mary b 1985); *Heir* s, Hon Benjamin Ralph Moore-Brabazon b 15 March 1983; *Career* memb London Stock Exchange 1972-84; a Lord in Waiting (Government Whip) 1984-86; spokesman for Dept of Transport 1984-85, and for Treasury, Dept of Trade and Industry, Energy 1985-86; Parly Under-Sec of State for Transport 1986-, and Min for Aviation and Shipping; *Recreations* sailing; *Clubs* White's, Royal Yacht Sqdn; *Style*— The Rt Hon the Lord Brabazon of Tara; 35 Cloncurry St, London SW6 6DR (☎ 01 736 3705); 3 Swains Villas, Swains Road, Bembridge IW (☎ IOW 872258)

BRABHAM, Sir John Arthur (Jack); OBE 1966; father Cyril Thomas Brabham; *b* 2 April 1926; *Educ* Hurstville Technical Coll Sydney; *m* 1951 Betty Evelyn; 3 s; *Career* racing driver ret 1970; md: Jack Brabham (Motors) Ltd, Jack Brabham (Worcester Park) Ltd, Jack Brabham Racing Ltd, Engine Dev Ltd; three times World Motor Racing Champion 1959, 1960, 1966; kt 1979; *Books* When the Flag Drops; *Recreations* flying, boating, skindiving; *Clubs* BRDC, RAC; *Style*— Sir Jack Brabham, OBE; c/o 248 Hook Rd, Chessington, Surrey (☎ 01 397 4343)

BRABOURNE, 7 Baron (UK 1880); John Ulick Knatchbull; 16 Bt (E 1641); s of 5 Baron Brabourne, GCSI, GCIE, MC, JP, MP (d 1939, sometime viceroy and actg govr-gen India) by his w, Lady Doreen Browne (Dowager Lady Brabourne, d 1979, da of 6 Marquess of Sligo); suc er bro, 6 Baron (d 1943, shot by the Germans after escaping from a prison train in Italy and recaptured); *b* 9 Nov 1924; *Educ* Eton, Brasenose Coll Oxford; *m* 1946, Lady Patricia Edwina Victoria Mountbatten (Countess Mountbatten of Burma, *qv*), da of 1 Earl Mountbatten of Burma; 4 s (and 1 s decd), 2 da; *Heir* s, Lord Romsey; *Career* dir: Thames TV plc, Mersham Productions Ltd; producer/co-producer feature films: Harry Black and the Tiger (1958), Sink the Bismarck (1960), HMS Defiant (1961), Othello (1966), Romeo and Juliet (1966), The Mikado (1967), Up the Junction (1968), The Dance of Death (1969), The Tales of Beatrix Potter (1971), Murder on the Orient Express (1974), Death on the Nile (1978), Stories from a Flying Trunk (1979), The Mirror Crack'd (1980), Evil under the Sun (1982); A Passage to India (1984); Little Dorrit 1987, TV productions: The Life and Times of Lord Mountbatten (1968), Royal Family (1969, memb advsy ctee), Romantic Versus Classic Art (1973), The National Gallery - A Private View (1974), A Much Maligned Monarch (1976), Royal Heritage (1977, memb advsy ctee) Leontype (1988); chm: Br Cncl Advsy Ctee on Film, TV and Video, cncl Caldecott Community, govrs of Norton Knatchbull Sch; govr: Gordonstoun, Nat Film Sch, Wye Coll, United World Coll of the Atlantic; memb: Br Screen Advisory Cncl; tstee: BAFTA, Science Museum, Nat Museum of Photography; dep pro chllr Kent Univ; pres Kent Tst for Nature Conservation; Br Film and Television Producers Assoc; vice-pres Royal Soc for Nature Conservation; *Style*— The Rt Hon the Lord Brabourne; Newhouse, Mersham, Ashford, Kent TN25 6NQ (☎ 0233 23466); 39/41 Montpelier Walk, London SW7 1JH (☎ 01 589 8829)

BRACEGIRDLE, Cyril; s of Thomas Bracegirdle (d 1939), and Mary Ann (d 1976); *b* 23 Dec 1920; *Educ* Moston HS and privately; *m* 6 June 1977, Lili Dyfyr, da of Henry Eryddon Roberts (d 1972); *Career* author; tutor for writing schs London; memb: Amateurs' Panel of NW Arts, Soc of Authors; *Books* A First Book of Antiques (1970), Zoos are News (1972), The Dark River (1973), Collecting Railway Antiques (1988); *Recreations* live theatre, music, environmental studies, antiques; *Style*— Cyril Bracegirdle, Esq; 7 Langdale Rd, Eastway, Sale, Cheshire M33 4EN (☎ 061 973 6215)

BRACEWELL, Her Hon Judge; Joyanne Winifred (Mrs Roy Copeland); QC (1978); da of Jack and Lilian Bracewell; *b* 5 July 1934; *Educ* Manchester Univ (LLB, LLM); *m* 1963, Roy Copeland, s of late Jack Copeland; 1 s (Adam b 1965), 1 da (Philippa b 1967); *Career* rec Crown Ct (Northern Circuit) 1975-83, circuit judge (Northern Circuit) 1983-; *Recreations* antiques, cooking, reading, walking, bridge; *Style*— Her Hon Judge Bracewell, QC

BRACEWELL SMITH, Sir Charles; 4 Bt (UK 1947), of Keighley, Co York; s of Sir George Bracewell Smith, 2 Bt, MBE (d 1976); suc bro, Sir Guy Bracewell Smith 1983; *b* 13 Oct 1955; *Educ* Harrow; *Heir* none; *Style*— Sir Charles Bracewell Smith; Park Lane Hotel, Piccadilly, London W1

BRACEY, Capt Norton Edward; TD; s of Maj Fredric Alfred Bracey (d 1966), of Cobham, Surrey, and Gladys Violet Lang (d 1969), da of E Whiteaway, of Bombay, Calcutta and Hong Kong; Maj Bracey pioneered the use of motor vehicles in Australia 1906, and supplied the Australian Govt with WW I motor transport; *b* 29 Oct 1911; *Educ* Bromsgrove, Neuchatel Univ Switzerland; *m* 24 Feb 1940, (Alice) Barbara, da of Noel Wilkinson (d 1956), of Ascot, Berks; 1 s (Ian Fredric d 1987), 1 da (Vanessa Jane); *Career* Capt Workshops Offr in N Africa and Italy; Lloyds Underwriting memb; dir: Norman & Bracey Lloyds Agencies (also chm) 1979-84, Viscose Devpt Co 1964-79, and Sponcel Ltd (ret); *Clubs* British Racing Drivers', RAC; *Style*— Capt Norton Bracey, TD; Shaldon, 26 Harebell Hill, Cobham, Surrey KT11 2RS (☎ 0932 64515)

BRACK, Peter Kenneth; s of Rev Martin Brack (d 1953), of Billingham, Co Durham, and Dorothea, *née* Martin (d 1977); *b* 13 April 1921; *Educ* Trent Coll Derbyshire; *m* 13 April 1961, Nora, da of Francis Kilmartin, MM (d 1956), of Cheadle, Cheshire; *Career* initial career with Rolls Royce Ltd Derby 1940-71; engineering apprenticeship followed by various duties home and abroad: Cordoba Argentina 1950-52, Venezuela 1953-56, France and Italy 1957-59, md Rolls Royce De Espana SA 1963-71 (pres Br Club Barcelona 1966-71); dir Bennett's Machine co 1973-75, TTI Ltd (Translations Co) 1975-77, md Brack & Assoc Ltd 1977-; CEng, FBIM; *Recreations* philately (recognised authority on Venezuela stamps), golf, chess, natural history; *Clubs* Canning, San Cugat Golf (Barcelona); *Style*— Peter K Brack, Esq; Chrysalis, Windley, Derbyshire DE5 2LP (☎ Cowers Lane 077 389 364); Brack & Associates Ltd, 66/66A Friar Gate, Derby DE1 1DJ (☎ 0332 360242, telex 377106, fax 0332 382028)

BRACKENBURY, Mark Hereward; s of Charles Hereward Brackenbury (d 1984), of Tweedhill, Berwick-upon-Tweed, and Elise, *née* Cuming (d 1984); *b* 19 April 1931; *Educ* Ampleforth, New Coll Oxford; *m* 18 Sept 1956, Virginia Catherine, da of Gibson Stott (d 1985), of 100 Hobson Street, Wellington, NZ; 1 s (David b 1961), 1 da (Claire b 1957); *Career* ptnr Sternberg Thomas Clarke & Co and predecessor firms 1964-76 London Stock Exchange; yachting author and journalist; *Books* Norwegian Cruising Guide (1978), S W Baltic Pilot (1983), Scottish West Coast Pilot (1980), Normandy & Channel Island Pilot (1983) and others; *Recreations* sailing (circumnavigated 1983-86), skiing, bridge; *Clubs* Garrick, Green Room, Royal Cruising; *Style*— Mark Brackenbury, Esq; Fallowfield, Stebbing, Dunmow, Essex CM6 3ST (☎ 037186 242)

BRACKETT, (Frederick John) Hugh; MBE (Mil 1941); s of Frederick Henry Brackett, of Pentrefechan, Wadhurst, Sussex (d 1930), and Mary, *née* Hughes-Parry (d 1945); Parry family owned extensive land in the Vale of Llangollen from Tudor times; *b* 6 July 1909; *Educ* St Michael's Sch Uckfield Sussex, Tonbridge, Coll of Estate Mgmnt; *m* April 1935 Shillinglaw (d 1973), da of Mr Thomas Hodgson of Derbyshire; 2 da (Jane b 1936, Belinda b 1939); had issue by Szuszanna Brackett (name changed from Fronkl 1967) out of wedlock 2 da (Nicola and Andrea (twins) b 1967); *Career* TA 6 AADiv, RASC commnd 3 Sept 1939 served Faroe Islands 1940-41, India 1942-45, Maj, staff combined Ops Beach control; chartered surveyor, Partner Debenham, Tewson & Chinnocks (DTC) 1934, conslt DTC 1970; ret 1985; FRICS; *Recreations* reading; *Clubs* East India; *Style*— Hugh Brackett, Esq; Rothbury, Brock Road, St Peter Port, Guernsey, C.I. (☎ 0481 711629)

BRACKFIELD, Peter; s of Julius Alexander Brackfield (d 1959); *b* 26 Sept 1922; *Educ* Berkhamsted Sch, Trinity Coll Cambridge (MA); *m* 1, 1954 (m dis), Odile, da of Louis de Koenigswarter, of Paris; 1 s; m 2, 1982, Beatrice, da of William Newton, of Kuala Lumpur; *Career* merchant banker; dir: Singer-Friedlander Ltd 1983- (md 1956-76, dep chm 1976-82), C T Bowring & Co 1971-80; cmmr Public Works Loans Bd; *Recreations* walking, tennis, skiing, gardening; *Style*— Peter Brackfield, Esq; Flat 6, 58 Rutland Gate, London SW7 (☎ 01 584 7432); Priory Stones, Lurgashall, Petworth, W Sussex (☎ 042 878 320)

BRACKLEY, Peter Gordon; s of Charles William Brackley (d 1979), of Northwood, and Ethel Florence Coster (d 1986); *b* 26 May 1923; *Educ* Watford GS, UCL (BSc); *m* 25 Oct 1948, Hettie Bewick, da of George Bewick Gibbins (d 1961); 1 s (Christopher b 1951), 1 da (Judith b 1956); *Career* with Anglo-Iranian Oil Co (now BP) 1943-82 (posts inc gen mangr Environmental Control Centre, refineries and mgmnt consultancy); former dir: BP Maatschappi, Nederland BV, BP Raffinaderi (Goteborg) AB, BP Overseas Refining Co Ltd; present dir Aberdeen Univ Marine Studies Ltd, The Emeritus Register; chm: ConCAWE 1976-78, Sullom Voe Environmental Advsy Gp 1974-76; memb Nature Conservancy Cncl 1976-86, vice-chm session World Petroleum Congress (Bucharest 1979, London 1983); Officier in der Ordre van Oranje-Nassau, FRSC, FRSA, FInstPet, assoc fell RIIA; *Recreations* music, sport; *Clubs* MCC; *Style*— Mr Brackley; Darwell Hill, Netherfield, Battle, E Sussex TN33 9QL (☎ 042 482 234)

BRADBEER, Sir (John) Derek (Richardson); OBE (1973), TD (1964), DL (1988); s of William Bertram Bradbeer, of Hexham, Northumberland, and Winifred, *née* Richardson (d 1985); *b* 29 Oct 1931; *Educ* Canford, Sidney Sussex Coll Cambridge (MA); *m* 6 April 1962, Margaret Elizabeth, da of Gerald Frederick Chantler, TD, of Ponteland, Northumberland; 1 s (Jeremy b 1962), 1 da (Amanda b 1963); *Career* cmmnd RA 1951, CO 101 (N) Med Regt RA (V) 1970-73, Dep Cdr 21 and 23 Bdes 1973-77, Hon Col 101 (N) FD Regt RA (V) 1986-; vice chm TAVR Assoc North of England 1988-; slr 1959, ptnr Wilkinson Maughan Newcastle 1961-, memb cncl of Law Soc 1973-, pres Newcastle Law Soc 1980, govr Coll of Law 1983-, pres Law Soc 1987-88 (vice pres 1986-87), memb Criminal Injuries Compensation Bd 1988-; dir: JT Dove Pensions Tst Ltd 1975-, Newcastle and Gateshead Water Co 1978-; kt 1988; *Recreations* gardening, reading, tennis, general sport; *Clubs* Army and Navy, Northern Counties; *Style*— Sir Derek Bradbeer, OBE, TD, DL; Forge Cottage, Shilvington, Northumberland NE20 0AP (☎ 067 075 214); Wilkinson Maughan, Sun Alliance House, 35 Mosley St, Newcastle upon Tyne NE1 (☎ 091 261 1841, fax 091 261 8267, telex 537477)

BRADBEER, Jonathan Linthorn; s of Leonard Harry Bradbeer (d 1983), and Grace Laura, *née* Whitting (d 1988); *b* 14 April 1938; *Educ* Clayesmore Sch Iwerne Minster Dorset, Guy's Hosp Dental Sch (BDS, LDS, RCS); *m* (m dis); *Career* Surgeon Lt (D) RN 1963-68; gen dental practice 1968-; Br Dental Assoc, RSM; *Recreations* ocean racing, skiing, flying; *Clubs* Royal Yacht Sqdn, Royal Ocean Racing (cdre), Royal Lymington Yacht, Island Sailing, Royal Yachting Assoc; *Style*— Jonathan Bradbeer, Esq; 14 Ashley Ct, Morpeth Terr, London SW1 (☎ 01 828 4779); 7 Harcourt House, 19A Cavendish Square, London W1 (☎ 01 580 2551)

BRADBROOK, Prof Muriel Clara; da of Samuel Bradbrook (d 1928), and Annie Wilson, *née* Harvey (d 1934); *b* 27 April 1909; *Educ* Oldershaw Sch Wallasey, Girton Coll Cambridge (BA, MA, PhD, LittD); *Career* war serv, Bd of Trade 1941-45; lectr Cambridge Univ 1945-64, reader 1964-66, prof 1966-76, mistress Girton Coll 1968-76; diocesan reader Diocese of Ely 1976-; author; Freedom of the City of Hiroshima (1964); Hon DLitt: Liverpool 1964, Sussex 1972, London 1973; Hon LLD Smith Coll USA 1965, Hon PhD Gothenburg 1975, Hon LHD Kenyon Coll USA 1977; foreign memb Norwegian Acad of Arts and Sciences 1966, hon memb Modern Language Assoc of America 1974; FRSL; *Recreations* theatre, travel; *Clubs* University Women's; *Style*— Prof Muriel Bradbrook; 91 Chesterton Rd, Cambridge CB4 4AP (☎ 0223 352765)

BRADBURN, Stephen Ernest; s of Ernest Bradburn, of Sheffield; *b* 24 Sept 1947; *Educ* Abbeydale Boys' GS Sheffield; *m* 1969, Geraldine, da of Albert Britton, of Woodley Berks; 1 s; *Career* dir Hargreaves Tport Ltd 1976-, Hargreaves Vehicle Distributors Ltd 1978-; *Style*— Stephen Bradburn, Esq; 10 Cottesmore Gdns, Hale Barns, Altrincham, Cheshire

BRADBURY, Surgn Vice Adm Sir Eric Blackburn; KBE (1971), CB (1968); s of late A B Bradbury, of Orchard House, Maze, Co Antrim; *b* 2 Mar 1911; *Educ* Royal Belfast Academical Instn, Queen's Univ Belfast; *m* 1939, Elizabeth Constance, da of late J G Austin, of Armagh; 3 da; *Career* RN Medical Service 1934, Surgn Capt 1959, Medical Offr i/c RN Hosp Haslar 1966, Surgn Rear Adm 1966, Surgn Vice Adm 1969, Med Dir-Gen of the Navy 1969-72; chm Tunbridge Wells District Health Authority 1981-84; FRCS 1972, Hon LLD Queen's Univ Belfast, CStJ, former QHP; *Style*— Surgn Vice Adm Sir Eric Bradbury, KB; The Gate House, Nevill Park, Tunbridge Wells, Kent TN4 8NN (☎ (0892) 27661)

BRADBURY, Hon John; s and h of 2 Baron Bradbury; *b* 17 Mar 1940; *Educ* Gresham's, Bristol Univ; *m* 1968 Susan, da of late W Liddiard, of East Shefford, Berks; 2 s; *Style*— The Hon John Bradbury; 10 Clifton Hill, London NW8

BRADBURY, 2 Baron (UK 1925); John Bradbury; s of 1 Baron, GCB (d 1950); *b* 7 Jan 1914; *Educ* Westminster, Brasenose Coll Oxford; *m* 1, 1939, Joan, o da of W D Knight, of Darley, Addlestone, Surrey; 1 s, 1 da; m 2, 1946, Gwerfyl, da of late E Stanton Roberts, of Gellifor, Ruthin, Denbigh; 1 da; *Heir* s, Hon John Bradbury; *Style*— The Rt Hon The Lord Bradbury; Wingham, Summerhays, Leigh Hill Rd, Cobham, Surrey (☎ Cobham 7757)

BRADBURY, John Howard Hullah; CBE (1986); s of Prof Fred Bradbury (d 1948), and Florence Jane, *née* Ratcliffe (d 1982); *b* 26 Feb 1940; *Educ* Friends' Sch Saffron Walden, Pomfret Sch Pomfret Connecticut USA, Jesus Coll Cambridge; *m* 31 Aug 1963, Christine Annette J, da of Rev Christopher Augustine Kelly, of Gargrave, Skipton, Yorks; 1 s (Michael b 2 Jan 1973), 1 da (Elizabeth b 19 Mar 1970); *Career* factory supt AEI Rugby 1965-67 (prodn devpt engr 1964-65), raw materials buyer Mars Ltd 1968-75 (shift prodn mangr 1967-68), UK buying dir Utd Biscuits (UK) Ltd 1978-87 (dep buying dir 1975-78) lay dir AFBD Ltd (non-exec dir); Tower Capt St Marys Farnham Royal; former pres Cake and Biscuit Alliance; *Recreations* fellwalking, flying, skiing, amateur radio, shooting, camponology; *Style*— John Bradbury, Esq, CBE; United Biscuits (UK) Ltd, Grant House, PO Box 40, Syon Lane, Isleworth, Middx TW7 5NN (car 0836 222399, fax 01 568 3505, telex UBISLE 8954657)

BRADBURY, John Keith; s of Ronald Charles Bradbury, of Knowle, Warwicks, and Gladys Marjorie, *née* Green (d 1971); *b* 18 Feb 1932; *Educ* King Henry VIII Sch Coventry; *m* 6 March 1954, Molly, da of Horace Reginald Woodbridge, of Coventry, (d 1973); 2 s (Andrew John b 1955, Richard Anthony b 1963), 1 da (Jennifer Ann 1958); *Career* Nat Serv RAF 1950-52, dep ed The Birmingham Post 1975-80, ed Sandwell Evening Mail 1980-84, ed Birmingham Post and Mail Weeklies 1984-85, ed Sunday Mercury Birmingham 1985-; chm Nat Cncl for the Trg of Journalists 1987-88; hon sec Birmingham district Newspaper Press Fund 1972-; past chm Birmingham Press Club, vice pres Walmley CC, former pres Wylde Green Bowling Club;memb Guild Br Newspaper Eds 1980 (cncl memb 1983-, regnl chm 1983-84); *Recreations* theatre, music, travel, gardening, railways; *Clubs* Birmingham Press; *Style*— John Bradbury, Esq; Farriers Cottage, Ebrington, Chipping Campden, Glos; and Eldon Dr, Sutton Coldfield, W Midlands (☎ 038 678 418); Sunday Mercury, Colmore Circus, Birmingham B4 6AZ (☎ 021 236 3366, fax 021 233 3958, telex 337 552)

BRADBURY, (Elizabeth) Joyce; CBE (1970); da of Thomas Edwin Bradbury (d 1943), and Anne, *née* Milburn (d 1929); *b* 12 Dec 1918; *Educ* Queen Elizabeth's GS Middleton Lancs, Univ of Leeds (BA, DipEd); *Career* various teaching appts 1941-57, dep head Stand GS for Girls Whitefield nr Manchester 1957-59; headmistress: Bede GS for Girls Sunderland 1959-67, Pennywell Sch Sunderland 1967-72, Thornhill Sch Sunderland 1972-78; ret 1978; memb Univ Grants Ctee 1967-72, nat pres Assoc of Head Mistresses 1974-76, Moir Cullis fellowship Br American Assocs 1979-; govr: Sunderland Poly 1968-87, Durham Univ 1972-87, Polam Hall Sch Darlington 1986-; memb local ctee Royal Soc of Arts 1977-, memb and former pres northern counties branch Assoc of Headmistresses, memb and former pres Soroptimist Int of Sunderland; FRSA 1977, hon memb Secdy Heads Assoc 1979; *Recreations* travel at home and abroad, pursuing some historical interests, domestic arts, photography; *Clubs* Soroptimist Int; *Style*— Miss Joyce Bradbury, CBE; 6 Cliffe Ct, Roker, Sunderland SR6 9NT (☎ 091 548 7773)

BRADBURY, Prof Malcolm Stanley; s of Arthur Bradbury, and Doris, *née* Marshall; *b* 7 Sept 1932; *Educ* Leicester Univ, QMC London (MA), Manchester Univ (PhD), Indiana Univ, Yale Univ;; *m* 1959, Elizabeth Salt; 2 s (Matthew, Dominic); *Career* lectr in english literature and language Univ of Birmingham 1961-65, lectr Univ of East Anglia 1965-70, prof of american studies UEA; visiting prof Univ of: Zürich, Washington, St Louis, Queensland; chm of judges Booker McConnell Prize 1981; Hon DLitt Univ of Leicester; *Publications* inc: Evelyn Waugh (1982), EM Forster: a collection of critical essays (ed, 1965), What is a novel (1963), The Social Context of Modern English Literature (1972), Modernism (1972), Saul Bellow (1982); The Modern World: Ten Great Writers (1988); fiction inc: Eating People is Wrong (1959), Stepping Westward (1965), The History Man (1975), Who Do You Think You Are (1976), Rates of Exchange (1982), Mensonge (1987), Cuts (1987); *Clubs* Royal Overseas League; *Style*— Prof Malcolm Bradbury; University of East Anglia, Norwich NR4 7TJ (telex UEANOR Norwich)

BRADBURY, Hon Paul; s of 1 Baron Bradbury, GCB (d 1950); *b* 28 Nov 1915; *Educ* Westminster, Brasenose Coll Oxford (MA); *m* 1940, Margaret Amy, da of John William Stammers; 3 s; *Career* company dir ret; *Style*— The Hon Paul Bradbury; Chelvey Batch, Brockley, Bristol BS19 3AP (☎ 027 583 2813)

BRADBURY, Robert Henry; s of William Henry Bradbury (d 1950), and Edith Minnie, *née* Talboys (d 1985); family spent 25 yrs in India, with Balmer Lawrie & Co Ltd (dir for 12 years), ret to UK 1932; *b* 10 April 1919, (in India); *Educ* Oundle; *m* 1, 1942, Jean Margaret, *née* Watson; 1 s (John Michael b 1943), 1 da (Suzanna b 1945); m 2, 24 March 1966, Enid Clement, da of William Vines (d 1965); *Career* RE (ret as Major) 1939-46; joined Crendon Concrete Co Ltd (family business founded by f 1933), dir 1948, mangr dir 1950; exec chm Crendon Hldgs Ltd chm of subsidiary companies and dir of Malaysian associate companies; FID 1956; *Recreations* tennis, swimming, gardening, travel; *Clubs* Inst of Directors; *Style*— Robert Bradbury, Esq; The Old Crown, 97 Bicester Road, Long Crendon, Aylesbury, Bucks HP18 9EF; Crendon Holdings Ltd, Long Crendon, Aylesbury, Bucks HP18 9BB (☎ 0844 208481, telex 83249G, fax 0844 201622)

BRADBURY, Rear Adm Thomas Henry; CB (1979); s of Thomas Henry Bradbury (d 1970), and Violet, *née* Buckingham; *b* 4 Dec 1922; *Educ* Christ's Hosp; *m* 1, 1945 (m dis 1979), Beryl Doreen Evans; 1 s, 1 da; m 2, 1979, Sarah Catherine, da of Harley Hillier; *Career* Flag Offr Admty Interview Bd 1977-79; gp personnel dir Inchcape Gp 1979-86; Mgmnt devpt advsr to Davy Corpn 1987-; *Recreations* sailing, gardening; *Style*— Rear-Adm Thomas Bradbury, CB; Churches Green, Dallington, Heathfield, Sussex (☎ 0435 830 657)

BRADFER LAWRENCE, Lt Col Philip Leslie; MC (1945); s of Harry Lawrence Bradfer Lawrence (d 1965), of Norfolk, and Violet Evelyn, *née* Bradfield (d 1919); *b* 6 Oct 1917; *Educ* Marlborough, RMA Woolwich, Cambridge Univ (BA); *m* 1945, Lyndsay Ann, William Watson (d 1928), of Scotland; 1 s (Roderick b 1950), 1 da (Harriet b 1955); *Career* cmmnd 2 Lt 1937; serv: France 1939-40, N Africa and Italy 1942-45; ret Lt-Col 1947; md: Hammonds United Breweries Ltd 1948-60, Charrington United Breweries Ltd 1962-67; dir: Hedges and Butler Ltd 1961-69, United Breweries Ltd 1960-65, United Caledonian Breweries Ltd 1960-63, Charrington and Co Ltd 1962-64, Nairn Williamson Ltd 1968-73, Zaehnsdorf Ltd 1972-, Guardian Assur plc 1965-87, Guardian Royal Exchange Assur plc 1968-87 (vice chm 1985-87), Bass plc 1967-82 (md 1967-74), Lake and Elliott plc 1972-82, British Field Products Ltd 1974-87 (chm 1984-87); chm Tennent Caledonian Breweries Ltd 1963-67; FSA, FRSA; *Recreations* shooting, previously cricket and golf; *Clubs* Boodles, Roxburghe, Saintsbury, MCC; *Style*— Lt-Col Philip Bradfer Lawrence; Little Turners, The Street, Warham, Wells-next-the-Sea, Norfolk NR23 1NH

BRADFIELD, Dr John Richard Grenfell; CBE (1986); s of Horace Bradfield (d 1959), of Cambridge, and Ada Sarah, *née* Houghton (d 1952); *b* 20 May 1925; *Educ* Cambridgeshire Co HS for Boys, Trinity Coll Cambridge (MA, PhD); *m* 23 June 1951, Jane, da of Capt Edgar W Wood, MC (d 1974); 1 s (Robert Andrew Richard b 1952); *Career* Univ of Cambridge: res fell in cell biol Trinity Coll 1947, sr bursar Trinity Coll 1956- (jr bursar 1951-56), hon fell Darwin Coll 1973-; Cwlth Harkness fell Chicago 1948, dir Cambridge Water Co 1965, Cambridge Bldg Soc 1968-, fndr Cambridge Sci Park 1970 and mangr since construction 1973-, bd memb Anglian Water Authy 1975-, chm Abbotstone Agric Property Unit Tst 1975-, dir Cambridge Control 1984-; former chm St Faith's Prep Sch Cambridge, govr Leys Sch; Associate Soc of Investmt Analysts 1970-; *Recreations* walking, sailing, arboretum-visiting; *Style*— Dr John Bradfield, CBE; Trinity College, Cambridge CB2 1TQ (☎ 0223 338 400, fax 0223 338 467)

BRADFORD, Archdeacon of; *see*: Shreeve, The Ven David Herbert

BRADFORD, Christopher Mark Newens (Chris); s of Marcus Newens Bradford, of Great Shelford, Cambs, and Hilda Muriel Annie Bradford, JP; *b* 4 Nov 1934; *Educ* Bedford Sch, Sidney Sussex Coll Cambridge (MA); *m* 9 Aug 1958, Lesley June, *née* Harvey; 2 s, 4 da; *Career* 2 Lt Nat Serv 1952-54, TA 1954-60; admitted slr 1960; partnerships: Saffron Walden 1963-65, Gainsborough 1965-67, Cambridge 1967-80 (conslt 1980-), farmer; cncllr: Cambridge City Cncl 1970-74, Cambs CC 1973-; memb 1985-: memb Nat Advsy Body on Public Sector Higher Educn, nat negotiating ctees on lectrs: and teachers' pay and conditions of serv; SLD educn spokesman ACC 1987-memb E Anglian Tourist Bd 1987-; author of various booklets on educn issues; memb Worshipful Co of Vitners; memb Law Soc 1960; *Recreations* cricket, walking, travelling; *Style*— Chris Bradford, Esq; 4 Cavendish Ave, Cambridge CB1 4US (☎ 0223 245796, 0223 211273)

BRADFORD, Donald Clifton; s of Col Sir Evelyn Bradford, 2 Bt (d 1914); hp of nephew, Sir Edward Bradford, 5 Bt; *b* 22 May 1914; *Educ* Eton, Oxford Univ (MA); *m* 1949, Constance Mary, yr da of late Richard Thomas Morgan, of Glyncorrwg, S Wales; 2 da (and 1 da decd); *Career* Capt Seaforth Highlanders 1939-46, served Europe; admin mangr with geophysical consultants 1954-79, ret; *Recreations* gardening, golf; *Style*— Donald Bradford, Esq; The Oast, Brightling, Robertsbridge, E Sussex TN32 5HD

BRADFORD, (Sir) Edward Alexander Slade; (5 Bt, UK 1902); s of 3 Bt (d 1952); suc half-bro, Sir John Ridley Evelyn Bradford, 4 Bt, 1954, but does not use title; *b* 18 June 1952; *Heir* unc, Donald Bradford; *Style*— Edward Bradford, Esq; Faith Cottage, Pett, Sussex

BRADFORD, Ian James; s of Alan James Bradford, of Tabor, 197 Willington St, Maidstone, Kent, and Ann, *née* Farley; *b* 2 April 1966; *Educ* Maidstone Sch; *Career* mangr Page & Wells, estate agents 1983-; *Style*— I J Bradford, Esq; 5 Bolingbroke House, London Rd, Maidstone, Kent (☎ 0622 52815); 9 Malling Rd, Snodland, Kent (☎ 0634 240672)

BRADFORD, Lady; Marjorie Edith; da of Samuel Bere, of Addiscombe, Surrey; *m* 1 (m dis), Stephen Chapman; m 2, 1950, as his 2 w, Maj Sir Edward Bradford, 3 Bt (d 1952); *Style*— Lady Bradford; Faith Cottage, Pett, Sussex

BRADFORD, 7 Earl of (UK 1815); The Rt Hon Richard Thomas Orlando Bridgeman; 12 Bt (E 1660); also Baron Bradford (GB 1794) and Viscount Newport (UK 1815); s of 6 Earl of Bradford, TD (d 1981); *b* 3 Oct 1947; *Educ* Harrow, Trinity Coll Cambridge (MA); *m* 1979, Joanne Elizabeth, da of Benjamin Miller, of 42 Pembroke Rd, W8; 3 s (Viscount Newport, Hon Henry Gerald Charles Orlando b 18 April 1982, Hon Benjamin Thomas Orlando b 1987); *Heir* er s, Viscount Newport; *Career* owner Porters Restaurant in Covent Garden; chm Unicorn Heritage plc; dep chm: Beacon Radio, Expedier Leisure plc; *Recreations* shooting, cooking, gardening; *Style*— The Rt Hon The Earl of Bradford; Woodlands House, Weston-under-Lizard, Shifnal, Shrops TF11 8LE

BRADFORD, Bishop of (cr 1920) 1984-; Rt Rev Robert (Roy) Kerr Williamson; s of late James Williamson, of Belfast, and late Elizabeth, *née* Kelly; *b* 18 Dec 1932; *Educ* Elmgrove Sch Belfast, Oak Hill Theol Coll London; *m* 1956, Anne Boyd, da of late John Smith of Belfast; 3 s (Stephen b 1958, Jonathan b 1965, Andrew b 1966), 2 da (Gillian b 1959, Katharine b 1968); *Career* ordained: deacon 1963, priest 1964, curate of Crowborough Sussex 1963-66, vicar: Hyson Green Nottingham 1966-71, St Ann with Emmanuel Nottingham 1971-76, Bramcote 1976-79, archdeacon of Nottingham 1978-84; Hon DLitt Bradford; *Recreations* home, family, bird watching, music, watching TV sport, reading; *Clubs* National; *Style*— The Rt Rev the Bishop of

Bradford; Bishopscroft, Ashwell Road, Heaton, Bradford, W Yorks BD9 4AU (☎ 0274 545414)

BRADFORD, Hon Mrs (Tatiana Sonia); *née* Lucas; da of 1 Baron Lucas of Chilworth (d 1967); *b* 10 Jan 1933; *Educ* Convent HS Southampton, Eastbourne sch of domestic economy; *m* 1964, Kenneth Bradford, s of Arthur Bradford (d 1961), of Charmouth, Dorset; 2 s (Adam, Justin); *Clubs* Royal Overseas League; *Style—* The Hon Mrs Bradford; Nashdom, 13 Woodlands Rd, Surbiton, Surrey KT6 6PR

BRADING, Philip William; s of Cdr WFJ Brading, OBE, RN (ret), of 10 Glebe Close, Burton upon Stather, South Humberside DN15 6BZ, and PE Brading, *née* Seymour; *b* 25 Jan 1952; *Educ* John Leggott GS, and Kent Univ (BSc Hons); *m* 14 June 1980, Lisa Mary Caroline, da of FW Bentley, of Brook Cottage, Underiver, Kent; 1 s (Benjamin b 1985), 1 da (Fleur b 1987); *Career* dir: Hill Samuel Bank Ltd 1985-, London Bridge Finance Ltd 1987-, Independence Insur Co Ltd (Bermuda) 1987-8, Neat Grooved Boards Ltd 1984-, Haringey Health Authy 1982-; *Recreations* skiing, music; *Style—* Philip Brading, Esq; 23 Highgate Close, London N6 4SD (☎ 01 340 8976); Hill Samuel Bank Ltd, 100 Wood St, London EC2P 2AJ (☎ 01 628 8011, telex: 888822, fax: 01 606 3319)

BRADISH, Martyn Henry Stewart; s of Edward Henry Bradish, and Florence Gertrude, *née* Tidman; *b* 10 Mar 1951; *Educ* Queen Elizabeth's Sch Barnet; *m* 1 March 1975, Linda Kay, da of George Squires; 3 da (Kirsty Linda b 1979, Samantha Elizabeth b 1982, Sarah Louise b 1984); *Career* ptnr: Wilkins Kennedy & Co CA; 1977-83, Foster Squires 1984-; area vice-chm Area 17 London NE Round Table; FCA 1973; *Clubs* Southgate Round Table; *Style—* Martyn Bradish, Esq; Rex House, 354 Ballards Lane, North Finchley, London N12 OEG (☎ 01 446 6055, fax 01 446 6964)

BRADISH-ELLAMES, Lt-Col Simon Edward Mountague; OBE (1973); s of Maj John Edward Mountague Bradish-Ellames (d 1984), of Little Marlow, and Helen Chambers, *née* Lehmann (d 1985); *b* 17 Jan 1930; *Educ* Eton, Mons OCS; *m* 1960, Cynthia Mary, step da of Air Chief Marshal Sir Hubert Patch of Marbella; 2 s (Peter b 1963, Andrew b 1965, d 1970), 1 da (Jane b 1961); *Career* joined The Royal Dragoons 1948, 2nd cmd RHG/D (The Blues and Royals) 1969, CO The Life Gds 1971 (ret 1974); dir Sabre Safety Ltd 1976; *Recreations* fishing, shooting, and labradors; *Clubs* Cavalry and Guards'; *Style—* Lt-Col Simon Bradish-Ellames; Velhurst Farm, Alfold, Cranleigh, Surrey (☎ 0403 752146); Sabre Safety Ltd, Matterson House, Aldershot, Hants (☎ 0252 344141)

BRADLAW, Prof Sir Robert Vivian; CBE (1950); s of Philip Archibald Bradlaw, of Blackrock, Dublin; *b* 14 April 1905; *Educ* Cranleigh, Guy's Hosp; *Career* consultant Royal Navy 1939-81; hon prof of oral pathology Royal Coll of Surgeons of England 1948-, emeritus prof Oral Medicine London Univ 1970-, chm Advsy Cncl on Misuse of Drugs, Home Office 1976-82; hon degrees: Belfast, Birmingham, Boston, Durham, Leeds, Malta, Melbourne, Meshed, Montreal, Newcastle-upon-Tyne; Chev de la Santé Publique (France) 1950, Kt Order of St Olaf (Norway), Cdr Order of Homayoun (Iran); FRCS (England, Edinburgh, Glasgow, Ireland); kt 1965; *Recreations* golf, fishing, orchids, oriental ceramics; *Clubs* Athenaeum; *Style—* Prof Sir Robert Bradlaw, CBE; The Manse, Stoke Goldington, Bucks (☎ 0908 55281)

BRADLEY, Clement Gordon; s of Lawrence Reginald Bradley (d 1988), and Clare Elizabeth, *née* Handsley (d 1953); *b* 11 Feb 1895; *Educ* Walton Sch, Deacon Sch Peterborough, Admty Apprenticeship Peter Brotherhood; *m* 4 Oct 1958, Ann Margaret, da of Alexander Grieve (d 1978); 1 s (James Handsley b 1964), 1 da (Elizabeth Ann b 1962); *Career* watchkeeping offr Mercantile Marine Royal Fleet Aux North Atlantic Mediterranean Pacific 1943-49; shipping ed South China Morning Post Hong Kong 1949-51, chief news broadcaster Rediffusion Hong Kong 1951-52, tv prodr chm and interviewer This Week Assoc Rediffusion London 1952-58, prodr Today TV Series Assoc TV 1958-60, film prodr chm md Gordon Bradley Ltd 1960-88; Freeman City of London 1983, Liveryman Worshipful Co of Shipwrights; FInstD 1962, MIPR 1981; *Clubs* Carlton, MCC, 1900; *Style—* Gordon Bradley, Esq; Gordon Bradley Ltd, 59 St James's St, London SW1A 1LB (☎ 01 499 7870, telex 268312 WESCOM G ATT'N BRADCO)

BRADLEY, Clive; s of Alfred Bradley (d 1970), and Annie Kathleen, *née* Turner; *b* 25 July 1934; *Educ* Felsted Sch, Clare Coll Cambridge (MA), Yale Univ; *Career* PO RAF 1953-55; called to the Bar Middle Temple 1961; BBC (1961-63 and 1965), broadcasting offr Lab Party 1963-64, political ed and broadcaster 1965-67, gp labour advsr IPC Newspapers 1967-69, dep gen mangr Daily and Sunday Mirror and controller of admin IPC 1969-71, project dir IPC 1971-73, dir The Observer 1973-76, chief exec The Publishers Assoc 1976-, dir Confedn Info Communication Industries 1984-; author of various pubns on politics, econs, media, indust relations and law; dep chm Central London Valuation Panel; gov Felsted Sch Essex; Liveryman Worshipful Co of Stationers; *Clubs* Reform, Groucho, Elizabethan; *Style—* Clive Bradley, Esq; 8 Northumberland Place, Richmond upon Thames, Surrey TW10 6TS (☎ 01 940 7172); 19 Bedford Square, London WC1B 3HJ (☎ 01 580 6321, fax 01 636 5375, telex 267 160 PUBASS G)

BRADLEY, (David) John; s of David John Bradley (d 1954), of 33 Priestfields, Rochester, Kent, and Dorothy Frances Mary *née* Black (d 1948); *b* 22 August 1924; *Educ* Rochester Cathedral Choir Sch, Kings Sch Rochester; *Career* RN 1942-46; dir Thomas Watson (shipping) ltd; consul for Sweden; tstee: Watts Charity (Rochester), Shafesbury Homes and Arethusa; cncl memb and former chm Friends of Rochester Cathedral, govr Sir John Hawkins Hosp, chm Lord Chancellor;s Advsy Ctee; Freeman: City of London 1971, Worshipful Co of Watermen & Lightermen; Inst of Chartered Shipbrokers : memb 1948, fell 1965), Fell Inst of Freight Forwarders; Knight Order of VASA (Sweden 1965) Knight First Class Order of Polar Star - (Sweden 1981); *Recreations* sailing, farming, fruit growing; *Clubs* Castle (Rochester), Danish; *Style—* John Bradley, Esq; Buck Hole Farm, High Halstow, Rochester, Kent ME3 8SE (☎ 0634 250 895); 252 High St, Rochester, Kent ME1 1HZ (☎ 0634 44632, telex 96109)

BRADLEY, Joseph Clyde; s of Joseph Richard and Ada Beatrice Bradley; *b* 21 May 1940; *Educ* Gt Yarmouth GS, Univ Coll London (BA, BSc); *m* 1962, Ute Brunhilde; 1 s (Martin b.1968), 1 da (Karen b.1971); *Career* with Unilever 1961-72, gen mangr Nationwide Building Soc 1972-81; ch exec 1981-, md 1982-87 (md Prudential Property Services 1988-; FICMA, FInstM, FRSA; *Recreations* music, chess, kayaking, cycling; *Style—* Joseph Bradley, Esq; Ravelston, 80 St Georges Rd West, Bickley, Bromley, Kent; Prudential Property Services Ltd, Winchmore House, 15 Fetter Lane, London EC4 1JJ (☎ 01 430 0176)

BRADLEY, Julia Anne (Mrs Keith Sharp); da of Herbert Bradley (d 1974), and Minnie Adelaide Amelia Doris, *née* King; *b* 22 Nov 1938; *Educ* Hove and Aldrington HS, Brighton Tech Coll; *m* 28 Sept 1963, Keith Lorenza Sharp, s of Frederick William Lorenza Sharp (d 1979); 2 s (Trevor b 1970, Martin b 1972); *Career* asst sec Atlas Homes Ltd 1959-64; ptnr: Bradley Kempton & Co 1966-69, WA Honey & Co 1977-85; sec: Br Engineerium 1985, Fedn Sussex Industs 1986-87; ptnr Bradley Soni & Co 1987-; cncl memb Inst Chartered Secs and Admins (former memb Sussex branch); govr: Davigdor first Sch, Hove Park Sch, Varndean HS; memb: Sussex branch Inst Taxation, Brighton and hove Business Enterprise Agency; involved in Sussex professional and mgmnt orgns, indust and young enterprise matters; memb Brighton and Hove Soc Miniature Locomotive Engrs; former memb Brighton and Hove Camesa Club, Sussex Car Club, Locomotive Club GB; Freeman City of London 1980, Liveryman Worshipful Co Chartered Secs and Admins 1980; FCIS, ATII; *Recreations* railways, photography, gardening, travel, bridge; *Style—* Miss Julia Bradley; 64 Palmeira Ave, Hove BN3 3GF (☎ 0273 734236); Bradley Soni & Co, 86 South Coast Rd, Peacehaven BN10 8SL (☎ 0273 582605, fax 0273 587745)

BRADLEY, Philip Herbert Gilbert; s of Herbert Bradley (d 1981), of S Ireland, and Phyllis Eleanor Josephine Marshall; *b* 11 Nov 1949; *Educ* Charterhouse, Trinity Coll Dublin (BA, BAI, ACA); *m* 1977, Charlotte Olivia Knollys, da of Lt-Col John Clairmont Wood, of Dorset; 3 s (William b 1980, Piers b 1982, Timonty b 1984); *Career* merchant banker; dir of Robert Fleming & Co Ltd 1984; chartered accountant; *Recreations* fishing, shooting, skiing; *Clubs* Kildare Street (Ireland), Lansdowne (UK); *Style—* Philip Bradley, Esq; 37 Cautley Avenue, London SW4 (☎ 675 5604); The Dairy House, Synderford, nr Chard, Somerset (☎ 046 030 245); 25 Copthall Avenue, London EC2 (☎ 638 5858, fax 638 9110)

BRADLEY, Roger Thubron; s of Ivor Lewis Bradley (d 1972), Bournemouth, and Elizabeth, *née* Thubron; *b* 5 July 1936; *Educ* Lancaster Royal GS, Oxford Univ (MA); *m* 19 Sept 1959, Ailsa Mary, da of Eric Walkden, of Bromley Cross; 1 da (Julia b 1960), 1 s (Mark b 1963); *Career* Forestry Cmmnr 1985; Dir Harvesting and Mktg 1983; Sr Offr Wales 1979, conservator N Wales 1977; dist offr Argyll 1970; *Recreations* sailing, wind surfing, skiing, gardening; *Clubs* Royal Commonwealth Soc, Royal Overseas League; *Style—* Roger T Bradley, Esq; 231 Corstorphine Rd, Edinburgh (☎ 031 334 0303)

BRADLEY, Stanley Walter; s of Walter Bradley (d 1955), and Laura, *née* Moss (d 1966); *b* 9 Sept 1966; *Educ* Boys' Br Sch Saffron Walden; *m* 6 Aug 1955, Jean Margaret, da of Alfred Brewster, of Low Park Farm, Kirbymoorside, York; 3 s (Nigel b 1957, Mark b 1959, Paul b 1962), 1 da (Jane b 1969); *Career* RAF 1945-48; md: Thorburn Bain & Co 1966-68, Spicers Stationery Co Ltd 1969-70 (gp personnel dir 1973-83); dir: Capital Spicers Ireland 1969-88, Harman Gp 1988-; dir gen Br Printing Industs Fedn 1983-88; pres E Anglian Printing Industs Alliance 1978-79; chm: Mfrg Stationery Indust Gp 1977-81, Printing Industs Sector Working Party 1981-87; *Recreations* fly fishing, painting; *Style—* S W Bradley, Esq; Dale House, Hogs Lane, Chrishall, Royston, Herts SG8 8RN (☎ (0763) 838820)

BRADLEY, Tom George; s of George Henry Bradley (d 1953), and Agnes Mason; *b* 13 April 1926; *Educ* Kettering Central Sch; *m* 15 Aug 1953, Joy Patricia, da of George Stramer (d 1964); 2 s (David b 1961, Peter b 1963); *Career* Northamptonshire ccncllr 1952-74; co alderman 1964-74; Kettering borough cncllr 1956-61; pres Transport Salaried Staffs Assoc 1964-76; acting gen sec 1977; memb NEC Lab Pty 1966-81; chm Labour Party 1976; memb of Parliament (Leicester East) 1962-83, Labour 1962-81, MP 1981-83, SDP MP; founder memb of SDP, PPS to Roy Jenkins at Ministries of Aviation, Home Off and Treasy 1964-70; front bench opposition spokesman on transport 1970-74; chm House of Commons Select Ctee on Transport 1979-83; dir Br Section of the European League for Economic Co-operation 1979-; *Recreations* watching football, cricket; *Clubs* Savile; *Style—* Tom Bradley, Esq; The Orchard, 111 London Rd, Kettering, Northants (☎ (0536) 513019)

BRADLEY-JONES, Hon Mrs (Susan Elizabeth); *née* Carr; eld da of Baron Carr of Hadley, PC (Life Peer); *b* 1947; *m* 1972, (Alun) Rhodri Bradley-Jones; *Style—* Hon Mrs Bradley-Jones; Gardener's Cottage, Kingscote, Glos

BRADMAN, Sir Donald George; AC (1979); s of late George Bradman and late Emily, *née* Whatman; *b* 27 August 1908; *Educ* Bowral Intermediate HS; *m* 1932, Jessie Martha, da of James Menzies, of Mittagong, NSW; 1 s (and 1 decd), 1 da; *Career* former cricketer, Capt Australia 1936-48, pres of S Australian Cricket Assoc 1965-73, chm Aust Cricket Board 1960-63 and 1969-72; kt 1949; *see Debrett's Handbook of Australia and New Zealand for further details*; *Recreations* golf; *Clubs* Commerce; *Style—* Sir Donald Bradman, AC; 2 Holden Street, Kensington Park 5068, S Australia

BRADMAN, Godfrey Michael; s of William Isadore Bradman (d 1973), and Anne Brenda, *née* Goldsweig; *b* 9 Sept 1936; *m* 2, 1975, Susan, da of George Bennett, of Slough; 1 s (Daniel b 1977), 2 da (Camilla b 1976, Katherine b 1976); *Career* chm and chief exec Rosehaugh plc; FCA; *Recreations* riding; *Style—* Godfrey Bradman, Esq; 53 Queen Anne St, London W1M 0LJ (☎ 01 486 7100, telex 28167)

BRADSHAW, Hon Mrs (Alison Margaret); *née* Herbert; yst da of Baron Tangley, KBE (Life Peer, d 1973); *b* 25 May 1943; *m* 1965, John Michael Bradshaw, s of Norman William Bradshaw, of Westcott, Surrey; 2 da (twins); *Career* LRAM, ARCM; *Style—* The Hon Mrs Bradshaw; Cherrydale, W Clandon, Surrey

BRADSHAW, Hon Mrs (Diana Mary); *née* Hepburne-Scott; 2 da of 10 Baron Polwarth, TD; *b* 30 June 1946; *m* 1977, Richard James Bradshaw; 1 s, 1 da; *Style—* The Hon Mrs Bradshaw; c/o Harden, Hawick, Roxburghshire TD9 7LP

BRADSHAW, Jonathan Burgess; s of Elston Burgess Bradshaw (d 1980), of Mill View, Beverley Rd, Driffield, and Dorothy, *née* Chambers; *b* 20 May 1924; *Educ* Woodhouse Grove Sch Apperley Bridge Bradford; *m* 11 June 1976, Carla Jannie, da of Cornelis Bertus Paap, of Iepenweg 14, Wormerveer, Zaanstad, Netherlands; 2 da (Kathryn b 1978, Holly b 1980); *Career* jt md Bradshaws Driffield (Hldgs) Ltd, chm and md E B Bradshaw & Sons Ltd 1988-; chm: Apea Farms Ltd 1988-, Bell Mills Garden Centre Ltd 1988-, Byass Ltd 1988-; pres Hull Corn Trade Assoc Ltd 1985-87; *Style—* Jonathan Bradshaw, Esq; The Mill House, Bells Mills, Driffield, E Yorks YO25 7XL (☎ 0377 431 63); Bell Mills , Driffield, E Yorks YO25 7XL (☎ 0377 431 63, telex 527 519)

BRADSHAW, Sir Kenneth Anthony; KCB (1986), CB (1982); s of late Herbert Leo and Gladys Margaret Bradshaw; *b* 1 Sept 1922; *Educ* Ampleforth, St Catharine's Coll Cambridge; *Career* clerk asst of House of Commons 1979-83, clerk of the House 1983-87 (ret); *Books* (with David Pring) Parliament and Congress (1982); *Recreations* opera, theatre, golf; *Clubs* Garrick; *Style—* Sir Kenneth Bradshaw, KCB

BRADSHAW, Kenneth Morton; s of Leonard Walter Bradshaw (d 1956), of Rushden, Northants, and Dorothy Gwendoline, *née* Walters (d 1983); *b* 27 June 1932; *Educ* Wellingborough GS, Manchester Univ (BA); *m* 29 Sept 1962, Veronica Ann, da of Sidney Arthur Steel Butcher, of Eastbourne; 1 s (Christopher b 1969), 3 da (Nicola b 1963, Carina b 1965, Deborah, b 1966); *Career* CA; sr ptnr Bradshaw & Co; dir Queens Hotel (Hastings) Ltd 1982-; FICA 1957; *Recreations* church and allied activities including Gideons International, philately; *Style—* Kenneth M Bradshaw, Esq; 7 Hyde Tynings Close, Eastbourne BN20 7TQ (☎ 0323 411243); Bradshaw & Co, 2 Upperton Gardens, Eastbourne BN21 2AH (☎ 0323 25244)

BRADSHAW, Maurice Bernard; OBE (1977); s of John Bradshaw, of Finchley, London, and Emma Munday; *b* 7 Feb 1903; *Educ* Christ's Coll London; *m* 1927, Gladys, da of Henry Harvey-Frost, of Finchley, and Kensington; 1 da (Lyndall); *Career* cmmnd RAFVR 1941, served in Far East (invalided 1945); jr clerk Messrs Furness Withy & Co 1918; self-employed 1926; Arts Exhibitions Bureau 1926; responsible for orgn Br Artists Exhibitions 1927-35; worked in co-op with FO to arrange exhibitions world-wide, organized floating art gallery in the Berengaria and Aquitania; sec Empire Art Loan Exhibition Soc; organising sec: exhibition for the Modern Architectural Res Gp 1938, Sea Power exhibition; planned orgn and inauguration of Soc of Marine Artists 1939 (Royal Soc 1969); pioneer in encouraging ind to sponsor the Arts arranged exhibitions for Richard Thomas, Baldwins, The Times, Shell Mex, BP Ltd, Arthur Rank Orgn, Charles Forte Orgn, Corpn of London; dep chief warden and incident offr borough of Finchley 1939-41; responsible for the formation of Soc of Wildlife Artists 1963; sec: RIOP, RI, RSBA, RSPP, CSA, Artists of Chelsea, Nat Soc, New Eng Art Club, Pastel Soc, Soc of Aviation Artists, Soc of Graphic Artists, Soc of Mural Painters, Soc of Wildlife Artists, Soc of Women Artists, Senefelder Gp; sec gen Mall Galleries; govr and dir Fedn of Br Artists; ret 1980; *Recreations* music, woodwork, philately; *Clubs* Eccentric, Chelsea Arts; *Style—* Maurice Bradshaw, Esq, OBE

BRADSHAW, Michael John; s of Harry Cosntantine Bradshaw (d 1979), original name Zalotynski of Warsaw, and Gladys *née* Church (d 1985); *b* 7 June 1935; *Educ* Peckham Sch, Camberwell Coll of Art; *m* 5 July 1958, Joyice Mary, da of James Albert Reid (d 1960); 1 s (Neil Christian b 1960), 1 da (Gabrielle Louise b 1962); *Career* deputy creative dir Dorland Advertising 1970-81; creative dir Chetwynd Haddons 1981, exec creative dir 1987 (memb Creative Circle Cncl 1976-79), CLIO 1981; 1982 (advertising award); gold award Dubonnet 1971, designers and art directors award, gold awards (int) film and TV festival New York 1984 (silver awards 1981-83), gold medal (New York Festival 1986); Freeman City of London 1983, MIPA, memb Creative Circle (1974); *Recreations* theatre, golf; *Clubs* Aquarius Golf, Le Beaujolais; *Style—* Michael Bradshaw, Esq; 75 Marmora Road, Dulwich, London SE22 0RY (☎ 01 693 6884); Chetwynd Haddons Ltd, s52-54 Broadwick St, London W1 (☎ 01 439 2288)

BRADSHAW, Paul Richard; s of Trevelyan William George Bradshaw and Beryl Mary; *b* 18 Jan 1950; *Educ* Huntingdon GS, Nottingham Univ (BSc 1971), FIA (Sir Joseph Burns Prize); *m* 28 July 1971, Sheila Margaret, da of Andrew John Broodbank; 1 s (Christopher b 1976), 1 da (Laura b 1980); *Career* md Skandia Life Assurance Co Ltd; dir: Skandia Investment Management Ltd, Skandia Financial Services Ltd, Skandia Life Business Services Ltd, Skandia Life Assurance (Hldgs) Ltd, Skandia Life (Pensions Tstee) Ltd, Skandia First Funding Ltd, Skandia Life America; *Recreations* chess; *Style—* Paul Bradshaw, Esq; 5 South End, Hursley, Nr Winchester, Hants; Frobisher House, Nelson Gate, Southampton SO9 7BX (☎ Southampton 334411)

BRADSHAW, (Hengist) Richard Edward; s of Thomas Claridge Bradshaw (d 1946), of The Mill House, Prestwood, Great Missenden, Bucks, and Emily Gertrude, *née* Hill (d 1948); *b* 29 Dec 1916; *Educ* Bryanston, Trinity Coll Cambridge (MA, LLM); *m* 20 Dec 1945, Anita Selma Margaret, da of Jagmastare Birger Ahlgren (d 1970), of Stockholm, Sweden; 2 s (Thomas Richard Gustaf b 1949, Richard Hengist William b 1953), 1 da (Cecilia Anita Clare b 1958); *Career* contributor satire articles in Swedish for: Stockholm's Tidningen 1945, Svenska Dagbladet Stockholm 1946-51, Sydsvenka Dagbladet Malmö 1951-64; chm Phyllis Ct Club Henley-on-Thames 1955-58, hon sec Swedish Lunch Club City of London 1958-65; memb: Stock Exchange 1952, Int Stock Exchange; *Recreations* foreign languages, writing, photography; *Clubs* Boodles, Carlton; *Style—* Richard Bradshaw, Esq; The Mill House, Prestwood, Gt Missenden, Bucks (☎ 02406 2525); Supercrans, Crans Montana, Switzerland; Blossoms Inn, 23 Lawrence Lane, London EC2V 8DA (☎ 01 600 7281)

BRADSHAW, Roger Joseph; MBE (1987); s of Joseph Tarver Bradshaw (d 1970), of Bramhall, and Dorothy Marian, *née* Ratcliffe; *b* 22 August 1937; *Educ* William Hulmes GS, St Albans Sch, Imperial Coll London (BSc); *m* 28 April 1962 (m dis), Janet, da of George Wilkins (d 1972), of Bushey Heath; 2 s (Anthony Paul b 1963, Kevin Michael b 1968), 1 da (Helen Elizabeth b 1965); m 2, 29 June 1984, Ruth Margaret, *née* Akass; *Career* mgmnt devpt mangr plastics div ICI 1969 (engr agric div 1960), started own business Roger Bradshaw Assocs Mgmnt Conslts 1973-; co fndr: Refugee Childrens Holiday Fund 1959, Childrens Relief Int 1959; fndr: Eastern Ravens Tst Stockton-on-Tres 1961; *Recreations* painting, golf, walking, gardening, bird watching; *Style—* Roger J Bradshaw, Esq, MBE; Orchard Cottage, Stanningfield, Suffolk IP29 4RS (☎ 0284 828436, FAX 0284 828798)

BRADSHAW, Prof William Peter (Bill); s of Leonard Charles Bradshaw (d 1978), of Wargrave Berks, and Ivy Doris, *née* Steele (d 1980); *b* 9 Sept 1936; *Educ* Slough GS, Univ of Reading (BA, MA); *m* 30 Nov 1957, Jill Elsie, da of James Francis Hayward, of Plastow Green, Hampshire; 1 s (Robert William b 1966), 1 da (Joanna b 1968); *Career* Nat Serv 1957-59; gen mangr (W Region) BR 1983-85 (mgmnt trainee 1959, div movements mangr Bristol 1967, div mangr Liverpool 1973, chief ops mangr London Midland Region 1976, dep gen mangr London Midland Region 1977, dir of ops BR HQ 1978, dir policy unit BR HQ 1980); sr visiting res fell Centre for Socio Legal Studies Wolfson Coll Oxford 1985-, prof of tport mgmnt Univ of Salford 1986-, chm Ulsterbus 1987-; dir NI Tport Hldg Co 1988-; FCIT 1986; *Recreations* growing hardy perennial plants, playing member of brass band; *Clubs* Nat Lib; *Style—* Prof Bill Bradshaw; Centre For Socio-Legal Studies, Wolfson College, Oxford OX2 6UD (☎ 0865 52967, 0865 274125)

BRADSTOCK, Hon Sara Victoria; da of 4 Baron Trevethin and 2 Baron Oaksey; *b* 1961; *m* 8 Aug 1987, Mark Fitzherbert Bradstock, eldest s of David Fitzherbert Bradstock, MC, of Clanville Lodge, Andover, Hants; *Style—* The Hon Sara Lawrence; Hill Farm, Oaksey, Malmesbury, Wilts SN16 9HS

BRADWELL, Bishop of 1976-; Rt Rev (Charles) Derek Bond; s of Charles Norman Bond (Flt-Lt RAF, despatches, d 1985), and Doris, *née* Rosendale; *b* 4 July 1927; *Educ* Bournemouth Sch, King's Coll London (AKC); *m* 4 July 1951, (Joan) Valerie, da of Ralph Meikle (Capt RAOC) of Bournemouth; 2 s (Stephen b 1957, Andrew b 1965), 2 da (Fiona b 1955, Elizabeth b 1963); *Career* Midlands area sec SCM in Schools 1955-58; vicar: Harringay 1958-62, Harrow Weald 1962-71; archdeacon of Colchester 1971-76; *Recreations* travel; *Style—* The Rt Rev the Bishop of Bradwell; Bishop's House, 21 Elmhurst Avenue, Benfleet, Essex SS7 5RY (☎ 0268 755 175)

BRADY, Hon Mrs (Charlotte Mary Thérèse); *née* Bingham; writes as Charlotte Bingham; da of 7 Baron Clanmorris; *b* 29 June 1942; *Educ* The Priory Hayward's Heath, The Sorbonne; *m* 1964, Terence Joseph Brady, son of Frederick Arthur Noel Brady (d 1985), of Montacute, Somerset; 1 s (Matthew b 1972), 1 da (Candida b 1965); *Career* playwright, novelist, journalist; *Books* Coronet Among the Weeds (1963), Lucinda (1965), Coronet Among the Grass (1972), Belgravia (1983), Country Life (1984), At Home, (with husb Terence Brady) Rose's Story (1973), Yes Honestly (1977); *TV series include* with Terence Brady: Take Three Girls, Upstairs Downstairs, No Honestly, Yes Honestly, Play for Today, Thomas and Sarah, Nanny, Pig in the Middle; *Recreations* horse breeding, riding, gardening, racing, swimming; *Style—* The Hon Mrs Brady; c/o A D Peters, Literary Agents, 10 Buckingham Street, London WC2 (☎ 01 839 2556)

BRADY, Janet Mary; *née* Mount; da of Allan Frederick Mount, of Oxford, and Doreen Margaret, *née* Hicks; *b* 26 Feb 1956; *Educ* Rochester GS, Medway and Maidstone Coll of Technol; *Career* legal asst Mobil Oil 1974-77, tax asst Marathon Oil 1977-81, exec McCann Erickson Advertising 1987, account dir Sterling PR 1982-85, dir PR American Express (UK and Ireland) 1985-87; founding dir Kinnear PR 1988-; voluntary trainer St John Cadets; publicity advsr: St John Ambulance Brig, GLF for the Blind, RAM; memb: Euro Womens Mgmnt Dvpt Gp 1986-88, Brit Assoc Travel Eds (1987-88); *Recreations* ballooning, stonemasonry, landscape gardeing, writing; *Clubs* IOD; *Style—* Ms Janet Brady; Barcheston Ho, Northside, Steeple Aston, Oxon OX5 3SE (☎ 0869 476 33); Flat 1, 18 Daventry St, London NW1; Kinnear PR, 25-28 Old Burlington St, London W1X 1LB (☎ 01 499 8650, fax 01 493 2558, telex 266512 KIN COM G)

BRADY, Terence Joseph; s of (Frederick Arthur) Noel Brady (d 1985), of Monacute, Somerset, and Elizabeth Mary Moore (d 1986); *b* 13 Mar 1939; *Educ* Merchant Taylors', Trinity Coll Dublin (BA); *m* 1964, Hon Charlotte Marie Thérèse, da of Lord Clanmorris, of London; 1 s (Matthew), 1 da (Candida); *Career* writer; television plays with Charlotte Bingham (spouse) incl: Take Three Girls, Upstairs Downstairs, Play for Today, 6 Plays of Marriage, No-Honestly, Yes-Honestly, Thomas and Sarah, Nanny, Pig in the Middle, Take Three Women, Love with A Perfect Stranger, Father Matthew's Daughter, This Magic Moment (1989); stage play I Wish I Wish 1989; contrib: Daily Mail, Country Homes and Interiors, Punch; *Books* The Fight against Slavery (1976), Roses Story (1973), Yes - Honestly (1977); *Recreations* racing, riding, music, painting; *Clubs* PEN; *Style—* Terence Brady, Esq; John Farquharson Ltd, 162-168 Regent St, London W1R 5JB

BRAGG, Henry John; s of Henry Bragg, of Torquay; *b* 28 Nov 1929; *Educ* Torquay GS, London Univ; *m* 1972, Anthea, da of Kew Shelley, QC; 3 children; *Career* md Calor Group Ltd 1980-; dir Imperial Continental Gas Ltd 1980; FCIT 1979; *Recreations* golf, hunting; *Clubs* Royal St George's Golf; *Style—* Henry Bragg Esq; 22 Thamespoint, Fairways, Teddington, Middx (☎ 01 977 9852); Hideway House, St George's Rd, Sandwich, Kent (☎ 12364)

BRAGG, Melvyn; s of Stanley Bragg, of Wigton, Cumbria and Mary Ethel, *née* Parks; *b* 6 Oct 1939; *Educ* Nelson-Tomlinson GS Wigton, Wadham Coll Oxford (MA); *m* 1, 1961, Marie-Elisabeth Roche (decd); 1 da; m 2, 1973, Catherine Mary, da of Eric Haste, of Crantock, Almondsbury, Avon; 1 s, 1 da; *Career* writer and broadcaster; began career on Monitor (BBC), presenter 2nd House 1973-77; presenter and ed: Read All About It (BBC) 1976-77, South Bank Show (ITV) 1978-; head Arts Dept LWT; memb: Arts Cncl (and chm Literature Panel) 1977-80, RSL 1977-80, exec ctee Fabian Soc 1983-; contributor to Punch; pres Nat Campaign for the Arts, BAFTA Richard Dimbleby Award 1987; DLitt Liverpool Univ 1986, hon Fell Lancs Poly; FRSL, ACTT; *Novels* For Want of a Nail (1965), The Second Inheritance (1966), Without a City Wall (1968), The Hired Man (1969), A Place in England (1970), The Nerve (1971), Josh Lawton (1972), The Silken Net (1974), Autumn Manoeuvres (1978), Kingdom Come (1980), Love and Glory (1983), The Maid of Buttermere (1987), Rich (1988 biog of Richard Burton), Speak for England (oral history of England since 1900), Land of the Lakes (1983); *Plays*: Mardi Gras, Prince of Wales (musical, 1976), Orion (TV, 1977); *Screenplays*: Isadora, Jesus Christ Superstar, (with Ken Russell) Clouds of Glory; musical: The Hired man (Westend 1984); *Recreations* walking, books; *Clubs* Garrick; *Style—* Melvyn Bragg, Esq; 12 Hampstead Hill, London NW3; South Bank Television Centre, Kent House, Upper Ground, London SE1 9LT (☎ 01 261 3434, telex 918123)

BRAGG, Stephen Lawrence; eld s of Sir (William) Lawrence Bragg, CH, MC, FRS (Nobel Laureate, d 1971), and Alice Grace Jenny, CBE, *née* Hopkinson; *b* 17 Nov 1923; *Educ* Rugby, Trinity Coll Cambridge (MA), MIT (MSc); *m* 1951, Maureen Ann, da of D R E Roberts, FRCS (d 1953), of Darlington; 3 s; *Career* chartered engineer, chief research engr Rolls-Royce 1963-70, vice-chllr Brunel Univ 1971-81, chm Cambridge Health Authority 1982-86, dir Industrial Co-operation Cambridge Univ 1984-87; admin American Friends of Cambridge Univ 1988-; FEng, FIMechE, FRAeS; *Books* Rocket Engines (1962); *Recreations* railway history; *Clubs* Athenaeum; *Style—* Stephen Bragg, Esq; 22 Brookside, Cambridge CB2 1JQ (☎ 0223 62208); American Friends of Cambridge Univ, The Pitt Building, Trumpington St, Cambridge CB2 1RP (☎ 0223 311021)

BRAGGE, Nicolas William; s of Norman Hugh Bragge, of The Towers, Brabourne, nr Ashford, Kent, and Nicolette Hilda, *née* Simms; *b* 13 Dec 1948; *Educ* S Kent Coll of Technol Ashford, Holborn Coll of Law London Univ (LLB), Inns of Ct Sch of Law; *m* 22 Dec 1973, Pamela Elizabeth, da of Ronald Gordon Brett; 3 s (Thomas Hereward b 1976, Christopher Joseph b 1980, Alasdair Charles b 1986); *Career* called to the Bar Inner Temple 1972, in practice at Patent Bar 1973-, Examiner of the Supreme Ct 1978-88; author of various articles on legal and historial subjects; Freedom City of London 1969, Liveryman Worshipful Co of Cutlers 1974; memb Br Gp AIPPI; *Recreations* my family, gardening; *Clubs* City Livery; *Style—* Nicolas Bragge, Esq;

New Court, Temple, London EC4Y 9BL (☎ 01 353 1769/8719, fax 01 583 5885)

BRAGGINS, Lt-Col Charles Willison; TD (1945), JP (1959 Beds), DL (1961); s of E Braggins (1960), of Bedford; *b* 27 June 1910; *Educ* Mill Hill; *m* 1936, Hilda, da of John A Heys (d 1966), of St Just-in-Roseland, Cornwall; 2 s, 1 da; *Career* cmmr Inland Revenue 1960-; Lt-Col cmdg Beds Yeomanry RA 1954-57; *Clubs* Army & Navy, Bedford; *Style*— Lt-Col Charles Braggins, TD, JP, DL; 29 Pemberley Av, Bedford (☎ 53711); Arden Close, Overstrand, Norfolk

BRAGGINS, Maj-Gen Derek Henry; CB (1986); s of Albert Edward Braggins (d 1988), of Pagham, Sussex, and Hilda Mary, *née* Pearce; *b* 19 April 1931; *Educ* Rothesay Acad, Hendon Tech Coll; *m* 10 April 1953, Sheila St Clair, da of George Stuart (d 1969), of Kirkwall, Orkney; 3 s (Geoffrey b 1953, Nigel b 1959, Mark b 1965); *Career* cmmnd RASC 1950, transferred RCT 1965, regtl and staff appts: Korea, Malaya, Singapore, Ghana, Aden, Germany, UK, Staff Coll Camberley 1962, Jt Servs Staff Coll Latimer 1970, CO 7 Regt RCT 1973-75, Col AQ Commando Forces RM 1977-80, cmd tport and movements BAOR 1981-83, dir gen tport and movements and head of RCT 1983-86; Col Cmdt RCT 1986-; pres RASC/RCT Assoc 1988-; Freeman City of London 1983, Liveryman Worshipful Co of Carmen 1983; FBIM 1979, FCIT 1983; *Recreations* running, shooting, fishing, gardening, country life; *Style*— Maj-Gen Derek Braggins, CB

BRAILEY, Michael Carl; s of Walter Carl Brailey (formerly Schumacher) (d 1969), and Marguerite Brailey; *b* 7 June 1932; *Educ* St George's Coll, Weybridge, Surrey, Institut Auf Dem Rosenberg, St Gallen, Switzerland, Lausanne Univ Switzerland; *m* 1, 4 June 1960 (m dis 1976), Valerie Norma, da of Edward Payne (d 1977); 1 s (Michael Anthony b 20 April 1961); m 2, 3 April 1979, Carol Ann, da of Robert Bithell, of Leven, Humberside; 1 s (James Ashley b 23 April 1980), 1 da (Camila Rose b 9 July 1981); *Career* dir: Brailey GMBH and Co KG Erkrath W Germany 1955-, Brailey and Co Ltd Crawley Sussex 1969-, Gabro Engng Ltd sussex 1981-; FCIS 1969; *Recreations* classical music, tennis; *Style*— Michael Brailey, Esq; Fox Vane House, Sandpit Hall Rd, Chobham, Surrey GU24 8AN (☎ 09905 8559); Brailey and Co Ltd, 16 Royce Rd, Fleming Way, Crawley, Sussex RG10 2XN (☎ 0293 510227, fax 0293 31932, telex 878158)

BRAIN, 2 Baron (UK 1962); Sir Christopher Langdon Brain; 2 Bt (UK 1954); s of 1 Baron, DM, FRS, FRCP, FRCPI, FRCPE (d 1966); *b* 30 August 1926; *Educ* Leighton Park Sch, New Coll Oxford (MA); *m* 1953, Susan Mary, da of George Philip Morris; 3 da (Hon Nicola Dorothy b 1955, Hon Fiona Janice (Hon Mrs Proud) b 1958, Hon Naomi Melicent b 1960); *Heir* bro, Hon Michael Brain DM FRCP(CAN); *Career* mgmnt conslt; also various posts in photographic indust; Liveryman Worshipful Co of Weavers; upper bailiff 1984-85; *Recreations* sailing, fly fishing; *Clubs* Oxford and Cambridge Sailing Soc, Royal Photographic Soc (ARPS); *Style*— The Rt Hon The Lord Brain; The Old Rectory, Cross Street, Moretonhampstead, Devon TQ13 8NL

BRAIN, Hon Mrs (Elizabeth Ann); *née* Herbert; el da of Baron Tangley, KBE (Life Peer) (d 1973); *b* 17 Nov 1933; *Educ* Oxford Univ (MA, BM, BCh); *m* 10 Dec 1960, Hon Michael Cottrell Brain, *qv*, yr son of 1 Baron Brain (d 1966); 1 s, 2 da; *Career* Assoc Prof McMaster Univ Faculty of Health Sciences, Canada; *Books* Learning Resources (medical editor 1970-); *Style*— The Hon Mrs Brain; 131 Northshore Blvd E, Burlington, Ontario, Canada L7T 4A4

BRAIN, Hon Michael Cottrell; s of 1 Baron Brain (d 1966), and hp of bro, 2 Baron; *b* 6 August 1928; *Educ* Leighton Park Sch, New Coll Oxford (MA, BCh, DM), London Hospital; *m* 1960, Hon Elizabeth Ann, da of Baron Tangley, KBE (Life Peer); 1 s (Thomas Russell b 1965), 2 da (Hilary Catherine (Mrs Guido Dino De Luca) b 1961, Philippa Harriet b 1963); *Career* Capt RAMC 1956-58; physician Hammersmith Hosp 1966-69; prof of medicine McMaster Univ of Canada 1969-; FRCP Canada; *Books* Current Therapy Hematology and Oncology (3 edn), Current Therapy of Internal Medicine (2 edn); *Recreations* tennis, sailing; *Style*— Dr Michael Brain; 131 North Shore Blvd E, Burlington, Ontario, Canada L7T 4A4

BRAIN, Dr The Hon Naomi Melicent; yst da of 2 Baron Brain, *qv*; *b* 27 May 1960; *Educ* Chelmsford HS, Millfield, Fitzwilliam Coll Cambridge (MA), The London Hosp Med Coll (MB, BS); *Career* trainee in general practice N London; *Recreations* squash, reading, walking; *Style*— The Hon Naomi Brain; 84 Selby Road, London E11 3LR

BRAIN, Hon Nicola Dorothy; eld da of 2 Baron Brain, *qv*; *b* 26 Oct 1955; *Style*— The Hon Nicola Brain; Laragh, Belmont Road, Combe Down, Bath BA2 5JR; 52 Boue Town, Glastonbury, Somerset BA6 8JE

BRAIN, Sir (Henry) Norman; KBE (1963, OBE 1947), CMG (1953); s of Bert Brain, of Rushall Staffs, and Ann Gertrude Swaffer; *b* 19 July 1907; *Educ* King Edward's HS Birmingham, Queen's Coll Oxford; *m* 1939, Nuala Gertrude (d 1988), da of Capt Archibald W Butterworth, of Ryde, IOW; 1 s (and 1 s decd); *Career* ambass Cambodia 1956-58 and Uruguay 1961-66; Pres Br-Uruguayan Soc 1973-; *Recreations* music, golf; *Clubs* Canning; *Style*— Sir Norman Brain, KBE, CMG; St Andrews, Abney Court, Bourne End, Bucks (☎ 20509)

BRAIN, Ronald; CB (1967); s of Trevelyan Thomas George Brain, RN (d 1964), and Edith Caroline, *née* Fruin (d 1957); *b* 1 Mar 1914; *Educ* Trowbridge HS; *m* 3 June 1943, Lilian Rose, da of Thomas Ravenhill (d 1915); 1 s (John b 1947), 1 da (Pamela b 1946); *Career* under-sec Min of Housing and Local Govt 1961-66, dep sec (later Department of the Environment) 1966-74, chm London & Quadrant Housing Tst 1977-80; *Recreations* chess; *Style*— Ronald Brain, Esq, CB; 4 Badminton, Galsworthy Rd, Kingston upon Thames, Surrey KT27BU (☎ 01 549 4191)

BRAINE, Rt Hon Sir Bernard Richard; PC (1985), DL (Essex 1978), MP (C) Castle Point 1983-; s of Arthur Ernest Braine (d 1933), of Kew Gdns; *b* 24 June 1914; *Educ* Hendon Co GS; *m* 1935, Kathleen Mary (d 1982), da of late Herbert William Faun, of East Sheen; 3 s (Richard, Michael, Brendan); *Career* WWII 1939-45 cmmnd N Staffs Regt, serv: W Africa, N W Europe, S E Asia, Cmberley Staff Coll; Temp Lt-Col; MP (C): Billericay 1950-55, Essex SE 1955-1983; Parly sec Miny of Pensions and Nat Insur 1960-61, under-sec of state Cwlth Rels 1961-62, parly sec Miny of Health 1962-64; Cons front bench spokesman Cwlth Affrs and Overseas Aid 1967-70, chm Parly Select Ctee on Overseas Aid 1970-74; dep chm Cmwlth Parly Assoc 1863-64 and 1970-74 (tres 1974-78); chm: Nat Cncl on Alcohol 1974-82, Br-German Parly Gp 1970-, Br-Greek Parly Gp 1979-, UK Chapter Soc for Int Devpt; ldr Parly Mission to: India 1963, Mauritius 1971, Ethiopia 1971, W Germany 1973, Greece 1982, Poland 1986, Australia 1988; pres: UK Ctee Defence of the Unjustly Prosecuted, Gtr London Alcohol Advsy Service 1983-; chm Br 'Solidarity with Poland' Campaign 1981, tstee (and former govr) Cwlth Inst, assoc Inst of Devpt Studies Sussex Univ; chm: All Party Ctee on the Misuse of Drugs, All Party Pro-Life Ctee, Nat Cncl on Alcoholism 1974-82: vice-chm All Party Parly Human Rights Gp: Health Visitors Assoc; vis prof Baylor Univ Texas USA; FRSA; kt 1972; Europe Peace Medal (1979), Cdr Polonia Restituta (Polish Govt in Exile, 1983), Kt Cdr Order of Merit (W Germany 1984), KCSG (1987), Cdr Order of Honour (Greece 1987); KStJ 1985; GCLJ 1987; *Recreations* reading, history, gardening; *Clubs* Beefsteak; *Style*— The Rt Hon Sir Bernard Braine, DL, MP; King's Wood, Great Wheatley Road, Rayleigh, Essex

BRAININ, Norbert; OBE (1960); s of Adolph, and Sophie Brainin; *b* 12 Mar 1923,, Vienna; *Educ* High Sch, Vienna; *m* 1948, Kathe Kottow; 1 da; *Career* leader of Amadeus String Quartet; *Style*— Norbert Brainin Esq, OBE,; 19 Prowse Ave, Bushey Heath, Herts (☎ 01 950 7379)

BRAITHWAITE, His Honour Judge; Bernard Richard Braithwaite; s of Bernard Leigh Braithwaite, of Great House, Newchurch, Mon, and Emily Dora Ballard, *née* Thomas; *b* 20 August 1917; *Educ* Clifton, Peterhouse Cambridge; *Career* barr 1946, circuit judge 1972-; *Recreations* hunting, sailing; *Clubs* Boodle's; *Style*— His Hon Judge Braithwaite; Summerfield House, Owlpen, Uley, Glos

BRAITHWAITE, Brian; s of Joseph Greenwood Braithwaite and Dorothea, *née* Swinbanks (d 1976); *b* 15 May 1927; *Educ* Mercers' Sch; *m* 1, 6 June 1959 (m dis 1962), Patricia, *née* Moore; m 2,1962, Gwendolin Phyllis, da of John Trevor Everson (d 1976), 2 s (Simon Guy b 1963, Christopher Brian b 1968), 1 da (Philippa Kate b 1964); *Career* Gordon Highlanders Trg Bn and Forces Broadcasting Service, Italy and Austria 1945-48; Associated Newspapers 1948-53; advertisement exec: Hulton Press 1953-56, Harrison Raison 1956-64; advertisement and bd dir Stevens Press 1964-69; joined Nat Magazine Co 1969; publisher Harpers Bazaar 1969, Harper & Queen, Cosmopolitan 1972; publishing dir Good Housekeeping 1984; bd dir 1979; vice-pres Publicity Club of London; *Books* Business of Womens Magazines (1978, 2 edn 1988), Ragtime to Wartime (1986), Home Front (1987), Christmas Book (1988); *Recreations* golf, theatre, cinema; *Style*— Brian Braithwaite; 1 Narbonne Avenue, London SW4 (☎ 01 673 4100); National Magazine Co Ltd, National Magazine House, 72 Broadwick Street, London W1 (☎ 01 439 5259)

BRAITHWAITE, Sir (Joseph) Franklin (Madders); DL (Cambs 1983); s of Sir John Braithwaite (d 1973, sometime chm Stock Exchange Cncl), and Martha Janette, *née* Baker; *b* 6 April 1917; *Educ* Bootham Sch, King's Coll Cambridge; *m* 1939, (Charlotte) Isabel, da of Robert Elmer Baker, of New York; 1 s (Peter Franklin Braithwaite (b 1942), m 1968, Patricia Neville-O'Brien), 1 da (Virginia Louise (b 1940) m 1966, Comte Geoffroy de Vitry d'Avaucourt); *Career* chm Baker Perkins Hldgs plc 1980-84 (joined Baker Perkins 1946, dir 1950-, md (B P Hldgs) 1971-79); pres Process Plant Assoc 1977-79; dir (east counties regnl bd) Lloyds Bank 1979-87; dep chm Peterborough Devpt Corpn 1982-88; chm: Peterborough Independent Hosp plc 1981-87; kt 1980; *Recreations* music, golf; *Clubs* Army and Navy; *Style*— Sir Franklin Braithwaite, DL; 7 Rutland Terrace, Stamford, Lincs PE9 2QD (☎ 0780 51244)

BRAITHWAITE, Michael; *b* 10 Dec 1937; *Educ* City Univ (BSc); *m* 4 Feb 1967, (Pamela) Margaret; 1 s (James b 7 Jan 1971), 1 da (Sally b 4 Oct 1969); *Career* UKAEA 1958-69, ptnr responsible for info tech consulting Touche Ross & Co 1969-; Freeman Worshipful Co of Info Technologists 1988; MBCS, MInstMC; *Recreations* skiing, gardening; *Style*— Michael Braithwaite, Esq; The Manor House, Thriplow, Royston, Herts; Touche Ross and Co, 1 Little New St, London EC4A 3TR (☎ 01 936 3000)

BRAITHWAITE, Roderick Clive; s of Thomas Braithwaite (d 1965), and Winifred (d 1983); *b* 11 June 1932; *Educ* Mill Hill, Queens' Coll Cambridge (MA); *m* 10 Aug 1956, Joan, da of Dr Francis Friend; 1 s (Nicholas b 1960), 1 da (Clare b 1959); *Career* Nat Serv Intelligence Corps 1954-56; chief exec Charles Barker Human Resources 1973-87; management consultant; memb Central Blood Laboratories Authority; *Books* How to Recruit (B.I.M.), Communications and the Job-Seeker (Advertising Association); *Recreations* languages, geology; *Clubs* Reform, Old Millhillians; *Style*— Roderick Braithwaite, Esq; Vineyard Cottages, Cavendish, Suffolk

BRAITHWAITE, Sir Rodric Quentin; KCMG (1988); s of (Henry) Warwick Braithwaite (d 1971), and Lorna Constance, *née* Davies; *b* 17 May 1932; *Educ* Bedales, Christ's Coll Cambridge (BA); *m* 1 April 1961, Gillian Mary, da of Patrick Robinson (d 1975); 4 s (Richard b 1962, Julian b 1968, Mark (twin b 1968, d 1971, David b 1972), 1 da (Katharine b 1963); *Career* Nat Serv 1950-52; Foreign Serv 1955-: Djakarta 1958-59, Warsaw 1959-61, FO 1961-63, Moscow 1963-66, Rome 1966-69, FO 1969-72, Oxford 1973-75, UK permanent rep to Euro Community Brussels 1975-78, FO 1978-82, Washington 1982-84, FO 1984-88, Moscow 1988-; visiting fell All Souls Coll Oxford 1972-73; *Recreations* music, sailing, walking, reading, Russia; *Clubs* United Oxford and Cambridge; *Style*— Sir Rodric Braithwaite, KCMG; c/o FCO, King Charles St, London SW1A 2AH

BRAMALL, Sir (Ernest) Ashley; DL (Gtr London 1982); er s of Maj Edmund Haselden Bramall, RA (d 1964), of 2 Symons St, Chelsea, and Katharine Bridget, *née* Westby (d 1985); bro of Field Marshal Sir Edwin Bramall; *b* 6 Jan 1916; *Educ* Westminster, Canford, Magdalen Coll Oxford (MA); *m* 1, 2 Sept 1939 (m dis 1950), Margaret Elaine, da of Raymond Taylor (d 1942), of Teddington, Middx; 2 s (Christopher b 1942, Richard b 1944); m 2, 23 Sept 1950, Germaine (Gery) Margaret, da of late Dr Victor Bloch (d 1968), of 48 Queen's Gate, London SW7; 1 s (Anthony b 1957); *Career* serv WWII 1940-46, Maj RAC 1943, psc; called to the Bar Inner Temple 1949; MP (Lab) Bexley 1946-50; memb (Lab): LCC Bethnal Green 1961, Westminster City Cncl 1959-68, GLC Tower Hamlets 1964-73, Bethnal Green & Bow 1973-86, ldr ILEA 1970-81, chm GLC 1982-83, chm ILEA 1984-86; chm Nat Cncl for Drama Trg; govr Museum of London; memb Cncl of City Univ; Freeman of City of London, Liveryman of Worshipful Co of Skinners 1951; Grand Offr Order of Orange Nassau (Netherlands) 1982; kt 1975; *Recreations* opera; *Style*— Sir Ashley Bramall, DL; 2 Egerton House, 59/63 Belgrave Rd, London SW1V 2BE (☎ 01 828 0973); 3 Dr Johnson's Buildings, Temple, London EC4 (☎ 01 353 4854)

BRAMALL, Baron (Life Peer UK 1987) Edwin Noel Westby; GCB (1979, KCB 1974), OBE (1965), MC (1945); yr s of Maj Edmund Haselden Bramall, and Katherine Bridget, *née* Westby; bro of Sir Ashley Bramall, *qv*; *b* 18 Dec 1923; *Educ* Eton; *m* 1949, Dorothy Avril Wentworth, only da of Col Henry Albemarle Vernon, DSO, JP (ggggs of Henry Vernon by his w Lady Henrietta Wentworth, yst da of 1 Earl of Strafford, Henry Vernon being himself 2 cous of 1 Baron Vernon); 1 s, 1 da; *Career* 2 Lt KRRC 1943, serv WWII NW Europe, occupation Japan 1946-47, Middle E 1953-58, Instr Army Staff Coll 1958-61, involved in re-organising MOD 1963-64, served

Malaysia during Indonesian confrontation 1965-66 (CO 2 Greenjackets KRRC), comd 5 Air portable Vde 1967-69, idc 1970, GOC 1 Div BAOR 1971-73, Lt-Gen 1973, Cdr Br Forces Hong Kong 1973-76, Gen 1976, C-in-C UKLF 1976-78, Vice-Ch Defence staff (Personnel and Logistics) 1978-79, Chief General Staff 1979-82, ADC Gen to HM the Queen 1979-82, Field Marshal 1982-, Chief of the Defence staff 1982-85; Col Cmdt 3 Bn Royal Green Jackets 1973-84, Col 2 Gurkhas 1976-86; tstee Imperial War Museum 1983-; HMS Lord Lt of Greater London 1986-; pres MCC 1988-89; *Recreations* MCC, Travellers, Pratts; *Style*— The Rt Hon Lord Bramall, GCB, OBE, MC, JP; c/o National Westminster Bank, 34 Lower Sloane Street, London SW3

BRAMBLE, Roger John Lawrence; DL (1986); s of Courtenay Parker Bramble CIE (d 1987), of Childer Thornton, Cheshire, and Margaret Louise Bramble, MBE, da of Sir Henry Lawrence, KCSI; *b* 3 April 1932; *Educ* Eton, King's Coll Cambridge (MA); *Career* chm Chandler Hargreaves Ltd; cncllr City of Westminster 1968-, Lord Mayor of Westminster 1985-86; dir ENO 1986-, dir London Festival Ballet 1986-, chm Benesh Inst; Order Aztec Eagle Mexico 1985, Order of Merit Qatar 1985; *Recreations* music, farming, language; *Clubs* Turf; *Style*— Roger Bramble, Esq, DL; 2 Sutherland Street, London SW1V 4LB; Chandler House, 3/7 Marshalsea Road, London SE1 1EF (fax, 01 407 1420, car tel 01 407 8000)

BRAMLEY, Colin; s of John William Bramley (d 1965), of Pickering, N Yorks, and Charlotte Elizabeth, *née* Watson (d 1966); *b* 1 May 1932; *Educ* Malton GS N Yorks; *m* 11 May 1963, Christine, da of Duncan Nichol Watson (d 1947), of Scarborough, N Yorks; 1 da (Carol b 1964); *Career* CA 1955, ptnr Gardiners CAs N Yorks 1965-85, private practice 1985-; fndr memb and tres Scarborough and Dist Fuchsia Soc; FCA 1955, ATII 1956; *Recreations* horticulture; *Style*— Colin Bramley, Esq; 29 Westfield Ave, Newby, Scarborough, N Yorks (☎ 0723 365246)

BRAMLEY, (Colin) Ian Coulson; s of William Bramley, of Cawthorne, Barnsley, Yorks, and Violet, *née* Coulson; *b* 18 April 1944; *Educ* Ecclesfield GS Sheffield, Wadham Coll Oxford (BCL, MA), Univ of Pennsylvania USA; *m* Aug 1970, Janet Susan, da of William Thomas Wood, (d 1976), of Chiswick, London; 2 s (Tom b 1971, Ben b 1974); *Career* slr 1970; asst slr Slaughter and May 1970-76, ptnr Hepworth and Chadwick Leeds 1977-; sec Weston-with-Denton PCC Bradford, organist All Saints Church Weston; memb: Oxford Soc 1962-, Law Soc 1970-; *Recreations* music, gardening, walking, travel; *Clubs* The Leeds; *Style*— Ian Bramley, Esq; Hepworth and Chadwick Solicitors, Cloth Hall Court, Infirmary St, Leeds LS1 2JB (☎ 0532 430391, fax 0532 456188, telex 557917)

BRAMLEY, Michael George; s of Arnold George Bramley (d 1973), and Violet, *née* White; *b* 9 July 1927; *Educ* Mountford House Neville Holt, Nottingham HS; *m* 17 Feb 1953, Kathleen Octavia, da of Robert Henry (d 1969); 1 s (Jonathan b 1967), 1 da (Jane b 1968); *Career* slr, admitted 1951; dir: GB (Nottingham) Ltd 1973-, Brough Superior (coachworks) Ltd 1975-, TB (Investmts) Ltd 1973-, TB (Nominees) Ltd 1981-; life memb: British Olympic Assoc, IEC Wine Soc; memb: The Nat Tst, The Woodland Tst, Nottinghamshire Tst for Nature Conservation, English Heritage; *Recreations* walking, swimming, theatre, travel, gardening; *Clubs* Notts CC, Caravan; *Style*— Michael G Bramley, Esq; 420 Bedling Road, Arnold, Nottingham NG5 6PD (☎ 0602 269147); 1 Oxford Street, Nottingham NG1 5BH (☎ 0602 475792, fax 0602 480853)

BRAMLEY, Prof Sir Paul Anthony; s of Charles Bramley (d 1962), and Constance Victoria Bramley (d 1983); *b* 24 May 1923; *Educ* Wyggeston Leicester, Birmingham Univ (MB, ChB, BDS); *m* 1952, Hazel Morag, da of Harold Arthur Boyd (d 1964), of Glasgow; 1 s, 3 da; *Career* Capt RADC 1946-48; conslt oral surgn Southwest Regnl Hosp Bd 1954-69; Sheffield Univ: prof of dental surgery 1969-88, dean dental sch 1972-75; dean faculty RCS 1980-83; pres: Sands Cox Soc, Br Dental Assoc; memb: cncl Med Protection Soc, Gen Dental Cncl; chm Standing Dental Advsy Ctee DHSS; FDSRCS, HOA, FRACDS, FRCS HonDDS; Bronze Medal Univ of Helsinki Finland, Collier Gold Medal RCS; kt 1984; *Style*— Prof Sir Paul Bramley; Greenhills, Back Lane, Hathersage S30 1AR (☎ 0433 50502)

BRAMLEY, Robin Thomas Todhunter; s of E A Bramley, of Boundary Farm, Gillingham, Norfolk, and M A M Bramley *née* Todhunter; *b* 16 June 1950; *Educ* Ampleforth, Exeter Univ (LLB); *m* 20 Oct 1973, Patricia Anne, da of Maj E S L Mason of Dunburgh House, Geldeston, Beccles, Suffolk; 1 s (George b 1982), 1 da (Henrietta b 1979); *Career* Landowner and Farmer Gillingham Estate, ptnr Francis Hornor and Son chartered surveyors Norwich 1976-, md Norfolk Landfill Ltd; chm Broads Soc 1986-87 (and memb 1984-), ctee memb Norfolk Branch CLA; memb the Broads Authy; JP; FRICS 1978; *Recreations* shooting, riding; *Clubs* Norfolk; *Style*— Robin T T Bramley, Esq; Gillingham Hall, Norfolk (☎ (0502) 717 247); Old Bank of England Court, Queen Street, Norwich, (☎ (0603) 629 871), fax (0502) 716 856

BRAMMA, Harry Wakefield; s of Fred Bramma (d 1983), of Guiseley, W Yorks, and Christine, *née* Wakefield; *b* 11 Nov 1936; *Educ* Bradford GS, Pembroke Coll Oxford (MA); *Career* master King Edward VI GS E Retford 1961-63, asst organist Worcester Cathedral 1963-76, dir of music The Kings Sch Worcester, organist Three Chorus Festival in 1966, 1969, 1972, 1975); conductor, Kidderminster Choral Soc 1972-79, organist and dir of music Southwark Cathedral 1976-89, hon tres Royal Coll of Organists 1987- dir The Royal Sch of Church Music 1989-; chm S London Soc of Organists; Liveryman, Worshipful Co of Musicians; memb FRCO; *Style*— Harry Bramma, Esq; Addington Palace, Croydon, Surrey (☎ 01 654 7676)

BRANCH, Prof Michael Arthur; s of Arthur Frederick Branch (d 1986), of Hornchurch, Essex, and Mahala, *née* Parker; *b* 24 Mar 1940; *Educ* Shene London, Sch of Slavonic and East Europe Studies London Univ (BA, PhD), Univ of Helsinki; *m* 11 Aug 1963, (Ritva-Riitta) Hannele, da of Erkki Lauri Kari (d 1982), of Heinola, Finland; 3 da (Jane, Jean, Ann); *Career* Univ of London: lectr Finno-Ugrian Studies 1971-73 (asst lectr 1967-71), dir Sch of Slavonic and East Euro Studies 1980-, prof Finnish 1986- (lectr 1973-77, reader 1977-86); chm library bd Univ of London; govr: Sch Oriental and African Studies, Warburg Inst, Br Inst Paris, GB-USSR Assoc, GB-East Europe Centre; Hon DPhil Univ of Oulu Finland 1983; Commander of the Finnish Lion Finland 1980; *Books* A J Sjögren: Travels in the North (1973), Finnish Folk Poetry: Epic (jtly 1977), Student's Glossary of Finnish (jtly 1981); *Recreations* walking, gardening; *Clubs* Athenaeum; *Style*— Prof Michael Branch; 33 St Donatt's Rd, New Cross, London SE14 6NU; Hämeentie 28 A3, 00530 Helsinki, Finland; Sch of Slavonic and East Europe Studies, Univ of London, Senate House, Malet St, London WC1E 7NU (☎ 01 637 4934, fax 01 436 8916, telex 269400 SHULG)

BRANCH, Sir William Allan Patrick; *b* 17 Feb 1915; *m* Thelma, *née* Rapier; 1 s; *Career* md and Grenada rep Windward Islands Banana Assoc; kt 1977; *Style*— Sir William Branch; Dougaldston, Gouyave, St John's, Grenada

BRANCKER, Sir (John Eustace) Theodore; QC (1961); s of Jabel Eustace and Myra Enid Vivienne Brancker; *b* 9 Feb 1909; *Educ* Harrison Coll Barbados; *m* 1967, Esmé Gwendolyn, da of Victor Walcott, of Barbados; *Career* barr, pres Barbados Senate 1971-76; kt 1969; *Recreations* chess, classical music, drama; *Clubs* Rotary Barbados, Empire Barbados, Challoner (London), Bridgetown Barbados; *Style*— Sir John Brancker, QC; Valencia, St James, Barbados (☎ 04138)

BRAND, Hon Lord; David William Robert; s of James Gordon Brand (d 1933), advocate, sheriff-substitute, of Huntingdon, Dumfries, and Frances Jessie, *née* Bull (d 1955); *b* 21 Oct 1923; *Educ* Stonyhurst, Edinburgh Univ (MA, LLB); *m* 1, 1948, Rose Josephine (d 1968), da of James Devlin, of Co Tyrone; 4 da; m 2, 1969, Brigid Veronica, da of Garrett Russell, of Co Limerick, and wid of Thomas Patrick Lynch; *Career* cmmnd in Argyll & Sutherland Highlanders 1942, Capt 1945; advocate 1948, QC (Scot) 1959, Sheriff Dumfries and Galloway 1968-70, slr-gen Scotland 1970-72, senator Coll of Justice Scotland (Lord of Session) 1972-; Kt SMO Malta; *Recreations* golf; *Clubs* New (Edinburgh), Hon Co of Edinburgh Golfers; *Style*— The Hon Lord Brand; Ardgarten, 6 Marmion Road, N. Berwick, E. Lothian (☎ 0620 3208)

BRAND, Lady - Doris Elspeth; da of H McNeill, of Arrino, W Australia; *m* 1944, Hon Sir David Brand, KCMG (d 1979); 2 s, 1 da; *Style*— Lady Brand; 24 Ednah St, Como, W Australia

BRAND, Hon Mrs (Laura Caroline Beatrice); *née* Smith; da of 3 Viscount Hambleden and Lady Patricia Herbert, da of 15 Earl of Pembroke; *b* 9 Sept 1931; *m* 1953, Michael Charles Brand, yr s of late Lt-Col John Charles Brand, DSO, MC, Coldstream Guards; 1 s, 2 da; *Style*— The Hon Mrs Brand; 6 Howley Place, London W2

BRAND, Prof (Charles) Peter; s of Charles Frank (d 1972), of Cambridge, and Dorothy Lois, *née* Tapping; *b* 7 Feb 1923; *Educ* Cambridgeshire HS, Trinity Hall Cambridge (MA); *m* 5 Aug 1948, Gunvor, da of Col Inge Hellgreen (d 1976), of Stockholm; 1 s (Simon Charles b 1965), 3 da Jane Marianne b 1949, Barbara Anne b 1952, Catharine b 1961); *Career* Intelligence Corps 1944-46, Lt 1945; fell Trinity Hall Cambridge (lectr 1952-66), prof of italian Edinburgh Univ 1966-88 (vice-princ 1984-88, ret 1988); Commendature Della Republica Italana; *Books* Italy and the English Romantics (1957) T Tasso (1965), L Ariosto (1974), Modern Language Review (ed 1970-76); *Recreations* gardening, sport; *Style*— Prof Peter Brand; 21 Succoth Park, Edinburgh EH12 6BX

BRAND, Capt Terence Edwin; s of Edwin Albert Thomas Brand (d 1980), and Ethel Louise, *née* Stoneham; *b* 18 Oct 1924; *Educ* State; *m* 6 Nov 1949 (m dis 1983), Linda Pasqualia Ceruti, step da of Maj Donald Thomas, of Sunbury On Thames; 2 s (Mark Edwin b 1959, Anthony Quentin b 1962); *Career* WWII RAF 1943-47: Fl Lt, Navigator, Staff Coll, Coastal, Transport and Trng Cmds; Pilot BA (formerly BOAC) 1947-79: sr Capt Boeing 747 1954-, 3 Royal flights, involved trg and devpt VC10 and Concord, dir and trustee Airways Pension Scheme involved with TV and Advertising BA image in UK, USA and Australia (presentations and 3 films); business conslt 1979-, dep chm OPAS 1983-, dir Collins-Wilde plc 1984-, chm Collins-Wilde Enterprises Ltd, chm Brittania and General plc 1984-; trustee BACPA Benevolent Ctee, trustee Guild of Air Pilots Benevolent Ctee, govr Crossways Tst; Queens Commendation 1977; Freeman City of London 1970, Liveryman Guild of Air Pilots and Air Navigators 1970; FIN 1948, FRMETS 1948, ABAC 1988; *Recreations* squash, bridge; *Clubs* RAF, City Livery, MCC; *Style*— Capt Terence Brand; 126 The Avenue, Sunbury on Thames, Middx TW16 5EA (☎ 09327 82704); Collins-Wilde plc, Wyeth House, Hyde St, Winchester, Hants SO23 7DL (☎ 0962 840555, fax 0962 840367, telex 677830 COWILD G)

BRANDER, Lady (Evelyn) Jean Blanche; da of 3 Earl of Balfour (d 1968); *b* 22 Mar 1929; *m* 1948, Michael William Brander, yr s of Francis R Brander, of 80 Iverna Court, W8; 1 s, 2 da; *Style*— Lady Evelyn Brandler; Whittingehame Mains, Haddington, E Lothian

BRANDON, (Oscar) Henry; CBE (1985); *b* 9 Mar 1916; *Educ* Prague Univ, Lausanne Univ; *m* 1970, Mabel Hobart Wentworth; 1 da; *Career* assoc ed and chief American correspondent Sunday Times, ret; columnist for New York Times News Service; guest scholar Brookings Instn Washington DC, CBE; *Style*— Henry Brandon, Esq, CBE; c/o Brookings Institution, 1775 Massachusetts Ave NW, Washington DC 20036, USA; International Consulting Services, 3604 Winfield Lane, NW, Washington DC 20007, USA (☎ 202 338 8506)

BRANDON, Hon James Roderick Vivian; eld s of Baron Brandon of Oakbrook, MC, PC (Life Peer); *b* 1956; *Style*— The Hon James Brandon

BRANDON, Hon Richard Henry; 2 s of Baron Brandon of Oakbrook, MC, PC (Life Peer); *b* 1961; *Educ* Winchester, Bristol Univ Drama Dept; *m* 15 May 1988, Jean Patricia, da of R B Horsfield, of Eccles, Manchester; *Career* theatre director; assoc dir Liverpool Playhouse 1984-85; artistic director, Hebden Bridge Festival Theatre 1987; *Style*— The Hon Richard Brandon

BRANDON, Hon Mrs - Hon Signe Evelyn; *née* Gully; da of 2 Viscount Selby (d 1923); *b* 1909; *m* 1938, Max Brandenstein, who assumed the name Mark Leslie Brandon; 1 s, 1 da; *Style*— The Hon Mrs Brandon; 2 Tyrawley Rd, London SW6

BRANDON, Hon William Roland; yst s of Baron Brandon of Oakbrook, MC, PC (Life Peer); *b* 1964; *Style*— Hon William Brandon

BRANDON OF OAKBROOK, Baron (Life Peer UK 1981); Sir Henry Vivian; MC (1942), PC (1978); yr s of Capt Vivian Ronald Brandon, CBE, RN (d 1944), of 33 Argyll Rd, Kensington, and Joan Elizabeth Maud, *née* Simpson (d 1979); *b* 3 June 1920; *Educ* Winchester, King's Coll Cambridge; *m* 1955, Jeanette Rosemary, da of Julian Vivian Breeze Janvrin, late Indian Police (d 1968); 3 s, 1 da; *Career* serv WWII RA: Madagasgar 1942, India and Burma 1942-45; barr 1946; QC 1961; High Court judge: Probate, Divorce and Admlty Div 1966-71, Family Div 1971-78; judge of Admiralty Court 1971-78, judge of Commercial Court 1977-78; Lord Justice of Appeal 1978-81; Lord of Appeal in Ordinary 1981-; kt 1966; *Recreations* watching cricket, travel, bridge; *Clubs* MCC; *Style*— The Rt Hon the Lord Brandon of Oakbrook, MC, PC; 6 Thackeray Close, Wimbledon, London SW19 (☎ 01 947 6344); House of Lords, London SW1 (☎ 01 219 3119)

BRANDON-BRAVO, Martin Maurice; MP (C) Nottingham South 1983-; s of Alfred (Issac) Brandon Bravo (d 1984), of London, and Phoebe Brandon Bravo (d 1967); of Sephardic origin with family records in Bevis Marks Synagogue dating back to late

1600s; *b* 25 Mar 1932; *Educ* Latymer Upper Sch, Trent Poly; *m* 1964, Sally Anne, da of Robert Wollwin, of Elton, Cambs; 2 s (Paul b 1967, Joel b 1971); *Career* md Richard Stump Ltd to 1983; non-exec dir: Richard Stump Ltd, Halland Earl Ltd, subsidiaries of Readson plc; Nottingham city cncllr 1968-70 and 1976-87; FBIM; *Recreations* rowing; *Clubs* Leander, Nottingham and Union Rowing, Carlton; *Style—* Martin Brandon-Bravo Esq, MP; House of Commons, London SW1 (☎ 01 219 4429)

BRANDRAM, Lady Katherine; HRH Princess Katherine of Greece and Denmark; yst da of HM King Constantine I of the Hellenes (d 1923), and HM Queen Sophie, *née* HRH Princess Sophie of Prussia (d 1932), 3 da of Friedrich III, German Emperor and King of Prussia; ggda of HM Queen Victoria; granted the style, title and precedence of a Duke's da in Great Britain by Royal Warrant of HM King George VI 9 Sept 1947; *b* 4 May 1913; *m* 21 April 1947, Maj Richard Campbell Andrew Brandram, MC, TD, RA, o s of late Richard Andrew Brandram, of The Well House, Bickley, Kent; 1 s (Paul); *Career* formerly HRH Princess Katherine of Greece and Denmark; Gd Cross Order of SS Olga and Sophia (Greece); *Style—* Lady Katherine Brandram; Croft Cottage, Pound Lane, Marlow, Bucks (☎ 062 84 3974)

BRANDRETH, Gyles Daubeney; s of Charles Daubeney Brandreth (d 1972), of London, and Alice, *née* Addison; *b* 8 Mar 1948; *Educ* Bedales, New Coll Oxford (MA); *m* 8 June 1973, Michele, da of Alec Brown; 1 s (Benet Xan b 1975), 2 da (Saethryd Charity b 1976, Aphra Kendal Alice b 1978); *Career* author, broadcaster, producer; journalist and tv presenter 1973-; chm: Victorama Ltd 1974-, Completer Editions Ltd; dep chm Unicorn Heritage plc, dir Newarke Wools Ltd; fndr: Royal Britain Exhibition Barbican, Nat Teddy Bear Museum Stratford upon Avon; chm (former appeals chm 1984-88) National Playing Fields Assoc 1989-; *Books* various incl Created in Captivity (1972), Everyman's Modern Phrase and Fable (1990); *Recreations* some time holder of world record for longest-ever after-dinner speech (12 1/2 hours); *Style—* Gyles Brandreth, Esq; Britannia Ho, Glenthorne Rd, London W6 0LF (☎ 01 938 1948, fax 01 748 3163, telex 619107)

BRANDT, Peter Augustus; s of Walter Augustus Brandt, of Saffron Walden, and Dorothy Gray, *née* Crane; *b* 2 July 1931; *Educ* Eton, Trinity Coll Cambridge; *m* 1962, Elisabeth Margaret, da of Frans ten Bos, of Holland; 2 s, 1 da; *Career* chm Atkins Fulford Ltd 1977- chief exec William Brandt's Sons & Co 1966-; dir William Brandt's Sons & Co, London Life Assoc, Corpn of Argentine Meat Producers' London Cos,; *Recreations* rowing, sailing, watercolours; *Clubs* Carlton, Leander, Royal Harwich Yacht; *Style—* Peter Brandt, Esq; 13 Kensington Place, London W8 (☎ 01 727 8449); Spout Farm, Boxford, Colchester, Essex (☎ (0787) 210297)

BRANDT, Richard; s of Edmund Hubert Brandt (d 1965), of London, and Norah, *née* Toole (d 1971); *b* 7 August 1929; *Educ* Downside, Lincoln Coll Oxford (BA, MA); *m* 4 July 1964, Margaret, da of Philip Archibald Campbell Adamson (d 1977), of Broadstairs; 2 s (Edmund Richard Adamson b 1967, William Robert Aldhelm b 1973), 1 da (Charlotte Louise b 1968); *Career* Nat Serv 1948-49, articled to Annan Dexter & Co 1953-57, CA 1957; ptnr: G Dixey & Co 1957-61, Dearden Harper Miller & Co 1962-68, mangr Arthur Andersen & Co 1969-72, ptnr Grant Thornton (formerly Thornton Baker & Co) 1972-; memb cncl and fin ctee Save the Children Fund 1975-(tres 1982-87); ACA 1957, FCA 1962; *Recreations* sailing, collecting antiques (particularly drinking glasses); *Clubs* Sea View YC; *Style—* Richard Brandt, Esq; 13 Richborne Terrace, London SW8 1AS (☎ 01 735 4127); The Anchorage, Ryde Rd, Seaview, Isle of Wight PO34 5AB (☎ 0983 613 769); Grant Thornton House, Melton St, Euston Sq, London NW1 2EP (☎ 01 383 5100, fax 01 383 4715, telex 28984 GT LDNG)

BRANIGAN, Sir Patrick Francis; QC (Gold Coast 1949); eldest s of Daniel Branigan (d 1923) and Teresa Alice, *née* Clinton (d 1921); *b* 30 August 1906; *Educ* Newbridge Coll Co Kildare, Trinity Coll Dublin, Downing Coll Cambridge; *m* 1935, Prudence, da of Dr Arthur Avent (d 1953), of Seaton, Devon, 1 s, 1 da; *Career* barr; Colonial Legal Service 1931-54; attorney gen and min of justice Gold Coast 1948-54; dep chm Devon QS, rec Crown Ct; chm: Pensions Appeal Tbnl, Agric Land Tbnl, Med Appeal Tbnl, Mental Health Review Tbnl, ret 1978; chm Suflex Ltd, ret 1983; kt 1954; *Style—* Sir Patrick Branigan, QC; C'an San Juan, La Huerta de la Font, Pollensa, Mallorca (☎ 010 3471 530767)

BRANN, (William) Norman; OBE (1967), ERD, JP; s of Rev William Brann, LLB (d 1945), of Ballyeaston, Ballycare, Co Antrim, and Francesca Euphemia Brann (d 1968); *b* 16 August 1915; *Educ* Campbell Coll Belfast NI; *m* 1950, Anne Elizabeth, da of Maj Thomas William Hughes of Dalchoolin, Craigavad, Co Down, NI; 1 s (Stephen), 2 da (Victoria, Catherine); *Career* Col RA 1939-45, served France and Far East; Hon ADC to HE Govr of NI 1952-72; DL Co Down 1974-79, Ld Lt 1979, High Sheriff 1982; Belfast Harbour Cmmn 1960-79; pres Burma Star Assn NI chm UVF Hospital for ex Service Men & Women chm Beck & Scott Ltd 1984-; *Recreations* hunting, gardening, farming; *Clubs* Reform (Belfast); *Style—* Col Norman Brann, OBE, ERD, JP; Drumavaddy, Craigantlet, Newtownards, Co Down, NI BT23 4TG

BRANNAN, Anthony Victor Frederick (Tony); s of (Thomas) Martin Brennan, OBE, of Portinscale, Keswick, Cumbria, and Phillys May, *née* Venebles; *b* 21 Feb 1944; *Educ* St Bees Sch; *m* 27 Feb 1965, Irene Elizabeth, da of William Irving (Bill) Tolson, of High Harrington, Workington, Cumbria; 2 da (Juliet b 13 May 1966, Emma b 12 Oct 1968); *Career* Ward & Pridmore CAs 1951-53, S Brannan & Sons Ltd Thermometer Mfrg 1953- (dir 1970); *Recreations* spectator football, cooking; *Style—* Tony Brannan, Esq; Finkle Lodge, Portinscale, Keswick, Cumbria CA12 5RF (☎ 07687 73244); S Brannan & Sons Ltd, Cleator Moor, Cumbria CA25 5QE (☎ 0946 810413, telex 64248)

BRANSOM, Brig Harold Ian; CBE (Mil 1965), DSO (1942), TD (1947), DL (Northumberland 1968); s of George Clements Bransom (d 1961), of Newcastle; *b* 29 August 1912; *Educ* Ackworth Sch; *m* 1945, Sonia, da of George Edwin Tinn, dentist, of Newcastle; 2 da; *Career* slr 1936; dep lord mayor Newcastle 1959; chm: United Europe Assoc (NE) 1962-72, DHSS Tribunal 1967-, N Cons 1975-82 Nth. Cons 1975-78; pres Nth. Area Con Clubs 1979-; *Recreations* golf, politics, bridge; *Clubs* Nothumberland Golf; *Style—* Brig Harold Bransom, CBE, DSO, TD, DL; 29 Moor Court, Gosforth, Newcastle-upon-Tyne (☎ (091) home: 2853264, work: 2612651)

BRANSON, Lady Noreen; *née* Browne; yr da of late Lt-Col Lord Alfred Browne, DSO (ka 1918), s of 5 Marquess of Sligo; sis of 10 Marquess of Sligo; *b* 16 May 1910; *m* 1931, Clive Ali Chimmo Branson (ka 1944), s of Maj L H Branson; 1 da; *Career* granted the style and precedence of a Marquess's da 1953; *Style—* Lady Noreen Branson; 46 Southwood Ave, N6

BRANSON, Hon Mrs (Stephana); *née* Warnock; da of Sir Geoffrey James Warnock, of Brick House, Axford, nr Marlborough, Wilts, and Baroness Warnock (Life Peeress), *qv*; *b* 9 July 1956; *Educ* Downe House nr Newbury, Oxford HS, Guildhall Sch of Music and Drama (GGSM); *m* 1 Aug 1987, David Ernest Branson, s of William Ernest Branson, of 53/54 High Street, Southill, nr Biggleswade, Beds; 7 St Ruald/s Close, Wallingford, Oxon (☎ 0491 34983)

BRANT, Colin Trevor; CMG (1981), CVO (1979); *b* 2 June 1929; *Educ* Christ's Hosp, Sidney Sussex Cambridge; *m* 1954, Jean Faith, *née* Walker; 1 s, 2 da; *Career* joined FO 1952, asst head oil dept FCO 1969-71, cnsllr (commercial) Caracas 1971-73, cnsllr (energy) Washington 1973-77, ambass Qatar 1978-81, consul-gen Johannesburg 1982-87, ret 1987; FCO fell St Antony's Coll Oxford 1981-82; *Clubs* Travellers'; *Style—* Colin Brant, Esq, CMG, CVO; The Old School House, Horcott, Fairford, Glos

BRASH, Robert; CMG (1980); s of Frank Brash (d 1978), and Ida Brash; *b* 30 May 1924; *Educ* Portsmouth Southern GS, Trinity Coll Cambridge (BA); *m* 1954, Barbara Enid, da of Brig Frederick William Clarke, of Bexhill (d 1966); 3 s, 1 da; *Career* Lt Burma, served 1943-46; Foreign Service 1949-84: consul gen Düsseldorf 1978-81, ambass to Jakarta 1981-84; chm Guildford Rambling Club; *Recreations* golf, walking, gardening, stained glass; *Clubs* RAC; *Style—* Robert Brash, Esq, CMG; Woodbrow, Woodham Lane, Woking, Surrey (☎ 093 23 43874); c/o Foreign and Commonwealth Office, King Charles St, London SW1

BRASHER, Christopher William; s of (William) Kenneth Brasher, CBE (d 1972), and Katie, *née* Howe (d 1987); *b* 21 August 1928; *Educ* Rugby, St John's Coll Cambridge; *m* 1959, Shirley Bloomer; 1 s, 2 da; *Career* Olympic Gold Medallist 1956; sports ed The Observer 1957-61, BBC TV reporter Tonight 1961-65; ed Time Out and Man Alive 1964-65; head Gen Features TV 1969-72; columnist and Olympic correspondent The Observer 1972-; chm Brasher Leisure Ltd 1977-, md Fleetwood Ltd 1979-, race dir London Marathon 1981-; *Recreations* mountains, fly fishing, orienteering, social running; *Clubs* Alpine, Hurlingham, Ranelagh Harriers; *Style—* Christopher Brasher, Esq; The Navigator's House, River Lane, Richmond, Surrey TW10 7AG (☎ 01 940 0296/8822)

BRASS, John; CBE (1968); s of John Brass (d 1961), of New Hall, Ardsley, Yorks, and Mary, *née* Swainston; *b* 22 Oct 1908; *Educ* Oundle, Birmingham Univ (BSc); *m* 1934, Jocelyn Constance, da of Lionel Thomas Cape (d 1962), of Stroud, Glos; 3 s, 1 da (dec'd); *Career* mining engineer; various appointments in mining 1929-; chm Amalgamated Construction Co Ltd 1977-84; memb NCB 1971-73; FEng, FIMinE, FRSA; *Recreations* gardening; *Style—* John Brass Esq, CBE; 2 Fledborough Rd, Wetherby, W Yorks LS22 4AB (☎ 0937 62949)

BRASSEY, Hon Edward; s and h of 3 Baron Brassey of Apethorpe; *b* 9 Mar 1964; *Educ* Eton, RMA Sandhurst; *Career* 2 Lieut Grenadier Guards 1985; *Style—* The Hon Edward Brassey; The Manor House, Apethorpe, Peterborough

BRASSEY, Col Sir Hugh Trefusis; KCVO (1985), OBE (1959), MC (1944), JP (Wilts 1951); s of Lt-Col Edgar Brassey, MVO, of Dauntsey Park, Chippenham (yr bro of 1 Baron Brassey of Apethorpe, JP, DL), by his w, Margaret (herself da of Col Hon Walter Trefusis, CB, who was in his turn 3 s of 19 Baron Clinton; the Col's w was Lady Mary Montagu Douglas Scott, yst da of 5 Duke of Buccleuch); *b* 5 Oct 1915; *Educ* Eton, Sandhurst; *m* 1939, Joyce, da of Capt Maurice Kingscote, of Kingscote Park, Dursley, Glos; 2 s, 2 da (and 1 da decd); *Career* DL Wilts 1955, High Sheriff Wilts 1959, Vice Lord-Lt 1968-81, Lord-Lt 1981-; Lt Queen's Bodyguard of Yeomen of the Guard 1978; regional dir Lloyds Bank Salisbury 1964; pres Chippenham Cons Assoc 1968-80; *Recreations* hunting, shooting, wondering why; *Clubs* Guards & Cavalry; *Style—* Colonel Sir Hugh Brassey, KCVO, OBE, MC, JP; Manor Farm, Little Somerford, Wilts (☎ 066 62 2255)

BRASSEY, Lt-Col Hon Peter Esmé; JP (1947); yst s of 1 Baron Brassey of Apethorpe (d 1958), and Lady Violet Mary Gordon-Lennox (d 1946), da of 7 Duke of Richmond and Gordon; *b* 5 Dec 1907; *Educ* Eton, Magdalene Coll Cambridge; *m* 12 Dec 1944, Lady Romayne, *née* Cecil, da of 5 Marquess of Exeter, KG, CMG, TD 2 s, 1 da; *Career* Northants Yeomanry 1938-46 (wounded 1944), control cmmn for Germany (legal div) 1945-46; barr 1930; chm Essex Water Co; high sheriff Huntingdon and Peterborough 1966; Lord-Lt Cambs 1975-81; KStJ 1975; *Recreations* fishing; *Clubs* Carlton; *Style—* Lt-Col The Hon Peter Brassey, JP; Pond House, Barnack, Stamford, Lincs (☎ 0780 740238)

BRASSEY, Lady Romayne Elizabeth Algitha; *née* Cecil; OBE, ARRC; yr da of 5 Marquess of Exeter, KG, CMG, TD (d 1956), and Hon Myra Orde-Powlett (d 1973), o da of 4 Baron Bolton; *b* 22 Mar 1915; *m* 12 Dec 1944, Lt-Col Hon Peter Brassey, *qv*; *Style—* Lady Romayne Brassey, OBE, ARRC; Pond House, Barnack, Stamford, Lincs (☎ 0780 740238)

BRASSEY, Hon Thomas Ian; s of 2 Baron Brassey of Apethorpe, MC, TD (d 1967); *b* 14 June 1934; *Educ* Stowe; *m* 1960, Valerie Christine Finlason, da of Mrs F F Powell (d 1964) and step da of F F Powell (d 1975), 1 s (Thomas b 1971), 3 da (Miranda b 1963, Louise b 1964, Davina b 1969); *Career* Lt Grenadier Gds 1953-58; company director; *Clubs* Boodles; *Style—* The Hon Thomas Brassey; The Coach House, Duncote, Towcester, Northamptonshire NN12 8AQ (Tel: 0327 52855)

BRASSEY OF APETHORPE, Barbara, Lady; Barbara; da of late Leonard Jorgensen, of West Tytherley; *b* 19 Dec 1911; *m* 1, 1934 (m dis 1948), Lt-Col Herbert Campbell Westmorland, DSO, MC; m 2, 1963, 2 Baron Brassey of Apethorpe, MC, TD (d 1967); *Style—* The Rt Hon Barbara, Lady Brassey of Apethorpe; The Forge, 23 Bull Lane, Ketton, Stamford, Lincs PE9 3TB (☎ 0780 720920)

BRASSEY OF APETHORPE, 3 Baron (UK 1938); Sir David Henry Brassey; 3 Bt (UK 1922); JP (Northants 1970), DL (1972); s of 2 Baron Brassey of Apethorpe, MC, TD (d 1967, whose maternal gf was 7 Duke of Richmond and Gordon); *b* 16 Sept 1932; *Educ* Stowe; *m* 1, 15 Oct 1958, Myrna Elizabeth (d 1974), da of Lt-Col John Baskervyle-Glegg, of Withington Hall, Cheshire; 1 s; m 2, 17 Oct 1978, Caroline, da of Lt-Col Godfrey Evill, of Chepstow; and step-da of Sir George Dunze, 6 Bt; 2 da (Hon Zara b 29 Feb 1980, Hon Chloe b 26 Feb 1982); *Heir* s, Hon Edward Brassey b 9 March 1964; *Style—* The Rt Hon the Lord Brassey of Apethorpe, JP, DL; The Manor House, Apethorpe, Peterborough PE8 5DL (☎ Kingscliffe 231)

BRASSINGTON, (Alexander) Kim; s of Thomas Young Brassington (d 1947), and Catherine Marjorie St Clair, *née* Bower (d 1968); *b* 31 Dec 1943; *Educ* Lechampton Ct Sch, NGTC; *m* 21 March, Ruth; 1 s (Thomas b 1971); *Career* farmer and writer; history of cruising serialized in Yachting Press; current Ms a biography of gu Sir Graham Bower, scapegoat for 1896 Jameson Raid; solo crossing Sahara 1964; London/

Sydney marathon 1968, London/Mexico World Cup Rally 1970, Chelt Area Rep for Op Raleigh 1983-; *Recreations* books, gardening, yachting; *Clubs* Cruising Assoc; *Style*— Alexander Brassington, Esq; Court Farm House, Whittington, nr Cheltenham, Glos GL54 4HB (☎ 0242 820495)

BRATBY, John Randall; s of George Alfred Bratby (d 1948), and Lily Beryl Randall (d 1946); *b* 19 July 1928; *Educ* Tiffin Boys Sch, Royal Coll, Kingston Art Sch; *m* 1, 1953, Jean Esme Oregon, da of Alfred O Cooke (d 1960); 3 s (David b 1955, Jason b 1960, Dayan b 1968), 1 da (Wendy b 1970); m 2, 1977, Darling Patti, da of Laurence Prime (d 1960); *Career* artist & writer; painting Venice Bienalle 1956; Guggenheim Nat Award 1956 & 1958, won John Moore's junior section 1957, picture for film 'Horses Mouth' 1958, works in Tate & Museum of Modern Art and countless public galleries, pictures for film Mistral's Daughter; *Books* Breakdown (1960), Breakfast & Elevenses (1961), Brake-Pedal Down (1962), Break 50 Kill (1963), Stanley Spencer (1965); *Recreations* gardening, walking, TV, talking about drinking, photography, writing, traveling; *Style*— John Bratby, Esq; The Cupola & The Tower of the Winds, Belmont Road, Hastings, East Sussex TN35 5NR (☎ 0424 434037)

BRATT, Guy Maurice; CMG (1977), MBE (1945); s of Ernst Lars Gustaf Bratt (decd), and Alice Maud Mary, *née* Raper (decd); *b* 4 April 1920; *Educ* Merchant Taylors', London Univ (BA); *m* 1945, Francoise Nelly, da of Robert Girardet; 2 s, 1 da; *Career* WWII Royal Signals 1939-46 (Major 1945); solicitor 1947; asst sec Colonial Devpt Corpn, HM Foreign Service 1952; served FO 1952-54, Berlin 1954-56, Brussels 1956-58, FO 1958-62, Vienna 1962-66, FCO 1966-70, Geneva 1970-72, FCO 1972-74, Washington 1974-77, cncllr FCO 1977-80, ret; *Recreations* music, railways, mountaineering; *Clubs* Travellers'; *Style*— Guy M Bratt, Esq, CMG, MBE; 2 Orchehill Rise, Gerrards Cross, Bucks SL9 8PR (☎ 0753 883106)

BRAUER, Irving; s of Jack Brauer (d 1972), of Hackney, London, and Lily, *née* Croll (d 1978); *b* 8 August 1939; *Educ* Davenant Fndn, Northern Poly (Dip Arch); *m* 21 April 1964, Stephanie Margaret, da of Edwin Sherwood Florida USA; 1 s (Marlow b 1975), 1 da (Amelia b 1965); *Career* architect and designer, worked in London and NY 1960-63, partnership Beryl Gollins 1963-76, princ Brauer Assocs 1976-; elected memb Chartered Soc of Designers 1967 (elected fell 1976); visiting tutor: Canterbury Sch of Architecture 1967-70, Central London Poly 1968-71; RIBA; *Recreations* house renovation, theatre, reading, travel; *Style*— Irving Brauer, Esq; Mount Stuart, Westgrove Lane, Greenwich, London SE10 8QP (☎ 01 692 3210); Brauer Associates, 20 Dock St, London E1 8JP (☎ 01 481 2184, fax 01 481 3368)

BRAUNE, Rudi Helmut; s of Wilhelm Friedrich Braune (d 1962), of E Germany, and Berta, *née* Riedel (d 1982); *b* 4 Sept 1925; *m* 23 July 1955, Diana, da of Harold Sheldon (d 1950), of Albert Rd, Southport, Lancs; 1 s (Jeremy b 1962), 3 da (Lindsey b 1956, Janet b 1958, Sara b 1961); *Career* dir Braune (Stroud) Ltd 1954-60, Wunda Machine Co Ltd 1955-57, Braune Batricar Ltd 1975-80; inventor of numerous patents worldwide; RASE; Int Riding and Driving (Bronze Medal 1942); Patent Expdn New York (Gold Medal 1975); *Recreations* driving, riding, landscaping; *Style*— Rudi Braune, Esq; R H Braune, Consultant, 113 Stratford Road, Stroud, Glos GL5 4AL (☎ 04536 5898)

BRAY, Denis Campbell; CMG (1977), CVO (1975), JP (1960-84 Official, 1987 Non-Official); s of Rev Arthur Henry and Edith Muriel Bray; bro of J W Bray, MP, *qv*; *b* 24 Jan 1926; *Educ* Chefoo Sch China, Kingswood Sch Bath, Jesus Coll Cambridge; *m* 1952, Marjorie Elizabeth, da of John Bottomley; (1 s decd), 4 da; *Career* chm: Denis Bray Conslts Ltd 1985-, Jubilee Sports Centre HK, English Schools Fndn Hong Kong; sec home affairs Hong Kong 1973-77 and 1980-84; Hong Kong cmmr London 1977-80; *Recreations* ocean cruising; *Clubs* Travellers', Royal Ocean Racing, Royal Hong Kong Yacht; *Style*— Denis Bray, Esq, CMG, CVO, JP; 8A-7 Borrett Mansions, 8-9 Bowen Rd, Hong Kong

BRAY, Derek William; s of Charles Bray, of Stratford House, Milford Haven; *b* 20 Sept 1926; *Educ* Milford Haven GS, Univ Coll Swansea (BSc); *m* 1948, Christina, da of Minard Hooper; 1 s, 1 da; *Career* chm: BICC Metals Ltd, BICC Connollys Ltd, Brookside Metal Co Ltd, Prescot Rod Rollers Ltd, Thomas Bolton & Sons (dir 1964-), Elsy & Gibbons 1979-; dir: BICC Industl Products 1980-82, BICC Cables Ltd, Br Kynoch Metals Ltd; pres Br Non-Ferrous Metals Fedn; *Recreations* work, golf; *Style*— Derek Bray Esq; Third Acre, Mottram Rd, Alderley Edge, Cheshire SK9 7JH (☎ 0625 582609); BICC Cables Ltd, PO Box 1, Prescot, Merseyside L34 5SZ (☎ 051 430 2202, telex 628811 BPILP)

BRAY, Dr Jeremy William; MP (Lab) Motherwell South 1983-; s of Rev Arthur Henry Bray and Edith Muriel Bray; bro of D C Bray, CMG, CVO, *qv*; *b* 29 June 1930; *Educ* Aberystwyth GS, Kingswood Sch, Jesus Coll Cambridge, Harvard Univ; *m* 1953, Elizabeth, da of Rev Dr Hubert Carey Trowell, OBE, MD, of Salisbury; 4 da; *Career* tech offr Wilton Works of ICI; contested (Lab) Thirsk and Malton 1959, MP (Lab): Middlesbrough West 1962-70, Motherwell and Wishaw 1974-83; memb select ctee: Nationalised Industs 1962-64, Treasury and Civil Serv 1979-83 (chm sub-ctee 1981-82); chm: Lab Sci and Tech Gp 1964-66, Econ Affrs Estimates Sub-Ctee 1964-66; parly sec Miny of Power 1966-67, jt parly sec Miny of Tech 1967-69; chm Fabian Soc 1971-72, dir Mullard Ltd 1970-73, conslt Battelle Res Centre Geneva 1973; visiting prof Strathclyde Univ 1975-79 (sr res fell 1974), dep chm Christian Aid 1972-84, oppn front bench spokesman Sci and Technol 1983-; *Publications* Decision in Government (1970), Production Purpose and Structure (1982); *Recreations* sailing; *Style*— Dr Jeremy Bray, MP; House of Commons, London SW1A 0AA

BRAY, John Frederick; s of John Bray (d 1970), of Goosnargh, Lancs, and Doris Hilda, *née* Brewin, of Preston, Lancs; *b* 5 Sept 1934; *Educ* Preston GS, Victoria Univ of Manchester (BA, Dip Town and Country Planning), Univ of Illinois USA (M Architecture); *m* 27 May 1958 (m dis 1988), Anne Christine Townley, da of Walter Kershaw, (d 1980), of Preston; 2 s (Andrew b 1962, Anthony b 1966), 1 da (Susan b 1961); *Career* RNVR 1954-57, dep launching authy RNLI 1976-79 and 1985-87 (launching authy and station sec 1979-85); asst architect and town planner London CC 1957-58; Central Mortgage and Housing Corpn (CMHC) Canada 1958-64; teaching asst Univ of Illinois USA 1959-60; sr architect and town planner private practice 1964-65, princ and ptnr architectural practice 1965-83, princ Bray Singleton Ptnrship 1983-; examiner: in Professional Practice Univ of Manchester, Architects Registration Cncl UK; lectr and dir Expert Witness Course for CIArb, former Cdre Ribble Cruising Club, past memb Rotary and Round Table; Liveryman Worshipful Co of Arbitrators 1982, Freeman City of London 1981; FRIBA 1970, FRTPI 1972, FCIArb 1981, FBIM 1983; *Recreations* golf, fly fishing, reading, music, photography; *Style*— John Bray, Esq; Tuesday Cottage, Church Lane, Mellor, nr Blackburn, Lancashire BB2 7JL (☎ 0254 81 2747); Bray Singleton Partnership, 50 Wood St, Lytham St Annes, Lancashire FY8 1QG (☎ 0253 712544, 0253 727769, fax 0253 723477, car 0836 601177, telex 677457 FOSBY G)

BRAY, Julian Charles; s of Flt Lt Reginald Charles Julian Bray, and Irene Audrey, *née* Stewart; *b* 23 May 1945; *Educ* Ayr Acad Ayr Scotland; *m* 1, 1971 (m dis 1981), Judith Marina; 2 s (Dominic Julian b 13 Oct 1977, Oliver William b 13 June 1980), m 2, Vivienne Margaret, da of John Carlton; *Career* md Leadenhall Assoc Ltd 1986-; non-exec dir CNS - City News Service 1986-, dir NTN TV News Ltd 1988, head of personal fin Granfield Rork Collins Fin, dir bus devpt Extel PR dir corp servs Editorial Servs Ltd, head of media relations Welbeck PR Ltd, broadcaster and journalist for BBC radio; memb NUJ; *Books* Information Technology in the Corporate Enviroment (1980); *Recreations* theatre, travel, motor sport, radio; *Clubs* Bloggs, Scribes; *Style*— Julian Bray, Esq; Leadenhall Assocs (Corporate Fin Servs PR) Ltd, Lindsey House, 40-42 Charterhouse St, London EC1M 6JH (☎ 01 253 5523 (10 lines), fax 01 253 5523, ext 34)

BRAY, Kelvin Arthur; OBE (1982); s of Arthur William Stretton Bray (d 1979), of Leicester, and Clarice May, *née* Perrin (d 1985); *b* 4 Feb 1935; *Educ* Leicester City Boys' Sch, King's Coll Cambridge (MA); *m* 1959, Grace Elizabeth, da of Dr Matthew Millar Tannahill (d 1981), of Lincoln; 2 s; *Career* sales mangr (gas turbine div) Ruston & Hornsby Ltd 1963; md: Ruston Gas Turbines Ltd 1969- (Queen's Award for Export 1969, 1977, 1978, 1982 Queens Award for Technology 1986), GEC Gas Turbines Ltd 1983-, GEC-Ruston Gas Turbines Ltd 1983-; chm Napier Turbochargers Ltd; Royal Soc Esso Medal 1974; Mac Robert Award 1983, FEng, FIMechE; *Recreations* squash, swimming; *Style*— Kelvin Bray, Esq, OBE; 17 Cherry Tree Lane, Nettleham, Lincoln LN2 2PR; GEC-Ruston Gas Turbines Ltd, PO Box 1, Lincoln LN2 5DJ (☎ (0522) 512612)

BRAY, Michael Peter; s of Sqdn Ldr William Charles Thomas Bray, DFC (d 1985), and Ivy Isobel, *née* Ellison (d 1986); *b* 27 Mar 1947; *Educ* Caterham Sch, Liverpool Univ (LLB); *m* 25 July 1970, Elizabeth-Ann, da of Hubert John Harrington (d 1981); 2 da (Natasha Jane b 13 April 1977, Samantha Louise b 13 April 1984); *Career* Clifford Chance 1970-76 (ptnr 1976-); memb: banking law sub-ctee City of London Slr's Co, jt working pty on banking law of the law reform ctees of the Law Soc and Bar Soc; Freeman City of London Slrs Co 1976; memb Law Soc; *Recreations* theatre, reading, skiing, photography; *Style*— Michael Bray, Esq; Blythe, Butlers Dene Rd, Woldingham, Surrey CR3 7HE (☎ 0888385 2225); Clifford Chance, Royex House, Aldermanbury Sq, London, EC2V 7LD (☎ 01 600 0808 x 2104, fax 01 726 8561, telex 8959991 COWARD G)

BRAY, Sir Theodor Charles; CBE (1964); s of Horace Turner Bray (d 1950), of Adelaide, and Elsie Maude Bray (d 1957); *b* 11 Feb 1905; *Educ* Norwood HS, Adelaide Univ; *m* 1931, Rosalie Irene, da of Rev Arthur Martin Trengove (d 1936); 3 s, 2 da (and 1 s, 1 da decd); *Career* ed-in-chief Courier Mail and Sunday Mail 1953-68, dir Qld Newspapers Pty Ltd 1956-81, jt md Qld Press 1968-70, memb Aust Cncl for Arts 1969-73; chllr Griffith Univ Brisbane 1975-85; chm: Aust Assoc Press 1968-70; Aust chm: Int Press Inst 1961-70; kt 1975; *Recreations* bowls; *Clubs* Queensland, Johnsonian, Journalists; *Style*— Sir Theodor Bray, CBE; 10/64 Macquarie St, St Lucia, Qld 4067, Australia (☎ 8707442)

BRAY, William Neil; s of Brig-Gen Robert Napier Bray, CMG, DSO (d 1921), and Ruth Ellinor, *née* Boys; *b* 11 Oct 1909; *Educ* Gresham's, Emmanuel Coll Cambridge (BA); *m* 1938, Mabel Cynthia, da of Cecil George Gorham Gee, of Rothley, Leics; 3 s (and 1 s decd); *Career* asst chief engr Armaments Design 1944-45; Br Utd Shoe Machinery Co: dir of research 1945-54, dir 1954-71, vice-chm and dep md 1971-74; dir Nashua Copycat Ltd 1967-84; chm Loughborough Conslts Ltd 1972-83; CEng, FIMechE, MIEE; *Recreations* sailing, shooting, fishing; *Clubs* Cruising Assoc; *Style*— William Bray, Esq; Whitcroft, Ulverscroft, Markfield, Leics (☎ 0530 242942)

BRAYBROOK, Edward John; CB (1972); s of Prior Wormsley Braybrook (d 1953), and Kate, *née* Canham (d 1957); *b* 25 Oct 1911; *Educ* Edmonton Latymer Secdy Sch; *m* 1937, Eva Rosalin, da of Reginald George Thomas (d 1916); 1 s (Nigel), 2 da (Susan, Elizabeth); *Career* superintending Naval Store Offr: Levant 1943-44; Ceylon and Southern India 1944-46; Supt RNSD Perth 1946-47, superintending Naval Store Offr Chatham 1953-55, Dir of Stores (Naval) MOD 1964-70, Dir-Gen of Supplies and Tport (Naval) MOD 1970-72; Cdr/Capt (SP) RNVR and SNSO E Indies 1945-46; *Recreations* painting; *Style*— Edward Braybrook, Esq, CB; 22 Church Drive, North Harrow, Middlesex HA2 7NW (☎ 01 427 0838)

BRAYBROOK, Nigel John Reginald; s of Edward Braybrook, CB, of North Harrow, and Rosalind, *née* Thomas; *b* 14 April 1939; *Educ* Merchant Taylors', Coll of Estate Mgmnt; *m* 14 Sept 1968, Lynne Christine, da of Leslie George Hardy (d 1987), of Mitcham; 1 s (Nicholas Edward b 1973), 1 da (Sarah Louise b 1970); *Career* Chartered Surveyor; Weatherall Green & Smith 1957-63, ptnr Montagu Evans & Son 1973 (joined 1963); Freeman City of London 1980, Liveryman Worshipful Co of Glass Sellers 1980; FRICS 1973, FRVA 1973; *Recreations* squash, photography; *Clubs* Bucks, Wig and Pen; *Style*— Nigel Braybrook, Esq; Tall Trees, Paines Lane, Pinner HA5 3BX; 11 Kingsway, London WC2B 6YE (☎ 01 240 2444)

BRAYBROOKE, 9 Baron (GB 1788); Henry Seymour Neville; JP (Saffron Walden 1953), DL (1950); hereditary visitor Magdalene Coll Cambridge; patron of three livings; s of Rev Hon Grey Neville (d 1920, descended from a yr branch of the Nevilles who were Lords Abergavenny; 1 Baron Braybrooke was also 4 Baron Howard de Walden, the Howard de Walden title descended through the female line whereas the Braybrooke title had a special remainder to his kinsman, a Neville); suc cous, 8 Baron (ka 1943); *b* 5 Feb 1897; *Educ* Shrewsbury, Magdalene Coll Cambridge (MA); *m* 1, 1930, Muriel (d 1962), da of William Manning and widow of Euan Cartwright; 1 s; m 2, 1963, Angela (d 1985), da of late W Hollis and widow of John Ree; *Heir* s, Hon Robin Neville; *Career* served as pilot in RNAS (Flt Cdr) and RAF (Capt) 1915-19, active service in France 1915-17; ADC and asst private sec to Lord Weir and Winston Churchill (secs of state for Air 1918-19); with BP 1919-29, Shell 1935-44; chm Diocesan Bd of Finance 1950-68; *Style*— The Rt Hon the Lord Braybrooke, JP, DL; Bruncketts, Wendens Ambo, Saffron Walden, Essex CB11 4JL (☎ 0799 40200)

BRAYBROOKE, Rev Marcus Christopher Rossi; s of Lt-Col Arthur Rossi Braybrooke, of Box Cottage, Cranleigh, Surrey, and Marcia Nona, *née* Leach; descended on female side from a brother of Robert Braybrooke, Bishop of London (d 1404); *b* 16 Nov 1938; *Educ* Cranleigh Sch, Magdalene Coll Cambridge (BA, MA),

London Univ (MPhil), Madras Christian Coll India, Wells Theological Coll; *m* 1964, Mary Elizabeth, da of George Walker, of 15 Sedley Taylor Rd, Cambridge; 1 s (Jeremy b 1966), 1 da (Rachel b 1965); *Career* curate St Michael's Highgate 1964-67, memb Strood Team Miny 1967-73, rector Swainswick with Langridge and Woolley 1973-79, dir of training diocese of Bath and Wells 1979; chm World Congress of Faiths: 1978-1983, Int Ctee 1987-; exec dir Cncl of Christians and Jews 1984-87; priest i/c Christ Church Bath 1984-; *Books* Together to the Truth, The Unknown Christ of Hinduism, Interfaith Organisations, A Historical Directory; ed (journals): World Faiths Insight, Common Ground; *Recreations* gardening, travel, tennis, swimming, home decorating, local history; *Style—* The Rev Marcus Braybrooke; Brookwalk, 2 The Bassetts, Box, Corsham, Wilts SN14 9ER (☎ 0225 742827)

BRAYBROOKE, Neville Patrick Bellairs; s of Patrick Philip William Braybrooke (d 1966), and Lettice Marjorie, *née* Bellairs (d 1986); *b* 30 May 1928; *Educ* Ampleforth; *m* 5 Dec 1953, June Guesdon, da of John Mayne Jolliffe (d 1962); step da (Victoria Mary Guesdon Orr-Ewing b 1942); *Career* author; dir Phoenix Press 1946-51, ed Chamber's Encyclopaedia 1947-48, lit ed Catholic Herald 1965-66; *Books* This is London (1953), London Green: The Story of Kensington Gardens, Hyde Park, Green Park, and St James's Park (1959), London 1961, The Idler (1961), The Delicate Investigation BBC Play (1969), Four Poems for Christmas (1986) ed The Wind and the Rain, Quarterly 1941-51, ed staf Chambers Encyclopaedia 1947-48, literary ed Catholic Herald 1964-66; edited: T S Eliot A Symposium for his 70th Birthday 1958, A Partridge in a Pear Tree: A Celebration for Christmas 1960, Pilgrim of the Future Teilhard de Chardin Symposium 1966, The Letters of JR Ackerley 1975, Seeds in the Wind: 20th Century Juvenilia from H G Wells to Ted Hughes 1989; *Recreations* little reviews, hats, animals,; *Clubs* Island SC Cowes, Pen; *Style—* Neville Braybrooke, Esq; 10 Gardnor Rd, London NW3 1HA (☎01 435 1851); Grove House, Castle Rd, Cowes, Isle of Wight PO31 7QZ (☎0983 293950)

BRAYE, Baroness (8 holder of the title); (Mary Penelope); *née* Verney-Cave; JP (Northants); da of 7 Baron Braye, DL (d 1985); *b* 28 Sept 1941; *Educ* Assumption Convent, Hengrave Hall, Warwick Univ; *m* 1981, Lt-Col Edward Henry Lancelot Aubrey-Fletcher, DL, *qv* Gren Gds, s of Maj Sir Henry Lancelot Aubrey-Fletcher, 6 Bt, CVO, DSO, JP, HM Lord-Lieut for Bucks; *Heir* co-heiresses; *Career* High Sheriff Northamptonshire 1983; *Style—* The Rt Hon Baroness Braye, JP; Stanford Hall, Lutterworth, Leics LE17 6DH (☎ Rugby 0788 860250)

BRAYLEY, Hon Avril Gay; da of Baron Brayley (Life Peer, d 1977); *Style—* Hon Avril Brayley

BRAYLEY, Hon Tessa Ann; da of Baron Brayley (Life Peer, d 1977); *Style—* Hon Tessa Brayley

BRAYNEN, Sir Alvin Rudolph; JP (Bahamas 1975); s of William Rudolph Braynen and Lulu Isabelle, *née* Griffin; *b* 6 Dec 1904; *Educ* in the Bahamas; *m* 1969, Ena Estelle, *née* Elden; (1 s, 1 da by a previous m); *Career* consultant to Shell Bahamas 1969-, Bahamas high cmmr in London 1973-77; kt 1975; *Style—* Sir Alvin Braynen, JP; PO Box N42, Nassau, Bahamas

BRAZEL, Hon Mrs; Lucinda Maria; *née* Stanley; only da of 8 Baron Stanley of Alderley; *b* 21 Feb 1958; *m* 1983, Peter Brazel, s of late Benedict Brazel of Lyndhurst, S Australia; *Style—* The Hon Mrs Brazel

BRAZENDALE, Alan Courtenay; s of Capt George William Ernest Brazendale (d 1970), of 12 Hall Drive, Greasby, Wirral, and Alice Annie, *née* Courtenay (d 1981); *b* 15 Dec 1924; *Educ* Birkenhead Sch; *m* 13 July 1946, Elizabeth Ewan, da of William Stewart Carr (d 1969), of Shieldaig, Stanley, Perthshire; 1 da (Elizabeth Ann b 1953); *Career* Fleet Air Arm 1943-47; CA; mayor of Gateshead MBC 1980-81; chm Gateshead Educ Ctee 1982-; dir: N Regnl Examinations Bd, Town Teacher Ltd, Alton Assocs Ltd; memb: Cncl of Local Educn Authorities, Assoc of Met Authorities Educn Ctee, Northern Cncl of Educn Ctees, Northern Cncl for Further Educn, ct of Newcastle Univ, cncl of Newcastle Poly; chm of govrs Gatehead Tech Coll; FCA, MBIM, MInstAM, MIIM; *Recreations* golf, local history, reading, writing, gardening; *Style—* Alan Brazendale, Esq; 8 The Orchard, Whickham, Newcastle upon Tyne NE16 4HD (☎ 091 4881622); Gateshead Civic Centre, Gateshead, Tyne and Wear NE8 1HH (☎ 091 4771011)

BRAZENDALE, George William; CMG (1958); s of Percy Ridout Brazendale (d 1915), of Lymm, Cheshire, and Edith Mary, *née* Maystre (d 1953); *b* 25 April 1909; *Educ* Arnold Sch Blackpool; *m* 1938, Madeleine (d 1981), o da of Thomas Wroe, of Lymm Cheshire; 2 da (Elizabeth, Inga); *Career* asst sec BOT 1946; Br Trade cmmnr in Calcutta 1950-60; princ Br Trade cmmnr in Fedn of Rhodesia and Nyasaland 1961-65; econ advsr to Special Br Rep in E and Central Africa 1964-67; FCA; *Recreations* fishing; *Clubs* Oriental; *Style—* George Brazendale, Esq, CMG; 4 Princes St, Sandy Bay, Hobart 7005, Tasmania (☎ 23 6244)

BRAZIER, Julian William Hendy; MP (C) Canterbury (1987-); s of Lt-Col Peter Hendy Brazier, and Patricia Audrey Helen, *née* Stubbs, ggd of Bishop Stubbs of Oxford noted lectr and author of the Constituted History of England; *b* 24 July 1953; *Educ* Dragon Sch, Wellington, Brasenose Coll Oxford (MA); *m* 21 July 1984, Katharine Elizabeth, da of Brig Patrick Blagden; *Career* late RE and TA (Capt); Charter Consolidated Ltd 1975-84, H B Maynard Mgmnt Cnslts 1984-87; *Recreations* cross country runner, science, philosophy; *Style—* Julian W H Brazier, Esq, MP; c/o House of Commons, London SW1A 0AA

BRAZIER-CREAGH, Maj-Gen Sir (Kilner) Rupert; KBE (1962, CBE 1947), CB (1954), DSO (1944); s of Lt-Col Kilner Brazier-Creagh, TD (d 1956); *b* 12 Dec 1909; *Educ* Rugby, RMA Woolwich; *m* 1, 1938, Elizabeth Mary (d 1967), da of Edward Magor (d 1954); 1 s, 2 da; *m* 2, 1968, Marie, da of Edward O'Keeffe; *Career* served NW Europe 1944-45, Malayan Emergency 1952-55; Asst Cmdt Staff Coll 1955-57, COS E Cmd 1957-59, Dir Staff Duties War Office 1959-61; sec Horse Race Betting Levy Bd 1961-65; *Recreations* gardening, travel; *Style—* Maj-Gen Sir Rupert Brazier-Creagh, KBE, CB, DSO; Travis Corners Rd, Garrison, New York 10524, USA

BRAZINGTON, Edward Stanley; s of George T Brazington (d 1934); *b* 2 Oct 1926; *Educ* Hemel Hempstead GS, King's Coll London (BSc); *m* 1956, Jeanne Margaret; *Career* Lt RE served Palestine; dir Wiggins Teape Gp; chm: Wiggins Teape (Belgium) SA, Wiggins Teape (Europe) Ltd; chief exec Carbonless Papers Operations of Wiggins Teape 1981; Chev de L'Ordre de Leopold; *Recreations* landscape gardening, woodwork, painting, shooting, literature, music; *Style—* Edward Brazington Esq; c/o Wiggins Teape Group, PO Box 88, Gateway House, Basing View, Basingstoke, Hants RG21 2EE (☎ 0256 20262, telex 858031 WTBSTK G)

BREACH, Peter John Freeman; s of Andrew Breach, of Pensford, nr Bristol, and Christine Ruth, *née* Watson (d 1973); *b* 12 Jan 1942; *Educ* Clifton, Univ of Bristol (BA); *m* 17 Dec 1966, Joan, da of (William) Raymond Livesey, of Clitheroe, Lancashire; 2 s (Harry William Freeman b 1972, Christopher (Kit) Andrew Talbot b 1974); *Career* Coopers & Lybrand 1963-68, Hoare Govett 1968-69, County Bank Ltd 1969-70, JH Vavasseur & Co Ltd 1970-73, pres and chief exec offr Major Hldgs & Devpts Ltd 1972-73, divnl md Bath & Portland Gp Ltd 1974-78, md James Dixon/ Viners Ltd 1978-82, fin dir Bristol & West Bldg Soc 1988- (dir 1976-, exec dir 1983-87); govr and dep chm Redland High Sch for Girls; Freeman: City of London, City of Bristol; Liveryman Worshipful Co of Basketmakers; FCA, ATII, ACT, ASIA; *Recreations* sailing, skiing; *Clubs* Royal Dart; *Style—* Peter Breach, Esq; Bristol & West Building Soc, Broad Quay, Bristol BS99 7AX (☎ 0272 294 271, fax 0272 211 632, car tel 0836 728 587, telex 44741)

BREADALBANE AND HOLLAND, 10 Earl of (S 1677); Sir John Romer Boreland Campbell; 14 Bt (NS 1625); also Viscount of Tay and Paintland (S 1677), and Lord Glenorchy, Benederaloch, Ormelie and Weick (S 1677); s of 9 Earl, MC (d 1959); *b* 28 April 1919; *Educ* Eton, RMC Sandhurst, Edinburgh Univ; *m* 1949 (m dis), Coralie, da of Charles Archer; *Heir* none known; *Career* formerly Lt Black Watch, served in France 1939-42 (despatches, invalided); *Style—* The Rt Hon The Earl of Breadalbane and Holland; 29 Mackeson Rd, NW3

BREADEN, Very Rev Robert William; s of Moses Breaden (d 1958), of Drummons, Magheracloone, Carrickmacross, Co Monaghan, and Martha Jane, *née* Hall; *b* 7 Nov 1937; *Educ* The King's Hosp Dublin, Edinburgh Theol Coll; *m* 3 July 1970, Glenice Sutton, da of Douglas Martin, of Dundee; 1 s (Patrick b 1971), 4 da (Sarah b 1973, Kathleen b 1979, Christina b 1981, Ann-Louise b 1987); *Career* ordained 1961, asst curate St Mary's Broughty Ferry 1961-65; rector: Church of the Holy Rood Carnoustie 1965-72, St Mary's Broughty Ferry 1972-; canon of St Paul's Cathedral Dundee 1977, dean of the Diocese of Brechin 1984-; *Recreations* gardening, horse-riding; *Clubs* Rotary of Abertay (pres 1979-80); *Style—* The Very Rev the Dean of Brechin; 46 Seafield Road, Broughty Ferry, Dundee DD5 3AN (☎ 0382 77477)

BREALEY, Prof Richard Arthur; s of Albert Brealey (d 1974), and Irene Brealey; *b* 9 June 1936; *Educ* Queen Elizabeth's Sch Barnet, Exeter Coll Oxford (MA); *m* 10 Feb 1967, Diana Cecily, da of Derek Brown-Kelly, of Oddington, Glos; 2 s (David Andrew b 1970, Charles Richard b 1972); *Career* investmt mangr Sun Life Assur Co of Canada 1959-66, mangr computer applications Keystone Custodian Funds of Boston 1966-68; London Business Sch: dir Inst Fin and Accounting 1974-84, memb body govrs dep princ and academic dean 1984-88, currently Midland Bank prof of corporate fin; visiting prof: Univ of California, Berkeley, Univ of Br Colombia, Univ of Hawaii, Aust Graduate Sch of Mgmnt; dir Helvetia Fund Inc; pres European Fin Assoc, dir American Fin Assoc; *Books* incl: Introduction to Risk and Return from Common Stocks (second edn 1983), Principles of Corporate Finance (with S C Myers, third edn 1987); *Recreations* rockclimbing, skiing, pottery; *Style—* Prof Richard Brealey; Haydens Cottage, The Pound, Cookham, Berks (☎ 06285 20143); London Business Sch, Sussex Place, Regent's Park, London NW1 (☎ 01 262 5050, fax 01 724 7875, telex 27461 LOND IS KOL)

BREAM, Hon Mrs (Catherine Frances Lilian Berry); yst da of 2 Viscount Kemsley; *b* 9 June 1944; *m* 19 April 1969, Richard Douglas Fowler Bream, yr s of Clifford Ellett Bream, of The Manor Farm, Grace Dieu, Leics; 1 s, 1 da; *Career* co pres for St John Leicestershire; *Style—* The Hon Mrs Bream; The Manor Farm, Grace Dieu, Whitwick, Leics LE6 3UG

BREAM, Richard Douglas Fowler; DL (Leicestershire 1984); s of Clifford Ellett Bream (d 1987), of Grace Dieu, Leics, and Elaine Mary, *née* Fowler (d 1980); *b* 25 July 1936; *Educ* The Kings Sch Canterbury; *m* 19 April 1969, Catherine Francis Lilian, yst da of 2 Viscount Kemsley, *qv*, of Market Harborough, Leics; 1 s (Tamerlane Douglas Fowler b 1972), 1 da (Atlanta Mary b 1971); *Career* TAVR 1970; dir D H Bream and Co Ltd 1963-; farmer; OStJ; *Recreations* hunting, shooting, fishing; *Clubs* Naval and Military; *Style—* Richard D F Bream, Esq; The Manor Farm, Grace Dieu, Leics LE6 3UG (☎ 0530 222277); D H Bream and Co Ltd, Spinney Hill Works, Prospect Road, Leicester LE5 3RP (☎ 0553 517385, telex 342162, car tel 0836 510661)

BREAM, Roland Ellett; TD (1967); s of Clifford Ellett Bream, MBE (d 1987), of Leics, and Elaine Mary, *née* Fowler (d 1980); *b* 15 Feb 1931; *Educ* Loughborough GS, Queens' Coll Cambridge (MA); *m* 8 Sept 1962, (Elizabeth) Gay, da of E L Whiteman, MC (d 1970), of Leics; 1 s (Charles b 1968), 2 da (Lindamina b 1964, Lucinda b 1966); *Career* Nat Serv cmmn RHA 1954, Maj S Notts Hussars Yeomanry 1955-67; mgmnt conslt logistics and distribution 1967-75; exec dir Harold Whitehead & Ptnrs 1970-75; dir and ptnr M M Distribution Conslts 1976-82; princ Roland Bream & Assocs; FIMC, FILDM, FIPC; *Recreations* gardening, reading, classical music, fine wine, travel; *Clubs* Naval and Military; *Style—* Roland E Bream, Esq, TD; Cruck Meole House, Cruck Meole, Shrewsbury SY5 8JN (☎ 0743 860295)

BREARE, William Robert Ackrill; s of late Robert Ackrill Breare, and Emily, *née* Waddington; *b* 5 July 1916; *Educ* Charterhouse, Wadham Coll Oxford; *m* 1942, Sybella Jessie Macduff, da of John Roddick, of Annan; 1 s, 2 da; *Career* chm Ackrill Gp; memb: Press Cncl, Cncl of Newspaper Soc; *Recreations* music, sailing; *Style—* William Breare, Esq; Harrison Hill House, Starbeck, Harrogate, N Yorks (☎ 883302)

BREARLEY, Dr Arthur; TD (1960); s of Leonard Brearley, of Lancs, and Mary Brearley; *b* 31 August 1928; *Educ* Queen Elizabeth I GS Middleton, Manchester Univ (BSc, MSc, PhD); *m* 1955, Margaret, da of Ben Lee, of Manchester; 2 s (John b 1961, Mark b 1963); *Career* professorial fell in mgmnt devpt Bradford Univ; chm R L Martindale Liverpool; dir Lawtex Manchester; dir Broadbents Southport; dir Toy and Hobby St Helens; dir Production Gp Chelford; *Recreations* flying, fell walking; *Style—* Dr Arthur Brearley, TD; Sheringham House, Ladybrook Road, Bramhall, Stockport, Cheshire (☎ 061 485 3944); Arthur Young, Commercial Union House Albert Sq, Manchester (☎ 061 831 7854)

BREARLEY, Christopher John Scott; s of Geoffrey William Brearley (d 1968), and Winifred Marion, *née* Scott; *b* 25 May 1943; *Educ* King Edward VII Sch Sheffield, Trinity Coll Oxford (MA, BPhil); *m* 1971, Rosemary Nanette, da of Lt-Col Wilfred Sydney Stockbridge; 2 s (Thomas b 1973, William b 1976); *Career* civil servant; under sec Planning and Devpt Control DOE 1988-; previously: dir Scottish Services, Property Services Agency 1981-83, under sec Cabinet Office 1983-85, dir local govt fin DOE 1985-88; *Recreations* walking, crosswords; *Clubs* New (Edinburgh); *Style—*

Christopher Brearley, Esq; Dept of Environment, 2 Marsham St, London SW1 (☎ 01 276 3854)

BREARLEY, Sir Norman; CBE (1965), DSO (1916), MC (1915), AFC (1918); s of Robert Hillard Brearley (d 1950), and Mary Karen Brearley (d 1950); *b* 22 Dec 1890; *Educ* state and private schs, Tech Coll Perth; *m* 1917, Violet Claremont, da of Hon Sydney Stubbs, CMG, MLA WA (d 1953), of Perth; 1 s, 1 da; *Career* WW 1 RFC and RAF also Maj Liverpool Regt Eng, France (wounded, MID), Gp Capt FAAF WW 11 1939-45; fndr W Aust Airways 1921; company dir ; FRAeS; kt 1971; *Recreations* golf; *Clubs* Weld (Perth); *Style*— Sir Norman Brearley, CBE, DSO, MC,AFC; 6 Esplanade, Cottesloe, W Australia 6011

BRECHIN, Bishop of, 1975-; Most Rev Lawrence Edward Luscombe; s of Reginald John Luscombe (d 1970), and Winifred Luscombe; *b* 10 Nov 1924; *Educ* Kelham Theological Coll, King's Coll London; *m* 1946, Doris Carswell, da of Andrew Morgan; 1 da; *Career* serv WWII Indian Army, India and Burma; formerly chartered accountant, ptnr in Watson Galbraith CA Glasgow 1952-63; ordained deacon 1963, priest 1964; rector St Barnabas Paisley 1966-71, provost of St Paul's Cathedral Dundee 1971-75; hon canon Trinity Cathedral Davenport Iowa 1983-, primus of the Scottish Episcopal Church 1985-90; OStJ; Hon LLD Univ of Dundee, Hon DLitt Geneva Theol Coll; *Style*— The Most Rev the Lord Bishop of Brechin; Woodville, Kirkton of Tealing, by Dundee (☎ 082 621 331)

BRECKNOCK, Earl of; James William John Pratt; s and h of 6 Marquess Camden; *b* 11 Dec 1965; *Educ* Eton, Edinburgh Univ; *Style*— Earl of Brecknock

BRECKNOCK, Marjorie, Countess of; Marjorie Minna; DBE (1967); da of Col Atherton Edward Jenkins, of Wherwell Priory Andover; *b* 28 Mar 1900; *Educ* Heathfield; *m* 1920 (m dis 1941), as his 1 w, Earl of Brecknock (later 5 Marquess Camden; d 1983); 1 s (6 Marquess Camden, *qv*), 1 da (Lady Mary Pawle, *qv*); *Career* serv WWII Sr ATS Offr SHAEF 1944-45 (despatches); lady-in-waiting to Princess Marina, Duchess of Kent 1937-39; supt-in-chief St John Ambulance Bde 1960-70, chief pres 1972, GCStJ 1971; Bronze Star (USA) 1945; *Recreations* gardening, fishing, shooting; *Style*— Marjorie, Countess of Brecknock, DBE; 2 Kinnerton St, London SW1 (☎ 01 235 9362); Wherwell Priory, Andover, Hants (☎ Chilbolton (026 474) 388)

BRECON, Baroness; Mabel Helen; CBE (1964), JP; da of John McColville (d 1946), of Abergavenny, and Martha McColville (d 1944); *b* 8 May 1910; *Educ* St Alban's Convent; *m* 1933, 1 and last Baron Brecon, PC (d 1976), s of Alfred William Lewis (d 1955); 2 da (Hon Mrs Price, Hon Mrs Foss, *qqv*); *Career* cllr Brecknock RDC 1949-74 (chm 1972), magistrate 1957-80, High Sheriff Breconshire 1971-72; chm: Wales Women Cons Advsy Ctee 1955-62, Wales World Refugee Year 1959, Freedom from Hunger Campaign 1961-66; *Recreations* gardening, reading; *Style*— The Rt Hon the Lady Brecon, CBE, JP; Greenhill, Cross Oak, Brecon, Powys (☎ Talybont-on-Usk (087 487) 247)

BREDIN, Brig Alexander Edward Craven; DSO (1945), MC (1944), DL (Devon 1966); s of Lt-Col Alexander Bredin, IA (d 1943), of Ballymahon, Co Longford, and Canterbury, Kent, and Ethel, *née* Homan (d 1975); bro of Maj-Gen H E N Bredin, *qv*; *b* 6 Jan 1911; *Educ* King's Sch Canterbury, RMC Sandhurst; *m* 1950, Désirée Ida, da of Robert Mills, of Straffan, Co Kildare; 1 s, (1 da decd); *Career* cmmnd Dorsetshire Regt 1931, served Egypt and Palestine 1936, NW Frontier India 1937-39; WWII: MEF, CMF, NW Europe, (CO 1 and 5 Dorset 1944-45); FARELF (CO 1/6 GR 1954-56); cmd 156 Lowland Infantry Bde TA and insp PT War Off; Col Devonshire & Dorset Regt 1967-77; pres Dorset Regt Assoc 1962-88; memb Cncl ACF Assoc; chm Nat Sports Ctee; Cdr Devon ACF 1964-70; pres D-Day and Normandy Fellowship 1978-86; county vice-chm (E) Devon Emergency Volunteers 1978-, (pres Dev 1988-), chm Army Benevolent Fund Appeals (Devon) 1978-85; churchwarden; *Books* Three Assault Landings (Dorset Regt), The Happy Warriors (Gurkhas), The Devonshire and Dorset Regiment 1958-83 (record for the Regt), History of the Irish Soldier (1014-1985); *Recreations* outdoor and country pursuits, shooting, beagling, cricket, writing on military subjects; *Clubs* Army & Navy; *Style*— Brig Alexander Bredin, DSO, MC, DL; Castle Cottage, Hawkchurch, nr Axminster, Devon EX13 5UA (☎ 02977 237)

BREDIN, Maj Gen Humphrey Edgar Nicholson; CB (1970), DL (Essex 1985-), DSO (1944), bars (1945, 1957), MC (1938), bar (1939); s of Lt-Col Alexander Bredin (d 1943), of Ballymahon Ireland, and Ethel, *née* Homan (d 1975); bro of Brig A E C Bredin, *qv*; *b* 28 Mar 1916; *Educ* Kings Sch Canterbury, RMC Sandhurst; *m* 1, 1947 (m dis 1961) Jacqueline, da of J Geare, of Rogart, Sutherland; 1 da (Corynne); m 2, 1965, Anne Finch, da of Robert Hardie (d 1980), of Edinburgh; 2 da (Jane, Sarah); *Career* cmmnd Royal Ulster Rifles 1936; serv: Palestine 1937-39, Dunkirk 1940, N Africa 1943, Italy 1943-45, Palestine 1946-47, Sudan 1949-53, Cyprus 1956-57, Suez 1956, Malaya 1959-62, cmd 6 Inniskilling Fus 1944, 2 London Irish Rifles 1944-45, Eastern Arab Corps Sudan Def Force 1949-53, 2 Bn The Parachute Regt 1956-58, 99 Gurkha Bde 1959-62, Chief of Br Mission to Soviet (C-in-C in D.D.R. 1963-65, District Cdr Lancashire Div and District 1965-67, dir TA 1968-71, Maj-Gen 1965, ret 1971, Col Royal Irish Rangers 1979-85, Hon. Col London Irish Rifles 1979-86; Field Sec Cancer Res Campaign for Essex and Suffolk 1871-83, chm Army Benevolent Fund for Suffolk 1985-; *Recreations* shooting, gardening; *Clubs* Army & Navy; *Style*— Maj-Gen Humphrey Bredin, CB, DSO, MC, D.L.; Bovills Hall, Ardleigh, Essex (☎ 0206 230217)

BREDIN, James John; s of John Francis Bredin (d 1981), and Margaret Bredin; *b* 18 Feb 1924; *Educ* Finchley Catholic GS, London Univ; *m* 1958, Virginia, da of John Meddowes; 1 s, 2 da; *Career* serv WWII Fleet Air Arm RNVR Sub-Lt, Europe, M East, Far East; producer: BBC TV 1950-55, ITN 1955-59, Associated Television (documentaries) 1959-64; chm Guild of Televison Producers and Directors 1961-64; dir ITN 1970-72; md Border Television Ltd 1964-82; specialist in television archives 1982-; FRTS 1983-; *Clubs* Beefsteak; *Style*— James Bredin, Esq; 25 Stack House, Cundy Street, London SW1W 9JS (☎ 01 730 2689)

BREEN, Geoffrey Brian; s of Ivor James Breen, of Cowbridge, S Wales, and Doreen Odessa Breen; *b* 3 June 1944; *Educ* Harrow HS, Coll of Law; *m* 8 April 1976, Lucy, da of Serafin Cabrera (d 1984), of Bogota, Colombia; 1 s (Christopher b 1977), 1 da (Deborah b 1979); *Career* articled clerk Stiles Breen & Ptnrs 1962-67 (previously Stiles Wood Head & Co Formerly Stiles Wood & Co): admitted slr 1967, ptnr 1970-75, sr ptnr 1976-86; ptnr Blaser Mills & Newman 1976-86; former ctee memb: Central and S Middx Law Soc, London Criminal Cts Slrs' Assoc; appointed metropolitan stipendary magistrate 1986; *Recreations* classical guitar, reading; *Style*— Geoffrey Breen, Esq; Camberwell Green Magistrates Ct, 15 D'Eynsford Rd, Camberwell, London SE5 7UP (☎ 01 703 0909)

BREEN, Dame Marie Freda; DBE (1979, OBE 1958); da of Frederick and Jeanne Chamberlin; *b* 3 Nov 1902; *Educ* St Michael's C of E Girls' GS; *m* 1928, Robert Tweedale Breen (d 1968); 3 da; *Career* senator for Victoria 1962-68; *see Debrett's Handbook of Australia and New Zealand for further details*; *Style*— Dame Marie Breen, DBE; 51 Carpenter St, Brighton, Victoria 3186, Australia (☎ 592 2314)

BREEZE, Alan Leonard; s of William John Richard Breeze, and Ivy Lorretta, *née* Bird; *b* 11 Nov 1950; *Educ* Eastbourne GS; *m* 7 July 1973, Barbara Caroline, da of Edwin Frederick Hope; 2 s (Jonathan b 1980, Thomas b 1983); *Career* CA 1973-, ptnr Breeze Ralph & Co; *Style*— Alan L Breeze, Esq; 75 Ratton Drive, Eastbourne, East Sussex; 69 Church Rd, Hove, (☎ 739592); 5 Cornfield Terrace, Eastbourne (☎ 411416)

BREITMEYER, Brig Alan Norman; DL (Cambridgeshire 1979); only s of L(ouis) Cecil Breitmeyer (himself 2 s of Ludwig Breitmeyer, originally of Stuttgart, a dir De Beers and chm Diamond Syndicate) by his w Clarice, da of Norman Herbert-Smith, of Hickling Hall, Norfolk; *b* 14 Mar 1924; *Educ* Winchester, RMA; *m* 1952 (m dis 1977), Hon June Jane Coupar Barrie, eldest da of 1 and last Baron Abertay; 1 s (Timothy b 1959), 1 da (Patricia b 1954); m 2, 1978, Susan Anne, da of Brig Humphrey Lipscomb, of Minterne Magna, Dorset; *Career* served WW II Gren Gds N W Europe, Capt 1946, Maj 1953, Lt-Col 1962, Col 1966, Brig 1972, served Palestine 1946-48, Egypt & Libya 1955-57, Malaya 1960-62; memb Hon Corps Gentlemen-at-Arms 1976-; *Clubs* Boodle's; *Style*— Brig Alan Breitmeyer, DL; Bartlow Park, Bartlow, Cambs (☎ 0223 891609)

BREMRIDGE, Sir John Henry; KBE (1983, OBE 1976); *b* 12 July 1925; *Educ* Dragon Sch, Cheltenham, St John's Coll Oxford (MA); *m* 1956, Jacqueline Everard, MBE; 2 s, 2 da; *Career* chm Swire Gp to 1980; fin sec Hong Kong 1981-86, dir Swire Gp 1986; Hon DSSc Chinese Univ, Hon LLD Hong Kong Univ; *Style*— Sir John Bremridge, KBE; Church House, Bradford on Avon, Wilts

BRENCHLEY, (Thomas) Frank; CMG (1964); s of Robert Ballard Brenchley (d 1967), and Alice, *née* Brough (d 1974); *b* 9 April 1918; *Educ* Oxford (MA), Open Univ (BA); *m* 1946, Edith Helen (d 1980), da of Moritz Helfand (d 1938), of Vienna, Austria; 3 da (Hilary, Victoria, Clare); *Career* RCS 1939-46, ME cmd, Actg Lt-Col; first sec: Singapore 1950-53, Cairo 1953-56, FO 1956-58, Mecas 1958-60; cnsllr Khartoum 1960-63, charge d'affaires Jedda 1963, head of Arabian dept FO 1963-67, under sec FCO 1967-68, ambass: Norway 1968-72, Poland 1972-74; dep sec (head of oversea and def sec) Cabinet Off 1974-76, ret HM Dip Serv 1976; chm Inst for Study of Conflict 1984-, dir center for security studies Washington DC 1988-; *Recreations* collecting books; *Clubs* Travellers; *Style*— Frank Brenchley, Esq, CMG; 19 Ennismore Gdns, London SW7 1AA (☎ 01 584 7981)

BRENDEL, Alfred; s of Albert Brendel, of Graz, and Ida, *née* Wieltschnig; *b* 5 Jan 1931; *Educ* London Univ; *m* 1, 1960 (m dis 1972), Iris Heymann-Gonzala; 1 da (Doris); m 2, 1975, Irene, da of Dr Johannes Semler, of Munich; 1 s (Adrian), 2 da (Anna-Sophie, Katharina); *Career* pianist and writer; concert career since 1949; recordings for Vox, Turnabout, Vanguard, Philips; Hon RAM; Hon DMus: London 1978, Sussex 1980, Oxford 1983; Cdr of Arts and Letters (France); *Books* Musical Thoughts and Afterthoughts (essays 1976); *Recreations* reading, theatre, films, unintentional humour, kitsch; *Style*— Alfred Brendel, Esq; c/o Ingpen & Williams, 14 Kensington Court, London W8 (☎ 01 937 5158)

BRENNAN, Daniel Joseph; QC (1985); s of Daniel Brennan, of Bradford (d 1969), and Mary, *née* Amearne (d 1966); *b* 19 Mar 1942; *Educ* St Bede's GS Bradford, Univ of Manchester (LLB); *m* 21 Aug 1968, Pilar, da of Luis Sanchez Hernandez, of Madrid (d 1980), and Nieves Moya Dominguez; 4 s (Daniel b 1971, Patrick b 1972, Michael b 1977, Alexander b 1980); *Career* Barr; recorder of Crown Court 1982; *Publications* Provisional Damages (1986); *Style*— Daniel J Brennan, Esq, QC; Brook House, Brook Lane, Alderley Edge, Cheshire SK9 7RU; 18 St John Street, Manchester (☎ 061 834 9843, fax 061 835 2051)

BRENNAN, Hon Justice; Sir (Francis) Gerard; AC (1988), KBE (1981), QC (1965); s of Hon Mr Justice Frank Tenison Brennan (d 1949), and Gertrude Mary Koenig; *b* 22 May 1928; *Educ* Christian Brother's Coll Rockhampton, Downlands Coll Toowoomba, Qld Univ (BA, LLB); *m* 1953, Patricia, da of Dr Joseph O'Hara; 3 s, 4 da; *Career* Justice of the High Court of Australia 1981-; *see Debrett's Handbook of Australia and New Zealand for further details*, hon LLD Trinity Coll Dublin 1988; *Recreations* gardening; *Clubs* Cwlth (Canberra); *Style*— The Hon Sir Gerard Brennan, AC, KBE; 10 Kurundi Place, Hawker, ACT 2614, Australia (☎ 062 54 6794)

BRENT, Allan Arthur; s of Lawrence Arthur Brent (d 1975); *b* 10 August 1931; *Educ* Woodhouse Sch, City of London Coll; *m* 1, 1963 (m dis 1980), Sheila Moira, da of James Patrick Caird MacKinlay; 3 s, 1 da; m 2, 1983, Alberta Joy, da of Albert Coisant; *Career* md Grendon Tst Ltd 1969-71, chm Camco (Machinery) Ltd 1975-80, sr conslt Alpha Beta Consultants Ltd 1975-, pres Dania Securities Inc 1983-; FCIS (memb of cncl 1974-80), FCIArb, FTII (memb of cncl 1966-8l, pres 1969-70); *Recreations* tennis, sailing, bridge, travel; *Clubs* Athenaeum, City Livery, Balboa Bay (USA); *Style*— Allan Brent, Esq; c/o David Moate Esq, Moate Thorpe & Co, CA, 40 Curzon St, W1; 1221 West Coast Highway, Newport Beach, CA 92660, USA; 10 Old Burlington St, London W1

BRENT, Prof Leslie; s of Arthur Baruch, of Köslin, (d 1943/4) of Germany, and Charlotte *née* Rosenthal (d 1943/4); *b* 5 July 1925; *Educ* Bunce Ct Sch Kent, Birmingham Central Tech Coll, Univ of Birmingham (BSc), UCL (PhD); *m* 16 April 1955, Joanne Elisabeth, da of Oates Manley of Todmorden, Lancs; 1 s (Simon b 1956), 2 da (Susanna b 1958, Jennifer b 1963); *Career* serv UK, Italy and Germany 1943-47 (acting Capt); lectr in zoology UCL, 1954-62; Rockefeller res fell 1956-57, scientist Nat Inst for Med Res 1962-65, Prof zoology Southampton Univ 1965-69, prof immunology St Mary's Hosp Med Sch London 1969-; ed: Transplantation 1962-67, Immunology Letters 1983-; fndr chm Wessex Branch of Inst Biol 1966-68, memb of WHO expert advsy ctee on Immunology 1970-, fndr sec Br Transplantation Soc 1972-75 (pres 1976-78), chm: organising ctee of 9 Int Transplantation Congress 1982, fellowships cmmn Inst of Biol 1979-85, Univ of London jt advsy cmmn in Immunology 1987-, chm British Univ Vietnam Orphans Appeal Fund 1967-69, convenor res and action gp of the Soc Serv, Haringey Lab Pty 1970-79, tres Haringey Community Relations Cncl 1974-79 (chm 1979-80), fndr memb and vice chm of exec ctee of Haringey Cncl for Voluntary Serv 1974-79; fndr chm of Haringey SDP 1981-83; memb of SLD 1987; Vice-Chllr Prize 1951, Scientific Medal Zoological Soc of London 1964; memb: Br Soc for Immunology, Br Transplantation Soc (hon memb 1988), Hon MRCP 1986, FIBiol 1964; *Books* Progress in Immunology II (ed 1974), Proceedings of the 9 Int Congress of The Transplantation Soc (2 vols ed 1983), Organ Transplantation (ed 1989); *Recreations* formerly hockey (Brit Univ & Staffordshire); fell walking, cricket, music, novels, singing (Crouch End Festival Chorus); *Style*— Professor Leslie Brent; 8 Wood Vale, London, N10 (☎) 01 883 5904); Department of Immunology, St Mary's Hospital Medical School, London, W2, (☎ 01 723 1252)

BRENT, Lucy Elizabeth; da of Allan Henry David George Brent (d 1978), and Irene Dorothy, *née* Jameson; *b* 7 Jan 1947; *Educ* Oak Hall; *Career* dep chm Trimite Ltd; FBIM; *Recreations* skiing, bridge, golf, theatre, opera; *Clubs* Wentworth Golf; *Style*— Miss Lucy Brent; c/o Midland Bank, 28 High St, PO Box 41, Uxbridge, Middx

BRENT, Michael Hamilton; s of Allan Henry David George Brent, (d 1978) Irene Dorothy, *née* Jameson; *b* 18 Mar 1943; *Educ* Charterhouse; *m* 1973, Janet, da of Irvine McBeath; 1 s, 2 da; *Career* chm and md Trimite Ltd 1974-; FCA; *Recreations* bridge, chess, golf, sailing, skiing, tennis; *Clubs* Carlton, Wentworth GC; *Style*— Michael Brent, Esq; Trimite Ltd, Arundel Rd, Uxbridge, Middx UB8 2SD (☎ 0895 51234, telex 934444 TRIMIT G); c/o Midland Bank, 28 High St, PO Box 41, Uxbridge, Middx

BRENT, Michael Leon; QC (1983); *b* 8 June 1936; *Educ* Manchester GS, Manchester Univ (LLB); *m* 22 Aug 1965, Rosalind, *née* Keller; 2 da (Sasha b 1970, Ella b 1972); *Career* called to the Bar Gray's Inn 1961; practised: Northern circuit 1961-67 (circuit jr 1964), MO circuit 1967-; *Style*— Michael Brent, Esq, QC; 2 Dr Johnson's Bldgs, Temple, London EC4Y 7AY (☎ 01 353 5371, fax 01 353 1344)

BRENTFORD, 4 Viscount (UK 1929), of Newick, Sussex; Sir Crispin William Joynson-Hicks; 4 Bt of Holmbury (UK 1919), 2 Bt of Newick (UK 1956); s of 3 Viscount Brentford, DL (d 1983), and Phyllis, *née* Allfrey (d 1979); *b* 7 April 1933; *Educ* Eton, New Coll Oxford; *m* 1964, Gillian Evelyn, er da of late Gerald Edward Schluter, OBE, of Nairobi, Kenya; 1 s, 3 da (Hon Emma b 1966, Hon Rowena b 1967, Hon Amy b 1978); *Heir* s, Hon Paul William Joynson-Hicks b 1971; *Career* late Lt 9 Lancers; slr 1960; ptnr in legal firm of Joynson-Hicks 1961-; master Girdlers Co 1983-84; *Style*— The Rt Hon the Viscount Brentford; Newick Park, East Sussex BN8 4SB (☎ Newick 082 572 3633)

BRENTNALL, Dr (Timothy) David; s of Dr Sam Boyer Brentnall (d 1944), and Ellen Meredyth *née* Lowe (d 1973); *b* 10 June 1923; *Educ* Bryanston Sch, Manchester Univ; *m* 1, 1950, Gwyneth Joyce Trinder (decd); 1 s (William Timothy Boyer 1955), 1 da (Meredyth Anne Proby b 1953); m 2, 1977, Angela Patricia, da of Maj William Frank Adams, of Oakham; *Career* formerly Temp Maj RAMC, Br Troops Austria Cambridge FA (TA); memb Rutland CC 1957-73; British Legion, tstee Uppingham Sch 1970-76; Gentlemen of Leicestershire CC MRCS, LRCP; *Recreations* hunting, shooting, fishing, painting; *Clubs* MCC, Army and Navy; *Style*— Dr David Brentnall; Corner Cottage, Preston, nr Uppingham, Rutland, Leicestershire LE15 9NN; Manton 230, 23 Burley, nr Oakham, Oakham (☎ 2621)

BRENTON, Howard John; s of Donald Henry Brenton, and Rose Lilian, *née* Lewis; *b* 13 Dec 1942; *Educ* Chichester HS for Boys, St Catherine's Coll Cambridge (BA); *m* 31 Jan 1970, Jane Margaret, da of William Alfred Fry; 2 s (Samuel John b 23 Sept 1974, Harry William Donald b 6 Sept 1976); *Career* plays include: Christie in Love Portable Theatre 1969, Revenge Royal Court Theatre Upstairs 1969, Hitler Dances Traverse Theatre Workshop Edinburgh 1972, Measure for Measure (after Shakespeare) Northlott Theatre Exeter 1972, Magnificence Royal Court Theatre 1973, Brassneck (with David Hare) Nottingham Playhouse 1973, The Churchill Play Nottingham Playhouse 1974 and twice revived by the RSC in 1978 and 1988, Government Property Aarhus Theatre Denmark 1975, Weapons of Happiness The National Theatre 1976 (winner of the Evening Standard Best Play of the Year Award) Epsom Downs Jt Stock Theatre Co 1977, Sore Throats RSC 1979, The Romans in Britain Nat Theatre 1980, Thirteenth Night RSC 1981, The Genius Royal Court Theatre 1983, Bloody Poetry Folo Novo Theatre 1984 and revived by the Royal Court Theatre 1988, Pravda with David Hare The Nat Theatre 1985 (winner of the Evening Standard Best Play of the Year Award), Greenland Royal Court Theatre 1988; TV plays include: A Saliva Milkshake BBC 1975, The Paradise Run Thames 1976, Desert of Lies BBC 1984, the four part series Dead Head BBC 1986; Freedom City of Buffalo, NY State USA; *Recreations* painting; *Clubs* Crystal Palace Football; *Style*— Howard Brenton, Esq; c/o Margaret Ramsay Ltd, 14A Goodwin's Ct, St Martin's Lane, London WC2N 4LL

BRENTWOOD, Bishop of 1980; Rt Rev Thomas; s of Ernest William McMahon (d 1969), and Mary Elizabeth, *née* Corbett (d 1978); *b* 17 Jun 1936; *Educ* St Bede's Coll Manchester, St Sulpice Seminary Paris; *Career* asst priest: Colchester 1959-64, Westcliffe-on-Sea 1964-69; parish priest Stock 1969, chaplain Essex 1972-80 ; *Style*— The Rt Rev the Bishop of Brentwood; Bishop's House, Stock, Ingatestone, Essex CM4 9BU

BRESLAND, Richard Charles; s of Charles William Bresland (d 1941), and Frances Ellen, *née* Fisher (d 1968); *b* 7 April 1926; *Educ* Bristol GS, Wadham Coll Oxford (MA); *Career* staff dir National Coal Bd, dir Coal Trade Benevolent Assoc 1972; Freeman of the City of London 1986, Liveryman of the Worshipful Company of Fuellers 1986; FIPM; *Recreations* walking, music, reading; *Style*— Richard Bresland, Esq; 3 Cedar Falls, Bishop's Lydeard, Taunton, Somerset TA4 3HR (☎ 0823 433487)

BRETT, Hon Christopher Lionel Baliol; el s, and h of 4 Viscount Esher; *b* 23 Dec 1936; *Educ* Eton, Magdalen Coll Oxford; *m* 1, 1962 (m dis 1970), Camilla Charlotte, da of Sir (Horace) Anthony Claude Rumbold, 10 Bt, KCMG, CB; 1 s (Matthew b 1963), 2 da (Miranda b 1964, Rebecca b 1966); m 2, 1971, F Valerie, da of Maxwell Maurice Harrington; 2 s (Oliver b 1972, William b 1982), twin da (Susannah and Clare b 1973); *Style*— The Hon Christopher Brett; Watlington Park, Watlington, Oxon (☎ 049 161 2302)

BRETT, Hon Guy Anthony Baliol; s of 4 Viscount Esher; *b* 18 Oct 1942; *Educ* Eton; *Style*— The Hon Guy Brett; Watlington Park, Oxon (☎ 302)

BRETT, (Peter) Jeremy William Huggins; s of Col HW Huggins, DSO, MC, DL (d 1964), and Elizabeth, *née* Cadbury Butler (d 1959); *b* 3 Nov 1935; *Educ* Eton; *m* 1, 28 May 1958 (m dis 1962), Anna, da of Raymond Massey; 1 s (David b 1959); m 2 Joan Wilson (d 1985), 1 step s (Caleb), 1 step da (Rebekah); *Career* actor; stage and film: War and Peace (American film version) 1956, Hamlet Strand Theatre London 1961, The Kitchen Royal Ct Theatre London Broadway 1964, My Fair Lady (film version) 1964, A Month in the Country Cambridge Theatre 1965, As you like it NT 1967, Tartuffe NT 1967, Any Just Cause Adeline Green Theatre London 1967, Edward II NT 1968, Much Ado About Nothing NT 1968, Love's Labours Lost NT 1969, The Merchant of Venice NT 1970, Hedda Gabler NT 1970, A Voyage Round My Father Haymarket Theatre London 1971, Traveler Without Luggage Thorndicke Theatre London 1972, Design for Living Phoenix Theatre London 1973-74, The Way of the World Stratford Festival Theatre Canada 1976, A Midsummer Night's Dream Stratford Festival Theatre Canada 1976, Robert & Elizabeth England and Canada 1976-77, Dracula 1978-79, Seagull Island (film) 1980, The Crucifer of Blood Ahmanson Theatre 1981, Noel Goodspeed Opera House Connecticut 1981, The Tempest 1982, The Secret of Sherlock Holmes Wyndham Theatre; TV: The Typewriter 1962, The Three Muskateers 1967, The Incantation of Casanova 1967, An Ideal Husband 1969, A Portrait of Katherine Mansfield 1973, A Legacy 1974, Jennie 1974, The Picture of Dorian Gray 1976, Piccadilly Circus 1976-77, Rebecca 1979, Madame X 1981, Macbeth 1982, Number 10 1982, Sherlock Holmes 1983-88 ; *Recreations* archery; *Style*— Jeremy Brett, Esq; The Penthouse, 47 Clapham Common, London SW4(☎ 01 622 7745)

BRETT, Sir Lionel; s of Very Rev Henry Brett, sometime Dean of Belfast; *b* 19 August 1911; *Educ* Marlborough, Magdalen Coll Oxford; *Career* served WW II; barr Inner Temple 1937, joined Colonial Legal Serv Nigeria 1946, Justice Supreme Court Nigeria 1958-68; kt 1961; *Style*— Sir Lionel Brett; Lower Ground Floor, 12, Sydney Place, Bath BA2 6NR

BRETT, Hon Michael Jeremy Baliol; 2 s of 4 Viscount Esher, CBE; *b* 26 April 1939; *Educ* Eton, Architectural Assoc London; *m* 1971, Sarah Calloway; *Career* ARIBA; *Style*— The Hon Michael Brett; Shelbyville, Kentucky, USA

BRETT, Michael John Lee; s of John Brett and Margaret, *née* Lee; *b* 23 May 1939; *Educ* King's Coll Sch Wimbledon, Wadham Oxford; *Career* dir Throgmorton Publications and Financial Times Business Publishing Div; ed Investors Chronicle 1977-; *Style*— Michael Brett, Esq; 134 Offord Rd, N1 (☎ 01 609 2362)

BRETT, Hon Olivia Clare Teresa; o da of 4 Viscount Esher; *b* 29 Nov 1947; *Style*— The Hon Olivia Brett; Watlington Park, Oxon (☎ 302)

BRETT, Hon (Maurice) Sebastian Baliol; 4 s of 4 Viscount Esher; *b* 16 May 1944; *Educ* Eton, Trinity Oxford; *m* 1968 (m dis), Pauline, da of Lt-Cdr Paul Murray-Jones, RN (ret); *Style*— The Hon Maurice Brett; Cordwainers, Titchfield, Hants

BRETT, Hon Stephen Patrick Baliol; yst s of 4 Viscount Esher; *b* 26 August 1952; *Educ* Bryanston Sch; *Style*— The Hon Stephen Brett; Watlington Park, Oxon

BRETT, Hon Virginia Charlotte Anne; eldest da of 3 Viscount Esher, GBE (d 1963); *b* 18 June 1916; *Style*— The Hon Virginia Brett; Watlington Park, Oxon (☎ 302)

BRETT-JONES, Antony Tom (Tony); CBE (1979); s of Lt David Tom Jones, DCM (d 1969), of London, and Mary, *née* Brett Needham; *b* 4 Mar 1922; *Educ* Cranbrook Sch; *m* 30 Aug 1952, Ann, da of Sir Lionel Wray Fox, MC (d 1961); 1 s (Harry Anthony Lionel b 1964), 3 da (Lucy Katharine b 1955, Sarah Josephine b 1956, Jane Rosalind b 1959); *Career* WWII Flt Offr RAF Bomber (md 1942-46); chartered Quantity Surveyor, ptnr Dearle & Henderson 1957-87; RICS: memb cncl 1952-, memb div cncl 1955- (pres 1969-70), govr Coll of Estate Mgmnt 1964- (chm govrs 1980-85), chm educn ctee 1973-78; vice pres Cruising Assoc 1985-, ed Cruising Assoc Handbook 1982-; Freeman City of London 1977, memb Worshipful Co of Chartered Surveyors 1977; ARICS 1947, FRICS 1962, FCIArb, FRSA, FCIArb; *Books* 4 Aqua books (contrib 1960-); *Recreations* sailing; *Clubs* Reform; *Style*— Tony Brett-Jones, Esq, CBE; 5 Inverness Gardens, London W8 4RN (☎ 01 229 1950)

BRETTEN, George Rex; QC (1980); s of Horace Victor Bretten (d 1954), and Kathleen Edna Betty Bretten; *b* 21 Feb 1942; *Educ* King Edward VII Sch King's Lynn, Sidney Sussex Coll Cambridge (MA, LLB); *m* 1965, Maureen Gillian, *née* Crowhurst; 1 da; *Career* called to the Bar 1970; *Style*— Rex Bretten Esq, QC; Church Farm, Great Eversden, Cambs (☎ 0223 263538)

BRETTLE, Robert Harvey Linton; s of Robert Edward Brettle (d 1974), and Mabel, *née* Linton, of Willingdon, nr Eastbourne, Sussex; *b* 3 April 1935; *Educ* Highgate Sch London, Christ Church Oxford (MA); *m* 27 May 1964, Lindsay Mary, da of the late Sydney Howson; 3 s (Thomas b 1966, Oliver b 1969, Adrian b 1972); *Career* Nat Serv: cmmnd 1955 Middx Regt, Royal West Africa Frontier Force 3 Bn Nigeria Regt (later Queen's Own Nigeria Regt 1955-56, intelligence and recruitment offr Asst Adj); slr 1963, ptnr Peard Son and Webster of Croydon 1966 (sr ptnr 1983), sr ptnr Peard Webster Pringle and John 1986- (insolvency practitioner), memb London Legal Aid Area Appeals Ctee; pres Croydon and Dist Law Soc 1972-73, chm of govrs St Margaret's Sch for Spastics and Physically Handicapped Children 1972-74; memb: Law Soc of England and Wales 1963-; *Recreations* bridge, gardening and travel; *Clubs* RAC; *Style*— Robert Brettle, Esq; 42 Brownlow Rd, Croydon, Surrey CRO 5JT (☎ 01 688 3307); Peard Webster Pringle and John, Suffolk House, College Rd, Croydon CR9 1DR (☎ 01 680 5262, fax 01 686 4560, telex 9180263 PWPJ G)

BREW, Richard Maddock; CBE (1981); s of late Leslie Maddock Brew, of Suffolk, and Phyllis Evelyn, *née* Huntsman (d 1949); *b* 13 Dec 1930; *Educ* Rugby, Magdalene Coll Cambridge (BA); *m* 1953, Judith Anne, da of Dr Percy Ellis Thompson Hancock; 2 s (Antony b 1957, Timothy b 1961), 2 da (Charlotte b 1955, Sophie b 1967); *Career* barr Inner Temple 1955; dep chm Brew Bros Ltd 1955-72, chm Monks Dormitory Ltd 1979-, memb NE Thames RHA 1982-, chm Budget Boilers Ltd 1984-, regnl dir (Eastern counties) Lloyds Bank plc 1988-; memb: Royal Borough of Kensington cncl 1959-65, Royal Borough of Kensington and Chelsea Cncl 1964-70, GLC 1968-86: alderman 1968-73, vice chm strategic planning ctee 1969-71, memb for Chingford 1973-86, dep ldr of Cncl and ldr policy and resources ctee 1977-81, dep ldr Cons Pty and opposition spokesman on finance 1974-77 and 1981-82, ldr of the opposition 1982-83; memb Nat Theatre Bd 1982-86; High Sheriff Greater London 1988-89; *Recreations* The Pony Club, gardening; *Clubs* Carlton, MCC; *Style*— Richard Brew, Esq, CBE; The Abbey, Coggeshall, Essex CO6 1RD (☎ 0376 61246)

BREW, William Raymond Thomas; s of William Brew; *b* 27 Mar 1915; *Educ* Palmers Coll Essex; *m* 1940, Peggy, da of William Farmer; 1 s; *Career* serv WWII Actg Lt-Col RA 14 Army S Africa and Burma; md Moody Gp 1975-80 (co dir 1980-), conslt to oil industry; *Recreations* philately, racing; *Clubs* IOD, Oil Indust; *Style*— William Brew, Esq; 4 Coombe Bank, Kingston-upon-Thames, Surrey (☎ 01 942 3178); office: Ewbank Preece Ltd., 5th Floor, Greencoat House, Francis Street, London SW1P 1DH (☎ 01 828 2192).

BREWER, David; s of William Watson Brewer (d 1968), and Eileen, *née* Hall; *b* 24 July 1946; *Educ* Briggs GS, Emmanuel Coll Cambridge (BA); *m* 26 May 1973, Elizabeth Margaret, da of John William Ferguson (d 1986); 1 da (Jane b 1975); *Career* Br Coal Corpn: area chief accountant South Midlands 1979-85, chief accountant 1985-87, hd of fin servs 1987-; ACMA 1978; *Style*— David Brewer, Esq; Westwinds, 2 Church Hill, Aspley Guise, Milton Keynes, Buck MK17 8HW (☎ 0908 585 700); British Coal Corporation, Hobart House, Grosvenor Place, London SW1X 7AE (☎ 01 235 2020/ 0302 66 111, fax 0302 34682, 0302 36144, telex 882161 HOB)

BREWER, David John; s of Raymond Bennett (d 1982), of Padstow, Cornwall, and Patricia Mary, *née* Key; *b* 29 Jan 1949; *Educ* Bodmin Co GS, Bath Univ (BSc); *m* 31 Mar 1973, Kate, da of Mitchell Scatterty Milne; 1 da (Rebecca b 1977); *Career* CA; Deloitte Haskins and Sells: London 1970-78, Dubai UAE 1978-86, ptnr 1980-, ptnr in charge Arabian Gulf Practice 1982-, sr ptnr (CI Firm) 1986-; tres: Assoc Jersey Charities, Jersey Amateur Swimming Assoc; memb Inst Dir (Jersey branch), FCA; *Recreations* bridge, sailing, supporting amateur swimming; *Clubs* United, St Helier; *Style*— David Brewer, Esq; Clos du Coin, La Haule, St Brelade, Jersey (☎ 0534 46432); Deloitte Haskins and Sells, Whiteley Chambers, 41 Don St, St Helier, Jersey (☎ 0534 75151, fax 0534 24321, telex 4192035)

BREWER, Dr Derek Stanley; s of Stanley Leonard Brewer, and Winifred Helen Forbes; *b* 13 July 1923; *Educ* The Crypt GS, Magdalen Coll Oxford; *m* 1951, Lucie Elisabeth Hoole; 3 s, 2 da; *Career* academic publisher; master of Emmanuel Coll Cambridge 1977-, prof of english 1983-; FSA; *Style*— Dr Derek Brewer; The Master's Lodge, Emmanuel College, Cambridge (☎ (0223) 350484)

BREWER, Rear Adm George Maxted Kenneth; CB (1981); s of Capt George Maxted Brewer (d 1954), of Dover Kent, and Cecilia Victoria Jessie (d 1987), *née* Clark; paternal gf served in HMS Basilisk under the then Capt Moresby during his discoveries in New Guinea in 1873, hence Brewer Island shown on Admiralty Chart 1873. For details of the voyage and discoveries *see* Two Admirals published in London by Murray 1909; *b* 4 Mar 1930; *Educ* The Nautical Coll Pangbourne; *m* 1989, Betty Mary, o da of Cdr Claude Harold Welton, RN; *Career* cmd: HMS Carysfort (Home, Mediterranean and Far East) 1964-65, HMS Agincourt (Home) 1967, HMS Grenville (Home, Mediterranean and Far East) 1967-69, HMS Juno and Capt 4 Frigate Sqdn (Home and Mediterranean) 1973-74; course student at Roy Coll of Def Studies 1975; cmd: HMS Tiger (Far East deployment) and Flag Capt to the Flag Offr Second Flotilla 1978, appointed ADC to HM The Queen 1980, HMS Bulwark (NATO area) 1978-80, flag offr Medway and Port Admiral Chatham 1980-82; *Recreations* watercolour painting; *Style*— Rear Adm George Brewer, CB; 14 St Helens Ct, St Helens Parade, Southsea, Hants PO4 0RR; c/o Nat Westminster Bank, Portchester, Fareham, Hants

BREWIN, Hon Mrs Anne Sheridan; *née* Walston; resumed use of former married name, Brewin; da of Baron Walston (Life Peer); *b* 4 Nov 1937; *m* 1, 6 Aug 1960 (m dis 1972), Charles Edward Brewin, s of late Ma Clement Noel Brewin, MC, RA; 1 s, 4 da; m 2, 1978 (m dis 1982), Edward McCririe-Hallman; *Style*— The Hon Mrs Brewin; Clare Cottage, 30 Northfield End, Henley on Thames, Oxon RG9 2JL (☎ (0491) 572910)

BREWIN, Daniel Robert (Dan); s of John Stuart Brewin (d 1968), of Sheffield, and Elsie Mary Brewin, *née* Timm; *b* 22 August 1946; *Educ* King Edward VII Sch Sheffield, Univ of Salford (BSc), Cranfield Sch of Mgmnt (MBA); *m* 1974, Sylvia Mary Frances, da of Roland Jones Sale Cheshire; 2 s (John b 1976, Timothy b 1980), 1 da (Anna b 1978); *Career* British Airways various 1964-81; dir of operations Manchester Airport 1981-84, gen mangr UK sales Br Caledonian 1984-87, sr gen mangr commerical British Caledonian 1987; *Recreations* tennis, cinema; *Style*— Daniel Brewin, Esq; 5 Old Martyrs, Crawley, W Sussex (☎ 0293 511980); British Caledonian, Caledonian House, Crawley (☎ 0293 583694)

BREWIS, Lady Anne Beatrice Mary; *née* Palmer; da of 3 Earl of Selborne, CH, PC (d 1971); *b* 26 Mar 1911; *Educ* Queen's Coll Harley St, Somerville Coll Oxford; *m* 3 July 1935, Rev John Salusbury Brewis (d 1972), s of George Robert Brewis, of Oxford; 2 s, 2 da; *Recreations* nature conservation, botany; *Style*— Lady Anne Brewis; Benham's House, Benham's Lane, Greatham, Hants GU33 6BE (☎ Blackmoor 348)

BREWIS, (Henry) John; s of Lt-Col Francis Bertie Brewis, of Norton Grove, Malton, Yorks; *b* 8 April 1920; *Educ* Eton, New Coll Oxford; *m* 1949, Faith Agnes Devorguilla, da of Sir Edward MacTaggart-Stewart, 2 and last Bt (d 1948); 3 s, 1 da; *Career* barrister 1946; MP (C) Galloway 1959-74, PPS to Lord Advocate 1960-61, MEP nominee 1973-75; regnl chm Scottish Landowners' Fedn 1978-80, chm Scottish Woodland Owners 1980-83; md Ardwell Estates Stranraer; dir Border TV Ltd 1977-; DL Wigtownshire 1966-81, HM Lord-Lieut (Wigtown) 1981-; *Recreations* shooting, golf; *Clubs* Caledonian, New (Edinburgh); *Style*— John Brewis, Esq; Ardwell House, Stranraer (☎ Ardwell (077 686) 227)

BREWIS, Pearl Paulina; *née* Beaumont-Thomas; da of Col Lionel Beaumont-Thomas, MC (d 1942), of Great Brampton House, Madley, Herefordshire, and Pauline Grace, *née* Marriott (d 1954); *b* 21 June 1921; *Educ* Downe House Sch nr Newbury Berks; *m* 21, 17 Aug 1940, Capt Peter Robert Sandham Bankes, MC (d 1943), s of Rev Conrad Douglas Richard Oakley Bankes (d 1940), of Morningthorpe, Long Stratton, Norfolk; 1 s (Peter Bankes b 14 July 1944); m 2, 9 Aug 1947 (m dis 1955), Richard Henry Ridgway, s of Henry Ridgway, of Rossmore, Mallow, Co Cork, Republic of Ireland; m 3, 13 Oct 1956 (m dis 1960), Lt-Col Charles Richard Wynn Brewis, DSO, MC, s of Capt Charles Richard Wynn Brewis, CBE, RN (d 1953), of Tuffs Hard, Bosham, nr Chichester; 1 s (Samuel Charles b 19 Nov 1957), 1 da (Susan Pauline b 30 Aug 1959); *Career* cmmnd 2 Lt Womens Auxiliary Serv Burma, promoted 1 Lt 1943 (despatches 1945); farmer 1958-88; memb Lloyds 1978-; alternately hon sec and chm New Forest and Dist Cancer Relief Macmillan Fund 1973-; memb PC and New Forest Consultative Panel 1979-83; *Recreations* equestrian, sailing, painting, sculpture, gardening, music; *Clubs* Royal Lymington YC; *Style*— Mrs Pearl P Brewis; Arnewood Manor, Arnewood Bridge Rd, Sway, nr Lymington, Hampshire SO41 6ER (☎ 0590 682 214)

BREWSTER, David Edward; s of Clement James Brewster (d 1959), of Essex, and Ruth Amelia Briggs, *née* Carver (d 1959); *b* 24 Feb 1918; *Educ* Highgate Sch; *m* 23 May 1942, Nancy, da of Arthur Thomas Winter (d 1953), of Enfield, Middx; 4 s (Richard b 1946, James b 1948, John b 1952, Paul b 1958); *Career* cmmnd 136 Field Regt RA, Major, served Far East; CA, dir various cos; pres: Old Cholmeleian Soc 1978-79, Enfield Lawn Tennis Club; FCA; *Recreations* tennis; *Clubs* HAC, FICA; *Style*— David E Brewster, Esq; Edge House, Kentish Lane, Hatfield, Herts AL9 6NH (☎ 0707 54703); Pridie Brewster, Carolyn House, 29/31 Greville Street, London EC1N 8RB (☎ 01 831 8821, telex 296326, fax 01 404 3069)

BREWSTER, David John; s of Dr Leslie George Brewster (d 1974), and Evangeline, *née* Creed (d 1976); *b* 16 June 1936; *Educ* Whitgift Sch, St John's Coll Cambridge (MA); *m* 9 May 1964, Christine, *née* Booth; 1 s (Jonathan b 27 March 1967), 3 da (Sarah b 6 March 1965, Louise b 10 Jan 1969, Emma b 22 Dec 1971); *Career* called to the Bar Grays Inn 1961, practising barrister in England 1961-63, ptnr Appleby Spurling and Kempe (barristers and attorneys) Bermuda 1964-74, dir Tyndall Gp 1974-86, sec and dir legal services Investmt Mgmnt Regulatory Orgn 1986-; chm St Peters Hospice Bristol 1984-88; *Style*— David Brewster, Esq; Investmt Mgmnt Regulatory Orgn Ltd, Centre Point, 103 New Oxford St, London WC1A 1PT

BREWSTER, Richard David; s of David Edward Brewster; *b* 5 Jan 1946; *Educ* Highgate; *m* Susan Ann; 2 s (Edward, William), 2 da (Emily, Rachel); *Career* CA; fin dir Giltspur plc to 1983, chief exec David S Smith (Hldgs) plc 1983-; FCA 1968; FInstD; *Recreations* gardening, sailing, tennis; *Clubs* Island Cruising, Richmond Cricket and Tennis, Institute of Directors; *Style*— Richard Brewster, Esq; c/o David S Smith (Holdings) plc; 16 Great Pater St, London SW1 (☎ 01 222 8855)

BREYER, Hon Mrs; Joanna Freda; da of 1 Viscount Blakenham, OBE, PC, and Hon Beryl Nancy Pearson, da of 2 Viscount Cowdray; *b* 27 July 1942; *m* 1967, Judge Stephen Breyer (prof Harvard Law Sch 1967-), of San Francisco, California, USA; 1 s (Michael b 1974), 2 da (Chloe b 1969, Nell b 1971); *Style*— The Hon Mrs Breyer; 12 Dunstable Rd, Cambridge, Mass, USA

BRIANCE, John Albert; CMG (1960); s of late Albert Percival and Louise Florence Briance; *b* 19 Oct 1915; *Educ* King Edward VII Sch Lytham, London Univ; *m* 1950, Prunella Mary, da of Col Eric Haldane Chapman; 1 s, 1 da; *Career* dep supt Colonial Police Palestine 1936-48; Foreign Service 1950-70; *Recreations* tennis, walking, reading; *Clubs* Naval & Military, Hurlingham; *Style*— John Briance, Esq, CMG; 14 Pitt St, London W8 (☎ 01 937 4140)

BRIANCE, Richard Henry; s of John Albert Briance, CMG, and Prunella Mary, *née* Chapman; *b* 23 August 1953; *Educ* Eton, Jesus Coll Cambridge (BA); *m* 13 Oct 1979, Lucille Hardin; 1 s (Henry b 1984), 2 da (Zoe b 1982, Clementine b 1987); *Career* merchant banker; exec dir: Credit Suisse First Boston Ltd; *Clubs* Hawks, Hurlingham, RA; *Style*— Richard Briance, Esq; The Old House, Holland Street, London W8 4NY (☎ 01 937 2113); Credit Suisse First Boston, 2A Great Titchfield Street, London W1

BRIANT, Bernard Christian; CVO (1977), MBE (1945); s of Bernard Briant, of London (d 1977), and Cecily, *née* Christian (d 1971); *b* 11 April 1917; *Educ* Stowe, Oxford Univ (MA); *m* 22 Oct 1942, Margaret Emslie, da of Arthur Strong Rawle, of Walton Heath (d 1964); 1 s (Richard b 1952), 2 da (Sarah b 1947, Elizabeth b 1949); *Career* WWII 1940-45 Maj Intelligence Corps (despatches) Tunisia, Italy, Austria; conslt Daniel Smith Chartered Surveyors 1952- (sr ptnr 1976-82); land steward Manor of Kennington of the Duchy of Cornwall 1963-76; agent All Souls Coll Oxford 1966-79, dir Church of Eng Building Soc 1953-87, Anglia Building Soc 1983-87, Nationwide Anglia Building Soc 1987-; memb various RICS ctee 1948-70, RICS cncl 1962-70; Clerk Co of Chartered Surveyors 1980-85, memb Ctee Mgmnt Lambeth Southwark Housing Soc 1971-; *Recreations* golf, reading, walking; *Clubs* United Oxford and Cambridge, Aldeburgh Golf, Rye Golf; *Style*— Bernard C Briant, Esq; c/o 32 St James's St SW1A HT

BRIARS, Colin Hubert; s of Hubert Alfred Briars (d 1958); *b* 8 July 1926; *Educ* Christ's Hosp; *m* 2, 1975, Susan, da of James Douglas Frail, CBE; 1 s, 1 da; *Career* conslt Pirbic Orgn Ltd; dir: Brush Switchgear Ltd 1960-70, Allenwest Ltd 1970-79, Westinghouse Electric MK Ltd 1979-83, Ottermill Ltd; chm Control and Automation Manufacturers Assoc; CEng; *Recreations* squash, tennis, skiing; *Clubs* RAC; *Style*— Colin Briars Esq; Shannon House, Kings Rd, Sunninghill, Berks (☎ Ascot (0990) 22448)

BRIAULT, Dr Eric William Henry; CBE (1976); s of Henry George Briault (d 1932), of Brighton, Sussex, and Beatrice Mary Emmaline, *née* Day (d 1961); *b* 24 Dec 1911; *Educ* Brighton Hove and Sussex GS, Peterhouse Cambridge (MA); Univ of London (PhD); *m* 3 Aug 1935, (Alice) Marie, da of Arthur Ernest Knight (d 1948), of Brighton; 2 s (Timothy b 1938, Stephen b 1952) 1 da (Anthea b 1943); *Career* sch teacher 1933-47, inspr of schs London CC 1948-56, dep educn offr London CC 1956-71, the educn offr ILEA 1971-76, visiting prof Univ of Sussex 1977-80 and 1984-85; chm of govrs: Storrington First Sch, Rydon Community Sch; Freeman City of London, Liveryman Worshipful Co of Goldsmiths; Hon D Litt Univ of Sussex 1975; FRGS (hon sec 1953-63); *Books* Introduction to Advanced Geography (jtly 1957), Geography in and out of School (jtly second edn 1967), Falling Rolls in Secondary Schools (jtly 1980); *Recreations* theatre, ballet, travel; *Clubs* Athenaeum; *Style*— Dr Eric Briault, CBE; Woodedge, Hampers Lane, Storrington, W Sussex, (☎ 090 66 3919)

BRICE, Edward St John; s of W Brice, OBE, TD, DL, of Highover Hoo, Rochester; *b* 15 Feb 1936; *Educ* Tonbridge, Clare Coll Cambridge; *m* 1960, Elizabeth, da of G Grieve; 1 s, 1 da; *Career* farmer; Lloyd's underwriter; memb Kent CC 1977; High Sheriff Kent 1980-81; chm Kent Co Agric Soc 1984-; Freeman Worshipful Co of Skinners 1985; *Recreations* golf, tennis; *Clubs* Royal and Ancient, Royal St George's Golf, MCC; *Style*— Edward Brice, Esq; Hoo Lodge, Hoo, Rochester, Kent

BRICE, Geoffrey James Barrington Groves; QC (1979); s of Lt Cdr John Edgar Leonard Brice, MBE (d 1971), and Winifried Ivy, *née* Field; *b* 21 April 1938; *Educ* Magdalen Coll Sch Brackley, UCL; *m* 1963, Ann Nuala, da of William Connor (d 1958); 1 s (Paul); *Career* barr Middle Temple 1960, arbitrator Lloyd's 1978-, cmmr wrecks 1979-, rec of Crown Ct 1980-, master of the Bench 1986; chm London Common Law and Commercial Bar Assoc 1988-, memb Gen Cncl of the Bar 1988-; *Books* Maritime Law of Salvage (1983); *Recreations* listening to music; *Clubs* Athenaeum; *Style*— Geoffrey Brice, Esq, QC; 15 Gayfere St, Smith Square, London SW1P 3HP (☎ 01 799 3807); Queen Elizabeth Building, Temple, London EC4Y 9BS (☎ 01 353 9153, telex 262762 INREMG)

BRICE, (Ann) Nuala; *née* Connor; da of William Connor (d 1957), of Manchester, and Rosaleen Gertrude, *née* Gilmartin; *b* 22 Dec 1937; *Educ* Loreto Convent Manchester, UCL (LLB, LLM, PhD); *m* 1 June 1963, Geoffrey James Barrington Groves, s of Lt Cdr John Edgar Leonard Brice, MBE; 1 s (Paul Francis b 17 March 1964); *Career* admitted slr 1963; asst sec-gen The Law Society 1987- (asst slr 1963, asst sec 1964, sr asst sec 1973, deptl sec 1982); Freeman City of London, Liveryman City of London Slrs Co; memb Law Soc 1963; *Recreations* reading, music, gardening; *Style*— Mrs Muala Brice; Yew Tree House, Spring Coppice, Lane End, Bucks HP14 3NU (☎ 0494 881810); 15 Gayfere Street, Smith Square, Westminster SW1P 3HP (☎ 01 794 3807);

The Law Society, 113 Chancery Lane, London WC2A 1PL (☎ 01 242 1222)

BRICKWOOD, Sir Basil Greame; 3 Bt (UK 1927); s of Sir John Brickwood, 1 Bt; suc half bro, Sir Rupert Brickwood, 2 Bt, 1974; *b* 21 May 1923; *Educ* King Edward's GS Stratford, Clifton; *m* 1, 1947, Betty Cooper; m 2, 1956, Shirley Anne, da of Richard Wallace Brown; 2 da; *Heir* none; *Clubs* RAF; *Style—* Sir Basil Brickwood, Bt; c/o RAF Club, 128 Piccadilly, London W1

BRICKWOOD, Richard Ian; s of Basil Arthur Brickwood (d 1979), and Hilary Joan; *b* 22 Dec 1947; *Educ* Wesley Coll Dublin, Hele's GS Exeter Devon; *m* 6 March 1971, Susan Vanessa Mary, da of Donald Hugh Galpin (d 1971); 1 s (Stephen James b 1979), 1 da (Sarah Louise b 1977); *Career* Lloyds broker, memb Lloyds 1986; dir: C.T. Bowring (Insur) Ltd 1985, Bowring Non-Marine Insur Brokers Ltd 1983; *Recreations* sailing, canoeing, fishing; *Clubs* Lloyds Yacht, British Level Rating Assoc, Junior Offshore Group; *Style—* Richard I Brickwood, Esq; Swan House, Widford, nr Ware, Herts SG12 8SJ (☎ (027 984) 2425; 01 283 3100)

BRIDEN, Professor James Christopher; s of Henry Charles Timberblake Briden, and Gladys Elizabeth Jefkins, of High Wycombe, *qv*; *b* 30 Dec 1938; *Educ* Royal GS High Wycombe, St Catherine's Coll Oxford (MA), Australian Nat Univ Canberra (PhD); *m* 20 July 1968, Caroline, da of Kenneth Gillmore (d 1988); 1 s (Benjamin b 1977), 1 da (Hannah b 1974); *Career* res fell Univs of: Rhodesia 1965-66, Oxford 1966-67, Birmingham 1967-68; hon prof Univ of Leeds 1986- (prof of geophysics 1975-86, reader 1973-75, lectr 1968-73); Canadian Cwlth fell and visiting prof Univ of W Ontario 1977-80, dir of earth sciences NERC 1986-; memb: governing cncl Int Seismological Centre 1979-83, NERC 1980-86, RAS cncl 1978-79, Cncl Euro Geophysical Soc 1976-84; awarded Murchison Medal of Geological Soc 1984; FGS 1961 FRAS 1963; *Books* joint author of 2 books on past position of the continents and contributor of over 70 geological and geophysical papers to learned journals; *Style—* Prof James Briden; Natural Environment Research Council, Polaris House, North Star Avenue, Swindon, Wilts, SN2 1EU (fax 0793 411 501, telex 444 293 ENVRE G)

BRIDGE, Very Rev Antony Cyprian (Tony); s of Cyprian Dunscomb Charles Bridge (Cdr RN, d 1952), and Gladys, *née* Steel (d 1969); *b* 5 Sept 1914; *Educ* Marlborough, Royal Acad Sch of Art; *m* 10 May 1937, Brenda Lois, da of Dr Raymond Streatfeild; 1 s (Cyprian b 1955), 2 da (Victoria b 1944, Charlotte b 1946); *Career* served WWII, demob Maj 1945; artist/painter; ordained: dean 1955, priest 1956; curate Hythe Kent 1955-58, vicar Christ Church Lancaster Gate London 1958-68, dean of Guildford 1968-86, dean emeritus 1986-; FSA 1980; *Books* Images of God (1960), Theodora: Portrait in a Byzantine Landscape (1978), The Crusades (1980), Suleiman the Magnificent (1983), One Man's Advent (1985), Richard the Lionheart (1989); *Recreations* bird watching; *Style—* The Very Rev Tony Bridge; 34 London Rd, Deal, Kent CT14 9TE (☎ 0304 366792)

BRIDGE, Christopher Charles Cyprian; ERD, DL (E Sussex 1983); s of Brig Charles Edward Dunscombe Bridge, CMG, DSO, MC (d 1961), of Hale House, De Vere Gardens, Kensington, and Georgena Canning, *née* Hall; gs of Brig-Gen sir Charles Henry Bridge, KCMG, CB; *b* 23 Oct 1918; *Educ* Eton, Trinity Coll Cambridge; *m* 1953, Hon Dinah, yr da of 1 and last Baron Brand, CMG (d 1963, s of 2 Visc Hampden), of Eydon Hall, Daventry, and former w of Lyttelton Fox; 1 s, 1 da (and 1 step s, 1 step da); *Career* Maj Coldstream Gds 1939-45; ptnr Akroyd & Smithers 1953-66; md Seccombe Marshall & Campion 1967-79, dir Hambros Investmnt Tst 1979-; high sheriff E Sussex 1979-80; *Recreations* gardening, racing, reading; *Clubs* Buck's, Beefsteak; *Style—* Christopher Bridge Esq, ERD, DL,; 18 The Street, Firle, Lewes, E Sussex (☎ 079 159 507. 74 Melton Court, Old Brompton Rd, London SW7 3JH (☎ 01 581 4166)

BRIDGE, Hon Mrs (Dinah); yr da of 1 and last Baron Brand, CMG (d 1963); *b* 1920; *m* 1, 1943 (m dis 1950), Lyttleton Fox; 1 s, 1 da; m 2, 1953, Christopher Charles Cyprian Bridge, *qv*; 1 s, 1 da; *Style—* The Hon Mrs Bridge; 18 The Street, Firle, Sussex (☎ 079 159 507); 74 Melton Court, Old Brompton Rd, London SW7 3JH (☎ 01581 4166)

BRIDGE, (Walter) John Blencowe; DL; s of Walter Bridge (d 1969), of Bury St Edmunds, Suffolk; *b* 8 Mar 1920; *Educ* Repton; *m* 1948, Susan Mary, da of Capt Robert Basil Wyndham Rushbrooke (d 1972), of Bury St Edmunds, Suffolk; 2 s, 1 da; *Career* chm Greene King and Sons (brewers) 1979-; *Style—* John Bridge, Esq, DL; Greene King and Sons plc, Westgate Brewery, Bury St Edmunds, Suffolk (☎ 0284 763222)

BRIDGE, Nicholas Anthony; s of Herbert Charles Bridge, of Essex, and Josephine Maisie Evelyn, *née* Mackee (d 1974); *b* 16 Jan 1948; *Educ* Southend and Southchurch Hall HS; *m* 2 Sept 1972, Valerie Christine, da of Joseph James Smith, of Leigh-on-Sea, Essex; 1 s (Andrew b 1975), 1 da (Lianne b 1977); *Career* dir: Alexander Howden Reinsur Brokers Ltd 1985; *Recreations* angling; *Style—* Nicholas Bridge, Esq; 32 Glebelands, Benfleet, Essex SS7 4LT (☎ (0268) 751944); 8 Devonshire Square, London EC2M 4PL (telex: 882171, fax: 01 626 3586)

BRIDGE OF HARWICH, Baron (Life Peer UK 1980); Nigel Cyprian Bridge; PC (1975); s of Cdr Cyprian Dunscombe Charles Bridge, RN (d 1938); bro of Very Rev Antony Cyprian Bridge, Dean of Guildford; *b* 26 Feb 1917; *Educ* Marlborough; *m* 1944, Margaret, da of Leonard Heseltine Swinbank, of Weybridge, Surrey; 1 s, 2 da; *Career* chm Permanent Security Cmmn 1982-85; barr 1947-68, High Court judge 1968-75, Ld Justice of Appeal 1975-80, Ld of Appeal in Ordinary 1980-; kt 1968; *Style—* The Rt Hon Lord Bridge of Harwich, PC; c/o House of Lords, London SW1

BRIDGEHOUSE, Edward; s of Joseph Bridgehouse (d 1965); *b* 19 May 1939; *Educ* Audenshaw GS; *m* 1, 1962, Brenda Elizabeth (d 1979); 1 s, 1 da; m 2, 1981, Muriel Winifred;; *Career* managing ptnr Boardman Woolrich 1964-, co sec United Engrg Industries plc 1970-82, dir and co sec Br Thornton Industries Ltd 1983; CA; *Recreations* golf; *Style—* Edward Bridgehouse, Esq; Trefin, Hilda Road, Gee Cross, Hyde, Cheshire (☎ 061 368 3649)

BRIDGEMAN, Hon Alexander Michael Orlando; s and h of Viscount Newport; *b* 6 Sept 1980; *Style—* Hon Alexander Bridgeman

BRIDGEMAN, Hon Charles Gerald Orlando; 2 s of 6 Earl of Bradford (d 1981), and Mary Willoughby, *née* Montgomery; *b* 25 June 1954; *Educ* Harrow, Warwick Univ (BA); *m* 1982, Nicola Marie-Thérèse, only da of Brian Denyer Sales, of Congleton; 2 s (James b 1978, Robert b 1983); *Career* landowner; *Style—* The Hon Charles Bridgeman; Albion Hayes Farm, Bomere Heath, Shrewsbury, Shropshire (☎ 0939 290246)

BRIDGEMAN, Hon Mrs Henry; Joan; da of late Hon Bernard Constable-Maxwell; *m* 1930, Col Hon Henry George Orlando Bridgeman, DSO, MC (d 1972); 2 s, 2 da; *Style—* The Hon Mrs Henry Bridgeman; 50 Lennox Gdns, London SW1

BRIDGEMAN, John Stuart; s of James Alfred George Bridgeman (d 1961), of Whitchurch, Cardiff, and Edith Celia, *née* Watkins; *b* 5 Oct 1944; *Educ* Whitchurch Sch Cardiff, Univ Coll Swansea (BSc); *m* 1967, Lindy Jane, da of Sidney Wesley Fillmore, of Gidea Park; 3 da (Victoria b 1972, Philippa b 1974, Annabel b 1980); *Career* cmmnd TA 1978, Major 1981-84 REME (V); md Extrusion Div Br Alcan Aluminium 1982-; chm: Alcan Building Extrusions Ltd, Alcan Extrusions Ltd, Alcan Systems Ltd, Almetex Ltd, Br Alcan Extrusions Ltd, Br Aluminium Extrusions Ltd, Minalex Ltd; tstee Magnesium Indust Cncl 1977-; memb BA Consumer Cncl 1978-; cncl memb Aluminium Extruders Assoc 1982-; pres Banbury Business and Ind Gp 1984-; govr North Oxon Technical Coll 1985-; memb TAVRA for Eastern Wessex 1985-; FBIM; *Recreations* Queen's Own Yeomanry, natural history, gardening, swimming, music; *Clubs* Glamorgan County Cricket; *Style—* John Bridgeman, Esq; Eastgate House, Hornton, Banbury, Oxon OX15 6BT (☎ 0295 87 282); Br Alcan Aluminium Ltd, Extrusion Division, Southam Rd, Banbury, Oxon OX16 7SN (☎ 0295 4444, telex 83645)

BRIDGEMAN, (John) Michael; CB (1988); s of John Wilfred Bridgeman, CBE, formerly of Loughborough, Leics, and Mary Jane, *née* Wallace (d 1961); *b* 26 April 1931; *Educ* Marlborough, Trinity Coll Cambridge (BA); *m* 13 Sept 1958, June, da of Gordon Forbes (d 1976); 1 s (Francis b 1968), 4 da (Clare (Mrs Sinha) b 1959, Teresa b 1961, Imogen b 1966, Cressida b 1969); *Career* Nat Serv RA 1949-51, 2 Lt 1950-51; 579 LAA Regt RA TA 1951-54, HQ 148 Inf Bde TA 1955-65, Maj 1962-65; asst princ BOT 1954-56; HM Treasy 1956-81: under sec home fin gp (fin inst and monetary policy) 1975-80, under sec gen expenditure gp 1980-81; chief registrar Friendly Societies 1982-, Building Societies Cmmn: first cmmr and chm 1986-; Tunbridge Wells Deanery Synod: memb 1970-76, lay chm 1973-76; *Clubs* Reform; *Style—* Michael Bridgeman, Esq, CB; Building Societies Commission, 15 Great Marlborough St, London W1V 2AX (☎ 01 437 9992)

BRIDGEMAN, 3 Viscount (UK 1929); Robin John Orlando Bridgeman; s of Brigadier Hon Geoffrey John Orlando Bridgeman, MC (d 1974, 2 s of 1 Viscount Bridgeman, sometime Home Sec and First Ld of the Admlty and gs of 2 Earl of Bradford), and Mary Meriel Gertrude (d 1974), da of Rt Hon Sir George Talbot, a High Court Judge and gs of John Chetwynd Talbot, QC (4 s of 2 Earl Talbot); suc his uncle, 2 Viscount 1982; *b* 5 Dec 1930; *Educ* Eton; *m* 10 Dec 1966, (Victoria) Harriet Lucy; 3 da of Ralph Meredyth Turton, TD, of Kildale Hall, Whitby, by his w Mary Blanche, da of Brig-Gen Bryan Chetwynd Stapylton, CBE; 4 s (Hon William, Hon Luke Robinson Orlando b 1 May 1971, Hon Esmond Francis Ralph Orlando b 3 Oct 1974, Hon Orlando Henry Geoffrey b 11 April 1983); *Heir* s, Hon William Orlando Caspar b 15 Aug 1968; *Career* 2 Lt Rifle Bde 1950-51; CA 1958; ptnr Henderson Crosthwaite & Co Stockbrokers; *Recreations* gardening, shooting, music; *Clubs* MCC, Beefsteak; *Style—* The Rt Hon Viscount Bridgeman; 19 Chepstow Rd, London W2 5BP (☎ 01 229 7420)

BRIDGER, Rev Canon Gordon Frederick; s of Dr John Dell Bridger (d 1955), and Hilda, *née* Piddington (d 1968); *b* 5 Feb 1932; *Educ* Christ's Hosp Horsham, Selwyn Coll Cambridge (BA, MA), Ridley Hall Cambridge; *m* 29 Sept 1962, Elizabeth Doris, da of Rev Canon Thomas Francis Cecil Bewes, of 10 Farm Lane, Chase Side, Southgate, London; 3 da (Rachel b 1963, Sarah b 1965, Mary b 1969); *Career* curate: Islington Parish Church 1956-59, Holy Sepulchure Church Cambridge 1959-63; vicar St Mary North End Fulham 1962-69, chaplain St Thomas's Episcopal Church Edinburgh 1969-76, rector Holy Trinity Church Heigham Norwich 1976-87, rural dean Norwich (south) 1981-86, examining chaplain to Bishop of Norwich 1981-86, hon canon Norwich Cathedral 1984-87 (emeritus 1988-), princ Oak Hill Theol Coll 1987-; memb Principal's Conf 1987-; *Books* The Man from Outside (1969), A Day that changed the World (1975), A Bible Study Commentary (1985); *Recreations* music, sport, reading, walking; *Clubs* Christ's Hosp; *Style—* Rev Canon Gordon Bridger; 10 Farm Lane, Chase Side, Southgate, London N14 4PP (☎ 01 441 7091); Oak Hill Theological College, Chase Side, Southgate, London N14 (☎ 01 449 0467)

BRIDGES, Alan James Stuart; *b* 28 Sept 1927; *Educ* Holt HS Shrewsbury, Rhyl GS, Oxford Univ, RADA London (Dip RADA); *m* 31 July 1954, Eileen Middleton, da of Ridgeway Proctor Morton Brown (d 1965), of Newcastle and London; 1 s (Adam Patrick Ridgeway Bridges b 1965), 1 da (Emma Ann Bridges b 1962); *Career* Army service Capt; film, theatre and TV dir; work incl: Too Late for the Mashed Potato (by John Mortimer), The Brothers Karamazov (BBC), Great Expectations and Les Miserables (TV), Let's Murder Vivaldi (with Glenda Jackson), The Lie (SFTA Award 1970), Crown Matrimonial (SFTA Award), Rain on the Roof, The Return of the Soldier, Pudd'nhead Wilson, The Shooting Party, Displaced Person (Emmy Award 1985); *Recreations* reading, music, theatre, film and sport; *Style—* Alan Bridges, Esq; The Old Manor Farm, Church Street, Sunbury-on-Thames, Middlesex TW16 6RG (☎ 0932 780166)

BRIDGES, Ian Scott; s of Joseph Edward Bridges, and Margaret Mackintosh, *née* McCarue; *b* 24 April 1947; *Educ* Lenzie Acad, Univ of Glasgow Mackintosh Sch of Architecture (Dip Arch Glasgow); *m* 12 Nov 1976, June Margaret; *Career* architect; dir Ian Bridges (Architects); RIBA; ARIAS; *Clubs* Glasgow Arts; *Style—* Ian S Bridges, Esq; 13 Ruskin Terrace, Glasgow G12 8DY; 4 Royal Terrace, Glasgow G3 7NT (☎ 041 332 9838); car telephone 0860 414000

BRIDGES, Prof James Wilfrid; s of Wilfrid Edward Seymour Bridges, of Cuxton, nr Rochester, Kent, and Mary Winifred, *née* Camerson (d 1987); *b* 9 August 1938; *Educ* Bromley GS, Kings College Univ of London (BSc), St Mary's Hosp Med Sch Univ of London (PhD); *m* 2 Feb 1963, Daphne, da of Langston Rose Hammond, of Exmouth, Devon; 1 s (Jonathan Michael b 15 April 1965), 1 da (Lynne Fiona b 3 April 1967); *Career* res asst St Mary's Hosp Med Sch London Univ 1960-62 (lectr 1962- 68), sr lectr and reader Univ of Surrey 1968-78; visiting prof: Univ of Texas 1973 and 1979, Univ of Rochester NY 1974; visiting sr scientist Nat Inst of Environmental Health Sciences USA 1976, founding dir Robens Inst of Industl and Environmental Health and Safety 1978-, prof of toxicology Univ of Surrey 1978-, dean of faculty of science Univ of Surrey 1988-; chm Br Toxicology Soc 1980-81, first pres Fedn of Euro Socs of Toxicology 1985-88, memb exec ctee of Euro Soc of Biochemical Pharmacology 1983-, fndr Euro Drug Metabolisms Workshops; memb: Veterinary Products Ctee (MAFF) 1982-, Advsy Ctee on Toxic Substances (HSE) 1986-, Air Soil and Water Contaminants Ctee (DHSS, DOE) 1984-, UK Shadow GP on Toxicology (DHSS)

1984-, Advsy Ctee on Irradiated and Novel Foods (MAFF) 1982-88, Maj Hazards Ctee (HSE) 1982-84; MRCPath 1984, CChem, FRSC, FIBiol, CBiol 1981, MInstEnvSci 1980; *Books* Progress in Drug Metabolism (ed with Dr L Chasseaud, vols 1-10); *Recreations* running, theatre going; *Style—* Prof James Bridges; Liddington Lodge, Aldershot Road, Guildford; The Robens Institute of Industrial and Environmental Health and Safety University of Surrey, Guildford, Surrey GU2 5XH (☎ 0483 509 203, fax 0483 503 517, telex 859331)

BRIDGES, Hon Mark Thomas; er s and h of 2 Baron Bridges, GCMG, *qv*; *b* 25 July 1954; *Educ* Eton, Corpus Christi Coll Cambridge; *m* 1978, Angela Margaret, da of J L Collinson, of Mansfield, Notts; 3 da (Venetia Rachel Lucy b 1982, Camilla Frances Iona b 1985, Drusilla Katharine Anne b 1988); *Career* slr; ptnr Farrer & Co; *Recreations* walking, sailing (yacht 'Bitter Sweet'), reading; *Style—* The Hon Mark Bridges; 4 Bushnell Road, London SW17

BRIDGES, Dame Mary Patricia; DBE (1981); *m* 1951, Bertram Marsdin (d 1988); 1 s, (1 da decd); *Career* Devon family practitioner, dir Home Care Tst; tstee: Exmouth Lympstone Hospice Care, Exmouth Adventure Tst for Girls; fndr chm Exmouth Cncl of Voluntary Serv, chm Devon County and S Western Electricity consumer cncl, county chm Royal Br Legion Womans Section, memb central ctee (NAT), Cons Pty worker, exec memb St Loyee Coll Exeter; *Recreations* cricket; *Clubs* Exmouth CC, Retford CC; *Style—* Dame Mary Bridges, DBE; Walton House, 3 Fairfield Close, Exmouth, Devon EX8 2BN (☎ 0395 265317)

BRIDGES, Hon Nicholas Edward; yr s of 2 Baron Bridges, GCMG (1988, KCMG 1983, CMG 1975), *qv*; *b* 29 Mar 1956; *Educ* Eton, Bath Univ (BSc, BArch); *m* 1985, Susan, da of Peter Guggenheim, of Bridge Cottage, Woodbury Salterton, Devon; 1 s (Matthew Orlando b 1988), 1 da (Alice Clementine b 1986); *Career* ARIBA; *Style—* The Hon Nicholas Bridges; 21 Alvington Crescent, London E8 2NN

BRIDGES, Ven Peter Sydney Godfrey; s of Sidney Clifford Bridges and Winifred, *née* Livette; *b* 30 Jan 1925; *Educ* Raynes Park GS, Kingston-upon-Thames Sch of Arch, Lincoln Theol Coll, Univ of Birmingham; *m* 1952, Joan Penlerick, *née* Madge; 2 s; *Career* ordained 1958, archdeacon: Southend Dio of Chelmsford 1972-77, Coventry 1977-83, Warwick 1983-; dir Chelmsford Diocesion Res and Devpt Unit 1972-79; ARIBA; *Clubs* Royal Cwlth Soc; *Style—* The Ven the Archdeacon of Warwick; 'Saint Clare' 50 Beverley Road Leamington Spa, Warwickshire CV32 6PJ (☎ 0926 003421)

BRIDGES, Sir Phillip Rodney; CMG (1967); eldest s of Capt Sir Ernest Arthur Bridges (d 1953), of Bedford, and Agnes Ida, *née* Conyers; *b* 9 July 1922; *Educ* Bedford Sch; *m* 1, 1951 (m dis 1961), Rosemary Ann, da of late Rev Canon Arthur Herbert Streeten, MC, of Bury St Edmunds; 2 s, 1 da; m 2, 1962, Angela Mary, da of Frederick George Dearden, of Appledore, and wid of James Huyton; *Career* RA, served 1941-47: UK, W Africa, India, Burma; Capt, Actg Maj TA (Beds Yeomanry) 1947-54; slr (England) 1951, barr (Gambia) 1954, slr gen Gambia 1961, QC (Gambia) 1964, attorney gen Gambia 1964, chief justice Gambia 1968-83; kt 1973; *Clubs* Travellers'; *Style—* Sir Phillip Bridges, CMG; Weavers, Coney Weston, Bury St Edmunds, Suffolk IP31 1HG (☎ 035 921 316)

BRIDGES, Hon Mrs (Susan Constance); da of 6 Baron Auckland (d 1941); *b* 5 Sept 1918; *m* 1, 1942, Jose Diaz de Rivera (m dis 1956); 1 s; m 2, 1957, Guillermo Pakenham Bridges, OBE (d 1980, HM hon vice-consul at Rio Grande Argentina); *Style—* The Hon Mrs Bridges; Hotel Lombardy, 111 East 56th St, New York, NY 10022, USA

BRIDGES, 2 Baron (UK 1957), of Headley, Co Surrey and of St Nicholas-at-Wade, Co Kent; Sir Thomas Edward Bridges; GCMG (1988, KCMG 1983, CMG 1975); s of 1 Baron Bridges, KG, GCB, GCVO, MC (d 1969), and Hon Katherine, da of 2 Baron Farrer (d 1986); *b* 27 Nov 1927; *Educ* Eton, New Coll Oxford (MA); *m* 1953, Rachel Mary, da of Sir Henry Bunbury, KCB (d 1968), of Ewell, Surrey; 2 s, 1 da; *Heir* s, Hon Mark Bridges; *Career* entered HM For Serv 1951; served: Bonn, Berlin, Rio de Janiero, Athens, Moscow; private sec (overseas affrs) to the PM 1972-74, min (commercial) Washington 1975-79, dep sec FCO 1979-83, ambass to Italy 1983-87, ret 1987; *Style—* The Rt Hon the Lord Bridges, GCMG; 73 Church Street Orford, Woodbridge, Suffolk 1P12 2NT.

BRIDGES-ADAMS, John Nicholas William; s of William Bridges-Adams, CBE (d 1965), of Stratford-Upon-Avon. and Marguerite Doris Wellsted (d 1963); *b* 16 Sept 1930; *Educ* Stowe, Oriel Coll Oxford (MA, Dip Ed); *m* 1962, Jenifer Celia Emily, da of David Hugh Sandell; *Career* cmmnd RA 1949, RAFVR 1951; barr Lincoln's Inn 1958 (Grays Inn 1979), head of chambers 1979, memb: exec ctee Soc of Cons Lawyers 1967-69 (chm Criminal Law sub Ctee 1983-86), House of Lords Reform Ctee 1982-; Parly candidate (C) West Bromwich West 1974; govr St Benedicts Upper Sch 1980-83; memb RIIA, IISS, FCIArb; *Recreations* shooting, sailing, skiing; *Clubs* Savile, Garrick; *Style—* Nicholas Bridges-Adams, Esq; Fornham Cottage, Fornham St Martin, Bury St Edmunds, Suffolk; 4 Verulam Buildings, Grays Inn, London WC1

BRIDGETT, John Alan Charles; s of Eric Bridgett (d 1987), of Rickmansworth, and Gwendoline, *née* Powell; *b* 13 Feb 1948; *Educ* Watford GS; *m* 28 June 1973, Christine Jennifer, da of Willen Arie Verkerk,of London; 1 s (Mark Peter John b 27 Oct 1969), 1 da (Claire b 2 May 1972); *Career* Br Movietone News 1965-68, Attos Film & TV Prodns 1968-84, BBC TV 1984-; BAFTA Sound Award Dubbing Ed for The Duty Men 1987; *Recreations* music, gardening; *Clubs* BBC; *Style—* John Bridgett, Esq; Chalklands, Bourne End, Bucks SL8 5TJ (☎ 06 285 223 36); BBC Film Dept, Ealing Studios, Ealing W5

BRIDGEWATER, Allan; *b* 26 August 1936; *Educ* Wyggestons GS, Leicester; *m* Janet, 3 da; *Career* Norwich Union Insur Gp 1979-; dep gen mangr: Norwich Union Fire Insur Soc Ltd 1983-; gen mngr: Norwich Union Fire Insur Soc Ltd 1984-89, gp chief exec 1989-; chm Endeavor Training; govr Norwich HS, dep pres Chartered Insur Inst 1988-89; *Style—* Allan Bridgewater, Esq; Norwich Union Insurance Group, PO Box 6, Surrey Street, Norwich (☎ 0603 622200)

BRIDGEWATER, Geraldine Diana Noelle; da of William Reay Bridgewater, of London, and Sheila Rosemary, *née* Burke; *b* 26 Dec 1952; *Educ* Holland Park Comprehensive; *Career* first woman dealer on floor London Metal Exchange 1976 (ring dealer 1976), first women individual subscriber London Metal Exchange 1986, commodity broker; Freeman City of London; *Recreations* metaphysics, philosophy, alternative medicine, reading; *Clubs* CND, Greenpeace, UNICEF, Action Aid, Network, Financial Initiative; *Style—* Miss Geraldine Bridgewater; 48 New River Crescent, Palmers Green, London N13; London Metal Exchange, Plantation House, Fenchurst St, London EC3

BRIDGMAN, Peter Thomas; s of Thomas William Bridgman; *b* 11 Nov 1924; *m* 1950, Eileen Mary, da of Albert Alexander Free (d 1956); 4 s; *Career* serv WWII Sub Lt RNVR Far East; accountant; md: Urwick Dynamics 1970-81, Urwick Orr & Ptnrs (mgmnt conslts) 1981-84; The Urwick Gp, Price Waterhouse 1984-; *Recreations* gardening, golf, fishing, music; *Style—* Peter Bridgman, Esq; Baysham Cottage, Sellack, Ross-on-Wye, Herefordshire HR9 6QP (☎ 0989 64990); Urwick Mgmnt Centre, Stoke Poges Lane, Slough, Berkshire S11 3PF (☎ 0753 34111, telex 848146 PRIWAT)

BRIDGWATER, Arthur Brian; MBE (1971); s of Arthur John Bridgwater, OBE (d 1975), and Kathleen, *née* Burton (d 1950); *b* 20 Nov 1923; *Educ* Bristol GS, Bristol Univ (BSc); *m* 1949, Olive, da of William Edward Bracher (d 1929); 1 s (Nicholas b 1953), 1 da (Jennifer b 1956); *Career* Flt Lt RAFVR - Coastal Cmd 1941-45; chm London and South Eastern Section of the Federation of Civil Engineering Contractors 1968; chartered civil engr, chm Bridgwater Bros Hldgs Ltd 1982-; *Recreations* philately, golf; *Clubs* RAC; *Style—* Brian Bridgwater, Esq, MBE; Merlin, Pleasure Pit Rd, Ashtead, Surrey KT21 1HR (☎ 0372 274 290)

BRIDPORT, 4 Viscount (UK 1868); Alexander Nelson Hood; also Baron Bridport (I 1794) and 7 Duke of Bronte in Sicily (cr 1799 by Ferdinand IV, the 'Lazzarone' King of the Two Sicilies, largely for Nelson's role in exterminating the Parthenopean Republic); in 1801 a Br Royal Licence was issued to Admiral Lord Nelson allowing him to accept for himself and his heirs the Dukedom of Bronte; s of 3 Viscount (d 1969, fourth in descent from the union of 2 Baron Bridport (2 s of 2 Viscount Hood) and Lady Charlotte Nelson, da of 1 Earl and niece of the great Admiral); *b* 17 Mar 1948; *Educ* Eton, Sorbonne; *m* 1, 1972 (m dis 1979), Linda Jacqueline, da of Lt-Col Vincent Rudolph Paravicini, of Nutley Manor, Basingstoke; 1 s; m 2, 1979, Mrs Nina Rindt; 1 s; *Heir* s, Hon Peregrine Hood; *Career* Kleinwort Benson Ltd 1967-80, Robert Fraser & Ptnrs 1980-83, Chase Manhattan Ltd 1983-85; (exec dir) dir Chase Manhattan Bank (Suisse) 1985-86 (gen mangr 1986-), md Shearman Lehman Hutton Fin (Switzerland); *Recreations* skiing, sailing; *Clubs* Brooks's,; *Style—* The Rt Hon the Viscount Bridport; Villa Jonin, 1261 Le Muids, Vaud, Switzerland (☎ 022 66 17 05)

BRIEN, Alan; s of late Ernest Brien, and Isabella, *née* Patterson; *b* 12 Mar 1925; *Educ* Bede GS Sunderland, Jesus Coll Oxford; *m* 1, 1947, Pamela Mary Jones; 3 da; m 2, 1961, Nancy Newbold Ryan; 1 s, 1 da; m 3, 1973, Jill Sheila, da of Patrick Grahame Tweedie, CBE, and former w of (1) Count Bela Cziraky (1 s, 1 da) and (2) Robert d'Ancona (1 s); *Career* Punch columnist 1972-, Sunday Times film critic 1976-; *Style—* Alan Brien, Esq; Blaen-y-Glyn, Pont Hyndwr, Llandrillo, Clwyd

BRIER, James Allan; s of James George Brier (d 1951), of Chesterfield, and Clara Annie, *née* Booth (d 1969); *b* 17 April 1925; *Educ* Chesterfield GS; *Career* WWII RN served coastal forces UK and Far East Sub Lt RNVSR 1943-46, Lt RNR 1962-72, Lt RNVR 1972-; CA sr ptnr Samuel Edward Short & Co; *Recreations* tennis, badminton, mountain walking, skiing, member of jazz band; *Clubs* Royal Overseas League; *Style—* James Brier, Esq; Samuel Edward Short & Co, Chartered Accountants, 6 Fairfield Road, Chesterfield S40 4TP

BRIERLEY, Hon Mrs (Caroline); *née* Gordon Walker; da of Baron Gordon-Walker, CH, PC; *b* 22 Dec 1937; *Educ* Cheltenham Ladies Coll, Lady Margaret Hall Oxford (BA); *m* 1960, David Brierley, s of John Brierley (d 1965), of Durban, South Africa; 1 da (Margaret b 1970); *Career* economist Int Sugar Cncl; political and economic planning; head of foods and services unit Nat Economic Devpt Off; *Books* Food Prices and the Common Market, The Making of European Policy, Lifting barriers to trade; *Recreations* travel, gardening; *Style—* The Hon Mrs Brierley; Old Farm, Harthall Lane, King's Langley, Herts WD4 8JW (☎ 092 77 62507); NEDO, Millbank Tower, Millbank, London SW1P 4QX (☎ 01 211 6114)

BRIERLEY, Christopher Wadsworth; CBE (1987); s of Eric Brierley (d 1978), and Edna Mary, *née* Lister (d 1980); *b* 1 June 1929; *Educ* Whitgift Middle Sch Croydon; *m* 1, 24 Aug 1951 (m dis), Dorothy, da of Jack Scott (d 1987); 2 da (Lesley Jeanne b 1956, Alison Jane b 1958); m 2, 20 Nov 1984, Dilwen Marie, da of John Morgan (d 1969); *Career* Nat Serv 1947-49; Sgt: RAEC, UK, BAOR; chief accountant: EMI Records Ltd 1960-68, Br Gas E Midlands Region 1970-74; dir of fin: Br Gas Eastern Region 1974-77, Br Gas plc 1977-80; dir of econ planning Br Gas plc 1980-82 (md 1982-87); dir: Br Gas Corpn 1984-86, Br Gas plc 1986- (md resources and new business 1987-); *Recreations* music; *Clubs* RAC; *Style—* Christopher W Brierley, Esq, CBE; 6 Stobarts Close, Knebworth, Herts SG3 6ND (☎ 0438 814988); 152 Grosvenor Rd, Rivermill House, London SW1 (☎ 01 821 1444, telex 938529)

BRIERLEY, David; s of John Paul Brierley (da 1965), of South Africa, and Ruth Mary, *née* Richmond; *b* 30 July 1936; *Educ* Hilton Coll SA, Univ of Natal, Oxford Univ (BA); *m* 23 April 1960, Caroline, da of Baron Patrick Gordon-Walker (Life Baron 1974, d 1980); 1 da (Margaret b 1970); *Career* teacher in France 1958-59, advertising 1960-75, author 1975-; *Books* Cold War (1979), Blood Group O (1980), Big Bear Little Bear (1981), Shooting Star (1983), Czechmate (1984), Skorpion's Death (1985), Snowline (1986), One Lives One Dies (1987); *Style—* David Brierley, Esq; Old Farm, Harthall Lane, Kings Langley, Herts WD3 8JW (☎ 092 77 625 07)

BRIERLEY, David; CBE (1946); s of Ernest William Brierley (d 1982), of Romiley, Stockport, Cheshire, and Jessie, *née* Stanway ; *b* 26 July 1936; *Educ* Stockport GS, Clare Coll Cambridge (MA, Cert Ed); *m* 7 Dec 1962, Ann Fosbrooke, da of Charles Rossell Fosbrooke Potter; 2 s (Benedict b 1964, Crispin b 1966); *Career* teacher 1959-61; Royal Shakespeare Theatre: stage mangr 1961, gen stage mangr 1963, asst to the dir 1966, gen mangr 1968; *Recreations* reading; *Style—* David Brierley, Esq, CBE; The Chestnuts, Upper Quinton, Stratford upon Avon, Warwickshire CV37 8SX (☎ 0789 720423); Royal Shakespeare Theatre, Stratford upon Avon, Warwickshire CV37 6BB (☎ 0789 296655, fax 0789 294810)

BRIERLEY, John David; CB (1978); s of late Walter George Brierley, and Doris, *née* Paterson; *b* 16 Mar 1918; *Educ* Whitgift Sch Croydon, Lincoln Coll Oxford; *m* 1956, Frances Elizabeth Davis; 1 s, 1 da (both adopted); *Career* under-sec DES 1969-77, dean of studies Working Men's Coll 1978-81; *Style—* David Brierley, Esq, CB; Little Trees, Winterbourne, nr Newbury, Berks (☎ 0635 24 8870)

BRIERLEY, Sir Zachry; CBE (1978, MBE 1969); s of late Zachry Brierley, of Rhos, and Nellie, *née* Ashworth; *b* 16 April 1920; *Educ* Rydal Sch Colwyn Bay N Wales; *m* 1946, Iris, da of Arnold Macara; 1 da; *Career* chm: Z Brierley Ltd 1972- (dir 1952-, chm and md 1957-72), Australia Pty 1973-; pres Z Brierley USA Inc 1972-; memb: CBI Central Cncl 1970-82, Welsh Devpt Agency 1975-86, Design Cncl 1976-86, Nat Broadcasting Cncl Wales 1981-85; pres Cons Political Centre Wales 1981-, chm Wales

Cons and Unionist Assoc 1982-86; vice-chm Mostyn Art Gallery 1979-85; kt 1987; *Recreations* philately, reading, sketching; *Clubs* Carlton; *Style—* Sir Zachry Brierley, CBE; West Point, Gloddaeth Ave, Llandudno, Gwynedd (☎ 0492 76970)

BRIERS, Richard David; OBE (1989); s of Joseph Benjamin (d 1980), and Morna Phyllis, *née* Richardson; *b* 14 Jan 1934; *Educ* Ridgeways Sch; *m* 1957, Ann Cuerton, da of H Ronald Davies (d 1980); 2 da (Katy, Lucy); *Career* actor; *Style—* Richard Briers, Esq; ICM Ltd, 388-396, Oxford St, London W1N 9HE (☎ 01 629 8080)

BRIGGS, Baron (Life Peer UK 1976); Asa Briggs; o s of William Walker Briggs (d 1952), of Keighley, and Jane Briggs; *b* 7 May 1921; *Educ* Keighley GS, Sidney Sussex Coll Cambridge (BA), LSE (BSc); *m* 1955, Susan Anne, da of Donald Ivor Banwell (d 1980), of Keevil, Wilts; 2 s, 2 da; *Career* served Intelligence Corps (Bletchley) 1942-45; historian and writer; prof of history Sussex Univ 1961-76, (vice-chllr 1967-76); provost Worcester Coll Oxford 1976-; chm advsy bd for Redundant Churches 1983-; recipient of French Academy of Architecture's Medal for 'formation and teaching' 1982; *Recreations* travel; *Clubs* Beefsteak, Oxford and Cambridge; *Style—* The Rt Hon the Lord Briggs; The Provost's Lodgings, Worcester College, Oxford (☎ 0865 247251); The Caprons, Keere St, Lewes, Sussex (☎ 079 16 4704)

BRIGGS, Hon Daniel Nicholas; s of Rt Hon Lord Briggs of Lewes, *qv*; *b* 13 Dec 1958; *Educ* Lancing Coll, Bristol Univ (BA); *Career* co dir The Flower Corpn Ltd; *Publications* The Bristol Post Office in The Age of Rowland Hill (1984); *Style—* The Hon Daniel Briggs; 132 Bennerley Road, London SW11 6DY; Elms Gardens, Glaziers Lane, Normandy, Guildford GU3

BRIGGS, David Muir; s of Maj Brian Ridsdale Briggs (d 1966), of Allt-Grianach Lochearnhead, and Elizabeth Hope, *née* Greenlees (d 1946); *b* 18 June 1944; *Educ* Ardvreck Sch Crieff Perthshire, Loretto Sch; *m* 5 July 1974, Julie Marilyn, da of Milton George Webber, of 10 Sortie Port, Castlecrag, Sydney, Australia; 1 s (Ian b 6 Jan 1979), 1 da (Alison b 15 Nov 1976); *Career* qualified CA 1967, Peat Marwick Mitchell (Paris) 1967-70, ptnr Messrs Turner Hutton & Lawson 1977-77; dir: GN Fund Mgmnt Ltd 1977-82, J Rothschild Investmt Mgmnt Ltd 1982-84, Murray Johnstone Ltd 1987; auditor Gartocharn CC; *Recreations* fishing, golf, hill-walking, gardening, reading; *Clubs* Prestwick GC; *Style—* David Briggs, Esq; Claddoch, Gartocharn, Dunbartonshire, G83 8NQ (☎ 038 983 210); Murray Johnstone Ltd, 7 West Nile St, Glasgow (☎ 041 226 3131, fax 041 248 5420, telex 778667)

BRIGGS, (Aidan) Favell; s of John Aidan Briggs (d 1969), of Blackwell Farm, Latimer, Chesham, Bucks, and Alice Mary Molyneux, *née* Favell; *b* 29 Oct 1942; *Educ* Eton, Trinity Hall Cambridge (MA); *m* 20 Feb 1971, Helen Ormsby, da of Dr Clive Ormsby Barnes (d 1977), of Coniston House, Hadleigh, Suffolk; 1 s (Jocelyn b 1972), 1 da (Emily b 1974); *Career* slr, under sheriff of Cornwall; *Recreations* fishing, gardening, shooting, fine arts; *Style—* Favell Briggs, Esq; Carwinnick Farm, Grampound, nr Truro, Cornwall (☎ 0726 882488); Graham & Graham, High Cross St, St Austell, Cornwall

BRIGGS, Sir Geoffrey Gould; 2 s of Late Rev C E Briggs, of Amersham, Bucks; *b* 6 May 1914; *Career* barr 1938; QC (Nigeria) 1955, former Puisne judge Sarawak, N Borneo and Brunei, chief justice W Pacific 1962-65, Puisne judge Hong Kong 1965-73, chief justice: Hong Kong 1973-79, Brunei 1973-79; pres: Brunei Court of Appeal 1979-87, Pensions Appeal Tbnls for England and Wales 1980-86; kt 1974; *Clubs* Wig & Pen; *Style—* Sir Geoffrey Briggs; 1 Farley Ct, Melbury Rd, Kensington, London W14 8LJ (☎ 01 602 2541)

BRIGGS, Wing Cdr Geoffrey Harry; DFC (1944), DL (Sussex 1970); s of Henry Hilton Briggs, of Holton Park, Oxon; *b* 22 Mar 1918; *Educ* Eton, Sandhurst, RAC Cirencester; *m* 1, 1947, Elizabeth Anne (d 1982), da of Crossley Swithinbank, of Newbury; 3 s, 1 da; m 2, 1983, Barbara Wilkinson, *née* Horsfield; *Career* ret farmer; county chief warden Civil Defence 1964; cmdt Special Constabulary W Sussex 1967; High Sheriff W Sussex 1974; *Recreations* shooting, fishing, sailing (yacht 'Soubrette'); *Clubs* Household Division Yacht, Itchenor Sailing; *Style—* Wing Cdr Geoffrey Briggs, DFC, DL; The Farm House, Strettington, Chichester, W Sussex (☎ Chichester 0243 773331)

BRIGGS, John; s of John Briggs, of Bolton, and Mabel, *née* Edwards; *b* 30 May 1933; *Educ* Stowe, Selwyn Coll Cambridge (MA, LLM); *m* 21 May 1960, Celia Rosalind, da of Henry Cecil Wild (d 1975), of Bury; 1 s (Paul Dudley John b 30 June 1964), 2 da (Nicola Rosalind b 6 July 1961, Angela Rosemary b 2 Aug 1965); *Career* slr 1960, Notary Public 1965; princ: Claude Leatham & Co, Brown Wilkin & Scott Wakefield, Owen & Briggs, Cartwright & Cliffe & Co Huddersfield; past pres: Huddersfield Incorporated Law Soc, Union Discussion Soc, Huddersfield Borough Club; hon sec The Royal Soc of St George Huddersfield branch; memb: Law Soc, Provincial Notaries Soc; *Recreations* fell walking, stock rearing (Blonde d'Aquitaine cattle and Texel sheep); *Clubs* Huddersfield Borough ; *Style—* John Briggs, Esq; office: 13 Railway St, Huddersfield, W Yorks HD1 1JX (☎ 0484 519999, fax 0484 544099, telex 517191 LEX G)

BRIGGS, (Frederick) John; s of Frederick John Briggs (d 1969), of Bournemouth, and Jessie Catherine, *née* Creighton; *b* 24 Oct 1923; *Educ* Christ Coll Finchley, William Hulme GS Manchester; *m* 1949, Margaret Jessie, da of Maj Percy Libbis Smout, MC (d 1960); 3 s (John, Norman, Stewart); *Career* served RAF 1942-46; chm: Manston Devpt Gp Ltd 1978-81, Duckry Ltd 1980-, Wiljay plc 1981-84, Pavion Int plc 1982-87, Bullers plc 1983-, Cauldon Gp plc 1985-, SI Gp plc 1985-88; dep chm Wheway plc 1984-; dir: Norcros plc 1966-83, Reading FC Ltd 1978-83, Bunzl plc 1978-88, Blagden Indust plc 1980-, Tudor plc 1982-, Erskine House plc 1983-, Reece Ltd 1986-; memb Br Rail (Western Bd) 1981-89; fndr pres World Packaging Orgn 1968-72; chm organising ctee: Pakex '77, Pakex '80, Pakex '83; memb: cncl PIRA 1971-81 (chm 1975-77), Euro Trade Ctee 1974-83; Court memb and Liveryman: Worshipful Co of Tylers and Bricklayers 1954- (Master 1982-83), Worshipful Co of Marketors 1973-; FInstM (nat chm 1976, pres 1978-81), FInstPkg (nat chm 1970, pres 1972-81), CBIM (pres Reading branch 1978-81, dir BIM Fndn 1980-83), FInstD, FRSA; *Recreations* tennis; *Clubs* Carlton, City Livery, Honourable Artillery Company, Phyllis Court, RAC, RAF, MCC; *Style—* John Briggs, Esq; Huish Cross, Finchampstead, Berks RG11 3SU (☎ 0734 733156, fax 0734 733182)

BRIGGS, (Peter) John; s of Percy Briggs CBE (d 1980), of Wansford, Peterborough, and Annie Maud (Topsy), *née* Folker; *b* 15 May 1928; *Educ* Kings Sch Peterborough, Balliol Coll Oxford (MA, BCL); *m* 24 July 1956, Sheila Phyllis, da of George Walton (d 1981), of Grimsby, Lincs; 1 s (Simon b 1963), 3 da (Ann b 1957, Abigail b 1960, Helen b 1961); *Career* Warrant Offr RA and RAEC 1946-48; barr 1953-; legal memb Mersey Mental Health Review Tbnl 1969 (dep chm 1971-79, chm 1979-), deputy circuit judge 1973, recorder of the Crown Ct 1978-; *Recreations* music, especially amateur operatics, golf; *Style—* John Briggs, Esq; Peel House, Harrington Street, Liverpool L2 9XN (☎ 051 236 0718, fax 051 255 1085)

BRIGGS, Hon Matthew William Banwell; s of Baron Briggs (Life Peer); *b* 1964; *Style—* The Hon Matthew Briggs

BRIGGS, Gp Capt Nelson; CBE (Mil 1968), AFC (1946); s of late Nelson Briggs; *b* 15 August 1915; *Educ* Swanwick Hall; *m* 1941, Linda Ellen, da of late Herbert Hunt; 1 s, 1 da; *Career* admin mangr Beecham Gp 1968-69; dir admin 1969-73, employee servs 1973-78, central servs 1978-79 Borough of Hammersmith & Fulham; *Clubs* RAF; *Style—* Gp Capt Nelson Briggs, CBE, AFC; 2 Baronsmead, Henley-on-Thames, Oxon

BRIGGS, Raymond Redvers; s of Ernest Redvers Briggs, and Ethel Bowyer; *b* 18 Jan 1934; *Educ* Rutlish Sch Merton, Wimbledon Sch of Art, Slade Sch of Fine Art London Univ (DFA); *m* 1963, Jean Patricia (d 1973), da of Arthur Taprell Clark; *Career* book illustrator, designer ; *Books* Father Christmas (1973), Fungus the Bogeyman (1977), The Snowman (1978), When the Wind Blows (book, radio play and stage play 1982-83); *Clubs* Groucho's; *Style—* Raymond Briggs, Esq; Weston, Underhill Lane, Westmeston, nr Hassocks, Sussex

BRIGGS, Robert Keith; s of Alfred Briggs; *b* 29 August 1926; *Educ* Cheltenham, Queen's Coll Oxford; *m* 1959, Jill, da of Charles Chapman; 1 s, 3 da; *Career* former jt md Holden Surface Coatings; former chief exec Arthur Holden & Sons;; *Recreations* walking; *Clubs* RAC; *Style—* Robert Briggs Esq; Croft Cottage, Bakers Lane, Knowle, W Midlands B93 8PR (☎ 0569 772702)

BRIGGS, Rear Adm Thomas Vallack; CB (1958), OBE (1945); s of Adm Sir Charles John Briggs, KCB (d 1951), and Frances, *née* Wilson; *b* 6 April 1906; *Educ* Imperial Serv Coll Windsor, RNC Greenwich, Imperial Def Coll, US Naval War Coll Rhode Island; *m* 1947, Estelle Burland, da of James Willing, of Boston, USA; 1 step s; *Career* vice-patron RN Assoc (pres 1971-76); joined RN 1924, advanced gunnery specialist 1934, WWII served in HMS: Ark Royal 1939-40, Excellent (AA Cmdre) 1941-42, Newcastle 1942-43, Renown, Queen Elizabeth and Nelson as staff Ops and gunnery offr afloat East Indies Station 1943-45; CO HMS Comus 1946, dep dir Naval Ordnance (G) 1947-48, Capt (D) 5 Destroyer Flotilla, HMS Solebay 1949-50, chief of staff Plymouth 1952-53, CO HMS Cumberland (trials cruiser) 1954, Rear Adm 1956, COS Home Fleet and Eastern Atlantic 1956-57, asst controller of Navy 1957-58, ret; FIM, DL Gtr London 1970-82; dir: Hugh Stevenson & Sons Ltd 1958-68, Bowater Packaging 1969-71, Free-Stay Holidays plc, Int Consumer Incentives plc, Meru Gp plc 1971-76; life govr Haileybury & ISC; *Recreations* golf, RNGS Capt: Aldeburgh GC (Capt 1981-82), shooting, RN sailing Assn, RN Ski Assoc; *Clubs* White's, Madison Winter USA; *Style—* Rear Adm Thomas Briggs, CB, OBE; 29 Twin Bridge Rd, Madison, Conn 06443, USA

BRIGHAM, Peter; s of Arthur Peter Donald Brigham (d 1964), of Scarborough, and Florence Drusilla, *née* Robson (d 1973); *b* 4 Nov 1928; *Educ* Bootham Sch York, Liverpool Univ; *m* 5 Sept 1953, Sheila Margaret, da of Henry John Riding (d 1971), of Ormskirk; 2 da (Catherine b 1957, Erica b 1960); *Career* lectr and conslt; former mgmnt conslt and architect; memb Nat Cncl Inst of Marketing, former conslt to OECD Paris; memb RIBA, FCIOB, FBIM, FInstM; *Recreations* riding, travel, conservation of historic houses & gardens; *Style—* Peter Brigham, Esq; Redcliff, 9 Lower Park Road, Chester CH4 7BB (☎ Chester 679276)

BRIGHT, Andrew John; s of Joseph Henry Bright (d 1970), of Wells, Somerset, and Freda Madeleine Phyllis, *née* Cotton; *b* 12 April 1951; *Educ* Wells Cathedral Sch, UCL (LLB); *m* 3 Jan, 1976, Sally Elizabeth, da of Charles Carter of Rochester, Kent; 2 s (Daniel b 1980, Charles b 1981); *Career* called to the Bar (Middle Temple) 1973, practised from the chambers of Mr Louis Blom-Cooper QC 1974-86; in practice from chambers of Mr H Michael Self QC 1986-; memb Criminal Bar Assoc; *Recreations* music; *Clubs* Chorleywood Round Table; *Style—* Andrew Bright, Esq; Gayfield, Loudhams Wood Lane, Chalfont St Giles, Bucks HP8 4AR (☎ 02404 2302); 4 Brick Court, Temple, London EC4 (☎ 01 583 8455)

BRIGHT, Brig Douglas Richard Lucas; OBE (1960); s of Maj Richard George Tyndal Bright, CMG (d 1944), of Arnewood Ct, Sway, Hants, and Murielle Dorothea, *née* Lucas-Tooth (d 1968); *b* 4 Sept 1918; *Educ* Eton, RMC Sandhurst; *m* 6 Nov 1948, (Charlotte) Rosemary, da of The Hon Mr Justice P A Farrer Manby (d 1938), of Manorfield, Lower Pennington, Lymington, Hants; 1 s (Richard b 1954), 1 da (Rosamond b 1951); *Career* cmmnd 1938 Oxfordhsire & Buckinghamshire LI, WWII serv: France, Belgium, India, Burma; subsequent serv: Far E, ME, USA, Kenya, Italy, UK; cmd Kenya Regt 1961-63, cmd 143 Inf Bde 1965-67, COS UK mil rep NATO 1967-69, ret 1971; chm Lymington RNLI Branch 1981-85, cdre Royal Lymington Yacht Club 1983-86; *Recreations* bird watching, natural history, sailing, field sports; *Clubs* Army & Navy, Royal Lymington Yacht; *Style—* Brig Douglas Bright, OBE; Willow Tree Cottage, Barnes Lane, Milford-on-Sea, Hants SO41 0RR

BRIGHT, Graham Frank James; MP (C) Luton South 1983-; s of Robert Frank Bright, and Agnes Mary, *née* Graham; *b* 2 April 1942; *Educ* Hassenbrook Comp Sch, Thurrock Tech Coll; *m* 16 Dec 1972, Valerie, da of late Ernest Henry Woolliams; 1 s (Rupert b 1984); *Career* chm and md Dietary Foods Ltd 1977-; pps: David Waddington, QC, MP and Patrick M·ayhew, QC, MP Mins of State Home Off 1983, David Waddington QC, MP and Douglas Hird, MP 1983, David Waddington QC, MP and Giles Shaw, MP 1984-86, Earl of Caithness DOE 1988; sec back bench Cons Smaller Business Ctee 1979-80 (vice chm 1980-83), sec back bench Aviation Ctee 1980-83, vice chm Cons Aviation Ctee 1983-85, sec back bench Food and Drink Sub-Ctee 1983-85, memb select ctee on House of Commons Servs 1982-84, introduced Private Mamber's Bill (Video Recordings Act) 1984, jt sec Parly Aviation Gp 1984-, vice chm Aviation Ctee 1987-88, chm Cons Smaller Businesses Ctee 1983-84 and 1987-88; memb: Thurrock Borough Cncl 1966-79, Essex 1967-70; nat vice chm Young Cons; *Recreations* gardening, golf; *Clubs* Carlton; *Style—* Mr Bright; House of Commons, London SW1A 0AA (☎ 01 219 5156)

BRIGHT, Sir Keith; s of Ernest William, and Lilian Mary Bright; *b* 30 August 1931; *Educ* London Univ (BSc, PhD); *m* 1, 1959, (m dis), Patricia Anne; 1 s, 1 da; m 2, 1985, Margot Joan Norman; *Career* former scientist, chm and co dir, dir and gp chief exec Huntley & Palmer Foods to July 1982; dir: Extel Gp Ltd, London & Continental Advertising Hldgs; formerly with: De La Rue (md of Formica), Hill Samuel, Sime Darby (Singapore trading house); chm and chief exec London Regnl Tport 1982-88;

FRSC, FCIT; kt 1987; *Style—* Sir Keith Bright; London Regional Transport, 55 Broadway, London SW1H 0BD (☎ 01 222 5600)

BRIGHT, Michael John; s of John Thomas Bright (d 1984), and Alice Hearne; *b* 10 August 1944; *Educ* Bromley GS Kent; *m* 15 July 1966, Catherine Ellen, da of Clifford Brown, of Sheffield; 1 s (James Michael b 1972), 1 da (Victoria Jane b 1970); *Career* chief exec and md: New Scotland Insur Gp plc, Independent Insur Co Ltd 1987-; dir and gen mangr Lombard Elizabethan Insur Co plc (subsequently Lombard Continental Insur plc) 1982-87; Orion Insur Co Ltd 1967-82 (gp asst gen mangr 1980); memb Lloyds of London; memb Worshipful Co of Insurers, Freeman of The City of London; ACII; *Recreations* gardening, reading, holidays; *Clubs* Marylebone Cricket (memb); *Style—* Michael J Bright, Esq; The Oasts, Biddenden Rd, Smarden, Kent (☎ (023) 377 289); Independent Insurance Co Ltd, 12th Floor, Fountain House, 130 Fenchurch St, London EC3M 5AU (☎ 01 623 8877, fax 01 283 8275)

BRIGHT, Brig Robert Henry; CBE (1965), OBE (1946); s of Lt-Col Richard Bright (d 1938), and Frances Eva, *née* Batten (d 1950); *b* 20 Nov 1912; *Educ* Wellington, RMA Woolwich; *m* 1, 12 Sept 1937 (m dis), Rachel, da of J S Helmer; 2 s (John b 1946, Charles b 1949); m 2, 18 Sept 1952, Elsie Rosina May, MBE, da of James Henry Mussel White (d 1942); *Career* army offr, cmmd RTC 1932; WWII 1939-45: UK and NW Europe, Lt-Col 1943; USA 1947-50, Col 1952, dir of inspection of fighting vehicles 1957-61, Brig 1960, dir of fighting vehicles War Off 1961-64; *Recreations* country sports, pheasant shooting; *Clubs* Farmers; *Style—* Brig Robert H Bright, CBE, OBE; 2 Uplands, Yetminster, Sherborne, Dorset DT9 6JZ (☎ 0935 872600)

BRIGHTMAN, Hon Christopher Anthony John; s of Baron Brightman, PC (Life Peer), *qv*; *b* 18 Mar 1948; *Educ* Marlborough, St John's Coll Cambridge, Middlesex Hosp (MA, MB BChir, MSc), MRCPath); *m* 1975, Elisabeth Justina, yr da of Jonkheer I R Willem Justinus de Beyer; 3 da (Louisa b 1978, Justina b 1980, Eugenie b 1982); *Career* medical practitioner, sr registrar in clinical bacteriology; memb BMA; *Recreations* woodwork, Tudor and Stuart history, egyptology; *Style—* Dr the Hon Christopher Brightman; 26 Glamorgan Road, Hampton, Wick KT1 4HP

BRIGHTMAN, Baron (Life Peer UK 1982); John Anson Brightman; PC (1979); 2 s of William Henry Brightman (d 1951), of St Albans, Herts; *b* 20 June 1911; *Educ* Marlborough, St John's Coll Cambridge (MA, hon fell 1982); *m* 1945, Roxane Guilda Hyacinth, da of Gerasimo Ambatielo (d 1958), of Cephalonia; 1 s (Hon Christopher, *qv*); *Career* serv WWII Lt Cdr RNVR Mediterranean and Atlantic, asst naval attaché Ankara 1944, staff SEAC 1945; barr Lincoln's Inn 1932, QC 1961, attorney-gen Duchy Lancaster and attorney and serjeant within Co Palatine of Lancaster 1969-70, High Court judge (Chancery div) 1970-79, judge Nat Industl Relations Court 1971-74, Lord Justice of Appeal 1979-82, Lord of Appeal in Ordinary 1982-86; govr Tancred's Fndn 1982-; kt 1970; *Recreations* sailing, skiing; *Style—* The Rt Hon the Lord Brightman, PC; Ibthorpe, Hants SP11 OBY

BRIGHTMORE, Neil James John; s of James Joseph Edmund Brightmore (d 1964), of Stoke on Trent, Staffs and Ethel Lettice, *née* Goode, MBE (d 1986); *b* 21 Jan 1937; *Eauc* The Lymes Ptd Sch Newcastle under Lyme, Stoke on Trent Coll of Art Stoke on Trent; *m* 1, m 1961 (m dis), Sheila Charsley; 2 s (Adrian Neil b 1963, Roger Jason b 1967); m 2, 5 Sept 1979, Vivienne Brenda Margaret, da of John Anthony Augustus Ireson; 1 da (Verity Abigail b 1981); *Career* Nat Serv RAF, trained in photography; press photographer; BIPP Fellow of the Year 1985, Peter Grugeon Jubilee Award 1985, Patrick Lichfield Portfolio Award 1985, Nat BIPP Portrait Photographer of the Year 1985, Kodak Portrait Photographer 1986, and 1988; 5 times winner Curzon Regnl BIPP Trophy; memb: Nat Cncl BIPP 1984-86, qualification Bd RPS 1986-; chm BIPP NW Regn 1987-88; FBIPP 1985, FMPA 1988, FRPS 1986, FRSA 1987; *Style—* Neil Brightmore, Esq; Highlands, 71 James St, Penkhull, Stoke on Trent, Staffs (☎ 0782 621839); 25 Ironmarket, Newcastle, Staffs ST5 1RH (☎ 0782 621 839, fax 0782 611 957)

BRIGHTY, (Anthony) David; CMG (1984), CVO (1985); s of C P J Brighty, and W G Turner; *b* 7 Feb 1939; *Educ* Northgate GS Ipswich, Clare Coll Cambridge (BA); *m* 1, 1963 (m dis 1979), Diana Porteous; 2 s, 2 da; m 2, 1982, Jane Docherty; *Career* entered Foreign Office 1961; Brussels 1962-63, Havana 1964-66, FO 1968-69, resigned; joined S G Warburg & Co 1969; rejoined FCO 1971, Saigon 1973-74, UK Mission to UN NY 1975-78, RCDS 1979, head of personnel operations dept FCO 1980-83, counsellor Lisbon 1983-86; dir of private office of Sec Gen of NATO 1986-87; *Style—* David Brighty, Esq, CMG, CVO; c/o Foreign and Commonwealth Office, London SW1

BRIGINSHAW, Baron (Life Peer UK 1974); Richard William Briginshaw; married; *Career* gen sec Nat Soc of Operative Printers, Graphical and Media Personnel 1951-75, memb Gen Cncl TUC 1965-75, memb ACAS 1974-76, former memb Br Nat Oil Corpn; *Style—* The Rt Hon The Lord Briginshaw; House of Lords, SW1

BRIGNELL, Gp Capt John Aubrey; OBE (1955), DFC (1945); s of John Brignell (d 1939), of Cambridge, and Gladys Georgina, *née* Butcher (d 1972); *b* 19 May 1918; *Educ* Perse Sch, Sidney Sussex Cambridge (MA); *m* Dulcis Doreen Margaret, da of Frederic Upton, of Caton, Lancaster; *Career* WWII Bomber Cmd (No 622), ldr of No 3 Gp G-H daylight raids, Air Force ADC to HE Govr of NI 1951-54, cdr RAF Sqdn Boscombe Down 1955-57; dep dir OPS Air Defence Air Miny 1958-61, cdr RAF Watton surface to air missile wing 1961-63, cdr RAF Bawdsey 1963-64, chief air defence planner 1964-67, Supreme HQ Europe, int staff NATO Air Defence Ground Environment Implementation Team 1968-74, ret; former tres (now reader) Holy Trinity Pro-Cathedral Bruxelles; *Recreations* squash, bridge, theology; *Clubs* Royal Automobile, Leander, RAF, Prince Albert (Bruxelles); *Style—* Gp Capt John A Brignell, OBE, DFC; Ave W, Churchill 202 Bte 3, B1180 Bruxelles, Belgium (☎ 02 3450812)

BRIGSTOCKE, Heather Renwick; da of Sqdn Ldr John Renwick Brown, DFC, and Mrs May Brown; *b* 2 Sept 1929; *Educ* Abbey Sch Reading, Girton Coll Cambridge; *m* 1952, Geoffrey Brigstocke (d 1974); 3 s, 1 da; *Career* classics mistress Francis Holland Sch (Graham Terrace), Godolphin & Latymer Sch; Latin teacher Nat Cathedral Sch Washington DC, headmistress Francis Holland (Clarence Gate) 1965-74, high mistress St Pauls' Girls' Sch 1974-; former memb: cncl of Middlesex Hosp Med, cncl of the City Univ, cncl of the Royal Holloway Coll; former tstee: Nat Gallery, Kennedy Meml Tst; cncl of St Georges House Windsor, non exec dir London Weekend Television; Royal Ballet Sch, Forest Sch; former govr Wellington Coll; former cncl memb of the Royal Soc of Arts; *Style—* Mrs Heather Brigstocke; St Paul's Girls' School, Brook Green, London W6 7BS

BRIGSTOCKE, Nicholas Owen; s of Mervyn Owen Brigstocke, of 12 Deep Acres, Chesham Bois, Amersham, Bucks, and Janet Mary, *née* Singleton; *b* 25 June 1942; *Educ* Epsom Coll; *m* 17 May 1969, Carol Barbara, da of Air Marshal Sir Walter Philip George Pretty, CB, KBE (d 1975), 2 s (Marcus b 1973, Henry b 1981), 1 da (Lucinda b 1971); *Career* Shell Mex and BP Ltd 1961-69, De Zoete and Gorton Ltd 1969-78, ptnr De Zoete and Bevan Ltd 1978-86, dir Barclays De Zoete Wedd Securities Ltd (head of UK equity sales) 1986-; *Recreations* tennis, cricket; *Clubs* MCC, City of London, Escorts SPR; *Style—* Nicholas Brigstocke, Esq; Linchmere House, Linchmere, Nr Haslemere, Surrey GU27 3NG (☎ 0428 722 134); Barclays De Zoete Wedd Ltd, Ebbgate House, 2 Swan Lane, London EC4R 3TS (☎ 01 623 2323, fax 01 626 1753, car telephone 0860 834 485, telex 888221)

BRIGSTOCKE, (Alexander) Sandy (Julian); s of Major Arthur Montagu Brigstocke (d 1928), and Doris Mamie, *née* Butler (d 1982); *b* 11 Nov 1922; *Educ* Wellington, Univ of London (BA); *m* 14 Dec 1949, Diana Mavis, da of John Arundel Evershed (d 1984); 1 s (Timothy b 1951), 2 da (Jennifer b 1953, Juliet b 1962); *Career* WWII Capt Rifle Bde served N Africa and Italy 1941-45; jt headmaster Boxgrove Sch Guildford 1953-64; elected Surrey CC 1970 (vice-chm 1987-, vice-chm social servs ctee 1977-81, chm planning 1981-85, vice-chm educn ctee 1987-89); chm: Guildford Cons Assoc 1978-81, Nat Tst Winkworth Arboretum Mgmnt Ctee 1981-89, W Surrey Centre Nat Tst 1985-89, Surrey Historic Bldgs Tst 1985-; govr: Kingston Poly, Guildford Coll of Technol, W Surrey Coll of Art & Design 1973-89; *Recreations* music, sport, travel; *Clubs* MCC, Greenjackets; *Style—* Sandy Brigstocke, Esq; Granton House, Shackleford, Godalming, Surrey GU8 6AX (☎ 0483 422545); County Hall, Kingston-upon-Thames (☎ 01 541 9016)

BRILL, John; s of Eric William Brill, of Bramhall, Cheshire, and Barbara Brill; *b* 21 August 1935; *Educ* Kings Sch Macclesfield, Jesus Coll Cambridge (MA); *m* 10 Sept 1960, Elizabeth, da of late David James Hughes-Morgan; 3 s (Timothy, Jonathon, James); *Career* chm Sterling Public Relations Ltd 1976-89; md Brian Dowling Ltd 1965-76; *Recreations* golf, tennis, travel; *Clubs* Savile; *Style—* John Brill, Esq; Rookhurst Coast Hill Lane, Westcott, Dorking, Surrey (☎ 0306 882344); Sterling Public Relations, 1 Chelsea Manor Gardens, London SW3 (☎ (01) 351 2400)

BRIMACOMBE, Michael William; s of Lt-Col Winston Brimacombe, OBE of Marine Lodge, Cliff Rd, Livermead, Torquay, S Devon, and Marjorie Gertrude, *née* Ling; *b* 6 Mar 1944; *Educ* Kelly Coll, Univ of London (LLB); *m* 9 April 1968, Pamela Jean, da of Charles mark Stone, of Choisie, Mont Cochon, St Helier, Jersey C1; 1 s (John Mark b 1969), 2 da (Ruth Michelle b 1972, Helen Marie-Anne b 1976); *Career* ptnr: Norman Allport & Co 1972-, Price Waterhouse (UK and Jersey 1975-85; md Legal Tstees (Jersey) Ltd 1985-, non exec dir The CI Knitwear Co Ltd trading as Pierre Sangan Int 1986-, past chm Jersey Assoc of practising Chartered and Certified Accountants; FID, FCA 1968, FRSA 1987; *Recreations* reading, travelling, walking; *Clubs* Royal Western YC of Eng; *Style—* Michael Brimacombe, Esq; Temple View, Rue des Marettes, Faldouet, St Martin, Jersey, Channel Isalnds (☎ 0534 51087); Norman Allport & Co, Hill Street Chambers, 6 Hill St, St Helier, Jersey C1 (☎ 0534 75544, fax 0534 78118, telex 4192123)

BRIMACOMBE, Rodney John; s of Lt-Col Winston Brimacombe, OBE, of Torquay, and Majorie Gertrude *née* Ling; *b* 22 Dec 1940; *Educ* Kelly Coll; *m* 16 Nov 1968, Susan Jane, da of John Stredwick, of Burrow Cottage, Livermead, Torquay; 2 s (Simon Rodney b 28 Jan 1970, Justin John b 22 May 1972); *Career* gen mangr Pophams Ltd Plymouth 1964-69, md Jollys Ltd Bath 1970-72, gp asst md E Dingle & Co Plymouth 1972-79, non exec dir Westwood TV Ltd 1979-81, gen mangr sales and devpt Harrods Ltd 1979-86, mktg conslt of England 1986-; chm Knightsbridge Gp 1985-86, vice pres and cncllr French C of C 1986, sec 20 Club 1986; *Recreations* sailing; *Clubs* Royal Western YC, Itchenor Sailing; *Style—* Rodney Brimacombe, Esq; The Penthouse, 25 Dolphin Hse, Sutton Harbour, Plymouth PL4 0DW (☎ 0752 222 852)

BRIMACOMBE, Lt-Col Winston; OBE (1959); s of John Brimacombe (d 1947), of Penradden, Lifton, Devon, and Louisa Beatrice, *née* Tubb (d 1956); *b* 23 Dec 1908; *Educ* Dunheved Coll Launceston Cornwall; *m* 8 June 1935, Marjorie Gertrude, da of Herbert Stephen Ling (d 1955), of Leamington Spa; 3 s (Peter b 1936, Rodney b 1940, Michael b 1944); *Career* Army Serv 1940-45; (Lt-Col 1943); chm: Nat Savings Ctee Plymouth 1955-74, Commercial Union Assur Gp Plymouth and Cornwall 1959-83, SW Region and Nat Indust Ctees of Nat Savings 1960-74; memb and nat chm Assoc Retail Distributors Cncl 1958-82; gen cmmr Income Tax Plymouth 1970-85; chm and md E Dingle Gp 1954-76; founder bd memb Westward TV 1961-80; chm: Chiesman Gp plc, Army & Navy Stores plc; main bd dir House of Fraser (90 stores in UK incl Harrods) 1971- (ret 1981); life pres: E Dingle Gp Cos 1981-, Mayflower Tst Ltd; chm FH Dingle Tst Ltd; govr Kelly Coll Tavistock 1960-85; FRSA 1972; *Recreations* golf, gardening; *Clubs* Royal Western YC of England; *Style—* Lt-Col Winston Brimacombe, Esq, OBE; Marine Lodge, Cliff Road, Livermead, Torquay, Devon (☎ Torquay 24000)

BRIMELOW, Hon Alison Jane; da of Baron Brimelow, GCMG, OBE

BRIMELOW, Hon Elizabeth Anne; da of Baron Brimelow, GCMG, OBE

BRIMELOW, Baron (Life Peer UK 1976); Thomas Brimelow; GCMG (1975, KCMG 1968, CMG 1959), OBE (1954); s of William Brimelow (d 1951), of New Mills, Derbys, and Hannah, *née* Smith; *b* 25 Oct 1915; *Educ* New Mills GS, Oriel Oxford; *m* 1945, Jean E, da of late John William Underwood Cull, of Glasgow; 2 da; *Career* FO 1938; cnsllr Washington 1960-63, min Br Embassy Moscow 1963-66, ambass to Poland 1966-69, dep under-sec of state FCO 1969-73, perm under-sec of state FO and head of Diplomatic Service 1973-75; MEP 1977-78; chm Occupational Pensions Bd 1978-82; *Style—* The Rt Hon The Lord Brimelow, GCMG, OBE; 12 West Hill Court, Millfield Lane, London N6 (☎ 01 340 8722)

BRIMS, Charles David; s of David Vaughan Brims, of Northumberland, and Eve Georgina Mary, *née* Barrett; *b* 5 May 1950; *Educ* Winchester, Brasenose Coll Oxford; *m* 1973, Patricia Catherine, da of John Desmond Henderson, of Berks; 2 s (David b 1980, Edward b 1982); *Career* dir: Courage (Western) Ltd 1980-83, Imperial Inns and Taverns Ltd 1983-86, Imperial Leisure and Retailing Ltd 1985-86, chief exec Portsmouth and Sunderland Newspapers plc 1986-; *Recreations* cricket, tennis, shooting; *Clubs* MCC, Vincent's Oxford; *Style—* Charles Brims, Esq; Pond House, Ramsdell, nr Basingstoke, Hants RG26 5PR; Buckton House, 37 Abingdon Rd, London W8 6AH (☎ 01-938 3039, telex 261091, fax 01-937 1479)

BRINCKMAN, Rosemary, Lady; Rosemary Marguerite; *née* Hope-Vere; da of late

Lt-Col James Hope-Vere, and ggggda of 1 Earl of Hopetoun; *b* 9 Feb 1907; *m* 1, 1930 (m dis 1933), Lt-Col John Drury Boteler Drury-Lowe, Scots Guards (d 1960); 1 s; m 2, 1933 (m dis 1942), Quintin Holland Gilbey; 1 s; m 3, 1942, as his 2 w, Col Sir Roderick (Napoleon) Brinckman, 5 Bt, DSO, MC (d 1985); 1 da; *Style—* Rosemary, Lady Brinckman; 7 Mallord Street, London SW3; Cross Keys, Sandwich, Kent

BRINCKMAN, Hon Lady; (Greta) Sheira Bernadette; *née* Grant-Ferris; da of Baron Harvington, PC (Life Peer); *b* 1937; *m* 1, 1956, John Frederick Edward Trehearne; 1 s (Edward b 1963), 2 da (Lucinda b 1957, Petrina b 1959); m 2, 1970 (m dis), Christopher Mark Henry Murray; m 3, 1983, as his 2 w, Sir Theodore (George Roderick) Brinckman, Bt, *qv*; *Style—* The Hon Lady Brinckman; Somerford Keynes House, Cirencester, Glos GL7 6DN

BRINCKMAN, Sir Theodore (George Roderick); 6 Bt (UK 1831); s of Col Sir Roderick Brinckman, 5 Bt, DSO, MC, the Grenadier Guards, (d 1985) and his 1 w, Margaret Wilson (d 1977), da of Wilson Southam, of Ottawa, Canada; *b* 20 Mar 1932; *Educ* Millfield, Trinity Coll Sch Port Hope Ontario, Christ Church Oxford, Trinity Coll Toronto Univ; *m* 1, 11 June 1958 (m dis 1983), Helen Mary Anne, da of late Arnold Elliot Cook, of Toronto, Canada; 2 s (Theodore, Roderick), 1 da (Sophia); m 2, 1983, Hon (Greta) Sheira Bernadette Grant-Ferris, *qv*, da of Baron Harvington; *Heir* s, Theodore Jonathan Brinckman; *Career* publisher and antiquarian bookseller; *Clubs* White's, Buck's, University (Toronto); *Style—* Sir Theodore Brinckman, Bt; Somerford Keynes House, Cirencester, Glos GL7 6DN (☎ 0285 861562); office (☎ 0285 860554)

BRIND, (Arthur) Henry; CMG (1973); o s of late Thomas Henry Brind, of Barry, and N W B Brind; *b* 4 July 1927; *Educ* St John's Coll Cambridge (MA); *m* 1954, Barbara, da of late George Frederick Harrison, of Bedford; 1 s, 1 da; *Career* HMOCS 1950-60; joined Diplomatic Service 1960; actg high cmmr Uganda 1972-73, high cmmr Mauritius 1974-77, ambass Somalia 1977-80, high cmmr Malawi 1983-87; *Clubs* Reform; *Style—* Henry Brind Esq, CMG; 20 Grove Terrace, London NW5 1PH (☎ 01 267 1190)

BRIND, Brigadier (ret) James Lindesay; DSO (1946); s of Gen Sir John Brind KCB, KBE, CMG, DSO (d 1954), and Dorothey Swire Frodsham (d 1924); descended from Walter Brind, prime warden of Goldsmith's Co (1820) and his s Gen Sir James Brind, GCB (1808-88) whose descendants were mostly Naval and Military; *b* 29 August 1909; *Educ* Wellington, RMM Sandhurst; *m* 21 Aug 1946, Evelyn Elizabeth, da of Stanley Lake Mann, of Leamington Spa (d 1972); 1 s (Christopher Markham b 1949); *Career* cmmnd Somerset Light Infantry (UK) 1929, Adjutant Depot Somerset LI (UK) 1936, Staff Coll Camberley 1943-44 (UK), staff and regimental offr (France, Belgium and Holland) 1944-45, CO 5 Wiltshire Regt (Germany) 1945-45, CO 4th Devonshire Regt (Austria) 1945-46, staff offr Sch of Infantry (UK) 1946-48, Staff Offr Middle East GHQ (Egypt) 1948-52, CO 1st Somerset Light Infantry (Germany and Malaya) 1952-55, bde cdr 159 TA Inf Bde (UK) 1955-58, cdr Rhine Area Germany 1958-61, ret from regular Army 1961, appointed Ret Offr II, in charge training areas East Midlands (UK) 1963-75; *Recreations* music, fishing, writing; *Clubs* Army and Navy, Pall Mall London; *Style—* James L Brind, DSO

BRIND, Maj-Gen Peter Holmes Walter; CBE (1962, OBE 1948), DSO (1945), DL (Surrey 1970); s of Gen Sir John Brind, KCB, KBE, CMG, DSO (d 1954), of Dorchester, and Dorothy Margaret Swire Frodsham (d 1924); *b* 16 Feb 1912; *Educ* Wellington, RMC Sandhurst; *m* 1942, Patricia Stewart, da of Cdr Stewart M Walker, DSC (d 1944), of Harrietsham Kent; 3 s (Robin, Michael, Nigel); *Career* cmmnd Dorsetshire Regt 1932, ADC to Govr of Bengal 1936-39, Adj NW Europe 1940 (wounded 1940), GSO3 War Off 1940-41, DAAG HQ 12 Corps and HQ Canadian Corps 1941-42, GSO2 (mil operations) War Off 1942, cmdt Battle Sch 1944, cmdg 2 Devonshire Regt NW Europe 1944-45, GSO1 War Off, Palestine 1948, Egypt 1949, Lt-Col 1952, cmdg 5 KAR (Kenya) 1954-56, Lt-Col 1954, Col 1955, cmdg 5 Inf Bde Gp (BAOR) 1956-58, IDC 1959, Brig 1960, Brig AQ ME 1960-62, BGS Eastern Cmd 1962-65, ADC to HM The Queen 1964, Maj-Gen 1965, COS Northern Cmd 1965-67; dir BRCS (Surrey Branch) 1968-77 (dep-pres 1977-83); govr public and prep schs 1968; *Recreations* gardening, music; *Style—* Maj-Gen Peter Brind, CBE, DSO, DL; Milestones, Hill Rd, Haslemere, Surrey

BRINDLE, Hon Mrs Joan Kathleen; *née* Davies; da of 1 Baron Darwen (d 1950); *b* 26 Oct 1917; *m* 1940, Walter Higham Brindle, MBE, TD, s of Walter Brindle, of St Annes-on-Sea; 1 s, 1 da; *Style—* The Hon Mrs Brindle; 27 Abbotsford Court, Colinton Rd, Edinburgh EH10 5EH

BRINDLEY, Rev Canon Brian Dominick Frederick Titus; s of Frederick Benjamin Brindley (d 1973) of Wood Way, Bushey Heath, and Violet, *née* Williams (d 1975); *Educ* Stowe, Exeter Coll Oxford (BA, MA); *Career* ordained: deacon 1962, priest 1963; asst curate Clewer St Andrew 1962-67, parish priest Most Holy Trinity Reading 1967-, hon canon Christ Church Oxford 1986-, proctor in convocation 1975-; memb: Standing Ctee of Gen Synod 1980- (policy sub-ctee 1980-85, chm business sub ctee), exec ctee and Gen Cncl Church Union, former chm Church Literature Assoc and Soc of St Peter and St Paul; *Books* Porci Ante Margaritam (1954); *Recreations* cooking, garden design and history, bridge, opera, sacred music; *Clubs* Athenaeum; *Style—* The Rev Canon Brian Brindley; Holy Trinity Presbytery, 32 Baker Street, Reading, Berks RG1 7XY (☎ 0734 572 650); Flat 1, 17 Devonshire Place, Brighton BN2 1QA (☎ 0273 608 895)

BRINSMEAD, Barry Michael; s of Lt Cdr Alfred Charles Brinsmead, RN (d 1965), and Gladys Ella, *née* Knight; *b* 13 Feb 1954; *Educ* Royal Hosp Sch Holbrook; *m* 20 July 1974, Deborah, da of Wing Cdr Owen Leslie Hardy, DFC, AFC, RAF; 1 s (Simon b 1980), 1 da (Jennifer b 1983); *Career* ptnr Hunt Ptnrs (Portsmouth, Chichester, IOW); dir: Winkelhopper (UK) Ltd 1985, Solent Accountancy Trg Ltd 1986, S Coast Aviation Ltd 1987, Griffin Fin Services (Southern) Ltd 1989; private pilot (PPL); FCA; *Style—* Barry Brinsmead, Esq; Te Gatehouse, Castlemans Lane, Hayling Island, Hants (☎ 0705 461971); 29/31 Guildhall Walk, Portsmouth (☎ 0705 815342, fax 0705 291019, telex 86475, car phone 0860 536591)

BRINTON, Michael Ashley Cecil; s of Maj Sir Tatton Brinton, DL (d 1985), of Queen's Gate, London SW7, and his 1 wife Mary Elizabeth, *née* Fahnestock (d 1960); *b* 6 Oct 1941; *Educ* Eton, Vienna, Perugia, Aix-en-Provence; *m* 1966, Angela, da of John Ludlow, of High Wycombe; 2 s, 1 da; *Career* dir Brintons Ltd 1970- (mktg and sales dir 1988-); pres: Confedn Int des Tapis et Tissus D'Ameublement; *Recreations* shooting, fishing; *Style—* Michael Brinton, Esq; Park Hall, nr Kidderminster, Worcs (☎ 0562 700268)

BRINTON, Tim(othy) Denis; s of Dr Denis Hubert Brinton (d 1986) (whose mother was Dorothea, gda of Sir William Bowman, 1 Bt; the Dr's 1 cousins include late Sir Tatton Brinton and late Lady (Life Baroness) Stocks), and his 1 wife Joan Violet, *née* Hood (d 1971); *b* 24 Dec 1929; *Educ* Eton, Geneva Univ, Central Sch of Speech and Drama; *m* 1, 1954 (m dis), Jane-Mari, da of Air-Marshal Sir Arthur Coningham; 1 s, 3 da; m 2, 1965, Jeanne Frances Wedge; 2 da; *Career* 2 Lt Royal Scots (UK); broadcaster: BBC 1951-59, ITN 1959-62; media conslt, presenter and commentator; memb Kent CC 1974-81; MP (C) Gravesend 1979-83, Gravesham 1983-87; memb select ctee Educn 1979-83, chm Cons Pty Media Cmmn 1983-87; memb court London Univ 1979-; *Recreations* fishing; *Style—* Tim Brinton, Esq; 78 Lupus Street, London SW1V 3EL (☎ 01 834 1181)

BRINTON, (Charles) Topham Cecil; s of Maj Sir (Esme) Tatton Cecil Brinton (d 1985), and Mary Elizabeth, *née* Fahnestock (d 1960); *b* 10 Sept 1939; *Educ* Eton, Brown Univ USA (BA); *m* 26 June 1965, Rosemary Anna, da of Alfred Peter Wilson, 2 da (Catharine Elizabeth b 18 Aug 1966, Annabelle Mary b 4 Feb 1968); *Career* Brintons Ltd: dir 1966, asst md 1977, vice chm 1978, chm 1981, chm and jt md 1988; memb: Carpet Indust Trg Bd 1969-71, Jt Advsy Cncl for the Carpet Indust 1971-83: chm dist jt cncl 1972-84, chm nat jt cncl 1972-; pres Kidderminster and Dist C of C 1977-78, memb Br Carpet Mfr's Assoc Ltd 1978- (pres 1981-86); chm: Kidderminster area bd Young Enterprise 1981-83, Kidderminster Dist Carpet Mfrs and Spinners Assoc 1981-83, (tax cmmr 1983-); chm W Mids Region CBI 1986-88 (vice chm 1988-); fell Royal Soc of Arts and Mfrs; *Recreations* squash, shooting, tennis; *Style—* Topham Brinton, Esq; Gothersley Hall, Stourton, Stourbridge, Worcs (☎ 0384 873974); Brintons Ltd, PO Box 16 Exchange St, Kidderminster, Worcs DY10 1AG (☎ 0562 820000, fax 0562 515597, car 0860 747934, telex 338586)

BRISBANE, Archbishop of; Most Rev John Basil Rowland Grindrod; KBE (1983); s of Edward Basil Grindrod and Dorothy Gladys Grindrod; *b* 14 Dec 1919; *Educ* Repton, Queen's Coll Oxford; *m* 1, 1949, Ailsa W (d 1981), da of G Newman; 2 da; m 2, 1983, Mrs Dell Cornish, da of S J Caswell; *Career* former RM commando; former curate of Bundaberg, Archdeacon of Rockhampton 1965, vicar of S Yarra 1965, bishop of Riverina 1966, bishop of Rockhampton 1971, archbishop of Brisbane and Metropolitan of the Province of Queensland 1980-, primate of the Anglican Church of Australia 1982-; *Style—* The Most Rev the Lord Archbishop of B; Bishopsbourne, 39 Eldernell Ave, Hamilton, Qld 4007, Australia

BRISBANE, Lady Marguerite Mary; *née* Chetwynd-Talbot; yst da of 21 Earl of Shrewsbury (d 1980); *b* 12 June 1950; *m* 1970, Guy William Brisbane; 1 s (Duncan b 1975); *Style—* Lady Marguerite Brisbane; 228 Meadvale Rd, Ealing, London W5 (☎ 01 997 5527)

BRISBOURNE, Richard; OBE (1971); s of Percy George Brisbourne (d 1957), of Uttoxeter, Staffs, and Beatrice Mabel, *née* Smith (d 1969); *b* 8 June 1920; *Educ* Alleynes GS Uttoxeter; *m* 7 Dec 1942, Joan, da of William Henry Smith (d 1959), of Uttoxeter, Staffs; 2 s (Richard Paul b 19 Nov 1943, Giles b 20 July 1948); *Career* Lt Leics Yeo 1942-46, served NW Europe; chm: Africa Timber and Plywood 1961-70, Ghana Timber Assoc 1961-65, pres Nigeria Timber Fedn 1965-70; conslt on tropical timber industs (ind) to World Bank and FAO 1970-79, advsr on forest concessions (Sarawak Govt) and timber industs 1979-80; Bucks CC rep Chalfont St Giles 1981-, chm Schs sub-ctee, vice-chm Educn Ctee; *Books* Sawmilling in the Tropics, Forest Development in Midwest Nigeria; Liveryman Worshipful Co of Loriners, Freeman City of London; *Recreations* golf, bridge, travel; *Clubs* Beaconsfield Golf; *Style—* Richard Brisbourne, OBE; c/o Lloyds Bank plc, The Broadway, Wycombe End, Beaconfield, Bucks

BRISBY, John Constant Shannon McBurney; s of Michael Douglas James McBurney Brisby (d 1965), of London, and Rada Liliana, *née* Daneva; *b* 8 May 1956; *Educ* Westminster, Christ Church Oxford (MA); *m* 20 April 1985, Claire Alexandra Anne, da of Sir Donald Arthur Logan, KCMG, of 6 Thurloe St, London SW7; *Career* 2 Lt 5 Royal Inniskilling Dragoon Gds 1974, transferred Res 1975-77; barr Lincoln's Inn 1978; *Style—* John Brisby, Esq; 40 St Dunstan's Rd, Baron's Court, London; Stockings Farm, nr Helmdon, South Northamptonshire; 4 Stone Bldgs, Lincoln's Inn, London WC2A 3XT

BRISBY, Liliana; *b* 2 Feb 1923; *Educ* Bulgaria and Univ of Lausanne, Switzerland; *m* 1946, M D J Brisby (d 1965); 2 s, 1 da; *Career* contributor BBC's East Euro Service 1947-60, memb of staff information and research dept FO, dep ed The World Today 1971 (ed 1975), asst ed Yearbook of European Law 1984; contributor: Soviet Survey, China Quarterly, New Leader, Encyclopeadia Britannica, The Spectator; *Books* Les relations russo-bulgares 1878-1886 (1946), co-ed: Contemporary History in Soviet Mirror (co-ed 1964), The Truth that Killed by Georgi Markov (translator 1983); *Style—* Liliana Brisby

BRISCO, Sir Donald Gilfrid; 8 Bt (GB 1782), JP (1967); s of Sir Hylton Musgrave Campbell Brisco, 7 Bt (d 1968); *b* 15 Sept 1920; *Educ* Wairapa Coll New Zealand; *m* 5 Aug 1945, Irene, o da of Henry John Gage, of Ermine Park, Brockworth, Glos; 3 da; *Heir* cousin, Campbell Howard Brisco b 1947; *Career* serv WWII, pilot RNZAF and RAF; sheep farmer (ret); *Style—* Sir Donald Brisco, JP; PO Box 165, Havelock North, Hawke's Bay, New Zealand

BRISCOE, (John) James; s and h of Sir John Leigh Charlton Briscoe, 4 Bt, DFC; *b* 15 July 1951; *Educ* Oratory Sch, UCL; *m* 1985, Felicity Mary, eldest da of D M Watkinson, of Gowthorpe Manor, Swardeston, nr Norwich, Norfolk; *Career* Beavis Walker; ACA 1978; FCA 1988; *Recreations* vintage cars, ocean racing; *Clubs* Royal Ocean Racing; *Style—* James Briscoe, Esq; 10 Hopgood St, London W12

BRISCOE, Dr John Hubert Daly; s of Dr Arnold Daly Briscoe, TD, of Seckford Lodge, Woodbridge, Suffolk, and Doris Winifred, *née* Nicholson (d 1985); *b* 19 Mar 1933; *Educ* Winchester, St John's Coll Cambridge, St Thomas's Hosp London (BA, BChir, MB, MA); *m* 1 Feb 1958, Janet Anne, da of James Douglas Earlam ((d 1958), of Bayfield, Warlingham, Surrey; 1 s (James b 1964), 4 da (Sarah b 1959, Emma b 1960, Lucy b 1961, Martha b 1967); *Career* med offr Overseas Civil Serv Basutoland 1959-62, asst in gen prac Aldeburgh Suffolk 1963-65, princ in gen practice Eton Berkshire 1965-; med offr: Eton Coll 1965-, St George's Sch Windsor Castle 1976-; apothecary to: HM Household Windsor, HM the Queen Mother's Household Royal Lodge 1986-; memb Windsor and Dist Med Soc 1965-, hon med offr The Guards Polo Club 1966-83, bridgemaster Baldwin's Bridge Tst Eton 1988, pres Med Offrs of Schools Assoc 1989- (hon sec 1980-85), hon auditor Euro Union of Sch and Univ Health and Medicine 1981-; Freeman City of London 1956, Asst of Worshipful Soc of Apothecaries of London 1984- (apprentice 1952, Yeoman 1956, Liveryman 1966);

DObst RCOG 1959, MRCGP 1968; *Recreations* growing vegetables; *Clubs* Omar Khayyam; *Style*— Dr John Briscoe; Eton Court House, Eton, Windsor, Berkshire SL4 6AQ

BRISCOE, Sir John Leigh Charlton; 4 Bt (UK 1910), of Bourn Hall, Bourn, Co of Cambridge, DFC (1945); s of Sir J Charlton Briscoe, 3 Bt, (d 1960), of Lakenheath Hall, Suffolk; *b* 3 Dec 1911; *Educ* Harrow, Magdalen Coll Oxford (MA); *m* 1948, Teresa Mary Violet, da of Brig-Gen Sir Archibald Home, KCVO, CB, CMG, DSO; 2 s, 1 da; *Heir* s, James Briscoe; *Career* served RAFVR 1942-46; dir of aerodromes Miny of Aviation 1961-66, dir ops BAA 1966-73; ACA, FCIT; *Recreations* old cars; *Clubs* RAF, Royal Ocean Racing; *Style*— Sir John Briscoe, Bt, DFC; Little Acres, Stoke Poges, Bucks (☎ 02814 2394)

BRISE; *see*: Ruggles-Brise

BRISON, Ven William Stanley (Bill); s of William P Brison (d 1967), of Glen Rock, New Jersey, USA, and Marion, *née* Wilber (d 1953); *b* 20 Nov 1929; *Educ* Ridgewood New Jersey HS, Alfred Univ NY (BSc), Berkeley Divinity Sch New Haven, Conn (now Berkeley with Yale Divinity Sch MDiv, STM); *m* 16 June 1951, Marguerite (Peggy), da of Leroy Nettleton; 2 s (Paul b 1958, Daniel b 1961), 2 da (Sarah b 1964, Martha b 1965); *Career* active serv US Marine Corps 1951-53, Capt; engr Norton Co Mass USA 1953-54, rector Christ Episcopal Church Bethany Conn USA 1957-69, archdeacon of New Haven Dio of Conn 1967-69, rector Emmanuel Episcopal Church Stamford Conn 1969-72, vicar Christ Church Davyhulme Dio of Manchester 1972-81, rector All Saints New Heath Manchester and area dean N Manchester Deanery 1981-85, archdeacon of Bolton 1985-; *Recreations* squash, gardening; *Style*— The Ven the Archdeacon of Bolton; 2 Myrrh Street, Bolton BL1 8XE (☎ 0204 27269)

BRISTER, Graeme Roy; s of Royston George Brister, of Loughton, Essex, and Eileen Gladys Brister; *b* 5 May 1955; *Educ* Forest Sch Essex, Phillips Exeter Academy Exeter New Hampshire USA, Brasenose Coll Oxford (MA); *m* 26 July 1986, Ashley Fiona, da of Frank Michael Ashley Hines (Wing Cdr RAF ret), of Welton, Lincolnshire; 1 da (Leander b 1988); *Career* slr 1979, ptnr Linklaters and Paines 1985-; memb Law Soc 1979; *Recreations* buying country houses, sport, travel, wine; *Style*— Graeme R Brister, Esq; 12 Belsize Mews, Hampstead, London, NW3 5AT (☎ 01 435 0626); Linklaters & Paines, Barrington House, 59-67 Gresham Street, London, EC2V 7JA (☎ 01 606 7080), fax 01 606 5113, telex 884 349

BRISTER, William Arthur Francis; CB (1984); s of Gp Capt Arthur John Brister, OBE (d 1985), and Velda Mirandoli (d 1974); *b* 10 Feb 1925; *Educ* Douai Sch, Brasenose Coll Oxford (MA); *m* 1949, Mary, da of John Speakman (d 1936); 1 s (and 1 s decd), 1 da; *Career* asst govr class II HM Borstal Lowdham Grange 1949-52, asst princ Imperial Training Sch Wakefield 1952-55, asst govr II HM Prison Parkhurst 1955-57; dep govr HM Prison: Camp Hill 1957-60, Manchester 1960-62; govr HM Borstal: Morton Hall 1962-67, Dover 1967-69; govr II Prison Dept HQ 1969-71, govr HM Remand Centre Ashford 1971-73, govr I Prison Dept HQ 1973-75, asst controller 1975-79, chief inspector of the Prison Service 1979-81, HM dep chief inspector of Prisons 1981-82, dep dir gen Prison Service 1982-85; Nuffield Travelling Fellow Canada and Mexico 1966-67; memb: Parole Bd 1986, bd of govrs New Hall Sch 1986; *Recreations* shooting, music, venetian history; *Clubs* United Oxford & Cambridge University, English-Speaking Union; *Style*— William Brister, Esq, CB

BRISTOL, Archdeacon of; *see*: Balmforth, Ven Anthony James

BRISTOL, Bishop of, 1985-; Rt Rev Barry Rogerson; s of Eric Rogerson (d 1986), and Olive Hooper; *b* 25 July 1936; *Educ* Magnus GS Newark Notts, Univ of Leeds (BA); *m* 1961, Olga May, da of Wilfred Gibson (d 1982); 2 da (Susan Claire b 1963, Deborah Jane b 1966); *Career* Midland Bank 1952-57; Nat Serv RAF 1955-57 (Corpl); Midland Bank 1952-57; curate: St Hilda with St Thomas South Shields 1962-65, St Nicholas Bishopwearmouth 1965-67; lectr Lichfield Theological Coll 1967-71, vice-princ Lichfield Theol Coll 1971-72, lectr Salisbury/Wells Theol Coll 1972-75, vicar St Thomas Wednesfield 1975-79, team rector Wednesfield Team 1979, bishop of Lichfield Wolverhampton 1979-85; chm Advsy Cncl for the Church's Ministry 1987-; *Recreations* cinema, stained glass, photography; *Clubs* Royal Cwlth Soc; *Style*— The Rt Rev the Lord Bishop of Bristol; Bishop's House, Clifton Hill, Clifton, Bristol BS8 1BW

BRISTOL, 7 Marquess of (UK 1826); (Frederick William) John Augustus Hervey; also Baron Hervey of Ickworth (E 1703), Earl of Bristol (GB 1714) and Earl Jermyn (UK 1826); Hereditary High Steward of the Liberty of St Edmund; patron of thirty livings; s of 6 Marquess of Bristol (d 1985), and his 1 w, Pauline Mary (now Mrs Edward G Lambton), da of late Herbert Coxton Bolton; *b* 15 Sept 1954; *Educ* Harrow, Neuchâtel Univ Switzerland; *m* 1984, Francesca, formerly w of Phillip Jones, of USA, and da of Douglas H Fisher, of Marbella, Spain; *Heir* half-bro, Lord Nicholas Hervey; *Career* ptnr in Mogee Investments (owner 55,000 hectare sheep stud in West Queensland); governing ptnr Jermyn Shipping; MInstD; *Recreations* horse racing, flying helicopters, snooker; *Clubs* Royal Thames Yacht, House of Lords Yacht, Travellers (Paris); *Style*— The Most Hon the Marquess of Bristol; Ickworth, Bury St Edmunds, Suffolk (☎ 028 488285)

BRISTOL, Hon Mrs (Lavinia Mary); da of 9 Baron Hawke (d 1985); *b* 15 June 1945; *Educ* Hatherop Castle, Queensgate London; *m* 1965, Maj Nicholas Maclean Verity Bristol; 3 s; *Career* administrator Project Tst 1973-; *Recreations* Army & Navy, New (Edinburgh); *Style*— The Hon Mrs Bristol; Breacachadh Castle, Isle of Coll, Argyll (☎ 087 93 378)

BRISTOL, Paul Lanfear Harold; s of Arnold Charles Verity Bristol; *b* 10 Nov 1937; *Educ* Wellington; *m* 1968, Polly Elizabeth, da of Gen Sir George Watkin Eban James Erskine, GCB, KBE, DSO; 3 children; *Career* short service cmmn King's Own Scottish Borderers; chief exec OIS Gp plc; *Recreations* work; *Clubs* Buck's; *Style*— Paul Bristol, Esq; OIS Gp plc, 1 Rozel Terrace, Mount Durand, St Peter Port, Guernsey, Channel Islands (☎ 0481 713571, fax 0481 71369)

BRISTOL, Timothy Arnold Neil; s of Arnold Charles Verity Bristol (d 1984), of Wotton, Surrey, and Lillias Nina Maud, *née* Francis-Hawkins; *b* 21 Feb 1941; *Educ* Cranleigh, Guildford Art Sch, RMA Sandhurst; *m* 7 Sept 1968, Elizabeth Olivia, da of John Gurney, of Walsingham Abbey, Norfolk; 2 s (Benjamin T F b 7 Nov 1972, Samuel F J b 3 Sept 1983), 1 da (Arabella F A 19 Aug 1970); *Career* 1 BN KOSB 1960-67, service in the Radfan, Borneo, South-Arabia and Dhofar Campaigns, seconded to the Sultan of Muscat's Forces 1966-67, ret as Capt; diamond valuer De Beers, seconded to the Sierra Leone Govt Diamond Off 1967-70; publishing mangr Medici Soc Ltd 1970-73, chm and chief exec Eastern Counties Printers and Publishing GP 1972-86, dir Marlow Int Ltd 1986-; *Recreations* riding, flying, travel; *Style*— Timothy Bristol, Esq; 12 Well Court, London EC4M 9DN (☎ 01 248 9614, fax 01 489 8316, telex 261260 ASH G)

BRISTOL, Dowager Marchioness of; Yvonne Marie; *née* Sutton; only da of Anthony Sutton, of Woodstock, The Glen, Farnborough Park, Kent; *m* 1974, as his 3 w, 6 Marquess of Bristol (d 1985); 1 s (Lord Frederick b 19 Oct 1979), 2 da (Lady Victoria b 6 Oct 1976, Lady Isabella b 9 March 1982); *Style*— The Most Hon the Dowager Marchioness; Sun Tower, Square Beaumarchais, Monte Carlo, Principality of Monaco

BRISTOW, Alan Edgar; OBE (1966); *b* 3 Sept 1923; *Educ* Portsmouth GS; *m* 1945, Jean Catherine; 1 s, 1 da; *Career* chm Bristow Helicopters Ltd 1953-85; FRAeS; Croix de Guerre; *Recreations* flying, shooting, sailing, farming, four-in-hand driving; *Style*— Alan Bristow Esq, OBE; Baynards Park Estate, Cranleigh, Surrey (☎ 0483 274674)

BRISTOW, Hon Mrs (Caroline Jean); da of 2 Baron Luke, KCVO, TD, JP, DL; *b* 25 Dec 1935; *m* 1958, James Bristow, *qv*; 3 s, 1 da; *Clubs* Sea View YC (IOW); *Style*— The Hon Mrs Bristow; Grange Farmhouse, Odell Bedford MK43 7AE (☎ 0234 720354); Penmorfa, Sea View, IOW (☎ 0983 613248)

BRISTOW, James; s of James Percy Bristow, of Aldeburgh; *b* 25 May 1934; *Educ* Oakham Sch; *m* 1958, Hon Caroline Jean, *qv*, da of 2 Baron Luke, KCVO, TD, JP, DL; 3 s, 1 da; *Career* dir Charles Wells Ltd; High Sheriff Beds 1982-83; horologist; Queen's Silver Jubilee Medal; *Recreations* music, sailing; *Clubs* Seaview Yacht; *Style*— James Bristow, Esq,; Grange Farmhouse, Odell, Bedford MK43 7AE (☎ 0234 720354); Penmorfa, Sea View, Isle of Wight (☎ 0983 613248)

BRISTOW, Air Cdre Nicholas Roger Lyell; s of Edward Lyell Bristow (d 1949), of London, and Margaret Emily, *née* Ekin (d 1963); *b* 13 April 1924; *Educ* Wellington; *m* 29 July 1950, Una Claire Margaret, da of Sir Anthony Francis Vincent, Bt (d 1936); 2 s (Robert b 1954, Edward b 1954), 2 da (Jane b 1953, Clare b 1951); *Career* RAF 1944-79; *Recreations* riding, walking, garden, travel; *Clubs* RAF; *Style*— Air Cdre Nicholas R L Bristow

BRISTOW, Hon Sir Peter Henry Rowley; s of Walter Rowley Bristow (d 1947), of London, and Florence, *née* White; *b* 1 June 1913; *Educ* Eton, Trinity Coll Cambridge (MA); *m* 1, 1940, Josephine Noel (d 1969), da of Bertram Leney, of Wateringbury, Kent; 1 s, 1 da; m 2, 1975, Elsa, da of Edwin Reynolds (d 1949), of Warwick, and wid of H B Leney; *Career* served WWII Sqdn Ldr RAF; barr 1936, QC 1964, dep chm Hants QS 1964-70, judge of Courts of Appeal of Guernsey and Jersey 1965-70, judge of the High Court Queen's Bench div 1970-85, presiding judge Western circuit 1979-82; kt 1970; *Books* Judge for Yourself; *Recreations* fishing, gardening; *Style*— The Hon Sir Peter Bristow; The Folly, Membury, Axminster, Devon EX13 7AG

BRITTAIN, Clive Edward; s of Edward John Brittain (d 1948), of Calne, Wilts, and Priscilla Rosalind, *née* Winzer; *b* 15 Dec 1933; *Educ* Calne Secdy Mod Sch; *m* 23 Feb 1957, Maureen Helen, da of Percy Russell Robinson (d 1987); *Career* Nat Serv 1954-56; racehorse trainer 1972-; won 1000 Gns 1984, Eclipse Stakes, Dubai Champion Stakes and Breeders Cup Turf USA 1985 with Pebbles; won Japan Cup Tokyo 1986 with Jupiter Island, won St Leger 1988 with Julio Mariner; *Recreations* shooting; *Clubs* Jockey Club Rooms; *Style*— Clive Brittain, Esq; Carlburg, 49 Bury Rd, Newmarket, Suffolk (☎ 0638 663739); Carlburg Stables (☎ 0638 664347, fax 0638 661744, car 0860 327118, telex 817160)

BRITTAIN, Dr John; s of Patrick Brittain (d 1962), of Warlingham. Surrey, and Anne, *née* Daly (d 1965); *b* 25 May 1923; *Educ* Slough GS, St Mary's Hosp and London Univ (MB BS); *m* 29 Oct 1955, Sheila Farnham, da of Albert George Wick (d 1961), of E Sheen; 2 s (Paul John b 1956, Jonathan b 1961), 1 da (Wendy Frances b 1958); *Career* RCS transferred RAMC Reserve; gen practice 1954-78, chief med offr Fred Olsen Shipping 1974-, attending physician Sus Allen Memorial Hosp Eldorado Kansas USA 1977; med advsr: Laporte Fluorides 1984, Wendstone Chemicals (Laporte) 1985-88, Laporte Industries R & D Div 1988; Laporte Interox 1988; memb sub ctee Gen Cncl for Shipping Code of Practice Hygiene of Food and Fresh Water Supplies in Passenger Ships 1979, memb Comité Technique Européan du Fluor 1987-; Freeman Worshipful Co of Apothecaries (Liveryman 1963); MRCS, LRCP, AFOM, DIH , FRSM; memb Medical Soc of London, BMA, Br Toxicology Soc, Soc Occupational Medicine; *Recreations* golf, reading; *Clubs* Savile, RSM, Tandridge GC; *Style*— Dr John Brittain; Research Division, Laporte Industries, P O Box 2, Moorfield Rd, Widnes, Cheshire WA8 0JU (☎ 051 495 2222 ext 2425, fax 051 420 4089, telex 82221)

BRITTAIN, Nicholas John; s of Denis Jack Brittain, MBE (d 1977), of Hungerford, Berks, and Irene Jane Williams (d 1945); *b* 8 Sept 1938; *Educ* Lord Wandsworth Coll, Jesus Coll Oxford (MA); *m* 1964, Patricia Mary, da of Alan Francis John Hopewell (d 1957); 1 s (James b 1969), 2 da (Charlotte b 1971, Rebecca b 1973); *Career* Unilever plc 1960-82; head of gp finance and dir of various subsidiary cos Legal and General plc 1983-86, chief accountant Barclays plc and Barclays Bank plc 1986-, chm Limebank Property Co Ltd and Bardco Property Investments Ltd 1986-; chm SW Surrey Cons Political Centre 1984-87; govr Alexandra Tst 1980-; memb Providence Row Housing Assoc Council mgmnt ctee (chm fin ctee 1986-), Fullemploy 500 Executive Ctee 1987-; memb cncl and educnl ctee CACA 1988-; chm British Bankers Assoc accounting ctee 1987-; *Recreations* politics, singing, cricket, gardening; *Clubs* Cannons, Brook CC, Privateers CC, Warbrook Ward, "59", FCCA; *Style*— Nicholas J Brittain, Esq; Churchfields, Church Lane, Witley, Godalming, Surrey GU8 5PP; Barclays Bank plc, 54 Lombard Street, London EC3P 3AH (☎ 01-626 1567)

BRITTAN, Rt Hon Sir Leon; PC (1981), QC (1978); s of Dr Joseph Brittan, and Rebecca, *née* Lipetz; yr bro of Samuel Brittan, *qv*; *b* 25 Sept 1939; *Educ* Haberdashers' Aske's, Trinity Coll Cambridge (MA), Yale Univ; *m* 1980, Diana Peterson; *Career* barr Inner Temple 1962 (bencher 1983); chm Bow Gp 1964-65; editor Crossbow 1966-68; Parly candidate (C) Kensington N 1966 and 1970; MP (C): Cleveland and Whitby Feb 1974-83, Richmond Yorkshire 1983-88; oppn spokesman: Devolution 1976-79, House of Commons Affairs 1976-78, Employment 1978-79; min of state Home Office 1979-81, chief sec to Treasury 1981-83, sec of state for the Home Dept 1983-86; sec of state for Trade and Industry 1985-86; chm Soc of Conservative Lawyers 1986-88; vice pres Cmmn to Euro Communities 1989-; kt 1989; *Clubs* Carlton, MCC; *Style*— The Rt Hon Sir Leon Brittan, QC; Commission of European Communities, Place de la Loi, 200, 1049 Brussels, Belgium

BRITTAN, Peter John; s of John Arthur Brittan, of 76 Norfolk Road, Erdington, Birmingham, and Joyce Barbara, *née* Dayman; *b* 29 June 1952; *Educ* King Edward's GS Birmingham; *m* 15 Sept 1984, Sally Hamilton, da of David Hamilton Jacob, of 3 Dunchurch Close, Balsall Common, Coventry; 2 da (Samantha, Stephanie); *Career* CA

1978-, managing ptnr Brittan & Bevan Chartered Accountants Birmingham; memb Birmingham Chamber of Commerce; FCA 1975; *Recreations* sports generally, stamp collecting; *Clubs* Birmingham Welsh RFC; *Style*— Peter Brittan, Esq; 43 Vesey Road, Wylde Green, Sutton Coldfield, West Midlands (☎ 021 355 3217); 18th Floor, Metropolitan House, 1 Hagley Road, Birmingham (☎ 021 456 2141, fax 021 452 1422)

BRITTAN, Samuel; s of Dr Joseph Brittan, and Rebecca, *née* Lipetz; er bro of Rt Hon Leon Brittan, QC, MP, *qv*; *b* 29 Dec 1933; *Educ* Kilburn GS, Jesus Coll Cambridge; *Career* with Financial Times 1955-61, economics ed Observer 1961-64, advsr Dept of Economic Affairs 1965, princ economic commentator Financial Times 1966-, asst ed Financial Times 1978-; visiting fell Nuffield Coll 1974, visiting prof Chicago Law Sch 1978; memb: Peacock Ctee on the Finance of the BBC 1985-86; awards: Wincott Prize for Finance Journalism 1971, George Orwell Prize for 1980, Ludwig Erhard Prize for Economic Writing 1988; Hon DLitt Heriot Watt Univ 1985, hon prof of politics Warwick Univ 1987, hon fell Jesus Coll Cambs 1988-; *Books* Left or Right: The Bogus Dilemma (1968), The Price of Economic Freedom: A Guide to Flexible Rates (1970), Steering the Economy (1971), Is There an Economic Consensus? (1973), Capitalism and the New Permissive Society (1973), A Restarting of Economic Liberalism (revised edn, 1988), The Delusion of Incomes Policy (1977, with Peter Lilley), The Economic Consequences of Democracy (1977), The Role and Limits of Government: Essays in Political Economy (1983); *Style*— Samuel Brittan, Esq; The Financial Times, 10 Cannon Street, London EC4 (☎ (01) 248 8000)

BRITTEN, Alan Edward Marsh; s of Robert Harry Marsh Britten (d 1987), and Helen Marjorie, *née* Goldson; *b* 26 Feb 1938; *Educ* Radley, Emmanuel Coll Cambridge (MA), Williams Coll Massachusetts, Princeton Univ NJ USA; *m* 23 Sept 1967, Judith Clare, da of Cdr Anthony Charles Akerman, OBE, DSC, of Edinburgh; 2 da (Tamara b 22 July 1970, Sophie b 29 Feb 1972); *Career* Northamptonshire Regt 1956-57, 2 Lt Cheshire Regt 1957-58, served Malaya; md Mobil Oil Co Ltd UK 1987- (joined 1961), co assignments USA and Italy; mangr: Mobil Oil Kenya Gp, Mobil Oil A/S Denmark, Mobil Oil Portuguesa SARL, Mobil Oil BV Gp Rotterdam; memb: cncl Aldeburgh Fndn, Crafts Cncl; cncl Royal Warrant Holders Assoc; *Recreations* music, travel, gardening; *Clubs* Garrick; *Style*— Alan Britten, Esq; Mobil Oil Co Ltd, Mobil House, 54-60 Victoria St, London SW1E 6QB (☎ 01 828 9777, fax 01 828 9777, ext 2659, telex 8812411 MOBIL (A-J) G)

BRITTEN, Brig George Vallette; CBE (1945, OBE, 1943, MBE 1940); s of John Britten (d 1938), of Bozeat Manor, Wellingborough, Northamptonshire, and Elizabeth Franziska, *née* Vallette (d 1956); *b* 19 Mar 1909; *Educ* Wellingborough and Sandhurst; *m* 1937, Shirley Jean, da of Charles Stewart Wink (d 1927), of 32 High St, Halstead, Essex; 3 s (John, Stewart, Neville); *Career* Army 1928-61: regimental duty Colchester and Aldershot 1929-36, instr Small Arms Sch Hythe 1936-38, regimental duty NI 1938, student Staff Coll 1939, GSO3 HQ II Corps BEF France and Belgium 1939-40, GSO2 HQ Southern Cmd Wilton 1940-41, GSO1 HQ Home Forces London 1941-42, cmdt Young Offrs Tactical Sch NI 1942-43, regimental duty N Africa and Sicily 1943, Col HQ 5 (US) Army, Italy 1943-44, HQ 21 Army Gp Planning Staff 1944-45, Brig DCOS Mil Govt (later Control Cmmn) Germany 1945-47, regimental duty Berlin and Austria 1947-48, GSO1 War Off 1949-52, cmdt Sch of Infantry Hythe 1952-54, Br instr US Army Staff Coll 1954-56, chm Inter-Serv Operational Planning Staff Central Region NATO Fontainebleau 1956-58, military attaché Br Embassy Bonn 1958-61; joined Diplomatic Serv 1961; princ: FO, Nigeria, Enugu, Kaduna, The Gambia, Berne until ret 1971; Offr American Legion of Merit 1946, Cdr W German Legion of Merit 1960; *Recreations* gardening; *Style*— Brig George Britten, CBE; 41 Bosville Drive, Sevenoaks, Kent (☎ 0732 455690)

BRITTEN, Rae Gordon; CMG (1972); s of Leonard Arthur Britten (d 1965), of Twickenham, Middx, and Elizabeth Percival, *née* Taylor (d 1975); *b* 27 Sept 1920; *Educ* Liverpool Inst HS, Magdalen Coll Oxford (MA); *m* 1, 1952 (m dis 1974), Valentine, da of Brig George Frederick Hill Alms , CBE; 1 s (Clive), 3 da (Nicola, Hilary, Anne); m 2, 1977, Mrs Joan Dorothy Bull, da of Robert Roughley (d 1980); *Career* served Army 1941-45, Lieut; appointed Cwlth Rels Off 1948, served Br High Cmmr's Off India and Pakistan 1948-62; dep high cmmr: Lahore 1962-64, Kingston Jamaica 1964-68; head trade policy dept FCO 1968-71, dep high cmmr Dacca E Pakistan and head Br Mission Bangladesh 1971-72, consul-gen and cnsllr Oslo 1973-76, head SW Pacific Dept FCO 1976-79, cnsllr in Special Duties 1979-80; ret 1980; *Clubs* Roy Cwlth Soc; *Style*— R G Britten, Esq, CMG; 4 Albany Crescent, Claygate, Esher, Surrey KT10 0PF

BRITTEN, Maj-Gen Robert Wallace Tudor (Bob); CB (1977), MC; s of Lt-Col Wallace Ernest Britten, OBE (d 1947), of Spindlestone, Belford, Northumberland, and Elizabeth Jane, *née* Thorp (d 1971); *b* 28 Feb 1922; *Educ* Wellington Coll, Trinity Coll Cambridge; *m* 1947, Elizabeth Mary (Jane), da of Edward H Davies, of Pentre, Rhondda; 1 s (Simon), 1 da (Sian); *Career* 2 Lt RE 1941, served WWII, Madras Sappers and Miners, 19 Indian Div in India and Burma, Cmd 21 Fd Pk Sqdn and 5 Fd Sqdn RE 1947-50, WO 1951-53, Br liaison offr to US Corps of Engrs 1953-56, cmd 50 Fd Sqdn RE 1956-58, WO 1958-61, on staff 1 (BR) Corps BAOR 1961-64, Lt-Col i/c 1 Trg Regt RE 1964-65, GSO1 (DS) JSSC 1965-67, Brig 1967, cmd 30 Engr Bde (v) and chief engr Western Cmd 1967, dir equipment mgmnt MOD (Army) 1970-71, Maj-Gen 1971, DQMG 1971-73, GOC W Midlands Dist 1973-76, ret 1976; Col Cmdt RE 1977-82, chm RE Assoc 1978-83; Hon Col Birmingham Univ OTC 1978-87; defence conslt Taylor Woodrow Ltd, chm IR Mgmnt Ltd, dir R & E Coordination Ltd, assoc dir Carmichael & Sweet Ltd; CBIM, Companion Inst of Civil Engrs; *Recreations* bridge, building, fishing, dowsing (vice pres Br Soc of Dowsers); *Clubs* Army & Navy; *Style*— Maj-Gen Robert Britten, CB, MC; Birch Trees, Fernden Lane, Haslemere, Surrey GU27 3LA (☎ 0428 2261)

BRITTENDEN, (Charles) Arthur; s of late Tom Edwin Brittenden, and Caroline, *née* Scrivener; *b* 23 Oct 1924; *Educ* Leeds GS; *m* 1, 1953 (m dis 1960), Sylvia Penelope Cadman; m 2, 1966 (m dis 1972), Ann Patricia Kenny; m 3, 1975, Valerie Arnison; *Career* ed Daily Mail 1966-71, dep ed The Sun 1972-1981, dir corporate relations News International plc 1982-, gen mangr (editorial) and dir Times Newspapers Ltd 1982-; jt vice-chm Press Cncl 1983-86; *Style*— Arthur Brittenden, Esq; News International plc, P.O. Box 481, Virginia Street, London E1 9BD. (☎ 01 481 4100, telex 925088); 22 Park St, Woodstock, Oxon

BRITTON, David George; *b* 3 August 1946; *Educ* The GS For Boys Weston Super Mare; *m* 4 Nov 1967, Linda Diana; 1 s (Stephen b 7 May 1973), 1 da (Rachel b 11 Sept 1970); *Career* chief dealer: American Express Int Banking Corpn London 1967-74, Nordic Bank Ltd 1975-78; dir: Banque Belge Ltd 1978-, Quin Cope Ltd 1985-, Belgian & Generale Investmts 1989; memb: membership and rules ctee London Int Fin Futures Exchange, euro advsy ctee The Chicage Mercantile Exchange; *Recreations* fell walking, oriental antiques, sport; *Clubs* Anglo Belgian, Knightsbridge; *Style*— David Britton, Esq; Generale bank, 4 Bishopsgate, London EC2N 4AN (☎ 01 621 9441, fax 01 626 7741, telex 927 948)

BRITTON, Sir Edward Louis; CBE (1967); s of George Edwin Britton (d 1956), and Ellen Alice Britton; *b* 4 Dec 1909; *Educ* Bromley GS, Trinity Coll Cambridge (MA); *m* 1936, Nora, da of Thomas Gregory Arnald (d 1912); *Career* headmaster Warlingham Co Secdy Sch 1952-60; gen sec: Assoc of Teachers in Technical Insts 1960-68, Nat Union of Teachers 1969-75; memb TUC Gen Cncl 1970-74, sr res fell Sheffield Univ 1975-79, lectr Christ Church Coll Canterbury 1979-86; Hon DEd (CNAA); kt 1975; *Style*— Sir Edward Britton, CBE; 40 Nightingale Rd, Guildford, Surrey GU1 1ER (☎ 0483 572084)

BRITTON, Dr John Henshaw; CBE (1972); s of George Bryant Britton (d 1959; MP for Bristol 1918-23), and Anne, *née* Henshaw (d 1959); *b* 17 August 1904; *Educ* Clifton, Trinity Coll Oxford (MA); *m* 16 July 1947, Monica, da of Robert Milne, of London; *Career* chm: CB Britton and Sons Ltd, Bristol Watermarks Co, Bristol Magistrates; pres Clifton Coll (chm of cncl); Hon LLD Univ of Bristol, hon fell Trinity Coll Oxford; *Recreations* cricket, golf, athletics (represented Oxford 1923); *Style*— Dr John Britton, CBE; Shortwood Lodge, Pucklechurch, Glos (☎ 2288)

BRITTON, Jonathan; s of Gerald Percy Britton (d 1978), and Jean, *née* Bowler; *b* 23 May 1954; *Educ* Kings Sch Worcester, Keble Coll Oxford (MA); *m* 21 Sept 1985, Dr Helen Florence, da of Reginald Gorge Drake; 1 s (Thomas b 1987); *Career* CA, Peat Marwick Mitchell & Co 1977-80, Financial Trg Ltd 1980-82; mgmnt conslt: Arthur Anderson & Co 1982-84, Morgan Stanley Int 1984-86; fin dir Swiss Bank Corpn Int Ltd 1986-; memb ICAEW; *Recreations* opera, golf, sailing, running, DIY, wine; *Clubs* Vincents, Malden GC; *Style*— Jonathan Britton, Esq; 29 Morella Rd, London SW12 8UQ (☎ 01 675 1546); Swiss Bank Ho, 1 High Timber St, London (☎ 01 329 0329, fax 01 329 8700, telex 887434)

BRIXWORTH, Bishop of (First) 1989-; Rt Rev Paul Everard Barber; s of Cecil Arthur Barber (d 1981), and Marye (Mollie), *née* Hardingham; *b* 16 Sept 1935; *Educ* Sherborne, Cambridge (MA), Wells Theol Coll; *m* 1959, Patricia Jayne, da of Hubert Jack Walford, of Penygroes, Pen y Lan, Bassaleg, Gwent; 3 s (Andrew, Philip (decd), David), 2 da (Jane, Thi Lien Clare adopted); *Career* ordained: deacon 1960, priest 1961; asst curate St Francis Westborough Guildford 1960-66; vicar: St Michael's Yorktown Camberley 1966-73, St Thomas-on-the Bourne Farnham 1973-80; rural dean of Farnham 1974-79, archdeacon of Surrey 1980-89; *Recreations* cricket, theatre, walking; *Style*— The Rt Rev the Bishop of Brixworth; 4 The Avenue, Dallington, Northampton NN5 7NA

BROACKES, Sir Nigel; s of late Donald Broackes, and Nan Alford; *b* 21 July 1934; *Educ* Stowe; *m* 1956, Joyce Edith Horne; 2 s, 1 da; *Career* Nat Serv cmmnd 3 Hussars 1953-54; chm: Trafalgar House Ltd, London Docklands Devpt Corpn 1981-84; tstee Royal Opera House Tst, dir Horserace Totalisator Bd 1976-81; Guardian Young Businessman of the Year 1978, Stewart & Hughman Ltd, Lloyds under-writing agents 1952-55; various property devpts 1955-57; Trafalgar Ho Investmts Ltd: md 1958, dep chm and jt md 1968; chm: 1969, Ship and Marine Technol Requirements Bd 1972-77; dep chm Offshore Energy Technol Bd 1975-77; hon tres Kensington House Tst 1963-69; vice-chm: Mulberry Housing Tst 1965-69, London Housing Tst 1967-70; memb: cncl Nat Assoc of Property Owners 1967-73; govr Stowe Sch 1974-81; memb: advisory cncl Victoria and Albert Museum 1980-83; kt 1984; *Books* A Growing Concern (1979); *Recreations* silversmith; *Style*— Sir Nigel Broackes; 41 Chelsea Sq, SW3; Checkendon Court, Checkendon, Oxon

BROAD, Sidney Thomas; CBE (1972); s of Francis Alfred Broad, JP (d 1956; sometime MP for Edmonton), and Eliza, *née* Macer; *b* 12 Nov 1911; *Educ* Latymer, Queen's Coll Oxford; *m* 1944, Mary, da of Peter Johnston; 2 s, 1 da; *Career* sometime pres County Educn Offrs Soc; county educn offr Herts 1958-74, first pres Soc of Educn Offrs 1971; *Clubs* United Oxford and Cambridge; *Style*— Sidney Broad, Esq, CBE; The Manor House, Ugborough, S Devon PL21 0NW (☎ Plymouth 0752 892279)

BROADBENT, Dr Donald Eric; CBE (1974); s of Herbert Arthur Broadbent (d 1963), and Hannah Elizabeth, *née* Williams (d 1965); *b* 6 May 1926; *Educ* Winchester, Pembroke Cambridge (BA, ScD); *m* 1, 1949, Margaret Elizabeth, da of Frederick Holden Wright (d 1952); 2 da (Patricia b 1951, Judith d 1979); m 2, 1972, Margaret Hope, da of Romney Moncrief Pattison Muir (d 1963); *Career* experimental psychologist; scientific staff Medical Res Cncl 1949-, memb Applied Psychology Unit Cambridge 1949-50, dir Apu 1958-74, memb external staff Oxford Univ; hon doctorate: Univ of Southampton 1973, Univ of York 1979, City Univ 1983, Free Univ of Brussels 1985; hon fell : Faculty of Occupational Med 1981, Royal Coll of Psychiatrists 1985, Br Psychological Soc 1986 (pres 1965); *Books* Perception and Communication (1958), Behaviour (1961), Decision and Stress (1971), In Defence of Empirical Psycology (1973), plus 200 papers in scientific journals; *Recreations* reading, camping, photography, motor-cycling; *Style*— Dr Donald Broadbent; Dept of Experimental Psychology, South Parks Rd, Oxford OX1 3UD (☎ 0865 27444)

BROADBENT, Prof Edward Granville; s of Joseph Charles Fletcher Broadbent (d 1963), and Lucetta, *née* Riley (d 1968); *b* 27 June 1923; *Educ* Huddersfield Coll, St Catharine's Coll Cambridge (MA, ScD); *m* 7 Sept 1949, Elizabeth Barbara, da of Percy Charles Puttick (d 1975); *Career* govt scientist RAE 1943-83 (dep CSO 1969-); vis prof mathematics dept Imperial Coll 1983-; author numerous scientific papers to learned jls on theory of aero-elasticity, aerodynamics, magneto hydrodynamics, propulsion; FRAeS 1959, FIMA 1965, FRS 1977, FEng 1978, FRSA 1984; *Books* The Elementary Theory of Aeroelasticity (1953); *Recreations* gardening, theatre, concerts, bridge, chess; *Style*— Prof Edward Broadbent, ScD; 11 Three Stiles Rd, Farnham, Surrey GU9 7DE (☎ 0252 714 621); Mathematics Dept, Imperial Coll, Huxley Bld, Queens Gate, London SW7 2BZ (☎ 01 589 5111, ext 5733)

BROADBENT, Sir Ewen; KCB (1984), CB (1973), CMG (1965); s of Rev Wilfred Broadbent (d 1945), of London, and Mary, *née* Ewen (d 1972); *b* 9 August 1924; *Educ* King Edward Sch VI Nuneaton, St John's Coll Cambridge (MA); *m* 1951, Barbara, da of F A David (d 1974), of Weston-Super-Mare; 1 s (Christopher); *Career* Capt Gordon Highlanders 1943-47; civil servant Air Miny and Miny of Def 1949-84, second perm sec 1982-84; dir: Int Mil Servs 1984-, Carrall Indust Corpn; tstee RAF Museum 1985-, vice chm Farnborough Aerospace Devpt Corpn, chm Look Ahead Housing

Assoc; *Books* The Military and Government, from Macmillan and Heseltine (1988); *Recreations* golf; *Clubs* Royal Cwlth, Army & Navy; *Style*— Sir Ewen Broadbent KCB, CB, CMG; 18 Park Hill, Ealing, London W5 2JN (☎ 01 997 1978); 2-6 Catherine Place, Westminster SW1E 6HF (☎ 01 828 6842)

BROADBENT, Prof Geoffrey Haigh; s of Albert Broadbent (d 1962), of Nether End, Meltham, Yorks, and Florence, *née* Haigh (d 1962); *b* 11 June 1929; *Educ* Holme Valley GS, Huddersfield Sch of Art, Univ of Manchester (BA); *m* 25 June 1955, Anne Barbara (d 1985), da of Edgar Sheard, of Glen Royd, Beaumont Park Rd, Huddersfield; 2 s (Mark b 22 April 1960, Antony b 27 Feb 1962); *Career* asst architect Harry S Fairhurst & Sons 1956-69, lectr in architecture Univ of Manchester 1959-61, sec Inst of Advanced Architectural Studies Univ of York 1961-62, lectr in architecture Univ of Sheffield 1963-67, head Sch of Architecture Portsmouth Poly 1967-88, prof of architecture Portsmouth Poly 1980-; Br Cncl and other lecture tours to: USA, Canada, Central America, S America, Middle East, S Africa, Europe, SE Asia, Australasia, China; pres Portsmouth Soc 1973-; chm Int Year of the Homeless Portsmouth Ctee 1981-86 and 1987, memb cncl ARCUK 1974-79; Br Sch at Rome: memb Faculty of Architecture 1969-85, memb Faculty of Architecture and Fine Arts 1985-, memb appointing bd Rome Scholar in Architecture 1985-; memb Cirque Int des Critiques d'Architecture 1986-; Professor Honorario Universidad Antonoma de Santo Domingo 1975, Huespedad de Honor Universidad Nacional di Rosario Argentina 1981, Dr Honoris Causa Universidad di Tucuman Argentina 1981; FRIBA 1955, FRSA 1983; *Books* Design in Architecture (second edn 1987), Emerging Concepts in Urban Space Design (1989); co-editor and contrib: Design Methods in Architecture (with A Ward, 1969), Signs, Symbols and Architecture (with C Jencks and R Bunt, 1980), Meaning and Behaviour in the Built Environment (with T Llorens and R Bunt, 1980); *Recreations* music, fine arts, travel, photography; *Clubs* Architectural Assoc; *Style*— Prof Geoffrey Broadbent; 11 Hereford Rd, Southsea, Hants PO5 2DH (☎ 0705 828 787); School of Architecture, Portsmouth Polytechnic, King Henry 1 St, Portsmouth, Hants PO1 2DY (☎ 0705 842 081/0705 827 681, fax 0705 842 351)

BROADBENT, Sir George Walter; 4 Bt (UK 1893); AFC; s of John Broadbent (d 1967), and Elizabeth Mary Beatrice, *née* Dendy (d 1976); suc kinsman Sir William Francis Broadbent, 3 Bt (d 1987); *b* 23 April 1935; *m* 1962, Valerie Anne, only da of Cecil Frank Ward, of York; 1 s, 1 da; *Heir* s, Andrew George Broadbent b 26 Jan 1963; *Career* Sqdn Ldr RAF; *Style*— Sir George Broadbent, Bt, AFC; 98 Heworth Green, York YO3 7TR

BROADBENT, Col (Herbert) Henry; OBE (1955), TD (1945), DL (Gtr Manchester 1974, Lancs 1973); s of Harry Broadbent (d 1942), and Dorothy, *née* Hatchman (d 1978); *b* 26 April 1914; *Educ* Ashton-u-Lyne GS; *m* 17 Aug 1938, Mary *née* Clark; 1 da (Jillian b 1942); *Career* Manchester Regt TA 1933, served WWII Africa (Sudan Def Force 1940-42), India and Burma 1942-45, Lt-Col (TA REME) 1957-62; foundryman; chm: Triangle Int Ltd 1975-79, Asco (UK) Ltd 1975-, Trind Pension Tst Ltd 1975-; chm: Steel Castings Res Assoc 1975-77, Prestbury branch Br Legion 1985-, Greater Manchester ACF Welfare Ctee; Liveryman Worshipful Co of Founders; *Style*— Col Henry Broadbent, OBE, TD, DL; Glebe House, Prestury Village, Cheshire SK10 4DG (☎ 0625 827734)

BROADBENT, John Michael (Mike); s of Ronald William Percy Broadbent (d 1979), of Huddersfield, Yorks, and Timperly Ches, and Marion, *née* White (d 1963); *b* 24 Nov 1923; *Educ* Manchester GS; *m* 29 July 1961, Sandra Elizabeth, da of Lewis Phillips (d 1966), of Runcorn, Cheshire; 2 s (Adam b 1971, Simon b and d 1967), 3 da (Maryan b 1965, Jane b 1969, Philippa b 1971, d 1972); *Career* Nat Serv Bombardier RA 1953-55; journalist: Kemsley Newspapers 1950-57, Star Newspaper 1957-59; with BBC 1959-: scriptwriter TV News, prodr (later ed) Westminster 1968-72, ed Nine O'Clock News, ed Sixty Minutes, founding ed One O'Clock News, current ed Commons TV; fndr sec and former chm Whitehill Ave Luton Res Assoc, memb Luton Town Supporters Club; *Recreations* supporting Luton Town FC everywhere; *Style*— Mike Broadbent, Esq; 1 Whitehill Avenue, Luton Beds (☎ 0582 20494); c/o Room 6202, BBC TV Centre, Woodland, London W12 7RJ (☎ 01 927 4143)

BROADBENT, William Benedict; ERD (1959); s of William Keighley Benedict Broadbent (d 1948), of Huddersfield; *b* 10 Jan 1924; *Educ* Rugby; *m* 1954 (m dis 1980), Joy Valerie, da of Ernest Wilkinson, CBE; 4 da; *Career* Capt TA and Army Emergency Reserve UK; chm Severn Valley Railway Hldgs plc 1975-, SVR Holdings plc 1975-87 (dir 1988-); dir: Festiniog Railway Co 1954-86 (also dir Sales Ltd), Staveley Industs Ltd 1968-71; md Br Salt Ltd 1966-71; chief ops exec Greater Manchester PTE 1973-76; engr, mgmnt conslt and florist/nurseryman; *Recreations* hill climbing, cruise sailing; *Clubs* Mountain Rangers Assoc; *Style*— William Broadbent Esq, ERD; Pembroke Cottage, Long Compton, Warwicks

BROADBRIDGE, Hon Mrs Ralph - Emma Rose Hancock; da of Henry Van der Weyden, of London; *m* 1925, Hon Ralph George Cameron Broadbridge (d 1983), s of 1 Baron Broadbridge; 3 da; *Style*— The Hon Mrs Ralph Broadbridge

BROADBRIDGE, Hon Howard Eustace; 4 s of 1 Baron Broadbridge, KCVO (d 1952); *b* 17 Nov 1904; *m* 1935, Margaret Ada Marion, da of Capt H H Witherington, of St Michaels, Natal; 1 da; *Style*— The Hon Howard Broadbridge; 12 Texel, Alexandra Rd, Pietermaritzburg, Natal, S Africa

BROADBRIDGE, Hon Hugh Trevor; 3 s of 1 Baron Broadbridge, KCVO (d 1952); hp of nephew, 3 Baron Broadbridge; *b* 22 July 1903; *Educ* Shoreham GS; *m* 1927, Anne Marjorie, da of late J Locke Elfick, of Purley, Surrey; 1 s, 1 da; *Career* regional works advr to regional cmmr Midland Region 1939-42, employed Miny of Supply 1942-44; *Style*— The Hon Hugh Broadbridge; 19 Hanover Close, Sturminster Newton, Dorset

BROADBRIDGE, 3 Baron (UK 1945); Sir Peter Hewett Broadbridge; o s of 2 Baron Broadbridge (d 1972), and Mabel Daisy, *née* Clarke (d 1966); *b* 19 August 1938; *Educ* Hurstpierpoint, St Catherine's Coll Oxford (MA, BSc); *m* 1 April 1967 (m dis 1980), Mary, o da of Wilhelm Otto Busch; 2 da (Hon Jemima Louise b 1970, Hon Sophie Mary b 1972); m 2, 1989, Sally Finn; *Heir* cousin, Martin Broadbridge; *Career* directorships within Ravendale Gp of Cos; formerly conslt: Coopers & Lybrand, Peat Marwick Mitchell & Co; mktg appts with: Gallaher, Colgate-Palmolive, Unilever; Liveryman Worshipful Co of Goldsmiths; pres Nat Assoc of Allotment Gardeners 1977-80; FRSA; *Recreations* early English watercolours, old English silver, silversmithing, tennis, squash; *Style*— The Rt Hon The Lord Broadbridge

BROADHURST, Air Chief Marshal Sir Harry; GCB (1960, KCB 1955, CB 1944), KBE (1945), DSO (and bar 1941), DFC (1940 and bar 1942), AFC (1937); s of Capt Harry Broadhurst, of Emsworth, Hants; *b* 28 Oct 1905; *Educ* various Serv Colls; *m* 1, 1931 (m dis 1945), Doris Kathleen French; 1 da; m 2, 1946, Jean Elizabeth, da of Dr J E Townley, MC, of Kinnersley, Hereford, 1 da; *Career* C-in-C 2 Tactical Air Force Germany 1954-56, Air Offr C-in-C Bomber Cmd 1956-59, cdr Allied Forces Central Europe 1959-61, md AVROE and Co 1961-66; dir Hawkley Siddeley Gp Ltd 1968-76 (former 1966-76, dir and dep md Hawker Siddeley Aviation Ltd), pres SBAC 1974-75; American Legion of Merit 1943, Kt Grand Cross Order of Orange-Nassau 1948; *Recreations* music, sailing; *Clubs* RAF; *Style*— Air Chief Marshal Sir Harry Broadhurst, GCB, KBE, DSO, DFC, AFC; Lock's End House, Birdham, Chichester, W Sussex PO20 7BB (☎ 0243 512717)

BROADHURST, (Ian) Kevan Averill; s of Samuel Broadhurst (d 1974), of Stoke-on-Trent, and Gladys, *née* Averill; *b* 30 Dec 1935; *Educ* Coll of Commerce Stoke-on-Trent; *m* 18 June 1966, Maureen, da of James Haddon, of Stoke-on-Trent; *Career* chartered accountant; Bourner Bullock and Co Certified Accountants 1951-67, Stratham and Co Chartered Accountants 1967-70, sr ptnr Harding Higgins Ptnrship (formerly Geo E Harding and Co Chartered Accountants) 1971-, md Harding Services Ltd; FCA 1962, FCCA 1971, ATII 1957, FRSA 1962; *Recreations* film making, photography, travel; *Style*— Kevan Broadhurst, Esq; Langenfeld, Meadow Way, Church Lawton, Stoke-on-Trent, Staffs (☎ 0270 873 832); Harding Higgins Partnership, 6 Marsh Parade, Newcastle under Lyme, Staffs ST5 1DU (☎ 0782 617 868)

BROADLEY, Lady; Kathleen May; da of late Alfred J Moore, of Camden Sq, London; *m* 1927, Sir Herbert Broadley, KBE (d 1983); *Style*— Lady Broadley; Hollingsworth, Redlands Lane, Ewshot, Farnham, Surrey

BROATCH, (Michael) Donald; s of Dr Alexander Donaldson Broatch (d 1982) of Folkestone, Kent and Nancy Dorothea, *née* Beatty (d 1953); *b* 28 May 1948; *Educ* Felsted, Queen Mary Coll London (LLB, LLM); *m* 1 June 1974, Catherine Margaret, da of Barry John Block (d 1968), of Shirley, Croydon; 2 s (Neil b 1978, Ian b 1980); *Career* called to the Bar 1971; in practice 1972-; *Style*— Donald Broatch, Esq; 5 Paper Buildings, Temple, London EC4 (☎ 01 353 8494, 01 583 4555), fax (01 583 1926, 01 583 2031), telex 8956431 Anton G LDE Box 415

BROCAS, Viscount; Patrick John Bernard Jellicoe; s (by 1 m) and h of 2 Earl Jellicoe, DSO, MC, PC; *b* 29 August 1950; *Educ* Eton; *m* 1971 (m dis 1981), Geraldine Ann FitzGerald Jackson; 1 s (Hon Justin Amadeus b 1970); *Heir* bro, Hon Nicholas Charles; *Career* engineer; *Style*— Viscount Brocas; Pantglas, Llanwoda, Dyfed

BROCK, Baroness; Chrissie Palmer; *née* Palmer Jones; da of John Alfred Jones, of Leeds; *b* 1 June 1903; *Educ* Leeds Girls HS, Royal Sch Needlework; *m* 1979, as his 2 w, Baron Brock (d 1980); 2 step da; *Career* private sec; *Style*— The Rt Hon the Lady Brock; 39 Chancellor House, Tunbridge Wells TN4 8BT

BROCK, John Hedley; OBE (1976); s of John Brock, JP (d 1949), of Kelly Bray, Cornwall, and Mary, *née* Priest (d 1960); *b* 18 Jan 1912; *Educ* Callington Sch; *m* 1, Vera Wonnacott (d 1972); 1 s; m 2, 1973, Ann Felicity, da of Harry Laity, JP; *Career* served RN 1940-46, Lt-Cdr; mangr Lloyds Bank plc 1950-74, dir South Crofty Ltd 1972-85; chm: China Clay Cncl 1972-, Cornwall Indust Devpt Assoc 1975-83; pres Cornish Mining Dvpt Assoc 1972-; *Recreations* music; *Style*— John Brock, Esq, OBE; Chy an Mor, Coverack, Helston, Cornwall TR12 6SZ (☎ 0326 280417)

BROCK, Michael George; CBE (1981); s of Sir Laurence George Brock, CB (d 1949), and Ellen Margery, *née* Williams; *b* 9 Mar 1920; *Educ* Wellington, Corpus Christi Coll Oxford; *m* 1949, Eleanor Hope Morrison; 3 s; *Career* historian; pro-vice-chllr Oxford Univ 1980-88; warden: Nuffield Coll Oxford 1978-88, St George's House Windsor Castle 1988-; hon fell: Wolfson Coll Oxford 1977, Corpus Christi Coll Oxford 1982, Nuffield Coll 1988; Hon DLitt Exeter 1982; FRHistS, FRSL, FRSA; *Style*— Dr Michael Brock, CBE; 24 The Cloisters, Windsor Castle SL4 1NJ (☎ 0753 866444; St Georges House, Windsor Castle SL4 1NJ (☎ 0753 861341)

BROCKBANK, (John) Bowman; s of Thomas Brockbank (d 1966), of Larkstone, Hilton, Bridgnorth, Shropshire, and Alice, *née* Peile (d 1961); *b* 24 June 1903; *Educ* Wolverhampton GS, Ackworth Sch nr Pontefract, Bootham Sch York, Univ of Birmingham (BSc); *m* 27 March 1937, Alice Margaret (d 1987), da of Frederick Parker (d 1962), of Tickenhill, Bewdley, Worcs; 2 s (Thomas b 1938, Richard b 1945), 1 da (Jane (Mrs Fox) b 1942); *Career* Auxiliary Fire Service (1938 until nationalisation), National Fire Service (until disbanded 1948) divisional officer; engr Bostock and Hargrove Ltd Wolverhampton (conslt engrgs) 1923-35, chm and md (formerly dir) Wolverhampton Steam Laundry Ltd 1935-79; former pres Wolverhampton Soc of Applied Sci, pres Wolverhampton and Dist Engrg Soc 1970-71; MIEE; *Recreations* gardening, motoring, handicrafts, photography; *Style*— Bowman Brockbank, Esq; Larkstone, Hilton, Bridgnorth, Shropshire WV15 5PD (☎ 074 64 207)

BROCKBANK, Mark Ellwood; s of John Ellwood Brockbank, of Westward Park, Wigton, Cumbria, and Elizabeth, *née* Allen; *b* 2 April 1952; *Educ* Bootham Sch York; *Career* appointed Lloyds Underwriter 1983; dir: Alston Brockbank Agencies Ltd 1982, Energy Entertainment Co Ltd 1987, Hayter Brockbank Ltd 1988, Haytor Brockbank Agencies Ltd 1988, John Hayter Motor Underwriting Agencies Ltd 1988, Charles Howard Underwriting Ltd 1988; *Recreations* the arts, cinema, shooting, bridge; *Style*— Mark Brockbank, Esq; 18 Rood Lane, London EC3M 8AP (☎ 01 283 6977, fax 283 5124, telex 8951858)

BROCKBANK, Thomas Frederick; s of John Bowman Brockbank, of Hilton, and Alice Margaret, *née* Parker (d 1987); *b* 6 Mar 1938; *Educ* Bootham Sch York, Loughborough Coll (DLC Mech Engrg); *m* 16 Dec 1967, Joan Emma, da of Martin Israelski, of Leamington; 3 da (Eleanor Clare b 1970, Laura Katherine b 1973, Harriet Elisabeth b 1975); *Career* merchant banker; Courtaulds Ltd 1960-65, mgmnt conslt Arthur Andersen & Co London 1965-68, RTZ Conslts (part of RTZ Corpn) 1968-73, Hill Samuel & Co Ltd 1973-87 (dir corporate fin 1985-, jt head of smallers cos team); mechanical engr Internal Consultancy Operational Res; FRSA 1986; *Books* numerous lectures and articles, particularly on finance for growing companies, flotation and general strategy; *Recreations* music, theatre, art, photography, travel; *Style*— Thomas Brockbank, Esq; Hill Samuel Bank Ltd, 100 Wood St, London EC2P 2AJ (☎ 01 628 8011)

BROCKBANK, (James) Tyrrell; DL (Durham 1970); yr s of late James Lindow Brockbank, of York; *b* 14 Dec 1920; *Educ* St Peter's York, St John's Coll Cambridge; *m* 1950, Pamela Margaret Oxley, yr da of late Lt-Col John Oxley Parker, TD, of The Old Rectory, Faulkbourne, Witham, Essex; 4 s; *Career* clerk of the peace Durham

1961-71, clerk of Durham CC 1961-74, clerk to Durham Ltcy 1984-88; memb Local Govt Boundary Cmmn England 1976-85, High Sheriff Durham 1989; *Recreations* fishing, shooting, golf; *Clubs* Travellers', Durham County; *Style—* Tyrrell Brockbank, Esq, DL; The Orange Tree, Shincliffe Village, Durham DH1 2NN (☎ 09138 65569)

BROCKET, 3 Baron (UK 1933); Sir Charles Ronald George Nall-Cain; 3 Bt (UK 1921); s of late Hon Ronald Charles Manus Nall-Cain, er s of 2 Baron; suc gf 1967; *b* 12 Feb 1952; *Educ* Eton; *m* 1982, Isabell (Isa) Maria only da of Gustavo Lorenzo, of Whaleneck Dve, Merrick, Long Island, NY, USA; 1 s; *Heir* s, Hon Alexander Christopher Charles b 30 Sept 1984; *Career* late 14/20 King's Hussars; Gen Service Medal, UN Medal; *Style—* The Rt Hon The Lord Brocket; Brocket Hall, Welwyn, Herts

BROCKHOFF, Sir Jack Stuart; s of Frederick Douglas Brockhoff; *b* 1908; *Educ* Wesley Coll Victoria; *m* 1980, Ursula Edith; *Career* chm and md Brockhoff's Biscuits Pty Ltd, Arnott-Brockhoff-Guest Pty Ltd, dir Arnotts Ltd, chm Jack Brockhoff Organisation; kt 1979; *Recreations* golf, bowls, fishing; *Clubs* Vic Golf, Woodlands Golf, Sandringham Yacht; *Style—* Sir Jack Brockhoff; 113 Beach Rd, Sandringham, Victoria 3191, Australia (☎ 598 9227)

BROCKHURST, Rowan Benford; s of Geoffrey Thomas Brockhurst, of 1 Lumby Drive, Ringwood, Hants, and Barbara, *née* Wickens; *b* 23 June 1936; *Educ* Sutton Valence Sch Kent, Coll of Law London; *m* 1, 8 April 1961 (m dis 1984), Eve, da of Maj William Tristram (d 1942); 1 s (Nicholas b 1965), 1 da (Harriet b 1963); m 2, 13 May 1987, Fiona Daphne, da of John Cunningham (d 1985); *Career* Nat Serv 2 Lt RASC 1959-60, Capt Army Emergency Res of Offrs; slr, sr ptnr Meesons Ringwood & Fordingbridge Hants, pres Hants Inc Law Soc 1978-79, dir Slrs Benevolent Assoc 1982; chm: Ringwood and Dist Community Assoc, Ringwood and Fordingbridge Footpath Soc; pres Ringwood Philatelic Soc, vice chm Ringwood Meeting House Assoc; govr Moyles Ct Sch Ringwood and Holme Grange Sch Wokingham; memb Law Soc 1958; *Recreations* walking, gardening, reading, inland waterways; *Style—* Rowan Brockhurst, Esq; 78 Allen Water Drive, Fordingbridge, Hants (☎ 0425 53748); New House Market Place, Ringwood, Hants (☎ 0425 472 315, fax 0425 470 912)

BROCKLEBANK, Sir Aubrey Thomas; 6 Bt (UK 1885); s of Sir John Montague Brocklebank, 5 Bt, TD (d 1974), and Pamela, *née* Pierce; *b* 29 Jan 1952; *Educ* Eton, Univ Coll Durham (BSc); *m* 1979, Dr Anna-Marie, da of Dr William Dunnet; 2 s (Aubrey William b 1980), Hamish John b 1987); *Heir* s, Aubrey William b 15 Dec 1980; *Career* dir Augill Castle Antiques Ltd; ACA; *Style—* Sir Aubrey Brocklebank, Bt; 37 Kyrle Rd, London SW11

BROCKLEBANK, Edward; s of Flt Lt Fred Brocklebank, of Ballater, Grampian, and Nancy Mitchell, *née* Ainslie (d 1969); *b* 24 Sept 1942; *Educ* Madras Coll St Andrews Fife; *m* 21 Aug 1965 (m dis 1978), Lesley Beverley, da of Dr Ronald Beverley Davidson (d 1973), of Dundee; 2 s (Andrew Edward b 4 Feb 1967, Jonathan Ainslie b 31 Dec 1967); *Career* trainee journalist DC Thomson & Co Ltd Dundee 1960-63, freelance 1963-65, journalist Scottish TV Glasgow 1965-70, in vision journalist/presenter Grampian TV Aberdeen 1970-77 (head of news and current affrs 1977-); prodns incl: Oil Channel 4 (8 pt prog on world oil business awarded AMANDA best documentary series Norway), What Price Oil (BAFTA award for Best Industl Prog of Year 1974), Last of the Hunters 1987, The Blood is Strong 1988 (3 pt prog on Gaelic Scots), The Sea Farmers 1988; head of documentaries Grampian TV 1986; *Recreations* walking, reading, music, rugby football; *Clubs* New GC St Andrews, Aberdeen Petroleum; *Style—* Edward Brocklebank, Esq; Grampian Television, Queen's Cross, Aberdeen, Scotland (☎ 0224 646464)

BROCKLEBANK, Pamela, Lady; Pamela Sue; da of late William Harold Pierce, OBE of Bidston, Cheshire; *m* 1, Maj Leslie Forshaw-Wilson; m 2, 1950, Maj Sir John Brocklebank, TD, 5 Bt (d 1974); *Style—* Pamela, Lady Brocklebank

BROCKLEBANK, Ralph Wilfrid; s of Cdr Denys Royds Brocklebank RN (d 1947), of Longbridge House, Warminster, Wilts, and Kathleen, *née* Lindsay (d 1985); *b* 18 July 1927; *Educ* Lakefield Sch Ontario, Michael Hall Sch Sussex, Millfield Sch, Trinity Coll Cambridge (MA); *m* 8 Feb 1954, Beryl, *née* Seabury; 1 s (Guy b 1954), 2 adopted s (Mark b 1959, Leo b 1965), 2 adopted da (Susan b 1956, Keren b 1960); *Career* Goethean Science Foundation 1951- (now tstee); chm The Colour Gp (GB) 1971-73, Sunfield Children's Homes 1985- (dir 1973-85); *Recreations* heraldry; *Clubs* English-Speaking Union; *Style—* Ralph Brocklebank, Esq; Orland, Clent, Stourbridge, West Midlands DY9 9QS (☎ 0562 730285); Sunfield Childrens Homes, Clent Grove, Clent, Stourbridge, West Midlands DY9 9PB (☎ 0562 882253)

BROCKLEBANK-FOWLER, Christopher; s of Sidney Straton Brocklebank Fowler (d 1954), of Oakham, Rutland; *b* 13 Jan 1934; *Educ* Perse Sch Cambridge; *m* 1, 1957 (m dis 1975), Joan, da of Louis Raymond Nowland (d 1961), of Kalgoorlie, W Australia; 2 s; m 2, 1975, (m dis 1985), Mary Berry; 1 step da;; *Career* served RN (submarines) 1952-54, Sub Lt RNVR; farm mangr Kenya 1954-57; Parly candidate (C) West Ham N 1964, MP (C) King's Lynn 1970-74, MP (C then SDP from 1981) Norfolk NW 1974-83, MP (SDP), Norfolk NW 1983 and 1987; memb Bow Gp 1961-81 (chm 1968-69), vice-chm Cons Parly Foreign and Cwlth Affrs Sub-Ctee 1979-81, Cons Parly Trade Ctee 1979-81; chm UN Parly Gp 1979-83, Overseas Dvpt Sub-Ctee 1979-83, memb Select Parly Ctee Foreign Affrs 1979-83; SDP spokesman Agric and Foreign Affrs 1981-83; chm SDP Overseas Devpt Policy Ctee 1981-83; vice-chm: SDP Agric Policy Ctee 1981-83, SDP Communications Ctee 1982-83; memb Cncl for Social Democracy 1982-; dir: Creative Conslts Ltd 1966-, Bow Publications 1968-71, SOS Children's Villages UK Trading 1981-84 (chm SOS Children's Villages UK 1978-84); fndr and non-exec chm Overseas Trade and Devpt Agency Ltd 1979-83; md: ACP Development Agency Ltd 1984-, Cambridge Corporate Conslts Ltd 1985-87; govr Inst of Devpt Studies Sussex Univ 1978-81, memb cncl Centre for World Devpt 1979-88; hon fellow Inst of Dvpt Studies Sussex U; MCAM MInstM, FInstD, FRGS; *Recreations* swimming, shooting, fishing, painting; *Clubs* Roy Cwlth Soc; *Style—* Christopher Brocklebank-Fowler Esq; The Long Cottage, Flitcham, King's Lynn, Norfolk PE31 6BU (☎ 0485 600255)

BROCKLEHURST, Maj-Gen Arthur Evers; CB (1956), DSO (1944); s of Ernest Brocklehurst (d 1935), of Knapton Hall, N Walsham, Norfolk, and Kathleen Brocklehurst; *b* 20 July 1905; *Educ* King's Sch Canterbury, RMA Woolwich; *m* 1940, Joan Beryl, da of Lt-Col Charles Douglas Parry-Crooke, CMG (d 1948), of Newe House, Pakenham, Suffolk; 2 twin da (Sally, Anne); *Career* 2 Lt RA 1925, served 1939-45: UK, France, Canada, N Africa, Italy; Col 1951, Brig 1955, Maj-Gen 1957, chief of staff Malaya Cmd 1956-57, GOC Rhine District BAOR 1958-59, dep cmd BAOR 1959, ret 1961; chm Devizes Constituency Cons Assoc 1963-66; *Recreations* gardening, painting; *Clubs* Army and Navy; *Style—* Maj Gen Arthur Brocklehurst, CB, DSO; Woodborough Manor, Pewsey, Wilts SN9 5PL

BROCKLEHURST, Aubrey Bernard; s of Clement George Bernard Brocklehurst (d 1937), of Chorlton-cum-Hardy, Manchester, and Ellen, *née* Davies (d 1943); *b* 29 June 1913; *Educ* Chorlton HS Manchester; *m* 1, 23 Nov 1940 (m dis 1983), Joan, da of James Rowbotton (d 1945), of Woodland Way, Middleton, Lancs; 2 s (Kevin b 7 Nov 1943, Edwin (twin) b 7 Nov 1943), 1 da (Ruth b 14 Jan 1955); m 2, Hazel Victoria (d 1984), da of Henry James Bryan (d 1931), of Liverpool; m 3, 11 Dec 1987, Helen, da of Charles Lawrence Pryal (d 1940), of San Francisco; *Career* laboratory asst and observer in an experimental machinery laboratory Br Cotton Indust Res Assoc 1931-37, calculator in drawing off Henry Wallwork & Co Ltd 1937-38, mechanical designer Ferguson Pailin Ltd 1938-42, travel organiser for overseas workers Friend's Relief Serv 1946-49, self employed watch and clock repairer 1950-63, proprietor (retailing and repairing) antique clock shop 1963-; chm London section Fell and Rock Climbing Club 1986-88, chm North London branch Br Horological Inst 1978-, ctee memb Nat Benevolent Soc of Watch and Clockmakers 1985-; Freeman City of London 1970, Liveryman Worshipful Co of Clockmakers 1973; FBHI 1960, memb BR Antique Dealers Assoc 1973; *Recreations* walking, mountaineering, skiing, travel; *Clubs* Ski, Fell and Rock Climbing; *Style—* Aubrey Brocklehurst, Esq; Flat 1, 124 Cromwell Rd, S Kensington, London SW7 4ET (☎ 01 373 0319); 12 Beaconsfield Rd, Hastings, E Sussex TN34 3TN; Aubrey Brocklehurst, 124 Cromwell Rd, London SW7 4ET (☎ 01 373 0319)

BROCKLEHURST, Ben Gilbert; s of Ernest (d 1935), and Kathleen (d 1965); *b* 18 Feb 1922; *Educ* Bradfield; *m* 1, March 1947 (m dis 1957), Mary; m 2, June 1962, Belinda, da of William S Bristowe; 3 s, 1 da; *Career* 10 Devon Regt 1940, Maj 16 FF Rifles Indian Army 1942, Lt-Col 4/12 FF Regt LA 1946 served Burma; dairy farmer Berks 1947, joined advertisement dept Country Life 1957, advertisement mangr Tothill Press 1961, advertisement dir Mercury House Pubns (md 24 Magazines Mercury House 1970), proprietor The Cricketer 1972, fndr Cricketer Holidays; Somerset County Cricket Club 2 XI 1951, Somerset County Cricket IXI 1952-54 (Capt 1953 and 1954); *Recreations* cricket, golf, tennis, squash; *Clubs* Naval and Military, Piccadilly, MCC, Free Foresters, IZ; *Style—* Ben Brocklehurst, Esq; Beech Hanger, Ashurst, nr Tunbridge Wells, Kent (car ☎ 089274 256)

BROCKLEHURST, Prof John Charles; CBE (1988); s of Harold John Brocklehurst (d 1981), and Dorothy, *née* Harrison; *b* 31 May 1924; *Educ* Glasgow HS, Ayr Acad, Univ of Glasgow (MB ChB, MD); *m* 24 July 1956, Gladys Florence (Susan); 2 s (Paul b 20 Aug 1958, Neil b 20 June 1961), 1 da (Morag b 1 May 1957); *Career* RAMC 1949-51 (Maj); Christine Hansen res fell Univ of Glasgow 1948- 49, med offr Grenfell Mission N Newfoundland and Labrador 1955-57, jr hosp appts 1957-61 (1951-55), conslt geriatrician Bromley Hosp Gp 1961-69, conslt geriatric gen medicine Guys Hosp 1969-70, hon conslt geriatrician NW Regnl Health Authy 1970-, prof of geriatric medicine Univ of Manchester 1970- (dir unit for biological ageing res 1974-), visiting prof and head of dir of geriatric Med Univ of Sarkatchewan 1978-79; pres Soc of Chiropodists 1977-83, tstee CIBA Geigy Educnl Tst 1977-, govr Res into Ageing 1980-, vice pres Age Concern England 1980- (vice-chm 1971-73, chm 1973-77); pres: Age Concern Lancs 1977 (chm 1972-77), Manchester and Salford Med Engrg Club 1976-77; pres British Geriatrics Soc 1983-85, chm Age Concern Macclesfield 1988-; Hon MSC Univ of Manchester 1974, MRCPS (Glasgow) 1959, FRCPS (Glasgow) 1972, RCPE 1961, FRCPE 1970, FRCP 1984; *Books* Incontinence in Old People (1951), The Geriatric Day Hospital (1971), Testbook of Geriatric Medicine & Gerontology (jtly third edn 1985), Geriatric Care in Advanced Societies (jtly 1975), Geriatric Medicine For Students (jtly third edn 1985), Progress in Geriatric Day Care (1980), Urology in Old Age (1984), Geriatric Pharmocology & Therapeutics (1984), Atlas of Geriatric Medicine (1985), British Geriatric Medicine in the 1980's (1987), Case Studies in Medicine For the Elderly (jtly 1987); *Recreations* art, music; *Clubs* East India and Devonshire, Royal Soc of Medicine; *Style—* Prof John Brocklehurst; 59 Stanneylands Rd, Wilmslow, Cheshire SK9 4EX (☎ 0625 525 795)

BROCKLEHURST, (John) Michael; s of John Mark Brocklehurst (d 1946), and Emily Victoria, *née* Burnet (d 1983); *b* 21 Nov 1929; *Educ* Ripon GS, Manchester Coll of Technology; *m* 1, 18 July 1959 (m dis 1984), Maureen Palles, da of Robert Bulloch Waddell; 1 s (Andrew b 1964), 1 da (Catherine b 1961); m 2, 18 April 1985, Lieselotte Tozer, da of Engelbert Jeibmann; *Career* cmmnd RASC; dir: Loch Long Estates Ltd 1972-81, Quarnford Estates Ltd 1987; chm: Craven DC 1979-80, Skipton Cons Assoc 1980-83; MBIM; *Clubs* Royal Scottish Automobile; *Style—* Michael Brocklehurst, Esq

BROCKLEHURST, Peter James; s of late John Gleave Brocklehurst, and Blanche Brocklehurst, *née* Hampson; *b* 30 Jan 1923; *Educ* Uppingham, Sandhurst; *m* 17 June 1950, Dinah Millicent, da of the late George Oldham, of Cheshire; 1 s (John George David Brocklehurst b 1953); *Career* WWII Capt Grenadier Gds; chartered loss adjuster, memb Lloyds, High Sheriff of Cheshire 1986-87; *Recreations* gardening, opera, riding; *Clubs* City of London, Guards; *Style—* Peter J Brocklehurst, Esq; Peover Cottage, Peover Superior, Knutsford, Cheshire WA16 9HG (☎ 056-581-2210); Suite 655, Lloyds, 1 Lime Street, London EC3 7DQ (☎ 01-626-5243)

BROCKLESBY, Donald Ian; s of William Brocklesby, of Hull, N Humberside, and Brenda Margaret, *née* Russell; *b* 8 Sept 1948; *Educ* Cottingham Co Secdy Sch Hull, Bradford Univ (Post Graduate Dip in Fin & Ind Admin) 1973-74; *m* 21 Sept 1974, Gillian, da of James Alexander Sutherland, of Whitley Bay, Tyne & Wear; 1 s (Mark Russell b 1979), 2 da (Laura Jayne b 1977, Hannah Gillian 1983); *Career* CA 1972; ptnr White & Hoggard, Chartered Accountant 1979; chm ST Peters Church Boys Club 1985-; FCA, FCCA; *Recreations* assoc football (Hull City Supporter), Cricket (Yorkshire); *Style—* Donald Brocklesby, Esq; 3 The Avenue, Norton, Malton, North Yorks YO17 9EF (☎ 0653 692 603); 1-3 Wheelgate, Malton, North Yorks YO17 0HT (☎ 0653 693 005)

BROCKLESBY, Ian; s of Harold Brocklesby (d 1967), of Doncaster, and Eleanor May Berry; *b* 5 Mar 1944; *Educ* Pocklington, Durham Univ (BA), Liverpool Univ; *m* 1978, Anna-Kay Elizabeth, da of Peter Eversley Evelyn, of Florida; 2 s (Benjamin b 1979, Matthew Ian b 1981); *Career* dir: Wholesale Supply Ltd 1967, Ogilvy & Mather Ltd 1984; *Recreations* golf, opera; *Style—* Ian Brocklesby, Esq; "The Nines", Village Way, Little Chalfont, Buckinghamshire HP7 9PX (☎ 02404 2868); Ogilvy & Mather Ltd, Brettenham House, Lancaster Place, London WC2E 7EZ (☎ 01-836 2466, fax 01 836 9899)

BROCKMAN, *see*: Drake-Brockman

BROCKMAN, Vice Adm Sir Ronald Vernon; KCB (1965), CSI (1947), CIE (1946), CVO (1979), CBE (1943), DL (Devon 1968); sr s of Rear Adm Henry Stafford Brockman, CB (d 1958), and Edith Mary, *née* Sheppard (d 1974); *b* 8 Mar 1909; *Educ* Weymouth Coll; *m* 1932, Marjorie Jean, da of Charles James Butt; 1 s, 3 da; *Career* served RN 1927-65: private sec to Govr Gen of India 1947-48, princ SO to Chief of Def Staff Adm of The Fleet The Earl Mountbatten of Burma 1959-65; extra gentleman usher to HM The Queen 1979- (gentleman usher 1967-79); KstJ 1984; *Recreations* sailing; *Clubs* White's, MCC, Royal Western Yacht of England; *Style—* Vice Adm Sir Ronald Brockman, KCB, CSI, CIE, CVO, CBE, DL; 3 Court House, Basil St, London SW3 1AJ (☎ 01 584 1023); 12 Blueberry Downs, Coastguard Road, Budleigh Salterton, Devon EX9 6 NU (☎ 03954 2687)

BROCKWAY, Hon Christopher Fenner; s of Baron Brockway (Life Peer, d 1988) and his 2 w, Edith Violet, *née* King; *b* 24 Nov 1946; *Educ* Magdalen College Oxford; *Style—* The Hon Christopher Brockway; 42 Chemin d'Eysins, CH-1260 Nyon, Switzerland

BROCKWAY, Baroness; Edith Violet; *née* King; da of late Archibald Herbert King, of Catford, London SE6; *m* 5 April 1946, as his 2 w, Baron Brockway (Life Peer, d 1988); 1 s (Hon Christopher Fenner, *qv*); 67 Southway, Totteridge, London N20

BRODEY, John; s of Richard Brodey (d 1957) of London E18, and Emily Caroline, *née* Humphriss (d 1954); *b* 24 Nov 1920; *Educ* Bow Central Sch; *Career* WWII reserved ocupation, enlisted 2 Bn Middx Regt 1945, demobbed Sgt 1948; Sgt Army Emergency Reserve 1952-56, RN Aux Serv 1969-85; self employed blacksmith and engr 1950-85, made and donated ornamented ironwork panels as contribution to Bexhill on Sea Charter Year Celebrations (unveiled by HRH Princess Alexandra), dip of merit for outstanding Craftmanship Worshipful Co of Blacksmiths; Queens Commendation for Brave Conduct (for rescue of small child from drowning in River Thames) 1976; Freeman City of London, Liveryman Worshipful Co of Blacksmiths 1974 (associate 1988); *Recreations* genealogical research, scottish country dancing, classical music; *Style—* John Brodey, Esq

BRODIE, Sir Benjamin David Ross; 5 Bt (UK 1834); s of Sir Benjamin Collins Brodie, 4 Bt, MC (d 1971); *b* 29 May 1925; *Educ* Eton; *m* m; 1 s, 1 da; *Heir* s, Alan Brodie; *Style—* Sir Benjamin Brodie, Bt

BRODIE, Colin Alexander; QC (1980); s of Sir Benjamin Collins Brodie, MC, 4 Bt (d 1971); *b* 19 April 1929; *Educ* Eton, Magdalen Oxford; *m* 1955, Julia Anne Irene, da of late Norman E Wates, of Elmore, Chipstead, Surrey; 2 s (Christian Norman, Alexander Colin); *Career* barr 1953; *Recreations* polo; *Style—* Colin Brodie, Esq, QC; 24 Old Bldgs, Lincoln's Inn, London WC2

BRODIE, Air Cdre Ian Eustace; OBE (1940), DL (Bucks 1964); s of William Alexander Brodie, of Fernhill, Wootton Bridge and La Cima, San Remo; *b* 17 Sept 1898; *Educ* Ovingdon, Oundle, St John's Coll Cambridge (with RN); *m* 1925, Mary Gonville, da of William Coristine Coates, JP (d 1914), of Knockanally, sometime High Sheriff Co Kildare; 3 da; *Career* RN 1917-23, RAF 1923-52, Acting Air Vice-Marshal Italy 1945-47; in Intelligence Security 1952-66, county cmmnr Scouts (Bucks) 1961-65; *Recreations* equestrian, sailing, gardening; *Style—* Air Cdre Ian Brodie, OBE, DL; Briar Well, Moons Hill, Freshwater, IOW (☎ 0983 752835)

BRODIE, Robert; s of Robert Brodie, MBE (d 1966), and Helen Ford Bayne, *née* Grieve; *b* 9 April 1938; *Educ* Morgan Acad Dundee, St Andrews Univ (MA, LLB); *m* 26 Sept 1970, Jean Margaret, da of Sheriff Princ Thomas Pringle McDonald, QC (d 1969); 2 s (Robert b 1971, James b 1980), 2 da (Alison b 1973, Ruth b 1978); *Career* legal asst to Sec of State for Scotland 1965 (dep slr 1984-87, slr 1987-), dep dir of Scottish cts admin 1975-82; memb: Sheriff Ct Rules Cncl 1975-82, Scottish Ctee on Jurisdiction and Enforcement 1977-80, working party on Divorce Procedure 1979-80, session clerk Wardie Parish Church; memb Law Soc of Scotland; *Recreations* music, hill walking, making jam; *Style—* Robert Brodie, Esq; 45 Stirling Rd, Edinburgh EH5 3JB (☎ 031 552 2028); Solicitors Office, New St Andrews House, Edinburgh EH1 3TE (☎ 031 244 5247)

BRODIE, Stanley Eric; QC (1975); s of Dr Abraham Brodie, of Allerton Bradford (d 1978), and Cissie Rache, Garstein; uncle Sir Israel Brodie, former chief rabbi of GB and The Cwlth; *b* 2 July 1930; *Educ* Bradford GS; Balliol Coll Oxford (MA); *m* 1, 31 July 1956, Gillian Rosemary, da of Sir Maxwell Joseph; 2 da (Henrietta b 1957, Charlotte b 1960); m 2, 29 Oct 1973, Elizabeth, da of Peter Gloster; 1 da (Sophie b 1978), 1 s (Samuel b 1981); *Career* barr: recorder Crown Court 1975, bencher Inner Temple 1984, Bar Cncl 1987; *Recreations* fishing, boating, opera, holidays; *Clubs* Flyfishers; *Style—* Stanley E Brodie, QC; Skeldon House, Dalrymple, Ayshire; 37 Addison Ave, London W11; 2 Hare Court, Temple, London EC4 (☎ 01 583 1770)

BRODIE, Hon Mrs (Vanessa Nathalie Mary); *née* Hawke; da of 10 Baron Hawke; *b* 20 June 1957; *m* 1985, (Peter) Adam William Brodie, s of Maj-Gen Thomas Brodie, CB, CBE, DSO, of Camberley, Surrey; 1 da (Nathalie b 30 July 1986); *Style—* The Hon Mrs Brodie; The Old Rectory, Tallarn Green, Malpas, Cheshire

BRODIE OF BRODIE, (Montagu) Ninian Alexander; JP (Morayshire 1958), DL (Nairn 1970); 25 Chief of Clan Brodie; s of Ian Brodie of Brodie (d 1943); *b* 12 June 1912; *Educ* Eton; *m* 1939, Helena, da of Janssen Budgen, of Wendover; 1 s, 1 da (d 1972); *Heir* Alastair Brodie, younger of Brodie; *Career* professional actor 1935-40 and 1945-50, market gardener and landowner 1953-80, ret; now involved in voluntary work (as a guide etc) at Brodie Castle which has been owned by the Nat Tst since 1980; *Recreations* shooting, bridge, backgammon, bird watching; *Style—* Ninian Brodie of Brodie, JP, DL; Brodie Castle, Forres, Moray IV36 0TE (☎ 030 94 202)

BRODIE, YOUNGER OF BRODIE, Alastair Ian Ninian; s and h of Ninian Brodie of Brodie, JP, DL; *b* 7 Sept 1943; *Educ* Eton, Balliol Coll Oxford; *m* 1968 (m dis 1986), Mary Louise Johnson; 2 s, 1 da; *Career* Turnkey Systems Pty Sydney Australia; *Recreations* squash, chess; *Style—* Alastair Brodie, yr of Brodie; c/o Ninian Brodie of Brodie, JP, DL, Brodie Castle, Forres, Moray IV36 OTE

BRODIE-HALL, Sir Laurence Charles; CMG (1976); *b* 10 June 1910; *Educ* Sch of Mines Kalgoorlie (Dip Metallurgy, DipME); *m* 1, 1940, Dorothy Jolly (decd); 3 s, 2 da; m 2, 1978, Jean Verschuer; *Career* tech asst to md Western Mining Corpn 1950-51; gen supt: Gt Western Consolidated 1951-58, Western Mining Corp 1958-62 (exec dir 1962-75, ret 1975, dir 1975-82); dir ALCOA of Aust 1972-83; chm of dir Central Norseman Gold Corp 1974-82; chm Gold Mines of Kalgoorlie 1974-; memb bd of mgmnt West Aust Sch of Mines 1982-; dir ANSETT (WA) 1983-; citizen of the year award (WA) 1975; chm Westintech Innovation Corpn Ltd 1984-former dir Alcoa of Aust Ltd, pres WA Chamber of Mines 1970-75, former pres Aust Inst of Mining and Metallurgy (Institute Medal 1977); chm WA State Ctee CSIRO 1971-78; Hon DTech WA Inst Technology 1978; kt 1982; *Style—* Sir Laurence Brodie-Hall; 2 Cliff St, Perth, WA 6000, Australia

BRODRIBB, Dr Arthur Gerald Norcott; s of Arthur Williamson Brodribb, JP (d 1950), and Violet Sybil Swainson (d 1970); *b* 21 May 1915; *Educ* Eastbourne Coll, Univ Coll Oxford (MA, DipEd), London Univ (PhD); *m* 3 April 1954, Jessica, da of Col Henry Vere Barr (d 1968); 1 s (Michael Brien b 1956); *Career* schoolmaster, writer, archaeologist; co-dir Excavations at Beauport Park 1966-; *Books* The English Game (1947), Cricket in Fiction (1950), All Round the Wicket (1951), Next Man In (1952), The Bay and Other Poems (1953), Hastings and the Men of Letters (1954), Hit for Six (1960), Felix on the Bat (1962), The Croucher (1974), Maurice Tate (1976), The Art of Nicholas Felix (1985), Roman Brick and Tile (1987), Cricket at Hastings (1989); *Recreations* cricket, golf, Royal tennis, music, archaeology; *Clubs* Marylebone Cricket, Rye Golf, Fell of Soc of Antiquaries (London), Cricket Writers; *Style—* Dr Gerald Brodribb; Stubbles, Ewhurst Green, E Sussex TN32 5TD (☎ 058 083 510)

BRODRICK, His Hon Judge; Michael John Lee; s of His Hon (Norman John Lee) Brodrick, QC, *qv*; *b* 12 Oct 1941; *Educ* Charterhouse, Merton Coll Oxford; *m* 1969, Valerie Lois, da of Gerald Max Stroud, of Pond House, Rogate, Petersfield, Hants; 2 children; *Career* barr Lincoln's Inn 1965, Western circuit; elected to Senate of Inns of Court and The Bar 1979, served 1979-82, recorder 1981-87, memb Wine Ctee Western circuit 1982-86; judicial memb Tport Tbnl 1986; circuit judge 1987; special panel memb of The Tport Tribunal 1986 1987; *Recreations* gardening; *Clubs* Hampshire; *Style—* His Hon Judge Brodrick

BRODRICK, His Hon Norman John Lee; QC (1960), JP; 4 s of (William John) Henry Brodrick, OBE (d 1964), of 12 Frognal Gdns, Hampstead, NW3; *b* 4 Feb 1912; *Educ* Charterhouse, Merton Coll Oxford; *m* Ruth Severn, da of Sir Stanley Unwin, KCMG; 3 s (*see* Brodrick, Michael), 1 da; *Career* circuit judge, (ret); *Style—* His Hon N J L Brodrick, QC, JP; Slade Lane Cottage, Slade Lane, Rogate, Petersfield, Hants GU31 5BL

BRODWELL, John Shenton; s of Joseph Brodwell (d 1964), and Blanche, *née* Shenton (d 1984); *b* 3 May 1945; *Educ* Woodhouse Grove Sch, Southampton Univ (LLB); *Career* admitted slr 1970; ptnr: Harrisons 1975-87, Harrison Jobbings 1987-; Immigration Appeal adjudicator 1976-; govr Woodhouse Grove Sch 1980-, chm Horsforth Civic Soc 1973-, hon sec Leeds Philharmonic Soc 1982-; *Recreations* music, choral singing, conservation of the environment; *Clubs* East India, Wig and Pen, Horsforth; *Style—* J S Brodwell, Esq; 30 Jackman Drive, Horsforth, Leeds LS18 4HS (☎ 0532 582744); 31/32 Park Row, Leeds LS1 5JT (☎ 0532 433311)

BROERS, Prof Alec Nigel; s of Alec William Broers (d 1987), of Melbourne, Victoria, Australia, and Constance Amy, *née* Cox; *b* 17 Sept 1938; *Educ* Geelong GS, Melbourne Univ (BSc), Cauis Coll Cambridge (BA) (PhD); *m* 1964, Mary (Therese), da of Michael Phelan (d 1944); 2 s (Mark b 1965, Christopher b 1967); *Career* numerous managerial positions inc mangr Photon and Electron Optics IBM T J Watson Res Lab 1965-81; mangr: Lithography and Technology Tools 1981-82, Advanced Devpt 1983-84 IBM E Fishkill Lab; prof of electrical engry and head of electrical divn, Cambridge Univ Engrg Dept 1984-; IBM fell 1977, fell Trinity Coll 1985, memb IBM Corp Tech Ctee 1984; IEEE Cledo Brunetti Award 1985, American Inst of Physics Prize for Industial Applications of Physics 1982; FIEE, FEng, FRS; numerous papers, book chapters and patents on integrated circuit microfabrication and related subjects; *Recreations* music, sailing, skiing, tennis; *Style—* Prof Alec Broers; Oak House, Hinxton, Essex CB10 1RF (☎ 0799 30245); Cambridge Univ Engineering Dept, Trumpington Street, Cambridge CB2 1PZ (☎ 0223 332675, fax 0223 332662, telex 81239)

BROGAN, Lt-Gen Sir Mervyn Francis; KBE (1972, CBE 1964, OBE 1944), CB (1970); s of Bernard Brogan, of Manly, NSW (d 1969), and Hilda Marcelle, *née* Richards (d 1965); *b* 10 Jan 1915; *Educ* Sydney Tech HS, Royal Military Coll of Aust, Sydney Univ (BE), Imperial Defence Coll; *m* 1941, Sheila, da of David Samuel Jones, of Canberra (d 1943); 2 s (Edward b 1944, Daryl b 1948); *Career* Chief Gen Staff (Australian Army) 1971-73 (ret); GOC Northern Command 1962-65; QMG 1965-68; GOC Eastern Command 1969-71; Brig Gen Staff Br GHQ Far East Land Forces 1956-58; OC Supplementary Reserve RE (Ripon) 1950-52; dir: Austmark Internat Ltd, Arabex Petroleum, Garina Pty Ltd, Resource and Mineral Equities; *Recreations* swimming, surfing, tennis, golf, formerly rugby (Blue Sydney Univ); *Clubs* Union, City Tattersalls, Australian Jockey, Royal Sydney Golf, Rose Bay Surf (all Sydney); *Style—* Lt-Gen Sir Mervyn Brogan, KBE, CB; 71/53 Ocean Avenue, Double Bay, NSW 2028, Australia (☎ 32 9509)

BROGDEN, John Patrick Newton; s of Lt Alban Thomas Brogden, RFC (d 1943), and Mabel Le Butt, *née* Newton (d 1976); *Educ* Hull GS; *m* 7 June 1952, Eileen Norah Mary, da of Henry Mahony (d 1976), of 16 St Colman's Ave, Cosham, Portsmouth; 1 s (Richard b 1956), 2 da (Teresa b 1953, Veronica b 1962); *Career* Nat Serv RN 1946-48; CA 1952; ptnr Jones Avens Portsmouth 1956-, chm Radio Victory Ltd 1974-84; dir: Day Hartley Pembroke Bishops Walthan (fin planning conslts) 1989-, Hants Bldg Soc 1989-; city cncllr Portsmouth 1967-76, Lord Mayor City of Portsmouth 1973-74; chm: Cncl Community Serv Portsmouth 1977-82, mgmnt ctee Citizens Advice Bureau Portsmouth 1983-; Freeman City of London, Liveryman Worshipful Co Carmen; FCA 1952; *Recreations* bridge; *Style—* John Brogden, Esq; 70 Links Lane, Rowlands Castle, Hants (☎ 0705 41 2990); 53 Kent Rd, Southsea, Portsmouth, Hants (☎ 0705 820726, fax 0705 291224)

BROKE, Lt-Col George Robin Straton; LVO (1977); s of Maj-Gen Robert Straton Broke, *qv*, of Ivy Farm, Holme Hale, Norfolk; *b* 31 Mar 1946; *Educ* Eton; *m* 1978, Patricia Thornhill, da of Thomas Thornhill Shann (d 1983), of Trenoweth, Feock, Cornwall; 1 s; *Career* Major; equerry-in-waiting to HM The Queen 1974-77; Lt-Col; Commanding Officer 3 RHA 1987-89; *Recreations* country sports, photography; *Clubs* Lansdowne; *Style—* Lt-Col George Broke, LVO; Ivy Farm, Holme Hale, Thetford, Norfolk IP25 7DJ (☎ 0760 440225)

BROKE, Michael Haviland Adlington; s of Philip Adlington Broke, of 167 Broadway, Peterborough, and Jean, *née* Hiley; *b* 9 Mar 1936; *Educ* Eton, Corpus Christi Coll Cambridge (MA), London Business Sch; *m* 1961, Vera Antonjeta, da of Nikola Gjuracic (d 1972); 1 s (Philip b 9 Sept 1962), 1 da (Nicola b 17 June 1964); *Career* dir J Rothschild & Co Ltd 1975-84, chief exec Stockley plc 1984-87, dep chm Chelsfield plc 1987-; *Recreations* cricket, theatre, music; *Clubs* Buck's, Cavalry &

Guards, Savile, MCC; *Style*— Michael Broke, Esq; 67 Brook St, London W1

BROKE, Maj-Gen Robert Straton; CB (1967), OBE (1946), MC (1940); s of Rev Horatio George Broke (d 1931), and Mary Campbell, *née* Adlington (d 1949); *b* 15 Mar 1913; *Educ* Eton, Magdalene Coll Cambridge; *m* 1939, Ernine Susan Margaret, da of Rev William Henry Bonsey (d 1951); 2 s (*see* Lt-Col George Broke); *Career* RA 1933-66, served M East, N Africa, Europe, Maj-Gen 1964, Northern Army Gp 1964-66; farmer; dir Wellman plc 1968-88, pres Metallurgical Plantmakers Fedn 1977-79; Col Cmdt RA 1968-78; *Recreations* country sports; *Clubs* Army and Navy, MCC; *Style*— Maj-Gen Robert Broke, CB, OBE, MC; Ivy Farm, Holme Hale, Thetford, Norfolk IP25 7DJ (☎ 0760 440225)

BROLLY, Brian Thomas; s of late Thomas Henry Brolly, and Winifred Louise, *née* Christie; *b* 21 Oct 1936; *Educ* St Dunstans Coll London; *m* 1 June 1963, Gillian, da of late William Adams; 2 s (Sarsfield Kean b 1967, Tristan Patrick b 1970); *Career* MCA Inc (USA) md 7 founder MCA UK & Europe: Records Ltd, Films Ltd, Universal Pictures Ltd; sr vice pres MCA TV, dir Universal Pictures Ltd 1957-61 and 1963-73, exec asst to dir gen Radio Telefis Eireann 1961-63, md MPL Communications Ltd (Paul McCartney: recording, TV, films, music, photography, books; Wings: recording, world concert tour) 1973-78; md Really Useful Co (now The Really Useful Gp plc, Andrew Lloyd Webber's company) 1978-; *Recreations* sport, rugby London Irish, Surrey; *Clubs* Hurlingham; *Style*— Brian T Brolly, Esq; The Really Useful Group, 20 Greek Street, London W1V 5LF (☎ 01 734 2114, telex 8953151, fax 01 734 6230)

BROMAGE, Hon Jaqumine; *née* Thellusson; da of 8 Baron Rendlesham by his 2 w, Clare; *b* 21 August 1960; *m* 11 June 1987, Charles N Bromage, s of Col Nigel Bromage, of Powys; *Style*— The Hon Mrs Bromage; c/o Colonel Nigel Bromage, Barland House, Presteigne, Powys

BROME, Ronald Frederick; OBE (1983); s of Edgar Broome (d 1977), and Ida, *née* Richardson (d 1975); *b* 29 Dec 1932; *Educ* Hemsworth GS; *m* 2 Oct 1954, Kathleen, da of Jack Lyon (d 1962); 3 s (Christopher b 31 Oct 1956, Graham Mark b 21 Nov 1957, Michael Antony b 2 May 1964) 2 da (Deborah Elizabeth b 4 Aug 1960, Helen Lucy b 7 June 1968); *Career* RAF police 1950-54; West Riding Constabulary 1954, asst chief constable West Midlands Police 1977 (dep chief constable 1977), chief constable Avon and Somerset Constabulory 1983; vice-chm: Polic Police Athletic Assoc, Royal Life-Saving Soc, memb Cncl of St John in Avon; *Recreations* tennis, badminton; *Clubs* Bristol Savages, Shakespeare

BROMET, Lady; *see*: Conan Doyle, Dame Jean

BROMET, John Anthony; s of Maj Henry Anthony Bromet (d 1982), of Wighill, Tadcaster, N Yorks, and Margaret Cicely, *née* Rishworth; *b* 4 July 1927; *Educ* Winchester, Oxford Univ (MA); *m* 122 April 1966, Charlotte Imogen Woollcombe, da of Geoffrey Roy Holland Smith (d 1964), of Oxton Hall, Tadcaster, N Yorks; 1 s (Edward Anthony b 1950), 3 da (Emma Charlotte and Mary Rose (twins) b 1967, Fiona Jane b 1975); *Career* Rifle Brigade 1945-48, Lt; solicitor, admitted 1956, clerk to the Cmmnr of Taxes Barkston Ash Div, sr ptnr Messrs Bromet & Sons; *Recreations* fishing, shooting, forestry; *Style*— John A Bromet, Esq; Brook Hall, Wighill, Tadcaster, N Yorkshire LS24 8BG; Messrs Bromet & Sons, Solicitors, Kirkgate House, Tadcaster, N Yorkshire LS24 9AD

BROMHEAD, Lt-Col David de Gonville; LVO (1984); 2 s of Lt-Col Edmund de Gonville Hosking Bromhead (d 1977, himself yr bro of Sir Benjamin Bromhead, 5 Bt, OBE, and great nephew of Lt-Col Gonville Bromhead, VC, who defended Rorke's Drift in the Zulu War of 1879), and Joan, da of late Brig Sir Henry Scott, CB, DSO, MC; bro of John Bromhead, *qv*; *b* 16 Sept 1944; *Educ* St Andrew's Grahamstown (S Africa), RMA; *m* 1970, Susan, da of Cdr Richard Furley Fyson, DSC, JP, RN; 1 s (James b 1974), 2 da (Annabel b 1973, Antonia b 1978); *Career* Royal Regt of Wales, Gen Service Medal (Clasps) S Arabia and NI; took part in expeditions under John Blashford-Snell down Blue Nile (1968) and led reconnaissance party through Darien Gap during Trans-America Expedition 1971; equerry to HRH The Prince of Wales 1982-84, Lt-Col 1983; *Recreations* fishing; *Style*— Lt-Col David Bromhead, LVO, Equerry to HRH The Prince of Wales; Buckingham Palace, London SW1; Old Bell House, Coulston, Westbury, Wilts

BROMHEAD, Sir John Desmond Gonville; 6 Bt (UK 1806), of Thurlby Lincs; s of Sir Benjamin Bromhead, 5 Bt, OBE (d 1981); *b* 21 Dec 1943; *Educ* Wellington; *Heir* cous, John Bromhead; *Style*— Sir John Bromhead, Bt; Thurlby Hall, Thurlby, nr Lincoln LN5 9EG

BROMHEAD, John Edmund de Gonville; s of late Lt-Col Edmund de Gonville Hosking Bromhead (d 1973) and Joan, da of late Brig Sir Henry Scott, CB, DSO, MC; bro of Lt-Col David Bromhead, *qv*; first cous and hp of Sir John Bromhead, 6 Bt; *b* 10 Oct 1939; *Educ* St Andrew's Coll Grahamstown S Africa, RAF Coll Cranwell; *m* 1965, Janet, da of Henry Brotherton, of Moreton-in-Marsh, Glos; 1 s, 1 da; *Career* Capt Br Airways, served RAF until 1964 (when ret); *Style*— John Bromhead, Esq; Duiker House, Fencott, Islip, Oxford

BROMHEAD, Lady; Nancy Mary; da of late T S Lough, of Buenos Aires; *m* 1938, Sir Benjamin Bromhead, 5 Bt, OBE (d 1981); 1 s, 2 da; *Style*— Lady Bromhead; Thurlby Hall, Lincoln

BROMLEY, Archdeacon of; *see*: Francis, Edward Reginald

BROMLEY, Charles Howard; s and h of Sir Rupert Bromley, 10 Bt; *b* 31 July 1963; *Style*— Charles Bromley, Esq; PO Box 249, Rivonia 2128, Transvaal

BROMLEY, (Amey) Ida; MBE; da of William Gordon Bromley (d 1967), and Amy Elizabeth, *née* Marsden (d 1973); *b* 18 July 1929; *Educ* Saxonholme Sch Birkdale Lancs, Royal Liverpool Utd Hosps Sch of Physiotherapy; *Career* various hosps in England and Royal N Shore Hosp Sydney Aust 1952-65, supt physiotherapist Stoke Hardeville Hosp Ayresbury 1966-77, supt King's Coll Hosp London 1977-79, dist supt physiotherapy Hampstead Health Dist 1979-86; chm cncl of Chartered Soc of Physiotherapy 1978-82 (memb 1952); memb: Br Sports Assoc for the Disabled 1973-76, cncl Western Cerebral Palsy Clinic 1980-, NHS Health Advsy Serv 1983, cncl Mobility for the Disabled; memb editorial bds: Paraplegia, Clinical Rehabilitation, Physiotherapy Practice; accompanied Br team to Olympic Games for the paralysed: Japan, Israel, Germany; frequent lectr at nat and int confs; memb: Soc for Res in Rehabilitation 1978 (fndr memb and former pres), Int Soc of Paraplegia; FCSP (1986); *Books* Paraplegia and Tetraplegia (1976), International Perspectives in Physical Therapy (series ed 1984-); *Recreations* music, bridge, country pursuits, conservation, foreign travel, entertaining, bird watching; *Style*— Miss Ida Bromley, MBE; 6 Belsize Grove, London NW3 4UN (☎ 01 722 1794)

BROMLEY, Sir Rupert Charles; 10 Bt (GB 1757), of East Stoke, Nottinghamshire; s of Maj Sir Rupert Bromley, 9 Bt, MC (d 1966, fifth in descent from Sir George Bromley, 2 Bt, who changed his name to Bromley from Smith); *b* 2 April 1936; *Educ* Rhodes Univ, Ch Ch Oxford; *m* 26 April 1962, Priscilla Hazel, o da of late Maj Howard Bourne, HAC; 3 s; *Heir* s, Charles Howard Bromley, b 31 July 1963; *Career* co exec Murray & Roberts Ltd; Diocesan Registrar, Diocese of Johannesburg; *Recreations* squash; *Clubs* Western Province Sports; *Style*— Sir Rupert Bromley, Bt; PO Box 249, Rivonia 2128, Transvaal

BROMLEY GARDNER, Lt-Col Richard; MC (1944); s of Richard Bromley Gardner (d 1934), and Evelyn Doris, *née* Walker (d 1977); *b* 21 June 1921; *Educ* Wrekin Coll, RMA Sandhurst; *m* 11 June 1949, Jean Dorothy, da of Theodore Bower (d 1967); 2 s (Michael b 1952, Charles b 1960), 1 da (Caroline b 1950); *Career* 2 Lt Highland LI 1939, war serv Western Desert, Sicily, Italy, Greece, Dalmation Islands (MC, despatches), instr RMA Sandhurst 1947-49, Capt King's Guard Balmoral 1949, Staff Coll 1950, serv Korea, Malaya 1954-56 (despatches), Lt-Col 1961, ret 1968; steward's sec Jockey Club 1969-87 (sr steward's sec 1987), pres Jockey Club Officials' Assoc, steward Bath and Salisbury racecourses; *Recreations* fox hunting, bloodstock breeding, music; *Clubs* Army and Navy; *Style*— Lt-Col Richard Bromley Gardner, MC; Kingscote Park, Tetbury, Glos (☎ 0453 860223)

BROMLEY-DAVENPORT, Lt-Col Sir Walter Henry; TD, DL (Cheshire 1949); s of Walter Arthur Bromley-Davenport (d 1942), of Capesthorne, Macclesfield, and Dame Lilian Emily Isabel Jane, DBE, JP (d 1972), da of Lt-Col John Henry Bagot Lane; *b* 1903; *Educ* Malvern; *m* 1933, Lenette Ford, da of Joseph Yerkes Jeanes, of Philadelphia, USA; 1 s (William Arthur, *qv*), 1 da (Lenette); *Career* Grenadiers Gds 1922, raised and commanded 5 Bn Cheshire Regt, Lt-Col 1939, MP (C) Cheshire (Knutsford Div) 1945-70, Conservative whip 1948-51; memb Br Boxing Bd of Control 1953; kt 1961; *Clubs* Carlton, Pratts, Whites; *Style*— Lt-Col Sir Walter Bromley-Davenport, TD, DL; 39 Westminster Gardens, Marsham St, London SW1 (☎ 01 834 2929); Capesthorne Hall, Macclesfield, Cheshire SK11 9JY (☎ Chelford 0625 861 221); Fiva, Aandalsnes, Norway

BROMLEY-DAVENPORT, William Arthur; DL (Cheshire 1982); only s of Lt-Col Sir Walter Bromley-Davenport, *qv*; *b* 7 Mar 1935; *Educ* Eton, Cornel Univ; *m* 1962, Elizabeth Boies, da of John Watts, of Oldwick, NJ, USA; 1 s; *Style*— William Bromley-Davenport, Esq, DL; The Kennels, Capesthorne, Macclesfield, Cheshire

BRON, Eleanor; da of Sydney Bron and Fagah Bron; *Educ* North London Collegiate Sch, Newnham Coll Cambridge (BA); *Career* actress and writer; De La Rue Co 1961, appearences incl: revue, Establishment nightclub Soho 1962, NY 1963; Not So Much a Programme More a Way of Life BBC TV 1964, several TV series written with John Fortune also TV series incl: Making Faces (by Michael Frayn) 1976, Pinkerton's Progress 1983; TV plays incl: Nina 1978, My Dear Palestrina 1980, A Month in the Country 1985, Quartermaine's Terms 1987; stage performances incl: The Doctor's Dilemma (Jennifer Dubedat) 1966, The Prime of Miss Jean Brodie (Jean Brodie) 1967, 1984, Hedda Gabler (title role) 1969, The Merchant of Venice (Portia) 1975, Private Lives (Amanda) 1976, Uncle Vanya (Elena) 1977, The Cherry Orchard (Charlotte) 1978, A Family (Margaret) 1978, On Her Own 1980, Goody Biddy Bean, The Amusing Spectacle of Cinderella and her Naughty, Naughty Sisters 1980, Betrayal 1981, Heartbreak House 1981, Duet for One 1982, The Duchess of Malfi 1985, The Real Inspector Hound and the Critic (double bill) 1985, Oedipus and Oedipus at Colnus (Jocasta and Ismene) 1987, Infidelities 1987; films incl: Help!, Alfie, Two for the Road, Bedazzled, Women in Love, The National Health, The Day that Christ Died 1980, Turtle Diary 1985, Little Dorrit; composer of song-cycle with John Dankworth 1973, also verses for Saint-Saens' Carnival of the Animals 1975;; *Publications* Is Your Marriage Really Necessary (with John Fortune 1972), My Cambridge (contrib 1976), More Words (contrib 1977), Life and Other Punctures (1978), The Pillow Book of Eleanor Bron (1985), Eleonora Duse (1988); *Style*— Miss Eleanor Bron; c/o Jeremy Conway, Eagle House, 109 Jermyn St, London SE1 (☎ 01 839 2121)

BRONDER, Peter Johann; s of Johann Bronder, and Gertrude, *née* Kastl; *b* 22 Oct 1953; *Educ* Letchworth GS, RAM; *Career* tenor; Bayreuth Festival Chorus 1983, Glyndebourne Festival Chorus 1985, debut Royal Opera Covent Garden 1986, princ tenor WNO 1986-; BBC: TV Lawrence Olivier Awards 1985, Radio 3 Snape Maltings Concert (live) 1987, radio Salome R Strauss (live) 1988; and many other appearances on TV and radio, recitatives on Philips' recording Kiri Ti Kanawa recitals 1988; LRAM, LGSM; *Recreations* sports, photography, electronics, motorcycling; *Style*— Peter Bronder, Esq; c/o Allied Artists, 42 Montpelier Sq, London SW7 1JZ (☎ 01 589 6243)

BROOK, Anthony Donald; s of Donald Charles Brook (d 1976), and Doris Ellen, *née* Emmett (d 1987); *b* 24 Sept 1936; *Educ* Eastbourne Coll; *m* 18 March 1964, Ann Mary, da of Edwin Reeves, of 51 Albert Road, New Milton, Hampshire BH25 6SP; 2 da (Clare b 30 June 1966, Joanne b 24 April 1970); *Career* joined Assoc Television Ltd 1966; fin controller ATV Network Ltd 1966-74; dir External Finance IBA 1974-78; fin dir/gen mangr ITC Entertainment Ltd 1978-81; md TVS Television Ltd and co sec TVS Entertainment plc 1981-; dir: Independent Broadcast Telethon Tst, TVS Telethon Tst; govr of the Out of Town Centre; FCA 1970; *Recreations* sailing, golf; *Clubs* Royal Southern Yacht; *Style*— Anthony Donald Brook, Esq; 18 Brookvale Road, Highfield, Southampton SO2 1QP; Television Centre, Southampton SO9 5HZ (☎ 0703 634211, telex 477217, fax 0703 834340)

BROOK, Hon Mrs; Catherine Mary; *née* Hawke; da of 10 Baron Hawke, and Angela Margaret Griselda, *née* Bury (d 1984); *b* 11 July 1940; *Educ* Tudor Hall, London Univ (BEd); *m* 16 March 1963, Charles Groves Darville Brook, s of Air Vice-Marshal Sir William Arthur Darville Brook, CB, CBE (d 1953); 2 da (Charlotte b 1965, Henrietta b 1968); *Career* teacher now working as a volunteer organiser for Richmond upon Thames; *Style*— The Hon Mrs Brook; 7 The Hermitage, Richmond, Surrey TW10 6SH

BROOK, Dr Charles Groves Darville; s of Air Vice-Marshal William Arthur Darville Brook, CB, CBE (d 1953), and Marjorie Jean Hamilton, *née* Grant; *b* 15 Jan 1940; *Educ* Rugby, Magdalene Coll Cambridge (BA, MA, MD), St Thomas's Hosp Med Sch (MB BChir); *m* 16 March 1963, Hon Catherine Mary, da of Lord Hawke, of Old Mill House, Cuddington, Northwich, Cheshire; 2 da (Charlotte b 1965, Henrietta b 1968); *Career* resident posts: St Thomas's Hosp 1964-68, Hosp for Sick Children St Ormond St 1968-74; Wellcome Travelling res fell Kinderspital Zurich 1972-73, conslt paediatrician Middx Hosp 1974-, reader in paediatric endocinology Univ of London

1987-; chm Richmond Soc 1968-74, tstee Richmond Parish Land Charity 1988-; memb: ctee of mgmnt Royal Med Benevolent Fund 1976-, RSM; MRCP 1967, FRCP 1979, DCH 1968; *Books* Practical Paediatric Endocrinology (second edn 1978), Clinical Paediatric Endocrinology (1989), Growth assessment in childhood & Adolescence (1982), All about Adolescence (1985), Current Concepts in Paediatric Endocrinology (1988); *Recreations* DIY, gardening, fishing; *Style*— Dr Charles Brook; 7 The Hermitage Richmond, Surrey, TW10 6SH (☎ 07 940 2581) The Middlesex Hospital, Mortimer St, London W1N 8AA (☎ 01 380 9450, fax 01 636 9941)

BROOK, Air Vice-Marshal David Conway Grant; CBE (1983); s of Air Vice-Marshal William Arthur Darville Brook, CB, CBE (d 1953) and Marjorie Jean Hamilton, *née* Grant; *b* 23 Dec 1935; *Educ* Marlborough, RAF Coll Cranwell; *m* 14 Jan 1961, Jessica Rose, da of Col Michael Ronald Lubbock, of Ottawa 1 s (William b 1965), 1 da (Julie b 1961); *Career* Pilot- Nos 263, 1 (Fighter) and 14 Sqdns (Hunter aircraft), 1957-62, ADC to AOC-in-C Near East Air Force 1962-64, Co No 1 (Fighter) Sqdn (Hunter MK 9) 1964-66, RN Staff Course 1967, RAF Advsr to Dir Land/Air Warfare (MOD Army) 1968-69, Wing Cdr Offensive Support (Joint Warfare Establishment) 1970-72, Co No 20 (Army Cooperation) Sqn (Harrier) 1974-76, Station Cdr RAF Wittering (Harrier) 1976-78, Royal Coll of Defence Studies 1979, princ staff officer to Chief of Defence Staff 1980-82, SASO HQ RAF Germany 1982-85, Air Offr Scotland and NI 1986- ; Ex-Officio Patron of wide variety of Scottish Service Charities; Royal Utd Inst 1956; *Recreations* golf, music, hill-walking; *Clubs* RAF Extraordinary memb of Royal and Ancient GC St Andrews; *Style*— Air Vice-Marshal D C G Brook, CBE,; Bendameer House, Burntisland, Fife, KY3 0AG (☎ 0592 873 266); Royal Air Force, Pitreavie Castle, Dunfermline, Fife, KY11 5QF (☎ 412 161 ext 400), fax 0383 709 392; car tel 0836 709 392

BROOK, Lady; Helen; eldest da of John and Helen Knewstub, of Chelsea, SW3; *b* 12 Oct 1907; *Educ* Convent of Holy Child Jesus, Mark Cross, Sussex; *m* 2, 1937, Sir Robin Brook, CMG, OBE, *qv*; 2 da (and 1 da of previous m); *Career* fndr (1963) and pres Brook Advsy Centre for Young People; opened the first birth control sessions for the unmarried woman in 1960 in the Marie Stopes Centre; founded 1963 The Brook Advisory Centres for young people; vice-pres Family Planning Assoc, chm Family Planning Sales 1974-80; *Style*— Lady Brook; 31 Acacia Rd, London NW8 6AS (☎ 01 722 5844); Claydene Garden Cottage, Cowden, Kent (☎ Cowden 367)

BROOK, Leopold; s of Albert and Kate Brook, of Hampstead; *b* 2 Jan 1912; *Educ* Univ Coll London (BSc(Eng), fellow 1970); *m* 1, 1940, Susan (d 1970), da of David Rose, of Hampstead; 2 s; m 2, 1974, Elly, wid of Gilbert G Rhodes, FCA; 2 step s, 1 step da; *Career* chm: Simon Engineering plc 1970-77, Associated Nuclear Services Ltd 1977-, Brown & Sharpe Gp Ltd 1979-; dir Renishaw plc 1981-; FICE, FIMechE; *Clubs* Athenaeum, Hurlingham; *Style*— Leopold Brook, Esq; 55 Kingston House North, Prince's Gate, London SW7 1LW (☎ 01 584 2041)

BROOK, Sir Robin (Ralph Ellis); CMG (1954), OBE (1945); s of Francis Brook, of Harley St, London W1; *b* 19 June 1908; *Educ* Eton, King's Cambridge; *m* 1937, Helen, *qv*; 2 da; *Career* serv WWII, Brig, W Europe 1945; former dir Bank of England; former chm: Gordon Woodroffe & Co, Leda Investment Tst, Carlco Engrg Gp; dir United City Merchants, BP 1970-73; vice pres Assoc of Br Cs of C (formerly pres), président d'honneur Conf Permanente of EEC Cs of C; vice pres London C of C and Industry (formerly chm then pres); memb City and Hackney Health Authy (formerly City and E London HA) 1974-85; govr St Bartholomew's Hosp 1962-74 (tres and chm 1969-74, chm special tstees 1974-, pres Medical Coll 1969-, chm research tst); former chm Sports Cncl and Sport Devpt Ctee; govr exec ctee Sports Aid Fund; chm Colson Tst; memb: cncl and finance ctee City U, cncl and mgmnt ctee King's Fund, cncl Festival of Britain; pres London Homes for the Elderly; high sheriff London 1950; past master and wine warden Haberdashers' Co; Br Sabre Champion 1936 (Olympic Games 1936 and 1948); Cdr Legion of Merit, Legion of Honour, Croix de Guerre and bars, Offr Order of Leopold, Belgian Croix de Guerre; kt 1974; *Style*— Sir Robin Brook, CMG, OBE; 31 Acacia Rd, London NW8 (☎ 01 722 5844); Claydene Garden Cottage, Cowden, Kent (☎ Cowden 367)

BROOK, Rosemary Helen; da of Charles Rex Brook (d 1971), and Nellie Beatrice, *née* Yare; *b* 7 Feb 1946; *Educ* Gravesend Sch for Girls, Newnham Coll Cambridge (MA); *m* 1, 1970 (m dis 1979) Roger John Gross; m 2 22 Sept 1984, late Richard Winston Arbiter; 1 step da (Victoria b 1974); *Career* account mangr McCann Erickson Ltd 1975-77, head of public affrs Wiggins Teape Gp Ltd 1977-82 (Euro mktg coordinator 1986-75), dep chm Daniel J Edelman Ltd 1982-; Freeman City of London 1985-; MIPR 1977, MIPRA 1979; *Recreations* opera, ballet, reading, gardening, swimming; *Clubs* Reform; *Style*— Rosemary Brook; Kingsgate House, 536 King's Rd, London SW10 OTE (☎ 01 835 1222, fax 01 351 7676, car tel 01 835 1222, telex 929478)

BROOK-PARTRIDGE, Bernard; s of Leslie Brook-Partridge (d 1933), and Gladys Vere, *née* Brooks (later Mrs Burchell d 1989); *Educ* Selsdon Co GS, Cambs Tech Coll, Cambridge Univ, London Univ; *m* 1, 3 Nov 1951 (m dis 1965), (Enid) Elizabeth da of Frederick Edmund Hatfield (d 1951), of Sanderstead; 2 da (Eva Katherine Helen (Mrs New) b 6 Dec 1952, Katrina Elizabeth Jane (Mrs Gannon) b 18 Aug 1954); m 2, 14 Oct 1967, Carol Devonald, da of Arnold Devonald Francis Lewis, of Gower, S Wales; *Career* Military Service 1944-48; member of Gray's Inn 1950, cashier and accountant Dominion Rubber Co Ltd 1950-51, asst export mangr Br & Gen Tube Co Ltd 1951-52, asst sec Assoc of Int Accountants 1952-59, sec gen Inst of Linguists 1959-62, various teaching posts FDR 1962-66, special asst to md M G Scott Ltd 1966-68, business conslt (incl various directorships) 1968-72, memb Peterborough Devpt Corpn 1972-88, ptnr Carsons Brook-Partridge & Co 1972-, dir and sec Roban Engrg Ltd 1975-, chm Queensgate Mgmnt Servs Ltd 1981-87; dir: Brompton Troika Ltd 1985-, Pugh Carmichael Conslts Ltd 1988-, Alan Wooff Assocs Ltd 1986-, Edmund Nuttall Ltd 1986-, Thermocare Energy Servs Ltd 1986-; local government and political advisor Transmanche-Link 1988-; Parly candidate (C) St Pancras N LCC 1958, memb (C) St Pancras Met Borough Cncl 1959-62, prospective parly candidate (C) Shoreditch and Finsbury 1960-62, contested (C) Nottingham Central 1970; GLC: memb for Havering 1967-73, memb for Havering (Romford) 1973-85, chm 1980-81; chm: Enviromental Planning (NE) area ctee 1967-71, town devpt ctee 1971-73, arts ctee 1977-79, public servs and safety ctee 1978-79; opposition spokesman: for Arts & Recreation 1973-74, for Policy matters 1983-85; memb: exec ctee Greater London Arts Assoc 1973-78, exec cncl Area Museums serv for SE Eng 1977-78, cncl and exec Greater London and SE Cncl for Sport and Recreation 1977-78, GLC Leaders Ctee with special responsibility for Law and order and police liaison matters 1977-79; dep ldr recreation and community servs policy ctee 1977-79; memb: exec ctee Exmoor Soc 1974-79, BBC Radio London Advsy Cncl 1974-79, gen cncl Poetry Soc 1977-86 (tres 1982-); tstee: London Festival Ballet 1977-79, Sadler's Wells Fndn 1977-79; chm: London Symphony Chorus Devpt Ctee 1981-88, The Young Vic Theatre 1983-87 (dir 1977-88), London Music Hall Tst Ltd 1983-, Samuel Lewis Housing Tst 1985- (tstee 1976-), St George's Housing Assoc Ltd 1985-, Shipworkers Jubilee Housing Tst 1985-, Spearhead Housing Tst 1986-; memb London Orchestral Concert Bd Ltd 1977-78, dir ENO 1977-79, memb LCDT 1979-84, govr and tstee SPCK 1976-, vice chm London Music Hall Protection Soc Ltd (Wilton's Music Hall) 1983- (bd memb 1978-, chm 1981-83); pres: Br Sch of Osteopathy Appeal Fund 1980-84, Witan (Co Hall) Rifle Club 1979-, City of London Rifle League 1980-, Greater London Horse Show 1982-86, Greater London Co Hall branch of the Royal Br Legion 1988-, Hon FIE, Hon Fell and PhD Columbia Pacific Univ USA 1984; FCIS 1970, FCPU, MBIM 1978, FRSA; Order of Gorkha Dakshina Bahu (2 class, Nepal 1981); *Books* Europe - Power and Responsibility: Direct Elections to the European Parliament (with David Barker, 1972), numerous contribs to learned jls and periodicals on various subjects; *Recreations* hunting, conversation, opera, ballet, classical music, being difficult; *Clubs* Athenaeum, United and Cecil (Nikaeau), Surrey CCC; *Style*— Bernard Brook-Partridge, Esq; 14 Redcliffe St, London SW10 9DT (☎ 01 373 1223, bus 01 244 7541, 01 770 2690, fax 01 835 1335, telex 946918 (A/B: LIQUID G))

BROOKE, Sir Alistair Weston; 4 Bt (UK 1919), of Almondbury, W Riding of Yorkshire; s of Sir John Weston Brooke, 3 Bt (d 1983), by 1 w Rosemary (m dis 1963), da of late Percy Llewelyn Nevill (gs of 4 Earl of Abergavenny); *b* 12 Sept 1947; *Educ* Repton, RAC Cirencester; *m* 1982, Susan Mary, only da of Barry Griffiths, of Church House, Norton, Powys; 1 da (Lorna b 1983); *Heir* bro, Charles Weston Brooke, *qv*; *Style*— Sir Alistair Brooke, Bt; Wootton Farm, Pencombe, Hereford; Fearn Lodge, Ardgay, Ross-shire

BROOKE, Prof Bryan Nicholas; s of George Cyril Brooke (d 1934), of Croydon, and Margaret Florence, *née* Parsons; *b* 21 Feb 1915; *Educ* Bradfield, Corpus Christi Coll Cambridge, St Bartholomew's Hosp London (MB BChir, MChir (Cantab), MD (Birm)); *m* 23 Dec 1940, Naomi Winefride, da of Charles E Mills (d 1972), of Richmond; 3 da (Marian Esther b 5 May 1942, Nicola Sarah b 23 Jul 1943, Penelope Frances b 16 April 1947); *Career* RAMC 1943-46: Capt 1943, Maj Surgical specialist 1944, Ltd Col 1945; sr lectr in surgery Aberdeen Univ 1946, reader in surgery Birmingham Univ 1947-63 (sr lectr), prof of surgery London Univ at St George's and St James's Hosps 1976-80, conslt ed World Medicine 1980-82; memb Medical Appeals Tribunal for Industl Injury Benefit 1948-87; awards: Copeman Medal for Sci Res, Award of NY Sac of Colon and Rectal surgeons, AB Graham Award of American Soc of Colon and Rectal surgeons; ed Clinics in Gastroenterology 1972-86; pres Medical Art Soc 1979-83; memb cncl: Malvern Girls Coll 1959-87 (chm 1972-82), C of E Coll for Girls Birmingham 1948-65, Malvern Coll 1983-87; fndr and pres Ileostomy Assoc of GB and Ireland; MRCS 1939, LRCP 1939, FRCS 1942, FRACS (hon) 1977; *Books* You and Your Operation (1955), Understanding Cancer and Ulcerating Colitis (1972), The Troubled Gut (1986), A Garden of Roses (1987), various books on Crohn's Disease; *Clubs* Athenaeum; *Style*— Prof Bryan N Brooke; 112 Balham Park Road, London, SW12 8EA (☎ 01 767 0130)

BROOKE, Charles Weston; s (by 1 m) of Sir John Weston Brooke, 3 Bt; hp of bro, Sir Alistair Brooke, 4 Bt, *qv*; *b* 27 Jan 1951; *Educ* Repton; *m* 1984, Tanya Elizabeth, da of Anthony Thelwell Maurice, of Lloran, Robertson, NSW, Australia; 2 da (Nicola Margery b 1985, Emily Grace b 1988); *Style*— Charles Brooke, Esq; Midfearn, Ardgay, Ross-shire

BROOKE, Hon Christopher Arthur; yr s of 2 Viscount Brookeborough, PC, DL; *b* 16 May 1954; *Educ* Gordonstoun; *Career* served with 5 Inniskilling Dragoon Guards, ret Capt 1980; served Sultans Special Forces 1980-83; md Int Real Estate Dubai and Al Madfai Trading 1983-88; *Recreations* shooting, fishing, riding, diving, photography; *Clubs* Special Forces, Cavalry and Guards; *Style*— The Hon Christopher Brooke; Ashbrooke, Brookeborough, Co Fermanagh, N Ireland

BROOKE, Christopher Roger Ettrick; s of Ralph Brooke (d 1985), and Marjorie Lee; *b* 2 Feb 1931; *Educ* Tonbridge Coll Oxford (MA); *m* 1958, Nancy Belle, da of Eugene M Lowenthal (d 1985); 3 s (Christopher b 1962, Kenneth b 1966, Stephen b 1973), 1 da (Jenny b 1960); *Career* HM Dip Serv 1955-61, served at HM Embassies Bonn, Washington, Tel Aviv and at the FO London 1966-69; dep md Industl Reorganization Corpn London 1969-71, md Scienta SA Brussels 1971-79, cncllr Royal Borough of Kensington and Chelsea 1973-79; exec dir Pearson Gp, vice-chm Pearson Longman, chm Longman 1979-80, gp md EMI; chief exec Candover Investmts plc 1980-, dir Slough Estates plc 1980-; *Recreations* golf, tennis, music, theatre; *Clubs* Brooks', Woking Golf; *Style*— Roger Brooke; Water Meadow, Swarraton, nr Alresford, Hants (☎ 0962 732259); Candover Investmts plc, Cedric House, 8/9 East Harding Street, London EC4A 3AS (☎ 01 583 5091, telex 928035, fax 01 583 0717)

BROOKE, David; s of Alec Brooke, of Huddersfield (d 1959); *b* 18 Dec 1940; *Educ* Uppingham, Leeds Univ, Sorbonne; *m* 1967, Ann Margaret, da of William Stork, of Kirkburton, W Yorks; 1 s, 1 da; *Career* dir: C & J Hirst & Sons 1977, Market Devpt Int Ltd 1983-, Scandinavian Selections Ltd 1983-; sole trader David Brooke Int marketing and cmmn agent 1983-; *Style*— David Brooke, Esq; Mount Annan, Annan, Dumfriesshire DG12 5LN (☎ 04612 2186)

BROOKE, (Richard) David Christopher; s and h of Sir Richard Neville Brooke, 10 Bt, by his 1 w, Lady Mabel, *née* Jocelyn, da of 8 Earl of Roden; *b* 23 Oct 1938; *Educ* Eton; *m* 1963 (m dis 1978), Carola Marion (*see* Stormonth-Darling, R A), da of Sir Robert Erskine-Hill, 2 Bt, *qv*; 2 s; *Style*— David Brooke, Esq; Cedar House, Shurlock Row, Twyford, Berks

BROOKE, Sir Francis George Windham; 4 Bt (UK 1903), of Summerton, Co Dublin; s of Sir George Brooke, 3 Bt, MBE (d 1982), and Lady Melissa Brooke, *qv*; *b* 15 Oct 1963; *Educ* Eton; *m* 8 April 1989, Katherine Elizabeth, o da of Marmaduke James Hussey, *qv*; *Heir* kinsman, Geoffrey A G Brooke, *qv*; *Clubs* Turf, Kildare Street (Dublin); *Style*— Sir Francis Brooke, Bt

BROOKE, Lt Cdr Geoffrey Arthur George; DSC; s of Capt John Brooke, DSC, RN (d 1974, 6 s of Sir George Frederick Brooke, 1 Bt, who was govr of Bank of Ireland); hp of kinsman, Sir Francis Brooke, 4 Bt; *b* 25 April 1920; *Educ* RNC Dartmouth; *m* 1956, Venetia Mabel, only da of late Capt Hon Oswald Wykeham Cornwallis, OBE, RN; 3 da; *Career* Lt Cdr RN (ret); publicity (Press Union, Racal, ret 1985, currently conslt); *Books* Alarm Starboard! (Patrick Stephens 1982), Radar Mate (Adlard Coles 1986); *Recreations* shooting, fishing, painting, photography, gardening; *Clubs* Army and Navy; *Style*— Lt-Cdr Geoffrey Brooke, DSC; Beech House, Balcombe, Sussex RH17 6PS

BROOKE, Lord; Guy David Greville; s and h of 8 Earl of Warwick, JP; *b* 30 Jan 1957; *Educ* Eton, Ecole des Roches; *m* 1981, Mrs Susan (Susie) Cobbold, formerly w of Nicholas Cobbold; 1 s, 2 step children; *Heir* s, Hon Charles Fulke Chester Greville, b 27 July 1982; *Career* runs soft drinks bottling company; *Style*— Lord Brooke; 4 Walter Street, Claremont, Perth, W Australia 6010

BROOKE, Hon Mr Justice; Hon Sir Henry; yr s of Baron Brooke of Cumnor, CH, PC (Life Peer) (d 1984), and Baroness Brooke of Ystradfellte, DBE (Life Peeress, *qv*); br of Rt Hon Peter Brooke, MP, *qv*; *b* 19 July 1936; *Educ* Marlborough, Balliol Coll Oxford; *m* 1966, Bridget Mary, da of Wilfrid George Kalaugher, of Appledene, Marlborough, Wilts; 3 s, 1 da; *Career* barr Inner Temple 1963, jr counsel to the Crown (Common Law) 1978-81, QC 1981, counsel to Sizewell B Nuclear Reactor Inquiry 1983-85, recorder SE circuit 1983-88, appointed inspr into the affairs of House of Fraser Hldgs plc 1987, chm Professional Standards Ctee of the Bar Cncl, master of the Bench (Inner Temple) 1987, Justice of the High Court (Queen's Bench Div) 1988-; *Books* Brooks's; *Style*— The Hon Henry Brooke, QC; Fountain Court, Temple, London EC4 9DH (☎ (01) 353 7356)

BROOKE, John Alan De Leighton; s of Capt Ronald De Leighton Brooke, DSO, DSC, (bar), of Winchester, and Jocelyn Pelham Brooke, *née* Kent; *b* 6 June 1944; *Educ* Lancing, Trinity Hall Cambridge (BA); *m* 1969, Lyn, da of William Ewan Catto (d 1983); 1 s (Thomas b 1973), 1 da (Heloïse b 1970); *Career* book publisher; editorial dir Michael Joseph Ltd 1974-80; md Michael Joseph Ltd 1980-; dir Penguin Gp 1987-; *Recreations* Horseracing, skiing, tennis; *Style*— Alan Brooke, Esq; 75 West Hill Road, London SW18 (☎ 01 874 9067); 27 Wrights Lane, London W8 5TZ (☎ 01 937 7255, telex 917181/2, fax 01 937 8704)

BROOKE, Martin Montague; s of Montague Brooke (d 1957), of Kew Gardens, Surrey, and Sybil Katharine Martin (d 1959); *b* 25 August 1923; *Educ* Eastbourne Coll, Magdalene Coll Cambridge (MA); *m* 1950, Judith Mary, da of Rev Truman Tanqueray (d 1960), of Peaslake, Surrey; 2 s (Anthony, Samuel), 1 da (Katharine); *Career* Lt RNVR, served Atlantic and Indian Oceans 1942-45; banker; dir: Guinness Mahon 1963-72, Emperor Fund NV 1968-; Cannon Assurance 1969-84; chm Druidale Securities 1972-; cncl memb Distressed Gentlefolk's Assoc 1969-; *Recreations* gardening, walking; *Clubs* Naval; *Style*— Martin Brooke Esq; Duxbury House, 53 Chantry View Rd, Guildford, Surrey GU1 3XT (☎ 0483 504777); Johnson's Cottage, Druidale, Michael, Isle of Man; 41/42 King William Street, London EC4R 9ET (☎ 01 623 6064, telex 888542)

BROOKE, Lady Melissa Eva Caroline; *née* Wyndham-Quin; da of 6 Earl of Dunraven, CB, MBE, MC (d 1965); *b* 16 Feb 1935; *m* 25 June 1959, Maj Sir George Cecil Francis Brooke, 3 Bt, MBE (d 1982); 1 s, 1 da; *Style*— Lady Melissa Brooke

BROOKE, Michael Eccles Macklin; s of Reginald Eccles Joseph Brooke (d 1978), and of Beryl Cicely, *née* Riggs (d 1988); *b* 8 May 1942; *Educ* Lycee Francais de Londres, Edinburgh Univ (LLB); *m* 21 Oct 1972 (m dis 1985), Annie Sophie, da of Andre Vautier; 3 s (Nicholas b 1975, Anthony b 1977, Benjamin b 1979); *Career* called to the Bar of England and Wales and in practice 1968-; admitted avocat a la Cour d'Appel de Paris and in practice 1987-; *Recreations* boating, England and France; *Style*— Michael Brooke, Esq; 46 Molyneux St, London W1 (☎ 01 723 8652); 2 Crown Office Row, Temple, London EC4 (☎ 01 583 8155, fax 01 583 1205); 250 Bis Blvd St Germain, Paris 75007 (☎ 1 4544 3805, fax 1 4544 6226)

BROOKE, Hon Mrs - Hon Nancy Marion; *née* Allsopp; da of 3 Baron Hindlip (d 1931); *b* 15 Oct 1910; *m* 1936, Peter Geoffrey Brooke, s of Maj-Gen Geoffrey Francis Hereman Brooke, CB, DSO, MC (d 1966); 1 s; *Style*— The Hon Mrs Brooke; Dial House, Chilmark, Wilts

BROOKE, Rt Hon Peter Leonard; PC (1988), MP (C) City of London and Westminster S 1977-; s of Baron Brooke of Cumnor, CH, PC (Life Peer) (d 1984), and Baroness Brooke of Ystradfellte, DBE (Life Peeress, *qv*); br of Hon Sir Henry Brooke, *qv*; *b* 3 Mar 1934; *Educ* Marlborough, Balliol Coll Oxford, Harvard Business Sch (MBA); *m* 1964, Joan, da of Frederick Smith, of São Paulo, Brazil; 3 s (and 1 s decd); *Career* former RE (invalided out); Res Assoc IMEDE Lausanne and Swiss correspondent *Financial Times* 1960-61; chm Spencer Stuart Management Consultants 1974-79; asst govt whip 1979-81, Lord Cmmr Treasury (govt whip) 1981-83; under-sec state Educn and Science 1983-; *Recreations* cricket, walking; *Clubs* Brooks's, City Livery, I Zingari, MCC, St George's (Hanover Sq), Conservative; *Style*— The Hon Peter Brooke MP; 110a Ashley Gdns, London SW1 (☎ 01 834 1563)

BROOKE, Piers Leighton; s of Sir Richard Brooke, Bt and Lady Mabel Cheetham, *née* Jocelyn (da of Lord Roden) (d 1985); *b* 28 Dec 1940; *Educ* Eton; *m* 15 July 1967, Susan W, da of John Davenport of Middletown, New Jersey, USA (d 1987); 1 s (Sebastian b 1974), 1 da (Arabella b 1973); *Career* Lt Scots Gds 1960-63, regional dir SE Asia Chase Manhattan Bank 1978-79; (dir USA 1979-82); exec dir Lloyds Bank Int 1982-85; md: Lloyds Merchant Bank 1985-88; special project dir Midland bank plc 1988-; *Recreations* fishing, skiing, bridge, shooting; *Clubs* Boodle's; *Style*— Piers Brooke Esq; 37 Yeomans Row, London SW3 (☎ 01 584 7823); Midland bank plc, Poultry, London EC2P 2BX (☎ 01 260 7235)

BROOKE, Sir (Norman) Richard (Rowley); CBE (1958); s of late William J Brooke, JP, of Crosby, Lincs, and Eleanor, *née* Wild; *b* 23 June 1910; *Educ* Charterhouse; *m* 1, 1948 (m dis 1957), Julia Dean; 1 s, 1 da; m 2, 1958, Nina Mari Dolan; *Career* dir Guest Keen and Nettlefolds 1961-67; dir/chm GKN (S Wales) until 1967; former dir: Eagle Star Insur Co (S Wales), L Ryan Hldgs; former pres Cardiff Chamber of Commerce, former jt vice pres Br Iron and Steel Fedn; hon vice pres (and fndr dir) Devpt Corpn for Wales until dissolution, hon life vice pres Wales Cons and Unionist Cncl; former memb cncl Univ Coll Cardiff (vice pres 1965-81); JP Glamorgan 1952-74, OStJ 1953; FCA; kt 1964; *Style*— Sir Richard Brooke, CBE; New Sarum, Pwllmelin Lane, Llandaff, Cardiff (☎ Cardiff 563692)

BROOKE, Sir Richard Neville; 10 Bt (E 1662), of Norton Priory, Cheshire; s of Sir Richard Christopher Brooke, 9 Bt (d 1981) by his 1 w, Marian Dorothea (d 1965), da of late Arthur Charles Innes-Cross; *b* 1 May 1915; *Educ* Eton; *m* 1937 (m dis 1959), Lady Mabel Kathleen Jocelyn, da of 8 Earl of Roden; 2 s; m 2, 1960, Jean Evison, da of late Lt-Col Arthur Cecil Corfe, DSO, and formerly w of Sir Nicolas John Cheetham, KCMG; *Heir* s, (Richard) David Christopher Brooke; *Career* former Lt Scots Gds, serv WWII (POW escaped); sr ptnr Price Waterhouse & Co European Firms 1969-75, ret; FCA; *Recreations* racing, fishing; *Clubs* Boodle's; *Style*— Sir Richard Brooke, Bt; Moulin de Mourachonne, 06370 Mouans Sartoux, France (☎ 93 75 65 17); Pond Cottage, Crawley, Nr Winchester, Hants (☎ 096 272 272)

BROOKE, Rodney George; s of George Sidney Brooke (d 1967), of Morley, Yorks, and Amy, *née* Grant; *b* 22 Oct 1939; *Educ* Queen Elizabeth's GS Wakefield; *m* 2 Sept 1967, Clare Margaret, da of William Martin Cox (d 1985), of Windermere Rd, Moseley, Birmingham; 1 s (Magnus b 1971), 1 da (Antonia b 1973); *Career* asst slr: Rochdale County Borough Cncl 1962-63, Leicester City Cncl 1963-65; sr asst slr Stockport County Borough Cncl 1965-67 (asst town clerk 1967-69, dep town clerk 1969-71, dir of admin 1971-73), dir of admin West Yorks CC 1973-81 (chief exec and clerk 1981-84), clerk to West Yorkshire Lieutenancy 1981-84; chief exec Westminster City Cncl 1984-, clerk to Greater London Lieutenancy 1987-; hon sec London Boroughs' Assoc 1984-; chm London NE Royal Jubilee and Prince's Tsts 1984-, hon fell Inst of Local Govt Studies Birmingham Univ 1987-; OM (France) 1984, Order of Aztec Eagle (Mexico) 1985, Medal of Merit (Qatar) 1985; Order of Merit (Germany 1986), Order of Merit (Senegal) 1988; *Books* Managing the Enabling Authority (1989); *Recreations* skiing, opera, Byzantium; *Clubs* Ski of GB; *Style*— Rodney Brooke, Esq; Stubham Lodge, Middleton, Ilkley, W Yorks LS29 0AX (☎ 0903 601 869); 706 Grenville House, Dolphin Sq, SW1V 3LX; City Hall, Victoria St, SW1 (☎ 01 798 8086, telex 8950917, West OCG DX 2310 Victoria)

BROOKE, Hon Susanna Cynthia; The Hon; da of 2 Viscount Brookeborough, PC, DL; *b* 17 April 1962; *Career* secretary; *Recreations* tennis, riding, swimming, travelling; *Style*— The Hon Susanna Brooke

BROOKE OF YSTRADFELLTE, Baroness (Life Peeress 1964); Barbara Muriel Brooke; *née* Mathews; DBE (1960); yst da of Rev Canon Alfred Augustus Mathews (d 1946), of Llanwern, Gwent, and Ethel Frances, *née* Evans (d 1951); *b* 14 Jan 1908; *Educ* Queen Anne's Sch Caversham, Glos Training Coll of Domestic Sci; *m* 1933, Baron Brooke of Cumnor, CH, PC (d 1984); 2 s (Rt Hon Peter Brooke, PC, MP, *qv*, The Hon Sir Henry Brooke, Kt, QC, *qv*), 2 da; *Career* memb Hampstead Borough Cncl 1948-65, vice-chm Cons Pty Orgn 1954-64, memb N W Met Regnl Hosp Bd 1955-66; chm: governing body of Godolphin and Latymer Sch 1960-78, exec ctee Queen's Inst of Dist Nursing 1961-71; memb mgmnt ctee King Edward's Hosp Fund for London 1967-70; *Style*— The Rt Hon The Lady Brooke of Ystradfellte, DBE; Romans Halt, Mildenhall, Marlborough, Wilts

BROOKE TURNER, Alan; CMG (1980); s of Capt Arthur Brooke Turner, MC (d 1953), of Bournemouth, and Ella Gladys, *née* Jackson, formerly Ella Gladys Rabone (d 1978); *b* 4 Jan 1926; *Educ* Marlborough, Balliol Coll Oxford; *m* 9 Oct 1954, Hazel Alexandra Rowan, da of Wilfred Alexander Henderson, CIE (d 1958), of Argyll; 2 s (Peter b 1958, James b 1960), 2 da (Prudence b 1955, Clarissa b 1964); *Career* served in RAF 1944-48 (pilot offr); head of Southern European dept FCO 1972-73, counsellor HM Embassy Rome 1973-76, dir of studies and dep cmdt NATO Defence Coll Rome 1976-78, minister HM Embassy Moscow 1979-82, Ambass to Finland 1983-86, dir GB/E Europe Centre 1987-; fell of Center for Int Affairs Harvard Univ 1968-69; res assoc Int Inst for Strategic Studies 1978-79; memb Working Gp on Peacemaking in a Nuclear Age (Church of England Bd for Social Responsibility) 1986-88; memb: Cncl of Anglican Centre Rome 1976-77, cncl of Sch of Slavonic and E European Studies (Univ of London) 1987-; *Recreations* skiing, sailing; *Clubs* Travellers', Nylands Yacht Helsinski; *Style*— Alan Brooke Turner, CMG; 11 Marsham Court, Marsham Street, London SW1P 4JY (☎ 01 834 8863); Great Britain/East Europe Centre, 31 Knightsbridge, London SW1X 7NH (☎ 01 245 9771)

BROOKE-HITCHING, Hon Mrs (Emma Caroline); *née* Blades; da of 2 Baron Ebbisham, TD; *b* 28 May 1954; *Educ* St Mary's Calne, Univ of Tours France; *m* 1977, Franklin Brooke-Hitching; 3 s (Edward Robert b 1982, Matthew Thomas b 1985, William Franklin b 1987); *Style*— The Hon Mrs Brooke-Hitching; Osmington House, Kintbury, Newbury, Berks

BROOKE-LITTLE, John Philip Brooke; CVO (1984, MVO 1969); s of Raymond Brooke-Little (d 1961), late of Unicorns House, Swalcliffe, Oxon, and Constance Marie, *née* Egan; *b* 6 April 1927; *Educ* Clayesmore Sch, New Coll Oxford (MA); *m* 1960, Mary Lee, o da of late John Raymond Pierce; 3 s, 1 da; *Career* fndr Heraldry Soc and chm 1947, hon editor-in-chief The Coat of Arms 1950-; on Earl Marshal's Staff 1952-53, served as Gold Staff Offr Coronation 1953, Bluemantle Pursuivant 1956-67, Richmond Herald 1967-80, Norroy and Ulster King of Arms 1980-; registrar Coll of Arms 1974-81, librarian 1974-, tres 1978-; an advsr on Heraldry to Nat Tst 1983-, dep dir Herald's Museum at Tower of London 1983-; fellow Soc of Genealogists 1969, hon fellow Inst of Heraldic and Genealogical Studies, FSA; Freeman, Liveryman Scriveners' Co (Master 1985-86); govr Clayesmore Sch 1960-85 (chm 1961-83), pres English Language Literary Tst 1985-; Kt of Malta 1955 (chllr 1973-77), KStJ 1976, Knight Grand Cross of Grace Constantinian, Order of St George, Cruz Distinguiola (1st Class) of the Order of S Raimundo de Peñafart; *Books* Royal London (1953), Pictorial History of Oxford (1954), Boutell's Heraldry (1963 and 1966 with C W Scott-Giles, 1970, 1973, 1978, 1983), Knights of the Middle Ages (1966), Prince of Wales (1969), Fox-Davies' Complete Guide to Heraldry (1969), Kings and Queens of Great Britain, An Heraldic Alphabet (1973), Beasts in Heraldry (co-author, 1974), The Br Monarchy in Colour (1976), Royal Arms, Beasts and Badges (1977), Royal Ceremonies of State (1979); *Clubs* City Livery, Chelsea Arts; *Style*— John Brooke-Little, Esq, CVO, Norroy and Ulster King of Arms; Heyford House, Lower Heyford, Oxford OX5 3NZ (☎ Steeple Aston 40337); College of Arms, Queen Victoria St, EC4V 4BT (☎ 01 248 1310)

BROOKE-ROSE, Prof Christine; da of Alfred Northbrook Rose (d 1934), and Evelyn Brooke (d 1984); *b* 16 Jan 1923; *Educ* St Stephen's Coll Folkestone (now Broadstairs), Oxford (BA, MA), London Univ (PhD); *m* 1948 (m dis 1975), Jerzy Peterkiewicz; *Career* Flt Offr WAAF 1941-45; freelance journalist 1955-68; prof of lit theory Univ of Paris 8 1968-; author; *Books* A Grammar of Metaphor (1958), A ZBC of Ezra Pound (1971), A Rhetoric of the Unreal (1981), The Languages of Love (1957), The Sycamore Tree (1958), The Dear Deceit (1960), The Middlemen (1961), Out (1964), Such (1965), Between (1968), Thru (1975), Amalgamemnon (1984), Xorandor (1986), Brooke-Rose Omnibus (1986), also short stories and essays; *Style*— Prof Christine Brooke-Rose; c/o Carcanet Press Ltd, Manchester

BROOKEBOROUGH, 3 Viscount (UK 1952); Sir Alan Henry Brooke; 7 Bt (UK 1822), DL (Co Fermanagh 1987); er s of 2 Viscount Brookeborough, PC, DL (d

1987), and Rosemary, Viscountess Brookeborough, *qv*; *b* 30 June 1952; *Educ* Harrow, Millfield; *m* 12 April 1980, Janet Elizabeth, o da of John Cooke, of Ballyvoy Lodge, Doagh, Co Antrim; *Heir* bro, Hon Christopher Arthur Brooke, *qv*; *Career* cmmnd 17/21 Lancers 1972, transferred to UDR part-time 1977, Capt Permanent Cadre 4 Bn UDR 1980-83, transfer UDR pt/t 1983, Maj-Co Cdr 1988-; farmer; *Recreations* riding, fishing, shooting, skiing; *Clubs* Cavalry and Guards; *Style*— The Rt Hon the Viscount Brookeborough; Colebrooke, Brookeborough, Co Fermanagh, NI (☎ 036 553 402)

BROOKEBOROUGH, Rosemary, Viscountess- Rosemary Hilda; eldest da of Lt-Col Arthur O'Neill Cubitt Chichester, OBE, MC (d 1972), and Hilda Grace, *née* Young; *b* 12 Feb 1926; *m* 4 March 1949, 2 Viscount Brookeborough, PC, DL (d 1987); 2 s, 3 da; *Style*— The Rt Hon Rosemary, Viscountess Brookeborough; Ashbrooke, Brookborough, Co Fermanagh, N Ireland

BROOKEBOROUGH, Eileen, Viscountess - Sarah Eileen Bell; *née* Healey; da of Henry Healey, of Belfast; *b* 30 July 1906; *Educ* Princess Gardens Sch Belfast; *m* 1, Cecil Armstrong Calvert, FRCS, dir of neuro-surgery, Royal Victoria Hosp Belfast; m 2, 1971, as his 2 w, 1 Viscount Brookeborough, KG, PC, CBE, MC (d 1973); *Style*— The Rt Hon Eileen, Viscountess Brookeborough; Carnbeg, Spa, Ballynahinch, Co Down, Northern Ireland

BROOKER, Dr Arthur Edward William; s of Edward John Brooker (d 1963), of London, and Mary Harriett, *née* Fuller (d 1953); *b* 12 Dec 1912; *Educ* Roan Sch Greenwich, Univ of London St Bartholomew's Hosp Med Coll (MRCS, LRCP, MB BS, MD, FRCGP); *m* 14 Nov 1942, Kathleen Elma, da of George Alexander Raw (d 1973), of Isle of Wight; 2 s (John b 1946, Stephen b 1956), 1 da (Catherine b 1950); *Career* Capt RAMC 1939-45; jr scholarship St Bartholomew's Hosp Med Coll 1932, exern-intern St Bartholomew's Hosp 1938, sr med registrar RPMS 1946-47, asst med professorial unit Royal Hosp Sheffield 1947-48, GP principal Cliftonville 1948-76, locum conslt rheumatology SE Thames Regnl Health Authy 1976-85, examining MO DHSS 1978-87, occasional ship's surgn on various shipping lines; sometime memb Kent Local Medical Ctee; life memb Assoc of Men of Kent and Kentish Men, veteran memb Royal Temple Yacht Club; Freeman City of London 1970, Liveryman Worshipful Soc of Apothecaries 1970; life memb BMA 1937-, memb Br Assoc for Rheumatology 1958-; *Books* Cervical Spondylosis (thesis in two volumes 1963), Cervical Spondylosis - A Clinical Study with Comparative Radiology (jtly, in BRAIN 1965); *Recreations* photography, motoring, sailing; *Clubs* Royal Temple Yacht; *Style*— Dr Arthur Brooker; Six Elms, Lanthorne Rd, Broadstairs, Kent CT10 3NA (☎ 0843 68741)

BROOKER, Margaret Anne; da of James Gibson Wood (d 1977), of Station House, Ashurst, Hants, and Joan Ivy Grace, *née* Young; *b* 19 Mar 1946; *Educ* Brockenhurst Co HS, Univ of Texas at Austin (BSc), Univ of Pennsylvania (MSc); *m* 23 June 1965, Robin Christopher, s of Harry Frederick Brooker (d 1974), of Spinney Cottage, Chestfield, Kent; 1 da (Joanna Marta b 1966); *Career* botanical advsr Anglo American Expedition to Mount Roraima Venezuela 1970, botanist Estacian Central de Ecologia Madrid 1971-74, ldr Univ of Texas Botanical Expedition to Mount Tacaha Guatemala 1975, dir Nat Survey of Flora Ecuador 1975-77, conslt botanist Servicios Parques Nacionales de Costa Rica 1978-83, botanical advsr Int Union for Conservation of Nature and Natural Resources 1984-; memb: Real Sociedad Espanola de Historia Natural Madrid, Portuguese League for Protection of Nature Lisbon, Fedn Francaise des Sociétés de Protection de la Nature Paris, Nat Geographic Soc, Sociedad de Ciencas Naturales Aranzadi San Sebastian; *Books* Alpine Flora of Iberia (1975), Insect Pollinators at High Altitudes (1978), Flora of the High Andes (1980), The Conservation of Alpine Habitats in Europe (1985); *Recreations* travel, entomology, hot air ballooning, rock climbing; *Style*— Mrs Margaret Brooker

BROOKES, Beata Ann; MEP (EDG) N Wales 1979-; da of George Brookes, JP (d 1983), of Cwybr Farm, Rhyl, and Gwen Brookes; *b* 21 Jan 1931; *Educ* Lowther Coll Abergele, Univ of Wales Bangor, USA scholarship; *m* (m dis 1963); *Career* former social worker; farmer and company secretary; *Recreations* swimming, working; *Style*— Ms Beata Brookes, MEP; The Cottage, Wayside Acres, Bodelwyddan, N Wales

BROOKES, Hon John David; s of Baron Brookes (Life Peer); *b* 22 Sept 1940; *Educ* Malvern, Oriel Coll Oxford; *m* 1970 (m dis 1982), Faith, da of late John Redman, of Bidford on Avon, Warwicks; 2 s; m 2, 1986, Susan Nemeth; *Career* (md GKN Transmissions 1974-78), vice pres GKN Automotive Components (USA) 1978-; *Recreations* fishing, conflict simulation; *Clubs* Lansdowne; *Style*— The Hon John Brookes; 30425 S Greenbriar, Franklin, Mich 48025, USA (☎ 313 626 7738)

BROOKES, Nicola; da of Leon Bernard (d 1954), of Ruislip, and Violet Charlotte, *née* Farrar; *b* 25 Dec 1951; *Educ* Wycombe HS, Univ of Warwick (BSc); *m* 27 Sept 1980, Ian Thomas Burns, s of Thomas George Burns, West Kirby Wirral; 1 da (Laura Kathryn b 1988); *Career* trainee accountant Arthur Andersen & Co 1973-76, Amari plc 1976-: US controller 1978-79, mgmnt buyout mangr 1983 corporate devpt dir 1984, fin dir 1986; selected by Business magazine as one of Brs top 40 young business ldrs 1986, finalist Business Woman of the Year 1988; FCA 1981; *Recreations* swimming, skiing, reading, music and opera; *Style*— Ms Nicola Brookes; Amadeus, 26A Holloway Lane, Chesham Bois, Amersham, Bucks HP6 6DJ (☎ 0494 728 520); Amari Plc, Amari House, 52 High St, Kingston, Surrey KT1 1HN (☎ 01 549 6122, fax 01 546 0637, car tel 0836 500506, telex 262 937)

BROOKES, Baron (Life Peer UK 1975); Raymond Percival Brookes; s of William Percival Brookes, of W Bromwich, Staffs, and Ursula Brookes; *b* 10 April 1909; *Educ* Kenrick Tech Coll W Bromwich; *m* 1937, Florence Edna, da of Isaac William Sharman; 1 s; *Career* former memb cncl CBI; chm and chief exec Guest Keen & Nettlefolds Ltd 1965-74 (life pres 1975-); dir The Plessey Co Ltd, memb Dubai Aluminium Authority 1981-; kt 1971 ; *Style*— The Rt Hon the Lord Brookes; Mallards, Santon, Isle of Man (☎ 0624 822451)

BROOKES, Sir Wilfred Deakin; CBE (1972), DSO (1944), AEA (1945); s of Herbert Robinson Brookes and Ivy Deakin; *b* 17 April 1906; *Educ* Melbourne GS, Melbourne Univ; *m* 1928, Bertha (Betty) (d 1968), da of Albert Henry Heal; 1 s; *Career* former chm and dir various Industrial, Commercial and Mining Cos, chm Deakin Univ Fndn and Edwards Wilson Chartered Tst; vice-chm: Corps of Commissionaires; DLitt (honoris causa Deakin) chm Deakin Fndn 1982-; kt 1979; *Style*— Sir Wilfred Brookes CBE, DSO, AEA; 20 Heyington pla, Toorak, Victoria 3142, Australia (☎ 20 4553)

BROOKHOUSE, Graham Raymond; s of Raymond Nuttall Brookhouse, and Phyliss Adeline Teresa, *née* Hart; *b* 19 June 1962; *Educ* King Edward VI Camphill Sch for Boys Birmingham, Coll of St Paul and St Mary Cheltenham (BEd); *Career* teacher of swimming Stowe Sch 1985-87, Br Modern Pentathlon champion 1987, Bronze Medal Team Modern Pentathlon Seoul Olympics 1988; pt/t coach Cheltenham Swimming Club, active memb Cheltenham Harriers; *Recreations* horses, coaching, running, swimming; *Clubs* Spartan Modern Penthatlon; *Style*— Graham Brookhouse, Esq; 137 Village Rd, Cheltenham, Gloucs (☎ 0242 572 930)

BROOKING, Maj-Gen Patrick Guy; CB (1988), MBE (1975); s of the Capt CAH Brooking, CBE, RN, and GMJ White, *née* Coleridge; *b* 4 April 1937; *Educ* Charterhouse Sch, Alliance Francaise Paris, (Dip French Lang); *m* 11 April 1964, Pamela Mary da of the late Lt Col JES Walford, MBE; 1 s (Jonathan b 1967), 1 da (Samantha b 1965); *Career* cmmd 5 Royal Inniskilling Dragoon Gds 1956, served: Eng, W Germany, NI, Cyprus; Camberley Staff Coll 1969, Maj 39 Bde Belfast 1974-75, Regtl Cdr 1975-77, instr Army Staff Coll 1978, COS 4 Armd Div 1979-80, RCDS 1981, Cdr 33 Armd Bde 1982-83, asst COS UK Land Forces 1984-85, Cmdt and GOC Br sector Berlin 1986-88, dir gen Army Manning and Recruiting 1988-; Freeman City of London 1979, memb Worshipful Co of Broderers; *Recreations* tennis, skiing, golf, music; *Clubs* Cavalry and Guards; *Style*— Maj-Gen P G Brooking, CB, MBE; c/o National Westminster Bank, 26 Haymarket, London, SW1

BROOKNER, Dr Anita; da of Newson Brookner, and Maude Schisska; *b* 16 July 1928; *Educ* James Allen's Girls' Sch, King's Coll London (BA); *Career* lectr then reader Courtauld Inst of Art 1964-88; PhD (Courtauld Inst); FRSL; *Books* Watteau (1964), J B Grevze (1971), The Genious of the Future (1972), J L David (1980); has also written eight novels incl Hotel du Lac (1984 Booler McConnell prize and filmed for TV 1986), A Friend from England (1987) and many articles in Apollo, Burlington Magazine,TLS; *Recreations* walking, reading; *Style*— Dr Anita Brookner; 68 Elm Park Gardens, London SW10 (☎ 01 352 6894)

BROOKS, Alastair Groves; s of Rev Ronald Groves Brooks (d 1979), of The Rectory, Bow Brickhill, Milton Keynes, Bucks, and Mabel MacNair, *née* Melvin; *b* 23 August 1947; *Educ* Swanbourne House Sch Bucks, St Edward's Sch Oxford; *m* 27 July 1974, Nora Elizabeth, da of John Brendan Browne; 4 s (Sean Nicholas b 18 March 1966, Simon David b 6 March 1967, Robert Groves 2 Oct 1976, Richard Ronald b 21 July 1979); *Career* slr and NP, sr ptnr Brooks and Co Slrs Milton Keynes; Rotarian; memb Law Soc; *Recreations* golf; *Clubs* The Rugby, Woburn GC; *Style*— Alastair Brooks, Esq; Fairview, 63 Church Rd, Aspley Heath, Milton Keynes MK17 8TJ (☎ 0908 582207); Sovereign Ct, 209 Witan Game East, Centl Milton Keynes MK9 2HP (☎ 0908 665968, fax 0908 678722, car 0836 244922, telex 827542)

BROOKS, Hon Mrs; Hon Ann; *née* Fremantle; da of 4 Baron Cottesloe, GBE, TD, and his 1 w, Lady Elizabeth Berwick (d 1983), da of 5 Earl of Malmesbury; *b* 21 Oct 1930; *m* 29 Nov 1951, Timothy Gerald Martin Brooks, JP, s of Hon Herbert Brooks (s of 2 Baron Crawshaw); 3 s (Richard m 1985, Diana, yr da of Sir Michael Thomas, 11 Bt, Andrew b 1966, Michael b 1969), 2 da (Lucy m 1978, Keith Charlton; 1 s, 2 da, Nicola m 1978, Gerald A Michel; 2 da); *Style*— The Hon Mrs Brooks; Wistow Hall, Leicester (☎ Great Glen 2000)

BROOKS, (Kathleen) Claire; OBE (1986); da of Arthur Graham (d 1969) of The Mains, Giggleswick, Settle, N Yorks, and Clara Grace, *née* Grisedale; *b* 20 June 1931; *Educ* Settle PS, Aberaham Lincoln Sch NJ, Settle Girls HS, Skipton Girls HS, UCL (LLB); *m* 28 Sept 1963 (m dis 1971), Herbert Berwick, s of Herbert Berwick Brooks Sr (d 1959), of Superior, Wisconsin and Louisville, Kentucky; *Career* slr: S Kitching Walker & Co 1956-61, Medley Drawbridge & Co 1961-64, Victor D Zermansky & Co 1973-75; live o'seas 1964-1973; propr K Claire Brooks & Co, slrs, 1975-; dir Settle Carlisle joint Action Ctee Ltd; tstee: Skipton & Craven Assoc for Disabled (pres 1988-89), Craven Museum, Petyt Library, Heap Parkinson Homes; memb Lancaster Univ Ct and Univ Cncl; govr Skipton GHS and others; lifelong Liberal; memb: Craven DC 1976- (chm 1988-89), Skipton Town Cncl 1976 (Mayor 1985-86); contested: 6 party elections (4 Lib, 2 Alliance), 2 Euro party elections; memb: Lib Pty Nat Exc Ctee 1975-88, Lib Pty Cncl 1973-88, Nat Exec Ctee The Liberal Movement 1988-; memb The Law Soc, Br Legal Assoc; *Recreations* local history and archaeology, genealogy; *Clubs* Nat Lib; *Style*— Mrs Claire Brooks, OBE; The mains, Giggleswick, Settle, N Yorks (☎ 0756 749 528); Mesdames K Claire Brooks & Co Solicitors, 43 Otley Street, Skipton, N Yorks BD23 1EL (☎ 0756 5069 & 3328, fax 0756 68243)

BROOKS, Hon David Gerald; s of 3 Baron Crawshaw (d 1946); hp of bro, 4 Baron; *b* 14 Sept 1934; *Educ* Eton; RAC, Cirencester; *m* 1970, Belinda Mary, da of G P H Burgess, of Sandringham, Melbourne, Australia; 4 da (Susanna b 1974, Amanda b 1975, Elizabeth b 1975, Katharine b 1978); *Style*— The Hon David Brooks; Little Rise, Long Whatton, Loughborough, Leics (☎ Loughborough 842392)

BROOKS, Donal Meredith; *b* 10 April 1917; *Career* conslt orthopaedic surgn King Edward VII Hosp of Officers London, emeritus civilian conslt orthopaedic surgn in hand surgery to RN, hon civilian conslt orthopaedic surgn in hand surgery RAF; conslt orthopaedic surgn: UCH, Royal Nat Orthopaedic Hosp London (surgn i/c of peripheral nerve injury & hand unit); past chm ct of examiners RCS; past pres: orthopaedic section RSM, Chelsea Clinical Soc; pres Combined Servs Orthopaedic Soc, fell Br Orthopaedic Assoc (travelling fell 1954-), past memb Hand Club; memb: Br Soc for Surgery of the Hand, Gp d'Etude de la Main; hon memb S African Hand Soc; guest lectr: American Assoc of Neurosurgeons 1977, S African Soc for Surgery of the Hand 1978, Italian Soc for Surgery of the Hand, Portugese Soc for Surgery of the Hand; visiting lectr: Jordan, Egypt, Kuwait, Iraq; Wattie visiting prof New Zealand 1983, Robert Jones lectr RCS 1979, fndr lectr of American Soc for Surgery of the Hand 1983; Jackson Burrows Lecture & Medal Award 1983, Ruscoe Clarke Meml Lecture 1984, former memb ed bd Br Journal of Bone & Joint Surgery; memb: RSM, BDA, GEM; *Books* papers on peripheral nerve injuries and hand surgery in books & jls;; *Recreations* farming, gardening, travelling; *Clubs* Landsdowne, Royal Irish YC; *Style*— Donal Brooks, Esq; Errislannan Manor, Clifden, Co Galway

BROOKS, Douglas; s of Oliver James Brooks (d 1977) and Olive, *née* Davies (d 1980); *b* 3 Sept 1928; *Educ* Newbridge GS, Univ Coll Cardiff; *m* 1952, June Anne, da of Hedley Branch (d 1965); 1 s, 1 da; *Career* assoc dir Hoover Ltd 1972-78, cncl memb Economic and Social Res Cncl 1976-82, chief personnel exec Tarmac Ltd 1978-79, chm Wooburn Festival Soc Ltd 1978-86; dir: Walker Brooks and Ptnrs Ltd 1980-, Flexello Castors & Wheels plc 1987-; visiting sr fell Policy Studies Inst 1982-84; *Recreations* talking, cooking, music, gardening; *Clubs* Reform; *Style*— Douglas Brooks, Esq; Bull Farm House, Park Lane, Beaconsfield, Bucks (☎ 049 46 675253, telex 849462 TELFAC G)

BROOKS, Harry; eldest s (adopted) of Harry Brooks (d 1979), of Peover Hall, Knutsford, Cheshire, and Norah Brooks; *b* 16 Feb 1936; *Educ* Macclesfield GS, St

John HS Canada; *m* 23 July 1977, Mileva, da of Capt Dŭan Babic, of Yugoslavia, who fought in Tito's partisan army; 1 da (Milanka b 8 Sept 1983); *Career* actor, prodr and writer; began acting in Liverpool Playhouse 1958 before appearing on tv and in films incl: The Dirty Dozen, The Quiller Memorandum, Colditz and Wings; photographer, producing many classical photographs notably The Lady of Light; writer and exec prodr of an original screenplay Disguise; involved with Invalid Children's Aid Nationwide; *Style*— Harry Brooks, Esq; Hamlet Enterprises Ltd (☎ 01 235 1811); c/o Wright Webb Syrett, 10 Soho Square, London W1V 6EE

BROOKS, John; s of Lewis Russell Brooks, of Norfolk, and Alice Evelyn, *née* Boast (d 1978); *b* 25 Oct 1939; *Educ* Norwich Sch, Gonville Caius Coll Cambridge (MA); *m* 1 July 1966, Francine Andrée, da of Rémi Tridon of Auxerre France (d 1977); 2 da (Sylvie b 1969, Stephanie b 1972); *Career* chm Phonographic Performance Ltd, Video Performance Ltd 1986; dir CBS United Kingdom Ltd 1978; *Recreations* messing about in boats; *Clubs* RAC, ARA; *Style*— John Brooks Esq; Glenwood, River Avenue, Thames Ditton; 17/19 Soho Square, London W1V 6HE (☎ 01 734 8181)

BROOKS, John Ashton; *b* 24 Oct 1928; *Educ* Merchant Taylors'; *m* 1959, Sheila, *née* Hulse; 1 s, 1 da; *Career* dir & dep gp chief exec Midland Bank plc; pres Chartered Inst of Bankers; *Recreations* rugby, walking; *Clubs* IOD, Overseas Bankers; *Style*— John Brooks, Esq; c/o Midland Bank plc, Head Office, Poultry, EC2 (☎ 01 260 8000)

BROOKS, Hon John Patrick; yst s of 3 Baron Crawshaw (d 1946); *b* 17 Mar 1938; *Educ* Loughborough Coll; *m* 1967, Rosemary Vans Agnew, da of C Vans Agnew Frank, of Hunmanby, E Yorks; 1 s, 1 da; *Style*— The Hon John Brooks; 25 Cadogan St, SW3

BROOKS, Hon Mary Aletheia; da of 3 Baron Crawshaw (d 1946); *b* 12 Mar 1931; *Style*— The Hon Mary Brooks; Whatton, nr Loughborough, Leics

BROOKS, Nigel John; s of Norman John Leslie Brooks, of Southfield, Helen's Bay, Co Down, and Sheila, *née* Mercer; *b* 20 Mar 1959; *Educ* Campbell Coll Belfast, Pembroke Coll Cambridge (MA); *Career* Price Waterhouse 1980-84, merchant banker asst dir Charterhouse Bank 1984-; ACA; *Style*— Nigel J Brooks, Esq; 91 Warwick Rd, London SW5(☎ 01 244 9738); 1 Paternoster Row, St Paul's, London EC4 (☎ 01 248 4000)

BROOKS, Robert; s of William Frederick Brooks, of Bishopswood House, Bishopswood, Herefordshire, and Joan Patricia, *née* Marshall; *b* 1 Oct 1956; *Educ* St Benedict's Sch Ealing; *m* 30 May 1981, Evelyn Rachel, da of Prof John William Durnford; 2 s (Charles b 24 Aug 1984, John b 21 June 1987), 1 da (Sarah b 11 May 1983); *Career* dir Christies S Kensington Ltd 1984-87 (joined 1975), dir Christie Manson and Woods Ltd 1987- present; *Recreations* flying; *Style*— Robert Brooks, Esq; London W9 1AN; Christie Manson & Woods Ltd, 8 King St, London SW1Y 6QT (☎ 01 839 9060)

BROOKS, (Richard) Simon; s of Maj Richard Clement Brooks, TD, JP (d 1980), of Wrington, Nr Bristol, and Edith Mary, *née* Shellard (d 1950); *b* 29 Mar 1931; *Educ* Radley; *m* 8 Aug 1959, Helen Rosemary, da of Frederick James Weeks, of Wrington, Bristol; 1 s (Adam Brooks b 1965), 2 da (Victoria (Mrs Botsford) b 1961, Emma Brooks b 1962); *Career* Nat Serv RAF, PO Royal Auxiliary Air Force 1955 (Flying Offr 1959); CA 1954, former pres Br Textile Rental Assoc, chm and md Brooks Serv Gp plc; memb W Eng Ctee ILD, tstee Clifton Suspension Bridge, govr Clifton Coll, chm Clifton Club, tres Anchor Soc; Freeman City of: London 1971, Bristol 1969; Liveryman: Dyers Co Launderers Co; ACA 1954, FCA 1965; *Recreations* reading, music, food and drink, motor sport, occasional squash, skiing, riding, sailing, golf, tennis, bridge, travel; *Clubs* Clifton; *Style*— Simon Brooks, Esq; Aztec West, Almondsbury, Bristol, Avon BS12 4SN (☎ 0454 614668)

BROOKS, William Donald Wykeham; CBE (1956); s of Arthur Edmund Brooks (d 1954), of Maidenhead, and Alice, *née* Swatton; *b* 3 August 1905; *Educ* Reading Sch, St John's Coll Oxford (MA, DM), Rochester Univ NY USA; *m* 1934, Phyllis Kathleen, da of Frank Anderson Juler, CVO (d 1962), of Harley St, London; 2 s, 2 da; *Career* Surgn Capt RNVR; Rockefeller medical fell 1931-32, Fereday fell St John's Coll Oxford 1931-34; conslt physician: St Mary's and Brompton Hosps 1935-70, to RN 1940-70; editor Quarterly Journal of Medicine 1946-67, sr censor and sr vice pres RCP 1965, Goulstonian lectr RCP 1940-, Marc Daniels Lectr RCP 1957-, asst registrar 1946-50, cncllr RCP 1959-61; FRCP; *Recreations* gardening, golf, bridge, shooting; *Style*— William Brooks, Esq, CBE; Two Acres, Fryern Rd, Storrington, Sussex (☎ 090 66 2159)

BROOKS OF TREMORFA, Baron (Life Peer UK 1979); John Edward Brooks; s of Edward George Brooks and Rachel, *née* White; *b* 12 April 1927; *m* 1, 1948 (m dis 1956); 1 s, 1 da; m 2, 1958, Margaret Pringle; 2 s; *Career* parliamentary agent to Rt Hon James Callaghan, MP, 1970 and 1979 gen elections; *Style*— The Rt Hon the Lord Brooks of Tremorfa; 57 Janet St, Slott, Cardiff (☎ 40709)

BROOKSBANK, Ann, Lady; Ann; da of Col Thomas Claud Clitherow, DSO, of Hotham Hall, Brough, Yorks; *m* 1943, Sir (Edward) William Brooksbank, 2 Bt, TD, JP, DL (d 1983); 1 s; *Style*— Ann, Lady Brooksbank; Menethorpe Hall, Malton, N Yorks

BROOKSBANK, Sir (Edward) Nicholas; 3 Bt (UK 1919), of Healaugh Manor, Healaugh, W Riding of Yorks; Lord of the Manor of Healaugh; s of Sir William Brooksbank, 2 Bt, TD, JP, DL (d 1983), and Ann, Lady Brooksbank, *qv*; *b* 4 Oct 1944; *Educ* Eton; *m* 1970, Hon Emma Myrtle Mary Anne, da of Baron Holderness, PC, DL, *qv*; 1 s, 1 da; *Heir* s, Florian Tom Charles b 9 Aug 1982; *Career* Capt the Blues and Royals, ret; Christie's rep York; *Style*— Sir Nicholas Brooksbank, Bt; Ryton Grange, Malton, N Yorks (☎ 065 386 270)

BROOKSHAW, Sarah Caroline (Sally); da of John Latter Barratt (d 1988), of Minsterley Hall, Shrewsbury, Shropshire and Pauline Monica, *née* Gapp; *b* 10 Jan 1956; *Educ* Shrewsbury HS, Aberystwyth Univ (LLB); *m* 6 June 1987, Oliver Chitty Brookshaw, s of Herbert Philip Brookshaw MC, of Old House Farm, Saunderton, Princes Risborough, Buckinghamshire; *Career* slr, ptnr William Sturges and Co 1986; *Recreations* riding and hunting; *Clubs* HAC Saddle, South Shropshire Hunt, Lansdowne; *Style*— Mrs Sally Brookshaw; 14 Tonsley Street, London SW18 (☎ 01 870 9370); William Sturgess and Co, 12 Caxton Street, London SW1H OQY (☎ 01 222 1391, fax 01 222 0361)

BROOM, Prof Donald Maurice; s of Donald Edward Broom (d 1971), of Tatsfield, Surrey, and Mavis Edith Rose, *née* Thompson; *b* 14 July 1942; *Educ* Whitgift Sch, St Catharine's Coll Cambridge (MA, PhD); *m* 31 May 1971, Sally Elizabeth Mary, da of Thomas Edward Fisher (d 1969), of Ufton Nervet, Berkshire; 3 s (Oliver b 1973, Tom b 1976, Giles b 1981); *Career* lectr (later reader) dept of pure and applied zoology Univ of Reading 1967-86, Colleen Macleod Prof of Animal Welfare dept of clinical veterinary med Univ of Cambridge 1986-, visiting asst prof zoology dept Univ of California 1969, visiting lectr biology dept Univ of West Indies Trinidad 1972, invited expert Cmmn of Euro Communities Farm Animal Welfare Expert Gp 1981, visiting sci div of animal prodn Cwlth Sci and Industl Res Orgn Perth 1983, hon res assoc Animal and Grassland Res Inst 1985, tstee Farm Animal Care Tst 1986, invited expert Cncl of Euro Standing Ctee on Welfare of Animals kept for Farming Purposes 1987-; fell St Catharine's Coll Cambridge 1987-; hon tres Assoc for the Study of Animal Behaviour 1971-80 (cncl memb 1980-83), pres Soc for Veterinary Ethology 1987-89 (cncl memb 1981-84, vice-pres 1986-87); memb: Int Ethological Ctee 1976-79, Br Tst for Ornithology, Br Soc of Animal Prodn, Zoological Soc of London, Assoc of Veterinary Teachers and Res Workers; FIBioL 1986; *Books* Birds and their Behaviour (1977) Biology of Behaviour (1981), Encyclopaedia of Domestic Animals (ed, with P A Messent 1986), Farmed Animals (ed, 1986), Farm Animal Behaviour and Welfare (with A F Fraser, 1989); *Recreations* squash, modern pentathlon, ornithology; *Clubs* Hawks (Cambridge); *Style*— Prof Donald Broom; Department of Clinical Veterinary Medicine, University of Cambridge, Madingley Rd, Cambridge CB3 OES; St Catharine's College, Cambridge (☎ 0223 337 697, fax 0223 337 610)

BROOM, Air Marshal Sir Ivor Gordon; KCB (1975, CB 1972), CBE (1969), DSO (1945), DFC (1942 and two bars 1944 and 1945), AFC (1956); s of Alfred Godfrey Broom, of Southport, and Janet Broom; *b* 2 June 1920; *Educ* W Monmouth Sch, Pontypridd GS; *m* 1942, Jess Irene, da of William Joseph Cooper, of Ipswich; 2 s, 1 da; *Career* served WW II bomber pilot, Cmdt Central Flying Sch 1968-70, controller of Nat Air Traffic Servs and bd memb CAA 1974-77, ret RAF 1977; int aerospace conslt 1977-; chm Gatwick Handling Ltd 1982-; dir Plessey Airports Ltd 1982-86, chm Farnborough Aerospace Devpt Corpn 1985-; *Recreations* golf; *Clubs* RAF, Moor Park Golf; *Style*— Air Marshal Sir Ivor Broom, KCB, CBE, DSO, DFC, AFC; Cherry Lawn, Bridle Lane, Loudwater, Rickmansworth, Herts WD3 4JB (☎ 0923 778878)

BROOMAN, John Cresswell; s of Benjamin Wallis Brooman (d 1940), of Wallington; *b* 11 Jan 1922; *Educ* Bec Sch SW17; *m* 1948, Doris Gwen, da of Horace John Robert Gisby, of Folkestone; 2 children; *Career* Lt RNVR, served Europe; chm Black and Decker Grouping (pres Black & Decker 1978-82), dir BSR (UK) 1983-; chm Freemans plc May 1984-; chm: London Ctee first National Bank of Maryland; CBIM, FCA; *Recreations* tennis, gardening; *Clubs* Moor Park; *Style*— John Brooman Esq; Emoyeni, Batchworth Hill, London Rd, Rickmansworth, Herts (☎ Rickmansworth (0923) 772327; office: 01 735 1378)

BROOME, David; OBE (1970); s of Fred and Amelia Broome, of Chepstow; *b* 1 Mar 1940; *Educ* Monmouth GS; *m* 1976, Elizabeth, da of K W Fletcher, of Thirk, N Yorkshire; 1 s; *Career* show jumper and farmer; World Show Jumping Champion 1970; MFH; *Style*— David Broome Esq, OBE; Mount Ballan Manor, Crick, Chepstow, Gwent (☎ Caldicot 42077)

BROOME, Ronald Frederick; OBE (1983); s of Edgar Broome (d 1977), and Ida, *née* Richardson (d 1975); *b* 29 Dec 1932; *Educ* Hemsworth GS; *m* 2 Oct 1954, Kathleen, da of Jack Lyon (d 1962); 3 s (Christopher b 31 Oct 1956, Graham Mark b 21 Nov 1957, Michael Antony b 2 May 1964) 2 da (Deoborah Elizabeth b 4 Aug 1960, Helen Lucy b 7 June 1968); *Career* RAF police 1950-54; West Riding Constabulary 1954, asst chief constable West Midlands Police 1977 (dep chief constable 1980), chief constable Avon and Somerset Constabulory 1983; vice-chm: Police Athletic Assoc, Royal Life-Saving Soc; memb Cncl of St John in Avon; *Recreations* tennis, badminton; *Clubs* Bristol Savages, Shakespeare; *Style*— Ronald F Broome, Esq, OBE; Police HQ, PO Box 188, Bristol (☎ 0272 277 777)

BROOMER, James Vincent; s of Vincent Walter Mason Broomer (d 1951), and Christina, *née* Joyce (d 1974); *b* 27 Feb 1927; *Educ* Lancaster Royal GS, Manchester Univ; *m* 24 March 1955, Averil Mary, da of Frank Crapper; 2 s (Charles, Jason), 1 da (Alison); *Career* RN 1946-49, asst to legal aid offr 1947-49; slr 1951, dep clerk to magistrates Howden 1952-63, ptnr Taylor Broomer & Co Goole; fndr pres Rotary Club of Howden; memb Law Soc; *Recreations* law, music; *Style*— James Broomer, Esq; 20 Riversdale Drive, Goole, North Humberside DN14 5LT, (☎ 0405 2219); 157 Boothferry Rd, Goole, DN14 6AL, (☎ 0405 3853, fax 0405 720246)

BROOMFIELD, Graham Martin; s of Herbert Broomfield, of W Sussex, and Muriel Joyce, *née* Robinson; *b* 12 Feb 1945; *Educ* Dorking County GS, Chelsea Coll, London Univ (BSc); *m* 5 Oct 1974, Wai Yu (Miranda), da of Leung Fu Ping (d 1972); 1 s (Lee b 1978), 1 da (Amy b 1981); *Career* CA; Charles Comins & Co 1967-72, Peat Marwick Mitchell & Co 1972-76, Watner Communications Inc 1977-81, Prager & Fenton 1981-87, Broomfield & Co 1983-, Stylus Music Ltd 1987; *Recreations* politics, squash; *Style*— Graham M Broomfield, Esq; 17 Cromwell Grove, London W6 (☎ 01 603 4487); Stylus Music Ltd, Media House, 3 Burlington Lane, Chiswick, London W4 (☎ 01 742 1662, telex 916848, fax 7421469)

BROOMFIELD, Nigel Hugh Robert Allen; CMG (1986); s of Col Arthur Allen Broomfield, OBE, MC (d 1970), and Ruth Sheilagh, *née* Anderson (d 1974); *b* 19 Mar 1937; *Educ* Haileybury, Trinity Coll Cambridge (BA); *m* 8 June 1963, Valerie, da of G Fenton, of Garden Court, Noirmont, Jersey, CI; 2 s (Alexander Allen b 29 April 1970, Nicholas Richard Allen b 2 Oct 1976); *Career* Maj 17/21 Lancers 1958-68; first sec: FCO 1969, Bonn 1970, Moscow 1973, FCO 1975; RCDS 1978, cnsllr and head of Chancery BMG Berlin 1979, head E Euro and Soviet Dept FCO 1981, dep high cmmr New Delhi 1986, ambass to GDR E Berlin 1988; Br Amateur Squash Champion 1957-58; *Recreations* reading, music, sport; *Clubs* MCC, RAC; *Style*— Nigel Broomfield, Esq, CMG; c/o FCO, Whitehall, London SW1A 2AA

BROOMHALL, Maj Gen (William) Maurice; CB (1950), DSO (1945), OBE (1932); o s of Alfred Edward Broomhall (d 1947), of London, and Florence Mary, *née* Chalk; *b* 16 July 1897; *Educ* St Paul's, RMA Woolwich, Christs Coll Cambridge; *Career* WW I Western Front (wounded twice), served NW Frontier India 1924 and 1928 (MBE and despatches), served WWII NW Europe, Chief Engr: CMF 1946, BAOR 1947-48, MELF 1948-51, ret 1951; chm Cellulose Devpt Corpn 1964-73; *Clubs* Army & Navy; *Style*— Major-General Maurice Broomhall, CB, DSO, OBE; The Cottage, Park Lane, Beaconsfield, Bucks HP9 2HR (☎ 0494 673562)

BROOMHEAD, Ivor William; s of Frederick William Broomhead (d 1970) and Florence Elizabeth *née* Percival; *b* 7 Dec 1924; *Educ* Doncaster GS, St John's Coll Cambridge (MA), Univ Coll Hospital London (MB, MChir); *m* 18 Dec 1950, Dorothea Primrose, da of John Edward Pretty Wagstaff (d 1963), Emeritus Prof of Physics, Univ of Durham; 1 s (Anthony b 1954), 2 da (Amanda b 1951, Susan b 1963); *Career*

National Service: medical officer, RAF 1950-2; consultant plastic surgeon: The Hospital for Sick Children 1964-87, Guy's Hospital 1968-87, Royal Masonic Hospital 1974-86; FRCS; pres: Royal Society of Medicine (plastic surgery section) 1981, memb British Assoc of Plastic Surgeons 1985; consultant adviser in plastic surgery to DHSS chief medical officer 1978-88; *Books* specialist publications on cleft lip and palate, and other congenital malformations; *Recreations* horology (skeleton clocks); *Clubs* Athenaeum; *Style*— Ivor Broomhead, Esq; 36 Highgate West Hill, Highgate, London N6 6LS (☎ 01 340 8769); 79 Harley Street, London W1N 1DE (☎ 01 935 0224)

BROPHY, Brigid Antonia; o da of John Brophy (d 1965, author), and Charis Weare, *née* Grundy; *b* 12 June 1929; *Educ* St Paul's Girls' Sch, St Hugh's Coll Oxford; *m* 1954, Sir Michael Levey, *qv*; 1 da; *Career* author and playwright; FRSL; *Books* 11 fiction volumes and 10 non-fiction; *Style*— Miss Brigid Brophy; Flat 3, 185 Old Brompton Rd, London SW5 0AN (☎ 01 373 9335)

BROPHY, Michael John Mary; s of Gerald Mary Brophy, and Mary Brophy; *b* 24 June 1937; *Educ* Ampleforth Coll, RN Coll Dartmouth; *m* 1962, Sarah Myrtle, da of Captain G B Rowle RN.; 3 s (James, Jonathan, Thomas), 1 da (Lucy); *Career* RN (Lt Cdr) 1953-66; assoc dir J Walter Thompson 1962-74, appeals dir The Spastics Society 1975-81, dir Charities Aid Foundation 1982-; *Recreations* travel, walking; *Clubs* Athenaeum; *Style*— Michael Brophy Esq; Pond House, Isfield, E Sussex

BROSTER, Brenda Maeve; *née* Shaw; da of Col F O J Shaw, of Wingham, Kent, and Catherine Maeve Power, *née* McCaul, of Guildford, Surrey; *b* 11 Nov 1944; *Educ* St Mary's Priory Warwicks, St Godric's Coll Hampstead; *m* 9 Oct 1965, David George, s of H F Broster (d 1973), of Bursledon, Hants; 2 s (Oliver b 1971, Humphrey b 1979), 2 da (Natalie b 1974, Georgette b 1975); *Career* md: Sales Promotions Agency, Powergirls Ltd Int Agency; *Recreations* horses, gemology, astronomy, the arts; *Style*— Mrs Brenda M Broster; The Hermitage, 193 Lower Road, Gt Bookham, Surrey; Powergirls Ltd, 59d Church Road, Gt Bookham, Surrey KT23 3JJ

BROTHERHOOD, James; s of Frederick Arthur (d 1974), and Isabel, *née* Bradley; *b* 5 June 1946,,; *Educ* King's Sch Chester; *m* 2 Aug 1969, Susan Elizabeth, da of Thomas Ian Jodrell Toler, of Cheshire; 3 s (Jonathan Alexander Jodrell b 1973, Philip Richard Thomas b 1975, Michael Rupert Benjamin b 1981), 2 da (Katherine Mary b 1978, Eleanor Elizabeth b 1984); *Career* architect, dip arch (Hons) 1973, RIBA 1974, pres Cheshire Soc of Architects 1978-80, NW Region chm RIBA 1983, Ancient Monuments and Historic Buildings Restoration Specialist; *Recreations* golf, shooting; *Clubs* City (Chester), St James (Manchester), Pitt; *Style*— James Brotherhood, Esq; 7 Selkirk Road, Curzon Park, Chester CH4 OHU (☎ 0244 683983); 33 Bold Square, Chester CH1 3LZ (☎ 0244 47557)

BROTHERHOOD, Air Cdre (Willem) Rowland; CBE (1953); s of James Brotherhood (d 1930), of Tintern, Monmouth, and Maria van Stockum (d 1950); *b* 22 Jan 1912; *Educ* Monmouth Sch, RAF Coll Cranwell; *m* 1939, Margaret, (d 1981) da of Ernest Sutcliffe of Stewton House, Louth, Lincs; 1 s (John), 1 da (Ann); *Career* station cdr RAF Chedburgh, Bomber Cmd 1944-45, sr personnel staff offr AHQ India 1946-47, dep dir Weapons Air Miny 1948-50, gp dir RAF Staff Coll Bracknell 1950-53, stn cdr Bomber Cmd Bombing Sch 1953-54; dir: Operational Requirements (C) AM 1955-58; Guided Weapons (Trials) Miny of Aviation 1959-60; *Recreations* fishing, gardening, travelling; *Style*— Air Cdre Rowland Brotherhood, CBE; Inglewood, Llandogo, Monmouth, Gwent (☎ 0594 530333)

BROTHERS, Brian Peter; s of Ernest Norman, and Frances Ruth (d 1987); *b* 18 May 1929; *Educ* Dauntsey's Sch; *m* 1, 1950, Diana Elizabeth, da of Edward J Tucker (d 1986); 3 s (Timothy b 1951, Jeremy b 1955, Toby b 1961), 1 da (Anne b 1956); m 2, 1974, Jacquelin Ann; 1 da (Katharine b 1975); *Career* fin advsr; arranged fin over 150 Hosps/Health Schemes, mainly S America with Economist Intelligence Unit 1975-80; dir: W Sussex Area Enterprise Centre Ltd, Voice of Progress, Seacourt Press, Oxford Initiative Investmts, Individual Fin, Individual Television, Arroyo Real Int Bowls Centre Ltd; Talking Newspaper for the Blind, chm govrs George Pringle Sch, memb ctee League of Friends of Worthing Hospitals, tres Children's Surgical Suite Appeal Worthing Hospital; FInstD (memb S ctee); *Clubs* Worthing: Golf, Rotary, Tennis; *Style*— Brian P Brothers, Esq; 4 Parklands Avenue, Goring-by-Sea, West Sussex BN12 4NH

BROTHERS, Air Cdre Peter Malam; CBE (1964), DSO (1944), DFC (1940, Bar 1943); s of John Malam Brothers (d 1953), of Prestwich, Lancs and Maude Elizabeth Owen (d 1969); *b* 30 Sept 1917; *Educ* N Manchester Sch; *m* 1939, Annette, da of James Wilson (d 1959), of Hutton House, Birmingham; 3 da (Caroline, Wendy, Hilary); *Career* Pilot Offr RAF 1936, Flt Lt 1939, served WW II, Battle of Britain 1940, Sqdn Ldr 1941, Wing Cdr 1942, Tangmere Wing Ldr 1942-43, Staff HQ No 10 Gp 1943, Exeter Wing Ldr 1944, US Cmd and Gen Staff Sch 1944-45, Central Fighter Estab 1945-46; joined HM Colonial Serv 1947 (dist off: Meru 1947-48, Kisumu 1948-49); rejoined RAF 1949, cmd Bomber Sqdn 1949-52, HQ No 3 Gp 1952-54, RAF Staff Coll 1954, HQ Fighter Cmd 1955-57, Bomber Stn 1957-59, Gp Capt and staff offr SHAPE Paris 1959-62, dir of ops (overseas) Air Miny 1962-65, Air Cdre and AOC Mil Air Traffic Ops 1965-68, dir PR (RAF) MOD (AIR) 1968-73, ret 1973; chm and md Peter Brothers Conslts Ltd 1973-; Master Guild Air Pilots & Air Navigators 1974-75 (Freeman 1966, Liveryman 1968, Warden 1971); Freeman City of London 1967; patron Spitfire Assoc Australis; vice pres; Spitfire Soc, chm Devon Emergency Vols; *Recreations* flying, fishing,swimming, sailing (yacht 'Atla'); *Clubs* RAF, RAF Yacht, Honiton Golf; *Style*— Air Cdre Peter Brothers, CBE, DSO, DFC; c/o National Westminster Bank, Topsham, Devon

BROTHERTON, Ian Dryhurst; TD (1964), DL (Middx 1964, Greater London 1967); s of Thomas D Brotherton, of Hampton, Middx; *b* 16 Nov 1920; *Educ* Hampton Sch, London Univ; *m* 1943, Margaret, da of Sidney F Ponting, of Shepperton; 3 da; *Career* Middx Regt 1939-46 (despatches), Bt Col 1962, ADC (TAVR) to HM The Queen 1968-73; md: S Daval & Sons 1968-69, Br American Optical Co 1970-72, Hadley Co 1972-85; princ Cruise Training 1985-; Croix de Guerre; *Recreations* photography, yachting (yacht 'Jimpa'); *Clubs* Army & Navy, Royal Lymington YC; *Style*— Ian Brotherton Esq, TD, DL; The Moorings, 6 Cranfield Ave, Wimborne, Dorset BH21 1DE (☎ 0202 886887)

BROTHERTON, Michael Lewis; s of late Capt John Basil Brotherton and Maud Brotherton; *b* 26 May 1931; *Educ* RNC Dartmouth; *m* 1968, Julia, da of Austin Gerald Comyn King, of Bath; 3 s, 1 da; *Career* Lt-Cdr RN to 1964; with Times Newspapers 1967-74; MP (C) Louth 1974-83; pres Hyde Pk Tories 1975; proprietor Michael Brotherton Assocs PR Consultants 1986; *Recreations* cricket, cooking; *Clubs* Army and Navy, MCC; *Style*— Michael Brotherton, Esq; The Old Vicarage, Wrangle, Boston, Lincs (☎ 0205 870 688)

BROUGH, Dr Colin; s of Peter Brough (d 1964), and Elizabeth Cassels Collison, *née* Charlmers; *b* 4 Jan 1932; *Educ* Bell Baxter Sch Cupar Fife, Univ of Edinburgh (MB, ChB, DPH, DIH); *m* 28 Dec 1957, Maureen (Jenny), da of late William Frederick Jennings; 4 s (Hamish b 1960, Ewan b 1963, Angus b 1967, Dugald b 1969), 1 da (Catriona b 1959); *Career* Surgn Lt RN 1957-60; house offr Leicester Gen Hosp 1956-57, GP Leith and Fife 1960-64, dep superintendent Royal Infirmary Edinburgh 1965-67 (house offr 1956-57); S Eastern Regnl Hosp Bd Scotland 1967-74: ASMO, PASMO, dep SAMO; chief admin MO Lothian Health Bd 1980-88 (community medicine specialist 1974-80); FFCM 1978, FRCPE 1982; *Recreations* golf, shooting, fishing; *Style*— Dr Colin Brough; The Saughs, Gullane, E Lothian EH31 2AL (☎ 0620 842179)

BROUGH, Michael David; s of Kenneth David Brough, of Highgate, London, and Frances Elizabeth, *née* Davies; *b* 4 July 1942; *Educ* Westminster Sch, Christs Coll Cambridge, Middx Hosp Med Sch (MA, MB, BChir); *m* 8 June 1974, Dr Geraldine Moira, da of Ernest Alfred Sleigh, of Sutton, Coldfield; 2 s (Jonathan b 1977, Nicholas b 1983), 2 da (Charlotte b 1978, Veronica b 1981); *Career* med post 1968-71: Middx Hosp, Centl Middx Hosp; surgical trg posts Birmingham Hosps 1971-74, plastic surgery trg posts 1975-80: Mt Vernon Hosp London, Odstock Hosp Salisbury, Withington Hosp Manchester; conslt in plastic surgery 1980-82: St Andrews Hosp Billericay, Queen Elizabeth Hosp Hackney, Whipps Cross Hosp, conslt plastic surgery 1982-: Univ Coll Hosp, Royal Free Hosp, Whittington Hosp, Royal Northern Hosp; Freeman City of London 1974, Liveryman: Worshipful Co of Tin Plate Workers (memb Ct of Assistants), Worshipful Co of Apothecaries; FRCS; *Recreations* family, skiing; *Clubs* Hawks Cambridge; *Style*— Mr M D Brough; 6 Stormont Rd, London N6 4NL; The Consulting Suite, 82 Portland Place, London WIN 3DH (☎ 01 935 8910)

BROUGHAM, Hon Charles William; s and h of 5 Baron Brougham and Vaux; *b* 9 Nov 1971; *Style*— The Hon Charles Brougham; Yew Tree Cottage, North Heath, Chieveley, nr Newbury, Berks

BROUGHAM, Hon David Peter; s of 4 Baron Brougham and Vaux (d 1967); *b* 22 August 1940; *Educ* Sedbergh; *m* 1, 1969, Moussie Christina Margareta Hallström, da of Sven Hörnblad, of Stockholm, Sweden; 1 s (Henry, b 1971); m 2, 1977, Caroline Susan, only da of Lt. Col James Michael Heigham Royce Tomkin, MC, of Red House, Wissett, Halesworth, Suffolk (by his w Margaret Elinor, da of Sir Charles Henry Napier Bunbury, 11 B), and former w of Julian Dixon; 1 s (Oliver, b 1978); *Style*— The Hon David Brougham; Flat D, 10 Girdlers Rd, London W14

BROUGHAM, Hon Henrietta Louise; da of 5 Baron Brougham and Vaux and Olivia Hicks, *née* Gray; *b* 23 Feb 1965; *Educ* Cranborne Chase Sch, Cambridgeshire Coll of Arts & Technology; *Style*— The Hon Henrietta Brougham; North Bohetherick, St Dominick, Saltash, Cornwall

BROUGHAM AND VAUX, 5 Baron (UK 1860); Michael John Brougham; s of 4 Baron (d 1967) by his 2 w, Jean, da of late Brig-Gen Gilbert Follett, DSO, MVO, and Lady Mildred, *née* Murray, da of 7 Earl of Dunmore, DL; *b* 2 August 1938; *Educ* Lycée Jaccard Lausanne, Millfield, Northampton Inst of Agric; *m* 1, 1963 (m dis 1968), Olivia Susan, da of Rear Adm Gordon Thomas Seccombe Gray, DSC, of Midhurst; 1 da; m 2, 1969 (m dis 1981), Catherine (who m 1981 Rupert Edward Odo Russell, gs of Sir Odo Russell, KCMG, KCVO, CB, himself 2 s of 1 Baron Ampthill), da of William Gulliver; 1 s; *Heir* s, Hon Charles Brougham; *Career* senior marketing exec and company dir; pres ROSPA; *Recreations* rugger, tennis, photography; *Style*— The Rt Hon the Lord Brougham and Vaux; 11 Westminster Gardens, Marsham Street, London SW1P 4JA

BROUGHSHANE, 2 Baron (UK 1945); Patrick Owen Alexander Davison; s of 1 Baron, KBE (d 1953), by his 1 w, Beatrice Mary, da of late Sir Owen Roberts; *b* 18 June 1903; *Educ* Winchester, Magdalen Coll Oxford; *m* 1929, Bettine, da of late Sir Arthur Edward Montague Russell, 6 Bt (cr 1812); 1 s; *Heir* s, Hon Alexander Davison; *Career* Irish Gds 1939-42, asst sec (mil) War Cabinet 1942-45; barr Inner Temple 1926; Legion of Merit (U.S.A.); *Clubs* White's; *Style*— The Rt Hon The Lord Broughshane; 21 Eaton Sq, London SW1; 28 Fisher St, Sandwich, Kent

BROUGHTON, Air Marshal Sir Charles; KBE (1965, CBE 1952), CB (1961); s of Charles and Florence Gertrude Broughton, of Christchurch, NZ; *b* 27 April 1911; *Educ* New Zealand, RAF Coll Cranwell; *m* 1939, Sylvia Dorothy Mary, da of late Col C H de St P Bunbury; 1 da (and 1 da decd); *Career* cmmnd RAF 1932, dir-gen of orgn Air Miny 1961-64, UK rep in Ankara Perm Mil Deputies Gp of Central Treaty Orgn 1965-66, air memb for Supply and Orgn Miny of Defence 1966-68; *Style*— Air Marshal Sir Charles Broughton, KBE, CB; c/o Shrewsbury House, Cheyne Walk, London SW3

BROUGHTON, David Delves; s of Lt Cdr Peter John Delves Broughton, RN (d 1963); hp to Btcy of kinsman, Sir Evelyn Delves Broughton, 12 Bt; *b* 7 May 1942; *Style*— David Broughton Esq

BROUGHTON, Sir (Evelyn) Delves; 12 Bt (E 1660), of Broughton, Staffs; s of Sir John Delves Broughton, 11 Bt (d 1942), and Vera Edyth, *née* Boscawen (d 1966); *b* 2 Oct 1915; *Educ* Eton, Trinity Coll Cambridge; *m* 1, 28 Jan 1947 (m dis 1953), Hon Elizabeth Florence Marion Cholmondeley, da of 4 Baron Delamere, JP, by his 1 w, Phyllis, da of Lord George Montagu-Douglas-Scott, OBE, 3 s of 6 Duke of Buccleuch, KG, KT, PC; m 2, 1955 (m dis 1974), Helen Mary, da of J Shore, of Wilmslow; 1 s (John b 12 July 1963, d 1965) 3 da (Isabella Delves b 19 Nov 1958, Julia Helen Delves b 11 Feb 1961, Lavinia Mary b 14 Feb 1965); m 3, 1974, Rona, da of E Clifford Johns, of Wargrave, and previously w of Donald Crammond, of London; *Heir* kinsman, David Delves Broughton; *Career* former 2 Lt Irish Gds; farmer and landowner; *Recreations* shooting, travel; *Clubs* Brooks's, White's, Tarporley Hunt; *Style*— Sir Delves Broughton, Bt; 37 Kensington Square, London W8 5HP (☎ 01 937 8883); Doddington Cottage, Nantwich, Cheshire (☎ 0270 841 258)

BROUGHTON, Hon James Henry Ailwyn; s and h of 3 Baron Fairhaven, JP; *b* 25 May 1963; *Educ* Harrow; *Career* Capt Blues and Royals; *Recreations* polo, skiing, hunting; *Clubs* Cavalry and Guards'; *Style*— The Hon James Broughton

BROUN, Sir Lionel John Law; 12 Bt (NS 1686), of Colstoun, Haddingtonshire; s of Sir (James) Lionel Law 11 Bt (d 1962), and Lady Broun, *qv*; *b* 25 April 1927; *Style*— Sir Lionel Broun, Bt; 89 Penshurst St, Willoughby, NSW 2068, Australia

BROUN, William Windsor; s of William Arthur Broun (d 1925); hp to Btcy of kinsman, Sir Lionel Broun, 12 Bt; *b* 1917; *m* 1952, D'Hrie, da of Frank R King, of Bingara, NSW; 2 da; *Style*— William Broun, Esq; 23 Clanalpine St, Mosman, NSW,

Australia

BROUN LINDSAY, Captain Colin George; s of Sir Humphrey George Maurice Broun Lindsay, KB, DSO (d 1964), of East Lothian, and Edith Christian, *née* Broun Baird (d 1981); *b* 4 Nov 1926; *Educ* Eton, RMA Sandhurst; *m* 4 Aug 1952, Beatrice Marie-Thérèse Ferdinande Yvonne Ghislaine Comtesse d'Ursel, da of Conrad Comte d'Ursel, of Belgium; 1 s (Ludovic b 1954), 1 da (Christian b 1956); *Career* Capt Grenadier Gds 1945-48, Lothian & Border Horse TA 1948-55; *Clubs* Boodles, New Edinburgh; *Style—* Captain Colin G Broun Lindsay

BROUWER, Egbert; CBE (1980); s of Jan Hendrick Brouwer, and Margaretha M E Dyjers; *b* 14 Feb 1927; *Educ* Nederlands Lyceum, The Netherlands Beatrix Coll Switzerland; *m* 14 Oct 1953, Dorine, da of Cornelis van Holst Pellekaan (d 1952); 3 s (Maarten b 1956, Egbert b 1959, Reinier b 1961), 1 da (Florentine b 1957); *Career* Capt Dutch Army 1947-49; branch mangr Internatio NV in SE Asia 1949-56; Roosendaal Commodity Brokers Rotterdam 1957-65; gen mangr BP Maatschappy Nederland BV Amsterdam 1965-80; md BP Nutrition Ltd London 1978-87; cncl memb VNO 1973-78; Bd Govrs Maritime Ryksmuseum 1972-80; ctee of Honour, William and Mary Tercentenary 1986-; chm Supervisory Bd Atlas COPCO Amsterdam 1975-80; Bd memb: Atlas Copco (GB) Hemel Hempstead 1980-, Purina Mills Inc 1986-, BP Nutrition Ltd 1987-; Supervisory Bd; memb: Merrem and Laporte 1974-80, Morgan Bank 1977-, BP Maatschappy 1980; dep chm Supervisory Bd Hendrix Internat 1979-; Knight Netherlands Lion (1987); *Recreations* sailing, skiing; *Clubs* Royal Netherlands Yacht; *Style—* Egbert Brouwer, Esq, CBE; Howick Farm, Balls Cross, nr Petworth, GU28 9JY (☎ Kirdford 548); BP Nutrition Ltd, 90 Longacre, London

BROW, John David Bromfield; s of Keith Phorson Brow, MBE, of 71 Albert Rd, Caversham, Reading, Berks (d 1979), and Mary Brow, *née* Bromfield; *b* 8 Oct 1930; *Educ* Aldenham; *m* 19 July 1958, Loelia Alfreda, da of Alfred Douglas Lewis, of 20 Priest Hill, Caversham, Reading, Berks (d 1962); 3 s (Jeremy b 1960, Robert b 1963, Alastair b 1966), 1 da (Elizabeth b 1978); *Career* Military Service Lt RNVR; CA, sr ptnr of Ensors CA's of Ipswich 1966-68; regnl conslt Square Mile Gate Ltd; chm: Bridget Collett Educnl Fndn, Ipswitch Suzuki Assoc; hon tres Suffolk Wildlife Trust; *Recreations* gardening, the arts, local history; *Clubs* Marylebone Cricket, The Naval; *Style—* J D B Brow, Esq; Lea Bank, Westerfield, Ipswich, Suffolk IP6 9AJ (☎ 0473 51207); Widford House, 5/7 Robjohns Rd, Chelmsford, Essex CM1 3AG (☎0245 492442, 0245 492443)

BROWELL, Col Jasper Miles; MBE (1968); s of Capt Jasper Geoffrey Browell, MC (d 1960), of Silanchia, Norham-on-Tweed, and Eleanor Mary, *née* Faulkner (d 1985); *b* 4 June 1928; *Educ* Loretto Sch; *m* 9 March 1957 (m dis 1979), Elizabeth Pamela Anne, da of Rev Canon T E G Morris, of Llanfrynach, nr Brecon, Powys; 2 s (Quentin b 1958, Marcus b 1959); *Career* cmmnd RA 1948, RA Trg Bde 1948-51, IFD Battery RWAFF Nigeria 1951- 53, Capt ADC to GOC Central W Africa 1953-56, Adj 20 FD Regt 1956-59, 3 Regt RHA 1959-61, Maj instr gunnery Larkhill 1961-65, CO Kings Troop RHA 1965-68, 2 i/c 40 FD Regt RA 1968-70, Lt-Col CO 42 Regt RA 1970-73, sr instr gunnery UKLF 1973-76, chief instr gunnery Larkhill 1977, Col Dep Cmdt Larkhill 1978-83; *Recreations* shooting, walking; *Clubs* Army and Navy; *Style—* Col Jasper Browell, MBE; Sandway House, Bourton, Nr Gillingham, Dorset (☎ 0747 840 538); Delgaty Ranch, Bellevue, Idaho, USA

BROWN; *see*: Crichton-Brown, Holden-Brown, Pigott-Brown, Richmond Brown

BROWN, (Francis) Adam; s of David Brown, of Flayosc, France, and Mrs R Y Preston-Jones, *née* Auckland; *b* 13 Mar 1955; *Educ* Harrow, Oxford Univ (MA); *Career* dir David Brown Hldgs Ltd 1978, dep chm David Brown Corpn plc 1986; *Recreations* foxhunting; *Style—* Adam Brown, Esq; David Brown Corporation plc, Park Works, Huddersfield HD4 5DD (☎ 0484 221 80, fax 0484 514 732, telex 51562/3)

BROWN, Adrian James; s of Rev Stanley George Brown, of The Vicarage, Tillingham, Southminster, Essex CM9 6ST, and Gabrielle Mary, *née* Holmes; *b* 25 Nov 1946; *Educ* The Friends' Sch, Saffron Walden, Essex, Birmingham Univ (BSc); *m* 21 Feb 1976, Jill, da of George Charles Harmsworth, of Crossways, Hullbridge Road, Rayleigh, Essex; 1 s (Gregory b 1985), 2 da (Hilary b 1980, Fiona b 1984); *Career* dir: MIM Ltd 1986-, Britannia Asset Mgmnt Ltd 1985-86; *Recreations* reading; *Style—* Adrian Brown, Esq; Colts Pightle, Post Office Road, Woodham Mortimer, Maldon, Essex (☎ 024541 5381); 11 Devonshire Square, London EC2A 4YR (☎ 01 626 3434, telex: 886108)

BROWN, Alan Edward; s of Edward George Brown, and Irene Frances, *née* Blower; *b* 8 Jan 1946; *Educ* St Peter's Coll Oxford (MA); *m* 7 Sept 1968, Diane June, da of Walter Oakley, of 3 Wolverhampton Road, Bridgnorth, Shropshire; 2 da (Michelle b 1974, Alison b 1976); *Career* dir Barclays Merchant Bank Ltd 1981-86, corporate finance dir Barclays Bank plc 1982-86, (corp dir 1986-), dir Barclays Devpt Capital Ltd 1987-; Freeman Town of Bridgenorth; ACIB; *Recreations* golf, windsurfing; *Clubs* Pinner Hill GC, Rickmansworth Windsurfing, Oxford & Cambridge Golfing Soc; *Style—* Alan Brown, Esq; Grasmere, 12 Moor Lane, Rickmansworth, Herts WD3 1LG; Barclays Bank plc, 54 Lombard Street, London EC3P 3AH (☎ 01 626 1567, telex: 894076; fax: 01 621 0386)

BROWN, Alan Reginald; *b* 10 Jan 1932; *m* and has issue, 2 s and 2 da; *Career* chm and chief exec Matthew Hall Mechanical & Electrical Engrs Ltd, chm Franklin Hodge Industries Ltd, and Matthew Hall Pension Fund Ltd; dir Matthew Hall plc, Matthew Hall Business Developments Ltd, and Travel Places (International) Ltd; tstee Matthew Hall Staff Tst Fund; govr Polytechnic of the S Bank, Liveryman Plumbers Co; *Recreations* sailing, fly fishing; *Clubs* East India, Royal Corinthian Yacht; *Style—* Alan Brown, Esq; Matthew Hall Mechanical & Electrical Engineers Ltd, PO 309, 7-14 Great Dover St, London SE1 4YR (☎ 01 407 7272, telex 88114622)

BROWN, Alan Thomas; CBE (1978), DL (Oxon 1978); s of Thomas Henry Brown, of Cromer, and Lucy Lilian, *née* Betts; *b* 18 April 1928; *Educ* Wyggeston GS Leicester, Sidney Sussex Coll Cambridge; *m* 1962, Marie Christine, da of Hubert York East, late of Blackburn; 2 da; *Career* chief exec Oxon CC 1973-88; *Recreations* reading, chess, cliff walking; *Style—* Alan Brown Esq, CBE, DL; 7 Field House Drive, Oxford

BROWN, Hon Mrs (Alison de Bois); da of 2 Baron Clwyd, JP (d 1987); *b* 24 Feb 1939; *m* 1, 1965 (m dis 1972), George Stricevic; 1 s (Milorad b 1967); m 2, 1972, Anthony H Brown; 3 s (Barnaby Joseph b 1973, Benedict Joseph b 1975, Lionel Trevor b 1978); *Style—* The Hon Mrs Brown; 9 Royal Terrace, Glasgow G3 7NT

BROWN, Sir Allen Stanley; CBE (1953); s of Robert Stanley Brown (d 1965) and late Harriett May Brown; *b* 3 July 1911; *Educ* Wesley Coll Melbourne, Melbourne Univ (MA, LLM); *m* 1936, Hilda May, da of Henry Herbert William Wilke (d 1958); 1 s, 2 da; *Career* Aust cmmr for Br Phosphate Cmmn and Christmas Island Phosphate Cmmn 1970-76; kt 1956; *see Debrett's Handbook of Australia and New Zealand for further details*; *Recreations* tennis; *Clubs* Melbourne; *Style—* Sir Allen Brown, CBE; 3 Devorgilla Ave, Toorak, Vic 3142, Australia (☎ (03) 20 7277)

BROWN, Andrew David; s of Frank Brown, of Prestwich, Manchester, and Marion Evelyn, *née* Brown; *b* 1 Mar 1953; *Educ* Stand GS Whitefield Manchester; *m* 18 April 1981, Pamela Edith, da of Eric Howarth, of Bury, Lancs; 2 s (Christopher Gary Howarth b 15 May 1975, Dominic David Howarth b 7 July 1982); *Career* ptnr Thomson Morley Jackson & Co (formerly Neild Hulme & Co) 1981-; ACA 1979, FCCA 1986; *Recreations* golf; *Clubs* Prestwich GC; *Style—* Andrew Brown, Esq; 9 Royston Close, Greenmount, Bury BL8 4BZ (☎ 0204 88 6312); Brook House, 64/72 Spring Gdns, Manchester M2 2BQ (☎ 061 236 8880, fax 061 236 9921)

BROWN, Hon Angus John Duncan; yst s of Baron Brown, MBE, PC (Life Peer) (d 1985); *b* 13 Jan 1951; *Educ* Bryanston, Newcastle Univ (BA); *m* 1974, Maya B Polonca, da of Janez Baloh, of Ljubljana; 1 child; *Career* designer; AADipl; *Style—* The Hon Angus Brown; 39 Clifton Road, London N8 8JA

BROWN, Anthony Cecil; OBE (1984); s of Cecil Philip Brown, of Dartmouth, Devon, and Bronwen Delia Llewella, *née* Lloyd-Griffiths (d 1980); *b* 16 Feb 1928; *Educ* Whitgift, Imperial Coll London (BSc); *m* 1974, Lesley Ann, da of Frederick Collings, of Broxbourne, Herts; 4 s (Simon, Tobias b 1965, Matthew b 1968, Patrick b 1978), 2 da (Katherine b 1966, Genevieve b 1971); *Career* chm and md Spirax-Sarco Engineering plc 1971-; dep chm Turriff Corpn plc 1978-83; dir Sale Tilney plc 1982-83; local dir (Bristol) Barclays Bank 1977-; ACGI, FCIBS, CBIM; *Recreations* skiing, sailing, motor racing, reading, travel; *Clubs* St Stephen's, MCC; *Style—* Anthony Brown, Esq; Longwood House, Bishops Cleeve, Glos; Avonmouth, Bigbury-on-Sea, Devon; Spirax-Sarco Engineering plc, Charlton House, 14 Cirencester Rd, Cheltenham, Glos GL53 8ER (☎ (0242) 521361, telex 43123)

BROWN, Prof Arthur Joseph; CBE (1974); s of Joseph Brown (d 1957), of Meliden, Prestatyn, Flintshire, and Adelene, *née* Lyles (d 1960); *b* 8 August 1914; *Educ* Bradford GS, Queen's Coll Oxford (BA, MA, DPhil); *m* 28 Dec 1938, Joan Hannah Margaret, da of Rev Canon Bertham Eustace Taylor (d 1961), of Walton Breck, Liverpool; 3 s (John Richard b 1940, d 1959, Henry Joseph b 1942, William Arthur b 1945); *Career* fell All Souls Coll Oxford 1937-46, lectr Hertford Coll Oxford 1937- 40, Foreign Res and Press Serv 1940-43, Foreign Office Res Dept 1943 -45, Cabinet Office economic section 1945-47, prof economics Univ of Leeds 1947-79 (emeritus 1979); visiting prof Columbia Univ NY 1950, Australian Nat Univ Canberra 1963; memb: East Africa Economic and Fiscal Cmmn 1960, Central Africa Office Sec of State's Advsy Gp 1962, Hunt Ctee on Intermediate Areas 1967-69, Univ Grants Ctee 1968-78 (vice chm 1977-78); memb: Thoresby Soc, Leeds Civic Tst, Art collections Fund; Hon DLitt Bradford Univ 1975, Hon DLitt Kent Univ 1979, Hon Litt D Sheffield Univ 1979, Hon LLD Aberdeen 1978, Hon fell Queen's Coll Oxford 1985; FBA 1972, pres Royal Economic Soc 1976-78, memb Royal Statistical Soc 1940; *Books* Applied Economics (1948), The Great Inflation 1939-51 (1955), The Framework of Regional Economics in the UK (1972), World Inflation Since 1950 (1985); *Recreations* gardening, walking; *Clubs* Athenaeum; *Style—* Prof Arthur Brown; 24 Moor Dr, Leeds LS6 4BY (☎ 0532 755 799)

BROWN, Arthur Robert (Bob); s of Arthur Brown; of Gawsworth, Macclesfield, Cheshire (d 1973), and Winifred Brown, *née* Poulson (d 1975); *b* 18 July 1945; *Educ* Sandbach GS; *m* 1, Dec 1966 (m dis 1977), Kim, *née* Mahoney; 2 s (Philip b 1964, Michael b 1968), 4 da (Fenella b 1963, Samantha b 1965, Claire b 1967, Justine b 1970); m 2, 22 July 1977, Maureen, da of Percy Valentine Law; *Career* formerly with: Thames TV Ltd, William Cory & Sons Ltd, Int Computers Ltd; gen mangr computer mktg Cable & Wireless plc 1970-76, assoc ptnr Touche Ross & Co 1976-82, mktg dir Software Sciences Ltd 1982- (currently dir i/c Tokyo subsid); *Books* Optimun Packing and Depletion (1971), VAT for the Computer User (1972), Program Debugging (1973); *Recreations* music (the twentieth century symphony); *Style—* Bob Brown, Esq; 103 Ishikawa Homes, Rokubancho 2, Chiyoda-ku, Tokyo 102, Japan (☎ 03 261 1346); Software Sciences Japan, Kowa Bldg No 1, 1-11- 41 Akasaka, Minato-ku, Tokyo 107, Japan (☎ 03 583 9601, fax 03 582 1176)

BROWN, Brig Athol Earle; CMG (1964), OBE (1956); s of late W J C G Brown, of Armidale, NSW, Australia; *b* 2 Jan 1905; *Educ* Armidale Sch, Royal Australian Naval Coll, Sydney Univ; *m* 1928, Millicent Alice, da of late Herman Marcus Heesh, of Sydney; 2 s, 1 da; *Career* WW II Royal Aust Artillery, Lt-Col 1944, Brig 1946; sec-gen Cwlth War Graves Cmmn (Pacific Regn) 1960-69, sec-gen Br Cwlth-Japanese Jt Ctee 1957-69; *Clubs* RAC; *Style—* Brig Athol Brown, CMG, OBE

BROWN, Aubrey; MBE (1975); s of Robert Brown (d 1963), of Dunmurry, Co Antrim, and Emily *née* Dillon; *b* 4 Dec 1927; *Educ* Queen's Univ Belfast (BSc), Univ of Northern Colorado (MA); *m* 30 June 1962, Catherine, da of Francis McHugh (d 1973), of Blackrock, Co Louth; *Career* colombo plan advsr on tech educn Pakistan 1963-65, sr inspr of schs (tech and commercial Swaziland 1971-78, inspt of educn (tech) Transkei SA 1979, educn offr southern educn and library bd NI 1979-81, conslt on tech educn Univ of Papua New Guinea 1986-88;; *Books* A Technical Teachers' Training Manual (published for Univ of Papua New Guinea, 1988); *Style—* Aubrey Brown, Esq, MBE; Tornabodagh Cottage, Drumaroan Rd, Ballycastle, County Antrim, NI, BT54 6QU (☎ 02657 63 685)

BROWN, Dr (James) Barry (Conway); GBE (1978); s of Frederick Clarence Brown, of Stroud, Glos, and Alys Brown, *née* Bleackley; *b* 3 July 1937; *Educ* King's Coll Taunton, Clare Coll Cambridge (MA), Birmingham (MSc, PhD); *m* 7 Sept 1963, Anne Rosemary, da of Frederick Clough (d 1970); 2 s (Andrew b 1964, Phillip b 1967), 1 da (Clare b 1971); *Career* res offr CEGB 1963-67, sci offr Br Cncl: London 1967-69, Spain 1969-72, France 1972-78; head Sci and Tech Gp Br Cncl London 1978-81 rep (head) Br Cncl and cultural cnsllr Br Embassy Mexico 1981-85; dep controller Higher Educn Div Br Cncl London 1985-89, dir Euro Cmmn Liason Unit (Higher Educn) Br Cncl Brussels 1989-; memb: Thames Vale Singers, GB USSR Assoc 1960-; *Recreations* singing, reading, foreign travel; *Style—* Dr Barry Brown, OBE; 42 Hazel Rd, Purley-on-Thames, Reading RG8 8BB (☎ 0734 417 581); Br Cncl, 10 Spring Gardens, London SW1A 2BN (☎ 01 930 8466, telex 8952201 BRICON G)

BROWN, Bernard Joseph (Joe); CBE (1981), JP (1970); s of William Goulson Brown (d 1935), and Kate Alice Brown (d 1960); *b* 27 Feb 1916; *Educ* Ealing Co Sch, Southall Tech Coll; *m* 9 Sept 1939, Vera, da of Clarence Douglass (d 1918); 4 s (Peter b 1941, Christopher b 1945, Roger b 1949, Philip b 1955), 1 da (Felicity b 1947);

Career WWII vol RA 1939 (cmmnd Survey 1941), Staff Capt Combined Ops 1942-46; asst Barry and Vernon Estate Agents London 1933-39, offr Air Miny Lands Branch 1946-49, fndr BJ Brown and Ptnrs Chartered Auctioneers and Estate Agents 1949-84; pres Ruislip Round Table 1961-63 (vice chm 1947, chm 1948), chm Ruislip Cons 1955-60 and 1965-70; memb Ruislip Northwood UDC 1949-55, Mayor London Borough of Hillingdon 1969-70 (Alderman 1964-74), vice chm GLC 1970- 71 (memb 1967-77), memb Ct of Common Cncl City of London 1972-86, Sheriff City of London 1977-78, chief commoner Corpn of London 1981, govr Christs Hospital, pres City Livery Club 1984-85, former pres W Middx and S Bucks Assoc of Surveyors and Estate Agents; Freedom City of Quito Equador 1981, Master Worshipful Co of Fletchers 1986-87 (memb 1970); FAI 1939, FRICS 1970; Order of King Abdul al Aziz (Class 2) 1981; *Recreations* gardening, music; *Clubs* City Livery, United Wards, Royal Soc of St George; *Style*— Joe Brown, Esq, CBE, JP; 1 Lunsford Manor, Ninfield Rd, Bexhill-on-Sea, E Sussex (☎ 0424 892 513)

BROWN, Vice Admiral Brian Thomas; CBE (1983); s of Walter Thomas Brown (d 1984), and Gladys, *née* Baddeley (d 1989); *b* 31 August 1934; *Educ* Peter Symonds' Sch; *m* 1 Aug 1959, Veronica Mary Elizabeth, da of Wing Cdr J D Bird (d 1982); 2 s (Mark b 1960, Matthew b 1962); *Career* joined RN (Dartmouth) 1952, pilot 898 and 848 sqdns 1958-62, dep supply offr HMY Britannia 1966-68, supply offr HMS Tiger 1973-75; secretary to VCNS 1975-78, 1 Sea Lord 1979-82; RCDS 1983, Capt HMS Raleigh 1984-86, DGNPS 1986, DGNMT 1987-88; 2 Sea Lord and Adm Pres RNC Greenwich 1988; *Recreations* cricket, gardening, ornithology; *Clubs* Army and Navy; *Style*— Vice-Admiral Brian Brown, CBE; c/o Lloyds Bank, High St, Winchester, Hants

BROWN, Bryan William; s of William James Brown (d 1958), and Beatrice Cutugno (d 1980); *b* 7 Oct 1938; *Educ* Salesian Coll; *m* 12 Dec 1975, Florie Therese, da of Anthony Stravens, of Seychelles; 3 s (Paul b 1976, Colin b 1977, Ian b 1979), 1 da (Liza b 1986);; *Career* CA; dir Joe Smith (conslts) Ltd; memb MICA Tax Legislation Ctee; *Recreations* gardening, walking, entertaining; *Clubs* Gresham; *Style*— Bryan Brown, Esq; Briar House, Fairfield Lane, W End, Woking, Surrey GU24 9QX (☎ 09905 8434)

BROWN, Lt-Col Sir Charles Frederick Richmond; 4 Bt (UK 1863), TD, DL (N R Yorks 1962); s of late Frederick Richmond Brown, 2 s of 2 Bt; suc unc, Sir Melville Richmond Brown, 3 Bt, 1944; *b* 6 Dec 1902; *Educ* Eton; *m* 1, 1933 (m dis 1948), Audrey, da of late Brig-Gen the Hon Everard Baring, CVO, CBE; 1 s, 2 da; m 2, 1951 (m dis 1968), Hon Gwendolin Carlis Meysey-Thompson, da of 1 Baron Knaresborough; m 3, 1969, Pauline Emily Gwyneth Mansel, da of late Arden Henry William Llewelyn Morgan, and wid of Edward John Westgarth Hildyard, FSA, FRES, of Middleton Hall, Pickering, Yorks; *Heir* s, George Francis Richmond Brown; *Career* Capt (ret) Welsh Gds, and Lt-Col cmdg 7 Bn Green Howards (TA); *Style*— Lt-Col Sir Charles Richmond Brown, Bt, TD, DL; Middleton Hall, Pickering

BROWN, Christopher David; s of Edward Kenneth Brown and Iris, *née* Hoddell; *b* 8 July 1944; *Educ* Plymouth Coll, Fitzwilliam Coll Cambridge (MA); *m* 1972, Caroline, da of Dr Arthur Dunkerley (d 1980); 2 da (Katharine b 1979, Jennifer b 1981); *Career* head of eng Radley Coll 1975-84, head master Norwich Sch 1984-; *Style*— Christopher Brown, Esq; 70 The Close, Norwich

BROWN, Colin Ian; s of Sidney Brown (d 1986), and Marion Esther, *née* Surrey; *b* 3 Dec 1933; *Educ* Raynes Park Co GS; *m* 15 May 1965, Lorna Louise, da of Albert Jarrett (d 1975); 3 da (Philippa b 8 April 1967, Rachel b 14 Dec 1968, Hilary b 17 June 1970); *Career* Nat Serv RAPC 1956-58; CA, trg James Worley and Sons 1951-56, dir of fin (ptnr) Price Waterhouse 1987- (joined 1958, nat recruitment ptnr 1966-72, ptnr i/c audit tax gp and memb UK policy ctee 1972-79, seconded to PW World Firm 1979-87); chm: IASC Steering Gp, IFAC jt sub-ctee; ICA 1956 chm banking ctee; *Books* The Institute Guide on Accounting and Auditing for Banks (jt author); *Recreations* golf, sailing, ski-ing and photography; *Clubs* Royal Lymington Yacht, North Downs and Edenbridge Golf; *Style*— Colin Brown, Esq; Gabilan House, Park View Road, Woldingham, Surrey CR3 7DN (☎ 088 385 2005); Price Waterhouse, Southwark Towers, 32 London Bridge Street, London SE1 9SY (☎ 01 4078989, fax 01 3780647, telex 884657/8)

BROWN, (William) Colin; JP; s of James Chalmers Brown, MC, and Annie Oman, *née* Shaw; *b* 20 Feb 1923; *Educ* Imperial Serv Coll (now Haileybury); *m* 25 July 1952, Mary Elizabeth, da of Sir Charles G Connell, WS, of Edinburgh; 3 s (Peter b 24 Oct 1953, Timothy b 14 Dec 1955, Roy b 26 April 1961); *Career* Capt Parachute Regt 1943-52; dir Dunfermline Bldg Soc 1964, md Furnishing Co 1968-88, dir Ski Sch 1970; chm: investmt co 1979, property co 1982, dir Cairngorm Chairlift Tst 1982; chm Br Ski Fedn 1980-84, former memb Ctee Fedn Internationale de Ski; memb: Co Merchants Edinburgh, Magistrates Ctee and Ct; former FNAEA; Croix de Guerre (Silver); *Recreations* skiing, fishing; *Clubs* New (Edinburgh); *Style*— Colin Brown, Esq, JP; 4 Blackbarony Rd, Edinburgh (☎ 031 667 1894); Bruach, Carrbridge, Inverness-shire

BROWN, Hon Mrs (Cordelia); *née* Fraser; er da of late 2 Baron Strathalmond, CMG, OBE, TD; *b* 12 Dec 1949; *m* 1981 (m dis 1986), Ralph Lyman Brown, s of Ralph Lyman Brown (d 1978); *Style*— The Hon Mrs Brown; 47 Aynhoe Road, London W14 0QA. (☎ 01 603 3551)

BROWN, Sir David; s of Francis (Frank) Edwin Brown (d 1941), of Huddersfield, and Caroline Brown; *b* 10 May 1904; *Educ* Rossall, Huddersfield Tech Coll; *m* 1, 1926 (m dis 1955), Daisie Muriel Firth; 1 s, 1 da; m 2, 1955 (m dis 1980), Marjorie, da of Frederick Herbert Deans, of Leeds; m 3, 1980, Paula Elizabeth, da of John Benjamin Stone (d 1974); *Career* chm David Brown Hldgs and Vosper Ltd to 1978; dir of all overseas cos in David Brown Gp; Grand Cdr of Royal Crown of Johor; made 'Chief Flying Sun' of the Iroquois Tribe, Mohawk Nation 1959; FIMechE; kt 1968; *Recreations* tennis, yachting, My Flying Sun; *Clubs* Monte Carlo Country, Yacht Club de Monaco, Club International des Anciens Pilotes de Grand Prix, Automobile Club de Monaco; *Style*— Sir David Brown; L'Estoril, 31 Avenue Princesse Grace, Monte Carlo, MC98000 Monaco

BROWN, David John Bowes; CBE (1982); s of Matthew Brown (d 1977), and Helene Brown; *b* 2 August 1925; *Educ* King James Sch Knaresborough, Leeds Coll of Technology; *m* 1954, Patricia Robson; 2 s, 2 da; *Career* chm and md Artix Ltd and Archer Components Ltd; *Style*— David J B Brown, Esq, CBE

BROWN, Vice Adm Sir David Worthington; KCB (1984); s of Capt John Ronald Stewart Brown, RN, of Cheltenham, and Mrs D M E Brown; *b* 28 Nov 1927; *Educ* HMS Conway; *m* 1958, Etienne Hester, da of Col Dick Boileau, DSO (d 1978), of Bradford-on-Avon; 3 da; *Career* joined RN 1945; cmd HM Ships: MGB 5036, MTB 5020, Dalswinton, Chailey, Cavendish, Falmouth, Hermione, Bristol; dir Naval Ops and Trade 1971-72, dir of Offr Appointments (Exec) 1976-78, ACDS (Ops) 1980-82, Vice Adm 1982, Flag Offr Plymouth, Port Admiral Devonport, Cdr Plymouth Sub Area Channel 1982-85; chm Broadmoor Special Hosp Bd; Fell Inst of Personnel Management 1985; *Recreations* sailing, fishing; *Clubs* Army & Navy; *Style*— Vice Adm Sir David Brown, KCB; c/o Barclays Bank, 107 Commercial Rd, Portsmouth PO1 1BT, Hants

BROWN, Maj Denis Frederick Spence; MC (1945), TD (1950); s of Frederick William Brown (d 1965), of Woodhall Spa, Lincolnshire, and Violet Spence Brown *née* Hubbard (d 1976); *b* 24 Feb 1917; *Educ* Trent Coll, Nottingham; *m* 13 Jan 1945, Margaret, da of Frederick Harry Shutler (d 1973), of London; 2 s (Nigel Denis Spence b 1946, Peter Frederick Spence b 1951), 1 da (Rosemary Spence b 1949); *Career* cmmn TA 1939, served RA, field and anti-tank, France, Mid East, Western Desert, Sicily, Italy, Major 1944 (despatches 1945); joined family firm now Brown Butlin Gp 1933, dir and chm 1965, resigned as chm 1987, and appointed pres; *Recreations* travel, gardening, reading; *Clubs* Inst of Dirs; *Style*— Maj Denis Brown, MC, TD; The Close, Dorrington, Lincoln LN4 3PX (☎ 0526 832282); Brown Butlin Group, Brook House, 0526 Ruskington 832771)

BROWN, Denise Jeanne Marie Lebreton (Mrs F Waters); da of Lt Frederick Peter Brown (d of wounds 1918), and Jeanne Marie Louise Lebreton (d 1974); *b* 8 Jan 1911; *Educ* Lyzeum Nonnenwerth im Rhein, RCA (ARCA); *m* 1938, Frank William Eric Waters (d 1986), s of Frank Waters (d 1922); 1 s (Peter); *Career* Br Inst scholarship in engraving 1932, prox. acc. Rome Scholarship in engraving 1936, RCA travelling scholarship 1936; has exhibited regularly: Royal Acad 1934-, Royal Soc of Painte-etchers & Engravers 1941-, Royal West of England Acad 1979-; has also exhibited in Canada, USA, S Africa; works represented: Br Museum, V&A, Ashmolean Museum, Sheffield Art Gallery, perm collection RWA; RE 1959, ARWA 1980 (elected cncl memb 1984) RWA 1986; *Books illustrated* many in the Famous Childhoods series, several gardening books; also illustrations for Farmers Weekly and designs for book jackets; *Recreations* music, gardening; *Clubs* RAF; *Style*— Miss Denise L Brown; 7 Priory Lodge, Nightingale Pl, Rickmansworth, Herts WD3 2DG (☎ 0923 773515)

BROWN, Sir Douglas Denison; s of Robert Brown (d 1968), and Alice Mary Brown; *b* 8 July 1917; *Educ* Bablake Sch Coventry; *m* 1941, Marion Cruickshanks, da of James Emmerson (d 1935); 1 s, 1 da; *Career* served RA WW II M East, N Africa, Italy, retired Major; chm James Corson Co; chm: North West Leeds Conservative Assoc 1961-74, Yorkshire Area Conservative Assoc 1978-83 (tres 1971-78), Jacob Kramer Coll of Further Education 1978-; v-chm PCC St Edmund's Church Roundhay 1980-, bd memb Yorkshire Water Authority 1983-1986; chm Leeds and Northern Clothing Assoc 1975-77; kt 1983; *Recreations* gardening, golf, rugby, cricket; *Style*— Sir Douglas Brown; Bankfield, 6 North Park Rd, Roundhay, Leeds LS8 1JD (☎ (0532) 66 2151); James Corson & Co Ltd, Corsonia House, Easy Rd, Leeds LS9 8TS (☎ (0532) 480033)

BROWN, Hon Mrs (Edna); da of 1 and last Baron Lawson (d 1965); *b* 1912; *m* D Brown; 1 s; *Style*— The Hon Mrs Brown

BROWN, Sir Edward Joseph; MBE (1958), JP; s of Edward Brown (d 1932), of Camberwell; *b* 15 April 1913; *Educ* Greencoat Elementary, Morley Coll; *m* 1940, Rosa, da of Samuel Feldman, of Stepney; 1 s, 1 da; *Career* company dir; chm Nat Union of Cons and Unionist Assocs 1959 and 1960, chm Cons Pty Conf 1960, MP (C) for Bath 1964-79 (contested Stalybridge and Hyde 1959); kt 1961; *Style*— Sir Edward Brown, MBE, JP; 71 Holly Walk, Enfield, Middx (☎ 01 363 3450)

BROWN, Edwin Percy; CBE (1981); s of James Percy Brown (d 1949), of Nottingham, and Hetty, *née* Walker (d 1984); *b* 20 May 1917; *Educ* Mundella GS Nottingham, Univ of Nottingham (Cert in Soc Studies), Teesside Poly (BA); *m* 28 June 1958, Margaret Anne, da of Thomas Walter Askey (d 1984), of Buxton, Derbys; 1 s (Paul b 1963), 1 da (Jacqui b 1961); *Career* WWII Gunner RA 1939-46; indust trainee 1933-38, factory foreman 1938-39 (1946-47), sr socl worker: Notts CC 1953-54 (socl worker 1951-53), Lancs CC 1954-59; children's offr: Southampton CC 1959-65, Wiltshire CC 1965-71; dir soc servs: North Riding CC 1971-74, Yorkshire CC 1973-82; memb Supplementary Benefits Cmmn 1976-80, advsr Assoc of Co Cncls 1974-81; pres: Assoc of Child Care Offrs 1958-59, Nat Assoc of Nursery and Family Care 1984-88 (vice-pres 1988); *Recreations* creative writing, political science, watching cricket; *Clubs* National Liberal, Nottingham & Notts Utd Servs; *Style*— Edwin Brown, Esq, CBE; Larkfield House, 5 Woodland Way, Eastwood, Nottinghamshire NG16 3BU (☎ 0773 714 461)

BROWN, Hon Mrs (Emily Rose); da of Baron Eden of Winton (Life Peer); *b* 26 Feb 1959; *m* 30 June 1984, Ronald Etienne Brown, s of James Brown; 1 s (Nicholas James b 1986), 1 da (Charlotte Lucy b 1985); *Style*— Hon Mrs Brown; Combebelle le Haut, Villespassons, St Ghinian 34360, Herault, France

BROWN, Prof Eric Herbert; s of Samuel Brown (d 1970), and Ada, *née* Hewes (d 1966); *b* 8 Dec 1922; *Educ* King Edward VII GS Melton Mowbray, Kings Coll Univ of London (BSc), Univ Coll of Wales Aberstwyth (MSc), Univ of London (PhD); *m* 30 Oct 1945, Eileen (d 1984), da of Phillip ap John Reynolds (d 1946); 2 da (Jane, Megan); *Career* pilot Coastal Cmnd 517 Sqdn RAF 1940-45; lectr geography Univ Coll of Wales Aberystwyth 1947-50, lectr reader and prof geography UCL 1950-88; chm governing body Longdean Sch Hemel Hempstead, church warden St Peters Berkamsted; FRGS 1947, hon fell Geographic Soc Argentina 1968; *Books* Relief and Drainage of Wales (1961); *Recreations* travel, rugby, wine; *Clubs* Athenaeum, Geographical; *Style*— Prof Eric Brown; Monterey, Castle Hill, Berkamsted, Herts HP4 1HE (☎ 0442 864 077); Dept of Geography, Univ College, 26 Bedford Way, London WC1H 0AP (☎ 01 380 7050, fax 380 7565)

BROWN, Capt Eric Melrose; CBE (1970, OBE 1945, MBE 1944), DSC (1942), AFC (1947); s of Robert John Brown (d 1947), of Edinburgh, and Euphemia Dorothy, *née* Melrose (d 1933); *b* 21 Jan 1919; *Educ* Royal HS Edinburgh, Edinburgh Univ (MA 1947); *m* 17 Jan 1942, Evelyn Jean Margaret, da of Robert Macrory (d 1946), of Belfast; 1 s (Glenn b 1 March 1948); *Career* Capt RN; served WW II, Fleet Air Arm Fighter Pilot 1939-42, Naval Test Pilot 1942-42, Chief Naval Test Pilot 1944-49, resident British Naval Test Pilot in USA 1951-52, CO No 804 (F) Sqdn 1953-54, Cdr (Air) RN Air Station Brawdy 1954-56, Head British Naval Air Mission to Germany 1958-60, dep dir Gunnery Divn Admiralty 1961, Naval Air Warfare Admiralty 1962-64,

Naval Attaché Bonn 1965-67, CO RN Air Station Lossiemouth 1967-70, ADC to HM The Queen 1969-70; chief exec British Helicopter Advsy Bd 1970-87 (vice-pres 1988-); chief exec European Helicopter Assoc 1980-; pres: Royal Aeronautical Soc 1982-83, Royal Naval Assoc (E Grinstead Branch); chm Br Aviation 1984 Bicentenary Exec Ctee 1983-84; Freeman of City of London 1975, Liveryman of Worshipful Co of Air Pilots and Air Navigators 1978; Hon FEng Inst of Engrs Pakistan, Hon Fell Soc of Experimental Test Pilots 1984; FRAeS 1964; *Books* Wings on My Sleeve (1961), Aircraft Carriers (jtly 1969), Wings of the Luftwaffe (1977), Wings of the Navy (1980), The Helicopter in Civil Operations (1981), Wings of the Weird and Wonderful, Vol I (1982), Vol II (1985), Duels in the Sky (1989); *Recreations* golf, skiing, bridge, philately; *Clubs* Naval and Military, Explorers' (New York), City Livery; *Style—* Capt Eric Brown, CBE, DSC, AFC, RN; Carousel, New Domewood, nr Copthorne, Sussex RH10 3HF (☎ 0342 712610)

BROWN, Prof Ewan; s of John Moir Brown (d 1971), of Perth, and Isobel, *née* Crerar; *b* 23 Mar 1942; *Educ* Perth Acad, St Andrews Univ (MA, LLB); *m* 1966, Christine Robertson, da of Hugh Douglas Robertson Lindsay; 1 s (Philip b 1968), 1 da (Kirsty b 1971); *Career* CA and merchant banker; exec dir 1970 Noble Grossart Ltd, princ dir Scottish Business Sch 1972-80 (memb exec ctee 1974-80), Church of Scotland Tst 1981-87; dir: Pict Petroleum plc 1974-, Scottish Devpt Fin 1982-, John Wood Gp plc 1982-, Scottish Tport Gp 1983-87, Aberdeen Tst plc 1982-85, Stagecoach Hldgs Ltd; govr Edinburgh Coll of Art 1986-; Hon Prof Heriot Watt 1988-; *Recreations* golf, music, family; *Clubs* New (Edinburgh); *Style—* Prof Ewan Brown; 18 Merchiston Crescent, Edinburgh EH10 5AX; 15a The Links, St Andrews, Fife; Office: 48 Queen St, Edinburgh EH2 3NR (☎ 031 226 7011, telex 72536, fax 031 226 6032)

BROWN, Prof Fred; s of Fred Brown (d 1982), of Burnley, Lancs, and Jane Ellen, *née* Fielding (d 1975); *b* 31 Jan 1925; *Educ* Burnley GS, Univ of Manchester (BSc, MSc, PhD); *m* 1 May 1948, Audrey Alice, da of Ernest Doherty; 2 s (Roger b 21 Nov 1949, David b 17 Oct 1953); *Career* asst lectr Univ of Manchester 1946-48, lectr Univ of Bristol 1948-50, sr sci offr Hannah Dairy Res Inst 1950-53, sr scientist Christie Hosp Manchester 1953-55; Animal Virus Res Inst: sr sci offr 1955-58, princ scientific offr 1958-64, sr princ scientific offr 1964-71, dep chief scientific offr 1971-83, dep dir 1980-83; hd of virology dept Wellcome Fndn 1983; Soc of Gen Mircrobiology, FRS 1981; *Recreations* fell walking, listening to classical music; *Style—* Prof Fred Brown; Syndal, Glaziers Lane, Normandy, Guildford, Surrey GU3 2DF (☎ 0483 811 107); Wellcome Biotechnology, Langley Ct, Beckenham, Kent BR3 3BS (☎ 01 658 2211, fax 01 650 9055, telex 23937)

BROWN, Rev Canon Geoffrey Harold; s of Harry Charles Brown, MBE (d 1972), and Ada Ethel, *née* Holiday; *b* 1 April 1930; *Educ* Monmouth Sch, Trinity Hall Cambridge (MA); *m* 24 Aug 1963, (Elizabeth) Jane, da of Jack Watson Williams (d 1981), of Dudley, Worcs; 2 da (Alison, Frances (twins) b 14 May 1964); *Career* RA 1949-51; asst curate: St Andrew's Plaistow London E13 1956-60, St Peter's Spring Hill Birmingham 1960-63; rector: St George's Birmingham 1963-73, Grimsby 1973-85; vicar St Martin-in-the-Fields 1985-; chm Humberside Cncl on Alcoholism 1977-87, vice chm Humberside Local Radio Cncl 1983, exec memb Nat Cncl on Alcoholism 1980-83; *Recreations* theatre, photography, the countryside; *Style—* The Rev Canon Geoffrey Brown; St Martin-in-the-Fields, Trafalgar Square, London WC2N 4JJ (☎ 01 930 1862)

BROWN, Hon George Arthur; CMG (1962); s of Samuel Austin Brown and Gertrude Brown; *b* 25 July 1922; *Educ* St Simon's Coll Jamaica and LSE (BSc); *m* 1, 1951, Jean, da of J T Farquharson; 1 s, 1 da; m 2, 1964, Leila Leonie, da of late Gerald Martin Gill; 2 da; *Career* govr Bank of Jamaica 1967-78, dep administrator UN Devpt Programme 1978-; assoc administrator UNDP 1978; *Recreations* hiking, boating, fishing; *Clubs* Jamaica, Kingston; *Style—* The Hon George Brown, CMG; 500 E 77th St, Apt 1432, New York, NY 10162 (☎ (212) 772 9107); One, UN Plaza, DC1-2118, New York, New York 10017 (☎ (212) 906 5788)

BROWN, George Francis Richmond; s and h of Sir Charles Brown, 4 Bt; *b* 3 Feb 1938; *Career* Lt Welsh Guards, extra equerry to HRH The Duke of Edinburgh 1961-63, ADC to Gov of Queensland 1963-65; *Style—* George Brown, Esq

BROWN, George Frederick William; CMG (1974); s of late G Brown; *b* 12 April 1908; *Educ* Phahran Tech Coll, Royal Melbourne Inst of Technol; *m* 1933, Catherine Mills, 1 da (and 1 da decd); *Career* memb Melbourne Underground Railway Loop Authority 1971-; *Style—* George F W Brown, Esq, CMG; Unit 1, 10 Lucas St, East Brighton, Victoria 3187, Australia

BROWN, George Mackay; OBE (1974); s of John Brown (d 1940), and Mary Jane, *née* Mackay (d 1967); *b* 17 Oct 1921; *Educ* Stromness Acad, Newbattle Abbey Coll, Univ of Edinburgh (MA); *Career* author; MA Open Univ 1973, LLD Univ of Dundee 1974, DLitt Univ of Glasgow 1985; *Books* Fiction: A Time To Keep (1969), Greenvoe (1972), Magnus (1973), Hawkfall (1974), The Two Fiddlers (1975), Andrina (1983), The Golden Bird (1987), The Masked Fisherman (1989); plays: A Spell for Green Corn (1970), Three Plays (1984); poetry: Fisherman With Ploughs (1971), Selected Poems (1976), Christmas Poems (1984), The Wreck of the Archangel (1989); *Recreations* ale tasting, watching tv, reading; *Style—* George MacKay Brown, Esq, OBE; 3 Mayburn Ct, Stromness, Orkney, KW16 3DH

BROWN, (James) Gordon; MP (Lab) Dunfermline East 1983-; s of Rev Dr John Brown and J Elizabeth Brown; *b* 20 Feb 1951; *Educ* Kirkcaldy HS, Edinburgh Univ (PhD); *Career* journalist Scottish TV, chm Scottish Lab Pty (memb exec ctee 1977-); memb Shadow Cabinet 1987-, shadow chief sec to the Treasy 1987-; opposition spokesman Regional Affairs 1985-87; rector Edinburgh Univ 1972-85; *Books* Maxton (1986); *Recreations* golf, tennis, reading; *Style—* Gordon Brown, Esq, MP; House of Commons, London SW1

BROWN, Hon Mrs (Gweneth Mary); da of 1 and last Baron Williams (d 1966); *b* 22 June 1927; *m* 1, 1947 (m dis 1958), Hugh Sharp Eadie, s of David Anderson Eadie, of Markinch; 1 s, 1 da; m 2, 1961, Donald Walker Alexander Brown, MB, ChB, only son of Archibald Donald Brown, MB, ChB (d 1958); *Style—* The Hon Mrs Brown

BROWN, Harold Arthur Neville; CMG (1963), CVO (1961); s of Stanley Raymond Brown, of Penarth, and Gladys Maud Brown; *b* 13 Dec 1914; *Educ* Cardiff HS, Univ Coll Cardiff; *m* 1939, Mary McBeath, da of late Alan Urquhart, of Cardiff; 1 s, 1 da; *Career* entered Miny of Labour 1939, transferred FO 1955, ambass Liberia 1960-63, FO 1963, ambass Cambodia 1966-70, consul-gen Johannesburg 1970-73, min Pretoria/Cape Town 1973-74, ret 1975; *Style—* Harold Brown, Esq, CMG, CVO; 14 Embassy Court, King's Rd, Brighton, Sussex BN1 2PX (☎ (0273) 734623)

BROWN, Hon Mrs (Helen Jean); er da of Baron Todd, OM, *qv*; *b* 13 July 1941; *Educ* Perse Sch for Girls Cambridge, Westonbirt, Somerville Coll Oxford (MA, BSc); *m* 21 Sept 1963, Philip Edgar Brown, s of Lawrence Felix Brown, of Stretford, Lancs; 2 s, 1 da; *Style—* The Hon Mrs Brown; 124 Edge Hill, Darras Hall, Ponteland, Newcastle-upon-Tyne (☎ 0661 24533)

BROWN, Sir (Ernest) Henry Phelps; MBE (1945); o son of Edgar William Brown, of Calne, Wilts; *b* 10 Feb 1906; *Educ* Taunton Sch, Wadham Coll Oxford; *m* 1932, Dorothy Evelyn Mostyn, yst da of Sir Anthony Alfred Bowlby, 1 Bt, KCB, KCMG, KCVO (d 1929); 2 s, 1 da; *Career* prof Economics of Labour Univ of London 1947-68, now emeritus; kt 1976; *Style—* Sir Henry Phelps Brown, MBE; 16 Bradmore Rd, Oxford (☎ (0865) 56320)

BROWN, Howard Roger; s of Leslie John Brown (d 1975), of Portsmouth, and Ruth Ethel, *née* Smith; *b* 25 Feb 1945; *Educ* Portsmouth GS; *m* 17 Oct 1970, Elizabeth Jane, da of Sidney Douglas Hillyar (d 1985), of Emsworth Hants; 3 da (Sally b 1974, Judith b 1976, Helen b 1979); *Career* trainee accountant Grant Thornton, 1963-69, sr to ptnr Ernst & Whinney 1969-, dir UK Banking GP Ernst & Whinney 1985-, chm inter banking ctee Ernst & Whinney 1986-; FCA 1969; deacon Bloomsbury Central Church, London, 1981-; *Books* Leasing, Accounting & Tax Implications (1978), International Bank Accounting (1987); *Recreations* badminton, tennis, reading; *Style—* Howard Brown, Esq; Ernst & Whinney, 1 Lambeth Palace Rd, London, SE1 7EU, (☎ 01 928 2000, fax 01 928 1345)

BROWN, Hugh Dunbar; s of Neil Brown and Grace, *née* Hargrave; *b* 18 May 1919; *Educ* Whitehill Secdy Sch; *m* 1947, Mary Glen Carmichael; 1 da; *Career* parly under-sec of state Scottish Off 1974-79; MP (Lab) Glasgow Provan 1964-87; *Style—* Hugh Brown, Esq; 29 Blackwood Road, Milngavie, Glasgow

BROWN, Col Hugh Goundry; TD (1968), DL (1986, QHS 1972); s of Charles Franc Brown, of Newcastle, and Edith Temple *née* Smithson (d 1952); *b* 25 Feb 1927; *Educ* St Peter's School York, Durham Univ (MBBS); *m* 26 Aug 1961, Ann Mary, da of Thomas Coburn Crump (d 1982); 1 s (Andrew b 1963), 2 da (Catherine b 1962, Elizabeth b 1967); *Career* Nat Serv RMO ATT 1(NY) Bn KAR 1950-52; TA 1 (N) Gen Hosp 1952-75, oc 201 (N) Gen Hosp 1970-73; conslt plastic surgn and sr lectr 1968-; pres: Br Soc for Surgery of the Hand 1985, Br Assoc of Plastic Surgns 1988, Br Assoc of Clinical Anatomists 1989; FRCS 1958; *Style—* Col Hugh Brown, TD, DL, QHS; Royal Victoria Infirmary, Newcastle (☎ 232 5131)

BROWN, Ian James Morris; s of Bruce Beveridge Brown (d 1957), of Alloa Scotland, and Eileen Frances, *née* Carnegie (d 1986); *b* 28 Feb 1945; *Educ* Dollar Acad, Edinburgh Univ (MA, Dip Ed, M Litt); *m* 8 June 1968, Judith Ellen, da of George Woodall Sidaway, of Adelaide; 1 s (Joshua b 1977), 1 da (Emily b 1972); *Career* playwright 1967-; sch teacher 1967-69 and 1970-71, lectr in drama Dunfermline Coll Edinburgh 1971-76, Br Cncl Edinburgh and Istanbul 1976-78, princ lectr Crewe & Alsager Coll 1978-86 (seconded as sec Cork Enquiry into Professional Theatre 1985-86); drama dir Arts Cncl of GB 1986-; *plays incl*: Mother Earth (1070), The Bacchae (1972), Positively the Last Final Farewell Performance (ballet senario 1972), Carnegie (1973), The Knife (1973), Rabelais (1973), The Fork (1976), New Reekie (1977), Mary (1977), Runners (1978), Mary Queen and the Loch Tower (1979), Joker in the Pack (1983), Beatrice (1989); *Recreations* theatre, sport, travel; *Style—* I J M Brown, Esq; Arts Council, 105 Piccadilly, London W1V 0AY (☎ 01 629 9495)

BROWN, Jack Reginald Valentine; s of Reginald Brown; *b* 14 Feb 1922; *Educ* Taunton Sch; *m* 1945, Margaret, *née* Mustard; 2 s, 1 da; *Career* slr; sec and slr Stone-Platt Industries until 1982; *Recreations* golf; *Clubs* Frinton-on-Sea Golf, RAF; *Style—* Jack Brown Esq; 4 Inner Court, 48 Old Church St, London SW3

BROWN, Maj-Gen James; CB (1982); s of late James Brown; *b* 12 Nov 1928; *Educ* Methodist Coll Belfast, RMA Sandhurst; *m* 1952, Lilian May Johnson; 2 s; *Career* dir gen Ordnance Servs 1980-83, current dir Mgmnt Info Servs Div London Univ; *Style—* Maj-Gen James Brown, CB; c/o Royal Bank of Scotland, Holt's Branch, Kirkland House, Whitehall, London SW1

BROWN, James David Denholm (Tim); s of Lt Col Robert Louis Brown (d 1988), of Torwood, Kilmacolm, Renfrewshire, Scotland, and Katherine, Lang, *née* Denholm (d 1983); *b* 9 Oct 1932; *Educ* St Marys Melrose, Merchiston Castle Sch Edinburgh; *m* 2 Oct 1965, Judith Elaine, da of Roland Edmund Dangerfield (d 1964), of Hoe Farm, Peaslake, Surrey; 1 s (Duncan b 1969), 3 da (Diana b 1966, Camilla b 1968, Kirsty b 1974); *Career* Nat Serv Pilot Offr RAF 1951-53; dir Denholm Gp of Cos in London (joined Denholms Glasgow 1953, based in London as Denholm Coates 1954-); FICS 1962; *Recreations* bridge; *Clubs* Baltic Exchange; *Style—* Tim Brown, Esq; Swains, Bonfire Hill, Southwater, Horsham, Sussex; Denholm Coates & Co Ltd, 26 Great Tower St, London EC3R 5AQ (☎ 01 626 0816, fax 01 283 9509, telex 885337)

BROWN, James Richard; s of James Leonard Brown, MD (d 1972), of Lenham Kent, and Kathleen Mary, *née* Wild; *b* 28 August 1940; *Educ* Mill Hill Sch; *m* 20 April 1985, Sally Karen, da of (Percival) Richard Day, of West Meon, Hants; *Career* CA, Arthur Young 1959-68, NM Rothschild 1969-71, Rothschild Invest Tst and successor cos 1971-86, Electra Mgmnt Serv 1987-; tstee Childrens' Med Charity; Freeman City of London 1985; FCA; *Recreations* golf, swimming; *Clubs* RAC; *Style—* Richard Brown, Esq; The Oast Hse, Dale Hill, Ticehurst, E Sussex; Electra Management Services Ltd, 65 Kingsway, London WC2B 6QT (☎ 01 831 6464, fax 01 404 5388, telex 265525)

BROWN, Hon Mrs (Jennifer Mary); *née* Bethell; da of 2 Baron Bethell (d 1965), and Veronica (d 1981), da of Hon Sir James Connolly; *b* 26 August 1930; *Educ* St Mary's Convent Ascot; *m* 1954, Edward Peter Moncrieff Brown (ret stockbroker), s of Andrew Moncrieff Brown, of Wooder Manor, Widecombe, Devon; 4 s (Alistair, Craig, Jamie, David); *Recreations* tennis, sailing; *Style—* The Hon Mrs Brown; Wotton, Grove Lane, Petworth, Sussex (☎ 0798 43146)

BROWN, John David; s of Alfred Stanley Brown, 24 Valley Rd, Little Billing, Northampton, and Joan Mary, *née* Ogle; *b* 13 Oct 1942; *Educ* Northampton GS, Nottingham Univ (BSc); *m* 24 Sept 1967, Diane Elaine, da of Eric Edmund Hatton (d 1987); *Career* entered patent agent profession 1964, qualified patent agent 1969, ptnr Forrester Ketley & Co London 1972, fndr ptnr Forrester & Boehmert London, Munich, Bremen 1977; memb: Kiwanis Club Welwyn, Cncl of the Chartered Inst of Patent Agents (chm parly ctee), Parly & Scientific Ctee; substitute memb Cncl of Euro Patent Inst; memb: Scl 1964, RSC 1964, CIPA 1966; *Recreations* walking, skiing, squash; *Style—* John D Brown, Esq; Forrester Ketley & Co, Forrester House, 52 Bounds Green Rd, London N11 2EY (☎ 01 889 6622, fax 01 881 1088)

BROWN, Sir John Douglas Keith; er s of Ralph Douglas Brown (d 1972), of Manor

Hotel, Hindhead, and Rhoda Miller Keith; *b* 8 Sept 1913; *Educ* Glasgow Acad; *m* 1940, Margaret Eleanor, da of William Alexander Burnet (d 1942); 2 s; *Career* chartered accountant to 1948; chm: Jardine Henderson Ltd 1957-63, McLeod Russell & Co Ltd London 1972-79; chm and dir other cos; kt 1960; *Style*— Sir John Brown; Windover, Whitmore Vale Rd, Hindhead, Surrey (☎ 042 873 4173)

BROWN, Sir John Gilbert Newton; CBE (1966); s of John Brown, of Kent (d 1986) and Mary Edith, *née* Purchas (d 1974); *b* 7 July 1916; *Educ* Lancing, Hertford Coll Oxford (MA); *m* 1946, Virginia, da of late Darcy Braddell, of Holland Park, London W11; 1 s, 2 da; *Career* 2 Lt RA Malaya; The publisher OUP 1956-80; chm: B H Blackwell 1980-83, Basil Blackwell Publishers 1983-85 (dep chm 1983-87); dir: Blackwell Gp, Basil Blackwell Publishers, Book Tokens; chm Univ Bookshop Oxford; kt 1974; *Clubs* Garrick; *Style*— Sir John Brown, CBE; Milton Lodge, Great Milton, Oxford (☎ 084 46 217)

BROWN, John Granger; s of Frank Brown, of Birkenhead; *b* 24 Nov 1939; *Educ* Birkenhead Sch, Birmingham Univ; *m* 1964, Averil, da of Arthur Jones, of Birkenhead; 2 da; *Career* chartered accountant; corpn dir/sec Bernard Matthews plc 1977-; *Recreations* squash, cricket, golf, bridge; *Style*— John Brown, Esq; Rose Cottage, West End, Old Costessey, Norwich (☎ 0603 744477)

BROWN, John Stevenson; s of Stanley Brown (d 1978), of Sanderstead, Surrey, and Agnes Campbell, *née* Stevenson; *b* 28 Dec 1929; *Educ* Whitgift Middle Sch Croydon, Coll of Estate Mgmnt; *m* 1953, Catherine Mary, da of Maurice Ludlam-Taylor (d 1981); 1 s, 1 da; *Career* Nat Service RE UK, served E Africa 1948-49; FRICS; vice-chm and md Artagen Properties Ltd 1966-76, md Peachey Property Corpn plc 1977-; dir: A Peachey plc, Frankswood Property Co Ltd and subsids; non exec dir Property Services Agency DOE; pres: Br chapter FIABCI 1975-76, Br property Fdn 1986-87; liveryman Worshipful Cos of: Basketmakers, Paviors; *Recreations* sailing (sloop 'Conclusion'); *Clubs* Royal Thames Yacht, Royal Lymington Yacht; *Style*— John Brown, Esq; Peachey Property Corporation plc, 19 Sloane St, London SW1X 9NE (☎ 01 235 2080)

BROWN, Joseph Lawler; CBE (1977), TD (1953), DL (W Midlands 1975); s of Neil Brown, of Peebles; *b* 22 March 1921; *Educ* Peebles, Heriot-Watt Coll Edinburgh, Open Univ (BA); *m* 1950, Mabel, da of Alderman Pearson Smith, BEM; 1 s, 1 da; *Career* served WW II, Europe, Maj 7/9 The Royal Scots, TA 1946-57; dir: Coventry Newspapers 1960-69 (md 1964-69), BPM Hldgs 1971-81, Reuters 1972-75; chm & md Birmingham Post and Mail 1971-77; pres Newspaper Soc 1976-77, memb Press Assoc 1968-75 (chm 1971), pres Birmingham Chamber of Industry & Commerce 1979; warden Neidpath Castle Peeble 1983, bailiff The Schs of King Edward VI in Birmingham 1987; Cdr Order of Merit (Italy) 1973, Kt of Mark Twain Soc (USA) 1979; *Recreations* Japanese woodcuts; *Style*— Joseph Brown, Esq, CBE, TD, DL; 37 Mearse Lane, Barnt Green, Birmingham B45 8HH (☎ 021 445 1234)

BROWN, Hon Mrs (Juliet); yst da of Dr Geoffrey Tyndale Young and Baroness Young, PC (Life Peer); *b* 1962; *m* 7 June 1986, Stephen P Brown, er s of Dr Stanley Brown, of Harborne, Birmingham; *Style*— Anthony Boswood Esq, QC

BROWN, Keith Clark; s of George Harold Brown (d 1970), and Sophie Eleanor, *née* Clark; *b* 14 Jan 1943; *Educ* Forest Sch, City of London Coll; *m* 16 April 1972, Rita Hildegard, da of Jack Stanley Rolfe (d 1977); 1 s (Timothy b 1979), 1 da (Lucy b 1976); *Career* stockbroker; ptnr: W Greenwell & Co 1978-86, md Greenwell Montague Securities 1987; bd memb London Regnl Tport 1984-; cncllr: London Borough Havering 1968-74 and Brentwood Dist Cncl 1976-86; chm Brentwood Dist Cncl 1983-84; memb of Lloyds'; md: Morgan Stanley Int 1988-; liveryman Worshipful Co Coopers; *Recreations* public and charitable affairs; *Clubs* Cordwainer; *Style*— Keith C Brown, Esq; Fryerning House, Ingatestone, Essex CM4 0PF (☎ 0277 352959); Morgan Stanley International, 1A Wimpole Street, London W1 (☎ 01 709 3000)

BROWN, Keith John; JP (1979); s of Frederick Charles Brown, and Doris Lilian, *née* French; *b* 21 June 1949; *Educ* Forest Hill Sch, City and East London Coll, London Univ; *Career* oculist: Moorfields Eye Hosp 1970, Kent Co Opthalmic and Aural Hosp Maidstone 1973, Kent and Sussex Hosp Tunbridge Well 1975; private practise ownership: Brown Poole & Ptnrs Tunbridge Wells 1972, Brown and Gimpel Southborough 1979; ind private practice: Southborough, Maidstone, West Malling 1981; Opticians: Keelers (Cromwell Hosp) 1984, Trotters Edinburgh 1986; conslt oculist: Dolland and Aitchison Gp 1987, Chaucer Hosp Canterbury 1988; chm Democrat Pty Cranbrook and dist; Freeman: City of London, Spectacle Makers Co; fndn fell Br Assoc Dispensing Opticians 1986; *Recreations* cooking, walking, shooting; *Clubs* Nat Liberal; *Style*— Keith Brown, Esq, JP; Linnet House, Hawkhurst, Kent (☎ 0580 753 668); 23-27 Swan St, West Malling, Kent (☎ 0732 848 384); 100 London Rd, Southborough Tunbridge Wells, Kent (☎ 0892 31004, telex prestel MBX 580 211167)

BROWN, Kenneth Edward Lindsay; s of Col Thomas Pyne Brown, OBE (d 1957); *b* 17 Oct 1940; *Educ* Sherborne; *m* 1968, Mary Ruth, da of Thomas Forrester (d 1969); 3 s; *Career* chm A R Brown McFarlane & Co Ltd 1972- (dir 1967-); FCA; *Recreations* sailing, skiing; *Clubs* Royal Ocean Racing; *Style*— Kenneth Brown Esq; 65 St Andrews Drive, Glasgow G41 4HP (☎ 041 423 8381); A R Brown McFarlane & Co Ltd, 239 Myreside St, Glasgow G32 6DR (☎ 041 551 8281, telex 779595)

BROWN, Leslie; s of late W H Brown and late Eliza J, *née* Fiveash; *b* 29 Oct 1902; *Educ* Selhurst GS; *m* 1930, Frances V, da of T B Lever; 2 s, 1 da; *Career* dep chm Prudential Assur Co Ltd 1970-74 (joined Prudential 1919, ch investment mangr 1955-64, dir 1965-77); FIA; *Style*— Leslie Brown Esq; 12 Park View, Christchurch Rd, Purley, Surrey CR2 2NL (☎ 01 668 8645)

BROWN, Prof Lionel Neville; OBE; s of Reginald Percy Neville Brown (d 1978), of York Crescent, Wolverhampton, and Fanny, *née* Carver (d 1980); *b* 29 July 1923; *Educ* Wolverhampton GS, Pembroke Coll Cambridge (MA, LLM), Lyons Univ France (Dr en Droit); *m* Mary Patricia, da of Charles Dennis Vowles (d 1984), of Heathcote, Great Barr, West Bromwich; 3 s (Roger b 1961, Simon b 1963, Adrian b 1965) 1 da (Rachel b 1967); *Career* WWII RAF 1942-45; slr 1951, lectr law Sheffield Univ 1953-55; Birmingham Univ: lect 1955-57, sr lectr 1957-64, reader 1964-66, prof of comparative law 1966-, dean of Faculty of Law 1970-74; sr res fell Univ of Michigan 1960; visiting prof: Tulane Univ New Orleans 1968; Nairobi Univ 1974, Laval Univ Quebec 1975, 1979, 1983, 1987, Limoges Univ 1987-88, Univ of Mauritius 1988-89; Cwlth Fndn Lectureship Caribbean 1976; reader C of E Lichfield Diocese 1972-; memb Cncl on Tribunals 1982-88, chm Birmingham Social Security Appeal Tribunal 1988-, Docteur Honoris Causa Limoges University France 1988; memb Law Soc 1951; Officier Dans L'Ordre Des Palmes Académiques France 1987; *Books* Amos & Walton's Introduction to French Law (3rd edn with FH Lawson & AE Anton 1967), French Administrative Law (3 edn with JF Garner 1983), Court of Justice of European Communities (3 edn with FG Jacobs 1989); *Recreations* landscape gardening, country walking, music; *Clubs* United Oxford and Cambridge; *Style*— Prof Neville Brown, OBE; 14 Waterdale, Compton, Wolverhampton WV3 9DY (☎ 0902 26 666); Faculty of Law, Univ of Birmingham, Edgbaston, Birmingham B15 2TT (☎ 021 414 6284)

BROWN, Maggie; da of Cecil Walter Brown and Marian, *née* Evans; *b* 7 Sept 1950; *Educ* Colston's Girls' Sch, Univ of Sussex, Univ of Bristol (BA), Univ of Cardiff (Dip in Journalism); *m* 22 June 1979, Charles John Giuseppe Harvey, s of Hon John Wynn Harvey, of Coed-y-Maen, Meifod, Powys (s of 1 Baron Harvey of Tasburgh); 2 da (Elena b 27 Dec 1982, Nina b 11 Aug 1985); *Career* trainee journalist Birmingham Post & Mail 1972-74; staff writer: Birmingham Post 1974-77, Reuters 1977-78; news editor: Financial Weekly 1979-80, The Guardian 1980-86; media editor The Independent 1986-; contributor to magazines and BBC radio; memb Victorian Soc; *Recreations* reading, gardening, being a mother; *Style*— Ms Maggie Brown; 162 East Dulwich Grove, London SE22 (☎ 01 693 5838); office, The Independent, 40 City Rd, London EC1Y 2DB (☎ 01 253 1222)

BROWN, Prof Sir (George) Malcolm; s of George Arthur Brown (d 1937), and Anne Brown (d 1987); *b* 5 Oct 1925; *Educ* Coatham Sch Redcar, Durham Univ (BSc, DSc), Oxford Univ (MA, DPhil), Princeton Univ, Univ of California, Univ of Berne; *m* 1, 1963 (m dis 1977); m 2, Sally Jane Marston, eld da of Alan Douglas Spencer, *qv*; 2 step da (Polly Marston b 1969, Verna Marston b 1971); *Career* served RAF (aircrew) 1944-47; Cwlth fell (Harkness) Princeton Univ 1954-55; Univ lectr; coll lectr Lincoln New Coll, fell St Cross Coll, Oxford Univ 1955-66, sr res fell Geophysical Lab Washington DC USA 1966-67, prof of geology, dean of science, pro vice chllr Durham Univ 1967-79; NASA princ investigator Apollo Moon Exploration programme 1967-75; dir of Br Geological Survey, Geological Museum and Geological Survey of N Ireland; conslt geologist 1985; geological advsr MOD 1979-85; Hon DSc Leicester Univ; FRS, FRSE, FGS; kt 1985; *Books* Layered Igneous Rocks (1968), Origin of the Solar System (1978, contrib), Planet Earth (1977, contrib); *Recreations* exploration, classical guitar; *Clubs* Royal Overseas League; *Style*— Prof Sir Malcolm Brown; 4 The Glebe, Wheatley, Oxford OX9 1YN (☎ 086 77 5127)

BROWN, Malcolm Ronald; s of Ronald Ernest Charles Brown, MBE (d 1988), of Orpington, Kent, and Peggy Elizabeth, *née* Mitchener; *b* 2 August 1946; *Educ* Quintin GS, London Univ (BSc); *m* 3 Oct 1970, Lyntina Sydnie, da of Clinton Sydney Squire; 1 s (Philip Clinton b 18 May 1975), 1 da (Samantha Anne b Feb 1972); *Career* construction analyst: de Zoete & Gorton 1968-72, James Capel & Co 1972-(ptnr 1981, sr exec 1984); chm repair and maintenance gp construction indust forecasting body Nat Econ Devpt Off; tres E Berks Cons Assoc; author numerous specialist papers and pubns; ASIA; *Recreations* ocean racing, chess, gardening; *Style*— Malcolm Brown, Esq; Carbery Ho, Carbery Lane, Ascot, Berks (☎ 0990 22 620); James Capel House, 6 Bevis Marks, London EC3N 7BQ (☎ 01 621 0011 ext 2644)

BROWN, Hon Mrs (Marjorie Elizabeth); *née* Palmer; da of 2 Baron Palmer (d 1950); *b* 24 April 1910; *m* 1945, Frederick Richard Brown, CBE, s of Roger Grounds Brown (d 1947), of Liverpool; 3 s, 1 da; *Style*— The Hon Mrs Brown; 13 Islescourt, Ramsbury, nr Marlborough, Wilts SN8 2QW (☎ 0672 20740)

BROWN, Sir (Cyril) Maxwell Palmer; KCB (1969, CB 1965), CMG (1957); s of Cyril Palmer Brown, of Wanganui, NZ; *b* 30 June 1914; *Educ* Wanganui Collegiate Sch, Victoria Univ NZ, Clare Coll Cambridge; *m* 1940, Margaret May, da of late W Edward Gillhespy, of Hathersage, Derbyshire; 3 s, 1 da; *Career* second perm sec BOT 1968-70, DTI 1970-74; dir: ERA Technol Ltd 1974-86, John Brown & Co 1975-82, Ransome Hoffman Pollard (later RHP Gp) 1975-88; dep chm Monopolies & Mergers Cmmn 1976-81; *Style*— Sir Maxwell Brown, KCB, CMG; 20 Cottenham Park Rd, London SW20 (☎ 01 946 7237)

BROWN, Sir Mervyn; KCMG (1981, CMG 1975), OBE (1963); s of William Brown, of Murton, Co Durham; *b* 24 Sept 1923; *Educ* Ryhope GS Sunderland, St John's Coll Oxford (MA); *m* 1949, Elizabeth, da of Harry Gittings, of Shipley, Derby; *Career* HM Foreign Service 1949-83; ambassador to Madagascar 1967-70 (non-resident 1976-78), high cmmr Tanzania 1975-78, min and dep perm rep to UN 1978, high cmmr Nigeria and ambass to Benin 1979-83, chm Visiting Arts and Anglo-Malagasy Soc;; *Books* Madagascar Rediscovered (1978); *Recreations* music, tennis, history; *Clubs* Royal Cwlth Soc, Hurlingham, All England Lawn Tennis; *Style*— Sir Mervyn Brown, KCMG, OBE; 195 Queen's Gate, London SW7 5EU

BROWN, (Charles) Michael; s of Richard Charles Brown (d 1982), of Minchinhampton, Glos; *b* 11 June 1930; *Educ* Clifton; *m* 1, 1954, Sonia Teresa, da of Harvey Valency Schwalm (d 1959), of Angmering, Sussex; 3 s, 1 da; m 2, 1977, (Pauline) Anne, da of John Robinson (d 1981), of Allanton, Berwicks; *Career* chm Vinten Gp plc 1975-87; dir: Pauls plc 1980-85, Domino Printing Scis plc 1985-89; FCA; *Recreations* shooting; *Style*— Michael Brown, Esq; 301 Lonsdale Road, Barnes, London SW13 9PY (☎ 01 878 7783, work 0284 2121); Fort Fredrick, Port Royal, Roatan Island, Honduras

BROWN, Hon Michael Colin Duncan; s of Baron Brown, PC, MBE (Life Peer) (d 1985); *b* 11 July 1944; *Educ* Bryanston Sch, Architectural Association; *m* 1970, Fenella, da of Peter Barnard, of Dorking; 1 s (Jago), 2 da (Merrilees, Clio); *Career* ptnr Brown Ibbotson Partnership (architects); *Style*— The Hon Michael Brown

BROWN, Michael John; s of Lt Cdr S R Brown (d 1976), of Aylesbury, and Ada Phyllis, *née* Evett; *b* 23 Sept 1932; *Educ* Berkhamsted Sch, New Coll Oxford (MA); *m* 20 Sept 1963, Margaret Jordan, JP (d 1988), da of William C Jordan; 4 s (Edward b 1964, Thomas b 1966, Robert b and d 1968, Adam b 1970); *Career* slr 1957, ptnr Denton Hall and Burgin 1959-80, sr ptnr Brown Cooper 1981-; dir: Urwick Orr and Ptnrs Ltd (chm 1981-84), Channel TV 1972-77, Purcell Graham and Co 1978-88, Paulstra Ltd 1977-; chm: Soc Eng and American Lawyers 1985-88, Pooh Properties Tst 1972-; hon slr Variety Club of GB 1968-; *Recreations* diverse; *Clubs* Garrick; *Style*— Michael Brown, Esq; The Master's House, The Common, Chorleywood, Herts; 7 Southampton Place, London WC1 (☎ 01 404 0422, fax 01 831 9856, telex 265471)

BROWN, Michael Russell; MP (C) Brigg and Cleethorpes 1983-; s of Frederick Alfred Brown, and Greta Mary, *née* Russell; *b* 3 July 1951; *Educ* Littlehampton, York Univ; *Career* memb Middle Temple; mgmnt trainee Barclays Bank 1972-74; lectr Swinton Cons Coll 1974-76, research asst to Michael Marshall MP 1975-77, parly res asst to Nicholas Winterton MP 1977-79; MP (C) Brigg and Scunthorpe 1979-83; sec parly N Ireland ctee 1981-87 (vice-chm 1987); memb Energy select ctee 1986-; *Style*— Michael Brown, Esq, MP; House of Commons, London SW1

BROWN, Nicholas Hugh; MP (Lab) Newcastle-upon-Tyne East 1983-; s of late R C Brown and G K Brown, *née* Tester; *b* 13 June 1950; *Educ* Tunbridge Wells Tech HS, Manchester Univ; *Career* memb: Newcastle-upon-Tyne Cncl 1980-, housing sub-ctee on slum clearance; *Style*— Nicholas Brown Esq, MP; House of Commons, London SW1

BROWN, Nicholas Warriner; s of Byron Warriner George Brown, and Constance Louise, *née* Austin; *b* 5 Nov 1938; *Educ* Oundle; *m* 13 July 1962, Margaret Joan, da of Charles Robert Smurthwaite; 1 s (David b 1964), 1 da (Sophia b 1963); *Career* fndr and chm Wallcoverings Int Ltd; ch exec Walker Greenbank plc; *Recreations* golf, art; *Style*— Nicholas W Brown, Esq; c/o Wallcoverings Int Ltd, 79/89 Pentonville Road, London N1 9LW (☎ 01 837 3666, telex 24798)

BROWN, Nigel Denis Spence; s of Denis Frederick Spence Brown, MC, of Dorrington, Lincoln, and Margaret, *née* Shutler; *b* 6 May 1946; *Educ* Uppingham, Manchester Business Sch; *m* 18 Sept 1971, Gillian Elizabeth Ann, da of Dr GHP Drake, of Appleshaw, Hants; 2 s (Thomas b 1980, James b 1982), 1 da (Juliet b 1986); *Career* chartered accountant 1966-71, merchant banker 1971-74, joined Brown Butlin Gp 1974 (gp chm 1987-); FCA 1968; *Style*— Nigel Brown, Esq; The Old Rectory, Fulbeck, Grantham, Lincs NG32 3JS (☎ 0450 75101); Brown Butlin Group Ltd, Brook House, Lincs (☎ 0526 832771)

BROWN, Dr Norman John; s of William John Brown (d 1983), of Bristol, and Lilian Rose, *née* Hackney (d 1935); *b* 2 Mar 1918; *Educ* Bristol GS, Univ of Bristol (MB, CHB); *m* 7 March 1942, Enid Rhoda, da of Samuel Gale (d 1961), of Portishead, Avon; 2 s (Christopher b 1943, Peter b 1952), 2 da (Pamela b 1947, Catherine b 1955); *Career* RAMC Lt 1942, Capt 1943, serv UK, M East, Italy, Regtl MORA 1943-45, specialist in pathology 1946-47; house physician casualty offr Bristol Royal Infirmary 1941-42, registrar in pathology Utd Bristol Hosps 1947-49, lectr in pathology Univ of Bristol 1949-51; conslt pathologist: Southmead Hosp Bristol 1951-83; Bristol Royal Hosp Sick Children, clincal teacher in pathology Univ of Bristol 1955-83, temp advsr WHO 1971-74; ed Bristol Medico-Chirurgical Jl 1961-74 (asst ed 1955-61), pres Bristol Medico-Chirurgical Soc 1980-81; chm: SW Regnl Lab Med Ctee 1979-82, med educn ctee Southmead Hosp Bristol 1958-82; parish cncllr Portbury Avon 1966-76, chm parish cncl 1973-76; memb Int Acad of Pathology 1965, Assoc of Clinical Pathologists 1952-; memb Br Paediatric Assoc 1977-, Paediatric Pathology Soc 1955-; FRCP, FRC Path (fndr fell 1963); *Books* Pathology of Testis (co ed 1975), Tumours of Children (co ed 1968, second edn 1975), Prematurity By Corner (1960); *Recreations* music (french horn player 40 years), gardening, photography; *Style*— Dr Norman Brown; The Old Vicarage, Harford Square, Chew Magna, Bristol BS18 8RA (☎ 0272 333 126)

BROWN, Percy Arthur Albert; s of Percy Brown (d 1954), and Elsie, *née* Massey (d 1978); *b* 28 Jan 1916; *Educ* Sir George Monoux GS; *m* 5 April 1947, Katherine Stanley, da of Samuel Potter (ka 1917); 2 da (Rosemary Anne b 1949, Susan Alison b 1954); *Career* WWII Western Desert 1941-43, Spears Mission to Syria and Lebanon (Beirut) 1943-46; Nat Building Soc 1934-38, mangr Co-op Permanent Building Soc (York, Hull, Ilford) 1938-61, asst gen mangr Gateway Building Soc (formerly Temperance Perm Building Soc) 1962-76, memb cncl Chartered Building Socs Inst 1963-76 (pres 1968-69, vice pres 1976-); former chm local review ctee HM Prison Ford; memb: exec ctee Worthing Area Guild for Vol Serv, fin ctee County Scout Assoc; Freeman City of London, life memb Guild of Freemen; FCBSI 1949; *Recreations* cricket watching, conservation; *Clubs* Sussex CCC, Offington, Findon; *Style*— Percy Brown, Esq; Overdale, Sullington Gdns, Findon Valley, Worthing, W Sussex (☎ 090 671 2316)

BROWN, Peter Eric; s of Eric Henry Ibbetson Brown (d 1951), of Yoxford House, Kings Lynn, Norfolk, and Violet Mary, *née* Phipps (d 1931); *b* 3 Oct 1931; *Educ* Cheltenham; *m* 23 Aug 1958, Sylvia Mary Ethel, da of Rev Charles Henry Watson (d 1949), of Lilleshall Vicarage, Lilleshall, Shropshire; 1 s (Richard Henry b 1967), 3 da (Vanessa Mary (Mrs Perkins) b 1960, Melanie Lucy b 1963, Camilla Susan b 1964); *Career* Nat Serv Capt 1952, RAOC 1950-52; mktg dir Martin Cadbury Ltd 1966-70, dep chief exec Andercroft Ltd 1970-73, md Brown Knight & Truscott Ltd 1977-79, chm and md Claremont Press Ltd 1979-; Freeman City of London 1974, Liveryman Worshipful Co of Stationers & Newspaper Makers 1975; memb Inst of Printing 1977, FInstM 1985; *Recreations* golf, tennis, badminton, theatre; *Clubs* City Livery; *Style*— Peter Brown, Esq; Claremont Press, Foundry Close, Horsham, W Sussex (☎ 0403 61387, fax 0403 55593)

BROWN, Peter John; s of John Jesse Brown (d 1942), of London, and Alice Irene, *née* Magnus (d 1978), of London; *b* 12 April 1934; *Educ* Finchley GS, Harrow, City Lit Inst; *m* 8 Feb 1963, Marie-France, da of Stephanie Albert Chasles (d 1958), of France; 2 s (Philippe John b 3 Dec 1967, Christopher Mark b 5 Oct 1974), 1 da (Natalie Christina 17 March 1964); *Career* RAF 1953-55; COI 1951-52, HMSO 1952-53, Utd Africa Co 1955-59, Lintas Ltd 1959-61, Greenlys 1961-63, The Times 1963-65, J Walter Thompson 1965-67, The Leslie Bishop Co 1967-68, Harris and Hunter 1968-69; chief exec PB Communications Int (PR and mktg consultancy); Inst PR, MIPR, PRCA; *Recreations* classical music, skiing, cricket, tennis; *Clubs* MCC, Arts; *Style*— Peter J Brown, Esq; 13 Colinette Rd, Putney London SW15 6QG; 2 Lansdowne House, Lansdowne Rd (☎ 01 229 8225, fax 01 221 3446)

BROWN, Peter Michael; s of Michael George Harold Brown (d 1969), of Sussex, and Dorothy Margaret Brown, *née* Douty; *b* 11 July 1934; *Educ* Rugby; *m* 1963, Rosemary Anne, da of Hubert Simon Baden-Baden (d 1979), of Geneva; 2 s (Hugo Michael Hubert b 1964, Dominic Peter b 1965); *Career* nat serv 2 Lt Somerset Light Infantry; chm/dir: Associated Br Industries plc, ABI Inc (USA), Synergy Hldgs Ltd, The Reward Gp, William Dawson Hldgs plc, Stag Jointings, Stag (USA); chm: Thomas Coram Fndn, Thames Help Tst, Charities Effectiveness Review Tst; *Recreations* charity work, squash; *Clubs* Carlton, Lansdowne; *Style*— Peter Michael Brown, Esq; 12 Hyde Park Place, London W2 2LH; 1 Lancaster Place, London WC2E 7EB (☎ 01-836 5831)

BROWN, Peter Wilfred Henry; s of Rev Wilfred George Brown (d 1968), and Joan Margaret Brown, *née* Adams; *b* 6 June 1941; *Educ* Marlborough Coll 1953-59; Jesus Coll, Cambridge 1960-63, MA (Cantab); *m* 29 March 1969 (m dis), Kathleen, da of Hugh Clarke, of Freetown (d 1982); 1 da (Sonya b 1971); *Career* asst master in Classics, Birkenhead Sch 1963-66; lectr in Classics, Fourah Bay Coll, Univ of Sierra Leone 1966-68; asst sec Sch of Oriental and African Studies, Univ of London 1968-75; sec of the Br Academy 1983- (dep sec 1975-83, acting sec 1976-77); memb: Br Library Advsy Cncl 1983-, Cncl Sch of Slavonic and E European Studies Univ of London 1984-, advsy ctee Inst of Archaeology Univ of London 1987-, Warburg Inst Univ of London 1987- ; *Recreations* sedentary pursuits, musical, bookish; *Style*— Peter Brown, Esq; 34 Victoria Rd, London NW6 6PX; The British Academy, 20-21 Cornwall Terrace, London NW1 4QP (☎ 01 487 5966, telex 263194)

BROWN, Philip Nicholas; s of Reginald F Brown (d 1970), and Margaret E Gladwell, *née* Simmons (d 1988); *b* 24 June 1942; *Educ* Cheshunt GS, Albion HS, Hobart Coll (BA), Columbia Univ (LLB); *m* 27 Dec 1975, Geraldine Lynn, da of Frederick Grover, of New Malden, Surrey; 2 da (Naomi b 1982, Emily b 1983); *Career* Vol Serv Peace Corps 1966-68; worked on New Jersey Law Reform Project 1969-71, managing ptnr Wilde Sapte 1988-(ptnr 1975); memb: Law Soc 1975, NY Bar 1966, New Jersey Bar 1969; *Recreations* pottery; *Style*— Philip Brown, Esq; Wilde Sapte, Queensbridge House, 60 Upper Thames St, London EC4V 3BD (☎ 01 236 3050, fax 01 236 9624, telex 88773)

BROWN, Ralph; s of Walter Wesley Brown, and Minnie, *née* Clay; *b* 24 April 1928; *Educ* Leeds GS, Leeds Sch of Art, Hammersmith Sch of Art, RCA; *m* 1, 1952 (m dis 1962), Margaret Elizabeth Taylor; 1 s (Matthew b 1953), 1 da (Sara b 1955); m 2, Feb 1964, Caroline Ann, da of Graham Clifton-Trigg (d 1983), of Jersey; 1 s (Jasper b 1965); *Career* artist; exhibited widely in UK and Europe 1953-; pt/t tutor RCA 1958 -69; work purchased by many public collections incl: Tate Gallery, Leeds, Liverpool, Bristol, Arts Cncl of GB, RCA, Cardiff, Rijkes Museum Kröller-Müller, Stuyvesant Fndn SA, Art Gallery of NSW, Contemporary Art Soc; ARA 1968, RA 1972; *Style*— Ralph Brown, Esq; Seynckley House, Amberley, Stroud, Glos GL5 5BB

BROWN, Hon Sir Ralph Kilner; OBE (1945), QC (1958), TD (1952), DL (Warwicks 1956); s of Rev Arthur Ernest Brown, CIE (d 1952), of The Manor House, Churchdown, Glos, and E Gertrude, *née* Parsons (d 1971); *b* 28 August 1909; *Educ* Kingswood Sch, Trin Hall Camb; *m* 1943, Cynthia Rosemary, da of Lt-Col George Vernon Breffit, MC; 1 s, 2 da; *Career* served WW II Brig HQ 21 Army Gp 1945; barr 1934; judge of the High Court, Queen's Bench Div 1970-84, judge of Employment Appeal Tribunal 1976-84; kt 1970; *Recreations* watching cricket and athletics (rep Camb Univ, England and Great Britain); *Clubs* Naval and Military, Hawks Cambridge; *Style*— The Hon Sir Ralph Kilner Brown, OBE, QC, TD, DL; 174 Defoe House, Barbican, London EC2Y 8DN

BROWN, Sir Raymond Frederick; OBE (1966); s of Frederick Brown (d 1944), and Susan Evelyn Brown; *b* 19 July 1920; *Educ* Morden Terrace LCC Sch, SE London Tech Coll, Morley Coll; *m* 1, 1942 (m dis 1949), Evelyn Jennings; 1 da (decd); m 2, 1953, Carol Jacquelin Elizabeth, da of Henry Robert Sprinks, of Paris; 2 s, 1 da; *Career* jt fndr Racal Electronics 1950 (chm, md and pres 1950-66); head of defence sales miny of Technol/Def 1966-69, conslt advsr (commercial policy and exports) to sec of state DHSS 1969-72; chm: Racecourse Tech Servs 1970-85, Muirhead plc 1972-85 (ch exec and md 1970-82); indust advsr to NEDC 1976-85, dir Nat Westminster Bank Outer London Region 1978-85, exec dir STC plc 1985-; memb Soc of Pilgrims; Liveryman Worshipful Co of: Scriveners', Scientific Instrument Makers'; Hon DSc (Bath) 1980; kt 1969; *Recreations* polo, farming, shooting, golf; *Clubs* Sunningdale Golf, Guards Polo (life memb), Swinley Forest Golf, City Livery, Travellers' (Canada, Australia, Ends of the Earth); *Style*— Sir Raymond Brown, OBE; Witley Park House, Haslemere Road, Witley, Surrey GU8 5PX (☎ 042 879 3859)

BROWN, Hon Richard Banks Duncan; s of Baron Brown, MBE (Life Peer) (d 1985), and Marjorie Hershel Skinner, of 9 Blenheim Road, London; *b* 31 May 1942; *Educ* Bryanston Sch, Brunel Univ (B Tech); *m* 1968, Gillian Mary, da of John Kennedy Carter; 1 s (Cameron b 6 June 1974) 1 da (Emma 3 Aug 1971); *Style*— The Hon Richard Brown; Alderholt Lodge, Alderholt, Fordingbridge, Hants

BROWN, His Hon Judge Robert; s of Robert Brown (d 1966), and Mary Lily, *née* Pullen; *b* 21 June 1943; *Educ* Downing Coll Cambridge (BA, LLB); *m* 1, 1964 (m dis 1971) Susan; 1 s (Andrew Juston b 20 June 1964), 1 da (Jocelyn Fiona 15 Sept 1970); m 2, 3 Nov 1973, Carole, *née* Tait; 2 step s (James Francis 12 May 1965, Benjamin William b 1 May 1967); *Career* barr Inner Temple 1968, standing counsel to DHSS Northern Circuit 1983-88, recorder Crown Ct 1983-88, circuit judge 1988; *Recreations* golf; *Clubs* Royal Lytham St Annes GC; *Style*— His Hon Judge Robert Brown; Chambers, 2 Old Bank St, Manchester M2 7PE (☎ 061 832 3791)

BROWN, Robert Alan; s of Charles Alan Brown, of Beverley, N Humberside, and Marion, *née* Lidgett; *b* 24 June 1954; *Educ* Beverley GS; *m* 1, May 1978, (m dis 1985), Marilyn Clare, da of Eric Sack; m 2, 17 Sept 1988, Deborah Anne, da of Harry Hodgkiss; *Career* Phillips and Drew: investment mangr 1972-77 (1980-88), ptnr 1984; investment mangr N M Rothschild and Sons 1977-80, vice pres Union Bank of Switzerland 1988-; memb Stock Exchange; *Recreations* music, fell walking, motor racing; *Style*— Robert Brown, Esq; Flat D, 40 Whistlers Ave, London SW11 3TS (☎ 01 350 2113); Union Bank of Switzerland, 122 Leadenhall St, London EC3 (☎ 01 929 4111)

BROWN, Robert Crofton; DL (Tyne and Wear 1988); s of William Brown (d 1954), of Newcastle-upon-Tyne; *b* 16 May 1921; *Educ* Atkinson Rd Tech Sch, Rutherford Tech Coll; *m* 1945, Marjorie, da of Anne Hogg, of Slaithwaite, Yorks; 1 s, 1 da; *Career* served in Royal Signals 1942-46; Gas Bd official; memb Newcastle Corpn 1958-88, sec of constituency Lab Pty and election agent 1950-66, sponsored by GMWU, MP (Lab): Newcastle upon Tyne West 1966-83, Newcastle upon Tyne North 1983-87; parly sec Min of Tport 1968-70; vice-chm: Trade Union Gp of Lab MPs 1970, Parly Lab Pty Tport Gp 1970; parly under-sec state: Dept of Health and Social Security 1974, Defence (Army) 1974-79; memb (Newburn Ward) Newcastle upon Tyne CC; *Style*— Robert Brown, Esq; 1 Newsham Close, The Boltons, N Walbottle, Newcastle upon Tyne, NE5 1QD

BROWN, Robert Glencairn; s of William Brown (d 1958), of Glasgow, and Marion, *née* Cockburn (d 1965); *b* 19 July 1930; *Educ* Hillhead HS Glasgow; *m* 25 May 1957, Florence May, da of William Stalker (d 1967), of Glasgow; 2 s (Gordon b 1959, Stewart b 1960); *Career* cmmnd 2 Lt Royal Signals 1949-51, served Austria; Forestry Cmmn 1947-63, seconded Civil Service Pay Research Unit 1963-64; princ: Miny of Land and Natural Resources 1964-67, Miny Housing & Local Govt 1968-71; seconded Nat Whitley Cncl 1969; asst dir Countryside Cmmn 1971-77; asst sec DOE 1977-83, under sec DOE 1983-86; dir Housing Corpn 1986-; chm W Middx Centre Nat Tst;

Recreations gardening, skiing, reading; *Clubs* Ski Club of GB; *Style*— Robert Glencairn Brown, Esq; 2 The Squirrels, Pinner, Middx HA5 3BD (☎ 01 886 8713); Housing Corporation, 149 Tottenham Court Road, London W1P 0BN (☎ 01 387 9466)

BROWN, Roland; s of Fred Brown (d 1982), of 14 Park Ave, Burnley, Lancs, and Jane Ellen, *née* Fielding (d 1975); *b* 16 Nov 1922; *Educ* Burnley Municipal Coll; *m* 24 Sept 1949, Anne, da of Owen Taylor (d 1975), of 39 Melville St, Burnley, Lancs; 1 s (Peter Anthony b 20 April 1951), 1 da (Wendy Elizabeth b 11 Dec 1956); *Career* WWII RAF 1942-46, Corpl 1946; CA; gp accountant Bury & Masco Industs Ltd 1961-66, fin dir Coloroll Ltd 1966-76, md Learoyd Packaging Ltd 1976-; memb: Burnley Enterprise Tst, Burnley C of C; ACA 1949, FCA 1959; *Recreations* golf; *Style*— Roland Brown Esq; 14 Park Avenue, Burnley, Lancs (☎ 0282 38016); Learoyd Packaging Ltd, Heasandford Mill, Queen Victoria Rd, Burnley, Lancs (☎ 0282 38016, fax 0282 30289)

BROWN, Ron(ald); MP (Lab) Edinburgh Leith 1979-; s of James Brown and Margaret McLaren; *b* 1940; *Educ* Ainslie Pk HS, Bristo Engrg Inst (both Edinburgh); *m* 1963, May Smart; 2 s; *Career* formerly served Royal Signals; former AUEW branch chm and shop stewards convener; memb Campaign Gp Lab MPs 1982-; *Style*— Ron Brown Esq, MP; House of Commons, London SW1

BROWN, Rt Rev Ronald; *see*: Birkenhead, Bishop of

BROWN, Ronald Hedley; OBE (1945); s of Reginald Hedley Brown (d 1967), and Lilian, *née* Howard (d 1963); *b* 2 Feb 1914; *Educ* Cambridgeshire HS, Univ of London (BSc, DipED); *m* 1, 12 Aug 1939, Margaret Caroline Linforth (d 1982), da of Edward Clifford Pitman (d 1963), of Alpheton, Suffolk; 1 s (Richard Hedley b 1951), 1 da (Patricia Carol b 1947); m 2, Rosemary Dorothy, *née* Carter; *Career* RAF: Educn Offr 1938-39, Intelligence Offr 1939-46, Fl Lt Bircham Newton 1939-41, Sqdn Ldr Iceland 1941-42, Sqdn Ldr N Russia 1943, Staff Coll (graduated WS) 1942, Gibraltar 1943-45 (despatches 4 times); Colonial Serv 1947-63: dir educn N Rhodesia 1959-63; pres Devon Beekeepers Assoc, former ed Beekeeping; *Books* 1000 Years of Devon Beekeeping (1973), Beeeswax (1981), Beekeeping - A Seasonal Guide (1985), Honey Bees - A Guide to Management (1988); *Recreations* beekeeping, foreign travel; *Style*— Ronald Brown, Esq, OBE; 20 Parkhurst Rd, Torquay, Devon (☎ 0803 37563)

BROWN, Ronald William; JP (County of London 1961); s of George Brown; yr bro of late Lord George-Brown; *b* 7 Sept 1921; *Educ* Borough Poly; *m* 1944, Mary Munn; 1 s, 2 da; *Career* MP (Lab) Shoreditch and Finsbury 1964-74, Hackney S and Shoreditch 1974-83 (resigned from Lab Party 1981, SDP MP from 1981), asst govt whip 1966-67, former chm London Gp Parly Lab Party, former memb House of Commons Select Ctee Science & Technol, alderman and ldr Southwark 1964, ldr Camberwell Borough Cncl 1956, former memb Greater London Labour Pty Exec; former sr lecturer electrical engrg and princ industl training sch; memb Cncl of Europe Assembly & WEU 1965-68, 1970-73, 1975-77 and 1980-83, memb Euro Parl 1977-79; rapporteur on Economic Affairs, Science and Technol, Tport, Nuclear Power, Environment and Public Health, Data Protection, and Defence; memb of bd Estate Govrs Alleyn's Coll of God's Gift (chm 1976-78), former memb bd of govrs St Bartholomew's Hosp, memb bd of govrs and tres St Bartholomew's Med Coll, memb NW Thames Regnl Health Authy 1974-; memb policy ctee, nat ctee and cncl for Social Democracy 1981-83, parly advsr to Furniture Timber & Allied Trades Union 1968-81, former parly conslt to nat and local govt offrs; dep dir gen FBIM, JP, memb Fedn of Master Builders; *Style*— Ronald Brown Esq, JP; 45 Innings Drive, Pevensey Bay, East Sussex BN24 6BH (☎ (0323) 764808)

BROWN, Russell Milton; s of Harry Louis Brown (d 1974), and Murielle Katherine, *née* Wartski (d 1983); *b* 20 May 1929; *Educ* Stowe; *Career* Nat Serv RAPC 1951-53; fin offr and clerk to the Govrs Sadlers Wells Theatre 1956-63, chief accountant and prodn controller RSC 1963-66, bursar RCA 1966-86; dir Scottish Ballet; tstee: Royal Ballet Benevolent Fund, Dancers Resettlement Fund, Areopagitica Educnl Tst; hon fell RCA 1986, FCA; Chevalier de L'Ordre Nationale de Merite 1970; *Books* ed Sadlers Wells Theatre Ballet (1955); *Recreations* ballet, opera, music, theatre, foreign travel; *Style*— Russell Brown, Esq; Flat 8, 284 Old Brompton Rd, London SW5 9HR; Oak Tree Cottage, Thornborough, Bucks (☎ 01 373 3141)

BROWN, The Hon Mr Justice; Sir Simon Denis; s of Denis Baer Brown (d 1981), and Edna Elizabeth, *née* Abrahams; *b* 9 April 1937; *Educ* Stowe Sch, Worcester Coll Oxford (BA); *m* 31 May 1963, Jennifer, da of (Robert) Prosper (Gedye) Buddicom (d 1968); 2 s (Daniel b 1966, Benedict 1969), 1 da (Abigail b 1964); *Career* barr Middle Temple 1961 (Harmsworth Scholarship), master of the bench, Hon Soc of Middle Temple 1980-; rec 1979-84, first jr tres counsel Common Law 1979-84, Judge of the High Court of Justice Queen's Bench Div 1984-; kt 1984; *Recreations* golf, skiing, theatre, reading; *Clubs* Denham GC; *Style*— The Hon Mr Justice Simon Brown; Royal Courts of Justice, Strand, London WC2

BROWN, Sir (Frederick Herbert) Stanley; CBE (1959); s of Clement and Annie S Brown, of Birmingham; *b* 9 Dec 1910; *Educ* King Edward's Sch Birmingham, Birmingham Univ; *m* 1937, Marjorie Nancy (d 1989), da of William Astell Brown, of Sutton Coldfield; 2 da; *Career* chm Central Electricity Generating Bd 1965-72; FEng, FIEE, FIMechE; kt 1967; *Style*— Sir Stanley Brown, CBE; Cobbler's Hill, Compton Abdale, Glos GL54 4DR (☎ Withington (024 289) 233)

BROWN, Sir (Arthur James) Stephen; KBE (1967); s of Arthur Mogg Brown, and Ada Kelk, *née* Upton; *b* 15 Feb 1906; *Educ* Taunton, Bristol Univ; *m* 1935, Margaret Alexandra, da of late D L McArthur; 1 s, 1 da; *Career* former dir Fairey Co; chm: Molins Ltd 1971-78, Stone-Platt Industries Ltd 1968-73; dep chm Chloride Gp 1965-73; pres: Engrng Employers Fedn 1964-65, CBI 1966-68; fndr memb Export Cncl for Europe 1960; dir Porvair Ltd 1971-; memb Nat Economic Devpt Cncl 1966-71; *Style*— Sir Stephen Brown, KBE; Cut Hedges, Bolney, Sussex (☎ (044 482) 225)

BROWN, Rt Hon Lord Justice; Stephen Brown; PC (1983); s of Wilfrid Brown (d 1972), of Longdon Green, Staffs, and Nora Elizabeth Brown. Staffs; *b* 3 Oct 1924; *Educ* Malvern, Queens' Coll Cambridge; *m* 1951, Patricia Ann, da of Richard Good, of Tenbury Wells, Worcs; 2 s (twins), 3 da; *Career* served WW II as Lt RNVR; barr Inner Temple 1949; bencher 1974; dep chm Staffs QS 1963-71, QC 1966; recorder W Bromwich 1965-71, recorder and hon recorder 1972-75, High Court judge (Queen's Bench) 1977-83 (Family Div 1975-77), presiding judge Midland and Oxford Circuit 1977-81, former memb Parole Bd England & Wales, Lord Justice of Appeal 1983-, pres Family Div 1988; memb advsy cncl on Penal System 1977; chm Cncl Malvern Coll 1976-; kt 1975; *Recreations* sailing; *Clubs* Garrick, Naval, Birmingham; *Style*— The Rt Hon Lord Justice Brown, QC; 3 King's Bench Walk, Temple, EC4; 78 Hamilton Ave, Harborne, Birmingham B17 8AR

BROWN, Sir Thomas; s of Ephraim Hugh and Elizabeth Brown; *b* 11 Oct 1915; *Educ* Royal Belfast Academical Inst; *m* 2 Sept 1988, Dr Eleanor A Thompson; *Career* slr 1938; chm Eastern Health and Social Services Bd, NI 1973-84; kt 1974; *Style*— Sir Thomas Brown; Westgate, Portaferry, Co Down, Northern Ireland (☎ (024 77) 28309)

BROWN, Dr Thomas Walter Falconer; CBE (1958); s of Walter Falconer Brown, of Tayvallich, Montgomery Terrace, Ayr, and Catherine Edith, *née* McGhie; *b* 10 May 1901; *Educ* Ayr Academy, Glasgow Univ (BSc, DSc) Harvard Univ (SM); *m* 1947, Lucy, da of William Stewart Dickie, OBE; 1 s (Charles), 1 da (Catherine); *Career* dir of Parsons and Marine Engrg Turbine Research and Devpt Assoc 1945-65, which included dir of Marine Engrg (BSRA); ret; *Style*— Dr Thomas Brown, CBE; 12 The Dene, Wylam, Northumberland, NE41 8JP (☎ (06614) 2228)

BROWN, Timothy Colin; s of Peter Brindley Brown, of Isles Court, Ramsbury, Wilts, and Margaret Jean, *née* McIntosh; *b* 20 Sept 1957; *Educ* Eton, RMA Sandhurst; *m* 24 Jan 1987, Lady Vanessa Petronel Pelham, yst da of 7 Earl of Yarborough; *Career* 4/7 Royal Dragoon Guards 1976-82 (A/Capt 1980); dir City & Commercial Communications plc; *Recreations* skiing, shooting, backgammon; *Clubs* Cavalry and Guards', Lansdowne; *Style*— Timothy Brown, Esq; 56 Hugh Street, London SW1V 4ER (☎ 01 630 1194); office, Bell Court House, 11 Blomfield Street, London EC2 (☎ 01 588 6050, fax 01 628 1861, car ☎ 0836 592452, telex 883502 CCCG)

BROWN, Tina (Christina Hamley); da of George H Brown, of San Pedro de Alcantana, Spain; *m* 1981, Harold Evans, *qv*; *Career* former ed The Tatler; ed Vanity Fair 1984-; *Style*— Ms Tina Brown

BROWN, Lady Vanessa Petronel; 3 da of 7 Earl of Yarborough, JP; *b* 21 Sept 1961; *m* 24 Jan 1987, Timothy C Brown, o s of Peter Brown; *Style*— Lady Vanessa Brown

BROWN, (Harold) Vivian Bigley; s of Alec Sidney Brown, of Leeds, and Joyce *née* Bigley; *b* 20 August 1945; *Educ* Leeds GC, St Johns Coll Oxford (BA), St Cross Coll Oxford (BPhil); *m* 25 July 1970, Jean Josephine, da of Sir Eric Blacklock Bowyer, KCB, (d 1963); 2 s (Matthew, b 1973, Oliver, b 1974); *Career* entered Min of Technol 1970, private sec to Permanent Sec DTI 1972-74, commercial sec: Br Embassy Jedda 1975-79, DTI 1979-86; under sec and head of Sci and Technol Assessment Off Cabinet Off 1986; chm Leander Sea Scouts Kingston upon Thames; *Books* co wrote with S M Stern and A Itourani; Islamic Philosophy and The Classical Tradition (1972); *Recreations* cycling, canoeing, piano; *Style*— Vivian Brown, Esq; Whitehall, London SW1 (☎ 01 270 0320)

BROWN, William; CBE (1971); s of Robert Brown, of Ayr; *b* 24 June 1929; *Educ* Ayr Acad, Edinburgh Univ; *m* 1955, Nancy Jennifer, da of Prof George Hunter, of Edmonton, Alberta; 1 s, 3 da; *Career* Scottish TV: London sales mangr 1958 sales dir 1961, dep md 1963, md 1966-, dep chm 1974-; dir: Indep TV Cos' Assoc (chm of cncl 1978-80), Indep TV Pubns Ltd, Radio Clyde Ltd, Independent TV News Ltd; Scottish Opera Theatre Royal Ltd, Scottish Amicable Life Assur Soc; gold medalist Royal TV Soc 1984; *Recreations* golf, gardening, films; *Clubs* Caledonian, Prestwick gol, Royal & Ancient G.C. of St Andrews; *Style*— William Brown, Esq, CBE; Scottish Television plc, Cowcaddens, Glasgow G2 3PR (☎ 041 332 9999, telex 77388)

BROWN, Prof William Arthur; s of Prof Arthur Joseph Brown, of Leeds, and Joan Hannah Margaret Brown; *b* 22 April 1945; *Educ* Leeds GS, Wadham Coll Oxford (BA); *Career* dir Industrial Relations Res Unit of the Economic & Social Res Cncl; prof Univ of Warwick; Montague Burton prof of Industrial Relations Univ of Cambridge 1985-; *Books* Piecework Bargaining (1973), The Changing Contours of British Industrial Relations (1981); *Recreations* gardening, walking; *Style*— Prof William A Brown; Wolfson Coll, Cambridge CB3 9BB (☎ 0223 335900); Faculty of Economics & Politics, Cambridge CB3 9DD (☎ 0223-334236)

BROWN, William Charles Langdon; OBE (1982); s of Charles Leonard Brown, (d 1952), and Kathleen May, *née* Tizzard (b 1988); *b* 9 Sept 1931; *Educ* John Ruskin Sch Croydon, Ashbourne GS Derbyshire; *m* 14 Feb 1959, Nachiko, da of Dr Eiji Sagawa (d 1952), of Tokyo, Japan; 1 s (Carl b 1959), 2 da (Lillian b 1963, Naomi b 1967); *Career* Nat Serv RAF 1949-51; Westminster Bank 1947-54, Standard Chartered Bank (formerly Chartered Bank of India, Aust and China): Tokyo 1954-59, Bangkok 1959-62, Hong Kong 1962-69, Singapore 1969-72, Bangkok 1972-75, area gen mangr Hong Kong 1975-87, sr gen mangr (London) for Asia Pacific Region 1987, exec dir SC plc 1987, md 1988, dep gp chief exec 1988; unofficial memb of legislative cncl of Hong Kong 1980-85; Hon Doctorate in Social Science Chinese Univ Hong Kong 1987; FCIB; *Recreations* mountain walking, skiing, yoga, philately, photography, clasical music; *Clubs* Oriental, RAC; *Style*— William Brown, Esq, OBE; 38 Bishopsgate, London EC2N 4DE (☎ 01 280 7500, fax 01 280 7112); Flat 4, 19 Inverness Terrace, Kensington Gardens, London W2 3TJ; Appleshaw, 11 Central Avenue, Findon Valley, Worthing, Sussex BN14 ODS

BROWN, William Ernest; s of William Brown (d 1941); *b* 9 Dec 1923; *Educ* Christ's Hosp and Grocers' Co Sch; *m* 1950, Catherine, *née* McColgan; 1 s, 1 da; *Career* md E G Cornelius and Co Ltd, dir Cornelius Chemical Co Ltd; *Style*— William Brown Esq; 8 Elm Grove, Hornchurch, Essex

BROWN, William Paterson; s of William Brown, of Cambuslang; *b* 18 Mar 1923; *Educ* Lenzie Acad, Glasgow Univ; *m* 1948, Nancy, da of William Palmer, of Cambuslang; 1 s, 1 da; *Career* dir Thomas Meadows UK Hldgs and subsidiaries, ret 1983; *Recreations* golf, reading; *Clubs* RAF; *Style*— William Brown Esq; 38 Cuckoo Hill Rd, Pinner, Middx (☎ 01 866 8973)

BROWNE; *see*: Gore Browne

BROWNE, Anthony George; s of Aloysious Browne of London, and Frances, *née* Gurney; *b* 18 June 1950; *Educ* Downside, Brasenose Coll Oxford (MA); *m* 15 Nov 1969, Monique Odette, da of Maxime Marnat (d 1965), of Paris; 2 da (Geraldine b 1970, Emily b 1972); *Career* CA 1974; Price Waterhouse: joined 1971, exechequer and audit dept 1980-82, ptnr dept privatisation servs 1983-; tres Wimbledon Ho Res Assoc; FCA 1975; *Books* Guide to Evaluating Policy Effectiveness; *Recreations* sailing, opera, art, literature; *Clubs* Reform, Royal Cruising, Royal Southern YC; *Style*— Anthony Browne, Esq; Caley House, Leopold Rd, London SW19 7JQ (☎ 01 946 8196), Price Waterhouse, Southwark Towers, 32 London Bridge St, London SE1 9SY (☎ 01 407 8989, fax 01 378 0647)

BROWNE, Charles Egerton; s of John Charles David Browne (d 1952), of Isle of Wight, and Emmie Marie, *née* Egerton (d 1922); *b* 15 Jan 1910; *Educ* Heatherley Sch of Art, Herts Coll of Art and Design; *m* 28 May 1941, Violet Mary Ellen (d 1977), da of Francis William James Squire (d 1947), of Luton, Beds; 1 s (Nicholas Egerton b

1949); *Career* aerospace engr; chm The Egerton Gp of Cos 1941-88; sculptor; distinctions incl: hon mention Paris Salon 1969, bronze medal Paris Salon 1970, silver medal Paris Salon 1971, gold medal Paris Salon 1984, diplome d'honneur Galerie Vallombreuse Biarritz, Halliday Prize for Portraiture; works exhibited: Whitbread & Co London, Shire Horse Soc Peterborough, Farmers Club London, Watford Museum, Lucy Kemp-Welch Meml St James' Church Bushey; princ The Frobisher Sch of Art, govr The Heatherley Sch of Art; Freeman City of London, Liveryman Worshipful Co of Gunmakers 1963; MIProdE, CEng, memb Societe des Artistes Francais; *Recreations* fishing, shooting; *Clubs* Fly Fishers; *Style*— Charles Browne, Esq; Haydon Dell, Merry Hill Rd, Bushey, Herts (☎ 01 950 2035); Egerton Fine Art, The Gallery, Haydon Dell Farm, Merry Hill Rd, Bushey, Herts (☎ 01 950 4769)

BROWNE, (John) Colin Clarke; s of Ernest Browne JP (d 1964), of Lisburn, Co Antrim, N Ireland, and Isobel Sarah, *née* McVitie; *b* 25 Oct 1945; *Educ* Wallace HS Lisburn, Trinity Coll Dublin (BA); *m* 3 March 1984, Karen Lesley, da of Ian Barr, of Edinburgh; *Career* BT: dir chms off 1981-85 (PO 1980-81), chief exec Broadband Servs 1985-86, dir corporate relations 1986-; chm Starstream Ltd 1986-; former cncl memb Royal TV Soc, cncl memb ISBA; MIPR; *Recreations* sprot, music, reading; *Clubs* Tugle Hill Hockey; *Style*— Colin Browne, Esq; Wandsworth Bridge Rd, London SW6; British Telecom Centre, 81 Newgate St, London EC1A 7AJ (☎ 01 356 5350, fax 01 356 6630, telex 8811510)

BROWNE, Coral Edith; *née* Browne; da of Leslie Clarence Browne, and Victoria Elizabeth, *née* Bennett; *b* 23 July 1913; *Educ* Claremont Ladies' Coll Melbourne; *m* 1, 1950, Philip Westrope Pearman (d 1964); m 2, 1974, Vincent Price; *Career* actress; *Style*— Miss Coral Browne; 16 Eaton Pl, London SW1

BROWNE, Hon Dominick Geoffrey Thomas; s and h of 4 Baron Oranmore and Browne; *b* 1 July 1929; *m* 25 Oct 1957 (m dis 1974), Sara Margaret, da of late Dr Herbert Wright, of 59 Merrion Sq, Dublin; *Style*— The Hon Dominick Browne

BROWNE, Donald John Woodthorpe; JP (1977); s of Harold Browne; *b* 1 Dec 1924; *Educ* Dulwich, Hertford Coll Oxford; *m* 1965, Dinah, da of Arthur Gurling, MC, of London W1; 1 s, 2 da; *Career* Sub-Lt RNVR; chm Hays Oils & Chemicals and assoc cos 1980-; *Recreations* penal matters, country living; *Clubs* Western, Ulster; *Style*— Donald Browne Esq, JP; Hays Oils & Chemicals Ltd, Redding-Muirhead, Falkirk FK2 9TS (☎ (0324) 712712, telex 779314)

BROWNE, Lady Enid Doreen Grace; da of Hon Evelyn Scudamore-Stanhope (d 1925), and gda of 9 Earl of Chesterfield; *b* 25 Jan 1899; *m* 1926, as his 2 w, Maj Alexander Browne (d 1961); 1 s; raised to the rank of an Earl's da 1938; *Style*— Lady Enid Browne; Marodze-Riversdale Farms, Harare, Zimbabwe

BROWNE, Lady Ulick - Fiona; *née* Glenn; *m* 1962, as his 2 w, Lord Ulick Browne, s of late Lt-Col Lord Alfred Eden Browne, DSO, s of 5 Marquess of Sligo, who was raised to the rank of a Marquess' son (1953) and who d 1980; 1 s, 1 da,; *Style*— Lady Ulick Browne; 32 The Little Boltons, SW10

BROWNE, Hon Garech Domnagh; s of 4 Baron Oranmore and Browne and Oonagh Lady Oranmore and Browne, *née* Guinness; *b* 25 June 1939; *Educ* Castle Park (Dublin), Le Rosey (Switzerland); *m* 1980, Princess Harshad Purna Devi, *née* Jadeja, da of HH Sri Mahendra Sinhji, Maharaja of Morvi (d 1957), and H H Sri Vijaykuverba, Maharani of Morvi, *née* Jhala; *Career* chm: Claddagh Records Ltd, Woodtown Music Publications Ltd; landowner (6,000 acres); *Style*— The Hon Garech Browne; 13 Rue de la Douzaine, Fort George, St Peter Port, Guernsey; Luggala, Rundwood, Co Wicklow, Ireland (☎ 81 81 50); Claddagh Records Ltd, Dame House, Dame St, Dublin 2 (☎ 77 80 34)

BROWNE, Henry Buxton; s of Richard Buxton Browne (d 1922), of Durban, S Africa, and Mary Hill Ryrie (d 1949); kinsman of 5 Baron Denman; *b* 28 Oct 1919; *Educ* Private Sch; *m* 4 April 1953, Enid Dorothy, da of George Cuthbert Jarvis FCA (d 1965), of Petts Wood, Kent; *Career* served 1940-46, RA, RAOC and REME in UK, France and Germany; FICA; *Recreations* golf, genealogical research; *Clubs* Chislehurst Golf; *Style*— Henry Browne, Esq; 1 Moorlands, Wilderness Rd, Chislehurst, Kent BR7 5HB

BROWNE, John Ernest Douglas de la Valette; MP (C) Winchester 1979-; s of Col Ernest Coigny de la Valette Browne, OBE, of Woodside House, Freshford, nr Bath, and late Victoria Mary Eugene, *née* Douglas; *b* 17 Oct 1938; *Educ* Malvern, RMA Sandhurst, Cranfield Inst of Technol (MSc), Harvard Business Sch (MBA); *m* 1965 (m dis 1983), Elizabeth Jeannette Marguerite, *née* Garthwaite; m 2 1986, Elaine Boylen, *née* Schmidt; *Career* served Grenadier Gds, Br Guyana (Bn pilot), Cyprus, BAOR 1959-67; Capt 1963; TA Grenadier Gds (Vol) 1981- Maj 1986; assoc Morgan Stanley & Co NY 1969-72, assoc Pember & Boyle London 1972-74, dir ME ops, Euro Banking Co 1974-78, md Falcon Fin Mgmnt 1978-; dir: The Churchill Clinic 1980-, Worms Investmt Ltd 1981-83, Scan Sat Bdcasring Ltd 1987-; advsr Barclays Bank 1978-83; memb: Westminster City Cncl 1974-78, court Southampton Univ 1979-; govr Malvern Coll 1981-; memb Treasy Select Ctee 1982-87; chm: Cons Backbench Smaller Business Ctee 1984-87, vice-chm: 1983-84; sec Cons Backbench: Finance Ctee 1981-84, Defence Ctee 1982-84; UK del to N Atlantic Assembly 1986-; Liveryman Worshipful Co of Goldsmiths 1982; OStJ; *Recreations* riding, sailing, skiing, shooting, golf; *Clubs* Boodle's, Turf; *Style*— John Browne Esq, MP; House of Commons, London SW1A 0AA

BROWNE, Lady Karen Lavinia; 2 da of Earl of Altamont; *b* 3 July 1964; *Style*— Lady Karen Browne

BROWNE, Lady Lucinda Jane; yst da of Earl of Altamont; *b* 18 May 1969; *Style*— Lady Lucinda Browne

BROWNE, Hon Martin Michael Dominick; s of 4 Baron Oranmore and Browne by his 1 w, Mildred, da of Hon Thomas Egerton, s of 3 Earl of Ellesmere, JP, DL; *b* 27 Oct 1931; *Educ* Eton; *m* 1958, Alison, Margaret, o da of John Bradford 1 s (Shaun), 1 da (Cara); *Career* stockbroker; *Clubs* White's; *Style*— The Hon Martin Browne; Berghane Hall, Castle Camps, Cambridge CB1 6TN (☎ Ashdon 079 984 304)

BROWNE, (Edward) Michael Andrew; QC (1970); yr s of Prof Edward Granville Browne (d 1926), of Cambridge, and Alice Caroline, *née* Blackburne Daniell (d 1925); bro of Rt Hon Sir Patrick Browne, *qv*; *b* 29 Nov 1910; *Educ* Eton, Pembroke Coll Cambridge (MA); *m* 1937, Anna Florence Augusta, da of James Little Luddington (d 1935), of Wallington, King's Lynn; 2 da (Maria, Alice); *Career* served WWII 1939-45, RA Capt, Adjt 82 HAA Regt Gibraltar, GSO III Directorate of Mil Ops War Off; barr Inner Temple 1934, bencher 1964; *Clubs* Athenaeum; *Style*— Michael Browne, Esq, QC; 19 Wallgrave Rd, London SW5 0RF

BROWNE, Lady Moyra Blanche Madeleine; *née* Ponsonby; DBE (1977, OBE 1962); o da of 9 Earl of Bessborough, GCMG, PC (d 1956); *b* 2 Mar 1918; *Educ* privately; *m* 10 Dec 1945, as his 2 w, Sir Denis John Wolko Browne, KCVO, FRCS (d 1967), s of late Sylvester Browne, of Australia; 1 s, 1 da; *Career* SEN 1946; chm hospitality ctee Victoria League 1956-62, vice-chm central cncl Victoria League 1961-65; supt-in-chief St John Ambulance Bde 1970-83 (dep supt-in-chief 1964-70), vice pres: Royal Coll of Nursing 1970-85, nat chm support gps Res into Ageing 1987, govr 1988; DGStJ 1984 (DS+J 1970, CS+J 1968); *Recreations* music, fishing, travel; *Style*— Lady Moyra Browne, DBE; 16 Wilton St, London SW1 (☎ 01 235 1419)

BROWNE, Hon Mrs - Noreen Anne; da of Sean MacSherry, of Co Down; *m* 1963, Hon Tara Browne (d 1966), s of 4 Baron of Oranmore and Browne; 2 s; *Style*— The Hon Mrs Tara Browne; 19 Eaton Row, SW1

BROWNE, Rt Hon Sir Patrick (Reginald Evelyn); OBE (1945), TD (1945), PC (1974); er s of Prof Edward Granville Browne, Arabic and Persian scholar at Cambridge (d 1926, himself s of Sir Benjamin Browne, JP, DL, an engineer & sometime Mayor Newcastle), and Alice Caroline, *née* Blackburne Daniell; bro of Michael Browne, QC, *qv*; *b* 28 May 1907; *Educ* Eton, Pembroke Coll Cambridge (hon fellow 1975-); *m* 1, 1931, Evelyn Sophie Alexandra (d 1966), o da of Sir Charles Walston and sis of Baron Walston; 2 da (*see* Sir Peter Swinnerton-Dyer); m 2, 1977, Lena, da of James Atkinson; *Career* served Army 1939-45, GSOI, Lt Col; barr Inner Temple 1931, bencher 1962, QC 1960, judge of the High Court of Justice, Queen's Bench Div 1965-74, a Lord Justice of Appeal 1974-80; controller Royal Opera House Devpt Land Tst 1981-84; kt 1965; *Clubs* Garrick, Cambridge County; *Style*— The Rt Hon Sir Patrick Browne, OBE, TD; Thriplow Bury, Thriplow, Cambs (☎ Fowlmere (076 382) 234)

BROWNE, Percy Basil; DL (Devon, 1984); s of Capt W P Browne, MC, of Higher Hougton, Blandford, Dorset (d 1970), and M R Hoare (d 1953); *b* 2 May 1923; *Educ* Eton; *m* 1, 1947, Pamela Iwerne (d 1951), da of Lt-Col Harold Exham, DSO, of Iwerne Minster, Dorset (decd); 1 s (Anthony b 1949); m 2, 1953, Jenefer Mary, da of Major Gerald Petherick, of The Mill House, St Cross, Winchester, Hants (decd); 2 s (Benjamin b 1954, Toby b 1955), 1 da (Mary Alice b 1959); *Career* served WW II Italy and NW Europe, (cmmnd Royal Dragoons); MP (C) Torrington Div of Devon 1959-64; dir Aggledore Shipbuilders 1965-72 (former chm); N Devon dist cncllr 1973-79 (vice-chm 1978-79); memb SW Regnl Hosp Bd 1967-70; vice-chm N Devon Hosp Mgmnt Ctee 1967-74; chm: N Devon Meat Ltd 1982-86; Miny of Agric's SW Regnl Panel 1985-; chm West of England Bldg Soc 1986- (vice-chm 1985-86, dir Western Counties Building Soc 1965-85); farmer, rode in Grand Nat 1953; High Sheriff Devon 1978; *Style*— Percy B Browne, Esq, DL; Wheatley House, Dunsford, Exeter (☎ Christow 52037)

BROWNE, Peter Kilmaine; s of Noël Francis Howe Browne (d 1943), and hp of 7 Baron Kilmaine; *b* 1920; *m* 1948, Grace Dorothy Robson, of Nakuru, Kenya; 2 da; *Style*— Peter Browne Esq; Morningside Farm, P O Box 692, Rustenburg, Transvaal

BROWNE, Prof Roger Michael; s of Arthur Leslie Browne (d 1974), of Birmingham, and Phyllis Maud, *née* Baker (d 1942); *b* 19 June 1934; *Educ* Berkhamsted Sch, Univ of Birmingham (BSc, BDS, PhD, DDS); *m* 31 May 1958, Lilah Hilda, da of Isaac Harold Manning (d 1960), of Leek; 1 s (Andrew b 1963), 1 da (Nicola b 1960); *Career* Univ of Birmingham: lectr in dental surgery 1960-64, lectr in dental pathology 1964-67, sr lectr in oral pathology 1966-67, prof 1977-, head of dept of oral pathology 1979-, dir of dental sch 1986-, postgrad advsr in densistry 1977-82; visiting prof Univ of Lagos Nigeria 1969; pres: Br Dental Assoc Hosps Gp 1986-87, Br Soc for Oral Pathology 1985-86, section of odontology Birmingham Med Inst 1975-76; memb City of Birmingham Health Authy; FDS, RCS (England) 1962, FRCPath 1979; *Books* Colour Atlas of Oral Histopathology (with E A Marsland, 1975), A Radiological Atlas of Diseases of the Teeth and Jaws (with H D Edmondson and P G J Rout, 1983); *Recreations* walking, rugby football; *Style*— Prof Roger Browne; Dept of Oral Pathology, Dental School, St Chad's Queensway Birmingham B4 6NN (☎ 021 236 8611)

BROWNE, Lady Sheelyn Felicity; eldest da of Earl of Altamont; *b* 1 June 1963; *Style*— Lady Sheelyn Browne

BROWNE, Sheila Jeanne; CB (1977); da of Edward Elliott Browne; *b* 25 Dec 1924; *Educ* Lady Margaret Hall Oxford, Ecole des Chartes, Paris; *Career* asst lectr Royal Holloway Coll London Univ, tutor and fell St Hilda's Coll Oxford and lectr in French Oxford 1951-61 (hon fellow St Hilda's 1978, Lady Margaret Hall 1978); sr chief inspr DES 1974-83 (formerly staff inspr/chief inspr Secondary Educn, dep sr chief inspr DES 1972-74), principal Newnham Coll Cambridge 1983- (succeeding Mrs J E Floud); Hon DLitt (Warwick) 1981; *Style*— Miss Sheila Browne, CB; Newnham College, Cambridge

BROWNE-CLAYTON, Capt Robert Bruce; s of Lt-Col William Patrick Browne-Clayton (d 1971), of 13 Nutley Rd, Dublin, and Janet Maitland Broce, *née* Jardine; direct decendant of Robert Browne of Browne's Hill, Carlow (d 1677) and of James Bruce, who discovered source of Blue Nile; *b* 25 April 1940; *Educ* Loretto, RMA Sandhurst, Royal Agric Coll Cirencester; *m* 1 March 1969, Jane Evelyn Reine, da of Eric Peter Butler, of Orchard Close, Blagdon, nr Bristol; 1 s (Benedict (Ben) John b 1970), 1 da (Clare Louise b 1973); *Career* Capt Royal Green jackets KRRC, served in Germany, Br Guiana and 1960-68; dir and co sec Economy Car Hire Ltd 1968-71, fin conslt 1971-74; desk offr responsible for agric, fisheries, food, forestry and rural affrs Cons Res Dept 1976-84; dir economic and public affairs The Building Employers Conf; fndr and first sec Nat Agric and Countryside Forum; cncllr London Borough of Greenwich 1978-82; vice chm Greenwich Cons Assoc 1983-84 and 1987-; *Recreations* shooting, fishing, painting, music, reading, tennis, golf; *Clubs* University and Kildare Street; *Style*— Robert Browne-Clayton, Esq; 34 Park Vista, Greenwich, London SE10 9LZ

BROWNE-WILKINSON, Rt Hon Sir Nicolas Christopher Henry Browne-Wilkinson; PC (1983); s of late Canon Arthur R Browne-Wilkinson and Molly Browne-Wilkinson; *b* 30 Mar 1930; *Educ* Lancing, Magdalen Oxford; *m* 1955, Ursula, da of Cedric de Lacy Bacon (d 1987); 3 s, 2 da; QC 1972; judge of Court of Appeal Jersey & Guernsey 1976-77, High Court judge (Chancery) 1977; Lord Justice of Appeal 1983-85; vice-chllr of the Supreme Court 1985; *Recreations* gardening, music; *Clubs* Garrick; *Style*— The Rt Hon Sir Nicolas Browne-Wilkinson; Royal Courts of Justice, The Strand, WC2

BROWNING, (Walter) Geoffrey; s of Lieut Walter Samuel Browning, RNAS, of Highleaden, Mere, Knutsford, Cheshire, and Dorothy Gwendoline, *née* Hill (d 1987); *b*

6 Nov 1938; *Educ* Burnage GS Manchester; *m* 1, 20 June 1964 (m dis 1982), Barbara; 1 s (Matthew b 18 Sept 1967), 2 da (Helen b 11 May 1965, Claire b 22 April 1969), 1 s adopted (Jon b 16 Mar 1967); m 2, 17 Aug 1983, Pauline Ann da of William Wilkinson of Lockgate West Runcorn Cheshire; 2 da (Alexandra b 7 June 1984, Danielle b 9 Sept 1985); *Career* CA, asst gp sr Peat Marwick Mitchell and Co 1961-63 (articled clerk 1955-60), div co sec The Steetly Co Ltd 1963-64, fin dir Syd Abrams Ltd 1964-69, jt md Boalloy Ltd 1969-; underwriting memb Lloyds 1980-; FCA; *Recreations* sailing, golf; *Clubs* Duquesa GC Spain Duquesa Sailing; *Style—* Geoffrey Browning, Esq; Cherry Rise, Lynwood, Hale, Cheshire WA15 ONF (☎ 061 980 5884); Boalloy Ltd, Radnor Park, Congleton, Cheshire CW12 4QA (☎ 0260 275151, fax 0260 279696, telex 669849)

BROWNING, Michael Lovelace; s of Harold Louis Browning (d 1963), of Exmouth; *b* 18 Mar 1937; *Educ* Kelly Coll Tavistock; *m* 1965, Anna Lynne, da of late Lawrence Clifford White, of Sampford Peverell; 3 da; *Career* dir HAT Group plc 1976-89; FCA, FBIM; *Style—* Michael Browning, Esq; Elm Tree Farm, Harts Lane, Hallatrow, Bristol BS18 5EA (☎ (0761) 52218)

BROWNING, (David) Peter James; CBE (1984); s of Frank Browning (d 1950) and Lucie Audrey, *née* Hiscock (d 1986); *b* 29 May 1927; *Educ* Christ's Coll Cambridge (MA), Sorbonne, Strasbourg Univ, Perugia Univ; *m* 1953, Eleanor Berry, da of John Henry Forshaw, CB, MC, (d 1973); 3 s (Paul, Jonathan, Nicholas); *Career* educator; asst dir of educn Cumberland LEA 1962-66, dep chief educn offr Southampton LEA 1966-69, chief educn offr: Southampton 1969-73, Beds 1973-89; memb: Schs Cncl Governing Cncl and 5-13 Steering Ctee 1969-75, cncl Univ of Southampton 1970-73, C of E Bd of Educn Schs Ctee 1970-75, cncl Nat Youth Orch 1972-77, Br Educnl Admin Soc (chm 1974-78, fndr memb cncl of mgmnt), UGC 1974-79, Taylor Ctee of Enquiry into Mgmnt and Govt of Schs 1975-77, governing body Centre for Information on Language Teaching and Res 1975-80, Euro Forum for Educnl Admin (fndr chm 1977-84), Library Advsy Cncl (England) 1978-81, Cambridge Inst of Educn Govrs (vice-chm 1980-89), Univ of Cambridge Faculty Bd of Educn 1983-, Br Sch Technol Cncl of Mgmnt 1984-88, Univ of Lancaster Cncl 1988-; govr: Gordonstoun Sch 1985-, Lakes Sch Windermere 1988-, Charlotte Mason Coll of Higher Educn Ambleside 1988-; conslt Miny of Educn: Sudan 1976, Cyprus 1977, Italy 1981; Sir James Matthews Memorial Lecture (Southampton Univ) 1983; Cavaliere Order of Merit (Republic of Italy) 1985; Offr Order of Palmes Académiques (France); FRSA 1981; *Publications* Julius Caesar for German Students (ed 1957), Macbeth for German Students (ed 1959); *Recreations* music, travel, gardening; *Style—* Peter Browning Esq, CBE; Park Fell, Skelwith, nr Ambleside, Cumbria LA22 9NP (☎ 05394 33978)

BROWNING, Ralph Morgan; s of Lt-Col John Morgan Browning (d 1974), of Coventry, Warwicks, and Anne, *née* Chalker (d 1971); *b* 9 August 1925; *Educ* Cheltenham, The Queen's Coll Oxford (MA); *m* 6 Dec 1950, Mary Louise, da of Capt Martinelle McLachlin (d 1925), of St Thomas, Ontario, Canada; *Career* Lt 1/7 Rajput IA 1945-47; mktg mangr The Procter and Gamble Co (UK, France, Italy, USA) 1950-66, mktg dir Reynolds Tobacco Co (Europe and ME) 1967-70, dir L'Oreal (UK) 1970-75, jt md Remy and Asociés (with responsibility for Europe, Canada, S America, Africa and ME) 1976-; memb Chelsea Cons Assoc; Freeman Worshipful Co of Distillers 1987; *Recreations* fishing, stalking, tennis; *Clubs* Turf, Hurlingham, Carlton, Oxford & Cambridge; *Style—* Ralph M Browning, Esq; Rémy Europe & Atlantic, 14 Curzon St, London W1Y 7FH (☎ 01 499 8701, fax 409 2988, telex 262902)

BROWNJOHN, John Nevil Maxwell; s of Gen Sir Nevil Charles Dowell Brownjohn (d 1973), and Isabelle, *née* White (d 1984); *b* 11 April 1929; *Educ* Sherborne, Lincoln Coll Oxford (MA); *m* 19 Nov 1968, Jacqueline Sally; 1 s (Jonathan b 1971), 1 da (Emma b 1969); *Career* cmmnd Somersetshire LI 1948, served Royal W African Frontier Force 1948-49; chm exec ctee Translators Assoc Soc of Authors 1976; Schlegel-Tieck Special Award 1979; US PEN Goethe-House Prize 1981; *literary works*: The Night of the Generals (1962), Memories of Teilhard de Chardin (1964), Klemperer Recollections (1964), Brothers in Arms (1965), Goya (1965), Rodin (1967), The Interpreter (1967), Alexander the Great (1968), The Poisoned Stream (1969), The Human Animal (1971), Hero in the Tower (1972), Strength Through Joy (1973), Madam Kitty (1973), A Time for Truth (1974), The Boat (1974), A Direct Flight to Allah (1975), The Manipulation Game (1976), The Night of the Long Knives (1976), The Hittites (1977), Willy Brandt Memoirs (1978), Canaris (1979), Life with the Enemy (1979), A German Love Story (1980), Richard Wagner (1983), The Middle Kingdom (1983), Solo Run (1984), Momo (1985), The Last Spring in Paris (1985), Invisible Walls (1986), Mirror in the Mirror (1986), Assassin (1987), The Battle of Wagram (1988), Daddy (1989), The Marquis of Bolibar (1989), and some fifty other titles; *screen credits*: Tess (in collaboration with Roman Polanski and Gérard Brach 1980), The Boat (1981), Pirates (1986), The Name of the Rose (1986); *Recreations* music; *Style—* John Brownjohn, Esq; The Vine House, Nether Compton, Sherborne, Dorset DT9 4QA (☎ 0935 814553, telex 46172 CONTEC G, fax 0963 34246)

BROWNLIE, Alistair Rutherford; OBE (1987); s of James Rutherford Brownlie (d 1966), of Edinburgh, and Muriel, *née* Dickson (d 1971); ancestors were dependents of the Dukes of Hamilton and Brandon; *b* 5 April 1924; *Educ* George Watson's Coll, Edinburgh Univ (MA, LLB, Dip Admin Law); *m* 20 June 1970, Martha Barron Mounsey, da of Thomas Mounsey (d 1964); *Career* served WW II as Bombardier RA and radio operator with 658 Sqdn RAF in Europe and India; slr in private practice; memb Lord Merthyr's Ctee of House of Lords on the Bastardy (Blood Tests) Bill and thereafter of Lord Amulree's Ctee, memb of Cncl of Law Soc of Scotland 1966-78, slr for the poor in High Ct (immediately prior to introduction of Criminal Legal Aid in Scotland), served Legal Aid Central Ctee 1970-86; fndr memb and sometime pres Forensic Science Soc (silver medal 1977); lectr and author on legal aspects of Forensic Science; co-author Drink Drugs and Driving; elder N Morningside United Church, Edinburgh; sec Soc of Solicitors, Supreme Courts of Scotland etc; *Recreations* the spade, the saw and the pen; *Style—* Alistair R Brownlie, Esq, OBE; Cherrytrees, 8 Braid Mount, Edinburgh EH10 6JP (☎ 031 447 4255); 2 Abercromby Place, Edinburgh EH3 6JZ (☎ 031 556 4116)

BROWNLIE, Prof Ian; QC (1979); s of John Nason Brownlie (d 1952), and Amy Isabella, *née* Atherton (d 1975); *b* 19 Sept 1932; *Educ* Alsop HS Liverpool, Oxford (MA, DPhil DCL); *m* 1, 1957, Jocelyn Gale; 1 s, 2 da; m 2, 1978, Christine Apperley; *Career* barr 1958, in practice 1967-, bencher Gray's Inn 1968; fell Wadham Coll Oxford 1963-76, prof of Int Law LSE 1976-80, Chichele prof of Public Int Law Oxford 1980-; fell All Souls Coll Oxford 1980-; FBA 1979; various works on public int law; co-ed, British Year Book of International Law, dir of studies, Int Law Assoc; *Style—* Prof Ian Brownlie, QC; 43 Fairfax Rd, Chiswick. London W4 1EN (☎ 01 995 3647); 2 Hare Court, Temple London EC4Y 7BM (☎ 01 583 1770); All Souls Coll, Oxford (☎ 0865 279 342)

BROWNLOW, Air Vice-Marshal Bertrand; CB (1982), OBE (1967), AFC (1962); s of Robert John Brownlow and Helen Louise Brownlow; *b* 13 Jan 1929; *Educ* Beaufort Lodge Sch; *m* 1958, Kathleen Shannon; 2 s, 1 da; *Career* joined RAF 1947, defence and air attaché Stockholm 1969-71, CO Experimental Flying (Royal Aircraft Estab) Farnborough 1971-73, dir Flying (research and devpt) MOD 1974-77; Cmdt: Aeroplane and Armament Experimental Estab Boscombe Down 1977-80, RAF Coll Cranwell 1980-82 (AOC; Asst Cmdt Office and Flying Training 1973-74); dir-gen Training RAF 1982-83, ret 1984; joined Marshall of Cambridge (Engineering) Ltd 1984, (exec dir 1987-), awarded Silver Medal of the Royal Aero Club for services to gliding 1984; FRAeS; *Style—* Air Vice-Marshal Bertrand Brownlow, CB, OBE, AFC; 'Woodside', Abbotsley Rd, Croxton, Huntingdon, Cambridgeshire (☎ Croxton (048087) 663)

BROWNLOW, 7 Baron (1776 GB), of Belton; Sir Edward John Peregrine Cust; 10 Bt (1677 E); s of 6 Baron Brownlow (d 1978) by his 1 w, Katherine, da of Brig-Gen Sir David Kinloch, 11 Bt, CB, MVO; *b* 25 Mar 1936; *Educ* Eton; *m* 1964, Shirlie, da of late John Yeomans, of The Manor Farm, Hill Croome, Upton-on-Severn ; 1 s; *Heir* s, Hon Peregrine Edward Quintin Cust b 9 July 1974; *Career* md Harris and Dixon (Underwriting Agencies) Ltd 1976-82, dir Hand-in-Hand Fire and Life Insur Soc (branch of Commercial Union Assurance Co Ltd) 1962-82; High Sheriff of Lincs 1978-79; memb Lloyds; *Clubs* White's, Pratt's; *Style—* The Rt Hon the Lord Brownlow; La Maison des Prés, St Peter, Jersey, CI

BROWNLOW, James Christy; s of Col Guy James Brownlow, DSO, DL (d 1960), of Ballwhite, Portaferry, Co Down, NI, and Elinor Hope Georgina, *née* Scott (d 1978); *b* 12 Dec 1922; *Educ* Eton; *m* 28 July 1951, Susan Honor Rushton, da of James Parkinson Barnes (d 1975), of Springfield, Alderley Edge, Cheshire; 1 s (William James b 1952), 2 da (Elisabeth Susan b 1955, Joanna Sarah b 1957); *Career* 60 Rifles 1941-47 (serv Western Desert, Italy and Greece), Cheshire Yeomanry 1947-53; dir: W M Christy and Sons Ltd 1950-55, Christy and Co 1951-72; High Sheriff Co Down 1971; *Clubs* Army & Navy; *Style—* James Brownlow, Esq; Chelworth Farm House, Crudwell, Nr Malmesbury, Wilts (☎ 066 67 237)

BROWNLOW, James Hilton; CBE (1984), QPM (1978); s of late Ernest Cuthbert Brownlow and Beatrice Annie Elizabeth Brownlow; *b* 19 Oct 1925; *Educ* Worksop Central Sch; *m* 1947, Joyce Key; 2 da; *Career* served WW II, RAF Flt-Sgt 1943-47; slr's clerk 1941-43, police constable Leicester City Police 1947, from police constable to det chief supt with Kent Co Constabulary 1947-69, asst chief constable Hertfordshire Constabulary 1969-75, asst to HM chief insp of Constabulary Home Office 1975-76, dep chief constable Greater Manchester Police 1976-79, chief constable S Yorks Police 1979-82, HM Inspector of Constabulary for NE England 1983-; *Recreations* golf, music, gardening, travel; *Clubs* Sheffield Club; *Style—* James Brownlow, Esq, CBE, QPM

BROWNLOW, Peter; s of Frederick Brownlow, of Leeds, and Margaret Brownlow (d 1985); *b* 4 June 1945; *Educ* Rothwell GS; *m* 1971, da of Douglas Alton, of Leeds; 2 s (Nicholas Simon b 1975, James Mark b 1978); *Career* accountant; fin dir Border Television plc; *Recreations* sports; *Style—* Peter Brownlow; Quarry Bank, Capon Hill, Brampton, Cumbria CA8 1QN; Border Television plc, The Television Centre, Carlilse CA1 3NT (fax 0228 511193)

BROWNLOW, Maj William Stephen; JP (Co Down 1956), DL (Co Down 1961); er s of Col Guy James Brownlow, DSO, DL (d 1960), of Ballywhite, Portaferry, Co Down, and Elinor Hope Georgina (d 1978), 2 da of Col George John Scott, DSO; descended from a jr branch of Lord Lurgan's family (*see* Burke's Irish Family Records 1976); *b* 9 Oct 1921; *Educ* Eton; *m* 11 Jan 1961, Eveleigh Finola Margaret, o da of Lt-Col George William Panter, MBE (d 1946), of Enniskeen, Newcastle, Co Down; 1 s (James George Christy b 20 Sept 1962), 2 da (Camilla Jane b 29 July 1964, Melissa Anne b 8 May 1968); *Career* Maj Rifle Bde 1940-54, (wounded, despatches), psc 1951, Hon Col 4 Bn Royal Irish Rangers TAVR 1973-78; High Sheriff Co Down 1959; memb: Down CC 1969-72, NI Assembly 1973-75; memb Irish Nat Hunt Ctee 1956; master E Down Foxhounds 1959-62; chm: Downpatrick Race Club 1960-, NI region Br Field Sports Soc 1971-; memb Irish Turf Club 1982; *Recreations* field sports; *Clubs* Army and Navy; *Style—* Maj William Brownlow, JP, DL; Ballywhite House, Portaferry, Co Down, N Ireland BT22 1PB (☎ 02477 28325)

BROWNRIGG, Deva; da of Sir Charles William Cayzer, Bt (d 1940), of Kinpurnie Castle, Newtye, Angus, Scotland, and Lady Cayzer OBE (d 1980); *b* 22 Jan 1923; *Educ* Miss Spalding's Queensgate London, Queens Secretarial Coll, WRNS; *m* 20 July 1946, John Studholme, s of late Lt-Cdr John Studholme Brownrigg RN, RTD, DSC; 1 s (Henry John Studholme b 20 May 1961); *Career* 3 Offr WRNS 1943-46, Hove HMS Lizard Staff of C in C Plymouth, Staff of FOLEM Lt Egypt, Staff of C in C Med, Italy and Malta; *Recreations* painting, pottery, gardening; *Clubs* The Lansdowne, Royal Lymington YC, Royal Yachting Assoc, RNSA Island Sailing Cowes; *Style—* Mrs Deva Brownrigg; Badgers Wood, Lymore Lane, Milford-on-Sea, Lymington, Hants SO4 10TX (☎ 42063)

BROWNRIGG, Michael Gawen; s and h of Sir Nicholas Brownrigg, 5 Bt; *b* 11 Oct 1961; *Style—* Michael Brownrigg Esq

BROWNRIGG, Sir Nicholas Gawen; 5 Bt (UK 1816); s of late Gawen Egremont Brownrigg, 2 s of 4 Bt; suc gf, Rear Adm Sir Douglas Egremont Robert Brownrigg, 4 Bt, CB, 1939; *b* 22 Dec 1932; *m* 1, 1959 (m dis 1965), Linda Louise, da of Jonathan B Lovelace, of Beverly Hills, California, USA; 1 s, 1 da; m 2, 1971, Valerie Ann, da of Julia A Arden, of Livonia, Michigan, USA; *Heir* s, Michael Gawen Brownrigg; *Style—* Sir Nicholas Brownrigg, Bt; PO Box 548, Ukiah, Calif 95482, USA

BROWNRIGG, Philip Henry Akerman; CMG (1964), DSO (1945), OBE (1953), TD (1945); s of Charles Edward Brownrigg (d 1942), of Oxford, and Valerie, *née* Akerman (d 1929); *b* 3 June 1911; *Educ* Eton, Magdalen Coll Oxford; *m* 1936, Marguerite Doreen, da of Capt C R Ottley (d 1936); 3 da; *Career* served WW II Reconnaissance Corps (RAC) NW Europe, Lt-Col 1944; journalist 1934-52, ed Sunday Graphic 1952, Anglo American Corpn of South Africa 1953, dir in Rhodesia 1961-63, Zambia 1964-65, Nchanga Consolidated Copper Mines Ltd and Roan Consolidated Mines Ltd 1969-80; pres Zambia Soc 1980-; Insignia of Honour (Zambia) 1981; *Recreations* writing biography of Kenneth Kaunda, golf, sport on TV; *Style—* Philip Brownrigg, Esq, CMG, DSO, OBE, TD; Wheeler's, Checkendon, nr Reading, Berks (☎ Checkendon

0491 680328)

BROWSE, Prof Norman Leslie; s of late Reginald Dederic Browse, BEM, and late Margaret Louise, *née* Gillis; *b* 1 Dec 1931; *Educ* East Ham GS, St Bart's Hosp Med Coll (MB, BS), Bristol Univ Med Sch (MD); *m* 6 May 1957, Jeanne Audrey, da of Lt-Col Victor Richard Menage, RE (d 1952); 1 s (Dominic James b 1962), 1 da (Sarah Lesley b 1960); *Career* Capt RAMC 1957-59; lectr in surgery Westminster Hosp 1962-64, res assoc Harkness Cwlth fell Mayo Clinic 1964-65, prof of surgery St Thomas' Hosp London 1982- (conslt surgn and reader in surgery 1965-72, prof of vascular surgery 1972-82); pres Euro Soc for Cardiovascular Surgery 1982-84; chm: Assoc of Profs of Surgery 1983-87, Specialist Advsy Ctee in Surgery 1985-88, Br Atherscelerosis Discussion Gp 1988-; cncl memb: Assoc of Surgns of GB and Ireland 1985-88, Royal Coll of Surgns 1986-, Marlborough Coll 1989-; hon memb: American Soc for Vascular Surgery, Australian Vascular Soc; pres elect Surgical Res Soc; *Books* Physiology and Pathology of Bed Rest (1964), Symptoms and Signs of Surgical Disease (1978), Reducing Operations for Lymphoedema (1987), Diseases of the Veins (1988); *Recreations* golf, sailing, marine painting; *Clubs* St Jame's; *Style*— Prof Norman Browse; Blaye House, 8 Home Farm Close, Esher, Surrey KT10 9HA; Dept of Surgery, St Thomas' Hospital, London SE1 (☎ 01 928 9292 x 2516)

BROXBOURNE, Baron (Life Peer UK 1983), of Broxbourne, Co Herts; Sir Derek Colclough Walker-Smith; 1 Bt (UK 1960), of Broxbourne, Co Herts, TD, PC (1957), QC (1955); s of late Sir Jonah Walker-Smith; *b* 13 April 1910; *Educ* Rossall, Ch Ch Oxford (BA); *m* 1938, Dorothy, da of Capt Louis John Walpole Etherton, of Rowlands Castle, Hants; 1 s, 2 da; *Heir* (to btcy only) s, John Jonah Walker-Smith; *Career* served WW II, Lt-Col RA (TA); barr Middle Temple 1934, bencher 1963; MP (C): Hertford 1945-55, Hertfordshire East 1955-83; chm: Cons Members (1922) Ctee 1951-55, Cons advsy ctee on Local Govt 1954-55, parly sec to Bd of Trade 1955-56, econ sec to HM Treasury 1956-57, min state Bd of Trade Jan to Sept 1957, min Health 1957-1960; *Clubs* Carlton; *Style*— The Rt Hon the Lord Broxbourne, TD, PC, QC; 25 Cavendish Close, London NW8 (☎ 01 286 1441)

BRUCE; *see*: Cumming-Bruce, Hovell-Thurlow-Cumming-Bruce

BRUCE, Hon Alastair John Lyndhurst; s and h of 4 Baron Aberdare, PC; *b* 2 May 1947; *Educ* Eton, Ch Ch Oxford; *m* 1971, Elizabeth Mary Culbert, da of John F Foulkes; 1 s, 1 da; *Style*— The Hon Alastair Bruce; 16 Beverley Road, London SW13 0LX

BRUCE, Lady Antonia Katherine; da of 11 Earl of Elgin; *b* 30 August 1964; *Educ* North Foreland Lodge, Edinburgh Univ; *Style*— Lady Antonia Bruce

BRUCE, Hon Charles Benjamin; yst s of 4 Baron Aberdare, PC; *b* 29 May 1965; *Educ* Eton; *Career* chartered accountant; *Clubs* Queen's; *Style*— The Hon Charles Bruce

BRUCE, Lord; Charles Edward Bruce; s and h of 11 Earl of Elgin, and Kincardine, Broomhall, Dunfermline KY11 3DU; *b* 19 Oct 1961; *Educ* Eton, St Andrew's Univ (MA); *Career* page of honour to HM Queen Elizabeth, The Queen Mother 1975-77; *Style*— Lord Bruce

BRUCE, Hon (Edward) David; yst s of 10 Earl of Elgin (d 1968); *b* 29 Feb 1936; *Educ* Eton, Balliol Oxford; *m* 1960, Sara Elizabeth Wallop, yr da of Capt Newton James Wallop William-Powlett, DSC, RN, of Cadhay, Ottery St Mary, Devon; 1 s, 1 da; *Career* formerly Lt Intelligence Corps; *Style*— The Hon Edward Bruce; Blairhill, Rumbling Bridge, Kinross

BRUCE, David Ian Rehbinder; s of Ian Stuart Rae Bruce, MC (d 1967), and Reinhildt Hilda Henriette Reinholdtsdotter, *née* Baroness Rehbinder; *b* 16 August 1946; *Educ* Eton, Oriel Coll Oxford (MA); *m* 4 Dec 1976, Anne Margaret Turquand, da of Col David Frank Turquand Colbeck, OBE; 2 s (Edward b 1984, Ian (twin) b 1984); *Career* CA; Peat Marwick Mitchell & Co 1968-72; Cazenove & Co: investmt analyst 1972-79, conslt Ctee to Review the Functioning of Fin Inst 1977-79; Royal Dutch/Shell Gp: asst tres advsr Shell Int Petroleum Co Ltd 1979-80, mangr fin planning Shell Canada Ltd 1980-83, tres & controller Shell UK Ltd 1983-86; exec dir fin and admin The Int Stock Exchange 1986-; The Hundred Gp, memb 1982 and tech ctees of the Assoc of Corporate Treasurers 1988-; Freeman City of London 1977, Liveryman Worshipful Co of Merchant Taylors 1980; FCA, ASIA, FCT; *Recreations* shooting, fishing; *Clubs* Turf, Pratt's, City of London, White's; *Style*— David Bruce, Esq; The International Stock Exchange, London EC2N 1HP (☎ 01 588 2355, fax 01 628 1055, telex 886 557)

BRUCE, Hon George John Done; yr s of 11 Baron Balfour of Burleigh (d 1967), and Violet Dorothy Done; *b* 28 Mar 1930; *Educ* Westminster, Byam Shaw Sch of Drawing and Painting; *Career* vice-pres RSPP 1984 (memb 1959-); cmmnd works include: three portraits of Archbishop Ramsey for the Church of England, Baron Lane as Lord Chief Justice, speaker George Thomas for the House of Commons, Baron Butler of Saffron Walden for Trinity Coll Cambridge; Sir Alan Cottrell vice chllr Cambridge; *Recreations* windsurfing, skiing, hang gliding; *Clubs* Athenaeum; *Style*— The Hon George Bruce; 6 Pembroke Walk, London W8 6PQ (☎ (01) 937 1493)

BRUCE, Lady Georgiana Mary; da of 11 Earl of Elgin; *b* 4 June 1960; *Educ* North Foreland Lodge; *Style*— Lady Georgiana Bruce

BRUCE, Hon Henry Adam Francis; s of 4 Baron Aberdare, PC, DL; *b* 5 Feb 1962; *Educ* Eton, Trinity Coll Oxford; *Career* slr 1988; esquire Order of St John 1982; *Clubs* Royal Tennis Ct, Hampton Ct, Lansdowne; *Style*— The Hon Henry Bruce; 23 Campana Rd, London SW6 4AT

BRUCE, Sir Hervey James Hugh; 7 Bt (UK 1804); s of Sir Hervey John William Bruce, 6 Bt (d 1971); *b* 3 Sept 1952; *Educ* Eton, Mons OCS; *m* 1979, Charlotte Sara Jane, da of John Temple Gore (s of late Capt Christopher Gore and Lady Barbara, da of 16 Earl of Eglinton); 1 s (Hervey Hamis Peter Bruce b 1984), 1 da (Laura Crista b 1984); *Career* Maj Grenadier Gds; *Recreations* Tapestry, polo; *Clubs* Cavalry and Guards; *Style*— Sir Hervey Bruce, Bt

BRUCE, Ian Cameron; MP South Dorset (1987-); s of Henry Bruce (d 1970), and (Ellen) Flora, *née* Bingham of "Cobblers", Kirby le Soken, Frinton, Essex; *b* 14 Mar 1947; *Educ* Chelmsford Tech HS, Bradford Univ, Mid-Essex Tech Coll (MInst Mgmnt Servs); *m* 6 Sept 1969, Hazel, da of Edward Sidney Roberts (d 1981); 1 s (James b 1974), 3 da (Kathleen b 1975, Maxine b 1977, Tasmin b 1978); *Career* apprentice Marconi; work study engnr: Sainsbury's, Pye & Marconi; work study mangr: Pye; factory mgnr: Pye, E.S.I., Sinclair, md Ian Bruce Associates Ltd - Employment & Management Consultancy, formerly md BOS Recruitment Gp; contested Burnley (C) 1984, euro-candidate 1984 for Yorkshire West; chm Cons Candidates Assoc 1986-87; *Recreations* badminton, sailing, hill walking, scouting, camping; *Style*— Ian c Bruce, Esq, MP; 14 Preston Road, Weymouth, Dorset DT3 6PZ (☎ 0305 833320); House of Commons, London SW1A 0AA (☎ 01 219 5086)

BRUCE, Capt Ian Norton Eyre; s of Lt Col Eyre Bruce, MC (d 1961), of Norton-Sub-Hamdon, Somerset, and Nona Elland *née* Norton (d 1944); *b* 28 Feb 1928; *Educ* Wellington, RMA Sandhurst; *m* 10 July 1959, Elizabeth Mary, da of JD Lyon-Smith (d 1986), of Inkberrow, Worcestershire; 2 s (Andrew b 1961, Rupert b 1963); *Career* 11 Hussars (PAO) 1948-58, served BAOR, Malaya and UK, ADC to HE The Govr Gen of NZ 1953-55; exec J Walter Thompson Co Ltd 1958-59 (dir 1969-79); chm: Lexington Int PR Ltd 1974-81 (md 1969-74), JWT Recruitment Advtg Ltd 1977-81; dir J Walter Thompson Gp Ltd 1974-81, PR Conslts Assoc 1970-80; regnl dir The British Horse Soc 1982-; MIPR 1969, MIPA 1974; *Recreations* painting, field sports, photography; *Clubs* Cavalry and Guards; *Style*— Capt Ian Bruce; Netherwood House, Dumfries DG1 4TY (☎ 0387 53 090)

BRUCE, Ian Waugh; s of Thomas Waugh Bruce (d 1980), and Una Nellie, *née* Eagle (d 1987); *b* 21 April 1945; *Educ* King Edward VI Sch Southampton, Central HS Arizona, Univ of Birmingham (BA); *m* 19 June 1971, Anthea Christine (Tina), da of Dr P R Rowland, of London; 1 s (William Waugh (Tom) b 18 May 1967), 1 da (Hannah b 20 Dec 1970); *Career* apprentice chem engr Courtaulds 1964-65, mktg trainee then mangr Unilever 1968-70; chm Coventry Int Centre 1964, memb Arts Cncl of GB (art panel, art film ctee, new activities ctee) 1967-71, Sir Raymond Priestley Expeditionary Award Birmingham Univ 1968, conslt UN div of social affairs 1970-72, appeals and PR offr then asst dir Age Concern England 1970-74, spokesman Artists Now 1973-77, dir Nat Volunteer Centre 1975-81, Nat Good Neighbour Campaign 1977-79; memb: exec ctee Nat Cncl for Voluntary Orgns 1978-81, cncl Ret Execs Action Clearing House 1978-83; sec volunteurope Brussels 1979-81, advsr BBC Community Progs Unit 1979-81, memb advsy cncl Centre for Policies on Ageing 1979-83, controller of secretariat then asst chief exec Borough of Hammersmith and Fulham 1981-83, memb Educn Advsy Cncl IBA 1981-83; dir gen RNIB 1983-; memb steering ctee Disability Alliance 1985-, exec ctee Age Concern England 1986-, Nat Advsy Cncl on Employment of Disabled People 1987-; memb ICA, MBIM 1975, FBIM 1981; *Books* Public Relations and the Social Services (1972), Patronage of the Creative artist (jtly 1974, 2 edn 1975); papers on: visual handicap, voluntary and community work, old people, contemporary art and mktg; *Recreations* The arts, the countryside; *Style*— Ian Bruce; 54 Mall Road, London W6

BRUCE, Hon James Henry Morys; s of 4 Baron Aberdare; *b* 28 Dec 1948; *Educ* Eton; *m* 1977, Grace, da of Allen Jao Wu; 1 da; *Style*— The Hon James Bruce; 99 Eaton Terrace, SW1 (☎ 01 730 6873)

BRUCE, Hon James Michael Edward; JP (Perthshire 1962); 2 s of 10 Earl of Elgin and 14 of Kincardine (d 1968); *b* 26 August 1927; *Educ* Eton, RMC, RAC Cirencester; *m* 1, 1950, Hon (Margaret) Jean Dagbjørt Coats, da of 2 Baron Glentanar, KBE (d 1971); 2 s (and 1 s decd), 1 da; m 2, 1975, Morven-Anne, da of Alistair Macdonald; 2 s, 2 da; *Career* served Scots Gds; chm: SWOAC Hldgs Ltd, Scottish Woodlands Ltd, Flintshire Woodlands Ltd; memb Home Grown Timber Advsy Ctee, vice pres Scottish Opera, chm RSA in Scotland; FRSA, FInstD; *Clubs* New (Edinburgh), Pratts; *Style*— The Hon James Bruce, JP; Dron House, Balmanno, by Perth PH2 9HG (☎ 073881 2786)

BRUCE, Hon Katherine Gordon; *née* Bruce; da of late 7 Lord Balfour of Burleigh; *b* 27 Nov 1922; *Educ* Oxford; *m* 1946 (m dis 1961), Thomas Riviere Bland, MC; 1 s, 2 da; reverted by deed poll 1975 to surname of Bruce; *Style*— The Hon Katherine Bruce; 25 Kew Green, Kew, Richmond, Surrey TW9 3AA

BRUCE, Malcolm Gray; MP (Lib) Gordon 1983-; s of David Stewart Bruce of White Wold, Mere Lane, Heswall, Wirral and Kathleen Elmslie, *née* Delf; *b* 17 Nov 1944; *Educ* Wrekin Coll Shropshire, St Andrews and Strathclyde Univs (MA, MSc); *m* 1969, Veronica Jane, da of Henry Coxon Wilson, of West Kirby, Wirral; 1 s (Alexander b 1974), 1 da (Caroline b 1976); *Career* contested (Lib): North Angus and Mearns Oct 1974, West Aberdeenshire 1979; rector of Univ of Dundee 1986-89; *Clubs* National Liberal; *Style*— Malcolm Bruce, Esq, MP; House of Commons, London SW1

BRUCE, Hon Mrs Victor; Margaret Charlotte; da of Alfred Ernest Beechey, of Hilgay, Downham Market, Norfolk; *m* 1941, as his 2 w, Hon Victor Austin (d 1978), yst s of Col 2 Baron Aberdare (d 1929); 1 s, 2 da; *Style*— The Hon Mrs Victor Bruce; Cranmore, 1 Frog Grove Lane, Wood Street Village, Guildford, Surrey

BRUCE, Lady Martha Veronica; OBE (1958), TD, DL (Co of Fife) 1987; da of late 10 Earl of Elgin and (14 of) Kincardine, KT, CMG, TD, CD, and Hon Dame Katherine Cochrane, DBE, da of late 1 Baron Cochrane of Cults, and Lady Gertrude Boyle, OBE, da of 6 Earl of Glasgow; *b* 7 Nov 1921; *Educ* Downham; *Career* Lt-Col WRAC (TA), CWRAC 51 Highland Div (TA); lady-in-waiting to HRH the late Princess Royal Jan to March 1965; govr: Greenock Prison 1969-75 (asst govr 1967-69), HM Instn Cornton Vale 1975-83; *Recreations* gardening, hill walking; *Style*— Lady Martha Bruce, OBE, TD, DL; Gardener's Cottage, The Old Orchard, Limekilns, Dunfermline KY11 3HS

BRUCE, Hon Mrs Bernard; Mary Patricia Macdonald; *m* as his 3 w, Hon Bernard Bruce (d 1983), s of 9 Earl of Elgin and Kincardine; *Style*— The Hon Mrs Bernard Bruce; Cauldhame, Sheriffmuir, Perths

BRUCE, Hon Michael Gordon; s of Baron Bruce of Donington (Life Peer); *b* 1952; *Style*— The Hon Michael Bruce; c/o 24-27 Thayer St, London W1

BRUCE, Sir (Francis) Michael Ian; 12 Bt (NS 1628)· s of Sir Michael William Selby Bruce, 11 Bt (d 1957); discontinued use of Christian name Francis; *b* 3 April 1926; *m* 1, 1947 (m dis 1957), Barbara Stevens, da of Francis J Lynch; 2 s; m 2, 1961 (m dis 1963), Frances Keegan; m 3, 1966 (m dis 1976), Marilyn Anne, da of Carter Mullaly; *Heir* s, Michael Ian Richard Bruce; *Career* US Marine Corps 1943-46, memb Sqdn A 7 Regt NY 1948 (ret); Master's Ticket 1968; pres: Newport Sailing Club and Academy of Sail 1977-, American Maritime Co 1980-; *Clubs* Balboa Bay, Vikings of Orange (both NewportBeach); *Style*— Sir Michael Bruce, Bt; 106 Via Antibes, Lido Isle, Newport Beach, Calif 92663, USA; Newport Sailing Club and Academy of Sail, 3432 Via Oporto, Suite 204, Newport Beach, Calif 92663, USA (☎ (714) 675 7100)

BRUCE, Michael Ian Richard; s (by 1 m) and h of Sir (Francis) Michael Bruce, 12 Bt; *b* 10 Dec 1950; *Style*— Michael Bruce Esq

BRUCE, Michael Jonathan; s of Oliver Bruce (d 1954), and Helen Marjorie, *née* King-Stephens; *b* 22 Mar 1920; *Educ* Sherborne Sch Dorset; *m* 26 April 1942, Joyce Irene, da of George John Pepper (d 1984); 2 s (Colin b 1948, Timothy b 1951); *Career*

WWII Gunner RA 1940, cmmnd 2 Lt 1941, Lt 1943, invalided out 1944; admitted slr 1946, joined a family firm 1949, sole proprieter thereof 1951, amalgamated with Halsey Lightly London 1985, conslt 1987-; memb Royal Br Legion Droxford Hants; memb Law Soc; *Recreations* jazz music, collection of nostalgia, theatre, railways; *Style—* Michael Bruce, Esq; Flat 11, 41 Craven Hill Gardens, London W2 3EA; office: 10 Carteret St, Queen Annes Gate, London SW1 (☎ 01 222 8844, fax 01 222 4123)

BRUCE, Col (Robert) Nigel Beresford Dalrymple; CBE (1972, OBE 1946), TD (and Clasp 1946); s of Maj Robert Nigel Dunlop Bruce (d 1921), of Hampstead, and Adelaide Frances, *née* Firth (d 1921); *b* 21 May 1907; *Educ* Harrow, Magdalen Coll Oxford (BA, BSc); *m* 1945, Elizabeth Brogden, da of John Gage Moore; 2 s (Patrick, Kenneth, twins), 2 da (Jane, Susan); *Career* 2 Lieut The Rangers (KRRC) TA 1931,WWII Maj 1939, Lt Col 1942 cmdg 9 KRRC, Greece 1941, Western Desert 1941-42, dir of materials MEF GHQ Cairo Middle East Supply Centre, Col 1942-45; staff controller Gas Light & Coke Co 1945-49 (res chem 1929-35, asst to gen mangr 1936-39), dep chm N Thames Gas Bd 1956-60; (staff controller 1949-56); chm: SE Gas Bd 1960-72, Cncl Engrg Inst 1968-78; pres: Inst Gas Engrgs 1968, sec Tennis and Rackets Assoc 1974-81; govr Westminster Coll 1946-70 (chm of Governing Body 1957-70); CEng;; *Recreations* walking, golf; *Clubs* Queen's; *Style—* Nigel Bruce Esq, CBE, TD; Fairway, 57 Woodland Grove, Weybridge, Surrey

BRUCE, Robert Charles; s of Maj James Charles, MC, of Salisbury, and Enid Lilian, *née* Brown; *b* 5 May 1948; *Educ* Belmont House, Solihull Sch, City of London Coll (BSc); *Career* trainee accountant Edward Moore and Sons 1971-75, ed Accountancy Age 1981- (staff writer and news ed 1976-81); memb: Indust Soc Employee Involvement Working Pty, Indust Achievement Award Judging Panel; *Books* Winners - how small businesses achieve excellence (1986); *Recreations* cricket, buying books; *Clubs* Surrey CC, Ronnie Scotts; *Style—* Robert Bruce, Esq; 87 Marylands Road, London W9 2DS (☎ 286 0211); Accountancy Age, 32-34 Broadwick Street, London W1A 2HG (☎ 439 4242, fax 437 7001)

BRUCE, Robert Peel (Alister); AFC (1943); s of Col Kenneth Hope Bruce, DSO (d 1968) and Lorna, *née* Burn-Murdoch (d 1948), of Trevereux Hill, Limpsfield; *b* 27 August 1915; *Educ* Eton; *m* 1941, Monica, da of R H A Jeff (lost at sea 1941), of Kuala Lumpur; 3 da (Claudia, Linda, Claire); *Career* WWII RAF Trg Cmd, 2 TAF, served Canada, Europe and USA; dir: Practical Investmt Co plc 1953-, London & St Lawrence Investmts plc 1954-, Pennant Properties plc 1961-, Tst of Property Shares plc 1980-; FCA; *Recreations* tennis, golf, shooting, fishing; *Clubs* Army & Navy; *Style—* Alister Bruce, Esq, AFC; Cinderhill, Chailey, E Sussex (☎ 0825 72 2603; office: 01 407 8000)

BRUCE, Ronald Cecil Juckes; s of late Sir Hervey Bruce, 5 Bt; hp of n, Sir Hervey Bruce, 7 Bt; *b* 22 August 1921; *m* 22 Aug 1960, Jean, da of Lewis James William Murfitt; 1 s; *Style—* Ronald Bruce Esq; 24 Fairfax Rd, Teddington, Middx

BRUCE, William Henry; s of William Bruce, of Grangewood, Ellon; *b* 17 Sept 1933; *Educ* Ellon Acad; *m* 1957, Margaret, da of Albert Wyness; 1 s, 2 da; *Career* dep chm Barratt Devpts, chm Barratt Devpts (Scotland) Ltd; *Recreations* riding, golf, badminton, shooting; *Clubs* Roy Aberdeen Golf; *Style—* William Bruce Esq; Logie House, Ellon, Aberdeenshire (☎ 0358 20531)

BRUCE LOCKHART, John Macgregor; CB (1960), CMG (1951), OBE (1944); s of John Harold Bruce Lockhart (d 1956; headmaster Sedbergh Sch, Yorkshire), and Mona Alwine, *née* Brougham (d 1980); *b* 9 May 1914; *Educ* Rugby, St Andrews Univ (MA); *m* 1939, Margaret Evelyn, da of Rt Rev Bishop Campbell Hone DD, (d 1967; Bishop of Wakefield 1938-45); 2 s (James, Alexander), 1 da (Sarah); *Career* TA commd Seaforth Highlanders, served UK, ME, Italy; master Rugby Sch 1937-39, Lt-Col 1944; HM Foreign Service 1945-65, served Paris, Germany, Washington and FO; dir staff personnel Courtaulds 1966-71, advsr Post Exp Prog City Univ 1971-80, chm business educn cncl 1974-80, visiting fellow St Andrew Univ 1981, Rand Afrikaans U 1983; *Recreations* golf, real tennis, fishing; *Clubs* Reform; *Style—* John Bruce Lockhart, Esq, CB, CMG, OBE; 37 Fair Meadow, Rye, Sussex, (☎ Rye 0797 223410)

BRUCE LOCKHART, Logie; s of John Harold Bruce Lockhart (d 1956), of Drum Manor, Bemersyde, and Mona Alwine, *née* Brougham (d 1981); *b* 12 Oct 1921; *Educ* Sedbergh, St John's Coll Cambridge (MA); *m* 6 Oct 1944, Josephine, da of Reginald Colville Agnew (d 1970), of Boscombe, Hants; 2 s ((Rhuraidh Agnew b 1949, Duncan Roderick McGregor b 1961), 3 da (Jennifer Morag b 1945, Kirsty Amanda b 1953, d 1960, Fiona Jacqueline (Mrs Drye) b 1957); *Career* WWII serv: RMC Sandhurst 1941, Lt 9 Sherwood Foresters 1942-43, 2 Household Cav 1944 (invasion NW Europe); asst master Tonbridge Sch 1948-55, headmaster Gresham's Sch 1955-82; former chm HMC Eastern Div; memb: RAF Educn Ctee, Int Educnl Sub ctee; played: rugby football for Scotland 1948, 1950 and 1953, squash Cambridge; *Books* Pleasures of Fishing (1981), Tribute to a Norfolk Naturalist (1987); *Recreations* writing, painting, fishing, sport, France; *Clubs* East India, Public Schools; *Style—* Logie Bruce Lockhart, Esq; Church Farm House, Lower Bodham, Nr Holt, Norfolk NR25 6PS (☎ 0263/ 712137)

BRUCE LOCKHART, Robin Norman; s of Sir Robert Hamilton Bruce Lockhart, KCMG (d 1970) and the late Jean Haslewood *née* Turner; paternal grandmother descended from King James II of Scotland; *b* 13 April 1920; *Educ* Royal Naval Coll Dartmouth, Pembroke Coll Cambridge (Econ); *m* 1, 1941, Margaret Crookdake; 1 da (Sheila Margaret b 1951); m 2, 1955, Ginette de Noyelle (d 1985); m 3 1987, Eila Owen; *Career* WWII Lt RNVR 1939-46; asst to Br Naval Attache Paris, naval intelligence Admiralty, Flag Lt to C-in Cs: China, Eastern Fleet, Ceylon; staff C in C Plymouth; foreign mangr Financial Times 1946-53; memb London Stock Exchange 1962-; dep chm Central Wagon Co Ltd 1965-69; chm: Moorgill Properties Ltd 1967-72, Chasebrook Ltd 1967-72, 37/38 Adelaide Cres (Hove) Ltd 1983-; author Reilly Ace of Spies (1967-) TV series 1984-85 Halfway to Heaven (1985), Reilly the First Man (1967); *Books* Reilly Ace of Spies (1967-), TV series 1984-85, Halfway to Heaven (1985), Reilly the First Man (1967); *Recreations* salmon fishing, travel; *Clubs* MCC, Royal Scottish Automobile Club; *Style—* Robin Bruce Lockhart, Esq; 37 Adelaide Crescent, Hove, Sussex (☎ 0273 777962; Quand Meme, Rue Rumain Rulland, Collioure, Pyrenees Orientales, France (☎ 68 82 29 14)

BRUCE OF DONINGTON, Baron (Life Peer UK 1974); Donald William Trevor Bruce; s of William Trevor Bruce (d 1934), of Norbury, Surrey; *b* 3 Oct 1912; *Educ* The Grammar School Donington Lincs; *m* 1, 1939 (m dis 1980), Joan Letitia, da of late H C Butcher, of London; 1 s, 2 da (and 1 da decd); m 2, 1981, Cyrena Heard, *née* Shaw; *Career* sits as Lab Peer (oppn spokesman on Trade and Industrial Matters 1983-); served WWII Maj UK and France; chartered accountant 1936-; economist, author; MP (Lab) Portsmouth N 1945-50, PPS to min of Health 1945-50; MEP 1975-79; *Recreations* swimming; *Clubs* Eccentric; *Style—* The Rt Hon the Lord Bruce of Donington; 310/305 Euston Road, London NW1 (☎ 01 388 2456)

BRUCE-GARDNER, Bryan Charles; s of Sir Charles Bruce-Gardner, 1 Bt (d 1960); bro of Sir Douglas Bruce-Gardner, 2 Bt; *b* 4 July 1924; *Educ* Uppingham, Trinity Coll Cambridge (MA); *m* 1952, Rosemary, da of Digby Sowerby, of Kirmington House, Kirmington, Lincs (d 1974); 4 s; *Career* md Patent Shaft Steel Works 1961-81; dir Laird Gp 1963-81; *Recreations* golf; *Style—* Bryan Bruce-Gardner, Esq; Stedefield, Church Lane, Flyford Flavell, Worcester (☎ 038 682 451)

BRUCE-GARDNER, Sir Douglas Bruce; 2 Bt (UK 1945); s of Sir Charles Bruce-Gardner, 1 Bt (d 1960); *b* 27 Jan 1917; *Educ* Uppingham, Trinity Coll Cambridge; *m* 1, 27 July 1940 (m dis 1964), Monica Flumerfelt, o da of late Prof Sir Geoffrey Jefferson, CBE; 1 s, 2 da; m 2, 18 March 1964, Sheila Jane , da of late Roger Stilliard, of Seer Green, Bucks; 1 s, 1 da; *Heir* s, Robert Henry Bruce-Gardner, *qv*; *Career* chm: GKN Steel 1965-67, GKN Rolled and Bright Steel 1968-72, GKN (S Wales), Miles Druce & Co 1974-77; dep chm GKN Gp 1974-77; dir: BHP GKN Hldgs 1977-78, GKN Ltd 1960-82, Iron Trades Employers Insur Assoc, Iron Trades Mutual Insur Co 1977-87; prime warden Blacksmiths' Co 1983-84; *Style—* Sir Douglas Bruce-Gardner, Bt; Stocklands, Lewstone, Ganarew, nr Monmouth (☎ 0600 890 216)

BRUCE-GARDNER, Robert Henry; s & h of Sir Douglas Bruce-Gardner, 2 Bt, by his 1 w, Monica; *b* 10 June 1943; *Educ* Uppingham, Reading Univ; *m* 1979, Veronica Hand-Oxborrow, da of late Rev W E Hand; 1 s (Thomas Edmund Peter b 28 Jan 1982); *Style—* Robert Bruce-Gardner Esq; 6/11 Sinclair Rd, W14 (☎ 01 602 3690)

BRUCE-GARDYNE, Hon Adam George John; yr s of Baron Bruce-Gardyne (Life Peer); *b* 7 Sept 1967; *Educ* Marlborough; *Style—* The Hon Adam Bruce-Gardyne; 13 Kelso Place, London W8

BRUCE-GARDYNE, Baron (Life Peer UK 1983), of Kirkden, District of Angus; John (Jock) Bruce-Gardyne; 2 s of Capt Evan Bruce-Gardyne, 13 Laird of Middleton, DSO, RN, of Middleton, by Arbroath, Angus, and Joan, *née* McLaren; the family has owned land in the Parish of Kirkden since before 1306; *b* 12 April 1930; *Educ* Winchester, Magdalen Coll Oxford (BA); *m* 1959, Sarah Louisa Mary, da of Cdr Sir John Francis Whitaker Maitland, RN, of Harrington Hall, Spilsby, Lincs; 2 s, 1 da; *Career* Lt Royal Dragoons 1948-50; writer and journalist HM Foreign Service 1953-56, Paris correspondent Financial Times 1957-60, foreign editor Statist 1961-64, former features editor The Spectator, columnist Sunday Telegraph 1979-81, editorial writer Daily Telegraph 1977-81; MP (C) S Angus 1964-74, Knutsford 1979-83; PPS to sec of state Scotland 1970-72, vice-chm Cons Parly Finance Ctee 1972-74, and 1979-80; min of state Treasury 1981, economic sec 1981-83; dir: NEI Inter, Central Tstee Savings Bank 1983-86; TSB England & Wales 1986-, TSB Gp plc 1986-; London & Northern Gp plc 1984-87; *Books* Whatever Happened to the Quiet Revolution (1974), The Power Game (with Nigel Lawson, 1976); *Recreations* fishing; *Clubs* Garrick, Beefsteak; *Style—* The Rt Hon the Lord Bruce-Gardyne; 13 Kelso Place, London W8 (☎ 01 937 6953); The Old Rectory, Aswardby, Spilsby, Lincs (☎ 0790 52652)

BRUCE-GARDYNE, Hon Thomas Andrew; er s of Baron Bruce-Gardyne (Life Peer); *b* 22 Mar 1962; *Educ* Marlborough; *Style—* The Hon Thomas Bruce-Gardyne; 13 Kelso Place, London W8

BRUCE-JONES, Tom Allan; s of Tom Bruce-Jones (d 1984), of Blairlogie, Stirlingshire, and Rachel Inglis, *née* Dunlop; *b* 28 August 1941; *Educ* Charterhouse, Lincoln Coll Oxford (BA); *m* 1, 1965 (m dis 1980), R Normand; 1 s (Tom b 8 Sept 1968), 1 da (Caroline b 23 Nov 1966); m 2, 6 March 1981, Stina Birgitta, da of Harry Ossian Ahlgren (d 1982), of Helsinki; *Career* dir Price and Pierce (Woodpulp) Ltd 1973-77, vice pres Georgia-Pacific Int Inc 1977-79, md James Jones and Sons Ltd 1987 (jt md 1979-87); dir: Jones and Campbell (Hldgs) Ltd 1988-, Jones Buckie Shipyard Ltd 1988-, Timber Processors plc 1985-, dir Highland Sawmillers plc 1988-; *Recreations* fishing, golf; *Clubs* Hon Co of Edinburgh Golfers; *Style—* Tom Bruce-Jones, Esq; 15 Queen's Gate, Dowanhill St, Glasgow; The Glebe, Killin, Perthshire; James Jones & Sons Ltd, Broomage Ave, Larbert, Stirlingshire (☎ 0324 562 241, fax 0324 558 755)

BRUCE-SMYTHE, Simon Carrington; s of Capt Reginald Oliver Bruce-Smythe (d 1969), and Jane Bruce-Smythe (d 1976); *b* 1 August 1942; *Educ* Downside; *m* 22 Oct 1966, Caroline Ann, da of Derek Godfrey Leach; 2 s (Charles Oliver b 19 Feb 1971, Peter Carrington b 30 Sept 1976); *Career* CA 1966, ptnr i/c Price Waterhouse SE at Redhill (joined 1965); memb ICAEW; *Recreations* horse racing, shooting, fishing; *Style—* Simon Bruce-Smythe, Esq; Bridge Gate, High St, Redhill, Surrey (☎ 0737 766 300)

BRUCE-WHITE, Frank; s of Bernard Frank White (d 1979), and Amy Beatrice, *née* Pitt (d 1970); *b* 16 Jan 1917; *Educ* Cheltenham, Univ of Southampton; *m* 2 Oct 1948, Olive, da of John Russell (d 1958); 2 s (Bernard Roger b 1949, Richard Stuart b 1951); *Career* WWII Capt RE; serv: France, Assam, Burma, Punjab, Maldive Is; articled City Engr Salisbury 1935-38, jr engr Southampton 1938-39 and 1945-46, dist engr Sudan 1947-49, farmer 1949-51, dist engr Tanganyika 1951-53, farmer 1953-; competed motor sports since 1949; CEng, AMICE; *Recreations* motor sport, cricket; *Clubs* BARC Vintage Sports Car, Vintage Motor Cycle, Tanganyika CC, Wilts Queries CC; *Style—* Frank Bruce-White, Esq; Ivy Cottage, Garters Lane, Winterbourne Dauntsey, Salisbury, Wilts SP4 6ER

BRUCK, Steven Mark; s of Herbert Martin Bruck, of London, and Kathe Margot Bruck; *b* 30 Sept 1947; *Educ* Hendon GS, Southampton Univ (BSc), LSE (MSc); *m* 1 July 1971, Mirela, da of Alexander Izsak; 1 s (Jonathan b 1977), 1 da (Tamara b 1974); *Career* articled clerk Chalmers Impey CAs 1969-72, special projects accountant Overseas Containers Ltd 1972-73, gp accountant Halma plc 1973-75, audit mangr Pannell Fitzpatrick 1975-78, ptnr Mercers Bryant 1978-84, ptnr and nat dis Pannell Kerr Forster 1984-; bd memb Belize Square Synagogue; FCA 1972; *Recreations* family, theatre, eating; *Style—* Steven Bruck, Esq; Pannell Kerr Forster, New Garden House, 78 Hatton Garden, London EC1N 8JI (☎ 01 831 7393, fax 01 405 6736, telex 295928)

BRUCKHEIMER, Nathan Norbert; s of Simon Bruckheimer; *b* 6 Nov 1933; *Educ* Alleyne's Stevenage, Holloway Sch London, Edinburgh Univ; *Career* exec dir Jacob Metals Ltd (A Cohen group); *Recreations* theatre, music (particularly opera); *Style—* Nathan Bruckheimer, Esq; Jacob Metals Ltd, Clareville House, 25-27 Oxendon St, London SW1Y 4EL (☎ 930 6953, telex: 918034/23 111)

BRUCKNER, Dr Felix Ernest; s of William Bruckner, of London, and Anna, *née*

Hahn; *b* 18 April 1937; *Educ* London Hosp Med Coll, Univ of London (MB BS); *m* 24 June 1967, Rosalind Dorothy, da of George Edward Farley Bailey, of Herts; 2 s (James b 1974, Thomas b 1976), 1 da (Catherine b 1981); *Career* conslt physician and rheumatologist St George's Hosp London 1970-; FRCP; *Books* numerous papers on rheumatology; *Recreations* chess, music; *Clubs* Royal Society of Medicine; *Style—* Dr Felix Bruckner; 12 Southwood Avenue, Kingston upon Thames, Surrey KT2 7HD (☎ 01 949 3955); 152 Harley St, London W1N 1HH (☎ 01 935 1858)

BRUDENELL, Edmund Crispin Stephen James George; DL (Northants 1977); s of George Brudenell (2 s of Cdr Lord Robert Brudenell-Bruce, RN, 4 s of 3 Marquess of Ailesbury); *b* 24 Oct 1928; *Educ* Harrow, RAC Cirencester; *m* 8 Nov 1955, Hon Marian Cynthia, *née* Manningham-Buller, eldest da of 1 Viscount Dilhorne, PC; twin s (Robert, Thomas b 1956), 1 da (Anna Maria b 1960); *Career* contested (C) Whitehaven 1964; High Sheriff of: Leics 1969, Northants 1987; landowner, farmer; *Recreations* shooting, deer stalking, travelling; *Clubs* Carlton, Pratt's; *Style—* Edmund Brudenell, Esq, DL; 18 Laxford House, Ebury St, London SW1 (☎ 01 730 8715); Deene Park, Corby, Northants (☎ Bulwick (078 085) 223)

BRUDENELL, Hon Mrs; Marian Cynthia; *née* Manningham-Buller; JP; eldest da of 1 Viscount Dilhorne, PC (d 1980); *b* 26 Nov 1934; *m* 8 Nov 1955, Edmund Brudenell, *qv*; 2 s (twin), 1 da; *Style—* The Hon Mrs Brudenell; 18 Laxford House, Ebury Street, London SW1 (☎ 01 730 8715); Deene Park, Corby, Nottinghamshire (☎ Bulwick (078 085) 223)

BRUDENELL, (John) Michael; s of Clement Shenstone Brudnell (d 1964), of Ashford, middx and Elizabeth Marjery *née* James; *b* 13 April 1925; *Educ* Hampton Sch, King's Coll London and King's Coll Hosp London (MB BS); *m* 6 April 1957, Mollie, da of Arthur Herbert Rothwell (d 1974) of Audenshaw, Lancs; 4 s (Timothy b 1958, Jeremy b 1960, Marcus b 1962, Edward b 1967); *Career* Capt RAMC 1950-52, Maj AER field surgical team 1953-63; sr conslt obstetrician and gynaecologist: Bradford Royal Infirmary Yorks 1961-64, King's Coll Hosp London 1964-; conslt gynaecologist King Edward VIII Hosp London 1980-, sr conslt gynaecologist Queen Victoria Hosp 1964-; fell RSM (former pres section of obstetrics and gynaecology); Freeman City of London 1974, Liveryman Worshipful Co of Apothecaries 1967; hon fell Royal Soc of Med Barcelona 1979; FRCS 1956, FRCOG 1973 ; *Recreations* reading, tennis, skiing; *Clubs* Gynaecological Travellers; *Style—* Michael Brudenell, Esq; 31a Sydenham Hill, London SE26 6SH; 73 Harley St London W1N IDE, (☎ 01 670 0743, 01 435 5098, car tel 0732 863 086)

BRUDENELL, Robert Edmund; s of Edmund Crispin Stephen James George Brudenell, of Deene Park, Corby, Northants, and Hon Mrs Brudenell, *née* Manningham-Buller; *b* 12 August 1956; *Educ* Barcote Manor Faringdon Berks, Stanbridge Earls Sch Romsey Hants, RAC Cirencester; *Career* shipbroker Escombe McGrath & Co 1977-79, estate agent: Matthews & Goodman 1979-82, Messrs Daniel Smith 1982-85; estate agent: John D Wood & Co 1985-87, Ashton Steele & Day 1987-; memb Hammersmith & Fulham Cons Assoc; Freeman City of London, Liveryman Worshipful Co of Fishmongers 1981; *Recreations* current affairs, shooting, stalking, fishing, reading; *Clubs* Pratts; *Style—* Robert Brudenell, Esq; 14A Wellesley Mansions, Edith Villas, London W14 9AH (☎ 01 602 4628); 138 Shepherds Bush Rd, London W6 7PB (☎ 01 602 8611, fax 01 603 4772)

BRUDENELL-BRUCE, Lord Charles Adam; s of 7 Marquess of Ailesbury (d 1974), and his 3 w, Jean, *née* Wilson; *b* 23 Mar 1951; *Educ* Eton; *Career* former Lt Royal Hussars, with COI 1976; formerly with Chestertons (until 1987), subsequently a self-employed property advsr; *Recreations* tennis, squash, shooting; *Clubs* Cavalry and Guards'; *Style—* Lord Charles Brudenell-Bruce; Little Lye Hill, Savernake Forest, Marlborough, Wilts (☎ 0672 810261)

BRUDENELL-BRUCE, Lady Kathryn Juliet; da of 8 Marquess of Ailesbury, of Sturmy House, Durley, Nr Marlborough, Wiltshire; *b* 24 August 1965; *Educ* St Mary's Sch Calne, Bristol Univ; *Style—* Lady Kathryn Brudenell-Bruce

BRUDENELL-BRUCE, Lady Louise; da of 8 Marquess of Ailesbury, of Sturmy House, Durley, Nr Marlborough, Wiltshire; *b* 13 July 1964; *Educ* St Mary's Sch Calne; *Style—* Lady Louise Brudenell-Bruce

BRUDENELL-BRUCE, Lady Piers; Nelida Garcia Otero; da of Mariano Garcia Villalba, of Madrid; *m* 1958, as his 2 w, Lord (Chandos Gerald) Piers Brudenell-Bruce (d 1980; 2 s of 7 Marquess of Ailesbury); 2 da; *Style—* Lady Piers Brudenell-Bruce; Cortijo de la Plata, Zahara de los Atunes, Cadiz, Spain

BRUDENELL-BRUCE, Lady Sylvia Davina; da of 8 Marquess of Ailesbury; *b* 19 June 1954; *Educ* Lawnside, Redlynch Park; *Style—* Lady Sylvia Brudenell-Bruce; Sturmy House, Savernake Forest, Marlborough, Wilts

BRUFORD-DAVIES, Maj (Edmund) Robin; s of Brig Edmund Davies; *b* 29 June 1928; *Educ* Radley, Sandhurst; *m* 1969, Sheelagh, da of Dr Norman Patterson; *Career* Royal Ulster Rifles 1948-69; dir Wm Bruford & Sons, Gowland Bros; *Recreations* tennis, skiing; *Clubs* Special Forces; *Style—* Maj Robin Bruford-Davies; 13A Marlborough Road, Exeter, Devon. EX2 4TJ

BRUGES, (Charles) James Long; s of Maj (Charles) Eric Lond Bruges (d 1967), of Brook House, Semington, Trowbridge, Wilts, and Beatrice Rose Campbell, *née* Leighton Stevens; *b* 25 August 1933; *Educ* Sheikh Bagh Kashmir, Kelly Coll Devon, Architectural Assoc London (Dip); *m* 4 June 1971, Anthea, da of (Oliver) Maldwyn Davies, of Bath; 1 s (Benedict b 1961), 3 da (Clare b 1963, Kate b 1972, Beatrice b 1974); *Career* asst architect Trevor Dannatt Assocs 1958-60, resident architect Khartoum Univ 1960-63, assoc Whicheloe Macfarlane 1963-69, ptnr Towning Hill and Ptnrs 1969-73, princ Brugers Tozer Architects 1973-; fndr memb Concept Planning Gp 1988; memb: Bristol City Docks Gp, Civic Soc, Bristol Visual & Environmental Gp; RIBA; *Recreations* painting, tennis, music; *Style—* 40 Cornwallis Crescent, Bristol, Avon BS8 4PH (☎ 0272 738 634); Bruges Tozer Partnership, 7 Unity St, Bristol, Avon BS1 5HH (☎ 0272 279 797)

BRUGGEMEYER, (William) James; s of Lt William Charles Bruggemeyer (d 1972), of London, and Kathleen, *née* Mangan (d 1983); *b* 16 June 1934; *Educ* St Joseph's Coll Beulah Hill, British Sch of Osteopathy (DO, MRO); *Career* Nat Serv 1952-54, private soldier 4 star, first class Malaya 1953, GSM and Clasp; *Recreations* music (singing), gardening, travel; *Style—* James Bruggemeyer, Esq; 99 Herne Hill, London SE24 9LY

BRUINVELS, Peter Nigel Edward; er s of Stanley Bruinvels and Ninette Maud, *née* Kibblewhite, of Dorking, Surrey; *b* 30 Mar 1950; *Educ* St John's Sch Leatherhead, London Univ (LLB), Cncl of Legal Educn; *m* 20 Sept 1980, Alison Margaret, da of Maj David Gilmore Bacon, RA (ret), of Lymington, Hants; 2 da (Alexandra Caroline Jane b 6 April 1986, Georgina Emma Kate b 20 Oct 1988); *Career* news bdcaster, columnist, media mgmnt and public affrs advsr; dir Aalco Nottingham 1983-, public affrs dir Abel Gp Ltd 1988-, princ Peter Bruinvels Assocs 1987-; corporate affrs dir 1988: The Brombard Gp plc, Brombard Devpts Ltd, Brombard Assocs Ltd; chm SOLAR Gp plc 1988-; co sec BPC Publishing Ltd 1978-81; MP (C) Leicester East 1983-87, memb Cons Home Office & NI ctees 1983-87; jt vice chm: Cons Urban Affrs and New Towns Ctee 1984-87 (jt sec 1983), Cons Educn Ctee 1985-87 (jt sec 1984-85); fndr chm Br- Malta Parly Gp 1984-87, jt chm Br Parly Lighting Gp 1983-87, promoter Crossbows Act 1987, sec E Midlands Cons MPs 1985-87, fndr chm Law and Order Soc 1985, chm Law students Cons Assoc of GB 1974-76, memb Cons NUEC 1976-79, vice chm Dorking Cons Assoc 1979-83, chm Dorking Cons Political Centre 1979-83, chm SE Area YC 1977-79, vice pres Surrey YC 1985-; memb: Guildford Diocesan Synod elected to Gen Synod C of E 1985, Bishops Cncl and Bd of Patrons 1985-; vice pres Dorking St Pauls Athletic Club 1984; memb Ct Univ of Leicester and Loughborough 1983-; ILEA and Surrey sch govr; memb Soc of Cons Lawyers; MIPR, FRSA, FInstD, MInstM, MCIM ; *Books* Zoning in on Enterprise (co-author), Light up the Roads (co-author), Sharing in Britains Success: A Study of Privatisation (1987), Investing in Enterprise (1989); *Recreations* politics in the C of E, lawn tennis umpire, cricket; *Clubs* Carlton, Inner Temple, Leicestershire Far and Near, Leicestershire CCC; *Style—* Peter Bruinvels, Esq; 14 High Meadow Close, Dorking, Surrey RH4 2LG (☎ 0306 887082);

BRUNNER, Elizabeth, Lady; (Dorothea) Elizabeth; OBE (1965), JP (Oxon 1946); o da of Henry Brodribb Irving (d 1919), and Dorothea, *née* Baird; gda of Sir Henry Irving, the actor; *m* 1926, Sir Felix Brunner, 3 Bt (d 1982); 3 s (and 2 s decd); *Career* chm: Nat Fedn of Women's Insts 1951-56, Keep Britain Tidy Gp 1958-67 (pres 1967-85); *Style—* Elizabeth, Lady Brunner, OBE, JP; Greys Court, Henley-on-Thames, Oxon RG9 4PG (☎ 049 17 296)

BRUNNER, Hugo Laurence Joseph; s of Sir Felix John Morgan Brunner, 3 Bt (d 1982), of Greys Court, nr Henley-on-Thames, Oxon, and Elizabeth, Lady Brunner OBE, *qv*; *b* 17 August 1935; *Educ* Eton, Trinity Coll, Oxford (MA); *m* 7 Jan 1967, Mary Rose Catherine, da of Arthur Joseph Lawrence Pollen (d 1968), of Harpsden Wood, Henley-on-Thames, Oxon; 5 s (Joseph b 1967, Samuel b 1972, Magnus b 1974, Philip b 1977, Francis b 1982), 1 da (Isabel b 1969); *Career* publisher, various appointments Oxford Univ Press 1958-65, and 1977-79, dir Chatto and Windus 1967-76, and 1979-85 (md 1979-82, chm 1982-85); dir Caithness Glass 1966- (chm 1985-), dir Brunner Investmt Tst 1987-; Parly candidate (Lib) for Torquay 1964 and 1966, chm Oxford Diocesan Advsy Ctee for Care of Churches 1985-, High Sheriff Oxfordshire 1988-89; *Recreations* hill walking, church crawling; *Clubs* Reform; *Style—* Hugo Brunner, Esq; 26 Norham Rd, Oxford OX2 6SF (☎ 0865 54821)

BRUNNER, Sir John Henry Kilian; 4 Bt (UK 1895), of Druids Cross, Little Woolton, Lancashire; Winnington Old Hall, Winnington, Cheshire; and Ennismore Gardens, Westminster, Co London; s of Sir Felix Brunner, 3 Bt (d 1982); *b* 1 June 1927; *Educ* Eton, Trinity Coll Oxford; *m* 1955, Jasmine Cicely, da of late John Wardrop-Moore by his w Janet (da of Sir James Erskine, JP, MP, himself gs of Sir David Erskine, 1 Bt, of Cambo); 2 s, 1 da; *Heir* s, Nicholas Felix Minturn, b 16 Jan 1960; *Career* with Political & Economic Planning (now Policy Studies Inst) 1950-53, talks producer BBC 1953, ec advsr with HM Treasury 1958-61, asst mangr with *Observer* (UK) 1961; formerly Lt RA & ADC to GOC 2 Infantry Div; *Style—* Sir John Brunner, Bt; 13 Glyndon Ave, Brighton, Victoria, Australia 3186

BRUNSKILL, Dr Ronald William; s of William Brunskill (d 1986), of Morecambe, Lancs, and Elizabeth Hannah, *née* Gowling; *b* 3 Jan 1929; *Educ* Bury HS, Univ of Manchester (BA, MA, PhD); *m* 20 June 1960, Miriam, s of late Joseph Allsop, of Weirsdale, Florida, USA; 2 da (Lesley (Mrs Glass) b 27 Oct 1961, Robin b 9 Sept 1963); *Career* Nat Serv 1953-55, 2 Lt RE serv in Suez Canal Zone; studio asst in architecture Univ of Manchester 1951-53; architectural asst: London CC 1955, Univ of Manchester 1955-56, Harkness fell and visiting fell MIT Boston Mass USA 1956-57, architect to Williams Deacon Bank Manchester 1957-60, reader in architecture Univ of Manchester 1983 (lectr 1960-, sr lectr 1973-83) visiting prof Univ of Florida Gainesville Florida USA 1969-70; architect in private practice, ptnr Carter Brunskill Assocs 1965-70; memb: Royal Cmmn on Ancient and Historical Monuments of Wales 1983-, Historic Bldgs Cncl for Eng 1978-84, advsy ctees Ancient Monuments and Historic Bldgs of Historic Buildings and Monuments Cmmn for Eng 1984-, Cathedrals advsy cmmn for Eng 1981-, Cathedral Fabric Ctee Manchester, Diocesan Advsy Ctee Manchester; govr Bolton Inst for Higher Educn 1982-89; vice pres: Cumberland and Westmorland Archaeological and Antiquaririan Soc, Weald and Downland Museum Tst; tstee Br Historic Bldgs Tst, vice-chm Ancient Monuments Soc; RIBA 1951, FSA 1975; *Books* Illustrated Handbook of Vernacular Architecture (1971 2 edn 1978 3 edn 1987), Vernacular Architecture of the Lake Counties (1974), English Brickwork (with Alec Clifton-Taylor 1978), Houses (1982), Traditional Buildings of Britain (1981), Traditional Farm Buildings of Britain, (1982, 2 edn 1987), Timber Building in Britain (1985); *Recreations* enjoying the countryside; *Style—* Dr Ronald Brunskill; Three Trees, 8 Overhill Road, Wilmslow, SK9 2BG (☎ 0625 522099); Glan Gors, Harlech, Gwynedd; School of Architecture, University of Manchester, Manchester M13 9PL (☎ 061 275 6909)

BRUNT, Dr Peter William; s of Harry Brunt, of Prestatyn, Clwyd, and Florence Jane Josephine Airey; *b* 18 Jan 1936; *Educ* Manchester GS, King George V Sch, Liverpool Univ; *m* 1961, (Marina Evelyn) Anne, da of Rev Reginald Henry Lewis (d 1974), of Liverpool; 3 da (Kristin, Nicola, Coralie); *Career* house surgn and house physician Liverpool Royal Infirmary 1959-60, medical registrar hosps in Liverpool region 1960-64, res fell dept of Medical Genetics John Hopkins Hosp and Sch of Medicine Baltimore USA 1965-66, lectr in medicine Univ of Edinburgh 1967-68, sr registrar in gastroenterology Western Gen Hosp Edinburgh 1968-69, hon lectr in medicine Univ of London 1969-70, conslt physician and gastroenterologist Aberdeen Royal Infirmary, clinical sr lectr in medicine Univ of Aberdeen, physician to HM The Queen (in Scotland); *Books* Diseases of Liver and Biliary System (1984), Gastroenterology (1984), numerous chapters in books and articles mainly on liver and alimentary diseases; *Recreations* mountaineering, music; *Clubs* Association of Physicians; *Style—* Dr Peter Brunt; 17 Kingshill Rd, Aberdeen AB2 4JY (☎ 0224 314204); Aberdeen Roy Infirmary, Forsterhill, Aberdeen

BRUNTISFIELD, 1 Baron (UK 1942); Sir Victor Alexander George Anthony Warrender; 8 Bt (GB 1715), MC (1918); s of Vice Adm Sir George John Scott, 7 Bt,

KCB, KCVO (d 1917) and Lady Ethel Maud Ashley-Cooper, da of 8 Earl of Shaftesbury; *b* 23 June 1899,, Queen Victoria stood sponsor at christening; *Educ* Eton; *m* 1, 1920 (m dis 1946), Dorothy Etta (d 1975), da of late Col Richard Hamilton Rawson, MP, by his w Lady Beatrice, *née* Anson (da of 2 Earl of Lichfield); 3 s; m 2, 1948, Tania, da of Dr M Kolin, of St Jacob, Dubrovnik, Yugoslavia; 1 s, 1 da; *Heir* s, Hon John Warrender, OBE, MC, TD; *Career* private sec to Sir Robert S Horne, GBE, KC, MP 1920-22; MP (C) Kesteven and Rutland Grantham Div 1923-42; pps (unpaid) to Parly Under-Sec of State for India 1924, asst Cons whip 1928-31, chm Young Cons Union 1929-30, jr lord of the Treasury 1931-32, vice-chamberlain of the Household 1932-35, comptroller of HM's Household 1935, parly and fin sec to Admiralty 1935, fin sec to War Dept and memb Army Cncl 1935-40, parly sec to Admiralty 1940-45; *Clubs* Turf; *Style—* The Rt Hon The Lord Bruntisfield, MC; Residence le Village 1B, 1837 Chateau-d'Oex, Switzerland (☎ 029 47117)

BRUNTON, Sir Gordon Charles; s of late Charles Arthur Brunton and Hylda Pritchard; *b* 27 Dec 1921; *Educ* Cranleigh Sch, LSE; *m* 1, 1946 (m dis 1965), Nadine Lucile Paula Sohr; 1 s, 2 da (and 1 s decd); m 2, 1966, Gillian Agnes Kirk; 1 s, 1 da; *Career* cmmnd RA 1942, joined IA 1942, served in India, Assam and Burma 1942-46; joined Tothill Press (appointed to bd 1954); md Tower Press Gp of Cos 1958-61; pa to md Tothill Press (renamed Odhams Press) 1961; md Thomson Pubns Ltd 1961, appointed dir Thomson Orgn Ltd 1963, md and ch exec Thomson Orgn 1968, pres Int Thomson Orgn Ltd, md and ch exec Int Thomson Org plc, ret 1984; chm: Bemrose Corpn plc, Martin Currie Pacific Tst plc 1985-, The Racing Post plc 1985-, Euram Consulting Ltd 1985-, John Silver Hldgs Ltd 1985-, Appeals Ctee of the Ind Adoption Soc; dir: Cable and Wireless plc, Mercury Communications Ltd, Yattendon Investmt Tst Ltd, Community Ind Ltd, Arts Cncl South Bank Bd, Sports Bureau Int Ltd, Times Newspapers; memb Ct of Govrs, cncl of Templeton Coll, Finance Ctee of Oxford Univ Press; fell LSE; former pres: Nat Advertising Benevolent Soc, Periodical Publishers Assoc Ltd, Printers' Charitable Corpn; govr Ashridge Mgmnt Coll; patron History of Advertising Tst; kt 1985; *Recreations* breeding horses, books; *Style—* Sir Gordon Brunton; North Munstead, Godalming, Surrey

BRUNTON, James Lauder; s and h of Sir (Edward Francis) Lauder Brunton, 3 Bt; *b* 24 Sept 1947; *Educ* MD; *m* 1967, Susan, da of Charles Hons; 1 s, 1 da; *Career* FRCP (Canada); *Style—* James Brunton, Esq; Apt 104, 1000 McGregor St, Montréal, Québec, Canada

BRUNTON, Sir (Edward Francis) Lauder; 3 Bt (UK 1908), of Stratford Place, St Marylebone; s of Sir (James) Stopford (Lauder) Brunton, 2 Bt (d 1943); *b* 10 Nov 1916; *Educ* Trinity Coll Sch Port Hope Ontario, Bryanston Sch, McGill Univ; *m* 1946, Marjorie Grant, only da of David Sclater Lewis, MSc, MD, FRCP (Canada), of Montreal; 1 s, 1 da; *Heir* s, James Brunton; *Career* hon attending physician Royal Victoria Hosp Montreal; fell: Int Soc of Hematology, American Coll of Physicians; memb American Soc of Hematology; *Style—* Sir Lauder Brunton, Bt; PO Box 140, Guysborough, Nova Scotia, Canada

BRUNTON, Ronald (Ron); s of John White Brunton, of Town Green, Whitfield, Northumberland, and Magaret Brunton, *née* Snowball; *b* 8 May 1949; *m* 20 Oct 1979, Helen Deira, da of Frederick William Hutchinson; 2 s (James Ronald b 5 July 1985, Andrew Ian b 31 Aug 1988); *Career* gen and sales mgmnt Mills & Allen Plc 1974-85, co dir Brunton Curtis Outdoor Advertising 1985-; *Style—* Ron Brunton, Esq; Brunton Curtis Outdoor Advertising Ltd, 34-36 Oxford St, London W1N 9FL (☎ 01 323 4957/4967, fax 01 255 1234)

BRUTON, Dr Dudley Malcolm; s of David Idris Bruton (d 1979), and Catherine, *née* Jones (d 1977); *b* 26 June 1933; *Educ* Aberdare Co Sch, Reading Sch Berks, The London Hosp Med Coll, Univ of London, The London Sch of Hygiene and Tropical Med, Univ of London (MB BS, MSc); *m* 5 May 1956, Joan, da of Cyril David Lewis (d 1977); 2 s (David b 1960, James b 1963), 1 da (Elizabeth b 1958); *Career* Flt Lt RAF Med Branch UK and Malta 1957-60; princ med offr BEA BOAC and BA 1969-79, dir med servs Rothmans Int Tobacco (UK) Ltd 1979-; hon sec Soc of Occupational Medicine 1976-79; bd memb Faculty of Occupational Med RCP 1978-83; cncl memb RSM 1981-86; memb specialist advsy ctee on Occupational Medicine jt ctee on Higher Med Trg 1982-86; regnl specialty advsr occupational med NW Thames Region 1986-; area surgn St John Ambulance Brigade (Bucks); memb Bucks Cncl on Alcohol and Drug Abuse; DIH 1964, MFOM 1978, FFOM 1979; *Recreations* art, music, various sports; *Clubs* Leander; *Style—* Dr Dudley M Bruton; Wildwood, Rotherfield Rd, Henley-on-Thames, Oxon RG9 1NN, (☎ 0491 575143)

BRUTON, Prof Michael John; s of (Patrick) John Bruton, of Hertford, and Louise Ann, *née* Roberts; *b* 28 Mar 1938; *Educ* Richard Hale Sch Hertford, Univ Coll London (BA), Imperial Coll London (MSc, DIC), Regent St, Poly (Dip TP); *m* 2 March 1963, Sheila Grace, da of Alexander Kyle Harrison; 2 da (Suzy b 1969, Catherine b 1972); *Career* princ planning offr Bucks CC 1966-67 (Lanarkshire CC 1965-66), princ lectr town planning Oxford Poly 1967-72, head school planning and landscape Birmingham Poly 1972-77, dep princ and register UWIST 1985-88 (prof town planning 1977-85), registar Univ of Wales Coll of Cardiff 1988-; govr Centre for enviromental Studies 1978-81, chm CNAA town planning bd 1978-84; memb: Countryside Cmmn for Wales 1981-85, Univ Grants Ctee social studies sub-ctee 1985-, ESRC post graduate bd 1985-; MRTPI, MCIT, MIHT; *Books* Introduction to Transportation Planning (1970, 1975, 3rd Edn 1985), Spirit and Purpose of Planning (1974, 1984), Local Planning in Practice (1987); *Recreations* watching rugby and cricket, travel; *Clubs* Royal Commonwealth; *Style—* Prof Michael Bruton; University of Wales, College of Cardiff, P O Box 68, Cardiff CF1 3XA (☎ 0222 874792, fax 0222 874478, telex 497368)

BRYAN, Sir Arthur; s of William Woodall Bryan, and Isobel Alan, *née* Tweedie; *b* 4 Mar 1923; *Educ* Longton HS Stoke-on-Trent; *m* 1947, Betty, da of F G Ratford, of Essex; 1 s, 1 da; *Career* pres and dir Waterford Wedgwood 1986-88, chm Wedgwood 1968-86 (joined Wedgwood 1947, gen sales mangr 1959, dir 1960, md 1963); dir Friends' Provident Life Office 1985- and Rank Organisation 1985-; dir UK Fund Inc (USA), chm consumer & vehicle mkts advsy ctee DTI; HM Lord-Lt Staffs 1968; memb ct Keele Univ; Hon MUniv (Keele) 1978; CBIM, FInstM, CICeram, FRSA 1964; KStJ; kt 1976; *Recreations* walking, tennis, reading; *Style—* Sir Arthur Bryan; Parkfields Cottage, Tittensor, Stoke-on-Trent, Staffs (☎ 078 139 2686); Josiah Wedgwood & Sons Ltd, Barlaston, Stoke-on-Trent, Staffs (☎ 078 139 4141, telex 36170)

BRYAN, Felicity Anne (Mrs Alexander Duncan); da of Sir Paul Bryan, DSO, MC, and Betty Mary, *née* Hoyle (d 1968); *b* 16 Oct 1945; *Educ* Courtauld Inst of Art, Univ of London; *m* 23 Oct 1981, Alexander Duncan, s of Patrick Duncan (d 1967); 1 da (Alice Mary b 1982), 2 s (Maxim Paul b 1983, Benjamin Patrick b 1987); *Career* journalist: Financial Times 1968-70, The Economist 1970-72; literary agent and dir Curtis Brown Ltd 1972-88, fndr The Felicity Bryan Agency 1988; *Books* The Town Gardener's Companion (1982), A Garden for Children (1986), Nursery Style (1989); *Recreations* opera, gardening, travel, entertaining; *Clubs* Groucho; *Style—* Ms Felicity Bryan; The Old Rectory, Mill St, Kidlington, Oxford OX5 2EE (☎ 043 684 2355); 2 A North Parade, Banbury Rd, Oxford OX2 6PE (☎ 0865 513 816, fax 0865 310055)

BRYAN, Gerald Jackson; CMG (1964), CVO (1966), OBE (1960), MC (1941); s of George Bryan, OBE, of Belfast (d 1929), and Ruby Evelyn, *née* Pollexfen (d 1975); *b* 2 April 1921; *Educ* Wrekin, RMA Woolwich, New Coll Oxford; *m* 1947, Georgiana Wendy Cockburn, da of William Barraud Hull, of Mbabane, Swaziland (d 1967); 1 s (Caesar), 2 da (Diana, Mary); *Career* Maj RE, served with 11 (Scottish) Commando in M East; Colonial Service 1944-67: Swaziland, Barbados, Mauritius; Administrator: Virgin Islands 1959-62, St Lucia 1962-67, ret 1967; govt sec and head of Civil Service Isle of Man 1967-69; gen-mangr Londonderry Devpt Cmmn 1969-73, Bracknell Dvpt Corpn 1973-82; lord chllr's panel 1982; dir Lovaux Engrg Co 1982; sec-gen Assoc of Contact Lens Mfrs 1983; memb (C) Berks CC 1983-85; FBIM 1969 MDSL 1988; CStJ 1964, KStJ 1985; *Recreations* walking, swimming; *Style—* Gerald Bryan, Esq, CMG, CVO, OBE, MC; Whitehouse, Murrell Hill Lane, Binfield, Berks RG12 5BY (☎ Bracknell 0344 425447)

BRYAN, James Robert Emmett; s of James Edward Bryan (d 1985), of Bristol, and Florence May, *née* Miller (d 1960); *b* 27 Jan 1913; *Educ* St Mary-on-the-Quay Bristol, St Brendan's Coll Bristol; *m* 31 Aug 1936, Kathleen Alice (d 1966), da of James Joseph McNally (d 1969), of Bristol; 1 s (Michael James b 1937), 2 da (Jaqueline Mary b 1939, Valerie Jean b 1942); *Career* chm and md: family firm of Bryan Bros, Motor Distributors Bristol 1929; dir 1941; md and chm Bryan Bros Hldgs Ltd, controlling Bryan Bros Ltd, Bryan Bros Trucks Ltd, Bryan Bros (Hanham) Ltd, Bryan Bros (St Austell) Ltd, Bristol Auto Centre Ltd, Bryan Bros (Contract Hire) Ltd; main Ford dealer 1933; chm Bristol Football Club (RU) 1956-74 (pres 1975-84); *Recreations* rugby, cricket; *Clubs* Bristol Football (RFU), Glos County Cricket; *Style—* James R E Bryan, Esq; The Grange, Tytherington, Wotton-under-Edge, Glos GL12 8QB (☎ 0454 412255); Bryan Bros Ltd, College Green, Bristol BS1 5XN (☎ 0272 293881, fax 225839, telex 449662); car ☎, 0860 357381

BRYAN, Sir Paul Elmore Oliver; DSO (1943), MC (1943); s of Rev John Thomas Ingram Bryan, PhD (d 1953), of Milton Ernest, Bedford; *b* 3 August 1913; *Educ* St John's Sch Leatherhead, Gonville and Caius Coll Cambridge; *m* 1, 1939, Betty Mary (d 1968), da of James Cars Hoyle; 3 da; m 2, 1971, Cynthia Duncan, da of late Sir Patrick Ashley Cooper, of Hexton Manor, Herts; *Career* MP (C) Howden 1955-83, Boothferry 1983-87, min of state Dept of Employment 1970-72; dir: Granada Television, Granada Theatres, Greater Manchester Independent Radio Ltd 1972-, Furness Withy Ltd 1983-; dep chm: Furness Withy Ltd 1984-, Croydon Cable Television Ltd 1985-; kt 1972; *Style—* Sir Paul Bryan, DSO, MC; 5 Westminster Gdns, Marsham St, London SW1 (☎ 01 834 2050); Park Farm, Sawdon, nr Scarborough, N Yorks (☎ 0723 85370)

BRYAN, (Percival Charles) Rex; s of Percival George Bryan, of Suffolk (d 1962), and Lilian Georgina (d 1983); *b* 25 Feb 1924; *Educ* Coll of Technol Cambridge, Northampton Coll of Art, Coll of Preceptors; *m* 20 May 1944, Vera Nellie; 2 s (Peter b 1944, Alan b 1946); *Career* CA; sr ptnr Rex Bryan Son & Pennock; formerly with Dept of Arch & Planning Cambridge City and Northants Borough Cncl; memb RIBA; *Recreations* golf; *Clubs* Northamptonshire County Golf, Cheyne Walk (Northampton), Northampton and County, Farmers; *Style—* Rex Bryan, Esq; The Lodge, High Street, Great Houghton, Northampton; Great Houghton House, Great Houghton, Northampton (☎ 0604 764051)

BRYAN, Rex Victor; s of Bertram Henry Bryan (d 1970), of Purley, Surrey, and Annie Ella Margaret, *née* King; *b* 2 Dec 1946; *Educ* Wallington GS, Jesus Coll Oxford (MA); *m* 1, 31 July 1971 (m dis 1981), Catherine, da of Samuel Carbery, of Ballymena, Co Antrim, NI; 1 s (Roland Patrick b 1977); m 2, 9 Aug 1982, Mary Elizabeth, da of Brendan Joseph O'Toole, of Woodford Green, Essex; 2 s (Adam Francis b 1985, Thomas Edward b 1988), 1 da (Victoria Louise b 1986); *Career* called to the Bar Lincoln's Inn 1971, Barb 1978-, head of chambers 1986-; *Recreations* carpentry, languages; *Style—* Rex Bryan, Esq; 5 Pump Ct, Temple, London EC4 (☎ 01 353 2532, fax 353 5321)

BRYAN, William Alexander (Bill); s of Andrew Bryan (d 1928), and Margaret Ann Bryan (d 1965); *b* 21 July 1924; *Educ* Newton Park Higher Grade Sch Ayr Scotland; *m* 30 June 1950, Margaret Aitken Jess, da of William Muir Morton (d 1951); 2 s (David b 1956, Gordon b 1959); *Career* accountant; dir The Builders Accident Insur Ltd 1984- (co sec 1972-83), dir and gen mangr 1984-88), co sec Tennant Budd and Roderick Pratt Ltd 1970-73; FCA; *Recreations* golf, reading; *Clubs* Caledonian; *Style—* William A Bryan, Esq; Glenayr, 1A Anglesey Ave, Loose, Maidstone, Kent ME15 9SH (☎ 0622 744941); 31/32 Bedford St, Strand, London WC2E 9EL (☎ 01 836 9885, telex 297311, fax (010 379 5329)

BRYANS, Dame Anne (Margaret); *née* Gilmour; DBE (1957, CBE 1945); da of Col Rt Hon Sir John Gilmour, 2 Bt, GCVO, DSO, MP (d 1940); *b* 29 Oct 1909; *Educ* privately; *m* 1932 Lt Cdr John Reginald Bryans, RN, s of Rev R du F Bryans (d 1922); 1 s; *Career* HQ Staff Br Red Cross Soc 1938, dep cmmr Br Red Cross and St John War Orgn, M East cmmn 1943, cmmr Jan-June 1945, dep chm 1953-64, vice-chm 1964-76, exec ctee BRCS; lay memb Cncl for Professions Supplementary to Med until 1979; memb: ethical practices sub-ctee Royal Free Hosp 1974-, Royal Free Hosp Sch Cncl 1968-83, bd of govrs Eastman Dental Hosp 1973-79, Camden and Islington AHA 1974-79; vice-pres Open Sect RSM 1975 (pres 1980-82), former memb ITA (later IBA); memb: Govt Anglo-Egyptian Resettlement Bd, BBC/ITA Appeals Ctee, Med Sch St George's Hosp, special tstee and former chm Royal Free Hosp and Friends of Royal Free Hosp, former chm bd of govrs Royal Free Hosp; cncl Florence Nightingale Hosp, tstee Florence Nightingale Aid in Sickness Tst 1979-; govr Royal Star and Garter Home 1975-89; memb exec ctee Royal Soc of Medicine 1982-84; vice-pres Royal Coll of Nursing, former govr Westminster Hosp, FRSM 1976; chm Order of St John of Jerusalem (DStJ) and BRCS Service Hosp Welfare Ctee and VAD Ctee 1960-; vice-chm jt ctee Order of St John and BRCS 1976-81; chm: Grants Ctee Nations Fund for Nurses; *Clubs* Royal Lymington YC, New Cavendish; *Style—* Dame Anne Bryans, DBE; 57 Elm Park House, Elm Park Gardens, London SW10 9QD (☎ 01 352 7436)

BRYANS, John Reginald (Jack); s of Reginald du Faur Bryans (d 1922), and Mildred Violet, *née* Doxat (d 1918); *b* 19 June 1906; *Educ* RNC Osborne, RNC Dartmouth; *m* 23 June 1932, Anne Margaret, da of Rt Hon Sir John Gilmour, Bt (d 1940), of Montrave; 1 s (John Patrick Gilmour b 1933); *Career* served two cmmns on China Station in cruisers and submarines, learned to fly when on foreign service leave, ran own airline 1934-37, broker Lloyds of London 1932-35, served reserve occupation on design and manufacture of aircraft instrument test and calibration equipment 1939-45; chm and md Bryans Ltd 1945-65; made study on origins of religious teachings FRGS, FRAeS; *Recreations* sailing, golf, flying; *Clubs* RYS, RORC, Senior Golfers Soc, Rye GC; *Style*— Jack Bryans, Esq; 57 Elm Park House, Fulham Rd, London SW10 9QD (☎ 01 352 7436)

BRYANT, Rear Adm Benjamin; CB (1955), DSO and two bars (1942, 1943), DSC (1940); s of John Forbes Bryant, MA, FRGS, ICS (ret) (d 1963), and Mary Ada, *née* Genge (d 1961); *b* 16 Sept 1905; *Educ* Oundle, RNC Osborne, RNC Dartmouth; *m* 1, 1929, Marjorie Dagmar Mynors (d 1965), da of Reginald Mynors Symonds (d 1945); 2 s (David d 1937, Joseph), 1 da (Patricia); m 2, 1966, Heather Elizabeth Williams, da of Julian Henry Reginald Hance (d 1959); *Career* RN 1939-41, CO HMS Sea Lion, served in Norway, Biscay, CO HM S/M Safari Mediterranean 1941-43, Capt S/M Sch HMS Dolphin 1947, Flag Offr Submarines 1948-49, Cdre Devonport 1951-53, Flag Capt to C-in-C Med 1953-54, DCNP; *Recreations* shooting, fishing, golf; *Style*— Rear Adm Benjamin Bryant, CB, DSO, DSC; Quarry Cottage, Kithurst Lane, Storrington, West Sussex RH20 4LP (☎ 090 66 3374)

BRYANT, David John; CBE (1980, MBE 1969); s of Reginald Samuel Harold Bryant (d 1978), of Avon, and Evelyn Clair, *née* Weaver (d 1987); *b* 27 Oct 1931; *Educ* Weston GS, St Paul's Coll Cheltenham, Redland Coll Bristol; *m* 1960, Ruth Georgina, da of George Roberts (d 1971), of Avon;2 da (Jacqueline b 1962, Carole Jayne b 1965); *Career* schoolmaster 1955-71; dir: Sporting Boutiques 1971-78, Drakelite Ltd (Bowls conslts 1978-); professional bowler 1980-, World Singles champ 1966, 1980 and 1988, Cwlth Games Gold Medallist 1962, 1970, 1974, 1978, Embassy World Indoor Singles Champ 1979, 1980, 1981, other titles include 26 national and 14 Br Isles; *Recreations* angling, gardening, watching most sports; *Clubs* Clevedon Cons, Clevedon Bowling; *Style*— David Bryant, Esq, CBE; 47 Esmond Grove, Clevedon, Avon BS21 7HP (☎ 0272 875423); Drakelite Ltd, 81 High Street, Southwold, Suffolk (☎ 0502 722002)

BRYANT, Air Vice-Marshal Derek Thomas; CB (1987), OBE (1974); s of (Joseph) Thomas Bryant (d 1957), and (Daisy Elizabeth) Mary, *née* Thurley; *b* 1 Nov 1933; *Educ* Latymer Upper GS Hammersmith; *m* 4 Aug 1956, Patricia, da of William Dodge (d 1977); 1 s (Iain David b 1957), 1 da (Janine b 1960); *Career* fighter pilot 1953, qualified flying instr 1957, Sqdn Cdr 228-OCU and 14 Sqdn 1968-74, Station Cdr RAF Coningsby 1976-78, Sr Air Staff Offr (SASO) 38 Gp 1982-84; Dep Cmdr RAF Germany 1984-87, Cmdt RAF Staff Coll 1987-88; *Recreations* gardening, golf; *Clubs* RAF; *Style*— Air Vice-Marshal D T Bryant, CB, OBE; Manor Stables, Lower Swell, Fivehead, Taunton, Somerset TA3 6PH (☎ 04608 209)

BRYANT, Edward James; s of Edward Bryant, of Minister House, Shaw, Wilts, and Alma Mary, *née* James (d 1955); *b* 24 April 1910; *Educ* The Abbey Portishead, Leamington Coll Warwicks; *m* 16 Aug 1948, Suzanne, da of Gp Capt John de Courcy, MC (d active service 1940), of The Manor House, Barton, Cambridge; 2 s (Edward b 1951, David b 1955); *Career* RAFVR 1940-46, Actg Wing Cdr; elected: W Suffolk Co Cncl 1963-73, St Edmunds Bury Borough Cncl 1979-87; min's rep on Eastern Region Sports Cncl 1972-76, chm W Suffolk Marriage Guidance Cncl to 1976; volunteer memb Probation After Care Serv Bury St Edmunds, community emergency advsr Hundon Centre, vice-chm Fuffolk War Pensioners Ctee; *Recreations* shooting, cricket, tennis; *Clubs* Royal Overseas League; *Style*— Edward Bryant, Esq; Marsh Morgen House, Stradishall, Newmarket, Suffolk (☎ 0440 820 287)

BRYANT, Prof Greyham Frank; s of Ernest Noel Bryant (d 1981), and Florence Ivy, *née* Russell (d 1974); *b* 3 June 1931; *Educ* Reading Univ (BSc), Imperial Coll Lond (PhD); *m* 2 July 1955, Iris Sybil, da of Albert Edward Jardine (d 1980); 2 s (Mark Greyham b 2 Jan 1963, David Nicholas b 18 Aug 1966); *Career* sr sci offr Br Iron and Steel Res 1959-64, prof of control Imperial Coll London 1982- (res fell 1964-67, reader in industl control 1975-82), chm Broner Conslts 1979-88, md Greycon Conslts 1985-; MIEE, FIMA, FEng; *Books* Automation of Tandem Mills (jtly); *Recreations* music; *Style*— Prof Greyham Bryant; 18 Wimborne Ave, Norwood Green, Middx (☎ 01 574 5648); Dept Electrical Engineering, Imperial College, London SW7 (☎ 01 589 5111)

BRYANT, John Beaton; TD (1963 and clasp 1975), JP (Bristol 1979), DL (Avon 1974); s of Arthur Bryant, of Bristol; *b* 9 July 1930; *Educ* Bristol GS; *m* 1960, Shirley, da of Henry Hopley, of Bristol; 2 s; *Career* dir Joseph Bryant Ltd 1956, Blacks Camping & Leisure Ltd 1978; *Recreations* fishing, shooting, hill walking; *Clubs* Army and Navy; *Style*— John Bryant, Esq, TD, JP, DL; Aelbryn, Bancyffordd, Llandyssul, Dyfed; 11 Sion Hill, Clifton, Bristol, Avon (☎ 0272 311868)

BRYANT, Jonathan Nicholas; JP (1979); s of Basil Stuart Bryant (d 1976); *b* 12 Jul 1944; *Educ* Cheltanham; *m* 1966, Sandra Anne, da of Alexander Kendrick (d 1984); 2 s, 1 da; *Career* chm and md Brymor Ltd and Bryant Corpn plc 1969-; tax cmmr 1977-; memb of Lloyds 1981; Liveryman: Worshipful Co of Curriers (Master 1983-84); *Recreations* family, weeding; *Style*— Jonathan Bryant, Esq, JP; Greenwood, Frant, East Sussex TN3 9DR (☎ 089 275 462); Brymor Ltd, East Peckham, Tonbridge, Kent (☎ 0622 871384)

BRYANT, Kenneth Marrable; s of Philip Harry Bryant (d 1979), of Guildford, Surrey, and Hilda Gertrude, *née* Linch (d 1988); *b* 13 June 1927; *Educ* Latymer Upper Sch, King's Coll London, Charing Cross Hosp Med Sch (MB BS); *m* 26 July 1952, Rosemary, da of Thomas Hawkins (d 1962), of Ealing London; 1 s (richard b 1962), 2 da (Elizabeth b 1957, Angela b 1959); *Career* Flt Lt 1952-55: RAF Orthopaedic Serv, RAF Hosp Ely; conslt orthopaedic surgn: St James Hosp 1965, Bolingbroke Hosp 1972, St George's Hosp 1980; hon sr lectr St George's Hosp Med Sch 1976, hon orthopaedic surgn Cheyne Centre for Spastic children 1978, visiting orthopaedic surgeon HM Prison Serv 1979; lay chm Deanery Synod, Churchwarden; Freeman city of London 1966, Liveryman Worshipful Co of Apothecaries 1966; FRSM, FBOA, FRCS, AKC; *Recreations* gardening, fine bookbinding; *Style*— Kenneth Bryant, Esq; Orthopaedic Dept, St George's Hosp, London SW17 OQT (☎ 01 672 1255); Mitchell Mews, Truro, Cornwall

BRYANT, Martin Warwick; s of Douglas William Bryant, of Chichester, Sussex, and Elsie Marjorie Sylvia, *née* Simpkins; *b* 30 June 1952; *Educ* Chicester HS, Christ Church Oxford (MA), Leeds Univ, Cranfield Sch of Mgmnt (MBA); *m* 26 May 1979, Hilary May, da of Philip Readhead Southall, of Rednal Worcs; 1 s (Laurence Michael b 1984), 1 da (Emily Anna b 1981); *Career* Swaziland ODI 1975-77, business analyst Foster Wheeler ltd 1978-82, planning mangr BOC GP Plc 1983-86, dir corporate devpt Charles Barker Plc 1986-89, dir of strategic planning Boots Co plc 1989-; tres Crondall Sch Asoc, ctee memb Village CC; *Recreations* golf, skiing; *Clubs* Ski (GB); *Style*— Martin Bryant, Esq; Boots Co plc, Head Office, Nottingham, NG3AA (☎ 0602 592935)

BRYANT, Michael Dennis; CBE (1988); s of William Frederick Bryant (d 1954), of London, and Ann Mary Kerrigan, *née* Jackson (d 1965); *b* 5 April 1928; *Educ* Battersea GS; *m* 1958 (m dis 1980), Josephine Martin; 2 s (Kerrigan, Simon), 2 da (Sarah, Josephine); *Career* ordinary seaman MN 1945, 2Lt 7 Queen's Own Hussars 1947-49; actor; RSC 1964-65, Nat Theatre player 1977-, assoc of Nat Theatre 1984-88; memb cncl RADA 1982-; *Recreations* walking; *Style*— Michael Bryant, Esq, CBE; The Nat Theatre, South Bank, London SE1 9PX

BRYANT, Michael Sydney; s of Sydney Cecil Bryant (d 1977), of Keynsham, Avon, and Lily May, *née* Jefferies; *b* 16 Mar 1944; *Educ* Bristol GS, Exeter Univ, City of London Coll; *Career* estate duty off Inland Revenue 1965-70, assoc dir Bevington Lowndes Ltd 1970-75, dir Rathbone Bros plc (formerly Comprehensive Financial Services plc) 1975; contrib: Daily Telegraph, Sunday Times, Money Mktg; cncl memb Fimbra 1986-88, chm Insur and Compensation ctee FIMBRA, memb tax ctee BIIBA; IBRC 1977; *Recreations* food, wine, travel; *Style*— Michael Bryant, Esq; 50 Hans Place, London SW1X 0LA (☎ 01 225 0759); University Hse, Lower Grosvenor Place, London SW1W 0EX (☎ 01 630 5611, fax 01 821 1437, telex 262257)

BRYARS, Donald Leonard; s of Leonard Bryars (d 1961), of Goole, Yorks, and Marie, *née* Purcell (d 1977); *b* 31 March 1929; *Educ* Goole GS, Leeds Univ (BA); *m* 18 July 1953, Joan, da of Jonathan Charles Noble Yealand (d 1967), of Goole, Yorks; 1 da (Anne b 1954); *Career* Nat Serv Royal Signals 1951-52; HM Customs and Excise 1953-84: princ 1964, asst sec 1971, on loan to Cabinet Office 1976-78, cmmr 1978-84, dir 1978, dir personnel 1979-84, ret 1984; dir Customs Annuity and Benevolent Fund 1986-; memb: ctee (ed) Focus Magazine, Chalfont St Giles Res Assoc; *Clubs* Civil Service (chm 1981-85); *Style*— Donald Bryars, Esq; 15 Ellwood Rise, Chalfont St Giles, Bucks HP8 4SU (☎ 02407 5466)

BRYCE, Sir (William) Gordon; CBE (1963); s of late James Chisholm Bryce and Emily Susan, *née* Lees; *b* 2 Feb 1913; *Educ* Bromsgrove, Hertford Coll Oxford (MA); *m* 1940, Molly Mary, da of late Arthur Cranch Drake; 2 da; *Career* Chief Justice of the Bahamas 1970-73 (formerly attorney-gen Gibraltar, Aden, Bahamas); kt 1971; *Style*— Sir Gordon Bryce, CBE; Broom Croft, Lydeard St Lawrence, Taunton, Somerset

BRYCE-SMITH, Prof Derek; s of Charles Philip Smith (d 1938) of Wanstead, London and Amelia, *née* Thick (d 1962); *b* 29 April 1926; *Educ* Bancrofts Sch Woodford Wells, SW Essex Tech Coll, West Ham Municipal Coll, Bedford Coll, Univ of London (BSc, PhD, DSc); *m* 1, 5 Sept 1956, Marjorie Mary Anne (d 1966), da of Maj Eric Stewart, MC (d 1937), of London; 2 s (Duncan b 1959, David b 1963), 2 da (Madeleine b 1957, Hazel b 1961); m 2, 21 June 1969, Pamela Joyce Morgan, da of Marius Andreas Thorndahl (d 1942), of Denmark; 2 step da (Pamela b 1948, Diana b 1953); *Career* ICI postdoctoral fell King's Coll 1951-55 (asst lectr 1955-56), lectr Univ Reading 1956-63 (reader 1963-65, prof 1965-), sr reporter Royal Soc Chem; formerly conslt to: Shell, Esso, EI Du Pont de Nemours (USA), Dutch state mines; currently conslt Lamberts Dietary Prods; endowed lectrship Royal soc chem 1984 (John Jeyes Silver Medal); numerous radio and television broadcasts in UK and abroad, largely on enviromental chemistry topics; FRSC (chm Photochemistry Subject Gp), C Chem, memb American Chem Soc, chm Roy Soc; *Books* Lead or Health (with R Stephens, 1980), The Zinc Solution (with L Hodgkinson, 1986); *Recreations* singing, piano playing, gardening, debating; *Style*— Prof Derek Bryce-Smith; Chemistry Dept, University of Reading, Whiteknights Park, Reading, Berks, (☎ 0734 318449/875123)

BRYDEN, Hon Mrs; Hon (Monica) Deborah; *née* Morris; da of 3 Baron Killanin, MBE, TD; *b* 24 Feb 1950; *Educ* Convent of the Assumption Hengrave, Byam Shaw Sch of Drawing and Painting; *m* 1970, Bill Bryden, *qv*; 1 s (Dillon), 1 da (Mary); *Style*— The Hon Mrs Bryden

BRYDEN, Bill - William Campbell Rough; s of George Bryden; *b* 12 April 1942; *Educ* Greenock HS, Glasgow Univ; *m* 1970, Hon Deborah, *née* Morris, *qv* da of 3 Baron Killanin, MBE, TD, and Mary, MBE, da of Rev Canon Douglas Dunlop; 1 s, 1 da; *Career* theatre director and writer; *Style*— Bill Bryden, Esq; c/o National Theatre, South Bank, SE1 9PX (☎ 01 928 2033)

BRYDON, Donald Hood; s of James Hood Brydon (d 1975) of Edinburgh and Mary Duncanson, *née* Young; *b* 25 May 1945; *Educ* George Watson's Coll Edinburgh, Univ of Edinburgh (BSc); *m* 16 Aril 1971, Joan Victoria *née* Rea; 1 s (Angus b 1977), 1 da (Fiona b 1975); *Career* res asst dept economics Univ of Edinburgh; investmt mangr: Airways Pension Scheme (BR Airways), Barclays Bank; dir Barclays Investmt Mgmt, md BZW Investmt Mgmt; ldr Bracknell DC 1977-80; vice chm Nat Assoc of Pension Funds 1988-, chm Instl Shareholders Ctee 1989-; AMSIA 1972; *Books* Economics of Technical Information Services (co-author 1972), Pension Fund Investment (co-author 1988); *Recreations* golf; *Clubs* Caledonian; *Style*— Donald Brydon, Esq; BZW Investment Management Ltd, Seal House, 1 Swan Lane, London EC4R 3UD, (☎ 01 623 7777 fax 01 621 9411)

BRYENTON, Michael John; s of Benjamin Bryenton (d 1958), of Heveningham, and Hilda, *née* Roberts, of Wenhaston, Suffolk; *b* 3 April 1946; *Educ* Walpole, Halesworth; *Career* fndr tres Halesworth Cancer Research Campaign Ctee 1977, church warden and church treas St Margaret's Church Heveningham, sch govr Walpole 1988; citizen of the year for Halesworth & Dist for work on cancer research; *Recreations* reading, the countryside, fund raising for charities; *Style*— Michael J Bryenton, Esq; Rose Cottage, Heveningham, Halesworth, Suffolk

BRYERS, Brig Richard Hugh Castellain; CBE (1963); s of Rev John Shaw Bryers (d 1945), of Bowers Gifford Rectory, Essex, and Charlotte Susan, *née* Newman (d 1959); *b* 12 Sept 1911; *Educ* Harrow, St John's Coll Cambridge (BA); *m* 1, July 1938, Phyllis (d 1964), da of Major David Lewis Hankin (d 1949), of N Rhodesia; 2 s (Humphrey b 1941 d 1941, John Richard Feneran b 1944), 1 da (Eliane Susan Gray b 1942); m 2, 22 May 1965, Isabella Marjorie, da of Percy Cromwell Clark (d 1928), of Wallington, Surrey; *Career* King's Own Royal Regt 1933-63, serv WWII: India, Iraq, Burma, Korea 1953-54; cmd 5 Bn Malay Regt Malayan Emergency 1954-56, Staff Appts War Off 1945-48 and 1957-60, BJSM Washington 1950-52, Instr Staff Coll 1942-44, Cdr Land Forces Persian Gulf 1960-63; memb Red Cross Suffolk Branch

1968-89 (branch dir 1974-76, dep pres 1977-89), holder of Red Cross Badges of Honour for Devoted Serv and Distinguished Serv; *Recreations* shooting, gardening; *Clubs* Army and Navy, Western India; *Style*— Brig Richard Bryers, CBE; Thorndon Old Rectory, nr Eye, Suffolk IP23 7LX (☎ 037 971 284)

BRYMER, Jack; OBE (1960); s of Jack Brymer, of South Shields, Co Durham (d 1975), and Mary, *née* Dixon (d 1960); *b* 27 Jan 1915; *Educ* South Shields GS; Goldsmiths Coll London (Dip Ed); *m* 21 Oct 1939, Joan, da of Jack Richardson (d 1924), of Lancaster, Lancs; 1 s (Timothy b 1951); *Career* principal clarinet RPO 1947-63; BBC Symphony 1963-71; LSO 1971-86; prof Royal Acad 1952-58, Kneller Hall 1963-67, Guildhall Sch of Music; dir Shell LSO Scholarship 1982-; dir London Wind Schoists; broadcaster: On a personal note, Music you love, At Home J B Presents; has recorded complete works Mozart, Bach, Haydn, Beethoven; MA Newcastle, Hon RAM, Hon FGSM; awarded Cobbett Medal by Worshipful Soc of Musicians 1989; *Books* The Clarinet (Menuhin Guides) Macdonald, From Where I Sit (autobiog) Cossell, In The Orchestra, Hutchinson; *Recreations* golf, gardening; *Clubs* Croham Hurst Golf; *Style*— Jack Brymer, Esq, OBE; Underwood, Ballards Farm Rd, South Croydon, Surrey CR2 7JA (☎ 01 657 1698)

BRYNING, Charles Frederick; s of Frederick Bryning (d 1982), of 58 Mossom Lane, Norbreck, Blackpool, and Dorothy Edith Bryning; *b* 17 July 1946; *Educ* Arnold Sch, Blackpool Lancs; *m* 29 April 1983, Katrina Carol, da of John Carole Boris Ely, of 52 Worsley Rd, Lytham, St Annes; 1 s (Simon b 1983); *Career* CA; certified and corporate accountant FCCA, ptnr Jones, Harris & Co CA 1972-, chief exec the Alexander Walker Gp of cos 1987-; FCA; *Style*— Charles Bryning, Esq; Holly Lodge, 1 The Avenue, Carleton, Poulton-le-Fylde; 17 St Peters Place, Fleetwood, Lancs (☎ 039 4255)

BRYSON, Col (James) Graeme; OBE (Mil 1954), TD (1949), JP (Liverpool 1956), DL (1968); s of John Conway Bryson, slr (d 1959), of Liverpool, and Oletta, *née* Olsen; *b* 4 Feb 1913; *Educ* St Edward's Coll Liverpool, Liverpool Univ; *m* 1938, Jean (d 1981), da of Walter Cook Glendinning, of Liverpool; 2 s (and 1 s decd), 4 da; *Career* slr 1935, sr dist registrar High Court of Justice at Liverpool 1947-78, dep circuit judge 1978-82; chm Med Appeal Tbnl 1978-86; pres Royal Br Legion (NW England) 1979; HM Vice-Lord-Lieut Merseyside 1979-; Queen's Commendation for Brave Conduct 1961; kt of Holy Sepulchre 1974; *Books* Execution in Halsbury's Laws of England (jtly 3 edn 1976); *Recreations* ex-service interests, local history, boating; *Clubs* Athenaeum (Liverpool, pres 1969); *Style*— Col Graeme Bryson, OBE, TD, JP, DL; Sunwards, Thirlmere Rd, Hightown, Liverpool L38 3RQ (☎ 051 929 2652)

BRYSON, Adm Sir Lindsay Sutherland; KCB (1981); s of James McAuslan Bryson (d 1976), and Margaret, *née* Whyte (d 1946); *b* 22 Jan 1925; *Educ* Allan Glen's Sch Glasgow, London Univ (BSc); *m* 1951, Averil, da of W T Curtis-Willson (d 1957); 1 s, 2 da; *Career* joined RN 1945, dir Naval Guided Weapons 1973, dir Surface Weapons Project (Navy) 1974-77, dir-gen Weapons (Naval) 1977-81, chief naval engr offr 1979-81, controller of the Navy 1981-84; pres IEE 1985-86; dir ERA Technol Ltd (non-exec) 1985; chm Marine Technol Directorate Ltd 1987, dep chm GEC Marconi Ltd 1987, non exec dir Molins plc 1988; hon fell Paisley Coll of Technol 1986; Hon DSc: Univ of Strathclyde 1987, Univ of Bristol 1988; FEng, FRSE, FRAeS, FIEE, OSc; *Recreations* sailing, opera; *Clubs* Army and Navy, MCC, Royal Yacht Sqdn; *Style*— Adm Sir Lindsay Bryson, KCB; 74 Dyke Road Ave, Brighton, Sussex BN1 5LE (☎ 0273 553638)

BUBB, Nicholas Henry (Nick); s of John William Edward Bubb, of Orsett, Essex, and Diana Rosemary, *née* Willetts; *b* 24 Mar 1955; *Educ* Gillingham GS, Christ Church Oxford (MA); *m* 6 April 1982, Susan Mary, da of Francis Dare, of Chichester, Sussex; 1 s (Alexander Benjamin Thomas b 1985), 1 da (Amy Louise Harriet b 1988); *Career* retailing analyst: Rowe & Pitman & Co 1977-79, Citicorp Scrimgeour Vickers (formerly Kemp-Gee & Co and Scrimgwour Kemp-Gee) 1979-88, (ptnr 1982), retailing analyst and exec-dir Morgan Stanley 1988; memb Stock Exchange, AMSIA; *Recreations* cricket, squash, running, gym, swimming, travel, reading, films, wine; *Clubs* Riverside Sports Chiswick; *Style*— Nicholas Bubb, Esq; 6 Orchard Rise, Richmond, Surrey TW10 5BX (☎ 01878 1155); Kingsley House, 1 A Wimpole St, London W1M 7AA (☎ 01 709 3707, fax 01 709 3907, car telephone 0860 643158, telex 8812564)

BUCCLEUCH AND QUEENSBERRY, Mary, Duchess of; (Vreda Esther) Mary; da of Maj William Frank Lascelles (gn of 3 Earl of Harewood), and Lady Sybil de Vere Beauclerk (2 da of 10 Duke of St Albans); *b* 17 Sept 1900; *m* 1921, 8 Duke of Buccleuch and (10 of) Queensberry, KT, GCVO, TD, PC (d 1973); 1 s (9 Duke), 2 da (Duchess of Northumberland, w of 10 Duke; Lady Caroline Gilmour, w of Sir Ian Gilmour, 3 Bt, MP); *Career* held the Queen's (now HM Queen Elizabeth The Queen Mother) canopy at the Coronation in 1937; *Style*— Her Grace Mary, Duchess of Buccleuch and Queensberry; Boughton Manor, Kettering, Northants

BUCCLEUCH AND QUEENSBERRY, 9 and 11 Duke of (S 1663 and 1684); Walter Francis John Montagu Douglas Scott; KT (1978), VRD (1970), JP (Roxburgh 1975); also Lord Scott of Buccleuch (S 1606), Lord Scott of Whitchester and Eskdaill, Earl of Buccleuch (both S 1619), Earl of Dalkeith (S 1663), Earl of Doncaster, Baron Scott of Tynedale (both E 1663), Lord Douglas of Kinmont, Middlebie and Dornoch, Viscount of Nith, Thorthorwald and Ross, Earl of Drumlanrig and Sanquhar, and Marquess of Dumfriesshire (all S 1706); s of 8 and 10 Duke of Buccleuch and Queensberry, KT, GCVO, TD, PC (d 1973) and Mary, da of Maj William Lascelles (ggs of 2 Earl of Harewood); *b* 28 Sept 1923; *Educ* Eton, Christ Church Oxford; *m* 1953, Jane, da of John McNeill, QC, Drumavuic, Argyll; 3 s, 1 da; *Heir* s, Earl of Dalkeith, DL; *Career* served RNVR & RNR 1942-71 Lt Cdr; Roxburgh CC 1958-; MP (C) Edinburgh N 1960-73, PPS to Sec of State Scotland 1961-64; chm Cons Forestry Ctee; hon memb Co of the Merchants of the City of Edinburgh 1981-; Ld-Lt Roxburghshire 1974-75, Selkirk 1975, Roxburgh, Ettrick and Lauderdale 1975-; Royal Highland & Agricultural Soc for Scotland 1969-; St Andrews Ambulance Assoc 1973-; Royal Blind Asylum & Sch; chm: Royal Assoc for Disability & Rehabilitation 1973-; pres: E of England Ag Soc 1976, Royal Scot Agric Benevolent Inst, Scot Nat Inst for War Blinded; chm Cwlth Forestry Assoc 1979-; Capt Royal Co Archers (Queen's Body Guard for Scotland); chm Benevolent Heritage Tst 1985-, chm Living Landscape Tst 1986-; *Recreations* music, painting, field sports, photography; *Clubs* New (Edinburgh); *Style*— His Grace the Duke of Buccleuch and Queensberry, KT, VRD, JP; Drumlanrig Castle, Thornhill, Dumfriesshire (☎ 0848 30248); Boughton House, Kettering, Northants; 46 Bedford Gdns, W8 (☎ 01 727 4358); Bowhill, Selkirk (☎ 20732)

BUCHAN, (Charles) Edward Ralph; s of the Hon William James De L'Aigle Buchan, and Barbara Howard, *née* Ensor (d 1969); *b* 5 August 1951; *Educ* Magdalen Coll Sch Oxford, Univ of Southampton (BSc); *m* 27 Nov 1982, Fiona Jane, da of Capt E P Carlisle, of Llanigon, Hay-on-Wye; 1 s (William b 1984), 2 da (Annabel b 1986, Laura b 1988); *Career* dir Hill Samuel Bank Ltd 1985- (joined 1977); FCA 1976; *Clubs* Travellers'; *Style*— Edward Buchan, Esq; Hill Samuel Bank Ltd, 100 Wood St, London EC2P 2AJ (☎01 628 8011, fax 01 588 5111, telex 888822)

BUCHAN, Lady Evelyn Rose; *née* Phipps; da of 4 Marquess of Normanby, CBE; *b* 1955; *m* 1986, James Buchan, s of Hon William Buchan, of Hornton, Oxon, *qv*; *Style*— Lady Evelyn Buchan; 5 Clover Mews, London SW3

BUCHAN, Hon Mrs Alastair; Hope; da of late David Gordon Gilmour, of Ottawa, Canada; *m* 1942, Prof the Hon Alastair Francis Buchan, CBE (d 1976); 2 s, 1 da; *Style*— The Hon Mrs Alastair Buchan; 10, The Firs, Brill, Bucks

BUCHAN, Janey (Jane O'Neil); MEP (Lab) Glasgow 1979-; da of Joseph and Christina Kent, of Glasgow; *b* 30 April 1926; *m* 1945, Norman Buchan, MP, *qv*; 1 s; *Career* former chm Scottish Gas Consumers' Cncl, Scottish Cncl of Labour Party; former memb Scottish Arts Cncl; *Style*— Mrs Norman Buchan, MEP; 72 Peel St, Glasgow G11 5LR (☎ 041 339 2583)

BUCHAN, 17 Earl of (S 1469); Malcolm Harry Erskine; JP (Westminster 1972); also Lord Auchterhouse (S 1469), Lord Cardross (S 1610), and Baron Erskine (UK 1806); s of 16 Earl of Buchan, and Christina, *née* Woolner; *b* 4 July 1930; *Educ* Eton; *m* 1957, Hilary Diana Cecil, da of late Sir Ivan McLannahan Cecil Power, 2 Bt; 2 s (Henry Thomas Alexander (Lord Cardross) b 1960, Hon Montagu John b 1966), 2 da (Lady Seraphina Mary b 1961, Lady Arabella Fleur b 1969); *Heir* s, Lord Cardross; *Style*— The Rt Hon The Earl of Buchan, JP; Newnham House, Newnham, Basingstoke, Hants

BUCHAN, Norman Findlay; MP (Lab) Paisley South 1983-; s of John Buchan, of Fraserburgh, Aberdeenshire; *b* 27 Oct 1922; *Educ* Kirkwall GS, Glasgow Univ; *m* 1945, Janey, *qv*; 1 s; *Career* former schoolmaster; serv WWII Royal Tank Regt: N Africa, Sicily and Italy; MP (Lab) Renfrewshire W 1964-83, Parly under-sec Scottish Office 1967-70, oppn front bench spokesman Agric Fish and Food 1970-74 (min of state March-Oct 1974) and 1981-83, shadow min Arts 1983-87; *Style*— Norman Buchan, Esq, MP; 72 Peel St, Glasgow G11 5LR (☎ 041 339 2583)

BUCHAN, Hon William James De L'Aigle; s of 1 Baron Tweedsmuir, PC, GCMG, GCVO, CH (d 1940; the author John Buchan), and hp of bro, 2 Baron Tweedsmuir, CBE, CD; *b* 10 Jan 1916; *Educ* Eton, New Coll Oxford; *m* 1, 1939 (m dis 1946), Nesta Irene, da of Lt-Col C D Crozier; 1 da; m 2, 1946 (m dis 1960), (d 1969), Barbara Howard, da of Ernest Nash Ensor of Wimbledon; 3 s, 3 da (of whom 2 are twins); m 3, 1960, Sauré Cynthia Mary, da of late Maj G E Tatchell, Royal Lincs Regt; 1 s; *Career* Sqdn Ldr RAFVR; *Books* author of biography of father: John Buchan, a Memoir (1982); *Clubs* Travellers'; *Style*— The Hon William Buchan; West End House, Hornton, Banbury, Oxon OX15 6DA (☎ Edge Hill 608);

BUCHAN OF AUCHMACOY, Capt David William Sinclair; JP (Aberdeenshire 1959-, Westminster 1972); s of Capt Stephen Lloyd Trevor, JP (d 1959), and Lady Olivia, *née* Sinclair, da of 18 Earl of Caithness, CBE (d 1947); suc maternal gf (18 Earl) as Chief of the Name of Buchan and recognised as such by Lord Lyon 1949; *b* 18 Sept 1929; *Educ* Eton, Sandhurst; *m* 1961, Jon (Blanche) Susan Fionodhbar, *née* Scott-Ellis, da and co-heiress of 9 Baron Howard de Walden; 4 s, 1 d; *Heir* s, Charles Buchan of Auchmacoy the younger; *Career* cmmnd Gordon Highlanders 1949, served Berlin, BAOR and Malaya, Capt and ADC to GOC-in-C Singapore 1951-53, ret 1955; memb London Stock Exchange, sr ptnr Gow & Parsons 1961-68; memb: Queen's Body Guard for Scotland, The Pilgrims, Friends of Malta GC, Alexandra Rose Day Cncl, cncl Royal Sch of Needlework 1987, Cons Industl Fund Ctee 1988; govr London clinic 1988; vice pres: Aberdeenshire CCC 1962-, Bucks CCC 1984-; memb Worshipful Co of Broderers, Freeman City of London; KStJ 1987 (OStJ 1981), cncl memb for London Order of St John; FIOD; *Recreations* cricket, tennis, squash; *Clubs* White's, Turf, City of London, Pratt's, RAC, MCC, Puffin's (Edinburgh); *Style*— Capt David Buchan of Auchmacoy, JP; Auchmacoy House, Ellon, Aberdeenshire (☎ 20229); 28 Little Boltons, SW10 (☎ 01 373 0654) and D-310, Puenta Romana, Marbella, Spain

BUCHAN OF AUCHMACOY, Hon Mrs; Hon (Blanche) Susan Fionodhbar; *née* Scott-Ellis; da of 9 Baron Howard de Walden and (5 Baron) Seaford; co-heiress to Barony of Howard de Walden; *b* 6 Oct 1937; *m* 1961, Capt David William Sinclair Buchan of Auchmacoy; 4 s, 1 da; *Style*— The Hon Mrs Buchan of Auchmacoy; Auchmacoy House, Ellon, Aberdeenshire; 28 The Little Boltons, London SW10

BUCHAN OF AUCHMACOY YR, (John) Charles Augustus David; s and h of Capt David Buchan of Auchmacoy, JP, and Hon Susan, *née* Scott-Ellis, da of 9 Baron Howard de Walden, to which Barony he is in remainder through his m; *b* 1 Mar 1963; *Educ* Ampleforth, RAC Cirencester; *Career* Banker; *Recreations* cricket, tennis, shooting; *Clubs* RAC; *Style*— Charles Buchan of Auchmacoy Yr

BUCHAN-HEPBURN, John Alastair Trant Kidd; s of John Trant Buchan-Hepburn (d 1953), and Edith Margaret, *née* Robb, of Atale Estate Ceylon, and Chagford, St Andrews Fife; hp of kinsman, Sir Ninian Buchan-Hepburn of Smeaton-Hepburn, 6 Bt; *b* 27 June 1931; *Educ* Charterhouse, St Andrews Univ, RMA Sandhurst; *m* 1957, Georgina Elizabeth, SRN, da of Oswald Morris Turner, MC (d 1953), of Armathwaite, Cumberland; 1 s (John Christopher Alastair b 1963), 3 da (Caroline Georgina (Mrs Thompson) b 1958, Sarah Elizabeth (Mrs Cox) b 1960, Louise Mary b 1966); *Career* Capt 1 King's Dragoon Gds, ADC to GOC-in-C Malaya Cmd 1956-57, attached to Swiss Army Cav, served BAOR and Far East; attached Household Cav; brewing sr exec Arthur Guinness & Co Ltd 1958-86, ret; agent Hill Samuel and Royal Insur Co, divnl dir Broughton Brewery Ltd; memb: Inst of Brewing, Burgess and Guild Bros of Glasgow, Incorpn of Maltmen; life memb St Andrew Presentation Tst; Freeman Citizen of Glasgow; *Recreations* gardening, shooting, fishing, walking, old china and glass, golf, tennis, travel in Scottish Islands; *Clubs* New (Edinburgh), Royal and Ancient Golf (St Andrews); *Style*— John Buchan-Hepburn, Esq; Chagford, Argyle St, St Andrews, Fife KY16 9BU; (☎ 0334 72161, 08994 345) office: Broughton Brewery Ltd, Broughton, By Biggar, Lanarkshire ML12 6HQ

BUCHAN-HEPBURN, Sir Ninian Buchan Archibald John; 6 Bt (UK 1815), of Smeaton Hepburn, Haddingtonshire; s of Sir John Karslake Thomas Buchan-Hepburn, 5 Bt (d 1961); *b* 8 Oct 1922; *Educ* Canford; *m* 1958, Bridget (d 1976), da of Sir Louis (Leisler) Greig, KBE, CVO (d 1952); *Heir* kinsman, John Alistair Buchan-Hepburn;

Career served Burma 1943-46 with Queen's Own Cameron Highlanders (wounded 1944); painter (RA and RSA exhibitor); memb Queen's Body Gd for Scotland (Royal Co of Archers); *Recreations* opera, gardening, shooting; *Clubs* New (Edinburgh), Puffin's (Edinburgh); *Style—* Sir Ninian Buchan Hepburn of Smeaton-Hepburn, Bt; Logan, by Stranraer, Scotland DG9 9ND

BUCHANAN; *see*: Leith-Buchanan, Macdonald-Buchanan

BUCHANAN, Alistair John; s of John James Buchanan (d 1983), and Phoebe Leonora, *née* Messel (d 1952), of Grosvenor Square, London; *b* 13 Dec 1935; *Educ* Eton, New Coll Oxford; *m* 1963, Ann Hermione, da of Raymond Alexander Baring (d 1967); 3 da (Katie, Tessa, Helen); *Career* 2 Lt 2 Bn Coldstream Guards 1954-56; Layton-Bennett, Billingham & Co 1959-62; Allen Harvey & Ross Ltd 1962-81; chm and md Mees & Hope Securities Holdings Ltd 1987-; Cater Allen Hldgs plc 1981-85, LIFFE 1981-84, A Sarasin & Co Ltd 1980-; md: Morgan Grenfell Govt Securities, 1985-87: Mannin Industs Ltd, Feathercombe Farm Ltd; Heritage of London Trust Ltd; MIOD; FCA Heritage of London Trust Ltd 1982; *Recreations* golf, gardening, shooting, stalking; *Clubs* White's, Livery, Swinley Forest Golf; *Style—* Alistair Buchanan, Esq; Hillbarn House, Great Bedwyn, Marlborough, Wilts;

BUCHANAN, Sir Andrew George; 5 Bt (UK 1878), of Dunburgh, Stirlingshire; DL (Notts 1985); s of Maj Sir Charles Buchanan, 4 Bt (d 1984), and Barbara Helen (d 1986), da of Lt-Col Rt Hon Sir George Frederick Stanley, GCSI, GCIE, CMG; *b* 21 July 1937; *Educ* Eton, Trinity Coll Cambridge, Wye Coll London; *m* 26 April 1966, Belinda Jane Virginia, JP Notts, da of Donald Colquhoun Maclean, KStJ, of Thurloe Sq, London SW7, and widow of Gresham Vaughan (d 1964); 1 s (George), 1 da, (Laura b 1967), 1 step s, 1 step da; *Heir* s, George Charles Mellish, *qv*; *Career* 2 Lt Coldstream Guards 1956-58, Maj cmdg A Sqdn Sherwood Rangers Yeo (TA) 1971-74; farmer, chartered surveyor, land agent; high sheriff Nottinghamshire 1976-77; chm Bd of Visitors HM Prison Ranby 1983-84; dir Bucentaur Gallery Ltd 1982-; *Recreations* skiing, shooting; *Clubs* Boodle's; *Style—* Sir Andrew Buchanan, Bt, DL; Hodsock Priory, Blyth, Worksop, Notts (☎ Blyth 090 976 204)

BUCHANAN, Dr (Robert) Angus; s of Robert Graham Buchanan (d 1975), of Sheffield and Bertha *née* Davis MBE JP, (d 1975); *b* 5 June 1930; *Educ* High Storrs GS Sheffield, St Catharines Coll Cambridge (BA, MA, PhD); *m* 10 Aug 1955, Brenda June, da of George Henry Wade (d 1975), of Sheffield; 2 s (Andrew Nassau b 1958, Thomas Claridge b 1960); *Career* Nat Serv RAOC 1948-50, GHQ far East Land Forces 1949-50; educ off Royal Fndr of St Katharine, Stepney, 1956-60, co-opted memb London cc Educ Ctee 1958-60, reader Bath univ (lectr, sr lectr) 1960-, dir centre for the History of Technol sci & soc 1964-, Royal cmmr Royal cmmn for Historial Monuments 1979-, properties ctee memb Nat Tst 1974-; pres: Assur for indust Archaeology 1975-77, Newcomen Soc for History of Engrg and Technol 1981-83, visiting prof Aust Nat Univ 1981, Jubilee prof Chalmers Univ Sweden 1984, visiting lectr Wuhan People's Republic of China 1983, chm Bath branch Historical Assoc 1987-, dir Nat Catalogving Unit for the Archives of Contemporary Scientist 1987-; DSc (Engr) Chalmers Univ Sweden 1986; FR Hist S 1978; *Books* Technology and Social Progress (1965), Industrial Archaeology in Britain (1972), History and Industrial Civilisation (1979); *Recreations* walking, travelling; *Style—* Dr Angus Buchanan; Centre for the History of Technology Science and Society, University of Bath, Claverton Down, Bath BA2 7AY, (☎ 0225 826826, telex 449097)

BUCHANAN, Arhcie; s of James Adams Buchanan, of Broadhayne, Dorset, and Aileen Elizabeth, *née* Thompson (1940); *b* 5 July 1928; *Educ* Winchester, St Peter's Coll Oxford, (BA); *m* 7 Jun 1952, Margaret Jean, 1 s (Jamie b 1955), 1 da (Massie b 1953); *Career* served RTR 1946-48, 2 LT; Foote Conc and Belding Ltd 1951-63, dir David Williams and Ptnrs Ltd 1963-68, MD Rodway Smith Advertising Ltd 1969-83, chm Buchanan and Ptnrs 1983-; former chm Royal Cosmetics Branch Inst of Mkting; former Liveryman Worshipful Company of Marketors; FInstD, MInstM; *Style—* Archie Buchanan, Esq; Buchanan & Partners, Buchanan House, Church Sq, Princes Risborough, Bucks, HP17 9AQ, (☎ 08444 2033 fax 08444 2997)

BUCHANAN, Prof Sir Colin Douglas; CBE (1964); s of William Ernest Buchanan (d 1946), of Simla, India, and Laura Kate Buchanan; *b* 22 August 1907; *Educ* Berkhamsted Sch, Imperial Coll London (BSc); *m* 1933, Elsie Alice (d 1984), da of Edward Mitchell (d 1978), of Fulbourn, Cambridge; 2 s, 1 da; *Career* Lt-Col RE, Sudan and N Africa; civil engr, architect and town planner; urban planning advsr Miny of Tport 1960-63, prof of tport Imperial Coll London 1963-72, prof of urban studies and dir Sch for Advanced Urban Studies Bristol Univ 1973-75; conslt in urban affairs; kt 1972; *Recreations* caravans, carpentry; *Clubs* RAC; *Style—* Prof Sir Colin Buchanan, CBE; Appletree House, Lincombe Lane, Boars Hill, Oxford OX1 5DU (☎ 0865 739458)

BUCHANAN, Maj (Harry Alexander) Desmond; MC (1942); s of Lt-Col James Claud Buchanan (d 1952), of Hales Hall, Market Drayton, N Staffs; *b* 10 Nov 1920; *Educ* Imperial Serv Coll (now Haileybury and ISC), RMC Sandhurst; *m* 1, 1948 (m dis 1954), as her 2 husb, Maureen, Marchioness of Dufferin and Ava (*see* Maude, Mrs John); m 2, 1974, Susan Margaret, only da of Lt Cdr Norman Macpherson, of Bearsted, Kent, and gda of Adm of the Fleet Sir Roger Backhouse Bart, GCB, GCVO, CMG, sometime First Sea Lord; 1 s (Harry Alexander b 12 March 1980); *Career* enlisted Gren Gds 1939, cmmnd Gren Gds 1940, no 8 Commando LAYFORCE 1940-41, Special Boat Section Middle East 1941-42, captured Sicily 1942, escaped 1943, 3 Bn Gren Gds Palestine 1945, joined Arab Legion 1947, wounded Jerusalem War 1948, ret 1948; special constable B Div Metropolitan Police 1965-76, prison visitor HM Prison Winchester 1979-; proprietor Mary John Interior Design, sometime dir George Spencer Decorations; *Recreations* shooting, fishing, gardening; *Clubs* MCC, Household Brigade Yacht; *Style—* Maj H A D Buchanan, MC; Keepers, Totford, Alresford, Hants (☎ 0962 732840)

BUCHANAN, Gary Church; s of Robert Smith Buchanan, Kirkcaldy, and Winifred Margery, *née* Church; *b* 30 June 1954; *Educ* George Watsons' Coll Edinburgh, Aberdeen Univ (BSc); *Career* conslt to travel orgns incl BA; travel writer and contributor to numerous pubns; dir: Jersey Artists 1984-, Communecosse 1983-; *Books* Night Ferry (with George Behrend, 1985), Dream Voyages (1989); *Recreations* travel, food and wine; *Style—* Gary Buchanan, Esq; 18 Raith Gardens, Kirkcaldy, Fife KY2 5NJ Scotland (☎ 0592 264 964)

BUCHANAN, George Charles Mellish; s and h of Sir Andrew George Buchanan, 5 Bt, and Belinda Jane Virginia (JP Notts), da of Donald C Maclean; *b* 27 Jan 1975; *Style—* George Buchanan, Esq; c/o Hodsock Priory, Blyth, Worksop, Notts

BUCHANAN, George Henry Perrott; s of Rev Charles H L Buchanan (d 1939), of Kilwaughter, Co Antrim, and Florence Moore; *b* 9 Jan 1904; *Educ* Campbell Coll Belfast, Belfast Univ; *m* 1, 1938 (m dis 1945), Winifred Mary (d 1971), yr da of Alfred H Corn (d 1916); m 2, 1949, Noel Pulleyne (d 1951), yr da of William G Beasley (d 1921), and wid of Maj John A Ritter, RA; m 3, 1952, Hon Janet (d 1968), da of 1 Viscount Margesson; 2 da; m 4, 1974, Sandra Gail McCloy, of Vancouver; *Career* poet and novelist; editorial staff The Times 1930-35, critic News Chronicle 1935-38; pres London Centre Euro Soc of Culture 1954-80; *Clubs* Savile; *Style—* George Buchanan, Esq; 27 Ashley Gdns, London SW1 (☎ 01 834 5722)

BUCHANAN, Nigel James Cubitt; s of Rev Basil Roberts Buchanan, (d 1987), of Cambridge, and Elene, *née* Cubitt; *b* 13 Nov 1943; *Educ* Denstone Coll; *m* 6 July 1968, (Katherine) Mary, da of Prof Sir Arthur Llewellyn Armitage; 1 s (James b 20 Nov 1979), 2 da (Katherine Lucy b 21 Sept 1975, Elizabeth Mary b 15 May 1978); *Career* Price Waterhouse: ptnr 1978-, dir fin servs 1988-; memb FCA; *Books* jt author: Accounting for Pensions, Euromoney Debt - Enquiry Swap Guide; *Recreations* tennis, golf; *Clubs* Carlton; *Style—* Nigel Buchanan, Esq; Longwood, 16 Park Avenue, Harpenden, Herts AL5 2EA (☎ 058 27 63076); Southwark Towers, 32 London Bridge St, London SE1 9SY (☎ 01 401 8989, fax 01 407 0545, telex 884657)

BUCHANAN, Vice Adm Sir Peter William; KBE (1980); s of Lt-Col Francis Henry Theodore Buchanan, and Gwendolen May Isobel, *née* Hunt; *b* 14 May 1925; *Educ* Malvern; *m* 1953, Audrey Rowena Mary, da of Dr Dunstan Edmondson, of Huddington Ct, Droitwich; 3 s, 1 da; *Career* RN 1943-82; COS to Cdr Allied Naval Forces S Europe 1979-82, ret 1982; *Recreations* sailing, walking; *Clubs* Caledonian, Royal Yacht Sqdn; *Style—* Vice Adm Sir Peter Buchanan, KBE

BUCHANAN-BARROW, Paul M; s of Rev Dr H R Buchanan-Barrow, of Henley, Oxon; *b* 23 April 1945; *Educ* Univ of St Andrews (MA); *m* 12 July 1969, Eithne A, da of G W M O'Shea, of Richmond, Surrey; 2 da (Perdita b 1972, Jessica b 1974); *Career* exec search conslt and md Goddard Kay Rogers and Assoc 1986-; merchant banker and dir County Bank Ltd 1981-86; *Recreations* politics, squash, chess; *Clubs* Reform, Honourable Artillery Co, MCC; *Style—* Paul Buchanan-Barrow, Esq; 127 Queens Rd, Richmond, Surrey; Newhouse Cottages, Luxborough, Somerset; Old London House, 32 St James Sq SW1Y 4JR

BUCHANAN-DUNLOP, Brig (Archibald) Ian; CBE (1959), DSO (1944); 2 s of Lt-Col Archibald Henry Buchanan-Dunlop, 18 Laird of Drumhead, Dunbartonshire (d 1947), and Mary Agnes, *née* Kennedy (d 1964); *b* 3 Mar 1908; *Educ* Loretto, RMC Sandhurst; *m* 1938, Renée Caroline Frances, da of John Charles Serjeant, of Hextable, Kent; 1 s, 1 da; *Career* psc, jssc, idc; cmd 6 Cameronians (SR) 1944-45, 1 Royal Scots Fus 1946-47, 2 Royal Scots Fus 1947-48 (N W Europe); DAG FARELF 1956-58, Col Royal Scots Fusiliers 1958-59, dir Boys' Trg WO 1958-60, princ Scottish Off 1960-75; professional artist 1975-; CStJ 1968; *Recreations* gardening, reading, writing; *Clubs* British Water Colour Soc; *Style—* Brig Ian Buchanan-Dunlop, CBE, DSO; Broughton Place, Broughton, by Biggar, Lanarks ML12 6HJ (☎ 379)

BUCHANAN-JARDINE, John Christopher Rupert; s and h of Sir Andrew Rupert John Buchanan-Jardine, 4 Bt, MC, JP, DL; *b* 20 Mar 1952; *Educ* Harrow, RAC Cirencester; *m* 1975, Pandora, da of Peter Murray Lee; 5 da (Tessa b 1979, Katie b 1980, Lorna b 1984, Juliet b 1986, a da b 1988); *Style—* John Buchanan-Jardine, Esq

BUCHANAN-JARDINE, Prudence, Lady; Prudence Audrey; da of William Haggie, of Knayton, Thirsk, Yorks; *m* 1944, as his 2 wife, Capt Sir John William Buchanan-Jardine, 3 Bt (d 1969); 1 s (Charles James), 1 da (Caroline Anne); *Style—* Prudence, Lady Buchanan-Jardine; Moulin de la Mourachonne, 06370 Mouans Sartoux, France AM

BUCHANAN-JARDINE, Sir (Andrew) Rupert John; 4 Bt (UK 1885), MC (1945), JP (Dumfriesshire 1957), DL (1978); s of Sir John Buchanan-Jardine, 3 Bt, JP (d 1969), by his 1 w, Jean, da of Lord Ernest Hamilton, sometime MP N Tyrone (7 s of 1 Duke of Abercorn, KG, PC, and Lady Louisa Russell, 2 da of 6 Duke of Bedford, KG); *b* 2 Feb 1923; *Educ* Harrow, RAC Cirencester; *m* 1950 (m dis 1975), Jane, da of Sir Archibald Edmonstone, 6 Bt, and Gwendolyn, da of Marshall Field, of Chicago; 1 s, 1 da; *Heir* s, John Buchanan-Jardine; *Career* farmer and landowner, formerly Maj RHG; master Dumfriesshire Foxhounds 1950-; KASG; *Recreations* country pursuits; *Clubs* MCC; *Style—* Sir Rupert Buchanan-Jardine, Bt, MC, JP, DL; Dixons, Lockerbie, Dumfriesshire (☎ 05762 2508)

BUCHANAN-SMITH, Rt Hon Alick Laidlaw; PC (1981), MP ((C) Kincardine and Deeside 1983-); 2 s of late Baron Balerno, CBE, TD, JP, DL (Life Peer); *b* 8 April 1932; *Educ* Edinburgh Acad, Trinity Coll Glenalmond, Pembroke Coll Cambridge, Univ of Edinburgh; *m* 1956, Janet, da of Thomas Lawrie, CBE, 1 s (James b 1962), 3 da (Jean b 1957, Margaret b 1960, Fenella b 1965); *Career* Nat Serv in Gordon Highlanders, later Capt 5/6 Gordon Highlanders (TA); farmer; contested (C) West Fife 1959, MP (C) N Angus and Mearns 1964-83, Parly under-sec Scottish Office 1970-74, oppn spokesman Scottish Affrs and memb of Shadow Cabinet from which he resigned over devolution issue 1977, Min of State Ag Fish and Food 1979-83, Min of State Energy 1983-87; *Style—* The Rt Hon Alick Buchanan-Smith, MP; House of Commons, London SW1A 0AA

BUCHANAN-SMITH, Hon Jock Gordon; 4 s of late Baron Balerno (Life Peer); *b* 3 Mar 1940; *Educ* Trinity Coll Glenalmond, Aberdeen Univ, Iowa State Univ USA, Texas Tech Coll, Oklahoma State Univ (PhD); *m* 1964, Virginia Lee, el da of John S Maxson, of Dallas, Texas, 1 s (Peter b 1972), 1 da (Rachel b 1975); *Career* Lt Gordon Highlanders 1963; prof Univ of Guelph, Ontario; *Style—* The Hon Jock Buchanan-Smith; Pitcaple Farm, RR22, Cambridge, Ontario N3C 2V4, Canada

BUCHANAN-SMITH, Hon Mrs George; (Isobel Angela) Margaret; da of Edward Bowden, of Oxshott, Surrey; *m* 1, Stuart McIntosh (decd); m 2, 1961, Rev Hon George Adam Buchanan-Smith (d 1983, sometime housemaster Fettes Coll Edinburgh), eldest s of Baron Balerno (Life Peer); 2 s, 1 da; *Style—* The Hon Mrs George Buchanan-Smith; Woodhouselee, Easter Howgate, Midlothian EH26 0PF

BUCHANAN-SMITH, Rev the Hon Robert Dunlop; 3 s of late Baron Balerno (Life Peer); *b* 1 Feb 1936; *Educ* Edinburgh Acad, Trinity Coll Glenalmond, Pembroke Coll Cambridge (BA), New Coll Edinburgh, Princeton Theol Seminary USA (ThM); *m* 1966, Sheena Mary, da of late Alexander W Edwards, of Duncraggan, Oban, Argyll; 2 s; *Career* minister Christ's Church Dunollie, Oban 1962-66, chaplain to 8 Bn Argyll and Sutherland Highlanders 1963-67, to St Andrews Univ 1966-73, to Highland Volunteers 1967-68, commodore Royal Highland Yacht Club 1977-81, chllr's assessor St Andrews Univ 1981-85, dir Scottish Television 1982-; *Recreations* sailing; *Clubs* Caledonian,

Royal Highland Yacht; *Style*— The Rev the Hon Robert Buchanan-Smith; Eriska, Ledaig, By Oban, Argyll (☎ Ledaig 205)

BUCK, Sir (Philip) Antony (Fyson); QC (1974), MP (C) Colchester N 1983-; yr s of late A F Buck, of Ely; *b* 19 Dec 1928; *Educ* King's Sch Ely, Trin Hall Cambridge; *m* 1955, Judy Elaine, o da of late Dr C A Grant, of Cottesloe, Perth, W Australia; 1 da; *Career* MP (C) Colchester 1961-83, Min for RN 1972-74; chm Cons Party Defence Ctee; chm select ctee on Parly Cmmr for Administration (Ombudsman) 1977-; kt 1983; *Recreations* most sports, reading; *Clubs* Utd Oxford and Cambridge; *Style*— Sir Antony Buck, QC, MP; Pete Hall, Langenhoe, Colchester, Essex (☎ 020 635 230) 23 Cardigan Street, London SE11 5PE

BUCK, Charles Gerard; JP (1966); s of Walter Gerard Buck (d 1934); *b* 21 Sept 1910; *Educ* Trent Coll; *m* 1946, Georgette Forrest, da of John Hamilton Shepherd Raeside (d 1957); 1 da (and 1 da decd); *Career* served Maj RA in UK, India, Africa; CA 1934-; chm: Buck & Lloyd (Sheffield) Ltd 1969-87, Sheffield Brick Gp plc 1975-80; pres Sheffield Amateur Sports Club Ltd; gen cmmr Taxes 1970-82; High Sheriff S Yorks 1980-81; *Recreations* cricket, hockey, golf; *Clubs* MCC, Sheffield (pres); *Style*— Charles Buck, Esq, JP; The Grange, Bradway Road, Sheffield S17 4PF (☎ 0742 363585);

BUCK, David Howard; s of Maj Glyn Howard Buck (d 1977), of Ipswich, Suffolk and Snape, Suffolk, and Mary Elizabeth, *née* Blackburn; *b* 16 Oct 1946; *Educ* St Edmunds Sch Kesgrave Suffolk, Greshams Sch; *m* 10 July 1971, Doreen Jeannette, da of Henry John Slater Wright, of Ispwich, Suffolk; 3 da (Rachel b 1977, Sarah b 1978, Heather b 1980); *Career* articled Ensor Son & Goult Ipswich 1966, qualified chartered accountant and joined Peat Marwick Mitchell Norwich 1972, mangr Ensor Son & Goult Felixstowe 1975-78 (joined 1973); ptnr: Hemming Graham & Poole Norwich 1979-, Stoy Hayward Norwich 1985-, HGP Management Services 1988-; vice pres Gresham Schs 1988 appeal, chm (past tres) Gt Plumstead New Village Hall Assoc 1980-88 (Hall opened 1988); FCA; *Recreations* tennis, swimming; *Clubs* Oasis Sports, Felixstowe Lawn Tennis (vice pres, former tres); *Style*— David Buck, Esq; Oakdene, Church Rd, Great Plumstead, Norwich, Norfolk NR13 5AB (☎ 0603 714 789); 58 Thorpe Rd, Norwich, Norfolk NR1 1RY (☎ 0603 620 241, fax 0603 630 224)

BUCK, David Shuttleworth; s of Douglas Shuttleworth Buck (d 1960), and Gladys May, aka Pearl (d 1988); *b* 8 April 1934; *Educ* Ashville Coll Harrogate N Yorks, Queen Elizabeth GS Gainsborough Lincs, Emmanuel Coll Cambridge (BA); *m* 16 Aug 1958, Jennifer, da of Clifford Kenneth Boundy, of Stratford-on-Avon; 1 s (Stephen b 1963), 3 da (Vanessa b 1961, Katherine b 1964, Margaret b 1969); *Career* Nat Serv FEAF Hong Kong 1952-54, PO RAF Fighter Control; mktg mangr ICI Ltd Fibres Div 1957-76, commerical mangr J Bibby & Sons Henry Cooke 1976-77, assoc ptnr textile analyst Laing & Cruickshank 1978-83, ptnr textile analyst De Zoete and Bevan 1983-86; dir res Barclays De Zoete Wedd 1986-, leading city textile analyst 1984-88, Star Analyst: 1986, 1987, 1988; Top Star Analyst 1987 and 1988, memb of Stock Exchange 1982; FTI 1985, FCFI 1986, ASIA 1981; *Recreations* golf, fell walking, bridge, travel; *Clubs* Inst of Chartered Accountants, Welwyn Garden City Golf; *Style*— David S Buck, Esq; 124 Parkway, Welwyn Garden City, Herts AL8 6HN (☎ 0707 336 827); Barclays De Zoete Wedd, Ebbgate House, 2 Swan Lane, London EC4R 3TS (☎ 01 623 2323, fax 01 626 1753, telex 888221)

BUCK, (Harry) Grant; s of Harry Reuben Buck, OBE, JP (d 1970), of Newmarket; *b* 17 June 1921; *Educ* Perse Sch, Clare Coll Cambridge (MA); *m* 1950, Nancy Elizabeth, da of Frederick Boyton Taylor (d 1959), of Dullingham House, Newmarket; 3 da; *Career* served 1941-46 N Africa and Europe, Maj Royal Inniskilling Fusiliers; Royal Dutch Shell Gp 1947-79 (dir Shell Venezuela 1964-66); chm Star Offshore Services plc 1979-81; int oil conslt and memb bd of advsrs Northville Indust Corpn USA 1981-; *Recreations* travel, swimming, horseracing; *Style*— Grant Buck, Esq; 10 Park Lane, Saffron Walden, Essex CB10 1DA (☎ 0799 21687)

BUCK, Michael Bernard Langdale; s of Horace Kitchen Buck (d 1953); *b* 25 May 1923; *Educ* Cockburn HS; *m* 1956, Brenda, da of Harry Simpson (d 1977); 3 s; *Career* CA, div chm Hargreaves Gp (dir 1971-85), ret; *Recreations* gardening, bird watching, short walks; *Style*— Michael Buck, Esq; Langdale, 55 Breary Lane, East Bramhope, Leeds

BUCKEE, His Hon Henry Thomas (Harry); DSO (1942); s of Henry Buckee (d 1972), and Sarah Emma, *née* Hutton (d 1959); *b* 14 June 1913; *Educ* King Edward VI Sch Chelmsford; *m* 20 May 1939, Margaret Frances, da of Frank Chapman (ka 1915), 2 da (Sarah Alison b 1942, Gillian Frances Mary b 1945); *Career* barr Middle Temple 1939; RNVR 1940-46; Lt Cmdr (Dieppe, DSO) 1942; Staff Course 1944; Arakan and Burma, Malaya 1944-45; Co ct judge 1961; circuit judge 1979 (ret); *Style*— His Hon H T Buckee, DSO; Rough Hill House, East Hanningfield, CM3 5AA (☎ 0245 400226)

BUCKINGHAM, Archdeacon Hugh Fletcher; s of Rev Christopher Leigh Buckingham (d 1963), of Alciston, Sussex, and Gladys Margaret, *née* Shellabear (d 1984); *b* 13 Sept 1932; *Educ* Lancing, Hertford Coll Oxford (MA), Westcott House, Cambridge; *m* 7 Jan 1967, Alison Mary, da of John Heywood Cock, of Norwick; 1 s (William Hugh b 28 Sept 1971), 1 da (Harriet Jane b 10 Dec 1969); *Career* curate: Halliwell St Thomas Bolton 1957-60, St Silas Sheffield 1960-65; incumbent: Hindolveston and Guestwick Norfolk 1965-70, Fakenham Norfolk 1970-88; rural dean Burnham Walsingham Norfolk 1981-87, chm Diocesan Bd for Social Responsibility Diocese of Norfolk 1981-88, hon canon Norwich Cath 1985, archdeacon of the Eat Riding and canon York Minster 1988-; *Books* How To Be A Christian In Trying Circumstances (1985); *Recreations* pottery, gardening; *Style*— The Ven the Archdeacon of East Riding; Brimley Lodge, Beverley, N Humberside HU17 7DX (☎ 0482 881659)

BUCKINGHAMSHIRE, Margot, Countess of; Margot Macrae; da of John Storey Rodger, of NSW, Australia, landowner and timber mill owner; *Educ* privately in Australia and Noumea, New Caledonia; *m* 1, F C Bruce Hittman, MD, FRACS (decd), of Sydney, Australia; m 2, 1972, 9 Earl of Buckinghamshire (d 1983); *Career* Int columnist for Australian gp and various int newspapers (fashion, social, famous people) 1960-70; public relations rep Nina Ricci UK 1971-87; charity work with Cancer Research and Leukemia Research Fund and Royal Manor Hosp; *Recreations* writing poetry, collecting memorabilia; *Clubs* English Speaking Union, UK and USA; *Style*— The Rt Hon Margot, Countess of Buckinghamshire; c/o Barclays Bank, 160 Piccadilly, London W1; 21a Hanover Sq, London W1

BUCKINGHAMSHIRE, 10 Earl of (GB 1746); Sir (George) Miles Hobart-Hampden; 14 Bt (E 1611); Baron Hobart (GB 1728); s of Cyril Langel Hobart-Hampden (d 1972), ggs of 6 Earl of Buckinghamshire; suc kinsman 1983; *b* 15 Dec 1944; *Educ* Clifton, Exeter Univ (BA), London Univ (MA); *m* 1, 1968 (m dis), Susan Jennifer, o da of Raymond W Adams, of Halesowen, Worcs; m 2, 1975, Alison Wightman, da of late William Forrest, of Edinburgh; 2 step s; *Heir* kinsman, Sir Robert Hampden Hobart, 3 Bt *qv*; *Career* dir: Scottish Pension Tstees Ltd 1979-81, Antony Gibbs Pension Services 1981-86, The Angel Tstee Co 1983-86; Hong Kong and Shanghai Banking Corpn 1963-64, Hudsons Bay Co 1968-70, Noble Lowndes & Ptnrs Ltd 1970-81, Wisli Investmt Services Int Ltd, Wardley Unit Tst Mangrs Ltd 1988-, Wisuk Nominees Ltd 1986-, Wardley Fund Mangrs (Jersey) Ltd 1988-, Wardley Investmt Services (Luxembourg) SA 1988-, Gota Global Selection (SICAV) 1988; patron Hobart Town (1804) Early Settlers Assoc (Tasmania); FInstD; *Recreations* squash, fishing, music, reading, walking, rugby football; *Clubs* Western (Glasgow), West of Scotland Football; *Style*— The Rt Hon The Earl of Buckinghamshire; The Old Rectory, Church Lane, Edgcott, Bucks HP18 0TR (☎ 029 677 Underwood 357); Wardley Investment Services International Ltd, 99 Bishopsgate, London EC2P 2LA (☎ 01 626 4811)

BUCKLAND, Ross; s of William Arthur Haverfield Buckland, and Elizabeth Schmitzer; *b* 19 Dec 1942; *Educ* Sydney Boys' HS; *m* 22 Jan 1966, Patricia Ann, da of William Stephen Bubb, of Warriewood, NSW, Aust; 2 s (Sean William b 1968, Mark Charles b 1970); *Career* held various positions in companies engaged in banking, engrg, off equipment and food industry 1958-66; dir fin and admin Elizabeth Arden Pty Ltd 1966-73; Kellogg (Aust) Pty Ltd (various positions) 1973-77; md Kellogg (Aust) Pty Ltd 1978; pres and chief exec offr Kellogg Salads Canada Inc 1979-80; vice-pres Kellogg Co USA; chm Kellogg Co of GB Ltd; dir euro ops Kellogg Co 1981; pres Food & Drink Fedn 1986; *Recreations* walking; *Style*— Ross Buckland, Esq; Beam House, 8 Bucklow View, Bowdon, Cheshire WA14 3JP (☎ 061 941 1319); Kellogg Company of Great Britain Ltd, Park Road, Stretford, Manchester M32 8RA (☎ 061 869 2202, fax 061 869 2795)

BUCKLAND-WRIGHT, Dr (John) Christopher; s of John Buckland-Wright (d 1954), of London, and Mary Elizabeth, *née* Anderson (d 1976); *b* 19 Nov 1945; *Educ* Lycée Francais De Londres, King's Coll London (BSc, AKC, PhD); *m* 11 Nov 1975, Rosalin, da of Charles W G T Kirk, OBE (d 1986), of Hemel Hempstead; 2 da (Helen b 1977, Alexandra b 1978); *Career* asst head dept of comparative osteology Centre of Prehistory and Paleontology Nairobi Kenya 1966-67, teacher Lycée Francais de Londres 1971-72, anatomy lectr St Mary's Hosp Med Sch of London 1973-76, sr lectr Guy's Hosp Med Sch London Univ 1980- (lectr 1976-80), head of macroradiographic res unit Guy's Hosp 1981-; memb Int Cmmn on Radiation Units and Measurements 1987, author of over 60 scientific pubns on microfocal radiography and its application to the study of bone and arthritis; Freeman City of London 1980, Liveryman and Hon Librarian Worshipful Co of Barbers 1980; FZS 1971, memb Anat Soc 1974, memb Br Soc Rheumatism 1984; *Books* Cockerel Cavalcade (1988); *Recreations* fine art and antiquarian books, drawing, painting, walking, sailing; *Clubs* City Livery; *Style*— Dr Christopher Buckland-Wright; 50 Beechwood Ave, Kew, Richmond, Surrey TW9 4DE (☎ 01 876 2011); Anatomy Dept, Utd Medical and Dental Sch of Guys' and St Thomass' Hosps, London SE1 9RT (☎ 01 407 7600, fax 01 407 3913)

BUCKLEY, Anthony James Henthorne; s of William Buckley (d 1956), and Nancy, *née* Stott; *b* 22 May 1934; *Educ* Haileybury and ISC, St John's Coll Cambridge (MA, LLB); *m* 9 March 1964, Celia Rosamund, da of Charles Sanderson (d 1971); 1 s (William b 9 Aug 1964), 2 da (Anna b 24 April 1966, Camilla b 25 Nov 1970); *Career* CA 1959; Peat Marwick Mitchell & Co 1959-62, Rank Orgn Ltd 1962-62, Slater Walker Securities Ltd 1966-75 (md 1972-75), conslt 1975-; memb Worshipful Co of Makers of Playing Cards; *Clubs* MCC; *Style*— Anthony Buckley, Esq; 2 St Mary's Grove, Barnes, London SW13 0JA

BUCKLEY, Rt Hon Sir Denys Burton; MBE (Mil 1945), PC (1970); 4 s of 1 Baron Wrenbury (d 1935); *b* 6 Feb 1906; *Educ* Eton (OS), Trinity Coll Oxford (BA, MA, Hon Fell); *m* 1932, Gwendolen Jane, yr da of Sir Robert Armstrong-Jones, CBE, JP, DL, FRCS, FRCP (d 1943); 3 da (Jane, Catherine, Miranda); *Career* served 1939-45 in RAOC (temp Maj GSO2, Sigs Directorate, WO); barr Lincolns Inn 1928, bencher 1949, pro-treasurer 1967, treasurer 1969), High Ct judge (Chancery) 1960-70, Lord Justice of Appeal 1970-81; Master Worshipful Co of Merchant Taylors' 1972-73; Medal of Freedom (USA) 1945; pres: Senate of Inns of Court 1970-72; Treasury Jnr Counsel (Chancery) 1949-60; Hon Fell American Coll of Trial Lawyers 1970; CStJ 1966, Medal of Freedom (USA) 1945, kt 1960; *Clubs* Brooks's, Beefsteak; *Style*— Rt Hon Sir Denys Buckley, MBE; Stream Farm, Dallington, E Sussex (☎ 0435 830223); 105 Onslow Sq, London SW7 (☎ 01 584 4735)

BUCKLEY, James; s of Harold Buckley (d 1966), and Mabel, *née* Taylor; *b* 5 April 1944; *Educ* Sheffield City GS, Imperial Coll of Sci & Technol (BSc, ARCS); *m* 15 Aug 1972, Valerie (Elizabeth), da of Ivor Powles, of Newport, Gwent; 1 da (Louise b 1976); *Career* scientific offr RAF Coastal Cmd MOD 1965, princ CSD 1971, pte sec to Min for CS and Ldr House of Lords successively Lord Peart, Lord Soames and Baroness Young 1979-82, pte sec to govr Rhodesia 1979-80, sec CS Coll 1982-85, chief exec BVA 1985-87; dep dir-gen, Gen Cncl Br Shipping 1987-; MSAE; *Recreations* photography, squash, tennis; *Style*— James Buckley, Esq; 29 Spenser Ave, Weybridge, Surrey KT13 0ST (☎ 0932 843 893); General Council of British Shipping, 30-32 St Mary Axe, London EC3A 8ET (☎ 01 283 2922, fax 01 626 8135, telex 884008)

BUCKLEY, (Guy) James McLean; s of John McLean Buckley (d 1972), of 46 Chelsea Park Gdns, London SW3, and Oonah Pamela, *née* Thesiger (d 1982); *b* 25 May 1936; *Educ* Eton, Magdalen Coll Oxford (BA); *m* 24 Feb 1968, Elena Rose, da of Hamish Holdsworth Deans, of Auchenflower, Darfield, Canterbury, NZ; 2 da (Virginia b 1969, Elizabeth b 1972); *Career* Nat Serv 2 Lt Rifle Bde 1954-56; slr; ptnr MacFarlanes 1963-; *Recreations* sailing, hill farming; *Clubs* Garrick, City of London; *Style*— James Buckley, Esq; 10 Norwich St, London EC4 (☎ 01 831 9222)

BUCKLEY, Sir John William; s of John William and Florence Buckley; *b* 9 Jan 1913; *m* 1, 1935 (m dis 1967), Bertha Bagnall; 2 s; m 2, 1967, Molly Neville-Clarke, chm MENCAP (Royal Soc for Mentally Handicapped Children and Adults); 1 step s (and 1 step s decd); *Career* gen mangr George Kent 1945-50 (joined 1934); md: Emmco Pty 1950-55, BMC Pty 1955-60; vice-chm and dep chm Winget Gloucester Ltd 1961-68, chm Alfred Herbert 1975-79; memb BSC 1978-, pres Anglo-Soviet Chamber of Commerce 1977-83, former dir BOTB; chm: Alfred Herbert 1975-79, Davy Corpn 1973-82 (formerly Davy Int: md and dep chm 1968-73), Oppenheimer Int 1983- (*see*

Sir David Nicolson); FRSA, Hon FIChemE, FIProdE; kt 1977; *Style*— Sir John Buckley; 21 Mulberry Walk, London SW3

BUCKLEY, Rear Adm Sir Kenneth Robertson; KBE (1961); 2 s of Llewellyn Eddison Buckley, CSI, VD, JP (d 1944), of Heydon, Graffham, Petworth, Sussex, and Innes Elphinston, *née* Robertson; *b* 24 May 1904; *Educ* RNC: Osborne, Dartmouth; *m* 1937, Bettie Helen Radcliffe, da of late Capt E R Dugmore, RN, of Alverstoke, Hants; 1 s, 2 da; *Career* RN 1918; Rear Adm 1958, ADC to HM The Queen 1956-58, Dir of Engineering and Electrical Training Navy and Sr Naval Electrical Offr 1959-62; *Style*— Rear Adm Sir Kenneth Buckley, KBE; Meadow Cottage, Cherque Lane, Lee-on-Solent, Hants (☎ 550646)

BUCKLEY, Dr Richard Anthony; s of Alfred Buckley, of Southampton, and Dorothy Iris, *née* Neale; *b* 16 April 1947; *Educ* Queen Elizabeth GS Wakefield, Merton Coll Oxford (MA, DPhil); *Career* called to the Bar Lincoln's Inn 1969; lectr in laws King's Coll London 1970-75, fell and tutor in law Mansfield Coll Oxford 1975-; writer of various articles for legal periodicals; *Books* The Law of Nuisance (1981), Salmond and Heuston on Torts (19th edn with RFV Heuston, 1987), The Modern Law of Negligence (1988); *Recreations* walking, swimming, working; *Style*— Dr Richard Buckley; 14 Hobson Road, Oxford OX2 7JX (☎ 0865 510537); Mansfield Coll, Mansfield Road, Oxford OX1 3TF (☎ 0865 270999)

BUCKLEY, Lt Cdr Sir (Peter) Richard; KCVO (1982, CVO 1973, MVO 1968); 2 s of Alfred Buckley (d 1952), and Elsie Gwendoline Buckley; *b* 31 Jan 1928; *Educ* Wellington; *m* 1958, Theresa Mary, da of Charles Peter Neve, OBE; 2 s, 1 da; *Career* joined RN as Cadet 1945, invalided 1961, Lt Cdr; private sec to TRH The Duke and Duchess of Kent 1961-; *Recreations* sailing, fishing, beekeeping; *Clubs* Army and Navy, Royal Dartmouth Yacht; *Style*— Lt Cdr Sir Richard Buckley, KCVO; Coppins Cottages, Iver, Bucks (☎ 0753 653004); York House, St James's Palace, London SW1 (☎ 01 930 4872)

BUCKLEY, Vivian Charles John (Pat); s of Charles Mars Buckley (d 1945), of 4 Hans Crescent, London SW1, and Ida, *née* Fennings (d 1955); *b* 21 June 1901; *Educ* Eton, Trinity Hall Cambridge; *Career* WWII Capt Intelligence Corps 1940-45 (mission to USA 1943); Blue Star Line (freight) 1920-24 (helped launch passenger serv 1946-49), Hollywood reporter Sunday Chronicle 1935-38; memb orignial ctee Dockland Island Settlement; Freeman Worshipful Co of Fishmongers; fell RGS 1932-39; *Books* With a Passport and Two Eyes, Tickets Please, Stop and Go, Happy Countries; *Recreations* squash, rackets, golf; *Clubs* Brooks's; *Style*— Pat Buckley, Esq

BUCKLEY, Maj William Kemmis; MBE (1959), DL (Carmarthenshire, latterly Dyfed 1969); o s of Lt-Col William Howell Buckley, DL, of Castell Gorfod, Dyfed, and Karolie Kathleen, *née* Kemmis; *b* 18 Oct 1921; *Educ* Radley, New Coll Oxford; *Career* Lt-Col Welsh Gds, served WWII (despatches) and Suez 1956, mil asst to Vice-CIGS 1958-59; chm Buckley's Brewery 1972-83 (pres 1983-86); dir: Rhymney Brewery (now Whitbread) 1962, Felinfoel Brewery 1975; High Sheriff Carmarthenshire 1966-67; KStJ 1983; *Recreations* gardening; *Clubs* Brooks's, Cardiff and County; *Style*— Maj William Buckley, MBE, DL; Briar Cottage, Ferryside, Dyfed (☎ 026 785 359)

BUCKMAN, Hon Mrs Griselda Rosalind; *née* Eden; 2 da of 6 Baron Henley (d 1962); *b* 16 Jan 1917; *m* 1939 (m dis 1964), John Buckman, late Sqdn Ldr RAFVR, 3 s of late Isaac Buckman; 1 s, 1 da; *Style*— The Hon Mrs Griselda Buckman; 8 High St, West Haddon, Northampton NN6 7AP

BUCKMASTER, Hon Colin John; s of late 2 Viscount Buckmaster, and his 1 w, Joan, da of Dr Garry Simpson; hp of bro, 3 Viscount; *b* 17 April 1923; *Educ* Winchester; *m* 1946, May, da of late Charles Henry Gibbon, of The Lodge, Great Bentley, Essex; 3 s, 2 da; *Career* late Flt Lt RAF; *Clubs* Brooks's; *Style*— The Hon Colin Buckmaster; Ryece Hall, Brettenham, Ipswich, Suffolk

BUCKMASTER, 3 Viscount (UK 1933); Martin Stanley Buckmaster; OBE (1979); also Baron Buckmaster (UK 1915); s of 2 Viscount (d 1974), and his 1 w, Joan, da of Dr Garry Simpson; *b* 11 April 1921; *Educ* Stowe; *Heir* bro, Hon Colin Buckmaster; *Career* FO 1946, first sec Br High Cmmr Kampala 1969-71, Beirut 1971-73, FCO 1973-77, head of chancery Yemen Arab Republic 1977-; FRGS; *Style*— The Rt Hon The Viscount Buckmaster, OBE; 8 Redcliffe Sq, SW10

BUCKMASTER, Colonel Maurice James; OBE (1943); s of Henry James Buckmaster (d 1942), of Fulmer Grange, Stoke Poges, Bucks, and Eva Matilda, *née* Nason (d 1944); *b* 11 Jan 1902; *Educ* Eton; *m* 1, 20 July 1927 (m dis 1941), Dorothy May, da of Otho Steed; m 2, Anna Cecilia, *née* Reinstein; 1 s (Michael Henry), 2 da (Sybil (Mrs Beaton), Tina (Mrs Cullen)); *Career* 2 Lt Intelligence Corps 1939, Capt 50 (4) Div 1939-40 (intelligence offr), Col SOE 1940-45; Ford Motor Co Ltd 1929-60; head of European Dept, md Ford SA (France), dir PR rep CIVC (Champagne Orgn) in UK 1960-83; Officier de la Légion D'Honneur (France, 1977), Croix de Guerre (France, 1945), Officer Legion of Merit (USA, 1947); *Books* Specially Employed (1951); *Style*— Col Maurice Buckmaster, OBE; c/o Walhatch Country Hotel, Forest Row, E Sussex

BUCKNALL, Derek Edwin; s of William Ralph Bucknall, of Norton House, Vision Hill Rd, Budleigh Salterton, Devon, and Nellie, *née* Aston (d 1938); *b* 23 Sept 1936; *Educ* Durham Sch, St John's Coll Cambridge (MA); *m* 26 June 1965, Pamela Marianne, da of James Chalmers Miller (d 1967), of Orchard Brae, Edinburgh; 1 s (Graham b 1970), 1 da (Jane b 1967); *Career* personnel dir ICI Petrochemicals & Plastics Div 1978-86, dir Weston-Hyde Ltd 1983-86, personnel dir Br Aerospace plc 1986-; personnel dir and gen mangr (successively): Polyolefine & Engrg Plastics Business Gp, ICI Fibres Div 1961-77; *Recreations* golf, gardening, enjoying a developing family, watching cricket and rugby; *Clubs* Utd Oxford and Cambridge Univ; *Style*— Derek Bucknall, Esq; Allerton, 27 Orchard Rd, Tewin, Herts AL6 0HL (☎ 043 879 228); Br Aerospace plc, 11 Strand, London WC2N 5JT (☎ 930 1020, telex 919221, fax 389 3986, car ☎ 0860 353 198)

BUCKNER, Jack Richard; s of Rev Richard Pentland Buckner, of Northumberland, and Anne Margaret, *née* Ferguson; *b* 22 Sept 1961; *Educ* St Petroc's Sch Bude, Worksop Coll, Loughborough Univ (BSc); *m* 10 Sept 1983, Kerin, da of Anthony John Wilson; *Career* 5000m runner; Silver Commonwealth Games 1986, Gold Euro Championships 1986, Bronze World Championships 1987, sixth Olympic Games 1988; *Recreations* reading, theatre, cinema, walking, writing; *Style*— Jack Buckner, Esq; 42 Leconfield Rd, Loughborough, Leics LE11 35P (☎ 0509 267772)

BUCKS, Peter; s of Nathan Bucks (d 1959), and Winifred José Beryl, *née* Hooper (d 1959); *b* 30 Sept 1947; *Educ* Sevenoaks Sch, Univ of Southampton (BSc); *m* 1973, Sarah Ann, da of Leslie Bernard Dobson (d 1983); 2 s (Oliver b 1978, Toby b 1982), 1 da (Eleanor b 1980); *Career* merchant banker; dir Hill Samuel Bank Ltd 1987; *Style*— Peter Bucks, Esq; 104 Addison Gdns, London W14 0DS (☎ 01 603 9629); 100 Wood St, London EC2P 2AJ (☎ 01 628 8011)

BUCKWELL, Anthony Basil; s of Maj B A Buckwell, DSO, MC, of Biddestone, Wiltshire, and Y E S Buckwell, *née* Tomlin; *b* 23 July 1946; *Educ* Winchester, RAC Cirencester; *m* 27 April 1968, Henrietta Judith, da of Ronald K Watson, WS, of Yew Tree Cottage, Ham, Marlborough, Wilts; 2 da (Tara b 1970, Alexia b 1971); *Career* merchant banker, dir Kleinwort Benson Ltd London 1985; dir: Centro Internationale Handels Bank AG, Vienna 1985, ABK Spa, Milan 1986; *Recreations* fishing, riding; *Clubs* Brooks's; *Style*— Anthony B Buckwell, Esq; Craven Keep, Hamstead Marshall, Newbury, Berkshire; 20 Fenchurch St, London EC3 (☎ 01 623 8000)

BUCKWELL, (John) Jeremy (Beaumont); s of John Beaumont Buckwell (d 1987), and Margaret Elaine, *née* Lindsay; *b* 12 April 1934; *Educ* Bedford Sch, Cambridge Univ (MA); *m* 1, 30 Mar 1964 (m dis 1977), Cynthia Jane, da of William Denis Heymanson (d 1988); 2 s (Oliver Charles Beaumont b 1966, William Dominic Heymanson b 1967), 1 da (Rebecca Geraldine b 1970); m 2, 4 Jan 1978, Gilda, da of William Hyde Clarke; *Career* Nat Serv Sub Lt RNVR 1952-54; slr, sr ptnr Gates & Co 1986-88 (ptnr 1961-86); sr ptnr Fitzhugh Gates 1988-; chm: Brighton Round Table 1972-, Dist Nursing Assoc Tst 1974-85, Somerset Day Centre Brighton 1978-85; pres Brighton & Hove C of C & Trade 1985; memb Nat Chamber of Trade Legislation & Taxation Ctee 1984-, sec Nat Young Slrs 1967-69, Freeman City of London 1960, liveryman Worshipful Co of Skinners 1960, memb Law Soc 1960- (memb planning ctee 1988-); RTPI 1964- (memb Cncl 1978-); *Recreations* skiing, sailing, golf; *Clubs* Brighton Marina Yacht, Itchenor Sailing, W Sussex Golf, SCGB, Kandahot Ski, Dyke Golf; *Style*— Jeremy Buckwell, Esq; 19 Cornwall Gardens, Brighton BN1 6RH (☎ 0273 552000); 3 Pavilion Parade, Brighton BN2 1RY (☎ 0273 686811, fax 0273 676837)

BUCKWORTH-HERNE-SOAME, Sir Charles John; 12 Bt (E 1697) of Sheen, Surrey; s of Sir Charles Burnett Buckworth-Herne-Soame, 11 Bt (d 1977), and Elsie May, *née* Lloyd (d 1972); *b* 28 May 1932; *m* 1958, Eileen Margaret Mary, da of late Leonard Minton, of Caughley, Shrops; 1 s (Richard b 1970); *Heir* s, Richard John Buckworth-Herne-Soame b 17 Aug 1970; *Career* Nat Serv 4 Regt RHA, RA (TA) (30 years); *Style*— Sir Charles Buckworth-Herne-Soame, Bt; Sheen Cottage, Coalbrookdale, Shropshire

BUDD, Prof Alan Peter; s of Ernest Frank Budd (d 1981) and Elsie Nora *née* Hambling (d 1985); *b* 16 Nov 1937; *Educ* Oundle, LSE (BSc), Churchill Coll Cambridge (PhD); *m* 18 July 1964, Susan, da of Prof Norman Millott, of Millport, Isle of Cumbrae; 3 s (Joel b 1973, Nathaniel b 1976, Saul b 1978); *Career* lectr Southampton Univ 1966-69, Ford visiting prof Carnegie-Mellon Univ of Pittsburgh 1969-70, sr econ advsr HM Treasy 1970-74, prof of economics London Business Sch 1981-88 (sr res fell 1974), Res Bank of Australia res prof Univ of New S Wales 1983, econ advsr 1988-, high level conslt OECD 1976, memb Securities and Inv Bd 1987-88; memb Bloomsbury DHA 1986-; *Books* The Politics of Economic Planning (1976); *Recreations* music, gardening; *Clubs* Reform; *Style*— Professor Alan P Budd; 30 Laurier Rd, London NW5 1SG (☎ 01 485 3779); Barclays Bank 54 Lombard St, London EC3P 3AH (☎ 01 626 1567)

BUDD, Bernard Wilfred; QC (1969); s of Rev William Robert Arscott Budd (d 1955), and Florence Daisy, *née* Hewson (d 1970); *b* 18 Dec 1912; *Educ* Cardiff HS, W Leeds HS, Pembroke Coll Cambridge (MA); *m* 29 April 1944, (Margaret) Meg Alison, MBE, da of Rt Hon E Leslie Burgin PC, MP, of Alpins Close, Harpenden, Herts (d 1945); 2 s (Colin b 1945, Andrew b 1952); *Career* ICS: joined 1935, asst collector Ahmedabad 1935-38, asst collector Thar Parkar Dist Sind 1938-39, special magistrate Sukkur 1939-40, asst collector Thar Parkar 1940-41, dep cmmr Upper Sind Frontier 1941-43, collector Thar Parkar 1943-45, collector Karachi 1945-46, special enquiry offr into corruption 1946-47, dep sec Govt of Pakistan 1947-49, anti-corruption offr and inspr gen of prisons 1949-51; barr 1952, ceased practice 1982; methodist lay preacher; Parly candidate (Lib) elections: Dover 1964 and 1966, Folkestone and Hythe 1974 and 1979; cncl candidate: Shepway Dist Cncl 1983 and 1984, Kent CC 1985; vice-pres Br Gp Int Assoc for Protection of Industl Property; *Recreations* hill walking, birds; *Clubs* Utd Oxford and Cambridge, Nat Lib; *Style*— Bernard Budd, Esq, QC; Highlands, Elham, Canterbury (☎ 030 384 350)

BUDD, Robert Fleming; s of Hal Fleming Budd (d 1976), of Brighton, and Eva, *née* Smith (d 1940); *b* 20 Dec 1930; *Educ* Varndean GS, LSE (BSc); *m* 26 April 1954, Margaret Irene, da of Harold Stenning (d 1976), of Brighton; 3 s (Kevin Robert b 1956, d 1959, Melvin Robert b 1959, Colin Robert b 1961), 1 da (Trudi Lisa b 1961); *Career* 3 Trg Bn RAOC: asst adj and trg offr, 2 Lt 1952-54, 1 Lt 1954; Frank Wright & Son Ltd: trainee mangr 1955-, branch mangr 1957, dir 1967, md 1968; Freeman City of London 1977, Liveryman Worshipful Co Builders Merchants 1977; memb Inst Builders Merchants; *Recreations* golf, squash; *Clubs* Naval; *Style*— Robert Budd, Esq; 3 Hillbrow Rd, Brighton BN1 5JP (☎ 0273 607 044); 124 Lewes Rd, Brighton BN2 3LU (☎ 0273 607 044, fax 0273 685 208)

BUDD, Stanley Alec; s of Henry Stanley Budd, of Edinburgh (d 1968), and Anne, *née* Mitchell (d 1981); *b* 22 May 1931; *Educ* George Heriot's Sch Edinburgh; *m* 5 Nov 1956, Wilma McQueen (d 1985), da of late Thomas Cuthbert, of Dundee; 3 s (Michael b 1959, Christopher b 1965, Benjamin b 1967), 1 da (Jocelyne b 1961); *Career* Nat Serv RAF 1949-51; newspaperman D C Thomson, Dundee and Edinburgh 1947-57; res writer FO 1957-60; second sec HM Embassy Beirut 1960-63; first sec British High Cmmn, Kuala Lumpur 1963-70; asst Euro Integration Dept, FCO 1970-72; dep dir: Scottish Info Off, 1972-73; press sec to Chllr of the Duchy of Lancaster 1973-74; chief info offr Cabinet Office 1974-75; Scottish rep Cmmn of the Euro Communities 1975-88; *Books* The EEC - A Guide to the Maze (1986, 1987); *Recreations* oriental antiques, music, bridge; *Style*— Stanley Budd, Esq; 2 Bellevue Crescent, Edinburgh EH3 6ND (☎ 031 556 7085)

BUDDS, Alan Roy; s of Leonard Frederick George Budds, of Hants, and Olive Miriam, *née* Bone (d 1964); *b* 26 April 1934; *Educ* Luton GS; *m* 28 June 1958, Dorothy Blanche, da of Stephen John Lower, of Luton (d 1980); 2 s (Jonathan Paul b 1963, Richard Mark b 1965), 1 da (Andrea Lorraine b 1960); *Career* admitted slr (1957), cmmr for oaths 1962; pres Luton and Dunstable Law Soc 1983, memb Nat Exec British Legal Assoc, dep registrar Co Ct SE circuit 1985; *Recreations* tennis, ecology, gardening, travel; *Style*— Alan R Budds, Esq; 6 Salisbury Ave, Harpenden, Herts AL5 2QG; Alan Budds & Co, 2 King Street, Luton LU1 2DN (☎ 30544/22194)

BUDGE, Anthony Frederick; OBE (1985); s of Frederick Thomas Frank Budge (d 1985), and Charlotte Constance Annie *née* Parker; *b* 9 August 1939; *Educ* Boston GS; *m* 1960, Janet, da of Harry Cropley (d 1983); 1 s (Karl), 3 da (Elizabeth, Karen, Lindsay); *Career* UK chm and md A F Budge (Contractors) Ltd and Gp Cos 1962-, US chm and md A F Budge (Mining) Ltd and Gp Cos 1977-; FICE, FIHT; *Clubs* Carlton, Turf; *Style—* Tony Budge, Esq, OBE; Osberton Hall, Worksop, Notts S81 0UF

BUDGEN, Nicholas William; MP (C) Wolverhampton S W Feb 1974-; s of Capt G N Budgen (d 1942), of Lichfield; *b* 3 Nov 1937; *Educ* St Edward's Oxford, Corpus Christi Coll Cambridge; *m* 1964, Madeleine Elizabeth, only da of Col Raymond Kittoe, OBE, by his w Rosalind, *née* Arbuthnot (a distant cousin of the Viscounts of Arbuthnott); 1 s, 1 da; *Career* barr Gray's Inn 1962; asst govt whip 1981-82; *Recreations* farming, hunting; *Style—* Nicholas Budgen, Esq, MP; Malt House Farm, Colton, nr Rugeley, Staffs (☎ 088 94 77059)

BUDGEN, Hon Mrs - Hon (Anne) Patricia Rosamund; *née* Wynn; er da of 7 Baron Newborough, DSC; *b* 14 Sept 1947; *Educ* St Mary's Sch Wantage; *m* 1970, Anthony George Budgen; 1 s, 1 da; *Style—* The Hon Mrs Budgen; Boreatton House, Baschurch, Shrewsbury, Shropshire SY4 2EP

BUERK, Michael Duncan; s of Capt Gordon Charles Buerk (d 1974), and Betty Mary Buerk (d 1960); *b* 18 Feb 1946; *Educ* Solihull Sch, Warwickshire; *m* 9 Sept 1968, Christine, da of late Bernard Joseph Lilley, of Hereford; 2 s (Simon, Roland (twins) b 30 Nov 1973); *Career* BBC TV News Corr 1973-: Energy 1976-79, Scotland 1979-81, special 1981-82, Africa 1983-87; corr/presenter BBC TV News 1987- (1982-83); Awards: Royal Television Soc Television Journalist of the Year 1984, Royal Television Soc Int News Award 1984, George Polk Award (US) Foreign TV Reporting 1984, Nat Headlines Award (US) 1984, Int News/Documentary Award Monte Carlo Festival 1984, BAFTA News & Documentary Award 1985, James Cameron Meml Award 1987; *Recreations* oenophily; *Style—* Michael Buerk, Esq; c/o BBC TV News, London W12 (☎ 01 576 7779)

BUFTON, Air Vice-Marshal Sydney Osborne; CB (1945), DFC (1941); 2 s of Alderman James Osborne Bufton, JP, CC (d 1942), of Llandrindod Wells, Radnorshire, and Florence, *née* Peters (d 1936); *b* 12 Jan 1908; *Educ* Llandrindod Wells County Sch, Dean Close Sch Cheltenham; *m* 1 Jan 1943, Maureen Anthony Osra Susanna, da of Col Edgar Monteagle- Browne, DSO (d 1950), of Chelsea; 2 da (Carol Denise b 1945, Marilyn Susan b 1949); *Career* cmmnd RAF 1927, RAF Staff Coll 1939, serv WWII 1939-45, cmd No 10 and 76 Bomber Sqdns, RAF Station Pocklington 1940-41, dep dir Bomber Ops Air Miny 1941-43, dir Bomber Ops Air Miny 1943-45, AOC Egypt 1945-46, Imp Def Coll 1946, Central Bomber Estab RAF Marham 1946-48, dep COS (Ops and Plans) Air Forces W Europe 1948-51, dir Weapons Air Miny 1951-52, AOA Bomber Cmd 1952-53, AOC Br Forces Aden 1953-55, Sr Air Staff Offr Bomber Cmd 1955-58, Asst Chief Air Staff (Intelligence) 1958-61; High Sheriff of Radnorshire 1967; dir: Radionic Products Ltd, Stewart Aeronautical Supply Co Ltd 1962-70; FRAeS 1970; Cdr Legion of Merit (USA) 1945, Cdr Order of Orange Nassau with swords (Netherlands) 1948; *Recreations* hockey (Welsh Int 1931-37), golf; *Clubs* RAF; *Style—* Air Vice-Marshal Sydney Bufton, CB, DFC, FRAeS; 1 Castle Keep, Reigate, Surrey RH2 9PU (☎ 0737 243707)

BUGGLES-BRISE, Rosemary Elizabeth; *née* Craig; da of John Sommerville Craig, of Belsize Park London NW3 4EB, and Agnes Marchbank, *née* Marshall; *b* 23 Oct 1949; *Educ* St Leonards Sch St Andrews Fife; *m* 3 May 1975, Timothy Edward Ruggles-Brise, s of Capt Guy Edward Ruggles-Brise, of Housham Tye, Harlow, Essex; 2 s (ARchie b 1979, Charlie b 1983), 2 da (Olivia b 1977, Felicity b 1984); *Career* HM Dip Serv 1971-75; ptnr Spains Hall Forest Tree Nursery 1979-; *Style—* Mrs Rosemary Ruggles-Brise; Spains Hall Farmhouse, Finchingfield, Essex CM7 4NJ (☎ 0371 810232)

BUJAKOWSKI, Peter Jan; s of Jan Bujakowski (d 1978), and Cora, *née* Leece; *b* 26 April 1952; *Educ* Lancaster Royal GS, Univ of Liverpool, College of Law (LLB Hons); *m* 2 May 1982, Karen Elisabeth, da of Robert Ashton, LRAM, LTCL, of Morecambe; 1 da (Elinor b 1987); *Career* slr; *Recreations* wine, chess, running; *Style—* Peter J Bujakowski, Esq; 6 Grange View, Bolton-Le-Sands, Carnforth, Lancashire LA5 8JQ (☎ 0524 822170); 16 Lancaster Road, Carnforth, Lancashire LA6 9LD (☎ 0524 733691)

BULFIELD, Peter William; s of Wilfred Irving Roden Bulfield (d 1969), of Midhurst, and Doris Margaret, *née* Bedford (d 1974); *b* 14 June 1930; *Educ* Beaumont Sch; *m* 21 June 1958, Pamela June, da of Arthur Henry Frederick Beckett (d 1963), of Buenos Aires; 2 da (Julia Therese b 1960, Marion Louise b 1963); *Career* CA Scotland 1953; dir: Newsphere Trading Co 1963, J Henry Schroder Wagg 1967-86, Darling Hldgs Australia 1973-82; vice-chm Mitsubishi Tst and Banking Corpn (Europe) SA 1973-84; jt dep chm Schroder Int 1977; exec dir Yamaichi Int (Europe) Ltd 1986-88; md and chief exec Yamaichi Bank (UK) plc 1988-; dep chm Crown Agents for Overseas Govts and Admins 1982-85 (memb 1978-85); memb: Overseas Projects Bd 1983-86, Export Guarantees Advsy Cncl 1986-88; *Recreations* music, sailing (yacht 'Keiko IV'), shooting, painting; *Clubs* Kildare Street and Univ, Royal Thames Yacht; *Style—* Peter Bulfield, Esq; 14 Lower Sloane Street, London SW1W 8BJ (☎ 01 730 2493); Yamaichi Bank (UK) plc, Guildhall House, Gresham Street, London EC2V 7NQ (☎ 01 600 1188, fax 01 600 1169, telex 919549 YBKLDN)

BULGIN, Ronald Arthur; s of Wing Cdr Arthur Bulgin, OBE, of Essex; *b* 20 August 1935; *Educ* Westminster, Merton Coll Oxford; *m* 1, 1958 (m dis), Margaret Gray; 2 s, 1 da; m 2, 1969, Elaine Harvey; 1 s, 1 da; *Career* chm Bulgin Gp; *Recreations* riding, golf; *Clubs* Essex Farmers Hunt, Chigwell Golf, RAC; *Style—* Ronald Bulgin, Esq; Norton Manor, Norton Mandeville, Blackmore, Essex (☎ 822211)

BULKELEY; see Williams-Bulkeley

BULL, Anthony; CBE (1968, OBE Mil 1944); s of Rt Hon Sir William Bull, MP, JP (d 1931), of London, and Lady Bull, *née* Lilian Hester Brandon (d 1963); *b* 18 July 1908; *Educ* Gresham's Sch Holt, Magdalene Coll Cambridge (MA); *m* 5 Oct 1946, Barbara (d 1947), da of Peter Donovan (d 1962), of Yonder, Rye, Sussex; 1 da (Caroline (m 1974 Sir Robin Chichester-Clark) b 11 July 1947); *Career* RE 1939-45, staff Capt, Maj WO 1939-42, Lt-Col Trans African lines of communication 1942-43, Lt Col GHQ M East 1943, staff of Supreme Cdr SE Asia 1943-45, Col Tport Div Berlin 1945-46; London Underground gp of cos: joined 1929, serv in staff publicity and p/r depts and in chms off 1929-36, sec to vice-chm London Passenger Tport Bd 1936-39; war service 1939-46; chief staff and welfare offr LPTB 1946, memb: London Tport Exec 1955-62, London Tport Bd 1962-65, vice chm London Tport 1965-71; advsr to House of Commons Tport Ctee 1981-82, tport conslt 1971-89; chm London Regnl Cncl for Technol Educn 1953-62; FCIT (pres 1969-70); Bronze Star (USA); *Recreations* travel; *Clubs* Utd Oxford and Cambridge; *Style—* Anthony Bull, Esq, CBE; 35 Clareville Grove, London SW7 5AU (☎ 01 373 5647)

BULL, Christopher; s of William Albert Bull (d 1984), of Taunton, Somerset, and Norah Bull; *b* 6 Sept 1936; *Educ* Taunton Sch; *m* Patricia Marcelline Barbara, da of Henry John Gardner (d 1983), of Paris; 1 s (James b 1965), 2 da (Helen b 1963, Fiona b 1974); *Career* CA, Goodland Bull & Co Taunton 1957-68, Price Waterhouse Trinidad 1968-71, Price Waterhouse London 1971- (ptnr 1974-); memb: Florence Nightingale Museum Tst Appeals Ctee 1987-88, Guildford Diocesan Bd of Fin 1988; memb ICAEW 1962 (fell 1972); *Recreations* golf, choral singing; *Clubs* Carlton, North Hants GC; *Style—* Christopher Bull, Esq; Kantara, Reading Road North, Fleet, Hampshire GU13 8AQ (☎ 0252 615 008); Price Waterhouse, Southwark Towers, 32 London Bridge St, London SE1 9SY (☎ 01 407 8989, fax 01 378 0647)

BULL, Christopher Robert Howard; s of Robert Golden Bull, of Settle, N Yorkshire, and Audrey, *née* Ineson; *b* 14 May 1942; *Educ* Christ's Hosp, CCC Cambridge (MA); *m* 1 April 1967, Rosemary Anne, da of Frank Coltman (d 1979), of Bromley, Kent; 2 s (Jeremy b 1969, Andrew b 1972), 1 da (Stephanie b 1976); *Career* CA Whinney Murray & Co 1964-68, centre for Interfirm Comparison 1968-71, industl gas div controller Air Products Ltd 1971-75, head of gp fin analysis BICC plc 1975-80, fin dir BICC Technologies Ltd, corporate tres Br Telecom, fin dir BTR plc 1988-, FCA 1968; *Recreations* music, sailing; *Style—* Christopher Bull, Esq; BTR Plc, Silvertown House, Vincent Square, London SW1P 2PL (☎ 01 834 3848/01 821 3752, fax 01 834 2279, telex 22524)

BULL, George Anthony; s of George Thomas Bull (d 1937), and Bridget Philomena *née* Nugent (d 1983); *b* 23 August 1929; *Educ* Wimbledon Coll, Brasenose Coll Oxford (MA); *m* 2 March 1957, Dido Marjorie, *née* Griffin; 2 s (Julian, Simon), 2 da (Catherine, Jennifer); *Career* Nat Serv Royal Fus 1947-49; for news ed Financial Times 1956-59, news ed McGraw Hill World News 1959-60, dep ed The Director magazine 1960-84 (ed in chief), dir Anglo-Japanese Econ Inst 1986-; author pubns incl: translations for Penguin Classics and OUP, Inside The Vatican (1982, translated into many languages); memb Soc of Art Historians; FRSL, FRSA; *Style—* George A Bull, Esq; 19 Hugh St, London SW1V 1QJ; Morley House, 314-322 Upper Regent St, London W1R 5AD (☎ 01 637 7872)

BULL, George Jeffrey; s of Michael Herbert Perkins Bull (d 1965), and Hon Noreen Madeleine Hennessy, da of 1 Baron Windlesham; *b* 16 July 1936; *Educ* Ampleforth; *m* 7 Jan 1960, Jane Fleur Thérèse, da of Patrick Freeland (d 1977); 4 s (Sebastian b 1960, Rupert b 1963, Justin b 1964, Cassian b 1966), 1 da (Tamsin b 1972); *Career* Lt Coldstream Gds 1954-57, served in Germany and UK; joined Dorland Advertising Ltd 1957, joined Twiss Browning & Hallowes wine merchants 1958, md Gilbey Vintners Ltd 1970, dir IDV (Home Trade) and IDV Ltd (Int Distillers and Vintners) 1973, md IDV Europe Ltd 1977, dep md IDV Ltd 1982, dir Grand Metropolitan Ltd 1985, ch exec IDV Ltd 1987, chm and ch exec IDV Ltd and chm Grand Metropolitan plc drinks sector 1988-; *Recreations* golf; *Clubs* Cavalry and Guards', Royal Worlington Golf; *Style—* George Bull, Esq; The Old Vicarage, Arkesden, Saffron Walden, Essex (☎ 0799 550 445); IDV Ltd, 1 York Gate, Regent's Park, London NW1 (☎ 01 935 4446, fax 01 486 2583, telex 261161 INDIST G)

BULL, John William Charles; TD (1960); s of Cdr William Robert Bull, DSC, DSM (d 1975), of Bridlington, Yorks, and Miriam, *née* Bartlett; *b* 3 Nov 1924; *Educ* St Michael's Sch Otford Kent, Kings Coll Taunton Som, Hymers Coll Hull Yorks, King's Coll London; *m* 8 Nov 1947, Cynthia Alicia, *née* Foster; 4 s (Jeremy Miles b 10 Jan 1955, Simon Foster b 20 may 1957, Mark Jonathan b 19 July 1958, Julian Charles b 14 June 1960); *Career* The E Yorks Regt: Private/lance Corpl 1943, 2 Lt/Lt 1946, Capt 4 Bn (TA) 1950, Maj 1952; advertising exec Reckitt & Colman (Overseas) Ltd 1950-55, mktg brands mangr Unilever Export Ltd 1955-60, product devpt mangr Batchelors Foods Ltd 1960-64, gp sales and mktg mangr G Brazil & Co Ltd 1965-68; chm: Bull Holmes Ltd 1968-, White Bull Holmes Gp; memb Hull and E Riding RUFC; *Recreations* cricket, swimming; *Style—* John Bull, Esq, TD; Alliance Ho, 63 St Martin's Lane, London WC2N 4JX (☎ 01 836 4466, fax 01 836 2164, telex 299701)

BULL, Hon Mrs (Judith Florence); *née* Gurdon; DL (1980 Suffolk); yr da of late 2 Baron Cranworth, KG, MC; *b* 8 May 1914; *m* 1943, Maj Thomas Henry Bull, TD, late Lt RA (d 1984), yst s of late William Perkins Bull, KC, of Toronto, Canada; *Style—* The Hon Mrs Bull, DL; Park Farm, Grundisburgh, Suffolk

BULL, Lady; Megan Patricia; OBE (1982); da of Dr Thomas Jones (d 1954), and Letitia Jones; *b* 17 Mar 1922, Naanpoort S Africa; *Educ* Good Hope Seminary Cape Town, Cape Town Univ (MB, ChB), Queen's Univ Belfast (MSc); *m* 1947, Sir Graham Bull, *qv*; 3 s, 1 da; *Career* medical offr Holloway Prison 1966-71, gov 1971-82, ret; DCH, DPM, MRCP; *Recreations* book collecting; *Style—* Lady Bull, OBE; 29 Heath Drive, London NW3 7SB (☎ 01 435 1624)

BULL, Hon Mrs; Noreen Madeleine Mary; *née* Hennessy; 3 da of 1 Baron Windlesham, OBE, JP; *b* 1910; *m* 1931 (m dis 1948), Michael Bull (d 1962), 3 s of late William Perkins Bull, KC, of Lorne Hall, Rosedale, Toronto, Canada; 2 s; *Style—* The Hon Mrs Bull; Flat 25, Belgravia Court, 33 Ebury St, London SW1

BULL, (Oliver) Richard Silvester; s of Walter Haverson Bull, of Shilling Orchard, Lavenham, Suffolk (d 1975), and Margaret Bridget, *née* Horne (d 1983); *b* 30 June 1930; *Educ* Rugby, Oxford Univ (MA); *m* 18 Aug 1956, Anne Hay, da of Hubert Fife, of 19 Bloxam Gardens, Rugby; 2 s (Matthew b 1970, Leroy b 1973), 4 da (Kate b 1960, Alice b 1962, Philippa b 1964, Hannah b 1964); *Career* asst master Eton 1955-77 (housemaster 1967-77); headmaster: Oakham Sch 1977-84, Rugby 1985-; *Recreations* music, reading, walking, sport; *Style—* Richard Bull, Esq; St John's, 13 Horton Crescent, Rugby; School House, Rugby (☎ 0788 3465)

BULL, Sir Simeon George; 4 Bt (UK 1922), of Hammersmith, Co London; s of Sir George Bull, 3 Bt (d 1987), and Gabrielle Muriel, *née* Jackson; *b* 1 August 1934; *Educ* Eton, Innsbruck (Law Faculty), Ecole de Notariat Paris; *m* 17 June 1961, Annick Elisabeth Geneviève Renée, da of late Louis Bresson (d 1960), of Château des Masselins, Chandai, Orne, France; 1 s (Stephen Louis), 2 da (Jacqueline Hester b 15 Oct 1964, Sophia Ann b 2 March 1971); *Heir* s, Stephen Louis Bull b 5 April 1966; *Career* admitted a slr 1959; snr ptnr legal firm of Bull & Bull; Cdre London Corinthian Sailing Club 1968-71; fndg hon sec Assoc of Thames Valley Sailing Clubs 1972-78; memb Cncl Royal Yachting Assoc 1977- 79; Freeman City of London 1955, Liveryman Worshipful Co of Fishmongers; *Recreations* sailing, foreign travel, gardening, carpentry, reading; *Clubs* Royal Thames Yacht, MCC; *Style—* Sir Simeon Bull, Bt; Pen Enez Tremeocx, Pont L'Abbé, Finistère S, France; Oakwood, 97 Island Road, Sturry, Canterbury, Kent (☎ 0227 710241); 24 Albert Square, London E15; 199 Piccadilly, London W1V 9LE (☎ 01 405 7474, fax 01 494 0863)

BULL, Tony Raymond; s of Henry Albert Bull (d 1963), and Phyllis Rosalie, *née* Webber; *b* 21 Dec 1934; *Educ* Monkton Combe Sch, London Univ, London Hosp Med Coll; *m* June 1959, Jill Rosemary Beresford, da of Air Vice-Marshal Albert Frederick Cook, CBE; 1 s (Antony b 1965), 2 da (Amanda b 1960, Karen b 1962); *Career* consultant surgeon: Charing Cross Hosp, Royal Nat Throat, Nose & Ear Hosp; FRCS; *Recreations* tennis (Somerset County) hockey (Essex County); *Clubs* MCC, Queens, Hurlingham; *Style—* Tony Bull, Esq; 26 Scarsdale Villas, London W8 (☎ 01 937 3411); 107 Harley Street, London W1 (☎ 01 935 3171)

BULL, Sir Walter Edward Avenon; KCVO (1977, CVO 1964); s of Walter Bull, of Walton-on-Thames, Surrey, and Florence Bull; *b* 17 Mar 1902; *Educ* Gresham's; *m* 1933, Moira Christian, da of William John Irwin, of N Ireland; 1 s; *Career* chartered surveyor; sr ptnr Vigers 1942-74, dir City of London Building Soc 1957-74, conslt Walter Bull and Co chartered surveyors 1987; memb cncl Duchy of Lancaster 1957-74; Liveryman Worshipful Co of Merchant Taylors; pres Royal Inst of Chartered Surveyors 1956; *Recreations* music, bowls; *Clubs* Naval and Military, Gresham; *Style—* Sir Walter Bull, KCVO; The Garden House, 1 Park Crescent, Brighton, Sussex BN2 3HA (☎ 0273 681196)

BULLARD, Sir Giles Lionel; KCVO (1985), CMG (1981); 2 s of Sir Reader Bullard, KCB, KCMG, CIE (d 1976), and Miriam, *née* Smith (d 1973); bro of Sir Julian Bullard, *qv*; *b* 24 August 1926; *Educ* Blundell's, Balliol Coll Oxford; *m* 1, 1952, Hilary Chadwick Brooks (d 1978); 2 s, 2 da; m 2, 1982, Linda Rannells Lewis; *Career* Foreign Serv: entered 1955, consul-gen Boston 1977-80, ambass Bulgaria 1980-83, high cmmr Barbados 1983-86; *Style—* Sir Giles Bullard, KCVO, CMG; Manor House, West Hendred, Wantage, Oxon OX12 8RP

BULLARD, His Excellency Sir Julian Leonard; GCMG (1987, KCMG 1982, CMG 1975); s of Sir Reader Bullard, KCB, KCMG, CIE (d 1976), sometime Ambass Teheran, and Miriam (d 1973), da of late A L Smith, sometime Master Balliol Coll Oxford; bro of Sir Giles Bullard, *qv*; *b* 8 Mar 1928; *Educ* Rugby, Magdalen Coll Oxford; *m* 1954, Margaret Stephens; 2 s, 2 da; *Career* served HM Forces 1950-52; FO 1953-; serv: Vienna, Amman, Bonn, Moscow, Dubai; head E Euro and Soviet Dept 1971-75, min Bonn 1975-79, dep under-sec FCO 1979- and dep to perm under-sec and political dir 1982-84, ambass Bonn 1984-88; fell All Souls Coll Oxford, hon fell St Anthony's Coll Oxford, memb cncl Univ of Birmingham; *Style—* HE Sir Julian Bullard, GCMG; 18 Northmoor Road Oxford OX2 6VR

BULLEID, Henry Anthony Vaughan; s of Oliver Vaughan Snell Bulleid, CBE (d 1970), of Boxhurst, Dorking, Surrey, and Marjorie Campbell, *née* Ivatt (d 1985); *b* 23 Dec 1912; *Educ* Ampleforth, Cambridge Univ (MA); *m* 11 April 1942, Margery Ann Mary, da of Laurence Dorian McCann (d 1931), of Sutton, Surrey; 1 s (David b 1945), 2 da (Susan b 1948, Hilary b 1958); *Career* prodn and engrg dir ICI Fibres Ltd 1965-72; FIMechE 1949, ARPS 1946, FRPSL 1985; *Books* Special Effects in Cinematography (1954), Master Builders of Steam (1963), The Aspinall Era (1967), Bulleid of the Southern (1977), Brief Cases (1977), Cylinder Musical Box Design & Repair (1987); *Clubs* Athenaeum; *Style—* Anthony Bulleid, Esq; Cherrymead, Ifold, Billingshurst, West Sussex RH14 0TA (☎ 0403 752 309)

BULLEN, James Edward; s of Albert Edward Bullen (d 1977), and Doris Josephine, *née* McHale; *b* 26 Mar 1943; *Educ* London Univ Hampton (LLB); *m* 1, 1973 (m dis 1984); m 2, 27 Sept 1985, mary, da of late Patrick Keane, 1 s (William James b 1986); *Career* called to Bar Gray's Inn 1966, senate of Inns of Ct and Bar 1979-82; *Recreations* music, reading, walking; *Style—* James Bullen, Esq; 5 Kings Bench Walk, Temple, London EC4 (☎ 01 353 2882)

BULLEN, Michael Fitzherbert Symes; s of Lt-Col John Fitzherbert Symes Bullen (d 1966), and Anne, *née* St John (d 1963); *b* 20 May 1937; *Educ* Millfield; *m* 28 April 1962, Sally Elizabeth, da of Frank Forbes Beazley, of Broncroft Parks, Craven Arms, Shropshire; 2 s (Edward b 1966, Henry b 1970), 1 da (Lucinda b 1963); *Career* Nat Serv 3rd Hussars later Queen's Own Hussars 1955-58 (ret as Capt); Olympic Rider Three Day Event Rome 1960, Tokyo 1964; dir Int Bloodstock Shipping Co 1961-; *Recreations* riding, shooting, talking, skiing, motor racing; *Clubs* Cavalry and Guards'; *Style—* Michael Bullen, Esq; Borough Court, Hartley Wintney, Hampshire RG27 8JA (☎ 025126 2592); Peden International, Orchard Garage, Chievely, Newbury, Berks (☎ 0635 24 8911)

BULLEN, Air Vice-Marshal Reginald; CB (1975), GM (1945); s of Henry Arthur Bullen (d 1932), of London, and Alice May, *née* Quaife (d 1947); *b* 19 Oct 1920; *Educ* Grocers' Co Sch, Gonville and Caius Coll Cambridge (MA); *m* 12 March 1952, (Doreen) Christiane, da of Eric Kenneth Phillips (d 1958), of Marseilles, France; 1 s (Michael b 1958), 1 da (Danielle b 1953); *Career* 39 Sqdn Malta 1942-44, 458 Sqdn N Africa, Air Miny 1945-50, RAF Coll Cranwell 1952-54, RAF Staff Coll Bracknell 1955, Exchange USAF Washington DC 1956-58, DSD RAF Staff Coll 1959-61, admin staff Coll Henley 1962, PSO to CAS 1962-64, NATO Def Coll Paris 1965, Adj-Gen AAFFCE 1965-68, Dir of Personnel RAF 1968-69, IDC 1970, Dep AOA maintenance Cmd 1971, AOA RAF Trg Cmd 1972-75; fell and sr bursar Gonville and Caius Coll Cambridge 1975-87, since when life fell and property devpts conslt Gonville and Caius Coll Cambridge; chm Huntingdon Health Authy 1981-; FBIM 1979 (MBIM 1971); *Recreations* work, travel; *Clubs* RAF; *Style—* Air Vice-Marshal Reginald Bullen, CB, GM; Gonville and Caius Coll, Cambridge CB2 1TA (☎ 0223 332437/332455)

BULLEN, Dr William Alexander; s of Francis Lisle Bullen, and Amelia, *née* Morgan; *b* 22 Sept 1918; *Educ* Merchant Taylors', London Hosp Med Coll; *m* 1, 1942 (m dis 1956), Phyllis, da of George Leeson; 3 da (Susan b 1943, Penelope b 1944, Virginia b 1950); m 2, 1956 (m dis 1983), Mary, da of Leigh Crutchley; m 3, 10 June 1983, Rosalind Margaret, da of Lawrence Reginald Gates; *Career* WWII cmmnd RTR (SR) 1939, resigned Major 1946; med dir Boehringer-Pfizer 1957-62, pres Pfizer Canada 1962-64, pres GM Pfizer Consumer Options UK 1964-66, chm Coty (England) 1965-66, md Scribbans Kemp 1966-67, chm Thos Borthwick & Sons plc 1975-81 (md 1967-77), chm Whitburgh Investmts 1976-80, Président Boucherie Bernard Paris 1977-81; memb Canterbury Wine Growers, assoc memb English Vineyards Assoc; Freeman City of London 1975, Liveryman Worshipful Co of Butchers 1975; FBIM 1976, MRCS, LRCP, MRCGP; *Recreations* sailing, music, viticulture; *Clubs* Royal Thames Yacht; *Style—* Dr William Bullen

BULLEY, Philip Marshall; s of Alfred Whishaw Bulley (d 1976), of Carpenters, Udimore, nr Rye, Sussex, and Eileen Mary, *née* Prentice; *b* 1 August 1934; *Educ* Radley, Corpus Christi Coll (MA); *m* 11 Dec 1963, Anne Dione, step da of Samuel Carson Fitzwilliam Allen (d 1987), of Lathbury Park, Newport Pagnell, Bucks; 2 da (Charlotte b 1965, Isabel b 1967); *Career* Nat Serv Intelligence Corps 1953, cmmnd 2 Lt 1954, SMIS served in Malaya 1954-55; dir: J Weiner Ltd 1962-69, City Magazines 1963-69, Berrows of Worcester Ltd 1963-69; md J Weiner Ltd 1967-69, dir Bees Ltd 1967-73, ptnr Theodore Goddard 1987-; *Recreations* golf, opera; *Clubs* Rye Golf; *Style—* Philip Bulley, Esq; Sackville Ct, Kennington Park Rd, London SE11 4JS (☎ 01 735 0503); Theodore Goddard, 16 St Martin's-le-Grand, London EC1A 4EJ (☎ 01 606 8855, fax 01 606 4390)

BULLICK, John; s of James Bullick (d 1951), of Co Monaghan, and Irene Waring McCunn (d 1956); *b* 2 Jan 1902; *Educ* Coleraine Acad Instn; *m* 6 Oct 1934, Helen Mary, da of Samuel Martin, of Belfast; 3 s (Michael b 1937, Peter b 1940, John b 1944), 3 da (Gillian b 1936, Caroline b 1942, Christine b 1946); *Career* banking mangr Northern Bank Coleraine 1956, business interests in New York; High Sheriff Londonderry 1963; *Recreations* shooting; *Clubs* New (Edinburgh); *Style—* John Bullick, Esq; Torsonce by Stow, Galashiels, Selkirkshire (☎ 057 83 235)

BULLIVANT, Col Anthony Stanley; MBE (1944); s of (Bernard) Stanley Bullivant (d 1959), late of Barton Lodge, Cerne Abbas, Dorset (launched Blondin across Niagara), and Mildred Adelaine, *née* Bucknall (d 1956); *b* 9 Feb 1915; *Educ* Harrow, RMC Sandhurst; *m* 18 June 1949, Elizabeth Christian, da of Capt William Martin (d 1947), late of Came, Dorchester; 1 s (George b 1951), 1 da (Caroline b 1952); *Career* Army Offr Cmmns 16/5 The Queens Royal Lancers 1955, Staff Coll 1943, Cdr 1954-57, Col 1969-76, ret Reg Army 1959; elected: Gen Assembly of the C of E 1965, Gen Synod of C of E 1970-75, Salisbury Theol Coll 1967, chm Diocesan Redundant Churches Uses Ctee 1965-, beef farmer 1972-86, memb Cncl Royal Bath and W and S Counties Soc 1969-, memb Magic Circle 1932, extensive Horticultural activities attracting tourism; *Recreations* hunting, shooting, skiing, travel, horticulture, conjuring; *Clubs* Magic Circle (MMC), Cavalry and Guards'; *Style—* Col Anthony Bullivant, MBE; Stourton House, Stourton, Warminster, Wiltshire BA12 6QF (☎ 0747 840417)

BULLMORE, George Hilary Lanyon; s of Edward Augustus Bullmore (d 1948), of Wisbech and Falmouth, and Hilda Maud, *née* Lanyon (d 1922); *b* 23 Mar 1912; *Educ* Oundle, Oriel Coll Oxford (MA, BM, BCh), University Coll Hosp London (LMSSA, DPM (Eng)); *m* 25 May 1948, Kitty, *née* Dedman; 2 s (Christopher b 1949, Theodore b 1950); *Career* Capt 1941-45 RAMC (Lt 1940-41) served India 1943-45; memb med advsy ctee Br Epilepsy Assoc 1951-77 (chm employment ctee), sec PsychoEndocrine Assoc 1957-62, dep physician supt St Ebba's Hosp Epsom 1957-77; pres Kingston Numismatic Soc; Freeman City of London, Liveryman Worshipful Co Apothecaries; *Recreations* numismatics; *Clubs* City Livery; *Style—* George Bullmore, Esq; 12 Portsmouth Rd, Kingston, Surrey KT1 2LU (☎ 01 546 9262)

BULLMORE, (John) Jeremy David; CBE (1985); s of Francis Edward Bullmore, and Adeline Gabrielle, *née* Roscow; *b* 21 Nov 1929; *Educ* Harrow, Christ Church Oxford; *m* 1958, Pamela Audrey Green; 2 s, 1 da; *Career* chm J Walter Thompson 1976- (joined 1954, dir 1964, dep chm 1975), dir J Walter Thompson (USA) 1980-; chm Advertising Assoc; memb Nat Ctee Electoral Reform 1978-; *Style—* Jeremy Bullmore, Esq, CBE; 20 Embankment Gdns, SW3 (☎ 01 351 2197)

BULLOCK, Hon Adrian Charles Sebastian; 2 s of Baron Bullock (Life Peer); *b* 1944; *m* 1970 (m dis 1984), Susan Elizabeth Swindlehurst; 1 da (Hannah b 1977); *Style—* The Hon Adrian Bullock; 46 Walton Crescent, Oxford OX1 2JQ

BULLOCK, Baron (Life Peer UK 1976); Alan Louis Charles Bullock; s of Rev Frank Allen Bullock, of Bradford, Yorks; *b* 13 Dec 1914; *Educ* Bradford Sch, Wadham Coll Oxford (MA, DLitt); *m* 1940, Hilda Yates, da of Edwin Handy, of Bradford; 3 s, 1 da; *Career* historian and writer; fell, dean and tutor New Coll Oxford 1945-52, founding master St Catherine's Coll Oxford 1960-80, vice-chllr Oxford Univ 1969-73; chm tstees Tate Gallery 1973-80; FBA; kt 1972; *Books* Hitler, A Study in Tyranny (1952), The Life and Times of Ernest Bevin (Vol I 1960, Vol II 1967), Ernest Bevin, Foreign Secretary (1983), The Humanist Tradition (1955); *Style—* The Rt Hon The Lord Bullock; The Old Manse, Leafield, Oxon

BULLOCK, David Graham; s of Ernest Cyril Bullock, of Shropshire, and Joyce Eliza Grace, *née* Bailey; *b* 21 July 1941; *Educ* Coalbrookdale HS, Univ of Nottingham (BA); *m* 4 April 1970, Georgina Alexandra Elizabeth, da of Michael Edward Fawcus, of Kenya; 2 s (Piers b 1974, Miles b 1981), 1 da (Romayne b 1977); *Career* dist admin and sec Trade and Econ Relations Ctee (TERC) Southern Rhodesia Govt 1963-64, with Unilever 1965-81, Lever Bros SA 1967-73; dir: Unilever Indonesia 1973-78, Batchelors Foods 1978-81, BP Int 1982-84, PA Consulting Gp 1986-87; chm David Bullock Assocs 1984, formed Warmington Gp 1984; exec memb Cons Foreign and Cwlth Cncl, Br Atlantic Ctee, Peace Through NATO; FInstD; *Recreations* eastern culture, old motor cars, fishing, falconry; *Clubs* Oriental, RREC; *Style—* David G Bullock, Esq; Warmington Manor, South Warwickshire OX17 1BU (☎ 029 589 239); David Bullock Associates Ltd, nr Banbury OX17 1BU (telex 837333)

BULLOCK, Gareth Richard; s of George Haydn Bullock, of Richmond, Surrey, and Veronica, *née* Jackson; *b* 20 Nov 1953; *Educ* Marling Sch Stroud, St Catharine's Coll Cambridge (MA); *m* 3 Sept 1983, Juliet Lucy Emma, da of Maj Cyril Vivian Eagleson Gordon MC, of Winterbourne Gunner, Wilts; 2 s (Joshua b 1985, Marcus b 1987); *Career* vice-pres Citibank NA London 1984-86 (joined 1977), exec dir Swiss Bank Corpn Investment Banking Ltd 1986-; memb ctee St Catherine's Coll Soc; RSPB; *Books* Euronotes and Euro-Commercial paper (1987); *Recreations* second-hand book collecting, ornithology

BULLOCK, Hazel Isabel; *née* MacNaughton-Jones; da of Henry MacNaughton-Jones, MD (d 1950), and Isabel Jessie, *née* Pownceby (d 1929); *b* 12 June 1919; *Educ* Kingsley Sch Hampstead, RADA, St Martin's Sch of Art, Sir John Cass Coll of Art; *m* 1, 8 March 1945 (m dis 1950), Vernon Kelso (d 1959); m 2, 13 Feb 1951, Ernest Edgar Bullock, s of Ernest Peter Bullock (d 1962); *Career* actress and painter (stage name Hazel Lawrence) BBC TV and London Stage 1943-51; exhibitions in London at: Loggia Gallery 1973, Judd St Gallery 1985, Phoenix Gallery 1989; gp exhibitions in London at Browse and D'Arby, Whitechapel Art Gallery, Nat Soc, RBA, HAC, FPS; memb Free Painters & Sculptors Soc; *Recreations* travel; *Clubs* Arts; *Style—* Mrs Hazel Bullock; 32 Devonshire Place, London W1N 1PE (☎ 01 935 6409); Las Cancelas, La Herradura, Granada, Spain

BULLOCK, John; s of Robert Arthur Bullock (d 1960), of London, and Doris Edith

Jane, *née* Thomas; *b* 12 July 1933; *Educ* Latymer Upper Sch; *m* 1960, Ruth Jennifer, da of Vernon William Bullock (d 1979), of Coulsdon Surrey; 3 s (Mark d 1982, Alastair, Robert); *Career* cmmnd RAF 1956-58; Smallfield Fitzhugh Tillet & Co 1949-56 and 1958-61; Robson Morrow 1961 (ptnr 1965-70, Robson Morrow merged with Deloitte Haskins & Sells), ptnr i/c Deloitte Haskins & Sells Mgmnt Conslts 1971-79; Deloitte Haskins & Sells: managing ptnr 1979-85, dep sr ptnr 1984-85, sr ptnr 1985-, vice-chm Deloitte Haskins & Sells Int, chm Deloitte Europe; pt time memb UK Atomic Energy Authy; FCA, FCMA, FIMC; *Recreations* opera, theatre, skiing, sailing, tennis; *Clubs* RAC, Gresham; *Style*— John Bullock, Esq; Deloitte Haskins & Sells, 128 Queen Victoria St, London EC4P 4JX (☎ 01 248 3913, telex 894941)

BULLOCK, John Charles Ernest; s of Ernest Henry Bullock (d 1957), of Kingston Upon Hull, and Emily, *née* Boodie (d 1974); *b* 15 August 1942; *Educ* Hymers Coll Hull; *m* 23 May 1969, Dilys Rosalyn Cross, da of Francis Robert Metcalfe (d 1970), of Kirk Ella; 1 s (Richard), 1 da (Amanda); *Career* slr 1969; clerk to Justices S Hunsley Beacon Div 1971-72; dir: Derwent Valley Railway Co 1976-86, Derwent Valley Hldgs plc 1984-86; underwriting memb of Lloyds 1981-; cncl memb Hull Incorporated Law Soc 1979-85; memb Law Soc 1969; *Recreations* sailing, golf, walking; *Clubs* Royal Yorkshire Yacht, Lloyds Yacht; *Style*— John Bullock, Esq; Westwood hall, Westwood Rd, Beverley, Humberside HU17 8EN; Wilston House, Manor St, Kingston Upon Hull HU1 1YX, (☎ 0482 236017, fax 0482 28132)

BULLOCK, Hon Matthew Peter Dominic; yst s of Baron Bullock (Life Peer); *b* 9 Sept 1949; *Educ* Magdalen Coll Sch Oxford, Peterhouse Cambridge; *m* 1970, Anna-Lena Margareta, da of Sven Hansson, of Uppsala, Sweden; 2 da; *Career* banker; regnl dir Leeds Regn Barclays Bank; *Recreations* gardening, reading; *Clubs* Utd Oxford and Cambridge; *Style*— The Hon Matthew Bullock; 6 Meynell Rd, Hackney, London E9 (☎ 01 986 2833); The Cottage, Kings Lane, Elmdon, Essex (☎ (0763) 838619); Barclays Bank plc, Leeds Regional Office, 6 East Parade, Leeds LS1 1HA (☎ 0532 440232)

BULLOCK, Hon (Oliver) Nicholas Alan; eldest s of Baron Bullock (Life Peer); *b* 28 April 1942; *Educ* King's Coll Cambridge (MA, PhD, DipArch); *m* 1, 1967 (m dis); m 2, 1972 (m dis), Ellen J Blatt; 2 children, 2 step children; m 3, 1984 Sally Todd, da of late Sinclair Holmes, of Bolden; *Career* fell and tutor King's Coll Cambridge, lectr and dir of studies in architecture Cambridge Univ; *Recreations* squash, cycling (competitive), guitar; *Style*— The Hon Nicholas Bullock; King's College, Cambridge

BULLOCK, Peter Bradley; s of William H Bradley Bullock, of Benson, Oxon; *b* 9 June 1934; *Educ* Dudley GS, QMC London (BSc); *m* 1958, Joyce Frances Muriel, da of Horace Rea (d 1957); 2 children; *Career* md Flymo Ltd (memb of Electrolux Gp of Sweden; mfr of lawnmowers; Queen's Award for Export 1982, Queen's Award for Technol 1983) to 1983, jt md Electrolux Gp UK to 1983, gp ch exec James Neill Hldgs plc (Queen's Award for Export 1966 and Queen's Award for Technol 1979) 1983-, and Spear & Jackson Int plc 1985-; CEng, MInstE; *Recreations* sailing; *Clubs* Arts (London), Phyllis Court, Leander (Henley-on-Thames); *Style*— Peter Bullock, Esq; James Neill Hldgs plc, Handsworth Road, Sheffield S13 9BR (☎ 0742 449911, telex J Neill G 54278); The Cottage, Queenwood, Christmas Common Watlington, Oxford OX9 5HW (☎ 049161 2406); The Mill Cottage, Glade, Via Sheffield, Derbyshire, S3O 2ZE (☎ 0433 70231)

BULLOCK, Hon Rachel Anne; only da of Baron Bullock (Life Peer); *b* 1946; *Style*— The Hon Rachel Bullock; St Catherine's College, Oxford

BULLOCK, Richard Henry Watson; CB (1971); s of Sir Christopher Llewellyn Bullock, KCB, CBE (d 1981), of Kensington, London, and Barbara May, *née* Lupton (d 1974); *b* 12 Nov 1920; *Educ* Rugby, Trinity Coll Cambridge; *m* 20 Dec 1946, Beryl, da of John Markes Haddan (d 1950), of Ipoh, Federated Malay States and Shripney; 1 s (Osmund Haddan Watson b 1951), 1 da (Susan Amaryllis Watson b 1947); *Career* War Serv 1940-46, 102 OCTU RAC 1940-41, cmmnd 2 Co of London Yeomanry/ Westminster Dragoons 1941, served England, NW Europe, Italy, Germany 1941-45, instr Armd Corps Offr's Trg Sch India 1945-46, demob 1947 (Maj); joined CS 1947: asst sec Min of Supply 1956-60 (asst princ 1947-49, principal 1949-56), on loan to WO 1960-61, Min of Aviation 1961-64, under sec 1963, Min of Technol 1964-70 (head of space divn 1969-70), dep sec DTI 1970-80, ret 1980; dir-gen Electronic Components Indust Fedn 1984- (conslt dir 1981-84); dir: Berkeley Seventh Round Ltd 1981-87, Grosvenor Place Amalgamations Ltd; vice pres Westminster Dragoons Assoc 1972- (welfare offr 1950-72, chm 1978-82), dir Rugby Sch Devpt Campaign 1981-86, pres Old Rugbeian Soc 1984-86 (memb exec ctee 1950-), vice pres CS Hockey Ctee (pres 1978-84); pres: Rugby Alternatives Hockey Club 1976-, Dulwich Hockey Club 1962-; *Recreations* watching cricket, playing tennis, playing and administering hockey, fishing; *Clubs* Army & Navy, MCC, Hurlingham, Cambridge Union, Dulwich Hockey; *Style*— Richard Bullock, Esq, CB; 12 Peterborough Villas, London SW6 2AT (☎ 01 236 5132); Electronic Components Industry Federation, Romano House, 399-401 Strand, London WC2 (☎ 01 497 2311)

BULLOCK, (James) Rodney; s of James Mayou Bullock (d 1986), of Worchester, and Evelyn Maxine Buckley Bullock; *b* 3 Dec 1945; *Educ* Cheltenham; *m* 1 s (John James b 1979), 1 da (Miriam Catherine b 1983); *Career* slr; *Recreations* squash, racing; *Style*— Rodney Bullock, Esq; 22 College Mews, Stratford-on-Avon, Warwickshire CV37 6FF (☎ 0785 298715); R J Evans Bullock Co, 1266 Stratford Road, Hall Green, Birmingham B28 6BG (☎ 021 777 7222)

BULLUS, Wing Cdr Sir Eric Edward; s of Thomas Bullus (d 1961), of Leeds, and Anna Louise, *née* Dodson; *b* 20 Nov 1906; *Educ* Leeds Modern Sch, Leeds Univ, Lincoln's Inn; *m* 1949, Joan, da of Capt Hector Macdonald Denny (d 1966), of Herne Bay, Kent; 2 da (Rosemary Jane b 1961, Jennifer Joan Davina b 1963); *Career* journalist; MP (C) Wembley N 1950-74, PPS to Min Overseas Trade Aviation and to Sec of State Def 1953-64; memb Church Assembly 1960-70; lay reader Ripon, London St Albans and Canterbury 1929-; kt 1964; *Recreations* swimming; *Clubs* MCC; *Style*— Wing Cdr Sir Eric Bullus; Westway, Herne Bay, Kent

BULMAN, Cdr Arthur Denis; s of H F Bulman, of Morwick Hall; *b* 18 June 1919; *Educ* RNC: Dartmouth, Greenwich; *m* 1940, Katharine, da of Col D McVean; 2 da; *Career* served RN 1937-61, ret as Cdr; with Texaco 1961-81, dir Texaco, md Regent Oil; *Recreations* sailing, shooting, fishing; *Clubs* RN Sailing Assoc, New (Edinburgh); *Style*— Cdr Arthur D Bulman; The Old Manse, Midlem, by Selkirk TD7 4QB (☎ 08357 294)

BULMER, (James) Esmond; MP (C) Wyre Forest 1983-; s of Edward Bulmer and Margaret, *née* Rye; *b* 19 May 1935; *Educ* Rugby, King's Coll Cambridge; *m* 1959, Morella Kearton; 3 s, 1 da; *Career* cmmnd Scots Gds 1954; H P Bulmer Hldgs: dir 1962-, dep chm 1980-82, chm 1982-; dir Nat West Bank (W Midlands and Wales regnl bd) July 1982-; memb exec ctee National Tst 1977-87; MP (C) Kidderminster Feb 1974-83; *Clubs* Boodle's; *Style*— Esmond Bulmer, Esq, MP; 56 Warwick Square, London SW1

BULMER, Ian Lowes; s of Eric Lowes Bulmer, MBE, TD (d 1980), and Monica Evelyn, *née* Head; *b* 16 Oct 1948; *Career* chm Bulmer Travel Associates 1977-; involved various charity works; IATA 1979; *Recreations* art in general, the art of living in particular; *Clubs* Windermere Island (Bahamas); *Style*— Ian Bulmer, Esq; 110 Strand, London WC2R 0AA (☎ 01 836 5244, fax 01 497 9106, telex 916 933)

BULMER, Lady Marcia Rose Aileen; *née* Leveson Gower; da of 5 Earl Granville, MC; *b* 10 Feb 1961; *m* 15 Oct 1986, Jonathan C Bulmer, yst s of late Edward Charles Bulmer; *Style*— Lady Marcia Bulmer

BULMER, Oliver Frederick; s of Robert Harold Bulmer (d 1985), of Hereford, and Pamela Mary Pleasance, *née* Dudding; *b* 29 Oct 1948; *Educ* Hereford Cathedral Sch, Univ of Bristol (BA); *m* 8 Sept 1980, Mary Rose, da of Ian Francis Henry Sconce, OBE, of Westerham, Kent; 3 da (Claire Olivia b 23 July 1981, Felicity Helena b 21 Oct 1982, Alison Rosemary b 2 Aug 1984); *Career* ptnr Pannell Kerr Forster 1979; vice-chm Cottered and Throcking Cons Assoc; FCA 1974, MBCS; *Recreations* tennis, skiing; *Style*— Oliver Bulmer, Esq; Wilding, Cottered, Buntingford, Herts S99 9QB (☎ 076 381 249); Pannell Kerr Forster, 78 Hatton Gdn, London (☎ 01 831 7393)

BULMER-THOMAS, Ivor; CBE (1984); s of Alfred Ernest Thomas (d 1918), of Cwmbran, Gwent, and Zipporah, *née* Jones (d 1952); assumed the additional surname of Bulmer by Deed Poll 1952; *b* 30 Nov 1905; *Educ* W Monmouthshire Sch Pontypool, St John's Coll Oxford (Hon Fell 1985), Magdalen Coll Oxford; *m* 1, 5 April 1932, Dilys Primrose (d 1938), da of Dr William Llewelyn Jones (d 1931), of Merthyr Tydfil; 1 s (Michael Alcuin); m 2, 26 Dec 1940, (Margaret) Joan, da of Edward Frederick Bulmer (d 1941), of Breinton, Herefordshire; 1 s (Victor Gerald), 2 da (Jennifer Elizabeth (Mrs Patten), Miranda (Mrs Wilson)); *Career* served in Royal Fusiliers 1939-40 and Royal Norfolk Regt 1940-42, Capt 1941; sub-ed The Times 1930-37; leader writer News Chronicle 1937-39; leader writer and acting dep ed Daily Telegraph 1952-56; MP Keighley 1942-50, Parly sec for Civil Aviation 1945-46, parly under-sec state for the Colonies 1946-47, delegate to gen assembly of UN 1946, first UK memb of trusteeship cncl 1947; hon dir Friends of Friendless Churches 1957-; chm Ancient Monuments Soc 1978-; memb Parish Clerks' Co 1963; Hon Fell St John's Coll Oxford 1985, Hon DSc Warwick Univ 1979; FSA 1970; Stella della Solidarietà Italiana 1948; *Books* Coal in the New Era (1934), Gladstone of Hawarden (1936), Top Sawyer (1938), Greek Mathematical Works (Loeb Library 1939, 1942), Warfare By Words (1942), The Problem of Italy (1946), The Socialist Tragedy (1949), The Party System in Great Britain (1953), The Growth of the British Party System (1965), Dilysia: A Threnody (1987); *Recreations* ski-ing; *Clubs* Athenaeum, Vincent's (Oxford); *Style*— Ivor Bulmer-Thomas, Esq, CBE; 12 Edwardes Square, London W8 6HG (☎ 01 602 6267); The Old School House, Farnborough, Wantage, Oxon

BULPITT, (Cecil Arthur Charles) Philip; s of Arthur Ernest Bulpitt (d 1943), of Birmingham, and Elsie Louise, *née* Moy (d 1976); *b* 6 Feb 1919; *Educ* Hounslow Coll, Spring Grove Sch, Bradford Univ, Columbia Univ USA; *m* 1943, Joyce Mary, da of R M Bloomfield, of Sussex; 1 s (Michael b 1944), 1 da (Gillian b 1947); *Career* RA (TA) 1939, cmmnd 1941, Capt 1943; West African Field Force 1945, RMA; joined Carrera Ltd 1936, dir 1958, dep chm and chief exec 1967, chm 1969; sr exec Thomas Tilling Ltd 1971, dir 1972 chm 1979-81;dir BIM Foundation Ltd 1977-84 (chm 1979-82); memb: London Regnl Cncl CBI 1978-81, BBC Consultative Gp Indus and Business Affairs 1978-82; Freeman City of London; *Recreations* golf, fishing, climbing, walking, reading, photography; *Clubs* Lansdowne, Stoke Poges Golf, Las Brisas Golf (Spain); *Style*— Philip Bulpitt, Esq; Apt 308, Casa 3, Bloque 1, Andalucia del Mar, Neuva Andalucia, Malaga, Spain

BULTEEL, Christopher Harris; MC (1943); s of Maj Walter Bulteel (d 1965), of Charlestown, Cornwall, and Constance, *née* Gaunt (d 1976); *b* 29 July 1921; *Educ* Wellington, Merton Coll Oxford (MA); *m* 1958, Jennifer Anne, da of Lt-Col Kenneth Previté (d 1974), of Marnhull, Dorset; 1 s (James), 2 da (Cynthia, Nicola); *Career* Coldstream Gds 1940-46, Capt, served in North Africa and Italy; sr hist teacher and head of dept Wellington Coll 1949-54 and 1956-61, chm Abbeyfield Soc 1956-59, headmaster Ardingly Coll Sussex 1962-80; GAP Activity Projects dir 1982-; *Recreations* sailing, natural history, collecting antiques; *Style*— Christopher Bulteel, Esq, MC; 3 Coastguard Cottages, Mevagissey, St Austell, Cornwall PL26 6QP (☎ 0726 843928)

BUMPUS, Bernard Sydney Graham; s of John Graham Bumpus (d 1949), of Sidmouth, Devon, and Gladys Louise, *née* White (d 1976); *b* 10 May 1921; *Educ* Oundle; *m* 30 July 1966, Judith Harriet, da of Robert Collison, of Budleigh Salterton, Devon; 2 da (Nicola b 1967, Francesca b 1968); *Career* Royal Corps of Signals 1940-46; T/Maj on Demobilisation Burma; admin offr Colonial Admin Service Gold Coast/ Ghana 1946-; head of int broadcasting and audience research dept BBC 1960-82; ceramic historian 1982-; organizer Rhead Artists and Potters Exhibition 1986-87; *Books* Charlotte Rhead Potter and Designer; *Style*— Bernard S G Bumpus, Esq

BUNBURY; *see*: Richardson-Bunbury

BUNBURY, Sir Michael William; 13 Bt (E 1681); s of Sir (John) William Napier Bunbury, 12 Bt (d 1985), and Margaret Pamela, *née* Sutton; *b* 29 Dec 1946; *Educ* Eton, Trinity Coll Cambridge (MA); *m* 1976, Caroline Anne, da of Col Anthony Derek Swift Mangnall, OBE, of Bradley Court, Chieveley, Berks; 2 s (Henry b 1980, Edward b 1986), 1 da (Katherine b 1978); *Heir* s, Henry Michael Napier Bunbury b 4 March 1980; *Career* farmer and company director; dir Smith and Williamson Securities; landowner (1100 acres); *Recreations* shooting; *Clubs* Boodle's; *Style*— Sir Michael Bunbury, Bt; Naunton Hall, Rendlesham, Woodbridge, Suffolk IP12 2RD (☎ 0394 460235); No1 Riding House Street, London W1 (☎ 01 637 5377)

BUNBURY, Pamela, Lady; (Margaret) Pamela; *née* Sutton; da of Thomas Alexander Sutton (gs of Sir Richard Sutton, 4 Bt); *b* 22 April 1919; *m* 1940, Sir (John) William Napier Bunbury, 12 Bt (d 1985); 4 s (Sir Michael William, 13 Bt *qv*, Charles Thomas b 1950, Christopher Henry b (twin) 1950, Peter Charles Napier b 1941, d 1964); *Style*— Pamela, Lady Bunbury; 9, Lee Rd Aldeburgh, Suffolk

BUNCE, Michael John; s of Roland John Bunce (d 1977), and Dorothy, *née* Woods; *b* 24 April 1935; *Educ* St Paul's, Kingston Coll; *m* 1 April 1961, Christina, da of Capt Sims (d 1939); 2 s (Charles b 1962, Rupert b 1966), 2 da (Miranda b 1968, Arabella b

1970); *Career* ed: The Money Programme 1968-70, BBC Nationwide 1970-75; BBC chief asst Current Affairs 1976-78, head of TV Information 1978-82, head of Information Div 1982-83, controller Information Services 1983-; visiting ed in residence Univ of Alabama 1987-, Marshall Fund Fell USA 1975; memb of Cncl of Royal TV Soc (chm Pr Ctee); *Recreations* gardening, visiting interesting buildings; *Clubs* Reform; *Style—* Michael Bunce, Esq; BBC, Broadcasting House, London W1A 1AA (☎ 01 580 4468)

BUNCE, Dr Ross John; s of Ross Frederick Bunce, BSc, DFC, of Iver, Bucks, and Gwendoline Janet, *née* Fox; gf played cricket for Sussex CC; *b* 28 Mar 1948; *Educ* Kingsbury Co GS, Univ Coll London (BSc, PhD); *m* 29 Dec 1972, Monique Irene, da of Pierre Roy; former Chief of Police in Sens, of Sens, France; 2 s (Philippe Ross b 27 Oct 1978, John Marc Alexander b 26 April 1980); *Career* asst vice-pres Investmt Mgmnt Bankers Tst Co London 1974-81, Mercury Asset Mgmnt 1981-; dir: Mercury Asset Mgmnt Ltd 1983, Mercury Asset Mgmnt Hldgs 1987; assoc memb Soc of Investmt Analysts ; *Recreations* squash, tennis, golf; *Clubs* Radlett Tennis and Squash, Porters Park Golf; *Style—* Dr Ross J Bunce, Esq; 6 Lamorna Close, Radlett, Hertfordshire; 33 King William St, London EC4R 9AS (☎ 01 280 2800)

BUNCH, Sir Austin Wyeth; CBE (1978, MBE 1974); s of Horace William Bunch (d 1953), and Winifred Ada Bunch; *b* 20 Mar 1918; *Educ* Christ's Hosp; *m* 1944, Joan Mary, *née* Peryer; 4 da; *Career* Lt Essex Regt 1941-44; with Deloite Plender Griffiths 1935-48, S Electricity Bd 1949-76 (chm 1974-76), chm The Electricity Cncl 1981-83 (dep chm 1976-81); nat pres Br Limbless Ex-Service Men's Assoc 1983-; kt 1983; *Recreations* sports for the disabled; *Clubs* Victory (Services); *Style—* Sir Austin Bunch, CBE; Sumner, School Lane, Cookham, Berks

BUNDY, Christopher; *b* 7 Oct 1945; *Educ* Cheshunt GS; *m* 8 Aug 1970, Wendy Constance Bundy; 1 s (Dominic b 1973), 2 da (Phillipa b 1975, Prudence b 1979); *Career* CA; fin accountant Caravans Int Ltd, fin dir subsidiary cos Ley Service Gp; chm and md E J Arnold and Son; chm Br Educnl Equipment Assoc; FCA; *Recreations* wine, computers; *Style—* Christopher Bundy, Esq; Brook House, Elvington, York YD4 5AA (☎ 0904 85 297); E J Arnold and Sons Ltd, Parkside Lane, Dewsbury Road, Leeds LS11 5TD (☎ 0532 772 112, fax 0532 710 487, telex 556347)

BUNFORD, (Max Adolph) Edward; s of Adolph John Tassillo Bunford (d 1939); *b* 10 Nov 1920; *Educ* Coll of Theresianum Vienna, Univ of Vienna (Dr Rerum Pol), LSE; *m* 1, 1946; m 2, 1967, Marie-Claude Blanche, da of André Elysée Bidoire (d 1964; gynaecologist and prof of medicine Paris); 2 s, 1 da; *Career* serv WWII Capt (actg Maj) Middle E, Africa, Europe; chm Layford Gp 1953-74, NSU (GB) Ltd 1955-73, Gestam Guinness Peat Int Realty Ltd 1980-; dir: Bank Gebr Gutmann AG Austria, Comotor SA Luxembourg 1964, Gestam Inc New York (USA) 1976-; *Recreations* yachting (yacht 'Amalia'), dressage; *Clubs* Royal Thames Yacht, Automobile Club de France, Cercle Interallié (Paris), Lyford Cay (Nassau Bahamas); *Style—* Edward Bunford, Esq; 16 Eaton Sq, London SW1 (☎ 01 235 2623); 91 Avenue Henri-Martin, Paris 75116, France; 860 Fifth Ave, New York, NY, USA

BUNKER, Albert Rowland; CB (1966); s of Alfred Francis Bunker (d 1961), and Ethel, *née* Trudgian (d 1938); *b* 5 Nov 1913; *Educ* Ealing GS; *m* 19 Aug 1939, Irene Ruth Ella, da of Walter Henry Lacey (d 1930); 2 s (Richard b 1942, Robert b 1945); *Career* RAF 1943-45, cmmnd air crew 1944; Home Off: asst sec 1948-61, asst under sec of state 1961-72, dep under sec of state 1972-75; served also: Cabinet Off, HM Treasy, Miny of Home Security; *Recreations* golf; *Clubs* RAF, Denham GC; *Style—* Albert Bunker, Esq, CB; 35 Park Ave, Ruislip, Middx HA4 7UQ (☎ 0895 635331)

BUNKER, Christopher Jonathan; s of Jonathan William Bunker, and Beryl Kathleen Rose, *née* Wood; *b* 16 Dec 1946; *Educ* Ilford Co HS, King's Coll London; *m* 9 Sept 1972, Julia Doris, da of Arthur James Seymour Russell (d 1954); 2 da (Jennifer b 1978, Elizabeth b 1982); *Career* accountant; fin dir Westland Gp plc; *Style—* Christopher Bunker, Esq; Westland Group plc, Yeovil, Somerset

BUNKER, Peter John; OBE (1988); s of Leslie John Daniel Bunker (d 1985), of Hove, and Rosa Amelia, *née* Sands (d 1961); *b* 26 Feb 1928; *Educ* Brighton Hove and Sussex GS, Gonville and Caius Coll Cambridge (MA, LLM); *m* 31 May 1952, Angela Elizabeth, RSCN, SCM, da of David Higham (d 1957), of Brighton; 1 s (John b 1957), 3 da (Elizabeth b 1955, Margaret b 1960, Catherine b 1965); *Career* Nat Serv as Acting Petty Offr (radio electrician) Fleet Air Arm 1946-48; slr; pres Sussex Law Soc 1979-80; memb Law Soc's Slr's Assistance Panel; fndr chm PACT; past chm of govrs: Goldstone Junior Sch Hove, Blatchington Mill Comprehensive Sch Hove; fndr chm: Martlet Housing Assoc, E Sussex Cncl on Alcoholism; chm Frederick Soddy Tst; memb Nat Exec United Reformed Church; FRGS 1978; *Recreations* gardening, skiing, listening to music; *Style—* Peter Bunker, Esq, OBE; 38 Shirley Drive, Hove, East Sussex (☎ 0273 503729); Bunker & Co, Solicitors, 9 The Drive, Hove, East Sussex (☎ 0273 29797)

BUNNEY, John Herrick; *b* 2 June 1945; *m* 1970, Pamela Anne Simcock; 1 s, 1 da; *Career* 2 Sec FCO 1971, MECAS 1971, 1 sec Damascus 1974-78, consul Sana'a 1981-; *Style—* John Bunney, Esq; c/o FCO, SW1

BUNTING, Gerald Leeson; DL (1988); s of Charles Gilbert Bunting (d 1967), of Northbrook, Hartlepool, and Edith Joyce, *née* Hopkinson; Landed Gentry family long resident in Kent until 17 C. From thence onwards found as Landed Woolcombers in Northants and Durham. Thomas Bunting of Lydd mentioned in Chamberlains Account Books of Lydd 1429. His gs John (attainted of High Treason for supporting Duke of Buckingham's Rebellion 1493), landed with Henry Tudor of Milford Haven and fought at Bosworth receiving a manor as reward; John Bunting (b 1490, d 1546) was Jurat and MP for New Romney as was his eld s Richard (d 1574); *b* 1 Mar 1928; *Educ* Uppingham; *m* 16 June 1956, Diana, da of Richard Henry Middleton, of Friars Lodge, Bamburgh; 2 s (Gerald) Nigel b 1957, Mark Charles b 1959), 1 da (Diana) Jane b 1962); *Career* cmmd 1947, serv Mid East; TA Capt 508 field squad RE TA 1952-60; slr; sr ptnr Gilbert Bunting & Co; dep Coroner Cleveland N 1968; pres Hartlepool Law Soc 1972-73; pres Durham and N Yorks Law Soc 1988-89; memb: Hartlepool Hosp Mgmnt Ctee 1969-74, Hartlepool Community Health Council 1974-82, Cleveland Family Practitioner Ctee 1985-87; vice-chm Hartlepool Health Authy 1982-89; *Recreations* golf, shooting; *Style—* Gerald Bunting, Esq, DL; Otterington House, Northallerton, N Yorks DL7 9EP (☎ 0609 2545); Gilbert Bunting & Co, Solicitors, Exchange Building, Church St, Hartlepool (☎ 0429 267032)

BUNTING, Sir (Edward) John; AC (1982) KBE (1977, CBE 1960); s of late G B Bunting, of Melbourne, Australia; *b* 13 August 1918; *Educ* Trinity GS Melbourne, Trinity Coll Melbourne Univ (BA); *m* 1942, (Pauline) Peggy, da of late D C MacGruer, of Melbourne; 3 s; *Career* Australian civil servant (ret); chm: Official Establishments Tst 1983-, nat co-ordinator Sir Robert Menzies Memorial Tst 1978-; kt 1964; *see Debrett's Handbook of Australia and New Zealand for further details*; *Books* R G Menzies: A Portrait (1988); *Recreations* cricket, golf, reading; *Style—* Sir John Bunting, AC, KBE; 3 Wickham Cres, Red Hill, ACT 2603, Australia

BUNTING, Michael Geoffrey; s of James Norman Bunting, of 88 Kenilworth Rd, St Annes on Sea, Lancs, and Dorothy, *née* Lowndes; *b* 20 May 1947; *Educ* King Edward VII Sch Lytham, Trinity Coll Cambridge (BA, MA), Manchester Business Sch (MBA); *m* 18 Feb 1984, Sheila Carolyn, da of George Herbert Booth, of Haxby, York; 2 s (Adrian b 1986, Richard b 1988), 1 da (Julia b 1984); *Career* gp tres: Tootal Gp plc 1982-84, The Boots Co plc 1984-; *Recreations* mountaineering; *Style—* Michael Bunting, Esq; 7 Highgrove Gdns, Edwalton, Nottingham, NG12 4DF (☎ 0602 231 406); The Boots Co plc, Head Office, Notts NG2 3AA (☎ 0602 506 111, fax 0602 592 727)

BUNTON, Christopher John; s of John Bunton, and Marion Helen, *née* Gotobed; *b* 22 Feb 1948; *Educ* Charterhouse, Trinity Coll Cambridge (MA), London Graduate Sch of Business Studies (MSc); *m* 10 May 1975, Jane Melanie, da of Antony J S Cartmell; 2 s (Anthony, Michael); *Career* with Gulf Oil Corpn 1973-1985, gp tres Saatchi & Saatchi plc 1986-; *Recreations* music; *Clubs* Hawks; *Style—* Christopher Bunton, Esq; Saatchi & Saatchi Co plc, 15 Lower Regent St, London SW1Y 4LR (☎ 01 930 2161)

BUNYAN, Stephen Alexander; TD (1968); s of Herbert Sandilands Bunyan (d 1974), of Melrose, and Alma Brooker; *b* 29 Oct 1933; *Educ* Galashiels Acad, Edinburgh Univ (MA, DipEd FSA Scot); *m* 3 Aug 1963, Diana Clare (d 1983), da of Dr Bernard William Paine (d 1985), of Rushden, Northants; 1 s (Alasdair James b 1970), 2 da (Alexandra Jane b 1964, Eleanor Anne b 1967); *Career* Co Cdr A (East Lothian) Company in TA service in Edinburgh Univ Contingent the OTC 357, Light Regt RA (TA) and 278 Field Regt RA (TA); cmd the City of Edinburgh Battery in the Lowland Regt Territorials (AVR III) 1967-69; schoolmaster, princ teacher of History Dublin GS; hon sec East Lothian Antiquarian and Field Naturalist Soc; hon vice pres East Lothian Conservative Assoc; chm Dunbar Community Cncl; *Books* A Walk Round Historic Dunbar; *Clubs* Lothian Battalion the ACF, Local History; *Style—* Stephen Bunyan, Esq, TD; Inchgarth, East Links, Dunbar EH42 1LT (☎ 0368 63335)

BUNYARD, Robert Sidney; CBE (1986), QPM (1978); s of Albert Percy Bunyard, and Nellie Maria, *née* Mount; *b* 20 May 1930; *Educ* Queen Elizabeth GS Faversham, Regent Street Polytechnic Mgmnt Sch, Open Univ (BA Hons); *m* 1948, Ruth; 2 da (Anne, Christine); *Career* joined Met Police 1952, chief superintendent: Lewisham 1969-71, Greenwich 1971-72; asst chief constable Leicestershire 1972-77; Royal Coll of Defence Studies 1977, dep chief constable Essex 1977 (chief constable 1978); chm: ACPO Computer Ctee 1980-82, ACPO Training Ctee 1984-87, No 5 Regional Crime Squad Ctee 1980-87; HM inspector of constabulary 1988-, cmdt Police Staff Coll 1988-; MIPM, CBIM; *Books* Police Organisation and Command (1978), Police Management Handbook (1979); *Recreations* music, opera, painting; *Style—* Robert Bunyard, Esq, CBE, QPM; The Police Staff College, Bramshill, Bramshill House, Hartley Witney, Hampshire RG27 0JW (☎ 025 126 2931)

BUNZL, Thomas F; s of Dr Max Bunzl; *b* 13 Dec 1934; *Educ* Bembridge Sch IOW, Glasgow Univ, Univ of California; *m* 1959, Marian, da of Walter Strauss; 2 da; *Career* md Electrautom Ltd 1965-; MIEE, MIEEE, FISM, FIPM; *Style—* Thomas Bunzl, Esq; 126 West Heath Rd, London NW3 (☎ 01 458 2691)

BURBIDGE, Sir Herbert Dudley; 5 Bt (UK 1916); s of late Herbert Edward Burbidge, 2 s of 1 Bt; suc kinsman, Sir John Richard Woodman Burbidge, 4 Bt, 1974; *b* 13 Nov 1904; *Educ* University Sch Victoria BC Canada; *m* 1933, Ruby, da of Charles Ethelbert Taylor, of Comox, Vancouver 1, BC; 1 s; *Heir* s, Peter Burbidge; *Career* mangr Silverwood Industries (Vancouver) 1931-70; *Style—* Sir Herbert Burbidge, Bt; 12549, 27th Avenue, Surrey, Br Columbia, Canada

BURBIDGE, Peter Dudley; s and h of Sir Herbert Burbidge, 5 Bt; *b* 20 June 1942; *m* 1967, Peggy Marilyn, da of Kenneth Anderson, of Ladner, BC; 1 s, 1 da; *Style—* Peter Burbidge, Esq; 3809 West 24th Ave, Vancouver, BC, Canada

BURBRIDGE, Very Rev (John) Paul; s of John Henry Gray Burbridge (d 1980), of Warninglid, Sussex, and Dorothy Vera, *née* Pratt (d 1981); *b* 21 May 1932; *Educ* Kings Sch Canterbury, Kings Coll Cambridge (MA), New Coll Oxford (MA), Wells Theol Coll; *m* 7 July 1956, Olive Denise, da of Denis Arthur Grenfell, of Holcombe, Dawlish, S Devon; 4 da (Rachel (Mrs Howgego) b 1960, Deborah (Mrs Johnson) b 1962, Sarah b 1966, Felicity b 1969); *Career* Nat Serv Cmmn RA 1957, Asst Adj 80 LAA Regt RA; curate Eastbourne Parish Church 1959-62, chamberlain York Minster 1962-76 (canon residentiary and presentor 1966-76), archdeacon of Richmond 1976-83, dean of Norwich 1983-; *Style—* The Very Rev the Dean of Norwich; The Deanery, Norwich, Norfolk (☎ 0603 760140)

BURBRIDGE, Stephen Nigel; s of John Henry Gray Burbridge (d 1980), and Dorothy Vera, *née* Pratt (d 1981); *b* 18 July 1934; *Educ* King's Sch Canterbury, Christ Church Oxford (MA); *Career* Nat Serv 2Lt RA 1953-55; asst princ BOT 1958; first sec: commercial Karachi 1963, economic Rawalpindi 1965; DTI: princ 1967, asst sec 1971, under sec 1980; sec to the Monopolies and Mergers Cmmn 1986; *Recreations* sport, reading, collecting; *Clubs* Rye Golf, West Sussex Golf; *Style—* Stephen Burbridge, Esq; Monopolies and Mergers Commission, New Court, 48 Carey Street, London WC2A 2JT, (☎ 01 324 1427, fax 01 324 1400)

BURBURY, Lt Cdr Nigel Hawkesly; s of Wing Cdr William Hawkesly Burbury, DFC, AFC (d 1986), of Henlow, and Esme Mary, *née* Cantrell; *b* 29 Dec 1937; *Educ* Wellington Coll Berks, Naval Coll Dartmouth; *m* 12 Nov 1960, Jean Mary, da of Major Frank Murdoch (d 1982); 2 s (Ian b 1961, Nicola b 1963, Duncan b 1966); *Career* naval offr 1956-81, Lt Cdr Active Serv 845 Sqdn Borneo 1963-65, (awarded AFC 1970); CO 772 Sqdn 1974-75; farmer 1981-87 (ret, ill health 1987); *Recreations* shooting; *Clubs* Fleet Air Arm Offrs Assoc; *Style—* Lt-Cdr Nigel H Burbury; Isca Villa, 28 Denmark Road, Exeter, Devon EX1 1SE (☎ 0392 73313)

BURBURY, Hon Mrs (Sarah Dingle); *née* Foot; o da of Baron Caradon, GCMG, KCVO, OBE, PC (Life Peer), *qv*; *b* 24 Sept 1939; *m* 1961, Maj Timothy Nicholas Percival Winter Burbury, The Blues and Royals, s of Surgn-Col Dermot Roland Winter Burbury; 1 s (Charles b 1964), 1 da (Camilla (Mrs Mark Lindfield) b 1962); *Career* author and editor of Cornish Scene magazine under maiden name Sarah Foot; *Books Incl:* Following the River Fowey, Following the Tamar, My Grandfather Isaac Foot, The Cornish Countryside; *Style—* The Hon Mrs Burbury; Ince Barton, Saltash, Cornwall (☎ Saltash (075 55) 7709)

BURBURY, Hon Sir Stanley Charles; KCMG (1981), KCVO (1977), KBE (1958), QC (1950); s of Daniel Charles Burbury and Mary, *née* Cunningham; *b* 2 Dec 1909; *Educ* Hutchins Sch Tasmania, Univ of Tasmania (LLB); *m* 1934, Pearl Christine, da of late Wallace Barren; *Career* barr 1934, slr-gen Tas 1952, chief justice Supreme Ct of Tas 1956-73, governor of Tasmania 1973-82; Hon LLD Univ of Tasmania; KStJ 1974; *Recreations* lawn bowls, music; *Clubs* Royal Hobart Bowls; *Style*— Hon Sir Stanley Burbury, KCMG, KCVO, KBE; 3 Mona St, Kingston, Tas 7150, Australia

BURCH, Maj-Gen Keith; CB (1985), CBE (1977, MBE 1965); s of Christopher Burch, of Saltdean, Sussex, and Gwendoline Ada, *née* James; *b* 31 May 1931; *Educ* Bedford Modern Sch, RMA Sandhurst; *m* 12 June 1957, Sara Vivette, da of Reginald Thomas Hales (d 1974); 2 da (Amanda b 1958, Emma b 1960), 1 s (Giles St John b 1966); *Career* cmmnd Essex Regt 1951, directing staff Staff Coll Camberley 1968-69, cmd 3 Bn The Royal Anglian Regt 1969-71, asst sec Chiefs of Staff Ctee MOD 1972-75, Col GS HQ 2 Armoured Div 1975-78, dir Administrative Planning (Army) MOD 1978-80, Indian Nat Defence Coll New Delhi 1981, dep dir Army Staff Duties MOD 1981-83, asst chief of the Defence Staff (personnel and logistics) MOD 1984, dir personnel MOD, 1985; chapter clerk York Minster 1985; *Recreations* country pursuits; *Clubs* Yorkshire (York); *Style*— Maj Gen Keith Burch, CB, CBE; Mayfield, Sandy Lane, Stockton on the Forest, York YO3 9US

BURCHFIELD, Dr Robert William; CBE (1975); s of Frederick Burchfield (d 1979), and Mary Lauder (d 1974), *née* Blair; *b* 27 Jan 1923; *Educ* Wanganui Tech Coll NZ, Victoria Univ Coll Wellington NZ, Magdalen Coll Oxford; *m* 1, 1949 (m dis 1976), Ethel May Yates; 1 s (Jonathan), 2 da (Jennifer, Elizabeth); m 2, 1976, Elizabeth Austen, da of Cedric Hankinson Knight (d 1983); *Career* RNZA 1941-46, NZ and Italy, Sgt 1941-44; lectr in English language CC Oxford 1953-57, fell and tutor in English language St Peter's Coll Oxford 1963-79, sr res fell 1979-; ed A Supplement to the Oxford English Dictionary 1957-86; *Books* The Oxford Dictionary of English Etymology (with C T Onions and G W S Friedrichsen, 1966), A Supplement to the Oxford English Dictionary Vol 1 A-G (1972), Vol 2 H-N (1976), Vol 3 O-Scz (1982), Vol 4 Se-Z (1986), The Spoken Word (1981), The English Language (1985), Studies in Lexicography (1987), Unlocking the English Language (1989); *Recreations* investigating English Grammar, travelling; *Style*— Dr Robert Burchfield, CBE; 14 The Green, Sutton Courtenay, Oxfordshire OX14 4AE (☎ Abingdon 848645); St Peter's Coll Oxford OX1 2DL

BURDEN, Hon Adrienne Gail; yst da of 2 Baron Burden; *b* 22 Jan 1957; *Style*— The Hon Adrienne Burden

BURDEN, Hon Carol Mary; el da of 2 Baron Burden; *b* 30 June 1952; *Style*— The Hon Carol Burden

BURDEN, Hon Fraser William Elsworth; 2 s of 2 Baron Burden; *b* 6 Nov 1964; *Style*— The Hon Fraser Burden

BURDEN, Hon Ian Stuart; yst s of 2 Baron Burden; *b* 1967; *Style*— The Hon Ian Burden

BURDEN, Norman; s of Walter Burden (d 1975), of Sefton Park, Liverpool, and Margaret Jane, *née* Thomas (d 1979); *b* 24 Sept 1934; *Educ* Liverpool Collegiate Sch, Christ's Coll Cambridge (MA); *m* 29 March 1958, Margot Asquith, da of George Lowe Tennant (d 1947); 3 da (Sarah b 1960, Xanthe b 1963, Celia b 1965); *Career* RAF 1956-58, Pilot Offr 1956, Flying Offr 1957; dir gp mktg Compair Ltd 1971-77, int chief exec Burmah Indust Prods Ltd 1979-81, chief exec The Rawlplug Gp 1981-85, ptnr Templewood Assocs 1985-; singing memb The Windsor and Eton Choral Soc: nat chm Inst of Mktg 1985 and 1986 (former vice-chm and tres), Br rep The European Mktg Cncl 1980-86; Freeman City of London 1982, Liveryman Worshipful Co of Marketors 1982; FInstM 1974, FRSA 1984, FInstD 1986; *Recreations* choral music, running; *Style*— Norman Burden, Esq; Penwern, 23 Mayflower Way, Farnham Common, Bucks SL2 3TU (☎ 02814 2325)

BURDER, (John) Robert; s of Edward Russell Burder (d 1965), and Elspeth Anne, *née* Little; *b* 27 Dec 1929; *Educ* Ashbury Coll Ottawa Canada, Tonbridge Sch Kent; *m* 30 Oct 1954, Diana Mary, da of Thomas Henry Beckett (d 1954); 1 s (Simon), 1 da (Susie); *Career* nat serv 1948-49, 4 Royal Tank Regt; slr 1955, ptnr Batchelor Fry Coulson and Burder 1960, sr ptnr Batchelor Street Longstaffe (now Batchelors) 1986; govr St Christopher's Sch Farnham Surrey, churchwarden Seale and Sands Parish Surrey; Liveryman City of London Solicitors Co 1964; memb Law Soc 1955; *Recreations* gardening, walking; *Style*— Robert Burder, Esq; Point House, Lynch Road, Farnham, Surrey GU9 8BT (☎ 0252 713717); Batchelors, The Outer Temple, 222-225 Strand, London WC2R 1BG (☎ 01 353 5134, fax 01 353 2766, telex 262363)

BURDETT, Crispin Peter; s and h of Sir Savile Burdett, 11 Bt; *b* 8 Feb 1967; *Style*— Crispin Burdett, Esq

BURDETT, Noel Henry; OBE (1986); s of Frederick Deane Burdett, of Philippine Islands, bro of Sir Henry Burdett KCB, KCVO, fndr of Nat Pension Fund for Nurses, and Janet Grant, *née* Chavasse (d 1959) (great niece of the writer George Eliot (Mary Ann Evans)); *b* 24 Mar 1920; *Educ* Christ's Hosp Horsham, Peterhouse Cambridge (BA, MA); *m* 17 May 1941, Rachel Mary, da of Capt William Dobson Womersley, of Westwick, Cambs; 1 s (Francis b 1952), 2 da (Christina b 1955, Jane b 1956); *Career* Capt RA 1940-45, served in N Africa and W Europe (despatches); dir of Richard Haworth & Co Ltd 1951-53, md of Cluett Peabody and Co (UK) Ltd 1959-65 (dir of euro servs 1954-59, 1965-85), chm Abbeyfield Cambridge Soc 1961, vice pres Abbeyfield (National) Soc 1985 (chm 1977-85, dir 1972), dep chm The Housing Corpn 1983-86 (bd memb 1980), chm First Cambridge Assured Properties plc 1988; *Recreations* painting, reading, travelling, voluntary housing; *Clubs* Savile, Pitt; *Style*— Noel H Burdett, Esq, OBE; Westwick Hall, Oakington, Cambridgeshire CB4 5AR (☎ Cambridge 2477); The Office, Westwick (as resident): (☎ Cambridge 2240 and 4517, telex 81502, fax Cambridge 235248)

BURDETT, Robert Pierpoint; s of Scott Langshaw Burdett, CBE, MC (d 1961), and Frances Eileen Davis, *née* Workman (d 1976); *b* 23 May 1935; *Educ* Marlborough; *m* 11 April 1959, Robina Clare Lindsay, da of Rear Adm Ralph Lindsay Fisher, CB, DSO, OBE, DSC (d 1988); 2 s (John b 1962, James b 1967), (Clare b 1961, Helen b 1965); *Career* RN 1953-72, ret as Lt Cdr; slr in private practice 1975-80, ptnr Dyer Burdett & Co 1980-; *Recreations* sailing; *Clubs* Royal Cruising, RN Sailing Assoc;; *Style*— Robert P Burdett, Esq; 64 West Street, Havant PO9 1PA (☎ 0705 492472)

BURDETT, Sir Savile Aylmer; 11 Bt (E 1665); s of Sir Henry Aylmer Burdett, 10 Bt, MC (d 1943); *b* 24 Sept 1931; *Educ* Wellington, Imperial Coll London; *m* 1962, June Elizabeth Campbell, o da of late Dr James Mackay Rutherford, of Knowl Hill, Woking, Surrey; 1 s, 1 da (Felicity Susan b 1963); *Heir* s, Crispin Peter Burdett b 8 Feb 1967; *Career* late temporary Sub-Lt RNVR; md: Rapaway Energy Ltd 1977-, Rydraulic Compressors Ltd 1979-; *Style*— Sir Savile Burdett, Bt; Farthings, 35 Park Ave, Solihull, W Midlands

BURDITT, Geoffrey Boulter; s of Col Howard Burdit, MC, TD (d 1963), and Norah Consitt, *née* Boulter (d 1972); *b* 2 Feb 1924; *Educ* Kimbolton Sch; *m* 5 April 1951, Cynthia Mary, da of Leslie John Wright (d 1972); 1 s (Philip b 1956), 1 da (Susan b 1954); *Career* served WWII 56 Reconnaissance Corps 1943-47; chm Rigid Containers Holdings Ltd 1973- (md 1965-73), dir Marker Harborough Building Soc 1974-; FICA; *Recreations* music, bowls; *Clubs* Rotary; *Style*— Geoffrey B Burditt, Esq; Steeping House, Glendon, Kettering, Northants NN14 1QE (☎ (0536) 712255); Rigid Containers Holdings Ltd, Rushton Road, Desborough, Kettering

BURDON-COOPER, Alan Ruthven; s of Sqdn Ldr Ruthven Hayne Burdon-Cooper (d 1970), of Radlett, and Anna Kathleen Beverley, *née* Farquharson; *b* 27 June 1942; *Educ* Oundle Sch, Emmanuel Coll Cambridge (MA, LLB); *m* 2 Sept 1967, Virginia Louise, da of Archibald George Mobsby, of Radlett; 1 s (John b 1968), 1 da (Sarah b 1970); *Career* admitted slr 1968, sr ptnr Collyer-Bristow 1985-; Liveryman Worshipful Co of Dyers; fndr memb The Int Ctee of the Olympiad of Art, memb Law Soc 1968, life memb Cambridge Union 1961; *Recreations* sport, music, gardening, philately; *Style*— Alan Burdon-Cooper, Esq; 30 Newlands Ave, Radlett, Herts (☎ 0923 856961); 4 Bedford Row, London WC1R 4DF (☎ 01 242 7363, fax 01 405 0555, telex 21615)

BURFORD, Earl of; Charles Francis Topham de Vere Beauclerk; s and h of 14 Duke of St Albans, *qv*; *b* 22 Feb 1965; *Educ* Eton, Sherborne, Edinburgh Univ, Hertford Coll Oxford; *Career* apptd Brig-Gen of Louisiana by Governor Edwin Edwards 1986; chm and fndr De Vere Soc of Oxford Univ; tstee Shakespearian Authorship Tst; *Recreations* literature; *Style*— Earl of Burford; c/o Viscount Exmouth, Canonteign House, nr Exeter, Devon EX6 7RH

BURFORD, Jeremy Michael Joseph; QC (1987); s of Major Alexander Joseph Burford, and Constance Grace Arlene, *née* Blakeley; *b* 3 June 1942; *Educ* Rondebosch Boys HS S Africa, Diocesan Coll S Africa, Univ of Cape Town (BA), Emmanuel Coll Cambridge (MA, LLB), Harvard Law Sch (LLM); *Career* barr 1968; *Style*— Jeremy Burford, Esq, QC; 2 Mitre Court Building, Temple, London EC4 (☎ 01 583 1355)

BURG, Gisela Elisabeth; Hon CBE (1987); da of Oberstudiendirektor Friedrich Schlüsselburg, of Langen, Germany, and Gerda Schlüsselburg; *b* 12 Oct 1939; *Educ* Gymnasium Philippinum Weilburg Germany, Ladies' Coll Wetzlar Germany; *Career* fndr and md Expotus Ltd; chm Fedn of Br Audio 1976-78 (vice-pres 1978-82); memb: NEDO Electronic SWP 1979-82, Br Overseas Trade Bd 1982-87; named Times/Clicquot Businesswoman of the Year 1981; *Recreations* golf, horseracing; *Style*— Ms Gisela Burg; 82 Kensington Heights, Campden Hill Rd, London W8; Expotus Ltd, 95 Grays Inn Rd, London WC1 (☎ 01 405 9665)

BURGEN, Sir Arnold Stanley Vincent; s of late Peter Burgen, and Elizabeth, *née* Wolfers; *b* 20 Mar 1922; *Educ* Christ's Coll Finchley, London Univ; *m* 1946, Judith, da of Frederick Browne; 2 s, 1 da; *Career* medical scientist, dir Nat Inst Med Res 1971-82; master Darwin Coll Cambridge 1982-89; pres Academia Europaea 1988-; FRS; kt 1976; *Recreations* sculpture, music; *Style*— Sir Arnold Burgen; 2 Stukeley Close, Cambridge CB3 9LT (☎ 0223 323014)

BURGES, Dr (Norman) Alan; CBE (1979); s of Lt James Clement Burges (d 1917), of E Maitland Australia, and Jessie Wilhelmina, *née* Thompson (d 1973); ggs of George Burges, a noted eccentric classicist (See DNB); *b* 5 August 1911; *Educ* Sydney Tech HS, Univ of Sydney (MSc), Emmanuel Coll Cambridge (PhD); *m* 1940, Florence Evelyn, da of Mathias Moulton (d 1957), of March, Cambs; 1 s (Andrew, decd), 3 da (Judith b 1946, Jennifer b 1948, Anne b 1950); *Career* RAF 1940-45, Signals branch, Wing Cdr Bomber Cmd (despatches); res fell Emmanuel Coll Cambridge 1938-47; prof of Botany: Univ of Sydney 1947-52, Univ of Liverpool 1952-66; vice chllr New Univ of Ulster 1966-1976; *Books* Micro-Organisms in the Soil (1958), Soil Biology (with F Raw 1967), Flora Europaea 5 vols (jt ed 1964-1980); *Recreations* sailing (yacht 'Singing Swan'); *Clubs* RAF; *Style*— Dr Alan Burges, CBE; Glenkeen Rd, Aghadowey, Coleraine, NI BT51 4BN

BURGES, Maj-Gen Rodney Lyon Travers; CBE (1963), DSO (1946); s of Dr Richard Burges (d 1948), of Stoke Bishop, Bristol, and Hilda Christine, *née* Lyon; *b* 19 Mar 1914; *Educ* Wellington, RMA Woolwich; *m* 1946, Sheila Marion Lyster, da of Howard L Goldby, of Birchington, Kent; 1 s (d 1987), 1 da; *Career* Maj-Gen RA: Lt 1934, Burma Assam Java 1939-45, CO Berks Yeomanry 1945-46, CO 3 RHA 1955-58, GOC Cyprus 1964-66, VQMG MOD 1966-67; Grieveson Grant and Co 1968-78, ptnr and memb of the Stock Exchange 1971-78, conslt Pat Simon Wines Ltd 1978-85, dir Caroline Fine Wine Ltd 1983-85; *Recreations* racing, drinking wine in the sun; *Clubs* Buck's, Army and Navy; *Style*— Maj-Gen Rodney Burges, CBE, DSO; Freemantle, Over Wallop, Hampshire (☎ Andover 0264 781469);

BURGESS, Alfred Leslie; JP (Westminster 1976); s of Alfred James Burgess (d 1967); *b* 7 Jan 1925; *Educ* Archbishop Tenison's Sch Croydon; *m* 1947, Mabel Millicent Davis; 2 s, 1 da; *Career* CA, sr ptnr Barker Hibbert and Co (qualified 1952, admitted to ptnrship 1962); FSA; *Recreations* music, reading; *Clubs* City of London; *Style*— Alfred Burgess, Esq, JP; 175 Amesbury Ave, Streatham Hill, SW2 3BJ (☎ 01 674 0050)

BURGESS, Dr Anthony; s of Joseph Wilson (d 1938), of Manchester, and Elizabeth, *née* Burgess (d 1918); *b* 25 Feb 1917; *Educ* Xaverian Coll Manchester, Univ of Manchester (BA); *m* 1, 12 Jan 1942, Llewela Isherwood (d 1968), da of Edward Jones Major, MC (d 1963), of Leicester; 1 s (Paolo Andrea b 9 Aug 1964); m 2, 9 Oct 1968, Liliana Macellaro, da of Contessa Lucrezia Maria Pasi Piani della Pergola; *Career* RAMC 1940-42, warrant offr Army Educnl Corps 1942-46; lectr: Univ of Birmingham 1946-49, Bamber Bridge Trg Coll 1949-51; master Banbury GS 1951-54, educn offr Malaya and Borneo 1954-59, prof Princeton Univ 1969-70, distinguished prof City Coll of NY 1971-73; Hon DLitt Univ of Manchester 1979, Hon LLD Univ of Birmingham 1986; FRSL 1964; ASCAP 1970; Foreign Orders: Commandeur des Arts et des Lettres 1983, Commandeur de Merite Cultural Monaco 1982; *Books* incl: Time for a Tiger (1956), The Enemy in the Blanket (1958), The Worm and The Ring (1961), A Clockwork Orange (1961, filmed 1971), The Wanting Seed (1962), Nothing Like The Sun (1964), A Shorter Finnegan's Wake, Enderby Outside (1968), Shakespeare (1970), Joysprick (1973), The Clockwork Testament (1974), Moses (1976), Ernest Hemingway and His World (1978), The Land Where the Ice Cream Grows (1979), Earthly Powers (1980), Enderby's Dark Lady (1984), The Kingdom of the Wicked

(1985), Little Wilson and Big God (autobiog 1987); translation of stage plays incl: Cyrano de Bergerac (1971), Oedipus the King (1973); as Joseph Kell: One Hand Clapping (1961), Inside Mr Enderby (1963); as John Burgess Wilson: Engish Literature: A Survey for Students (1958); TV Scripts: Moses the Lawgiver (1977), Jesus of Nazareth (1977), Blooms of Dublin (radio musical 1982); contrib to: Observer, Spectator, Listener, Queen, Times Literary Supplement, Playboy, Le Monde; *Recreations* music, philosophy, motoring; *Clubs* Monaco Automobile; *Style—* Dr Anthony Burgess; 44 Rue Grimaldi, Monaco; 63 Via Cantonale, Savosa, Switzerland

BURGESS, Anthony Jack; s of late Edgar Jack Burgess, and late Emma Marie, *née* Shafe; *b* 27 June 1925; *Educ* Lewes Co GS, Hertford Coll Oxford (MA); *m* 24 Sept 1949, Barbara Evelyn, da of late Bertram Tofts; 3 s (Quentin b 1950 Rupert b 1958, Jeremy b 1963), 2 da (Charlotte b 1955, Emma b 1961); *Career* Capt RA 1943-48; sr ptnr Cheeswright Murly & Co, memb Baltic Exchange 1987, Notary Public 1958; cncllr Colchester Borough Cncl 1962-65; Freeman Worshipful Co of Scriveners 1958 (Master 1969-70); *Recreations* reading, history, music, theatre (Shakespeare), wine, golf; *Style—* Anthony Burgess, Esq; 33 Riverside Court, Nine Elms Lane, London SW8; Henpools House, Lower Littleworth, Stroud, Gloucestershire; Los Limoneros, Mijas Costa, Malaga, Spain; Cheeswright, Murly & Co, Baltic Exchange Chambers, 24 St Mary Axe, London EC4 (☎ 01 623 9477, fax 01 623 5428, car tel 0860 330 479, 0860 330 481, telex 883806)

BURGESS, Anthony Reginald Frank (Tony); CVO (1983); *b* 27 Jan 1932; *Educ* Ealing GS, Univ Coll London (BSc); *m* 21 May 1960, Carlyn, da of Harold Samuel Shawyer d (1942); 1 s (Paul b 1971); *Career* Nat Serv 1953-55 cmmnd RAOC, parachutist, TA 16 Airborne Div 1955-57; journalism 1955-62, Euro Community Civil Serv 1962-65; HM Dip Serv 1966-: 1 sec Euro Econ Orgn Dept FCO 1966-67, 1 sec (Political) Dhaka 1967-69, 1 sec SE Asia Dept FCO 1970-72, 1 sec (Econ) Ottawa 1972-76, head of Chancery HM Consul Bogota 1976-79, 1 sec Rhodesia Dept FCO 1979-80, asst head of Info Dept FCO 1980-82, dep high cmmr Dhaka 1982-86, (cnsllr) head of chancery Havana 1986-; *Books* The Common Market and the Treaty of Rome Explained (jtly 1967); *Recreations* travel, photography, shooting, scuba diving; *Clubs* Brooks's; *Style—* Tony Burgess, Esq, CVO; c/o FCO, King Charles St, London SW1A 2AH

BURGESS, (Dilys) Averil; da of David Evans, of Berthlwyd, Nantmor, Nantgwynant, Gwynedd, and Dorothy, *née* Owen; *b* 8 July 1938; *Educ* Ashby de la Zouch Girls' GS Leics, Queen Mary Coll, Univ London (BA); *m* 5 Dec 1959, (m dis 1973), Clifford Charles Antony Burgess, s of Sidney Burgess, of Boreham Wood, Herts; *Career* Fulham Co Sch 1965-69, head of history and second mistress Wimbledon HS GPDST 1969-74, headmistress South Hampstead HS GPDST 1975-; memb: bursaries mgmnt ctee GPDST 1979-86, exec ctee GS Assoc 1984-, (chm edcn sub ctee 1986-87, pres 1988-89), Secdy Heads Assoc; govr Central Sch of Speech and Drama; *Recreations* reading, mountain walking, cross-country ski-ing; *Style—* Mrs Averil Burgess; South Hampstead High School, 3 Maresfield Gardens, London NW3 5SS (☎ 01 435 2899)

BURGESS, Claude Bramall; CMG (1958), OBE (1954); s of George Herbert Burgess, of Weaverham Cheshire (d 1956), and Martha Elizabeth, *née* Gilbert (d 1966); *b* 25 Feb 1910; *Educ* Epworth Coll, Christ Church Oxford (MA); *m* 1, 1952 (m dis 1965), Margaret Joan, da of Reginald Charles Webb; 1 s (Tobias); m 2, 1969, Linda Nettleton Beilby, da of William Grothier Beilby (d 1973), of New York, USA; *Career* cmmnd RA 1940 (POW 1941-45), demobilised with rank of Lt-Col 1946; Colonial Office 1946-48; Imp Def Coll London 1951; govt posts in Hong Kong 1952-57, colonial sec (and actg govr on various occasions) Hong Kong 1958-63; head of co-ordination and devpt dept Euro Free Trade Assoc Geneva 1964-73, min for Hong Kong Commercial Rels with Euro Communities and Memb States Br Embassy Brussels 1974-82; *Style—* Claude Burgess, Esq, CMG, OBE; 75 Chester Row, London SW1W 8JL (☎ 01 730 8758)

BURGESS, Dr Colin Gordon; s of Ernest Arthur Walter Burgess (d 1976), of Henfield, Sussex, and Evie, *née* Evans (d 1983); *b* 02 Feb 1940; *Educ* Epsom Coll, South Bank Poly (BSc, PhD); *m* 10 Aug 1963, Rosalind Ann, da of Sydney George Gray (d 1964), of 6 Springhead Rd, North Fleet, Kent; 1 s (Alastair Mark b 5 May 1973), 1 da (Claire Louise b 11 Dec 1969); *Career* tech mangr Castrol Plastics Ltd 1966-69, export mangr Cray Valley Products (Coaetes Inks Ltd) 1969-72, tech dir Swan Plastics 1972-76, md Kent Chemical Co 1980- (commercial and tech dir 1977-80), chm Ian Young Aerosols Ltd 1988; Freeman City of London 1981, Liveryman Worshipful Co of Horners 1981; FRSC, MPI, FInstDir; *Style—* Dr Colin Burgess; Kent Chemical Co, George House, Bridewell Lane, Tenterden, Kent TN3 9DL (☎ 05806 4244, fax 05806 5652, car tel 0860 307576, telex 95508)

BURGESS, David Charles William; s of Leonard Cecil Burgess (d 1970), and Comfort, *née* Horler; *b* 25 Sept 1947; *Educ* Ermysted GS Skipton Yorks, St Catherines Coll Cambridge (MA); *m* 4 July 1987, Youdon, *née* Lhamo; 1 s (Tenzin b 21 May 1981), 2 da (Dechen b 21 June 1978, Kusang b 7 Aug 1985); *Career* admitted slr 1972, ptnr Winstanley-Burgess 1975; *Style—* David Burgess, Esq; Winstanley-Burgess, 378 City Rd, London EC1V 2QA (☎ 01 278 7911, fax 01 833 2135)

BURGESS, Rev David John; s of Albert Burgess, of the Pinfold, Ailsworth, Cambs, and Mary *née* Kelsey; *b* 4 August 1939; *Educ* The King's School Peterborough, Trinity Hall Cambridge (MA), Cuddesdon Theol Coll Oxford, Halki Studentship Istanbul; *m* 17 Feb 1976, Katherine Louise, da of Brig Lindsay Costeloe (d 1978); 1 s ((Patrick) Rollo (Lindsay) Burgess b 25 May 1978), 1 da (Frances Mary (Fanny) b 26 July 1981); *Career* curate All Saints Maidstone 1965-66, domestic bursar Univ Coll Oxford 1971 (asst chaplain Univ Coll Oxford 1966, chaplain and fell 1969) canon of Windsor 1978-87, tres Windsor Castle, guild vicar St Lawrence Jewry Next Guildhall 1987; govr Pangbourne Coll; tstee: Univ Coll Appeal, Holy Cross Appeal; Freeman of the City of London; Hon Chaplain: The Haberdashers Co, The Loriners Co, The Distillers Co, The Insurers Co, The Constructors Co, The Actuaries Co; Hon Fell Inst of Clerk of Works; Chaplain to HM The Queen 1987; *Books* Signs of Faith, Hope, and Love (contrib 1988); *Clubs* The Aula, The Omar Khayyam; *Style—* The Rev David Burgess; The Vicarage, St Lawrence Jewry Next Guildhall, London EC2V 5AA (☎ 01 600 9478)

BURGESS, Gen Sir Edward Arthur; KCB (1982), OBE (1972); s of Edward Burgess, and Alice Burgess; *b* 30 Sept 1927; *Educ* All Saints Sch Bloxham, Lincoln Coll Oxford, RMA Sandhurst; *m* 1954, Jean Angelique Leslie, *née* Henderson; 1 s, 1 da; *Career* cmmnd 1948 RA, served BAOR, Far East and M East, GSO1 Staff Coll 1968-70, CO 25 Light Regt RA 1970-72, Cdr RA 4 Div 1972-74, dir Army Recruiting 1975-77, dir Combat Devpt 1977-79, GOC Artillery Div 1979-82, Cdr UK FD Army and Inspr Gen TA 1982-84, Col Cmdt RA 1982-, Dep Supreme Allied Cdr Europe 1984-87 ADC Gen 1985-87; Welsh Gantleman Usher to the Sword of State 1988; pres Army Football Assoc 1982-88; pres Royal British Legion 1987-; *Recreations* sailing, fishing, music, wines; *Clubs* Army & Navy; *Style—* Gen Sir Edward Burgess, KCB, OBE; c/o Lloyds Bank, Winton, Bournemouth

BURGESS, Brig John Robert; MBE; s of Robert Burgess, DSO, MC (d 1969), of Tiverton, Devon, and Marjorie Constance, *née* Fetherstonhaugh (d 1988); *b* 27 Jan 1920; *Educ* Winchester, RMC Sandhurst; *m* 3 July 1946, Susan Deborah, da of Hugh Somerset Kevill-Davies (d 1957), of Hays Mews, Berkeley Square, London; 1 s (Peter b 4 Sept 1949), 1 da (Lorna b 2 July 1947); *Career* active serv Somerset LI NW Frontier India and Arakan in Burma 1940-44, memb Supreme HQ Allied Powers Europe 1951-52, military asst to CIGS of Imp Gen Staff 1954-56, serv Somerset LI Malaya (anti-terrorists opns) 1957-58, cmd 1 DLI 1961-63, memb jt planning staff MOD 1964-66, cmd TA Inf Bde 1966-67, Div Brig HQ Light Div 1968-69, ret 1969; joined wife's dog breeding and showing activities, judge at Crufts and Worldwide; *Style—* Brig John Burgess, MBE; The Rhea House, Bromyard, Herefordshire HR7 4PA (☎ 0885 482 281)

BURGESS, Michael John Clement; s of David Clement Burgess (d 1966), and Dr Ethne Nannette Moira Barnwall, *née* Ryan, of Kingston-Upon-Thames; *b* 31 Mar 1946; *Educ* Beaumont Coll Old Windsor Berks, King's Coll London; *m* 31 July 1971, Catherine Vivian, da of Vivian John Du Veluz Gout, of Mulhausen, W Germany; 1 s (Peter b 1980), 2 da (Alexandra b 1974, Nicola b 1976); *Career* admitted slr 1970, conslt McNamara Ryan Weybridge 1986- (ptnr 1972-86), coroner Surrey 1986- (asst dep coroner 1979-86); pres West Surrey Law Soc 1985-86 (hon tres 1979-84), memb Catholic Union 1974-, chm fin ctee and parish cncl memb St Francis de Sales RC Church Hampton, helper (ex gp ldr and regnl chm) Handicapped Children's Pilgrimage Tst, advsr to several local charities and trusts; Freeman: City of London, Worshipful Co of Feltmakers 1967; memb: Law Soc 1970, Coroner's Soc; *Recreations* reading, art, music, gardening; *Clubs* Surrey Law; *Style—* Michael Burgess, Esq; c/o McNamara Ryan, Ashburton House, 3 Monument Green, Wembridge, Surrey KT13 8QR (☎ 0932 846041, fax 0932 857709)

BURGESS, Paul Graham; s of James Cooke Burgess (d 1987), and Marian, *née* Ellison (d 1987); *b* 5 May 1953; *Educ* Wallasey GS; *m* 11 Oct 1975, Christine Anne, da of Derek Sidney Carey, of 6 Redcar Rd, Wallasey, Wirral; 2 s (Graham John b 1983, Jonathan b 1988), 1 da (Anne Marie b 1980); *Career* dir: Lifecycle Biorhythms Ltd 1982-, Rinksport plc 1985-, Rinksport Wirral Ltd 1985-, Mykonos Holidays Ltd 1987-, Horby F Lowe Ltd 1988-, Bontrane Ltd 1988-, BKN Int Ltd 1988-; ACA 1979; *Style—* Paul Burgess, Esq; 259 Wallasey Village, Wallasey, Wirral L45 3LR (☎ 051 630 6404, fax 051 691 2846)

BURGESS, (Ian) Peter; s of Samuel Richard Burgess (d 1985), and Gladys Eugenie, *née* Blake; *b* 27 August 1923; *Educ* Ellesmere Coll; *m* 22 May 1948, Roberta Helen, da of Mark Stott (d 1970); 2 da (Eugenie b 1949, Victoria b 1952); *Career* RN 1942-45; gen cmmr of Income Tax 1971, chm McCartneys Livestock Auctioneers 1977; surveyor and farmer; *Recreations* shooting; *Style—* Peter Burgess, Esq; Whitcliffe Lodge, Ludlow, Shropshire; 19 Britannia House, Marina Bay, Gibraltar; 25 Corve Street, Ludlow (☎ 0584 2659)

BURGESS, (Robert Lawie Frederick) Robin; s of Sir John Burgess (d 1987), of Carlisle, and Lady Burgess, *née* Gilleron; *b* 31 Jan 1951; *Educ* Trinity Coll, Glenalmond; *m* 20 Sept 1986, Alexandra Rosemary, da of W A Twiston-Davies, of Herefordshire; *Career* 2 Lt The Kings Royal Border Regt 1969-72; md Cumbrian Newspapers Gp Ltd 1985-, dir Cumberland and Westmorland Herald Printing Co Ltd 1985-, dir Border TV plc 1987-; *Clubs* Army and Navy, Border and County (Carlisle); *Style—* R L F Burgess, Esq; Cumbrian Newspapers Gp Ltd, Dalston Rd, Carlisle, Cumbria CA2 5UA (☎ 0228 23488)

BURGESS, Sydney; s of Charles Ernest Burgess (d 1935), and Dorothy Iris Burgess; *b* 14 Oct 1926; *Educ* Wrangle County Sch, Kings Sch Peterborough; *m* 7 June 1947, Christine Rose, da of James Harper, of Hubberts Bridge, Boston, Lincolnshire (d 1948); 1 s (Maxwell b 1948); *Career* memb Farm Animal Welfare Cncl 1979-; md Buitelaar Gp of Cos 1968; Queens Award for Exports 1978; dir: Frams Buitelaar Ltd and various subsidiary companies, Bands of Perth Ltd, Lincolnshire Rabbits Ltd, Sydney Burgess & Ptnrs Ltd, Sydney Burgess (Life & Pensions) Ltd, Community Guarantee Insurance Co Ltd (Guernsey), GB Biomedical Products Ltd, Societie Transformation Viandes (Tunis), Boston United FC Ltd, Br Meat Exporters Consortium Ltd, Bury St Edmunds Meat Co Ltd, Bonecosse Viande Ltd, Colelle Skin Care Products Ltd, Snacks and Treats Ltd, Karim SA (Panama); *Recreations* all sports; *Clubs* County Farmers (Boston), Wig and Pen; *Style—* Sydney Burgess, Esq; Beck Lodge, Wyberton Fen, Boston, Lincs (☎ 0205 63104); Buitelaar Gp of Companies, Wyberton Fen; Boston, Lincs (☎ 0205 52020, car ☎ 0860 413 574)

BURGH, 7 Baron (E 1529); Alexander Peter Willoughby Leith; s of 6 Baron (d 1959); *b* 20 Mar 1935; *Educ* Harrow, Magdalene Cambridge; *m* 29 Aug 1957, Anita Lorna, da of Frederick Charles Eldridge, of Gillingham, Kent; 2 s, 1 da; *Heir* s, Hon Gregory Leith; *Career* formerly RAF Pilot Offr; *Style—* The Rt Hon The Lord Burgh; Santa Cruz, California, USA

BURGH, Sir John Charles; KCMG (1981), CB (1975); *b* 9 Dec 1925; *Educ* Friends' Sch Sibford, LSE; *m* 1957, Ann Sturge; 2 da; *Career* under-sec Employment Dept 1968-71 (formerly with BOT, Colonial Off, DEA), dep chm Community Rels Cmmn 1971-72; dep sec: CPRS 1972-74, Prices and Consumer Protection 1974-79, Dept of Trade 1979-80; dir-gen Br Cncl 1980-87, pres Trinity Coll Oxford 1987-; sec Nat Opera Coordinating Ctee 1972-, sec opera ctee Royal Opera House Covent Garden 1972-80; memb exec Political and Econ Planning 1970-78; chm of govrs LSE 1985-87 (govr 1980-, hon fell 1982); memb cncl: Policy Studies Inst 1978-85, VSO 1980-, RSA 1982-86; FRSA; Hon LLD Bath, Hon RNCM; *Style—* Sir John Burgh, KCMG, CB; Trinity Coll, Oxford OX1 3BH (☎ 0865 279900)

BURGHERSH, Lord; Anthony David Francis Henry Fane; s and h of 15 Earl of Westmorland, KCVO; *b* 1 August 1951; *Educ* Eton and Spain; *m* 1985, Mrs Caroline E Fairey, da of Keon Hughes; 1 da (Daisy Caroline b 18 Jan 1989); *Career* insurance broker, life pres St Moritz Sporting Club; *Style—* Lord Burghersh; 10 Peterborough Villas, London SW6

BURGHLEY, Lord; Anthony John Cecil; s and h of 8 Marquess of Exeter; *b* 9 August 1970; *Educ* Eton; *Style—* Lord Burghley; 100 Mile House, PO Box 8, Br

Columbia V0K 2E0, Canada (☎ (604) 395 2767)

BURGIN, Adrian Gwyn John; s of Arthur Carver Burgin (d 1985), of Lincs, and Anne Mary, *née* Hassall; *b* 23 Sept 1950; *Educ* St James Sch Peterborough; *m* 8 Sept 1973, Susan Georgina, da of George Falconer McLean (d 1980), of Lincs; 2 s (John b 1979, Thomas b 1982), 1 da (Holly b 1981); *Career* CA; princ Burgin and Co CA; tres Stamford Festival Assoc Ltd 1983; FICA; *Recreations* mountaineering, cricket, literature; *Clubs* Daniel Lamberts, Lyke Wake, Motley Crew Cricket; *Style*— Adrian Burgin, Esq; The Warden's House, 4 Broad St, Stamford, Lincs (☎ 0780 51315)

BURGIN, Patrick Leslie; s of The Rt Hon Edward Leslie Burgin, MP (d 1945, the first Min of Supply), of South Beds and Dorothy Theresa, *née* Cooper (d 1975); *b* 28 Nov 1919; *Educ* St George's Sch Harpenden, Le Rosey Rolle Gstaad Switzerland, Gonville & Caius Coll Cambridge; *m* 27 April 1950, Elizabeth Lavender, da of Benjamin John Uren (d 1972), of St Ives, Cornwall; 1 s (Mark b 1954), 2 da (Caroline b 1952, Rosemary b 1957); *Career* WWII joined The Beds & Herts (Pte) 1940, Northamptonshire Regt (2/Lt) 1941, Intelligence Sch Karachi India (Capt Instructor) 1941-42, GIII(I) Lucknow Dist HQ 1943, GIII(I) Army HQ New Delhi (major in security intelligence planning sect) 1943, Burma E Gp 1944 45 (despatches), repatriated UK GII(I) Scottish Cmd HQ Edinburgh until June 1946; admitted slr, ptnr Denton Hall & Burgin 1948; chm Rentokil Gp plc 1969-81 (dir 1953-85), dir Assoc Br Picture Corp 1964-72, chm Dentsply Ltd (formerly Amalgamated Dental Co) 1970-85, chm Val de Travers Asphalte Ltd (alternate dir Iraq, Basrah, Mosul & Qatar Petrol Cos) 1970-73; sr ptnr Dental Hall and Burgin (now Denton Hall Burgin & Warrens) 1978-88; conslt; chm Govrs St George's Sch Harpenden; memb: Herts County Cncl 1966-76, The Law Society 1948; Order of Dannebrog Denmark 1967, Legion d'Honneur France 1988; *Recreations* hunting, gardening, skiing, reading; *Clubs* Oriental, RAC; *Style*— Patrick Burgin, Esq; 10 Park Ave South, Harpenden, Herts (☎ 058 27 2035); Denton Hall Burgin & Warrens, 5 Chancery Lane, London WC2A 1LF (☎ 01 242 1212, fax 01 404 0087, telex 263567 BURGIN G)

BURGIN, Peter Brinton; s of George Burgin, of Huddersfield; *b* 3 August 1934; *Educ* Holme Valley GS Holmfirth; *m* 1960, Jean, da of Donovan Hartshorne, of Tamerton Foliat; 1 s, 1 da; *Career* mktg dir: Crittall Windows 1974-78, Dow-Mac Concrete 1985-88; dir and sec Dow-Mac Concrete 1978-81; md Lion Foundry Co Ltd 1981-85; practice mangr Landscape Design Assocs 1988-; ACMA, MBCS, MInstM; *Recreations* golf, gardening; *Style*— Peter Burgin, Esq; 5 Priors Gate, Werrington, Peterborough PE4 6LZ (☎ 0733 77384); Landscape Design Associates, 17 Minster Precincts, Peterborough PE1 1XX (☎ 0733 310471)

BURGON, Geoffrey Alan; s of Alan Wybert Burgon (d 1983), and Ada Vera Isom; Huguenot descent; *b* 15 July 1941; *Educ* Pewley Sch Guildford, Guildford Sch of Music and Drama; *m* 1963 (m dis), Janice Elizabeth, da of Frank Garwood; 1 s (Matthew b 1967), 1 da (Hannah b 1965); *Career* composer and conductor; dramatic works include: Joan of Arc 1970, Orpheus 1982; orchestral music includes: Concerto for String Orchestra 1963, Gending 1968; orchestral music with voices includes: Requiem 1976, The World Again 1983, Revelations 1984, Mass 1984; ballet music includes: The Golden Fish 1964, Songs, Lamentations and Praises 1979, The Trials of Prometheus 1988; chamber music includes: Gloria 1973, Six Studies 1980; chamber music with voices includes The Fire of Heaven 1973, Dos Coros 1975; film and tv scores include: The Changeling 1973, Dr Who and the Terror of the Zygons 1975, Monty Python's Life of Brian 1979, Tinker Tailor Soldier Spy 1979, The Dogs of War 1980, Brideshead Revisited 1981, Turtle Diary 1985, The Death of the Heart 1985, The Chronicles of Narnia 1988; *Recreations* cricket, jazz, wasting money on Bristol cars; *Style*— Geoffrey Burgon, Esq; 8-9 Frith St, London W1V 5TZ (☎ 01 434 0066)

BURGOYNE, Rev Geoffrey; s of Edward Godfrey Burgoyne (d 1968), and Florence Mildred, *née* Lloyd (d 1968); *b* 18 Nov 1927; *Educ* UC of Wales Aberystwyth (BA), St Michael's Coll Llandaff; *Career* asst priest: Aberavon 1951-55, Ynyshir 1955-63; vicar Bockleton with Leysters and Hatfield 1963-70, housemaster The Bishops Bluecoat Hereford 1970-, licensed under seal of Bishop of Hereford; *Recreations* game fishing, pottery; *Style*— The Rev Geoffrey Burgoyne; Lawnswood, Tupsley, Hereford HR1 1UT (☎ 0423 268860); Bluecoat Sch, Hereford (☎ 0423 57481, ext 215)

BURGOYNE, Dr John Henry; CBE (1980); s of Sir John Burgoyne, OBE, JP (d 1969), of Luton, and Florence Emily Burgoyne, *née* Farrow (d 1964); *b* 4 August 1913; *Educ* Luton Modern GS, London Univ (BSc, PhD, DSc); *m* 8 March 1944, Margaret Graves, da of Herbert Beeston Tupholme (d 1963), of Sheffield; 1 s (John b 1944); *Career* lectr in chem engrg Imp Coll London 1946-64 (latterly sr lectr, and reader), ind conslt 1964-68, sr ptnr Dr J H Burgoyne ptnrs 1968-78, conslt Burgoyne Gp 1978-; visiting prof and sr fell City Univ 1972-83, visiting prof Univ of Sheffield 1986-; chm safety in mines res advsy bd Miny of Fuel & Power 1970-75, memb advsy ctee on major hazards Health and Safety Cmmn 1976-83, chm inquiry into offshore safety Dept of Energy 1979-80, pres Assoc of Consulting scientists 1987-; CChem 1948, FEng 1982, FCGI 1984; *Recreations* music, photography, travel; *Style*— Dr J H Burgoyne, CBE; The Lodge, 2 Silverdale Rd, Sheffield S11 9JL, (☎ 0742 352600); The Burgoyne Group, 39A Bartholomew Close, London EC1A 7JN, (☎ 01 726 4951, fax 01 726 8980, telex 884957 BGOYNE G)

BURJA'N, Imre Josef; s of Imre Burja'n (d 1986), of Hungary, and Vilma, *née* Szebik (d 1956); descendant of old Hungarian family, arrived in England 1956, naturalised Br 1968; *b* 24 Mar 1935; *Educ* Technical Univ Budapest (DipArch), Coll of Art Manchester (awarded distinction by RIBA); *m* 20 Nov 1956, Julianna, da of Imre Teilinger (d 1980), of Hungary; 1 s (Attifa Imre Winston b 1958); *Career* chartered architect, memb of ARCUK and Royal Inst of British Architects; former ptnr Turner Buttres Architects, now solo practitioner architect; *Recreations* general drawing, water colours; *Style*— Imre J Burja'n, Esq; 51 South Drive, Chorlton Ville, Manchester

BURKE, Major (Edward) Bernard (Plunkett Mary); s of Major Edward Bernard Mary Burke, MBE (d 1976), of Staffordshire, and Eileen Jane Josephine, *née* MacCarthy (d 1973); ggs of Sir John Bernard Burke - Ulster King of Arms 1853-92; *b* 15 Jan 1927; *Educ* St Bedes Hawkesyard, Stonyhurst; *m* 8 July 1967, Gillian Alexander, da of Alan Gilbert James (d 1955), of Yorkshire; 1 s (Edward Bernard Gilbert b 1969), 1 da (Clare Mollie b 1968); *Career* Reg Army Offr cmmnd into RA 1947, served UK, BAOR, Far East, Korea, Hong Kong, Malaya; MOD 1969-71, Br Honduras 1972, ret as Major 1982; *Recreations* field sports; *Style*— Major Bernard Burke; The Cottage, Lichfield, Staffordshire WS13 7BZ (☎ 0543 263950)

BURKE, James Stanley Gilbert; s and h of Sir Thomas Burke, 8 Bt; *b* 1 July 1956; *m* 1980, Laura, da of Domingo Branzuela, of Philippines; 1 s (Martin b 1980), 1 da (Catherine); *Style*— James Burke, Esq; Linoenbergstr 231, Ch-5618 Bettwil (☎ 057 273124)

BURKE, John Kenneth; QC (1985); s of Kenneth Burke (d 1960), of Stockport, and Madeline Lorina, *née* Eastwood; *b* 4 August 1939; *Educ* Stockport GS; *m* 30 March 1962, Margaret Anne, da of Frank Scattergood, of Nottingham; 3 da (Virginia b 1963, Joanna b 1967, Geraldine b 1969); *Career* nat serv with Cheshire Regt in Far East 1958-60, Capt 12/13 Bn The Parachute Regt (TA) 1962-67, Capt/Actg Maj 4 Bn The Parachute Regt (TAVR) 1974; barr Middle Temple 1965, recorder of Crown Court 1980-; *Recreations* walking, drawing, painting; *Style*— John Burke, Esq, QC; 1 Hawthorn View Cottage, Knutsford Road, Mobberley, Cheshire WA16 7BA (☎ 0565 872627); 18 St John Street, Manchester M3 4EA (☎ 061 834 9843, fax 061 835 2051); 12 South Square, Grays Inn WC1R 5JP (☎ 01 242 0858)

BURKE, Sir Joseph Terence Anthony; KBE (1980, CBE 1973, OBE 1946); s of late R M J Burke; *b* 14 July 1913; *Educ* Ealing Priory Sch, King's Coll London Univ (MA), Courtauld Inst of Fine Arts, Yale Univ; *m* 1940, Agnes, da of late Rev James Middleton; 1 s; *Career* private sec to PM Rt Hon C R Atlee 1945-46, The Herald prof of fine arts Melbourne Univ 1947-79, prof emeritus Melbourne Univ 1979-; *Books* various art publications; *Recreations* golf, swimming; *Clubs* Melbourne, Athenaeum; *Style*— Sir Joseph Burke, KBE; Dormers, Falls Rd, Mt Dandenong, Vic 3766, Australia

BURKE, Michael John; s of Illick Burke (d 1986), and Dorothy Margaret, *née* Clark; *b* 22 June 1934; *Educ* Westcliff Sch, Nottingham Univ (LLB); *m* 9 Nov 1959, Margaret, da of Harry Charles (d 1988), of 43 Leasway, Westcliff; 1 s (Anthony b 1961), 3 da (Jane b 1962, Henrietta b 1964, Sophia b 1970); *Career* admitted slr 1958; Layton & Co: assoc slr 1962-64, ptnr 1967- (merged to become Cameron Markby 1981); govr Westcliffe Girls Sch 1966-, hon slr Essex YC 1978-; memb: City Livery Club Cncl 1976-, City Slrs Co; dep clerk Carmen's Co 1974-; clerk: Farriers Co 1962-70, Downgate Ward 1974-; memb Livery Consultative Ctee 1981-; Freeman City of London 1962, Liveryman Worshipful Co of: Solicitors 1962, Farriers 1963, Carmen 1984; *Recreations* sailing, golf, walking; *Clubs* Essex, City Livery; *Style*— Michael Burke, Esq; 66 Undercliff Gardens, Leigh on Sea, Essex, Barbican EC2 (☎ 0702 79 871); Sceptre Ct, 40 Tower Hill, EC3N 4BB (☎ 01 702 2345, 688, 6937, fax 01 702 2303, telex 925779)

BURKE, Richard Sylvester; s of David Burke (d 1948), and Elizabeth, *née* Kelly (d 1987); *b* 29 Mar 1932; *Educ* Christian Brothers Sch Thurles and Dublin Ireland, Nat Univ of Ireland (BA, MA, HDipEd); *m* 1961, Mary Josephine, da of John J Freeley (d 1934); 3 s (Joseph (d 1962), David Joseph b 1964, Richard Anthony b 1969), 3 da (Mary Carmel b 1963, Audrey Elisabeth b 1966, Avila Therese b 1971); *Career* taught at: Presentation Coll 1953-55, Blackrock Coll 1955-72; govr Univ Coll Dublin 1967-70; memb Dublin County Cncl 1967-73 (chm 1972-73); barr at law King's Inns 1973-; TD 1969-77, and 1981-82, opposition chief whip and spokesman on Posts and Telegraphs 1969-73, min for Educn 1973-76; memb and vice-pres Cmmn of Euro Communities 1977-81 and 1982-85; chm Player and Wills 1981-82; dir: Abbey Life 1981-82, Sedgwick Europe BV 1985-86; special advsr Euro Community Off Ernst and Whinney 1985-; assoc fell Harvard Univ Centre for Int Affairs 1980-81; Pro Merito Europa Medal (European Parliament 1980), Order of Leopold II (Grand-Cross) Belgium 1981, Order of Phoenix (Grand-Cross) Greece 1983; *Books* Anthology of Prose (ed 1967); *Recreations* golf, music, travel; *Clubs* Royal Golf Club De Belgique Brussels; Portmarnock Golf Club Dublin; Elm Park Golf Club Dublin, Grange Golf Club Dublin, Hibernian United Serviced Dublin; *Style*— Richard Burke, Esq; 67 Ailesbury Road, Dublin 4 (☎ 1692520); Avenue Louise 300, BTE6, 1050 Brussels (☎ 32 26471880, fax 32 26406820)

BURKE, Sheila; da of Maurice Burke, and Eileen, *née* McKenna; *b* 26 May 1956; *Educ* Notre Dame RC GS for Girls; *Career* dir of studies KMG Thomson McLintock 1980-86; recruitment mangr Binder Hamlyn BDO 1987-88, md SB Business Services 1989; *Recreations* art, music, antiques, photography, theatre, tennis, badminton; *Clubs* Country Gentleman's Assoc, Club Cognac, International Teddy Bear; *Style*— Ms Sheila Burke; Ridley Hall, Honington, Suffolk (☎ 035 96 362);

BURKE, Sir Thomas Stanley; 8 Bt (I 1797), of Marble Hill, Galway; s of Capt Sir Gerald Burke, 7 Bt, DL (d 1954), and his 1 wife Elizabeth Mary, *née* Mathews (d 1918); *b* 20 July 1916; *Educ* Harrow, Trinity Coll Cambridge; *m* 17 Aug 1955, Susanne Margarete (d 1983), da of Otto Theodor Salvisberg, of Thun, Switzerland; 1 s, 1 da; *Heir* s, James Stanley Gilbert Burke b 1 July 1956; *Career* technical translation agent (ret 1984); *Style*— Sir Thomas Burke, Bt; Ellern Mede Nursing Home, 31 Totteridge Common, London N20 (☎ 01 959 4221)

BURKE, (David Thomas) Tom; s of J V Burke, DSM, of Plymouth, Devon, and Mary, *née* Bradley; *b* 5 Jan 1947; *Educ* St Boniface's Coll Plymouth, Liverpool Univ (BA); *Career* lectr: W Cheshire Coll 1970-71, Old Swan Tech Coll 1971-73; Friends of the Earth: local gps coordinator 1973-75, exec dir 1975-80, dir special projects 1979-80, vice chm 1980-81; non-exec dir Earth Resources Res 1975-87, memb Waste Mgmnt Advsy Cncl 1976-80, memb Packaging Cncl 1978-82, policy advsr Euro Environment Bureau 1978-86, memb exec ctee 1987-, dir Green Alliance 1982- (memb exec ctee 1979-83), memb exec ctee and chm planning and enviroment gp NCVO 1984-, memb UK nat ctee Euro Year of the Enviroment 1986-, dir Sustain Ability 1987-; contested (SDP): Brighton Kemptown general election 1983, Surbiton gen election 1987; Royal Humane Soc Testimonial Parchment 1969 (Vellum 1966); Hon Visiting Fell Manchester Business Sch 1984-86; *Books* Euro Environment (jtly, 1981), Pressure Groups in the Global System (1982), Ecology 2000 (jtly, 1984), The Gaia Atlas of Planetary Management (contrib, 1984), The Green Capitalists (jtly, 1987), Green Pages (jtly, 1988); *Clubs* Reform; *Style*— Tom Burke, Esq; 36 Crewdson Road, London SW9 (☎ 01 735 9019); The Green Alliance, 60 Chandos Place, London WC2N 4HG (☎ 01 836 0341, 01 836 8670, fax 240 9205)

BURKE-GAFFNEY, John Campion; s of Dr Henry Joseph O'Donnell Burke-Gaffney, tropical medicine expert (d 1973) and Constance Mary, *née* Bishop (d 1986); *b* 27 Feb 1932; *Educ* Douai Sch; *m* 7 July 1956, Margaret Mary Jennifer, da of Lt-Col Humphrey Herbert Stacpoole (d 1971); 2 s (Jonathan b 1959, Rupert b 1962), 2 da (Sarah b 1957, Frances b 1964); *Career* nat serv cmmnd RAC 1950-52, TA East Riding Yeo (Lt-Actg Capt) 1952-56; called to the Bar (Gray's Inn) 1956; Shell Mex & BP Ltd 1956-75, Shell UK Ltd 1975-77, md Shell & BP Zambia Ltd 1977-81, Shell Int Petroleum Co Ltd 1981-85; dir gen Br Red Cross Soc 1985-; *Style*— John Burke-Gaffney, Esq; c/o Lloyds Bank, Aldwych, London WC2R 0HR; 9 Grosvenor Crescent,

London SW1 (☎ 01 235 5454)

BURKETT, John; s of Alfred Burkett, MC, (d 1986), of Stoke Bishop, Bristol, and Marjorie, *née* Wingfield (d 1972); *b* 17 Feb 1926; *Educ* Eltham Coll, Jesus Coll Cambridge, Architectural Association Sch (AA Dipl); *m* 24 April 1948, Patricia Ann (d 1988), da of Stanley Walter Mack (d 1985), of Chislehurst, Kent; 2 da (Deborah Jane b 1953, Sarah Louise b 1955); *Career* served Flt Lt RAF 1945-48; lectr Architectural Assoc 1955-57; ptnr: D J McLennan & ptnrs 1958-63, John Burkett Assoc 1963-70, Scarlett Burkett Assoc 1970-86; ptnr Scarlett Burkett Griffiths 1986-; cncl memb and hon sec Assoc of Conslt Architects; Financial Times Award 1971, civic Tst awards 1968 and 1972, Heritage Landscape Award 1976, memb various ctees connected with youthwork in Bromley; Hereditary Freeman of Dover (1947), Freeman City of London (1981), Liveryman Worshipful Company of Arbitrators; *Recreations* gardening, skiing; *Clubs* Ski Club Great Britain, Architectural Association; *Style—* J Burkett, Esq; Maxbys, Raggleswood, Chislehurst, Kent (☎ 01 467 3802); Scarlett Burkett Griffiths, 10-14 Macklin St, London WC2B 5NF (☎ 01 242 1374, fax 01 242 5108)

BURKETT, Mary Elizabeth; OBE (1978); da of Ridley Burkett (d 1965), of Canet Place, PO, France, and Mary Alice Gaussen (d 1965); The Gaussens were a Huguenot family from Lunel, this branch settled at Loughneagh; *Educ* Musgrave Sch, Durham Univ (BA); *Career* art teacher Wroxhall Abbey 1942-55; art lectr Charlotte Mason Coll Ambleside 1955-62; dir Abbot Hall Art Gallery and Museums Kendal 1966-; memb: Arts Cncl Art Finance Ctee 1978-80, Nat Tst NW Regional Exec Ctee 1978-85, N Western Museums & Art Gallery Servs Area Cncl 1975-; Cumbria CC: Museums Advsy Gp 1975, Museum Offrs Working Party 1975-; memb Cumbria-Westmorland Fedn of WI's Art Sub-Ctee 1977-; judge for the Scottish Museum of the Year Award 1977-; memb: Museum Accreditation Panel for the Museums Assoc to examine Cheltenham Museum 1980-, Br Tourist Authy Museums Mission to USA 1981-, Hawkshead GS Ctee 1981; tstee: Carlisle Cathedral Appeal 1981, Armitt Tst 1982; Senhouse Tst 1985; memb bd of Border Television 1982, pres Feltmakers Assoc 1984, FRSA, FMA, FRGS; *Books* William Green of Ambleside (1984), Kurt Schwitters and the Art of the Feltmaker; *Recreations* travelling, writing, photography; *Style—* Miss Mary Burkett, OBE

BURLETSON, Bryan Richard; s of Bryan Burletson (ka 1941, Fleet Air Arm), and Evelyn Loveday Sharp, *née* Bradshaw; *b* 28 June 1941; *Educ* Harrow, Dublin Univ (MA hon); *m* 20 March 1965, Prudence Margaret, da of Henry Wheatley Ridsdale; 1 s (Richard b 1966), 1 da (Louise b 1968); *Career* chm and chief exec Clayform Properties plc; *Recreations* sailing, skiing, tennis, riding; *Style—* Bryan Burletson, Esq; 24 Bruton Street, Mayfair, London W1X 7DA (☎ 01 491 8400, fax: 01 499 1053)

BURLEY, Hon Mrs (Laura Blackstock); *née* Butterworth; yr da of Baron Butterworth, CBE (Life Peer); *Educ* Benenden, Westfield Coll London; *m* 1985, John Laughton Burley, s of John Burley, of Pocklington, York; *Style—* Hon Mrs Burley; The Coffee House, Everingham, York

BURLEY, Cdr Malcolm Keith; MBE (1966); s of Leonard Lancelot Burley (d 1976), and Edythe Emmeline Hasluck, *née* Baker (d 1968); *b* 28 Sept 1927; *Educ* Solihull Sch, RNC Dartmouth; *m* 29 May 1965, Fiona Mairi, da of Rev James Fergus Macdonald, TD, of Perthshire; 3 da (Ailsa b 1966, Leonie b 1969, Erica b 1972); *Career* served RN, Med, Far East (Korean War), E Indies, Antarctic and S Atlantic 1945-73; ldr 2 Arctic expdns 1958-60; ldr jt servs expdn: S Georgia 1964-65, Elephant Island, Br Antartica 1970-71; bursar Stowe Sch 1973-86, mgmnt Anchor Estate 1986-; vice-chm Br Schs Exploring Soc, past pres RN Assoc (Buckingham); chm Peasenhall and Sibton Cons Assoc, vice-pres Saxmundham Rotary Club, Past Pres Buckingham Rotary Club; Freeman City of London 1986; FRGS, FRSA; *Recreations* offshore cruising (Navy Colours), travelling, gardening; *Style—* Cdr Malcolm Burley, MBE; Bay House, Peasenhall, Suffolk IP17 2NQ (☎ 072 879 221); The Anchorage, Iken, Suffolk IP12 2ER (☎ 072 888 262)

BURLEY, Stephen Rodney; s of Ronald Gordon Burley, of Beckenham, Kent, and Marjorie, *née* Methuen; *b* 9 July 1947; *Educ* BA (hons); *m* 1 June 1974, Katherine Mary, da of Stanley Dransfield; 1 s (Robert b 1979), 1 da (Elizabeth b 1977); *Career* Commerical Union Assur 1971-82, investmt RTZ Pension Investmts Ltd, non-exec dir Strata Investmts Plc 1985; hon tres Ranfurly Library 1985; *Recreations* riding, walking; *Style—* Stephen Burley, Esq; 6 St James's Square, London SW1Y 4LD

BURLEY, Sir Victor George; CBE (1969); s of late G H Burley, of Bristol, and M A Luby; *b* 4 Dec 1914; *Educ* High Sch Tas, Univ of Tas (BE); *m* 1941, Alpha Loyal Batt, da of David Lord; 1 s, 3 da; *Career* chm advisory cncl of Cwlth Scientific and Research Organization 1979-81; kt 1980; *see Debrett's Handbook of Australia and New Zealand for further details*; *Style—* Sir Victor Burley, CBE; Montaigne, 553 Sandy Bay Rd, Hobart, Tasmania 7005 (☎ 002 25 2583)

BURLIN, Terence Eric; s of Eric Jonas Burlin, and Winifred Kate, *née* Thomas; *b* 24 Sept 1931; *Educ* Acton Co Sch, Univ of Southampton (BSc), Univ of London (BSc, PhD, DSc); *m* 23 Mar 1957, Plessey Pamela, da of John William Carpenter; 1 s (Adrian b 1962), 1 da (Helen b 1965); *Career* physicist Mount Vernon Hosp and Radium Inst 1953-57, sr physicist Hammersmith Hosp 1957-62, pt/t princ physicist St Johns Hosp for Diseases of Skin 1960-, sr lectr Poly of Central London 1969-71 (reader 1969-71, pro dir 1971-74, sr pro rector 1974-82, rector 1982-); govr: Quintin Kynaston Sch 1971-73, Central Sch of Speech and Drama 1980; memb: Harrow Coll of Higher Educn Academic Bd 1979-84, Longfield Sch Managing Body 1973-76, Paddington Coll Governing Body 1986-, cncl Inst for Study of Drug Dependence 1974-86; FInstP 1969, CPhys 1976; FIEE, FIPSM 1988; *Recreations* tennis, music; *Clubs* Athenaeum; *Style—* Prof Terence Burlin; Polytechnic of Central London, 309 Regent St, London W1 (☎ 01 580 2020, fax 01 436 7367)

BURLINGHAM, Lt-Col Richard Geoffrey; OBE (1977), TD (1944), JP (1960), DL (Hereford and Worcester 1976); s of Capt Richard Henry Burlingham (d 1969), of Fladbury, Pershore, Worcs; *b* 11 Nov 1912; *Educ* Malvern; *m* 1939, Evelyn Marjorie, da of Theodore Armstrong, of Rudgewick; 1 s, 3 da; *Career* Lt-Col WW II; agric and builders merchant; Mayor Evesham Borough Cncl 1960-62, chm Wychavon Dist Cncl 1974-77; *Recreations* music, genealogy, gardening; *Style—* Lt-Col Richard Burlingham, OBE, TD, JP, DL; 19 Mount Road, Evesham, Worcs (☎ 0386 6541)

BURLINGTON, Earl of; William Cavendish; s of Marquess of Hartington, *qv*; *b* 6 June 1969; *Style—* Earl of Burlington

BURMAN, Sir (John) Charles; JP (Birmingham 1942), DL (Warwicks 1967); s of Sir John Bedford Burman, JP (d 1941), of Tibbington House, Edgbaston, and Elizabeth Vernon, *née* Pugh; *b* 30 August 1908; *Educ* Rugby; *m* 1936, Ursula, *qv* da of John Herbert Hesketh-Wright, and Millicent Ella, *née* Pickering, of Bournemouth; 2 s, 2 da; *Career* lord mayor Birmingham 1947-49, memb govt ctee on Admin Tbnls 1955; High Sheriff Warwicks 1958-59, memb Royal Cmmn on Police 1960; chm: S Staffs Waterworks Co 1959-79, Tarmac Ltd 1961-71; chm Birmingham Cons Assoc 1963-72, chm of tstees Barber Inst of Fine Arts Birmingham Univ; hon LLD (Birmingham Univ) 1986; KStJ 1961; kt 1961; *Recreations* gardening; *Style—* Sir Charles Burman, JP, DL; Little Bickerscourt, Danzey Green, Tanworth-in-Arden, Warwicks B94 5BL (☎ 056 44 2711)

BURMAN, Richard; s of Robert Burman (d 1938), of Alvechurch, Worcs, and Margaret Harriet, *née* Shaw (d 1960); *b* 22 Jan 1916; *Educ* Bromsgrove; *m* 5 April 1947, Joan Edith, da of James Louis Dearne (d 1972), of Hunnington, Worcs; 2 s (Paul Robert James b 12 June 1948, David Richard b 27 Sept 1951); *Career* HG; CA 1939, ptnr Burman and Co 1939- (sr ptnr Roberts Hall and Co); chm: Darby and Co Hldgs 1960-, Worcestershire Metal Hldgs Ltd 1970-; further overseas directorships in USA, Singapore, Nigeria and formerly in Aust and NZ; trade missions to: Hong Kong, Malaysia, Kenya, Zimbabwe; ldr Birmingham C of C, clerk Alvechurch PC 1945-; former dir: Birmingham FC, Worcs Co Cricket 2XI, Bart Green CC, Alvechurch CC, Hopwood CC; FICA; *Style—* Richard Burman, Esq; Shepley Gables, Barnt Green, Worcs (☎ 021 445 1988); Golg-Y-Mor, Llwylgwrill, Gwynedd; Burman House, 39 George Rd, Edgbaston, Birmingham B15 1PL (☎ 021 454 3894, telex 337820)

BURMAN, Sir Stephen France; CBE (1954, MBE 1943); s of Henry Burman, of 103 Harborne Road, Edgbaston, Birmingham; *b* 27 Dec 1904; *Educ* Oundle; *m* 1931, Joan Margaret, da of John Henry Rogers, of Edgbaston; 2 s (1 decd); *Career* former dir: Midland Bank Ltd, Averys Ltd, ICI Ltd, Imperial Metal Industries Ltd, J Lucas Industries Ltd; chm Serck Ltd Birmingham 1962-70; kt 1973; *Style—* Sir Stephen Burman, CBE; 12 Cherry Hill Rd, Barnt Green, Birmingham B45 8LJ (☎ 021 445 1529)

BURMAN, Lady Ursula; JP (1949-); da of John Herbert Hesketh-Wright (d 1967), and Ella Millicent, *née* Pickering (d 1959); *b* 26 Feb 1914; *Educ* Benenden Sch Kent; *m* 26 Sept 1936, Sir (John) Charles Burman JP, DL, qv, s of Sir John Bedford Burman, JP (d 1941); 2 s (John Hesketh b 8 Sept 1939, Michael Charles b 16 June 1944), 2 da (Elizabeth Ursula (Mrs Landale) b 22 Dec 1937, Rosanne Margaret (Mrs Corben) b 26 Nov 1941); *Career* WWII Civil Nursing Res (St John) and WVS 1939-46; chm (formerly memb, chm and vice chm) Juvenile Ct Panel 1949-79, memb Nat cncl Magistrates Assoc 1957-75, pres Birmingham branch Magistrates Assoc 1975-84 (chm 1970-75); memb: bd of visitors Winson Green Prison, Home Off Ctee Legal Aid in Criminal Proceedings 1964-66, cncl Benenden Sch 1972-83; Lady Mayoress Birmingham 1947-49; *Recreations* riding, reading; *Style—* Lady Burman, JP; Little Bickerscourt, Danzey Green, Tanworth-in-Arden, Warwicks B94 5BL, (☎ 05644 2711)

BURN, Hon Mrs (Anne Catherine); *née* Wilberforce; da of Baron Wilberforce, CMG, OBE, PC; *b* 5 Sept 1948; *m* 1975, Lindsay Stuart Burn; *Style—* The Hon Mrs Burn

BURN, Edward Hector; s of Edward Burn (d 1982), and Bertha Maud, *née* Hector (d 1976); *b* 20 Nov 1922; *Educ* St Edward's Oxford, Wadham Coll Oxford (BCL, MA); *m* 21 Dec 1948, Helen Joyce, da of Maj Merrick Hugh McConnel RHA (ka 1917); *Career* cmmnd 1 Bucks Bn, Oxford Bucks, Capt GSO 3 1 Airborne Corps, Maj GSO 2 26 Indian Div (despatches Normandy 1944 and Sumatra 1946); barr Lincolns Inn 1951; student and tutor jurisprudence Christ Church 1954-, censor of Christ Church 1959-64, lectr in law Inns of Ct 1965-80, hon master of the bench Lincolns Inn 1980; visiting prof City Univ 1983-; govr St Edwards Sch Oxford; *Books* Maudsley and Burn Land Law (jtly 1986), Cheshire and Burn Modern Law of Real Property (jrly 1988); *Clubs* Athenaeum, MCC; *Style—* Edward Burn, Esq; Christ Church, Oxford

BURNABY-ATKINS, Maj Andrew Graham; MC (and bar 1945); s of John Burnaby-Atkins (d 1946), of Halstead Place, Kent, and Dorothy Dalrymple, Graham-Watson (d 1982); *b* 29 Dec 1922; *Educ* Eton; *m* 8 Jan 1966 (Anne) Caroline, da of Christopher Thomas Dalgety, of Broomy Lodge, Ringwood, Hants; 1 s (Hugh b 5 Jan 1968), 1 da (Joanna b 17 Aug 1969); *Career* enlisted Green Jackets 1941, cmmnd KRRC 1942, served 12 Bn Normandy Landings to the Baltic, Adj 2 Bn 1946, ADC to Field Marshal Viscount Montgomery 1947-49; Adj Eton Cadet Force 1951-53; dir Whitbread & Co 1960 (joined 1953), ret 1974; dir Burghley Horse Trials 1976-78; *Style—* Maj Andrew Burnaby-Atkins; Manton Lodge Farm, Oakham, Rutland LE15 8SS (☎ 057285 269)

BURNABY-ATKINS, Lt-Col Frederick John; s of John Burnaby-Atkins (d 1946), of Stamford, and Dorothy Dalrymple, *née* Graham Watson (d 1983); see Burkes Landed Gentry 18 Edn, Vol I, p 26 and Kelly's Handbook 1971, p 368; *b* 9 Nov 1920; *Educ* Eton, RMC Sandhurst; *m* 13 Oct 1951, Hon Anne Jennifer Lawrence, da of 3 Baron Trevethin and Oaksey, PC, DSO, TD (d 1971); 1 s (John b 1961), 3 da (Charlotte b 1951, Catherine b 1954, Rosamond b 1957); *Career* cmmnd The Black Watch 1939, (POW Germany 1940-45), ADC and dep comptroller to Viceroy and Govr Gen India (Earl Wavell and Earl Mountbatten of Burma) 1946-48, regtl and staff serv 1949-49, cmd depot The Black Watch Perth 1960-61, mil attaché Lisbon 1961-64, comptroller and mil sec Govr Gen New Zealand (Sir Bernard Ferguson) 1964-67, def attaché Rabat 1968-70, private sec HRH The Princess Margaret 1970-73, MOD 1974-85, ret; *Recreations* travel, fishing, shooting; *Clubs* Army and Navy; *Style—* Lt-Col Frederick J Burnaby-Atkins; 3 The Street, Oaksey, Malmesbury, Wilts SN16 9TH

BURNABY-ATKINS, Hon Mrs; Hon (Anne) Jennifer; *née* Lawrence; da of 3 Baron Trevethin and 1 Oaksey, DSO, TD, PC (d 1971); *b* 1926; *m* 1951, Lt-Col Frederick John Burnaby-Atkins, er s of John Burnaby-Atkins (d 1946), of Tolethorpe Hall, Stamford, Rutland; 1 s, 3 da; *Style—* The Hon Mrs Burnaby-Atkins; 11 Rupert House, Nevern Sq, London SW5; 3 The Street, Oaksey, Malmesbury, Wilts

BURNAND, Arthur; s of Col Montagu Berthon Burnand, OBE (d 1936), and late Ethel Elizabeth Mary, *née* Blake; *b* 31 July 1905; *Educ* Felsted, Coll of Est Mgmnt; *m* 1, 1941, Hilda, da of George Bates (d 1950), of Essex; m 2, 1974, Patricia, da of Maj Patrick Martin Hall, MC, FRICS (d 1941), of Hants; *Career* chartered quantity surveyor, chartered arb; sr ptnr Harris & Porter Chartered Quantity Surveyors 1950-70; Inspector Metropolitan Police Special Constabulary 1926-51; memb Govt Ctee on Placing & Mgmnt of Contracts for Building & Civil Engrg 1962-64, memb cncl Royal Cwlth Soc 1950-55; dep chm London Assoc for the Blind 1960-70, former chm govrs Princess Helena Coll; Freeman City of London 1936, Liveryman Worshipful Co of Merchant Taylors (memb Ct of Assistants 1957, Master 1965-66); FRICS, FCIArb; *Recreations* gardening, walking, horology, philately; *Clubs* The Athenaeum, Naval & Mil; *Style—* Arthur Burnand, Esq; Garden Cottage, Shipton Moyne, Tetbury, Gloucestershire

BURNAND, Paul William; s of Guy Matthey Burnand (d 1985), and Mary Veronica (d 1986); *b* 24 Nov 1944; *Educ* Downside Sch, RMA Sandhurst; *m* 13 May 1967 (m dis 1979), Fiona Mary, da of late Anthony Kenneth Forbes; 1 s (Edward b 1969), 1 da (Louise Mary b 1970); *Career* cmmnd KRRC (60 Rifles) 1964, resigned 1968; insur broker Sedgwick Collins & Co Ltd 1968-69, joined Astley & Pearce Ltd 1969: dir Hong Kong 1977, gen mangr Japan 1978; dir Exco Int plc 1982-; *Recreations* book collecting, clock and watch collecting, skiing; *Clubs* MCC; *Style—* Paul Burnand, Esq; Exco Int Plc, 80 Cannon St, London EC4N 6LJ (☎ 01 623 4040)

BURNELL, Digby McLaren; s of Charles McLaren Burnell; *b* 25 Feb 1920; *Educ* Stonyhurst, Harvard USA; *m* 1958, Maureen, da of Dr Moray Melvin, of Fraserburgh; 3 s; *Career* served RN 1939-46, N Atlantic, Mediterranean and Br Admiralty Delgn to Washington DC; chm: AAA Industs Ltd, Agil Hldgs Ltd, London Leisure Ltd, TVL Ltd and other companies; Liveryman Worshipful Co of Coachmakers and Coach Harness Makers, Freeman City of London; *Recreations* reading, music; *Clubs* Army & Navy; *Style—* Digby Burnell Esq; AAA Industries, Wokingham, Berkshire RG11 2QL

BURNELL, (Susan) Jocelyn Bell; Dr; da of George Philip Bell (d 1982), of Solitude, Lurgan, N Ireland, and Margaret Allison Bell, MBE, JP, *née* Kennedy; *b* 15 July 1943; *Educ* The Mount Sch York, Univ of Glasgow (BSc), New Hall Cambridge (PhD); *m* 21 Dec 1968, Martin Burnell, s of Arnold Burnell, of London; 1 s (Gavin b 1973); *Career* Univ of Southampton: SRC Fellowship 1968-70, jr teaching fell 1970-73; Mullard Space Sci Lab UCL: pt/t graduate programmer 1974-76, pt/t assoc res fell 1976-82; Royal Observatory Edinburgh: pt/t sr res fell 1982-86, astronomer i/c of visitor centre 1985-86, sr sci offr and hd of James Clerk Maxwell Telescope Section 1986-; ed The Observatory 1973-76; Open Univ 1973-88: tutor, conslt, guest lectr; cncl memb RAS 1978-81, memb various ctees and panels SERC 1978- (incl vice chm Astronomy 1 Ctee 1983-84), hon fell Univ of Edinburgh 1988-; memb Br Cncl of Churches Assembly 1978-; memb Scottish Churches Cncl 1982- (exec ctee 1984-88); Michelson Medal Franklin Inst Philadelphia 1973, J Robert Oppenheimer Memorial Prize Center for Theoretical Studies Miami 1978, Beatrice Tinsley Prize American Astronomical Soc (first recipient) 1987, Herschel Medal RAS London 1989; FRAS 1969, memb Internat Astronomical Union 1979; *Recreations* swimming, learning dutch, knitting & sewing, ecumenical activities; *Style—* Dr Jocelyn Burnell; Royal Observatory, Blackford Hill, Edinburgh EH9 3HJ, (☎ 031 668 8100, fax 031 668 8264, telex 72383 ROEDIN G)

BURNESS, Hon Mrs (Marie Louise); *née* Forte; 2 da of Baron Forte (Life Peer), *qv*; *b* 16 Sept 1950; *m* 3 May 1975, Robert Alexander Burness; 2 da (Georgina Gerda b 21 Sept 1976, Julia Irene b 6 Oct 1978); *Style—* The Hon Mrs Burness; 4 Clarendon Close, London W2 4NS

BURNET, David Stewart; s of Alexander James Findlay Burnet, of Ilfracombe, Queensland, Aust (ka 1944), and Bonnie Jean McNair, *née* Stewart (d 1974); *b* 7 April 1927; *Educ* Scotch Coll Melbourne Victoria Aust, Melbourne Univ (BCom); *m* 2 Feb 1951, Elizabeth Joan Phyllis, da of Frederick William Haig, AFC, of Portsea, Victoria, Aust (d 1984); 2 s (Gregory b 1953, John b 1958), 2 da (Sue b 1957, Katarina b 1964); *Career* chm: Bardsey plc, Testlink Hldgs Ltd, Microvitec plc; non exec dir: Vikingate Ltd, Havelock Europa plc, Armstrong Equip plc; *Recreations* tennis, swimming, skiing, farming; *Clubs* RAC; *Style—* David Burnet, Esq; Westland Farm, Ewhurst, Surrey; Bardsey plc (☎ (☎ 01 405 9082, fax 0483 267216)

BURNET, George Wardlaw; LVO (1981), DL Midlothian (1975); s of Sheriff John Rudolph Wardlaw Burnet, KC (d 1941), and Lucy Margaret Ord, *née* Wallace (d 1962); *b* 26 Dec 1927; *Educ* Edinburgh Academy, Lincoln Coll Oxford Univ (BA), Edinburgh Univ (LLB); *m* 26 July 1951, Jane Elena Moncrieff, da of Malcolm Moncrieff Stuart, CIE, OBE, ICS (ret) of Smeaton Dower, Inveresk, Midlothian; 2 s (Peter b 1957, Andrew b 1962), 1 da (Sarah b 1955); *Career* served Black Watch (RNR) TA, ret Capt 1957; Writer to the Signet 1954; snr partner Murray Beith & Murray WS; chm: The Life Association of Scotland Ltd, Smaller Companies International Trust plc; dir Hibernian Life Assoc Ltd and other co's; hon fell Royal Incorporation of Architects in Scotland 1980; county cnsllr Midlothian 1967-76; convener Church of Scotland Finance Ctee 1980-83; Brigadier Royal Company of Archers (HM The Queen's Bodyguard for Scotland); KStJ; *Recreations* shooting, gardening, architecture; *Clubs* New (Edinburgh), East India; *Style—* George Burnet, Esq, LVO, DL; Rose Court, Inveresk, Midlothian; 39 Castle Street, Edinburgh (☎ 031 225 1200)

BURNET, Sir Alastair - James William Alexander; s of late Alexander and Schonaid Burnet, of Edinburgh; *b* 12 July 1928; *Educ* The Leys Sch Cambridge, Worcester Coll Oxford; *m* 1958, Maureen Campbell Sinclair; *Career* former editor: The Economist, Daily Express; news presenter ITN 1976- (News at Ten), assoc ed News at Ten 1982-; dir Times Newspaper Hldgs; kt 1984; *Style—* Sir Alastair Burnet; 43 Hornton Court, Campden Hill Rd, London W8

BURNET, Pauline Ruth; CBE (1970), JP (1957); da of Rev Edmund Willis (d 1946), and Constance Marjorie, *née* Bostock (d 1968); *b* 23 August 1920; *Educ* St Stephens Coll Kent; *m* 1940, John Forbes Burnet, s of William Hodgson Burnet (d 1932); 1 s (David) and 1 s (Martin, decd), 1 da (Susan); *Career* housewife, memb Windsor & Eton HMC 1948, Fulbourn & Ida Darwin HMC 1951-74, chm: Cambridgeshire Area Health Authy (Teaching) 1974-82, Cambridge Mencap; pres Cambridgeshire Mental Welfare Assoc; *Recreations* walking, swimming; *Style—* Mrs Pauline Burnet, CBE, JP; Grange Ho, Selwyn Gardens, Cambridge CB3 9AZ (☎ 0223 350726)

BURNETT, (Robert) Andrew; s of Wing-Cdr Robert Leslie Burnett, AFC, of Barton-on-Sea, and Barbara Noel, *née* Pink; *b* 20 Feb 1942; *Educ* St Lawrence Coll Kent; *m* 8 Feb 1964, Patricia, da of John Holden, of Bournemouth; 2 s (Robert Gwyer b 27 Nov 1966, Richard John b 14 April 1969), 2 da (Sarah Louise b 6 Sept 1965, Ann-Marie Frances b 23 Aug 1970); *Career* served HAC 1960-65; joined Price Waterhouse 1960 (ptnr 1974, nat dir of Info Technol); dir American C of C, Br affiliate tstee Br America Fndn; FCA 1965; *Recreations* computers, skiing, golf, jogging; *Clubs* North Hants Golf (Fleet), Hon Artillery Co; *Style—* Andrew Burnett, Esq; Sutherland, 75 Elvetham Rd, Fleet, Hants GU13 8HL (☎ 0252 621 419); Price Waterhouse, Southwark Towers, 32 London Bridge St, London SE1 9GY (☎ 01 407 8989, fax 01 378 0647, car tel 0836 525 432, telex 884657/8)

BURNETT, Lt Cdr Arthur Noel Stuart, RN; s of Alexander Douglas Gilbert Burnett (d 1962), of Kemnay, Aberdeenshire and London, and Margaret Irene *née* Kennedy (d 1978); *b* 16 Dec 1922; *Educ* Cheltenham, RN Engrg Coll Devonport; *m* 6 Sept 1952, Elizabeth Gwynne, da of Rev Arthur Molony of Cragg, Co Clare, Eire (d 1976); 2 s (Andrew (Andy), Robin), 2 da (Penelope (Penny), Joanna (Joey)); *Career* cadet 1941, midshipman (E) Russian Convoy 1942: HMS Belfast, HMS Duke of York, HMS Manxman (Far East Pacific Fleet) 1944-45, HMS Duke of York (Flagship For East Fleet) 1945-46; RN Sch of Physical Trg Portsmouth 1947 PT and recreational trg offr: HMS Imperieuse, HMS Raleigh 1946-49; HMS Devonshire (cadet trg cruiser) 1949-50, engr in chief Admirality Bath 1950-52, chief engr HMS Cygnet 1952-54, PT and recreational trg offr HMS Thunderer and RN Engrg Coll Plymouth 1955-57, sqdn engr offr MTBS HMS Hornet (Gosport) 1958, chief engr HMS Puma (S Atlantic Sqdn) 1958-60, dir gen ship dept Admirality Bath 1960-63, ret 1963; sales mangr Elliott Marine Automation Greenwich 1963-65, marine mangr FA Hughes & Son (Epsom) 1965-69; pres and chief exec: Int Marine Servs 1970-81, Offshore & Marine Int Servs & Assoc 1981; memb Devon CCC 1949-57, Rugby Union referee Somerset Co 1960-63; memb MCC 1957 (main ctee 1983-86, memb Bicentenary Sub-Ctee 1985-87); memb: Soc of Petroleum Engrs, Soc of Underwater Technol; C Eng, FIMarE, MIMech E, MRINA, MCIM; *Clubs* RAC; *Style—* Lt Cdr Arthur Burnett; Castleton, Hookwood Park, Limpsfield, Surrey RH8 0DU (☎ 0883 712637) Inst of Directors, 116 Pall Mall, London (☎ 0883 712637, fax 01 930 1949, telex 21614 IOD G)

BURNETT, Air Chief Marshal Sir Brian Kenyon; GCB 1970, (KCB 1965, CB 1961), DFC (1942), AFC (1939); s of Kenneth Burnett (d 1959), of Hurley, Maidenhead, Berks, and Anita Catherine, *née* Evans (1969); *b* 10 Mar 1913; *Educ* Charterhouse, Wadham Coll Oxford (BA); *m* 4 Nov 1944, Valerie Mary, da of Joseph St Ludger (d 1952), of Bromsgrove, Worcs; 2 s; *Career* joined RAF 1934, served WWII, dir Bomber and Reconnaissance Ops Air Miny 1956-57, IDC 1958, Air Offr Admin HQ Bomber Command 1959-61, AOC No 3 Gp Bomber Cmd 1961-64, vice-chief of Air Staff 1964-67, air sec MOD 1967-70, C-in-C Far East Command Singapore 1970-71, ret 1972; ADC to HM The Queen 1953-57 and Air ADC 1969-72; pres Squash Racquets Assoc 1972-75; vice-pres All England Lawn Tennis Club Wimbledon 1984- (chm 1974-83); *Recreations* lawn tennis, golf, skiing; *Clubs* RAF, International Lawn Tennis of GB, Hankley Common Golf; *Style—* Air Chief Marshal Sir Brian Burnett, GCB, DFC, AFC,; Heather Hill, Littleworth Cross, Seale, Farnham, Surrey GU10 1JN (☎ 025 18 2165)

BURNETT, Carl Joseph; s of Carl Joseph Burnett, Sr, and Elizabeth, *née* Smith (d 1976); *b* 4 Jan 1927; *Educ* US Naval Acad, Harvard Sch of Mgmnt; *m* 1; 1 s (Michael), 1 da (Kathryn); m 2, 1980, Patricia, da of Percy B Cooke; *Career* served US Navy WWII, Lt, Atlantic and Euro theatre, Pacific; chm and pres Mobil N Sea 1985-88, chm Burnett Assocs and Clarion Petroleum Ltd 1988-; FIOD, fell Nigerian Mining and Geoscience Soc; *Recreations* golf, tennis; *Clubs* Highgate, RAC; *Style—* Carl J Burnett, Jr; 1A Akenside Rd, London NW3; office: Greybrook House, 28 Brook St, London W1

BURNETT, Charles David; s and h of Sir David Burnett, 3 Bt, MBE, TD; *b* 18 May 1951; *Educ* Harrow, Lincoln Coll Oxford; *Career* underwriting memb of Lloyd's; *Recreations* wine, fishing, travel; *Clubs* Brooks's, Turf, 106 (pres); *Style—* Charles Burnett, Esq

BURNETT, David Henry; s of George Dawson Burnett, CBE, TD, of Surrey, and Ferdinanda Anna Van Den Brandeler; *b* 16 Dec 1951; *Educ* Tonbridge, Churchill Coll Cambridge (MA); *Career* dir Capital Markets - New Issues, Samuel Montagu & Co Ltd; *Style—* David H Burnett, Esq; Faircroft, Vale of Health, London NW3 1AN; Samuel Montagu & Co Ltd, 10 Lower Thames St, London EC3R 6AE (☎ 01 260 9000, telex 889213)

BURNETT, Sir David Humphery; 3 Bt (UK 1913), of Selborne House, Co Borough of Croydon; MBE (1945), TD; s of Col Sir Leslie Trew Burnett, 2 Bt, CBE, TD, DL (d 1955) and Joan, Lady Burnett, *qv*; *b* 27 Jan 1918; *Educ* Harrow, St John's Coll Cambridge (MA); *m* 21 July 1948, Geraldine Elizabeth Mortimer, da of late Sir Godfrey Arthur Fisher, KCMG; 2 s (and 1 s decd); *Heir* s, Charles David Burnett b 18 May 1951; *Career* served WW II (despatches) France, N Africa, Sicily and Italy, Temp Lt-Col GSO1 1945; memb Port of London Authority 1962-75; chm: Proprietors of Hay's Wharf Ltd 1964-80, London Wharfingers Assoc 1964-71, S London Botanical Inst 1964-80 (pres 1985-); Master Co of Watermen and Lightermen 1964; dir Guardian Royal Exchange Assurance Ltd; one of HM Lts of City of London; memb cncl Brighton Coll; FRICS, FLS; *Style—* Sir David Burnett, Bt, MBE, TD; Tandridge Hall, nr Oxted, Surrey; Tillmouth Park, Cornhill-on-Tweed, Northumberland

BURNETT, David John Stuart; s of J E Burnett; *b* 6 Feb 1958; *Educ* Oundle, Peterhouse Cambridge; *m* 1988, Anne, da of C J C Humphrey; *Career* stockbroker; former ptnr at Rowe & Pitman, dir Warburg Securities; *Style—* David Burnett, Esq; The Old Rectory, Steeple Gidding, Huntingdon, Cambs (☎ 08323 488); 70 Holland Park, London W11 (☎ 01 243 0887)

BURNETT, Ernest John; s of Ernest Burnett, MBE, of Staplehurst Manor, Staplehurst, Kent, and Norah Agnes, *née* Davis (d 1982); *b* 7 Oct 1931; *Educ* Liverpool Collegiate Sch, Colfe's GS; *m* 17 Dec 1955, Anne, da of Walter Hazell (d 1946), of IOW; 2 s (Jonathan b 1959, David b 1963), 1 da (Brigitte b 1956); *Career* CA 1955, ptnr Victor Stewart & Co 1959-69, princ John Burnett & Co (later John Burnett McMahon & Co) 1969-; cncllr Maidstone Borough 1972-84; Freeman City of London, Ct of Assts Worshipful Co of Bowyers; FCA, FCCA, ATII; *Recreations* philosophy, restoration of Elizabethan timbered house; *Style—* John Burnett, Esq; Chequers, High St, Headcorn, Ashford, Kent TN27 9NE (☎ 0622 890 052); 103 Newgate St, London EC1A 7AP (☎ 01 606 4861, fax 01 606 4862)

BURNETT, George Dawson; CBE (1985, TD; s of George Alexander Burnett (d 1952, of Belsay, Northumberland, and Fanny Louisa Evelyn, *née* Dawson; *b* 3 Sep 1917; *Educ* Pocklington Sch; *m* 2 Jan 1951, Ferdinanda Anna (Nan, da of Jonkheer Bastiaan Van Den Brandeler (197, of Zeist, The Netherlands; 2 s (David Henry b 1951, Daniel George b 1954); *Career* WWII 2 Lt 1939 (POW 1942, escaped 1943, despatches, demob Maj RA 1946; gen mangr Nat Provincial Bank Ltd 1967-68 (sec 1963-67, gen mangr Nat West Bank Ltd 1969-77 (dir 1973-77, chm Jt Ctee on Gilt Edged Settlements 1977-79, dir TSB (England and Wales plc 1979-87 (dep chm 1983-87), dir London Italian Bank Ltd 1989; FCIB 1970; *Recreations* fishing, golf; *Clubs* Richmond GC; *Style—* George Burnett, Esq, CBE, TD; The Warren, Fitzgeorge Ave, New Malden, Surrey KT3 4SH (☎ 01 949 2245)

BURNETT, Joan, Lady; Joan; da of late Lt-Col Sir John Humphery (d 1938), and his 1 wife, Amy Constance, *née* Rixon; *m* 1917, Col Sir Leslie Trew Burnett, 2 Bt, CBE, TD, DL (d 1955); 2 s, 2 da (and 1 da decd); *Style—* Joan, Lady Burnett; Stratton Cottage, Godstone, Surrey

BURNETT, Sir John (Harrison); s of Rev T Harrison Burnett, of Paisley; *b* 21 Jan 1922; *Educ* Kingswood Sch Bath, Merton Coll Oxford; *m* 1945, Enid Margaret, er da of Rev Dr Edgar W Bishop; 2 s; *Career* served WW II Lt RNVR Atlantic, Channel, Mediterranean; fellow Magdalen Coll Oxford 1949-54; prof botany: St Andrews 1955-60, Newcastle 1960-68; Regius prof botany Glasgow 1968-70, Sibthorpian prof of rural economy and fellow St John's Oxford 1970-79; princ and vice-chllr Edinburgh Univ 1979-87; Hon FRSC Edin 1983, Hon LLD (Dundee) 1982, (Strathclyde) 1983 (Glasgow) 1987; Hon DSc: Buckingham 1981, Pennsylvania 1983; exec sec World Cncl for the Biosphere 1987-; kt 1987; *Books* Vegetation of Scotland (1964), Fundamentals of Mycology (1968, 1976), Mycogenetics (1975), Edinburgh Univ Portaits II (1985), Speciation in Fungi (1988); *Recreations* writing, walking, gardening; *Clubs* Athenaeum (London); *Style—* Sir John Burnett; c/o Agricultural Science Building, Department of Plant Sciences, Parks Road, Oxford OX1 3PR (☎ 0865 270880)

BURNETT, Paul Arthur Brian; s of Brian Walter Burnett, of Wittersham, Kent, and Eve Catherine Anne, *née* McHaffie, JP; *b* 24 June 1957; *Educ* Tonbridge, RCM (GRSM, ARCM); *Career* freelance conductor, horn player, organist and harpsichordist; asst dir of music Downside 1980-, freelance hornplayer BBC Symphony Orchestra, English Chamber Orchestra, English Wind Ensemble 1980-, fndr and music dir Purley Philharmonic Soc 1980-, conductor Dulwich Orchestra 1982-, don Winchester Coll 1983-87; Freeman City of London 1982-, Liveryman Worshipful Co of Musicians 1982-; memb Royal Coll of Organists 1981-; *Recreations* tennis, squash, interest in Homeopathy; *Style—* Paul Burnett, Esq; Flat 3, Arndell House, 48 Benhill Wood Road, Sutton Surrey SM1 4HN (☎ 01 642 7484)

BURNETT, Timothy Adrian John; s of late Lt-Col Maurice John Brownless Burnett, DSO, DL, of Dunsa Manor, Dalton, Richmond, North Yorks, and Crystal Henrietta Deschamps, *née* Chamier; *b* 12 April 1937; *Educ* Eton, Trinity Coll Cambridge (BA); *m* 15 Jul 1961, (Catherine Barbara) Jean, da of Dr Julius Harald Beilby (d 1978), of Aiskew House, Bedale, North Yorks; 1 s (James b 1964), 1 da (Henrietta b 1962); *Career* 2 Lt Coldstream Gds 1956-58; asst keeper Dept of Manuscripts British Museum 1961, Manuscripts Librarian British Library 1986; *Books* The Rise and Fall of a Regency Dandy, The Life and Times of Scrope Berdmore Davies (1981), Byron, Childe Harold Canto III (1988); *Recreations* architectural history, travel, sailing, shooting, fishing; *Clubs* Beefsteak, Pratts, Royal Yacht Sqdn; *Style—* Timothy Burnett, Esq; 11 Highbury Place, London N5 (☎ 01 226 6234); Dunsa Manor, Dalton, Richmond, North Yorks; Dept of Manuscripts, British Library, Great Russell Street, London WC1 (☎ 01 323 7523)

BURNETT ARMSTRONG, Lady (Christine) Caroline Catherine; *née* Rous; eld da of 5 Earl of Stradbroke (d 1983), and Hon Mrs Mary April Rous, *née* Asquith, *qv*; *b* 27 April 1946; *Educ* Stella Maris Convent Bideford, Croft House Sch Dorset, Cramborne Chase Sch Wiltshire; Univ of Zambia, Inst of Educ, Univ of London (BSc, PGCE, DipEd); *m* 1978, John Francis Burnett Armstrong, of Dalby, Terrington, N Yorks, s of Capt Burnett Armstrong, MC (d 1982); 2 s (Henry b 1978, George b 1982) 1 da (Catherine Julia b 1986); *Career* ptnr in JF Armstrong Farms; *Recreations* riding; *Clubs* The Yorkshire; *Style—* Lady Caroline Burnett Armstrong; Dalby, Terrington, N Yorks (☎ Brandsby 666)

BURNETT OF KEMNAY, Madam Susan Letitia; da of Arthur Moubray Burnett (d 1948), of Kemnay, and Muriel, *née* Andrew Speed (d 1963); family granted charter for Kemnay by James VII 1688, Baronage of Scotland; *b* 16 Oct 1922; *Educ* Heatherley, Inverness and Kemnay Secondary Sch; *m* 19 Aug 1946, Fredrick James Milton, s of Edwin Barnes Milton (d 1959), of S Africa; *Career* leading Wren, WRNS Rosyth Cmd; *Recreations* music, drama, gardening, art; *Style—* Burnett of Kemnay; Kemnay House, Kemnay, Aberdeenshire AB5 9LH (☎ 0467 42220)

BURNETT-HALL, Richard Hamilton; s of Basil Burnett-Hall (d 1982), and Kathleen Ruth, *née* Wilson; *b* 5 August 1935; *Educ* Marlborough, Trinity Hall Cambridge (MA); *m* 25 April 1964, Judith Diana (Judy), da of Robert Newton, CMG (d 1983); 2 s (John b 1967, Graham b 1970), 1 da (Louisa b 1965); *Career* Nat Serv RCS 1954-56 (2 Lt 1955); Carpmaels & Ransford 1960-68, Int Synthetic Rubber Co Ltd 1968-71, McKenna & Co Slrs 1971- (admitted slr 1974, ptnr 1974-); chm laws ctee and cncl memb Licensing Executives Soc, cncl memb UK Environmental Law Assoc; chartered patent agent 1966; Freeman Berwick-upon-Tweed 1965; memb Law Soc; *Recreations* music; *Clubs* United Oxford & Cambridge; *Style—* Richard Burnett-Hall, Esq; McKenna & Co, Inveresk House, 1 Aldwych, London WC2R 0HF (☎ 01 836 2442, fax 01 379 3059, telex 27251)

BURNETT-HURST, Clive Robert; s of Lt Alexander Robert Burnett-Hurst (d 1973), of Parbold, and Winifred Gladys, *née* Thompson (d 1983); *b* 21 June 1932; *Educ* Clitheroe Royal GS; *m* 30 July 1966, Marjorie, da of Thomas Allen, of Wigan; 1 s (Peter Robert b 1970) 2 da (Caroline Ann b 1973, Alexandra Jill b 1974); *Career* princ managing clerk Wilkinson & Freeman CAs Preston 1957-60, lectr on accountancy Wigan and Dist Mining and Tech Coll 1960-74; ptnr CR Bernett Hurst & Co CAs Parbold 1959-, Stubbs Parkin CAs Formby 1979-; vice chm Friends of Kingswood Schs Birkdale Southport, rep for Merseyside and Sefton on Independant Schs Action ctees, memb Liverpool Soc of CAs Educn Ctee; FCA 1958, ATII 1958, ACIS; *Recreations* photography, philately, railway preservation, numismatism; *Style—* Clive R Burnett-Hurst, Esq; 5A The Common, Parbold, Nr Wigan, Lancs WN8 7HA (☎ 02576 2482/ 4403)

BURNEY, Sir Cecil Denniston; 3 Bt (UK 1921), of Preston House, Preston Candover, Co Southampton; s of Sir Charles Dennistoun Burney, 2 Bt, CMG (d 1968), and Gladys, *née* High (d 1982); *b* 8 Jan 1923; *Educ* Eton, Trinity Coll Cambridge; *m* 5 Sept 1957, Hazel Marguerite, yr da of Thurman Coleman (d 1939), of Weymouth, Dorset, and former w of Trevor de Hamel; 2 s; *Heir* s, Nigel Dennistoun Burney; *Career* served WW II Special Branch RNVR, Lt; chm: Energy Capital plc, Independent Resources Ltd (Australia), Hampton Tst plc 1975-87 memb Legislative Cncl N Rhodesia 1959-64, MP Zambia 1964-68; chm Public Accounts Ctee Zambia 1964-67; *Recreations* tennis, skiing; *Clubs* White's, Turf, Carlton, Buck's, Leander, Harare, Ndola; *Style—* Sir Cecil Burney, Bt; 5 Lyall St, London SW1 (☎ 01 235 4014); Energy Capital plc 4 Lowndes Pr SW1X 9ET London W1H 4AU (☎ 01 245 6655 telex PROFIT G 8812521)

BURNEY, Nigel Dennistoun; s and h of Sir Cecil Burney, 3 Bt; *b* 6 Sept 1959; *Educ* Eton, Trinity Coll Cambridge; *Clubs* Turf, Annabels; *Style—* Nigel Burney, Esq; 5 Lyall St, London SW1 (☎ 01 235 4014)

BURNHAM, Peter Michael; s of Frank Burnham (d 1980), of Chislehurst, and Winifred Eileen, *née* Fyson (d 1972); *b* 13 May 1935; *Educ* Eltham Coll Univ of Bristol (BA, JDip, MA); *m* 6 Feb 1963, Jill, da of Langton Gowlland, of Godalming, Surrey; 2 da (Sarah Jane Reily b 6 June 1964, Emma Elizabeth Reily b 6 April 1965); *Career* Nat Serv, Pilot Offr RAF 1959-61 (Sword of Honour 1960); articled clerk Sturges, Fraser, Cave & Co 1956-59; Coopers & Lybrand 1961-: dir 1970-83, dep md 1983-88, sr dir key accounts 1988-; cmmr Historic Bldgs & Monuments Cmmn 1984-88; dir UK Cncl for Computing Devpt 1984-88; parish cncllr East Clandon PC 1973-78, church warden East Clandon PCC 1976-82, memb ctee Royal Thames YC 1988-; Freeman City of London, memb Worshipful Co of Information Technologists; ACA 1959, FCA 1969, FCMA 1963; *Recreations* sailing; *Clubs* Reform, Royal Thames YC, RAF; *Style—* Peter Burnham, Esq; Tilthams House, Meadrow, Godalming, Surrey GU7 3BX (☎ 04868 4889); Las Terrazas No 21, La Herradura, Grenada, Spain; Plumtree Court, London EC4A 4HT (☎ 01 583 5000, 01 822 4520, fax 01 822 4652, telex 887470)

BURNHAM, 5 Baron (UK 1903); Sir William Edward Harry Lawson; 5 Bt (UK 1892), JP (Bucks 1970), DL (1977); s of Maj-Gen 4 Baron Burnham, CB, DSO, MC, TD (d 1963, he was ggs of Joseph Moses Levy, fndr proprietor of The Daily Telegraph as the first London penny daily), and Marie Enid, CBE, *née* Scott-Robson; *b* 22 Oct 1920; *Educ* Eton; *m* 1942, Anne (DL for Bucks 1985-), da of Maj George Gerald Petherick, of St Cross, Winchester; (1 s decd), 3 da; *Heir* bro, Hon Hugh Lawson; *Career* landowner; served Royal Bucks Yeomanry 1939-41, Scots Gds 1941-68 (cmd 1 Bn 1959-62), ret as Lt-Col 1968; chm: Sail Trg Assoc 1977-, Masonic Housing Assoc 1979-; *Recreations* sailing, shooting; *Clubs* Royal Yacht Sqdn, Turf, Garrick; *Style—* The Rt Hon the Lord Burnham, JP, DL; Hall Barn, Beaconsfield, Bucks (☎ 0494 673315)

BURNIER, Hon Mrs; Hon Kamala; da of late 1 Baron Sinha (*see Sinha, Hon Tarun*); *b* 1892; *m* 1, 1910 (m dis 1943), Ashoke Chandra Gupta, OBE, Accountant-Gen (ret) Central Revenue India; 1 s; m 2, 1943, J Burnier; *Style—* The Hon Mrs Burnier; Paris

BURNS, David Allan; s of Lt Col Allan Robert Desmond Burns, GM (d 1968), of New Station House, Bagshot, Surrey, and Gladys Frances, *née* Dine; *b* 20 Sept 1937; *Educ* Brentwood Sch, Sch of E Euro and Slavonic Studies London Univ; *m* 15 June 1971, Inger Ellen, da of Nils Gustav Kristiansson, of Stockholm, Sweden; 1 s (Paul b 1971), 1 da (Anna b 1974); *Career* 2 Lt RCS 1956-58; jr appts FO Belgrade and Bangkok 1959-71, head of chancery Br Embassy Belgrade 1972-75, asst head Arms Control Dept FCO 1976-79, political cnsllr Br Embassy Bangkok 1979-83, HM consul gen NZ 1983-87, head N America Dept FCO 1988-; memb Marshall Scholarships Selection Ctee for New Eng 1983-87; Freedom City of Lowell Massachusetts 1987; *Recreations* fell walking, sport; *Clubs* Travellers, Royal Bangkok Sports; *Style—* David Burns, Esq; Foreign and Commonwealth Office, King Charles St, London SW1A 2AH (☎ 01 270 2661)

BURNS, Maj-Gen Sir (Walter Arthur) George; KCVO (1962), CB (1961), DSO (1944), OBE (1953), MC (1940); s of Walter Spencer Morgan Burns (d 1929), (whose mother was Mary, sister of J Pierpont Morgan, the celebrated American financier), of North Mymms Park, Hatfield, Herts, by his w Ruth (herself 2 da of William Cavendish-Bentinck, MP, who was in his turn ggs of 3 Duke of Portland); *b* 29 Jan 1911; *Educ* Eton, Trinity Coll Cambridge; *Career* served Coldstream Gds from 1932-: CO 3 Bn (Italy) 1943-44 and Palestine 1947-50, Bde Maj Household Bde 1945-47, CO 3 Bn 1948-50, DAG London Dist 1950-52, Regtl Lt-Col 1952-55, cdr 4 Gds Bde 1955-59, GOC London Dist and Household Bde 1959-62, Col 1966-; Lord-Lt Herts 1961-1986; also served as ADC to Viceroy India 1938-40 and Staff Coll Camberley 1945; steward Jockey Club 1964-67; KStJ; *Style—* Major-General Sir George Burns, KCVO, CB, DSO, OBE, MC Lord-Lt for Hertfordshire; (☎ 0707 45117)

BURNS, Iain Keatings; s of Edward Burns (d 1962), and Mary Ann, *née* Keatings; *b* 6 April 1948; *Educ* St Mungos Acad Glasgow, Univ of Glasgow, (BSc Hons); *m* 1972, Adrienne Mary Elizabeth, *née* Kelly; 2 s (Jonathan b 1975, Nicholas b 1981), 1 da (Jennifer b 1977); *Career* dir: Glasses Guide Service Ltd 1982-85, William Collins plc 1973-82, Pan Books Ltd 1986-; finance dir: Octopus Publishing Gp, Int Thomson Publishing Ltd; ACMA; *Recreations* music, reading, painting; *Style—* Iain Burns, Esq; 30 Greystone Gdns, Kenton, Middx HA3 0EG (☎ 01 907 8585); 59 Grosvenor Street, London W1X 9DA (☎ 01 493 5841)

BURNS, Ian Morgan; s of Donald George Burns, PhD and Margaret Brenda, *née* Morgan, MBE, BA (d 1979); *b* 3 June 1939; *Educ* Bootham Sch York, King's Coll London (LLM); *m* 2 April 1965, Susan Rebecca, da of Col Harold Tidbury Wheeler, ERD; 2 da (Juliet b 1969, Annabel b 1971); *Career* Nat Serv cmmnd RASC (served Duke of Wellington's Regt, Intelligence Corps) 1957-59; examiner Estate Duty Office 1960-65, princ Home Office 1969-72 (asst princ 1965-69), asst sec NI Office 1974-77 (princ 1972-74), asst sec Home Office 1977-79, asst under sec of State NI Office 1979-84, under sec (2 gen mangr disablement serv) DHSS 1986-87; dep under sec of State NI Office 1987-; *Recreations* listening to music, constructive gardening; *Clubs* Royal Cwlth Soc; *Style—* I M Burns Esq; Northern Ireland Office, Whitehall, London, SW1 2AZ (☎ 01 210 3000)

BURNS, James; JP (Motherwell 1972); s of James Burns (d 1980), and Mary, *née* Magee; *b* 8 Feb 1931; *Educ* St Patrick's Sch Shotts, Coatbridge Tech Coll; *m* 1959, Jean, da of John Ward (d 1951); 2 s (James, Colin); *Career* engr NCB 1948-71; memb: Lanark CC 1967-75, Lanarkshire Health Bd 1973-77, Strathclyde Regnl Cncl 1974-; vice-convener 1978-82, convener Strathclyde Regnl Cncl 1982-; chm: Gen Purposes Ctee 1975-82, visiting Ctee HM Prison Shotts 1980-; memb: Cwlth Games Cncl for Scotland 1982-, Main Organising Ctee Cwlth Games 1982-86; hon pres: Strathclyde Community Rels Cncl 1982-, The Princess Louise Scottish Hosp (Erskine Hosp) 1982, tstee The Pearce Inst 1983-; vice-pres: Glasgow Western St Andrew's Youth Club 1982-, St Andrew's Ambulance Assoc 1984-; patron: Strathclyde Youth Club 1982-, YMCA Sports Centre 1982-, The Scottish Pakistani Assoc 1984-, and Indo-Scottish Friendship Soc 1985-, Scottish Retirement Cncl 1984-; *Recreations* fishing, golf; *Clubs* Roy Scottish Automobile (Glasgow); *Style—* James Burns, Esq; 57 Springhill Rd, Shotts ML7 5JA (☎ Shotts 20187); Strathclyde Regnl Cncl, Strathclyde Ho, India St, Glasgow G2 4PF (☎ 041 227 3395, telex 777237)

BURNS, Dr James; GM (1941), CBE (1967); s of William Wilson Burns (d 1941), of Inverness-shire, and Isabella MacDonald (d 1941); *b* 27 Feb 1902; *Educ* Inverness Royal Acad, Aberdeen Univ, Cambridge Univ (Kings Coll), BSc (Hons) PhD; *m* 1934, Kathleen Ida, s of Henry Holt (d 1911), of London; 1 s (Ian MacDonald d 1943), 1 da (Gillian b 1935); *Career* joined Gas Light & Coke Co as research worker 1929, worked in Germany 1930-32, seconded to Messrs Chemical Reactions Ltd: station engr 1940, dep chief engr 1944, chief engr North Thames 1949; dir Br Carbo Norit Union 1954-59; pres: Inst of Gas Engrs 1958, Inst of Fuel 1959, Br representative Int Gas Union

1958-63, dep chm North Thames Gas Bd 1959-62, fndr pres Pipe Line Industries Guild 1962; Chm: Northern Gas Bd 1962-67, Southern Gas Bd 1967-69, ret 1969; works with Cheshire Fndn; *Recreations* country pursuits now confined to bird watching; *Clubs* Royal Motor Yacht Club Poole; *Style*— Dr James Burns, CBE; Flat 4, 14 Chaddesley Glen, Canford Cliffs, Poole, Dorset BH13 7PG (☎ 0202 707370)

BURNS, Sir John Crawford; s of William Barr Burns and Elizabeth Crawford; *b* 29 August 1903; *Educ* Glasgow HS; *m* 1941, Eleanor Margaret Haughton, da of late Rev Montague G James; 1 s, 3 da; *Career* served WW II, Capt; dir James Finlay & Co 1957-74; kt 1957; *Recreations* golf, fishing; *Clubs* Oriental; *Style*— Sir John Burns; Blairalan, Dargai Terrace, Dunblane, Perthshire (☎ 0786 822367)

BURNS, HE Kevin Francis Xavier; CMG (1984); *b* 18 Dec 1930; *Educ* Finchley GS, Trinity Coll Cambridge (BA); *m* 1963, Nan Pinto (d 1984); 1 s , 1 da; *Career* Br high cmmr to Ghana and ambass (non-resident) to Togo 1983-; *Style*— HE Mr Kevin Burns, CMG; Foreign and Commonwealth Office, King Charles St, London SW1

BURNS, Hon Mrs (Mary Margaret); *née* Addington; da of 7 Viscount Sidmouth; *b* 27 July 1956; *m* 1978, James Alexander Burns; 1 da (Julia b 1985); *Style*— The Hon Mrs Burns; Travessa da Portugesa No 5, Lisbon, Portugal

BURNS, Michael James; s of William James Burns (d 1977), and Belle Evelyn, *née* Harrison (d 1970); *b* 18 June 1925; *Educ* St Paul's, Hertford Coll Oxford (MA); *Career* gen mangr and dir Equity & Law Life Assur Soc 1974-86 (joined 1948); non-exec dir: Nat Home Loans Corpn 1985-, Ecclesiastical Insur Off 1987-; memb cncl Inst Actuaries 1973-82 (tres 1979-81); hon tres: Nat Fedn Music Socs 1981-88, Insur Benevolent Fund 1987-; Freeman City of London 1979; Liveryman: Worshipful Co Musicians 1981, Worshipful Co Actuaries 1984; FIA 1955; *Recreations* music, walking; *Style*— Michael Burns, Esq; 7 Laverton Mews, London SW5 OPB (☎ 01 370 4709)

BURNS, Paul; s of Edward Burns, of Hamilton, and Gertrude, *née* Press; *b* 28 May 1947; *Educ* St Aloysius Coll Glasgow, Glasgow Univ (LLB); *m* 11 Sept 1977, Diana Mary, da of Thomas Taylor (d 1986); 1 da (Madeleine Kirsty b 1985); *Career* Lt RCT; slr; sr ptnr Hamilton Burns Moore 1987-; fndr and chm Legal Defence Union 1986-, fndr and ed Glasgow Legal Review; *Recreations* flying, fencing, writing, philosophy, archaeology; *Clubs* RSAC, Royal Cwlth Soc; *Style*— Paul Burns, Esq; 17 Winton Drive, Glasgow; Hamilton Burns & Moore, 111 Union Street, Glasgow (☎ 041 248 6668)

BURNS, Simon Hugh McGuigan; s of Maj Brian Stanley Burns, MC, of Wilts, and Shelagh Mary *née* Nash; *b* 6 Sept 1952; *Educ* Christ the King Sch, Accra Ghana, Stamford Sch, Worcester Coll Oxford (BA); *m* 1982, Emma Mary, da of David Clifford, of London W8; 1 da (Amelia b 1987); *Career* political asst to Rt Hon Mrs Sally Oppenheim MP 1975-81, dir What to Buy Ltd 1981-83, conf organiser IOD 1983-87; *Recreations* photography, travelling, swimming, antiques; *Clubs* Chelmsford Cons (patron); *Style*— Simon Burns, Esq; House of Commons, London SW1 (☎ 01 219 3000)

BURNS, Sir Terence; s of Patrick Owen Burns, and Doris Burns; *b* 13 Mar 1944; *Educ* Houghton-le-Spring GS, Univ of Manchester (BA Econ), London Business Sch; *m* 1969, Anne Elizabeth Powell; 1 s, 2 da; *Career* chief econ advsr to Treasy and head Govt Econ Serv 1980-; vice-pres Soc of Business Economists 1985-; memb cncl Royal Econ Soc 1986-; kt 1983; *Recreations* soccer spectator, golf, music; *Clubs* Reform; *Style*— Sir Terence Burns; c/o HM Treasury, Parliament St, London SW1P 3AG (☎ 01 270 5203)

BURNSIDE, Dame Edith; DBE (1976, OBE 1957); *m* W K Burnside; 1 s, 1 da; *Career* pres Prince Henry's Hosp Central Cncl of Auxiliary 1952; awarded DBE for services to hospitals and the community; *Style*— Dame Edith Burnside, DBE; Flat 6-1, 9 Struan St, Toorak, Vic 3142, Australia

BURNSTOCK, Prof Geoffrey; s of James Burnstock (d 1947), and Nancy, *née* Green (d 1978); *b* 10 May 1929; *Educ* Greenford Co GS, King's Coll London (BSc), King's Coll and UCL (PhD), Melbourne Univ (DSc); *m* 9 Apr 1957, Nomi, da of Sigmund Hirschfeld (d 1988), 3 da (Aviva b 1959, Tamara b 1960, Dina b 1964); *Career* Nat Serv 1947-48; Nat Inst for Med Res London 1956-57, dept of pharmacology Oxford Univ 1957-59, dept of physiology Univ of Illinois (Rockefeller Travelling Fellowship) 1959; Univ of Melbourne Aust: sr lectr dept of zoology 1959-62, reader in physiolgical zoology 1962-64, prof of zoology and chm of dept 1964-75, assoc dean (biological sci) 1969-72; visiting prof dept of pharmacology Univ of California LA 1970; UCL: prof of anatomy and head of dept of anatomy and developmental Biology 1975-, convenor centre for neuroscience 1979-, vice dean (faculty of med sci) 1980-83; author of over 550 pubns in scientific and medical jls and books; memb: Gt Barrier Reef Ctee, Faculty Victorian Coll of Pharmacy; memb IUPS cmmn on: Transmitters and Modulators, the Autonomic Nervous System; fndr memb Int Cncl for Scientific Devpt and Int Acad of Sci, memb cncl The Euro Neuroscience Assoc, chm the Scientific and Engrg Res Cncl Invertebrate Neuroscience Initiative Panel, memb cncl The Bayliss and Starling Soc, bd memb MRC; MSc (Hon) 1962, FAA 1971, FRS 1986, MRCP (Hon) 1987; memb: Br Physiological Soc, Aust Physiological and Pharmacological Soc, Int Soc for Biochemical Pharmacology, Br Pharmacological Soc, Br Anatomical Soc, Euro Artery Club, Int Brain Res Orgn, Int Soc for Devptal Neuroscience, Euro Neuroscience Assoc, Serotonin Club; ed-in-chief Journal of the Autonomic Nervous System, memb ed bd of 15 other Journals; *Books* How Cells Work (1972), Adrenergic Neurons: Their Organisation, Function and Development in the Peripheral Nervous System (jtly 1975), An Atlas of the Fine Structure of Muscle and its Innervation (jtly 1976), Vascular Neuroeffector Mechanisms (jt-ed 1976), Purinergic Receptors (ed 1981), Somatic and Autonomic Nerve-Muscle Interactions (co-editor 1983), Non edrenergic Innervatios of Blood Vessels (jt-ed 1988); *Recreations* wood sculpture and tennis; *Style*— Prof Geoffrey Burnstock; Dept of Anatomy and Developmental Biology, UCL, Gower St, London WC1E 6BT (☎ 01 387 7050 ext 3344, fax 01 380 7349)

BURNTON, Stanley Jeffrey; QC (1982); s of Harry Burnton, of London, and Fay, *née* Levy; *b* 25 Oct 1942; *Educ* Hackney Downs GS, St Edmund Hall Oxford (MA); *m* 26 Feb 1971, Gwenyth, da of Frank Castle, of Aust; 1 s (Simon b 1974), 2 da (Abigail b 1972, Rebecca b 1976); *Career* called to Bar Middle Temple 1965; *Recreations* theatre, wine, travel, reading, music; *Style*— Stanley Burnton, Esq, QC; 9 Kidderpore Ave, London NW3 7SX (☎ 01 431 2819; 1 Essex Ct, Temple, London EC4Y 9AR (☎ 01 583 2000, fax 01 583 0118, telex 889109 Essex G)

BURR, John Perry Underwood; MBE (1944); s of John Perry Burr (d 1929), of St Neots, Cambs, and Evelyn Mabel, *née* Underwood (d 1945); *b* 18 July 1918; *Educ* Bedford Sch; *m* 2 June 1945, Kathleen Mary (Billie), da of Arnold Gladstone Palmer (d 1967), of Great Paxton, Cambs; 2 s (David John b 17 Jan 1947, Christopher Stephen b 10 Aug 1951); *Career* served WW II BEF, MEF, Eighth Army (despatches 1943), BAOR, Lt-Col RAOC; brewer; dir Bass Ltd; chm: Bass Prod, Bass Europe, Charrington & Co, Crest Hotels, ret 1982; dir Carling-O'Keefe (Toronto) Canada 1977-83; pres Common Market Brewers Cncl 1980-84, vice-chm Food and Drinks Ind Cncl 1981-83; chm Sidney C Banks Ltd 1980-, Brewing Research Fndn Cncl 1980-84; memb Inst of Brewing; Bronze Star (USA) 1944; Royal Warrant Holder (1975-78); *Recreations* racing, music; *Style*— John Burr Esq, MBE; Greenacres, Cleat Hill, Ravensden, Bedford MK41 8AN (☎ 0234 771245); Sidney C Banks plc, St Neots Road, Sandy, Beds (☎ 0767 80351)

BURRELL, Denis James; CBE (1982); s of Edwin Charles Merrick Burrell (d 1950); *b* 25 May 1930; *Educ* Rugby, Clare Coll Cambridge (MA); *m* 1977, Susan, da of Eric Alwyn Ingham (d 1978); 1 child; *Career* chm and md Martin Baker Aircraft Co Ltd 1981- (mfr of ejection seats for use in military aircraft; Queen's Award for Export 1969, 1982); *Recreations* squash, tennis; *Style*— Denis Burrell Esq, CBE; Denham Mount, Denham, nr Uxbridge, Middx; Martin-Baker Aircraft Co Ltd, Higher Denham, nr Uxbridge, Middx UB9 5AJ (☎ 0895 832214)

BURRELL, Derek William; s of Thomas Richard Burrell (d 1960), and Flora Frances (d 1986), *née* Nash; *b* 4 Nov 1925; *Educ* Tottenham GS, Queens' Coll Cambridge (MA); *Career* asst master Solihull Sch 1948-52, head of Eng Dollar Acad 1952-59, headmaster Truro Sch 1959-86; memb Headmaster's Conference and Secondary Heads Assoc; fully accredited local preacher (Methodist) 1948-; vice-chm: Cornwall Ctee of Voluntary Service Overseas, Governors of Luton Industrial Coll; chm: Mid Cornwall Branch of Leprosy Mission, Methodist Day Sch Ctee; vice-pres Br Methodist Conf 1987-88; FRSA; *Recreations* music, drama, walking in London or deep countryside; *Clubs* East India, Devonshire, Sports & Public School; *Style*— Derek Burrell, Esq; 2 Strangways Tce, Truro, Cornwall TR1 2NY (☎ 0872 77733)

BURRELL, Mark William; yr s of Sir Walter Burrell, 8 Bt, CBE, TD, DL (d 1985); *b* 9 April 1937; *Educ* Eton, Pembroke Coll Camb (BA); *m* 1966, Margot Rosemary, yr da of Westray Pearce, of Killara, NSW, Australia, and former w of Mackenzie Munro; 2 s, 1 da; *Career* dir: Pearson plc, Lazard Bros & Co Ltd, British Satellite Broadcasting; *Style*— Mark Burrell, Esq; c/o Pearson plc, Millbank Tower London SW1P 4QZ (☎ 01 828 9020)

BURRELL, Sir (John) Raymond; 9 Bt (GB 1774), of Valentine House, Essex; s of Lt-Col Sir Walter Burrell, 8 Bt, CBE, TD, DL (d 1985), by his w, Hon Anne Judith, OBE, da of 3 Baron Denman, GCMG, KCVO, PC, JP; *b* 20 Feb 1934; *Educ* Eton; *m* 1, 1959 (m dis 1971), Rowena Frances, da of Michael H Pearce; 1 s ; m 2, 1971, Margot Lucy, da of F E Thatcher, of Sydney; 1 s (Andrew b 1974), 1 da (Catherine b 1977); *Heir* s, Charles Raymond Burrell b 27 Aug 1962; *Style*— Sir Raymond Burrell, Bt; c/o Knepp Castle Estate Office, West Grinstead, Horsham, sussex

BURRENCHOBAY, Sir Dayendranath; KBE (1978), CMG (1977), CVO (1972); s of Mohabeer Burrenchobay, MBE, and Anant Kumari Burrenchobay; *b* 24 Mar 1919; *Educ* Roy Coll Curepipe Mauritius, Imp Coll London (BSc Eng), Inst of Education London; *m* 1957, Oomawatee Ramphul; 1 s, 2 da; *Career* Mauritius min of external affrs, tourism and immigration 1968-76; sec to cabinet and head Mauritius Civil Service 1976-78, govr-gen Mauritius 1978-83; *Style*— Sir Dayendranath Burrenchobay, KBE, CMG, CVO; Government House, Le Réduit, Mauritius

BURRETT, (Frederick) Gordon; CB (1974); s of Frederick Harold John Burrett, of London (d 1957),and Marion, *née* Knowles (d 1956); *b* 31 Oct 1921; *Educ* Emanuel Sch, St Catharine's Coll Cambridge (BA); *m* 17 April 1943, Margaret Joan, da of Edward George Giddings of Petersfield, Hants (d 1969); 1 s (John b 1954), 2 da (Ann b 1948, Jill b 1949); *Career* serv in RE, N Africa, Italy, Yugoslavia, Greece 1942-45 Capt (despatches); Dip Serv 1946: 3 sec Budapest 1946-49, FO 1949-51, vice consul NY 1951-54, FO 1954-57, 1 sec Rome 1957-60; transferred to HM Treasy 1960; private sec to chief sec Treasy 1963-64, asst sec HM Treasy 1964; Cabinet Office 1967-68; sec of review body on Doctors' and Dentists' Remuneration 1967-68, sec of review body on Pay of Higher Civil Serv 1967-68, under sec Civil Serv Dept 1969, memb of Civil Serv Pay Res Unit Bd 1978-81, dep sec Civil Serv Dept 1972-81; conducted Govt Scrutiny of V and A and Science Museums 1982; advsr to Govt of Oman on Civil Serv reorganisation 1984; led Govt review of policies and operations of Cwlth Inst 1987, leader of review team on responsibilities of the directors of the nat museums and galleries 1987, led review of grading of Sr Arts Cncl Br Film Inst Posts 1988, chm ctee of inquiry into Civil Serv Pay Hong Kong 1988-89; chm of the Wagner Soc 1984-87; *Books* article on the Watercolours of J.M. Wright (1777-1866) in vol 54 of the Old Water Colour Society's Club Annual; *Recreations* reading, music, walking; *Clubs* Athenaeum; *Style*— Gordon Burrett, Esq; Trinity Cottage, Church Rd, Claygate, Surrey (☎ 0372 62783)

BURRILL, Mark Hurlbutt; elder s of Lyonel Peckover Burrill, OBE (d 1983), and Marjorie Sybil, *née* Hurlbutt (d 1976); *b* 10 Sept 1927; *Educ* Eton, and RMC Sandhurst; *Career* Capt Gren Gds 1956 (RARO), Suez Crisis; ptnr Peckover Burrill and Owen, Chartered Surveyors and Land Agents, Denbigh, N Wales, until 1978, external underwriting memb of Lloyds 1960; memb Aled RDC 1959-74 (chm 1971, chm fin ctee 1966-69), chm N Wales branch RDC assoc 1966-68, memb: Merseyside & N Wales electricity consultative cncl 1963-74 (tariff ctee 1964-74), W Denbighshire and W Flintshire Water Bd 1967-72, Denbighshire Local Valuation Panel 1962-72; last High Sheriff for co Denbighshire 1972; Memb Central Assoc of Agric Valuers (chm Denbigh and Flint Branch 1969-70), memb exec ctee Sports Cncl for Wales 1965; Liveryman Guild of Air Pilots and Air Navigators 1968; Freeman City of London 1961; FRICS; *Clubs* First Guards, Farmers; *Style*— Mark H Burrill, Esq; 10 Le Clos Galliotte, Icart, St Martin's, Guernsey CI (☎ 0481 36655)

BURRILL, Timothy Peckover; yr s of Lyonel Peckover Burrill OBE (d 1983), and Marjorie Sybil, *née* Hurlbutt (d 1976); *b* 8 June 1931; *Educ* Eton, Sorbonne Univ; *m* 1, 1959 (m dis 1966) Philippa, o da of Maurice Hare; 1 da (Rebecca Nina b 1961); m 2, 1968, Santa, er da of John Raymond; 1 s (Joshua Hal Peckover b 1973), 2 da (Jemima Lucy b 1970, Tabitha Sara b 1974),; *Career* served Grenadier Gds 1949-52, 2 Bn 1950-52; jr mgmnt Cayzer Iruine & Co 1952-56; entered film indust 1956, joined Brookfield Prodns 1965, md Burrill Prodns 1966-, dir World Film Services 1967-69, first prodn admin Nat Film Sch 1972, md Allied Stars (resp for Chariots of Fire) 1979-80, dir Dovemead Ltd 1977- and Artistry Ltd 1982 (resp for Superman and Supergirl films), conslt Nat Film Devpt Fund 1980-81; chm BAFTA 1981-83 (vice-chm 1979-81); memb gen cncl ACTT 1975-76; prodr memb Cinematograph Films Cncl 1980-83, exec ctee Br Film and TV Prodrs Assoc 1981-, govr Nat Film and TV Sch 1981-; govr Nat Theatre 1982-88, chm Film Asset Devpt plc 1987-, dir Central Casting 1988-; *Recreations* theatre; *Style—* Timothy P Burrill, Esq; 19 Cranbury Rd, London SW6 2NS (☎ 01 736 8673, fax 01 371 5775, car tel 0836 200 559)

BURRINGTON, Ernest; s of Harold Burrington (d 1978), of Chadderton, Lancs, and Laura, *née* Slater; *b* 13 Dec 1926; *m* 5 Jan 1950, Nancy, da of Fred Crossley (d 1988), of Lees, Oldham; 1 s (Peter), 1 da (Jill); *Career* Army 1943-47; reporter and sub-ed Oldham Chronicle 1947-49 (reporter 1941-43), sub-ed Bristol Evening World 1950; Daily Herald: sub-ed Manchester 1950, night ed 1955, London night ed 1957; IPC Sun: night ed 1964, asst ed 1965, asst ed and night ed 1969; dep night ed Daily Mirror 1970, assoc ed Sunday People 1972 (de ed 1971), ed The People 1985-88, dep chm and dep publisher and dir Mirror Gp Newspapers 1988; exec Int Press Inst, Foreign Press Assoc; tstee Int Inst of Child Studies; *Recreations* travel, tennis, bridge; *Style—* Ernest Burrington, Esq; Mirror Gp Newspapers, Holborn Circus, London EC4A 1AR (☎ 01 822 2599, fax 01 353 5811, telex 896713)

BURROUGH, John Outhit Harold; CB (1975), CBE (1963); s of Adm Sir Harold Martin Burrough, GCB, KBE, DSO (d 1977), and Nellie Wills Outhit (d 1972); *b* 31 Jan 1916; *Educ* Manor House Horsham; RNCs Dartmouth and Greenwich; *m* 1944, Suzanne Cécile, da of Philip James Jourdan (d 1961), of Cape Town, SA; 1 s, 1 da; *Career* RN 1929-46, Lt Cdr; GCHQ (FCO) 1946-76, student IDC 1964; under-sec Cabinet Office 1967-69, dir GCHQ (FCO) 1969-73 and 1973-76, dir Racal Communications Systems Ltd 1976-80, dir Racal Communications Ltd 1980-82; *Recreations* reading, defence and foreign affairs, politics, racing, music, househusband, gardening; *Clubs* Naval & Military (chm 1969-72); *Style—* John Burrough, Esq, CB, CBE; The Old Vicarage, Guiting Power, Glos (☎ 045 15 596)

BURROUGH, (Anthony) Paul; s of Evan Jerome Ridgway Burrough (d 1987), of Oxford, and Elaine Shelton, *née* Bliss; *b* 14 Dec 1943; *Educ* Beaumont Coll, RAC Cirencester; *m* 1, 7 June 1968, Veronica Ann, da of Lt-Col Reginald Walter (d 1982); 1 s (Daniel b 7 March 1969), 1 da (Kirsty b 19 Feb 1971); m 2, Gillian Olivia Courtenay, da of Alfred Edward Courtenay Snell (d 1985); *Career* fndr Burrough & Co Estate Agents 1979; MICAC; *Recreations* shooting, riding, racing; *Style—* Paul Burrough, Esq; Rose Cottage, Marten, Marlborough, Wilts (☎ 0264 89 279); Kennet House, High St, Hungerford, Berks (☎ 0488 82349, car tel 0836 292 976)

BURROW, Prof John Wyon; s of Charles Wyon Burrow, of Exeter, and Amy Alice, *née* Vosper; *b* 4 June 1935; *Educ* Exeter Sch, Christ's Coll Cambridge (MA, PhD); *m* 11 Oct 1958, Diane Margaret, da of Harold William Dunnington (d 1983), of Cambridge; 1 s (Laurence b 1961), 1 da (Francesca b 1968); *Career* res fell Christ's Coll Cambridge 1959-62, fell Downing Coll Cambridge 1962-65, lectr Univ of East Anglia 1965-69, Reader in History Univ of Sussex 1969-82, prof Univ of Sussex 1982-; Dr in Scienze Politiche (Bologna) 1988; FRHistS, FBA ; *Books* Evolution and Society (1966), Aliberal Descent (1981), Gibbon (1985), Whigs and Liberals (1988); *Style—* Prof John Burrow; 7 Ranelagh Villas, Hove, East Sussex (☎ 0273 731296); Arts Building, Univ of Sussex, Falmer, Brighton, East Sussex (☎ 0273 606755)

BURROW, Robert Philip; s of Robert F Burrow, of 51 The Woodlands, Market Harbrough, Leics, and Rosalind, *née* Hughes; *b* 24 Mar 1951; *Educ* St Georges Coll Weybridge, Fitzwilliam Coll Cambridge (MA); *m* 21 July 1984, Angela Mary, da of Henry Cornelius Bourne Hill, of 11 Lambourne Ave, London SW19; 2 s (Matthew Robert Henry b 5 June 1985, Simon Richard Philip b 20 July 1987); *Career* articled clerk Clifford Turner 1973-75, (slr 1975-76), slr Linklater & Paines 1976-78, dir RIT Mgmnt Ltd 1979; md: J Rothschild & Co 1981-85 (dir 1978-81), Transcontinental Serv Gp NV (dir 1983-88); non-exec dir: Control Components Ltd 1983, Applied Power Tech Inc 1984, Wickes plc 1989; ptnr S J Berwin & Co 1985-; memb Law Soc; *Style—* Robert P Burrow, Esq; 11 Lambourne Ave, London, SW19 7OW (☎ 01 947 5875); 236 Grays Inn Rd, London, WC1 (☎ 01 278 0444, fax 01 833 2860)

BURROWES, Norma Elizabeth (Mrs Emile Belcourt); da of Henry Burrowes (d 1973), of Bangor, Co Down, N Ireland, and Caroline Mathers, *née* Irwin (d 1987); *b* 24 April 1946; *Educ* Sullivan Upper Sch Holywood Co Down, Queen's Univ Belfast (BA), Royal Acad of Music (ARAM); *m* 23 Dec 1969 (m dis 1979), Steuart John Rudolph Bedford, s of Leslie Herbert Bedford; m 2, 27 Feb 1987, Emile Adrien Belcourt, s of Adrien Joseph Belcourt; 1 s (Sébastien), 1 da (Romilly); *Career* opera and concert singer (soprano); debut: Glyndebourne 1970, ENO 1971, Royal Opera House Covent Garden 1970, Salzburg Fesival 1973, Paris Opera 1975, Met Opera New York 1979, La Scala Milan 1982; numerous other performances world wide incl: Berlin, Buenos Aires, Geneva, Lyons; recordings incl: Die Entführing alls dem Serail, Die Schöpfung, Carmina Burana, Fauré Requiem, Semele, Acis and Galatea; hon Doctor of Music Queen's Univ Belfast 1979; *Recreations* swimming, needlework; *Style—* Miss Norma Burrowes

BURROWS, Anthony (Richard) Brocas; s of Lt-Gen Montagu Brocas Burrows (d 1966) and Molly Rose *née* Le Bas; *b* 27 Jan 1939; *Educ* Eton; *m* 6 Oct 1966, Angela Margaret, da of John Vincent Sheffield; 1 s (Brocas b 1975), 3 da (Carey b 1968, Joanna b 1969, Petra b 1972); *Career* chm: Le Bas Investment Trust, Tex Holdings, I.S & G. Steel Stock Holders; *Recreations* golf, tennis, travel; *Clubs* Whites; *Style—* Richard Burrows, Esq; Barham Hall, Ipswich, Suffolk (☎ 0473830315 (home), 0473830055 (office)); Le Bas Investment Trusts, Claydon, Ipswich, Suffolk (☎ 0860 315114)

BURROWS, Sir Bernard Alexander Brocas; GCMG (1970, KCMG 1955, CMG 1950); s of Edward Henry Burrows (d 1910), and Ione, *née* MacDonald; *b* 3 July 1910; *Educ* Eton, Oxford (BA); *m* 1944, Ines, da of late John Walter, of St Catherines, Bear Wood, Wokingham, Berks; 1 s (Rupert), 1 da, (Antonia); *Career* Foreign Service 1934: ambass to Turkey 1958-62, dep under-sec of state FO 1963-66, perm Br rep N Atlantic Cncl 1966-70; conslt Fed Tst for Educ and Res (former dir-gen); *Style—* Sir Bernard Burrows, GCMG; Rubens West, East Dean, Chichester, W. Sussex

BURROWS, (Robert) David; s of Sir Robert Burrows (d 1961); *b* 12 May 1929; *Educ* Shrewsbury; *m* 1973, Erica, da of Louis Simonds; 1 s, 3 da; *Career* formerly 2 Lt 9 Lancers; chm and md Fieldgrove Developments Ltd; *Recreations* shooting; *Style—* David Burrows, Esq; Waste Barn, Knockdown, Tetbury GL8 8QY (☎ (Leighterton 361))

BURROWS, General Eva Evelyn; AO; da of Robert John Burrows (d 1970), and Ella Maria Watson (d 1967); *b* 15 Sept 1929; *Educ* Brisbane HS, Queensland Univ (BA), London Univ (PGCE), Sydney Univ (MEd); *Career* Zimbabwe - missionary educator Howard Inst 1952-57, princ Usher Inst 1967-69; vice-princ Int Coll for Officers 1970-73 (princ 1974-75); ldr Women's Social Services in GB and Ireland 1975-77; Territorial Cdr: Sri Lanka 1977-79, Scotland 1979-82, Australia 1982-86; General (International Leader) of the Salvation Army 1986; Hon Doctorate of Liberal Arts EHWA Women's Univ Seoul Korea 1988, Hon LLD Asbury Coll USA 1988; *Recreations* classical music, reading, travelling; *Style—* General Eva Burrows, AO; Salvation Army International Headquarters, 101 Queen Victoria Street, London EC4P 4EP (telex 8954847)

BURROWS, Joseph Brian; s of Joseph Ronald Burrows, of Bramhope, Leeds (d 1976), and Lady Joyce Doreen Woodeson, *née* Haste, of Overcliffe Foxton, Northumberland; step f Sir James Brewis Woodeson OBE 1917-1980,; *b* 12 May 1943; *Educ* Oundle and Leeds Univ (Dip Textiles Industs); *m* 1, 14 Sept 1968 (m dis Nov 1982), Suzanne, da of Charles Henry Vince (d 1982); 1 s (Niel b 1975), 2 da (Vanessa b 1971, Georgina b 1972); m 2, 6 March 1986, Linda Louise, da of John Duncan Raper, of Dunstran Farm, Leeds; *Career* dir: J & F Burrows Ltd, R & B Textiles Ltd (and co-fndr) 1965-73; chm Burmatex Gp (formerly R & B Textiles 1973-87); *Recreations* golf, cricket, rugby; *Clubs* Alwoodley GC, Ganton GC, Headingley Taverners; *Style—* Joseph Burrows, Esq; Hallcroft Hall, Addingham, Ilkley, W Yorks LS29 0QN (☎ 0943 830349)

BURROWS, Reginald Arthur; CMG (1964); s of Arthur Richard Burrows (d 1947), and Nellie Gertrude, *née* Oxley (d 1963); father was first dir of Programmes of BBC in 1923, subsequently sec-gen The Int Bdcasting Union Geneva; *b* 31 August 1918; *Educ* Mill Hill Sch, St Catharine's Coll Camb (MA); *m* 1952, Jenny Louisa Henriette (d 1985), da of Maurice Campiche, of Lausanne, Switzerland; 1 s (Stephen), 1 da (Susan); *Career* served WW II RAF in Europe, SE Asia, Wing Cdr, cmmnd 13 Sqdn; Diplomatic Serv 1947-78, served: France, Pakistan (twice), Iran, Vietnam, Netherlands, Turkey; asst under-sec of state 1976-78; *Recreations* skiing, tennis, mountain walking; *Style—* Reginald Burrows, Esq, CMG; 9 Summer Court, Summer Hill, Hambledown, Canterbury, Kent, CT2 8NP (☎ 0227 457394)

BURROWS, Rt Rev Simon Hedley; s of Very Reverend Hedley Robert Burrows (d 1983), and Joan Lumsden, *née* Lovett; *b* 8 Nov 1928; *Educ* Eton, Kings Scholar, Kings Coll Cambridge (MA); *m* 25 June 1960, Janet, da of Rev Canon Frederick Hampden Basil Woodd (d 1986); 2 s (Giles b 1965, Jeremy b 1969), 3 da (Philippa b 1961, Frances b 1962, Rebecca b 1967); *Career* clerk Holy Orders, curate St John's Wood 1954-57, vicar Holy Trinity Fareham 1967-74, chaplain Jesus Coll Cambridge 1957-60, vicar Wyken Coventry 1960-67; suffragan bishop of Buckingham 1974-; *Style—* Right Reverend Simon H Burrows; Sheridan, Grimms Hill, Great Missenden, Bucks HP16 9BD

BURSTALL, Dr Clare; da of Alfred Wells (d 1958), and Lily, *née* Humphreys; *b* 3 Sept 1931; *Educ* Ribston Hall HS for Girls Gloucester, Univ of London (BA, PhD); *m* 1955 (m dis 1977), Michael Lyle Burstall, s of Dr Francis Hereward Burstall (d 1956); 1 s (Francis), 1 da (Lindsay); *Career* psychologist; dir: Nat Fndn for Educnl Res 1983- (dep dir 1972-83), Nfer-Nelson Publishing Co 1983-; *Books* French in the Primary School (1970), Primary French in the Balance (1974); *Recreations* art collection, sailing, needlework; *Clubs* IOD, Royal Overseas League; *Style—* Dr Clare Burstall; 26 Lennox Gardens, London SW1X 0DQ (☎ 01 584 3127); Nat Fndn for Educational Res, The Mere, Upton Park, Slough, Berks SL1 2DQ (☎ 0753 74123)

BURSTON, Sir Samuel Gerald Wood; OBE (1966); s of Maj-Gen Sir Samuel Roy Burston, KBE, CB, DSO, VD (d 1960), and Helen Elizabeth, *née* Culross (d 1958); *b* 24 April 1915; *Educ* St Peter's Coll Adelaide; *m* 1940, Verna Helen Peebles (d 1980); 1 s, 1 da; *Career* grazier 1945-; memb Nat Employers Policy Ctee 1970-78; pres: Aust Woolgrowers & Graziers Cncl 1976-79, Aust Science & Technol Cncl 1977-85; vice-pres Confedn of Aust Industry 1978-83; dir Reserve Bank of Australia 1977-87; kt 1977; *see Debrett's handbook of Australia and New Zealand for further details*; *Recreations* golf, tennis, swimming; *Clubs* Melbourne, Adelaide, Naval and Military (Adelaide); *Style—* Sir Samuel Burston, OBE; 43-52 Brougham Place, North Adelaide, South Australia 5006, Australia (☎ 08 267 3783)

BURT, Alistair James Hendrie; MP (C) Bury North 1983-; s of James Hendrie Burt and Mina Christie Robertson; *b* 25 May 1955; *Educ* Bury GS, St John's Coll Oxford; *m* 1983, Eve Alexandra Twite, 1 s, 1 da; *Career* slr, memb Haringey Borough Cncl 1982-84, vice-pres: Tory Reform Gp, patron Lawyers Assoc working for Soviet Jewry; memb: All Party Paper Ind Gp, of All Party Textile Gp; sec of Parly Christian Fellowship; PPS to Rt Hon Kenneth Baker MP Sec of State for Educ; *Recreations* family, modern art, music, sport, church affairs; *Style—* Alistair Burt, Esq, MP; House of Commons, London SW1

BURT, David Lyndon; s of Maj Robert Frederick Burt (d 1969); *b* 13 Jan 1930; *Educ* Tonbridge; *m* 1961, Prunella Mary, *née* Antrobus, of Johannesburg, S Africa; 1 s, 1 da; *Career* joined Lewis & Peat Gp 1958, former dep chm Guinness Peat Gp; dir: Lewis & Peat Ltd, Wilson Smithett & Cope Ltd, Multigerm Int Ltd; *Recreations* skiing, shooting, gardening, farming, horses; *Clubs* Cavalry; *Style—* David Burt, Esq; Silton, Peaslake, Surrey GU5 9SR (☎ 0306 730792, fax 0306 730027)

BURT, Hon Sir Francis Theodore Page; KCMG (1977); s of Archibald Francis Gustavus Burt (d 1941), of Western Aust; *b* 14 June 1918; *Educ* Guildford GS, Univ of WA (LLB, LLM, LLD (Hon)); *m* 1943, Margaret, da of Brig J E Lloyd; 2 s, 2 da; *Career* RAN and RAAF 1940-45; barr WA 1941, QC 1960, pres Law Soc WA 1960-62, Bd of Management Charles Gairdner Hosp 1962-72, chief justice of WA 1977- (judge of Supreme Ct 1969-), lt-govr of Western Aust 1977-; *Style—* The Hon Sir Francis Burt, KCMG; 64 Leake St, Cottesloe, W Australia 6011

BURT, Hilary Rose; *née* Garnett; da of Onslow Garnett (d 1958), of Wainstalls, Yorkshire (whose maternal gf was Maj-Gen Reginald Onslow Farmer, RA, bro of William Francis Gamul Farmer, High Sheriff of Surrey 1849, owner of Nonsuch Palace, Surrey, a former royal residence, *see* Burke's Visitation of Seats and Arms, vol I, p 214), and Elaine Mary (who m 2, Brig Percival de Courcy Jones, OBE, *qv*), da of Harry Charles Connatty, of Co Cork (whose mother was Amelia Lovejoy, a Gaiety Girl); *b* 4 Dec 1943; *Educ* Byam-Shaw Sch of Art; *m* 1966, Timothy Lyndon Burt, writer, linguist and economist, s of Oliver Burt, actor, and first cousin of David Lyndon Burt, *qv*; 2 da (Sophie Jane Caroline b 1967, Olivia Lucy b 1974); *Career* artist and equestrian sculptor in bronze, work exhibited in York; *Recreations* tennis, riding, music, theatre, arts; *Style—* George A Dowse Esq; Jack's Cottage, West Tanfield, Ripon, N Yorkshire; 41 Elm Park Gardens, London SW10

BURT, Terence William; s of Terence William, of Walgrave, Northants, and Dorothy Evelyn, *née* Jones; *b* 21 June 1956; *Educ* Pilgrim GS, Hatfield Poly; *m* 20 Sept 1980,

Susan, da of John Hudson of Bedford; 3 s (Michael b 1983, Philip b 1984, Nicholas b 1986); *Career* md Star Computers Ltd 1985-, sec & gp finance dir Star Computer Gp plc 1985-, resigned 1988, formed K2 Systems plc, dir Complete Intruder Alarms Ltd; ACMA; *Style—* Terence Burt, Esq; 17 Farnham Way, Bedford (☎ 0234 58919); 70 Bells Rd, Gorleston, Norfolk; 64 Great Eastern St, London EC2A 3QR (☎ 0923 816266, fax 0923 816260); 4 Colonial Business Park, Colonial Way, Watford WD2 4PT

BURT, Hon Mrs; Hon Vanessa Mary Linda; *née* Russell; only da of 4 Baron Ampthill; *b* 18 Sept 1960; *m* 24 June 1983, Charles Burt, elder s of Ivor Burt; 1 s (James Ivor Geoffrey b 1984); 1 da (Emma Louise Victoria b 1986); *Style—* The Hon Mrs Burt; 21 Macaulay Road, London SW4 0QP

BURTON, Sir Carlisle Archibald; OBE (1968); *b* 29 July 1921; *Educ* Harrison Coll Barbados, Univ of London (BA), Sch of Librarianship Leeds (ALA), Univ of Pittsburgh (MS); *m* 1946, Hyacinth Marjorie Adelle Barker; *Career* perm sec PM's Office and head of Civil Service, Barbados 1972-81; chm Public Service Cmmn, Barbados 1981-; chm Cave Hill Campus Cncl, Univ of the W Indies 1984-; co dir; kt 1979; *Style—* Sir Carlisle Burton, OBE; Caradelle, Mountjoy Avenue, Pine Gardens, St Michael, Barbados, West Indies

BURTON, Frances Rosemary; da of Maj Richard Francis Heveningham Pughe, DFC, ERD, of Ridlington, Norfolk, and Pamela Margaret, *née* Coates (d 1978);; *b* 19 June 1941; *Educ* St Mary's Convent Herts, Tortington Park Arundel Sussex, Lady Margaret House Cambridge, St Anne's Coll Oxford, Univ of London (LLB); *m* 1, 26 Oct 1963 (m dis 1973), Robert Scott Alexander (now Lord Alexander of Weedon, PC), s of Samuel James Alexander (d 1965), of Fleet, Hants; 2 s (Hon David Robert James b 1964, William Richard Scott b 1969), 1 da (Mary Frances Anne b 1966); m 2, 28 Nov 1975, David Michael Burton, s of Frank Raymond Burton (d 1965), of Wellington Shropshire; 2 da (Jane Richenda Frances b 1979, Charlotte Alice Octavia b 1981); *Career* barr Middle Temple 1970 (ad eundem Lincoln's Inn 1972), practiced Chancery Bar until 1975; tutor for Bar and Law Soc examinations, author legal text books; govr Westminster Coll until 1973; numerous fundraising activities incl: Justice (Br section Int Cmmn of Jurists) 1963-, Peckham Settlement 1973-, Jubilee Sailing Tst 1985-, Cancer Res Campaign 1986-, Duke of Edinburgh's Award Scheme 1987; chm ctee Justice Ball 1983 and 1985, exec ctee memb Big Bang City Hall 1986; memb Soc of Cons Lawyers; *Books* Family Law Textbook (1988, companion vol 1989); *Recreations* RAF (assoc memb); *Style—* Mrs David Burton; 41 Crescent Wood Rd, Sydenham Hill, London SE26 6SA (☎ 01 299 2154); 10 Old Square, Lincoln's Inn, London WC2A 3SU(☎ 01 405 0758, fax 01 831 8237)

BURTON, Sir George Vernon Kennedy; CBE (1972, MBE Mil 1945), DL (Suffolk) 1980; s of George Ethelbert Earnshaw Burton, and Francesca, *née* Holden-White; *b* 21 April 1916; *Educ* Charterhouse, Weimar Univ; *m* 1, 1945 (m dis), Sarah Katherine Tcherniavsky; 2 s; m 2, 1975, Priscilla Margaret, da of Cecil Harmsworth King *qv*, and formerly w of St John Gore *qv*; *Career* formerly Capt RA WW II; chm Fisons 1973-86; dir: Barclays Bank Int 1976-82, Thomas Tilling 1976-82, Rolls-Royce 1976-83; memb Cncl CBI 1970-84, chm CBI Overseas Ctee 1975-83; memb BOTB 1972-82, NEDC 1975-79, Assoc Br Sponsorship of the Arts 1978-84; FRSA; Br Nat Ctee of Int Chamber of Commerce 1979-86, govr Suttons Hosp in Charterhouse 1979-; Cdr Order of Quissan Alaouts, Morroco (1968), Cdr Order of Leopold II, Belgium (1974), FRSA; kt 1977; *Recreations* music; *Clubs* Farmers, Oriental; *Style—* Sir George Burton, CBE, DL; Aldham Mill, Hadleigh, Suffolk IP7 6LE

BURTON, Gerald; s of Edward Neville Burton (d 1985), of Kelsall, Nr Chester, Cheshire, and Mary Elizabeth, *née* Bull (d 1977); *b* 12 August 1938; *Educ* Liverpool Collegiate GS; *m* 4 May 1963, Gillian Margaret, da of John Dean Wilson (d 1986), of W Kirby, Cheshire; 3 s (John, James, Andrew), 1 da (Deborah); *Career* articled clerk Sheard Vickers & Winder CAs Liverpool 1955-61; ptnr 1987- Hodgson Impey CAs, Predecessor Firms (joined 1961, ptnr 1965); chm Beaconsfield Scout Gp; Freeman City of London 1980, memb Worshipful Co of Basketmakers 1982; FCA; *Recreations* golf, music; *Clubs* City Livery, Wig & Pen, Cricketers, Vagabonds; *Style—* Gerald Burton, Esq; Hilbre, Old Farm Close, Knotty Green, Beaconsfield, Bucks (☎ 0494 671560); Hodgson Impey, CAs, Spectrum House, 20-26 Cursitor St, London EC4A 1HY (☎ 01 405 2088, fax 01 831 2206)

BURTON, Graham Stuart; CMG (1987); s of Cyril Stanley Richard Burton (d 1982), and Jessie Blythe Burton; *b* 8 April 1941; *Educ* Sir William Borlase's Sch Marlow; *m* 30 Jan 1965, Julia Margaret Lappin; 1 s (b 1967), 1 da (b 1966); *Career* HM consul-gen San Francisco since 1987, FO 1961, Abu Dhabi 1964, ME Centre for Arabic Studies 1967, Kuwait 1969, FCO 1972, Tunis 1975, UK Mission to United Nations 1978, cnsllr: Tripoli 1981, FCO 1984; *Recreations* golf, watching all sports, opera; *Clubs* MCC; *Style—* Graham Burton, Esq, CMG; c/o Foreign and Commonwealth Office, London SW1

BURTON, Air Marshal Sir Harry; KCB (1971, CB 1970), CBE (1963, MBE 1943), DSO (1941); s of Robert Reid Burton (d 1975), of Rutherglen, Lanarkshire; *b* 2 May 1919; *Educ* Glasgow HS; *m* 1945, Jean (d 1987), da of Tom Dobie (d 1930), of Whitehaven, Cumberland; 1 s, 1 da; *Career* RAF 1937, served Europe, Burma, Pacific (despatches 1942), CO RAF Scampton 1960-63, SASO 3 Bomber Group, air exec to Dept for Nuclear Affrs SHAPE NATO 1965-67, AOC 23 Gp RAF 1948-70, AOC-in-C Air Support Command 1970-73; co dir; *Recreations* squash; *Clubs* RAF; *Style—* Air Marshal Sir Harry Burton, KCB, CBE, DSO; Mayfield, West Drive, Middleton-on-Sea, Sussex PO22 7TS (☎ Middleton-on-Sea 2976)

BURTON, Humphrey McGuire; s of Harry Philip Burton (d 1980), and Kathleen Alice, *née* Henwood (d 1982); *b* 25 Mar 1931; *Educ* Long Dene Sch Chiddingstone Kent, The Judd Sch Tonbridge, Cambridge (BA); *m* 1, 1957, Gretel, *née* Davis; 1 s (Mathew), 1 da (Clare); m 2, 1970, Christina, da of Svante Hellstedt; 1 s (Lukas), 1 da (Helena); *Career* ed Performance Programmes BBC-TV, former head Music and Arts BBC-TV 1965-67 and 1975-81, chm TV Music Working Pty, Euro Broadcasting Union 1976-85, TV dir 1985 Requiem by Lloyd Webber, prod Omnibus (Bernstein's West Side Story); Chevalier de l'Ordre des Arts et Lettres (France); *Recreations* tennis, travel; *Clubs* Garrick; *Style—* Humphrey Burton, Esq; 123 Oakwood Court, London W14 8LA, BBC-TV Kensington House, Richmond Way, London W14 0AX (☎ 01 743 1272)

BURTON, Iris Grace; da of Arthur Robert Burton, of Lewisham, London, and Alice Elizabeth Burton (d 1980); *b* 7 Mar 1940; *Educ* Roan Girls GS, City of London Coll; *m* Joseph Thomas Lucas, s of Elio Lucas (d 1987), of Spain; 1 s (Joseph b 8 Aug 1976), 1 da (Rachel b 12 April 1971); *Career* asst ed TV Times 1978-80; ed: Woman's Own Magazine 1980-86, Prima Magazine 1986-87, Best Magazine 1987-88; ed dir and publisher G & J UK 1988-; *Recreations* walking, gardening; *Style—* Ms Iris Burton; G & J of the UK, Portland House, Stag Place, Victoria, London SW1 (☎ 01 245 8700, fax 01 630 5509)

BURTON, 3 Baron (UK 1897); Michael Evan Victor Baillie; s of Brig Hon George Evan Michael Baillie, MC, TD (s of Baroness Burton, to whom Barony passed from 1 Baron by special remainder, and her 1 husband, Col James Baillie, MVO, JP, DL, sometime MP Inverness-shire), by his w, Lady Maud, *née* Cavendish, CBE, JP, widow of Capt Angus Mackintosh, RHG, and da of 9 Duke of Devonshire, KG; through Lady Maud Lord Burton is 1 cous to late Maurice Macmillan, MP, and 2 Viscount Stuart of Findhorn; suc grandmother 1962; *b* 27 June 1924; *Educ* Eton; *m* 1, 1948 (m dis 1977), Elizabeth, da of late Capt Anthony Wise; 2 s, 4 da; m 2, 1978, Coralie, da of Claude Cliffe, of S Africa; *Heir* s, Hon Evan Baillie; *Career* sits as Conservative in House of Lords; formerly Lt Lovat Scouts and Scots Gds; landowner and farmer; memb Inverness CC 1948-75, JP 1961-75, DL 1963-65; *Recreations* stalking, shooting, fishing, hunting; *Clubs* Cavalry & Guards, Brooks's, Pratt's, New (Edinburgh); *Style—* The Rt Hon the Lord Burton; Dochfour, Inverness IV3 6JY (☎ Dochgarroch 046 386 252)

BURTON, Michael John; QC (1984); s of Henry Burton, QC (d 1952), and Hilda, *née* Shaffer (d 1986); *b* 12 Nov 1946; *Educ* Eton, Balliol Coll Oxford (MA); *m* 17 Dec 1972, Corinne Ruth, da of Dr Jack Cowan, MC, of Putney; 4 da (Josephine b 1977, Isabel b 1979, Genevieve b 1982, Henrietta b 1986); *Career* barr (Gray's Inn) 1970, rec Crown Ct 1989, lectr-in-law Balliol Coll 1972-74, cand (L) Kensington Cncl 1971, Parly cand (L) Stratford-on-Avon 1974, cand (SD) GLC Putney; *Recreations* amateur theatricals, lyric writing, singing, bridge, watching Wimbledon FC; *Style—* Michael Burton, Esq, QC; 125 Howards Lane, Putney, London SW15; 2 Crown Office Row, Temple, London EC4 (☎ 01 583 2681, fax: 01 583 2850)

BURTON, Michael St Edmund; s of Brig WS Burton, DSO (d 1981), of Linton, Kent, and Barbara, *née* Kemmis Betty; *b* 18 Oct 1937; *Educ* Bedford Sch, Magdalen Coll Oxford (MA); *m* 1 Apr 1967, Henrietta Jindra, da of Joseph Hones, of Nicopia, Cyprus; 1 s (Nicholas b 1969), 2 da (Amanda b 1971, Samantha b 1968 d 1971); *Career* joined FCO 1960, asst political agent Dubai and Trucial States 1962-64; served: Khartoum 1967-69, Paris 1969-77, Kuwait 1977-79; Br min and dep cmdt Berlin 1985-; secondment to BP as head of Policy Review Unit 1984-85; *Recreations* tennis, travel, opera; *Clubs* United Oxford and Cambridge Univ, Hurlingham; *Style—* M S Edmund, Esq, CMG, CVO; c/o Foreign & Commonwealth Office, King Charles St, London SW1

BURTON, Nigel Foster; s of Kenneth Burton, of Nottingham, and Margaret Valerie, *née* Foster; *b* 20 Sept 1951; *Educ* Leeds GS, Cheltenham GS, Pembroke Coll Oxford (MA); *m* 17 Aug 1973, Alwyn, da of Brian Robson, of Cheltenham; 3 s (Thomas b 1978, William b 1980, Edward b 1984); *Career* dep actuary Lloyds Life Assur Ltd (now Royal Heritage) until 1983, currently exec dir Allied Dunbar Assur plc; dir Allied Dunbar: Mortgages Ltd, Int Funds Ltd, Int Ltd; FIA 1977; *Style—* Nigel Burton, Esq; Manor Farmhouse, Broad Blunsdon, nr Swindon, Wilts (☎ 0793 721 260); Allied Dunbar Assur plc, Allied Dunbar Centre, Station Rd, Swindon, Wilts SN1 1EL (☎ 0793 514 514, fax 0793 512 371)

BURTON, Richard Hilary; s of Robert Claud Burton (d 1971), of Sussex, and Theodora Constance Helen, *née* Hill (d 1957); *b* 28 Dec 1923; *Educ* Lancing, Brasenose Coll Oxford (MA); *m* 1962, Priscilla Jane, da of Geoffrey Coode-Adams (d 1985), of Essex; 1 s (Edward David Fowler b 1963), 1 da (Sarah Catherine b 1964); *Career* WWII Capt 60 Rifles 1942-46 (despatches), memb mil cts Palestine 1946; called to Bar Inner Temple 1951, barr 1951-54; mangr legal dept Gillette Industs Ltd 1954-65 (legal dir 1965-78, chm 1978-84), dep to chm The Gillette Co (USA) 1984-88; chm: Cable Authy 1984-, Nestor-BNA 1986-; chm West Middx Arts Devpt Tst 1978-86, ctee memb MCC 1989; Freeman City of London; FRSA; *Recreations* cricket, real tennis, shooting, ornithology, lepidoptery; *Clubs* Boodle's; *Style—* Richard Burton, Esq; Danmoor House, Heckfield, Basingstoke, Hants (☎ 0734 326233); Cable Authority, Gillingham House, Gillingham Street London SW1 (☎ 8216161)

BURTON, Richard St John Vladmir; s of Percy Basil Harmsworth Burton, and Vera, *née* Poliakoff Russell; *b* 3 Nov 1933; *Educ* Bryanston, Architectural Assoc Sch of Architecture (AA Dip); *m* 3 April 1956, Mireille, da of Joseph Dernbach-Mayen; 3 s (Mark b 24 April 1957, David b 25 Oct 1958, Jonathan b 2 Jan 1960), 1 da (Catherine b 7 Jan 1962); *Career* ptnr & dir Ahrends Burton & Koralek Architects 1961-, principle works include; Trinity Coll Dublin (Berkeley library 1972, arts faculty bldg 1979), residential bldg Keble Coll 1976, Templeton Coll Oxford 1969-88, St Mary's Hosp Newport IOW 1981-, British Embassy Moscow 1988-, stations for extension Docklands Railway; govr Bldg Centre Tst, chm percent for art steering gp Arts Cncl of GB 1989; RIBA 1957, FRSA 1980; *Recreations* building, writing; *Style—* Richard Burton, Esq; Ahrends Burton and Koralek, Unit 1, 7 Chalcot Rd, London NW1 8LH (☎ 01 586 3311)

BURTON OF COVENTRY, Baroness (Life Peeress UK 1962); Elaine Frances Burton; da of late Leslie Aubrey Burton, of Harrogate, and Frances Burton; *b* 2 Mar 1904; *Educ* Leeds Modern Sch, Leeds Trg Coll; *Career* teacher Leeds 1924-35; memb: S Wales Cncl of Social Welfare 1935-37, Nat Fitness Cncl 1938-39, MP (L) Coventry S 1950-59; former conslt John Waddington Ltd, Courtaulds Ltd; memb: ITA 1964-69, Cncl of Industrial Design 1963-68, Sports Cncl 1965-71; chm Mail Order Publishers' Authy 1970, pres Inst of Travel Managers in Industry and Commerce; joined SDP 1981; *Style—* The Rt Hon The Lady Burton of Coventry; 47 Molyneux St, W1 (☎ 01 262 0864)

BURTON STEWART, Colin; s of Gavin Burton Stewart, CBE (d 1973), of Appin Argyll, and Joyce Irene *née* Middleton, MBE (d 1977); *b* 21 Jan 1948; *Educ* Milton Abbey, Univ of Paris; *m* March 1985, Avril, da of Capt John Ogilvie Munro (d 1980), of Banchory, Aberdeenshire; 1 s (John b 1985); *Career* dir: Anglo-Swiss Reinsur Brokers Ltd 1977-85, The Number Two Oil Co Ltd 1985-; chm: The Stewart Transport & Trading Co Ltd 1984-; *Recreations* travelling, fishing, shooting, reading, model railways; *Clubs* Caledonian, Special Forces; *Style—* Colin Burton Stewart, Esq; c/o Bank of Scotland plc, 16-18 Piccadilly, London W1; 7 Westminster Palace Gardens, London SW1

BURTON-CHADWICK; *see*: Chadwick

BURTON-TAYLOR, Sir Alvin; s of Alvin Alfred Wheatley Taylor, of Aelaide, and Ruby Ella Burton; *b* 17 August 1912; *Educ* Sydney C of E GS; *m* 1949, Joan Lorraine, da of Herbert Toole; 2 s, 1 da (and 1 decd); *Career* chm and dir: NSW Div Nat Heart Fndn of Australia, O'Connell St Associates Pty Ltd; life govr Aust Inst of Mgmnt; FCA (Aust), FAIMr; kt 1972; *Recreations* fishing, bowls, gardening, surfing; *Clubs* Union, Royal Sydney Yacht Sqdn, Elanora Country; *Style—* Sir Alvin Burton-Taylor; 6/50 Upper Pitt St, Kirribilli, NSW 2061, Australia (☎ 920 5807)

BURY, Diana Mary; *née* Incledon-Webber; Lady of the Manors of Croyde and Putsborough, Devon; eldest da of Lt-Col Godfrey Sturdy Incledon-Webber, TD, DL (d 1986), of Buckland Manor, Braunton, N Devon, and Angela Florence, 4 da of Sir Pierce Thomas Lacy, 1 Bt; descended from John Webber, Mayor of Barnstaple (17 cent), ggs Philip Rogers Webber, JP, DL; m 1759, Mary, er da and co-heir of John Incledon, of Buckland, Braunton, Devon (*see* Burke's Landed Gentry, 18 edn, vol I, 1965, Incledon-Webber of Buckland); *b* 27 Sept 1932; *Educ* Stoodley Knowle Convent Torquay; *m* 28 June 1961, John Edward Bury, o s of Col John Bury, OBE (d 1969), of Berden Lodge, Berden, Herts; 1 s (Henry Incledon b 5 May 1962), 5 da (Mary Helen b 1964 (m 1987 Marc Cumberlege), Anne b 1965, Eleanor b 1967, Jane b 1971, Clare b 1972); *Career* sec in Foreign Office 1955-60; ctee memb: DGAA, NADFAS, St Brannoc's RC Church, Braunton; *Recreations* tennis, swimming; *Clubs* Lansdowne; *Style—* Mrs Diana Bury; Buckland Manor, Braunton, N Devon EX33 1HN (☎ 0271 812016)

BURY, Lady Mairi (Elizabeth); *née* Vane-Tempest-Stewart; JP (Co Down); da of 7 Marquess of Londonderry, KG, MVO, TD, PC (d 1949); *b* 25 Mar 1921; *Educ* private; *m* 10 Dec 1940 (m dis 1958), Lt-Col Viscount Bury (d 1968), s of 9 Earl of Albemarle, 2 da (Elizabeth, Rose); *Career* farmer and estate owner, pres Co Down branch Br Red Cross Soc, former pres and chm of Ards Womens Unionist Assoc N Ireland; Liveryman Worshipful Co of Air Pilots and Air Navigators; fell Royal Philatelic Soc London; *Clubs* North of Ireland Flying; *Style—* Lady Mairi Bury, JP; Mount Stewart, Newtownards, Co Down, NI BT22 2AD (☎ 024 774 217)

BURY, Viscountess; Marina; *née* Orloff-Davidoff; da of Count Serge Orloff-Davidoff and Hon Elisabeth, *née* Scott-Ellis, da of 8 Baron Howard de Walden and 4 Baron Seaford; *b* 30 Dec 1937; *m* 1964, as his 2 w, Viscount Bury (d 1968), s and h of 9 Earl of Albemarle, MC, who d 1979); 1 s (10 Earl of Albemarle, *qv*); *Career* ARIBA, AA Dip; *Style—* Viscountess Bury; Piazza di Bellosguardo 10, Florence 50124, Italy (☎ 055 222055)

BURY, Lt(-Col) Ralph James; OBE (1945), TD (1947); s of William George Bury (d 1974), and Ethel Mary, *née* Swann (d 1949); *b* 31 Jan 1920; *Educ* Beckenham GS; *m* 17 Aug 1940, Winifred Muriel, da of Cecil Henry Coppard (d 1945); 1 s (Dr Michael Colin b 1942), 2 da (Jacqueline Mary b 1947, Maureen Claire b 1948); *Career* WW II: N Africa, Sicily, Burma, Singapore; attached RAF Malayan Campaign 1952; attached Fleet Air Arm Korean War 1953; div: United City Merchants 1963-66, Cope Allman Int plc 1966-77; vice chm Clothing Export Cncl of Gt Britain 1969-75; non exec dir: English Continental Ltd merchant bankers 1977-82, Financial & General Securities Ltd, merchant bankers 1978-86, 94 Piccadilly Ltd 1985-; Liveryman Gold & Silver Wyre Drawers Co; *Clubs* Naval & Military; *Style—* Lt-Col Ralph Bury, OBE, TD; Yeomans, Woodbridge Park, East Preston, West Sussex BN16 1NL (☎ 0903 783331)

BUSBRIDGE, Raymond John; s of John Charles Busbridge (d 1968), and Marie Ida, *née* Stratton; *b* 11 Dec 1946; *Educ* Woodside Secdy Sch; *m* 1, June 1966 (m dis 1979), Dianne Rosemary, *née* Webster; 1 s (Phillip James b 8 May 1970), 1 da (Claire Nanette b 21 Nov 1974); m 2, 13 March 1982, Mary Claire, da of Paul Fennelly, of Kilkenny, Ireland; *Career* Leslie & Godwin 1963-64, aviation asst underwriter RW Sturge 1964-75, aviation underwriter Assicurazioni Generali 1975-80, JFC Dugdale (later Octavian Underwriting): fndr AJM Drake (later Busbridge Aviation Syndicate); exec dir Octavian Gp plc, exec memb Lloyd's ctee for Lloyds Aviation Claims Centre, memb Lloyd's 1985-; *Recreations* shooting, fishing, painting; *Style—* Raymond Busbridge, Esq; 84 Fenchurch St, London EC3M 4BY (☎ 01 265 0071, telex 8951200)

BUSBY, (Thomas Samuel) Charles; CBE (1977 OBE 1971), AE (1946), DL (Kent 1981); Thomas William Busby (d 1974) and his w Alice (*née* Feaver) (d 1972); *b* 28 July 1919; *Educ* Cranbrook Sch, Kent; *m* 1949, Diana Daun, da of William Cruickshank Dalgarno (d 1954); *Career* joined 500 Sqdn (co Kent) AAF 1939, served Coastal Cmd Sqdns as Flt Lt (demobilised 1946); FSVA incorporated surveyor, auctioneer and estate agent (ret 1984); nat chm Royal British Legion 1975-78, chm Royal British Legion Village 1965-; *Recreations* gardening, rugby football and cricket; *Clubs* RAF, Royal Overseas League; *Style—* Thomas Busby, Esq CBE, AE, DL; Willow Cottage, Benenden, Cranbrook, Kent TN17 4DB (☎ 0580 240466)

BUSBY, John Philip; s of Eric Alfred Busby, MBE (d 1983), and Margaret Elizabeth, *née* Ware; *b* 2 Feb 1928; *Educ* Ilkley GS, Leeds Coll of Art (NDD), Edinburgh Coll of Art (DA Edin); *m* 18 July 1959, Joan, da of Fred Warriner, of Cleveland; 1 s (Philip b 1960), 2 da (Rachel b 1962, Sarah b 1966); *Career* Nat Serv RAF 1946-48; lectr Edinburgh Coll of Art 1956-88; pres Soc of Scottish Artists 1973-76, fndr memb Soc of Wildlife Artists; RSW 1983, ARSA 1987; *Books* The Living Birds of Eric Ennion (1982), Drawing Birds (1986), Birds in Mallorca (1988); *Recreations* ornithology, travel, music; *Style—* John P Busby, Esq; Easter Haining, Ormiston Hall, Ormiston, E Lothian EH35 5NJ (☎ 0875 340512)

BUSCALL, Robert Edmond; s of Lt-Col V H Buscall (d 1979), of Carbrooke Hall, Thetford, Norfolk, and Gwendolene Mary Angela, *née* Mahony; *b* 2 April 1935; *Educ* Downside, RAC Cirencester (MRAC); *m* 7 Oct 1961, Livia, da of Sir Stephen Lycett Green, Bt, CBE, DL, of Ken Hill, Snettisham, Kings Lynn; 2 s (Harry Charles b 1963, Patrick Edward b 1965); *Career* serv Irish Guards (Lt) 1953-56; farmer; JP 1971-, cnclr Breckland DC 1983-, gen cmmr of income tax 1983-; memb: Bd of Visitors Wayland Prison 1984-87, Agric Land Tbnl (E area) 1983; *Recreations* fishing, shooting, gardening; *Clubs* Whites, Allsorts; *Style—* Robert Buscall Esq; Carbrooke Hall, Thetford, Norfolk (☎ 0953 881 274)

BUSH; *see*: de L'Isle Bush

BUSH, Dr Alan Dudley; s of Alfred Walter Bush, (d 1966), and Alice Maud, *née* Brimsley (d 1987); *b* 22 Dec 1900; *Educ* Highgate Sch, Royal Academy of Music, (AKAM, FRAM), Univ of Berlin; *m* 1931, Nancy Rachel, da of Frederick D Head; 2 da (Rachel b 1931, Catherine b 1937) and 1 da dec'd (twin Alice b 1937, d 1952); *Career* WWII served RAMC 1941-45; prof of composition RAM 1925-30 and 1946- 78; concert pianist, orchestral and operatic conductor 1925-84; examiner Assoc Bd RSM 1947-78; musical compositions incl: 4 full length operas (of which Wat Tyler, Men of Blackmoor and The Sugar Reapers aka Guyanz Johnny had libretti written by his w), num orchestral, solo and instrumental works; hon D Mus (Dunedin) 1965; RSA 1960; *Books* In My Eighth Decade and Other Essays (1980), Strict Counterpoint in the Style of Palestrina; *Recreations* chess, walking; *Style—* Dr Alan Bush; 25 Christchurch Crescent, Radlett, Hertfordshire (☎ Radlett 856 422)

BUSH, Adm Sir John Fitzroy Duyland; GCB (1970, KCB 1965, CB 1963), DSC and Two Bars (1941, 1941 and 1944); s of Fitzroy Bush (d 1949), of Beach, Bitton, Glos; *b* 1 Nov 1914; *Educ* Clifton Coll; *m* 1938, Ruth Kennedy, da of Capt Herbert K Horsey, RN, of Foreham, Hants; 3 s, 2 da; *Career* RN, C-in-C Western Fleet, Allied C-in-C Channel, Allied C-in-C E Atlantic 1967-70, Vice-Adm of UK and Lt of Admiralty 1979-84; pres Clifton Coll 1982-87 (chm cncl 1978-81, memb 1971-87); *Recreations* fishing, gardening; *Style—* Adm Sir John Bush, GCB, DSC**; Becksteddle House, Colemore, nr Alton, Hants (☎ Tisted 367)

BUSHE, Peter Dalwyn Scott; s of Louis Alfred Bushe (d 1986), of Surrey, and Marion Howard, *née* Wing (d 1970); *b* 17 August 1924; *Educ* Lodge Sch Barbados, Lancing Coll; *m* 14 April 1951, Margaret, da of Major Frank Walter Mace (d 1975), of Surrey; 2 s (Andrew b 1952, David b 1956); *Career* RNVR Sub Lt Normandy and Far East 1943-46, Royal Sch of Mines 1946-47; Trinidad Petroleum Dvpt Ltd 1948-60, BP (Trinidad) Ltd 1960-68, BP Libya 1968-71, technical co-ordinator BP London 1971-76, co-ordinator Abu Dhabi Marine Areas 1976-83; dir: Ilex Lubricants Ltd 1968-, Cadmuir Dvpts Ltd 1983-, Headston Contracts Ltd 1985-; FInstPet; *Recreations* tennis, golf; *Clubs* Naval; *Style—* Peter Bushe, Esq; Little Fairhall, Colley lane, Reigate, Surrey RH2 9JA (☎ 0737 245193); Headston Contracts Ltd, Little Fairhall, Colley Lane, Reigate, Surrey RH2 9JA (☎ 0737 240001)

BUSHELL, John Hudson; s of (Charles) Harold Bushell, OBE, of Reigate, Surrey, and Bessie Mary, *née* Smith; *b* 13 Oct 1941; *Educ* Haileybury; *m* 8 Oct 1966, Marian Elisabeth, da of Eric Percival Marsh, of Woking, Surrey; 1 s (Alistair b 1970), 2 da (Emma b 1968, Heather b 1978); *Career* dir J Henry Schroder Wagg & Co Ltd 1975-85, chm and chief exec London Shop plc 1986-89 (dir 1982-89, exec vice chm 1985-86); FCA 1964; *Recreations* cricket, tennis; *Clubs* Walton Strollers Cricket, Inst of Dirs; *Style—* John Bushell, Esq; Oxshott, Surrey

BUSK, Sir Douglas Laird; KCMG (1959, CMG 1948); s of John Laird Busk, of Westerham, Kent, and Eleanor, *née* Joy; *b* 15 July 1906; *Educ* Eton, New Coll Oxford, Princeton USA; *m* 1937, Bridget Anne Moyra, da of Brig-Gen William George Hemsley Thompson, CMG, DSO (d 1944), of Warminster, Witts; 2 da; *Career* Diplomatic Service 1929; ambass: Ethiopia 1952-56, Finland 1958-60, Venezuela 1961-64; chm Mount Everest Foundation to 1983; *Style—* Sir Douglas Busk, KCMG; Broxton House, Chilbolton, nr Stockbridge, Hants (☎ Chilbolton 272)

BUSSE, Hon Mrs (Susan Anne); er da of Baron Trevelyan (Life Peer; d 1985); *b* 10 Jan 1941; *m* 1961, Harald Busse, s of Gerhard Busse, of Cologne; 2 s, 1 da; *Style—* The Hon Mrs Busse; c/o Ministry of Foreign Affairs, Bonn, W Germany

BUSTON, Maj Roger; TD (1985); s of Russell Buston, of Parkstone, Dorset, and Kathleen, *née* Williams (d 1955); *b* 24 May 1953; *Educ* Colchester RES, Poole ES, Queen Mary Coll London Univ (LLB); *Career* London Univ OTC 1971-74; 36 Signal Regt (TA): Troop Cdr 1974, Sqdn Cdr 1986-, Regtl Ops Offr 1988-; slr 1977, sole practitioner Asmer Prior & Son 1981-86, ptnr Asmer Prior Bates 1986-; MBIM; *Recreations* skiing; *Style—* Roger Buston, Esq, TD; New House, Wellesley Rd, Colchester CO3 3HH (☎ 0206 45986); Asmer Prior Bates (Solicitors), Blackborn House, 32 Crouch St, Colchester, Essex CO3 3HF (☎ 0206 573089, fax 0206 760096, car tel 0860 833483, telex 987750 ASHBAT G)

BUSWELL, Hon Mrs; Hon (Barbara); *née* Fisher; yr da of 2 Baron Fisher (d 1955); *b* 1 Oct 1925; *m* 1961, Leslie Charles Croft Buswell, s of Gerald Buswell (d 1959), of Johannesburg, S Africa ; 1 s, 1 da; *Style—* The Hon Mrs Buswell; Jersey, CI; Normandie Farm, PO Box 6, Firgrove, Cape 7110 S Africa

BUTCHER, Ian George; s of George Wilfred Robert Butcher, of Winchmore Hill, London, and Joyce Patricia, *née* Payne; *b* 13 April 1950; *Educ* Winchmore Sch, City of London Coll; *m* 15 Sept 1978, Sarah Jane, da of Donald Percy Jeffery, of Aston Hill Farmhouse, Halton, Bucks; 1 s (Harry b 1987), 2 da (Emma b 1981, Kellie b 1984); *Career* exec dir County Bank Ltd 1974-84, fin dir Addison Page plc 1984-86, corp devpt dir Addison Conslt Gp plc 1986-87, gp fin dir Charles Baker plc 1987-89, chm Lefax Publishing Ltd 1984-89; dir Whitehead Mann plc 1989-; FCA; *Recreations* hockey, cricket, tennis, music, reading; *Clubs* MCC, RAC; *Style—* Ian G Butcher, Esq; Aston Hill Farmhouse, Aston Hill, Halton, nr Aylesbury, Bucks HP22 5NQ (☎ 0296 630643); 44 Welbeck Street, London W1 (☎ 01 935 8978)

BUTCHER, Nicholas Andrew Christopher; s of Reginald Herbert Butcher, of Norwich, and Elsie May, *née* Balls; *b* 11 Nov 1945; *Educ* City of Norwich Sch, Trinity Hall, Cambridge (MA, LLM); *m* 12 May 1973, Pamela Ann, da of Harry Roberts (d 1987), of Coventry; 1 s (David Simon b 27 May 1980); *Career* slr 1971; memb nat exec Nat Assoc of Round Table GB and Ireland 1982-84; *Recreations* Gastronomy, sport (squash, hockey), music; *Clubs* Strangers', Norwich, Rotary; *Style—* Nicholas Butcher, Esq; The Weavers' Barn, Squires Road, Halvergate, Norfolk BR13 3PZ (☎ 0493 701122); 4 Cathedral Street, Norwich (☎ 0603 660701, fax 0603 616302, telex 975649)

BUTCHER, Thomas Edmund; s of Lt.Col Osborne Arthur Butcher (d 1934) and Beatrice Viola *née* Hodgson (d 1968); *b* 28 May 1924; *Educ* Oundle Sch 1938-42; *m* 8 June 1957, Jean Audrey (d 1963), da of Ernest Leonard Warren (d 1986); 2 da (Alison b 1959 (now Mrs Huntrods), Fiona b 1962); *Career* Lt RNVR 1942-46; solicitor; *Style—* Thomas Butcher, Esq; 19 Lee Grove, Chigwell, Essex (☎ 01 500 2587); 20 Queen Anne Street, London W1 (☎ 01 580 8021)

BUTE, Dowager Marchioness of; Lady Eileen Beatrice; *née* Forbes; da of 8 Earl of Granard; *b* 1 July 1912; *m* 1932, 5 Marquess of Bute (d 1956); 3 s (including 6 Marquess), 1 da; *Style—* The Most Hon the Dowager Marchioness of Bute; Dumfries House, Cumnock, Ayrshire

BUTE, 6 Marquess of (GB 1796); Sir John Crichton-Stuart; 11 Bt (S 1627), JP (Bute 1967); Lord Crichton (S 1488), Earl of Dumfries, Viscount of Air, Lord Crichton of Sanquhar and Cumnock (S 1633), Earl of Bute, Viscount Kingarth, Lord Mountstuart, Cumra(e) and Inchmarnock (S 1703), Baron Mountstuart of Wortley (GB 1761), Baron Cardiff of Cardiff Castle (GB 1776), Earl of Windsor and Viscount Mountjoy (GB 1796); Hereditary Sheriff and Coroner of Co Bute, Hereditary Keeper of Rothesay Castle; patron of 9 livings (but being a Roman Catholic cannot present); s (twin) of 5 Marquess (d 1956), and Lady Eileen, *née* Forbes, da of 8 Earl of Granard; *b* 27 Feb 1933; *Educ* Ampleforth, Trinity Coll Cambridge; *m* 1, 1955 (m dis 1977),

(Beatrice) Nicola Grace, da of late Lt-Cdr Wolstan Beaumont Charles Weld-Forester, CBE, RN, gs of 5 Baron Forester; 2 s, 2 da; m 2, 1978, Jennifer, da of J B Home-Rigg and former w of Gerald Percy (of the family of the Duke of Northumberland); *Heir* s, Earl of Dumfries; *Career* Lord-Lieut for Bute 1967-75 (DL 1961); chm Nat Tst for Scotland Exec Ctee 1969-84; convenor Buteshire CC 1967-70; memb: Countryside Cmmn for Scotland 1970-78, Dvpt Cmmn 1973-78, Oil Dvpt Cncl for Scotland 1973-78; chm Historic Buildings Cncl Scotland 1983-; tstee Nat Galleries Scotland 1980-; chm National Museums of Scotland 1985-; *Clubs* Turf, White's, New (Edinburgh), Puffin's (Edinburgh); *Style*— The Most Hon the Marquess of Bute, JP; Mount Stuart, Rothesay, Isle of Bute (☎ Rothesay 2730)

BUTLER, Sir Adam Courtauld; PC (1984),; s of Baron Butler of Saffron Walden (d 1982), KG, CH, PC, by his 1 w, Sydney, da of Samuel Courtauld; *b* 11 Oct 1931; *Educ* Eton, Pembroke Coll Cambridge; *m* 1955, Felicity, da of Kemyel Molesworth-St Aubyn (s of Sir Hugh Molesworth-St Aubyn, 13 Bt, JP, by his w, Emma, da of Adm Charles Wake, 2 s of Sir Charles Wake, 10 Bt; Adm Charles Wake m Emma, da of Sir Edward St Aubyn, 1 Bt, and sis of 1 Baron St Levan); 2 s, 1 da; *Career* 2 Lt KRRC 1950-51 (National Service); dir: Kayser Bondor 1966-73, Aristoc Ltd 1966-73, Capital & Counties Property Co Ltd 1973-79; MP (C) Bosworth 1970-87, Cons Whip 1974-75, PPS to Rt Hon Margaret Thatcher 1975-79; min of state: Industry 1979-81, NI 1981-4, Defence 1984-5; farmer; kt 1986; *Recreations* field sports, music, pictures; *Style*— The Rt Hon Sir Adam Butler, PC; The Old Rectory, Lighthorne, Warwick (☎ 0926 651214)

BUTLER, Alan Edward; s of Albert Frederick Butler (d 1978), of Clacton-on-Sea, and Lillian Elizabeth, *née* Carlson (d 1969); *b* 6 Dec 1940; *Educ* Raine's Foundation GS, UCL, (BSc); *m* 27 Nov 1981, Gail Katharine; 1 s (Richard b 1984); *Career* md: Carl Byoir and Assocs Ltd 1975- (dir 1970), Communications Strategy Ltd 1985-, Countrywide Communications Ltd 1987-; past chm and memb Strangers Gallery NW Surrey House of Commons Dining Club, past chm PR Conslts Assoc; Freeman City of London: Liveryman: Worshipful Co of Gold and Silver Wyre Drawers 1982, Worshipful Co of Marketers 1988; MBCS, MIPRA, FIPR; *Recreations* most sports; *Clubs* Wentworth, Wig and Pen; *Style*— Alan Butler, Esq; Greenway Cottage, Abbey Road, Virginia Water, Surrey (☎ 09904 2385); Countrywide Communications Ltd, Bowater House East, 68 Knightsbridge, London SW1 (☎ 01 225 0311, fax 01 584 6655)

BUTLER, Rt Rev Arthur Hamilton Butler; MBE (1944); s of George Booker and Anne Maude Butler, of Dublin; *b* 8 Mar 1912; *Educ* Friars Sch Bangor, Trinity Coll Dublin; *m* 1, 1938, Betty Pringle (d 1976), da of Seton Pringle, FRCSI, of Dublin; 1 s; m 2, 1979, Dr Elizabeth Mayne; *Career* ordained 1935, bishop of Tuam Killala and Achonry 1958-69, bishop of Connor 1969-81, ret; *Style*— The Rt Rev Arthur Butler, MBE; 1 Spa Grange, Ballynahinch, Co Down, N Ireland BT24 8PD (☎ 0238 562966)

BUTLER, Arthur William; ERD (1964); s of Frederick Butler (d 1975), and Elizina, *née* Bond; *b* 20 Jan 1929; *Educ* Wanstead HS, LSE (BSc); *m* 3 May 1958, Evelyn Mary, da of Thomas Alexander Luetchford (d 1988), of South Island Place, London SW9; 1 da (Caroline b 7 May 1966); *Career* Offr Cadet India Cadet Co 1946, 2 Lt RAOC 1947-48, Capt AER 1957-64 (Lt 1953); trainee Kemsley Newpapers Graduate Trg Course 1951-55, political corr News Chronicle 1956-60, political ed Reynolds News 1960-62, political corr Daily Express 1963-69, political ed Daily Sketch 1969-71, md Partnerplan Public Affrs 1971-74, dir Public Affrs Div John Addey Assocs 1974-77, vice-chm Charles Barker Watney and Powell (jt md 1978-87), sec Parly and Scientific Ctee 1978-, fndr sec All Pty Motor Indust Gp 1978-; sec Roads Campaign Cncl 1974-86, memb Middlesbrough Trades Cncl 1952-55, govr Sch for Disabled Putney 1975-79; fndr sec Party Info Technol Ctee 1981-84, sec Parly All Pty Roads Study Gp 1974-86; Liveryman Worshipful Co of Tobacco Pipe Makers, Freeman City of London 1976; memb: The Royal Institution of Great Britain 1980; *Books* No Feet to Drag (with Alfred Morris MP 1972), The First Forty Years- A History of the Parliamentary and Scientific Committee (1980), Lobbying in the British Parliament (with Douglas Smith 1986); *Recreations* walking, gardening, collecting books and militaria, travel; *Style*— Arthur Butler, Esq, ERD; 30 Chester Way, Kennington, London SE11 4UR (☎ 01 582 2350); McAvoy Wreford Bayley, 36 Grosvenor Gardens, London SW1W OEB (☎ 01 730 4500, fax 01 730 9364, telex 886827)

BUTLER, Audrey Maude Beman; da of Robert Beman Minchin (d 1972), and Vivien Florence Fraser, *née* Scott (d 1976); *b* 31 May 1936; *Educ* Queenswood Sch Herts, St Andrews Univ Scotland (MA); *m* 1959, (m dis 1981), Anthony Michael Butler, s of Michael John Butler; 2 da (Clare, Siobhan); *Career* geography teacher; head of geography St Michael's Burton Park 1970-73 and 1976-78, housemistress Manor House Lancing Coll 1978-81, headmistress Queenswood Hatfield Herts 1981-; govr Aldenham Sch Tockington Manor; memb: Girls Schs Assoc, RGS; MInstD; *Recreations* golf, tennis, swimming, walking, theatre; *Style*— Mrs Audrey Butler; Queenswood, Shepherd's Way, Brookmans Park, Hatfield, Herts AL9 6NS

BUTLER, Basil Richard Ryland; OBE (1976); s of Hugh Montagu Butler, (d 1971), of Churchdown, Glos, and Annie Isabelle, *née* Wiltshire (d 1969); *b* 1 Mar 1930; *Educ* Denstone Coll Staffs, St John's Coll Cambridge (MA); *m* 26 June 1954, Lilian Joyce, da of Reginald Merryweather Haswell, of Amersham, Bucks; 1 s (Richard b 1957), 2 da (Clare b 1960, Helen b 1964); *Career* 2 Lt 5 Royal Inniskilling Dragoon Guards 1948-50; reservoir engr Trinidad Leaseholds Ltd 1954, petroleum engr to Chief Petroleum Engr and Supt Prodn Planning Divn Kuwait Oil Co 1958-68, ops mangr BP (Colombia) 1968, ops mangr and gen mangr (BP Alaska Inc 1970, seconded to Kuwait Oil Co as gen mangr ops 1972, mangr Ninian Devpts, BP Petroleum Devpt Co Ltd (London) 1975, Sullom Voe Terminal Shetland Islands 1976; BP Petroleum Devpt Ltd: gen mangr exploration and production (Aberdeen) 1978, chief exec (London) 1980, gen mangr exploration and prodn dept 1980; dir BP Int Ltd, md and chief exec BP Exploration Co Ltd 1981, md The BP Co plc 1986; Freeman City of London (1987), Worshipful Co of Shipwrights (1988); FEng (1985), FIMM (1985); *Recreations* sailing, music; *Clubs* IOD; *Style*— Basil Butler, Esq, OBE; The British Petroleum Co plc, Britannic House, Moor Lane, London EC2Y 9BU (☎ 01 920 6165, fax 01 920 4232)

BUTLER, Christopher John; MP (C) Warrington South 1987-; s of Dr John Lynn Butler, of Cardiff, and the late Eileen Patricia Butler; *b* 12 August 1950; *Educ* Cardiff HS, Emmanuel Coll Cambridge (MA); *m* 25 March 1989, Jacqueline Clair, *née* Harper, of Lymm, Cheshire; *Career* mkt res conslt 1972-77, Cons Res Dept 1977-80, Political Off 10 Downing St, special advsr Sec of State for Wales 1983-85, mkt res conslt 1985-86, special advsr Min for Arts 1986-87; *Recreations* writing, tennis; *Style*— Christopher J Butler, Esq; Flat 2, 48 Clifton Gardens, London W9 1AU (☎ 01 219 3000); 27 Kildonan Rd, Grappenhall, Warrington, Cheshire; Conservative Hall, Grappenhall Rd, Stockton Heath, Warrington, Cheshire (☎ 0925 601 534, car tel 0860 419611)

BUTLER, Sir Clifford Charles; s of C H J and O Butler, of Earley, Reading; *b* 20 May 1922; *Educ* Reading Sch, Reading Univ (BSc, PhD); *m* 1947, Kathleen Betty Collins; 2 da; *Career* former physics lectr Manchester Univ, prof physics and head physics dept Imperial Coll London 1963-70, dean Royal Coll Science 1966-69, dir Nuffield Fndn 1970-75; vice-chllr Loughborough Univ of Technol 1975-85; memb: Schools Cncl 1965-, Univ Grants Ctee 1966-71, OU Cncl 1971-, Br Cncl Science Advsy Ctee 1980-; chm: Cncl Educn & Training Health Visitors 1977-83, Advsy Cncl Supply & Educn Teachers 1980-85; Steering Ctee for DES Educnl Counselling & Credit Transfer Info Serv Project; chm into Geologise Surveying 1985-87; Hon DSc Reading, Hon D Univ (Open Univ), Hon D Tech (Longhborough); FRS; kt 1983; *Clubs* Athenanum; *Style*— Sir Clifford Butler; Low Woods Farm House, Low Woods Lane, Belton, nr Loughborough, Leics (☎ 0530 223125)

BUTLER, David; s of James Charles Butler, of Woodford Green Essex, and Ethel Violet, *née* Newell (d 1967); *b* 1 Feb 1936; *Educ* Mill Hill Sch, Keble Coll Oxford (BA); *m* 1, 15 Dec 1956, Catherine Anita, da of Glynn Harry, of Leamington Spa, Warwicks; 1 s (Gideon b 1957), 2 da (Alison b 1960, Justine b 1963); m 2, 18 March 1975, Frances Mary, da of Bernard Francis McMahon, of Melbourne, Australia; 1 da (Rebecca b 1982); *Career* computer programmer, analyst, project ldr Hert CC 1960-64, computer mangr NW Metropolitan Hosp Bd 1964-65, mgmnt conslt Urwick Orr 1965-72; dir: Diebold Europe 1972-77, Istel Ltd 1983-, Octagon Services Ltd 1986-, JMI Advsy Services Ltd 1986-; investmt advsr Utd Bank of Kuwait 1985-, chm Butler Cox and Ptnrs 1977-; vice pres Br Computer Soc 1981-83, chm Humantec Fndn for the Disabled 1986-, memb Fraud Trials Ctee 1984-85; *Books* The Convergence of Technologies (1977), Britain and the Information Society (1981), A Director's Guide to Information Technology (1982), Trends in Information Technology (1984), Information Technology and Realpolitik (1986), The Men Who Mastered Time (novel, 1986), Senior Management IT Education (1987); *Recreations* cricket, rugby, literature; *Clubs* Oxford and Cambridge; *Style*— David Butler, Esq; 12 Laurel Rd, London SW13 0EE (☎ 01 876 1810); Butler Cox House, 12 Brloomsbury Square, London WC1A 2LL (☎ 01 831 0101)

BUTLER, Denis William Langford; s of William Henry Butler (d 1965), and Kitty Langford, *née* Sweeney; *b* 26 Oct 1926; *Educ* Repton; *m* 17 Oct 1953, Margaret (Marna), da of Charles Donald Taylor (d 1962); 3 da (Wendy b 1955, Susan b 1957, Katharine b 1957); *Career* comptroller and city solicitor to the City of London 1981-, solicitor 1951, ass solicitor Norfolk CC 1953-54, ass solicitor Shropshire CC 1954-57, s assist solicitor Lindsey (Lincs) CC 1957-60, dep clerk Wiltshire CC 1960-74, county solicitor and clerk Wiltshire CC 1974-81, chm County Secretaries Soc 1974-76; Freeman City of London 1981, Liveryman Solicitors Co 1983; *Recreations* gardening and travel; *Style*— Denis Butler, Esq; 5 Stone House, 9 Weymouth Street, London W1N 3FF (☎ 01 580 2707; Guildhall, London EC2P 2EJ (telex: 265608 London G; fax: 01 260 1119)

BUTLER, Lady Denyne Gillian Patricia; only surv da of 9 Earl of Lanesborough, TD, DL; *b* 23 Feb 1945; *Style*— Lady Denyne Butler; Alton Lodge, Kegworth, Derby

BUTLER, Hon Edmund Henry Richard; s of 17 Viscount Mountgarret; *b* 1 Sept 1962; *Educ* Stowe; *m* 7 May 1988, Adelle, only da of M Lloyd, of New York; *Style*— The Hon Edmund Butler

BUTLER, Hon Mrs (Elizabeth Olson); *née* Erskine; da of 1 Baron Erskine of Rerrick, GBE (d 1980); *b* 2 July 1923; *m* 1944, Gilbert Butler, s of Harry John Butler, of 39 Duffryn Av, Cardiff; 2 s, 1 da; *Career* Subaltern ATS 1939-45; *Style*— The Hon Mrs Butler; Gatehouse, 8B Churchfields Ave, Weybridge, Surrey KT13 9YA

BUTLER, His Honour Judge Gerald Norman; QC (1975); s of Joshua Butler (d 1978), and Esther, *née* Lampel; *b* 15 Sept 1930; *Educ* County HS Ilford, LSE (LLB), Magdalen Coll Oxford (BCL); *m* 2 April 1959, Stella, da of Harris Isaacs (d 1975); 1 s (Mark b 28 Feb 1963), 2 da (Jane b 26 Oct 1960, Charlotte b 29 April 1967); *Career* 2 Lt RASC 1954-56; barr Middle Temple 1955; recorder of Crown Court 1977-82; circuit judge 1982, sr judge of Southwark Crown Court 1984-; *Recreations* opera, rugby, reading; *Clubs* MCC; *Style*— His Honour Judge Butler, QC; Southwark Crown Court, London SE1 (☎ 01 403 4141)

BUTLER, Hon Henrietta Elizabeth Alexandra; da of 17 Viscount Mountgarret; *b* 4 Nov 1964; *Style*— The Hon Henrietta Butler

BUTLER, Maj-Gen Hew Dacres George; CB (1975), DL (Hants 1980); s of Maj-Gen Stephen Seymour Butler, CB, CMG, DSO (d 1964), of Bury Lodge, Hambledon, and Phyllis, *née* Critchley-Salmonson; *b* 12 Mar 1922; *Educ* Winchester; *m* 1954, Joanna Christiane Aline, da of Geoffrey Puckridge, CMG, ED (d 1975), of Worton, Wilts; 2 s, 1 da; *Career* GOC Near East Land Forces 1972-74, COS Contingency Planning SHAPE 1975-76, ret 1977; underwriting memb Lloyds, sec Beit Tst 1978-; High Sheriff Hampshire 1983; *Recreations* shooting, racing, skiing, horticulture; *Clubs* Boodle's, Royal Cwlth Soc, MCC; *Style*— Maj-Gen Hew Butler, CB, DL; Bury Lodge, Hambledon, Hants (☎ 070 132 507)

BUTLER, Hubert Arthur James; s of Charles Butler, MBE, of Newport, Essex; *b* 24 Sept 1937 yds;; *Educ* Eton, RAC Cirencester; *m* 1968 (m dis 1984), Anne, da of Capt Peter Robert Churchward, of Devon; 1 s, 2 da; *Career* formerly Lt 17/21 Lancers; dir Winchmore plc 1963; ARICS; *Recreations* shooting, cricket; *Clubs* Cavalry & Guards, Farmers; *Style*— Hubert Butler, Esq; Le Pavillon, Newport, Essex (☎ 0799 40225)

BUTLER, Ian Geoffrey; s of Hubert Desramaux Butler, of Cumbria; *b* 12 April 1925; *Educ* Stowe, Trinity Coll Oxford; *m* 1973, Anne, da of James Robertson, of Dunbartonshire; 2 da; *Career* Lt Coldstream Gds 1945-47; ptnr Tansley Witt 1951-55; chm: Cookson Gp plc (formerly Lead Industries Gp, mfr of specialist industl materials) 1976- (md 1973-84), Tioxide Gp plc; dir: Barclays Bank plc, Nurdin & Peacock plc; FCA; *Recreations* yachting (National Swallow 'Dart'), skiing; *Clubs* Royal Yacht Sqdn, Royal Thames Yacht (vice cdre), Itchenor Sailing; *Style*— Ian Butler, Esq; Wyke House, Ellanore Lane, W Wittering, Sussex (☎ 0243 513269); 105 Abingdon Rd, London W8 (☎ 01 937 5220)

BUTLER, James Morris; s of Frederick Thomas Butler; *b* 15 June 1926; *Educ* Hull GS, Cambridge Univ; *m* 1950, Freda; 1 s, 2 da; *Career* chm McKechnie plc; former pres Br Non-Ferrous Metals Fedn; chm Int Wrought Copper Cncl; *Recreations* golf; *Style*— Dr James Butler; 2 Old Hall, Whittington, Staffs (☎ 0543 432323)

BUTLER, (Percy) James; CBE (1981); s of Percy Ernest Butler (d 1944), and Phyllis

Mary, *née* Bartholomew (d 1950); *b* 15 Mar 1929; *Educ* Marlborough, Clare Coll Cambridge (MA); *m* 1954, Margaret Prudence, da of Percy Copland (d 1970); 1 s, 2 da; *Career* chartered accountant; dir (Govt appt) Mersey Docks & Harbours Co 1972- (dep chm 1987-); managing ptnr London region Peat Marwick Mitchell & Co 1981-85, sr ptnr Peat Marwick McLintock 1986-; memb: Serpell Ctee on Railway Finance 1982, Klynveld Peat Marwick Goerdeler Exex ctee and cncl 1987-; advsr Treasury and Civil Service Ctee 1980-82; memb Marlborough Coll Cncl 1975-; memb Lloyd's; FCA; *Recreations* farming, shooting, bridge; *Clubs* Carlton, Pilgrims; *Style*— P James Butler, Esq, CBE; Littleton House, Crawley, Winchester SO21 2QF (☎ (0962) 880206); Flat 8, 3 Lennox Gdns London SW1X 0DA (☎ 01 581 8759); office: 1 Puddle Dock, Blackfriars, London EC4V 3PD (☎ 01 236 8000, telex 8811541)

BUTLER, Hon (Samuel) James; yst s of Baron Butler of Saffron Walden, KG, CH, PC (Life Peer) (d 1982) and his 1 w, Sydney, da of Samuel Courtauld; *b* 13 Dec 1936; *Educ* Eton, Pembroke Coll Cambridge; *m* 1, 24 June 1960 (m dis 1977) Lucilla Blanche, yr da of late Algernon Malcolm Borthwick, MC, TD, of Wethersfield Pl, Braintree, Essex; 2 s, 4 da; m2, 4 July 1986, Jennifer, o da of Dr George Gladston of Almeria NY State USA; *Career* late 2 Lt RHG; head features Rediffusion 1966-68, exec producer Granada TV 1968-70, freelance TV producer 1970-, memb cncl Univ of Essex, chm arts ctee Univ of Essex; *Recreations* talking, walking; *Style*— The Hon James Butler; Gladfen Hall, Halstead, Essex

BUTLER, Hon John Fitzwalter; s and h of 28 Baron Dunboyne; *b* 31 July 1951; *Educ* Winchester, Trinity Cambridge (MA), London Business Sch (Sloan Fellow),; *m* 1975, (Diana) Caroline, da of Sir Michael Sanigear Williams, KCMG *qv*; 1 s (Richard b 1983), 3 da (Genevieve b 1977, Imogen b 1979, Cleone b 1986); *Style*— The Hon John Butler; c/o C. Hoare & Co, 37 Fleet Street, London, EC4P 4DQ

BUTLER, John Sherburng; s of Thomas George Butler (d 1961), of Oswaldtwistl, Lancashire, and Isabella, *née* Lord (d 1972); *b* 7 Dec 1931; *Educ* Accrington GS, Manchester Municipal Sch of Art (Goudsy medal for architecture 1960), Manchester Poly; *m* 19 May 1956, (Beryl) Eurwen, da of Richard Jones (d 1963), of Oswaldtwistle; 1 da (Ursula Anne b 1959); *Career* sr ptnr Grimshaw and Townsend Chartered Architects 1975- (joined as ptnr 1962); the Methodist Church N Lancs Dist 1962-73: sec Home Missions and Redundancy Cmmn, memb Home Missions Bd, exec ctee Connechional Property Div Bd; memb exec ctee Round Table and Rotary Clubs of Accrington; JP Accrington Bench 1976-86; FAMS, FRIBA 1971 (Assoc 1961), FCI Arb 1978 (Assoc 1977), FRSA 1979; *Recreations* gardening, painting, reading, birdwatching, walking; *Style*— John Butler, Esq; Grimshaw and Townsend, 24 Willow St, Accrington, Lancashire BB5 1LS (☎ 0254 320 07/320 30)

BUTLER, Lady Juliana Mary Philomena; da of 9 Earl of Carrick, and Belinda, da of Maj David Turville-Constable-Maxwell , TD (s of Hon Bernard Constable-Maxwell, 4 s of 10 Lord Herries of Terregles, by his 2 w, Hon Alice, *née* Fraser, da of 15 Lord Lovat), by his w, Mary, da of Lt-Col Oswald Turville-Petre, TD, JP, DL (gggs of 9 Baron Petre); *b* 20 Dec 1960; *Educ* Univ of Sussex, St Andrews Coll Cambridge; *Career* flt instr; neurobiologist; *Clubs* IAM (elected memb), MENSA; *Style*— Lady Juliana Butler; 10 Netherton Grove, London SW10

BUTLER, Keith Stephenson; CMG (1977); s of Raymond Renard Butler (d 1972), of St Leonards on Sea, Sussex, and Gertrude, *née* Stephenson (d 1972); *b* 3 Sept 1917; *Educ* Liverpool Coll, Oxford Univ (MA), Canadian Nat Def Coll (NDC); *m* 1, 1952, Geraldine Marjorie Clark (d 1979); m 2, 1979, Mrs Priscilla Wittels, da of Cdr John Boldero, DSC (Bar) RN (d 1984), of Bridport, Dorset; *Career* HM Forces 1939-46: Maj RA, North Africa, Greece and Crete, POW in Germany 1941-45 (despatches); HM Diplomatic Serv 1950-77 (HM consul gen, Seville 1968-69, Bordeaux 1969-74, Naples 1974-77), appeal dir for charities 1978-; *Recreations* historical research; *Clubs* Oxford Union Soc; *Style*— Keith Butler, Esq, CMG; Easter Cottage, Westbrook, Boxford, Newbury, Berkshire RG16 8DN (☎ 048838 557)

BUTLER, Prof Marilyn Speers; da of Sir Trevor Maldwyn Evans, CBE (d 1981), of Kingston-on-Thames, and Margaret Speers, *née* Gribbin; *b* 11 Feb 1937; *Educ* Wimbledon HS, St Hilda's Coll Oxford (MA, D Phil); *m* 3 Mar 1962, David Edgeworth, s of Harold Edgeworth Butler (d 1951); 3 s (Daniel b 1963, Gareth b 1965, Edmund b 1967); *Career* trainee and talks producer BBC 1960-62; res and teaching Oxford Univ 1962-70, jr res fell St Hilda's Coll 1970-73, fell and tutor St Hugh's Coll 1973-85; King Edward VII Prof of Eng Lit Univ of Cambridge 1986-; *Books* Maria Edgeworth, a Lit Biography (1972), Jane Austen and the War of Ideas (1975), Peacock Displayed (1979), Romantics Rebels and Reactionaries (1981, 1985), Burke Paine Godwin and the Revolution Controversy (1984); *Style*— Prof Marilyn Butler; 151 Woodstock Road, Oxford OX2 7NA (☎ 0865 58323); Kings College, Cambridge (☎ 0865 58323)

BUTLER, Lt Cdr Michael (Mike); s of Humphrey Daniel Butler, of Eglwysbach, Clywd, and Lucy, *née* Mills; *b* 15 Nov 1952; *Educ* Ellesmere Coll Shrop; *m* 6 March 1974, Jennifer (Jenny) Catherine, da of Thomas Ramsey Sharpe; 1 s (Ben b 2 May 1977), 1 da (Anna b 1 March 1979); *Career* RN 1972-82; offr i/c Devonport Field Gun Crew 1981; served Sultan of Oman's Navy 1982-85, security cnslt and md SECON Ltd 1985-87, md Thompson Butler Assocs Ltd (exec search and mgmnt cnslts) 1988-; memb Int Pro Security Assoc; Sultan of Oman Peace Medal (1983); *Recreations* shooting, sailing; *Style*— Lt Cdr Mike Butler, RNR; Thompson Butler Associates Ltd, 1 A Market Place, Southwell, Notts (☎ 0636 812 200, fax 0636 815 230, car tel 0860 810 038)

BUTLER, Sir Michael Dacres; GCMG (1984, KCMG 1979, CMG 1975); s of T D Butler, of Almer, Blandford, Dorset, and Beryl May, *née* Lambert; *b* 27 Feb 1927; *Educ* Winchester, Trinity Coll Oxford; *m* 1951, (Margaret) Ann, da of Rt Hon Lord Clyde, PC (d 1975, MP (C) North Edinburgh 1950-54, Lord Justice-Gen of Scotland 1954-72); 2 s, 2 da; *Career* Diplomatic Service 1950: under-sec in charge of EEC Affairs FCO 1974-76, dep under-sec of state FCO 1976-79, UK perm rep to EEC 1979-85, dep chm Bd of Tstees Victoria & Albert Museum 1985-; exec dir Hambros Bank 1986-; dir: Wellcome Fndn 1986-, Oriental Aut Mag 1987-; advsr Euro Affairs to chm ICL 1986-; *Books* Europe; More Than a Continent (1986); *Recreations* collecting Chinese porcelain, tennis, skiing; *Clubs* Brooks; *Style*— Sir Michael Butler, GCMG; 36A Elm Park Rd, London SW3; 6 Rond-Point Robert Schumann, Brussels, Belgium

BUTLER, Michael Howard; s of Howard Butler, of Beech Ct, Mapperley, Notts, and Constance Gertrude, *née* King; *b* 13 Feb 1936; *Educ* Nottingham HS; *m* 27 July 1961, Christine Elizabeth, da of Sidney Frank Killer, of West Bridgeford Notts; 2 s (Ian Michael b 1965, Andrew John b 1967) 1 da (Ruth Elizabeth b 1971); *Career* dir gen of fin NCB 1980- (tres 1978), corpn memb Br Coal Corpn 1986- (fin dir 1985) FCA 1958, CBIM 1987; *Recreations* tennis, music, gardening, assoc football; *Style*— Michael Butler, Esq; British Coal Corporation, Hobart House, Grosvenor Place, London, (☎ 01 235 2020)

BUTLER, Michael James; s of late Lt-Col James Dighton Butler (1987), formerly of Bath, Pamela Elizabeth, *née* Pickwoad (d 1987); *b* 1944; *Educ* Eastbourne Coll, RMA Sandhurst, RAC Cirencester; *m* 1981, Jennifer, da of late Percy Williams, of Dundee; 1 da (Elizabeth b 1985); *Career* cmmnd 15/19 The King's Royal Hussars 1965, served Germany 1965-67, Army Outward Bound Sch Towyn 1967-68; area mangr Watney Mann Ltd 1968-71, RAC Cirencester 1971-74; asst agent: Nidd Estate Harrogate 1974-76, Savile Estate Dewsbury 1976-79; sole princ James Butler & Co Huddersfield 1979-86, ptnr Hunter & Butler Tiverton 1986-88, sole princ Axworthy Chartered Surveyors Tiverton 1988-; memb: Royal Forestry Soc, Taunton Operatic Soc, Tiverton Operatic Soc; FRICS 1980, FAAV 1978; *Recreations* singing, work; *Clubs* Farmers; *Style*— James Butler, Esq; Axworthy Chartered Surveyors, 32 St Peter St, Tiverton, Devon EX16 6NR (☎ 0884 258010, fax 0884 258344)

BUTLER, Sir (Reginald) Michael Thomas; 3 Bt (UK 1922), of Old Park, Devizes, Wilts; QC (Can 1967); s of Sir (Reginald) Thomas Butler, 2 Bt (d 1959); *b* 22 April 1928; *Educ* Brentwood Coll Victoria BC, Univ of BC (BA), Osgoode Hall Sch of Law Toronto; *m* 1, 1952 (m dis 1967), Marja Margaret Elizabeth, da of Ewen H McLean, of Toronto; 3 s; m 2, 1968 (m dis 1974), Barbara Anne, da of Kevin Cahill, of Dublin; 1 s (adopted); *Heir* s, (Reginald) Richard Michael Butler; *Career* barr and slr Ontario 1954 and BC 1967; ptnr Messrs Butler, Angus (Victoria, BC); *Clubs* Vancouver; *Style*— Sir Michael Butler, Bt, QC; (☎ 604 388 6155); 736 Broughton St, Victoria, Br Columbia V8W 1E1, Canada

BUTLER, Prof Neville Roy; s of Dr Cuthbert John Butler (d 1937), of Harrow, Middx, and Ida Margaret, *née* Soman (d 1959); *b* 6 July 1920; *Educ* Epsom Coll, Charing Cross Hosp Med Sch (MB, BS, MRCP, DCH); *m* 14 May 1954 (m dis 1979), Jean Ogilvie, da of John McCormack (d 1983); 2 da (Claire b 1957, Fiona b 1959); *Career* Capt RAMC; first asst Paediatric Unit UCH 1950, med registrar and pathologist Hosp for Sick Children Gt Ormond St 1953, conslt paediatrician Oxford and Wessex RHB 1957-63, dir Perinatal Mortality Survey (Birthday Tst Fund 1958); conslt physician Hosp for Sick Children Gt Ormond St and sr lectr Inst of Child Health London Univ 1963-65; co-dir Nat Child Devpt Study (1958 Cohort) 1965-69, prof Child Health at Bristol Univ 1965-85 (emeritus prof 1985-), dir Child Health and Educn Study (1970 Cohort) 1970-85, dir Int Centre for Child Studies 1982-; dir Youthscan UK 1985-; vice pres: RCM 1972-, HVA 1975-; memb BPA 1958, Neonatal Soc 1961-, Cuban Paediatric Soc 1973, Hungarian Paediatric Soc 1979-; FRCP, FRCOG; *Books* (jointly) Perinatal Mortality (1963), 11,000 Seven Year Olds (1966), Perinatal Problems (1969), From Birth to Seven (1972), ABO Haemolytic Disease of the Newborn (1972), The Social Life of Britain's Five Year Olds (1984), From Birth to Five (1986); *Clubs* Savage; *Style*— Prof Neville Butler; 16 Cotham Park, Bristol BS6 6BU (☎ 0272 429961)

BUTLER, Hon Mrs Penelope Cynthia; *née* Dewar; yr da of Maj 3 Baron Forteviot, MBE; *b* 29 April 1935; *m* 1959 (m dis 1978), Norman Frank Paul Butler; 2 s, 1 da; *Style*— The Hon Mrs Penelope Butler; 73 Duchess Drive, Newmarket, Suffolk

BUTLER, Hon Piers James Richard; s and h of 17 Viscount Mountgarret; *b* 15 April 1961; *Educ* Eton; *Style*— The Hon Piers Butler

BUTLER, Hon Sir Richard Clive; DL (Essex 1972); s of late Baron Butler, of Saffron Walden, KG, CH, PC (Life Peer) by his 1 w, Sydney, da of Samuel Courtauld; *b* 12 Jan 1929; *Educ* Eton, Pembroke Coll Cambridge; *m* 1952, Susan Anne Maud, da of Maj Patrick Walker, MBE (s of Sir James Walker, 3 Bt); 2 s, 1 da; *Career* 2 Lt RHG BAOR 1948-49; farmer; pres NFU 1979-86 (memb cncl 1962-); kt 1981; *Recreations* hunting, shooting, tennis; *Clubs* Farmers'; *Style*— The Hon Sir Richard Butler, DL; Penny Pot, Halstead, Essex (☎ 0787 472828)

BUTLER, Richard Pierce; s and h of Sir Thomas Pierce Butler, 12 Bt, CVO, DSO, OBE; *b* 22 July 1940; *Educ* Eton, NY Univ, Inst of CA in England and Wales; *m* 21 Oct 1965, Diana Anne, yr da of Col Stephen John Borg (d 1971); 3 s (Thomas b 1966, Stephen b 1968, Rupert b 1971), 1 da (Anne b 1973); *Career* ptnr Charles Wakeling & Co 1964-66, dir The First Boston Corp (NY) 1967-78; dir Paine Webber Int Bank 1978-; memb cncl Pestalozzi Childrens Village Tst 1983-; govr Summerfields Sch Oxford 1984-; MBA, FCA; *Style*— Richard Butler, Esq; 18 Chapel Street, London SW1X 7BY

BUTLER, Capt Robert George Danhaive (Bob); s of George Keating Butler (d 1967), of Brussels, and Germaine Helene Caroline, *née* Danhaive (d 1966); *b* 27 Jan 1916; *Educ* Col St Michel Brussels, Ecole Abbat Maredsous Belgium, Sch of Law; *m* 14 July 1951, (Dorothy) Elyzabeth, da of Walter James Keates (d 1958), of Hong Kong; 1 s (Alan b 4 April 1955), 1 da (Carole (Mrs Coulson-Gilmaur) b 28 Nov 1956); *Career* Trooper Inns of Ct Regt TA 1937, Sandhurst 1939, cmmnd RAC 1940, 47 RTR, seconded Hobsons Horse IA 1940, Capt and Tech Adj served Iraq and Persia 1941, offr i/c D & M Wing Abbassia Egypt 1942, seconded Spears Mission in Syria and Lebanon 1943-45, UK and demob 1945; Hedleys (originally A M Longhurst & Butler): articled clerk 1935-39, asst slr 1948-51, ptnr 1951, sr ptnr 1978-85, ret 1985, conslt 1985-; Notary Public 1974; sec chartered shipbrokers Protection and Indemnity Assoc Ltd 1961, fndr chm and md Int Shipbrokers and Agents P & I Club Ltd 1983-86 (hon life memb 1986-), memb cncl Notaries Soc 1988; Liveryman Worshipful Co of Slrs of the City of London; memb: Law Soc 1948, Baltic Exchange 1963-85; assoc Lloyds, fell Inst of Linguists 1963, FCIArb, FICS 1986;; *Recreations* piano, organ, DIY, languages, geneology; *Clubs* Victory Serv, Anglo Belgian Soc; *Style*— Capt Bob Butler; Merrilea, ivy Lane, Woking, Surrey GU22 7BY, (☎ 04862 60493)

BUTLER, Sir (Frederick Edward) Robin; KCB (1988); s of Bernard Daft Butler, and Nora Butler, *née* Jones, of St Annes on Sea, Lancs; *b* 3 Jan 1938; *Educ* Harrow, Univ Coll Oxford (BA); *m* 1962, Gillian Lois, da of Dr Robert Galley, of Cranleigh, Surrey; 1 s (Andrew b 1968), 2 da (Sophie b 1964, Nell b 1967); *Career* private sec: Rt Hon Edward Heath 1972-74, Rt Hon Harold Wilson 1974-75; princ private sec to Rt Hon Margaret Thatcher 1982-85; second perm sec HM Treasy 1985-87; sec to the Cabinet and head of the Home Civil Service 1988-; *Recreations* competitive games and sport, opera; *Clubs* Anglo-Belgian; *Style*— Sir Robin Butler, KCB; Cabinet Office, 70 Whitehall, London SW1 (☎ 01 233 3000)

BUTLER, Roger John; *b* 19 June 1947; *Educ* Cheltenham GS; *m* 31 Aug 1968, Kathleen Teresa, 1 s (David b 1983) 1 da (Caroline b 1979); *Career* ptnr Fryer Whitehill & Co 1971-80; Arthur Young: ptnr 1981-, nat dir of tax practice 1983-85, regnl managing ptnr London 1986-; FCA 1969; *Recreations* golf; *Style*— Roger Butler, Esq; Far End, Wagon Way, Loudwater, Herts WD3 4JE (☎ 0923 774 110); Rolls House, 7 Rolls Bldgs, Fetter Lane, London EC4A 1NH (☎ 01 831 7130, fax 01 405 2147)

BUTLER, Dr Rohan D'Olier; CMG (1966); s of Sir Harold (Beresford) Butler , KCMG, CB (d 1951), of Little Court, Sonning, Berks, and Olive Augusta Newnham, *née* Waters (Lady Butler); *b* 21 Jan 1917; *Educ* Eton, Balliol Coll Oxford (BA, MA, DLitt); *m* Lucy Rosemary, da of Eric Byron, Lord of The Manor of White Notley (d 1964), of White Notley Hall, nr Witham, Essex; *Career* WW II RAPC 1941-42, HG 1942-44; fell All Souls Coll Oxford 1938-84, sub warden 1961-63, fell emeritus 1984-; staff Miny of Info 1939-41, and 1942-44, special ops exec 1941, FO 1944-45, ed Documents on Br Foreign Policy (1919-39) 1945-65, (sr ed 1955- 65), sr ed Documents on Br Affairs 1963-68, for Foreign Policy Overseas 1973-82; historical advsr: sec of state for Foreign & Cwlth Affairs 1968-82; govr Felsted Sch 1959-77 (rep GBA 1964-77), tstee Felsted Almshouses 1961-77, memb Ct Univ of Essex 1971-; FRHistS 1966: Laureate of Institut de France 1982; *Books* The Roots of National Socialism 1783-1933 (1941), Choiseul (1980); *Recreations* idling; *Clubs* Beefsteak, The Lunch; *Style*— Dr Rohan Butler, CMG; White Notley Hall, nr Witham, Essex

BUTLER, (Stanley) Roy; s of Harry Butler (d 1950) of Epsom, and Emily, *née* Whiteing (d 1950); *b* 16 Feb 1923; *m* 14 July 1951, Jessie, da of Edward James Fletcher (d 1966), of Brixton; 1 s (Glenn b 1961), 1 da (Deborah b 1958); *Career* administrator Hawker Aircraft 1940-42, RN ordnance corps 1942-47, serv M East 1943-46; ptnr Wallis & Wallis The Militaria (arms and armour auctioneers) 1962-, dir Arms Fairs Ltd 1967-, fndr The Mil Heritage Museum (Lewes) 1977; TV appearances: Going for a Song (1973), BBC Antiques Roadshow (arms & militaria expert, 1977-89), ITV Heirlooms (1987 and 1988), BBC Heirs and Graces (1988); pres St John Ambulance (Lewes div), benefactor and life memb Soc of Friends of RN Museum, life memb HMS Warrior Assoc, memb Rotary Club of Lewes; Freeman City ofLondon 1981, memb Worshipful Co of Pipermakers 1979; *Recreations* swimming, snooker; *Clubs* IOD; *Style*— Roy Butler, Esq; Wallks & Wallis, West Street, Auction Galleries, Lewes, Sussex BN7 2NJ (☎ 0273 480208, fax 0273 476562, telex 896691 TLXIR G)

BUTLER, Col Sir Thomas Pierce; 12 Bt (I 1628), CVO (1970), DSO (1944), OBE (1954); s of Lt-Col Sir Richard Pierce Butler, 11 Bt, OBE (d 1955); *b* 18 Sept 1910; *Educ* Harrow, Trinity Coll Cambridge (BA); *m* 1937, Rosemary Liège Woodgate, da of late Maj James Hamilton Davidson-Houston (d 1961), of Pembury Hall, Kent and of Thurloe Sq, SW7; 1 s, 2 da (Caroline m Maj-Gen Richard Keightley, *qv*); *Heir* s, Richard Pierce Butler; *Career* Army 1933-61: cmd Gds Composite Bn Norway 1945-46, cmd 2 Bn Grenadier Gds BAOR 1949-52, AQMG London Dist 1952-55, Col, Lt-Col Cmdg Grenadier Gds 1955-59, mil advr to High Cmmr for UK in New Zealand 1959-61, Maj and resident govr of HM Tower of London 1961-70, keeper of Jewel House Tower of London 1968-70, pres London (Prince of Wales's) Dist St John Ambulance Bde 1967-70; CStJ 1969, former JP Co London; *Recreations* fishing, gardening, travel, sketching; *Clubs* Cavalry and Guards; *Style*— Col Sir Thomas Butler, Bt, CVO, DSO, OBE; 6 Thurloe Sq, London SW7 (☎ 01 584 1225); Ballin Temple, Ardattin, Co Carlow, Eire (☎ 0503 56662)

BUTLER, Vincent Frederick; s of Frederick Butler (d 1956), of Manchester, and Rose Ann, *née* Duffy (d 1973); *b* 27 Oct 1933; *Educ* St Bedes Coll Manchester, Edinburgh Coll of Art (DA), Acad of Fine Art Milan; *m* 21 Aug 1961, Camilla Luisa, da of Cavaliere Giuseppe Meazza (d 1971), of Milan; 2 s (Angus, Adam); *Career* language tutor Milan 1956-60, hd of sculpture dept Univ N Nigeria 1960-63, lectr sculpture and art history Edinburgh Coll of Art 1960-, now leading Scottish figurative sculptor; SSA 1966, RSA 1971; *Recreations* hillwalking, travel; *Style*— Vincent Butler, Esq; 17 Deanpark Crescent, Edinburgh EH4 1PH (☎ 031 332 5884)

BUTLER, Prof William Elliott; s of William Elliott Butler, of Black Mountain, N Carolina, US, and Maxine Swan Elmberg; *b* 20 Oct 1939; *Educ* The American Univ (BA), The Johns Hopkins Univ (MA), Harvard Law Sch (JD), The Johns Hopkins Univ (PhD), London Univ (LLD); *m* 2 Sept 1961, Darlene Mae Johnson; 2 s (William Elliott III, Bradley Newman); *Career* res asst Washington Centre of Foreign Policy Res John Hopkins Univ 1966-68, res assoc in law Harvard Law Sch and Assoc 1968-70, reader in comparative law London Univ 1970-76; visiting scholar: Moscow State Univ 1972(1980), USSR Acad of Sci 1976 (1981, 1983, 1984, 1988), Mongolian State Univ 1979; memb SSEES 1973-88 (vice chm 1983-88), prof of comparative law London Univ (1976-), dean Faculty of Laws Univ Coll London 1977-79; visiting prof: NY Univ Law Sch 1978, Ritsumeikan Univ 1985, Harvard Law Sch 1986-87; coordinator UCL-USSR Acad of Sci Protocol on Co-operation in Social Sci 1981-, dir Centre for Study of Socialist Legal systems Univ Coll London 1982-, lectr Hague Acad of Int Law 1985, memb Ctee of Mgmnt Inst of Advanced Legal Studies London Univ 1985-88, govr City of London Poly 1985-89, dean Faculty of Laws London Univ 1988-90, author of more than 60 books, 450 articles, reviews, and translations on int and comparitive law, especially Soviet Law and other socialist legal systems, bookplates, and bibliography; sec The Bookplate Soc 1978-86 (foreign sec 1988-), fndr ed The Bookplate Jl 1983-86, vice-pres Fed Int des Sociétés d'Amateurs d'Ex-Libris 1984-86 (exec sec 1988-); memb: Dist of Columbia Bar, Bar of US Ct of Appeals for Dist of Columbia, Bar of US Supreme Ct; memb: Associé Int Acad of Comparative Law 1986, FRSA 1986; *Recreations* book collecting, bookplate collecting; *Clubs* Cosmos; *Style*— Prof William Butler; 20 Ainger Road, London NW3 3AS (☎ 01 586 2454); Faculty of Laws, Univeristy College London, Bentham House, Endsleigh Gardens, London WC1H OEG (☎ 01 380 7017, fax 01 387 8057, telex 28722 UCPHYS G)

BUTLER-HENDERSON, Edward; 3 s of Hon Eric Brand Butler-Henderson (d 1953), 6 s of 1 Baron Faringdon, CH, JP), of Faccombe Manor, Andover, and Hon Sophia Isabelle Massey (2 da of 5 Baron Clarina, DL); *b* 9 June 1916; *Educ* Eton, Trinity Coll Cambridge; *m* 1939, Elizabeth Marjorie (d 1988), da of Henry George Dacres Dixon (d 1948), of Ireland; 1 s, 1 da; *Career* formerly Lt-Col 99 Bucks Yeo RA (TA); md Henderson Admin Ltd 1951-69, chm Naydale Servs; *Recreations* shooting, escapism; *Clubs* City of London; *Style*— Edward Butler-Henderson, Esq; Flat 11, 3 West Halkin St, London SW1X 8jj (☎ 01 235 5888; 01 235 9308)

BUTLER-HENDERSON, Kenneth; yst s of late Capt Hon Eric Brand Butler-Henderson (6 s of 1 Baron Faringdon, CH, JP), and Hon Sophia Isabelle Massey (da of 5 Baron Clarina, DL); *b* 19 May 1929; *Educ* Eton; *m* 1952, Phyllis Daphne, 1 da of late Lt-Col Alfred Edward Cartmel, CIE, of Hertford; 2 s, 1 da; *Career* memb Stock Exchange; dir Strauss Turnbull & Co Ltd; *Recreations* shooting, golf; *Clubs* City of London, Farmer's, Frilford Heath G; *Style*— Kenneth Butler-Henderson, Esq; 11 Egerton Place, London SW3 2EF (☎ 01 589 2648); Strauss Turnbull & Co, Ltd Stockbrokers, 3 Moorgate Place, London EC2R 6HR (☎ 01 638 5699)

BUTLER-SLOSS, Rt Hon Lord Justice; Rt Hon Dame (Ann) Elizabeth Oldfield Butler-Sloss; DBE (1979), PC (1987); da of Sir Cecil Havers, QC (d 1977), and Enid, *née* Snelling (d 1956), and sister of Baron Havers, *qv*; *b* 10 August 1933; *Educ* Wycombe Abbey; *m* 1958, Joseph William Alexander Butler-Sloss, *qv*; *Career* barr 1955, registrar Princ Registry Probate (subsequently Family Div) 1979-88, a Lord Justice of Appeal 1988-; Parly candidate (Cons) Lambeth Vauxhall 1959; a vice-pres Medico-Legal Soc, memb Judicial Studies Bd 1985-, chm Cleveland Child Abuse Inquiry 1987-88; Hon Fell St Hilda's Coll Oxford; *Style*— The Rt Hon Mrs Justice Butler-Sloss, DBE; Royal Courts of Justice, Strand, London WC2

BUTLER-SLOSS, Joseph William Alexander; s of Francis Alexander Sloss (d 1952); *b* 16 Nov 1926; *Educ* Bangor GS Co Down, Hertford Coll Oxford; *m* 1958, Dame (Ann) Elizabeth Oldfield, DBE, *qv*; 2 s, 1 da; *Career* Sub Lt RNVR; barr 1952, rec Crown Ct 1972-, judge High Ct Kenya 1984-; *Recreations* violin, hunting; *Clubs* Carlton, Muthaiga (Nairobi); *Style*— Joseph Butler-Sloss, Esq; Higher Marsh Farm, Marsh Green, Rockbeare, Nr Exeter, Devon

BUTLIN, Martin Richard Fletcher; s of Kenneth Rupert Butlin (d 1965), and Helen Mary, *née* Fletcher, MBE; *b* 7 June 1929; *Educ* Rendcomb Coll, Trinity Coll Cambridge (MA), Courtauld Inst of Art London Univ (DLit); *m* 31 Jan 1969, Frances Caroline, da oi Michael Anthony Chodzko, of France; *Career* Nat Serv RAMC; asst keeper Tate Gallery 1955-67, keeper Historic Br Collection Tate Gallery 1967-; pubns incl: A Catalogue of the Works of William Blake in the Tate Gallery (1957, 2 edn 1971, 3 edn forthcoming), Samuel Palmers Sketchbook of 1824 (1962), Turner Watercolours (1962), Turner (with Sir John Rothenstein 1964); with Mary Charrot and Dennis Farr: Tate Gallery Catalogues, The Modern British Paintings, Drawings and Sculpture (1964); The Later Works of JMW Turner (1965), William Blake (1966), The Blake-Varley Sketchbook of 1819 (1969); The Paintings of JMW Turner (with Evelyn Joll 1977); num articles and reviews for magazines etc; FBA 1984; *Recreations* opera, ballet, travel; *Style*— Martin Butlin, Esq; The Tate Gallery, Millbank, London SW1P 4RG (☎ 01 821 1313, fax 01 931 7512, telex 944010 TATGAL G)

BUTLIN, Bobbie - Robert Frank; s of Sir William (Billy) Butlin (d 1980, pioneer of holiday camps in the 1930s); *b* 30 April 1934; *Educ* Stowe; *Career* chm and md Butlin's Ltd 1968-; dir Rank Organisation, md Rank Hotels and Holiday Div; CStJ; *Style*— Bobbie Butlin, Esq; c/o Butlin's Ltd, 441 Oxford St, London W1A 1BH (☎ 01 629 6616)

BUTT, Geoffrey Frank; s of Frank Thomas Woodman Butt (d 1946), of Exeter, and Dorothy Rosamond, *née* Graseman (d 1968); *b* 5 May 1943; *Educ* Royal Masonic Sch Bushey, Univ of Reading (BA); *m* 8 Jul 1972, Lee Anne, da of Frederick Arthur Davey, of Exmouth; 2 s (David b 1973, Richard b 1976 twin), 1 da (Anne b 1976 twin); *Career* joined Off Slr for Customs and Excise 1971 (qualified slr, sr legal asst 1974, asst slr 1982, princ asst slr 1986); memb Law Soc 1970; *Recreations* family life, gardening, classical music, literature and art; *Style*— Geoffrey Butt, Esq; Office of the Solicitor for the Customs and Excise, New King's Beam House, 22 Upper Ground, London SE1 9PJ (☎ 01 382 5126)

BUTT, Henry Arthur; s of Capt Robert Arthur Butt, of South Rd, Weston-super-Mare (d 1963), and Annee Matilda, *née* Willis; gs of Robert Henry Coate Butt, Charter Mayor and first Freeman, Borough of Weston-super-Mare; *b* 8 Mar 1928; *Educ* Dulwich Coll; *m* 5 Sept 1953, Barbara Mary, da of Arthur MacDonald Perks, of Chipping Sodbury (d 1976); 2 da (Patricia b 1960, Ann b 1964); *Career* articled J & W Sully & Co 1948-51; nat dir Local Govt Services Price Waterhouse 1983- (ind 1952, ptnr since 1969); ind memb econ devpt ctee for Shipbldg and Repairing 1972-74; FICA, FIMC, FBIM, MIM; *Recreations* travel, gardening, DIY; *Style*— Henry Butt, Esq; Court Barn, Upton Snodsbury, Worcester WR7 4NN (☎ 090 560 557); Price Waterhouse, Office of Local Government Services, Berwick House, 35 Livery Street, Birmingham B3 2PD (☎ 021 200 3000, fax 021 200 2464)

BUTT, Sir (Alfred) Kenneth Dudley; 2 Bt (UK 1929), of Westminster, Co London; s of Sir Alfred Butt, 1 Bt (d 1962); *b* 7 July 1908; *Educ* Rugby, BNC Oxford; *m* 1, 1938 (m dis 1948), Kathleen Breen, da of E Farmer, of Shanklin IOW; m 2, 1948, Marie Josephine, da of John Bain, of Wadhurst, and widow of Lt-Col Ivor Watkins Birts; *Career* bloodstock breeder and farmer; Lloyd's underwriter 1931-74, dir Brook Stud Co 1949 (md and chm 1962-81); chm Thoroughbred Breeders Assoc 1973; pres Aberdeen Angus Cattle Soc 1967-68; *Recreations* shooting, paintings, racing; *Clubs* Carlton; *Style*— Sir Kenneth Butt, Bt; Wheat Hill, Sandon, Buntingford, Herts SG9 0RB (☎ 076 387 203); Flat 29, 1 Hyde Park Sq, London W2 (☎ 01 262 3988)

BUTT, Michael Acton; s of late Gp-Capt Leslie Butt; *b* 25 May 1942; *Educ* Rugby, Magdalen Coll Oxford, INSEAD Fontainebleau France (MBA); *m* 1, 1965 (m dis 1986), Diana Lorraine, da of Sir Robin Brook, *qv*; m 2, 1986, Zoe Bennett; *Career* dir Bland Payne Holdings 1970, chm Sedgwick Ltd 1983, dep chm Sedgwick Gp 1985, chief exec Eagle Star Holdings (chm 1988); memb of bd of BAT Industries 1987; *Recreations* opera, skiing; *Style*— Michael Butt, Esq; 4 Maida Av, Little Venice, London W2 (☎ 01 723 9657); Eagle Star Gp, 1 Threadneedle St, London EC2R 8BE (☎ 01 588 1212; telex 885867)

BUTT, Richard Bevan; s of Roger William Bevan Butt, of Latimer, Winchester Close, Esher, Surrey and Jean Mary, *née* Carter; *b* 27 Feb 1943; *Educ* Magdalen Coll Oxford (BA), Lancaster Univ (MA); *m* 25 July 1976, Amanda Jane, da of His Hon Judge John Finlay, QC, of Thornhill, Golf Road, Bickley, Kent; 2 s (Matthew b 1979, Nicholas b 1983); *Career* head of conservation, English Heritage 1986-, formerly asst sec HM Treasury 1978-86 on secondment to Diplomatic Service as fin cnsllr, UK rep to Euro Community 1981-84; *Recreations* ceramics, music, travel, books; *Style*— Richard Butt, Esq; 35 Gloucester Circus, London SE10 8RY (☎ 01 858 5066); Fortress House, 23 Savile Row, London WC1 (☎ 01 734 6010)

BUTT, Ronald Herbert; CBE (1987); s of Herbert Butt (d 1965), and Elizabeth Clare, *née* Morley (d 1948); *b* 17 Feb 1920; *Educ* St Dunstan's Coll, St Catherine's Coll Oxford (BA, MA); *m* 20 Oct 1956,(Daphne) Margaret Forfar, da of Theodore William Chaundy (d 1966), of Oxford; 2 s (Oliver b 1960, Edmund b 1963), 2 da (Bridget b 1959, Elizabeth b 1966); *Career* Army Intelligence Corps; ldr writer, political corr and political ed The Financial Times 1951-67, res fell Nuffield Coll Oxford 1964-65, asst ed and political commentator The Sunday Times 1967-85, assoc ed The Times 1983-85 (columnist on public affrs 1968-); memb: Butler Ctee on Mentally Abnormal Offenders 1972-75, Cncl Westfield Coll London Univ 1971-; *Books* The Power of Parliament (1967), A History of Parliament The Middle Ages (1989); *Recreations* music, reading, walking, history; *Clubs* Carlton; *Style—* Ronald Butt, Esq, CBE; The Times, 1 Pennington Street, London E1 9XN (☎ 01 782 5038)

BUTTENSHAW, Brig Cedric George; CBE (1967, OBE 1953, MBE 1943), DSO (1945); s of Brig Alfred Sidney Buttenshaw, DSO, of Stonebarrow Lodge, Charmouth, Dorset, and Constance Mary, *née* Garlick; *b* 17 June 1912; *Educ* Sherborne, RMA Woolwich; *m* 1939, Barbara Burnett, da of Hubert de Burgh Wooldridge, of Chiswick; 3 da; *Career* served WW II, CO 142 Field Regt Royal Devon Yeomanry 1944-45, Brig 1961, provost marshal War Office 1962-65, cmmnd Salisbury Plain Sub-Dist 1965-67; *Recreations* following hounds, gardening; *Style—* Brig Cedric Buttenshaw, CBE, DSO; The Coach House, Worton, Devizes, Wilts

BUTTER, Maj David Henry; MC (1942); s of Col Charles Adrian James Butter, OBE, JP, DL (d 1944), of Cluniemore, Pitlochry, Perth, and Agnes Marguerite, *née* Clark, of New Jersey, USA (d 1972); *b* 18 Mar 1920; *Educ* Eton, Oxford; *m* 1946, Myra Alice, yr da of Maj-Gen Sir Harold Augustus Wernher, 3 Bt, GCVO, of Luton Hoo, Luton, Beds, and Lady Zia Wernher, da of HIH Grand Duke Michael of Russia and his morganatic wife Countess Torby; 1 s, 4 da; *Career* landowner, farmer, co dir; 2 Lt Scots Gds 1940, served WW II in N Africa, Italy and Sicily, Temp Maj 1946; Brigadier Queen's Body Guard for Scotland (Roy Co of Archers); DL Perthshire 1956, vice-Lieut 1960, HM Lieut Perthshire 1971-75, Kinross 1974-75, Lord-Lieut Perth and Kinross 1975-; pres Highland TAVR 1979-1984, co cncllr Perthshire 1955-74; govr Gordonstoun; *Clubs* R&A St Andrews, Turf Club; *Style—* Major David Butter, MC; Cluniemore, Pitlochry, Perthshire (☎ Pitlochry 2006); 64 Rutland Gate, London SW7 (☎ 01 589 6731)

BUTTER, His Hon Judge (Neil McLaren); QC (1976); s of late Andrew Butter, MD, of London, and late Ena Butter; *b* 10 May 1933; *Educ* The Leys Sc' Queens Coll Cambridge; *m* 1974, Claire Marianne, da of A Miskin, of Ifield Court Farm, Ifield, Kent; *Career* barr 1955, asst and dep recorder Bournemouth 1971, Crown Court recorder 1972-, Circuit judge 1982-; tstee Kingdon-Ward Speech Therapy Tst 1980-; *Recreations* holidays, motoring; *Clubs* Oxford & Cambridge, Hampshire (Winchester); *Style—* His Honour Judge Butter, QC; Carpmael Building, Temple, EC4 (☎ 01 353 5537)

BUTTERFIELD, Baron (Life Peer UK 1988), of Stechford in the Co of W Midlands (William) John (Hughes) Butterfield; OBE (1953); s of late William Hughes Butterfield, of Hampton-in-Arden, Warwicks, and Mrs Doris North; *b* 28 Mar 1920; *Educ* Solihull Sch, Exeter Coll Oxford, Johns Hopkins Univ USA; *m* 1, 1946, Ann (d 1948), da of late Robert Sanders, of New York, USA; 1 s (Hon Jonathan West Sanders b 23 Oct 1948); m 2, 1950, Isabel-Ann, da of Dr Foster Kennedy (d 1952), neurologist, of New York City; 2 s (Hon Jeremy John Nicholas b 23 Dec 1954, Hon Toby Michael John b 6 Dec 1965), 1 da (Hon Sarah Harriet Ann (Hon Mrs Willetts) b 28 Aug 1953); *Career* Maj RAMC; Regius prof of physics Cambridge 1975-87, master Downing Coll Cambridge 1978-87, vice-chllr Cambridge Univ 1983-85; chm: E Midlands Economic Dvpt Cncl 1973-75, Medicines Cmmn 1976-81, Health Promotion Research Tst 1982-; kt 1978; *Recreations* real tennis, cricket; *Clubs* Athenaeum, Beefsteak, MCC, Oxford & Cambridge, Vincents; *Style—* Prof Sir John Butterfield, OBE; 39 Clarendon St, Cambridge CB1 1JX (☎ 0223 328854)

BUTTERFIELD, John David; s of Leslie John Butterfield (d 1983); *b* 20 Jan 1930; *Educ* King's Coll Sch Wimbledon, Nautical Coll Pangbourne; *m* 1981, Anita Marie, da of late Edward Marek; 1 child; *Career* asst sales man Raithby Lawrence & Co 1948-54, print buyer Lonsdale-Hands Orgn 1954-56; owner & md The Norman Press Ltd 1956-61, world wide dir of printing Ambassador Press (Los Angeles) 1961-73, owner and chm The Euroweb Gp of Cos High Wycombe 1973-; *Recreations* boating; *Style—* John Butterfield, Esq; 3a Fernhills, Kings Langley, Herts, WD4 8PT (☎ Kings Langley 67367); Business (☎ High Wycombe 450445)

BUTTERFIELD, Keith Oldham; s of Edwin Butterfield (d 1966), and Edna Mary Oldham (d 1986); *b* 1 July 1931; *Educ* Merchant Taylors Sch, Lincoln Coll Oxford (MA); *m* 1 Sept 1962, Susan Felicity, da of Alwyn Rigby Hughes (d 1981); 1 s (John Charles b 1969), 1 da (Ann Mary b 1966); *Career* admitted slr 1958; asst slr Bd of Inland Revenue 1981-; *Books* The Countryside and the Law (1971, under pen name Charles Fox); *Recreations* reading, writing, travel; *Clubs* United Oxford and Cambridge Univs; *Style—* Keith Butterfield, Esq; 6 Priors Barton, Kingsgate Road, Winchester SO23 9QF (☎ 0962 63297); Solicitors Office, Inland Revenue, Somerset House, Strand, London WC2R 1LB (☎ 01 438 7087)

BUTTERFIELD, Hon Sarah Harriet Anne (Mrs Willetts); da of Baron Butterfield, OBE, *qv* of 39 Clarendon St, Cambridge, and Isabel Ann Foster, *née* Kennedy; *b* 28 Aug 1953; *Educ* Sherborne Sch for Girls, Univ of Edinburgh (BA), Ruskin Sch of Fine Art and Drawing Oxford Univ, Univ of Bristol (Dip Arch); 19 April 1986, David Lindsay, s of John Roland Willetts, of 35 Marchmount Rd, West Midlands; 1 da (Imogen Anna Kennedy b 12 June 1988); *Career* artist, illustrator 1978-86; illustrator for experimental psychology dept Cambride Univ 1976-78, art critic Oxford Mail 1978; practised as architect 1979-86: California, Bristol, London; exhibitions incl: RCA 1978, Mall Galleries 1980, 1984 and 1986, Royal Soc of Br ARtists 1988, Young Comtemporaries Agnews 1988; Egerton Coghill Landscape award 1976, Windsor & Newton award 1978, finalist Hunting Gp Art Competition 1986, commended Spectator Three Cities Competition 1988; ARCUK; *Books* Ward Order Comprehension Test (with Dr Gillian Fenn); *Recreations* tennis; *Clubs* Queen's; *Style—* The Hon Sarah Butterfield; 21 Ashchurch Grove, London W12 9BT (☎ 01 740 8595)

BUTTERFILL, John Valentine; MP (C) Bournemouth West 1983-; s of George Thomas Butterfill (d 1980), and Elsie Amelia, *née* Watts (d 1974); *b* 14 Feb 1941; *Educ* Caterham Sch, Coll of Estate Mgmnt London; *m* 1965, Pamela Ross, da of Frederick Ross Ross-Symons; 1 s (James b 1975), 3 da (Natasha b 1969, Samara b 1974, Jemima b 1976); *Career* chartered surveyor; valuer Jones Lang Wooton 1962-64, sr exec Hammerson Gp 1964-69, dir Audley Properties Ltd (Bovis Gp) 1969-71, md St Paul's Securities Gp 1971-76, dep chm Euro Democrat Forum 1981-; vice-chm: Guidford Cons Assoc 1980-82 (chm Guidford CPC 1976-82), Foreign Affairs Forum 1983-; sr ptnr Curchod and Co Chartered Surveyors 1977-; sec: Backbench Tourism Ctee 1983-85 (u chm 1985-88), Backbench Trade and Industry Ctee 1987-88; memb: Nat Cncl Euro Foreign Affairs Forum, Cons Gp for Europe; ctee memb London Europe Soc; contested London South Inner in Euro Parl 1979; contested Croydon North West 1981 by-election; memb for Bournemouth West 1983; PPS to Sec of State for Energy 1988-; FRICS 1974; *Recreations* skiing, tennis, riding, bridge, music; *Clubs* Carlton; *Style—* John Butterfill, Esq, MP; 16a Branksome Towers, Westminster Road, Poole, Dorset; House of Commons, London SW1; Churchod & Co, Chartered Surveyors, Portmore House, 54 Church Street, Weybridge, Surrey KT13 8DP (☎ 0932 854370)

BUTTERICK, Peter Stephen; s of Stephen Butterick (d 1987), of Epsom, and Josephine Kathleen, *née* Ansell (d 1958); *b* 1 Dec 1933; *Educ* Ealing GS; *m* 1958, Audrey, da of Raymond St Quintin Bates (d 1986), of Watford; 2 s (Ian, Howard); *Career* dir and sec Macmillan Bloedel Containers Ltd 1975-1983, dir UK Corrugated Ltd 1983-; FCA; *Recreations* church, gardening, motoring, DIY; *Style—* Peter Butterick, Esq; Openfields, Love Lane, King's Langley, Herts (☎ 092 77 64085, office ☎ 0923 242306)

BUTTERS, Francis Arthur; s of Arthur Butters (d 1968), of Westcliff-on-sea, Essex, and Elsie Beatrice Annie, *née* Wood (d 1975); *b* 4 Mar 1920; *Educ* Lindisfarne Coll; *m* 20 July 1946, Heather Margaret, JP, da of Gilbert Harris (d 1969), of Stone, Staffordshire; 1 s (Richard b 8 Jan 1948), 3 da (Margaret b 20 Dec 1949, Rosalind b 9 Aug 1952, Veronica b 14 Sept 1957); *Career* mobilised RNV (W) R telegraphist, served minesweeping trawlers, cmmnd 1940, served armed merchant cruisers coastal forces Ops Dir Admty 1941, ADC and priv sec (Lt RNVR) to Lord Swinton res min W Africa 1942, Miny of civil Aviation 1944-45 (memb UK delegation Int Civil Aviation Confs Chicago 1944, Cape Town 1945), i/c PR private off Civil Aviation Miny 1945, info work HQ Miny Civil Aviation 1945, 1 PR Off Heathrow Airport 1949; joined firm PR Conslts 1950, fndr own PR cos 1957; Berkshire CC 1956-: former ldr cncl and vice-chm cncl, former chm gen purpose ctee; chm educn and social servs Thames Valley Police Authy; memb: ct and cncl Univ of Reading 1973-, indust tbnls 1976-88, ACC 1962-77 and 1984-(former chm police ctee); chm People's Dispensary for Sick Animals 1987-(memb cncl mgmnt 1976-) former chm Police Cncl UK, served various Home Off Working Parties (incl Miny Tport); dir Thames Valley Broadcasting, various int radio appearances; FIPR 1969 (MIPR 1949, chm educn ctee), memb Soc Tech Analysts 1988; *Books* The Government Explains (with study gp Royal Inst Pub Admin 1965); various pubns incl articles and photographs (Encyclopaedia Britannica, world exclusive pictures of Prince of Wales Crown); *Recreations* still and video photography, music, information technology, travel, sleeping; *Clubs* Carlton; *Style—* Francis Butters, Esq; Cornerstone, Fifield, Maidenhead, Berks SL6 2PF (☎ 0628 27112)

BUTTERWICK, Antony James; s of (James) Cyril Butterwick (d 1966), and Hon (Agnes) Désirée, *née* Dickinson, OBE (d 1986), da of 1 Baron Dickinson, KBE; *b* 27 Sept 1930; *Educ* Eton, Trin Coll Oxford (BA); *m* 8 Oct 1958, Joanna Vivien, yr da of Col Hugh A G Vanderfelt (d 1982); 2 s (James Hugo b 1962, (Antony) Guy b 1966), 1 da (Henrietta b 1960); *Career* Nat Serv cmmn Rifle Bde; Grieveson Grant & Co stockbrokers 1953-58, chief passenger mangr Union Castle Line 1958-65, jt md P & O Containers Ltd (formerly Overseas Containers Ltd) 1965-; govr: Gresham's Sch Holt, North Foreland Lodge Sch; chm local ctee Nat Tst; Warden Fishmongers' Co; *Recreations* golf, shooting; *Style—* Antony Butterwick, Esq; Pinkneys House, Pinkneys Green, Berks SL6 6QD (☎ 0628 21726); P & O Containers Ltd, Beagle House, Braham St, London E1 8EP (☎ 01 488 1313, fax 01 481 3459, telex 883947)

BUTTERWICK, John Newton; TD (1961); s of (James) Cyril Butterwick (d 1966), of Old Park, Beaconsfield, and Hon (Agnes) Désirée Butterwick O.B.E. (d 1986), da of 1 Baron Dickinson, KBE; *b* 3 Mar 1923; *Educ* Eton, Trinity Coll Oxford; *m* 1956, Marcia, o da of John Scott, of Pittsburgh, USA (d 1969); 3 s , (Nicholas Scott b 1959, Christopher Hugh b 1963, William Toby b 1965), 1 da (Sarah b 1958); *Career* Capt WW II NW Europe 1942-46, TA 1949-62, ret with rank Bt-Col; vice-chm Lazard Bros & Co 1981-83 (dir 1972-80); dir Glyn Mills & Co (later Williams & Glyn's Bank) 1961-72; chm: Baker St Investmt Co plc 1983-; dir: London Merchant Securities plc 1963-, Lazard Unquoted Companies Fund Ltd 1986-, NDL Int Ltd 1986-, Duncan Lawrie Bank Ltd 1987-; *Recreations* golf, gardening; *Clubs* Royal West Norfolk Golf; *Style—* John Butterwick, Esq, TD; Danyells, Sandon, Buntingford, Herts (☎ 0763 87 312); The Gables, Brancaster, King's Lynn, Norfolk (☎ Brancaster 210242); Suite 10 Westminster Palace Gardens, Artillery Row, London SW1 P1RL (☎ 01 2227686, telex LJMCN 291018)

BUTTERWORTH, Henry; s of Henry Butterworth (d 1955), and Wilhelmena Butterworth (d 1931); *b* 21 Jan 1926; *Educ* St Mary's Leyland Lancs, Preston Tech Coll, Birmingham Univ (CEng MIMechE); *m* 28 Oct 1948, Ann, da of late Patrick Joseph Smith; 2 s (Peter b 1951, James b 1956); *Career* engr; dir gen Royal Ordnance Factories MOD 1979-84, md Royal Ordnance Factories MOD 1984-86, md Royal Ordnance plc 1986-88; *Recreations* fishing, dancing, boating; *Style—* Henry Butterworth, Esq; 5 Vicarsfield Rd, Worden Park, Leyland, Lancs (☎ 0772 436073); Royal Ordnance plc, Chorley, Lancs (☎ 02572 65511)

BUTTERWORTH, Baron (Life Peer UK 1985), of Warwick, Co Warwick; John Blackstock Butterworth; CBE (1982), DL (Warwicks 1967-74, W Midlands 1974-), JP (City of Oxford 1962, Coventry 1963-); only s of John William Butterworth, by his wife, Florence, da of John Blackstock, of Dumfries; *b* 13 Mar 1918; *Educ* Queen Elizabeth's GS Mansfield, Queens' Coll Oxford; *m* 1948, Doris Crawford, da of George Elder, of Edinburgh; 1 s (Hon John William Blackstock b 1952), 2 da (Hon Anna Elizabeth Blackstock (Hon Mrs Walker) b 1951, Hon Laura Blackstock (Hon Mrs Burley) b 1959); *Career* Maj RA 1939-46; barr Lincoln's Inn 1947; fell New Coll Oxford 1946-63, bursar 1956-63, managing tstee Nuffield Fndn 1964-85 (tstee 1985-); chm Univs Ctee for Non-teaching staffs 1970-85, memb Bd of Br Cncl 1981-86, vice-chllr Warwick Univ 1963-85; govr Royal Shakespeare Theatre 1964-, dir Melapraxis Ltd 1986-; memb: Jarratt Ctee on Univ Efficiency 1986, Croham Ctee on review of U.G.C. 1987; univ cmmr (under Educn Reform Act 1988) 1988-; Hon DCL Sierra Leone 1976, Hon DSc Aston Univ 1985, Hon LLD Univ of Warwick 1986; *Clubs* Athenaeum; *Style—* The Rt Hon Baron Butterworth, CBE, JP, DL; The Barn, Barton, Guiting Power, Glos GL54 5US

BUTTERWORTH, Sir (George) Neville; DL (Gtr Manchester 1974); s of (George) Richard Butterworth, and Hannah, *née* Wright; *b* 27 Dec 1911; *Educ* Malvern, St John's Coll Cambridge (MA); *m* 1947, Barbara Mary, da of Frank William Briggs; 2 s; *Career* former chm: NW cncl CBI, Tootal Ltd (was previously chm English Sewing Cotton Co Ltd, merged with The Calico Printers' Assoc); former memb Royal Cmmn on the Distribution of Income Wealth; High Sheriff Gtr Manchester 1974; kt 1973;

Style— Sir Neville Butterworth, DL; Oak Farm, Ollerton, Knutsford, Cheshire (☎ 0565 3150)

BUTTERWORTH, Peter John; s of John Bielby Butterworth (d 1981), of Bridgwater, Somerset, and Olive Gwendoline, *née* Stevens (d 1978); *b* 12 Nov 1927; *Educ* Monkton Combe Sch Bath; *m* 25 Aug 1956, Carolyn Mary, da of Antony Squibbs (d 1971), of Bridgwater; 2 s (Philip b 30 May 1957, Michael John b 12 Aug 1960), 1 da (Gillian Mary Jane 28 Aug 1963); *Career* KRRC 1945, REME 1946-48 (WOII 1948); sr ptnr Butterworth Jones & Co Bridgwater 1983- (ptnr 1953-83); tres: Bridgwater Cancer Res Campaign 1954-84, County Club Bridgwater 1955-75 (chm 1977-80); sec Bridgwater C of C 1956-; ACA 1951, FCA 1956, ACCA 1968, FCCA 1973; *Recreations* golf, philately, local history res; *Clubs* County Club (Bridgwater), Ivel (Yeovil), Rotary (Sedgemoor); *Style*— Peter Butterworth, Esq; Brooklands, 5 Durleigh Rd, Bridgwater, Somerset (☎ 0278 423948); 7 Castle St, Bridgwater, Somerset (☎ 0278 428251, fax 0278 428 358, telex 46616)

BUTTFIELD, Dame Nancy Eileen; *née* Wheewall Holden; DBE (1972); da of Sir Edward Wheewall Holden (d 1947), and Hilda May Lavis; *b* 12 Nov 1912; *Educ* Woodlands C of E Girls' GS Adelaide, Adelaide Univ, Cauposenea Paris; *m* 1936, Frank Charles Buttfield; 2 s; *Career* senator for S Australia 1955-65 and 1968-74; dir co-op Retirement Services; *Books* So Great a Change (Story of Holden Family); *Recreations* embroidery, wood carving and polishing; *Clubs* Queen Adelaide and Lyceum; *Style*— Dame Nancy Buttfield, DBE; 52 Strangeways Terrace, N Adelaide, S Australia 5006

BUTTON, Air Vice-Marshal Arthur Daniel; CB (1976), OBE (1959); s of Leonard Victor Daniel Button (d 1966), of Eastbourne, and Ann Agnes, *née* Derbyshire (d 1981); *b* 26 May 1916; *Educ* County HS for Boys Ilford Essex, Univ of Southampton (BSc London); *m* 1944, Eira Guelph, da of Reginald Waterhouse Jones (d 1955); 1 s (John Daniel b 1945, d 1945); *Career* RAF offr in GD 1941-46, Educn 1938-41 and 1946-76; dir: RAF educnl servs 1972-76, ARELS Examinations Tst 1976-86; active in RAF and other serv charities; *Recreations* music; *Clubs* RAF; *Style*— Air Vice-Marshal Arthur D Button, CB, OBE; 7 Parsonage Ct, Trgin, Herts HP23 5BG (☎ 044 282 6017)

BUTTON, Roger Martin; s of Frederick Charles Button, of High Dell, Harrow-on-the-Hill, Middx (d 1970), and Una Florence, *née* Martin; *b* 7 Feb 1931; *Educ* Winchester Coll, Pembroke Coll Cambridge (MA Arch); *m* 2 April 1955, Shirley Gwynfryd, da of Dr Rodney Howell Holt, of Eastbourne, Sussex (d 1970); 2 s (Rupert b 1959, Benjamin b 1962, d 1978), 1 da (Myfanwy b 1969); *Career* Lt RE 1949-51; ptnr: Adie, Button & Ptnrs 1963-, Waterhouse Ripley 1968-; asst architect to Sir Basil Spence for Coventry Cathedral Reconstruction 1955-62; *Recreations* sailing, swimming, gardening; *Clubs* Royal Ocean Racing, Royal Engineer Yacht, Artworkers Guild; *Style*— Roger M Button, Esq; The Old Stores, Ashampstead, Reading, Berkshire RG8 8RT (☎ 0635 578 559); 50 Charlotte St, London W1P 1LW (☎ 01 637 0881)

BUTTRESS, Donald Reeve; s of Edward Crossley Buttress, of Manchester, and Evelyn Edna, *née* Reeve-Whaley; *b* 27 April 1932; *Educ* Stockport Sch, Univ of Manchester (MA); *m* 15 Dec 1956, Elsa Mary, da of Herbert Bardsley, of Bramhall (d 1964); 2 s (Richard b 1960, John b 1966), 3 da (Helen b 1958, Fiona b 1962, Lucy b 1973); *Career* Flying Offr RAF 1958-61; architect and ecclesiastical surveyor; architect: Sheffield and Bangor Cathedrals 1978-88, Llandaff Cathedral 1986; surveyor Chichester Cathedral 1985, Surveyor of the Fabric Westminster Abbey 1988; FSA, FRIBA; *Recreations* walking, countryside conservation, books; *Clubs* RAF; *Style*— Donald R Buttress, Esq; 2B, Little Cloister, Westminster Abbey, London SW1; 176Oxford Rd, Manchester M13 9QQ (☎ 061 273 5405)

BUXTON, Andrew Edward; s of Desmond Gurney Buxton (d 1987), of Hoveton Hall, Norfolk, and gggs of Sir Edward Buxton, 2 Bt, MP; *b* 3 Mar 1935; *Educ* Eton, Magdalene Coll Cambridge; *m* 1967, Barbara, da of Capt Cyril Gascoigne Lloyd; 1 s, 2 da; *Career* dir RTZ Corpn plc, Corpu plc; *Recreations* shooting, tennis, cricket; *Clubs* Boodle's; *Style*— Andrew Buxton, Esq; 36 Burnsall St, London SW3; Hoveton Hall, Norfolk

BUXTON, Andrew Robert Fowell; s of Capt Joseph Gurney Fowell Buxton, Grenadier Gds (ka 1943, gggs of Sir Thomas Buxton, 1 Bt), and Elizabeth (da of late Maj Robert Barbour, of Bolesworth Castle, Tattenhall, Chester) who m subsequently Alexander Grant (half-bro of Lt-Col Ian Grant - *see below*); *b* 5 April 1939; *Educ* Winchester, Pembroke Coll Oxford; *m* 1965, Jane Margery, da of Lt-Col Ian (John Peter) Grant of Rothiemurchus, MBE, and Lady Katherine Grant, *qv*; 2 da; *Career* 2 Lt Grenadier Gds; vice chm Barclays Bank; *Style*— Andrew Buxton, Esq; Bentley Park, Ipswich, Suffolk

BUXTON, Edward John Mawby; s of Alfred Mellor Buxton, OBE (d 1963), of Cheshire, and Ethel Marion Mawby (d 1954); *b* 16 Dec 1912; *Educ* Malvern, New Coll Oxford (MA); *m* 12 April 1939, Emilie Marjorie (d 1977), da of Harry Lockley (d 1950); *Career* WWII serv Lt 1 Commando Norway 1940 (POW 1940-45); fell New Coll Oxford 1949- (emeritus fell and reader 1979-), reader English Lit Univ of Oxford 1972-, visiting fell Wesleyan Univ Connecticut 1966; Atlantic Award Eng Lit (Rockefeller Fndn) 1946, Warton Lectr Br Acad 1970; FSA; *Books* Island of Skomer (ed 1950), Sir Philip Sidney & the English Renaissance (1954, 64, 65, 87), Elizabethan Taste (1963, 83), A Tradition of Poetry (1967), Byron & Shelley (1968), The Grecian Taste (1978), New College Oxford 1379-1979 (ed 1979), Poems of Charles Cotton (ed 1958), The Compleat Angler (ed 1978), The Redstart (1950 Swedish trans 1953) The Birds of Wiltshire (1981) *Poems*: Such Liberty (1944); *Recreations* ornithology, gardening, travel; *Style*— John Buxton, Esq; The Grove, East Tytherton, Chippenham, Wiltshire SN15 4LX (☎ 0249 74200)

BUXTON, Gervase Michael; s of Lt-Cdr Michael Buxton, RNVR, sometime High Sheriff Rutland (himself s of Henry Fowell Buxton, 7 ggs of Sir Thomas Buxton, 1 Bt, by his 1 w, Katharine, da of Rt Hon James Round, JP, DL; *b* 2 Jan 1939; *Educ* Harrow, Trin Cambridge; *m* 1965, Susan Margaret, er da of Kenneth Malcolm McKenzie, of Kensington; 2 s (Matthew b 1967, Jocelyn b 1972), 2 da (Lucy b 1966, Cara b 1969); *Career* 2 Lt Royal Scots Greys; exec dir Barclays Merchant Bank, on secondment int finance dir Barclays Bank Int 1982-; *Style*— Gervase Buxton, Esq; Swangles Farm, Cold Christmas, Ware, Herts

BUXTON, Hon (Aubrey) James Francis; yr s of Baron Buxton of Alsa; *b* 20 Mar 1956; *Educ* Ampleforth, Royal Agricultural Coll Cirencester; *m* 1981, Melinda D M, da of Peter Henry Samuelson, of Ugley Hall, Essex; 1 s (Henry b 19 May 1988), 2 da (Emma Lucy Maria b 1984, Olivia Louise b 1986); *Career* ptnr Bidwells, Chartered Surveyor's, Cambridge; *Recreations* shooting, painting, music; *Clubs* White's; *Style*— The Hon James Buxton; Church Farm, Carlton, Newmarket, Suffolk (☎ 0223 290511)

BUXTON, James Geoffrey Pease; s of Maj Peter Stapleton Buxton (ka 1944), and Julia Victoria, *née* Pease; *b* 24 Oct 1939; *Educ* Eton, Trinity Coll Cambridge (MA); *m* 20 June 1970, Meriel Jessica, da of Maj Denis Joseph Cowen, OBE (d 1986), of E Farndon Manor, Market Harborough, Leics; 1 s (Hugh b 1975), 1 da (Rose b 1973); *Career* local dir Barclays Bank: Peterborough 1970-79, Norwich 1979-87; fin admin Shuttleworth Agric Coll 1988-; hon tres: Fernie Hunt, Fernie Point to Point; AIB 1967; *Recreations* hunting, stalking, beekeeping; *Style*— James Buxton, Esq; Manor Farm House, Lubenham, Market Harborough, Leicestershire LE16 9TD (☎ 0858 31758); Shuttleworth Agricultural College, Old Warden Park, Biggleswade, Bedfordshire (☎ 076 727 441, fax 076 727 561)

BUXTON, Hon Jane Elizabeth Noel; da of 1 Baron Noel-Buxton, PC (d 1948); *b* 22 May 1925; *Career* relinquished surname of Noel by public declaration, 1957; *Style*— The Hon Jane Buxton; 27 Redington Rd, Hampstead, NW3

BUXTON, Jocelyn Charles Roden; VRD; s of late Capt Roden Buxton, CBE, RN, 2 s of 4 Bt, by 1 w, Dorothy, da of late Col Charles St John, RE; hp of kinsman, Sir Thomas Buxton, 6 Bt; *b* 8 August 1924; *m* 1960, Ann Frances, da of Frank Smitherman, MBE; 3 da; *Career* WW II Lt-Cdr RNVR (despatches); *Style*— Jocelyn Buxton, Esq, VRD; Rodwell House, Loddon, Norwich

BUXTON, John Burns; s of Alan Thomas Buxton, of NZ; *b* 31 Oct 1933; *Educ* Takapuna GS, Massey Univ, Lincoln Coll; *m* 1961, Helen, da of Sir Douglas Robb; 1 s, 3 da (and 1 s decd); *Career* gen mangr W Richmond Ltd (NZ) 1968-72, exec chm Towers & Co 1972-81, md Riverlands Foods 1983-, vice-pres Imported Meat Trade Assoc 1977-81; pres: NZ Soc 1980-81, London Meat Trades and Inairers Benevolent Inst 1977, cncllr NZ Meat indust Assoc 1988-; memb: cncl Lincoln Coll Canterbury NZ, Worshipful Co of Butchers London; *Recreations* gardening, music, sport, art; *Clubs* RAC, Canterbury (Christchurch); *Style*— John Buxton, Esq; Amwell, 166 Papanui Road, Christchurch 1, New Zealand

BUXTON, Prof John Noel; s of John William Buxton (d 1971), and Laura Frances, *née* Whitehead; *b* 25 Dec 1933; *Educ* Bradford GS, Trinity Coll Cambridge (MA); *m* 8 Feb 1958, Moira Jean, da of William E C O'Brien (d 1972); 2 s (Nigel b 1961, Patrick b 1965), 2 da (Jocelyn b 1959, Delia b 1963); *Career* flight trials eng de Havilland Prepellers 1955-59, ops res scientist Br Iron & Steel Res Assoc 1959-60, applied sci rep IBM UK 1960-62, lectr Inst of Computer Sci London Univ 1962-66, chief software conslt SCICON (formerly CEIR) 1966-68, prof of computer sci Warwick Univ 1968-84, UNDP project mangr Int Computer Educn Centre Budapest 1975-77, visiting scholar Harvard Univ 1979-80, prof of info technol King's Coll London 1984-; memb various ctees SERC 1987-; FBCS 1968; *Books* Simulation Programming Languages (ed 1968), Proc NATO Software Engineering Conf (ed jtly 1970), The Craft of Software Engineering (jtly 1987); *Recreations* mountaineering, music, restoration of medieval Homes; *Clubs* Climbers; *Style*— Prof John Buxton; Bull's Hall, Yaxley, Eye, Suffolk IP23 8BZ; Kings Coll, Strand, London WC2R 2LS

BUXTON, Jonathan James; s of Cdr Michael Buxton (s of Henry Fowell Buxton by his 1 w, Katharine, da of Rt Hon James Round, of Birch Hall, Essex; Henry Buxton was 1 s of John Henry Buxton, DL, by his w, Emma, da of Capt Richard Pelly, DL, RN, 5 s of Sir John Pelly, 1 Bt; John Henry Buxton was 1 s of Thomas Buxton, JP, 2 s of Sir Thomas Buxton, 1 Bt); *b* 2 July 1943; *Educ* Harrow; *m* 1972, Rosaleen, da of Sir John Bagge, 6 Bt; 3 da; *Career* formerly Maj 17/21 Lancers; co dir; *Recreations* sailing, skiing; *Clubs* Cavalry; *Style*— Jonathan Buxton, Esq; 62 Endlesham Rd, SW12 (☎ 01 675 4242)

BUXTON, Hon Lucinda Catherine; 2 da of Baron Buxton, of Alsa, and Pamela Mary, *née* Birkin; *b* 21 August 1950; *Educ* New Hall Sch Chelmsford; *Career* wildlife photographer; tstee Falkland Islands Appeal, wildlife advsr Falkland Islands Fndn; Media Award 1982; ctee memb United Kingdom Falkland Islands Ctee; 50 acres in Falkland Islands; FRGS; *Books* Survival in the Wild (1980), Survival - South Atlantic (1983); *Recreations* tennis, flying, diving; *Style*— The Hon Lucinda Buxton; The Old House, Langham, Holt, Norfolk (☎ 032 875 352); 69 Archel Rd, London W14 (☎ 01 381 9922)

BUXTON, Hon Mrs (Margaret Evelyn); *née* Bridges; da of 1 Baron Bridges, KG, GCB, GCVO, MC (d 1969), and Hon Katharine, da of 2 Baron Farrer; *b* 9 Oct 1932; *Educ* Downe House Newbury, Lady Margaret Hall Oxford (MA, DPhil); *m* 1, 1954 (m dis 1969), Trevor Aston; m 2, 1971, as his 2 w, Paul William Jex Buxton, s of Denis Alfred Jex Buxton (d 1964) and gggs of Sir Thomas Buxton, 1 Bt; 2 da; *Career* lectr St Anne's Coll Oxford 1956-59, research fell Newnham Coll Cambridge 1961-66, hon sr research fell Queen's Univ Belfast 1984-85; FRHS, FSA; *Books* (under name of Margaret Aston) Thomas Arundel (1967), The Fifteenth Century (1968), Lollards and Reformers (1984), England's Iconoclasts (1988); *Style*— The Hon Mrs Buxton; Castle House, Chipping Ongar, Essex (☎ 0277 362642)

BUXTON, Paul William Jex; s of Denis Buxton (d 1964), of Gt Yarmouth, and Emily, *née* Hollins (d 1970); gggs of Sir Thomas Towell Buxton carried Bill abolishing Slavery through Commons 1835; *b* 20 Sept 1925; *Educ* Rugby Sch, Balliol Coll Oxford (BA 1st class Lit, Hum) MA; *m* 1, 1950, (m dis 1971), Katharine (d 1977); 2 s (Charles b 1951, Toby b 1953), 1 da (Mary b 1956); m 2, 1971, Margaret, da of Rt Hon Lord Bridges, KG (d 1969), of Hendley, Surrey; 2 da (Sophie b 1972, Hero b 1974); *Career* Capt Coldstream Gds Germany 1945-47; Foreign/Diplomatic Service 1950-71 (served India, United Nations New York, Guatemala, United States: Washington) cnsllr 1967-71, Northern Ireland Office 1974-85; under sec Belfast 1981-85; tres (Hon) Anti-Slavery Soc; memb of cncl Howard League for Penal Reform; *Recreations* forestry, gardening; *Clubs* Brooks's; *Style*— Paul Buxton, Esq; Castle House, Chipping Ongar, Essex CM5 9JT

BUXTON, Hon Richard Christopher; s of 2 Baron Noel-Buxton (d 1980); *b* 15 Feb 1950; *Educ* Bryanston; *Style*— The Hon Richard Buxton

BUXTON, Ronald Carlile; s of Murray Barclay Buxton, and Janet Mary Muriel, *née* Carlile; *b* 20 August 1923; *Educ* Eton, Trinity Coll Cambridge (MA); *m* 1959, Phyllida Dorothy Roden; 2 s, 2 da; *Career* dir H Young & Co London and assoc cos; MP (C) Leyton 1955-66; FIStructE; *Recreations* travel, music, riding; *Clubs* Carlton; *Style*— Ronald Buxton, Esq; Kimberley Hall, Wymondham, Norfolk; 67 Ashley Gdns, SW1

BUXTON, Hon Simon Campden; 2 s of 2 Baron Noel-Buxton (d 1980); *b* 9 April 1943; *Educ* Bryanston, Balliol Coll Oxford; *m* 1981, Alison, da of S J Liddle, of Exmouth; 1 s (Christopher John Noel b 11 June 1988), 1 da (Katherine Helen b 1983);

Career editor, social action programmes Thames Television; *Clubs* MCC; *Style*— The Hon Simon Buxton

BUXTON, Hon Timothy Leland; er s of Baron Buxton of Alsa; *b* 20 Nov 1948; *Educ* Ampleforth; *m* 1972, Julie Mary, da of Lt-Cdr (John) Michael Avison Parker, CVO; 1 s (Edward Leland b 1976), 1 da (Alexandra Louise b 1973); *Style*— The Hon Timothy Buxton; The Dower House, Heydon, Norfolk

BUXTON, Hon Victoria Jane; 4 da of Baron Buxton of Alsa, *qv*; *b* 4 June 1960; *Educ* St Mary's Convent, Ascot; *Career* commercial pilot; *Style*— The Hon Victoria Buxton; Burntwalls Farm, Daventry, Northants

BUXTON OF ALSA, Baron (Life Peer UK 1978), of Stiffkey, Co Norfolk; Aubrey Leland Oakes Buxton; MC (1943), DL (Essex 1975); s of late Leland William Wilberforce Buxton, s of Sir Thomas Fowell Buxton, 3 Bt, GCMG, JP, DL; *b* 15 July 1918; *Educ* Ampleforth, Trinity Coll Cambridge; *m* 1946, Pamela Mary (d 1983), da of Sir Henry Ralph Stanley Birkin, 3 Bt, and wid of Maj Samuel Luckyn Buxton, MC, 17/21 Lancers; 2 s, 4 da; m 2, 16 July 1988, Mrs Kathleen Peterson, of Maine, USA; *Career* Maj Supplementary Reserves; chief exec Anglia TV Gp (dir 1958-88, chm 1986-88), chm ITN 1981-86; vice-pres World Wildlife Fund 1968-, pres Royal TV Soc 1973-77, tres London Zoological Soc 1977-83, chm Survival Anglia 1986-; memb: Countryside Cmmn, Royal Cmmn on Pollution, Nature Conservancy Cncl 1988-; prodr of television and wildlife films; Queens Award for Industry 1974; extra equerry to HRH The Duke of Edinburgh 1964, High Sheriff of Essex 1972; *Style*— The Rt Hon the Lord Buxton of Alsa; Old Hall Farm, Stiffkey, Wells-next-the-Sea, Norfolk NR23 1QJ (☎ 032 875 347)

BUZZARD, Hon Mrs (Ann Sophia Madeline); *née* Whitfield; da of 1 Baron Kenswood (d 1963); *b* 14 Feb 1928; *m* 1948, Richard Bethune Buzzard, s of Brig-Gen Frank Anstie Buzzard, DSO (d 1950), of Haxted house, Edenbridge, Kent; 1 s, 3 da; *Style*— The Hon Mrs Buzzard; Villa les Terrasses, 10 Avenue de Rigaud, 893240 Cavalaire-sur-Mer, France

BUZZARD, Sir Anthony Farquhar; 3 Bt (UK 1929), of Munstead Grange, Godalming, Co Surrey; s of Rear Adm Sir Anthony Wass Buzzard, 2 Bt, CB, DSO, OBE (d 1972), and Margaret, da of Sir Arthur Knapp, KCIE, CSI, CBE; *b* 28 June 1935; *Educ* Charterhouse, Ch Ch Oxford; *m* 1970, Barbara Jean, da of Gordon Arnold, of Michigan; 2 da, (Sarah b 1971, Claire b 1974); *Heir* Timothy MacDonnell; *Career* modern languages teacher at American School in London 1974-81; lectr Theology Oregon Bible Coll Illinois 1982-; articles on Christology & Eschatology in various theological journals; fndr of Restoration Fellowship; *Books* The Coming Kingdom of the Messiah: A Solution to the Riddle of the New Testament, (1987); *Recreations* music, tennis; *Style*— Sir Anthony Buzzard, Bt; Box 100, Oregon, Ill 61061, USA; (☎ 815 734 4344), 815 732 7991

BUZZARD, Timothy Macdonnell; s of Rear Adm Sir Anthony Wass Buzzard, 2 Bt, CB, DSO, OBE (d 1972); hp of bro, Sir Anthony Buzzard, 3 Bt; *b* 28 Jan 1939; *Educ* Royal Acad of Music; *m* 1970, Jennifer, da of Peter Patching (d 1971); 1 s, 1 da; *Career* dir of music; LRAM, GRSM; *Style*— Timothy Buzzard, Esq; Kennel Cottage, East Mascalls, Lindfield, West Sussex (☎ Lindfield 044 47 3420)

BYAM SHAW, (John) James; CBE; s of John Byam Liston Shaw (d 1919), of London, and Caroline Evelyn Eunice, *née* Pyke-Nott (d 1960); *b* 12 Jan 1903; *Educ* Westminster, Christ Church Oxford (MA, DLitt); *m* 1, 1929 (m dis 1938), Eveline, da of Capt Arthur Dodgson RN; m 2, 1945 Margaret (d 1965), da of Arthur Saunders; 1 adopted s (James Frederick 1950); m 3, 1967, Christine Pamela, wid of W P Gibson; *Career* WWII The Royal Scots 1940-46: cmmnd 2 Lt, Capt 1941, Maj 1944, served UK, India, Burma; lectr and asst to dir Courtauld Inst of Art 1933-34, dir P & D Colnaghi & Co 1937-68 (joined 1934); Christ Church Oxford: lectr 1964-73, assoc curator of pictures 1973-74, hon student fell 1976; Hon DLitt Oxford Univ; FSA, FRSA; hon fell: Pierpont Morgan Library New York, Ateneo Veneto Venice, Grande Ufficiale, Order of Merit of the Rep of Italy 1982; *Books* The Drawings of Francesco Guardi (1951), The Drawings of Domenico Tiepolo (1962), Catalogue of Paintings at Christ Church Oxford (1967), Catalogue of Drawings at Christ Church (1976), Catalogue of Italian Drawings in the Lugt Collection Fondation Custodia Institut Néerlandais Paris (1983), Catalogue of Italian 18th Century Drawings in the Robert Lehman Collection Metro Museum New York (with George Knox 1987); *Clubs* Athenaeum; *Style*— James Byam Shaw, Esq, CBE; 4 Abingdon Villas, London W8 6BX (☎ 01 937 6128)

BYAM SHAW, Nicholas Glencairn; s of Lt-Cmdr David Byam Shaw, OBE, RN (ka 1941), and Clarita Pamela Clarke; gf, a painter who started the Byam Shaw Art Sch early in 20th century (John Byam Eston Shaw, d 1919); *b* 28 Mar 1934; *Educ* RNC Dartmouth; *m* 1, 1956, Joan, da of Major Hedley Edmund Dennis Elliott, of Roundabout, West Chittington, Sussex (d 1958); 2 s (Justin b 1960, Matthew b 1963), 1 da (Clare b 1957); m 2, 1987, Constance, da of Rev Serson Clarke, of Ottawa Canada (d 1979); *Career* Lieut RN (cmmnd 1953) promoted 1955; publisher; md: Macmillan Publishers Ltd 1969-, Macmillan Ltd 1983-; chm Pan Books Ltd 1986-; dir St Martins Press NY and other Macmillan cos; *Recreations* gardening, music, theatre; Macmillan Ltd, 4 Little Essex St, London WC2 (☎ 01 836 6633)

BYATT, Antonia Susan; da of His Hon Judge John Frederick Drabble, QC (d 1983), of Martlesham Suffolk, and Kathleen Marie Bloor (d 1984); *b* 24 August 1936; *m* 1959 (m dis 1969) ICR Byatt, 1 s decd (Charles d 1961), 1 da (Antonia b 1960); m 2, 1969, Peter John Duffy; 2 da (Isabel b 1970, Miranda b 1973); *Career* teacher: Westminster Tutors 1962-65, extra-mural dept of London Univ 1962-71; part-time lectr dept of Lib Studies Central Sch of Art and Design 1965-69; lectr dept of Eng UCL 1972-, asst tutor for Admissions Dept of Eng UCL 1977-80, tutor for Admissions Dept of Eng 1980-82; sr lectr Dept of Eng UCL 1981-; full time writer 1983-; regular reviewer: for various newspapers, The Times Literary Supplement, BBC Kaleidoscope; external assessor in literature Central Sch of Art and Design, external examiner Univ of East Anglia; judge Booker Prize 1973; memb: panel of judges Hawthornden Prize, CNAA Communications and Cultural Studies Bd 1978-83, Creative and Performing Arts Bd 1984, BBC's Social Effects of TV Advsy Gp 1974-77, Kingman Ctee on Eng Language 1987; assoc late Newnham Coll Cambridge (chm 1986-), chm Ctee of Mgmnt Soc of Authors 1986- (dep chm 1985-); Hon DLitt Bradford 1987; FRSL; *Books* Shadow of a Sun (1964), Degrees of Freedom (1965), The Game (1967), The Virgin in the Garden (1978), Still Life (1985), Sugar and Other Stories (1987) also various literary criticisms, articles, prefaces, reviews, articles and broadcasts; *Style*— Mrs A S Byatt; 37 Rusholme Rd, London SW15 3LF (☎ 01 789 3109)

BYATT, Sir Hugh Campbell; KCVO (1985), CMG (1979); s of Sir Horace Archer Byatt, GCMG (d 1938), and Lady Byatt, MBE, (d 1943), *née* Olga Margaret Campbell; *b* 27 August 1927; *Educ* Gordonstoun, New Coll Oxford (MA Oxon); *m* 1954, Fiona, da of Ian Pountney Coats, DL; 2 s, 1 da; *Career* served RNVR 1945-48; Nigerian Political Serv 1952-57; CRO; India; and Cabinet Office 1957-67, head of chancery Lisbon 1967; asst head South Asia Dept FCO 1970; consul-gen Mozambique 1971-73, inspector HM Diplomatic Service 1973-75, Royal Coll of Defence Studies 1976, dep high cmmr Kenya 1977-78, first ambass to Angola 1978-81, Portugal 1981-86; chm of governors, Centre for Information of Language Teaching and Research (CILT); dir Dragon Tst plc (Edinburgh Fund Managers); KtGCM O of Christ (Portugal 1985); *Recreations* sailing, fishing, gardening; *Clubs* New (Edinburgh), Royal Ocean Racing, Leander (Henley-on-Thames); *Style*— Sir Hugh Campbell Byatt, KCVO, CMG; Leargnahension, By Tarbert, Argyll

BYATT, Dr Ian Charles Rayner; s of Charles Rayner Byatt (d 1944), and Enid Marjorie Annie, *née* Howat (d 1977); *b* 11 Mar 1932; *Educ* Kirkham GS, St Edmund Hall Oxford, Nuffield Coll Oxford, Harvard Univ; *m* 4 July 1959 (m dis 1969), Antonia Susan, da of His Hon Judge J F Drabble, QC; 1 s (Charles Nicholas John b 1961, d 1972), 1 da (Helen Antonia b 1960); *Career* served RAF 1950-52; lectr in economics Durham Univ 1958-62, econ conslt HM Treasy 1962-64, lectr LSE 1964-67, sr econ advsr DES 1967-69, dir economics and statistics miny of Housing (later DOE) 1969-72, dep chief econ advsr HM Treasy 1978- (head of pub sector 1972-78); memb: Holy Cross Ch, Holy Cross Centre Tst; *Books* British Electrical Industry 1875-1914 (1979); *Recreations* painting; *Clubs* Oxford and Cambridge; *Style*— Dr Ian Byatt; 17 Thanet St, London WC1H 9QL (☎ 01 388 3888); H M Treasury, Parliament St, London SW1P 3AG (☎ 01 270 4409, fax 01 270 5653)

BYERS, Hon Charles William; o s of Baron Byers, OBE, PC, DL (Life Peer, d 1984), and Baroness Byers, *qv*; *b* 24 Mar 1949; *Educ* Westminster, Ch Ch Oxford; *m* 8 July 1972, Suzan Mary, o da of Aubrey Kefford Stone (d 1980); 2 s (Jonathan Charles b 11 April 1975, George William b 19 Nov 1977); *Career* barr Gray's Inn 1973; *Style*— The Hon Charles Byers; 3 Clayford, Dormansland, Surrey

BYERS, Baroness; Joan Elizabeth; da of late William Oliver, of Alfriston, Wayside, Golders Green, NW11; *m* 1939, Baron Byers, OBE, PC, DL (Lib Life Peer, cr 1964, a former chief whip, chm of the Pty, and ldr of Libs in House of Lords, who died 1984); 1 s (Charles, *qv*), 3 da (Elizabeth Malcolm, Luise Nandy, Sara Somers, *qqv*); *Style*— The Rt Hon the Lady Byers; Hunters Hill, Blindley Heath, Lingfield, Surrey

BYERS, Sir Maurice Hearne; CBE (1978), QC (1960); s of Arthur Tolhurst Byers (d 1950), and Mabel Florence, *née* Hearne (d 1950); *b* 10 Nov 1917; *Educ* St Aloysius Coll Sydney, Sydney Univ (LLB); *m* 1949, Patricia Therese, da of Henry Gilbert Davis (d 1947); 2 s, 1 da; *Career* barr, slr-gen of Australia 1973-83, ldr Aust delegation to UN Cmmn on Int Trade Law 1974, 1976-81; chm Police Bd of NSW 1984-, Australian Constitutional Cmmn 1987-; kt 1982; *see Debrett's Handbook of Australia and New Zealand for further details*; *Style*— Sir Maurice Byers, CBE, QC; 14 Morella Rd, Clifton Gdns, NSW 2088, Australia (☎ 969 8257, 6/180 Phillip St. Sydney (☎ 232-4766)

BYFORD, Sir Lawrence; CBE (1979), QPM (1974, DL 1987); s of George Byford (d 1949), of Normanton, Yorks, and Monica Irene Byford; *b* 10 August 1925; *Educ* Leeds Univ; *m* 1950, Muriel Campbell Massey; 2 s, 1 da; *Career* barr; joined W Riding Police 1947, divnl cdr Huddersfield 1966-68, asst chief constable Lincs 1970-73, chief constable Lincs 1973-77, HM inspr of constabulary for SE region 1977-78, for NE region 1978-83; HM chief inspr of Constabulary 1983-87; now engaged as mgmnt and security conslt; Hon LLD Univ of Leeds 1987; kt 1984; *Clubs* MCC, Royal Overseas League; *Style*— Sir Lawrence Byford, CBE, QPM, DL; Dalefield, Riseholme, Lincoln

BYGRAVE, Clifford; s of Fred Bygrave, of Caddington, nr Luton, and Beatrice Rose Bygrave; *b* 24 May 1934; *Educ* Luton GS; *m* 15 July 1961, Jean Elizabeth, da of Edward Neale (d 1986); 3 da (Angela Joy b 1964, Paula Jane b 1968, Heather Alison b 1972); *Career* RNVR 1955-59; chartered accountant, ptnr Hillier Hills Frary & Co 1962, memb cncl Inst of Chartered Accountants 1980; ptnr Arthur Young 1981; chm Bd of Govrs Ashton Middle Sch, vice chm Ashton Schs Fndn Dunstable, pres of Beds Bucks and Herts Soc of Chartered Accountants 1975-76 (memb mgmnt ctee 1971-); tstee and tres Friends of Luton Parish Church, vice pres Luton Town FC; memb Worshipful Co of Chartered Accountants; Freeman City of London; FCA 1958, ATII 1964; *Recreations* golf, soccer, athletics; *Clubs* Farmers, Dunstable Downs Rotary, Ashridge GC; *Style*— C Bygrave, Esq; The Rustlings, Valley Close, Studham, Dunstable, Beds (☎ 0582 872070); St Nicholas House, 15/17 George St, Luton Beds (☎ 0582 410011, fax 0582 452127, telex 826574 AYLU)

BYGRAVES, Max Walter William; OBE (1983); s of Henry Walter (d 1974), and Lilian Mary (d 1985); *b* 16 Oct 1922; *Educ* St Joseph's London; *m* 1942, Blossom Mary; 1 s (Anthony b 1947), 2 da (Christine b 1943, Maxine b 1953); *Career* fitter RAF 1940-45; performed as entertainer shows for troops; turned professional 1946, has appeared all over world; 11 Royal Command Performances; 29 Gold Disc recordings; host Family Fortunes TV show; *Books* I Wanna Tell You a Story (1976), The Milkman's on his Way (1977), After Thoughts (1988); *Recreations* golf, travel, short story writing; *Clubs* St James, East India, RAC; *Style*— Max Bygraves, Esq, OBE; 32 Stafford Mansions Place, SW1 (☎ 01 828 4595)

BYLLAM-BARNES, Joseph Charles Felix Byllam; s of Cyril Charles Byllam-Barnes (d 1976), of Boothby House, Ashtead, Surrey, and Barbara Isabel, *née* Walls; *b* 30 August 1928; *Educ* The Modern Sch Streatham, Shaftesbury, City of London Freemen's Sch; *m* 1 April 1978, Maureen Margaret Mary, da of Maj Claude Montague Castle, MC (d 1940), of Hampstead, London; *Career* RAMC 1946-49, i/c Mil and Public Health Servs Eritrea 1948-49; with Barclays Bank plc 1945- (inspr 1940-76, head office inspr 1976-); vice pres Farringdon Ward Club; memb: cncl City Livery Club, cncl Royal Soc of St George City of London Branch, Utd Wards Club of the City of London, Ward of Cheap Club, Guild of Freeman of the City of London; local covenant organiser RC Diocese of Arundel and Brighton, Oblate of Quarr Abbey 1963; fell: Chartered Inst of Bankers, Inst of Financial Accountants; Freeman: City of London 1983, Worshipful Co of Upholders 1984 (tres 1985, Ct of Assts 1986); FCIB, FIFA; *Recreations* music, opera, walking, study of Law and Theology; *Clubs* Guards Polo, City Livery Yacht, Surrey County Cricket; *Style*— Joseph Byllam-Barnes, Esq; Walsingham House, Oldfield Gardens, Ashtead, Surrey; 16/17 Old Bailey, London EC4M 7DN (☎ 01 489 1998, fax 01 248 5875, telex 884670 INSPBB G)

BYNG, Hon Julian Francis; yr s of 7 Earl of Strafford (d 1984), by his 1 w; *b* 3 May

1938; *Educ* Eton; *m* 1, 1966 (m dis 1983), Ingela Brita, da of Axel Berglund, of Stockholm; 2 s (Francis b 1968, Alexander b 1973); m 2, 1984, Prudence Mary, da of Albert Edward Delany (d 1980), of Qld, Australia, and former w of David Kent; *Career* Capt Queen's R Rifles (TA); *Clubs* Boodle's; *Style—* The Hon Julian Byng; 8, Elm Park Rd, London SW3 6BB (☎ 01 351 4750)

BYNG, Julian Michael Edmund; assumed surname of Byng by Deed Poll 1952 in lieu of his patronymic, and was granted Royal Licence to bear the arms of Byng 1969 in accordance with the Will of his grandfather the 6th Earl of Stafford; s of Capt Michael William Millicent Lafone (d 1966), of Lusaka Turf Club N Rhodesia, by his first w, Lady (Florence) Elizabeth Alice Byng (resumed her maiden surname by Deed Poll 1952, in accordance with her father's will and d 1987), da of 6 Earl of Strafford; descended from Adm Sir George Byng (1 Viscount Torrington), Hon Robert Byng (Govr of Barbados), and FM Sir John Byng (1 Earl of Strafford, Col of Coldm Gds and Cdr of Gds Bde at Waterloo); *b* 20 Oct 1928; *Educ* Eton, Lausanne Univ, Kings Coll Cambridge; *m* 1960, Eve Finola, da of Captain Michael St Maur Wellesley-Wesley (d 1982), of Doon, Tahilla, Co Kerry; 3 s (Robert, Patrick, Thomas), 1 da (Georgiana); *Career* barr, farmer, thoroughbred breeder; landowner (in excess of 1000 acres); *Recreations* skiing, shooting; *Clubs* Brooks's, Jockey (Paris), Pratt's; *Style—* Julian Byng, Esq; Wrotham Park, Barnet, Hertfordshire EN5 4SB (☎ 01 449 1499)

BYNG, Rupert Wingfield; s of Leonard Harold Robert Byng (d 1974), of The Salutation, Sandwich, Kent, and Lady Mary Anne Denham, *née* Stuart; *b* 5 June 1946; *Educ* Harrow, New Coll Oxford (MA), Sorbonne; *m* 28 April 1987, Francesca, da of Arthur Ivor Stewart Liberty, MC TD, of The Lee, Bucks ; *Career* mangr Internation Dept, Joseph Sebag 1969-75, W I Carr & Sons (Overseas) 1981-86, dir int Equities Barclays De Zoete Wedd 1986-; Br Camelid Owners & Breeders Assoc; *Recreations* tennis, sailing, Alpaca breeding; *Clubs* Annabels; *Style—* Rupert W Byng, Esq; Langley Farm, Cowden, Kent; 17 Burton Ct, London, SW3; Barclays De Zoete Wedd, Ebbgate Hse, 2 Swan La, London, EC4 (☎ 01 623 2323)

BYNOE, Dame Hilda Louisa; DBE (1969); da of Thomas Joseph Gibbs, CBE, JP and Louisa, *née* La Touche; *b* 18 Nov 1921,Grenada,; *Educ* St George's Grenada, Roy Free Hosp Med Sch Univ of London, MB, BS 1951; *m* 1947, Peter Cecil Alexander Bynoe, ARIBA; former RAF Officer; 2 s; *Career* teacher St Joseph's Convents Trinidad and Grenada 1939-44, hospital and private practice London 1951-53, public service with Govt of Trinidad and Tobago 1958-65; govr of Associated State of Grenada WI 1968-74, chm Nat Fndn for Arts and Culture Trinidad and Tobago 1980-; patron Caribbean Women's Assoc 1970-; General Med Practice Port of Spain Trinidad 1975-; MRCS, LRCP; *Recreations* swimming, music, reading, poetry-writing; *Style—* Dame Hilda Bynoe, DBE; 5A Barcant Avenue, Maraval, Trinidad

BYRNE, Anthony John; s of Benjamin James Byrne, of Dublin, and Ruby Anne, *née* O'Brien (d 1975); *b* 9 August 1947; *Educ* Oakham Sch Rutland, Lancaster Univ, Colorado Univ, Sidney Sussex Coll Cambridge; *m* 5 Sept 1971, Kathy, da of Carl Strain, of Denver, Colorado; 2 da (Rachel, Jenny); *Career* PA to gen mangr Central Lancs Devpt Corpn 1973-77, Inst of Advanced Architectural Studies Univ of York 1977-78, dir Bicentenary of the Iron Bridge Ironbridge Gorge Museum Tst 1978-80, project dir Watershed Media Centre Bristol 1980-83, dir Bristol Mktg Bd 1983- 87, dir BAFTA; chm Sci-Tech Film and TV Festivals 1987 and 1989; tstee: Brunel Tst Temple Meads Bristol, Vivat Tst, Wildscreen Tst; Parly candidate (Lab) Rutland and Stamford 1972-74; *Style—* Anthony Bryne, Esq; 6 Kensington Place, Clifton, Bristol BS8 3AH; BAFTA, 195 Piccadilly, London W1V 9LG (☎ 01 734 0022)

BYRNE, Sir Clarence Askew; OBE (1964), DSC (1945); s of George Patrick Byrne (d 1931), of Brisbane, Queensland, and Elizabeth Emma, *née* Askew (d 1963); *b* 17 Jan 1903; *Educ* Brisbane Tech Coll; *m* 1928, Nellie Ann Millicent, da of late Hon A J Jones, MLA former Lord Mayor of Brisbane; 1 s, 1 da; *Career* dir of several companies concerned with: mining and oil exploration, uranium, insurance, engrg, ship building and construction; pres Queensland Chamber of Mines for 9 years, chm Queensland Alumina Ltd 1978-81; kt 1969; *see Debrett's Handbook of Australia and New Zealand for further details*; *Style—* Sir Clarence Byrne, OBE, DSC; Culverston, Dingle Ave, Caloundra, QLD 4551, Australia (☎ 071 91 1228)

BYRNE, John Napier; s of Christopher Thomas Byrne (d 1973), and Christian McDougall, *née* Napier; *b* 28 August 1953; *Educ* Bangor GS, Gonville and Caius Coll Cambridge (MA); *m* 16 may 1981, (Birgit) Marita, da of Arne Gotthard Westberg; 1 s (Daniel 1986); *Career* slr, joined Freshfields 1978 (ptnr 1985); Freeman City of London Slrs Co; *Clubs* Landsdowne; *Style—* J N Byrne, Esq; Grindall House, 25 Newgate St, London EC1 (☎ 01 606 6677, fax 01 248 3487/8/9)

BYRNE, Michael Sean Richmond; s of Kenneth Arthur Richmond Byrne, of Anglesey, and Beryl Margaret, *née* Halsall; *b* 31 May 1947; *Educ* Rydal Sch Colwyn Bay, Trinity Coll Dublin; *m* 7 March 1970, Pamela Kerry, da of Albert Ivor Roberts, of Wirral; 1 da (Melissa b 1973); *Career* banker (ret ill health); after Univ had cricket trials for Kent and Lancs, captained Cheshire Colts CC and played for Cheshire (capped 1969) and Ireland; AIB; *Recreations* golf, cricket; *Clubs* Royal Liverpool Golf, Cheshire CC, Cheshire Gents CC; *Style—* Michael S R Byrne, Esq

BYRNE, Hon Mrs; Hon Nona Georgette; *née* Lawrence; yst da of 3 Baron Lawrence (d 1947); *b* 10 Sept 1922; *Educ* F H S Graham Ter; *m* 8 Feb 1945, Wing Cdr Vincent George Byrne (d 1978), yst s of late James Byrne, of Malahide, Co Dublin; 5 s (Nicholas, James, Patrick, Dominic, Roy), 4 da (Teresa, Dierdre (decd), Clare, Fiona); *Career* chm Catholic Bldg Soc; *Clubs* RAF; *Style—* The Hon Mrs Byrne; West Broyle Place, Chichester, W Sussex PO19 3PL

BYROM, Richard John; JP (1973); s of Richard Byrom (d 1961), of Bury, and Bessie, *née* Jardin; *b* 12 Oct 1939; *Educ* Denstone Coll, Manchester Univ (BA Hons); *m* 4 April 1964, Susan Hope, da of Richard Clegg (d 1985), of Gwydir; 2 s (Peter b 1965, David b 1968), 1 da (Joy b 1967); *Career* sr ptnr Byrom Clark Architects Surveyors and Consulting Engineers Manchester 1985-; practicing arbitrator; cncl memb Incorporated Soc of Valuers and Auctioneers; chm Building Surveying Ctee 1986, Industrial Archaeologist; General Synod of The Church of England 1970-75; reader Hawkshaw Parish Church; memb Manchester Soc of Architects; RIBA, FCIArb, FSVA, FBIM; *Books* The Building Society Valuer (1979); *Recreations* industrial archaeology, antiquarian books; *Style—* Richard J Byrom, Esq, JP; 3 Hawkshaw Lane, Bury, Lancs BL8 4JZ (☎ 020 488 3110); Byrom Clark, The Building Centre, 115 Portland St, Manchester M1 6DW (☎ 061 236 9601, fax 061 763 1739, car tel 0836 603 521)

BYRON, Kathleen Elizabeth; *née* Fell; da of Richard John Fell (d 1981), of Herne Bay, Kent, and Eleanor Mary, *née* Macaree; *b* 11 Jan 1922; *Educ* GS, Old Vic Theatre Sch; *m* 1, 1944 (m dis 1951), Daniel John Bowen, s of D J Bowen (d 1955), of Atlanta, Georgia; m 2, 23 Sept 1953, Alaric Jacob, s of Col Harold Jacob, CSI (d 1937), of Aden; 1 s (Jasper Alexander b 2 July 1958), 1 da (Harriet Christina Mary b 20 April 1954); *Career* actress; entered profession 1946; films incl: Matter of Life and Death 1946, Black Narcissus 1947, Small Back Room 1948; TV incl: Emergency Ward 10 1961-64, Portrait of a Lady 1969, The Golden Bowl 1971, Dearly Beloved 1983; *Recreations* pottery; *Style—* Ms Kathleen Byron; 30 Glengall Rd, London SE15 6NN (☎ 01 231 9316)

BYRON, Pauline, Baroness; Pauline Augusta; *née* Cornwall; da of late T J Cornwall, of Wagin, W Australia; *m* 1931, 11 Baron Byron (d 1983); 1 da; *Style—* The Rt Hon Pauline, Lady Byron; 1/12 Mount Street, Claremont, WA

BYRON, 12 Baron (E 1643); Richard Geoffrey Gordon Byron; DSO (1944); s of late Col Richard Byron, DSO, who shares a common descent with the 6 Baron (the poet) from 4 Baron Byron; suc kinsman, 11 Baron, 1983; *b* 3 Nov 1899; *Educ* Eton; *m* 1926 (m dis 1946), Margaret Mary, only da late of Francis Gerald Steuart; m 2, 1946, Dorigen Margaret (d 1985), only da of Percival Kennedy Esdaile; 1 s (and 1 s decd); *Heir* s, Hon Robin Byron; *Career* Lt-Col 4/7 Royal Dragoon Gds (cmdg 1941-44), ADC to govr of Bombay 1921-22, mil sec to govr-gen and C-in-C New Zealand 1937; *Style—* The Rt Hon the Lord Byron, DSO; 62 Burton Court, London SW3 (☎ 01 730 2921)

BYRON, Hon Robert James; 2 (but only surviving) s and h of 12 Baron Byron by his 2 w, Dorigen Margaret, *née* Esdaile (d 1985); *b* 5 April 1950; *Educ* Wellington; *m* 1979, Robyn Margaret, da of John McLean, of Hamilton, NZ; 3 da (Caroline b 1981, Emily b 1984, Sophie b 1986); *Style—* The Hon Robin Byron; 19 Spencer Park, London SW18

BYRT, His Hon Judge Henry John; QC (1976); s of Albert Henry Byrt, CBE (d 1966), and Dorothy Muriel Thorne (d 1972); *b* 5 Mar 1929; *Educ* Charterhouse, Meston Coll Oxford; *m* 1957, Eve Hemione, da of Lt-Col Gordon McLaurin Bartlet (d 1964); 1 s (Charles b 1966), 2 da (Frances b 1962, Hermione b 1964); *Career* barr 1953; SE Circuit QC 1976, circuit judge 1983; vice-pres The Working Mens Coll 1978 (principal 1982-87), memb of Corporation 1978-, Queens Coll Harley St (memb of Cncl 1982-); pres of the Social Security Appeal Tribunals & Medical Appeal Tribunals 1983-; *Clubs* Leander; *Style—* His Hon Judge John Byrt, QC; 65 Gloucester Crescent, London NW1 7EG (☎ 01-485-0341); Almack House, 26-28 King Street, London SW1 (☎ 01-839-1621)

BYSTRAM, Charles Anthony; s of Baron Cyprian Bystram, sometime Col in Polish Army (d 1961); *b* 23 Dec 1929; *Educ* Douai Sch, Cambridge Univ; *m* 1958, Jean, da of Col Ian Hardie, DSO, RA; 1 s, 2 da; *Career* dir United Biscuits Hldgs 1972-85, md United Biscuits Int 1978-85 (dir gp corporate devpt 1980-83, dir external affairs 1983-85), chm Ortiz SA 1975-85; dir: Lewmar plc 1985-87, Stakis plc 1987-; chm Geest plc 1986-; *Recreations* travel, food and wine, various sports; *Style—* Charles Bystram, Esq; 53 Drayton Gdns, London SW10, (☎ 01 373 8840); Geest plc, White House Chambers, Spalding, Lincs, (☎ 0775 61111)

BYWATER, James Edward; s of Elam Bywater; *b* 22 May 1921; *Educ* Morley GS Yorks; *m* Margaret, da of Leonard Fry; 1 da; *Career* engineering; dir Ford of Britain 1965, chm and chief exec Sime Darby Hldgs 1975, chm Thermal Syndicate 1980; dir: Associated Biscuits 1979-83, Varity Hldgs Ltd 1983-; *Recreations* archaeology, prehistory; *Clubs* Oriental; *Style—* James Bywater, Esq; 27 Park CLose, Old Hatfield, Herts

C

CABARRUS; *see*: de Cabarrus

CABBELL MANNERS, Hon Richard Neville; s of 4 Baron Manners, MC (d 1972), and Mary Edith, *née* Gascoyne-Cecil; *b* 4 April 1924; *Educ* Eton; *m* 14 July 1945, Juliet Mary, eldest da of Lt-Col Sir Edward Hulton Preston, 5 Bt, DSO, MC (d 1963), of Beeston Hall, Neatishead, Norwich; 3 s, 1 da; *Career* farmer; *Recreations* hunting; *Style*— The Hon Richard Cabbell Manners; Cromer Hall, Cromer, Norfolk (☎ 2506)

CABLE, Sir James Eric; KCVO (1976), CMG (1967); s of Eric Grant Cable, CMG (d 1970), and Nellie Margaret, *née* Skelton; *b* 15 Nov 1920; *Educ* Stowe, CCC Cambridge; *m* 1954, Viveca, da of Dr Ragnar Hollmerus, of Helsinki; 1 s; *Career* entered Foreign Office 1947, asst under-sec of state FCO 1972-75, ambassador to Finland 1975-80, ret; writer on International Relations and Naval Affairs; *Style*— Sir James Cable, KCVO, CMG; c/o Lloyds Bank, 16 St James's St, London SW1

CABLE-ALEXANDER, Margaret, Lady; Margaret Mabel; da of late John Leopold Burnett, of Dublin; *m* 1941, as his 2 w, Sir Desmond William Lionel Cable-Alexander, 7 Bt (d 1988); 2 da (Jacqueline (Mrs Dillon Godfrey Welchman) b 1942, Susan (Mrs Richard Humphrey Hardwicke) b 1948); *Style*— Margaret, Lady Cable-Alexander; c/o Barclays Bank, Cocks Biddulp Branch, 16 Whitehall, London SW1

CABLE-ALEXANDER, Lt-Col Sir Patrick Desmond William; 8 Bt (UK 1809), of the City of Dublin; s of Sir Desmond William Lionel Cable-Alexander, 7 Bt (d 1988), and his 1 w Mary Jane, *née* O'Brien; *b* 19 April 1936; *Educ* Downside, RMA Sandhurst; *m* 1, 1961 (m dis 1976), Diana Frances, eldest da of late Col Paul Heberden Rogers, of Bushey, Herts; 2 da (Melanie Jane b 1963, Louise Fenella b 1967); m 2, 1976, Jane Mary, da of Dr Anthony Arthur Gough Lewis, MD, FRCP, of York; 1 s (Fergus William Antony b 1981); *Heir* s, Fergus William Antony Cable-Alexander b 19 June 1981; *Career* former Lt-Col Royal Scots Dragoon Guards (Carabiniers and Greys), cmmnd 1956, serv BAOR, UK, Aden, Army Staff Coll 1967, asst mil attaché Saigon 1968-70, BAOR, MOD, Nat Defence Coll 1975-76, cmd Duke of Lancaster's Own Yeomanry 1978-80, Chief of Staff HQ NW Dist 1981-83, ret 1984; bursar and clerk to the cncl Lancing Coll 1984-; *Recreations* the arts, painting, gardening, cricket, reading; *Style*— Lt-Col Sir Patrick Cable-Alexander; Windrush House, Hoe Court, Lancing, W Sussex BN15 OQX

CABORN, Richard George; MP (Lab) Sheffield Central 1983-, MEP (Lab) Sheffield 1979-; s of George and Mary Caborn; *b* 6 Oct 1943; *Educ* Hurlfield Comprehensive Sch, Granville Coll of Further Education, Sheffield Polytechnic; *m* 1966, Margaret; 1 s, 1 da; *Career* engineer; convenor of shop stewards Firth Brown Ltd 1967-79; *Style*— Richard Caborn, Esq, MP, MEP; 29 Quarry Vale Rd, Sheffield (☎ 0742 393802); office: 54 Pinstone St, Sheffield S1 2HN (☎ 0742 737947)

CABOT, (Richard) Murray de Quetteville; s of Dr Philippe Sidney de Quetteville Cabot, of Totnes, Devon; *b* 20 June 1936; *Educ* Dartington Hall, Emmanuel Coll Cambridge (BA); *m* 1960, Janet, da of James MacGibbon, of Manningtree; 1 s, 2 da; *Career* vice chm W & A Gilbey Ltd 1976-82; dir: IDV Export Ltd 1976-82, marketing London Business Sch 1982-85; asst v-pres Brown-Forman Int Ltd 1985-; memb Worshipful Co of Distillers; *Recreations* tennis, sailing, skiing; *Clubs* Royal Harwich Yacht; *Style*— Murray Cabot, Esq; 44 Courthope Rd, London NW3 (☎ 01 485 2755; work 01 439 6531)

CACCIA, Hon Mrs Antonia Catherine; da of Baron Caccia (Life Peer); *b* 25 Feb 1947; *m* 1970 (m dis 1974), Barton Midwood, 1 s (Jacob b 1972); *Style*— The Hon Mrs Antonia Caccia; 21 Westwood Rd, Barnes, SW13

CACCIA, Baron (Life Peer UK 1965); Harold Anthony Caccia; GCMG (1959), KCMG (1950, CMG 1945, GCVO 1961, KCVO 1957); s of Anthony Mario Felix Caccia, CB, MVO (d 1962, s of Fabio Caccia, of a Tuscan family long politically active (they are mentioned in Dante's Inferno canto 29; Count Alessandro Caccia, whose arms were recorded 1576, was an ancestor of Lord Caccia) by his w and 1 cous, Fanny Theodor Birch (d 1960), da of Azim Salvador Birch, of Pudlicote House, Oxon and later of Erewhon, NZ, an area from which Samuel Butler derived the setting for his homonymous novel); *b* 21 Dec 1905; *Educ* Eton, Trinity Oxford (Hon Fellow 1963), Queens' Oxford (Hon Fellow 1974); *m* 1932, Anne Catherine, o da of late Sir George Lewis Barstow, KCB, of Chapel House, Builth Wells, by his w Hon Enid Lilian Lawrence, da of 1 Baron Trevethin; 1 s, 2 da; *Career* joined Foreign Office 1929, dep under-sec of State 1949 and 1954-56, ambass to Austria 1951-54 (pres Anglo-Austrian Soc), Washington 1956-61, permanent under-sec FO 1962-65, head of Diplomatic Serv 1964-65, ret; provost of Eton 1965-77; chm ITT (UK) Ltd to 1982, dir Prudential Assurance Co Ltd, National Westminster Bank, F & C Eurotrust; Lord Prior of the Order of St John of Jerusalem 1969-80; pres of MCC 1973-74; GCStJ; *Style*— The Rt Hon the Lord Caccia, GCMG, KCMG, CMG, GCVO, KCVO; Abernant, Builth-Wells, Powys, Wales LD2 3YR (☎ 098 23 233)

CADBURY, Sir George (Adrian) Hayhurst; s of Laurence John Cadbury, OBE (d 1982), of Birmingham, and Joyce, *née* Mathews, OBE; *b* 15 April 1929; *Educ* Eton, King's Coll Cambridge (MA); *m* 1956, Gillian Mary, da of Edmund Drane Skepper (d 1962), of Neuilly-sur-Seine, France; 2 s, 1 da; *Career* chm: Cadbury Gp 1965-69, Cadbury Schweppes plc 1975- (dep chm and md 1969-74); dir: Bank of England 1970-, IBM (UK) Ltd 1975-; memb Covent Garden Market Authority 1974-; chm: W Midlands Economic Planning Ctee 1967-70, CBI Economic and Financial Policy Ctee 1974-80, Food and Drink Industries Cncl 1981-83; chllr Aston U 1979-; Hon DSc (Aston) 1973; Freeman City of Birmingham 1982; chm PRO NED (Promotion of non-exec dirs) 1984-, Hon DSc (Cranfield) 1985, Hon LLD (Bristol) 1986; vice-pres Birmingham Chamber of Industry and Commerce, pres Soc of Business Economists; CBIM, FIPM, Hon FInstM; kt 1977; *Recreations* Boodle's, Hawks, Leander; *Style*— Sir Adrian Cadbury; Rising Sun House, Baker's Lane, Knowle, Solihull, W Midlands B93 8PT (☎ 021 458 2000)

CADBURY, Kenneth Hotham; CBE (1974), MC (1944); s of Joel Hotham Cadbury, of Birmingham; bro of Michael Hotham Cadbury, *qv*; *b* 19 Feb 1919; *Educ* Bootham Sch York, Birmingham Univ; *m* 1, 1944 (m dis 1964), Margaret Rosamund King; 1 s, 1 da; m 2, Marjorie Iris Lille; 3 da; *Career* asst princ Post Office 1946, princ Cabinet Office 1950-53, sr dir Planning and Purchasing Post Office 1970, asst md Telecommunications 1976-; *Style*— Kenneth Cadbury, Esq, CBE, MC; Pendle, Burdenshott Hill, Worplesdon, Surrey (☎ Worplesdon 2084)

CADBURY, Michael Hotham; DL (W Midlands 1975); s of Joel Hotham Cadbury, of Birmingham; bro of Kenneth Hotham Cadbury, *qv*; *b* 16 Dec 1915; *Educ* Leighton Park Sch Reading, Munich and Freiburg Us; *m* 1939, Margaret Heather, *née* Chambers; 2 s, 1 da; *Career* former dir Cadbury Bros Ltd, Friends Ambulance Unit 1940-46, American Relief for France 1945-46, dir Friends Provident Life Office 1950-75; elected memb Council Nat Tst 1978, vice pres Birmingham Branch English Speaking Union 1975, pres Scout Assoc Birmingham 1981, tstee Selly Oak Colleges 1975, chm Friends of Birmingham Museum and Art Gallery 1983; Gold Medal Birmingham Civic Soc 1984; High Sheriff W Midlands 1974; cncl Winston Churchill Memorial Tst, pres Birmingham Assoc Youth Clubs 1987; *Style*— Michael Cadbury, Esq, DL; 54 Ramsden Close, Selly Oak, Birmingham B29 4JX

CADBURY, Peter Egbert; s of Sir Egbert Cadbury, DSC, DFC, JP, DL (d 1967), and Mary Forbes, *née* Phillips (d 1968); gs of George Cadbury, founder of Cadbury Bros, Bournville; *b* 6 Feb 1918; *Educ* Leighton Park Sch, Trinity Coll Cambridge (MA) ; *m* 1, 13 Dec 1947 (m dis 1968), (Eugenie) Benedicta, da of late Maj Ewen Cameron Bruce, DSO, MC, of Montpelier Gdns, Cheltenham, and former w of St John Donn-Byrne; 1 s (Justin Peter b 13 April 1951), 1 da ((Eugenie Mary) Felicity (Mrs Michael Wigan) b 14 Dec 1948); m 2, 1970 (m dis 1976), Jennifer Victoria, da of Maj Michael William Vernon Hammond-Maude, of Amerdale House, Arncliffe, Yorks, and former w of Capt David Gwyn Morgan-Jones, The Life Guards; 1 s (Joel Michael b 28 July 1971); m 3, 1976, Angela Jane, *née* Thoyts, former w of Humphrey Mead, of Moyaux, Normandy; 2 s; *Career* experimental test pilot 1941-45; contested (Lib) Stroud 1945; barr Inner Temple 1946-54; exec chm of various cos 1954-71: Keith Prowse Ltd, Ashton & Mitchell, Alfred Hays 1954-71, Westward Television 1960-80, Air Westward 1976-78, Prowest Ltd, Preston Estates, George Cadbury Tst 1979-, Westward Travel Ltd 1981-84, Educnl Video Index Ltd 1982-; Freeman City of London 1946, Liveryman Curriers' Co 1946; *Recreations* flying (Cessna 340 'G-Pete', Helicopter (Squirrell) 'G-Jany'), sailing (express 55' motor cruiser 'Colinette VI'), golf, tennis, shooting, travelling; owner of racehorses: Cool Million, Egbert, Westward Lad, Westward Ho; *Clubs* MCC, Buck's, Royal Motor Yacht, RAF Yacht, Island Sailing; *Style*— Peter Cadbury, Esq; Armsworth Hill, Alresford, Hampshire SO24 9RJ (☎ 0962 734656); 42 Cadogan Sq, London SW1 (☎ 01 589 8755)

CADBURY, Peter Hugh George; 3 s of (John) Christopher Cadbury, of Beaconwood, Rednal, nr Birmingham, by his 1 w, Honor Mary (d 1957), *née* Milward; *b* 8 June 1943; *Educ* Rugby; *m* 1969, Sally, er da of Peter Frederick Strouvelle, of Cape Town, S Africa; 1 s (Simon b 1975), 1 da (Eleanor b 1973); *Career* slr; dir Morgan Grenfell; *Clubs* City of London; *Style*— Peter Cadbury, Esq; Morgan Grenfell & Co Ltd, 23 Great Winchester St, London EC2 (☎ 01 588 4545)

CADDICK, Col Godfrey Armstrong; OBE (1952), TD (1948, DL (Staffs 1953, W Midlands 1974)); s of Charles John Caddick, MD, FRCS(E) (d 1939), of Sotik, Kenya; *b* 31 May 1912; *Educ* Malvern, Emmanuel Cambridge; *m* 1941, Kathleen Marcelle, MRCVS, da of Stanley Bourne Jagger, of Walsall, Staffs; 2 s, 1 da; *Career* slr, 1937; private practice, 1937-77; *Style*— Col Godfrey Caddick, OBE, TD, DL; Rydal, 62 Streetly Lane, Sutton Coldfield (☎ 021 353 7585)

CADDY, David Henry Arnold Courtenay; s of Colonel John Caddy, of Ivy House, Highgate Village, London N6, and Elizabeth, *née* Day; *b* 22 June 1944; *Educ* Eton; *m* 24 July 1971, Valerie Elizabeth Margaret, da of Dr Kelly Swanston, of Tillypronie, Mill Lane, Helmsley, N Yorks; 1 s (Julian b 1972), 1 da (Henrietta b 1978); *Career* articled to Layton Bennett Billingham and Co London 1962-68, CA 1968, Coopers and Lybrand 1968-, ptnr Liberia 1974, managing ptnr Liberia 1974-77, ptnr UK 1977-; ctee memb: London Soc of CAs 1980; memb: ICAEW 1968-, ICA (Ghana) 1983-, ICA (Nigeria) 1983-; *Recreations* golf, swimming, walking, reading, theatre; *Clubs* Boodles, Leander; *Style*— David Caddy, Esq; Oakfield House, Station Rd, Wargrave, Berks RG10 8EU (☎ 0735 22 2502); Coopers and Lybrand, Harman House, 1 George St, Uxbridge UB8 1QA (☎ 0895 73305, fax 0895 56413, car 0860 710730, telex 887470)

CADE, David Patrick Gordon; s of Richard William Poole Cade, FCA, of Lyme Regis, Devon, and Mabel *née* Norah; *b* 17 Nov 1942; *Educ* The Leys Sch, Queens' Coll Cambridge Univ (MA hons econ); *m* 18 June 1966, Julia Christine, da of Commander William Percy Cooper, OBE, of Guildford, Surrey; 2 da (Heather b 1969, Angela b 1973); *Career* fell Institute of Chartered Accountants in England and Wales 1967; ptnr: Arthur Anderson & Co Chartered Accountants 1976-; FCA 1967; *Recreations* sailing, music; *Clubs* RAC; *Style*— David Cade, Esq

CADELL, Alan Henry; s of Lt- Col John George Cadell, DSO (d 1950), of South Ct, Finchamstead, Berks, and Muddlebridge Hse, Fremington, Barnstaple, Devon, and Clara Margaret Annie, *née* Hunt (d 1963); *b* 2 Feb 1926; *Educ* Marlborough, Clare Coll Cambridge; *m* 27 Aug 1960, Valentine Frances, da of Charles Ernest St John Evers, OBE, of Bell Cottage, Bury Gate, nr Pulborough, Sussex; 1 s (Andrew b July 1966), 1 da (Iona b Feb 1969); *Career* Lt The Royal Scots 1945-48; trainee accountant McClelland Kerr 1950, CA 1952, Peat Marwick Mitchell & Co 1952-55 (a year spent in Sinapore), Scruttons plc 1955-86 (fin dir 1971-86); Freeman City of London, Liveryman of the Worshipful Co of Gunmakers 1966; *Recreations* shooting, dog handling, beagling, sailing; *Clubs* Utd Oxford and Cambridge, Bembridge SC, Keyhaven YC; *Style—* Alan Cadell, Esq; Heatherside, Bennetts Lane, Burley, nr Ringwood, Hants BH24 4AT

CADELL, Air Cdre Colin Simson; CBE (1944); s of late Lt-Col John Macfarlane Cadell, DL, JP, MB, CM, IMS, of Foxhall, Kirkliston, W Lothian, and Avoncrook, Stirling; *b* 7 August 1905; *Educ* Merchiston, Edinburgh Univ, Ecole Supérieur de l'Electricité Paris (MA AMIEE); *m* 1939, Rosemary Elizabeth, da of Thomas Edward Pooley, of Victoria, BC, Canada; 2 s (*see* Ian Victor Cadell), 1 da; *Career* Air Cdre RAF, ret; md International Aeradio Ltd 1947-58; chm Edinburgh Airport Consultative Ctee 1972-83; DL Linlithgowshire 1963-72, vice-lieut W Lothian 1972-, memb Roy Co of Archers (HM The Queen's Body Guard for Scotland); Legion of Merit (USA) 1943; *Clubs* New Club; *Style—* Air Cdre Colin Cadell, CBE; 2 Upper Coltbridge Terrace, Edinburgh EH12

CADELL, Ian Victor; s of Air Cdre Colin S Cadell, CBE (*qv*); *b* 3 July 1940; *Educ* Eton; *m* 11 Oct 1966, Teresa, da of Philip German-Ribon; 2 s (Piers b 1970, Charlie b 1978), 2 da (Olivia b 1968, Lucy b 1981); *Career* chm: MCP Hldgs Ltd, Mining & Chemical Products Ltd, MCP Electronic Materials Ltd, MCP-Peko Ltd; memb Roy Co of Archers (The Queen's Body Guard for Scotland); *Clubs* New (Edinburgh); *Style—* Ian Cadell, Esq; Foliejon Park, Winkfield, Berks; Alperton, Wembley, Middx HA0 4PE (☎ 01 902 1191)

CADELL, Vice-Adm Sir John Frederick; KBE (1983); s of Henry Dunlop Mallock Cadell, and Violet Elizabeth, *née* Van Dyke; *b* 6 Dec 1929; *Educ* RNC Dartmouth; *m* 1958, Jaquetta Bridget Nolan; 1 s, 2 da; *Career* dir-gen Naval Personal Services 1979-81, COS to Commander Allied Naval Forces Southern Europe 1982-85; dist gen mangr Canterbury and Tranet Health Authority; *Recreations* skiing, tennis; *Style—* Vice Adm Sir John Cadell, KBE; 6 St Martins Rd, London SW9

CADELL OF GRANGE, William Archibald; DL (W Lothian 1982); el s of Col Henry Cadell, OBE, JP (d 1967), HM Lord-Lt for W Lothian 1952-63, and Christina Rose, *née* Nimmo; descended from William Cadell, burgess of Haddington, b 1668 and sr rep of the family of Cadell of Grange and Banton and formerly of Banton and Cockenzie; *b* 9 Mar 1933; *Educ* Merchiston, Trin Coll Cambridge (MA), London Poly (Dip); *m* 1960, Mary-Jean, da of Cdr Arthur Harold Carmichael, RN (ret), of Gozo, Malta; 3 s (John, Patrick, Benjamin); *Career* former Lt RE; architect in private practice with related occupation of estate mgmnt; RIBA, FRIAS; *Style—* William Cadell of Grange, DL; Grange, Linlithgow, W Lothian EH49 7RH (☎ 0506 842946)

CADIEUX, Hon Léo; PC (1965), OC (1975); s of Joseph E Cadieux and Rosa Paquette; *b* 28 May 1908; *Educ* Quebec; *m* 1962, Monique, da of Placide Plante; 1 s; *Career* journalist 1930-44, Canada MP 1962-70, min of Nat Defence 1967-70, ambass to France 1970-75; *Style—* Hon Léo Cadieux, PC, OC; 20 Driveway, Appt 1106, Ottawa, Canada

CADMAN, Hon James Rupert; yr s of 2 Baron Cadman (d 1966); *b* 9 June 1944; *Educ* Harrow; *Style—* The Hon James Cadman; Overlands, 157 Church Rd, Combe Down, Bath, Somerset

CADMAN, 3 Baron (1937 UK); John Anthony Cadman; s of 2 Baron Cadman (d 1966); *b* 3 July 1938; *Educ* Harrow, Selwyn Coll Cambridge, RAC Cirencester; *m* 1975, Janet, da of Arthur Hayes, of Morecambe; 2 s (Hon Nicholas, Hon Giles Oliver Richard b 5 Feb 1979); *Heir* s Hon Nicholas Anthony James Cadman b 18 Nov 1977; *Career* farmer; *Style—* The Rt Hon The Lord Cadman; Heathcourt House, Ironmould Lane, Brislington, Bristol, BS4 5RS, Avon (☎ Bristol 775706

CADMAN, Kenneth John; o s of Herbert (d 1957), and Phyllis, *née* Knaggs; da of Sir Samuel William Knaggs Govr of Trinidad; nephew of 1 Baron Cadman; *b* 31 August 1925; *Educ* Berkhamsted Sch, Queens Univ Belfast (BSc Civil Eng, MICE); *m* 1, 12 March 1953, Marie, da of David R Bates, JP; 1 s (James b 1964), 1 da (Janet b 1960); m 2, 23 May 1980, Inger, da of Dr Med Eric Mogensen (d 1957); *Career* flying offr RAF WWII; dir Robert M Douglas Hldgs plc 1978-, md Rapid Metal Devpts Ltd; MICE; *Recreations* gliding, pres of the coventry gliding club; *Clubs* Priory Tennis; *Style—* Kenneth J Cadman, Esq; 27 Barlows Rd, Edgbaston, Birmingham 15 (☎ 021 455 7433); Rapid Metal Developments Ltd, Stubbers Green Rd, Aldridge, Staffs (☎ 0922 743 743)

CADMAN, Marjorie, Baroness; Marjorie Elizabeth; *née* Bunnis; da of Byron William Bunnis; *m* 1936, 2 Baron Cadman (d 1966); 2 s (3 Baron, Hon James Cadman); *Style—* The Rt Hon Marjorie, Lady Cadman; Overlands, 157 Church Rd, Combe Down, Bath, Somerset

CADMAN, Hon Mrs (Sybil Mary); yr da of 1 Baron Cadman, GCMG, FRS (d 1941); *b* 1916; *m* 1, 1938, Maj-Gen William Pat Arthur Bradshaw, CB, DSO, late Scots Gds (d 1966), s of Arthur Bradshaw; 2 s, 2 da; m 2, 1968, her 1 cous James Simon Cadman (whose 1 w was Kathleen, da of Sir John Ferguson, KBE, MP), o son of James Cadman, DSC, JP, DL (d 1947), of Walton Hall, Staffs; *Style—* The Hon Mrs Cadman; Rhagatt Hall, Corwen, Clwyd LL21 9HY

CADOGAN, Hon Anna-Karina; da of Viscount Chelsea (s and h of 7 Earl Cadogan), and Philippa Dorothy Bluet, *née* Wallop (d 1984); *b* 4 Feb 1964; *Educ* St Mary,s Sch Wantage, Bryanston, St Andrews Univ; *Style—* The Hon Anna-Karina Cadogan; Marndhill, Ardington, Wantage, Oxon (☎ 0235 833273)

CADOGAN, Peter William; s of Archibald Douglas Cadogan (d 1947), of Newcastle-on-Tyne, and Audrey, *née* Wannop (d 1978); *b* 26 Jan 1921; *Educ* Kings Sch Tynemouth, Kings Coll Newcastle-on-Tyne, Newcastle Univ (BA, Dip Ed); *m* 1949 (m dis) 1969, Joyce, da of the late William Stones, MP for Ansett; 1 da (Claire b 1950); *Career* WWII Coxswain RAF Air Sea Rescue Service served Orkneys, D Day Arnhem 1941-46; with Atlas Assur Co Ltd 1936-40, undergraduate 1946-51; hist teacher: Kettering 1951-53, Cambridge 1953-65; sec Nat Ctee of 100 1965-68; fdg sec Save Biatra Campaign 1968-70, gen sec Place Ethical Soc 1970-81, extra mutral lectr Univ of London 1981-; fdr E W Peace People 1978, co-chm Anglo-Afghan circle 1986, memb Cncl of the Gandhi Fndn; *Books* Early Radical Newcaster (1975), Direct Democracy (1976), writer of many acad and polemical papers; *Recreations* gardening, social inventions; *Style—* Peter Cadogan, Esq; 3 Hinchinbrook House, Greville Row, London NW6 5UP (☎ 01 328 3709)

CADOGAN, Lady (Mary) Veronica; *née* Lambart; er da of late 11 Earl of Cavan (d 1950); *b* 12 April 1908; *m* 1934, Col Edward Henry Cadogan, CBE, late Royal Welch Fusiliers, o son of Lt-Col Henry Osbert Samuel Cadogan, Royal Welch Fusiliers (ka 1914); 3 s (Henry Michael Edward b 1935, Alexander John b 1937, Oliver Roger b 1946); *Style—* Lady Veronica Cadogan; Field Head, Hollywood Lane, Lymington, Hants

CADOGAN, 7 Earl (1800 GB) William Gerald Charles Cadogan; MC (1943), DL (County of London 1958); also Baron Cadogan of Oakley (GB 1718), Viscount Chelsea (GB 1800), and Baron Oakley of Caversham (UK 1831); s of 6 Earl (d 1933), and Lilian (d 1973), *née* Coxon, who m 2, 1941, Lt-Col H E Hambro; the name Cadogan, of Welsh origin, was spelt Cadwgan to *c* 1600; *b* 13 Feb 1914; *Educ* Eton, Sandhurst; *m* 1, 1936 (m dis 1959), Hon Primrose Yarde-Buller, da of 3 Baron Churston and sis of Viscountess Camrose, Denise Lady Ebury (ex-w of 5 Baron) and Lydia, Duchess of Bedford (ex-w of 13 Duke); 1 s, 3 da; m 2, 1961, Cecilia, da of Lt-Col Henry K Hamilton-Wedderburn, OBE; *Heir* s, Viscount Chelsea; *Career* Capt Coldstream Guards (rtd), Lt Col Royal Wiltshire Yeomanry (TA); patron of four livings; pro grand master of United Grand Lodge of Freemasons 1969-82; landowner, mayor of Chelsea 1964, chm Cadogan Estates Ltd and subsidiaries 1935-; *Style—* The Rt Hon the Earl Cadogan, MC, DL; 28 Cadogan Sq, London SW3 2RP (☎ 01 730 4567); Snaigow, Dunkeld, Perthshire (☎ 073 871 223)

CADWALLADER, Anthony Robin; s of F A Cadwallader, and M K Cadwallader, *née* Stone; *b* 16 June 1944; *Educ* King Edward II GS Lichfield; *m* 26 May 1973, Mary Gwendoline, da of Rev Kenneth C Sawyer (d 1986); 1 s (Martin Anthony b 1976), 1 da (Tina Mary b 1974); *Career* md Cadwallader Ltd 1971-, dir Cadwallader (Metal Fittings) Ltd 1979-; past pres Midland Reg Assoc of Shopfitters; exec memb Nat Assoc of Shopfitters; ACIS; *Recreations* family, computer programming; *Style—* Anthony R Cadwallader, Esq; 119 Beacon Street, Lichfield, Staffs WS13 7BG (☎ 0543 254494); Cadwallader Ltd, 400 Aldridge Road, Perry Barr, Birmingham B44 8BJ (☎ 021 356 6211, fax 021 3566212)

CAESAR, Rev Canon Anthony Douglass; LVO (1987); s of Rev Canon Harold Douglass Caesar (d 1961), and Winifred Kathleen Caesar; *b* 3 April 1924; *Educ* Cranleigh Sch, Magdalene Coll Cambridge (MA, MusB), St Stephen's House Oxford; *Career* Flying Offr RAF 1943-46; asst music master Eton Coll 1948-51, precentor Radley Coll 1952-59, asst curate St Mary Abbots Kensington 1961-65, asst sec ACCM 1965-70, chaplain Roy Sch of Church Music 1965-70, dep priest-in-ordinary to HM The Queen 1967-68, priest-in-ordinary 1968-70, resident priest St Stephen's Church Bournemouth 1970-73; precentor and sacrist Winchester 1974-79, residentiary canon 1976-79, Honorary Canon 1979-; sub-dean of HM Chapels Roy, deputy clerk of the Closet and sub-almoner, domestic chaplain to HM The Queen 1979-; FRCO; *Style—* The Rev Canon Anthony Caesar, LVO; Marlborough Gate, St James's Palace, London SW1 (☎ 01 930 6609)

CAFFIN, Albert Edward; CIE (1947), OBE (1946); s of Claud Carter Caffin (d 1971), of Southsea, and Lilian Edith Caffin; *b* 16 June 1902; *Educ* Portsmouth; *m* 1929, Hilda Elizabeth, da of Walter George Wheeler; *Career* joined Indian Police 1922; asst inspector-gen Poona 1939, cmmr of police Bombay, 1947 (formerly dep cmmr); *Style—* Albert Caffin, Esq, CIE, OBE; C22 San Remo Towers, Sea Road, Boscombe, Bournemouth, Dorset (☎ 0202 36408)

CAFFIN, (Arthur) Crawford; s of Charles Crawford and Annie Rosila Caffin; *b* 10 June 1910; *Educ* King's Sch Rochester; *m* 1933, Mala Pocock; 1 da; *Career* slr 1932, former ptnr R L Frank & Caffin Truro, rec of the Crown Ct 1972-82; *Style—* A Crawford Caffin, Esq; Cove Cottage, Portloe, Truro

CAFFYN, Brig Sir Edward Roy; KBE (1963), CBE (1945, OBE 1942, CB 1955, TD 1950, JP (Eastbourne 1948, E Sussex 1960), DL (Sussex 1956)); s of Percy Thomas Caffyn, of Hay Tor, Eastbourne; *b* 27 May 1904; *Educ* Eastbourne Coll, Loughborough Coll; *m* 1, 1929 (m dis 1945), Elsa Muriel, da of William Henry Nurse, of Eastbourne; 2 s; m 2, 1946, Delphine Angelique, da of Maj William Chilton-Riggs; *Career* dir Mech Engrg Field Marshal Montgomery's Staff 1943-45; chm Sussex TAFA 1947-67, vice chm cncl TAFA 1961-66; v-chm E Sussex CC 1967, chm Sussex Police Authority 1971-74; pres Caffyns 1981- (chm to 1981); *Style—* Brig Sir Edward Caffyn, KBE, CB, CBE, OBE, TD, JP, DL; Norman Norris, Vines Cross, Heathfield, E Sussex (☎ 043 53 2674)

CAFFYN, Robert James Morris; s of Sir Sydney Morris Caffyn, CBE (1976), and Annie, *née* Dawson; *b* 1 June 1935; *Educ* Eastbourne Coll, Peterhouse Cambridge (MA); *m* 1961, Gillian Mabel Ann, *née* Bailey; 1 s, 2 da; *Career* jt md Caffyns plc 1972-; hon tres: Free Church Federal Cncl 1976-82, Br Cncl of Churches 1982-; FCA; *Style—* Robert Caffyn, Esq; Field House, Old Willingdon Rd, Friston, nr Eastbourne, E Sussex (☎ 032 15 3100)

CAHILL, Christina Tracy,; *née* Boxer; da of Raymond Walter Boxer, and Joan Eleanor, *née* Almond; *b* 25 Mar 1957; *Educ* Yateley Comprehensive, Loughborough Univ of Technol (BSc, PGCE); *m* 27 Sept 1986, Séan Cahill, s of Robert Cahill, of Leeds; *Career* middle distance runner, Cwlth Games 1982 Gold Medallist 1500m, Olympic Games 1984 sixth place 1500m, Europa Cup 1985 Silver Medallist 1500m, Olympic Games 1988 fourth place 1500m; formerly Br record holder: 800m, 1500, mile; hon life memb Br Sports Assoc for the Disabled; *Recreations* athletics, gardening, birdwatching, walking, countryside pubs; *Clubs* Gateshead Harriers; *Style—* Mrs Christina Cahill; Student Services (Sport & Recreation), Sunderland Poly Sports Centre, Chester Road, Sunderland SR1 3SD (☎ 091 5140831 ext 8)

CAHILL, John Conway; s of Francis Conway Cahill (d 1969), of London, and Dorothy Winifred, *née* Mills; *b* 8 Jan 1930; *Educ* St Pauls Sch; *m* 5 July 1956, Giovanna (Vanna) Caterina, da of Riccardo Lenardon, (d 1972), of Valvasone, Italy; 3 da (Karen Lavina b 5 May 1961, Ann Catherine b 6 Dec 1963, Mary Elizabeth b 24 March 1965); *Career* Nat Serv 1948-50; BTR Industs Ltd: joined 1955, dep overseas gen mangr 1963, dir 1968, dep md 1975; vice pres BTR Inc USA 1976, pres and chief exec BTR Inc 1976, chm BTR Pan American Ops 1979, chief exec BTR plc 1987; *Recreations* tennis, reading, walking, music; *Style—* John Cahill, Esq; BIR plc, Silvertown House, Vincent Sq, London SW1P 2PL (☎ 01 821 3700, 01 821 3701, fax 01 834 2279, telex 22524)

CAHILL, Michael Leo; s of John Cahill, MBE (d 1980), and Josephine, *née* Bergonzi (d 1964); *b* 4 April 1928; *Educ* Beaumont Coll, Magdalen Coll Oxford (MA); *m* 1961, Harriette Emma Clemency, da of Christopher Gilbert Eastwood, CMG (d 1983), of Oxfordshire; 2 da (Lydia b 1964, Jessica b 1967); *Career* civil servant (FO colonial office and overseas dvpt admin), UK permanent delegate to UNESCO 1972-74, head of Central and Southern Africa Dept, overseas dvpt admin 1983-; chm Woldingham Sch

Parents' Assoc 1981-83; *Recreations* history of art, pianism; *Style—* Michael Cahill, Esq; 9 Murray Rd, London SW19 4PD (☎ 01 947 0568); Overseas Development Administration, Eland House, Stag Place, London SW1E 5DH (☎ 01 213 3000)

CAHILL, Michael Melland; s of Brig Michael John Cahill, OBE, KHS (d 1968), of Coachford Co Cork, and Joan, *née* Melland (d 1965); *b* 18 Sept 1927; *Educ* Winchester, Trinity Coll Dublin (MA, LLB); *m* 11 Aug 1972, Jean Alma, da of Allister Jackson Charles Mackenzie Lowe (d 1959), of Alexandria, Egypt; *Career* Lt Irish Guards 1945-48; called to the Bar Middle Temple 1953-64; asst co sec and communications offr Express Dairy 1955; chm Henry Melland Ltd (publishers) 1965-; fndn fell Br Assoc of Indust Eds 1966 (senator 1972-81), winner Industl Ed's Trophy 1962; FAIE; *Recreations* word-processing, swimming, spoiling pets; *Style—* Michael Cahill, Esq; Bourton Orchard, Penselwood, Wincanton, Somerset BA9 8LL (☎ 0747 840423); Henry Melland Ltd, 23 Ridgmount St, London WC1E 7AH (☎ 01 636 3529)

CAHILL, Teresa Mary; da of Henry Daniel Cahill, of Rotherhithe (d 1948), and Florence, *née* Dallimore (d 1964); *b* 30 July 1944; *Educ* Notre Dame HS Southwark, Guildhall Sch of Music & Drama (AGSM Piano, LRAM Singing), London Opera Centre; *m* 1971 (m dis 1978), John Anthony Kiernander; *Career* opera and concert singer: Glyndebourne debut 1969, Covent Garden debut 1970; La Scala Milan 1976, Philadelphia Opera 1981, specialising in Mozart & Strauss; concerts: all the London orchestras, Boston Symphony Orchestra, Chicago Symphony Orchestra, Berlin Festival 1987, Vienna Festival 1983, Rotterdam Philharmonic 1984, Hamburg Philharmonic 1985, West Deutscher Rundfunk Cologne 1985; promenade concerts BBC Radio & TV; recordings including Elgar, Strauss (and Mahler) for all major cos; recitals and concerts throughout Europe, USA and the Far East; Silver Medal Worshipful Co of Musicians, John Christie Award 1970; *Recreations* cinema, theatre, travel, reading, collecting antique furniture; *Clubs* Roy Overseas League; *Style—* Teresa Cahill; c/o Ibbs & Tillett, 18B Pindock Mews, Little Venice, London W9 2PY (☎ 01 286 7526)

CAHN, Sir Albert Jonas; 2 Bt (UK 1934), of Stanford-upon-Soar, Co Nottingham; s of Sir Julien Cahn, 1 Bt (d 1944); *b* 27 June 1924; *Educ* Harrow; *m* 1948, Malka, da of Reuben Bluestone (d 1961); 2 s, 2 da; *Heir* s, Julien Cahn; *Career* company dir, marriage guidance cnsllr; *Style—* Sir Albert Cahn, Bt; 10 Edgecombe Close, Warren Rd, Kingston-upon-Thames, Surrey (☎ 01 942 6956)

CAHN, Julien Michael; s and h of Sir Albert Cahn, 2 Bt; *b* 15 Jan 1951; *Educ* Harrow; *Style—* Julien Cahn, Esq

CAICEDO; *see*: de Caicedo

CAILLARD, Air Vice-Marshal (Hugh) Anthony; CB (1981); s of Col Felix Caillard, MC (d 1955), and Monica Yoland; mother, yr da of Count & Countess Riccardi-Cubitt, Italian title recognised as ranking as Viscountcy at Court of James by King Edward VII in 1903; *b* 16 April 1927; *Educ* Downside, Oriel Coll Oxford, RAF Coll Cranwell; *m* 20 Aug 1957, Margaret Ann, da of Kenneth Malcolm Crawford, Palm Beach, NSW, Australia; 4 s (Richard b 1958, Andrew b 1959, David b 1961, John b 1963); *Career* RAF 1945-82. ret as dir of operations central region air forces NATO; 1982 dir-general Brit Australia Soc, 1985 air adviser House of Commons Defence Ctee, chm Ex-Forces Fellowship 1987; *Recreations* gardening, travel; *Clubs* RAF, Royal Commonwealth, Royal Overseas League; *Style—* Air Vice-Marshal Anthony Caillard, CB; 114 Ashley Road, Walton on Thames KT12 1HW; Cleveland House, 19 James' Square, London SW1Y 4JG

CAIN, Sir Edward Thomas; CBE (1966); s of Edward Victor Cain and Kathleen Teresa, of Maryborough, Queensland; *b* 7 Dec 1916; *Educ* Nudgee Coll Qld, Qld Univ; *m* 1942, Marcia Yvonne, da of N F Parbery, of Canberra; 1 s, 1 da; *Career* commissioner of Taxation Australia 1964-76; kt 1972; *Style—* Sir Edward Cain, CBE; 99 Buxton St, Deakin, Canberra, Australia (☎ 811462)

CAIN, John Clifford; s of William John Cain (d 1940), and Florence Jessie, *née* Wood (d 1975); *b* 2 April 1924; *Educ* Emanuel Sch, London Univ (BSc, MSc), Open Univ (BA); *m* 1954, Shirley Jean, da of Edward Arthur Roberts, of Amblecote, Brierley Hill, West Midlands; 2 da (Charlotte, Susannah); *Career* RAF Aircrew Fl Sgt 1943-47; mathematics and science teacher 1950-59, science museum lectr 1959-61, asst head sch of bdcasting Assoc Rediffusion 1961-63, BBC prodr and sr prodr 1963-71, asst head Further Educn Television BBC 1971-72 (head 1972-77), asst controller Educnl Bdcasting 1977-80, controller Pub Affairs BBC 1981-84, res historian BBC 1984-; chm Bdcasting Support Servs 1980-85, tstee 1985-, memb Health Educn Cncl 1977-83, dir Bdcasters Audience Res Bd 1982-84; memb: Royal Television Soc, BAFTA; *Books* Talking Machines (1961), Mathematics Miscellany (1966, with others), numerous articles and reviews; *Recreations* reading, music, gardening, theatre, study; *Style—* John Cain, Esq; 63 Park Rd, London W4 3EY (☎ 01 994 2712); BBC Bdcasting Ho, London W1 (☎ 01 927 4956)

CAIN, (Thomas) William; s of James Arthur Cain (d 1956), of IOM, and Mary Edith Cunningham Robertson, *née* Lamb (d 1965); *b* 1 June 1935; *Educ* Marlborough, Worcester Coll Oxford (BA, MA); *m* 25 Nov 1961, Felicity Jane, da of Rev Arthur Stephen Gregory, of Ivie Cottage, Kirk Michael, IOM; 2 s (Patrick Arthur b 18 June 1964, Simon Thomas Hugh b 10 July 1966) 1 da (Joanna Penelope b 14 Jan 1963); *Career* Nat Serv RAC 1953-55, cmmnd 2 Lt 1954, served Middle East 1954-55; called to the Bar Gray's Inn 1959, advocate Manx Bar with TW Cain & Sons Douglas IOM 1961-79, HM attorney gen IOM 1980-; pres IOM Law Soc 1986-; chm Manx Nature Conservation Tst 1973-, pres Friends of Manx Youth Orchestra; *Recreations* sailing; *Clubs* Ellan Vannin; *Style—* William Cain, Esq; Ivie Cottage, Kirk Michael, IOM (☎ 0624 87 266); Attorney General's Chambers, Government Office, Douglas IOM (☎ 0624 26 262 ext 2000)

CAINE, Michael (né Maurice Joseph Micklewhite); s of late Maurice Micklewhite and Ellen Frances Marie Micklewhite; *b* 14 Mar 1933; *Educ* Wilson's GS Peckham; *m* 1, 1955 (m dis), Patricia Haines; 1 da; m 2, 1973, Shakira Baksh; 1 da; *Career* actor in TV, theatre, films; *Style—* Michael Caine, Esq; c/o Jerry Pam, 120 El Camino Drive, Beverly Hills, Calif 90212, USA

CAINE, Sir Michael Harris; s of Sir Sydney Caine, KCMG, *qv*; *b* 17 June 1927; *Educ* Bedales, Lincoln Coll Oxford, George Washington Univ (Washington DC); *m* 1, 1952 (m dis 1987), Janice Denise, *née* Mercer; 1 s (Richard b 24 Nov 1955), 1 da (Amanda b 7 Feb 1954); m 2, 1987, Emma Harriet Nicholson, MP (*qv*), da of Sir Godfrey Nicholson, 1 Bt; *Career* RNAS 1945-47; joined Booker plc 1952, dir 1964-, ch exec 1975-79, chm 1979-; memb Independent Broadcasting Authority 1984-; dir Cwlth Devpt Corpn 1985-; memb: Cncl Inst of Race Relations 1962-72, Cncl of Bedford Coll London 1966-85; chm: management ctee Booker Prize for Fiction 1972-, Cncl for Technical Educ and Training for Overseas Countries (TETOC) 1973-75, Cncl UK Cncl for Overseas Student Affairs 1979-86, Cncl Royal African Soc 1984-, Cwlth Scholarship Cmmn in UK 1987-; memb governing body: Inst of Devpt Studies Sussex 1975-, Nat Inst of Economic & Social Research 1979-, Queen Elizabeth House Oxford 1983-; CBIM, FRSA; kt 1988; *Recreations* reading, gardening; *Clubs* Reform; *Style—* Sir Michael Caine; c/o Booker plc, Portland House, Stag Place, London SW1E 5AG (☎ 01 828 9850, fax 01 630 8029, telex 88169)

CAINE, Sir Sydney; KCMG (1947), CMG (1945); s of Harry Edward Caine, of St Bees, Church Grove, Little Chalfont, Bucks, and Jane Harker, *née* Buckley; *b* 27 June 1902; *Educ* Harrow County Sch, LSE; *m* 1, 1925, Muriel Ann (d 1962), da of Abner H Harris, MA, of 18 Hervey Close, N3; 1 s (Michael Harris Caine, *qv*); m 2, 1965, Doris Winifred (d 1973), da of Walter Folkard, of Forest Gate, Essex; m 3, 1975, Elizabeth Crane, da of late J Crane Nicholls, and widow of Sir Eric Bowyer, KCB, KBE; *Career* dir LSE 1957-67, served Colonial Off 1940-48, Treasury 1948-51; *Books* Foundation of the London School of Economics (1963), British Universities; Purpose and Prospects (1969); *Clubs* Reform; *Style—* Sir Sydney Caine, KCMG, CMG; Buckland House, Tarn Rd, Hindhead, Surrey

CAIRNCROSS, Sir Alec (Alexander Kirkland); KCMG (1967), CMG (1950); 3 s of Alexander Kirkland Cairncross (d 1948), of Lesmahagow, Lanark, and Elizabeth Andrew Cairncross; *b* 11 Feb 1911; *Educ* Hamilton Acad, Glasgow Univ, Cambridge (PhD); *m* 1943, Mary Frances, da of Maj Edward Francis Glynn, TD (d 1948), of Ilkley; 3 s, 2 da; *Career* economic advsr to HM Govt 1961-64, head Govt Econ Service 1964-69; master St Peter's Coll Oxford 1969-78; chllr Glasgow Univ 1972-; *Recreations* travelling, writing; *Style—* Sir Alec Cairncross, KCMG, CMG; 14 Staverton Rd, Oxford (☎ 0865 52358)

CAIRNCROSS, Neil Francis; CB (1971); s of James Cairncross (d 1964), and Olive Hunter, *née* Amner (d 1969); *b* 29 July 1920; *Educ* Charterhouse, Oriel Coll Oxford (MA); *m* 26 July 1947, Eleanor Elizabeth, da of Herbert Walter Leisten (d 1927); 2 s (Ian b 1950, David b 1951), 1 da (Julia (Mrs Pearce) b 1948); *Career* served in Royal Sussex Regt 1940-45; barr Lincoln's Inn 1948; joined Home Office 1948, a private sec to Prime Minister 1955-58, sec Royal Cmmn on the Press 1961-62, dep sec Cabinet Office 1970-72, dep sec Northern Ireland Office 1972; dep under-sec of state Home Office 1972-80; memb: Parole Bd 1982-85, Home Grown Timber Advsy Ctee 1981-, Avon Probation Ctee (co-opted) 1983-; *Recreations* painting; *Clubs* United Oxford and Cambridge University; *Style—* Neil Cairncross, Esq, CB; Little Grange, The Green, Olveston, Bristol BS12 3EJ (☎ 0454 613060)

CAIRNS, Hon (Hugh) Andrew David; yr s of 5 Earl Cairns; *b* 27 August 1942; *Educ* Wellington, Trinity Coll Dublin (BA); *m* 1966, (Celia) Elizabeth Mary, da of Lt-Col Francis Cecil Leonard Bell, DSO, MC, TD, of Cross Glades, Chiddingfold, Surrey; 1 s, 1 da; *Career* banker; regnl dir Barclays Bank plc; dir United Services Tstee; *Recreations* shooting, fishing, golf; *Clubs* Pratt's, Royal St George's Golf; *Style—* The Hon Peter Cairns; Knowle Hill Farm, Ulcombe, nr Maidstone, Kent (☎ 0622 850240)

CAIRNS, 5 Earl (1878 UK); David Charles Cairns; GCVO (1972), (KCVO 1969, CB 1960); also Baron Cairns (UK 1867) and Viscount Garmoyle (UK 1878); s of 4 Earl Cairns, CMG (d 1946), and Olive (d 1952), da of late J P Cobbold, MP; *b* 3 July 1909; *Educ* RNC Dartmouth; *m* 1936, Barbara Jeanne Harrisson, da of late Sydney Harrisson Burgess, of Heathfield, Bowden, Cheshire; 2 s, 1 da; *Heir* s, Viscount Garmoyle; *Career* served RN, Rear Adm, ret; pres Navy League 1966-77, HM Marshal of Diplomatic Corps 1962-71, extra equerry to HM The Queen 1972-; *Style—* Rear Adm The Rt Hon The Earl Cairns, GCVO, KCVO, CB; The Red House, Clopton, nr Woodbridge (☎ Grundisburgh 262)

CAIRNS, David Howard; s of David Lauder Cairns, of Mulberry Road, Birmingham, and Edith Rose, *née* Cairns; *b* 4 June 1946; *Educ* Cheadle Hulme Sch, LSE (MSc); *m* 1 May 1980, Stella Jane, da of Stanley Cecil Askew, DSO, DFC; *Career* CA; Pannell Kerr Forster 1964-71, Carlsberg Brewery Ltd 1971-72, Black & Decker Ltd 1972-75; PD Leake fell LSE 1973-75, ptnr Stoy Hayward 1975-85; sec gen Int Accounting Standards Ctee 1985-, pres Thames Valley Soc CA's 1979-80; ACA 1969, FCA 1969, FBIM 1982; *Books* Current Cost Accounting after Sandilands (1976), Financial Times Survey of 100 Major European Companies Reports and Accounts (1979), Financial Times World Survey of Annual Reports (1980), Survey of Accounts and Accountants (1983-84); *Recreations* cricket, cycling, music; *Clubs* RAC; *Style—* David Cairns, Esq; Bramblewood, Turville Heath, Henley-on-Thames, Oxon RG9 6JY (☎ 049 163 296); International Accounting Standards Committee, 41 Kingsway, London WC2B 6YU (☎ 01 240 8781, fax 01 379 1148, telex 295177 IASC G)

CAIRNS, Air Vice-Marshal Geoffrey Crerar; CBE (1970), AFC (1960); s of James William Cairns, MD, BCh (d 1949), and Marion, *née* Crerar; *b* 21 May 1926; *Educ* Loretto, Gonville and Caius Coll Cambridge; *m* 1948, Carol (d 1985), da of Ivan Evernden (d 1979); 4 da (Madeline b 1949, Claudia b 1952, Catherine b 1960, Eliza b 1964); *Career* RAF 1944-80 (AVM), Cmdt A+AEE Boscombe Down 1971-74, asst chief of Air Staff (Operational Requirements) 1975-76; Cmdt Southern Maritime Air Region 1976-77, chief of Staff 18 Gp 1978-80; dir Trago Aircraft Ltd, defence conslt Marconi Avionics 1980-81; FRAeS (1979), FBIM; *Recreations* golf, music, railways; *Clubs* RAF; *Style—* Air Vice-Marshal Geoffrey Cairns, CBE, AFC; Powells Kenn, Exeter, Devon EX6 7UG (☎ 0392 832886); Orca Aircraft Ltd, Bodmin Airfield, Cardinham, Bodmin, Cornwall PL30 4BU (☎ 020 882 485/511)

CAIRNS, Lady; Helena; da of George McCullough; *m* 1944, Sir Joseph Foster Cairns, JP (d 1981, former Lord Mayor of Belfast and memb Senate of Northern Ireland); 1 s, 1 da; *Style—* Lady Cairns; c/o S Cairns Esq, Amaranth, Craigdarragh Rd, Helens Bay, NI

CAIRNS, Hon Hugh Sebastian Frederick; s and h of Viscount Garmoyle and gs of 5 Earl Cairns; *b* 26 Mar 1965; *Educ* Eton; *Style—* The Hon Hugh Cairns

CAIRNS, Dr James Ford; s of James John Cairns and Letitia, *née* Ford; *b* 4 Oct 1914; *Educ* Melbourne U; *m* 1939, Gwendolyn Olga Robb; 2 s; *Career* MHR (ALP) for Yarra 1955-69, for Lalor 1969-78, min for Overseas Trade 1972-74, Fed tres 1974-75, dep PM 1974-75, min for Environment 1975; author; *Books* The Eagle and the Lotus (1969), Silence Kills (1970), The Quiet Revolution (1972), Survival Now; numerous articles in journals and press; *Style—* Dr James Cairns

CAIRNS, Peter Granville; s of Maj H W Cairns, MC (gs of 1 Earl Cairns); *b* 3 Sept 1940; *Educ* Eton; *Career* Lt Royal Scots Greys, ret; banker; dir: Cater Ryder 1976-81, Cater Allen 1981-; *Recreations* fox-hunting; *Clubs* Turf, White's; *Style—* Peter

Cairns, Esq; 11 St Mary Abbots Court, London W14 (☎ 01 603 7356)

CAIRNS, Robert James; s of Robert Mons Cairns, of Birkenhead, and Rita Mary, *née* Crocker (d 1985); *b* 1 June 1951; *Educ* Wirral County GS, Univ of Sussex (BA); *m* 4 Nov 1971, Julia Ann, da of Leslie Miles Richardson, of Whickham, Newcastle upon Tyne; 2 da (Rebecca b 1972, Abby-Louise b 1979); *Career* branch mangr Britannia Bldg Soc 1980-83, dep gen mangr Cumberland Bldg Soc 1987- (asst sec 1983-86, asst gen mangr of admin and sec 1987); chm: Carlisle Area Bd of Young Enterprise, Northern Gp Chartered Bldg Socs Inst (memb ctee Cumberland centre); memb Round Table; FCBSI 1985; *Recreations* sport, music; *Style*— Robert Cairns, Esq; Allendale House, Armathwaite, Carlisle (☎ 06992 239); Cumberland Bldg Soc, Cumberland House, 38 Fisher St, Carlisle (☎ 0228 41341, fax 0228 25309)

CAIRNS, Dr Roger John Russell; s of Arthur John Cairns (d 1982), and Edith Ann, *née*, Russell (d 1979); *b* 8 Mar 1943; *Educ* Ranelagh Sch Berks, Durham Univ (BSc), Bristol Univ (MSc, PhD); *m* 20 July 1966, Zara Corry, da of Herbert Bolton (d 1970); 2 s (Nigel b 1969, Alistair b 1973), 1 da (Kirsten b 1975); *Career* oilfield water mgmnt BP 1978-81, planner Qatar Gen Petroleum Corpn 1981-83, tech and commercial dir Trafalgar House Oil & Gas Ltd 1983-; FRCS; memb: IOD, MENSA; *Recreations* wine making, tennis, reading, chess; *Style*— Dr Roger Cairns; High Larch, Lewis Lane, Chalfont Heights, Gerrard's Cross, Bucks SL9 9TS (☎ 01 724 5655, GX 885881); 20 Eastbourne Terr, London W2 6LE

CAIRNS, William James; s of Lt Col Robert William Cairns, MBE, TD, MA (d 1972), and Marjory Helen, *née* Dickson (d 1983); *b* 13 Mar 1936; *Educ* George Heriot's Edinburgh, Durham Univ (Dip Landscape Design), MIT (Master of City Planning); *m* 3 Oct 1962, Barbara Marjory, da of Lt Col George Stuart Russell, OBE, WS, CA, of 59 Braid Rd, Edinburgh; 1 s (Alastair b 1966), 1 da (Sarah b 1966 twin); *Career* Nat Serv: Royal Military Police, Cyprus 1954-56; TA 7/9 & 8/9 Bat The Royal Scots 1958-62 (Lieut); landscape architect, environmental planner; chief landscape architect Craigavon Dev Cmmn 1966-68, snr assoc Land Use Conslts London 1968-72, chm W J Cairns & Ptnrs Ltd (environmental conslts Edinburgh, Belfast, Manchester) 1972-87; Whitney fell MIT 1964-66, asst prof Univ of Georgia 1962-64, exec chm Int Cncl Oil & The Environment, ed North Sea Oil Environment Review, BBC design award, Assoc Preservation of Rural Scotland; FLI, FInstPet, FID, FRSA; *Recreations* golf, hill walking, gardening, skiing; *Clubs* New (Edinburgh), Scottish Arts, Bruntisfield Golfing Soc; *Style*— William Cairns, Esq; 32 Garscube Terr, Edinburgh EH12 6BR; 16 Randolph Crescent, Edinburgh EH3 7TT (☎ 031 225 3241, telex 72277, fax 031 225 5016)

CAITHNESS, 20 Earl of (S 1455); Malcolm Ian Sinclair; 15 Bt (S 1631); also Lord Berriedale (S 1592); s of 19 Earl of Caithness (d 1965), by his 2 w Madeleine Gabrielle, *née* de Pury; *b* 3 Nov 1948; *Educ* Marlborough, RAC Cirencester; *m* 1975, Diana Caroline, da of Maj Richard Coke, DSO, MC, DL (gs of 2 Earl of Leicester); 1 s, 1 da (Lady Iona b 1978); *Heir* s, Lord Berriedale, *qv*; *Career* a Lord in Waiting and Government whip 1984-85; under-sec for transport 1985-86, minister of state Home Office 1986-88, minister of state Dept of the Environment 1988-; FRICS; *Style*— The Rt Hon the Earl of Caithness; c/o The House of Lords, London SW1

CAKEBREAD, Frank Ingram; s of Alfred George Watson (d 1969), of London, and Dorothy Evelyn, *née* Cakebread (d 1929); *b* 15 Mar 1919; *Educ* Aldenham; *m* 1960, Berenice Mary, da of Col Hugh James Mortimer, MC (d 1955), of S Devon; 2 s (Nicholas b 1961, Robin b 1965), 2 da (Sally b 1963, Susan b 1966); *Career* WWII: 1 Bn Herts Regt 1939, cmmnd 1 Bn Beds & Herts Regt 1940, Egypt 8 Army Syrian Campaign 1941, trained LRDG Phantom Patrol 1942, Adj Capt Moascar Camp Egypt 1943-44, demob 1945; chm Savay Investmts Ltd 1950-, dep chm Cakebread Robey & Co plc 1962-87; Bucks county cncllr 1971-80, chm Bucks Assoc of Youth Clubs; memb Lloyds; memb Worshipful Co Builders Merchants; *Recreations* tennis, travel; *Style*— Frank Cakebread, Esq; Savay Farm, Denham, Bucks (☎ 0895 832262)

CAKOBAU, Ratu Sir George Kadavulevu; GCMG (1973), GCVO (1977, OBE 1953); s of Ratu Popi Epeli Seniloli Cakobau; descendant of King Cakobau of Fiji; *b* 1911; *Educ* Newington Coll Australia, Wanganui Technical Coll NZ; *m* 1, 1937, Adi Veniana Gavoka; m 2, 1956, Adi Seruwala Lealea Balekiwai; *Career* memb of Legislative Council of Fiji 1951-70, min Fijian Affairs and Local Govt 1970-71, min without Portfolio 1971-72, govr-gen Fiji 1973-83, KStJ 1973; *Style*— His Excellency Ratu Sir George Cakobau, GCMG, GCVO, OBE; Government House, Suva, Fiji

CALCUTT, David Charles; QC (1972); s of Henry Calcutt (d 1972), of Peterborough; *b* 2 Nov 1930; *Educ* Cranleigh, King's Coll Cambridge, Stewart of Rannoch Sch; *m* 1969, Barbara Ann, da of Vivian Walker (d 1965), of Fenny Stratford, Bucks; *Career* barr 1955, dep chm Somerset QS 1970-71, recorder 1972-, dept of Trade Inspr Cornhill Consolidated 1974-77; chm: Civil Service Arbitration Tribunal 1979-, Inst of Actuaries' Appeal Bd 1985-, Provincial Tribunal of Enquiry 1979, Falklands Islands Cmmn of Enquiry 1984, Cyprus Servicemen Inquiry 1985-86; master Magdalene Coll Cambridge 1986-, chllr dioceses of Exeter and Bristol 1971, Europe 1983, vice chm cncl Cranleigh and Bramley Schs 1983-, govr: SPCK 1980-, Blundells' Sch 1981-, Br Inst of Human Rights 1983-, dir Edington Music Festival 1956-64; memb: Criminal Injuries Compensation Bd 1977-, cncl of Tribunals 1980-86, Gen Cncl of the Bar 1968-72, Crown Ct Rules Ctee 1971-77, Senate of the Inns of Court and the Bar 1979-85 (chm of the Senate 1984-85, chm of the Bar 1984-85), UK Delgn Consultative Ctee Bars and Law socs EEC 1979-83; cncl RSCM 1967-, RCM 1980-, Colliery Ind Review Body 1985-; hon memb: American Bar Assoc 1985-, Canadian Bar Assoc 1985-; fell commoner Magdalene Coll Cambridge, fell Int Acad of Trial Lawyers (NY); *Recreations* living on Exmoor; *Clubs* Athenaeum, New (Edinburgh); *Style*— David Calcutt, Esq, QC; Magdalene Coll, Cambridge; Lamb Building, Temple, London EC4

CALDECOTE, 2 Viscount (UK 1939); Sir Robert (Robin) Andrew Inskip; KBE (1987), DSC (1941); s of 1 Viscount Caldecote (Rt Hon Sir Thomas Walker Hobart Inskip, CBE, d 1947), and Lady Augusta Orr Ewing (d 1967), wid of Charles Orr Ewing, MP, and er da of 7 Earl of Glasgow; *b* 8 Oct 1917; *Educ* Eton, King's Coll Cambridge (MA), RNC Greenwich; *m* 22 July 1942, Jean Hamilla, da of Rear Adm Hugh Dundas Hamilton (d 1963); 1 s, 2 da; *Heir* s, Hon Piers James Hampden Inskip; *Career* served RNVR 1939-45; chm: EDC Movement of Exports 1965-72, Export Cncl for Europe 1970-71, Design Cncl 1972-80, Delta Gp plc 1972-82, Legal and General Gp 1977-80, BBC Gen Advsy Cncl 1982-85, Investors in Indust Gp plc 1980-87, Mary Rose Tst 1983-; dir: Eng Electric Co 1953-69, Br Aircraft Corpn 1960-69 (dep md 1961-67), Consolidated Gold Fields 1969-78, Lloyds Bank 1975-88, W S Atkins Ltd 1985-; pres: Parly and Scientific Ctee 1966-69, Fellowship of Engrg 1981-86, Royal Inst Naval Architects 1987-; memb: Review Bd for Govt Contracts 1969-76, Inflation Accounting Ctee 1974-75, Engrg Industs Cncl 1975-82, BR Bd 1979-85, advsy cncl for Applied Research and Devpt 1981-84, Engrg Cncl 1982-85; pro-chllr Cranfield Inst of Technol 1976-84; fell: King's Coll Cambridge 1948-55 (and lectr in engrg), Eton Coll 1953-72; tstee: Princess Youth Business Tst 1986-, Church Urban Fund 1987-; FEng, Hon FIEE, Hon FICE, Hon FIMechE, FRINA, Hon FSIAD 1976; Hon DSc: Cranfield, Aston, Bristol, City; Hon LLD London, Cantab; *Recreations* sailing (yacht 'Citara III'), shooting, golf; *Clubs* Pratt's, Royal Yacht Sqdn, Royal Ocean Racing, Royal Cruising, Athenaeum; *Style*— The Rt Hon Viscount Caldecote, KBE, DSC; Orchard Cottage, South Harting, Petersfield, Hants (☎ 073 085 264); Office: 91 Waterloo Rd, London SE1 8XP (☎ 01 928 7822, telex 917844)

CALDECOTT, (John) Andrew; s of Sir Andrew Caldecott, GCMG, CBE (d 1951), and Olive Mary, *née* Inness (d 1943); *b* 25 Feb 1924; *Educ* Eton, Trinity Coll Oxford (BA); *m* 7 July 1951, Zita Ursula Mary, da of Capt Peter Belloc, RM (ka 1941); 3 s (Andrew b 1952, Rupert b 1953, Dominic b 1956), 1 da (Mary b 1957); *Career* Capt KRRC 1942-46, served in Italy and Greece; admitted slr 1951; ptnr Druces and Attlee 1955-69, dir Kleinwort Benson 1970- (vice-chm 1974-83); chm M & G Gp plc; dir: Kleinwort Benson Gp plc, Blue Circle Industs plc, Whitbread & Co plc, Chloride Gp plc, Blick plc; memb Bank of England Bd of Supervision; *Recreations* fishing, music; *Clubs* Boodle's; *Style*— Andrew Caldecott, Esq; 137B Ashley Gardens, Thirleby Rd, London SW1P 1HN; 20 Fenchurch St, London EC3P 3DB (☎ 01 623 8000, telex 888531)

CALDER, Dr Allan Balfour; s of Alexander Angus Calder (d 1986), of Crewe, and Jane Calder, *née* Balfour (d 1973); *b* 13 Sept 1920; *Educ* Montrose Acad, St Andrews Univ (Bsc), Edinburgh Univ (PhD); *m* 6 Nov 1954, (Janet) Netta Kerr, da of William Law Cockburn Scullion (d 1969), of Linlithgow; 2 da (Mary b 1955, Jane b 1955); *Career* metallurgical chemist Colvilles Ltd Motherwell 1943-47, sr spectroscopist Edinburgh and East of Scotland Coll of Agri 1947-56, sr analyst Br Titan Products Co Ltd Billingham 1956-57, sr lectr in inorganic chemistry Newcastle upon Tyne Poly 1957-81; former elder and lay preacher Jesmond Utd Reform Church; fell Victoria Inst; CChem, FRSC 1954, FIS 1959; *Books* Photometric Methods of Analysis (1969), Statistics from Modern Methods of Geo-chemical Analysis (contrib chptr Statistics, 1971); papers: Operational Statistics in Instrumental Analysis (1961), The Use of Discriminant Functions in Biological Sampling (1961), How Substances are Formed (1966), The Use of Nomograms in Purity Control Analysis (1968),; *Recreations* walking, listening to music; *Style*— Dr Allan Calder; 8 Crossway, Jesmond, Newcastle upon Tyne NE2 3QH (☎ 091 281 4424)

CALDER, Hon Allan Graham Ritchie; 3 s of Baron Ritchie-Calder, CBE (d 1982); *b* 4 Jan 1944; *Educ* Ewell Tech Coll, Birkbeck Coll London Univ (BSc, PhD); *m* 1, 1967, Anne Margaret, da of Robert Allan Wood; 1 s; m 2, 1983, Lilian Lydia, da of Edward Godfrey; *Career* commercial balloon pilot and mathematician; asst prof: Carlton U Ottawa 1970-71, Louisiana State U 1971-72, Univ of Missouri 1975-76; lecturer in mathematics: Univ of Essex 1972-73, Birkbeck Coll 1972-83; assoc prof New Mexico State U 1979-81; chief pilot: Sunrise Balloons California 1981-82, Bombard Soc France 1983- (sr pilot 1982); *Recreations* classic cars, sailing, hot air ballooning; *Clubs* Savile, Bentley Drivers, Porsche GB, Br Balloon and Airship; *Style*— The Hon Allan Calder; Château de Laborde, 21200 Beaune, France (☎ 80 22 51 61); Roy Bank of Scotland, 15 Kingsway, London WC2

CALDER, Barry Clifford; s of George Cruickshank Calder (d 1935), of Stonehaven, Kincardineshire, and Evangeline *née* Turton (d 1964); *b* 15 Dec 1922; *Educ* Mackie Acad Stonehaven, Andover GS Coll of Estate Mgmnt; *m* 3 Sept 1949, Sheila Avis da of Percy Charles Wells (d 1959), of London NW8; 1 s (Neil Timoth John b 1960), 1 da (Sara Elizabeth b 1961); *Career* Armament Des Dept Miny of Supply Fort Halstead Sevenhoaks kent, articled to FW Charity, started own practice 1949 (which now has o/s in London, Manchester, Glasgow, Edinburgh, Chichester, Sawbridgeworth with assoc o/s in Belfast & Dublin); former: tres Mod Pentathlon Assoc of Great Br, pres bldg surveyors div RICS 1980-81, hon memb American Soc of Home Inspectors 1980; Freeman City of London 1970; memb: Worshipful Co of Horners 1972, Worshipful Co of Surveyors 1979; FRICS 1949, ACIArb 1983, FFB 1970, MRSH 1950, FRIBA; *Recreations* riding, gardening, philately; *Clubs* City Livery, Royal Scottish Automobile; *Style*— Barry Calder, Esq; Scearnbank, Kent Hatch Rd, Crockham Hill, Edenbridge, Kent, TN8 6SZ (☎ 0883 722233); Calder Ashby, Rochester House, Belvedere Rd, London SE19 2HL (☎ 01 653 8866, fax 01 771 8612)

CALDER, Hon Isla Elizabeth Ritchie; *née* Calder; resumed surname of Calder by deed poll; yr da of Baron Ritchie-Calder (Life Peer), CBE (d 1982); *b* 7 Sept 1947; *Educ* Nonsuch Co Sch Cheam, St George's Edinburgh, Froebel Inst of Education; *m* 1971 (m dis 1983), Alan Evans; *Career* business consultant; *Style*— The Hon Isla Calder

CALDER, John; DL (West Lothian 1976); s of late John Calder; *b* 11 July 1914; *Educ* Morgan Acad Dundee, Univ Coll Dundee, Edinburgh Univ; *m* 1940, Vida Campbell, *née* Carmichael; 1 s, 1 da; *Career* slr; co clerk W Lothian CC 1950-75, dist govr Rotary Int Dist 102 1962-63; Hon Sheriff Substitute of the Sheriffdom of the Lothians and Peebles, pres W Lothian Area Scouts; Verdienstkreuz am Bande (FDR) awarded by Bundespräsident Dr Karl Carstens 1983; *Style*— John Calder, Esq, DL; Woodlands, 8 Dundas St, Bo'ness, W Lothian EH51 0DG (☎ 0506 822311)

CALDER, John Mackenzie; s of James Calder, of Ardargie, Forgandenny, Perthshire, and Lucianne Wilson; *b* 25 Jan 1927; *Educ* McGill Univ, Sir George Williams Coll, Zürich Univ; *m* 1, 1949, Mary Ann Simmonds; 1 da; m 2, 1960 (m dis 1975), Bettina Jonic; 1 da; *Career* publisher, ed, author; fndr and md John Calder (Publishers) Ltd 1950-, dir of other associated publishing and opera cos; co-fndr Def of Lit and the Arts Soc, chm Fedn of Scottish Theatres 1972-74; contested (Lib): Kinross and W Perthshire 1970, Hamilton 1974, Centl Scotland (Euro election) 1979; Chev des Arts et des Lettres, chev Ordre de Mérite Nat; FRSA; *Books* ed: A Samuel Beckett Reader, Beckett at 60, The *Nouveau Roman* Reader, Gambit International Drama Review, William Burroughs Reader, Henry Miller Reader As No Other Dare Fail: For Samuel Beckett on his 80th Birthday; author The Defence of Literature, fiction and plays; *Clubs* Caledonian, Scottish Arts; *Style*— John Calder, Esq; John Calder (Publishers) Ltd, 18 Brewer St, London W1R 4AS (☎ 01 734 3786)

CALDER, Michael John; s of Geoffrey Charles Calder, Dulwich (d 1974), and Mary Patricia Calder (d 1982); *b* 28 Nov 1931; *Educ* Dulwich, Christ Church Oxford (MA); *m* 10 June 1965, Sheila, da of Herbert Maughan (d 1962), of Sunderland; 2 s (James b

1966, Andrew b 1968); *Career* Lt RA 1950-56; Shell 1956-57; CA 1959-; sr ptnr W J Calder, Sons & Co (gs of fndr), FCA; *Recreations* music, travel, cricket; *Clubs* Travellers; *Style—* Michael Calder, Esq; 42 Carson Rd, Dulwich, London SE21 8HU (☎ 01 670 6207); W J Calder Sons & Co, 25 Lower Belgrave St, London SW1W 0LS (☎ 01 730 8632, fax 01 730 7372)

CALDER, Hon Nigel David Ritchie; eldest s of Baron Ritchie-Calder, CBE (Life Peer, d 1982); *b* 2 Dec 1931; *Educ* Merchant Taylors', Sidney Sussex Coll Cambridge (MA); *m* 1954, Elisabeth, da of Alfred James Palmer; 2 s, 3 da; *Career* writer New Scientist 1956-66 (ed 1962-66); freelance author and TV scriptwriter; author of over 20 books; *Books Incl:* Einstein's Universe (1979), Nuclear Nightmares (1979), The Comet is Coming (1980), Timescale (1983), The English Channel (1986); *Recreations* sailing (ketch, 'Charmed'); *Clubs* Athenaeum, Cruising Assoc; *Style—* The Hon Nigel Calder; 8 The Chase, Furnace Green, Crawley, Sussex (☎ 0293 26693)

CALDERWOOD, Richard Johnston; s of Alistair Lawton Calderwood, DFC, AFC, of Aulaways, Zimbabwe, and Inex Annandale, *née* Johnston; *b* 18 April 1946; *Educ* St Stephen's Coll Bulaways Rhodesia; *m* 10 Sept 1976, Susan Elizabeth, da of David Basil Jones (d 1988), of Sevenoaks, Kent; 3 s (Alistair b 1977, William b 1978, Peter b 1982); *Career* articled clerk Coopers & Lybrand London, chief accountant and head of Corporate Finance Standard Merchant Bank of Rhodesia 1973-76, owner of professional CA firm 1983-; ACA 1970, FCA; *Recreations* sailing, flying; *Style—* Richard Claderwood, Esq; c/o Sun Alliance House, St George's Place, Canterbury, Kent CT1 1UW (☎ 0227 766666, fax 0227 766667)

CALDERWOOD, Robert; s of Robert Calderwood (d 1952), and Jessie Reid, *née* Marshall; *b* 1 Mar 1932; *Educ* Darrel HG Sch, William Hulme's Sch Manchester, Univ of Manchester (LLB); *m* 6 Sept 1958, Meryl Anne, da of David Walter Fleming (d 1977); 3 s (Robert b 1959, David b 1965, Iain b 1968), 1 da (Lyn b 1962); *Career* slr Supreme Ct of Judicature 1956; town clerk and cheif exec: Salford 1966-69, Bolton 1969-73, Manchester 1973-79; chief exec Strathclyde Regnl Cncl 1980-; UN Assocs, Discharged Pensioners Aid Orgns; dep pres NUS 1954, memb Parole Bd (England) 1971-73, memb advsy ctees on community rels and crime prevention for Sec of State for Scot; memb Glasgow Trades House; memb Indust Soc 1981, CBIM 1981, Companion Inst of Water and Envionmental Mgmnt 1987; *Recreations* walking, swimming, garden, reading, theatre; *Style—* Robert Calderwood, Esq; 6 Mosspark Ave, Milngavie, Glasgow G62 8NL (☎ 041 956 4585); Strathclyde Regional Council, 20 India St, Glasgow G2 4PF (☎ 041 227 3415, fax 041 227 2870, telex 77428)

CALDICOTT, Hon Sir John Moore; KBE (1963), CMG (1955); *b* 1900; *Educ* Shrewsbury; *m* 1945, Evelyn Macarthur; 1 s, 2 step da; *Career* farmer Rhodesia, MP Rhodesia Parliament Mazoe 1948, min of Economic Affairs 1958-62, then of the Common Market and of Finance, Fedn of Rhodesia and Nyasaland; *Style—* The Hon Sir John Caldicott, KBE, CMG; 24 Court Rd, Greendale, Harare, Zimbabwe

CALDIN, Prof Edward Francis Hussey; s of Edward Caldin (d 1951), and Agnes Mary, *née* Hussey (d 1948); *b* 05 Aug 1914; *Educ* St Paul's Sch, Queen's Coll Oxford (BA, MA, DPhil, DSc); *m* 17 April 1944, mary, da of Joseph Francis Parker (d 1960); 2 s (Hugh b 1946, Giles b 1948); *Career* armaments res dept Miny of Supply 1941-45; Univ of Leeds: lectr 1945-54, sr lectr 1954-64, reader 1964-65; Univ of Kent: reader 1965-66, prof of physical chemistry 1966-79, emeritus prof 1979-; memb Royal Soc of Chemistry; *Books* The Power and Limits of Science (1949), Science and Christian Apologetic (1953), Chemical Thermodynamics (1958), Fast Reactions in Solution (1964), The Structure of Physical Science (1961), Proton - Transfer Reactions (jt ed with V Gold 1975); *Style—* Prof Edward Caldin; c/o University Chemical Laboratory, Canterbury, Kent CT2 7NH

CALDOW, William James; CMG (1977); s of William Caldow (d 1981), and Mary Wilson Grier (d 1979); *b* 7 Dec 1919; *Educ* Marr Coll Glasgow Univ (MA), Sorbonne; *m* 1950, Monique Henriette, da of Gaétan Hervé, Chevalier de la Légion d' Honneur, memb of French Resistance (executed 1944); 2 s (Mark (d 1976), Charles); *Career* WWII 1940-45, serv: Scots Gds, Intelligence Corps, France, Belgium, Holland, Germany, demob Capt; Colonial Admin Serv Gold Coast, later Ghana 1947-59; War Off, later MOD 1959-80, conslt ICI plc 1981-86; *Recreations* reading, music, ornithology; *Clubs* Royal Commonwealth Soc, County (Guildford); *Style—* William James Caldow, Esq, CMG; Hillsboro, 3 Pilgrims Way, Guildford, GU4 8AB (☎ 0483 62183)

CALDWELL, Surg Vice Adm Sir (Eric) Dick; KBE (1969), CB (1965); s of late Dr John Colin Caldwell; *b* 6 July 1909; *Educ* Edinburgh Acad, Edinburgh U; *m* 1942, Margery Lee Abbott; *Career* medical dir-gen of RN 1966-69, former exec dir Medical Cncl on Alcoholism; CStJ; *Style—* Surg Vice Admiral Sir Dick Caldwell, KBE, CB; 9a Holland Park Rd, Kensington, London W14

CALDWELL, Edward George; s of Prof A F Caldwell, of Herts, and Olive Gertrude, *née* Riddle; *b* 21 August 1941; *Educ* St Andrews Singapore, Clifton, Worcester Coll Oxford (Jurisprudence Hons); *m* 1965, Bronwen Anne, da of Dr J A Crockett, of Oxford; 2 da (Bronwen (Lucy) b 1968, Sophie b 1971); *Career* slr Fisher Dowson and Wasbrough 1966, Law Cmmn 1967, office of the parly counsel, Law Cmmn 1974-76 and 1987-88; *Style—* Edward Caldwell, Esq; Office of the Parliamentary Counsel, 36 Whitehall, London SW1

CALDWELL, Maj-Gen Frank Griffiths; OBE (1953), MBE (1945, MC 1941 and Bar 1942); s of Maj William Charles Francis Caldwell, of Guernsey, and Violet Marjorie Kathleen Caldwell; *b* 26 Feb 1921; *Educ* Elizabeth Coll Guernsey, RMA Woolwich; *m* 1945, Betty Palmer, da of Capt Charles Palmer Buesden, of Bournemouth; 1 s, 1 da; *Career* cmmnd RE 1940, Col 1965, Brig 1966, Maj-Gen 1970, Engr-in-Chief 1970-72, Asst Chief Gen Staff 1972-74, ret 1974; Croix de Guerre, Croix de Guerre, Croix Militaire (Belgium) 1945; *Clubs* MCC, Army and Navy; *Style—* Maj-Gen Frank Caldwell, OBE, MBE, MC; Le Courtil Tomar, Rue des Pres, St Peters, Guernsey, C.I. (☎ 0481 65292)

CALDWELL, Prof John Bernard; OBE (1979); s of Dr John Revie Caldwell (d 1968), of Barkbooth, Winster, Cumbria, and Doris, *née* Bolland (d 1929); *b* 26 Sept 1926; *Educ* Botham Sch York, Liverpool Univ (B Eng), Bristol Univ (PhD); *m* 12 Aug 1955, Jean Muriel Frances, da of Leonard Francis Duddridge, of 6 Dene Garth, Ovingham, Northumberland; 2 s (Philip b 1959, Michael b 1961); *Career* shipbuilding apprentice Vickers-Armstrong 1943-48 (ship tech draughtsman 1948-49), res fell in naval architecture Bristol Univ 1953-55, sr sci offr then princ sci offr RN Scientific Serv 1955-60, asst prof of applied mechanics RNC Greenwich 1960-66, visiting prof MIT 1962-63; Univ of Newcastle Upon Tyne: prof and head of dept of naval architecture 1966-83, dean faculty of engrg 1983-86, head sch of marine technol 1975-80 and 1986-; visiting lectr: Norway 1969, Singapore 1970, Brazil 1973, SA 1974, Hong Kong 1975, Canada 1976, Egypt 1979, China 1980, Malaysia 1981, Yugoslavia 1985, Aust 1986, USA, Holland, Italy, Poland, Japan; David Taylor Medal American Soc of Naval Architects and Marine Engrs 1987; memb Tyne Port Authy 1973-75; non-exec dir: Nat Maritime Inst Ltd 1983-85, Marine Technol Directorate Ltd 1986-, Marine Design Conslts Ltd 1985-, Newcastle Technol Centre 1985-; memb Engrg Cncl 1988-; memb of various ctees for: MOD Def Sci Advsy Cncl; Dept of Energy, Offshore Energy Technol Bd, Dept of Indust, Dept of Tport Marine Div, DES SERC; memb tech ctee Lloyds Register of Shiping; memb Br Ship Res Assoc: naval architecture ctee, co-ordinating ctee on ship structures; RINA: memb cncl, gen purposes and fin ctee, chm educn and trg ctee; Int Ship and Ocean Structures Congress: UK memb of standing ctee, chm ctees on design philosphy superstructures and plastic analysis; chm W Euro Grad Educn in Marine Technol: exec ctee, annual conference; memb ed bd: Jl of Soc of Underwater Technol, Euro Shipbuilding Progress, Int Jl of Marine Structures; conslt for various marine orgns incl: Br Shipbuilders, MOD; author of numerous papers and articles on marine matters; Hon DSc Tech Univ of Gdansk Poland 1985; FRINA 1966 (Froude Medal 1984, pres 1984-87), MIStruct E 1966, F Eng (fndr memb) 1976, FNECInst 1977 (Gold Medal 1973 pres 1976-78), hon memb Soc of Naval Architects and Marine Engrs Singapore 1978; *Recreations* reading, listening, seeing, thinking; *Clubs* Nat Lib; *Style—* Prof John Caldwell, OBE; The White House, 18 Cadehill Rd, Stocksfield, Norhtumberland NE43 7PT (☎ 0661 843 445); University of Newcastle Upon Tyne, Newcastle Upon Tyne NE1 7RU (☎ 091 232 8511 ext 6722, fax 091 261 1182, telex 563654 UNINEW G)

CALDWELL, Dr (James) Richard; s of late James Caldwell, JP, of The White House of Speen, Aylesbury, Bucks, and late Anne Blanche, *née* Young; *b* 25 Feb 1916; *Educ* Uppingham (MB, BS), St Thomas's Hosp London; *m* 14 Feb 1948, Phyllis Doreen, da of late Geofrey Reynolds, of Nakuru, Kenya; 4 da (Janet, Nancy, Helen, Carol); *Career* WWII RAFVR 1939-45, served Europe, ME and FAR E (despatches); med practioner 1946-83; Hunterian gold medal 1963; memb: Mid-Sussex Hosp Mgmnt Ctee, E Sussex Local Med Ctee, E Sussex Fam Practioner Ctee, gen med ctee of BMA; Freeman City of London, Liveryman Worshipful Co of Shipwrights; FRCGP, BMA; *Recreations* gardening, being a grandfather; *Style—* Dr Dick Caldwell; Silver Birches, 26 Newick Hill, Newick, Sussex BN8 4QR (☎ 02572 2572)

CALDWELL, Wilfrid Moores (Bill); s of Col Wilfrid Caldwell (d 1935), and Mabel Gertrude, *née* Moores; *b* 14 Oct 1935; *Educ* Marlborough, Magdalene Coll Cambridge (MA); *m* 8 April 1972,Linda Louise, da of Robert Ian Hamish Sievwright (d 1978); 2 s (William b 1978, James b 1981), 1 da (Fiona b 1976); *Career* Nat Serv 2 Lt RA 1954-56, Lt (TA) 1956-59; CA, ptnr Price Waterhouse 1970- (joined 1959); chm of govrs: Redcliffe Sch Fulham 1979-, Arundale Sch Pulborough 1985-; FCA 1963; *Recreations* golf, skiing, bridge, philately; *Clubs* Carlton; *Style—* Bill Caldwell, Esq; The Grange, Hesworth Lane, Fittleworth, Pulborough, W Sussex (☎ 079 882 384); Price Waterhouse, Southwark Towers, 32 London Bridge St, London SE1 9ST (☎ 01 407 8989, fax 01 378 0647, telex 884657/8)

CALEDON, Elisabeth, Countess of; Marie Elisabeth Burton; *née* Allen; da of Maj Richard Burton Allen, 3 Dragoon Guards, of Benvheir House, Ballachulish, Argyll; *m* 1, 1955 (m dis 1964), Maj Hon Iain Maxwell Erskine, later 2 Baron Erskine of Rerrick; m 2, 1964, as his 3 w, 6 Earl of Caledon (d 1980); *Style—* The Rt Hon Elisabeth, Countess of Caledon; The Gate House, Hunsdon, nr Ware, Hertfordshire

CALEDON, 7 Earl of (I 1800); Nicholas James Alexander; s of 6 Earl of Caledon (d 1980), by his 2 w, Baroness Anne (d 1963), da of Baron Nicolai de Graevenitz (Dukedom of Mecklenburg-Schwerin 1847, Russia (Tsar Nicholas I) 1851); *b* 6 May 1955; *Educ* Gordonstoun; *m* 1979 (m dis 1985), Wendy Catherine, da of Spiro Nicholas Coumantaros, of Athens; *Heir* kinsman, 2 Earl Alexander of Tunis; *Career* HM Lord Lieutenant for Co Armagh 1989-; *Style—* The Rt Hon the Earl of Caledon; Caledon Castle, Co Tyrone, Ireland (☎ 232)

CALLADINE, Prof Christopher Reuben; s of Reuben Callandine (d 1968), of Stapleford, Nottingham, and Mabel, *née* Boam (d 1963); *b* 19 Jan 1935; *Educ* Nottingham HS, Peterhouse Cambridge (BA), Massachusetts Inst of Technol (SM), Univ of Cambridge (ScD); *m* 4 Jan 1964, Mary Ruth Howard, da of Alan Howard Webb, of Bengeo, Hertford; 2 s (Robert James b 1964, Daniel Edward b 1967), 1 da (Rachel Margaret b 1966); *Career* devpt engr English Electric Co 1958-60; Univ of Cambridge: univ demonstrator 1960-63, univ lectr 1963-78, reader in Structural Mechanics 1978-86, prof of Structural Mechanics 1986-; fell Peterhouse Coll 1960-; govr Cherry Hinton Infants Sch, formerly govr Richard Hale Sch Hertford, memb gen bd Univ of Cambridge; FRS 1984; *Style—* Prof Christopher Calladine; Peterhouse, Cambridge CB2 1RD (☎ 0223 338 200, fax 0223 338 202)

CALLAGHAN, Sir Allan Robert; CMG (1945); s of late Phillip George Callaghan, of Perthville, NSW, Australia; *b* 24 Nov 1903; *Educ* St Paul's Coll Sydney Univ, St John's Oxford; *m* 1, 1928, Zillah May (d 1964), da of late E E Sampson, or Orange, NSW; 2 s, 1 da (and 1 s decd); m 2, 1965, Doreen Winifred Rhys, da of late E R Draper, of Regent, Victoria; *Career* princ Roseworthy Agric Coll SA 1932-49, dir of Agriculture South Australia 1949-59, commercial counsellor Australian Embassy Washington DC 1959-65, former chm Australian Wheat Bd 1965-71, agricultural consultant; kt 1972; *Books* Wheat Industry in Australia (with A J Millington); *Style—* Sir Allan Callaghan, CMG; Tralee, 22 Murray St, Clapham, SA 5062, Australia (☎ 276-6524)

CALLAGHAN, Austin; s of Austin Callaghan (d 1957); *b* 3 Nov 1926; *Educ* St Martin's Coll Bootle, CBS Dublin; *m* 1949, Maureen, da of Joseph Morgan (d 1965); 1 s, 6 da; *Career* Mersey Docks and Harbour Co: mgmnt accountant 1966-69, dep chief accountant 1969-73, chief accountant 1974-76, controller (finance) Port Servs 1976-80, fin controller Royal Liverpool Philharmonic Soc 1980-88; hon tres Bluecoat Soc of arts 1988-, pres Chartered Inst of Mgmnt Accountants 1981-82 (admitted 1951, memb of cncl 1973-85, chm fin ctee, vice pres 1979-81); FCMA;; *Recreations* choral singing, fell walking, wine making, badminton; *Style—* Austin Callaghan, Esq; 4 Stanley House, Stanley Rd, Hoylake, Wirral L47 1HY (☎ 051 632 2471); Royal Liverpool Philharmonic Society, Hope Street, Liverpool L1 9BP (☎ 051 709 2895)

CALLAGHAN, Sir Bede Bertrand; CBE (1968); s of Stanislaus K Callaghan (d 1950), of Sydney, NSW, and Amy M Ryan; *b* 16 Mar 1912; *Educ* Newcastle HS Australia; *m* 1940, Mary T (Mollie), da of late G F Brewer; 3 da; *Career* exec dir IMF and IBRD 1954-59, gen mangr Commonwealth Devpt Bank of Australia 1959-65, md Commonwealth Banking Corpn 1965-76; chllr Newcastle Univ 1977- (dep chllr 1973-

77); kt 1976; *Clubs* Union (Sydney); *Style*— Sir Bede Callaghan, CBE; 69 Darnley St, Gordon, NSW 2072, Australia (☎ 498 7583)

CALLAGHAN, Rear Adm Desmond Noble; CB (1970); s of Edmund Ford Callaghan, of London, and Kathleen Louise, *née* Noble; *b* 24 Nov 1915; *Educ* RNC Dartmouth; *m* 1948, Patricia Munro, da of Peter Geddes, of London; 1 s, 2 da; *Career* joined RN 1929, Capt 1958, Rear Adm 1968, pres Ordnance Bd 1968-71, ret 1971; dir-gen Nat Supervisory Cncl for Intruder Alarms 1971-77; FRSA; *Style*— Rear Adm Desmond Callaghan, CB; Willand, Boyn Hill Rd, Maidenhead, Berks (☎ 0628 26840)

CALLAGHAN, James; MP (Lab) Heywood and Middleton 1983-; s of James Callaghan; *b* 28 Jan 1927; *Career* lecturer St John's Coll Manchester 1959-74; former borough councillor Middleton; MP (Lab) Middleton and Prestwich 1974-1983, oppn front bench spokesman on Euro and Community Affairs 1983-; *Style*— James Callaghan, Esq, MP; 17 Towncroft Ave, Middleton, Manchester M24 3LA (☎ 061 643 8108)

CALLAGHAN, Hon Michael James; o s of Baron Callaghan of Cardiff, KG, PC (Life Peer), *qv*; *b* 1945,; *Educ* Dulwich, Univ of Wales Cardiff, Manchester Business Sch; *m* 1968, Jennifer Mary, *née* Morris; 1 s (Joseph Edwin James b 1981), 2 da (Kate Elizabeth b 1970, Sarah Jane b 1972); *Style*— The Hon Michael Callaghan; 3515 Maxwell Court, Birmingham, Michigan 48010, USA

CALLAGHAN OF CARDIFF, Baron (Life Peer UK 1987), of the City of Cardiff co S Glamorgan; Rt Hon Sir (Leonard) James Callaghan; PC (1964), MP (Lab) Cardiff South and Penarth 1983-87, KG (1987); s of James Callaghan, Chief Petty Officer RN, of Portsmouth; *b* 27 Mar 1912; *Educ* Portsmouth Northern Secondary Sch; *m* 1938, Audrey Elizabeth, da of Frank Moulton, of Loose, Kent; 1 s, 2 da; *Career* joined Civil Service 1929, asst sec Inland Revenue Staff Fedn 1936-47; MP (Lab) South Cardiff 1945-50, South East Cardiff 1950-83; parly Sec Min of Transport 1947-50, parly and fin sec Admiralty 1950-51, chllr of the Exchequer 1964-67, home sec 1967-70, sec of state for Foreign and Commonwealth Affairs 1974-76, min of Overseas Dvpt 1975-76, prime minister and first lord of the Treasury 1976-79, leader of Oppn 1979-80, father of the House (of Commons) 1983-; *Books* A House Divided: the dilemma of Northern Ireland (1973), Time and Chance (memoirs, 1987); *Style*— The Rt Hon Lord Callaghan of Cardiff, KG, PC; Upper Clayhill Farm, Ringmer, E Sussex; 5 Temple West Mews, West Square, London SE11 4TJ

CALLAHAN, J Loughlin; s of John G P Callahan, Lt-Col US Air Force (ret), of 661 Garden Road, Dayton Ohio 45419, and Marie Loughlin, *née* Loughlin, of USA; *b* 18 Jan 1948; *Educ* Holy Cross Coll Worcester, Massachusetts (BA), Harvard Law Sch, Cambridge, Massachusetts, (Juris Dr cum laude); *m* 5 May 1973, Mary da of Vincent Reilly (d 1969), of 25 Lennox Drive, Tinton Falls, New Jersey, USA; 1 s (Christopher b 1974), 1 da (Denise b 1976); *Career* lawyer 1972-80, Davis Polk & Wardwell, New York; investment banker S G Warburg Securities (London) 1980-; dir: S G Warburg & Co Ltd 1983-86, S G Warburg Securities 1986-, Int Primary Mkts Assoc 1986-; *Recreations* art collecting; *Style*— J L Callahan, Esq; 7 Spencer Hill, London SW19 4PA (☎ 01 947 7726); S G Warburg Securities, 1 Finsbury Ave, London EC2 (☎ 01 280 2743)

CALLAN, Maj-Gen Michael; CB (1979); s of Maj John Callan, and Elsie Dorothy, *née* Fordham; *b* 27 Nov 1925; *Educ* Farnborough GS, Army Staff Coll, JSSC, RCDS; *m* 1948, Marie Evelyn, *née* Farthing; 2 s; *Career* 1 Gurkhas IA 1944-47, RAOC 1948, Cdr Rhine Area BAOR 1975-76, Dir gen Ordnance Servs (MOD) 1976-80, Col Cmdt RAOC 1981- (Rep Col Cmdt 1982, 1985, 1988) Hon Col SW London ACF 1982-; conslt Def Logistics & Admin; *Recreations* sailing, gardening, DIY; *Style*— Maj-Gen Michael Callan, CB; c/o Royal Bank of Scotland Ltd, Kirkland House, Whitehall, London SW1A 2EB

CALLANDER, Lady Mary Pamela; *née* Douglas; da of 21 Earl of Morton; *b* 12 Nov 1950; *m* 1973, Richard Callander; 1 s (James Edward b 1979), 2 da (Sarah Mary b 1977, Emma Louise b 1981); *Style*— Lady Mary Callander; Saughland House, Pathhead, Midlothian

CALLARD, Sir Jack (Eric John); s of Frank Callard (d 1951), of Torquay; *b* 15 Mar 1913; *Educ* Queen's Coll Taunton, St John's Coll Cambridge (MA); *m* 1938, Pauline Mary, da of Rev Charles Pengelly (d 1941); 3 da; *Career* chartered mechanical engr; chm: ICI Ltd 1971-75, Br Home Stores 1976-82; dir: Midland Bank 1971-87, Commercial Union Assur 1975-83, Ferguson Indust Hldgs 1975-86, Equity Capital for Industry 1976-84; Hons DSc Cranfield Inst of Technol; FEng, Hon FIMechE; kt 1974; *Recreations* fly fishing, gardening; *Clubs* Fly Fishers; *Style*— Sir Jack Callard; Crookwath Cottage, High Row, Dockray, nr Penrith, Cumbria CA11 0LG

CALLAWAY, Emeritus Prof Sir Frank Adams; CMG (1975), OBE (1970); s of Archibald Charles Callaway (d 1956), and Mabel, *née* Adams Callaway; *b* 16 May 1919; *Educ* W Christchurch HS, Otago Univ (Mus B), Dunedin Teachers' Training Coll, Royal Acad of Music London; *m* 1942, Kathleen Jessie, da of Ronald Allan; 2 s, 2 da; *Career* RNZAF Central Band 1940-42; Hon MusD (WA and Melb), FRAM, ARCM, FTCL, FACE; head music dept King Edward Tech Coll Dunedin 1942-53, conductor Univ of WA Orchestral Soc 1953-65, Univ of WA Choral Soc 1953-79; guest conductor: NZ Symphony Orchestra, WA Symphony Orchestra, Adelaide Philharmonic Choir, SA Symphony Orchestra and Manila Symphony Orchestra; memb Perth Festival Ctee 1953-75, reader in Music Univ of WA 1953-59, memb Aust Music Exams Bd 1955- (chm 1964-66 and 1977-79), memb bd Int Soc for Music Educn 1958- (pres 1968-72, tres 1972-87, hon pres 1988-), founding pres and life memb Aust Soc for Music Educn 1966-71, founding ed Aust Journal of Music Educn 1967-83, and Int Journal of Music Educn 1983-85, chm Aust UNESCO Ctee for Music 1968-71, memb Aust UNESCO Arts Ctee 1971-77, pres Int Music Council of UNESCO 1980-82, life memb of Honour 1985-, memb exec Aust UNESCO Ctee 1977-82, chm WA Arts Advsy Bd 1970-73, chm WA Arts Cncl 1973-79, pres Indian Ocean Arts Assoc 1980-, pres Lord's Taverners (WA) 1984-; prof and head dept of music Univ of WA 1959-84; W Australian of the Year 1975; Sir Bernard Meinze Award, service to Australian Music 1988; kt 1981; *Books* Challenges in Music Education 1975 (gen ed), Australian Composition in the Twentieth Century 1978 (ed with D E Tunley); *Recreations* cricket, gardening, reading; *Style*— Emeritus Prof Sir Frank Callaway, CMG, OBE; 16 The Lane, Churchlands, W Australia 6018 (☎ 09 387 3345)

CALLAWAY, (Norman) Keith; s of Victor George Charles Callaway (d 1980), and Edna Alice Josephine, *née* Pedley; *b* 20 August 1930; *Educ* Collyers Sch Horsham Sussex; *Career* CA 1964-; formerly with Peat Marwick Mitchell & Co London Off; dir Anscon Ltd; *Recreations* walking, gardening, travel; *Style*— Keith Callaway, Esq; 121 Cromwell Tower, London EC2 (☎ 01 588 2691); Callaways, 1 Whites Row, London E1 7NF (☎ 01 628 5988)

CALLAWAY-FITTALL, Betty Daphne; *née* Roberts; MBE (1984); da of William Arthur Roberts (d 1965), and Elizabeth Theobald, *née* Hayward (d 1972); *b* 22 Mar 1928; *Educ* St Pauls Convent, Graycoat Sch London; *m* 1, 1949, E Roy Callaway; m 2, 1978, Capt William Percival Fittall, Br Airways (ret); *Career* ice skating trainer; nat trainer W Germany 1969-72; pupils include: Angelika and Erich Buck Euro Champions and second in the World Championships 1972, Chrisztine Recoczy and Andras Sally Hungarian and World Champions and Olympic Silver Medallists 1980, Jayne Torvill and Christopher Dean World and Euro Champions 1981, 1982, 1983-84, also Olympic Champions 1984; Hon citizen Ravensburg Germany 1972, Gold Medal Nat Skating Assoc 1955, Hungarian Olympic Medal 1980, now skating dir Slough Ice Arena; *Recreations* water ski-ing, music, gardening; *Style*— Betty Callaway-Fittall, MBE; 35 Long Grove, Seer Green, Beaconsfield, Bucks (☎ 04946 6370)

CALLEY, Sir Henry Algernon; DSO (1945), DFC (1943, DL (Wilts 1968)); yst s of Rev Algernon Charles Mainwaring Langton (d 1948), and Elizabeth Ina, *née* Calley (d 1960); assumed the surname of Calley in lieu of Langton 1974; *b* 9 Feb 1914; *Educ* St John's Sch Leatherhead; *Career* Met Police 1938-41; former teacher; former chm: Cncl and Fin Ctee Wilts CC, Wessex Area Cons Assoc; stud owner and mangr: kt 1964; *Style*— Sir Henry Calley, DSO, DFC, DL; Overtown House, Wroughton, Swindon, Wilts (☎ 0793 812208)

CALLINAN, Sir Bernard James; AC (1986), CBE (1971, DSO 1945, MC 1943); s of Michael Joseph Callinan (d 1958), and Mary, *née* Prendergast; *b* 2 Feb 1913; *Educ* Melbourne Univ (BCE, Diploma of Town and Regnl Planning); *m* 1943, Naomi Marian, da of Thomas Cullinan (d 1953); 5 s (Nicholas, Christopher, Stephen, Matthew, Andrew); *Career* consulting engr; chm and md Gutteridge Haskins & Davey Pty Ltd 1971-78 (later conslt); dir: BP Co of Australia Ltd 1969-85, CSR Ltd 1978-85;chm CCI Insur Ltd 1984-; memb and chm West Gate Bridge Authy 1968-81, cmmr Royal Inquiry of Aust Post Office 1973-74, memb Royal Humane Soc Australia 1978- (pres 1986-); chm: Inst Catholic Educn Victoria 1974-, Nat Catholic Educn Comm 1984-88; author Independent Company (1953, 1954, 1984, 1989); Hon LLD (Melb) 1987, Hon DEng (Mon) 1984; kt 1977; *Clubs* Melbourne, Australian (Melb), Naval and Military (Melb), Melb Cricket (pres 1980-85); *Style*— Sir Bernard Callinan, AC, CBE, DSO, MC; 111 Sackville St, Kew Victoria, Australia 3101 (☎ 03 817 1230), 97 Franklin St, Melbourne, Australia 3000

CALLINAN, Raymond Clive; s of Jeremiah Callinan (d 1959); *b* 13 Mar 1934; *Educ* Clifton Coll, BNC Oxford; *m* 1962 (m dis 1977), Gita, da of Satish Gore of Calcutta; 1 s, 1 da; *Career* banker; md Singer & Friedlander Ltd 1970-; *Recreations* cricket, motor racing, reading; *Style*— Raymond Callinan, Esq; 19 Westbourne St, London W2

CALLINICOS, Hon Mrs (Aedgyth Bertha Milburg Mary Antonia Frances); *née* Lyon-Dalberg-Acton; OBE Decorated by Greek Government for work in (1986) Annexion with Ionian Islands Earthquakes 1953; 7 da of 2 Baron Acton, KCVO (d 1924); *b* 15 Dec 1920; *Educ* various convents and finishing schs in the United Kingdom and Europe; *m* 1949, John Alexander Callinicos, yst s of Alexander Theodore Callinicos, of Ithaca, Greece; 2 s; *Career* FO 1942-49; public relations and hotel management Zimbabwe; engaged in political and welfare work Zimbabwe; chm Prankerd Jones Memorial Fnd, hon sec and co fndr Br Zimbabwe Soc; *Style*— The Hon Mrs Callinicos; Villa Ithaki, Hatfield, Harare, Zimbabwe (☎ 50065)

CALLMAN, His Hon Judge; Clive Vernon Callman; o s of Felix Callman, DMD, LDS, RCS, and Edith Callman; *b* 21 June 1927; *Educ* Ottershaw Coll, St George's Coll Weybridge, LSE (BSc Econ); *m* 1967, Judith Helen, o da of Gus Hines, OBE, JP, of Adelaide, S Australia; 1 s, 1 da; *Career* barrister Middle Temple 1951, practiced in London and Norwich 1951-73, dep circuit judge in Civil and Criminal Jurisdiction 1971-73, circuit judge (SE Circuit) 1973-; sitting Royal Courts of Justice, Family Division Mayor's and City of London Court and in Crown Courts London U; memb standing ctee on Convocation 1954-79, senator 1978-; memb: Careers Advsy Bd 1979-, advsy ctee for Magistrates' Courses 1979-; memb cncl Anglo-Jewish Assoc 1956-; memb editorial bd Media Law and Practice, and Professional Negligence; govr Birbeck Coll London U; *Recreations* the arts, travel, reading; *Clubs* Bar Yacht; *Style*— His Hon Judge Callman; 11 Constable Close, London NW11 6UA (☎ 01 458 3010)

CALMADY-HAMLYN, Lt-Col (Vincent) Warwick; o s of Maj Charles Hamlyn Hunt Calmady-Hamlyn, TD, JP (d 1963), of Leawood and Paschoe, Devon, and Grace (d 1948), yst da of Rev Sabine Baring-Gould (the author of 'Onward Christian Soldiers'); descended from an Exeter family which acquired Paschoe early 15 cent and Leawood by the marriage of Christopher Hamlyn to Elizabeth Mary Calmady in the 18 cent (*see* Burke's Landed Gentry, 18 ed, vol III, 1972); *b* 5 Dec 1915; *Educ* Cheltenham, RMC Sandhurst; *m* 1, 25 Jan 1945 (m dis 1957), (Marguerite) Kilmeny Sarah, o da of Lt-Col Peter Calvert Lord, OBE, RE (d 1960); m 2, 20 Nov 1958, Madeleine Joan, o da of Henry Albert Moulden, of New Malden, Surrey; 2 da (Laura Dawn b 16 April 1960, Angela Grace b 6 July 1961); *Career* cmmnd Royal Sussex Regt 1936, served in Palestine, Cyprus, Egypt, Iraq, 8 Army (despatches India), ret 1951; memb Bridestowe Parish Cncl (sometime chm); former memb Okehampton RDC; former dist cmmr Lamerton Hunt (Devon) Pony Club; former Master Delhi and Meerut (India) Hunts; *Recreations* steeple chasing, hurdle racing, polo, hunting; *Clubs* Delhi Gymkhana; *Style*— Lt-Col Calmady-Hamlyn; Leawood, Bridestowe, Okehampton, Devon EX20 4ET (☎ 083 786 203)

CALMAN, Montague; s of Clement Calman (d 1946), and Anna Marcus (d 1961); *b* 18 June 1917; *Educ* Grocers' Co Sch; *m* 24 Oct 1957, Deecie Campbell, da of Gordon Lyall (d 1960); *Career* served WW II 1940-46; asst press offr Miny of Supply 1947, press offr NCB 1947; ballet, music and opera critic London Evening Standard; columnist LA Times, feature columnist Ballet Today; PR conslt; FRSA 1947, MJI 1947, MIPR 1956; *Clubs* Royal Cwlth Soc; *Style*— Montague Calman, Esq; 1E Carlisle Place, London SW1P 1NP (☎ 01 828 6665)

CALNE, Prof Sir Roy Yorke; s of Joseph Robert Calne (d 1984), and Eileen Calne; *b* 30 Dec 1930; *Educ* Lancing, Guy's Hosp Med Sch; *m* 2 March 1956, Patricia Doreen; 2 s (Russell b 1964, Richard b 1970), 4 da (Jane b 1958, Sarah b 1959, Deborah b 1962, Suzanne b 1963); *Career* Nat Serv RAMC BMH Singapore RMO to KEO 2 Gurkhas 1954-56; conslt and sr lectr (surgery) Westminster Hosp London 1962-65, prof of surgery Univ of Cambridge 1965-, conslt surgn Cambridge Health Authy 1965-; kt 1986; *Books* Renal Transplantation (1963), Lecture Notes in Surgery (with H Ellis 1965), A Gift of Life (1970), Clinical Organ Transplantation (ed 1971), Organ Grafts (1974), Liver Transplantation (ed & contrib 1983), A Colour Atlas of Transplatation:

Renal (1984), Pancreas (1985), Liver (1985), Transplant Immunology (ed & contrib 1984), Living surgical anatomy of the abdomen (1988); *Recreations* squash, tennis, painting; *Style*— Prof Sir Roy Calne; 22 Barrow Road, Cambridge (☎ 0223 242708); Dept of Surgery, Addenbrooke's Hills Rd, Cambridge CB2 2QQ (☎ 0223 336975)

CALNE AND CALSTONE, Viscount; Simon Henry George Petty-Fitzmaurice; s and h of Earl of Shelburne and gs of 8 Marquess of Lansdowne, PC; *b* 24 Nov 1970; *Style*— Viscount Calne and Calstone

CALTHORPE; *see*: Anstruther-Gough-Calthorpe

CALTHORPE, 10 Baron (GB 1796); Sir Peter Waldo Somerset Gough-Calthorpe; 11 Bt (1728); s of Hon Frederick Gough-Calthorpe (d 1935), and Dorothy, *née* Vernon-Harcourt (d 1985); suc bro, 9 Baron, 1945; *b* 13 July 1927; *Educ* Stowe; *m* 1, June 1956 (m dis 1971), Saranne Frances (d 1984), only da of James Harold Alexander, of Dublin; m 2, 1979, Elizabeth, da of James Young, of Guildford, Surrey; *Career* late Lt Welsh Gds Palestine; airline pilot (free-lance, later for Aer Lingus, then Jersey Airlines) 1951-59, md Mercury Airlines 1960-65; author of two novels published under pseudonym Peter Somerset 1966-67; gp investment mangr 1970-81; *Recreations* theatre, paintings (not modern); *Style*— The Rt Hon the Lord Calthorpe; c/o IOM Bank Ltd, 2 Athol St, Douglas, Isle of Man

CALTON, (Frederick) George; s of Harold Percy Calton (d 1968), of Waterlooville, Hants, and Ethel May, *née* Ching; *b* 11 July 1925; *Educ* Price's Sch Fareham, Queen's Univ Belfast; *m* 28 March 1956, Pamela Margaret, da of Clarence Thomas Church, CBE (d 1963), of Goring-by-Sea; 1 s (Grant b 8 April 1960); *Career* RAF 1944-47; CA; Joseph Lucas Ltd 1951-53, chm Cross and Herbert Ltd 1953-; memb Cncl Br Retailer's Assoc, dir Co Chemists' Assoc; FCA 1951; *Recreations* reading, music, walking; *Style*— George Calton, Esq; Hangmoor, Callow Hill, Virginia Water, Surrey GU25 4LD (☎ 09904 3246); 41 High St Egham, Surrey TW20 9DS (☎ 0784 32444)

CALVER, Gordon Anthony; s of late Ernest Walter Calver; *b* 12 Jan 1921; *Educ* Sutton Valence Sch; *m* 1959, Yvonne Margaret, *née* Burnside; 2 da; *Career* int banker; gen mangr and dir Br Bank of the ME 1970-77 (dir 1977-79), memb London Advsy Ctee 1979-85; FIB; *Books* The Bankers Guide to the Marine Insurance of Goods; *Recreations* gardening, reading, swimming; *Clubs* RAC; *Style*— Gordon Calver, Esq; Darband House, Blackdown Ave, Pyrford, Nr Woking, Surrey GU22 8QG (☎ 093 23 47602)

CALVERLEY, 3 Baron (UK 1945) Charles Rodney Muff; s of 2 Baron Calverley (d 1971); *b* 2 Oct 1946; *Educ* Moravian Boys' Sch Fulneck; *m* 1972, Barbara Ann, da of Jonathan Brown, of Colne, Lancs; 2 s (Hon Jonathan, Hon Andrew b 1978); *Heir* s, Hon Jonathan Edward Muff b 16 April 1975; *Career* memb W Yorkshire Metropolitan Police; formerly with City of Bradford Police; 110 Buttershaw Lane, Wibsey, Bradford, W Yorkshire BD6 2DA (tel 0274 676414)

CALVERLEY, 3 Baron (UK 1945); Charles Rodney Muff Calverley; s of 2 Baron Calverley (d 1971); *b* 2 Oct 1946; *Educ* Moravian Boys' Sch Fulneck; *m* 1972, Barbara Ann, da of Jonathan Brown, of Colne, Lancs; 2 s (Hon Jonathan, Hon Andrew b 1978); *Heir* s, Hon Jonathan Edward Muff b 16 April 1975; *Career* memb W Yorks Police; formerly with City of Bradford Police; *Style*— The Rt Hon the Lord Calverley; 110 Buttershaw Lane, Wibsey, Bradford, W Yorks BD6 2DA (☎ 0274 676414)

CALVERT, Barbara Adamson; *née* Parker; QC (1975); er da of Albert Parker, CBE (d 1980), and Lilian Maud, *née* Midgley (d 1972); *b* 30 April 1926; *Educ* St Helen's Northwood, London Univ (BSc Econ); *m* 1948, John Thornton Calvert, CBE (d 1987), s of Harry Thornton Calvert, MBE (d 1947); 1 s, 1 da; *Career* barr Middle Temple 1959, pt/t chm Industl Tbnl 1974-, recorder SE Circuit 1980, bencher Middle Temple 1982, memb Matrimonial Causes Rule Ctee 1983-86, full-time chm Industl Tbnl 1986-; *Recreations* swimming, gardening, poetry; *Clubs* Royal Fowey Yacht; *Style*— Mrs John Calvert, QC; 4 Brick Court, Temple, London EC4 (☎ 01 353 5392); 158 Ashley Gdns, London SW1P 1HW (☎ 01 828 0530)

CALVERT, Maj Edmund Archibald; s of Lt-Col C A Calvert DSO (d 1956), and Winifred Susan, *née* Cholmeley (d 1960); *b* 21 April 1909; *Educ* Winchester, Cambridge; *m* 24 Jan 1944, Elizabeth, da of Brig H C Clifton Brown (d 1946); 1 s (Henry b 1948), 1 da (Jennifer b 1947); *Career* Maj 1 Royal Dragoons, served M East and Europe 1931-46; JP W Sussex 1949-79 (chm Crawley Bench 1964-79), DL W Sussex; *Recreations* outdoor sports; *Style*— Maj Edmund Calvert; Rose Cottage, Farm House, Faygate, Sussex RH12 4SE (☎ 029383 277)

CALVERT, Louis Victor Denis; CB (1985); s of late Louis Victor Calvert, of Belfast, and Gertrude Cherry, *née* Hobson (d 1985); *b* 20 April 1924; *Educ* Belfast Royal Academy, Queens Univ Belfast BSc (Econ), Administrative Staff Coll, Henley-on-Thames; *m* 24 Aug 1949, Vivien Millicent, da of George Albert Lawson (d 1958); 2 s (David b 1951, Steven b 1952), 1 da (Jacqueline b 1961); *Career* RAF 1943-57, FO navigator (UK, Europe, S Africa), N Ireland Civil Service 1947-80, Miny of Agriculture 1947-56, dep principal 1951, principal Miny of Finance 1956-63, min of Health and Local Govt 1963-65, asst sec 1964, Miny of Devpt 1965-73, sr asst sec 1970, dep sec 1971, Miny of Housing Local Govt and Planning 1973-76, DOE for N Ireland 1976-80; comptroller and auditor gen for N Ireland 1980-; *Recreations* gardening, golf, reading, television; *Style*— L V D Calvert, Esq, CB; Northern Ireland Audit Office, Rosepark House, Upper Newtownards Road, Belfast BT4 2NS

CALVERT, Margaret Ada Tomsett; JP; da of Donald Arthur Hodge, of 69 Stratheden Ct, Seaford, Sussex, and Ada Constance Jannette, *née* Tomsett (d 1973); *b* 8 Jan 1924; *Educ* Haberdashers Askes, UCL (BA); *m* 4 July 1953, Dr Jack Maxwell, s of Albert Henry Calvert (d 1978), of Selby, Yorks; 4 s (David b 1955, Ian b 1956, Jonathan b 1958, Alastair b 1967); *Career* WWII WRNS 1942-46; CA; princ accountant (first woman) Univ of Oxford 1952-53, public practice as int tax specialist 1954-, lectr comparative taxation Univ of Manchester 1958-88, memb taxation advsy panel ICEAW 1984-; memb and one time div pres Br Red Cross Cheshire Branch, cmmr and cncl memb Girl Guides Assoc, pres Br Fedn of Univ Women; formerly tres: Int Fedn Univ Women, World Assoc of Girl Guides and Girl Scouts; FCA 1959; memb: VAT tribunal, Nat Insur tribunal, Community Health Cncl; JP; *Recreations* travel, photography; *Clubs* University Womens; *Style*— Mrs Margaret Calvert, JP; 3 Chyngton Place, Seaford, E Sussex BN25 4HQ (☎ 0323 490 685)

CALVERT, Michael John; JP (1972), DL (Surrey 1974); s of John Charles Calvert (d 1974); *b* 15 Sept 1930; *Educ* Eton, RMA Sandhurst; *m* 1963, Sally Noel, da of Noel Victor Sharpe Cannon (d 1958); 3 da (Clare, Nicola, Celia); *Career* 60 Rifles 1949-62, Adjt Queen's Royal Rifles 1962-64; farmer and market gardener 1964-; chm: Surrey TAVRA 1980-87, Surrey Community Devpt Tst 1982-; high sheriff Surrey 1979-80; non exec dir Seeboard 1985-; *Recreations* shooting, cricket, golf; *Clubs* Farmers'; *Style*— Michael J Calvert, Esq, JP, DL; Ockley Court, Ockley, nr Dorking, Surrey (☎ 0306 711160)

CALVERT, Phyllis (Mrs Hill); da of Frederick Bickle (d 1964), and Annie Williams (d 1957); *b* 18 Feb 1915; *Educ* French Lycee, Margaret Morris Sch Dancing and Acting; *m* 1941, Peter Auriol Murray Hill (d 1957), s of George Murray Hill (d 1941); 1 s (Piers), 1 da (Auriol); *Career* actress; first appeared in London in A Woman's Privilege (Kingsway Theatre 1939), Punch without Judy (Embassy 1939), Flare Path (Apollo 1942) Escapade (St James's 1953), It's Never Too Late (Strand 1954), River Breeze (Phoenix 1956), The Complaisant Lover (Globe 1959), The Rehearsal (Globe 1981), Ménage à Trois (Lyric 1963), Portrait of Murder (Savoy and Vaudervílle 1963), A Scent of Flowers (Duke of York's 1964), Present Laughter (Queen's 1965), A Woman of No Importance (Vaudervílle 1967), Blithe Spirit (Globe 1970), Crown Matrimonial (Haymarket 1973), Dear Daddy (Ambassadors 1976), Mrs Warren's Profession (Worcester 1977), She Stoops to Conquer (Old World Exeter 1978), Suite in Two Keys (tour 1978), Before the Party (Queen's 1980); started films 1939; Kipps, The Young Mr Pitt, Man in Grey, Fanny by Gaslight, Madonna of the Seven Moons, They were Sisters, Time out of Mind, Broken Journey, My Own True Love, The Golden Madonna, A Woman with No Name, Mr Denning Drives North, Mandy, The Net, It's Never too Late, Child in the House, Indiscreet, The Young and The Guilty, Oscar Wilde, Twisted Nerve, Oh! What a Lovely War, The Walking Stick; tv series include: Kate 1970, Month in the Country 1984, PD James' Cover Her Face 1984, Death of the Heart 1985, All Passion Spent, Killing on The Exchange 1986, Old Wives Tale 1987; *Style*— Mrs Phyllis Calvert; Hill Ho, Waddesdon, Bucks (☎ 0296 651291); agent Jeremy Conway (☎ 01 839 2121)

CALVOCORESSI, Hon Mrs; (Barbara Dorothy); *née* Eden; da of 6 Baron Henley (d 1962); *b* 1915; *m* 1938, Peter John Ambrose Calvocoressi, s of Pandia Calvocoressi (d 1965), of 31 Albion Gate, London W2; 2 s; *Style*— The Hon Mrs Calvocoressi; 1 Queen's Parade, Bath, Avon BA1 2NJ

CALVOCORESSI, Maj Ion Melville; MBE (1945), MC (1942); s of Matthew Calvocoressi and Agnes Hermione, da of late Judge Robert Melville, of Sussex and Salop; *b* 12 April 1919; *Educ* Eton, Magdalen Coll Oxford (MA); *m* 1947, Katherine, da of Capt Edward Coverley Kennedy, RN (d on active serv 1939, ggs of Hon Robert Kennedy, bro of 1 Marquess of Ailsa and 3 s of 11 Earl of Cassillis), and Rosalind, da of Sir Ludovic Grant, 11 Bt; 3 s, 1 da; *Career* Scots Gds 1939-46; Middle East, Sicily, Italy, SE Asia 1941-45, ADC, GOC 8 Army 1944, Mil Asst, CGS ALFSEA 1945; memb London Stock Exchange 1949; High Sheriff Kent 1978-79; *Recreations* cricket, gardening; *Clubs* Cavalry & Guards, City of London, Pratt's, MCC, Kent CC; *Style*— Maj Ion Calvocoressi, MBE, MC; Court Lodge, Westerham, Kent (☎ 0959 63358); Garrard House, Gresham St, London EC2 (☎ 01 600 4177)

CALVOCORESSI, Peter John Ambrose; s of Pandia John Calvocoressi (d 1965), of 31 Albion Gate, London W2, and Irene, *née* Ralli; *b* 17 Nov 1912,Karachi; *Educ* Eton, Balliol Coll Oxford; *m* 1938, Hon Barbara Dorothy Eden, da of late 6 Baron Henley; 2 s; *Career* served WW II Wing Cdr RAFVR (Air Intelligence); barrister Inner Temple 1935; contested (Lib) Warwicks (Nuneaton Div) 1945; author; dir Chatto & Windus Ltd and The Hogarth Press Ltd 1954-65; reader in Int Relations Sussex U 1966-71, editorial dir and chief exec Penguin Books 1972-76; chm Open University Educational Enterprises 1979-; memb cncl: Roy Inst of Int Affairs, Inst of Strategic Studies; *Clubs* Garrick; *Style*— Peter Calvocoressi Esq; 1 Queen's Parade, Bath, Avon

CAMARA, His Excellency Ousmane; *b* 1933; *Educ* Université de Dakar (Lic en Droit); *Career* director Sûreté Nationale (Senegal) 1964-68, cncllr Supreme Court (Senegal) 1968; min: Fonction Publique et du Travail 1970, l'Information Chargé des relations avec les Assemblées 1970-71, l'Enseignement Supérieur 1971-80; Senegalese Ambass to UK 1981-; *Style*— HE Monsieur Ousmane Camara; Embassy of Republic of Senegal, 11 Phillimore Gdns, London W8 (☎ 01 937 0925)

CAMBER, Hon Mrs; Angela Felicity; *née* Birk; JP; only da of Baroness Birk (Life Peeress) by her husband Ellis Samuel Birk; *b* July 1947; *Educ* Camden Sch for Girls, London Univ; *m* 1970, Richard Camber (*qv*); 1s (Thomas b Sept 1980), 2 da (Alice b Aug 1974, Chloe b Sepy 1980); *Style*— Hon Mrs Camber

CAMBER, Richard Monash; s of Maurice Camber, of Glasgow and Libby Camber (d 1981); *b* 22 July 1944; *Educ* Glasgow HS, Edinburgh Univ (MA), Paris Univ, London Univ; *m* 26 Oct 1970, The Hon Angela Felicity, da of Ellis Birk, of London; 1 s (Thomas b 1980), 2 da (Alice, b 1974, Chloe b 1980); *Career* asst keeper dept of medieval and latet antiquities Br Museum 1970-78; dir: Sotheby's London 1983-87, Sotheby's, Sotheby's Int; conslt Euro Works of Art 1988-; FSA; *Recreations* reading, listening to music, particularly opera; *Style*— Richard Camber, Esq; 28 Heath Drive, Hampstead, London NW3 7SB (☎ 01 435 5250, 01 431 4553)

CAMBRIDGE, Alan John; s of Thomas David Cambridge (d 1969), and Winifred Elizabeth, *née* Jarret (d 1970); *b* 1 July 1925; *Educ* Beckenham GS; *m* 1947, Thelma, da of Francis Elliot (d 1960); 3 s, 1 da; *Career* RAF 1943-47, Fl Sgt rear gunner, 150 Sqdn Bomber Cmd; War Pensions Off and MPNI 1948-55; joined Cwlth Relations Off 1955, Madras 1956-58, Kuala Lumpur 1959-62, Rhodesia and Nyasaland 1962-65; HM Dipl Serv 1965, first sec UN Dept FCO 1966-69, del UN Gen Assembly 1968, first sec Prague 1969, first sec (consular aid) Suva 1970-72, consul Milan 1972-74, asst head Info Dept FCO 1974-78, first sec (info) Ankara 1978-81, asst head then head Migration and Visa Dept FCO 1981-85, ret 1985; assessor FCO 1985-; *Recreations* photography, tennis, swimming; *Clubs* Civil Service; *Style*— Alan Cambridge Esq; 9 The Ferns, Carlton Rd, Tunbridge Wells, Kent TN1 2JT (☎ 0892 31223): Foreign and Commonwealth Office, King Charles St, London SW1

CAMBRIDGE, (Sydney) John Guy; CMG (1979), CVO (1979); o s of late Jack and Mona Cambridge; *b* 5 Nov 1928; *Educ* Marlborough, King's Coll Cambridge; *Career* joined HM Dipl Serv 1952; first sec UK Mission NY 1960, head of Chancery Jakarta 1964; cnsllr: Rome 1970, Nicosia 1975; ambass: to Kuwait 1977-82, to Morocco 1982-84; *Style*— John Cambridge, Esq, CMG, CVO; 9 Craven Hill, London W2 3EN

CAMDEN, 6 Marquess (UK 1812); David George Edward Henry Pratt; also Baron Camden (GB 1765), Earl Camden and Viscount Bayham (GB 1786), and Earl of Brecknock (UK 1812); s of 5 Marquess Camden, JP, DL (d 1983), and 1 w, Marjorie (Marjorie, Countess of Brecknock, DBE, *qv*), da of late Col Atherton Edward Jenkins; *b* 13 August 1930; *Educ* Eton; *m* 1961 (m dis 1985), Virginia Ann, only da of late Francis Harry Hume Finlaison, of Windsor; 2 s (1 decd), 1 da; *Heir* s, Earl of Brecknock; *Career* late 2 Lt Scots Gds; *Style*— The Most Hon the Marquess Camden;

Cowdown Farm House, Andover, Hants SP11 6LE (☎ 52085)

CAMELL, Lt-Col (Martin) Charles; s of John Camell (d 1955), and Beryl Evelyn, *née* Liddell (d 1985); *b* 17 Jan 1919; *Educ* Marlborough, RMA Woolwich; *m* 24 Feb 1943, Nora Pauline, da of James Richard Tayler (d 1964); 2 da (Gillian Nonie Coleman b 1946, Judith Patricia Munro b 1953); *Career* cmmnd RA 1939, war serv France, Belgium, N Africa, Italy and Greece 1939-45, Gunnery Instr Sch of Artill Larkhill 1946-48, Army Staff Coll 1951, RAF Staff Coll 1958, ret Lt-Col 1966; princ Civil Serv (bd of Trade and Dept Ind) 1966-82; *Recreations* walking, shooting; *Style*— Lt-Col Charles Camell; The Bell House, Kingston Deverill, Warminster, Wilts BA12 7HE

CAMERON, Maj Allan John; MBE (1988), (JP (Ross & Cromarty 1960), DL); s of Col Sir Donald Cameron of Lochiel, CMG (d 1951) and Lady Hermione Graham (d 1978), da of 5 Duke of Montrose; *b* 25 Mar 1917; *Educ* Harrow, RMC Sandhurst; *m* 1945, (Mary) Elizabeth, da of Col Arthur Vaughan-Lee, MVO (d 1933), of Dillington, Somerset; 2 s (and 1 s decd), 2 da; *Career* served WW II Maj Queen's Own Cameron Highlanders (POW 1942), ret 1948; landowner and farmer; served on: BBC Cncl for Scotland, Countryside Cmmn of Scotland, Red Deer Cmmn, Ross-shire CC 1955- (chm County Educn Ctee 1962-75); pres Roy Caledonian Curling Club 1963-64; vice Lord-Lieut Ross and Cromarty, Highland Region, 1977-; *Recreations* shooting, fishing, curling, golf, gardening; *Clubs* Naval and Military; *Style*— Maj Allan Cameron, MBE, JP, DL; Allangrange, Munlochy, Ross and Cromarty (☎ 046 381 249)

CAMERON, Lt-Col Angus Ewen; MC, DL (Inverness-shire 1967); s of Capt Allan George Cameron, of Lochiel (ka 1914), and Hester Vere, *née* Fraser-Tytler (d 1949); *b* 20 Jan 1914; *Educ* Eton Trinity Coll Cambridge; *m* 1949, Hon Judith Evelyn Maud, da of Brig Hon George Evan Michael Baillie, MC, TD, and sis of 3 Baron Burton; 1 s (Angus Iain b 1952), 1 da (Hester Caroline b 1950); *Career* 2 Lt Scots Gds 1936, Lt-Col 1950, ret; *Style*— Lt-Col Angus Cameron, MC, DL; Aldourie Castle, Inverness (☎ 046 375 309)

CAMERON, Lt-Col Charles Alexander; MC (1944), TD (1947, JP 1961, DL 1956); s of Sir Donald Walter Cameron of Lochiel, KT, CMG (d 1951); bro of Col Sir Donald Cameron of Lochiel and of Maj Allan John Cameron, *qv*; *b* 29 Sept 1920; *Educ* Loretto; *m* 1953, Felicia Margaret, er da of Col Kenneth Macdonald, of Tote, Skye; 1 s, 1 da; *Career* served 1939-45 Cameron Highlander TA, Maj 1944, Lt-col 1957, CC 1952-75 (Inverness-shire), Highland Regional Cncl 1975-82; Highland Regional rep Nat Tst for Scotland 1982-86; *Style*— Lt-Col Charles Cameron, MC, TD, JP, DL; 3 Marine Cottages, Nairn, Scotland

CAMERON, Ewen James Hanning; s of Maj Alland J Cameron, JP, DL, MBE, of Allangrange, Munlochy, Ross and Cromarty, and Mary Elizabeth *née* Vaughan-Lee; *b* 24 Nov 1949; *Educ* Harrow, Christ Church Oxford (MA); *m* 5 April 1975, Caroline Anne, da of Derek Ripley (d 1966), of Hurst Farm, Privett, Alton, Hants; 3 s (Ewen b 10 July 1977, James b 14 May 1979, Angus b 19 March 1983), 1 da Flora b 13 Oct 1986); *Career* memb: CLA, NFU, Nat, Tst, Rural Devpt Cmmn; High Sheriff of Somerset 1986; *Recreations* shooting, windsurfing, tennis; *Style*— Ewen Cameron, Esq; Whitelackington Manor, Ilminster, Somerset Rutland Mews South, London SW7 (☎ 0460-52448); Dillington Estate Office, Ilminster, Somerset (☎ 0460 54614, fax 0460)

CAMERON, Ewen William; OBE, JP; s of William Tulloch Cameron (d 1955), of Lochearnhead Hotel, Perthshire, and Christine Mabon (d 1944); *b* 23 Dec 1926; *Educ* Trinity Coll Glenalmond; *m* 27 April 1955, Davina Anne, da of Mr Morton Frew (d 1983), of the Shieling, Race Course Rd, Ayr; 1 s (Angus James b 1957), 1 da (Elaine Tootie b 1959); *Career* Ordinary Seaman RNVR 1944-47; md: Lochearn Devpt Co 1951-, Lochearnhead Hotel 1955, Lochearnhead Water Sports Co 1970-; vice chm: Cumbernauld New Town Devpt Corpn 1963-77, Royal Highland Shaw 1981; chm Br Water Ski Fedn 1966-70; pres: Edinchip Curling Club 1950-82, Lochearnhead Highland Games 1978-; memb: Perth CC 1963-75, Stirling DC 1974-77, Perth abd Kinross DC 1980- (dep provost 1982-84), Scottish Sports Cncl 1980-88, Perth Prison Bd 1980-, Scottish Electricity Cncl 1981-87, Tayside Health Bd 1982-, Scottish Tourist Bd; Scottish champion Highland Games Field Events 1953; *Recreations* shooting, rugby, golf, curling, dominos; *Clubs* Kandahar, Royal Perth, Saints and Sinners (Scotland), Elie GC; *Style*— Ewen Cameron, Esq, OBE, JP; Ben Ouhr Lochearnhead, Perthshire (☎ 05673 231); Admiralty House, Elie, Fife (☎ 033 3330 686); Lochearnhead Hotel, Perthshire

CAMERON, George Edmund; CBE (1970); s of William Cameron and Margaret, *née* Craig; *b* 2 July 1911; *Educ* Ballymena Acad; *m* 1939, Winifred Audrey, da of James Brown; 2 s; *Career* sr ptnr Wright Fitzsimmons and Cameron (CA); chm Northern Ireland Carriers Ltd, dir Cameron Investmts Ltd, Lombard & Ulster Banking Ltd, Ulster Bank Unit Tst Mangrs Ltd; *Style*— George Cameron, Esq, CBE; Ardavon, Glen Rd, Craigavad, Co Down, N Ireland

CAMERON, Hugh Forbes; MC, TD, WS; s of late James Cameron, WS; *b* 27 Dec 1917; *Educ* Edinburgh Acad, Sidney Sussex Coll Cambridge, Edinburgh Univ; *m* 1941, Jean Robertson, *née* Kydd; 1 s, 1 da; *Career* writer to the signet Edinburgh, former vice chm Fraser Westfield Motor Gp, dir The Edinburgh and Dundee Investmt Co Ltd 1964-77, dir The Appleyard Gp of Cos Ltd 1969-80; *Clubs* Army and Navy, New (Edinburgh); *Style*— Hugh Cameron, Esq, MC, TD, WS; Laighfield, New Galloway, Castle Douglas, Kirkcudbrightshire DG7 3SB (☎ 064 429336)

CAMERON, Ian Donald; s of Ewen Donald Cameron, and Enid Agnes Maud Levita; *b* 12 Oct 1932; *Educ* Eton; *m* 1962, Mary Fleur, *née* Mount; 2 s (Allan b 1963, David b 1966), 2 da (Tania b 1963, Clare b 1971); *Career* memb Stock Exchange 1955, senior ptnr Panmure Gordon and Co (stockbrokers); high sheriff of Berkshire 1978-79; *Clubs* White's; *Style*— Ian Cameron, Esq; The Old Rectory, Peasemore, Newbury, Berks; Panmure Gordon & Co, 9 Moorfields Highwalk, London EC2Y 9DS (☎ 01 638 4010, telex 883832)

CAMERON, James Brough; s of John Henderson Cameron, and Jessica Lillias, *née* Brough; *b* 3 Nov 1910; *Educ* Hamilton Acad Glasgow and West of Scotland Commercial Coll; *m* 25 March 1937, Margaret Mitchell MacLaren, 1 da (Annabel Jane (Mrs Baker) b 7 Dec 1946); *Career* RA 1941, London Scottish HAA Regt 1942, served RA (HAA) on Gunsites, Glasgow, Belfast, Windsor Great Park, Manchester, Hull 1941-43, Capt trg AA Cmd HQ 1943, Capt Intelligence 11 AA Mobile Trg Bde, Maj 21 Army Gp Rear HQ i/c Bdcasting Troops & distribution of radios Br Liberation Army 1944, Lt-Col i/c Br Forces Network Germany 1945, (despatches); advertising dept Hamilton Advertiser 1929-34, publicity dept J Lyons & Co Ltd 1934-37, advertising mangr Metal Box Co Ltd 1937-38, publicity mangr IBC Radio Normandy 1938-40, freelance advertising and pr conslt 1940-41, gen mangr Voice & Vision (MIPR) Ltd 1945-48, pa to md Alexander Films Ltd Johannesburg 1948-49, sr account exec Mather & Crowther Ltd 1950-57, dir M&C Ltd, O & M Ltd, chm Mathers Pr Ltd 1957-67, conslt to bd Ogilvy & Mather 1967-70, mktg conslt to FAO World Health Orgn (Poland & Iran), memb N Ireland Livestock Mktg Cmmn 1969-77, mktg res USA, Sweden, Jugoslavia, Italy; MCAM, MIPA; *Recreations* golf, painting, music, ceramics; *Style*— James B Cameron, Esq; Cnoc Mhor, Camserney, Aberfeldy, Perthshire PH15 2JF (☎ 0887 20210); Monte Estoril, Portugal

CAMERON, Sir James Clark; CBE (1969), TD (1947); s of Malcolm Clark Cameron, of Rannoch, Perthshire; *b* 8 April 1905; *Educ* Perth Acad, St Andrews Univ (MB ChB); *m* 1933, Irene Maud (d 1986), da of Arthur Ferguson, of Perth; 1 s, 2 da; *Career* serv WWII Capt RAMC attached 1 Bn The Rifle Bde, Calais (POW 1940, despatches 1945); chm Gen Med Servs Ctee BMA 1964-74 (hon life memb); visitor to cncl BMA (former chm cncl 1976-79); hon memb cncl Cameron Fund Ltd; FRCCP; Gold Medal for distinguished merit BMA 1974; kt 1979; *Recreations* medical politics; *Style*— Sir James Cameron, CBE, TD; 62 Haven Green Court, Haven Green, Ealing W5 2UY (☎ 01 997 8262)

CAMERON, (Mark) James Walter; CBE (1979); s of William Ernest Cameron; *b* 17 June 1911; *m* 1, 1938, Eleanor Mara Murray (decd); 1 da; m 2, 1944 (m dis) Elizabeth O'Conor; 1 s, 1 step s; m 3, 1971, Moneesha Sarkar; 1 step s, 1 step da; *Career* journalist; TV film producer; author; Prix Italia for Drama 1973, journalist of the Year Granada Award 1965; Hon DLitt Lancaster 1970, Hon LLD Bradford 1977, Hon DUniv Essex 1978; *Style*— James Cameron, Esq, CBE; 3 Eton College Rd, London NW3 (☎ 01 586 5340)

CAMERON, John Alastair; QC (Scotland 1979); s of William Philip Legerwood Cameron (d 1977), of Edinburgh, and Kathleen Milthorpe, *née* Parker (d 1966); *b* 1 Feb 1938; *Educ* Glenalmond Coll Perth, Pembroke Coll Oxford (MA); *m* 1968, Elspeth Mary Dunlop, da of James Bowie Miller, of E Lothian; 3 s (Hamish b 1970, Neil b 1972, Iain b 1975); *Career* Nat Serv, 2 Lt RASC Aldershot & Malta 1956-58; barr Inner Temple 1963; advocate 1966, advocate-depute 1972-75; standing jr counsel Dept of Energy 1976-79; Scottish Devpt Dept 1978-79; pres legal chm Pensions Appeal Tbnls for Scotland 1985-(legal chm 1979-), chm Faculty Services Ltd 1983-, (dir 1979-); vice-dean Faculty of Advocates 1983-; *Publications* Medical Negligence: An Introduction (1983); *Recreations* sport, travel, Africana; *Style*— Alastair Cameron, Esq, QC; 4 Garscube Terrace, Edinburgh EH12 6BQ (☎ 031 337 3460); Advocates' Library, Parliament House, Edinburgh EH1 1RF (☎ 031 226 5071)

CAMERON, John Bell; CBE; s of Capt John Archibald, MC (d 1960), and Margaret (d 1974); *b* 14 June 1939; *Educ* Dollar Acad; *m* 24 July 1964, Margaret, da of James Clapperton OBE (d 1977); *Career* pres NFU of Scotland 1979-84 (first long term pres); chm: EEC Sheepmeat Ctee 1983-, World Meats Gp 1983-, Bd of Govrs Dollar Acad, UK Sheep Consultative Ctee 1984-86, BR (Scotland) Bd 1988-; memb BR Bd 1988-; FRAgS; *Recreations* flying, shooting, swimming; *Style*— John Cameron, Esq, CBE; Balbuthie Farm, Leven, Fife, Scotland (☎ 03331210)

CAMERON, Hon Lord; Sir John Cameron; DSC (1944), DL (Edinburgh 1953); s of John Cameron, SSC (d 1943), of Edinburgh; *b* 8 Feb 1900; *Educ* Edinburgh Acad, Edinburgh Univ; *m* 1, 1927, Eileen Dorothea (d 1943), da of Harry Milburn Burrell; 1 s (Rt Hon Lord Cameron of Lochbroom, PC, *qv*), 2 da; m 2, 1944, Iris Eunice, da of late Eric Alfred Henry, Indian Police, and wid of Lambert C Shepherd; *Career* advocate Scotland 1924, KC 1936, appointed a lord of session with title Lord Cameron 1955, ret from bench 1985; former Sheriff of Inverness, Elgin and Nairn and of Inverness, Moray, Nairn and Ross and Cromarty; Hon: RSA, FRSE, FBA; Hon LLD: Edinburgh, Aberdeen, Glasgow; LittD Heriot-Watt, Hon DUniv Edinburgh; kt 1954; *Style*— The Hon Lord Cameron, DSC, DL; 28 Moray Place, Edinburgh (☎ 031 225 7585)

CAMERON, Sir (Eustace) John; CBE (1970); s of Eustace Noel Cameron (d 1939), and Alexina Maria Cameron (d 1953); *b* 8 Oct 1913; *Educ* Geelong GS, Trinity Coll Cambridge (MA); *m* 1934, Nancie Ailsa Cameron, OBE (d 1988), da of John Sutherland (d 1951); 1 da; *Career* pastoralist 1946-, state pres Liberal Party 1948-52; pres Tas Stockowners Assoc 1965-68; chllr Tasmania Univ 1973-81, memb Cwlth Housing Loan Insurance Corpn 1973-75; kt 1977; *see Debrett's Handbook of Australia and New Zealand for further details*; *Recreations* gardening, Australiana; *Clubs* Tasmanian, Launceston; *Style*— Sir John Cameron, CBE; Lochiel, Ross, Tas 7209, Australia (☎ Ross 81 5253)

CAMERON, Prof John Robinson (Robin); s of Dr George Gordon Cameron (d 1980), of Edinburgh, and Mary Levering, *née* Robinson; *b* 24 June 1936; *Educ* Dundee HS, Univ of St Andrews (MA, B Phil); *m* 1, 19 Aug 1959, Mary Elizabeth (d 1984), da of Charles Wesley Ranson (d 1988), of Lakeville Ct, USA; 1 s (Ian b 1967), 2 da (Margaret b 1962, Catherine b 1965); m2, 25 June 1987, Barbara Elizabeth, da of James Moncur (d 1967), of Newport-on-Tay; *Career* lectr in philosophy Queen's Coll Dundee 1963-67 (asst lectr 1962-63), sr lectr Univ of Dundee 1973-78 (lectr 1967-72); regius prof of logic Univ of Aberdeen 1979-; edler Ch of Scotland; *Recreations* bricolage; *Style*— Prof Robin Cameron; 70 Cornhill Rd, Aberdeen AB2 5DH (☎ 0224 486700); Dept of Philosophy, Univ of Aberdeen, Kings Coll, Old Aberdeen AB9 2UB (☎ 0224 2722365)

CAMERON, John Taylor; QC (Scot, 1973); s of late John Reid Cameron, MA, former Dir of Education, Dundee; *b* 24 April 1934; *Educ* Fettes Coll, CCC Oxford, Edinburgh Univ; *m* 1964, Bridget Deirdre Sloan; *Career* advocate 1960, lectr Edinburgh Univ 1960-64, advocate-depute 1977-79, keeper of the Advocates' Law Library 1977-; *Style*— John Cameron, Esq, QC; 17 Moray Pla, Edinburgh (☎ 031 225 7695)

CAMERON, Sir John Watson; OBE (1960); s of Capt Watson Cameron and Isabel Mann; *b* 16 Nov 1901; *Educ* Lancing; *m* Lilian Florence, *née* Sanderson; 1 s, 2 da; *Career* cmmd Durham RGA 1920; memb Northern Area Econ League 1950-80 (chm 1964-69), tres Northern Area Con Pty 1967-72, pres and patron Hartlepool Con Pty 1978- (chm 1942-45, pres 1945-76, patron 1976-78), pres J W Cameron & Co Brewery 1977- (joined 1922, md 1940, chm 1943-75); kt 1981; *Style*— Sir John Cameron, OBE

CAMERON, Joseph Gordon Stuart; WS; s of James Douglas Cameron (d 1973), of Edinburgh, and Josephine Gordon Cameron, *née* Stuart (d 1955); *b* 4 Feb 1927; *Educ* George Watson's Boys' Coll, Univ of Edinburgh (MA, LLB); *m* 24 July 1956, Celia Margaret, da of Hugh Alexander Russell Niven (d 1981), of Rugby; 3 s (Gordon b 1957, Hugh b 1960, James b 1962), 1 da (Lucy b 1965); *Career* Nat Serv Corpl Wilts

Regt 1948-49, 1953-, lectr in conveyancing Edinburgh Univ 1955-66; govr St Leonards Sch 1969-88; *Books* part author Paton and Cameron Law of Landlord and Tenant in Scotland (1967); *Style*— Joseph Cameron, Esq, WS; 23 Rutland St, Edinburgh EH1 2RN (☎ 031 228 6449)

CAMERON, Hon Mrs; Judith Evelyn Maud; *née* Baillie; o da of Brig the Hon George Evan Michael Baillie, MC, TD, RA (ka 1941), by his wife, Lady Maud, CBE, JP (d 1975), wid of Capt Angus Alexander Mackintosh, RHG, and e da of 9 Duke of Devonshire, KG; sis of 3 Baron Burton; raised to rank of a Baron's da 1964; *b* 12 Nov 1925; *m* 1949, Lt-Col Angus Ewen Cameron, MC, Scots Gds, *qv*, gs of late Donald Cameron of Lochiel, 24 Chief of Clan Cameron; 1 s, 1 da; *Career* in ATS 1944-47; *Style*— Hon Mrs Cameron; Aldourie Castle, Inverness (☎ 046 375 309)

CAMERON, Prof Kenneth; CBE 1987; s of Angus Whittaker Cameron (d 1948), of Habergham, Burnley, Lancs and Elizabeth Alice, *née* Hargreaves; *b* 21 May 1922; *Educ* Burnley GS, Univ of Leeds (BA), Univ of Sheffield (PhD); *m* 8 Dec 1948, Kathleen (d 1977), da of Frank Ewart Heap, of Burnley, Lancs; 1 s (Iain b 1955), 1 da (Susan (Mrs Cole) b 1949); *Career* WWII Fl Lt RAF 1941-45; prof of english language Univ of Nottingham 1963-87 (reader 1962-63, sr lectr 1959-62); head dept english studies 1984-87, prof emeritus 1988; hon dir English Place Name Soc; Hon Fil Dr Univ of Uppsala 1977; FBA 1976, FRHS 1970, FSA 1984; *Books* The Place-Names of Derbyshire (3 vols 1959), English Place-Names (1961, 1988), The Place-Names of Lincolnshire (1985), Studies in Honour of Kenneth Cameron (1987), Place-Name Evidence for the Anglo-Saxon Invasion and Scandinavian Settlements (1975); *Recreations* sports (supporting); *Style*— Prof Kenneth Cameron, CBE; 292 Queens Road, Beeston, Nottingham NG9 1JA (☎ 0602 254 503); The University of Nottingham, Nottingham, NG5 2RD (☎ 0602 484 848, ext 2892)

CAMERON, Michael David; s of Alec Leslie Cameron (d 1950), of Calcutta, and Evelyn Grace, *née* Sandifer (d 1979); *b* 1 August 1928; *Educ* Rottingdean Sch, Michaelhouse, S Africa, Pembroke Coll Cambridge (MA,MBBChir); *m* 2 Aug 1952, Enid Mary, da of Frank Burge; 1 s (Ian Sandifer b 1953), 2 da (Patsy b 1958, Nicola (twin)); *Career* Nat Serv Fl Lt RAF 1952-54; sr obstetrician and gynaecologist: St Thomas' London 1967-79, Royal Masonic Hosp 1979-; FRCS, FRCOG, memb RSM; *Recreations* fishing, shooting, egyptology; *Clubs* Oriental; *Style*— Michael Cameron, Esq; 1 St Stephens Close, Avenue Rd, London NW8 6DB; 92 Harley St, London W1 (☎ 01 935 7473)

CAMERON, Hon Neil; s of Baron Cameron of Balhousie (Life Peer) (d 1985); *b* 1949; *Educ* Dean Close Sch, London U (external), Bath U (BA, DEd); *Style*— The Hon Neil Cameron

CAMERON, Sheila Morag Clark; da of Sir James Clark Cameron, CBE, TD, of 62 Haven Green Court, Ealing, London, and Lady Irene Maud, *née* Ferguson (d 1986); *b* 22 Mar 1934; *Educ* Commonwealth Lodge Sch Purley Surrey, St Hugh's Coll Oxford (MA); *m* 3 Dec 1960, Gerard Charles Ryan; 2 s (Andrew b 21 Aug 1965, Nicholas b 6 Dec 1967); *Career* called to the Bar Middle Temple 1957, Harmsworth Law Scholar 1958, pt/t lectr law Univ of Southampton 1960-64, pt/t tutor Cncl of Legal Educn, memb Bar Cncl 1967-70, QC 1983, rec Crown Ct, memb cncl on Tribunals 1986-, memb boundary Cmmn for England 1989-, chllr Diocese of Chelmsford 1969, memb Legal Advsy Cmmn Gen Synod C of E 1975, vicar Gen Province of Canterbury 1983, memb cncl Wycombe Abbey Sch 1972-86, Middle Temple Bencher 1988; *Style*— Miss Sheila Cameron, QC; 2 Harcourt Bldgs, Temple, London EC4Y 9DB (☎ 01 353 8415, fax 01 353 7622)

CAMERON, Stuart Gordon; MC (1943); s of James Cameron, and Dora Sylvia, *née* Godsell; *b* 8 Jan 1924; *Educ* Chigwell; *m* 1946, Joyce Alice, da of Roland Ashley Wood; 3 s, 1 da; *Career* chm and chief exec Gallaher Ltd 1980- (md 1976-78, dep chm 1978-80), dir American Brands Inc 1980-; *Style*— Stuart Cameron, Esq, MC; Gallaher Ltd, 65 Kingsway, London WC2B 6TG (☎ 01 242 1290, telex 25505)

CAMERON OF BALHOUSIE, Lady; Patricia Louise; *née* Asprey; da of late Maj Edward Asprey, RE; *m* 1947, Marshal of the RAF Baron Cameron of Balhousie, KT, GCB, CBE, DSO, DFC, AE (Life Peer) (d 1985); 1 s, 1 da; *Style*— The Rt Hon Lady Cameron of Balhousie; c/o King's College, Strand, London WC2

CAMERON OF LOCHBROOM, Baron (Life Peer UK 1984); Kenneth John Cameron; PC (1984), QC (1972); s of Hon Lord (John) Cameron, KT, DSC, *qv*; *b* 11 June 1931; *Educ* Edinburgh Acad, Oxford U (MA), Edinburgh U (LLB); *m* 1964, Jean Pamela, da of late Col Granville Murray; 2 da (Hon Victoria Christian b 1965, Hon Camilla Louise b 1967); *Career* served RN 1950-52; advocate 1958; chm Indust Tribunals (Scotland) 1966-81, pres Pensions Appeal Tribunal (Scotland) 1976-84 (chm 1975), chm ctee for Investigation in Scotland of Agricultural Marketing Schemes 1980-84; Lord Advocate of Scotland 1984-; *Clubs* Scottish Arts, New (Edinburgh); *Style*— The Rt Hon the Lord Cameron of Lochbroom, PC, QC; 10 Belford Terrace, Edinburgh EH4 3DQ (☎ 031 332 6636)

CAMERON OF LOCHIEL, Col Sir Donald Hamish; KT (1973), CVO (1970), TD (1944), JP; 26 Chief of the Clan Cameron; s of Col Sir Donald Walter Cameron of Lochiel, KT, CMG, 25 Chief of the Clan of Cameron (d 1951), and Lady Hermione Graham (d 1978), da of 5 Duke of Montrose; *b* 12 Sept 1910; *Educ* Harrow, Balliol Coll Oxford; *m* 1939, Margaret, da of Lt-Col Hon Nigel Gathorne-Hardy, DSO; 2 s, 2 da; *Heir* s, Donald Angus Cameron yr of Lochiel b 1946; *Career* dir: Royal Bank of Scotland 1954-80 (vice-chm 1969-80), Scottish Widows Fund 1955-81, Save & Prosper Securities 1968-85; Lt-Col cmdg Lovat Scouts 1945; Hon Col: 4/5th Bn QO Cameron Highlanders 1958-69, 2 Bn 51 Highland Volunteers 1970-75; Scottish Railways Bd 1964-72 (chm Scottish Area Bd 1959-64); pt/t memb BR Bd 1962-64; Crown Estate Cmmr 1957-69, govr Harrow Sch 1967-77, pres Royal Highland Agric Soc of Scotland 1971, 1979, 1987; Ld-Lt of County of Inverness 1971-85 (formerly Vice-Lt); FCA; *Clubs* New (Edinburgh), Pratt's; *Style*— Col Sir Donald Cameron of Lochiel, KT, CVO, TD, JP; Achnacarry, Spean Bridge, Inverness-shire (☎ 039 781 208)

CAMERON OF LOCHIEL, yr, Donald Angus; DL (Lochaber, Inverness and Badenoch and Strathspey, 1986); s and h of Col Sir Donald Cameron of Lochiel, KT, CVO, TD, Chief of Clan *qv*, and Margaret, *née* Gathorne-Hardy; *b* 2 August 1946; *Educ* Harrow, ChCh Oxford (MA); *m* 1 June 1974, Lady Cecil Nennella Therese Kerr, da of 12 Marquess of Lothian, KCVO *qv*; 1 s (Donald Andrew John b 26 Nov 1976), 3 da (Catherine Mary b 1 March 1975, a bridesmaid to HRH The Princess of Wales, Lucy Margot Therese b 5 July 1980, Emily Frances b 18 Jan 1986); *Career* 2 Lt 4/5 Queen's Own Cameron Highlanders (TA) 1966-68; dir J Henry Schroder Wagg & Co Ltd 1984-; FCA 1971; *Clubs* Pratt's; *Style*— Donald Cameron of Lochiel, yr; 26 The Little Boltons, London SW10 (☎ 01 373 0999); c/o J Henry Schroder Wagg & Co Ltd, 120 Cheapside, London EC2 (☎ 01 382 6000)

CAMERON WATT, Prof Donald; s of Robert Cameron Watt (d 1982), and Barbara, *née* Bidwell (d 1977); *b* 17 May 1928; *Educ* Rugby, Oriel Coll Oxford (BA, MA); *m* 1, 1951, Marianne Ruth, *née* Grau (d 1962); 1 s (Ewen b 24 June 1956); m 2, 29 Dec 1962, Felicia Cobb Stanley; 1 step da (Cathy b 19 June 1951); *Career* Nat Serv Sgt BTA 1946-48; FO res dept 1951-54, lectr LSE 1956-62 (asst lectr 1954-56), Rockefeller res fell Washington Centre for Policy Res 1960-61; LSE: sr lectr 1962-65, reader 1966-71, titular prof of int history 1972-82, Stevenson prof of int history 1982-; official historian Cabinet Off 1977-; sec and chm Assoc of Contemporary Historians 1966-85, chm Greenwich Forum 1974-84, sec and tres Int Cmmn for the History of Int Rels; memb ed bd: Political Quarterly, Int History Review, Marine Policy, Intelligence and Nat Security; FRHistS; *Books* Britain and the Suez Canal (1956), Britain Looks to Germany (1965), Personalities and Policies (1965), Survey of Int Affairs 1961-1963 (ed 1965-71), A History of the World in the Twentieth Century Pt 1 (1967), Contemporary History in Europe (ed 1969), Hitler's Mein Kampf (ed 1969), Current British Foreign Policy (annual vols 1970-72), Too Serious a Business (1975), Succeeding John Bull: America in Britain's Place 1900-1975 (1984); *Recreations* exploring London; *Clubs* Players Theatre; *Style*— Prof Donald Cameron Watt; c/o London School of Economics, London WC2A 2AE (☎ 01 405 7686, fax 01 242 0392, telex 24655 DLPES G)

CAMERON WATT, Ewen; s of Prof Donald Cameron Watt, and Marianne Ruth Grau; *b* 24 June 1956; *Educ* St Pauls, Oriel Coll Oxford (BA); *m* 8 Jan 1983, Penelope Ann, da of Robert Henry Weldon, Stone, Bucks; *Career* ptnr E B Savory Milln 1983-85 (1979-83), divnl dir Warburg Securities (formerly Rowe & Pitman) 1986- (1983-86); memb Int Stock Exchange; *Recreations* walking, travel, Scottish watercolours; *Clubs* Vincents (Oxford); *Style*— Ewen Cameron Watt, Esq; 18 Cambridge Park, Twickenham, Middx, TW1 2JE (☎ 01 891 2590); Warburg Securities, 1 Finsbury Ave, London EC2M 2PA (☎ 01 606 1066, fax 01 382 4800)

CAMERON WATT, Penelope Ann; *née* Weldon; da of Robert Henry Weldon, and Brenda Marianne, *née* Jones; *b* 10 May 1959; *Educ* Clifton HS Bristol, St Hugh's Coll Oxford (BA); *m* 8 Jan 1983, Ewen Cameron Watt, s of Prof Donald Cameron Watt, of London; *Career* EB Savory Milln 1980-82, Wico Galloway and Pearson 1982-84, Kleinwort Benson 1984-87, Investmt mangr Robert Fleming 1987-; *Recreations* travel, walking, Japanese language; *Style*— Mrs Ewen Cameron Watt; 18 Cambridge Pk, Twickenham, Middx TW1 2JE; Robert Fleming & Co, 25 Copthall Ave, London EC2 (☎ 01 638 5858)

CAMERON-HAYES, Colonel John; MVO; s of Hugh Cameron-Hayes (d 1967), and Mabel Henrietta, *née* Jones (d 1971); *b* 30 July 1925; *Educ* Clifton Coll; *m* 11 Aug 1951, Patricia Mary, da of Lt-Col Geoffrey Hartley Yates, OBE (d 1983); 1 s (Jonathan b 1953), 1 da (Nicola b 1957); *Career* RHA, active service Middle and Far East The Kings Troop RHA, i/c Guncarriage funeral HM King George VI, 1 army offr instr Britannia RNC 1964-66, cmmd regt BAOR 1966-68, RAf Staff Coll Bracknell 1969, asst dir def policy MOD 1970-72, ret 1972; amateur rider Nat Hunt Steeplechases, hurdle and flat races, competitor Badminton; show jumping, Prince of Wales Cup winner Earls Ct; chief exec Racecourse Assoc 1972-; *Recreations* racing, polo, three-day events; *Style*— Col John Cameron-Hayes, MVO; Worplesdon Chase, Worplesdon, Surrey GU3 3LA; The Racecourse Assoc, Winkfield Road, Ascot, Berkshire (telex 848887, fax 0990-27233)

CAMERON-HEAD OF INVERAILORT, (Lucretia Pauline Rebecca Ann); *née* Farrell; CBE, JP (Inverness-shire), DL (1974); elder da of late Charles Bennett Farrell, of Archargle, Argyll; *m* 1942, Francis Somerville Cameron-Head of Inverailort (decd); *Style*— Mrs Cameron-Head of Inverailort, CBE, JP, DL; Inverailort, Lochailort, Inverness

CAMERON-ROSE, Hon Mrs; Caroline Patricia; *née* Bagot; da of 9 Baron Bagot, and Patricia Muriel, *née* Moore-Boyle; *b* 6 May 1942; *m* 1962 (m dis 1985), Hugh Alexander James Cameron-Rose; 1 s (Hugh b 1962), 1 da (Georgina b 1968); *Recreations* flying, sailing, shooting; *Style*— The Hon Mrs Cameron-Rose; c/o Silvermans, 11 High Street, Barnet, Herts

CAMILLERI, His Honour Sir Luigi Antonio; s of late Notary Giuseppe Camilleri, and Matilde, *née* Bonello; *b* 7 Dec 1892; *Educ* Gozo Seminary, Malta U; *m* 1914, Erminia, da of Prof G Cali'; 5 s, 3 da; *Career* Malta Legislative Assembly 1921-24, magistrate 1924-30, one of HM judges in Malta 1930-52, chief justice and pres Court of Appeal 1952-57; examiner in Civil, Criminal and Roman Law at Malta Univ 1931-70; knight SMO Malta 1952; kt 1954; *Style*— His Honour Sir Luigi Camilleri; 27 Victoria Ave, Sliema, Malta (☎ 513532)

CAMM, John Sutcliffe; s of Thomas Camm; *b* 18 Jan 1925; *Educ* Wycliffe Coll, Bristol U; *m* 1956, Barbara Kathleen Small; 3 s, 3 da; *Career* former schoolmaster; chm and chief exec DRG plc (Dickinson Robinson Group; paper stationery and packaging gp); *Style*— John Camm, Esq; c/o DRG plc, 1 Redcliffe Street, Bristol (☎ Almondsbury 613207)

CAMOYS, 7 Baron (E 1264; called out of abeyance 1839); (Ralph) Thomas Campion George Sherman Stonor; s of 6 Baron Camoys (d 1976), and Mary Jeanne, *née* Stourton (d 1987); the Stonors inherited the Barony through a Mary Biddulph who m Thomas Stonor 1732, descended from an earlier Thomas Stonor and Jeanne, da of John de la Pole, Duke of Suffolk, thus descending from Geoffrey Chaucer, the poet; *b* 16 April 1940; *Educ* Balliol Coll Oxford; *m* 11 June 1966, Elisabeth Mary Hyde, o da of Sir William Hyde Parker, 11 Bt; 1 s, 3 da (Alina b 1967, Emily b 1969, Sophia b 1971); *Heir* s, Hon (Ralph) William Robert Thomas Stonor b 10 Sept 1974; *Career* sits as Conservative Peer in House of Lords; dir Barclays plc 1985-, chief exec Barclays de Zoete Wedd Holdings Ltd 1986-88, dep chm 1988-; md Barclays Merchant Bank Ltd 1978-85, vice-chm 1985-86; dir: National Provident Institution 1981-, Barclays Bank International Ltd, Mercantile Credit Co Ltd; chm: Robert Jackson & Co Ltd 1968-85, Amex Bank 1977-78 (md 1975-77); memb Royal Cmmn Historical MSS 1987-, cmmr English Heritage 1984-87; memb Court of Assts Fishmongers' Co; 1 cl Order of Gorkha Dakshina Bahu (Nepal) 1980; *Recreations* the arts, shooting; *Clubs* Boodle's, Pratt's, Leander; *Style*— The Rt Hon the Lord Camoys; Stonor Park, Henley-on-Thames, Oxon RG9 6HF (☎ 049 163 644); Barclays de Zoete Wedd Ltd, Ebbgate House, Swan Lane, London (☎ 01 623 2323)

CAMP, Anthony John; s of Henry Victor Camp (d 1954), of Walkern Lodge, Hertfords, and Alice Emma, *née* Doidge (d 1973); *b* 27 Nov 1937; *Educ* Alleyne's Sch

Stevenage, UCL (BA); *m* 24 Aug 1976 (m dis 1978), Deborah Mary, da of Joseph Donald Jeavens, of Bristol; 1 s (Gavin b 1977); *Career* Soc Genealogists: res asst 1957, librarian 1959, dir res 1962, dir 1979, hon fell 1982; lectr: yearly Nat Genealogical Confs USA 1981-, Australasian Congress Canberra 1986, English Genealogical Confs 1975-; contrib daily Dairy Family Tree Magazine 1984-; Award of Merit Nat Genealogical Soc 1984; hon genealogical advsr Assoc to Combat Huntingons Chorea 1974-; Assoc Genealogists and Record Agents: fndr memb 1968, memb cncl 1968-75, chm 1973-75, vice-pres 1980-; memb cncl: Br Record Soc 1967-71 and 1983-, Br Archaeology 1973-, English Genealogical Congress 1975-, Br Records Assoc (records preservation section) 1980-83 and 1985-88, Friends of Public Record Off 1988-; pres Hertfords Family History and Population Soc 1982-; Freeman City of London 1984; *Books* Genealogists Handbook (1964), Tracing Your Ancestors (1964), Wills and Their Whereabouts (secondedn 1974), Everyone Has Roots (1978), Index to Wills Proved in Prerogative Court of Canterbury 1750-1800 (4 Vols 1976-88), My Ancestor was a Migrant (1987), My Ancestors came with the Conqueror (1988); *Style—* Anthony Camp, Esq; 65 Fursecroft, George St, London W1H 5LG (☎ 01 723 3758); 14 Charterhouse Bldgs, Goswell Rd, London EC1M 7BA (☎ 01 251 8799)

CAMP, Clarence Victor (Larry); JP (City of London 1974); s of George Victor Camp (d 1955), of Colless Rd, London, and Marjorie Minnie, *née* Salmon (d 1977); *b* 7 May 1920; *Educ* Down Lane Sch London; *m* 17 Nov 1945, Kathleen, and Walter Moody (d 1948), of Shouldham St, London; 2 s (Stuart b 26 March 1949, Stephen b 8 Feb 1954); *Career* RAOC 1940-46: 8 Army 1941-44, served Malta 1944-45, NI 1946; Bank of England 1947-80: edcon intelligence dept 1952-63, mangr mgmnt servs dept 1963-74, memb delegation to Australia and NZ 1967, princ job evaluation div 1974-80; dep chm: City of London Magistrates Cts Ctee, probation ctee, licensing ctee, ct uses gp; Freeman City of London 1957, Liveryman Worshipful Co Carmen 1976; *Books* contrib to Bankers Management Handbook (1976); *Recreations* reading, gardening, walking; *Clubs* Guildhall, Aldgate Ward, Probus; *Style—* Clarence Camp, Esq, JP; Headley Cottage, Grays Lane, Ashtead, Surrey KT21 1BZ (☎ 0372 274000)

CAMP, Jeffery Bruce; s of George Camp, and Caroline Camp; *b* 17 April 1923; *Educ* Lowestoft and Ipswich Art Schs, Edinburgh Coll of Art; *m* 1963, Laetitia, *née* Yhap; *Career* artist; pt/t lectr Slade Sch of Fine Art Univ of London; public collections incl: Arts Cncl of GB, City Art Gallery Bradford, Br Cncl, Contemporary Arts Soc, DOE, Fermoy Art Gallery King's Lynn, Univ of London, Manchester Educn Dept, Norwich Castle Museum, The Nuffield Orgn, Tate Gallery, Towner Art Gallery Eastbourne, Harris Museum and Art Gallery Preston; One Man Exhibitions: Edinburgh Festival 1950, Galerie de Seine London 1958, Beaux Arts Gallery London 1959/61/63, New Art Centre London 1968, Fermoy Art Gallery Kings Lynn 1970, South London Art Gallery (Retrospective) 1973, Royal Shakespeare Theatre Stratford 1974, Serpentine Gallery (Arts Cncl) 1978, Bradford City Art Gallery 1979, Browse and Darby 1984, The 29 Aldeburgh Festival in assoc with the Arts Cncl of GB 1986, Nigel Greenwood Gallery 1986-87, The Library Gallery Univ of Surrey 1988, Royal Albert Museum Exeter (Retrospective) 1988, Royal Acad of Arts London 1988, Manchester City Art Gallery 1988, Laing Art Gallery Newcastle 1988; Group Exhibitions include: Aldeburgh Festival 1958/61/63, Cafe Royal Centenary 1965, Marlborough Gallery London 1968, Br Painting 1974, Hayward Gallery London 1974, Br Painting 1952-77 Royal Acad Drawings at Burlington House 1977, Drawing and Watercolours for China (Edinburgh, Br Cncl Touring) 1982, Br Cncl Exhibition Delhi and Bombay 1985, Proud and Prejudiced Twining Gallery NY 1985, The Self Portrait A Modern View Artside Gallery Bath and tour 1987; ARA 1974, RA 1984; *Style—* Jeffrey Camp, Esq; c/o Nigel Greenwood Gallery, 4 New Burlington Street, London W1

CAMPBELL; *see*: Cockburn-Campbell, Montgomery Campbell

CAMPBELL, Agnes, Lady; Agnes Louise; da of late William Henry Gerhardi; *m* 1, Victor Vsevolod Watson, MBE; m 2, 1941, as his 3 wife Sir Ian Vincent Hamilton Campbell, 7 Bt, CB (d 1978); 1 s; *Style—* Agnes, Lady Campbell; Barcaldine Castle, Ledaig, Argyllshire; White Rose, Hawkhurst, Kent

CAMPBELL, Sir Alan Hugh; GCMG (1979, KCMG 1976, CMG 1964); s of late Hugh Elphinstone Campbell, of Bantham, S Devon, and Ethel, *née* Warren; *b* 1 July 1919; *Educ* Sherborne, Gonville and Caius Coll Cambridge; *m* 1947, Margaret Jean, da of Gilbert Taylor, of Sydney, NSW; 3 da; *Career* Dipl Serv 1946-: ambass to Ethiopia 1969-72, dep under-sec of state FO 1973-76, ambass to Italy 1976-79, ret; dir Nat West Bank and other cos; *Clubs* Beefsteak, Brooks's; *Style—* Sir Alan Campbell, GCMG; 45 Carlisle Mansions, Carlisle Place, London SW1

CAMPBELL, Alan Keir; s of Alastair Magnus Campbell (d 1930), of Auchendarroch, Ardrishaig, Argyll, and Evelyn, *née* Sanderson (d 1954); *b* 8 Oct 1908; *Educ* Fettes Coll Edinburgh; *m* 12 Aug 1938, Elizabeth Mary, da of Lt Col AC Adderley, DSO, RAMC (d 1943); 1 s (Keir Charles b 1942), 1 da (Fiona Evelyn Bridget b 1939); *Career* WWII Maj Intellingence Corps (despatches twice); Coats Viyella plc (formerly JTP Coats Ltd) Glasgow, Africa,ME and Scandinavia; ret ; *Style—* Alan Campbell, Esq; Drover Hse, Riccal, York YO4 6QE (☎ 075 784 209)

CAMPBELL, Hon Alastair Colin Leckie; s (by 1 m) and h of 3 Baron Colgrain; *b* 16 Sept 1951; *Educ* Eton, Trin Coll Cambridge; *m* 1979, Annabel Rose, da of Hon Robin Hugh Warrender (s of 1 Baron Bruntisfield, MC); 2 s (Thomas Colin Donald b 9 Feb 1984, Nicholas Robin b 12 Dec 1986); *Style—* The Hon Alastair Campbell; The Stables, Everlands, Sevenoaks, Kent

CAMPBELL, Hon Alastair James Calthrop; yr s of Baron Campbell of Croy, MC, PC (Life Peer); *b* 6 Jan 1952; *Educ* Eton, Oxford (BA); *Career* commissioned Queen's Own Highlanders 1973, Capt 1976, Maj 1984; FRGS; Sultan of Oman's Commendation Medal; *Recreations* bagpipes, squash, skiing; *Style—* The Hon Alastair Campbell

CAMPBELL, Alastair Lorne; s of Brig Lorne Campbell of Airds, VC, DSO, OBE, TD, *qv*, and Amy Muriel Jordan, *née* Campbell (d 1950); *b* 11 July 1937; *Educ* Eton, Sandhurst; *m* 1960, Mary Ann, da of Lt-Col (George) Patrick Campbell-Preston, MBE; 4c; *Career* md Waverley Vintners Ltd 1977-; chm Christopher and Co Ltd 1975-; *Style—* Alastair Campbell, Esq; Rosehill, Inveresk, by Musselburgh, Scotland

CAMPBELL, Alexander Buchanan; s of Capt Hugh Paterson Campbell (d 1948), of 49 St Kilda Dr, Jordanhill, Glasgow, and Elizabeth, *née* Flett (d 1954); *b* 14 June 1914; *Educ* Hyndland Sedcy Sch, Glasgow Sch of Architecture, Strathclyde Univ (BArch); *m* 24 March 1939, Sheila Neville, da of John Smith (d 1964), of Comley Cottage, Kirn, Argyll; 1 s (Euan Buchanan b 1948), 1 da (Alexis Louise Leech b 1954); *Career* WWII joined RA 1940, cmmnd RE 1941, serv dir of fortifications and works WO, chief enspr engr and signal stores 1942, chief inspr electrical and mech equipment 1943-45; cmmnd Maj RE TA 1950; asst to Prof T H Hughes G Grey Wornum city architects Glasgow 1938-40, inspr CIEME 1946, cheif tech offr Scottish Building Centre 1948 (later dep dir), commenced private practice 1950; works incl: St Christopher's church and Priesthill church Glasgow, Callendar Park and Carigle Colls of Educn (Civic Tst awards), Ascot Flats Glasgow; former pres: Glasgow Inst of Architects 1974-76, Royal Incorpn of Architects in Scotland, Glasgow Art Club; ARSA 1973, FRIBA; *Recreations* music, art, golf, dog showing and breeding; *Clubs* Glasgow Art, Isle of Man YC; *Style—* Alexander Campbell, Esq; 15 Craigmillar Ave, Milngavie, Glasgow (☎ 041 956 1233); Harbourside Apts, Port St Mary, Isle of Man (☎ 0624 832756); 1 Royal Cres, Glasgow G3 7SL (☎ 041 332 3553)

CAMPBELL, Alexander Rennie; s of Alexander Rennie Campbell (d 1959), of Edgware, Middx, and Mary Isobel, *née* Hayes (d 1976); *b* 2 Sept 1936; *Educ* Univ Coll Sch Hampstead, Gonville & Caius Coll Cambridge (BA MA); *m* 1 May 1970, Marilyn Daphne, da of Capt Robert Cyril Kerfoot, of Cheshire; 1 s (Rennie b 1972), 2 da (Kate b 1972, Anna b 1976); *Career* dir London Midland & Scottish Contractors Ltd 1974-77, chm and md AR Campbell Construction Ltd 1977-; pres Forth Valley Bldg Trades Employers Assoc, vice pres Airthey Castle Curling Club, govr Beaconhurst Grange Sch; memb Area Manpower Bd Central Scotland and Fife 1986-88; MICE 1963; *Recreations* curling; *Clubs* Stirling & County; *Style—* Alexander Campbell, Esq; Old Farm, Blair Drummond, By Stirling FK9 4UP (☎ 0786 841601); Burghmuir Industrial Estate, Stirling FK7 7PY (☎ 0786 50500, fax 0786 50413, cartel 0860 734446)

CAMPBELL, Alida, Lady - Alida Virginie (Lilian); da of Augustus Peeters van Nieuwenrode, of Pachtof, Nieuwenrode, Belgium; *m* 1, F A S Allan (decd); m 2, 1955, as his 2nd wife, Maj Sir Guy Colin Campbell, 4 Bt (d 1960); *Style—* Alida, Lady Campbell; c/o Cavalry & Guards Club, 127 Piccadilly W1

CAMPBELL, Dr Angus Scott; s of Archiebald Campbell, CBE (d 1978), and Jane, *née* Russell (d 1976); *b* 16 June 1929; *Educ* Wallington Co GS, Royal Sch of Mines Imperial Coll, London Univ (BSc, ARSM), Kings Coll Univ of Durham (Phd); *m* 1, 15 March 1952 (m dis 1977), May Ethel Campbell, da of Harold Slight (d 1976), of Carlisle, Cumbria; 1 s (Ian b 1956), 2 da (Susan b 1952, Alison b 1960); m 2, 5 Feb 1977, Anne, da of William Heslam (d 1982) of North Shields, Tyne and Wear; *Career* RAF: Pilot Offr 1954, Flying Offr 1955; geologist Conorada Petroleum Corpn Somaliland 1956-58; Oasis Oil: sr geologist Tripoli: Libya 1958-62, dir geological lab 1962-66, mangr geology Libya 1967-72; staff geologist Continental Oil Stamford USA 1974-76; Conoco Inc: mangr exploration Houston Texas 1976-82, md (UK Ltd) London 1982-87, area mangr (Europe, Asia) Houston Texas 1987-88-; memb Amercan Assoc Petroleum Geologists; *Recreations* travel, jogging, theatre; *Clubs* RAC; *Style—* Dr Angus Campbell; c/o Conoco (UK) Ltd, 116 Park St, London, W1Y 4NN (☎ 01 408 6000)

CAMPBELL, Archibald; CMG (1966); s of Archibald Campbell (d 1950), of Amersham, Bucks, and Jessie Sanders, *née* Halsall; *b* 10 Dec 1914; *Educ* Berkhamsted Sch, Hertford Coll Oxford; *m* 1939, Peggy Phyllis, da of Herbert Neville Hussey, of E Sheen; 2 s, 1 da; *Career* barr 1947; joined Colonial Serv 1936, colonial attaché Washington 1952-56, chief sec Malta 1959-62, asst sec Colonial Off 1956-67, asst under-sec MOD 1970-74, ret; *Style—* Archibald Campbell, Esq, CMG; Bransbury, Long Park, Chesham Bois, Bucks (☎ 0494 7727)

CAMPBELL, (Mary Lorrimer) Beatrix; da of James William Barnes, of Carlisle, Cumbria, and Catarina Johanna Lorier Barnes; *b* 3 Feb 1947; *Educ* Haraby Secdy Mod Sch, Carlisle HS, Architectural Assoc; *m* 28 Oct 1968 (m dis 1978), Bobby Campbell; *Career* journalist: Morning Star 1967-76, Time Out 1979, City Limits 1981-87; freelance reporter: New Statesman, Guardian, Marxism Today; broadcaster I Shot My Husband and No One Asked Me Why Documentary Channel 4 TV; memb : Communist Pty, Women's Liberation Movement; bd memb of Marxism Today; *Books* Sweet Freedom (with Anna Cooke 1981), Wigan Pier Revisited (1984 Winner of Cheltenham Literary Festival Prize), The Iron Ladies Why Women Vote Tory (1987 Winner of Fawcett Prize), Unofficial Secrets Childabuse The Cleveland Case (1988); *Recreations* movies, food, friends; *Style—* Ms Beatrix Campbell

CAMPBELL, Sir Bruce Colin Patrick; 3 Bt (UK 1913, with precedence of 1804), of Ardnamurchan, Argyllshire; name does not, at time of going to press, appear on the Official Roll of Baronets; s of Lt-Col Sir John Bruce Stuart, 2 Bt, DSO (d 1943, whilst prisoner in Palembang Camp, Sumatra); *b* 2 July 1904; *Educ* Edinburgh Acad, Glenalmond and Pangbourne Nautical Colls; *Career* no information concerning this baronet has been received since 1943; *Style—* Sir Bruce Campbell, Bt

CAMPBELL, Christopher James; s of Dr David Heggie Campbell (d 1979), and Nettie Phyllis, *née* Burgess; *b* 2 Jan 1936; *Educ* Epsom Coll Surrey; *Career* Nat Serv 2 Lt RAPC 1958-60, Capt paymaster Inf Bn HAC 1960-63; md Hardy Amies Ltd 1979-81; dir Harvey Nicholls Ltd 1973-78, Lotus Ltd 1973-78, Debenhams Fashion Dir 1981-84, Debenhams Dept Store Bd 1984-86, Debenhams Fin Ltd 1984-86; exec memb Nat Bus Co 1986-88 (non-exec memb 1988-) fin dir Nat Rivers Authy Advsy Ctee 1988-; tres Bow Gp 1966; FCA 1959; *Recreations* reading, listening to music, entertaining, indifferent bridge; *Clubs* Brooks's; *Style—* Christopher Campbell, Esq; 19 Morpeth Mansions, Morpeth Terrace, London SW1P 1ER (☎ 01 630 7527); 30 Albert Embankment, London SE1 7TL (☎ 01 820 0101)

CAMPBELL, Sir Clifford Clarence; GCMG (1962), GCVO (1966); s of late James Campbell and Blanche, *née* Ruddock; *b* 28 June 1892; *Educ* Mico Training Coll Jamaica; *m* 1920, Alice Esthephene, CStJ, da of William Jolly; 2 s, 2 da; *Career* former headmaster, MHR Jamaica 1944-45, speaker of the House of Representatives 1950-55, pres of the Senate 1962, govr-gen of Jamaica 1962-73; KStJ; *Style—* Sir Clifford Campbell, GCMG, GCVO; 8 Cherry Gdns Ave, Kingston 8, Jamaica

CAMPBELL, Cochrane Highet; CBE (1967); s of late James Campbell, of Kerelaw, Stevenston, Ayrshire; *b* 23 June 1912; *Educ* Edinburgh Acad; *m* 1946, Lesley Margaret Frances, da of late Capt L J Graham, RN; 3 da; *Career* served WW II, Maj 19 King George V's Own Lancers IA; dir James Finlay plc 1968-82; Cdr Order of the Finnish Lion 1967; *Clubs* Oriental; *Style—* Cochrane Campbell, Esq, CBE; 49 Colquhoun St, Helensburgh, Dunbartonshire G84 9JR (☎ 0436 3740)

CAMPBELL, Lord Colin Ivar; yr s of 11 Duke of Argyll (d 1973), by his 2 w, Louise (d 1970), only da of late Henry Clews, of Château de la Napoule, AM, France; *b* 14 May 1946; *Educ* in USA, Trinity Coll Glenalmond; *m* 1974 (m dis 1975), Georgia Ariana, da of Michael Ziadie; *Style—* Lord Colin Campbell; c/o Inveraray Castle, Inveraray, Argyll

CAMPBELL, Colin John Bruce; s of Capt Richard Galbraith Campbell (d 1975), and

Margaret Kathleen, *née* Spoor (d 1970); *b* 6 April 1939; *Educ* Gordonstoun, Royal Marines; *m* 15 Aug 1964, Angela Rosemary, da of the late Lt-Col Colin Gordon Irving-Bell; 2 da (Shuna Catherine Islay b 1965, Ffyona Jane Alison b 1967); *Career* Nat Serv cmmnd RM 1959-61, regular commn 1961, troop cdr 45 commando Aden 42 Commando Borneo 1962-63, Flying Trg RAF Linton on Ouse and RNAS Culdrose 1964-65, Fleet Air Arm Helicopter Pilot 845 NACS HMS Bulwork 1965-67, qualified Helicopter Flying Instr 1967, Flying Instr RNAS Culdrose 1967-69, Exchange Appt USMC New River N Carolina 1969-71, Display Pilot 1971-72, Helicopter Standards Instr RAE Farnborough 1972-74, VIP Pilot RNAS Lee-on-Solent 1974-76; capt Br Airways Helicopters 1976, hotelier 1989; memb Rotary Int; *Recreations* sailing, hillwalking, skiing; *Clubs* Argyllshire Gathering; *Style—* Capt Colin Campbell; Hazelhurst Lodge, Aboyne, Aberdeenshire (☎ 0339 2921)

CAMPBELL, Sir Colin Moffat; 8 Bt (NS *ca*1668), of Aberuchill, Perthshire; MC (1945); s of Sir John Campbell, 7 Bt (d 1960); *b* 4 August 1925; *Educ* Stowe; *m* 1952, Mary Anne Chichester, da of Brig George Alexander Bain, OBE (d 1982); 2 s, (and 1 da decd); *Heir* James Alexander Moffat Bain; *Career* employed with James Finlay and Co Ltd Calcutta 1948-58, Nairobi 1958-71, dir 1971-, dep chm 1973-75, chm (James Finlay & Co Ltd and associated cos) 1975-; pres Fedn of Kenya Employers 1962-70; chm: Tea Bd of Kenya 1961-71, E African Tea Trade Assoc 1960-61, 1962-63 and 1966-67; memb: Scottish cncl CBI 1979-85, cncl CBI 1981-, Commonwealth Dvpt Corpn 1981- (dep chm 1983-); FRSA; *Recreations* gardening, racing, cards; *Clubs* Boodle's, Western (Glasgow), Royal Calcutta Turf, Yollygunge (Calcutta), Nairobi, Muthaiga (Kenya); *Style—* Sir Colin Campbell, Bt, MC; Kilbryde Castle, Dunblane, Perthshire (☎ 0786 823104)

CAMPBELL, Hon David Anthony; o s and h of 6 Baron Stratheden and Campbell, *qv*; *b* 13 Feb 1963; c/o The Rt Hon Lord Stratheden and Campbell, Ridgewood, M5 1064, Cooroy, Queensland 4563, Australia

CAMPBELL, Donald le Strange; MC (1944); s of Donald Fraser Campbell (d 1964), of Summerhill, Heacham, Norfolk, and Caroline, *née* Henry; *b* 16 June 1919; *Educ* Winchester, Clare Coll Cambridge (BSc); *m* 6 Sept 1952, Hon Shona Catherine Greig, da of 1 Baron Macpherson of Drumochter (d 1965); 1 s (Bruce Donald le Strange b 10 July 1956), 1 da (Victoria Louise b 3 April 1959); *Career* 2 Lt RA 1939, Maj 1945, demobilised 1945; dir: Project Servs Overseas Ltd, Hovair Systems Ltd, Beechdean Farms Ltd; Liveryman of Worshipful Co of Blacksmiths 1968; *Recreations* field sports, sailing, countryside conservation; *Clubs* Boodle's, Royal Yacht Sqdn; *Style—* Donald Campbell, Esq, MC; Little Dartmouth House, Dartmouth, Devon TQ6 0JP (☎ 08043 2120)

CAMPBELL, Hon Mrs; Elisabeth Joan; *née* Adderley; da of 6 Baron Norton (d 1961), and Elizabeth, *née* Birkbeck (d 1952); *b* 12 June 1919; *m* 1943, Prof (Alexander) Colin Patton Campbell, MB, ChB, MSc, FRCP, FRCPath, s of Alexander Callender Campbell (d 1952), of Edinburgh; 2 s, (Andrew, Richard), 1 da (Rosamund); *Career* served VAD RAF Hosp Ely 1940-43; *Style—* The Hon Mrs Campbell; The Priory House, Ascott-under-Wychwood, Oxon (☎ 0993 830626)

CAMPBELL, Hon Mrs (Elizabeth Janet); *née* Mackay; da of Baron Mackay of Clashfern (Life Peer), *qv*; *b* 1961; *m* 1983, James Campbell; *Style—* The Hon Mrs Campbell; Milton of Ness Side, Inverness

CAMPBELL, Lady Elizabeth Lucy; 2 da of 6 Earl Cawdor; *b* 24 Sept 1959; *Style—* Lady Elizabeth Campbell

CAMPBELL, Hon Fiona; yst da (by 1 m) of 4 Baron Stratheden and Campbell, CBE (d 1981); *b* 1932; *Style—* The Hon Fiona Campbell; 158 Lambeth Rd, London SE1 (☎ 01 928 1633)

CAMPBELL, Lady Fiona; *née* Erskine; da of 13 Earl of Mar and 15 of Kellie, *qv*; *b* 5 April 1956, (twin with Hon Michael Erskine); *Educ* St Leonards Sch, St Andrews Fife; *m* 30 Aug 1980, Maj Andrew P W Campbell, Argyll & Sutherland Highlanders, yr s of late Prof Wilson Campbell, of Coquet House, Warkworth, Northumberland; 1 s (Barnabas b 1983), 2 da (Poppy b 1985, Rosanna b 1986); *Style—* Lady Fiona Campbell; c/o Claremont House, Alloa, Scotland FK10 2JF (☎ 0259 212020)

CAMPBELL, Hon Frederick William; yr s of 6 Earl Cawdor; *b* 29 July 1965; *Style—* The Hon Frederick Campbell; Cawdor Castle, Nairn, Scotland

CAMPBELL, Graham Gordon; CB (1984); s of late Lt-Col P H Campbell; *b* 12 Dec 1924; *Educ* Cheltenham Coll, Caius Coll Cambridge (BA); *m* 1955, Margaret Rosamond Busby; 1 da; *Career* served WW II, RA 1943-46; Miny of Fuel and Power: asst princ 1949, private sec to parly sec 1953-54, princ 1954; asst sec Miny of Power 1965, under-sec Dept of Trade and Industry 1973, under-sec Dept of Energy 1974-84; *Style—* Graham Campbell, Esq, CB; 3 Clovelly Avenue, Warlingham, Surrey CR3 9HZ (☎ 088 32 4671)

CAMPBELL, Col Sir Guy Theophilus Halswell; 5 Bt (UK 1815), OBE (1954), MC (1941); s of Maj Sir Guy Colin Campbell, 4 Bt (d 1960), and Mary Arabella Swinnerton Kemeys-Tynte (d 1948), sis of 8 Baron Wharton; *b* 18 Jan 1910; *Educ* Eton, St Andrew's Univ; *m* 1956, Elizabeth (stage name Lizbeth Webb), da of Frederick Holton (d 1956); 2 s (Lachlan, Rory); *Heir* s, Lachlan Philip Kemeys Campbell; *Career* KOYLI and Col late 60 Rifles, Camel Corps, Sudan Defence Force, served WW II (wounded), A/Brig 1945, Palestine 1948, mil advsr to Count Folke Bernadotte and Dr Ralph Bunche UN Mediation Force of Advsrs Mediation of Palestine in Cairo, Civil Affairs Office Cairo, British Mil Mission to Ethiopia 1948-52, Mau Mau 1952-56 (cmd Kenya Regt), head British Mil Mission to Libya 1956-60, ret 1960; former chm Anglo-Sudanese Soc in UK; *Books* The Charging Buffalo (a history of the Kenya Regt) (1986); *Recreations* writing, heraldry, painting ; *Clubs* Army & Navy, Special Forces, Puffin's, Royal and Ancient; *Style—* Col Sir Guy Campbell, Bt, OBE, MC; 18 Lansdown Terrace, Malvern Road, Cheltenham, Glos GL50 2JT (☎ 0242 43320)

CAMPBELL, Maj-Gen Sir Hamish Manus; KBE (1963), CB (1961); s of late Maj Arthur Crawford Julian Campbell (d 1940), Middx Regt and Army Pay Dept, and Alice, *née* O'Keeffe; *b* 6 Jan 1905; *Educ* Downside, New Coll Oxford; *m* 1929, Marcelle Amelie Alice (d 1983), da of Charles Ortlieb (d 1922), of Neuchâtel, Switzerland; 1 s; *Career* commissioned Argyll and Sutherland Highlanders 1927, transfd RAPC 1937, Maj-Gen 1959, Paymaster-in-Chief 1959-63, ret 1963; Col Cmdt RAPC 1963-70; professed in Order of Canons Regular of Prémontré 1984; *Style—* Rev Brother Hamish; Our Lady of England Priory, Storrington, Pulborough, W Sussex RH20 4LN (☎ 090 66 2150)

CAMPBELL, Hugh Hall; QC (1983); s of William Wright Campbell, of Cambuslang, Lanarkshire, and Marianne Doris Stewart, *née* Hutchison; *b* 18 Feb 1944; *Educ* Glasgow Acad, Glenalmond Coll, Exeter Coll Oxford (BA), Edinburgh Univ (LLB); *m* 1969, Eleanor Jane, da of Sydney Charles Hare, of Stoke Poges; 3 s (Benjamin b 1972, Timothy b 1975, Thomas b 1978); *Career* advocate Scottish Bar 1969, standing jr counsel to Admty 1976; dir Scottish Ensemble; FCIArb 1986; *Recreations* music, hill-walking, golf; *Clubs* HCEG (Muirfield); *Style—* H H Campbell, Esq, QC; 12 Ainslie Place, Edinburgh EH3 6AS (☎ 031 225 2067)

CAMPBELL, Iain Chalmers; s of Peter Campbell (d 1988), and Janet McVey Milton Fraser Lauder; *b* 27 May 1951; *Educ* Ringwood GS, Manchester Poly (BA Hons); *m* 7 Sept 1974, Valerie, da of Alfred Neville Downer (d 1957); 1 s (James b 1978), 2 da (Anna b 1976, Beth b 1984); *Career* slr and princ: Bowen Symes Weymouth, Trinity House Dorchester; *Recreations* windsurfing; *Style—* Iain C Campbell, Esq; Rowans, Osmington, Weymouth DT3 6EE; 7 Frederick Place, Weymouth DT4 8DP (☎ 0305 783555)

CAMPBELL, Ian; s of William Campbell (d 1968), and Helen Crockett; *b* 26 April 1926; *Educ* Dumbarton Acad, Royal Tech Coll Glasgow; *m* 1950, Mary, da of late Alexander Millar; 2 s, 3 da; *Career* test engr power stations S of Scotland Electricity Bd Local Authy 1958-70, ptnr C & W Conslts; provost of Dumbarton 1962-70 dir Dumbarton Dist Enterprise Tst; memb Strathclyde Regnl Cncl Valuation Appeal ctee; MP (Lab) W Dunbartonshire 1970-83 and 1983-87, to Sec of State for Scotland 1976-79; MIMechE, CEng; *Recreations* family; *Style—* Ian Campbell, Esq; The Shanacles, Gartocharn, Alexandria, Dunbartonshire (☎ 0389 52286)

CAMPBELL, Col Ian Clement; OBE (1962), DFC (1944, TD 1951, JP 1980, DL (Renfrewshire 1970)); s of S Campbell, MC, of Glasgow; *b* 26 April 1922; *Educ* Hurst Grange, The Leys Sch; *m* 1, 1945, Nadine Lilian (decd), da of H Wesley Steel, of Glasgow; 3 da; m 2, 1972, Kathleen Mary, *née* Bagot; *Career* RAF 1940-46, TA 1947-68; dir Scotcros plc; *Style—* Col Ian Campbell, OBE, DFC, TD, JP, DL; Scotcros plc, 3 Woodside Place, Glasgow (☎ 041 248 5822); Barcapel Holm Farm, Newton Mearns, Renfrewshire (☎ 041 639 3735)

CAMPBELL, Ian James; s of Thomas Wight Campbell (d 1966), and Doris Ada Campbell (d 1960); *b* 21 Oct 1931; *Educ* Haileybury; *m* 11 May 1957, Ann Elizabeth, da of Stanley Vernon Hardiman (d 1980); 2 s (Robert Anthony b 1958, Neil David b 1960); *Career* CA; ptnr Waugh Haines Rigby 1986, now admin Harnhull Centre of Christian Healing; *Recreations* ornithology; *Style—* Ian Campbell, Esq; Harnhill Manor Harnhill, Cirencester, Glos (☎ 0285 87283)

CAMPBELL, Ian James; s of Allan Campbell (d 1968), and Elizabeth, *née* Gamble (d 1986); *b* 9 June 1923; *Educ* George Heriot's Sch, Edinburgh Univ (MA); *m* 14 Dec 1946, Stella Margaret, da of Matthew Baird Smith, MB, ChB (d 1924); *Career* scientist; head of torpedo res div Admty Underwater Weapons Estab 1961-68, chief scientist Naval Construction Res Estab 1969-73, head of weapons dept and dep dir AUWE 1973-76, MOD: dir of res (Ships) 1976-78, scientific advsr to ship dept 1976-81, dir gen res (Maritime) 1978-81; tech dir CAP Scientific 1983-87, dir of studies Centre for Operational Res and Def Analysis 1987-; author of various res pubns and numerous MOD internal reports, tech memoranda, and other papers of a classified nature on various aspects of undersea warfare; *Style—* Ian Campbell, Esq; Claremont, North St, Charminster, Dorchester, Dorset (☎ 0605 64270); Scientific House, 40-44 Coombe Rd, New Malden, Surrey KT3 4QF (☎ 01 942 9661)

CAMPBELL, Ian Matthew; s of John Strange Campbell (d 1978), and Mary Brown, *née* Wright; *b* 4 April 1952; *Educ* Coatbridge HS, Univ of Glasgow (BSc Hons Maths); *m* 1975, Carolyn Jean, da of Robin Dalziel Vanstone, of Coatbridge; 2 s (Andrew b 1978, Jamie b 1985), 1 da (Deborah b 1980); *Career* actuary: life assurance, pensions and investmt; snr asst gen mangr of FS Assurance Ltd 1987, dir FS Investmt Services Ltd 1987, FS Investmt Managers 1984-, FS Assurance Tstees Ltd 1986-; Northern Mortgage Corp 1986; *Recreations* golf, gardening; *Clubs* Royal Scottish Automobile, Lenzie Golf; *Style—* Ian Campbell, Esq; 6 Grove Park, Lenzie, Glasgow G66 5AH (☎ 041 775 0481); FS Assurance Ltd, 190 West George St, Glasgow G2 2PA (☎ 041 332 6464, telex 779921, fax 041 332 3343)

CAMPBELL, Air Vice-Marshal Ian Robert; CB (1976), CBE (1964, AFC 1948); s of late Maj Duncan Elidor Campbell, DSO (gs of 2 Earl Cawdor) and Hon Florence Evelyn, *née* Willey, da of 1 Baron Barnby; *b* 5 Oct 1920; *Educ* Eton, RAF Coll Cranwell; *m* 1, 1953, Beryl Evelyn (d 1982), da of Brig Thomas Kennedy Newbigging, MC (d 1968), of Thaxted, Essex; 1 s; m 2, 1984, Elisabeth Lingard-Guthrie; *Career* joined RAF 1939, air attaché Bonn 1968-70, DMSI MOD 1970-72, Air Cdre 1965, Air Vice-Marshal 1970, Chief of Staff No 18 (Maritime) Gp 1973-75; *Clubs* Boodle's, Royal Air Force; *Style—* Air Vice-Marshal Ian Campbell, CB, CBE, AFC; Pike Farm, Fossebridge, Cheltenham, Glos GL54 3JR (☎ 028 572 537)

CAMPBELL, Sir Ilay Mark; 7 Bt (UK 1808), of Succoth, Dunbartonshire; s of Capt Sir George Ilay Campbell, DL, JP, 6 Bt (d 1967) and Clematis Elizabeth Denys, *née* Waring (d 1986); *b* 29 May 1927; *Educ* Eton, Christ Church Oxford (MA); *m* 22 July 1961, (Margaret Minette) Rohais, da of (James) Alasdair Anderson, of Tullichewan (d 1982); 2 da (Cecilia (Mrs MacGregor, younger of MacGregor) b 1963, Candida b 1964); *Career* Scottish agent Christie's 1968, jt Scottish agent 1973-, chm Christie's Scotland 1978-; pres Assoc for the Protection of Rural Scotland; convener Church of Scotland Ctee for artistic matters 1987-, hon vice-pres Scotland's Garden Scheme 1983-, Scottish rep Nat Art Collections Fund 1972-83; dir High Craigton Farming Co; *Recreations* heraldry, family history, collecting bookplates; *Clubs* Turf, Arts (Glasgow); *Style—* Sir Ilay Campbell, Bt; Crarae Lodge, Inveraray, Argyll PA32 8YA (☎ 0546 86274); office, Cumlodden Estate Office, Inveraray, Argyll PA32 8YA (☎ 0546 86633)

CAMPBELL, Hon James Alexander; yr s of 5 Earl Cawdor (d 1970), and his 1 wife Wilma Mairie, *née* Vickers; *b* 21 July 1942; *Educ* Eton, Royal Coll of Art; *m* 1, 14 Nov 1964 (m dis 1973) Brigid Carol Dolben, da of late Major Patrick Owen Lyons, RA; 2 da (Slaine Catherine b 1966, Clara Jenny b 1968); m 2, 1973 (m dis 1986), Ann Elizabeth, da of late Col Argyle Henry Gillmore, OBE; 2 da (Lucy Georgia Elizabeth b 1973, Sarah Ann b 1977); *Career* designer and maker of ceramics; draughtsman; work exhibited and in private and public collections in UK, USA, Europe and Japan; lecturer: Gloucestershire Coll of Arts and Technol, Herefordshire Coll of Art and Design; ARCA; *Recreations* music; *Style—* The Hon James Campbell; 141 Bath Rd, Cheltenham, Glos

CAMPBELL, James Alexander Moffat Bain; s and h of Sir Colin Moffat Campbell, 8 Bt; *b* 23 Sept 1956; *Educ* Stowe; *Career* Capt Scots Gds ret 1983, Capt London Scottish 1/51 Highlanders 1984- 87; insurance broker 1983-; *Recreations* motorcycling, gliding; *Clubs* Boodle's; *Style—* James Campbell, Esq; Kilbryde Castle, Dunblane,

Perthshire (☎ 0786 823104)

CAMPBELL, Dr James Grant; CMG (1970); s of John Kay Campbell (d 1949), of Nova Scotia, and Wilna Archibald, *née* Grant; *b* 8 June 1914,Springville NS,; *Educ* Mount Allison Univ Canada (BSc); *m* 1941, Alice Isobel, da of Robert Dougall, of Montreal; 1 da; *Career* chemical engr; chm and md Alcan Guyana 1955-71, vice pres Alcan Ore Ltd 1971-77, overseas rep Alcan Int 1977-79, conslt Atlantic Div Alcan Aluminium 1979-; Hon LLD Mount Allison 1967; *Recreations* golf, travel, gardening; *Clubs* Brooks's, Traveller's, Oriental, University (NY, Montreal); *Style—* Dr James Campbell, CMG; 45 Eaton Sq, London SW1 (☎ 01 235 2188); Shortridge, Balcombe, Sussex (☎ 0444 811 386); Palm Desert, California (☎ 619 346 7723)

CAMPBELL, Hon Mrs (Jennet Parker); da of 1 Baron Adrian, OM; *b* 16 Oct 1927; *m* 1953, Peter Watson Campbell, s of Peter Watson Campbell (d 1959), of W Kensington; 1 s (Richard), 2 da (Sally, Emma); *Style—* The Hon Mrs Campbell; St Anthony in Roseland, Portscatho, Truro, Cornwall, TR2 5EY (☎ 087 258 229)

CAMPBELL, Hon Mrs Angus; Joan Esther Sybella; JP (Cheshire); da of late Col Hercules Arthur Pakenham, CMG (d 1937), and Lilian Blanche Georgiana, *née* Ashley (d 1939); *b* 2 Feb 1904; *m* 1926, Hon Angus Dudley Campbell, CBE, JP (d 1967), yr s of 1 Baron Colgrain; 3 da; *Style—* The Hon Mrs Angus Campbell, JP; Doddington Cottage, Nantwich, Cheshire

CAMPBELL, Hon John Charles Middleton; er s (by 1 m) of Baron Campbell of Eskan (Life Peer), *qv*; *b* 1940; *Educ* Eton; *m* 1965, Patricia Ann, er da of late Tom Webster, of Bishopwood, Highgate, N6; 2 da and 1 adopted da; *Style—* The Hon John Campbell; 39 Gondar Gardens, London NW6

CAMPBELL, John Davies; CVO (1980), CBE (1981, MBE 1957, MC and Bar 1945); s of late Maj William Hastings Campbell, and Hon Eugenie Anne Westenra, *née* Plunkett, da of 14 Baron Louth; *b* 11 Nov 1921; *Educ* Cheltenham Coll, St Andrews Univ; *m* 1959, Shirley Bouch; 1 s, 2 da; *Career* despatches 1957; joined HM Diplomatic Service 1961 (formerly with Colonial Service), cnsllr Ottawa 1972-77, consul-gen Naples 1977-81; Commendatore dell'ordine al merito della Repubblica Italiana 1980; *Style—* John Campbell, Esq, CVO, CBE, MBE, MC; Ridgeway, Ludlow Road, Leominster, Herefs HR6 0DH

CAMPBELL, John Donington; da of Maj John Donington Campbell, of Heathfield, Sussex, and Edith Jean, *née* Crick; *b* 23 April 1959; *Educ* Harrow, RMA Sandhurst; *m* 4 June 1988, Catriona Helen Cecilia, s of John Spence Swan, of Letham, Fife; *Career* cmmnd Royal Scots Dragoon Guards 1979, ADC to Gneral Offr cmd Scotland and Govr of Edinburgh Castle 1985-87; Phoenix Burners Ltd 1977-79, Ivory and Sime plc 1987-; *Recreations* country pursuits, tobogganing, tennis; *Clubs* Carlton, St Moritz Tobogganing; *Style—* John Campbell, Esq; Currburn, Yetholm, Roxburghshire; Ivory and Sime plc, 1 Charlotte Sq, Edinburgh EH2 (☎ 031 225 1357, fax 031 225 2375)

CAMPBELL, John Lorne; s of Lt-Col Duncan Campbell of Inverneill (d 1954), by his 1 w Ethel Harriet, *née* Waterbury; *b* 1 Oct 1906; *Educ* Rugby, abroad, St John's Coll Oxford (MA, DLitt); *m* 1935, Margaret Fay, da of late Henry Clay Shaw, of Glenshaw, Pennsylvania, USA; *Career* ret farmer; presented Isle of Canna to the Nat Trust for Scotland 1981; author; pres Folklore Inst Scotland 1947-51, chief Inverness Gaelic Soc 1965; Hon LLD St Francis Xavier, NS 1953, Hon DLitt Glasgow 1965, DLitt Oxford 1965; *Books* Canna, the Story of a Hebridean Island (1984); *Recreations* entomology, music, sea fishing, listening to old Gaelic stories; *Style—* John L Campbell, Esq; Canna House, Isle of Canna, Scotland PH44 4RS

CAMPBELL, John Park; JP; s of Keith Campbell (d 1950), and Joan Rank *née* Park (d 1985); *b* 1 April 1934; *Educ* Strachur Public Sch Argyll, Strathallan Sch Perth; *m* 3 April 1957, Catherine Mary Sutherland; 3 s (Ian b 1960, Keith b 1962, Colin b 1968), 1 da (Karen b 1958); *Career* farmer, chm and md Glenrath (Farms) Ltd; convener Tweeddale Dist Cncl 1979-; FRAGS; *Style—* John Campbell, Esq, JP; Glenrath Manor, Peeblesshire (☎ 07214 221); The Whim Poultry Farm, Lamancha, West Linton, Peeblesshire

CAMPBELL, John Quentin; s of John McKnight Campbell, OBE, MC (d 1959), and Katharine Margaret, *née* Grant (d 1983); *b* 5 Mar 1939; *Educ* Loretto Sch, Wadham Coll Oxford (MA); *m* 1, 1960, Penelope Jane Redman; 3 s (James Alistair b 1962, John Marcus b 1964, Matthew b 1967), 1 da (Jessica Louise b 1970); m 2, 1977, Ann Rosemary, da of Sqn-Ldr Richard Henry Beeching (ret); 1 s (Frederick b 1982), 1 da (Anabella b 1977); *Career* Metropolitan Stipendiary Magistrate 1981-; chm Governors Bessels Leigh Sch, Oxford 1977-; *Clubs* Chelsea Arts, Frewen (Oxford); *Style—* J Q Campbell, Esq; 12 Park Town, Oxford; Marylebone Magistrates Court, 181 Marylebone Road, NW1

CAMPBELL, (Alastair) John Wilson; s of Wilson William Campbell (d 1975), of Warkworth, Northumberland, and Pearl Gray, *née* Ackrill; *b* 18 Feb 1947; *Educ* Kings Sch Canterbury, Sidney Sussex Coll Cambridge (MA); *m* 25 Feb 1972, Sarah Jane, da of Patrick Philip Shellard (d 1982); 2 s (Milo b 1974, Rollo b 1978), 1 da (Coco b 1976); *Career* exec NM Rothschild and Sons Ltd 1969-72, dir Noble Grossart Ltd 1973-86, md McLeod Russel MC 1979-82, md Campbell Lutyens and Co 1988-; *Clubs* Reform, New (Edinburgh); *Style—* John Campbell, Esq; 25 Lansdowne Rd, London W11 3AG (☎ 01 229 6768); Campbell Lutyens & Co, 4 Clifford St, London W1X 1RB (☎ 01 439 7191, fax 01 437 0153, telex 21 888)

CAMPBELL, Lachlan Philip Kemeys; s and h of Sir Guy Campbell, 5 Bt, OBE, MC, *qv*; *b* 9 Oct 1958; *m* 1986, Harriet Jane Sarah, o da of F E Jex Girling, of W Malvern, Worcs; *Career* The Royal Green Jackets, served in N Ireland (short service cmmn), Queen Victoria's Rifles (TA); *Style—* Lachlan Campbell, Esq

CAMPBELL, Lady Laura Jane; yst da of 6 Earl Cawdor; *b* 26 Dec 1966; *Style—* Lady Laura Campbell; 19 Grove Court, Drayton Gardens, London SW10

CAMPBELL, Louis Auchinbreck; s and h of Sir Robin Auchinbreck Campbell, 15 Bt; *b* 17 Jan 1953; *Style—* Louis Campbell, Esq

CAMPBELL, Lucy; *née* Barnett; da of James Allen Barnett, of Portland, Oregan, USA, and Jane, *née* Dodge (d 1952); *b* 26 Jan 1940; *Educ* Nightingale Bamford Sch NYC, The Garland Coll Boston Mass; *m* 1, 1959 (m dis 1963), Clifford Smith Jr, s of Clifford Smith (d 1961), of Rockpart, Maine, USA; 2 s (Clifford Allen b 24 Aug 1960, Grafton Dodge b 3 Dec 1961); m 2, 1965 (m dis 1981), Colin Guy Napier Campbell, s of Archibald Campbell (d 1975), of London; 2 da (Georgina Dorothy b 24 Jan 1969, Tessa Sylvia b 3 April 1971); *Career* art dealer in antiquarian prints and watercolours; owner of Lucy B Campbell Gallery London (founded 1984) and Georgina Fine Arts NY and Toronto; *Style—* Mrs Lucy Campbell; 80 Holland Park Ave, London W11 3RE (☎ 01 727 2205, car tel 0836 741 487)

CAMPBELL, Malcolm; s of Malcolm Brown Campbell (d 1940), and Helen Munro, *née* Carruthers; *b* 3 Jan 1934; *Educ* Glenalmond Coll; *m* 1, 25 Sept 1960 (m dis 1977), Fiona, *née* McLaren; 3 s (Colin b 30 Sept 1961, David b 19 April 1963, Graham b 6 March 1967); m 2, 18 Feb 1983, Susan Elizabeth Patten, da of Sydney David (d 1965), of Mid Glamorgan; 1 s (James b 29 June 1984), 1 step da (Elizabeth b 7 Oct 1975); *Career* Nat Serv RA 1953-55; chm and md Malcolm Campbell Ltd 1969-(joined 1955, sales mangr 1959, sales dir 1961, md 1966); dir: Glasgow C of C, Br Retailers Assoc (cncl memb); winner Scottish Special Free Enterprise Award by Aims of Indust 1988; memb bd of govrs Queen's Coll Glasgow 1989-; Freeman City of London 1978, Liveryman Worshipful Co of Fruiterers 1978; *Recreations* golf, motor boating; *Clubs* Royal and Ancient St Andrews, Prestwick; *Style—* Malcolm Campbell, Esq; Malcolm Campbell Ltd, Glasgow Rd, Rutherglen, Glasgow G73 1SJ (☎ 041 647 2141, fax 041 647 0451, telex 779256)

CAMPBELL, Malcolm Godfrey Wilson; s of Wilson William Campbell (d 1975), of Northumberland, and Pearl Gray, *née* Ackrill; *b* 30 July 1945; *Educ* The King's Sch Canterbury, Jesus Coll Oxford (MA); *Career* Oxford Univ Air Sqdn 1963-66; slr; ptnr Linklaters and Paines 1977-; memb Law Soc 1970; *Recreations* sport, flying, travel, photography; *Style—* Malcolm Campbell, Esq; Barrington House, 59-67 Gresham Street, London EC2V 7JA (☎ 01 606 7080, fax 01 606 5113, telex 884349)

CAMPBELL, Margaret Letitia; da of John Campbell; *b* 13 July 1947; *Educ* Newnham Coll Cambridge (MA), Manchester Business Sch (MBA); *m* 1973, John Sinclair Gillespie, s of John H H Gillespie, OBE; 1 s (Iain); *Career* vice pres Morgan Guaranty Tst Co of New York; *Recreations* reading, theatre, gardening; *Style—* Miss Margaret Campbell; Aldavhu, Garelochhead, Scotland (☎ 0436 810221)

CAMPBELL, Hon Mrs Margaret Taylor Young; *née* Westwood; MBE; yr da of 1 Baron Westwood, OBE (d 1953); *b* 15 Dec 1913; *m* 1, 1934 (m dis 1943), William Blackbird Lynn, s of John Lynn, of S Shields; m 2, 1945 (m dis 1974), John Bruce Campbell, s of George Howard Campbell, of Port Hope, Ontario, Canada; 1 s (Robert b 1948), 1 da (Helen b 1946); *Style—* The Hon Mrs Campbell, MBE; 2 Ethorpe Crescent, Gerrards Cross, Bucks

CAMPBELL, Sir Matthew; KBE (1963), CB (1959); s of Matthew Campbell (d 1952), of High Blantyre, Lanarkshire; *b* 23 May 1907; *Educ* Hamilton Acad, Glasgow Univ; *m* 1939, Isabella, da of late John Wilson, of St Conans, Rutherglen, Lanarkshire; 2 s (Colin, John); *Career* Civil Serv 1928-: (under-sec 1953-58) sec Dept of Agric and Fisheries 1958-68 (under-sec 1953-58); dep chm White Fish Authy 1968-78; *Style—* Sir Matthew Campbell, KBE, CB; 10 Craigleith View, Edinburgh (☎ 031 337 5168)

CAMPBELL, Michael David Colin Craven; s of Bruce Colin Campbell (d 1980), and Doris, *née* Craven-Ellis; *b* 12 Dec 1942; *Educ* Radley; *m* 6 April 1967, Linda Frances, da of Charles Brownrigg (d 1982); 1 s (Jamie b 1970), 2 da (Alexandra b 1968, Laura b 1977); *Career* chm Ellis Campbell Gp 1987- (md 1977-), dir Authority Investments plc 1986-, vice-pres Small Business Bureau 1983-; memb Hampshire CC 1983-87; *Recreations* sailing, shooting, skiing; *Clubs* Buck's, Boodle's, Royal Yacht Sqdn; *Style—* Michael Campbell, Esq; 7 The Gateways, London SW3; Shalden Park House, Shalden, Alton, Hants; Edradynate, Strathtay, Aberfeldy, Perthshire; office: Craven House, Arundell Place, West Street, Farnham, Surrey (☎ 0252 722333, fax 0252 714189, car tel 0836 590003)

CAMPBELL, Hon Moyra Jean; eld da (by 1 m) of late 4 Baron Stratheden and Campbell, CBE; *b* 1924; *Style—* The Hon Moyra Campbell; Scraesburgh, Jedburgh, Roxburghshire (☎ 0835 62416)

CAMPBELL, Lady Moyra Kathleen; *née* Hamilton; CVO (1963); only da of 4 Duke of Abercorn (d 1979); *b* 22 July 1930; *m* 1966 Cdr Peter Colin Drummond Campbell, LVO, DL *qv*, s of Maj-Gen Sir Douglas Campbell, KBE, CB, DSO, MC (d 1980); 2 s; *Career* a train bearer to HM The Queen at Coronation 1953, lady-in-waiting (temp) to HRH Princess Alexandra of Kent 1954-64, a lady-in-waiting 1964-66, and an extra lady-in-waiting 1966-69; *Style—* Lady Moyra Campbell; Hollybrook House, Randalstown, Co Antrim, N Ireland BT41 2PB (☎ 084 94 72224)

CAMPBELL, Hon Neil Donald; DSC (1945); yst s of 2 Baron Colgrain (d 1973); *b* 24 August 1922; *Educ* RNC Dartmouth; *m* 1951, Angela Louise Vereker, da of Rt Hon Sir Ronald Hibbert Cross, 1 Bt, KCMG, KCVO; 2 s (and 1 s decd), 1 da; *Career* late Lt RN, ret 1947; dir: Geo & R Dewhurst 1947-56, James Capel 1956-77; *Style—* The Hon Neil Campbell, DSC; Yorks Hill Farm, Ide Hill, Sevenoaks, Kent

CAMPBELL, Sir Niall Alexander Hamilton; 8 Bt (UK 1831), of Barcaldine and Glenure, Argyllshire; 15 Chieftain, Hereditary Keeper of Barcaldine Castle; s of Sir Ian Campbell, 7 Bt, CB (d 1978), and Madeline Lowe Reid, *née* Whitelocke (d 1929); *b* 7 Jan 1925; *Educ* Cheltenham, CCC Oxford; *m* 1949 (m dis 1956), *née* Turner; m 2, 1957, Norma Joyce, da of W N Wiggin; 2 s, 2 da; *Heir* s, Roderick Duncan Hamilton; *Career* barr 1951, hospital administrator 1953-70, dep chief clerk Inner London Magistrates' Courts 1970-76, clerk to Justices of Barnstaple, Bideford and Great Torrington and S Molton (N Devon Divs) 1976-; *Style—* Sir Niall Campbell, Bt; The Old Mill, Milltown, Muddiford, Barnstaple, Devon (☎ Shirwell 341); The Law Courts, Civic Centre, Barnstaple, Devon (☎ Barnstaple 72511); Barcaldine Castle, Benderloch via Connel, Argyllshire

CAMPBELL, Maj-Gen (Charles) Peter; CBE (1977); s of Charles Alfred Campbell (d 1975), and Blanche, *née* Appleton (d 1983); *b* 25 August 1926; *Educ* Gillingham GS, Emmanuel Coll Cambridge; *m* 1, 11 May 1949, Lucy (d 1986), da of William David Kitching (d 1960); 2 s (Murray b 2 July 1951, Colin b 16 May 1954); m 2, 22 Nov 1986, Elizabeth Barbara, da of Maj William Barington Tristram (ka 1942); *Career* cmmnd RE 1945, army staff course 1957, OC 11 Independent Field Sqdn RE in Far East 1960-62, Jt Services Staff Course 1963, co cdr RMA Sandhurst 1965-67, CRE 1 Divn BAOR 1967-70, GSO1 Plans MOD 1970-71, CRE 3 Divn UK 1971, cmd 12 Engrg Bde UK 1972-73, Royal Coll of Defence Studies 1974, Chief of Staff Northern Ireland 1975-77, Engr-in-Chief (Army) 1977-80, Col Comdt RE 1981-86, Hon Col 101 (London) Engr Regt (EOD) 1986-; chm RE Assoc 1983-; dir Quicks Gp plc 1982-, conslt Terex Equipment 1983-; FBIM 1971; *Recreations* painting, collecting militaria; *Clubs* Naval and Military; *Style—* Maj-Gen Peter Campbell, CBE; Corner Cottage, Donhead St Andrew, Shaftesbury, Dorset SP7 9EG (☎ 0747 88201)

CAMPBELL, Cdr Peter Colin Drummond; LVO (1960), DL (Antrim 1984); s of Maj-Gen Sir (Alexander) Douglas Campbell, KBE, CB, DSO, MC (d 1980), and Patience Loveday, *née* Carlyon; *b* 24 Oct 1927; *Educ* Cheltenham, RNC Dartmouth; *m* 1966, Lady Moyra Kathleen, *qv*, da of 4 Duke of Abercorn (d 1979); 2 s; *Career* late Cdr RN; equerry to HM the Queen 1957-60; farmer; Ireland rep Irish Soc 1974-;

memb NI advsy bd Abbey Nat Bldg Soc 1982-, life vice pres RN Assoc 1979-; DL and High Sheriff Co Antrim 1985, Freeman City of London 1975; *Recreations* field sports, boating; *Clubs* Army & Navy; *Style*— Cdr Peter Campbell, LVO, DL; Hollybrook House, Randalstown, Co Antrim, NI (☎ 084 94 72224); Rathlin Island, Co Antrim (☎ 02657 63911)

CAMPBELL, Hon Peter Mark Middleton; yr s (by 1 m) of Baron Campbell of Eskan (Life Peer); *b* 4 Mar 1946; *Educ* Eton; *m* 1972, Anne Susan, da of John E Cuthbert, of Enfield Middx; 2 s, 1 da; *Style*— The Hon Peter Campbell; Tudor Cottage, Magpies, Nettlebed, nr Henley, Oxon

CAMPBELL, Prof Peter Walter; s of Walter Clement Howard Campbell (d 1958), of Bournemouth, and Lillian Muriel, *née* Locke (d 1978); *b* 17 June 1926; *Educ* Bournemouth Sch, New Coll Oxford (MA), Nuffield Coll Oxford; *Career* lectr in govt Manchester Univ 1949-60; Reading Univ: prof of political economy 1960-64, prof of politics 1964-, dean of faculty of letters and socl scis 1966-69, chm graduate sch of contemp Euro studies 1971-73; vice chm Socl Serv Reading DC 1966-71; chm Reading Romilly Assoc 1965-69, Berks Electoral Reform Gp 1979-80, Reading Campaign for Homosexual Equality 1979-80; sec-tres Political Studies Assoc of UK 1955-58, chm Inst of Electoral Res 1958-65, memb cncl Hansard Soc for Parliamentary Govt 1962-77, ed Political Studies 1963-69; memb: Cwlth Scholarship Cmmn's Advsy Panel 1964-73, Soc Sci Res Cncl's Political Sci Ctee 1968-72; memb CNAA Bds and Panels 1969-78, UGC's Soc Studies Sub-Ctee 1973-83, vice pres Electoral Reform Soc 1973-, chm Cons Gp for Homosexual Equality 1982-88 (vice pres 1988-); *Books* Encyclopaedia of World Politics (1950 with W Theimer), French Electoral Systems and Elections 1789-1957 (1958), The Constitution of the Fifth Republic (1958); *Recreations* idling, ambling; *Clubs* Oxford and Cambridge, English-Speaking Union; *Style*— Prof Peter Campbell; Department of Politics, The University Reading, Reading, Berkshire RG6 2AA (☎ 0734 875 123)

CAMPBELL, Hon Mrs Phyllis Audrey; *née* Thomson; er da of 1 Baron Thomson of Fleet, GBE (d 1976); *b* 6 July 1917; *m* 1947, Clarence Elwood Campbell, s of late George Brown Campbell; 3 da; *Style*— The Hon Mrs Campbell; c/o Thomson Organisation Ltd, PO Box 4YG, 4 Stratford Place, W1A 4YG

CAMPBELL, Sir Ralph Abercromby; 2 s of Maj William Orr Campbell, MC, JP, of Burton Hall, Christchurch, Hants; *b* 16 Mar 1906; *Educ* Winchester, Univ Coll Oxford; *m* 1, 1936 (m dis 1967), Joan Childers, da of Lionel Blake, of Canford Cliffs, Dorset; 1 s, 1 da; m 2, 1968, Mrs Shelagh J Moore, of New York; *Career* barr 1928; res magistrate Kenya 1945; chief justice: Aden 1952-60, Bahamas 1960-70; kt 1961; *Style*— Sir Ralph Campbell; 12 Frere Ave, Fleet GU13 8AP (☎ 0252 615364)

CAMPBELL, Robert; s of Robert Stewart Campbell (d 1966), of Booking Hall, Coughton, Warwickshire, and Isobella Frances, *née* Nettleton (d 1957); *b* 18 May 1929; *Educ* Loughborough Univ (DLC, MSc); *m* 1950, Edna Maud, da of Thomas Henry Evans (d 1949); *Career* chartered engineer 1954-69, various appointments in Water Industry; ministry inspector 1969-74, asst dir Anglian Water 1974-77; chief exec Epping Forest District Cncl 1977-79; sec Inst of Civil Engineers; dir Watt Ctee on Energy Ltd; md Thomas Telford Ltd; Tstee ICE Benevolent fund 1979-82; chm REM Campbell Int Mgmnt Conslts 1982-; FICE; *Recreations* music, gardening, watching cricket; *Clubs* MCC; *Style*— Robert Campbell, Esq; 8 Tansy Close, Northampton NN4 9XW; 320 Wellingborough Road, Northampton NN1 4EP (☎ 0604 250959, telex 265871)

CAMPBELL, Hon Robert (Robin) Dudley; 2 s of late 2 Baron Colgrain (d 1973); *b* 6 July 1921; *Educ* Eton, Trin Coll Camb; *m* 1, 1954 (m dis 1978), Cecilia Barbara, da of late Cdr Alexander Leslie, RN; 2 da; m 2, 1983, Mrs Muriel Anne Kendal; *Career* late Scots Gds; dep chm and dir C E Coates & Co 1981-, md Baltic Investments (London) Ltd; *Style*— The Hon Robin Campbell; Sharp's Place, Boughbeech, Edenbridge, Kent

CAMPBELL, Robin Alexander; s of Robert Campbell (d 1986), of Sway, Hants, and Marion Steele, *née* Davidson; *Educ* Aldenham, Wadham Coll Oxford (MA); *m* 1968, Heather-Ann, da of Gordon Henderson Munro TD (d 1980), of Inverness; 1 s (Alexander b 1972), 1 da (Fiona b 1974); *Career* Nat Serv 2 Lt: Gordon Highlanders, 4 King's African Rifles (Kenya and Uganda); dist offr HM Overseas Civil Serv N Rhodesia 1961-64, magistrate Zambia 1964-65; called to the bar Middle Temple 1967; *Books* Seneca: Letters from a Stoic (translation 1969), Lumley's Public Health Acts (jt ed 1970-72); *Recreations* travel, mountain walking, sea canoeing, drawing and watercolours, wildlife; *Style*— Robin Campbell, Esq; 5 Arlington Sq, London N1 7DS (☎ 01 359 2334); Pollanaich, Nedd, Drumbeg by Lairg, Sutherland IV27 4NN (☎ 05 713 292); 4-5 Gray's Inn Square, Gray's Inn, London WC1R 5AY (☎ 01 404 5252, fax 01 242 7803, telex Gralaw 895 3743)

CAMPBELL, Sir Robin Auchinbreck; 15 Bt (NS 1628), of Auchinbreck; s of Sir Louis Hamilton Campbell, 14 Bt (d 1970), and Margaret Elizabeth Patricia (d 1985), da of Patrick Campbell; *b* 7 June 1922; *Educ* Eton; *m* 1, 1948, Rosemary (Sally) (d 1978), da of Ashley Dean, of Christchurch, New Zealand; 1 s, 2 da; m 2, 1978, Elizabeth, da of Sir Arthur Colegate, MP, and formerly w of Richard Wellesley Gunston; *Heir* s, Louis Auchinbreck Campbell; *Career* late Lt (A) RNVR; *Style*— Sir Robin Campbell, Bt; Greta Valley, RMD, N Canterbury, New Zealand

CAMPBELL, Roderick Duncan Hamilton; s and h of Sir Niall Campbell, 8 Bt, *qv*; *b* 24 Feb 1961; *Style*— Roderick Campbell, Esq

CAMPBELL, Ronnie; MP (Lab Blyth Valley 1987-); s of Ronald Campbell, and Edna, *née* Howes; *b* 14 August 1943; *Educ* Ridley HS; *m* 17 July 1967, Deirdre, da of Edward McHale (d 1976); 5 s (Edward b 1968, Barry b 1971, Shaun b 1973, Brendan b 1973, Aiden b 1977), 1 da (Sharon b 1969); *Career* former miner; memb Blyth Borough Cncl 1969-74, dist cnllr 1969-88, memb Blyth Valley Cncl 1974-; chm Bates NUM; *Style*— Mr Ronnie Campbell, Esq, MP; House of Commons, London SW1A 0AA

CAMPBELL, Hon Rosalind Leonora Middleton; da (by 1 m) of Baron Campbell of Eskan (Life Peer); *b* 8 July 1942; *Educ* Down House Newbury; *Career* bookbinder and restorer; *Style*— The Hon Rosalind Campbell; 13 Alma Green, Stoke Row, Oxon (☎ 0491 681349)

CAMPBELL, Ross; s of George Albert Campbell (d 1972), and Jean Glendinning, *née* Ross (d 1965); *b* 4 May 1916; *Educ* Farnborough GS, Univ of Reading (CEng); *m* 1, 9 Feb 1939 (m dis 1948), Emmy Teresa, *née* Zoph; 1 s (John Andrew), 1 da (Rita); m 2, 9 Feb 1951, Dr Diana Stewart (d 1977); 2 da (Jane (Klarli) b 1952 d 1976, Rosalie); m 3, 25 July 1979 (m dis 1984), Mrs Jean Margaret Turner; *Career* Sqdn Ldr RAF 1944-47 (section offr Palestine); municipal engr for various local authys 1936-39, civil engr Air Miny 1939-44, superintending engr Gibraltar 1952-55, Air Miny London 1955-59 (1947-52); chief engr: Far East Air Force 1959-62, Bomber Cnd 1962-63; chief res engr Persian Gulf 1966-68, dir staff mgmnt MPBW 1968-69 (professional personal mgmnt 1963-66), dir of works Air Miny 1969-72, under sec and dir defence servs PSA DOE 1972-75, bd memb crown agents and non-exec dir Int Military Servs Ltd 1979-83 (dir and dep chief exec 1975-79); FICE; *Recreations* golf, music; *Clubs* RAF, Denham Golf; *Style*— Ross Campbell, Esq; 41 Nightingale Road, Rickmansworth, Herts WD3 2DA (☎ 0923 773744)

CAMPBELL, Hon Mrs; (Shona Catherine Greig); *née* Macpherson; da of 1 Baron Macpherson of Drumochter (d 1965); *b* 31 July 1929; *m* 1952, Donald le Strange Campbell, MC, *qv*; 1 s, 1 da; *Recreations* sailing, horse racing; *Clubs* Boodles; *Style*— The Hon Mrs Campbell; Little Dartmouth House, Dartmouth, Devon TQ6 0JP (☎ (08043) 2120)

CAMPBELL, Steven MacMillan; s of George Campbell, of Glasgow, Scotland, and Martha Dallas, *née* MacMillan; *b* 19 Mar 1953; *Educ* Rutherglen Acad, Glagow Sch of Art (BA), Pratt Inst NY; *m* 4 July 1975, Carol Ann, da of Andrew Crossan Thompson, of Glasgow, Scot; 1 s (Rory b 6 June 1988), 2 da (Lauren b 22 May 1984, Greer b 25 Feb 1987); *Career* artist; collections at Hirshorn Museum, Tate Br Cncl, Wardsworth Atheneum, Metropolitan Museum; shows at: Barbara Tull NYC 1982, Riverside Studios London 1984, Walker Art Gallery Minneapolis 1985, Marlborough Fine Art London 1987 (NYC 1988); Scot Spagtics Assoc; *Recreations* angling, reading, mathematics, detective novels; *Style*— Steven Campbell, Esq; Inchwood Cottage, by Milton of Campsie, Glasgow G65 8AL; Riverbank Studio, Stirling Rd, Dunblane, Scot (☎ 0236 822 930)

CAMPBELL, Thomas; s of Thomas Campbell (d 1965), of Edinburgh, and Mary Frances, *née* Young (d 1971); *b* 13 August 1924; *Educ* Melville Coll Edinburgh, Manchester Univ; *m* 19 Nov 1955, Sheila Margaret, da of Sir George Campbell, KCIE (d 1965); 3 s (Hamish and Niall b 1957 (twins), Iain b 1958); *Career* served W Africa 1954-69; sr exec Unilever Gp of Cos 1954-74, chm George Campbell and Sons 1983-, Cons Cncllr Perth and Kinross Dist Cncl, ldr Cons Gp, chm Perthshire Tourist Bd; *Recreations* golf, gardening; *Clubs* Royal Perth Golfing Soc, Perth Hunt; *Style*— Thomas Campbell, Esq; Balnabeggan, Bridge of Cally, Perthshire (☎ 025 086 305)

CAMPBELL, Maj-Gen Victor David Graham; CB (1956), DSO (1940, OBE 1946, JP 1962, DL (Devon 1962)); s of Gen Sir David Graham Muschet Campbell, GCB (d 1936), and Janet Mary, da of Sir Robert Smith Aikman, LLD; *b* 9 Mar 1905; *Educ* Rugby, Sandhurst; *m* 1947, Dulce Beatrix, da of George B Collier (d 1953), of Whinfield, S Brent, Devon, and widow of Lt-Col John Abingdon Goodwin; *Career* 2 Lt Cameron Highlanders 1924, instructor RMC Sandhurst 1935-37, psc 1938; BM 152 Inf Bde France 1940, AQMG and Brig A/Q HQAFNEI 1945-46, cmdg 1 Cameron Highlanders Malaya 1947, Lt-Col cmdg 1 Bn Gordon Highlanders 1949, Brig cmdg 31 Lorried Inf Bde 1951-52, idc 1953, COS HQ Scottish Cmd 1954-57, Maj-Gen 1955, ret 1957; High Sheriff Devon 1968; chm: Totnes Magistrates Court 1971-75, Totnes RDC 1973; *Recreations* beagling; *Style*— Maj-Gen Victor Campbell, CB, DSO, OBE, DL; Beggar's Bush, South Brent, South Devon TQ10 9JE (☎ 036 47 3264)

CAMPBELL, Hon Sir Walter Benjamin; QC (1960); s of Archie Eric Gordon Campbell, DSO, MC (d 1963), and Leila Mary, *née* Murphy (d 1933); gggs of John Campbell of Lochend, who emigrated to Australia in 1821 (fully documented); *b* 4 Mar 1921; *Educ* Downlands Coll, Queensland Univ Australia (MA, LLB); *m* 1942, Georgina Margaret, da of George Pearce (d 1970); 2 s (Peter decd, Wallace) 1 da (Deborah); *Career* barr 1948, judge of Supreme Court of Queensland 1967-85, chief justice of Queensland 1982-85; govr of Queensland 1985-, chllr Queensland Univ 1977-85; Hon LLD Queensland Univ 1980; kt 1979; *Recreations* golf, reading; *Clubs* Queensland, Australasian Pioneers; *Style*— The Hon Sir Walter Campbell, QC; Government House, Brisbane, 4001, Australia (☎ 07 3697744)

CAMPBELL, Maj-Gen William Tait; CBE (1945), OBE (1944); s of late Robert B Campbell, of Edinburgh; *b* 8 Oct 1912; *Educ* Fettes Coll, RMC Sandhurst; *m* 1942, Rhoda Alice, da of Adm Algernon Walker-Heneage-Vivian, CB, MVO; 2 da; *Career* 2 Lt The Royal Scots (The Royal Regt) 1933; Lt-Col cmdg 1 Bn The Royal Scots 1954-57 (despatches), Brig i/c admin Malaya 1962, Maj-Gen 1964, DQMG MOD (Army Dept) 1964-67, ret 1967; Col The Royal Scots 1964-74; dir The Fairbridge Soc 1969-78; *Style*— Maj-Gen William Campbell, CBE, OBE; Ashwood, Boarhills, St Andrews, Fife (☎ 033 488 394)

CAMPBELL GOLDING, (Frederick) Keith; s of Dr Frederick Campbell Golding (d 1984), of The Barn, Hursley, Winchester, Hants, and Barbara, *née*, Hubbard; *b* 17 May 1947; *Educ* Mill Hill Sch; *m* 26 July 1980, Davina, da of Sir David Lancaster Nicolson, of Howicks, Dunsfold, Godalming, Surrey; 1 s (Angus b 1987), 3 da (Amy b 1981, Tania b 1981, Juliette b 1984); *Career* md Campbell Golding Assocs Ltd 1977-84, exec dir EBC AMRO Bank Ltd 1986-88, md EBC AMRO Asset Mgmnt Ltd 1986-88; *Recreations* field sports, wine collecting; *Clubs* Bucks; *Style*— Keith Campbell Golding, Esq; Queens Court, Tockenham, Wootton Bassett, Wilts (☎ 0793 853186); EBC AMRO Bank Ltd, 10 Devonshire Square, London EC2M 4HS (☎ 01 621 0101, fax 01 626 7915, telex 8811001)

CAMPBELL OF AIRDS, Brig Lorne Maclaine; VC (1943), DSO (1940, and Bar 1943, OBE 1968, TD 1941); s of Col Ian Maxwell Campbell, CBE, TD (d 1954), and Hilda Mary Wade (d 1969); *b* 22 July 1902; *Educ* Dulwich, Merton Coll Oxford (MA); *m* 1935, Amy Muriel Jordan (d 1950), da of Alastair Magnus Campbell of Auchendarroch; 2 s (Alastair, *qv*, Patrick); *Career* 8 (Argyllshire) Bn Argyll and Sutherland Highlanders 1921-42, Hon Col 1954-67, cmd 7 Bn 1942-43, cmd 13 Inf Bde 1943-44, BGS Br Army Staff Washington 1944-45, WWII 1939-45 (despatches four times); wine shipper; master Vintners Co 1958-59 (Liveryman hc); Lieutenancy City of London 1958-68; offr US Legion of Merit (1945); *Clubs* New (Edinburgh); *Style*— Brig Lorne Campbell of Airds, VC, DSO, OBE, TD; 95 Trinity Rd, Edinburgh EH5 3JX (☎ 031 552 6851)

CAMPBELL OF AIRDS BAY, Maj Michael McNeil; yr twin s of Rear Adm Keith McNeil Campbell-Walter, CB (d 1976), and Frances Henriette, eldest da of Sir Edward Campbell of Airds Bay, 1 Bt, MP (d 1945); *b* 3 Mar 1941; *Educ* Wellington, RMA Sandhurst; *m* 1963, Anne Catriona, da of late Capt Ian Andrew Tait, Queen's Own Cameron Highlanders; 1 s, 2 da; *Career* 2 Lt Scots Gds 1961, Adjt 1 Bn 1967-69, Maj 1970, ret 1971; recognized by Lord Lyon 1954 as representor of family of Campbells of Airds Bay and matriculated as successor and representor to his uncle Sir Duncan Campbell of Airds Bay, 2 and last Bt (d 1954); memb Queen's Body Guard for

Scotland (Royal Co of Archers); Hon ADC to Lt-Gov of Jersey 1973-80; sec-gen Confederation of Jersey Indust 1976-85; *Style—* Major Michael Campbell; Fonthill, Trinity Hill, St Helier, Jersey, CI (☎ 0534 70 681)

CAMPBELL OF ALLOWAY, Baron (Life Peer UK 1981), of Ayr, in the District of Kyle and Carrick; Alan Robertson Campbell; QC (1965); s of late John Kenneth Campbell; *b* 24 May 1917; *Educ* Aldenham, Trinity Hall Cambridge, Ecole des Sciences Politiques Paris; *m* 1957, Vivien, yr da of late Cdr A H de Kantzow, DSO, RN; *Career* sits as Conservative in House of Lords; late Lt RA supp reserve, served in BEF France during WW II (prisoner); barr Inner Temple 1939, bencher 1972; practised on Western Circuit; conslt to sub- ctee of legal ctee of Cncl of Europe on industrial espionage 1965-74; chm: Legal Research Ctee, Soc Cons Lawyers 1968-80; memb: law advsy ctee British Cncl 1974-80, management ctee Assoc for European Law 1975-, Old Carlton Club, Political ctee 1967-79; Rec of Crown Court 1976-89 ; *Clubs* Carlton, Pratt's, Beefsteak; *Style—* The Rt Hon Lord Campbell of Alloway, QC; 2 King's Bench Walk, Temple, London EC4 7DE (☎ 01 353 9276)

CAMPBELL OF CROY, Baron (UK Life Peer 1974); Gordon Thomas Calthrop Campbell; MC and Bar (1944, 1945), PC (1970); s of Maj-Gen James Alexander Campbell, DSO (d 1964), and Violet Constance Madeline Calthrop; *b* 8 June 1921; *Educ* Wellington; *m* 1949, Nicola Elizabeth Gina, da of Capt Geoffrey Spencer Madan, by his w Marjorie, er da of Sir Saxton Noble, 3 Bt; 2 s, 1 da; *Career* regular army 1939-46, Major 1942 (wounded and disabled); HM Diplomatic Service 1946-57; MP Moray and Nairn 1959-74, lord cmmr of the Treasury 1962-63, parly under-sec of state for Scotland 1963-64, oppn spokesman on Defence and Scottish Affairs 1966-70, sec of state for Scotland 1970-74; chm Alliance Building Soc (Scottish Bd), dir Alliance Building Soc (main bd) 1983-; ptnr Holme Rose Farms and Estate; conslt Chevron Cos; chm: Scottish Cncl of Independent Schs 1974-78, Stoic Insurance Services 1979-, Advsy Ctee on Pollution of the Sea 1979-81 and 1987-; tstee Thomson Foundation 1978-; chm Int Year of Disabled People in Scotland 1981; first fell Nuffield Provincial Hospital Tst, Queen Elizabeth the Queen Mother Fellowship 1981; DL Nairnshire 1985; Vice Lieut Nairnshire 1988; *Books* Disablement: Problems and Prospects in the United Kingdom; *Style—* The Rt Hon the Lord Campbell of Croy, MC, PC; Holme Rose, Cawdor, Nairn (☎ 066 78 223)

CAMPBELL OF DUNSTAFFNAGE, The Captain of; Michael John Alexander Campbell; 22 Hereditary Capt and Maor of Dunstaffnage; s of Michael Eadon Campbell of Dunstafnage, and Kathleen Weddall, *née* Lundon; s of Michael Eadon Campbell of Dunstaffnage; *b* 22 Nov 1953; *Educ* Stowe; *m* 1977, Anne Ingrid, da of Charles Arthur McIntyre; 1 s (Angus Arthur Eadon b 1983), 1 da (Claire Ingrid b 1981); *Career* yacht capt 1973-77; chm Bencamp Ltd; dir: Halfway House Enterprises Ltd, Dunstaffnage Yacht Haven Ltd; proprietor Dunstaffnage Seafoods; *Recreations* sailing, shooting; *Style—* The Captain of Dunstaffnage; Dunstaffnage, Connel, Argyll, Scotland

CAMPBELL OF ESKAN, Baron (Life Peer UK 1966); Jock (John) Middleton Campbell; s of Colin Algernon Campbell (d 1957), 4th of Colgrain, Dunbartonshire, and late of Underriver House, Sevenoaks, Kent, and Mary Charlotte Gladys, *née* Barrington; *b* 8 August 1912; *Educ* Eton, Exeter Coll Oxford (hon fell 1973); *m* 1, 8 Jan 1938 (m dis 1948), Barbara Noel, da of late Leslie Arden Roffey, of Hayesden House, nr Tonbridge, Kent; 2 s, 2 da; m 2, 7 May 1949, Phyllis Jacqueline Gilmour (d 1983), da of late Henry Boyd, CBE, of St Germain-en-Laye, France, and formerly w of James Edward John Taylor; *Career* former chm Booker McConnell Ltd and Statesman and Nation Publishing Co Ltd, former dir London Weekend TV Ltd, chm Commonwealth Sugar Exporters' Assoc 1950-84, dir Commonwealth Devpt Corpn 1968-81, chm Milton Keynes Dvpt Corpn 1967-83, pres Town and Country Planning Assoc 1980-; first Freeman of Milton Keynes 1982; D Open Univ 1973; kt 1957; *Style—* The Rt Hon Lord Campbell of Eskan; 15 Eaton Sq, London SW1 (☎ 01 235 5695); Lawers, Crocker End, Nettlebed, Oxon (☎ Nettlebed 641202)

CAMPBELL OF STRACHUR, (Ian) Niall Macarthur; 24 Chief of the Macarthur Campbells of Strachur and Representor of Baronial House of Campbell of Strachur, who held their Barony of Strachur direct from the Crown, for galley service; s of Lt-Col Kenneth John Campbell of Strachur (d 1965); *b* 23 Nov 1916; *Educ* Beaumont Coll; *m* 1947, Diana Susan, da of of Ernest Albert Sursham, JP, Lord of the Manor of Markyate, Herts; 1 s, 1 da; *Career* 2 Lt Black Watch 1939-45, Maj 1945; GRA Property Trust 1951-64; hon sec British Field Sports Soc (Berwickshire) 1980-; on Scottish Committee 1984-; *Recreations* fishing, shooting, skiing; *Clubs* Puffin's (Edinburgh); *Style—* Niall Campbell of Strachur; Newtonlees, Kelso, Roxburghshire (☎ 057 37 229)

CAMPBELL OF STRACHUR yr, David Niall MacArthur; s of (Ian) Niall MacArthur Campbell of Strachur, and Diana Susan, da of Ernest Albert Sursham; *b* 15 April 1948; *Educ* Eton, Exeter Coll Oxford; *m* 1974, Alexandra, Marquesa de Muros, da of Sir Charles Wiggin, Marques de Muros, KCMG (d 1977); 1 s, 1 da; *Career* int publishing dir of Hachette, Paris; *Style—* David Campbell of Strachur yr; 8 Rue Garanciere, Paris 6, France; Bavbreck House, By Lochgilphead, Argyll (☎ Barbreck 239)

CAMPBELL REGAN, (Maurice David) Brian; s of Maurice O'Regan, LRCPI & SI, FRSM, DLO, Fl Lt RAFMS, and Margaret, *née* McElearney; *b* 7 Nov 1936; *Educ* Ampleforth, Sorbonne Paris; *m* 1 Aug 1970, Jasmine, da of Ivor Elystan Campbell-Davys, JP (d 1965), of Neuaddfawr, Llandovery, Dyfed; 1 s (Justin), 2 da (Ciaran, Alice); *Career* CA, ptnr Buzzacott & Co; FICA; *Recreations* fishing, shooting, reading, painting; *Clubs* Reform; *Style—* Brian Campbell Regan, Esq; Beauchamps, Wyddial, Buntingford, Herts SG9 OEP (☎ 0763 71382); Buzzacott & Co, 4 Wood Street, London EC2V 4JJ (☎ 01 600 0336)

CAMPBELL-GRAY, Hon Andrew Godfrey Diarmid Stuart; *see*: Gray, Master of

CAMPBELL-GRAY, Hon Cailain Douglas; yr s of late Maj Hon Lindsay Stuart Campbell-Gray (Master of Gray), MC (d 1945); bro of 22 Lord; raised to rank of a Baron's son, 1950; *b* 14 July 1934; *Educ* Eton; *m* 1963, Wendy Helen Katharine, yr da of late William Herbert Dunlop, of Doonside, Ayr; 1 s, 1 da; *Style—* The Hon Cailain Campbell-Gray; Fanamor, Taynuilt, Argyll PA35 1HR

CAMPBELL-GRAY, Hon Cethlyn Isobell; yst da of 22 Lord Gray; *b* 14 June 1969; *Style—* Hon Cethlyn Campbell-Gray

CAMPBELL-GRAY, Hon Iona Doreen; 2 da of 23 Lord Gray; *b* 4 Sept 1962; *Educ* St Martins Sch of Art, Winchester Sch of Art (BA), Chelsea Sch of Art (MA); *Career* artist; *Style—* Hon Iona Campbell-Gray; c/o Rt Hon Lord Gray, Airds Bay House, Taynuilt, Argyll

CAMPBELL-GRAY, Hon Lucinda Margaret; eld da of 22 Lord Gray; *b* 13 May 1961; *Style—* Hon Lucinda Campbell-Gray; c/o Rt Hon Lord Gray, Airds Bay House, Taynuilt, Argyll

CAMPBELL-HARRIS, Alastair Neil; s of Maj Arthur Edward Campbell-Harris, MC, of London (d 1970), and Doris Marie, *née* Robson (d 1964); *b* 9 Feb 1926; *Educ* Sunningdale Sch, RNC Dartmouth; *m* 9 Jan 1962, Zara Carolyn, da of William Herbert Harrison, of Staffs (d 1975); 1 s (James Neil b 1966), 2 da (Clare Louise b 1963, Lucinda Zara b 1968); *Career* RN 1943-55, midshipman in Atlantic and East Indies 1943, Sub Lt in Med 1945, Lt Far East 1947-50, home waters 1950-52, ADC to Govr Gen of NZ 1952-55, ret Lt 1955; fin PR conslt; chm Citigate Communications Gp Ltd 1987; dep chm Streets Fin Strategy Ltd 1986 (dir Streets Financial Ltd 1975-86); *Recreations* shooting, fishing, golf, gardening; *Style—* Alastair Campbell-Harris, Esq; Gattendon Lodge, Goring-on-Thames, Nr Reading, Berks RG8 9LU (☎ 0491 872292); Citigate Communications Group Ltd, 7 Birchin Lane, London EC3M 2PA (☎ 01 623 2737)

CAMPBELL-JOHNSON, Alan; CIE (1947), OBE (1946); s of Lt-Col James Alexander Campbell-Johnson (d 1918), of S Australia, and Gladys Susanne Campbell-Johnson; *b* 16 July 1913; *Educ* Westminster, Ch Ch Oxford; *m* 1938, Imogen Fay de la Tour, da of Ernest Alexander Dunlap (d 1921), of Jacksonville, Illinois, USA; 1 s (decd), 1 da; *Career* political sec to Rt Hon Sir Archibald Sinclair Leader of the Lib Pty 1937-39; contested (Lib) Salisbury and S Wilts 1945 and 1950; press attaché to Viceroy and Govr-Gen of India 1947-48; PR consultant; founder and chm Campbell-Johnson Ltd 1953-78, dir Hill and Knowlton (UK) Ltd 1978-85; past pres Inst of Public Relations; US Legion of Merit; FRSA; *Books* Peace Offering (1936), Anthony Eden (1938 revised 1955), Viscount Halifax (1941), Mission with Mountbatten (1951); *Recreations* cricket; *Clubs* Brooks's, National Liberal, MCC; *Style—* Alan Campbell-Johnson, CIE, OBE; 21 Ashley Gdns, London SW1P 1QD (☎ 01 834 1532)

CAMPBELL-ORDE, Eleanor, Lady; Eleanor Hyde; *née* Watts; da of late Col Humphrey Watts, OBE, TD, and G Mary Parkes; *b* 25 August 1908; *Educ* St Winifred's, Eastbourne and Lady Margaret Hall Oxford; *m* 1938, Maj Sir Simon Campbell-Orde, 5 Bt, TD (d 1969); 2 s, 1 da; *Career* decorator with de Basil's Russian Ballet, Festival Ballet etc: painter; exhibited RA & RWS etc as 'E.Watts' Cncl of Mgmnt, Arts Educnl Sch; dir Royal Caledonian Sch Hon Citizen Tennesseee US; *Recreations* gardening, travel; *Clubs* Caledonian; *Style—* Eleanor, Lady Campbell-Orde; Westgate House, Dedham, Colchester, Essex CO7 6HJ (☎ 0206 322496)

CAMPBELL-ORDE, Sir John Alexander; 6 Bt (GB 1790), of Morpeth, Northumberland; s of Maj Sir Simon Arthur Campbell-Orde, 5 Bt, TD (d 1969) and Eleanor, Lady Campbell-Orde, *qv*; *b* 11 May 1943; *Educ* Gordonstoun; *m* 1973, Lacy Rals, da of T Grady Gallant, of Nashville, Tennessee, USA; 1 s, 3 da; *Heir* s, John Simon Arthur Campbell-Orde, b 15 Aug 1981; *Career* art dealer; *Clubs* Caledonian, Lansdowne; *Style—* Sir John Campbell-Orde, Bt; Beeswing Farm, Box 380, Route 2, Kingston Road, Fairview, TN 37062, USA

CAMPBELL-PRESTON, Lt-Col Robert Modan Thorne; OBE (1955), (MC 1943, TD and 2 Bars 1944, JP 1950, DL 1951); s of Lt-Col R W P Clarke Campbell-Preston, JP, DL (d 1929), of Ardchatton Priory, by Orban, Argyll, and Mary Agusta Margaret, *née* Nicol Thorne, MBE (d 1964); *b* 7 Jan 1909; *Educ* Eton, Christ Church Oxford (MA); *m* 6 June 1950, Hon Angela Murray, wid of Lt-Col G A Murray, OBE, TD (ka Italy 1945) and da of 2 Viscount Cowdray, DL (d 1933); 1 da (Sarah Hope (Mrs Troughton) b 7 March 1951); *Career* 2 Lt Scottish Horse 1927, Lt-Col 1945, Hon Col Fife Forfar Yeo/Scottish Horse 1962-67; md Alginate Indust Ltd 1949-74; former memb CBI Scotland; chm Argyll and Bute Tst, Vice Lord Lieut Argyll and bute 1976, memb Royal Co of Archers, Queens Bodyguard for Scotland; American Silver Star 1945; *Recreations* shooting, fishing, gardening; *Clubs* Puffins; *Style—* Lt-Col Robert Campbell-Preston, OBE, MC, TD, JP, DL; Ardchattan Priory, by Oban, Argyll (☎ 063 175 274)

CAMPBELL-PRESTON OF ARDCHATTAN, Lt-Col Robert Modan Thorne; OBE (1955), MC (1943, JP 1950, DL (Argyll and Bute 1951);; s of Col Robert William Piggott Clark-Campbell-Preston (d 1929), JP, DL, of Ardchattan and Valleyfield, Fife, and Mary Augusta Thorne, MBE (d 1964); *b* 7 Jan 1909; *Educ* Eton, ChCh Oxford; *m* 1950, Hon Angela (d 1981), *née* Pearson, 3 da of 2 Viscount Cowdray (d 1933) and wid of Lt-Col George Murray, OBE, RA; 1 da, 1 step s (*see* Duke of Atholl); *Career* Lt Scottish Horse, Lt-Col 1945, Hon Col Fife and Forfar Yeo/Scottish Horse 1962-67; memb Royal Co of Archers (Queen's Body Guard for Scotland), vice lt Argyll and Bute 1976-; Silver Star (USA); *Recreations* fishing, shooting, gardening; *Clubs* Puffins; *Style—* Lt-Col Robert Campbell-Preston of Ardchattan, OBE, MC, JP, DL; 31 Marlborough Hill, London NW8 (☎ 01 586 2291); Ardchattan Priory Connel, Argyll (☎ 063 175274)

CAMPBELL-SAVOURS, Dale Norman; MP (Lab) Workington 1979-; s of John Lawrences, and Cynthia Lorraine Campbell-Savours; *b* 23 August 1943; *Educ* Keswick Sch, Sorbonne; *m* 1970, Gudrun Kristin Runolfsdottir; 3 s; *Career* former co dir; contested (Lab) Darwen Lancs 1974, Workington Cumbria 1976; *Style—* Dale Campbell-Savours Esq, MP; House of Commons, London SW1A 0AA

CAMPBELL-SHARP, Noelle; *b* 24 Dec 1943; *m* (m dis 1987), Neil Campbell-Sharp; 1 da (Tara b 1 May 1971; *Career* clerk typist, moved into PR, freelance fashion writer for Irish newspapers, bought half share in Irish Tatler 1977 (bought out ptnrs 1979), founded Irish business magazine Success 1981, bought Social and Personal 1985; prodr of on board magazines for: Ryan Air 1986, Swansea-Cork Ferries 1988, Irish Rail 1989, Irish Ferries 1989; appeared many times on Irish TV and radio (hosting own show at one stage); *Recreations* collecting antique cars, collecting Napoleonic paraphenalia; *Style—* Ms Noelle Campbell-Sharp; Campanella, Marino Ave West, Killiney, Co Dublin

CAMPBELL-WALTER, Richard Keith; s of Rear-Adm Keith McNiel Campbell-Walter CB (d 1976), of 19a Princes Gate Mews, London SW7, and Frances Henriette, da of Sir Edward Taswell Campbell, 1 Bt, MP (d 1945); *b* 3 Mar 1941; *Educ* Milton Abbey, RAC Cirencester; *m* 1, 1963 (m dis), Marion Clare, o da of F G Minter, MBE; 2 da (Lavinia b 1964, Petrina b 1967); m 2, Dorothy Ann, yst da of late T W Oliver; 1 s (Jamie Oliver b 1972); *Career* 2 Lt Argyll and Sutherland Highlanders 1958-1964 TA; gp public relations dir Dans Simpson Gp plc 1982, dir Simpson Piccadilly Ltd 1982; *Style—* Richard K Campbell-Walter, Esq; 9 Passmore Street, London SW21 (☎ 01 823 4299); Simpson Piccadilly Ltd, 203 Piccadilly, London W1 (☎ 01 734 2002), (car

☎ 0860 360096)

CAMPDEN, Viscount; Anthony Baptist Noel; s and h of 5 Earl of Gainsborough; *b* 16 Jan 1950; *Educ* Ampleforth, RAC Cirencester; *m* 1972, Sarah Rose, er da of Col Thomas Foley Churchill Winnington, MBE; 1 s; *Heir* s, Hon Henry Robert Anthony Noel b 1 July 1977; *Style*— Viscount Campden; 105 Earls Court Rd, London W8 (☎ 01 370 5650); Exton Park, Oakham, Rutland, Leics. (☎ 0572 812209)

CAMPION, Barry Barry David Bardsley; s of Norman Campion (d 1987), of Southport, Lancs, and Enid Mary, *née* Bardsley; *b* 20 Mar 1938; *Educ* Shrewsbury; *m* 1, 1962 (m dis 1972), Victoria Wild; 1 s (Mark), 1 da (Sarah); m 2, 1979, Sally Manning, da of Frank Walter Manning Arkle; *Career* dir: Wheatsheaf Distribution and Trading 1968-78, BAF Securities Ltd 1972- (chm), Linfood Hldgs 1978-81; chm Food Div CWS Ltd 1982-87, chief exec Monarchy Foods Ltd 1987-; *Recreations* golf, cricket; *Clubs* MCC, Delamere Forest GC, Royal Birkdale GC; *Style*— Barry Campion, Esq; Monarchy Hall Farm, Utkinton, Tarporley, Ches CB6 OJZ (☎ 0829 51363); Monarchy Foods Ltd, James House, 1 Babmaes St, St James, London SW1Y 6HD (☎ 901 925 0555)

CAMPION, David Gifford; CBE (1975), TD (1963); s of Charles Aldworth Gifford Campion (d 1963), of Brasted, Kent and Margery Frances Mary, *née* Farrington (d 1956); *b* 9 Nov 1924; *Educ* Stowe, Trinity Coll Cambridge (MA); *m* 26 April 1958, Elisabeth Mary, da of Aubery Richmond Bishop Phelp, OBE, RN, of Bath, Avon; 1 s (Charles Richmond Gifford b 29 June 1963), 1 da (Alexandra Mary b 15 April 1959); *Career* WWII Lt Rifle Bde 1943-47, Maj London Rifle Bde Rangers 1951-65; called to the Bar Inner Temple 1950; Seccombe, Marshal & Campion Ltd (billbrokers) 1950-85: dir 1951-56, md 1956-77, chm 1977- 85 (Bank of England broker 1975-85); *Recreations* fishing, travel, gardening; *Clubs* Army and Navy, Green Jacket; *Style*— David Campion, Esq, CBE, TD; Littleworth Cottage, Milton Lilbourne, Pewsey, Wilts SN9 5LF

CAMPION, Sir Harry; CB (1949), CBE (1945); s of John Henry Campion, of Worsley, Lancs; *b* 20 May 1905; *Educ* Farnworth GS, Manchester; *Career* former dir central statistical off Cabinet Off; pres Int Statistical Inst 1963-67; kt 1957; *Style*— Sir Harry Campion, CB, CBE; Rima, Priory Close, Stanmore, Middx (☎ 01 954 3267)

CAMPION-SMITH, (William) Nigel; s of H R A Campion-Smith, of Gerrards Cross, Bucks, and Moyra, *née* Campion; *b* 10 July 1954; *Educ* King George V Sch Southport, Royal GS High Wycombe, St John's Coll Cambridge (MA); *m* 31 July 1976, Andrea Jean, da of Edward Willacy, of Hale Barns, Ches; 1 s (Jonathan b 1985), 1 da (Joanna b 1983); *Career* slr 1978, ptnr Travers Smith Braithwaite 1982-; memb Law Soc 1978; *Style*— Nigel Campion-Smith, Esq; Travers Smith Braithwaite, 6 Snow Hill, London EC1A 2AL (☎ 01 248 9133, fax 01 236 3728, telex 887117)

CAMPLING, The Very Reverend Christopher Russell; s of Rev Canon William Charles Campling (d 1972), and Phyllis Russell, *née* Webb; *b* 4 July 1925; *Educ* Lancing, St Edmund Hall Oxford (MA); *m* 1953, Juliet Marian, Hughes; 1 s, 2 da; *Career* temp Sub-Lt (special cypher) RNVR 1943-47; curate Basingstoke 1951-55, chaplin King's Sch Ely and minor canon Ely 1955-60, chaplain Lancing Coll 1960-67, vicar of Pershore 1968-76, rural dean Pershore 1970-76, hon canon Worcs Cathedral 1974-84, memb Gen Synod from inception, Archdn of Dudley; priest-in-charge St Augustine's Church, Dodderhill and dir of religious educn Worc dio 1976-84; dean of Ripon 1984-; memb Gen Synod 1970-; *Books* The Way, the Truth and the Life (6 volumes: a series for schools), Words for Worship, The Fourth Lesson (editor); *Recreations* music, golf, theatre; *Clubs* Naval; *Style*— The Very Rev Christopher Campling; The Minster House, Ripon, North Yorkshire HG4 1PE, (☎0765 3615)

CAMPLING, Dr Graham Ewart George; s of Reginald Ewart Campling, of Lindfield Sussex, and Elsie Clara, *née* Wodhams; *b* 27 August 1938; *Educ* Birkbeck and Imperial Colls Univ of London (BSc, PhD); *m* 1 April 1961, Zena Margaret, da of George William Birkbeck (d 1969); 2 s (Noel b 1963, Jeremy b 1969); *Career* Lt TA 1959-62; Bank of England 1956-63, Selfridges Ltd 1963-65, lectr and sr lectr in computing Brighton Poly 1965-69, head of dept of mgmnt S Bank Poly 1969-72, vice-princ Kilburn Poly 1973-77, princ Dacorum Coll Hemel Hempstead 1978-; memb Cuckfield UDC 1968-74 (ctee chm 1969-73, vice chm of cncl 1971-72), memb Mid Sussex DC 1974-76, chm of govrs Lindfield Primary Sch's 1971-79, chm of govrs Oathall Comprehensive Sch 1972-81; hon sec 1985-88, and vice pres 1988-89 of Assoc of Princ's of Colls, chm educn ctee Inst of Administrative Mgmnt 1973-81 (inst medal 1982); Freeman City of London; MBCS 1970, FBIM 1980; *Books* Can You Manage Statistics? (1968); *Recreations* transport organisation, music, film-making; *Style*— Dr Graham Campling; 46 Hickmans Lane, Lindfield, Haywards Heath, Sussex RH16 2BY (☎ 04447 3539); Dacorum Coll, Marlowes, Hemel Hempstead, Herts HP1 1HD (☎ 0442 63771)

CAMROSE, Viscountess; Joan Barbara; *née* Yarde-Buller; er da of 3 Baron Churston, MVO, OBE (d 1930); *b* 22 April 1908; *m* 1, 1927 (m dis 1936), Gp Capt Loel Guinness, OBE (d 1988); m 2, 1936 (m dis 1949), Prince Aly Khan (d 1960), s of HH Aga Khan, GCSI, GCIE, GCVO, PC; 2 s (HH Aga Khan, Prince Amyn Aga Khan); m 3, 1986, 2 Viscount Camrose, *qv*; *Style*— The Rt Hon the Viscountess Camrose; Hackwood Park, Basingstoke, Hants (☎ 0256 64630)

CAMROSE, 2 Viscount (UK 1941); Sir (John) Seymour Berry; TD; 2 Bt (UK 1921), also Baron Camrose (UK 1929); eldest s of 1 Viscount Camrose (d 1954), and Mary Agnes (d 1962), eldest da of Thomas Corns, of Bolton Street, London W; *b* 12 July 1909; *Educ* Eton, Ch Ch Oxford; *m* 1986, Hon Joan Yarde-Buller, eldest da of 3 Baron Churston, MVO, OBE (d 1930), formerly w of (i) Gp Capt Loel Guinness (d 1988), and (ii) Prince Aly Khan (d 1960); *Heir* bro, Baron Hartwell, *qv*; *Career* served WW II as Maj City of London Yeo (despatches); MP (C) Hitchin 1941-45; dir Daily Telegraph plc; a Younger Brother of Trinity House; *Clubs* White's, Buck's, Beefsteak, Pratt's, MCC, Royal Yacht Sqdn (tstee); *Style*— The Rt Hon the Viscount Camrose, TD; Hackwood Park, Basingstoke, Hants RG25 2JY (☎ 0256 464630); 8a Hobart Place, London SW1W 0HH (☎ 01 235 9900)

CAMROUX-OLIVER, Timothy Patrick; s of Wing Cdr George Leonard, DFC, AFC (d 1984), and Patricia Rosamund, *née* Douglas; *b* 02 Mar 1944; *Educ* Christs Hosp; *m* 18 July 1966, Susan Elizabeth, da of Maj Frederick Wilson Hanham, of The Cottage Chipps Manor Lane End Bucks; 2 s (James Richard b Sept 1967, Cahrles Guy b 1 April 1970), 1 da (Alexa Kate Louise b 25 Dec 1974); *Career* asst gen mangr IGI (SA) 1969-71; dir: Manson Byng Gp 1971-, Hampden Russell plc 1987-; chm: Hampden Insur Hldgs Ltd 1973-, Market Run-Off Servs Ltd 1984-; Freeman City of London 1966, memb Worshipful Co of Ironmongers 1966, FRGS 1963; *Style*— Timothy Camroux-Oliver, Esq; Gallery Ten, Lloyd's of London, One Lime St, London EC3M 7DQ (☎ 01 626 3036, fax 01 929 0044, car tel 0860 515552, telex 83688 Market G)

CANAVAN, Dennis Andrew; MP (Lab) Falkirk West 1983-; s of Thomas Canavan (d 1974), of Cowdenbeath, and Agnes Canavan; *b* 8 August 1942; *Educ* St Columba's HS Cowdenbeath, Edinburgh Univ (BSc, DipEd); *m* 1964, Elnor, da of late Charles Stewart, of Montrose; 3 s, 1 da; *Career* former head of maths dept, former assistant head Holyrood HS Edinburgh; MP (Lab) West Stirlingshire 1974-83, chm Scottish Parly Lab Gp 1980-81 (educn convener 1976-80, convener of Devolution Ctee 1985-87); memb House of Commons Select Ctee on Foreign Affairs, Scottish chm of Liberation; hon pres Milton Amateurs Football Club; *Recreations* walking, marathon running, swimming, football; *Clubs* Camelon Labour, Bannockburn Miners' Welfare; *Style*— Dennis Canavan, Esq, MP; 15 Margaret Road, Bannockburn, Stirlingshire (☎ 0786 812581); House of Commons, London SW1A 0AA (☎ 01 219 3000)

CANBY, Guy Richard; s of Arthur John Canby (d 1985), of Cottingham, Humberside, and Ivy Gladys, *née* Hutton; *b* 13 April 1950; *Educ* Hymers Coll Hull, RAC; *m* 19 July 1975, Diana Mary, da of Capt John Buckingham Segrott, of E Lothian; 2 s (Michael John b 1978, James Guy b 1981), 1 da (Charlotte Mary b 1984); *Career* asst factor Lothian Estates 1973-83; resident land agent: Thonock and Somerby Estates 1983-86; Fitzwilliam (Wentworth) Estates 1986-; FRICS, MRAC; *Recreations* shooting, fishing, squash, tennis, golf; *Style*— Guy Canby, Esq; Cortworth House, Wentworth, Rotherham, S Yorks (☎ 0226 742288); Estate Off, Clayfields Lane, Wentworth, Rotherham, S Yorks (☎ 0226 742041)

CANBY, Michael William; s of Clarence Canby, and Mary Frances, *née* Drake; *b* 11 Jan 1955; *Educ* Buckhurst Hill County HS, Cambridge Univ (BA, MA, LLB); *m* 6 Sept 1980, Sarah, da of John Houghton Masters (d 1965); 1 s (Philip Charles Houghton b 1988); *Career* admitted slr 1980, ptnr Linklaters & Ptnrs 1986-; memb: Law Soc; *Style*— Michael Canby, Esq; Barrington House, 59/67 Gresham St, London EC2V 7JA

CANDLER, Janet Elizabeth; da of Col Kenneth David Treasure, CB, CBE, TD, DL (d 1983), and Jean Treasure, *née* Mitchell, of Gwent; *b* 3 Aug 1942; *Educ* Norfolk House Sch Cardiff, Alice Ottley Sch Worcester; *m* 5 Nov 1966 (m dis 1977); 1 da (Kate b 1972); m 2, 30 Jan 1988, Nicolas Pycock Candler; *Career* slr and ptnr Treasures, Blackwood, clerk to Gen Cmmrs of Income Tax 1983-; *Recreations* theatre, seq watching, domesticity; *Style*— Mrs J P Candler; 14 Oakfield Rd, Newport, Gwent (☎ 0633 213915); 114A High St, Blackwood, Gwent (☎ 0495 223328)

CANDY, Thomas Frank; s of Frank Patrick Candy and Jacqueline Honoreen, *née* Vroome; *b* 18 Dec 1955; *Educ* Eastbourne Coll, Surrey Univ; *Career* banker; dir Eurobond Dept Hambros Bank Ltd; *Recreations* tennis, squash, windsurfing, skiing; *Clubs* Queen's; *Style*— Thomas Candy, Esq; Witley Ct, 68 Worple Rd, Wimbledon, London; Hambros Bank Ltd, 41 Tower Hill, London (☎ 01 480 5000)

CANEDO, Lady Rosemary Millicent; *née* Ward; da (twin, by 1 m), 4 Earl of Dudley, and Stella Carcano; *b* 26 May 1955; *m* 1980, Castor Cañedo, s of Castor Cañedo Pidal (d 1974); 1 da (Gabriela b 1982); *Style*— Lady Rosemary Cañedo

CANHAM, (Bryan Frederick) Peter; MC (1943); s of Frederick William Canham (d 1961), and Emma Louisa, *née* Martin (d 1971); *b* 11 April 1920; *Educ* Trinity Co Sch; *m* 1944, Rita Gwendoline, *née* Huggett, 1 s (Richard); *Career* Capt 1 RTR, N Africa, Italy, NW Europe 1939-46; controller S Europe and N Africa Shell Int Petroleum 1956-60; fin dir: Shell Co Philippines and assoc cos 1960-63, Shell Co Malaysia and assoc cos 1963-68; div head loans directorate DGXVIII EEC 1973-76 (dir investmt and loans 1976-80), chm Eurofi (UK) Ltd 1980-; FCIS, ACIS; *Style*— Peter Canham, Esq, MC; The Old Laundry, Penshurst, Kent (☎ 0892 870 239); The Cottage, Stedhamhall, nr Midhurst, W Sussex (☎ 073081 2947); Eurofi plc Ltd, Guildgate House, Newbury Berks (☎ 0635 31900)

CANN, (John William) Anthony; s of Dr John Cann, of 1 Meadowhead Rd, Southampton, and Enid Grace, *née* Long; *b* 21 July 1947; *Educ* Old Malthouse Sch Swanage, Shrewsbury, Southampton Univ (LLB); *m* 6 Jan 1973, Anne, da of Harold Thorswald Clausen, of Johannesburg; 2 s (John Harold b 25 Nov 1973, Robert Charles b 13 Aug 1984), 1 da (Sally Elizabeth b 10 Jan 1978); *Career* admitted slr 1972; Linklater & Paines 1970-: asst slr 1972-78, New York off 1975-82, ptnr 1978-; memb advsy ctee CAB (Battersea) 1973-75; Freeman City of London Slrs Co 1978; memb Law Soc; *Books* Mergers & Acquisitions Handbook (Part D); *Recreations* photography, sports; *Clubs* MCC, Wimbledon; *Style*— Anthony Cann, Esq; Langrick, 13 Murray Rd, Wimbledon, London SW19 4PD (☎ 01 946 6731); Linklaters & Paines, Barrington Ho, 59-67 Gresham St, London EC2V 7JA (☎ 01 606 7080, fax 01 606 5113, telex 884349, 888167)

CANNAN, Rt Rev Edward Alexander Capparis; s of Alexander Capparis, and Mabel, *née* Harris (d 1973); *b* 25 Dec 1920; *Educ* St Marylebone GS, King's Coll London (BD, AKC); *m* 31 May 1941, Eunice Mary, da of Arthur Blandford, (d 1964); 3 s (Jeremy b 1943, Stephen b 1949, Nigel b 1951); *Career* RAF 1937-46 (despatches 1941), cmmnd Tech Branch 1942, RAF Chaplains' Branch 1953-74, RAF Cosford 1953-54, RAF Padgate 1954-57, HQ 2 Gp Germany 1957-58, lectr RAF Chaplains' Sch 1958-60, RAF Gan Maldive Is 1960-61, RAF Halton 1961-62, RAF Hereford 1962-64, RAF Khormak sar Aden 1964-66, vice princ RAF Chaplains' Sch 1966-69, asst chaplain-in-chief 1969-74, FEAF Singapore 1969-72, HQ Trg Cmd 1972-73, princ RAF Chaplains' Sch 1973-74, hon chaplain to HM The Queen 1972-74; ordained: deacon 1950, priest 1951; curate Blandford Forum Dorset 1950-53, chaplain St Margaret's Sch Bushey 1974-79, bishop of St Helena (S Atlantic) 1979-85, asst bishop Diocese of Hereford 1986-; *Books* A History of the Diocese of St Helena 1502-1984 (1985); *Recreations* house maintenance, gardening; *Clubs* RAF; *Style*— The Rt Rev Edward Cannan; Church Cottage, Allensmore, Hereford HR2 9AQ (☎ 0432 277357)

CANNING, Hon Spencer George Stratford de Redcliffe; s and h of 5 Baron Garvagh; *b* 12 Feb 1953; *m* 1979, Julia Margery Morison, da of Col F C E Bye, of Twickenham, Middx; 1 da (Cordelia Louise Morison b 1985); *Style*— The Hon Spencer Canning; 24 Cobbold Rd, London W12 (☎ 01 749 4360)

CANNINGS-BUSHELL, David John; s of Thomas Meredith Cannings-Bushell, of Cirencester, Glos, and Julia Dorothy, *née* Dawe; *b* 8 April 1949; *Educ* Cirencester GS; *m* 31 July 1971 (sep 1981), Jennifer Ann, da of Meurig Jones, of Meifod, Powys; 2 da (Catherine Sarah b 5 Feb 1974, Louisa Frances b 24 Nov 1976); *Career* lighting dir TV drama Pebble Mill BBC 1983 (engr 1968, lectr 1978); maj prodns: Deadhead 1985, Lizzies Pictures 1986, Vanity Fair 1987, Franchise Affair 1988; BAFTA nomination Video Lighting 1987; tenor singer Pershore Choral Soc; memb: Vale of Evesham Amateur Radio Soc, Soc of TV Lighting Dirs 1981; *Recreations* choral singing, photography, painting, walking, amateur radio; *Style*— David Cannings-Bushell, Esq; Tanglewood, Bridge St, Lower Moor, Pershore, Worcs (☎ 0386 860 922); BBC, Pebble Mill, Birmingham (☎ 021 414 8418)

CANNON, George Anthony; s of Lt-Col Douglas Rabbetts Cannon, of Poole, Dorset (d 1973), and Olivia Lumley, *née* Robins, of Poole, Dorset (d 1963); *b* 9 Feb 1925; *Educ* Westminster, Christ Church Oxford (MA); *m* 9 Sept 1950, Jacqueline Hélène Edmée Charlotte, da of Dr Werner Hoedemakers, of Brussels (d 1975); 1 s (Robin b 1953), 3 da (Joy b 1955, Carolyn b 1960, Alison b 1962); *Career* Capt RA Far East; dep chm Fitch Lovall 1977-79; dir: Portsmouth and Sunderland plc, Midsummer Leisure plc, Resources International plc, Esk Food Hldgs Ltd; *Style*— George A Cannon, Esq; Princhetts, Chelsworth, Ipswich IP7 7HU; 1 Smyrna Mansions, Smyrna Road, London NW6 74LY (☎ 01 328 3552)

CANNON, Prof John Ashton; CBE (1985); s of George Ashton Cannon, and Gladys Violet; *b* 8 Oct 1926; *Educ* Hertford GS, Peterhouse Cambridge (BA, MA), Univ of Bristol (PhD); *m* 1, 1948 (m dis 1953), Audrey Elizabeth, da of G R Caple, of Bristol; 1 s (Marcus b 1948), 1 da (Hilary b 1952); m 2, 1953, Minni Sofie, da of Frederick Pedersen of Denmark; 1 s (Martin b 1966), 2 da (Susan b 1955, Annelise b 1962); *Career* RAF Flt-Lt 1947-49 and 1952-55; reader Univ of Bristol 1970-75 (lectr 1961-67, sr lectr 1967-69), prof mod history Univ of Newcastle upon Tyne 1976- (dean Faculty of Arts 1979-82, pro vice chllr 1983-86); chm Radio Bristol 1970-74, memb Univ Grants Ctee 1983-89 (vice-chm 1986-89 chm Arts sub ctee 1983-89); FRHistS; *Books* The Fox-North Coalition (1970), Parliamentary Reform (1973), The Letters of Junius (ed 1978), The Historian at Work (1980), The Whig Ascendancy (1981), Aristocratic Century (1984), Dictionary of Historians (ed 1988), Oxford illustrated History of The Monarchy (with R Griffiths 1988); *Recreations* music, sailing, tennis; *Style*— Prof John Cannon, CBE; 17 Haldane Terr, Jesmond, Newcastle upon Tyne (☎ 091 281 5186); Alma House, Grosmont, Gwent; Dept of History, Univ of Newcastle upon Tyne (☎ 091 232 8511, ext 6694)

CANNON, Nicholas Charles; s of Dr Ronald Cannon, of W Sussex, and Anita, *née* Foux; *b* 21 April 1951; *Educ* Northease Manor Lewes Sussex, Davies's Tutors Hove Sussex, King's Coll London (LLB), Inns of Court Sch of Law; *Career* barr Gray's Inn 1973, lectr Inns of Ct Sch of Law 1974-77, legal advsr Br Bankers Assoc 1978-80; memb legal ctee EEC Banking Comm, legal advsr Scandinavian Bank Gp plc 1980- (Gp legal advsr and exec dir 1987); memb: Inst of Strategic Studies, London, Bar Assoc of Commerce and Indust; *Books* various articles on int fin law; *Recreations* opera, art history, int politics and relations, tennis, travel; *Clubs* St James's; *Style*— Nicholas C Cannon, Esq; 13 Wilton Mews, London SW1X 7AT; Scandinavian Bank Group plc, Scandinavian House, 2/6 Cannon Street, London EC4M 6XX (☎ 01 236 6090, fax 01 248 6612, telex 889093)

CANNON, Simon Adrian; s of Henry Leigh Cannon (d 1987), of Bristol, and Frances Mary; *b* 5 June 1952; *Educ* Clifton, Nottingham Univ (LLB, MIL); *m* Aug 1978, Gunda, da of Paul Kern, of Remscheid, W Germany; *Career* dir: John Martin Publishing Ltd 1978- (and co sec), Planning Research and System plc 1983-; *Recreations* languages (translations), script writing, music; *Style*— Simon A Cannon, Esq; PRS plc, 44-48 Dover Street, London W1 (☎ 01 409 1635, fax 01 629 0221)

CANNON-BROOKES, Dr Peter; s of Victor Montgomery Cannon-Brookes, and Nancy Margaret, *née* Markham Carter; *b* 23 August 1938; *Educ* Bryanston, Trinity Hall Cambridge (MA), Courtauld Inst of Art Univ of London (PhD); *m* 13 April 1966, Caroline Aylmer, da of Lt Col John Aylmer Christie-Miller, CBE, TD, DL, of Manor House, Bourton-on-the-Hill, Gloucs; 1 s (Stephen William Aylmer b 1966), 1 da (Emma Wilbraham Montgomery b 1968); *Career* keeper dept of art: City Museum and Art Gallery Birmingham 1965-78, Nat Museum of Wales 1978-86; Int Cncl of Museums: memb exec bd UK ctee 1973-81, pres Int Art Exhibitions Ctee 1977-79 (exec bd 1975-81), vice pres Conservation Ctee 1978-81 (exec bd 1975-81); Welsh Arts Cncl 1978-87: Art Ctee 1978-84, Craft Ctee 1983-87; projects and organisations ctee Crafts Cncl 1985-87, pres Welsh Fedn of Museums 1980-82, pres S Wales Art Soc 1980-87, ed Int Jl of Museum Mgmnt and Curatorship 1981-, dir museum servs Stipple Database Servs Ltd 1986-, conslt curator The Tabley House Collection 1988-; town twinning ctee Birmingham Int Cncl 1968-78, Birmingham Diocesan Synod 1970-78, Birmingham Diocesan ADU Ctee for Care of Churches 1972-78, Edgbaston Deanery Synod 1970-78 (lay jt chm 1975-78); JP: Birmingham 1973-78, Cardiff 1978-82; Liveryman Worshipful Co of Goldsmiths 1974 (Freeman 1969); FMA, FIIC, FRSA; *Books* European Sculpture (with H D Molesworth, 1964), Baroque Churches (with C A Cannon-Brookes, 1969), Lombard Painting (1974), After Gulbenkian (1976), The Cornbury Park Bellini (1977), Michael Ayrton (1978), Emile Antoine Bourdelle (1983), Ivor Roberts-Jones (1983), Czech Sculpture 1800-1938 (1983); *Recreations* cooking, growing vegetables, photography; *Clubs* Athenaeum, Birmingham (Birmingham); *Style*— Dr Peter Cannon-Brookes; Thrupp Hse, Abingdon, Oxon OX14 3NE (☎ 0235 205 95); Warren Hse, Thame Lane, Culham, nr Abingdon, Oxon OX14 3DT (☎ 0235 246 76)

CANOSA MONTORO, Francisco Octavio (Frank); s of Dr Francisco Canosa Lorenzo, and Elisa, *née* Montoro de la Torre; *b* 28 May 1951; *Educ* Columbia Univ NY (BA), Fordham Univ NY (JD); *m* 1, Dec 1972 (m dis 1975), Gloria de Avagon; m, 2 15 Sept 1979, Belinda Mary, da of Lt-Col Charles Reginald Clayton Albrecht, OBE, TA, of Pulborough, Sussex; 2 da (Alexandra Elisa b 12 Jan 1983, Isabel Christina b 20 June 1985); *Career* asst to pres Bank of America Ny 1975, asst vice pres Mfrs Hanover Tst Co NY 1978; Bank of America Int Ltd London: vice pres 1980, exec dir 1985, currently head of corporate fin UK and Europe; *Clubs* RAC; *Style*— Frank Canosa Montoro, Esq; 38 St Mary's Grove, London W4 (☎ 01 994 6827); Bank of America International Ltd, 1 Watling St, London EC4P 4BX (☎ 01 634 4511, fax 01 634 4532, telex 884552)

CANSDALE, George Soper; yst s of George William Cansdale (d 1973), of Paignton, Devon, and Alice Louisa Cansdale (d 1948); *b* 29 Nov 1909; *Educ* Brentwood Sch, Oxford (BA, BSc); *m* 1940, Margaret Sheila, o da of Robert Marshall Williamson, Indian Forest Service; 2 s (David, Richard); *Career* Colonial Forest Serv Ghana 1934-48, supt Zoological Soc of London 1948-53, TV presenter 1948-; TV Soc Silver Medal 1952; *Books* Animals of West Africa (1946), West African Snakes (1960), Animals of Bible Lands (1970); *Recreations* gardening, birdwatching, fishing; *Clubs* Royal Cwlth Soc; *Style*— George Cansdale, Esq; Dove Cottage, Great Chesterford, Essex CB10 1PL (☎ 0799 30274)

CANT, Frank Edward Frederick; s of Frank Edward Cant (d 1970), of Paignton, and Daisy Beatrice Pitts (d 1984); *b* 10 Sept 1909; *Educ* Merchant Taylors' Crosby; *m* 29 June 1940, Elizabeth Muriel, da of Henry Bernard Pinnington (d 1955), of Blundellsands, Lancashire; 1 s (Anthony Pinnington b 1941); *Career* joined Br American Tobacco Co Ltd on leaving school in 1927, transferred to India 1934, retired from India as district mangr 1960; *Recreations* photography, carpentry, rugby, cricket, walking; *Clubs* Nat Trust and Country Gentlemans Assoc; *Style*— Frank Cant, Esq; The Croft, Well lane, Mollington, Chester CH1 6LD (☎ 0244 851208)

CANTACUZINO, Sherban; CBE (1988); s of Prince Georges Matei Cantacuzino (d 1960), and Princess Alexandra, *née* Princess Stirbey; *b* 6 Sept 1928; *Educ* Winchester, Magdalene Coll Cambridge (MA); *m* 29 Jan 1954, Anne Mary Trafford, da of Maj Cecil Edward Trafford, MC (d 1948); 1 s (Sherban d 1978), 2 da (Ilinca, Marina); *Career* ptnr Steane Shipman & Cantacuzino Chartered Architects 1956-65, private practice as Sherban Cantacuzino Assocs 1965-73, asst ed Architectural Review 1967-73 (exec ed 1973-79), sr lectr Dept of Architecture Coll of Art Canterbury 1967-70; tstee: Thomas Cubitt Tst 1978-, Design Museum (Conran Fndn) 1981-; memb: Arts Panel Arts Cncl 1977-80, steering ctee Aga Khan Award for Architecture 1980-83 (memb of Master Jury 1980), cncl RSA 1980-85, Design Ctee London Tport 1981-82, advsy panel Railway Heritage Tst 1986-; chm Int cncl of Monuments and Sites (ICOMOS) UK Ctee; memb Fabric Ctee Canterbury Cathedral 1987; ARIBA 1956, FRIBA 1969; *Books* Modern Houses of the World (1964, 3rd edn 1966), Great modern Architecture (1966, 2nd edn 1968), European Domestic Architecture (1969), New Uses for Old Buildings (1975), Architectural Conservation in Europe (ed 1975), Wells Coates, a monograph (1978), Saving Old Buildings (1980 with Susan Brandt), The Architecture of Howell, Killick, Partridge and Amis (1981), Charles Correa (1984), Architecture in Continuity: building in the Islamic world today (ed 1985), articles in Arcitectural Rev; *Clubs* Garrick; *Style*— Sherban Cantacuzino, Esq, CBE; 140 Iffley Rd, London W6 0PE, (☎ 01 748 0415); Royal Fine Art Commission, 7 St James's Square, London SW1Y 4JU, (☎ 01 839 6537)

CANTERBURY, Archdeacon of; *see*: Till, Ven Michael Stanley

CANTERBURY, 102 Archbishop of; Most Rev and Rt Hon Robert Alexander Kennedy Runcie; MC (1945), PC (1980); Primate of all England and Metropolitan; patron of 179 livings, Archdeaconries of Canterbury and Maidstone (each of which is endowed with a canonry), and 6 Cathedral Preacherships; province (contains 29 sees) founded by St Augustine (under Ethelbert King of Kent) 597; s of Robert Dalziel Runcie (d 1945), of Crosby, Merseyside, and Ann Edna, *née* Benson (d 1949); *b* 2 Oct 1921; *Educ* Merchant Taylors' Crosby, BNC Oxford (MA), Westcott House Cambridge (Dip Theol); *m* 5 Sept 1957, (Angela) Rosalind, da of J W Cecil Turner, MC (d 1968), of Cambridge; 1 s (James b 1959), 1 da (Rebecca b 1961); *Career* served WW II Scots Gds, tank offr Normandy, Baltic, PA to Br Rep Italy/Yugoslavia Boundary Cmmn 1945-46; ordained 1949, curate All Saints Gosforth 1950-52, chaplain and vice princ Westcott House Cambridge 1953-56, dean Trinity Hall Cambridge 1956-60, princ Cuddesdon Theol Coll 1960-70, bishop St Albans 1970-80; Anglican chm Anglican-Orthodox Joint Doctrinal Cmmn 1973-; pres: Church Army, C of E Children's Soc, Royal Sch of Church Music, Churches Cncl for Health and Healing, BCC, Help the Hospices, Corpn of the Sons of the Clergy; hon memb Canterbury Rotary Club 1981-; Freeman City of: London, Canterbury, St Albans; Freeman: Co of Merchant Taylors, Grocers, Butchers; Hon DD: Univ of Oxford 1980, Univ Cambridge 1981, Univ of the South Sewanee 1981, St Andrew's Univ 1989, New Raday Coll Budapest 1987, Univ of South Carolina 1987; Hon DLitt: Univ of Keele 1981, Rikkyo Univ Tokyo 1987; Hon DCL Univ of Kent 1982, Hon LittD Univ of Liverpool 1983; Cross of the Order of the Holy Sepulchre 1986, Order of St Vladimin Class II 1975; *Books* Cathedral and City: St Albans Ancient and Modern (ed 1978), Windows onto God (1983), Seasons of the Spirit (1983), One Light for One World (1988), Theology, University and the Modern World (1988), Authority in Crisis? (1988); *Recreations* opera, reading history and novels, owning Berkshire pigs; *Clubs* Athenaeum, Cavalry and Guards; *Style*— The Most Rev and Rt Hon the Lord Archbishop of Canterbury, MC; Lambeth Palace, London SE1 7JU (☎ 01 928 8282, fax 01 261 9836); The Old Palace, Canterbury, Kent

CANTLAY, Charles Peter Thrale; s of Peter Allen Cantlay, and Elizabeth Ann Cantlay; *b* 4 Feb 1954; *Educ* Radley Coll, Oriel Coll Oxford (BA); *m* 1985, Sandra Jane; *Career* Alexander Howden Reinsur Brokers 1976-: dir marine div 1983-86, md Marine Div 1986; *Recreations* golf, hockey, skiing; *Clubs* Tandridge Golf, Oxted Hockey; *Style*— Charles P T Cantlay, Esq; 10 Killieser Ave, London SW2 4NT (☎ 01 674 1136); Alexander Howden Reinsurance Brokers Ltd, 8 Devonshire Square, London EC2M 4PL (☎ 01 623 5500, telex 882171, fax 01 621 1511)

CANTLAY, George Thomson; CBE (1973); s of George Thomson Cantlay (d 1939); *b* 2 August 1907; *Educ* HS Glasgow; *m* 1934, Sibyl Gwendoline Alsop, da of John Alsop Stoker (d 1965); 1 s, 1 da; *Career* stockbroker; memb Stock Exchange, ptnr Murray and Co; dir: AB Electronic Products Gp plc, Welsh Nat Opera; *Recreations* opera; *Clubs* Carlton, Cardiff and County; *Style*— George Cantlay, Esq, CBE; 9 Park Road, Penarth, S Glamorgan CF6 2BD (☎ 0222 704588)

CANTLEY, Sir Joseph Donaldson; OBE (1945); s of Dr Joseph Cantley (d 1926), of Crumpsall, Manchester, and Georgina, *née* Kean (d 1968); *b* 8 August 1910; *Educ* Manchester GS, Manchester Univ; *m* 1966, Hilda Goodwin, da of Arthur George Jones (d 1954), of Fyling Hall, Robin Hood's Bay, Yorks, and wid of Sir (Albert) Denis Gerrard (d 1965); 1 step s; *Career* served WW II Lt-Col N Africa and Italy; barrister 1933, QC 1954, rec of Oldham 1959-60, judge of the Court of Record for the Hundred of Salford 1960-65, judge of appeal IOM 1962-65, a judge of the High Court of Justice (Queen's Bench Div) 1965-85, presiding judge of the Northern Circuit 1970-74, presiding judge of the South Eastern Circuit 1980; Hon Col OTC Manchester Univ and Salford Univ 1971-77; Hon LLD Manchester; kt 1965; *Recreations* music, golf, reading books; *Clubs* Travellers'; *Style*— Sir Joseph Cantley, OBE

CAPARROS, Miguel; s of Miguel Caparros, of Fuengirola, Spain, and Francisca; *b* 7 April 1944; *Educ* Ecote des Hautes Etudes Commerciales France (HEG), Graduate Sch of Business Univ of Chicago (MBA); *m* 2 Dec 1967, Nancy, da of Paul Vogeler, of Chicago, USA; 1 s (Alexander b 1978), 2 da (Elizabeth b 1968, Marie-Laure b 1972); *Career* Continental Illinois Nat Bank 1970-83, md Morgan Stanley Int 1985-, inv banking in France and Spain; *Clubs* Queen's Tennis; *Style*— Miguel Caparros, Esq; Morgan Stanley Int, Kingsley House, 1A Wimpole St, London W1M 7AA (☎ 01 709 3039, fax 01 709 3944, telex 8812 564)

CAPE, Donald Paul Montagu Stewart; CMG (1977); s of late John Scarvell Cape, and Olivia Millicent Cape; *b* 6 Jan 1923; *Educ* Ampleforth, BNC Oxford; *m* 1948, Cathune Agnes Johnston; 4 s, 1 da; *Career* entered Foreign Office 1946; counsellor: Washington 1970-73, Brasilia 1973-75; ambass to Laos 1976-78, ambass and UK permanent rep Cncl of Europe 1978-83, consultant to Community Service Volunteers, administrator Anglo-Irish Encounter, chm Anglo- Portuguese Soc; *Style*— Donald Cape, Esq, CMG; Hilltop, Wonersh, Guildford GU5 0PB (☎ 0483 893407)

CAPE, Maj-Gen Timothy Frederick; CB (1972), CBE (1966, DSO 1946); s of Charles Scarvell Cape, DSO, of Edgecliff, NSW, and Maude, *née* Want; *b* 5 August 1915; *Educ* Cranbrook Sch Sydney, RMC Duntroon; *m* 1961, Elizabeth, da of Brig Reginald Lee Rex Rabbett, CMG; 1 da; *Career* 1939-45 war in New Guinea, Timor and Borneo (MBE, DSO), GSO I (ops) Br Cwlth Occupation Force Japan 1946-47, GSO 1 (Plans) Army HQ Melbourne 1948-49; instructor: Sch of Combined Operations UK 1950, and Staff Coll Camberley 1951-52; Comdt Off Cadet Sch Portsea Victoria 1954-56, and Staff Coll Queenscliff Victoria 1956-57, Dep Master Gen of the Ordnance Army HQ Melbourne 1957-59, Chief of Staff N Command Brisbane 1961, Dir of Staff Duties Army HQ Canberra 1962, Cdr Central Command Adelaide 1964, GDC Northern Command Brisbane 1965-67, Master-Gen the of Ordnance Army HQ Canberra 1968-72, ret 1972; memb Nat cncl Aust Red Cross 1975-85; nat pres R United Services Inst of Australia 1980-83; US Bronze star, FAIM; *Style*— Maj-Gen Timothy Cape, CB, CBE, DSO; 20 Charlotte St, Red Hill, ACT 2603, Australia

CAPEL, David John; s of John Capel and Angela Janet Capel; *b* 6 Feb 1963; *Educ* Roade Comprehensive Sch; *m* 1985, Deborah Jane; *Career* pro-cricketer Northants CCC and England; *Style*— David Capel, Esq; c/o Northants CCC, County Ground, Wantage Rd, Northampton

CAPEL CURE, George Ronald; s of George Nigel Capel Cure, *qv*; *b* 21 Oct 1936; *Educ* Eton; *m* 1968, Caroline Ann, who d 1986, only da of Giles Yarnton Mills, of Puys sur Dieppe, France; 3 s; *Career* dir CT Bowring and Co (Insur) Ltd 1985; *Style*— George Capel Cure, Esq; Blake Hall, Ongar, Essex (☎ 0277 362652)

CAPEL CURE, (George) Nigel; TD, (JP 1947, DL 1947); s of late Maj George Edward Capel Cure, JP (d 1943); the family, Capel Cure of Blake Hall, descends from Thomas Cure, of Southwark, Surrey, saddler to Edward VI, Mary I and Elizabeth I, arms granted 1588; *b* 28 Sept 1908; *Educ* Eton, Trinity Coll Cambridge; *m* 1935, Nancy Elizabeth, da of William James Barry (d 1952), of Great Witchingham Hall, Norwich; 2 s, 1 da; *Career* insurance broker ret; landowner and farmer; High Sheriff of Essex 1951-52; Vice Ld-Lt of Essex 1958-78; *Clubs* City University, MCC; *Style*— G. Nigel Capel Cure, Esq, TD, JP, DL; Ashlings, Moreton Rd, Ongar, Essex CM5 0EZ (☎ 0277 362634)

CAPLAN, Harold; s of Samuel Caplan (d 1981), of Manchester, and Gertrude, *née* Freeman (d 1972); *b* 13 Mar 1927; *Educ* Queen Elizabeth Hosp Bristol, Wimbledon Tech Coll (HNC), Coll of Aeronautics Cranfield (MSc); *m* 22 Nov 1968, Isabel, da of Stephen Randall (d 1980), of Richmond Surrey; *Career* Br Aviation Insur Co Ltd 1948-69 (head legal dept 1958-), md Internat Insur Servs 1981- (jt gen mangr 1969-81), legal advsr to Internat Union of Aviation Insurers 1985-, jt dir Airclaims Insur Servs Ltd 1987-; C Eng, FRAeS, FCIArb, MIMechE, ACII; *Recreations* reading and writing; *Clubs* Athenaeum, City of London; *Style*— Harold Caplan, Esq; 3 The Pennards, Sunbury on Thames, TW16 5JZ; 15 St Helen's Place, Bishopsgate, EC3A 6DE (☎ 01 638 7208, fax 01 374 0460, telex 887 857 IIS G)

CAPLAN, Leonard; QC (1954); s of late Henry Caplan, of Liverpool; *b* 28 June 1909; *m* 1, 1942, Tania (d 1974); 2 da; m 2, 1977, Mrs Korda Herskovits, of New York; *Career* WWII Lt Col Allied Land Forces SE Asia; barr 1935, master of the bench Gray's Inn 1964 (tres 1979), memb Senate of Inns of Ct 1975-; chm: College Hal London Univ 1956-67, Mental Health Tbnl 1960-63; vice chm NI Retention Appeals Tbnl 1972-74, pres Medico-Legal Soc 1979-81; Parly candidate (C): Pontypool 1935, Hammersmith 1945, Kensington North 1950 and 1951; *Clubs* Savage, Authors, Hurlingham, RAC; *Style*— Leonard Caplan, Esq, QC; 1 Pump Court, Temple, London EC4 (☎ 01 353 9332); 40 East 66th St, New York, USA (☎ 744 9392); Skol, Marbella, Spain

CAPLAN, The Hon, Lord (Philip Isaac); QC; s of Hyman Caplan (d 1962), of Glasgow, and Rosalena Silverstone (d 1985); *b* 24 Feb 1929; *Educ* Eastwood Sec Sch, Glasgow Univ (MA, LLB); *m* 1, 1953, Elaine Marcia, da of Abraham Gelfer, of Glasgow; 2 s, 1 da; m 2, 1974, Joyce Ethel, da of Walter Stone, of London; 1 da; *Career* admitted Faculty of Advocates 1957-; former standing jr counsel to the Accountant of Court, former chm Plant and Seeds Tbnl (Scot); sheriff of Lothian and Borders at Edinburgh 1979-83, sheriff principal of North Strathclyde 1983-88, sheriff Court Rules Cncl 1984-88, senator of the Coll of Justice 1980; chm Scottish Association for the Study of Deliquency 1985-, commissioner of the Northern Lighthouse Board 1983-88; FRPS, AFIAP; *Recreations* photography, music, reading, sailing; *Clubs* Royal Northern and Clyde YC (Rhu), New (Edinburgh); *Style*— The Hon Lord Caplan; Auchenlea, Torwoodhill Rd, Rhu, Dunbartonshire (☎ 0436 820359)

CAPLAN, Simon Anthony; JP (1986); s of Malcolm Denis Caplan, and Jean Hilary, *née* Winroope (d 1984); *b* 13 Dec 1946; *Educ* Carmel Coll Wallingford; *m* 6 Sept 1970, Yolande Anne, da of Simon Albert (d 1978); 1 s (Benjamin b 1974), 1 da (Amanda b 1971); *Career* Touche Ross 1970, jt fndr Financial Advice Panels (within Citizen Advice Bureaux), fndr Caplan, Montagu, Shamash Assoc, chm and md of Stagestruck Gp of Co's; barker of the Variety Club of GB; memb BAFTA, Soc of West End Theatre, Royal TV Soc, Royal Inst, fndr dir Criterion Fund Mgmnt Ltd, gen cmmr income tax 1988; Freeman City of London 1980; FCA FTII; *Recreations* art and antique collecting, theatre; *Clubs* Reform, IOD; *Style*— Simon Caplan, JP; Stowe March, Barnet Lane, Elstree, Herts; 57 Duke Street, Grosvenor Square, London W1 (☎ 01 629 2334, fax 01 493 3808)

CAPLAT, Moran Victor Hingston; CBE (1968); s of Roger Armand Charles Caplat (d 1958), of Herne Bay, Kent, and Norah, *née* Hingston (d 1972); *b* 1 Oct 1916; *Educ* privately, RADA; *m* 29 May 1943, Diana Murray, da of Capt Arthur Murray Downton (d 1964), of West Malling, Kent; 1 s (Marc Charles b 25 May 1948), 2 da (Simone b 10 May 1945, Dominique b 22 June 1952); *Career* Lt Cdr Northern Patrol destroyers and submarines RNVR 1939-45; former actor; gen admin Glyndebourne Festival Opera 1949-81; *Books* Dinghies to Divas (autobiography, 1985), Glyndebourne Festival Programme Book; *Recreations* sailing, rough gardening, European travel; *Clubs* Royal Ocean Racing, Garrick; *Style*— Moran Caplat, Esq, CBE; Mermaid Cottage, 6 Church Road, Newick, Lewes, East Sussex BN8 4JU (☎ 082 572 2964)

CAPLE, (John) Anthony; s of William Ambrose Caple (d 1977), and Lillian Flora Caple (d 1984); *b* 2 May 1930; *Educ* Gateway Sch Leics; *Career* works in family printing firm William Caple and Co Ltd; *Recreations* steam railways; *Style*— Anthony Caple, Esq; Barclays Bank, Town Hall Square, 40 Sybil Road, Leicester LE3 2EY (☎ 891379); William Caple and Co Ltd, Morledge Street, Leicester LE1 1TF (☎ 0533 292417)

CAPPER, Rt Rev Edmund Michael Hubert; OBE (1961); s of Arthur Charles Capper (d 1958), of Torquay, and Mabel Lavinia, *née* Barnett (d 1961); *b* 12 Mar 1908; *Educ* St Joseph's Acad Blackheath, St Augustine's Coll Canterbury, LTh (Durham); *Career* ordained: deacon 1932, priest 1933; RA Chaplains Dept (EA) 1942-46, HCF 1946-, officiating chaplain to King's African Rifles 1954-62; memb Univs Mission to Central Africa 1936-62, archdeacon of Lindi and canon of Masasi Cathedral 1947-54, archdeacon of Dar es Salaam and canon of Zanzibar Cathedral 1954-58, provost Collegiate Church of St Alban the Martyr Dar es Salaam 1957-62, bishop St Helena 1967-73; chaplain: Palma de Mallorca 1962-67, St Georges Malaga 1973-76; auxiliary bishop in the Diocese of Gibraltar in Europe 1973-, asst bishop Southwark 1981-; chm Tanganyika Br Legion Benevolent Fund 1956-62, pres Tanganyika Br Legion 1960-62; *Clubs* Travellers'; *Style*— The Rt Rev Edmund Capper, OBE; Morden Coll, Blackheath, London SE3 0PW (☎ 01 858 9169)

CAPRON, (George) Christopher; s of Lt-Col George Theodore Herbert Capron (d 1970), of Southwick Hall, Peterborough, and Hon Edith Christian Hepburne-Scott, 3 da of 9 Baron Polwarth; *b* 17 Dec 1935; *Educ* Wellington, Trin Hall Cambridge (BA); *m* 1958, Edna Naomi, da of Chanania Goldrei (d 1973); 1 s (David), 1 da (Naomi); *Career* 2 Lt 12 Royal Lancers (POW) 1954-56; BBC TV 1959-87, ed Tonight 1976-77, Panorama 1977-79, asst head current affrs programmes 1979-81 (head 1981-85), head of parly bdcasting 1985-87, ind TV prodr Capron Prodns Ltd 1987-; memb: BAFTA, Royal TV Soc; *Recreations* tennis, village cricket; *Clubs* Northamptonshire CCC; *Style*— Christopher Capron, Esq; 32 Amerland Rd, London SW1F (☎ 01 874 4829)

CAPRON, Hon Mrs; (Edith Christian); *née* Hepburne-Scott; 3 da of 9 Baron Polwarth (d 1944); *b* 20 August 1901; *m* 1926, Lt-Col George Theodore Herbert Capron, RE (d 1970), eldest s of George Herbert Capron, of Southwick Hall; 1 s, 3 da; *Style*— The Hon Mrs Capron; Southwick Hall, Oundle, Peterborough (☎ 0832 74013)

CAPSTICK, Brian Eric; QC (1973); o s of (Norman) Eric and Betty Capstick; *b* 12 Feb 1927; *Educ* Sedbergh, Queen's Coll Oxford; *m* 1960, Margaret Elizabeth Harrison; 1 s, 1 da; *Career* barr 1952, recorder of the Crown Court 1980-; dir Hartley Main Farms Ltd 1950-; *Style*— Brian Capstick, Esq, QC; 2 Crown Office Row, Temple, London EC4 (☎ 01 583 2681); 71 South End Rd, NW3 (☎ 01 435 3540)

CAPSTICK, Charles William; CMG (1972); s of William Capstick and Janet Frankland; *b* 18 Dec 1934; *Educ* King's Coll Durham Univ, Kentucky Univ; *m* 1962, Joyce Alma, da of William Dodsworth; 2 s; *Career* former under-sec Milk and Milk Products Miny of Ag Fish and Food, dir Economics and Statistics 1977-89, dep sec (Fisheries and Food) Miny of Agric, Fisheries and Food 1989-; *Style*— Charles Capstick, Esq, CMG; 7 Dellfield Clo, Radlett, Herts (☎ Radlett 7640)

CARADON, Baron (Life Peer UK 1964); Hugh Mackintosh Foot; GCMG (1957), KCMG (1951, CMG 1946, KCVO 1953, OBE 1939, PC 1968); 2 s of late Rt Hon Isaac Foot (d 1960), of Pencrebar, Callington, Cornwall, and his 1 wife Eva, *née* Mackintosh (d 1946); bro of Lord Foot and Rt Hon Michael Foot; *b* 8 Oct 1907; *Educ* Leighton Park Sch, St John's Coll Cambridge; *m* 1936, (Florence) Sylvia (d 1985), er da of Arthur White Millar Tod, OBE, of Lasswade, Midlothian, and Haifa, Palestine; 3 s, 1 da; *Career* Colonial Service Palestine, Trans-Jordan, Nigeria, Cyprus and Jamaica, ambassador to United Nations 1962, min of state for Foreign and Commonwealth Affairs and perm UK rep to UN 1964-70, conslt to UN Dvpt Programme 1971-75; hon fellow St John's Coll Cambridge; KStJ; *Style*— The Rt Hon the Lord Caradon, GCMG, KCMG, CMG, KCVO, OBE, PC; House of Lords, London SW1A 0AA

CARANCI, Lady Georgina Joceleyn; da of late 8 Earl of Chichester; *b* 7 June 1942; *m* 27 June 1974, Halios Alberto, s of Helios Jorge Caranci, of Buenos Aires, Argentina; 1 s (Helios Nicolás b 1983), 2 da (Cecilia Catalina b 1976, Ursula Claudia b 1978); *Style*— Lady Georgina Caranci; La Catalina, Diego de Alvear, Santa Fe, Argentina

CARBERRY, (Hon) Juanita Virginia Sistare; *née* Carberry; da of 10 Baron Carbery (d 1970), and his 2 wife, Maïa Ivy, *née* Anderson (d 1928); *b* 7 May 1925; *Educ* Roedean Johannesburg, Wickham Pietermaritzburg Switzerland; *Career* seaman; *Style*— Ms Juanita Carberry; Anchorage, PO Box 96094, Likoni, via Mombasa, Kenya, East Africa (☎ Mombasa 451076)

CARBERY, 11 Baron (1715); Sir Peter Ralfe Harrington Evans-Freke; 7 Bt (I 1768); s of Maj the Hon Ralfe Evans-Freke, MBE (d 1969), 2 s of 9 Baron; suc unc, 10 Baron, 1970; *b* 20 Mar 1920; *Educ* Downside; *m* 1941, Joyzelle Mary, o da of late Herbert Binnie, of Sydney, NSW; 3 s, 2 da; *Heir* Hon Michael Evans-Freke; *Career* served WWII 1939-45 as Capt RE in India and Burma; former memb London Stock Exchange; author of novels, plays and poetry; MICE; *Clubs* Kennel, Ski Club of Great Britain; *Style*— The Rt Hon the Lord Carbery; 2 Hayes Court, Sunnyside, Wimbledon, London SW19 4SH (☎ 01 946 6615)

CARBONELL, William Leycester Rouse; CMG (1956), QPM (1949); s of John Carbonell (d 1936), of Eastaway, Westleigh, N Devon; *b* 14 August 1912; *Educ* Shrewsbury, St Catharine's Coll Cambridge; *m* 1937, Elsa Agnes, da of John William Curdie, of Camperdown, Victoria, Australia; 2 s; *Career* entered Colonial Police Service 1935, asst cmmr 1952, cmmr Police Fedn of Malaya 1953-58; PMN (Malaya) 1957; OStJ; *Style*— William Carbonell, Esq, CMG, QPM; Amery End, Tanhouse Lane, Alton, Hants

CARBUTT, Billy (Francis); s of George H Carbutt (d 1956), and Ann M, *née* de Montmorency (now Mrs E W Swanton); *b* 16 July 1936; *Educ* Eton Coll; *m* 1, 19 July 1958, Sally Fenella, da of James C Harris, of Ampfield, Hants; 1 s (George Henry b 1963), 1 da (Emma Louise (Mrs Swinton) b 1961); *Career* Nat Serv Lt Rifle Brig 1954-56; chartered acct; ptnr Ernst Whinney 1967- (joined 1956); chm Ct of the Mary Rose; memb Ct Worshipful Co of Grocers'; FCA (1961); *Recreations* swimming, photography, gardening, all kinds of music; *Clubs* Boodles, City of London, MCC; *Style*— Billy Carbutt, Esq; The White House, Langham, Colchester, Essex CO4 5PY (☎ 0206 323 182); Ernst & Whinney, Becket House, 1 Lambeth Palace Rd, London SE1 7EU (☎ 01 928 2000, fax 01 928 1345, telex 885234

CARD, Gp Capt Leslie Thomas; CBE (1957); s of Herbert Henry Card, of Redhill, Surrey; *b* 1905; *Educ* Reigate GS; *m* 1946, Evelyn Maud, da of Mark Hill, of Monmouth; 1 da; *Career* served RAF 1922-60, Gp Capt, ret; *Style*— Gp Capt Leslie

Card, CBE; 88 Riverview Rd, Ewell, Surrey (☎ 01 337 4123)

CARD, Philip Haven; s of Oliver Card (d 1962), of Caldicot, Gwent, and Alice Mary, *née* Summerfield (d 1982); *b* 12 August 1933; *Educ* Latymer Fndn Sch Hammersmith; *m* 19 Sept 1959, Barbara Rose, da of Charles William Hanslow (d 1987), of Barnes; 1 da (Christine Judith b 10 May 1972); *Career* Nat Serv RAF 1951-53; Morris Ashby Ltd 1948-79, chm and md Philip Card Ltd 1980-; special constable City of London Police 1966-88; Liveryman Worshipful Co of Pattenmakers; *Recreations* shooting, clockmaking and restoration; *Clubs* Hitchin Cons, Victory Servs; *Style*— Philip Card, Esq; Philip Card Ltd, 10a Bucklersbury, Hitchin, Herts SG5 1BB (☎ 0462 342 81, telex 94011290 CARD G)

CARDALE, William Tyndale; s of Brig W J Cardale, OBE, ADC (d 1986), and Vere Audrey, *née* Parry-Crooke; *b* 10 Dec 1945; *Educ* Eton; *m* 13 Aug 1968, Lynn Muriel, da of Alan Thomas Brown, CBE, DL, *qv*; *Career* CA; managing tax conslt Tst Dept Price Waterhouse Birmingham, W Midlands and S of England; lectures in taxation at Birmingham Univ on secondment from Price Waterhouse and at various Insts of Chartered Accountants courses; FCA, ATII; *Recreations* riding, (hunter trials and events), tennis; *Style*— William T Cardale, Esq; West Lodge, Bradfield St George, Bury St Edmunds, Suffolk; 39 Clarence Road, Harborne, Birmingham (☎ 021 200 3000)

CARDEN, Christopher Robert; s (by 1 m) and h of Sir Henry Carden, 4 Bt, OBE; *b* 24 Nov 1946; *Educ* Eton, Aberdeen Univ (BSc); *m* 1, 1972 (m dis 1979), Sainimere Rokotuibau, of Suva, Fiji; m 2, 1981, Clarita Peralta Eriksen, of Manila, Philippines; 1 step s (Johnny Eriksen b 1975); *Career* Forestry 1970; Govt of Papua New Guinea 1970-74, Fiji Pine Cmmn 1976-79, dir C R Forestry Services 1979-82, Usutu Pulp Co Swaziland 1982-86, cwlth Fund for Tech Co-operation Solomon Is 1986-88, forestry conslt 1989-; *Recreations* tennis, squash, bowls, travel, philately, uftology; *Style*— Christopher Carden Esq; 39 St Cuthbert St, Wells, Somerset BA5 2AW (☎ 0749 79282, fax 0749 75096)

CARDEN, Dowager Lady (Dorothy Mary); da of Charles Luckraft McKinnon; *m* 1925, as his 2 wife, Sir John Valentine Carden, 6 Bt, MBE (d 1935); 1 s; *Style*— Dowager Lady Carden

CARDEN, Lt-Col Sir Henry Christopher; 4 Bt (UK 1887), of Wimpole Street, Middlesex, and of Mole Lodge, Surrey; OBE (1945); s of Maj Sir Frederick Henry Walter Carden, 3 Bt (d 1966), and Winifred Mary, *née* Wroughton (d 1972); *b* 16 Oct 1908; *Educ* Eton, RMC Sandhurst; *m* 1, 5 June 1943 (m dis 1961), Jane St Clare, da of late Thomas Edward St Clare Daniell, OBE, MC; 1 s, 1 da (Melinda Jane (Mrs A Wilson) b 1950); m 2, 8 Nov 1962, Gwyneth Sybil, da of late Herbert Arthur Dyke Acland, and widow of F/Lt Roderick Stanley Emerson, RAFVR (ka 1944); *Heir* s, Christopher Robert Carden, *qv*; *Career* cmmnd 17/21 Lancers 1928, serv Egypt and India 1930-39, Staff Coll 1941, cmd 2 Armoured Delivery Regt France 1944-45, CO 17/21 Lancers in Greece and Palestine 1947-48, WO 1948-51, mil attaché Stockholm 1951-55, ret 1956; Order of the Sword (Sweden) 1954; *Recreations* most field sports, cricket; *Clubs* Cavalry and Guards'; *Style*— Lt-Col Sir Henry Carden, Bt; Moongrove, East Woodhay, Newbury, Berks (☎ 0635 253661)

CARDEN, Sir John Craven; 7 Bt (I 1787), of Templemore, Tipperary; s of Capt Sir John V Carden, 6 Bt, MBE (d 1935); *b* 11 Mar 1926; *Educ* Eton; *m* 1947, Isabel Georgette, yst da of late Robert de Hart; 1 da; *Heir* kinsman, Derrick Charles Carden, *qv*; *Style*— Sir John Carden, Bt; PO Box N7776, Lyford Cay, Nassau, Bahamas

CARDEN, Peter Maurice Arthur; s of Paul Carden (d 1985), and Lilias Kathleen, *née* Wills; *b* 18 June 1931; *Educ* Harrow; *m* 3 Dec 1966, Sheila Joan, da of Richard Vevers Matson (d 1957); 1 s (Tom b 1972) 2 da (Alice b 1968, Kate b 1969); *Career* Nat Serv 1949-51, 2 Lt RHA 1950; dir: Thos and Jas Harrison Ltd 1967 (Caribbean rep 1953-60, mangr Liverpool 1960), Charente Steam-Ship Co Ltd 1971; chm: Prentice, Service & Henderson Ltd 1980 (dir 1965), Caribbean Overseas Lines (CAROL) 1975; dir Associated Container Transportation Ltd (ACT) 1985; govr Liverpool Sch of Tropical Med 1962-72; *Recreations* sailing, tennis, gardening; *Clubs* Liverpool Racquet; *Style*— Peter Carden, Esq; Croughton Ho, Chester CH2 4DA (☎ 0244 383 162); Thos & Jas Harrison Ltd, Mersey Chambers, Liverpool L2 8UF (☎ 051 236 5611, fax 051 236 1200, telex 628 404)

CARDEN, Philippe O'Neill; s of Dick Guy Carden, of London, and Françoise Jeanne, *née* Domerc; *b* 22 Sept 1950; *Educ* Wimbledon Coll, Bellarmine Coll (Kentucky), St John's Coll Cambridge (BA); *m* 20 Sept 1975, Julia Francesca, da of Austin Raymond Lindon, of London; 2 da (Mondane b 1979, Genevieve b 1981); *Career* CA; dir Carden Martin Ltd 1985-88, tres Amnesty Int Kingston Gp 1984-88; *Recreations* theatre, music, gastronomy; *Style*— Philippe Carden, Esq; 12 Lintons Lane, Epsom, Surrey KT17 1DD; 38A High St, Ewell, Epsom, Surrey KT17 1RW

CARDEN, (Graham) Stephen Paul; CBE (1986), TD 1968, DL (Greater London 1983); s of Paul Carden (d 1985), of Colchester, and Lilias Kathleen, *née* Wills; *b* 14 May 1935; *Educ* Harrow Sch; *Career* 9 Lancers 1954-56, City of London Yeo (Rough Riders) and on amalgamation Inns of Ct and City Yeo 1956-74, TA Col 1976-78; stockbroker Cazenove & Co 1956, ptnr 1964-, chm Outback Tst Co Ltd 1969-, dir Greenfriar Investmnt 1966-; Hon Col 71 (Yeo) Signal Regt 1989-; vice-pres Greater London TAVR 1988- (vice-chm Cncl TAVRAs 1984-88), cmmr Royal Hosp Chelsea 1986-, vice-pres Yeomanry Benevolent Fund 1986-, vice chm and hon tres Fairbridge Drake Society 1987- (hon tres Fairbridge Soc 1964-87), vice-chm London House for Overseas Graduates 1985-; *Recreations* equestrian (mainly hunting), fishing, sailing, watching cricket; *Clubs* Cavalry and Guards, White's, City of London, MCC, Royal Yacht Squadron; *Style*— Stephen Carden, Esq, CBE, TD, DL; 12 Warwick Square, London SW1V 2AA (☎ 01 834 8919); 12 Tokenhouse Yard, London EC2R 7AN (☎ 01 588 2828, telex 886758, fax 01 606 9205)

CARDEW, Anthony John; s of Lt Col Martin Philip Cardew, of Rookley Manor, Rookley, IOW, and Anne Elizabeth, *née* Foster; *b* 8 Sept 1949; *Educ* Bishop Wordsworth's Sch Salisbury Wiltshire, Marlborough Coll Marlborough Wiltshire; *m* 10 Dec 1971, Janice Frances, da of Alec Anthony Smallwood (d 1985); 1 s (James), 1 da (Sarah); *Career* chief reporter Surrey Mirror 1968-70, news reporter UPI 1970-71, fin corr Reuters 1972-74, dir then head of fin pr Charles Barker Ltd 1974-83, chm Grandfield Rork Collins Financial 1985- (dir 1983-); *Recreations* book collecting, walking; *Clubs* Reform, Thunderers; *Style*— Anthony Cardew, Esq; Horns Farm House, Eversley, Hampshire (☎ 0734 732 200); Grandfield Rork Collins Financial Ltd, Prestige House, 14-18 Holborn, London EC1 (☎ 01 242 2002, fax 01 405 2208, telex 8956158)

CARDEW, Lt Cdr Philip Peel; s of Evelyn Philip Cardew (d 1978), of Middleton on Sea, Sussex, and Dorothy Lilian Cardew, *née* Nuttall (d 1946); *b* 5 June 1929; *Educ* Dragon Sch, Reigate GS; *m* 5 Oct 1957, Anne Florence, da of Lt-Col Henry Baker (d 1975), of Hartley Wintney; 1 s (Geoffrey b 1958), 1 da (Caroline b 1965); *Career* RN Fleet Air Arm 1947-69, Lieut-Cdr; professional pilot, BEA 1969-72, Corporate Aviation 1972-, md Br Car Auctions (Aviation) 1976-, airport dir Blackbushe 1984-, chm Farnham Fleet Aldershot Sea-Cadets 1977-; cncl memb: GAMTA, ATOA, BAUA; Freeman Worshipful Co of Air Pilots and Navigators; *Recreations* golf, tennis, sailing, squash, riding; *Clubs* Offs (Aldershot); *Style*— Lt Cdr Philip Cardew; Woodside, Broad Oak, Odiham, Basingstoke, Hants (☎ 025 671 2609, fax 0252 874444, telex 858858 BLKBG); Terminal Bldg, Blackbushe Airport, Camberley, Surrey (☎ 0252 879 449, car tel 0836 277 722)

CARDIFF, Archbishop of (RC), 1983-; Most Rev John Aloysius Ward; OFM Cap; s of Eugene Ward and Hannah, *née* Cheetham; *b* 24 Jan 1929; *Educ* Prior Park Coll Bath; *Career* Bishop Coadjutor of Menevia 1980-81, Bishop of Menevia 1981-83; *Style*— His Grace the Archbishop of Cardiff, OFM Cap; Archbishop's House, 41-43 Cathedral Road, Cardiff, South Glamorgan CF1 9HD (☎ 0222 20411)

CARDIFF, Maurice Henry; CBE (1973), OBE (1970); yst s of Lt-Col Richard Henry Wingfield Cardiff (d 1945); bro of Brig Ereld Boteler Wingfield Cardiff, *qv*; *b* 27 July 1915; *Educ* Eton, Worcester Coll Oxford; *m* 1939, Leonora Rachel, *née* Freeman; 3 s; *Career* Br Cncl rep 1952-: Belgium 1963-67, Thailand 1968-71, France 1971-73; author under pseudonym John Lincoln; *Style*— Maurice Cardiff Esq, CBE; Stone House, Little Haseley, Oxford

CARDIGAN, Earl of; David Michael James Brudenell-Bruce; s and h of 8 Marquess of Ailesbury; *b* 12 Nov 1952; *Educ* Eton, Rannoch, RAC Cirencester; *m* 1980, Rosamond Jane, er da of Capt W R M Winkley, of Wyke Champflower Manor, Wyke Champflower, Bruton, Somerset; 1 s (Thomas b 1982), 1 da (Catherine b 1984); *Heir* s, Viscount Savernake; *Career* owner mangr Savernake Forest; *Style*— Earl of Cardigan; Savernake Lodge, Savernake Forest, Marlborough, Wilts (☎ 0672 52161)

CARDROSS, Lord; Henry Thomas Alexander Erskine; s and h of 17 Earl of Buchan, JP, *qv*; *b* 31 May 1960; *Educ* Eton, Central Sch of Art and Design; *m* 28 Feb 1987, Charlotte Catherine Lucinda, da of Hon Matthew Beaumont, *qv*; *Career* stained glass designer and photographer; *Recreations* cars, photography, video, travel; *Style*— Lord Cardross

CARDY, Peter John Stubbings; s of Gordon Douglas Stubbings, of Gosport, Hants, and Eva, *née* Walker; changed name to Cardy by Deed 1987; *b* 4 April 1947; *Educ* Price's Sch, Univ Coll Durham (BA), Cranfield Inst of Technol (MSc); *m* 5 Sept 1987, Christine Mary, da of Ronald Edward Francis Doyle, of Manchester; *Career* dist sec WEA North of Scotland 1971-77, dep dir Volunteer Centre UK 1977-87, dir Motor Neurone Disease Assoc 1987-; chm Nat Assoc of Volunteer Bureaux 1988-; *Recreations* sailing, conversation, travel; *Clubs* Reform, Royal Cwlth Soc; *Style*— Peter Cardy, Esq; Motor Neurone Disease Assoc, 61 Derngate, Northampton NN1 1UE (☎ 0604 22269, 0604 250505)

CARELESS, Col William Paget; DSO, JP (1963, DL Salop 1962); *b* 1907; *m* 1937, Beatrice Delitia; 1 da; *Career* former cmmr St John's Ambulance; CStJ; High Sheriff Radnorshire 1964; *Style*— Col William Careless, DSO, JP, DL; 3 Russell Ridge, Shrewsbury, Salop

CAREW, Hon Gavin George; MBE (1945), TD; 2 s of late 5 Baron Carew (d 1927); *b* 21 Sept 1906; *Educ* Clifton; *m* 1932, Aileen Hilda Frances (d 1974), o da of late Ean Francis Cecil, of Hilltop, Sunningdale, Berks; 1 da; *Career* late Maj Co London Yeo; *Style*— The Hon Gavin Carew, MBE, TD; Gellillyndu, Llanio, Tregaron, Dyfed

CAREW, Sir Rivers Verain; 11 Bt (E 1661), of Haccombe, Devonshire; s of Sir Thomas Palk Carew, 10 Bt (d 1976), and his 2 wife, Phyllis Evelyn, *née* Mayman; *b* 17 Oct 1935; *Educ* St Columba's Coll, Dublin Univ (MA, BAgrSc Hort); *m* 1968, Susan Babington, yr da of late Harold Babington Hill, of London; 1 s (and 1 s decd), 3 da; *Heir* s, Gerald de Redvers Carew b 24 May 1975; *Career* ed, journalist, author; asst ed Ireland of The Welcomes (Irish Tourist Bd magazine) 1964-67, jt ed The Dublin Magazine 1964-69, journalist Irish Television 1967-, BBC World Service 1987-;; *Books* Figures out of Mist (poems with T Brownlow Dublin 1966); *Recreations* reading, music, reflection; *Style*— Sir Rivers Carew, Bt

CAREW, 6 Baron (I 1834 and UK 1838); William Francis Conolly-Carew; CBE (1966); s of 5 Baron Carew (d 1927); *b* 23 April 1905; *Educ* Wellington, Sandhurst; *m* 1937, Lady Sylvia Gwendoline Eva Maitland, da of 15 Earl of Lauderdale; 2 s, 2 da; *Heir* Hon Patrick Thomas Conolly-Carew; *Career* assumed by Deed Poll 1938 additional surname of Conolly; Maj Duke of Cornwall's LI (ret); former ADC to Govr and CIC of Bermuda; former National chm Br Legion; CStJ; *Clubs* Armyand and Navy, Kildine Street Dublin; *Style*— The Rt Hon the Lord Carew, CBE; Oakville, Donadea, Co Kildare, Eire (☎ Naas 69171)

CAREW, William James; CBE (1937); s of late James and Mary Carew, of St John's, Newfoundland; *b* 28 Dec 1890; *Educ* St Patrick's Hall, St John's, Newfoundland; *m* 1920, Mary Florence (decd), da of James Channing; 1 s, 3 da; *Career* former sec Prime Minister's Office, dep min for External Affairs 1932, clerk of Exec Cncl and dep min of Provincial Affairs Newfoundland, ret; Hon LLD Newfoundland Univ 1985; Kt Cdr of Order of St Silvester (Papal) 1976; *Style*— William Carew Esq, CBE; 74 Cochrane St, St John's, Newfoundland, Canada

CAREW POLE, Col Sir John Gawen; 12 Bt (E 1628), DSO (1944), TD, JP (Cornwall 1939), DL (1947); s of late Lt-Gen Sir Reginald Pole-Carew, KCB and Lady Beatrice, *née* Butler, er da of 3 Marquess of Ormonde, and kinsman of Sir Frederick Arundell de la Pole, 11 Bt (d 1926); assumed by deed poll 1926 the name of John Gawen Carew Pole in lieu of John Gawen Pole-Carew; *b* 4 Mar 1902; *Educ* Eton, RMC Sandhurst; *m* 1, 1928, Cynthia Mary, OBE (d 1977), da of Walter Spencer Morgan Burns, of North Mymms Park, Hatfield, Herts; 1 s, 2 da; m 2, 1979, Joan Shirley, da of Rear Adm Charles Maurice Blackman, DSO, of Peak Cottage, Bishop's Waltham, Hants, and wid of Lt-Col (Francis Edgar) Anthony Fulford, and previously of Maj Jocelyn Arthur Persse, Rifle Bde; *Heir* s (John) Richard (Walter Reginald) Carew Pole; *Career* Coldstream Gds 1923-39, cmd 5 Bn Duke of Cornwall's Light Infantry TA 1939-43, cmd 2 Devonshire Regt 1944 (Normandy, Belgium, Holland, Germany), Col Second Army HQ 1944-45, raised and cmd post-war TA Bn 4/5 Bn DCLI 1946-47, Hon Col 4/5 Bn DCLI (TA) 1958-60, Hon Col DCLI (TA) 1960-67; former dir: Lloyds Bank Ltd (and chm Devon and Cornwall Regnl Bd), English China Clays, Keith Prowse, Westward TV Ltd (vice chm); memb Western Region BR; chm Cornwall CC

1946-57, CA 1954-66 Cornwall, High Sheriff 1947-48, Vice-Lt 1950-62, Ld-Lt 1962-77, a Gentleman of HM Bodyguard of the Hon Corps of Gentlemen-at-Arms 1950-72, Standard Bearer 1968-72, memb Prince of Wales's Cncl 1952-68, steward Nat Hunt Ctee 1953-56, memb Jockey Club 1969-, Prime Warden Worshopful Co of Fishmongers' 1969-70; KStJ 1972; Hon LLD Exeter 1979; *Clubs* Army and Navy, Pratt's, MCC; *Style*— Col Sir John Carew Pole, Bt, DSO, TD, JP; Horson House, Torpoint, Cornwall PL11 2PE (☎ 0752 812406)

CAREW POLE, (John) Richard Walter Reginald; s and h of Sir John Gawen Carew Pole, DSO, TD, 12 Bt; *b* 2 Dec 1938; *Educ* Eton, RAC Cirencester; *m* 1, 1966 (m dis 1973), Hon Victoria Marion Ann Lever, da of 3 Viscount Leverhulme; m 2, 1974, Mary, LVO, da of Lt-Col Ronald Dawnay; 2 s; *Heir* Tremayne John Carew Pole; *Career* late Coldstream Gds; memb: CC for Cornwall, Devon and Cornwall Ctee, Nat Tst 1978-83; pres Surf Life Saving Assoc of GB 1978-87; High Sheriff of Cornwall 1979; part-time dir SW Electricity Bd 1981-, regnl dir West of England Building Soc 1989-; pres Royal Cornwall Agric Show 1981, chm Devon and Cornwall Police Authy 1985-87; govr: Seale Hayne Agric Coll 1979-, Plymouth Coll 1981-; dir Theatre Royal Plymouth 1985-, Cornwall CC chm of Planning and Employment Comm 1980-84, chm of Finance Comm 1985-89; Liveryman Fishmongers' Co; *Recreations* walking, travelling, contemporary pictures, gardening; *Clubs* White's, Pratt's; *Style*— Richard Carew Pole, Esq; Antony House, Torpoint, Cornwall PL11 2QA (☎ 0752 814914)

CAREY, Gp Capt Alban Majendie; CBE (1943); s of Henry N Carey, of Norfolk; *b* 18 April 1906; *Educ* Bloxham; *m* 1934, Enid Morten, da of E M Bond, of Woking, Surrey; 1 s; *Career* Gp Capt RAF 1942; chm Maden Park Property Investment Co Ltd and Chirit Investment Co Ltd; *Style*— Gp Capt Alban Carey, CBE; Shaway House, Lower Sydenham, SE266; Town Green Farm, Englefield Green, Surrey (☎ Egham 213)

CAREY, Dennis Charles Peter; *b* 28 July 1931; *Educ* Sherborne Sch, Cambridge Univ (MA); *m* 1957 (m dis), Ann, m 2 (m dis) 1971, Michele; 1 s, 2 da; *Career* industrialist; md Coates Brothers and Co Ltd 1972-74, European vice pres Morton Chemical Co Inc 1975-80, ch exec Borthwicks plc 1981-; dir 1981-:Thomas Borthwick and Son (Pacific Hldgs) Ltd, Barnett and Foster Ltd, Burton Son and Sanders Ltd, Broadland Foods Ltd; *Recreations* travel, languages; *Style*— D.C.P. Carey, Esq; Borthwicks plc, Priory House, St John's Lane, London EC1M 4BX (☎ 01 253 8661, telex 23716 BOWSTRING)

CAREY, George Leonard; *see*: Bath and Wells, Bishop of

CAREY, John; s of Charles William Carey (d 1965), of Barnes SW13, and Winifred Ethel, *née* Cook (d 1967); *b* 5 April 1934; *Educ* Richmond and East Sheen County GS, St John's Coll Oxford (MA, DPhil); *m* 1960, Gillian Mary Florence, da of Reginald Booth (d 1968), of Wilmslow, Cheshire; 2 s (Leo b 1974, Thomas b 1977); *Career* 2 Lieut E Surrey Regt 1953-54; Harmsworth sr scholar Merton Coll Oxford 1957-58, lectr ChCh Oxford 1958-59, Andrew Bradley jr res fell Balliol Oxford 1959-60, tutorial fell: Keble Coll Oxford 1960-64, St John's Coll Oxford 1964-75; princ book reviewer Sunday Times 1977-; FRSL; *Books* The Poems of John Milton (ed with Alastair Fowler 1968), Milton (1969), The Violent Effigy: a study of Dickens' imagination (1973), Thackeray: Prodigal Genius (1977), John Donne: Life, Mind and Art (1981), The Private Memoirs and Confessions of a Justified Sinner (ed 1981), Original Copy: Selected Reviews and Journalism 1969-1986 (1987), The Faber Book of Reportage (ed 1987), articles in Modern Language Review; *Recreations* swimming, gardening, bee-keeping; *Style*— John Carey, Esq; Brasenose Cottage, Lyneham, Oxon; 57 Stapleton Rd, Headington, Oxford (☎ 0865 64304); Merton Coll, Oxford (☎ Oxford 276389)

CAREY, Sir Peter Willoughby; GCB (1982), KCB (1976, CB 1972); s of Jack Delves Carey, of Portsmouth, Hants, and Sophie Carey; *b* 26 July 1923; *Educ* Portsmouth GS, Oriel Coll Oxford; *m* 1946, Thelma, da of John Brigham Young, of Portsmouth; 3 da; *Career* dep sec: Cabinet Office 1971, Dept of Trade and Indust 1972-73; second perm sec Dept of Trade and Indust 1973-76, perm sec Dept of Indust 1976-83; exec dir Morgan Grenfell Hldgs 1983-; chm: Dalgety 1986, Morgan Grenfell Gp 1987; *Clubs* United Oxford and Cambridge Univs; *Style*— Sir Peter Carey, GCB, KCB. CB; Rose Cottage, 67 Church Rd, Wimbledon, London SW19 (☎ 01 947 5222)

CAREY JONES, Norman Stewart; CMG (1965); s of Samuel Carey Jones (d 1963), of Swansea, and Jessie Isabella Stewart; *b* 11 Dec 1911; *Educ* Monmouth Sch, Merton Coll Oxford (MA); *m* 1946, Stella, da of Maj Claud Myles (d 1961), of Cape Town, S Africa; 2 s; *Career* Colonial Audit Service 1934-54, Colonial Admin Service 1954-65, perm sec Miny of Lands and Settlement Kenya 1962-65, dir in devpt admin Leeds Univ 1965-77; *Books* The Pattern of a Dependent Economy, The Anatomy of Uhuru Politics, Public Enterprise and the Industrial Development Agency; *Clubs* Royal Commonwealth Soc; *Style*— Norman Carey Jones Esq, CMG; Mawingo, Welsh St Donats, nr Cowbridge, South Glam CF7 7SS (☎ 04463 2841)

CAREY-EVANS, David Lloyd; OBE (1983); s of Sir Thomas Carey-Evans MC, FRCS, and 2 Lady Olwen OBE, *née* Lloyd George, DBE; *b* 14 August 1925; *Educ* Rottingdean Pref Sch, Oundle, Univ of Wales (BSc agric); *m* 14 Nov 1959, Annwen, da of William Williams, Craig, Llanerchymedd, Anglesey; 3 s (Thomas Robert b 1961, William Lloyd b 1962, Richard Huw b 1968), 1 da (Davina b 1964); *Career* WW II, Sub-Ltd RNVR 1943-46; farmer 1947- ; chm: Welsh Cncl NFU 1978-81, WAOS Cncl 1984- ; JP 1969, DL 1988; *Clubs* Sloane Club, London; *Style*— David Carey-Evans Esq, OBE; Eisteddfa, Criccieth, Gwynedd

CAREY-EVANS, Lady Olwen Elizabeth; *née* Lloyd George; DBE (1969); el da of 1 Earl Lloyd George of Dwyfor, PM of Great Britain 1916-22 (d 1945), and his 1 w, Dame Margaret, GBE, *née* Owen (d 1941); *b* 3 April 1892; *m* 19 June 1917, Maj Sir Thomas John Carey-Evans, MC, FRCS, IMS (d 25 Aug 1947); 2 s, 2 da; *Style*— Lady Olwen Carey-Evans; Eisteddfa, Criccieth, Gwynedd

CAREY-FOSTER, George Arthur; CMG (1952), DFC (1944, AFC 1941); s of George Muir Foster, FRCS, MRCP (d 1935), and Marie Thérèse Mutin; *b* 18 Nov 1907; *Educ* Clifton; *m* 1936, Margaret Aloysius Egan, da of Barry M Egan, of Cork; 1 da; *Career* RAF 1929-46; entered FO 1946; head of Security Dept 1946-53, cnsllr: Rio de Janciro 1953-55, Warsaw 1953-58; consul-gen Hanover 1959-61, cnsllr Br Embassy The Hague 1961-64, asst under-sec FO 1965-68, ret; *Style*— George Carey-Foster Esq, CMG, DFC, AFC; Kilkeran, Castle Freke, Co Cork

CARFRAE, Maj Michael James Fergus; s of Maj Cecil Carfrae, RA (d 1958), and Gertrude Hilda, *née* Fergusson (d 1977); *b* 4 Mar 1914; *Educ* Wellington Coll; *m* 4 July 1953, Maureen Edith, da of Guy Anmson Maunsell (d 1961); 1 s (Guy Martin b 1956), 2 da (Bryony Frances b 1954, Caroline Harriet (twin) b 1956); *Career* RA 1934-55; WWII 1939-45; ret as Maj; chm Lignacite Hldgs 1958-68; *Recreations* antiques, gardening; *Clubs* Army and Navy; *Style*— Maj Michael Carfrae, Esq; The Old Vicarage, Vicarage Lane, Farnham, Surrey (☎ 0252 715141)

CARINGTON, Hon Rupert Francis John; s and h of 6 Baron Carington; *b* 2 Dec 1948; *Educ* Eton, Bristol Univ; *Style*— The Hon Rupert Carington; The Manor House, Bledlow, Nr Aylesbury, Bucks (☎ 084 44 3499)

CARLESS, Bruce; s of Raymond Carless, of 23 Westgate Rd, Rugby, Warwickshire, and Irene, *née* Bingley; *b* 7 Mar 1945; *Educ* Lawrence Sheriff Sch, Rugby; *m* 21 March 1970, Felicity Mary, da of William John Snell, of Vicarage Farm, Church Lawford, Rugby; 2 s (Jeremy Paul b 1972, Benjamin John b 1974), 1 da (Rosemary Susan b 1982); *Career* CA; pres Warwicks Soc of CAs, tstee Coventry and Warwicks Cancer Treatment Fnd; *Recreations* cricket, golf; *Style*— Bruce Carless, Esq; Westfields, Leamington Rd, Long Itchington, nr Rugby, Warks (☎ 092681 2928); Crompton and Co CAs, 42 Queens Rd, Coventry CV1 3DX

CARLESS, Hugh Michael; CMG (1976); s of Henry Alfred Carless, CIE (d 1975), and Gwendolen Mary, *née* Pattullo; *b* 22 April 1925; *Educ* Sherborne, Sch of Oriental and African Studies London, Trinity Hall Cambridge; *m* 1957, Rosa Maria, eld da of Martino Frontini, of São Paulo, Brazil; 2 s; *Career* Dipl Serv 1950-85; served at Kabul, Rio de Janeiro, Tehran, Budapest, Luanda and Bonn; head of Latin America Dept FCO 1973-77, chargé d'affaires Buenos Aires 1977-80, seconded to Northern Engrg Industs Int 1980-82, ambass to Caracas 1982-85; int conslt and co dir; exec vice pres Hinduja Fndn, dep chm S Atlantic Cncl; *Recreations* golf; *Clubs* Travellers, Royal Mid Surrey; *Style*— Hugh Carless, Esq, CMG; 15 Bryanston Sq, London W1H 7FF

CARLETON-SMITH, Maj Gen Michael Edward; CBE (1979), MBE (1966); s of Lt Col Dudley Lancelot Guy Carleton-Smith (himself gggs (through female line) of Gen Sir Guy Carleton, KB, 1 Baron Dorchester who was first Lt-Govr of Canada 1766-70) and Barbara Leticia Camilla, *née* Popham (d 1980), descended from Rear Adm Sir Home Popham, who captured Buenos Aires 1807 (with William Beresford, later Viscount Beresford), becoming C-in-C on the Jamaica Station until his death in 1820; *b* 5 May 1931; *Educ* Radley Coll, RMA Sandhurst psc, JSSC, NDC, RCDS; *m* 1963, Helga Katja, da of Josef Stoss (d 1973); 3 s; *Career* Cdr Gurkha Field Force Hong Kong 1977-79, dep dir staff duties MOD 1981-82, Maj Gen def advsr and mil advsr Canberra Aust and mil advsr Wellington NZ 1982-85; dir gen Marie Curie Meml Fndn 1985-; *Recreations* riding; *Style*— Maj-Gen Michael Carleton-Smith, CBE, MBE; 28 Belgrave Square, London SW1

CARLETON-SMITH INGLIS, Lt-Col Dudley Guy; DL (Ayrshire 1972); s of Lt-Col Dudley Lancelot Guy Carleton-Smith; bro of Maj-Gen Michael Edward Carleton-Smith, *qv*; *b* 8 Sept 1918; *Educ* Lancing, Sandhurst and Camberley; *m* 1947, Barbara Anne, da of Air Cdre Henry Le Marchant Brock, CBE (d 1964); 1 s, 1 da; *Career* cmmnd Royal Scots Fusiliers 1939, Lt-Col Madagascar, N Africa, Sicily, Italy and Palestine; served 2 and 4/5 Bns RSF and on staff XIII Corps HQ 8 Army, War Office and MOD as memb personal staff of CDS; cmd 4/5 Bn RSF (TA) 1960-62; cncllr: Royal Burgh of Ayr 1967, Baillie 1968; ret 1972; *Style*— Lt-Col Dudley Carleton-Smith Inglis, DL; Dooncroft, Doonfoot, Ayrshire

CARLEY, James; s of Arthur William John Carley (d 1972), of Leyton, London; *b* 2 Oct 1913; *Educ* Leyton Co HS; *m* 1938, Helen; 1 s, 1 da; *Career* WW II RASC Middle East and Western Cmmnd (despatches 1942); Lt in Home Guard 1953; chartered accountant; chm: Meopham Parish Council 1973-, Meopham Historical Society 1976-; *Recreations* country walking, writing history of the parish, writing guided walks leaflets, gardening; *Clubs* Gravesend Conservative; *Style*— James Carley Esq; Wrenbury, Wrotham Rd, Meopham, Kent (☎ 812110)

CARLIER, Maj-Gen (Anthony) Neil; OBE (1982); s of Geoffrey Anthony George Carlier (d 1966), and Sylvia Maude, *née* Emerson; *b* 11 Jan 1937; *Educ* Highgate Sch, RMA Sandhurst, RMCS (BSc), RCDS; *m* 18 May 1974, Daphne Kathleen, da of Capt Langley Humphreys, of Church View, Coombe Cross, Bovey Tracey, S Devon; 1 s (Christopher b 18 May 1975), 1 da (Donna b 27 June 1980); *Career* cmmnd RE 1957, RMCS 1958-61, Troop Cdr RE 1961-63, GSO3 1964-65, instr RMA Sandhurst 1966-69, RNC and Army Staff Coll Shrivenham 1970-71, GSO2 RN 1972-73, Sqdn Cdr 50 Field Sqdn 1974-75, 2 i/c 2 Armed Div Engr Regt 1976-77, CO 39 Engr Regt 1978-79, MA to Army Bd Memb (MGO) 1980-82, Col ASD 2 MOD 1982-83, Cdr 11 Engr Gp 1984-85, RCDS 1986, Cdr Br Forces Falkland Islands 1987-88; Capt Army Team Round the World Yacht Race 1977-78, Flag Offr Army Sailing Assoc 1978-87, Cdre RE YC 1984-87; memb Inst of RE 1958; *Recreations* sailing (offshore), fly fishing, DIY, gardening; *Clubs* Int Soc of Cape Horners RHS; *Style*— Maj-Gen Neil Carlier, OBE; Warren House, Doras Green, Ewshot, Farnham, Surrey GU10 5BL (☎ 0252 850 303)

CARLILE, Alexander Charles; QC, MP (Lib) Montgomery 1983-; s of Erwin Falik, MD, and Sabina Falik; *b* 12 Feb 1948; *Educ* Epsom Coll Surrey, King's Coll London, Inns of Court Sch of Law; *m* 1968, Frances, da of Michael Soley; 3 da; *Career* contested (Lib) Flintshire East: Feb 1974, 1979; chm Welsh Liberal Party 1980-2; *Clubs* Reform, National Liberal, Bristol Channel Yacht; *Style*— Alexander Carlile Esq, QC, MP; House of Commons, London SW1

CARLILE, Lady; Katharine Elizabeth Mary; *née* Field; JP; o da of Rev George Hawkes Field (d 1954), Rector of Milton Keynes, Bletchley, Bucks, and Frances Georgiana, *née* Cadogan (d 1970); *b* 11 Nov 1908; *m* 1, 30 Nov 1940, as his 2 w, Sir (William) Walter Carlile, 1st and last Bt (d 1950); m 2, 24 April 1973, as his 2 w, Geoffrey Dover (d 1984, s of Thomas Dover); has reverted to her former style; *Career* JP Bucks 1948-78; *Recreations* shooting, natural history; *Style*— Lady Carlile; The Old Cottage, Gayhurst, Newport Pagnell, Bucks MK16 8LG (☎ 0908 55248)

CARLILL, Rear Adm John Hildred; OBE (1969); s of Dr Hildred Bertram Carlill (d 1942), and Mildred Constance, *née* Godfrey (d 1984); *b* 24 Oct 1925; *Educ* RNC Dartmouth; *m* 1955, (Elizabeth) Ann, da of Lt-Col Willis Southern (d 1968), of Guildford, Surrey; 3 da (Jennifer, Gale, Joanne); *Career* RN 1939-82, HMS Mauritius 1943-45; war serv: Med, Normandy, N Atlantic, Arctic; psc 1961, jssc 1967, Capt 1972, sec to Flag Offr Naval Air Cmd, dir Naval Manning and Trg (S) MOD, sec to Second Sea Lord MOD, bd pres Admty Interview Bd, Cdre HMS Drake, Rear Adm 1980, Adm Pres RN Coll Greenwich; sec of The Engrg Cncl 1983-87; *Recreations* walking, skiing, DIY, gardening, water colour painting; *Clubs* Army and Navy; *Style*— Rear Adm John Carlill, OBE; Crownpits Barn, Crownpits Lane, Godalming, Surrey GU7 1NY (☎ 048 68 5022)

CARLILL, Vice Adm Sir Stephen Hope; KBE (1957), CB (1954, DSO 1942); s of Harold Flamank Carlill (d 1959), of Caterham, Surrey; *b* 23 Dec 1902; *Educ* RNC

Osborne, RNC Dartmouth; *m* 1928, Julie Fredrike Elisabeth Hildegarde, o da of Rev F W Rahlenbeck (d 1912), of Hohensyburg, Westphalia; 2 s; *Career* joined RN 1916, Cdr 1937, Capt 1942, Rear-Adm 1952, Flag Offr Home Fleet Tning Sqdn 1954-55, Vice-Adm 1954, Chief of Naval Staff Indian Navy 1955-58, ret 1959; West Africa Ctee rep Ghana 1960, advsr to West Africa Ctee 1966-67; *Style—* Vice Adm Sir Stephen Carlill, KBE, CB, DSO; 22 Hamilton Ct, Milford on Sea, Lymington, Hants (☎ 0590 42958)

CARLINE, Gordon David; s of David Smith Carline (d 1961), and Helen Louise, *née* Carpenter (d 1941); *b* 25 June 1933; *Educ* BEC GS, Westminster Tech Coll London; *m* 14 Aug 1954, Doreen Margaret, da of Albert Edward Brown (d 1941); 1 s (David Stuart b 1961), 1 da (Denise Elizabeth b 1959); *Career* trainee draughtsman Laidlaw Smith 1949-51; draughtsman/designer: Johnson Ireton 1951-54, Moore and Tucker 1954-55; engr John F Farquharson and Ptnrs 1955-61, ptnr Andrews Kent and Stone 1972- (assoc 1965-72, engr 1961-65); FIStructE 1959, FICE 1966, FCIOB 1979, FFS 1963 (pres 1986-87), MWeldI 1959, ACIArB 1977, FRS 1987, FIHospE 1972; *Recreations* reading; *Clubs* Clarendon Oxford; *Style—* Gordon D Carline, Esq; "Chaumont", 55 Clifden Rd, Worminghall, Nr Aylesbury, Bucks, HP18 9JR (☎ 08447 209); Andrews Kent & Stone, Seacourt Tower, West Way, Botley, Oxford, OX2 0JJ (☎ 0865 240071, fax 0865 248 006, car 0860 531 586)

CARLISLE, Brian Apcar; CBE (1974), DSC (1945); 2 s of Capt Frederick Montagu Methven Carlisle, MC (d 1973); *b* 27 Dec 1919; *Educ* Harrow, CCC Cambridge; *m* 1953, Elizabeth Hazel Mary, da of Cdr J A Binnie, RN (d 1945); 1 s, 3 da; *Career* served WW II Lt RNVR (HMS Hood and subsequently destroyers); Sudan Political Service 1946-54, Royal Dutch/Shell Gp 1955-74, regnl co-ordinator Oil and Gas Middle East, conslt Lloyds Bank 1975-80, dir Home Oil UK Ltd 1977-80, chm Saxon Oil plc 1980-85; *Clubs* Athenaeum, MCC; *Style—* Brian Carlisle Esq, CBE, DSC; Heath Cottage, Hartley Wintney, Hants (☎ 025 126 2224)

CARLISLE, 12 Earl of (E 1661); Charles James Ruthven Howard; MC (1945), DL (Cumbria, 1984); also Viscount Howard of Morpeth, Baron Dacre of Gillesland (both E 1661) and 12 Lord Ruthven of Freeland (S 1651) (suc mother, Lady Ruthven of Freeland, who m as her 2 husb 1 Viscount Monckton of Brenchley and d 1982); s of 11 Earl (d 1963, whose ancestor, 1 Earl, was gggs of 4 Duke of Norfolk) and Lady Ruthven of Freeland; *b* 21 Feb 1923; *Educ* Eton; *m* 3 Oct 1945, Hon Ela Hilda Aline, *née* Beaumont (*see* Carlisle, Countess of); 2 s, 2 da; *Heir* Viscount Morpeth; *Career* late Lt Rifle Bde; former forestry cmmr; chartered surveyor; FRICS; *Clubs* Boodle's, Pratt's; *Style—* The Rt Hon the Earl of Carlisle, MC; Naworth Castle, Brampton, Cumberland (☎ 06977 2621)

CARLISLE, Countess of; Hon Ela Hilda Aline; *née* Beaumont; da of 2 Viscount Allendale, KG, CB, CBE, MC (d 1956); *b* 27 May 1925; *m* 1945, 12 Earl of Carlisle, *qv*; 2 s, 2 da; *Career* OStJ; *Style—* The Rt Hon the Countess of Carlisle; Naworth Castle, Brampton, Cumberland

CARLISLE, Hon Mrs; Hon Elizabeth Mary; *née* McLaren; er da of 2 Baron Aberconway, CBE (d 1953); *b* 31 May 1911; *m* 9 June 1938, Maj Kenneth Ralph Malcolm Carlisle (d 1983); 1 s (Kenneth Carlisle, MP, *qv*), 3 da (Christabel b 1939, m 1965 Sir James Watson, Bt, *qv*; Katharine (twin with Kenneth) b 1941, m 1970 Victor Newell; Barbara b 1951); *Career* over fifty years in St John Ambulance Bde; OStJ; *Style—* The Hon Mrs Carlisle; 7 Laurie House, Airlie Gdns, London W8 (☎ 01 229 1714); Wyken Hall, Stanton, Bury St Edmunds, Suffolk IP31 2DW (☎ 0359 50240)

CARLISLE, Esmé, Countess of; Esmé Mary Shrubb; da of Charles Edward Iredell; *b* 7 Feb 1914; *m* 1947, as his 2 w, 11 Earl of Carlisle (d 1963); 1 da (Lady Susan Ankaret de Meyer); *Style—* The Rt Hon Esmé, Countess of Carlisle; West Wing, Duns Tew Manor, Oxford OX5 4JS (☎ 0869 40721)

CARLISLE, 64 Bishop of, 1972-; Rt Rev Henry David Halsey; patron of 63 Livings, the Archdeaconries of Carlisle, Westmorland and Furness and W Cumberland and the Canonries in his Cathedral; this See was established by Henry I in 1133, soon after the fndn of the Cathedral by William Rufus; s of late George Halsey, MBE, and Gladys W Halsey, DSc; *b* 27 Jan 1919; *Educ* King's Coll Sch Wimbledon, London Univ, Wells Theol Coll; *m* 1947, Rachel Margaret Neil Smith; 4 da; *Career* hon canon of Rochester 1964-68, rural dean of Bromley 1965-66, archdeacon of Bromley 1966-68, bishop suffragan of Tonbridge 1968-72; *Style—* The Rt Rev the Lord Bishop of Carlisle; Rose Castle, Dalston, Carlisle, Cumbria (☎ 069 96 274)

CARLISLE, Hugh Bernard Harwood; QC (1978); s of William Harwood Carlisle, (d 1979), and Joyce Carlisle; *b* 14 Mar 1937; *Educ* Oundle, Downing Coll Cambridge (MA); *m* 1964, Veronica Marjorie, da of George Arthur Worth, MBE, DL, of Manton, Rutland; 1 s, 1 da; *Career* Nat Service 2 Lt RA; barr Middle Temple 1961 (bencher 1985), jr treasury counsel (personal injuries cases) 1975-78, inspr Dept of Trade Inquiry into Bryanston Finance Ltd 1978-87, memb Criminal Injuries Bd 1982-, recorder S E Circuit 1983-; inspr Dept of Trade Inquiry into Milbury plc 1985-87; *Recreations* fishing, croquet; *Clubs* Garrick, Hurlingham (chm 1982-85); *Style—* Hugh Carlisle Esq, QC; 18 Ranelagh Ave, London SW6 3PJ (☎ 01 736 4238)

CARLISLE, John Russell; MP (C) North Luton 1987-; s of Andrew Russell Carlisle (d 1967), and Edith Carlisle (d 1964); *b* 28 August 1942; *Educ* Bedford, St Lawrence Coll Ramsgate, London Univ; *m* 1964, Anthea Jane Lindsay, da of Cedric May; 2 da; *Career* memb London Corn Exchange 1970-, former tres British/Gibraltar Gp, sec S Africa Gp, dir Granfin Agric Ltd 1979-86; MP (C): Luton West 1979-83, Luton N 1983-; vice chm Parly Party Football ctte; non exec dir: Bletchley Motor Gp plc, Sinai Airlines Ltd; chm Cons Back Bench Sports Ctee 1981-; pres Luton 100 Club, pres Luton Band, govr Sports Aid Fndn (Eastern Area), memb Select Ctee on Agriculture 1986-88, chm S Africa Gp 1987-; *Recreations* watching sport; *Clubs* Farmers', Rugby, MCC, XL; *Style—* John Carlisle, Esq, MP; House of Commons, London SW1A 0AA

CARLISLE, Kenneth Melville; MP (C) Lincoln 1979-; s of Maj Kenneth Ralph Malcolm Carlisle, TD, (d 1983) and Hon Mrs Carlisle, *qv* ;*b* 21 March 1941; *Educ* Harrow, Magdalen Oxford; *m* July 1986, Carla, da of A W Haffner, of Maryland USA; *Career* with Brooke Bond Liebig 1966-74; barr 1965; farmer; Government Whip 1987; *Style—* Kenneth Carlisle, Esq, MP; Wyken Hall Farm, Stanton, Bury St Edmunds, Suffolk (☎ 0359 50240)

CARLISLE, Sir (John) Michael; s of John Hugh Carlisle (d 1958), and Lilian Amy, *née* Smith; *b* 16 Dec 1929; *Educ* King Edward VII Sch Sheffield, Sheffield Univ (BEng); *m* 1957, Mary Scott, da of Robert Magnus Young (d 1972); 1 s (Andrew b 1962), 1 da (Janet b 1960); *Career* pres Sheffield Jr C of C 1967-68; memb cncl: Sheffield C of C 1967-79, Prodn Engrg Res Assoc 1968-73; chm: Sheffield Productivity Assoc 1970, N Sheffield Univ Hosp Mgmnt Ctee 1971-74, Sheffield Area Health Authy (Teaching) 1974-82, Sheffield Health Authy April-July 1982; memb: bd of govrs Utd Sheffield Hosps 1972-74, Sheffield U Careers Advsy Bd 1973-82; govr: Sheffield City Poly 1979-82 (hon fell 1977), Sheffield HS; dir: Torday and Carlisle plc, Diesel Marine Int Ltd, (non-exec) Fenchurch (Midlands); former dir: gp subsidiary cos in Norway, Holland, Greece, Singapore and Hong Kong, Eric Woodward (Electrical) Ltd; chm Trent Regional Health Authy 1982; Freeman Worshipful Co of Cutlers Hallamshire; memb of Ct: Univ of Sheffield, Univ of Nottingham; FRSA, FIMechE, FIMarE, FBIM; kt 1985; *Recreations* horse riding, golf, walking in N Yorkshire; *Clubs* Sheffield, Sickleholme GC; *Style—* Sir Michael Carlisle; 7 Rushley Ave, Dore, Sheffield S17 3EP; St Ovins, Lastingham, N Yorks YO6 6TL; Lockwood, Torday and Carlisle Ltd, Stalkerlees Rd, Sheffield S11 8NN (☎ 0742 686101, telex 54182)

CARLISLE, Stanley Charles; s of Chalres Alfred Carlisle, 1 Lt RNAS (d 1922), and Elizabeth Ann, *née* Edwards (d 1971); *b* 27 Dec 1919; *Educ* Bradford GS, Bradford Univ; *m* 1, 12 Dec 1942, Margaret, da of Oliver Kitcheman (d 1970); 1 s (Paul Gregor b 1944), 1 da (Margaret Gillian b 1947); m 2, 13 Jan 1972, Penelope, da of Arthur Heron Lowes, of Blackpool; *Career* RAF Actg Sqdn-Ldr, Battle of Atlantic 1942, air crew Europe (despatches); md: Bearder Ltd (Bradford), Cohen and Wilks, Parkland Manufacturing (Bradford), Parkland Textile Hldg 1983-87; *Recreations* amateur acting, directing, travel; *Clubs* Bradford Civic Playhouse, Gold Fish; *Style—* Stanley C Carlisle, Esq; High Gables, Wetherby Rd, Scarcroft, Nr Leeds; Parkland Textile Holdings plc, Albion Mills, Greengates, Bradford (☎ Bradford 611161, fax 0274 618398)

CARLISLE OF BUCKLOW, Baron (Life Peer UK 1987), of Mobberley, Co Cheshire; Mark Carlisle; PC (1979), QC (1971, DL Cheshire, 1983); 2 s of late Philip Edmund Carlisle, of Alderley Edge, Cheshire, and Mary Carlisle; *b* 7 July 1929; *Educ* Radley, Manchester Univ; *m* 1959, Sandra Joyce, da of John Hamilton Des Voeux (d 1963), of St Ives, Cornwall; 1 da (Hon Vanessa Lucy); *Career* barr Gray's Inn 1954, bencher 1980, rec of the Crown Court 1976-79 and 1981-, and Warrington South 1983-87, parly under-sec of state Home Office 1970-72, min of state Home Office 1972-74, sec of state for Educn and Science 1979-81; chm Criminal Injuries Compensation Bd 1989- chm Review Ctee on the Parole System in England and Wales 1988; *Style—* The Rt Hon Lord Carlisle of Bucklow, PC, QC, DL; Queen Elizabeth Building, Temple, London EC4 (☎ 01 583 5766); 3 Holt Gardens, Mobberley, Cheshire (☎ 056 587 2275)

CARLOW, Viscount; Charles George Yuill Seymour Dawson-Damer; eldest s and h of 7 Earl of Portarlington; *b* 6 Oct 1965; *Educ* Eton, Univ of Edinburgh (MA); *Career* page of honour to HM The Queen 1979-81; *Style—* Viscount Carlow; 19 Coolong Rd, Vaucluse, NSW 2030, Australia; c/o Yuills Ltd, 95 Aldwych, London WC2B 4JF; c/o John Swire & Sons Ltd, GPO Box 1, Hong Kong

CARLTON, Vivienne Margaret; da of John Carlton, and Phyllis Florence Kaye *née* Minchin; *b* 28 Sept 1947; *Educ* Herts & Essex HS Bishop's Stortford, Trent Park Coll Cockfosters Univ of London; *Career* account dir: Biss Lancaster plc 1980-82, Opus PR Ltd 1982-84, Osca Plc 1985-87, Leadenhall Assocs Ltd 1987-, NTN Television News Ltd 1988-; MIPR, IOD; *Recreations* theatre, reading; *Style—* Miss Vivienne Carlton; Leadenhall Associates Ltd, Lindsey House, 40/42 Charterhouse Stre(et, London, EC1M 6JH (☎ 253 5523, fax 253 5523, telex T-GOLD 87:CQQ033 and 87:CQQ034)

CARLTON-PORTER, Robert William; s of Francis William Porter, of Derbyshire, and Cyrilla, *née* Carlton; *b* 29 Nov 1944; *Educ* St Helens Derby; *m* 9 Oct 1987, Angela, da of William Jenkins, of Ledbury, Herefords; 1 s (Alexander William b 8 Aug 1988); *Career* dir fin: Hoechst UK Ltd 1973-83, Eng China Clays plc 1983-; chm ECC Overseas Investmts Ltd 1983-, pres Eng China Clays Inc (USA) 1983-, dir and chm Assoc of Corporate Tres, non-exec dir Western Tst & Savings Ltd; ACIB 1968, MInstM 1973, FBIM 1976, FCT 1979 (fndn fell); *Recreations* antiques, philately, gardening, Nat Kidney Res Fund; *Style—* Robert Carlton-Porter, Esq; Eng China Clays plc, John Keay Ho, St Austell, Cornwall PL25 4DJ (☎ 0726 74482, fax 0726 623 019, telex 45526 ECCSAU G)

CARLYLE, Nigel Stewart; s of Thomas Edward Carlyle (d 1982), of Scothern, Lincoln, and Gertrude Ellen, *née* Strutt; *b* 14 July 1938; *Educ* Queen Elizabeth Boys' GS Mansfield, Leeds Univ (LLB); *m* 22 Sept 1962, Susan Margaret, da of Capt John Hugh Storey (d 1975), of Harrogate; 2 s (Nicholas Stewart b 1963, Jonathan Stuart b 1967), 2 da (Helen Margaret b 1965, Kathryn Margaret b 1970); *Career* slr; John Barran Ltd 1968-69, mangr of financial analysis Rolls Royce Motors Ltd 1971-73, snr ptnr Hodgson Carlyle and Co Slrs 1979-; cncl memb Lincolnshire Law Soc 1985-, chm Lincoln Ramblers Assoc, Scothern CC, tres Lincoln Branch Gideons Int 1985-; FICA; *Recreations* rambling, badminton, classical music; *Style—* Nigel S Carlyle, Esq; Churchside House, Scothern, Lincoln LN2 2UA (☎ 0673 62412); Hodgson Carlyle and Co, Slrs, 46 Silver St, Lincoln LN2 1EH

CARMAN, George Alfred; QC (1971); o s of Alfred George Carman, of Blackpool, and late Evelyn Carman; *b* 6 Oct 1929; *Educ* St Joseph's Coll Blackpool, Balliol Coll Oxford (BA); *m* 1, 1960 (m dis 1976), Cecilia Sparrow; 1 s; m 2, 1976 (m dis 1984), Frances Elizabeth, da of Thomas Venning, MBE, of Ilkley, N Yorks; *Career* acting Capt RAEC 1948-49; barr 1953, recorder of the Crown Court 1972; *Clubs* Garrick; *Style—* George Carman Esq, QC; 1 Red Lion Cottages, Little Missenden, Bucks (☎ 02406 4560); 12 Old Square, Lincoln's Inn, London WC2 (☎ 01 242 8456); chambers: New Court, The Temple, London EC4 (☎ 01 583 6166)

CARMICHAEL; *see*: Gibson-Craig-Carmichael

CARMICHAEL, Andrew James; s of James Horsfall Elliott Carmichael, MD, FRCR, DMRD, of Liverpool, and Maureen Catherine, *née* McGowan, JP; *b* 8 August 1957; *Educ* St Edwards Coll Liverpool, Downing Coll Cambridge (MA); *Career* articled to Ralph Bonnett of Linklaters & Paines 1979, slr of the Supreme Ct 1981, ptnr Linkcaters & Paines 1987; special minister of St Thomas More Catholic Church; *Recreations* cooking, theatre; *Style—* Andrew Carmichael, Esq; 69 Therapia Rd, London SE22 0SD (☎ 01 693 4432); Linklaters & Paines, Barrington House, 59-67 Gresham St, London EC2V 7JA (☎ 01 606 7080, fax 01 606 5113)

CARMICHAEL, Ian Gillett; s of Arthur Denholm Carmichael (d 1958), of North Ferriby, North Humberside, and Kate, *née* Gillett (d 1962); *b* 18 June 1920; *Educ* Scarborough Coll, Bromsgrove Sch, RADA; *m* 6 Oct 1943, Jean Pyman (d 1983), da of Donald Pyman MacLean (d 1970), of Sleights, Yorks; 2 da (Carol Lee (Mrs West) b 2 April 1946, Sally Maclean (Mrs Hennen) b 9 Sept 1949); *Career* serv WWII 22 Dragoons Maj NW Europe (despatches); film, theatre, television and radio actor; TV performances include The World of Wooster and Lord Peter Wimsey; Hon DLitt Univ of Hull 1987; *Books* Will the Real Ian Carmichael...(autobiography, 1979); *Recreations* gardening, walking, reading; *Clubs* MCC; *Style*— Ian Carmichael, Esq; c/o London Management, 235/241 Regent Street, London W1A 2JT (☎ 01 493 1610)

CARMICHAEL, Ian Leslie; s of Henry Carmichael (d 1972), of Hilton House, Claines, Worcester, and Alice Muriel, *née* Brown; *b* 4 Oct 1941; *Educ* Oundle Northampton, Univ of Wales (BSc); *m* 29 Jan 1966, Myra Phillips, da of Myrfyn Reginald Jones (d 1980), 10A Mount Pleasant, Troedyrhiw, Mid Glam, South Wales; 1 s (Edward), 2 da (Annabel, Camilla); *Career* grad trainee Rootes Gp 1963-64, PA to md Dodge Trucks (UK) Ltd 1964-66, PA to prodn dir commercial vehicle Div Chrysler (UK) Ltd 1966-67 (PA to gp dir diversified products 1967-69), dir and gen mangr mfrg div Carmichael & Sons Ltd 1975-77 (sales mangr 1969-75), chm and md Carmichael Fire & Bulk Ltd 1977-; govr and a Six Master Royal GS Worcester, chm Worcs Assoc, tres Worcs Hunt, vice prod Worcs Horses; I Mech E 1964; *Recreations* skiing, riding, tennis; *Clubs* Br Ski Worcs Hunt; *Style*— Ian Carmichael, Esq; Morton Hall, Holberrow Green, Redditch, Worcs B96 6SJ (☎ 0386 792244); Carmichael Holdings Ltd, Gregory's Mill Street, Worcester WR3 8BE (☎ 0905 21381, fax 0905 20596, car tel 0836 281667, telex 0905 338039)

CARMICHAEL, James; s of James Carmichael (d 1976), of Glasgow, and Margaret, *née* Pettigrew (d 1970); *b* 14 July 1933; *Educ* Whitehill Sch Glasgow, Glasgow Coll of Printing, London Coll of Printing; *m* 28 June 1958, Isabelle Pettigrew, da of William Barr (d 1979), of Glasgow; 3 s (Alistair James b 1959, Gordon William b 1962, Andrew David b 1965); *Career* md: The Cavendish Press Ltd 1972-, The Cavendish Collection Ltd 1977-, chm Fotofit Ltd 1987; dir: Clondalkin Group (UK) Ltd 1988-, A P Burt & Sons Ltd 1988-; vice chm Leicester Guild of Printers, past pres Publicity Assocn of Leicester 1984; *Recreations* golf, bridge, gardening; *Clubs* National Liberal; *Style*— James Carmichael, Esq; Linwood House, Willoughby Waterleys, Leicestershire LE8 3UD (☎0533 478313, car phone 0860 339953); Gibson Place, St Andrews, Fife (☎ 0334 76240)

CARMICHAEL, Dr James Armstrong Gordon; CB (1978); 2 s of Dr Donald Gordon Carmichael (d 1940), and Eileen Mora Carmichael; *b* 28 July 1913; *Educ* Epsom Coll, Guy's Hosp; *m* 1936, Nina Betty Ashton (d 1981), da of Edmond Ashton Heape (d 1942); 2 s; *Career* served Army in India, Iraq, Egypt, Austria, Singapore attained rank of Col; conslt physician MELF 1953-55, conslt physician and prof of tropical medicine Royal Army Med Coll 1956-58, chief med advsr DHSS 1973-78 (dep chief 1971-73); MRCS, FRCP; *Style*— Dr James Carmichael, CB; Adcote, Branksomewood Road, Fleet, Hants (☎ 025 14 5434)

CARMICHAEL, Sir John; KBE (1955); s of late Thomas Carmichael, of Kinburn Terrace, St Andrews, and Margaret Doig Coupar; *b* 22 April 1910; *Educ* Madras Coll St Andrews, St Andrews and Michigan Univs; *m* 1940, Cecilia Macdonald, da of late Joseph Edwards, of Kingask, St Andrews; 1 s, 3 da; *Career* entered Sudan Civil Service 1936, under-sec Min of Finance Sudan Govt 1955-59, memb Br delegation to 19th United Nations 1959, chm Herring Advsy Bd 1960-63, dep chm Ind Tr Authy (acting chm 1963), former dep chm and chief exec Fison's, chm Sidlaw Industries Ltd 1970-80; dir: Abbey National Bldg Soc 1968-81, Royal Bank of Scotland 1966-80; memb Scottish Devpt Advsy Bd 1972-82, cncllr EEC Social and Econ Ctee 1972-74; Captain Royal and Ancient Golf Club 1974-75; chm, St Andrews Link Tst 1983-; *Clubs* Royal and Ancient GC, Augusta National GC, Pine Valley GC; *Style*— Sir John Carmichael, KBE; Hayston Park, Balmullo, St Andrews, Fife (☎ 0334 870268)

CARMICHAEL, Keith Stanley; CBE (1981); s of Stanley Carmichael (d 1949), of Bristol, and Ruby Dorothy, *née* Fox (d 1980); *b* 5 Oct 1929; *Educ* Charlton House Sch, Bristol GS; *m* 1958, Cynthia Mary, da of John David Robert Jones (d 1971); 1 s (Richard John Carmichael b 1968); *Career* qualified CA 1951, ptnr Wilson Bigg and Co 1957-69; dir: H Foulks Lynch & Co Ltd 1957-69, Radio Rentals Ltd 1967-69; sole practitioner 1968-81, managing partner Longcrofts 1981-; memb Monopolies and Merger Cmmn 1983-, Lloyds underwriter 1979-; pres Hertsmere Cons Assoc, chm bd of govrs and tstees of Rickmansworth Masonic Sch, memb ed bd of Simons Taxes 1970-82; FCA, FInstD, FTII; *Books* Spicer and Peglers Income Tax (ed 1965), Corporation Tax (1966), Capital Gains Tax (1966), Ranking Spicer and Peglers Executorship Law and Accounts (ed 1965-87), Taxation of Lloyds Underwriters (with P Wolstenholme 1988); *Recreations* gardening, reading, golf, tennis; *Clubs* Carlton, MCC, Lords Taveners, City of London; *Style*— Keith Carmichael, Esq, CBE; 117 Newberries Avenue, Radlett, Herts WD7 7EN (☎ 0923 855098); Longcroft House, Victoria Avenue, London EC2M 4NS (☎ 01 623 6626, fax 0836 207 206)

CARMICHAEL, Peter; CBE (1981); s of Robert Carmichael (d 1986), of Perthshire, and Elizabeth Paterson (d 1987); *b* 26 Mar 1933; *Educ* Univ of Glasgow (BSc, DSc); *m* 1 (m dis); 2 s (Colin David b 1957, Angus Robert b 1961), 4 da (Sheena Elizabeth, b 1956, Fiona Helen b 1959, Morag Isobel b 1964, Heather Jane b 1967); m 2, 1980, June, da of Ronald D Philip, of Perthshire; *Career* design engr Ferranti Ltd 1958-65, project ldr Hewlett-Packard 1965-68 (production engrg mangr 1968-69, quality assur mangr 1969-72, R and D mangr 1972-74, manufacturing mangr 1974-75, gen mangr 1975-78, jt md Hewlett-Packard 1978-81); dir of small business and electronics Scottish Devpt Agency 1981-87, exec dir for East of Scotland, Scottish Dvpt Agency 1987- (i/c instrument design which won Queen's Award to Industry 1967); *Recreations* music, gardening, antique clock restoration; *Style*— Peter Carmichael, Esq, CBE; 86 Craiglea Drive, Edinburgh EH10 5PH (☎ 031 447 6334); Scottish Dvpt Agency, Rosebery House, Haymarket Terrace, Edinburgh (☎ 031 337 9595)

CARMICHAEL, Maj Peter Oliphant; JP (Perthshire 1962), DL (1966); s of late Col James Louis Carmichael, TD, JP (d 1953), of Arthurstone, Perthshire; *b* 25 August 1921; *Educ* Stowe, Peterhouse Cambridge, RAC Cirencester; *m* 1948, Pamela Muriel, da of Col Maurice James Hartley Wilson, OBE (d 1977), of Ashmore; 3 s, 1 da; *Career* served with 79 (Scottish Horse) Medium Regt RA 1942-45, with Scottish Horse RAC TA 1951-61; *Clubs* New (Edinburgh); *Style*— Maj Peter Carmichael, JP, DL; Arthurstone, Meigle, Perthshire PH12 8QY (☎ 082 84 217)

CARMICHAEL OF KELVINGROVE, Baron (Life Peer UK 1983), of Camlachie in the Dist of the City of Glasgow; Neil George Carmichael; s of James Carmichael (d 1966, former MP Glasgow Bridgeton); *b* 1921,Oct; *Educ* Estbank Acad Glasgow, Royal Coll of Science and Technology Glasgow; *m* 1948, Catherine McIntosh, da of John Dawson Rankin, of Glasgow; 1 da; *Career* memb Glasgow Corpn 1962; MP (Lab) Glasgow Woodside 1962-74, Glasgow Kelvingrove 1974-83; PPS to min of Technology 1966-67, parly sec to min of Technology and Power 1969-70, parly under-sec of state: min of Transport 1967-69, DOE 1974-75, Dept of Industry 1975-76; memb select ctee on Transport 1980-83; *Style*— The Rt Hon the Lord Carmichael of Kelvingrove; 53 Partick Hill Rd, Glasgow G11 5AB (☎ 041 334 1718)

CARNAC; see Rivett-Carnac

CARNARVON, 7 Earl of (GB 1793); Henry George Reginald Molyneux Herbert; KCVO (1982), KBE (1976, DL Hants 1965); also Baron Porchester (GB 1780); o s of 6 Earl (d 1987), and his 1 w Anne Catherine Tredick, *née* Wendell; *b* 19 Jan 1924; *Educ* Eton, RAC Cirencester (Dip Ag); *m* 7 Jan 1956, Jean Margaret, er da of Hon Oliver Malcolm Wallop (s of 8 Earl of Portsmouth); 2 s (Lord Porchester, Hon Henry Malcolm b 1959), 1 da (Lady Carolyn Penelope b 1962); *Heir* s, Lord Porchester, *qv*; *Career* late Lt Royal Horse Gds, Hon Col 115 (Hants Fortress) Engineer Regt (TA) 1963-67; appointed racing mangr to HM The Queen 1969; pres Thoroughbred Breeders' Assoc 1969-74 and 1986-, chm Agricultural Research Cncl 1978-82, vice-pres Game Research Assoc 1967-, chm Stallion Advsy Ctee to Betting Levy Bd 1974-, pres Royal Agric Soc 1980-81, CC Hants 1954, county alderman 1965-74, vice-chm County Cncl 1971-74, chm 1973-77, vice-chm County Cncls Assoc 1972-74, chm South East Economic Planning Cncl 1971-79, chm Sports Cncl Planning Ctee 1965-70, pres Hants and IOW Naturalist Tst 1987-; chm: Newbury Racecourse plc 1985-, Equine Virology Research Foundfation 1986-, Basingstoke and North Hants Medical Tst 1981-; memb: Nature Conservancy Cncl 1963-66, Forestry Cmmn 1967-70; Verderer of the New Forest 1961-65; High Steward of Winchester 1977, Jockey Club (chm Race Planning Ctee 1967-84); hon fell Portsmouth Poly 1976; Hon DSc Reading 1980; *Clubs* White's, Portland; *Style*— The Rt Hon the Earl of Carnarvon, KCVO, KBE, DL; Milford Lake House, Burghclere, Newbury, Berks RG15 9EL (☎ 0635 253387)

CARNEGIE, Lady Alexandra Clare; da of 3 Duke of Fife and Hon Lady Worsley; *b* 20 June 1959; *Style*— Lady Alexandra Carnegie

CARNEGIE, Hon James Duthac; TD (1944); yst s of 10 Earl of Southesk (d 1941); *b* 26 Sept 1910; *Educ* Eton, Trinity Cambridge (BA Eng); *m* 1935, Claudia Katharine Angela, da of Hon Lord Blackburn (d 1941), Scottish Lord of Session, by his w, Lady Constance, da of 13 Earl of Strathmore and Kinghorne; 1 s (Robin, *see* Selina, Marchioness of Lansdowne); *Career* Maj 4/5 Bn Black Watch RHR (TA); *Style*— The Hon James Carnegie, TD; Balloch, Alyth, Perths PH11 8JN (☎ 082 83 2339)

CARNEGIE, Hon Jocelyn Jacek Alexander Bannerman; s of Countess of Erroll (d 1978), and 2 husband, Maj Raymond Alexander Carnegie, gs of late 10 Earl of Southesk; half-bro of Earl of Erroll; *b* 21 Nov 1966; *Style*— The Hon Jocelyn Carnegie; Crimonmogate, Lonmay, Aberdeenshire

CARNEGIE, Maj Raymond Alexander; o s of Hon Alexander Bannerman Carnegie (d 1989; s of 10 Earl of Southesk), and his 1 w, Susan Ottilia (d 1968), da of Maj Ernest Rodakowski and Lady Dora Susan, *née* Carnegie, da of 9 Earl of Southesk; *b* 9 July 1920; *Educ* Eton; *m* 1, 1943 (m dis 1953), Patricia Elinor Trevor, da of Cdr Sir Hugh Trevor Dawson, 2 Bt (cr 1920), RN; 2 da; m 2, 1964, Diana Denyse Hay, Countess of Errol (who m 1 (m dis), Capt Sir (Rupert) Iain Kay Moncreiffe of that Ilk, 11 Bt (d 1985), and who d 1978); 1 s (*see* Carnegie, Hon Jocelyn); *Career* late Scots Gds, wounded 3 times and despatches WW II; *Style*— Maj Raymond Carnegie; Crimonmogate, Lonmay, Aberdeenshire

CARNEGIE, Lt-Gen Sir Robin Macdonald; KCB (1979), OBE (1968); yr s of Sir Francis Carnegie, CBE (d 1946), and Theodora, *née* Matthews; *b* 22 June 1926; *Educ* Rugby; *m* 1955, Iona, da of Maj-Gen Sir John Sinclair, KCMG, CB, OBE (d 1977); 1 s, 2 da; *Career* cmmnd The Queen's Own Hussars 1946, cmd 1967-69, cmd 11 Armoured Bde 1971-72, student Royal Coll Defence Studies 1973, GOC 3 Div (Maj-Gen) 1974-76, COS HQ BAOR 1976-78, mil sec 1978-80, Col dir-gen Army Training MOD 1981-82, ret 1982; *Style*— Lt-Gen Sir Robin Carnegie, KCB, OBE

CARNEGIE, Sir Roderick Howard; s of Douglas Howard and Margaret F Carnegie; *b* 27 Nov 1932; *Educ* Geelong GS, Trinity Coll Melbourne Univ, New Coll Oxford, Harvard Business Sch; *m* 1959, Carmen Sandra, da of W J T Clarke; 3 s; *Career* former dir McKinsey and Co, former chm and chief exec CRA Ltd; pres Business Cncl of Australia 1987; kt 1978; *Style*— Sir Roderick Carnegie; 2 Floor, 135 Collins Street, Melbourne, Victoria 3000, Australia (☎ 03 658 3310, 658 3311)

CARNEGY, Derek Francis; s of Francis Anthony Roberts Carnegy; *b* 23 August 1928; *Educ* Pangbourne Coll; *m* 1961, Judith Frances; 2 s; *Career* former submarine specialist RN; joined Hambros Bank 1968, dir Hambros Unit Tst Mngrs Ltd; *Style*— Derek Carnegy, Esq; 14 Ranelagh Rd, Winchester, Hants (☎ 66077)

CARNEGY OF LOUR, Baroness (UK Life Peeress 1982); Elizabeth Patricia Carnegy of Lour; eld da of Lt-Col Ughtred Elliott Carnegy Carnegy of Lour, 11 of Lour, DSO, MC and Bar, JP, DL (d 1973), sometime CC Angus and Baron (Scottish territorial Barony) of Lour, formerly memb of Hon Corps of Gentlemen at Arms and Royal Co Archers. The Col's mother's gggggf in the male line was Patrick Carnegy, yr bro of 3 Earl of Northesk. The Col's wife was Violet, MBE (d 1965), da of Henry Henderson, himself yr bro of 1 Baron Faringdon; *b* 28 April 1925; *Educ* Downham Sch Essex; *Career* worked in Cavendish Lab Cambridge 1943-46; Girl Guide Assoc: joined 1947, Co cmmr Angus 1956-63, tning advsr Scotland 1958-62, training advsr Cwlth HQ 1963-65, pres Angus 1971-84, pres Scotland 1979-; coopted onto Angus Co Cncl Educn Ctee 1967-75; chm: Working Party on Professional Tning for Community Educn in Scotland 1975-77, Scottish Cncl Community Educn 1981- (memb 1978-), Manpower Servs Cmmn for Scotland 1981-83; memb: Cncl Tertiary Educn Scotland 1979-83, Manpower Servs Cmmn 1979-82, Scottish Economic Cncl 1981-; cncllr Tayside Regnl Cncl 1974-82 (convener Recreation and Tourism Ctee 1974-76 and Educn Ctee 1977-81); Hon Sheriff 1969-84; memb: Cncl of Open Univ 1984-, Admin Cncl Royal Jubilee Tsts 1984-; tstee Nat Museums of Scotland 1987-; *Style*— The Rt Hon the Lady Carnegy of Lour; Lour, Forfar, Angus DD8 2LR (☎ Inverarity 0307 82 237)

CARNEGY-ARBUTHNOTT, Brevet Col David; TD (1969), DL (Co of City of Dundee 1973); s of Lt-Col Wilmot Boys Carnegy-Arbuthnott (d 1973), and Enid Carnegy-Arbuthnott (d 1986), *née* Carnegy-Arbuthnott, thirteenth of Balnamoon and thirteenth of Findowrie; Alexander Carnegy, 5 of Balnamoon, took part in 1715 rebellion, captured, imprisoned, pardoned 1721, estates forfeited, repurchased 1728. James Carnegy, subsequently 6 of Balnamoon, took part in 1745 rebellion, captured, tried but not convicted, because of misnomer - he had married Margaret Arbuthnott who became 5 of Findowrie and added her name to his; *b* 17 July 1925; *Educ* Stowe; *m* 1949, Helen Adamson, da of Capt David Collier Lyell, MC (d 1970); 2 s (James, Hugh), 2 da (Sarah, Bridget); *Career* emergency cmmn Black Watch 1944-47, TA 1955-69, Bt-Col 1969; Honorary Col First Bn 51 Highland Volunteers (TA) 1980-89;

CA 1953, in practice in Dundee 1956-; pres Dundee C of C 1971-72; memb of court Dundee Univ 1977-85, Royal Co of Archers (Queen's Body Guard for Scotland) 1959-; landowner through family cos (3000 acres); hon LLD (Univ Dundee 1982); *Recreations* shooting, country pursuits; *Clubs* New (Edinburgh), Army and Navy, Puffins (Edinburgh); *Style*— Bt-Col David Carnegy-Arbuthnott of Balnamoon, TD, DL; Balnamoon, Brechin, Angus DD9 7RH (☎ 035 66 208); City House, 16 Overgate, Dundee DD1 9PN (☎ 0382 202561)

CARNELL, Rev Canon Geoffrey Gordon; *b* 5 July 1918; *Educ* City of Norwich Sch, St John's Coll Cambridge (BA, MA, Lightfoot Scholar); *m* 1945, Mary Elizabeth Boucher, da of John Smith (d 1946), of Abington, Northampton; 2 s (Martin, Andrew); *Career* asst curate Abington Northampton 1942-48, chaplain and lectr St Gabriel's Coll Camberwell 1949-53; rector: Isham with Gt and Little Harrowden 1953-71, Boughton Northampton 1971-85; chaplain to the High Sheriff of Northants 1972, dir post-ordination trg, examining chaplain to the Bishop of Peterborough 1962-86, non-residentiary canon of Peterborough Cathedral 1965-85, canon emeritus 1986-, chaplain to the Mayor of Kettering 1988-89; librarian Ecton House Conf and Retreat Centre 1968-, memb Ecclesiastical History Soc 1978-, vice chm Northamptonshire Record Soc 1981-; chaplain to HM The Queen 1981-88; *Recreations* walking, music, reading (especially biography), visiting art collections; *Style*— The Rev Canon Geoffrey Carnell; 52 Walsingham Ave, Barton Woods, Kettering, Northants NN15 5ER (☎ 0536 511415)

CARNELLEY, The Ven Desmond; *b* 29 Nov 1929; *Educ* St John's Coll York (Cert Ed), Univ Coll of Southwest Exeter (Cert Rel Ed), Ripon Hall Oxford, Open Univ (BA); *m* 6 June 1954, Dorothy (d 1986); 3 s (Philip b 1957, John b 1961, David b 1965), 1 da (Elizabeth Amy b 1964); *Career* teaching 1951-59; curate of Aston Sheffield 1960, p-in-c St Paul Ecclesfield 1963, vicar of Balby Doncaster 1967; p-in-c (later vicar) of Mosborough Sheffield 1973, archdeacon of Doncaster 1985-; *Recreations* reading, theatre, walking in Derbyshire; *Style*— The Venerable the Archdeacon of Doncaster; 1 Balmoral Road, Town Moor, Doncaster DN2 5BZ

CARNEY, Michael; s of Bernard Patrick Carney (d 1988), of Panton Place, Holywell, Clwyd, and Gwyneth Carney, *née* Ellis; *b* 19 Oct 1937; *Educ* The Grammar Sch Holywell, Clwyd, Univ Coll of N Wales Bangor (BA); *m* 22 Apr 1963, Mary Patricia Carney, da of Robert Ingmam Davies (d 1983), of Wern Isaf, Llanfairfechan, Gwynedd; 2 s (Owen, Gwyn), 1 da (Bethan); *Career* staff offr to dep chm NCB 1963-67, asst sec Electricity Cncl 1971-74 (admin offr 1968-71), personnel mangr Midlands Regn CEGB 1980-82 (sec SW Regn 1974-82); personnel dir Oxfam 1982-87; sec Water Authys Assoc 1987-; MIPM; *Recreations* book collecting, reading; *Clubs* Royal Cwlth; *Style*— Michael Carney Esq; 344B Woodstock Road, Oxford OX2 8BZ (☎ Oxford 515325); WAA, 1 Queen Anne's Gate, London SW1H 9BT (☎ 01 222 8111, fax 01 222 1811, telex 918518)

CARNEY, Adm Robert Bostwick; Hon CBE (1946), DSM (1942 US); s of Robert E and Bertha Carney; *b* 26 Mar 1895; *Educ* US Naval Academy (BS); *m* 1918, Grace Stone Craycroft, of Maryland; 1 s, 1 da; *Career* Adm US Navy 1950, CIC Allied Forces S Europe NATO 1951-53, Chief of Naval Operations 1953-55, ret; pres US Naval Inst 1947-49 and 1953-55, chm Bath Iron Works Shipbuilders 1956-67, chm Naval History Fndn 1961-81; LLD (Loras); *Clubs* Chevy Chase (DC), Alibi (DC), The Brook (New York); *Style*— Adm Robert Carney, CBE, DSM; 2801 New Mexico Ave (NW), Washington, DC 2007, USA

CARNOCK, 4 Baron (UK 1916); Sir David Henry Arthur Nicolson; 14 Bt (NS 1637), of Carnock, Co Stirling; recognised by Lord Lyon 1984 as holder of the Baronetcy of Lasswade (NS 1629) and as chief of the Clan Nicolson and Nicolson of that Ilk; s of Captain 3 Baron Carnock, DSO, JP, RN (d 1982), by his w, Hon Katharine Lopes (d 1968), da of 1 Baron Roborough; *b* 10 July 1920; *Educ* Winchester, Balliol Coll Oxford; *Heir* 1 cous, Nigel Nicolson, MBE; *Career* served 1940-46 with Royal Devon Yeo Staff, DAQMG HQ Land Forces Hong Kong, Maj 1945; slr 1949; ptnr Clifford-Turner Slrs 1955-86; *Recreations* shooting, fishing, gardening, foreign travel; *Clubs* Travellers', Beefsteak; *Style*— The Rt Hon the Lord Carnock; 90 Whitehall Court, London SW1A 2EL (☎ 01 839 5544); Ermewood House, Harford, Ivybridge, Devon PL21 0JE (☎ 075 54 2519)

CARNWATH, Sir Andrew Hunter; KCVO (1975), DL (Essex 1972); s of Dr Thomas Carnwath, DSO (d 1954), Dep CMO, Min of Health, and Margaret Ethel, *née* McKee; *b* 26 Oct 1909; *Educ* Eton (King's Scholar); *m* 1, 1939, Kathleen Marianne (d 1968), da of late William Anderson Armstrong, of Westoe, Co Durham; 5 s, 1 da (Felicity, now Hon Mrs Diarmid Guinness, *qv*); m 2, 1973, Joan Gertrude (author writing as Joan Alexander), da of Maj-Gen Henry Lethbridge Alexander, CB, CMG, DSO (d 1944), and widow of D S Wetherell-Pepper; *Career* served WW II Fl-Lt RAF; ret merchant banker; with Baring Bros and Co Ltd 1928-74 (md 1955-74); chm: Save and Prosper Gp 1961-80, London Multinational Bank 1971-74; dir Equity and Law Life Assur Soc 1955-83, Scottish Agric Industs 1969-75, Great Portland Estates 1977-; memb London ctee Hongkong Shanghai Bank 1967-74, pres Inst of Bankers 1970-72; chm: Central Bd of Fin C of E Investmt Mgmnt Ctee 1960-74, Chelmsford Diocesan Bd of Finance 1969-75; govr: King Edward's Hosp Fund for London 1976-85 (tres 1965-74), Felsted Sch 1965-81; tstee Imperial War Graves Endowment Fund 1963-74 (chm 1964-74), memb Royal Cmmn for Exhibition of 1851 1964-85; tres: Friends of Tate Gallery 1966-82, Essex Univ 1973-82; High Sheriff of Essex 1965, CC 1973-77; Master Worshipful Co of Musicians 1981-82; hon fell Eton 1981, Hon DUniv (Essex 1983); *Recreations* music (playing the piano), pictures; *Clubs* Athenaeum, Essex; *Style*— Sir Andrew Carnwath, KCVO, DL; Garden Flat, 39 Palace Gardens Terrace, London W8 4SB (☎ 01 727 9145)

CARNWATH, Francis Anthony Armstrong; s of Sir Andrew Hunter Carnwath, KCVO, and Kathleen Marianne, *née* Armstrong (d 1968); *b* 26 May 1940; *Educ* Eton (Oppidan Scholar), Trin Camb (BA); *m* 1975, Penelope Clare, da of Sir Charles Rose (d 1965); 1 s (Alexander Patrick b 1980), 2 da (Flora Helen b 1976, Catriona Rose b 1978, d 1985); *Career* dir Baring Bros and Co Limited 1979-; Shelter Nat Campaign for the Homeless (tres and later dep chm and chm of exec ctee 1968-76), tres VSO 1979-84; chm: Ravensbourne Registration Services Ltd 1981- Spitalfields Historic Building Tst 1984-, Henley Soc (Civic Tst Amenity Soc) 1984-; memb Exec Ctee Friends of Tate Gallery (tres 1985-), co sec Foreign Anglican Church and Educnl Assoc Ltd 1973-85 (dir 1973-); *Recreations* music, gardening, walking; *Clubs* Royal Commonwealth Soc; *Style*— Francis Carnwath; The Old Rectory, Rotherfield Greys, Henley on Thames (☎ 04917 255); 8 Bishopsgate, London EC2N 4AE (☎ 01 283 8833)

CARNWATH, Robert John Anderson; QC (1985); s of Sir Andrew Carnwath KCVO, and K M *née* Armstrong (d 1968); *b* 15 Mar 1945; *Educ* Eton, Trinity Coll Cambridge (MA, LLB); *m* 18 May 1974, Bambina, da of G D'Adda, of Bergamo, Italy; *Career* called to Bar 1969, jr consel to Revenue 1980-85, QC 1985-, Attorney-General to Prince of Wales 1988-; various legal publications; chm Shepherds Bush Housing Assoc; Musicians Co; *Recreations* violin, singing, tennis; *Clubs* Garrick; *Style*— Robert Carnwath, Esq, QC; 2 Paper Building, Temple, London, EC4 (☎ 01 353 5835)

CARO, Anthony Alfred; CBE (1969); s of Alfred and Mary Caro; *b* 8 Mar 1924; *Educ* Charterhouse, Christ's Coll Camb, Regent St Poly, Royal Acad Schs; *m* 1949, Sheila May Girling; 2 s; *Career* asst to Henry Moore 1951-53, taught pt/t St Martin's Sch of Art 1953-79, taught sculpture at Bennington Coll Vermont 1963 and 1965, initiated and attended first Triangle Workshop Pine Plains NY 1982; memb: cncl RCA 1981-, cncl Slade Sch of Art 1982-; William Townsend Meml lectr 1982, tstee Tate Gall 1982-; most recent one-man exhibitions: Aspects of Br Art, Solomon R Guggenheim Museum NY 1983, Six in Bronze, Williams Coll Museum of Art, Williamstown Massachusetts 1984 (also shown at Museum of Art, Carnegie Int Pittsburgh, Columbus Museum of Art Ohio, Brooklyn Museum NY); Transformations in Sculpture: Four Decades of American and European Art, Solomon R Guggenheim Museum NY 1985-86, Between Object and Image Br Cncl Touring Exhibition: Madrid, Barcelona, Bilbao 1986; works also in a number of public collections including: Nat Gallery of Victory Melbourne, The Tate Gallery London and UCLA Art Cncl; given key to City of NY 1976, cmmnd by Nat Gallery of Art Washington 1978, hon memb American Academy and Inst of Arts and Letters 1979, Hon DLitt; East Anglia, York Univ, Toronto; kt 1987; *Recreations* listening to music; *Style*— Anthony Caro Esq, CBE; 111 Frognal, Hampstead, London NW3 6XR

CAROE, Martin Bragg; s of Alban Douglas Rendall Caroe, OBE, of 15 Campden Hill Square, London, and Gwendolen Mary, *née* Bragg (d 1984); *b* 15 Nov 1933; *Educ* Winchester, Trinity Coll Cambridge (BA), Kingston on Thames School of Architecture (DipArch); *m* 15 Sept 1962, Mary Elizabeth, da of Capt Stephen Wentworth Roskill, CBE, DSC, RN (d 1982), of Frostlake Cottage, Malting Lane, Cambridge; 2 s (William b 1967, d 1974, Oliver b 1968), 3 da (Rebecca b 1965, Ruth b 1972, Emily b 1976); *Career* Lance Corpl KRRC 1952, 2 Lt 1 Royal Fus 1952-53, Capt 8 Royal Fus 1954-62; ptnr Caroe and Martin 1962; third generation conservation workind: specialising in care of historic buildings, architect St Davids Cathedral 1966, Wells Cathedral West Front Sculpture Conservation 1981-86, repair on accession to Nat Tst Kingston Lacy 1982-84, surveyor Rochester Cathedral 1982-; Civic Tst Award Wells Vicars Close 1984; pres EASA (Ecclesiastical Architects & Surveyors Assoc) 1978-79; memb: Faculty Jurisdiction Cmmn 1980-84, exec ctee Cncl for the Care of Churches 1986-; Freeman Worshipful Co of Plumbers (Master 1986); ARIBA 1960, FSA 1988; UN Medal Korea; *Recreations* gardening, punting; *Style*— Martin Caroe, Esq; Vann, Hambledon, Nr Godalmuig, Surrey GU8 4EF (☎ 042 879 3413); 90 Eversholt St, London NW1 1BT (☎ 01 387 0477, car tel 0836 211 142)

CARPENTER, David Iain; s of Jeffrey Frank Carpenter, of Epsom, Surrey, and Joyce Cumming, *née* Mitchell; *b* 14 Oct 1951; *Educ* Sutton GS, Kingston upon Thames Sch of ARchitecture, Britannia RN Coll, Heriot-Watt Sch of Architecture Edinburgh (Dip Arch); *m* 20 Jan 1979, Anne Richmond, da of Dr Norman John McQueen, of Appin, Argyll; 4 s (Angus b 1980, Edward b 1981, Alexander b and d 1983, Simon b 1984); *Career* Sub Lt HMS Hermes and HMS Monkton (Hong Kong) 1975, secretarial and short legal course HMS Pembroker 1976, asst sec to Capt Mine Countermeasures and Fishery Protection Rosyth 1976, Lt 1977, asst sec HMS Hermes 1977, acquaint course RN Coll Greenwich 1987, supply offr HMS Edinburgh 1988; J & F Johnson and Ptnrs: project architect 21982, sr architect 1986, assoc dir 1987, resigned 1988; established own practice David Carpenter ARchitect Edinburgh 1988, dir Plan Shop (Edinburgh) Ltd 1987; memb: RIBA 1984, RIAS 1985, Edinburgh Architectural Assoc; *Recreations* sailing, sketching, readingk; *Clubs* Royal Scots (Edinburgh); *Style*— David Carpenter, Esq; David Carpenter Architect, 9-14 Maritime St, Edinburgh EH6 6SB (☎ 031 554 3041, fax 031 553 5358)

CARPENTER, Very Rev Edward Frederick; s of Frederick James and Jessie Kate Carpenter; *b* 27 Nov 1910; *Educ* Strodes Sch Egham, King's Coll London Univ; *m* 1951, Lilian Betsy Wright; 3 s, 1 da; *Career* ordained 1935; Archdn of Westminster 1963-74, Dean of Westminster 1974-85; *Style*— The Very Rev Edward Carpenter; 6 Selwyn Avenue, Richmond, Surrey TW9 2HA

CARPENTER, James Montagu; s of Edward Harry Osmund Carpenter (d 1974), of Holbeache, Trimpley, Worcs; *b* 28 Dec 1924; *Educ* Eton; *m* 1961, Mary Morris, o da of Brig Geoffrey William Auten, OBE (d 1981), of Knockholt, Kent; 3 s; *Career* served WW II Sub-Lt RNVR, Far East and Med; High Sheriff of Worcestershire 1965; chm Hereford and Worcs Ctee of COSIRA 1983-; dir South Staffordshire Waterworks Co 1983-, chm Milcort Ltd 1984-; *Recreations* farming, tennis, shooting; *Style*— James Carpenter, Esq; Holbeache House, Trimpley, nr Bewdley, Worcs (☎ 029 97 256)

CARPENTER, Maj-Gen (Victor Harry) John; CB (1975), MBE (1945); s of Harry and Amelia Carpenter; *b* 21 June 1921; *m* 1946, Theresa McCulloch; 1 s, 1 da; *Career* 2 Lt RASC 1939, Tport Offr in Chief MOD 1971-73, Maj-Gen 1971, Dir of Movements (Army) MOD 1973-75, ret; chm Traffic Cmmrs Yorks Traffic Area 1975-; *Style*— Maj-Gen John Carpenter, CB, OBE; Traffic Commrs, Yorkshire Traffic Area, 386 Harehills Lane, Leeds

CARPENTER, Leslie Arthur; s of William and Rose Carpenter; *b* 26 June 1927; *Educ* Hackney Tech Coll; *m* 1952, Stella Louise Bozza; 1 da; *Career* chm and chief exec International Publishing Corpn Ltd, chief exec Reed International plc 1982-, dir IPC Investmts (Pty) Ltd; *Style*— Leslie Carpenter, Esq; Reed House, Piccadilly, London W1A 1GJ

CARPENTER, Robert David Evans; s of Ernest Henry Carpenter (d 1973), of Reading, and Muriel Carpenter; *b* 22 Jan 1940; *Educ* Mill Hill Sch; *m* 16 Sept 1967, Gloria Faith Davie, da of Gordon Stuart Clarke (d 1980); 1 s (James Nicholas b 9 June 1970), 1 da (Caroline Claire b 18 Dec 1972); *Career* with Montagu Loebl Stanley & Co 1968-85 (ptnr 1979-85), dir investment research Kitcat & Aitken 1985-; AIB 1962; *Recreations* squash; *Style*— Robert Carpenter, Esq; Kitcat & Aitken, 71 Queen Victoria St, London EC4V 4DE (☎ 01 489 1966)

CARPENTER-GARNIER, Col (Leonard) George; OBE (1949), DL (1971); s of late George William Carpenter-Garnier (d 1960), of Rookesbury Park, Hants, and his 1 wife Helen, *née* Gregory (d 1911); *b* 1 Nov 1911; *Educ* Radley, Sandhurst; *m* 1937,

Eileen Florence Tufnell (d 1987), da of Geoffrey Turbett (d 1967), of Hale Place, Farnham, Surrey; 1 da; *Career* cmmnd Devonshire Regt 1932, Col 1958, ret; memb Droxford RDC 1967-1973 and City of Winchester Cncl 1974-86; High Sheriff of Hants 1968; chm Rooksbury Park Sch Wickham 1962-; *Clubs* MCC, Naval and Military; *Style—* Col George Carpenter-Garnier, OBE, DL; Beverley, Wickham, Fareham, Hants PO17 6HR (☎ 0329 833125)

CARR; *see*: Baker-Carr

CARR, Lady Anne Mary; *née* Somerset; da of 11 Duke of Beaufort; *b* 21 Jan 1955; *m* 26 March 1988, Matthew Carr, yr s of Sir Raymond Carr, of Burch, N Molton, Devon; *Style—* Lady Anne Carr

CARR, Very Rev Dr Arthur Wesley; s of Arthur Eugene Carr, and Irene Alice, *née* Cummins; *b* 26 July 1941; *Educ* Dulwich Coll, Jesus Coll Oxford (MA), Jesus Coll Cambridge (MA), Ridley Hall Cambridge, Sch of Ecumenical Studies Geneva, Univ of Sheffield (PhD); *m* 20 April 1967, Natalie Gay, da of Norman Robert Gill; 1 da (Helga b 1973); *Career* curate Luton Parish Church 1967-71, tutor Ridley Hall 1970-71, chaplain Ridley Hall 1971-72, Sir Henry Stephenson fell in biblical studies Univ of Sheffield 1972-74, hon curate Ranmoor Parish Church Sheffield 1972-74, chaplain Chelmsford Cathedral 1974-78 (canon residentiary 1974-87); dep dir and programme dir Chelmsford Cath Centre for research and trg 1974-82, Bishop of Chelmsford's dir of trg 1976-84, examining chaplain to Bishop of Chelmsford 1976-86, hon fell dept of christian ethics and applied theology New Coll Edinburgh 1986-88; dean of Bristol 1987-; *Books* Angels and Principalities (1981), 'Angels' and 'The Devil' in A Dictionary of Christian Spirituality (1983), The Priestlike Task (1985), Brief Encounters. Pastoral Ministry through the Occasional Offices (1985), The Pastor as Theologian (1989), articles in various journals; *Recreations* reading, writing, music, gardening; *Style—* The Very Rev the Dean of Bristol; The Deanery, 20 Charlotte St, Bristol BS1 5PZ (☎ 0272 262443); Bristol Cathedral, College Green, Bristol BS1 5TJ (☎ 0272 264879/ 250692)

CARR, Charles Francis; CBE (1973); s of Edward Crossley Carr; *b* 1913; *Educ* Nottingham HS, Hertford Oxford; *m* 1951, Florian, *née* Winslow; *Career* dep chief inspr of Factories DOE 1965, sr dep chief Inspr of Factories Dept of Employment; *Style—* Charles Carr Esq, CBE; 64 Malborough Place, London NW8

CARR, David; s of Samuel Carr (d 1940), of Liverpool, and Lily, *née* Marks (d 1958); *b* 20 June 1922; *Educ* Oulton HS, Univ of Liverpool; *m* 13 Jan 1954, Adele, da of Israel Karp (d 1980), of Liverpool; 3 s (Nigel b 1955, Colin b 1957, Timothy b 1964); *Career* Sgt wireless operator (serv Normandy 1944-) RCS 1942-47; slr 1949, sr ptnr David Carr & Roe Birkenhead 1949-, chm Social Security Appeal Tbnl 1980; sr warden Liverpool Old Hebrew Congregation 1972-74, life govr Imperial Cancer Res Fund; memb: Law Soc 1949, Slrs Benevolent Assoc; *Recreations* bridge, swimming, travel; *Style—* David Carr, Esq; 1 Merrilocks Green, Blundellsands, Liverpool L23 6XR (☎ 051 924 4883); 34 Hamilton St, Birkenhead, Merseyside L41 5AJ (☎ 051 647 7401)

CARR, Donald Bryce; OBE (1985); s of Col John Lillingston Carr (d 1963), and Constance Ruth, *née* Smith (d 1987); *b* 28 Dec 1926; *Educ* Repton, Worcester Coll Oxford (MA); *m* 1953, Stella Alice Vaughan, da of Rev Francis Vaughan Simpkinson; 1 da (Diana b 1958), 1 s (John b 1963); *Career* Lt Royal Berks Regt; capt Derbyshire CCC (asst sec 1953-59, sec 1959-62), asst sec MCC 1962-74, sec Test and Co Cricket Bd 1974-86; soccer Blue Oxford; played cricket for England; *Recreations* golf, gardening; *Clubs* MCC Vincents, Porters Park Golf; *Style—* Donald B Carr Esq, OBE; 28 Aldenham Ave, Radlett, Herts (☎ 092 76 855602)

CARR, Dorothy; da of Daniel Greenwood (d 1976), of Harrow, Middx, and Elvina, *née* Stanworth (d 1968); *b* 8 Feb 1921; *Educ* Harrow Co Sch for Girls, LSE, Univ of London (BA); *m* 1948, David Carr, s of Alfred Edward Carr (d 1958), of Bath; 1 da (Susan b 1951); *Career* historian; lectr and adult educn tutor (ret); tutorial studentship King's Coll London 1965-69, corr tutor London region Open Univ 1970-71; memb panel of tutors dept of extra-mural studies Univ of London 1970-85 (various classes in different areas); *Books* The Reformation in England to the Accession of Elizabeth I (ed with A G Dickens 1967); *Recreations* music, reading, walking; *Style—* Mrs David Carr; 18 Roundwood View, Banstead, Surrey SM7 1EQ (☎ 0737 355267)

CARR, Dr Eric Francis; s of Edward Francis Carr (d 1963), and Maude Mary Carr (d 1954); *b* 23 Sept 1919; *Educ* Mill Hill Sch, Emmanuel Coll Cambridge (BA), London Hosp (MBBCh, Cantab 1943, MA Cantab 1946, DPM 1952); *m* 23 Jan 1954 (m dis 1980), Janet Gould, da of Rev Trevor Gilfillan; 2 s (Anthony James b 1955, Nicholas Francis b 1956), 1 da (Sara Jane b 1958); *Career* Nat Serv 1944-46, Capt RAMC, Regnl Mo 1 RTR, served India, W Africa; conslt psychiatrist: St Ebba's Hosp 1955-61, KCH 1961-70, Epsom Dist and KCH 1970-76, sr princ MO DHSS 1976-78, Lord Chllrs visitor 1978-, mental health act mmnr 1983-89, memb Mental Health Review Tribunal, Parole Bd memb 1988-; MRCP 1948, FRCP 1971, FRCPsych 1972; *Recreations* music, french language; *Style—* Dr Eric Carr; 116 Holly Lane East, Banstead, Surrey SM7 2BE (☎ 0737 353 675)

CARR, Frank George Griffith; CB (1967), CBE (1954); s of Frank Carr, (d 1957), and Agnes Maud, *née* Todd (d 1956); *b* 23 April 1903; *Educ* Perse Sch, Trinity Hall Cambridge (LLB, MA); *m* 1932, Ruth, da of Harold Hamilton Burkitt, ICS (d 1961), of Ballycastle, Co Antrim; *Career* Acting Lt-Cdr RNVR, WWII RN N Atlantic Convoys and Coastal Forces; Yacht Master's (deep sea) Certificate BOT 1927, mate of Thames sailing barge 1928, asst librarian House of Lords 1929-47, dir Nat Maritime Museum Greenwich 1947-66, chm Cutty Sark Ship Mgmnt Ctee 1953-72, int chm American Ship Tst Ctee 1978-, chm World Ship Tst 1979-89 ; FSA, FRAS, ARINA, FRInstNav; *Recreations* nautical research, historic ship preservation; *Clubs* Athenaeum, Royal Cruising, Cruising Assoc, Cambridge Univ Cruising; *Style—* Frank Carr, Esq, CB, CBE; 10 Park Gate, Blackheath, London SE3 9BX (☎ 01 852 5181)

CARR, Ian Cufaude; DL (Cumbria 1988); s of Laurence Carr (d 1938), and Beryl, *née* Cufaude (d 1979); *b* 12 August 1928; *Educ* Rugby; *m* 1, 24 May 1952 (m dis 1975), Doreen, *née* Hindle; 2 s (Jonathan Michael Ian b 12 April 1954, Dominic David b 11 Oct 1966), 2 da (Melanie Elizabeth b 3 Nov 1956, Stephanie Clare b 31 May 1960); m 2, 1976, Mrs Rilla Cameron Diggle, *née* Carr; 1 step s (Peter), 1 step da (Alison); *Career* chm: Carr's Milling Industries plc 1964-, E Cumbria Health Authy 1986-, Penrith and Border Conservative Assoc 1970-75; *Recreations* shooting, golf; *Clubs* Royal and Ancient GC, Silloth GC, Southerness GC, Border and County (Carlisle); *Style—* Ian Carr Esq; Brown Hill, Walton, Brampton, Cumbria CA8 2JW (☎ 06977 2540); Carr's Milling Industries plc, Stanwix, Carlisle (☎ 0228 28291)

CARR, Ian Henry Randell; s of Thomas Randell Carr (d 1979), of Gosforth, Newcastle-on-Tyne, and Phyllis Harriet Carr (d 1985); *b* 21 April 1933; *Educ* Barnard Castle Sch, Kings Coll Newcastle-on-Tyne (BA, DipEd); *m* 1, 28 June 1963, Margaret Blackburn (d 1967), da of John Lowery Bell (missing presumed dead 1943), of Annefield, Co Durham; 1 da (Selena b 29 July 1967); m 2, 9 Dec 1972 (m dis 1989), Sandra Louise, *née* Major; *Career* Nat Serv 2 Lt Royal Nothumberland Fusiliers 1956-58 served NI and W Germany; performer: Emcee Five Quintet 1960-62, Rendell-Carr Quintet 1963-69, Ian Carr's Nucleus 1969-, The Utd Jazz and Rock Ensemble 1975- (worldwide tours); composed: Solar Plexus 1970, Labyrinth 1973, Will's Birthday Suite (for the Globe theatre Tst) 1974, Out of the Long Dark (1978), Northumbrian Sketches (1988); assoc prof Guildhall Sch of Music and Drama; many presentations BBC Radio 3; memb Gtr London Arts Assoc 1975-80; patron: live Theatre Co Newcastle-upon-Tyne 1985-, Art at the Whittington Hosp Appeal Islington; PRS 1970, Royal Soc of Musicians of GB 1982, Assoc of Professional Composers 1983, Central music Advsy Ctee BBC Radio and TV; Italian Calabria Award 1982; *Books* Music Outside (1973), Miles Davis: A Critical Biography (1982), Jazz: The Essential Companion (jtly 1987); *Recreations* music, the visual arts, world literature, travel; *Style—* Ian Carr, Esq; 34 Brailsford Rd, London SW2 2TE, (☎ 01 671 7195)

CARR, Brig James Gouinlock; CBE (1965); s of George Patton Carr; *b* 1 Sept 1911; *Educ* Upper Canada Coll, RMC Canada, Cambridge Univ; *m* 1941, Joyce Maud, da of late Alfred Ranicar, JP, of Wigan; 3 s; *Career* 2 Lt RE 1931, NWEF and 7 Armd Div 1939-45, Brig 1960, CE Northern Command 1959-62, Cmdt Royal Sch of Mil Engineering 1962-65, ADC to HM the Queen 1963-65; *Style—* Brig James Carr, CBE; Wicks Field, Yateley, Camberley, Surrey

CARR, Rear Adm Lawrence George; CB (1971), DSC (1954); s of late George Henry Carr; *b* 31 Jan 1920; *Educ* Wellington Tech Coll New Zealand; *Career* Cdre Auckland 1966-68, 2 Naval Memb NZ Naval Bd 1968-69, Chief of Naval Staff NZ 1969, ret 1972; *Style—* Rear Adm Lawrence Carr, CB, DSC; 57 Pigeon Mountain Rd, Half Moon Bay, Auckland, New Zealand

CARR, Peter Derek; CBE (1989); s of George William (d 1972), of Mexborough Yorkshire, and Marjorie, *née* Taylby; *b* 12 July 1930; *Educ* Fircroft Coll Birmingham, Ruskin Coll Oxford Univ; *m* 12 April 1958, Geraldine Pamela, da of Alexander Graham Ward, of Babbacombe; 1 s (Steven John b 1959), 1 da (Alyce (Mrs Austin) b 1942); *Career* Nat Serv Mountain Rescue Serv RAF 1951-53; site mangr Construction Indust 1944-60, sr lectr in mgmnt Thurrock Coll Essex 1964-69, dir cmmn on Industl Rels 1969-74, section dir ACAS 1974-78, dip serv cncllr Br Embassy Washington DC 1978-83, presently regnl dir DOE Northern and ldr Govt City Action Team; *Books* Worker Participation and Collective Bargaining in Europe, Industrial Relations in the National Newspaper Industry; *Recreations* cabinet making, walking, cooking; *Style—* Peter Carr, Esq, CBE; Corchester Towers, Corbridge, Northumberland NE45 5NR (☎ 043471 2841); Broadacre House, Market St, Newcastle-upon-Tyne NE1 6HH (☎ 091 232 4181, fax 091 261 7407)

CARR, Sir (Albert) Raymond Maillard; s of Reginald Maillard Carr, of Bath; *b* 11 April 1919; *Educ* Brockenhurst Sch, Christ Church Oxford; *m* 1950, Sara, da of Algernon Strickland, of Apperley, Glos; 3 s, 1 da; *Career* former fell of All Souls' and New Coll Oxford, prof of latin american history Oxford 1967-68; warden of St Antony's Coll Oxford 1968-1987; author; D.Litt, FBA; kt 1987; *Recreations* foxhunting; *Style—* Sir Raymond Carr; Burch, North Molton, South Bolton, Devon EX36 3JU (☎ 07697 267)

CARR, Dr Stephen Paul; s of Denis Carr, and Muriel Betty, *née* Jamieson; *b* 1 May 1955; *Educ* Marple Hall GS, Univ of Warwick (BA), Univ of Oxford (DPhil); *m* 9 Jul 1977, Pamela Susan, da of Prof Harold Leslie Rosenthal; *Career* food mfrg analyst Rowe and Pitman 1979-86; div dir Warburg Securities Ltd 1986-; memb Woolhampton Parish Cncl 1982-83; *Style—* Dr Stephen Carr; 4 Sandford House Cottages, Knowl Hill, Kingsclere, Newbury RG15 (☎ 0635 298 817); Warburg Securities, 1 Finsbury Ave, London EC2 (☎ 01 606 1066)

CARR, Dr Thomas Ernest Ashdown; CB (1977); s of Laurence Hudson Ashdown Carr (d 1959), and Norah E V, *née* Taylor; *b* 21 June 1915; *Educ* Co HS For Boys Altrincham, Victoria Univ Manchester (BSc, MB, ChB); *m* 1940, Mary Sybil, da of Percy Harold Enoch Dunkey (d 1979); 1 s, 2 da; *Career* served WW II Maj RAMC NW Europe; princ medical offr DHSS 1966, sr princ med offr GP and Regnl Med Serv 1967-79, part-time med referee 1979-87; chm: Nat Soc of Non-Smokers 1982-1986 (vice-pres 1986-), Guildford div Br Med Assoc 1988-89; DObstRCOG, FRCGP, FFCM; *Recreations* music, photography, foreign travel, country walks; *Clubs* Civil Service, Royal Soc of Medicine, Yvonne Arnaud Theatre (Guildford).; *Style—* Dr Tommy Carr, CB; Tollgate House, 2 Pilgrims Way, Guildford, Surrey GU4 8AB (☎ 0483 63012)

CARR, Air Cdre William George; CBE (1968, MBE 1948); s of William George Carr (d 1937), and Alice Ellen, *née* Humphries (d 1975); *b* 12 Nov 1916; *Educ* Freemantle and Univ Coll Southampton; *m* 1949, Marion Ethel, da of late Capt Joseph Archibald Martin Hislop; 1 s (Martin b 1952), 1 da (Rosemary b 1955); *Career* entered RAF in 1939, served in Maintenance, Trg, Tport, Air Support, Far East and Middle East Cmds, RAF Coll, Cranwell, and in MOD, ret Dir of Movements (RAF) in 1972; with Br Tport Hotels 1972-81; *Recreations* gardening, bridge, travel; *Clubs* Royal Air Force; *Style—* Air Cdre William Carr, CBE; High Oaks, Wonersh Park, nr Guildford, Surrey GU5 0QS (☎ 0483 892289)

CARR OF HADLEY, Baron (Life Peer UK 1975); (Leonard) Robert Carr; PC (1963); s of late Ralph Edward and Katie Elizabeth Carr, of Totteridge, Herts; *b* 11 Nov 1916; *Educ* Westminster Sch, Gonville and Caius Cambridge; *m* 1943, Joan Kathleen, da of Dr E W Twining, of Cheadle, Cheshire; 1 s (decd), 2 da; *Career* MP (C) Mitcham 1950-74, Sutton (Carshalton) 1974-75; former PPS to Sir Anthony Eden; parly sec to Min of Lab and Nat Service 1955-59, sec for Tech Co-operation 1963-64, sec of state for Employment 1970-72, lord pres of the Cncl and ldr of the House of Commons 1972, sec of state for Home Affairs 1972-74; dir: Prudential Corpn plc (chm 1980-85); former dir: Prudential Assur Co Ltd (chm 1980-85), Securicor Ltd, SGB Gp Ltd, Cadbury Schweppes Gp plc; former govr and dep chm of governing body Imperial Coll of Science and Technol (fellow 1985); chm Business in the Community 1984-87; *Recreations* tennis, music, gardening; *Clubs* Brooks, Surrey County Cricket (pres 1985-86), All England Lawn Tennis and Croquet; *Style—* The Rt Hon the Lord Carr of Hadley, PC; 14 North Court, Great Peter St, London SW1

CARR-ELLISON, Col Sir Ralph Harry; TD (1962), ED (TAVR 1974); s of Maj John Campbell Carr-Ellison (d 1956), of Hedgeley Hall, and his 1 wife, Daphne Hermione

Indica, *née* Cradock (m dis 1946, d 1984); *b* 8 Dec 1925; *Educ* Eton; *m* 1951, Mary Clare McMorrough, da of Maj Arthur Thomas McMorrough Kavanagh, MC (d 1953), of Borris House, Co Carlow; 3 s, 1 da; *Career* served CMF 1945-46, BAOR 1946-49, TA and TAVR 1949-73; Lt-Col cmdg Northumberland Hussars 1966-69, Hon Col Queens Own Yeomanry 1988-; Territorial Col (TAVR) NE Dist 1969-73, Hon Col Northumbrian Univs OTC 1982-86, Northumberland Hussar Sqns 1986-88, ADC (TAVR) to HM The Queen 1970-75; chm: Northumbrian Water Authority 1973-82, North Tyne Area Manpower Bd MSC 1983-84, North of England Territorial Assoc 1976-80, AA 1986- (vice-chm 1985-86), Newcastle Univ Devpt Tst 1979-81; memb court Newcastle Univ 1979-, vice-chm Nat Union of Cons and Unionist Assoc 1969-71; govr Swinton Cons Coll 1967-81, dir: Newcastle and Gateshead Water Co 1964-73, Trident Television 1972-81 (dep chm 1976-81); pres northern area Cons Cncl 1974-78 (tres 1961-66, chm 1966-69); memb cncl The Scout Assoc 1982- (co cmmr Northumberland 1958-68); former JP Northumberland, High Sheriff 1972, DL 1981-85, Vice-Ld Lt 1984 Northumberland, Ld Lt for County of Tyne and Wear 1984-; FRSA 1983; KStJ 1984; kt 1973; *Recreations* jt master West Percy Foxhounds 1950-; *Clubs* Cavalry and Gds, Pratt's, White's, Northern Counties (Newcastle); *Style—* Col Sir Ralph Carr-Ellison, TD, ED; Hedgeley Hall, Powburn, Alnwick, Northumberland (☎ 066 578 273; office: 091 2610181)

CARR-GOMM, Richard Culling; OBE (1985); s of Mark Culling Carr-Gomm (d 1965) and Thea, *née* Heming (d 1961); *b* 2 Jan 1922; *Educ* Stowe; *m* 21 Oct 1957, Susan, da of Ralph Gibbs (d 1957); 2 s (Adam b 1965, David b 1967), 3 da (Anna b 1958, Elizabeth b 1959, Harriet b 1964); *Career* cmmnd Coldstream Gds 1941; served with 6 Gds Tank Bde in NW Europe (twice wounded, despatches), Palestine 1945, Cyprus, Canal Zone and Tripoli, Major resigned cmmn 1955; fndr: Abbeyfield Soc 1956, Carr-Gomm Soc 1965, Morpeth Soc 1972; Croix de Guerre (Silver Star) France 1944, KStJ 1981, Templeton UK Project Award 1984; *Books* Push On the Door (autobiog, 1979), Loneliness - The Wider Scene (1987); *Recreations* golf, drawing; *Style—* Richard Carr-Gomm, Esq, OBE; 9 The Batch, Batheaston, Avon BA1 7DR (☎ 0225 858434); 38 Gomm Road, Bermondsey, London SE16 2TX (☎ 01 231 9284)

CARREL, Philip; CMG (1960), OBE (1954); s of late Louis Raymond Carrel, and Lucy Mabel, *née* Cooper; *b* 23 Sept 1915; *Educ* Blundell's, Balliol Oxford; *m* 1948, Eileen Mary Bullock, da of F V Hainworth; 1 s, 1 da; *Career* entered Colonial Admin Service (Zanzibar) 1938, admin officer Somaliland 1947, chief sec 1959-60, ret; *Style—* Philip Carrel, Esq, CMG, OBE; Lych Gates, Chiltley Lane, Liphook, Hants (☎ 722150)

CARRELL, Prof Robin Wayne; s of Ruane George Carrell, of Christchurch, NZ, and Constance Gwendoline, *née* Rowe; *b* 5 April 1936; *Educ* Christchurch Boys HS NZ, Univ of Otago (MB, ChB), Univ of Canterbury (BSc), Univ of Cambridge (MA, PhD); *m* 27 Jan 1962, Susan Wyatt, da of John Leonard Rogers (d 1975), Christchurch, New Zealand; 2 s (Thomas Wyatt George b 1968, Edward Robin William b 1970), 2 da (Sarah Anne b 1963, Rebecca Susan b 1964); *Career* MRC Abnormal Haemoglobin Unit Cambridge 1965-68, dir clinical biochemistry Christchurch NZ 1968-75, lectr and conslt Addenbrookes Hosp and Univ of Cambridge 1976-78, prof of pathology Christchurch Clinical Sch Univ of Otago 1978-86, prof of Haematology Cambridge Univ 1986-; cwlth fell St John's Coll Cambridge 1985-86, fell Trinity Coll Cambridge 1987-; memb gen bd Cambridge Univ 1989; FRACP 1973, FRCPath 1976, MRCP 1985, FRSNZ 1980; *Recreations* gardening, walking; *Style—* Prof Robin Carrell; 19 Madingley Rd, Cambridge CB3 0EG (☎ 0223 312 970); Haematology Dept, Univ of Cambridge, MRC Centre, Hills Rd, Cambridge CB2 2QL (☎ 0223 336 788, fax 0223 336 709, telex 81240 CAMSPL G)

CARRERAS, Sir James; KCVO (1979), MBE (1944); s of Henry and Dolores Carreras; *b* 30 Jan 1909; *m* 1927, Vera St John, *née* Smart (d 30 Oct 1986); 1 s (Michael b 1928, film producer and director with Hammer Films); *Career* served Army 1938-46, Lt-Col RA; former chm and chief exec Hammer Film Productions Ltd; kt 1969; *Style—* Sir James Carreras, KCVO, MBE; Queen Anne Cottage, Friday Street, Henley-on-Thames, Oxon (☎ (049 57) 2170)

CARRICK, 9 Earl of (I 1748); Brian Stuart Theobald Somerset Caher Butler; also Viscount Ikerrin (I 1629) and (sits as) Baron Butler of Mount Juliet (UK 1912); s of 8 Earl (d 1957), by his 1 w Marion; *b* 17 August 1931; *Educ* Downside; *m* 1, 1951 (m dis 1976), (Mary) Belinda, da of Maj David Constable-Maxwell, TD; 1 s, 1 da; m 2, 4 June 1986, Gillian, da of Leonard Grimes; *Heir* s, Viscount Ikerrin; *Career* dir: Cargill UK Ltd, Ralli Bros and Coney Ltd, Bowater Indust plc, Bowater Incorporated; *Recreations* horse racing; *Clubs* Brooks's, Pratt's, White's; *Style—* The Rt Hon the Earl of Carrick; 10 Netherton Grove, London SW10 (☎ 01 352 6328)

CARRICK, Hon Sir John Leslie; KCMG (1982); s of Arthur James Carrick (d 1940) and Emily Ellen, *née* Terry (d 1970); *b* 4 Sept 1918; *Educ* Sydney Tech HS, Sydney Univ (BEc); *m* 1951, Diana Margaret, da of Alexander Hunter (d 1939); 3 da; *Career* senator Cwlth Parliament of Australia 1971-87 (ldr of the Govt in the Senate 1978-83); chm NSW State Govt Ctee of Review of Schools; Hon DLitt Sydney; *see Debrett's Handbook of Australia and New Zealand for further details*; *Style—* The Hon Sir John Carrick, KCMG; 8 Montah Ave, Killara, NSW 2071, Australia (☎ 498 6326)

CARRICK, Roger John; CMG (1983), LVO (1972); s of John Horwood Carrick, of Whitchurch Hants, and Florence May, *née* Pudner; *b* 13 Oct 1937; *Educ* Isleworth GS, London Univ Sch of Slavonic and Euro Studies; *m* 1962, Hilary Elizabeth, da of Terence Verdun Blinman; 2 s (John, Charles); *Career* RN 1956-58; HM Diplomatic Serv FO 1958-61, Br Legation Sofia 1962-65, FO 1965-67, Br Embassy Paris 1967-71, Head of Chancery Br High Cmmn Singapore 1971-73, FCO 1973, cnsllr and dep head Personnel Ops Dept 1976, visiting fell Inst of Int Studies Univ of California Berkeley 1977-78, cnsllr Br Embassy Washington 1978-82, head Overseas Estate Dept, FCO 1982-85, HM consul-gen Chicago 1985-; *Books* East-West Technology Transfer in Perspective (1978); *Recreations* sailing, some racquet games, music, reading, avoiding gardening, collecting walking sticks; *Clubs* Royal Cwlth Soc, Univ (Chicago), Tavern, Cliff Dwellers' (Chicago); *Style—* Roger Carrick, Esq, CMG, LVO; 1260 N Astor St, Chicago, Illinois 60610; c/o FCO (Chicago), King Charles St, London SW1A 2AH; Br Consulate-Gen, 33 N Dearborn St, Chicago, Illinois 60602, USA (☎ 312 346 1810, telex 254432 a/b Britain GGO

CARRICK, Ruth, Countess of; Ruth; *née* McEnery; da of Francis T M McEnery, of Chicago, Ill, USA; *b* 1918; *m* 1954, as his 3 w, 8 Earl of Carrick (d 1957); *Style—* The Rt Hon Ruth, Countess of Carrick; PO Box 1190, Pinehurst, N Carolina 28374, USA (☎ 919 295 6337)

CARRICK, Maj-Gen Thomas Welsh; OBE (1959); s of late George Carrick, and late Mary, *née* Welsh; *b* 19 Dec 1914; *Educ* Glasgow Acad, Glasgow Univ (MB, CHB), London Sch of Hygiene and Tropical Medicine (DPH, DIH); *m* 1948, Nan Middleton Allison; 1 s; *Career* prof Army Health RAMC 1970-71, dir Army Health and Res MOD 1971-73, Cmdt Post-Graduate Dean RAMC 1973-75, ret; specialist in community medicine (medical staffing) Camden and Islington Area Health Authy 1975-78; pres Blackmore Vale and Yeovil Centre the National Trust 1978-85; FFCM QHS (1973), OStJ (1947); *Style—* Maj-Gen Thomas Carrick, OBE; Little Chantry, Gillingham, Dorset SP8 4NA

CARRICK-BUCHANAN, Lt-Col David Richard; JP (1952), DL (Wigtownshire 1949); s of Lt-Col Arthur Louis Hamilton Buchanan, MP (d 1925), of Drumpellier, Lanarkshire, and Adeline Musgrave, *née* Harvey; *b* 1906; *Educ* Eton, Trinity Coll Cambridge; *m* 1937, Cinderella Beatrix, da of Lt-Col Charles Staveley, of Roadend, Newton Ferrers, S Devon; 1 s, 1 da; *Career* Lt 2 Bn Gordon Highlanders 1929, Capt 1938, Lt-Col 1945; *Style—* Lt-Col David Carrick-Buchanan JP DL; Corsewall, Stranraer, Wigtownshire (☎ Kircolm 209)

CARRINGTON, Charles Edmund; MC; s of Very Rev Charles Walter Carrington (d 1941), and Margaret Constance, *née* Pughe (d 1930); *b* 21 April 1897; *Educ* Christ's Coll NZ, Christ Church Oxford (BA, MA); *m* 1, 1932 (m dis 1954), Cecil Grace MacGregor; 1 da (decd); m 2, 1955, Maysie Cuthbert Robertson (d 1983); *Career* served in WWI and WWII; first cmmn 1915, Capt 5 Royal Warwicks Regt 1917, served France and Italy, Maj TA 1927, Lt-Col Gen Staff 1941-45; educnl sec CUP 1929-54, prof Chatham Ho 1954-62, organized unofficial Cwlth confs NZ 1959, and Nigeria 1962, visiting prof USA 1964-65, memb: LCC Educn Ctee, Classical Assoc Cncl, Publishers Assoc Educnl Gp, Royal Cwlth Soc Cncl, Inter-Univ Cncl, Overseas Migration Bd, Islington Soc; chm Shoreditch Housing Assoc 1961-67; *Books* The 1/5 Royal Warwickshire Regt (1922), A Subaltern's War (1929), A History of England (with J Hampden Jackson, 1932), T E Lawrence (1935), An Exposition of Empire (1947), The British Overseas (1950), J R Godley of Canterbury (1951), The Liquidation of the Br Empire (1961), Soldier from the Wars Returning (1965), The Complete Barrack Room Ballads of Rudyard Kipling (1973), Kiplings Horace (1978), contrib: Cambridge History of the Br Empire (1959), An African Survey (1957), surveys of Int Affairs (1957-58 and 1959-60), Soldier Bomber Command (1987);; *Recreations* historical studies, travel; *Clubs* Travellers'; *Style—* Charles Carrington Esq, MC; 31 Grange Rd, London N1 2NP (☎ 354 2832)

CARRINGTON, Hon Mrs; Jennifer Michelle; *née* Souter; da and co-hp of 25 Baron Audley; *b* 23 May 1948; *m* Michael Carrington; 2 s (Jesse Michael b 1978, Jonah David b 1980), 1 da (Holly b 1975); *Style—* The Hon Mrs Carrington; 2050 North Rodeo Gulch Drive, Soquel, California 95067, USA

CARRINGTON, Matthew Hadrian Marshall; MP (C) Fulham 1987-; s of Walter Hadrian Marshall Carrington, of 18 Lansdowne Rd, London W11, and Dilys Mary Gwyneth Carrington; *b* 19 Oct 1947; *Educ* French Lycee London, Imperial Coll, London Univ (BSc), London Business Sch (MSc); *m* 29 March 1975, Mary Lou, da of Robert Darrow, of Columbus, Ohio, USA; 1 da (Victoria b 11 June 1981); *Career* production foreman GKN Sankey 1969-72; banker: The First National Bank of Chicago 1974-78, Saudi Int Bank 1978-87; *Recreations* cooking, political history; *Style—* Matthew H M Carrington, Esq, MP; 34 Ladbroke Square, London W11 3NB (☎ 01 221 4243); House of Commons London SW1A 0AA (☎ 01 219 6855)

CARRINGTON, 6 Baron (I 1796, GB 1797); Peter Alexander Rupert Carrington; KG (1985), CH (1983), KCMG (1958), MC (1945), PC (1959), JP (Bucks 1948), DL (1951); s of 5 Baron Carrington, JP, DL (d 1938, n of 3 Baron, KG, GCMG, PC, JP, DL, sometime MP High Wycombe, and also 1 and last Marquess of Lincolnshire, Govr of New South Wales, Lord Great Chamberlain of England and Lord Privy Seal) by his w, Hon Sybil, da of 2 Viscount Colville of Culross.; *b* 6 June 1919; *Educ* Eton, RMC Sandhurst; *m* 1942, Iona, yr da of Sir Francis Kennedy McClean, AFC (d 1955); 1 s, 2 da (Hon Mrs de Bunsen, Virginia Lady Ashcombe); *Heir* s, Hon Rupert Carrington; *Career* served as Maj Gren Gds NW Europe; parly sec Miny of Agric and Fisheries 1951-54, MOD 1954-56; high cmmr Australia 1956-59; first lord of Admiralty 1959-63; min without portfolio and ldr of House of Lords 1963-64, ldr of oppn House of Lords 1964-70 and 1974-79, sec of state for Defence 1970-74, sec of state Dept of Energy 1974, Miny of Aviation Supply 1971-74, chm Cons Party 1972-74, sec of state for Foreign and Cwlth Affrs and min of Overseas Devpt 1979-82; sec-gen NATO 1984-; chm GEC 1983-84 (dir 1982-84); fellow Eton 1966-81; hon fellow St Antony's Coll Oxford 1982-; memb int bd United World Colls 1982-84; chm of tstees V and A Museum 1983-; Chancellor of the Order of St. Michael and St. John (1984); Hon Bencher of Middle Temple 1983; Hon Elder Brother Trinity House 1984; Hon LLD: Leeds, Cantab, Philippines, S Carolina, Cambridge 1981, Hon LLD Univ. Aberdeen 1985, Hon DUniv Essex; *Clubs* Pratt's, White's, Melbourne; *Style—* The Rt Hon the Lord Carrington, KGCH, KCMG, MC, PC, JP, DL; 32A Ovington Sq, London SW3 1LR (☎ 01 584 1476); The Manor House, Bledlow, nr Aylesbury, Bucks (☎ (084 44) 3499)

CARRINGTON, Simon Robert; s of Robert Carrington, of Suffolk, and Jean, *née* Hill, of Wiltshire; *b* 23 Oct 1942; *Educ* Ch Ch Cathedral Choir Sch Oxford, The King's Sch Canterbury, King's Coll Cambridge, New Coll Oxford; *m* 2 Sept 1969, Hilary Elizabeth Stott, da of Leslie Stott (d 1962); 1 s (Jamie b 1973), 1 da (Rebecca b 1971); *Career* dir The King's Singers 1968-; teacher and adjudicator Double Bass, dir Choral Summer Sch, Marlborough Coll Wilts and Berwang, Austria; with The King's Singers: 40 LP's for EMI, Tours Worldwide, regular TV Appearances Worldwide, inc Live at the Boston Pops 1983, BC TV Series The King's Singers Madrigal History Tour 1984, ABC TV (USA) The Sound of Christman from Salzburgh 1987; festival dir Barbican Summer in the City Festivals 1988-89, 20 Anniversary Concerts Worldwide 1988, Grammy nomination USA 1986; *Books* The King's Singers - a Self Portrait (1981); *Recreations* vintage cars, inland waterways, gardens, trees, walking, jogging; *Clubs* Royal Soc of Musicians, Inc Soc of Musicians; *Style—* Simon R Carrington, Esq; The Old House, Rushall, Pewsey, Wiltshire SN9 6EN (☎ 0980 630 477); The King's Singers Mgmnt, Gillian Newson Associates, 13 Norfolk Mansions, Prince of Wales Drive, London SW11 4HL (☎ 01 720 7678)

CARRITT, Rodney Lorraine Blasson; s of Hugh Blasson Carritt (d 1928), of 18 Sloane Gdns, London, and Audrey Browning (d 1970); *b* 26 Mar 1927; *Educ* Rugby; *m* Nov 1957 (m dis 1973), Madeleine Frances, da of Harold Dabell (d 1941), of Egypt; 1 s (Tony b 1958); *Career* RN 1945-48; dir: Alexander Howden & Swann Ltd 1968-70, Thos Nelson (Insur) Ltd 1970-76; chm: Kingsley Carritt & Co Ltd 1976-86, London &

Solent Ltd 1986-, Carritt & Ptnrs 1986-; Freeman City of London 1948, Liveryman Worshipful Co of Grocers 1958; memb Lloyd's; *Recreations* yacht racing, sailing, hunting; *Clubs* Royal Yacht Squadron, Sea View YC, City of London; *Style—* Rodney Carritt, Esq; 40 Lamond Rd, London SW10 0JA; 14 Fenchurch Ave, London EC3M 5BS (☎ 01 626 2641, fax 01 283 5063, telex 8813423)

CARROL, Charles Gordon; s of Charles Muir Carrol (d 1974), of Edinburgh, and Catherine Gray *née* Napier; *b* 21 Mar 1935; *Educ* Melville Coll Edinburgh, Edinburgh Univ (MA, DipEd); *m* 1970, Frances Anne, da of John A Sinclair, of Edinburgh; 3 s (Simon b 1971, Christopher b 1974, David b 1979); *Career* educn offr: Govt Northern Nigeria 1959-65, Cwlth Inst Scotland 1965-71; dir Cwlth Inst Scotland 1971-; lay memb Press Cncl 1978-83; *Recreations* hill walking, angling; *Clubs* Rotary (Edinburgh); *Style—* Charles Carrol Esq; 11 Dukehaugh, Peebles, EH45 9DN (☎ 0721 21296); Commonwealth Institute Scotland, 8 Rutland Square, Edinburgh EH1 2AS (☎ 031 229 6668)

CARROLL, Gerald John Howard; s of John Robert Carroll, of London and Frinton-on-Sea, Essex, and Catherine Florence Howard; lineal descendant of ancient Sept O'Carroll Princes of Ely, Barons of Ely O'Carroll, co Offaly, Eire; *b* 9 Oct 1951; *Educ* Herrington House, Ipswich Sch; *Career* tstee Carroll Fndn 1972-; chm The Carroll Gp and Associated cos 1972-, chief exec Farnborough Aerospace Devpt Corpn Ltd 1985-; dir: Strategic R & D Corpn Ltd 1985-, The Manchester Canal and Business Park Devpt Corpn Ltd 1985-, Carroll Aircraft Corpn Ltd 1985-, Solid State Securities Ltd 1973-, Dukes Park Industl Estates Ltd 1974-78, Culver Devpts Ltd 1980-, Longfeld Investment Co Ltd 1972-, Westbury Investmt Co Ltd 1972-, Galleria Devpt Corpn Ltd 1986-, London and Central Properties Ltd 1980-, Automated Machine Industs Ltd 1980-, Anglia Fine Arts Ltd 1980-; memb Br Helicopter Advsy Bd 1984-; *Recreations* racing, sailing, shooting; *Clubs* Royal Thames YC, Guards, Cirencester Park Polo, Race Horse Owners Assoc, Old Ipswichian; *Style—* Gerald Carroll, Esq; 29 Eaton Sq, Belgravia, London SW1W 9DF; Villa Borghese, 06230 Cap Ferrat, France; Carroll House, 2-6 Catherine Place, Westminster, London SW1E 6HF (☎ 01 828 6842)

CARROLL, Robin David; s of William George Carroll, of Putney and Mary Jenny *née* Crane; *b* 29 Feb 1948; *Educ* Elliot Sch, Kingston Coll of Art (BA); *Career* sr art dir: Ogilvey and Mather 1972-79, Mathers Allders and Marchant 1979-84; creative dir Bastabl Dailey 1984-; RSA 1970-72; *Recreations* antique collecting, writing; *Style—* Robin Carroll, Esq; Bastable Dailey, 18 Dering Street, London, W1, (☎ 01 408 1818 fax 629 5501)

CARROLL, Terence Patrick (Terry); s of George Daniel Carroll, of Upchurch, Kent, and Betty Doreen, *née* Holmes; *b* 24 Nov 1948; *Educ* Gillingham GS, Bradford Univ Mgmnt Centre (BSc); *m* 1, 4 April 1971 (m dis 1984), Louise Mary, da of Leslie Charles Smith; 1 s (Mark George b 1979); m 2, 12 Oct 1984, Penelope Julia (Penny), da of Walter John Berry; *Career* auditor and computer auditor Armitage & Norton 1970-76, mgmnt accountant Bradford & Bingley Bldg Soc 1976-80, exec and memb of stock exchange Sheppards & Chase 1980-82, tres Halifax Bldg Soc 1982-85, fin dir Nat & Provincial Bldg Soc 1985-89; FCA 1980, MBIM 1979, MCT 1985, FCBSI 1986; *Recreations* golf, hockey, bridge; *Clubs* Bradford, Ilkley GC; *Style—* Terry Carroll, Esq; National & Provincial BS, Provincial Hse, Bradford, W Yorks BD1 1NL (☎ 0274 733 444, fax 0274 733 858, car tel 0836 620 716)

CARRON, Byron Richard; s of Arthur Carron (d 1966), and Gladys Irene, *née* Richards; *b* 18 Mar 1942; *Educ* Swindon HS; *m* 1965, Joan Olive, da of Archibald John Scott (d 1973); 1 s (Richard b 1967), 4 da (Louise b 1968, Annette b 1970, Rebecca b 1971, Sarah b 1971 twin); *Career* slr; ptnr Messrs Townsends Swindon; former memb Nat Young Slrs Gp; former chm Glos and Wiltshire Young slrs; former chm Devizes Constituency Liberal Assoc, Wilts CC 1981-, vice chm and chm of Finance (Wilts CC) 1985-; *Recreations* gardening, walking, music; *Clubs* Swindon Rotary; *Style—* Byron R Carron, Esq; The Gables, Lower Wanborough, Swindon, Wilts (☎ (0793) 790294); Townsends, 42 Cricklade Street, Swindon, Wilts (☎ (0793) 354231)

CARRUTHERS, James Edwin; s of James Carruthers (d 1964), and Dollie Carruthers (d 1968); *b* 19 Mar 1928; *Educ* George Heriot's Sch, Edinburgh Univ (MA); *m* 5 March 1955, Phyllis May, *née* Williams; 1 s (James Alexander b 1964); *Career* Queen's Own Cameron Highlanders 1949-57; with: Air Miny 1951-60, Miny of Aviation 1960-62, MOD 1962-68, chief offr Sovereign Base Areas Admin Cyprus 1968-71, MOD 1971-73, Cabinet Office 1973-74, Br Aerospace 1975-79, Royal Ordnance Factories 1980-83, chm Civil Serv Selection Bd 1983-84, asst under sec of state MOD 1984-88, asst sec Royal Hosp Chelsea; *Style—* James Carruthers, Esq

CARRUTHERS, Philip Anthony (Tony); s of Donald Carruthers (d 1983), of Torquay, Devon, and Beatrice Ada, *née* Tremain (d 1987); *b* 29 Nov 1934; *Educ* Homelands Tech HS Torquay. S Devon Tech Coll Torquay; *m* 4 April 1964, Sheila Mary, da of Rowdon Atkins (d 1956), of St Marychurch, Torquay, Devon; 1 da (Anne-Marie Carole b 1966); *Career* RN 1951-54, RNR 1954-59; dir: Charles Moxham & Co Ltd 1960 (joined 1954), Moxhams of Torquay Ltd (Barlow Gp) 1968, Thos Barlow Motors Ltd 1970, Barlow Handling Ltd 1972 (co sec 1975), Thos Barlow Hldgs Ltd (Material Handling Div of J Bibby & Sons plc) 1985; supporter: Henley Royal Regatta, Henley Festival of Music and Art; FID 1968; *Clubs* Leander (Henley), Phyliss Court (Henley); *Style—* Tony Carruthers, Esq; St Marymead, Wargrave on Thames, Berks (☎ 073 522 2693); Moongates, Torquay, Devon; Thos Barlow Holdings Ltd, Airfield Estate, Maidenhead, Berks SL6 3QN (☎ 062 882 6401, fax 062 882 5745, telex 848191)

CARRUTHERS, Robert; s of John Robert Carruthers (d 1987), of Middx, and Mabel, *née* Walshaw (d 1974); *b* 29 Jan 1921; *Educ* Harrow Co Sch, Univ of London, City and Guilds Coll (BSc); *m* 7 Sept 1945, Phyllis Kathleen, da of William John Deal (d 1958), of Cardiff; 2 da (Jane b 1946, Frances b 1952); *Career* worked on devpt of radar RRE Malvern 1941-46, subsequently with UKAEA (Harwell and Culham laboratories), sr princ scientist and head of applied physics and technol div Culham (working on nuclear fusion) 1961-79; MIEE 1939, FIEE 1961 (former cncl memb and chm Oxford Area 1985-87), ACGI, fell Royal Soc for the Encouragement of Arts Manufacture and Commerce 1972; *Style—* Robert Carruthers, Esq; 11 Badgers Copse, Radley, Abingdon, Oxon OX14 3BQ (☎ 0235 20386)

CARRUTHERS, Valerie Marie; *née* Bürli; da of Ernst Bürli (d 1984), and Constance May, *née* Cartwright; *b* 15 May 1943; *Educ* Notre Dame Convent, Oxford Poly; *m* 18 July 1965, John Carruthers; 1 s (Bruce b 1964), 1 da (Lydia b 1962); *Career* property mgmnt exec; *Recreations* painting, music; *Clubs* Conservative Party; *Style—* Mrs Valerie M Carruthers; Kirtlington House, Crowcastle Lane, Kirtlington, Oxford (☎ 0869 50222)

CARSBERG, Prof Sir Bryan Victor; s of Alfred Victor Carsberg, of Chesham Bois Bucks, and Maryllia Cicelyn *née* Collins; *b* 3 Jan 1939; *Educ* Berkhamsted, LSE (MSc), Univ of Manchester (MA); *m* 1960, Margaret Linda, da of Capt Neil McKenzie Graham (d 1966); 2 da (Debbie, Sarah); *Career* CA, sole practice 1962-64, lectr in accounting LSE 1964-68, visiting lectr Graduate Sch of Business Univ of Chicago 1968-69, prof of accounting Univ of Manchester 1969-81 (dean faculty of econ and social studies 1977-78), visiting prof of business admin Univ of Calif Berkeley 1974; asst dir of res and technical activities Financial Accounting Standards Bd USA 1978-81, memb cncl ICA 1975-79; dir: Economists Advsy Gp 1976-84, Economist Bookshop 1981-, Philip Allan Publishers 1981-; Arthur Anderson prof of Accounting LSE 1981-87, dir of research (pt/t) ICA 1981-87, visiting prof of accounting LSE 1987-; dir gen of telecommunication OFTEL 1984-; CAs Founding Socs' Centenary Award 1988; kt 1989; *Books* An Introduction to Mathematical Programming for Accountants (1969), Modern Financial Management (with H C Edey, 1969), Analysis for Investment Decisions (1974), Indexation and Inflation (with E V Morgan and M Parkin, 1975), Economics of Business Decisions (1975), Investment Decisions under Inflation (with A Hope, 1976), Current Issues in Accountancy (with A Hope, 1977), Topics in Management Accounting (with J Arnold and R Scapens, 1980), Current Cost Acccounting (with M Page 1983) Small Company Financial Reporting (with M Page and others, 1985); *Recreations* road running, theatre, opera, music; *Style—* Prof Sir Bryan Carsberg; Office of Telecommunications, Atlantic Ho, Holborn Viaduct, London EC1N 2HQ (☎ 01 822 1601)

CARSLAW, Major (Francis) William Lochhead; s of Frank Henderson Carslaw, VD (d 1956), of Abingdon, Berks, and Evelyn Victoria, *née* Powell (d 1962); *b* 20 August 1912; *Educ* Sutton Valence Sch, RMA Woolwich; *m* 1 May 1939, (Louise) Dora (d 1978), da of the late Joseph Mathison, of Thornhill and Wearne, Somerset; 1 s (James Alan Mathison b 1941, d 1955), 1 da (Joanna Frances (Mrs Hadfield) b 25 Oct 1947); *Career* RMA Woolwich 1930-31, RA 1931-58; served Malaya (POW 1942-45), Suez Canal Zone; instr in Gunnery 1949; schoolmaster (Dip Ed 1958): Millfield 1958-66, Ansford 1967, All Hallows PS 1968072, Wells Cathedral Jr Sch 1973-76; Red Cross Centre organiser Glastonbury & Street 1977-82; churchwarden; rugby football: sch capt, RMA blue, rep Army Malaya; *Recreations* field sports; *Style—* Major William Carslaw; Yew Cottage, West Pennard, Somerset BA6 (☎ 0458 328 06)

CARSON, Air Cdre Robert John; CBE (1974), AFC (1964, QC 1962); er s of Robert George, and Margaret Etta Carson; *b* 3 August 1924; *Educ* Regent House Sch Newtownards, RAF; *m* 1945, Jane, *née* Bailie; 3 da; *Career* Air Cdre; served in Far East, M East, Europe, NATO, Rhodesia, Africa, Canada, USA; air advsr Br High Cmmn Ottawa 1974-75, def advsr to Br High Cmmr in Canada 1975-78; mangr (Panavia Office) Grumman Aerospace Corpn Bethpage 1978-80; dir Leics Medical Res Fndn Leicester Univ 1980-; MRAeS, MBIM, memb Inst of Admin mgmnt; *Recreations* golf, tennis, rugby, gardening; *Clubs* RAF, Royal Ottawa, Leicestershire Golf Club; *Style—* Air Cdre Robert J Carson, CBE, AFC, QC; 20 Meadow Drive, Scruton, Nr Northallerton, N Yorks DL7 0QW (☎ 0609 748656); Leicestershire Medical Research Foundation, Leicester University, Leicester LE1 7RH (☎ 0533 556662 or 556665)

CARSON, (Edward) Rory; s of The Hon Edward Carson, MP (d 1987), of Hastings, Sussex, and Hon Mrs Heather Carson, *née* Slater; *b* 25 May 1949; *Educ* Ludgrove Prep, Radley Coll Berks; *m* 19 April 1975, Araminta, da of Sir John Horlick, Bt, of Scotland; 3 s (Toby b 1977, Jonathen b 1979, Oliver b 1982); *Career* dir Seift 103 Ltd 1984-; *Recreations* tennis, walking, exotic pets; *Clubs* Raffles; *Style—* Rory Carson, Esq; Perseverance Cottage, Harpsden, Henley-on-Thames, Oxon R59 4AS; BAnk Messrs Coutts and Co, 15 Lombard Street, London EL3; 1 Shortlands, Hammersmith, London W6 (☎ 01 370 1595)

CARSS, Gordon; s of Herbert Jackson Carss, Seaham, Co Durham, and Florence May Carss; *b* 12 Mar 1931; *Educ* Argyle House Sch, Sunderland; *m* 31 March 1954, Doreen; 1 da (Amanda Jayne b 1966); *Career* gen mangr and md sec Mid Sussex Bldg Soc (sec 1972); asst sec: Harrow Bldg Soc 1970-, Chesham Bldg Soc 1971; chm Brighton and Dist CBSI 1983-84; FCIS, FCBSI, MBIM; *Clubs* Rotary, Burgess Hill and District; *Style—* Gordon Carss, Esq; 'Hurzanmyne, 70C Ferndale Road, Burgess Hill, West Sussex RH15 0HD (☎ (04446) 42330); 66 Church Road, Burgess Hill, West Sussex RH15 9AU

CARSTAIRS, Charles Young; CB (1968), CMG (1950); eldest s of Rev Dr George Carstairs, DD (d 1948), of Edinburgh; *b* 30 Oct 1910; *Educ* Glasgow Acad, George Watson's Boys' Coll Edinburgh, Edinburgh Univ (MA); *m* 1939, Frances Mary (d 1981), da of Dr CLaude Lionel Coode, of Stroud, Glos; 1 s, 1 da; *Career* Home Gd; entered Civil Serv 1934: admin sec Off of Comptroller for Devpt and Welfare West Indies 1947-50, dir Infor Servs Colonial Off 1950-53, asst under-sec of State 1953, dep sec MRC 1962, under-sec Miny of Public Bldgs and Works 1965, special advsr Expenditure Ctee House of Commons 1971, clerk to Select Ctee on Commodity Prices House of Lords 1976-77; *Recreations* water colours, reading, idling; *Clubs* Athenaeum; *Style—* C Y Carstairs, Esq, CB, CMG; 4 Church Ct, 31 Monks Well, Surrey RH2 (☎ 0737 224 896)

CARSTAIRS, Ian Andrew; s of Alexander Gordon Carstairs, of Leics, and Dorothy Mary, *née* Carr; *b* 13 Feb 1951; *Educ* Hinckley GS (now John Cleveland Coll), St Johns Coll Cambridge (MA); *m* 1973, Kay, da of Keith Reginald Muggleton, of Leics; 3 s (Thomas Andrew b 1979, Benjamin James b 1980, Joseph William b 1983); *Career* investmt fund mangr; dir: Target Investmt Mgmnt Ltd 1985-, Target Residential Property Fund SA 1986-; *Recreations* tennis, squash, swimming, fine food and wine, crosswords; *Style—* Ian Carstairs, Esq; Target Group plc, Alton House, 174/177 High Holborn, London WC1 (☎ 01 836 8040, telex 269879, fax 01 836 4012)

CARSWELL, John Patrick; CB (1977); s of Donald Carswell (d 1940), and Catherine Roxburgh Macfarlane (d 1946); *b* 30 May 1918; *Educ* Merchant Taylors' Sch, St John's Coll Oxford (MA); *m* 1945, Ianthe, da of Capt Eric Bramley Elstob, RN (d 1946); 2 da; *Career* served WW II Maj India and E Bengal; Civil Service 1946-77, Miny of Pensions National Insurance 1946-60, HM Treasury 1960-64, under-sec DES 1964-74, sec Univ Grants Ctee 1974-77; sec Br Academy 1978-83; author; FRSL; *Recreations* writing, war on a small scale; *Clubs* Garrick; *Style—* John Carswell, Esq, CB; 5 Prince Arthur Rd, London NW3 (☎ 01 794 6527); Berins Hill, Ipsden, Oxfordshire

CARSWELL, Hon Mr Justice; Sir Robert Douglas; QC (1971); s of Alan Edward Carswell (d 1972), of Belfast, and Nance Eileen, *née* Corlett; *b* 28 June 1934; *Educ* Royal Belfast Acad Inst, Pembroke Coll Oxford (MA), Univ of Chicago Law Sch; *m*

1961, Romayne Winifred, da of James Ferris, JP, of Co Down; 2 da (Catherine, Patricia); *Career* NI 1957, barr Gray's Inn 1972, counsel to Attorney-Gen for NI 1970-71, sr Crown counsel in NI 1979-84, bencher Inn of Ct of NI 1979, pro-chllr and chm Cncl Univ of Ulster 1984, judge of High Court of NI 1984; kt 1988; *Recreations* golf; *Clubs* Ulster Reform (Belfast); *Style*— The Hon Mr Justice Carswell, QC; c/o Royal Cts of Justice, Belfast BT1 3JF (☎ Belfast 235111)

CARTE, Brian Addison; TD (1976); s of late James Carte; *b* 7 August 1943; *Educ* St Lawrence Coll Ramsgate; *m* 1969, Shirley Anne, da of Lt-Col W H Brinkley; 2 da; *Career* Co Cdr Queen's Regt TA, Maj GSO II HQ London Dist; asst project offr DTA and C; RARO (1987); md Nat Westminster Insur Servs Ltd; pres Assoc of Corporate Treasurers; *Recreations* Golf, opera; *Clubs* New Zealand Golf; *Style*— Brian Carte, Esq, TD; Mariners, Mariners Drive, Stoke Bishop, Bristol BS9 1QQ (☎ 0272 687352)

CARTER; *see*: Bonham-Carter

CARTER, Alan Barham; s of Edwin Carter (d 1953), of Belvedere, Kent, and Laura Emily Edith, *née* Mead (d 1960); *b* 5 Feb 1907; *Educ* Tonbridge Sch, St Olave's GS London, Gonville and Caius Coll Cambridge (MA, MD, BCH); *m* 10 June 1937, Mollie Christina, da of Alderman Sidney Sanders (d 1944), of Streatham, London; 2 s (Clive b 1942, Stephen b 1953), 2 da (Clare b 1946, Jane b 1949); *Career* RAMC, Maj 1947, Lt-Col, 1949, conslt neurologist mil hosps and advisor neurology WO 1950, Hon Col, civilian conslt neurologist Cambridge mil hosp 1960; conslt physician: Middx Hosp 1938-43, Ashford Hosp 1943-74; hon conslt: Atkinson Morleys Hosp 1960-76, St Georges Hosp 1976-80; Freeman City of London 1965, Liveryman Worshipful Co of Clockmakers 1965; Coronation Medal 1936; FRCP 1961, FRSM (cllr 1950-60); *Books* Cerebral Infarction (1964), All About Strokes (1968), The Art of Ageing (1983); *Recreations* cricket, golf; *Clubs* Royal Soc Medicine; *Style*— Dr Barham Carter; The Bracken, St Georges Hill, Weybridge, Surrey KT13 0NU (☎ 0932 64422); Nuffield Hosp, Woking, Surrey (☎ 048 62 63511)

CARTER, Alan Ponsford; s of William Howard Carter (d 1971), of Bishop's Cannings, Devizes, Wilts, and Brenda, *née* Ponsford; *b* 10 Dec 1941; *Educ* Devizes GS, RVC London; *m* 28 Dec 1968, Margaret Lyon, da of Col Thomas Henry Band, of Stratford Upon Avon; 1 s (Benjamin b 1978), 2 da (Clare b 1972, Lucy b 1974); *Career* vet surgn gen practice 1967-70, dep regnl offr Milk Mktg Bd 1979-81 (vet offr 1970-81), ptnr in gen practice Longmead 1981-; memb: local PCC, BVA, ctee SCVS; *Style*— Alan Carter, Esq; Castleton House, Breach Lane, Shaftesbury, Dorset (☎ 0747 52820); Longmead Vet Practice, Shaftesbury, Dorset (☎ 0747 52064)

CARTER, Bernard Thomas; s of Cecil Carter (d 1962), and Ethel, *née* Darby (d 1961); *b* 6 April 1920; *Educ* Haberdashers' Aske's, Goldsmiths Coll of Art London Univ (NDD, ATD); *m* 1952, Eugenie Mary, da of Capt David William Alexander, RNR (d 1952); 1 s (John); *Career* RAF 1939-46; art lectr 1952-68; Nat Maritime Museum: asst keeper (prints and drawings) 1968, dep keeper (head of picture dept) 1970, keeper (head of picture dept) 1970, keeper head of dept of pictures and conservation 1972-77); full-time artist 1977-; one-man exhibitions: Arthur Jeffress Gallery 1955, eleven one-man exhibitions Portal Gallery Grafton St W1; pictures in many pub collections in UK and abroad; Hon RE; *Recreations* music, theatre, restaurants, gardening, travel, reading, tv; *Style*— Bernard Carter, Esq; 56 King George St, Greenwich London SE10 8QD (☎ 01 858 4281)

CARTER, Hon Mrs (Brenda Ruby); *née* Pearson; 4 da of 2 Visc Cowdray (d 1933), and Agnes Beryl (d 1948), da of Lord Edward Spencer-Churchill; *b* 15 Nov 1912; *m* 1, 1934 (m dis 1948), Gp-Capt Paul Willert, RAF, o son of Sir Arthur Willert, KBE; 2 da (Pauline m John, s of Sir Maurice Dorman, *qv*, Wanda m John Rix); m 2, 1948, Hugh Carter; 1 s (Harold m Theresa Silkstone); *Style*— The Hon Mrs Carter; Mallards, Duck Lane, Midhurst, W Sussex GU29 9DE

CARTER, His Hon Judge (Frederick) Brian; QC (1980); s of late Arthur Carter, and late Minnie Carter; *b* 11 May 1933; *Educ* Stretford GS, Kings Coll London (LLB); *m* 1960, Elizabeth, JP, da of late W B Hughes; 2 s (1 decd), 3 da; *Career* barr Gray's Inn 1955, practised Northern circuit 1957-, prosecuting counsel for Inland Revenue Northern circuit 1973-80, rec of The Crown Ct 1978-85, circuit judge 1985-; *Recreations* golf, travel; *Clubs* Chorlton-cum-Hardy GC, Big Four (Manchester); *Style*— His Hon Judge Brian Carter, QC

CARTER, Sir Charles Frederick; yst s of Frederick William Carter, FRS (d 1950), of Rugby; *b* 15 August 1919; *Educ* Rugby, St John's Coll Cambridge (MA); *m* 1944, Janet, da of Edward Shea (d 1923), of Newcastle; 1 s, 2 da; *Career* lectr in statistics Cambridge Univ 1947-51, fellow Emmanuel Coll Cambridge 1947-51 (now hon fell); prof of economics Queen's Univ Belfast 1950-59, Manchester Univ 1959-63; vice-chllr Lancaster Univ 1963-79; pres Policy Studies Inst 1989-; vice-chm Rowntree Memorial Tst 1981- (tstee 1966-), chm, Sir Halley Stewart Tst 1986-; chm N Ireland Econ Cncl 1977-87; former jt editor Economic Journal and Journal of Industrial Economics; former pres Manchester Statistical Soc and Br Assoc for Advancement of Science; former chm Schools' Broadcasting Cncl, NW Econ Planning Cncl, Centre for Studies in Social Policy; Hon DSc: Lancaster, Queen's Belfast, New (Ulster): Hon LLD Liverpool, Trinity Coll Dublin; Hon DEconSc National Univ Ireland; CBIM, FBA; kt 1978; *Recreations* gardening; *Clubs* United Oxford and Cambridge Univ, National Liberal; *Style*— Sir Charles Carter; 1 Gosforth Rd, Seascale, Cumbria CA20 1PU (☎ 09467 28359)

CARTER, Christopher John; s of Wilfred Lawrence Carter, of Broadwater House, Burwood Park, Walton on Thames, Surrey, and Betty Mary, *née* Vavasour; *b* 7 August 1945; *Educ* Uppingham Sch, Interpnbeten's Institute, Munich;; *m* 17 June 1978, Emma Caroline, da of Sir Robin Kinahan, ERD, JP, of Castle Upton, Templepatrick, Co Antrim, NI; 3 s (Thomas b 7 Jan 1981, Alastair b 14 March 1983, Nicholas b 16 March 1987); *Career* HAC 1964-66; ED & FMan Gp of Co's 1964-85: At New York 1969-71, Hong Kong 1974-76, dir (London) 1976-85; dir: London Int Fin Futures Exchanges 1982-85, Channel Island Money Brokers Ltd 1985-; md GNI (Jersey) Ltd 1986-; Liveryman Worshipful Co of Grocers 1977-; *Recreations* tennis, fishing, skiing; *Clubs* United, St Helier; *Style*— Christopher Carter, Esq; Maufant Manor, St Saviour's, Jersey, CI (☎ office 0534 210 86)

CARTER, David Alexander; CBE (1968); s of late John Howard Carter, JP (d 1956), of Ardeley Bury, nr Stevenage; *b* 25 April 1910; *Educ* Repton, Reading Univ; *Career* chm: Herts Branch NFU 1953, Herts and Middlesex Branch Country Landowners Assoc 1955-57; JP Herts 1944, CC 1954-61; chm of magistrates Buntingford Court 1959-68; *Style*— David Carter Esq, CBE; Bancroft Farm, Cottered, Buntingford, Herts (☎ Cottered 253)

CARTER, (William) David Antony; s of William Henry Newton Carter, CBE (d 1981) and Joan Stuart Carter (d 1983); *b* 21 Feb 1938; *Educ* Oundle, Oriel Coll Oxford (MA); *m* 27 April 1964, Angela Mary, da of Archibald Elliot Peel; 2 s (Justin Mark b 1965, Dominic William b 1968), 3 da (Catherine Sarah (Kate) b 1966, Emma Rachel b 1971, (Mary) Jessica b 1975); *Career* 2 Lt RA 1956-58; CA 1964, ptnr Peat Marwick Mitchell & Co 1975, head of corporate fin serv Peat Marwick McLintock 1986- (mgmnt buyout specialist 1981-); memb fin ctee Ampleforth Abbey; FCA 1974; *Recreations* opera, cricket, redundant Devon farmhouse; *Clubs* Oxford & Cambridge; *Style*— David Carter, Esq; 7 Bois Ave, Amersham, Bucks HP6 5NS (☎ 0494 727 109); Peat Marwick McLintock, 1 Puddle Dock, London EC4V 3PD (☎ 01 236 8000)

CARTER, David Ewart; s of Maj Ewart Grattan Carter, MC, TD (d 1978), of Ilkley, W Yorks, and Joan Elizabeth Carter; *b* 4 Feb 1946; *Educ* The Leys Cambridge, Leeds Univ (BA); *m* 29 Aug 1978, Claire Noel Raffles, da of Alexander Maben (d 1981), of Leeds; 1 step s (Christian b 25 March 1974), 1 da (Alice b 9 Sept 1980); *Career* chm: Carter and Parker Ltd 1978, chm Sharow and Capt Hewick Cons Assoc; *Recreations* shooting, tory politics, reading; *Style*— David Carter, Esq; Sharow Close, Ripon, N Yorks (☎ 0765 701474); Carter and Parker Ltd, Guiseley, W Yorkshire LS20 9PD (☎ 0943 72264, fax 0943 78689, telex 51234 WENDY G)

CARTER, Baron (Life Peer UK 1987), of Devizes, Co Wilts; Denis Victor Carter; s of Albert William Carter (d 1973), of Sussex, and Annie Julia, *née* Tynan (d 1972); *b* 17 Jan 1932; *Educ* Xaverian Coll Brighton, East Sussex Coll of Agriculture, Essex Coll of Agriculture (Nat Dip in Agric), Worcester Coll Oxford (B Litt); *m* 1957, Teresa Mary, da of Cecil William Walter Greengoe (d 1972), of Sussex; 1 s (Andrew Peter b 1963, d 1982), 1 da (Hon Catherine Mary b 1959); *Career* army, sergeant, Suez Canal zone; farmer and agricultural conslt; dir/fndr AKC Ltd (Agricultural Accounting and Mgmnt) 1957-; dir: United Oilseeds Ltd 1968-, Cave Hldgs/W E and D T Cave Ltd 1976-; *Recreations* reading, walking, supporting Southampton football club; *Clubs* Farmers, Turners, Grasshoppers; *Style*— The Rt Hon the Lord Carter; c/o House of Lords, London

CARTER, Sir Derrick Hunton; TD (1952); s of Dr Arthur Hunton Carter (d 1961), of Sedbergh, and Winifred Carter; *b* 7 April 1906; *Educ* Haileybury, St John's Coll Cambridge (MA); *m* 1, 1933, Phyllis, da of Denis Best, of Worcester; 1 s, 1 da; m 2, 1948, Madeline, da of Col Denis Moriarty O'Callaghan, CMG, DSO; 1 da; *Career* served WWII RA Lt-Col 1942; civil engr Dominion Bridge Co (Canada) 1927-28, research engr ICI 1928-33 (sales mangr 1933-39, md 1953); chm: Gen Chem Div ICI 1961, Mond Div ICI Ltd 1963-67, Remploy Ltd 1972-76; kt 1975; *Recreations* gardening, woodworking; *Clubs* Army and Navy; *Style*— Sir Derrick Carter, TD; Withington House, Withington, Cheltenham, Glos GL54 4BB (☎ 024 289 286)

CARTER, Douglas; CB (1969); 3 s of late Albert and Mabel Carter, of Bradford; *b* 4 Dec 1911; *Educ* Bradford GS, St John's Cambridge; *m* 1935, Alice Mary Clare, da of Capt Charles Edward Le Mesurier, CB, RN (d 1917), of Southsea, Hants; 3 s, 1 da; *Career* entered Bd of Trade 1934, under-sec 1963-71, ret; under-sec Dept of Trade and Industry 1969-71; *Style*— Douglas Carter Esq, CB; 12 Garbrand Walk, Ewell Village, Epsom, Surrey (☎ 01 394 1316)

CARTER, Eric Stephen; CBE 1986; s of Albert Harry Carter, MBE (d 1973), of Cheltenham, and Doris Margaret Carter, *née* Mann (d 1983); *b* 23 June 1923; *Educ* The GS Lydney Glos, Reading Univ (BSc); *m* 1948, Audrey, da of Joseph Windsor (d 1970), of Glos; 1 s (Michael b 1958); *Career* dist agric offr Nat Agric Advsy Serv Gloucestershire 1945-47, sr dist agric advsr Lincolnshire 1957-63, county agric offr Lincoln 1963-69, dep regnl dir Yorks/Lancs Regn and regnl agric offr 1969-74, chief regnl offr MAAF 1974-75, dep dir general Agric Dvpt and Advsy Service MAAF 1975-81, advsr Farming and Wildlife Tst 1981-88; memb: Royal Agric Soc of England 1976-, Welsh Plant Breeding Stn advsy ctee, Long Ashton Research Station Agric Ctee, govr body Grassland Res Inst 1976-87, selection ctee Nuffield Farming Scholarships Tst 1982-) Assoc of Agric 1985-; convener Standing Conference on Countryside Sports 1988-; visiting lectr Univ of Nottingham 1984-; hon fell RAS 1988, CBiol 1974, FIBol, FRAGS; *Recreations* countryside, reading, music; *Clubs* Farmers'; *Style*— Eric Carter, Esq, CBE; 15 Farrs Lane, East Hyde, Luton LU2 9PY (☎ 05827 60504)

CARTER, Lady Frances Elizabeth; *née* Bernard; yr da of Air Ch Marshal 5 and last Earl of Bandon, GBE, CB, CVO, DSO (d 1979), and his 1 w, (Maybel) Elizabeth (*see* Holcroft, Elizabeth, Lady); *b* 4 Feb 1943; *m* 1967, Paul Mark Carter, o son of Flt Lieut Mark Carter, DFC (d 1940); 1 s (Philip b 1979), 2 da (Emma b 1969, Annabelle b 1971); *Style*— Lady Frances Carter; Woodsprings, Snelsmore Common, Newbury, Berks

CARTER, Frank Ernest Lovell; CBE (1956); s of late Ernest C and Florence Carter, of Ilford, Essex; *b* 6 Oct 1909; *Educ* Chigwell Sch, Hertford Oxford; *m* 1966, Gerda, *née* Gruen; *Career* former dir-gen of Overseas Audit Service, ret 1972; *Style*— Frank Carter, Esq, CBE; 8 The Leys, London N2

CARTER, (Francis Jackson) Frank; CMG (1954), CVO (1963), CBE (1946); s of late Francis Henry Carter, of Bendigo, Victoria, Australia; *b* 9 Sept 1899; *Educ* Hobart HS, Tasmania Univ; *m* 1926, Margaret Flora, da of William Thomas Walker, of Launceston, Tasmania; 2 s, 1 da; *Career* state under-sec and perm head of Premier's Dept Tasmania 1952-64, official sec for Tasmania in London 1949-50; chm Fire Brigades Cmmn of Tasmania 1946-70; former Grand Master Freemasons Grand Lodge of Tasmania; *Style*— Frank Carter, Esq, CMG, CVO, CBE; Tavistock, 568 Churchill Avenue, Sandy Bay, Hobart, Tas, Australia (☎ 252382)

CARTER, (William) George Key; Lt-Col William Tom Carter, OBE, JP (d 1956), and Georgina Margaret, *née* Key (d 1986); *b* 29 Jan 1934; *Educ* Warwick Sch; *m* 30 June 1965, Anne Rosalie Mary, da of Trevor Acheson-Williams Flamagan (d 1987); 1 s (Alexander Corfield b 1971), 1 da (Louisa Mary-Anne b 1968); *Career* 2xxnd Lt 16/5 The Queens Royal Lancers 1958-60 (Adj 1959); qualified CA 1957; Price Waterhouse: joined 1956, mangr 1963, ptnr 1966, sr ptnr (W Midlands) 1982-; non exec dir W Midlands Industl Devpt Assoc; cncl memb: Birmingham Chamber of Indust and Commerce (memb gen purposes ctee), W Midlands CBI; judge W Midlands Business of the Year Award; memb: Ferrous Foundry Indust Advsy Ctee, Pharmacist Review Bd; FCA 1957; *Books* The Work of the Investigating Accountant; *Recreations* golf, shooting, sailing, gardening; *Clubs* Cavalry and Guards; *Style*— George Carter, Esq; The Old Rectory, Elmley Lovett, Droitwich, Worcs WR9 OPS; 28 Westmorland Ter, London SW1 (☎ 029 923 251); Price Waterhouse, Livery House, 169 Edmund St, Birmingham B32JB (☎ 021 200 3000, fax 200 2464, car tel 0836 245 455, telex

338684)

CARTER, Air Cdre Gerald Paul Halliley; CBE (1946); s of William Fowler Carter (d 1942), of Maidsmere, nr Bromsgrove; *b* 18 Feb 1900; *Educ* Bromsgrove Sch, St Catharine's Cambridge; *m* 1930, Esther Mary Douglas (d 1982), da of Maj-Gen Sir Henry John Milnes MacAndrew, KCB, DSO (d 1919); 2 da; *Career* joined RAF 1918, Air Cdre 1944, cmdg RAF Base Seletar 1946-49, ret 1950; bursar Ardingly Coll 1953-65; *Clubs* Royal Air Force; *Style—* Air Cdre Gerald Carter, CBE; Pryor House, East Hanney, Wantage, Oxon OX12 0HU (☎ (023 587) 233)

CARTER, Godfrey James; CBE (1984); s of Capt James Shuckburgh Carter, Grenadier Gds (ka 1918) and, Diana Violet Gladys, *née* Cavendish (d 1962); *b* 1 June 1919; *Educ* Eton, Magdalene Coll Cambridge (MA, LLM); *m* 15 June 1946, Cynthia, da of Eric Strickland Mason, of Park Farm, Iden, Rye, Sussex; 3 s (James b 1948, Simon b 1953, Hugh b 1960); *Career* WWII Capt Rifle Bde 1940-45 served 8 Army M East (twice wounded); barr Inner Temple 1946; Parly Counsel Off 1949-56 and 1964-79 (ret); commercial depts, Bristol Aeroplane Co and Bristol Siddeley Engines 1956-64; draftsman of: Companies Act 1985, Insolvency Act 1986, Insolvency Rules 1986; *Clubs* Travellers'; *Style—* Godfrey J Carter Esq, CBE; Old Bournstream House, Wotton-under-Edge, Glos GL12 7PA (☎ (0453) 843246)

CARTER, Jeffrey Alan; s of George Thomas Carter and Frances Lily Carter, of London; *b* 9 April 1938; *Educ* Whitgift Sch, Imperial Coll London Univ (BSc), Harvard Graduate Sch; *m* 1962, Diana Shirley, da of Harry Aukett; 1 s, 2 da (1 decd); *Career* md: Babcock Woodall Duckham Ltd 1978-, Babcock Engineering Contractos (Pty) Ltd Johannesburg SA 1980-; dir: Coal Processing Consultants Ltd 1979-, Fluidised Combustion Contractors Ltd 1979-, Babcock Contractors Ltd 1979-, Babcock Africa (Pty) Johannesburg 1980-, GEC Diesels Ltd 1983-; MIMechE, CEng; *Recreations* ornithology, music; *Style—* Jeffrey Carter Esq; 36 Hurst View Rd, Croham Hurst, South Croydon, Surrey CR2 7AG (☎ 01 688 6203, work 09252 5151, telex 627131 GECDUK G)

CARTER, Sir John; QC (Guyana 1962); s of Kemp R Carter, of Guyana; *b* 27 Jan 1919; *Educ* Queen's Coll Guyana, London Univ; *m* 1959, Sara Lou, da of James Harris, of N Carolina, USA; 2 s, 2 da; *Career* barr 1942; pro-chllr Univ of Br Guyana 1962-66; high cmmr for Guyana in UK 1970-76; ambassador of Guyana to China 1976-; kt 1966; *Style—* Sir John Carter, QC; Embassy of Guyana, No 1 Hsui Hsueh Tung Chieh, Chien Kuo Men Wai, China

CARTER, John Alan; s of Kenneth Carter, of Batley West Yorkshire, and Mary June, *née* Anderson; *b* 20 May 1951; *Educ* Carlton GS Bradford, Prince Henry's GS Otley; *m* 9 July 1977, Angela, da of David Andrew Tipper, of Salisbury, Wiltshire; *Career* chartered accountant; FICA England and Wales; *Recreations* philately, ballroom dancing, swimming; *Style—* John A Carter, Esq; Park Dale, Womersley Road, Knottingley, West Yorkshire WF11 8DH (☎ (0977) 86094); 15 The Arcade, Hill Top, Knottingley, West Yorkshire WF11 8EA (☎ (0977) 87338)

CARTER, Dr John Timothy (Tim); *b* 12 Feb 1944; *Educ* Dulwich Coll, Corpus Christi Coll Cambridge (MA, BA, BChir), Univ Coll Hosp London, London Sch of Hygiene and Tropical Med (MSc); *Career* lectr London Sch of Hygiene 1974-75, med advsr BP 1975-83, dir of Med Servs Health and Safety Exec 1983-; FRCP, FFOM; *Style—* Dr Tim Carter; Health and Safety Executive, Baynards House, 1 Chepstow Place, London W2 4TF (☎ 01 243 6100)

CARTER, (Thomas) Mark; JP (1971), DL (Staffs 1983); s of William Edward Carter, JP (1965), of Stafford, and Rose Margaret Eleanor, *née* Morris-Eyton (d 1982); *b* 20 May 1936; *Educ* Harrow, RAC Cirencester (MRAC); *m* 3 July 1965, Cecilia Catherine, da of Maj Henry Cecil Winger, of Staffs; 2 da (Melissa Margaret b 1966, Catherine Elizabeth b 1973); *Career* Lt Grenadier Gds Suez Canal Zone, Kenya 1954-56; chartered surveyor; former dir: Sneyd Brickworks Ltd, Keates Ltd; former ptnr John German Hughes & Wilbraham: farmer and landowner; gen cmmr Inland Revenue; memb; Agric Lands Tbnl, cncl Historic Houses Assoc 1 986-, bd of mgmnt Heart of England Tourist Bd 1986-; engaged in opening Eccleshall Castle to the public; High Sheriff Staffs 1974-75; hunt sec and master N Staffs Hunt 1963-76; *Recreations* hunting, tennis, shooting; *Clubs* Cavalry and Guards, MCC; *Style—* Mark Carter, Esq, JP, DL; Eccleshall Castle, Stafford ST21 6LS (☎ 0785x 850204); Estates Office, Eccleshall Castle, Stafford ST21 6LS (☎ 0785 850250)

CARTER, Lt-Col Maurice Fitzgerald; TD (1952) DL (Glos 1960); s of Maurice Frederic Carter, of The Castle House, Newnham, Glos; *b* 1 August 1913; *Educ* Cheltenham; *Career* Maj 43 Recce Regt NW Europe (despatches); C O Royal Glos Hussars 1958; slr; *Style—* Lt-Col Maurice Carter Esq, TD, DL; The Castle House, Newnham, Glos

CARTER, Michael James Frederick; CBE (1987); s of Dr David Michael Frederick Carter (Surgn Lt RN, d 1975), and Alice, *née*, McNally (d 1941); *b* 23 Mar 1941; *Educ* Downside; *m* 29 April 1967, Camilla Gillian, JP, da of Arthur Gordon Taylor; 2 s (James Gordon Frederick b 15 Nov 1968, David John b 29 Dec 1971), 1 da (Rachel Jane b 16 April 1970); *Career* memb: Somerset Health Authy 1978-, Nat Union of Cons and Unionist Assocs 1979-, Royal Bath and West Show Arts Ctee; High Sheriff of Somerset 1987-88; *Books* Modern British Painters 1900-40 (1978); *Recreations* gardening; *Style—* Michael Carter, Esq, CBE

CARTER, Hon Lady Nichola Jane Eleanora (Minervina); *née* Boyle; da of Rear Adm 9 Earl of Glasgow, CB, DSC (d 1984); *b* 21 Dec 1946; *m* 1976, Thomas G Carter, 1 s (Matthew b 1978); *Style—* Lady Nichola Carter

CARTER, Air Cdre North; CB (1948), DFC (1935); s of Lt-Col Godfrey Lambert Carter, CIE, IA (d 1932), of Cookstown, Co Tyrone, and Nellie, *née* Wiseman; *b* 26 Nov 1902; *Educ* Wellington, RAF Coll Cranwell; *m* 1931, Kathleen Graham, da of Charles MacHattie, of Keith, Banff; 1 s, 1 da; *Career* joined RAF 1921, Air Cdre 1948, SASO No 205 Group MEAF 1951, Provost Marshal and Chief of Air Force Police 1953, ret 1954; admin offr in public service N Region Nigeria 1955-63; *Style—* Air Cdre North Carter, CB, DFC; Gould's Bay, Hawkesbury River, PMB Brooklyn, NSW 2253, Australia

CARTER, Peers Lee; CMG (1965); s of Peers Owen Carter (d 1966), and Edith, *née* Lee (d 1982), of Bolton, Lancs; *b* 5 Dec 1916; *Educ* Radley, Ch Ch Oxford (MA); *m* 1940, Joan Eleanor, da of Capt Alfred Victor Robertson Lovegrove, DSO, RD, RNR, of Vancouver; 1 s; *Career* served WW II Fezzan and North Africa, Southern Europe, Maj; entered HM Foreign S ervice 1939, 2/1 sec Baghdad 1945-49, 1 sec cmmr-gen's office Singapore 1951-54, cnsllr Washington 1958-61, head Perm Delgn to UN Geneva 1961-63, inspr/chief inspr HM Diplomatic Service 1963-68, ambass Afghanistan 1968-72, asst under-sec of state and ministerial interpreter FCO 1973-76, ret; memb Int Assoc of Conference Interpreters; memb: Afghanistan Support Ctee (former dir), Afghan Aid, Sardar-e A'ala (1971); *Recreations* mountain walking, beekeeping, photography; *Clubs* Special Forces, Travellers'; *Style—* Peers Carter, Esq, CMG; Dean Land Shaw, by Jobes, Balcombe, Haywards Heath, W Sussex RH17 6HZ (☎ 0444 811205)

CARTER, Peter Basil; JP (1959); s of Albert George Carter (d 1961), and Amy Kathleen FitzGerald Carter (d 1973); *b* 10 April 1921; *Educ* Loughborough, Oriel Coll Oxford (BCL, MA); *m* 1, 1960, Elizabeth Maxwell Ely (decd); m 2, 1982, Lorna Jean Sinclair; *Career* served WW II Capt; barr 1947, hon bencher Middle Temple 1981; jt ed Int and Comparative Loan Quarterly 1961-; fell Wadham Coll Oxford 1949-88 (emeritus fell 1988-); former visiting prof various Cwlth and United States Univs; chm Univ Life Assur Soc 1980- (dir 1969-); Croix de Guerre 1944; FIOD 1984-; *Recreations* criticising bad architecture; *Clubs* United Oxford and Cambridge University; *Style—* Peter Carter Esq, JP; Wadham College, Oxford (☎ 0865 277900)

CARTER, Philip David; CBE (1981); s of Percival Carter and Isobell, *née* Stirrup; *b* 8 May 1927; *Educ* Waterloo GS Liverpool; *m* 1946, Harriet Rita, *née* Evans; *Career* md Littlewoods Orgn 1976-83 ret; chm Empire Tst 1986; pres Football League 1986-88; chm: Everton FC 1977, Merseyside Tourism Bd 1986, Liverpool Cons Assoc 1985, Merseyside Devpt Corpn 1987;; *Style—* Philip Carter, Esq, CBE; Oak Cottage, Noctorum Rd, Noctorum, Wirral, Merseyside L43 9UQ

CARTER, Air Cdre Robert Alfred Copsey; CB (1956), DSO (1942, DFC 1943); s of late Sidney Herbert Carter (d 1961), and S Carter, *née* Copsey (d 1949); *b* 15 Sept 1910; *Educ* Portsmouth GS, RAF Coll Cranwell; *m* 1947, Sarah Ann, da of Florence Booker Peters, of Hampton, Virginia, USA; 2 s, 1 da; *Career* joined RAF 1927, Air Cdre 1956, SASO Tport Cmd 1955-58, DPS (A) Air Min 1958-61, AOA RAF Germany 1961-64, ret; CEng, MRAeS; *Clubs* RAF; *Style—* Air Commodore R A C Carter, CB, DSO, DFC; The Old Cottage, Castle Lane, Whaddon, Salisbury, Wilts SP5 3EQ

CARTER, Prof Robert Lewis; s of Edwin Christopher Carter (d 1964); *b* 23 August 1932; *Educ* London Univ (BSc), Sussex Univ (DPhil); *m* 1954, Pearl Rita; 1 s, 2 da; *Career* prof Nottingham Univ (holds Britain's only chair of insur studies); govt nominee to Insur Brokers Registration Cncl 1979-82 and 1986-; cncl memb Insur Ombudsman Bureau 1981-; govr Inst of Risk Mgmt; visiting prof of Insur American Graduate Sch of Int Mgmnt 1982-83; FCII, FIRM, FRSA; *Recreations* reading, pottering in garden, travelling, walking; *Style—* Prof Robert Carter; 4 Bramcote Lane, Beeston, Nottingham NG9 5EN; Department of Industrial Economics, Accounting and Insurance, Nottingham University, Nottingham NG7 2RD (☎ 0602 484848)

CARTER, Robert Owen; CBE (1970); s of late Joseph Charles William Carter and late Laurie Ethel, *née* Plant; *b* 1906; *Educ* Bancroft's Sch, London Univ (MSc); *Career* research branch GPO Engrg Dept 1933-65, asst dir (research and dvpt) London Communications (Electronic) Security Agency 1965-70; FIEE, ACGI, DIC; *Style—* Robert Carter Esq, CBE; 8 Grange Ave, Woodford Green, Essex IG8 9JT (☎ 01 504 2522)

CARTER, Robert William Bernard; CMG (1964); s of William Joseph Carter (d 1961), of Heywood, Wilts, and Lucy, *née* How (d 1950); *b* 19 Dec 1913; *Educ* St Bees Sch, Trinity Coll Oxford (MA); *m* 1945, Joan Violet, da of Theodore Allingham Magnus (d 1955), of Grands Vaux, Jersey; 1 s, 2 da (and 1 da decd); *Career* former trade cmmr Calcutta, Delhi, Accra, Colombo (princ); sr trade cmmr Karachi 1961-66, min FCO 1966, dep high cmmr Karachi 1966-68, Melbourne 1969-72, consul-gen Melbourne 1972-73, ret 1974; *Recreations* reading, travelling, collecting beer-mugs; *Clubs* Oriental; *Style—* Robert Carter, Esq, CMG; The Old Parsonage, Heywood, Westbury, Wilts (☎ 0373 822194)

CARTER, Roger Hayward; s of Harry Edgar Carter (d 1964), of London, and Hannah Carter; *b* 28 August 1936; *Educ* Glendale GS; *m* 1958, Jeanne Florence; 1 s (Antony b 1967), 1 da (Jacqueline b 1970); *Career* RN - Able Seaman; dir weekly newspaper; publishers and printers; *Recreations* squash, football, cricket; *Style—* Roger Carter; 8 New Farm Drive, Abridge, Essex (☎ Theydon Bois 3290); London and Essex Guardian Newspapers Ltd, News Centre, Fulbourne Road, Walthamstow, London E17 (☎ 01 531 4141, fax 01 527 3696)

CARTER, Roger James; s of Frank William Carter (d 1959), of Finchley, London, and Eva Grace, *née* Howard (d 1968); *b* 29 Nov 1941; *Educ* Christs Coll Finchley, Northern Poly Sch of Architecture (Dip Arch); *m* 5 Oct 1963, Margaret, da of Frederick Walker, of Mill Hill; 1 s (Jeffrey Richard b 1972), 1 da (Victoria Eve); *Career* registered architect ARCUK 1965, assoc memb RIBA 1966, fell Faculty of Architects and Surveyors 1984, princ Roger Carter Architects; asst dir of architecture London Borough of Newham 1979-84; memb Nat Assoc of Round Tables 1972-82, chm Hornsey Round Table 1976, vice-chm London NW NSPPCC Centenary Appeal Ctee 1983; *Recreations* flat green bowls; *Clubs* Hatfield Bowls, Hertfordshire Indoor Bowls Assoc; *Style—* Roger J Carter, Esq; 47 The Ryde, Hatfield, Hertfordshire AL9 5DQ

CARTER, Stephen McCart; s of Dr Ralph Harlan Carter (d 1962), of Burwash Common, East Sussex and Dorothy Maud *née* Williams of Vain Cottage, Burwash Common, East Sussex; *b* 3 July 1935; *Educ* Clayesmore Sch Iwerne Minister Dorset, Cranfield Mgmnt Coll, Harvard Business Sch ; *m* 13 Oct 1962, Diana Mary, da of Eric James Foice, of Station Lane, Tewesbury, Glos; 1 s (Julian b 1964), 1 da (Philippa b 1966); *Career* gen mangr - P & O Bulk Shipping 1976-77, head of P & O Deep Sea Cargo Div; md: P & O Bulk Shipping Ltd 1981-83, Boyle Fin Services 1984-; chief exec Biffex Ltd 1985-87; sec gen The Baltic Futures Exchange Ltd 1987-; FICS 1960, memb The Baltic Exchange 1972;; *Recreations* golf, shooting, fishing; *Style—* Stephen Carter, Esq; 19A The Vale, Coulsdon, Surrey CR3 2AU, (☎ 01 660 9010), 24/28 St Mary Axe, London EC3A 8EP, (☎ 01 626 7985, fax 01 623 2917, telex 916434 BALFUT G

CARTER, Air Vice-Marshal Wilfred; CB (1963), DFC (1943); s of Samuel Carter (d 1943), of Nottingham; *b* 5 Nov 1912; *Educ* Witney GS; *m* 1950, Margaret Enid, da of Herbert Jones Bray, of Gainsborough, Lincs; 1 s (decd), 1 da; *Career* joined RAF 1929, Air Cdre 1960, AOA Bomber Command 1965-67, Air Vice-Marshal 1965, ret 1967; dir Australian Counter Disaster Coll 1969-78, int disaster conslt 1978-; Officer of Order of Cedars of Lebanon (1954); *Books* Disaster Preparedness and Response; *Recreations* swimming, walking; *Style—* Air Vice-Marshal Wilfred Carter, CB, DFC; Blue Range, Macedon, Vic 3440, Australia

CARTER, William Henry Newton; CBE (1964); s of William Henry Carter, of Mansfield, Notts; *b* 1903; *Educ* Dean Close Sch, Nottingham Univ; *m* 1936, Joan

Stuart, da of J West, of Ashton-under-Lyne; 2 s; *Career* princ inspector of mines and quarries Miny of Power 1954, pres S Cos Instn of Mining Engineers 1954-65; *Style*— William Carter Esq, CBE; 21 Clifton Rd, Chesham Bois, Bucks

CARTER, Sir William Oscar; s of Oscar Carter (d 1952), of Norwich, and Alice Carter; *b* 12 Jan 1905; *Educ* Swaffham GS, City of Norwich Sch; *m* 1934, Winifred Rose, da of Sidney Charles Thompson (d 1952), of Wymondham, Norfolk; *Career* served WW II Wing Cdr RAF; slr 1931; conslt Daynes Hill and Perks (Slrs) Norwich, memb cncl Law Soc 1954-75 (vice-pres 1970, pres 1971-72); pres: East Anglian Law Soc 1952-80, Norfolk and Norwich Inc Law Soc 1959, Int Legal Aid Assoc 1974-80; life memb cncl Int Bar Assoc (first vice-pres 1976-78); memb: Co Ct Rules Ctee 1956-60, Supreme Ct Rules Ctee 1960-75, Criminal Injuries Compensation Bd 1967-82 (dep chm 1977-82); hon memb The Fellows of the American Bar Fndn; Liveryman Co of Glaziers (Master 1985); kt 1972; *Recreations* swimming, foreign travel; *Clubs* Army and Navy, Norfolk (Norwich); *Style*— Sir William Carter; 83 Newmarket Road, Norwich (☎ 0603 53772); Holland Court, The Close, Norwich NR1 4DX (☎ 0603 611212; telex 97197)

CARTER-CAMPBELL, Lt-Col Duncan Machlan; OBE (1958); o s of Maj-Gen George Tupper Campbell Carter Campbell, CB, DSO (d 1921), of Fascadale, Ardrishaig, Argyllshire, and Frances Elizabeth, *née* Ward (d 1960), (see Burkes Landed Gentry, 18 edn, Vol III, 1972); *b* 06 Dec 1911; *Educ* Malvern, RMC Sandhurst; *m* 31 July 1948, Margaret Elliot (Peggie), yr da of Norman Thain Davidson (d 1940), of Ashstead, Surrey; 2 s (Lorne George Tupper b 20 May 1951, Colin Duncan b 17 May 1958), 3 da (Jean Frances b 10 Aug 1949, Mary Elizabeth b 21 Jan 1953, Anne Catherine b 28 May 1954); *Career* cmmnd The Cameronians (Scottish Rifles) 1932, served WWII Italy and NW Europe, cmd 1 Bn The Cameronians 1956-58, ret 1960; dist cmmr Linlithgow and Stirling Poly Club 1967-72, tres Dumfries Br Red Cross 1979-83; *Recreations* gardening, horses; *Style*— Lt-Col Duncan Carter-Campbell of Possil, OBE; The Clachan, Newton Airds, Dumfriesshire (☎ 038 782 340)

CARTER-CLOUT, Derrick Gilbert; s of Leslie Douglas Carter-Clout (d 1969), of 20 Saffrons Ct, Compton Place Rd, Eastbourne, Sussex, and Hilda Elizabeth, *née* Kendall; *b* 13 August 1920; *Educ* Cranleigh, Sch of Bldg Brixton; *m* 1, 8 April 1945 (m dis), Joyce Elizabeth (d 1975), da of Percy Welford Davidson (d 1961), of Cloverlands, Birthwaite Rd, Windermere; 1 s (Anthony b 1948), 1 da (Catherine b 1946), m 2, 1964, Joan Dane, da of George Robert Gummery (d 1929); *Career* HAC 1938, RE OCTU 1939, cmmnd 2 Lt RE 1940, India Royal Bombay Sappers & Miners 1940, Maj RBS Malaya 9 India div 1941, India Co Cmd 1941, invalided out of serv 1944; jt pres G & S Allgood Ltd (Architectural Ironmongers) 1980 (propentor 1947, md 1948-80); pres Executives Assoc of Great Br 1979-84 (dir 1967-69, chm 1969-70), chm local Cons branch Ashford Kent 1984; fell Faculty of Bldg; cncl memb City Livery Club 1988; memb Guild of Freeman City of London 1984 (Freeman 1960), Freeman Worshipful Co of Ironmongers 1979; *Recreations* golf; *Clubs* Ashford GC (Kent), City Livery, Rugger, Wellington, IOD, Henley Royal Regatta, Henley-on-Thames; *Style*— Derrick Carter-Clout, Esq; The Grange, Mersham, Nr Ashford, Kent (☎ 023 372 314); Flat 30, Silsoe House, 50 Park Village East, London NW1 (☎ 01 388 0645); G & S Allgood Ltd, Carterville House, Euston Rd, London NW1 (☎ 01 387 9951, fax 01 380 1232, telex 261817)

CARTER-JONES, Lewis; s of Thomas Jones (d 1950), and Elizabeth Jones (d 1946), of Kenfig Hill, Bridgend, Glam; *b* 17 Nov 1920; *Educ* Kenfig Hill Cncl Sch, Bridgend County Sch, Univ Coll of Wales Aberystwyth (BA, DipEd); *m* 1945, Patricia Hylda, da of Alfred Bastiman (d 1962), of Scarborough; 2 da; *Career* served RAF 1940-45 Fl-Sgt Navigator; former chm student finance ctee Univ Coll of Wales, former head of Business Studies Dept Yale Tech Sch Wrexham; contested (Lab) Chester 1956 (by-election) and 1959; sec all-party gp: India, BLESMA; parly advsr to RNIB and other orgns linked with disability MP (Lab) Eccles 1964-87; *Recreations* rugby, reading, gardening; *Style*— Lewis Carter-Jones Esq; Cader Idris, 5 Cefn Rd, Rhosnesni, Wrexham, Clwyd; House of Commons, London SW1

CARTER-PEGG, Hallam; s of Carter Pegg (d 1970), of Manor Way, S Croydon, Surrey, and Helen Elise, *née* Johnson (d 1975); f played cricket for the London Counties with W G Grace; *b* 7 May 1932; *Educ* Whitgift Sch, Croydon; *m* 16 April 1960, Margaret Edith, da of Norman Dale Mant (d 1957), of Hurst Way, S Croydon, Surrey; 2 s (Nicholas Hallam b 1964, Christopher Norman b 1973), 1 da (Karen Margaret b 1967); *Career* sr ptnr Pegg, Robertson, CAs; chm dir: Peckham Bldg Soc, S London Investmt and Mortgage Corpn Ltd; FCA; *Recreations* scouting, gardening, shooting; *Style*— Hallam Carter-Pegg, Esq; 47 Wandle Rd, Croydon, Surrey CR0 1DF (☎ 01 686 8011, telex 8813096 PEGROB, car ☎ (0860) 516 793)

CARTER-RUCK, Peter Frederick; s of Frederick Henry Carter-Ruck (d 1968), of Gerrards Cross, Bucks and Nell Mabel, *née* Allen; *b* 1914; *Educ* St Edward's Oxford; *m* 6 July 1940, Pamela Ann, only da of Gp Capt Reginald Stuart Maxwell, MC, DFC, AFC (d 1960), of Thorney Island, Emsworth; 1 s (Brian b 1943, d 1973), 1 da (Julie b 1941); *Career* served RA 1939-44, Capt Instructor in Gunnery; slr 1937; sr ptnr: Oswald Hickson Collier & Co 1945-81, Peter Carter Ruck & Ptnrs 1981-; dir Kwik-Serve Business Systems Ltd 1988; Private Property Mortgage Co Ltd; specialist memb Cncl Law Soc 1971-84; pres: City of Westminster Law Soc 1976, Media Soc 1981-82 and 1984-86; chm: Law Soc Law Reform Ctee 1980-83, Media Ctee Int Bar Assoc 1983-85; memb: Cncl of Justice, Intellectual Property Ctee of Law Soc; hon constlg slr: Inst of Journalists, Media Soc; Lloyd's Underwriter; govr St Edward's Sch Oxford 1950-78, past chm and fndr govr Shiplake Coll Henley; memb City of London Solicitors' Co 1949; *Books* Libel and Slander (1953, 1985 3 edn), The Cyclist and the Law (with Ian Mackrill, 1953), Copyright: Modern Law and Practice (with Edmund Skone James, 1965); *Recreations* writing, cinematography, wood-turning, ocean racing and cruising; *Clubs* Carlton, Garrick, Press, Royal Yacht Sqdn, Lloyd's Yacht, Law Soc Yacht, (past Cdre) Royal Ocean Racing and Ocean Cruising (past Cdre); *Style*— Peter Carter-Ruck, Esq; Latchmore Cottage, Great Hallingbury, Bishop's Stortford, Herts (☎ 0279 54357); Eilagadale, N Ardnamurchan, Argyll (☎ 097 23 267); Essex House, Essex St, Strand, London WC2R 3AH (☎ 01 379 3456, fax 01 240 1486/01 583 2115/01 497 9287, telex 265277 Libel G)

CARTIER, Rudolph; s of Joseph Cartier (d 1939), and Hermine, *née* Bohm (d 1942); *b* 19 April 1904; *Educ* Vienna Acad of Arts and Music; *m* 1, Ilse Prochnow (m dis), m 2, Trudy Binar (m dis); 1 da (Yolanda Poppoviv b 1933); m 3, 30 Dec 1949, Margaret Pepper; 1 da (Corinne b 1955); *Career* sr prodr of drama and opera BBC TV 1952-76; Oscar for best drama prdn by Guild of Br Producers and Directors 1957; *Style*— Rudolph Cartier, Esq; 26 Lowther Rd, Barnes, London SW13 (☎ 01 748 1475)

CARTLAND, Barbara (Hamilton); da of late Maj Bertram Cartland, Worcs Regt; *b* 9 July 1901; *m* 1, 1927 (m dis 1932), Alexander George McCorquodale (d 1964); 1 da (Countess Spencer); m 2, 1936, Hugh McCorquodale (d 1963), 2 son of Harold McCorquodale, of Forest hall, Ongar, Essex; 2 s (*see* Ian McCorquodale); *Career* best selling authoress in the World (Guinness Book of Records 1983) has also published plays, poems, biography and autobiography; former chm St John Ambulance Exhibition Ctee; founder Barbara Cartland Onslow Romany Gypsy Fund; pres Nat Assoc of Health 1966; awarded Woman of Achievement by Nat Home Fashions League 1981; received Bishop Wright Air Ind Award for the development of aviation 1984; dep pres St John Ambulance Bde for Herts, chm St John Cncl for Herts; FRSA; DStJ 1972; *Books* 450; *Style*— Miss Barbara Cartland; Camfield Place, Essendon, Nr Hatfield, Herts (☎ 0707 42612, 42657)

CARTLAND, Sir George (Barrington); CMG (1956); s of late William Arthur Cartland (d 1933), of West Didsbury, Manchester, and Margaret Cartland; jt author with son, J B Cartland 'The Irish Cartlands and Cartland Genealogy' (1978); *b* 22 Sept 1912; *Educ* Manchester HS, Manchester Univ, Hertford Oxford; *m* 1937, Dorothy, da of Ambrose Rayton; 2 s; *Career* Colonial Service (Gold Coast) 1935; Colonial Office 1944-49; Uganda: admin sec 1949, min of social servs 1955, min of educn and info 1958, cheif sec 1960, dep govr 1961-62; registrar Birmingham Univ 1963-67, vice-chllr Tasmania Univ 1968-77; chm: Aust Nat Accreditation Authy for Translators and Interpreters 1977-83, ctee of Review Library and Archives Legislation in Tasmania 1977; reported on Tasmanian Govt Admin 1981; memb of ctee to advise on proposed changing the size of both houses of the Tasmanian Parly 1984; KStJ 1971; kt 1963; *Clubs* Athenaeum, Tasmanian, RYCT; *Style*— Sir George Cartland, CMG; 5 Aotea Rd, Sandy Bay, Hobart, Tasmania 7005

CARTLEDGE, Sir Bryan George; KCMG (1985, CMG 1980); s of Eric Montague George Cartledge, and Phyllis, *née* Shaw; *b* 10 June 1931; *Educ* Hurstpierpoint Coll, St John's Coll Cambridge (hon fell 1985), St Antony's Coll Oxford (hon fell 1987); *m* 1960, Ruth Hylton, da of John Gass; 1 s, 1 da; *Career* Lt Queen's Royal Regt 1950-52; Dip Serv 1960-: private sec (Overseas Affairs) to PM 1977-79, ambassador to Hungary 1980-83, asst under sec of state (Def) 1983-84, dep-sec of the Cabinet 1984-85, ambassador to Soviet Union 1985-88; princ Linacre Coll Oxford 1988-; *Clubs* Utd Oxford and Cambridge; *Style*— Sir Bryan Cartledge, KCMG; Linacre College, Oxford OX1 3JA

CARTLIDGE, Hon Mrs; (Mary Cecilia); *née* Wigg; eld da of Baron Wigg, PC (d 1983), and Florence, *née* Veal; *b* 25 June 1930; *m* 1958, Robert George Cartlidge; 3 da; *Style*— The Hon Mrs Cartlidge; Abilene, Princes Street, Huntly, Aberdeenshire AB5 5HA (☎ 0466 3445)

CARTTISS, Michael Reginald Harry; MP (C) Great Yarmouth 1983-; s of Reginald Carttiss and Doris Culling; *b* 11 Mar 1938; *Educ* Great Yarmouth Tech HS, London Univ, LSE; *Career* former constituency agent for Yarmouth, memb Norfolk CC 1966-; *Style*— Michael Carttiss Esq, MP; House of Commons, London SW1

CARTWRIGHT, Lady Betty (Elizabeth Constance); *née* Bertie; OBE (1938); da of 7 Earl of Abingdon (d 1928); *b* 12 Mar 1895; *m* 1 1914, Maj Sigismund William Joseph Trafford, JP, DL (d 1953); 1 s (Edward m 1951 June Harding), 3 da (Helen m 1936 Capt Peter Fanshawe CBE, DSC, RN; Sophie m 1938 2 Baron Lyell of Kinnordy; Diana m 1, 1952 John Reford, m 2, Col L M Collins); m 2 1956, as his 2 wife, Col Henry Antrobus Cartwright, CMG, MC (d 1957); *Career* Sr Cmdt ATS 1938-44; *Style*— Lady Betty Cartwright, OBE; 30 Lennox Gdns, London SW1

CARTWRIGHT, Christopher Egerton; s of Herbert Edward Cartwirght (d 1978), and Ruth, *née* Collins; *b* 19 Oct 1944; *Educ* Kings Sch Worcester, Bristol Univ; *m* 30 Dec 1967, Susan Lois, da of Anthony John Mindham, of Brighton, Sussex; 1 s (James Egerton b 1971), 1 da (Sarah Elizabeth b 1974); *Career* Stockbroker; ptnr and dir Wood Mackenzie & Co, memb Stock Exchange, ACA 1969; *Recreations* gardening, microcomputing, angling, guitar; *Clubs* Chiselhurst GC; *Style*— Christopher Cartwright, Esq; Hostye Farm, Cudham Lane North, Cudham, Kent TN14 7QT (☎ 0959 73163, car tel 0860 619 295); County Nat West Securities Ltd, Draper Gardens, 12 Throgmarton Ave, London EC2P 2ES (☎ 01 382 100)

CARTWRIGHT, Rt Rev (Edward) David; see Southampton, Bishop of

CARTWRIGHT, (William) Frederick; CBE (1977), DL Glamorganshire (1946); s of late Rev William Digby Cartwright, of Aynho, nr Banbury, and Lucy Harriette Maud,*née* Bury; bro of Dame Mary Cartwright *qv*; *b* 13 Nov 1906; *Educ* Dragon Sch, Rugby; *m* 1937, Sally Chrystobel, da of Wyndham Ware, of Penarth; 2 s (Nigel, Peter), 1 da (Lucy); *Career* engr; former dep chm Br Steel Corpn; former md Steel Co of Wales Ltd; dir Davy Corp Ltd, BSC (Int) Ltd; High Sheriff 1961; OStJ; *Recreations* hunting, yachting 'Lucy of Lynington; *Clubs* Royal Yacht Squadron, Royal Ocean Racing, Royal Cruising; *Style*— Frederick Cartwright, Esq, CBE, DL; Castle-upon-Alun, St Brides Major, nr Bridgend, Mid Glam (☎ Southerndown 298)

CARTWRIGHT, Harry; CBE (1979, MBE Mil 1946); s of Edwin Harry Cartwright, and Agnes Alice, *née* Gillibrand; *b* 16 Sept 1919; *Educ* William Hulme's GS, St John's Coll Cambridge; *m* 1950, Catharine Margaret Carson Bradbury; 2 s; *Career* Dept of Atomic Energy 1949: chief engineer 1955, dir Water Reactors 1964-70, dir Fast Reactor Systems 1970-73; Atomic Energy Establishment Winfrith 1973-83; pres Euro Nuclear Soc 1983-85; *Style*— Harry Cartwright Esq, CBE; Tabbit's Hill House, Corfe Castle, Wareham, Dorset (☎ 0929 480582)

CARTWRIGHT, John Cameron; MP (SDP) Woolwich 1983-; JP (1970); s of late Aubrey John Randolph Cartwright and Ivy Adeline Billie Cartwright; *b* 29 Nov 1933; *Educ* Woking County GS; *m* 1959, Iris June Tant; 1 s, 1 da; *Career* exec civil servant 1952-55; Lab Party Agent 1955-67; political sec Royal Arsenal Co-op Soc Ltd 1967-72, dir 1972-74; MP (Lab changed to SDP 1981) Greenwich Woolwich E 1974-83, Woolwich 1983-, pps to Sec of State for Educ and Science 1976-77, founding memb SDP March 1981, parly spokesman on housing, local govt and the environment, SDP whip 1983-, SDP pres 1988- (vice pres 1987-88), SDP spokesman on defence 1983-; former tstee Nat Maritime Museum; *Books* Cruise, Pershing and SS20, with co author (1985), View from the House, with others (1986); *Style*— John Cartwright, Esq, MP; 17 Commonwealth Way, London SE2 (☎ 01 311 4394)

CARTWRIGHT, Capt John Cecil; DSC (1942, and bar 1953); s of Edward Cartwright (d 1948), of Bristol, and Gertrude, *née* Ellershaw (d 1953); *b* 22 May 1914; *Educ* private and RNC Dartmouth; *m* 17 Aug 1946, Alice Susan Gillespie, da of John Jagoe, of Liskeard and Buenos Aires; 2 da (Elizabeth b 1949, Charlotte Mary b 1956); *Career* entered RNC Dartmouth 1928, ret RN 1965, served mainly in destroyers (despatches 1940 and 1942); cmd HM Ships: Puckeridge 1942-43, Raider 1944-45, Contest 1946-47, Consort 1947-48, Opossum 1952-53, Plymouth and 4 Frigate Sqn 1960-63, Sea Eagle as dir of Jt Anti-Submarine Sch and Sr Naval Offr NI 1963-65; Bursar Portora Royal Sch 1965-69, Gentleman Usher of the Black Rod (N Ireland parliament) 1969-73; *Recreations* shooting, fishing; *Style*— Capt J C Cartwright, DSC; 29 High St, Sydling St Nicholas, Dorset (☎ 030 03 357)

CARTWRIGHT, Brig John Mael Fox; CBE (1946); s of Rev George Frederick Cartwright; *b* 1904; *Educ* King's Sch Canterbury, RMA; *m* 1940, Pamela (d 1981), o da of Lt-Col Wellesley Hutcheson; 1 s, 2 da; *Career* 2 Lt RA 1924, Staff Coll 1938, Brig 1954, ret 1956; bursar Welbeck Coll 1957-67; *Style*— Brig John Cartwright, CBE; Barn House, Kingston, Cambridge

CARTWRIGHT, John Wallace; s of Reginald Cartwright (d 1982), of Cambridge, and Iris Marion, *née* Dear; *b* 10 Mar 1946; *Educ* Bedford Sch, Cranfield Mgmnt Sch (MBA); *m* 1973, Christine Elsie, da of Jack Whitaker, of Newbury; 1 s (Timothy b 1975), 2 da (Genevieve b 1978, Bethany b 1980); *Career* merchant banker, dir corporate fin ANZ McCaughan 1989- (formerly dir ANZ Merchant Bank Ltd 1985), dir Indian Investmt Fund 1989; FCIB; *Recreations* gardening, golf; *Style*— John Cartwright, Esq; 16 Millfield, Berkhamsted HP4 2PB (☎ 04427 4984); 65 Holborn Viaduct, London EC1A 2EU (☎ 01 248 3331)

CARTWRIGHT, Dame Mary Lucy; DBE (1969); da of Rev William Digby Cartwright (d c1926), sometime Rector of Aynho, and Lucy Harriette Maud, *née* Bury (d 1950); *b* 17 Dec 1900; *Educ* Godolphin Sch Salisbury, St Hugh's Coll Oxford (MA, DPhil), ScD Cantab; *Career* lectr mathematics 1935-59, reader 1959-68, emeritus reader Cambridge Univ 1968, mistress of Girton 1946-68 (and former staff fell, life fell 1968); Hon LLD (Edin) 1953, Hon DSc Leeds 1958, Hull 1959, Wales 1962, Oxford 1966, (Brown) USA 1969; Cdr Order of the Dannebrog 1961; FRS; *Style*— Dame Mary Cartwright, DBE; 38 Sherlock Close, Cambridge (☎ 0223 352 574)

CARTWRIGHT, Nigel John Frederick; s of William Frederick Cartwright of Castle-upon-Alun, St Brides Major Glamorgan, and Sally Christobel, *née* Ware; *b* 12 August 1939; *Educ* Rugby, Christchurch Oxford; *m* 20 Dec 1968, Penelope Dolce Amber Constantia, da of Rear Adm Sir Morgan Morgan Giles DSO, OBE, of Frenchmoor Farm, W Tytherly, Salisbury Wilts; 2 s (Frederick Fairfax Agar b 1974, Edward John Chauncey b 1981), 1 da (Henrietta Julia Hester (b 1972); *Career* 2 Lt Grendadier Gds 1958-60; stockbroker London; *Style*— Nigel Cartwright, Esq; Trotton Place, Petersfield, Hampshire GU3 15EN (☎ 0730 813 672); City Merchants Investmt Mgmnt Ltd, 9 Devonshire Square, London EC2 M4YL (☎ 01 929 5269, fax 01 929 5889/8, telex 883621/886108)

CARTWRIGHT, Rt Rev Richard Fox; s of Rev George Frederick Cartwright (Vicar of Plumstead, d 1938), and Constance Margaret, *née* Clark (d 1975); *b* 10 Nov 1913; *Educ* The King's Sch Canterbury, Pembroke Coll Cambridge (BA, MA), Cuddesdon Theol Coll; *m* 6 Sept 1947, Rosemary Magdalen, da of Francis Evelyn Bray (d 1973), of Woodham Grange, Surrey; 1 s (Andrew Martin b 1948), 3 da (Rosemary Jane (Mrs Turner) b 1951, Mary Katharine (Mrs Bradley) b 1953, Susan Margaret (Mrs Meikle) b 1958); *Career* curate St Anselm Kennington Cross 1936-40, princ Lower Kingswood 1940-45; vicar: St Andrew Surbiton 1945-52, St Mary Redcliffe Bristol (with Temple 1956- and St John Bedminster 1965-) 1952-72; hon canon Bristol 1960-72, suffragan bishop of Plymouth 1972-81, asst bishop Diocese of Truro 1982-, proctor in convocation 1950-52, memb Gen Synod 1976-80; chm Govrs Kelly Coll Tavistock 1973-88, govr Summer Fields Oxford 1964-88; dir: Ecclesiastical Insurance Gp 1964-85, All Churches Tst 1985-; Grand Chaplain Utd Grand Lodge of England 1973-75, OStJ 1957; Hon DD Univ of the South Tennesee 1969; *Recreations* fly fishing, gardening, water colour painting; *Clubs* Army and Navy; *Style*— The Rt Rev Richard Cartwright; 5 Old Vicarage Close, Ide, nr Exeter, Devon EX2 9RT (☎ 0392 211 270)

CARTWRIGHT, Ronald Casper; s of late Joseph William Cartwright; *b* 21 Nov 1919; *Educ* King's Coll Sch Wimbledon; *m* 1, 1947, Ella Margaret, *née* Trinnear (d 1978); 1 s, 1 da; m 2, 1980, Isobel Andrews, *née* Stevenson; *Career* chartered sec; chm Martonair Int plc 1980-86; *Clubs* RAC, Burhill GC; *Style*— Ronald Cartwright, Esq; Tanglewood, 27 Sandown Road, Esher, Surrey

CARTWRIGHT, Stephen John; s of Cyril Cartwright, of Dorset; *b* 5 Dec 1953; *Educ* King's Coll London (BSC, AKC), Oxford Univ, Cncl of Legal Educn; *Career* writer and photographer; winner of William Stebbing Prize 1975; joined Hon Soc Gray's Inn 1974, chm and md Bloomsbury Times Ltd 1987-; *Recreations* ballet; *Style*— Stephen J Cartwright, Esq; 103 Warwick Rd, London SW5 9EZ

CARUS, Louis Revell; s of Lt Col Martin MacDowall Carus-Wilson, RAEC (ret) (d 1969), and Enid Madeleine Thaxter, *née* Revell (d 1973); *b* 22 Oct 1927; *Educ* Rugby, Burrels Conservatoire of Music, Peabody Conservatory of Music (USA); *m* 11 July 1951, Nancy Reade, da of Percival Edward Noell (d 1981), of Durham, N Carolina, USA; 2 s (Kenneth Edward b 20 Feb 1953, Colin Martin b 4 Sept 1956), 1 da (Alison Noell (Mrs L J Du Cane) b 29 May 1955); *Career* violinist, teacher and admin: memb Scottish Nat Orchestra 1950-55, head of strings Royal Scottish Acad of Music and Drama 1955-75, dean of faculty Birmingham Sch of Music 1975-87, artistic dir Int String Quartet Week 1987-, admin Benslow Tst Musical Instrument Loan Scheme 1987-; former pres Inc Soc of Musicians; chm Euro String Teachers Assoc (Br Branch); FRCM, FRSAMD, FBSM, hon RAM; *Recreations* gardening, walking, painting; *Style*— Louis Carus, Esq; 15 Kings End Rd, Powick, Worcs WR2 4RA (☎ 0905 831715)

CARUTH, Major Michael James; s of Major R A Caruth (d 1939), and Ruby Duncal Hodgson (d 1980); *b* 23 Nov 1928; *Educ* RMA Sandhurst, Wellington; *m* 7 June 1958, Anne, da of Brig J N Lumley (d 1965); 1 s (Patrick b 1959), 1 da (Camilla b 1962); *Career* 4/7 Royal Dragoon Guards 1949-66; md Wightman-Mountain Co 1975-; M F H Weser Hunt 1957-59; *Recreations* hunting, shooting; *Clubs* Cavalry and Guards; *Style*— Maj Michael J Caruth; Hardington Lodge, Hardington-Mandeville, Yeovil, Somerset; 142 Vauxhall Street, London SE11 5RU (☎ 01 582 6522, fax 582 4431, car telephone 0860 343738)

CARVER, Hon Andrew Richard; er s of Baron Carver, GCB, CBE, DSO, MC (Life Peer); *b* 1950; *m* 1973, Anne Rosamunde, da of Brian Stewart, of The Broich, Crief, Perthshire; *Style*— The Hon Andrew Carver; 18 Hayter Rd, London SW2

CARVER, James; CB (1978); s of late William and Ellen Carver; *b* 29 Feb 1916; *Educ* Wigan Mining and Tech Coll; *m* 1944, Elsie, *née* Sharrock; 1 s (twin); 2 da; *Career* former asst mine mangr; inspector of Mines and Quarries from 1943-, HM chief inspector of Mines and Quarries 1975-77, memb Health and Safety Exec 1976-77; int mining conslt; *Style*— James Carver, Esq, CB; 196 Forest Rd, Tunbridge Wells, Kent (☎ 0892 26748)

CARVER, Hon John Anthony; s of Baron Carver (Life Peer); *b* 1961; *Educ* Winchester Coll, Durham Univ (BA); *Career* financial management in FMCG Co; *Style*— The Hon John Carver

CARVER, Baron (Life Peer 1977); Field Marshal (Richard) Michael Power Carver; GCB (1970, KCB 1966, CB 1957), CBE (1945), DSO (1943) and Bar (1943), MC (1941); 2 s of late Harold Power Carver, of Ticklerton, Salop, and Winifred Anne Gabrielle, *née* Wellesley; *b* 24 April 1915; *Educ* Winchester, RMA Sandhurst; *m* 1947, Edith, da of Lt-Col Sir Henry Lowry-Corry, MC (gs of 3 Earl Belmore); 2 s, 2 da; *Career* sits as Ind peer in House of Lords; 2 Lt R Tank Corps 1935, Command 4 Armoured Bde 1944-47, Lt-Col 1942, Brig 1944; GOC 3 Div (Maj-Gen) 1962-64, Dep Cdr UN Force in Cyprus 1964, DSD MOD 1964-66, C-in-C Far East 1967-69, GOCIC Southern Command 1969-71, CGS 1971-73, Field-Marshal 1973, CDS 1973-76; Col Cmdt REME 1966-76, Col Cmdt RAC 1973-77; British Resident Cmmr (Designate) in Rhodesia 1977-78; *Books* El Alamein (1962), Tobruk (1964), The War Lords (ed 1976), Harding of Petherton (1978), The Apostles of Mobility (1979), War Since 1945 (1980), A Policy for Peace (1982), The Seven Ages of The British Army (1984), Dilemmas of the Desert War (1986) Twentieth Century Warriors (1987); *Recreations* sailing, tennis, gardening; *Clubs* Anglo-Belgian, Cavalry and Guards; *Style*— Field Marshal The Rt Hon The Lord Carver, GCB, CBE, DSO, MC; Wood End House, Wickham, Fareham, Hants (☎ 0329 832143)

CARVER, Gp Capt Neville John (Mike); OBE (1986), AFC (1961); s of Bertie John Carver (d 1952), of Norfolk, and Rose Harriett, *née* Bloom (d 1970); *b* 5 August 1922; *Educ* Norwich Sch; *m* 1950, Caroline Mary, da of Arthur Henry Whewell (d 1966), of Lincs; 1 s (Michael Christopher b 1955), 2 da (Sarah Jane b 1953, Carolyn Rebecca b 1963); *Career* RAF 1941, cmmnd 1942, flying operations Mediterranean, North Africa, Atlantic 1943-46, ret 1963 Gp Capt; joined: Ford Motor Co 1963, British Leyland 1969; dir: Rover Gp plc (exec), UGC Ltd, ISTEL Ltd, BLMC Ltd, Br Motor Heritage Ltd, Lloyds Register Quality Assurance Ltd; *Recreations* golf, gardening, squash, reading; *Clubs* RAF; *Style*— Group Capt Neville Carver, OBE, AFC; Weirdown, Blackthorn, Bicester, Oxon OX6 0TH (☎ 0869 244 911); Rover Gp plc, 7-10 Hobart Place, London SW1W 0HH

CARVER, Peter William John; JP (1973), DL (Humberside 1983); 23 patron of North Cave living, and churchwarden since 1969; s of Maj John Henton Carver, JP, TD (d 1968), and Juliet (d 1969), er da of Col T C Clitherow, DSO (d 1963), of Hotham Hall, York; *b* 18 June 1938; *Educ* Uppingham; *m* 1963, Jacqueline Sarah, da of James Boyce, of Fornham All Saints, Suffolk (d 1984); 1 s (Christian Henton James); *Career* Nat Serv 2 Lt DCLI; staff broadcaster with Br Forces Network, Germany 1959-62, Radio Luxembourg 1962-64; farmer and landowner; underwriting memb of Lloyd's 1971-; cncllr E Riding Yorks CC 1971-74; contested (C) Hull Central 1974 (twice); pres Humberside Euro Constituency 1983-88, (chm 1978-83); chm Humberside Scout Assoc 1978-83, (co cmmr 1983-); memb ctee of the Cncl Scout Assoc 1986-; dir: Hull City AFC 1981, Viking Radio; memb Yorks regnl ctee Nat Tst; landowner (1500 acres), dep chm S Hunsley Magistrates; *Recreations* shooting, gardening, historic houses; *Clubs* Royal Overseas; *Style*— Peter Carver, Esq, JP, DL; The Croft, North Cave, East Yorks (☎ 043042 2203); work: Hotham Estate Farms, North Cave, East Yorks HV15 2NG

CARVER, Hon Susanna Mary; da of Baron Carver (Life Peer); *b* 1948; *Style*— The Hon Susanna Carver; 16 Kelso Place, London W8

CARVER, Wyndham Houssemayne; s of Capt Edmund Squarey Carver, DSC, RN, and Freda Wilmot Houssemayne, *née* Du Boulay (d 1970); *b* 4 May 1943; *Educ* Malvern Coll, Harvard Business Sch (PMD); *m* 11 May 1984 (m dis 1984), Jocelyn Mary Anne, da of Graham Rogers, of Hungerford House, Hyde, Fordingbridge, Hants; m 2, Shona Leslie, da of Maj Ian McKillop, of Ladys Walk, East Cholderton, Nr Andover, Hants; 1 da (Tamsin b 7 Sept 1985); *Career* md Wyvern Int (subsidiary of Int Distillers & Viners Ltd of Grand Met plc) 1982- (joined 1965); *Recreations* squash, tennis, golf, forestry, travel; *Clubs* Annabels, Lansdowne; *Style*— Wyndham Carver, Esq; Rondle Wood House, Nr Milland, Liphook Hants (☎ 073 080 397); 1 York Gate, Regents Park, London NW1 4PU (☎ 01 487 3412, fax 01 487 3882, telex 262548 SPIRIT G)

CARY, Hon Mrs (Clare Louise Katharine); da of Baron Elworthy, KG, GCB, CBE, DSO, MVO, DFC, AFC (Life Peer); *b* 1950; *m* 1975, Anthony Joyce Cary, s of Sir (Arthur Lucius) Michael Cary, GCB; 3 s (Sam Michael b 1978, Thomas Joyce b 1980, Arthur Lucius b 1983), 1 da (Harriet Maude b 1985); *Style*— The Hon Mrs Cary

CARY, Hon Mrs (Daphne Helen); er da of late Capt Edward Westcott King, RA; *m* 1932, Hon Byron Godfrey Plantagenet Cary (d 1971), 2 s of 13 Viscount Falkland, OBE; 1 s, 2 da; *Style*— The Hon Mrs Byron Cary; The Cottage, 26 Dorset Rd South, Bexhill-on-Sea, E Sussex

CARY, Nicolas Robert Hugh; s and h of Sir Roger Cary, 2 Bt; *b* 17 April 1955; *Educ* St Paul's, London Univ (BA); *m* 1979, Pauline Jean, da of Thomas Ian Boyd, of Grays, Essex; 2 s (Alexander b 1981, Nathaniel b 1983); *Career* with Sotheby's 1977-82, production asst catalogue dept 1979-82; city print rep Westerham Press 1982-; *Recreations* book collecting, typography, cookery; *Style*— Nicolas Cary Esq; 232 Ongar Rd, Brentwood, Essex CM15 9DX (☎ (0277) 225424)

CARY, Sir Roger Hugh; 2 Bt (UK 1955); s of Sir Robert Cary, 1 Bt, sometime MP for Eccles and Manchester (Withington), PPS to Capt Harry Crookshank 1951-55; *b* 8 Jan 1926; *Educ* Ludgrove, Eton, New Coll Oxford; *m* 1, 1948 (m dis 1951), Marilda, da of Maj Philip Pearson-Gregory, MC; 1 da; m 2, 1953, Ann Helen Katharine, da of Blair Brenan, OBE; 2 s, 1 da; *Heir* s, Nicolas Cary; *Career* former sub-ed and leader writer The Times and dep ed The Listener; sr asst then special asst (Public Affairs) BBC 1972-77, special asst to md BBC TV 1977-82, chief asst to dir of Programming BBC TV 1983-86, asst to dir gen BBC 1986-; *Recreations* looking at pictures; *Clubs* Pratt's; *Style*— Sir Roger Cary, Bt; 23 Bath Rd, London W4 (☎ 01 994 7293); BBC, Broadcasting House, London W1A 1AA (☎ 01 580 4468, ext 5026)

CARY-ELWES, Charles Gervase Rundle; s of Lt-Col Oswald Aloysius Joseph Cary-Elwes, and Elizabeth Pamela, *née* Brendon; *b* 8 Nov 1939; *Educ* Ampleforth Coll, Sorbonne Paris, Trin Coll Oxford (MA); *m* 2 April 1972, Angela Jean, da of Maj Eric Rowland, TD, TA (d 1960); 1 s (James b 1976), 1 da (Lucy b 1974); *Career* stockjobber Durlacher Oldham Mordaunt Godson 1962-65, self-employed 1965-74,

Peat Marwick Mitchell & Co CA 1975-79, corporate fin exec Grievson Grant & Co 1980-83, PA to Exco Int plc 1983-85, exec dir Br & Cwlth Hldgs plc 1986-; ACA, ATII; *Recreations* golf, music, theatre, travel; *Clubs* Dulwich and Sydenham Hill Golf; *Style—* Charles Cary-Elwes, Esq; British & Commonwealth Holdings plc, Kings House, 36/37 King Street, London EC2V 8BE (☎ 01 600 3000, fax 01 600 0734, telex 884095)

CASE, Air Vice-Marshal (Albert) Avion; CB (1964), CBE (1957, OBE 1943); s of Gp-Capt Albert Edward Case, RAF (d 1965), of Barn Cottage, Amesbury, Wilts, and (Florence) Stella Hosier Case (d 1981); *b* 5 April 1916; *Educ* Collegiate Coll Malta, Imperial Service Coll; *m* 11 June 1949, (Brenda) Margaret, da of Maj Arthur George Andrews, HAC (d 1969), of Brenarth, Enfield, Middx; 1 s (Geoffrey b 7 Aug 1952), 1 da (Gillian b 19 March 1951); *Career* joined RAF 1934, Gp Capt 1953, Air Cdre 1959, Air Vice-Marshal 1962, AOC No 22 Gp Tech Training 1963-66, SASO HQ Coastal Command 1967-69, ret; gen sec Hosp Saving Assoc 1969-82; hon sec Br Hosp Contributory Schemes Assoc 1970-80; vice-pres Hosp Saving Assoc 1983; dir RAF Yacht Club Ltd 1986-; Adm RAF Yacht Club 1986; memb ctee Meadway House (Winchester) Ltd (homes for the elderly) 1986-88; FBIM; *Recreations* sailing, swimming; *Clubs* RAF, RAF Yacht, RAF Sailing Assoc, RYA; *Style—* Air Vice-Marshal Avion Case, CB, CBE; High Trees, Dean Lane, Winchester, Hants SO22 5LS (☎ 0962 55625)

CASE, David Charles; s of Charles Kendal Case and Grace Tennent, *née* Smith; *b* 18 Oct 1943; *Educ* Oakham Sch, Oxford Univ (MA); *m* 3 June 1967, Anthea Fiendley, da of Thomas Fiendly Stones, OBE; 2 da (Melissa Katherine b 1977, Laura Alexandra b 1983); *Career* with ICI 1967-68; export mangr British Sidac 1968-72; dir CCA Galleries plc (formerly Christie's Contemporary Art); *Clubs* Arts; *Style—* David Case Esq; 58 Gibson Sq, London N1 ORA (☎ 01 359 2267); CCA Galleries, 8 Dover Street, London W1 (☎ 01 499 6701)

CASE, David James; s of James Henry Case (d 1935), and Kathleen Nora Savory (d 1971); *b* 1 Sept 1923; *Educ* King Edward VII King's Lynn, Paston Sch; *m* 16 Oct 1956, Ruth; 1 s (James b 1958, 1 da (Gillian b 1957); *Career* RN 1941-46, Lt RNVR; assoc of Agric Valuers; station hon sec Wells Station Branch RNLI 1969-, lifeboatman 1953-; past pres Norfolk Assoc of Agric Valuers; memb Eastern Sea Fisheries Jt Ctee, harbour cmmr Wells Next The Sea Norfolk; FRICS, FAAV; *Recreations* shooting, sea fishing, gardening; *Style—* David J Case, Esq; Saxons, Northfield, Wells Next The Sea, Norfolk NR23 1JZ (☎ 0328 710234); Case and Dewing, Church Street, Dereham, Norfolk NR19 2DJ (☎ 0362 692004)

CASE, Humphrey John; s of late George Reginald Case, and Margaret Helen, *née* Duckett; *b* 26 May 1918; *Educ* Charterhouse, St John's Coll Cambridge; *m* 1 1943 Margaret Adelia, *née* Eaton; m 2 1949 Jean Alison, *née* Orr, 2 s; m 3, 1979, Jocelyn, *née* Herickx; *Career* keeper Dept of Antiquities Ashmolean Museum Oxford 1973-82; chm Charles Case & Son Ltd 1959-84; *Recreations* working for Cncl for the Protection of Rural England, gardening; *Style—* Humphrey Case Esq; Pitts Cottage, 187 Thame Rd, Warborough, Oxford

CASE, Janet Ruth; da of James Anthony Simpson, of Exeter and Cathleen, *née* King; *b* 29 June 1943; *Educ* Bishop Blackall Sch Exeter, Durham Univ (LLB); *m* 1965 (m dis 1982), Jeremy David Michael Case, s of Glyn Pryce (d 1980), of Gunley; 1 s (Edwin, b 1969), 1 da (Charlotte b 1966); *Career* barr Inner Temple 1975, Wales and Chester circuit 1975; chm Med Appeals Tbnl; *Recreations* gardening; *Clubs* Lansdowne; *Style—* Mrs Janet Case; Croeswylan, Oswestry, Shropshire (☎ 0691 653726); 40 King St, Chester (☎ 0244 323886)

CASE, Richard Vere Essex; DSO (1942), DSC (1940 and Bar) RD (1940 and Clasp 1955); s of Robert Hope Case (d 1944), of Liverpool, and Hilda Annie, *née* Trew (d 1946); *b* 13 April 1904; *Educ* Thames Nautical Tning Coll, HMS Worcester; *m* 1940, Olive May, da of Henry William Griggs, of Preston, nr Canterbury, Kent; 1 s (Robert), 1 da (Jocelyn); *Career* served WW II Norway 1940, North Africa Invasion 1942, Battle of the Atlantic 1940-45; Master Mariner; ADC to Queen 1958-59, chief supt Coast Lines and Assoc Cos 1953-69; *Recreations* bowls; *Clubs* Athenaeum (Liverpool), Liverpool CC; *Style—* Capt Richard Case, DSO, DSC, RD; 14 Aigburth Hall Rd, Liverpool L19 9DQ (☎ 051 427 1016)

CASEY, Lady Arabella; 2 da of 7 Earl of Yarborough, JP; *b* 20 Jan 1960; *Educ* Heathfield, L'Institut Alpin Videmanette Switzerland; *m* 2 June 1984, Christopher Casey, o s of Ronald Casey, of Pecklands, Stansted, Kent; 2 da (Laura Alexandra b 1 Aug 1986, Emma Olivia b 13 April 1988); *Style—* Lady Arabella Casey

CASEY, Jayne; da of John Casey (d 1988), of Bidston, Wirral, and Sonia Georgette, *née* Burden-Green (d 1963); *b* 12 Sept 1956; *Educ* Wallasey Tech HS; 1 s (Ra Jojo Cole); *Career* singer and songwriter; work incl: Big in Japan, A to Z and Never Again 1978, Pink Military, Blood and Lipstick 1979, Pink Military, Do Animals Believe in God? 1980, Pink Industry, Low Technology 1982, Pink Industry, New Beginnings 1984; dir Zulu Records 1981-87; script reader Liverpool Playhouse, assessor Merseyside Arts (memb Asian Music Panel) dir performing arts Bluecoat Arts centre Liverpool; *Clubs* Arts; *Style—* Ms Jayne Casey; Bluecoat Arts Centre, Bluecoat Chambers, School Lane, Liverpool L1 3BX (☎ 708 8877)

CASEY, Kevin Lawrence; s of James Casey, of Hillingdon, and Theresa, *née* Daly; *b* 2 Oct 1949; *Educ* Gunnersbury GS; *m* 5 Aug 1972, Theresa Margaret, da of Patrick Rooney, of Galway, Eire; 2 da (Emma b 1977, Claire b 1979); *Career* served 10 Bn(V) Para Regt 1970-74; qualified CA 1973, Price Waterhouse: ptnr 1984-, ptnr i/c UK Customs and VAT 1985, chm world customs specialists 1988, ptnr i/c Euro VAT 1989; fdr VAT Practitioners Gp 1982, former memb: London Soc of CAs VAT Ctee, ICAEW VAT Ctee; govr St Bernadette's PS Hillingdon; FCA; *Recreations* shooting, marathon running, cooking; *Style—* K L Casey, Esq; 12 Arlington Drive, Ruislip, Middx HA4 7RL (☎ 0895 635041); Price Waterhouse, Southwark Towers, 32 London Br St, London SE1 9SY (☎ 01 407 8989, fax 01 407 0545 or 01 403 2315, telex 88465718)

CASEY, Michael Bernard; s of Joseph Bernard Casey OBE (d 1985), and Dorothy, *née* Love (d 1949); *b* 1 Sept 1928; *Educ* Colwyn Bay GS, LSE (LLB); *m* 1963, Sally Louise, da of James Stuart Smith; 2 s (Dominic b 1966, Matthew Damian b 1967), 2 da (Louise Dorothy b 1964, Charlotte Hanna b 1971); *Career* offr: MAFF 1954-63, Miny of Sci 1963-64, Dept Econ Affrs 1964-69, Miny of Technol 1969-71; asst sec DTI 1971-72, under sec head shipbuilding policy div Dept Indust 1975-77; chief exec and dep chm Br Shipbuilders 1977-80, chm and md Mather and Platt Ltd 1980-82, dir Marlar Int Ltd 1982-87, chm and chief exec Sallingbury Casey Ltd 1986-; *Recreations* golf, chess, bridge; *Clubs* Reform; *Style—* Michael B Casey, Esq; 10 Phillimore Terrace, Allen Street, London W8 (☎ 01 937 4268); 25 Victoria St, London SW1 (☎ 01 222 1566, fax 01 222 3220, telex 268456)

CASEY, Michael Vince; s of Charles John Casey (d 1966), of Exmouth, Devon, and May Louise, *née* Yeulett (d 1981); *b* 25 May 1927; *Educ* Glossop GS, Univ of London (BSc); *m* 1954, Elinor Jane (d 1987), da of Alfred George Harris (d 1982), of Purton, Wilts; 2 s (William, Edward), 2 da (Annabel, Angela); *Career* Lt-Col RE (TA) Engrg and Tport Staff Corps; various engrg posts with BR 1944-78; engrg dir BR Engrg Ltd 1978-82; dir of mech and electrical engrg BR Bd 1982-87, project dir (privatisation) BR Bd 1987-;; *Recreations* gardening, philately; *Style—* M V Casey, Esq; Hunters Ride, Stoke Row Rd, Peppard, Henley-on-Thames, Oxon (☎ 0734 722653); British Railways Bd, Departure Offices, Paddington Station, London (☎ 01 922 6675)

CASEY, Thomas William; CBE (1950, OBE 1945), MC (1918); s of late Thomas Worrall Casey, of Sheffield; *b* 25 June 1896; *Educ* Mexborough GS; *m* 1922, Mabel Eliza, da of late James Ray, of Cumnor Hill, Oxford; 1 s, 1 da (both decd); *Career* Lt Royal Fusiliers 1916-19 in France, Belgium and Italy; asst sec Min of Pensions and National Insurance 1945-61; *Style—* Thomas Casey, Esq, CBE, MC; Flat 8, Lavington Court, 77 Putney Hill, London SW15

CASH, Sir Gerald Christopher; GCMG (1980), GCVO (1985, KCVO 1977), OBE (1964), JP (Bahamas 1940); s of late Wilfred Gladstone Cash and late Lillian Cash; *b* 28 May 1917; *Educ* Govt HS Nassau; *m* 1950, Dorothy Eileen, *née* Long; 2 s, 1 da; *Career* barr Middle Temple 1948, gen law practice to 1976; memb House of Assembly of Bahamas 1949-62, chm Labour Bd (Bahamas) 1950-52; memb: Bd of Educn 1950-62, Immigration Ctee 1958-62, Road Traffic Ctee 1958-62, Air Tport Licensing Authy 1958-62, HM Exec Cncl 1958-62; memb Police Service Cmmn 1964-69; memb and then pres Senate of Bahamas 1969-72, Govr-Gen Bahamas 1979-88 (Acting Govr-Gen 1976-79), memb bd of dirs Central Bank of the Bahamas; vice-chllr Anglican Diocese of the Bahamas to 1976; chm nat ctee United World Coll 1977-81; patron: Bahamas Red Cross (with Lady Cash), Bahamas Humane Soc, Bahamas Boy Scout Assoc, Bahamas Boys Bde, Bahamas branch Royal Life Saving Soc, Freeport Friends of the Arts, Bahamas Air Sea Rescue Assoc; silver medal Olympic Order 1983; *Style—* Sir Gerald Cash, GCMG, GCVO, OBE, JP; PO Box N 476, Nassau, Bahamas (☎ 393 4767; 393 2062)

CASH, William Nigel Paul; MP (C) Stafford 1984-; s of Capt Paul Trevor Cash, MC (ka Normandy 1944), and Moyra Margaret Elizabeth, *née* Morrison; *b* 10 May 1940; *Educ* Stonyhurst, Lincoln Coll Oxford (MA); *m* 1965, Bridget Mary, da of James Rupert Lee; 2 s (William, Samuel), 1 da (Letitia); *Career* slr William Cash and Co 1967-; vice chm: Cons Constitutional Ctee 1986, Cons Small Business Bureau, backbench ctee on Smaller Business; memb Select Ctee on Euro Legislation; chm All Pty Parly Ctee: on Widows, on E Africa; hon sec Lords and Commons Cricket, bd memb Ironbridge Gorge Tst; *Recreations* cricket, tennis, the heritage, cutting lawns, cutting red tape; *Clubs* Carlton, Vincent's (Oxford), Free Foresters CC; *Style—* William Cash, Esq, MP; Upton Cressett Hall, nr Bridgnorth, Shropshire (☎ (074 631 307); 37 St George's Sq, London SW1 (☎ 01 821 6237); 10 Little College St, London SW1 (☎ 01 222 7040, telex 919302)

CASHEL AND OSSORY, Bishop of (901) 1980-; Rt Rev Noel Vincent Willoughby; 58 Bp of Cashel (901), 89 Bp of Ossory (441), 63 Bp of Waterford (1096), 70 Bp of Lismore (631); s of George and Mary Jane Willoughby; *b* 15 Dec 1926; *Educ* Tate Sch Wexford, Trin Dublin; *m* 1959, Valerie Moore, of Dungannon, Tyrone; 2 s, 1 da; *Career* deacon 1950, ordained Armagh Cathedral 1951; curate: Drumglass Parish 1950-53, St Catherine's Dublin 1953-55, Bray Parish 1955-59; rector: Delgany Parish 1959-69, Glenageary Parish 1969-80; hon sec General Synod 1976-80, tres St Patrick's Cathedral Dublin 1976-80, archdn of Dublin 1979-80; *Books* What We Believe (1985); *Style—* The Rt Rev the Bishop of Cashel and Ossory; The Palace, Kilkenny, Ireland (☎ (056) 21560)

CASPARI, Prof Fritz Edward Wilhelm Carl; hon KCVO (1972); s of Dr Eduard Caspari (d 1973), and Elli, *née* Klussmann (d 1947); *b* 21 Mar 1914; *Educ* Gymnasium Heidelberg, Heidelbdeg Univ, Oxford Univ (MLitt), Hamburg Univ (DPhil); *m* 1944, Elita Galdos, da of Irving Miller Walker (d 1969); 2 s (Conrad b 1952, Hans Michael b 1945 d 1980), 2 da (Elisabeth b 1954, Andrea b 1956); *Career* asst prof South Western Univ Memphis, Scripps Coll California, Univ of Chicago; Foreign Serv FDR: joined 1954, i/c Br Irish Cwlth Affrs 1955-58, cnsllr London 1958-63, cnsllr and min off of perm observer to UN NY 1963-68, asst under sec of state FO Bonn 1968-69, off of fed pres Bonn 1969-74, ambass Portugal 1974-79; hon prof Univ of Grand Cross Order: of St Sylvester 1973; *Books* Humanism and the Social Order in Tudor England (1954, 1968); *Recreations* walking, skiing; *Clubs* Boodles, Gremio Literario (Lisbon), Swiss Alpine; *Style—* Prof Fritz Caspari; Casa das Nogueiras, Malveira da Serra, 2750 Cascais, Portugal (☎ Lisbon 285 0293); 3 Chilgrove House, Chilgrove, Chichester, W Sussex PO18 9HU (☎ 0243 59297, 0243 59215)

CASS, Geoffrey Arthur; s of Arthur Cass (d 1982), of Darlington and Oxford, and Jessie, *née* Simpson (d 1967); *b* 11 August 1932; *Educ* Queen Elizabeth GS Darlington, Jesus Coll, Univ of Oxford (BA MA) Nuffield Coll Univ of Cambridge, Jesus Coll and Clare Hall Camb (MA); *m* 1957, Olwen Mary, da of late William Leslie Richards, of Brecon; 4 da (Fiona b 1961, Karen b 1962, Miranda b 1965, Fleur b 1969); *Career* cmmnd Pilot Offr RAFVR (Oxford Univ Air Sqdn) 1954, Nat Serv Pilot Offr 1958, Flying Offr 1960 Air Ministry Directorate Work Study RAF 1958-60; conslt PA Mgmnt Conslts 1960-65; private mgmnt conslt Br Communications Corpn, Controls and Communications Ltd, 1965; md George Allen & Unwin 1967-71 (dir 1965-67), dir: Controls and Communications Ltd 1966-69, Chicago Univ Press (UK) Ltd 1971-86, chief exec Cambridge Univ Press 1972-; dir: Weidenfeld Publishers Ltd 1972-74, Newcastle Theatre Royal Tst 1984-89, American Friends Royal Shakespeare Theatre 1985-, Cambridge Theatre Co 1986-; tstee and guardian Shakespeare Birthplace Tst 1982-; chm: Royal Shakespeare Theatre Tst 1983- (dir 1967-), Royal Shakespear Co 1985- (govr 1975-), Br Int Tennis and Nat Trg 1985-; memb bd Lawn Tennis Assoc GB 1985- (memb cncl 1976-); memb governing syndicate Fitzwilliam Museum Cambridge 1977-78, chm govrs Perse Sch for Girls Cambridge 1978-88, memb: Univ of Cambridge ctee and exec sub ctee Mgmnt Fenners 1976-, exec ctee Univ of Cambridge Careers Service Syndicate 1982- (memb 1977-); chm Cambridge Univ Lawn Tennis Club 1977-, pres Cambridgeshire Lawn Tennis Assoc 1980-82; played Wimbledon Championships 1954, 1955, 1956, 1959, Br Veterans Singles Champion Wimbledon 1978, Oxford Tennis Blue 1953, 1954, 1955, hon Cambridge Tennis Blue 1980; Fell of Clare Hall Camb 1979; FInstD 1968, FIWM 1979, FIIM 1979, CBIM

1980; Chevalier de L'Ordre des Arts et des Lettres France 1982; *Recreations* lawn tennis, theatre, running; *Clubs* Hurlingham, Queen's, Int Lawn Tennis of GB, The 45, Cambridge Univ Lawn Tennis, Veterans Lawn Tennis GB; *Style—* Geoffrey Cass, Esq; Middlefield, Huntingdon Rd, Cambridge CB3 0LH; The Edinburgh Bldg, Shaftesbury Rd, Cambridge CB2 2RU (☎ 0223 312393)

CASS, (Edward) Geoffrey; CB (1974), OBE (1951); s of Edward Charles and Florence Mary Cass; *b* 10 Sept 1916; *Educ* St Olave's, Univ Coll London, Queen's Coll Oxford; *m* 1941, Ruth Mary Powley; 4 da; *Career* economist and statistician; asst under-sec of state MOD 1965-72, dep under-sec of state 1972-76; govr Reserve Bank of Rhodesia 1978-9; *Style—* Geoffrey Cass Esq, CB, OBE; 60 Rotherwick Rd, London NW11 (☎ 01 455 1664)

CASS, Sir John Patrick; OBE (1960); s of Philip and Florence Cass; *b* 7 May 1909; *Educ* Christian Bros Coll NSW; *m* 1932, Velma Mostyn; 2 s; *Career* former sr vice-pres Australian NFU; dir: Farmers and Graziers Co-op Co 1962-; The Land Newspaper Ltd 1964, Queensland Country Life Newspaper 1977; kt 1978; *Style—* Sir John Cass, OBE; Stoney Ridge, Crowther, NSW 2692, Australia

CASS, Richard Martin; s of Edward Charles Cass, of Cheshire, and Hazel Rosemary; *b* 25 May 1946; *Educ* High Wycombe GS, Sheffield Univ (BArch, MA); *m* 1977, Judith Claire, da of Dr Linton Morris Snaith, of Newcastle upon Tyne; 2 s (Simon b 1983, Alexander b 1986); *Career* architect and landscape architect; dir Brian Clouston and Ptnrs 1979-82; princ Cass Assocs 1982-; *Recreations* music, theatre, gardening, sailing, reading; *Style—* Richard M Cass, Esq; Osborne House, Fullwood Park, Liverpool (☎ 051 727 7614); Cass Associates, Albion House, 30 James St, Liverpool (☎ 051 236 9074, fax 051 236 1582)

CASSAB, Judy; CBE (1969); da of late Imre Kaszab; *b* 15 August 1920; *Educ* Budapest and Prague; *m* 1939, John Kampfner; 2 s; *Career* artist; one-man shows 1953-76; works in galleries in UK, Hungary and Australia; *Style—* Miss Judy Cassab, CBE; 156 Victoria Rd, Bellevue Hill, NSW 2023, Australia (☎ 389 4466)

CASSEL, His Hon Judge Sir Harold Felix; 3 Bt (1920 UK), TD (1975), QC (1970); s of Sir Felix Cassel, 1 Bt, PC, QC (d 1953); suc bro, Sir Francis Cassel, 2 Bt (d 1969); *b* 8 Nov 1916; *Educ* Stowe, CCC Oxford; *m* 1, 1940 (m dis 1963), Ione Jean, *née* Barclay; 3 s, 1 da; m 2, 1963, Mrs Eileen Elfrida Smedley, *née* Faulkner; *Heir* s, Timothy Cassel; *Career* barr 1946; dep chm Herts Quarter Sessions 1959-62; rec of Great Yarmouth 1968-71; Crown Court Recorder 1972-76; circuit judge 1976-88; JP Herts 1959-62; *Style—* His Honour Sir Harold Cassel, Bt; 49 Lennox Gdns, London SW1 (☎ 01 584 2721)

CASSEL, Jeremy James; s of Sir Harold Cassel, Bt, QC, TD, of 49 Lennox Gardens, London SW1, and Ione Jean, *née* Barclay; *b* 07 June 1950; *Educ* Eton, Sorbonne; *m* 7 June 1982, Vivien Helen, da of David John Hayter, of Kinghams Farm, Highclere, Berks; 2 s (Hugo b 1982, Felix b 1988), 1 da (Sieglinde b 1984); *Career* mangr Perroquet Restaurant 1975, gen mangr Compleat Angler Marlow 1978, hotels and restaurants conslt 1982, md Cassel Hotels and Restaurants plc 1989; tstee King Edward VII British-German Fndn; *Recreations* racing; *Clubs* Bucks; *Style—* Jeremy Cassel, Esq; Manor Hse, Kirbyunderdale, York (☎ 075 96 519); The Grange Hotel, Clifton, Yorks (☎ 0860 360 194, fax 07596 519)

CASSEL, Timothy Felix Harold; QC (1988); s and h of His Hon Judge Sir Harold Cassel, Bt, TD, QC; *b* 30 April 1942; *Educ* Eton; *m* 1971 (m dis 1975), Jenifer Samuel; 1 s, 1 da; m 2, 1979, Ann, only da of Sir William Mallalieu; 2 da; *Career* barr Lincoln's Inn 1965, jr prosecutor for the Crown of the Central Criminal Ct; asst boundary cmmr 1979; sr prosecutor for the Crown 1986; *Style—* Timothy Cassel, Esq, TD; Studdridge Farm, Stokenchurch, Bucks

CASSELS, Gervase de la Poer; CBE (1971, OBE 1960, MBE 1951); s of late Walter Seton Cassels; *b* 1915; *Educ* Marlborough, St John's Coll Oxford; *m* 1947, Mary Edith, da of James Cresswell; 2 s, 1 da; *Career* Colonial Admin Service Nigeria and Cyprus 1938-60 (dir secondments also to British Mil Admin Ethiopia and British Admin in Libya); with UNRWA for Palestine Refugees in Near East 1967-71 (joined 1960) OStJ 1971; *Style—* Gervase de la Poer Cassels Esq, CBE; 17 Five Mile Dve, Oxford

CASSELS, Field Marshal Sir (Archibald) James (Halkett); GCB (1961, CB 1950), KBE (1952, CBE 1944), DSO (1944); s of late Gen Sir Robert Archibald Cassels, GCB, GCSI, DSO (d 1959), and Florence Emily, *née* Jackson; *b* 28 Feb 1907; *Educ* Rugby, Sandhurst; *m* 1, 1935, Joyce (d 1978), da of late Brig-Gen Henry Kirk; 1 s; m 2, 1978, Joy, wid of Kenneth Dickson; *Career* 2 Lt Seaforth Highlander 1926 (Col 1957-61), Adj-Gen to Forces 1963-64, CGS 1965-68, FM 1968; Col Cmdt: Corps of Royal Mil Police 1957-68, Army Physical Trg Corps 1961-66; Col Queen's Own Highlander (Seaforth and Camerons) 1961-66; ADC (Gen) to HM the Queen 1960-63; *Style—* Field Marshal Sir James Cassels, GCB, KBE, DSO; Hamble End, Higham Rd, Barrow, Bury St Edmunds, Suffolk IP29 5BE (☎ 0284 810895)

CASSELS, John Seton; CB (1978); s of Alastair Macdonald Cassels and Ada White, *née* Scott; *b* 10 Oct 1928; *Educ* Sedbergh Sch Yorks, Trin Cambridge; *m* 1956, Mary Whittington; 2 s, 2 da; *Career* min of Labour 1954, former under-sec Nat Bd for Prices and Incomes, chief exec Trg Services Agency 1972-75, dir Manpower Services Cmmn 1975-81, 2 perm sec 1981-83, dir-gen NEDO 1983-; *Style—* John Cassels Esq, CB; 10 Beverley Rd, Barnes, London SW13 (☎ 01 876 6270)

CASSIDI, Adm Sir (Arthur) Desmond; GCB (1982, KCB 1978); s of Cdr Robert Alexander Cassidi, RN (d 1966), and his 1 wife Clare Florinda, *née* Alexander (d 1925); *b* 26 Jan 1925; *Educ* RNC Dartmouth; *m* 1, 1950, (Dorothy) Sheelagh Marie Scott (d 1974), da of Rev Canon Robert Francis Scott, of Garvagh, Co Derry; 1 s, 2 da; m 2, 1982, Deborah Marion, *née* Bliss; *Career* War Service as Midshipman and Sub-Lt 1942-45, CO HMS Ark Royal 1972-73, Flag Offr Carriers and Amphibious Ships 1974-75, Dir-Gen Naval Manpower Trg 1975-77, Flag Offr Naval Air Cmd 1978-79, Chief of Naval Personnel and Second Sea Lord 1979-82, C-in-C Naval Home Command 1982-85; Flag ADC to HM The Queen 1982-85; pres FAA Museum Yeovilton, tstee Science Museum S Kensington, pres Royal Naval Assoc, dep grand pres Br Cwlth Ex Services League; *Recreations* country pursuits; *Style—* Adm Sir Desmond Cassidi, GCB; c/o Barclays Bank Ltd, 16 Whitehall, London SW1

CASSIDY, Bryan Michael Deece; s of William Francis Deece Cassidy (d 1986) and Kathleen Selina Patricia, *né* Geraghty; *b* 17 Feb 1934; *Educ* Ratcliffe Coll Leicester, Sidney Sussex Coll Cambridge (MA Law); *m* 27 Aug 1960, Gillian Mary, da of Austen Patrick Bohane (d 1988); 1 s (Dominic b 1964), 2 da (Katherine b 1961, Siobhan b 1962); *Career* Cmmnd RA, 1955-57 (Malta and Libya); HAC 1957-62, with Ever Ready, Beechams and Reed Int (dir Euro Associates); memb cncl of the CBI 1981-84, dir-gen Cosmetic, Toiletry and Perfumery Assoc 1981-84; contested Wandsworth Central 1966, memb GLC (Hendon North) 1977-85 (Opposition Spokesman on indust and employment 1983-84); MEP (C) Hampshire West and Dorset East 1984-; *Recreations* country pursuits; *Clubs* Carlton; *Style—* Bryan Cassidy Esq, MEP; 11 Esmond Ct, Thackeray St, London W8 5HB

CASSIDY, Ven George Henry; s of Joseph Abram Cassidy (d 1979), and Ethel, *née* McDonald (d 1973); *b* 17 Oct 1942; *Educ* Belfast HS, Queen's Univ Belfast (BSc), Univ Coll London (MPhil), Oak Hill Theol Coll (MRTPI); *m* 17 Dec 1966, Jane Barling, da of Rev Frank Hayman Stevens; 2 da (Sarah, Gael); *Career* civil servant: NI 1967-68, Govt of Kenya 1968-70; curate Christ Church Clifton Bristol 1972-75; vicar: St Edyth's Sea Mills Bristol 1975-82, St Paul's Portman Sq W1 1982-87; archdeacon of London and canon residentiary of St Paul's Cathedral 1987-; Freedom of the City of London 1988, Liveryman Worshipful Co of Tylers and Bricklayers 1988; *Recreations* rugby football, art, chamber music; *Clubs* National; *Style—* The Ven the Archdeacon of London; 2 Amen Ct, Warwick Lane, London EC4M 7BU (☎ 01 248 3312, fax 01 489 8579)

CASSIDY, Mark Anthony; s of Anthony Roland Richard Jessie Patrick Cassidy, of Fownehope, Herefordshire, and Pauline Joyce Cassidy; *b* 27 Mar 1953; *Educ* King Edward VI Sch Bath, Univ of York (BA); *m* 25 Sept 1982, Lynne Kezia, da of Herbert Reginald Grainger (d 1978); 1 s (David b 1983), 1 da (Sarah b 1985); *Career* slr to the Bromyard and Winslow Town Cncl 1982-; sr ptnr Rutter & Senior Slrs Bromyard and Wedbury; *Recreations* rugby; *Style—* Mark A Cassidy, Esq; The Old Rectory, Putley, Ledbury, Herefordshire (☎ 0531 83 288); 38 High St, Bromyard, Herefordshire (☎ 0885 82323)

CASSIDY, Michael Warren Arkinstall; s of George Edward Cassidy, of Kew, Richmond, Surrey, and Kathleen Mary, *née* Roberts; *b* 22 Mar 1939; *Educ* Latymer Upper Sch Hammersmith, UCL (BA Arch), Univ of California (Harkness Fellowship MCP); *m* 1, 5 Jan 1963 (m dis) Mary Madeline, da of Joseph Burnhill; m 2, 13 Nov 1981, Marianthi, da of Constantino P Constantinu (d 1969); 1 da (Melina b 1982); *Career* architect and town planner; head planner environmental studies gp GLC 1970-75, ptnr Cassidy Taggart Ptnrship; work includes until 1983: Warwick Univ, John Radcliffe Hosp, teaching hosp Enugu Nigeria, med coll Basrah Univ Iraq (large commissions: Bahrain, Hong Kong, Jordan) 1983-: residences for heads of State, Govt Conf Centre Kuwait, maj ind commercial and planning projects UK, Middle and Far East; visiting prof (arch) Washington Univ St Louis, lectr Univ Coll, dir Mantra Ltd; RIBA (chm NE Thames architectural soc), MRTPI; *Books* frequent tech papers in architectural jls; *Recreations* walking, travelling; *Style—* Michael Cassidy, Esq; 47 Highpoint, North Hill, London N6 4BA (☎ 01 341 4884); Cassidy Taggart Ptnrship, 22 Little Portland St, London W1N 5AF (☎ 01 580 5791, telex 23152, fax 01 323 0630)

CASSIDY, Thomas Daniel; s of Joseph Cassidy (d 1963), and Mary *née* Gilligan (d 1974); *b* 3 May 1920; *Educ* St Dunstan's RC Elementary Sch Manchester; *m* 16 Sept 1944, Bridget Mary (Bridie), da of the late Joseph Donnelly, of Belfast NI; 2 s (Paul b 1945, Timothy b 1958), 4 da (Bernadette b 1949, Patsy b 1951, Frances b 1961, Michelle b 1963); *Career* started Cassidy Brothers in 1946 (now chm and md); former memb Lions Club, Rotary Club; current memb Catenian Assoc (past pres) Blackpool & Fylde Soc for the blind; past sr master Vale of Lune Harriers; former chm & vice pres of Br Toy & Hobby Assoc; *Recreations* hunting, shooting, fishing, photography; *Style—* Thomas Cassidy, Esq; Calder House, Garstang, Nr Preston, Lancs PR3 1ZE (☎ 09952 3345); Cassidy Brothers Plc, Casdon Works Mitcham Road, Blackpool, Lancs FV4 4QW (☎ 0253 66411, fax 0253 691486, telex 67293 CASDON G)

CASSILLIS, Earl of; Archibald Angus Charles Kennedy; s and h of 7 Marquess of Ailsa, OBE, DL, *qv*; *b* 13 Sept 1956; *m* 1979 (m dis 1989), Dawn Leslie Anne, o da of David A Keen, of Paris; 2 da (Lady Rosemary Margaret b 1980, Lady Alicia-Jane Lesley b 1981); *Heir* bro, Lord David Kennedy; *Recreations* shooting, skiing, youth work; *Clubs* New (Edinburgh); *Style—* Earl of Cassillis; Cassillis House, Maybole, Ayrshire (☎ Dalrymple 310)

CASSON, Sir Hugh Maxwell; CH (1985), KCVO (1978); s of late Randal Casson, and late May Caroline, *née* Man; *b* 23 May 1910; *Educ* Eastbourne Coll, St John's Coll Cambridge; *m* 1938, Margaret MacDonald, da of Dr James MacDonald Troup, of Pretoria; 3 da; *Career* architect; dir of architecture Festival of Britain 1948-51, Prof Royal Coll of Art 1953-75, memb Royal Fine Art Cmmn 1960-83, pres Royal Acad 1976-84, architectural advsr to Commons Servs Ctee 1983-; hon fell UCL 1983; kt 1952; *Books* Hugh Casson's London Diary (1980), Hugh Casson's London, Hugh Casson's Oxford (1987); *Style—* Sir Hugh Casson, CH, KCVO; 6 Hereford Mansions, Hereford Rd, London W2 5BA; office: 35 Thurloe Place, London SW7 (☎ 01 584 4581)

CASSTLES, Col David Stewart; TD, DL (Essex 1983); s of Joseph Cecil Casstles (d 1956); *b* 5 Mar 1936; *Educ* Brentwood Sch, Cambridge Univ; *m* 1964, Lynne Frances, *née* Alexandre; 1 s (Andrew b 1969), 1 da (Amanda b 1966); *Career* Col TA 1983-; investment banker; *Recreations* opera-going, dining, shooting, volunteer soldiering; *Clubs* Army and Navy; *Style—* Col David Casstles, TD, DL; Sandylay House, Great Leighs, Essex CM3 1PS (☎ 0245 361258, Leighs 034 534 258)

CASSWELL, Hon Mrs (Helen Jennifer Frances); *née* Annesley; yst da of 14 Viscount Valentia, MC, MRCS, LRCP; *b* 13 Oct 1935; *m* 1957, Simon FitzRoy Casswell, yst s of His Honour Joshua David Casswell, QC (d 1963); 1 s, 2 da; *Style—* The Hon Mrs Casswell; The Limes Farm, Smarden, nr Ashford, Kent

CASTENSKIOLD, Holger; s of Ludvig Helmuth Frederik Holger Castenskiold (d 1957), of Gyllingnaes, Denmark, and Gudrun, *née* Thorsen; *b* 5 April 1931; *Educ* Oester Farimagsgade Sch Oester Borgerdyd Copenhagen, Commercial HS Copenhagen, City of London Coll ; *m* 27 Oct 1962, Gurli Bering, da of Capt Arthur Hermann Franz Pittelkow (d 1964), of Copenhagen; 1 s (Erik b 1 Feb 1967), 1 da (Birgitte b 14 Dec 1963); *Career* Royal Danish Navy 1951-52; The East Asiatic Co Ltd (Copenhagen, London, Manila, Singapore) 1949-72; md: Utd Baltic Corpn Ltd 1972-, MacAndrews & Co Ltd 1973-, Bank Line Ltd 1989- (dir 1977-), Andrew Weir Shipping Ltd 1989-; dir Andrew & Co Ltd 1989-; chm Philippines Europe Conf Manila 1957-59, actg hon Royal Danish Consul Manila 1960-61; chm Assoc of Int Steamship Lines Manila 1961, London Steamship Owners Mutual Insur Assoc 1985-; memb Baltic Exchange 1972; *Recreations* golf, gardening, travels, reading; *Clubs* Moor Park Golf, Les Ambassadeurs, Wig and Pen; *Style—* Holger Castenskiold, Esq; 1 The Broad Walk, Northwood, Middx HA6 5AU (☎ 09274 22875); 21 Bury St, London EC3A 5AU (☎ 01 283 1266, fax 01 623 6024, telex 892728)

CASTLE, Rt Hon Barbara Anne; PC (1964), MEP (Lab) Gtr Manchester N 1979-84, Gtr Manchester W 1984-89; Baroness Castle; da of Frank and Annie Rebecca Betts; *b* 6 Oct 1910; *Educ* Bradford Girls' GS, St Hugh's Coll Oxford; *m* 1944, Edward (Ted) Cyril Castle (d 1979), cr Baron Castle (Life Peer) 1974; *Career* MP (Lab): Blackburn 1945-50, Blackburn E 1950-55, Blackburn 1955-79; memb nat exec ctee of Labour Party 1950-85, chm Labour Party 1959; min of Overseas Dvpt 1964-65, min of Transport 1965-68, first sec of state and sec of state Employment and Productivity 1968-70, oppn spokesman on Employment 1971, sec of state for Social Servs 1974-76; vice-chm Socialist Gp European Parl 1979-85; *Publications* The Castle Diaries 1974-76 (1981), The Castle Diaries 1964-70 (1984), Sylvia and Christabel Pankhurst (1987); *Style*— The Rt Hon Barbara Castle, MEP; Headland House, 308 Gray's Inn Rd, London WC1 (☎ 01 833 4898)

CASTLE, Geoffrey Ellis Trevor; s of Richard Basil Trevor Castle, OBE (d 1986), of Cuckfield, West Sussex, and Geraldine Therese, *née* Ellis; *b* 12 August 1936; *Educ* Uppingham. Coll of Estate Mgmnt; *m* 5 Oct 1963, Sarah Margaret Sherwin, da of Francis (Frank) Neville (d 1986), of Cookham, Berks; 2 da (Frances b 1966, Helen b 1968); *Career* asst surveyor Jones Lang Wootton 1961-69, ptnr BA James and Co 1970- 72, dir Herring Daw 1972-76, ptnr Dron and Wright 1976- (sr ptnr since 1984); Freeman: City of London, Worshipful Co of Chartered Surveyors 1984, ARICS 1961, FRICS 1973; *Recreations* gardening, arts; *Style*— Geoffrey Castle, Esq; St George's House, 12a St George St, London W1 (☎ 01 491 7332)

CASTLE, Norman Henry; s of Hubert William Castle, MBE, and Elizabeth May Castle; *b* 1 Sept 1913; *Educ* Ludlow GS; *m* 1939, Ivy Olive Watson; 1 da (decd); *Career* chm: Wace Gp Ltd, Condale Investments Ltd, Smith Castle and Co Ltd, Hookcastle Ltd; underwriting memb of Lloyds; *Style*— Norman Castle Esq; The Penthouse, 39 Courcels, Black Rock, Brighton, E Sussex BN2 5UB (☎ 0273 681039)

CASTLE STEWART, 8 Earl (I 1800) Arthur Patrick Avondale; 15 Bt (S 1628); also Baron Castle Stuart (I 1619 I), and Viscount Castle Stuart (I 1793); s of 7 Earl Castle Stewart, MC (d 1961), and Eleanor, da of Solomon R Guggenheim; *b* 18 August 1928; *Educ* Eton, Trinity Coll Cambridge; *m* 1952, Edna, da of William Edward Fowler; 1 s, 1 da; *Heir* s, Viscount Stuart; *Career* late Lt Scots Gds; farmer; FBIM; *Clubs* Carlton; *Style*— The Rt Hon the Earl Castle Stewart; Stone House, East Pennard, nr Shepton Mallet, Somerset BA4 6RZ (☎ Ditcheat 240); Stuart Hall, Stewartstown, Co Tyrone (☎ Stewartstown 208)

CASTLE STEWART, Eleanor, Countess Eleanor May; er da of Solomon R Guggenheim, of New York; *b* 1896; *m* 1920, 7 Earl Castle Stewart (d 1961); 2 s; *Style*— The Rt Hon Eleanor, Countess Castle Stewart; Old Lodge, Nutley, Sussex

CASTLEMAINE, 8 Baron (I 1812); Roland Thomas John Handcock; MBE; s of late 7 Baron (d 1973); *b* 22 April 1943; *Educ* Campbell Coll Belfast; *m* (m dis); *Heir* kinsman, Terence Robin Handcock, *qv*; *Career* Lt.Col Army Air Corps; *Style*— The Rt Hon the Lord Castlemaine; c/o Lloyds Bank, Aldershot, Hants

CASTLEMAN, Christopher Norman Anthony; s of James Stanley Phillips (d 1969), and Joan Doris, *née* Srring-Rice Pyper; *b* 23 June 1941; *Educ* Harrow, Clare Coll Cambridge (MA); *m* 1, 1967, Sarah Victoria (d 1979), da of Judge Frank Alleyne Stockdale, of Gwent; 1 s (Jonathan b 1971), 1 da (Amanda b 1967); m 2, 1980, Caroline Clare, da of Thomas Norman Westcott, of S Africa; 2 da (Alexandra b 1982, Georgia b 1984); *Career* corporate fin dept Hill Samuel & Co Ltd (formerly H Samuel & Co Ltd) 1965-69, gen mangr Hill Samuel Aust Ltd 1970-72, corporate fin dir Hill Samuel & Co Ltd 1973-75; md: Hill Samuel Int Ltd 1976-77, Hill Samuel Gp (SA) Ltd 1978-80; chief exec Hill Samuel Gp plc 1980 (resigned from the bd 1987), chief exec Blue Arrow plc 1987 (resigned from the bd 1988); fin advsr Christopher Castleman & Co 1988; *Recreations* travel, sports; *Clubs* MCC (Associate); *Style*— Christopher Castleman, Esq; 190 Strand, London WC2R 1DT (☎ 01 379 5040)

CASTLEREAGH, Viscount; Frederick Aubrey Vane-Tempest-Stewart; s (by 2 m) and h of 9 Marq of Londonderry; *b* 6 Sept 1972; *Style*— Viscount Castlereagh

CASTONGUAY, Lady Marina June; da of 7 Marquess of Exeter by his 2 w, Lillian; *b* 16 June 1956; *Educ* Vancouver City Coll; *m* 1980, Peter Castonguay, s of Nelson Castonguay, of Ottawa; 1 s (Dylan b 1984), 1 da (Majessa b 1983); *Career* shop owner, mangr and mother; *Recreations* tennis, cross-country skiing, swimming; *Style*— Lady Marina Castonguay; PO Box 8, 100 Mile House, Br Columbia V0K 2E0, Canada (☎ 604 395 3717, work 395 4311)

CASWELL, Gp Capt Arthur William; CBE 1961, (OBE 1946); s of late William George Caswell; *b* 8 August 1906; *Educ* Swindon & North Wilts Secdy Sch and Tech Inst (Swindon Coll); *m* 7 July 1934, Rhoda Mary; 1 s (Alan Godfrey); *Career* 3 Entry Halton Aircraft Apprentices 1923-25; Fleet Air Arm 1927-29 and 1935-37; WWII 1939-45; (despatches 1945) Devp Choir West Europe Est Com RAF 1947/8; Asst Cmdt No 2 S of TT RAF Cosford 1956-59 (Cmdt and Station Cdr 1959-61); diocesan sec and sec bd of fin Hereford Diocese 1961-74; hon admin Hereford Cathedral 1974-82 (emeritus 1982); memb Gen Synod C of E 1965-80; life vice pres Hereford Branch RAF Assoc; CEng, MRAeS, FInstBE; *Clubs* RAF; *Style*— Gp Capt Arthur Caswell, CBE; Tralohr, 5 Pentaloe Close, Mordiford, Hereford HR1 4LS (☎ 0432 73 425)

CASWELL, Donald; s of late George Clement Caswell; *b* 17 April 1926; *Educ* Wilsons; *m* 1, 1952, Margaret Sheila, *née* Nurse-Lewis (d 1969); 1 s, 1 da; m 2, 1970, Susan Ann, *née* Thompson; *Career* chartered accountant; gp dep dir of finance and tres Inchcape Gp 1953-84 (ret); FCA, FCT, FBIM; *Clubs* Oriental; *Style*— Donald Caswell, Esq; Old Linkfield, Hatchlands Rd, Redhill, Surrey RH1 6AE (☎ 0737 763417)

CATCHPOLE, Nancy Mona; OBE (1987); da of George William Page (d 1980), of New Eltham, and Mona Dorothy, *née* Cowin (d 1979); *b* 6 August 1929; *Educ* Haberdashers' Aske's Hatchman Girls Sch, Bedford Coll London Univ (BA); *m* 1959, Geoffrey David Arthur Catchpole; 1 s, 1 da; *Career* pres Br Fedn of Univ Women 1981-84, co-chm Women's Nat Cmmn 1985-88; conslt to indust matters for women's trg roadshow programme 1989; memb of Wessex Regnl Health Authy 1986-; FRSA 1986; *Clubs* Crosby Hall; *Style*— Nancy Catchpole, OBE; 66 Leighton Rd, Weston, Bath BA1 4NG (☎ 0225 23338); Industry Matters, Royal Soc for Arts, 8 John Adam St, London WC2M 6EZ (☎ 01 930 9129/39)

CATER, Sir Jack; KBE (1979, CBE 1973, MBE 1956); yr s of Alfred Francis Cater and Pamela Elizabeth Dukes; *b* 21 Feb 1922; *Educ* Sir George Monoux GS Walthamstow; *m* 1950, Peggy Gwenda Richards; 1 s, 2 da; *Career* Colonial Admin Service Hong Kong 1946, dir Commerce and Industry 1970-72, sec for Information 1972, for Home Affairs and Information 1973, chief sec 1978-; *Style*— Sir Jack Cater, KBE; Victoria House, Hong Kong (☎ 5 96696)

CATER, Sir Robin John Robert; s of Sir John James Cater (d 1962), of Edinburgh, and Jessie Sheila MacDonald, *née* Moodie (d 1948); *b* 25 April 1919; *Educ* George Watson's Coll Edinburgh, Jesus Coll Cambridge (MA); *m* 1945, Isobel Calder Ritchie; 1 da; *Career* chm: The Distillers Co 1976-83, The Scotch Whisky Assoc 1976-1983; kt 1984; *Style*— Sir Robin Cater; Avernish, Elie, Fife, Scotland KY9 1DA (☎ (0333) 330 667)

CATES, Armel Conyers; s of Conyers Seely Cates (d 1965), of Guildford, and Jacqueline Maude, *née* Geoffroy (d 1988); *b* 3 May 1943; *Educ* Charterhouse, Southampton Univ (LLB); *m* 8 July 1967, Pamela Susan, da of Colin Huson Walker, of Fowlmere, Cambs; 2 s (Tom b 1974, Sam b 1978), 1 da (Ilaria b 1980); *Career* articled to Theodore Goddard (London) and Vinters (Cambridge) 1967-69, slr 1969; asst slr Coward Chance 1970-72, Clifford Turner 1972-76, ptnr Clifford Chance 1976-; tstee Charterhouse Mission in Southwark, memb of City of London slrs Co; memb: Law Soc 1969, Int Bar Assoc; ed advsr Int Financial Law Review; *Recreations* golf, tennis, photography; *Style*— Armel Cates, Esq; Graves Farm, Catmere End, Saffron Walden, Essex CB11 4XG; Clifford Chance, Royex House, Aldermanbury Sq, London EC2V 7LD (☎ 01 600 0808, fax 01 726 8561, telex 8959991 G)

CATES, Dr Joseph Elmhirst; s of Dr Henry Joseph Cates (d 1969), and Rosa, *née* Elmhirst; *b* 22 June 1914; *Educ* Clifton, St Bartholomews (MD); *m* 6 Aug 1955, Dr Mary Elizabeth, da of Frank Willoughby Moore (d 1953); 4 s (Christopher J, Robert J W, Michael E, Andrew T), 2 da (Anne R, Kathleen M); *Career* RNVR Surgn Lt 1940, Lt Cdr 1943-46; house physician and chief asst med prof unit St Bartholomews 1936-40 and 1946-50, conslt physician Bristol Royal Infirmary 1951-79, med postgrad dean Univ of Bristol 1957-80, emeritus conslt physician Avon AHA; Hon MD Univ of Bristol 1981; FRCP; *Style*— Dr Joseph Cates; 11 Cedar Park, Bristol BS9 1BW

CATFORD, Gordon Vivian; s of Harry George Bascombe (d 1984), of 19 Uphill Rd, North, Weston-super-Mare, and Gladys Annie, *née* Horton (d 1951); *b* 23 Nov 1927; *Educ* Clifton, Bristol Univ (MB ChB); *m* 10 June 1955, June Crichton, da of Robert Baxter (d 1983), of 8 Craigleith View, Edinburgh 4; 2 s (Gordon Baxter b 1958, Paul Nicholas b 1961); *Career* Nat Serv Sqdn Ldr RAF Med Br CME 1954-56; house appts: Bristol Infirmary 1951-52, Bristol Eye Hosp 1952-54; chief clinical asst Moorfields Eye Hosp 1960-64, (house appt 1958-60); conslt ophthalmic surgn: St Georges Hosp London 1963-88 (first asst 1961-63), Royal London Homoeopathic Hosp 1969-88, Royal Masonic Hosp London 1973-, St Lukes Hosp for the Clergy 1988-; ophthalmologist: Linden Lodge Sch for the Blind 1978-89, Greenmead Sch for Multiple Handicapped 1978-89, John Aird Sch 1978-; memb Med Appeals Tbnl London South 1988-, advsr Br Orthoptic Soc; govr Linden Lodge Sch 1978-89, Clifton Coll; hon fell of orthoptics Br Orthoptic Soc 1988; Freeman City of London 1963, Liveryman Soc of Apothecaries 1963; memb BMA 1952-, FRSM 1961-, FRCS 1961-, fell Coll of Opthalmology 1988-; *Recreations* gardening; *Style*— Gordon Catford, Esq; 9 St Johns Wood Park, London NW8 6QP; 11 Devonshire Place, London W1N 1PB, (☎ 01 935 9523)

CATFORD, (John) Robin; er s of Adrian Leslie Catford, MIAE (d 1979), and Ethel Augusta *née* Rolfe (d 1988); *b* 11 Jan 1923; *Educ* Hampton GS, St Andrews Univ (BSc), St Johns Coll Cambridge (Dip Agric); *m* 21 Aug 1948, Daphne Georgina, da of Col John Francis Darby, CBE, TD (d 1950); 3 s (John Charles b 1949, Simon Leslie b 1956, Francis James Robin b 1959), 1 da (Lucy Georgina b 1952); *Career* Sudan CS Dept of Agric and Forests 1946-55, commercial appts in UK 1955-66; MAFF 1966-82 (princ 1966, asst sec 1972, under sec 1979); transfered to PM's Off 1982, sec for appts to PM and ecclesiastical sec to Lord Chllr 1982-; *Recreations* sailing, travel, theatre, arts; *Clubs* United Oxford and Cambridge University; *Style*— Robin Catford, Esq; 27 Blackthorns, Lindfield, Haywards Heath, West Sussex, RH16 2AX (☎ 0444 451896); 10 Downing St, London SW1A 2AA

CATHCART, 6 Earl (UK 1814); Alan Cathcart; CB (1973), DSO (1945), MC (1944); also 15 Lord Cathcart (S *circa* 1447), Baron Greenock and Viscount Cathcart (both UK 1807); s of 5 Earl Cathcart (d 1927), and Vera Estelle, *née* Fraser (now Dowager Lady Hodge); *b* 22 August 1919; *Educ* Eton, Magdalene Coll Cambridge; *m* 1, 1946, Rosemary Clare Marie Gabrielle (d 1980), da of late Air-Cdre Sir Henry Smyth-Osborne, CMG, CBE; 1 s, 2 da; m 2, 1984, Marie Isobel, da of late Hon William Joseph French (3 s of 4 Baron de Freyne), and widow of Sir Thomas Brian Weldon, 8 Bt; *Heir* s, Lord Greenock (*qv*); *Career* sits as Cons in House of Lords; 2 Lt Scots Gds 1939; Brig Operations Div SHAPE 1967-69, Maj-Gen 1969, GOC Yorks Dist 1969-70, GOC Berlin (Br Sector) 1970-73, ret; dep speaker House of Lords 1976-89; pres ROSPA 1982-86; Brig Queen's Body Guard for Scotland (Royal Co of Archers); Commodore Royal Yacht Sqdn 1974-80; dep grand pres Br Cwlth Ex-Services League 1975-86; Lord Prior Order of St. John of Jerusalem 1985-88; pres Army Cadet Force Assoc 1976-82; *Clubs* Brooks's, Royal Yacht Squadron; *Style*— The Rt Hon the Earl Cathcart, CB, DSO, MC; 2 Pembroke Gardens Close, London W8 (☎ 01 602 4535); Moor Hatches, W Amesbury, Salisbury, Wilts

CATHERWOOD, Sir (Henry) Frederick Ross; MEP (EDG) Cambridgeshire 1979-; s of late Harold Matthew Stuart, and late Jean Catherwood, of Co Londonderry; *b* 30 Jan 1925; *Educ* Shrewsbury, Clare Coll Cambridge; *m* 1954, Elizabeth, er da of Rev Dr D Martyn Lloyd-Jones, of Westminster Chapel, London; 2 s, 1 da; *Career* chm: Br Inst of Mgmnt 1974-76, Br Overseas Trade Bd 1975-79, Euro Parl Ctee on External Economic Relations 1979-84; dir The Goodyear Tyre and Rubber Co (GB) Ltd; dep ldr Cons Euro MPs 1983-87; kt 1971; *Books* The Christian in Industrial Society (1964), The Christian Citizen (1969), A Better Way (1976), First Things First (1979), God's Time God's Money (1987); FCA (1951); *Recreations* music, gardening, reading; *Clubs* United Oxford and Cambridge; *Style*— Sir Fred Catherwood, MEP; Sutton Hall, Balsham, Cambridgeshire

CATHIE, Dr Ian Aysgarth Bewley; DL (Warwickshire 1973-); s of George Ernest Cathie (d 1968), of Ewell, Surrey, and Lilly Jane Pickford-Evans (d 1969); *b* 3 Jan 1908; *Educ* Guy's Hosp, London and Zürich Univs (MD, BS); *m* 1938, Marian Josephine (d 1982), da of Joseph Cunning, FRCS (d 1947), of Broome Park, Betchworth Surrey; 1 s (Hamish), 3 da (Janet, Alison, Kyle); *Career* Maj RAMC 1940-45; clinical pathologist The Hosp for Sick Children Gt Ormond St 1938-60; jt-ed Archives of Disease in Childhood 1949-62; hon fell Inst of Child Health 1983; Warwickshire CC 1963-77 (chm 1973-76); MRCP, FRCPath; landowner (750 acres); *Recreations* hunting, gardening; *Clubs* Chelsea Arts, Saintsbury; *Style*— Dr Ian Cathie, DL; Barton Ho, Barton-on-the-Heath, Moreton-in-Marsh, Glos (☎ 0608 74303)

CATHIE, Kyle Anne Bewley; da of Dr Ian Aysgarth Bewley Cathie of Warwickshire and Dr Marion Josephine *née* Cunning (d 1983); *b* 10 Oct 1948; *Educ* Chipping Norton GS, Cheltenham Ladies Coll; *m* 21 April 1973, David Charles ap Simon; 2 s (Thomas b 1978, Nicholas b 1980), 1 da (Josephine b 1985); *Career* former sr ed Pan Books, ed dir Elm Tree Books 1983-86; Papermac publisher; dir MacMillan London Ltd 1987-; *Books* Complete Calorie Counter (1978), Complete Carbohydrate Counter (1980), The Corgi Calorie Counter (1989); *Recreations* bee keeping, opera, reading; *Style—* Ms Kyle Cathie; 4 Little Essex Street, London WC2 (☎ 01 836 6633)

CATO, Senator the Hon Sir Arnott Samuel; KCMG (1983), PC (1976 Barbados); *b* 24 Sept 1912; *Educ* St Vincent GS, Edinburgh Univ; *Career* formerly surgeon in private practice; memb and pres Senate of Barbados 1976-; kt 1977; *Style—* Senator the Hon Sir Arnott Cato, KCMG; Arndale, Government Hill, St Michael, Barbados (☎ 4293962); Senate House, Bridgetown, Barbados

CATO, Brian Hudson; s of Thomas Cato (d 1972), and Edith Willis Hudson (d 1976); *b* 6 June 1928; *Educ* LEA Elementary and GS, Trinity Coll Oxford (MA) London Univ LLB; *m* 1963, Barbara Edith, da of Harry Myles (d 1977); 1 s (Paul Marcus b 1964); *Career* pilot offr RAF 1952-54; barr NE circuit 1954-75, rec Crown Ct 1974-75; industl tbnl chm 1975-; Freeman: Newcastle upon Tyne 1950, City of London 1985; *Recreations* bibliomania, antiquarian studies and family life; *Style—* Brian Cato, Esq; 46 Bemersyde Drive, Jesmond, Newcastle Upon Tyne NE2 2HJ (☎ 091 281 4226); 2 Croft Place, High Newton-by-the Sea, Alnwick Northumberland (☎ 066 576 334); Plummer House, Market Street East, Newcastle Upon Tyne NE1 6NF

CATO, Michael John; s of William Henry Cato (d 1978), and Cladys Annie Hayes; *b* 13 Dec 1933; *Educ* Mercers Sch London; *m* 1, 1959, Rosemary (d 1978), da of Thomas Tapping; 2 s (Timothy b 1961, Alastair b 1963), 2 da (Jane Rosalind b 1960, Catherine b 1966); m 2, 1985, Helen Peeples, da of Col Leonard Frederick Butler (d 1968); 1 step son (Benson b 1977), 2 step da (Lesley b 1976, Emily b 1979); *Career* chm and md William Cato and Sons Ltd 1971- (dir 1961); chm and dir Br Hardware Fedn Merchandising Co 1981-85; memb nat ctee Br Hardware Fedn 1974- (memb Bd of Mgmnt 1976-85, chm Marketing Gp 1981-85); memb Royal Metal Trades Bd of Mgmnt 1982-87; churchwarden Benefice of Farnham Royal St Mary's Hedgerley 1974-84, Burnham Deanery Synod 1970-84; fell Nat Inst of Hardware; *Recreations* cricket, sailing, association football; *Clubs* MCC, Old Mercers', Farnham CC (pres 1988-89); *Style—* Michael Cato, Esq; Lawday House Farm, Follyhill, Farnham, Surrey GU10 5AB (☎ Farnham 715562); William Cato and Sons Ltd, 6 Alexandra Terrace, Alexandra Rd, Aldershot, Hants (☎ Aldershot 334871)

CATOR, Albemarle John; s of John Cator, of Woodbastwick, Norfolk, and Elizabeth Jane, *née* Kerrison; *b* 23 August 1953; *Educ* Harrow; *m* 27 Nov 1980, Fiona Mary, da of Robert Edgar Atheling Drummond; 2 s (John b 1983, Robert Henry b 1985); *Career* Lt Scots Guards 1971-74; with Samuel Montagu 1975-84; exec dir Chemical Bank Int Ltd 1984-88; exec dir Chemical Securities Ltd 1988-; vice-pres Chemical Bank 1988-; *Recreations* sailing, shooting, skiing; *Clubs* RYS, Pratts; *Style—* Albemarle Cator, Esq; Whitehouse Farm, Woodbastwick, Norwich, Norfolk; Chemical Bank House, 180 Strand, London WC2R 1EX (☎ 01 379 7474)

CATOR, Hon Jacquetta; *née* Storey; only da of Baron Buckton (Life Peer), who d 1978, and sis of the Hon Sir Richard Storey, 2 Bt *qv*; *b* 19 April 1930; *m* 1956, Francis Cator, yr s of Lt-Col Henry John Cator, OBE, MC (d 1965), of Woodbastick Hall, Norwich, Norfolk; 3 s, 1 da; *Style—* The Hon Mrs Cator; 12 Warwick Square Mews, London SW1 (☎ 01 821 0920); The Old House, Ranworth, Norfolk (☎ 060 549 300)

CATOR, Lady (Wilhelmina) Joan Mary; *née* Fitz-Clarence; raised to rank of an Earl's da 1928; da of late Maj the Hon Harold Edward Fitz-Clarence, MC, and sis of 5 Earl of Munster (d 1975); *b* 1904; *m* 1, 1928, Oliver Birkbeck (d 1952); 2 s (*see* Birkbeck, Edward Harold, John Oliver) 1 da; m 2, 1961, Lt-Col Henry John Cator, OBE, MC (d 1965); *Style—* Lady Joan Cator; Little Massingham House, King's Lynn, Norfolk

CATOR, Peter John; s of Sir Geoffrey Cator, CMG (d 1973), and Elizabeth Margaret Wynne, *née* Mostyn; *b* 26 Oct 1924; *Educ* Shrewsbury Sch, CCC Cambridge; *m* 23 Jan 1951, Katharine Verd, da of Capt the Hon Reginald Coke, DSO (d 1969); 1 s (Charles Henry b 1952), 1 da (Caroline Sarah b 1954); *Career* WW II RAFVR and Welsh Gds (Lt) 1943-47; HM Overseas Civil Serv 1949-62; Nigeria sr District Offr Petroleum Indust Trg Bd 1967-82; *Style—* Peter J Cator, Esq; Paxton House, Blockley, Moreton Marsh, Glos GL56 9BA (☎ 0386 700213)

CATTELL, George Harold Bernard; s of Harold William Kingston Cattell (d 1955); *b* 23 Mar 1920; *Educ* Royal GS Colchester, Staff Coll Camberley, Royal Mil Coll of Science; *m* 1951, Agnes Jean, da of Brig John Hardy (d 1969); 3 s (Jonathan, Jeremy, Simon), 1 da (Sarah); *Career* served with RA Maj; asst dir London Engrg Employers Fedn 1958-60; with Rootes Gp and Chrysler Organisation 1960-68 (former dir of manufacturing UK Chrysler); dir of Manpower and Productivity Services Dept of Employment and Productivity 1968-70; dir-gen Nat Farmers' Union 1970-78; chief exec (former gp md) FMC Gp plc (meat wholesalers) 1978-, chief exec NFU Hldgs Ltd 1978-84; FBIM, FRSA; *Recreations* tennis, fishing; *Clubs* Institute of Directors; *Style—* George Cattell, Esq; Little Cheveney, Yalding, Kent (☎ Hunton 365)

CATTERALL, (Robert) Christopher Fielden; s of Rev Robert Catterall (d 1914), and Sarah, *née* Fielden (d 1958); *b* 5 April 1910; *Educ* Rugby, Trinity Coll Cambridge, Univ Coll Hosp (MB, BCh (Cantab) 1938, MCh (Cantab) 1941); *m* 31 July 1934, (Phyllis) Joyce Margery, da of Arthur Sykes (d 1928); 2 s (Anthony b 1936, Richard Ian Robert b 1943), 1 da ((Penelope) Jane b 1939); *Career* vice-pres Br Orthopaedic Assoc 1972, pres Section of Orthopaedics in Royal Soc of Med 1971 (Hon Memb of the Section 1986), pres Medical Protection Soc 1978-82, ed Br Vol, Journal of Bone and Jt Surgery 1973-83; MRCS LRCP 1034, FRCS 1938; *Recreations* amateur gardening; *Style—* Christopher Catterall, Esq; Heath Lodge, Headley, Epsom KT18 6NJ (☎ 0372 377336)

CATTERALL, John Stewart; s of John Bernard Catterall (d 1965), and Eliza, *née* Whitiker; *b* 13 Jan 1939; *Educ* Blackpool Tech Coll Sch of Art; *m* 18 Sept 1965, (Ann) Beryl, da of Edgar Watkin Hughes; 2 s (Andrew b 4 Aug 1969, Stewart b 3 Feb 1971); *Career* Nat Serv band memb 12 Royal Lancers 1958-60; dep auditor Preston Co Borough Cncl: 1966-68, sr accountant Derby Co Borugh Cncl 1968-70, mgmnt and chief accoutant Cambs and Isle of Ely CC 1970-73, asst co tres Cambs CC 1973-76, dist tres Southampton & SW Hants Health Authy 1976-78, area tres Hants AHA 1978-82, regnl tres NE Thames RHA 1982-85; CIPFA: dep dir fin mgmnt and head health serv 1985-88, dir health gp 1988-; *Recreations* golf, tennis; *Style—* John Catterall, Esq; Birkdale, Green Lane, Chilworth, Hants (☎ 0703 769402); Heron House, 10 Dean Farrar Street, London SW1H 0DX (☎ 01 222 3433, fax 01 222 2988, car tel 086052 3068)

CATTLE, Walter Edmund (Tony); s of Lt-Col Edward Arthur Cattle (d 1969), of Pinner, and Margret Doris Williams (d 1952); *b* 12 July 1937; *Educ* Westminster Tech Coll, Regent St Poly; *m* 1, 4 May 1963 (m dis 30 June 1988), Linda, da of Sidney James Theobold (d 1970); 2 da (Joy Dawn b 22 May 1968, Anne Julia b 7 Sept 1970); m 2, 10 Aug 1988, Catriona McLean, da of John Challen (d 1988); *Career* RAF marine engr Air Sea Rescue 1955-60, Pilot Offr Volunteer Reserve Trg 1961-63; dir (later chm) Higgins & Cattle (int building servs) 1960-; capt of Br Flight Team 1977, holder world record for the most number of landings at different airports in a day 1976; holder world speed record London/Spitzburgh 1977; memb Runnymede Borough Cncl: former chm enviromental health and gen purposes ctees, vice chm highway ctee; pres League of Friends of St Peters Hosp Chertsey; Freeman City of London 1970; memb: Worshipful Co of Glaziers, Worshipful Co of Lightmongers (master 1975); FIAA 1987, FIEEE 1969; *Recreations* clay pigeon shooting; *Style—* Tony Cattle, Esq; Linton Lodge, Fan Ct Gardens, Longcross Rd, Longcross, Chertsey, Surrey KT16 0DJ (☎ 093287 2571); 12 Guildford St, Chertsey, Surrey KT16 9DA (☎ 0932 568 666, fax 0932 567 882, car tel 0836 584 021)

CATTO, Hon Alexander Gordon; 2 s (by 1 m) of 2 Baron Catto; *b* 22 June 1952; *Educ* Westminster, Trinity Coll Cambridge; *m* 1981, Elizabeth Scott, da of Maj T P Boyes, of Brookvale Cottage, Whitford, Devon; 2 s (Thomas Innes Gordon b 18 Oct 1983, Alastair Gordon b 1986), 1 da (Charlotte Gordon b 1988); *Career* vice-pres Morgan Guaranty Tst Co of New York 1980-; dir Yule Catto and Co 1981-; *Style—* The Hon Alexander Catto; 3 Edenhurst Avenue, London SW6 3PD; c/o Yule Catto and Co, 1 New Bond St, London W1Y 0SD (☎ 01 493 6567)

CATTO, Hon Ariane Madeleine Gordon; da (by 1 m) of 2 Baron Catto; *b* 22 August 1960; *Educ* Westwood House Peterborough, Aiglon Coll Switzerland; *Style—* The Hon Ariane Catto

CATTO, Hon Innes Gordon; s (by 1 m) and h of 2 Baron Catto, *qv*; *b* 7 August 1950; *Educ* Grenville Coll, Shuttleworth Agric Coll; *Style—* The Hon Innes Catto; House of Schivas, Ythanbank, Ellon, Aberdeenshire (☎ 03587 224)

CATTO, Hon Isabel Ida Gordon; OBE (1952); da of late 1 Baron Catto; *b* 1912; *Career* govr PNEU Schs; world pres YWCA 1955-63, pres YWCA of Gt Britain 1966-72; *Clubs* Oriental; *Style—* The Hon Isabel Catto, OBE; Holmdale, Holmbury St Mary, Surrey; 61 Cadogan Gdns, London SW3

CATTO, Hon James Stuart Gordon; s (by 2 m) of 2 Baron Catto; *b* 20 Dec 1966; *Style—* The Hon James Catto

CATTO, 2 Baron (UK 1936); Sir Stephen Gordon Catto; 2 Bt (UK 1921); s of 1 Baron Catto, PC, CBE (d 1959), and Gladys Forbes, *née* Gordon (d 1980); *b* 14 Jan 1923; *Educ* Eton, Trinity Coll Cambridge; *m* 1, 28 July 1948 (m dis 1965), Josephine Innes, er da of late George Herbert Packer, of Alexandria, Egypt; 2 s, 2 da; m 2, 27 Jan 1966, Margaret, da of James Stuart Forrest, of Dilston, Tasmania; 1 s, 1 da (Hon Georgina Lucinda Gordon b 21 May 1969); *Heir* s, Hon Innes Catto; *Career* served RAFVR 1943-47; chm: Yule Catto and Co 1971-, Australian Mutual Provident Soc (UK branch) 1972-; Morgan Grenfell and Co Ltd 1973-79 (dir 1957, ch exec 1973-74), pres Morgan Grenfell Group plc 1987- (joined 1980); dir: GEC plc 1959-, News International plc 1969-, The News Corpn Ltd 1979-, Times Newspaper Hldgs Ltd 1981-; memb: advsy cncl ECGD 1959-65, London Transport Bd (pt/t) 1962-68, London advsy ctee Hong Kong and Shanghai Banking Corpn 1966-80; chm cncl RAF Benevolent Fund 1978-; tstee and chm exec ctee Westminster Abbey Tst 1973-; FCIB; *Recreations* music, gardening; *Clubs* Oriental, Melbourne (Australia); *Style—* The Rt Hon the Lord Catto; 41 William Mews, Lowndes Square, London SW1X 9HQ; Morgan Grenfell Group plc, 23 Great Winchester St, London EC2P 2AX (☎ 01 588 4545, fax 01 826 6155, telex 8953511 MG LDN G)

CATTRALL, Peter Jeremy; s of Ralph W Cattrall, of Westwood, Old Green Road, Cliftonville, Margate, Kent, and Sally, *née* Lunn; *b* 8 Jan 1947; *Educ* Kings Sch Canterbury, Trinity Coll Oxford Univ (MA); *m* 26 April 1975, Amanda Jane Maria, da of Maj Gen W N J Withall, CB, of Wiltshire; 1 s (Charles David b 1 March 1980), 1 da (Sarah Louise b 21 Sept 1982); *Career* sch master Holmewood House Kent, slr 1974, asst slr Knocker and Faskett Kent 1974-77, slr to Esso UK plc (formerly Esso Petroleum Co Ltd) 1977-88; memb: Kent Co Squash Side, Beckenham Cricket Club, Law Soc, IBA, Oxford Union; *Recreations* cricket, squash, golf, tennis, swimming, cycling, reading, music, current affairs; *Clubs* Utd Oxford and Cambridge, MCC, Rye GC, Free Foresters, Izingari, Arabs, Jesters, Bank of Brothers, Harlequins, Vincents; *Style—* Peter Cattrall, Esq; 21 Whitmore Road, Beckenham, Kent (☎ 01 658 7265, 01 245 2150)

CAUGHEY, Sir (Thomas) Harcourt Clarke; KBE (1972), JP; s of James Marsden Caughey; *b* 4 July 1911; *Educ* King's Coll Auckland, Univ of Auckland; *m* 1939, Patricia Mary, da of Hon Sir George Finlay; 1 s, 2 da; *Career* dep chm: South Br Insur Co Ltd 1978-81, NZ Insur Co 1981-86; exec chm Smith and Caughey Ltd 1975- (md 1962-85); former chm: Auckland Hosps Bd, Social Cncl of NZ, NZ Med Res Cncl, by Preston Tst Bd, All Blacks (Rugby) 1932-37; pres Auckland Medical Fndn 1978-84; Hon LLD Auckland 1986, CStJ; *Recreations* gardening, walking; *Clubs* Northern; *Style—* Sir Harcourt Caughey, KBE, JP; 7 Judges Bay Rd, Auckland, New Zealand

CAULFEILD, James Alexander Toby; s of Wade Toby Caulfeild, of Honeysuckle Cottage, Redford, Midhurst, Sussex, and Philippa Mary, *née* Brocklebank; *b* 30 Mar 1937; *Educ* Eton, New Coll Oxford (MA); *m* 20 March 1976, (Diana) Penelope, da of Col Martin Pound, of Duke House, Robert St, Deal, Kent; 4 da (Harriet Katharine, Victoria Louise, (Charlotte) Frances, Sophie Elizabeth); *Career* Nat Serv 2 Lt KRRC; asst investment mangr Provincial Insur 1967-70; dir M & G Investment Mgmnt 1970-89; FCA; *Recreations* skiing; *Clubs* Ski; *Style—* James Caulfeild, Esq; Hookland, Redford, Midhurst, Sussex (☎ 042 876 415); 3 Quays, Tower Hill, London EC3 (☎ 01 626 4588)

CAULFEILD, John Day; s of Eric St George Caulfeild (d 1975), and hp of uncle, 13 Viscount Charlemont; *b* 19 Mar 1934; *m* 1, 1964, Judith Ann (d 1971), da of James Dodd; 1 s, 1 da; m 2, 1972, Janet Evelyn, da of Orville Nancekivell; *Style—* John Caulfeild Esq; 39 Rossburn Drive, Etobicoke, Ontario M9C 2P9, Canada

CAULFEILD, Hon Patricia St George; da of 9 Visc Charlemont (d 1964); *b* 17 Sept 1920; *Career* 3 Officer WRNS 1939-45; *Style—* The Hon Patricia Caulfeild; 55 New Rd, Lewes, E Sussex

CAULFIELD, Hon Mr Justice; Hon Sir Bernard; QC (1961); s of late John Caulfield, of St Helens, Lancs, and Catherine Quinn; *b* 24 April 1914; *Educ* St Francis Xavier's Coll, Liverpool Univ; *m* 1953, Sheila Mary, da of Dr John F J Herbert, of London; 3 s, 1 da; *Career* slr 1940, barr 1947; rec of Coventry 1964-68, judge of the High Court of Justice (Queen's Bench Div) 1968-, presiding judge N Circuit 1976-80; kt 1968; master of the walks Lincoln's Inn 1984; *Style*— The Hon Mr Justice Caulfield; Royal Courts of Justice, WC2

CAUSLEY, Charles; CBE (1986); s of Charles Causley and Laura Bartlett; *b* 24 August 1917; *Educ* Launceston Nat Sch, Horwell GS, Launceston Coll, Peterborough Training Coll; *Career* RN, served WWII; poet; hon visiting fellow in Poetry Exeter Univ, Hon DLitt Exeter Univ, Hon MA Open Univ; former literary ed Signature and Apollo BBC W Region Radio; Queen's Gold Medal for Poetry 1967, Cholmondeley Award 1971, Signal Poetry Award 1986, Kurt Maschler Award 1987; has contributed to numerous anthologies of verse UK, USA; FRSL; *Publications include* Hands to Dance (1951), Union Street (1957), Underneath the Water (1968), The Puffin Book of Magic Verse (ed, 1974), Collected Poems 1951-75 (1975), The Last King of Cornwall (1978), The Puffin Book of Salt-Sea Verse (ed, 1978) 25 Poems by Hamdija Demirovic (trans 1980), The Ballad of Aucassin and Nicolette (1981), The Sun, Dancing (ed 1982), Secret Destinations (1984), 21 Poems (1986), King's Children (trans 1986), Early in the Morning (1986), Jack the Treacle Eater (1987), A Field of Vision (1988); *Recreations* travel, piano, the re-discovery of his native town; *Style*— Charles Causley, Esq, CBE; 2 Cyprus Well, Launceston, Cornwall (☎ 0566 2731)

CAUTE, (John) David; *b* 16 Dec 1936; *Educ* Edinburgh Acad, Wellington, Wadham Oxford; *m* 1, 1961 (m dis 1970), Catherine Shuckburgh; 2 s; m 2, 1973, Martha Bates; 2 da; *Career* former fellow All Souls Oxford and reader in Social and Political Theory Brunel Univ; literary ed New Statesman 1979-80; playwright and author; *Style*— David Caute, Esq; 41 Westcroft Sq, London W6

CAUTLEY, Edward Paul Ronald; s of Lt Cdr Ronald Lockwood Cautley, KSG, RNVR (d 1981), of 9 North End Rd, London NW11, and Ena Lily, *née* Medwin (d 1966); *b* 1 Mar 1940; *Educ* Downside Sch Somerset, Harvard Business Sch (advtg and mktg mgmnt prog); *m* 3 Sept 1966, (Sandra) Elizabeth (Liz), da of Capt Fred Erick David Baker; 2 da (Victoria Louise b 20 April 1968, Emma Jane b 20 Dec 1972); *Career* trained soldier 4 CY Inf Bn Hon Artillery Co 1958-60, cmmnd 2 Lt City of London Unit RMR Res 1960-62, Lt-Actg Capt (SCC) CO Sherborne House Marine Cadet Unit London 1962-68; sales rep Central Press Features 1958-60, retail servs mangr ICI Paints 1960-62, fin negotiator Goode Durrant & Murray 1962-64, gen mangr Marling Industs Ltd 1964-66, account dir S H Benson Ltd 1966-70, dir New Prod Devpt BR Bd 1970-73; chm and chief exec Strategy Int Ltd 1974-, dir Inward Int Business Devpt Urban Transportation Devpt Corpn Ltd Canada 1979-87, mktg dir The Economist Intelligence Unit 1981-82, dir Inward Investmt Programme London Docklands Devpt Corpn 1982-88, mktg dir Br Urban Devpt Ltd 1988-; memb ctee and cncl: Downside Settlement London 1958-, Centre Charles Peguy London 1960-63, Sherborne House London 1962-68, Licensing Exec Soc (currently); currently govr South of Eng Agric Soc; *Books* The Cautley Chronicle (1986), Change (int technol paper, publisher 1986-); *Recreations* veteran hockey, photography, watercolour painting, philately, fell walking; *Style*— Paul Cautley, Esq; 14 The Ivory House, St Katharine Docks, London E1 9AT (☎ 01 480 5562); Strategy Int Ltd, World Trade Centre, London E1 9AA (☎ 01 488 2400, fax 01 488 9643)

CAVAN, 13 Earl of (I 1647); Roger Cavan Lambart; also Viscount Kilcoursie (I 1647) and Lord Lambart, Baron of Cavan (I 1617); o s of Frederick Cavan Lambart (d 1963; o s of Maj Charles Edward Kilcoursie Lambart, 4 s of Maj Frederick Richard Henry Lambart, 2 s of Cdr Hon Oliver Matthew Lambart, RN, 2 s of 7 Earl of Cavan), and Audrey May, *née* Dunham; s kinsman, 12 Earl of Cavan, TD 1988; *b* 1 Sept 1944; *Educ* Wilson's Sch Wallington Surrey; *Heir* kinsman, Arthur Liver Reid Lambart b 28 Jan 1909; *Style*— The Rt Hon the Earl of Cavan; 34 Woodleigh Gdns, London SW16

CAVANAGH, Ann; *née* Fairbairn; da of Kenneth Huntsman Fairbairn, of Labourne Fell Farm, Chopwell, Newcastle upon Tyne, and Aileen Fairbairn, *née* Thompson; *b* 7 May 1954; *Educ* Newcastle upon Tyne (BSc hons); *m* 20 Sept 1975 (m dis 1989), George Cavanagh, s of George Cavanagh; 2 s (Neal George b 22 Aug 1980, Ross b 2 Jan 1984); *Career* asst accountant Assoc Br Foods 1978-84; co sec Romag Hldgs plc 1988-; fin dir: Romag Glass Products Ltd, Romag Hldgs plc 1988, Romag Security Laminators 1987-, Romag Electro-Optics Ltd 1988; tres Romag Inc 1988-; ACMA 1983; *Recreations* riding; *Style*— Ms Ann Cavanagh; Broomfield House, Derwent View, Chopwell, Newcastle upon Tyne NE17 7AN (☎ 0207 561 001); Patterson St, Blaydon, Tyne & Wear NE21 5SG (☎ 091 414 5511, fax 091 414 0545, telex 53570)

CAVANAGH, Rev Charles Terrence Stephen; s of Arthur Lawrence Cavanagh (d 1963), of USA, and Coleen, *née* Ludrick; *b* 29 July 1949; *Educ* Univ of Oklahoma (BLitt), Univ of Cambridge (BA, MA), Univ of Oxford (Cert in Theol); *Career* with Hedderwick Stirling Grumbar & Co 1978-81; pres: SG Warburg & Co 1981-, Mercury Asset Mgmnt plc 1981- (dir 1984-); ordained priest 1980; hon curate: St Peter's Clapham 1980-84, St Peter's Streatham 1985-; dir and tres Extemporary Dance Theatre Ltd 1985-; *Recreations* modern dance, cooking, wine; *Clubs* Athenaeum; *Style*— The Rev Charles Cavanagh; 34 Tasman Rd, London SW9 9LU (☎ 01 737 2269); Mercury Asset Mgmnt plc, 33 King William St, London EC4 (☎ 01 280 2800)

CAVANAGH, John Bryan; s of Cyril Cavanagh (d 1941), and Annie Frances, *née* Murphy (d 1966); *b* 28 Sept 1914; *Educ* St Paul's Sch, trained with Capt Edward Molyneux in London and Paris 1932-40; *Career* Intelligence Corps 1940, Capt GS Camouflage 1944; on demobilization travelled throughout USA studying fashion promotion, PA to Pierre Balmain Paris 1947-51; opened: own business 1952, John Cavanagh Boutique 1959; elected to Incorporated Soc of London Fashion Designers 1952 (vice-chm 1956-59); took own complete collection to Paris 1953, designed clothes for late Princess Marina and wedding dresses for the Duchess of Kent and Princess Alexandra; chm and md John Cavanagh Ltd; ret; Gold Medal Munich 1954; *Recreations* theatre, swimming, travelling; *Style*— John Cavanagh, Esq; 10 Birchlands Ave, London SW12 8ND (☎ 01 673 1504)

CAVAZZA, Lady Charlotte Sarah Alexandra; *née* Chetwynd-Talbot; da of 21 Earl of Shrewsbury and Waterford (d 1980), and his 1 w, Nadine Muriel, yr da of late Brig-Gen Cyril Randell Crofton, CBE; *b* 18 Nov 1938; *m* 1965, Camillo Cavazza dei Conti Cavazza (d 1981); 4 s, 3 da; *Style*— Lady Charlotte Cavazza; S Felice del Benaco, Brescia, Italy

CAVE; *see*: Haddon-Cave

CAVE, Sir Charles Edward Coleridge; 4 Bt (UK 1896), JP (Devon 1972), DL (1977); only s of Sir Edward Cave, 3 Bt (d 1946), by his w Betty Christabel (da of Maj Rennell Coleridge, himself ggn of S T Coleridge, the poet, and 3 cous of 2 Baron Coleridge); *b* 28 Feb 1927; *Educ* Eton; *m* 1957, Mary Elizabeth, da of John Francis Gore, CVO, TD (d 1983, 3 s of Sir Francis Gore, KCB, who in his turn was nephew of 4 Earl of Arran) by his w Lady Janet Campbell (er da of 4 Earl Cawdor); 4 s (John b 1958, Nicholas b 1961, Thomas b 1964, Richard b 1967); *Heir* s, John Cave; *Career* formerly Lt Devonshire Regt; ADC to Govr Punjab 1947; High Sheriff of Devon 1969; FRICS; *Style*— Sir Charles Cave, Bt, JP, DL; Sidbury Manor, Sidmouth, Devon (☎ 039 57 207)

CAVE, Francis Joseph (Frank); ERD (1968); s of Joseph Cave (d 1950), of Leicester, and Emily, *née* Potter (d 1938); *b* 11 June 1912; *Educ* Mill Hill Boys Sch Leicester, Leicester Coll Art and Technol, Northampton Poly London, Univ of Liverpool, London Univ (BSc); *m* 14 Nov 1939, (Sophia) Joan, da of Tom Herrick (d 1947), of Leicester; 1 s (Anthony b 13 Oct 1946), 1 da (Frances b 9 Sept 1942); *Career* Res Cmmn RE 1936, 105 Corps FD Park Co Liverpool 1937-39, WWII active serv, FD Co RE Dunkirk 1940, Maj 62 FD Co RE, Maj 58 Mech Equipment Co RE (serv India, Assam, Burma) returned from Rangoon 1945; trainee and articled civil engr 1928-33, asst engr (Willesden, Birkenhead, Oxford) 1933-39, chief asst engr Willesden 1946-48, dep borough engr West Ham 1948-52, borough engr Northampton 1952-58, borough surveyor Hendon Middx 1958-65, city engr Westminster 1965-74, md Halcrow Carribean Ltd WI 1975-78, conslt engr and surveyor 1978-; memb and chm tech and advsy ctees: RICS, Inst Municiple Engrs, Inst Civil Engrs Method of Measurement (Inst Civil Engrs); Br Standards Inst: memb cncl codes of practise for bldg and codes of practice for mechanical engrs, memb drafting ctees; memb: examination panel London Dist Surveyors, bd govrs Westminster Tech Coll; chm cncl Royal Soc of Health 1969, pres Rotary Club Westminster West 1973; hon memb: American Public Health Assoc 1969, Inst Public Health 1971; Freeman City of London, Liveryman Worshipful Co of Paviors 1966; FRSH 1948 (memb 1935), FIMunE 1952 (memb 1936), FICE 1955 (1938), FRICS 1955 (memb 1948), FRTPI 1958 (memb 1949), FRSA 1972,; *Recreations* travelling, art, DIY; *Clubs* RAC; *Style*— Frank Cave, Esq, ERD; 8 Borodale, Kirkwick Ave, Harpenden, Herts AL5 2QW (☎ 0582 72666)

CAVE, Hugh Walford Melville; s of Alexander Melville Cave (d 1964), and Mary Elizabeth Cave, *née* Bennett (d 1987); *b* 10 July 1932; *Educ* Shrewsbury Sch; *m* 14 Oct 1961, Diana Patricia, da of Brig Edward Antrobus James, OBE, TD, DL (d 1976); 2 s (Timothy b 1962, Andrew b 1964), 1 da (Victoria b 1966); *Career* Nat Serv RA; Lt TA; chartered surveyor; ptnr Chesshire Gibson Chartered Surveyors of Birmingham, London and LA 1961-88 (sr ptnr 1982-88) dir Debenham, Tewson & Chinnocks plc 1988-, chm Debenham, Tewson, Chesshire 1988-; chm: Rhodes Almsdhouse Tst, Old Salopian Club 1978-79; Freeman of the City of London, memb Worshipful Co of Chartered Surveyors; surveyor to Sutton Coldfield Municipal Charities; *Recreations* golf; *Clubs* Army and Navy, Birmingham, Little Aston Golf; *Style*— Hugh W M Cave, Esq; 2 Heather Court Gardens, Four Oaks, Sutton Coldfield, W Midlands (☎ 021 308 2004); 10 Colmore Row, Birmingham (☎ 021 200 2050) 4292, fax 021 632 4302)

CAVE, John Arthur; s of Ernest and Eva Mary Cave; *b* 30 Jan 1915; *Educ* Loughborough GS; *m* 1937, Peggy Pauline, yst da of Frederick Charles Matthews Browne; 2 s, 2 da; *Career* Capt Royal Tank Regt (UK and India); dir Midland Bank 1975-80; chm Forward Tst Ltd, Midland Bank Fin Corp Ltd, Midland Montagu Leasing Ltd 1975-80; memb Cncl Chartered Inst Bankers 1967-75 (dep chm 1973-75); FCIB; *Style*— John Cave, Esq; Dolphin House, Centre Cliff, Southwold, Suffolk IP18 6EN (☎ 0502 722232)

CAVE, John Charles; s and h of Sir Charles Cave, 4 Bt; *b* 8 Sept 1958; *Educ* Eton; *m* 1984 Carey Diana, er da of John Lloyd, of Barrymore Farm, Langport, Somerset; 1 s (George b 1987);; *Style*— John Cave Esq; Buckley, Sidbury, Sidmouth, Devon (☎ 039 57 212)

CAVE, Dr Terence Christopher; s of Alfred Cyril Cave (d 1979), and Sylvia Norah, *née* Norman; *b* 1 Dec 1938; *Educ* Winchester, Gonville and Caius Coll Cambridge (BA, MA, DPhil); *m* 31 July 1965, Helen Elizabeth; 1 s (Christopher b 1969), 1 da (Hilary b 1970); *Career* lectr Univ of St Andrews 1963-65 (asst lectr 1962-63), sr lectr Univ of Warwick 1970-72 (lectr 1965-70), fell and tutor St John's Coll Oxford 1972-; visiting posts: Cornell Univ 1967-68, Univ of California Santa Barbara 1976, Univ of Virginia 1979, Princeton Univ 1984; visiting fell All Soul Coll Oxford 1971; *Books* Devotional Poetry in France (1969), The Cornucopian Text (1979), Recognitions (1988); *Style*— Dr Terence Cave; St John's Coll, Oxford OX1 3JP (☎ 0865 277 345)

CAVE-BROWNE-CAVE, Dorothea, Lady; Dorothea Plewman; da of Robert Greene Dwen; *m* 1923, Sir Clement Charles Cave-Browne-Cave, 15 Bt (d 1945); 1 s; *Style*— Dorothea, Lady Cave-Browne-Cave

CAVE-BROWNE-CAVE, John Robert Charles; s and h of Sir Robert Cave-Brown-Cave, 16 Bt; *b* 22 June 1957; *Style*— John Cave-Brown-Cave Esq

CAVE-BROWNE-CAVE, Sir Robert; 16 Bt (1641 E); s of Sir Clement Cave-Browne-Cave, 15 Bt (d 1945); *b* 8 June 1929; *Educ* St George's Sch Vancouver, Univ Sch Victoria, British Columbia Univ; *m* 1, 1954 (m dis 1975), Lois Shirley, da of John Chalmers Huggard, of Winnipeg; 1 s, 1 da; m 2, 1977, Joan Shirley, da of Dr Kenneth Ashe Peacock, of W Vancouver, BC; *Heir* s, John Cave-Brown-Cave; *Career* pres Cave and Co Ltd, Seabord Chemicals Ltd; *Style*— Sir Robert Cave-Browne-Cave, Bt; 6087 Wiltshire St, Vancouver, British Columbia, Canada

CAVELL, The Right Rev John Kingsmill; o s of William H G Cavell, of Deal Kent, and Edith May, *née* Warner; *b* 4 Nov 1916; *Educ* Sir Roger Manwood's GS Kent, Queens' Coll Cambridge (MA), Wycliffe Hall Oxford; *m* 1942, Mary Grossett, da of Christopher Penman, of Devizes, Wilts; 1 da (Margaret); *Career* ordained 1940; vicar Christ Church Cheltenham 1952-62, St Andrew's Plymouth 1962-72 (formerly prebendary of Exeter Cathedral and rural dean of Plymouth); bishop: Southampton 1972-84, HM Prisons 1975-85; *Recreations* genealogy, local history; *Style*— The Right Rev John Cavell; 5 Constable Way, West Harnham, Salisbury SP2 8LN (☎ 0722 334782)

CAVENAGH, Winifred Elizabeth; OBE; da of Arthur Speakman (d 1960), and Ethel Speakman (d 1969); *Educ* Broughton & Crumpsall HS, Univ Coll & LSE (BSc Econ), Univ of Birmingham (PhD); *m* 5 Nov 1938, Hugh Cavenagh (d 1967), s of Edward Cavenagh (d 1931); *Career* with Miny of Labour 1941-45; Univ of Birmingham 1946-76 (Prof Emeritus 1976); visiting prof Ghana Univ 1971, Moir/Cullis lecture fellowship USA 1977 and Canada 1980, chm (pt/t) Industl Tbnl 1974-77; memb: Utd Birmingham

Hosps Bd 1958-64, Home Off Probation Recruitment & Trg Ctee 1958-67, advsy ctee on Juvenile Deliquency 1964-65, Lord Chllr ctee on Legal Aid 1960-71 and Trg of Magistrates 1965-73; nat chm Assoc of Social Workers 1955-57, Magistrates Assoc cncl 1965-78, Birmingham Educn Ctee 1946-66, W Midlands Econ Planning Cncl 1967-71; *Style—* Prof W E Cavenagh, OBE; 25 High Point, Richmond Hill Rd, Edgbaston, Birmingham B15 3RU (☎ 021 454 0109)

CAVENAGH-MAINWARING, Charles Rafe Gordon; s of Capt Maurice Kildare Cavenagh-Mainwaring, RN, DSO, and Iris Mary, *née* Denaro; *b* 11 Mar 1944; *Educ* Downside; *m* 20 Oct 1973, Rosemary Lee, da of Capt Thomas Lee Reay Hardy (d 1982), of London; 1 s (Rupert William b 1976); *Career* Lt RM Reserve 1964-67, Lt HAC (RHA) 1967-73, transferred to RARO 1974; dir Hinton Hill Underwriting Agents Ltd, Underwriting Memb Lloyd's; Knight of Honour and Devotion Sovereign Mil Order of Malta, Knight of Justice of the Sacred Military Order of Constantine of St George 1986 (Spain); *Recreations* shooting, skiing, watching rugby union football, tennis; *Clubs* Hurlingham; *Style—* Charles Cavenagh-Mainwaring, Esq; 3 Bridge Lane, London SW11 3AD; (☎ 01 223 2237); 47 Cadogan Gardens, London SW3 (☎ 01 480 5152 x275, fax 01 480 6403, telex 883422)

CAVENAGH-MAINWARING, Guy; s of Rafe Gordon Dutton Cavenagh-Mainwaring, of Whitmore Hall, Staffs (High Sheriff of Staffs 1954), by his w Rosemary Mainwaring, da of Sir Arthur Murray Cudmore, CMG, MB; *b* 22 Feb 1934; *Educ* private; *m* 1961, Margery Christine Rachel, da of Eric Rowland James Robbins; 1 s (Edward Rowland b 1962), 3 da (Tara Rose b 1964, Fleur Amicia b 1970, Rosanna Rachel b 1972 (decd)); *Heir* Edward Rowland Cavenagh-Mainwaring; *Career* landowner and farmer; High Sheriff of Staffs 1977-78; *Style—* Guy Cavenagh-Mainwaring Esq; Hillside Farm, Whitmore, Staffs (☎ 0782 680478), 22 Lakeman St, N Adelaide, S Australia (☎ Adelaide 267-4294)

CAVENAGH-MAINWARING, Capt Maurice Kildare; DSO (1940); s of Maj James Gordon Cavenagh-Mainwaring (d 1938), of Whitmore Hall, Staffs;; *b* 13 April 1908; *Educ* Dartmouth; *m* 1933, Iris Mary, da of Col Charles Albert Denaro, OBE, of Valletta, Malta; 1 s; *Career* Capt RN 1951, naval attaché Paris 1957-60, ADC to HM the Queen 1960, Cdr Legion d'Honneur 1960, ret 1960; joined Simpson (Piccadilly) Ltd 1961; *Clubs* Naval and Military, Union Malta; *Style—* Capt Maurice Cavenagh-Mainwaring, DSO, RN; 47 Cadogan Gdns, London SW3 (☎ 01 584 7870); Apollo Court, St Julians, Malta (☎ 312712)

CAVENAGH-MAINWARING, Rafe Gordon Dutton; er s of late Maj James Gordon Cavenagh-Mainwaring (d 1938), of Whitmore Hall, and Evelyn Dutton, *née* Green (d 1963); *b* 20 July 1906; *Educ* Cheltenham Coll; *m* 1931, Rosemary Mainwaring, er da of Sir Arthur Murray Cudmore, CMG, MB, FRCS (d 1951), of Adelaide, S Australia; 1 s (Guy, *qv*); *Career* landowner; JP Staffs 1932-55, High Sheriff 1954-55, Patron of the Living of Whitmore, 33 Hereditary Lord of the Manors of Whitmore and Biddulph; *Clubs* Naval and Military; *Style—* Rafe Cavenagh-Mainwaring Esq; Whitmore Hall, Whitmore, Newcastle-under-Lyme, Staffs ST5 5HW (☎ 0782 680235); 22 Lakeman St, N Adelaide, S Australia 5006 (☎ Adelaide 267 4294)

CAVENDISH, Anthony John; s of George Henry Frederick Cavendish (d 1932); *b* 20 July 1927; *Educ* Lyceum Alpinum, London Univ (BA); *m* 1980, Elspeth Gail, da of Montagu Frank Macdonald, of Poole; 1 s (Julius b 1981), 1 da (Charlotte b 1984); *Career* Maj Army 1945-48; foreign serv 1948-1953; foreign corr UPI 1953-60; France, Poland, Hungary, Middle East: banker; dir: Brandts 1972-1975, Hong Kong Shanghai Bank 1975-78; Overland Tst Bank 1986-, Overland Tst Ltd, Overland Tst Int plc; chm: Contship (UK) Ltd 1987-, Lonham Servs Ltd, Arrow Freight Ltd 1989-, The Fountain head Gp SA; parly candidate (Cons) Harlow 1973; govr Pierrepoint Sch; Freeman City of London;; *Books* Inside Intelligence; *Recreations* cooking, music, winter sports, power boating; *Clubs* Carlton, Cavalry and Guards, Special Forces, Royal Southern YC, Travellers' (Paris), St Moritz Tobogganing; *Style—* Anthony Cavendish, Esq; Lowfields, Hartley Wintney, Hants (☎ 3124)

CAVENDISH, Lady Elizabeth Georgiana Alice; LVO (1976); da of late 10 Duke of Devonshire, KG, MBE, TD; *b* 24 April 1926; *Career* JP London 1961; appointed an extra lady-in-waiting to HRH Princess Margaret 1954; chm: North Westminster PSD1980-83, Inner London Juvenile Court 1983-86, Board of Visitors, Wandsworth Prison 1970-73, Board of Advertising Standards Authority 1981-; lay memb: the Senate of the Inns of Court Professional Conduct Ctee, the Bar Council, the senates Disciplinary Ctee Tribunal 1983-; chm: Cancer Research Campaign 1981-; memb Maire Ctee on the Future of Legal Profession 1986-.; *Style—* Lady Elizabeth Cavendish, LVO, JP; 19 Radnor Walk, SW3 (☎ 01 352 0774); Moor View, Edensor, Bakewell, Derbyshire (☎ Baslow 2204)

CAVENDISH, Hon John Charles Gregory; s of 5 Baron Chesham; *b* 23 Nov 1952; *Educ* Eton, Jesus Cambridge; *m* 1976, Lucinda Mary, da of Richard Hugh Corbett (d 1974); *Career* shipbroker; with Tradax England Ltd (grain shippers) 1974-81, E D and F Man Ltd (sugar shippers) 1981-85; Braemar Chartering Ltd 1985-88, shooting instr, princ Cavendish Sporting 1988-; *Recreations* motor sports, country life and sports; *Style—* The Hon John Cavendish; Hall Farm, Farringdon, Alton, Hants (☎ Tisted 275)

CAVENDISH, Hon Juliet Enid; da of 7 Baron Waterpark; *b* 17 Oct 1953; *Style—* The Hon Juliet Cavendish

CAVENDISH, Hon Nicholas Charles; s and h of 5 Baron Chesham; *b* 7 Nov 1941; *Educ* Eton; *m* 1, 1965 (m dis), Susan Donne, eldest da of Frederick Guy Beauchamp, MB, ChB, of 119 Harley St, W1; m 2, 1973, Suzanne Adrienne, eldest da of late Alan Gray Byrne, of Sydney; 2 s; *Career* ACA; *Style—* The Hon Nicholas Cavendish; 132 Fletcher Street, Woollahra, Sydney, NSW 2025, Australia

CAVENDISH, Maj-Gen Peter Boucher; CB (1981), OBE (1969); s of Brig Ronald Valentine Cecil Cavendish, OBE, MC (ka 1943, gs of Lt-Col William Cavendish, Groom-in-Waiting to Queen Victoria, by his w Lady Emily Lambton, da of 1 Earl of Durham. William was in turn gs of 1 Earl of Burlington of the 1831 creation and 1 cous of 7 Duke of Devonshire), and Helen, *née* Boucher; *b* 26 August 1925; *Educ* Abberley Hall Worcester, Winchester Coll, New Coll Oxford; *m* 1952, Marion Loudon, 2 da of Robert Constantine, TD, JP, by his w Marie, *née* van Haaren (descended from William the Silent, Prince of Orange); 3 s (Ronald b 1954, Mark b 1955, Rupert b 1962); *Career* enlisted 1943, commissioned Royal Dragoons 1945, 3 King's Own Hussars 1946, Queen's Own Hussars 1958, 14/20 Hussars (CO 1966-69 and Hon Col 1976-81); Cmdt RAC Centre 1971-74, Sec to Mil Ctee Int Mil Staff HQ NATO 1975-78, Dir Armaments Standardisation and Interoperability Div 1978-81 and Chm Mil Agency for Standardisation NATO HQ 1978-81; Hon Col Queen's Own Mercian Yeo TAVR 1982-87; Col Cmdt the Yeomanry 1986-; High Sheriff of Derbyshire 1986; Peak Park Planning Bd 1982- (vice-chm 1987-); *Style—* Maj-Gen Peter Cavendish, CB, OBE; The Rock Cottage, Middleton-by-Youlgrave, Bakewell, Derby DE4 1LS (☎ (0629 636 225)

CAVENDISH, Hon Roderick Alexander; s and h of 7 Baron Waterpark; *b* 10 Oct 1959; *Style—* The Hon Roderick Cavendish

CAVENDISH-BENTINCK, Lady (Alexandra Margaret) Anne; da of 7 Duke of Portland, KG (d 1977); *b* 6 Sept 1916; *Career* CStJ; *Style—* Lady Anne Cavendish-Bentinck; Welbeck Woodhouse, Worksop, Notts

CAVENDISH-TRIBE, Hon Mrs; Hon Winifred; *née* Cavendish; da of 6 Baron Waterpark (d 1948), by his 2 w, May (d 1969), da of William Ernest Burbidge; *b* 1 June 1909; *Educ* St Monicas Priory Dorset; *m* 13 Dec 1929, Capt Albert Frank Tribe, who later assumed additional surname of Cavendish (d 1962), 4 s of late Lt Cdr Arthur Ernest Tribe, RNR; 1 s; *Style—* The Hon Mrs Cavendish-Tribe; Saxons Beech Hill, Bridge, nr Canterbury, Kent

CAWDOR, 6 Earl (1827 UK); Hugh John Vaughan Campbell; also Baron Cawdor of Castlemartin (GB 1796) and Viscount Emlyn (UK 1827) (the full designation of the Earldom in its patent of 1827 was Earl Cawdor of Castlemartin); s of 5 Earl Cawdor (d 1970), by his 1 w Wilma Mairi (d 1982), da of Vincent Cartwright Vickers, of Aldenham; *b* 6 Sept 1932; *Educ* Eton, Magdalen Coll Oxford, RAC Cirencester; *m* 1, 1957 (m dis 1979), Cathryn, da of Maj-Gen Sir Robert Hinde, KBE, CB, DSO, by his w Evelyn, 3 da of Henry Fitzherbert, JP, of Yeldersley Hall, Derbyshire; 2 s, 3 da; m 2, 1979, Countess Angelika Ilona Lazansky von Bukowa; *Heir* s, Viscount Emlyn; *Career* High Sheriff of Carmarthenshire 1964; FSA, FRICS; *Style—* The Rt Hon the Earl Cawdor; Cawdor Castle, Nairn; Cawdor Estate Office, Nairn (☎ 06677 666, telex 75225)

CAWLEY, Hon Charles Michael; 5 s of 3 Baron Cawley, *qv*; *b* 9 Feb 1955; *Educ* Milton Abbey, Univ of Manchester; *m* 1980; *Style—* The Hon Charles Cawley

CAWLEY, Sir Charles Mills; KB (1965), CBE (1957, OBE 1946); s of John Cawley (d 1938), of Gillingham, Kent, and Emily Cawley; *b* 17 May 1907; *Educ* Sir Joseph Williamson's Mathematical Sch Rochester, Imperial Coll of Science and Technol (ARCS, DIC, MSc, PhD, DSc); *m* 1934, Florence Mary Ellaline, da of James Shepherd (d 1925), of York; 1 da; *Career* Capt Army (Special Service) 1945; temporarily employed with the rank of Col by the Control Cmmn for Germany 1946-47, Imperial Defence Coll 1949; employed Fuel Research Station DSIR 1929-53, seconded to the Petroleum Warfare Dept 1939-45, dir DSIR HQ 1953-59, chief scientist Miny of Power 1959-67, a Civil Serv Cmmr 1967-69, (ret); fell of Imperial Coll of Sci and Technol; ARCS, FRSC, FInstE, FRSA; *Style—* Sir Charles Cawley, KB, CBE; 8 Glen Gdns, Ferring-by-Sea, Worthing, W Sussex BN12 5HG (☎ 0903 501850)

CAWLEY, 3 Baron (1918 UK); Sir Frederick Lee Cawley; 3 Bt (UK 1906); s of 2 Baron Cawley (d 1954), and Vivienne (d 1978, aged 100), da of Harold Lee, of Manchester and sis of Sir Kenneth Lee, 1 and last Bt; *b* 27 July 1913; *Educ* Eton, New Coll Oxford (BA 1935, MA 1942); *m* 1944, Rosemary Joan, da of Reginald Edward Marsden, former bursar of Eton, and Hon Vere Dillon (sis of 18 and 19 Viscounts Dillon), and whose twin sis Iris m Lord Cawley's yr bro, Hon Stephen Cawley, *qv*; 6 s, 1 da; *Heir* s, Hon John Francis Cawley; *Career* served WW II Capt RA Leics Yeo (wounded) NW Europe; barr Lincoln's Inn 1938, practised 1946-73; dep chm Ctees House of Lords 1958-67, and chm of many select ctees; farmer; *Style—* The Rt Hon Lord Cawley; Bircher Hall, Leominster, Herefordshire HR6 OAX (☎ 056 885 218)

CAWLEY, Hon John Francis; s and h of 3 Baron Cawley, *qv*; *b* 28 Sept 1946; *Educ* Eton; *m* 1979, Regina Sarabia, da of late Marques de Hazas (cr of 1873 by King Amadeus I), of Juan Bravo 10, Madrid 6; 3 s (William Robert Harold b 2 July 1981, Thomas Frederick José-Luis b 1982, Andrew David b 1988), 1 da (Susan Mary b 1980); *Style—* The Hon John Cawley; Castle Grounds, Ashton, Leominster, Herefordshire HR6 0DN (☎ 058 472 209)

CAWLEY, Hon Justin Robert; 4 s of 3 Baron Cawley; *b* 15 June 1953; *Educ* Milton Abbey; *m* 1986, Margaret Lee Davies; *Recreations* game shooting, antique watching; *Style—* The Hon Justin Cawley; 24 Malta Close, Popley, Basingstoke RG24 9PD

CAWLEY, Hon Mark Andrew; 6 s of 3 Baron Cawley; *b* 3 Nov 1957; *Educ* Eton, New Coll Oxford (MA); *Clubs* Eton Vikings, Joshua Lipschitz; *Style—* The Hon Mark Cawley

CAWLEY, Hon Richard Kenneth; 3 s of 3 Baron Cawley; *b* 14 April 1949; *Educ* Eton, Durham Univ (BA), City Univ (MBA); *m* 1976, Tsugumi, da of S Ota, of Takarazuka, Japan; *Style—* The Hon Richard Cawley

CAWLEY, Hon Stephen Robert; 2 s of 2 Baron Cawley, JP, by his w Vivienne, da of Harold Lee; *b* 22 Oct 1915; *Educ* Eton, New Coll Oxford (MA, BSc); *m* 1952, Iris Edrica, da of Reginald Marsden and Hon Vere, aunt of late 20 Viscount Dillon; 3 s (Alec b 1954, James b 1956, Martin b 1959; 1 da (Yoland b 1957); *Career* served WW II with Royal Signals; JP Lancashire 1951-53, Surrey 1955-74, Hereford and Worcester 1978-83; Lib Candidate: Stretford (Gen Election) 1950, High Peak 1951, 1955 and 1959, Esher 1964 and 1966; prime warden Dyers' Co 1970-71; dir bleaching, dyeing and printing of calico piece goods and manufacture of plastic chemical plant, ret; *Style—* The Hon Stephen Cawley; Woodhay, Tilford Road, Hindhead, Surrey GU26 6QY (☎ 042 873 6856)

CAWLEY, Hon William Frederick; 2 s of 3 Baron Cawley, *qv*; *b* 7 Dec 1947; *Educ* Eton, New Coll Oxford (MA); *m* 1979 (m dis 1988), Philippa J, er da of Philip Hoare, DFC, of The Playle, Weycombe Rd, Haslemere, Surrey; 1 s (Edward Frederick b 1980), 1 da (Elizabeth Lena b 1982); *Style—* The Hon William Cawley

CAWS, Richard Byron; CBE (1984); s of Maxwell Caws, of London (d 1976) and Edith S (d 1979); *b* 9 Mar 1927; *m* 28 May 1948, Fiona Muriel Ruth Elton, da of Lt Col Edwin Darling, MC, RA (d 1949); 2 s (Eian b 1950, Andrew b 1952 (decd)), 2 da (Genevra b 1949, Alexandra b 1953); *Career* chm: Caws Morris, Chartered Surveyors, London 1987-; sr conslt (Real Estate), Goldman Sachs Int Corpn (London) 1987-; ptnr: Nightingale, Page and Bennett, Chartered Surveyors, Kingston upon Thames, 1944-60, Debenham Tewson and Chinnocks, Chartered Surveyors, London 1961-87; Crown Estate Cmmr 1971-; memb Cmmn for the New Towns, 1976- (chm Property Ctee, 1978-); Dobry Ctee on Review of the Development Control System, 1973-75; DoE advsy gp on Commercial Property Development, 1973-77; dep chm: DoE Property Advsy Gp 1978-88; govr Royal Agric Coll, 1985-88; Master Worshipful Co of Chartered Surveyors, 1982-83; chm jnr org, RICS 1959-60; *Recreations* sailing, travel; *Clubs* Boodles, Royal Thames Yacht, Little Ship; *Style—* Richard Caws, Esq; 36

Mount Park Rd, Ealing, London W5 2RS (☎ 01 997 7739); Caws Morris Assoc Ltd, Chancery House, 53/64 Chancery Lane, London WC2A 1QU (☎ 01 404 4303, fax: 01 831 0390)

CAYFORD, Dame Florence Evelyn; DBE (1965), JP (Co of London 1941); da of late George William and Mary SA Bunch; *b* 14 June 1897; *Educ* County Secondary Sch St Pancras, Paddington Tech Inst; *m* 1923, John Cayford, s of Alfred Cayford; 2 s; *Career* chm London CC 1960-61, memb GLC 1964-67, Mayor of London Borough of Camden 1969; Freeman of Hampstead; chm Metropolitan Water Bd 1966-67; *Style*— Dame Florence Cayford, DBE, JP; 26 Hemstal Rd, Hampstead, London NW6 (☎ 01 624 6181)

CAYLEY, Sir Digby William David; 11 Bt (UK 1661); o s of William Arthur Seton Cayley (d 1964), ggs of 7 Bt; suc his kinsman Maj Sir Kenelm Henry Ernest Cayley, 10 Bt 1967; *b* 3 June 1944; *Educ* Malvern, Downing Coll Cambridge; *m* 19 July 1969, Christine Mary, o da of late Derek Francis Gaunt, of Ilkley; 2 da; *Heir* kinsman, George Paul Cayley b 23 May 1940; *Career* asst classics master Stonyhurst Coll 1973-; *Style*— Sir Digby Cayley, Bt; 12 Lensfield Rd, Cambridge

CAYLEY, George Paul; s of late Capt Charles Cayley, ggs of 7 Bt; hp of kinsman, Sir Digby Cayley, 11 Bt; *b* 23 May 1940; *Educ* Felsted; *m* 1967, Shirley Southwell, da of Frank Woodward Petford, of Kirby Cane, Norfolk; 2 s; *Style*— George Cayley Esq; Applegarth, Brewers Green, Roydon, Diss, Norfolk

CAYZER, Hon (Michael) Anthony Rathborne; s of late 1 Baron Rotherwick; *b* 28 May 1920; *Educ* Eton, Sandhurst; *m* 1952, Hon Patricia Browne (d 1981), da of 4 Baron Oranmore and Browne by his 1 w Mildred (late Hon Mrs Hew Dalrymple); 3 da; m 2, 1982, Baroness Sybille de Selys Longchamps; *Career* cmmnd Royal Scots Greys, ME 1939-44 (despatches); chm: tstees of Nat Maritime Museum, Liverpool Steamship 1977-87 Owners' Assoc 1956-57, Missions to Seamen (London Cncl) 1963-67 (hon tres 1974-84, vice-pres 1984-); dep chm: Chatham Historic Dockyard Tst 1958-87, Caledonia Investmts plc; Br and Cwlth Shipping Co plc; pres: Inst of Shipping and Forwarding Agents 1963-64, Chamber of Shipping of UK 1967-68, Hertfordshire Agric Soc 1974; past memb Mersey Docks and Harbour Bd, past vice-pres Br Light Aviation Centre; *Style*— The Hon Anthony Cayzer; Great Westwood, King's Langley, Herts; Cayzer House, 2 and 4 St Mary Axe, London EC3A 8BP (☎ 01 283 4343)

CAYZER, Hon Avon Arthur; s of 2 Baron Rotherwick; *b* 13 Sept 1968; *Style*— The Hon Avon Cayzer

CAYZER, Hon Charles William; s of 2 Baron Rotherwick; *b* 26 April 1957; *m* 1985, Amanda C S, 2 da of John Squire, of Marbella, Spain; *Style*— The Hon Charles Cayzer

CAYZER, Hon Elizabeth; yr da of Baron Cayzer; *b* 16 Jan 1946; *Style*— The Hon Elizabeth Cayzer

CAYZER, Sir James Arthur; 5 Bt (UK 1904), of Gartmore, Co Perth; s of Sir Charles William Cayzer, 3 Bt, MP (d 1940), and Eileen, OBE (d 1981), da of James Meakin (d 1912), and Emma Beatrice (d 1935), later wife of 3 Earl Sondes; suc his bro, Sir Nigel John Cayzer, 4 Bt, 1943; *b* 15 Nov 1931; *Educ* Eton; *Heir* kinsman, Lord Cayzer; *Career* dir Caledonia Investments 1958-88 Cayzer Tst Co 1988-; *Clubs* Carlton; *Style*— Sir James Cayzer, Bt; Kinpurnie Castle, Newtyle, Angus PH12 8TW (☎ 082 85 207)

CAYZER, Baron (Life Peer UK 1981); Sir (William) Nicholas Cayzer; 2 Bt (UK 1921), of Roffey Park, Horsham, Co Sussex; er s of Sir August Cayzer, 1 Bt, JP (d 1943, himself 3 s of Sir Charles Cayzer, 1s Bt, of Gartmore) by his w Ina (d of William Stancomb, JP); hp of 1 cous once removed, Sir James Cayzer, 5 Bt, of Gartmore; *b* 21 Jan 1910; *Educ* Eton, CCC Cambridge; *m* 1935, Elizabeth Catherine, *née* Williams; 2 da; *Heir* (to Btcy only) none; *Career* pres: Br and Cwlth Holdings plc; chm: Caledonia Investmt, Clan Line Steamers 1928-87, Coyzer Irvine and Co Ltd 1929-87, Union Castle Mail Steamship Co Ltd 1955-87; *Style*— The Rt Hon The Lord Cayzer; 95J Eaton Sq, London SW1 (☎ 01 235 5551); The Grove, Walsham-le-Willows, Suffolk (☎ 035 98 263)

CAYZER, Nigel Kenneth; s of Anthony Galliers-Pratt, of Mawley Hall Worcs, and Angela, da of Sir Charles Cayzer, 3 Bt (decd); *b* 30 April 1954; *Educ* Eton; *m* 1986, Henrietta, da of Sir Richard Sykes 7 Bt (d 1978); 1 s (b 24 March 1988); *Career* chm Film Finances Ltd; *Clubs* Turf, White's; *Style*— Nigel Cayzer, Esq; Thriepley Ho, Lundie, Dundee DD2 5PA (☎ 0382 581268); 15 West Halkin Street, London SW1 (☎ 01 235 1478)

CAYZER, Hon (Herbert) Robin; er s and h of 2 Baron Rotherwick; *b* 12 Mar 1954; *Educ* Harrow; *m* 1982, Sara J M, da of R J McAlpine, of Swettenham Hall, Swettenham, Cheshire, and Mrs J McAlpine, of Lower Carden Hall, Malpas, Cheshire; 1 da (Harriette b 1986); *Style*— The Hon Herbert Cayzer

CAZALET, Hon Lady (Camilla Jane); *née* Gage; da of 6 Viscount Gage, KCVO, by his 1 w, Hon Imogen Grenfell; *b* 12 July 1937; *Educ* Benenden; *m* 24 April 1965, Hon Sir Edward Stephen Cazalet (Hon Mr Justice Cazalet), *qv*; 2 s, 1 da; *Career* dir Lumley Cazalet 1967-; tstee Glyndebourne Arts Tst 1978-; *Recreations* tennis, music; *Clubs* Queen's; *Style*— The Hon Lady Cazalet; Shaw Farm, Plumpton Green, Lewes, Sussex; 58 Seymour Walk, London SW10 (☎ 01 352 0401)

CAZALET, Hon Mr Justice; Hon Sir Edward Stephen; QC (1980); s of Peter Victor Ferdinand Cazalet, JP, DL (d 1973), the race horse trainer, and his 1 w, Leonora, *née* Rowley, step da of Sir P G Wodehouse; *b* 26 April 1936; *Educ* Eton, Ch Ch Oxford; *m* 24 April 1965, Hon Camilla Jane, da of Viscount Gage, KCVO; 2 s (David b 1967, Hal b 1969), 1 da (Lara b 1973); *Career* subaltern Welsh Guards 1954-56; barr; chm Horse Race Betting Levy Appeal Tribunal 1979-88; QC 1980-88, bencher Inner Temple 1985, recorder of Crown Court 1985-88, judge of the High Court of Justice 1988-; kt 1988; *Recreations* riding, ball games, chess; *Clubs* Garrick, White's; *Style*— The Hon Mr Justice Cazalet; Royal Courts of Justice, Strand, London WC2A 2LL

CAZALET, Lady; Elise; da of James Percival Winterbotham, of Cheltenham; *m* 1928, Vice-Adm Sir Peter Grenville Lyon Cazalet, KBE, CB, DSO and bar, DSC (d 1982); 4 s; *Style*— Lady Cazalet; 16 High Hurst Close, Newick, Lewes, E Sussex

CAZALET, (Charles) Julian; s of Vice-Adm Sir Peter Grenville Lyon Cazalet, KBE, CB, DSO, DSC (d 1982), of Newick, E Sussex, and Lady Beatrice Elise, *née* Winterbotham; *b* 29 Nov 1947; *Educ* Uppingham, Magdalene Coll Cambridge (MA); *m* 29 Nov 1986, Jennifer Clare, da of Maurice Nelson Little (d 1985), of Laverton, Gloucs; 1 s (Charles b 1987); *Career* ptnr Cazenove and Co Stockbrokers 1978-; FCA 1977; *Recreations* sailing, skiing; *Clubs* City Univ; *Style*— Julian Cazalet, Esq; 38 Norland Sq, London W11 4PZ (☎ 01 727 1756); Cazenove and Co, 12 Tokenhouse Yard, London EC2R 7AN (☎ 01 588 2828, fax 01 606 9205)

CAZALET, Sir Peter (Grenville); s of Vice-Adm Sir Peter Grenville Lyon Cazalet, KBE, CB, DSO, DSC (d 1982), and Beatrice Elise, *née* Winterbotham,*qv*; *b* 26 Feb 1929; *Educ* Uppingham, Magdalene Coll Cambridge (MA); *m* 1957, Jane Jennifer, yr da of Charles Harry Rew (d 1972), of Guernsey; 3 s; *Career* dep chm BP Petroleum Co plc 1986- (md 1981-); dir: P and O Steam Navigation Co Ltd 1980-, Thomas De la Rue Co plc 1983-; dep chm GKN plc 1989-; kt 1989; *Recreations* theatre, travel; *Clubs* Brooks's, Royal Wimbledon Golf, MCC; *Style*— Sir Peter Cazalet; c/o British Petroleum Co plc, Britannic House, Moor Lane, London EC2 9BN(☎ 01 920 7011, telex 888811)

CAZALET, Raymond Percival Saint George; s of Vice Adm Sir Peter Genville Lyon Cazalet, KBE, CB, DSO, DSC; *b* 23 April 1931; *Educ* Uppingham Sch; *m* 1962, Deborah Caroline, *née* Fuggles-Couchman; 3 s; *Career* chief accountant Marshall-Andrew and Co Ltd 1959-61, chm Henderson Administration Ltd 1961-, ACA, FCA; *Recreations* tennis; *Clubs* City of London; *Style*— Raymond Cazalet Esq; 4 Kelso Pla, London W8 (☎ 01 937 6446)

CAZENOVE, Bernard Michael de Lerisson; TD; s of David Michael de Lerisson Cazenove, of 79 Ebury St, London, and Euphemia, *née* MacLean RRC; *b* 14 June 1947; *Educ* RMA Sandhurst; *m* 19 Dec 1971, Caroline June, da of Richard Moore (d 1963), of Wellington, NZ; 2 s (Richard b 1974, George b 1977), 1 da (Edwina b 1985); *Career* cmmnd Coldstream Guard 1967, ADC to HE Governor General of New Zealand 1970, transfered Parachute Regt (TA) 1973, 2 i/c 10 (V) BN The Parachute Regt 1983-; joined Cazenove and Co (Stock Brockers) 1973; ptnr Cazenove and Co 1982-; memb Int Stock Exchange; *Clubs* Whites, Pratts; *Style*— Bernard de Lerisson Cazenove, Esq, TD; 20 Edenhurst Ave, London SW6 3PB; Cazenove & Co, 12 Tokenhouse Yard, London EC2 7AN (☎ 01 588 2828)

CAZENOVE, Christopher de Lerisson; s of Brig Arnold de Lerisson Cazenove, CBE, DSO, MVO (d 1969; descended from Arnaud de Cazenove, Seigneur de Lerisson, of Guienne, France who m 1, 1578, Anne de Bruil, and m 2, 1596, Marie de Laumond), and Elizabeth Laura, 3 da of late Sir Eustace Gurney, JP, of Walsingham Abbey, Norfolk; *b* 17 Dec 1943; *Educ* Eton, Bristol Old Vic Theatre Sch; *m* 8 Sept 1973, Angharad Mary Rees, the actress, da of Prof Linford Rees, CBE, FRCP, FRCPsych; 2 s (Linford b 20 July 1974, Rhys William b 12 Dec 1976); *Career* actor; West End: The Lionel Touch 1969, My Darling Daisy 1970, The Winslow Boy 1970, Joking Apart 1979; Broadway: Goodbye Fidel 1980; TV incl: The Regiment 1971-72, The British Hero, The Pathfinders, K is for Killer 1973, Duchess of Duke Street 1976-77, Jenny's War, Lace II, Dynasty 1986-87, Ticket to Ride 1988-89; Films incl: Royal Flash 1975, East of Elephant Rock 1976, Zulu Dawn 1979, Eye of the Needle 1980, From A Far Country 1980, Heat and Dust 1982, Until September 1984, The Fantasist 1985, Souvenir 1987, Hold My Hand I'm Dying 1988; *Style*— Christopher Cazenove, Esq; Michael Whitehall, 124 Gloucester Rd, London SW1

CAZENOVE, Henry de Lerisson; s of Maj Philip Henry de Lerisson Cazenove, TD, of Cottesbrooke Cottage, Northampton (d 1978), and Aurea Ethelwyn Allix; *b* 13 Jan 1943; *Educ* Eton; *Career* Lt Northamptonshire Yeo TA (now disbanded) 1963-69; ptnr Cazenove and Co 1972- (joined 1963); memb Stock Exchange; govr and tstee St Andrews Hosp, Northampton; Freeman City of London 1980; *Books* A Short History of The Northamptonshire Yeomanry (1966); *Recreations* shooting, travel, gardening; *Clubs* Whites, Pratts, City of London, MCC; *Style*— Henry Cazenove, Esq; Cottesbrooke Cottage, Northampton; Milner Street, London, SW3; Cazenove and Co, 12 Tokenhouse Yard, London, EC2 (☎ 01 588 2828)

CECIL, Hon Anthony Henry Amherst; yr s of 3 Baron Amherst of Hackney, CBE (d 1980); *b* 1 April 1947; *Educ* Eton; *m* 1, 1969 (m dis 1974), Fenella Jane, da of David George Crichton, MVO; m 2, 1974, Jane Elizabeth, da of Philip Norman Elston Holbrook; 2 s (Henry Edward Amherst b 1976, Thomas b 1981), 1 da (Georgiana Helen Amherst b 1979); *Style*— The Hon Anthony Cecil; Bucks Farm, Shorewell, Isle of Wight

CECIL, Hon Anthony Robert; s and h of 3 Baron Rockley and Lady Sarah Primrose Beatrix, da of 7 Earl Cadogan, MC; *b* 29 July 1961; *Educ* Eton, Cambridge; *m* 9 Jan 1988, Katherine Jane, da of G A Whalley, of Chipperfield, Herts; *Recreations* rugby, squash, tennis; *Style*— The Hon Anthony Cecil; Lytchett Heath, Poole, Dorset (☎ 0202 622228)

CECIL, Hon Aurelia Margaret Amherst; da of 4 Baron Amherst of Hackney; *b* 19 July 1966; *Educ* Prior's Field, Queensgate; *Style*— The Hon Aurelia Cecil

CECIL, Hon Camilla Sarah; da of 3 Baron Rockley; *b* 8 Feb 1965; *Educ* North Foreland Lodge, Cambridge Coll of Arts; *Career* magazine journalist; *Style*— The Hon Camilla Cecil

CECIL, Lord Charles Edward Vere (Gascoyne); s of 6 Marquess of Salisbury; *b* 13 July 1949; *Educ* Eton, Ch Ch Oxford; *Career* dir Schroder Wagg (merchant bank); pres Herts Assoc Youth Clubs; cncl memb Children's Society; *Clubs* Turf, Beefsteak, Pratts; *Style*— Lord Charles Cecil; 21 Hollywood Rd, London SW10 (☎ 01 352 1169)

CECIL, Hon Charles Evelyn; 2 s of 2 Baron Rockley; *b* 15 Nov 1936; *Educ* Eton; *m* 1965, Jennifer, da of Duncan Mackinnon and Pamela, da of Capt Robert Brassey, JP, DL (nephew of 1 Earl Brassey, JP, DL, and 1 cous of 1 Baron Brassey of Apethorpe, JP, DL; Pamela's mother was the Capt's 1 w, Violet Lowry-Corry, great niece of 3 Earl Belmore; the Capt's mother was Hon Matilda Bingham, OBE, da of 4 Baron Clanmorris) and 2 cous of the writer Charlotte Bingham; 1 s, 2 da; *Style*— The Hon Charles Cecil; Wilcote House, Charlbury, Oxon (☎ 099 386 355)

CECIL, Henry Richard Amherst; 4 s (twin) of Hon Henry Kerr Auchmuty Cecil (ka 1942), and Elizabeth Rohays Mary, *née* Burnett of Leys (later Lady Boyd-Rochfort); *b* 11 Jan 1943; *Educ* Canford, RAC Cirencester; *m* 18 Oct 1966, Julia, da of Sir (Charles Francis) Noel Murless (d 1987); 1 s (Noel b 3 Feb 1973), 1 da (Katrina b 17 June 1971); *Career* leading racehorse trainer on the flat; trained 2 Derby winners, 2 Oaks winners, 2 2000 Guineas winners, 3 1000 Guineas winners, and 3 St Leger winners; *Books* On The Level; *Recreations* gardening; Warren Place, Newmarket, Suffolk CB8 8QQ (☎ 0638 662387); office (☎ 0638 662192; fax, 0638 669005; telex, 817759 CECIL G)

CECIL, Jonathan Hugh; s of Lord Edward Christian David Gascoyne Cecil, CH (d 1986), of Red Lion House, Cranborne, and Rachel Mary Veronica, *née* McCarthy (d 1982); *b* 22 Feb 1939; *Educ* Eton, New Coll Oxford (BA), London Acad of Music and Dramatic Art; *m* 1, 1963, Vivien Sarah Frances da of David G Heilbron, of Glasgow; m

2, 3 Nov 1976, Anna Sharkey; *Career* actor; theatre incl: A Heritage and its History 1965, Halfway Up the Tree 1967, The Ruling Class 1969, Lulu 1971, Cowardy Custard 1972, The Bed Before Yesterday 1976, The Orchestra 1981, Good Morning Bill 1987, Uncle Vanya 1988; films incl: The Great St Trinian Train Robbery 1965, Otley 1968, Catch Me a Spy 1971, Barry Lyndon 1973, Joseph Andrews 1976, History of the World Part 1 1980, E la Nave Va (Fellini) 1983; tv incl: Maggie 1964, Love Labours Lost 1975, Gulliver in Lilliput 1981, The Puppet Man 1984, 13 at Dinner 1985, Murder in 3 Acts 1987; has also starred in numerous comedy series; *Recreations* writing, reading, history of theatre & music hall; *Clubs* Garrick; *Style—* Jonathan Cecil, Esq; c/o Kate Feast Management, 43A Princess Rd, London NW1 (☎ 01 586 5502)

CECIL, Lord Michael Hugh (Gascoyne); s of 6 Marquess of Salisbury; *b* 1960; *m* 1986, Camilla, da of late Richard Scott; *Career* commissioned Gren Gds 1980; *Style—* Lord Michael Cecil

CECIL, Rear Adm Sir (Oswald) Nigel Amherst; KBE (1979), CB (1978); s of Cdr the Hon Henry Cecil, OBE, RN (d 1962; himself 4 s of Baroness Amherst of Hackney by her husb Lord William Cecil, CVO, 3 s of 3 Marquess of Exeter) and Hon Yvonne Cornwallis (d 1983), 3 da of 1 Baron Cornwallis; *b* 11 Nov 1925; *Educ* Ludgrove, RNC Dartmouth; *m* 1961, Annette, (CStJ 1980) er da of Major Robert Barclay TD, of Bury Hill, Dorking, Surrey; 1 s (Robert b 1965); *Career* joined Navy 1939, Flag Lt to Adm Br Jt Services Mission Washington DC 1948-50, Cdr 1959. Chief Staff Officer London Division RNR 1959-61; commanded: HMS Corunna 1961-63, HMS Royal Arthur 1963-66, Capt 1966; Central Defence Staff 1966-69; Capt (D) Dartmouth Trg Sqdn and in command HM Ships Tenby and Scarborough 1969-71, Cdre Sr Br Naval Offr S Africa and naval attaché Cape Town 1971-73, dir Naval Operational Requirements 1974-75, Naval ADC to HM The Queen 1975, Rear Adm 1975, Cdr Br Forces Malta and Flag Offr Malta 1975-79, Cdr NATO S Eastern Mediterranean 1975-77, Rear-Adm 1975, ret 1979; Lt-Govr IOM 1980-85; KStJ 1980 (OStJ 1971); *Clubs* White's, MCC; *Style—* Rear Adm Sir Nigel Cecil, KBE, CB; c/o C Hoare and Co, 37 Fleet St, London EC4P 4DQ

CECIL, Lord Valentine William (Gascoyne); s of 6 Marquess of Salisbury; *b* 13 May 1952; *Educ* Eton; *Career* a page of honour to HM Queen Elizabeth The Queen Mother 1966-67, Major Gren Gds; *Recreations* flying; *Clubs* Turf, Beefsteak; *Style—* Lord Valentine Cecil; c/o Hatfield House, Hatfield, Herts; 11 Shalcomb Street, London SW10

CECIL, Hon (Hugh) William Amherst; s and h of 4 Baron Amherst of Hackney; *b* 17 July 1968; *Educ* Ludgrove, Eton; *Style—* The Hon Hugh Cecil

CELLAN-JONES, (Alan) James Gwynne; s of Cecil John Cellan-Jones, OBE (d 1968, Lt-Col RAMC), of Swansea, and Lavinia Alicia Sophia, *née* Johnson-Dailey, MBE (d 1963); *b* 13 July 1931; *Educ* Dragon Sch, Lycée Jaccard Lausanne, Charterhouse, St John's Coll Cambridge (BA, MA); *m* 2 April 1959, Margaret Shirley, da of Ernest William Eavis (d 1972), of Burnham on Sea; 3 s (Rory b 1960, Simon b 1962, Deiniol b 1965), 1 da (Lavinia b 1967); *Career* Nat Serv cmmnd RE 1953, Troop Cdr Korea, TA; dir BBC 1963 (joined as callboy 1950); freelance dir: Forsyte Saga, Portrait of a Lady, Jennie (with Lee Remick), Casesar and Cleopatra (with Alec Guinness); dir: The Kingfisher (with Rex Harrison), Bequest to the Nation (with Peter Finch and Glenda Jackson), Much Ado About Nothing (Royal Lyceum Edinburgh), The Adams Chronicles NY ;1976-; head of plays BBC TV 1976-79; dir: School Play, The Day Christ Died, A Fine Romance, Oxbridge Blues, Comedy of Errors, Fortunes of War; writer screenplay: Rates of Exchange, Arms and The Man; DGA Award 1976, Cable Award 1985; memb: cncl DGGB, British Academy of Film Television Arts (chm 1983-85); *Recreations* scuba diving, wine making; *Clubs* Garrick; *Style—* James Cellan-Jones, Esq; 19 Cumberland Ave, Kew, Surrey; Worthy Cottage, Pilton, nr Shipton Mallet, Somerset (☎ 01 940 8742); c/o Jane Annakin, Wm Morris (UK) Ltd, 20th Century House, Soho Square, London W1 (☎ 01 434 2192)

CELY TREVILIAN, Maj Richard Edwin Fearing; TD, DL (Somerset 1982); Lord of the Manors of Midelney and Drayton; el s of Maj Maurice Fearing Cely Trevilian, JP, DL (d 1932), and Mary, *née* Athill; *b* 25 Dec 1912; *Educ* Radley; *m* 26 Sept 1936, Daphne Olive, o da of Sir Digby Lawson, 2 Bt, TD, JP; 1 s, 3 da; *Career* served WW II as Maj in N Somerset Yeo in M East, Mediterranean, NW Europe (despatches); High Sheriff Somerset 1961; hon fellow Woodard Corpn; *Recreations* country pursuits; *Clubs* Army and Navy, MCC; *Style—* Major Richard Cely Trevilian, TD, DL; Midelney Manor, Drayton, Langport, Somerset (☎ 0458 251229)

CENTNER, Hon Mrs (Anne Catherine); da of 2 Viscount Leathers; *b* 1 Jan 1944; *Educ* Benenden; *m* 1977, Arthur Sydney Centner; 1 da (Lucy b 1977); *Style—* The Hon Mrs Centner; 11 Orchard Rd, Orchards, Johannesburg 2192, South Africa

CHACKSFIELD, Air Vice-Marshal Sir Bernard Albert; KBE (1968, OBE 1945), CB (1961); s of Edgar Chacksfield (d 1919), of Ilford, Essex; *b* 13 April 1913; *Educ* County HS, RAF Halton, RAF Cranwell; *m* 1, 1937, Myrtle Elsa Alexena (d 1984), da of Walter Matthews (d 1947), of Rickmansworth, Herts; 2 s, 2 da; *m* 2, 1985, Elizabeth Beatrice, da of James Meek (d 1969), and wid of Frederick Ody (d 1982); *Career* joined RAF 1928, Gp Capt 1951, Air Cdre 1956 (Fighter Cmd), Acting Air Vice-Marshal SASO Tech Trg Cmd 1960, AOC No 22 Group 1960-62, Cmdt-Gen RAF Regt and Inspr Ground Defence 1963-68, ret 1968; chief cmmr Scouts for England 1968-80; pres Soc Aeronautical Engrs 1969-; chm Burma Star Assoc 1979-, chm Bd Royal Masonic Hosp 1988-; CEng, FRAcS; *Recreations* travelling, youth work, flying, sailing, music, drama; *Clubs* RAF; *Style—* Air Vice-Marshal Sir Bernard Chacksfield, KBE, CB; No 8 Rowan House, Bourne End, Bucks SL8 5TG (☎ 062 85 20829)

CHADD, David Francis Lanfear; s of Joseph Chadd (d 1976), and Hilda Birica Lanfear (d 1983); *b* 10 Sept 1943; *Educ* Keble Coll Oxford (MA); *m* 23 Sept 1983, Julia Mary Martin, da of Dr Alan John Rowe, OBE, of Haughley Grange, Stowmarket, Suffolk; 2 s (Alexander b 1984, Tobias b 1988), 1 da (Helena b 1986); *Career* asst lectr Univ of Durham 1966-67, lectr Univ of E Anglia 1967-79 (sr lectr 1979); dean Sch of Art History and Music 1987-; sec Henry Bradshaw Soc 1985-; *Recreations* gardening, mountaineering, visual arts, repairing old houses; *Style—* David F L Chadd, Esq; Thornage Old Rectory, Holt, North Norfolk (☎ 0263 861096); University of East Anglia, Norwich (☎ 0603 592454, fax 0603 58553)

CHADD, Margaret Ruth; JP (Suffolk, 1968); da of Sir Henry Collet, 2 Bt, of The Knoll, Stone Rd, Bromley, Kent, and Ruth Mildred, *née* Hatch; *b* 07 June 1922; *Educ* Kinnaird Park Sch Bromley, LSE, Inst of Hosp Almoners (AIMSW); *m* 10 June 1950, Col George V N Chadd, OBE, TD, JP, DL, s if George Bertie Chadd (d 1940), of Four Stones, Corton, nr Lowestoft, Suffolk; 4 s (Christopher George Andrew b 1951, d 1974, Richard Jonathan b 1953, Timothy Charles b 1955, d 1976, Nicholas Martyn Phillip b 1958); *Career* hosp almoner Queen Victoria Hosp E Grinstead Sussex, 1941-45, county almoner E Sussex CC Lewes Sussex 1948-50, dir GB Chadd (Hldgs) Ltd Lowestoft Suffolk; joined BRCS 1941 (now welfare offr and hon vice pres Suffolk branch); hon organising sec Waverney & N Suffolk CRUSE (bereavement care) 1978-, fndr tstee PACT Suffolk (parents conciliation tst) 1987; BASW; *Books* The Collett Saga (1988); *Recreations* skiing, sailing, tennis, gardening, swimming; *Clubs* VAD, Women of the Year Assoc; *Style—* Mrs Margaret Chadd, JP; Mardle House, Wangford, Nr Beccles Suffolk NR34 8AU (☎ 0502 78334; G B Chadd (Holdings) Ltd, London Rd, North Lowestoft, Suffolk (☎ 0502 588085)

CHADWICK, Donald; s of Rennie Chadwick (d 1944); *b* 12 Mar 1934; *Educ* Bury GS; *m* 1955, Sheila Mary, da of Norman Jackson, of Lilliesleaf; 3 children; *Career* accountant; fin dir Carrington Viyella Ltd 1962-80, md Claridge Mills Ltd 1980-86 (weavers of wool, silk, cashmere; Queen's Award for Export 1982 and 1987); md Ledatec Ltd (mfrs of non-woven textiles); FCMA; *Recreations* golf; *Clubs* Selkirk Rotary; *Style—* Donald Chadwick, Esq; Ruberslaw, Midlem, Selkirk (☎ 083 57 469); Ledatec Ltd, Blackburn, Lancs (☎ 0254 56 413)

CHADWICK, Very Rev Prof Henry; 3 s of late John Chadwick (d 1931), of Bromley, Kent, and Edith, *née* Horrocks; bro of late Sir John and Prof Owen Chadwick, *qv* and of Lady McNicoll (w of Vice Adm Sir Alan McNicol, former Australian Ambass to Turkey); *b* 23 June 1920; *Educ* Eton, Magdalene Coll Cambridge (DD, fell 1979); *m* 1945, Margaret Elizabeth, da of late W Pemell Brownrigg, of Moorhill, Co Kildare; *Career* former regius prof of divinity and canon of Christ Church Oxford, dean 1969-79, hon canon of Ely 1979-, regius prof of divinity Cambridge Univ 1979-82 ; master of Peterhouse Cambridge 1987-; *Recreations* music; *Clubs* Oxford and Cambridge, Royal Commonwealth, Cambridge Univ Wanderers (hockey); *Style—* The Very Rev Prof Henry Chadwick; Peterhouse, Cambridge (☎ 0223 338201)

CHADWICK, Lady Burton-; (Beryl) Joan; da of Stanley Frederick J Brailsford; *m* 1950, as his 2 w, Sir Robert (Peter) Burton-Chadwick, 2 Bt (d 1983); 1 s, 1 da; *Style—* Lady Burton-Chadwick; 102 Meadowbank Rd, Remuera, Auckland 5, New Zealand

CHADWICK, (Gerald William St) John; CMG (1961); s of John Frederick Chadwick; *b* 28 May 1915; *Educ* Lancing, St Catharine's Coll Cambridge; *m* 1938, Madeleine, da of René Boucheron; 2 s; *Career* Colonial Office 1938, Dominions Office 1940; Commonwealth Relations Office asst under-sec of state 1960-66 (formerly asst sec); govr Commonwealth Inst 1967-; first dir Commonwealth Fndn 1966-; author; *Style—* John Chadwick Esq, CMG; 11 Cumberland House, Kensington Rd, London W8

CHADWICK, John Murray; ED (1979), QC (1980); s of Capt Hector George Chadwick, 3 Kings Own Hussars (ka 1942), and Margaret Corry, *née* Laing (d 1977); *b* 20 Jan 1941; *Educ* Rugby, Magdalene Coll Cambridge (MA); *m* 5 Dec 1975, Diana Mary, da of Maj Charles Marshall Blunt, DL (d 1986), of March, Cambs; 2 da (Jane b 1976, Elizabeth b 1978); *Career* Maj (TAVR) 4 bn Royal Green Jackets 1973-76; barr Inner Temple 1966, Bencher 1986; jr cnsl Dept of Trade 1974-80; Judge of the Cts of Appeal of Guernsey and Jersey 1986; memb Wine Standards Bd of Vintners' Co 1983-; rec Crown Cts; *Recreations* sailing; *Clubs* Cavalry and Guards', Royal Yacht Sqdn; *Style—* John Chadwick Esq, QC; Queen Elizabeth Building, Temple, London EC4Y 9BS (☎ 01 936 3131, fax 01 353 1937, car ☎ 0860 204 658)

CHADWICK, Sir Joshua Kenneth Burton-; 3 Bt (UK 1935), of Bidston, Co Palatine of Chester; s of Sir Robert Burton-Chadwick, 2 Bt (d 1983), and Lady Burton-Chadwick, *qv*; *b* 1 Feb 1954; *Style—* Sir Joshua Burton-Chadwick, Bt

CHADWICK, Rev Prof (William) Owen; OM (1983), KBE (1982); s of John Chadwick (d 1931), of Bromley, Kent; er bro of Very Rev Prof Henry Chadwick, *qv*, yr bro of Sir John Chadwick (d 1987), and also bro of Lady McNicoll (w of Vice Adm Sir Alan McNicoll (d 1987), former Australian ambass to Turkey); *b* 20 May 1916; *Educ* Tonbridge, St John's Coll Cambridge; *m* 1949, Ruth Romaine, eldest da of Bertrand Leslie Hallward, formerly Vice-Chancellor of Nottingham Univ; 2 s, 2 da; *Career* former dean and fellow of Trinity Hall Cambridge, sometime chm tstees University Coll (subsequently Wolfson Coll) Cambridge, hon fellow 1977, regius prof of modern history Cambridge Univ 1968-83, vice-chllr 1969-71, master of Selwyn Coll 1956-83; tstee Nat Portrait Gallery 1978- (chm 1988-), memb Royal Cmmn on Historical Manuscripts 1984-, chllr Univ of East Anglia 1985-; Hon DD: St Andrews, Oxford; Hon DLitt: Kent, Bristol, London, E Anglia Cambridge; Hon DLett Columbia USA; FBA (pres 1981-85); *Books* Newman (1983), Hensley Henson (1983), Britain and the Vatican During the Second World War (1987); *Style—* Prof Owen Chadwick; 67 Grantchester Street, Cambridge (☎ 0223 314000)

CHADWICK, Peter; s of Kenneth Fred Chadwick (d 1985), and Grace Jean, *née* Holden; *b* 19 August 1946; *Educ* St Pauls, Churchill Coll Cambridge (BA, MA); *m* 27 Oct 1971, Diana Kathryn Lillian, da of Frank Richard Stanford Kellett; 1 da (Lindsey Nicola b 1974); *Career* princ Dept of Indust 1977-79, ptnr Peat Marwick Mitchess and Co (now Peat Marwick McLintock) 1982-(currently managing ptnr Kent); ACA 1970, FCA 1979; *Style—* Peter Chadwick, Esq; The Old Rectory, Little Chart, Ashford, Kent TN27 0QH; Peat Marwick McLintock, Barnham Ct, Terton, Maidstone, Kent ME18 5ZL (☎ 0622 814 814, fax 0622 814 888); 16-17 Lower Bridge St, Canterbury, Kent CT1 2LG (☎ 0227 762 800, fax 0227 762 810)

CHADWICK, Prof Peter; s of Jack Chadwick, Huddersfield, and Marjorie, *née* Castle (d 1982); *b* 23 Mar 1931; *Educ* Huddersfield Coll, Univ of Machester (BSc), Univ of Cambridge (PhD, ScD); *m* 2 Apr 1956, Sheila (Gladys), da of Clarence Frederick Slater (d 1939), of Colchester; 2 da (Jancie b 1958, Susan b 1970); *Career* sr scientific offr AWRE Aldermaston 1957-59 (scientific offr 1955-57), sr lectr mathematics Univ of Sheffield 1964-65 (lectr 1959-64); prof of mathematics Univ of E Anglia Norwich 1965-(Dean Sch of Maths & Physics 1979-82); vis prof Univ of Queensland 1972; FRS; *Books* Continuum Mechanics (1976), Concise Theory and Problems (1976); *Recreations* walking, music; *Style—* Prof Peter Chadwick; 8 Stratford Crescent, Cringleford, Norwich NR4 7SF (☎ 0603 51655); School of Mathematics, Univ of East Anglia, Univ Plain, Norwich NR4 7TJ (☎ 0603 56161, ext 2848)

CHADWICK, Robert; s of Jack Chadwick, of Inchkeith Court, Cadham, Glenrothes, Fife, and Margaret, *née* Lyons; *b* 18 August 1949; *Educ* Lathallan, Montrose Acad; *m* 9 May 1988, Eileen Joan, da of Flying Offr Leo Hubert Skelton (d 1938); *Career* RA: 22 Battery Sch of Artillery Larkhill 1966-70; Meteorological Off: joined 1970, Prestwick Airport 1970-83, forecaster 1984, Glasgow Weather Centre 1984-88, higher forecaster 1988, RAF Honington 1988-; memb: Trollope Soc, Br Field Sports Soc,

BASC, Game Conservancy; CGA FRMetS 1987; *Recreations* shooting, fishing, reading, following the hunt; *Clubs* Naval, Sloane; *Style—* Robert Chadwick, Esq; Oakacre, Fen St, Hopton, Diss, Norfolk

CHADWICK, Robert Everard; s of Robert Agar and Aline Chadwick; *b* 20 Oct 1916; *Educ* Oundle, Leeds Univ (LLB); *m* 1948, Audrey Monica Procter; 2 s, 1 da; *Career* former chm J Hepworth and Son; former Leeds district dir Barclays Bank; former pres Leeds Permanent Building Soc 1983-85 (dir-pres 1981-83); LLB; *Style—* Robert Chadwick Esq; Leeds Permanent Building Society, Permanent House, The Headrow, Leeds (☎ 0532 438181 7241)

CHADWICK, Terry; s of Parker Chadwick (d 1966), and Helen Elizabeth *née* Hooler (d 1956); *b* 21 Jan 1933; *Educ* Clitheroe Royal GS, Leeds Univ (BSc), King George VI Memorial fell (1956), Univ of California Berkeley (MS); *m* 22 April 1957, Marguerite Elizabeth, da of Arthur Ashworth of Penrhyn Bay, Llandudno; 4 s (Iven b 1960, Stephen b 1962, Martin b 1963, Aran b 1966), 1 da (Lynn b 1958); *Career* conslt civil and structural engr, fndr Deleuw Chadwick Oheocha 1959, estab related practice in Nigeria 1960 (responsible for bridges bldgs and highways); in UK designed: underground railway proposed for Manchester, precint centre Manchester Univ, new HQ Barclays Bank Knutsford; chm Parkside Scout and Guides 1979-82; M Cons E, FICE, MICEI; *Recreations* fellwalking, skiing, golf, classical music; *Clubs* Bramall Park GC; *Style—* Terry Chadwick, Esq; 5 Ladybrook Road, Bramhall, Stockport (☎ 061 485 2868), Clemence House, Mellor Road, Cheadle Hulme, Stockport (☎ 061 486 0011, fax 061 486 0014)

CHADWYCK-HEALEY, Sir Charles Edward; 5 Bt (UK 1919); s of Sir Charles Chadwyck-Healey, 4 Bt, OBE, TD, (d 1986), and Viola, *née* Lubbock; *b* 13 May 1940; *Educ* Eton, Trinity Coll Oxford (MA); *m* 16 Sept 1967, Angela Mary, eldest da of late John Metson of Little Dunmow, Essex; 1 s, 2 da; *Heir* s, Edward Alexander b 2 June 1972; *Career* publisher; chm and md Chadwyck-Healey Ltd 1973-; pres Chadwyck-Healey Inc 1981-, dir Chadwyck-Healey France SARL 1985-; *Clubs* Brooks's; *Style—* Sir Charles Chadwyck-Healey, Bt; Manor Farm, Bassingbourn, Cambs (☎ 0763 242447)

CHAGRIN, Hon Mrs (Elizabeth Constance); *née* Mackintosh; da of (by 1 m) 2 Visc Mackintosh of Halifax, OBE, BEM (d 1980); *b* 4 May 1950; *m* 1, 1972, Timothy Cutting; m 2, 1980, Nicholas Chagrin; 1 da; *Style—* The Hon Mrs Chagrin

CHAITOW, Christopher John Adam; s of Boris Reuben Chaitow, of Stellenbosch, Cape Province, S Africa, and of Elizabeth, *née* Rice (d 1980); *b* 19 Jan 1943; *Educ* Worthing HS; *m* 18 May 1974, Susan Patricia, da of George Joseph Foley, of Keystone Rd, Cardiff; 1 s (Daniel b 1984), 1 da (Ella b 1983); *Career* trainee Northcote & Co 1964-68, res/institutional sales 1968-70, ptnr Beamish & Co 1970-75, institutional sales Northcote & Co 1975-79; tech analysis: Simon & Coates 1979-86, Chase Manhattan Securities 1986, Morgan Grenfell Securities 1986-; contributor: Market Perspective (weekly market comment), UK Equity Market Turnover Analysis (monthly journal); STA; *Recreations* music, golf; *Style—* Christopher Chaitow, Esq; Caroline House, 29/30 Alwyne Rd, London N1 (☎ 01 226 4471); Morgan Grenfell Securities, 20 Finsbury Circus, London EC2M 7BB (☎ 01 256 6278, fax 01 628 7966, telex 939022)

CHALDECOTT, (Oswald) Harry; s of Lt-Col Oswald Arthur Chaldecott (d 1964), of Lonsdale, and Margaret Ursula, *née* Worsley-Taylor (d 1959); Sir Henry Worsley-Taylor, Bt (1924), was MP for Blackpool 1901-13; *b* 29 June 1928; *Educ* Wellington, Peterhouse Camb (BA); *m* 1 July 1960, Grizel Mary Virginia, da of Rear Adm John Grant, of London; 2 da (Perilla b 1961, Alexandra b 1964); *Career* stockbroker; investmt advsr J A Scrymgeour 1953-67, ptnr: J A Scrimgeour 1968-75, Stock and Co 1976-85; assoc dir Stock Beech and Co 1985-; *Recreations* travel, walking, gardening; *Clubs* City Univ, Hurlingham; *Style—* Harry Chaldecotte, Esq; c/o Aitken Home Ltd, 30 City Road, London EC1Y 2AY; Stock Beech and Co, Warnford Court, Throgmorton Street, London EC2N 2AY (☎ 01 638 8471)

CHALFONT, Baron (Life Peer UK 1964); Alun Arthur Gwynne Jones; OBE (1961), MC (1957), PC (1964); s of Arthur Gwynne Jones (d 1982), and Eliza Alice, *née* Hardman (d 1975); *b* 5 Dec 1919; *Educ* West Monmouth Sch, Sch of Slavonic Studies London Univ; *m* 1948, Mona, MB ChB, da of late Harry Douglas Mitchell, of Grimsby; 1 child decd; *Career* sits as Independent in House of Lords, chm Lords All-Party Defence Gp; Brevet Lt-Col (ret) S Wales Borderers (Regular Army Officer 1940-61) served Burma, Ethiopia, Malaya, Cyprus, Egypt; former defence and mil correspondent The Times; min of state Foreign Office 1964-70, Br perm rep to WEU 1969-70; foreign editor New Statesman 1970-71; dir IBM United Kingdom Hldgs Ltd, IBM United Kingdom Ltd; non-exec dir Lazard Bros 1981-, pres Nottingham Building Soc 1983-; chm Euro Atlantic Gp, exec ctee Pilgrims Soc; pres Royal Nat Inst for Deaf; *Books* The Sword and the Spirit (1963), The Great Commanders (1973), Montgomery of Alamein (1976), Waterloo: Story of Three Armies (1979), Star Wars: Suicide or Survival (1985); *Recreations* music, theatre; *Clubs* Garrick, MCC; *Style—* The Rt Hon the Lord Chalfont, OBE, MC, PC; 65 Ashley Gdns, London SW1 (☎ 01 834 5485); c/o IBM (UK) Ltd, 103 Wigmore Street, London W1H 0AB (☎ 01 935 6600)

CHALK, Gilbert John; s of Ronald Arthur Chalk, of Herts, and Elizabeth, *née* Talbot; *b* 21 Sept 1947; *Educ* Lancing, Southampton Univ (BSc), Lancaster Univ (MA), Columbia Univ New York; *m* 9 June 1975, Gillian Frances Audrey, da of Sir Gervase Blois, 10 Bt (d 1967); 2 s (Alexander John Gervase b 1976, Christopher Harry Gilbert b 1985), 1 da (Nicola Elizabeth b 1978); *Career* dir: Centaur Communications Ltd 1981-, Hambros Bank Ltd 1984-, Melville Technology Ltd 1985-, Tranwood plc 1986-88, Bear Brand plc 1988-; MBA; *Recreations* tennis, riding, skiing; *Clubs* Queens; *Style—* Gilbert Chalk, Esq; 103 Elgin Crescent, London W11 2JF (☎ 1091 727 1981); Foxcote Grange, Foxcote, Andoversford, Glos (☎ 0242 820322); Hambros Bank Ltd, 41 Tower Hill, London EC3N 4HA (☎ 01 480 5000)

CHALK, Hon Sir Gordon (William Wesley); KBE (1971); s of late Samuel Chalk; *b* 1913, Britain; *Educ* Queensland; *m* 1937, Ellen Clare, da of William Grant; 1 s, 1 da; *Career* MP Queensland Australia 1947-76, leader Australian Liberal Party (Queensland) 1965-76, dep premier and treasurer Queensland State Govt 1965-76, ret; *Style—* The Hon Sir Gordon Chalk, KBE; 277 Indooroopilly Rd, Indooroopilly, Queensland 4068, Australia (☎ Brisbane 3711598)

CHALK, John Howard; MBE (1945); s of Rupert Ridley Chalk (d 1931), of Port Talbot, and Constance Wing, *née* Bennett; *b* 4 August 1901; *Educ* Oswestry GS; *m* 1, 14 Dec 1927 (m dis), Rowena Jenny Hargest; 2 da (Mary b 1930, Jan b 1931, d 1987); m 2, 11 May 1972, Joan (d 1981), da of late Ben Robinson; 1 s (Mark b 1954); *Career* works engr Damard Lacquer Co Ltd 1933-40, chief engr Bakelite Ltd 1940-66; FIMechE, MIChemE; *Recreations* bee-keeping, wildlife study; *Style—* John H Chalk, MBE; Faraway, Kingston, Kingsbridge, Devon (☎ 0548 810461)

CHALK, Philip Alexander Forbes; s of Charles Philip Chalk, of Much Hadham, Herts (d 1954), and Ann, *née* Forbes (d 1974); *b* 1 May 1930; *Educ* Selwyn Coll Cambridge, The London Hosp Med Coll (MA, MB, BChir); *m* 17 May 1958, Jean Graham, da of Bertram Doughty (d 1978), of Gt Dunmow, Essex; 1 s (David b 1959), 2 da (Alison b 1961, Hilary b 1963); *Career* consult obstetrician and gynnaecologist The Royal Free Hosp London 1969-; formerly resident accoucheur The London Hosp 1958; registrar and sr registrar The Middlesex Hosp 1964-69; govr Queen Mary Coll London; Ct Asst Worshipful Co of Drapers; FRCS, FRCOG; *Recreations* fishing, campanology, Suffolk sheep; *Clubs* Royal Society of Medicine; *Style—* Philip Chalk, Esq; 5 Devonshire Mews North, London W1; The Old Rectory, Whepstead, Bury St Edmunds; 90 Harley St, London W1N 1AH (☎ 01 486 2445)

CHALKER, Rt Hon Lynda; MP (C) Wallasey Feb 1974-; PC (1987); da of late Sidney Henry James Bates and late Marjorie Kathleen Randell; *b* 29 April 1942; *Educ* Roedean, Heidelberg Univ, Westfield Coll London, Central London Poly; *m* 1, 1967 (m dis 1973), Eric Robert Chalker (sometime chm Greater London Young Conservatives, also fndr memb Set the Party Free charter movement within Cons Party, who in Feb 1982 called for one-memb one-vote selection procedure for party and local cncl candidates); m 2, 1981, Clive Landa (chm Tory Reform Gp 1979-82 and chm Young Conservatives 1972-74); *Career* former statistician with Unilever subsidiary, market researcher with Shell Mex and BP, chief exec Louis Harris Int (int div); chm Gtr London YCs 1969-70 (nat vice-chm YCs 1970-71); memb BBC Gen Advsy Ctee 1975-79; oppn spokesman social services 1976-79; parly under-sec state: DHSS 1979-82, Transport 1982-Oct 1983; min state Transport 1983-86; Min of State Foreign and Commonwealth Office Jan 1986-; *Recreations* cooking, driving; *Style—* Rt Hon Lynda Chalker, MP; House of Commons, London SW1A 0AA (☎ 01 219 5098)

CHALLIS, George Hubert; s of Hubert William Challis (d 1969); *b* 26 May 1921; *Educ* King Edward VI Sch Stourbridge; *m* 1946, Margaret Beatrice, da of Reginald Percy Bonner (d 1965); 1 s, 1 da; *Career* served 1940-46 1/9 Gurkha Rifles (despatches twice); banker and co dir; with Lloyds Bank plc 1938-81 (head of premises div 1974-81); dir: Lloyds Bank Property Co 1974-81, Towco Gp Ltd 1982-84, Westminster Property Gp plc 1983-84; memb: Court of Common Cncl (City of London) 1978-, chm Port and City Health and Social Servs Ctee 1988-; cncl London Chamber of Commerce and Industry 1979-, Thames Water Authy 1982-83; dep govr The Hon Irish Soc 1983-84; Fourth Warden Worshipful Co of tobacco Pipe Makers and Tobacco Blenders 1988-89; Hon Clerk Worshipful Co of Chartered Secretaries and Administrators 1984- Cdr of the Order of Merit (Federal Republic of Germany) 1986; *Recreations* travel, reading, music; *Clubs* RAC, MCC, Guildhall, City Livery; *Style—* George Challis, Esq; 77 West Hill Ave, Epsom, Surrey KT19 8JX (☎ Epsom 21705)

CHALMERS, George Buchanan; CMG (1978); s of George Chalmers (d 1938), of Glasgow, and Anne Buchanan Chalmers (d 1981); *b* 14 Mar 1929; *Educ* Hutchesons' GS Glasgow, Glasgow and Leiden Univ (MA, Dr Econ Sc); *m* 1954, Jeanette Donald, da of Alexander Cant (d 1963), of Glasgow; *Career* RAF 1950-52, Flt Lt; HM Diplomatic Serv 1952-82: min Br Embassy Tehran 1975-79, consul gen Chicago 1979-82; *Recreations* gardening, golf, bridge; *Style—* George Chalmers, Esq, CMG; East Bank Ho, Bowden, Melrose, Roxburghshire TD6 0ST (☎ 0835 22316)

CHALMERS, Dr James Alexander (Hamish); s of William Chalmers (d 1928), of Southcote, Inverness , and Catherine Florence Munro, of Old Thacky, Monks Risborough, Bucks; *b* 11 Jan 1912; *Educ* Inverness Royal Acad, Univ of Edinburgh (MB, ChB, MD); *m* 23 Dec 1940, Lois Guille, da of Charles Humphries Taudevin (d 1963), of Gipsy Corner, Willaston in Wirral, Cheshire; 2 s (Iain b 1943, Robert b 1950), 1 da (Penelope b 1946); *Career* WWII Wing Cdr med branch RAF 1939-45; conslt obsterician gynaecologist, Northern Counties Scotland 1947-51, Worcester Royal Infirmary 1951-77; author several books and pubns (mainly obstetrical); FRCS Edinburgh 1945, MRCOG 1940, FRCOG 1954; *Recreations* music, history; *Clubs* RAF; *Style—* Dr James Chalmers; 44 Observatory St, Oxford OX2 6EP

CHALMERS, Hon Mrs; (Lydia Elizabeth Palmer); *née* MacDermott; da of Baron MacDermott, MC, PC (Life Peer, d 1979); *b* 6 June 1939; *Educ* Wycombe Abbey Sch, Belfast Coll of Art; *m* 1964, David McKenzie Chalmers, yr s of Dr Robert Miller Chalmers (d 1954), of Wandsworth; 2 s (Douglas b 1966, John b 1969); *Career* artist; *Style—* The Hon Mrs Chalmers; Old School House, Beech Hill, Reading, Berks RG7 2BE

CHALMERS, Norman Ashley; s of Reginald Chalmers (d 1984), of Berkhamsted, and Francis, *née* Flynn (d 1980); *b* 19 June 1933; *Educ* Berkhamsted Sch, RMA Sandhurst; *m* 12 July 1958, Susan, da of Leslie Bradford Harvey (d 1984), of Nantwich, Cheshire; 2 da (Caroline b 3 March 1964, Sarah b 23 Oct 1966); *Career* The Black Watch Royal Highland Regt 1951-58, cmmnd 1953; sr ptnr Arthur Andersen & Co CAs, dep chm Nat Mutual Life Assur Soc 1980-; chm: London & Clydeside Hldgs plc 1974-, Siver Estates Gp 1980-, City & Commerical Comms plc 1988-; chm Families at Risk 1987-, dir World Family of Foster Parents Plan 1983-; memb Worshipful Co of Gardeners (memb ct), Freeman City of London; FCA; *Recreations* golf, shooting, fishing; *Clubs* Wentworth, Stoke Poges GC, City Livery; *Style—* Norman Chalmers, Esq; Beechwood, Egypt Lane, Farnham Common, Bucks SL2 3D; 1 Surrey St, London WC2R 2PS (☎ 01 438 3743)

CHALMERS, William Gordon; CB (1980), MC (1944); s of Robert Wilson Chalmers, and Mary Robertson, *née* Clark; *b* 4 June 1922; *Educ* Robert Gordon's Coll Aberdeen, Aberdeen Univ; *m* 1948, Margaret Helen McLeod; 1 s, 1 da; *Career* slr; asst Crown Office 1963-67, dep crown agent 1967-74, crown agent for Scotland 1974-84; *Recreations* bridge, golf; *Clubs* Royal Overseas League; *Style—* William Chalmers, Esq, CB; 3/4/ Rocheid Park, East Fettes Avenue, Edinburgh EH4 1RP

CHALONER, John Seymour; s of Ernest Joseph Chaloner (d 1954), and Lenore Maud, MBE, *née* Barling (d 1974); *b* 5 Nov 1924; *Educ* Beltane Sch Wimbledon, Carleton Coll Ottawa Canada; *m* 1, 1952; 2 s (Nicholas b 1956, Ben b 1960); m 2, 1978, Patricia Ann; *Career* served as Maj Westminster Dragoons in NW Europe 1944-45; founded Post War German Newspapers, incl Der Spiegel 1946; founder and chm Seymour Press Gp London 1948-76; memb Wandsworth Borough Cncl 1961-68; govr St George's Hosp London 1961-68; author: Three for The Road, To Europe with Love, To The Manor Born, Bottom Line, 9 illustrated childrens titles; chm Publishing

Div Inst of Dirs 1984-; *Recreations* shooting, hunting, sailing, skiing; *Style*— John Chaloner, Esq; 4 Warwick Square, London SW1 (☎ 01 834 9871); Sandfold Farm, Selmeston, Sussex (☎ 0323 870391)

CHALONER, Hon Robert Toby Long; s of 3 Baron Gisborough; *b* 13 July 1966; *Style*— The Hon Robert Chaloner

CHALONER, Hon Thomas Peregrine Long (Perry); s and h of 3 Baron Gisborough; *b* 17 Jan 1961; *Educ* Univ of Buckingham (LLB), Barrister at Law (Inner Temple); *Career* pilot; *Recreations* diving, windsurfing, aerobatics; *Style*— The Hon Perry Chaloner; 114 Lupus St, London SW1

CHALSTREY, Leonard John; s of Leonard Chalstrey, of Tipton, Staffordshire, and Frances Mary, *née* Lakin; *b* 17 Mar 1931; *Educ* Dudley Sch, Queens' Coll Cambridge, St Bartholomew's Hosp Med Coll (MA, MD, BChir, FRCS); *m* 6 Sept 1958, Aileen Beatrice, da of Harold Bayes (d 1984); 1 s (Jonathan b 1962), 1 da (Susan b 1959); *Career* conslt surgn St Bartholomew's and Homerton Hosps 1969-, sr lectr in surgery St Bartholomew's Med Coll 1969-, examiner in surgery Univ of London 1976- and Univ of Cambridge 1988-, hon cnslt surgn St Luke's Hosp for the Clergy; Alderman (Ward of Vintry) Corpn City of London 1984- (memb Common Cncl 1981-), memb Ct of City Univ; memb Ct of Assts Worshipful Soc of Apothecaries of London, memb Ct of Assts Worshipful Co of Barbers 1987; memb Guild of Freemen City of London, Fell Hunterian Soc, memb Br Soc of Gastro Enterology; memb Assoc of Surgeons of Gt Britain and Ireland, FRSM; *Books* Gastro-Intestinal Disorders (1986); contributor: numerous papers on surgical subjects to medical press GB and USA, Maingot's Abdominal Operations (7 edn 1980, 8 edn 1985); *Recreations* painting in oils; *Clubs* United Oxford and Cambridge Univ, The City Livery; Guildhall; *Style*— L J Chalstrey, Esq; Danebury, The Chine, London N21 2EG (☎ 01 360 8921); 116 Harley Street, London W1N 1AG (☎ 01 935 7413)

CHAMBERLAIN, Lady Catharine Laura; *née* Chetwynd-Talbot; 3 da (by 1 m) of late 21 Earl of Shrewsbury and Waterford; *b* 4 August 1945; *m* 1966, Richard Sebastian Endicott Chamberlain, eldest s of Lawrence Endicott Chamberlain, of The Dairy House, Tonerspuddle, Dorset; 1 s, 2 da; *Style*— Lady Catharine Chamberlain; Stocks Farm, Burley St, Nr Ringwood, Hants

CHAMBERLAIN, Prof Geoffrey Victor Price; RD (1974); s of Albert Victor Chamberlain, MBE (d 1978), of Penylan, Cardiff, and Irene May, *née* Price, MBE, of Westgate St, Cardiff; *b* 21 April 1930; *Educ* Llandaff Cathedral Sch, Cowbridge GS, Unversity Coll London, University Coll Hosp Med Sch (MB, BS, MD); *m* 23 June 1956, Prof Jocelyn Olivia Peter, da of Sir Peter Kerley, KCVO (d 1979), of Putney London; 3 s (Christopher b 1957, Mark b 1959, Patrick b 1962), 2 da (Hilary b 1961, Virginia b 1966); *Career* Surgn Lt: RNVR 1955-57, RNR 1957-70, (surgn lt -cmdr 1961-, surgn cdr 1970-74); ret 1974; demonstrator in Anatomy Royal Univ of Malta 1956-57; res: Royal Postgraduate Med Sch, Hosp for Sick Children Great Ormond Street (and others) 1958-62, sr registrar, King's Coll Hosp 1962-69 (registrar), visiting res fell George Washington Univ USA 1966-67, conslt Obstetrician & Gynaecologist Queen Charlotte's Hosp for women 1970-82, head of dept Obstetrics & Gynaecology St George's Hosp med Sch 1982- (prof); visiting prof: USA 1984, Hong Kong 1985, Brisbane 1987, SA 1988; med examiner: London Univ 1972-, Liverpool Univ 1973-75, Manchester Univ 1979-83, Birmingham Univ 1979-82, Cambridge Univ 1981-86, Glasgow Univ 1985-87, Kuala Lumpur Univ 1986-87, Nottingham Univ 1987-, Wales 1988-, Malta 1988-, examiner RCOG 1972-, chm medical ctee nat birthday tst, former chm Blair Bell Res Soc, Hon Gynaecologist Br Airways, fell Univ Coll London, former VP RCOG, tres RSM, inspector of Nullity; Freeman City of London 1982; FRCS 1960, MRCOG 1063, FRCOG 1978; *Books* Lecture Notes in Obstetrics (1984), Practice of Obstetrics and Gynaecology (1985), Pregnancy Survival Manual (1986), Birthplace (1987), Lecture Notes in Gynaecology (1988), Manual of Obstetrics (1988), Obstetrics (1989); *Recreations* opera, gardening, writing, travel; *Clubs* Perinatal, Blair Bell Soc, McDonald; *Style*— Prof Geoffrey Chamberlain; Department of Obstetrics & Gynaecology, St George's Hospital Medical Sch, Cranmer Terr, London, SW17 ORE, (☎ 01 672 9944 ext 55956, fax 767 4696, telex 945291 SAGEMS G)

CHAMBERLAIN, Air Vice-Marshal George Philip; CB (1946), OBE (1941); s of George Arthur Raddon Chamberlain (d 1953), of Enville, Stourbridge, Worcs; *b* 18 August 1905; *Educ* Denstone Coll, RAF Cranwell; *m* 1930, Alfreda Rosamond da of F M Kedward, of Swingfield, Kent; 1 s, 1 da; *Career* cmmnd RAF 1925, AOA Fighter Command 1954-57, Air Vice-Marshal 1955, Dep Controller of Electronics Miny of Supply 1957, Miny of Aviation 1959-60, ret 1960; md Collins Radio Co of England Ltd 1962-66, aviation and electronics consultant and non-exec dir 1966-75; *Recreations* gardening; *Style*— Air Vice-Marshal Philip Chamberlain, CB, OBE; Little Orchard, 12 Adelaide Close, Stanmore, Middx (☎ 01 954 0710)

CHAMBERLAIN, Kevin John; s of Arthur James Chamberlain, of Purley, Surrey, and Gladys Mary, *née* Harris; *b* 31 Jan 1942; *Educ* Wimbledon Coll, Kings Coll London (LLB); *m* 23 Sept 1967, Pia Rosita, da of Jean Frauenlob, of Geneva, Switzerland; 1 da (Georgina b 26 Aug 1975); *Career* barr Inner Temple 1965; FCO: asst legal advsr 1965-73, legal advsr Br Mil Govt Berlin 1973-76, 1 sec (legal advsr) HM Embassy Bonn 1976-78, legal cnsllr 1979-83, cnsllr (legal advsr) Off of the UK permanent rep to the euro community 1983-87, legal cnsllr 1987-; *Recreations* opera, riding, tennis, skiing; *Style*— Kevin Chamberlain, Esq; Foreign and Commonwealth Office, London SW1 2AH (☎ 01 270 3084)

CHAMBERLAIN, (Leslie) Neville; s of Leslie Chamberlain, (d 1970), and Doris Anne, *née* Thompson; *b* 3 Oct 1939; *Educ* King James GS Bishop Auckland, King's Coll Univ of Durham; *m* 13 April 1971, Joy Rachel, da of Capt William Wellings (d 1979); 1 s (Andrew b 1984), 3 da (Louise b 1972, Elizabeth b 1974, Christina b 1981); *Career* UKAEA: mgmnt trainee 1962-64, health physicist Springfields 1964-67, res scientist Capenhurst 1967-71; mangr URENCO 1971-77; BNFL: works mangr Springfields 1977-81, enrichment bus mangr Risley 1981-84, dir enrichment divn Risley 1984-86; chief exec British Nuclear Fuels plc Risley 1986-; FInstM, CBIM, MInstPh; *Recreations* horse racing, swimming, music; *Style*— Neville Chamberlain, Esq; Spring House, 56 Brimstage Road, Heswall, Wirrall L60 1XG (☎ 051 342 5981); British Nuclear Fuels plc, Risley, Warrington, Cheshire (☎ 0925 835 006, fax 0925 817625, car 0860 388846, telex 627581)

CHAMBERLAIN, Peter Edwin; s of Dr Eric Alfred Charles Chamberlain, OBE, FRSE, and Susan Winifred Louise, *née* Bone; *b* 25 July 1939; *Educ* Royal HS, Edinburgh Univ (BSc), RN Coll Manadon, RN Coll Greenwich, UCL, RCDS; *m* 27 July 1963, Irene May, da of Dr David B Frew, of Craigielea, 87 Whitehouse Road, Barnton, Edinburgh; 2 s (Mark b 1964, Paul b 1965), 1 da (Louise b 1970); *Career* asst construction ship and submarine design M East and Bath 1963-68, constructor 1968-69, submarine construction Birkenhead 1969-72, Ship Structures RCD Dunfermline 1972-74, Ship Design Bath 1977-78, Chief Constructor and head of Secretariat Bath 1978-80, Surface Ship Forward Design Bath 1980-82, asst sec Head of Secretariat to MGO London 1984-85, Under Sec dir gen, Future Material Programmes 1985-88; Chief Underwater Systems Executive 1988-; RNCN, FEng 1988; *Recreations* jogging, music, visual arts, poetry; *Style*— Peter Chamberlain, Esq; Ministry of Defence, Main Building, Whitehall, London SW1A 2HB

CHAMBERLAIN, Hon Sir (Reginald) Roderic (St Clair); QC (1945); s of late Henry Chamberlain; *b* 17 June 1901; *Educ* St Peter's Coll, Adelaide Univ; *m* 1929, Leila Macdonald, da of George James Haining; 1 da; *Career* former Crown solicitor and Crown prosecutor; judge of the Supreme Court of South Australia 1959-71; kt 1970; *Style*— The Hon Sir Roderic Chamberlain, QC; 72 Moseley St, Glenelg South, SA 5045, Australia (☎ 95 2036)

CHAMBERLAIN, William Richard Frank; s of Lt-Cdr Richard Chamberlain (d 1967), and Elizabeth, *née* Robson (d 1965); *b* 13 April 1925; *Educ* Uppingham ; *m* 1960, Gillian Diarmid, da of Laurence Malcolm Trevor Castle; 1 s, 1 da; *Career* chm Stead and Simpson plc 1983-, eastern regnl dir Nat West Bank plc 1983-; chm Northants CCC, memb Test and County Cricket Bd; *Recreations* shooting, cricket; *Clubs* Naval and Military, MCC; *Style*— William Chamberlain Esq; Manor House, Swineshead, 0234 MK44 2AF (☎ Bedford 708283)

CHAMBERLAYNE, Lt-Col John Edward Stanes; DL (1967); s of Col Edward Tankerville Chamberlayne, DSO, DL, JP (d 1963), of Chipping Norton, Oxon, and Susan Katherine, *née* Scott MacKirdy (d 1945); *b* 26 Nov 1910; *Educ* Eton, Christ Church Oxford (MA); *m* 29 Oct 1936, Daphne Helena, da of Col George Henry Barnett, CMG, DSO (d 1942), of Glympton Park, Woodstock, Oxon; 2 s (Simon John b 1940, Mark Edward b 1942); *Career* 16/5 Lancers 1931; Res of Offrs 1948; Mayor of Chipping Norton 1953-55, High Sheriff 1966 (Oxfordshire), hon sec MFHA 1956-76, JP (Oxon) 1953-80; *Recreations* hunting, racing; *Clubs* Jockey Club, Cavalry and Guards; *Style*— Lt-Col John Chamberlayne, Esq, JP, DL; Old Rectory, Churchill, Oxford (☎ 060 871 601)

CHAMBERLAYNE-MACDONALD, Major Nigel Donald Peter; LVO (1960), OBE (1980), DL (1975); s of Sir Geoffrey Bosville Macdonald of the Isles, 15 Bt, MBE (d 1951), and Hon Rachael Audrey, *née* Campbell (d 1978); *b* 10 June 1927; *Educ* Radley; *m* 15 April 1958, Penelope Mary Alexandra, da of Tankerville Chamberlayne; 2 s (Alexander Nigel Bosville b 1959, Thomas Somerled b 1969), 2 da (Diana Mary b 1961, Frances Penelope b 1965 d 1985); *Career* cmmnd Scots Gds 1946, served Italy 1946-47 and Malaya 1950-51, Canal Zone 1952-53; equerry to HRH The Duke of Gloucester 1954-55, and asst private sec 1958-60; High Sheriff Hampshire 1974-75; chm Hants Assoc of Boys Clubs 1967-82, a vice chm Nat Assoc of Boys Clubs 1969; pres: The Coaching Club 1982, Eastleigh and Chandlers Ford Boys Scouts Assoc; a Gentleman Usher to HM The Queen 1979; memb The Queen's Body Guard for Scotland (Royal Co of Archers); OStJ 1958; *Recreations* coaching, shooting, stalking; *Clubs* White's, Brooks's, Pratt's, Royal Yacht Squadron; *Style*— Major Nigel Chamberlayne-MacDonald, LVO, OBE, DL; Cranbury Park, Winchester, Hants SO21 2HL (☎ 0703 252617); Glaschoille House, Knoydart, Mallaig (☎ 0687 2244); 17 William Mews, London SW1 (☎ 01 235 5867)

CHAMBERLEN, Captain Christopher John Tankervills; LVO (1972); s of Leonard Saunders Chamberlen (d 1987), and Lillian Margaret Chamberlen, *née* Webley; *b* 3 Sept 1933; *Educ* RNC Dartmouth; *m* 6 Aug 1967, Eila Margaret, da of Maj George Dannielsen, MBE (d 1943); 3 da (Venetia b 1968, Annabel b 1969, Jessica b 1972); *Career* RN Capt; QHM Porstmouth 1984-87; ret 1988; *Recreations* painting, shooting, riding, racing; *Clubs* RN, Boodles, Farmers; *Style*— Capt Christopher J T Chamberlen, LVO; West Hall, Upham, Hants SO3 1JD (☎ 04896 674)

CHAMBERLEN, Nicholas Hugh; s of Rev Leonard Saunders Chamberlen, MC (d 1987), of Heathfield, Sussex, and Lillian Margaret, *née* Webley; *b* 18 April 1939; *Educ* Sherborne, Lincoln Coll Oxford (BA); *m* 18 Sept 1962, Jane Mary, da of Paul Lindo (d 1970); 3 s (Julian b 1964, Mark b 1965, Alexander b 1970), 1 da (Camilla b 1967); *Career* nat serv RN 1957-59, Lt RNR; with NCR 1962-67; Clive Discount Co Ltd 1967-: dir 1969, chm 1977-; chm London Discount Market Assoc 1985-87; *Recreations* shooting, golf, cricket; *Style*— Nicholas Chamberlen, Esq; 9 Devonshire Square, London EC2M 4HP (☎ 01 548 4042, fax 01 548 4642, telex 8958901)

CHAMBERLIN, Lt-Col Peter Guy; s of Guy Ronald Chamberlin, and Geraldine Mary, *née* Payne Cook (d 1963); *b* 23 June 1942; *Educ* Eton Coll, Aix-en-Provence Univ, RMA Sandhurst; *m* 30 Nov 1968, Marion Jacqueline, da of Lt-Col John Alan Burns (d 1987); 1 s (Edward b 1974), 2 da (Lucinda b 1970, Vanessa b 1977); *Career* army offr; cmmnd Green Jackets 1963; served Far East, Berlin, W Germany, N Ireland, Canada, Hong Kong, Lt-Col CO Light Div Depot Winchester, SHAPE MA D/Saceur, UKLO Heeresamt, Cologne; *Recreations* cricket, golf, tennis and raquets, military history; *Clubs* MCC, I Zingari; *Style*— Lt-Col Peter G Chamberlin; Coldharbour House, St Mary Bourne, Andover, Hants (☎ 0264 738283)

CHAMBERS, Antony Craven; s of Brig Samuel Craven Chambers, CBE, of 45 Hillhead Rd, Fareham, and Mary Agnes, *née* McAllister; *b* 8 Dec 1943; *Educ* Ampleforth, St Catherine's Coll Oxford (MA), Manchester Business Sch (MBA); *m* 24 July 1965, Rosemary Isabel, da of Wing Cdr Gerald Constable Maxwell DFC, AFC, AEM (d 1959), of Alresford House, Alresford, Hants; 3 s (Dominic b 1966, Sebastian b 1967, Mungo b 1977), 2 da (Antonia b 1974, Alexandra b 1979); *Career* joined Grenadier Gds 1966, platoon cdr Cyprus and UK, signals offr 1 Bn served Muscat and Trucial States 1968, 2 i/c Rifle Company NI 1969 -70; asst investmt mangr Hill Samuel & Co Ltd 1970-71; First Chicago 1972: North Sea project fin 1972-74, business devpt UK branch network 1975-77, mangr mktg divs 1978-81, gp head banking and mktg 1982-83, head strategic planning Europe 1984; dir Robert Fleming & Co Ltd (responsible for commercial banking) 1984-; memb: exec ctee and control bd Army Benevolent Fndn 1979, Offrs Assoc 1985; tstee Help the Aged 1987; *Recreations* sailing; *Style*— Antony Chambers, Esq; Lake House, Alresford, Hampshire (☎ 0962 733148); Robert Fleming & Co Ltd, 25 Copthall Ave, London EC2R 7DR (☎ 01 638 5858, fax 01 256 5036, telex 297451)

CHAMBERS, David John; s of George Alfred Chambers, of Middlesex, and Marie Louise Chambers, *née* Ackerman; *b* 19 April 1930; *Educ* Lower Sch of John Lyon Harrow; *m* 1956, Preto Hermione, da of George Chick Aggett (d 1971), of Kenya; 1 s

(Peter b 1958), 2 da (Clare b 1960, Susan b 1964); *Career* non-marine underwriter Lloyds 1966-1987; md Gilliat Scotford and Hayworth Ltd 1987 (previously jt md 1966-86); dir Bain Dawes underwriting agency 1980-86; *Books* Cock-A-Hoop, A Bibliography of the Golden Cockerel Press 1949-61 (with Christopher Sandford 1976); Joan Hassall engravings and drawings 1985; ed: private Press Books, An Annual Bibliography 1963-79; The Private Library, Quaterly Jl of the Private Libraries Assoc (1979-); *Recreations* book collecting, printing; *Clubs* Double Crown Club, Private Libraries Association, Bibliographical Soc; *Style*— David John Chambers, Esq; Ravelston, South View Rd, Pinner, Middx HA5 3YD

CHAMBERS, Dr Douglas Robert (Bob); s of Douglas Henry Chambers, of East Sheen (d 1979), and Elizabeth Chambers, *née* Paterson, of Richmond (d 1987); *b* 2 Nov 1929; *Educ* Sheen GS, Kings Coll London (AKC, MB BS), Univ London (external LLB), Bar 1965 Lincoln's Inn; *m* 8 Jan 1955, Barbara (June) Rowe; 1 s (Robert Mark b 1958), 2 da (Barbara Lynn b 1955, Judith Elizabeth b 1961); *Career* Flt Lt RAF Medical Branch (1955-1958) Jordan 1956-57, medical dir Hoechst Pharmaceuticals 1965-70, HM Coroner Inner North London 1970-, Hon lectr, City University, University Coll and Royal Free Hospitals (legal medicine); *Recreations* history of coroners, scouting; *Clubs* Auriol-Kensington Rowing, Wig and Pen; *Style*— Dr Bob Chambers; 4 Ormond Avenue, Richmond, Surrey TW10 6TN (☎ 01 940 7745); Coroners Court, St Pancras, London NW1 (☎ 01 387 4882)

CHAMBERS, Lady; Edith; da of Robert Philips Lamb, of Workington; *m* 1, 1940 (m dis 1954), Morris Pollack; m 2, 1955, as his 2 w, Sir (Stanley) Paul Chambers, KBE, CB, CIE, taxation expert, sometime chm Royal Insurance, ICI (d 1981); 2 da; *Style*— Lady Chambers; 1a Frognal Gdns, Hampstead, London NW3 (☎ 01 794 6906)

CHAMBERS, Lucinda Anne; da of Michael Chambers, and Anne Chambers; *b* 17 Dec 1959; *Educ* Convent of the Sacred Heart Woldingham; *Career* sr fashion ed Elle Magazine UK 1986-88, exec fashion ed Vogue Magazine 1988- (former asst ed); *Style*— Miss Lucinda Chambers; 29 Oaklands Grove, London W12 (☎ 01 743 3678); Cobblestones, Shipton-U-Wychwood, Oxon; Vogue, Vogue House, Hanover Sq, London W1 (☎ 01 499 9080)

CHAMBERS, Nicholas Mordaunt; s of Marcus Mordaunt Bertrand Chambers, and Lona Margit, *née* Gross (d 1987); *b* 25 Feb 1944; *Educ* King's Sch Worcester, Hertford Coll Oxford; *m* 1966, Sarah Elizabeth, da of Thomas Herbert Fothergill Banks; 2 s (William b 1968, Roland b 1970), 1 da (Jane b 1973); *Career* barr 1966, QC 1985, rec 1987; *Recreations* sketching; *Clubs* Garrick, Lansdowne; *Style*— Nicholas Chambers, Esq, QC; 1 Brick Court, Temple, London EC4 (☎ 01 583 0777)

CHAMBERS, Sidney Hamilton Beadnall; CBE (1972); Sidney Harry Chambers (d 1971), and Marjorie Kathleen (d 1985); *b* 9 Jan 1932; *Educ* Chatsworth HS Wahroonga; *m* 1955, Marguerite Sinclair, da of John Keith Shirley (d 1952); 3 s (Sidney b 1961, John b 1966, William b 1971); *Career* fndr Whale Three Minute Car Wash Pty Ltd; chm: Kruger Mining Co Pty Ltd, Rand Mining Co Pty Ltd, Foundation Constructions Pty Ltd; *Recreations* cricket, tennis, running; *Clubs* Australian American, Tattersalls (Sydney), Sydney Cricket Ground, Royal Agriculture Soc; *Style*— Sidney Chambers, Esq, CBE; Ellerslie, 3 Cross Street, Mosman, NSW 2088, Australia

CHAMPION, John Stuart; CMG (1977), OBE (1963); s of Rev Sir Reginald Stuart Champion, KCMG, OBE (d 1982), of Tunbridge Wells, Kent, and Margaret, da of late Very Rev W M Macgregor; *b* 17 May 1921; *Educ* Shrewsbury, Balliol Coll Oxford (BA); *m* 1944, Olive Lawrencina, da of Lawrence Durning Holt (d 1961), of Liverpool (Lord Mayor 1930); 5 s (David, Lawrence, William, Peter, Richard), 2 da (Sally, Catherine); *Career* cmmnd Lt 11 Hussars (PAO) 1941-46, served in Western Desert, Italy, and NW Europe; Colonial Serv (later HMOCS) Uganda 1946-63, dist cmmr 1954, asst financial sec 1956, actg perm sec Min of Health 1959, perm sec Min of Internal Affrs 1960, ret 1963; princ CRO 1963, 1 sec FCO 1965, head of chancery Tehran 1968, cncllr Amman 1971 (charge d'affaires 1972), FCO 1973, Br resident cmmr Anglo/French Condominium of the New Hebrides 1975-78, ret 1978; memb W Midlands RHA 1980-81, chm Herefordshire Health Authy 1982-86; govr Royal Nat Coll for the Blind 1980- (vice-chm 1985-), chm St John Council for Hereford and Worcester 1987-; OStJ (1987); *Recreations* hill walking, golf, music; *Clubs* Royal Cwlth Soc; *Style*— John Champion, Esq, CMG, OBE; Farmore, Callow, Hereford HR2 8DB (☎ 0432 274875)

CHAMPION, Baroness; Mary Emma; *née* Williams; da of David Williams, of Pwllgwaun, Pontypridd, Glam; *m* 1930, Baron Champion (Life Peer; d 1985); 1 da (Hon Mrs Chubb, *qv*); *Style*— The Rt Hon Lady Champion; 22 Lanelay Terrace, Pontypridd, Mid Glam CF37 1ER (☎ 0443 402349)

CHAMPKIN, Peter; s of Cyril Champkin (d 1949), and Gwendoline Wilson (d 1919); *b* 1 Sept 1918; *Educ* Kings Sch Canterbury, St Catharines Coll Cambridge; *m* 21 oct 1950, Edna Kathleen, da of George Wilton (d 1976); 1 s (Julian Guy b 1954), 1 da (Clare Wendy b 1952); *Books* In Another Room (1960), Poems of Our Time (1962), The Emnity of Noon (1964), For the Employed (1970), The Waking Life of Aspern Williams (1976), The Sleeping Life of Aspern Williams (1988); *Recreations* clock making; *Style*— Peter Champkin, Esq; Hemingfold Oast, Telham, Battle, E Sussex TN33 0TU

CHAMPNESS, John Ashley; *b* 17 April 1938; *m* Sandra; 2 da (Joanna Louise, Charlotte Helen); *Career* dir Lowndes Lambert Group Ltd, chm & md Lowndes Lambert Marine Ltd, dir Wallem Lambert (Hong Kong) Ltd; *Style*— John Champness, Esq; Stoneraise, Plummers Plain, Horsham, Essex; 53 Eastcheap, London EC3P 3HL (☎ 01 283 2000)

CHAMPNESS, Philip Harvey; s of Clement Maurice Champness (d 1960), of Surrey, and Constance Harriet Duder (d 1959); *b* 30 August 1919; *Educ* Rugby, King's Coll Camb (MA); *m* 26 April 1952, Elizabeth Jean, da of Air Marshal Sir Philip Babington, KCB, MC, AFC (d 1965), of Surrey; 2 s (Henry b 1953, Peter b 1955); *Career* WWII cmmnd Duke of Cornwall's LI 1940, 6 Rajputana Rifles 1941-45, served in India Cmd (Maj); CA, sr ptnr Champness Cowper and Co (ret 1977); common councilman Corpn of London, Walbrook Ward 1966-87, dep Walbrook Ward 1975-87; Liveryman The Worshipful Co of Barbers 1962, (Master 1983), appointed Barber Emeritus 1987; *Recreations* history, music, gardening; *Clubs* Guildhall; *Style*— Philip Champness, Esq; Croylands, Hindon, Salisbury, Wiltshire SP3 6DP (☎ 074 789 285)

CHAN, Rt Hon Sir Julius; KBE (1980, CBE 1975), PC (1981); s of Chin Pak Chan, and Tingoris Chan; *b* 29 August 1939; *Educ* Marist Brothers Coll Ashgrove Qld, Queensland Univ; *m* 1966, Stella Ahmat; 3 s, 1 da; *Career* Parly ldr People's Progress Party PNG 1970-, min fin 1972-77, Dep PM and Min for Primary Indust 1977-78, prime minister of PNG 1980-82, opposition 1982-85, dep pm and min for fin and planning 1985-86, dep pm and min for trade and indust 1987-88, dep ldr of opposition 1988; *Recreations* swimming, walking, boating; *Style*— The Rt Hon Sir Julius Chan, KBE; PO Box 717, Rabaul, Papua New Guinea

CHANCE, Alan Derek; s of Derek Arthur Chance, of The Grange, Funtington, Chichester, W Sussex, and Kay, *née* Renshaw (d 1988); *b* 12 April 1951; *Educ* Eton, Merton Coll Oxford (BA); *m* 30 May 1981, Sarah Elizabeth, da of(William) Dennis Delany, of Chelwood, West Broyle Drive, n Chichester, W Sussex; 2 s (Benjamin b 1984, Thomas b 1987); *Career* dir Streets Financial Ltd 1979-83, chm Chance Plastics Ltd 1978-87, dir Money Mktg Ltd 1983-86, md The Moorgate Gp plc 1988- (dir 1986); *Recreations* skiing, backgammon, croquet; *Clubs* Hurlingham; *Style*— Alan Chance, Esq; The Moorgate Group plc, 56/58 Artillery Lane, London E1 7LS (☎ 01 377 2400)

CHANCE, Lady (Hilda) Ava Fiona Nancy; *née* Baird; 3 and yst da of 1 Viscount Stonehaven, GCMG, DSO, PC (d 1941), and Countess of Kintore (d 1974); *b* 20 April 1919; *m* 12 June 1945, Lt-Col Ronald Fulton Lucas Chance, MC, er s of Walter Lucas Chance, JP (d 1962), of Mill Green House, Wargrave, Berks; 1 s, 1 da; *Style*— Lady Ava Chance; Lower Moor Farm, Charlton, Malmesbury, Wilts (☎ 0666 822185)

CHANCE, Derek Arthur; TD (1941); s of Walter Lucas Chance (d 1962), and Rosa Edith *née* Fulton (d 1966); ggs of Robert Lucas Chance of Chance Bros, glass mfrs 1824, glaziers of the Crystal Palace; *b* 26 Feb 1914; *Educ* Eton Coll, Konsularakademie, Vienna; *m* 15 Jan 1944, Kay Kathleen, da of John Frederick Renshaw (d 1935); 1 s (Alan b 1951), 2 da (Susan b 1947, Gillian b 1952); *Career* WWII Capt (A/Maj) RA served France, Belgium, Holland, Germany 1940-45; glass mfr 1934-39, 1945-51; fruit farmer 1951-; *Recreations* tennis, walking, photography; *Style*— Derek Chance, TD; The Grange, Funtington, Chichester, W Sussex PO18 9LN (☎ 0243 573701); Grange Farm, Funtington, Chichester W Sussex (☎ 0243 575372)

CHANCE, Sir (George) Jeremy (ffolliott); 4 Bt (UK 1900), of Grand Avenue, Hove, Co Sussex; s of Sir Roger James Ferguson Chance, 3 Bt, MC (d 1987), and Mary Georgina, *née* Rowney (d 1984); *b* 24 Feb 1926; *Educ* Gordonstoun, Ch Ch Oxford (MA); *m* 4 March 1950, his cousin, Cecilia Mary Elizabeth, 2 da of Sir Hugh Chance, CBE; 2 s, 2 da; *Heir* s, John Sebastian Chance, b 2 Oct 1954; late Lt RNVR, former dir Massey-Ferguson Ltd Coventry; *Recreations* making lakes, planting trees, choral singing, painting; *Style*— Sir Jeremy Chance, Bt; Rhosgyll Fawr, Chwilog, Pwllheli, Gwynedd (☎ 0766 810584)

CHANCE, Michael Edward Ferguson; s of John Wybergh Chance (d 1984), of 59 Lyall Mews, London, and Wendy Muriel Chance (d 1970); *b* 7 Mar 1955; *Educ* Eton, King's Coll Cambridge (MA); *Career* opera singer; BBC Promenade Concerts 1985-, Lincoln Centre New York 1985, La Scala Milan 1985, Lyon Opera 1985, Stuttgart Opera 1986, Paris Opera 1988, princ singer Kent Opera 1984-88, debut Glyndebourne Festival 1989; *Style*— Michael Chance, Esq; (☎ 0233 76 558); c/o Kent Opera, Pembles Cross, Egerton, Asford, Kent TN27 9EN

CHANCE, Michael Spencer; s of Ernest Horace Chance (d 1980), of Church Stretton, Shrops, and Florence, *née* Kitson; *b* 14 May 1938; *Educ* Rossall Sch; *m* 9 June 1962, Enid Mabel, da of Harry Carter (d 1958), of West Hagley, Worcs; 3 da (Karen b 1963, Helen b 1965, Susan b 1965); *Career* slr; asst dir pub prosecutors 1981-85, chief corwn prosecutor for N London 1986-87; dep dir Serious Fraud Office 1987-; *Style*— Michael Chance, Esq; 16 Frithsden, Hemel Hempstead, Herts (☎ 0442 875 687); Serious Fraud Office, Elm House, Elm St, London EC1X 0BJ (☎ 01 833 1616)

CHANCELLOR, Alexander Surtees; s of Sir Christopher Chancellor, CMG, and Sylvia, e da of Sir Richard Paget, 2 Bt, by Sir Richard's 1 w, Lady Muriel Finch-Hatton, CBE (only da of 12 Earl of Winchilsea and Nottingham); *b* 4 Jan 1940; *Educ* Eton, Trinity Hall Cambridge; *m* 1964, Susanna, da of Martin Debenham, JP (3 s of Sir Ernest Debenham, 1 Bt, JP, by Cecily, niece of Rt Hon Joseph Chamberlain); 2 da; *Career* Reuters News Agency 1964-74, ed The Spectator 1975-84, asst edit Sunday Telegraph 1984-86; dep e Sunday Telegraph 1986, US ed The Independent 1986-88, ed The Independent Magazine 1988-; *Style*— Alexander Chancellor Esq; The Independent Magazine, 40 City Rd, London EC1

CHANCELLOR, Sir Christopher John; CMG (1948); s of late Sir John Chancellor, GCMG, GCVO, GBE, DSO (d 1952), and Elsie, *née* Thompson; *b* 29 Mar 1904; *Educ* Eton, Trinity Coll Cambridge; *m* 1926, Sylvia Mary, OBE, da of Sir Richard Paget, 2 Bt, and Lady Muriel Finch-Hatton, da of 12 Earl of Winchilsea and Nottingham; 2 s (*see* Chancellor, Alexander), 2 da; *Career* gen mangr Reuters 1930-59, then tstee; former chm Odhams Press Ltd; chm and chief exec The Bowater Paper Corpn Ltd 1962-69; Offr Legion of Honour 1951; kt 1951; *Style*— Sir Christopher Chancellor, CMG; The Priory, Ditcheat, Shepton Mallet, Somerset (☎ 074 986 295)

CHANDLER, Charles Henry; s of late Charles Chandler; *b* 6 Mar 1940; *Educ* Highgate; *m* 1965, Christine Elizabeth, *née* Dunn; 2 s; *Career* md: GRA Ltd 1983-, Greyhound Racing Assoc Ltd 1972-; chm Walthamstow Stadium Ltd 1976-; *Style*— Charles Chandler, Esq; Mymfield, Kentish Lane, Brookmans Park, Herts AL9 6NQ (☎ office 01 902 8833, home 0707 52478)

CHANDLER, Sir Geoffrey; CBE (1976); s of Dr Frederick George Chandler (d 1942), and Marjorie, *née* Raimes, of Newdigate, Surrey (d 1988); *b* 15 Nov 1922; *Educ* Sherborne, Trinity Coll Cambridge (MA); *m* 1955, Lucy Bertha, da of Prof Patrick Buxton, CMG, (d 1956); 4 da; *Career* Financial Times 1951-56; Royal Dutch/Shell Gp 1956-78 (chm and md Shell Trinidad Ltd 1964-69; dir: Shell Int, Shell Petroleum, Shell Petroleum NV); dir-gen NEDO 1978-83; dir Industry Year 1986; Industry Advsr to Royal Soc of Arts 1987- (ldr in indust matters); kt 1983; *Recreations* gardening, music; *Clubs* Athenaeum; *Style*— Sir Geoffrey Chandler, CBE; 46 Hyde Vale, Greenwich, London SE10 8HP (☎ 01 692 5304)

CHANDLER, Godfrey John; *b* 4 July 1925; *Educ* Clarks Coll London; *m* 1948, Audrey Haydee; 3 s (Timothy b 1952, Graham b 1953, Henry b 1960), 1 da (Susan b 1949); *Career* ptnr Cazenove and Co 1957-85; dep chm W H Smith Gp 1982-88; dir: Globe Investmt Tst plc 1980-88, Strata Investmt Tst plc 1985-88; Stratton Investmt Tst plc 1986-88, Lloyds Devpt Capital Ltd 1986-88, Halifax Bldg Soc (London Bd 1981-87); hon fell Darwin Coll Cambs, visiting fell Henley Coll of Mgmnt; *Recreations* gardening, chess; *Clubs* City of London; *Style*— Godfrey Chandler; Stormont Court, Godden Green, Sevenoaks, Kent

CHANDLER, (William) John; s of Harold Grant Chandler (d 1985), of Bollington, Cheshire; *b* 31 May 1932; *Educ* Welwyn Garden City GS, Jesus Coll Cambridge (MA),

Brunel Univ (PhD); *m* 1956, Margaret Rosa, da of Herbert B Thomas (d 1977); 3 children; *Career* barr Middle Temple; co sec Int Publishing Corpn 1963, admin dir Int Publishing Corpn 1970; exec and planning dir Reed Int 1975; strategic mgmnt conslt 1988; chm: Global Electronic Fin (UK) Ltd, Chandlers Ltd; md Stewkie Systems Ltd, dir Natural Resources Gp plc; prof dept of cybernetics Brunel Univ; ASCA; FCybS; *Books* Techniques of Scenario Planning (with Reed economist Paul Cockle; 1982), Science of History (1984) Practical Business Planning (1987); *Recreations* yachting, music, history; *Clubs* Royal Thames YC, Lansdowne; *Style*— John Chandler, Esq; 3 Willow Grove, Welwyn Garden City, Herts (☎ 0707 324600); 85a Great Portland St, London W1 (☎ 01 436 0241)

CHANDLER, Laurence George; JP (1985); s of Frederick Arthur Chandler (d 1986), of 24 Wingrave Rd, London W6, and Daisy Annie, *née* Hollingbery; *b* 19 Sept 1937; *Educ* Balham and Tooting Coll of Commerce; *m* 25 May 1963, Beryl Celia, da of Cecil Charles Richards, of 8 Hayling Ave, Feltham, Middx; 2 s (Barry Laurence b 1967, Robert Alun b 1970), 1 da (Anne-Marie b 1965); *Career* CA; dir: Beryl Properties (Kingston) Ltd 1976, Adastral Aircraft Ltd 1976, Indent Aviation (UK) Ltd 1977, Kerry Tree Ltd 1982, Stoic Insurance Services Ltd 1986, Stoic Financial Services Ltd 1986; hon auditor: Kingston Onward Tst, Peterborough Benevolent Soc, South Lodge Housing Assoc; *Recreations* cricket umpire, duplicate bridge, gardening; *Clubs* chm Kingston YMCA, Duplicate Bridge, pres Hurlingham Oddfellows Cricket; *Style*— Laurence Chandler, JP; 25 Church Meadow, Long Ditton, Surbiton, Surrey KT6 5EP (☎ 01 398 1295); Parman House, 30-36 Fife Rd, Kingston upon Thames, Surrey KT1 1SU

CHANDLER, Robert William; s of Robert Samuel (d 1970), of Tylers Green, Bucks, and Amy Lilian, *née* Glascoe; *b* 19 Mar 1920; *Educ* NW Poly; *m* 29 Jan 1944, Elizabeth, da of William Greenham (d 1966), of Hants; 1 s (Dennis b 1946); *Career* war serv: Royal Signals; business conslt, freelance journalist; dir: Brax Ltd, Palmer Brackenbury Ltd 1965-, NSS Newsagents 1965-, Good News 1973-, RS McColl Ltd 1975-; addressing business seminars for gps of retailers; memb Inst of Journalists; *Books* Just Imagine (1986), Story of W Lavington Church (1988); *Recreations* writing; *Clubs* IOD; *Style*— Robert W Chandler, Esq; Woodpeckers, Pinewood Way, Midhurst, W Sussex GU29 9LN (☎ 073081 5187)

CHANDLEY, (Charles William) Duncan; s of Samuel Chandley (d 1978), of Stockport, Cheshire, and Annie, *née* Kemp (d 1965); *b* 23 June 1940; *Educ* Stockport Sch; *m* 3 Aug 1963, Anne, da of George Robert Forster (d 1957), of Macclesfield, Cheshire; 2 da (Victoria b 1965, Elizabeth b 1967); *Career* CA 1962, certified accountant 1972, ptnr Thomas Silvey Campbell and Bowden 1964-68, divnl internal auditor organics and pharmaceuticals divs ICI 1968-70, ptnr Proud Goulbourn and Co 1972- (sr ptnr 1985-); dir: Leafstan Ltd 1972-, Clevebrook Ltd 1979-, Bribow Ltd 1982-, Northwest Mgmnt Servs Ltd 1984-; sec Blackstock (financiers) Ltd 1974-; *Recreations* chess, swimming; *Clubs* Bramhall chess; *Style*— Duncan Chandley, Esq; 14 Avondale Ave, Hazel Grove, Stockport, Cheshire (☎ 061 483 7626); 103 Castle Street, Edgeley, Stockport SK3 9AR (☎ 061 480 1928)

CHANDOS, 3 Viscount (1954 UK); Thomas Orlando Lyttelton; s of 2 Viscount Chandos (d 1980, himself ggs of 4 Baron Cobham), and Caroline (da of Sir Alan Lascelles, who was in his turn gs of 4 Earl of Harewood); *b* 12 Feb 1953; *Educ* Eton, Worcester Coll Oxford; *m* 19 Oct 1985, Arabella Sarah Lucy, da of Adrian Bailey, by his 1 wife Mary Katherine (now Lady Mary Russel), o da of 12 Earl of Haddington, KT; 2 s (Hon Oliver, Hon Benedict b 30 April 1988); *Heir* s, Hon Oliver Antony Lyttelton b 21 Feb 1986; *Career* assist dir Kleinwort Benson Jan 1982-; sat in Lords as Cross Bencher to Nov 1981 when joined SDP; *Style*— The Rt Hon the Viscount Chandos; The Vyne, Sherborne St John, Basingstoke, Hants (☎ 0256 881227)

CHANDOS-POLE, Lt-Col John; CVO (1979), OBE (1951), JP (1957); s of Brig-Gen Harry Anthony Chandos-Pole, CBE, JP, DL (d 1934), of Heverswood, Brasted, Kent, and Ada, *née* Ismay (d 1955); *b* 20 July 1909; *Educ* Eton, Magdalene Coll Cambridge (MA); *m* 1952, Josephine Sylvia, da of Brig-Gen Cyril Randell Crofton, CBE (d 1941), of Limerick House, Milborne Port, nr Sherborne, Dorset, and formerly w of Lt-Col Peter Heber-Percy, OBE, RA (TA); 2 step da; *Career* 2 Lt Coldstream Gds 1933; ADC: to Govr of Bombay 1937, to Govr of Bengal 1937-39, to Viceroy of India 1938; served WW II (wounded), Lt-Col 1947, cmd 1 Bn Coldstream Gds 1947-48, Palestine 1948 (despatches, wounded), cmd Gds Depot 1948-50, cmd 2 Bn 1950-52, ret 1953; Gentleman-at-Arms 1956-79 (Harbinger 1966-79); Lord-Lt Northants 1967-84, DL 1965, JP 1957; KStJ 1975; *Recreations* travel, racing; *Clubs* Boodle's, Pratt's; *Style*— Lt-Col John Chandos-Pole, CVO, OBE, JP; Newnham Hall, Daventry, Northants NN11 6HQ (☎ 0327 702711)

CHANDOS-POLE, Maj (John) Walkelyne; JP (Derbyshire 1951), DL (1961); s of Col Reginald Walkelyne Chandos-Pole, TD, JP (d 1930), and his 2 wife, Inez Blanche Marie Clotilde Eva, *née* Arent (d 1941); *b* 4 Nov 1913; *Educ* Eton, RMC; *m* 1947, Ilsa Jill Barstz, er da of late Emil Ernst Barstz, of Zürich; 1 da (and 1 s decd); *Career* Maj late Grenadier Gds; ADC to Viceroy of India 1938-39; High Sheriff of Derbyshire 1959; *Recreations* shooting; *Clubs* Army and Navy, Lansdowne, Derby County, MCC; *Style*— Maj Walkelyne Chandos-Pole, JP, DL; Radburne Hall, Kirk Langley, Derby DE6 4LZ (☎ 033 124 246)

CHANEY, Sir Frederick Charles; KBE (1982, CBE 1970), AFC (1945); s of Frederick Charles Chaney (d 1932), and Rose Templar Chaney (d 1957); *b* 12 Oct 1914; *Educ* Aquinas Coll; *m* 1938, Mavis Mary, da of Albert Herbert Bond; 4 s, 3 da; *Career* Flt Lt RAAF, serv Australia, New Guinea and Borneo 1941-45; MHR (Lib) Perth 1955-69, chm Public Works Ctee 1966-69, chm: Home Building Soc 1977-87, Territory Building Soc 1977-85; Lord Mayor of Perth 1978-82; *see Debrett's Handbook of Australia and New Zealand for further details*; *Recreations* golf; *Clubs* Mt Lawley Golf; *Style*— Sir Frederick Chaney, KBE, AFC; 9A Melville St, Claremont, W Australia 6010 (☎ 384 0596)

CHANNING, Leslie Thomas; s of Richard Channing (d 1958), of 30 Pembridge Avenue, Twickenham, and Salome Charlotte, *née* Munns (d 1956); *b* 24 April 1916; *Educ* Wandsworth Co Sch, Regent St Poly Sch of Architecture; *m* 30 March 1940, Florence Helen (d 1986), da of Thomas Cole, of 30 Hounslow Gardens, Hounslow; 1 s (Richard b 1946), 1 da (Elaine b 1941); m 2, 5 June 1987, Audrey Joan, *née* Glanvill; *Career* WWII serv Flying Offr RAF Vol Res (BEF camouflage and intelligence) 1940-44, SEAC 1944-46; asst architect: London CC 1946-48, Middx CC 1948-55, offical architects dept Church Cmmrs 1955-77; work incl: bishops houses, churches, parsonages, Bishop's House Manchester 1964, new Church of St Richard's Hanworth 1963; artist; exhibited regularly in: Art Soc's Exhibitions, Mall Galleries, United Soc, Nat Soc; one man exhibition of landscapes and watercolours Fairfield Hall Croydon 1980; memb Thames Valley Arts Club; ARIBA; memb United Soc of Artists, assoc memb Nat Soc of Painters Sculptors and Printmakers; *Recreations* water colour and landscape painting, rambling; *Style*— Leslie Channing, Esq; 4 Raleigh Way, Hanworth, Middlesex TW13 7NX (☎ 01 890 3110)

CHANNON, Derek French; s of John French Channon; *b* 4 Mar 1939; *Educ* Eastbourne GS, Univ Coll London (BSc), Manchester Univ (MBA), Harvard Grad Sch of Business Admin (DBA); *m* 1963, Ann Lesley (m dis 1987); 1 s, 1 da; *Career* formerly with Royal Dutch Shell Gp, md Evode Hldgs 1976-77, prof of marketing Manchester Business Sch 1978, associate dir Manchester Business Sch 1986-7; dir Royal Bank of Scotland 1988; pres Strategic Mgmnt Soc 1986-88; *Books* Strategy and Structure of British Enterprise (1973), The Service Industries (1976), British Banking Strategy (1977), Multinational Strategic Planning (1979), Bank Strategic Mgmnt and Marketing (1986), Global Banking Strategy (1988); *Style*— Prof Derek Channon

CHANNON, Michael Ronald (Charles); s of Ronald Arthur Channon (d 1970), and Kathleen, *née* Gamblin; *b* 7 June 1936; *Educ* Battersea GS, Jesus Coll Camb (MA Hons); *Career* assoc dir Br Market Res Bureau 1961-70, account dir J Walter Thompson 1970-72 (creative mangr and sr assoc dir 1972-74), dir res and planning Ayer Barker Ltd 1974-85 (vice-chm 1977-85), special advsr Charles Barker Gp 1985-88; dir of studies Inst of Practitioners in Advertising 1985-; FIPA; memb: Market Res Soc, Advertising Assoc Res Ctee, London Diocesan Synod; guardian Shrine of Our Lady of Walsingham; *Publications* numerous papers on res, account planning and advertising; editor: Advertising Works 3 (1975), Advertising Works 4 (1987); *Recreations* decorative arts, architecture, gardens; *Clubs* Reform; *Style*— M R Channon, Esq; Lower Ground Floor Flat, 21 Edith Rd, London W14 0SU (☎ 01 602 8009); Institute of Practitioners in Advertising, 44 Belgrave Square, London SW1X 9QS (☎ 01 235 7020)

CHANNON, Rt Hon (Henry) Paul (Guinness); PC (1980), MP Southend W 1959-; s of late Sir Henry ('Chips') Channon, MP,(d 1958), ofKelvedon Hall, Brentwood, Essex, and Lady Honor Svejdar, *née* Guinness, da of 2 Earl of Iveagh; *b* 9 Oct 1935; *Educ* Eton, Ch Ch Oxford; *m* 1963, Ingrid, formerly w of Hon Jonathan Guinness, *qv*, and da of Maj Guy Wyndham, MC (gs of Hon Percy Wyndham, 2 s of 1 Baron Leconfield), by his 2 w Grethe, da of G Wulfsberg, of Bergen, Norway; 1 s (Henry b 1970), 2 da (Olivia d 1986, Georgia b 1966); *Career* served RHG 1954-56; Min of Power 1959-60; PPS to: Home Sec 1960-62, Foreign Sec 1963-64; oppn spokesman Arts and Amenities 1967-70, parly sec Miny Housing and Local Govt 1970, parly under-sec Environment 1970-72, min of state N Ireland 1972, min Housing and Construction Environment Dept 1972-74, oppn spokesman Prices and Consumer Protection 1974, oppn spokesman Environmental Affairs 1974-75, min of state CSD 1979-81, min for the Arts 1981-83, min for Trade 1983-86; sec of state for trade and indust 1986-87, currently min for transport; *Style*— The Rt Hon Paul Channon, MP; House of Commons, London

CHANT, Anthony; s of Percival James Chant, and Ethel Eleanor, *née* Quick (d 1987); *b* 21 Feb 1938; *Educ* Hitchi GS, London Univ (BSc, MB, BS, MS); *m* 21 March 1959, Ann Nadia, da of Edwin Venning (d 1940); 3 s (Ben b 1963, Harvey b 1964, Thomas b 1966); *Career* conslt Vascular Surgn Wessex Med Sch, FRCS, author of works on Vascular Physiology, Vascular and General Surgery, Med Mgmnt and Ethics; *Recreations* fishing; *Style*— Anthony Chant, Esq; Royal South Hants Hospital, Southampton (☎ 0703 634288 ext 2405/2654)

CHANT, (Leonard Ernest) John; CBE (1986); s of Leonard Joseph Chant (d 1949), of Chard, Somerset, and Dorothy Frances Chant (d 1938); *b* 23 April 1938; *Educ* Huish Episcopi, Yeovil Tech Coll, Bristol Poly, Edinburgh Univ (Cert PSW, CSW); *m* 31 Aug 1963, Catherine Joyce, da of John Orr (d 1977), of Moffat, Scotland; 1 s (Eric John), 2 da (Catriona, Laura); *Career* dir social servs Somerset CC 1975-88 (supt mental welfare offr 1970-72, asst dir 1972-75), dir social work Lothian Regnl Cncl 1988; social servs assessor Cleveland Child Abuse Enquiry 1988; vice pres Somerset Alcoholism Cncl, branch welfare advsr Br Red Cross Soc; SRN, RMN; *Recreations* fly fishing, collecting vintage pens, english watercolours; *Style*— John Chant, Esq, CBE; c/o Lothian Regional Council, Edinburgh

CHANT-SEMPILL, Hon Ian David Whitemore; s (by 2 m) of Lady Sempill, *qv*; *b* 2 April 1951; *Educ* Oratory Sch; *m* 1980, Amanda, yr da of Anthony Dallas, of Blackmoor, Burghfield, Berks; 1 s (Hamish b 1987), 1 da (Clementine b 1985); *Career* Maj Gordon Highlanders; ADC to GOC Scotland 1975-76, Adj 1 Bn The Gordon Highlanders 1976-78, SO3 G3 HQ33 Armd Bde 1983-84, SO2 DS JDSC 1987-; *Recreations* shooting, fishing, cooking, country pursuits; *Style*— The Hon Ian Chant-Sempill

CHANTER, Rev Canon Anthony R; s of Charles Harry Chanter, of Jersey, CI, and Eva Marjorie, *née* Le Cornu (d 1966); *b* 24 Oct 1937; *Educ* Hautlieu Sch Jersey, Salisbury Theo Coll, Open Univ (BA), Univ of London (MA); *m* 10 Sept 1966, Yvonne, da of Flt Lt William Reid (ka 1944); 2 da (Fiona b 31 May 1968, Alison b 15 May 1975); *Career* priest vicar Lincoln Cath 1970-73; headmaster: Bishop King Sch Lincoln 1970-73, Grey Court Sch Ham Richmond upon Thames 1973-77, Bishop Reindorp Sch Guildford 1977-84; dir of educn Diocese of Guildford 1984-, hon canon Guildford Cath 1984-; memb Surrey CCncl Educn Ctee 1984-, dir Guildford Diocesan Bd of Finance; memb Nat Assoc of Headteachers; *Books* Student Profiling (co-author 1980); *Recreations* golf, cricket, squash, windsurfing, music, opera; *Clubs* Sion Coll, Worplesdon Golf; *Style*— The Rev Canon Anthony Chanter; Grasshoppers, Woodland Ave, Cranleigh, Surrey GU6 7HU (☎ 0483 571826); Diocesan House, Quarrey St, Guildford, Surrey (☎ 0483 571836)

CHANTRY, Dr George William; s of George William Chantry (d 1981), of Wallasey, Merseyside, and Sophia Veronica, *née* Johnson (d 1979); *b* 13 April 1933; *Educ* St Francis' Coll Liverpool, Christ Church Oxford (MA, DPhil); *m* Diana Margaret Rhodes, da of William Rhodes Martin, (d 1969), of Little Hampton, Sussex; 2 s (Richard b 1959, Paul b 1967), 1 da (Catherine b 1961); *Career* res assoc Cornell Univ 1958-60; NPL Teddington: sr res fell 1960-62, sr sci offr 1962-67, princ sci offr 1967-73, sr princ sci offr 1973-82; cnsllr (sci and technol) HM Embassy Bonn 1982-85, asst dir (indust) SDIPO/MOD 1985-; FInstP 1973, FIEE 1976, CEng 1976, CPhys 1985; *Books* Long-Wave Optics (1982), and others; *Recreations* music, philately, bridge, gardening; *Style*— Dr George Chantry; 42 Cranwell Grove, Shepperton, Middx TW17 0JR (☎ 0932 560524); Research and Technology Policy Division, Dept of Trade and

Industry, Ashdown House, 123 Victoria St, London SW1E 6RB (☎ 01 218 0545, fax 01 218 4081)

CHAPLIN, Hon Mrs Niall; Angela Marjory; only da of Hon Claud Lambton (d 1945, 7 s of 2 Earl of Durham) by his w Lettice (herself 2 da of Edward Wormald); *b* 12 Oct 1902; *m* 1961, as his 2 w, Hon Niall Greville Chaplin (d 1963, yr s of 2 Viscount Chaplin); *Style*— The Hon Mrs Niall Chaplin; Flat 4, 34 Ennismore Gdns, London SW7 (☎ 01 589 7997)

CHAPLIN, Hon Christina Susanna; 3 da (but yr by his 2 w) of 3 Viscount Chaplin (d 1981); *b* 16 Dec 1958; *Style*— The Hon Christina Chaplin

CHAPLIN, John Cyril; CBE (1988); s of Ernest Stanley Chaplin, of Beckthorns, Keswick, Cumbria (d 1966), and Isobel, *née* Mackereth (d 1944); *b* 13 August 1926; *Educ* Keswick Sch Cumbria; *m* 17 Sept 1949, Ruth Marianne, da of Raymond Livingstone, of Village Farm, Owslebury, Winchester, Hants (d 1961); 2 s (Peter b 1951, Alistair b 1965), 2 da (Rosalind b 1954, Sarah b 1958); *Career* aeronautical engr; CAA: dir gen airworthiness 1979-83, gp dir safety regulation 1983-88; bd memb 1983-88, chm ops advsy ctee 1984-; FEng; *Recreations* sailing, photography; *Clubs* Cruising Assoc; *Style*— John Chaplin, Esq, CBE; Norman Croft, Vicarage Lane, Mattingley, Basingstoke, Hampshire RG27 8LF (☎ 0734 326 207)

CHAPLIN, Lady; Oona; da of Eugene Gladstone O'Neill (d 1953), the American Playwright, and his 3 wife Agnes Boulton (d 1968); *m* 1943, as his 4 wife, Sir Charles Spencer Chaplin, KBE (Charlie Chaplin, d 1977, actor and producer); 3 s (Michael b 1946, Eugene b 1953, Christopher b 1962), 5 da (Geraldine b 1944, Josephine b 1949, Victoria b 1951, Jane b 1957, Annette b 1959); *Style*— Lady Chaplin; c/o United Artists Ltd, 142 Wardour St, London W1

CHAPLIN, Viscountess; Hon Rosemary; *née* Lyttelton; only da of 1 Viscount Chandos, DSO, MC (d 1972), by his w Lady Moira Osborne (herself 4 da of 10 Duke of Leeds) (d 1972); *b* 30 May 1922; *m* 1951, as his 2 w, 3 and last Viscount Chaplin (d 1981); 2 da (Hon Miranda and Hon Christina Chaplin, *qqv*); *Style*— The Rt Hon the Viscountess Chaplin; Wadstray House, Blackawton, Totnes, S Devon (☎ 080 421 232); 61 Ladbroke Rd, London, W11 3PN

CHAPLIN, William John Montague; s of late Rev Canon William Robert Moffett Chaplin; *b* 28 Feb 1932; *Educ* Shrewsbury, St Edmund Hall Oxford; *m* 1957, Claire Mary, *née* Pedder; 3 s, 1 da; *Career* farmer and company director; chm Titus Wilson and Sons Ltd 1975-; dir Hawker Marris Ltd 1966-79, Thomas Reed Ltd 1969-, S Cumbria and N Lancs Management Ltd 1984-; High Sheriff of Cumbria 1982-83; memb: Lake District Special Planning Bd 1982-85, National Tst Regional Ctee 1985-; chm exec ctee Abott Hall Art Gallery 1986-; *Style*— W J M Chaplin Esq; Finsthwaite House, nr Ulverston, Cumbria (☎ Newby Bridge 31339)

CHAPMAN; *see*: Dugan-Chapman

CHAPMAN, Barbara, Lady; Barbara May; *née* Tonks; da of Hubert Tonks, of Delmar, Halgranoya, Ceylon, and Harvington, nr Evesham, Worcs; *m* 18 Jan 1941, Sir Robin (Robert Macgowan) Chapman, 2 Bt, CBE, TD, JP, DL (d 1987); 2 s, 1 da; pres: Jarrow Cons Assoc, St Clare's Hospice South Shields, South Shields Ladies Lifeboat Guild; vice pres: YWCA North East Area, Tyne & Wear SSAFA; *Style*— Barbara, Lady Chapman; Pinfold House, Cleadon, Sunderland (☎ 091 536 7451)

CHAPMAN, Prof Christopher Hugh; s of John Harold Chapman, of Vicarage Fields, Church Road, Milton-under-Wychwood, Oxford, and Margaret Joan Weeks; *b* 5 May 1945; *Educ* Latymer Upper Sch, Christ Coll Cambridge (BA, PhD, MA); *m* 1 June 1974, Lillian, da of Michael Tarapaski, of Redwater, Alberta, Canada; 1 s (Timothy b 26 May 1978), 1 da (Heather b 24 June 1981); *Career* asst prof dept of geology and geophysics Univ California Berkley 1972-73, assoc prof dept of physics Univ of Alberta Canada 1973-74 (asst prof 1969-72), prof dept of physics Univ of Toronto Canada 1980-84 and 1988- (assoc prof 1974-80), Green scholar Univ of California San Diego 1978-79, prof of geophysics dept of earth sciences Cambridge 1984-88; FRAS, FAGU, SEG, SSA; *Recreations* sailing, photography; *Style*— Prof Christopher Chapman; 7 Spinner Drive, Great Shelford, Cambridge, CB2 5LY (☎ 0223 845007); Dept of Physics, Univ of Toronto, Toronto, Ontario M5S 1A7, Canada (☎ 416 978 3658)

CHAPMAN, Colin; s of Charles Stocker Chapman (d 1974), and Norah Veronica, *née* Onions (d 1982); *b* 3 April 1935; *Educ* Malet Lambert GS Kingston Upon Hull, Keele Univ (BA), UEA (MA), Cambridge Inst of Educn (Adv Dip Ed); *m* 1962, Shelagh Margaret, da of Walter McCann; 1 s (Michael b 1963); *Career* prospecting offr NCB Opencast Exec 1957-60; teacher: Kingston GS and Elizabethan Hall, Kingston upon Hull, Silver Jubilee and County Upper Schs Bury St Edmunds; educational cnslt; asst chief examiner E Anglian Bd 1957-60, examiner, London and E Anglian Gp, sci advsr Suffolk CC 1976-86 (Home Office, Home Defence Coll 1978); sec Horticultural Soc shows; *Recreations* cricket (chm village cricket), collecting trees and lilacs, trout fishing, music; *Clubs* MCC, Arboricultural Assoc, Soil Assoc; *Style*— Colin Chapman, Esq; Norman's Farm, Wyverstone, Stowmarket, Suffolk IP14 4SF (☎ 0449 780 081); Thurleston High Sch, Defoe Rd, Ipswich

CHAPMAN, His Honour Judge; Cyril Donald; QC (1965); s of Cyril Chapman and Frances Elizabeth, *née* Braithwaite; *b* 17 Sept 1920; *Educ* Roundhay Sch Leeds, BNC Oxford; *m* 1, 1950 (m dis 1959), Audrey Margaret Fraser, *née* Gough; 1 s; m 2, 1960, Muriel Falconer Bristow; 1 s; *Career* RNVR 1940-45; barr 1947; contested (C) E Leeds 1955, Goole 1964, Brighouse and Spenborough 1966; recorder: Huddersfield 1965-69, Bradford 1969-71; circuit judge 1972-, ret 1986; *Style*— His Honour Judge Chapman, QC; Hill Top, Collingham, Wetherby, W Yorks (☎ Collingham Bridge 2813)

CHAPMAN, Sir David Robert Macgowan; 3 Bt (UK 1958), of Cleadon, Co Durham; s of Sir Robin Chapman, 2 Bt, CBE, TD, JP, DL (d 1987), and Barbara May, *née* Tonks; *b* 16 Dec 1941; *Educ* Marlborough, McGill Univ Montreal (B Comm); *m* 19 June 1965, Maria Elizabeth de Gosztony-Zsolnay, da of Dr N de Mattyasovsky-Zsolnay, of Montreal, Canada; 1 s (Michael b 1969), 1 da (Christina b 1970); *Heir* s, Michael Nicholas Chapman, b 21 May 1969; *Career* stockbroker; dir Wise Speke Ltd; James Hogg and Sons (North Shields) Ltd, North of England Building Soc; chm Northern Unit of the Stock Exchange; *Recreations* travel, tennis, reading; *Clubs* Lansdowne, Northern Counties (Newcastle); *Style*— Sir David Chapman, Bt; Westmount, 14 West Park Rd, Cleadon, Sunderland SR6 7RR (☎ 091 536 7887); Wise Speke Ltd, Commercial Union House, 39 Pilgrim St, Newcastle upon Tyne NE1 6RQ (☎ 091 261 1266)

CHAPMAN, Denis Henry Clarke; s of Alderman R F Chapman, JP (d 1963), of Scarborough, and Henrietta *née* Stothard (d 1985); *b* 26 May 1934; *Educ* Scarborough Coll; *m* 4 April 1959, Mavis Lee da of Robert Duncanson (d 1961); 1 s (Robert b 1971), 2 da (Fiona b 1966, Lisa b 1968); *Career* RAF 1952-54; chartered surveyor; chief exec H C Chapman & Son; memb: Gen Cncl RICS 1984-, Lloyd's 1979-; FRICS, FSVA, FRVA; *Recreations* farming, shooting, gardening, walking; *Clubs* Farmers; *Style*— Denis H C Chapman, Esq; Stoneway House, Scalby, Scarborough YO13 0RU (☎ 0723 372 428) H C Chapman & Son, The Auction Mart, North St, Scarborough YO11 1DL (☎ 0723 372 424, fax 0723 500 697)

CHAPMAN, Dennis; s of George Henry Chapman, da of Katherine Hannah Beckwith, *née* Magnus; *b* 6 May 1927; *Educ* London (BSc), Liverpool (PhD), London (DSc); *m* 1948, Elsie Margaret, da of Capt William Stephenson; 2 s (Michael, Paul), 1 da (Alison); *Career* Comyns Berkeley fell Caius Coll Cambridge 1960-63, head gen res div Unilever Ltd 1963-69, assoc prof Sheffield Univ 1968-76, sr Wellcome Tst fell 1976-77, prof biophysical chem Royal Free Hosp Sch of Med (head of Dept of Protein and Molecular Biol) 1977-, fndr and dir Biocompatibles Ltd; visiting prof Univ of: California, Bologna Meml, Penn State USA, Royal Free Hosp Sch of Med medal 1987; hon DSc: Utrecht Univ, Memorial Univ; hon MRCP, FRS, FRSC; *Books* Biological Membranes Volume I-V, 400 sci pubns; *Recreations* golf, spanish; *Clubs* Athenaeum; *Style*— Prof Dennis Chapman; 103 Gregories Rd, Beaconsfield, Bucks, HP9 1HZ (☎ 0494 672 051); Royal Free Hospital School of Medicine, Dept of Protein & Molecular Biology, Rowland Hill Street, London, NW3 2PF (☎ 01 794 0500 ext 3246)

CHAPMAN, Derek Reginald; s of Reginald Chapman (d 1986), of Romney, Lee Grove, Chigwell, Essex, and Ethel Maud, *née* March (d 1982); *b* 17 May 1932; *Educ* Buckhurst Hill GS, Univ Coll Oxford (BA Jurisprudence), London Univ External Student (LLB); *m* 21 June 1958, Joan Marjorie, da of Thomas Bartram (d 1976), of Grange Farm, Stillingfleet, Yorks; 2 s (Peter b 1961, Michael b 1965), 1 da (Helen b 1959); *Career* E Edwards Son & Noice: articled clerk 1954-57, asst slr 1957-59, ptnr 1959-; sec Mid Essex Law Soc 1967-69 (pres 1972), memb Eastern area ctee Legal Aid 1981- (chm 1989); chm: Billericay Round Table, Billericay Chamber of Trade, Mayflower 70 (to commemorate the 350 anniversary of the Mayflower sailing to the New World); vice chm Carnival Ctee, past memb Nat Freedom of Info Ctee; gen cmmr for taxes 1982-; sec and chm Basildon and Billericay Lib Assocs (Agent General Election Oct 1974); Freeman City of London 1982, Liveryman Worshipful Co of Painters-Stainers 1982; memb Law Soc 1958; *Recreations* tennis, bridge, music; *Style*— Derek Chapman, Esq; Hill House, 39 Stock Rd, Billericay, Essex CM12 OAR (☎ 0277 652 443); Three Horseshoes House, 139 High St, Billericay, Essex CM12 9AF (☎ 0277 658 551, fax 0277 630 024)

CHAPMAN, Ernest; s of Arthur Leslie Chapman (d 1983), of 7 Gainford Road, Moorends, Doncaster, S Yorkshire, and Alice, *née* Lucas (d 1978); *b* 2 Dec 1933; *Educ* Thorne GS Nr Doncaster, St John's Coll, Oxford Univ (BA); *m* 4 Aug 1956, Dorothy, da of Alfred Sutton (d 1978), of 3 Hollingthorpe Court, Hall Green, Wakefield; 3 s (Michael b 1958, Neil b 1960, Alexander b 1963), 1 da (Sarah b 1966); *Career* nat serv; Sgt RAEC 1952-54; qual slr 1961 and in private practice; sr ptnr Dixon, Coles and Gill, Walkefield 1979-; Registrar Wakefield Diicese 1979- (dep registrar 1969-79), dep asst Coroner 1984-; memb Wakefield Festival Chorus; pres: Wakefield Amateur Operatic Soc, Stanley Falcon Cricket Club, Yorks Cricket Cncl 1982-84; Law Soc; *Recreations* cricket, singing, languages, sport in general; *Style*— Ernest Chapman, Esq; 1 Pennine View, Darton, Barnsley, S Yorkshire S75 5AT (☎ 0226 282 796); Bank House, Burton Street, Wakefield, W Yorkshire WF1 2DA (☎ 0924 373 467, fax 0924 366 234)

CHAPMAN, Hon Mrs; Hon (Catherine) Fiona; *née* Robertson; da of 1 Baron Robertson of Oakridge, GCB, GBE, KCMG, KCVO, DSO, MC; *b* 13 August 1939; *m* 1965, Allan Claude Chapman, er s of Claude Frederick Chapman, of Accrington, Lancs; 2 da (twins); *Career* dist concllr Mid Bedfordshsire DC; *Style*— The Hon Mrs Chapman; 23 Church End, Milton Bryan, Milton Keynes MK17 9HR

CHAPMAN, Frank Watson; s of Thomas Chapman (d 1965), of Bournemouth, and Beatrice, *née* Padgett (d 1976); *b* 7 Nov 1929; *Educ* Swindon Coll, Marine Sch of South Shields; *m* 18 March 1955, Wendy Joanna, da of Roger Philip Holly (d 1972), of Switzerland; 1 s (Thomas b 1963), 1 da (Susie b 1956); *Career* MN: cadet 1946; deck offr: Union Steamship Co NZ 1951-54, Royal Mail Lines 1954-58, Cunard Steamship Co 1958-62; salesman Telephone Rentals 1962, fndr and md 1964: Bahamas Properties Ltd, Sovereign Travel Ltd; purchased Lord Rannoch and Forest Hills Hotels Scotland 1974, fndr Multi-Ownership & Hotels Ltd 1975 (thereby becoming fndr of timeshare in UK), 2 devpt in Wales 1978, 3 devpt Forest Hills Hotel 1980, sold co to Barratt Devpts plc 1982 (md until 1988), fndr and chm Sovereign Travel & Leisure Gp plc 1988-; memb Lloyd's, vice pres Timeshare Devpt Assoc 1987; *Recreations* travel, reading, swimming; *Style*— Frank Chapman, Esq; Norbury Pk, Mickleham, Surrey RH5 6DN (☎ 0372 372633); Sovereign Travel & Leisure Gp plc, 2 Chertsey St, Guildford, Surrey GU1 4HD, fax 0483 506721, telex 858623)

CHAPMAN, Frederick John; s of Reginald John Chapman (d 1981), and Elizabeth, *née* Hughes (d 1946); *b* 24 June 1939; *Educ* Sutton GS; *m* 4 Nov 1964, Paula Brenda Chapman, da of Victor Lewis Waller, of Capdepera, Majorca, Spain; 1 s (Daniel b 1979), 2 da (Emma b 1966, Melissa b 1968); *Career* 2 Lt Queens Royal Surrey Regt 1960-62; joined Export Credits Guarantee Dept 1958: princ 1969, asst sec 1977, princ estab and finance offr (under sec) 1982, tres Europe Varity Corpn 1988, tres Varity Corpn 1989; *Recreations* reading, music; *Style*— Frederick Chapman, Esq; Varity House, 35 Davies St, London W1Y 2EA (☎ 01 7000 5222, fax 01 491 5271, telex 28 346)

CHAPMAN, (Francis) Ian; CBE (1988); s of late Rev Peter Chapman, and Frances Burdett; *b* 26 Oct 1925; *Educ* Shawlands Acad Glasgow, Ommer Sch of Music; *m* 1953, Marjory Stewart, *née* Swinton; 1 s, 1 da; *Career* Air Crew Cadet RAF 1943-44, Nat Serv Coal Mines 1945-47; William Collins Sons & Co Ltd: joined as mgmnt trainee 1947, trainee sales rep NY branch 1950-51, gen sales mangr London 1955, gp sales dir 1959; jt md William Collins (Holdings) Ltd 1967 (chm 1976); dir: Hatchards Ltd 1961, Pan Books Ltd 1962-84, Ancient House Bookshop (Ipswich) Ltd, Scottish Opera Theatre Royal Ltd 1974-79, Book Tokens Ltd 1981, IRN Ltd 1983-85, Stanley Botes Ltd 1985; chm: Radio Clyde Ltd 1972-, Hatchards Ltd 1976, Harvill Press Ltd 1976, William Collins Publishers Ltd 1979, The Listener 1988; chm and gp chief exec William Collins plc 1981, non exec dir Guinness plc 1986, jt chm Harper and Row NY 1987; Scottish Free Enterprise award 1985; Publisher Assoc: memb cncl 1962-77, vice pres 1978, pres 1979, vice pres 1981; dir Book Devpt Cncl 1967, tstee Book Trade Benevolent Soc 1982, memb governing cncl SCOTBIC 1983; chm advsy bd Strathclyde Univ Business School 1985-88; CBIM 1982, FRSA 1985; *Recreations* music, golf, reading, skiing; *Clubs* Garrick, Royal Wimbledon Golf, MCC, Prestwick; *Style*— Ian Chapman, Esq, CBE; Kenmore, 46 The Avenue, Cheam, Surrey (☎ 01 642 1820); William Collins Sons and Co Ltd, Grafton St, London W1 (☎ 01 493 7070)

CHAPMAN, John Clifford; Dr; s of James Clifford Crossley Chapman (d 1983), and Marion, *née* Harrison; *b* 21 Feb 1923; *Educ* Ilford HS, Imperial Coll London (BSc, PhD); *m* 18 Oct 1947, Roberta Blanche, da of Robert Broughton Gingell; 1 s (Andrew b 1958), 1 da (Sarah b 1953); *Career* Capt RE 1942-46; res fell and reader in structural engrg Imperial Coll 1950-71, dir Constructional Steel R and D Orgn 1971-73, gp tech dir George Wimpey plc 1973-81, dir Chapman Dowling Assoc Ltd Consulting Engrs, F Eng 1979, FCGI 1988, FICE, FRINA, FIStructE, MConsE; *Books* Many papers on Structural Engrg in professional jls; *Recreations* tennis, squash, mountain walking, music; *Clubs* Athenaeum; *Style*— Dr John Chapman; Chapman & Dowling Assocs, 41 Oathall Rd, Haywards Heath, West Sussex RH16 3EG

CHAPMAN, Kenneth Herbert; s of Herbert Chapman and Anne Bennett, *née* Poxon; *b* 9 Sept 1908; *Educ* St Peter's York; *m* 1937, Jean Martha Mahring; 1 s; *Career* slr 1931, former md Thomas Tilling Ltd, chm Goodliffe Garages Ltd, dir: Br Steam Specialities Gp Ltd, Ready Mixed Concrete Ltd, Société Générale; *Style*— Kenneth Chapman Esq

CHAPMAN, Leslie Charles; eldest s of Charles Richard Chapman (d 1977), and Lilian Elizabeth Chapman (d 1934); *b* 14 Sept 1919; *Educ* Bishopshalt Sch Hillingdon; *m* 1947, Beryl Edith, da of Bertram George England, of Leighton Buzzard; 1 s (Robin); *Career* army 1939-45; civil servant; regnl dir Southern Region Dept of Environment; memb exec London Tport; memb: Nat Cncl of Freedom Assoc, Freedom of Info Assoc Nat Cncl; chm Campaigning Against Waste in Public Expenditure; *Books* Your Disobedient Servant (1979), Waste Away (1982); *Recreations* music, gardening; *Style*— Leslie Chapman, Esq; Caradog, Ffarmers, Llanwrda, Dyfed

CHAPMAN, Mark Fenger; CVO (1979); er s of Geoffrey Walter Chapman, of Dyfed, and Esther Maria Hauch, *née* Fenger; *b* 12 Sept 1934; *Educ* Cranbrook Sch, St Catharine's Coll Cambridge (BA), Sch of Oriental and African Studies London Univ; *m* 28 July 1959, Patricia Mary, da of Henry Nelson Long, of Norfolk; 4 s (Giles b 1960, Jeremy b 1962 (d 1983), Julian b 1965, Adrian b 1971); *Career* Nat Serv 1953-55 Royal Sussex Regt, Nigeria Regt, Lt 1955; entered HM Diplomatic Serv 1958: 3 (later 2) sec Bangkok 1959-63, 2 (later 1) sec FO 1963-67, head Chancery Maseru 1967-71, asst head Dept FCO 1971-74, head Chancery Vienna 1975-76, dep high cmmr Lusaka 1976-79, Diplomatic Serv inspr 1979-82, cnsllr The Hague 1982-86, ambass Reykjavik 1986-; *Clubs* Royal Cwlth Soc; *Style*— Mark Chapman, Esq, CVO; Half Moon House, Briston, Melton Constable, Norfolk NR24 2LG (☎ 0263 860651); c/o FCO, London SW1 (☎ 010 354 1 13113)

CHAPMAN, Nigel Peter; s of Lt Col Sidney Rex Chapman, MC, of Lincolnshire, and Joan Mary, *née* Bates; *b* 31 Jan 1950; *Educ* Kimbolton Sch; *m* 26 Sept 1981, Heather Elizabeth, da of James Lindsay, of London; 2 s (Nicolas b 1982, Daniel b 1984), 1 da (Jennifer b 1987); *Career* CA; sr ptnr Chapman Wong CA (joined firm 1975); *Recreations* tennis, cricket; *Clubs* RAC, Lansdowne; *Style*— Nigel P Chapman, Esq; 10 Ripple Vale Grove, London N1 (☎ 01 607 1353); Chapman Wong, Chartered Accountants, New Concordia Wharf, Mill Street, London SE1 2BA (☎ 01 231 8761, fax 01 237 5946)

CHAPMAN, Peter Richard; s of Lt Ernest Richard Chapman RNVR (d 1974), and Edith Winifred, *née* Softly; *b* 1 April 1942; *Educ* St Paul's Cathedral Choir Sch, St John's Sch Leatherhead; *m* 1 Jun 1974, Stephanie Daynel, da of Kenneth Paul Alexander Watson; 2 s (Richard b 1975, Philip b 1978); *Career* CA 1964; Ogden Parsons & Co: 1959-69, ptnr 1970-71; ptnr: Harmood Banner & Co 1972-73, Deloitte Haskins & Sells 1974-; chm DH&S: Banking Indust Gp 1983, Int Fin Indust Gp 1985; memb: CCAB Banking sub-ctee, sch cncl St Paul's Cathedral Choir Sch, Ct of advsrs St Paul's Cathedral, Surrey Hockey Assoc, Tadworth Church Choir; ctee memb: Gresham Club, Info Technol Skills agency 1985-88; FCA; CMI; *Recreations* golf, music, hockey; *Style*— Peter Chapman, Esq; Deloitte Haskins & Sells, 128 Queen Victoria St, London EC4P 4JX, (☎ 01 248 3913 fax 01 248 3623)

CHAPMAN, Hon Mrs (Rhiannon Elisabeth); *née* Philipps; da (by 1 m) of 2 Viscount St Davids; *b* 21 Sept 1946; *Educ* Tormead Sch, King's Coll London Univ (LLB); *m* 1974, Donald Hudson Chapman, s of late Francis Robert Chapman; 2 step s; *Career* head of personnel The Stock Exchange 1980-; dir VAD Club; ptnr Pennyloaf Wines; FIPM; *Recreations* golf, good food and wine, handcrafts; *Clubs* VAD, Woburn Golf and Country; *Style*— The Hon Mrs Chapman; Pennyloaf, Odsey, Ashwell, Herts (☎ 046 274 2725); The Stock Exchange, London EC2N (☎ 01 588 2355)

CHAPMAN, Roy de Courcy; s of (Edward Frederic) Gilbert Chapman and Aline de Courcy Ireland; *b* 1 Oct 1936; *Educ* St Andrews Univ, Moray House Coll of Educn Edinburgh; *m* 1959, Valerie Rosemary Small; 2 s, 1 da; *Career* former head of modern languages Marlborough Coll, rector of Glasgow Academy 1975, headmaster of Malvern Coll 1983-; *Books* Le Français Contemporain (1972); Le Français Contemporain: Passages for Comprehension and Translation (with D. Whiting, 1975); *Style*— Roy de Courcy Chapman, Esq; Malvern College, Malvern, Worcs (☎ 068 4892333)

CHAPMAN, Roy John; *née* Holdsworth; s of William George Chapman (d 1978), of Kettering, and Frances Harriet, *née* Yeomans (d 1981); *b* 30 Nov 1936; *Educ* Kettering GS, St Catharine's Coll Cambridge (MA); *m* 23 Sept 1961, Janet Gibbeson, da of Roy Gibbeson Taylor (d 1955) of Worthing; 2 s (William b 1962, Henry b 1972), 1 da (Lucy b 1964); *Career* chartered accountant Arthur Andersen & Co 1958- (ptnr 1970-, managing ptnr (London) 1984-); memb advsy cncl London Enterprise Agency; FCA, FIMC, FBIM, FBPICS; *Recreations* cricket, walking, opera, literature, idling; *Clubs* Utd Oxford and Cambridge Univ, Hawks, MCC; *Style*— Roy Chapman, Esq; Arthur Andersen & Co, 1 Surrey Street, London WC2 (☎ 01 836 1200), fax 01 831 1133, telex 8812 711)

CHAPMAN, Sir Stephen; s of late Sir Sydney John Chapman, KCB, CBE (d 1951), and Mabel Gwendoline, JP *née* Mordey (d 1958); *b* 5 June 1907; *Educ* Westminster, Trinity Coll Cambridge; *m* 1963, Pauline da of Lt-Col Allcard (d 1970), and wid of Dimitri de Lobel Niewiarowski; *Career* barrister 1931, former rec Rochester, Cambridge, Liverpool; judge of the Crown Ct Liverpool 1963-66, a judge of the High Ct of Justice (Queen's Bench Div) 1966-81, ret; kt 1966; *Books* contrib: Atkins Encyclopedia of Court Forms (1938), Halsbury's Laws of England (1958), Statutes on the Law of Torts (1962); *Clubs* Utd Oxford and Cambridge; *Style*— Sir Stephen Chapman; 72 Thomas More House, Barbican, London EC2 (☎ 01 628 9251);

CHAPMAN, Sydney Brookes; MP (Cons Chipping Barnet 1979-); s of W Dobson Chapman (d 1965), of Prestbury, Cheshire, and Edith Laura, *née* Wadge (d 1978); *b* 17 Oct 1935; *Educ* Rugby, Univ of Manchester; *m* 1976 (m dis 1987), Claire Lesley, *née* Davies; 2 s, 1 da; *Career* nat chm Young Cons 1964-66, memb exec ctee Nat Union of Cons and Unionist Assocs 1961-70, contested Stalybridge and Hyde 1964, MP Birmingham Handsworth 1970-74; PPS: Sec State Tport 1979-81, Sec State Social Servs 1981-83; appt govt whip 1988; memb select ctee; Environment 1983-87, House of Commons Servs 1983-87; non-practising chartered architect and chartered town and country planner; memb Cncl RIBA 1972-77 (vice-pres 1974-76); pres: Arboricultural Assoc (until 1989), London Green Belt Cncl (until 1988); initiator Nat Tree Planting Year 1973; Patron Tree Cncl; Queen's Silver Jubilee Medal 1977; FRTPI, Hon FIAAS, Hon FFB, FRSA; *Clubs* United and Cecil (vice-chm); *Style*— Sydney Chapman Esq, MP; House of Commons, London SW1A 0AA

CHAPPEL, Lt-Col William Arthur Brian; s of Maj-Gen Brian Herbert Chappel, DSO (d 1964), and Irene Mabel, *née* Maltby (d 1978); *b* 30 June 1925; *Educ* Marlborough, Jesus Coll Cambridge; *m* 3 Nov 1951, Sheila Margaret, da of George Foster Ibbotson (d 1969), of Ainsdale, Southport, Lancs; 2 s (Christopher b 1952, Nicholas b 1957); *Career* served RE 1943-77 retiring as Lt-Col; sr exec Sir William Halcrow and Ptnrs Ltd 1977-; *Recreations* golf, reading, gardening; *Style*— Lt-Col William Chappel; The Old Manor, Chirton, Devizes, Wilts SN10 3QS (☎ 038084 777); Sir William Halcrow & Partners Ltd, Burderop Park, Swindon, Wilts SN4 0QD (☎ 0793 812479, fax 0793 812089)

CHAPPELL, Edwin Brian Horst; s of Edwin Barnard Henry Chappell (d 1957), of London, and Vera Vita Muriel, *née* Karr de Karroff (d 1975); *b* 11 Feb 1929; *Educ* Royal Masonic Sch; *m* 3 Oct 1953, Yvonne Audrey, da of Wilfrid John Nolan (d 1968), of Twickenham; 1 s (Edwin b 1962); *Career* property registrar Royal Dutch (oblique) Shell Gp; hon steward Westminster Abbey, clerk of the Guild of St Bride, memb exec ctee London Soc, sec Omnibus Soc; Freeman City of London 1950, Liveryman Worshipful Co of Makers of Playing Cards 1984; FRSA 1950; *Recreations* transport esp road transport, London esp City of London; *Clubs* City Livery; *Style*— EBH Chappell, Esq; The Spinney, Meadow Rd, Ashtead, Surrey KT21 1QR (☎ 0372 272 631)

CHAPPELL, Helen Diane; da of George Chappell, and Olivia Patricia, *née* Spellman; *b* 5 Mar 1955; *Educ* The Downer Sch Middx, New Hall Cambridge (BA, MA); *Career* journalist; feature writer New Society magazine 1981-84, winner Catherine Packenham Award 1980-81, Third Person Columnist Guardian, contrib to New Statesman and Society magazine; memb New Hall Soc; *Books* The Other Britain (contrib 1982); *Style*— Ms Helen Chappell; c/o The Guardian, 119 Farringdon Rd, London EC1R 3ER (☎ 01 278 2332)

CHAPPELL, (Edwin) Philip; CBE (1976); s of Rev Claude Roland Chappell (d 1972), of Oakwood Lodge, Lambourn, Berks, and Laura Harland, *née* Hudson (d 1980); *b* 12 June 1929; *Educ* Marlborough, Christ Church Oxford (MA 1953); *m* 10 Feb 1962, Julia Clavering, da of (Harry) Wilfred House, DSO, MC (d 1987), of The Old Rectory, Stutton, Suffolk; 1 s (Luke b 1968), 3 da (Miranda b 1963, Lucy b 1969, Jessica b 1973); *Career* dir Morgan Grenfell 1964-85 (joined 1954), vice-chm 1976-85; non-exec dir: Bank of New Zealand (London Bd) 1967-, Fisons plc 1969-; chm Nat Ports Cncl 1971-77, non-exec dir GLN plc 1974-, advsr Assoc of Investment Tsts 1986-, Finance Ctee Int Chamber of Commerce 1986-; non-exec dir: Forestry Investment Management Ltd 1986-, British Rail Property Bd 1986-, Interallianz (London) Ltd 1987-; tres: City Univ 1988-, Georgian Gp 1988-, Royal Soc of Arts 1982-87; dir RSA Examinations 1987-; memb Barbican Centre Ctee 1977-; dir City Arts Tst Ltd 1977-; govr BBC 1976-81; chm EDC Food & Drink Manufacturing 1976-80; Freeman of City of London; CBIM 1974, FCIB 1968, FCIT 1972; *Books* Pensions and Privilege (1988); *Recreations* sailing, music; *Clubs* Athenaeum, Garrick; *Style*— Philip Chappell, Esq; 22 Frognal Lane, London NW3 7DT (☎ 01 435 8627); Association of Investment Trust Companies, Park House (6 floor), 16 Finsbsury Circus, London EC2M 7JJ (☎ 01 588 5347, fax 01 638 1803)

CHAPPELL, Lt Col Robert Henville; OBE (1973); s of Lt Col Hereward Chappell, OBE (d 1970), and Aileen, *née* Davis; *b* 19 Jan 1931; *Educ* Wellington RMA Sandhurst, Staff Coll Camberley; *m* 1 April 1959, Joanell Vera, da of Bernard Studd (d 1967); 2 s (Bruce b 1961 (d 1976), Gavin b 1963), 1 da (Kathryn b 1966); *Career* Army Offr Queen's Regt, CO 2 (Co Armagh) Bn UDR 1971, Co 11 (Craigaron) Bn UDR 1972, def attaché Sofia 1974-76, ret 1988; *Recreations* cricket, squash, tennis, golf, shooting; *Clubs* Army and Navy; *Style*— Lt Col Robin Chappell, OBE; c/o Lloyds Bank Ltd, 37 Market Place, Warminster, Wilts; HQ DINF (TDG), Sch of Infantry, Warminster, Wilts (☎ 0985 214000 ext 2459)

CHAPPELL, William Evelyn; s of Archibald Walter Chappell, and Edith Eva Clara Blair-Staples (d 1952); *b* 22 Sept 1907; *Educ* Chelsea Sch of Art, studied dancing under Marie Rambert; *Career* Army Serv 1940-45 (two years overseas), Capt RA; dancer, designer, theatre dir, painter, illustrator, writer; first appearance on stage 1929, joined Sadlers Wells Co 1934, (designed scenery and costumes 1934-); designed costumes and scenery Covent Garden 1947- including Les Rendezvous, Les Patineurs, Coppelia, Giselle, Handel's Samson, Frederick Ashton's Walk to the Paradise Garden and Ashton's Rhapsody (costumes); produced Lyric Revue 1951, Globe Revue 1952, High Spirits Hippodrome 1953, At the Lyric 1953, Going to Town St Martin's 1954 (with Orson Welles), The Buccaneer Lyric (Hammersmith) 1955, The Rivals Saville, Beaux' Stratagem Chichester, Violins of St Jacques Sadler's Wells, English Eccentrics, Love and a Bottle, Passion Flower Hotel, Travelling Light, Espresso Bongo, Living For Pleasure, Where's Charley?; appeared in and assisted Orson Welles with film The Trial, The Chalk Garden 1971, Offenbach's Robinson Crusoe 1973, Cockie 1973, Oh Kay! 1974, Nat Tour In Praise of Love 1974, Fallen Angels 1975, Marriage of Figaro 1977, The Master's Voice 1977, Memoir 1978, Gianni Schicci 1978, Nijinsky (film) 1979, Same Time Next Year 1980, A Little Bit on the Side (revue with Beryl Reid 1983), Speak of the Devil (musical), Arsenic and Old Lace Dublin Theatre Festival 1985; designs for Giselle including two prodns for Anton Dolin; choreographed: Travesties 1974, Bloomsbury 1974; directed, designed costumes and choreographed: Purcells Fairy Queen 1974, Donizetti's Torquato Tasso 1975, Lully's Alceste 1975, A Moon for the Misbegotten 1976, The Rivals 1976; teacher and advsr for: Nureyev season 1979, Joffrey Ballet NY 1979; tv shows; illustrator of several books; *Books* Studies in Ballet (ed and jt author), Edward Burra: a painter remembered by his friends (1982), Well Dearie: the letters of Edward Burra (ed); *Style*— William Chappell, Esq

CHAPPLE, Hon Barry Joseph; s of Baron Chapple (Life Peer); *b* 1951; *Educ* Hawes Down Comprehensive; *m* 1980, Angela Christine, da of Kenneth R Medgett; *Style*— Hon Barry Chapple; c/o The Rt Hon Lord Chapple, EETPU, Hayes Court, West Common Road, Bromley BR2 7AU

CHAPPLE, Brian Bedford; s of Richard Chapple, of The Cottage, Heatherhurst Grange, Deepcut, Surrey, and Violet Elizabeth, *née* Groves (d 1973); *b* 6 Feb 1939; *Educ* St Clement Danes GS; *m* 30 Sept 1961, Wendy Ann, da of Kenneth Andrew Cole; 1 da (Amanda b 27 March 1967); *Career* CA 1963 Clark Whitehill (formerly Clark Battams); ptnr Arthur Young & Co (prev Jasolyne Layton Bennett formerly Angus Campbell & Co); dep chm Minet Hldgs plc 1983 (gp fin dir 1977); FCA 1973, FICT 1983; *Recreations* golf, motor boats, horses; *Clubs* RAC, Crockford, Army GC; *Style*— Brian Chapple, Esq; Minet Holdings plc, 100 Leman St, London E1 8HG (☎ 01 481 0707, fax 01 488 9786, telex 8813901)

CHAPPLE, Baron (Life Peer UK 1985); Francis Joseph; s of Frank Chapple, of Shoreditch and his w, Emily, da of Joseph Rook, of Hoxton; *b* 1921,Aug; *Educ* Elementary Sch; *m* 1944, Joan Jeanette, da of James Nicholls; 2 s; *Career* electrician; memb TUC Gen Council 1971, gen sec Electrical, Electronic, Telecommunication and Plumbing Union 1966-84; dir: National Nuclear Corpn 1980-, Southern Water Authority 1983-, Inner City Enterprises 1983-; chm TUC 1982-83; memb NEDC; *Style*— The Rt Hon Lord Chapple; EETPU, Hayes Court, West Common Rd, Bromley, Kent

CHAPPLE, Hon Roger Francis; s of Baron Chapple (Life Peer); *b* 1947; *Educ* Brooke House Comprehensive; *m* 1969, Susan Audrey, da of Charles F W Brown; 2 s (David b 1974, Robin b 1981), 1 da (Rachel b 1972); *Style*— Hon Roger Chapple; c/o The Rt Hon Lord Chapple, EETPU, Hayes Court, West Common Road, Bromley BR2 7AU

CHAPRONIERE, Kenneth Roger; s of Arthur James Chaproniere (d 1978), and Joyce Marion, *née* Cook; *b* 25 July 1948; *Educ* Peckham Manor Sch, Guild Hall Sch of Music and Drama; *m* 1, 29 July 1967 (m dis 1972), Sally Carlsson; *Career* BBC Radio 3 1971-75 and 1978-79, English Bach Festival 1975-77, Liszt Festival of London 1977, Victor Hochhausor Ltd 1978, The Stables Wavendon 1979-, London Bach Orchestra 1988- ; *Recreations* swimming, food and wine, antiques; *Clubs* Royal Overseas League; *Style*— Kenneth R Chaproniere, Esq; The Old Rectory, Milton Keynes Village, Milton Keynes, Bucks MK10 9AF; The Stable, Wavendon, Milton Keynes, Bucks MK17 8LT

CHARAP, Prof John Michael; s of Samuel Lewis Charap, of Stanmore, Middx, and Irene, *née* Shaw (d 1984); *b* 1 Jan 1935; *Educ* City of London Sch, Trinity Coll Cambridge (MA, PhD); *m* 11 June 1961, Ellen Elfrieda, da of Eric Kuhn (d 1986); 1 s (David b 1965); *Career* res assoc: Univ of Chicago 1959-60, Univ of California (Berkeley) 1960-62; memb Inst for Advanced Study Princeton NJ, lectr in Physics Imperial Coll London 1964-65 (sr scientific offr 1963-64); Queen Mary Coll London: reader in theoretical physics 1965-78, prof of theoretical physics 1978-, head of dept of physics 1980-85, dean of faculty of sci 1982-85, pro-princ1987-; Univ of London: chm bd of studies in physics 1976-80, memb senate 1981-; memb: American Physical Soc 1960-, European Physical Soc 1980-; FInstP 1979; *Recreations* walking, talking; *Style*— Prof John Charap; 67 South Hill Park, London NW3 2SS (☎ 01 975 5039, fax 01 981 7517, telex 893750)

CHARITY, William Brian; s of Arthur William Charity (d 1977), of Merseyside, and Gertrude, *née* Hopley (d 1983); *b* 10 Oct 1934; *Educ* Kirkham GS; *m* 1961, Jean Mary, da of Thomas Rennison (d 1969); 2 da (Claire Michelle b 1964, Mandy Jane b 1965); *Career* ptnr Parker Edwards and Co 1961-64, chief exec of overseas ops Norcros plc 1977-79, Edward Le Bas Ltd 1979-, Tex Hldgs plc 1985-; chm: Edward Le Bas Properties Ltd 1979-, Woolamay Bungalows Ltd 1979-, BSP Int Fndn Ltd 1979-, BSP Ltd 1979-, Tex Abrasives (UK) Ltd 1985-, AK Precision Mouldings Ltd 1986-, Quinton-Kaines Ltd 1987; memb Deanery Synod of Ipswich and St Edmundsbury C of E; FCA; *Recreations* philately, sports; *Clubs* Eastern Counties Rugby Union, Lancashire County Rugby Football Union, Essex CCC, Oriental,; *Style*— William B Charity, Esq; The Deans, Newton Green, Sudbury, Suffolk CO10 0QS (☎ 0787 79992); c/o Edward Le Bas Ltd, Claydon, Ipswich, Suffolk (☎ (0473) 830055, fax 0473 832545)

CHARKHAM, Jonathan Philip; s of Louis D London (d 1962), and Phoebe Beatrice Barquet, *née* Miller; *b* 17 Oct 1930; *Educ* St Pauls Sch, Jesus Coll Cambridge (MA); *m* 1954, Moira Elizabeth Frances, da of Barnett Alfred Salmon (d 1965); 2 s (Graham, Rupert twins), 1 da (Fiona); *Career* barr 1953; md Morris Charkham Ltd 1953-63; divnl dir Rest Assured 1963-69, civil service 1969-81; on secondment from Bank of England as dir PRO NED 1982-85, chief advsr Bank of England 1985-88; advsr to the Govrs 1988-; *Recreations* music, wine, antique English furniture, golf, shooting; *Clubs* Athenaeum, City Livery, Roehampton; *Style*— Jonathan Charkham Esq; c/o Bank of England, Threadneedle St, London EC2 8AH (☎ 01 601 4497)

CHARLEMONT, Dorothy, Viscountess; Dorothy Jessie Caulfeild; da of Albert A Johnston (d 1936), of Ottawa, Canada; *m* 1930, 13 Viscount Charlemont (d 1985); *Style*— The Rt Hon Dorothy, Viscountess Charlemont; Apt 915, 2055 Carling Avenue, Ottawa, Ontario, Canada K2A 1G6

CHARLEMONT, 14 Viscount (I 1665); John Day Caulfeild; also Lord Caulfeild, Baron of Charlemont (I 1620); s of Eric St George Caulfeild (d 1975) and Edith Evelyn, da of Frederick William Day, of Ottawa; suc unc, 13 Viscount (d 1985); *b* 19 Mar 1934; *m* 1, 1964, Judith Ann (d 1971), da of James Dodd, of Ontario; 1 s, 1 da (Hon Janis Ann b 1968); m 2, 1972, Janet Evelyn, da of Orville Nancekivell, of Ontario; *Heir* s John Dodd Caulfeild b 15 May 1966; *Style*— The Rt Hon the Viscount Charlemont; 39 Rossburn Drive, Etobicoke, Ontario M9C 2P9, Canada

CHARLES, Colonel Anthony Harold; ERD, TD; s of Hary Percy Charles (d 1962), of London W1, and the late Kate Elize, *née* Cousins; *b* 14 May 1908; *Educ* Dulwich Coll, Gonville and Caius Coll Cambridge (MA, MB); *m* 21 Nov 1962, Rosemary Christine, da of Frederick Theophily Hubert (d 1949), of Hampstead, London; 3 da (Alyson b 1964, Kate b 1966, Harriet b 1969); *Career* WWII, surgical specialist served Aldershot, Malta, M East 1939-45, offr i/c Surg Divn 15 Scottish Gen Hosp 1945, Col Ams, hon Col late OC 308 Co of London Gen Hosp AER, hon Surgeon to the Queen 1957-59; late Vice Dean of St George's Hosp Med Sch, sr obstetric and gynaecoligical surgeon St George's Hosp, surgeon Samaritan Hosp for Women, cnlst gynaecologist Roy Nat Orthopaedic Hosp, hon gynaecologist King Edward VII Hosp for Offrs, examiner; Univ of Cambridge, London Univ, Hong Kong Univ; patron RCOG 1988; Freeman City of London, memb Apothecaries Soc; past pres Alleyns, Rosalyn Park FC; FRCS, FRCOG; *Recreations* golf, boxing (middle weight, Cambridge v Oxford 1930), horse racing; *Clubs* Army and Navy, Buck's, Hawks, MCC; *Style*— Col Anthony Charles, ERD, TD; Gaywood Farm, Gay Street, Pulborough, W Sussex RH20 2HL (☎ 079 83 2223); Humana Hosp, Wellington Place, London NW8 9LE (☎ 01 586 5959)

CHARLES, Bernard Leopold (Leo); QC (1980); s of Chaskiel Charles (d 1960), of 48 Grosvenor Sq, London W1, and Mary, *née* Harris (d 1980); *b* 16 May 1929; *Educ* Kings' Coll Taunton; *m* 13 Aug 1958, (Margaret) Daphne, da of Arthur Lawrence Abel (d 1978), of 48 Harley St, London W1; 1 s Edward Duncan b 1963), 2 da ((Margaret) Lucy b 1966, Katriona Mary (Katy) b 1968); *Career* Nat Serv 1948-50, Capt RAEC 1949; barr Gray's Inn 1955, rec SE circuit 1985; *Recreations* music, gardening; *Style*— Leo Charles, Esq; 8 Henniker Mews, London SW3; Eaton Lodge, 2 Crossbush Rd, Felpham, West Sussex; Lamb Building, Temple, London EC4 (☎ 01 353 6701, fax 01 353 4686, telex 261511 JURIST G)

CHARLES, Lady; Gipsy Joan; da of late Sir Walter Lawrence (d 1939), of Hyde Hall, Sawbridgeworth, Herts, and Mabel, *née* Woollard; *m* 1957, as his 2 w, Sir Noel Hughes Havelock Charles, 3 Bt, KCMG, MC (d 1975, when title became extinct); *Style*— Lady Charles; St Christophe, Châteauneuf-de-Grasse, France, AM

CHARLES, Rev Canon Sebastian; s of Gnanamuthu Pakiannathan Charles and Kamala David; *b* 31 May 1932, at Rangoon; *Educ* Madras and Serampore Univs, Lincoln Theol Coll; *m* 1967, Frances Rosemary Challen; 2 s (Tagore Mark, Ashok Dominic), 2 da (Shanti Deborah, Lalitha Rachel); *Career* former vicar St Barnabas' Pendleton and chaplain Salford Univ, asst gen sec and sec Br Cncl of Churches (Community Affairs) 1974-78, residentiary canon Westminster Abbey 1978-, tres 1982-; *Style*— The Rev Canon Sebastian Charles; 5 Little Cloister, Westminster Abbey, London SW1 3PL (☎ 01 222 6939)

CHARLES, Lady; Winifred Marie; *née* Heath; *m* 1959, as his 2 w, Sir John Pendrill Charles, KCVO, MC (d 1984), partner Allen and Overy 1947-78; 3 da; *Recreations* travel, walking, theatre, studying people, psychology, politics; *Style*— Lady Charles; 42 Belgrave Mews South, London SW1X 8BT (☎ 01 235 5792)

CHARLESWORTH, David Anthony; s of David Harold Charlesworth, MBE (d 1970), and Jessie Vilma, *née* Waldron (d 1970); *b* 19 July 1936; *Educ* Haileybury and ISC; *m* 1970 (m dis 1975), Carol Ann, *née* Green; *Career* Capt RAPC; dir and sec: Sika Contracts Gp of Cos 1965-76, Surban Trading Co Ltd 1968-; dir: SGB Gp 1973-76, Johnson and Avon Ltd 1977-82, Michael Ashby Fine Art Ltd 1978-84, NHM Agency Hldgs Ltd 1982-, Michael Watson (Mgmnt) Ltd 1983-87, P J Dewey (Agencies) Co 1983-, Shaftesbury Mews Co Ltd 1984-, Nelson Hurst of Marsh Agencies Ltd 1985-; underwriting memb of Lloyd's 1975-; *Recreations* bridge, listening to Mozart, motor cycling, reading biographies; *Clubs* IOD; *Style*— David Charlesworth, Esq; 1 Shaftesbury Mews, Stratford Rd, London W8 6QR (☎ 01 937 3550); 41 Seawest Boulevard De La Plage, Le Touqet, 62520, France

CHARLESWORTH, Peter James; s of Joseph William Charlesworth (d 1969), of N Humberside, and Florence Mary, *née* Fisher; *b* 24 August 1944; *Educ* Hull GS, Univ of Leeds (LLB, LLM); *m* 1967, Elizabeth Mary, da of Ronald Herbert Postill (d 1945), of N Humberside; 1 s (Robin b 1972), 1 da (Caroline b 1975); *Career* barr, recorder 1982; *Recreations* tennis, skiing, rugby (spectating), walking; *Clubs* Hull Rugby League (vice-pres), Otley Rugby Union, Leeds YMCA (tennis); *Style*— Peter Charlesworth, Esq; Daleswood, Creskeld Gdns, Bramhope, Leeds LS16 9EN (☎ 0532 674377); 10 Park Sq, Leeds LS1 2LH (☎ 0532 455438); 53 Piecefields Threshfield, nr Skipton BD23 5HR (☎ 752046)

CHARLTON, Clive Arthur Cyril; s of Harold Arthur Charlton (d 1965), of Bexhill, Sussex, and Hilda Gertrude, *née* White (d 1968); *b* 30 Sept 1932; *Educ* Kings Coll Taunton, St Bart Hosp Med Coll and London Univ (MB BS, MS); *m* 9 July 1960, Sheelagh Jennifer, da of Gordon Edward Price (d 1986), of London; 3 s (Simon b 1961, Jason b 1968, Harry b 1970), 1 da (Clare b 1963); *Career* res fell dept of surgery Univ of Kentucky Med Sch USA 1965-66, sr registar St Paul's Hosp and Inst of Urology London 1967-68, conslt urological surgn Royal United Hosp Bath 1972-(St Bart's Hosp London 1968-72); memb cncl: section of Urology RSM 1973-76, Br Assoc of Urological Surgns 1979-82 and 1984-87; memb editorial ctee Br Journal of Surgery 1979-86, asst ed Br Journal of Urology 1981-, hon sr clinical lectr Inst of Urology 1984-, memb of bd of examiners Royal Coll of Surgeons 1988-; memb Bath Dist Health Authy 1982-84; Freeman City of London 1973, Yeoman Worshipful Co of Apothecaries 1971; memb RSM 1968; FRCS 1963; *Books* The Urological System (second edn 1984); contributor in: Calculus Disease (1988), New Trends in Urinary Tract Infections (1988), Operative surgery and Management (1987), Textbook Of Genito-Urinary Surgery (1986); *Recreations* golf, theatre, biographies, medical history; *Style*— Clive Charlton, Esq; Radford Villa, Timsbury, Near Bath (☎ 0761 70658); Department Of Urology, Royal United Hospital, Bath BA1 3NG; The Bath Clinic, Claverton Down Rd, Bath BA2 7BR (☎ 0225 825555)

CHARLTON, David; s of Robert Charlton (d 1968), of Kenilworth, and Alice Jane Stephenson, *née* Pescod; *b* 17 Oct 1936; *Educ* Dame Allan's Sch Newcastle upon Tyne, Durham Univ Law Sch; *m* 4 Aug 1975, Doreen, da of Joseph Woodward, of Kenilworth; 1 s (Angus b 1964); *Career* slr and arbitrator; snr ptnr Angel and Co Coventry and Kenilworth; chm of Tribunals, memb Panel of Arbitrators Chartered Institute of Arbitrators; liveryman Worshipful Co of Arbitrators; chm Talisman Theatre Kenilworth; co slr to European Ferries plc 1962-66; memb Kenilworth UDC 1970-74; *Recreations* performing arts, golf; *Clubs* World Trade Centre; *Style*— David Charlton, Esq; Charnwood, 59 Queens Road, Kenilworth, Warwickshire CV8 1JS (☎ 0926 54453); 42 The Square, Kenilworth, Warwickshire CV8 1GZ (☎ 0925 56214)

CHARLTON, Prof Graham; s of Simpson Rutherford Charlton, (d 1981), of Newbiggin-by-Sea, Northumberland, and Georgina, *née* Graham; *b* 15 Oct 1928; *Educ* Bedlington GS Northumberland, St John's Coll York, Durham Univ (BDS), Bristol Univ (MDS), RCS Edinburgh; *m* 14 July 1956, Stella, da of George W Dobson, 2 s (Bruce b 1959, Fraser b 1967), 1 da (Penelope b 1960); *Career* Nat Serv; gen dental practice Torquay 1958-64, lectr Bristol Univ 1964-72, conslt sr lectr Bristol Univ 1972-78, (clinical dean 1975-78), dean of dental studies Edinburgh Univ 1978-83 (prof of conservative dentistry 1978-), memb gen Dental Cncl 1978-84; memb: FDS, RCS Edinburgh; *Style*— Prof Graham Charlton; Carnethy, Bog Road, Penicuik, Edinburgh EH26 9BT (☎ 0968 73639), Dental School, Chambers Street, Edinburgh EH1 1JA (☎ 031 225 9511)

CHARLTON, (Thomas Alfred) Graham; CB (1970); 3 s of Frederick William Charlton (d 1973), of Purley, Surrey, and Marian, *née* Butterworth (d 1974), bro of F

Noel Charlton, *qv*; *b* 29 August 1913; *Educ* Rugby, CCC Cambridge (MA); *m* 1940, Margaret Ethel, yr da of Albert E Furst, of Chesham Bois, Bucks; 3 da; *Career* War Off 1936, asst private sec to Sec of State 1937-39, Cabinet Off 1947-49, loaned to NATO 1950-52, cmd sec BAOR 1952-55, asst under-sec of state WO 1960, Air Miny 1963, Navy Dept 1968; sec Trade Marks Patents and Designs Fedn 1973-84; *Recreations* golf, gardening; *Clubs* Beaconsfield Golf ; *Style—* Graham Charlton Esq, CB; Victoria House, Elm Rd, Penn, Bucks

CHARLTON, John Fraser; s of late Dr Paul Henry Charlton, of Cardigan, Dyfed, and Margaret, *née* Smith, of Ditchling, Sussex; *b* 23 April 1940; *Educ* Winchester, Magdalene Coll Cambridge (BA); *m* 1966, Susan Ann, da of Walter Herbert Allan, of Esher Surrey; 1 s (David b 1969), 2 da (Anna b 1967, Lisa b 1971); *Career* publisher, chm: Great Gardens of England Investmts Ltd, Chatto and Windus Ltd 1985; dir: Chatto and Windus 1967-, The Hogarth Press 1970, Chatto Bodley Head and Jonathan Cape Ltd 1977 (co name changed to Random House UK Ltd 1988); *Recreations* sport; *Clubs* Garrick, Groucho, Hurlingham; *Style—* John Charlton Esq; 4 Selwood Place, London SW7 3QQ (☎ 01 370 1711); Chatto and Windus Ltd, 30 Bedford Square, London WC1B 3SG (☎ 01 255 2393)

CHARLTON, Maj (Frederick) John; JP (1957); s of Maj George Charlton Anne, OBE (d 1960), of Burghwallis Hall, Doncaster, Yorks (gf assumed name of Anne on inheriting Burghwallis Hall; reverted to Charlton by deed poll 1951), and Amy Violet, *née* Montagu (d 1935); *b* 9 Nov 1914; *Educ* Ampleforth, RMC Sandhurst; *m* 4 Mar 1944, Mary Ellen (Mamie), da of William Henry Charlton (d 1950), of Hesleyside, Bellingham, Northumberland; 5 da (Jenny b 1946, d 1976, Kate b 1948, d 1976, Henrietta b 1951, Teresa b 1953, Josephine b 1961); *Career* cmmnd 2 Lt KOYLI 1934, serv Burma 1936-42 (despatches), Staff Coll Quetta 1942-43, HQ Combined Ops India 1943, served France, Holland, Germany 1944-45, DAQMG 1 Airborne Div 1945, Inst Sch of Land/Air Warfare 1946-48, Hong Kong 1948-49; ret 1949; pres N Tyne and Redesdale Agric Soc 1950-; memb Bellingham RDC 1951-79; High Sheriff Northumberland 1957; *Style—* Maj John Charlton, JP; Hesleyside, Bellingham, Hexham, Northumberland (☎ 0660 202 12)

CHARLTON, Prof Kenneth; s of George charlton (d 1952), and Lottie, *née* Little (d 1976); *b* 11 July 1925; *Educ* Chester GS, Univ of Glasgow (MA, MEd), Jordanhill Coll of Educn Glasgow; *m* 2 April 1953, Maud Tulloch, da of Peter Renwick Brown, MBE (d 1955); 1 s (Peter b 3 Feb 1957), 1 da (Shelagh b 3 June 1955); *Career* Sub Lt RNVR 1943-46; history master Daljiel HS Motherwell 1950, sr history master Uddington GS Lanarkshire 1950-54, sr lectr in educn Univ of Keele 1964-66 (lectr 1954-64), prof of history and philosophy of educn Univ of Birmingham 1966-72, prof of history of educn and dean of the faculty of educn King's Coll Univ of London 1972-83, prof emeritus of history of educn London Univ 1983-, Leverhulme tst emeritus res fellowship 1984-86; *Books* Education in Renaissance England (1955); *Recreations* gardening, listening to music; *Style—* Prof Kenneth Charlton; 128 Ridge Langley, Sanderstead, Croydon, Surrey CR2 OAS (☎ 01

CHARLTON, Prof (Thomas) Malcolm; s of William Charlton (d 1974), of Great Wyrley, Staffs, and Emily May, *née* Wallbank (d 1950); *b* 1 Sept 1923; *Educ* Doncaster GS, Univ Coll Nottingham (BSc), Univ of Cambridge (MA); *m* 18 Sept 1950, Valerie, da of Dr Colin McCulloch (d 1947), of Hexham; 3 s (Richard b 1951, William b 1956, d 1956, Edward b 1958); *Career* jr sci offr min of aircraft production TRE Malvern 1943-46, asst engr Merz and McLellan 1946-54, lectr in engrg Univ of Cambridge 1945-63), (fell and tutor Sidney Sussex Coll 1959-63, prof of civil engrg Queen's Univ Belfast 1963-70 (Dean Faculty of Applied Sci 1967-70), Jackson prof of Engrg Univ of Aberdeen 1970-79 (professor emeritus 1979-), historian of engineering science 1979-; memb: advsy cncl UDR 1969-71, bd of Fin Diocese of Hereford 1980; hon for memb Finnish Acad of Tech Sciences (1967); FRSE 1973; *Books* Model Analysis of Structures (1954-66), Energy Principles in Applied Statics (1959), Analysis of Statically-Indeterminate Frameworks (1961), Principles of Structural Analysis (1969,1977), Energy Principles in Theory of Structures (1973), A History of Theory of Structures in the Nineteenth Century (1982); *Recreations* walking, ecclesiastical history; *Clubs* New (Edinburgh); *Style—* Prof Malcolm Charlton; 8 Lambourn Close, Trumpington, Cambridge CB2 2JX (☎ 0223 840 228)

CHARLTON, (Frederick) Noel; CB (1961), CBE (1946); s of Frederick William Charlton (d 1973), of Purley, Surrey, and Marian, *née* Butterworth (d 1974); bro of T A Graham Charlton, *qv*; *b* 4 Dec 1906; *Educ* Rugby, Hertford Coll Oxford (MA); *m* 1932, Maud Helen, da of Charles Walter Rudgard, of Davington, Faversham, Kent; *Career* slr 1932, Slr's Dept Treasury 1946-71, princ asst slr (Litigation) 1956-71; sec Lord Chllr's Ctee on Defamation 1971-74; Dept of Energy (Legal Branch) 1975-81; *Recreations* golf, travel; *Clubs* Army and Navy; *Style—* Noel Charlton Esq, CB, CBE; 4 Newton Rd, Purley, Surrey (☎ 01 660 2802)

CHARLTON, Philip; OBE (1987); s of George Charlton (d 1953), of Chester, and Lottie, *née* Little (d 1976); *b* 31 July 1930; *Educ* City GS Chester; *m* 1953, Jessie, da of Joseph Boulton (d 1966), of Chester; 1 s (Philip), 1 da (Margaret); *Career* gen mangr: Chester Savings Bank 1966-75, TSB Wales and Border Counties 1975-81; memb and dep chief gen mangr Tstee Savings Banks Central Bd 1981-82 (chief gen mangr 1982-); dir: TSB Computer Servs (Wythenshawe) Ltd 1976-81, TSB Tst Co Ltd 1979-82, TSB Hldgs Ltd 1982-, TSB Gp Computer Servs Ltd 1981-84, Central Tstee Savings Bank 1982-; chief gen mangr TSB England and Wales 1983-85, dir TSB England and Wales 1985-, vice pres and gp chief exec TSB Group plc 1986-; cncl memb The Inst of Bankers 1982-; memb bd of Admin of the Int Savings Banks Inst Geneva 1985-; FCIB, CBIM; *Style—* Philip Charlton, Esq, OBE; 62 Quinta Drive, Arkley, Herts (☎ 01 440 4477); TSB Gp plc, 25 Milk St, London EC2V 8LU (☎ 01 606 7070, telex 8812487)

CHARLTON, Richard Wingate Edward; s of Col Wingate Charlton, OBE, DL, of Great Canfield Park, Takeley, Essex, and Angela Margot, *née* Windle; *b* 3 May 1948; *Educ* Eton, Univ of Neuchatel; *m* 1 Feb 1979, Claudine Marie Germaine, da of Maître Hubert Maringe (d 1988), of Champlin, Premery, Nievre, France; 1 s (Andrew b 9 Nov 1981), 1 da (Emma b 29 Sept 1985); *Career* Frere Cholmeley & Co slrs 1968-78, Swaks & Co 1974-76, Hambros Bank 1977-81, exec dir Banque Paribas London 1981-88, chief exec Banque Internationale A Luxembourg London 1988, Slr of the Supreme Ct 1976; Freeman City of London, Liveryman Merchant Taylors memb Solicitor of the Supreme Court 1975; *Recreations* theatre, cinema, tennis, football, travel; *Clubs* Whites, Turf; *Style—* Richard Charlton, Esq; Banque Internationale A Luxembourg, Priory House, 1 Mitre Sq London EC3A 5BS (☎ 01 623 3110, telex 884 032)

CHARLTON, (Robert Joseph) Robin; *née* Watson; s of James Charlton, MM (d 1978), of 32 Wareing Street, Tyldesley, Manchester, and Mary Eliabeth, *née* Crompton (d 1977); *b* 27 May 1933; *Educ* Manchester GS, Manchester Univ (BA); *m* 31 Mar 1962, Joan Charlton, da of George Sydney Firth, of 26 Schofield Lane, Atherton, Manchester; 1 da (Helen b 1964); *Career* adm chartered accountant 1957; ptnr: mellor Snape & Co 1970-76, Josolyne Layton-Bennett & Co 1976-81, Arthur Young 1981-87; ptnr Alexander Layton 1987-; fdr pres of Cheshire Jr Chamber 1969-70, pres Crewe Dist Chamber of Trade 1975-76; tres: Crewe Constituency Con Assoc 1974-83, Crewe & Nantwich Con Assoc 1983-88; memb Crewe Rotary Club 1979-, Br Jr Chamber 1973, senator Jr Chamber Int 1974-; FCA; *Recreations* watching cricket, lecturing on the peerage; *Clubs* Lancashire County Cricket; *Style—* Robin Charlton, Esq; Roldal, 43 Pit Lane, Hough, Crewer, Ches CW2 5JH (☎ 0270 841 759); 130-132 Nantwich Road, Crewe, Cheshire CW2 6AZ (☎ 0270 213 475)

CHARLTON, Lt-Col (Richard) Wingate (COLLINS-); OBE (1975, MBE 1961), DSC, DL (Essex 1971); o s of Brig-Gen Claud Edward Charles Graham Charlton, CB, CMG, DSO (d 1961), of Great Canfield Park, Takeley, Essex, and Gwendoline Sylvia, *née* Whitaker (d 1964); gs of Lt-Col Richard Granville Charlton (d 1912), who served in Indian Mutiny; *b* 30 July 1913; *Educ* Eton, RMC Sandhurst; *m* 26 May 1945, Angela Margot, da of late Norman Whitmore Windle, of Mells Lodge, Hailsworth, Suffolk; 2 s (Richard Wingate Edward b 3 May 1948, William Wingate Hugo b 23 Sept 1951); *Career* 2 Lt 8 Hussars 1933, served Palestine 1936, Capt 1938, Transjordan Frontier Force 1938; WWII 1939-45 in Syria (wounded, despatches) and NW Europe, cmd 2 Bedouin Mechanised Regt Arab Legion; ME Staff College 1943, served Para Regt SOE NW Europe & Hussars 1944; 2 i/c Hussars 1946, Trg Directorate WO 1947, GSO11 RASC Offrs' Sch, 2 i/c Northants Yeo; Mil and air attaché British Embassy Damascus 1958-61; HQ Allied Land Forces Central Europe; Sec chm Royal Humane Soc 1977- (sec 1962-74, ctee memb 1975-); memb: Chelmsford and Deanery Synods; Court and Cncl Essex Univ; Pres SSAFA; Pres Essex County Playing Fields; chm Essex Army Benevolent Fund; dep cmmr St John Ambulance Essex; High Sheriff of Essex 1976-77; Freeman of the Merchant Taylors' Co; FRSA 1947; OStJ 1979; DSC (US Army), 3 cl Order of the Istiqlal (Jordan) 1943; *Books* Verses (1937), More Verses (1938); *Recreations* fox and hare hunting (in England), stag hunting (in France); *Clubs* Cavalry and Guards'; *Style—* Lt-Col Wingate Charlton, OBE, DL; Great Canfield Park, Takeley, nr Bishop's Stortford, Herts CM22 6SS (☎ 0279 870256)

CHARMAN, Michael; s of Edwin Henry Charman (d 1969), and Doris Ada Charman, *née* Whitehead (d 1985); *b* 28 May 1920; *Educ* St Pauls; *m* 13 April 1946, Florence Joyce (Joy), da of The Rev Prebendary Thomas Harry Philips Hyatt (d 1941), Prebendary of Lichfield Cathedral; 1 s (David Michael b 1948), 1 da (Philippa Joyce b 1951); *Career* TA 1938; War Serv 1939-43 44th Leicesters, invalided out; admitted slr 1945, HM Coroner City of Leicester and S Leics 1969-; hon lay canon Leicester Cathedral 1963-; chm: The Royal Leicesters, Rutland and Wycliffe Soc for the Blind 1975-; hon slr The Samaritans 1975-88; chm Glebe Ctee Leicester Diocesan Bd of Finance 1980-; *Recreations* books, bridge, golf; *Clubs* Leicestershire Book Soc, The Leicestershire, The Leicestershire Golf, The Far and Near; *Style—* Michael Charman, Esq; 40 Bankart Ave, Leicester LE2 2DB (☎ 0533 707789); Freer Bouskell Solicitors, 10 New St, Leicester LE1 5ND (☎ 0533 516624)

CHARNLEY, Lady; Jill Margaret; *née* Heaver; *m* 1957, Sir John Charnley, CBE, FRCS, FRS (d 1982), sometime prof orthopaedic surgery Manchester Univ; 1 s, 1 da; *Style—* Lady Charnley; Birchwood, Moss Lane, Mere, Knutsford, Cheshire (☎ 0565 2267)

CHARNLEY, Sir (William) John; CB (1973); s of George Edward Charnley (d 1983), and Catherine Charnley; *b* 4 Sept 1922; *Educ* Oulton HS Liverpool, Univ of Liverpool (MEng); *m* 1945, Mary, da of Richard Paden (d 1933); 1 s, 1 da; *Career* aeronautical engr; controller Guided Weapons and Electronics MOD 1972-73, chief scientist RAF 1973-77, controller R and D Establishments and Res MOD 1977-82, technical consult 1982-; conslt: King Bros plc, CAA, Graviner Ltd; pres Royal Inst of Navigation 1987-, tstee Richard Ormonde Shuttleworth Rememberance Tst; FRAeS 1966 (silver medal 1973, gold medal 1980), FRIN 1963 (bronze medal 1960), Cumberbatch Trophy (Guild of Air Pilots, Air Navigators) 1964; Hon DEng Univ of Liverpool 1988; kt 1981; *Recreations* all sport, hill walking, chess; *Clubs* RAF; *Style—* Sir John Charnley, CB; Kirkstones, 29 Brackendale Close, Camberley, Surrey GU15 1HP (☎ 0276 22547)

CHARRINGTON, Gerald Anthony; JP (Essex 1982), DL (Essex 1977); o s of Brig Harold Vincent Spencer Charrington, DSO, MC, of Winchfield House, Hants, and Eleanor Sophia Campbell, *née* Jeffreys; *b* 14 July 1926; *Educ* Eton, Sandhurst, Staff Coll; *m* 28 Sept 1957, Susannah Elizabeth, da of late Brig Ord Henderson Tidbury, MC, of The Greate House, Layer de la Haye, Essex; 3 s, 1 da; *Career* 9/12 Royal Lancers 1946-67, ret as Maj; farmer 1969-; memb Gen Synod 1970-, lay chm Chelmsford Diocesan Synod 1976-, memb Redundant Churches Fund 1977-, church cmmr 1978-; High Sheriff of Essex 1981-82; *Recreations* shooting, beagling, Tudor brickwork, church architecture; *Clubs* Athenaeum; *Style—* Gerald Charrington, Esq, JP, DL; Layer Marney Tower, Colchester, Essex (☎ 0206 330202)

CHARRINGTON, Timothy Somerset; s of Maj Edward Craven Charrington (d 1971), of Alton, and Betty, *née* Bowles (d 1987); *b* 18 Mar 1938; *Educ* Malvern, Harper Adams Agric Coll, Oxford Air Trg Sch; *m* 16 Nov 1974, Elisabeth Anne Fiennes da of Dr John Ley Greaves, of E Worldham Manor, Alton (d 1987); 2 s (Oliver b 1980, Hugh b 1983), 1 da (Sarah b 1977); *Career* Airline Pilot, Capt with BA; *Recreations* fishing, tennis, windsurfing; *Style—* Timothy Charrington, Esq; The Croft, Farringdon, Alton, Hants GU34 3DT (☎ 042 058 200)

CHARTERIS, Hon Andrew Martin; er s of Baron Charteris of Amisfield (Life Peer); *b* 19 August 1947; *Educ* Milton Abbey; *Style—* The Hon Andrew Charteris

CHARTERIS, Hon Harold Francis; yr s of Baron Charteris of Amisfield; *b* 11 Jan 1950; *Educ* Eton, Pembroke Coll Oxford; *m* 1984, Blandine Marie, elder da of Roger Desmons, of 14 rue Wilhelm, Paris, 16; 1 da (Zoe France b 1984, Julia Marie b 29 Nov 1985); *Style—* The Hon Harold Charteris

CHARTERIS, Hon Mrs Guy; Violet; da of Alfred Charles Masterton Porter, of Dundee; *m* 5 Oct 1945, as his 2 w, Capt Hon Guy Laurence Charteris (d 21 Sept 1967), 2 s of 11 Earl of Wemyss and (7 of) March; *Style—* The Hon Mrs Guy Charteris; The Old House, Didbrook, Nr Cheltenham, Glos (☎ 0242 621236)

CHARTERIS OF AMISFIELD, Baroness; Hon (Mary) Gay Hobart; da of 1 Visc Margesson (d 1965); *b* 3 May 1919; *m* 16 Dec 1944, Baron Charteris of Amisfield, GCB, GCVO, QSO, OBE, PC, *qv*; 2 s, 1 da; *Style—* The Rt Hon The Lady Charteris of Amisfield; Provost's Lodge, Eton College, Windsor, Berks (☎ 0753 66304); Wood Stanway Hse, Wood Stanway, Cheltenham, Glos (☎ 038 673 480)

CHARTERIS OF AMISFIELD, Baron (Life Peer UK 1977); Hon Martin Michael Charles Charteris; GCB (1977, KCB 1972, CB 1958), GCVO (1976, KCVO 1962, MVO 1953), QSO (1978), OBE (1946), PC (1972); s of late Capt (Hugo Francis Charteris) Lord Elcho (d 1916), and bro of 12 Earl of Wemyss and March; *b* 7 Sept 1913; *Educ* Eton, Sandhurst; *m* 16 Dec 1944, Hon (Mary) Gay Hobart Margesson, da of 1 Viscount Margesson; 2 s, 1 da; *Career* Lt KRRC 1936, serv WWII Middle East, Palestine, Lt-Col 1944; private sec to HRH The Princess Elizabeth 1950-52, asst private sec to HM The Queen 1952-72, private sec to HM The Queen and keeper of HM's Archives 1972-77, a permanent lord in waiting to HM The Queen 1978-; dir: De La Rue Co 1978-85, Rio Tinto Zinc Corpn 1978-84, Claridge's and Connaught Hotels; provost of Eton 1978-; tstee British Museum 1979, chm tstees Nat Heritage Meml Fund 1980; Hon DCL (Oxon) 1978, Hon LLD (London) 1981; *Style*— The Rt Hon the Lord Charteris of Amisfield, GCB, GCVO, QSO, OBE, PC; Provost's Lodge, Eton College, Windsor, Berks (☎ 0753 866304); Wood Stanway House, Wood Stanway, Cheltenham, Glos (☎ 038 673 480)

CHARVET, Richard Christopher Larkins; JP; s of Patrice Edouard Charvet, and Eleanor Margaret; *b* 12 Dec 1936; *Educ* Rugby; *m* 30 Sept 1961 (m dis 1988), Elizabeth Joan, da of Hubert Johnson; 2 s (Charles Richard de Merle b 1963, Edward Bryan Nugent b 1972), 1 da (Alexandra Mary Dashwood b 1965); *Career* clerk Union Castle Line 1956-58, clerk Killick Martin and Co Ltd 1958-67 (dir 1967-81), dir Vogt and Maguire Ltd 1981-88, assoc dir Anglo Soviet Shipping Ltd 1988-; City of London: Common Councilman 1973-78, Ald Aldgate Ward 1978-85, Queens Sheriff 1984; chm Royalist Appeal 1985, chm St John's Ambulance Centenary Appeal 1987-, chm RNLI London 1988; Freeman City of London 1962, Prime Warden Worshipful Co of Shipwrights 1985; memb: Guild of World Traders 1976, FRSA, FBIM, MITT, ACIArb, FICS; JSM 1979, OStJ 1984, RD; *Books* Peter and Tom in the Lord Mayors Show (1981); *Recreations* sailing, gardening, people; *Style*— Richard Charvet, Esq, RD, JP; Anglo Soviet Shipping Ltd, 10 Lloyds Ave, London EC3 (☎ 01 488 1399)

CHASSELS, (James) David Simpson; s of Robert Brown Chassels, and Frances Amelia, *née* Simpson; *b* 2 April 1947; *Educ* Rannoch Sch; *m* 21 May 1976, Angela Elizabeth, da of James Nicol Martin Bulloch; 2 s (Ross b 30 Nov 1977, Scott b 29 March 1980), 1 da (Nicola b 28 Feb 1983); *Career* CA: French & Cowan Glasgow 1965-70, Arthur Young Edinburgh 1970-74, 3i Investmt Exec Glasgow & Edinburgh (formerly ICFC) 1974-81 (dir 3i Corporate Fin 1981-); govr Rannoch Sch 1972-, memb Polmont Borstal visiting ctee 1978-83; former Deacon Incorpn of Barbers Trades House of Glasgow 1985-86; MICAS 1973; *Recreations* sailing, skiing; *Clubs* RSAC, CCC; *Style*— David Chassels, Esq; 10 Duart Drive, Newton Mearns, Glasgow G77 5DS (☎ 041 639 3914), 3i Corporate Finance Ltd, 20 Blythswood Squ, Glasgow, G2 4AR (☎ 041 248 4456, fax 041 248 3245, car tel 0836 706604, telex 917844)

CHASTNEY, John Garner; s of Alec Richardson Chastney (d 1981), and Constance Mary, *née* Edwards; *b* 5 Jan 1947; *Educ* Henry Mellish GS Nottingham, Univ of Lancaster (MA); *m* 4 Aug 1973, Susan Thirza, da of Norman Dunkerley; 2 s (Martin Richard, b 1980, David Paul, b 1982), 1 da (Catherine Jane, b 1978); *Career* qual accountant 1973, princ lectr Sheffield City Poly 1974-79, sr nat trg mangr Neville Russell 1979-83, dvpt ptnr Neville Russell 1983-88; on secondment: under sec DTI, dir Indus Devpt Unit 1988-; FCA 1973; *Books* True and Fair View (1974), European Financial Reporting: The Netherlands (with J H Beeny, 1976); *Clubs* Square Mile; *Style*— John Chastney, Esq; 246 Bishopsgate, London EC2M 4PB (☎ 01 377 1000, fax 01 377 8931)

CHATAWAY, Rt Hon Christopher John; PC (1970); s of James Denys Percival Chataway, OBE (d 1953), of 46 De Vere Gdns, W8; *b* 31 Jan 1931; *Educ* Sherborne, Magdalen Coll Oxford; *m* 1, 1959 (m dis 1975), Anna Maria, da of H Lett; 2 s, 1 da; m 2, 1976, Carola Cecil Walker, da of Maj Charles Ashton, DSO; 2 s; *Career* Olympic runner 1952 and 1956 (world record holder 5,000 metres 1954); TV News reporter 1955-59; MP (C) Lewisham N 1959-66, Chichester 1969-74; min: Posts and Telecommunications 1970-72, Industrial Devpt 1972-74; chm: United Medical Enterprises 1980-83, London Broadcasting Co 1981-; v-chm Orion Royal Bank 1974-; dir: British Electric Traction Co 1974-, Int Gen Electric (USA) Ltd 1979-, Petrofina UK Ltd 1985-; chm Crown T.V. Productions P.L.C. 1987-; *Style*— The Rt Hon Christopher Chataway; 40 Addison Rd, London W14

CHATAWAY, Michael Denys; s of James Denys Percival Chataway OBE (d 1983), and Margaret Pritchard, *née* Smith (d 1988);; *b* 23 July 1934; *Educ* Sherborne, Magdalen Coll Oxford (BA); *m* 1 Aug 1970, Caroline Mary; da of Lt Col E H Colville OBE (d 1980); 1 s (James b 1973), 1 da (Charlotte b 1977); *Career* Nat Serv 2 Lieut 1 Bn KRRC 1953; chm C Czarnikow Ltd 1985- (dir 1970-); *Style*— Michael Chataway, Esq; The Old Rectory, Tichborne, Nr Alresford, Hants; C Czarnikow Ltd, 66 Mark Lane, London, EC3P 3EA (☎ 01 480 9300);

CHATER, Dr Anthony Philip John; *b* 21 Dec 1929; *Educ* Northampton GS, Queen Mary Coll London; *m* 1954, Janice, *née* Smith; 3 s; *Career* biochemist; former teacher and lectr; contested Luton (Com) 1963, 1964, 1966, 1970; National Chm Communist Party 1967-69; ed Morning Star 1974-; *Style*— Dr Tony Chater; 8 Katherine Drive, Dunstable, Beds (☎ 64835)

CHATFIELD, Dennis; s of Reginald Herbert Chatfield (d 1985), and Delia, *née* Gale (d 1982); *b* 15 July 1927; *m* 5 April 1952, Bess May, da of William Pearce, RA, ISM (d 1978); 2 s (Jeremy Dennis b 1956, Christopher Leo b 1960); *Career* PA to F Fortescue Brickdale (ptnr of Gregory Rowcliffe Ltd, solicitors) 1949-53, tax conslt Country Gentlemen's Assoc 1953-55, Alliott Pierson - Chartered Accountants 1955-67, Kidsons Chartered Accountants (int tax man) 1967-70; hd of tax dept Towry Law Insurance Brokers Ltd 1970-71; dir County Town Investmts plc, Seagrove Corporate Services, Tenco Industries Ltd, J M S Associates Ltd; memb: Inst of Taxation, Int Fiscal Assoc; *Recreations* snooker (1986 RAC snooker handicap champion); *Clubs* RAC, Naval; *Style*— Dennis Chatfield, Esq; The Cotswold House, Landsdown, Bourton on the Water, Gloucestershire GL54 2AR (☎ 0451 20474); 78 Buckingham Gate, London SW1E 6PD (☎ 01 222 1522, fax 222 0741)

CHATFIELD, 2 Baron (1937 UK); Ernle David Lewis Chatfield; s of 1 Baron Chatfield, GCB, OM, KCMG, CVO, PC (Admiral of the Fleet, d 1967); *b* 2 Jan 1917; *Educ* Dartmouth, Trinty Cambridge; *m* 16 May 1969, (Felicia Mary) Elizabeth, da of late Dr John R Bulman, of Hereford; *Career* ADC to Govr-Gen of Canada 1940-44; *Style*— The Rt Hon the Lord Chatfield; 535 Island Road, Victoria, BC V8S 2T7, Canada

CHATFIELD, John Freeman; CBE (1982), DL (E Sussex 1986); s of Cecil Freeman Chatfield (d 1974), of The Lodge, Blackwater Rd, Eastbourne, and Florence Dorothy, *née* Greed (d 1985); *b* 28 Oct 1929; *Educ* Southdown Coll Eastbourne, Roborough Sch Eastbourne, Lawrence Sheriff Rugby, Lewes GS, Sch of Law London; *m* 18 Sept 1954, Barbara Elizabeth, da of Frank Hubert Trickett (d 1969), of Montford, nr Shrewsbury, Shropshire; *Career* slr, sr ptnr private practice; ldr East Sussex CC 1981-85 (chm 1985-87, vice chm 1987-); chm: Sussex Police Authy, Police Ctee Assoc CC, Official Side Police Negotiating Bd UK 1982-85, Cons SE Area Local Govt Advsy Ctee; pres Eastbourne Cons Assoc 1975-, vice chm exec cncl ACC (ldr Cons Gp) 1986-; memb: ct of cncl Sussex Univ 1981-85, Police Advsy Bd England and Wales 1980-85, Cons Nat Local Govt Advsy ctee 1982-, Nat Union of Cons and Unionist Assocs Nat Exec Ctee, of cncl Pestalozzi Tst; *Recreations* music, theatre; *Style*— John F Chatfield, Esq, CBE, DL; Underhill House, Went Way, East Dean, Eastbourne, E Sussex BN20 0DB (☎ 0323 423 397); 306 Nell Gwynne House, Sloane Ave, London SW3 (☎ 01 589 1627); 104 South St, Eastbourne, E Sussex BN21 4LW (☎ 0323 27321)

CHATMAN, William C; s of Edgar T Chatman (d 1939), and Gertrude Hewett (d 1977); *b* 20 Nov 1930; *Educ* Drexel Univ (BSc) 1952; *m* 6 Sept 1952, Helen S, da of August Siefert (d 1981); 3 da (Linda (Mrs Thomsen) b 1954, Sandra (Mrs Loether) b 1957, Susan (Mrs Webb) b 1960); *Career* engr; dir of ops Societe Foster Wheeler Francaise 1983-86, chm and chief exec Foster Wheeler Ltd 1986-; CEng, FICHE, CBIM; *Recreations* singing (London Philharmonica Choir), skiing; *Style*— William C Chatman, Esq; 12A Hornton Street, London W8 4NR; c/o Foster Wheeler Ltd, Foster Wheeler House, Station Road, Reading, Berks RG1 1LX

CHATT, Joseph; CBE (1978); s of Joseph Chatt (d 1929), of Caldbeck, Cumbria, and M Elsie, *née* Parker (d 1972); *b* 6 Nov 1914; *Educ* Nelson Sch Wigton Cumbria, Emmanuel Coll Cambridge (BA, PhD, MA, ScD); *m* 31 May 1947, Ethel, *née* Williams; 1 s (Joseph b 16 May 1951), 1 da (Elizabeth b 12 March 1948); *Career* res chemist Woowich Arsenal 1941-42, chief chemist Peter Spence and Sons Ltd Widnes 1942-46, ICI res fell Imperial Coll london 1946-47, head inorganic chemistry dept Butterwick (later Akers) res laboratories ICI Ltd Welwyn 1947-60, gp mangr Akers Gp, heavy organic chemicals div ICI Ltd 1961-62, prof inorganic chemistry Queen Mary Coll Univ of London 1964, prof of chemistry Univ of Sussex 1964-80 emeritus prof 1980-, dir Unit of Nitrogen Fixation Agric Res Cncl 1963-80; active in int and nat bodies concerned with chemistry especially Int Union of Pure and Applied Chemistry 1950-; hon memb: Nat Acad of Portugal 1978, Indian Nat Sci Acad 1980, NY Acad of Sciences 1978, Royal Physiological Soc of Lund 1984, American Acad of Arts and Sciences 1985; Hon DSc: Univ of E Anglia 1974, Sussex Univ 1982; Hon Dr Pierre et Marie Curie Paris 1981, Filasofie Dr Lund Sweden 1986; Wolf Fndn Prize Chemistry FRSC (memb cncl 1952-65 and 1972-76, hon sec 1956-62, vice pres 1962-65 and 1972-74, pres Dalton Div 1972-74), FRS 1961 memb cncl, Davy Medal Chemistry, parly and scientific ctee 1961-62, fell American Chemcial Soc 1961, IUPAC 1984; *Recreations* numismatics, art, history; *Clubs* Civil Service; *Style*— Prof Joseph Chatt, CBE; 16 Tongdean Road, Hove, E Sussex BN3 6QE (☎ 0273 554 377); School of Chemistry & Molecular Sciences, Univ of Sussex, Falmer, Brighton BN1 9QJ (☎ 0273 606 755)

CHATTERJEE, Mira; da of Dr Haradlan Chatterjee (Capt IMS/IAMC Seac, Burma Star), of Maya Cottage, Chase Lane, Lambourne Rd, Chigwell, Essex, and Kamala, *née* Banerjee; *b* 19 April 1948; *Educ* City of London Sch for Girls; *m* 19 April 1980, Dr Gautam Chaudhuri, s of Dr Punendu Chandhuri, of Calcutta; 1 da (Sandra b 28 Jan 1981); *Career* called to the bar Middle Temple 1973, South East Circuit; *Recreations* reading, philosophy; *Clubs* Wig and Pen; *Style*— Miss Mira Chatterjee; 4 Brick Court, Middle Temple, London EC4 (☎ 01 353 1492/3/4, fax 01 583 8645)

CHATTERJEE, Dr Satya Saran; OBE (1971); s of Basanta Kumar Chatterjee (d 1956), of Patna India, and Sabani Chatterjee (d 1924); *b* 16 July 1922; *Educ* Patna Univ; *m* 1948, Enid May, da of Joseph Adlington (d 1965), of Birmingham; 1 s (Nigel), 2 da (Camille, Petula); *Career* Capt Indian Army 1944; conslt chest physician i/c Dept of Respiratory Physiology Wythenshawe Hosp Manchester 1959-87; pres Overseas Doctors' Assoc; memb North Western Regional Health Authy 1976-86; memb: Standing Advsy Cncl on Race Relations 1977-86, Gen Medical Cncl 1979-; res papers on various projects related to cardio/pulmonary disorders; *Recreations* gardening, bridge; *Clubs* Manchester Bridge, Rotary (Wythenshawe); *Style*— Dr Satya Chatterjee, OBE; March, 20 Macclesfield Rd, Wilmslow, Cheshire SK9 2AF (☎ 0625 522559); Dept of Respiratory Physiology, Wythenshawe Hosp, Southmoor Rd, Manchester M23 9LT (☎ 061 998 7070 ext 78)

CHATTERTON, (Charles) Robert; s of Charles Chatterton (d 1952), of Penarth, Glam, and Lilian, *née* Saunders (d 1972); *b* 30 Sept 1913; *Educ* Cardiff GS, Cardiff Tech Coll, Bloggs Coll Cardiff; *m* 21 Aug 1937, Lilian May, da of Howard Henry Sladen (d 1959), of Cardiff; 1 s (Peter b 1939), 1 da (Susan b 1947); *Career* TA 1937-45, Welsh Regt 1939, cmmnd Queen's Own Royal West Kents 1940, A/Maj, served overseas (despatches twice); chm: Reardon Smith Gp of Cos 1970-85 (jr accountant 1929, asst co sec 1961, dir and co sec 1963), Cardiff Ship Mgmnt & Services Ltd 1987- (dir 1985); dir Bank of Wales plc 1974-; chm: Horton and Port Eynon Lifeboat Ctee, Cardiff Station The Missions to Seamen; Queens Silver Jubilee Medal; FInstD; *Recreations* ornithology, walking, fishing; *Clubs* Cardiff County, Cardiff Business; *Style*— Robert Chatterton, Esq; Green Meadow, Ger y Llan, St Nicholas, Cardiff CF5 6SY (☎ 0446 760723); Dominions House South, Queen St, Cardiff

CHATWIN, Charles Leslie; DSC (1945); s of Leslie Boughton Chatwin (d 1933), of Birmingham, and Isobel, *née* Milward (d 1952); *b* 2 Dec 1908; *Educ* King Edwards VI Sch Stratford-upon-Avon, Univ of Birmingham (LLB); *m* 30 Aug 1938, Mary Margharita, da of Samuel Edward Turnell (d 1953), of Sheffield: 2 s (Bruce (writer) b 1940 d 1989, Hugh b 1944); *Career* slr; served RN 1940-45, acting Lt Cdr Home Waters and Med; ptnr Wragge and Co, ret; gen cmmnr of taxes 1952-80, memb Birmingham Teaching Hospital Bd 1948-66, vice-pres and pres West Rent Assessment Panel 1965-80; life govr Birmingham Univ 1964-; *Recreations* sailing, European travel; *Clubs* Royal Crusing; *Style*— Charles Chatwin, Esq, DSC; 16 College St, Stratford-upon-Avon CV37 6BN (☎ 0789 293575)

CHATWOOD, Albert Rawsthorne; s of Albert Chatwood (d 1972), of Devon, and Jessie Dunbar, *née* Wilson (d 1979); *b* 9 July 1931; *Educ* Holloway Sch, St John's Newfoundland, Prince of Wales Coll St John's; *Career* statistician Iron Ore Co of Canada Labrador City 1962-79; tres and chm Labrador City Library Bd 1964-78, hon tres Anglican Charitable Fndn for Children 1980-; *Recreations* walking, music, reading, gardening; *Clubs* Royal Overseas League; *Style—* Albert R Chatwood, Esq; 8 Prince William Place, St John's, Newfoundland, Canada A1B 1A5 (☎ 709 722 8261); Chesterblade, Chamberlains, CBS, Newfoundland, Canada, A0A 2YO (☎ 709 834 2815)

CHAU, Hon Sir Sik-Nin; CBE (1950), JP (1940); s of late Cheuk-Fan Chau, of Hong Kong; *b* 13 April 1903; *Educ* St Stephen's Coll Hong Kong, London, Vienna State Univ; *m* 1927, Ida Hing-Kwai, da of late Lau Siu-Cheuk; 2 s (Kai-Yin, Kai-bong); *Career* memb Hong Kong Exec Council 1947-62, company director; pres: Firecrackers and Fireworks Co Ltd (Taiwan), State Trading Corp (Far East) Ltd; hon chm Hong Kong Chinese Bank Ltd; kt 1960; *Style—* Hon Sir Sik-Nin Chau, CBE, JP; IL 3547 Hatton Rd, Hong Kong (☎ 433695)

CHAVASSE, Christopher Patrick Grant; s of Alban Ludovick Grant Chavasse (d 1953), of Colne House, Rickmansworth, and Maureen Shingler, *née* Whalley; *b* 14 Mar 1928; *Educ* Bedford Sch, Clare Coll Cambridge (MA); *m* 1955, Audrey Mary, da of the late Hugh Robert Leonard, of Ladywalk, Heronsgate; 2 s (Nicholas Robert Grant b 1956, Timothy James Grant b 1960), 1 da (Kathryn Margaret Grant b 1957); *Career* cmmnd The Rifle Bde 1947, served in Palestine (despatches) 1948, RAFVR 1949; Slr 1955; Ptnr: Jacobs and Greenwood 1960, Woodham Smith 1970; pres Holborn Law Soc 1977-78, Trustee Nat Assoc of Decorative and Fine Art Societies 1986-, chm NADFAS Tours Ltd 1986-, Hon Steward Westminster Abbey 1950-, tres St Mary le Bow church 1981-88, clerk Worshipful Co of Grocers 1981-88; Sec Governing Body of Oundle and Laxton Schs 1981-88, The memb Ct Corp of Sons of the Clergy 1985;; *Publications* Conveyancing Costs (1971), Non Conentious Costs (1975), The Discretionary Items in Contentious Costs (1980); articles in Law Soc Gazette, New Law Journal and Slrs Journal; *Recreations* sailing; *Style—* Christopher Chavasse, Esq; Duncannon House, Stoke Gabriel, nr Totnes, S Devon TQ9 6QY (☎ 080428 291); Grocers' Hall, Princes St, London EC2R 8AD (☎ 01 606 3113)

CHAWORTH-MUSTERS, Hon Mrs (Mary Victoria); *née* Monckton; eldest da of 8 Viscount Galway, PC, GCMG, DSO, OBE (d 1943); *b* 20 August 1924; *m* 1, 20 Aug 1947 (m dis 1972), David Henry Fetherstonhaugh, Coldstream Gds, s of late Lt-Col Timothy Fetherstonhaugh, DSO, of Kirkoswald, Penrith; 2 s (Hugh Simon b 1949, m 1971 Louise, adopted da of Hon Hanning Phillips, m s of 1 Baron Milford; Henry George b 1954, m 1978 Nicola Payne-Gallwey), 1 da (Victoria Bronwen b 1951); m 2, 1974, Maj Robert Patricius Chaworth-Musters, yr s of Lt-Col John Neville Chaworth-Musters, DSO, OBE, TD, of Annesley Park, Notts; *Style—* The Hon Mrs Chaworth-Musters; Felley Priory, Jacksdale, Notts

CHAWORTH-MUSTERS, Maj Robert Patricius; s of Col John Nevile Chaworth-Musters, DSO, OBE (d 1970), of Annesley Park, Nottinghamshire, and Daphne *née* Wilberforce Bell, OBE (d 1973); *b* 7 May 1923; *Educ* Eton, RMC Sandhurst; *m* 1, 22 Feb 1951; Diana Margaret (d 1973), da of Col Edward Robert Clayton, of Northmoor, Pulverton, Somerset; 2 da (Venetia b 6 June 1954, Sophia b 28 Oct 1957, d 1972); m 2, 30 March 1974, Mary Victoria Fetherstonhaugh, da of Viscount George Vere Arundel Morkton Arundel, of Galway; *Career* Coldstream Gds 1942-60, served N Africa and Italy 1943-45, ADC to GOC Malta 1948, Malaya 1949; farming; *Recreations* fishing, shooting; *Clubs* Bucks and Pratts; *Style—* Maj Robert Chaworth-Musters; Felley Priory, Jacksdale, Notts NG16 5FL (☎ 0773 810 230)

CHAYTOR, Sir George Reginald; 8 Bt (UK 1831), of Croft, Yorkshire, and Witton Castle, Durham; s of William Richard Carter Chaytor (d 1973), gs of 2 Bt, and Anna Laura, *née* Fawcett (d 1947); suc kinsman, Sir William Chaytor, 7 Bt, 1976; *b* 28 Oct 1912; *m* 1970, Mrs Elsie Magdeline Rogers; *Heir* cousin, (Herbert) Gordon Chaytor; *Career* patron (alternatively) of Witton-le-Wear Vicarage; *Style—* Sir George Chaytor, Bt; 32 Bonny Ave, Chilliwack, British Columbia, Canada

CHAYTOR, (Herbert) Gordon; s of Herbert Archibald Chaytor (d 1979); hp of cous, Sir George Chaytor, 8 Bt; *b* 1922; *m* 1947, Mary Alice, da of Thomas Craven; 3 s (Bruce Gordon b 1949, Kenneth Reginald b 1952, Robert David b 1958); *Style—* Gordon Chaytor, Esq; Honeymoon Bay, British Columbia, Canada

CHAYTOR, Patricia, Lady; Patricia Nora; da of Loftus Joseph McCaffry and former w of George Walkley Alderman; *m* 28 July 1947, Sir William Henry Clervaux Chaytor, 7 Bt (d 1976); 1 da; *Style—* Patricia, Lady Chaytor

CHAZAL; *see*: de Chazal

CHEADLE, Sir Eric (Wallers); CBE (1973), DL (1985); s of late Edgar Cheadle and Nellie, *née* Pimley; *b* 14 May 1908; *Educ* Farnworth GS; *m* 1938, Pamela, da of Alfred Hulme; 2 s; *Career* served RAFVR 1941-46, Sqdn Ldr; joined Evening Chronicle and Daily Dispatch 1924; dep md Thomson Orgn 1959-74 (dir 1949-74, ret 1974); dir: Thomson Int Press Consultancy Ltd; pres: Newspaper Soc 1970-71 (memb cncl 1959-78), Assoc of Lancastrians in London 1959 and 1973, Manchester Publicity Assoc 1972-74 (gold medal 1973); memb: Newspaper Publishers' Assoc Cncl 1947-74, cncl Imperial Soc of Knights Bachelor 1979-, St Brides', Fleet St Restoration Appeal Ctee; tstee Printers' Charitable Corpn 1981- (pres 1974, chm 1975-81); chm: Chest Heart and Stroke Assoc Appeal advsy ctee 1982-, Nat Stroke Campaign 1986-, St Albans Cathedral Trust and Appeal 1982-, dir Herts Groundwork Tst, Hon Life Memb Friends of St Albans City Hospital; lay canon St Albans Cathedral 1989, local tstee Hospital Tst; kt 1978; *Books* The Roll of Knights Bachelor 1981, ed Chivalry (Knights Bachelor Newsletter); *Recreations* golf, cricket, reading, talking about newspapers; *Clubs* Wig and Pen, Press, Variety, MCC; *Style—* Sir Eric Cheadle, CBE, DL; The Old Church House, 172 Fishpool St, St Albans, Herts AL3 4SB (☎ 0727 59 639)

CHEADLE, (Eric) Neville; s of Sir Eric W Cheadle, CBE, DL, of St Albans, Herts, and Lady Pamela Cheadle; *b* 10 May 1940; *Educ* Mill Hill Sch (Dip Comm Admin), London Poly, NATO Res Fell Stanford Graduate Sch of Business; *m* 1 Sept 1964, Hilary Ann; 3 s (Timothy b 1968, Jeremy b 1969, Duncan b 1971); *Career* graduate apprentice Standard Telephones & Cables Ltd 1959-64, sales and admin mangr Elliot Automation Ltd 1965-68; joined Price Waterhouse 1968: mangr 1973, ptnr 1977, exchange visit to Kuwait 1977; ptnr London Mgmnt Cnslty Services 1981-88, (nat dir 1985-88, Euro sr ptnr 1988-); FIMC 1985; *Recreations* sailing, cricket, amateur radio; *Clubs* MCC; *Style—* Neville Cheadle, Esq; Price Waterhouse Management Consultants, No 1 London Bridge, London SE1 9QL (☎ 01 378 7200, fax 01 403 5265, telex 931709 and 934716)

CHEALES, Maxwell Bellingham; s of late Lt-Col Ralph Cheales; *b* 4 Nov 1929; *Educ* Michaelhouse S Africa, Pembroke Coll Cambridge; *m* 1960, Hermione Ann, *née* Hogarth; 1 s, 2 da; *Career* dir Hill Samuel and Co Ltd 1965-77, chm Hogarth Shipping Co Ltd Glasgow 1978- (md 1971-); FCA; *Style—* Maxwell Cheales, Esq; Blewburton Hall, Aston Upthorpe, Didcot, Oxon OX11 9EE (☎ 0235 850772)

CHEAPE, John Ronald; JP; s of Brig Gen George Ronald Hamilton Cheape, CMG, DSO, MC (d 1957), and Margaret Bruce, *née* Ismay (d 1967); *b* 16 Oct 1929; *Educ* Cargilfield Sch Harrow, RAC Cirencester; *m* 15 Oct 1960, Gillian, da of Robert Mercer (d 1977); 3 s (Ewan Ronald b 1962, Malcolm John b 1964, Robert Neil (d 1985); *Career* farmer; *Recreations* fishing, shooting, photography; *Style—* John R Cheape, JP; Letham, Glenfarg, Perthshire PH2 9GF (☎ 0577 3215)

CHECKETTS, Sir David John; KCVO (1979, CVO 1969, MVO 1966); 3 s of late Reginald Ernest George Checketts, and late Frances Mary Checketts; *b* 23 August 1930; *m* 1958, Rachel Leila Warren Herrick; 1 s, 3 da; *Career* RATG Rhodesia 1948-49, 14 Sqn Germany 1950-54; FWS Leconfield 1954-57; Air ADC AFMED Malta 1957-59; 3 Sqdn Germany 1960-61, ret Sqdn-Ldr 1961; equerry to HRH the Duke of Edinburgh 1961-66, equerry to HRH the Prince of Wales 1967-70 and extra equerry 1979- (private sec 1970-78); dir: Global Aviation Printing Ltd, Brieftag Ltd, Seatic Co Ltd; md: ISC Technologies Ltd, Penselworth Ltd; chm: Rainbow Boats Tst, Young Enterprise, The Wilderness Foundation UK; FInstD, memb IISS; *Style—* Sir David Checketts, KCVO; Church Cottage, Winkfield, Windsor, Berks

CHECKETTS, Ronald Harry George; MBE (1981); s of Reginald Ernest George Checketts (Flt-Lt RAF, d 1948), and Francis Mary, *née* Hagger (d 1965); *b* 30 May 1921; *Educ* Salters Hill Rd Sch West Norwood London, Gipsy Rd Sch West Norwood London; *m* 16 Aug 1947, Joan Rose, da of Henry Castle (d 1966); 1 s (Adrian Michel b 7 Sept 1958); *Career* RN ships: HMS Ganges, Ramillies, Glorious, Arethusa, Capetwon, Liverpool, Manxman, Sheffield Rnella W/T Station Malta, HMS Loch Shin, Mercury, Phoebe, Manxman; RN 1936-53; Reuters News Agency 1953-56, HM Dip Serv 1956-81; auxiliary coastguard Lands End Cornwall 1981-86, town clerk Marazion Cornwall 1985; memb: RSGB 1983, RNARS 1983; *Recreations* sailing, amateur radio; *Clubs* Royal Overseas League, The White Elephant; Mounts Bay Sailing Cornwall; *Style—* Ronald Checketts, Esq, MBE; c/o The Manor, Turweston, Nr Brackley, Northants NN13 5JX (☎ 0280 703 777)

CHECKLAND, Michael; s of Leslie and Ivy Florence Checkland; *b* 13 Mar 1936; *Educ* King Edward's GS Birmingham, Wadham Coll Oxford; *m* 1, 1960 (m dis 1983), Shirley Corbett; 2 s, 1 da; m 2, 1987, Mrs Sue Zetter; *Career* dir Resources BBC TV 1982-, controller Planning and Resource Management BBC TV 1977-82, controller Finance 1976-77, chief accountant BBC TV 1971-76 (Central Finance Servs 1969-71, head Central Finance Unit 1967-69, sr cost accountant 1964-67); formerly with Parkinson Cowan and Thorn Electronics; *Style—* Michael Checkland, Esq; 5 Springfield Crescent, Horsham, W Sussex (☎ 0403 4845)

CHECKLEY, Jonathan Richard Parknell; s of Stephen Henry Cooper Checkley (d 1984), and Beryl, *née* Parnell; *b* 4 Dec 1951; *Educ* Warwick Sch, St Peter's Coll Oxford (BSc); *m* 20 May 1978, Amanda Ellen, da of Frank Reuben Rubens (d 1985); 2 s (Edward b 1984, Timothy b 1987), 1 da (Laura b 1981); *Career* ptnr Clay and Ptnrs consulting actuaries 1977-; FIA; *Recreations* reading, walking, music, water colour painting, gardening; *Style—* Jonathan Checkley, Esq; Clay & Partners, 61 Brook Street, London W1Y 2HN (☎ 01 408 1600, fax 01 499 0711, telex 27167 CLAYCO G)

CHEDLOW, Barry William; QC (1969); *b* 8 Oct 1921; *Educ* Burnage HS, Univ of Manchester; *m* 1944, Anne Sheldon; 1 s, 1 da; *Career* Flt-Lt RAF 1943; barr 1947, rec of the Crown Ct 1974-; memb Criminal Injuries Compensation Bd 1976; *Style—* Barry Chedlow Esq, QC; 12 King's Bench Walk, Temple, London EC4 (☎ 01 583 0811); Little Kimblewick Farm, Finch Lane, Amersham, Bucks (☎ 024 04 2156)

CHEESBROUGH, John Wright; AEA (1958); s of George Cheesbrough, of Thorne, Yorks (d 1971), and Edith, *née* Wright (d 1935); *b* 26 May 1914; *Educ* Thorne GS, Sheffield Univ; *m* 3 Nov 1946, Muriel Mary, da of Richard Finney Wain (d 1953); 1 s (John Stephen b 31 Dec 1952), 1 da (Mary Ruth (Mrs Peck) b 3 Nov 1948); *Career* WWII RAF 1939-45; RA TA 1947-52, Royal Auxiliary Air Force 1952-61; admitted slr 1936, sr ptnr Coles & James 1967-87; clerk to gen cmmrs of income tax: Upper Pevensey and Pevensey Liberty 1957-72, Pevensey Div 1972; dep dist registrar High Ct 1959-87, notary public 1948; dir: Hydro Hotel (Eastbourne) plc 1957-(chm 1974-), Abbeyfield (Eastbourne) Soc Ltd 1962-87; Liveryman City of London Slrs' Co 1979; memb Law Soc, FIOD 1981; *Clubs* City Livery, Devonshire (Eastbourne, chm 1983-86); *Style—* John Cheesbrough, Esq, AEA; 47 Osborne Rd, Eastbourne, East Sussex (☎ 0323 29002); Claremont Chambers, 1 Trinity Trees, Eastbourne, East Sussex BN21 3LB (☎ 0323 644 683, fax 0323 20670)

CHEESMAN, Dr (Anthony David) Tony; s of Leslie Charles Cheesman, of Shoreham-by-Sea (d 1968), and Eileen, *née* Griggs; *b* 14 Nov 1939; *Educ* Steyning GS, Charing Cross Hosp Medical Sch, Univ of London (BSc, MB, BS); *m* 26 Sept 1966, Janet, da of Eric James Bristow, of Haywards Heath, Sussex; 2 s (David b 1969, James b 1972), 1 da (Katherine b 1974); *Career* conslt surgn; ENT surgn Univ Hosp of W Indies Jamaica 1972-74, otolaryngologist head and neck surgn Charing Cross Hosp, Royal Nat Throat Nose and Ear Hosp; memb Ct of Examiners RCS; *Books* numerous papers and chapters on otolaryngology; FRCS; *Recreations* yachting, skiing, flying, avoiding correspondence; *Clubs* Royal Soc of Medicine, Sussex Yacht, Politzer Soc; *Style—* Dr Tony Cheesman, Esq; 6 Thornhill Bridge Wharf, Islington, London N1 0RU (☎ 01 837 0709); 128 Harley St, London W1N 1AH (☎ 01 486 9400)

CHEETHAM, Francis William; OBE (1979); s of Francis Cheetham (d 1966),and Doris Elizabeth Cheetham (d 1939); *b* 5 Feb 1928; *Educ* King Edward VII Sch Sheffield, The Univ of Sheffield (BA); *m* 19 April 1954, Monica, da of Arthur Fairhurst (d 1963); 3 s (Paul b 1958, Dominic b 1960, Mark b 1964), 1 da (Claire b 1968); *Career* dep art dir and curator Castle Museum Nottingham 1960-63; dir: City of Norwich Museums 1963-74, Norfolk Museums Serv 1974-; pres Museums Assoc 1978-79, Museums advsr to Assoc of CCs 1976-84; pres Norfolk Contemporary Crafts Soc 1985- (chm 1972-85), chm Norfolk and Norwich Film Theatre 1968-70; memb: mgmnt ctee Norfolk and Norwich Triennial Festival 1966-, bd of Norwich Puppet Theatre 1981-87, mgmnt ctee of Eastern Arts Assoc 1987-, exec bd ICOM UK 1981-85, bde of Radio Broadland 1983-; Winston Churchill Fell 1967, FMA 1966, FRSA 1986; *Books* Medieval English Alabaster Carvings in the Castle Museum, Nottingham (1962), English Medieval Alabasters: catalogue of the collection in the Victoria and Albert Museum (1984); *Recreations* hill walking, listening to music especially early and baroque; *Clubs* Rotary (Norwich); *Style—* Francis Cheetham, Esq, OBE; 25 St Andrews Ave, Thorpe St Andrew, Norwich, Norfolk (☎ 0603 340 91); Castle Museum, Norwich NR1 3JU (☎ 0603 611 277)

CHEETHAM, John Frederick Thomas; CB (1978); s of James Oldham Cheetham (d 1965), and Gwendoline, *née* Hambly (d 1968); *b* 27 Mar 1919; *Educ* Penarth GS, Univ of Wales; *m* 1943, Yvonne Marie, da of James Alexander Smith (d 1968); 1 s (David), 1 da (Jane); *Career* former dep sec Exchequer and Audit Dept, sec 1975-79; *Recreations* gardening, family genealogy; *Clubs* MCC; *Style*— John Cheetham Esq, CB; 70 Chatsworth Rd, Croydon, Surrey (☎ 01 688 3740)

CHEETHAM, Prof Juliet; da of Col Harold Neville Blair, of London, and Isabel, *née* Sanders (d 1988); *b* 12 Oct 1934; *Educ* St Andrews Univ (MA), Oxford Univ; *m* 26 April 1965, (Christopher) Paul Cheetam, s of Robert Cheetham, of Wallasey; 1 s (Matthew b 1969), 2 da (Rebecca b 1972, Sophie b 1983); *Career* probation offr 1959-65, lectr in applied social studies and fell Green Coll Oxford Univ 1965-85; memb: ctee of enquiry into the working of the Abortion Act 1971-74, cmmn for racial equality 1977-84, social security advsy ctee 1983-; currently prof and dir social work res centre Stirling Univ; BASW; *Books* Social Work with Immigrants (1972), Unwanted Pregnancy and Counselling (1977), Social Work and Ethnicity (1982), Social Work with Black Children and their Families (1986); *Recreations* canal boats; *Style*— Professor Juliet Cheetham; 101 Woodstock Rd, Oxford; 4/2 Advocates Close, High St, Edinburgh EH1 1PS (☎ 031 225 5639); Social Work Research Centre, Stirling University (☎ 0786 73171, fax 0786 63060)

CHEETHAM, Sir Nicolas John Alexander; KCMG (1964, CMG 1953); s of late Sir Milne Cheetham, KCMG (d 1938) and his 1 wife (m dis 1923) Anastasia, CBE, DStJ (later Mrs Nigel Law), *née* Mouravieff; *b* 8 Oct 1910; *Educ* Eton, Ch Ch Oxford; *m* 1, 1937 (m dis 1960), Jean Evison, da of Col Arthur Cecil Corfe, DSO (d 1949); 2 s; m 2, 1960, Lady Mabel Kathleen (d 1985), da of 8 Earl of Roden and formerly w of Richard Neville Brooke; *Career* joined HM Diplomatic Service 1934, min to Hungary 1959-61, asst under-sec FO 1961-64, ambass to Mexico 1964-68; *Books* A History of Mexico, New Spain, Mediaeval Greece, Keepers of the Keys; *Style*— Sir Nicolas Cheetham, KCMG; 50 Cadogan Square, London SW1

CHEKE, Dudley John; CMG (1961); s of Thomas William Cheke, (d 1960), and Bertha Elizabeth, *née* Boyten (d 1964); *b* 14 June 1912; *Educ* St Christopher Sch Herts, Emmanuel Coll Cambridge (MA); *m* 1944, Yvonne Carmen, da of Rear Adm Martin John Coucher de Méric, MVO (d 1943); 2 s (Anthony, Robert); *Career* HM Diplomatic Service: min HM Embassy Tokyo 1963-67, ambass to the Ivory Coast, Niger and Upper Volta 1967-70; chm Japan Soc of London 1979-82; *Recreations* gardening, bird-watching, theatre, opera; *Clubs* United Oxford and Cambridge, Union Soc Cambridge; *Style*— Dudley Cheke, Esq, CMG; Honey Farm, Bramley, Basingstoke, Hants

CHELMER, Baron (Life Peer UK 1963); Eric Cyril Boyd Edwards; MC (1944), TD, JP (Essex 1950), DL (1971); s of Col Cyril Ernest Edwards, DSO, MC, TD, JP, DL (d 1953), of Bullwood Hall, Hockley, Essex, and Jessie, *née* Boyd; *b* 9 Oct 1914; *Educ* Felsted; *m* 2 June 1939, Enid, da of Frank W Harvey, of Leigh-on-Sea, Essex; 1 s; *Career* served WW II Lt Col Essex Yeo; solicitor 1937; former chm National Union of Conservative Assocs 1957-64, tres Conservative Party 1965-77; chm Provident Financial Gp 1977-83; dir NEM Gp of Cos 1977-; chm Greycoats Estates Ltd; kt 1954; *Recreations* improving; *Clubs* Carlton, Buck's, Royal Ocean Racing; *Style*— The Rt Hon the Lord Chelmer, MC, TD, JP, DL; Peacocks, Margaretting, Essex

CHELMSFORD, 3 Viscount (UK 1921); Frederic Jan Thesiger; also Baron Chelmsford (UK 1858); s of 2 Viscount (d 1970), and Gillian Lubbock (great niece of 1 Baron Avebury); 1 cous once removed of Wilfrid Thesiger, the Arabist and traveller; *b* 7 Mar 1931; *m* 16 Aug 1958, Clare Rendle, da of Dr George Rendle Rolston, of Crofts, Haslemere, Surrey; 1 s, 1 da (Hon Tiffany b 23 April 1968); *Heir* Hon Frederic Thesiger, *qv*; *Career* late Lt Inns of Court Regt; Lloyd's insurance broker; *Style*— The Rt Hon the Viscount Chelmsford; 26 Ormonde Gate, London SW3 (☎ 01 352 5636); Hazelbridge Court, Chiddingfold, Surrey

CHELMSFORD, 7 Bishop of (cr 1914) 1986-; Rt Rev John Waine; s of late William Waine; *b* 20 June 1930; *Educ* Prescot GS, Manchester Univ (BA), Ridley Hall Cambridge; *m* 1957, Patricia Zena, da of late Bertram Stephenson Haikney; 3 s; *Career* Pilot Offr RAF; ordained deacon 1955, priest 1956; vicar: Ditton 1960-64, Holy Trinity Southport 1964-69; rector Kirkby 1969-75, bishop suffragan of Stafford 1975-78, bishop of St Edmundsbury and Ipswich 1978-86; Chaplain OStJ; *Clubs* RAF; *Style*— The Rt Rev the Bishop of Chelmsford; Bishopscourt, Margaretting, Ingatestone, Essex CM4 0HD; (☎ 0277 352001)

CHELSEA, Viscount; Charles Gerald John Cadogan; s and h of 7 Earl Cadogan; *b* 24 Mar 1937; *Educ* Eton; *m* 6 June 1963, Lady Philippa Dorothy Bluett Wallop (d 31 Aug 1984), 2 da of 9 Earl of Portsmouth (d 1984); 2 s (Hon Edward b 1966, Hon William b 1973), 1 da (Hon Anna-Karina b 1964); *Heir* s, Hon Edward Charles Cadogan b 10 May 1966; *Career* dir Cadogan Estates and Gp Cos; *Style*— Viscount Chelsea; 7 Smith St, London SW3 (☎ 01 730 2465); Marndhill, Ardington, Wantage, Oxon (☎ 0235 833 273)

CHELTON, Capt Lewis William Leonard; RN; s of Lewis Walter Chelton (d 1959), and Doris May, *née* Gamblin (d 1961); *b* 19 Dec 1934; *Educ* RNC Dartmouth; *m* 11 May 1957, Daphne Joan, da of Lt Col R P Landon, MC, RA (d 1936); 3 s (Simon Roger Lewis b 1958, Roderick Charles Dominic b 1960, Hugo Rupert Philip b 1966); *Career* RN: Naval Cadet 1951, Midshipman 1953, Sub-Lt 1955, Lt 1956, staff of Flag Offr Flying Trg 1956-57; serv in: HMS Torquay, HMS Scarborough (5 Frigate Sqdn) 1958-59; staff of C in C Med 1960-61, HMS Caprice (8 Destroyer Sqdn) 1962-64, Lt-Cdr 1964, legal trg 1964-66, barr Inner Temple 1966, sec to Cdr Naval Forces Gulf (Sr Naval Offr Persian Gulf) 1967-69, asst sec to Flag Offr Scotland and NI 1970-71, serv HMS Hampshire 1972 Cdr 1972, sec to Flag Offr Carriers and Amphibious Ships 1973-74, NDC Latimer 1975, HMS Fearless 1976-77, naval admin plans MOD 1978-79, Fleet Supply Offr 1979-81, Capt 1981, Chief Naval Judge Advocate 1982-84, dep dir Naval Serv Conditions, ret 1987; sec Engrg Cncl; *Recreations* shooting, gardening, country pursuits; *Clubs* Farmers; *Style*— Capt Lewis Chelton, RN; Palmers Green House, Hatch Beauchamp, Nr Taunton, Somerset (☎ 0823 480 221); 51 Badminton Rd, London SW12; The Secretary of the Engrg Cncl, 10 Maltravers St, London WC2 (☎ 01 240 7891, fax 01 240 7517, telex 279177)

CHEMPIN, Beryl Margaret; da of Authur Harold Jordan Perry, MM, of Birmingham, and Ada Dora, *née* Banner; *Educ* King Edward's HS, Birmingham Secretarial Sch, Birmingham Sch of Music; *m* 1, the late Arnold Chempin; 2 da (Jenny Margaret (Mrs Renowden), Judith Ursula (Mrs Wallis)); m 2, the late Bernard While; m 3, Prof Denis Matthews, CBE; *Career* freelance sec and translator, pianist, music lectr adjudicator (home and abroad); piano teacher: Birmingham Sch of Music, Birmingham Jr Sch of Music; private music teacher; contrib: Musical Times, Music Teacher, Music Jnl; memb lecturing panel Int Piano Teachers Conslts, Nat Award for Piano Teaching 1983; ISM Birmingham Centre: memb cncl 1969-71 and 1982-84, sec 1964-74, chm 1975-85, warden and chm private teachers section 1969; lectr Euro Piano Teachers Assoc; memb: City of Birmingham Symphony Orch Soc, Br Fedn of Music Festivals, King Edwards HS Old Edwardians; Midland Woman of the Year 1977; FTCL LRAM, ARCM, LTCL, ABSM; *Recreations* reading, languages, art, cooking; *Style*— Ms Beryl Chempin; 10 Russell Road, Moseley, Birmingham B13 8RD (☎ 021 449 3055)

CHEN, Shwing Chong; s of Ping Liem Chen (d 1963), of Sri Lanka, and Chu Lan Chen (d 1977); *b* 1 Sept 1934; *Educ* Wesley Coll Colombo (Hill Medal for best scholar 1954); Univ of Ceylon (BA MBBS); *m* 24 Nov 1957, Ai Bow, da of Chang Yung Yoe, of India (d 1975); 3 s (Terng Fong b 1960, Terng Weng b 1962, Terng Bhing b 1965), 1 da (Hui Fong b 1958); *Career* conslt orthopaedic surgn Enfield Gp of Hosps 1972-; sr orthopaedic registrar: St Bartholomew's Hosp, Royal Nat Orthopaedic Hosp Norfolk and Norwich Hosp 1968-72 (Benjamin Gooch Prize 1969-70); orthopaedic registrar Hammersmith Hosp 1967-68; designer of: Chen Tennis Elbow Strap, Enfield Total Knee Prosthesis; FRCS; *Recreations* skiing, sailing, swimming; *Clubs* Royal Society of Medicine; *Style*— S C Chen, Esq; 66 Mymms Drive, Brookmans Park, Herts AL9 7AD (☎ 0707 58538); 152 Harley St, London W1N 1HH (☎ 01 935 3834)

CHENEVIERE, Lady Selina Clare; *née* Shirley; yst da of 13 Earl Ferrers, PC, DL, *qv*; *b* 1958; *m* 11 March 1989, Antoine R B Chenevière, yr s of Bertrand Chenevière, of Geneva, and Madame Harritina Panitza-Yablansky, of Florence; *Style*— Lady Selina Chenevière; c/o The Rt Hon the Earl Ferrers, PC, DL, Ditchingham Hall, Bungay, Suffolk

CHENEVIX-TRENCH, Timothy Christopher John; s of Christopher John Chenevix-Trench, MBE, and Mary Elizabeth, *née* Allen; *b* 5 Oct 1938; *Educ* Kings Sch Canterbury, Corpus Christi Coll Oxford (MA); *m* 1, 3 Sept 1961 (m dis 1972), Penelope Mary, *née* Travers; 3 da (Katherine Rae (Mrs Slater) b 8 June 1964, Alison Mary (Mrs Hill) b 20 Aug 1965, Phillida b 26 May 1967); m 2, 1974, Stella Mavis, *née* Henderson; *Career* ICI 1961-67, Mgmnt Dynamics 1967-69, Scicon 1969-72, dir Miles Ronan Ltd 1972-73, advsr HM Treasy 1973-76, Shell Int Petroleum Co 1976-82, Heidrick & Struggles 1982-85, dir Richdata Ltd 1985-; Liveryman Worshipful Co Mercers; *Recreations* family, head hunting; *Clubs* Naval & Military; *Style*— Timothy Chenevix-Trench, Esq; Richdata Ltd, 13 Camden Passage, London N1 8EA (☎ 01 359 1200, car tel 0836 311112)

CHENEY, Donald Harvey; s of Arthur Stanley Cheney (d 1975), and Jessie Cheney (d 1986); *b* 16 Jan 1931; *Educ* Eggars GS Alton Hants, Harrow Weald Co GS Middx, Regent St Poly Sch of Architecture (Dip Arch); *m* 13 Feb 1956, Gillian Evelyn Florence Frances, JP, da of Guy Holman Tatum (d 1969); 3 da (Frances b 1956, Fiona (Mrs Ford) b 1960, Claire b 1968); *Career* qualified as architect 1955; in practice: NZ 1956-62, S Coast of England 1963-(ptnr 1970-); cncl memb RIBA 1983, external examiner Canterbury Sch of Architecture 1982-87, memb Franco British Union of Architects 1977-; chm Hythe Venetian Fete 1978-86, Hythe town cncllr 1981-86; Freeman City of London 1983; memb: Worshipful Co of Arbitrators 1983, Co of Architects 1985; RIBA 1956, assoc memb NZ Inst of Architects 1956, CIArb 1976; *Recreations* sailing, photography; *Clubs* Royal Cinque Ports YC, St John House; *Style*— Donald Cheney, Esq; Crosstrees, North Rd, Hythe, Kent (☎ 0303 68720); La Lande Du Burgos, Guehenno 56, France; The Tramway Stables, Rampart Rd, Hythe, Kent CT21 5BG (☎ 0303 260 515, fax 0303 68214, car tel 0860 729 904)

CHERNIAVSKY, Andrew Scott; s of David Blythe Cherniavsky (d 1954), and Peggy Claire, *née* Scott; *b* 27 April 1949; *Educ* Lycee Francais London, Edinburgh Univ (MA Hons); *m* 1 Jul 1977, Caroline (Maria Aviva), da of Josef Schuck, of London; 1 s (Paul Alexander b 1982), 1 da (Kate Isabella b 1980); *Career* dir Prolific Gp plc 1988-(Prolific Fin Mgmnt 1986), chm Prolific Unit Tst Mangrs 1988-; *Recreations* music, squash, tennis, fishing, sailing; *Clubs* Hampstead Cricket; *Style*— Andrew Cherniavsky Esq; 222 Bishopsgate, London EC2M 4JS (☎ 01 247 6544, telex 8814339)

CHERRY, Alan Herbert; MBE (1985); *Career* chm and gp md Countryside Properties plc 1981; pres Housebuilders Fedn 1988; memb: Inquiry into Br Housing 1984-85, Inner City Cmmn; govr Essex Inst of Higher Educn; Freeman City of London, memb Worshipful Co of Blacksmiths; FRICS, FSVA; *Style*— Countryside House, The Warley Hill Business Park, Brentwood, Essex CM13 3AT (☎ 0277 260 000, fax 0277 260 175)

CHERRY, (George) Anthony; s of Capt Harold Edward Cherry (d 1930), of Rolleston, Burton-on-Trent, and Agnes Irene, *née* Bairstow (d 1963); *b* 20 May 1918; *Educ* Elms Sch Colwall, Denstone Coll Staffordshire; *m* 10 July 1946, Ellan Angus, da of David George Thompson (d 1985), of Rosyth, Fife; 2 s (Christopher b 1947, Iain b 1956), 1 da (Elizabeth b 1950); *Career* served in army Sherwood Foresters 1940-47; major ME 1941-42, POW 1942-45, War Office Mil Intelligence 1945-46; chartered accountant Price Waterhouse 1946-81, nat dir 1974-79, dep chm Price Waterhouse Int 1979-81; Liveryman Worshipful Co of Gardeners of London; *Recreations* gardening, golf; *Style*— Anthony Cherry, Esq; Forge House, Nyton Road, Eastergate, Chichester, W Sussex (☎ 0243 543086)

CHERRY, Colin; s of Reginald Cherry (d 1970), of Hull, and Dorothy Cherry, *née* Brooks (d 1939); *b* 20 Nov 1931; *Educ* Hymers Coll; *m* 2 Aug 1988, Marjorie Rose, da of Thomas Harman, of Holderness; 2 da (Nicola (Mrs Gatt) b 1962, Jacqueline b 1964); *Career* Nat Serv RAEC 1950-52, Lt TA E Yorks Regt 1952-58; Inland Revenue 1952, HM Insp of Taxes 1958-85, under sec Dir of Operations Inland Revenue 1985-; *Clubs* Reform; *Style*— Colin Cherry, Esq; Operations Division, Bush House, Strand WC2R 4RD (☎ 01 438 6067)

CHERRY, John Roy; s of Arthur Hal Cherry (d 1969), and Doris Mildred, *née* Kerley; *b* 17 Mar 1948, Worthing; *Career* CA, ptnr LEV Masters and Co; FCA; *Recreations* breeder St Bernard Dogs; *Style*— John Cherry, Esq; 6 New Cottages, Washington, W Sussex RH20 4AW (☎ Ashington 892912); 46A Goring Road, Worthing, W Sussex BN12 4AD (☎ Worthing 46544)

CHESHAM, 5 Baron (UK 1858); John Charles Compton Cavendish; PC (1964) TD; s of 4 Baron Chesham, MC (d 1952), himself ggs of 1 Baron (4 s of 1 Earl of Burlington); *b* 18 June 1916; *Educ* Eton, Zuoz Coll Switzerland, Trinity Coll Cambridge; *m* 28 Sept 1937, Mary Edmunds, 4 da of late David Gregory Marshall, MBE, of White Hill, Fen Ditton, Cambridgeshire; 2 s, 2 da (Hon Mrs Price, Hon Mrs Tufnell); *Heir* s, Hon Nicholas Cavendish, *qv*; *Career* served WW II Capt RA; former

JP Bucks; a lord-in-waiting to HM The Queen 1955-59; parly sec Miny of Transport 1959-64; exec vice-chm RAC 1966-70, pres Fellowship of Motor Indust 1969-71, vice-pres British Road Fedn 1972- (formerly chm), chm Int Road Fedn Geneva 1973-76; Hon FInstHE 1970, Hon FIRTE 1974; *Recreations* living; *Clubs* Carlton; *Style—* The Rt Hon the Lord Chesham, PC; Manor Farm, Preston Candover, nr Basingstoke, Hants RG25 2EN (☎ 025 687 230)

CHESHIRE, Lt-Col Colin Charles Chance; s of ACM Sir Walter Graemes Cheshire, GBE, KCB, CBE (d 1978), and Mary Cheshire, DL, of 14 St James's Villas, Winchester; *b* 23 August 1941; *Educ* Worksop; *m* 1, 8 Aug 1968, Cherida Evelyn, da of ACM Sir Wallace Kyle, GCB, KCVO, CBE, DSO, DFC, *qv*; 1 s (Christopher b 1971), 1 da (Philippa b 1969); m 2, 2 Oct 1976, Angela Mary, da of D Fulcher, of Bury St Edmunds, Suffolk; 2 step da (Sarah McMillen b 1968, Emma McMillen b 1970); *Career* Lt-Col RTR (ret 1981); serv: Aden, Borneo, Singapore, Malaysia, BAOR, N I and UK; Armour Sch Bovington Camp 1968 (tt), RMC of Science 1972-73 and Staff Coll Camberley 1974- (psc); sales and mktg mgr: defence equipment, Vickers Instruments Ltd, York 1981-83, army systems, Ferranti Computer Systems Ltd, Cwmbran 1983-85, and Wallop Gp, Andover (md Walloptonics Ltd) 1985-87, since when bursar Oundle Sch, sec Oundle Schs Ctee, dir Oundle Sch Bldg Co and Oundle Sch Servs Co; rifle shooting: internat full bore, rep GB 1970- (vice capt 1982, adj 1988), rep England 1970-, Army 1967-81, Yorks, Herefords and Worcs and Hants (capt 1987-); FBiM, MBIM; *Recreations* shooting; *Clubs* Army and Navy, HAC; *Style—* Lt-Col Colin Cheshire; Bear Lodge, Glapthorn Road, Oundle, Peterborough PE8 4JA (☎ 0832 73537); Bursar's Office: Church Street, Oundle, Peterborough PE8 4EE (☎ 0832 73434)

CHESHIRE, Hon ('Gigi') Elizabeth Diana; da of Baroness Ryder of Warsaw and Gp Capt Leonard Cheshire, *qqv*; *b* 1962; *Style—* The Hon Elizabeth Cheshire

CHESHIRE, Hon Mrs (Isobel Gray); 2 da of 1 Viscount Addison, KG, PC, MD, FRCS (d 1951); *b* 1907; *m* 29 Aug 1932, Nicholas Cheshire, s of Francis Augustus Cheshire, of St Petersburg; 1 s (Paul b 1941), 2 da (Susan (Mrs Peter Howell) b 1933, Isobel (Mrs David William Ingham Brooke) b 1936); *Style—* The Hon Mrs Cheshire; 9 Mansfield Road, Reading, Berks RG1 6AL

CHESHIRE, Hon Jeromy Charles; s of Baroness Ryder of Warsaw and Gp Capt Leonard Cheshire, *qqv*; *b* 1960; *Style—* The Hon Jeromy Cheshire

CHESHIRE, Group Captain (Geoffrey) Leonard; VC (1944), OM (1981), DSO (1940, and Bar 1942, 1943), DFC (1941); s of late Geoffrey Chevalier Cheshire, FBA, DCL, LLD (d 1978), and his 1 wife Primrose, *née* Barstow (d 1962); *b* 7 Sept 1917; *Educ* Stowe, Merton Coll Oxford; *m* 2, 1959, Susan Ryder (Baroness Ryder of Warsaw, *qv*); 1 s, 1 da; *Career* joined Oxford Univ Sqdn 1936, RAFR 1937, Pilot Offr RAF 1939, Wing Cdr 1944, Gp Capt 1944, ret 1946; fndr Leonard Cheshire Foundation, co-fndr Ryder-Cheshire Mission for the Relief of Suffering; hon master of bench of Gray's Inn 1983, Hon DCL Oxford Univ; Hon LLD: Liverpool Univ 1973, Manchester Polytech 1979, Nottingham Univ 1981, Bristol Univ 1985, Kent Univ 1986; *Publications* The Light of Many Suns (1985), The Hidden World (1981), The Face of Victory (1961), Pilgrimage to the Shroud (1956), Bomber Pilot (1943); *Style—* Group Capt Leonard Cheshire, VC, OM, DSO, DFC; Cavendish, Suffolk; The Leonard Cheshire Foundation, 26-29 Maunsel St, London SW1P 2QN (☎ 01 828 1822)

CHESHIRE, (Christopher) Scott; JP Stoke on Trent (1977); s of Christopher Cheshire (d 1955), and Elizabeth Ann, *née* Brown (d 1977); *b* 16 Nov 1927; *Educ* Radley Coll, Trinity Coll Oxford (MA Hons); *m* 2 Jan 1968, Marie Josephine, da of Samuel Ephraim Moss Simpson (d 1945), of Staffs; 4 step-s (Philip b 1952, William b 1954, Sam b 1956, Timothy b 1958); *Career* asst master Repton Sch 1953-74 and 1985-86 (housemaster 1955-74); author Chelsea Football Club 1905-85, Chelsea Football Club Who's Who (1987), Barclays World of Cricket (contrib, 1986); Oxford Univ Assoc Football 'blue' 1952; FRGS; *Recreations* cricket, association football; *Clubs* MCC, IZ; *Style—* Scott Cheshire, Esq, JP; Lane End, Longton Road, Barlaston, Stoke-on-Trent Staffs ST12 9AU (☎ 078 139 2627)

CHESSHYRE, (David) Hubert Boothby; s of Col Hubert Layard Chesshyre of Whatmer Hall, Sturry, Canterbury (d 1981), and Katharine Anne, *née* Boothby; *b* 22 June 1940; *Educ* King's Sch Canterbury, Trinity Coll Cambridge (MA), Christ Church Oxford (DipEd); *Career* former vintner and language teacher; Green Staff Offr at Investiture of Prince of Wales 1969; memb cncl: Heraldry Soc 1973-85, Rouge Croix Pursuivant 1970-78; on staff of Sir Anthony Wagner as Garter King of Arms 1971-78, Chester Herald of Arms 1978-; memb Hon Artillery Co 1964-65; memb: Bach Choir, Madrigal Soc, Soc of Genealogists; Freeman City of London, lay clerk Southwark Cathedral; Lecturer for NADFAS; FSA; *Books* edited: Heraldry of the World (Blandford 1973), author of The Identification of Coats of Arms on British Silver (1978), (with A J Robinson), The Green, A History of the Heart of Bethnal Green (1978), (with Adrian Ailes), Heralds of Today (1985), jt ed Dictionary of British Arms (in progress); *Recreations* singing, gardening, motorcycling; *Style—* Hubert Chesshyre, Esq, Chester Herald of Arms; Hawthorn Cottage, 1 Flamborough Walk, London E14 7LS; College of Arms, Queen Victoria St, EC4V 4BT (☎ 01 248 1137)

CHESTER, 39 Bishop of, 1982-; Rt Rev Michael Alfred Baughen; patron of 114 livings, Canonries of his Cathedral, the Archdeaconries of Chester and Macclesfield, and the Chancellorship of the Diocese. The See, anciently part of the diocese of Lichfield, was erected into a distinct Bishopric by Henry VIII in 1541, and the abbey-church of St Werburgh became its Cathedral; s of Alfred Henry Baughen (d 1956), and Clarice Adelaide Baughen; *b* 7 June 1930; *Educ* Bromley County GS, London Univ, Oak Hill Theol Coll (BD); *m* 1956, Myrtle Newcomb Phillips; 2 s, 1 da; *Career* served in Royal Signals 1948-50; with Martins Bank 1946-48 and 1950-51; ordained: deacon 1956, priest 1957; curate in Nottingham and Reigate, candidates sec Church Pastoral Aid Soc 1961-64, rector Holy Trinity Rusholme 1964-70, vicar All Souls Langham Place 1970-75 (next to Broadcasting House and whence BBC transmitted daily services), rector 1975-82, area dean St Marylebone 1978-82, prebendary St Paul's 1979-82; memb Gen Synod 1975-; *Style—* The Rt Rev the Lord Bishop of Chester; Bishop's House, Abbey Sq, Chester CH1 2JD (☎ 0244 350864)

CHESTER, Prof Theodore Edward; CBE (1967); *b* 28 June 1908; *Educ* Univ of Manchester (MA, Dip Commerce); *m* 1940, Mimi; 1 s; *Career* teaching and res in law and admin 1931-39, asst mangr London city firm 1946-48, dir Acton Soc Tst 1952-55 (sr res worker 1948-52); Univ of Manchester: prof of social admin 1955-75, dean faculty of econ and social studies 1962-63, sr res fell and emeritus prof 1976-78, dir mgmnt prog for clinicians 1979-; memb cncl fin and gen purposes ctee Manchester Business Sch 1964-86; Kenneth Pray visiting prof Univ of Pa 1968, first Kellogg visiting prof Washington Univ St Louis 1969 and 1970, memb summer faculty sloan inst of health servs admin Cornell Univ 1972-, Ford Fndn Travelling fellowships 1960 and 1967, WMO staff trg programme 1963-, UN Res Inst for Econ and Social Studies 1968; memb: nat selection ctee for the recruitment of sr hosp admin staff 1956-66, advsy ctee on mgmnt efficiency in the Health Serv 1959-65, trg and Social Workers and Health Visitors 1963-65, ctee on tech coll resources 1964-69, Inter Agency Inst of Fed Health Execs (USA) 1980-84; pres corpn of Secs 1955-66; advsr: social affairs div OECD 1965-66, Turkish State Planning Orgn on Health and Welfare Problems 1964; *Books* Golden Needle of Honour (Austrian Hosp Dirs Assoc, 1970), The Grand Gold Komturcross for servs to the Health Serv (Austria, 1980) numerous publications incl: Patterns of Organisation (1952), Management under Nationalisation (1953), the Central Control of the Service (1958), Post War Growth of Management in Western Europe (1961), The British NHS (1970), The Swedish NHS (1970), Management for clinicians (1982), Alternative Systems in organising and Controlling Health Services: public health systems in a democratic society (1985), The Prospects for Rationing - an international view (1986); *Recreations* travel, music, swimming, detective stories; *Style—* Prof Theodore Chester, CBE; 189 Grove Lane, Hale, Altrincham, Cheshire (☎ 061 980 2828)

CHESTERFIELD, The Ven Archdeacon of; see: Phizackerley, The Ven Gerald Robert Phizackerley

CHESTERFIELD, Arthur Desborough; CBE (1962); s of Arthur William Chesterfield (d 1947), of Hastings, and Ellen Harvey Chesterfield; *b* 21 August 1905; *Educ* Hastings GS; *m* 1932, Betty (d 1980), da of John Henry Downey, of St Leonards-on-Sea; 2 s, 3 da; *Career* joined Westminster Bank 1923, chief gen mangr 1950-65, dir 1963-69; dir: Singer and Friedlander (Hldgs) Ltd 1967-86, Singer and Friedlander Ltd 1967-86; chm: Clifford Property Co Ltd 1972-87, Percy Bilton Ltd 1983- (dir 1977-); dir Woolwich Equitable Building Soc 1966-80 (vice-chm 1976-80); *Style—* Arthur Chesterfield Esq, CBE; Two Trees, Crowborough Road, Nutley, Sussex TN22 3HU (☎ 9907 12410)

CHESTERMAN, (Henry) David; s of Sir Clement Chesterman (d 1983), and Winifred, *née* Spear (d 1981); *b* 17 April 1920; *Educ* Monkton Combe Sch Bath; *m* 5 Sept 1945, Jean, da of Sir Harold Kenward (d 1947); 2 s (Andrew b 1946, Daniel b 1954), 1 da (Clare b 1949); *Career* served army 1940-45; Dunlop Rubber Co Ltd 1945-66; PA to Sir Robert Mayer chm of Youth and Music, mangr Ernest Read Music Assoc 1971-76, dir Br Cncl for Prevention of Blindness 1976-; *Recreations* music, tennis, walking, theatre, getting to know 6 grandchildren; *Style—* David Chesterman, Esq; 15 Shire Lane, Chorleywood, Herts WD3 5NQ; 12 Harcourt Street, London W1H 1DS (☎ 01 724 3716)

CHESTERMAN, Sir Ross; s of Dudley Edmund Chesterman (d 1950), of Bexhill, Sussex, and Ettie Esther, *née* Thorington; *b* 27 April 1909; *Educ* Hastings GS, Imperial Coll of Sci London (BSc, MSc, PhD); *m* 1, 1938, Audrey Mary (d 1982), da of Rev Arthur Herbert Horlick (d 1950), of Portishead; 1 s (John), 1 da (Jane); m 2, 1985, Patricia, da of Frederic Burns Bell; *Career* sci master in various grammar schs, former headmaster Meols Cop Secdy Sch Southport, chemistry lectr Woolwich Poly, sch inspr, chief county schs inspr Worcs 1948-53; warden Goldsmiths' Coll London Univ 1953-74 (hon fell 1980), dean Coll of Craft Educn 1958-60 (hon fell 1958), master Coll of Craft Design and Technol 1982-; chm: Nat Cncl for Supply and Trg of Teachers Overseas 1971, advsy ctee for Teacher Trg Overseas FCO (ODA) 1972-74; Ford Fndn Travel Award to American Univ 1966; educnl conslt to numerous overseas countries 1966-73; Freeman and Liveryman Worshipful Co Goldsmiths'; kt 1970; chm: Nat Cncl for Supply and Training of Teachers Overseas 1971, chm advsy ctee for Teacher Trng Overseas FCO (ODA) 1972-74; Ford Foundation Travel Award to American Univ 1966; educational consultant to numerous overseas countries 1966-73; *Books* Teacher Training in some American Universities (1967), scientific papers in chemical jls and jls of natural history, articles in educnl periodicals; *Recreations* music, painting, natural history, travel; *Style—* Sir Ross Chesterman; The Garden House, 6 High St, Lancaster LA1 1LA (☎ 0524 65687)

CHESTERS, Ven Alan David; s of Herbert Chesters (d 1982), of Huddersfield, W Yorks, and Catherine Rebecca, *née* Mountfort (d 1984); *b* 26 August 1937; *Educ* Elland GS, St Chad's Coll Durham (MA), St Catherine's Coll Oxford (BA), St Stephen's House Oxford; *m* 23 July 1975, Jennie, da of Thomas Davison Garrett (d 1973), of Sunderland, Tyne and Wear; 1 s (David b 1977); *Career* curate St Anne Wandsworth London 1962-66, chaplain Tiffin Sch Kingston upon Thames 1966-72, hon curate St Richard Ham 1967-72, dir of Educn Diocese of Durham 1972-85, rector of Brancepeth 1972-85, hon canon Durham Cathedral 1955-75, archdeacon of Halifax 1985-; C of E Gen Synod: memb 1975-, memb Standing Ctee 1985-, vice chm Bd of Educn 1984-, chm Bd of Educn Schs Ctee 1984-; church cmmr 1982-, govr St Chad's Coll Durham 1980-, memb advsy cncl Radio Leeds 1987-; *Recreations* railways, walking; *Style—* The Ven the Archdeacon of Halifax; 9 Healey Wood Gdns, Brighouse, W Yorks HD6 3SQ (☎ 0484 714 553)

CHESTERTON, (John Sydney) Keith; s of Maj Hugh Chesteron, MBE (d 1962), of Sussex, and Phyllis Mary, *née* Harries (d 1986); *b* 26 April 1927; *Educ* Sherborne, Corpus Christi Coll Cambridge; *m* 1, 29 March 1953, Penelope Ann (m dis); 1 s (Christopher b 1957), 1 da (Venetia b 1955); m 2, 19 Aug 1964, Diana Margaret; *Career* Lt RN 1945-56; admitted slr 1961; HM Coroner Isle of Wight 1980-; *Recreations* sailing, gardening; *Clubs* Royal Victoria Yacht (past Cdre), Seaview Yacht; *Style—* Keith Chesterton, Esq; Shirley's Yard, Yafford, Shorwell, Isle of Wight; 36 Union Street, Ryde, Isle of Wight (☎ 0983 63305)

CHESTERTON, Sir Oliver Sidney; MC (1943); s of Frank Sidney and Nora Chesterton; *b* 28 Jan 1913; *Educ* Rugby; *m* 1944, Violet Ethel, yst da of Henry Robert Jameson, of Dublin; 2 s (Michael, Sam), 1 da (Jane); *Career* served WW II Irish Gds; Crown Estate Cmmn 1969-83; qualified as chartered surveyor 1934, sr ptnr Chesterton and Sons; chm Woolwich Equitable Building Soc 1976-84 (formerly vice-chm), dir Property Growth Assur 1972-85, London Life Assoc 1975-84, Estates Property Investmt Co 1979-; FRICS, hon sec RICS 1972-74 (formerly pres); govr Rugby sch 1972-; kt 1969; *Clubs* White's; *Style—* Sir Oliver Chesterton, MC; Hookfield House, Abinger Common, Dorking, Surrey

CHESWORTH, Donald Piers; OBE (1987); s of Frederick Gladstone Chesworth (d 1975), and Daisy, *née* Radmore (d 1987); *b* 30 Jan 1923; *Educ* King Edward VI Sch Camp Hill Birmingham, LSE; *Career* WWII NFS, RAF 1939-45; lab advsr Tanganyika

Govt (and chm territorial miniimum wages bd) 1961-62; Mauritius Govt: lab advsr (and chm sugar wages cncls) 1962-65, pt/t chm salaries cmmn 1973-77, chm enquiry into position of families without wage earners 1981, govt salaries cmmr 1987-89; memb econs branch ILO Geneva 1967, dir Notting Hill Social Cncl 1968-77, warden Toynbee Hall (univs settlement in East London) 1977-87, conslt social affrs Kumagai Gumi UK 1987-, dir Citicare St Clements plc 1988-; parly candidate (Lab): Warwick and Leamington 1945, Bromsgrove 1950 and 1951; memb (Lab) LCC Kensington North Div 1952-65 (whip and memb policy ctee), co-opted memb educnl ctee ILEA 1970-77, cncl memb War on Want 1965-76 (chm 1967, 1968, 1970-74), Alderman Royal Borough Kensington and Chelsea 1971-77; memb ct of govrs LSE 1973-78; tstee: Mutual Aid Centre London 1977, Hilden Charitable Fund 1978-, Aldgate Freedom Fndn 1978-; govr City and East London Coll 1978-, dir Attlee Meml Fndn 1979-81 (tstee 1977-); chm: govrs Tower Hamlets Adult Educn Inst 1987-, Spitalfields Heritage Centre 1988-; *Books* Contrib: Statutory Wage Fixing in Developing Countries (ILO Geneva 1968), International Labour Review (ILO); *Recreations* travel; *Clubs* Reform; *Style*— Donald Chesworth, Esq, OBE; 16 Evershed House, Old Castle St, London E1 7NU (☎ 01 247 4580)

CHETWODE, Hon Christopher Roger; s of late Capt Roger Charles George Chetwode and bro of 2 Baron Chetwode; raised to rank of baron's son 1951; *b* 24 Mar 1940; *Educ* Eton; *m* 25 July 1961, Hon Philippa Mary Imogen, *née* Brand, yr da of 5 Visc Hampden; 5 s; *Style*— The Hon Christopher Chetwode; Hill House, Cheriton, Alresford, Hants

CHETWODE, 2 Baron (UK 1945); Sir Philip Chetwode; 8 Bt (E 1700); s (by 1 m) of Capt Hon Roger Chetwode (d 1940, s of 1 Baron) and Hon Molly, *née* Berry, da of 1 Visc Camrose; suc grandfather 1950; *b* 26 Mar 1937; *Educ* Eton; *m* 10 Aug 1967 (m dis 1979), Susan Janet, da of Capt Voltelin James Howard Van der Byl, DSC, RN (ret), and formerly wife of Alwyn Richard Dudley Smith; 2 s (Hon Roger b 1968, Hon Alexander b 1969), 1 da (Hon Miranda b 1974); *Heir* s, Hon Roger Chetwode b 29 May 1968; *Career* Capt (ret) Royal Horse Guards; *Clubs* White's; *Style*— The Rt Hon the Lord Chetwode; The Mill House, Chilton Foliat, Hungerford, Berks

CHETWODE, Hon Mrs; (Philippa Mary Imogen); *née* Brand; yr da of 5 Viscount Hampden; *b* 7 April 1942; *m* 25 July 1961, Hon Christopher Roger Chetwode, yr bro of 2 Baron Chetwode; 5 s; *Style*— The Hon Mrs Chetwode; Hill House, Cheriton, Alresford, Hants

CHETWODE, Lady Willa; *née* Elliot; yst da of 5 Earl of Minto (d 1975); *b* 21 Mar 1924; *m* 9 Oct 1946, Maj (George) David Chetwode, MBE, 2 s of Adm Sir George Knightley Chetwode, KCB, CBE (d 1957), who was bro of 1 Baron Chetwode; 1 s, 5 da; *Style*— Lady Willa Chetwode; Swiss Farm House, Upper Slaughter, Cheltenham, Glos GL54 2JP

CHETWOOD, Sir Clifford Jack; s of Stanley Jack Chetwood and Doris May Palmer; *b* 2 Nov 1928; *m* 1953, Pamela Phyllis Sherlock; 1 s, 3 da; *Career* FCIOB, FRSA, FRSH; chm George Wimpey from Jan 1984- (md and ch exec 1982); tstee Victoria and Albert Museum and Zoological Soc London Devpt Tst; Prince Philip Medal for Exceptional Service to Industry 1987 (City and Guilds Inst); kt 1987; *Style*— Sir Clifford Chetwood; c/o George Wimpey Plc, 27 Hammersmith Grove, W6 7EN (☎ 01 748 2000)

CHETWYN, Robert; s of Frederick Reuben Suckling (d 1963), and Eleanor Lavinia, *née* Boffee; *b* 7 Sept 1933; *Educ* Rutlish Sch Merton, Central Sch of Drama; *Career* actor with Dundee Rep Co 1952; in rep at Hull, Alexandra Theatre Birmingham 1954, Birmingham Rep Theatre 1954-56; various tv plays 1956-59; first prodn Five Finger Exercise, Salisbury Playhouse 1960; dir of prodns Opera House Harrogate 1961-62; artistic dir Ipswich Arts 1962-64; assoc dir Mermaid 1966; *plays* The Beaver Coat-3 one-act plays by Shaw; There's A Girl in my Soup, Globe 1966; Music Box (NY) 1967; A Present For The Past, Edinburgh Festival 1966; The Flip Side, Apollo 1967; The Importance of Being Earnest, Haymarket 1968; What the Butler Saw, Queens 1968; The Country Wife, Chichester Festival 1968; The Band-Waggon, Mermaid 1968 and Sydney 1970; Cannibal Crackers, Hampstead 1969; When We Are Married, Strand 1970; Hamlet, in Rome, Zurich, Vienna, Antwerp, Cologne, Cambridge 1971; The Sandboy, Greenwich; Parents Day, Globe 1972; Restez Donc Jus q'au Petit Dejeuner Belgium, 1973; Who's Who, Fortune 1973; At The End Of The Day, Savoy 1973; Chez Nous, Globe 1974; Qui Est Qui, Belgium 1974; The Doctors Dilemma, Mermaid 1976; Getting Away with Murder, Comedy 1976; A Murder is Announced, Vauderville 1977; Arms and the Man, Greenwich 1978; Bent, Royal Ct and transferred to Criterion 1979; Pygmalion, Nat Theatre of Belgium; Moving, Queens 1981; Beethoven's Tenth, Vaudeville, Los Angeles and NY 1983; Number One, Queens 1984; Why Me?, Strand 1985; Selling the Sizzle, Hampstead; major TV work: Private Shultz 1980-81, The Irish RM 1982, Tropical Moon Over Dorking 1984, That Uncertain Feeling 1985, Born in the Gardens 1985-86, Small World 1987; *Recreations* sport, gardening; *Style*— Robert Chetwyn, Esq; 1 Wilton Ct, Eccleston Sq, London SW1V 1PH (☎ 01 834 6485)

CHETWYND, 10 Viscount (I 1717); Adam Richard John Casson; also Baron Rathdown (I 1717); s of 9 Viscount (d 1965); *b* 2 Feb 1935; *Educ* Eton; *m* 1, 19 Feb 1966 (m dis 1974), Celia Grace, er da of Cdr Alexander Robert Ramsay, DSC, RNVR; 2 s (Hon Adam, Hon Robert Duncan b (twin) 26 Feb 1969), 1 da (Hon Emma Grace b 5 May 1967); m 2, 1975, Angela May, da of Jack Payne McCarthy (d 1982), of Nottingham; *Heir* s, Hon Adam Douglas Chetwynd b 26 Feb 1969; *Career* Lt Queen's Own Cameron Highlanders; life assurance agent Prudential Assurance Co of SA Ltd 1978-; fellow Inst of Life and Pension Advsrs; Freeman Guild of Air Pilots and Air Navigators; *Recreations* squash, travel, flying; *Clubs* Rand; *Style*— The Rt Hon the Viscount Chetwynd; c/o J G Ouvry, Lee Bolton and Lee, 1 The Sanctuary, Westmister, London SW1; Prudential Assurance Co of SA Ltd, Sandton Branch, Johannesburg, South Africa (☎ 011 783 7125)

CHETWYND, Sir Arthur Ralph Talbot; 8 Bt (GB 1795), of Brocton Hall, Staffordshire; s of Hon (William) Ralph Chetwynd, MLA, MC (d 1957), bro of 7 Bt; and Frances Mary Jupe (d 1986); suc unc 1972; *b* 28 Oct 1913; *Educ* Vernon Prep Sch, Provincial Normal Sch, UBC; *m* 26 Aug 1940, Marjory May MacDonald, da of Robert Bruce Lang (d 1940), of Vancouver; 2 s (Robin, William Richard); *Heir* s, Robin John Talbot Chetwynd, b 21 Aug 1941; *Career* served RCAF 1943-45; rancher in BC 1928-35; teacher 1935-38; physical rehabilitation 1939-42; chief instructor medical reconditioning RCAF, assoc in physical and health educn Univ of Toronto 1946-52, pres and gen mangr Chetwynd Productions Ltd (Toronto) 1950-78, chm bd Chetwynd Publications Inc (1985); pres Brocton Hall Communications (Toronto) 1978- Order of Barbados (Silver Crown of Merit) Hon 1984, Queen's Jubilee Medal 1977 Voluntary Serv and Victory Medals 1945; pres Brocton Hall Communications Ltd 1978-, has served in Red Cross Soc and many other organizations; memb: Nat Cncl Royal Cwlth Soc, Churchill Soc, Monarchist League, Heraldry Soc; *Recreations* swimming, golf, travel; *Clubs* The Toronto Hunt, Albany (Toronto), Empire (Canada) Royal Cwlth Soc (Toronto (chm 1982-87), and London); *Style*— Sir Arthur Chetwynd, Bt; 117 King St East, Cobourg, Ontario K9A 1LZ

CHETWYND, Hon Catherine Sophia Marianne; da (by 2 m) of 9 Viscount Chetwynd (d 1965); *b* 5 Oct 1956; *Style*— The Hon Catherine Chetwynd; Ford Farm Cottage, Aldbourne, Marlborough, Wilts

CHETWYND, Dorothea, Viscountess; Dorothea Marianne; MBE (1974); da of late Lt-Col Angus Colin Duncan-Johnstone, MBE, ED, of Oakwood, Hermitage, Berks; *m* 17 Jan 1952, as his 2 w, 9 Visc Chetwynd (d 12 June 1965); 2 da; *Career* OStJ; *Style*— The Rt Hon Dorothea, Viscountess Chetwynd, MBE; Ford Farm Cottage, Aldbourne, Marlborough, Wilts SN8 2DR

CHETWYND, Hon (Mary Diana) Eve; da of 8 Viscount Chetwynd (d 1936); *b* 19 July 1908; *Educ* privately and in Paris, St Thomas's Hosp; *Career* SRN, SCM, MTD, HVCert; nurse, midwife, health visitor, now retired; pres East Herts Branch Royal Coll of Midwives; *Recreations* travelling, meeting people, gardening; *Style*— The Hon Eve Chetwynd; 6 Hulton Drive, Emberton, nr Olney, Bucks MK46 5BY (☎ 0234 711457)

CHETWYND, Hon Frances Diana Dorothea; da (by 2 m) of 9 Visc Chetwynd (d 1965); *b* 19 Jan 1959; *Educ* The Royal Masonic Sch for Girls, Durham Univ (jt hons applied physics and chemistry); *Career* WRAF Offr 1982-89 (Sash of Merit 1982); *Style*— The Hon Frances Chetwynd; c/o Ford Farm Cottage, Aldbourne, Marlborough, Wilts SN8 2DR

CHETWYND, Lady; Laura Ellen; da of John Mallaby, JP; granted rank and precedence of a knight's widow; *m* 1968, as his 2 wife, George Roland Chetwynd, CBE (kt 1982, d 2 Sept 1982); *Style*— Lady Chetwynd

CHETWYND, Hon Mrs John; Margaret Agnes; da of Maj-Gen Hugh Clement Sutton, CB, CMG (d 1928), and his 2 wife, Hon Alexandra Mary Elizabeth, *née* Wood (d 1965), eldest da of 2 Viscount Halifax; *m* 6 April 1937, Hon John Julian Chetwynd (s of late 8 Viscount Chetwynd and who d 22 April 1966); 2 s; *Style*— The Hon Mrs John Chetwynd; 3 Cadogan Sq, London SW1 (☎ 01 235 7612)

CHETWYND-TALBOT, Capt (Edward) Hugh Frederick; MBE (1945); s of Gilbert Edward Chetwynd-Talbot (d 1950), and Geraldine Mary Murray (d 1953); *b* 19 Jan 1909; *Educ* Haileybury, RMA Woolwich; *m* 27 July 1936, Cynthia Phoebe, da of Noel McGrigor Phillips (d 1942), of Surrey; 1 s (Mark b 1941), 2 da (Anthea b 1939, Meriel b 1944); *Career* cmmnd RA 1929, served India and WW II (disabled 1939); asst sec Irish Turf Club 1947-55, bursar Worksop Coll 1955-63, chm Kiplin Estate (Charitable) Tst 1970-; author; *Books* The English Achilles: Life of John Talbot, First Earl of Shrewsbury 1383-1453 (1981); *Recreations* travel, genealogy, historical research (medieval); *Style*— Capt Hugh Chetwynd-Talbot, MBE; Mead Acre, Milton Lilbourne, Pewsey, Wilts SN9 5LQ (☎ 0672 62229)

CHETWYND-TALBOT, Hon Paul Alexander Anthony Bueno; yr s (by 1 m) of late 21 Earl of Shrewsbury and Waterford, and Nadine Muriel, *née* Crofton-Atkins; *b* 25 Nov 1957; *Educ* Eton, Christ Church Oxford (modern history); *m* 1982, Sarah Elizabeth, da of Simon Hildebrand Melville Bradley, of 35 Ballingdon Rd, London SW11; 2 s (Harry b 1985, Jack b 1987); *Career* insurance broker; *Style*— The Hon Paul Chetwynd-Talbot; Lloyds Chambers, 1 Portsoken Street, London E1

CHETWYND-TALBOT, His Hon Richard Michael Arthur; s of late Rev Arthur Talbot (s of Rev Hon Arthur Chetwynd-Talbot, 3 s of 2 Earl Talbot); 2 cous twice removed of 21 Earl of Shrewsbury and Waterford, the Premier Earl (on the Roll) of England and Ireland; *b* 28 Sept 1911; *Educ* Harrow, Magdalene Coll Cambridge; *Career* barr Middle Temple 1936, dep chm Salop QS 1950-67 (chm 1967-71), bencher 1962, former rec Banbury (hon rec 1972), circuit judge 1972-83; *Style*— His Honour Richard Chetwynd-Talbot; 7 St Leonard's Close, Bridgnorth, Salop (☎ 074 62 3619)

CHEVALLIER GUILD, John Marjoribanks; s of Cyril Harrower Guild (d 1978), and Perronelle Mary, *née* Chevallier; *b* 23 August 1933; *Educ* RN Coll Dartmouth; *m* 18 Dec 1965, Jennifer Isobel, da of Col Brian Sherlock Gooch, DSO, TD, DL, JP: 2 s (John Barrington b 1967, Henry b 1968); *Career* Lt Cdr RN serv at sea 1951-63, HM Yacht Britannia 1959, Staff Coll Camberley 1964, cmd HM Ships Badminton, Upton, Bronington 1965-67, served BRNC Dartmouth 1967-69; ret RN to take over family owned cyder, apple juice and cyder vinegar business Aspall Cyder (estab 1728), first in Good Housekeeping Tests 1985, equal first BBC Food and Drink Tests 1985, Gold Medal Br Bottling Inst Soft Drinks Competition 1987, first and second of all Supermarket Apple Juices tested by Daily Mail 1987, first Marden Fruit Show Kent 1987; *Recreations* country pursuits; *Style*— John Chevallier Guild, Esq; Aspall Hall, Stowmarket, Suffolk IP14 6PD (☎ 0728 860492); Aspall Cyder, Aspall Hall, Stowmarket, Suffolk IP14 6PD (☎ 0728 860510, fax 0728 861031)

CHEWTON, Viscount; James Sherbrooke; s and h of 12 Earl Waldegrave, KG, GCVO, TD; *b* 8 Dec 1940; *Educ* Eton, Trinity Coll Cambridge; *m* 12 April 1986, Mary Alison Anthea, da of Sir Robert Allason Furness, KBE, CMG (d 1954), of South Lodge, Little Shelford, Cambs; 1 s (Edward Robert b 1986); *Clubs* Beefsteak; *Style*— Viscount Chewton; West End Farm, Chewton Mendip, Bath (☎ 076 121 666)

CHEYNE, David Watson; s of Brig William Watson Cheyne, DSO, OBE (d 1970), and Laurel Audrey, *née* Hutchinson; *b* 30 Dec 1948; *Educ* Stowe, Trinity Coll Cambridge (BA); *m* 22 April 1978, (Judith) Gay McAuslane, da of David Anstruther Passey, of 3 Gregory Place, London W8; 2 s (Alexander William David b 25 Nov 1980, Rory Alistair Watson b 22 Aug 1984); *Career* ptnr Linklaters and Paines 1980- (articled clerk 1972-74, asst slr 1974-80); memb City of London Solicitors Co 1980; memb Law Soc; *Recreations* shooting, fishing, collecting antiques; *Style*— David Cheyne, Esq; 25 Edge St, London W8 7PN (☎ 01 727 3780); Linklaters and Paines, 59-67 Gresham St, London EC2V 7JA (☎ 01 606 7080, fax 01 606 5113, telex 884349,888167)

CHEYNE, (William) Gerald; s of Brig William Watson Cheyne, DSO, OBE (d 1970), and Laurel Audrey, *née* Hutchinson; b 13 April 1950; *Educ* Stowe, Trinity Coll Cambridge (BA); *m* 29 July 1978 (m dis 1984), Clare Rosdew, *née* van der Stegen-Drake; 1 da (Kate b 1980); *Career* 1 Bn Queens Own Highlanders 1972-77, Lt platoon cdr 1973, intelligence offr 1974, Capt mortar platoon cdr 1975, ops and trg offr 1977; supervising sr Peat Marwick Mitchell & Co CAs 1977-82, exec Larpent Newton & Co

Ltd 1982-84; dir: Henderson Crosthwaite & Co 1987-88, Guinness Mahon & Co Ltd 1988, Henderson Crosthwaite Corporate Fin Ltd 1988; ACA 1981; *Recreations* golf, tennis, bridge, piano; *Style—* Gerald Cheyne, Esq; 32 Ringmer Ave, London SW6 5LW (☎ 01 731 1806); Guinness Mahon & Co Ltd, 32 St Mary At Hill, London EC3 3AJ (☎ 01 623 9333, fax 01 929 3398)

CHEYNE, Major Sir Joseph Lister Watson; 3 Bt (UK 1908), OBE (1976); s of Col Sir Joseph Cheyne, 2 Bt, MC (d 1957); *b* 10 Oct 1914; *Educ* Stowe, CCC Cambridge; *m* 1, 14 Jan 1938 (m dis 1955), Mary Mort (d 29 Oct 1959), er da of Vice Adm John Derwent Allen, CB (d 1958); 1 s, 1 da; m 2, 6 Aug 1955, Cicely, da of Thomas Metcalfe, of Padiham, Lancs; 2 s, 1 da; *Heir* s, Patrick John Lister Cheyne, *qv*; *Career* served WW II North Africa and Italy, Maj; former first sec British Embassy Rome; curator Keats Shelley Memorial House Rome 1976-; *Clubs* Boodle's, Circolo della Caccia (Rome); *Style—* Major Sir Joseph Cheyne, Bt, OBE; Piazza di Spagna 29, Rome, Italy (☎ 6782334); Leagarth, Fetlar, Shetland

CHEYNE, Cdr Mark Edmonstone; DSC, DL (Norfolk 1977); s of Col Reginald Edmonstone Cheyne, and Sybil, sole surviving grandchild of Sir Henry Rider Haggard DBE; *b* 14 Mar 1917; *Educ* Cheltenham; *m* 9 July 1947, Nada Helen Angela, adopted da of Mrs Thomas Barker Amyand Haggard (d 1973); 2 s (Rider b 1948, Jonathan b 1957), 2 da (Dorothy b 1951, Judith b 1955); *Career* Naval Offr (ret 1961); county cncllr for Norfolk 1967-82; peoples warden St Mary's Church Ditchingham; *Recreations* village affairs; *Style—* Cdr Mark E Cheyne, DSO, DL, RN; Ditchingham Lodge, Bungay, Suffolk NR35 2JN (☎ 6986 2319)

CHEYNE, Patrick John Lister; s (by 1 m) and h of Sir Joseph Cheyne, 3 Bt, OBE; *b* 2 July 1941; *Educ* Lancing; *m* 8 June 1968, Helen Louise Trevor, yr da of Louis Smith, of Marine Lodge, 25 Driftwood Gardens, Southsea; 1 s, 3 da; *Career* short service cmmn Lt RN; Fine Art valuer and auctioneer; FSVA; *Recreations* squash, photography, gardening; *Style—* Patrick Cheyne Esq; 37 Chapel Lane, Hale Barns, Cheshire WA15 0AG (☎ home 061 980 3094; work 061 941 4879)

CHIANDETTI, Gian Battista (Tito); s of Giovanni Battista Chiandetti (d 1942), and Pauline, *née* Caron (d 1982); *b* 17 Mar 1935; *Educ* Douai Sch Woolhampton Berks, Harvard Business Sch; *m* 18 Mar 1968, (Maria) Elisa, da of Mario Bulferi-Bulferetti, of Lugano, Switzerland; 1 s (Marco Paolo Angelo b 25 Aug 1973), 1 da (Corinna Elena Paola b 13 Nov 1970); *Career* Trusthouse Forte: md THF Products 1973-75, dir THF Ltd 1975-77, THF Catering Ltd 1979-84 (md 1977-79), dep chief exec THF plc 1984-; FHCIMA; *Recreations* mountain walking, swimming, rock collecting; *Style—* Tito Chiandetti, Esq; Daneswood, Monks Walk, South Ascot, Berks SL5 9AZ (☎ 0990 26036); Trusthouse Forte plc, 166 High Holborn, London WC1V 6TT (☎ 01 836 7744, fax 01 240 9993, telex 264678 THFPLC)

CHIARI, Dr Joseph; s of Nicolas Chiari (ka 1914), of Corsica, and Marie, *née* Dominici (d 1930); *b* 12 Jan 1911; *Educ* Lycée de Bastia, Lycée Thiers Marseille, Univ of Aix-Marseille (Licenceès-Lettres, Diplôme d'Etudes Supérieures, Doctorat d'Etat); *m* 1, 11 May 1940, Margaret (decd), da of John Henderson; 3 s (Jean-Antoine b 1941 (decd), Nicholas b 1946, Alain b 1949), 1 da (Margaret b 1942); m 2, 30 April 1970, Joyce, da of Harold Cannon; *Career* writer, lectr, diplomat; teacher 1938-40, lectr Min of Information 1940-42, hd of Information Service French Nat Ctee Scotland 1942-45, French vice-consul then consul Edinburgh 1945-49, lectr Manchester Univ and London Univ 1949-55, translator Western European Union 1955-56, French vice-consul Southampton 1956-69; *Books* Mary Stuart (a verse play, 1955), Symbolisme from Poe to Mallarmè (1956), Corsica, Columbus's Isle (1960), Realism and Imagination (1960), Religion and Modern Society (1964), The Aesthetics of Modernism (1970), T S Eliot, Poet and Dramatist (1972), The Necessity of Being (1973), Twentieth Century French Thought (1975), Art and Knowledge (1977), Reflections on Life and Death (1977), Collected Poems (1978), Christopher Columbus (a play, 1979), T S Eliot, A Memoir (1982); *Recreations* country walks, music; *Style—* Dr Joseph Chiari; 15A Westleigh Ave, London SW15 6RF

CHIBBETT, Geoffrey John; s of Ernest James Chibbett (d 1955), barrister, of Hoylake, Ches; *b* 2 Sept 1928; *Educ* Stowe, Liverpool Univ (BCom); *m* 1977, Diana Leslie, da of Frederick Green (d 1963), of London; 1 s, 1 da; *Career* chm: Kango Wolf Power Tools Ltd, Ralliwolf Ltd (Bombay), Dobson Park Industries plc (engrg div); FCA; *Recreations* lawn tennis, golf; *Clubs* Royal Liverpool Golf; *Style—* Geoffrey Chibbett Esq; Withamside, Church Street, Long Bennington, nr Newark, Notts (☎ 0400 81249); Dobson Park Industries Ltd, Dobson Park House, Colwick Industrial Estate, Notts NG4 2BX

CHICHESTER, 99 Bishop of (680) 1974-; Rt Rev Eric Waldram Kemp; Bishopric founded in Isle of Selsey by Wilfrid, 2 Archbishop of York, removed to Chichester by Stigand after 1075; patron of 96 livings and 9 alternatively, the Archdeaconries of Chichester, Lewes and Hastings, and Horsham, and the Prebends (including the three residentiaries) in the Cathedral; s of Tom Kemp and Florence Lilian, *née* Waldram, of Grove House, Waltham, Grimsby, Lincs; *b* 27 April 1915; *Educ* Brigg GS Lincs, Exeter Coll Oxford, St Stephen's House Oxford; *m* 1953, Leslie Patricia, 3 da of late Rt Rev Kenneth Escott Kirk, former Bishop of Oxford (d 1954); 1 s, 4 da; *Career* deacon 1939, fell and chaplain Exeter Coll Oxford 1946-69, dean of Worcester 1969-74; author; Hon DD Berne Univ 1987, Hon DLitt Sussex Univ, DD Oxon; *Style—* The Rt Rev the Lord Bishop of Chichester; The Palace, Chichester, Sussex (☎ 0243 782161)

CHICHESTER, Hon Lady; Hon Anne Rachel Pearl; *née* Douglas-Scott-Montagu; da of 2 Baron Montagu of Beaulieu, KCIE, CSI (d 1929), and his 2 w, Alice Pearl, er da of late Major Edward Barrington Crake; *b* 4 Oct 1921; *m* 1, 2 March 1946, Maj Howel Joseph Moore-Gwyn, Welsh Guards (d 20 Sept 1947), only s of late Major Joseph Gwyn Moore-Gwyn, of Duffryn, Glamorgan, and Abercrave, Brecknock; 1 s; m 2, 23 Sept 1950, Sir (Edward) John Chichester, 11 Bt; 2 s, 2 da (and 1 da decd); *Career* serv Red Cross WWII; JP Hants 1968-80; *Style—* The Hon Lady Chichester; Battramsley Lodge, Boldre, Nr Lymington, Hants SO41 8PT

CHICHESTER, Archdeacon of; *see*: Hobbs, Ven Keith

CHICHESTER, Lord Desmond Clive; MC (1944); s of 4 Baron Templemore (d 1953), and bro of 7 Marquess of Donegall; raised to the rank of a Marquess's son 1977; *b* 27 Jan 1920; *Educ* Harrow, Christ Church Oxford (MA); *m* 1, 7 March 1946, Lorna Althea, MBE (d 9 April 1948), da of Capt Montagu Hamer Ravenhill, and wid of Capt Richard Cecil Twining, Welsh Guards, and previously of P/O Geoffrey Christopher Appleby Holt, RAF; 1 s; m 2, 12 April 1951, Felicity Stella, 6 da of Maj John Fenwick Harrison, JP, DL, of King's Walden, Bury, Herts; 1 s; *Career* served WW II, Maj Coldstream Gds (ret); ADC to Govr-Gen of Canada 1948-50; chm Colne Valley Water Co 1983-88 (dir 1956-); *Recreations* shooting, racing; *Clubs* Whites; *Style—* Major Lord Desmond Chichester, MC; Preston Hill, Preston, Hitchin, Herts (☎ 0462 56965); Colne Valley Water Co, Blackwell House, Aldenham Road, Watford, Herts (☎ 0923 23333)

CHICHESTER, James Henry Edward; s and h of Sir Edward John Chichester, 11 Bt, *qv*; *b* 15 Oct 1951; *Educ* Eton; *Career* fndr of Chichester Trees and Shrubs; *Recreations* shooting, fishing, big game hunting and dendrology; *Style—* James Chichester, Esq; The Mill House, Beaulieu, Brockenhurst, Hants SO42 7YG (☎ 0590 612198)

CHICHESTER, Sir (Edward) John; 11 Bt (E 1641), of Raleigh, Devonshire; s of Cdr Sir Edward Chichester, 10 Bt, RN (ret, d 1940); *b* 14 April 1916; *Educ* Radley, Sandhurst; *m* 23 Sept 1950, Hon Anne Rachel Pearl Douglas-Scott-Montagu, da of 2 Baron Montagu of Beaulieu; 2 s, 2 da (1 da decd); *Heir* s, James Chichester, *qv*; *Career* serv WWII former Capt Royal Scots Fusiliers, Lt RNVR, King's Foreign Serv Messenger 1947-50, ICI Ltd 1950-60; patron of one living; *Style—* Sir John Chichester, Bt; Battramsley Lodge, Boldre, Lymington, Hants

CHICHESTER, 9 Earl of (UK 1801); Sir John Nicholas Pelham; 14 Bt (E 1611); also Baron Pelham of Stanmer (GB 1762); s of 8 Earl of Chichester (ka 1944), and Ursula Pannwitz, of Buenos Aires; *b* 14 April 1944,(posthumously); *Educ* Stanbridge Earls Sch, Mozarteum Salzburg; *m* 1975, Mrs June Marijke Hall, da of Gp-Capt E D Wells, DSO, DFC, of Marbella; 1 da (Lady Eliza b 12 May 1983); *Heir* kinsman, Richard Pelham; *Career* farmer; *Recreations* music, theatre, tennis, riding; *Style—* The Rt Hon the Earl of Chichester; 53 Shawfield St, London SW3 (☎ 01 352 1516); Little Durnford Manor, Salisbury, Wilts

CHICHESTER, Maj (Oscar) Richard Herschel; s of Shane Randolph Chichester(d 1969), of Farnham, and Madeline, *née* Whately (d 1977); *b* 17 Oct 1915; *Educ* Wellington, Trinity Coll Camb (BA); *m* 29 Sept 1951, Margaret Edmondson, da of Charles Edgar Farr, JP; 1 s (Timothy Arthur Shane b 1956), 2 da (Jane Caroline Sheelah b 1952, Sara Arabella Kathleen b 1958); *Career* Major (ret) Rifle Bde, ADC to High Cmmr for Palestine 1946-48; *Recreations* travel, motor racing, farming; *Clubs* Pratts, Army and Navy; *Style—* Major Richard Chichester; Wiscombe Park, Colyton, Devon (☎ M Farway 252); Drummond's, 49 Charing Cross SW1

CHICHESTER-CLARK, Hon Fiona; da of Baron Moyola (Life Peer); *b* 1960; *Educ* Knighton House Blandford, Cranborne Chase Wilts; *Career* antique furniture restorer and cabinet maker; *Recreations* shooting, fishing, tennis; *Style—* The Hon Fiona Chichester-Clark

CHICHESTER-CLARK, Sir Robin Robert; s of Capt James Jackson Lenox-Conyngham Chichester-Clark, DSO, DL, MP, and Marion Caroline Dehra, *née* Chichester (later Mrs Charles Edward Brackenbury); bro of Rt Hon Lord Moyola, PC, DL, *qv*; *b* 10 Jan 1928; *Educ* Magdalene Coll Cambridge (BA); *m* 1, 6 Nov 1953 (m dis 1972), Jane Helen, o child of Air Marshal Sir (Robert) Victor Goddard, KCB; 1 s, 2 da; m 2, 1974, Caroline, o da of Col Anthony Bull, CBE, RE, of 35 Clareville Grove, London SW7; 2 s; *Career* MP (UU) for Londonderry City and Co 1955-74, Lord Cmmr of the Treasy 1960-61, Comptroller of HM Household 1961-64, Chief Opposition Spokesman on NI 1964-70, on Public Building and Works and The Arts 1965-70, Min of State, Dept of Employment 1972-74; mgnmt consult; dir: Alfred Booth and Co, Welbeck Gp Ltd; Hon FIWM; kt 1974; *Clubs* Brooks's; *Style—* Sir Robin Chichester-Clark

CHICK, Charles Richard; s of Edgar Percy Chick; *b* 6 April 1941; *Educ* Sir Robert Pattinson Sec Mod, Lincoln Tech Coll; *m* 1963, Janet Yvonne; 2 da; *Career* dir: Howard Tenens Ltd 1976-79, Mansill Booth Ltd 1979-; *Style—* Charles Chick Esq; 423 Lichfield Rd, Four Oaks, Sutton Coldfield, W Midlands (☎ 021 308 2533)

CHIENE, John; *b* 27 Jan 1937; *Educ* Rugby, Queens' Coll Cambridge; *m* ; 1 s, 1 da; *Career* memb Stock Exchange 1964; sr ptnr Wood, Mackenzie and Co (stockbrokers); *Recreations* golf, music; *Clubs* Cavalry and Guards, City, New (Edinburgh); *Style—* John Chiene Esq; Stone House, Snowdenham Links Rd, Bramley, Guildford, Surrey; Wood, Mackenzie and Co, 62-63 Threadneedle St, London EC2R 8HP (☎ 01 600 3600; telex 883369)

CHIGNALL, John Horsley; s of Horace Victor Chignall (d 1952), of Uckfield Sussex, and Ethel Kate, *née* Godwin (d 1972); *b* 26 July 1926; *Educ* Regent St Poly London; *m* 26 Aug 1948, Esme Elizabeth, da of Sidney James Michel (d 1962); 1 da (Linda Susan b 20 July 1949); *Career* civilian attached to Special Service Division US Army 1944-46; dir: AE Medway & Co Ltd 1947-54, JH Chignall & Co Ltd 1954-82; chm: Pleasure Heating Ltd, Pleasure Heating Fin Dept Ltd, Pleasure Investmts Ltd; FBIM; *Recreations* shooting, golf, tennis, sailing; *Clubs* Stoke Poges GC, Pinner Hill GC (Capt 1966); *Style—* J Horsley Chignall, Esq; Cedar House, Camp Road, Gerrards Cross, Bucks; Vallee du Fournel, Roquebrune sur Argens, Cote D'Azur France

CHIGNELL, Anthony Hugh; s of Thomas Hugh Chignell (d 1965), and Phyllis Una, *née* Green; *b* 14 April 1939; *Educ* Downside, St Thomas Hosp London (MB BS, DO); *m* 16 June 1962, Phillipa Price, da of Rear Adm F B P Brayne-Nicholls, CB, DSC, RN, of 3 Tedworth Sq, London; 1 s (Christopher Damien b 1965), 2 da (Caroline Paula b 1963, Georgina Natalie b 1966); *Career* conslt ophthalmic surgn St Thomas' Hosp 1973-, civilian conslt in ophthalmology to Army 1983-, conslt surgn King Edward V11 Hosp for offrs 1985-, advsr in ophthalmology to met Police 1987-; numerous papers on retinal detachment surgery; govr Royal Nat Coll for the Blind 1987-, memb cncl Guide dogs for the Blind 1989-; memb: Oxford Ophthalmology, Club Jules Gonin; OstJ; memb Ct Worshipful Co Spectacle Makers 1987; FRCS 1968; *Books* Retinal Detachment Surgery (2 eds); *Recreations* fly fishing, golf, the country; *Clubs* Fly Fishers, Anglo Belgian; *Style—* Anthony Chignell Esq; 44 Wimpole St, London W1M 7DG, (☎ 01 935 7022, fax 01 224 3722)

CHILD, Alan Arthur; s of Walter Henry Child (d 1954); *b* 7 July 1912; *Educ* Alleyns Sch; *m* 1941, Olive Ella, da of Archibald Wood (d 1981); 1 s, 1 da; *Career* Capt RA UK Belgium and Germany; insurance and pension fund consultant; former chief exec dir C T Bowring and Layborn Ltd (chm 1974-78); pres Soc of Pension Consultants 1970-72, chm Hospital Saving Assoc 1975-, memb Occupational Pensions Bd 1973-84; Pres Croydon North East Conservative Assoc 1986-; *Clubs* Inst of Directors, Croydon Conservative; *Style—* Alan Child, Esq; 35 Campion Close, Coombe Road, Croydon, Surrey CR0 5SN (☎ 01 688 4126)

CHILD, (John) Christopher; s of Ernest Henry Child (d 1962), of Southwold, and Barbara Christobel, *née* Hebbert (d 1962); *b* 5 Mar 1927; *Educ* Orley Farm Sch

Harrow, Aldenham, de Havilland Aeronautical Sch Hatfield; *m* 26 Feb 1949, Elisabeth Anne, da of Frank Wilkinson Fish, MC; 1 s (Andrew b 1950), 1 da (Sarah b 1953); *Career* aeronautical engr 1970, specialist in design of cameras for harsh environments, student of Irish Folk Life, antique restorer and dealer 1970-; *Recreations* photography, wood turning, collecting artifacts; *Style*— Christopher Child, Esq; Meadowbank, Morchard Bishop Crediton, Devon (☎ 036 37 456)

CHILD, Denis Marsden; CBE (1987); s of Percival Snowden (d 1964), and Alice (d 1963); *b* 1 Nov 1926; *Educ* Woodhouse Grove Sch; *m* 1973, Patricia, da of Arthur Charlton (d 1979); 2 s (Richard b 1961, Nicholas b 1968), 1 da (Elizabeth b 1956); *Career* dir: Nat Westminster Bank 1986- (ret as dep gp ch exec 1986), Coutts and Co 1983-; bd memb: IBM UK Pensions Tst Ltd 1984-, Eurotunnel Gp, Civil Aviation Authy; chm Br Bankers Assoc Exec Ctee 1986-87; memb: Accounting Standards Ctee 1985-, The Securities and Investmts Bd 1986; FIB, FCT, FBIM; *Recreations* golf, gardening; *Clubs* Stoke Poges GC; *Style*— Denis Child, Esq; Hill House, Ascott, Shipston-on-Stour, Warwickshire CU36 5PP Civil Aviation Authority, 45/59 Kingsway, London WC2 6TE

CHILD, Graham Derek; s of Albert Edward Child, of Broadstone, Dorset, and Phyllis, *née* Wooldridge (d 1973); *b* 24 June 1943; *Educ* Bedford Sch, Worcester Coll Oxford (MA); *Career* Slaughter and May: asst slr 1968-75, ptnr 1976-; memb Law Soc; *Books* Common Market Law of Competition (with CW Bellamy QC, 1987); *Recreations* outdoor activities; *Style*— Graham Child, Esq; 35 Basinghall St, London EC2V 5DB (☎ 01 600 1200, fax 01 726 0038)

CHILD, Sir (Coles John) Jeremy; 3 Bt (UK 1919), of Bromley Palace, Bromley, Kent; s of Sir Coles John Child, 2 Bt (d 1971), and Sheila, *née* Mathewson (d 1964); *b* 20 Sept 1944; *Educ* Eton, Poitiers Univ (Dip); *m* 1, 1971 (m dis 1976), Deborah Jane, da of Henry Snelling; 1 da (Melissa b 1973); m 2, 1978 (m dis 1987), Jan, actress, yst da of Bernard Todd, of Kingston-upon-Thames; 1 s (Alexander b 10 May 1982), 1 da (Leonora b 1980); m 3 Elizabeth, yst da the Rev Grenville Morgan of Canterbury, Kent; *Heir* s, Coles John Alexander; *Career* actor; *TV*: Father dear Father, Wings, Glittering Prizes, Edward and Mrs Simpson, The Jewel in the Crown, Fairly Secret Army, First Among Equals, Game Set and Match; *Films*: High Road to China (1982), Give My Regards to Broad St (1982/83), A Fish Called Wanda 1987, Taffin 1987; *Recreations* flying, squash, travel, photography, cooking, gardening; *Clubs* Garrick, Roehampton; *Style*— Sir Jeremy Child, Bt; The Old Mill House, Mill Lane, Benson, Oxon

CHILD, John Frederick; s of Frederick George Child (d 1980) and Doris Frances *née* Henley; *b* 18 April 1942; *Educ* King Edward's Sch Bath, Univ of Southampton (BA), Sidney Sussex Coll Cambridge (BA, LLB), Univ of Columbia, Leiden (Dip American Law); *m* 2 Sept 1972, Dr Jean Alexander *née* Cunningham, da of Dr Albert Alexander Cunningham, of Glenone Haymeads Drive, Esher; 2 s (Andrew b 25 May 1974, Jeremy b 11 May 1977); *Career* Chancery Barr; Droop Scholar and Tancred Common Law Student, Hon Soc of Lincoln's Inn, Supervisor in Law Sidney Sussex Coll Cambridge 1966-1978; memb: Lincoln's Inn, Chancery Bar Assoc, Revenue Bar Assoc; *Books* Main Contrib Vol 19 (Sale of Land) Encyclopaedia of Forms and Precedents (4 edn); *Recreations* tennis, badminton; *Style*— John Child, Esq; 17 Old Buildings, Lincolns Inn, London, WC2A 3UP, (☎ 01 405 9653/01 831 1621, fax 01 405 5032)

CHILD-VILLIERS, Hon Charles Victor; s of 9 Earl of Jersey; *b* 10 Jan 1952; *m* 1975, Brigitte Elisabeth Germaine, da of Rolland Marchand; 2 da (Eleanor b 1979, Barbara b 1981); *Style*— The Hon Charles Child-Villiers; Springvale, La Route des Maltières, Grouville, Jersey, CI (☎ 0534 55051)

CHILD-VILLIERS, (Edward) John Mansel; s of Sqr-Ldr The Hon Edward Mansel Child-Villiers (d 1980), and Mary Barbara Emma Torrens, *née* Frampton; *b* 29 April 1935; *Educ* Harrow; *m* 2 June 1958, Celia Elinor Vadyn, da of Cyril Hail Green (d 1923) (see Debrett's Peerage, Blake Bt); 2 s (Alexander b 1961, Roderick b 1963); *Career* memb of Lloyd's, 1962-; literary executor 18 Baron Dunsany 1966-; *Recreations* Bordeaux wines; *Style*— John Child-Villiers, Esq; Stable House, Mystole, Canterbury, Kent CT4 7DB (☎ 0227 738729)

CHILDS, Richard; s of Henry Childs, of 9 Trinity Way, Bradpole, Bridport, Dorset, and Clara Emily, *née* Curruthers; *b* 7 May 1944; *m* 29 April 1974, Jayne Angela, da of Capt George Henry Lawrence, of Rydal-Mount, Petersfield Rd, Boscombe, Bournemouth, Dorset; 1 s (Simon Matthew b 1978), 1 da (Caroline Elizabeth b 1980); *Career* hotelier; *Recreations* horse racing; *Style*— Richard Childs, Esq; The Manor Hotel, Beach Rd, W Bexington, nr Dorchester, Dorset

CHILDS-CLARKE, (Arthur) John (Gordon); s of Canon Septimus John Childs-Clarke (d 1964), Rector of St Columb Major, Cornwall, and Harriet Ethel, *née* Taylor (d 1959); *b* 13 Dec 1908; *Educ* King's Sch Canterbury; *m* 7 Dec 1940, Agnes Gilchrist Walker, da of Dr Thomas Inglis (d 1947), of Fairmilehead, Edinburgh; 1 s (Richard b 1943); *Career* served RN 1942-46 in N Atlantic; insurance broker (ret), underwriting memb of Lloyds 1946-; *Recreations* rugby union football, lawn tennis, gardening; *Clubs* Rosslyn Park Football, Naval, British Sportsmans, Middlesex County Rugby Football Union; *Style*— John Childs-Clarke, Esq; Penhellick, Drews Park, Knotty Green, Beaconsfield, Bucks HP9 2TT

CHILSTON, 4 Viscount (UK 1911); Alastair George Akers-Douglas; s of late Capt Ian Stanley Akers-Douglas (gs of 1 Viscount Chilston), by his 2 w, Phyllis Rosemary; suc kinsman, 3 Viscount Chilston, 1982; *b* 5 Sept 1946; *Educ* Ashdown House, Eton; *m* 1971, Juliet Anne, da of late Lt-Col Nigel Lovett, of The Old Rectory, Inwardleigh, Okehampton, Devon; 3 s (Hon Oliver, Hon Alexander Hugh b 1975, Hon Dominic b 1979); *Heir* s, Hon Oliver Ian Akers-Douglas b 17 Oct 1973; *Career* film producer; *Style*— The Rt Hon the Viscount Chilston; The Old Rectory, Twyford, nr Winchester, Hants (☎ 0962 712300)

CHILTON, Air Marshal Sir (Charles) Edward; KBE (1959, CBE 1945), CB (1951); o s of Joseph Charles (d 1966), of Southsea, Hants, and Olive Minette, *née* Dowling; *b* 1 Nov 1906; *m* 1, 21 Sept 1929, Betty Ursula, (d 6 July 1963), 2 da of late Bernard Temple Wrinch, of Grove House, Denham, Suffolk; 1 s; m 2, 14 Sept 1964, (Margaret Elizabeth) Joyce, widow of A W Cornforth, *née* Fenwick; *Career* Air Cdre 1950, Air Marshal 1959, AOC-in-C Coastal Cmd and Maritime Air Cdr E Atlantic Area and Cdr Maritime Air Channel and S North Sea 1959-62; air historian and lectr on mil subjects; former conslt and dir IBM, Def Systems and Data Processing int conslt; fellow fndr Royal Inst of Navigation; Grand Cross of Prince Henry the Navigator (Portugal) 1960, Order of Polonia Restituta (Poland) 1945 air master navigator (1937), specialist navigator RAF 1931; *Books* biographies: Air Chief Marshal Sir Philip Jollbert, Air Chief Marshal the Hon Sir Ralph Cochrane, Rear Adm Sir Murray Sueter, Wing Cdr J C Porte; numerous published articles on navigation and maritime subjects; *Recreations* sailing, fishing, walking; *Clubs* Vice Admiral RAFSA, Vice Patron RGYC, RAF, Phyllis Court (Henley); *Style*— Air Marshal Sir Edward Chilton, KBE, CB; 11 Charles House, Phyllis Court Drive, Henley-on-Thames, Oxon (☎ 049 157 3836)

CHILTON, James Richard; s of Col Richard Chilton; *b* 2 Jan 1941; *Educ* Winchester; *m* 1964, Margaret Ann, *née* McKay; 1 s, 3 da; *Career* served 1 The Royal Dragoons, Arabian Peninsular 1960, Malaysia 1961-62; dir McKay Securities plc 1973-; *Recreations* skiing, plantsmanship, vinousness; *Clubs* Cavalry and Guards'; *Style*— James Chilton, Esq; Hyde House, Great Missenden, Bucks; Maufant Manor, Jersey, CI

CHILTON, (Frederick) Paul; s of Charles Frederick Chilton, of 167 Birling Rd, Erith, Kent, and Elizabeth, *née* Docherty; *b* 28 July 1946; *Educ* St Stephens Roman Catholic Sch, NW Kent Coll of Technol; *Career* dep chm Alexander Howden Ltd; ctee memb The UK Int Insur Brokers Ctee; *Recreations* equestrian sports; *Clubs* Les Ambassadeurs; *Style*— Paul Chilton, Esq; Alexander Howden Ltd, 8 Devonshire Sq, London EC2M 4PL (☎ 01 623 5500, fax 01 621 1511, telex 882171)

CHILVER, Brian Outram; s of Flt Lt Bertram Montagu Chilver RAF, of Harare, Zimbabwe, and Edith Gwendoline, *née* Adams (d 1984); *b* 17 June 1933; *Educ* Univ Coll Sch; *m* 23 June 1956, Erica Mary, da of Laurence Truella Howell, of 23 Bury Drive, Goring on Sea, Sussex; 2 s (Andrew b 1961, David b 1963), 2 da (Hazel b 1957, Heather b 1959); *Career* trainee CA Temple Gothard and Co 1949-55, (qualified 1954); Flying Offr RAF 1955-57; joined Barton Mayhew as a qualified accountant 1957-59, re-joined Temple Gothard 1959, apptd ptnr with Temple Gothard 1960, sr ptnr Temple Gothard 1974-85, conslt Touche Ross and Co 1985-87, non-exec dir Laing Properties plc 1982 (dep-chm 1986, exec chm 1987, non exec dir 1988); dir: Eskmuir Ltd 1987-, Regions Beyond Missionary Union 1960-, Yeovil Livestock Auctioners Ltd 1965-, Hildenborough Evangelistic Tst; FCA, ACWA; *Recreations* walking, swimming, reading, travel, involved in christian charitable activity in UK and overseas; *Style*— Brian Chilver, Esq; Bretaye, Limbourne Lane, Fittleworth, W Sussex RH20 1HR (☎ 079 882 366); Laing Properties plc, 34 Clarendon Rd, Watfords, Herts WD1 1JL (☎ 0293 244255, fax 0923 30180, telex 923501)

CHILVER, Elizabeth Leila Millicent; o da of Philip Perceval Graves (d 1953), of Bantry, Co Cork, and Leila Millicent Knox Gilchrist (d 1935); ggda of Charles Graves, DD, FRS, PRIA, and gda of Alfred Perceval Graves (see DNB Supplements); *b* 3 August 1914; *Educ* Benenden, Somerville Coll Oxford (MA); *m* 1937, Richard Clementson Chilver, CB (d 1985), s of late Arthur Farquhar Chilver; *Career* war-time Civil Servant 1940-44; Daily News Ltd 1944-47, Colonial Off 1947-57, dir Inst of Cwlth Studies Oxford 1957-61, sr res fell Inst of Cwlth Studies London 1961-64; princ: Bedford Coll London 1964-71, Lady Margaret Hall Oxford 1971-79; Médaille de la Reconnaisance Française 1946; *Style*— Mrs Elizabeth Chilver; 47 Kingston Rd, Oxford OX2 6RH (☎ 53082)

CHILVER, Baron (Life Peer UK 1987), of Cranfield, Beds; Sir (Amos) Henry Chilver; e s of Amos Henry Chilver, of Southend-on-Sea, and A E Chilver, *née* Mack; *b* 30 Oct 1926; *Educ* Southend HS, Bristol Univ; *m* 1959, Claudia Mary Beverley, o da of Sir Wilfrid Vernon Grigson, CSI (d 1948), of Pelynt, Cornwall; 3 s (Hon John b 1964, Hon Mark b 1965, Hon Paul b 1967), 2 da (Hon Helen (Hon Mrs Prentice) b 1960, Hon Sarah b 1962); *Career* prof civil engrg London Univ 1961-69, vice-chllr Cranfield Inst of Technology 1970-89, chm Milton Keynes Devpt Corp 1983-; dir: English China Clays 1973-, Powell Duffryn 1979-, BASE Int Hlgs 1988-; pres: Inst Mgmnt Servs 1982-, pres Inst Mats Mgmnt 1986-; Hon DSc: Leeds 1982, Bristol 1983, Salford 1983, Strathclyde 1986, Bath 1986; hon Fell CCC Cambridge 1981; FRS 1982; FEng; CBIM; kt 1978; *Clubs* Athenaeum, United Oxford and Cambridge; *Style*— The Rt Hon Lord Chilver; Lanlawren House, Trenewen, Looe, Cornwall PL13 2PZ; English China Clays plc, John Keay House, St Austell, Cornwall PL25 4DJ (☎ 0726 74482, fax 0726 623019)

CHILVERS, Donald Richard; s of Gordon Edward Chilvers (d 1988), of Limpsfield, and Caroline, *née* Nendick; *b* 1 Feb 1929; *Educ* Bancrofts Sch; *m* 25 Nov 1961, Rosemary, da of Archibald Watson (d 1979), of Edinburgh; 1 s (Angus b 1965), 3 da (Penelope b 1962, Felicity b 1967, Camilla b 1969); *Career* Nat Serv cmmnd 1951-53; ptnr Coopers and Lybrand 1961-; memb: Sandilands Ctee of Inflation 1977-78, Industl Advsy Bd 1979-82; chm: Invalid Children's Aid Nationwide, Charities Report Award Scheme; seconded to Miny of Energy 1961; FCA 1951, FCMA 1952; *Books* Receivership Manual (1971), Litigation Support (1988); *Recreations* golf, gardening; *Clubs* City Univ; *Style*— Donald Chilvers, Esq; The Priory, Denham Village, Bucks; 17 Callcott St, London WC8 (☎ 089 583 2430); Plumtree Court, London EC4 (☎ 01 583 5000)

CHIN, Dr Lincoln Li-Jen; s of Pun-Jian Chin, and Grace Chin, *née* Sun; *b* 2 Nov 1942; *Educ* Christ's Coll Cambridge (BA, MA), MIT USA (ScD); *m* 21 Jan 1971, Lillian Chen Ming, da of Wen Hsiung Chu; 1 s (Nicholas b 1973), 1 da (Tamara b 1975); *Career* dep chm Chindwell Co Ltd; *Recreations* walking, swimming, travelling, music; *Clubs* Utd Oxford and Cambridge; *Style*— Dr Lincoln Chin; Chindwell Co Ltd, Hyde House, The Hyde, London NW9 6JT (☎ 01 205 6171, telex 923441, fax 01 2058800)

CHINN, Trevor Edwin; CVO; s of Rosser Chinn, and Sarah *née* Feitelson; *b* 24 July 1935; *Educ* Clifton, King's Coll Cambridge; *m* 1965, Susan Avril, da of Louis Speelman; 2 s (David b 1966, Simon b 1969); *Career* Lex Serv plc: joined 1955, joined bd 1959, md 1968, chm and md 1973, chm and chief exec 1987; (memb governing cncl) Business in the Community 1983; memb ct of governors Royal Shakespeare Theatre, tstee and chm Friends of Duke of Edinburgh's Award Scheme 1978-88, memb Cncl Centre for Business Strategy London Business Sch, chief barker Variety Club of GB 1977 and 1978 (memb exec bd), memb cncl Prince's Youth Business Tst, vice-chm Great Ormond Street Hosp Redevpt Appeal; jt pres of the Joint Israel Appeal of GB; chm Br/Israel Public Affrs Ctee; Freeman: City of London, Worshipful Co of Painter-Stainers; *Recreations* fishing, scuba diving; *Clubs* RAC, Harvard Club of New York; *Style*— Trevor Chinn, Esq CVO; Lex Service plc, Lex House, 17 Connaught Place, London W2 2EL (☎ 01 723 1212, telex 23668 LEXGRP G, fax 01 723 5732)

CHINNERY, (Charles) Derek; s of Percy Herbert and Frances Dorothy Chinnery; *b* 27 April 1925; *Educ* Gosforth GS; *m* 1953, Doreen Grace Clarke; *Career* RAF trainee pilot 1943-47; jnr engr BBC 1941; studio mangr, producer, exec 1947, controller BBC Radio 1 1978-85; ret; *Style*— Derek Chinnery, Esq

CHIPP, David Allan; s of late Thomas Ford Chipp and late Isabel Mary Ballinger; *b* 6 June 1927; *Educ* Geelong GS, King's Coll Cambridge; *Career* served Middx Regt 1944-47; with Reuters 1950-68 (editor 1968); editor-in-chief The Press Assoc 1969-85; dir The Reuter Foundation; *Clubs* Garrick, Leander; *Style*— David Chipp, Esq; 2 Wilton Court, 59/60 Eccleston Square, London SW1V 1PH (☎ 01 834 5579)

CHIPPERFIELD, David Alan; s of Alan John Chipperfield, and Peggy *née* Singleton; *b* 18 Dec 1953; *Educ* Wellington Sch Somerset, Architectural Association (AA Dip); *m* (m dis), Susan Elizabeth, da of Leslie Hudson; 1 s (Chester); *Career* architect, principal Chipperfield Assocs, visiting lectr Harvard Univ 1986-87; designs for: Issey Miyake London, Japan 1986-87, Arnolfini Gallery Bristol 1987, private museum Tokyo 1987-; fndr and dir 9H Gallery London; AAdip RIBA; *Style*— David Chipperfield, Esq; 28 Cleveland Square, London W2 6DD (☎ 01 262 5238); Chipperfield Assocs, 26-28 Cramer Street, London W1M 3HE (☎ 01 486 1326, fax 01 486 1451)

CHIPPINDALE, Christopher Ralph; s of Keith Chippindale, and Ruth Chippindale; *b* 13 Oct 1951; *Educ* Sedbergh Sch, St John's Coll Cambridge (BA); *m* 1976, Anne, *née* Lowe; 2 s, 2 da; *Career* freelance ed: Penguin Books, Hutchinson Publishing Gp 1974-82; ed Antiquity 1987-; res fell in archaeology Girton Coll Cambridge 1985-87, asst curator Cambridge Univ Museum of Archeology and Anthropology 1987-; *Books* Stonehenge Complete (1983); *Recreations* archaeology, worrying; *Style*— Christopher Chippindale, Esq; 85 Hills Rd, Cambridge

CHIPPINDALE, Hon Mrs (Margaret Ruth); *née* Ritchie; da of 2 Baron Ritchie of Dundee (d 1948), and sis of 3, 4 and 5 Barons; *b* 13 Nov 1913; *m* 10 Sept 1943, Maj (William Arthur) Martin Chippindale, o child of Edgar John Chippindale (d 1937), of Flackley Ash, Peasmarsh, Sussex, and Hon Mary Cassandra, *née* Hill (d 1968, having been granted the title, rank and precedence of a baron's da which would have been hers had her father survived to succeed to the barony of Sandys); 1 s, 1 da; *Style*— The Hon Mrs Chippindale; Wintons, Peasmarsh, Rye, Sussex

CHISHOLM, Prof Alexander William John (Alec); s of Thomas Alexander Chisholm (d 1948), of Bryn Yr Efail Cwm Y Glo Gwynedd, and Maude Mary, *née* Robinson (d 1972); *b* 18 April 1922; *Educ* Brentwood Sch Essex, Northampton Poly, Manchester Coll of Sci and Technol, Royal Tech Coll Salford, Univ of London (BSc); *m* 29 March 1945, Aline Mary, da of Roy Eastwood; 1 s (Roger b 21 Oct 1951, 1 da (Diana b 4 June 1955); *Career* Nat Fire Service WWII; section 1 gp head res dept Met Vickers Electrical Co Ltd 1944-49, sr scientific offr (later princ scientific offr) Nat Engrg Laboratory 1949-57, UK scientific mission Br Embassy USA 1952-54, head of dept of mechanical engrg (later prof) Royal Coll of Advanced Technol Salford 1957-67, prof of mechanical engrg Salford Univ 1967-82, res prof (later professorial fell) Salford Univ 1982-; visitor engrg dept Cambridge Univ, visiting fell Wolfson Coll Cambridge 1973-74; chm Salford Univ Industl Centre Ltd 1976-82; chm: indust admin gp IMechE 1960-62, prodn engrg ctee Nat Cncl for Technol Awards (vice chm bd of studies in engrg, govr 1960-65), Engrg Profs Conf 1976-80; pres CIRP 1983-4 (hon memb 1987); memb technol ctee UGC 1969-74, memb of ct Cranfield Inst of Technol 1974-; numerous articles in tech and professional literature; FIMechE 1959, FIProdE 1963; *Recreations* hill walking, sailing; *Clubs* Athenaeum; *Style*— Prof Alec Chisholm; 12 Legh Road, Prestbury, Macclesfield, Cheshire SK10 4HX (☎ 0625 829 412); University of Salford, The Crescent, Salford M5 4WT (☎ 061 736 5843 ext 351, fax 061 745 7808, telex 668680 SULIB)

CHISHOLM, Hon Mrs (Annabel Jane); *née* Hennessy; da of 2 Baron Windlesham (d 1962); *b* 20 Dec 1937; *m* 4 May 1963, (Ian) Duncan Chisholm, MA, MB, MRCP, MRCPsych, DPM, o s of John Michael Chisholm (d 1946), of Westminster Gdns, SW1, and Nutley, Sussex; 4 s; *Style*— The Hon Mrs Chisholm; Bourton House, Flax Bourton, Somerset (☎ 2250)

CHISHOLM, Hon Mrs (Caroline Elizabeth); *née* Wyndham; da of 6 Baron Leconfield and (1) Egremont (d 1972), and Pamela Wyndham-Quin, gda of 5 Earl of Dunraven and Mountearl; *b* 23 Dec 1951; *m* 1976, Colin Chisholm, s of Archibald Hugh Tennent Chisholm, CBE, of 107 Hamilton Terrace, NW8; 2 s, 1 da; *Style*— The Hon Mrs Chisholm

CHISHOLM, Lady; Margaret Grace; *née* Brantom; da of J H Brantom; *m* 1, -- Crofton-Atkins; m 2, 1956, as his 3 wife, Sir Henry Chisholm, CBE, FCA, first chm Corby Devpt Corpn (d 20 July 1981); *Style*— Lady Chisholm; Scott's Grove House, Chobham, Woking, Surrey (☎ Chobham 8660)

CHISHOLM, Prof Michael Donald Inglis; s of Samuel Martin Chisholm (d 1985), of Norwich, and Alice Winfred, *née* Lee; *b* 10 June 1931; *Educ* St Christopher Sch Leicworth Herts, St Catherine's Coll Cambridge (MA); *m* 12 Sept 1959 (m dis 1981), Edith Gretchen Emma, da of Adolf Hoof (d 1984); 1 s (Andrew b 1966), 2 da (Annabel b 1960, Julia b 1962); m 2, 13 Dec 1987, Judith Carola, da of Henry Murray (d 1960); *Career* Nat Serv 1950-51, cmmnd 2 Lt 1950; dept demonstrations Inst for Agric Econ (Formerly Inst for Res in Agric Econs) 1954-59, lectr in geog Bedford Coll London 1962-64 (asst lectr 1960-62), visiting sr lectr in geog Univ of Ibadon Nigeria 1964-65, prof of econ and social goeg Univ of Bristol 1972-76 (lectr in geog 1965-, reader in econ geog 1967-72), prof of geog Univ of Cambridge 1976-, head of Dept of Geog Univ of Cambridge 1976-84; memb: SSRC 1967-72, Local Govt Boundary Cmmn for Eng 1971-78, Rural Devpt Cmmn 1981-; conservator for the River Cam 1979-; memb Inst Br Geographers 1954, RGS 1954; *Books* Rural Settlement and Land Use (1962), Modern World Devolopment (1982), Freight Flows and Spatial Aspects of the British Economy (jointly, 1973), The Changing Pattern of Employment (jointly, 1973), Inner City Waste Land (jointly 1987), Regional Forecasting (jointly ed 1971), Spatial Policy Problems of the British Economy (jt ed 1971); *Style*— Prof Michael Chisholm; University of Cambridge, Department of Geography, Downing Place, Cambridge CB2 3EN (☎ 333399, 333388, fax 0223 334748)

CHISM, Nigel William Michael Goddard; s of His Hon Judge Michael William McGladdery Chism, of Hong Kong, and May Elizabeth Collins, *née* Goddard; *b* 2 July 1954; *Educ* The John Lyon Sch Harrow, Poly of Central London; *m* Christine Pamela Chism, da of Eric Leonard Brown, of Berks; 1 s (William b 23 July 1982); *Career* TA 4 V Bn Royal Green Jackets 1972-75; CA, Arthur Young (formerly Josolyne Layton Bennett and Co) 1974-82, asst govt auditor Bermuda 1982-83; jt md Kingsway Rowland Ltd 1988- (chief accountant 1983-, fin dir 1985); memb ICEAW 1979; *Recreations* motoring and car restoration, travel, shooting, reading; *Style*— Nigel Chism, Esq; 98 Wakehurst Rd, London SW11 6BT (☎ 01 228 0226); Kingsway Rowland Ltd, 67-69 Whitfield St, London W1P 5RL (☎ 01 436 4060, fax 01 255 2131, telex 8953033)

CHISWELL, Maj-Gen Peter Irvine; CB (1985), CBE (1976, OBE 1972, MBE 1966); s of Col Henry Thomas Chiswell, OBE, late RAMC (d 1966), and Gladys Beatrice, *née* Mortimore; *b* 19 April 1930; *Educ* Allhallows, RMA Sandhurst; *m* 1958, Felicity Philippa, da of Roger Fenwick Martin (d 1970), of Esher Surrey; 2 s (Hugh, James); *Career* cmmnd Devonshire Regt 1951, served with 1 Devon in ME and Kenya during MauMau Campaign 1953-55, seconded to Para Regt 1955, served with 1 PARA Cyprus Emergency and Suez, adjutant 12/13 Bn Para Regt TA 1957-59, Instr Mons Offr Cadet Sch 1960, Student Army Staff Coll Camberley 1961, regimental duty 1 PARA Persian Gulf 1962-63, Dep Asst Adjutant Gen Berlin Infantry Bde 1963-65, regimental duty 3 Para Borneo Campaign 1965-66, Bde Maj 16 PARA Bde 1967; Lt Col 1968, memb Directing Staff Coll Camberley 1968; Cmdg Offr 3rd Bn The Para Regt 1969-71; Col 1971, Col Gen Staff Army Tning MOD 1971; Cdr Br Contingent UN Force Cyprus, Brig; Cdr 44 Para Bde (Vols) 1977-78, Asst Chief of Staff (Ops) HQ Northern Army Gp, Maj Gen; Cdr Land Forces NI 1982-83, GOC Wales 1984-85; ret; *Recreations* sailing, travel; *Style*— Maj-Gen Peter Chiswell, CB, CBE; c/o Lloyds Bank, 116 Victoria Rd, Aldershot, Hants

CHITNIS, Baron (Life Peer UK 1977); Pratap Chidamber Chitnis; s of late Chidamber N Chitnis, and Lucia Mallik; *b* 1 May 1936; *Educ* Penryn Sch, Stonyhurst, Univ of Birmingham, Univ of Kansas ; *m* 1964, Anne, da of Frank Mansell Brand; 1 s (decd); *Career* sits as ind peer in House of Lords, head of Liberal Pty Orgn 1966-69; chief exec Rowntree Soc Serv Tst 1974 (dir 1975-88); memb Community Relations Cmmn 1970-77, chm Br Refugee Cncl 1986-; author of ind reports on the elections in Zimbabwe 1979 and 1980, Guyana 1980, El Salvador 1982 and 1984 and 1988, and Nicaragua 1984; *Style*— The Lord Chitnis; House of Lords, London SW1A 0PW

CHITTENDEN, Keith Alan; s of Norman Jack Chittenden, of Uppingham, Rutland; *b* 26 Mar 1934; *Educ* Nottingham HS, Imp Coll London (BSc); *m* 1959, Sylvia June, da of Frederick Henry Wearing, of Dunmow; 1 s, 1 da; *Career* gen mangr Marconi Space and Defence Systems (Frimley) 1981-82; md Marconi Radar Systems (Chelmsford) 1982-; CEng; *Recreations* riding, golf, theatre; *Clubs* Royal Commonwealth Soc; *Style*— Keith Chittenden Esq; The Old Red Lion, Stebbing, Dunmow, Essex (☎ 037 186 272)

CHITTLEBURGH, Cdr Edward Hayden; MBE (1960); s of James Edward Chittleburgh, of Walton-on-Thames, Surrey, and Elsie Elizabeth (d 1981); *b* 25 July 1921; *Educ* Bedford Sch, Imp Coll (BSc Eng, DIC); *m* 3 July 1946, Winifred Margaret, da of Malcolm Myers (d 1950); 1 da (Julia b 1950); *Career* Cdr RN 1949-66; UNESCO Chief Technical Advsr, Kenya Poly, Nairobi 1966-73, Training Advsr, Chief Training Unit, World Bank 1973-80, Conslt 1980-; CEng, FIEE; *Recreations* golf, watching cricket; *Clubs* Army and Navy, MCC; *Style*— Cdr Edward Chittleburgh, RN (ret); The Mill House, Howsham, York (☎ 0653 81643); 35 Cranley Gdns, London SW7 (☎ 01 373 2941)

CHITTOCK, John Dudley; OBE (1982); s of James Hiram Chittock (d 1973), of Leytonstone, and Phyllis Lucy Milner (d 1985); *b* 29 May 1928; *Educ* Oxford and Elson House, Forestdene, SW Essex Technical Coll; *m* 1947, Joyce Kate, da of Roy Ayrton Winter (1969), of Kent; *Career* writer, film producer, publisher; exec ed Focal Press 1954-58; sr ptnr Films of Industry 1958-61, video and film columnist The Financial Times 1963-87, fndr chm Screen Digest 1971-; fndr The Grievson Tst 1974 (chm 1989-), deputy chm Br Screen Advsy Cncl 1986-; conslt ed Royal TV Soc Journal 1978-82; non-exec chm NVC Cable Ltd 1983-86, dir Nat Video Corp Ltd 1981-86; chm Screen Digest Ltd 1974-, prod and dir of over 30 documentary films; numerous books, articles, papers about films, TV, video; various chairmanships of film and TV indust ctees; Queens Silver Jubilee Medal 1977; *Recreations* period home and antiques, cooking, gardening, work, the arts; *Style*— John Chittock, Esq, OBE; The Old Vicarage, Wickhambrook, Suffolk (☎ 0440 820314); 37 Gower Street, London WC1E 6HH (☎ 01 580 2842)

CHITTOCK, Ronald Ernest; s of Reginald Ernest Chittock (d 1974), of London, and Clara Beatrice, *née* Jenkins; *b* 8 Feb 1931; *Educ* Borough Poly, Nat Coll; *m* 1, 1 Aug 1953 (m dis 1972), Betty, da of Erwin Short; 1 s (Barrie b 1956), 1 da (Diane b 1960); m 2, 16 Aug 1982, Irene Winifred, *née* Jackman; *Career* Nat Serv RN 1949-51; draughtsman Utilities London Ltd 1947-52, engr Troughton and Young (Heating) Ltd 1952-58, sr ptnr J E Greatorex and Ptnrs 1977-87 (ptnr 1958-76, ret 1987), freelance computer software mktg 1987-; author of various articles and papers on technical subjects; CEng, FIMechE, FCIBSE, MConsE, FRSA 1976; *Recreations* American automobiles, hi-fi, video, photography; *Style*— Ronald Chittock, Esq; St Martins, 68 Shelvers Way, Tadworth, Surrey KT20 5QF (☎ 0737 357086)

CHITTY, Andrew Edward Willes; s and h of Sir Thomas Chitty, 3 Bt; *b* 20 Nov 1953; *Style*— Andrew Chitty Esq

CHITTY, Dr Anthony; s of Ashley George Chitty (d 1980), of Surrey, and Doris Ellen Mary Buck; *b* 29 May 1931; *Educ* The Glyn GS Epsom, Imp Coll London BSc, PhD, DIC, CEng; *m* 1956, Audrey, da of Edward Charles Munro (d 1965); 2 s (Martin b 1958, David b 1962), 1 da (Claire b 1960); *Career* GEC Res Labs 1953-55; head Creep of Steels Lab ERA 1959-63, GEC Power Gp 1963-66, chief metallurgist CA Parsons 1966-73; dir: Advanced Technol Div Clarke Chapman-John Thompson 1973-78, Int Res and Devpt Co 1978-79; gen mangr engrg prods NEI Parsons 1979-84; regnl industl advsr DTI NE Regn 1984-88, dir Corporate Engrg Northern Engrg Industs 1989-; dep chm bd Newcastle Technol Centre 1985-88, chm bd Newcastle Technol Centre 1988-; visiting prof Univ of Aston 1977-84; *Style*— Dr Anthony Chitty; 1 Willow Way, Darras Hall, Ponteland, Newcastle Upon Tyne

CHITTY, Bernard Anthony; s of Edward Chitty (d 1970), of Broadstairs, Kent, and Anne Josephine, *née* Lowe; *b* 9 August 1951; *Educ* Chatham House County GS, Ramsgate, Univ of Reading (BA); *m* 20 Nov 1981, Vivienne Mandy, da of Mervyn Grant (d 1960), of Cardiff; 1 s (Jack b 1987), 1 da (Leanne b 1985); *Career* fin Coopers and Lybrand London 1974-77; Unilever: London 1978, Lagos Nigeria 1979, London 1980; fin controller PA Consulting Services Ltd 1980-86; dir: McAvoy Wreford Bayley Ltd 1986-, HR and H Consensus Res Int Ltd 1988-, Falcon Designs Ltd 1988-; gp co sec and asst gp fin dir The VPI Gp plc; memb of Eng Schoolboys Hockey XI 1969 (Capt 1970), memb Eng under 22 Hockey XI 1971 and 1972; FCA 1983; *Recreations* most sports, DIY, current affairs; *Clubs* Dulwich Hockey; *Style*— Bernard A Chitty, Esq; 36 Southwood Gardens, Hinchley Wood, Esher, Surrey, KT10 0DE (☎ 01 398 2292); 32 Grosvenor Gardens, London, SW1W 0DH (☎ 01 730 3456), fax 01 730 6663, telex 296 846 BIZOM G

CHITTY, (Thomas) David; s of Joseph Torrie Chitty (d 1952); *b* 4 Feb 1922; *Educ*

Haileybury, Glasgow Univ; *m* 1944, Patricia Pamela, da of Wing-Cdr Edward Leslie Magrath, MBE (d 1979); 1 da (Tessa); *Career* served WW II 1940-45, NW Europe (despatches), Capt Regular Commn RA 1945-52, Middle East 1949-52, ret 1952; Barclays Life Assurance Co Ltd (gen mangr 1974-82, dir 1977-82), Barclays Unicorn Ltd (dir 1977-82), Barclays Unicorn Group Ltd (dir 1977-82), ret 1982; *Recreations* golf; *Style*— David Chitty, Esq; Pippins, Mount Close, Hook Heath, Woking, Surrey GU22 0PZ (☎ 04862 63773)

CHITTY, Sir Thomas Willes; 3 Bt (UK 1924), of The Temple; s of Sir (Thomas) Henry Willes Chitty, 2 Bt (d 1955); *b* 2 Mar 1926; *Educ* Winchester, Univ Coll Oxford; *m* 23 Aug 1951, Susan Elspeth Russell (author), da of Rudolph Glossop; 1 s, 3 da; *Heir* s, Andrew Edward Willes Chitty b 20 Nov 1953; *Career* served RN 1944-47, Granada Arts fell Univ of York 1964-65, visiting prof Boston Univ 1969-70; novelist, biographer; *Style*— Sir Thomas Chitty, Bt; Bow Cottage, West Hoathly, Sussex

CHOLERTON, (Frederick) Arthur; CBE (1978); s of Frederick Arthur Cholerton (d 1968), of Stoke-on-Trent, and Charlotte, *née* Wagstaff (d 1968); *b* 15 April 1917; *Educ* Penkhull Sr Sch Stoke-on-Trent; *m* 25 Feb 1939, Ethel, da of late Albert Jackson, of Stoke-on-Trent; 1 s (Frederick Arthur b 1939, d 1940); *Career* footplate London Midland and Scotland Railway 1934, ret as engine driver from BR 1977; memb: W Mids Industl Devpt Assoc, W Mids Regnl Forum of Strategic Local Authorities, Stoke-on-Trent Postal Users Advsy Ctee; dir Keele Univ Sci Park Ltd; pres: Staffs Community Cncl, Staffs Forum of Voluntary Orgns; chm Staffs E Euro Constituency Lab pty; chm Staffs CC 1981- (memb 1973-, vice chm 1973-77, opposition ldr 1977-81), Lord Mayor Stoke-on-Trent 1971-72 (cncl memb 1951-87); Freedom of Accra (Ghana) 1988; M Univ (Keele) 1988; *Recreations* gardening, service with voluntary charitable organisations; *Style*— Arthur Cholerton, Esq, CBE; 12 Werburgh Drive, Trentham, Stoke-on-Trent, Staffs ST4 8JP (☎ 0782 657457); Staffordshire County Council, PO Box 11, County Buildings, Martin Street, Stafford, Staffs ST16 2LH (☎ 0785 223121, fax 0785 215153)

CHOLMELEY, Cecilia, Lady - Cecilia; da of William Henry Ellice, of Ewhurst Manor, Shermanbury, Horsham, Sussex; *m* 23 July 1931, Lt-Col Sir Hugh John Francis Sibthorp Cholmeley, 5 Bt, CB, DSO (d 1 Feb 1964); 1 s; *Style*— Cecilia, Lady Cholmeley; The Dower House, Easton, Grantham, Lincs

CHOLMELEY, Sir Montague John; 6 Bt (UK 1806), of Easton, Lincolnshire; s of Lt-Col Sir Hugh John Cholmeley, 5 Bt, CB, DSO (d 1964); *b* 27 Mar 1935; *Educ* Eton; *m* 18 Oct 1960, Juliet Auriol Sally, yr da of Maj-Gen Sir Eustace Nelson, KCVO, CB, DSO, OBE, MC, *qv*; 1 s, 2 da (Camilla b 1962, Davina b 1964); *Heir* s, Hugh John Frederick Sebastian Cholmeley b 3 Jan 1968; *Career* Grenadier Gds 1954-64; *Style*— Sir Montague Cholmeley, Bt; Church Farm, Burton le Coggles, Grantham, Lincs (☎ Corby Glen 329); Easton Hall, Grantham

CHOLMONDELEY, Lady Aline Caroline; da of 5 Marquess of Cholmondeley, GCVO (d 1968); *b* 5 Oct 1916; *Style*— Lady Aline Cholmondeley; Flat 5, 6 Strathearn Place, London W2 (☎ 01 723 6494)

CHOLMONDELEY, 6 Marquess of (UK 1815) George Hugh; Bt (I 1611), GCVO (1977), MC (1943), DL (Chester 1955); also Viscount Cholmondeley of Kells (I 1661), Baron Cholmondeley of Namptwich (E 1689), Viscount Malpas and Earl of Cholmondeley (GB 1706), Baron Newborough (I 1715), Baron Newburgh (GB 1716), and Earl of Rocksavage (UK 1815); s of 5 Marquess of Cholmondeley, GCVO (d 1968), and Sybil, da of Sir Edward Sassoon, 2 Bt, by his w Aline, da of Baron Gustave de Rothschild; *b* 24 April 1919; *Educ* Eton, Magdalene Coll Cambridge; *m* 14 June 1947, Lavinia Margaret, da of Col John Leslie, DSO, MC; 1 s, 3 da; *Heir* s, Earl of Rocksavage, *qv*; *Career* 1 Royal Dragoons Middle East, Italy, France, Germany 1939-45, ret Hon Maj Grenadier Guards 1949, Joint Hereditary Lord Great Chamberlain of England 1966-; *Clubs* Turf; *Style*— The Most Hon the Marquess of Cholmondeley, GCVO, MC, DL; Cholmondeley Castle, Malpas, Cheshire (☎ 082 922 202); Houghton Hall, King's Lynn, Norfolk

CHOLMONDELEY, Lady Rose Aline; eldest da of 6 Marq of Cholmondeley, GCVO, MC; *b* 20 Mar 1948; *Style*— Lady Rose Cholmondeley

CHOLMONDELEY, Dowager Marchioness of; Sybil Rachel Betty Cecile; CBE (1946), Legion of Honour (officier) (1985); da of Sir Edward Albert Sassoon, 2 Bt (d 1912); *b* 30 Jan 1894; *m* 6 Aug 1913, 5 Marquess of Cholmondeley, GCVO (d 1968); 2 s, 1 da; *Career* asst princ WRNS MIT 1914-18, supt WRNS 1939-45; *Style*— The Most Hon the Dowager Marchioness of Cholmondeley, CBE; 36 Eaton Sq, London SW1; Houghton Hall, King's Lynn, Norfolk

CHOLMONDELEY CLARKE, Marshal Butler; s of Maj Cecil Cholmondeley Clarke (d 1924), of Holycross, Co Tipperary, and late Fanny Ethel Carter; *b* 14 July 1919; *Educ* Aldenham; *m* 1947, Joan Roberta, da of late John Kyle Stephens, JP, of Holywood, Co Down; 2 s (Edward, Robert); *Career* slr 1943, ptnr Burton Yeates and Hart slrs 1946-72; pres City of Westminster Law Soc 1971-72, memb Cncl of Law Soc 1966-72; chm: Family Law Ctee 1970-72, Legal Aid Ctee 1972, Chancery Procedure Ctee 1968-72; master of the Supreme Ct of Judicature (Chancery Div) 1973-; ecclesiastical examiner Dioc of London; tstee Utd Law Clerks' Soc; memb cncl Inc Soc The Church Lads and Girls Bde; ed of The Supreme Ct Practice; *Recreations* reading; *Clubs* Turf; *Style*— Marshal Cholmondeley Clarke, Esq; 16 Cheyne Ct, Flood St, London SW3 5TP; Royal Cts of Justice, Strand, London

CHONG, Monica; da of Philip Chong (d 1981), and Margaret, *née* Lau; *b* 16 Jan 1958; *Educ* Maryknoll Sisters Sch Hong Kong, St Catherines Sch Sydney, Chelsea Sch of Art (BA); *Career* PA to Bridget Jacquetty 1977-78, first collection under own label 1978-79, exhibited London Designers Collections 1980-, Tricouille 1983-86; design conslt: Br Caledonian Airways 1985, BUPA 1986, Nat Hosp Nervous Diseases 1988; A Barbie Retrospective Exhibition Paris 1986, judged fashion design competition Portugal on invitation of Portuguese Govt 1987; collections exhibited: City of London presents Br Fashion in Aid of Action Res for Crippled Children 1988, The Clothes Show (BBC 1) 1988; career featured on Orient Express (Channel 4) 1986; *Recreations* collecting antique jewellery and art; *Style*— Ms Monica Chong; 51 Brompton Rd, 3rd Floor, London SW3 (☎ 01 581 9952, fax 01 581 3529, telex 8951859)

CHOPE, Christopher Robert; OBE (1983), MP (Cons Southampton, Itchen 1983-); s of His Hon Judge Robert Charles Chope (d 1988), and Pamela, *née* Durell; *b* 19 May 1947; *Educ* Marlborough, Univ of St Andrews (LLB); *m* Christine, *née* Hutchinson; *Career* barr; ldr Wandsworth Borough Cncl 1979-83 (memb 1974-83), parly under sec of state DOE 1986-; *Style*— Christopher Chope, Esq, OBE, MP; House of Commons, London SW1

CHORLEY, Richard Abdiel; VRD (1964); s of William Samuel Chorley (d 1971) of Bowdon, Cheshire and Grace Caroline Emma, *née* Moss (d 1982); *b* 4 Jan 1923; *Educ* Altrincham GS, Univ of Manchester (BScTech); *m* 26 July 1948, (Kathleen) Joanna, da of Gp-Capt Alfred Hugh Stradling, DSO, of Willingdon, Sussex; 1 s (Simon b 1953), 2 da (Susan b 1951, Alison b 1955); *Career* RNVR Electrical Sub-Lt 1944-46, Lt 1949-57, Lt-Cdr 1957-58; RNR Lt-Cdr 1958-64, res engr Metro Vickers Electrical Co 1947-51, asst chief electrical engr Br Messier Ltd 1951-55, res gp mangr Smiths Industs Aerospace & Def Systems Ltd 1955-84, memb Alvey Directorate Dept of Trade and Indust 1984-86; chm: Tewkesbury and Dist Choral Soc, Gloucs Organists' Assoc, Musica Vera Cheltenham; asst organist Tewkesbury Abbey; MIEE 1951; *Recreations* music, walking, swimming; *Style*— Richard Chorley, Esq; Monastery Cottage, Abbey Precinct, Tewkesbury, Gloucs GL20 5SR (☎ 0684 293 063)

CHORLEY, 2 Baron (UK 1945); Roger Richard Edward Chorley; s of 1 Baron Chorley, QC (d 1978); *b* 14 August 1930; *Educ* Stowe, Gonville and Caius Coll Cambridge (BA); *m* 31 Oct 1964, Ann Elizabeth, yr da of late Archibald Scott Debenham, of Ingatestone, Essex; 2 s (Hon Nicholas Rupert, Hon Christopher Robert Hopkinson b 1968); *Heir* s, Hon Nicholas Rupert Chorley b 15 July 1966; *Career* memb: Ordnance Survey Advsy Bd 1982- board British Cncl 1981-; partner Coopers and Lybrand (CA) 1967-, FCA; *Style*— The Rt Hon the Lord Chorley; House of Lords, London SW1

CHOULARTON, Stephen Derek; s of Cyril Choularton; *b* 29 Mar 1949; *Educ* Monte Rosa Montreux; *m* 1982, Elizabeth, *née* Taylor; 1 s; *Career* banker, William Deacons Bank Ltd 1965, Henry Cooke and Son 1968, md C P Choularton Sons and Ptnrs Ltd (dir 1970-83), chm Choularton plc; *Style*— Stephen Choularton, Esq; 24 Clavendon Gdns, London W9 1AZ (☎ 01 283 7671)

CHOYCE, Prof (David) Peter; s of Prof Charles Coley Choyce, CMG, CBE (Col RAMC WWI d 1937), and Gwendolen Alice *née* Dobbing (d 1957); *b* 1 Mar 1919; *Educ* Stowe, UCL (BSc, MB BS), UCH (MS), Moorfields Eye Hosp and Inst of Opthalmology London; *m* 3 Sept 1949, Diana, da of Thomas Nadin (d 1978), of Leigh on Sea; 3 s (Jonathan b 1951, David Gregory b 1955, Matthew Quentin b 1963); *Career* med offr HM Tp Tports 1942-46; served N and S Atlantic, Caribbean, Med, Indian Ocean; world authy on: intraocular lenses and implants, refractive surgery; recognised authy on tropical opthalmology; Hunterian Prof RCS; hon memb: Henry Ford Hosp Detroit, Int Intraocular Inplant Club, American UK Japanese and Yugoslav Implant socs; involved with Southend on Sea gp hosps 1953-84; Palealogus Award Kerato Refractive Soc 1986; Liveryman Worshipful Co Apothecaries; FRSM 1942, FRCS 1947, FCOPHTH 1988; *Books* Intra-Ocular Lenses and Implants (1964); *Recreations* golf, history, food and wine, the opposite sex; *Clubs* Rochford Hundred GC, Moor Park GC; *Style*— Prof Peter Choyce; 9 Drake Road, Westcliff on Sea, Essex (☎ 0702 343 810); 45 Wimpole St, London WIM 7DG (☎ 01 935 3411); Vila Colunata, Praia da Luz, Algarve, Portugal

CHRISTIAN, Hon Mrs (Margaret Anne); *née* Mackay; da of 13 Lord Reay; *b* 13 Mar 1941; *m* 1976, Allen Leslie Christian, of Chicago and Florida; *Style*— The Hon Mrs Christian; Buttonwood Bay AA8, Key Largo, Florida, USA; Upper Huntlywood, Earlston, Berwickshire

CHRISTIAN, Nigel Robin Gladwyn; s of Geoffrey Gladwyn Christian (d 1960), of 9 Cadogan Sq, London SW1, and Patricia Wynne Cavendish, *née* Shelly (d 1988); *b* 4 August 1942; *Educ* Harcourt Sch and Cranleigh; *m* 22 Jul 1972, Susan Anne Leila, da of Col Robert de Lisle King, CBE, of Amsterdam Cottage, Inkpen, nr Hungerford, Berks; 2 s (Alexander b 1974, Edward b 1981), 1 da (Annabel b 1977); *Career* with Price Forbes 1960-61, Lambert Bros 1962-64; dir Leslie & Godwin Ltd 1987- (asst dir 1972, joined 1964; dir Leslie & Godwin Aviation Ltd 1980); *Recreations* gardening, golf, tennis, sailing, skiing; *Clubs* Rye Golf; *Style*— N R G Christian, Esq; Leslie and Godwin, PO Box 219, 6 Braham St, London E1 8ED (☎ 01 480 7200, fax 01 480 7450, telex 8950221 CORPO G)

CHRISTIE, Campbell; s of Thomas Christie (d 1944), and Johnina, *née* Rolling (d 1965); *b* 23 August 1937; *Educ* Albert Senior Secdy Sch Glasgow, Langside Coll Glasgow, Woolwich Poly London; *m* 2 Feb 1963, Elizabeth Brown, da of Alexander Cameron (d 1968); 2 s (Andrew Cameron b 1963, Douglas Campbell b 1965); *Career* RN 1956-58; with Civil Serv 1954-72, Admiralty 1954-59, DHSS 1959- 72; with Soc of Civil and Public Servants 1972-85 (dep gen sec (1975-85), gen sec Scottish Trades Union Congress 1986-; bd memb: Wildcat Theatre Co, Scottish Nat Orchestra, Theatre Royal Opera, Lothian Enterprise Bd; memb: EEC Economic and Social Ctee, Scottish Economic Cncl, NEDC EDC for Electronic Industs; *Recreations* golf; *Clubs* Glenbeevir Golf; *Style*— Campbell Christie, Esq; 31 Dumyat Drive, Falkirk FK1 5PA (☎ 0324 24555); 16 Woodlands Terrace, Glasgow G5 (☎ 041 332 4946)

CHRISTIE, Sir George William Langham; DL (E Sussex 1983); s of John Christie, CH, MC (d 1962), and Audrey, *née* Mildmay (d 1953); *b* 31 Dec 1934; *Educ* Eton, Trinty Coll Cambridge; *m* 8 Aug 1958, (Patricia) Mary, da of late Ivor Percy Nicholson, and step da of Cdr Alan McGaw; 3 s (Hector b 1961, Augustus b 1963, Ptolemy (Tolly) b 1971), 1 da (Louise b 1966); *Career* exec chm Glyndebourne Productions Ltd 1956-89; fndr chm London Sinfonietta 1958; Cavaliere al Merito della Republica Italiana; kt 1984; *Style*— Sir George Christie, DL; Glyndebourne, Lewes, E Sussex BN8 5UU (☎ 0273 812321, fax 0273 812783, telex 877862 GLYOP G)

CHRISTIE, Prof Ian Ralph; s of John Reid Christie (d 1948), and Gladys Lillian, *née* Whatley (d 1987); *b* 11 May 1919; *Educ* Royal GS Worcester, Magdalen Coll Oxford (BA, MA); *Career* RAF Equipment Branch 1940-46, cmmnd 1942; Foreign Serv: W Africa 1943-44, India 1945-46; univ teacher; UCL: asst lectr History 1948, lectr 1951, reader 1960, prof Modern Br History 1966, dean of arts 1971-73, chm History Dept 1975-79, astor prof of Br History 1979-84; memb Ed Bd of The History of Parl Tst 1973-; FRHistS: literary dir 1964-70, cncl memb 1970-74; FBA 1977, FRHistS; *Books* The End of North's Ministry 1780-82 (1958), Wilkes, Wyvill and Reform (jtly with Lucy M Brown 1962), Bibliography of British History 1789-1851 (1977), Wars and Revolutions, Britain 1760-1815 (1982), Stress and Stability in Late Eighteenth-Century Britain (1984); *Style*— Prof Ian Christie; 109 Green Lane, Croxley Green, Herts WD3 3HR (☎ 0923 773008)

CHRISTIE, Lady Jean Agatha; *née* Dundas; yst da of 2 Marquess of Zetland; *b* 4 May 1916; *m* 2 Sept 1939, Capt Hector Lorenzo Christie, MBE (d 18 Oct 1969), o s of William Lorenzo Christie, JP, of Jervaulx Abbey; 1 s, 1 da; *Style*— Lady Jean Christie; Seven Springs, Upper Lambourn, Berks

CHRISTIE, John Belford Wilson; CBE (1981); s of John Aitken Christie (d 1928), and Mary, *née* Belford (d 1932); *b* 4 May 1914; *Educ* Merchiston Castle Sch, St John's Coll Cambridge (BA), Univ of Edinburgh (LLB); *m* 14 Sept 1939, Christine Isobel Syme, da of Rev John Thomas Arnott (d 1920); 4 da (Jennifer b 1940, Catrine (Mrs Waller) b 1942, Ann (Mrs Henry) b 1943, Francesca (Mrs Dawson) b 1955); *Career* WWII RNVR, Active Serv 1939-46, asst sec to Flying Offr Levant and E Med 1945; admitted Faculty of Advocates 1939, sheriff-subst Western Div Dumfries and Galloway 1948-55, sheriff Tayside Central and Fife (formerly Perth and Angus of Dundee) 1955-83; memb Queens Coll Cncl Univ of St Andrews 1960-67, memb Univ Ct Univ of Dundee 1967-75, hon lectr Dept of Private Law Univ of Dundee; memb Parole Bd for Scot 1967-73; Univ of Dundee LLd 1977; Knight of the Order of the Holy Sepulchre of Jerusalem 1988; *Recreations* golf; *Clubs* New (Edinburgh), Royal and Ancient (St Andrews); *Style*— John Christie, Esq, CBE; Annsmuir Farm, Ladybank, Fife (☎ 0337 304 80)

CHRISTIE, John Rankin; CB (1978); s of Robert Christie (d 1940), of Co Antrim, and Georgina, *née* Rankin (d 1934); *b* 5 Jan 1918; *Educ* Ormskirk GS, LSE; *m* 1941, Constance May, da of Henry Gracie (d 1939), of Rotherham; 1 s (Antony), 2 da (Alison, Hilary); *Career* entered CS 1936, War Off, served 1939-45 War as Capt RA, served in UK and India 1943-47, Miny of Supply 1947, Air Miny 1954, princ private sec to Mins of Supply 1955-57, asst sec 1957, Br Def Staffs Washington 1962-65, under-sec Min of Aviation 1965-67, Min of Technol 1967-70, Min of Aviation Supply 1970-71, asst under-sec of State MOD 1971-74; dep master and controller of Royal Mint 1974-77; *Recreations* travel, bird-watching; *Style*— John R Christie Esq, CB; Twitten Cottage, East Hill, Oxted, Surrey (☎ 088 33 3047)

CHRISTIE, Michael Alexander Hunter Christie; s of Alexander John Christie (d 1969), and Marjorie Jane Moore-Bayley b 1969; gf John Alexander Christie one of founding dirs of Midland Bank; unc Gp Capt M G Christie was very first Air Attaché in Washington and later in Berlin; *b* 31 Dec 1918; *Educ* Lickey Hills Sch, Malvern; *m* 1939, Pamela Mary (d 1987), da of Edward Frank du Sautoy, OBE, TD, DL (d 1962); 1 s (Timothy John Alexander b 1943), 1 da (Penelope Jane b 1942 d 1979); m 2 1988, Audrey Margaret Georgina, da of Cdr Murray Gordon Edwards (d 1961); *Career* Birmingham Stock Exchange 1936-39; RAFVR, dir Miny of Aircraft Prodn Film Unit 1943-45; sales dir Christie Tyler Ltd 1946-53, md/chm Alexander Engineering Co Ltd 1946-; motor racing success: runner-up British Hillclimb Championship 1953-57; *Clubs* British Racing Drivers, Royal London Yacht, Seaview Yacht, Island Sailing; *Style*— Michael Christie, Esq; Elmwood House, Ludgeshall, Bucks HP18 9WT (☎ 0844 238113); Alexander Engineering Co Ltd, Haddenham, Aylesbury, Bucks HP17 8BZ (☎ 0844 291345, telex 83504, fax 0844 291320)

CHRISTIE, Nigel Bryan; s of Wing Cdr George Edward Bryan Christie (d 1961), and Hilda Nevyth Sheila, *née* Warr; *b* 30 Dec 1948; *Educ* Trinity Coll Glenalmond, St Andrew's Univ (MA), Harvard Sch of Business Admin; *m* 1974, Catriona Rowena Beveridge, da of Capt Robert Ronald Beveridge Mackenzie; 2 s (Roderick b 1977, Gavin b 1979); *Career* dir: S G Warburg and Co Ltd, S G Warburg and Co Inc; FCA; *Recreations* golf, tennis, skiing; *Clubs* Royal and Ancient Golf, Hurlingham, Racquet (New York); *Style*— Nigel Christie, Esq; 19 Kenilworth Terrace, Greenwich, Connecticut 06830, USA (☎ 0101 203 622 8645); S G Warburg and Co Inc, 787 7th Avenue, New York, NY 10019 (☎ 0101 212 459 7000)

CHRISTIE, Mrs M J G; Philippa; *see*: Pearce, Miss Philippa

CHRISTIE, Dr Socrates Panteles; s of Pantele Christie, and Olga *née* Hellenas; *b* 26 Jan 1920; *Educ* Univ of Athens (Dip), Univ of London (BSc, PhD); *m* 1950, Erasmia, da of Sir R Stakis; 1 s (John Alexander), 4 da (Katrina Olga, Daphne Anastasia, Pandora Elisa, Latona Flora Anna); *Career* site engr Errochty Hydroelectric Scheme 1948-49, design and site engr Scottish Orlit 1949-50, sr civil/structural engr Br London Midland Region 1950-51, Ove Arup and Ptnrs and Richard Costain 1950-55, fndr SP Christie and Ptnrs (princ ptnr) 1950-, lectr in engrg Univ Coll London 1955-80; fndr of the Co of constuctors (former master) memb of the Company of Paviors; FICE, FISTtructE, MConsE, FFB, FIArb, MINSTHE, MSocCE, FRSA; St Andrews Cross of the Greek Orthodox Patriarch in Constantinople; *Recreations* fishing, gardening; *Clubs* St Stephens and Constitutional; *Style*— Dr Socrates Christie; 23 Bloomsbury Sq, London, WC1A 2PJ (☎ 01 636 3867, fax 01 631 0309, car tel 214999/371810, telex 23249 CRICON G)

CHRISTIE, Timothy John Alexander; s of Michael Alexander Hunter Christie, and Pamela Mary, *née* Du Sautoy (d 1987); *b* 2 June 1943; *Educ* Radley, London Business Sch; *m* 27 Jan 1966, Annabelle Bronson, da of Sir Donald Albery (d 1988); 3 s (Oliver b 1971, Nicholas b 1973, William b 1977); *Career* mktg exec London Press Exchange Ltd 1963-64, mkt res exec Honda (UK) Ltd 1964-65, account exec London Press Exchange Ltd 1966-67, account rep J Walter Thompson Co Ltd 1968-71; ALexander Engrg Co Ltd: mktg mangr 1971-75, mktg dir 1976-81, md 1981-; Freeman City of London 1968, Liveryman Coach makers and Coach Harness Makers 1968; *Recreations* sailing, tennis, skiing; *Clubs* Seaview Yacht; *Style*— Timothy Christie, Esq; Alexander Engrg Co Ltd, Haddenham, Bucks HP17 8BZ (☎ 0844 291 345, fax 0844 291 320, telex 83504)

CHRISTIE, Hon Sir Vernon Howard Colville; s of C Christie, of Sydney; *b* 17 Dec 1909; *m* 1936, Joyce, *née* Hamlin; 1 s, 2 da; *Career* memb Legislative Assembly (Lib) Ivanhoe Victoria Australia 1955-73, speaker 1967-73; dir: Aust Elizabethan Theatre Trust 1969-78, Aust Ballet Fndn, Qld Ballet; AASA, FCIS, AFAIM; kt 1972; *Recreations* bowls, sailing, music ballet and the arts, conservation, fly fishing; *Style*— The Hon Sir Vernon Christie; Gray St, Redlands Bay, Queensland 4165, Australia

CHRISTIE, Sir William; MBE (1970), JP (Belfast 1951), DL (Belfast 1977); s of Richard and Ellen Christie, of Belfast; *b* 1 June 1913; *Educ* Ward Sch Bangor N Ireland; *m* 1935, Selina, *née* Pattison; 1 s (and 1 s decd), 2 da; *Career* High Sheriff Belfast 1964-65, Lord Mayor 1972-75 (Dep Mayor 1969), alderman 1973-77; co dir; kt 1975; *Style*— Sir William Christie, MBE, JP, DL

CHRISTIE, (Eric) William Hunter; s of Harold Alfred Hunter Christie, QC, TD, tres Lincoln's Inn (d 1960), and Norah Agnes Veronica, *née* Brooks (d 1965); gs of Sir William Christie, FRS, Astronomer Royal (by his w Violette, 3 da of Sir Alfred Hickman, 1 Bt, MP), ggs of Prof Samuel Hunter Christie, and gggs of James Christie (b 1739), of Leicester Sq (collateral of Christie of Durie); *b* 18 August 1922; *Educ* Marlborough, RMA Sandhurst; *m* 20 May 1950, Dorothy Ursula Merle, da of Roderick Macleod, of Pippins Toft, Angmering, Sussex (d 1947); 2 s (Robert b 1951, Nial b 1960), 2 da (Fiona b 1956, Catriona b 1968); *Career* Lt Coldstream Gds 1941-43 (wounded); FO: S American Dept 1944-46, 3rd sec Br Embassy Buenos Aires 1946-48; Scott Polar Research Inst, Camb 1948-50, barr Lincoln's Inn 1952; bencher 1989; memb: cncl Inland Waterways 1950-52 (hon life memb 1968), Chelsea Metropolitan Borough Cncl 1956-65 and chm Ctees of Cncl; hon sec UK Falkland Is Ctee 1968-76, chm Falkland Is Research and Dvpt Assocn Ltd (The Falkland Is Off) 1976-83, chm S Atlantic Fisheries Ctee 1977-82, Falkland Is Assocn 1983-85; memb of Ct of Worshipful Co of Clockmakers 1968 (Master 1979), pres Br Horological Inst 1979, pres Nat Clock and Watchmakers Benevolent Soc 1979 (the first occasion that one person has held all 3 offs simultaneously); FBHI; *Books* The Antarctic Problem: An Historical and Political Study (1950), Portrait of Trent in Collection Portraits of Rivers by Dennis Dobson (1953); contributor to legal and specialist publications; *Recreations* country life; *Clubs* Flyfishers'; *Style*— William Christie, Esq; 13 Old Sq, Lincoln's Inn, London WC2A 3UA (☎ 01 404 4800, telex 22487 INNLAW G, fax Gps 2 and 3 01 405 4267)

CHRISTIE-MILLER, Andrew William Michael; o s of Maj Samuel Vandeleur Christie-Miller, CBE (d 1968), of Clarendon Park, Salisbury, and Esmée Antoinette Fraser, *née* Hutcheson; *see* Burke's Landed Gentry, 18 edn, vol II, 1969; *b* 22 Sept 1950; *Educ* Eton, RAC Cirencester (Dip Rural Estate Management, Dip Advanced Farm Management); *m* 6 Feb 1976, Barbara, da of Maj Charles Alexander Neil (d 1959), of 18 Lansdowne Road, London W11; 1 s (Alexander William Henry b 1982), 2 da (Rebecca Claire b 1976, Victoria Phoebe b 1978); *Career* with Spicer & Pegler 1970-73, Savills 1978-82; memb CLA exec; dep chm Timber Growers United Kingdom (TGUK); memb Wilts CC 1985-; ARICS 1979; *Recreations* shooting, travel, bicycling, conservation; *Clubs* White's, New (Edinburgh); *Style*— Andrew Christie-Miller, Esq;; Clarendon Park, Salisbury, Wilts SP5 3EP (☎ 0722 710217); Estate Office, Clarendon Park, Salisbury, Wilts SP5 3EW (☎ 0722 710233); car ☎ 0836 740220

CHRISTIE-MILLER, Lt-Col John Aylmer; CBE (1960, OBE 1944), TD (1946), DL (Cheshire 1963); s of Sir Geoffry Christie-Miller (d 1969), of Cheshire, and Kathleen Olive, *née* Thorpe (d 1965); *b* 12 August 1911; *Educ* Eton; *m* 28 Oct 1939, Bridget Wilbraham, da of Cdr Noel Wilbraham Dixon, OBE, RN (d 1960), of Cheshire; 3 da (Caroline (Mrs Cannon-Brookes) b 1942, Lydia (Mrs McClure) b 1947, Charlotte (Mrs Beatson) b 1949); *Career* co dir; mil serv; Lt-Col Cheshire Regt, W Desert, N Africa, Sicily, Italy, Germany 1939-45; dir: Christy and Co Ltd 1935-80, Swain and Co Ltd 1946-79, chm Cheshire T and A F Assoc 1965-68, High Sheriff 1974-75, JP 1949-74; pres Br Felt Hat Manufacturers Fed 1950-51, Master Worshipful Co of Feltmakers 1956-57, pres European Assoc of Hat Manufacturers 1957-64, pres Stockport and Dist TSB 1969-75; *Recreations* travel, gardening; *Clubs* Army and Navy; *Style*— Lt-Col Christie-Miller, CBE, TD, DL; Manor House, Bourton-on-the-Hill, Moreton-in-Marsh, Glos GL56 9AQ (☎ 0386 700642)

CHRISTIE-MURRAY, David Hugh Arthur; s of Dudley Christie-Murray (d 1921), and Mirian Violet Hume (d 1969); ggs of Gen Sir Hugh Rowlands, VC, KCB; *b* 12 July 1913; *Educ* St Lawrence Coll Ramsgate, UCL (Dip in Journalism), St Peter's Coll Oxford (BA, MA); *m* 1, 11 July 1942, Ena Louise Elisabeth, da of Edward Rainsford Mumford (d 1954), of Croydon; 3 da (Anne b 1946, Alison b 1951, Susan b 1952), 1 adopted s (Martin b 1949); m 2, 15 April 1972, Sheila Mary, da of Joseph Herbert Watson, of London; 2 step da (Karen b 1964, Laura b 1967); *Career* journalist 1934-37, schoolmaster 1937-38, ordained in Anglican Church 1942, youth organiser Diocese of Rochester 1942-46, asst master and asst to chaplain Harrow Sch 1946-67, associate prof Clarion State Coll Pennsylvania 1967-68 resigned Holy Orders 1968; asst master Harrow Sch 1968-73; currently author; *Books* Heraldry in the Churches of Beckenham (1954), Armorial Bearings of British Schools (1966), Illustrated Children's Bible (1974), Voices from the Gods; Speaking with Tongues (1978), A History of Heresy (1980), Reincarnation: Ancient Beliefs and Modern Evidence (1981); *Recreations* psychical research, genealogy, heraldry, philately, walking; *Clubs* Surrey Walking; *Style*— David Christie-Murray, Esq; Imber Court Cottage, Orchard Lane, East Molesey, Surrey KT8 0BN (☎ 01 398 2381)

CHRISTISON, Gen Sir (Alexander Frank) Philip; 4 Bt (UK 1871), of Moray Place, Edinburgh, GBE (1948, KBE 1944), CB (1943), DSO (1945), MC and Bar (1915, 1917), DL (Roxburghshire 1956); s of Surgn-Gen Sir Alexander Christison, 2 Bt (d 1918); suc half-bro, 3 Bt 1945; *b* 17 Nov 1893; *Educ* Edinburgh Acad, Univ Coll Oxford (BA); *m* 1, 29 Feb 1916, Lizzie Isobel (d 1974), da of Rt Rev Anthony Mitchell, Bishop of Aberdeen and Orkney (d 1917); 1 s (ka Burma 1942), 2 da (and 1 decd); m 2, 1974, Jessie Vida Wallace Smith, MBE; *Heir* none; *Career* 2 Lt Cameron Highlanders 1914, cmd 6 Seaforth Highlanders 1918-19, Lt-Col Duke of Wellington's Regt 1937 (Col 1947-57), cmd Gurkha Bde 1938,Cmdt Staff Coll 1940, Brig Gen Staff 1941, cmd 15 (Scottish) Div 1941-43, Burma Campaign 1943-45, cmd 15 Corps, 14 army and Allied Land Forces South East Asia, cmd Netherland E Indies Campaign 1945-46, Gen 1947, Col 10 (Princess Mary's Own) Gurkha Rifles 1947-57, ADC Gen to HM The King 1947-49, GOC-in-C Northern Cmd 1946-47, GOC in C Scottish Cmd and Gov Edinburgh Castle 1947-49; Hon Col Coast Regt RA 1950-57; dir Cochran and Co Ltd 1950-70, chm Alban Timber Ltd 1953-79; memb Nat Cncl BBC 1965-69; fruit farmer and ornithologist; hon fell Univ Coll Oxford; *Books* Birds of Baluchistan; *Recreations* field sports, ornithology; *Clubs* New (Edinburgh); *Style*— Gen Sir Philip Christison, Bt, GBE, CB, DSO, MC, DL; The Croft, Melrose, Roxburghshire (☎ 089 682 2456)

CHRISTOFAS, Sir Kenneth Cavendish; KCMG (1982, CMG 1969), MBE (1944); o s of late Edward Julius Goodwin (d 1921), and Lillian Christofas, step s of late Alexander Christofas; *b* 18 August 1917; *Educ* Merchant Taylors', UCL; *m* 1948, Jessica Laura, da of Thomas Sparshott (d 1953); 2 da; *Career* War Service 1939-46 (Lt-Col); joined Foreign Service 1948, min and dep head UK Delegation to the European Communities 1969-72; dir-gen Secretariat of Council of Ministers of the European Communities 1973-82, hon dir-gen 1982-; *Recreations* railways, music; *Clubs* East India, Devonshire, Sports and Public Schs; *Style*— Sir Kenneth Christofas, KCMG, MBE; 3 The Ridge, Bolsover Rd, Eastbourne, Sussex BN20 7JE (☎ 0323 22384)

CHRISTOPHER, (Phyllis) Ann; da of William Christopher (d 1986) of Rickmansworth, Herts, and Phyllis *née* Vennal; *b* 4 Dec 1947; *Educ* Watford Girls GS, Harrow Sch of Art, W of Eng Coll of Art (Dip Art and Design); *m* 19 July 1969, Kenneth Harold Cook, s of Harold Gilbert Cook, of Oldland Common, Nr Bristol; *Career* sculptor; numerous gp and solo exhibitions 1969-, works in public collections incl: Bristol City Art Gallery, Bristol Univ, Glynn Vivienne Art Gallery Swansea, Royal W of Eng Acad, Chantrey Bequest Royal Acad, Harrison Weir Collection London;

RWA 1983 (assoc 1972), ARA 1980; *Recreations* cinema, travel, architecture, gardens; *Style*— Miss Ann Christopher

CHRISTOPHER, Anthony Martin Grosvenor; CBE (1984); s of George Russell Christopher (d 1951), and Helen Kathleen Milford, *née* Rowley (d 1971); *b* 25 April 1925; *Educ* Cheltenham GS, Westminster Coll of Commerce; *m* 1962, Adela Joy Thompson; *Career* asst sec IRSF 1957-60 (asst gen sec 1960-74, jt gen sec 1975); dir Civil Serv Bldg Soc 1958-87, pres TUC 1988-89 (chm 1978); memb: bd Civil Serv Housing Assoc 1958 (vice-chm 1988), cncl of Nat Assoc for Care and Resettlement of Offenders 1956 (chm 1973), Home Sec's Advsy Cncl for Probation and After-Care Ctee 1966-79, Home Sec's Working Party on Treatment of Habitual Drunken Offenders 1969-71, cncl of Policy Studies Inst, cncl Inst of Manpower Studies, Econ Social Res Cncl 1985-88; memb: TUC Gen Cncl 1976, TUC Econ Ctee 1977, TUC Educn Ctee 1977, TUC Employment Policy and Orgn Ctee 1979, TUC Int Ctee, TUC Media Working Gp, TUC Finance Gen Purposes Ctee 1984, Tax Consultative Ctee 1974-88, Royal Cmmn on Distribution of Income and Wealth 1979-80, IBA 1978-83; chm: Trades Union Unit Tst Mangrs Ltd 1984, NEDO Tyre Ind Econ Dvpt Ctee, Alcoholics Recovery Project 1970-76; gen sec Inland Revenue Staff Fedn 1976-88; *Books* Policy for Poverty (1970), The Wealth Report (jtly 1979); *Recreations* gardening, reading, music; *Clubs* Wig and Pen; *Style*— A M G Christopher, Esq, CBE; Douglas Houghton House, 231 Vauxhall Bridge Rd, London SW1V 1EH (☎ 01 834 8254)

CHRISTOPHER, John Anthony; CB (1983); s of John William Christopher (d 1974), and Dorothy, *née* Southwell (d 1983); *b* 19 June 1924; *Educ* Sir George Monoux GS, London Univ (BSc); *m* 1947, Pamela Evelyn, da of Charles Hardy (d 1971); 1 s (Geoffrey), 1 da (Sheila) and 1 s decd (Richard); *Career* Flight Lt 1943-47; chartered surveyor; district valuer Lincoln 1965-72, chief valuer Valuation Off, Inland Revenue 1981-84; cncl memb RICS 1981-85, BSc memb Bd Surveyors Pubns 1984-; FRICS; *Recreations* golf, sailing, music; *Style*— John Christopher Esq, CB; 40 Svenskaby, Orton Wistow, Peterborough, Cambs. PE2 0YZ (☎ 0733 238199)

CHRISTOPHERSEN, (Gunnar) Rolf; DFC (1943); s of Oscar Christophersen (d 1940), of Bromley, Kent, and Sigrid, *née* Myhre (d 1971); *b* 20 Nov 1921; *Educ* Cranleigh, Corpus Christie Coll Oxford (MA); *m* 4 Feb 1966, Angela Gwen, da of James Harfield (d 1968), of Southport Lancs; 2 da ((Astrid) Miranda b 1969, Olvia Kirsten b 1971); *Career* Flt Lt RAF 1941-46; chm J John Masters Hldgs Ltd 1973-83; dir: Br match Corpn 1966-74, Wilkinson Match Ltd 1974-81; chm Pipesmakers Cncl 1982-, vice chm Anglo-Norse Soc 1956-; Master Worshipful Co of Tobacco Pipe Makers and Tobacco Blenders 1980-81; FIOD; *Recreations* sailing, squash; *Clubs* RAFYC; *Style*— Rolf Christophersen, Esq, DFC; 25 St Ann's Villas, London W11 4RT (☎ 01 503 9089)

CHRISTOPHERSON, Sir Derman Guy; OBE (1946); s of Rev Derman Christopherson (d 1945), of Blackheath, and Edith Frances Christopherson; *b* 6 Sept 1915; *Educ* Sherborne, Univ Coll Oxford (BA, DPhil), Harvard Univ (SM); *m* 1940, Frances Edith (d 1988), da of James Tearle (d 1940); 3 s (Oliver, James, Peter), 1 adopted da (Ann); *Career* engaged on scientific research in connection with the War effort 1939-45; univ staff 1945-; prof of mech engrg Leeds Univ 1949-55, of applied sci with reference to Engineering Imperial Coll of Sci and Technol 1955-60, vice-chllr Durham Univ 1961-78, master of Magdalene Coll Cambridge 1979-85 (former fell and bursar); chm Royal Fine Art Cmmn 1979-; FRS, FEng, MICE, MIMechE; kt 1969; *Recreations* university life in all its aspects; *Clubs* United Oxford and Cambridge; *Style*— Sir Derman Christopherson, OBE; 43 Lensfield Road, Cambridge, CB2 1EN (☎ (0223) 327729)

CHRISTOPHERSON, Hon Mrs (Griselda Etheldreda Clodagh); *née* O'Brien; 2 da of 15 Baron Inchiquin (d 1929); *b* 19 Oct 1906; *m* 14 March 1953, as his 2 wife, David Clifford Christopherson, DSC, yr s of Henry Clifford Christopherson, of Woodbury, Reigate, Surrey; 2 step-da; *Style*— The Hon Mrs Christopherson; The Dower House, 53 Firs Chase, West Mersea, Colchester, Essex CO5 8NN (☎ 0206 382868)

CHUBB, Hon Mrs; (Barbara); *née* Champion; da of Baron Champion (Life Peer) (d 1985); *b* 14 Dec 1931; *Educ* Pontypridd Girls' GS, Rachel McMillan Training Coll; *m* 10 Aug 1957, Trevor Chubb, s of Robert Rees Chubb (d 1962), of Pontypridd; 3 da (Alison b 1960, Judith b 1963, Claire b 1968); *Recreations* painting; *Style*— The Hon Mrs Chubb; 160 Redland Road, Redland, Bristol, BS6 6YG

CHUBB, Hon Charles Henry Thomas; s of 3 Baron Hayter, KCVO, CBE; *b* 1949; *Educ* Marlborough, King's Coll Cambridge; *m* 1979, Ann Nicola, da of Charles Manning, of Herts; *Style*— The Hon Charles Chubb; Tower Hill, 101 High Street, Kidlington, Oxford OX5 2DS

CHUBB, Cdr Hon David William Early, RN; s of 2 Baron Hayter (d 1967); *b* 31 May 1914; *Educ* RNC Dartmouth; *m* 2 Dec 1939, Veronica, da of William Clifton, of Shanghai; 1 s; *Career* Cdr RN (ret), Far East 1939-45 (despatches, prisoner); *Style*— Cdr The Hon David Chubb, RN (ret)

CHUBB, Hon John Andrew; s of 3 Baron Hayter, KCVO, CBE; *b* 20 April 1946; *Educ* Marlborough, Southampton Univ (BSc, MA); *m* 1975, Sandy, da of late Alfred E Brereton; 1 s, 1 da; *Career* dep chief accountant Oxford Univ; Liveryman of Worshipful Co of Weavers; FCA; *Recreations* windsurfing; *Style*— The Hon John Chubb; Manor Farm House, Warborough, Oxon

CHUBB, Hon (George) William Michael; s and h of 3 Baron Hayter, KCVO, CBE; *b* 9 Oct 1943; *Educ* Marlborough, Nottingham Univ (BSc); *m* 8 Jan 1983, Waltraud, yr da of J Flackl, of Sydney, Aust; 1 s (Thomas Frederik b 1986); *Style*— The Hon William Chubb; Mapledurwell House, Mapledurwell, nr Basingstoke, Hants RG25 2LT

CHUCK, Peter John; s of Albert Edward Chuck (d 1955), of London, and Ada Florence, *née* Heming (d 1947); *b* 23 Oct 1930; *Educ* Burstow Sch Horley Surrey; *m* 2 Feb 1957, Winnifred Kathleen, da of Capt Robert Michie (d 1983), of Cupar, Fife; 1 s (Robert Alistair b 9 Nov 1959), 1 da (Fiona Anne b 9 Nov 1957); *Career* RN 1959; surveyor; Edward Erdman & Co 1946-49, Healy & Baker 1949-58, Bernard Thorpe & Ptnrs 1958-86: ptnr Edin 1959 (ptnr Paris 1973, Westminster 1975, City of London 1979), sr ptnr 1986-; ctee memb Br Chapter Int Real Estate Fedn 1980-87; Freeman City of London; Liveryman: Worshipful Co of Chartered Surveyors 1979, Worshipful Co of Gold & Silver Wyre Drawers 1983; FRICS 1953; *Recreations* golf, philately, foreign travel; *Style*— Peter Chuck, Esq; 3 Broadhurst Close, Richmond, Surrey, TW10 6HU (☎ 01 948 4062)

CHUNG, Sir Sze-yuen; GBE (1989, CBE 1975, OBE 1968), JP (Hong Kong 1964); *b* 3 Nov 1917; *Educ* Hong Kong Univ, Sheffield Univ (PhD); *m* 1942, Nancy Cheung (d 1977); 1 s, 2 da; *Career* engr; chm Sonca Industries 1978- (formerly md); dir China Light and Power Co Ltd; memb Hong Kong Exec Council 1972-80 (sr unofficial memb 1980-); chm Hong Kong Poly 1972- (chm planning ctee 1982-);FEng, Hon FIMechE, FIPRodE; kt 1978; *Style*— Sir Sze-yuen Chung, CBE, JP; House 25, Bella Vista, Silver Terrace Rd, Clear Water Bay, Kowloon, Hong Kong (☎ 010 852 3719 2857)

CHURCH, Ian Berkeley; s of late Leslie Humphreys Church, DSO, TD, of Church Brampton, Northants, and Leila Grace, *née* Berkeley; *b* 23 Jan 1927; *Educ* Stowe; *m* 14 Feb 1956, Elizabeth Anne Linley, da of Lt-Col Linley Francis Messel, TD (d 1980); 1 s, 1 da; *Career* chm Church and Co plc (manufacturers and retailers of shoes); dir Chandler Henderson Financial Services Ltd and Faber Prest plc; *Clubs* Bucks; *Style*— Ian Church, Esq; 12 Cranley Mews, London SW7 (☎ 01 373 8278)

CHURCH, James Victor; s of James Haslem Church, BEM (d 1970), and Elsie Dorothy Church; *b* 22 Oct 1930; *Educ* Alleyn's Sch Dulwich, Rossall Sch Fleetwood; *m* 30 Mar 1957, Janice Violet, da of William Linton, of Hayes, Kent; 2 s (Andrew James b 1959, Jonathan Charles Linton b 1962); *Career* Nat Serv cmmnd RCS 1949-50, TA (Lt) 1950-55; James Capel & Co (incorporating Nathan & Rosselli) 1947- , (dir 1973-1987); dir James Capel Moneybroking Ltd 1986- ; dir & chm NHL First Funding plc, NHL Second Funding plc, NHL Third Funding plc, Blue Chip Mortgage Passthrough Ltd (No 1); memb: Community Advsy Bd, Sloan Hosp, Beckenham, Ravensbourne Light Operatic Soc; ACIS (1953); *Recreations* skiing, golf; *Clubs* City of London; *Style*— James Church, Esq; James Capel House, 6 Bevis Marks, London, EC3A 7JQ, (☎ 01 621 0011, fax 01 621 0496, telex 888866)

CHURCH, Richard Edmund; s of Cdr William John Patrick Church, DSO, DSC (d 1963), of Weybridge, Surrey, and Rosemary Mary Church (d 1963); *b* 23 June 1950; *Educ* Downside, Trinity Coll Dublin (BA, LLB); *m* 11 Dec 1976, Susan Primrose, da of Maurice Hall, of Farnham, Surrey; 3 s (Andrew b 1977, Francis b 1979, Philip b 1984); *Career* admitted slr 1976; ptnr: Richards Butler 1981-88, More Fisher Brown 1988-; memb Law Soc; *Recreations* cricket, (county cricketer Co Kildare), squash; *Style*— Richard Church, Esq; The Firs, Pangbourne Rd, Upper Basildon, Berkshire (☎ 0491 671 428); 1 Norton Folegate, London EC1 (☎ 01 247 0438, fax 247 0639)

CHURCH, William Edward; s of Dr William Edward Church, FSG, of Mannering House, Bethersden, Kent, and Enid Marjorie, *née* Wallace; *b* 11 August 1943; *Educ* Eton, Trinity Coll Cambridge (BA); *m* 7 Feb 1970, Bryony Susan Louise, da of Col Michael Botwell Adams, of Chichester, W Sussex; 2 s (Edward b 1971, Andrew b 1973); *Career* CA; capt 1 and 3 Trinity Boat Club Cambridge 1964-65; Cambridge Univ Boat Race Crew 1965; *Recreations* gardening, supporting the sport of rowing; *Clubs* Leander, Hawks, First & Third Trinity Boat, Cambridge Univ Boat; *Style*— William E Church, Esq; Hillside, Headcorn, Ashford, Kent TN27 9JE (☎ 0622 890248); 11 Station Road, Headcorn, Ashford, Kent TN27 9SB (☎ (0622) 890779)

CHURCHER, Maj-Gen John Bryan; CB (1952), DSO (1944) and Bar (1946); s of late Lt-Col Bryan Thomas Churcher, of Wargrave, Berks, and Beatrice Theresa Churcher; *b* 2 Sept 1905; *Educ* Wellington, Sandhurst; *m* 1937, Rosamond Hildegarde Mary, yst da of late Frederick Parkin, of Truro Vean, Truro, Cornwall; 1 s, 2 da; *Career* 2 Lt DCLI 1925, served WW II, cmd 43 Wessex Div 1946, 2 Div 1946, 3 Div 1947, Maj-Gen 1947, 5 Div 1947-48, 3 Div 1954-57, dir Mil Training WO 1957, ret 1959; ADC to HM The King 1949-52 and to HM The Queen 1952; dir and sec Independent Stores Assoc, ret 1971; *Style*— Maj-Gen John Churcher, CB, DSO*; 34 Oaks Drive, Colchester, Essex CO3 3PS (☎ 0206 574525)

CHURCHHOUSE, Prof Robert Francis; CBE (1982); s of Robert Francis Churchhouse, of Manchester, and Agnes, *née* Howard (d 1985); *b* 30 Dec 1927; *Educ* St Bede's Coll Manchester, Manchester Univ (BSc), Cambridge Univ (PhD); *m* 7 Aug 1954, Julia Gertrude, da of John McCarthy (d 1929), of Irlam, Lancs; 3 s (Gerard b 1955, Robert b 1956, John b 1960); *Career* RN sci serv RN 1952-63; head of programming Atlas Computer Laboratory 1963-71, prof of computing maths Univ Coll Cardiff 1971-; chm Computer Bd 1979-83, pres Inst of Maths and its Applications 1986-88; FRAS 1962, FIMA 1964, FBCS 1967; KSG 1988; *Books* Computers in Mathematical Research (with JC Herz, 1968), The Computer in Literary and Linguistic Studies (with A Jones, 1976), Numerical Analysis (1978), Handbook of Applicable Mathematics Vol III (1981); *Recreations* cricket, astronomy; *Clubs* Challenor; *Style*— Prof Robert Churchhouse, CBE; 15 Holly Grove, Lisvane, Cardiff CF4 5UJ (☎ 0222 750 250); Dept of Computing Mathematics, Univ of Wales Coll of Cardiff, Mathematics Inst, Senghennydd Rd, Cardiff CF2 4YN (☎ 0222 874 812, fax 0222 371 921, telex 498635)

CHURCHILL, John George Spencer; s of Maj John Strange Spencer Churchill (d 1947, gson of 7 Duke of Marlborough), and Lady Gwendoline Bertie (d 1941), da of 7 Earl of Abingdon; *b* 31 May 1909; *Educ* Harrow, Oxford, Central Sch of Arts and Crafts, Ruskin Sch Oxford (privately); *m* 1, 13 May 1934 (m dis 1938), Angela Mary, da of late Capt George Culme Seymour, KRRC; 1 da (Sarah); m 2, 20 May 1941 (m dis 1953), Mary, o da of late Kenneth Cookson, of Wynberg, Cape Province, S Africa; m 3, 5 March 1953, Mrs Kathlyn Maude Muriel Hall Tandy (d 25 June 1957), o da of Maj-Gen Watter Samuel Hall Beddall, CB, OBE; m 4, 27 Aug 1958 (m dis 1972), Anna Gunvor Maria, da of Johan Janson, of Kristianstad, Sweden, and wid of Granger Boston; *Career* artist, author; mural Marlborough Pavilion, Chartwell Westerham Kent (Nat Tst); piece carved incised relief on State 1949; mural London from the South Bank Simpsons Piccadilly 1957-; painting Save the Forests World Wildlife Fund 1985-; *Books* Crowded Canvas (1960), A Churchill Canvas (USA) (1961), Vanishing Day (1989); *Recreations* music, travel; *Clubs* Chelsea Arts, Press, Cincinnati (Washington DC, USA); *Style*— John G Spencer Churchill Esq; Domicile, 6 Place de Cros, Grimand, Var 83360, France (☎ 94 43 21 31); Work 6 Ashburnham Mansions, Ashburnham Rd, London SW10 0PA (☎ 01 352 2352)

CHURCHILL, Very Rev John Howard; s of John Lancelot Churchill (d 1945), and Emily Winifred Churchill d 1948); *b* 9 June 1920; *Educ* Sutton Valence Sch Kent, Trinity Coll Cambridge (BA, MA), Lincoln Theological Coll; *m* 28 Aug 1948, Patricia May, da of John Joseph Williams (d 1965); 1 s (John b 1951), 2 da (Elizabeth b 1949, Margaret b 1955); *Career* ordained deacon 1943, priest 1944; asst curate St George Camberwell 1943-48, All Hallows' Tottenham 1948-53, chaplain and lectr in technol King's Coll London 1953-60, vicar of St George Sheffield 1960-67, lectr in educn Univ of Sheffield 1960-67, canon residentiary St Edmundsbury 1967-73, dir of clergy trg St Edmundsbury and Ipswich 1967-73, Lady Margaret preacher Univ of Cambridge 1969, proctor in Convocation and Gen Synod 1970-87, dean of Carlisle 1973-87; fell King's Coll London; *Books* Prayer in Progress (1961), Going Up (1963), Finding Prayer

(1977), Finding Communion (1987); *Recreations* walking, listening to music; *Style*— The Very Rev John H Churchill; 43 City Road, Norwich NR1 3AD (☎ 0603 633878)

CHURCHILL, Maj-Gen Thomas Bell Lindsay; CB (1957), CBE (1949), MC (1931); s of late Alec Fleming Churchill, Ceylon and Hong Kong, and Elinor Elizabeth, *née* Bell; *b* 1 Nov 1907; *Educ* Dragon Sch, Magdalen Coll Sch Oxford, RMC Sandhurst; *m* 1, Gwendolen Janie (d 1962), da of late Dr Lewis Williams, of Carmarthenshire; 1 s, 1 da; m 2, 1968 (m dis 1974), Penelope Jane, da of C G Ormiston, of Shobley House, Ringwood, Hants; *Career* 2 Lt Manchester Regt 1927, Burma Rebellion 1930-31 (despatches), instr in interpretation of air photography RAF Sch of Photography 1934-39, serv WWII, GSO 1 Commando Bde Sicily and Salerno 1943, Cdr 2 Commando Bde 1943-44, served with Marshal Tito in Yugoslavia 1944, Bde Cdr Austria 1945-46, Zone Cdr Austria 1947-49, Col The Manchester Regt 1952-58, Col King's Regt 1958-62, Vice-Quartermaster-Gen to Forces 1957-60, Dep COS Allied Land Forces Central Europe 1960-62, ret; Partisan Star with Gold Wreath (Yugoslavia); *Books* The Interpretation of Air Photographs, The Churchill Chronicles, Commando Crusade; *Recreations* genealogy, heraldry, fine arts; *Style*— Maj-Gen Thomas Churchill, CB, CBE, MC; Treedown Farm, Spreyton, Credition, Devon EX17 5AS (☎03633 671)

CHURCHILL, 3 Viscount (UK 1902); Victor George Spencer; also Baron Churchill (UK 1815); s of 1 Viscount Churchill, GCVO (d 1934), by his 2 w Christine Sinclair (Lady Oliphant); suc half-bro 1973; *b* 31 July 1934; *Educ* Eton, New Coll Oxford; *Heir* (to Barony only) kinsman, Richard Spencer; *Career* Lt Scots Gds 1953-55; employed Morgan Grenfell and Co Ltd 1958-74; investment mangr The Central Bd of the Church of England and the Charities Official Investment Fund 1974; dir Local Authorities' Mutual Investment Trust 1978; *Style*— The Rt Hon the Viscount Churchill; 6 Cumberland Mansions, George St, London W1H 5TE (☎ 01 262 6223)

CHURCHILL, Winston Spencer; MP (C) Davyhulme (Manchester) 1983-; s of late Randolph Frederick Edward Spencer Churchill, MBE (s of Sir Winston Churchill) by his 1 w, Hon Pamela Digby (now Hon Mrs Harriman), da of 11 Baron Digby, KG, DSO, MC, TD; *b* 10 Oct 1940; *Educ* Eton, Christ Church, Oxford; *m* 15 July 1964, Mary Caroline, da of late Sir Gerard d'Erlanger, CBE; 2 s, 2 da; *Career* author, journalist and war correspondent 1964-, with The Times 1969-70; contested (C) Manchester (Gorton Div) 1967, MP (C) Stretford Lancs 1970-83, PPS: to min of Housing and Construction 1970-72, to min of state FCO 1972-72; Cons spokesman on Defence 1976-78, vice-chm Cons Pty Defence Ctee 1979-83, memb exec 1922 Ctee 1979-83, treas 1987-, Cons Party co-ordinator for Defence and Disarmament and chm of Campaign for Defence and Multilateral Disarmament 1982-84; *Books* First Journey (1964), The Six Day War (1967), Defending the West (1980); *Clubs* Buck's, White's, Press; *Style*— Winston Churchill, Esq, MP; House of Commons, London SW1A 0AA (☎ 01 219 3405)

CHURCHILL-DAVIDSON, Dudley; RD and Clasp; s of Dr Frederick Churchill-Davidson (d 1961), and Marie Peacock, *née* Jacques (d 1976); *b* 11 May 1927; *Educ* Charterhouse, Trinity Coll Cambridge, St Thomas' Hosp Medical Sch, (MA, MB, BCHIR); *Career* Nat Serv RN, Surgn Lt RNVR 1953-55; ret Surgn Capt RNR; Hon Col RM Reserve (City of London) 1982-; conslt orthopaedic surgn (now in private practice and conslt to BR Airways and the Automobile Assoc); Nat Health Service 1985 (ret); registrar and sr registrar in Orthopaedic Surgery at St Peters Hosp, Chertsey and at the Rowby Bristow Orthopaedic Hosp in Surrey 1958-61; first asst to Orthopaedic Dept St Georges Hosp London 1961-66; conslt orthopaedic surgeon to: Royal London Homoeopathic Hosp 1966, the Kensington and Chelsea Gp of Hosps 1967-72; FRCS; *Recreations* gardening, travel; *Clubs* Bucks; *Style*— Dudley Churchill-Davidson, Esq, RD; 1 Montagu Mews South, London W1H 1TE (☎ 01 724 0482); 79 Harley Street, London W1N 1DE (☎ 01 935 5916)

CHURCHWARD, (Peter) Robert Shordiche; s of Capt Paul Rycaut de Shordiche Shordiche-Churchward, Coldstream Gds (d 1981), explorer and writer, and Claire Isabel, *née* Whitaker (d 1981); *b* 3 Feb 1950; *Educ* Tabley House Knutsford Cheshire; *m* 22 May 1976, Ida Catherine Morwenna, da of Gp Capt Desmond Spencer, CBE (ret), *qv*, of Cornwall; 1 s (Matthew b 1977), 2 da (Victoria b 1981, Thomasina b 1984); *Career* wine specialist, auctioneer Phillips Gp Int 1985- (formerly Phillips wine conslt), contributor Law Soc Journal and numerous wine periodicals; head Bonhams Wine Dept 1974-83; *Recreations* riding, tennis, amateur mountaineering, most outdoor pursuits; *Style*— Robert Churchward, Esq; Phillips, 39 Park End St, Oxford OX1 1JD (☎ 0865 723524)

CHURSTON, 4 Baron (UK 1858); Sir Richard Francis Roger Yarde-Buller; 6 Bt (GB 1790), VRD; s of 3 Baron (d 1930); bro of Viscountess Camrose, Denise Lady Ebury, Lydia, Duchess of Bedford and late Primrose, Countess Cadogan; *b* 12 Feb 1910; *Educ* Eton; *m* 1, 5 Jan 1933 (m dis 1943), Elizabeth Mary (d 23 Sept 1951), da of Lt-Col William Baring Du Pre, JP, DL; 1 s, 1 da; m 2, 31 March 1949, Sandra (d 1979), da of Percy Needham, and former w of Jack Dunfee, and previously of Claud Harold Bertram (Arthur) Griffiths; m 3, Mrs Olga Alice Muriel Blair; *Heir* s, Hon John Yarde-Buller; *Career* Lt-Cdr RNVR, ret; patron of two livings; bore one of the Golden Spurs at Coronations of King George VI and Queen Elizabeth II; *Clubs* RYS; *Style*— The Rt Hon the Lord Churston, VRD; Pendragon, Fort George, Guernsey, Channel Islands (☎ 28550)

CHURTON, Hon Mrs (Katherine); *née* Tyrell-Kenyon; only da of 5 Baron Kenyon; *b* 21 April 1959; *m* 1985, David Nigel Vardon Churton, elder s of Col G V Churton, of The White House, Bunbury, Cheshire; 1 s (Oscar Vardon b 1987); *Style*— Hon Mrs Churton

CHUTE, Anthony Vere; s of Lawrence Vere, MC (d 1948), and Norah Lydia, *née* Boyd (d 1944); is sr surviving memb of family Chute of the Vyne (given to Nat Tst 1956) and descendant of Chaloner Chute, speaker of the House of Commons in Richard Cromwell's parliament; *b* 16 Sept 1920; *Educ* ISC, RMA Woolwich; *m* 29 June 1946, Daphne Gore, da of Cdr F C Darley (d China 1926); 3 s (Robin b 1947, Chaloner b 1949, Richard b 1953); *Career* WWII Capt RA served N Africa (POW) 1939-45; a dep chm Blything Bench 1987- (chm 1976-88), chm Suffolk Valuation Panel 1983- and rep for Home and Eastern Countries Gp on Nat Ctee 1985-; *Recreations* tennis, skiing; *Clubs* Ski (Great Britain); *Style*— Anthony V Chute, Esq; Bulhams, Wissett, Halesworth, Suffolk (☎ Ilketshall 239)

CHUTE, Robin Vere; Lord of the Manor of Sherborne St John; s of Anthony Vere Chute (d 1987), of Suffolk, and Daphne Gore, *née* Darley; family descends from Alexander Chute, living 1268; Philip Chute was standard bearer to Henry VIII, and Chaloner Chute (1595-1659) speaker of the House of Commons, and first Chute of The Vyne, Basingstoke (*see* Burke's Landed Gentry, 1937 edn); *b* 24 May 1947; *Educ* Winchester, RAC Cirencester; *m* 30 Sept 1978, Julia Mary Susan, da of Maj John Sylvester Perkins, of Chippenham, Wilts; 1 s (Charles John Vere b 1981), 1 da (Arabella Julia Handasy-de b 1984); *Career* Estates Bursar of Winchester Coll 1981; FRICS 1982; *Recreations* shooting, fishing, cricket, rackets; *Clubs* MCC; *Style*— Robin V Chute, Esq; 15 Kingsgate Street, Winchester, Hants (☎ 0962 56708); Winchester College, Winchester, Hants (☎ 0962 64242)

CHUTE, Terence Michael; s of George James Chute (d 1972), and Minnie Margaret Chute (d 1974); *b* 14 Mar 1936; *Educ* Clapham Xavarien Coll; *m* 28 June 1958, Pauline Gloria, *née* Prentice; 1 s (Julian b 1968), 1 da (Nicola b 1963); *Career* Photo-Me Int plc 1966-, appointed co sec, dir 1977, jnt md 1984, sole md and memb of bd exec Ctee 1985; FICA 1964; *Recreations* golf, reading, music, gardening; *Style*— Terence M Chute, Esq; edwoods, off Blacksmith Lane, Chilworth, Surrey GU4 8NU (☎ 0483 35781)

CHYNOWETH, David Boyd; s of Ernest Chynoweth (d 1982), and Blodwen, *née* Griffiths; *b* 26 Dec 1944; *Educ* Simon Langton Sch Canterbury, Univ of Nottingham (BA); *m* 15 June 1968, Margaret, da of Thomas Slater, of Park House, Edensor, Derbyshire; 1 s (Richard b 1981), 2 da (Susan b 1971, Claire b 1974); *Career* dep County Tres W Suffolk CC 1969-73; County Tres S Yorks CC 1973-85; dir of Finance Lothian Regl Cncl 1985; *Recreations* sailing, photography; *Clubs* Royal Overseas League; *Style*— David Chynoweth, Esq; Ardvulin, 37 Clifford Rd, N Berwick, E Lothian (☎ 0620 3652)

CIECHANOWIECKI, Count Andrew Stanislaus; s of Count George Ciechanowiecki (d 1930), Polish diplomat and landowner, and Matilda, *née* Countess Osiecimska-Hutten-Czapska, Dame of Hon and Dev SMOM, Dame Gd Cross of Justice, Constantinian Order of St George; *b* Warsaw 28 Sept 1924; *Educ* Lycée S Batory Warsaw, Higher Sch Ec Studies Kraków (BA), Jagiellonian Univ Kraków (MA), Karl Eberhard Univ Tübingen (PhD); *Career* anti-Nazi resistance in Poland 1942-45, Polish war decorations; cnsllr Polish Foreign Office, in govt of National Unity and chef de protocole Min Foreign Trade 1945-6; political prisoner 1950-56; former lectr Jagiellonian Univ Kraków; former museum curator in Poland; md Mallett at Bourdon House (London) 1961-65, md Heim Gallery (London) Ltd 1965-86; md Old Masters Gallery (London) Ltd 1986-; tstee various Polish charities abroad; mem various learned bodies; Kt Cdr Polonia Restituta, (govt in Exile), Kt Cdr Order of St Gregory the Great (Holy See), Kt Cdr Order of Merit (Italy), Cdr Grosses Silbernes Ehrenzeichen (Austria), Cdr Order of Merit (Senegal), Bundesverdienstkreuz (1 Class, Germany), Chev Légion d'Honneur (France), Kt Grand Cross of Hon and Dev and Kt Grand Cross of Merit SMOM, vice-pres Polish Assoc of SMOM, Kt Order of St Januarius, Bailiff Grand Cross of Justic Constantinian Order of St George (decorated with the Collar), (Royal House of Naples), Kt Cdr Order SS Mauritius and Lazarus (Royal House of Savoy); medal 'Merentibus' Jagiellonian Univ Krakow; *Books* author of several books and numerous articles in the field of art and history of culture; *Recreations* reading, travelling; *Clubs* Brooks's, Polish Hearth; *Style*— Count Andrew Ciechanowiecki; 44 Sydney St, London SW3 6PX (☎ 01 352 1395; office 01 930 1145)

CIERACH, Lindka Rosalind Wanda; da of Edek Cierach, MBE, of Starydom, St Just-in-Roseland, Truro, Cornwall, and Diana Rosemary, *née* Wilson; f mapped large tracts of Africa, decorated for Battle of Monte Cassino with highest Order of Virtuti Military, Kirzyz Walecznych, Star medal 1939-44, Star Italian Campaign, Star of Monte Cassino, Star Defense MBE; *b* 8 June 1952; *Educ* Primary Sch, Uganda, Convent of the Holy Child Jesus Sussex; *Career* fashion designer, designed wedding dress for Duchess of York's marriage on 23 July 1986; *Recreations* travelling, photography, swimming, cooking, music, opera; *Style*— Miss Lindka R W Cierach; 54 Hartismere Rd, London SW6 7UD (☎ 01 381 4436)

CITRINE, 2 Baron (UK 1946); Norman Arthur Citrine; s of 1 Baron Citrine, GBE, PC (d 1983, former chm Central Electricity Authority, pres World Fedn of Trade Unions and gen sec TUC), and Doris Helen (d 1973), da of Edgar Slade; *b* 27 Sept 1914; *Educ* Univ Coll Sch, LLB London; *m* 4 Jan 1939, Kathleen Alice, da of late George Chilvers, of Saxmundham, Suffolk; 1 da; *Heir* bro, Hon Ronald Eric Citrine; *Career* Lt RNVR 1940-46; slr and advocate 1937-84, author of legal and technical works, legal adviser to Trades Union Congress 1946-51; *Recreations* yachting, painting, rambling, music, literature, many constructional crafts; *Style*— The Rt Hon Lord Citrine; Casa Katrina, The Mount, Opua, Bay of Islands, Northland, NZ

CITRINE, Hon Ronald Eric; s of 1 Baron Citrine; hp to bro, 2 Baron Citrine; *b* 19 May 1919; *Educ* Univ Coll Sch, UCL; *m* 27 July 1945, Mary, da of Reginald Williams, of Wembley; *Career* MRCS, LRCP; *Style*— The Hon Ronald Citrine; Paihia, Bay of Islands, North Island, New Zealand

CLAGUE, Andrew Charlesworth; s of John Charlesworth Clague, of Canterbury, and Margaret Elsie, *née* Musgrave; *b* 15 May 1951; *Educ* St Edmunds Sch Canterbury, Canterbury Coll of Art (Dip Arch); *m* 23 June 1973, Alison Francesca, da of Dennis Arthur Land, of 6 Eversley Crescent, London; 2 s (James Charlesworth, Nicholas Charlesworth), 2 da (Anna Genevieve, Isabel Lucy); *Career* John Clague 1975, ptnr John Clague & Ptnrs 1977; fndr: Countryman Properties Ltd 1986, Harrison Clague Architects in Ashford Kent 1988, Betts Hanbury Clague Ltd Midhurst W Sussex 1988; sec St Edmunds Soc (of St Edmunds Sch Old Boys), chm Plant a Tree for Canterbury; memb: Round Table (Canterbury and Dist), Rotary Club (Canterbury), Canterbury conservation Advsy Ctee Canterbury Soc, PCC St John Bapist Church Barham; RIBA 1976 (chm Canterbury and Dist); *Recreations* windsurfing, music; *Clubs* Kent and Canterbury, Inst of Dirs; *Style*— Andrew Clague, Esq; Bonnie Bush, Black Robin Lane, Kingston, Kent CT4 6HR (☎ 0227 830 138); John Clague & Ptnrs, 62 Burgate, Canterbury, Kent CT1 2HJ (☎ 0227 762 060, fax 0227 762 149, car tel 0860 301 449)

CLANCARTY, 8 Earl of (I 1803); (William Francis) Brinsley Le Poer Trench; also (sits as) Viscount Clancarty (UK 1823), Baron Kilconnel (I 1793), Viscount Dunlo (I 1801), Baron Trench (UK 1815), Marqis of Heusden in the Netherlands (1818); s of late 5 Earl of Clancarty; suc his half-bro 1975; *b* 18 Sept 1911; *Educ* Nautical Coll Pangbourne; *m* 1, 6 June 1940 (m dis 1947), Diana Joan, da of Sir William Younger, 2 Bt; m 2, 16 June 1961 (m dis 1969), Wilma Dorothy Millen, da of S R Vermilyea, of USA, and former w of William Burke Belknap, Jr; m 3, 1974, Mrs Mildred Alleyn Spong (d 1975); m 4, 1976, May, o da of late E Radonicich, and widow of Cdr Frank M Beasley, RN; *Heir* nephew, Nicholas Le Poer Trench; *Career* chm House of Lords UFO Study Gp; author (as Brinsley Le Poer Trench); *Books* The Sky People, Men Among Mankind, Forgotten Heritage, The Flying Saucer Story, Operation Earth, The

Eternal Subject, Secret of the Ages; *Style*— The Rt Hon the Earl of Clancarty; 51 Eaton Place, London SW1

CLANCARTY, Cora, Countess of; Cora Maria Edith; *née* Spooner; er da of H H Spooner, of Thornton Hall, Surrey; *m* 12 March 1919, as his 2 w, 6 Earl of Clancarty (d 1971); 1 s (decd), 3 da; *Style*— The Rt Hon Cora, Countess of Clancarty; Old Vicarage, Moulsford, nr Wallingford, Oxon

CLANFIELD, Viscount; Ashton Robert Gerard Peel; s and h of 3 Earl Peel; *b* 16 Sept 1976; *Style*— Viscount Clanfield; Gunnerside Lodge, Gunnerside, Richmond, N Yorks

CLANMORRIS, 8 Baron (I 1800) Simon John Ward Bingham; s of 7 Baron Clanmorris (d 1988), and Madeleine Mary, da of Clement Ebel; *b* 25 Oct 1937; *Educ* Downside, Queens' Coll Cambridge (BA, MA); *m* 1971, Gizella Maria, da of Sandor Zverkó, of Budapest (d 1979); 1 da (Lucy Katherine Gizella); *Heir* kinsman, John Temple Bingham b 22 Feb 1923; *Career* 13/18 Royal Hussars (QMO) 1956-58; fin conslt; ACA 1965, FCA 1975; *Recreations* skiing, sailing; *Style*— Lord Clanmorris; 6 Zetland House, Marloes Rd, London W8 5LB

CLANWILLIAM, 6 Earl of (I 1776); Sir John Charles Edmund Carson Meade; 9 Bt (I 1703); also (sits as) Baron Clanwilliam (UK 1828), Viscount Clanwilliam and Baron Gilford (I 1766); s of 5 Earl (d 1953); *b* 6 June 1914; *Educ* Eton, Sandhurst; *m* 1 Dec 1948, Catherine, yst da of late Arthur Thomas Loyd, OBE, of Lockinge, Wantage; 6 da; *Heir* cousin, John Meade; *Career* Maj Coldstream Gds, ret; HM Lord-Lt Co Down 1975-79 (formerly HM Lt); OStJ; *Style*— The Rt Hon the Earl of Clanwilliam; Rainscombe Park, Oare, Marlborough, Wilts (☎ Marlborough 63491)

CLAPHAM, Adam John; s of Sir Michael Clapham, of 26 Hill St, London W1, and The Hon Lady Elisabeth, *née* The Hon Elisabeth Russell Rea; *b* 8 April 1940; *Educ* Bryanston, Univ of Grenoble; *Career* Anglia TV 1960-63, scriptwriter ABC TV 1963; BBC TV: prodr Man Alive 1965-69 (ed 1972-75), prodr Braden's Week 1969-71, exec prodr documentary features 1975-82; chief exec Griffin Prodns 1982-; Freeman City of London 1976, Liveryman Worshipful Co of Bowyers 1976; *Books* As Nature Intended (1982); *Clubs* Oriental; *Style*— Adam Clapham, Esq; 254 Alexandra Park Rd, London N22 4BG (☎ 01 889 9035); Griffin Prodns, Balfour House, 46-54 Great Titchfield St, London W1P 7AE (☎ 01 636 5066, fax 01 436 3232, telex 261799)

CLAPHAM, His Hon Brian Ralph; s of late Isaac Bleazard Clapham, and Laura Alice, *née* Meech; *b* 1 July 1913; *Educ* Tonbridge, Wadham Coll Oxford, UCL, Open Univ; *m* 1961, (Renata) Margaret, da of Dr Rudolph Pius Warburg; 2 s; *Career* barr 1936; contested (Lab) Tonbridge 1950, Billericay 1951 and 1955, Chelmsford 1959; a circuit judge 1974-85; Freeman City of London; govr West Kent Coll; ACI Arb; *Recreations* walking and talking; *Style*— His Hon Brian Clapham

CLAPHAM, Hon Lady (Elisabeth Russell); *née* Rea; JP (1956 supp 1981-); yr da of 1 Baron Rea of Eskdale PC (d 1948); *b* 2 May 1911; *Educ* Priorsfield Sch, Newnham Coll Cambridge (MA); *m* 18 May 1935, Sir Michael Clapham, KBE, *qv*; 3 s, 1 da; *Career* Welfare Officer, Min of Labour, 1940-42; chm Birmingham Settlement 1955-61, and SW Magistrates Court 1973-76; *Style*— The Hon Lady Clapham, JP; 26 Hill St, W1X 7FU

CLAPHAM, Sir Michael John Sinclair; KBE (1973); s of Prof Sir John Clapham, CBE, LittD, FBA (d 1946), of Storey's End, Cambridge, and Mary Margaret, *née* Green (d 1965); *b* 17 Jan 1912; *Educ* Marlborough, King's Coll Cambridge (BA, MA); *m* 18 May 1935, Hon Elisabeth Russell Rea, *qv*, da of 1st Baron Rea of Eskdale; 3 s (Adam, Charles, Giles), 1 da (Antonia); *Career* non-exec dir: Hoytesbury Hldgs Ltd 1988, Stok Moss Theatres Ltd 1986 former dep chm ICI, dir Lloyds Bank Ltd 1971-82 (dep chm 1974-79), Grindlays Bank Ltd 1975-84, chm BPM Hldgs plc 1974-81, IMI Ltd 1974-81; Hon DSc Aston (1973), Hon LLD CNAA (1978), Hon LLD London (1984); *Recreations* canal boating ('Thelema'), cooking; *Clubs* Royal Yacht Sqdn; *Style*— Sir Michael Clapham, KBE; 26 Hill St, London W1X 7FU (☎ 01 499 1240)

CLAPHAM, Brig Patrick John Eldred; OBE (1951); s of Col Douglas Clapham, DSO, OBE (d 1960), of Sparsholt, Winchester, and Frances Colledge, *née* Halton (d 1952); *b* 17 Mar 1907; *Educ* Winchester, New Coll Oxford (BA, MA); *m* 1, 20 May 1933, Jocelyn Carver (d 1986), da of Reginald Morgan Weld Smith (d 1964), of Seend Manor, Melksham, Wiltshire; 2 da (Catherine Hilary b 1936, Frances Mita b 1939); m 2, 24 Oct 1987, Mary Marguerite, da of Arthur Thomas Hodgson (d 1931), of Smallwood Manor, Uttoxeter; *Career* soldier, appointed Offr to RMC Sandhurst (the last appointment made to the RMC for Gunners); relinquished on outbreak of war, highest rank Brig; theatre of operations: NW Frontier of India 1930, France 1944; thereafter Common Cryer and Sgt-at-Arms to Lord Mayor of London 1960-70; OStJ; *Recreations* painting, shooting; *Clubs* Army and Navy; *Style*— Brig Patrick J E Clapham, Esq, OBE; The Willows, Lavenham, Sudbury, Suffolk (☎ 0787 297 204)

CLAPPERTON, (Alexander) Wallace Ford; s of Alexander Clapperton (d 1943), of Edinburgh, and Kathleen Nora, *née* Ford; *b* 22 July 1934; *Educ* Charterhouse; *m* 27 March 1965, Catherine Anne, da of Sir Henry Horsman, MC (d 1966), of Bermuda; 1 s (Graeme Alexander Ford b 1969), 1 da (Alison Nicola b 1967); *Career* Nat Serv RCS 1957-59; ptnr de Zoete and Bevan stockbrokers (formerly de Zoete and Gorton) 1963-86, dir Barclays de Zoete Wedd Securities Ltd 1986-; MICAS; *Recreations* golf, skiing; *Clubs* Hon Co of Edinburgh Golfers, Durham GC, Woburn GC, City of London Club; *Style*— Wallace Clapperton, Esq; Broomfield House, Broomfield Hill, Great Missenden, Bucks HP16 9HT (☎ 02406 2559); Ebbgate House, 2 Swan Lane, London EC4R 3TS (☎ 01 623 2323, fax 01 626 1879, telex 9413230)

CLARE, Prof Anthony Ward; s of Bernard Clare, and Agnes, *née* Dunne of 28 Albany Rd, Ranelagh, Dublin; *b* 24 Dec 1942; *Educ* Gonzaga Coll, Univ Coll Dublin, (MB, BCh, BAO, MD), London Univ (MPhil); *m* 4 Oct 1966, Jane, da of Gabriel Sarsfield Hogan, 3s (Simon John b 1970, Peter Tobias b 1975, Sebastian Patrick b 1985), 4 da (Rachel Judith b 1967, Eleanor Ruth b 1971, Sophie Carolyn b 1979, Justine Chiara b 1982); *Career* intern St Joseph Hosp Syracuse NY 1966-67, registrar: St Patrick's Hosp Dublin 1967-69, Bethlem Royal and Maudsley Hosps London 1970-72; dep dir gen practice res unit Inst of Psychiatry 1979-82 (sr registrar and res worker 1973-78), prof and head dept of psychological medicine, St Bart's Hosp Med Coll 1982-88; med dir St Patrick's Hosp Dublin and prof of clinical psychiatry Trinity Coll Dublin 1989- ; memb Health Educn Authy, chm Centre Ctee King Edward's Hosp Fund for London; num broadcasts inc Let's Talk About Me, In the Psychiatrists's Chair (BBC 1982), Stop the Week FRCPI (1983), FRCPsych (1986), MD (1982);; *Books* Psychiatry in Dissent (1976, 1980), Let's Talk About Me (1981), In the Psychiatrist's Chair (1983), Lovelaw (1986); *Recreations* tennis, broadcasting, travel; *Style*— Prof A W Clare; 87 Coper's Cope Road, Beckenham, Kent, BR3 1NR (☎ 01 650 1784); Delville, Lucan, Co Dublin, Republic of Ireland (☎ 0001 264 782); St Patrick's Hospital, James's Street, Dublin 8, Republic of Ireland (☎ 0001 775 423)

CLARE, (Adrian) George (Howe); s of Ernest Vivian Clare, and Betty Kennedy, *née* Hester; *b* 27 Sept 1937; *Educ* Bickley Park Sch, Radley; *m* Helen Aline da of late Edgar Frederick Shannon, of New Malden, Surrey; 3 da (Rosamund b 1964, Alison b 1966, Belinda b 1967); *Career* Nat Serv Royal Ulster Rifles 1957-58, TA London Irish Rifles 1958- 63; princ Euro Actuarial Consultancy Servs, dir int serv R Watson & Sons; memb: Effingham Housing Assoc, Horsley Choral Soc, King George Fifth Playing Fields Ctee; Master Joiners & Ceilers Co 1987- 88; FPMI, ACII, MBIM; *Recreations* singing, travel, politics; *Clubs* RAC; *Style*— George Clare, Esq; Old Vicarage, Church St, Effingham, Leatherhead, Surrey KT24 2LX (☎ 0372 58435); Watsons Europe, London Rd, Reigate

CLARE, Hon Mrs (Pauline Rosemary); *née* Addington; 4 da of 7 Viscount Sidmouth; *b* 18 Feb 1951; *m* 1973, Paul Christopher Clare; *Style*— The Hon Mrs Clare; Glenarth, Abernarth, Aberaeron, Dyfed

CLARENDON, 7 Earl of (GB 1776); George Frederick Laurence Hyde Villiers; also Baron Hyde (GB 1756); s of late Lord Hyde and late Hon Marion, *née* Glyn, da of 4 Baron Wolverton; suc gf 1955; *b* 2 Feb 1933; *Educ* Eton, Madrid Univ; *m* 1974, Jane Diana, da of Edward William Dawson (d 1979), of Idmiston, Salisbury, Wilts; 1 s (George Edward Laurence, Lord Hyde b 12 Feb 1976), 1 da (Lady Sarah Katherine Jane Villiers, b 1977); *Heir* s, Lord Hyde; *Career* page of hon to HM King George VI 1948-49; Lt RHG 1951-53; Glyn Mills and Co 1955-60, Seccombe Marshall and Campion 1960- (md 1962, chm 1985); *Style*— The Rt Hon the Earl of Clarendon; 5 Astell Street, London SW3 3RT (☎ 01 352 9131); Soberton Mill, Swanmore, Hampshire SO3 2QF (☎ 0329 833118)

CLARFELT, Hon Mrs (Christina Marjorie); o da of Baron Campbell of Croy, PC, MC (Life Peer), *qv*; *b* 24 Nov 1953; *Educ* West Heath; *m* 23 April 1980, Mark Michael Clarfelt, s of Jack Gerald Clarfelt, *qv*; 1 s (Max b 1986), 2 da (Alice Nicola Irene b 1982, Tessa b 1984); *Style*— The Hon Mrs Clarfelt; 8 Vicarage Gardens, London W8

CLARFELT, Jack Gerald; s of Barnett Clarfelt and Rene, *née* Frankel; *b* 7 Feb 1914; *Educ* Grocers' Co Sch, Sorbonne; *m* 1948, Baba Fredman; 1 s, 1 da; *Career* chm: Linhay Meats Ltd, chm Linhay Frizzell Insur Brokers Ltd; dir Alton Estates Ltd and other property cos; farmer;; *Style*— Jack Clarfelt, Esq; Linhay Meads, Timsbury, Romsey, Hants (☎ 0794 68243)

CLARINGBULL, Sir (Gordon) Frank; s of William Horace Claringbull and Hannah Agnes Cutting; *b* 21 August 1911; *Educ* Finchley GS, Queen Mary Coll London Univ (BSc, PhD); *m* 1, 1938, Grace Helen Mortimer (d 1953); 1 s, 1 da; m 2, 1953, Enid Dorothy Phyllis, da of late William Henry Lambert; *Career* Br Museum (Natural History): joined 1935, keeper of mineralogy 1953-68, dir 1968-76; memb museums and Galleries Cmmn 1976-83; kt 1975; *Style*— Sir Frank Claringbull; Westering, South Esplanade, Burnham-on-Sea, Somerset TA8 1BU (☎ 0278 780096)

CLARK *see also*: Chichester-Clark, Stewart Clark

CLARK, Hon Alan Kenneth McKenzie; MP (C) Plymouth Sutton Feb 1974-; s of Baron Clark, OM, CH, KCB (Life Peer, d 1983) and his 1 w Elizabeth, *née* Martin (d 1976); *b* 13 April 1928; *Educ* Eton, Christ Church Oxford; *m* 1958, Caroline Jane, da of Col Leslie Brindley Bream Beuttler (and ggda of Hon George Ogilvie-Grant, 6 s of 6 Earl of Seafield); 2 s (James, Andrew); *Career* served in Household Cavalry Trg Regt 1946 and RAuxAF 1952-54; barr Inner Temple; mil historian, memb Inst Strategic Studies and Royal United Services Inst for Def Studies; vice-chm Parly Def Ctee, memb Parly Home Affrs Ctee; under-sec of state Employment (responsibilities incl legislation on trade union's political levy) 1983-86, min for Trade 1986-; *Clubs* Brooks, Pratt's; *Style*— The Hon Alan Clark, MP; Saltwood Castle, Kent CT21 4QU (☎ 0303 67190)

CLARK, His Hon Judge Albert William; s of William Clark (d 1927), and Cissy, *née* Annis (d 1983); *b* 23 Sept 1922; *Educ* Christ's Coll Finchley, Cncl of Legal Education; *m* 1951, Frances Philippa, da of Dr Samuel Lavington-Hart of Cambridge (England) and Tientsin (China); 1 s (Adrian), 1 da (Susan); *Career* served WWII RN Patrol Serv N Atlantic 1941-45; barr 1949, metropolitan magistrate 1970, dep circuit judge 1972, circuit judge Inner London Crown Court (SE) 1981-; *Recreations* fishing, walking, boating (MY Pelham); *Style*— His Hon Judge Albert Clark; 31 Hill Court, Wimbledon Hill Rd, Wimbledon, London SW19 7PD (☎ 01 947 8041); Pelham, 45 West Parade, Worthing, Sussex BN11 5ES (☎ 0903 47472)

CLARK, (Wilfred) Allan; s of John Wilfred Clark (d 1969), and Lavinia Clark, *née* Light (d 1940); *b* 18 Nov 1927; *Educ* Shipley Central Sch, Manchester Sch of Art, Aston Univ; *m* 20 March 1954, Emmie Catherine, da of Albert Edward Hillman; 2 da (Catherine Joy b 1955, Lindsay Gail b 1958); *Career* mil serv RE (NCO) served Malaya, Singapore, UK; architect, ptnr Percy Thomas Partnership 1975-; FRIBA, DipLA, FFB; *Recreations* golf, walking, painting; *Clubs* Nottingham, Notts Utd Services; *Style*— Allan Clark, Esq; Woodlands, Bunny Hill, Bunny, Nottingham NG11 6QQ; Percy Thomas Partnership Architects, Imperial Buildings, 20 Victoria Street, Nottingham NG1 2JS (☎ 0602 587095, fax (0602) 414256, telex 449966)

CLARK, Hon Mrs; Hon Anna; eld da of late 2 Baron Fisher; *b* 27 July 1916; *m* 10 Aug 1936, Thomas Williams Clark, MD, s of Percy Hamilton Clark, of Cynwyd, Pennsylvania, USA; 2 s, 2 da; *Style*— The Hon Mrs Clark; 44 West Highland Ave, Philadelphia, PA, USA 19118

CLARK, Charles Anthony; s of Stephen Clark (d 1965), and Winifred Clark (d 1971); *b* 13 June 1940; *Educ* Kings Coll Sch Wimbledon, Pembroke Coll Oxford (BA); *m* 1968, Penelope Margaret, da of A John Brett (d 1975); 1 s (Jonathan b 1977), 2 da (Philippa b 1969, Joanna b 1971); *Career* head of fin branch (under sec and accountant general) Dept of Educn and Sci; *Recreations* running, sailing, reading; *Style*— Anthony Clark, Esq; The Paddock, Guildford Road, Effingham, Surrey (☎ 0372 52337); Dept of Educn and Sci, London SE1 7PH (☎ 01 934 9960)

CLARK, Charles Brian; ERD, DL; s of HJ Clark, MBE, DL (d 1958), of Ardtara, Upperlands, and Alice Warren, *née* Moore (d 1957); *b* 6 Nov 1907; *Educ* Shrewsbury; *Career* WWII Maj Colraine Battery 1939-45; High Sherriff Co Londonderry 1965; County Grand Master Orange; *Recreations* shooting; *Style*— Brian Clark, Esq, ERD, DL; c/o William CLark & Sons Ltd, Upperlands, Co Derry, N Ireland (☎ 0648 42 248)

CLARK, Christopher Harvey; s of Maj Harvey Frederick Beckford Clark, of The Hill, Loperwood Lane Calmore, Southampton and Winifred Julia, *née* Caesar; *b* 20 Dec

1946; *Educ* Taundon's GS Southampton, Queen's Coll Oxford (MA); *m* 25 March 1972, Gillian Elizabeth, da of Anthony Mullen, of The Long House, Ramridge Park, Weyhill, Andover, Hants; 1 s (Patrick Harvey b 1974), 2 da (Melanie Julia b 1976, Lucy Elizabeth b 1980); *Career* called to the Bar 1969; memb Western Circuit 1970-; asst rec 1982-86, rec Crown Ct 1986-; memb Wine Ctee of the Western Circuit 1985-; memb Longstock Parish Cncl 1979-; Youth Club orgnr (The Longstock Tadpoles) 1981-, chm Stockbridge (Hants) Dramatic Soc 1977-; *Recreations* amateur dramatics, golf, cricket, gardening, reading; *Style—* C H Clark, Esq; Halfway Cottage, Longstock, Stockbridge, Hampshire (☎ 0264 810 574); 3 Pump Ct, Temple, London EC4 (☎ 01 353 0111 , fax 01 353 3319); Wessex Lodge, 7 Upper High St, Winchester, Hampshire (☎ 0962 68161, fax 0962 67645)

CLARK, Clive Henry; s of Henry Stephen Clark, and Helena Cissie, *née* Hosegood; *b* 24 August 1941; *Educ* King Edward VI GS Chelmsford; *m* 6 July 1968, Gillian Moira, da of Oswald John Casey (d 1977); 3 da (Sharon, Melissa, Nicole); *Career* CA; ptnr Allfields 1973, dep managing ptnr Finnie Ross Allfields, exec ptnr Finnie & Co 1983; hon tres Abbey Menibs Against Flotation; FCA 1963; *Recreations* gardening, travel; *Style—* Clive Clark, Esq; Highport, 424 Baddow Rd, Great Baddow, Chelmsford (☎ 0245 72100); Lazenia, Torrevieja, Spain; Kreston House, 8 Gate St, London WC2A 3HJ (☎ 01 831 9100, fax 01 831 2666, car tel 0836 723976, telex 897205)

CLARK, Hon Colette Elizabeth Dickson; twin da of Baron Clark, OM, CH, KCB (Life Peer, d 1983), and (1 w) Elizabeth, *née* Martin (d 1976); *b* 1932; *Educ* Cheltenham, Lady Margaret Hall Oxford (BA); *Style—* The Hon Colette Clark; 34 Anhalt Rd, London SW11 4NX

CLARK, Hon Colin MacArthur; s of Baron Clark, OM, CH, KCB (Life Peer, d 1983) and (1 w) Elizabeth, *née* Martin (d 1976); *b* 1932; *Educ* Eton, Christ Church Oxford; *m* 1, 1961 (m dis 1969), Violette Verdy; m 2, 1971 (m dis), Faith Beatrice, formerly w of Julian Shuckburgh, and da of Sir Paul Hervé Giraud Wright, *qv*; m 3, Helena Sin, da of Cheung Wan Li (d 1969), of Hong Kong; *Style—* The Hon Colin Clark

CLARK, Dr David George; MP (Lab) South Shields 1979-; s of George Clark, and Janet, of Askham, Cumbria; *b* 19 Oct 1939; *Educ* Windermere GS, Manchester Univ (BA, MSc), Sheffield Univ (PhD); *m* 1970, Christine, da of Ronald Kirkby, of Grasmere; 1 da; *Career* former forester, lab asst, student teacher, univ lectr; contested (Lab) Manchester Withington 1966, MP Colne Valley 1970-74 (contested again Oct 1974), oppn spokesman (Agric and Food) 1973-74, oppn spokesman Def 1980-81, front bench oppn spokesman Environment 1981-7, princ oppn spokesman on Agriculture and Rural Affairs 1987-; *Books* Industrial Manager (1966), Radicalism to Socialism (1981), Victor Grayson (1985); *Style—* Dr David Clark, MP; House of Commons, London SW1A 0AA

CLARK, David Wincott; s of Jack Wincott Clark, of Halnackar W Sussex, and Winifred Mary, *née* Watley (d 1988); *b* 21 June 1947; *Educ* Archbishop Tenisons GS, QMC London (BSc); *m* 20 July 1974, Susan Margaret, da of Maj Kenneth McCrae Cowan, RA; 2 s (Matthew b 1980, Daniel b 1981), 1 da (Sarah b 1985); *Career* Bankers Trust Int 1969-76, dep gen mangr Commerzbank AG 1976-, chm Forex Assoc London 1987-88 (ctee memb 1982), sec gen Assoc Cambiste Internationale 1988-, memb euro advisory ctee Chicago Mercantile Exchange; Rotherfield Cons Assoc ctee memb; FRSA; *Recreations* rugby, angling, sailing; *Style—* David Clark, Esq; Readings Farm, Rotherfield, E Sussex (☎ 089 285 2360); 10-11 Austin Friars, London EC2N 2HE (☎ 01 638 5895)

CLARK, Derek John; s of Robert Clark (d 1970), of Eastbourne, and Florence Mary, *née* Wise (d 1960); *b* 17 June 1929; *Educ* Selhurst GS, SE London Tech Coll 1956-59; *m* 21 March 1949, Edna Doris, da of Alfred Coome (d 1966), of Croydon; 1 s (Paul Wesley b 1949), 1 da (Laura Alison b 1954); *Career* Nat Serv RAF 1948-49; asst sec (leter comptroller) RICS 1966-70, dir of admin Inst of Cost Mgmnt Accountants 1970-82, sec Inst of Structural Engrs 1982-; FCIS 1982; *Recreations* squash, athletics; *Style—* Derek Clark, Esq; 7 Elvington Green, Hayesford Park, Bromley, Kent BR2 9DE (☎ 01 460 9055); The Inst of Structural Engineers, 11 Upper Belgrave St, London SW1X 8BH (☎ 01 235 4535)

CLARK, Dr Douglas Henderson; s of William Robb Clark (d 1932), of Cummock, Ayrshire, and Jane Henderson Clark (d 1979); *b* 20 Jan 1917; *Educ* Ayr Acad, Glasgow Univ (MD, ChM, DSc), Johns Hopkins Hosp Baltimore USA; *m* 5 April 1950, Morag (d 1972), da of Capt Donald Kennedy, of Glasgow (d 1930); 3 s (William Robb Kennedy b 1951, Donald Kennedy b 1955, Alan Douglas b 1957); *Career* Capt RAMC 1941-46 served: India, Burma, Malaya; surgn Western Infimary, ret 1982; pres RCP Glas 1980-82, memb ct Glasgow Univ 1982-; Hon DSc Glasgow Univ; fell Acad Med Singapore 1982, hon FRCS 1983, hon FRCS Ireland, fell Coll of Surgns SA 1980; *Style—* Dr Douglas Clark; 36 Southbrae Dr, Glasgow G13 1PZ (☎ 041 959 3556)

CLARK, Francis Drake; s of late Sir Thomas Clark, 3 Bt and hp of bro, 4 Bt; *b* 16 July 1924; *Educ* Edinburgh Acad; *m* 14 Aug 1958, Mary, da of late John Alban Andrews, MC, FRCS; 1 s (Edward Drake b 27 April 1966); *Career* RN 1943-46; *Style—* Francis Clark, Esq; 2 Woodend Cottages, Burgh-next-Aylsham, Norfolk

CLARK, Geoffrey Mossop; TD (1962); s of Maj James John Clark (d 1947), and Muriel Rose, *née* Mossop (d 1976); *b* 23 Oct 1928; *Educ* Quarry Bank Sch Liverpool; *m* 1, 10 Aug 1956 (m dis 1979), Ruth, da of Llewellyn Merrick-Jones (d 1974); 3 da (Deborah b 17 March 1958, d 1970, Philippa b 30 June 1960, Rebecca b 19 June 1968); m2, 25 April 1981, Diana Celia, da of Ronald George Murphy (d 1971) ; *Career* cmmn Royal Signals 1948; TA 1949-68: cmd 307 Signal Sqdn 1963-66, 1 Sqdn 59 Signal Regt 1966-68; Royal Insur 1950-81 (mangr Leeds Life Branch 1973-81), md Stylo Insur Mgmnt Ltd 1981-; Insur Inst of Leeds: sec 1973-80, pres 1982-83, currently vice-pres; FCII 1958; *Recreations* golf, gardening; *Clubs* Pannal Golf; *Style—* Geoffrey Clark, Esq; Mill Cottage, Pannal, Harrogate, N Yorks GH3 1JY (☎ 0423 879 387); Stylo House, Apperley Bridge, Bradford BD10 0NW (☎ 0274 617 761)

CLARK, Sir George Anthony; 3 Bt (UK 1917), of Dunlambert, City of Belfast, DL (Belfast 1961); s of Sir George Ernest Clark, 2 Bt, DL, MA (d 1950); *b* 24 Jan 1914; *Educ* Canford; *m* 15 Feb 1949, Nancy Catherine, 2 da of George Wallis Newport Clark, of Carnabane, Upperlands, Co Londonderry; 1 da (Elizabeth b 1960); *Heir* bro, Colin Clark, MC; *Career* Capt Res of Officers Black Watch 1939-64, MP (U) Dock Div Belfast, N Ireland Parl senator 1951-69, high sheriff Co Antrim 1954; *Recreations* golf, tennis, fishing; *Clubs* Naval and Military, Royal Ulster Yacht; *Style—* Sir George Clark, Bt, DL; Tullygirvan House, Ballygowan, Newtownards, Co Down (☎ 0238 528267)

CLARK, George Thomas; s of George Clark (d 1938), of 33 Sedley Taylor Rd, Cambridge, and the late Daisy Elizabeth, *née* Jaques; *b* 24 May 1919; *Educ* Perse Sch Cambridge, Jesus Coll Cambridge (MA, LLB); *m* 10 Nov 1941, Barbara Elizabeth (Betty) (d 1986), da of the late Charles Frederick Morley, of 36 Barrow Rd, Cambridge; 1 s (Timothy Glanvil Clark), 1 da (Patricia Mary (Mrs Barnes)); *Career* cmmnd 1939, Arborfield 1939-40, Staff Lt 1940-41, posted: REMBR via Liverpool 1943 ended up in Beolali, 1 Indian Regt Muslim Hindu mix, 8 Sikh Regt, 9 Raj (demob Maj 1946), WWII Victory Medal; articled clerk Landons 1946-48, admitted slr 1948; Freshfields: manager 1949, ptnr 1952, ret ptnr 1982; chm Cowden Villiage Hall Ctee; pres: Cowden & Dist hort Soc, Copwden & Dist Sports Assoc; charitable work; Freeman City of London, Master City of London Slrs Co 1976-77; memb Law Soc, FRSA, Kentucky Colonel USA; *Recreations* gardening, walking, reading, writing letters, music; *Clubs* Oriental

CLARK, Rev (Charles) Gordon Froggatt; s of Rev Charles Clark (d 1940), and Amy, *née* Froggatt; *b* 21 April 1907; *Educ* Oakham Sch, Emmanuel Coll Cambridge (MA), Wycliffe Hall Oxford; *m* 10 Feb 1934, Joan, da of Capt Raleigh Hills (d 1938), of Wood End, Cromford, Derbys; 2 da (Ruth b 21 April 1935, Susan b 28 Aug 1938); *Career* ordained: deacon 1931, priest 1932; asst curate: St John Ealing 1931-33, St Matthew Bayswater 1933-35; rector Ilmington Diocese of Coventry 1935-40; curate: Somercotes Diocese of Derby 1940-43, Barton Seagrave Diocese of Peterborough 1943-48; vicar All Saints Crowborough Diocese of Chichester 1948-67, chaplain Kent Sussex Hosp Tunbridge Wells 1967-80, Diocese of Rochester commissary to Bishop of Ekiiti (Nigeria) 1967-, hon curate Tunbridge Wells Holy Trinity with Christ Church Rochester 1967-80, licence to officiate 1967-85; permission to officiate: Chichester 1967-, Canterbury 1967-; hon curate Penshurst and Fordcombe Rochester 1980-84, permission to officiate 1985-; govr Wadhurst Coll 1949-, vice-pres Church Missionary Soc (CMS); hon memb Tunbridge Wells Rotary Club; Freeman City of London 1928, Liveryman Worshipful Co of Grocers 1933; *Recreations* bowls; *Clubs* National, City Livery; *Style—* The Rev Gordon Clark; Froggatt Edge, Orchard Rise, Groombridge, Tunbridge Wells, Kent TN3 9RZ (☎ 0892 864 777)

CLARK, Graham Ronald; s of Ronald Edward Clark, of 17 Lea Road, Lea, Preston, Lancs, and Annie, *née* Eckersley (d 1984); *b* 10 Nov 1941; *Educ* Kirkham GS Lancs, Loughborough Coll of Educn (DLC), Loughborough Univ (MSc); *m* 1, 9 April 1966 (m dis 1975), Susan, da of late Walter George Fenn, of Oxford; m 2, 31 March 1979, Joan Barbara, da of Albert Frederick Lawrence (d 1956), of Dunstable, Beds; 1 step da (Sarah Elisabeth b 8 Oct 1965); *Career* opera singer, character tenor; teacher 1964-69 Mexborough GS Yorks, head PE dept 1966-69; sr regnl offr The Sports Cncl 1971-75; princ Scottish Opera 1975-77, debut London Bomarzo (Ginastera) 1976, princ ENO 1978-85; roles include: Alexey in The Gambler (Prokofiev), Mephistopheles in Doktor Faustus (Busoni); guest artist at: Bayreuther Festspiele Germany (performed David in Die Meistersinger, Mime and Loge in Ring) 1981-87, Met Opera NY, Vienna Staatsoper, Munich, Zurich, Paris, Barcelona, Amsterdam, Turin, Rome, WNO 1985-88; *Recreations* swimming, golf; *Clubs* Lansdowne; *Style—* Graham Clark, Esq; 21 Benyon Ct, Bath Rd, Reading, Berks (☎ 0734 507 983)

CLARK, Prof (John) Grahame Douglas; CBE (1971); s of Lt-Col Charles Douglas Clark and Maude Ethel Grahame, *née* Shaw; *b* 28 July 1907; *Educ* Marlborough, Peterhouse Cambridge (MA, PhD, ScD); *m* 1936, Gwladys Maude, da of William Llewellyn White; 2 s, 1 da; *Career* Disney prof of archaeology Cambridge Univ 1952-74, head of dept of archaeology and Anthropology 1956-61, master of Peterhouse 1973-80 (fell 1950, hon fell 1980); tstee Br Museum 1975-80; FBA; author of books on archaeology, incl The Identity of Man (1983), Symbols of Excellence (1985); *Style—* Prof Grahame Clark, CBE; 36 Millington Rd, Cambridge (☎ 0223 353287)

CLARK, Guy Wyndham Niall Hamilton; JP (1981), DL (Renfrewshire) 1987; s of Capt George Hubert Wyndham Clark (d 1978), and Lavinia Margaruita Smith, *née* Shaw Stewart (d 1971); *b* 28 Mar 1944; *Educ* Eton, Mons OCS; *m* 28 Jan 1968, Brighid Lovell, da of Maj Lovell Greene, of S Africa; 2 s (Charles, Guy Lovell Wyndham), 1 da (Nicola); *Career* cmmnd Coldstream Gds 1962-67; investmt mangr Murray Johnstone Ltd Glasgow 1973-77, ptnr RC Greig & Co (stockbrokers) Glasgow 1977-86, dir Greig Middleton & Co Ltd (stockbrokers) 1986-; memb exec ctee Erskine Hosp for Disabled Servicemen Renfrewshire; memb Int Stock Exchange 1983; *Recreations* shooting, racing, fishing; *Style—* Guy Clark, Esq; Braeton House, Inverkip, Renfrewshire, PA16 ODU (☎ 0475 520619); Greig, Middleton & Co Ltd, Pacific House, 70 Wellington St, Glasgow G2 6UD fax 041 221 5286, telex 776695)

CLARK, Henry Percival Bolton; *b* 4 Oct 1944; *Educ* Dragon Sch, Harrow; *m* 2 Dec 1978, Gill; 1 s (Austen b 1980), 1 da (Celia b 1982); *Career* managing ptnr Nottingham off Arthur Young; dir: Bridge Housing Soc Ltd, Notts Business Venture; tres Harby PCC, cncl memb Notts C of C and Indust; CA; *Recreations* avoiding all sport; *Style—* Henry Clark, Esq; 10/12 The Ropewalk, Nottingham NG1 5DT (☎ 0602 411861, fax 0602 483 369)

CLARK, Hugh Victor; s of Lt Cdr Phillip Neville Clark, VRD, RNR, of Gorsley, Herefords, and Winifred Betty, *née* Kiddle; *b* 18 May 1948; *Educ* Brewood GS Staffs; *m* 5 Dec 1970, Rosemary Anne, da of Kenneth Walter Solloway, of Wolverhampton; 1 s (Richard Ian b 1974), 1 da (Michelle Emma b 1977); *Career* Westminster Bank Ltd 1965-67, Canadian Imperial Bank of Commerce 1967-70, Nat Westminster Bank Ltd 1970-77; Tarmac plc: tres accountant 1978-83, asst gp tres 1983-87, gp tres 1987-; ACIB 1975, MCT 1982; *Recreations* photography, motor racing; *Style—* Hugh Clark, Esq; Tarmac plc, Hilton Hall, Essington, Wolverhampton WV11 2BQ (☎ 0902 307 407, fax 0902 307 408, telex 338544)

CLARK, Ian Robertson; CBE (1979); s of Alexander Clark and Annie Dundas, *née* Watson; *b* 18 Jan 1939; *Educ* Dalziel HS Motherwell; *m* 1961, Jean Scott Waddell, *née* Lang; 1 s, 1 da; *Career* chm: Ventures Div, Costain Gp, Sigma Resources plc, 1986-88, Br Nat Oil Corpn 1976-82, BNOC Ventures; jt md Britoil 1982-85; former co tres Zetland CC; chief exec Shetlands Islands Cncl 1974-76; memb: Court Glasgow Univ, Scottish Econ Cncl; *Books* Resevoir of Power (1979); *Recreations* reading, writing, walking; *Style—* Ian Clark, Esq, CBE; 16 Pan's Gardens, Camberley, Surrey GU15 1HY

CLARK, Sir John Allen; eld s of Sir Allen Clark (d 1962), and Jocelyn, *née* Culverhouse; bro of Michael William Clark, *qv*; *b* 14 Feb 1926; *Educ* Harrow (govr 1982-), Trinity Coll Cambridge; *m* 1, 1952 (m dis 1962), Deirdre Kathleen, da of Samuel Herbert Waterhouse; 1 s, 1 da; m 2, 1970, Olivia, da of H Pratt; 2 s (twins), 1 da; *Career* served WWII RNVR (Sub-Lt); received early industl training with Met Vickers and Ford Motor co; spent year in USA studying electronics indust; asst to gen mangr Plessey Int Ltd 1949, dir and gen mangr Plessey (Ireland) and Wireless

Telephone Co 1950; The Plessey Co Ltd: dir 1953, md 1962-70, dep chm 1967-70, chm and chief exec 1970-; dir: Int Computers Ltd 1968-79, Banque Nationale de Paris Ltd 1976-; pres Telecommunications Engrg and Mfrg Assoc 1964-66 and 1971-73; chm Wavertree Technol Park 1983-88 ; vice-pres: Inst of Works Mangrs, Engrg Employers' Fedn; memb: Nat Defence Industs Cncl, Engrg Industs Cncl 1975-; Order of Henry the Navigator (Portugal) 1973; kt 1971; *Recreations* shooting, riding; *Clubs* Boodle's; *Style—* Sir John Clark; The Plessey Co plc, Millbank Tower, 21-24 Millbank, London SW1P 4QP (☎ 01 834 3855)

CLARK, Sir John Douglas; 4 Bt (UK 1886), of Melville Crescent, Edinburgh; s of Sir Thomas Clark, 3 Bt (d 1977); *b* 9 Jan 1923; *Educ* Gordonstoun, Edinburgh Univ; *m* 1969, Anne, da of late Angus Gordon; *Heir* bro, Francis Clark; *Career* publisher; former ptnr T and T Clark Publishers Edinburgh; *Style—* Sir John Clark, Bt; 52 Ormidale Terrace, Edinburgh 12 (☎ (031 337) 5610)

CLARK, John Edward; s of Albert Edward Clark (d 1973), of Kent, and Edith, *née* Brown (d 1984); *b* 18 Oct 1932; *Educ* Clitheroe Royal GS, Keble Coll Oxford (MA, BCL); *m* 1969, Judith Rosemary, da of Dr Arnold Marklew Lester; 1 da (Katherine, decd), 1 s (Roy); *Career* barr; sec of Nat Assoc of Local Cncls 1978-, dep sec Nat Assoc of Parish Cncls 1961-78; *Recreations* board games, collecting detective fiction, walking; *Style—* John Clark, Esq; 113 Turney Rd, London SE21 7JB (☎ 01 274 1381); 108 Great Russell St, London WC1B 3LD (☎ 01 637 1865)

CLARK, Keith; s of Douglas William Clark (d 1967), of Chicester, Sussex, and Evelyn Lucy, *née* Longlands; *b* 25 Oct 1944; *Educ* Chicester HS for Boys, St Catherine's Coll Oxford (MA, BA); *m* 2 Nov 1976, Linda Sue, da of Eric Woodler, Ringwood, Hants; 1 s (Nicholas Howard Douglas b 1980), 1 da (Katherine Sara Amy b 1984); *Career* slr; ptnr (joined 1971, specialising fin law and sov debt restructuring, various mgmt appts) Clifford Chance 1977-; memb: Law Soc 1971, Slrs Benevolent Soc, Int Bar Assoc; *Recreations* hiking, family, drama; *Style—* Keith Clark, Esq; Royex Ho, Aldermanbury Sq, London EC2V 7LD (☎ 01 600 0808, fax 01 726 8561, telex 8959991)

CLARK, Ven Kenneth James; DSC (1944); s of Francis James Clark, OBE, of 15 Elizabeth Ct, Hempstead Rd, Watford, Herts, and Winifred Adelaide, *née* Martin (d 1984); *b* 31 May 1922; *Educ* Watford GS, St Catherine's Soc, Oxford Univ (MA), Cuddesdon Theol Coll Oxford; *m* 24 July 1948, Elisabeth Mary Monica Helen, da of Arthur St George Joseph McCarthy Huggett, FRS (d 1968); 3 s (Simon b 1954, Alistair b 1954, Jonathan b 1958), 3 da (Marguerite b 1949, Christine b 1951, Rachel b 1964); *Career* Cadet RN 1939, Midshipman 1940, Lt 1942, served in Submarines 1942-46, ret; baptist minster Forest Row Sussex 1950-52; ordained (C of E): deacon 1952, priest 1953; curate: Brinkworth 1952-53, Cricklade and Latton 1953-56; vicar: Holy Cross Inns Court Bristol 1956-61, Westbury-on-Trym Bristol 1961-72, St Mary Redcliffe Bristol 1972-82; rural dean Bedminster 1973-79, hon canon Bristol 1974-, archdeacon of Swindon 1982-; *Recreations* music, travel; *Style—* The Ven the Archdeacon of Swindon; 70 Bath Rd, Swindon, Wilts SN1 4AY (☎ 0793 695 059)

CLARK, His Hon Judge (Francis) Leo; QC (1972); s of Sydney John Clark (d 1969), of Oxford, and Florence Lilian, *née* Clark; *b* 15 Dec 1920; *Educ* Bablake Sch, St Peter's Coll Oxford; *m* 1, 1957, Denise Jacqueline, da of Raymond Rambaud, of Paris; 1 s; m 2, 1967, Dr Daphne Margaret, da of David Humphreys, of Hitchin; *Career* barr 1947, rec Crown Ct 1972-76, circuit judge 1976-; *Style—* His Honour Judge Leo Clark, QC; The Ivy House, Charlbury, Oxon (☎ 0608 810242)

CLARK, Leslie Joseph; CBE (1977, BEM 1942); s of late Joseph George Clark and Elizabeth, *née* Winslow; *b* 21 May 1914; *Educ* Stationers Company's Sch, King's Coll London U (BSc Eng, MSc); *m* 1940, Mary Myfanwy, da of Robert Peacock; 1 s, 1 da; *Career* chartered engineer; chm Northern Gas Bd 1967-75, chm Victor Products (Wallsend) Ltd 1976-79, former pres International Gas Union; FEng, FICE, FIMechE, FIGasE, FInstE MIEE MIChemE; *Style—* Leslie Clark Esq, CBE, BEM; Hillway, New Ridley Rd, Stocksfield, Northumberland NE43 7QB (☎ (066 15) 2339)

CLARK, Dr Michael; MP (Cons) Rochford 1983-; s of late Mervyn Clark and Sybilla Norma, *née* Winscott; *b* 8 August 1935; *Educ* King Edward VI GS Retford, King's Coll London, St John's Coll Cambridge, Univ of Minnesota; *m* 1958, Valerie Ethel, da of C S Harbord; 1 s, 1 da; *Career* mgmnt conslt and industl chemist; ICI 1960-66, Smiths Industs 1966-69, pa Mgmnt Conslts 1969-; Cambridge Cons Assoc Tres 1975-78, vice-chm 1978-80, chm 1980-83, Ilkeston 1979; House of Commons Select Ctee for Energy 1983-; hon tres Br-Malawi All Pty Gp 1987-, hon sec: Parly and Scientific Ctee 1985-, Anglo-Nepalese All Pty Gp 1985-, All-Pty Gp for the Chemical Indust 1985-; exec ctee Inter Parly Union 1987-; fell King's Coll London 1987, Royal Soc of Chemistry 1988;; *Recreations* golf, gardening, DIY; *Clubs* Carlton, Rochford Cons; *Style—* Dr Michael Clark, MP; House of Commons, London SW1A 0AA

CLARK, Michael William; CBE (1977), DL (1988 Essex); s of Sir Allen Clark (d 1962), of Braxted Park, Witham, Essex, and Jocelyn Anina Marie Louise, *née* Culverhouse (d 1968), bro of Sir John Clark, *qv*; *b* 7 May 1927; *Educ* Harrow; *m* 1, 1955, Shirley (d 1974), da of Alec MacPhayden (d 1938), of Toronto; 1 s (Duncan Allan b 1960), 1 step s (Matthew Harragin b 1952), 2 da (Marion b 1956 d 1988; Miranda b 1958); m 2, 1985, Virginia Ann, da of Dr Francis Harry Hume Finlaison (d 1968), and former w of 6 Marquess Camden; *Career* served Grenadier Guards 1945-48; joined Plessey Co 1950, dep chm and dep ch exec Plessey Co Ltd, fndr and chm Plessey Electronic Systems Ltd; ret 1987; *Recreations* shooting, fishing, forestry; *Clubs* Boodle's, Pratt's; *Style—* Michael Clark Esq, CBE, DL; Braxted Park, Witham, Essex CM8 3EN (☎ 0621 891393)

CLARK, Hon Mrs (Moira Muriel); o da of Baron Sorensen (Life Peer, d 1971); *b* 6 Oct 1917; *m* 13 Oct 1951, Derek Gerald Clark, JP, s of Wilfred Charles Clark (d 1971), of 12 Smeaton Rd, Woodford Bridge, Essex; 2 da; *Style—* The Hon Mrs Clark; 15 Crossing Rd, Epping, Essex

CLARK, Baroness; Nolwen Louise-Marie-Alix; *née* de Janzé; da of Frederic, Comte de Janzé and Alice Silverthorne; *b* 1922; *Educ* Sarah Laurence College Bronxville USA (BA); m 1 1947, (m dis 1949), Lionel Armand-DeLille, 1 s, 1 da; m 2, 1962, Edward Denis Rice (d 1973); m 3, 1977, as his 2 w, Baron Clark, OM, CH, KCB (Life Peer, d 1983); *Career* served with Free French Forces 1944-45; *Recreations* music, travel, reading; *Style—* The Rt Hon the Lady Clark; Chateau de Parfondeval, St Pierre des Jonquieres, 76660 Londinieres, France (☎ 35 93 83 36)

CLARK, Oswald William Hugh; CBE (1978); s of Rev Hugh Miller Allison Clark (d 1962), of Raynes Park, London SW20, and Mabel Bessie Clark (d 1969); *b* 26 Nov 1917; *Educ* Rutlish Sch Merton, Univ of London (BA, BD); *m* 23 July 1966, Diana Mary, da of William Alfred Hine, of New Milton, Hants; 1 da (Alison Mary Cynthia b 1967); *Career* WWII Maj 2 Derbyshire Yeomanry 8 Army ME NW Europe; asst dir gen GLC 1973-79 (formerly London Co Cncl, joined 1937); C of E: memb gen synod (formerly church assembly 1948-, memb standing and legislative ctees 1950, chm standing orders ctee 1950-, church cmmnr 1958-88, vice pres corpn of church house 1981-, memb crown appts cmmn 1987-; life fell Guild of Guide Lectrs 1982-, princ Soc of the Faith 1987-; memb Worshipful Co of Parish Clerks; *Recreations* history of London; goss china, heraldry; *Clubs* Cavalry and Guard's; Pratt's; *Style—* O W H Clark, Esq, CBE; 8 Courtlands Ave, Hampton, Middx TW12 3NT (☎ 01 979 1081)

CLARK, His Hon Judge Paul Paul Nicholas Rowntree; s of Henry Rowntree Clark (d 1975), and Gwendoline Victoria Clark; *b* 17 August 1940; *Educ* Bristol GS, New Coll Oxford (MA); *m* 9 Sept 1967, Diana Barbara, da of Maurice Stapenhill Bishop, of Lyme Regis, Dorset; 2 s (Oliver b 1972, Edward b 1977), 1 da (Harriet b 1970); *Career* called to the Bar Middle Temple (Harmsworth scholar) 1966, bencher 1982, barr practising on Oxford Circuit, later Midland and Oxford Circuit 1966-85, rec 1981, CJ 1985-; *Style—* His Hon Judge Paul Clark; 2 Harcourt Buildings, Temple, London EC4Y 9DB

CLARK, Raymond Vincent; s of Peter Clark, of Broxbourne, Herts, and Eileen, *née* Rothery; *b* 26 Feb 1946; *Educ* Tottenham Boys Sch, NE London Poly (Dip Arch); *m* 16 Aug 1969, Gillian Elizabeth, da of Henry Cook, of Frinton, Essex; 2 s (Simon b 15 May 1978, Iain b 22 July 1982); *Career* ptnr Clark Hatt Quirke partnership 1982- (co-fndr); memb: RIBA 1976, ARCUK 1976; *Style—* Raymond Clark, Esq; Knot's Foss, 73 Hall Lane, Gt Chishill, Royston, Herts (0763 838 785); Clark Hatt Quirke Partnership, The Maltings, 44 Whitehorse St, Baldock, Hertfordshire (☎ 0462 895 110, fax 0462 895 099, car tel 0860 341 878)

CLARK, Sir Robert Anthony; DSC (1944); yr s of John Clark and Gladys, *née* Dyer; *b* 6 Jan 1924; *Educ* Highgate, King's Coll Cambridge; *m* 1949, Andolyn Marjorie Beynon Lewis; 2 s, 1 da; *Career* ptnr Slaughter and May Slrs 1953; Hill Samuel Bank Ltd 1974-, TSB Hill Samuel Bank Hldg Co plc 1981- (joined 1961, later Philip Hill, Higginson, Erlangers Ltd), IMI 1981-, Alfred McAlpine plc 1958-, Marley plc 1985-, dir Shell Tport and Trading 1982-; chm: Doctors and Dentists Review Body 1979-86, Charing Cross Hosp Med Sch 1981-; Hon DSc (Cranfield) 1982; kt 1976; *Clubs* Pratt's; *Style—* Sir Robert Clark, DSC; Deputy Chairman, TSB Group plc, 100 Wood St, London EC2P 2AJ (☎ 01 628 8011); Munstead Wood, Godalming, Surrey (☎ 04868 7867)

CLARK, Prof Robert Bernard; s of Joseph Laurence Clark (d 1980), of London and Burrowbridge, Somerset, and Dorothy, *née* Halden (d 1988); *b* 13 Oct 1923; *Educ* St Marylebone GS, Univ of London (BSc), Univ of Exeter (BSc), Univ of Glasgow (PhD), Univ of London (DSc); *m* 1, 19 July 1956 (m dis 1969), Mary Eleanor, da of Walter Lawrence (d 1969), of San Francisco, USA; m 2 30 Dec 1970, Susan Diana, da of Lt-Col Leonard Smith (d 1971), of Haslemere, Surrey; *Career* asst in zoology Univ of Glasgow 1950-53, asst prof of zoology Univ of Calif at Berkeley USA 1953-55, lectr in zoology Univ of Bristol 1956-65, prof in zoology and dir The Dove Marine Laboratory Univ of Newcastle upon Tyne 1965-; memb NERC 1971-77 and 1982-85, Royal Cmmn on Environmental Pollution 1978-82, Advsy Commn on Pesticides 1985-; FiBiol 1966, FLS 1969, FRSE 1970; *Books* Dynamics in Metazoan Evolution (1964), Invertebrate Panorama (1971), Marine Pollution (1986), Marine Pollution Bulletin (ed); *Style—* Prof Robert Clark; Highbury House, Highbury, Newcastle Upon Tyne NE2 3LN (☎ 091 281 4672); Department of Biology, University, Newcastle Upon Tyne NE1 7RU (☎ 091 232 8511)

CLARK, Prof Ronald George; s of George Clark (d 1968), of Loanhead, Cairnie, Aberdeenshire, and Gladys, *née* Taylor (d 1987); *b* 9 August 1928; *Educ* Aberdeen Acad, Univ of Aberdeen (MB, ChB); *m* 10 Sept 1960, Tamar Welsh, da of Walter Erskine Harvie (d 1961), of Duntocher, Dumbartonshire; 2 da (Tamar Taylor b 1962, Deborah Harvie b 1964); *Career* lectr Univ of Glasgow 1961-65, surgical res fell Harvard Univ 1960-61; Univ of Sheffield: sr lectr of surgery 1966-71, prof surgery 1971-, dean of faculty med and dentistry 1982-85, pro vice-chllr 1988-; memb Gen Med Cncl 1982-, sci govr Br Nutrition Fndn 1983-, cncl memb Nutrition Soc 1981-84, exec chm Euro Soc of Parental and Enteral Nutrition 1982-87; FRCS, FRCS (Edinburgh); memb: Assoc of Surgns 1969, RSM 1979; *Recreations* golf, walking; *Clubs* RSM, Cwlth Soc; *Style—* Prof Ronald Clark; 2 Chesterwood Drive, Sheffield S10 5DU (☎ 0742 663 601); Clinical Sciences Centre, Northern General Hosp, Sheffield S5 7AU (☎ 0742 434 343 ext 4191)

CLARK, Terence George; OBE (1980); s of George Cyril Clark (d 1960); *b* 6 Mar 1922; *Educ* Southampton Poly, Regent Poly; *m* 1946, Patricia Eve, da of George Alfred Careford (d 1968), horticulturist; 2 s (Nigel, Graeme); *Career* military and civil airfield construction 1940-45; fndr memb Soil Mechanics Ltd 1944-61; md and chm ELE Ltd 1961-82; pres Soil-Test Inc Chicago 1980-82; dep chm and md Mowlem Eng Prods Div 1980-82; ret from Mowlem Gp 1982; dir: Terry Turner Ltd (Mgt conslts) 1980-, sr ptnr Terry Clark Assoc 1980-, chm Herts and Beds EEC Business Cncl 1980-83; dep chmn C Stevens and Son (Weighing Machines) Ltd 1985-; chm: Unimetrics Ltd 1985-, AWT Ltd 1985-, Dunwich Museum Charity 1985-; *Recreations* numismatics, horticulture, music, piano; *Style—* Terence Clark, Esq, OBE; St James House, Park Rd, Toddington, Beds (☎ 052 55 2060), Heathfield House, Westleton Road, Dunwich, Suffolk (☎ 0728 73578)

CLARK, Terence Joseph; CMG (1985), CVO (1978); s of Joseph Henry Clark (d 1971), of London, and Mary Ann Matilda Clark; *b* 19 June 1934; *Educ* Parmiter's Foundation Sch London, Univ of Grenoble, Cambridge Univ, London Univ, Freiburg Univ; *m* 1960, Lieselotte Rosa Marie, da of Lt Cdr Erich Ernst Müller, of Kiel; 2 s (Adrian, Martin), 1 da (Sonja); *Career* Pilot Offr RAF VR 1955, entered HM Foreign Serv 1955, ME Centre of Arab Studies Lebanon 1956-57; third sec Political Residency, Bahrain 1957-58, Br Embassy Amman Jordan 1958-60, vice consul Br Consulate Gen Casablanca 1960-62, FO 1962-65, asst political agent Dubai, Trucial States 1965-68; first sec (Info) Belgrade 1969-71; head of Chancery and Consul Muscat Oman 1972-73; asst head ME Depart FCO 1974-75; cncllr (Info); Bonn 1976-79, cllr Belgrade 1979-82; dep ldr of UK Delgn to Conf on Security and Cooperation in Europe (Madrid) 1982-83; head of Info Dept FCO 1983-85, ambass Rep of Iraq 1985-; hon vice-pres Br Archaeological Expdn to Iraq 1985-, memb Royal Cwlth Soc; *Recreations* salukis, tennis, walking; *Clubs* Hurlingham; *Style—* Terence Clark Esq, CMG, CVO; Baghdad c/o FCO, King Charles St, London SW1A 2AH

CLARK, (Alastair) Trevor; CBE (1976), LVO (1974); s of Dr William George Clark, CBE, KHP, (d 1957) and Gladys Catherine *née* Harrison (d 1969); *b* 10 June 1923;

Educ Glasgow and Edinburgh Acads, Magdalen Coll Oxford (MA); *m* 1 May 1965, Hilary Agnes, da of Dr John Binnie Mackenzie Anderson (d 1944); *Career* WWII, cmmnd Queen's Own Cameron Highlanders second RWAFF (temp Maj) served Nigeria, India, Burma 1942-46; served admin branch HM Colonial Serv (later HMOCS): Nigeria (sec to exec cncl, sr dist offr) 1949-59, Hong Kong (clerk of cncls, princ asst Colonial Sec, dir social welfare, dep and actg dir Urban Servs, acting chm Urban Cncl) 1960-72; W Pacific (chief sec W Pacific High Cmmn, dep and acting govr Solomon Islands) 1972-77; ret 1977; barr Middle Temple; USA State Dept Country ldr Fellowship 1972, UN Conf on Human Enviroment Stockholm 1972; memb: Scottish Museums Cncl 1980- (chm 1981-84, 1987-), Museums Assoc Cncl 1982-86, Sec of State for Scotlands' Museum Advsy Bd 1983-85, vice chm ctee Area Museum Cncls 1983-84, Nat Museums of Scotland Charitable Tst 1987; tstee Bd of nat Museum of Scotland 1985-87, jt fndr Hong Kong Outward Bound Sch 1966, chm Edinburgh Heritage Tst 1984-, memb Edinburgh Int Festival Cncl 1980-86, govr Edinburgh Filmhouse 1980-84 and 1987-, dir Edinburgh Acad 1979-84, cncllr Nat Tst for Scotland 1981-84 and 1987-; Leverhulme Tst Grant 1979-81 (biographer of Sir Abubakar Tafawa Balewa, late PM of Nigeria); memb: City of Edinburgh DC 1980-88; Lothian Health Bd 1981-, race relations panel (Scottish Sheriff Cts) 1983-; *Recreations* listening to music and opera, books, theatre, netsuke, cartophily; *Clubs* Athenaeum, New (Edinburgh); *Style*— Trevor Clark, Esq; 11 Ramsay Garden, Edinburgh, EH1 2NA (☎ 031 225 8070)

CLARK, Cdr Victor Cecil Froggatt; DSC (1940 and Bar 1942); s of Rev Charles Clark (d 1940), of The Valley House, Glassmill Lane, Bromley, Kent, and Amy, *née* Froggatt (d 1966); *b* 24 May 1908; *Educ* Haileybury; *m* 10 May 1975, Danae Heather, da of Frederick James Stileman (d 1982), of Broadwood Farm, Dunster, Somerset; 2 da (Jessica b 1976, Rosalind b 1980); *Career* RN: Cadet 1926, Midshipman Med Fleet (HMS Valiant, HMS Wren, HMS Warspite, HMS Courageous) 1927-29, Sub Lt courses Portsmouth and Greenwich 1930, Med Fleet HMS Anthony 1931-32, Home Fleet HMS Watchman 1932-34, Boys Trg Estab HMS Ganges 1935-37, HMS Wild Swan Jubilee Review 1937, Med Fleet HMS Warspite 1937-38, Home Fleet HMS Punjabi active serv Battle Narvik 1938-40, i/c HMS Anthony 1940-41, HMS Repulse (sunk in action off Singapore) organised commando raids (W Coast Raiders) during Malayan Campaign 1941-42 carried out secret evaluation of 2000 troops from behind Japanese lines, sunk in action with superior Japanese forces, wounded one and a half days in water with broken arm, 6 weeks in Sumatran jungle, betrayed to Japanese 1942, POW Sumatra and Singapore 1942-45), i/c HMS Loch Tralaig and HMS Loch Dunvegan 1946-47, Trg Offr Sea Cadet HQ London 1947-53, ret as Cdr 1953; circumnavigation (48000 miles) yacht Solace 1953-59, lectr tours 1960-61, sail trg i/c schooners Prince Louis and Capt Scott 1962-74; Freeman City of London 1930, Liveryman Worshipful Co of Grocers 1935; *Books* On The Wind of a Dream (1960); *Recreations* walking, riding, tennis, sailing; *Clubs* Royal Cwlth Soc, Ocean Cruising, RN; *Style*— Cdr Victor Clark, DSC, RN

CLARK, (Henry) Wallace Stuart; MBE (1970), DL (1963); s of Maj Harry Francis Clark, MBE, JP, RA (d 1977), of Rockwood, Upperlands, and Sybil Emily, *née* Stuart; director of family business (linen manufacturers in Upperlands since 1736, celebrated 250th anniversary in 1986); *b* 20 Nov 1926; *Educ* Shrewsbury; *m* 1956, June Elisabeth Lester, da of James Lester Deane, of Belfast; 2 s; *Career* Maj Ulster Defence Regt (NI), Lt RNVR Bomb and Mine Disposal UK, Dist Cmdt Ulster Special Constabulary, dir William Clark and Sons Ltd (Est 1736) Linen Mfrs 1972-,; *Publications* North and East Coasts of Ireland (1957), Guns in Ulster (1963), Linen on the Green (1982), Rathlin Island (1970), Sailing Round Ireland (1975); *Recreations* sailing (yacht Wild Goose of Moyle); *Clubs* Royal Cruising, Irish Cruising; *Style*— Maj Wallace Clark, MBE, DL; Gorteade Cottage, Upperlands, Maghera, Co Londonderry (☎ 0648 42737)

CLARK, Sir William Gibson; MP (C) S Croydon 1974-; s of Hugh Clark, of 17 Cautley Ave, SW4; *b* 18 Oct 1917; *m* 1944, Irene Dorothy Dawson, da of E F Rands, of Grimsby, Lincs; 3 s, 1 da; *Career* served WW II UK and India; contested (C) Northampton 1955, MP (C) Nottingham S 1959-66, E Surrey 1970-74, oppn front bench spokesman Economics 1964-66; jt dep chm Cons Pty Orgn 1975-77 (jt tres 1974-75), chm Cons Fin Ctee 1979-; ACA; kt 1979; *Clubs* Bucks, Carlton; *Style*— Sir William Clark, MP; 3 Barton St, London SW1 (☎ 01 222 5759); The Clock House, Box End, Bedford (☎ 0234 852361)

CLARK, William James; s of William Clark, of Glencarse, Scotland, and Elizabeth Shanks Clark; *b* 3 May 1950; *Educ* Dundee HS, Edinburgh Univ (BSc Agric), Univ of W Ontario Canada (MBA); *m* 28 Aug 1981, Karen Neergaard, da of HE Jorgen Holm, of Danish Embassy, Kuala Lumpur; 2 da (Camilla, Kristina); *Career* regnl mangr origination and corporate fin Chemical Bank London 1987- (regnl mangr energy and minerals 1984-87, gen mangr Singapore 1980-83, regnl mktg mangr Singapore 1979-80, mktg offr London 1974-79); represented GB at athletics 1973-75, UK Triple Jump champion 1974, Scottish Triple Jump champion 1974-76; *Recreations* sport, farming; *Clubs* RAC, Annabel's; *Style*— William J Clark, Esq; Chemical Bank, 180 Strand, London, WC2R 1EX (☎ 01 380 5151)

CLARK-MAXWELL, John William; s of Maj John Noel Clark-Maxwell (d 1987), and Anne Joan, *née* Fearnley-Whittingstall (d 1985); *b* 23 Sept 1933; *Educ* Eton, Magdalene Coll Cambridge (MA); *m* 27 Jan 1973, Juliet Nina, da of Charles Michael Stratton; 1 s (James b 1975), 1 da (Alice b 1979); *Career* CA; landowner; *Recreations* outdoor activities, shooting, music; *Style*— John W Clark-Maxwell, Esq; Speddoch, Dumfries DG2 9UB (☎ 0387 82 342)

CLARKE; *see*: Osmond-Clarke

CLARKE, Andrew Bertram; s of Arthur Bertram Clarke, and Violet Doris, *née* Lewis; *b* 23 August 1956; *Educ* Crewe Co GS, King's Coll London Univ (AKC), Lincoln Coll Oxford (BCL); *m* 1 Aug 1981, Victoria Clare, da of Kelsey Thomas; 1 s (Christopher Harding b 1985), 1 da (Judith Ellen b 1987); *Career* called to the Bar Middle Temple 1981; *Recreations* cricket watching, collecting modern prints; *Clubs* Gloucestershire CCC; *Style*— Andrew Clarke, Esq; 38 Albury Ride, Cheshunt, Herts (☎ 0992 31269); 2 Crown Office Row, Temple, London EC4Y 7HJ (☎ 01 583 2681, fax 01 583 2850)

CLARKE, Anthony Peter; QC (1979); s of Harry Alston Clarke (d 1979), and Isobel, *née* Kay; *b* 13 May 1943; *Educ* Oakham Sch, King's Coll Cambridge; *m* 7 Sept 1968, Rosemary, da of K W Adam, of Barnham, Sussex; 2 s (Ben b 7 Jan 1972, Thomas b 20 June 1973), 1 da (Sally b 3 June 1977); *Career* Arbitrator: Lloyds, ICC; Recorder, Wreck Cmmr, Membre de la Chambre Arbitrale Maritime; *Recreations* tennis, golf, holidays; *Style*— Anthony Clarke Esq QC; Lewis Heath, Horsmonden, Kent TN12 8EE (☎ 0892 723783) 2 Essex Court, Temple, London EC4Y 9AP (☎ 01 583 8381, fax 01 353 0998, telex 8812528 ADROIT)

CLARKE, Arthur C(harles); s of Charles Wright Clarke and Nora Mary, *née* Willis; *b* 16 Dec 1917; *Educ* Huish's GS Taunton, King's Coll London (BSc); *m* 1953 (m dis 1964), Marilyn Mayfield; *Career* serv WWII, Flt Lt RAF; scientist; underwater exploration Great Barrier Reef 1954-63; chllr Univ of Moratuwa Sri Lanka 1979-; Vikram Sarabhai prof PRL Ahmedabad India 1980; Marconi Int fell 1982; Lindbergh Award 1987, Vidya Jothi 1986; dir: Rocket Publishing Co (UK), Underwater Safaris (Sri Lanka); bd memb: Nat Space Inst (USA), Inst of Fundamental Studies, patron Arthur Clarke Centre for Modern Technologies (Sri Lanka); author of books on the Space Age, also science-fiction novelist; *Books include* Arthur C Clarke's Mysterious World (1980; with Simon Welfare and John Fairley; also YTV Series), Arthur C Clarke's World of Strange Powers (1984; with Simon Welfare and John Fairley), Ascent to Orbit (1984), *fiction* Childhood's End (1953), 2001: A Space Odyssey (1968), The Songs of Distant Earth (1986), 2061: Odyssey Three; *Style*— Arthur C Clarke, Esq; Leslie's House, 25 Barnes Place, Colombo 7, Sri Lanka (☎ Colombo 94255, 599757); Rocket Publishing Co, Dene Court, Bishop's Lydeard TA4 3LT (☎ 0823 432671); c/o David Higham Associates, 5-8 Lower John St, Golden Sq, London W1R 4HA

CLARKE, Arthur Grenfell; CMG (1953); s of late Henry Clarke, of Athlone; *b* 17 August 1906; *Educ* Trinity Coll Dublin (BA); *m* 1, 1934, Rhoda McLean (d 1980), da of late Henry William Arnott; m 2, 1980, Violet Louise Riley; *Career* col admin serv Hong Kong 1930-61, financial sec Hong Kong 1951-61; *Style*— Arthur Clarke, Esq, CMG; Foxdene, Brighton Rd, Foxrock, Dublin 18, Ireland (☎ 894368)

CLARKE, Sir (Henry) Ashley; GCMG (1962, KCMG 1952, CMG 1946), GCVO (1961); s of Henry Hugh Rose Clarke, MD (d 1962), of Rottingdean, Sussex, and Rachel Hill, *née* Duncan; *b* 26 June 1903; *Educ* Repton, Pembroke Coll Cambridge (MA, hon fell 1962); *m* 1, 15 June 1937 (m dis 1960), Virginia, Bell, of New York; m 2, Aug 1962, Frances Pickett, OBE (1984), da of John Molyneux of Stourbridge, Worcs; *Career* joined Dip Serv 1925, served Budapest, Warsaw, Constantinople, FO, League of Nations, Tokyo, min Lisbon 1944-46, min Paris 1946-49, dep under-sec of state FO 1949-53, ambass to Italy 1953-62, ret; memb Nat Theatre Bd 1962-66; govr BBC 1962-67; chm: Royal Acad of Dancing 1964-69, Italian Art and Archives Rescue Fund 1966-70; vice-chm Venice in Peril Fund 1970-84, (pres 1984-); dir Royal Acad of Music 1973-84 (hon fellow), vice-pres Ancient Monuments Soc; Pietro Torta Prize (Venice) 1976, Kt of St Mark (Venice) 1979; Kt Grand Cross Order of Merit (Italy) 1961, Kt Grand Cross Order of St Gregory the Great 1976; Freeman of the City of Venice 1985; FSA; *Recreations* music; *Clubs* Athenaeum, Garrick; *Style*— Sir Ashley Clarke, GCMG, GCVO; Bushy Cottage, The Green, Hampton Court, Surrey KT8 9BS (☎ 01 943-2709); Fondamenta Bonlini 1113, Dorsoduro, 30123 Venice, Italy (☎ Venice 5206530)

CLARKE, Lady Betty Jocelyne; *née* Bourke; da of 8 Earl of Mayo (d 1939), and his 2 wife Margaret Anah, *née* Harvey Scott (d 1964); *b* 18 August 1917; *Educ* Queen Anne's Caversham Berks; *m* 1, 21 May 1943, Capt Ronald Banon, late 60th Rifles (d 22 Aug 1943), oc of Brig-Gen Lionel Banon, CB; m 2, 27 April 1953, Samuel Clarke; 2 da (Elizabeth b 1955, Jocelyne b 1957); *Style*— Lady Betty Clarke; 361 Woodstock Rd, Oxford OX2 8AA

CLARKE, Bruce Robert Duncan; s of Robert Duncan Clarke (d 1936), of Elbury, Worcs, and Beatrice Gertrude, *née* Rose (d 1978); *b* 3 Oct 1924; *Educ* Clifton, Trinity Coll Cambridge (MA, LLM); *m* 24 July 1965, Margaret, da of Thomas Alfred Matthews (d 1947), of Canford Cliffs, Poole; *Career* WWII Royal Corps of Signals and Intelligence Corps 1943-46; serv: UK 19543-45, Egypt & India 1945-46; slr Elvy Robb & Co 1948-54; Br Oxygen Co Ltd 1954-62: asst sec 1956, sec 1958, admin offr tech div 1961-62; slrs office Inland Rev 1962-: legal asst 1962-67, sr legal asst 1967-80, asst slr 1980-88, princ legal offr 1988- (rating valuation); dir RN Ltd 1981-88; Fin Ctee RIAA 1958-70; memb Law Soc, MInstD; *Recreations* reading, wine, good talk; *Clubs* The Athenaeum; *Style*— Bruce Clarke, Esq; 7 Warwick Sq, London SW1V 2AA (☎ 01 834 2635); Solicitor of Inland Revenue, Somerset House, Strand, London WC2R 1LB (☎ 01 438 6449/7725)

CLARKE, Prof Bryan Campbell; s of Robert Campbell Clarke (d 1941), of Sywell Hall, Sywell, Northants, and Gladys Mary, *née* Carter (1987); *b* 24 June 1932; *Educ* Fay Sch Southborough Mass, Magdalen Coll Sch Oxford, Magdalen Coll Oxford (MA, DPhil); *m* 20 Aug 1960, Dr Ann Gillian, da of Prof John Jewkes, CBE (d 1988), of Boar's Hill, Oxford; 1 s (Peter b 1971), 1 da (Alexandra 1975); *Career* Pilot Off RAF 1951-52; Univ of Edinburgh: asst in zoology 1959-63, lectr in zoology, reader in zoology 1969-71; prof of genetics 1971- (vice-dean of sci 1986-89; SERC ser res fell 1976-81; vice pres: Genetical Soc 1981, Linnean Soc 1983-85; scientific expeditions: Morocco (1955), Polynesia (1962, 1967, 1968, 1980 and 1982), chm terrestrial life sciences ctee NERC 1983-86, memb biological sciences sub ctee UGC 1987-; ed: Heredity 1977-84, Proceedings of the Royal Soc, Series B 1989-; *Books* Berber Village (1959), The Evolution of DNA Sequences (ed 1986), Frequency-Dependent Selection (ed 1988); *Recreations* painting, archaeology; *Clubs* RAF; *Style*— Prof Bryan Clarke; Linden Cottage, School Lane, Colston Bassett, Nottingham NG12 3FD (☎ 0949 81243); Dept of Genetics, Queen's Medical Centre, Clifton Boulevard, Nottingham NG7 2UH (☎ 0602 420639)

CLARKE, Charles Nigel; CBE (1987); s of Charles Cyril Clarke (d 1968), of Gatcombe Court, Flax Bourton, and Olga Helena, *née* Robinson (d 1971); *b* 3 August 1926; *Educ* Radley; *m* 21 Jun 1952, Stella Rosemary, da of John Herbert King, of Somerlea, Langford, Somerset; 4 s (Giles b 1953, Nigel b 1957, Henry b 1959, Matthew b 1963), 1 da (Bridget b 1955); *Career* Lt Welsh Gds 1944-48, served Germany; slr 1951, notary public 1953, sr ptnr Osborne Clarke (slrs) Bristol 1985- (ptnr 1952); memb and chm various Health Bds and Authorities 1952-86; memb Cncl Nat Assoc of Health Authorities 1982-86, tstee Bristol Municipal Charities 1962-87 (chm 1976-87), special tstee United Bristol Hosp 1974- (chm 1974-82 and 1986-); memb cncl Bristol Univ 1969-86; maitre commanderie de Bordeaux Bristol 1980-, Lord of the Manor of Gatcombe and patron of the living of Wanstrow and Cloford; memb Soc of Merchant Venturers (master 1967); hon degree: D Litt Univ of Bristol; *Recreations* wine, military history, roses, shooting; *Clubs* Army and Navy; *Style*— Charles Clarke, Esq, CBE; Gatcombe Court, Flax Bourton, Bristol BS19 1PX (☎ 0272 393 141); 30 Queen Charlotte Street, Bristol BS99 7QQ (☎ 0272 230 220, fax

0272 279 209, car tel 0860 661 322, telex 44734G)

CLARKE, Charles St George Stephenson; s of John Philip Stephenson Clarke, of Broadhurst Manor, Sussex (d 1969), and Kathleen Adeline Jane Loftus St George (d 1979); *b* 19 April 1924; *Educ* Eton; *m* 20 Jan 1959, Therese Emilie Edwige Elvire, da of Gen Husson, of Toulon, France; 2 s (Edmund John b 1959, Richard Louis b 1961); *Career* Powell Duffryn Gp 1942 (now non-exec); chm for 15 years Shires Investment Co plc (now dep chm); chm Edric Property and Investment Co; fndr Maser Worshipful Co of Fuellers, Past Master Worshipful Co of Clothworkers; *Recreations* shooting, fishing, gardening; *Clubs* Boodles, Pratt's; *Style—* Charles Clarke, Esq; Mill House, Letcombe Regis, Oxon OX12 9JD

CLARKE, Christopher Alan; s of Harry Alston Clarke (d 1979), and Isobel Corsan Clarke, *née* Kay; gs of Henry R Clarke, brewer of Bury St Edmunds, Suffolk and of Sir James Reid Kay of Ayr; *b* 14 May 1945; *Educ* Oakham Sch, Oakham, Rutland BA (Cantab), MSC (London); London Graduate Sch of Business Studies; *m* 1, 1970, Jessica Mary, da of Maj Mark Pearson of Bulcote; m 2, 9 Dec 1978, Charlotte Edith, da of Major William Gordon Jenkins of Windlesham; 1 s (Henry William Anthony b 1984); 1 da (Katherine Sarah b 1981); *Career* dir Samuel Montagu and Co Ltd 1982; present dir Arbuthnot Latham and Co Ltd 1978-82; formerly with Shell International Petroleum Co Ltd; *Recreations* reading, fishing, golf, tennis, gardening, music; *Clubs* Berkshire; *Style—* Christopher A Clarke, Esq; Glebe House, Windlesham, Surrey, GU20 6AA; Samuel Montagu and Co Ltd, 10 Lower Thames St, London EC3R 6AE

CLARKE, Christopher Simon Courtenay Stephenson; QC (1984); yr s of Rev John Stephenson Clarke (d 1982), and Enid Courtenay, *née* Manico; *b* 14 Mar 1947; *Educ* Marlborough, Gonville and Caius Coll Cambridge (MA); *m* 14 Sept 1974, Caroline Anne, da of Prof Charles Montague Fletcher, CBE, *qv*; 1 s (Edward b 31 May 1981), 2 da (Henrietta b 16 Aug 1977, Louisa b 21 June 1979); *Career* barr Middle Temple 1969; advocate of the Supreme Ct of the Turks and Caicos Islands 1975; chm Ctee of Inquiry of States of Guernsey into Barnett Christie (Finance) Ltd 1985-87; cncllr Int Bar Assoc 1987-; *Clubs* Brooks's, Hurlingham; *Style—* Christopher Clarke Esq, QC; 42 The Chase, London SW4 0NH (☎ 01 622 0765); 1 Brick Court, Temple, London EC4 (☎ 01 583 0777, telex 892687)

CLARKE, Prof Sir Cyril Astley; KBE (1974, CBE 1969); s of Astley Vavasour Clarke, MD, JP, DL, and Ethel Mary, *née* Gee (d 1965); *b* 22 August 1907; *Educ* Oundle, Gonville and Caius Coll Cambridge, Guy's Hosp London; *m* 1935, Frieda (Féo) Margaret Mary, da of Alexander John Campbell Hart; 3 s; *Career* dir Research Unit RCP 1983-88; FRS 1970, hon fell Royal Soc of Medicine 1982, MD, DSc; prof of Medicine Liverpool Univ, dir Nuffield Unit of Medical Genetics 1965-72 (now Emeritus Prof and hon research fellow), pres Royal Coll of Physicians 1972-77, chm cncl Br Heart Fndn 1982-87; hon conslt physician Royal Infirmary, Broadgreen Hosp and United Liverpool Hosps; *Books* Genetics for the Clinician, Selected Topics in Medical Genetics, Rhesus Haemolytic Disease, selected papers and extracts, Human Genetics and Medicine (1970, 1972, 1987); *Recreations* sailing (yacht Hobby IV), butterfly genetics; *Clubs* Athenaeum, Oxford and Cambridge Sailing Soc, Explorers (New York); *Style—* Prof Sir Cyril Clarke, KBE; 43 Caldy Rd, W Kirby, Wirral, Merseyside L48 2HF (☎ 051 625 8811); Royal Coll of Physicians, Regent's Park, London NW1 (☎ 01 935 1174); Dept of Genetics, Univ of Liverpool, PO Box 147, Liverpool L69 3BX

CLARKE, David Clive; QC; s of Philip George Clarke, of Kilconquhar, Fife, and José Margaret, *née* Fletcher (d 1979); *b* 16 July 1942; *Educ* Winchester, Magdalene Coll Cambridge (BA, MA); *m* 2 Aug 1969, Alison Claire, da of Rt Rev (Percy) James Brazier, of Devizes, Wilts; 3 s (Andrew b 1970, Jonathan b 1972, Edward b 1975); *Career* barr Inner Temple 1965, Northern circuit (tres 1988), rec 1981; *Recreations* canals, sailing, swimming; *Style—* David Clark, Esq, QC; 5 Essex Ct, Temple, London EC4Y 9AH (☎ 01 353 4363, fax 01 583 1491); 25 Byrom St, Manchester M3 4PF (☎ 061 834 5238, fax 061 834 0394)

CLARKE, David Hilton; s of Hilton Swift Clarke, CBE, 4 Coverdale Ave, Couden, nr Bexhill, Sussex, and Sibyl Muriel, *née* Salter (d 1975); *b* 9 Jan 1938; *Educ* Hurst Pier Point Coll, Sussex; *m* 27 Feb 1965, Leonora Virginia, da of Capt Campbell Marshall (d 1971); 2 s (Edward Hilton b 23 Feb 1966, Campbell David Hilton b 10 Aug 1967); *Career* Nat Serv RN 1956-58, Leading Seaman RNR 1967-72; asst and trainee Anthony Gibbs and Sons Ltd 1958-67; dir: non-exec Falmouth Oil Servs, Gerrard and Nat Holdgs plc 1974- (joined 1967); Churchwarden Holy Trinity Roehampton, memb Roehampton Boys Club, chm fin ctee Middx Hosp Med Sch, memb fin ctee UCL; Freeman City of London 1984; *Recreations* sailing, skiing; *Clubs* Royal Ocean Racing; *Style—* David Clarke, Esq; 8 Parthenia Rd, Fulham, London SW6 4BD; Gerrard and National Holdings plc, 33 Lombard St, London EC3 (☎ 01 628 9981)

CLARKE, Douglas Hewitt; s of Reginald Douglas Clarke (d 1979), of Liverpool, and Mabel Hewitt, *née* Drew (d 1958); *b* 17 July 1934; *Educ* Liverpool Inst HS for boys, Birkenhead Tech Coll, Univ of Durham Kings Coll; *m* 1, 24 April 1963 (m dis 1968), Eileen Elizabeth Hilton; m 2, 21 May 1977, Christine Mary Jacobs; 1 s (Alexander Douglas b 19 March 1987), 1 da (Karen Mary b 11 April 1978); *Career* asst naval architect Cammell Laird & Co Ltd 1968-71, ship surveyor Lloyds Register of Shipping 1971-78, dir Bestgrange Ltd 1978-, Ship System Engrg Gp (SSEG) 1986-87; pres UK Assoc of Professional Engrs 1974-76; memb: Nautical Inst Computers and Communications Working Gp, Information Technol Working Gp; Inst Mechanical and Gen Technician Engrs: chm 1976-78, pres 1978-80, hon tres 1985-88; advsr to HM Princ Sec of State for Trade & Indust (Efficient Ship Programme) 1987-, memb IEC TC80 Working Gp on Digital Interfaces for Navigation Equipment 1987; memb and hon tres London branch Royal Inst of Naval Architects, memb Surrey ECRO and Engrg Cncl Assembly; author of numerous articles in journals and magazines and for nat institutions (Institution Gold Medal 'Powering of Ships' 1963, Instituition Silver Medal 'Some Notes on Escalators and their Use in Ships' 1959; Freeman City of London 1983, Liveryman Worshipful Co of Shipwrights 1983; CEng, FRINA 1983, FIMarE 1987, CNI 1988, FIMechIE; *Recreations* water colour painting; *Style—* Douglas Hewitt, Esq; 10 Treadwell Rd, Epsom, Surrey KT18 5JW (☎ 0372 729 910); Bestgrage Ltd, c/o 10 Treadwell Rd

CLARKE, Hon Mrs Eleanor Geraldine; *née* de Courcy; 4 da of 29 Baron Kingsale, DSO (d 1969); *b* 1919; *m* 10 April 1940 (m dis 1947), John Campbell Clarke (d 17 June 1966), s of late Dr Hugh Campbell Wilson Clarke, of Ashton-upon-Mersey, Cheshire; 1 s (Peter b 1945); *Style—* The Hon Mrs Eleanor Clarke; 48 Fore St, North Tawton, Devon

CLARKE, Sir Ellis Emmanuel Innocent; TC (1969), GCMG (1972, CMG 1960); o s of late Cecil El and Elma Clarke; *b* 28 Dec 1917; *Educ* St Mary's Coll Trinidad, London U; *m* 1952, Eyrmyntrude, eldest da of William Hurford Hagley, OBE, of St George's, Grenada; 2 s, 1 da; *Career* barr 1940, in private practice to 1954; former Permanent rep to UN for Trinidad and Tobago, ambass to US 1962-73, to Mexico 1966-73, gov len and CIC Repub of Trinidad and Tobago 1973-76, president 1976-; hon fell Univ Coll London 1983, (does not use title in Trinidad and Tobago), KStJ 1973; kt 1963; *Style—* Sir Ellis Clarke, TC, GCMG; President's House, Port of Spain, Trinidad

CLARKE, Frederick Edwin Lawson; s of Victor William Clarke (d 1947), of Whetstone, N London, and Ada Eliza, *née* Messenger (d 1949); *b* 28 May 1901; *Educ* Christs Coll, Church End, Finchley; *m* 1, 12 April 1930 (m dis) Audrey Evelyn, da of IF Cuthbert, (d 1972), of Elsenham Hall, Elsenham, Essex; 1 s (Christopher Lawson b 2 Feb 1933), 1 da (Carolyn b 20 Sept 1938); m 2, 14 Feb 1974, Frances Brenda, da of late Frank Lewis Cranmore; *Career* chm and md Wilson and Gill Jevellers 1947-67 (joined 1824); dir Rosenthal Studio House 1967-; fell Gemmological Assoc GB 1943, chm Nat Assoc Goldsmith 1975; Freeman City of London 1923, Liveryman Worshipful Co of Clockmakers 1956; *Style—* Lawson Clarke, Esq; d'Ayrel, 33 Mymms Drive, Brookhmans Park, Hatfield AL9 7AE (☎ 0707 52442); Rosenthal Studio House Ltd, 102 Brompton Rd, London SW3 1JJ (☎ 01 584 0683/4)

CLARKE, Gordon Oscar Burland; OBE (1980), TD (1957); s of Douglas Burland Clarke (d 1955), and Elsie Mary, *née* Wrigley (d 1972); *b* 23 Mar 1922; *Educ* Altrincham High, Manchester Univ (CEng); *m* 1950, Marion, da of Osmond Rutherford, of Norwich; 1 s (Jeremy), 1 da (Victoria); *Career* RE 1942-47, served in France, Germany and India, Capt; divnl mangr BR: Edinburgh 1968-70, Norwich 1970-83; regnl chm CBI 1978-80, memb CBI Cncl 1974-83, consulting engr 1983-; *Recreations* sailing, Times crossword; *Style—* Gordon Clarke, Esq, OBE, TD; 86 Charles Close, Wroxham, Norwich, Norfolk NR12 8TT (☎ (06053) 2610)

CLARKE, Graham Staward; TD (1971); s of Douglas Staward Clarke (d 1949), and Beatrice, *née* Auld; *b* 16 Mar 1937; *Educ* St Bees Sch Cumberland, Emmanuel Coll Cambridge (MA); *m* 1964, Rita Elisabeth Karoline, da of Oskar Becker (d 1961); 1 s (Douglas b 1968), 1 da (Tessa b 1965); *Career* Maj RA, Euro theatre; gp fin dir: Telex Computers Ltd 1972-75, Coles Cranes Ltd 1976-81, Fairey Hldgs Ltd 1981-84; md Energy and Military Engrg Div, Fairey Hldgs Ltd 1984-86; chm: Fairey Engrg Ltd 1984-86, Elequip Ltd 1984-86; dir: Fairey Hldgs Ltd 1981-86, Fairey Construction Ltd 1984-86, Mathews and Yates Ltd 1984-86, Fairey Nuclear Ltd 1984-86, Fairey Devpts Ltd 1981-86; chm Bourn Management Consultants Ltd 1985-, md Bourn Developments 1986-, proprietor Bourn Estates 1980-; FCA, FRSA; *Recreations* bridge, travel, business management; *Clubs* RAC, IOD; *Style—* Graham Clarke Esq, TD; Bourn Reach, Montrose Gdns, Oxshott, Surrey, KT22 0UU (☎ 037 284 3655); Bourn Management Consultants Ltd, Montrose Gardens, Oxshott, Surrey KT22 0UU (☎ 037 284 3445)

CLARKE, James Dudley Henderson; BEM (1988); s of James Dudley Clarke (d 1945), of Shepperton, Middx, and Ethel Eliza Hambly, *née* Johnson; *b* 14 May 1923; *Educ* Reay Sch London; *m* 15 May 1942, (Muriel) Jean, da of Clarence Carthew Quick (d 1966); 1 s (James), 2 da ('Tricia, Lynne); *Career* WWII Intelligence Corps 1941-46; md Zetters Gp plc 1965; vice chm: Zetters Int Pools Ltd, Metagraph Ltd, Zetters Mktg Ltd; govr The London Marathon, memb Sports Aid Fndn; churchwarden Frinton-on-Sea; Freeman City of London 1982, Liveryman Worshipful Co of Govrs 1982; *Recreations* cricket, golf, reading; *Clubs* MCC; *Style—* James Clarke, Esq, BEM; 86/88 Clerkenwell Rd, London EC1 (☎ 01 253 5376, fax 01 253 1584)

CLARKE, James Henry; s of Edward Clarke (d 1959), of Tynemouth, and Jane Elizabeth, *née* Turnbull (d 1921); *b* 27 June 1913; *Educ* Rutherford Tech Coll Newcastle, Marine Sch of South Shields; *m* 19 Oct 1938, Florence (d 1987), da of George Bell (d 1921), of Wylam, Northumberland; *Career* chief engr offr (formerly Junior-senior engr offr) merchant navy 1935-46; lines: Hopemount Shipping Co Ltd, Blue Funnel Line, C T Bowring & Co Ltd; WWII S Atlantic, France and N Atlantic convoys, seconded Royal Fleet Auxiliary (oiling RN ships at sea); Br Tanker Co served: UK, Egypt, Persian Gulf, Indian Ocean, India, Burma, Singapore, Iraq, Iran; sr asst J G Harrison (naval Architect-consulting engr) 1946-50, chief marine supt engr and tech conslt Chandris England Ltd and Chandris (London) Servs Ltd 1950-84; memb: Langbourn Ward Club, Lime St, Ward Club, Bishopsgate Ward Club; Freeman City of London 1963, Liveryman Worshipful Co of Shipwrights 1964; CEng 1968, FRINA 1960, FIMarE 1942, FCMS 1950;; *Recreations* maritime history, famous passenger ships, diy, Greece; *Clubs* City Livery, City Livery Yacht, City Livery Music; *Style—* James H Clarke, Esq; Greenacres, 8 Shalford Rd, Guildford, Surrey GU4 8BL, (☎ 0483 576384)

CLARKE, James Samuel; MC (1943 and bar 1944); s of James Henry Clarke (d 1955), of Horley, Surrey, and Deborah Florence, *née* Moliver (d 1984); *b* 19 Jan 1921; *Educ* Reigate GS, St Catharine's Coll Cambridge (MA); *m* 1949, Ilse, da of Herman-Max Cohen of Germany; 2 da (Jane, Susan); *Career* cmmnd Royal Irish Fusiliers 1941-45, served 1 Bn N Africa and Italy, demob Maj 1945; barr Middle Temple 1946, entered legal serv 1953, under sec and princ asst slr Inland Revenue 1970-81; ret; md Bishop and Clark Ltd 1981-; *Recreations* gardening, sailing; *Clubs* Nat Lib, RAC; *Style—* James Clarke, Esq, MC; Dormers, The Downs, Givons, Grove, Leatherhead, Surrey (☎ 0372 378254); Bishop and Clarke Ltd, Hereford House, Massetts Rd, Horley, Surrey (☎ 0293 782288)

CLARKE, Prof John Frederick; s of Frederick William Clarke (d 1974), and Clara Auguste Antonie, *née* Nauen (d 1975); *b* 1 May 1927; *Educ* Warwick Sch, QMC London (BSc, PhD); *m* 19 Dec 1953, Jean Ruth, da of Joseph Alfred Hector Roberts Gentle (d 1960), 2 da (Jenny b 1956, Julie b 1957); *Career* pupil pilot Naval Aviation RN 1946-48; aerodynamist Eng Electric Co Ltd 1956-57, lectr Coll of Aeronautics Cranfield 1958-65, Fulbright Scholar and visiting assoc prof of Stanford Univ California 1961-62, reader Cranfield Inst of Technol 1965-72 (prof theoretical gas dynamics 1972-), visiting prof at various UK, Euro and US Univ, memb various ctees for sci, contrib learned jls; FIMA 1965, FRAeS 1969, FRSA 1986, FRS 1987; *Books* The Dyamics of Real Gases (with M McChesney 1964), Dynamics of Relaxing Gases (with M McChesney 1976); *Recreations* Sunday painter; *Style—* Prof John Clarke; Field House, Green Lane, Aspley Guise MK17 8EN (☎ 0908 582234); Aerodynamics, Coll of Aeronautics, Cranfield Inst of Technology, Cranfield, Bedford MK43 0AL (☎ 0234 750 111, ext 2123, telex 825072 CITECH G)

CLARKE, Prof John Innes; s of Bernard Griffith Clarke, of 53 West Way, Bournemouth, and Edith Louie, *née* Mott; *b* 7 Jan 1929; *Educ* Bournemouth Sch, Univ of Aberdeen (MA, PhD), Univ of Paris; *m* 2 Apr 1955, Dorothy Anne, da of George May Watkinson (decd), of Ashbourne, Derbyshire; 3 d (Gemma b 1956, Anna b 1959, Lucy b 1969); *Career* Nat Serv FO RAF 1952-54; asst lectr in geog Univ of Aberdeen 1954-55, lectr in geog Univ of Durham 1955-63, prof of geog Univ Coll of Sierra Leone 1963-65; prof of geog Univ of Durham 1968- (reader 1965-68); pro vice-chllr and sub-warden Univ of Durham 1984-; chm exec ctee HESIN 1987-; FRGS; *Books* Population Geography (1965), Population Geography and Developing Countries (1971); ed: An Advanced Geography of Africa (1975), Geography and Population (1984), co-ed: Population & Development Projects in Africa (1985); *Recreations* hill walking, family history, travel; *Style*— Prof John Clarke; Tower Cottage, The Avenue, Durham DH1 4EB (☎ 091 384 8350); Univ of Durham, Old Shire Hall, Durham DH1 3LE (☎ 091 374 2948, fax 091 374 3740, telex 537 351 DURLIB G)

CLARKE, John Neil; s of George Philip Clarke (d 1969); *b* 7 August 1934; *Educ* Rugby, King's Coll London (LLB); *m* 1958, Sonia Heather, *née* Beckett; 3 s; *Career* dep chm Charter Consolidated plc 1982-88 (chief exec 1980-88), chm Johnson Matthey plc 1984-; FCA; *Clubs* MCC, Royal W Norfolk GC, Addington GC; *Style*— J Neil Clarke, Esq; High Willows, 18 Park Ave, Farnborough Park, Kent BR6 8LL (☎ 0689 51651; The Cottage, Hall Lane, Thornham, Norfolk (☎ 048 526 269); 35, Ely Place, London EC1N 6TD

CLARKE, His Hon Judge Sir Jonathan Dennis; eldest s of Dennis Robert Clarke (Master of the Supreme Court, d 1967) and Caroline Alice, *née* Hill; *b* 19 Jan 1930; *Educ* Kidstones Sch, Univ Coll London; *m* 1956, Susan Margaret Elizabeth Ashworth; 1 s, 3 da; *Career* Crown Court recorder 1972-82, circuit judge (Western) 1982-; ptnr Townsends 1959-82; pres Law Soc; kt 1981; *Style*— Sir Jonathan Clarke; c/o Midland Bank, 1 Wood St, Swindon, Wilts

CLARKE, Rt Hon Kenneth Harry; PC (1984), QC (1980), MP (C) Rushcliffe Notts 1970-; s of Kenneth Clarke, of Nottingham; *b* 2 July 1940; *Educ* Nottingham HS, Gonville and Caius Coll Cambridge; *m* 1964, Gillian Mary, da of Bruce Edwards, of Sidcup, Kent; 1 s, 1 da; *Career* former pres Cambridge Union; barr Gray's Inn 1963, bencher 1989; former oppn spokesman on Social Services and Industry, parly under-sec Dept of Transport 1979-82, min of state (Health) DHSS 1982-85, memb Health Services Supervisory Bd 1983-85; HM Paymaster Gen and Min for Employment 1985-87; Chllr of the Duchy of Lancaster and Min for Trade and Industry 1987-88; Sec of State for Health July 1988-; *Recreations* modern jazz, bird watching, watching football and cricket; *Style*— The Rt Hon Kenneth Clarke, QC, MP; House of Commons, London SW1A 0AA

CLARKE, Col (Henry) Leslie; TD (1949, 3 Clasps 1950, 1956, 1961); s of Harry Stanley Clarke, OBE, JP, (d 1969), 10 Cranbourne Court, Hermon Hill, London E18, and Lilian Margaret *née* Wells (d 1925); *b* 15 June 1920; *Educ* Brentwood Sch, Inst Exports (Dip M); *m* 1, 11 Nov 1950, Kathleen Doris (d 1973), da of George Forest Hoyles (d 1951), of Newton Hall, Wisbech, Cambs; m 2, 19 Jan 1974, Coral Norah, da of Frank Hollis Anthony (d 1975), of London; *Career* WWII cmmnd 2 Lt Essex Regt TA 1939, transferred RA 1940, served Africa and M East, demob Maj 1947; TA: Maj 599 Essex HAA Regt, Lt-Col 1958, Col GS Dep Cdr RA 1962, transferred on ret RARO 1965; ADC to HM The Queen 1966-71; ret from pharmaceutical industry; JP West Ham 1950; DL Essex 1961-77, Greater London 1977, rep DL Borough of Ealing 1983; pres: Royal Br Legion (Ealing Branch) 1988-, Ealing and Hanwell Dist Scouts 1988-; Liveryman Worshipful Co of Barbers 1974; MIM; *Recreations* walking; *Style*— Col Leslie Clarke, TD, DL; 11 Dalling Road, Ravenscourt Park, London W6 0JD (☎ 01 747 0837)

CLARKE, Martin Courtenay; s of Douglas Archibald Clarke, of London, and Marjorie, *née* Blinkhorn (d 1987); *b* 7 Jan 1941; *Educ* Winchester, Trinity Col Cambridge (MA); *m* 5 Sept 1974, Esmee Frances, da of Col J F Cottrell, OBE, MC (d 1972), of Exmouth; *Career* Touche Ross and Co CAs: ptnr 1973, nat dir res devpt 1982-87, nat dir of mktg 1987-, ptnr corporate fin gp 1988-; memb Auditing Practices Consultative Ctee of Accounting Bodies 1982-88, dir Haymills Hldgs Ltd; Liveryman: Worshipful Co of Merchant Taylors 1970, Worshipful Co of Loriners 1983; FICA 1973; *Recreations* sailing, diving, skiing, opera, reading; *Clubs* City of London, Landsdowne; *Style*— Martin Clarke, Esq; 91 Bedford Gardens, Kensington, London W8 7EQ; Hill House, 1 Little New Street, London EC4A 3TR (☎ 01 936 3000, fax 01 583 8517, telex 884739 TRLDNG)

CLARKE, Mary; da of late Frederick Clarke, and Ethel Kate, *née* Reynolds (d 1984); *b* 23 August 1923; *Educ* Mary Datchelor Girls Sch; *Career* ed The Dancing Times London 1963-, ballet critic The Guardian 1977-; author: The Sadler's Wells Ballet: A History and an Appreciation (1955), Dancers of Mercury: the Story of Ballet Rambert (1962); jtly with Clement Crisp: Design for Ballet (1978), The History of Dance (1981), contributor to Encyclopedia Britannica (1974); memb Grand Cncl The Royal Acad of Dancing; *Recreations* watching dancing, travel, reading; *Clubs* Gautier; *Style*— Ms Mary Clarke; 11 Danbury St, Islington, London N1 8LD (☎ 01 226 9209); The Dancing Times, 45-47 Clerkenwell Green, London EC1R OBE (☎ 01 250 3006, fax 01 253 6679)

CLARKE, (John) Michael; s of Harold Vivian Clarke (d 1983), and Orpah Clarke (d 1976); *b* 24 Feb 1932; *Educ* Scarborough Coll; *m* 1982, Susan Margaret, da of Herbert Wrigley (d 1973); 1 s (Jeremy b 1985), 1 da (Emily b 1984); *Career* financial investor; Cons memb: Rotherham Cncl 1966-74, South Yorkshire CC 1974-82; chm Rotherham Cons Assoc 1979-82; hon FRGS; Rotary (pres 1978-79), Sheffield Corinthian Sailing (cdre 1983-84); *Recreations* sailing, skiing; *Clubs* Rotherham; *Style*— Michael Clarke, Esq; Weetwood, 187 Moorgate Road, Rotherham, S Yorks S60 3AX (☎ 0709 382852); The White House, Belvedere Close, Bridlington, N Humberside YO15 3LZ (☎ 0262 679000)

CLARKE, Michael John Marshal; s of Adm Sir Marshal Llewelyn Clarke, KBE, CB, DSC (d 1959), and Ina Leonora, *née* Edwards; *b* 3 Feb 1927; *Educ* St Edward's Sch Oxford, Trinity Coll Oxford; *m* 1954, Flavia Dorothea, da of Air Chief Marshal Sir (William) Alec Coryton, KCB, KBE, MVO, DFC, *qv*; 1 s, 1 da; *Career* Capt (TA) Rifle Bde; dir Personnel Servs Br Steel Corpn; personnel consult; memb: Central Arbitration Ctee, Police Arbitration Tribunal, Arts Cncl of Great Britain, Welsh Arts Cncl, cncl of Nat Museum of Wales, High Sheriff of Gwent 1985-6; *Recreations* shooting, landscape painting, growing vines; *Style*— Michael Clarke, Esq; Osbaston House, Monmouth, Gwent NP5 4BB (☎ 0600 3596)

CLARKE, Orme Roosevelt; s of late Sir Humphrey Clarke, 5 Bt; half-bro and hp of Sir Tobias Clarke, 6 Bt; *b* 30 Nov 1947; *Educ* Eton; *m* 1971, Joanna Valentine, da of John Barkley Schuster, TD; 1 s; *Style*— Orme Clarke, Esq; 28 Marville Rd, London SW6

CLARKE, His Hon Judge Paul Henry Francis; s of Dr Richard Clarke, FRCP, of Clifton, Bristol; *b* 14 Oct 1921; *Educ* Clifton, Exeter Coll Oxford; *m* 1, 1955, Eileen Sheila (d 1987), da of Lt-Col J K B Crawford, of Clifton Coll; 2 s, 1 da; m2, 1988, Mary Charmian, da of Rev Canon NS Kidson, and wid of Kenneth Soddy; *Career* barr 1949, practised to 1974, a circuit judge 1974-; *Style*— His Hon Judge Paul Clarke; The Manor Cottage, Doccombe, Moretonhamstead, Devon

CLARKE, Maj Peter Cecil; CVO (1969, MVO 1964); s of late Capt Edward Denman Clarke, CBE, MC (d 1966), of Crossways, Binstead, Isle of Wight, and Maureen Cowie, *née* Leitch; *b* 9 August 1927; *Educ* Eton, RMC Sandhurst; *m* 1950, Rosemary Virginia Margaret Harmsworth, da of late T C Durham, of Appomattox, Virginia, USA; 1 s, 2 da; *Career* Maj (ret) 3 The King's Own Hussars and 14/20 King's Hussars 1945-64; asst priv sec then comptroller to HRH Princess Marina, Duchess of Kent 1961-68, comptroller and extra equerry to HRH Princess Alexandra, the Hon Mrs Angus Ogilvy 1964-69, ch clerk Duchy of Lancaster 1969-, JP Hants 1971-81; *Style*— Maj Peter Clarke, CVO; 6 Gordon Place, W8 (☎ home 01 937 0356, office 01 836 8277)

CLARKE, Peter Lovat; JP (1970); s of Harold Clarke (d 1945), of Warrington, and Alice Taylor; *b* 25 July 1934; *Educ* Ellesmere; *m* 1956, Audrey Christine, da of Walter Jonathan Elston, of Cheshire; 3 s (John b 1956, Simon and Timothy b 1964 (twins)), 1 da (Denise b 1959); *Career* dir: Greenall Whitley plc; chm: Gilbert and John Greenall Ltd, Cellar 5 Ltd, David Scatchard Ltd, G and J Wine Bars Ltd, Harvey Prince and Co Ltd, Drew and Co (Wine Cellars) Ltd, Sureweek Ltd, Thomas Threlfall and Co Ltd, Corry's Soft Drinks Ltd, B M and J Strauss Ltd, Bombay Spirits Co Ltd, Wilderspool Commercial Hldgs Ltd, Clansouth Ltd, Vladivar Vodka Ltd, Stanneylands Gp Ltd, Stretton Automatics Ltd, Stretton Leisure Clubs Ltd, Warrington Festival Tst Ltd, Warrington Industrial Training Tst Ltd, Laker Holidays (North) Ltd, Greenall Whitley Take-Home (sales) Ltd, Greenall Whitley Exports Ltd, Cambrian Soft Drinks Ltd; memb Worshipful Co of Distillers 1979; *Recreations* golf, music, reading, swimming; *Clubs* Warrington Golf, Wine and Spirit over 40 Club, Majority, Walton Investment; *Style*— Peter Clarke, Esq; Brook House, Cann Lane, Appleton, nr Warrington, Cheshire (☎ 61660); Gilbert and John Greenhall Ltd, PO Box No 3, Causeway Distillery, Warrington, Cheshire (☎ 50111)

CLARKE, Philip Michael; s of Gerald Michael Richard Clarke (d 1988), of Hagley, W Mids, and Phyllis Mary, *née* Adams; *b* 31 May 1954; *Educ* Oundle, Univ of Birmingham (BSc, B Comm); *m* 21 July 1986, Rachel Barbara Lucia, da of Bernard Laurence O'Hare (d 1988), of Burton-On-Trent, Derbys; 1 s (George b 1988); *Career* Clamason Ind Ltd 1977-: commercial dir 1981-86, md 1986; chm Providence Gp Trg Scheme Ltd; CEngMIProdE; *Recreations* golf; *Clubs* Stourbridge Golf ; *Style*— Philip Clarke, Esq; 25 Station Rd, Hagley, W Mids DY9 0NU (☎ 0562 886 062); Clamason Industries Ltd, Gibbons Industrial Park, Kingswinford, W Mids DY6 8XG (☎ 0384 400 000, fax 0384 279 222, telex 334 580)

CLARKE, Robert Charles; s of John Edward Kenyon Clarke (d 1980), and Elsie Mary, *née* Rand; *b* 15 April 1943; *Educ* John Lyon Sch, Harrow; *m* 11 April 1970, Christine Marjorie, da of Ronald Charles Gardner, of Knowle West Midlands; 2 s (Jonathan b 1970, Laurence b 1972), 2 da (Eleanor b 1974, Georgina b 1977); *Career* CA; Barton Mayhew 1962-70, Peat Marwick Mitchell 1970-72, Viney Merretts 1972-80, BDO Binder Hamlyn 1980-; Freeman: City of London 1976, Chartered Accountants Livery Co 1976; FCA 1971; *Recreations* golf; *Clubs* MCC; *Style*— Robert Clarke, Esq; Hudnall Farm, Little Gaddesden, Berkhamstead, Herts HP4 1QN (☎ 044 284 3214);BDO Binder Hamyln, 8 St Bride St, London EC4A 4DA (☎ 01 353 3020, fax 01 583 0031)

CLARKE, Robert Cyril; s of Robert Henry Clarke (d 1964), and Rose, *née* Bratton (d 1952); *Educ* Dulwich, Pembroke Coll Oxford (MA); *m* 12 July 1952, Evelyn Mary (Lynne), da of Cyrus Harper (d 1959); 3 s (Tristan b 26 May 1956, Jonathan b (twin) 26 May 1956, Ben b 13 July 1966), 1 da (Anna b 19 May 1969); *Career* Royal West Kent Regt 1947-49; trainee Cadbury Bros Ltd 1952-54; gen mangr John Forrest Ltd 1954-57; marketing dir Cadbury Confectionary 1957-62; md Cadbury Cakes Ltd 1962-69; chm Cadbury Cakes and dir Cadbury Schweppes Foods Ltd 1969-71; md McVitie & Cadbury Cakes Ltd 1971-74; joined bd of United Biscuits (UK) Ltd 1974; md UB Biscuits 1977; chm and md United Biscuits (UK) Ltd and dir United Biscuits (Hldgs) plc 1984; gp chief exec United Biscuits (Hldgs) plc 1986-; memb cncl: Cake & Biscuit Alliance 1965-83, ISBA 1977-84; memb resources ctee Food & Drink Fedn 1984; memb EDC for Food and Drink Industry 1984, non exec memb Thames Water Authy 1988; *Recreations* reading, walking, renovating old buildings, planting trees; *Style*— Robert C Clarke, Esq; United Biscuits (Holdings) plc, Grant House, Syon Lane, Isleworth, Middlesex TW7 5NN (☎ 01 560 3131, fax 01 895 4657, telex 8954657)

CLARKE, Robert MacDonald; s of Samuel Frank Clarke, of Bournemouth, and Anne *née* Franklin; *b* 16 Dec 1944; *Educ* High Storrs GS Sheffield; *m* 10 Sept 1967, Sandra Lynne, da of Leo Edwards Morgan, of Great Missenden; 1 s (Adam Edward b 1970), 1 da (Sarah Lyn b 1972); *Career* accountant Yorks Electricity Bd, mgmnt conslt Spicer & Pegler, chm and md Royce plc; FCCA 1968; *Style*— Robert Clarke, Esq; Royco Plc, Royco House, Liston Rd, Marlow (☎ 06284 6922, 0836 716666, 06284 3880)

CLARKE, Robert Sandifer; s of Robert Arthur Clarke (d 1988), of Abinger Manor, Abinger Common, Surrey, and Agnes Joyce, *née* Coventry (d 1987); *b* 9 May 1934; *Educ* Westminster, Christ Church Oxford (MA), College of Law; *m* 14 Sept 1964, Cherry June Leslie, da of William Attwood Waudby, of Mombasa, Kenya; 1 s (Damian Rupert b 4 Jan 1967), 2 da (Vanessa-Jane b 4 Sept 1965, Georgina Ann b 16 Sept 1975); *Career* Nat Serv RN 1952; cmmnd RNVR: Midshipman 1952, Sub Lt 1953, Lt 1955; slr 1962; ptnr Wood Nash (currently sr ptnr), UK ed Droit Et Affaires France 1968-75; chm: Fedn Field Sports Assocs (UK) of EEC 1978-83, Br Delgn to Int Cncl of Hunting and Conservation of Game UK 1983-; vice-pres and fell Game Conservancy Fordingbridge; Freeman City of London 1975, Liveryman Worshipful Co of Gunmakers 1975; memb Law Soc 1962; *Recreations* sailing, shooting, tennis, travel, skiing; *Clubs* Turf, Utd Oxford and Cambridge, Shikar; *Style*— Robert Clarke, Esq; Abinger Manor, Abinger Common, Surrey; 2 Cheyne Mews, Cheyne Walk, Chelsea, London SW3 (☎ 01 242 7322); 6 Raymond Bldgs, Gray's Inn, London (☎ 01 242 7322, fax 01 831 9041, telex 21143 WNANDW G)

CLARKE, Roger Eric; s o fFrederick Cuérel Clarke, of Petts Wood, Kent, and Hilda Josephine, *née* Holbrook (d 1980); *b* 13 June 1939; *Educ* UCS Hampstead, Corpus Christi Coll Cambridge (MA); *m* 8 Nov 1983, Elizabeth Jane, da of Gordon William Pingstone, of Beckenham, Kent; 1 da (Rebecca, b 1986); *Career* positions held: Civil Aviation divs of Miny of Aviation, BOT and Dept of Trade and Tport 1961-72 and 1980-85; air traffic rights advsr to Govt Fiji 1972-74, asst sec insur and overseas trade divs Dept of Trade 1975-80, under sec civil aviation policy directorate Dept of Trade 1985-; *Recreations* family, friends, church, garden, walking, theatre, music, languages, travel; *Clubs* Reform; *Style—* Roger Clarke, Esq; Dept of Tport, 2 Marsham St, London SW1P 3EB (☎ 01 276 5379/5365, fax 01 276 0818, telex 22221)

CLARKE, Roy H; s of Henry Clarke (d 1975), and Florence Ruth, *née* Bavage; *b* 14 July 1935; *Educ* Strodes Sch; *m* 3 Sept 1960, Sylvia Maud, da of Fred Snell (d 1985); 2 s (Martin b 1965, Simon b 1970); *Career* dir: Systems Ltd 1984-; govr BUPA 1984, md BUPA Insur 1987 Basic Ltd 1984-; *Recreations* sailing, fly fishing; *Clubs* RNSA; *Style—* R H Clarke, Esq; BUPA Ltd, Rowell House, Essex St, London WC2

CLARKE, Rupert Grant Alexander; s and h of Maj Sir Rupert Clarke, 3 Bt, MBE; *b* 12 Dec 1947; *m* 1978, Susannah, da of Sir (Richard) Robert Law-Smith; 1 s, 2 da; *Style—* Rupert Clarke, Esq

CLARKE, Maj Sir Rupert William John; 3 Bt (UK 1882), of Rupertswood, Colony of Victoria; MBE (1943); s of Sir Rupert Turner Havelock Clarke, 2 Bt (d 1926); *b* 5 Nov 1919; *Educ* Eton, Magdalen Coll Oxford (MA), FAIM; *m* 21 Jan 1947, Kathleen Grant, da of Peter Grant Hay (d 1961), of Melbourne; 2 s (and 1 s decd), 1 da; *Heir* s, Rupert Clarke; *Career* serv WWII, Maj Irish Gds (despatches); chm: Cadbury Schweppes Australia Ltd, P and O Australia Ltd, Nat Australia Bank Ltd; dir: Morganite Australia Pty Ltd, Custom Credit Hldgs Ltd; hon fell Trinity Coll Melbourne; Order of Grimaldis 1975, Légion d'Honneur (France) 1979; *Recreations* racing, swimming; *Clubs* Melbourne, Australian, Athenaeum (Melbourne), Union (Sydney), Queensland, Victoria Amateur Turf Club, Cavalry and Gds (London); *Style—* Maj Sir Rupert Clarke, Bt, MBE; Bolinda Vale, Clarkefield, Vic 3430, Australia (☎ 05 428 5111); Richmond House, 56 Avoca Street, Melbourne, Vic 3141, Australia (☎ 03 266 1045); office: Nat Bank House, 500 Bourke St, Melbourne, Vic 3000, Australia (☎ 03 602 3088

CLARKE, Samuel (Lawrence) Harrison; CBE (1988); s of Samuel Harrison Clarke, CBE, of Stevenage and Frances Mary, *née* Blowers (d 1976); *b* 16 Dec 1929; *Educ* Westminster, Trinity Coll Cambridge (BA); *m* 10 June 1952, Ruth Joan, da of Oscar William Godwin, OBE, of Old Colwyn (d 1958); 1 s (Christopher b 1958), 3 da (Susan b 1953, Mary b 1956, Janet b 1960); *Career* asst tech dir GEC plc 1981-, dir Alvey Programme 1987 (dep dir 1983-87), chm Zebra Parallel Ltd 1988-; visiting prof UCL 1983-; vice pres SERT; FIEE, FBCS; *Recreations* skiing, Scottish dancing; *Clubs* SCGB; *Style—* Laurence Clarke, Esq, CBE; 31 Craigweil Ave, Radlett, Herts WD7 7ET (☎ 092 76 2418); GEC plc, Hirst Reseatch Centre, East Lane, Wembley HA9 7PP (☎ 01 908 9018, fax 01 904 7582)

CLARKE, Thomas; CBE (1980), JP Lanark (1972), MP (Lab) Monklands West 1983-; s of James Clarke and Mary, *née* Gordon; *b* 10 Jan 1941; *Educ* Columba HS, Coatbridge and Scottish Coll of Commerce; *Career* former asst dir Scottish Film Cncl, memb Coatbridge Cncl 1964-74, Provost of Monklands District Cncl 1974-82; vice-pres Convention of Scottish Local Authorities 1976-78, pres 1978-80; MP (Lab) Coatbridge and Airdrie 1982 (by-election)-1983, sponsor of Disabled Persons' Act 1986; *Books* Managing Third World Debt (co-author); *Style—* Thomas Clarke, Esq, CBE, JP, MP; House of Commons, SW1

CLARKE, Thomas Sydney (Tom); s of Thomas William Clarke, of Stubbington, Hants, and Evelyn Elizabeth, *née* Hodge (d 1962); *b* 29 April 1939; *Educ* Isleworth GS; *m* 12 Sept 1961, Margaret Jean, da of Archibald Morgan (d 1953); 1 s (Morgan b 1968), 2 da (Heather b 1964, Donna b 1966); *Career* journalist: Hayes Chronicle, Herts Advertiser St Albans, The Chronicle Bulawayo Southern Rhodesia, Daily and Sunday Nation Nairobi, Kenya, Daily Express London, Queen Magazine Evening Standard; Sports ed: Evening Standard 1972-74, Daily Mail 1975-86, The Times 1986-; former capt Press Golfing Soc; *Recreations* watching sport, playing golf; *Clubs* Thorndon Pk GC, Sloane; *Style—* Tom Clarke, Esq; 11 Thorndon Hall, Ingrave, Brentwood, Essex CM13 3RJ (☎ 0277 811 835); The Times, 1 Pennington St, London E1 9XN (☎ 01 782 5944, fax 01 782 5046, telex 262141)

CLARKE, Sir (Charles Mansfield) Tobias; 6 Bt (UK 1831), of Dunham Lodge, Norfolk; adopted name Tobias 1962; s of Sir Humphrey Orme Clarke, 5 Bt (d 1973); *b* 8 Sept 1939; *Educ* Eton, Christ Church Oxford, Sorbonne, New York U; *m* 1, 1971 (m dis 1979), Charlotte, da of Roderick Walter; m 2, 1984, Teresa Lorraine Aphrodite, da of Somerset Struben de Chair, of St Osyth's Priory, Essex; 1 da (Theodora b 1985); *Heir* half-bro, Orme Clarke; *Career* vice-pres London Branch of Bankers Tst Co New York; hon tres Standing Cncl of the Baronetage 1980-; *Style—* Sir Tobias Clarke, Bt; 80a Campden Hill Rd, London W8 (☎ 01 937 6213); The Church House, Bibury, Glos (☎ 028 574 225)

CLARKE, (Thomas) Tom; *Career* founder and chm Silentnight Holdings; chm Buoyant (Nelson) Ltd, C B S Composite Bldg Services, Daco Productions, Foster-Len Ltd, H and N Binder Ltd, H Parkinson Ltd, The Heckmondwike Flock Co, J A Enser Co, Medical Research Bldgs, Sealy Sleep Products (UK), Transdrive Distributors; dir of various other cos; *Style—* Tom Clarke, Esq; c/o Silentnight Holdings Ltd, Wellhouse Rd, Barnoldswick, Colne, Lancs (☎ 0282 815888)

CLARKE, (Edmund) Walter Nunn Stephenson; TD (1950); Capt; s of Maj Edmund Stephenson Clarke, of Pickwell, Bolney, Sussex, and Invernesshire, and Frances Mary, *née* Whitehead; *b* 26 Jan1920; *Educ* St Peters Sch Seaford Sussex, St Michael's Sch Uckfield Sussex, Chillon Coll Switzerland; *m* 3 April 1956, Patricia Mary Glyn, da of Maj Richard Dean Russell, MC (d 1944), of Brians Orchard, Limpsfield, Surrey; *Career* cmmnd 4 Bn Royal Sussex Regt (ta) 1937; WWII serv: France 1939 (POW 1941, escaped), 1 Bn Royal Sussex Regt Western Desert (wounded twice), temp Maj Special ME Forces (special serv Turkey, Kurdistan); farmer S Rhodesia 1947-55, memb pub affrs ctee and main ctee BFSS, BFFS rep on CCPR Outdoor Ctee; Freeman City of London, Liveryman Worshipful Co of Clothworkers; *Books* numerous articles on country life for various magazines; *Recreations* fishing, shooting, stalking; *Clubs* Turf, Puffin's (Edinburgh), Kildare St (Dublin); *Style—* Capt Walter Stephenson Clarke, TD; 18 Lennox Gdns, London SW1X 0DG (☎ 01 584 4537)

CLARKE, William Malpas; CBE (1976); s of Ernest Clarke (d 1963), and Florence, *née* Wright (d 1973); *b* 5 June 1922; *Educ* Audenshaw GS, Univ of Manchester (BA); *m* 1, 1946, Margaret Braithwaite; 2 da (Deborah, Pamela); m 2, 1973, Faith Elizabeth, da of Lionel Dawson, of Bucks:; *Career* journalist: Manchester Guardian editorial staff 1948-56 (asst financial ed 1955-56), The Times editorial staff 1956-66 (dep city ed 1956-57, city ed 1957-62, financial and indust ed 1962-66), ed The Banker 1966 (conslt 1967-76), fndr dir Euromoney 1969-84, chm Harold Wincott Financial Journalist of the Year Award Panel 1972-; dir of Studies Ctee on Invisible Exports 1966-67, dir perm ctee on Invisible Exports 1968 (ctee became Br Invisible Exports Cncl 1983), dir-gen and dep chm Br Invisible Exports Cncl 1976-87, chm City Telecommunications Ctee 1972-87, dep chm City Communications Centre 1976-87; dir: Grindlays Bank 1966-87, dir ANZ Hldgs 1985-87, chm: Grindlays Bank (Jersey), ANZ Merchant Bank 1987-; dir Trade Indemnity, Swiss Re-Insur (UK); govr: Gt Ormond St Hosp for Sick Children 1982-, Greenwich Theatre 1984-87; chm Appeal Tstees Gt Ormond St Hosp 1984-; cncl memb RIIA 1970-83; tstee Harold Wincott Fndn 1970-; chm Harold Wincott Financial Journalist of the Year Award Panel 1971-; *Books* The City's Invisible Earnings (1958), Private Enterprise in Developing Countries (1966), The City in the World Economy (1965, 1967), Britains Invisible Earnings (for the Ctee on Invisible Exports 1967), The World's Money (1970, US edition 1972), Money Markets of the World (1971), Inside the City (1979, paperback 1983), How the City of London Works (1986); *Recreations* books, theatre; *Clubs* Reform; *Style—* William Clarke Esq, CBE; 37 Park Vista, Greenwich, London SE10 (☎ 01 858 0979); ANZ Merchant Bank, 55 Gracechurch Street EC3 (☎ 01 280 3100)

CLARKSON, Ven Alan Geoffrey; s of Geoffrey Archibald Clarkson, OBE (d 1980), of Lyndhurst, and Essie Isabel Bruce, *née* Bruce-Porter (d 1981); *b* 14 Feb 1934; *Educ* Sherborne, Christ's Coll Cambridge (MA), Wycliffe Hall Oxford; *m* 10 Sept 1959, Monica Ruth, da of Rev Harcourt Robert Henry Lightburne (d 1949), of Upchurch, Kent; 2 s (John b 1961, Michael b 1964), 1 da (Anne b 1960); *Career* Nat Serv 1952-54, cmmnd Lt; ordained deacon 1959, priest 1960; curate: Penn Wolverhampton 1959-60, St Oswald's Oswestry 1960-63, Wrington with Redhill 1963-65; incumbent vicar Chewton Mendip with Emborough 1965-74; vicar: St John's Glastonbury with Godney 1974-84, West Pennard 1981-84, Meare 1981-84, St Benedict Glastonbury 1982-84, Burley 1984-; archdeacon of Winchester and hon canon Winchester Cathedral 1984-; proctor in convocation 1970-75, diocesan ecumenical offr 1965-75; *Recreations* gardening, photography, do it yourself, sailing, singing; *Style—* The Ven the Archdeacon of Winchester; The Vicarage, Church Corner, Burley, Ringwood, Hants BH24 4AP (☎ 04253 2303)

CLARKSON, Prof Brian Leonard; s of Leonard Coleman Clarkson, of Driffield, E Yorks, and Gertrude Irene, *née* Shouler; *b* 28 July 1930; *Educ* Beverley GS E Yorks, The Univ of Leeds (BSc, PhD); *m* 5 Sept 1953, Margaret Elaine, da of Frank Bancroft Wilby (d 1976), of Hedge End, Southampton; 3 s (Stephen Anthony b 1955, John Michael b 1957, Paul Richard b 1965), 1 da (Carol Margaret b 1960); *Career* structural engr de Havilland Aircraft Co 1953-57, Sir Alan Cobham res fell Univ of Southampton 1957-58, lectr dept of aeronautics Univ of Southampton 1958-63, lectr and sr lectr Inst of Sound and Vibration Res 1963-66; Univ of Southampton: prof vibration studies 1966-82, dir Inst of Sound Vibration Res 1967-78, dean of engrg 1978-70, dep vice-chllr 1980-82; sr res asst NASA USA 1970-71, princ Univ Coll Swansea 1981-, vice chllr Univ of Wales 1987-89; memb Wintech Advsy Bd; sec Int Cmmn on Acoustics 1975-81, pres Inst of Acoustics 1980-82, pres Fedn of Acoustical Socs of Europe 1982-84, memb SERC; DSc Leeds 1984, DSC Southampton 1987; FEng 1986, FInst of Acoustics, FSoc of Environmental Engrgs, FRAeS; *Recreations* walking, gardening; *Clubs* Athenaeum; *Style—* Prof Brian Clarkson; Danver House, 236 Gower Rd, Sketty, Swansea SA2 9JJ (☎ 0792 202 329); The Univ Coll of Swansea, Singleton Pk, Swansea SA2 8PP (☎ 0792 295154, fax 0792 295 655, telex 0792 295618)

CLARKSON, His Hon Judge; Derek Joshua; QC (1969); s of Albert Clarkson (d 1955), of Pudsey, Yorks, and Winifred Charlotte, *née* James; *b* 10 Dec 1929; *Educ* Pudsey GS, King's Coll London, (LLB); *m* 1960, Peternella Marie-Luise Ilse, da of R Canenbley, of Leer, Germany; 1 s, 1 da; *Career* Nat Serv (RAF) 1952-54; barr 1951, rec: Rotherham 1967-72, Huddersfield 1972, the Crown Court 1972-77, circuit judge (SE) 1977-, Middx liason judge 1985-; *Recreations* walking, theatre, book-collecting; *Style—* His Hon Judge Clarkson, QC; 24 John Islip St, London SW1; 72A Cornwall Rd, Harrogate, N Yorks

CLARKSON WEBB, Hon Mrs (Ruth Isabel); *née* Wakefield; da of 1 Baron Wakefield of Kendal (d 1983), and Rowena Doris (d 1981), da of late Dr Llewellyn Lewis, OBE, JP; *b* 12 Oct 1932; *m* 1 June 1955, Maj Nigel James Clarkson Webb (d 1987), yst s of William Thomas Clarkson Webb (d 1966), of Shortlands, Shortheath, Farnham, Surrey, and 25 Weymouth St, W1; 1 s (Edward b 1966), 2 da (Georgina b 1957, Carolyn b 1958); *Style—* The Hon Mrs Clarkson Webb; Buckstone House, Carnforth, Lancs (☎ 0524 781585)

CLARRICOATS, Prof Peter John Bell; s of John Clarricoats OBE (d 1969), of London and Alice Cecilia, *née* Bell (d 1982); *b* 6 April 1932; *Educ* Minchenden GS, Imperial Coll London (BSc, PhD, DSc); *m* 1, 6 Aug 1955 (m dis 1963),(Mary) Gillian Stephenson, da of George Gerald Hall (d 1971), of Leeds; 1 s (Michael b 1960), 1 da (Alison b 1962); m 2, 19 Oct 1968, Phyllis Joan, da of Reginald Blackburn Lloyd, of Newton Abbot; 2 das (Angela b 1969, Caroline b 1969); *Career* scientific staff GEC 1953-59, lectr: Queens Univ Belfast 1959-62, Sheffield Univ 1962-63; prof: Univ of Leeds 1963-67, Queen Mary Coll Univ of London 1968-, dean of Engng 1977-80, head of Electrical and Electronic Engng 1979-, govr 1976-79 and 1987-90); chm: Int Confce on Ferrimagnetics and Plasmas 1964, Int Confce on Antennas and Propagation 1978, IEE Electronics Div 1979, Euro Microwave Confce 1979, Br Nat Ctee for Radio Science (1985),appt Distinguished Lectr IEEE Antennas and Propagation 1986- (chm Mil Microwaves 1988); FIEE 1968, FIEEE 1968, FInstP 1964, FCGI 1980, FEng 1983; *Books* Microwave Ferrites F(1960), Corrugated Horns for Microwave Antennas (1984); *Recreations* formerly mountaineering and squash, classical music and photography; *Style—* Professor Peter Clarricoats; 7 Falcon Close, Sawbridgeworth, Herts CM21 OAX (☎ 0279 723 561); Department of Electrical and Electronic Engineering, Queen Mary College, University of London, Mile End Road, London E1 4NS (☎ 01 975 5330, fax 01 981 0259, telex 893750)

CLATWORTHY, Peter Francis; s of Walter Stanley Clatworthy (d 1956), and May Henrietta, *née* Morley (d 1980); *b* 19 Mar 1921; *Educ* Whitgift, London Univ, Bristol Univ (BSc); *m* 24 Feb 1951, Muriel Patricia, da of Frank Bickford (d 1981), of Barnstaple; 1 s (Richard b 1953), 1 da (Ann b 1952); *Career* Fl Lt 1941-46 Fighter Cmd 1 and 131 Sqdns, served in Mid E; Dep Borough Surveyor for Barnstaple E

1949-57, sr engr Miny of Tport London and Exeter 1964-69 (engr Leeds and London 1957-64), supt engr DOE Midlands and SW 1969-75; MICE, FIMunE; *Recreations* sailing, making spinning wheels; *Style*— Peter F Clatworthy, Esq; Middle Weaver Farm, Plymtree, Cullompton, Devon EX15 2JW (☎ 08847 421)

CLATWORTHY, Robert Ernest; s of Ernest William Clatworthy (d 1985), of Bridgwater, Som, and Gladys, *née* Tugela; *b* 31 Jan 1928; *Educ* Dr Morgan's GS Bridgwater, W of England Coll of Art, Chelsea Sch of Art, Slade Sch of Fine Art; *m* 1954 (m dis 1966), Pamela, *née* Gordon; 2 s (Benn b 1955, Thomas b 1959), 1 da (Sarah Alexandra b 1957); *Career* Nat Serv head of fine art wing E Formation Coll 1949; lectr W of Eng Coll of Art 1967-71, visiting tutor RCA 1960-72, memb fine art panel Nat Cncl for Dips in Art and Design 1961-72, govr St Martin's Sch of Art 1970-71, head of dept of fine art Central Sch of Art and Design 1971-75; exhibitions: Hanover Gallery, Waddington Galleries, Holland Park Open Air Sculpture, Battersea Park Open Air Sculpture, Br Sculpture in the Sixties Tate Gallery, Br Sculptors Burlington House 1972, Basil Jacobs Fine Art Ltd, Diploma Galleries Burlington House, Photographer's Gallery, Quinton Green Gallery, Chapman Gallery; works in the collections of: Arts Cncl, Contemporary Art Soc, Tate Gallery V & A, GLC, Nat Portrait Gallery, Monumental Horse and Rider; ARA 1968, RA 1973; *Recreations* music; *Clubs* Chelsea Arts; *Style*— Robert Clatworthy, Esq; Moelfre, Cynghordy, Llandovery, Dyfed SA20 0UW (☎ 0550 20 201)

CLAUSON, Oliver Drake Husey; s of Sir Gerard Leslie Makins Clauson, KCMG, OBE (d 1974), and Honor Emily Mary, *née* Husey (d 1978); *b* 23 April 1927; *Educ* Eton, Corpus Christi Coll Oxford (MA); *m* 14 Jan 1955, Barbara Susan, da of Maj De Symons Harry Lewis-Barned (d 1964), of Maidstone; 3 s (Richard b 1956, Julian b 1960, Francis b 1964), 1 da (Antonia b 1958); *Career* insur clerk Lloyd's 1952-56, underwriting memb of Lloyd's 1956-, claims adjudicator leading Personal Accident and Travel Syndicate 1965-; *Recreations* amateur acting, producing, stage hand; *Clubs* Army and Navy, Lansdowne; *Style*— Oliver D H Clauson, Esq; Applegarth, Ogbourne St George, Marlborough, Wilts SN8 1SU (☎ 067284 219); W R Massey and Ors, Box 110, Lloyd's, 1 Lime St, London EC3M 7HL (☎ 01 623 71004 ext 3011)

CLAXTON, Lt-Col David John; LVO (1985), TD (1973); s of Rt Rev Charles Robert Claxton, Asst Bishop of Exeter, and Jane, *née* Stevenson; *b* 15 July 1933; *Educ* Haileybury, Queens' Coll Cambridge (BA); *m* 1, 30 Sept 1967 (m dis 1985), Elizabeth Anne, da of Maj Thomas Henry Baker Cresswell, DL, qv, of Preston Tower, Chathill, Northumberland; 3 s (Charles b 1968, Piers b 1970, Christopher b 1971), 1 da (Tassagrie b 1975); m 2, 27 Sept 1986, Pamela, da of Charles Mycock, of Grinlow Rd, Harpur Hill, Buxton, Derbys; 1 step da (Sharon b 1967); *Career* Duke of Lancaster's Own Yeo 1960-78: offr cadet 1960-61, cmmnd 2 Lt 1961, Co Lt Col) 1974-78; asst farm mangr 1952-54, ptnr Joshua Bury Earle & Co Manchester (chartered surveyors and land agents) 1957-73, surveyor of lands Crewe Survey of the Duchy of Lancaster 1973-89; formerly: hon sec Bow Gp (NW), chm Lancs Cheshire and IOM branch (land agency and agric div) RICS, pres Cheshire Agric Valuers Assoc; currently churchwarden Barthomley, FRICS 1963, FAAV 1971; *Recreations* skiing, sailing, mountaineering; *Style*— Lt-Col David Claxton, LVO, TD; Duchy House, Barthomley, Crewe, Cheshire CW2 5NX (☎ 0270 583818); 3 Ruskin Rd, Crewe, Cheshire CW2 7JR (☎ 0270 582119)

CLAXTON, John Francis; CB (1969); s of Alfred John Claxton OBE (d 1963), of Hove, Sussex, and Dorothy Francis Olive, *née* Roberts (d 1942) of Khartoum; *b* 11 Jan 1911; *Educ* Tonbridge, Alpine Coll Villars Switzerland, Exeter Coll Oxford (BA); *m* 24 July 1937, Norma Margaret, (d 1983), da of Alfred Rawlinson (d 1946), of Primrose Manisons, Battersea; *Career* barr Middle Temple 1935, jr legal asst Dir of Pub Protection Dept (civil serv cmmn) 1937 (asst dir 1956, dep dir 1966 ret 1971); *Recreations* model making, gardening; *Clubs* Oxford and Cambridge Univ (1942-1972); *Style*— John F Claxton, Esq, CB; The White Cottage, 9 Lock Rd, Marlow, Bucks, SL7 1QN (☎ 06284 2744)

CLAXTON, Maj-Gen Patrick Fisher; CB (1972), OBE (1946); s of late Rear Adm Ernest William Claxton, and Kathleen O'Callaghan, *née* Fisher; *b* 13 Mar 1915; *Educ* Sutton Valence Sch, St John's Coll Cambridge; *m* 1941, Jóna Gudrún Gunnarsdóttir (d 1980), da of Gunnar Gunnarsson, of Reykjavik, Iceland; 2 da; *Career* Cdt Sch of Transport and ADC to HM the Queen 1966-68, Transport Offr-in-Chief (Army) 1969-71, ret; gen mangr Regular Forces Employment Assoc 1971-81; *Style*— Maj-Gen Patrick Claxton, CB, OBE; The Lodge, Beacon Hill Park, Hindhead, Surrey (☎ 042 873 4437)

CLAY, Jennifer Mary Ellen; *née* Coutts; da of Dr William Ernest Coutts, MA, MB, ChB, of Wilts, and Nora Margaret Jane, *née* Grassick; *b* 27 Sept 1941; *Educ* Howell's Sch Llandaff, Univ Coll Cardiff, Univ of Wales (BA, MA), Cornell Univ NY (LTCL, MCIT); *m* 1972, John Peter Clay, s of late Harold Peter Clay; *Career* Br Airways: sales trg mangr 1974-79, mangr Western USA 1979-82 (Scotland 1982-84), controller Corporate Identity 1984-86, gen-mngr product design and devpt Pan Am 1986-; *Recreations* music, travel, royal tennis, squash, dress-making; *Clubs* IOD, The Queen's; *Style*— Mrs Jennifer Clay; Pan American World Airways, Inc, 200 Park Ave, New York, New York 10166

CLAY, Jeremy Arden; s of Henry Arthur Clay (d 1971), of Castle Hill, Lower Fulbrook, Warwick, and Daphne Sybil Pauline, *née* Atkinson; *b* 30 June 1938; *Educ* Eton, RAC Cirencester; *m* 12 June 1971, Susan Caroline, da of Frank Tate Chapman (d 1978); 1 s (Richard Henry Arden b 4 Feb 1977), 1 da (Nicola Olivia b 12 July 1974); *Career* RN 1957-59; farmer, dir Bencraft Ltd; MRAC 1961; *Recreations* shooting, sailing, gardening; *Clubs* MCC, RASE; *Style*— Jeremy Clay, Esq; Castle Farm, Lower Fulbrook, Warwick

CLAY, Jeremy Peter Foster; s of Gerard Leigh Clay, of Brockhampton Cottage, Nr Hereford, and Drucilla Madelaine, *née* Foster (d 1960); *b* 26 July 1932; *Educ* Eton, RAC Cirencester; *m* 1, 20 Oct 1956 (m dis), Ann Julie, da of Dr Basil Rathburn Fuller, MC (d 1962), of St Micheal's Lodge, St Cross Rd, Winchester; 1 s (Peter Robert b 1958); m 2, 1962, Mary Elizabeth Anne, *née* Pryce Jenkins; 1 da (Luccilla b 1964); *Career* farmer; ctee memb: CLA, NFU; *Recreations* fishing, shooting; *Style*— Jeremy Clay, Esq; Fawley Court, nr Hereford, HR1 4SP; 94 Eaton Place, London SW1 (☎ 043 270 247)

CLAY, His Hon John Lionel; TD (1961); s of Capt Lionel Pilleau Clay (ka 1918), of Rastrick House, Yorks and Mary Winifred Muriel, da of Ralph Walker; *b* 31 Jan 1918; *Educ* Harrow, Corpus College Coll Oxford (MA); *m* 30 Aug 1952, Elizabeth, 2 da of Rev Canon Maurice George Jesser Ponsonby, MC gs of 2 Baron de Mauley (d 1943), and the Lady Phyllis Sydney, OBE (d 1942), eldest da of 1 Earl Buxton; 1 s (Andrew b 1962), 3 da (Fiona b 1954, Catriona b 1955, Joanna b 1958); *Career* serv WWII 8 Army (despatches), Rifle Bde, served TA London Rifle Bde Rangers and SAS; barrister 1947, recorder 1975-77, Circuit Judge 1977-88; freeman City of London 1980, liveryman Worshipful Co of Gardeners; *Recreations* gardening, fishing; *Style*— His Hon John Clay, TD; Newtimber Place, Hassocks, Sussex (☎ 0273 833104)

CLAY, John Martin; s of Sir Henry Clay (d 1954), and his 1 wife Gladys, *née* Priestman; *b* 20 August 1927; *Educ* Eton, Magdalen Coll Oxford; *m* 1952, Susan Jennifer, da of Lt-Gen Sir Euan Miller, KCB, KBE, DSO, MC (d 1985); 4 s; *Career* chm Johnson and Firth Brown Ltd; former dir Bank of England, dir Hambro plc; *Style*— John Clay, Esq; 41 Tower Hill, London EC3

CLAY, John Peter; s of Harold Peter Clay (d 1970), and Mary Dansie Clay (d 1974); *b* 26 June 1934; *Educ* St Paul's, Queen's Coll Oxford (MA); *m* 1972, Jennifer Mary Ellen (*qv*), da of Dr William Ernest Coutts, of Wiltshire; 3 da (Teresa, Lalage, Xanthe); *Career* investmt mangr; joined Vickers da Costa Ltd 1957 (dep chm 1976-81), chm Globe Int Ltd 1981-; memb Cncl of the Stock Exchange 1974-77; *Recreations* real tennis, flying; *Clubs* City, Queen's; *Style*— John Clay, Esq; 54 Ebury Mews, London SW1W 9NY (☎ 01 730 5368); Maison de la Voûte, Place de l'Amour, La Garde-Freinet, 83310 Var (☎ 94 436571); 123 East 30th Street, New York, NY 10016

CLAY, Dowager Lady; Phyllis Mary; *née* Paramore; da of Richard Horace Paramore, MD, FRCS; *b* 19 April 1907; *m* 1933, Sir Henry Felix Clay, 6 Bt (d 1985); 1 s (Richard Henry) , 2 da (Jenny Elizabeth Murray, Sarah Richenda Wise); *Recreations* sailing, gardening, chatting; *Clubs* Aldeburgh Yacht, New Cavendish; *Style*— Dowager Lady Clay; Wheelwrights, Cocking, Midhurst, Sussex

CLAY, Sir Richard Henry; 7 Bt (UK 1841), of Fulwell Lodge, Middlesex; s of Sir Henry Felix Clay, 6 Bt (d 1985), and Phyllis Mary, *née* Paramore (*see* Clay, Dowager Lady); *b* 2 June 1940; *Educ* Eton; *m* 14 Sept 1963, Alison Mary, da of Dr James Gordon Fife, of Summerhill, Aldeburgh, Suffolk; 3 s (Charles Richard, Thomas Henry b 28 July 1967, James Felix b 13 April 1969), 2 da (Virginia Rachel 7 July 1964, Catherine b 9 June 1971); *Heir* s, Charles Richard Clay b 18 Dec 1965; *Career* FCA 1966; *Recreations* sailing; *Clubs* Aldeburgh Yacht; The Copse, Shiplate Rd, Bleadon, Avon BS24 ONX (☎ 0934 815203)

CLAY, Robert Alan; MP (Lab) Sunderland North 1983-; *b* 2 Oct 1946; *Educ* Bedford Sch, Gonville and Caius Coll Cambridge; *m* 1980, Uta Christa; *Style*— Bob Clay, Esq, MP; House of Commons, London SW1

CLAY, Trevor; s of Joseph Reginald George Clay (d 1970), and Florence Emma Steptoe; *b* 10 May 1936; *Educ* Nuneaton, Bethlem Royal and Maudsley Hosps, Brunel Univ; *Career* gen sec Royal Coll of Nursing of the UK 1982-; MPhil, RGN, RMN, FRCN; *Books* Nurses: Power and Politics (1987); *Recreations* music, good friends, theatre; *Style*— Trevor Clay, Esq; c/o Royal Coll of Nursing of the UK, 20 Cavendish Square, London W1M 0AB (☎ 01 409 3333)

CLAYMAN, Stanley Joseph; s of Norman Clayman (d 1983), and Sophie, *née* Chisell (d 1964); *b* 24 Nov 1935; *Educ* St Paul's, London Univ (LLB); *m* 6 Oct 1964, Joy Lilian Sally, da of Angel Dell (d 1970); 2 da (Linda b 1966, Helen b 1969); *Career* slr in private practice 1958-65, First Nat Fin Corpn 1965- (dir 1985); Gen Cmmr of Taxes; memb Law Soc 1958; *Recreations* music, theatre, cricket, horticulture; *Clubs* MCC, IOD; *Style*— Stanley Clayman, Esq; 127 The Reddings, Mill Hill, London NW7 4JP (☎ 01 959 7888); First Nat Fin Corpn plc, PO Box 505, St Alphage House, Fore St, London EC2P 2NJ (☎ 01 638 2855, fax 01 628 9963)

CLAYPOLE WHITE, Rev Douglas Eric; *b* 13 Jan 1929; *Educ* Clifton Coll, Monkton Combe; *m* 26 Dec 1953, Anne; 2 da (Susan b 1959, Barbara b 1961); *Career* CA and clerk in Holy Orders; former ptnr Grant Thornton (chartered accountants); currently priest in charge St Marys Felmersham Beds; *Recreations* swimming; *Style*— The Rev Douglas Claypole White; Homelands, Turvey, Bedford MK43 8DB (☎ 023064 661)

CLAYSON, Sir Eric Maurice; DL (W Midlands 1975); yr s of late Harry Clayson, of Westcliff-on-Sea, Essex, and Emily Clayson; *b* 17 Feb 1908; *Educ* Woodbridge Sch; *m* 1933, Pauline Audrey, da of John Ferguson Wright, of Westcliff-on-Sea; 2 s; *Career* CA 1932; former chm and md The Birmingham Post and Mail Gp of Cos; former dir: Reuters Ltd, Sun Alliance and London Insurance Gp, ATV and ATV Network; former chm The Press Assoc; kt 1964; *Style*— Sir Eric Clayson, DL; Clare Park, nr Farnham, Surrey

CLAYSON, Peter John; s of Francis Henry Clayson (d 1988), of Crewe, and Sarah Anne *née* Wyatt (d 1952); *b* 29 May 1933; *Educ* Crewe GS, Liverpool Univ (B Eng); *m* 29 Mar 1960, (m dis) 1981, Barbara, da of Hubert Coyne (d 1983); 1 s (Jonathan Mark b 1962), 3 da (Amanda Jane b 1961, Katherine Anne and Jacqueline Nancy b 1964 (twins)); m 2, 1986, RitaKotchinsky; *Career* Electrical offfr MN 1956-59, commissioning engr 1960-63, power station engr 1963-65, res engr 1915-68, chief engr 1968-74, ptnr Heap & Digby cnslts 1974-81; holdings dir Mott Hay & Anderson 1986- (dir 1981-86) and chm assoc co's: MHA (M&E), Mott Laverack, Haggie Patterson, MHA (Midlands); FIEE, FRSA; *Recreations* golf, squash; *Clubs* Lingfield, Squash Club; *Style*— Peter Clayson, Esq

CLAYTON, Sir David Robert; 12 Bt (GB 1732), of Marden Park, Surrey; s of Sir Arthur Harold Clayton, 11 Bt, DSC (d 1985), and his 2 w, Alexandra, *née* Andreevsky; *b* 12 Dec 1936; *Educ* HMS Conway, Sir John Cass Coll London; *m* 1971, Julia Louise, da of Charles Henry Redfearn (d 1969); 2 s (Robert, John Richard b 1978); *Heir* s, Robert Philip b 8 July 1975; *Career* Capt Merchant Navy; *Recreations* shooting, sailing; *Clubs* Royal Dart Yacht; *Style*— Sir David Clayton, Bt; Rock House, Kingswear, Dartmouth, Devon

CLAYTON, Diana, Lady; Diana Katherine Mary; da of Capt Charles Alverey Grazebrook, 60 Rifles (ka Givenchy 1915); *b* 19 May 1913; *m* 1, 1934, Peter Neve; m 2, - Bircham; m 3, 1965, as his 4 w, Sir Arthur Harold Clayton, 11 Bt, DSC (d 1985); *Style*— Diana, Lady Clayton; Colonsay, Kingswear, Dartmouth, Devon

CLAYTON, Francis Howard; s of Rev Arthur Clayton (d 1960), of Lichfield, and Frances Ella, *née* Warren (d 1974); *b* 20 May 1918; *Educ* St John's Sch Leatherhead, Univ of Birmingham (BCom); *m* 29 July 1942, Helen Margaret (d 1988), da of Dr Henry Doig, of Lennoxtown, Stirlingshire; 1 s (John b 1950), 2 da (Elizabeth b 1943, Margaret b 1948); *Career* WWII 1939-46: comm RA 1942, S Staffs Regt 1944 (wounded in action Holland 1944, leg amputated; asst sec Manor Hosp Walsall 1949-56; lectr: Wednesbury Coll of Commerce 1957-61, Tamworth Coll of Further Educn 1961-67; freelance writer 1967-; dir Lichfield Cathedral Arts Ltd 1980-; memb Lichfield DC 1976-87 (chm 1983-84); Lichfield: Sheriff 1978-79, Mayor 1987-88; *Books*

The Atmospheric Railways (1966), The Duffield Bank (1967), Eaton Railways (1967), Atlantic Bridgehead (1968), Coaching City (1970), Cathedral City (1976), The Great Swinfen Case (1980), Loyal and Ancient City (1986); *Recreations* historic res, music, reading; *Style*— Francis Clayton, Esq; 2a Brownsfield Rd, Lichfield, Staffs

CLAYTON, Air Marshal Sir Gareth Thomas Butler; KCB (1970, CB 1962), DFC (1940) and Bar (1944); s of Thomas Clayton, and Katherine, of The Beacon, Torquay, Devon; *b* 13 Nov 1914; *Educ* Rossall; *m* 1938, Elisabeth Marian, da of Thomas Keates, of Barons Court; 3 da; *Career* entered RAF 1936, Dir-Gen RAF Personal Services 1966-69, Chief of Staff HQ RAF Strike Command 1969-70, Air Sec MOD 1970-72, ret; chm RAFA 1978-81, pres NW Area RAFA 1983-88; *Clubs* RAF; *Style*— Air Marshal Sir Gareth Clayton, KCB, DFC; Greenacre, Polstead, nr Colchester CO6 5AD

CLAYTON, Dr John Pilkington; CVO (1986); s of Brig-Gen Sir Gilbert Falkingham Clayton, KCMG, KBE, CB (d 1929), and Enid Caroline, *née* Thorowgood; bro of Samuel Wittewronge Clayton (*see* Lady Mary Clayton); *b* 13 Feb 1921; *Educ* Wellington, Gonville and Caius Coll Cambridge; *Career* RAFVR Medical Branch 1947-49; sr resident Nottingham Children's Hosp 1950; medical offr: Holloway Coll London Univ 1953-81, Black and Decker Ltd 1955-70; surgn-apothecary to HM the Queen's Household at Windsor and to the Household of HM Queen Elizabeth the Queen Mother at Royal Lodge 1965-86, sr medical offr Eton 1965-86 (ret); MB, BChir; *Style*— Dr John Clayton, CVO; Knapp House, Market Lavington, nr Devizes, Wiltshire SN10 4DP (☎ 0380 813274)

CLAYTON, John Robert; CBE (1987); s of late John Clayton; *b* 29 Mar 1922; *Educ* Highgate, LSE; *m* 1, 1943 (m dis 1956) Doris Louise, *née* Usherwood; m 2, 1958, Aileen Bowen, *née* Morris (d 1981); m 3, 1984 Jean Olive, da of Ernest Marks (d 1978); 1 s; *Career* serv WWII, Capt RCS; industl advsr Fed Govt of Nigeria 1951-61, ptnr John Tyzack and Ptnrs Ltd 1961-69, gp md Pauls and Whites plc (maltsters and animal feed gp) 1970-82; dir: Nat Westminster Bank (SE regnl bd) 1974-, Richard Clay and Co plc 1977-86, Dewe Rogerson Gp Ltd 1981-; IPSENTA Ltd 1982- (chm 1982-85); chm: Agric Trg Bd 1983-, Thurlow Nunn Hldgs Ltd 1983-; memb Suffolk CC 1982-, (vice-chm educn ctee 1985-); gen commr of Income Tax 1976- memb IOD; CBIM; *Clubs* Oriental; *Style*— John R Clayton, CBE; Erie House, Hadleigh, Suffolk IP7 5AG (☎ 0473 823316)

CLAYTON, Prof Keith Martin; s of Edgar Francis Clayton (d 1978), and Constance Annie, *née* Clark (d 1985); *b* 25 Sept 1928; *Educ* Bedales, Univ of Sheffield (BSc MSc), Univ of London (PhD); *m* 1 1950 (m dis 1976); m2, 29 Dec 1976, Jennifer Nan 3 s, 1 da; *Career* Nat Serv, 2 Lt RE 1951-53; LSE 1953-67: asst lectr, lectr, reader; Univ of E Anglia Norwich: prof of enviromental sciences 1967-, dean 1967-71, pro vice-chllr 1971-73, dean 1987-); parish cncllr Thorpe St Andrew; memb: cncl NERC 1971-74, Univ Grants Ctee 1974-84; *Style*— Prof Keith Clayton, CBE; Well Close, Pound Lane, Norwich NR7 OVA (☎ 0603 33780); School of Environmental Sciences, University of East Anglia, Norwich NR4 7TJ (☎ 0603 592533)

CLAYTON, Margaret Ann; da of Percy Clayton (d 1970), and Kathleen, *née* Payne; *b* 7 May 1941; *Educ* Christs Hosp Hertford (BA), Birkbeck Coll London; *Career* dir Regimes and Services, Prison Dept, Home Off 1986-; civil servant Home Off 1960-, resident chm Civil Service Selection Bd 1983, establ offr Home Off 1984-86; *Recreations* reading, gardening, theatre, equitation; *Clubs* Reform; *Style*— Miss Margaret Clayton; Prison Dept, Cleland House, Page Street, SW1 (☎ 211 8294)

CLAYTON, Lady Mary Cecilia; *née* Leveson-Gower; only da of Vice-Adm 4 Earl Granville, KG, KCVO, CB, DSO (d 1953), and Lady Rose Constance Bowes-Lyon, GCVO (d 1967); niece (through her mother) of HM Queen Elizabeth the Queen Mother; *b* 12 Dec 1917; *m* 7 July 1956, Samuel Wittewronge Clayton, s of Brig-Gen Sir Gilbert Falkingham Clayton, KCMG, KBE, CB (d 1929), and bro of Dr John Pilkington Clayton, CVO, *qv*; 1 s (Gilbert Falkingham b 1958), 1 da; *Style*— Lady Mary Clayton; Broad Lea, Long Martin, Appleby, Westmorland

CLAYTON, Michael Aylwin; s of Aylwin Goff Clayton of Bournemouth, Dorset, and Norah Kathleen Joan, *née* Banfield (d 1978); *b* 20 Nov 1934; *Educ* Bournemouth GS; *m* 1, Mary 1 s (Marcus 6 1967), 1 da (Maxine (Mrs Butler-Gallie) b 1965); m 2, 1979, Barbara J Ryman; m 3, 28 Oct 1988, Marilyn Croshurst, da Ernest George Jolin Orring; *Career* journalist, author, broadcaster; news correspondent radio and TV BBC 1965-73, ed Horse and Hound 1973-; *Recreations* foxhunting; *Style*— Michael Clayton, Esq

CLAYTON, Michael Thomas Emilius; CB (1976), OBE (1958); s of Lt-Col Emilius Clayton, OBE, RA (ggs of George Clayton, who was gs of Sir William Clayton, 1 Bt; George's mother (his father William's 3 w) was Lady Louisa Fermor, da of 1 Earl of Pomfret by Henrietta, gda of Judge Jeffreys), and Irene Dorothy Constance, *née* Strong; *b* 15 Sept 1917; *Educ* Bradfield; *m* 1942, Mary Margery, da of Dr John Roberts Pate, of Oxford; 1 da (Amanda, m 1976 Peter Hobson); *Career* attached WO 1939-64, MOD 1964-76; *Recreations* philately, country pursuits; *Style*— Michael Clayton, Esq, CB, OBE; Hillside Cottage, Marshwood, Bridport, Dorset (☎ 029 77 452)

CLEALL, Charles; s of Sydney Cleall (d 1973), and Dorothy Bound (d 1978); *b* 1 June 1927; *Educ* Hampton Sch Middlesex, Univ of London (BMus), Univ of Wales (MA); *m* 1953, Mary, yr da of George Lee Turner (d 1979), of Archery Lodge, Ashford, Middlesex; 2 da (Anne, Alisoun); *Career* cmmnd music advsr RN 1946-48; prof of solo singing Voice Prod and Choral Repertoire TCL 1949-52, conductor Morley Coll Orchestra 1949-51, organist and choirmaster Wesley's Chapel London 1950-52, conductor Glasgow Choral Union 1952-54, BBC music asst Midland Region 1954-55; music master Glyn County Sch 1955-66, conductor Aldeburgh Festival Choir 1957-60; organist and choirmaster: St Paul's, Portman Sq, London W1 1957-61, Holy Trinity Guildford 1961-65, lectr in music Froebel Inst 1967-68, advsr in music London Borough of Harrow 1968-72, warden educn section Incorporated Soc of Musicians 1971-72, music specialist for the Northern Div of Her Majesty's Inspectorate of Schs in Scotland 1972-87, ed of Journal The Ernest George White Soc 1983-88, registered teacher The Sch of Sinus Tone 1985-; *Books* Voice Production in Choral Technique (1955, revised and enlarged edition 1970), The Selection and Training of Mixed Choirs in Churches (1960), Sixty Songs from Sankey (1960), John Merbecke's Music for the Congregation at Holy Communion (ed 1963), Music and Holiness (1964), Authentic Chanting (1969), Plainsong for Pleasure (1969), A Guide to 'Vanity Fair' (1982); *Recreations* reading, writing, genealogy; *Style*— Charles Cleall, Esq; 10 Carronhall, Stonehaven, Kincardineshire, Grampian AB3 2HF

CLEAR, Michael Charles; MBE (1943); s of Charles Arnold Clear (d 1945), and Ruth Clear, *née* Wilkinson (d 1966); *b* 12 Oct 1913; *Educ* Trent, Imperial Coll London (BSc) ; *m* 1945, Kathleen, da of Charles Mieville Chevalier (d 1951); 1 s (Jeremy b 1951), 1 da (Derryn b 1946); *Career* Lt Col REME 1939-45, (despatches 1942); Royal Cmmn Inventors Award Scorpion Flail Tank 1947, non exec dir Metal Box (overseas) Ltd 1958-61, md Brush Elec Eng Co Ltd Hawker Siddeley Gp 1945-64; gp md Tillotson and Sons Ltd 1964-71; md MK Electric Ltd 1971-75; non exec dir Dubilier plc 1976-87, dir Parkington Co Ltd 1977-; ACGI, CEng, FIMechE, FIEE; *Recreations* gardening, bridge, golf; *Style*— Michael Clear, Esq, MBE; 8 Paterson Drive, Woodhouse Eaves, Leicestershire LE12 8RL; Parkington Co Ltd, 44 Green Street, London W1Y 3FJ (☎ 01 629 8916, telex (9401) 6116 GRST, fax 01 493 3800)

CLEARY, (Owen) Alistair; s of Bernard Cleary (d 1968), and Mary Weir, *née* Hamilton (d 1985); *b* 20 June 1931; *Educ* Leith Acad, Royal HS of Edinburgh, Edinburgh Univ (MA, LLB); *m* 6 Aug 1960, (Elsie) Dylena, da of Adriaan Hendricus Stander Fourie (d 1960); 1 step s (Adrian James Cook b 1953), 1 step da (Mrs Arlene Dawn Shuttleworth b 1951, 1 da (Susan Mary Hamilton b 1966); *Career* slr and notary public; former: Dean of faculty of Procurators of Caithness (Caithness bar), former Depute Procurator Fiscal of Caithness; presently clerk to Gen Cmmnrs of Income Tax; memb: Aid to the Persecuted, Action Aid, Christian Aid, Help the Aged; ran Dublin, Boston, Paris and Natal SA marathons, silver medal Scottish Veteran Track and Field Championships 1986; First Caithness Sportsman of the Year 1983; *Recreations* rugby, cricket, athletes, photography, writing poetry, Scottish and Southern African Plitics, genealogy, int travel, gardening; *Clubs* Royal HS, Scottish Veteran Harriers, The TS; *Style*— Alistair Cleary, Esq; Elangeni, 5 Upper Dunbar Street, Wick, Caithness (☎ Wick 2447)

CLEARY, Denis Mackrow; CMG (1967); s of Francis Esmonde Cleary (d 1936), of Dublin, and Emmeline Marie, *née* Mackrow (d 1931); *b* 20 Dec 1907; *Educ* St Ignatius Coll, St Olave's Sch, St John's Coll Cambridge (MA); *m* 1, 1941, Barbara (d 1960), da of late Hereford Wykeham-George; m 2, 1962, Mary, widow of Harold Kent and da of late George Dunlop, of Church Farm, Hendon; 1 step da (Elizabeth); *Career* India Off 1931-46, seconded to Miny of Home Security 1940-44, asst sec FO (German Section) 1946-49, joined Cwlth Serv (subsequently HM Diplomatic Serv) 1949, cnsllr Delhi 1949-51; dep high cmmr: NZ 1955-58, Cyprus 1962-64; ret 1968; re-employed in DHSS 1968-72; *Recreations* gardening, walking; *Style*— Denis Cleary, Esq, CMG; High Gate, Burwash, E Sussex TN19 7LA (☎ 0435 882712)

CLEARY, Sir Joseph Jackson; JP (Liverpool 1936); s of Joseph Cleary, JP, of Liverpool; *b* 26 Oct 1902; *Educ* Holy Trinity C of E Sch Anfield, Skerry's Coll Liverpool; *m* 1945, Ethel McColl; *Career* contested (Lab) E Toxteth Div Liverpool 1929, W Derby 1931, MP (Lab) Wavertree Div of Liverpool Feb-Oct 1935; Lord Mayor of Liverpool 1949-50; Hon freeman City of Liverpool 1970; kt 1965; *Style*— Sir Joseph Cleary, JP; 115 Riverview Heights, Liverpool L19 OLQ (☎ 051 427 2133)

CLEAVER, Leonard Harry; JP; s of Harry Cleaver, OBE, JP (d 1969; pres Eng Rugby Union 1952), of Burleigh, Balsall Common, Warwickshire, and Edith Lucy Wootton (d 1968); *b* 27 Oct 1909; *Educ* Rugby; *m* 1938, Mary Richards, da of Frank Hart Matthews (d 1961), of Edgbaston; 1 s; *Career* chartered accountant; sec and chief accountant Chance Bros Ltd 1935-51, ptnr Heathcote and Coleman 1951-59; MP (C) Yardley Divn 1959-64, PPS to Parly sec to Miny of Housing and Local Govt 1963-64; tres Deritend Divn Unionist Assoc 1945-48; Yardley Divn Unionist Assoc: tres 1949-52, chm 1952-57, pres 1970-81, patron 1981-; city magistrate 1954; Birmingham City Cncl 1966-70; memb: Birmingham Probation Ctee 1955-73, Central Cncl of Probation and After Care Ctees for Eng and Wales 1966-73; govr Yardley Educnl Fndn 1968-74; *Recreations* rugby football; *Style*— Leonard Cleaver, Esq, JP

CLEAVER, Air Vice-Marshal Peter Charles; CB (1971), OBE (1945); s of William Henry Cleaver (d 1966), of Warwick; *b* 6 July 1919; *Educ* Warwick Sch, Coll of Aeronautics (MSc), Staff Coll Haifa, Imperial Def Coll; *m* 1948, Jean, da of John Edward Birkett Fairclough (d 1948), of Ledburg; 2 s; *Career* Offr cmdg RAF Swanson Morley 1962-63, Air Offr Engrg: Flying Training Cmd 1963-65, HQ FEAF 1967-69, Air Support Command 1969-72, ret; sec Cranfield Inst of Technology 1973-78; *Recreations* gardening, walking; *Clubs* RAF; *Style*— Air Vice-Marshal Peter Cleaver, CB, OBE; Willow House, Watling St, Little Brickhill, Milton Keynes, Bucks MK17 9LS

CLEAVER, William Benjamin; s of David John Cleaver (d 1963), of Rhondda, and Blodwen, *née* Miles (d 1948); *b* 15 Sept 1921; *Educ* Pentre GS Rhondda, Univ of Wales (BSc); *m* 1943, Mary Watkin, da of Watkin James (d 1951), of Dyfed; 1 s (John), 2 da (Pamela, Patricia); *Career* mining engr; NCB: area gen mangr 1958-67, dep dir (Mining) 1967-83, ret 1983; Welsh Rugby Int 1947-50 14 caps, Br Lion NZ and Aust 1950, fndr chm Welsh Youth Rugby Union 1949-57; vice-chm Welsh Arts Cncl 1977-83; memb Arts Cncl GB 1980-83; sec Contemporary Art Soc for Wales 1973-; memb Cncl Nat Museum Wales 1977-, chm Cncl Museums in Wales 1986-; FIMinE; OStJ; *Recreations* rugby football, fine arts, wine appreciation; *Clubs* Cardiff and County, Saville; *Style*— William Cleaver, Esq; 29 Lon-y-Deri, Rhiwbina, Cardiff CF4 6JN (☎ 0222 693242)

CLEDWYN OF PENRHOS, Baron (Life Peer UK 1979); Cledwyn Hughes; CH (1977), PC (1966); s of late Rev Henry David Hughes, of Frondeg, Holyhead, and Emily Hughes; *b* 14 Sept 1916; *Educ* Holyhead GS, Univ Coll of Wales Aberystwyth; *m* 1949, Jean Beatrice, da of Capt Jesse Hughes, of Holyhead; 1 s, 1 da; *Career* serv WWII RAFVR, memb Anglesey CC 1946-52, slr 1940, MP (L) Anglesey 1951-79 (also candidate 1945 and 1950), Min of Ag, Fish and Food 1968-70, Oppn Spokesman on Ag, Fish and Food 1970-72, Cmmnr of Ho of Commons 1979, chm Ho of Lords Select Ctee on Agric and Food 1980-83, dep ldr Oppn in Lords 1979-82, ldr 1982-, oppn spokesman (Lords) on Civil Serv, Foreign Affrs and Welsh Affrs 1983-; former chm Welsh Parly Pty and Parly Labour Pty 1974-79; dir: Shell UK Ltd 1980-, Anglesey Aluminium Ltd 1980-, Holyhead Towing Ltd 1980-; regnl advsr Midland Bank with responsibilities for Wales 1979-; memb C Cncls Assoc 1980-; pres Housing and Town Planning Cncl 1980-, Age Concern Wales 1980-, Soc of Welsh People Overseas 1980-, UCW Aberystwyth 1976-; Hon Freedom Beaumaris 1972, Freeman Borough of Anglesey 1976, Hon LLD Wales 1970, Alderman Anglesey CC 1973; Min of State for the Cwlth 1964-66, Sec of State for Wales 1966-68, pres Univ Coll of Wales 1975-85, pro-chllr Univ of Wales 1985-; *Style*— The Rt Hon the Lord Cledwyn of Penrhos, CH, PC; Swynol Le, Trearddur, Holyhead, Gwynedd (☎ Trearddur 544)

CLEERE, Dr Henry Forester; s of Christopher Henry John Cleere (d 1981), of

London, and Frances Eleanor, *née* King (d 1970); *b* 2 Dec 1926; *Educ* Beckenham GS, UCL (BA), Univ of London Inst of Archaeology (PhD); *m* 1, 1950 (m dis), Dorothy Percy; 1 s (Christopher), 1 da (Elizabeth); m 2, 1974, Pamela Joan, da of Stanley Vertue (d 1979), of Tadley Hants; 2 da (Josephine, Catherine); *Career* dep sec Iron and Steel Inst London 1952-71, indust devpt offr UN Indust Devpt Orgn Vienna 1972-73; archaeologist; dir Cncl Br Archaeology 1974-; memb exec ctee Int Cncl on Monuments and Sites; pres Sussex Archaeological Soc 1987-; hon visiting fell Univ of York 1988-, research fell Univ of Paris I (Sorbonne) 1989- FSA; *Clubs* Athenaeum; *Style—* Dr Henry Cleere; Acres Rise, Lower Platts, Ticehurst, Wadhurst, E Sussex TN5 7DD (☎ 0580 200752); 112 Kennington Rd, London SE11 6RE (☎ 01 582 0494)

CLEGG, (William, Gavin) Anthony; s of GH Clegg, of Poole Hall, Nantwich, Cheshire, and Francis May Angela, *née* Joynson (d 1987); *b* 15 Jan 1940; *Educ* Heatherdown Sch, Eton, Grenoble Univ France; *Career* ptnr Grieveson Grant and Co 1972-86; dir of Kleinwort, Benson Gilts Ltd; *Books* 3 Feb 1985, Caroline Janet, da of J Doniger; *Style—* A Clegg, Esq

CLEGG, Christopher; s of William Henry Clegg (d 1945), and Elinor Mary Constance Clement, *née* Bowen (d 1954); *b* 5 Jan 1926; *Educ* Eton, Guy's Hosp London (BDS); *m* 21 May 1955, Diana, da of John Brant Butland (d 1960), of West Byfleet, Surrey; 3 da (Fiona b 1956, Jane Louise b 1957, d 1959, Sophia Philipps b 1960); *Career* Inf in Ranks 1943-45, cmmnd RASC Serv Egypt and Palestine 1945, military mission Greece 1946-47, Fl Lt RAF Regt 1948, Aden Levies 1949, RAF Levies Iraq 1950, serv Uk 1950-56, Capt RADC (TA) 1970-75; dental surgn: Farnham 1967-76, City of Liverpool Field Ambulance (TA) 1970-74, Hants 1976-; memb local ctee Cons Party; memb Br Dental Assoc 1963-; *Recreations* archaeology, sailing, skiing, riding, gardening, sheep; *Clubs* Key Haven YC, Winchester Med and Dental Soc; *Style—* Christopher Clegg, Esq; Ryedown Farmhouse, Ryedown Lane, E Wellow, Romsey (☎ 0794 23393)

CLEGG, Jeremy Paul Jermyn; s of Maj Benjamin Beattie Clegg, MC, of The Lawn, Ridgeway, nr Sheffield, and Rosemary Anne, *née* Coles (d 1955); *b* 11 July 1948; *Educ* Fettes, Univ of Sussex (BSc); *m* 24 March 1973, Marilyn Anne, da of Edward Towndrow, of Barnet, Herts; 1 s (Oliver b 14 Feb 1980), 1 da (Anna-Louise b 6 March 1978); *Career* Commercial Union 1970, Leslie & Godwin 1974, MPA Ltd 1982, dir Baring Investmt Mgmnt (Baring Brothers & Co) 1986-; FIA; *Recreations* golf, tennis, photography; *Style—* Jeremy Clegg, Esq; The Moorings, Bowling Alley, Crondall, Farnham, Surrey (☎ 0252 850229; Baring Bros & Co Ltd, 8 Bishopsgate, London EC2N 4AE (☎ 01 283 8833, fax 01 283 2633, telex 8958761)

CLEGG, (William Edwin) Morris; s of Norman Clegg (d 1962), and Ada Nina Fisher; *b* 6 May 1930; *Educ* Cowley Sch, HMS Conway (trg ship); *m* 1958, Judith Anne, da of George Wardle (d 1983), of Liverpool; 2 s (Mark William Norman b 1959, Richard Henry Morris b 1962), 2 da (Rosemary Anne b 1960, Jane Amanda Judith b 1967); *Career* reader Anglican Church 1957-; chm: Cleggs of Prescot Ltd 1962-85 (dir 1957-62), Pioneer Replacement Servs Ltd 1970-83, Lancaster Ct (Chorley) Ltd 1970-83; dir: Knowsley Sports Club Ltd 1980-87, Charles Baynes plc 1984-, chm St Helens Comm Tst BES Investmt Appraisal Ctee 1984-; dir Job Ownership Ltd 1985-, underwriting name Lloyds 1985-, chm G M Bldg Systems Ltd 1985-; dir: Astra Ind Hldgs plc 1985-87, The Guy Pilkington meml Hosp Ltd 1986-; chm Gawsworth Fin Ltd 1986-, dir Holroyd and Meek Ltd 1987-, chm Royal Stafford China Ltd 1987-88; memb clergy Selection Panel Chester Diocese 1987-; *Recreations* reading, walking, gardening, piano; *Style—* Morris Clegg, Esq; The Old Rectory, Gawsworth, Cheshire SK11 9RJ; (☎ 0260 223372

CLEGG, Nicholas Peter; s of Dr Hugh Anthony Clegg, CBE (d 1983); *b* 24 May 1936; *Educ* Bryanston, Trinity Coll Cambridge (BA); *m* 1959, Eulalie, da of Herman van den Wall Bake; 3 s, 1 da; *Career* banker; with Royal Netherlands Blast Furnaces and Steelworks 1960-62, Proctor and Gamble Brussels 1962-64; dir Hill Samuel and Co Ltd 1970-; *Recreations* gardening, skiing, listening to music; *Style—* Nicholas Clegg, Esq; The Leather Bottle, Wainhill, Chinnor, Oxford OX9 4AB; Hill Samuel and Co, 100 Wood Street, London EC2P 2AJ (☎ 01 628 8011; telex 888822)

CLEGG, Richard Ninian Barwick; QC (1979); o s of Sir Cuthbert Barwick Clegg, TD, JP (d 1986), and Helen Margaret, *née* Jefferson (d 1987); *b* 28 June 1938; *Educ* Charterhouse, Trinity Coll Oxford (MA); *m* 3 Aug 1963, Katherine Veronica, da of Andrew Archibald Henry Douglas of Ashley, Shalbourne, Wilts; 2 s (Aidan b 1966, Sebastian b 1969), 1 da (Flavia b 1968); *Career* capt Oxford Pentathlon Team 1959; barr Inner Temple 1960, bencher 1985, rec Crown Ct 1978-; chm NW section Bow Gp 1964-66, v-chm Bow Gp 1965-66, chm Winston Circle 1965-66, pres Heywood and Royton Cons Assoc 1965-68; *Recreations* hunting, shooting, fishing, skiing, travel, music, books; *Clubs* Lansdowne; *Style—* Richard Clegg, Esq, QC; The Old Rectory, Brereton, via Sandbach, Cheshire (☎ 0477 32358); 5 Essex Court, Temple, London EC4 (☎ 01 353 4365, fax 01 583 1491)

CLEGG, Ronald Anthony (Tony); s of Stanley Clegg, and Cicely, *née* Bentley; *b* 8 April 1937; *Educ* Bickerton House, Southport, Lancs; *m* 9 March 1963, Dorothy Eve; 3 da (Virginia b 1965, Fiona b 1966, Victoria b 1970); *Career* mangr Mountain Mills Co Ltd 1961 (dir 1963), jt md Leigh Mills Co Ltd 1972 (merged with above to form Mountleigh Gp Ltd 1979); chm and chief exec Mountleigh Gp plc 1983-; memb: cncl Yorks Agric Soc, fin and gen purposes ctee Princes Youth Business Tst; patron Leeds Area Riding for the Disabled; memb Worshipful Co of Turners; CBIM, FInstD; *Recreations* riding, breeding highland cattle; *Style—* Tony Clegg, Esq; The Old Hall, Bramham, W Yorks LS23 6QR; Mountleigh Group plc, 49 Grosvenor St, Mayfair, London 41X 7FH (☎ 01 493 5555)

CLEGG, Hon Mrs; Hon Sally Mary; *née* Atkins; 3 and yst da of Baron Colnbrook (Life Peer), *qv*; *b* 18 Feb 1948; *m* 1970, William Field Clegg; 1 s, 1 da; *Style—* The Hon Mrs Clegg; Homer House, Ipsden, Oxon

CLEGG, Sir Walter; s of Edwin Clegg, of Blackpool; *b* 18 April 1920; *Educ* Bury GS, Arnold Sch Blackpool, Manchester U Law Sch; *m* 1951, Elise Margaret, da of J Hargreaves, of Blackpool; *Career* slr 1947, practising to 1961; MP (C) N Fylde 1966-83, MP(C) Wyre 1983-87; a lord cmmr HM Treasury 1970-72, vice-chamberlain HM Household 1972-73, Comptroller 1973-74, Opp Whip 1967-69 and 1974, kt 1980; *Style—* Sir Walter Clegg; Beech House, Raikes Rd, Little Thornton, nr Blackpool (☎ 0253 826131)

CLEGG-HILL, Hon Mrs Frederic; Alice Dorothy; yr da of Rear Adm Cuthbert Godfrey Chapman, MVO (d 1931), and Hon Dorothy Beatrix Wynn, da of 3 Baron Newborough; *b* 21 Sept 1910; *m* 18 Nov 1938, Maj Hon Frederic Raymond Clegg-Hill (ka 13 April 1945), yr s of 6 Viscount Hill (d 1957); 1 s (Peter David Raymond Charles, *qv*); *Style—* The Hon Mrs Frederic Clegg-Hill; The Old Forge, Stone in Oxney, nr Tenterden, Kent

CLEGG-HILL, Peter David Raymond Charles; s of Major Hon Frederic Raymond Clegg-Hill (ka 1945); 2 s of 6 Viscount Hill, and Hon Mrs Frederic Clegg-Hill, *qv*; hp to Viscountcy of cous, 8 Viscount Hill; *b* 17 Oct 1945, (posthumous); *Educ* Tabley House Sch; *m* 1973, Sharon Ruth Deane, of New Zealand; 2 s (Paul b 1979, Michael Clarke David b 1988), 5 da (Catherine b 1974, Jennifer b 1976, Susan b 1980, Rachelle 1984, Mellisa b 1986); *Career* farmer; *Style—* Peter Clegg-Hill, Esq; The Old Forge, Stone-in-Oxney, Tenterden, Kent

CLELAND, Dame Rachel; *née* Evans; DBE (1980, CBE 1966, MBE 1960); da of William H Evans, of Perth, W Australia; *b* 1906,Jan; *m* 1928, Brig Sir Donald (MacKinnon) Cleland, CBE (d 1975), former administrator of Territory of Papua New Guinea and pres Exec and Ligislative Councils of Papua New Guinea; *Career* pres Girl Guide Assoc and Red Cross NGP 1952-66; *Style—* Dame Rachel Cleland, DBE; Chester St, Port Moresby, Papua New Guinea

CLELLAND, David Gordon; MP Tynebridge 1985; s of Archibald (Clem) Clelland, of 157 Avenue Rd, Gateshead, and Ellen, *née* Butchart; *b* 27 June 1943; *Educ* Kelvin Grove Boys Sch Gateshead, Gateshead and Hebburn Tech Coll; *m* 31 March 1965, Maureen, da of William Potts; 2 da (Jillian, Vicki); *Career* apprentice electrical fitter 1959-64, electrical tester 1964-81; shop steward AEUW 1965-79, works ctee memb, sec Combine ctee, sec Health and Safety ctee; memb Lab Party 1970-, prospective Parly candidate Gateshead West 1981-83; memb Gateshead Cncl 1972-87 (chm Parks and Recreation 1976-84, leader 1984-86); nat sec Assoc of Cncllrs 1981-86; *Recreations* golf, music, reading; *Style—* David Clelland, Esq; House of Commons, Westminster, London SW1A NAA

CLEMENCE, (John) Alistair; TD (1972); s of L A Clemence (d 1978), of Bexhill-on-Sea, and Helen, *née* Gilles (d 1982); *b* 17 May 1937; *Educ* Tonbridge; *m* 8 April 1967, Heather May Kerr, da of Canon C A Offer (d 1964), of Ightham, Kent; 3 s (William b 1969, James b 1970, Jonathan b 1973); *Career* Nat Serv Seaforth Highlanders 1956-58, 2 Lt 1957; London Scottish Regt TA 1959-72, Lt 1959, Capt 1963, Maj 1970, regtl tres 1973-; CA; ptnr L A Clemence and Co (now finnie and Co) 1966-, dir Alfred Knight Ltd (piano manufacturers); ACA 1963, FInstD, FBIM; Liveryman Worshipful Co of Skinners 1969; *Recreations* gardening; *Clubs* Army and Navy; *Style—* A Clemence, Esq, TD; Bassetts, Mill Lane, Hildenborough, Kent TN11 9LX; 46 Church Ave, Beckenham, Kent BR3 1DT (☎ 01 658 7911)

CLEMENS, Brian Horace; s of Albert George Clemens (d 1988), of 5 Arthur St, Ampthill, Beds, and Susannah, *née* O'Grady; *b* 30 July 1931; *m* 23 Nov 1979, Janet Elizabeth, da of Filory Loveday East (d 1985), of 12 The Comyns, Bushey Heath, Herts; 2 s (Samuel b 1980, George b 1982); *Career* Nat Serv RAOC 1949-51; RN series: prodr and writer The Avengers 1964-70, prodr and writer The New Avengers 1976-78, creator My Wife Next Door 1975 (BAFTA Award), creator prodr and writer The Professionals 1978-82, creator and writer Blueblood 1988-89; feature films: writer Blind Terror/See No Evil 1973 (Edgar Alan Poe Award), prodr and writer Dr Jekyll and Sister Hyde 1973 (Cinema Fantastique Award), writer prodr and dir Captain KRO-NOS 1973, writer Golden Voyage of Sinbad 1974 (Fantasy Film Award); writer teleplay Scene of the Crime 1968 (Edgar Alan Poe Award; writer stage plays: Shock 1969, Edge of Darkness 1974, Sting in the Tale 1984, Inside Job 1988; co-prodr The Wicked Stage (amateur prodns to aid nominated charities); memb Writers Guilds of GB and America; *Recreations* Ferrari cars, swimming, writing (for pleasure), soccer, good wines; *Style—* Brian Clemens, Esq; Park Farm Cottage, Ampthill, Beds (☎ 0525 402215, telex 0234 826067); 5 Talbot Sq, London W2 (☎ 01 402 4048, fax 0525 402 3692)

CLEMENT, David Morris; CBE (1971); yr s of Charles William Clement (d 1944), of Swansea, and Rosina Wannell Fox (d 1966); *b* 6 Feb 1911; *Educ* Bishop Gores GS Swansea; *m* 1938, Kathleen Mary, da of Ernest George Davies, ACA (d 1946), of Swansea; 1 da (Mary); *Career* CA; ICI Lime Gp 1935-40, Chloride Electrical Storage Co Ltd 1941-46, NCB: sec NW Div 1946-49, chief accountant Northern and Durham Divs 1949-55, dep-dir gen of Finance 1955-61 and dir gen 1961-69 BD MEMB 1969-76; formerly chm: NCB (Ancilliaries) Ltd, Compower Ltd, Tredomen Engrg Ltd, Redwood-Corex Servs Ltd, and Jt Mission Hosps Equipment Bd Ltd; dep-chm Horizon Exploration Ltd; dir: NCB (Coal Products) Ltd, Assoc Heat Servs Ltd, J H Sankey and Son Ltd, Br Fuel Co, Western Fuel Co, Nypro (UK) Ltd, Scottish Brick Co Ltd; hon tres City and Guilds of London Inst; memb: Aircraft and Shipbuilding Industs Arbitration Tribunal, cncl Chartered Inst of Public Finance and Accountancy; Hon FCGI 1982; *Recreations* golf, walking, swimming; *Clubs* Royal Automobile, IOD; *Style—* David M Clement, Esq, CBE; 19 The Highway, Sutton, Surrey, SM2 5QT (☎ 01 642 3626)

CLEMENT, Hon Mrs (Diana Benda); *née* Richards; da of 1 Baron Milverton, GCMG (d 1978); *b* 9 August 1928; *Educ* Havergal Coll Toronto, Cheltenham Ladies' Coll, London Univ (BA), Sorbonne ; *m* 1 Sept 1960, Sqdn-Ldr Glyn John Clement, RAF (ret) (b 1 Nov 1920), s of Sydney Joseph Clement, of Dunraven, Gower, Glamorgan; 1 s, 1 da; *Style—* The Hon Mrs Clement; The Bell House, Kewstoke Rd, Worle, Weston-Super-Mare

CLEMENT-JONES, Timothy Francis; CBE (1988); s of Maurice Llewelyn Clement-Jones (d 1988), of Haywards Heath, Sussex, and Margaret Jean, *née* Hudson; *b* 26 Oct 1949; *Educ* Haileybury, Trinity Coll Cambridge (MA); *m* 14 June 1973, Dr Vicky Veronica (d 1987), fndr of Br Assoc of Cancer Utd Patients; da of Teddy Yip, of Hong Kong; *Career* slr; articled clerk Coward Chance 1972-74, assoc Joynson-Hicks & Co 1974-76, corporate lawyer Letraset Int Ltd 1976-80, asst head (later head) legal servs LWT Ltd 1980-83, legal dir retailing div Grand Met plc 1984-86, gp co sec and legal advst Woolworth hldgs plc 1986-; chm: Assoc of Liberal Lawyers 1982-86, Liberal Pty 1986-88,; dep chm federal exec Social and Liberal Democrats 1988-; tstee Br Assoc of Cancer Utd Patients, memb Crime Concern Advsy Bd; memb Law Soc; *Recreations* walking, travelling, reading, eating, talking; *Clubs* RAC, Nat Lib; *Style—* Timothy Clement-Jones, Esq, CBE; 10 Northbourne Road, London SW4 7DJ (☎ 01 627 0556); c/o Woolworth Hldgs plc 119, Marylebone Rd, London NW1 (☎ 01 724 7749)

CLEMENTI, David Cecil; s of Air Vice-Marshal Cresswell Montagu Clementi, CB, CBE, and Susan, da of late Sir (Edward) Henry Pelham, KCB; gs of Sir Cecil Clementi, GCMG (d 1947); *b* 25 Feb 1949; *Educ* Winchester, Oxford Univ (MA), Harvard Business Sch (MBA); *m* 23 Sept 1972, Sarah Louise (Sally), da of Dr Anthony Beach Cowley; 1 s (Tom b 17 April 1979), 1 da (Anna b 26 Nov 1976); *Career* with

Arthur Anderson & Co 1970-73; qualified as CA 1973; joined Kleinworth Benson Ltd 1975, dir 1981-; memb Mercers' Co; FCA; *Style*— David C Clementi, Esq; c/o Kleinwort Benson Ltd, 20 Fenchurch St, London EC3 3DB (☎ 01 623 8000)

CLEMENTS, Prof Geoffrey; s of William Frederick Clements (d 1987), and Molly *née* Chelmick; maternal grandfather, William George Hamar Chelmick, CBE, accountant and comptroller general Inland Revenue 1940-45, responsible for the development and introduction of PAYE; *b* 30 Dec 1948; *Educ* Shoreham GS Sussex, Collyers GS Horsham, Sussex Univ (BSc, DPhil); *m* 8 Aug 1979, Daphne Mary, da of Capt Edward Nathaniel Grace, MC, 6th Battalion, Gordon Highlanders, Coroner for E Sussex 1977-87, of 15 The Park Close, Eastbourne, Sussex; *Career* Prof of Physics Maharishi European Research Univ Seelisberg Switzerland 1975-82 (vice-chancellor 1977-82), vice-chancellor and prof of Physics Maharishi Univ of Natural Law, Mentmore, Bucks 1982; chm of Trustees World Govt of the Age of Enlightenment, GB, charity responsible for transcendental meditation, under the guidance of His Holiness Maharishi Mahesh Yogi 1982-, Governor-General of Age of Enlightenment for Europe 1983-; *Books* (co-author with wife): Science, Consciousness and the Reversal of Ageing, Proceedings of the International Conference (1981), Tour of Universities in the People's Republic of China (1985); *Style*— Prof Geoffrey Clements; Mentmore Towers, Mentmore, Bucks, LU7 0QH (☎ 0296 661 881)

CLEMENTS, Gilbert Edward Isaac; s of Gilbert Edward Clements, of 26 Abbotsford Rd, Redland, Bristol, and Violet Victoria, *née* Dean; *b* 23 Feb 1915; *Educ* Bristol GS, UCL (LLB); *m* 1950 (m dis 1961), Maureen Elizabeth Charlotte (Valerie), *née* Stitson; 1 da (Lady Anne Clements Eyre w of Sir Reginald Eyre); *Career* RAF 1940-47: pilot, sector controller, ops offr (Normandy invasion) special liaison offr 1 Allied Airborne Army SHAEF 3 American Army and SACSEA; barr Middle Temple 1946, fire mangr Bedford Gen Insur Co 1957-73, vice-chm Bedford Bldg soc 1965-86 (dir 1962-65), fire mangr Zurich Insur Co 1973-76 (fire and accident mangr 1970-72), sec Vectis Property Gp 1978-; Farringdon Without City Ward: common councilman 1960-, (dep 1965); memb MENSA 1959-) Lonon branch chm Chartered Inst; Freeman: City of London 1953; Liveryman Worshipful Co of: Scriveners (Memb Ct of Assts), Chartered Secs and Administrators (Memb Ct of Assts); FCIS 1948, FCII 1940; *Recreations* walking and reading; *Clubs* Reform, Guildhall, City Livery; *Style*— Edward Clements, Esq; 2 Plowden Bldgs, Temple, London EC4Y 9AS (☎ 01 353 0035)

CLEMENTS, Graham Charles; s of Eric Charles Clements (d 1972), and Barbara Mary, *née* Williams (d 1957); *b* 28 May 1931; *Educ* Wallington County GS; *m* 29 March 1952, Heather Janet, da of William Charles Townsend (d 1982); 1 s (Robert b 1955), 1 da (Joanna b 1957); *Career* md Bunten and Lancaster Ltd 1979- (dir 1964-79); *Recreations* lay-preaching (Christadelphians), tennis, swimming, skiing; *Style*— Graham Clements, Esq; c/o Nat-West Bank plc, 1 Mincing Lane, London EC3; PO Box 52, Coulsdon, Surrey (☎ 01 668 0318, telex 888159 932573)

CLEMENTS, Leslie Craig; s of Leslie Sidney Harold Clements (d 1960), and Annie Boomer Clements, *née* Rae; *b* 31 Dec 1940; *Educ* Selborne Sch; Ealing Tech Coll; Bristol Univ (BA); *m* 30 May 1970, Carole, da of Frederick Allen (d 1970); 1 s (Adam Craig b 4 May 1975); *Career* sr ptnr: Merchant and Co, FICA; *Recreations* badminton, bowling, aquatics; *Clubs* Saints Boat, Ealing CC, Perivale Boat ; *Style*— L C Clements, Esq; Matlock House, 229 High St, Acton, London W3 9BY (☎ 01 992 7811, telex 937052 MERLONG, fax 01 993 7109)

CLEMINSON, Sir James Arnold Stacey; MC (1945), DL (Norfolk 1983); s of late Arnold Russel Cleminson, JP, FCIS, himself sometime chm Reckitt and Colman, and Florence, da of James Stacey, of New Zealand; *b* 31 August 1921; *Educ* Rugby; *m* 1950, Helen Juliet Measor; 1 s, 2 da; *Career* served WW II Para Regt; chm Reckitt and Colman Ltd 1977-86 (ch exec 1973-80, joined 1946, dir overseas co 1957, ch exec 1973-80); dir Norwich Union 1979-, (vice-chm 1983-), non-exec dir United Biscuits (Hldgs) 1982-; memb and CBI 1978 (pres 1984-86), pres Food Manufacturers Fedn 1980-82, chm Food and Drink Industries Cncl 1983-84, pres Endeavour Training 1984-; chm BOTB 1986-; chm AP Bank 1986-; chm Jeyes Hygiene 1985-; London dir Toronto Dominion Bank; chm Nurses Pay Board 1986-; Hon Fell Royal Coll of General Practitioners; Hon Doctor of Law Hull Univ (1985); kt 1982; *Recreations* field sports, golf; *Clubs* Boodles; *Style*— Sir James Cleminson, MC, DL; Loddon Hall, Hales, Norfolk (☎ 0508 20717); 135 Cranmer Court, Whiteheads Grove, Chelsea

CLEMITS, John Henry; s of Cyril Thomas Clemits (d 1955), and Minnie Alberta Clemits (d 1968); *b* 16 Feb 1934; *Educ* Sutton HS for Boys Plymouth, Plymouth Coll of Art (Distinction in Thesis); *m* 14 June 1958, (Elizabeth) Angela, da of Frederick John Moon; 1 s (Roger b 1965), 1 da (Elizabeth b 1962); *Career* Capt RE (TA) 43 Wessex Div and Royal Monmouthshire RE (Militia) 1964-69; chartered architect, civil servant: New Works planning offr, Property Services Agency Germany 1975-79; dir of works (Army) PSA Chessington 1979-85; dir for Wales PSA Cardiff 1985-; FRSA, ARIBA; *Recreations* golf, choral singing, music, DIY; *Clubs* Civil Serv; *Style*— John Clemits, Esq; The Lodge, Hendrescythan Creigiau, Nr Cardiff CF4 8NN (☎ 0222 891786); Director for Wales, PSA, Block I Government Bldgs, St Agnes Road, Gabalfa, Cardiff (☎ 0222 726760, fax 0222 614288)

CLEMPSON, Vincent Richard; *b* 2 Oct 1953; *Educ* Churchill Coll Cambridge (BA, Dip Crim); *Career* admitted slr 1979, ptnr Freshfields 1986-; memb: intellectual property sub ctee City of London Slrs Co, London Young Slrs Gp; memb Law Soc; *Style*— Vincent Clempson, Esq; Freshfields, Grindall House, 25 Newgate St, London EC1A 7L (☎ 01 606 6677)

CLEOBURY, Nicholas Randall; s of Dr John Frank Cleobury, of Croft House, Street End, Lower Hardes, Canterbury, Kent, and Brenda Julie, *née* Randall; *b* 23 June 1950; *Educ* King's Sch Worcester, Worcester Coll Oxford (MA); *m* 4 Nov 1978, Heather Noelle, da of Noel Kay (d 1981), of 8 Station Rd, Upper Poppleton, York; 1 s (Simon Randall b 23 Oct 1979), 1 da (Sophie Noelle b 12 Dec 1981); *Career* asst organist: Chichester Cathedral 1971-72, Christ Church Oxford 1972-76; chorus master Glyndebourne Opera 1977-79, asst dir BBC Singers 1978-80, princ conductor of opera RAM 1981-87, dir Aquarius 1983-; 1980-: int conductor working throughout UK, Europe and Scandinavia, regular TV and BBC Radio and Prom appearances, numerous commercial recordings; princ guest conductor Gävle Orchestra (Sweden) 1989-; FRCO 1968, hon emmb RAM 1985; *Recreations* cricket, reading, walking, food, wine; *Clubs* Savage; *Style*— Nicholas Cleobury, Esq; China Cottage, Church Lane, Petham, Canterbury, Kent CT4 5RD (☎ 0227 70 584, fax 0227 70 827)

CLEOBURY, Stephen John; s of Dr John Frank Cleobury, of Croft House, Canterbury, and Brenda Julie, *née* Randall; *b* 31 Dec 1948; *Educ* King's Sch Worcester, St John's Coll Cambridge (MA, MusB); *m* 3 July 1971, Penelope Jane, da of William Francis Holloway (d 1984); 2 da (Suzannah b 1973, Laura b 1976); *Career* organist St Matthew's Church Northampton, dir of Music Northampton GS 1971-74, sub-organist Westminster Abbey 1974-78, master of music Westminster Cathedral 1979-82, fell organist and dir of music King's Coll Cambridge 1982-, hon sec Royal Coll of Organists 1981-; pres: Incoporated Assoc of Organists 1985-87, Cathedral Organist's Assoc 1988-90; memb Cncl Royal Sch of Church Music 1983-; FRCO, ISM; *Style*— S J Cleobury, Esq; 85 Gough Way, Newnham, Cambridge CB3 9LN; King's College, Cambridge (☎ 0223 350411 x 224)

CLEPHAN, Derek Peter; s of George Keith Clephan (d 1982), and Bertha Mary, *née* Speakman; *b* 27 June 1938; *Educ* Dudley GS Worcs, Birmingham Univ (LLM); *m* 21 Dec 1971, Joy, da of Sidney William Fryer, of Sheffield; 2 s (Mark b 20 Nov 1973, John b 25 Feb 1975), 1 da (Trudie b 14 July 1976); *Career* slr 1963, asst town clerk Sheffield 1971-74, dir of admin Barnsley 1974-; pres Assoc of Dist Secs 1983-84; *Style*— Derek Clephan, Esq; 21 Dewar Drive, Sheffield, S Yorks S7 2GQ (☎ 0742 369192); Town Hall, Barnsley, S Yorks S 70 2TA (☎ 0226 733232, fax 0226 733711)

CLERK, Sir John Dutton; 10 Bt (NS 1679), of Penicuik, Edinburgh, CBE (1966), VRD, FRSE (1977), JP; s of Sir George Clerk, 9 Bt (d 1943); *b* 30 Jan 1917; *Educ* Stowe; *m* 10 June 1944, Evelyn Elizabeth, er da of late William Robertson; 2 s, 2 da; *Heir* s, Robert Maxwell Clerk, *qv*; *Career* Cdre RNR ret; Ensign Queen's Body Guard for Scotland (Royal Co of Archers); lord-lt Midlothian 1972- (formerly vice-lt, DL 1956); FRSE 1977; *Style*— Sir John Clerk, Bt, CBE, VRD, JP; Penicuik House, Penicuik, Midlothian EH26 9LA (☎ 0968 74318)

CLERK, Robert Maxwell; s and h of Sir John Clerk, 10 Bt; *b* 3 April 1945; *Educ* Winchester, London Univ (BSc); *m* 1970, Felicity Faye, *née* Collins; 2 s, 1 da; *Career* FRICS; ptnr Smiths Gore chartered surveyors; Salman Advisory Ctee; *Recreations* fishing, stalking, skiing, gardening; *Clubs* New, Edinburgh; *Style*— Robert Clerk Esq; Lachlanwells, Forres, Morayshire

CLERKE, Francis Ludlow Longueville; s and h of Sir John Edward Longueville Clerke, 12 Bt, *qv*; *b* 25 Jan 1953; *Educ* Diocesan Coll Cape Town, Stellenbosch Univ (BA), Witwatersrand Univ (LLB); *m* 1982, Vanessa Anne, only da of Charles Cosman Citron (d 1974), of Mouille Point, Cape Town, S Africa; *Career* solicitor (South Africa); *Recreations* windsurfing, squash; *Clubs* Western Province Sports (Cape Town); *Style*— Francis Clerke, Esq

CLERKE, Sir John Edward Longueville; 12 Bt (E 1660), of Hitcham, Buckinghamshire; s of Francis William Talbot Clerke (ka 1916), s of 11 Bt; suc gf 1930; *b* 29 Oct 1913; *Educ* Eton, Magdalene Coll Cambridge (MA); *m* 1948, Mary, da of Lt-Col Ivor Reginald Beviss Bond, OBE, MC (d 1967); 1 s, 2 da; *Heir* s, Francis Clerke, *qv*; *Career* Capt Royal Wilts Yeo (TA); FCA 1948, ret; *Recreations* lawn tennis, shooting, fishing; *Clubs* Lansdowne; *Style*— Sir John Clerke, Bt; Holly Tree House, Pound Pill, Corsham, Wilts SN13 9HT (☎ 0249 713760)

CLERKE BROWN, Col Arthur; OBE (1944); s of John Clerke Brown (d 1964), and Gwen Clerke Brown *née* Bros (d 1969); family have owned Kingston Blount Estate since 1810; *b* 8 August 1912; *Educ* Eton, RMC Sandhurst; *m* 12 Feb 1944, Anne Carlotta *née* Rawle, da of late Capt William Rawle; 1 da (Angela b 1949); *Career* Army Offr and landowner; cmmnd Oxford and Bucks LI 1933-64; served: France 1940, France and Germany 1944-46, HQ Far East Land Forces 1946-48, HQ Rhine Army 1959-62; Jt master Colchester Garrison Beagles 1936-39, Master Catterick Garrison Beagles 1951-55, jt MFH S Oxfordshire Hounds 1967-70, chm Oxon Branch CLA 1976-79, memb Point-to-Point Secs Ctee 1971- (chm 1976-79); *Recreations* hunting, racing, cricket, shooting; *Clubs* Army and Navy, MCC; *Style*— Col Arthur Clerke Brown, OBE; Kingston Grove, Kingston Blount, Oxford (☎ 0844 51356)

CLEVERDON, Julia Charity; Mrs W J P Maxwell Garnett); da of Douglas Cleverdon (d 1987), of London, and Elinor Nest Lewis; *b* 19 April 1950; *Educ* Camden Sch for Girls, Newnham Coll Cambridge (BA); *m* 1, 30 June 1973 (m dis), Martin Ollard; m 2, 3 April 1985, William John Poulton Maxwell Garnett, CBE, s of Maxwell Garnett, of Horestone Point (d 1960); 1 da (Victoria b 1987); *Career* dir of Educn, The Industrial Soc 1981-87; Business in the Community 1988-; memb Sch Curriculum Dvpt Ctee 1984; chm Economic Awareness Ctee, Nat Curriculum Cncl Tstee 300 Gp; fndn govr Camden Sch for Girls; vice-pres Newnham Coll Roll; *Recreations* gardening, cooking, junk shops; *Clubs* Reform; *Style*— Julia C Cleverdon; 8 Alwyne Road, London N1 2HH; 48 Bryanston Square, London W1

CLEVERDON, Philip Henry; s of Kenneth Penwarden Cleverdon, of Nailsea, Bristol, and Lena, *née* Morgan (d 1985); *b* 15 Mar 1950; *Educ* Shebbear Coll North Devon; *m* 4 Aug 1973, Ruth Mary, da of Alan Towell, of Sandpipers, 3 Kenbury Cres, Cockwood, Starcross, Exeter; 1 s (Michael Philip b 1977), 1 da (Elizabeth Patricia b 1979); *Career* practising CA; area 12 chm Round Tables GB and Ireland; FICA; *Recreations* squash, orienteering; *Clubs* Round Table GB and Ireland; *Style*— Philip Cleverdon, Esq; 1 Scots Pine Ave, Nailsea, Bristol (☎ 0272 852528); 82A High St, Nailsea, Bristol (☎ 0272 854961)

CLEVERLEY FORD, Rev Preb Douglas William; yr s of Arthur James Ford (d 1918), and Mildred, *née* Cleverley (d 1969); *b* 4 Mar 1914; *Educ* Great Yarmouth GS, London Univ (BD, MTh); *m* 1939, Olga Mary, er da of Dr Thomas Bewley Gilbart-Smith (d 1955), and Elizabeth Girdler, *née* Eddison (d 1965); *Career* deacon 1937, priest 1938, vicar Holy Trinity London SW7 1955-74, rd of Westminster 1965-74, prebendary of St Paul's Cathedral 1968-74 (emeritus 1974-), provincial canon of York 1969-, chaplain to HM The Queen 1973-84, sr chaplain to the Archbp of Canterbury 1975-80, six preacher of Canterbury Cathedral 1982-; *Recreations* gardening; *Clubs* Athenaeum; *Style*— The Rev Prebendary Douglas Cleverley Ford; Rostrevor, Lingfield, Surrey RH7 6BZ (☎ 0342 832461)

CLEWS, Michael Graham; s of Reginald Alan Frederick Clews, of Bristol, and Alwine Annie, *née* Adams; *b* 11 Oct 1944; *Educ* Kingswood GS, Oxford Sch of Architecture (DipArch); *m* 24 July 1971, Heather Jane, da of Douglas Charles Sharratt, of Coventry; 2 s (Charles b 1978, Jonathan b 1983, d 1984), 2 da (Camilla b 1976, Helena b 1985); *Career* architect; fndr ptnr Clews Architectural Partnership 1972-; works incl historic buildings: Compton Verney, Croome Court, Boscobel House; conslt to PSA on Historic Buildings 1984-87 (Historic Buildings Surrey, Oxfordshire, Warwickshire and Northamptonshire for DOE); pilot project for computerisation of Historic Building Records for English Heritage; Oxford diocesian Surveyor; ARIBA; *Recreations* sailing, golf, squash; *Clubs* Tadmarton Heath GC, Beauchamp Squash; *Style*— Michael Clews, Esq; The Old Vicarage, Great Bourton, Banbury, Oxon (☎ 0295 75621); Clews

Architects Partnership, The Coach House, Great Bourton, Banbury, Oxon (☎ 0295 758101)

CLIBBORN, Donovan Harold; CMG (1966); s of Henry Joseph Fairley Clibborn (d 1930), and Isabel Sarah Jago (d 1933); *b* 2 July 1917; *Educ* County HS Ilford, St Edmund Hall Oxford (MA), Queen's Coll Oxford, (Laming Travelling fell); *m* 1, 1940, Margaret Mercedes Edwige (d 1966), da of John Clement Nelson (d 1952), of Oxford; 1 s (John), 2 da (Isabel, Enrica); m 2, 1973, Marina Victoria Ondiviela Garvi; *Career* served WW II Maj Western Desert 1941-43, Sicily, South Italy 1943-44, North West Europe 1944-45 (despatches); HM Diplomatic Serv 1939-75; cnsllr: (economic) Tehran 1963-64, Rio de Janeiro 1964-66; consul-gen Barcelona 1966-71, ambass San Salvador 1971-75; *Recreations* reading, music, perpetrating light verse; *Style—* Donovan Clibborn, Esq, CMG; Paseo del Dr Moragao 188, Atico la, Barberá del Vallés, 08210 Barcelona, Spain (☎ Barcelona 718 5377)

CLIFF, John Burnhill; s of Stanley Cliff (d 1957), and Doris, *née* Burnhill; *b* 24 April 1927; *m* 8 Sept 1956, Gillian Mary, da of Leslie Bell (d 1963); 1 s (Simon b 1957), 1 da (Trudie b 1959); *Career* mil serv Lieut RE Germany; motor trade insurance and finance; dir: R Garwood and Sons Ltd 1980-, Garwood Garages Ltd 1983-, DG and JG (Finance and Insurance) Ltd 1980-; *Recreations* football, tennis, squash; *Style—* John B Cliff, Esq; The Stables, 60 High Street, Barkway, Royston, Herts SG8 8EE; 419 High Road N22 4JD (☎ 01 888 6663)

CLIFF HODGES, Hon Mrs; (Linnéa Nilsson); *née* Birkett; da of 1 Baron Birkett, PC (d 1962); *b* 27 June 1923; *m* 25 June 1949, Gavin Cliff Hodges (b 26 Nov 1916), eldest s of late William Cliff Hodges, MD, of Perrydene, Hascombe, Godalming, Surrey; 1 s, 3 da; *Recreations* music, gardening, books; *Style—* The Hon Mrs Cliff Hodges; Briar Cottage, Packers Hill, Holwell, Sherborne, Dorset DT9 5LN (☎ 096 323 285)

CLIFFORD, Charles Joseph; s of Sir Roger Charles Joseph Gerrard Clifford, 6 Bt (d 1982); twin br and hp of Sir Roger Joseph Gerrard Clifford, 7 Bt; *b* 5 June 1936; *m* 1983, Sally Madeline, da of William Hartgill Pennefather Green; *Style—* Charles Clifford, Esq; 264 Te Moana Rd, Waikanae, New Zealand

CLIFFORD, David; s of late Robert Clifford; *b* 20 July 1940; *Educ* Friends' Sch Great Ayton, Sunderland Tech Coll, Newcastle Coll of Further Education; *m* 1963, Margaret; 2 s; *Career* gen mangr Econofreight Transport Ltd 1976-78; dir and gen mangr Seaham Harbour Dock Co 1978-; md Seaham Harbour Dock Co 1983-; memb of the Inst of Mgmnt Servs MMS; MCIT; memb Chartered Inst of Transport; chm Durham Groundwork Trust; *Clubs* Rotary of Seaham; *Style—* David Clifford, Esq; Rosedale, Dene House Road, Seaham, Co Durham (☎ 091 581 2230)

CLIFFORD, Sir Roger Joseph Gerrard; 7 Bt (UK 1887), of Flaxbourne, Marlborough, New Zealand; s (twin, by 1 m) of Sir Roger Clifford, 6 Bt (d 1982); *b* 5 June 1936; *m* 12 April 1968, Joanna Theresa, da of Cyril James Ward, of Christchurch, New Zealand, and gda of Sir Cyril Rupert Joseph Ward, 2 Bt; 2 da (Angela b 1971, Annabel b 1973); *Heir* bro, Charles Joseph Clifford, *qv*; *Style—* Sir Roger Clifford, Bt; 135 Totara Street, Christchurch 4, New Zealand

CLIFFORD, Hon Rollo Hugh; yr s of 13 Baron Clifford of Chudleigh, *qv*; *b* 15 Mar 1954; *Educ* Downside; *m* 1977, Fiona Margaret, da of Richard Todd, actor; 2 s (Christopher Rollo, Alasdair Rollo), 1 da (Elizabeth Alice); *Career* formerly with Rudolf Wolff and Co on London Metal Exchange; ptnr Mgmnt Training Consultant, The MAST Organisation; md RCA, memb Pacific Inst; *Recreations* sailing, gardening, fishing, shooting; *Clubs* Bucks, RYS, RORC, RTYC; *Style—* The Hon Rollo Clifford; Timewell House, Morebath, nr Tiverton, Devon EX16 QBY

CLIFFORD, Timothy Peter Plint; s of Derek Plint Clifford, of Sittingbourne Kent, and Ann, *née* Pierson (d 1984); cadet branch of Marcher family seated in Gloucestershire since 11th Century; *b* 26 Jan 1946; *Educ* Sherborne Dorset, Courtauld Instn, Univ of London (BA), Dip Fine Art Museums Assoc; *m* 1968, Jane Olivia, yr da of Sir George Paterson, QC, OBE, of Sherborne Dorset; 1 da (Pandora b 1973); *Career* asst keeper Dept of Paintings City Art Galleries 1968-72, acting keeper 1972; asst keeper: Dept of Ceramics Victoria and Albert Museum London 1972-76, Dept of Prints and Drawings British Museum London 1976-78; dir: Manchester City Arts Gallery 1978-84, Nat Galleries of Scotland 1984-; AMA, FRSA; *Recreations* shooting, birdwatching; *Clubs* Turf, Beefsteak, New (Edinburgh); *Style—* Timothy Clifford, Esq; The Hopetoun Estate, South Queensferry, West Lothian (☎ 031 331 3571); Nat Gallery of Scotland, The Mound, Edinburgh EH2 2EL (☎ 031 556 8921)

CLIFFORD OF CHUDLEIGH, Baroness; Hon Katharine Vavasseur; *née* Fisher; 2 da of 2 Baron Fisher (d 1955), and Jane, *née* Morgan (d 1955); *b* 3 Nov 1919; *m* 29 Jan 1945, 13 Baron Clifford of Chudleigh (d 1988); *Style—* Katharine, Lady Clifford of Chudleigh; La Colline, St Jacques, St Peter Port, Guernsey, CI (☎ 0481 25047)

CLIFFORD OF CHUDLEIGH, 14 Baron (E 1672) Thomas Hugh Clifford; Count of the Holy Roman Empire; s of 13 Baron Clifford of Chudleigh (d 1988), and Katharine, Lady Clifford of Chudleigh, *qv*; *b* 17 Mar 1948; *Educ* Downside; *m* 15 Dec 1980, (Muriel) Suzanne, yr da of Maj Campbell Austin; 2 s Hon Alexander Thomas Hugh b 24 Sept 1985, Hon Edward George Hugh b 1988), 1 da (Hon Georgina Apollonia b 1983); *Heir* s, Hon Alexander Thomas Hugh Clifford b 24 Sept 1985; *Career* late Capt Coldstream Gds, served Norway, Turkey, Berlin, Ireland, British Honduras (Belize); mangr: The Clifford Estate Co, Ugbrooke Enterprises, Ugbrooke Reception Enterprise; KSOM; *Style—* Capt the Hon Thomas Clifford; Ugbrooke Park, Chudleigh, S Devon TQ13 OAD (☎ 0626 852179)

CLIFT, Richard Dennis; CMG (1984); s of late Dennis Victor Clift, and Helen Wilmot, *née* Evans; *b* 18 May 1933; *Educ* St Edward's Sch Oxford, Pembroke Coll Cambridge (BA); *m* 1, 1957 (m dis 1982), Barbara Mary Travis; 3 da; m 2, 1982, Jane Rosamund Barker, *née* Homfray; *Career* FO 1956-57, office of Br chargé d'affaires Peking 1958-60, Br Embassy Berne 1961-62, UK delgn to NATO Paris 1962-64, FO 1964-68, head of chancery Br High Cmmn Kuala Lumpur 1969-71, FCO 1971-73, cnsllr (commercial) Peking 1974-76, Canadian Nat Defence Coll 1976-77, seconded to NI Office 1977-79, head of Hong Kong and Gen Dept FCO 1979-1984, Br high cmmr Freetown 1984-1986, political advsr Hong Kong 1987-; *Recreations* sailing, walking, woodwork; *Clubs* Hong Kong; *Style—* Richard Clift, Esq, CMG; c/o Foreign and Cwlth Office, London SW1A 2AL

CLIFTON, Gerald Michael; s of Frederick Maurice Clifton MA (d 1988), of Xanau, Hilltop Rd, Rainford, Lancs, and Jane, *née* Hayes (d 1986); *b* 3 July 1947; *Educ* Liverpool Coll, open classical scholar, Brasenose Coll Oxford (MA); *m* 21 Jul 1973, Rosemary Anne Vera, da of Reginald Edward Jackson, of Cornways, Selworthy Rd, Birkdale, Southport; 2 s (Rupert b 1977, Giles b 1980); *Career* barr 1970, rec Crown Court 1988-; *Recreations* sailing, tennis, walking, philately; *Clubs* West Kirby Sailing; *Style—* G M Clifton, Esq; Norton, Telegraph Rd, Heswall, Wirral; Peel House, 5/7 Harrington St, Liverpool L2 9QA (☎ 051 236 4321)

CLIFTON, Lt-Col Peter Thomas; CVO (1979), DSO (1945), DL (1954); s of Lt-Col Percy Clifton, CMG, DSO, TD (d 1945), of Clifton Hall, Nottingham who was twin bro of Sir Hervey Ronald Bruce, 5 Bt (he assumed the surname Clifton by Royal Licence 1919), and his 2 wife Evelyn Mary Amelia (d 1969), da of Maj Thomas Leith, DL (nephew of 5 Baron Burgh); *b* 24 Jan 1911; *Educ* Eton, RMC Sandhurst; *m* 1, 2 June 1934 (m dis 1936), Ursula Sybil, da of Sir Edward Hussey Packe, KBE, of Prestwold Hall, Leics; m 2, 1948, Patricia Mary Adela, DStJ, yr da of late Maj James Miller Gibson-Watt, and widow of Maj Robert Nevill Cobbold, Welsh Guards; 2 da (*see* Seddon-Brown, Georgina Anne); *Career* 2 Lt Grenadier Gds 1931, Lt-Col 1944; memb HM Body Guard of Hon Corps of Gentlemen at Arms 1960-, Clerk of the Cheque and Adjutant 1973-79, Standard Bearer 1979-81, ret; JP Notts 1952-59, Hants 1964-81; *Clubs* Royal Yacht Squadron, Cavalry and Guards, Whites; *Style—* Lt-Col Peter Clifton, CVO, DSO, DL; Dummer House, Basingstoke, Hants RG25 2AG (☎ Dummer 306)

CLIFTON OF RATHMORE, Lord; Ivo Donald Stuart Bligh; s and h of 11 Earl of Darnley; *b* 17 April 1968; *Style—* Lord Clifton of Rathmore

CLINCH, David John; s of Thomas Charles Clinch, of Surrey, and Madge Isobel, *née* Saker (d 1984); ancestors were brewers, bankers and blanket Weavers of Witney; *b* 14 Feb 1937; *Educ* Nautical Coll Pangbourne, Durham Univ (BA), Indiana Univ USA (MBA); *m* 1963, Hilary, da of John Herbert Jacques (d 1984), of Claxby, Lincs; 1 s (John), 1 da (Helen); *Career* Nat Serv 1955-57, RN Acting Sub Lt; admin Univ of Sussex 1963-69, dep sec and registrar Open Univ 1969-80, sec Open Univ 1981-; *Recreations* music, walking, bird watching; *Style—* Joe Clinch, Esq; 39 Tudor Gardens, Stony Stratford, Milton Keynes MK11 1HX (☎ 0908 562475); The Open University, Walton Hall, Milton Keynes MK7 6AA (☎ 0908 653213)

CLINTON, 22 Baron (E 1299); Gerard Neville Mark Fane Trefusis; JP (Bideford 1963), DL (Devon 1977); s of Capt Charles Fane (ka 1940), s of Hon Harriet Trefusis, herself da of 21 Baron Clinton (d 1957); assumed additional surname Trefusis by Deed Poll 1958 and suc to Barony 1965 on termination of abeyance; *b* 7 Oct 1934; *Educ* Gordonstoun; *m* 1959, Nicola Harriette, da of Maj Charles Robert Purdon Coote (d 1954); 1 s, 2 da; *Heir* s, Hon Charles Fane Trefusis; *Career* memb Prince of Wales's Councils 1968-79; landowner; *Style—* The Rt Hon the Lord Clinton, JP, DL; Heanton Satchville, nr Okehampton, N Devon (☎ Dolton 224)

CLINTON, Robert Alan; s of John (d 1972), of Birmingham, and Leah Millington (d 1986); *b* 12 July 1931; *Educ* George Dixon GS Birmingham, Manchester Business Sch; *m* 1956, Valerie Joy, da of Herbert Allan Falconer (d 1981), of Birmingham; *Career* joined PO 1948, asst dir (personnel) PO HQ 1975, asst dir (operations) 1976, regional dir Eastern Postal Region 1978, dir Postal Operations 1979, memb PO Bd London 1981-85, resigned 1985; gp md Picton House Ltd 1986; dir: Picton House (Leicester) Ltd, Picton House Properties Ltd, Picton Homes Ltd, Picton Homes (Wales) Ltd 1986, Picton Homes (Gwent) Ltd, HK Properties Ltd 1987, Pembroke Services Ltd 1988; Freeman City of London 1979, Liveryman Worshipful Co of Carmen 1981; FCIT 1982; *Recreations* music, walking, sailing; *Clubs* City Livery; Colne Yacht (Brightlinesea); *Style—* Alan Clinton, Esq; Binders, Colchester Rd, St Osyth, Clacton-on-Sea, Essex CO16 8HA (☎ 0255 820 375); Flat 19, No 4 Crane Court, Fleet St, London EC4A 2EJ (☎ 01 353 7509); Picton House Ltd, 108 Fenchurch St, London EC3M 5JJ (☎ 01 480 5740, fax 01 480 5745)

CLITHEROE, 2 Baron (UK 1955), also 3 Bt (UK 1945) Ralph John Assheton; DL (Lancs); Lord of the Honour of Clitheroe and Hundred of Blackburn; s of 1 Baron Clitheroe, KCVO, PC (d 1984), and Sylvia, Lady Clitheroe, *qv*, da of 6 Baron Hotham; *b* 3 Nov 1929; *Educ* Eton, Christ Church Oxford (MA); *m* 2 May 1961, Juliet, o da of Lt-Col Christopher Lionel Hanbury, MBE, TD; 2 s (Ralph, John), 1 da (Elizabeth); *Heir* s, Hon Ralph Christopher Assheton, *qv*; *Career* late 2 Lt Life Guards; dir and dep ch exec RTZ Corpn plc; dir: First Interstate Bank of California, Halliburton Co, Chemical Industry Assoc, American Mining Congress; chm: RTZ Borax; Liveryman Worshipful Co of Skinners' Co; *Clubs* Boodle's, Pratt's, RAC; *Style—* The Rt Hon Lord Clitheroe; 6 St James's Square, London SW1Y 4LD

CLITHEROE, Baroness; Hon Sylvia Benita Frances; *née* Hotham; er da of 6 Baron Hotham (d 1923), and Eliza Benita, nee Sanders; *b* 19 Sept 1903; *m* 24 Jan 1924, 1 Baron Clitheroe, KCVO, PC (d 1984); 2 s, 1 da; *Career* former govr Westminster Hosp and chm house ctees; memb: cncl Lancaster Univ, Lancs War Agric Exec Ctee 1941-48, Agric Exec Ctee 1948-59; FRICS; *Style—* The Rt Hon Sylvia, Lady Clitheroe; 85 Whitelands House, Cheltenham Terr, London SW3

CLIVE, Viscount; John George Herbert; eldest s and h of 7 Earl of Powis, *qv*; *b* 19 May 1952; *Educ* Wellington, McMaster Univ Ontario (MA); *m* 1977, Marijke, eldest da of Maarten N Guther, of Hamilton, Ontario, Canada; 1 son (Hon Jonathan Nicholas William), 2 da (Hon Stephanie Moira Christina b 1982, Hon Samantha Julie Esther b 1988); *Heir* s, Hon Jonathan Nicholas William Herbert b 5 Dec 1979; 284 Wilson Street West, Ancaster, Ontario, Canada

CLIVE, Lady Mary Katharine; *née* Pakenham; 2 da of 5 Earl of Longford, KP, MVO (d 1915); *b* 23 August 1907; *m* 30 Dec 1939, Major Meysey George Dallas Clive, Gren Gds (ka 1 May 1943), er s of late Lt-Col Percy Archer Clive, MP, JP, DL, of Whitfield, Hereford; 1 s, 1 da; *Books* Christmas with the Savages (1955), The Day of Reckoning (1964), This Son of York (1973); *Style—* Lady Mary Clive; Whitfield, Allensmore, Herefordshire

CLIVE, Nigel David; CMG (1967), OBE (1959), MC (1944), TD (1945); s of Horace David Clive (d 1962), and Hilda Mary, *née* Clive (d 1963); *b* 13 July 1917; *Educ* Stowe, Christ Church Oxford (MA); *m* 1949, Maria Jeanne, da of Ioannis Tambakopoulos (d 1963), of Sounion, Greece; *Career* cmmnd 2 Middx Yeo 1939, served ME, Greece SOE 1943-44, Maj 1945; joined FO, served Athens 1946-48, Jerusalem 1948, FO 1948-50, Baghdad 1950-53, FO 1953-58, Tunis 1958-62, Algiers 1962-63, FO 1964-65; head of Info Res Dept FCO (formerly FO) 1966-69, advsr to Sec Gen of OECD (Paris) 1970-80, ret; *Books* A Greek Experience 1943-48 (1985); *Clubs* Brooks's, Special Forces, MCC; *Style—* Nigel Clive, Esq, CMG, OBE, MC, TD; 41 Lowndes Sq, London SW1X 9JL (☎ 01 235 1186)

CLIVE-PONSONBY-FANE, Charles Edward Brabazon; JP (1979); s of late Nicholas Brabazon Clive-Ponsonby-Fane, 2 s of Edward Clive (1 cous four times removed of (Robert) Clive of India) by Edward's w Violet, ggda of 4 Earl of Bessborough by Lady Maria Fane (da of 10 Earl of Westmorland); Nicholas m, Petronilla Dunsterville, whose mother was Eveline, da of Sir Frederick Goldney, 3 and penultimate Bt, JP; *b* 10 August 1941; *Educ* Harrow, L'Institut de Touraine France, RAC Cirencester; *m* 1974, Judy Barbara, *née* Bushby; 1 s, 2 da; *Career* viticulturalist, distiller; High Sheriff of Somerset 1984; *Books* We Started a Stately Home (1980); *Recreations* cricket; *Clubs* I Zingari; *Style*— Charles Clive-Ponsonby-Fane, Esq, JP; Brympton d'Evercy, Yeovil, Somerset BA22 8TD (☎ 0935 862528)

CLOAKE, Graham Arthur; s of late Wilfred Cloake; *b* 1 Jan 1934; *Educ* Badingham Coll; *m* 1961, Jennifer Noel, da of late Frank Sidney Smith, of New Malden, Surrey; 2 s, 1 da; *Career* dir Greenwell Montagu Stockbrokers and Effess Farms Ltd; *Recreations* gardening, swimming; *Clubs* City of London; *Style*— Graham Cloake, Esq; 13 Preston Rd, Wimbledon, London SW20 (☎ 01 947 2962); Greenwell Montagu Stockbrokers, 114 Old Broad St, London EC2 (☎ 01 588 8817)

CLOAKE, John Cecil; CMG (1977); s of late Dr Cecil Stedman Cloake, of Wimbledon, and Maude Osborne, *née* Newling; *b* 2 Dec 1924; *Educ* KCS Wimbledon, Peterhouse Cambridge; *m* 1956, Margaret Thomure, *née* Morris, of Washington, DC, USA; 1 s; *Career* Army 1943-46; Dip Serv 1948-; cnsllr (commercial) Tehran 1968-72, head trade relations and exports dept FCO 1973-76, ambassador to Bulgaria 1976-80; hon treas Br Inst of Persian Studies 1982-; chm Richmond Local History Soc 1985-; Museum of Richmond 1986-; *Books* Templer, Tiger of Malaya (1985); *Style*— John Cloake, Esq, CMG; 4 The Terrace, Richmond Hill, Richmond, Surrey TW10 6RN

CLODE, Dame (Emma) Frances Heather; *née* Marc; DBE (1974, CBE 1969, OBE 1955, MBE 1951); da of Alexander Marc, and Florence Marc; *b* 12 August 1903; *Educ* privately; *m* 1927, late Col Charles Mathew Clode, MC, s of Sir Walker Baker Clode, KC (d 1937); 1 s (Walter); *Career* Joined WRVS 1939, serv Cambridge 1940-45, WRVS HQ 1945, chm WRVS 1971-74 (vice-chm 1967); CStJ 1973; *Style*— Dame Frances Clode, DBE; 19 Rushers Close, Pershore, Worcs, WR10 1HF

CLODE, Michael Leslie Hailey; s of Capt Roger Leslie Clode, RN, of Kynance, 22 Cheltenham Crescent, Lee-on-Solent, Hants, and Patricia Mary, *née* Kyd; *b* 5 Oct 1943; *Educ* St Edward Sch Oxford; *m* 4 Apr 1970, Isobel McLeod, da of Henry Watson Carrick (d 1976); 4 da (Fiona b 1972, Alison b 1974, Jennifer b 1977, Camilla b 1982); *Career* slr; ptnr Freshfields 1974-, memb cncl St Leonards Sch, St Andrews, Fife; Freeman: City of London, City of London Slrs Co; memb Law Soc; *Recreations* skiing, breeding Aberdeen Angus Cattle; *Style*— Michael Clode, Esq; 56 Brompton Square, London SW3; Chesters, Orchard Way, Esher, Surrey KT10 9DY; Little Kilry, By Blairgowrie, Perthshire PH11 8HY; Freshfields, Grindall House, 25 Newgate Street EC1A 7LH (☎ 01 606 6677, fax 01 248 3487, telex 889292)

CLOGG, Oliver John Bertram; s of Rev Prof Frank Bertram Clogg, MA (d 1955), and Jessie Winifred, *née* Stinson (d 1967); *b* 16 Dec 1919; *Educ* Colet Court, St Pauls Sch; *m* 15 July 1948, Margaret Doreen, da of Frank Ambrose Taylor (d 1967); 1 s (Jonathan b 1958), 4 da (Wendy Margaret b 1949, Elizabeth Angela b 1951, Melanie Anne b 1955, Fiona Penelope b 1958); *Career* Major RASC, CRASC 5 AA Gp; chartered surveyor former princ Reynolds and Eason; FRICS; *Recreations* walking, gardening, woodwork, model making; *Style*— Oliver J B Clogg, Esq; The Stables, Ballewan, Blanefield, Glasgow G63 9AT (☎ 0360 70918)

CLOGHER, Bishop of; Most Rev Joseph Augustine Duffy; s of Edward Duffy (d 1956), and Brigid MacEntee (d 1963); *b* 3 Feb 1934; *Educ* Maynooth (BD), Nat Univ of Ireland (MA, HDipEd); *Career* RC Bishop of Clogher 1979-; *Books* Patrick In His Own Words (1985), Lough Derg Guide (1978); *Recreations* history, travel; *Style*— The Most Rev Joseph Duffy; Bishop's House, Monaghan, Ireland (☎ (047) 81019)

CLOGSTOUN-WILLMOTT, Capt (Herbert) Nigel; DSO (1941), DSC (1942 and bar 1944); s of Herbert Morton Willmott, FCH (d 1951), of Langhaun Mansions London SW5, chief engr India Service of Engrs, and Bessie Beatrix de Perpigna Clogstoun (d 1970); *b* 12 July 1910; *Educ* Lambrook Sch, Marlborough, HMS Erebus trg ship, RNC Greenwich; *m* 1, 1944 (m dis) Prudence, da of Albert Leslie Wright, JP, of Butterly Hall Derby (d 1957); 1 s (Jonathan Nigel b 1945), 2 da (Teresa Leslie b 1949, Serena Jane b 1955); m 2, Pamela Armitage, da of Frederick Beach of Bournemouth (d 1975); *Career* RN 1928; Med, East Indies, Lt 1932, South Pacific 1937-39; WWII: 1940 N Atlantic and Norway Campaigns, Med 1941-42, Channel 1943-44, founder of Comb ined Ops Pilotage Parties (Commando for Beach Reconanisance and Pilotage (Top secret until 1956)) 1941-44, Admty Plans Q 1945-46; cmd HMS Yector, Wildfire 1946-48, Peacock 1948-50, Admty and FO founded Directorate of Naval MoD, Mgmnt Systems 1956-61 Dept FO 1967-74; despatches (twice); *Recreations* sailing, cruising, riding, shooting; *Clubs* Army and Navy, Royal Naval and Hayling Island SC, Royal Albert YC; *Style*— Capt N Clogstoun-Willmott, DSO, DSC, RN; PO Box 2136, Paphos, Cyprus

CLOKE, Anthony (Tony) John; s of Maj John Nicholas Cloke (d 1985), of Walsall and May Eddy, *née* Craghill; *b* 10 Jan 1943; *Educ* Queen Mary's GS Walsall, Clare Coll, Cambridge (MA); *m* 7 June 1969, Ann Gwendoline, da of Bertie Cordy (d 1981), of Usk; 2 s (John b 1970, Richard b 1972), 1 da (Caroline b 1974); *Career* solr 1970, ptnr Peter Peter and Wright (and its predecessors 1973-; widespread involvement in local organisations and activities; solr of the Supreme Ct 1970; *Recreations* farming, golf; *Style*— Tony Cloke, Esq; Peter, Peter and Wright, 1 West Street, Okehampton, Devon (☎ 0837 2379, fax 0837 3604)

CLOKE, Richard Owen; s of Owen William Cloke, MBE, of 25 Priests Lane, Brentwood, Essex, and Barbara Ethel Beatrice, *née* Abbott; *b* 3 May 1944; *Educ* Reading Sch; *m* 26 Jun 1969, Carol Ann, da of Frank Wadsworth; 2 s (Ian, Andrew), 1 da Jackie); *Career* branch mangr Barclays Bank plc 1979-83 (asst dis mangr 1976-79, joined 1960), asst dir Barclays Merchant Bank Ltd 1983-85, dir Barclays de Zoete Wedd Ltd 1986-; *Recreations* tennis, badminton, golf; *Style*— Richard Cloke, Esq; Barclays De Zoete Wedd Ltd, Ebbgate House, 2 Swan Lane, London, EC4R 3TS, (☎ 01 623 2323 fax 01 623 6075)

CLOSE, David John; s of John Edward Close (d 1969); *b* 10 May 1929; *Educ* Queen Elizabeth's GS Mansfield, King's Coll London; *m* 1971, Jan, *née* Wileman; 2 da; *Career* personnel offr NCB 1956-63, gp personnel mangr Sangamo Weston 1963-64, personnel mangr Pirelli 1965-69; personnel and admin dir: Davy and United Eng 1969-71, Kearney and Trecker 1971-73; gen personnel mangr Reliant Motor Co 1973-74; personnel dir: Simon Engrg (contracting gp) 1974-83, Simon Engrg plc 1983-; FIPM, FBIM, FIIM; *Recreations* walking, gardening, DIY, music; *Style*— David Close, Esq

CLOSE, Roy Edwin; CBE (1973); s of Bruce Edwin Close and Minnie Louise Close; *b* 11 Mar 1920; *Educ* Trinity GS N London; *m* 1947, (Olive) Joan, da of Robert George Forty; 2 s; *Career* served WWII SAS rising to rank of Capt; asst ed The Time Review of Indust 1949-57; dir Bookers Sugar Estates and exec Booker McConnell Gp 1957-66; industl dir NEDO 1970-73 (industl advsr 1966-70); dir: Broad St Gp, Kepner Treqoe Ltd, Kramer Int Ltd; dir gen BIM 1976-85; chm and dean Aston Univ Mgmnt Centre 1973-76; chm: OU Business Sch, bd Prof Advsy Ctee, Conservation Fndn; hon D Univ hon MSc, CBIM, MSC FRSA, FIIM; *Clubs* Reform, Special Forces; *Style*— Roy Close, Esq, CBE; Cathedral Cottage, North Elmham, Norfolk;

CLOTHIER, Sir Cecil Montacute; KCB (1982), QC (1965); s of Hugh Montacute Clothier (d 1961), of Blundellsands, Liverpool; *b* 28 August 1919; *Educ* Stonyhurst, Lincoln Coll Oxford (BCL, MA); *m* 1943, Mary Elizabeth (d 1984), da of Ernest Glover Bush (d 1962), of Aughton, Lancs; 1 s, 2 da; *Career* served WWII 51 Highland Div, Army Staff Washington DC, Hon Lt-Col Royal Signals; barr Inner Temple 1950, bencher 1972, rec Blackpool 1965-72, Appeal Judge IOM 1972-78; legal assessor to Gen Medical and Gen Dental Cncls 1972-78, Hon memb Assocn of Anaesthetists, memb Royal Cmmn on NHS 1976-78, parly cmmr Administration and Health Service Cmmr England Wales and Scotland 1979-84; chm Police Complaints Authority 1985-; Rook Carling Fellow 1988; hon fell Oxford Univ 1984, hon LLd Hull Univ 1983; kt 1981; *Clubs* Athenaeum; *Style*— Sir Cecil Clothier, KCB, QC; 10 Great George Street, London SW1P 3AE

CLOUDSLEY-THOMPSON, John Leonard; Prof; s of Dr Ashley George Gyton Thompson (d 1983), and Muriel Elaine, *née* Griffiths; *b* 23 May 1921; *Educ* Marlborough, Pembroke Coll Cambridge (BA, MA, PhD), Univ of London (DSc); *m* May 1944, (Jessie) Anne, da of Capt John Leslie Cloudsley (d 1968); 3 s (Hugh b 1944, Timothy b 1948, Peter b 1952); *Career* cmmnd 4QUH 1941, transferred 4 Co London Yeo (Sharpshooters), served N africa (Opn Crusader) 1941-42, Knightsbridge Tank Battle (serverly wounded), instr Sandhurst (Capt) 1943, rejoined regt for D Day (escaped from villers bocage), served Caen offensive (Opn Goodwood) 1944, hon rank of Capt on resignation; lectr zoology King's Coll London 1950-60, prof zoology Univ of Khartoum and keeper Sudan Natural History Museum 1960-71, prof Zoology (now emeritus prof) Birkbeck Coll London 1972-86 (Leverhulme emeritus fell 1987-89), sr res fell Univ of Mexico Albuquerque 1969; visiting prof: Univ of Kuwait 1978 and 1983, Univ of Nigeria 1981, Univ of Qatar 1986, Australian Nat Univ 1987; chm: Br Naturalists Assoc 1974-83 (vice-pres 1985-), Biological Cncl 1977-82 (medal 1983); pres: Br Arachnological Soc 1982-85 (vice-pres 1985-86), Br soc for Chronobiology 1985-87; vice-pres: Linnean Soc 1975-76 and 1977-78, first World Congress of Herpetology 1989; hon memb: Royal African Soc 1969- (medal 1969), Br Herpetological Soc 1983-; KSS Charter Award Inst of Biology 1981, JH Grundy Medal RAMC 1987; ed Journal of Arid Environments 1987-; Freeman City of London 1945, Liveryman Worshipful Co of Skinners 1952; Hon DSc Univ of Khartoum (and gold medal) 1091; FIBIol 1962, FWA 1962, FRES, FLS, FZS; *Books* 45 books incl: Spiders, Scorpions, Centipedes and Mites (1958), Zoology of Tropical Africa (1969), The Temperature and Water Relations of Reptiles (1971), Insects and History (1976), Why the Dinosaurs Became Extinct (1978), Tooth and Claw (1980), Evolution and Adaption of Terrestial Arthropeds (1988); *Recreations* music (especially opera), photography, travel; *Style*— Prof Cloudsley-Thompson; Flat 9, 4 Craven Hill, London W2 3DS (☎ 01 723 5214); Little Clarkes, Little Samford, Nr Saffron, Walden, Essex CB10 2SA; Dept of Biology (Medawar Bldg), UCL, Univ of London, Gower St, London WC1E 6BT (☎ 01 387 7050 ext 3587)

CLOUGH, (John) Alan; CBE (1972), MC (1945); s of John Clough (d 1982) and Yvonne, *née* Dollfus; *b* 20 Mar 1924; *Educ* Marlborough, Leeds Univ; *m* 1, 1949 (m dis 1961), Margaret Joy, da of A Catton, of Kirkby Overblow; 1 s, 2 da; m 2, 1961, Mary Cowan, da of Harold Mathew Stuart Catherwood; 1 s, 1 da; *Career* Capt, served N Africa and Italy 1943-47, Maj TA Yorks Hussars 1947-53; chm: Wool Industs Res Assoc 1967-69, Wool Textile delgn 1969-72; pres: Br Textile Confedn 1974-77, Comitextil-Brussels (co-ordinating ctee for textile industries in EEC) 1975-77, Textile Inst 1979-81, Confedn of Br Wool Textiles 1982-84; chm Br Mohair Spinners Ltd to 1984, Textile Res Cncl 1984-; Past Mayor Co of Merchants of the Staple of England; *Recreations* travelling, gardening, fishing; *Clubs* Boodle's; *Style*— Alan Clough, Esq, CBE, MC; The Hays, Monks Eleigh, Suffolk

CLOUSTON, James Brian; s of James Parker Clouston, of Durham City, and Dorothy Margaret, *née* Schrimsham; *b* 3 Feb 1935; *Educ* Durham Univ, Kings Coll (Dip in Landscape Design); *m* 23 July 1959, Karin Kelman, da of Dr William Kelman Macdonald (d 1945); 2 s (Charles Brian b 1961, William Stuart James b 1965), 2 da (Katherine Anna b 1972, Sally Karel Christine b 1963); *Career* landscape architect, chm: Brian Clouston and Ptnrs Ltd, BCP Asta Ltd; pres The Landscape Institute 1981-83; ed: Landscape Design with Plants, Landscape by Design with Tony Aldous, After the Elm; *Recreations* sailing, mountain bicycling, walking, horticulture, family history; *Clubs* National Liberal; *Style*— J B Clouston, Esq; Parkhill, Princess Street, Durham City, County Durham; St Cuthberts House, Framwellgate Peth, Durham DH1 5SU (☎ 091 3867226/0, telex 538216, fax 091 386 1703)

CLOUTMAN, Air Vice-Marshal Geoffrey William; CB (1980); s of Rev Walter Evans Cloutman and Dora Cloutman; *b* 1 April 1920; *Educ* Cheltenham GS, QMC, London, London Hosp; *m* 1949, Sylvia, *née* Brown; 3 da; *Career* joined RAFVR 1942, princ dental offr Strike Command 1973, dir of Dental Services RAF 1977-80; FDSRCS, QHDS 1976; *Style*— Air Vice-Marshal Geoffrey Cloutman, CB; Willow Bridge, Easton, Wells, Somerset

CLOVER, His Honour Judge; (Robert) Gordon; TD (1951), QC 1958 ; s of Lt-Col Henry Edward Clover (d 1964), and Catherine Clifford Clover (d 1965); *b* 14 Nov 1911; *Educ* Lancing, Exeter Coll Oxford (MA, BCL); *m* 1947, Elizabeth Suzanne, da of Archibald McCorquodale (d 1920); 2 s (Thomas, Stephen); *Career* served in RA 1939-45, N Africa and Italy (despatches 1944); barr 1935, practised on Northern Circuit 1936-61, rec Blackpool 1960-61, dep cmmr for purposes of National Insur Acts 1961-65, dep chm QS Bucks 1969-71, former County Courts Judge, circuit judge 1965-82; *Style*— His Honour Gordon Judge Clover, TD, QC; JP; 10 Westcliff, Sheringham, Norfolk NR26 8JT

CLOW, Robert Christopher; s of Ronald Robert Clow, of 16 Hudson Close, Dovercourt, Essex, and Esme Joan, *née* Street; *b* 27 Mar 1948; *Educ* Aloysius Coll Highgate; *m* 1, 2 Feb 1969 (m dis 1978), Monica Mary, *née* Stratta; 2 da (Sandra Monica b 1969, Sarah Jennifer b 1971); m 2, 21 July 1981, Philippa, da of Capt Edward Atkinson (d 1970); *Career* CA 1973, ptnr Gordon Kanter & Co 1975-81, sole practitioner 1981-; FCA 1978; *Recreations* squash, sub-aqua, sailing, bridge, theatre, gardening; *Clubs* RAC; *Style—* Robert Clow, Esq; Netherfield, 10 Batchworth Lane, Northwood, Middx (☎ 092 74 25715); 18a Northampton Square, London EC1 (☎ 01 428 4038)

CLOWES, Col Sir Henry Nelson; KCVO (1981, CVO 1977), DSO (1945), OBE (1953); yr s of Maj Ernest William Clowes, DSO (d 1951), of Bradley Hall, Ashbourne, Derbys, by his w Blanche, da of Rear Adm Hon Algernon Littleton, who was 2 s of 2 Baron Hatherton; the Admiral's w was Lady Margaret Needham, sis of 2 Earl of Kilmorey; *b* 21 Oct 1911; *Educ* Eton, Sandhurst; *m* 1941, Diana Katharine, MBE, da of Maj Basil Kerr, DSC (d 1957; himself ggs of 6 Marquess of Lothian by his 2 w, who was Lady Harriet Scott, da of 3 Duke of Buccleuch); 1 s (Capt Andrew Henry Clowes, Scots Gds (ret 1967), sometime Equerry to HRH The (1) Duke of Gloucester, m 1967, Georgiana, da of Richard Cavendish, of Holker Hall, Cumbria); *Career* served Scots Gds 1931-57 (cmd 2 Bn then 1 Bn, Lt-Col cmdg 1954-57, ret 1957); Lt Hon Corps Gentlemen at Arms 1976-81 (joined 1961, Clerk of the Cheque and Adj 1966, Standard Bearer 1973-76); *Recreations* gardening, shooting, fishing, travel; *Clubs* Cavalry and Guards, Shikar, Pratt's; *Style—* Colonel Sir Henry Clowes, KCVO, DSO, OBE; 57 Perrymead St, London SW6 3SN (☎ 01 736 7901)

CLUCAS, Sir Kenneth Henry; KCB (1976, CB 1969); o s of Rev J H Clucas (d 1963); *b* 18 Nov 1921; *Educ* Kingswood Sch, Emmanuel Coll Cambridge; *m* 1960, Barbara, da of Rear Adm R P Hunter, USN (retd), of Washington, DC, USA; 2 da; *Career* served WWII RCS; served as 2 sec labour HM Embassy Cairo 1950, under-sec Miny of Labour 1966-68, sec Nat Bd Prices and Incomes 1968-71, CSD 1971-73 (also First CS Cmmr), dep sec DTI 1974, perm sec Dept of Prices and Consumer Protection 1974-79, perm sec Dept of Trade 1979-82 (ret); memb Cncl on Tbnls 1983-; chm Nat Assoc of Citizens' Advice Bureaux 1984-; chm Nuffield Fndn ctee of inquiry into pharmacy 1983-6; cncl memb Fin Intermediaries, Managers and Brokers Regulatory Assoc 1986-; membs Ombudsman Lloyds of London 1988-;; *Style—* Sir Kenneth Clucas, KCB; Cariad, Knoll Rd, Godalming, Surrey (☎ 048 68 6430)

CLUFF, Algy (John Gordon); s of Harold Cluff, of Waldeshare House, Waldeshore, Kent; *b* 19 April 1940; *Educ* Stowe; *Career* served as 2 Lt Grenadier Gds 1959, Capt Gds Independent Parachute Co; founder, chm and chief exec Cluff Oil; contested (C) Ardwick Manchester 1966; md CCP North Seas Associates Ltd, dep chm Cluff Oil (Australia); proprietor The Spectator 1981-; *Style—* Algy Cluff Esq; 70 Arlington House, Arlington St, London SW1; Clova House, Lumsden, Aberdeenshire (☎ 046 48 331/335/336)

CLUGSTON, John Westland Antony; s of Leonard Gordon Clugston OBE, DL (d 1 May 1984), and Sybil Mark Bacon (d 1981); *b* 16 May 1938; *Educ* Sandroyd, Gordonstoun; *m* m 1, 6 June 1969, Patricia, da of Gordon Columba Harvey, of Chance Wood, Manby Louth, Lincs; 2 s (Alistair b 1970, David b 1972), 2 da (Linda b 1973, Christina b 1976); m 2, Jane Elizabeth Ann, da of Charles Burtt Marfleet (d 1967), of Wykeham Hall, Ludford, Lincs; *Career* six yrs in the TA with Sherwood Rangers Yeomany, Lt; apprentice at Huttenwerk Rheinhausen A G Iron and Steel Works 1958-60; Lorraine Escaut Iron and Steel Works at Mont-St-Martin and Senelle (France) 1960-61; dir: Clugston Hldgs Ltd 1964, Rhoadstone Div Activities 1965-68, (dir of all subsidiary co's 1970); chm: Roadstone Div 1969, Reclamation Div and St Vincent Plant Ltd 1980, gp vice-chm and md of Clugston Hldsgs Ltd 1978, Colvilles Clugston Shanks (Hldgs) Ltd and Colvilles Clugston Shanks Ltd 1984, Clydesdale Excavating and Construction Co Ltd 1987-; chm and md Clugston Hldgs Ltd 1984; has held and currently holds numerous dirships; past pres Humbeside Branch of the Br Inst of Mgmnt; govr Brigg Prep Sch; chm East Glanford Scouts; cncl memb: BACMI, Lincolnshire Iron and Steel Inst; Assoc of the Inst of Quarrying; Freeman of the City of London, Liveryman Worshipful Co of Paviors 1965, (elected to the Ct 1986); FIHT 1984; *Recreations* shooting, fishing, tennis, music; *Style—* J W A Clugston, Esq; The Old Vicarage, Scawby, Brigg, Lincs DN20 9LX (☎ 0652 57100); Clugston Hldgs Ltd, St Vincent House, Normanby Rd, Scunthorpe, S Humberside DN15 8QT (☎ 0724 843491, telex 527345, fax 0724 867680)

CLUTTERBUCK, Vice Adm Sir David Granville; KBE (1968), CB (1965); s of Charles Granville Clutterbuck (d 1957); *b* 25 Jan 1913; *Educ* HMS Conway; *m* 1937, Rose Mere, da of Hubert Earle Vaile, of Auckland, New Zealand; 2 da; *Career* joined RN 1929, Rear Adm 1963, Vice Adm 1966, Dep Supreme Allied Cdr Atlantic 1966-68, ret; admin dir Business Graduates Assoc Ltd 1969-83; *Style—* Vice Adm Sir David Clutterbuck, KBE, CB; 29 Elvaston Place, London SW7

CLUTTERBUCK, Edmund Harry Michael; OBE (1957); o s of Maj-Gen Walter Edmond Clutterbuck, DSO, MC, of Hornby Castle, Bedale, N Yorks, and Gwendolin Atterbury, *née* Younger (d 1975); *b* 22 July 1920; *Educ* Winchester Coll, New Coll Oxford; *m* 22 Sept 1945, Anne Agatha, yr da of late Dr Robert Noel Woodsend, of Corner Hourse, Catterick, Yorks; 1 s, 3 da; *Career* dir Scottish and Newcastle Breweries Ltd 1960-, dir Scottish Brewers Ltd, Brewers' Food Supply Co Ltd, Wm Younger and Co Ltd and others; *Style—* Edmund Clutterbuck, Esq, OBE; The Tower, Hornby Castle, Bemale, N Yorks

CLUTTERBUCK, Jasper Meadows; s of late Hugh Clutterbuck; *b* 5 Feb 1935; *Educ* Eton; *m* 1958, Marguerite Susan, *née* Birnie; 1 s, 1 da; *Career* Lt Coldstream Gds 1953-56; dir Whitbread & Co 1975-88, chief exec Morland & Co plc; *Style—* Jasper Clutterbuck, Esq; Mottisfont House, nr Romsey, Hants SO5 0LN

CLUTTERBUCK, Maj-Gen Richard Lewis; CB (1971), OBE (1958); s Col Lewis st John Rawlinson Clutterbuck, OBE, late RA (d 1965), and Isabella Jessie, *née* Jocelyn (d 1968), ggda of 2 Earl of Roden; *b* 22 Nov 1917; *Educ* Radley, Pembroke Coll Cambridge (MA, PhD); *m* 1948, Angela Muriel, da of Col Bernard Cole Barford, RA, of Bishop's Waltham; 3 s (Peter, Robin, Julian); *Career* 2 Lt RE 1937, Maj-Gen 1968, chief instr (Army) Royal Coll of Def Studies 1971-72, Col Cmdt RE 1972-77; reader in political conflict Exeter Univ 1972-83; author; BBC Gen Advisory Cncl 1975-81; *Books* The Media and Political Violence (1983), Industrial Conflict and Democracy (1984), Conflict and Violence in Singapore and Malaysia (1985), The Future of Political Violence (1986), Kidnap, Hijack and Extortion (1987); *Clubs* Army and Navy, Royal Cwlth Soc; *Style—* Maj-Gen Richard Clutterbuck, CB, OBE; Dept of Politics, Univ of Exeter EX5 5LT

CLUTTON, Rafe Henry; s of Robin John Clutton (d 1978), and Rosalie Muriel, *née* Birch (d 1978); *b* 13 June 1929; *Educ* Tonbridge; *m* 1954, Jill Olwyn, da of John Albert Evans, of Haywards Heath, Sussex ; 4 s (Owen b 1958, Gareth b 1960, Jonathan b 1962, Niall b 1964), 1 da (Helen b 1968); *Career* chartered surveyor; ptnr Cluttons 1955-; dir: Legal and General Gp Ltd 1972-, City Acre Property Investmt Tst Ltd 1973-85; memb Nat Theatre Bd 1976-; chm Royal Fndn of Greycoat Hospital; FRICS; *Recreations* reading, hill walking; *Clubs* Royal Thames Yacht, City of London; *Style—* Rafe Clutton, Esq; Fairfield, North Chailey, Sussex (☎ 082 572 2431), 45 Berkeley Square, London W1X 5DB (☎ 01 408 1010, telex 23620)

CLWYD, Ann (Ann Clwyd Roberts); MP (Lab) Cynon Valley 1984-; da of Gwilym Henri Lewis and Elizabeth Ann Lewis; *b* 21 Mar 1937; *Educ* Holywell GS, The Queen's Sch Chester, Univ Coll Bangor; *m* 1963, Owen Dryhurst Roberts, Assistant to Head of Programmes, BBC Wales; *Career* contested (Lab) Denbigh 1970, Gloucester Oct 1974, MEP (Lab) Mid and W Wales 1979-84; shadow: Educn jr min 1987-88; Women's Affairs min 1987-88; journalist The Guardian and The Observer; broadcaster; vice-chm Welsh Arts Cncl 1975-79, memb Lab NEC 1983-84;; shadow Educn Jr Min and shadow dep Min for Women 1987-; *Style—* Ann Clwyd, MP; House of Commons, London SW1; 70 St Michael's Rd, Llandaff, Cardiff (☎ 01 219 3000)

CLWYD, 3 Baron (UK 1919); Sir (John) Anthony Roberts; 3 Bt (UK 1908); o s of 2 Baron Clwyd (d 1987), and Joan de Bois, *née* Murray (d 1985); *b* 2 Jan 1935; *Educ* Harrow, Trinity Coll Cambridge; *m* 1969, (Linda) Geraldine, yr da of Charles Eugene Cannons, of Sanderstead, Surrey; 3 s (Hon (John) Murray, Hon Jeremy Trevor b 1973, Hon Hugh Gerald Arthur b 1977); *Heir* s, Hon (John) Murray Roberts b 27 Aug 1971; *Career* barr Gray's Inn 1970; civil servant; *Recreations* music, literature; *Style—* The Rt Hon Lord Clwyd; 24 Salisbury Avenue, Cheam, Sutton, Surrey (☎ 01 642 2527)

CLYDE, Lady Elizabeth; *née* Wellesley; da of 7 Duke of Wellington, KG; *b* 26 Dec 1918; *m* 18 Nov 1939 (m dis 1959), Maj Thomas Clyde, RHG, s of William Pancoast Clyde, of New York; 2 s (of whom the er is Jeremy Clyde, the actor) (and 1 s decd); *Style—* Lady Elizabeth Clyde; Oliver's Farm, Bramley, Basingstoke, Hants

CLYDE, The Hon Lord James John; QC (1971); s of Rt Hon Lord Clyde (d 1975), and Margaret Letitia Dubuisson (d 1974); *b* 29 Jan 1932; *Educ* The Edinburgh Acad, Oxford Univ (BA), Edinburgh Univ (LLB); *m* 1963, Ann Clunie, da of Donald Robert Armstrong Hoblyn (d 1975); 2 s (James b 1969, Timothy b 1973); *Career* advocate Scotland 1959, advocate depute 1973-74; chllr to bp of Argyll and the Isles 1972-85; memb Scottish Valuation Advsy Cncl 1972-, (vice-chm 1980-87, chm 1987-); ldr UK Delegation to the CCBE 1981-84; chm Medical Appeal Tribunals 1974-85; judge in the Cts of Appeal for Jersey and Guernsey 1979-85; senator Coll of Justice 1985-; tstee St Mary's Music Sch 1978-, dir Edinburgh Acad 1979-88, chm cncl St George's Sch for Girls 1989-, govr Napier Poly 1989-, tstee Nat Library of Scotland 1977-; *Recreations* music, gardening; *Clubs* New (Edinburgh); *Style—* The Hon Lord Clyde; 9 Heriot Row, Edinburgh EH3 6HU (☎ 031 556 7114)

CLYDESMUIR, 2 Baron (UK 1948); Ronald John Bilsland Colville; KT (1972), CB (1965), MBE (1944), TD; s of 1 Baron Clydesmuir, PC, GCIE, TD (d 1954); *b* 21 May 1917; *Educ* Charterhouse, Trinity Coll Cambridge; *m* 10 April 1946, Joan Marguerita, er da of Lt-Col Ernest Brabazon Booth, DSO, MD; 2 s, 2 da; *Heir* s, Hon David Colville; *Career* Lord-Lt Lanarkshire 1963 (formerly Vice-Lt, DL 1955), Capt Royal Co of Archers (Queen's Body Guard for Scotland), dep govr The British Linen Bank 1966-71, dir Bank of Scotland 1971-87 (govr 1972-81), Scottish Provident Instn, Barclays Bank 1972-82; chm North Sea Assets Ltd; *Style—* The Rt Hon the Lord Clydesmuir, KT, CB, MBE, TD; Langlees House, Biggar, Lanarkshire (☎ Biggar 20057)

COAD, Jonathan George; *b* 2 Feb 1945; *Educ* Lancing, Keble Coll Oxford Univ (BA); *m* 16 April 1976, Vivienne Jaques; 2 da (Jennifer b 1982, Felicity b 1986); *Career* historian, inspr of ancient monuments with Historic Bldgs and Monuments Cmmn; hon sec Royal Archaeological Inst, vice pres Soc for Nautical Res, cncl memb Navy Records Soc; FSA; *Books* Historic Architecture of The Royal Navy (1983); The Royal Dockyards 1690-1850, Architecture and Engineering Works of the Sailing Navy 1989;; *Recreations* reading, travel, woodworking; *Clubs* Eclectic; *Style—* Jonathan G Coad, Esq; Baileys Reed, Salehurst, Sussex TN32 5JP; 25 Savile Row, London W1X 2HE (☎ 01 734 6010 ext 711)

COAKER, Peter Brian; s of George William Coaker (d 1973), and Dorothy Elsie, *née* Watling (d 1984); *b* 23 June 1928; *Educ* Chingford Co HS, Tiffin Boys Sch, Imperial Coll London (BSc); *m* 22 Oct 1955, Phyllis Patricia, da of John Elborne (d 1983); 1 s (Paul James b 1967); *Career* RAF 1950-52 as Educn Offr and Flying Offr; BP 1949-83: operational res, computing, and mangr educnl affairs 1978-83; pres Mathematical Assoc 1984-85, chm Jt Schs Panel Confederation of Br Indust 1979-83, and memb of many mathematical ctees; ARCS, DIC, FIMA, FBCS, FOR; *Recreations* gardening, computing, photography; *Clubs* Royal Overseas League; *Style—* Peter B Coaker, Esq; Greenslades, Exford, Minehead, Somerset TA24 7QG (☎ 064 383 572)

COALES, Prof John Flavell; CBE (1974, OBE 1945); s of John Dennis Coales, DSc (d 1972), of Cobham, and Marion Beatrix, *née* Flavell, ARCM (d 1962); *b* 14 Sept 1907; *Educ* Berkhamsted Sch, Sidney Sussex Coll Cambridge (BA, MA, ScD); *m* 1 Aug 1936, (Mary) Dorothea Violet, da of Rev Henry Lewis Gutherie Alison (d 1958), vicar of Kintbury, Berks; 2 s (Edward b 16 May 1939, Martin b 16 Mar 1943), 2 da (Susan b 17 May 1937, Alison b 7 Jan 1942); *Career* Admiralty Dept of Sci Res and Experiment: jr sci offr 1929-32, sci offr 1933-39, sr sci offr 1940-43, princ 1944-46 (temp Cdr RNVR); res dir Elliott Bros (London) 1946-52; prof emerius of engrg Cambridge Univ 1974- (asst dir res 1952-55, lectr 1956-57, reader 1958-64, prof 1965-73); chm UK Automation Cncl 1963-66, Cncl of Engrg Insts 1975-76; pres Int Fedn of Automatic Control 1963-66; Freeman City of London, Liveryman Worshipful Co of Engineers; hon DSc City Univ (1971), hon DTech Univ of Loughborough (1977), hon DEng Univ of Sheffield (1978), hon fell Hatfield Poly (1971); FIEE (1943), FInstP (1946), FICE (1973), FIEEE (1968), FRS (1970), Hon FIEE (1985), Hon FInstMC (1971), FIAgrE (1975), FEng (1976); for mem Serbian Acadamy of Sciences; *Books* Automatic and Remote Control (ed 1967); many papers in tech jnls on elec engrg, systems engrg and educn; *Style—* Pof John Coales; Cambridge University Engineering Dept, Trumpington St, Cambridge CB2 1PZ

COATE, Lady; Frances Margaret; da of John Varley, of Leamington Spa; *m* 1939, Maj-Gen Sir Raymond Douglas Coate, KBE, CB (d 1983, sometime paymaster-in-chief and chm Royal Homes for Officers' Widows and Daughters); 2 s; *Style—* Lady Coate; 18 Roehampton Close, London SW15 5LU

COATES; *see*: Milnes-Coates

COATES, Caroline Mary; da of Clifford Coates, of Haworth, W Yorks, and Brenda Mary Coates; *b* 28 Mar 1954; *Educ* Keighley Girls GS, Wall Hall Coll (Cambridge Inst)

Alderham, W Herts; *m* 1 March 1987, Seamus Deane Potter, s of Maj John Deane Potter, (d 1982); *Career* fndr Amalgamated Talent (promotional gp for fashion designers), exec i/c Hyper Hyper High St Ken London 1986-87, opened Boyd Stevy 1987 Newburgh St London (now md Amalgated Boyd Stevy design ptnrship); dir Fashion Acts, exec on mgmnt bd Br Knitting and Cutting Expert Cncl, memb: designers Gp Br Fashion Cncl, BIC, CEC; *Style*— Ms Caroline Coates; Battersea, London; Juneva, Spain; 12 Newburgh St, London W1V 1LG (☎ 01 494 3188)

COATES, David Charlton Frederick; s and h of Brig Sir Frederick Coates, 2 Bt; *b* 16 Feb 1948; *Educ* Millfield; *m* 1973, Christine Helen, *née* Marshall; 2 s (James b 1977, Robert b 1980); *Style*— David Coates, Esq; 30 Hauxton Rd, Little Shelford, Cambridge

COATES, Sir Ernest William; CMG (1970); s of Thomas Atlee Coates; *b* 30 Nov 1916; *Educ* Ballarat HS, Melbourne Univ; *m* 1, 1943, Phylis E (d 1971), da of H W Morris, of Ballarat; 1 s, 3 da; m 2, 1974, Patricia Ann (d 1986), da of late Charles A Fisher, of Herts; *Career* state dir of Finance and perm head of Victoria Treasury Australia 1959-77, co dir; kt 1973; *see Debrett's Handbook of Australia and New Zealand for further details*; *Style*— Sir Ernest Coates, CMG; 64 Molesworth St, Kew, Vic 3101, Australia (☎ 03 8618226)

COATES, Brig Sir Frederick Gregory Lindsay; 2 Bt (UK 1921), of Haypark, City of Belfast; s of Sir William Frederick Coates, 1 Bt (d 1932); *b* 19 May 1916; *Educ* Eton, Sandhurst; *m* 1940, Joan Nugent, da of Maj-Gen Sir Charlton Spinks, KBE, DSO (d 1959); 1 s, 2 da; *Heir* s, David Coates; *Career* Royal Tank Regt 1936, served WWII Middle East and NW Europe (wounded 2), WO and Miny of Supply 1950-66, asst mil attaché Stockholm 1953-56, Brig Br Defence Staff Washington DC 1966-69, mil advsr Defence Sales MOD 1969-71, ret; *Recreations* yachting; *Clubs* Royal Yacht Sqdn, Royal Ocean Racing, Royal Motor Yacht, RAC Yacht, Royal Lymington Yacht; *Style*— Brig Sir Frederick Coates, Bt; Launchfield, Briantspuddle, Dorchester, Dorset DT2 7HN (☎ 0929 471229)

COATES, Michael Arthur; yr s of Joseph Michael Smith Coates, OBE (d 1984), of Elmfield, Wylam, Northumberland, and Lilian Warren, *née* Murray (d 1973); *b* 12 May 1924; *Educ* Uppingham; *m* 1, 1952 (m dis 1970), Audrey Hampton, da of Arthur William Thorne, of St Nicholas Close, Wimborne, Dorset; 1 s (Simon Michael b 1 July 1959), 2 da (Amanda b 23 March 1954, Catherine Lilian Mary b 28 March 1962); m 2, 1971 (m dis 1980), Mrs Hazel Ruth (Sally) Rogers, *née* Thorne; *Career* served WWII 1942-47 Mediterranean; employed by Price Waterhouse Newcastle 1947-54, London 1954-59, ptnr 1959-88; sr ptnr UK 1975-82; chm Price Waterhouse World Firm 1982-; memb Tribunal under Banking Act 1979; Freeman of the City of London, Liveryman Worshipful Co of Chartered Accountants in England and Wales; *Recreations* horticulture, antiques, reading, railways, photography; *Style*— Michael Coates, Esq; 20 Wilton Crescent, London SW1X 8SA (☎ 01 235 4423); Cantray House, Croy, Inverness-shire (☎ 066 78 204); Price Waterhouse World Firm Ltd, Southwark Towers, 32 London Bridge Street, London SE1 9SY (☎ 01 407 8989, fax 01 378 0647, telex 8846587/8)

COATES, Patrick Devereux; s of Hamish Hustler Howard Coates, OBE, (d 1976), of Bexhill-on-Sea, and Frederica Joy, *née* Connor, (d 1962); *b* 30 April 1916; *Educ* Trinity Coll Cambridge (MA); *m* 12 Aug 1946, Mary Eleanor, da of Capt Leveson Gordon Byron Alexander Campbell, DSO, RN, (d 1951) Younger, of Fairfield, Ayr; 1 s (Richard b 1950), 1 da (Elizabeth b 1948); *Career* attached Chinese 22 Div in Burma, (despatches), GSO2 II, and serv Chinese forces in India 1941-44; entered HM Consular Serv 1937, posted to Peking for language study, serv Canton and Kunming 1938-41, acting Chinese sec HM Embassy; Chungking and Nanking 1944-46, first sec FO 1946-50, transferred to Home Civil Serv 1950, asst sec 1955-65; Dept of Econ Affrs, Miny of Housing and Local Govt, DOE 1962-72; retd 1971; hon visiting fell Sch of Oriental and African Studies Univ of London 1973-76, pt/t ed Br Acad of Chinese-language records PRO London 1976-87; *Books* The China Consuls (1988); *Recreations* reading, writing and pottering; *Style*— Patrick Devereaux, Esq

COATES, Roger Frederick; s of Harry Coates, DCM (d 1962), and Grace, *née* Milnes (d 1963); *b* 12 Sept 1937; *Educ* St Peters Sch York, Sheffield Univ (LLB); *m* 11 June 1960, (Patricia) Anne, da of Aubrey Beresford; 2 da (Joanna Louise b 1965, Caroline Amanda b 1969); *Career* slr, sr ptnr Buller Jeffries 1973- (joined 1965-), dep coroner Birmingham 1971-80; member Law Soc 1961; *Recreations* antiques, fine art, photography; *Clubs* The Birmingham; *Style*— Roger Coates, Esq; Buller Jeffries, 48 Temple Street, Birmingham B2 5NL (☎ 021 643 8201)

COATES, William Muir Nelson; s of Victor Airth Coates; *b* 18 June 1934; *Educ* Fettes, Edinburgh Univ; *m* 1959, Christina, *née* MacLeod; 1 s, 1 da; *Career* civil engineer, CEng, MICE; md Curral Lewis and Martin Ltd 1976 (formerly contracts dir); *Style*— William Coates, Esq; Boxmoor, Meer End, Kenilworth, Warwicks (☎ 0676 32038)

COATESWORTH, Lt-Col David; MBE (1943); s of David Coatesworth (d 1971), and Sarah Ann, *née* Beevers (d 1986); *b* 3 Feb 1920; *Educ* Manchester GS, Manchester Univ (BSc, MSc), Grad Army Staff Coll; *m* 2 June 1945, Constance Ellen Mary, da of George Newson (d 1968); 1 s (David Philip Richard b 1949), 1 da (Sarah Ann b 1953); *Career* war serv Royal Signals and Gen Staff, Signal Offr to Gen Montgomery at El Alamein, then Chief Wireless Offr 8 Army HQ; instr ME Staff Sch 1944; regular army until 1962; snr Br offr NATO HQ SE Europe; Brevet Lt-Col 1959; princ Norfolk Coll of Arts and Technol 1965-73, dir of Educn Norfolk 1973-80, chm Cncl for BBC Radio Norfolk 1980-84; memb: Nat Advsy Bd Duke of Edinburgh Award Scheme 1976-80, cncl Nat Academic Awards 1970-73, City and Guilds of London Examinations Bd 1974-77, Technician Educn Cncl 1971-74, Construction Indust Trg Bd 1974-88; vice-chm Broadland Housing Assoc 1986-; past pres Rotary Club of Thorpe St Andrew Norwich; *Recreations* golf, trout fishing; *Style*— Lt-Col David Coatesworth, MBE; 3 Camberley Road, Norwich, Norfolk NR4 6SJ (☎ 0603 52391)

COATS, Sir Alastair Francis Stuart; 4 Bt (UK 1905), of Auchendrane, Maybole, Co Ayr; s of Lt-Col Sir James Coats, 3 Bt, MC (d 1966); *b* 18 Nov 1921; *Educ* Eton; *m* 6 Feb 1947, Lukyn, da of Capt Charles Gordon; 1 s, 1 da; *Heir* s, Alexander Coats; *Career* Capt Coldstream Gds 1939-45; *Style*— Sir Alastair Coats, Bt; Birchwood House, Durford Wood, Petersfield, Hants GU31 5AW (☎ 0730 892254)

COATS, Alexander James; s and h of Sir Alastair Coats, 4 Bt, *qv*; *b* 6 July 1951; *Educ* Eton; *Style*— Alexander Coats, Esq

COATS, David Jervis; CBE (1984); s of The Rev William Holms Coats, DD (d 1954), of Glasgow, and Muriel Gwendoline, *née* Fowler (d 1984); *b* 25 Jan 1924; *Educ* HS of Glasgow, Glasgow Univ (BSc); *m* 24 Mar 1955, Hazel Bell, da of John Livingstone (d 1979), of Glasgow: 1 s (Michael b 1960), 2 da (Gillian b 1956, Pamela b 1958); *Career* REME 1943-47, Maj cmdg Mobile Workshop in India 1947; ptnr Babtie Shaw and Morton 1962-79 (sr ptnr 1979-87, sr conslt 1988-); chm Assoc Consulting Engrs 1979-80, chm Br section Int Commn Large Dams 1980-83 (vice-pres 1983-86), vice-pres Inst Civil Engrs 1987-89; chm Scottish Construction Indust Gp 1986-; chm convenor Glasgow Univ Business Ctee of General Cncl 1982-85, chm Glasgow Univ Tst 1985-; hon DSc Glasgow Univ 1984; FICE, FEng, FRSE; *Recreations* walking, swimming; *Clubs* Caledonian (London), RSAC (Glasgow); *Style*— Dr David Coats, CBE; 7 Kilmardinny Cres, Bearsden, Glasgow G61 3NP (☎ 041 942 2593) Babtie Shaw and Morton, 95 Bothwell St, Glasgow G2 7HX (☎ 041 204 2511, fax 041 226 3109, telex 77202 BABTIEG)

COATS, Hon Lady (Elizabeth Lilian Graham); *née* MacAndrew; da of 1 Baron MacAndrew, TD, PC (d 1979), by his 1 wife Lilian Cathleen, *née* Curran; *b* 23 August 1929; *m* 8 Feb 1950, Sir William David Coats, *qv* 2 s, 1 da; *Style*— The Hon Lady Coats; The Cottage, Symington, Ayrshire

COATS, Lt Cdr James Alexander Pountney; s of Ian P Coats, DL (d 1980), of Carse, Tarbert, Argyll, and Hilda May, *née* Latta; *b* 31 Dec 1927; *Educ* Lockers Park, W Downs, Britannia Naval Coll Dartmouth, RNC Greenwich; *m* 26 Aug 1961, Sarah Margaret, da of Adm Sir Mark Pizey, GBE, CB, DSO, DL, of Burnham on Sea, Somerset; 3 da (Amanda b 1964, Fiona b 1966, Annie b 1969); *Career* Lt Cdr RN: torpedo and anti submarine specialist 1967; ret; hill farmer; hon sec and tres SSAFA Argyll and Bute branch; memb mid Argyll Crime Prevention Panel; *Recreations* trout fishing, pheasant shooting; *Clubs* Royal Naval Argyll; *Style*— Lt Cdr James A P Coats; Gorten, Carse, Tarbert, Argyll PA29 6YB

COATS, Percy Murray; s of Percy Murray Coats (d 1968), and Lizzie Burroughs Blance (d 1980); *b* 8 Jan 1941; *Educ* Highgate, Bishop Vesey's GS Warwickshire, London Univ, St George's Hosp (MB BS, DCH); *m* 20 Sept 1975, Margaret Elisabeth Joan, da of Donald Clarence Ashley; 1 s (Edward b 1980), 3 da (Louise b 1976, Caroline b 1978, Maria b 1981); *Career* Surgn Lt RN 1966-72; Queen Charlotte's and Chelsea Hosp for Women 1973-74, King's Coll Hosp 1974-80, conslt obstetrician and gynaecologist SW Surrey Health Dist 1980-, dist tutor in obstetrics and gynaecology SW Surrey, special professional interest Ultrasound Subfertility; Liveryman Worshipful Soc of Apothecaries; memb: BMA, Euro Assoc of Gynaecologists and Obstetricians, London Obstetrics and Gynaecological Soc; MRCP, FRCS (1974), FRCOG 1988; *publications*: Specialist Medical Papers; *Recreations* fly fishing; *Clubs* Royal Soc of Medicine Carlton; *Style*— Percy M Coats, Esq; Fairacre, Horsham Road, Bramley, Surrey GU5 0AW; Private Consulting Rooms, 8 Waterden Road, Guildford, Surrey (☎ 0483 68286)

COATS, Sir William David; s of Thomas Heywood Coats (d 1958), of Nitshall, Glasgow (nephew of 1 Baron Glentamar), and Olivia Violet, *née* Pitman; *b* 25 July 1924; *Educ* Eton; *m* 8 Feb 1950, Hon Elizabeth Lilian Graham, da of 1 Baron MacAndrew, PC, TD; 2 s, 1 da; *Career* former chm Coats Paton plc; dir Clydesdale Bank, South of Scotland Electricity Bd, Murray Caledonian Investmt Tst, Weir Gp; LLD; kt 1985; *Style*— Sir William Coats; c/o Coats Paton plc, 155 Vincent St, Glasgow, G2 5PA (☎ 041 221 8711)

COBB, Hon Mrs; Hon (Rosamond Stella) Frances; *née* Byng; 4 da of 10 Viscount Torrington (d 1961); *b* 28 Jan 1937; *m* 10 Sept 1960, Antony Brockington Cobb (b 5 April 1927), eldest s of Basil Brockington Cobb, of Merridale, East Wellow, hr Ramsey, Hants; 1 s (Dorian Byng b 1965), 1 da (Michelle Pandora b 1961); *Style*— The Hon Mrs Cobb; Highbury, Lane End, Bembridge, Isle of Wight

COBB, Henry (Harry) Stephen; yst s of Ernest Cobb (d 1945), of Wallasey, and Violet Kate, *née* Sleath (d 1975); *b* 17 Nov 1926; *Educ* Birkenhead Sch, London Univ (BA, MA); *m* 1969, Eileen Margaret, da of Alfred John Downer (d 1964), of London; *Career* clerk of the records House of Lords 1981- (asst clerk 1953-73, dep clerk 1973-81); FSA, FRHistS; *Style*— Harry Cobb, Esq, FSA; 1 Childs Way, London NW11 6XU (☎ 01 458 3688); Record Off, House of Lords, London SW1A 0PW (☎ 01 219 3073)

COBB, Cdr John Martin; RN; s of Richard Martin cobb (d 1966), of Rochester, Kent, and Ursula Joan, *née* Abell; *b* 28 Sept 1931; *Educ* Canford Sch; *m* 25 July 1959, Susan Mary Coeltrane, yst da of Roderick Watson (d 1975), of London; 1 s (James b 1964), 2 da (Mary b 1960, Philippa b 1962); *Career* seaman offr RN 1949-69; served Far East, Aust, Med, W Indies and the Persian Gulf cmdg a landing ship and anti-submarine frigate; dep policy staf MOD 1966-69, retd 1969; private clients dept Sheppards Stock Brokers 1969-88 (dir), dir Marine Adventure Sailing Tst Investmt Tst; memb: S of Ang Agric Soc, tstee Temple Grove Prep Sch Uckfield Sussex, Wealden Cons Assoc; City Liason Gp (former sec); memb: Stock Exchange; *Recreations* skiing, sailing, gardening,music; *Clubs* RN Ski, Itchenor Sailing; *Style*— Cdr John Cobb, RN; No 1 London Bridge, London SE1 9QU (☎ 01 378 7000, fax 01 378 7585)

COBB, Prof Richard Charles; CBE (1978); s of Francis Hills Cobb, Sudan CS, and Dora, *née* Swindale; *b* 20 May 1917; *Educ* Shrewsbury, Merton Coll Oxford; *m* 1963, Margaret Tennant; 4 s, 1 da; *Career* prof of modern history Oxford Univ 1973-84; sr research fell Worcester Coll Oxford 1984-; author; FBA 1967; *Books* Still Life: Sketches from a Tunbridge Wells Childhood (1983); *Style*— Prof Richard Cobb, CBE; Worcester College, Oxford

COBB, Timothy Humphry (Tim); s of Humphry Henry Cobb (d 1949), of Harrow Weald, Middx, and Edith Muriel, *née* Stogdon (d 1948); *b* 4 July 1909; *Educ* Harrow, Magdalene Coll Cambridge (BA, MA); *m* 23 April 1952, Cecilia Mary Josephine (Celia), da of Walter George Chapman (d 1974), of Dorset House London NW1; 2 s (Kenneth b 1954, Martin b 1959), 1 da (Josephine b 1955); *Career* asst master Middx Sch Concord Mass USA 1931-32, asst master Bryanston Sch 1932-47, head master King's Coll Budo Kampala Uganda 1947-58, headmaster Dover Coll Kent 1958-73; sec Uganda Headmasters Assoc; Headmasters Conf 1958-73; *Recreations* music, railways; *Clubs* MCC; *Style*— T H Cobb, Esq; Parkgate Farm, Framlingham, Woodbridge, Suffolk IP13 9JH (☎ 072 875 672)

COBBAN, Sir James (Macdonald); CBE (1971), TD (1950), JP (Berks 1950, Oxon 1974), DL (Berks 1966, Oxon 1974); s of Alexander Macdonald Cobban (d 1956), of Scunthorpe; *b* 14 Sept 1910; *Educ* Pocklington Sch, Jesus Coll Cambridge (MA), Vienna Univ, Pembroke Coll Oxford (MA); *m* 1942, Lorna Mary (d 1961), da of George Stanley Withers Marlow, of Sydenham; 4 da (and 1 decd); *Career* asst master

King Edward VI Sch Southampton 1933-36, classical sixth form master Dulwich Coll 1936-40 and 1946-47; 2 Lt TA (Gen List) 1937, Intelligence Corps 1941, GSO3 Directorate of Mil Intelligence 1941, DAQMG Combined Ops HQ 1943, Staff Offr CCG 1944, Lt-Col 1945; headmaster Abingdon Sch 1947-70; former chm Abingdon Cnty Bench, dep chm Governing Bodies Assoc 1976-82 (hon life memb 1981); former govr: Stowe Sch, Wellington Coll, Campion Sch (Athens), St Helen's Sch, St Stephen's House; former memb Gen Synod Church of England; kt 1982; *Recreations* walking; *Clubs* East India, Public Schools; *Style—* Sir James Cobban, CBE, TD, DL; 14 St Swithin's Close, Sherborne, Dorset DT9 3DW (☎ 0935 812094)

COBBE, Hon Mrs (Isabel Anne Marie Henrietta); eldest da of 20 Viscount Dillon (d 1979); *b* 6 Sept 1942; *m* 1970, Richard Alexander Charles Cobbe; 2 s, 2 da; *Style—* The Hon Mrs Cobbe; The Manor House, Yattendon, nr Newbury, Berks

COBBOLD, Anthony Alan Russell; s of Rowland Hope Cobbold, of Bristol (d 1986), and Mary Selby, *née* Parkin; descended from Robert Cobbold, of Tostock, Suffolk (d 1603), founder of the brewing family; ggs of Sir Harry Parkes, GCMG, KCB (d 1885), envoy extraordinaire and min plen in Japan and China; n of Vice-Adm Sir Charles Hughes Hallett, KCB, CBE (d 1985); *b* 15 Mar 1935; *Educ* Marlborough, Gonville and Caius Coll Cambridge (BA); *m* 1, 15 Aug 1959, Margaret Elizabeth, da of Prof J W Cecil Turner, (d 1968) of Cambridge; 3 s (Timothy b 1962, Humphrey b 1964, Jeremy b 1969); m 2, 25 April 1974, Jillianne Bridget, formerly wife of Capt Martin J Minter-Kemp, and da of Lt-Col Denis Lucius Alban Gibbs, DSO (d 1984), of Tavistock, Devon; 1 steps (Robin b 1963), 2 stepda (Emma b 1960, Claire b (twin) 1963); *Career* Lt Duke of Edinburgh's Royal regt 1953-55; w & T avery Ltd 1958-66, W D & H O Wills 1966-71, Evade Gp plc 1971-87, chief exec Regnl Bldg Centres Ltd 1988-; dir: Evade Roofing Ltd 1973-87, Evade Jt Sealing 1973-87, Evade Gp plc 1980-87, Tekurat Insulations Ltd 1980-87, Bldg Centre Gp Ltd 1985-88, Br Roof Mart Ltd 1986-87, Bldg Centre Tst 1986-; *Recreations* genealogy, woodland mgmnt; *Clubs* IOD; *Style—* Anthony Cobbold, Esq; The Vineyard, Weston under Redcastle, Shrewsbury SY4 5JY (☎ 063084 344, fax: 063084 506)

COBBOLD, 2 Baron (UK 1960), of Knebworth, Co Hertford; David Antony Fromanteel Lytton Cobbold; er s of 1 Baron Cobbold, KG, GCVO, PC (d 1987); assumed by Deed Poll 1960 the additional surname of Lytton before his patronymic; *b* 14 July 1937; *Educ* Eton, Trinity Coll Cambridge (BA); *m* 7 Jan 1961, Christine Elizabeth, 3 da of Maj Sir Dennis Frederick Bankes Stucley, 5 Bt (d 1983); 3 s (Hon Henry Fromanteel, Hon Peter Guy Fromanteel b 1964, Hon Richard Stucley Fromanteel b 1968, a Page of Honour to HM The Queen 1980-82), 1 da (Hon Rosina Kim b 1971); *Heir* s, Hon Henry Fromanteel Lytton Cobbold, b 12 May 1962; *Career* served in RAF 1955-57; Bank of London and S America 1962-72; Finance for Industry 1974-79; British Petroleum 1979-87; TSB England and Wales plc 1987-; dir Hill Samuel Bank Ltd 1988-; fell Assoc of Corporate Treasurers 1983; hon tres Historic Houses Assoc 1988-; *Style—* The Hon Lord Cobbold; Knebworth House, Knebworth, Herts

COBBOLD, (Michael) David Nevill; CBE (1983), DL (Gtr London); s of Geoffrey Wyndham Nevill Cobbold (d 1980), and Cicely Helen, *née* Middleton (d 1969); *b* 21 Oct 1919; *Educ* Charterhouse, Oxford Univ (MA); *m* 1949, Ann Rosemary, da of John Christopher Trevor (d 1960); 3 s (Charles-decd, Richard, Christopher), 1 da (Gillian); *Career* Maj The Buffs; slr; ptnr Stileman Neate and Topping 1949-83, conslt Messrs Beachcrofts 1983-; memb Westminster City Cncl 1949-86 (ldr 1964-65 and 1977-83), Mayor 1958-59, Lord Mayor 1973-74, chm Soc Responsibility Ctee for the London Episcopal Area 1988-; *Recreations* gardening, architecture; *Clubs* Wig and Pen; *Style—* David Cobbold, Esq, CBE, DL; 31 Ashley Ct, Morpeth Terrace, London SW1P 1EN (☎ 01 834 5020); Beachcroft Stanleys, 100 Fetter Lane, London EC4A 1BN (☎ 01 242 1011, telex 264607 BEALAW G)

COBBOLD, Baroness; Lady (Margaret) Hermione Millicent; *née* Lytton; da of 2 Earl of Lytton, KG, GCSI, GCIE, PC (d 1947); *b* 31 August 1905; *m* 3 April 1930, Cameron Fromanteel, 1 Baron Cobbold, KG, GCVO, PC; 2 s, 1 da (and 1 da decd); *Style—* The Rt Hon the Lady Cobbold; Lake House, Knebworth, Herts (☎ 0438 812310)

COBBOLD, Patrick Mark; s of Ivan Murray Cobbold (d 1944), of Glemham Hall, Woodbridge, Suffolk, and Lady Blanche Katharine, *née* Cavendish (d 1987), da of 9 Duke of Devonshire; *b* 20 June 1934; *Educ* Eton; *Career* short serv cmmn Scots Gds 1952-55; ADC Govr of the Bahamas 1957-60; non exec dir Tollemache & Cobbold Breweries Ltd; chm Ipswich Town FC; *Recreations* fishing, shooting; *Clubs* Whites, Pratts; *Style—* Patrick Cobbold, Esq; Glemham Hall, Woodbridge, Suffolk (☎ 0728 746219)

COBBOLD, Hon Rowland John Fromanteel; yr s of 1 Baron Cobbold, KG, GCVO, PC; *b* 20 June 1944; *Educ* Eton, Trinity Coll Cambridge (MA); *m* 3 June 1969, Sophia Augusta, da of the late B N White-Spunner, 1 s, 1 da; *Career* Lt Kent and County of London Yeo (TA); with BOAC/British Airways 1966-80; joined Cathay Pacific Airways 1980: gen mangr (Europe) 1981-85 Mktg 1985-86 dir Bd and Mktg 1987; *Clubs* Brooks's, RAC, Hong Kong, Shek-O; *Style—* The Hon Rowland Cobbold; Cathay Pacific Airways Ltd, Swire House, Hong Kong (☎ 5 8425100); 6 Deep Water Bay Road, Hong Kong; Lower Town Farmhouse, Clifton Hampden, Oxon

COBHAM, Baroness - Christina Jean; da of Albert Edward Honeybone; *b* 27 Sept 1887; *m* 1923 (m dis 1934, remarried 1949), 16 Baron Cobham (d 21 Feb 1951, when title went into abeyance); *Style—* The Rt Hon Lady Cobham; 246 Metella Rd, Prospect, NSW 2149, Australia

COBHAM, 11 Viscount (GB 1718); Sir John William Leonard Lyttelton; 14 Bt (E 1618); also Baron Cobham (GB 1718), Lord Lyttelton, Baron of Frankley (1756, renewed 1794), and Baron Westcote of Ballymore (I 1776); s of 10 Viscount, KG, PC, GCMG, GCVO, TD (d 1977); *b* 5 June 1943; *Educ* Eton, Christ's Coll New Zealand, RAC Cirencester; *m* 1974, Penelope Ann, eldest da of late Roy Cooper, of Moss Farm, Ollerton, nr Knutsford, Cheshire; *Heir* bro, Hon Christopher Lyttelton; *Career* ptnr Hagley Hall Farms 1976-; *Style—* The Rt Hon the Viscount Cobham; Hagley Hall, Stourbridge, W Midlands DY9 9LG (☎ 0562 885823); 20 Kylestrome House, Cundy St, Ebury St, London SW1 (☎ 01 730 5756)

COBHAM, Michael John; CBE (1981); s of Sir Alan John Cobham, KBE, AFC (d 1973), and Gladys Marie, *née* Lloyd (d 1961); *b* 22 Feb 1927; *Educ* Malvern, Trinity Coll Camb (BA, MA); *m* 1, 1954 (m dis 1972), June Oakes; m 2, 1973, Nadine Felicity, da of William Abbott, of Wimborne, Dorset; 1 da; *Career* chm and chief exec FR Group plc; chm: Flight Refuelling Ltd, Alan Cobham Engrg Ltd, Stanley Aviation Corp (Denver, USA), Hymatic Engineering Co Ltd, FR Aviation Ltd, WES Gp Ltd, Carleton Technologies Inc (Buffalo NY, USA); FRAeS, CBIM; *Recreations* sailing and skiing; *Clubs* Royal Thames Yacht, Royal Southern YC, Naval and Military; *Style—* Michael Cobham Esq, CBE; c/o FR Group plc, Wimborne, Dorset (☎ 0202 882121)

COBURN, Alfred Henry (Mick); CBE (1979); s of Alfred George Coburn (d 1977); *b* 12 Feb 1922; *Educ* Sidcup GS; *m* 1, 1944, Betty Winifred (d 1981), da of F/Lt Percy Robinson (d 1960); 2 da; m 2, 1984, Mary Vera, da of Harold Thomas Read; *Career* md Findus Ltd 1965-83, chm Findus UK Ltd (Hldg Co) to 1983, md Chambourcy Food Products Ltd 1973-83, dir The Nestle Co (UK) Ltd (Hldg Co) to 1983; chm Britfish 1959-69; past pres UK Assoc Frozen Food Producers; FRSA, FIGD; *Recreations* golf, horse racing, travel; *Clubs* Wellington, RAC; *Style—* Mick Coburn, Esq, CBE; Goodwood, Burnhams Rd, Bookham, Surrey KT23 3BB (☎ 0372 52970)

COCHRANE, (Alexander John) Cameron; MBE (1987); s of late Dr Alexander Younger Cochrane, of Edinburgh; *b* 19 July 1933; *Educ* The Edinburgh Acad, Univ Coll Oxford (MA); *m* 1958, Rosemary Aline, da of Robert Alexander Ogg (d 1974); 1 s (David), 2 da (Fiona, Sandra); *Career* asst master St Edward's Sch Oxford 1957-66, warden Brathay Hall Cumbria 1966-70, asst dir City of Edinburgh Educn Dept 1970-74; headmaster: Arnold Sch Blackpool 1974-79, Fettes Coll Edinburgh 1979-88; princ Prince-Willem-Alexander Coll The Netherlands 1988; *Recreations* games, mountains, music, people; *Clubs* Public Schools, New (Edinburgh), MCC; *Style—* Cameron Cochrane, Esq, MBE; Gravenallee 22, 7591 Pe Denekamp, The Netherlands (☎ home 05413 4485, office 05413 3485)

COCHRANE, (Alexander John) Cameron; MBE (1967); s of Alexander Younger Cochrane (d 1988), of Edinburgh, and Jenny Johnstonne, *née* Morris; *b* 19 July 1933; *Educ* Edinburgh Acad, Univk Coll Oxford (MA); *m* 14 Aug 1958, Rosemary Aline, da of Robert Alexander Ogg (d 1974), of Glasgow; 1 s (David Alexander Cameron b 1968), 2 da (Fiona b 1961, Sandy (Mrs Gamba) b 1964); *Career* Nat Serv 2 Lt RA 1952-54; Maj CCF St Edwards Sch 1957-66, Maj ACF Cumberland and Westmorland 1966-69; asst master St Edwards Sch Oxford 1957-66, warden Brathay Hall Ambleside Cumbria 1966-70, asst dir of educn City of Edinburgh 1970-74; headmaster: Arnold Sch Blackpool 1974-79, Fettes Coll Edinburgh 1979-88; princ Prince Willem-Alexander Coll The Netherlands 1988-; hon fell dept of educational studies Edinburgh Univ 1973-74, co-opted memb Lancs Educn Ctee 1976-79; chm of govrs: Ullswater Outward Bound Sch 1979-84, Loch Eil Outward Bound Sch 1984-88; chm: Lothian Fedn of Boys' Clubs 1981-84 (vice pres 1987), HMC servs sub-ctee Inter-Service Ctee 1982-88; cmdt XIII Cwlth Games Athletes' Village Edinburgh 1986; memb: Outward Bound Tst Cncl 1979-88, advsy ctee Duke of Edinburgh's Award 1982-87; elder Church of Scotland 1972-; MBIM 1987; *Recreations* games, mountains, beaches, music; *Clubs* Public Schools, MCC, Vincent's (Oxford), New (Edinburgh); *Style—* Cameraon Cochrane, Esq, MBE; Gravenallee22, 7591 Pe Denekamp, The Netherlands; Fersit House, Roy Bridge, Iverness-shire; Prince Willem-Alexander College, Gravenallee 11, 7591 Pe Denekamp, The Netherlands (☎ 010 31 05413 3485, fax 431 53 338705)

COCHRANE, Ian Andrew; s of Lt-Col W A Cochrane, of Haxby, York, and Rebecca Cochrane, *née* Segal; *b* 8 Feb 1951; *Educ* Bramcote Hall Prep Notts; Archibishop Holgates GS York; Manchester Univ (BSc, Physics) 1973; *m* 3 Aug 1974, Jennifer Wilna, da of Donald Edward Crisp (d 1983); 3 s (Mark b 1980, James b 1982, Adam b 1984); *Career* CA, Arthur Andersen 1973-78; md Fitch and Co Design Consultants plc 1981-87; FCA 1976; *Recreations* motor racing; *Clubs* Ferarri Owners, Oronettos; *Style—* Ian Cochrane, Esq; 4-6 Soho Square, London W1 (☎ 01 927 6413)

COCHRANE, Hon (John Douglas) Julian; 3 s of late 2 Baron Cochrane; *b* 12 June 1929; *Educ* Eton; *m* 25 Nov 1965, Vaila Rose, yr da of Cdr Robert Dalby, RN (ret), of Castle Donington, Leics; 1 s, 2 da; *Style—* The Hon Julian Cochrane; Townend House, Hopton, Derbys

COCHRANE, Sir (Henry) Marc (Sursock); 4 Bt (UK 1903); s of Sir Desmond Oriel Alastair George Weston Cochrane, 3 Bt (d 1979); *b* 23 Oct 1946; *Educ* Eton, Trinity Coll Dublin (BBS, MA); *m* 28 June 1969, Hala, 2 da of Fuad Mahmoud Bey es-Said, of Beirut; 2 s, 1 da; *Heir* s, Alexander Desmond Sursock Cochrane b 7 May 1973; *Career* hon consul gen for Ireland in Lebanon 1979-84; dir: Hambros Bank Ltd 1979-85, GT Management (UK) Ltd, 1985-; *Recreations* electronics, skiing, shooting; *Clubs* Annabel's; *Style—* Sir Marc Cochrane, Bt; Woodbrook, Bray, Co Wicklow, Eire (☎ 821421); Palais Sursock, Beirut, Lebanon (☎ 331607 334663)

COCHRANE, Lady Tanya Jean Farquhar; da (by 1 m) of 14 Earl of Dundonald; *b* 9 July 1964; *Educ* Benenden; *Style—* Lady Tanya Cochrane; 7 Campana Road, London SW6

COCHRANE, Hon (Ralph Henry) Vere; DL (Fife); s of 2 Baron Cochrane of Cults, DSO (d 1968) by 1 w, Hon Elin, *née* Douglas-Pennant (d 1934), da of 2 Baron Penrhyn; hp of bro, 3 Baron; *b* 20 Sept 1926; *Educ* Eton, King's Coll Cambridge (MA); *m* 18 Dec 1956, Janet Mary Watson, da of Dr William Hunter Watson Cheyne MB, MRCS, LRCP (d 1957); 2 s; *Heir* Thomas Hunter Vere C. b 1957; *Career* Lt RE Germany; farmer; gen cmmr of Income Tax, chm Craigtoun Meadows Ltd; underwriting memb Lloyd's 1965; memb Queen's Body Guard for Scotland (Royal Co of Archers); *Recreations* skiing; *Clubs* New (Edinburgh); *Style—* The Hon Vere Cochrane; Cults, Cupar, Fife KY15 5RD

COCHRANE OF CULTS, 3 Baron (UK 1919); Thomas Charles Anthony Cochrane; s of 2 Baron (d 1968, gs of 11 Earl of Dundonald through his father and gs of 6 Earl of Glasgow through his mother) by his 1 w Hon Elin Douglas-Pennant (da of 2 Baron Penrhyn); *b* 31 Oct 1922; *Educ* privately; *Heir* bro, Hon Vere Cochrane; *Career* fndr and tstee Gardeners' Meml Tst; *Style—* The Rt Hon the Lord Cochrane of Cults; Turret House, Crawford Priory Estate, nr Cupar, Fife; East Craigard, East Church Street, Buckie, Banffshire AB5 1LR

COCKBURN, (John) Alasdair Murray; s of James Ronald Murray Cockburn, of Westcroft, Knockbuckle Rd, Kilmacolm, and Evelyn Marguerite, *née* Mathieson; *b* 10 July 1946; *Educ* Glenalmond Coll, Aberdeen Univ (LLB); *m* 19 April 1976, Carole Agnes, da of Karl Godfrey Mohr (d 1972), of Bramhall, Cheshire; 1 s (Iain b 1980), 1 da (Gail b 1977); *Career* CA, ptnr Coopers & Lybrand; *Recreations* golf, sailing; *Clubs* Caledonian; *Style—* Alasdair Cockburn, Esq; Catherton, 5 Pine Ridge Dr, Lower Bourne, Farnham, Surrey (☎ 0252 715529); Plumtree Ct, London (☎ 01 583 5000)

COCKBURN, Charles Christopher; s and h of Sir John Eliot Cockburn, 12 Bt, of 48 Frewin Road, Wandsworth Common, London SW18, and Glory Patricia Cockburn, *née* Mullings; *b* 19 Nov 1950; *Educ* Emanuel Sch, City of London Poly (BA), Garnett Coll; *m* 1, 1978, Beverly J, o da of B Stangroom, of Richmond, Surrey; m 2, 1985,

Margaret Ruth, da of Samuel Esmond Bell, of 18 Portland Drive, Bury Green, Cheshunt, Herts; 1 s (Christopher Samuel Alexander b 24 March 1986), 1 da (Charlotte Elspeth Catherine b (twin) 24 March 1986); *Career* lectr; conslt in government relations; ed Fin Regulation Review; *Recreations* rowing, cycling, song writing, travelling; *Clubs* Twickenham Rowing; *Style*— Charles Cockburn, Esq; 4 Connaught Rd, Teddington, Middlesex TW11 0PS; DC Gardner and Co Ltd, 5-9 New Street, London EC2M 4TP (☎ 01 283 7962)

COCKBURN, Prof Forrester; s of Forrester Cockburn, and Violet Elizabeth, *née* Bunce; *b* 13 Oct 1934; *Educ* Leith Acad, Univ of Edinburgh (MB, ChB, MD); *m* 15 Jan 1960, Alison Fisher, da of Roger Lindsay Grieve; 2 s (David, John); *Career* Huntington - Hartford res fell Univ of Boston USA 1963-65, Nuffield sr res fell Univ of Oxford 1965-66, Wellcome sr res fell Univ of Edinburgh 1966-71, sr lectr dept of child life and health Univ of Edinburgh 1971-77, Samson Gemmell prof of Child health Royal Hosp for Sick Children Glasgow 1977-; *Books* Neonatal Medicine (with Drillien, 1974), Practical Paediatric Problems (with Hutchinson, sixth edn 1986), Craig's Care of the Newly Born Infant (with Turner and Douglas, 1988), Fetal and Neonatal Growth (1988); *Recreations* sailing; *Style*— Prof Forrester Cockburn; 53 Hamilton Dr, Glasgow G12 8DP (☎ 041 339 2973); Dept of Child Health, Royal Hosp for Sick Children, Yorkhill, Glasgow G3 8SJ (☎ 041 339 8888, ext 375)

COCKBURN, (George) Ian (Macloy); s of George William Macloy Cockburn, of 42 Anglesey Ct Rd, Carshalton Beeches, Surrey, and Jean Violet Cockburn; *b* 8 June 1945; *Educ* Pangbourne Coll Berks; *m* 10 June 1967, Joanna Mary, da of Paul Wallace Gibson, of Heath Antiques, 15 Flanchford Rd, Reigate, Surrey; 2 s (Mark b 13 Sept 1969, Ben b 25 Sept 1971), 1 da (Alexandra b 28 Feb 1975); *Career* chartered surveyor, property investmt dir Electricity Supply Pension Scheme; ARICS 1984; *Recreations* sport (watching and playing), music, wine; *Clubs* MCC; *Style*— Ian Cockburn, Esq; 20 Brokes Crescent, Reigate, Surrey RH2 9PS (☎ 0737 243 827); Electricity Supply Pension Scheme, 30 Millbank, London SW1P 4RD (☎ 01 834 2333, 01 828 8922)

COCKBURN, James Angus; s of Carleton Varty Cockburn, of 11 Craigmillar Ave, Milngavie, Glasgow, and Margaret Cockburn, *née* Robertson; *b* 6 Dec 1939; *Educ* George Heriots Hosp, Edinburgh Univ Sch of Arch; *m* 1 Aug 1964, Shirley Elizabeth, da of Walter Ronald Brotherstone (d 1967); 4 s (Christopher Dean b 1966, Jonathan James b 1968, Nicholas Carl b 1970, Jason Angus b 1972); *Career* chartered arch: Mowlem (Scotland) Ltd 1966-68, Lyon Gp (Scotland Ltd 1968-71; ptnr Robin Claton Ptnrship 1971-74; princ Cockburn Assocs 1974-; Major City Centre Devpts Scotland, Urban Renewal Projects; md Berkeley Estates (Scotland) Ltd; *Recreations* travel, sailing, skiing, fishing, swimming, golf, bridge, theatre; *Clubs* Merchants House, W of Scotland RF, Bearsden Ski, Chamber of Commerce, Douglas Park GC; *Style*— James Cockburn, Esq; Craigallander, 35 Craigmillar Ave, Milngavie, Glasgow (☎ 041 956 5167); Trinity House, Lynedoch St, Glasgow G3 6AB (☎ 041 248 3754, car tel 0836 664353)

COCKBURN, Sir John Elliot Cockburn; 12 Bt of that Ilk (NS 1671); s of Lt-Col Sir John Cockburn, 11 Bt, DSO (d 1949), and Isabel Hunter, *née* McQueen (d 1978); *b* 7 Dec 1925; *Educ* RNC Dartmouth, RAC Cirencester; *m* 7 Sept 1949, Glory Patricia, er da of late Nigel Tudway Mullings, of Sea Spray, The Lizard, Corwall; 3 s, 2 da; *Heir* s, Charles Cockburn; *Career* md Cellar Management Ltd; *Style*— Sir John Cockburn, Bt; 48 Frewin Rd, SW18

COCKBURN, Sir Robert; KBE (1960, OBE 1946), CB (1953); 2 s of late Rev Robert Tough Cockburn, of Columba Manse, Belford, Northumberland; *b* 31 Mar 1909; *Educ* Southern Secondary Sch, Municipal Coll Portsmouth, London Univ (MSc PhD), Cambridge Univ (MA); *m* 1935, Phyllis, da of late Frederick Hoyland; 2 da; *Career* scientific advsr to Air Miny 1948-53, chief scientist Miny of Aviation 1959-64, dir RAE Farnborough 1964-69, chm National Computing Centre 1970-77, sr res fell Churchill Coll Cambridge 1970-77; US Medal for Merit; FEng, Hon FRAeS, FIEE, FInst; *Style*— Sir Robert Cockburn, KBE, CB; 1 Firethorn Close, Longmead, Fleet, Hants GU13 9TR (☎ 0252 615518)

COCKBURN, William; TD (1980); s of Edward Cockburn (d 1986), of Edinburgh, and Alice, *née* Brennan (d 1983); *b* 28 Feb 1943; *Educ* Holy Cross Acad Edinburgh (Dip); *m* 25 Jul 1970, Susan Elisabeth, da of Maj William Phillpots, MBE; 2 da (Rachel b 1974, Rebecca b 1977); *Career* TA RE Postal and Courier Serv 1968, appt Col 1986; Post Off: joined Glasgow 1961, PA to chm 1971-73, asst dir of fin and planning 1973-77, dir of central planning 1977-78, dir postal fin 1978-79, dir London postal regn 1979-82, memb PO Bd 1981, memb for fin counter servs and planning 1982-84, memb for Royal Mail ops 1984-86, md Royal Mail Letters 1986-; non-exec dir VAT Watkins Hldgs Ltd 1985-; Freeman City of London 1980; *Style*— William Cockburn, Esq, TD; Post Office Headquarters, 33 Grosvenor Place, London SW1X 1PX (☎ 01 235 8000)

COCKBURN-CAMPBELL, Alexander Thomas; s and h of Sir Thomas Cockburn-Campbell, 6 Bt; *b* 16 Mar 1945; *m* 1969, Kerry Anne, eldest da of Sgt K Johnson; 1 s (Thomas Justin b 10 Feb 1974), 1 da (Felicity Anne b 9 June 1981); *Style*— Alexander Cockburn-Campbell, Esq; 29 Champlin Way, Ferndale 6155, W Australia

COCKBURN-CAMPBELL, Sir Thomas; 6 Bt (UK 1821), of Gartsford, Ross-shire; s of Sir Alexander Thomas Cockburn-Campbell, 5 Bt (d 1935), and Maude Frances Lorenzo, *née* Giles (d 1926); *b* 8 Dec 1918; *Educ* C of E GS Melbourne, Victoria, Aust.; *m* 1, 24 June 1944 (m dis 1981), (Josephine) Zoi, eldest da of Harold Douglas Forward, of Cunjardine, W Australia; 1 s (Alexander); m 2, 1982, Janice Laraine, da of William John Pascoe, of 2 Sutton Court, Bundoora 3038 Victoria, Australia; *Heir* s, Alexander Thomas Cockburn-Campbell; *Career* pastoralist, publican, nursery owner, now ret; landowner (4 acres); *Recreations* antique collecting, reading, writing (Autobiography); *Style*— Sir Thomas Cockburn-Campbell, Bt; Gartsford Cottage, 14 Lincoln St, York 6302, Western Australia

COCKCROFT, Maj (Jon) Barnaby Briggs; s of Maj Eric Briggs Cockcroft (d 1977), of Bryn Dinarth, Colwyn Bay, and Olive Mary, *née* Brown; *b* 27 August 1936; *Educ* Sherborne, RMA Sandhurst, Staff Coll Camberley; *m* 4 Oct 1960, Audrey Mary, da of Lt-Col Robert Charles Henry Kidd, OBE (d 1970), of Moat House, Fincham, Norfolk; 1 s (Capt Rupert b 1963), 1 da (Laura b 1967); *Career* Maj WG: served Aden 1965-66, NI 1973, Hong Kong 1979-81, ret 1983; HM Body Guard Hon Corps of Gentlemen-At-Arms 1987-; sec City of London TAVRA 1985-, underwriting memb Lloyds 1985-; Freeman City of London; *Recreations* gardening, shooting; *Clubs* Lansdowne, Army Rugby FC; *Style*— Maj Barnaby Cockcroft; Holt End House, Ashford Hill, Newbury, Berks (☎ 07356 3727); Duke of Yorks HQ, Chelsea, London SW3 4RY (☎ 01 730 8131)

COCKCROFT, Dr Frank; s of Ernest Edward Cockcroft (d 1963), of Luddendenfoot, Yorks, and Edith, *née* Thompson, MBE (d 1975); *b* 4 Oct 1918; *Educ* Bridlington Sch, Cambridge Univ (MA), Middx Hosp (LRCP, MRCS), Sch of Hygiene and Tropical Medicine (DPH); *m* 6 July 1945, Doris Mary, da of Samuel Sinclair (d 1975), of Belfast; 1 s (Michael b 1947), 4 da (Felicity b 1949 (d 1960), Zoe b 1954 (d 1982), Nicole b 1959, Avril b 1962); *Career* Surgn Lt RNVR 1943-46, med offr Health Glossop 1949-51, Littlehampton and Worthing 1951-79, dir Fairlea Mill Co Walsden 1974, med referee Worthing Crematorium 1979; *Recreations* golf, tennis, bridge; *Style*— Dr Frank Cockcroft; Thatchings, 28 Bushby Avenue, Rustington, Sussex BN16 2BY (☎ 0903 783644)

COCKCROFT, John Hoyle; s of Lionel Fielden Cockcroft, of Todmordern Yorks, and Jenny Hoyle; nephew of Sir John Cockcroft (d 1967), who was winner of Nobel prize for physics 1951 and first master of Churchill Coll Cambridge; *b* 6 July 1934; *Educ* Oundle, St John's Coll Cambridge (MA); *m* 1971, Tessa Fay, da of Dr William Shepley (d 1968); 3 da (Lucia b 1972, Gemma b 1974, Eloise b 1978); *Career* electronics economist; feature writer and investmt analyst financial The Times 1959-61, economist and analyst (acquisitions) GKN 1962-67, seconded to Treasy public enterprise div 1965-66, econ leader writer Daily Telegraph 1967-74, historian and conslt Guest Keen and Nettlefolds 1971-76; MP(Cons) Nantwich 1974-79, memb select ctee on Nationalised Industs (tport) 1975-79, Co Secretaries Bill (private memb) 1978-79; Parly conslt: Br Field Sports Soc 1975-76, ICS 1977-79; dir: RSJ Aviation (aircraft brokers) 1979-, Spalding Securities (investmt advsrs) 1982-, Communications Educnl Servs 1983-, BR (eastern region bd) 1984-89, BR Anglia bd 1987-89, Innovare (electronics) 1986-; conslt: Datsun (Nissan) UK 1980-81, Cray Electronics 1982-84, Wedgwood 1983-84, Crystalate Hldgs 1984-87, Camden Assocs (political PR) 1984-88; electronics economist and conslt stockbroking Laurence Prust Corporate Fin 1986-; columnist and contributor: Microscope 1982-, Banking World 1984-, Electronics Times 1985-; *Publications* Reforming the Constitution (jtly 1968), Self-Help Reborn (jtly 1969), Why England Sleeps (1971), Internal History of Guest Keen and Nettlefolds (jtly 1976), Microelectronics (second ed 1983), Microtechnology in Banking (1984); *Recreations* reading, writing, walking, entertaining; *Clubs* Europe House, IOD, Cannon's, Cambridge Union; *Style*— John Cockcroft, Esq; Mitchell's Farmhouse, Stapleford Tawney, Essex RM4 1SS (☎ 04028 254); 27 Finsbury Square, London EC2A 1LP (☎ 01 628 1111)

COCKCROFT, Sir Wilfred Halliday; s of Wilfred Cockcroft (d 1958), of Keighley, Yorks, and Bessie, *née* Halliday; *b* 7 June 1923; *Educ* Keighley Boys' GS, Balliol Coll Oxford (MA, DPhil); *m* 1, 1949, Barbara Rhona Huggan (d 1982); 2 s; m 2, 1982, Vivien, da of David Lloyd, of Warmington; *Career* prof of pure mathematics Hull Univ 1961-73, vice-chllr New Univ of Ulster 1976-82, chm Secondary Examination Cncl 1983-89; FRSA; FIMA; kt 1982; *Clubs* Athenaeum; *Style*— Sir Wilfred Cockcroft; The Old Rectory, Warmington OX17 1BU

COCKERAM, Eric Paul; JP (City of Liverpool 1960); er s of John Winter Cockeram (d 1977), of Birkenhead, Cheshire, and Mildred Edith, *née* O'Neill (d 1969); *b* 4 July 1924; *Educ* The Leys Sch Cambridge; *m* 2 July 1949, Frances Gertrude, da of Herbert Irving (d 1970), of Birkenhead; 2 s (Howard b 1950, James b (twin) 1955), 2 da (Susan b 1952, Julia b (twin) 1955); *Career* served 1942-46, Capt Gloucestershire Regt, D-Day landings (wounded 2); MP (C) Bebington 1970-Feb 1974, Ludlow 1979-87; former pps to: chllr of the Exchequer, min Industry, min Posts and Telecommunications; chm Watson Prickard Ltd; dir: TSB (NW) Ltd, Midshires Building Soc; memb Lloyds; Liveryman and memb of Ct Worshipful Co of Glovers: Freeman City of London, freeman City of Springfield (Illinois) USA; *Recreations* shooting, golf, bridge; *Clubs* Carlton; *Style*— Eric Cockeram, Esq, JP; Fairway Lodge, Links Hey Road, Caldy, Wirral L48 1NB (☎ 051 625 1100); Watson Prickard Ltd, North John Street, Liverpool L2 4SH (☎ 051 236 8841)

COCKERELL, Sir Christopher Sydney; CBE (1966); s of Sir Sydney Cockerell (d 1962), and Florence Kate, *née* Kingsford (d 1949); *b* 4 June 1910; *Educ* Gresham's, Peterhouse Cambridge (MA); *m* 1937, Margaret Elinor, da of John Horace Belsham (d 1947); 2 da; *Career* inventor of the hovercraft; pupil W H Allen's 1931-33; in charge of aircraft navigational and communications equipment Marconi's 1935-51 (filed 36 patents); started boat-building business on the Broads 1950 (chm Ripplecraft Co Ltd 1950-79); commenced work on hovercraft 1953, experimental craft operated crossing Channel 1959 (filed 56 patents), former dir and conslt Hovercraft Devpt Ltd; commenced work on extraction of power from sea waves 1972 (filed 3 patents), formed Wavepower Ltd 1974 (chm 1974-82); Royal Medal Royal Soc 1986, Inst of Mech Engrs James Watt Int Gold Medal 1983; Hon Doctorate RCA 1968; Hon DSc: Leicester 1967, Heriot-Watt 1971, London 1975; FRS 1967, RDI 1987; kt 1969; *Recreations* fishing, gardening, the visual arts; *Style*— Sir Christopher Cockerell, CBE, RDI, FRS; 16 Prospect Place, Hythe, Hants SO4 6AU (☎ 0703 842931)

COCKETT, Geoffrey Howard; s of William Cockett (d 1970), of Southampton, and Edith Gertrude, *née* Dinham (d 1957); *b* 18 Mar 1926; *Educ* King Edward VI Sch Southampton, Univ of Southampton (BSc); *m* 1951, Elizabeth Mary Florence, da of Stanley Frederick Bagshaw (d 1970), of Orpington; 2 da (Juliet, Jenny-Sarah); *Career* chartered physicist; res scientist: Royal Aircraft Establishment 1948-52, Armament Res Establishment 1952-68, Supt Physics Res Chem Def Establishment 1968-71; supt Optics and Surveillance System RARDE 1971-76; head Applied Physics Gp 1976-83; dep dir (Systems) and chief scientific offr RARDE 1983-; FInstP; *Recreations* opera, photography, under gardening; *Style*— Geoffrey Cockett, Esq; Rarde, Fort Halstead, Sevenoaks, Kent TN14 7BP

COCKFIELD, Baron (Life Peer UK 1978); (Francis) Arthur Cockfield; PC (1982); 2 s of Lt C F Cockfield (ka 1916), and Louisa, *née* James; *b* 28 Sept 1916; *Educ* Dover GS, LSE; *m* Aileen Monica Mudie, choreographer; *Career* barr 1942, former fin dir and chief exec Boots Pure Drug Co Ltd, dir of statistics and intelligence Bd of Inland Revenue 1944; Cmmn of Inland Revenue 1951; pres Royal Statistical Soc 1968; advisor on Fiscal Policy to Chllr of Exchequer 1970-73; chm Price Cmmn 1973-77; min of state Treasy 1979-82, sec state Trade 1982-83, Pres BOT; chllr Duchy of Lancaster 1983-; vice-pres Comm of European Communities 1985-; kt 1973; *Style*— The Rt Hon The Lord Cockfield, PC; House of Lords, Westminster, London SW1

COCKING, Maurice Douglas; s of Cecil Maurice Cocking (d 1967) of Hastings and Amelia *née* Shorter (d 1972); *b* 28 Oct 1930; *Educ* Beckenham GS, Exeter Univ (BA), London Univ (BSc); *m* 11 Sept 1954, Patricia da of James Charles Fowler (d 1966) of

Sevenoaks, 2 s (Crispian b 1961, Kester b 1962); *Career* Nat Serv BAOR 1949-51; fin journalist 1955; city ed: Empire News 1958, Daily Sketch 1964: fndr and chm FABUS Fin and Business PR Ltd 1967, fin journalist Sunday Times and Daily Express; Liveryman Worshipful Co: of Basketmakers (steward), of Tallow Chandlers; *Recreations* verse, oenology, equestrianism; *Clubs* City Livery, IOD, Farringdon Ward and Utd Wards Pickwick; *Style—* Maurice Cocking, Esq; Hind Court, 147 Fleet St, London (☎ 01 583 0265)

COCKRAM, Sir John; s of Alfred John Cockram (d 1956), of Highgate, and Beatrice Elizabeth Cockram; *b* 10 July 1908; *Educ* St Aloysius Coll Highgate; *m* 1937, Phyllis Eleanor, o da of Albert Henning, of Loughton, Essex; 1 s, 2 da; *Career* former gen mangr and dir Colne Valley Water Co; dir and chm Rickmansworth and Uxbridge Valley Water Co; memb: exec ctee Br Waterworks Ctee 1948-74 (pres 1957-58, memb Central advsy ctee 1955-74), Thames Conservancy 1954-74; life govr Haileybury; FCA; kt 1964; *Style—* Sir John Cockram; Rebels' Corner, The Common, Chorleywood, Rickmansworth, Herts WD3 5LT

COCKROFT, Richard Robert; s of Albert Hainsworth Cockroft, of Devon, and Jocelyn Courtney, OBE, *née* Dart; *b* 7 Mar 1939; *Educ* Exeter Sch, Trinity Coll Cambrdige (MA); *m* 1962, Judith Prunella, da of Cecil Victor Alexander Wearn (d 1964); 1 s (Timothy b 1967), 1 da (Georgina b 1965); *Career* dir Towry Law and Co Ltd 1966-84; md Towry Law (Hldgs) Ltd 1971-84; dir M and G Gp plc 1984-88; md M and G Assurance Gp Ltd 1984-88; chm Independent Market Assistance Gp Ltd 1987-, dir The Financial Intermediaries, Managers and Brokers Regulatory Assoc 1989-;; *Recreations* golf, real tennis; *Clubs* MCC, East Berks Golf, Real Tennis Club (Berks); *Style—* Richard R Cockroft, Esq; Arborfield House, Arborfield, nr Reading, Berkshire RG2 9JB;

COCKS, Rt Rev Francis William; CB (Mil 1959); s of Canon William Cocks, OBE (d 1963), of Felixstowe, and Ella Margaret, *née* Smith (d 1963); *b* 5 Nov 1913; *Educ* Haileybury, St Catharine's Coll Cambridge (rugby blue, MA); *m* 1940, Barbara Irene May, 2 da of Lieut Harry Thompson, RN (d 1953); 1 s (Michael), 1 da (Christine); *Career* chaplain: RAFVR 1939-45, RAF 1945-65, served as Cmd Chaplain at Air HQ India, HQ BAFO, HQ Bomber Cmd and HQ FEAF; hon chaplain HM the Queen 1959-65, Chaplain-in-Chief (Air Vice-Marshal) 1959-65; rector Wolverhampton 1965-70, bishop of Shrewsbury 1970-80; pres: Haileybury Soc 1976, Buccaneers CC 1964-; played rugby for E Counties and Hampshire; *Recreations* golf, reading, watching sport; *Clubs* RAF, MCC, Hawks (Cambridge); *Style—* The Rt Rev Francis Cocks, CB; 41 Beatrice Ave, Felixstowe, Suffolk IP11 9HB (☎ 0394 283574)

COCKS, Freda Mary; *née* Wood; OBE (1972), JP (1968); da of Frank Wood (d 1985), and Mary Turner (d 1968); *b* 30 July 1915; *Educ* St Peters Sch Birmingham, Queens Coll Birmingham; *m* 20 Oct 1942, Donald Francis Melvin (d 1979), s of Melvin Francis (d 1968); 2 da (Janet Mary b 2 July 1943, Christine Ann b 11 June 1944, d 1946); *Career* Hotelier 1949-79, nurse 1938-41; chm: Housing Birmingham 1968-72, gen purposes 1980-82; memb Area West Health Authy; Bromford Housing Assoc, pres League of Friends: Dudley Rd Hosp, Womens Hosp, Birmingham Eye Hosp; pres Mission to Seamen Birmingham Branch, fndr Birmingham Hosp Broadcasting Assoc, pres Edgbaston Cons Assoc; City Cncl 1957-, Lord and Mayor of Birmingham 1976-77; Freeman City of Birmingham 1986; Freedom of Du Panne Belgium 1978; *Recreations* hospitals, social services, walking; *Clubs* Soroptomist (Birmigham); *Style—* Mrs Freda Cocks, OBE, JP; 332-334 Hagley Rd, Edgbaston, Birmingham B16 8BH (☎ 021 420 1140); The Council House, Birmingham (☎ 021 235 2130)

COCKS, Dr Leonard Robert Morrison (Robin); TD (1979); s of Ralph Morrison Cocks (d 1970), and Lucille Mary, *née* Blackler; *b* 17 June 1938; *Educ* Felsted Sch, Hertford Coll Oxford (BA, MA, DPhil, DSc); *m* 31 Aug 1962, Elaine Margaret, da of Canon J B Sturdy; 1 s (Mark b 1964), 2 da (Zoe b 1967, Julia b 1970); *Career* 2 Lt RA 1957-59, active serv Malaya; scientist Br Museum (Nat Hist) 1965, keeper of palaeontology 1986; pres Palaeontological Assoc 1986-88, sec Geol Soc 1985-, cmmr Int Cmmn on Zoological Nomenclature 1980-; memb; FGS; *Books* The Evolving Earth (1981), contrib to over 80 articles in sci jls on geol and palaeontology; *Style—* Dr Robin Cocks, TD; 12 Winchester Park, Bromley BR2 OPY; British Museum (Nat Hist), Cromwell Road, London SW7 5BD (☎ 01 938 8845)

COCKS, Rt Hon Michael Francis Lovell; PC (1976); s of Dr Harry F Lovell Cocks (d 1983, sometime Moderator Free Church Federal Cncl and chm Congregational Union of England and Wales); *b* 19 August 1929; *Educ* Bristol Univ; *m* 1954, Janet Macfarlane; 2 s, 2 da; *Career* former lectr; contested: Bristol W 1959, S Glos 1964 and 1966; Lab chief whip and Parly sec Treasury 1976-79, MP (Lab) Bristol S 1970-87; *Style—* The Rt Hon Michael Cocks; House of Commons, London SW1A 0AA

COCKSHAW, Mr Alan; s of John Cockshaw (d 1986), and Maud, *née* Simpson; *b* 14 July 1937; *Educ* Farnworth GS; Leeds Univ (Hon Degree in Civil Engrg); *m* 17 Dec 1960, Brenda, da of Fred Payne; 1 s (John Nigel b 1964); 3 da (Elizabeth Ann b 1967, Sally Louise b 1970, Catherine Helen b 1979); *Career* gp chief exec AMEC plc 1984- (chm 1988-); formerly chief exec: Fairclough Civil Engr Ltd 1978-85, Fairclough-Parkinson Mining Ltd 1982-85, Fairclough Engr Ltd 1983-84; *Recreations* rugby (both codes); cricket, walking, gardening; *Style—* Alan Cockshaw, Esq; Red Hill House, 4 Waterbridge, The Green, Worsley, Manchester M28 4NL (☎ 061 794 5972); AMEC plc, Sandiway House, Northwich, Cheshire CW8 2YA (☎ 0606 883885, telex 669708, fax 0606 883996)

CODD, (Ronald) Geoffrey; s of Thomas Reuben Codd (d 1976), and Betty Leyster Justice, *née* Sturt; *b* 20 August 1932; *Educ* Cathedral Sch Llandaff, The College Llandovery, Presentation Coll Cobh Co Cork; *m* 2 April 1960, Christine Ellen Leone, da of Flt-Lt Reginald Arthur John Robertson, of Endways, The Tye, Barking, Needham Market, Suffolk; 1 s (Justin b 27 Oct 1968), 2 da (Louise b 11 May 1962, Emma b 19 July 1966); *Career* RAF Tport Command 1952-57; Rolls-Royce 1957-58, Int Computers 1958-61, Marconi Co 1961-70, J Bibby and Sons 1970-74, Weir Gp 1974-80, Brooke Bond Gp 1981-86, dir Info and Risk Mgmnt ECGD 1986-; involved with Info Technol Policy Gp; FBCS, FBIM, MIOD; *Books* contrib to business publications; *Recreations* sailing, theatre, practical pastimes; *Clubs* Royal Northern and Clyde YC; *Style—* Geoffrey Codd, Esq; Chesterton, Three Gates Lane, Haslemere, Surrey GU27 2LD (☎ 0428 2163); 50 Ludgate Hill, London EC4M 7AY (☎ 01 382 7015, fax 01 382 7649, telex 883601 ECGD HQ G)

CODRINGTON, Christopher George Wayne; s (by 2 m) and h of Sir Simon Codrington, 3 Bt; *b* 20 Feb 1960; *Educ* Hawtreys, Millfield Coll, Royal Agricultural Coll Cirencester; *Career* pres Codrington Oil and Gas Inc; dir Conservatives Abroad (Texas); MRAC; *Style—* Christopher Codrington Esq; 13405 Northwest Freeway, Suite 310, Houston, Texas 77040, U.S.A.

CODRINGTON, Giles Peter; s of late Lt-Cdr Sir William Codrington, 7 Bt and hp of bro, 8 Bt; *b* 28 Oct 1943; *Recreations* sailing; *Clubs* Antique Yacht; *Style—* Giles Codrington, Esq

CODRINGTON, John Ernest Fleetwood; CMG (1968); s of Stewart Codrington (d 1948), of Buntingford, Herts, and Kathleen, *née* Rawlins (d 1957); *b* 19 June 1919; *Educ* Haileybury, Trinity Coll Cambridge (MA); *m* 1951, Margaret, da of Sir Herbert Hall Hall, KCMG, of Walton-on-Thames; 3 da (Sarah, Joanna, Gillian); *Career* serv WWII: RNVR 1940-42, N Atlantic (Sub-Lt); RM 1942-46, 42 Commando (Capt) colonial admin serv Gold Coast and Ghana 1946-58, Nyasaland 1958-64; fin sec Bahamas 1964-70; cmmnr Bahamas in London 1970-73; acting high cmmnr 1973-74; fin sec Bermuda 1974-77, ret; *Clubs* Army & Navy, Royal Lymington YC; *Style—* John Codrington, Esq, CMG; Chequers Close, Lymington, Hants

CODRINGTON, Sir Simon Francis Bethell; 3 Bt (UK 1876), of Dodington, Gloucestershire; s of Sir Christopher Codrington, 2 Bt (d 1979), and his 1 wife Joan Mary, *née* Hague-Cook (d 1961); *b* 14 August 1923; *Educ* Eton; *m* 1, 3 May 1947 (m dis 1959) Joanne, da of John William Molineaux, of Rock Castle, Kilmacsimon, Co Cork, and widow of William Humphrey Austin Thompson; m 2, 1959 (m dis 1979), Pamela Joy Halliday, da of Maj George Walter Bentley Wise, MBE; 3 s; m 3, 1980 (m dis 1988), Mrs Sarah (Sally) Gwynne Gaze, *née* Pennell; *Heir* s, Christopher Codrington; *Career* formerly Maj Coldstream Gds, served WW II Italy; *Style—* Sir Simon Codrington, Bt; Dodington, Chipping Sodbury, Avon

CODRINGTON, Sir William Alexander; 8 Bt (GB 1721), of Dodington, Gloucestershire; s of Lt-Cdr Sir William Codrington, 5 Bt (d 1961); *b* 5 July 1934; *Educ* St Andrew Coll S Africa, S African Naval Coll; *Heir* bro, Giles Codrington; *Career* Merchant Navy 1952, Worldwide Shipping 1976, memb Hon Co of Master Mariners, FNI; *Style—* Sir William Codrington, Bt; 99 St James Drive, Wandsworth Common, SW17

COE, (Albert) Harry; *b* 28 May 1944; *m* ; 2 children; *Career* fin dir Granada Television 1981-88, Airtours plc 1988-; *Recreations* cricket, tennis, golf, skiing; *Style—* Harry Coe Esq; 48 Broad Walk, Wilmslow, Cheshire SK9 5PL (☎ 0625 522315); Granada TV, Manchester M60 9EA (☎ 061 832 7211)

COE, Sebastian Newbold; MBE (1981); s of Peter Coe, and Angela, *née* Swan; *b* 29 Sept 1956; *Educ* Tapton Sch Sheffield, Loughborough Univ (BSc DTech); *Career* athlete; broken 13 world records incl 800m (current holder 1987) 1500m and 1 mile, Olympic gold 1500m, silver 800m at Moscow Olympics in 1980 and Los Angeles Olympics 1984, World Cup gold 800m 1981, gold Euro 800m 1986; vice chm Sport Cncl of GB 1986 (memb since 1983), chm Sports Cncls Olympic Review 1985-86; memb Health Educn Cncl 1986 now memb Health Educn Authy, Athletes Cmmn and Med Cmmn of Int Olympic Ctee; assoc memb Academic Des Sports France 1982-; Kiphuth Fellowship Yale Univ 1982, memb Athletes Cmmn and Medical Cmmn of Int Olympic Ctee; *Books* 'Running Free', 'Running for Fitness with Peter Coe' (1983), 'The Olympians' (1984); *Clubs* East India and Sportsmans; *Style—* Sebastian Coe, Esq; Sports Council, 16 Upper Woburn Place, London WC1

COFFIN, Dr Brian John; s of John Francis Charles Coffin (d 1975), of Bournemouth, Dorset, and Marjorie Gwendoline, *née* Henson; *b* 24 August 1937; *Educ* Canford, King's Coll (BSc, PhD); *m* 22 Oct 1960, Paula Patricia, JP, da of Robert Thomas Ingham, of Normandy, nr Guildford, Surrey; 1 da (Linda-Jane b 24 Oct 1961); *Career* sr lectr in chemistry South Bank Poly 1968-; govr: Royal GS 1977-, Charterhouse 1981-, Tomlinscote Sch Frimley 1988; cncllr Heatherside and Parkside Div Surrey CC 1970-, memb exec cncl Assoc of CCs 1981-; chm: London and SE Region Library Cncl 1975-, Surrey Educn Ctee 1981-85, Surrey Fire Bde Ctee 1985-89; memb NW Surrey Cons Assoc; *Books* Chemistry of Organic Compounds (contrib 1976 and 1983); *Recreations* travel, gardening; *Style—*. Dr Brian Coffin; 37 High Beeches, Frimley, Camberley, Surrey GU16 5UG (☎ Camberley 243 90); South Bank Poly, Borough Rd, London SE1 (☎ 01 928 8989, ext 2226)

COFFIN, Cyril Edwin; CBE (1984); s of Percy Edwin Coffin (d 1962), of Timsbury, Romsey, Hants, and Helena Constance, *née* Carter; *b* 29 June 1919; *Educ* King's Coll Sch Wimbledon, King's Coll Cambridge (BA, MA); *m* 29 March 1947, Joyce Mary, da of Cyril Richmond Tobitt, MBE (d 1983) of Castle Hedingham, Essex; 1 s (Christopher b 1948), 2 da (Margaret b 1950, Philippa b 1952, d 1953); *Career* Gunner RA 1939, Royal Scots 1940, cmmnd RIASC 1941, Capt 1941, cmd Field Supply Depots at Imphal and Palel 1942-44, Stocks Offr Advanced Base Supply Depot Chittagong 1945, DADST HQ Allied Land Forces SE Asia 1945; princ Miny of Food 1948 (asst princ 1947), asst sec MAFF 1957, Office of Minister for Sci 1963, under sec Miny of Technol 1966 (later Dept of Prices & Consumer Protection), dir-gen Food Manufacturers' Fedn 1977-84; area co-ordinator local neighbourhood watch scheme; FRSA 1978; *Books* Working with Whitehall (1987); *Recreations* genealogy, music, learning languages; *Style—* Cyril Coffin, Esq, CBE; 54 Cambridge Ave, New Malden, Surrey KT3 4LE (☎ 01 942 0763)

COGGAN, Hon (Dorothy) Ann; da of Rt Rev and Rt Hon Lord Coggan, PC, DD, *qv*; *b* 1938; *Style—* The Hon Ann Coggan

COGGAN, Baron (Life Peer UK 1980); Rt Rev and Rt Hon (Frederick) Donald Coggan; PC (1961); s of late Cornish Arthur Coggan, of London, and Fannie Sarah Coggan; *b* 9 Oct 1909; *Educ* Merchant Taylors', St John's Cambridge (MA), Wycliffe Hall Oxford, DD Lambeth 1957; *m* 1935, Jean Braithwaite, da of Dr W Loudon Strain, of Wimbledon; 2 da; *Career* asst lectr in Semitic Languages and Literatures Manchester U 1931-34, ordained 1934, curate St Mary Islington 1934-37, prof of new testament Wycliffe Coll Toronto 1937-44 (BD, DD hc), princ London Coll of Divinity 1944-56, bp of Bradford 1956-61, Archbp of: York 1961-74, Canterbury 1974-80; chm Liturgical Cmmn 1960-64, pro-chllr York U 1962-74, Hull U 1968-74, pres Soc for Old Testament Studies 1967-68, prelate Order of St John of Jerusalem 1967-, hon pres Int Cncl of Christians and Jews; Hon DD: Cambridge, Leeds, Aberdeen, Tokyo, Saskatoon, Huron, Hull, Manchester, Moravian Theol Seminary, Virginia Theol Seminary; Hon LLD Liverpool, HHD Westminster Choir Coll Princeton, Hon DLitt Lancaster, STD (hc) Gen Theol Seminary NY, Hon DCL Kent, DUniv York, FKC; *Books Incl:* The Heart of the Christian Faith (1978), The Name above all Names (1981), Sure Foundation (1981), Mission to the World (1982), Paul: Portrait of a Revolutionary (1984), The Sacrament of the Word (1987); *Recreations* gardening, motoring, music; *Clubs* Athenaeum; *Style—* The Rt Rev and Rt Hon Lord Coggan,

PC; 28 Lions Hall, St Swithun Street, Winchester

COGGAN, Hon Ruth Evelyn; OBE (1984); da of Rt Rev and Rt Hon Lord Coggan of Sissinghurst and Canterbury, PC, DD, and Jean Braithwaite Coggan, *née* Strain; *b* 8 July 1940; *Educ* St Helen's Sch, Northwood, Leeds Univ, MB, ChB, FRCOG; *Career* gynaecologist, Pennell Meml Hosp, Bannu, N-W Frontier Province Pakistan since 1970; Sitara-i-Qaid-i-Azam (Pakistan) 1985; *Style—* The Hon Ruth Coggan; 28 Lions Hall, St Swithun St, Winchester SO23 9HW; Pennell Memorial Hospital, Bannu, NWFP, Pakistan

COGGINS, Alec Harold; s of Harold Coggins, and Margaret Mauchline Ironside, *née* Duncan; *b* 19 Jan 1934; *Educ* Wellingborough Sch; *m* m, Jennifer Mary, *née* Dickenson; 4 s (Andrew, Matthew, Timothy, Daniel); *Career* dir Headlam Sims and Coggins plc; chm and md Wilfley Mining Machinery Co Ltd; dir R Coggins and Sons Ltd, Cotton Oxford Ltd, RA Latter Ltd, and other cos; *Recreations* cricket, lost causes; *Clubs* Oakley; *Style—* Alec Coggins, Esq; c/o Wilfley Mining Machinery Co Ltd, Cambridge St, Wellingborough, Northants NN8 1DW (☎ 0933 226368)

COGHILL, Sir Egerton James Nevill Tobias (Toby); 8 Bt (GB 1778), of Coghill, Yorkshire; s of Sir Joscelyn Ambrose Cramer Coghill, 7 Bt (d 1983) and his 1 w Elizabeth Gwendoline, *née* Atkins (d 1980); *b* 26 Mar 1930; *Educ* Gordonstoun, Pembroke Coll Cambridge (MA); *m* 12 April 1958, Gabrielle Nancy, da of Maj Douglas Claud Dudley Ryder, of Rempstone, Corfe Castle, Dorset; 1 s, 1 da (Elizabeth b 1962); *Heir* s, Patrick Kendal Farley Coghill; *Career* architect 1952-56, industrial devpt 1956-59, mgmnt consultancy 1959-61, teacher 1961-64; headmaster Aberlour House 1964-89; chm: Scottish Schs Ski Assoc 1974-77, Assoc of Prep Schs (Scotland) 1984-87, Ind Schs Info Serv (Scotland) 1982-89; *Recreations* country pursuits; *Clubs* Royal Ocean Racing; *Style—* Sir Toby Coghill, Bt; (☎ (034 03) 208)

COGHILL, Hon Mrs (Patricia Mary); *née* St Clair; o da of 16th Lord Sinclair, MVO (d 1957); *b* 17 Mar 1912; *m* 15 March 1940, Lt-Col Charles Archibald Richard Coghill, OBE, Scots Gds (d 1975), s of Norman Coghill, of Almington Hall, Market Drayton; 1 s (Hugh b 1950, m 1973 Edwina Wells, 3 s), 2 da (Sarah b 1948, m 1972 Peter Hopkins; Jane b 1949, m 1970 Graham Merrison); *Style—* The Hon Mrs Coghill; Three Wags, Yelverta Rd, Framingham Earl, Norwich NR14 7SD

COGHILL, Patrick Kendal Farley; s and h of Sir Toby Coghill, 8 Bt; *b* 3 Nov 1960; *Career* specialized luxury catering; *Recreations* skiing, windsurfing, offshore sailing; *Style—* Patrick Coghill Esq; 26 Gowrie Road, London SW11, (☎ 01 350 1355)

COGHLAN, Gerard Anthony Dillon; OBE (1982), JP (Birmingham 1961-); s of Herbert George Coghlan (d 1943), and Norah Elizabeth, *née* Dillon (d 1976); *b* 6 Nov 1920; *Educ* St Philips GS Birmingham, Univ of Birmingham (BSc); *m* 13 Sept 1947, Mary Theresa, da of Ernest Arthur Eden (d 1956), of Birmingham; 2 s (Michael b 5 Nov 1951, Simon b 30 Oct 1959), 1 da (Louise b 21 July 1949); *Career* 2Lt RAOC, 2Lt and Lt REME 1942, Capt (EME 3 Class) 1943, EME (RA) Gds Div until 1946; asst chief engr Kenrick & Jefferson 1947-48, head of work study (head of corp planning, chief engr, works mangr) Richard Haworth & Co Ltd Manchester 1948-56, mgmnt conslt Tube Investmt Gp Servs 1956-58, exec Wrights Ropes 1958-60, mgmnt conslt Neville Industl Consults Ltd 1960-63, dir and gen mangr Midland Industl Issues Ltd 1963-67; Duport Ltd 1967-71: head of gp mgmnt servs, dir of personnel and industl rels, dep chm Duport Computer Servs, dir Duport Servs Ltd; memb Industl Tbnls 1979-, chm W Birmingham Health Authy 1981-, memb Police Complaints Bd 1983-85; tres Knutsford Cons Assoc 1956, chm Harborne Ward Cons Assoc 1960-71 (pres 1971-), guardian The Birmingham Proof House 1973-, cncl memb Univ of Birmingham 1975- (life govr 1978-), chm of cncl for School/Work Links 1979-, gen cmmr of Taxes; Freeman City of London, Liveryman Worshipful Co of Glovers 1978; FIPRodE, MIMechE, MIEE; KSG Knight of the Most Noble and Equestrian Order of St Gregory (Papal Award) 1980; *Recreations* golf; *Clubs* Naval & Military, The Birmingham (Birmingham) Edgbaston GC; *Style—* Gerard Coghlan, Esq, OBE, JP; 10 Hamilton Ave, Harborne, Birmingham B17 8AJ (☎ 021 429 1613); Chairman's Office, West Birmingham Health Authy, Dudley Rd Hosp, Dudley Rd, Birmingham B18 7QH (☎ 021 554 3801, fax 021 551 5562)

COGHLAN, Terence Augustine; s of Austin Coghlan (d 1981), of Horsted Keynes, Sussex, and Ruby, *née* Comrie; *b* 17 August 1945; *Educ* Downside, Univ of Perugia, Oxford Univ (MA); *m* 11 Aug 1973, Angela, da of Rev F E Westmacott (d 1987), of Barsham, Suffolk; 1 s (Thomas Alexander b 1975), 2 da (Candida Mary b 1978, Anna Frances b 1988); *Career* RAFVR (Oxford Univ Air Sqdn) 1964-67; called to the bar Inner Temple, practising barr 1968-, asst recorder of the Crown Ct 1985-; dir City of London Sinfonia; memb Inner Temple; *Recreations* music, cricket, windsurfing, astronomy, skiing, winemaking; *Style—* T A Coghlan, Esq; 1 Crown Office Row, Temple, London EC4Y 7HH (☎ 01 353 3150, fax 01 583 1700)

COGHLAN, Timothy Boyle Lake; *b* 29 Mar 1939; *Educ* Rugby, Pembroke Coll, Cambridge; *m* 1966, Elizabeth, da of Fredrick and Mary af Petersens; 1 s (Henry), 1 da (Melindy); *Career* partner de Zoete and Bevan; dir: Plantations and General Investment Trust Ltd, Tropical and Eastern Produce Co Ltd, Barclays de Zoete Wedd Holdings Ltd; *Style—* Timothy Coghlan Esq; Baclays de Zoete Wedd, Ebbgate House, 2 Swan Lane, London ECHR 3TS (☎ 01 623 2323, telex 888221)

COGSWELL, Dr Jeremy John; s of Dr Alan Philip Lloyd Cogswell (d 1973), and Audrey Sylvia, *née* Jackson; *b* 10 Sept 1937; *Educ* Radley Coll, St John's Coll, Cambridge Univ (MA, MB, BChic, MD); *m* 2 April 1972, Saranna Leigh, da of Bryan Leigh Heseltine, of Bath; 1 s (Oliver b 1974), 1 da (Katherine b 1975); *Career* paediatrician; formerly paediatric res fell Univ of Colorado Med Center; respiratory research fell Hosp for Sick Children Gt Ormond Street; sr registrar Dept of Paediatrics Guys Hosp; conslt paediatrician E Dorset Health Dist; author of papers on paediatric respiratory medicine; *Recreations* skiing, viticulture; *Style—* Dr Jeremy J Cogswell; Warmwell Farm, Flowers Drove, Lytchett Matravers, Poole, Dorset BH16 6BX (☎ 0258 857115); Poole General Hospital (☎ 0202 675100)

COHAN, Robert P; CBE (Hon 1988); s of Walter and Billie Cohan;; *b* 27 Mar 1925; *Educ* Martha Graham Sch, NY; *Career* joined Martha Graham Co 1946 (ptnr 1950, co-dir 1966); artistic dir Contemporary Dance Tst Ltd 1967, artistic dir and prime choreographer London Contemporary Dance Theatre 1969-, artistic advsr Batsheva Co Israel 1980; dir: York Univ, Toronto choreographic Summer Sch 1977, Gulbenkian Choreographic Summer Sch Univ of Surrey 1978, 1979 and 1982; Banff Sch of Fine Arts Choregraphic Seminar Canada 1980; choreographic seminar: NZ 1982, Vancouver 1985; with London Contemporary Dance Theatre (LCDT) has toured over 50 countries throughout: Europe, E Europe, S America, N America, USA; works incl: Cell 1969 (BBC TV 1982), Stages 1971, Waterless Method of Swimming Instruction 1974 (BBC TV), Class 1975, Stabat Mater 1975 (BBC TV) Masque of Separation 1975, Khamsin 1976, Nympheas 1976 (BBC TV 1983) Forest 1977 (BBC TV), Eos 1978, Songs Lamentations and Praises 1979, Dances of Love and Death 1981, Agora 1984, with music by Geoffrey Burgon, A Mass for Man broadcast Nov 1985, Ceremony 1986, Interrogations 1986, Video Life 1986; LCDT was only Br dance co invited to Olympic Arts Fest Los Angeles 1984 and Seoul 1988, performed at Karmiel Dance Fest Israel 1988; won Evening Standard Award for Most Outstanding Achievement in Ballet 1975, award from Soc of West End Theatres 1978;; *Books* Contemporary Dance Workshop (1986), ed Choreo and Dance Internl Jl; *Style—* Robert Cohan, Esq, CBE; The Place, 17 Dukes Road, London, WC1H 9AB, (☎ 01 387 0324)

COHEN; *see:* Waley-Cohen

COHEN, Alan Abraham; s of Tobias Cohen (d 1947), of London, and Rose Cohen, *née* Posner (d 1987); *b* 17 Nov 1935; *Educ* Elmhurst Sch, Hendon Technical Coll; *m* 14 June 1959, Karen Frances, da of Alfred Bernard Cold, of 7 York Ct, Alermans Hill, London N21; 1 s (Philip b 1962), 1 da (Susan b 1964); *Career* chartered accountant, sr ptnr Wilson Green Gibbs Chartered Accountants 1969-; *Recreations* squash, gardening, music; *Style—* Alan Cohen, Esq; 31 Camlet Way, Hadley Wood, Herts EN4 0LJ (☎ 01 441 9079); 5 Southampton Place, London WC1A 20A (☎ 01 404 4949, fax 01 405 3322)

COHEN, His Hon Judge (Nathaniel) Arthur (Jim); JP (Surrey 1958); 2 s of Sir Benjamin Arthur Cohen, KC (d 1942), and Margaret Abigail, *née* Cohen; *b* 19 Jan 1898; *Educ* Rugby, CCC Oxford; *m* 1, 1927 (m dis), Judith Alexandra Grace, da of Capt Sandford William Luard; 2 s (Christopher, Jeremy); m 2, 1936, Joyce, da of Harvey Collingridge, of Woking, Surrey; *Career* barr 1923, circuit judge 1955-70; *Style—* His Hon Judge Cohen, JP; Bay Tree Cottage, Crockham Hill, Edenbridge, Kent

COHEN, Christopher David Arthur; s of His Hon Nathaniel Arthur Jim Cohen, of Crockham Hill, Edenbridge, Kent, and Judith Alexandra Grace Luard (d 1974); *b* 23 June 1928; *Educ* Rugby; *m* 18 Sept 1954, Judith Mary Pyne; 2 s (Peter b 1961, Michael b 1961), 1 da (Virginia b 1959); *Career* Nat Serv 1946-48; articled clerk 1948, slr 1954, ptnr Holman Fenwick and Willan 1961-, dir of slrs: Indemnity Mutual Insur Assoc, Staff Pension Fund; memb of Law Soc, Liveryman Worshipful Co of Slrs, Freeman City of London; memb: Law Society; *Style—* Christopher Cohen, Esq; The Farmhouse, Winkhurst Green, Ide Hill, Kent (☎ 073 275 257); Marlow House, Lloyds Avenue, London EC3N 3AL (☎ 01 488 2300, fax 01 481 0316, telex 8812247)

COHEN, Dr (Johnson) David; s of John Solomon Cohen (d 1974), and Golda, *née* Brenner (d 1968); *b* 6 Jan 1930; *Educ* Chist's Coll Finchley, Lincoln Coll Oxford (MA), Brandeis Univ USA, King's Coll London, Westminster Hosp Medical Sch (MB BS MRCS LRCP); *m* 28 Aug 1962, Veronica Jane Addison, da of Felix Addison Salmon (d 1969), of London; 2 da (Imogen b 1964, Olivia b 1966); *Career* Nat Serv 1948-50; GP; memb: Camden and Islington Area Health Authy 1973-78, Hampstead Dist Health Authy 1983-87; govr Hosps for sick children Great Ormond St 1974-79, special tstee Royal Free Hosp 1984-88; chm: Camden and Islington Family Practioner Ctee 1982-87, Camden and Islington Local Medical Ctee 1983-86, Hampstead Dist Med Ctee 1983-84, John S Cohen Fndn 1974- (tstee 1965-), David Cohen Family Charitable Tst 1981-; govr Royal Ballet Schs 1978-; memb int bd of govrs Hebrew Univ of Jerusalem 1975-, exec ctee Prison Reform Tst 1985-88, bd Opera Factory 1986-, ballet bd Royal Opera House Covent Garden 1987-, bd ENO 1988-; chm Opera 80 1987-; Freeman City of London 1982; FRCGP; *Recreations* music, theatre, the arts; *Clubs* Savile; *Style—* Dr David Cohen; 33 Elsworthy Rd, London NW3 3BT (☎ 01 586 0460); 33a Elsworthy Rd, London NW3 3BT (☎ 01 722 0746)

COHEN, Edmund George; s of Henry Cohen; *b* 16 Sept 1926; *Educ* Harrow, Jesus Coll Cambridge (MA); *m* 1951, Daphne, *née* Froomberg; 2 s; *Career* chm Courts (Furnishers) Ltd 1976-86; *Style—* Edmund Cohen, Esq; 15 Somerset Rd, Wimbledon, London SW19 (☎ 01 947 0975)

COHEN, George Nigel; s of Anthony van den Burgh Cohen (d 1985), and Judy, *née* Tack; *b* 26 Dec 1959; *Educ* St Paul's Sch, City of London Poly (OND); *Career* CA, supervisor Arthur Young 1978-82, mangr Nyman Libson Paul 1984-86, ptnr Vandenburghs 1986; ACA 1983; *Recreations* photography, electronics; *Style—* G Nigel Cohen, Esq; Vandenburgh House, Pindock Mews, London W9 2PY (☎ 01 286 8052, fax 01 286 8048)

COHEN, Harry Michael; MP (Lab) Leyton 1983-; *b* 10 Dec 1949; *Style—* Harry Cohen Esq, MP; House of Commons, London SW1

COHEN, Hon Hugh Lionel; yr s of Baron Cohen (Life Peer, d 1973); *b* 14 Jan 1925; *Educ* Eton, New Coll Oxford; *m* 7 Oct 1953, Jane, da of Rt Hon Sir Seymour Edward Karminski; 3 s; *Career* RNVR 1939-68; *Style—* The Hon Hugh Cohen; Overbrook House, Devil's Highway, Crowthorne, Berks RG11 6BJ

COHEN, Ivor Harold; CBE (1985), TD (1968); s of Jack Cohen (d 1987), of 1 St Luke's Close, London SE25, and Anne, *née* Victor (d 1980); *b* 28 April 1931; *Educ* Central Fndn Sch London, UCL (BA); *m* 4 Jan 1963, Betty Edith, da of Reginald George Appleby (d 1974); 1 da (Elisabeth b 1966); *Career* Nat Serv Royal Signals 1952-54, 2/Lt 1953, TA 1954-69, Maj 1964; Arthur Lyon & Co (Engrs) Ltd 1954-55, Sturtevant Engrg Co Ltd 1955-57, md Mullard Ltd 1979-87 (joined 1957, divn/dir 1973-77), dir: Philips Lighting 1977-79, Philips Electronics Ltd 1984-87, chm Remploy Ltd 1987-; advsr: Allan Patricof Assocs Ltd 1987-, Comet Gp plc 1987-; AB Electronic Products Gp plc 1987-, Océ (UK) Ltd 1988-, Redifon Hldgs Ltd 1989-, Redifon Ltd 1989-, PA Holdings Gp Ltd 1989-; dir Radio Industs Cncl (RIC) 1980-87; memb: Teletext & Viewdata Steering Gp 1980-84, cncl Electronic Components Indust Fedn (ECIF) 1980-87, Info Technol Advsy Panel (ITAP) 1981-86, cncl of mgmnt Br Schs Technol 1984-87 (tstee dir 1987-), Computer Software and Communications Requirements Bd DTI 1984-88, Cncl Euro Electronic Components Assoc 1985-87, DTI Steering Gp on Telecommunications Infrastructure 1987-88, Schs Examination & Assessment Cncl 1988-; NEDO: memb Electronic Components EDC 1980-87, Electronic Industs EDC 1982-86 and 1988-, chm Electronic applications Sector Gp 1988-; memb: mgmnt advsy gp IT Res Inst Brighton Poly, ed bd Nat Electronics Review; Freeman City of London, Liveryman Worshipful Co of Scientific Instrument Makers; Fell UCL; FRSA 1981, CIEE 1988, FIOD 1988; *Recreations* reading, music, opera, sculpting (occasionally); *Clubs* Army & Navy; *Style—* Ivor Cohen, Esq, CBE, TD; 24 Selborne Rd, Croydon, Surrey CR0 5JQ (☎ 01 688 0981)

COHEN, Janet; da of George Edric Neel (d 1952), of 1 Oakhill Ave, London, and Mary Isobel, *née* Budge; *b* 4 July 1940; *Educ* Holy Trinity Church Sch, South Hampstead HS, Newnham Coll Cambridge (BA); *m* 1, 10 June 1964 (m dis 1968), Michael Rodney Newton Moore, s of Gen Sir (James) Rodney Newton Moore (d 1980); m 2, 18 Dec 1971, James Lionel Cohen, s of Dr Richard Henry Lionel Cohen, CB, of The End House South, Lady Margaret Rd, Cambridge; 2 s (Henry b 1973, Richard b 1975), 1 da (Isobel b 1979); *Career* articled clerk Frere Cholmeley 1963-65, admitted slr 1965, ABT Assoc Cambridge, Mass USA 1965-67 John Laing Construction 1967-69, princ (later asst sec) DTI 1969-82; dir F Chaterhouse Bank Ltd 1987- (joined 1982), dir Cafe Pelican 1983-; assoc fell Newnham Coll Cambridge 1988-; *Books* Deaths Bright Angel (as Janet Neel 1988), John Creasey Award for best first crime novel; *Recreations* writing, theatre, restaurants; *Style*— Mrs James Cohen; 50 Blenheim Terr, London NW8 0EH (☎ 01 625 5809); 1 Paternoster Row, St Pauls, London EC4M 7DH (☎ 01 248 4000, fax 01 248 1998)

COHEN, Jennifer Ann; *née* Page; da of Surgn Lt-Cdr John Percy Page (d 1972), and Katherine Isobel, *née* Maskry; *b* 13 April 1959; *Educ* Maidstone GS for Girls; *m* 10 Sept 1988, Peter Arthur David Cohen, s of Christopher David Arthur Cohen, of The Farmhouse, Winkhurst Green, Ide Hill, Kent; *Career* trainee buyer Harrods Ltd Knightsbridge 1976-78, advertsing mangr Kent Messenger Newspaper 1978-81, ad mangr C Cheney & Assocs Hong Kong 1981-84, sr sales exec Financial Times Magazines London 1986-; *Recreations* scuba diving, tennis, windsurfing; *Style*— Mrs Peter Cohen; 34A Duntshill Rd, London SW18 4QL (☎ 01 870 0271); Financial Times Magazines, 102-108 Clerkenwell Rd, Lonson EC1M 5SA (☎ 01 251 9321, fax 01 251 4686, telex 23700 FINBI G)

COHEN, Jeremy Sandford; s of His Hon Judge N A J Cohen, of Kent, and Judith A G Luard (d 1974); *b* 14 June 1930; *Educ* Rugby Sch, Trinity Coll Cambridge BA (Hons); *m* 1962, Susan Kirsteen, da of William Le B Egerton (d 1947); 1 s (Thomas b 1965), 1 da (Lucy b 1968); *Career* insurance broker, dir Willis Faber plc 1984; *Recreations* music, farming; *Clubs* United Oxford and Cambridge Univ; *Style*— Jeremy Cohen, Esq; Wiston Mill, Nayland, Suffolk (☎ 0206 262219); 10 Trinity Square, London EC3P 3AX (☎ 01 488 8380)

COHEN, John (Louis) Brunel; OBE (1989); yr s of Maj Sir (Jack Ben) Brunel Cohen, KBE (d 1965), and Vera Evelyn, er da of Sir Stuart Montague Samuel, 1 Bt (d 1926); *b* 13 June 1922; *Educ* Cheltenham; *m* 1, 4 March 1951, Simone Dolores Everitt (d 1969), da of late Robert L de Vergriette, of Paris; 2 s (Richard Stuart b 17 Aug 1954, David John (twin) b 17 Aug 1954), 1 da (Jane Caroline b 24 May 1952); m 2, 1972, Christine Bowman Blamey, da of late John Rothwell Dixon; *Career* Cunard Steamship Co 1946-59, C T Bowring (insur) 1959-87 (ret); underwriting memb Lloyd's 1960; chm Not Forgotton Assoc 1979- (memb ctee 1965-), memb benevolent ctee Royal Br Legion 1983-88; Master Worshipful Co of Gardeners 1977-78; *Recreations* sailing, travel, horse racing; *Clubs* Carlton, Royal Southern YC; *Style*— John Brunel Cohen, Esq; Flat 5, 17 Cheyne Gardens, London SW3 5QT (☎ 01 351 6505); Ayrmer View, Ringmore, Kingsbridge, South Devon TQ7 4HJ (☎ 0548 810 245)

COHEN, Hon John Christopher Coleman; s of Baron Cohen of Brighton (Life Peer, d 1966); *b* 13 July 1940; *Educ* Stowe, McGill Univ; *m* 20 Feb 1965, Anne-Marie, da of Eugene Krauss, of Paris; 1 s; *Style*— The Hon John Cohen; 47 Quickswood, Chalcots Pk, London NW3

COHEN, Jonathan; TD; s of Leonard Joseph Cohen (d 1948), and Elise Cohen, *née* Brewster (d 1983); *b* 28 Jan 1944; *Educ* St Albans' Sch, Queens' Coll Cambridge (MA Law); *m* 1973, Susan Margaret (now separated), da of Philip Andrews (d 1971); 1 s (Marc 1976), 1 da (Lisa b 1978); *Career* Price Waterhouse and Co 1967-71, SG Warburg and Co Ltd 1971-74; County Bank Ltd 1974-86; dir corporate fin 1976, dir int div Int Corporate Fin and Capital Mkts 1978, sr dir head of corporate advsy div 1982-83, dep chief exec 1984, chief exec 1985-; chief exec County Nat West Ltd, dep chief exec Nat West Investmt Bank Ltd 1986; *Recreations* opera, literature, sport; *Clubs* City of London, Army and Navy; *Style*— Jonathan Cohen, Esq, TD; 104 Ledbury Road, London W11; County Natwest Ltd, Drapers Gdns, 12 Throgmorton Avenue, London EC2P 2ES (☎ 01 382 1000, telex 882121, fax 01 628 2436)

COHEN, Lawrence Francis Richard; s of Harris Cohen of Willesden, and Sarah *née* Rich; *b* 4 Nov 1951; *Educ* Preston Manor Sch, Birmingham Univ (LLB), Inns of Court Sch of Law; *m* 24 May 1986, Alison Jane, da of Dr Rowland Patrick Bradshaw of Cobham, Surrey; 1 da (Sophie 1987); *Career* barr 1974-; ACIA 1986; *Recreations* reading, walking; *Style*— Lawrence F R Cohen, Esq; 24 Old Buildings, Lincoln's Inn, London, WC2A 3UJ (☎ 01 4040946)

COHEN, (Lewis) Lennard; s of late Cecil Cohen; *b* 2 Dec 1925; *Educ* Clifton, Peterhouse Cambridge; *m* 1953 (m dis 1973), Norma Beverley, *née* Cash; 2 da; *Career* dir Baird Textile Hldgs Ltd 1978-82; *Clubs* Royal Ocean Racing, Royal Southern Yacht; *Style*— Lennard Cohen, Esq; Flat 12, 9 Beaufort Gdns, London SW3 1PT (☎ 01 584 0040)

COHEN, Hon Leonard Harold Lionel; er s of Baron Cohen (Life Peer, d 1973); *b* 1 Jan 1922; *Educ* Eton, New Coll Oxford (BA, MA); *m* 14 July 1949, Eleanor Lucy, da of late Philip Quixano Henriques; 2 s, 1 da; *Career* Rifle Bde 1939-45; barr 1948; former dir Hill Samuel and Co; former md S Hoffnung and Co Ltd; chm Utd Serv Tstees 1976-81; dir-gen Accepting Hos Ctee 1976-82; chm: Ariel UK Ltd 1982-88, Secure Retirement plc 1987-, Royal Free Hosp Med Sch Cncl; governing body The Judd Sch Tonbridge; Liveryman Worshipful Co of Skinners (Master 1971-72); High Sheriff of Berkshire 1987-88; *Recreations* gardening, reading, shooting; *Clubs* White's, Swinley Forest Golf; *Style*— The Hon Leonard Cohen; Dovecote House, Swallowfield Park, Reading, Berks RG7 1TG (☎ 0734 884775)

COHEN, Leslie Samuel; s of Harold Leopold Cohen, JP (d 1936), of 5 Palace Green, London, and Barwythe, Studham, Beds, and Clara, *née* Stern (d 1963); *b* 24 August 1910; *Educ* Charterhouse, Christs' Coll Cambridge (BA); *m* 1, 16 March 1935 (m dis 1942), Joan Lucy Eggar, da of John Kyrke Smith; 1 da (Penelope Clare (Mrs Roy Gluckstein) b 17 Oct 1938); m 2, Dorothy Victoria Mary (d 1987), da of John De La Mare; *Career* WWII Capt 5 Kings Regt, motor contact offr HQ Br Troops NI 1940, jr staff Coll Course Oxford 1942, GSO3 area HQ Sleaford Lincs 1942, GSO3 WO 1943; trainee Macy's Dept Store NYC 1932; Lewis's Ltd 1933-: various mgmnt appts 1933-39, bd memb 1949, bd memb Lewis's Investment Tst 1964-, dep chm Lewis Ltd 1964-; chm: bd of govrs David Lewis Orgn Liverpool, bd of mgmnt Textile Benevolent Assoc 1968-86; pres Liverpool Jewish Youth and Community Centre; Freeman City of London 1964, memb Worshipful Co of Furniture Makers 1964; *Recreations* shooting, horse racing; *Clubs* Carlton; *Style*— Leslie Cohen, Esq

COHEN, Michael Alan; s of Harris Cohen, of London, and Cissie, *née* Rich; *b* 30 Jul 1933; *Educ* Ilford Co HS, UCL (LLB); 3 July 1955, Ann Cohen; 1 s (Julian Andrew b 1967), 1 da (Nicola Amanda b 1970); *Career* Flt Lt RAF 1955-58; md Avery Rich Assocs Ltd; ptnr: Michael Cohen Assocs, Ara Financial Servs; dir: ARA Assur Servs, ARA Conf Servs, ARA Life Assur Servs; practising arbitrator; vice pres Br Insur Law Assoc, chm Br Acad of Experts; memb: disciplinary tbnl Inst of Actuaries, cncl Friends of UCL, various ctees Chartered Inst of Arbitrators; Freeman City of London; Liveryman Worshipful Cos: Spectacle Makers, Insurers and Arbitrators; FCIArb, FBSC, FBAE, FRSA, barr Hon Soc of Gray's Inn; *Recreations* sailing, swimming, driving, collecting, yoga; *Clubs* Naval and Military, Royal Southern YC; *Style*— Michael Cohen, Esq; 90 Bedford Court Mansions, Bedford Ave, London WC1B 3AE (☎: 01 637 0333, fax 01 637 1893, telex 23873 ARA G)

COHEN, Lt-Col Mordaunt; TD (1954); s of Israel Ellis Cohen (d 1946), and Sophie, *née* Cohen; *b* 6 August 1916; *m* 1953, Judge Myrella Cohen QC, *qv*, da of Samuel Cohen (d 1948); 1 s (Jeffrey), 1 da (Sheila); *Career* RA 1940-46, seconded RWAFF (despatches), served TA 1947-55, CO 463 (M) HAA Regt, RA (TA) 1954-55; alderman Sunderland County Borough Cncl 1967-74; chm: Sunderland Educn Ctee 1970-72, NE Cncl of Educn Ctees 1971; cncllr Tyne and Wear CC 1973-74; dep chm Northern Traffic Cmmrs 1973-74; chm Mental Health Review Tribunal 1967-76; regional chm of Industl Tribunals 1976-, (chm 1974-76); memb Ct Univ of Newcastle upon Tyne 1968-72; pres Sunderland Law Soc 1970; tstee and past pres Sunderland Hebrew Congregation; memb bd of Deputies of Br Jews (chm provincial ctee); former memb Chief Rabbinate Cncl; tstee: Ajax Charitable Tst, Ashbrooke Fndn; *Recreations* watching sport, playing bowls, gardening, communal service, promoting inter-faith understanding; *Style*— Lt-Col Mordaunt Cohen, TD; c/o Regional Off of Industl Tribunals, Watson Ho, Pilgrim Street, Newcastle upon Tyne (☎ 328865)

COHEN, Her Hon Judge Myrella; QC (1970); da of Samuel Cohen (d 1948), of Manchester, and Sarah Cohen (d.1978); *b* 16 Dec 1927; *Educ* Manchester HS for Girls, Colwyn Bay GS, Manchester Univ; *m* 1953, Lt-Col Mordaunt Cohen, TD DL, *qv*, s of Israel Ellis Cohen (d 1948); 1 s, 1 da; *Career* barr 1950, recorder Kingston upon Hull 1971-72, circuit judge 1972-, memb Parole Bd 1983-86; *Clubs* Soroptomist Int; *Style*— Her Honour Judge Myrella Cohen, QC; c/o Crown Court, Kenton Bar, Newcastle upon Tyne

COHEN, Prof; Philip; s of Jacob D Cohen and Fanny *née* Bragman of London;; *b* 22 July 1945; *Educ* Hendon GS, University Coll London (BSc PhD); *m* 17 Feb 1969, Patricia Townsend, da of Charles H T Wade, of Greenmount, Lancs; 1 s (Simon Daniel, b 1977), 1 da (Suzanne (Emma) b 1974);; *Career* SRC/NATO fell Univ of Washington, Seattle 1969-71; Royal Soc res prof Univ of Dundee 1984-, (prof of enzymology 1981-84, reader in biochemistry 1978-81, lectr in biochemistry 1971-78); Colworth medal Br Bicohemical Soc 1977, Anniversary prize Fedn of Euro Biochemical Societies 1977; FRS (1984), FRSE (1984); *Books* Control of Enzyme Activity (1976, 2 edn 1983, trans into German, Italian, Russian and Malay), Series Edt of Molecular Aspects of Cellular Regulation, contrib over 200 articles to learned journals; *Style*— Philip Cohen Esq ; Inverbay II, Invergowrie, Dundee, DD2 5DG (☎ 0382 562 328); Dept of Biochemistry, Univ of Dundee, Dundee, Scotland (☎ 0382 23181), (fax 0382 201 063)

COHEN, Ronald Mourad; s of Michael Mourad Cohen, of Cadogan Gardens, London SW1, and Sonia Sophie, *née* Douek; *b* 1 August 1945; *Educ* Orange Hill GS London, Exeter Coll Oxford (BA), Harvard Business Sch (MBA); *m* 1, Dec 1972 (m dis 1975), Carol Marylene, da of Gerard Belmont of Geneva; m 2, Dec 1983 (m dis 1986), Claire Whitmore, da of Thomas Enders, of New York; m 3, 5 March 1987, Sharon Ruth, da of Joseph Harel, of New York and Tel Aviv; 1 da (Tamara b 7 Oct 1987); *Career* consIt McKinsey and Co (UK and Italy) 1969-71, chargé de mission Institut de Développement Industriel France 1971-72, fndr chm The MMG Patricof Gp plc 1972-; chm The Sterling Publishing Gp plc; fndr dir: Br Venture Capital Assoc (former chm), Euro Venture Capitol Assoc; dir My Kinda Town Gp; advsr Inter-Action Gp (charity), former memb Oxford Union Soc; Lib candidate Kensington North 1974 and London West for Euro Parl 1979; *Recreations* music, art, tennis, travel; *Clubs* RAC, RIIA; *Style*— Ronald Cohen, Esq; 23 Chester Terrace, Regent's Park, London NW1 4ND; 24 Upper Brook St, London W1Y 1PD (☎ 01 872 0017, fax 01 629 9035)

COHEN, Prof Samuel Isaac; s of Gershon Cohen (d 1963), of Cardiff, and Ada, *née* Samuel; *b* 22 Nov 1925; *Educ* Cardiff HS, Univ of Wales (BSc, MB, CHB), Univ of London (MD); *m* 24 May 1955, Vivienne, da of Samuel William Wolfson (d 1974), of London; 1 s (Michael Ben-Gershon b 1960), 1 da (Elizabeth Hacohen b 1962); *Career* conslt psychiatrist The London Hosp 1963-83, hon conslt psychiatrist The Brompton Hosp 1971-83, prof of psychiatry The London Hosp Med Coll Univ of London 1983-, chm med cncl of The London Hosp 1985-88; Royal Coll of Psychiatrists: memb cncl 1974-79, ct of electors 1975- 78, chm East Anglian Div 1981-86; regnl advsr NE Thames RHA 1982-88, med examiner Gen Med Cncl 1982-; FRCP, FRCPsych; *Books* contributed to Asthma (1977 and 1983), Medicine and Psychiatry (1982 and 1984), papers on Asthma, Cushing's Syndrome and Physical Symptoms in Psychiatric Disorders; *Style*— Prof Samuel I Cohen; 8 Linnell Drive, London NW11 7LT (☎ 01 455 4781); The London Hosp Med Coll, Turner St, Whitechapel, London E1 2AD (☎ 01 377 7344)

COHEN, Stanley; s of Thomas and Teresa Cohen; *b* 31 July 1927; *Educ* St Patrick's and St Charles' Schs Leeds; *m* 1954, Brenda Patricia, *née* Rafferty; 3 s, 1 da; *Career* RN 1947-49, British Rail 1951-70, contested (Lab) Barkston Ash 1966, MP (Lab) Leeds South East 1970-83, pps to Min of State DES 1976-79; *Style*— Stanley Cohen Esq; 164 Ring Rd, Halton, Leeds LS15 7AE (☎ (0532) 649568)

COHN, Michael William Hardy; s of E Cohn (d 1976), and Lotti Cohn; *b* 16 Nov 1939; *Educ* Mill Hill Sch, St Andrews Univ (BSc); *m* 4 Sept 1965, Pamela Gray; 2 s (Anthony b 1969, Timothy b 1972), 1 da (Lucy b 1971); *Career* md M W Hardy & Co Hldgs Ltd, cncl memb Br Chemical Distributors and Traders Assoc; *Recreations* walking, gardening; *Style*— Michael W H Cohn, Esq; Bidston, Burtons Lane, Chalfont St Giles, Bucks; M W Hardy & Co Ltd, Hardy House, Northbridge Rd, Berkhamsted, Herts (telex 825886, fax 04427 72 412)

COHN, Prof Paul Moritz; s of late James Cohn, and late Julia Mathilde, *née* Cohen; *b* 8 Jan 1924; *Educ* Trinity Coll Cambridge (BA, MA, PhD); *m* 27 March 1958, Deirdre Sonia Sharon, da of Arthur David Finkle (d 1968), of London; 2 da (Juliet, Ursula); *Career* Charge de Recherches (CNRS) Univ of Nancy France 1951-52, lectr Univ of

Manchester 1952-62, reader Queen Mary Coll Univ of London 1962-67, prof and head Dept of Maths Bedford Coll Univ of London 1967-84, prof UCL 1984-86 (Astor Prof 1986-); visiting prof: Yale Univ, Univ of California at Berkeley, Univ of Chicago, SUNY Stonybrook, Rutgers Univ, Univ of Paris, Tulane Univ, Indian Inst of Technol Delhi, Univ of Alberta, Carleton Univ, Haifa Technion, Univ of Iowa, Univ of Bielefeld, Univ of Frankfurt, Bar Ilan Univ, Univ d'Etat Mons; author; ctee memb SRC Maths 1977-79, convenor to select algebra speakers for Int Congress of Mathematicians 1974 (panel memb 1970) pres London Math Soc 1982-84 (memb 1957); FRS 1980 (cncl memb 1985-87); *Books* Lie Groups (1957), Linear Equations (1958), Solid Geometry (1961), Universal Algebra (1965, 1981), Free Rings and their relations (1971, 1985), Skew Field Constructions (1977), Algebra I (1974, 1982), Algebra II (1977, 1989), translations into Spainish, Italian, Russian, Chinese; *Recreations* language in all its forms; *Style*— Prof P M Cohn; Dept of Mathematics, Univ Coll London, Gower St, London WC1E 6BT (☎ 01 387 7050)

COIA, Ferdinando; s of Ernesto Coia (d 1938), of Glasgow, and Filomena Cocozza (d 1974); *b* 19 August 1928; *Educ* Camphill Sr Sec Sch Paisley, Glasgow univ (BSc); *m* 12 May 1954, Jane, da of James Lockhart (d 1961), of Glasgow; 3 s (Paul and Gerard b 1955, Martin b 1958), 1 da (Denise b 1958); *Career* Army Service BHA BAOR; dir of facilties Scottish TV; dir: Scottish TV plc, Theatrical Enterprises Ltd William Mutrie and Son; chm the Scottish Centre, the Royal Televison Society 1976; *Recreations* curling, golf; *Clubs* Royal Scottish Automobile; *Style*— Ferdinando Coia, Esq; Scottish Television plc, Cowcaddens, Glasgow (☎ 041 332 9999)

COKAYNE, Hon Edmund Willoughby Marsham; 2 s of late 1 Baron Cullen of Ashbourne, KBE (d 1932), and Grace Margaret (d 1971), da of Rev Hon John Marsham (s of 3 Earl of Romney); hp of bro, 2 Baron; *b* 18 May 1916; *Educ* Eton, Royal Sch of Mines; *m* 18 May 1943, Janet Manson, da of William Douglas Watson (d 1916), of Canterbury; 1 da; *Career* late Fl Lt RAF; mining engr (ret); *Style*— The Hon Edmund Cokayne; PRI Site 52 Comp 5, Merritt, BC VOK2BO, Canada (☎ 604 378 9462, 836 3155; office: 836 2141)

COKAYNE, (Hon) John O'Brien Marsham; does not use courtesy style; s of late 1 Baron Cullen of Ashbourne, KBE (d 1932), and Grace Margaret (d 1973), da of Rev Hon John Marsham (s of 3 Earl of Romney); *b* 11 Oct 1920; *Educ* Eton; *m* 1 May 1948, Anne Frances (d 1973), er da of late Bertram Clayton, of Wakefield, Yorks; 1 s (Michael John b 28 Nov 1950); *Style*— John Cokayne Esq; 14 St Omer Rd, Cowley, Oxford (☎ 0865 774867)

COKE, Cyril Edward Rigby; s of Edward Rigby Coke (d 1951), and Phyllis Muriel, *née* Austin (d 1979); *b* 29 July 1914; *Educ* Haileybury Coll; *m* 1, 5 may 1934, Suzanne Grasett; 1 s (Michael b 1938), 1 da (Judith b 1936); m 2, 1954 Muriel, da of Wilfred Young (d 1964); *Career* WW II 1941-45 Royal Canadian Artillery (Major) served Italy; worked on feature films as personal asst, prod mangr and casting dir with Frank Launder and Sidney Gilliat 1946-55; tv drama dir Assoc Rediffusion from 1955-65; freelance therafter; notable prodns incl: Crime and Punishment (best dir award), The Rat Catchers, Darkness at Noon, Malice Aforethought, Pride and Prejudice; *Recreations* golf; *Style*— Cyril E R Coke, Esq; 6 Stanhope Castle, Stanhope, Co Durham DL13 2LY (☎ 0388 528809)

COKE, Viscount; Edward Douglas; s and h of 6 Earl of Leicester, *qv*; *b* 6 May 1936; *Educ* St Andrew's Coll Grahamstown S Africa; *m* 28 April 1962 (m dis 1985), Valeria, el da of Leonard A Potter, of Berkhamstead, Herts; 2 s (Hon Thomas, Hon Rupert Henry John b 1975), 1 da (Hon Laura-Jane Elizabeth b 1968); *Heir* s, Hon Thomas Coke; *Style*— Viscount Coke; Holkham Hall, Wells, Norfolk (☎ 0328 710227)

COKE, Edward Peter; s of Lt-Cdr John Hodson Coke, of Tone Lodge, Birtley, Hexham, Northumberland, and Kathleen Mary, *née* Pennington; *b* 12 Oct 1948; *Educ* St John's Coll Southsea, Univ of Warwick (LLB Hons), Inns of Ct Sch of Law; *m* 6 July 1968, Josephine Linette, da of Frederick Francis Kennard (d 1987); 1 s (Dominic Francis), 2 da (Sarah Marie, Jessica Mary); *Career* trainee mangr W Woolworth 1966-69, postman PO 1969-71, barr 1976, sr advsy offr Consumer Protection Dept W Midlands CC, tenant St Ive's Chambers 1977-, ctee memb Legal Aid Ctee Area No 6; memb: Inner Temple, Midland cncl Oxford Circiut, Birmingham Medico Legal Soc, Assoc for Def of Unborn, Old Johannians Assoc, Warwick Univ Graduates Assoc; *Recreations* dry fly fishing, walking, snooker, theatre, reading, music; *Style*— Edward Coke, Esq; St Ive's Chambers, 9 Fountain Court, Steelhouse Lane, Birmingham B4 6DR (☎ 021 236 0863/0929/8952, fax 021 236 6961)

COKE, Hon Thomas Edward; er s, and h, of Viscount Coke, and gs of 6 Earl of Leicester; *b* 6 July 1965; *Career* page of honour to HM The Queen to 1981; *Style*— The Hon Thomas Coke

COKE, Hon Wenman John; s of 6 Earl of Leicester; *b* 24 May 1940; *Educ* St Andrew's Coll Grahamstown; *m* 1969, Carolyn May, er da of late D D Steuart Redler, of Cape Town , S Africa; 2 s, 1 da; *Style*— The Hon Wenman Coke; 106 Park St, Vryheid, Natal

COKE-STEEL, David; s of Ronald Coke-Steel (d 1963) of Trusley Old Hall, Derbyshire and Frances H *née* Coke; *b* 24 Jan 1944; *Educ* Wellington, London Univ, Coll of Estate Mgmnt (BSc); *m* 14 April 1979, Jane Elizabeth, da of Hon Dean J Eyre, of 517 Wilbrod St, Ottawa, Ontario, Canada; 1 s (Edward b 1983), 2 da (Celia b 1979, Sophie b 1982); *Career* land and estate agent John D Wood & Co 1971-76, landowner and farmer 1977-; and memb Derbyshire Historic Bldgs Tst; Nat Tst; Cncl for Preservation of Rural England; *Recreations* music esp opera, trout fishing, travelling especially third world, english art and architecture, early english porcelain; David Coke-Steel, Esq

COKER, Bryan Sydney; s of Sydney Orlando Coker (d 1954), of Grays, Essex, and Lilian Rose, *née* Harford-Roberts (d 1971); *b* 25 Dec 1924; *Educ* Palmer's Endowed Sch Essex; *m* 20 Aug 1949, Doreen Edith, da of Francis James Caton (d 1970), of Grays, Essex; 3 da (Jane b 1950, Gillian b 1955, Alison b 1964); *Career* chartered accountant; ptnr Rowland Hall & Co 1955-88, sec Thurrock District Assoc of Industries 1966-88; gen sec World Cncl of Young Men's Service Clubs 1973-79; fin dir Grays AFC, past pres Rotary Club of Grays Thurrock; past memb Essex CC Educn Ctee 1970-77; chm: Trustees of William Palmer's Charity, Govrs of Palmer's VI Form Coll, Thurrock Technical Coll; pres Nat Assoc of Round Tables 1963-64; cncl memb of Assoc Examining Bd; FCA; *Recreations* association football, rotary, canasta; *Clubs* Grays Athletic Football, Rotary Club of Grays Thurrock, Grays 41; *Style*— Bryan Coker, Esq; Alfriston, 14 College Avenue, Grays, Essex (☎ 0375 374949)

COKER, Frank Percival Charles; s of Frank Percival Coker (d 1972), of Broadclyst, Devon, and Winifrd Clara, *née* Pearse (d 1972); *b* 2 Nov 1927; *Educ* King Edward VI GS Totnes, Imp Coll London (BSc (Eng), DIC); *m* 7 Aug 1953, Mary, da of John Gerrard (d 1963), of Stoak, Cheshire; 3 s (John b 1955, Timothy b 1960, Richard (twin) b 1960), 1 da (Jane b 1954); *Career* engr Shell Petroleum Ltd 1948-50, section engr ICI Ltd 1951-60, dir Simon Engrg Gp 1961-74, chief exec Wormald Int Ltd 1974-77, dir Scientific Design Co Ltd 1977-80, mktg mangr Worley Engrg Ltd 1981-82, fndr and chm Tylatron Ltd 1982-; conslt Costain Gp 1984-85, chm Bofors Electronics Ltd 1984-; sch govr; ACGI Freeman City of London; FIMechE 1957, FIChemE 1957, FCIArb 1977; *Clubs* Dartmouth YC, IOD; *Style*— Frank Coker, Esq

COKER, (Herbert) Maxwell; s of Arthur Leonard Coker (d 1980), and Mildred, *née* Prior; *b* 28 April 1919; *Educ* Regent St Poly (TEng, FIElec, JE); *m* m, Daphne Elizabeth, da of Frederick Charles Stokes (d 1987); *Career* memb of Engrg Cncl Assembly, Eastern Regnl Ctee IEEEIE, Engrg Cncl Regnl Orgn; sr ptnr Max Coker Assoc Conslting Engrg 1960; sr lectr Norfolk Coll of Art and Tech 1957-84; *Recreations* golf, sailing; *Style*— Maxwell Coker, Esq; Highfields, Harpley, King's Lynn PE31 6TU (☎ (048 524) 397)

COKER, Michael Alexander O'Neil; s of Alexander Albert Coker, MBE (d 1986), of Oxford, and May Lucy, *née* Riley; *b* 13 Jan 1933; *Educ* Prince Henry's Sch Evesham, The Royal Liberty Sch, Romford, RAM, Univ of Birmingham (Advanced Supplementary Certificate for Teachers of Handicapped Children), Univ of Sussex; *Career* Bishop Otter Coll Chichester 1971-82: sr lectr in educn studies (special and remedial educn), course tutor (advanced dip for teachers of children with special needs); dir of computer servs Marlborough 1982-; contributor to books on computing; memb natural history ctee Wilts Archaelogical and Natural History Soc; LRAM, ARCM; *Recreations* gardening, music, astrology, early science, medicine; *Style*— Michael Coker, Esq; Bush Cottage, Brunton, Collingbourne Kingston, Marlborough, Wilts; Marlborough Coll, Marlborough, Wilts (☎ 0672 55511 ext 249)

COLAHAN, Air Vice-Marshal William Edward; CB (1978), CBE (1973), DFC (1945); er s of Dr W E Colahan (d 1946), and Dr G C J Colahan (1966); *b* 7 August 1923; *Educ* Templeton HS South Africa; *m* 1949, Kathleen Anne, da of Philip George Butler; 1 s, 2 da; *Career* S African Air Force 1941-46, RAF 1947, Air Vice-Marshal 1973, Asst Chief of Air Staff (Ops) 1973-75, Air Offr cmdg and Cmdt RAF Coll Cranwell 1975-78, ret; offr careers counsellor RAF 1978-83; Lord Chllr's panel of Independent Inquiry Insprs 1983-; memb cncl St Dunstan's 1978-; ret; Cdr St JA Lincolnshire 1985-88; OstJ 1986; *Clubs* RAF; *Style*— Air Vice-Marshal Colahan, CB, CBE, DFC; Northbeck House, Scredington, Sleaford, Lincs (☎ 0529 302489)

COLBECK-WELCH, Air Vice-Marshal Edward Lawrence; CB (1960), OBE (1948), DFC (1941); s of Major G S M Colbeck-Welch, MC, (d 1943), of Collingham, Yorks; *b* 29 Jan 1914; *Educ* Leeds GS; *m* 1938, Doreen (d 1988), da of T G Jenkin, LDS RCS, of Sliema, Malta; 1 s, 2 da; *Career* RAF 1933, No 22 Sqdn 1934-37, asst adj No 603 (City of Edinburgh) Sqdn AAF 1938, adj No 600 (City of London) Sqdn AAF 1939, CO No 29 (NF) Sqdn 1941-42, student RAF Staff Coll 1942, Ops Staff HQ No 10 Gp 1943-44, HQ 2 TAF and CO No 139 Wing 1944-45, dep dir of Ops Air Defence, Air Miny 1945-47, student US Armed Forces Staff Coll 1947, BJSM Washington 1948-49, OC RAF Coltishall 1950, OC RAF Horsham St Faith 1951-53, Gp Capt 1952, AMP's Dept Air Miny 1954-55, student IDC 1956, Cmdt Central Fighter Estab 1957-58, Air Cdre 1958, SASO HQ No 13 (F) Gp 1959, Air Vice-Marshal 1961, SASO HQ Fighter Command 1960-63, ret; *Recreations* sailing; *Clubs* Royal Channel Islands Yacht, St Helier Yacht; *Style*— Air Vice-Marshal Edward Colbeck-Welch; La Côte au Palier, St Martin, Jersey, CI (☎ Jersey 52962)

COLBORNE-MALPAS, Hon Mrs; Hon Venetia Jane; *née* Manners; er da of 4 Baron Manners; *b* 30 July 1950; *m* 1972, Alasdair John Colborne-Malpas; *Style*— Hon Mrs Colborne-Malpas; Keeper's Cottage, Ramsdell, Hants

COLBURN, Oscar Henry; CBE (1981), JP, DL (Glos 1982); *m* 1950, Helen Joan, *née* Garne; 1 s, 2 da; *Career* farmer; sheep (Colbred) and cattle (Poll Hereford) breeder; High Sheriff of Gloucestershire 1980-81; FRASE, FRAgS; *Style*— Oscar Colburn Esq, CBE, JP, DL; Crickley Barrow, Northleach, nr Cheltenham, Glos

COLCHESTER, Archdeacon of; *see*: Stroud, The Ven Ernest Charles Frederick

COLCHESTER, Rev Halsey Sparrowe; CMG (1968), OBE (1960); s of Ernest Charles Colchester (d 1937), and Henrietta Louise, *née* Colchester (d 1971); *b* 5 Mar 1918; *Educ* Uppingham, Magdalen Coll Oxford (MA); *m* 7 Jan 1946, Rozanne Felicity Hastings, da of Air Chief Marshal Sir Charles Medhurst, KCB, OBE, MC (d 1955); 4 s (Nicholas b 1946, Charles b 1950, Marcus b 1953, Jonathan b 1955), 1 da (Chloë b 1964); *Career* Oxfordshire and Buck LI 1940-43, 2 SAS Regt 1943-46 (despatches); joined Dip Serv 1947, FO 1948-50, second sec Instanbul 1950-54, FO 1954-56, consul Zurich 1956-60, first sec Athens 1960-64, FO 1964-68, cnsllr Paris 1968-72, ret 1972; trained as ordinand Cuddesdon Theol Coll 1972-73, deacon 1973, priest 1974, curate Minchinhampton Glos 1973-76, vicar Bollington Cheshire 1976-81, priest i/c Great Tew Oxfordshire 1981-87, ret 1987; *Recreations* theatre going, wild flowers; *Clubs* Travellers'; *Style*— The Rev Halsey Colchester, CMG, OBE; 18 Dale Close, Oxford OX1 1TU (☎ 0865 244 192)

COLCHESTER, Nicholas Benedick Sparrowe; s of Rev Halsey Sparrowe Colchester, CMG, OBE, *qv*, and Rozanne Felicity Hastings *née* Medhurst; *b* 20 Dec 1946; *Educ* Radley Coll, Magdalen Coll Oxford; *m* 28 May 1976, Laurence Lucie Antoinette, da of Jean Louis Armand Schloesing; 2 s (Max b 1983, Felix b 1985); *Career* joined Financial Times 1968 (NY corr 1970-73, Bonn corr 1973-77, for ed 1980-86), joined The Economist 1986 (business ed 1988, dep ed); Chevalier de L'ordre National du Merite 1988; *Recreations* travel, music, theatre; *Clubs* Garrick; *Style*— Nicholas B S Colchester, Esq; 37 Arundel Gardens, London, W11 (☎ 01 221 2829); Soulages, Lasalle, Gard, France; The Economist, 25 St James' Street, London, SW1 (☎ 01 839 7000)

COLCLOUGH, Christopher Gordon; s of George Dudley Colclough (d 1958), of 44 Manor House, Marylebone Rd, London NW, and Helen Scott, *née* Jenkins (d 1979); *b* 22 April 1914; *Educ* Charterhouse, Trinity Coll Cambridge (LLB); *m* 25 April 1942, Enid Coral, da of late James Stewart; 1 s (Christopher Angus b 1945), 1 da (Carol Ila b 1943); *Career* TA serv 3 Bn London Scottish 1939, OCTU Filey 1940, 2 Lt-Capt 151 Regt RA (Ayrshire Yeo) 1941-43, Maj 2 Corps Staff and 21 Army Gp Staff 1944-45; slr 1938, Linklaters & Paines 1939, ptnr Johnson Jecks & Landons 1946-63, md Bombay Burmah Trading Corpn Ltd Bombay 1964-68, chm Wallace Bros Trading & Industl Ltd 1968-72, conslt slr 1972-; chm and sec Wentworth Estate Roads Ctee; Freeman City of London, Liveryman Worshipful Co of Slrs; memb Law Soc 1938;

Recreations rowing, golf; *Clubs* Leander, Wentworth; *Style*— Christopher Colclough, Esq; 8 Virginia Beeches, Virginia Water, Surrey GU25 4LT (☎ 09904 2120); Wentworth Club, Virginia Water, Surrey GU25 4LS (☎ 09904 2819)

COLDSTREAM, Sir George Phillips; KCB (1955, CB 1949), KCVO (1968), QC (1960); s of Francis Menzies Coldstream (d 1958), of East Blatchington, Seaford, E Sussex, and Carlotta Mary, *née* Young (d 1940); *b* 20 Dec 1907; *Educ* Bilton Grange, Rugby, Oriel Coll Oxford (MA); *m* 1, 29 Sept 1934 (m dis 1948), (Mary) Morna, da of Maj Alistair Drummond Carmichael (d 1967), of Balendoch, Meigle, Perthshire; 2 da (Grizelda Morna b 1938 d 1945, Rosamund Charlotte b 1939); m 2, 1949, Sheila Hope, da of Lt-Col George Patrick Grant, DSO (d 1955), of Grove House, Woodbridge, Suffolk, and widow of Lt-Col John Henry Whitty, DSO, MC; *Career* barr Lincoln's Inn 1930; practiced at Chancery Bar 1931-34; asst to Parly Counsel HM Treasury 1934-39; legal asst Lord Chancellor's Office, House of Lords 1939-44; British War Crimes Exec 1942-46; Dep Clerk of the Crown in Chancery 1944-54; Clerk of the Crown in Chancery and Perm Sec Lord Chancellor's Office, House of Lords 1954-68; memb Royal Commn on Assizes and Quarter Sessions 1967-70; special conslt American Inst of Judicial Administration 1968-72; chm Cncl of Legal Educ 1970-73; memb Top Salaries Review Body 1971-83; Hon LLD Columbia Univ USA 1966; Hon Memb American Bar Assoc, Hon Memb American Coll of Trial Lawyers; *Recreations* sailing, golf; *Clubs* Athenaeum, Royal Cruising, Vincents (Oxford); *Style*— Sir George Coldstream, KCB, KCVO, QC; The Gate House, East Blatchington, Seaford, E Sussex BN25 2AH (☎ 0323 892801)

COLDSTREAM, Lady; Monica Mary; *née* Hoyer; da of A E Monrad Hoyer; *m* 1961, as his 2 w, Sir William Menzies Coldstream, CBE (d 1987); 1 s, 2 da; *Style*— Lady Coldstream

COLDWELLS, Rev Canon Alan Alfred; s of Alfred Carpenter Coldwells (d 1962), and Leila Philis Eugenie, *née* Livings; *b* 15 Jan 1930; *Educ* Haileybury and ISC, Univ Coll Oxford (BA, MA), Wells Theol Coll; *m* 5 Jan 1963, (Mary) Patricia, da of Arthur Leonard Hemsley, of Rugby; 1 s (Adam b 1969), 2 da (Katie b 1963, Lotti b 1966); *Career* Nat Serv, 1948-1950 Lt RASC; deacon 1955, priest 1956, curate Rugby St Andrew Diocese of Coventry 1955-62, curate i/c St George Rugby 1956-62, perpetual curate Sprowston Norwich 1962-73, rector Beeston St Andrew Norwich 1962-73; rural dean: Norwich North 1970-72, Rugby 1973-78; rector Rugby St Andrew 1973-87, hon canon Coventry Cathedral 1983-, canon of Windsor 1987-; dir Norwich Samaritans 1970-72; Freeman of the City of London 1954, Liveryman Worshipful Co of Vinters1954; *Books* The Story of St Andrew's Rugby (1979); *Recreations* art, painting, local history; *Style*— The Rev Canon Alan Coldwells; 6 The Cloisters, Windsor Castle, Berks SL4 1NJ (☎ 0753 866 313)

COLE, Viscount; Andrew John Galbraith Cole; s and h of 6 Earl of Enniskillen; *b* 28 April 1942; *Educ* Eton; *m* 3 Oct 1964, Sarah Frances Caroline, o da of the late Maj-Gen John Keith-Edwards, CBE, DSO, MC of Nairobi; 3 da (Hon Amanda Mary b 4 May 1966, Hon Emma Frances b 14 Feb 1969, Hon Lucy Caroline b 8 Dec 1970); *Career* late Capt Irish Gds; co dir; pilot; *Style*— Viscount Cole; c/o Royal Bank of Scotland, 9 Pall Mall, SW1

COLE, Hon Mrs (Cecilia Anne); *née* Ridley; da of 4 Viscount Ridley, TD, JP, DL; *b* 1 Dec 1953; *m* 1978, Berkeley Arthur Cole, s of Arthur Cole, bro of 6 Earl of Enniskillen, MBE, JP, DL; 1 s (b 1986); *Style*— The Hon Mrs Cole

COLE, Col Sir (Alexander) Colin; KCVO (1982, CVO 1979, MVO 1977), TD (1972); s of Capt Edward Harold Cole (d 1963), of Croham Hurst, Surrey, and Blanche Ruby Lavinia, *née* Wallis (d 1984); *b* 16 May 1922; *Educ* Dulwich, Brasenose Coll Oxford, (MA, BCL); *m* 1944, Valerie, o da of late Capt Stanley Walter Card; 4 s, 3 da; *Career* serv WWII Capt Coldstream Gds; Maj Inf Bn HAC, Bt Lt-Col, (later Hon Col) 6/7 Volunteer Bn The Queen's Regt TAVR 1981-86, Col RARO 1986-; barr Inner Temple 1949, hon bencher 1988; Fitzalan Pursuivant of Arms Extraordinary 1953, Portcullis Pursuivant of Arms 1957, Windsor Herald of Arms 1966, Garter Principal King of Arms 1978- (registrar and librarian Coll of Arms 1967-74); pres Royal Soc of St George, fell Heraldry Soc; kt princ Imperial Soc of Knights Bachelor 1983-; Sheriff City of London 1976-77; memb Ct of Common Cncl City of London Ward of Castle Baynard 1964-; govr Dulwich Coll, OStJ; memb Ct of Assistants HAC 1962-89; Freeman, Liveryman and memb Ct Worshipful Cos: Basketmakers, Scriveners', Painter Stainers; FSA, FRSA; *Clubs* Cavalry and Guards, City Livery; *Style*— Col Sir Colin Cole, KCVO, TD, Garter Principal King of Arms; College of Arms, Queen Victoria St, London EC4 (☎ 01 248 1188); Holly House, Burstow, Surrey

COLE, Sir David Lee; KCMG (1975, CMG 1965), MC 1944; s of late Brig David Henry Cole, CBE (d 1957), and Charlotte Louisa Ryles, *née* Wedgwood; *b* 31 August 1920; *Educ* Cheltenham, Sidney Sussex Coll Cambridge; *m* 1945, Dorothy, *née* Patton; 1s (David b 1950); *Career* served Royal Inniskilling Fusiliers 1940-45, Sicily and Italy; Dominions Office 1947; later Diplomatic Service: private sec to Rt Hon the Earl of Home 1957-60, high cmmr Malawi 1964-67, min (political) New Delhi 1967-70, asst under-sec of state FCO 1970-73, ambass Thailand 1973-78, ret; *Books* Rough Road to Rome (1983); *Recreations* watercolour painting; *Style*— Sir David Cole, KCMG, MC; 19 Burghley House, Somerset Rd, Wimbledon, London SW19 5JB

COLE, Maj-Gen Eric Stuart; CB (1960), CBE (1945); s of John William Cole (d 1947); *b* 10 Feb 1906; *m* 1941, Doris Hartley; *Career* Maj-Gen 1958, dir of Telecommunications War Off 1958-61, ret; conslt dir Granger Assocs Ltd Weybridge (formerly md), former pres Radio Soc of Great Britain; *Clubs* Army and Navy, MCC; *Style*— Maj-Gen Eric Cole, CB, CBE; 28 Roy Ave, London SW3

COLE, Frank (George Francis); *b* 3 Nov 1918; *Educ* Manchester GS; *m* 1, 1940, Gwendoline Mary Laver (decd); 2 s, 1 da; m 2, Barbara Mary Booth, *née* Gornall; *Career* chm Nat Exhibition Centre Ltd 1970-75; currently dir: Rical Ltd, William Mitchell (Sinkers) Ltd, Alexander Stenhouse UK Ltd, Frank Cole (Consultancy) Ltd; dep chm: Armstrong Equipment plc; past pres Birmingham Chamber of Industry and Commerce; *Style*— Frank Cole Esq; Northcot, 128 Station Rd, Balsall Common, Coventry, W Midlands CV7 7FF (☎ Berkswell 32105)

COLE, Frank Mortimore; s of Albert Percival Cole (d 1955), and Mary Flora Mortimore (d 1973); *b* 26 August 1904; *Educ* St Paul's Cathedral Choir Sch, Sutton Valence Sch, RN Coll Greenwich ; *m* 1934, Susanna Evelyn Norah, da of Thomas Alfred Capron (d 1931); 1 s (Christopher), 1 da (Rosalie); *Career* Lt RNVR; chm and md Cole & Son (holder of The Royal Warrant to HM as suppliers of wallpaper); *Recreations* sailing, painting pictures; *Clubs* Cruising Assoc; *Style*— Frank Cole Esq; The Old Rectory, Erwarton, Ipswich, Suffolk (☎ 047 334 223)

COLE, Geoffrey Christopher; s of Roy Cole, of Essex, and Rose, *née* Blanking (d 1981); *b* 4 Oct 1947; *Educ* Mayfield Sch for Boys; *m* 1971, Jennifer Mary, da of John Bertram Symonds (d 1965); 2 s (Martin b 1973, Stuart b 1974), 1 da (Victoria b 1977); *Career* advtg commercial dir Saatchi and Saatchi, (formerly dep media dir), chm Pinnacle Posters Ltd, chm and md Acme Media Ltd ; *Recreations* game fishing, chess, keen sportsman; *Clubs* Three Rivers GC, Cold Norton, Badminton, Sportsman, Tudor; *Style*— Geoffrey Cole, Esq; Glebe House, Fambridge Road, Althorne, Chelmsford, Essex CM3 6BZ; 80 Charlotte Sreet, London W1 (☎ 01 636 5060)

COLE, Howard Alfred Albury; s of Alfred Sidney Cole (d 1956), of Carshalton Beechs, Surrey, and Midred, *née* Albury (d 1953); *b* 18 Jan 1925; *Educ* Dulwich, Leeds Univ, City of London Coll; *m* 18 Dec 1954, Mary, da of Frank Earnest Woolveridge (d 1980); *Career* Lance Corpl HG 1942-46, Sgt RAEC 1947-48; teacher 1948-54, membership sec Br Inst of Radio Engrs 1954-62, asst sec Inst of Printing 1962-64, sr mangr insolvency Deloitte Haskins & Sells 1964-86, reader Chichester Diocese 1980-, tstee Runton Dolphin Tst 1969-, sec W Runton Camp 1950-56; Freeman: City of London 1979, Worshipful Co of Chartered Secretaries and Administrators 1979; FCIS 1970, FIPA 1985; *Recreations* gardening, walking; *Clubs* Royal Commonwealth Soc; *Style*— Howard Cole, Esq; 4 Highfield Drive, Hurstpierpoint, Hassocks, W Sussex BN6 9AT (☎ 0273 832 048)

COLE, Hon Jonathan Dare; s of Baron Cole (Life Peer, d 1979); *b* 12 Sept 1945; *Educ* Eton, Hertford Oxford; *Style*— The Hon Jonathan Cole

COLE, Joseph; s of Sidney Cole (d 1962), of Hurstwood Rd London NW11 and Millie, *née* Max; *b* 26 Dec 1936; *Educ* Regent St Poly London; *m* 25 June 1961, Helen, da of Morris Gorroway (d 1982) of Stanford Hill, London N16; 1 s (Simon b 25 Nov 1962), 3 da (Debra b 5 Jan 1964, Lisa b 27 April 1966, Rochelle b 29 Dec 1968); *Career* chm and md: S Cole Properties Ltd 1962-, J Cole Rentals Ltd 1980-, J Cole (Poulterers) Ltd 1983-, Courier Plan Ltd 1985-, Relay Postal Services 1987-; *Recreations* driving; *Style*— J Cole, Esq; White Ladyes, Totteridge Green, London N20 8PB (☎ 01 446 0775, fax 01 375 1203)

COLE, Hon Juliet Anthea; da of Baron Cole (Life Peer, d 1979); *b* 4 Jan 1951; *Career* interior designer; *Clubs* Chelsea Arts; *Style*— The Hon Juliet Cole; 24 Drayson Mews, London W8

COLE, Maggie; da of Robert Lawrence Cole, of NY, and Cyrella, *née* Golden (d 1972); *b* 30 Mar 1952; *Educ* Nyack HS NY, Juilliard Sch, Lawrence Univ, Geneva Conservatory of Music; *m* 21 March 1982, Richard Paul Macphail, s of Maj David Lamont Macphail, of Chichester; *Career* harpicordist; recordings made of Bach Scarlatti and other seventeenth and Eighteenth century composers for: Hyperion, Amon Ra, Virgin; performed at a series of Bach concerts at the Wigmore Hall 1985, numerous recordings for BBC Radio 3 and concerts throughout: Europe, USA, Poland, and Russia; active in organising music in local primary schs in Notting Hill fund raiser through charity concerts for London Lighthouse (the first hospice for AIDS sufferers in the UK); *Recreations* swimming, walking, reading, looking at paintings; *Style*— Miss Maggie Cole; c/o Robert White Artist Management, 182 Moselle Ave, London N22 6EX (☎ 01 221 4681)

COLE, Nicholas Stephen Edward; s of Col Sir Colin Cole, KCVO, TD, Garter Principal King of Arms, *qv*, of Holly House, Church Rd, Burstow, Horley, Surrey, and Valerie, *née* Card; *b* 23 August 1951; *Educ* Hurstpierpoint Coll, Central Sch of Art & Design, London (BA); *m* 30 Oct 1976, Suzanne Maryanne, da of John Duncan Rae; 2 s (Edward b 7 Sept 1979, Frederick b 14 Oct 1981), 1 da (Stephanie b 13 Aug 1977); *Career* assoc Jack Howe & Assoc 1975-76, art dir PD Design Co Ltd 1979-82; fndr and sr ptnr Cole Design Assocs (graphics, displays and interiors); Freeman City of London, Liveryman Worshipful Co of Scriveners 1975; MCSD 1974; *Style*— Nicholas Cole, Esq; Kenps House, E Chiltington, Lewes, E Sussex BN7 3QT (☎ 0273 890520); Cole Design Associates, Cambridge Grove, Hove, E Sussex BN3 3ED (☎ 0273 890590, 0273 822929, fax 0273 822939, car 0860 225969)

COLE, Robert Henry; s of Henry George (d 1960), and Anne Elizabeth, *née* Simmonds; *b* 5 May 1934; *Educ* Wilson's London, Ruskin Coll Oxford; *m* 26 April 1958, Pamela Jean, da of Stanley Arthur Figg (d 1960), of London; *Career* corrector of the press Kelihers London 1955-66, gp trg offr 1967-72, servs mangr Br Printing and Communication Corpn London 1973-86, pres servs mangr Maxwell Communication Corpn London 1987-; memb governing cncl Printers Charitable Corpn; Freeman City of London 1957; Liveryman: Worshipful Co of Makers of Playing Cards 1979, Worshipful Co of Stationers and Newspaper makers 1971; life memb Guild of Freemen of the City of London 1957; MBIM 1969, MITD 1969, FRSA 1970, MIOP 1971, MIIM 1979; *Recreations* walking, reading; *Style*— Robert H Cole, Esq; 11 Sheridan Crescent, Chislehurst, Kent BR7 5RZ, (☎ 01 467 9939); Maxwell Communication Corporation plc, Holborn Circus, London EC1P 1DQ, (☎ 01 377 4731, fax 01 353 0360, telex 888804)

COLE, Dr William Charles; LVO (1966); s of Frederick George Cole and Maria, *née* Fry; *b* 9 Oct 1909; *Educ* St Olave's GS, RAM; *m* 1, Elizabeth Brown Caw (d 1942); 3 da; m 2, Winifred Grace Mitchell; 1 s; *Career* former prof and lectr RAM and former lectr Royal Acad of Dancing; Master of the Music HM The Queen's Chapel of the Savoy 1954-; hon sec Royal Philharmonic Soc 1969-81; past pres and hon tres cncl Royal Coll of Organists (memb 1960-); chm Central Music Library 1972-; FRAM, FRCM, FRCO, FSA; *Books* The Form of Music (1969); articles on stained glass in learned journals; *Recreations* stained glass; *Clubs* Garrick; *Style*— Dr William Cole LVO; Barnacre, Wood Rd, Hindhead, Surrey (☎ 042 873 4917)

COLE, Sir (Robert) William; s of James Henry and Rita Sarah Cole; *b* 16 Sept 1926; *Educ* Northcote HS, Melbourne Univ (BCom); *m* 1956, Margaret Noleen, *née* Martin; 1 s, 1 da; *Career* sec Dept of Finance 1976-78, chm Public Service Bd 1978-; kt 1981; *see Debrett's Handbook of Australia and New Zealand for further details*; *Style*— Sir Robert Cole; 8 Scarborough St, Red Hill, ACT 2603, Australia

COLE, William Scott; CB (1949), CBE (1946); s of late William Scott Cole, of Jersey, C1; *b* 29 Mar 1902; *Educ* Victoria Coll Jersey, RMA Woolwich; *m* 1, 1948 (m dis 1970), Kathleen Winifred, yst da of late J Coleing; 1 da; m 2, 1971, Alice Rose, widow of Dr G T Pitts; *Career* Corps of Royal Engineers 1921, Dep Quartermaster-Gen War Office 1955, Maj-Gen 1956, ret 1958; *Clubs* Army and Navy; *Style*— Maj-Gen William Cole, CB, CBE

COLE-ADAMS, David John; s of Bernard Randall Cole-Adams (d 1945), step s of Brig Charles Frederick Cunningham Macaskie, CMG (d 1969), of Stanthorpe, Aust, and Doris, *née* Legg; *b* 21 May 1942; *Educ* The Southport Sch Southport Aust,

Queensland Univ Aust (B Arch); *m* 30 Nov 1968, Mary Theresa, Freeman da of Archibald Desmond Freeman, of Inverell, Aust; 2 s (Thomas b 1970, Oliver b 1972), 2 da (Elizabeth b 1968, Agnes b 1974); *Career* architect; Kenzie Lovell Ptnrship (formally Ronald Fielding Ptnrship), 1968-87; assoc 1972, sr assoc 1976, ptnr 1984; md Kenzie Lovell Architects Ltd 1987-; pres Cities of London & Westminster Soc of Architects 1982-84 (hon sec 1974-80); chm: London region RIBA 1986-88 (vice chm 1984086), London Devpt Control Forum 1986-; Freeman: City of London 1980, Worshipful Co of Tylers and Bricklayers (1984), Worshipful Co of Chartered Architects 1984 (Ct of Asst 1987); ARAiA 1967, FRIBA 1968; *Recreations* cooking, philately, walking; *Style*— David-Cole Adams, Esq; 134 Muswell Hill Rd, London N10 3JD (☎ 01 883 3665); Kenzie Lovell Architects, 113 Southwark St, London SE1 OJF (☎ 01 928 8201, fax 01 928 1828, telex 267592)

COLE-FONTAYN, Hon Mrs (Barbara Wendy Maia); *née* Latham; da of 1 Baron Latham (d 1970); *b* 7 Jan 1920; *Educ* Hendon Coll; *m* 1, 17 April 1941 (m diss 1945), Capt Denis Charles Wildish, RASC, s of Charles Albert Wildish; m 2, 26 Oct 1946 (m diss 1951), Peter Anthony Charles Kurt Bruckmann, er s of Kurt Bruckmann, of Linakers, Cookham Dean, Berks; 1 da; m 3, 1966, Malcolm Blundell Cole-Fontayn; *Career* 1942-44 war as 1 class Aircraft Woman WAAF; *Style*— The Hon Mrs Cole-Fontayn

COLE-HAMILTON, (Arthur) Richard; s of John Cole-Hamilton, CBE, DL, of Kilwinning, Ayrshire, and Gladys, *née* Cowie; *b* 8 May 1935; *Educ* Ardrossan Acad, Loretto Sch, Cambridge Univ (BA); *m* 16 Feb 1963, Prudence Ann, da of Dr Lindsay Lamb, of Edinburgh; 1 s (John Liston b 11 March 1971), 2 da (Patricia Joy b 17 Feb 1964, Sara Louise b 21 June 1967); *Career* Nat Serv, 2 Lt Argyll & Sutherland Highlanders; ptnr Brechin Cole-Hamilton CA's 1962-67; Clydesdale Bank plc: asst mangr 1967, hd off mangr 1976, chief gen mangr 1982, dir and chief exec 1987; memb cncl Inst of CA's (Scot) 1981-85, chm Ctee of Sco Cleaning Bankers 1985-87, memb bd of tstees Nat Galleries of Scot 1986, pres Inst of Bankers (Scot) 1988, dep chm Sco Cncl Devpt and Indust 1989, memb exec ctee Erskine Hosp, dir Glasgow C of C, chm bd of govrs Drumley House Sch, hon pres Ayrshire Chamber of Indust, memb cncl Strathclyde Business Sch; capt Prestwick GC 1987-88; FTIS (Scot); *Recreations* golf; *Clubs* Royal & Ancient, Prestwick GC, Western Highland Bde; *Style*— Richard Cole-Hamilton, Esq; Troon, Ayrshire; 30 St Vincent Pl, Glasgow G1 2HL (☎ 041 248 7070, fax 041 204 1527)

COLE-HAMILTON, Richard Arthur; s of the Ven Richard Meryn Cole-Hamilton (d 1959), formerly Archdeacon of Brecon, and Margaret, *née* Bennett (d 1954); *b* 24 Oct 1912; *Educ* Marlborough, Worcester Coll Oxford (BA, MA, Dip Ed); *m* 9 Aug 1947, (Ruth Kathleen) Betty, da of Sir William Lorenzo Parker, 3 Bt, OBE (d 1971), of Llangattock Ct, Crickhowell, Breconshire; 3 s (Robin b 1948, (Richard) Simon b 1951, (William Mervyn) John b 1954); *Career* TA Gen Serv Sch's OTC 1936-40, WWII, The Royal Scots Regt 1940-42, Maj 1 Bn The Cameronians (Scots Rifles) 1942-46, Adj, detached for course in Jap language SIMLA 1944-45, Wilton Pk German POW Rehabilitation Centre 1945-46; asst master St Albans Sch 1936-38; Fettes Coll Edinburgh: asst master 1938-55, housemaster 1955-69, second master 1969-77, acting headmaster 1978,79, keeper of the register 1978-; memb bd of dirs Royal Blind Asylum and Sch Edinburgh 1978-88; *Style*— Richard Cole-Hamilton, Esq; Hawthorn Villa, 386 Ferry Rd, Edbinburgh EH5 3QG (☎ 031 552 4423); Fettes College, Edinburgh (☎ 031 332 2281)

COLEBROOK, Miles William Merrill; s of Peter Merrill Colebrook, MC, JP, of Hawthorne Hill, Maidenhead, Berks, and Joyce Hay, *née* Rothven (d 1969); *b* 14 Jan 1948; *Educ* Shrewsbury, Ann Arbor Univ Michigan; *m* 1 Sept 1973, Jane Margaret, da of John Scott Findlay, of Widford, Herts; 2 s (Thomas b 1978, George b 1987) 1 da (Lucy b 1977); *Career* J Walter Thompson: media exec 1966-70, account exec 1970-78, bd dir 1978-85, md 1985-88, regnl pres Europe 1988-; MIPA 1978; *Recreations* shooting, skiing, cooking; *Style*— Miles Colebrook, Esq; 6 Whittingtall Rd, London, SW6; South Farm, Challow, Wantage, Oxon; J Walter Thompson, 40 Berkeley Sq, London W1X 6AD (☎ 01 6299496, fax 493 8432, telex 22871)

COLEBY, Anthony Laurie; s of Dr Leslie James Moger Coleby (d 1971), and Laurie, *née* Shuttleworth; *b* 27 April 1935; *Educ* Winchester, CCC Cambridge; *m* 1966, Rosemary Melian Elisabeth, da of Sir (Isham) Peter Garran KCMG, *qv*; 1 s, 2 da; *Career* personal asst to md IMF 1964-67, chief monetary advsr to govr Bank of England 1986- (dep chief cashier 1973-80, asst dir 1980-86); *Recreations* choral singing, railways, transport; *Clubs* Overseas Bankers; *Style*— Anthony Coleby Esq; Bank of England, London EC2 (☎ 01 601 4444)

COLECLOUGH, Peter Cecil; s of late Thomas James Coleclough, and Hilda Emma, *née* Ingram; *b* 5 Mar 1917; *Educ* Bradfield; *m* 1944, Pamela Beresford, *née* Rhodes; 2 s (1 decd); *Career* chm Howard Machinery Ltd 1969-82; dir: Nat Westminster Bank Ltd (chm SE regn) 1972-86, NCR Ltd 1971-87; chm SE regn CBI 1971-72; former pres; Royal Warrant Holders Assoc, Agric Engrs Assoc; *Recreations* fishing; *Clubs* Naval and Military; *Style*— Peter Coleclough Esq; Longlands Hall, Stonham Aspal, Stowmarket, Suffolk (☎ 0449 711 242)

COLEGATE, Raymond; CBE (1982); s of Ernest William Colegate, of 19 Arnold Rd, Gravesend, Kent and Violet Mary Dubettier Annett; *b* 31 August 1927; *Educ* Co Sch for Boys Gravesend, LSE (BA); *m* 6 April 1961, Cecilia Mary (Sally), da of James Healy (d 1970); 1 s (John b 1965), 1 da (Joanne b 1968); *Career* Bd of Trade 1949; Central Stat Off 1952-3, asst private sec to Pres BOT 1955-56 (Treasy 1957-59); EFTA Secretariat Geneva, Brussels 1960-64; CRE Dept BOT 1964-67; Aviation dept BOT/DTI 1967-72; head econ policy and licencing dept CAA 1972-75; head econ dept CAA 1975-77; gp dir Econ Regulation Civil Aviation Authy 1977-89; *Recreations* travel, music, reflection; *Style*— Raymond Colegate, Esq, CBE; CAA House, 45-59 Kingsway, London WC2B 6TE (☎ 01 379 7311, telex 883092, fax 01 379 3264)

COLEHAN, Barney; MBE (1981); s of Edward Colehan and Julia, *née* Mulkeen; *b* 19 Jan 1914; *Educ* Bradford Univ (MA); *m* 1935, Brett; 2 da (Margaret, Eileen); *Career* served WW II private 1940, served GB, Germany, demobbed 1946 (Maj); joined Br Forces Network Head of Light Entertainment Germany; joined BBC, produced Have a Go with Wilfred Pickles, Give 'im The Money Barney; joined BBC TV 1953, produced over 1000 programmes including Good Old Days (for thirty years), It's A Knock Out (for sixteen years), ret 1984; *Recreations* golf; *Style*— Barney Colehan Esq, MBE; 1 Tranfield Ave, Bradford Rd, Guiseley, Leeds LS20 8NL

COLEMAN, Prof Alice Mary; da of Bertie Coleman, DCM (d 1970), and Elizabeth Mary, *née* White (d 1959); *b* 8 June 1923; *Educ* Clarendon House Sch Ramsgate, Furzedown Coll, Birkbeck Coll (BA), King's Coll London (MA); *Career* teacher i/c geography Northfleet Central Sch Kent 1943-48, memb academic staff Kings Coll London 1948- (subsequently: asst lectr, sr lectr, reader, prof, emeritus prof 1988-, FKC 1980); sabbaticals: John Hopkins Univ Baltimore USA 1957-58, Canadian Federal Dept of Energy Mines and Resources 1965, Univ of Western Ontario (first holder of visiting professorship for Distinguished Woman Social Scientists) 1976,Hokkaido Univ of Educn Asahikawa Japan 1985 ; pres Isle of Thanet Geographical Assoc; dir Second Land Utilisation Survey of Britain 1960s, res contract DOE for Design Improvement of Problem Estates 1988; Gill Meml Award RGS 1963, Times/Veuve Clicquot Award 1974, Busk Gold Medal RGS 1987; memb RGS 1948; *Books* The Planning Challenge of the Ottawa Area (1969), Canadian Settlement and Enviromental Planning (1976), Utopia on Trial (1985); *Recreations* reading; *Style*— Prof Alice Coleman; King's College, Strand, London WC2R 2LS (☎ 01 836 5454 ext 2610)

COLEMAN, Donald Richard; CBE (1979), JP (Swansea 1962), MP (L) Neath 1964-; s of Albert Archer Coleman (d 1946), and Winified Marguerite Coleman; *b* 19 Sept 1925; *Educ* Cadoxton Boys' Sch Barry, Cardiff Tech Coll; *m* 1, 1949, Phyllis Eileen, *née* Williams (d 1963); 1 s; m 2, 1966, Margaret Elizabeth, da of William Thomas Morgan; 1 da; *Career* oppn front bench spokesman Welsh Affrs 1981-; tenor soloist, former metallurgist Steel Co of Wales Ltd; and lab technician at Welsh Nat Sch of Medicine in Cardiff, then sr technician at Swansea Tech and Univ Coll Swansea; pps to Min of State for Wales 1967-70, Opposition Whip 1970-74, a lord cmmr HM Tres 1974-79, vice-chamberlain of the Household 1978-79; *Style*— Donald Coleman Esq, CBE, JP, MP; Penderyn, 18 Penywern Rd, Bryncoch, Neath, W Glamorgan (☎ (0639) 4599)

COLEMAN, Gordon Barton; s of Walter Robert Granville Coleman, of Eastbourne, Sussex, and Olive May, *née* Buckenham; *b* 8 July 1900; *Educ* Brentwood; *m* 14 April 1956, Marie Jessie Thérèse (Moira), da of William Vogt; 2 da (Sylvia b 10 Dec 1957, Brenda b 28 Sept 1959); *Career* Army 1942-47, cmmnd Royal Welch Fusiliers 1943, Platoon Cdr Duke of Wellingtons Regt in Normandy 1944 (wounded Aug 1944), Capt 1945; gen mangr for Brazil FS Hampshire & Co Ltd 1960-61, fndr chm md Int Licensing (journal acknowledged as world ldr in field of technol transfer and licensing of patents) 1964-; *Recreations* equestrian sports, golf, gardening, antiques restoration; *Clubs* Northwood GC, Royal Eastbourne GC; *Style*— Gordon Coleman, Esq; 17 Farm Ave, Harrow, Middx HA2 7LP (☎ 01 868 9951) 92 Cannon Lane, Pinner, Middx HA5 1HT (☎ 01 866 2812, fax 01 831 9489, telex 262 433)

COLEMAN, John Ennis; s of Donald Stafford Coleman (d 1968), of 8 Carlisle Rd, Eastbourne, Sussex, and Dorothy Jean Balieff, *née* Ennis (d 1980); *b* 12 Nov 1930; *Educ* Dean Close Sch Cheltenham, Dulwich Coll London, Oxford Univ (MA); *m* 29 March 1958, Doreen Gwendoline, da of Percy Hellinger (d 1970), of Wimbledon; 1 s (David b 1968), 1 da (Kathryn b 1964); *Career* slr 1957; legal asst Treasy Slrs Dept 1958-64 (sr legal asst 1964-71, asst slr 1971-80) under sec (legal) Depts of Indust and Trade 1980-83, legal advsr Dept of Educn and Sci 1983-; *Style*— John Coleman, Esq; Department of Education and Science, Elizabeth House, York Rd, London SE1 7PH (☎ 01 934 9959)

COLEMAN, John Raymond; s of James Alexander Coleman (d 1967), and Cathleen Kelly, *née* Lucas; *b* 23 Jan 1948; *Educ* Univ of Strathclyde (BA, MSc); *m* 25 Nov 1972, Rose Ann, da of James William Johnson (d 1985); 3 s (Iain James b 1973, James Edward b 1975, Alan Stephen b 1981); *Career* sr ptnr: Coleman Ballantine Partnership 1977, Coleman Ballantine of Gibralter 1986; dir Mainhead Properties 1984, ptnr Property Marketing Conslts 1987; cncl memb of RIAS; FRIAS; *Style*— John R Coleman, Esq; "Waltry", Milton of Campsie, Glasgow G65 8AA; 9/10 Woodside Crescent, Glasgow G3 7UL (☎ (041 332) 1818, fax (041 332) 6433)

COLEMAN, Malcolm Jerry; s of Colin Coleman (d 1975), and Esta, *née* Joel; *b* 9 Dec 1938; *Educ* Whittinghame Coll Brighton, City of London Sch; *m* 17 June 1962, Deanne Elaine Bernice, da of Hilary Louis Clive, of London and Portugal; 2 s (Jeremy Andrew b 1963, Daniel Clive b 1964), 1 da (Sara Melanie b 1966); *Career* sr ptnr Jeffreys Henry Rudolf and Marks, dir Managed Growth Investmts Ltd, FCA; *Recreations* Golf, Bridge; *Clubs* Potters Bar Golf (Capt 1974-75, chm 1980-87); *Style*— Malcolm J Coleman, Esq; 37 Springfield Road, London NW8; Wilec House, 82/84 City Road, London EC1Y 2DA (telex 892907, fax 608 1983)

COLEMAN, (Elizabeth) Maryla Helen; s of Zygmunt Karol Lambert Chojecki (d 1983), of Bannisters, Ralade St, Woodcote, Oxon, and Caroline Elizabeth MBE, *née* Rowett; *b* 28 Mar 1954; *Educ* St Josephs Convent Reading Berks, Univ of London (BA); *m* 1 Dec 1973, (m dis 1981) Antony Gerard Coleman, s of Michael Coleman (d 1974), of Daly, Co Dublin, Ireland; *Career* md Champeson Bros (UK) Ltd 1979, dir Far East Pearls Ltd 1983, formed Maryla Coleman Assocs; *Style*— Mrs Maryla Coleman; 1 Coach and Horses Yd, Savile Row, London W1

COLEMAN, Bishop Suffragan of Crediton Peter Everard; s of Geoffrey Everard Coleman (d 1942), of Ware Herts, and Lilian Bessie, *née* Cook (d 1982); *b* 28 August 1928; *Educ* Haileybury, London Univ (LLB), Bristol Univ (MLitt); *m* 14 May 1960, HSH Princess Elisabeth Donata Regina Emma Clementine, yst da of HSH Prince Heinrich XXXIX Reuss (d 1946); 2 s (Basil b 1963, Benedict b 1965), 2 da (Antonia b 1961, Elena b 1969); *Career* military service RHG and RA, 2nd Lt 1947-49; barr Middle Temple 1965; ordained Bristol 1955, chaplain and lectr King's Coll London 1960-66, vicar St Paul's Clifton, chaplain Bristol Univ 1966-71; canon residentiary and dir of tning Bristol 1971-81, archdeacon of Worcester 1981-84, Bishop Suffragan of Creditor 1984- clerical memb Ct of Archers 1980-, memb Gen Synod 1974-81, jt ed Theology 1982-; *Books* Experiments with Prayer (1961), A Christian Approach to Television (1968), Christian Attitudes to Homosexuality (1980); *Recreations* film making, fishing; *Style*— The Rt Rev the Bishop of Crediton; 10 The Close, Exeter EX1 1EZ

COLEMAN, Prof Robert George Gilbert; s of George Gilbert Coleman (d 1953), of Wellington NZ, and Rosina Emily, *née* Warner (d 1964); *b* 2 Oct 1929; *Educ* St Mark's Sch, Rongotai Coll, Wellington Coll, Victoria Univ of Wellington (MA), Emmanuel Coll Cambridge (BA, MA); *m* 28 June 1958, Dorothy, da of Rufus Gabe (d 1956), of Ystalyfera; 1 s (Ian Gilbert b 1965); *Career* lectr in humanity Kings Coll Aberdeen 1955-60, fell Emmanuel Coll Cambridge 1960-, prof of comparative philology Cambridge Univ 1985- (lectr in classics 1960-65, tutor 1963-71, librarian 1980-85); *Books* The Eclogues of Vergil (ed with intro 1977); *Recreations* music, conversation, exploring strange towns; *Style*— Prof Robert Coleman; 60 Gilbert Rd, Cambridge CB4 3PE (☎ 0223 357 348); Emmanuel College Cambridge CB2 3A (☎ 0223 334 200)

COLEMAN, Rodney Bernard; s of Jacob Henry Coleman, of 3 Osterley Road, London, and Rosina, *née* Kelly; *b* 16 Nov 1945; *Educ* Joseph Priestley Secdy Tech Sch, Brooke House Sch, PCL (LLB); *m* 1 Nov 1986, Marijana, da of Jovo Skorupan of Vuceticev Prilaz No 3, 41000 Zagreb, Yugoslavia; *Career* with civil serv: Dept of Employment and Productivity 1967-68, Off of Population Censuses and Surveys 1969-71f, MOD 1971-79; barr Gray's Inn 1978; memb: Cons Pty Hackney 10973-, Hackney Cncl (C) Candidate 1974, 1982, 1986; govr: Princess May Primary Sch, Sir Thomas Abney Primary Sch; *Recreations* music, bridge; *Style—* Rodney Coleman, Esq; 169 Upper Street, Islington, London N1 1RG; 1 Stone Buildings, Lower Ground Floor, Lincoln's Inn, London WC2A 3XB (☎ 405 1673)

COLEMAN, Sylvia May; da of Capt Gordon Barton Coleman, of Harrow, Middx, and Marie Jessie Therese, *née* Vogt; *b* 10 Dec 1957; *Educ* Harrow Co GS for Girls, Univ of Birmingham (LLB), Coll of Law Lancaster Gate; *Career* slr Stephenson Harwood 1980-85, co lawyer Gallaher Ltd 1985-86, CBS Records 1987-, md The Entertainment Zone 1989-; jt UK promoter Ceroc Dance 1983-, co-organiser Annual Ceroc Charity Ball, memb Action Aid; memb Law Soc 1980; *Recreations* dance, music, entertaining; *Clubs* The Kensington Close; *Style—* Miss Sylvia Coleman; 20 Courtfield Gdns, London SW5 OPD (☎ 01 370 5161); 17/19 Soho Sq, London W1V 6HE (☎ 01 734 8181, ext 305, fax 01 734 4321, telex 24203 CBSREC G)

COLEMAN, Talbot Pascoe Hilbut; s of Jack Talbot Coleman (d 1966), of Bristol, and Amelia Marjorie *née* Butt; *b* 10 Oct 1934; *Educ* Cardiff HS; *m* 9 Aug 1958, (Kathryn) Ann Louise, da of Flt-Lt Hugh David McDougall, of Godalming, Surrey; 1 s (Nial Talbot b 1961), 1 da (Charlotte Ann Louise b 1962); *Career* Fl Offr RAF 1952-54, RAFVR 1959-65; Thames Bd Mills Ltd 1956-66, md Assi Pulp and Paper Sales UK Ltd 1966-; prcs UK Paper Agents Assoc 1984-86, chm Croydon Central Cons Assoc 1985-88; Freeman: Worshipful Co of Gold and Silver Wyre Drawers 1979, Worshipful Co of Stationers and Newspaper Makers 1984; *Recreations* golf, cricket, reading; *Clubs* Carlton, MCC; *Style—* Talbot Coleman, Esq; 1 Upfield, Croydon

COLEMAN, Terence Francis Frank (Terry); s of Jack Coleman (d 1978), of Poole, Dorset, and Doreen, *née* Grose; *b* 13 Feb 1931; *Educ* London Univ (LLB); *Career* journalist: Poole Herald, Savoir Faire (ed), Sunday Mercury, Birmingham Post; The Guardian: reporter, arts corr, chief feature writer 1961-74; special writer Daily Mail 1974-76; The Guardian: chief feature writer 1976-78, New York corr 1981, special corr 1982-89; assoc ed The Independent 1989-; Feature Writer of the Year, Br Press Awards 1983, Journalist of the Year, Granada Awards 1987; *Books* The Railway Navvies (1965 Yorkshire Post Prize for the best Book of the Year), A Girl for the Afternoons (1965), Providence and Mr Hardy (with Lois Deacon 1966), The Only True History (collected journalism 1969), Passage to America (1972), The Liners (1976), ed An Indiscretion in the Life of an Heiress (1976), The Scented Brawl (collected journalism 1978), Southern Cross (1979), Thanksgiving (1981), Movers and Shakers (collected interviews 1987), Thatcher's Britain (1987); *Recreations* cricket, opera, circumnavigation; *Clubs* MCC; *Style—* Terry Coleman, Esq; 18 North Side, London SW4

COLERAINE, 2 Baron (UK 1954); (James) Martin Bonar Law; s of 1 Baron, PC (d 1980, himself s of Andrew Bonar Law, Prime Minister 1922-23); *b* 8 August 1931; *Educ* Eton, Trin Oxford; *m* 1, 30 April 1958 (m dis 1966), Emma Elizabeth, o da of late Nigel Richards; 2 da; m 2, 21 Aug 1966, (Anne) Patricia, yr da of Maj-Gen Ralph Henry Farrant, CB, of King's Acre, Wareham, Dorset; 1 s (Hon James b 1975), 2 da (Hon Henrietta b 1968, Hon Juliana b 1971); *Heir* s, Hon James Law; *Career* sits as Cons in House of Lords; *Style—* The Rt Hon the Lord Coleraine; 3/5 Kensington Pk Gdns, W11 (☎ 01 221 4148)

COLERIDGE, David Ean; s of late Guy Cecil Richard Coleridge, MC, and Katherine Cicely Stewart Smith; *b* 7 June 1932; *Educ* Eton; *m* 1955, Susan, *née* Senior; 3 s; *Career* Lloyds underwriter; chm Sturge Gp of Cos 1978-, dep chm Lloyd's 1985, 1988, 1989; *Recreations* shooting, golf, early English Watercolours, family; *Style—* David Coleridge, Esq; 37 Egerton Terrace, London SW3 2BUA; Spring Pond, Wispers, nr Midhurst, W Sussex; Sturge Holdings PLC, 9 Devonshire Sq, London EC2M 4YL (☎ 01 623 8822, telex 894156 STURGE G, fax 623 3386)

COLERIDGE, Lady (Marguerite) Georgina Christine; *née* Hay; 2 da of 11 Marquess of Tweeddale (d 1967), and his 1 wife Marguerite Christine, *née* Ralli (d 1944); *b* 19 Mar 1916; *m* 20 Sept 1941, Capt Arthur Nicholas Coleridge, late Irish Gds, s of John Duke Coleridge, FRIBA (d 1934), of Darby Green House, Blackwater, Hants; 1 da; *Career* with National Magazine Co Ltd 1937-39, with Country Life 1945, editor Homes and Gardens 1949-63; dir: Country Life Ltd 1962-74, George Newnes Ltd 1963-69; publisher: Homes and Gardens, Woman's Journal 1969-71, Ideal Home 1970-71; dir special projects IPC Women's Magazines 1971-74, conslt IPC Women's Magazines 1974-82; dir Public Relations Cncl Ltd 1974-82; chm: Inst of Journalists (London Dist) 1954 (fell 1970), Women's Press Club 1959 (pres 1965-67);memb Int Assoc of Women and Home Page Journalists 1968-74, assoc Women in Public Relations 1972-, assoc memb Ladies Jockey Assoc of GB, fndr memb Media Soc Ltd (Inst of Journalists Fndn) 1973-76; vice-pres Greater London Fund for the Blind 1981, pres Friends of Moorfields 1981; freeman Worshipful Co of Stationers and Newspapermakers 1973; *Publications* Grand Smashional Pointers (cartoons, 1934), I Know What I Like (1959), That's Racing (1978), and various articles; *Recreations* racing, writing, cooking; nothing highbrow; *Style—* Lady Georgina Coleridge; 33 Peel St, London W8 (☎ 01 727 7732)

COLERIDGE, Hon John Seymour Duke; s of 3 Baron Coleridge (d 1955); *b* 1 Oct 1908; *m* 8 Sept 1934, Dora Lovelace, da of late George Coplestone Carter; *Style—* The Hon John Coleridge; 4 Angel Court, Shaftesbury, Dorset SP7 8HX

COLERIDGE, Nicholas David; s of David Ean Coleridge, and Susan, *née* Senior; *b* 4 Mar 1957; *Educ* Eton Coll Berks, Trinity Coll Cambridge; *Career* assoc ed Tatler, 1980-82, columnist Evening Standard 1982-84, assoc ed Harpers and Queen 1984-86 (ed 1986-); author: Tunnel Vision (collected joualism, 1982), Shooting Stars (1984), Aroun the World in 78 Days (1984), The Fashion Conspirancy (1988); Young Journalist of the Year 1984; *Recreations* travel, shuttlecock; *Clubs* Harry's Bar; *Style—* Nicholas Coleridge, Esq; 14 Wandon Road, London SW6 (☎ 01 731 3416); 72 Broadwick Street, London W1 (☎ 01 439 5000)

COLERIDGE, The Dowager Lady (Cecilia) Rosamund; *née* Fisher; The Dowager; er da of Adm Sir William Wordsworth Fisher, GCB, GCVO (d 1937), and Cecilia, *née* Warre-Cornish; *m* 28 Aug 1936, 4 Baron Coleridge, KBE, DL (d 1984); 2 s (5 Baron and Hon Samuel, *qqv*); *Clubs* Army and Navy; *Style—* The Rt Hon Dowager Lady Coleridge; The Manor House, Ottery St Mary, S Devon (☎ (040 481) 4201)

COLERIDGE, Lt-Col Hon Samuel John Taylor; yr s of 4 Baron Coleridge, KBE, DL (d 1984), and Dowager Baroness Coleridge, *qv*; *b* 5 Feb 1942; *Educ* Winchester, Trinity Coll Oxford; *m* 1973, Patricia Susan, yr da of John Basil Edwards, CBE, of Cradley, nr Malvern, Worcs; 2 da (Jessica Alice Seymour b 1974, Clara Emily Taylor b 1976); *Career* Lt-Col Grenadier Gds, attached Army Air Corps 1964-68; Military Attaché Algiers and Tunis 1985-88; *Style—* Lt-Col The Hon Samuel Coleridge; 43 Vogesenstrasse, 7570 Baden-Baden, W Germany

COLERIDGE, 5 Baron (UK 1873); William Duke Coleridge; er s of 4 Baron Coleridge, KBE, DL (d 1984; ggs of 1 Baron who was gn Samuel Taylor Coleridge, the poet), and Rosamund, Baroness Coleridge, *qv*; *b* 18 June 1937; *Educ* Eton, RMA Sandhurst; *m* 1, 17 Feb 1962 (m dis 1977), Everild Tania, da of Lt-Col Beauchamp Hambrough, OBE; 1 s, 2 da (Hon Tania Rosamund b 1966, Hon Sophia Tamsin b 1970); m 2, 1977, Pamela, da of George William Baker, CBE, VRD; 2 da (Hon Vanessa Layla b 1978, Hon Katharine Suzannah b 1981); *Heir* s, Hon James Duke Coleridge b 5 June 1967; *Career* Maj Coldstream Gds (ret), commanded Guards Independent Parachute Co 1970-72; chm Universal Energy; gov Royal West of England Sch for Deaf; patron Colway Theatre Trust; *Recreations* golf, tennis, water-skiing; *Style—* The Rt Hon the Lord Coleridge; The Chanter's House, Ottery St Mary, S Devon (☎ (040 481) 2417)

COLES, Adrian Michael; s of Kenneth Ernest Coles, and Constance Mary, *née* Sykes; *b* 19 April 1954; *Educ* Holly Lodge Smethwick, Univ of Nottingham (BA), Univ of Sheffield (MA); *m* 23 May 1981, Marion Alma da of Joseph Henry Hoare; 1 s (David), 1 da (Verity); *Career* economist: Electricity Cncl 1976-79, economist Electricity Cncl 1976-79, head of external rels dept Bldg Socs Assoc 1986- (economist 1979-81, head of econs and statistics dept 1981-86); examiner econ affairs CBSI 1984-87; regular contrib: CBSI jl, Building Soc Gazette, Housing Fin Int, Building Soc Yearbook; *Recreations* family, swimming; *Style—* Adrian Coles, Esq; 3 Savile Row, London, WIX 1AF (☎ 01 437 0655, fax 01 734 6416, telex 2438 BSAG)

COLES, Hon Mrs (Bridget Mary); *née* Hope; 1 da of 2 Baron Rankeillour, GCIE, MC (d 1958), by Grizel, da of Brig-Gen Sir Robert Gilmour, 1 Bt, CB, CVO, DSO; *b* 17 Oct 1920; *m* 25 Jan 1942, Lt-Col George Henry Hugh Coles, The East Yorks Regt, s of late Lt-Col James Hugh Coles, DSO, The East Yorks Regt; 3 da; *Style—* The Hon Mrs Coles; 25 Kings Court North, Kings Road, London SW3 (☎ 01 352 8570)

COLES, Prof Bryan Randell; s of Charles Frederick Coles (d 1974), of Cardiff, Wales and Olive Irene, *née* Randell (d 1975); *b* 9 June 1926; *Educ* Canton HS Cardiff, Univ of Wales Cardiff (BSc), Jesus Coll Oxford (DPhil); *m* 27 July 1955, Merivan, da of W Ace Robinson (d 1935), of Minneapolis USA; 2 s (Matthew b 1965, Jonathan b 1967); *Career* physics dept Imperial Coll London: lectr 1950-60, reader 1960-65, prof 1965-, pro rector 1986-; dean RCS 1984-86, visiting prof Univ of California 1969 (Univ of Minnesota 1983), bd chm Taylor & Francis Scientific publishers 1976-; chm: Physics Ctee SRC 1973-77, Neutron Beam Ctee SERC 1984-88; FInstP 1968; *Books* Atomic Theory for Students of Metallurgy (with W Hume-Rothery 1969), Electronic Structures of Solids (with A D Caplin, 1976); *Recreations* music, theatre, natural history; *Style—* Prof Bryan Coles; 61 Courtfield Gdns, London SW5 (☎ 01 373 3539); Shoe Cottage, Vines Cross, Horam, E Sussex; Imperial Coll, London SW7; Taylor & Francis Ltd, 4 John St, London WC1

COLES, His Hon Judge Gerald James Kay; QC (1976); s of James William Coles (d 1977), of Redcar, Yorkshire, and Jane Elizabeth Kay (d 1981); *b* 6 May 1933; *Educ* Coatham Sch, Sir William Turner's Sch Redcar, Brasenose Coll Oxford (BA, BCL), Harvard Law Sch USA (LLM); *m* 22 Feb 1958, Kathleen Yolande, da of Alfred John Hobson, FRCS (d 1970); 3 s (Andrew James b 1961, Christopher John Kay b 1963, Matthew Henry b 1970); *Career* called to the bar Middle Temple 1957, practised London and NE circuit 1957-85, prosecuting cncl to the Inland Revenue 1971-76, recorder 1972-85, circuit judge 1985; memb Mental Health Review Tribunal 1985; *Recreations* music, theatre, photography, opera; *Clubs* Yorkshire; *Style—* His Hon Judge Coles, QC; Redwood, Dean Lane, Hawksworth, Guiseley, Leeds LS20 8NY (☎ 0943 72688)

COLES, Joanna Louise; da of Michael Edward Coles, and Margaret Coles; *b* 20 April 1962; *Educ* Prince Henry's Comprehensive Sch Otley W Yorks, UEA (BA); *Career* grad trainee The Spectator (contrib The Guardian) 1984-86, dep literary ed The Spectator 1986-87, news/feature writer and rock reviewer Daily Telegraph 1987-; *Recreations* riding, theatre; *Clubs* Westminster Dining; *Style—* Miss Joanna Coles; Daily Telegraph, 181 Marsh Wall, South Quay, London E14 9SR (☎ 01 538 5000)

COLES, Sir (Arthur) John; KCMG (1989, CMG 1984); s of Arthur Strixton Coles, and Doris Gwendoline Coles; *b* 13 Nov 1937; *Educ* Magdalen Coll Sch Brackley, Magdalen Coll Oxford (BA); *m* 1965, Anne Mary Sutherland Graham; 2 s, 1 da; *Career* served HM Forces 1955-57; HM Diplomatic Serv 1960-: Middle Eastern Centre for Arabic Studies Lebanon 1960-62, third sec Khartoum 1962-64, FO 1964-68, asst political agent Trucial States (Dubai) 1968-71, FCO 1971-75, head of Chancery Cairo 1975-77, cnsllr (Developing Countries) UK Perm Mission to EEC 1977-80, head of S Asian Dept FCO 1980-81, private sec to the PM 1981-84, ambassador to Jordan 1984-88, High Cmmr Australia 1988-; *Style—* HE Sir John Coles, CMG; Br High Commission, Commonwealth Ave, Canberra, Australia

COLES, Dame Mabel Irene; DBE (1971, CBE 1965); da of late Edward Johnston; *m* 1927, Sir Edgar Barton Coles (d 1981); 1 s, 2 da; *Career* pres Australian Women's Liberal Club 1965-, dir Asthma Foundation of Victoria 1965, pres Royal Women's Hosp Melbourne 1968-72; *Style—* Dame Mabel Coles, DBE; Hendra, Williams Rd, Mount Eliza, Vic 3930, Australia

COLES, Norman; CB (1971); s of Fred Coles (d 1939), of Sutton Coldfield, and Emily, *née* Carr (d 1979); *b* 29 Dec 1914; *Educ* Hanson High Bradford, Imp Coll London (BSc, ACCS, DIC); *m* 1947, Una Valerie, da of Edwin Prestoe Tarrant (d 1934), of Australia; 5 s (Richard, Christopher, Simon, Jeremy, Robert); *Career* head armament dept RAE Farnborough 1959; dir gen Equipment Res and Devpt Miny of Aviation 1962; dep controller aircraft (RAF) Miny of Technol 1966-68; dep controller Guided Weapons Miny of Technol 1968-69; dep chief advsr (res and studies) MOD 1969-71; dep controller establisments and res MOD 1971-75; *Recreations* carpentry, crossword puzzles; *Style—* Norman Coles, Esq, CB; 27 Castle Hill, Banwell, Weston-Super-Mare, Avon BS24 6NX (☎ Banwell 822019)

COLFOX, Lady Frederica Loveday; da of Adm Sir Victor Crutchley, VC, KCB, DSC (d 1986), and Joan Elizabeth Loveday, *née* Coryton (d 1982); *b* 28 Dec 1934; *Educ*

Heathfield, Ascot; *m* 13 Jan 1962, Sir John, s of S W Philip Colfox, Brt, MC (d 1966); 2 s (Philip b 27 Dec 1962, Edward b 14 Jan 1969), 3 da (Victoria b 14 Jan 1964, Charlotte b 28 Jan 1966, Connie b 20 July 1971); *Career* The Witt Library, Courtauld Inst of Art until 1961; chm The Enviromental Med Fnd (acting chm 1987); *Recreations* childish pursuits; *Style*— Lady Colfox; Symondsbury House, Bridport, Dorset DT6 6HB, (☎ 0308 22956)

COLFOX, Sir (William) John; 2 Bt (UK 1939), of Symondsbury, Co Dorset, JP (Dorset 1962), and Mary Frances, *née* Symes-Bullen DL (d 1973); s of Sir Philip Colfox, 1 Bt, MC (d 1966); *b* 25 April 1924; *Educ* Eton; *m* 13 Jan 1962, Frederica Loveday, da of Adm Sir Victor Crutchley, VC, KCB, DSC, DL, of Mappercombe Manor, Bridport, Dorset, *qv*; 2 s, 3 da; *Heir* s, Philip Colfox, *qv*; *Career* Lt RNVR 1935-45; land agent 1950, chm Land Settlement Assoc 1979-81, dir TV South West 1981-; High Sheriff of Dorset 1969; *Style*— Sir John Colfox, Bt, JP, DL; Symondsbury House, Bridport, Dorset (☎ 0308 22956)

COLFOX, Philip John; s and h of Sir William John Colfox, 2 Bt; *b* 27 Dec 1962; *Educ* Eton; *Career* private industrialist; trained with Jardine Thompson Graham Ltd 1982-85; md Symondsbsury House Ltd 1987, Philip Colfox Ltd 1989; *Books* The Case for Environmental Medicine, The Environmental Med Fndn; *Recreations* writing, politics, anti-pollution; *Style*— Philip Colfox Esq; 715 Fulham Rd, London SW6 5UL (☎ 01 736 9293)

COLGATE, Dennis Harvey; MM (1944); s of Charles William Colgate (d 1977), and Marjorie, *née* Harvey (d 1979); *b* 9 Oct 1922; *Educ* Varndean Sch Brighton, Univ Coll of South West Exeter, Univ of London (LLB); *m* 8 April 1961, Kathleen, da of Rev Victor Marquis (d 1958); 1 da (Sarah b 1963); *Career* Army 1942-47; princ probate registry 1947-64 (estab offr 1959-64), district probate registrar Manchester 1964-74, registrar High Ct (family div) 1974-84, ret; *Books* conslt ed Tristram and Coote's Probate Practice (1976-84), jt ed : Rayden on Divorce (7 edn 1958, 8 edn 1960), Atkin's Court Forms (Probate) (2 edn 1974, and 1985); *Recreations* walking, DIY ; *Style*— Dennis Colgate, Esq, MM; 10 Frogmore Close, Hughenden Valley, High Wycombe, Bucks (☎ 024 024 2659)

COLGRAIN, 3 Baron (UK 1946); David Colin Campbell; s of 2 Baron Colgrain, MC (d 1973); *b* 24 April 1920; *Educ* Eton, Trinity Coll Cambridge; *m* 1, 20 June 1945 (m dis 1964), Veronica Margaret, da of late Lt-Col William Leckie Webster, RAMC; 1 s, 1 da; m 2, 1973, Mrs Sheila McLeod Hudson; *Heir* s, Hon Alastair Campbell; *Career* served WW II, Lt 9 Lancers, UK and ME (wounded Alamein 1942); exec Grindlays Bank: India and Pakistan 1945-48, London 1949; Antony Gibbs & Sons Ltd and successive cos 1949-83 (dir 1954-83, ret 1983); chm Alexander and Berendt Ltd 1967-; *Recreations* music, farming, forestry; *Clubs* Cavalry and Guards'; *Style*— The Rt Hon the Lord Colgrain; Bushes Farm, Weald, Sevenoaks, Kent (☎ 073 277 279)

COLHOUN, Prof John; s of James Colhoun (d 1935), of Castlederg, Co Tyrone, and Rebecca, *née* Lecky (d 1963); *b* 15 May 1913; *Educ* Edwards Sch Castlederg Co Tyrone, The Queen's Univ Belfast (BSc, B Agr, M Agr), Imperial Coll of Sci London (DIC), Univ of London (PhD, DSc); *m* 29 July 1949, Margaret Waterhouse, da of Prof Gilbert Waterhouse, of Belfast; 3 da (Lucy (Mrs Loerzer) b 1950, Georgiana (Mrs Golub b 1956, Jacqueline (Mrs Chaddock) b 1959); *Career* Miny of Agric for NI: res asst 1939-46, sr sci offr 1946-50, princ sec offr 1951-60; Queen's Univ of Belfast: asst lectr in agric botany 1940-42, reader in mycology and plant pathology 1954-60 (asst lectr 1942-45, jr lectr 1945-46, lectr 1946-54); Univ of Manchester: Barker prof of cryptogamic botany 1960-80, dean faculty of sci 1974 and 75, pro-vice chllr 1977-80, professor emeritus 1980; jt ed-in-chief Jl of Phytopathology (Phytopathologische Zeitschrift) 1973-; pres: The Queen's Univ Assoc 1960-61, Br Mycological Soc 1963, the Queen's Univ Club London 1983-85; chm: Fedn of Br Plant Pathologists 1968, int ctee of Fusarium Workers 1968-73, ctee of euro discussion gps in Plant Pathology 1968-75, sub ctee on res on cereals ARC 1973-78; memb: governing body Glasshouse Crops Res Int Littlehampton 1967-77, plants and soils ctee ARC 1968-78, Univ of Manchester cncl and ct 1973-76 and 1977-80; visiting prof State Univ of Washington USA 1969; govr: Hulme Hall Tst Fndn 1964-, Manchester HS for Girls 1961-85, City of Manchester Coll of HE 1978-83; chm bd for awards in affiliated colls Univ of Manchester 1977-80; chm of ctee: Ashburne Hall Manchester 1970-80, The Manchester Museum 1974-80 (memb ctee 1960-); président d'honneur Third Euro Congress of Myclology 1963; FLS 1955, FIBiol 1963; Univ of Manchester (MSc, ex-officio degree) 1964; *Books* Diseases of The Flax Plant (1947), Clubroot Disease of Crucifers caused by *Plasmodiophora brassicae* Woron. (1958); Numerous papers in: Annals of Applied Biology, Annals of Botany, Trans. British Mycological Soc, Nature, Phytopathologische Zeitschrift, Annales Academie Scientiarum Feenicae, Annales Agriculturae Fennaie, Annual Reviews of Phytopathology; *Clubs* Athenaeum; *Style*— Prof John Colhoun; 12 Southdown Cres, Cheadle Hulme, Cheshire SK8 6EQ (☎ 061 485 2084)

COLKER, Richard Frank; s of Frank Colker (d 1986), of St Clair Shores, Michigan, USA, and Marjorie, *née* Humphry; *b* 5 Oct 1945; *Educ* Michigan State Univ, E Lansing USA (BA); *m* 24 Nov 1979, Marie-Claude, da of Jean-Louis Fouché, of Carquefou, France, 3 da (Emilie b 1980, Jennifer b 1982, Stephanie b 1985); *Career* served US Army until 1968; Wells Fargo Bank San Francisco US 1969-72 (London 1973-75) vice-pres corp fin Banque de la Société Financière Europèenne Paris Fr (1976-83), md investment banking Kidder Peabody Int London 1984-; *Recreations* golf, classical music, european history; *Clubs* Royal St George's Golf (Kent), Union (New York NY); *Style*— Richard Colker, Esq; 6 Pelham Place, London SW7 (☎ 01 581 5631); 107 Cheapside, London EC2V 6DD (☎ 01 480 8419)

COLLACOTT, Peter Barrie; s of Dr Ralph Albert Collacott, of 1 Fordview Close, Great Glen, Leicester and Ruby Hilda, *née* Nash; *b* 19 June 1944; *Educ* King's Sch Rochester; *m* 4 Sept 1971, Frances Rosamond, da of LtC dr Hibbard (d 1983), of 585 Maidstone Road, Blue Bell Hill, Rochester, Kent; 2 s (Nicholas b 1973, Piers b 1978), 2 da (Esther b 1976, Hannah b 1985); *Career* articled clerk Jackson Pixley 1963-68, audit sr Price Waterhouse 1968-71; accountant: Keyser Ullman Ltd 1971-75, NM Rothschild & Sons Ltd 1976-79; accountant/sec MOD 1977-79, auditor gen Govt of Tonga 1979-80; fin controller 1980-85; fin dir: NM Rothschild Asset Mgmnt Ltd, NM Rothschild Fund Mgmnt Ltd, Rothschild Nominees Ltd; non exec dir NM Rothschild Asset Mgmnt (CI) Ltd; FICA; *Recreations* cricket, squash, tennis; *Style*— Peter B Collacott, Esq; Chart Cottage, Seal Chart, Sevenoaks, Kent; NM Rothschild Asset Management Ltd, Five Arrows House, St Swithins Lane, London, EC4N 8NR (☎ 01 280 5000), fax 01 929 1643, telex 888031)

COLLARD, Prof Patrick John; s of Rupert John Collard (d 1961), and Georgina Eveline, *née* Anderson (1967); *b* 22 April 1920; *Educ* St Barts Med Coll and Univ of London (MB BS, MD); *m* 1, 1948 (m dis 1955), Jessie, da of William Robertson; 1 s (Michael b 1952), 1 da (Deirdre b 1959,); m 2, Kathleen Sarginson; 1 s (James b 1960), 1 da (Ann b 1957); *Career* WWII RAMC 1944-48; lectr (later sr lectr) Guy's Hosp Med Sch 1950- 54; prof of bacteriology: Univ Coll Ibadon Nigeria 1954-62, Univ of Manchester 1962-80 (emeritus prof 1980); Short term conslt WHO 1960-80; fndr memb and hon pres Univ of the Third Age Oxford: JP Manchester City Bench 1973-80; Hon MSc Manchester 1965; FRCP 1972, FRCPath 1969; *Recreations* reading, bookbinding; *Clubs* Athenaeum; *Style*— Prof Patrick Collard; Honor Oak Cottage, Kingham, Oxon OX7 6YL (☎ 060 871 335)

COLLCUTT, Michael Francis; s of Edgar Hugh Collcutt, OBE (d 1967), of Robartes, Falmouth Rd, Truro, Cornwall, and Dorothy Marie, *née* Smith (d 1978); *b* 28 July 1928; *Educ* Truro Cathedral Sch, Pembroke Coll Cambridge (BA); *m* 6 March 1954, Iris Audrey, da of George Sowry, of Eastbourne; 1 s (Christopher b 1961), 1 da (Catherine b 1958); *Career* Mil Serv RA (2 Lieut) 1947-49; slr, dir numerous private Co's, underwriting memb of Lloyds; sr ptnr Toller Hales and Collcutt; HM Coroner of Northamptonshire; *Recreations* golf, fishing, shooting; *Clubs* IOD, Northampton County Golf, Luffenham Heath Golf, Kettering Golf (pres), Northampton and County, Hawks; *Style*— Michael F Collcutt, Esq; Isebrook Cottage, Finedon, Wellingborough, Northants; Toller Hales and Collcutt, 55 Headlands, Kettering, Northants NN15 7EY (☎ 0536 83671, telex 341861, fax 0536 410068)

COLLER, Mervyn Tarrant; s of Maj Raymond Geoffrey Coller, RA (d 1940), and Beryl Mary Lempriere, *née* Back (d 1950)1; *b* 7 Nov 1929; *Educ* Eton; *m* 22 Sept 1955, Cecilia Mary, da of Capt Stuart Cozens-Hardy Boardman (ka 1943); 2 s (Richard Stuart b 1959, Nicholas Lempriere b 1962); *Career* chm and md Pertwee and Back Ltd 1962-; pres Great Yarmouth Chamber of Commerce 1982-85; *Recreations* trout fishing, gardening; *Style*— Mervyn Coller, Esq; Loke House, Sutton, Stalham, Norwich, Norfolk (☎ 0692 80527); Pertwee and Back Ltd, Southgates Road, Great Yarmouth (☎ 0493 844922)

COLLESTATTE; *see*: Manassei di Collestatte

COLLET, Harald Johan Holger; s of Harald P O Collet (d 1972), of Estate Owner, Chamberlain, Denmark, and Else Collet, *née* Collett; *b* 13 Oct 1947; *Educ* St Gall Business Sch, Switzerland (BA), Wharton Sch of Fin, Univ of Penns, USA; *m* 30 Aug 1975, Marianne, da of Lars Erick Sundberg (d 1968), chief exec, Overums Bruk, Sweden; 1 s (Johan b 1986); 3 da (Michaela b 1980, Stephanie b 1982, Alexandra b 1985); *Career* Lt Danish Royal Guards; investmt banker Salomon Bro 1986; dir: Humbros Bank 1984-86, Nordic Bank 1982-84, V UK Hldgs Ltd; vice pres and dir Hanover Tst 1974-82; *Recreations* tennis, golf, shooting; *Clubs* Hurlingham, Royal Wimbldeon Golf; *Style*— Harald Collet, Esq; Salomon Brothers International Ltd, 111 Buckingham Palace Rd, London SW1W 0SB (☎ 01 721 3829)

COLLET, Robert Thomson (Robin); s of Robert Alan Collet (d 1979), of Epsom, and Jean Edith Isobel, *née* Thomson; *b* 26 Nov 1939; *Educ* Malvern, Pembroke Coll Cambridge (MA); *m* 6 May 1972, Olivia Diana Mary, da of Leonard Clough-Taylor; 1 s (Henry b 1977), 1 da (Eloise b 1974); *Career* CA; dir Tilhill Forestry Ltd 1979-; Freeman City of London 1964, memb Worshipful Co of Coopers 1964; FCA 1966; *Recreations* golf, skiing, walking; *Style*— Robin Collet, Esq; The School House, Wimble Hill, Crondall, Farnham, Surrey GU10 5KL (☎ 0252 850 824); Tilhill Forestry Ltd, Greenhills, Tilford, Farnham, Surrey (☎ 025 125 4771, fax 025 125 4758)

COLLETT, Sir Christopher; GBE (1988), JP (City of London 1979); 2 s of Sir Henry Seymour Collett, 2 Bt (d 1971), and hp of nephew, 3 Bt; *b* 10 June 1931; *Educ* Harrow, Emmanuel Cambridge (MA); *m* 1959, Christine Anne, da of Oswald Hardy Griffiths, of Nunthorpe, Yorks; 2 s, 1 da; *Career* Capt RA (TA); ptnr Arthur Young Chartered Accountants London; memb Court of Common Cncl Broad Street Ward City of London 1973-79, Alderman 1979-, Sheriff City of London 1985-86, Lord Mayor 1988-89; Master Worshipful Co of Glovers 1981; memb: Guild of Freemen, Worshipful Co of Chartered Accountants in England and Wales, City of London TAVR Ctee; govr: Bridewell Royal Hosp 1982-, Haberdashers' Aske's Schools Elstree 1982-; govr King Edwards Sch, Witley 1987-; cncl memb Action Research for the Crippled Child 1984-; pres Broad Street Ward Club 1979-; Hon DSc City Univ 1988; KStJ 1988; cdr Order of Merit Federal Republic of Germany 1986, Order of Merit (Class II) State of Qatar 1985, Order of Civil Merit (Class II) Spain 1986; *Recreations* gardening, fishing; *Clubs* City of London, City Livery; *Style*— Sir Christopher Collett, GBE; 121 Home Park Rd, Wimbledon, SW19

COLLETT, Sir Ian Seymour; 3 Bt (UK 1934), of Bridge Ward in the City of London; s of David Seymour Collett (d 1962), by his w, now Lady Miskin (w of His Honour Judge Sir James Miskin, QC); suc gf 1971; *b* 5 Oct 1953; *Educ* Lancing Coll; *m* 18 Sept 1982, Philippa, da of James R I Hawkins, of Preston St Mary, Suffolk; 1 s (Anthony b 1984), 1 da (Georgina b 1986); *Heir* s, Anthony Collett, b 1984; *Recreations* fishing, shooting, cricket; *Clubs* MCC; *Style*— Sir Ian Collett, Bt; Glebe House, Aspall, Debenham, Suffolk

COLLETT, Michael Frederick; s of Victor Valentine Collett (d 1986), of 24 Arleston Drive, Wollaton, Nottingham, and Jennie, *née* Truswell (d 1973); *b* 7 July 1933; *Educ* Whitgift Sch Croydon, Queens' Coll Cambridge (MA); *m* 1, 17 Aug 1957 (m dis 1973), Elizabeth Anne, da of Gerald Leon, of Toorak, Aust; m 2, 25 Feb 1978, Cynthia Barbara, da of Albert Henry Lee James (d 1973), of Erdington, Birmingham; 1 s (Christopher Andrew), 2 step s (Stuart James Hands, Michael Charles Hands), 1 step da (Claire Elizabeth Hands); *Career* Nat Serv RA 1951-53, 2 Lt; TA 1953-74: Lt 460 HAA Regt RA 1953-55, Capt 265 Light Air Defence Regt 1955-69, Maj London and Kent Artillery (CADRE Regt, Cdr), Maj 6 (Vol) Bn The Queens Regt 1971-74 (Co Cdr); Equity and Law Life Assoc Soc 1956- (staff mangr 1969-77, policy servicing mangr 1977-88), dir Chamber Devpt Assoc Br C's of C 1988-; pres Birmingham Actuarial Soc, former pres Warwick Avon Rotary Club (pres 1980/81), dep pres Coventry C of C (pres 1986/88); fndr Bd Coventry Poly; Freedom of the City of London 1974; FIA 1962; *Recreations* philately; *Clubs* Army and Navy; *Style*— Michael F Collett, Esq; "Stable Hollow", 50A Kenilworth Rd, Leamington Spa, Warwicks (☎ 0926 423641); "Trevan", Station Rd, Deganwy, nr Conwy, N Wales; Assoc of Br C of C, Unit 4 Westwood House, Westwood Business Park, Coventry (☎ 0203 694 492)

COLLETT, Lady; Ruth Mildred; *née* Hatch; er da of late William Thomas Hatch of Bromley, Kent; *m* 22 Nov 1920, Sir Henry Seymour Collett, 2 Bt (d 1971); 2 s (1 decd), 1 da; *Style*— Lady Collett; Flat 1, Sunset House, Godyll Road, Southwold,

Suffolk

COLLEY, Maj-Gen David Bryan Hall; CB, CBE (OBE 1977, MBE 1968); s of Lawson-Colley (d 1970), of Sutton Coldfield, and Alice, *née* Hall; *b* 5 June 1934; *Educ* King Edward's Sch Birmingham, RMA Sandhurst; *m* 30 Sept 1957, Marie Therese, da of Louis Auguste Prefontaine (d 1966), of Edmonton, Alberta, Canada; 1 s (John b 1961), 1 da (Michele b 1959); *Career* cmmnd: RASC 1954, RCT 1965; regtl appts in Germany, Belgium, UK, Hong Kong and Singapore; Student Staff Coll Camberley 1964, JSSC Latimer 1970, CO Gurkha Tport Regt & 31 Regt RCT 1971-74, Staff HQ 1 (Br) Corps 1974-77, Cmd Logistic Support Gp 1977-80, Col AQ (Ops & Plans) and dir Admin Planning MOD (Army) 1980-82, Cmd Tport 1 (Br) Corps 1983-86; dir gen: Tport and Movements (Army) 1986-88, Col Cmdt RCT 1988-; Road Haulage Assoc 1988-; Freeman City of London 1986, Hon Liveryman Worshipful Co of Carmen 1986; FCIT; *Recreations* travel, walking; *Clubs* Army & Navy; *Style—* Maj-Gen D B H Colley, CB, CBE; c/o Midland Bank plc, Church Green West, Redditch, Worcs, B97 4EA

COLLEY, Surgn Rear Adm Ian Harris; OBE (1963); s of Aubrey James Colley and Violet Fulford Colley; *b* 14 Oct 1922; *Educ* Hanley Castle GS, King's Coll London, King's Coll Hosp (MB BS); *m* 1952, Joy Kathleen, *née* Goodacre; *Career* RN Med Serv 1948-80; MO HMS Cardigan Bay and HMS Consort 1949-52, serv with Fleet Air Arm 1955-78, PMO HMS Centaur, MO i/c Air Med Sch, pres Central Air Med Bd, cmd MO to Flag Offr Naval Air Cmd, Surgn Rear Adm (ships and establishments) 1978-80, ret; QHP 1978-80, conslt in aviation med, former examiner to Conjoint Bd RCS and RCP for Dip Av Med, hon conslt in occupational med to RNLI, chm Med and Survival Ctee, RNLI 1984-88; CStJ 1980; *Books* papers in field of aviation med; *Style—* Surgn Rear Adm I H Colley, OBE; c/o Royal Bank of Scotland, Inveraray, Argyll PA32 8TY

COLLIE, George Francis; CBE (civil 1964, mil MBE 1943), JP (Aberdeen); s of late George Duncan Collie (d 1946), of Morkeu, Cults, Aberdeenshire; *b* 1 April 1909; *Educ* Aberdeen GS, Aberdeen Univ (BL); *m* 1949, Margery Constance Fullarton, OBE, da of Rev James Wishart, of Irvine, Ayrshire; 2 s; *Career* advocate Aberdeen; sr ptnr James and George Collie Slrs Aberdeen, ret; pres Aberdeen Univ Press (chm 1959-1979); Hon Col 51 Highland Div RASC and RTC 1964-72; hon sheriff of Grampian Highland and Islands at Aberdeen; *Clubs* Army and Navy, Royal Northern (Aberdeen); *Style—* George Collie Esq, CBE, JP; Morkeu, Cults, Aberdeen (☎ 0224 867636); A33 Le Surcouf, Cannes Marina, 06210 Mandelieu, France (☎ 93 49 36 24)

COLLIER, Andrew James; CB (1976); s of Joseph Veasy Collier (d 1963), of London, and Dorothy Murray (d 1981); *b* 12 July 1923; *Educ* Harrow, Ch Ch Oxford (MA); *m* 1950, Bridget, da of George Eberstadt (d 1963), of London; 2 da (Caroline b 1952, Lucy-Ann b 1955); *Career* served RHA Capt 1942-46; HM treasy 1948-70; private sec to Chancellors of the Exchequer: Rt Hon Macmillan, Rt Hon Thorneycroft, Rt Hon Heathcoat Amory, dep sec Dept of Health; now conslt and co dir; *Clubs* Athenaeum; *Style—* James Collier, Esq, CB; 10 Lambourne Avenue, Wimbledon SW19 7DW (☎ 879 3560)

COLLIER, Andrew John; s of Francis George Collier (d 1976), and Margaret Nancy, *née* Nockles; *b* 29 Oct 1939; *Educ* Univ Coll Sch, St Johns Coll Cambridge (MA); *m* 25 July 1964, Gillian Anne, da of George Thomas Ernest Churchill (ka 1945); 2 da (Susan b 1965, Sarah b 1968); *Career* asst master Winchester Coll 1962-68, Hampshire CC Educn Dept 1968-71, sr asst educn offr Buckinghamshire 1971-77, dep chief offr Lancashire 1977-79 (chief educn offr 1980-); cncl memb Univ of Lancaster 1981-86 and 1988-; pres Lancashire Fedn Young Farmers Clubs 1985-88; memb: visiting ctee Open Univ 1982-, Cncl for Accreditation of Teacher Educn 1984-; advsr Assoc of CCs and Cncl of Local Educn Authys, exec memb and hon tres of Educn Offrs 1974-; Liveryman Worshipful Co of Wheelwrights 1972; FRSA; *Recreations* opera, walking, the Greenhouse; *Clubs* Athenaeum, Leander; *Style—* Andrew Collier, Esq; Education Dept, PO Box 61, County Hall, Preston PR1 8RJ (☎ 0772 263646, fax 0772 263630)

COLLIER, Anthony; s of Anthony Collier (d 1983); *b* 4 Jan 1947; *Educ* St Mary's GS, Middlesbrough, Leics Poly (Dip Arch); *m* 23 Sept 1973, Judith Ann, da of Henry Reginald Page, of Yorks; 1 s (Stephen Benedict b 1977), 1 da (Louise Helen b 1979); *Career* architect and interior designer; DOE medal 'Good Design in Housing Awards' (1979), Civic Trust Commended (1978); has designed and supervised many projects for new buildings and refurbishment of existing or derelict buildings, especially in areas to be revitalised; RIBA; *Recreations* travel, golf, tennis, art, music; *Style—* Anthony Collier, Esq; Wadcrag, Wythop Mill, Embleton, Cockermouth, Cumbria (☎ Bassenthwaite Lake 634); work: South Quay Studios, 2-3 South Quay, Maryport, Cumbria CA15 8AB (☎ 0900 814271)

COLLIER, Benjamino; 3 s of William Adrian Larry Collier (disclaimed Barony of Monkswell for life 1964) (d 1984), and o s by his 3 wife Nora, *née* Selby; *b* 2 Feb 1958; *m* 24 Dec 1984, Clare Maria Murphy; 1 s (Daniel James William Paulo b 1987); *Style—* Benjamino Collier, Esq; Harford House Cottage, Chew Magna, Avon

COLLIER, John Spencer; s of James Bradburn Collier, of Bramhall Ches, and Phyllis Mary (d 1953); *b* 4 Mar 1945; *Educ* Cheadle Hulme Sch, Trinity Cambridge (BA), King's Coll London; *m* 1 (m dis 1969) Elizabeth Ann Hall Turner; m 2, 25 March 1972, Theresa Mary, da of Charles John Peers (d 1977), of Chislehampton, Oxon; 2 s (Barnaby James b 1973, Edward John b 1977), 1 da (Amy Louise b 1975); *Career* Price Waterhouse 1969- (ptnr 1981-); dep pres Northern Soc of CA's 1988-89; FCA 1973; *Recreations* running, climbing, windsurfing; *Clubs* Northern Counties (Newcastle); *Style—* John Collier, Esq; 32 Graham Park Rd, Gosforth, Newcastle Upon Tyne (☎ 091 232 8493, fax 091 261 9490, car telephone 0836 6912 759, telex 537222 PRIWAT)

COLLIER, Hon Mrs Muriel Joan Lowry; *née* Lamb; yst da of 1 Baron Rochester, CMG (d 1955); *b* 1921; *Educ* LMH Oxford; *m* 29 Aug 1947 (m dis 1957), William Oswald Collier, o s of Sir Laurence Collier, KCMG (sometime Ambass Oslo and s of Hon John Collier, OBE, 2 s of 1 Baron Monkswell, by John's 2 w Ethel, sis of his 1 w and 5 da of Rt Hon Thomas Huxley, PC, FRS), and 1 cous once removed of Aldous Huxley, the novelist, and Sir Julian Huxley, the biologist; 1 s, 1 da; *Career* sr lectr educn Loughborough Coll Educn; late 3 sec Br Embassy Oslo; *Style—* The Hon Mrs Muriel Collier; 26 George St, Cambridge

COLLIER, Neill Adrian José; s of William Adrian Larry Collier (disclaimed Barony of Monkswell for life 1964) (d 1984); *b* 20 August 1948; *Educ* George Heriot's Sch Edinburgh; *Style—* Neill Collier, Esq; Moora Moora, Box 214, Healesville, Vic 3777, Australia

COLLIER, Roy Sefton; s of Samuel Collier (d 1962), of Manchester, and Margaret Cordelia, *née* Bellis (d 1964); *b* 8 May 1931; *Educ* Whitworth St High Sch Manchester; *m* 1, 1 June 1957, Enid Mavis, s of Alderman A T Barratt (d 1965); 1 s (Christopher b 1954 (d 1978), 1 da (Helen b 1962); m 2, 2 April 1977, Margaret Ann, s of T S Rodger (d 1947); *Career* Nat Serv: Pay Corps Germany; CA; tres: N Counties Archery Soc 1972-, dir Grand Nat Archery Soc Cncl; Soc of Archers and Antiquaries 1979-; FCA; ATH; *Recreations* golf; *Clubs* Heaton Moor Golf, Bowmen of Bruntwood; *Style—* Roy S Collier, Esq; 488 Parrs Wood Road, East Didsbury, Manchester M20 0QQ (☎ 061 445 6508); 9 Park Rd, Heaton Moor, Stockport SK4 4PY (☎ 061 432 2588)

COLLIER, Tiaré Penelope Katherine; da of William Adrian Larry Collier (disclaimed Barony of Monkswell for life 1964) (d 1984); *b* 5 Sept 1952; *Educ* Friends' Sch Saffron Walden; *Style—* Miss Tiaré Collier; 176 Lansdowne Drive, Hackney, London E8

COLLIN, Lady Clarissa; *née* Duncombe; JP; da of 3 Earl of Feversham (d 1963, when the Earldom became extinct, but the Barony of Feversham passed to a kinsman); *b* 11 Oct 1938; *Educ* Heathfield, Paris France; *m* 14 Dec 1966, Nicholas Spencer Compton Collin, s of late Maj Francis Spencer Collin, of 42 Eaton Place, SW1 and Fullers Farm, West Grinstead, Horsham, Sussex; 1 s, 1 da; *Career* farming; *Recreations* gardening, country activities; *Style—* Lady Clarissa Collin; Wytherstone House, Pockley, York (☎ (0439) 70398)

COLLIN, Maj-Gen Geoffrey de Egglesfield; CB (1975), MC (1944), DL (N Yorks 1977); s of late Charles de Egglesfield Collin (d 1960), of Ripon, and Catherine Mary, *née* Smith; *b* 18 July 1921; *Educ* Wellington; *m* 1949, Angela Stella, da of Lt-Col Noel Charles Secombe Young (d 1966), of Roecliffe, York; 1 s, 3 da; *Career* 2 Lt RA 1941, Maj-Gen RA HQ BAOR 1971-73, GOC NE Dist York 1973-76, ret; Col Cmdt RA 1976-83; hon dir Great Yorks Show 1976-87: pres Yorks Agric Soc 1988-89; pt/t chm Civil Serv Selection Panel 1978-; *Recreations* fishing, ornithology, photography; *Clubs* Army and Navy; *Style—* Maj-Gen Geoffrey Collin, CB, MC, DL; Old Vicarage, Roecliffe, York

COLLIN, Jack; s of John Collin, and Amy Maud, *née* Burton; *b* 23 April 1945; *Educ* Consett GS, Univ of Newcastle (MB BS, MD), Mayo Clinic USA, Univ of Oxford (MA); *m* 17 July 1971, Christine Frances Collin, da of Albert Proud (d 1973), of Durham; 3 s (Neil b 1976, Graham b 1980, Ivan b 1985), 1 da (Beth b 1974); *Career* registrar in surgery Newcastle 1971-80, res fell Mayo Clinic USA 1977, Arris and Gale lectr RCS 1976, euro fell Surgical Res Soc 1979, Moynihan travelling fell assoc of Surgeons 1980, reader in surgery Oxon 1980-, conslt surgn John Radcliffe Hop, professorial fell Trinity Coll Oxford, Hunterian prof RCS 1988-89; memb dist research ctee; regnl med advsy ctee bd of faculty clinical medicine; examiner: in surgery Uinv of Oxford, in anatomy RCS; memb: governing body and bursarial ctee Trinity Coll, gen purposes ctee faculty of clinical med; Jacksonian Prizewinner RCS 1979; memb: vascular surgical soc 1982, euro vascular surgical soc 1988; FRCS 1972; *Recreations* food, family, gardening; *Style—* Jack Collin, Esq; Nuffield Department of Surgery, John Radcliffe Hospital, Oxford, OX3 9DU (☎ 0865 817 592, 817 591), fax 0865 726 753, telex 83147 VIAOR ATT : NDS

COLLIN, John Richard Olaf; s of Dr John Olaf Collin, of Broom Cottage, Ashdown Rd, Forest Row, E Sussex, and Ellen Vera, *née* Knudsen; *b* 1 May 1943; *Educ* Charterhouse, Cambridge Univ (MA, MB); *Career* ophthalmic surgeon with conslt appointments to Moorfields Eye Hosp and Hosp for Sick Children, Great Ormond Street 1981, special interest in eyelid surgery; FRCS, DO; *Books* publications on ophthalmic plastic surgery include: A Manual of Systematic Eyelid Surgery (1983); *Recreations* sailing, shooting, tennis, hunting, opera; *Clubs* Royal Ocean Racing, Hurlingham; *Style—* J R O Collin, Esq; 67 Harley Street, London W1N 1DE (☎ 01 486 2699)

COLLING, Ronald Norris; s of Archibald Robert Colling (d 1958), and Lily, *née* Norris; *b* 11 July 1936; *Educ* William Hulme's GS Manchester; *m* 22 Sept 1978, Lynne Patricia, da of Keith Martin Belcher, of Cheshire; 2 s (John b 1983, Peter b 1986); *Career* chm and fndr Norkem Holdings plc gp of cos; *Style—* Ronald N Colling, Esq; Meadow Lodge, School Lane, Ollerton, Knutsford, Cheshire WA16 8SJ; 15 Ruskin Ct, Knutsford, Cheshire WA16 6HN (☎ 0565 55550, telex 669629, fax 0565 55496)

COLLINGE, (Richard) Paul; s of Graham Collinge (d 1965), and Winifred Mary, *née* Farley (d 1969); *b* 26 June 1946; *Educ* (Architectural) Thames Poly (ATP); *m* 23 March 1968, Jean Mary, da of George Robert Dewey, of 235 Desborough Avenue, High Wycombe, Bucks; 2 s (Jake b 2 May 1974, Luke b 14 Sept 1976), 1 da (Emma b 23 Oct 1972); *Career* princ Aldington Craig & Collinge 1986- (ptnr from 1979); external examiner N London Poly sch of Architecture 1986-89, assessor: RIBA awards 1988; selected in 1985 as one of the 40 under 40 young architects; design awards received: RIBA 1978 (commendation) and 1987, DOE Good Housing Award 1978, Civic Tst Awards 1987 and 1988, Brick Devpt Assoc Biennial Award 1979; RIBA 1972, MCSD 1984; *Recreations* cricket, golf; *Clubs* Thame Cricket; *Style—* Paul Collinge, Esq; Aldington Craig & Collinge, 6 High St, Haddenham, Bucks HP17 6ER (☎ 0844 291228, fax 0844 292448)

COLLINGRIDGE, Barrie John; s of Leonard Cyril Collingridge, MBE (d 1968), and Constance Louise, *née* Overal; *b* 5 July 1905; *Educ* Ottershaw Sch; *m* 12 dec 1959, Ann Beatrice, da of Leonard Riddle; 2 da (Belinda Ann West b 2 Dec 1960, Lucinda Jane (Mrs Adams) b 6 June 1963); *Career* Nat Serv Royal Corp of Signals: cmmnd 1955, serv as 2 Lt Malaya, discharged 1956, dir J Collingridge Ltd 1967, bd memb Grower Magazine 1972-80, chm J Collingrdige and subsidiaries 1980, pres Covent Garden Tenants Assoc (CGTA) 1987 (chm 1980), fndr chm Conservation Area Advsy Ctee W End (Esher) memb Apple & Pear Devpt Cncl 1980; Freeman City of London Liveryman Worshipful Co of Fruiterers; FIFP; *Recreations* antique clocks, vintage cars, gardening; *Clubs* Farmers; *Style—* Barrie Collingridge, Esq; The Old Cottage, The St, W Horley, Surrey KT24 6HR (☎ 04865 4662); J Collingridge Ltd, 218-223 Flower Mkt, New Covent Garden, London SW8 5ND (☎ 01 720 6911)

COLLINGS, Peter Glydon; s of Alfred James Collings, of 3 Kenilworth Ct, Poole, Dorset BH13 7BB, and Margot Lavinia, *née* Harper; *b* 4 Nov 1942; *Educ* Worksop Coll; *m* 1 Sept 1967, Rosemary Anne, da of Henry William Wesley-Harkcom (d 1966); 2 da (Sarah Jane b 1968, Emma Louise b 1970); *Career* asst regnl mangr Old Broad St Securities Ltd Birmingham 1970-75, regnl mangr Grindlays Industl Fin Ltd Birmingham 1976-82, dep chief exec W Mids Enterprise Bd Ltd 1982-; dir: Tangye Ltd 1986-87, dir Raydyot Ltd 1987-, vice-pres Sutton Coldfield RFC; FCA 1966-; *Recreations* rugby football, tennis; *Clubs* Sutton Coldfield RFC, Four Oaks Tennis; *Style—* Peter

Collings, Esq; Squirrels Leap, 15 Oaklands Rd, Four Oaks, Sutton Coldfield, West Mids B74 2TB (☎ 01 308 5434); Wellington Ho, 31/34 Waterloo St, Birmingham B2 5TJ (☎ 021 236 8855, fax 021 233 3942)

COLLINGWOOD, Gp Capt Cuthbert John; DFC (1933), OBE (1944); s of Col C G Collingwood, CB (d 1933), of Northumberland, and Dorothy, *née* Fawcett (d 1973); *b* 12 Jan 1901; *Educ* RNC's Osborne and Dartmouth; *m* 9 Jan 1936, Sarah, da of Hon Archibald Dudley Ryder (d 1954), of Beaulieu, Hants; 1 da (Susan b 1939); *Career* Gp Capt RAF; midshipman HMS Ramilies 1917-, HMS Walpole 1919, Royal Oak 1920; RAF Coll Cranwell 1920, pilot offr 1920, NW Frontier Indian 1931-35, UK and Canada 1939-45, ret 1948; Glendale Rural District Cncl 1948 (chm 1954-63), hon Alderman Berwick-upon-Tweed Borough Cncl 1983; *Recreations* racing, shooting, fishing; *Clubs* MCC; *Style—* Gp Capt Cuthbert J Collingwood, DFC, OBE; West Lilburn House, Alnwick, Northumberland (☎ 066 87 226)

COLLINS, Adrian John Reginald; s of John Reginald Maulden Collins, MBE, and Jennifer Anne, *née* Wasey; *b* 29 May 1954; *Educ* Leys Sch Cambridge; *m* 6 Aug 1984, Ailie Ford, 1 s (Mark John Ford) 1 da (Seil Charlotte); *Career* chief exec: Gartmore Investmt 1974-84, Fincorp Int Ltd 1984-85, Royal Tst Asset Mgmnt Ltd 1985-; *Style—* Adrian Collins, Esq; 4 Campden Hill Sq, London W8 7LB (☎ 01 638 2433, fax 01 638 2655)

COLLINS, (John) Alford Kingswell; MC, TD; s of John Preedy Collins (d 1964), of IOW, and Marion Martha, *née* Kingswell (d 1951); *b* 19 June 1920; *Educ* Denstone Coll; *m* 3 April 1952, June, da of Stanley H Matthews (d 1985), of IOW; 1 s (David b 1956), 2 da (Diana b 1954, Angela b 1958); *Career* chm: Medens Tst Ltd 1973-85, Vectis Stone Group plc 1965-85, Upward and Rich plc 1952-74; dir: Bardon Hill Gp plc 1985-86, Brown Shipley and Co 1981-85, Blackgang Hotels Ltd, Celtic Oil Supplies Ltd, Channel Oil Ltd, Cheek Bros Ltd, Island Oils Ltd, Wall Bros (Piling) Ltd; chm Southern Vectis plc 1986-; FCA; *Recreations* travel, sailing, walking; *Clubs* Island Sailing, Royal Solent Yacht IOD; *Style—* Alford Collins, Esq, MC, TD; Tollacre, Watergate, Newport, Isle of Wight PO30 1YP (☎ 0983 523096); Lugley House, Lugley St, Newport, Isle of Wight PO30 5EX (☎ 0983 521236)

COLLINS, Andrew Seymoure; TD (1977); s of Seymour John Collins, JP (d 1970), and Nancye Westray *née* Yarwood; *b* 2 Nov 1944; *Educ* Radley, Coll of Law; *m* 1, 17 July 1971 (m dis 1985), Susan Lucretia, da of Cdr John Weston Chase, RN (d 1989); 3 s (Charles b 1972, James b 1975, Giles b 1977) 1 da (Amelia b 1974); m 2, 26 Nov 1986, Virginia Mary Crisp, da of John Richard Craik-White (d 1988); *Career* HAC 1964, cmmnd 1969, transferred 68 Signals Sqdn (Inns of Ct & City yeomanry) 1970 (cmd 1977-80), SO 2 Directorant of Army Reserves and Cadets 1983-88, transferred RARO 1988, serv as selected mil memb City of London TA & VRA 1978- (Greater London 1985-); slr of the Supreme Ct 1969, ptnr Walker Martineau 1986-, co dir in fields of investmt and hotels; gen cmmr of taxes 1983; Liveryman Worshipful Co of Tarmakers 1970 (asst 1985); memb: Law Soc, Holburn Law Soc, City of London Law Soc; *Recreations* sailing, hunting, shooting, tennis; *Clubs* Royal Thames Yacht ; *Style—* Andrew Collins, Esq, TD; The Old Rectory, Eydon, Daventry, Northants NN11 6QE (☎ 0327 60745); 38 Bellevile Road, London SW11 6QT (☎ 01 350 1452); 64 Quen Street, London EC4R 1AD (☎ 01 236 4232, fax 01 236 2525, car tel 0836 738 273, tlx 28843)

COLLINS, Sir Arthur James Robert; KCVO (1980, CVO 1963); s of Col William Fellowes Collins, DSO, JP, DL, of Cundall Manor, York, Lord of the Manor of Cundall and Patron of the living of Farnham, and Lady Evelyn Innes-Ker, OBE (4 da of 7 Duke of Roxburghe); *b* 10 July 1911; *Educ* Eton, Ch Ch Oxford (MA); *m* 1965, Elizabeth, da of Rear Adm Sir Arthur Bromley, 8 Bt, KCMG, KCVO, and widow of 6 Baron Sudeley killed in active serv (1941); *Career* WWII, Maj RHG, Adj 2 Household Cavalry Regt (despatches); slr, ptnr Withers and Co 1937, sr ptnr 1962-82; conslt 1982; *Clubs* Turf, White's; *Style—* Sir Arthur Collins, KCVO; Kirkman Bank, Knaresborough, N Yorks (☎ 0423 863136); 38 Clarence Terrace, London NW1 (☎ 01 723 4198)

COLLINS, Arthur John; OBE (1973); s of Reginald Collins, and Margery Collins; *b* 17 May 1931; *Educ* Purley GS; *m* 1952, Enid Stableford; 1 s, 1 da; *Career* served RAF 1949-51; joined FCO 1968 from Miny of Health (where priv sec to perm sec and Parly sec), asst head Latin America and Caribbean depts FCO 1974-77, cnsllr and head of chancery UK delgn to OECD Paris 1978-81, UK high cmmr PNG 1982-85, cnsllr and advsr on mgmnt FCO 1986-88, ret; appointed protocol rep of For and Cwlth Sec of State; *Style—* Arthur Collins, Esq, OBE; Foreign and Commonwealth Office, King Charles St, London SW1

COLLINS, Basil Eugene Sinclair; CBE (1983); s of Albert Collins (d 1971), and Pauline Alicia, *née* Wright; *b* 21 Dec 1923; *Educ* Great Yarmouth GS; *m* 1942, Doris, da of Harry Meyer Slott (d 1944); 2 da; *Career* Cadbury Schweppes plc: md 1974-80, dep chm and ch exec 1980-83; chm Nabisco Gp Ltd 1984-; dir: Thomas Cook Gp 1980-85, Br Airways 1982-, Royal Mint 1984-; Royal Coll of Nursing: life vice-pres, hon tres, chm of Finance Ctee 1970-86; memb Cncl Univ of E Anglia 1987, tstee and dir Inst of Econ Affairs 1987; FZS, CBIM, FID, FIGD, fell and dir American Chamber of Commerce, FRSA; *Recreations* music, languages, English countryside; *Clubs* Carlton; *Style—* Basil Collins Esq, CBE; Wyddial Parva, Buntingford, Herts SG9 0EL; c/o Nabisco Group Ltd, Bowater House, Knightsbridge, London SW1 7LT

COLLINS, Bryan; s of Leslie George Thomas Collins (d 1981), and Ivy Clara, *née* Biggs; *b* 21 April 1936; *Educ* Cambridge Central GS; *m* 1 March 1958, Mary Josephine, da of Walter George Cole (d 1970), of Cambridge; 1 s (Timothy Howard b 1961), 1 da (Louise Mary b 1963); *Career* md and chief exec Bristow Helicopter Group Ltd 1979-, chm Bromley Family Practitioner Ctee 1985-; *Recreations* cricket, badminton, tennis, squash; *Clubs* IOD, Royal Soc of Medicine; *Style—* Bryan Collins, Esq; Wymondley, Hookwood Park, Limpsfield, Surrey RH8 0SG (☎ 0883 723281); Bristow Helicopter Group Ltd, Redhill Aerodrome, Surrey RH1 5JZ (telex 21913, fax 0737 822694)

COLLINS, David Stuart; s of James Henry Collins, of Dalkeith, Midlothian, Scotland, and Hilda, *née* Oldfield (d 1977); *b* 24 Feb 1945; *Educ* Fazakerley Comprehensive Liverpool, Liverpool Coll of Commerce; *m* 14 Oct 1967, Penelope Noël, da of Herbert Lancelot Charters, of 36 Avondale Avenue, Maghull, Liverpool; 1 s (Mark Stuart b 1977), 1 da (Nicola Caroline b 1980); *Career* Granada Publishing Ltd; mangr: S Africa 1974-77, area sales mangr N Africa, M East, India and Pakistan 1977-81, trade mangr 1981-83; export sales mangr Harrap Ltd 1983-84 (sales dir 1984-); Columbus Books Ltd 1986-; *Recreations* travel, walking, reading, swimming, good conversation; *Style—* David Stuart Collins, Esq; 152A Park Street Lane, Park Street, St Albans AL2 2AU (☎ 0727 73866); Harrap Ltd, 19-23 Ludgate Hill, London EC4M 7PD (☎ 01 248 6444, telex: 28673, fax: 01 248 3357)

COLLINS, Edward Geoffrey Lissant; OBE (1983); s of George Geoffrey Collins (d 1978), of Rochdale, and Lucy May Capstick, *née* Squires (d 1980); *b* 1 May 1936; *Educ* Rossall and William Hulmes GS Manchester; *m* 16 April 1966, Hilary Elizabeth, da of William Dryland, of Rochdale; 3 s (William b 1967, David b 1968, Francis b 1972); *Career* slr 1959, sr ptnr Jackson Stoney & Co Rochdale 1976-; memb Rochdale: CC 1965-71, Met Borough Cncl 1973-86 (ldr of cncl 1976-80 and 1982-86); pres Rochdale and Dist Blind Welfare Soc; chm: Rochdale Music Soc, tstees Rochdale Curtain Theatre; vice chm Rochdale Parish Church PCC; *Recreations* reading, music, theatre, gardening, walking; *Style—* Edward Collins, Esq, OBE; Rose Villa, Edenfield Rd, Rochdale, Lancs (☎ 0706 42172); The Old Parsonage, 2 St Mary's Gate, Rochdale, Lancs (☎ 0706 44187)

COLLINS, Mrs Michael; (Lesley) Elizabeth; *see*: Appleby, (Lesley) Elizabeth

COLLINS, (John) Grenville; s of John Aloysius Collins (d 1969), of London, and Joan Leigh, *née* Price; *b* 24 Jan 1943; *Educ* St Edwards Oxford; *m* 22 Aug 1966, Susan Elizabeth Carr, da of Lt-Col Arthur Henry Carr Sutherland, OBE, MC, DL, (d 1962), of Cringletie, Peebles, Scotland; 1 da (Ika b 23 Nov 1974); *Career* head of islamic studies at Beshara Sch of Intensive Esoteric Educn Sherborne Gloucs 1975-78, G & A Kelly Ltd 1984-, Beshara Co Ltd 1986-, Breyberry Ltd 1987-; charity tstee: Beshara Tst 1971-, Chisholme Inst 1985; chm Muhyiddin Ibn Arabic Soc (Oxford, Istanbul, San Francisco, Sydney); author of papers on esoteric subjects; *Recreations* travelling, publishing; *Style—* Grenville Collins, Esq; Kingham House, Kingham, Oxford OX7 6YA; 82 St George's Sq, London SW1 (☎ 060871 520)

COLLINS, (Henry) Harry Ernest; s of Edwin Collins (d 1955), of 28 Hardinge Rd, London NW10, and Florence Louise, *née* Scarbrow (d 1969); *b* 19 Jan 1920; *Educ* Kilburn GS; *Career* cmmnd pilot RAF 1941, serv with 264 Sqdn Night Fighters (Boulton - Paul Defiants), test pilot attached to 1 CRU Aston Down, demobbed 1946; CA Morton Mollern Sheen & Co 1936, Sir WM Garthwaite & Co Ltd (Insur Brokers), Co-operative Permanent Bldg Soc (now Nationwide) 1938, A C Eaves Ltd 1946-55, F J Parsons Ltd 1955-62, Journal of Park Admin Ltd 1972, conslt Adam Publishing Ltd 1988- (fndr 1973, sold firm to Inst of Groundsmanship 1987); hon life memb: Constitutional, Bronderbury, Cricklewood and Willesdon Green Conservative Club Kensal Rise; memb Old Creightonians Assoc, vice pres The Lighthouse Club (former chm cncl); Freeman: City of London 1976, Worshipful Co of Paviors; *Books* Mining Memories and Musings: The Autobiography of a Mining Engineer (1985); *Recreations* cricket, golf, cooking; *Clubs* RAF, Rugby, The Lighthouse, South Hampstead CC, Sudbury Golf ; *Style—* Harry Collins, Esq; 82 Hawes Close, Northwood, Middlesex HA6 1EW (☎ 092 74 29570); Adam Publishing Ltd, Suite 52, 26 Charing Cross Rd, London WC2H 0DH (☎ 01 839 7151, 01 836 7844)

COLLINS, Hon Ian Grenville Victor; s of Baron Stonham (Life Peer, d 1971); *b* 24 Nov 1941; *Educ* Queen's Coll Taunton, Kingston GS; *m* 1968, Sandra Felicity da of Robert Ernest Henry Bell; children; *Style—* The Hon Ian Collins; Mallards, Mileham, Kings Lynn, Norfolk

COLLINS, Joan; da of Joseph William Collins (d 1988), and his 1 w, Elsa, *née* Bessant (d 1962); *b* 23 May 1933; *Educ* Francis Holland Sch St Margaret's Middx, RADA; *m* 1, 23 May 1954 (m dis 1957), Maxwell Reed, actor (d 1974); m 2, May 1963 (m dis), Anthony Newley, actor; 1 s (Alexander b 8 Sept 1965), 1 da (Tara b 12 Oct 1963); m 3, Feb 1972 (m dis 1983), Ron Kass, film prod; 1 da (Katyana b 20 June 1972); m 4, 6 Nov 1985 (m dis 1987), Peter Holm; *Career* film and TV actress since 1951; GB film incl: The Road to Hong Kong (1962), Can Hieronymus Merkin Ever Forget Mercy Humppe and Find True Happiness (1969), Tales From the Crypt (1972), The Big Sleep (1977), The Stud (1978), The Bitch (1979); US films incl: Land of the Pharaohs (1954), The Virgin Queen (1955), The Opposite Sex (1956), Rally Round the Flag, Boys (1958), Esther and the King (1960); Br TV incl: Tales of the Unexpected, The Persuaders; US TV incl: Star Trek (1975), Batman (1975), The Moneychangers (1976), Mission Impossible (1976), Police Woman (1976), Starsky and Hutch (1978), Space 1999 (1979), Fantasy Island (1981), The Making of a Male Model (1983), My Life as a Man (1984), Dynasty (1981-), Sins (1985), Monte Carlo (1986); awards: Hollywood Women's Press Club Golden Apple Award (1982), Golden Globe Award 'Best Actress in a TV Drama' (Alexis in Dynasty) (1983), People's Choice Award 'Most Popular Actress' (1983, 1984); *Books* Past Imperfect (1978), Joan Collins Beauty Book (1982), Katy: A Fight for Life (1983), Prime Time (1988); *Recreations* travelling, collecting antiques from art deco period, writing; *Style—* Miss Joan Collins; 15363 Mulholland Drive, Los Angeles, California 90077; c/o Rogers and Cowan, 27 Albemarle St, W1X 3FA (☎ 01 499 0691, fax 495 1275)

COLLINS, John Alexander; s of Maj John Constantine Collins of Bodmin Cornwall, and Nancy Isobel, *née* Mitchell; *b* 10 Dec 1941; *Educ* Campbell Coll Belfast, Reading Univ (BSc); *m* 24 April 1965, Susan Mary, da of Robert Reid Hooper, of Wimbourne, Dorset; 1 s (Robert b 18 May 1970), 1 da (Helen b 18 June 1968); *Career* Shell Int 1964-: mktg asst agric div London 1964-66, head of agric devpt Shell Chemical Co E Africa Nairobi 1966-71, head of devpt agric div London 1971-73, mktg oil assignment London 1973-74, chemicals mangr Shell Nigeria Lagos 1974-76, head of Polyolefins div London 1976-79, gen mangr Shell Colombia Bogota 1979-82, head of chemicals regnl Far East and Australasia London 1982-83, head of petrochemicals London 1983-84, md Shell chemicals UK and a md of Shell UK 1984-, supply and mktg co-ordinator 1989-; vice pres and cncl memb Chemical Industs Assoc; Freeman City of London, Liveryman Worshipful Co of Horners; memb BIM; *Recreations* family, sailing, riding, golf and tennis; *Style—* John Collins, Esq; Shell Centre, London SE1 7NA (☎ 01 934 1234, fax 01 934 5186, telex 919651 SHEL)

COLLINS, Vice Adm Sir John Augustine; KBE (1951), CB (1940); s of Michael John Collins, of Deloraine, Tasmania; *b* 7 Jan 1899; *Educ* Royal Australian Naval Coll; *m* 1930, Phyllis Laishley, da of Alexander Joseph McLachlan, of Sydney; 1 da; *Career* RAN 1913, Vice-Adm 1950, Chief of Naval Staff and First Naval Memb Aust Cwlth Naval Bd Melbourne 1948-55, ret; Aust high cmmr New Zealand 1955-62; *see Debrett's Handbook of Australia and New Zealand for further details*; *Style—* Vice Adm Sir John Collins, KBE, CB; Unit 31, 69 Roslyn Gardens, Elizabeth Bay, Sydney 2011, Aust (☎23 356 2479)

COLLINS, John Frederick Norman; OBE; s of Harry Norman Collins (d 1973) of Chester, and Doris Emily Collins (d 1972); *b* 15 Sept 1924; *Educ* King Edward's Sch Birmingham, Birmingham Sch of Architecture (Dip Arch), Sch of Planning and Res for

Regnl Devpt London (SP Dip); *m* 1, 27 July 1955, Angela Mary (Jill) (d 1973), da of Donald Hutton Cox (1973); 3 s (Timothy John b 12 Feb 1959, Dr Matthew James b 12 May 1960, Richard Studholme b 26 April 1971), 3 da (Emma Louise (Mrs M Hawkins) b 26 April 1962, Katharine Lucy b 8 June 1965, Joanna Mary b 11 Aug 1968); m 2, 14 May 1976, Mary Muriel; *Career* RAF 1944-47, leading aircraftsmen, served Africa and Aden project architect local authy housing Birmingham 1953-55, architect and town planner gp ldr, Coventry 1955-59, project architect works abroad (Cyprus) then sr architect R & D WO Works Directorate 1959-63, sr assoc Graeme Shankland Assocs Liverpool 1963-67, co planner Ches cc 1969-88 (2 dep co planning offr 1967-69), ptnr Long Collins Partnership Chester 1988-; pres Ches Soc of Architects 1983-85, chm NW regnl Cncl RIBA; memb RIBA 1951, FRTPI 1955 (cncl 1970-, pres 1980-82); *Recreations* theatre, sailing, travel; *Style*— John Collins, Esq, OBE; Greenlooms, Hargrave, Chester, Ches CH3 7RX; Glan Yr Aig, Borth, Ceredigion, Dyfed (☎ 0829 41070); Long Collins Partnership, Richmond Place, 125 Boughton, Chester, Ches CH3 5BJ (☎ 0244 312 387, fax 0244 320 072)

COLLINS, John Hardie; OBE (1966); s of William Smithson Collins (d 1949), of Rhiwbina, Cardiff, and Hannah Jane, *née* Wilson; *b* 26 Feb 1923; *Educ* Cowbridge GS, Univ Coll Cardiff (BSc); *m* 20 Dec 1947, Dorothy (d 1980), da of Lt Jack Archibald (d 1953), of Bristol; 1 da (Jean); m 2, 21 Feb 1981, Rona, da of Abraham Mottershedd, 1 s (Anthony d 1988); *Career* industl chemist 1943-81; ldr Cheshire CC, former ldr Widnes and Halton Borough Cncls, memb bd Warrington Runcorn Devpt Corpn; Hon Freeman Widnes 1973; *Recreations* golf, music; *Style*— John Collins Esq, OBE; 5 Shelley Rd, Widnes, Lancs; County Hall Chester

COLLINS, John Morris; s of Emmanuel Cohen, MBE (d 1980), of 1 Primley Park View, Leeds 17, and Ruby Cohen (d 1988); *b* 25 June 1931; *Educ* Leeds GS, Queens Coll Oxford (MA); *m* 19 March 1968, Sheila, da of David Brummer of 14 Raleigh Close, Hendon, London NW4; 1 da (Simone Natalie b 1974); *Career* barr Middle Temple 1956, dep co ct judge 1970-71, asst rec 1971, dep circuit judge 1972-80, crown ct rec 1980-; *Recreations* walking; *Style*— John M Collins, Esq; 14 Sandhill, Oval, Leeds LS17 8EA (☎ 0532 686 008); Pearl Chambers Leeds LS1 5BZ (☎ 0532 451 986)

COLLINS, Maj-Gen Joseph Clinton; CB (1953), CBE (1951, OBE 1946); s of Edward Collins; *b* 8 Jan 1895; *Educ* London Hosp; *m* 1925, Eileen Patricia, da of Dr E Williams, of Ealing; 2 da; *Career* RNVR and RAMC 1914-18, Maj-Gen 1951, Dir Medical Services 1953-54, ret; CStJ (1948); *Style*— Maj-Gen Joseph Collins, CB, CBE; 42 Staveley Rd, Chiswick, London W4 3ES

COLLINS, Julian Peter; s of Edward Arthur Burnette Collins, and Dorothy, *née* Wragg; *b* 15 Nov 1942; *Educ* Nottingham HS, Gonville and Caius Coll Cambridge (MA, LLM); *Career* slr 1967, hd of industl branch legal dept NCB 1973, legal advsr and slr Br Coal Corpn 1988; memb: Law Soc, Int Bar Assoc; *Recreations* theatre, travel; *Style*— Julian Collins, Esq; 59 Gilpin Avenue, E Sheen, London SW14 8QX (☎ 01 876 6347); Hobart House, Grosvenor Place, London SW1X 7AE (☎ 01 235 2020, fax 01 235 2020 ext 34309, telex 882161 (CBHOB 9))

COLLINS, Kenneth Darlington; MEP (Lab) E Strathclyde 1979-; s of late Nicholas Collins and Ellen Williamson; *b* 12 August 1939; *Educ* St John's GS, Hamilton Acad, Glasgow Univ, Strathclyde Univ; *m* 1966, Georgina Frances, *née* Pollard; 1 s, 1 da; *Career* former bd memb E Kilbridge Devpt Corpn, former tutor-organiser WEA; social geographer; lectr Paisley Coll of Technology 1969-79; dep ldr Labour Gp Euro Parl 1979-, chm Environment Ctee 1979-; memb Red Rose Gp 1982- (Lab gp formed to change party policy of withdrawal of UK from EEC); *Style*— Kenneth Collins Esq, MEP; 11 Stuarton Park, East Kilbride, Lanarkshire (☎ (035 52) 37282)

COLLINS, Michael Brendan; OBE (1983), MBE (1969); s of Daniel James Collins, GM, (d 1962), of Cardiff, and Mary Bridget, *née* Kennedy; *Educ* St Illtyd's Coll Cardiff, UCL; *m* 2 Apr 1959, Elena, da of Dr Mario Lozar, (d 1963), of Milan; *Career* HM Forces 1953-55; entered FO 1956, Santiago Chile 1959-61, Consul Cuba 1962-63, FCO 1964-66, consul (prev 2nd then first Sec) Prague 1967-69, dep Hrsh Commr The Gambia 1970-72, Head of Chancery Algiers 1972-74, First Sec FCO 1975-77, Consul Commercial Montreal 1978-80, Consul Atlantic Provinces of Canada 1981-82, Cnsllr Econ and Commercial Brussels 1983-87; HM Consul-General Istanbul 1988-; *Recreations* fishing, shooting, golf, walking, music, reading; *Clubs* Army and Navy; *Style*— Michael Collins, Esq, OBE, MBE; (Istanbul), c/o Foreign and Commonwealth Office, King Charles Street London, SW1 2AH

COLLINS, Michael Brian; s of Leslie Gerald Collins (d 1959), and Ada Florence Collins; *b* 12 Dec 1942; *Educ* Queen's Coll Taunton Somerset; *m* 1971, Rosalind, da of Dudley Grey Cooper (d 1986); 1 s (Timothy b 1975), 1 da (Annabelle b 1977); *Career* ptnr Micol and Partners, chartered accountants; dir Argonaut Ltd and other cos; underwriting memb of Lloyd's of London; elder Church of Scotland; pres Bermuda Hockey Assoc; former Int hockey player; FCA; *Recreations* golf, hockey, squash, tennis, cricket, sailing; *Clubs* Royal and Ancient Golf of St Andrews, MCC, RAC, Royal Bermuda Yacht, Coral Beach and Tennis, Annabel's; *Style*— Michael Collins, Esq; Les Adams, Rue Des Adams, St Peter, Guernsey (☎ 0481 63578); Eerie Castle, Southampton, Bermuda (☎ 809 298 0972); Pollet House, The Pollet, St Peter Port, Guernsey (☎ (0481 24136); Argyle House West, Cedar Avenue, Hamilton, Bermuda (☎ (809) 292 7979)

COLLINS, Air Vice-Marshal Peter Spencer; CB (1985), AFC (1961); s of Sqdn-Ldr Frederick Wildbore Collins, OBE (d 1962), of Essex, and Mary, *née* Spencer (d 1939); *b* 19 Mar 1930; *Educ* Royal GS High Wycombe, Univ of Birmingham (BA); *m* 25 June 1953, Sheila Mary, da of Sidney John Perks (d 1983), of Wolverhampton; 3 s (Timothy b 1955, Paul b 1960, Christopher b 1963), 1 da (Fiona b 1957); *Career* RAF 1951-85; cmd: No 111 Sqdn 1970-72, RAF Gutersloh 1974-76; Dir of Forward Policy (RAF) 1978-81; Sr Air Staff Offrs No 11 Gp 1981-83; Dir-Gen of Communications, Info Systems and Orgn 1983-85; non exec dir Marconi Radar Systems 1985-; conslt GEC-Marconi Research Centre 1989-; FBIM; *Recreations* golf, music; *Clubs* RAF; *Style*— Air Vice-Marshal Peter Collins, CB, AFC; MRSL, Writtle Road, Chelmsford, Essex (☎ 0245 267111)

COLLINS, Dr Peter Victor; s of Lewis John Collins (d 1982), and Diana Clavering, *née* Elliot; *b* 27 June 1948; *Educ* Eton, Trinity Coll Cambridge, (BA, PhD); *m* 29 Oct 1983, Dawn Elisabeth, *née* Grimshaw; 2 s (Tolomey John b 1986, Oscar Barnaby b 1988); *Career* div mangr GEC Hirst Res Centre Centre 1974-85, tech mangr Marconi Maritime Applied Res Lab 1985-88, mangr future technol Marconi Underwater Systems Ltd 1988-; *Recreations* bridge; *Style*— Dr Peter Collins; Yew Tree House, Hill Row, Haddenham, Cambridgeshire CB6 3TH (☎ 0353 740996); Marconi Underwater Systems, Croxley Mill, Blackmoor Lane, Watford, Herts WD1 8YR (☎ 0932 57719, fax 09235 7777, telex 893327)

COLLINS, Prof Philip Arthur William; s of Arthur Henry Collins, (d 1963), of Little Burstead, Essex, and Winifred Nellie, *née* Bowmaker (d 1968); *b* 28 May 1923; *Educ* Brentwood Sch, Emmanuel Coll Cambridge (BA, MA); *m* 1, 1952 (m dis 1963) Mildred, *née* Lowe; m 2, 18 Aug 1965, Joyce, da of James Wilfred Dickens; 2 s (Simon Charles Oliver, Marcus James Arthur), 1 da (Rosamund Patricia); *Career* Sgt RAOC 1942-44, Lt Royal Norfolk Regt 1944-45; Univ of Leicester 1947-: warden of Vaughan Coll 1954-62, prof of english 1964-82, public orator 1976-78, and 1980-82; visiting prof: Univs of California 1967, Columbia 1969, Victoria NZ 1974; scripted and appeared on BBC TV and Radio in The Canker and the Rose, Mermaid Theatre, London 1964, sec Leicester Theatre Tst 1962-87; memb; Arts Cncl Drama Panel 1970-75, Nat Theatre Bd of Dirs 1976-82; govr Br American Drama Acad 1983-, pres Dickens Fellowship 1984-86, chm Tennyson Soc 1983; *Books* Dickens and Crime (1962), Dickens; the Critical Heritage (1971), Thackeray: Interviews and Recollections (1983); *Recreations* theatre, music; *Style*— Prof Philip Collins

COLLINS, Lady; Priscilla Marian; eldest da of Lloyd, JP (d 1943), of Pipewell Hall, Kettering, and Margaret Ellen, *née* Philips; *b* 9 Oct 1901; *m* 1924, Sir William Alexander Roy Collins, CBE (d 1983, chm and md William Collins and Sons Co Ltd, Publishers); 2 s (*see* Lady Sarah Collins), 1 da (and 1 da decd - *see* Ziegler, Philip); *Style*— Lady Collins; 25 St James's Place, London SW1

COLLINS, Lady Sara Elena; *née* Hely-Hutchinson; o da of 7 Earl of Donoughmore; *b* 22 August 1930; *m* 2 Aug 1951, William Janson Collins (6 6 Oct 1929), er s of Sir William Alexander Roy Collins, CBE (d 1983); 1 s, 3 da; *Style*— Lady Sara Collins; House of Craigie, by Kilmarnock, Ayrshire

COLLINS, Terence Bernard; s of late George Bernard Collins and Helen Teresa, *née* Goodfellow; *b* 3 Mar 1927; *Educ* Marist Coll Hull, St Andrews Univ (MA); *m* 1956, Barbara, nee Lowday; 2 s, 2 da; *Career* md Berger Jenson Nicholson 1975-86, dir Hoechst UK 1979-86, A G Stanley 1979-86, Hoechst Aust investmts Pty 1980-86, Mayborn Gp plc 1986-, Cranfield Conf Servs 1986- (chm 1988-); chm: Phoenix Devpts 1987-, mgmnt ctee Kingline Consultancy Ltd 1989-; cncl memb Cranfield Inst of Technol 1980-, tstee Atlas Fndn 1986-, vice chm cncl Buckingham Univ 1987- (chm fin and gen purposes ctee 1987-); memb int panel Duke of Edinburgh's Award 1978-86 (int fellowship ctee 1987-); *Recreations* music, golf; *Clubs* Directors', Aldeburgh Golf, Cook Society; *Style*— Terence Collins, Esq; Aldehurst, Church Walk, Aldeburgh, Suffolk IP15 5DX

COLLINS, Brig Thomas Frederick James; CBE (1946), JP, DL (Essex); s of Capt James Adolphus Collins (d 1943), of Ashdon Hall, Essex, and Emily Truscott (d 1946); *b* 9 April 1905; *Educ* Haileybury, RMC Sandhurst; *m* 1942, Marjorie Morwenna, da of Lt-Col Thomas Donnelly; 1 da (Lucy); *Career* 2 Lt The Green Howards 1924; cncllr Essex CC 1960-81, chm 1968-71; Cdr Order of Leopold (Belgium) 1945; *Clubs* Army and Navy; *Style*— Brig Thomas Collins, CBE, JP, DL; Ashdon Hall, Saffron Walden, Essex (☎ 079 984 232)

COLLINSON, Alicia Hester; da of His Hon Judge Richard Jeffreys Hampton Collinson, BCL, MA (d 1983), and Gwendolen Hester, *née* Ward ; *b* 12 August 1956; *Educ* Birkenhead HS, St Hugh's Coll Oxford (MA, MPhil); *m* 23 Apr 1988, Damian Howard Green, s of Howard Green, KSG; *Career* barrister; *Clubs* Oxford Union; *Style*— Miss Alicia Collinson; 2 Harecourt Buildings, Temple, London EC4 (☎ 01 353 6961, fax 01 353 6968)

COLLINSON, Anthony Raymond; s of Jack Collinson, of Ballacregga Farm, Kirk Michael, Isle of Man, and Irene Collinson, of Burton Old Hall, Burton-in-Kendal, Cumbria; *b* 9 April 1949; *Educ* Lancaster Royal GS, Guildford Coll of Law; *m* 1 March 1975, Carol Ann, da of Patrick David Horsfall, of Poole House, Arkholme, Carnforth, Lancs (s of Sir (John) Donald Horsfall, Bt); 1 s (Jack b 4 Aug 1980), 1 da (Poppy b 9 Aug 1983); *Career* slr, sr ptnr Whiteside & Knowles, Morecambe 1983- (ptnr 1973-); hon sec Lancaster Morecambe and Dist Law Soc 1978; memb ctee Morecambe CAB, hon sec PCC St Mary's Borwick; memb: Law Soc, slrs Benevolent Assoc; *Recreations* riding to hounds, reading, walking, local history; *Style*— Anthony Collinson, Esq; The Coach House, Capernwray, Carnforth, Lancashire LA6 1AL (☎ 0524 734 333); 5/7 Skipton St, Morecambe, Lancashire LA4 4AW (☎ 0524 416 315, fax 0524 831 008)

COLLINSON, Capt Peter Robert Holt; s of Herbert Collinson (d 1951), of Manchester, and Elsie, *née* Holt (d 1978); *b* 25 Oct 1929; *Educ* Manchester GS, RNC Dartmouth, Jesus Coll Cambridge (MA); *m* 16 Aug 1952, Elaine Dora, da of Ernest Shawcross, of Cheshire; 1 da (Janet b 1956); *Career* RN 1947-82, dir Weapon Systems (Polaris) 1976-79, Capt HMS Collingwood 1979-81, ADC 1982; Marconi Underwater Systems Ltd (gen mangr 1982-85); dist gen mangr West Cumbria Health Authy 1985-; Lacrosse Half Blue 1948, 1949, 1950; RMCS, Advanced Guided Weapon Course 1957-58; pres: Whitehaven Sea Cadet Corps 1985-, Whitehaven RN Assoc 1985-; *Recreations* fly fishing; *Style*— Capt Peter Collinson; Skald How, Applethwaite, Keswick, Cumbria (☎ 07687 72245); West Cumberland Hospital, Whitehaven, Cumbria (☎ 0946 3181, telex and fax 0946 63931)

COLLIS, (Herbert Charles) Clive; OBE (1974), MC (1918); s of Frank Collis (d 1929), sometime Mayor of Stoke-on-Trent, and Mary Ellen, *née* Stevenson (d 1968); *b* 13 Oct 1898; *Educ* Denstone Coll Staffs; *m* 1, 1926, Dorothy Elizabeth, da of John Riley (d 1959); 1 child; m 2, 1962, Doris; *Career* served WWI, Capt Royal Field Artillery, BEF, France; slr, Notary Public; asst dep coroner for NW Staffs and City of Stoke-on-Trent 1936-66; clerk to the Justices, Petty Sessional Div Cheadle 1945-68; chm Stoke-on-Trent and Cheadle War Pensions Ctee 1950-70; pres: Stoke-on-Trent Br Legion, N Staffs Law Soc 1942-43, Staffs Justices Clerks Soc 1950; *Recreations* shooting, fishing, formerly hunting; *Style*— Clive Collis Esq, OBE, MC; Rosehill, Townend, Cheadle, Staffs (☎ 0538 753125)

COLLIS, Richard John; *b* 11 Nov 1904; *Educ* Newport GS Essex; *m* 1, 12 July 1930, Kathleen, *née* Hallett (d 1951), 1 s (John Richard b 1937), 1 da (Patricia Anne (Mrs F S Brazier) b 1939); m 2, 8 June 1957, Marjorie, da of late Sir Henry Ridpath; *Career* chm and dir Ridpath Bros Ltd (London) 1950-; pres: Imported Meat Trade Assoc 1968-69, Butchers & Drovers Charitable Inst 1959; Freeman Worshipful Co of Butchers 1951; Order of Merit (Poland) 1984;; *Clubs* City Livery, Canada, Royal Smithfield; *Style*— Richard Collis, Esq; Great Notts, Bovinger, Ongar. Essex CM5 0LU (☎ 0277 83227); Ridpath Bros Ltd, 228 Central Markets, Smithfield, London EC1A 9LH (☎ 01 248 8471)

COLLISON, Baron (Life Peer UK 1964); Harold Francis Collison; CBE (1961); *b* 10 May 1909; *Educ* Hay Currie LCC Sch, Crypt Sch Gloucester; *m* 1, 15 May 1940, Mary (d 9 Sept 1945), da of Frederick Smith, of The Hollies, Shepshed, Leics; m 2, 31 Jan 1946, Ivy Kate, da of Walter Frederick Hanks (d 1949), of Burleigh, nr Stroud, Glos; *Career* farm worker 1934-44; gen sec Nat Union of Agric Workers 1953-69 (official 1944-46, chm Supplementary Benefits Cmmn 1969-75); pres Int Fedn of Agric and Allied Workers 1960-76; chm TUC 1964-65 (memb gen cncl 1953-69); chm Agric Apprenticeship Cncl 1968-74; pres Assoc of Agric 1976-84; chm Land Settlement Assoc 1977-79 (vice-chm 1964-77); memb: governing body Int Labour Orgn 1960-69, Pilkington Ctee on Broadcasting 1960-62, Royal Cmmn on Trade Unions and Employers Assoc 1965-68; *Recreations* gardening, chess; *Style—* The Rt Hon the Lord Collison, CBE; Honeywood, 163 Old Nazeing Rd, Broxbourne, Herts EN10 6QT (☎ 0992 463597)

COLLIVER, Douglas John; s of Douglas John Colliver (d 1983), of Farnborough, Hants, and Alice Emily, *née* White; *b* 22 Mar 1947; *Educ* The GS Farnborough, Bristol Univ (LLB); *m* 27 Feb 1971, Lulu, da of Henry William Hayes (d 1983), of Camberley, Surrey; 3 s (Toby b 1972, Jasper b 1979, Giles b 1981), 1 da (Sophy b 1974); *Career* articles Durrant Cooper and Hambling 1969-71, slr Norton Rose 1973-78 (ptnr 1978); memb: Int Bar Assoc, Law Soc; *Recreations* reading, music, tennis, walking; *Clubs* St Georges Hill, Lawn Tennis; *Style—* Douglas Colliver, Esq; Kempson House, Camomile Street, London EC3A 7AN (☎ 01 283 2434, fax 01 588 1181, telex 883652)

COLLS, Alan Howard Crawfurd; s of Maj Derek Archibald Colls, MBE, of 4 Carlton Lodge, 37-39 Lowndes St, SW1, and Amy, *née* Christie-Crawfurd (d 1982); *b* 15 Dec 1941; *Educ* Harrow; *m* 20 March 1969, Janet Mary, da of Maj Michael Gillespie (d 1986); 1 s (Toby b 19 Dec 1970), 1 da (Nina b 15 Jan 1970); *Career* chm Stewart Wrightson Aviation Ltd 1975-86, dir Stewart Wrightson Holdings plc 1981-87; chm: Stewart Wrightson Int Gp 1981-85, chm Stewart Wrightson Ltd 1986-87; dep chm Lloyds Insur Brokers Ctee 1986-87, chm Nicholson Chamberlain & Colls Ltd 1988-; *Recreations* tennis, golf, travel; *Clubs* Annabels; *Style—* Alan Colls, Esq; 11 Drayton Gdns, London SW10 9RY (☎ 01 370 3427); Nicholson Chamberlain & Colls Ltd, Guild Ho, 36-38 Fenchurch St, London EC3M 3DQ (☎ 01 929 5252, ext 2158, fax 01 929 5484, telex 914561)

COLLUM, Hugh Robert; s of Robert Archibald Hugh (d 13 July 1976), and Marie Vivien *née* Skinner (d 1978); *b* 29 June 1940; *Educ* Eton Coll; *m* 24 July 1965, Elizabeth Noel, da of Gordon Stewart, of Pontefract, Yorks; 2 da (Lucinda Elizabeth b 1967, Melissa Jane b 1969); *Career* Coopers and Lybrand 1959-65; Plymouth Breweries Ltd and Courage Western Ltd 1965-72; fin dir: Courage Ltd 1973-81, Cadbury Schweppes plc 1983-86 (dep 1981-83), Beecham Gp plc 1987-; non exec dir Imperial Tobacco Ltd 1978-81, Ladbroke Courage Holidays Ltd 1976-81, Cncl of Brewers Soc 1978-81, Sedgwick Gp plc 1987-; FCA; *Recreations* sport, opera, shooting, travel; *Clubs* Boodles, MCC; *Style—* Hugh R Collum, Esq; Clinton Lodge, Fletching, E Sussex TN22 3ST (☎ 082 572 2952); Beecham Group plc, Beecham, Hse, Brentford, Middx TW8 9BD (☎ 01 975 3721, fax 01 847 6225)

COLLYEAR, Sir John Gowen; s of John Robert Collyear (d 1968), and Amy Elizabeth, *née* Gowen; *b* 19 Feb 1927; *Educ* Watford GS, Manchester Univ, Leeds Univ (BSc); *m* 1953, Catherine Barbara, da of William James Newman; 1 s (John), 2 da (Elizabeth, Kathryn); *Career* Lt RE; engr; chm AE plc 1981-86 (formerly Associated Engrg, gp md 1975-81); chm: MK Electric Gp plc 1987-88, Fulmer Ltd; chm United Machinery Gp Ltd, Glacier Metal Co Ltd 1972-76; FEng, FIMechE, FIProdE, FRSA, CBIM; kt 1986; *Books* Management Precepts (1975), The Practice of First Level Management (1976); *Recreations* golf, bridge, music; *Clubs* Athenaeum; *Style—* Sir John Collyear; Walnut Tree House, Nether Westcote, Oxon, OX7 6SD (☎ 0993 831247)

COLLYER, Lt Cdr Alan Wilfred Mervyn; s of Frederick Charles Collyer (d 1933), and Beatrice Anne Watson (d 1929); *b* 23 Dec 1908; *Educ* Blundell's, RN Engrg Coll Devonport; *m* 4 April 1959, Jennifer, da of Geoffrey Le Mare (d 1986), of Kelveden, Essex; 1 s (Charles Richard Julian b 1967), 2 da (Caroline Anne b 1960, Rosemary Jane b 1965); *Career* SO to C-in-C Pacific Fleet, Aust, Hong Kong 1945-46; Africa Star (Inshore Sqdn Bar); Atlantic Star; 1939-45 Star; cncllr City of Canterbury 1983-87; *Recreations* snooker, gardening; *Clubs* Naval and Military, Kent and Canterbury; *Style—* Lt Cdr Alan W M Collyer; The Manor House, Ford, Hoath, Canterbury, Kent CT3 4LS (☎ Chislet 217)

COLMAN, Anthony David; QC (1977); s of Solomon Colman, of Larchfield Manor, Harrogate, and Helen, *née* Weiss (d 1987); *b* 27 May 1938; *Educ* Harrogate GS, Trinity Hall Cambridge (BA, MA); *m* 23 Aug 1964, Angela Barbara, da of Hyman Glynn (d 1984), of London; 2 da (Deborah b 1967, Rosalind b 1971); *Career* Instr RAEC (Nat Serv) 1957-59; barr Gray's Inn 1962; in commercial practice 1963 (specialising in shipping, int trade and insurance); chm ctees of enquiry and disciplinary ctees at Lloyds; recorder of Crown Courts 1985; bencher Gray's Inn 1986; dep High Court judge 1987; memb of Bar Cncl 1989-; FCIArb 1978; *Books* Mathew's Practice of the Commercial Court (2nd edn 1965), The Practice and Procedure of the Commercial Court (1983; 2nd edn 1986); *Recreations* cricket, tennis, gardening; *Style—* Anthony Colman, Esq, QC; 4 Essex Ct, Temple, London EC4Y 9AJ (☎ 01 583 9191, fax 01 353 3421)

COLMAN, Hon Mrs (Cynthia); 2 da (twin) of 1 Baron Sherfield, GCB, GCMG; *b* 11 July 1935; *m* 4 March 1967, Oliver James Colman, yr s of Sir Jeremiah Colman, 2 Bt (d 1961), and bro of 3 Bt; 1 s, 1 da; *Style—* The Hon Mrs Colman; 35 Greville Rd, London NW6

COLMAN, Jeremiah Michael Powlett; s and h of Sir Michael Colman, 3 Bt; *b* 23 Jan 1958; *Educ* Eton, Leicester Univ (LLB); *m* 10 Oct 1981, Susan Elizabeth, da of John Henry Britland, of York; 1 s (Joseph Jeremiah b 31 Nov 1988), 1 da (Eleanor b 1985); *Career* slr; *Style—* Jamie Colman, Esq; 12 Eland Rd, London SW11

COLMAN, Jeremy Gye; s of Philip Colman, and Georgina Maude, *née*, Gye; *b* 9 April 1948; *Educ* John Lyon Sch Harrow, Peterhouse Coll Cambridge (MA), Imperial Coll London (MSc, DIC); *m* 10 Oct 1978, Patricia Ann, da of Willliam Walter Stewart; *Career* CS offr 1971-75, princ HM Treasy 1975-78, CS Dept 1978-81; private sec to head of Home CS 1980-81, princ HM Treasy 1981-84, pte sec to Permanent Sec and Joint Head of Home Civil Services 1981-82, asst sec HM Treasy 1984-87; dir County Nat West Ltd 1988-; *Recreations* cookery, opera, wine; *Clubs* United Oxford and Cambridge Univ, Ski Club of Great Britain; *Style—* J G Colman, Esq; 15 Linkfield Lane, Redhill, Surrey (☎ 0737 768 479); County Natwest Ltd, Drapers Gardens, 12 Throgmorton Ave, London EC2 (☎ 01 382 1000, fax 01 638 4679, telex 882121 COUNTY)

COLMAN, Keith Thomas; s of Thomas Aurthur Colman, of Melton Constable, Norfolk, and Lorna Margaret, *née* Warnes; *b* 30 August 1952; *Educ* Fakenham GS, London Univ (BSc); *m* 27 July 1974, Denise Jane, da of Jack Donald Matsell (d 1977); 2 s (Adam b 1978, Alistair b 1983), 2 da (Rebecca b 1980, Eleanor b 1987); *Career* trainee CA 1974-78, Ernst & Whinney 1978-81, ptnr Neville Russell 1982-86, ptnr The Colman Dring Ptnrship 1987-, md The Fin Advice Centre 1988-; govr Avenue Middle Sch Norwich, tstee of the Dove Tst Norwich, a ldr of Norwich Community Church, involved with Life for the World drug rehabilitation Centre Norwich, Matthew Project young peoples advice serv Norwich; FCA 1978; *Recreations* squash, DIY, soccer, family; *Style—* Keith Colman, Esq; The Colman Dring Ptnrship, 2 Dove St, Norwich, NR2 1DE (☎ 0603 617 009, fax 0603 620 213)

COLMAN, Lady Mary Cecilia; *née* Bowes-Lyon; da (twin) of Hon Michael Claude Hamilton Bowes-Lyon (d 1953), 5 s of 14 Earl of Strathmore; sis of 17 Earl; raised to the rank of an Earl's da 1974; *b* 30 Jan 1932; *m* 10 Nov 1951, Timothy James Alan Colman, *qv*; 2 s, 3 da; *Career* an extra lady-in-waiting to HRH Princess Alexandra, the Hon Mrs Angus Ogilvy 1970-; *Style—* Lady Mary Colman; Bixley Manor, Norwich, Norfolk NR15 8SJ

COLMAN, Sir Michael Jeremiah; 3 Bt (UK 1907), of Gatton Park, Surrey; s of Sir Jeremiah Colman, 2 Bt (d 1961); *b* 7 July 1928; *Educ* Eton; *m* 29 Oct 1955, Judith Jean Wallop, da of Vice Adm Sir Peveril William-Powlett, KCB, CBE, DSO; 2 s, 3 da; *Heir* s, Jeremiah Colman; *Career* chm Reckitt and Colman plc; memb cncl: Royal Warrant Holders 1977- (pres 1984); memb cncl Chemical Industries Assoc 1983-84; asst dir of Trinity House - memb Lighthouse Bd; memb Court of the Skinners' Co; memb cncl of the Scouts Assoc; memb gen cncl and finance ctee of King Edward's Hosp Fund for London; dir The UK Centre for Economic and Environmental Development; special tstee for St Mary's Hosp; dir Foreign & Colonial Ventures Advsrs Ltd; FRSA; *Recreations* farming, forestry, golf, shooting; *Clubs* Cavalry and Guards; *Style—* Sir Michael Colman, Bt; Malshanger, Basingstoke, Hants (☎ 0256 780241); Tarvie, Bridge of Cally, Blairgowrie, Perthshire (☎ 025 081 264); Reckitt and Colman plc, One Burlington Lane, London W4 2RW (☎ 01 994 6464, telex 21268)

COLMAN, (David) Stacy; s of Maj Horace Crakanthorp Colman, TD, of Broughty Ferry, and Nora, *née* Mackie; *b* 1 May 1906; *Educ* Shrewsbury, Balliol Coll Oxford (MA); *m* 29 Dec 1934, Sarah Alice, da of Maj Cyril Edwards, of Kidderminster; *Career* Lt gen list TA; asst master Shrewsbury 1928-31, 1935-36 and 1938-66 (master of dayboys, sch librarian), praelector classics and ancient history Queens Coll Univ of Oxford 1931-34 (fell), headmaster C of E GS Melbourne 1937-38; *Books* Sabrinae Corolla: The Classics at Shrewsbury School (1950); *Clubs* National Liberal, Leander, Salop (Shrewsbury); *Style—* Stacy Colman, Esq; 19 Woodfield Rd, Shrewsbury SY3 8HZ (☎ 0743 53749)

COLMAN, Timothy James Alan; JP (1958); s of Capt Geoffrey Russell Rees Colman, JP (d 1935), of Framlingham Chase, Norwich; *b* 19 Sept 1929; *Educ* RNC Dartmouth and Greenwich; *m* 10 Nov 1951, Lady Mary, *qv*; 2 s, 3 da; *Career* RN 1943-53, Lt 1950; chm Eastern Cos Newspaper Gp; dir: Reckitt & Colman plc, Whitbread & Co 1980-86; pro-vice-chllr UEA 1974- (chm cncl 1974-85), chm of tstees Norfolk and Norwich Triennial Festival 1974-, chm Royal Norfolk Agric Assoc 1985- (pres 1982); memb: Eastern regnl ctee Nat Tst 1967-71, Countryside Cmmn 1971-76, Water Space Amenity Cmmn 1973-76, advsy ctee England Nature Conservancy Cncl 1974-80 (pres Norfolk Naturalists Tst 1962-78); High Sheriff Norfolk 1970, Lord-Lieut Norfolk 1978- (DL 1968); Hon DCL UEA 1973; KStJ 1979; *Clubs* Turf, Pratt's, Royal Yacht Sqdn, Norfolk (Norwich); *Style—* Timothy Colman Esq; Bixley Manor, Norwich, Norfolk NR14 8SJ (☎ 0603 625298)

COLNBROOK, Baron (Life Peer UK 1987), of Waltham St Lawrence, Co Berks; Sir Humphrey Edward Gregory Atkins; KCMG (1983), PC (1973); o s of Capt Edward Davis Atkins (d 1925), of Nyeri, Kenya, and Mary Violet, *née* Preston (d 1975); *b* 12 August 1922; *Educ* Wellington; *m* 21 Jan 1944, (Adela) Margaret, yst da of Sir Robert Spencer-Nairn, 1 Bt, TD, JP, DL (d 1960); 1 s (Hon Charles Edward Spencer, *qv*), 3 da (Hon Mrs Schroeder, Hon Mrs Keay, Hon Mrs Clegg, *qqqv*); *Career* served WWII Lt RN Atlantic and Mediterranean; MP (C) Merton and Morden Surrey 1955-70, Spelthorne 1970-87; parly sec to Treasury and govt chief whip 1973-74, oppn chief whip 1974-79, sec of state for NI 1979-81, Lord Privy Seal and princ FCO spokesman in Commons 1981-82; chm Airey Neave Memorial Tst 1983-;pres Nat Union of Conservative and Unionist Assocs 1985-86; *Recreations* shooting, sailing, golf; *Clubs* Brooks's; *Style—* The Rt Hon Lord Colnbrook, KCMG, PC; Tuckenhams, Waltham St Lawrence, Berks RG10 0JH

COLONNA-CZOSNOWSKI, Karol Anthony; s of Eustace Colonna-Czosnowski (descended from Roscislaw, whose designation of Comes (which he appears to have born c 1250) was essentially a feudal one, in some ways comparable with W Euro seigneuries or lordships; a sr branch of the family was granted the title of Count by King Umberto I of Italy 24 Oct 1887 and by Pope Leo XIII 8 April 1897; *b* 24 Feb 1921; *Educ* St Joseph's Coll, Chyrow, Poland; *m* 1948, Maria, da of late Baron Stanislas Heydel of Siechow, Poland; *Career* Capt Italy 1944, chm Bishopsgate Steels Ltd and associated companies; *Recreations* foxhunting; *Clubs* Brooks's; *Style—* Karol Colonna-Czosnowski, Esq; Saddlecombe Stud, Hurst Lane, Headley, Surrey KT18 6DY (☎ 0372 379 443)

COLQUHOUN, Maj-Gen Sir Cyril Harry; KCVO (1968, CVO 1965), CB (1955), OBE (1945); s of late Capt Harry Colquhoun; *b* 16 August 1903; *Educ* RMA Woolwich; *m* 1930, Stella Irene, yr da of late W C Rose, of Kotagiri, India, and Cheam, Surrey; 1 s; *Career* cmmnd Royal Field Artillery 1923, served WW II, France 1939-40 (despatches), Europe 1944-45 (despatches), Palestine 1946-48 (despatches), cmd 1 and 6 Field Regts RA and 76 field Regt, CRA 6 Airborne Div 1946-48, CRA 61 Div 1945, CRA 1 Div 1948-50, Cmdt School of Artillery 1951-53, GOC 50 (Northumbria) Inf Div (TA) and Northumbrian Dist 1953-56, GOC troops Malta 1956-59, ret 1960; Col Cmdt: RA 1962-69, Royal Malta Artillery 1962-70; sec Central Chancery of the Orders of Knighthood 1960-68; extra gentleman usher to HM The Queen 1968-; *Recreations* shooting, gardening; *Clubs* Army and Navy; *Style—* Maj-Gen Sir Cyril Colquhoun, KCVO, CB, OBE; Longwalls, Shenington, Banbury, Oxon OX15 6NQ (☎ 029 587 246)

COLQUHOUN, Ernest Patrick; s of Wing Cdr Edgar Edmund Colquhoun, MBE (d 1953), of Staffs, and Elizabeth Colquhoun (d 1986); *b* 5 Jan 1937; *Educ* Shrewsbury,

Cambridge Univ; *m* 16 Jan 1964, (Patricia Susan) Alexandra , da of Frederick Versen (d 1953); 3 s (James b 1966, Harry b 1969, Freddy b 1980); *Career* Lt Scots Guards 1955-57; md Henderson Administration Ltd 1969-76; vice pres Swiss Bank Corpn 1983-88; memb Trading Ctee Royal Sch of Needlework 1988-;; *Recreations* shooting, cricket, antique collecting; *Clubs* Boodle's; *Style*— EP Colquhoun, Esq; 40 Markham St, London SW3 3NR (☎ 01 352 2737)

COLQUHOUN, (Ernest) Patrick; s of Wing Cdr Edgar Edmund Colquhoun, MBE (d 1953), of Staffordshire, and Elizabeth, *née* Makin (d 1986); *b* 5 Jan 1937; *Educ* Shrewsbury, Cambridge Univ; *m* 16 Jan 1964, Patricia Susan Alexandra, da of Flt Lt Frederick Versen (d 1953); 3 s (James b 1966, Henry b 1969, Frederick b 1980); *Career* Scots Guards 1955-59; banker; vice-pres Swiss Bank Corpn 1969-76; md Henderson Admin Ltd; *Recreations* shooting, cricket, antique collecting; *Clubs* Boodles; *Style*— Patrick Colquhoun, Esq; Swiss Bank Corpn, 30A Charles II Street, London SW1Y 4AE (☎ 606 4000, fax 606 4000, ext 4839)

COLQUHOUN OF LUSS, Capt Sir Ivar Iain; 8 Bt (GB 1786), JP (Dunbartonshire 1951), DL (1952); Chief of the Clan Colquhoun; s of Lt-Col Sir Iain Colquhoun, 7 Bt, KT, DSO, LLD (d 1948); *b* 4 Jan 1916; *Educ* Eton; *m* 17 April 1943, Kathleen, 2 da of late Walter Atholl Duncan, of 53 Cadogan Square, SW1; 1 s (and 1 s decd), 1 da; *Heir* s, Malcolm Colquhoun; *Career* Capt Grenadier Gds; hon sheriff (former hon sheriff substitute); *Clubs* White's, Puffin's, Royal Ocean Racing; *Style*— Capt Sir Ivar Colquhoun of Luss, Bt; 37 Radnor Walk, London SW3 (☎ 01 352 9510); Eilean da Mheinn, Crinan, Argyllshire; Camstraddan, Luss, Dunbartonshire (☎ 043 686 245)

COLQUHOUN, YR OF LUSS, Malcolm Rory; s and h of Capt Sir Ivar Colquhoun of Luss, 8 Bt; *b* 20 Dec 1947; *Educ* Eton; *m* 1978, Susan, da of Stewart W Timmerman, of Harrisburg, Penn, USA; *Style*— Malcolm Colquhoun, yr of Luss

COLQUHOUN-DENVERS, Nicholas John Arthur; s of H E John Dalrymple Colquhoun-Denvers, Australian Consul-Gen, of Bombay, India, and Winifred May, *née* Mitchell; *b* 5 Jan 1949; *Educ* Christ Church Coll, Perth; *m* 20 May 1978, Anne Patricia, da of Maj Charles Walter Douglas Wellesley Alexander, late of 3 Carabiniers and Royal Scots Dragoon Gds (d 1983); *Career* Offr RA served BAOR, Hong Kong, N Ireland Capt 1969-77, ret; sec to chm Australian Public Service Bd Canberra 1966-69, with Adnan Khashoggi's Triad Corpn 1977-85; md: CLC 1985-87, Hurlingham Int (Mgmnt) Ltd 1987-; dir Hurlingham Estates Ltd; Gen Service Medal 1971; *Recreations* polo, shooting, skiing; *Clubs* Carlton, Gds Polo, Ham Polo; *Style*— Nicholas Colquhoun-Denvers, Esq; 10 Catherine Place, London SW1E 6HF (☎ 01 834 1666/ 6646); 10 Belgrave Sq, London SW1X 8PH (☎ 01 259 6901/2) car (☎ 0836 220 339, 0836 220 439)

COLSON, Jeremy Richard; s of Cecil K W Colson, of London, and Hilda, *née* Richards; *b* 7 Nov 1947; *Educ* Oundle Sch; *m* 17 Oct 1970 (m dis 1980), Geraldine Louise, da of Philip Stevens, of Crediton, Devon; 1 da (Zoe Victoria b 1976); *Career* CA; gp fin dir Donald Macpherson Gp plc 1982-85, Bestwood plc 1985-; FCA 1970; FACT 1985; *Recreations* sailing, gardening; *Style*— Jeremy R Colson, Esq; 1 St Giles Ave, South Mimms, Herts EN6 3PZ (☎ 0707 45341); 99 Charterhouse St, London EC1 (☎ 01 490 2882, fax 01 608 2335)

COLSON, Maurice John; s of Louis-Philippe Colson (d 1984), and Kathleen, *née* Burke (d 1959); *b* 25 June 1942; *Educ* Loyola Montreal (BA 1963), McGill Univ (MBA), Oxford Univ; *m* Sept 1969 (m dis 1974); 1 s (Christopher Sean b 10 Feb 1974), 1 da (Kathryn b 22 April 1972); *Career* dir gen financing Montreal Olympics Organising Ctee 1974-77, vice pres McLeod Young Weir 1977-80, vice pres and dir First Marathon Securities 1980-86, md Richardson Greenshields of Canada 1986-; dir Northern Mines Ltd; Freeman City of London 1987; *Clubs* Annabels, United Oxford and Cambridge, Toronto Lawn Tennis; *Style*— Maurice Colson, Esq; 48 Cadogan Sq, London SW1 (☎ 01 584 7599); 1/9 City Rd, Lowndes House, London EC1Y 1BH (☎ 01 638 8831, fax 01 628 2114, telex 887439)

COLSTON, His Hon Judge; Colin Charles; QC; s of Eric Lawrence Colston, JP (d 1975), of Buckinghamshire, and Dr Catherine Colston; *b* 2 Oct 1937; *Educ* Rugby Trinity Hall Cambridge (MA); *m* 23 March 1963, Edith Helga, da of Dr Wilhelm Hille, of Austria; 2 s (Martin b 1965, Dominic b 1968), 1 da (Helen-Jane b 1970); *Career* Nat Serv 1956-58, cmmnd RNR 1957-64, Lt RNR; called to bar Gray's Inn 1962; Midland and Oxford circuit (formerly Midland Circuit); recorder of Midland Circuit 1968-69; member of the Senate of the Inns of Court and Bar 1977-80; recorder of Crown Court 1978-83; circuit judge 1983-; *Recreations* shooting, fishing, renovation of old house; *Style*— His Hon Judge Colston, QC; The Crown Court, St Albans, Herts

COLSTON, Michael; s of Sir Charles Blampied Colston, CBE, MC, DCM (d 1969), and Eliza, *née* Foster, MBE (d 1964), da of W A Shaw; *b* 24 July 1932; *Educ* Ridley Coll Canada, Stowe, Gonville and Caius Coll Cambridge; *m* 1, 1956 (m dis), Jane Olivia, da of Denys Kilham Roberts (d 1970); 3 da (Katrina b 1957, Quita b 1959, Melissa b 1961); m 2, 1977, Judith Angela, da of Gp Capt Nelson Briggs, CBE, AFC; *Career* served Korea, Lt 17/21 Lancers, seconded 1 RTR; chm Charles Colston Gp 1969-89, Tallent Engrg Ltd 1969-89, ITS Rubber Ltd 1969-85, Tallent Hldgs plc 1989-; chm and md Colston Domestic Appliances Ltd 1969-79; chm: Dishwasher Cncl 1970-75, Assoc Manufacturers of Domestic Electrical Appliances 1976-79; memb: Br Electrotechnical Approvals Bd 1976-79, cncl IOD 1977- (pres Thames Valley Branch), cncl CBI (chm Southern Region Cncl 1986-88), Soc of Motor Mfrs and Traders 1987-; fndr Cambridge Univ Water Ski Club; Freeman City of London, memb Worshipful Co of Coachmakers and Coach Harness Makers 1986; *Recreations* fishing, shooting, tennis; *Style*— Michael Colston, Esq; C6 Albany, Piccadilly, London W1V 9RF (☎ 01 734 2452); Tallent Holdings plc, c/o PO Box 15, Henley-on-Thames, Oxfordshire RG9 6HT (☎ 0491 641 668, fax 0491 641 938)

COLT, Sir Edward William Dutton; 10 Bt (E 1694), of St James's-in-the-Fields Liberty of Westminster, Middlesex; s of Major John Rochfort Colt, N Staffs Regt (d 1944), half-bro of 9 Bt; suc unc Sir Henry Archer Colt, 9 Bt, DSO, MC (d 1951); *b* 22 Sept 1936; *Educ* Stoke House Seaford, Douai Sch, Univ Coll London; *m* 1, 20 Aug 1966 (m dis 1972), Jane Caroline, da of James Histed Lewis; m 2, 1979, Suzanne Nelson, *née* Knickerbocker; 1 s (Tristan b 1983), 1 da (Angela Cecily b 1979); *Heir* s, Tristan Charles Edward, b 27 June 1983; *Career* asst attending physician St Luke's Hosp New York; MB, MRCP, FACP; *Style*— Sir Edward Colt, Bt; 12 East 88 St, New York, NY 10028, USA

COLTART, Col George John Letham; TD; s of George James Letham Coltart, MC (d 1974), and Augustine, *née* Claireaux (d 1973); *b* 2 Feb 1929; *Educ* George Watson Coll Edinburgh, RMA Sandhurst, King's Coll Cambridge (MA), Cornell Univ NY USA (MSc, King George VI Memorial Fell); *m* 17 Feb 1958, Inger Christina, da of Ivar-Ragnar Larsson (d 1974), of Gothenburg Sweden; 1 s (Neil b 1962), 1 da Karin b 1963); *Career* cmmnd RE 1949, Staff Coll Camberly 1962, DAA and QMG 5 Infantry Bde 1963-65, OC 51 Field Sqdn RE 1965-66, CO Edinburgh and Heriot-Watt UOTC 1972-74. TA Col Lowlands 1975-79, ret 1982; presently sr lectr and dep head Civil Engrg Heriot-Watt Univ Edinburgh (joined academic staff 1966); chm Lowland TA and VRA 1986; MICE 1961; *Recreations* walking, silvaculture, restoring buildings; *Clubs* Royal Commonwealth Soc; *Style*— Col George Coltart, TD; Napier House, 8 Colinton Rd, Edinburgh, EH10 5DS (☎ 031 447 6314); Polskeoch, Thornhill, Dumfriesshire DG3 4NN; Heriot-Watt Univ, Riccarton, Edinburgh EH14 4AS (☎ 031 449 5111, fax 031 449 5153)

COLTHURST, Caroline Romaine; *née* Combe; da of Cdr Antony Boyce Combe, of Grove Cottage, South Creake, nr Fakenham, Norfolk, and late Sibyl Barbara Grant, *née* Farquhar; *b* 29 Jan 1935; *Educ* Sydenham House; *m* 22 May 1958, George Silver Oliver Annesley Colthurst, yr s of Sir Richard St John Jeffreys Colthurst, 8 Bt, of Blarney Castle, Co Cork, Eire; 2 da (Romaine b 9 April 1969, Rowena b 15 Sept 1971); *Career* fashion ed 1958-67: Vogue, Sunday Times, Daily Mail, Harpers Bazaar; patron living of St Michaels & All Angels Pitchford, Acton Burnell, Codesley and Condonver; memb Shropshire charities incl Meals-on-Wheels; *Recreations* chess, bridge, fauna and flora conservation, ballet, classical music, computer adventure games, cats, logic problems, historic houses; *Style*— Mrs Oliver Colthurst; Pitchford Hall, nr Condover, Shropshire (☎ 06944 205)

COLTHURST, Charles St John; s and h of Sir Richard Colthurst, 9 Bt; *b* 21 May 1955; *Educ* Eton, Magdalene Cambridge, Univ Coll Dublin; *m* 31 Oct 1987, Nora Mary, da of Mortimer Kelleher, of Dooniskey, Lissarda, Co Cork; *Career* slr (Law Soc of Ireland); farmer; *Recreations* tennis, watersports, golf, skiing, reading; *Clubs* MCC, City Univ, Royal Irish Automobile, Royal Dublin Soc; *Style*— Charles Colthurst, Esq

COLTHURST, (George Silver) Oliver Annesley; s of Sir Richard St John Jefferyes Colthurst, 8 Bt (d 1955), of Blarney Castle, Co Cork, and Denys Maida Hanmer, *née* West (d 1965); *b* 1 Mar 1931; *Educ* Harrow, Trinity Coll Cambridge (MA); *m* 1, 10 Oct 1959 (m dis 1966), Hon Elizabeth Sophia Sidney, eldest da of 1 Viscount De L'Isle, VC, KG, PC, GCMG, GCVO; 1 da (Shaunagh Anne Henrietta b 1961, m Thomas Heneage); m 2, 22 May 1968, Caroline Romaine, 2 da of Cdr Anthony Boyce Combe, RN (ret), of Grove Cottage, South Creake, Fakenham, Norfolk; 2 da (Romaine Louisa b 1969, Rowena Barbara b 1971); *Career* late 2 Lt The Life Guards (National Service); memb London Stock Exchange (ptnr de Zoete and Bevan 1961-81); underwriting memb of Lloyd's; memb Court of Common Cncl (Broad Street Ward) 1976-80; Liveryman Goldsmith's Co; *Recreations* tennis, shooting, dendrology; *Clubs* Turf, Pratt's, MCC; *Style*— Oliver Colthurst, Esq; Pitchford Hall, Shrewsbury, Shropshire (☎ 06944 205); Charterhouse Tilney, 15 Pride Hill, Shrewsbsury, Shropshire (☎ 0743 51374)

COLTHURST, Sir Richard La Touche; 9 Bt (I 1744), of Ardrum, Cork; s of Sir Richard St John Jefferyes Colthurst, 8 Bt (d 1955), and Denis Maida Hanmer, *née* West (d 1965); *b* 14 August 1928; *Educ* Harrow, Peterhouse Cambridge; *m* 24 Oct 1953, Janet Georgina, da of Leonard Almroth Wilson-Wright (d 1971), of Coolcarrigan, Co Kildare; 3 s (Charles, *qv* James b 1957, Henry b 1959), 1 da (Georgina b 1961); *Heir* s, Charles St John Colthurst; *Career* underwriting memb of Lloyds; dir KC Webb Underwriting Ltd; Liveryman Worshipful Co of Grocers; *Recreations* cricket, gardening, forestry; *Clubs* City University, MCC; *Style*— Sir Richard Colthurst, Bt

COLTMAN, David Alexander; s of Col Thomas Alexander Hamilton Coltman, OBE, DL, RA, of Ayrshire, and Susan Stella Tufton; *b* 5 August 1942; *Educ* Eton, Edinburgh Univ; *m* 1972, Mary Cecilia, 3 da of 1 Viscount Whitelaw; 1 da (Susannah Lucy b 1987); *Career* md British Caledonian Airways 1984; *Recreations* shooting; *Clubs* Caledonian; *Style*— David A Coltman, Esq; Haystoun, Peebles; Caledonian House, Crawley, Sussex (☎ 0293 27890, telex 87161 BCAL G)

COLTMAN, (Arthur) Leycester Scott; s of Arthur Cranfield Coltman (d 1982), and Vera, *née* Vaid (d 1971); *b* 24 May 1938; *Educ* Rugby, Magdalene Coll Cambridge; *m* 21 March 1969, (Maria) Piedad Josefina, *née* Cantos Aberasturi, da of Excmo Sr Antonio Cantos Guerrero, of General Moscardo 20, Madrid 20, Spain; 2 s (Roland b 1974, Stephen b 1978), 1 da (Beatrice b 1971); *Career* FCO; joined 1961, third sec Copenhagen 1963-64; second sec: Cairo 1964-66, Madrid 1966-69; Manchester Business Sch 1969-70 (sabbatical year), FCO 1970-74, first sec Brasilia 1974-77, FCO 1977-79; cnsllr and head of chancery: Mexico City 1979-83, Brussels 1983-87; Head Mexico and Central American Dept FCO 1987-; *Recreations* squash, chess, books, music; *Style*— Leycester Coltman, Esq; FCO, King Charles St, London SW1A 2AH (☎ 01 270 2470)

COLTMAN, Hon Mrs; Hon Mary Cecilia; da of 1 Viscount Whitelaw; *b* 1947; *m* 1972, David Alexander Coltman, s of Col Thomas Alexander Hamilton Coltman, OBE, DL, RA, and Susan Stella, da of late Hon Charles Henry Tufton, CMG; 1 da (b 1987); *Style*— The Hon Mrs Coltman; Haystoun House, Peebles

COLTON, Mary Winifred; da of James Colton (d 1952), and Winifred Alice, *née* Smith; *b* 2 Jan 1933; *Educ* Kingsbury Co Sch, London Univ (LLB); *Career* barr Middle Temple 1955, SE circuit, dep circuit judge 1978-81, asst rec 1982-; *Style*— Miss Mary Colton; 4 Brick Ct, The Temple, London EC4Y 9Ad (☎ 01 583 8455)

COLTRANE, Robbie (formerly McMillan); s of Ian Bayter McMillan (d 1969), of Rutherglen, Glasgow, and Jean Ross, *née* Howie; *b* 31 March 1950; *Educ* Trinity Coll Glenalmond, Glasgow Sch of Art (Dip Drawing and Painting); *Career* actor; theatre: toured univs with the San Quentin Theatre Workshop 1974-75, Snobs and Yobs Edinburgh Festival 1980, Yr Obedient Servant (one man show on Dr Samuel Johnson) Lyric Hammersmith 1987; TV appearances incl: Jasper Carrot Live, Alfresco (2 series), Kick Up the Eighties, The Lenny Henry Show, The Comic Strip Presents ... (various programmes), Laugh I Nearly Paid My License Fee, The Young Ones (several guest roles), Saturday Night Live, Girls On Top, The Tube (guest spots), Hooray for Holyrood (documentary about Edinburgh Film Festival), Tutti Frutti (lead role), Blackadder III (guest role) and Blackadder Xmas Special, Emma Thompson Show; films incl: Scrubbers 1982, The Supergrass (Comic Strip Feature Film) 1984, Defence of the Realm 1985, Revolution 1985, Caravaggio 1985, Absolute Beginners 1985, Mona Lisa 1985, Eat the Rich 1987, The Fruit Machine 1987, Slipstream 1988, Danny Champion of the World 1988, Henry V (Falstaff) 1988; involved with: Labour Pty, Amnesty, Greenpeace, Friends of the Earth, CND, Freeze; hon pres Herriot-Watt Univ; *Recreations* vintage cars, painting, sailing, clubs, playing piano; *Clubs*

Groucho's, Colony Room, Moscow's Glasgow Arts, Zanzibar; *Style*— Robbie Coltrane, Esq;; c/o CDA, 47 Courtfield Rd, London SW7 (☎ 01 370 0708)

COLVILE, Maj Robert Asgill; TD; s of Arthur Montague Colvile (d 1952), and Phyllis Margaret Colvile (d 1974); *b* 4 July 1916; *Educ* Queen's Coll Oxford (MA); *m* 21 April 1974, Rosemary, da of Campbell Raleigh; 1 s (Robert b 1980), 1 da (Katharine b 1977); *Career* army offr (Maj) Italy; *Recreations* tennis; *Clubs* Naval and Military; *Style*— Major Robert A Colvile, TD; Weald Manor, Bampton, Oxford (☎ 0993 850224)

COLVILLE, Hon Alexander Fergus Gale; 3 s of 4 Viscount Colville of Culross, *qv*; *b* 9 July 1964; *Educ* Wellington Coll, Nottingham Poly (BSc); *Style*— The Hon Alexander Colville

COLVILLE, Hon Andrew John; 2 s of 2 Baron Clydesmuir, KT, CB, MBE, TD; *b* 30 May 1953; *m* 1978, Elaine Genevieve, *née* Davy; *Style*— The Hon Andrew Colville

COLVILLE, Hon Angus Richmond; yst s of Cdr 3 Visc Colville of Culross, RN (k on active service 1945); *b* 29 April 1939; *Educ* Rugby; *Career* Lt Grenadier Gds (Reserve); chartered surveyor; ptnr Michelmore Hughes at Tavistock; FRICS; *Style*— The Hon Angus Colville; 1 Bedford Place, Tavistock, Devon PL19 8AZ (☎ 0822 614206; office: 0822 614507)

COLVILLE, Hon (Elizabeth) Anne; yr da of 2 Baron Clydesmuir, KT, CB, MBE, TD; *b* 26 June 1955; *Style*— The Hon Anne Colville

COLVILLE, Hon (Charles) Anthony; 2 s of 3 Viscount Colville of Culross (ka 1945); *b* 5 August 1935; *Educ* Rugby, Magdalen Coll Oxford (BA); *m* 2 Oct 1965, Katherine, da of Humphrey John Sankey (d 1945), of Kinangop, Kenya; 2 s (Robert Quintin Oxnam b 1971, Charles Alexander b 1974); *Career* late Sub-Lt RNR; Overseas Civil Serv Kenya 1958-64; slr 1969; *Style*— The Hon Anthony Colville; Rydes, The Crossway, Neville Court, Tunbridge Wells, Kent TN4 8NL

COLVILLE, Master of; Hon Charles Mark Townshend Colville; s and h of 4 Visc Colville of Culross; *b* 5 Sept 1959; *Educ* Rugby, Durham Univ; *Style*— The Master of Colville

COLVILLE, Hon David Ronald; s and h of 2 Baron Clydesmuir, KT, CB, MBE, TD; *b* 8 April 1949; *Educ* Charterhouse; *m* 1978, Aline Frances, da of Peter Merriam, of Holton Lodge, Holton St Mary, Suffolk; 1 s, 2 da; *Style*— The Hon David Colville

COLVILLE, Lady Joan; *née* Child-Villiers; er da of 8 Earl of Jersey (d 1923); *b* 26 Sept 1911; *m* 21 Jan 1933, Lt David Richard Colville, RNVR, (d 1986), s of late Hon George Charles Colville, MBE (3 s of 1 Viscount Colville of Culross); 2 s; 3 da; *Style*— Lady Joan Colville; Old Vicarage, Dorton, nr Aylesbury, Bucks

COLVILLE, Lady Margaret; *née* Egerton; da of 4 Earl of Ellesmere; *b* 20 July 1918; *m* 20 Oct 1948, Sir John Colville, *qv*; 2 s, 1 da; *Career* ATS (Jr Subaltern) 1939-45; lady in waiting to HRH Princess Elizabeth 1946-49, pres Cecil Houses Inc, pres Friendly Almshouses; *Style*— Lady Margaret Colville; The Close, Broughton, nr Stockbridge, Hants (☎ 0794 301331)

COLVILLE, Hon Richmond James Innys; 2 s of 4 Viscount Colville of Culross, *qv*; *b* 9 June 1961; *Educ* Rugby, Bristol Univ (BSc), King's Coll London (MSc), Univ Coll and Middx Sch of Medicine; *Style*— The Hon Richmond Colville

COLVILLE, Hon Rupert George Streatfeild; 4 s of 4 Viscount Colville of Culross, *qv*; *b* 17 May 1966; *Educ* Milton Abbey; *Style*— The Hon Rupert Colville

COLVILLE OF CULROSS, 4 Viscount (UK 1902); John Mark Alexander Colville; QC (1978); also 14 Lord Colville of Culross (S precedency 1609) and 4 Baron Colville of Culross (UK 1885); s of 3 Viscount (k on active service 1945); 1 cous of Lord Carrington and 1 cous once removed of Sir John Colville, *qv*; *b* 19 July 1933; *Educ* Rugby, New Coll Oxford; *m* 1, 4 Oct 1958 (m dis 1973), Mary Elizabeth, da of Col Mostyn Hird Wheeler Webb-Bowen, RM; 4 s; m 2, 1974, Margaret Birgitta, LlB, JP (Inner London), barr 1985, da of Maj-Gen Cyril Henry Norton, CB, CBE, DSO, and former w of 2 Viscount Davidson; 1 s (Hon Edmund Carleton b 1978); *Heir* s, Master of Colville; *Career* sits as Conservative Peer in Lords; Lt Gren Gds (Reserve); barr 1960, bencher Lincoln's Inn 1986; min of state Home Office 1972-74, UK rep UN Human Rights Cmmn 1980-83, special rapporteur on Guatemala 1983-87; exec dir Br Electric Traction Co 1981-84, and cos in gp 1968-84; chm: Mental Health Act Cmmn 1983-1987, Alcohol Educn and Res Cncl 1984-, Parole Bd for England and Wales 1988-; memb Royal Co of Archers (Queen's Body Gd for Scotland); *Style*— The Rt Hon the Viscount Colville of Culross, QC; Worlingham Hall, Beccles, Suffolk (☎ 0502 713191); 2 Mitre Court Buildings, Temple, London EC4Y 7BX (☎ 01 583 1355)

COLVIN, David Hugh; s of Maj Leslie Hubert Boyd Colvin, MC, of Pk View, Gret Baddow, Essex, and Edna Mary, *née* Parrott; *b* 23 Jan 1941; *Educ* Lincoln Sch, Trinity Coll Oxford (MA); *m* 15 May 1971, Diana Caroline Carew, da of Gordon MacPherson Lang Smith, of 44 Devonshire St, London, W1; 1 s (Thomas b 1983); *Career* asst princ Bd of Trade 1966; HM For Serv 1967: central dept FO 1967, second sec Bangkok 1968-71, euro integration dept FCO 1971-75, first sec Paris 1975-77, first sec (press and info) UK perm representation to the Euro Community Brussels, 1977-82, cnsllr on loan to the Cabinet Office 1982-85, cnsllr and head of Chancery Budapest 1985-88, head SE Asian Dept FCO 1988-; *Recreations* squash, tennis, shooting; *Clubs* The Travellers; *Style*— David Colvin, Esq; c/o FCO, King Charles St, London, SW1 (☎ 01 270 2438)

COLVIN, Michael Keith Beale; MP (C) Romsey and Waterside 1983-; s of Capt Ivan Beale Colvin, RN, and Joy Frances, OBE, *née* Arbuthnot (*see* Burke's Landed Gentry, 18 edn, Vol I, 1965); *b* 27 Sept 1932; *Educ* Eton, RMA Sandhurst, RAC Cirencester; *m* 1956, Hon Nichola, da of Baron Cayzer (Life Peer), *qv*; 1 s (James b 1965), 2 da (Amanda b 1957, Arabella b 1960); *Career* served Gren Guards 1950-57: Queen's Co 1954-55, BAOR Berlin 1954, Suez Campaign, Cyprus 1956-57; with J Walter Thompson Co Ltd 1958-63; Andover RDC 1965-72; jt vice-chm Test Valley Borough Cncl 1972- 74; dep chm Winchester Cons Assoc 1973-76; MP Bristol NW 1979-83, PPS to Baroness Young FCO 1983-85 and Rt Hon Richard Luce FCO 1983-87, memb Select Ctee of Employment 1981-83; sec Cons Foreign Affairs Ctee 1987-; chm: Cons Aviation Ctee 1982-83 and 1987-, West Country MPs 1982-83, Br Gibraltar Gp, cncl for Country Sports 1987- ; vice-chm: Cons Smaller Business Ctee 1980-83, British Bophuthatswana Gp, Br Field Sports Soc 1987-; pres Hampshire Young Farmers Clubs 1973-75, govr Enham Village Centre 1965-; parly advsr nat Licenced Victuallers Assoc; landowner, farmer; *Books* Britain, a View from Westminster (jt); *Recreations* painting, field sports; *Clubs* Turf, Pratts; *Style*— Michael Colvin, Esq, MP; Tangley House, Andover, Hants SP11 0SH (☎ 026 470 215); c/o The House of Commons, London SW1 (☎ 01 219 4208)

COLVIN, Hon Mrs; (Nichola); *née* Cayzer; er da of Baron Cayzer (Life Peer); *b* 27 May 1937; *m* 15 Sept 1956, Michael Keith Beale Colvin, MP, *qv*; 1 s, 2 da; *Style*— The Hon Mrs Colvin; Tangley House, Andover, Hampshire

COLWYN, 3 Baron (UK 1917); Sir (Ian) Anthony Hamilton-Smith; 3 Bt (UK 1912); s of 2 Baron Colwyn (d 1966); *b* 1 Jan 1942; *Educ* Cheltenham Coll, London Univ; *m* 1, 30 May 1964 (m dis 1977), Sonia Jane, er da of Peter Henry Geoffrey Morgan; 1 s, 1 da (Hon Jacqueline b 5 March 1967); m 2, 1977, Nicola Jeanne, da of Arthur Tyers; 2 da (Hon Kirsten b 17 Jan 1981, Hon Tanya b 14 Jan 1983); *Heir* s, Hon Craig Peter Hamilton-Smith b 13 Oct 1969; *Career* sits as Conservative in House of Lords; BDS, LDS, RCS, dental surgeon 1966-; musician, leader of own dance band and orchestra; *Style*— The Rt Hon the Lord Colwyn; 53 Wimpole St, London W1M 7DF (☎ 01 935 6809)

COLWYN, Miriam, Lady; Miriam Gwendoline; o da of late Victor Bruce Ferguson, of Abbotsdene, Charlton Kings, Cheltenham; *m* 21 Dec 1940 (m dis 1951), as his 1 wife, 2 Baron Colwyn (d 1966); 2 s (3 Baron and Hon Timothy Smith); *Style*— Miriam, Lady Colwyn; Cantley, 32 Bafford Lane, Charlton Kings, Cheltenham, Glos GL53 8DL

COLYER, John Stuart; QC (1976); s of Stanley Herbert Colyer, MBE (d 1986), of Worthing, Sussex and Sevenoaks, Kent and Louisa, *née* Randle (d 1976); *b* 25 April 1935; *Educ* Dudley GS, Shrewsbury Sch, Worcester Coll Oxford; *m* 24 June 1961, Emily Warner, da of the late Stanley Leyland Dutrow, of Blue Ridge Summit, Pennsylvania, USA; 2 da (Elizabeth Emily b 13 April 1964, Mary Susan b 2 July 1969); *Career* Nat Serv 1953-55, 2 Lt RA, serv BAOR with T Battery (Shah Sujahs Troop) RA at Celle; called to the bar 1959; instr Univ of Pennsylvania Law Sch Philadelphia USA 1959-60 (asst prof 1960-61), practised at Eng Bar Oxford Midland and Oxford circuits 1962-, bencher Middle Temple 1983; Inns of Court Sch of Law: lectr in Law of Landlord and Tenant 1983-, hon reader 1982-; memb Cncl of Legal Educn 1983-, chm Lawyers' Christian Fellowship; *Books* Modern View Law of Torts (1966), Encyclopaedia Forms and Precedents (Landlord and Tenant) (ed jtly, 4 edn, vols 11 and 12), Megarry's Rent Acts (gen ed, 11 edn, 1988); *Recreations* travel, gardening (especially collecting & growing Lithops & cacti) opera; *Style*— John Stuart Colyer, Esq; 11 King's Bench Walk, London, EC4Y 7EQ (☎ 01 353 2484)

COLYER, Norman Frank; s of Sir Frank Colyer, KBE (d 1954), of Streatham Hill, London SW2, and Lucy, *née* Simpson (d 1950); *b* 19 April 1908; *Educ* Uppingham, Jesus Coll Cambridge (MA); *Career* schoolmaster HM Royal Wanstead Sch 1946-47, housemaster Epsom Coll 1947-67; memb: Epsom and Ewell Borough Cncl 1967-87 (chm housing ctee 1972-87), Epsom Downs Bd of Conservators; Freeman City of London 1932, Liveryman Worshipful Co Fishmongers 1936; *Style*— Norman Colyer, Esq; 15 Longdawn Lane, Ewell, Surrey KT17 3HY (☎ 01 393 4356)

COLYER-FERGUSSON, Sir James Herbert Hamilton; 4 Bt (UK 1866), of Spitalhaugh, Peeblesshire; s of Max Colyer-Fergusson, Capt RASC, s of 3 Bt (ka 1940); suc gf 1951; *b* 10 Jan 1917; *Educ* Harrow, Balliol Coll Oxford (BA, MA); *Heir* none; *Career* formerly Capt The Buffs; offr British Railways, ret; *Style*— Sir James Colyer-Fergusson, Bt; 61 Onslow Sq, London SW7 3LS

COLYTON, 1 Baron (UK 1956), of Farway, Co Devon and Taunton, Co Somerset; Henry Lennox d'Aubigné Hopkinson; CMG (1944), PC (1952); s of Sir Henry Hopkinson, KCVO (d 1936), of Duntisbourne Manor House, Cirencester, Glos, and 2 Hans St, SW1, by his w, Marie Ruan (d 1949), da of Francis Blake du Bois, of St Croix, Virgin Is, and Montclair, NJ, USA; *b* 3 Jan 1902; *Educ* Eton, Trinity Coll Cambridge; *m* 1, 10 Nov 1927, Alice Labouisse (d 30 April 1953), da of Henry Lane Eno (d 1928) of Maine, USA; 1 s (Hon Nicholas), 1 da (twins, da decd in infancy); m 2, 11 Dec 1956, Barbara Estella, da of Stephen Barb (d 1920) of New York, and formerly w of Charles Samuel Addams; *Heir* s, Hon Nicholas Hopkinson; *Career* HM Diplomatic Service 1924-1946, political advsr to min of state M East 1941-43, HM min Lisbon 1943, dep high cmmr and vice-pres Allied Control Cmmn in Italy 1944-46; dir Cons Parly Secretariat 1946-49; MP (C) Taunton Somerset 1950-56, sec for Overseas Trade 1951-52, min of state for Colonial Affairs 1952-55, delegate Gen Assembly UN 1952-55; chm: Anglo-Egyptian Resettlement Bd 1957-60, Joint East and Central Africa Bd 1960-65, Tanganyika Concessions Ltd 1966-72; awarded Royal Humane Soc's Award for Saving Life from drowning 1919; Grand Cross Order of Prince Henry the Navigator (Portugal), Grand Cordon of Order of Stia Negara (Brunei), Cdr Order of Zaire; OStJ 1959; *Recreations* hunting, polo, shooting; *Clubs* White's, Buck's, Beefsteak; *Style*— The Rt Hon The Lord Colyton, CMG, PC; Le Formentor, Av Princesse Grace, Monte Carlo, Monaco (☎ 33 93 30 92 96)

COMBE, Lady Mary Esther Constance; *née* Needham; da of late Maj the Hon Francis Edward Needham, MVO (d 1955, 2 s of 3 Earl of Kilmorey); sis of 5 Earl of Kilmorey; *b* 2 Dec 1918; *m* 14 July 1949, Cdr Anthony Boyce Combe, RN (ret), eldest s of late Maj Boyce Combe, of Great Holt, Farnham, Surrey; 3 s, 1 da; *Style*— Lady Mary Combe; Grove Cottage, South Creake, Fakenham, Norfolk

COMBE, Lady Silvia (Beatrice); *née* Coke; da of 4 Earl of Leicester (d 1949); *b* 1909; *m* 1932, Capt Simon Harvey Combe, MC (d 1965); 1 s, 1 da; *Career* JP; *Style*— Lady Silvia Combe, JP; The Manor House, Burnham Thorpe, Kings Lynn

COMBER, Ven Anthony James; s of Prof Norman Mederson Comber (d 1953), and Nellie, *née* Finch (d 1983); *b* 20 April 1927; *Educ* Leeds GS, Leeds Univ (MSc), Durham Univ (Dip Theol), Munich Univ; *Career* colliery dep Rossington 1952-53; vicar: Oulton 1960-69, Hunslet 1969-77; rural dean of Armley 1972-75 and 1979-82, rector of Farnley 1977-82, archdeacon of Leeds 1982-; *Recreations* walking in Bavaria, politics; *Clubs* Leeds; *Style*— The Ven the Archdeacon of Leeds; 712 Foundry Lane, Leeds LS14 6BL (☎ 0532 602069)

COMBERMERE, 5 Viscount (UK 1826); Sir Michael Wellington Stapleton-Cotton; 10 Bt (E 1677); Baron Combermere (UK 1814); s of 4 Viscount Combermere (d 1969); *b* 8 August 1929; *Educ* Eton, King's Coll London (BD, MTh); *m* 4 Feb 1961, Pamela Elizabeth, da of Rev Robert Gustavus Coulson, of The Old Vicarage, Moulsford, Nr Wallingford, Oxon 1 s, 2 da; *Heir* s, Hon Thomas Robert Wellington Stapleton-Cotton b 30 Aug 1969; *Career* short service cmmn pilot RAF 1950-58, ret as Fl-Lt; lectr Biblical and Religious Studies Birkbeck Centre for Extra Mural Studies London Univ 1972- (sr lectr 1988-); chm World Congress of Faiths 1983-88; *Clubs* RAC; *Style*— The Rt Hon the Viscount Combermere; 46 Smith St, London SW3 (☎ 01 352 1319)

COMBIE, Prof Alistair Cameron; s of William David (d 1949), of Maranthona, Longreach, Queensland, Australia, and Janet Wilmina, *née* Macdonald (d 1975); *b* 4 Nov 1915; *Educ* Geelong GS Victoria Australia, Trinity Coll Univ of Melbourne (BSc),

Jesus Coll Cambridge (PhD), Univ of Oxford (MA); *m* 3 Dec 1943, Nancy, da of Col Donald Hey, MC (d 1953), of Bramhope Manor, Nr Leeds; 3 s (Charles b 1947, James b 1951, Nicholas b 1954), 1 da (Sophie b 1946); *Career* res offr zoology laboratory Univ of Cambridge 1941-46; lectr: hist and philosophy of sci UCL 1946-53 (nominated reader), history of sci Univ of Oxford 1953-83 (fell Trinity Coll 1969-83); prof history of sci and medicine Smith Coll Mass 1983-85 (Kennedy prof in the Renaissance 1982); visiting prof: Univ of Washington 1953-54, Princeton 1959-60, Tokyo 1976, Sorbonne Paris 1982-83, Williams Coll Mass 1984, Ecole des Hautes Etudes Paris 1989; memb: cncl Sci Museum 1962-66, Br Nat Ctee History of Sci 1963-69; Hon DLitt Univ of Durham 1979; memb: Br Soc Hist of Sci 1946 (pres 1964-66), Académie Internationale d'Histoire des Sciences 1957 (pres 1968-71), Academia Leopoldina 1972; FRHistS 1970; *Books* Augustine to Galileo (1952 4 ed 1979), Robert Grosseteste (1953 3 ed 1971), Scientific Change (1963), Science Optics and Music in Medieval and Early Modern Thought (1989), Styles of Scientific Thinking in the European Tradition (1989); *Recreations* literature, travel, landscape gardening; *Clubs* Brooks; *Style—* Prof Alistair Crombie; Orchardlea, Boas Hill, Oxford OX1 5DF (☎ 0865 735 692)

COMBS, Sir Willis Ide; KCVO (1974), CMG (1962); s of Willis Ide Combs of Napier, NZ; *b* 6 May 1916; *Educ* Dannevirke HS, Victoria Coll NZ, St John's Coll Cambridge; *m* 1942, Grace Willis; 2 da; *Career* Foreign, later Diplomatic, Serv 1947-75; Paris, Rio de Janiero, Peking, counsellor Baghdad, Rangoon, asst under-sec of state FCO 1968, ambass to Indonesia 1970-75, ret; *Style—* Sir Willis Combs, KCVO, CMG; Sunset, Wadhurst Park, Wadhurst, E Sussex

COMER, Michael Edward Cowpland; s of Rev Ernest Comer (d 1948), and Agnes Millicent Enid Comer; *b* 2 May 1928; *Educ* St John's Sch Leatherhead, Balliol Coll Oxford (MA); *m* 6 April 1974, Shirley Patricia (formerly Long-Innes), da of Caryl Thain (d 1969); *Career* master Blundell's Sch 1951-64; master St John's Sch Leatherhead 1964 (housemaster 1975-83, rector 1984-); pres Assoc Reps of Old Pupils Socs 1974- (fndr chm and sec 1970-74); hon sec Old Johnian Soc 1964- (pres 1985); *Recreations* cricket, gardening, golf; *Clubs* MCC, Incogniti CC, St Enodoc GC; *Style—* Michael Comer, Esq; Barn Cottage, Church Rd, Leigh, Reigate, Surrey RH2 8RF (☎ 030 678 347); St John's School, Leatherhead (☎ 0372 376 077)

COMINS, Peter Crawford Melhuish; s of late Capt Dennis Comins, MC; *b* 25 Nov 1930; *Educ* Ampleforth, Lincoln Coll Oxford; *m* 1963, Dinah, *née* Collins; 3 s; *Career* dir: Borax Consolidated Ltd, Borax Hldgs Ltd 1969-, Lowestoft Enterprise Tst 1987-; *Recreations* shooting, skiing, swimming; *Style—* Peter Comins, Esq; Hornlie House, Wiveton, Holt, Norfolk (☎ 0263 740311)

COMLEY, Brett Nicholas; s of Ernest Phillip Comley, and Eve Annesley, *née* Brand; *b* 8 Dec 1958; *Educ* BCom SA; *Career* SAAF 1976-77; mangr Deloitte Haskins and Sells SA 1981-84 (London 1984-86), dir SBCI Savory Milln 1988- (chief fin offr 1986, bd dir 1986-87, memb exec ctee 1987-88); memb: Natal Soc of CAs 1983, SA Inst of CAs 1983; Civil Award for Bravery from the High Sheriff of London 1987; *Style—* Brett Comley, Esq; SBCI Savory Milln, 3 London Wall Buildings, London EC2

COMNINOS, Michael; s of John Michael Comninos (d 1976), of Holland Park, London, and Elsie Rose, *née* Turner; *b* 25 July 1931; *Educ* Malvern; *m* 14 Jan 1956, Ann, da of Stanley Graves (d 1985); 1 s (Charles b 1956), 1 da (Sarah Helen b 1962); *Career* Lt RTR 1950-52; clerk/mangr N M Rothschild & Sons 1954-65, ptnr 1965-70, exec dir N M Rothschild and Sons Ltd 1970-; FCIB, FCIS, FCT, ASIA; *Recreations* collecting antiquities, skiing; *Clubs* Brooks's; *Style—* Michael Comninos, Esq; Staithe House, Chiswick Mall, London W4 2PR (☎ 01 995 8026); New Court, St Swithin's Lane, London EC4P 4DU (☎ 01 280 5704, fax 01 929 1643, telex 888031)

COMPIGNÉ-ROGERS, Robin Christopher; s of Maj Leslie Rubert Sidney Rogers, CPM (mangr rubber plantation in Malaya 1927-64), and Patricia Dorothy Madeleine, *née* Compigné-Stone; *b* 12 Mar 1941; *Educ* Taunton Sch Som, Royal Tunbridge Wells Coll of Art; *m* 1, 18 March 1967 (m dis); 1 s (Julian Simon Compigné b 1969), 2 da (Samantha Compigné b 1968, Katherine Compigné b 1981); m 2, Sara Phillips, *née* Dawson Walker; *Career* trainee rubber planter 1960-61, P & O Passenger Servs London 1961-1962 P & O Agents Far East; Mackinnon MacKenzie Hong Kong 1962, Singapore 1962-70, Durban and S Africa 1970, mangr admin Western Bank Johannesburg 1970-71, special projects mangr Freemans Mail Order London 1971-73, graphic and commercial artist 1973-80, specialised as armorist, illustrator, calligrapher 1981-89; work incl: reproducing Coats of Arms on sheep and calf skins, commissions for family trees for old English and Euro families, illuminated addresses for presentations and religious dedications, illustrated mil records for individuals and Armed Servs Assocs; examples of work are kept in film archives on Heraldry and various illustrations are on permanent display at Kent Co Police HQ Maidstone; registrar the Most Hon Co of Armigers; memb: Heraldry Soc, Hugenot Soc of GB and Ireland; *Recreations* music, painting, genealogy; *Style—* Robin Compigné-Rogers, Esq; 17 Westwell Ct, Tenterden, Kent TN30 6TS (☎ 05806 2203)

COMPSTON, His Hon Judge Christopher Dean; s of Vice Adm Sir Peter Maxwell Compston, KCB, and Valerie Marjorie, *née* Bocquet; *b* 5 May 1940; *Educ* Epsom Coll, Magdalen Coll Oxford (MA); *m* 1, Bronwen, da of Martin Henniker Gotley, of Derwenlas, Machynlleth, Wales; m 2, Caroline Philippa, da of Paul Odgers, of Haddenham, Bucks; 3 s (Harry b 1969 (decd), Joshua b 1970, Rupert b 1987), 2 da (Emily b 1972, Harriet b 1985); *Clubs* The Arts; *Style—* His Honour Judge Christopher Compston; c/o 6 King's Bench Walk, Temple, London EC4

COMPSTON, Vice Adm Sir Peter Maxwell; KCB (1970, CB 1967); s of Dr George Dean Compston, of Halton, Yorks; *b* 12 Sept 1915; *Educ* Epsom Coll; *m* 1, 1939 (m dis), Valerie M Bocquet; 1 s, 1 da; m 2, 1954, Angela, da of late Harry Brickwood, of Bembridge, IOW; *Career* RN 1937, Rear Adm 1965, Chief of British Naval Staff and naval attaché Washington 1965-67, flag offr Flotillas W Fleet 1967-68, Dep SACLANT (Vice Adm) 1968-70, ret; *Style—* Vice Admiral Sir Peter Compston, KCB; Holmwood, Stroud, nr Petersfield, Hants

COMPTON, Earl; Daniel Bingham Compton; s and h of 7 Marquess of Northampton; *b* 16 Jan 1973; *Style—* Earl Compton; Compton Wynyates, Tysoe, Warwicks CV35 0UD

COMPTON, Sir Edmund Gerald; GCB (1971, KCB 1965, CB 1948), KBE (1955); er s of late Edmund Spencer Compton, MC, of Pailton House, Rugby; *b* 30 July 1906; *Educ* Rugby, New Coll Oxford; *m* 1934, Betty Tresyllian (d 1987), 2 da of Hakewill Tresyllian Williams, JP, DL (d 1929), of Churchill Court, Kidderminster, Worcs; 1 s, 4 da; *Career* Civil Service 1929, Colonial Office 1930, Treasury 1931-57, comptroller and auditor General Exchequer and Audit Dept 1958-66, parly cmmr for Admin 1967-71, Northern Ireland 1969-71; *Style—* Sir Edmund Compton, GCB, KBE; 1/80 Elm Park Gdns, SW10 9PD (☎ 01 351 3790)

COMPTON, Hon Mrs (Gillian Sarah); *née* Blease; o da of Baron Blease, JP (Life Peer), *qv*; *b* 1948; *m* 1972, John Compton; issue; *Style—* The Hon Mrs Compton; 17 Station Road, Craigavad, Co Down BT18 OBP, Northern Ireland

COMPTON, Ivor; s of Samuel Harry Cohen (d 1940), and Jane Anne, *née* Kanovich (d 1963); *b* 12 August 1933; *Educ* Hackney Down GS; *m* 3 July 1955, Lorna Frances, da of Lewis Greene (d 1985); 1 s (Stanford Harvey b 1957); 1 da (Michelle Alison b 1959); *Career* RAF 1951-53, chm and md Hall of Cards Ltd 1968-; chm: Lorimist Ltd, City Cards Ltd 1981-; *Recreations* golf, theatre, family and charitable works; *Clubs* Aldenham GC, MCC, IOD; *Style—* Ivor Compton, Esq; Letchmore Lodge, Aldenham Rd, Elstree, Herts WD6 3AB (☎ 01 953 1986); Hall of Cards Ltd, Stanford House, Oldfield Lane North, Greenford, Middx UB6 0AL (☎ 01 578 0293)

COMPTON, Lady Lara Katrina; da of 7 Marquess of Northampton; *b* 26 April 1968; *Style—* Lady Lara Compton; Compton Wynyates, Tysoe, Warwicks CV35 0UD

COMPTON, Robert Edward John; DL (N Yorks 1981); s of Maj Edward Robert Francis Compton, JP, DL (d 1977; s of Lord Alwyne Compton, DSO, DL, 3 s of 4 Marquess of Northampton), and his 1 w, Sylvia, *née* Farquharson (d 1950); *b* 11 July 1922; *Educ* Eton, Magdalen Coll Oxford; *m* 5 July 1951, as her 3 husb, (Ursula) Jane, 2 da of Maj Rodolph Kenyon-Slaney, JP, DL, and formerly w of (i) Lt-Col Peter Lindsay, DSO (d 1971), (ii) Sir Max Aitken, 2 Bt, DSO, DFC (d 1985), by whom she had 2 das; 2 s (James Alwyne b 30 May 1953 m 1978, Rebecca, da of Sir Alan Wigan, 5 Bt, *qv*, Richard Clephane b 16 April 1957); *Career* served WW II with Coldstream Guards 1941-46 (wounded), military asst to British Ambass Vienna 1945-46 with rank of Maj; sr account exec W S Crawford Ltd advertising agency 1951-54; Time Life Int 1954; advertsing dir Time UK 1958-62; dir Time Life Int Ltd 1958-; public affairs dir Time Life Int Europe 1965-70; chm: Newby Hall Estate Co Ltd 1965-69, CXL UK Ltd 1971-73; bd dir Extel Corp Chicago 1973-80; dir Transtel Communications Ltd 1974-83; chm Time Life Int 1979-, md 1985-87; vice-chm Nat Tst Yorkshire Ctee 1970- 85; pres: Ripon Tourist Assoc, Dales Centre Nat Tst; memb properties ctee and gardens panel Nat Tst; pres: N of England Horticultural Soc 1984-86, Northern Horticultural Soc 1986-; chm Nat Cncl for Conservation of Plants and Gardens 1988-; High Sheriff North Yorkshire 1977, FIOD 1951; *Recreations* gardening, music, golf, shooting; *Clubs* White's, Buck's, Swinley Forest Golf; *Style—* Robin Compton Esq, DL; 17 Brompton Square, London SW37; Newby Hall, Ripon, N Yorkshire (☎ 042332 3315); Time Life International Ltd, Time Life Building, New Bond St, London W1Y 0AA (☎ 01 499 4080, fax 01 499 9377, telex 22557)

COMPTON, Lord William James Bingham; s of 6 Marquess of Northampton, DSO (d 1978); *b* 26 Nov 1947; *Educ* Bryanston; *m* 1973, Marlene, da of late Francis Hosie; 1 s, 1 da; *Style—* Lord William Compton; 50 Bedford Gdns, London W8

COMRIE, Rear Adm Alexander Peter; CB (1982); s of late Robert Duncan Comrie (d 1957), and Phyllis Dorothy, *née* Jubb; *b* 27 Mar 1924; *Educ* Sutton Valence, RCDS; *m* 1945, Madeleine Irene (d 1983), da of Leslie Bullock (d 1956); 1 s, 1 da; *Career* RN 1945, Capt HMS Daedalus 1974-75, dir Weapons Co-ordination and Acceptance (Naval) 1975-77, dep controller Aircraft MOD (PE) 1978-81, dir-gen Aircraft (Naval) 1981-83, ret; memb cncl Instn of Electrical Engrs 1981-84 (vice pres 1988-), company dir and chm 1983-, def conslt 1984-, chm exec gp ctee 3 of the Engrg Cncl 1986-; CEng, FIEE, FRAeS, Eur Ing; *Recreations* sailing, gardening; *Clubs* Royal Commonwealth, Hayling Island Sailing, Birdham Yacht; *Style—* Rear Adm Alexander Comrie, CB; c/o National Westminster Bank plc, 23 West St, Havant, Hants PO9 1EU

COMYN, Hon Sir James Peter; o s of late James Comyn, QC, of Dublin, and late Mary Comyn; *b* 8 Mar 1921; *Educ* Oratory Sch, New Coll Oxford (MA); *m* 1967, Anne, da of late Philip Chaundler, MC, of Biggleswade, Beds; 1 s, 1 da; *Career* former pres Oxford Union, barr (I) 1947, QC 1961, recorder of the Crown Court 1972-77, judge of the High Court Family Div 1978-79, Queen's Bench Div 1979-85; kt 1978; *Style—* The Hon Sir James Comyn; Belvin, Tara, Co Meath, Ireland

COMYNS, Jacqueline Roberta; da of Jack Fisher (d 1979), and Belle, *née* Offenbach; *b* 27 April 1943; *Educ* Hendon Co GS, LSE (LLB); *m* 29 Aug 1963, Dr Malcolm John Comyns, s of Louis Comyns (d 1962); 1 s (David b 13 Aug 1975); *Career* barr Inner Temple 1969, SE Circuit, Met Stipendiary Magistrate 1982-; *Recreations* travel, theatre, bridge; *Style—* Mrs Jacqueline Comyns; Tower Bridge Magistrates Ct, Tooley St, London SE1 2JY (☎ 01 407 4232)

CONAN DOYLE, Air Cmdt Dme Jean Lena Annette (Lady Bromet); DBE (1963, OBE 1948), AE; da of late Sir Arthur Conan Doyle; *b* 21 Dec 1912; *m* 1965, Air Vice-Marshal Sir Geoffrey Bromet (d 1983, Lieut-Govr Isle of Man 1945-52); *Career* No 46 (Co of Sussex) ATS RAF Co 1938, dep dir WRAF 1952-54 and 1960-62, Air Cmdt 1963, dir WRAF 1963-66, Hon ADC to HM The Queen 1963-66, ret 1966; pres Not Forgotten Assoc, holder of father's USA copyright; *Style—* Air Cmdt Dame Jean Conan Doyle, DBE; Flat 6, 72 Cadogan Sq, London SW1;

CONANT, (Simon) Edward Christopher; s and h of Sir John Conant, 2 Bt; *b* 13 Oct 1958; *Educ* Eton, RAC Cirencester; *Career* chartered surveyor; *Style—* Edward Conant, Esq

CONANT, Guy Timothy Geoffrey; JP (Northants 1960), DL (Northants 1972); s of Sir Roger Conant, 1 Bt (d 1973), and Daphne Lorraine, *née* Learoyd (d 1979); *b* 7 Oct 1924; *Educ* Stowe; *m* 1, 27 June 1953 (m dis), Elizabeth, da of Alfred Trevor Handley, of IOW; 1 s (Rupert b 1964), 3 da (Sheena b 1954, Jane b 1955, Diana b 1960); m 2, 31 Jan 1981, Davina Huntley, da of Sir Guy Holland, 3 Bt; 1 da (Melissa b 1984); *Career* Fl Lt RAF; high sheriff of Northants 1969; landowner and farmer; *Recreations* shooting, fishing; *Clubs* Boodles; *Style—* Guy T G Conant, Esq, JP, DL; Bulwick Park, Corby, Northants (☎ 078 085 245)

CONANT, Sir John Ernest Michael Conant; 2 Bt (UK 1954), of Lyndon, Co Rutland; s of Sir Roger Conant, 1 Bt, CVO (d 1973); *b* 24 April 1923; *Educ* Eton, CCC Cambridge; *m* 16 Sept 1950, Periwinkle Elizabeth (d 1985), da of late Dudley Thorp, of Brothers House, Kimbolton, Hunts; 2 s (and 1 decd), 2 da; *Heir* s, (Simon) Edward Conant; *Career* farmer, high sheriff Rutland 1960; *Style—* Sir John Conant, Bt; Lyndon Hall, Oakham, Rutland (☎ 057285 275)

CONCANNON, Rt Hon John Dennis (Don); PC (1978); s of James Concannon, formerly of Rossington, Doncaster, subsequently of Somercotes, Derby; *b* 16 May 1930; *Educ* Rossington Secdy Sch, WEA; *m* 1953, Iris May, da of Charles Wilson, of Mansfield; 2 s, 2 da; *Career* served Coldstream Gds 1947-53; memb NUM 1953-66; memb Mansfield Borough Cncl 1963-; MP (Lab) Mansfield 1966-87; asst govt whip

1968-70, oppn whip 1970-74; vice-chamberlain HM Household 1974, parly under-sec of state NI Off 1974-76, min of state NI Off 1976-79, oppn spokesman for: Def 1979-81, NI 1981-83; Select Ctee for Energy 1983-87; memb Cwlth War Graves Cmmn 1986-; *Style*— The Rt Hon Don Concannon; 69 Skegby Lane, Mansfield, Notts (☎ 0623 27235)

CONCANON, (Brian) Anthony Ross; s of Austin Brian Concanon (d 1965), of Plymouth, and Joyce Ruth, *née* Chadderton; *b* 2 Mar 1943; *Educ* Worth Prep Sch, Downside ; *m* 1 (m dis); 2 s (Lee b 1966, Jonathan b 1977), 3 da (Tracey b 1961 Nina b 1964, Juliet b 1974); m 2, Annabel Concanon; *Career* with Deloitte Haskins & Sells 1961-71, qualified CA 1967, with Norton Rose 1971-76, admitted slr 1976, UK Tax attorney Texaco (UK) Ltd 1976-78; corporate tax ptnr McKenna & Co 1981-(joined 1978), ICEAW 1967, memb Law Soc 1976; *Recreations* english cartography; *Clubs* Royal Automobile Club; *Style*— Anthony Concanon, Esq; 71 Queen Victoria St, London EC4V 4EB (☎ 01 236 4340)

CONDER, Col Henry Roubiliac Reignier; OBE (1942); s of Rev Canon Edward Baines Conder (d 1936), and Eleanor Charlotte Henrietta, *née* Eames (d 1959); *b* 18 Nov 1907; *Educ* Haileybury, RMC Sandhurst, Staff Coll Camberley; *m* 20 April 1938, Mary, da of Clifford Needham Philpot (d 1944); 2 s (Edward b 1939, Rupert b 1942), 1 da (Jacqueline b 1946); *Career* Royal Norfolk 1927-50; served Egypt, China, India, UK, France, Gibraltar (despatches thrice); cmdr 2 KOSR 1943, Royal Leicesters 1950-52, Col 1953-60; post war served UK, Egypt, France, (Nato HQ) Japan and UK; local govt cnsllr Wainford RDC, E Suffolk and Suffolk Co 1962-79; *Recreations* gardening, DIY; *Clubs* Army and Navy; *Style*— Col Henry Conder, OBE; The Old Rectory, Weston, Beccles, Suffolk NR34 8TU (☎ 0502 712251)

CONDLIFFE, Gregor Stuart; s of Wilfred Condliffe (d 1984), of Exmouth, Devon, and Marion Condliffe (d 1983); *b* 28 May 1943; *Educ* Kingsmoor Sch Glossop, Hulme GS for Boys Oldham, Univ of Nottingham (DipArch); *m* 24 July 1971, Frances Gillian, da of Charles Edward Berry, of Titchfield, Hants; 2 s (Otto b 1973, Ivan b 1978), 1 da (Emma b 1974); *Career* with Corby New Town Corpn 1969-72, architect Salisbury Dist Cncl 1974-81, ed Assoc of Official Architects public authorities handbook 1981-84; started private practice in own name 1981; elected co cncllr (Lib) Salisbury-Harnham 1985, memb Alliance ldr Co Cncl, chm Tport and Waste Disposal Ctee, vice chm Property Ctee; RIBA; *Recreations* politics, community project work, gardening; *Clubs* Salisbury Liberal (fndr life memb); *Style*— Gregor S Condliffe, Esq; 14 Sussex Rd, Harnham, Salisbury, Wilts (☎ 0722 23833); Carter House, 6-10 Salt Lane, Salisbury (☎ 0722 331877)

CONGLETON, 8 Baron (UK 1841); Sir Christopher Patrick Parnell; 11 Bt (I 1766); s of 6 Baron Congleton (d 1932), and Hon Edith Mary Palmer Howard, MBE, da of late Baroness Strathcona and Mount Royal (in her own right) and R J B Howard; suc bro 1967; *b* 11 Mar 1930; *Educ* Eton, New Coll Oxford, (MA); *m* 19 Nov 1955, Anna Hedvig, er da of Gustav Adolf Sommerelt, of Oslo, Norway; 2 s, 3 da; *Heir* s, Hon John Parnell; *Career* Salisbury and Wilton RDC 1964-74 (chm 1971); chm Salisbury and S Wilts Museum 1972-77, pres Br Ski Fedn 1976-81, chm Sandroyd Sch Tst 1980-84, memb Advsy Bd for Redundant Churches 1981-87, tstee Wessex Med Sch Tst 1984-, chm Southampton Univ Devpt Tst 1986-; *Recreations* music, fishing, skiing; *Style*— The Rt Hon the Lord Congleton; Ebbesbourne Wake, Salisbury, Wilts

CONGREVE, Ambrose Christian; CBE (1965); only child of Maj John Congreve, JP, DL (d 1947, whose mother was Hon Alice Dillon, da of 3 Baron Clonbrock), by his w Lady Helena, *née* Ponsonby (d 1962), da of 8 Earl of Bessborough, KP, CB, CVO; *b* 4 April 1907; *Educ* Eton, Trin Coll Cambridge; *m* 1935, Margaret, da of Dr Arthur Graham Glasgow, of Richmond, Virginia, USA; *Career* served WW II Air Ministry Intelligence and Miny Supply; with Unilever 1929-36 in UK and China; chm Humphreys and Glasgow Ltd 1955-; *Clubs* Kildare Street (Dublin), Beefsteak; *Style*— Ambrose Congreve, Esq, CBE; Winkfield Manor, Ascot, Berks (☎ 034 47 2101); Mount Congreve, Waterford, Eire (☎ Kilmeaden 7403); c/o Humphreys and Glasgow Ltd, 22 Carlisle Place, SW1 (☎ 821 2328)

CONI, Peter Richard Carstairs; OBE (1987), QC (1980); s of Eric Charles Coni (d 1942) of Wellington, NZ, and Leslie Sybil Carstairs, *née* Pearson (d 1973); *b* 20 Nov 1935; *Educ* Uppingham, St Catharine's Coll, Cambridge (MA); *Career* barr Inner Temple 1960, recorder 1985, master of the bench Inner Temple 1986; memb: Amateur Rowing Assoc Cncl 1962- (exec ctee 1968-, chm 1970-77), London Rowing Club Ctee 1961- (pres 1988), Leander Club Ctee 1983-; steward Henley Royal Regatta 1974 (chm 1978-), chm 1986 World Rowing Championships; memb Thames Water Authy 1978-83; FISA Medal of Honour 1986; memb of court Worshipful Co of Needlemakers, Freeman City of London; *Recreations* sports admin, good food, modern art, English Literature; *Clubs* Athenaeum, Garrick, London Rowing, Leander; *Style*— Peter Coni, Esq, OBE, QC; 3 Churton Place, London SW1V 2LN (☎ 01 828 2135); 44 Vicarage Rd, Henley-on-Thames, Oxon RG9 1HW (☎ 0491 577930); 1 Gray's Inn Sq, Gray's Inn, London WC1R 5AG (☎ 01 404 5416, fax 01 405 9942)

CONINGSBY, Thomas Arthur Charles; QC (1986); s of Francis Charles Coningsby, PhD, of Guernsey, and Eileen Rowena, *née* Monson; *b* 21 April 1933; *Educ* Epsom, Queen's Coll Cambridge (MA); *m* 8 Aug 1959, Elaine Mary, da of Edwin Stanley Treacher (d 1983), of Sussex; 2 s (Andrew b 1960, James b 1964), 3 da (Sara b 1962, Elizabeth, Katharine b 1963 (twins)); *Career* Nat Serv Cmmn, RA 1951-53, TA, City of London Field Regt and Aerial Photographic Interpretation (Intelligence Corps) Capt 1953-67; called to the Bar (Gray's Inn) 1957, recorder of the Crown Court 1986-, chllr Diocese of York 1977-; sec Family Law Assoc 1986-88 (chm 1988-); memb: Gen Cncl of the Bar 1988-, Matrimonial Causes Rule Ctee 1985-; chm Chipstead Village Preservation Soc 1983-88; vicar-gen Province of York 1980-; memb: Gen Synod of C of E 1970-, Legal Advsy Cmmn of Gen Synod 1976-; *Recreations* lawn tennis; *Style*— Thomas Coningsby, Esq, QC; Leyfields, Elmore Road, Chipstead, Surrey (☎ 07375 53304); 3 Dr Johnson's Buildings, Temple, London EC4 (☎ 01 353 4854, fax 01 583 8784)

CONLAN, Bernard; MP (Lab) Gateshead E 1964-; *b* 24 Oct 1923; *Educ* Manchester Secdy Sch; *m* ; 1 da; *Career* memb AEU 1940-; contested High Peak 1959, vice-chm PLP Trade Union Gp 1974-, memb select ctee Defence 1979-83; *Style*— Bernard Conlan, Esq, MP; House of Commons, London SW1A 0AA

CONLAN, John Oliver; s of Eugene J Conlan, of Dublin, Ireland, and Bridgid, *née* Hayes; *b* 13 July 1942; *Educ* Thurles CBS, Ireland; *m* 19 March 1968, Carolyn Sylvia, da of Raymond Ingram, of Luton, Beds; 3 da (Tara Louise b 1972, Amanda Carolyn b 1973, Alison Theresa b 1980); *Career* md: First Leisure Corp plc 1983-, Trust House Forte Leisure 1981-83, EMI Leisure 1980-81; gen cmmr for Taxes (London) 1986-; *Recreations* golf; *Style*— John Conlan, Esq; First Leisure Corp, 7 Soho St, London W1V 5FA (☎ 01 437 9727, car tel 0836 231396)

CONNAUGHTON, Col Richard Michael; s of Thomas Connaughton (d 1981), of Huntingdon, and Joan Florence, *née* Lisher (d 1979); *b* 20 Jan 1942; *Educ* Duke of York's Royal Military Sch Dover; *m* 12 June 1971, (Annis Rosemary) Georgina, da of Capt George Frederik Matthew Best, OBE, of Dorset; 1 s (Michael b 1972), 1 da (Emma b 1974); *Career* RMA Sandhurst 1960-61, III Co RASC (guided weapons) W Germany 1962-64, 28 Co Gurkha Army Serv Corps Hong Kong 1965-67, Jr Ldrs' RCT Taunton 1967-69, 28 Sqdn Gurtha Tport Regt Hong Kong 1969-71 (Adj 1971-73), student Army Staff Coll Camberley 1974, G20 II Co-ord MUEE Chertsey 1975-76, cmd 2 Sqdn RCT W Germany 1977-79, 2 i/c Logistic Support Gp Regt Aldershot 1979-81, cmd 1 Armd Div Tport Regt RCT W Germany 1982-84, memb Directing Staff Army Staff Coll Camberley and Australian Army Cmd and Staff Coll Fort Queenscliff Victoria 1984-86, Col Tport HQ BAOR W Germany 1987-89; def fellowship St John's Coll Cambridge 1989; FBIM 1981, MCIT 1983; *Books* The War of The rising Sun and Tumbling Bear (1989); *Recreations* writing, tennis; *Clubs* Army and Navy; *Style*— Col Richard Connaughton; Tpt & Mov Dte, HQ BAOR, BFPO 140 (☎ 010 49 2161 472 305)

CONNELL, Lady Alexandra Victoria Caroline Anne; *née* Hay; da of Countess of Erroll (who retained her maiden name Hay under Scots Law and d 1978), and her 1 husband, Sir (Rupert) Iain Kay Moncreiffe of that Ilk, 11 Bt (d 1985); *b* 30 July 1955; *m* 22 Feb 1989, Jolyon C N Connell, eldest s of Christopher Connell, of Pitlochry, Perthshire 1 s (Ivar Francis Grey de Miremont Wigan b 1979); *Style*— Lady Alexandra Connell

CONNELL, David Allan Maclean; s of late John Maclean Connell; *b* 18 Jan 1930; *Educ* Stowe, Ch Ch Oxford; *m* 1954, Bridget Willink, *née* Fletcher; 3 children; *Career* md and vice-chm John Walker and Sons Ltd, dir Distillers Co plc; *Clubs* Vincents (Oxford), MCC; *Style*— David Connell, Esq; Windy Ridge, Effingham Common Rd, Effingham, Surrey; John Walker and Sons Ltd, 63 St James's St, London SW1 1NB (☎ 01 493 8155); distillery: Kilmarnock, Scotland (☎ 0563 23401)

CONNELL, Edward Arthur; s of Edward Connell (d 1950), of London, and Mary Ann, *née* Gadsby; *b* 26 Oct 1919; *Educ* Camberwell Sch of Arts and Crafts, London Coll of Printing; *m* 21 Aug 1949, May, da of Percy Godfrey Sims (d 1952), of London; 1 da (Janet May (Mrs Blackledge) b 1956); *Career* RAC 1940, W/Cpl 1944, demobbed 1946, discharged from Army Reserve on med grounds 1952; lectr Camberwell Sch of Arts and Crafts 1946-60; Colour Printing Co: mangr 1948-53, dir 1953-70, md 1970-75, chm 1975-84, ret; memb: Beckenham Cons Assoc, Bromley Art Soc, RSPB; Freeman City of London 1967, Freeman Worshipful Co of Feltmakers 1975; memb Inst of Printing 1950-85; *Recreations* oil painting, gardening, motoring; *Clubs* United Wards, Guild of Freemen; *Style*— Edward Connell, Esq; 41 Kenwood Drive, Beckenham, Kent BR3 2QY (☎ 01 650 9324)

CONNELL, John MacFarlane; s of late John Maclean Connell and Mollie Isobel MacFarlane; *b* 29 Dec 1924; *Educ* Stowe, Ch Ch Oxford; *m* 1949, Jean Matheson, da of late Maj George Sutherland Mackay; 2 s; *Career* joined Tanqueray Gordon 1946, md until 1971; dir Distillers Co 1965, memb DCL management ctee 1971, chm Distillers Co 1983-; *Style*— John Connell, Esq; The Distillers Co plc, Distillers House, 20 St James's Sq, London SW1Y 4JF (☎ 01 930 1040)

CONNELL, John William; s of William J Connell (d 1947), and Maud Emily Edge (d 1983); *b* 4 Feb 1933; *Educ* St Edwards Coll Liverpool; *m* 29 Sept 1958, Joan, da of Walter Bromley (d 1980); 3 da (Gillian b 1963, Janey b 1965, Elizabeth b 1966); *Career* chm Liverpool and London Steamship Protection and Indemnity Assoc Ltd; md Bibby Financial Services Ltd; dir of numerous cos incl: Bibby Bros (mgmnt) Ltd and assoc cos, Br Steamship Co Ltd, Liverpool and London Pal Mgmnt Ltd, Grayhill Ins Co (Bermuda) Ltd, Grayhill Ins (Cayman) Ltd, Overseas Trading Co Ltd (Gibralter), United Gas Carrier Corpn (Liberia); *Style*— John Connell, Esq; 401 Norwich House, Water Street, Liverpool L2 8UW (☎ 051 236 0492)

CONNELL, Dr Philip Henry; CBE (1986); s of George Henry Connell (d 1928), of Selby, Yorks, and Evelyn Hilda Sykes (d 1969); *b* 6 July 1921; *Educ* St Pauls, St Barts Hosp London Univ (MB BS, MRCS, LRCP, MD, DPM); *m* 1, April 1948 (m dis 1973) (Marjorie) Helen, da of John Gilham, of Ashford, Kent; 2 s (Michael Charles b 25 Jan 1953, David Nicholas b 19 Aug 1955); m 2, Cecily Mary (Celia), da of Edward Russell Harper, MC (d 1959); *Career* house physician St Stephens Hosp London 1951-53, registrar and sr registrar inst of psychiatry The Bethlem Royal Hosp and Maudsley Hosp 1953-58, conslt psychiatrist and physician i/c child psychiatry unit New Castle Gen Hosp in assoc with Kings Coll Durham Univ 1957-63, physician Bethlem Royal Hosp and Maudsley Hosp 1963-86; extensive nat and int work on drug addiction and dependence for: WHO, Cncl of Europe, CENTO and on maladjusted and psychiatrically ill children and adolescents; memb: standing mental health advsy ctee DHSS 1966-72 (vice chm 1967-72, standing advsy ctee drug dependence (Wayne ctee 1966-70 and sub-cttees), Wootton ctees on cannabis and LSD amphetamines and barbiturates); conslt advsr (addiction) DHSS 1966-71 and 1981-86, pres Soc for Study of Addiction 1973-78, vice pres Int Cncl on Alcohol and Addictions 1982 (chm scientific and prof advsy bd 1971-79) chm Inst for Study of Drug Dependence 1975-, chm advsy cncl on Misuse of Drugs 1982-88 (statutory body set up under the Misuse of Drugs Act 1977); memb cncl of Royal Medico Psychological Assoc 1962-67, Royal Coll of Psychiatrist 1971-81 (vice pres 1979-81) ctee mgmnt Inst of Psychiatry 1968-74, chm med ctee Bethlem Royal Hosp and Maudsley Hosp 1969-72 memb (bd of govrs 1966-73); memb: Trettonan ctee DHSS (the role of psychologists in Health Service) 1968-72, Gen Med Cncl 1979-; preliminary screener for Health 1982-, vice pres RCPsych 1979-81, Dent Meml lectr Kings Coll and Soc for Study of Addiction 1983, memb ed bds of med jls, emeritus physician Bethlem Royal Hosp and Maudsley Hosp 1986-; memb bd of govrs Mowden Hall Sch Northumberland 1976-82; FRCP 1971, FRC Psych 1971; *Books* Amphetamine Psychosis (1958), Cannabis and Man (1975); *Recreations* bridge, music; *Clubs* Athenaeum; *Style*— Dr P H Connell, CBE; 25 Oxford Rd, Putney, London SW15 2LG; 21 Wimpole St, London W1M 7AD (☎ 01 788 1416, 01 636 2220)

CONNELL, Stephanie Lee; da of George Saul (d 1982), of Yorks, and Tena, *née* Wheater (d 1987); *b* 21 August 1945; *Educ* London Univ (Dip Ed), Leeds Univ (Dip EFL), Bristol Univ (Med), NE London Poly (MA); *m* 30 Oct 1971 (m dis 1980); *Career* sr lectr NE London Poly 1972-, educn advsr conslt writer Thames TV plc 1975-, literary conslt contributor Anabas prods 1986-, freelance writer; *Recreations* learning and appreciating louis roederer cristal; *Style*— Miss Stephanie Connell; Thorndon Hall, Apt 46, Ingrave, Brentwood, Essex; SIS NE London Poly, Livingstone House, Stratford, London E15 (☎ 01 590 7722)

CONNELL, Lady Susan (Jean); *née* Carnegie; yr da of 12 Earl of Northesk (d 1975), and Dorothy Mary, *née* Campion (d 1969); *b* 20 August 1930; *Educ* Moreton Hall Sch, Courtauld Inst of Art London Univ; *m* 21 May 1955, David Blackall Connell, er son of Dr Arthur Blackall Connell; 2 s (Timothy b 1956, Alistair b 1960), 1 da (Caroline b 1958); *Career* picture restorer, memb Int Inst for Conservation, fund raiser for Pain Relief Fndn; *Recreations* sailing ('Blue Genie'); *Clubs* Brixham Yacht, Inst of Advanced Motorists; *Style*— Lady Susan Connell; Lower Wreyland, Lustleigh, Newton Abbot, Devon TQ13 9TS (☎ Lustleigh 262)

CONNERY, Sean (Thomas); s of Joseph Connery, and Euphamia; *b* 25 August 1930; *m* 1, 29 Nov 1962 (m dis 1974), Diane (who m 2, 1985, Anthony Shaffer, playwright), da of Sir Raphael West Cilento (d 1985), and former w of Andrea Volpt; 1 s (Jason b 1963 actor); m 2, Jan 1975, Micheline Roquebrune; *Career* actor; films incl: Tarzan's Greatest Adventure (1959), The Longest Day (1962), Dr No (1963), From Russia With Love (1964), Goldfinger (1965), Thunderball (1965), A Fine Madness (1966), You Only Live Twice (1967), Shalako (1968), Diamonds are Forever (1971), Murder on the Orient Express (1974), The Man Who Would be King (1975), Outland (1981), The Name of the Rose (1986), The Untouchables (1987); fell Royal Scottish Academy of Music and Drama; Hon DLitt Heriot-Watt Univ 1981; *Style*— Sean Connery Esq; Michael S Ovitz, Creative Artists Agency Inc, Suite 1400, 1888 Century Pk E, Los Angeles, Calif 90067, USA

CONNICK, Harold Ivor; s of Aaron Connick, of London (d 1963), and Raie, *née* Winner (d 1972); *b* 25 Jan 1927; *Educ* Ealing GS, LSE (LLB); *m* 16 Oct 1955, Claire Grace, da of John William Benson of 8 Roehampton Close, London SW15; 2 s (David b 1956, Jeremy b 1963), 1 da (Lesley b 1956); *Career* slr, sr ptnr Thornton Lynne and Lawson; attached Army War Crimes, Singapore 1946-48; dir: UDS Gp plc 1975-83 (dep chm 1983), Land Securities plc 1987-; chm Br ORT 1984-; *Recreations* golf, theatre, cricket; *Clubs* MCC Roehampton, IOD; *Style*— H I Connick, Esq; 54 Fairacres, Roehampton Lane, London SW15 5LX (☎ 01 876 7188); 56 Portland Place, London W1N 4BD (☎ 01 580 6688, fax 01 637 1558, telex 263200 TLLAWS)

CONNOCK, Stephen Leslie; s of Leslie Thomas Connock, of Peterborough, Cambs, and Gladys Edna, *née* Chappell; *b* 16 Nov 1949; *Educ* Sheffield Univ (BA), LSE (MPhil); *m* 18 Aug 1973, Margaret Anne, da of Richard Bolger, of Palmers Green, London; 2 s (Adrian b 1981, Mark b 1985); *Career* mgmnt devpt manager Philips Electronics 1985-87 (industl relations mangr 1979-85), gen mangr human resources Pearl Assur 1987-; MIPM 1973; *Books* Industrial Relations Training for Managers, Cost Effective Strategies in Industral Relations (1985); *Recreations* music, writing; *Style*— Stephen Connock, Esq; Pearl Assurance, High Holborn, London WC1V 7EB (☎ 01 405 8441)

CONNOLLY, Dr (Charles) Kevin; TD (1981); s of Dr Charles Vincent Connolly (d 1961), of Rothwell, Kettering, Northamptonshire, and Frances Elliott, *née* Turner; *b* 26 Sept 1936; *Educ* Ampleforth, Gonville and Caius Coll Cambridge, Middx Hosp Med Sch (MA, MB BChir); *m* 24 Oct 1970, Rachel Bronwen, da of Lewis Philip Jameson Evans (d 1972), of Bromsgrove, Worcs; 3 da (Kate b 1971, Celia b 1973, Clare b 1975); *Career* house physician Middx Hosp 1961, resident med offr Brompton Hosp 1963, sr med registrar St Georges Hosp 1967, conslt physician Darlington & Northallerton Hosp 1970-, clinical tutor Northallerton Health Dist 1974-82, examiner Temporary Registration/Provisional Licence Assessment Bd 1975-, hon clinical lectr dept of medicine Univ of Newcastle upon of Tyne 1988-; vice pres Nat Assoc of Clinical Tutors 1981-83, past and present memb various ctee RCP and Br Thoracic Soc; pres: Northallerton div Br Med Assoc 1974-76, Yorks Thoracic Soc 1982-84; memb: Darlington Health Authy 1981, exec and med ctees Breathe North Appeal; pres elect Northern Thoracic Soc; Liveryman Worshipful Co of Apothecaries 1964; MRCP 1964, FRCP 1977; memb: Thoracic Soc, Med Res Soc; *Recreations* tennis, skiing; *Style*— Dr C K Connolly, TD; Aldbrough Hse, Aldbrough St John, Richmond, N Yorks DL11 7TP (☎ 0325 374 244); 39 Stanhope Rd, Darlington (☎ 462 593)

CONNOLLY, Rainier Campbell; s of George Augustus Victor Connolly (d 1952), of Braeside, Garden Ave, Brighton, and Margaret Winifred, *née* Edgell (d 1981); *b* 15 July 1919; *Educ* Bedford Sch, St Bartholomews Medical Coll (FRCS (Eng) 1947); *m* 20 Nov 1948, Elizabeth Fowler, da of Prof Charles Gilbert Cullis (d 1944); 1 s (Richard b 1955), 2 da (Susan b 1949, Janet b 1952); *Career* 2 Lieut Royal Sussex Regt TA 1937-39; Major RAMC 1943-47, Italy 1943-45 (despatches), India 1945-46; neurosurgeon St Bartholomews Hosp 1959-84; conslt nuerosurgeon: Royal Nat Orthopaedic Hosp 1959-84, Midland Centre for Neurosurgery 1952-59, Royal Victoria Hosp 1948-52, King Edward VII Hosp for Offrs; civilian conslt in neurosurgery to RN 1971-84; Hunterian prof Royal Coll of Surgeons (Eng) 1961; pres of neurological section Royal Soc of Medicine 1981; *Recreations* foreign travelling; *Style*— Rainier Campbell Connolly, Esq; 149 Harley Street, London W1N 2DH (☎ 01 935 4444)

CONNOLLY, Terence Ralph; s of Ralph Dennis Connolly, of Esher, Surrey, and Doreen Mabel Connolly; *b* 28 Sept 1943; *Educ* Surbiton GS; *m* 16 July 1966, Kathryn Mary; 2 da (Emma Claire b 1970, Sarah Louise b 1976); *Career* gp md Chrysalis Gp plc 1973; FICA 1966; *Recreations* sailing; *Clubs* Reform; *Style*— Terence R Connolly, Esq; High Trees, Hydon Heath, Godalming, Surrey (☎ 04868 212261); 12 Stratford Place, London W1 (☎ 01 408 2355)

CONNOR, Howard Arthur; s of Arthur Albert William Connor (d 1969, Sgt RAF), of 10 Mansfield Hill, Chingford, London, and Winifred Edith, *née* Rugg (d 1983); *b* 31 Jan 1938; *Educ* Richmond House Sch Chingford, Chingford Co HS; *m* 23 July 1960, Dorothy Myrtle, da of Frederick Hobbs (d 1981), of 34 Elmfield Rd, Chingford, London; 2 da (Alison b 1964, Melinda b 1966); *Career* CA; princ G H Attenborough and Co, md The Business and Financial Advisory Co Ltd; life vice pres Hoddesdon and Broxbourne C of C; FCA, ATII; *Recreations* horse riding, skiing, badminton; *Clubs* Burford, Rotary of Hoddesdon (pres); *Style*— Howard Connor, Esq; Spinney House, The Spinney, Broxbourne, Hertfordshire (☎ 0992 468071); 34 Fawkon Walk, Hoddesdon, Herts (☎ 0992 460016)

CONNOR, Jeremy George; s of Joseph Connor (d 1975), and Mabel Emmeline, *née* Adams (d 1985); *b* 14 Dec 1938; *Educ* Beaumont, Univ Coll London (LLB, DRS); *Career* barr Middle Temple 1961, recorder SE circuit, Metropolitan Stipendiary Magistrate 1979-, appointed to Treasury List Central Criminal Court 1973, chm Inner London Juvenile Courts 1980-, chm Inner London Probation Area Liaison Ctee 1986-, memb Central Cncl of Probation Exec Ctee 1981, chm exec Cncl Br Acad of Forensic Sciences 1983; Freeman City of London 1980, memb of Livery Ctee of Fanmakers Co 1987-, underwriting memb of Lloyds; *Publications* Chapter (Jury) Archbold, Criminal Pleading Evidence and Practice 38 and 39 editions; *Recreations* travel, theatre, occasional broadcasting; *Clubs* Garrick, Royal Society of Medicine; *Style*— Jeremy Connor, Esq; Bow Street Court, London WC2

CONNOR, Leslie John; s of William John Connor (d 1980), of Lancs, and Doris Eliza, *née* Neild; *b* 23 April 1932; *Educ* St Mary's Coll Crosby, Liverpool Univ (BA), California Univ of Advanced Studies (MBA); *m* 1951, Jean Margaret, da of Roger Pendleton, of Lancashire; 2 da (Christine Lesley b 1964, Hilary Elaine b 1968); *Career* exec trainee C and A Modes 1956-58, Gt Universal Stores 1958-63, Connor Fin Corpn 1963-, md Leisure and General Hldgs Ltd 1970-73, fndr and chm First Castle Electronics plc 1973-86; dir: Connor Fin Corpn, L J Connor Conslts Ltd, W J Connor Properties (and Publishing) Ltd, Southern Litho Supplies Ltd, Manordale Devpts Ltd, Manordale (Southern) Ltd, Vidview Ltd; Br Show Pony Soc (BSPS): cncl memb 1978-83, tres 1979-83, tstee 1979-, vice pres 1983-; tstee Monks Ferry Trg Tst 1988-; *Books* The Managed Growth of a Quoted British Public Company, The Working Hunter Pony (co-author); *Recreations* showing horses, farming, antiques, porcelain and painting, walking, writing, golf; *Clubs* Farmers; *Style*— Leslie Connor, Esq; Greenbank, Prescot Rd, Aughton, Lancashire L39 5AG (☎ 0695 423573, fax 0695 423395); Connor Finance Corp Ltd, Bowker's Green Court, Bowker's Green Aughton, Lanchashire L39 6TA (☎ 0695 42400, fax 0695 424109)

CONNOR, (Patrick) Riordan; MBE (1967); s of John Connor and Bridget Riordan; *b* 19 Feb 1907; *Educ* Presentation Coll Cork; *m* 1942, Malinka Marie, da of Benjamin West Smith (d 1927), of Folkingham, Lincs; *Career* res and devpt dept of MOD; critic of fiction The Fortnightly 1935-37, reader of fiction for Cassell 1948-56; work has been included in: Best Short Stories anthology twice, Pick of Today's Short Stories, Whit Burnett anthology (USA); author; *Books* Shake Hands with the Devil (filmed 1958), Rude Earth, Salute to Aphrodite (USA), I am Death, Time to Kill (USA), Men Must Live, The Sword of Love, Wife to Colum, The Devil Among the Tailors, My Love to the Gallows, Hunger of the Heart, The Singing Stone, The House of Cain; under the pen name Peter Malin: To Kill Is My Vocation, River, Sing me a Song, Kobo the Brave; *Clubs* Soc of Authors; *Style*— Riordan Connor, Esq, MBE; 79 Balsdean Rd, Woodingdean, Brighton BN2 6PG (☎ Brighton 34032)

CONNOR, Roger David; s of Thomas Bernard Connor, of Aisby, Lincolns (d 1962), and Susie Violet, *née* Spittlehouse (d 1964); *b* 8 June 1939; *Educ* Merchant Taylors', Brunel Coll of Advanced Science and Technol; *m* 25 March 1967, Sandra Home, da of Eldred Rolef Holmes, of St Ouen, Jersey; 2 s (Hugh b 1969, Rupert b 1970); *Career* ptnr Messrs Hodders 1970-83, slr 1968, met stipendary magistrate 1983-, rec of Crown Ct 1987; memb Ctee of Magistrates 1986-; *Recreations* music, gardening, golf, bee keeping; *Style*— Roger Connor, Esq; Bourn's Meadow, Little Missenden, Amersham, Bucks HP7 0RF (☎ 02406 2760); Camberwell Green Magistrates' Court, London SE5 7UP (☎ 01 703 0909)

CONNOR, Bishop of, 1987-; Rt Rev Samuel Greenfield Poyntz; s of Rev James Poyntz (d 1968), and Katharine Jane Poyntz; *b* 4 Mar 1926; *Educ* Portora Royal Sch Enniskillen, Dublin Univ (MA, BD, PhD); *m* 1952, Noreen Henrietta Armstrong; 1 s, 2 da; *Career* deacon 1950, priest 1951, archdeacon of Dublin and examining chaplain to Archbishop of Dublin 1974-78, Bishop of Cork Cloyne and Ross 1978-87; chm Irish Council of Churches 1986-, vice-pres British Council of Churches 1987-; *Style*— The Rt Rev the Lord Bishop of Connor; Bishop's House, 22 Deramore Park, Belfast, Northern Ireland BT9 5JU

CONOLLY-CAREW, Hon Patrick Thomas; s and h of 6 Baron Carew, CBE; *b* 6 Mar 1938; *Educ* Harrow, RMA Sandhurst; *m* 30 April 1962, Celia Mary, da of Col Hon (Charles) Guy Cubitt, CBE, DSO, TD; 1 s, 3 da; *Career* late Capt Royal Horse Gds, former int show jumping rider memb Irish Olympic Three Day Event team Mexico 1968, Munich 1972, Montreal 1976; pres Equestrian Fedn of Ireland 1979-84; *Recreations* all equestrian sports, shooting, cricket, bridge; *Clubs* Cavalry and Guards, Kildare St and Univ (Dublin); *Style*— Capt The Hon Patrick Conolly-Carew; Donadea House, Naas, Co Kildare, Ireland

CONQUEST, (George) Robert Acworth; OBE (1955); s of Robert Folger Westcott Conquest (d 1959), of Vence, Alpes Maritimes, and Rosamund Alys, *née* Acworth (d 1973); *b* 15 July 1917; *Educ* Winchester, Univ of Grenoble, Magdalen Coll Oxford (MA, DLitt); *m* 1, 1942 (m dis 1948), Joan, *née* Watkins; 2 s (John b 1943, Richard b 1945); m 2, 1948 (m dis 1962), Tatiana Mikhailova; m 3, 1964 (m dis 1978), Caroleen, *née* Macfarlane; m 4, 1979, Elizabeth, da of late Col Richard D Neece, USAF; *Career* Oxf and Bucks Lt Inf 1939-46 Capt; HM For Serv 1946-56, 2 sec Sofia, 1 sec UK Delegation to the UN, princ FO, fell LSE 1956-58, visiting poet Univ of Buffalo 1959-60, lit ed The Spectator 1962-63, sr fell Columbia Univ 1964-65, fell The Woodrow Wilson Int Center 1976-77, sr res fell The Hoover Inst Stanford Univ 1977-79 and 1981-, visiting scholar The Heritage Fndn 1980-81, res assoc Harvard Univ 1983-; FRSL 1972, FBIS 1968, memb Soc for the Promotion of Roman Studies; *Books* Poems (1955), Power and Policy in the USSR (1961), Between Mars and Venus (1963), The Great Terror (1968), Lenin (1972), The Abomination of Moab (1979), Present Danger (1979), Forays (1979), The Harvest of Sorrow (1986), New and Collected Poems (1988); *Clubs* Travellers; *Style*— Robert Conquest, Esq, OBE; 52 Peter Coutts Circle, Stanford, California 94305, USA (☎ 415 493 5152); Hoover Institution, Stanford, California 94305, USA (☎ 415 723 1647)

CONRAD, Conrad John; s of Marc Scheinberg (d 1981), of London, and Martha, *née* Greenberg; *b* 25 May 1919; *Educ* Tollington GS, Muswell Hill London; *m* 25 July 1942, Florence Louisa Ellen (Flon), da of late George Webb; 1 s (Gary Kelvyn b 17 Aug 1945), 1 da (Lois Karyl b 10 April 1949); *Career* WWII section ldr NCC 1939-46; Merit Toys plc (formerly J & L Randall Ltd): joined 1946, chief buyer 1949, exec dir 1957, bd dir 1963, chief exec 1978, ret 1988; joined parent co Bluebird Toys plc 1988; qualified Samaritans; *Recreations* philately, photography, swimming; *Style*— Conrad Conrad, Esq; 'Ashmount', 81 Hatfield Rd, Potters Bar, Herts EN6 1N2 (☎ 0707 55 992); Merit Toys Ltd (Bluebird Devpts Ltd), Parsonage Rd, Swindon SN3 4RJ (☎ 0793 831 111, fax 0793 827 887, car tel 0836 722 847, telex 444 865)

CONRAN, Elizabeth Margaret; *née* Johnston; da of James Johnston (d 1954), and Elizabeth Russell, *née* Wilson (d 1987); *b* 5 May 1939; *Educ* Falkirk HS, Univ of Glasgow (MA); *m* 26 Nov 1970, (George) Loraine Conran (d 1986), s of Col George Hay Montgomery Conran (d 1940); 1 da (Violet b 1972); *Career* res asst Glasgow Univ

1959-60, asst curator The Iveagh Bequest Kenwood London 1960-63, keeper of paintings City Art Gallery Manchester 1963-74, arts advsr Greater Manchester Cncl 1974-79, curator The Bowes Museum Barnard Castle Co Durham 1979-; tstee Teesdale Preservation Tst, chm Teesdale Sch PTA, memb bd of mgmnt English Dance Theatre; FMA 1969, FRSA 1987; *Recreations* dance, gardens; *Style*— Mrs Elizabeth Conran; 31 Thorngate, Barnard Castle, Co Durham DL12 8QB (☎ 0833 31055); The Bowes Museum, Barnard Castle, Co Durham DL12 8NP (☎ 0833 690606)

CONRAN, Jasper Alexander; s of Sir Terence Conran, *qv*, and Shirley Ida, *née* Pearce; *b* 12 Dec 1959; *Educ* Bryanston, Parsons Sch of Design NY; *Career* md and designer Jasper Conran Ltd; British Fashion Cncl Designer of the Year Award 1986-87, Fashion Gp of America Award 1987; *Style*— Jasper Conran, Esq; 49-50 Gt Marlborough St, London W1V 1DB (☎ 01 437 0386 and 01 439 8572, fax 01 734 7761, telex 24517 JASPER G)

CONRAN, Shirley Ida; da of W Thirlby Pearce and Ida Pearce; *b* 21 Sept 1932; *Educ* St Paul's Girls' Sch; *m* 1955 (m dis 1962), as his 2 w, Terence Orby Conran (now Sir Terence), *qv*; 2 s; *Career* designer; co-fndr Conran Fabrics Ltd 1957; founded Textile Design Studio 1958; memb selection ctee Design Centre 1961; journalist, first woman's ed Observer Colour Magazine 1964, with Observer until 1969, woman ed Daily Mail 1969-70; *Books* Superwoman (1975), Superwoman Year Book (1976), Superwoman in Action (1977), Lace (1982), Shirley Conran's Magic Garden (1983), Lace 2 (1985); *Style*— Ms Shirley Conran; c/o Coutts Bank, 14 Lombard Street, London EC4

CONRAN, Sir Terence Orby; *b* 4 Oct 1931; *Educ* Bryanston; *m* 1, 1955 (m dis 1962), Shirley Ida Pearce (*see* Shirley Conran); 2 s; m 2, 1963, Caroline Herbert (the cookery writer Caroline Conran); 2 s, 1 da; *Career* chm Conran Holdings Ltd 1965-68, jt chm Ryman Conran Ltd 1968-71, dir: Conran Ink Ltd 1969, Conran Design Gp 1971; chm Habitat Gp Ltd 1971, dir The Neal Street Restaurant 1972, chm Habitat France SA 1973; dir: Conran Stores Inc 1977-, Electra Risk Capital Gp plc 1981-84; chm J Hepworth and Son Ltd 1981-83 (dir 1979-83), dir Conran Roche Ltd 1982; chm Habitat Mothercare plc 1982; dir Conran Octopus 1983; chm Richard Shops 1983-87, dir Heal and Son Ltd 1983-87, chm Butlers Wharf Ltd 1984, dir Michelin House Development 1985; vice-pres FNAC 1985, dir: BHS 1986, Bibendum Restaurant Ltd 1986; chm and chief exec Storehouse plc, following merger of Habitat/Mothercare and BHS 1986; FSIAD; presented with SIAD medal 1980; RSA Bicentenary Medal 1984; Hon FRIBA 1984; memb: cncl RCA, V and A Advsy Cncl 1979-83, tstee V and A 1984-; established Conran Foundation for design educ and research 1981; kt 1982; *Books* The House Book (1974), The Kitchen Book (1977), The Bedroom and Bathroom Book (1978), The Cook Book (with Caroline Conran, 1980), The New House Book (1985); Conran Director of Design (1985), Plants at Home (1986), The Soft Furnishings Book (1986), Terence Conran's France (1987); *Recreations* gardening, cooking; *Style*— Sir Terence Conran; Storehouse plc, The Heal's Building, 196 Tottenham Court Rd, London W1P 9LD (☎ 01 631 0101)

CONROY, Harry; *b* 6 April 1943; *m* Margaret; 3 children; *Career* trainee lab technician Southern Gen Hosp 1961-62, night messenger (copy boy) Scottish Daily Express 1962-63; reporter: Daily Record 1964-66, Scottish Daily Mail 1966-67, Daily Record 1967-69; financial corr Daily Record 1969-; dep father of chapel Daily Record and Sunday Mail Chapel 1968-69, father of chapel Daily Record and Sunday Mail NUJ Chapel 1975-77, Nat Exec Cncl memb for nat newspapers and agencies outside London 1982- (vice-pres 1980-81, pres 1981-82), chair Scotland W Area Cncl 1980-81, ADM delegate: 1970, 1971, 1972, 1973 and 1975; TUC delegate: 1981, 1982 and 1983; STUC delegate: 1981, 1982, 1983, 1984 and 1985; FOC Daily Record and Sunday Mail 1984-; memb ASTMS 1961-62; assoc memb Gen and Municipal Boilermakers Union 1984-85; memb NUJ 1963-, gen sec NUJ 1986-; *Style*— Harry Conroy Esq; NUJ, Acorn Ho, 314-320 Gray's Inn Rd, London WC1X 8DP

CONSETT, Lt Col (Montagu Charles Warcop) Peter; TD (1949 bar), JP (N Yorks 1952), DL (N Yorks 1960); s of Rear Adm MWWP Consett, CMG, JP, DL, of Brawith Hall, Thirsk, and Ethel Maud, *née* Wilson; *b* 20 July 1909; *Educ* RN Coll Dartmouth, RN Coll Greenwich; *m* 7 Feb 1944, Margaret Syssylt (d 1971), da of Sir John Storey Barwick, 2 Bt, of Thimbleby Halt, Osmotherley, Northallerton; 3 s (John b 10 March 1946, Christopher b 6 May 1948, Geoffrey b 1 May 1952); *Career* Midshipman 1927, Sub Lt 1929, Lt 1931, ret 1935; APWO Yorks Hussars: Lt 1935, Capt 1940, Maj 1941; Maj MO(4)SP 1943; E Riding Yeo: Capt 1944, Maj 1945; Alexandra Princess of Wales' own Yorkshire Hussars: Maj 1947, Lt Col (commanding) 1950-53; vice chm: NRYKS TA & AF Assoc 1966-68, N of England TA & VR Assoc 1968-74; farmer 1935-; High Sheriff N Yorks 1974-75; dist cncllr Thisk (chm 1959-74), RDC 1937-74, co cncllr NR Yorks 1952-81, dist cncllr Hambleton DC 1974- (chm 1984 & 1985), hon alderman N Yorks CC 1981; *Recreations* shooting, tennis; *Clubs* Naval & Military, Pratts, MCC; *Style*— Lt Col Peter Consett, TD, JP, DL; The Wing, Braiwth Hall, Thirsk, (☎ 0845 22187)

CONSTABLE; see Strickland-Constable

CONSTABLE, Prof (Charles) John; s of Charles Constable, of Bedford, and Gladys May, *née* Morris; *b* 20 Jan 1936; *Educ* Durham Sch, Cambridge Univ (MA), London Univ (BSc), Harvard Univ (DBA); *m* 9 April 1960, Elisabeth Mary, da of Ronald Light (d 1981); 3 s (Charles b 1962, Giles b 1965, Piers b 1971), 1 da (Harriet b 1961); *Career* mgmnt educator and conslt; visiting prof Cranfield Sch of Mgmnt and Manchester Business Sch; dir gen of the Br Inst of Mgmnt 1985-86; dir: Cranfield Sch of Mgmnt, Cranfield Inst of Techn 1982-85; prof of management Cranfield Sch of Mgmnt 1971-85; non exec dir: Lodge Ceramics Ltd, SIMAC Ltd 1982-, Int Military Services Ltd 1984-, Abbey Life plc 1987; govr Harpur Tst 1979-; memb: NEDO Heavy Electrical Machinery EDC 1977-87, N Beds DHA 1987-; *Books* Group Assessment Programmes (with D A Smith, 1966), Text and Cases in Operations Management (with C C New, 1976), Cases in Strategic Management (with J Stopford and D Channon, 1980), The Making of British Managers (with R McCormick, 1987); *Recreations* family, golf; *Clubs* Bedfordshire Golf; *Style*— Professor John Constable, Esq; 20 Kimbolton Rd, Bedford MK40 2NR (☎ 0234 212576); Gore Point, Porlock Weir, Minehead, Somerset

CONSTABLE, Gp Capt John Hurn; s of Prof F H Constable (d 1975), and Sance Helena, *née* Robson (d 1981); *b* 19 August 1934; *Educ* Hitchin GS, RAF Coll, RAF Staff Coll, Nat Def Coll, Open Univ (BA); *m* 12 Aug 1961, Karin, da of Karsten Emmanuel Amundsen, of Oslo, Norway; 1 s (Harald John Catherock b 6 June 1962), 1 da (Helen Katrine (Mrs Lindley) b 19 Nov 1964); *Career* cmmnd RAF (Sec Branch) 1956 (Sword of Honnour); early appointments on legal accounting, personnel duties including: Adj Br Element Heafnorth Oslo 1958-61, ADC to AOC and Cmdt RAF Tech Coll 1961-64, Staff of Air Sec MOD 1967-70; later OC Admin Wing RAF Wyton 1976-78, directing staff Nat Def Coll 1978-80, dep dir RAF Ground Trg MOD 1980-83, cmmnd accountant RAF Support Cmmnd 1983-87, ret 1987; Secondary of London, Under Sheriff and High Bailiff of Southwark 1987-; ed journals: RAF Coll, RAF Staff Coll and Nat Def Coll; sec St Boniface PCC 1970-73; St Marys PCC 1983-85; Freeman City of London 1982, memb Ct of Assts Worshipful Co Chartered Secs and Admins 1987; FRGS 1975, FRSA 1977, FCIS 1977 (2 prizes), FInstAM 1977, FBIM 1980; *Recreations* fell walking, travel, classical music and art, history; *Clubs* RAF; *Style*— Gp Capt John Constable; Central Criminal Ct, Old Bailey, London EC4M 7BS (☎ 01 248 3277)

CONSTABLE, Dr (Frank) Leonard; TD (1965), DL (1988), (QHP 1975); s of Francis Albert Constable (d 1974), and Mary, *née* Nichol (d 1979); *b* 28 May 1920; *Educ* Dame Allan's Sch, Univ of Durham (BSc, MB BS, MD); *m* 7 July 1951, Jean Margaret da of Cdr Ivor McIvor, RN (d 1956); 3 s (John b 1957, Christopher b 1959, Timothy b 1962); *Career* Lt REME 1942-46, Maj RAMC 1951-73 (latterly Lt-Col), Col cmmd 201 Gen Hosp 1973, Dep Cdr NE Dist TA 1973-79, cmdt Tyne & Wear Army Cadet force 1979-81, Hon Col 251 Field Ambulance 1978-84; house physician Royal Victoria Infirmary Newcastle upon Tyne 1951-53, lectr Univ of Edinburgh 1953-61, conslt microbiologist Royal Victoria Infirmary 1961-85; cdr Northumbria St John's Ambulance; Cdr Ost J; FRCPath 1963; *Recreations* fly fishing; *Style*— Dr Leonard Constable, TD, DL, QHP; 17 Roseworth Ave, Gosforth, Newcastle upon Tyne NE3 1NB (☎ 091 285 1223)

CONSTABLE-MAXWELL, Lt-Col Andrew; MBE (1945), MC; 6 s of Hon Bernard Constable-Maxwell (d 1938), 4 son of 10 Lord Herries, of Farlie House, Beauly, Invernesshire, and Hon Alice, *née* Fraser, da of 15 Lord Lovat; *b* 31 Jan 1906; *Educ* Ampleforth; *m* 26 Feb 1949, Nikki, da of Mark Kerkes (d 1972); 1 da (Andreina b 10 March 1950), 1 s (Mark b 16 d 18 Nov 1951); *Career* joined Scots Guards 1939, Staff Coll Haifa 1941, served Tobruk 1942, wounded, captured, escaped (MC), joined Col David Stirling in SAS 1942, instructing staff at Mountain Warfare Training Centre Lebanon 1943, joined Fitzroy Maclean as 2 i/c Yugoslavia 1944, Lt Col 1946; Southern States Devpt Co USA 1926-28; Dominick and Dominick Wall Street New York 1929-33, GMP Murphy Co Wall Street 1936-39; private fin cos 1946-58, int head of Hoffman Electronics Corpn California 1958-72; *Recreations* collecting ancient glass and rare books; *Clubs* Metropolitan NY, The Brook NY, White's, Cavalry and Guards, Turf, Pratt's; *Style*— Lt-Col Andrew Constable-Maxwell, MBE, MC; 1181 Vincy (Vaud), Switzerland (☎ 021 74 18 91)

CONSTANTINE, Air Chief Marshal Sir Hugh Alex; KBE (1958, CBE 1944), CB (1946), DSO (1942); s of Cdr Henry Constantine, RN, of Southsea, Hants, and Alice Louise Squire; *b* 23 May 1908; *Educ* Christ's Hosp, RAF Cranwell; *m* 1937, Helen, da of J W Bourke, of Sydney, Australia; 1 da; *Career* 56(F) Sqdn CFS instructor bomber cmd 1940-45; cmmnd RAF 1927, Air Marshal 1958, AOC-in-C Flying Training Cmd 1959-61, Cmdt IDC 1961-64, Air Ch Marshal 1961, ret 1964; co-ordinator Anglo-American Community Relations MOD (Air) 1964-77, Hon LLD Warwick (1978); *Style*— Air Chief Marshal Sir Hugh Constantine, KBE, CB, DSO; 14 Cadogan Ct, Draycott Ave, London SW3 3BX (☎ 01 581 8821)

CONSTANTINE, Joseph; s of Maj Robert Alfred Constantine, TD, JP (d 1968), and Marie Leonie Françoise Van Haaren, eleventh in descent through female line from William the Silent, Count of Nassau in the Netherlands and Prince of Orange; *b* 12 Feb 1928; *Educ* Eton; *m* April 1954, Mary Rose, da of late Harwood Lawrence Cotter, and Rosemary, Lady Ley (d 1977), yr da of Capt Duncan Macpherson, RN and sister of Francis Cameron Macpherson of Cluny, 26 Chief of Clan Macpherson; 2 da (Annette (Hon Mrs Jonathan Boyd) b 1956, Susannah b 1962); *Career* Lt Coldstream Gds 1946-48; chm and md Constantine Hldgs Ltd 1964-; FRICS 1955; *Recreations* painting; *Clubs* Brooks's, Turf; *Style*— Joseph Constantine, Esq; 9 Canning Place, London W8 (☎ 01 584 7640); The Priory, Knipton, Grantham, Lincs (☎ 047 6870 238)

CONSTANTINE, Hon Roy; only s of Baron Constantine of Stanmore, CBE (Life Peer); *b* 1936; *Style*— Hon Roy Constantine; 11 Grove Park Terrace, London W4

CONSTANTINE OF STANMORE, Baron (Life Peer UK 1981); Sir Theodore; CBE (1956), AE (1945), DL (Greater London 1967); s of Leonard Constantine, of London, and Fanny Louise Constantine; *b* 15 Mar 1910; *Educ* Acton Coll; *m* 1935, Sylvia Mary, yr da of Wallace Henry Legge-Pointing, of London; 1 s, 1 da; *Career* sits as Conservative Peer in the House of Lords; served WWII RAuxAF; dir of industrial hldg co 1956-59, chm of public companies 1959-85; chm Anscon Ltd; pres National Union Cons and Unionist Assocs 1980- (chm 1967-68); High Sheriff Greater London 1967; Master Worshipful Co of Coachmakers 1975, Freeman City of London; kt 1964; *Recreations* reading, walking, watching motor racing; *Clubs* Carlton, Buck's; *Style*— The Rt Hon Lord Constantine of Stanmore, CBE, AE, DL; Hunters Beck, Uxbridge Rd, Stanmore, Middx

CONTEH, John Anthony; s of Amadu Frank Conteh, and Rachel Hannah; *b* 27 May 1951; *Educ* Sacred Heart Jr Sch, St Kevins Comprehensive Kirkby Liverpool; *m* Veronica Anne, da of Stanley Smith; 1 s (James Alexander b 1977), 1 da (Joanna Louise b 1978); *Career* boxer; ABA Champion: Middleweight 1970, Light Heavyweight 1971; Cwlth Games Middleweight Champion Edinburgh 1970, Light Heavyweight Champion Br, Euro, Cwlth 1973, WBC World Light Heavyweight Champion 1974, Br Superstars Champion 1974; *Books* I Conteh (Autobiography 1982); *Recreations* golf, piano; *Clubs* Moor Park Golf ; *Style*— John Conteh, Esq; 13 Downalong, Bushey Heath, Herts WD2 1HZ (☎ 01 950 0106)

CONTI, Rt Rev Mario; *see*: Aberdeen, Bishop of (RC)

CONTI, Thomas A (Tom); s of Alfonso Conti (d 1961), of Paisley, Renfrewshire, and Mary McGoldrick (d 1979); *b* 22 Nov 1941; *Educ* Royal Scottish Acad of Music; *m* 1967, Katherine Drummond, da of Wilson George Drummond Tait, of Edinburgh; 1 da (Nina b 1973); *Career* actor 1960-; dir; London appearances incl: Savages (Royal Court and Comedy 1973), The Devil's Disciple (RSC Aldwych 1976), Whose Life is it Anyway? (Mermaid and Savoy 1978 and NY 1979, SWET Award for Best Actor in a new play, Variety Club of GB Award for Best Stage Actor 1978, Tony Award for Best Actor 1979), They're Playing Our Song (Shaftesbury 1980), Romantic Comedy (Apollo 1983); directed: Last Licks (Broadway 1979), Before the Party (Oxford Playhouse and Queen's 1980), The Housekeeper (Apollo 1982); films include: Galileo (1974), Flame

(1974), Eclipse (1975), Full Circle (1977), The Duelists (1977), The Wall (1980), Merry Christmas, Mr Lawrence (1983), Reuben, Reuben (1983), Miracles, Heavenly Pursuits, Beyond Therapy, Saving Grace, American Dreamer, Two Brothers Running, White Roses, Shirley Valentine; tv appearances incl: Madame Bovary, The Norman Conquests, Glittering Prizes 1984-87; tv films incl: The Quick and the Dead, The Beate Klarsfeld Story (tv mini series) etc; *Clubs* Garrick; *Style*— Tom Conti, Esq; c/o Plant & Frogatt, 4 Windmill St London W1; APA 9000 Sunset Bvd, Los Angeles, USA

CONVILLE, David Henry; OBE (1983); s of Lt-Col Leopold Henry George Conville, CBE (d 1979), of Convillepur Farm, Sahiwal, Pakistan, and Katherine Mary, *née* Gispert (d 1973); *b* 4 June 1929; *Educ* Marlborough, St John's Coll Oxford, RADA; *m* 1, Jean Margaret Bury (d 1967); 1 da (Clare b 14 Oct 1959); m 2, 2 Jan 1970, Philippa Juliet Antonia, da of Alfred John Gordge (d 1959); 1 s (Leo b 23 Jan 1979); *Career* Nat Serv 1947-49, cmmnd Royal Welsh Fus, 2 Lt 4 Bn Nigeria Regt Royal W African Frontier Force; Ipswich Rep Theatre 1952, Stratford Memorial Theatre Co 1955 and 1957, fndr David Conville Prodns (toured 1959), first London prodns 1960, Toad of Toad Hall West End Christmas 1960-84, fndr New Shakespeare Co 1962, dir New Shakespeare Co at open air theatre Regent's Park 1962-86, pres Soc of West End Theatre 1975, 1976, 1983; plays written include: The Wind in the Willows 1984, Look Here Old Son 1986, Obituaries 1988; awarded Coronation Medal 1953; chm: Drama Centre 1982-89, The New Shakespeare Co; memb Arts Cncl Drama panel 1988-89, exec memb Soc of West End Theatre; memb: Soc of West End Theatre, Theatre Managers Assoc; *Recreations* walking, reading, tennis, wine; *Clubs* Garrick, Roehampton; *Style*— David Conville, Esq, OBE; 17 Gwendolen Ave, London SW15 6ET (☎ 01 789 8327)

CONWAY, Derek Leslie; MP (C) Shrewsbury and Atcham 1983-; s of Leslie Conway, and Florence Gwendoline, *née* Bailes; *b* 15 Feb 1953; *Educ* Beacon Hill Boys' Sch; *m* 1980, Colette Elizabeth Mary, da of Charles Lamb; 2 s (Henry b 1982, Fredrick b 1985); *Career* Maj 5 Bn The LI TA; memb Cons Pty Nat Exec 1972-81, nat vice-chm Young Cons 1973-75, borough cncllr 1974-78, Parly candidate (C) Durham Oct 1974 and Newcastle upon Tyne East 1979, ldr Tyne and Wear Met CC 1979-82 (memb 1977-83); memb: bd Washington Devpt Corpn 1979-83, bd Newcastle Airport 1979-82, select ctee on Agric, select ctee on Tport; PPS to Min of State for Wales 1988-; *Recreations* Maj 5 Bn The Light Infantry, TA; *Clubs* Beaconsfield, Shrewsbury; *Style*— Derek Conway, Esq, MP; House of Commons, London SW1A 0AA

CONWAY, Prof Gordon Richard; s of Cyril Gordon Conway (d 1977), of Kingston, Surrey, and Thelma, *née* Goodwin; *b* 6 July 1938; *Educ* Kingston GS, Kingston Tech Coll, UCNW Bangor (BSc), Cambridge Univ (Dip Ag Sc), Univ of West Indies Trinidad (DTA), Univ of California, Davis (PhD); *m* 20 March 1966, Susan Mary, da of Harold Mumford, of Winchester, Hants; 1 s (Simon Goodwin b 10 Feb 1967), 2 da (Katherine Ellen b 2 March 1973, Zoe Martha (twin)); *Career* entomologist State of Sabah, Malaysia 1961-66, lectr (later reader and prof) Imperial Coll 1970-88; representative The Ford Fndn, New Delhi 1989-; memb Royal Cmmn Environmental Pollution 1984-88; FIBiol; *Books* Pest and Pathogen Control (1980); *Recreations* travel; *Style*— Prof Gordon Conway

CONWAY, (David) Martin; s of Lt-Col Geoffrey Seymour Conway, MC, (d 1984), of Portpatrick, Galloway, and Elsie, *née* Phillips; *b* 22 August 1935; *Educ* Sedbergh, Gonville and Caius Coll Cambridge Univ (BA, MA); *m* 10 March 1962, Ruth Fairey, da of Rev Richard Daniel (d 1983), of Audlem, Ches; 1 s (John b 1967), 2 da (Ann, Moira (Mrs Zheng)); *Career* int sec Student Christian Movement GB and Ireland 1958-61, study sec World Student Christian Fedn Geneva 1961-67, C of E's sec for Chaplaincies in Higher Educn London 1967-70, ed and pubns sec World Cncl of Churches Geneva 1970-74, asst gen sec Br Cncl of Churches London 1974-83, tutor in church and soc Ripon Coll Cuddesdon Oxford and dir Oxford Inst for Church and Soc 1983-86, pres Selly Oak Colls Birmingham 1986-; chm Birmingham Diocesan Cncl for Mission and Unity, vice-chm Friends of the Church in China; ed Oxford Papers on Contemporary Soc 1984-86, Christians Together newsletter; *Books* The Undivided Vision (1966), The Christian Enterprise in Higher Education (1971), Seeing Education Whole (1970), Look Listen Care: (1983); *Recreations* friends, travel, music; *Style*— Martin Conway, Esq; President's House, Selly Oak Colleges, Birmingham B29 6LQ (☎ 021 472 2462); President's Office, Selly Oak Colleges, Birmingham B29 6LQ (☎ 021 472 4231, telex 334349 SELLYO G)

CONWAY, Robert David; s of Walter Conway, of Guildford; *b* 11 Dec 1949; *Educ* London Univ (LLB); *m* 17 Jan 1976, Patricia Lock; 2 da (Anna b 6 Oct 1978, Laura b 20 Sept 1980); *Career* tax offr 1969, DPP 1973, barr Inner Temple 1974, SE circuit, lectr in law and legal conslt to Legal Protection Insur Co; writer and performer (as Walter Zerlin Jr); winner Edinburgh Festival Scotsman Award 1975 and 1980, own tv show on Granada, six plays published and performed worldwide; dir: Entertainment Machine Theatre Co, Coups De Theatre Ltd, Conway McGillivray Publishing House; legal advsr to A Fish Called Wanda, and Marlon Brando's A Dry White Season; *Books* Miss You've Dropped Your Briefs (cartoonist), The British Alternative Theatre Directory (ed yearly); *Recreations* art, music, swimming; *Style*— Robert Conway, Esq; 92 South Lane, New Malden, Surrey (☎ 01 949 1689); 7 Stone Buildings, Lincoln's Inn, London WC2A 3SZ (☎ 01 242 0961)

CONWAY, Robert John; s of Ernest Conway, and Jean Patricia; *b* 10 June 1951; *Educ* Univ of Salford (BSc); *m* 1 July 1972, Susan Mary; 1 s (Matthew James b 1975), 3 da (Claire Louise b 1977, Charlotte Elizabeth b 1979, Caroline Michele b 1980); *Career* CA, ptnr Price Waterhouse; FCA; *Recreations* Southampton Round Table; *Style*— Robert Conway, Esq; Primavera, Goodworth Clatford, nr Andover, Hampshire (☎ 0264 23454); Price Waterhouse, The Quay, 30 Channel Way, Ocean Village, Southampton, Hants (☎ 0703 330077)

CONWAY-GORDON, Col Ronald Cosmo; s of Col Ingram Cosmo Conway-Gordon (d 1930), of Lynwode Manor, Market Rasen, Lincs (d 1930), and Ethel Forbes Macbean (d 1924); *b* 6 Dec 1900; *Educ* Wellington, RMC Sandhurst; *m* 25 March 1925, Florita Gladys, da of Guillenmo de Udy, of Buenos Aires; 1 da (Stella Jean b 1926); *Career* Gazetted 1920, Highland LI, served Egypt, Palestine Chanak, Malta, transferred to Royal Signals 1938, served NW Europe and Germany, chief Signal Offr Lines of Communication, Brussels 1946 as Brig (ret 1948); *Style*— Col Ronald Conway-Gordon; 25 Cumberland Rd, Angmering, W Sussex

CONYERS, Nicholas Charles; s of Edwin Keith Conyers, and Elizabeth, *née* Manning; *b* 31 August 1955; *Educ* Ellesmere Coll Shropshire; *m* 29 March 1980, Shirley Anne, da of Thomas Leslie Barrowby; 1 s (John b 3 July 1987), 1 da (Alison b 28 June 1983); *Career* Mercantile Credit 1977-80, asst dir Towry Law Gp 1980-85, ptnr Pearson Jones & Co 1985-; memb: rules and regulations ctee Br Insur and Investmt Brokers Assoc, cncl FIMBRA; *Recreations* walking, cycling, classic cars; *Style*— Nicholas Conyers, Esq; Pearson Jones and Co, Clayton Wood Close, West Park Ring Rd, Leeds LS16 6QE (☎ 0532 304804, fax 0532 744365, car 0836 630381)

CONYNGHAM, 7 Marquess (I 1816); Frederick William Henry Francis Conyngham; also (sits as) Baron Minster (UK 1821), Earl Conyngham (I 1781), Baron Conyngham (I 1781), Viscount Conyngham (I 1789), Viscount Mount Charles (I 1797), Earl of Mount Charles and Viscount Slane (I 1816); patron of one living; s of 6 Marquess Conyngham (d 1974), by his 2 wife Antoinette Winifred, *née* Thompson (d 1966); *b* 13 Mar 1924; *Educ* Eton; *m* 1, 29 April 1950 (m dis 1970), Eileen Wren, o da of Capt Clement Wren Newsam; 3 s; m 2, 1971, Elizabeth Ann, yr da of late Frederick Molyneux Hughes, of Fareham, Hants, and formerly w of David Sutherland Rudd; m 3, 1980, Daphne Georgina Adelaide (d 24 Nov 1986), eldest da of R C Armour, and formerly w of C P V Walker; *Heir* s, Earl of Mount Charles; *Career* late Capt Irish Gds; *Style*— The Most Hon the Marquess Conyngham; Bifrons, nr Canterbury, Kent; Cronk Ghennie House, Ramsay, Isle of Man

CONYNGHAM, Lord Frederick William Patrick; 3 s of 7th Marquess Conyngham by his 1 w, Eileen; *b* 23 Mar 1959; *Style*— Lord Frederick Conyngham

CONYNGHAM, Lady Henrietta Tamara Juliet; da of Earl of Mount Charles, *qv*; *b* 1976; *Style*— Lady Henrietta Conyngham

CONYNGHAM, Lord Simon Charles Eveleigh Wren; 2 s of 7th Marquess Conyngham by his 1 w, Eileen; *b* 20 Nov 1953; *Educ* Harrow; *m* 1978, Emma S, da of Wing Cdr F W Breeze; 1 da (Chloe Wren b 1980); *Career* caterer, runs Staveley's (former fish and chip shop); *Style*— Lord Simon Conyngham

COODE-ADAMS, (John) Giles Selby; s of Geoffrey Coode-Adams (d 1986), and Cynthia Mildred, *née* Selby-Bigge; *b* 30 August 1938; *Educ* Eton; *m* 30 April 1960, Sonia Elisabeth, da of Laurence Frederick York (d 1965); 1 s (Ben b 1965), 1 da (Henrietta Guest b 1962); *Career* 2 Lt 16/5 Queens Royal Lancers 1956-58; joined L Messel (taken over by Shearson Lehman Hutton 1984) 1959 (ptnr 1967-), md Shearson Lehman Hutton 1985; memb of cncl Univ of Essex; *Recreations* fishing, shooting, music, gardening; *Clubs* Boodle's; *Style*— Giles Coode-Adams, Esq; Shearson Lehman Hutton Int, 1 Broadgate, London EC2 (☎ 01 260 2122)

COOGAN, Ven Robert Arthur William; s of Ronald Dudley Coogan (d 1965), and Joyce Elizabeth, *née* Roberts (d 1971); *b* 11 July 1929; *Educ* Launceston HS, Univ of Tasmania (BA), Univ of Durham (DipTheol); *Career* asst curate St Andrew Plaistow 1953-56, rector Bothwell Tasmania 1956-62; vicar: St John N Woolwich 1962-73, St Stephen Hampstead 1973-77; p-in-c All Hallows Gospel Oak 1974-77, vicar St Stephen with All Hallows Hampstead 1977-85; area dean: S Camden 1975-81, N Camden 1978-83; prebendary St Pauls Cathedral 1982-85, commissary for Bishop of Tasmania 1968-88, examining chaplain Bishop of Edmonton 1985-, archdeacon of Hampstead 1985-; *Recreations* reading, gardening, travel; *Clubs* The Oriental; *Style*— The Ven the Archdeacon of Hampstead; 27 Thurlow Rd, Hampstead, London NW3 5PP (☎ 01 435 5890, fax 01 435 6049)

COOK, Prof Sir Alan Hugh; s of late Reginald Thomas Cook, OBE, and Ethel Cook; *b* 2 Dec 1922; *Educ* Westcliff HS for Boys, CCC Camb (MA, PhD, ScD); *m* 1948, Isabell Weir Adamson, 1 s, 1 da; *Career* Cambridge Univ: Jackson prof of natural philosophy 1972-, head of Dept of Physics 1979-84, master of Selwyn Coll 1983-; FRSE memb Science and Engrg Res Cncl 1984-; FRSE 1969, FRSE 1970, memb Soc Sfraniero Acad Naz dei Lincei (Rome); kt 1988; memb Science and Engineering Research Council 1984-; *Books* Gravity and the Earth, Global Geophysics, Interference of Electromagnetic Waves, Physics of the Earth and Planets, Celestial Masers, Interiors of the Planets; *Recreations* travel, amateur theatre, painting, gardening; *Clubs* Explorers (NY), United Oxford and Cambridge; *Style*— Prof Sir Alan Cook; Selwyn College, Cambridge CB3 9DQ

COOK, Andrew Donald Douglas; s of Donald George Cook, JP (d 1988), of 15 Pointers Hill, Westcott, Dorking, Surrey, and Jean, *née* Douglas; *b* 25 Jan 1939; *Educ* Harrow; *m* 1, 4 July 1964 (m dis 1985), Venice Ann, da of Dane Henry Donaldson (d 1987), of 46 Barnmeadow Lane, Great Bookham, Surrey; 1 da (Isobel Christiane b 1 Nov 1969); m 2, 11 Dec 1985, Vivien Hamilton, da of Eric Sutcliffe Aspinall, of 4 Dixs Close, Heacham, Norfolk; *Career* Nat Serv E Surrey Regt (later Queens Surreys) 1958-60; C E Heath & Co Ltd 1957-63; James Walker & Co Ltd 1964-: tech trainee 1964-67, tech sales rep 1967-69, asst London sales mangr 1969-72, London sales mangr 1972-79, asst to bd of dir 1980-81, commercial off mangr 1981-83, dir 1984-; chm Leatherhad Round Table 1978-79; *Recreations* golf, motoring; *Clubs* RAC, Oil Industs, Effingham Golf ; *Style*— Andrew Cook, Esq; Pooks Hollow, Glendene Avenue, East Horsley, Leatherhead, Surrey KT24 5AY (☎ 048 652 707); James Walker & Co Ltd, Lion Works, Woking, Surrey GU22 8AP (☎ 0483 757 575, fax 0483 755 711, telex 859221 LIONWK G)

COOK, Beryl Frances; da of Adrian Stephen Barton Lansley, and Ella, *née* Farmer-Francis; *b* 10 Sept 1926; *Educ* Kendrick Sch Reading; *m* 1948, John Victor Cook, s of Victor Harry Cook (d 1980); 1 s (John); *Career* artist; *Books* The Works (1978), Private View (1980), One Man Show (1981), Beryl Cook's New York (1985), Beryl Cook's London (1988); illustrated: Seven Years and a Day (1980), Bertie and the Big Red Ball (1982), My Granny (1983); *Style*— Mrs Beryl Cook; 3 Athenaeum St, The Hoe, Plymouth PL1 2RQ

COOK, Charles Alfred George; MC (1944), GM (1944); s of Charles Frederick Cook (d 1939), of London, and Beatrice Alice Grist (d 1935); *b* 20 August 1913; *Educ* St Edward's Sch Oxford, London Univ, Aston Univ Birmingham (DSc); *m* 1939, Edna Constance, da of Herbert Dobson (d 1917), of London; 1 s (John), 1 da (Jill); *Career* served WWII 1939-45 Capt and Maj RAMC; conslt ophthalmic surgn emeritus Guys Hosp 1954; Moorfields Eye Hosp 1956-; Moorfields res fell Inst of Ophthalmology 1951-55; memb of ct of examiners Royal Coll of Surgns of Eng 1964-70; vice-dean Inst of Ophthalmology 1959-62, memb ctee of mgmnt Inst of Ophthalmology; govr: Moorfields Eye Hosp 1962-65, Royal Nat Coll for the Blind 1965-; *Recreations* reading, exploring countryside; *Clubs* Garrick, Athenaeum; *Style*— Charles Cook, Esq, MC, GM; 13 Clarence Terrace, Regents Park, London NW1 4RD

COOK, Christopher William Batstone; s of Cecil Batstone Cook (d 1965), and Penelope Mayall; *b* 21 Jan 1951; *Educ* Eton; *m* 15 July 1978, Margaret Anne, da of Maj John Christopher Blackett Ord, of Whitfield Hall, Hexham, Northumberland; 2 s (Edward b 1982, Benjamin b 1983), 1 da (Emma b 1980); *Career* Lloyds broker; exec dir Bowring Aviation Ltd 1985-; dir: C T Bowring and Co (Insurance) Ltd 1980-, Bowring Space Projects 1979-, md Marsh & McLenna Worldwide 1988; *Recreations* shooting, stalking, fishing; *Style*— Christopher W B Cook, Esq; 24 Granard Rd, London SW12 8UL (☎ 01 675 0239); The Bowring Building, Tower Place, London EC3P 3BE (☎ 01 283 3100, fax 01 623 5769, car ☎ 0860 331 075)

COOK, Sir Christopher Wymondham Rayner Herbert; 5 Bt (UK 1886) of Doughty House, Richmond, Surrey; s of Sir Francis Cook, 4 Bt (d 1978); *b* 24 Mar 1938; *Educ* King's Sch Canterbury; *m* 1, 1958 (m dis 1975), Mrs Malina Gunasekera; 1 s (Richard b 1959), 1 da (Priscilla b 1968); m 2, 1975, Mrs Margaret Miller, da of late John Murray; 1 s (Alexander b 1980), 1 da (Caroline b 1978); *Heir* s, Richard Cook; *Career* dir Diamond Guarantees Ltd 1980-; *Style*— Sir Christopher Cook, Bt; La Fontenelle, Ville au Roi, St Peter Port, Guernsey, CI

COOK, (Kenneth) Clifford; OBE (1979); s of George Kenneth Cook, JP (d 1963); *b* 4 Sept 1916; *Educ* The Leas Sch Hoylake, Oundle; *m* 1945, Hon Barbara Isabel, da of Rt Hon Lord Jamieson, PC, KC (d 1952); 2 s, 2 da; *Career* served RA (TA) 1939-40, Intelligence Corps 1940-46, Maj; FCA; KStJ (1966); *Recreations* lawn tennis, hockey; *Clubs* Athenaeum (Liverpool), Reform; *Style*— K. Clifford Cook, Esq, OBE; 8 Hill Rd, Birkenhead L43 8TL (☎ 051 652 1252)

COOK, Francis; MP (Lab) Stockton North 1983-; s of James and Elizabeth May Cook; *b* 3 Nov 1935; *Educ* Corby Sch Sunderland, De La Salle Manchester, Inst of Educn Leeds; *m* 1959, Patricia, da of Thomas Lundrigan; 1 s, 3 da; *Career* sponsored by MSF; memb select ctee for Employment 1983-87; oppn whip 1987-, memb: Select ctee on Procedure of the House 1988-, N Atlantic Assembly 1988-; *Style*— Frank Cook, MP; House of Commons, London SW1

COOK, (Brian) Francis; s of Harry Cook (d 1959), and Renia Maria, *née* Conlon (d 1962); *b* 13 Feb 1933; *Educ* St Bede's GS Bradford, Univ of Manchester (BA), Downing Coll & St Edmund's House Cambridge (BA, MA), British Sch at Athens; *m* 18 Aug 1962, Veronica Mary Teresa, da of Bernard Dewhirst (d 1974); *Career* Nat Serv 1956-58, 16/15 The Queens Royal Lancers; Dept of Greek and Roman Art Metropolitan Museum of Art NY: curatorial asst 1960, asst curator 1961, assoc curator 1965-69; keeper of Greek and Roman Antiquities Br Museum 1976- (asst keeper 1969-76); corr memb German Archaeological Inst 1977, FSA 1971; *Books* Inscribed Hadra Vases in The Metropolitan Museum of Art (1966), Greek and Roman Art in the British Museum (1976), The Elgin Marbles (1984), The Townley Marbles (1985), Greek Inscriptions (1987), The Rogozen Treasure (1989); *Recreations* reading, gardening; *Clubs* Challoner; *Style*— F Cook, Esq; 4 Belmont Avenue, Barnet, Herts, EN4 9LJ (☎ 01 440 6590); British Museum, London WC1B 3DG (☎ 01 636 1555 ext 8411, 01 323 8411)

COOK, Sir (Philip) Halford; OBE (1965); s of Rev R Osborne Cook (d 1923), and May Cook; *b* 10 Oct 1912; *Educ* Wesley Coll Melbourne, Queen's Coll Melbourne Univ (MA), UCL, Columbia Univ, Kansas Univ (PhD); *m* 1945, Myra Victoria, da of Marcus A Dean (d 1965); 1 s, 1 da; *Career* former industl rels lectr Melbourne Univ, Aust Dept of Labour and Nat Serv 1942-72; perm head (sec) 1968-72, ambass and special labour advsr in Europe Aust Perm Mission Geneva 1973-77; chm governing body Int Labour Orgn 1976; FBPsS, FAPsS, Hon FAPsS 1972; fell Queen's Coll Melbourne Univ; kt 1976; *Recreations* reading, travel; *Clubs* Athenaeum (Melbourne); *Style*— Sir Halford Cook, OBE; 11 Boisdale St, Surrey Hills, Vic 3127, Australia (☎ Melbourne 898 4793)

COOK, Cdre Henry Home; s of George Home Cook (d 1920), of 'Westfield', Bowden, Cheshire, and Lilian Eliza Anna Stewart, *née* Byng-Hall (d 1951); *b* 24 Jan 1918; *Educ* RNC Pangbourne (Dip Communication Advertising Mktg Fndn); *m* 26 June 1943, Theffania (Fania), da of Arthur Percival Saunders (d 1956), of Latchmore Cottage, Gerrards Cross, and Highlands Bolney Sussex; 2 s (Martin b 1944, Charles b 1958), 2 da (Sarah 1948, Alice 1955); *Career* RN: Cadet 1936, Cdre 1973, head Br Def Staff Canada 1970-72, ADC to HM The Queen 1971-72, dir PR RN 1966-70; HM naval attache 1963-66: Ankara, Teheran, Bagdad, Damascus, Amman; Cdr RNC Greenwich 1960-63; dir admin Ellerman Gp Shipping Div 1973-80, dir Christopher Gold Assocs Ltd 1974-87, assoc advsr Industl Soc 1980- 81, vice pres Cncl Inst Admin Mgmnt 1982 (chm 1981), gen cmmr of income tax 1982-, dir PR Operation Raleigh 1984-87, PR conslt 1987-; chm: The Chiltern Soc 1988-, Gerrards Cross and Chalfont Rotary 1986-; hon sec Missions to Seamen Gerrards Cross 1988-; memb Worshipful Co of Shipwrights 1968-, Freeman City of London 1967-; FInstAM, FBIM, MIPR; *Recreations* fishing; *Clubs* Army and Navy, Wig & Pen; *Style*— Cdre Henry Cook; Ramblers Cottage, Layters Green, Chalfort St Peter, Bucks SL9 8TH (☎ 0753 883 724)

COOK, Rear Adm James William Dunbar; CB (1975); s of James Alexander Cook (d 1970), of Pluscarden, Morayshire, and Edith Evangeline May, *née* Cameron (d 1951); *b* 12 Dec 1921; *Educ* Bedford Sch; *m* 1949, Edith, *née* Williams; 1 s, 2 da; *Career* RN 1940, Cdr 1957, Capt 1963, Rear Adm 1972, Asst Chief of Naval Staff (Ops) 1973-75, ret; *Clubs* Army and Navy; *Style*— Rear Adm Bill Cook, CB; Springways Cottage, Farnham Lane, Haslemere, Surrey (☎ 0428 3615)

COOK, Dr John Barry; s of Albert Edward Cook, of Gloucester, and Beatrice Irene, *née* Blake (d 1978); *b* 9 May 1940; *Educ* Sir Thomas Rich's Sch Gloucester, Kings Coll of London (BSc, AKC), Guy's Hosp Med Sch Univ of London (PhD); *m* 1964, Vivien Margaret Roxana, da of Capt Victor Lamb, CBE, RN, of St Albans, Hertfordshire; 2 s (David b 1967, Richard b 1972), 1 da (Susan b 1969); *Career* lectr in physics Guy's Hosp Med Sch 1964-65, sr sci master and head of physics dept Haileybury 1965-72; headmaster: Christ Coll Brecon 1973-82, Epsom Coll 1982-; *Books* Multiple Choice Questions in A-level Physics, Multiple Choice Questions in O-level Physics, Solid State Biophysics; *Recreations* most sports, philately, photography; *Clubs* East India, Devonshire, Sports and Public Schools; *Style*— Dr John Cook; Headmasters House, Epsom Coll, Surrey KT17 4JQ (☎ Epsom 22118); Epsom Coll, Surrey (☎ Epsom 23621)

COOK, Kathryn Jane; *née* Smallwood; MBE (1986); s of George Henry Smallwood, of Tadley, Hampshire, and Sylvia Phyllis, *née* Briggs; *b* 3 May 1960; *Educ* The Hurst Secondary Sch Baughurst, Queen Mary's VI Form Coll Basingstoke, West London Inst of Higher Educn, Birmingham Poly; *m* 1982, Garry Peter Cook, s of Eric Cook, of Walsall, W Midlands; *Career* Cwlth Games Gold Medalist 4 x 100m relay 1978 (WAAAs Champion 100 and 200m); Euro Championships Silver Medalist 4 x 100m 1978; Olympic Games Bronze Medalist 4 x 100m relay 1980 (WAAAs Champion 100 and 200m). World Cup Silver Medalist 100m 1981; Euro Championships Silver Medalist 200m and 4 x 100m relay 1982, Cwlth Games Silver Medalist 200, (Gold Medal 4 x 100m relay) 1982; World Championships Bronze Medalist 200m, Silver Medalist 4 x 100m relay 1983; WAAAs Champion 100m and 200m 1984, Olympic Games Bronze Medalist 400m and 4 x 100m relay 1984; UK records in: 100m, 200m, 300m, 400m and 4 x 100m relay; Cwlth record holder in the 400m; voted Female Athlete of the Year by Br Athletic Writers in 1980, 1981 and 1982; *Style*— Mrs Kathryn Cook, MBE; c/o TSB Eng and Wales, District Off, 19 West Bromwich St, Caldmore, Walsall, W Midlands (☎ 0922 615187)

COOK, Kenneth Anthony; s of Walter Cook (d 1953), and Marion Grace Berry, *née* Lovell (d 1988); *b* 11 Mar 1933; *Educ* Haberdasher's Aske's; *m* 5 July 1952, (Jeanne) Sylvia, da of Thomas Harris; 4 s (Martin b 1960, Ian b 1961, Simon b 1964, Brian b 1967); *Career* Pannell Kerr Forster 1954-63, ptnr Judkins CA's 1963-; FCA, FCIS, ATII, FBIM; *Recreations* swimming; *Clubs* Farmers, Castle (Rochester); *Style*— Kenneth Cook, Esq; Newham Court, Detling, Maidstone, Kent ME14 3ER (☎ 0622 37948); 16 Star Hill, Rochester, Kent ME1 1UU (☎ 0634 830321, fax 0634 830969, telex 9401 6714 JUDKE, car tel 0836 213163)

COOK, His Hon Judge Michael John; s of George Henry Cook (d 1947), and Nora Wilson, *née* Mackman; *b* 20 June 1930; *Educ* Leeds Grammar Sch, Worksop Coll, Leeds Univ; *m* 1, 1958, Anne Margaret Vaughan; 3 s, 1 da; m 2, 1974, Patricia Anne Sturdy; 1 da; *Career* Lt RA (Nat Serv Canal Zone); slr; sr ptnr Ward Bowie 1968-86, rec Crown Ct circuit 1986-; author and broadcaster; former pres London Slrs Litigation Assoc; *Recreations* gardening, reading, theatre; *Clubs* The Law Soc; *Style*— His Hon Judge Michael Cook

COOK, Peter Charles Henry; s of Leslie Cook; *b* 13 June 1935; *Educ* Manchester GS; *m* 1957, Olive, *née* Poulton; 2 s, 1 da; *Career* former div fin dir Tube Investments Ltd, dir Simon Engineering Ltd (fin dir until 1981); pres: Simon United States Corpn 1981-, Simon United States Holdings Inc 1981-; FICA, ACMA; *Style*— Peter Cook, Esq; c/o Simon Engineering, Bird Hall Lane, Cheadle Heath, Stockport; resident in USA

COOK, Richard Herbert Aster Maurice; s (by 1 m) and h of Sir Christopher Cook, 5 Bt; *b* 30 June 1959; *Style*— Richard Cook Esq

COOK, Robert (Robin) Finlayson; MP (Lab) Livingston 1983-; s of Peter Cook and Christina, *née* Lynch; *b* 28 Feb 1946; *Educ* Aberdeen GS, Edinburgh Univ; *m* 1969, Margaret K Whitmore; 2 s; *Career* formerly: chm Edinburgh Corpn Housing Ctee, memb Scottish Assoc Labour Student Organisations, tutor-organiser with WEA; memb Tribune Gp; MP (Lab) Edinburgh Central 1974-1983, oppn front bench spokesman Treasury and Econ Affrs 1980-Nov 1983, Lab leadership campaign mangr for Rt Hon Neil Kinnock 1983, elected to shadow cabinet and front bench spokesman European and Community Affrs Nov 1983-84; PLP campaign coordinator 1984-86; front bench spokesperson for Trade and the City 1986-87, shadow sec of state for Health and Social Security 1987-; *Style*— Robin Cook, Esq, MP; House of Commons, London SW1 (☎ 01 219 5120)

COOK, Roy Edward; s of Herbert Edward Cook (d 1972), of Horsforth, W Yorks; *b* 25 April 1927; *Educ* Dauntsey's Sch Devizes; *m* 1973, Shevaun Mary, da of John Knock of Howsham Hall, York; 3 s (and 1 s, 2 da by previous m); *Career* dir Derwent Valley Hldgs plc; *Recreations* sailing (yachts: 'Dicer'), country life; *Clubs* Royal Cruising, Royal Yorks Yacht (Cdre 1979-80); *Style*— Roy Cook, Esq; Kyreham House, Crambe, York (☎ 065 381 268)

COOK, Hon Mrs; Sarah Isobel; da of Baron Murray of Epping Forest (Life Peer); *b* 1959; *m* 1983, Ian Cook; *Style*— The Hon Mrs Cook; c/o 29 The Crescent, Laughton, Essex

COOK, Thomas Roger Edward; o s of Lt-Col Sir Thomas Russell Albert Mason Cook, JP (d 1970), of Sennowe Park, MP for N Norfolk, 1931-45, and Gweneth Margaret (CC Norfolk 1931-46), o da of Spencer Evan Jones, of Banwell Abbey; gggs of Thomas Cook (d 1884), fndr of the famous travel agency; *b* 21 August 1936; *Educ* Eton, RAC Cirencester; *m* 1, 14 Sept 1960, Virginia Margaret (d 1978), yr da of (Henry) Leslie Courtley Aked (d 1964), of Forest Manor, Knaresborough, Yorkshire; m 2, Carola Zara Lennox, da of Capt Roger Edward Lennox Harvey, Scots Guards (d 1976), of Parliament Piece, Ramsbury, Wilts; *Career* Lt Gren Guards 1954-56; farmer, forester and landowner; chm Royal Forestry Soc (E Anglian Branch) 1970-73; chm CLA (Norfolk Branch) 1979-81; memb: Rural Development Cmmn 1983, Regional Advsry Ctee Forestry Cmmn 1988-; *Recreations* country pursuits, flying; *Clubs* White's, Pratt's, Norfolk; *Style*— Thomas R E Cook, Esq; Sennowe Park, Guist, Norfolk (☎ 032878 202)

COOK, William Birkett; s of William James Cook (d 1980), of Headington, Oxford and Mildred Elizabeth, *née* Birkett; *b* 30 August 1931; *Educ* Dragon Sch, Eton, Trinity Coll Cambridge (BA, MA), Oxford Univ (MA); *m* 20 Dec 1958, Marianne Ruth, da of Albert Edward Taylor (d 1952), of Shrewsbury; 1 s (Andrew b 1965), 2 da (Susan b 1960, d 1965, Deborah b 1962); *Career* asst master Shrewsbury Sch 1955-67 (head of classics 1960-67), headmaster Durham Sch 1967-72, master of Magdalen Coll Sch Oxford 1972-; local govr Oxford HS 1979-; memb HMC 1967, SHA 1967, CSA 1972; *Recreations* music, gardening, scottish country dancing; 27 St Andrew's Rd, Headington, Oxford OX3 9DL (☎ 0865 63190); Magdalen Coll Sch, Oxford OX4 1DZ (☎ 0865 242191)

COOKE; *see*: Fletcher-Cooke

COOKE, Rear Adm Anthony John; CB (1980); s of Rear Adm John Ernest Cooke, CB (d 1980), and Kathleen Mary, *née* Haward (d 1976); *b* 21 Sept 1927; *Educ* St Edward's Sch Oxford; *m* 1951, Margaret Anne, da of Frederick Charles Hynard; 2 s, 3 da; *Career* RN 1945, Cdre in Cmd Clyde Submarine Base 1973-75, Rear Adm 1976, sr naval memb directing staff RCDS 1975-78, Adm Pres RNC Greenwich 1978-80; Freeman City of London, Liveryman Shipwrights' Co; private sec to Lord Mayor of London 1981-; *Recreations* philately; *Clubs* City Livery; *Style*— Rear Adm Anthony Cooke, CB; Chalkhurst, Eynsford, Kent (☎ Farningham 862789)

COOKE, Anthony Roderick Chichester Bancroft; yr (twin) of Maj-Gen Ronald Basil Bowen Bancroft Cooke, CB, CBE, DSO (d 1971), and Joan, da of late Maj Claude Chichester, of Tunworth Down House, Basingstoke; *b* 24 July 1941; *Educ* Ampleforth, London Business Sch (MSc); *m* 1972, Daryll, *née* Aird-Ross; 2 s, 1 da; *Career* FCA 1964; dir Ellerman Lines plc 1976 (chm and chief exec 1985-87) chm and chief exec Cunard Ellerman Ltd 1987-; *Style*— Anthony Cooke, Esq; Poland Ct, Odiham, Hants RG25 1JL (☎ (0256 702060); Cunard Ellerman Ltd, Ellerman House, 12-20 Camomile St, London EC3A 7EX (☎ 01 283 4311, telex 884771/2)

COOKE, Christopher Edward Cobden; s of Reginald Garforth Cooke, of Mudeford, Christchurch, Dorset, and Phylis Mary Blackburn, *née* Wilde; *b* 18 April 1944; *Educ* King Williams Coll IOM, Southampton Univ (LLB); *m* 26 July 1969, (Greta) Yvonne, da of Raymond Vere Alberto (d 1979); 3 da (Lisa b 25 May 1971, Lucy b 11 March 1973, Lindy b 19 Jan 1977); *Career* slr; ptnr Rooks Rider (formerly Rooks & Co) Lincoln's Inn London 1970-; memb: Law Soc 1969, Holborn Law Soc 1988; Freeman: City of London 1966, City of Monroe Louisiana 1986; Liveryman Worshipful Co of Makers of Playing Cards 1966; *Recreations* skiing; *Style*— Christopher Cooke, Esq; Chubbers, Sterings Field, Cookham Dean, Berks (☎ 062 84 736 42); Rooks Rider, 8/9 New Sq, Lincoln's Inn, London WC2A 3QJ (☎ 01 831 7767, fax 01 242 7149, mobile tel 0860 729 920/0836 284 560, telex 261302)

COOKE, David John; s of Matthew Peterson Cooke, of Rugby, and Margaret Rose; *b* 23 August 1956; *Educ* Lawrence Sheriff Sch Rugby, Trinity Coll Cambridge (MA); *m* 31 Mar 1979, Susan Margaret, da of Albert Arthur George, of Rugby; 1 s (Stephen b 1984), 1 da (Helen b 1986); *Career* ptnr Pinsent & Co slrs 1982-; memb Law Society; *Recreations* sailing; *Style*— D J Cooke, Esq; Pinsent & Co, Post & Mail House, 26 Colmore Circus, Birmingham B4 6BH (☎ 021 200 1050, fax (021) 200 1040, telex 335101 PINCO G)

COOKE, Col Sir David William Perceval; 12 Bt (E 1661), of Wheatley Hall, Yorks; s of Sir Charles Arthur John Cooke, 11 Bt, of Fowey, Cornwall (d 1978), and Diana, *née* Perceval; *b* 28 April 1935; *Educ* Wellington, RMA Sandhurst, Open Univ (BA); *m* 30 March 1959, Margaret Frances, da of Herbert Skinner (d 1984), of Knutsford; 3 da (Sara b 1960, Louise b 1962, Catherine b 1968); *Heir* kinsman, Edmund Cooke-Yarborough; *Career* 4/7 RDG 1955, RASC 1958, RCT 1965; CO 25 Tport and Movements Regt RCT 1977-80; MOD 1981-82, Cdr Tport and Movements Br Forces Hong Kong 1982-84, Col 1984, Cdr Tport and Movements HQ NW Dist, Western Dist and Wales 1984-87, Col Movements 1 (Army), MOD 1987-; *Recreations* bird-watching, walking, social and local history, fishing; *Style*— Col Sir David Cooke, Bt; c/o Midland Bank, 19 Princess Street, Knutsford, Cheshire WA16 6BZ

COOKE, Diana, Lady; Diana; o da of Maj-Gen Sir Edward Maxwell Perceval, KCB, DSO, JP (d 1955), of The Grange, Farnham, Surrey, and his 2 wife Norah, *née* Mayne; *m* 12 July 1932, Maj Sir Charles Arthur John Cooke, 11 Bt (d 1978); 1 s, 1 da; *Style*— Diana, Lady Cooke; 15 The Esplanade, Fowey, Cornwall

COOKE, George Venables; CBE (1978); s of William Geoffrey Cooke (d 1967), of Dean Bank, The Hill, Sandbach, Cheshire, and Constance Eva, *née* Venables (d 1976); *b* 8 Sept 1918; *Educ* Sandbach Sch Cheshire, Lincoln Coll Oxford (MA, Dip Ed); *m* 11 Oct 1941, Doreen, da of Harold Cooke (d 1984), of Riva, Barracks Lane, Ravensmoor, Nantwich, Cheshire; 1 s (Robin b 1946), 2 da (Susan (Mrs Wilson) b 1951, Prudence (Mrs James) b 1954); *Career* WWII 1939-46, 7 Cheshire Regt TA, RMC Sandhurst, 10 Lancashire Fusiliers, HQ XIV Army, Maj; teacher Manchester GS 1947-51, prof asst (educn) W Riding of Yorks CC 1951-53, asst dir of educn Liverpool 1953-58, dep dir of educn Sheffield 1958-64, dir of educn Lindsey (Lincs) CC 1965-74, co educn offr Lincs CC 1974-78, gen sec Soc of Educn Offrs 1978-84 (pres 1975-76); chm Sec of States advsy ctee on Handicapped Children 1973-74, vice chm Nat Ctee of Enquiry into Special Educn (Warnock Ctee) 1974-78, memb Parole Bd 1984-87; chm Lincs and Humberside Arts 1987-; *Books* Education Committees (with P Gosden, 1986); *Recreations* golf, gardening; *Clubs* Royal Overseas League; *Style*— George Cooke, Esq, CBE; White House, Grange Lane, Riseholme, Lincoln LN2 2LQ (☎ 0522 22667)

COOKE, Gilbert Andrew; s of Gilbert N Cooke, and Laurie Cooke; *b* 7 Mar 1923; *Educ* Bournemouth Sch; *m* 1949, Katherine Margaret Mary McGovern; 1 s, 1 da; *Career* chartered accountant, md C T Bowring and Co Ltd 1976 (dir 1969-, chm and chief exec 1982-); FCA; *Style*— Gilbert Cooke Esq; Kilmarth, 66 Onslow Rd, Burwood Park, Walton-on-Thames, Surrey (☎ Walton 240451)

COOKE, (John) Howard; s of Capt Jack Cooke, MC, of Exeter, Devon, and Ellen Jean, *née* Passmore; *b* 7 Jan 1952; *Educ* Exeter Sch, Queen Mary Coll London (LLB); *m* 1, July 1972 (m dis 1983), Sally-Anne da of Sydney Evans; m 2, 25 March 1983, Dr Jayne Elizabeth Munn; 2 da (Elena b 1983, Lauren b 1986); *Career* admitted slr 1976, ptnr Frere Chelmeley 1980; memb Law Soc; *Recreations* country pursuits; *Style*— Howard Cooke, Esq; 65 Stadella Rd, Herne Hill, London SE24; Cotleigh House, Elstone, nr Chulmleigh, Devon; 28 Lincoln's Inn Fields, London W2 (☎ 01 405 7878, fax 01 405 9056, telex 27 623)

COOKE, Lady Jenifer Patricia Evelyn; da of Evelyn King, Embley Manor, Romsey, Hants, and Hermione, *née* Crutchley; *b* 5 May 1945; *Educ* Fritham House, Queens Sec Coll; *m* 30 July 1966, Sir Robert Cooke (d 1987), s of Robert Victor Cooke (d 1979), of Bristol; 1 s (Patrick b 1967), 1 da (Louise b 1970); *Career* interior decorator 1981-87, owner and admin Athelhampton historic house and gdns (open to public); vice chm Historic Houses Assoc Wessex, exec of Winterbourne Hosp, memb Dorset and Somerset Theatre Co; *Books* Athelhampton Guide Book (1989); *Recreations* reading, walking, music; *Style*— Lady Jenifer Cooke; Athelhampton, Dorchester, Dorset DT2 7LG (☎ 0305 848 363)

COOKE, John Arthur; s of Arthur Hafford Cooke, MBE (d 1987), and Ilse Cooke, *née* Sachs (d 1973); *b* 13 April 1943; *Educ* Dragon Sch, Magdalen Coll Sch Oxford, Univ of Heidleberg, King's Coll Cambridge (BA, MA), LSE; *m* 21 Feb 1970, Tania Frances, da of Alexander Cochrane Crichton; 1 s (Alexander b 1975), 2 da (Olga b 1972, Beatrice b 1977); *Career* Civil Serv 1966: asst princ Bd of Trade 1966, second sec (later first sec) UK delgn to Euro Communities 1969-73, DTI 1973-76, off of the UK permanent rep to Euro Communities 1976-77, DTI 1977-80 institut int d'admin publique Paris 1979), asst sec DTI 1980-84, seconded asst dir Morgan Grenfell & Co 1984-85, DTI 1986-87, under sec DTI 1987-; tstee St Luke's Day Centre Tst; *Recreations* reading, travelling, looking at buildings; *Clubs* Utd Oxford and Cambridge, Cambridge Union; *Style*— John Cooke, Esq; Department of Trade and Industry, 1 Victoria St, London SW1H OET (☎ 01 215 7877, fax 01 222 2629, telex 8811074/5 DTHQ G)

COOKE, Air Vice-Marshal John Nigel Carlyle; CB (1984), OBE (1954); s of Air Marshal Sir Cyril Bertram Cooke, KCB, CBE (d 1972), and Elizabeth Amelia Phyllis, *née* Davies; *b* 16 Jan 1922; *Educ* Felsted, St Mary's Hosp Paddington (MD); *m* 1958, Elizabeth Helena Murray Johnstone; 2 s, 1 da; *Career* prof of aviation med 1974-79, dean of Air Force Medicine 1979-83, sr conslt RAF 1983-85, ret 1985; conslt CAA, conslt advsr to Sultan of Oman's Air Force 1985-; conslt physician King Edward VIII Hosp Midhurst 1988-; FRCP, FRCPE, MFOM; *Recreations* fly fishing, gliding; *Clubs* RAF; *Style*— Air Vice-Marshal John Cooke, CB, OBE; 4 Lincoln Close, Stoke Mandeville, Bucks (☎ 029 61 3852)

COOKE, John Patrick; s of Patrick Cooke (d 1967), of Kilkenny (d 1967), and Winifred Cooke; *b* 18 June 1933; *Educ* Good Cnsl Coll New Ross Co Wexford; *m* 26 Sept 1959, Avril, da of Alfred Palmer, of Croxley Green, Herts; 3 s (Andrew b 1962, Kevin b 1963, Jonathan b 1970); *Career* banking, vice-pres Citibank NA 1977-; exec dir Citicorp Investmt Bank Ltd 1979-; *Recreations* golf; *Clubs* Burhill Golf, Weybridge Surrey, Portmarnock Dublin, Aloha Golf, Marbella; *Style*— John P Cooke, Esq; Spinney Lodge, Firlands, Weybridge, Surrey (☎ 0932 847105); Citicorp Investment Bank Ltd, 335 Strand, London WC2; 71 St Stephens Green, Dublin, Ireland

COOKE, His Hon Judge; (Richard) Kenneth; OBE (1945); s of Richard Cooke, and Beatrice Mary; *b* 17 Mar 1917; *Educ* Sebright Sch Wolverley, Birmingham Univ; *m* 1945, Gwendoline Mary Black; *Career* slr 1939, practising 1945-52, clerk to Justices 1952-70, metropolitan stipendiary magistrate 1970, recorder of the Crown Court 1972-1980, a circuit judge (SE) 1980-; memb Lord Chllr's advsy ctee on Trg of Magistrates 1979-; hon dep chm Magistrates Assoc 1981-82 (chm legal ctee 1980-); licensed reader Rochester Diocese 1970-; pres South West London Branch Magistrates Assoc 1984-; *Style*— His Hon Judge Cooke, OBE; 8 St Paul's Sq, Church Rd, Bromley, Kent (☎ 01 464 6761)

COOKE, Michael Edmond; s of Michael Joseph Cooke, (d 1960), of Thornton Kingston Hill, Kingston-on-Thames, Surrey, and late Mary Margaret, *née* Donaghy; *b* 21 August 1929; *Educ* Beaumont Coll Old Windsor Berks, Lincoln Coll Oxford Univ (MA); *m* 11 March 1961, Jennifer Gwendoline, s of Earnest J Jack, (d 1981), of Crossbush, Summerley, Middleton-on-Sea, Sussex; 1 s (Tristan b 19 Jan 1966), 2 da (Olivia b 12 March 1964, Anastasia b 9 Jan 1968); *Career* 2 Lt RA 1948-49, serv M East; barr Middle Temple; Nat Bank Ltd 1961-69: chief account, sec, asst gen mangr; jt md Banque Paribas London; chm: Paribas Guernsey Ltd, PIL Petroleum & Energy Ltd, Triton Petroleum Ltd 1972-88; dir: Chiers HFC Int Ltd, Copdrex N Sea Petroleum Ltd, EC (Hldgs) Ltd, R & W Hawthorne Leslie & Co Ltd, Heurty Ltd, Heurty Furnaces Ltd, Nuclear Tport Ltd, Paibas Fin Ltd, Torhurst Ltd; md Third Triton Petroleum Ltd 1980-81; dir High Park Securities Inc (USA) 1981-85, Cordel Corp Devpt Ltd, Cordel Mgmnt Ltd 1982-; memb: Lloyds, Middle Temple; *Recreations* tennis, golf, cricket, Marylebone CC; *Clubs* City Univ, Hurlingham, Royal Wimbledon GC, MGC; *Style*— Michael Cooke, Esq; 14 Highbury Rd, Wimbledon, London SW19 7PR; (☎ 01 946 1533, 01 946 5821)

COOKE, Michael John; s of John Cooke (d 1981), and Renée Elizabeth, *née* Holmes; *b* 18 Nov 1945; *Educ* Riland, Bedford; *m* 31 Aug 1968, Janet Margaret, da of William Mason Fullerton; 3 s (James b 1970, Matthew b 1972, Alexander b 1985), 2 da (Melissa b 1976, Louise b 1978); *Career* CA; dir Eurolens Establissement 1983; Lord of the Manor of Edingale; specialist in Soviet Trade; CA; Lord of the Manor of Edingale; dir Euroleys Etablissement 1983; *Recreations* cricket, football, golf; *Style*— Michael Cooke, Esq; Whinrigg House, Borrowcop Lane, Lichfield, Staffs WS14 9DF; Eurolens Etablissement, 30 Monkspath Business Park, Solihull B90 5NZ (☎ 021 745 9111, telex 335307, fax 021 744 9744)

COOKE, Nigel Frank; s of Nigel Cuthbert Cooke (d 1951), of Kassa House, Kassa, Plateau Province, N Nigeria, and Catherine Cooke, *née* Woodhams (d 1964); *b* 25 April 1916; *Educ* Ipswich Sch, Gonville and Caius Coll, Cambridge Univ (MA); *m* 16 Nov 1957, Heather Elizabeth Seymour, da of Arthur Henry Seymour Vivian (d 1985), of 24 Sandy Lodge Rd, Moor Park, Rickmansworth, Herts; 2 s (Richard b 1958, Timothy b 1960), 1 da (Catherine b 1964); *Career* Lieut Nigeria Regt 1939-43, Admin Serv N Nigeria 1938-62, sr resident 1959-62, i/c Kano Province 1961-62, Courtaulds head of mgmnt recruitment 1964-80, chm Moor Park (1968) Ltd 1985; figured in Tales From the Dark Continent, by Charles Allen; *Recreations* reading, bridge, golf; *Clubs* United Oxford and Cambridge Univ, Moor Park Golf; *Style*— Nigel Cooke, Esq; 25 Russell Rd, Moor Park, Northwood, Middlesex HA6 2LP (☎ Northwood 21900)

COOKE, (William) Peter; s of Douglas Edgar Cooke, MC (Lt Durham LI, d 1964), of Gerrards Cross, Bucks, and Florence May, *née* Mills (d 1986); *b* 1 Feb 1932; *Educ* Kingswood Sch Bath, Merton Coll Oxford (MA); *m* 22 April 1957, Maureen Elizabeth, da of Dr E A Haslam-Fox (d 1975), of Holmes Chapel, Cheshire; 2 s (Nicholas b 1959, Andrew b 1964), 2 da (Caroline b 1960, Stephanie b 1970); *Career* Nat Serv RA 1951; joined Bank of England 1955; seconded: to Bank for Int Settlements Basle Switzerland 1958-59, as PA to md of Int Monetary Fund Washington DC 1961-65, as sec City Takeover Panel 1968-69; appointed first dep chief cashier 1970-73, advsr to Govrs 1973-76, head Banking Supervision 1976-85, assoc dir 1982-88; chm: City EEC Ctee 1973-80, ctee on Banking Regulations and Supervisory Practices at the Bank for Int Settlements Basle Switzerland 1977-88, Price Waterhouse World Regulatory Advsy Gp 1989-, chm Merton Soc 1979-; govr Pangbourne Coll 1982-, bd memb Housing Corpn 1988-, memb mgmnt ctee Church Housing Assoc 1977-; *Recreations* music, golf, travel; *Clubs* Overseas Bankers, Denham Golf; *Style*— Peter Cooke, Esq; Price Waterhouse, Southwark Towers, 32 London Bridge St, London SE1 9SY (☎ 01 407 8989, fax 01 378 0647, telex 884657/8)

COOKE, Raymond Edgar; OBE; s of late Edgar Jonathan Cooke; *b* 14 Feb 1925; *Educ* London Univ; *m* 1948 (m dis 1968), Marjorie Evelyn; 1 s, 1 da; m 2, 1987, Jennifer, da of Léon J Goossens CBE (d 1988); *Career* former designs engineer BBC; tech dir Wharfedale Wireless Works Ltd 1955-61; md KEF Electronics Ltd 1961-; FRSA, FBKSTS, FAES; *Style*— Raymond Cooke, Esq, OBE; Kingswood Lodge, Nevill Park, Tunbridge Wells, Kent (☎ 0892 31843; office: 0622 672261, telex Kefel G 96140)

COOKE, Rt Hon Mr Justice; Rt Hon Sir Robin Brunskill; KBE (1986), PC (1977); s of Hon Mr Justice (Philip Brunskill) Cooke, MC (d 1956), and Valmai Digby Gore; *b* 9 May 1926; *Educ* Wanganui Collegiate Sch, Victoria Univ Coll Wellington NZ (LLM), Gonville and Caius Cambridge (MA, PhD, hon fellow); *m* 1952, Phyllis Annette, da of Malcolm Balgownie Miller (d 1968); 3 s; *Career* called to the Bar NZ 1950, Inner Temple 1954 (hon bencher 1985), practised NZ 1955-72, QC 1964, judge of Court of Appeal of New Zealand 1976- (pres 1986-); kt 1977; *Clubs* United Oxford and Cambridge University (London), Wellington (NZ); *Style*— The Rt Hon Mr Justice Cooke; 4 Homewood Cres, Karori, Wellington, New Zealand (☎ 768 059), Court of Appeal (☎ 726 398)

COOKE, Roger Arnold; s of Stanley Gordon Cooke, of Nether Alderley, Cheshire, and Frances Mabel, *née* Reading; *b* 30 Nov 1939; *Educ* Repton, Magdalen Coll Oxford (BA, MA); *m* 16 May 1970, Hilary, da of Eric Robertson, of Shorwell, IOW; 2 s (James b 1972, Thomas b 1975), 2 da (Elizabeth b 1973, Mary b 1979); *Career* called to the Bar Middle Temple 1962, memb ad eundem Lincoln's Inn 1967; practice at the Channcery Bar 1963-, head of chambers 1985-88, jt head of Chambers 1988-, recorder 1987 (asst recorder 1982-87); hon sec Chancery Bar Assoc 1979-, memb Disciplinary Tbnls Bar 1988-; churchwarden Little Berkhamstead 1979-; memb fin and gen purpose ctee Broxbourne (C) Assoc 1986-; Freeman (by purchase) City of London 1986; *Recreations* gardening, photography, history, old buildings, food; *Clubs* Royal Inst of GB; *Style—* Roger Cooke, Esq; The Old Cottage, Howe Green, Hertford SG13 8LH (☎ 089277 61394); 11 New Square, Lincoln's Inn, London WC2A (☎ 01 831 0081, fax 01 405 2560)

COOKE, Prof Ronald Vewick; s of Ernest Oswald Cooke (d 1948), of Maidstone, Kent, and Lilian, *née* Mount (d 1949); *b* 1 Sept 1941; *Educ* Ashford GS, UCL (BSc, MSc, PhD, DSc); *m* 4 Jan 1968, Barbara Anne, da of Albert Henry Baldwin (d 1969), of Petts Wood, Kent; 1 s (Graham Stephen b 1971), 1 da (Emma Louise b 1974); *Career* reader UCL 1975 (lectr 1961-75), vice princ Bedford Coll London 1979-80 (prof 1975-81, dean of sci 1978-80), prof of geography and head of dept UCL 1981-; govr: Watford Boys GS, Watford Girls GS; memb: RGS, Inst Br Geographers, Geological Soc of London; *Books* incl: Geomorphology in Deserts (with A Warren, 1973), Geomorphology in Environmental Management (with J C Doorncamp, 1974), Arroyos and Environmental Change in the American Southwest (with R W Reeves, 1976), Environmental Hazards in Los Angeles (1984), Urban Geomorphology in Dry Lands (with D Brunsden, J C Doomkamp, and DKC Jones, 1982); *Clubs* Athenaeum; *Style—* Prof Ronald Cooke; Dept Geography, University Coll London, 26 Bedford Way, London WC1N OAP (☎ 01 380 7562)

COOKE, Roy; JP (Gravesend 1972, W Midlands 1976); s of Reginald Herbert Cooke, of Sale, Cheshire, and Alice, *née* Brown; *b* 6 May 1930; *Educ* Manchester GS (Scholar), Trinity Coll Oxford (MA); *m* 1957, Claire Marion Medlicott, da of Lt-Col Clifford Stanley Woodward, CBE, JP, DL (d 1974), of Bridgend, Glam; 3 s (Richard, Jeremy, Michael); *Career* mil serv, 1951-54 short serv cmmn RAEC, Acting-Maj Staff Offr, HQ N Army Gp, NATO; schoolmaster: Gillingham GS Kent 1955-56, Woking GS Surrey 1956-58, The Manchester GS 1958-64; head of for languages Stockport Sch 1964-68; headmaster: Gravesend GS 1968-74, King Henry VIII Sch Coventry 1974-77, Coventry Sch; dir Coventry Sch Fndn; memb Headmasters' Conf; *Recreations* reading, music, travel, gardening, photography, fell walking; *Clubs* East India and Public Schs; *Style—* Roy Cooke, Esq, JP; 10 Stivichall Croft, Coventry; Coventry Sch, King Henry VIII, Warwick Rd, Coventry CV3 6AQ (☎ 0203 75050)

COOKE, Hon Mrs (Sarah Myfida Mary); *née* Tyrell-Kenyon; MBE (1952); da of 4 Baron Kenyon (d 1927); *b* 13 Sept 1917; *m* 10 Oct 1966, Col Desmond Aubrey Robert Bancroft Cooke (d 1987), late 13/18 Hussars, yst s of late Lt-Col Sydney Fitzwyman Cooke, of Orwell Lodge, Horsham, Sussex; *Career* formerly in VAD; vice-chm Victoria League for Cwlth Friendship (prev gen hospitality sec); *Style—* The Hon Mrs Cooke; 10 Guthrie St, London SW3 6NU

COOKE, Simon Henry; s of George Bristow Cooke, DFC, of Gestinethorpe Hall, Halstead, Essex, and Frances Evelina, *née* Hopkinson; *b* 16 April 1932; *Educ* Dragon Sch, Marlborough, Caius Coll Cambridge (MA); *m* 9 June 1956, Anne Gillian De Horne, da of Brig John Theodore De Horne Vaizey (d 1982), of Attwoods, Halstead, Essex; 3 s (Jonathan b 1959, Adam b 1960, Matthew b 1964); *Career* admitted slr 1957, ptnr Bristows, Cooke & Carpmell 1960-, chm Critchley Ltd 1978; non exec dir: Trico Folberth Ltd, Bausch & Lomb UK Ltd, Western Electric Ltd; chm of govrs Newport Free GS Essex; memb Law Soc; *Recreations* bird watching, skiing, shooting, travel, gardening; *Style—* Simon Cooke, Esq; Deers, Clavering, Saffron Walden, Essex (☎ 02 7978342); 10 Lincolns Inn Fields, London WC2A 3BP (☎ 01 242 0462, fax 01 242 1232, 01 831 3537, telex 27487)

COOKE, Thomas Fitzpatrick; s of Thomas Fitzpatrick Cooke, Lord Lieut of County Londonderry (d 1926), and Aileen Frances Cooke, *née* Babington (d 1921); *b* 10 July 1911; *Educ* Stowe, Trinity Coll Dublin (Dip Comm); *m* 3 July 1946, Ruth Jones, da of Rt Hon Anthony Brutus Babington QC (d 1972), of Postrush, Co Antrim; 1 s (Stephen b 1955), 1 da (Priscilla b 1948); *Career* WWII RA (Capt) 1939-46, miller and farmer; Ald Londonderry Corpn 1946-52; County of Londonderry: High Sheriff 1949, DL 1950; chm Londonderry Port and Harbour 1967-73; City of Londonderry: High Sheriff 1971-72, Lord Lieut 1975-76; *Recreations* shooting, fishing, gardening; *Style—* Thomas Cooke, Esq; The Lodge, 5 Edenreagh Rd, Eglinton, Londonerry

COOKE-COLLIS, Brig Edward Cunliffe; CBE (1954), DSO (and bar); s of Col William Cooke-Collis, CMG (d 1933), of Castle Cooke, Kilworth, Co Cork, and his 2 wife Elizabeth Marion Shrubsole, *née* Cunliffe (d 1926); *b* 27 Oct 1902; *Educ* Cheltenham, RMC Sandhurst; *m* 23 June 1931, Elizabeth Grace (d 29 Oct 1983), da of Rev Canon John Henry Heigham, of Gilling West, Yorks; 2 da; *Career* 2 Lt Green Howards, Capt 1935, Lt-Col 1946, Col 1946, served WWII, N Africa, Sicily, NW Europe with Eighth Army (despatches 2), ret 1954; Silver Star (USA); *Style—* Brig Edward Cooke-Collis, CBE, DSO; 16 Lark Hill Crescent, Ripon, Yorks

COOKE-YARBOROUGH, Edmund Harry; s of George Eustace Cooke-Yarborough (d 1938); kinsman and hp of Sir David Cooke, 12 Bt; *b* 25 Dec 1918; *Educ* Canford, Ch Ch Oxford (MA); *m* 1952, Anthea Katharine, da of John Alexander Dixon (d 1976), of Market Harborough; 1 s, 1 da; *Career* head instrumentation and applied physics div UK Atomic Energy Authy 1957-80, chief res scientist 1980-82; FEng 1980, FInstP, FEng, FIEE; *Books* An Introduction to Transistor Circuits (1957, second ed 1960), Development of Stirling Engines; *Recreations* tracing archaeological alignments, digital computing, Stirling engines; *Style—* Edmund Cooke-Yarborough Esq; Lincoln Lodge, Longworth, nr Abingdon, Oxon

COOKSEY, David James Scott; s of Dr Frank Sebastian Cooksey, CBE, of Suffolk, and Muriel Mary, *née* Scott; *b* 14 May 1940; *Educ* Westminster, St Edmund Hall Oxford (MA); *m* 1973, Janet Clouston Bewley, da of Dr Ian Aysgarth Bewley Cathie, of Gloucs; 1 s (Alexander b 1976), 1 da (Leanda b 1974), 1 step da (Atlanta Wardell-Yerburgh); *Career* chm Advent Ltd 1987- (md 1981-87); dir: Agricultural Genetics Co 1983-, Br Venture Capital Assoc 1983- (chm 1983-84), European Silicon Structures 1985-, Advent Int Corpn 1985-; chm The Audit Cmmn for Local Govt in England and Wales 1986-, memb Innovation Advsy Bd Dept of Trade and Indust 1988-; *Recreations* sailing, performing and visual arts; *Clubs* Royal Thames Yacht, New (Edinburgh); *Style—* David Cooksey, Esq; Advent Ltd, 25 Buckingham Gate, London SW1E 6LD (☎ 01 630 9811)

COOKSON, Hon Mrs (Angela Mary Martyn); *née* Martyn-Hemphill; er da of 5 Baron Hemphill; *b* 26 Jan 1953; *m* 2 Oct 1982, Robert Edwin Cookson, s of Capt Peter Henry Cookson, MC, of Lower Slaughter, Glos; 1 s (Edward Peter b 1 May 1988), 1 da (Serena Louise b 16 Nov 1986); *Style—* The Hon Mrs Cookson; Manor Farm, Upper Slaughter, Cheltenham, Glos GL54 2JJ

COOKSON, Anthony John; s of John Cookson (d 1971), of Ipswich, and Joyce Creaser, *née* Hutchison; *b* 3 June 1940; *Educ* Northgate GS Ipswich; *m* 8 Oct 1967, Janet, da of Kenneth Noble, of Ipswich; 1 s (John Alexander b 1978), 2 da (Samantha Jo b 1970, Tara Danielle b 1971); *Career* Hadleigh Industs plc: joined 1961, md 1971, gp chief exec 1987; hon tres The Energy Industs Cncl; Freeman: City of London, Worshipful Co of Founders; FBIM 1986; *Recreations* golf, squash, travel, reading; *Clubs* Woodbridge Golf, Annabels; *Style—* Tony Cookson, Esq; Stonehurst, Elm Lane, Copdock, Ipswich (☎ 0473 865 74); No 14, Carmanso, Ampuriabrava, Gerona, Spain; Hadleigh Industs plc, No 1 Cromwell Ct, Greyfriars Rd, Ipswich, Suffolk IP1 1XG (☎ 0473 231 031, fax 0473 232 126, car tel 0860 627 421/0860 521 999, telex 98613)

COOKSON, Catherine Ann; OBE (1985); da of Catherine Fawcett; *b* 20 June 1906; *m* 1940, Thomas Henry Cookson; *Career* novelist, 68 novels published in English and 17 Foreign languages; *Publications include* Kate Hannigan (1950), Maggie Rowan (1954), A Grand Man (1954) (filmed as Jacqueline 1956), The Lord and Mary Ann (1956), Rooney (1957) (filmed 1958), The Menagerie (1958), The Devil and Mary Ann (1958), Fenwick Houses (1960), Love and Mary Ann (1961), Life and Mary Ann (1962), Marriage and Mary Ann (1964), Mary Ann's Angels (1965), Matty Doolin (1965), Katie Mullholland (1967), Mary Ann and Bill (1967), Our Kate (autobiog 1969), The Nice Bloke (1969), The Glass Virgin (1970), The Mallen Streak (1973), The Mallen Girl (1974), The Mallen Litter (1974), Our John Willie (1974), The Invisible Cord (1975), Go Tell It to Mrs Golightly (1977), The Cinder Path (1978), Tilly Trotter (1980), Tilly Trotty Wed (1981), Tilly Trotter Widowed (1982), A Dinner of Herbs (1985), Harold (1985), The Moth (1986), Catherine Cookson Country (memoirs, 1986), The Parson's Daughter (1987), The Cultured Handmaiden (1988), Let Me Make Myself Plain (A Personal Anthology, 1988), The Harrogate Secret (1989); Hon MA Univ of Newcastle upon Tyne 1983; *Recreations* painting; *Style—* Mrs Catherine Cookson; Bristol Lodge, Langley on Tyne, Hexham, Northumberland

COOKSON, Lt-Col Michael John Blencowe; OBE (1986), TD (1969), DL (Northumberland 1983); s of Col John Charles Blencowe Cookson, DSO, TD, DL (d 1987), and Mary Marjorie Banks (now Fanshawe), *née* Askew; *b* 13 Oct 1927; *Educ* Eton, RAC Cirencester; *m* 26 Sept 1957, Rosemary Elizabeth, da of David Aubry Haggie (d 1958), of Red Hall, Haughton-le-Skerne, Darlington; 1 s (James b 1965), 3 da (Jane b 1958, Sarah b 1960, Rosie-Anne b 1963); *Career* Army 1945, posted to E African Forces 1947, demobbed 1948; joined Northumberland Hussars TA 1952, cmd Cadre N Hussars 1969-71, Cadre enlarged to form part of Queens Own Yeomanry became 2 i/c, ret 1972; memb exec ctee Northumberland Assoc of Boys' Clubs 1964-86 (chm 1974-86); joint master: Haydon Foxhounds 1955-58, Morpeth Foxhounds 1960 and 1970-; Parly candidate (C) NW Durham Constituency 1977; memb Morpeth RDC 1965-74; High Sheriff of Northumberland 1976; Vice-Lieut for Northumberland 1987; chm Northumberland Hussar Regimental Assoc 1977-87; chm Queen's Silver Jubilee Appeal 1978; *Recreations* gardening, foxhunting; *Clubs* Northern Counties (Newcastle); *Style—* Col Michael Cookson, OBE, TD, DL; Meldon Park, Morpeth, Northumberland NE61 3SW (☎ 067 072 661)

COOKSON, Prof Richard Clive; s of Clive Cookson (d 1971), of Nether Warden, Hexham, Northumberland, and Marion Amy, *née* James (d 1961); *b* 27 August 1922; *Educ* Harrow, Trinity Coll Cambridge (BA, MA, PhD); *m* 4 Nov 1948, Ellen, da of Dr Amin Fawaz, of Lebanon; 2 s (Clive b 1952, Hugh b 1954); *Career* res fell Harvard Univ 1948, res chemist Glaxo Labs 1949-51, lectr Birkbeck Coll London Univ 1951-57, prof chemistry Southampton Univ 1957-85 (visiting prof Univ of California 1960); Freeman City of Newcastle upon Tyne; FRSC 1959, FRS 1968; *Style—* Prof R C Cookson; Manor House, Stratford Tony, Salisbury SP5 4AT

COOLEY, Sir Alan Sydenham; CBE (1972); s of Hector William Cooley (d 1970), and Ruby Ann Cooley (d 1969); *b* 17 Sept 1920; *Educ* Geelong GS, Melbourne Univ; *m* 1949, Nancie Chisholm, da of Ivan Sinclair Young (d 1968); 4 da; *Career* chm Aust Public Service Bd 1971-77; sec Dept of Productivity 1977-80, ret; kt 1976; *see Debrett's Handbook of Australia and New Zealand for further details*; *Style—* Sir Alan Cooley, CBE; 330 Canadian Bay Rd, Mt Eliza, Vic 3930, Australia

COOLS-LARTIGUE, Sir Louis; OBE (1955); s of Theodore Cools-Lartigue, of Roseau, Dominica, and Emily, *née* Giraud; *b* 18 Jan 1905; *Educ* Convents of St Lucia and Dominica, Dominica GS; *m* 1932, Eugene, da of Robert W Royer; 2 s, 4 da; *Career* Dominica Civil Service 1924, chief sec Windward Islands 1951, ret 1960, govr of Dominica 1967-78, KStJ 1975; kt 1968; *Style—* Sir Louis Cools-Lartigue, OBE; 7 Virgin Lane, Roseau, Commonwealth of Dominica, West Indies

COOMBE, Anthony Joseph; s of Edwin Harry Coombe (d Burma 1944), of Thorverton, Devon, and Kathleen Joyce Wellington, *née* Garland-Wells; *b* 23 May 1942; *Educ* Sherborne Sch, Sidney Sussex Coll Cambridge (BA, MA); *m* 3 Feb 1968, Helen Elizabeth, da of Hugh Campbell Crawford, of St Johns Wood; 4 da (Hannah b 1971, Tabitha b 1971, Thomasina b 1976, Tessa b 1978); *Career* mktg dir Sturtevant Welbeck Ltd 1973-78; Sturtevant Engrg Co Ltd: dep md 1978-83, md 1983-89; memb Westminster North Cons Assoc; FInstD 1974, MInstM 1974; *Style—* Anthony Coombe, Esq; 1 Woronzow Rd, St Johns Wood, London NW8 6QB (☎ 01 722 0234); 88 Les Oliviers, 1 Avenue Des Hellenes, Beaulieu Sur Mer, France AM; Sturtevant Engineering Co Ltd, Westergate Rd, Moulsecoomb Way, Brighton BN2 4QB (☎ 0273 601 666, fax 0273 570 549, telex 87658)

COOMBE, Denys Baynham; s of Arthur Edward (d 1936), and Phyllis Mina, *née* Baynham (d 1964); *b* 21 Nov 1918; *Educ* Blundell's Sch, Architectural Assoc Sch of Architecture London (AADip); *m* 30 Aug 1952, June Swinford, da of John Lindsay Lee-Jones (d 1974); 1 s (Nicholas b 1957), 1 da (Rosemary b 1953); *Career* architect; served Royal Bombay Sappers and Miners WWII, princ DB and JS Coombe Chartered Architects 1964; RIBA; *Recreations* music, gardening, walking; *Clubs* Architectural Assoc; *Style—* Denys B Coombe, Esq; 21 Petworth Rd, Haslemere, Surrey (☎ 0428 3572)

COOMBE, Donald Howard; JP (1973); *b* 21 Oct 1927; *Educ* Northbrook C of E Sch Lee, Roan Sch Greenwich, Univ of The World (MA); *m* 5 June 1948, Betty Joyce, da of George William Adie (d 1938); 2 s (Richard Howard b 25 April 1953, David Peter b 8 Oct 1958); *Career* RN 1942-47, hon cmmn Adm Texas Navy 1976; chm: RTC Ltd Lloyds Brokers 1971-, Portcullis Insur Servs Ltd 1985-; memb Lloyds 1974; fndr chm Coombe Tst Fund, fndr chm Coombe Holiday Tst Fund (all three registered charities for needy children), chm Victoria Wellesley Tst, dep pres Thanet Red Cross, former cmmr Scouts Assoc; hon attorney-gen N Carolina, chm of bench 1982, cmmr Income Tax 1978-85; Freeman: City of London 1970, City of Dallas Texas 1976; Liveryman Worshipful Co of Poulters 1978; Order of St George Sweden 1974; *Recreations* charity fund-raising, social work, boxing; *Clubs* National Sporting, Wig & Pen; *Style*— Donald H Coombe, Esq, JP; Sunarise, Beckenham Place Park, Kent BR3 2BN (☎ 01 658 2714); 7 Lovat Lane, London EC3R 8DT (☎ 01 283 7367, fax 01 283 3593)

COOMBE, His Hon Judge Gerald Hugh; s of Capt William Stafford Coombe, Merchant Marine (d 1962), and Mabel Florence, *née* Bullas (d 1983); *b* 16 Dec 1925; *Educ* Alleyn's, Hele's Sch Exeter; *m* 17 Aug 1957, Zoe Margaret, da of Sidney Ivor Richards, of Penarth, S Wales; 1 s (Robert b 1960), 1 da (Fiona b 1963); *Career* RAF Navigator 1944-48; slr Whitehead Monckton and Co Maidstone 1953-86, HM coroner Maidstone Kent District 1962-86, circuit judge 1986-; Hon MA Oxon; *Recreations* gardening; *Clubs* RAF; *Style*— His Hon Judge Coombe

COOMBE, John David; s of Sidney Coombe; *b* 17 Mar 1945; *Educ* Haberdashers' Aske's, London Univ (BSc); *m* 1970, Gail Alicia, *née* Brazier; 3 da; *Career* CA, financial controller Glaxo Holdings 1986- mangr fin and Treasy Charter Consolidated plc 1984-86, gp tres The Charterhouse Gp plc 1976-84; *Style*— John Coombe, Esq; Up Yonder, 76 Valley Rd, Rickmansworth, Herts (☎ 0923 776817)

COOMBE, (John) Kinred; s of G A Coombe, MC (d 1968), and Louise Marie, *née* Hockle (d 1984); *b* 15 Dec 1925; *Educ* Mill Hill Sch; *m* 7 June 1956, (Dorothy) Moira, da of Stanley Lockwood (d 1958), of Harrogate; *Career* Capt TA 1944-47; chm and md Leaf & Carver Ltd; gen cmmr for income tax; Freeman: City of London, Worshipful Co of Painter-Stainers 1955; *Recreations* rugby football admin, yachting, shooting, fishing; *Clubs* Royal Thames Yatch, Old Millhillian's; *Style*— Kinred Coombe, Esq; Etna House, 350 Kennington Rd, London SE11 4LH (☎ 01 735 8434, fax 01 793 0462, telex 919349)

COOMBE, His Hon Judge Michael Rew; s of John Rew Coombe (d 1985), of Hunton Bridge, King's Langley, Herts, and Phyllis Mary (d 1980); *b* 17 June 1930; *Educ* Berkhamsted, New Coll Oxford (MA); *m* 7 Jan 1961, (Elizabeth) Anne, da of Tom Hull, (d 1957); 3 s (Nicholas b Dec 1961, Jonathan b and d 1966, Peter b 1970), 1 da (Juliet b 1967); *Career* Nat Serv RAF; barr Middle Temple 1957, second prosecuting counsel to the Inland Revenue Centl Criminal Ct and 5 Cts of London Sessions 1971, second counsel to the Crown Inner London Sessions 1971-74, first counsel to the Crown Inner London Crown Ct 1974, second jr prosecuting counsel to the Crown Central Criminal Ct 1975-77, (fourth jr 1974-75), rec of the Crown Ct 1976-85, first jr prosecuting counsel to the Crown Central Criminal Ct 1977-78, a sr prosecuting counsel to the Crown at the Central Criminal Ct 1978-85, master of the bench Middle Temple 1984-, circuit judge 1985, Central Criminal Ct 1986-; Freeman City of London 1986; *Recreations* theatre, antiquity, art and architecture, printing; *Style*— His Hon Judge Coombe; Central Criminal Court, Old Bailey, City of London

COOMBE-TENNANT, Alexander John Serocold; s of Charles Coombe Tennant, JP (d 1928), of Cadoxton Lodge, Vale of Neath, S Wales, and Winifred Margaret, *née* Serocold, JP, (d 1956); *b* 20 Nov 1909; *Educ* Sherborne, Trinity Coll Cambridge (BA); *m* 10 Sept 1954, Jenifer Margaret, da of Frederic, JP; 3 s (Charles b 1955, John b 1957, Mark b 1958), 2 da (Rosalie b 1960, Susanna b 1964); *Career* min of econ warfare 1940-45, Army Gen List 2/Lt A/Major 1944; stockbroker, memb LSE; ptnr Cazenove & Co 1952-79; dir Societe Generale Merchant Bank Ltd 1979-89, GT Japan Investmt plc 1979-89, Freeman City of London, Liveryman Worshipful Co of Clothworkers (1955); *Clubs* Naval and Military; *Style*— A J S Coombe-Tennant, Esq; Gostrode Farm, Chiddingfold, Godalming, Surrey GU8 4SR (☎ 0428 4598); C/o G T Management plc, 8 Devonshire Square, London EC2

COOMBES, Lt-Col Brian John Nevill; s of Reginald Ernest Coombes (d 1965), of Ruislip, and Margaret Theodora, *née* Nevill (d 1980); *b* 1 Mar 1937; *Educ* The King's Sch Harrow; *m* 31 March 1973, Alana Stephannie, da of Maj Kenneth Clifford Dudley, of Chalfont St Peter, Bucks; 1 s (Dominic b 2 Oct 1975), 1 da (Kirsty b 6 Sept 1979); *Career* cmmnd Royal Tank Regt 1956, GSO 3 Ops HQ 7 Armd Bde 1969-71, 2 i/c 4 Royal Tank Regt 1976-77, Exec Offr and Mil Asst to Sr Br Staff Offr HQ Allied Forces Central Europe 1978-81, Lt-Col 1980, COS HQ Aldershot Garrison 1981-83, ret 1983; dep registrar Corpn of the Sons of the Clergy 1982-; memb Fleet Parochial Parish Cncl, govr All Saint's C of E Sch Fleet, parish clerk St John's Westminster; memb Worshipful Co of Parish Clerks; *Recreations* fly fishing, wine making, occasional shooting; *Style*— Lt-Col Brian Coombes; 37 Velmead Rd, Fleet, Hants GU13 9LJ (☎ 0252 622745); Corpn of the Sons of the Clergy, 1 Dean Trench St, Westminster SW1P 3HB (☎ 01 222 1138)

COOMBS, Anthony Michael Vincent; MP (C) Wyre Forest 1987-; s of Clifford Keith Coombs, of Stripes Hill House, Knowle, Nr Solihull, W Midlands, and Celia Mary Gostling, *née* Vincent; *b* 18 Nov 1952; *Educ* Charterhouse, Worcester Coll Oxford (MA); *m* 21 Sept 1984, Andrea Caroline, da of Daniel Pritchard, of 11 Exeter Rd, Netherton Dudley, W Midlands; 1 s (Alexander Graham David); *Career* founder and md Grevayne Properties Ltd; dir: Tweedies (Wolverhampton) Ltd 1976, Sartorial Shops Ltd 1976; sec: Back Bench Educn Ctee, All Party Human Rights Gp; *Recreations* tennis, golf, skiing, football, music; *Style*— Anthony M V Coombs, Esq, MP; 47 Clarence St, Kidderminster (☎ 0562 752 439); Grevayne Properties Ltd, 51/53 Edgbaston St, Birmingham B5 4QH (☎ 021 622 4881, car ☎ 0860 516400)

COOMBS, Derek Michael; s of Clifford Coombs (d 1975), and Elizabeth Mary, *née* Evans (d 1974); *b* 12 August 1937; *Educ* Bromsgrove Sch; *m* 1, 28 Jan 1959 (m dis 1985), Patricia Teresa, *née* O'Toole; 1 s (Fiann b 27 Sept 1968), 1 da (Siân b 1 Feb 1967); m 2, 14 June 1986, Jennifer Sheila, da of Lt Cdr Edward Lonsdale, DSO, RN, of Langness, Woodgaston Lane, Hayling Island, Hants; 1 s (Jack Edward Clifford b 21 Sept 1987); *Career* chm Hardanger Props plc 1972-, dir Metalrax Gp plc 1975-, chm and md S & U Stores plc 1976-, (Named as one of the top 100 in The British Entrepreneur 1988); political journalist; MP (Cons) Yardley 1970-74; govr Royal Hosp & Home Putney; *Recreations* friends, tennis, skiing; *Style*— Derek Coombs, Esq; Cheyne Row, London SW3

COOMBS, Prof Robert Royston Amos (Robin); s of late Charles Royston Amos Edris Owen Coombs (d 1972); *b* 9 Jan 1921; *Educ* Diocesan Coll Cape Town SA, Univ of Edinburgh (BSc), Univ of Cambridge (PhD, ScD); *m* 13 Sept 1952, Anne Marion, da of Charles Geoffrey Blomfield; 1 s (Robert Christopher b 30 Aug 1954), 1 da (Rosalind Edris Lucy b 13 Jan 1956); *Career* WWII volunteer Royal Scots 1939, reserved occupation; Univ of Cambridge: asst dir res dept pathology 1948, reader of immunology 1962, Quick prof biology immunology div dept pathology 1965, emeritus prof 1988; Stringer fell Kings Coll 1947-56, fell Corpus Christi Coll 1962-; for correspondent Royal Belgium Acad Medicine 1979; Hon MD Linköping Sweden 1973, Hon dr med vet Copenhagen 1979, Hon DSc Guelph Canada 1981, Hon DSc Edinburgh 1984; FRS 1965, FRCPath 1968, MRCVS 1943, Hon FRCP 1973; *Books* Serology of Conglutination (with AM Coombs and DG Ingram 1961), Clinical Aspects of Immunology (co-ed with PGH Gell 1963,1968,1975); *Style*— Prof Robert Coombs; 6 Selwyn Gdns, Cambridge CB3 9AX (☎ 0223 352681)

COOMBS, Simon Christopher; MP (C) Swindon 1983-; s of Ian Peter Coombs (d 1981), of Weston-super-Mare, and Rachel Margaret Anne, *née* Robins; *b* 21 Feb 1947; *Educ* Wycliffe Coll, Reading Univ (BA, MPhil); *m* 1983, Kathryn Lee Coe Royce; *Career* Reading: County Boro Cncl 1969-72, Boro Cncl 1973-84, chm Transportation Ctee 1976-83, dep Cons ldr 1976-81 (chief whip 1983); mktg exec Br Telecom and PO Telecommunications 1970-81, mktg mangr Telex Networks Br Telecom 1981-83; chm Cons Party Wessex Area 1980-83, memb Nat Exec Cons Pty 1980-83; chm Wessex YCs 1973-76; PPS: to Min for Info Technol 1984, PPS to Min for the Environment 1984-85; chm All Pty Cable TV Group, tres Parly Information Technol Ctee, chm All Party Food and Health Forum, memb Employment Select Ctee 1987-, vice chm Conservative Back bench tourism ctee, chm Anglo-Malawi Parly Gp; *Recreations* cricket, philately, music; *Clubs* Swindon Conservative; *Style*— Simon Coombs, Esq, MP; House of Commons, London SW1

COONEY, Raymond George Alfred (Ray); s of Gerard Joseph (d 1987), of London, and Olive Harriet, *née* Clarke (d 1975); *b* 30 May 1932; *Educ* Alleyns Coll Dulwich; *m* 8 Dec 1962, Linda Ann, da of Leonard Spencer Dixon (d 1985), of Epping; 2 s (Danny b 1964, Michael b 1966); *Career* Nat Serv RASC 1950-52; actor, writer, prodr, dir; acting debut Sons of Norway Palace Theatre 1946; playwright: One For The Pot (1961), Chase Me Comrade (1964), Charlie Girl (1965), Not Now Darling (1967), Move Over Mrs Markham (1969), Why Not Stay for Breakfast? (1970), There Goes the Bride (1974), Run for your Wife (1983), Two into One (1984), Wife Begins at Forty (1985), It Runs in the Family (1984); dir of most of the above; prodr: Lloyd George knew My Father (1972), Say Goodnight to Grandma (1973), At the End of the Day (1973), The Dame of Sark (1974), A Ghost on Tiptoe (1974), Bodies (1980), Whose Life Is It Anyway? (1980), They're Playing Our Song (1980), Elvis (1981), Duet for One (1981), Childres of a Lesser God (1982); fndr The Theatre of Comedy Co 1983 (artistic dir 1983-88); memb Actors Equity; *Recreations* tennis, swimming; *Style*— Ray Cooney, Esq; 1-3 Spring Gdns, London SW1 (☎ 01 839 5098)

COOP, Geoffrey Brian; s of Roy Coop, of Raymonds Hill, Axminster, Devon, and Doris, *née* Hall (d 1970); *b* 30 Mar 1933; *Educ* Cheltenham, Clare Coll (MA); *m* 20 July 1962, (Margaret) Valerie, da of Fredrick George Tanton; 1 s (Andrew Christopher b 1970), 1 da (Joanna Kate b 1968); *Career* ptnr Rowley Pemberton and Co 1960-81 (subsequently Rowley Pemberton Robertsi and Co), ptnr fin and admin Pannell Kerr Forster 1981- (on merger with Rowley Pemberton Roberts and Co); FCA; *Recreations* cdre Hayling Island Sailing Club, theatre, yacht racing; *Clubs* Royal Thames Yacht, Lloyd's Yacht, Hayling Island Sailing; *Style*— Geoffrey Coop, Esq; The Old Barn, 45 Bath Rd, Emsworth, Hants PO10 7ER (☎ 0243 374 376); Pannell Kerr Forster, Pannell House, Park St, Guildford, Surrey GU1 4HN (☎ 048 364 646)

COOP, Sir Maurice Fletcher; s of George Harry Coop (d 1922), and Ada Coop; *b* 11 Sept 1907; *Educ* Epworth Coll Rhyl, Emmanuel Coll Cambridge; *m* 1948, Elsie Hilda, da of Harry Robert Brazier; *Career* slr 1932; dir Dunlop Rubber Co Ltd 1966-70; kt 1973; *Recreations* association football, cricket; *Clubs* Utd Oxford and Cambridge Univ; *Style*— Sir Maurice Coop; 39 Hill St, Berkeley Sq, London W1 (☎ 01 491 4549); Brendon Cottage, Punchbowl Lane, Dorking, Surrey (☎ (0306) 882835)

COOPER *see also*: Ashley-Cooper, Astley Cooper, Mansfield Cooper

COOPER, Hon Artemis (Alice Clare Antonia Opportune); only da of 2 Viscount Norwich; *b* 22 April 1953; *m* 1 Feb 1986, Antony James Beevor, s of John Grosvenor Beevor, OBE (d 1987), of 161 Fulham Rd, London SW3; *Career* writer; *Style*— The Hon Artemis Cooper; 54 St Maur Rd, London SW6

COOPER, Dr Barrington Spencer; s of Maurice Lionel Cooper (d 1950), and Dena, *née* Orman (d 1959); *b* 15 Jan 1923; *Educ* Grocer's Co Sch, Queen's Coll Cambridge (external BA), St Bart Hosp Med Sch London (MB, BS), Cancer Meml Hosp NY Univ; *m* 1, Fay Helena, *née* Harman; 1 da (Victoria Ann b 18 Feb 1957); m 2, 16 Dec 1988, Jane Eva Livermore Wallace, da of Edward Charles Livermore (d 1976), of Knight's Hill Farm, Westhill, Buntingford, Herts; *Career* Capt RAMC 1947-49; formerly: house physician Whittington Hosp and Ashford Co Hosp, med registrar Oster House Hosp, clinical asst in psychiatry St Barts Hosp, London Jewist Hosp and Nat Hosp for Nervous Diseases, visiting physician Fndn for Manic Depression NYC, corr assoc WHO Psychosocial Centre Stockholm, psychosomatic investigator for WHO, med advsr for various hosp projects and private cos; currently: dir Allied Med Diagnostic Clinic, visitor Boston Univ Med Sch, consulting physician The Clinic of Psychotherapy and Bowden House Clinic, visiting physician The Strang Inst of Preventive Med NYC; med advsr: West One Prodns Inc, Fabyan Films Ltd, World Film Servs, New Media Med Univ; author of various specialist papers; dir Fabyan Ltd and Fabyan Films Ltd, independent film prodr: The One-Eyed Soldiers, The Doctor and the Devils; memb: Assoc of Independent Prodrs, BAFTA; involved with Salerno Int Youth Orchestra Festival; FRSH, fell Psychosomatic Res Soc, MRCGP; memb: med section Br psychological Soc, Soc of Clinical Psychiatrists, Br Assoc of Counselling, Assoc of Family Therapy, London Jewist Hosp Soc; affiliate RCPsych; *Books* Helix (Script, 1982), Cockpits (1987), Travel Sickness (1982), Consumer Guide to Prescription Medicines (1989); *Recreations* film, music, theatre, fine arts, swimming, sailing, rowing; *Clubs* Regency; *Style*— Dr Barrington Cooper; 21 Connaught Sq, London W2 2HJ (☎ 01 706 4191); Flat F, 21 Devonshire Place, London W1N 1PD (☎ 01 935 0113, fax 01 486 0505)

COOPER, Beryl Phyllis; QC (1977); o da of Charles Augustus Cooper (d 1981), and Phyllis Lillie, *née* Burrows; *b* 24 Nov 1927; *Educ* Surbiton HS, Birmingham Univ (BCom); *Career* recorder of the Crown Court 1977-; memb: Criminal Injuries Compensation Bd 1978, Nurses and Professions Allied to Medicine Pay Review Bd 1984; bencher Gray's Inn (1988); *Recreations* golf, swimming, theatre; *Clubs* English Speaking Union, Caledonian (Edinburgh); *Style*— Miss Beryl Cooper, QC; 31 Alleyn Park, Dulwich, London SE21 (☎ 01 670 7012); 8d South Cliff Tower, Eastbourne, Sussex; 2 Dr Johnson's Buildings, Temple, London EC4 (☎ 01 353 5371)

COOPER, Brian; s of Frederick Hubert Cooper, and Florence Mabel, *née* Field; *b* 1

Jan 1936; *Educ* St Albans Sch, De Havilland Aeronautical Techn Sch, Hatfield Poly, London Business Sch; *m* 21 Nov 1959, Marjorie Anne (Sue), da of Ronald John More (d 1973); 2 da (Jenny b 1962, Charlotte b 1967); *Career* Flying Offr RAF 1959-62; subsidiary co dir: Firth Cleveland GKN Gps (Germany, UK) 1962-74, Bowater Corpn Ltd (UK, France, Belgium, Holland, Germany) 1974-84; asst md Hargreaves Gp plc 1984-87, dir Coalite Gp plc 1987-; hon fell Brighton Poly 1987; CEng, MRAeS, FIMechE; *Recreations* squash, sailing, skiing; *Clubs* RAF; *Style—* Brian Cooper, Esq; Marton Cum Grafton, N Yorks; Coalite Gp plc, PO Box 21, Chesterfield, Derbys S44 6AB (☎ 0246 822281, fax 0246 240265)

COOPER, Prof Cary Lynn; s of Harry Cooper, of Los Angeles, Calif, USA, and Caroline Lillian, *née* Greenberg; *b* 28 April 1940; *Educ* Fairfax Sch Los Angeles, Univ of Calif (BS, MBA), Univ of Leeds (PhD); *m* 1, 1970 (m dis 1984), (Edna) June Taylor; 1 s (Hamish Scott b 1972), 1 da (Natasha Beth b 1974); m 2, 1984, Rachel Faith Davies; 2 da (Laura Anne b 1982, Sarah Kate b 1984); *Career* prof of mgmnt educn methods UMIST 1975-79, of organisational psychology UMIST; ed-in-chief Jl for Organizational Behavior 1980-, past advsr WHO and ILO 1982-84, memb bd of tstees American Inst of Stress, recipient BPS Myers lecture 1986, hon prof of psychology Univ of Manchester 1986-, pres Br Acad of Mgmnt 1986-, chm Professional Affairs Ctee (OPD) Int Assoc of Applied Psychology 1987-, past advsr Home Office on Police Stress 1982-84; Hon MSC Univ of Manchester 1979; FBPsS, BAM, IAAP, AM; *Books inc*: T-Groups (1971), Theories of Group Processes (1976), Developing Social Skills in Managers (1976), Stress at Work (jtly 1978), Executives Under Pressure (1978), Behavioural Problems in Organisations (1979), Learning From Others in Groups (1979), The Executive Gypsy (1979), Current Concerns in Occupational Stress (1980), The Stress Check (1980), Improving Interpersonal Relations (1981), Psychology and Management (1982), Management Education (jtly 1982), Stress Research (1983), Public Faces, Private Lives (jtly 1984), Working Women (jtly 1984), Psychology for Managers (jtly 1984), Man and Accidents Offshore (jtly 1986), Pilots Under Stress (jtly 1986), Women and Information Technology (jtly 1987), Pressure Sensitive (jtly 1988), High Flyers (jtly 1988), Living with Stress (1988), Organisational Stress (jtly 1988), Early Retirement (jtly 1989); *Recreations* swimming, reading, squash, writing children's books, following politics; *Clubs* St Jame's; *Style—* Prof C L Cooper; 25 Lostock Hall Rd, Poynton, Cheshire (☎ 0625 871 450); Manchester Sch of Management, Univ of Manchester Inst of Science & Tech, PO Box 88, Manchester M60 1QD (☎ 061 236 3311 ext 2272, fax 061 228 7040)

COOPER, David Jackson; s of late Charles Cooper; *b* 3 Feb 1929; *Educ* Churchers Coll Petersfield, Univ Coll Southampton, Univ Coll of N Wales; *m* 1954, Patricia Mary; 3 s, 2 da; *Career* md Forest Thinnings Ltd 1962-; dir: Economic Forestry (Hds) Ltd 1977-, Furniture and Timber Industry Training Bd 1979-; sr vice pres British Timber Merchants Assoc 1980-; *Style—* David Cooper, Esq; Candovers, Hartley Mauditt, Alton, Hants (☎ 042 050 293, office 0420 83504)

COOPER, Derek Macdonald; s of Stephen George Cooper (d 1958), and late Jessie Margaret Macdonald; *b* 25 May 1925; *Educ* Raynes Park Co Sch, Portree HS, Wadham Coll Oxford (MA); *m* 17 Oct 1953, Janet Marian, da of Robert Feaster; 1 s (Nicholas b 1957), 1 da (Penelope Jane b 1954); *Career* Leading Seaman RNVR 1943-47; broadcaster, journalist and author; prodr Radio Malaya 1950 (ret controller of progs 1960), prodr Roving Report ITN 1960-61; radio progs incl: Today, Ten O'Clock, Newstime, PM, Town and Country, A La Carte, Home This Afternoon, Frankly Speaking, Two of a Kind, You and Yours, Northbeat, New Worlds, Asian Club, Speaking for Myself, Conversations with Cooper, Friday Call, Its Your Line, Offshore Britons, Person to Person, Meridien Book Programme; tv progs incl: World in Action, Tomorrow's World, Breathing Space, A Taste of Britain, The Caterers, World About Us, I Am An engineer, Men and Materials, Apart from Oil, Money Wise, One in a Hundred, The Living Body, From the Face of the Earth; columnist: The Listener, The Guardian, Observer magazine, World Medicine, Scottish Field, Sunday Standard, Homes and Gardens, Saga magazine, Scotland on Sunday; contrib: Taste, A La Carte, The West Highland Free Press; Glenfiddich Trophy as wine and food writer 1973 and 1980, Broadcaster of the Year 1984; fndr memb and first chm Guild of Food Writers 1985- (pres 1988); *Books* The Bad Food Guide (1967), Skye (second edn 1977, third edn 1989), The Beverage Report (1970), The Gullibility Gap (1974), Hebridean Connection (1977), Guide to the Whiskies of Scotland (1978), Road to the Isles (1979, Scottish Arts Cncl Award 1980), Enjoying Scotch (with Diane Pattullo 1980), Wine with Food (1980, second edn 1986), The Whisky Roads of Scotland (with Fay Godwin 1982), The Century Companion to Whiskies (1983), Skye Remembered (1983), The World of Cooking (1983), The Road to Mingulay (1985), The Gunge File (1986), A Taste of Scotch (1989); *Style—* Derek Cooper, Esq; 4 St Helena Terr, Richmond, Surrey TW9 1NR (☎ 01 940 7051); Seafield House, Portree, Isle of Skye (☎ 0478 2380)

COOPER, Wing Cdr Donald Arthur; AFC (1961); s of Albert Arthur Cooper (d 1965), and Elizabeth Barbara, *née* Edmonds; *b* 27 Sept 1930; *Educ* Queen's Coll British Guiana, RAF Coll Cranwell, Open Univ (BA); *m* 5 April 1958, (Ann) Belinda, da of Adm Sir Charles Woodhouse, KCB (d 1978); 3 s (Andrew Cooper b 1959, Duncan Cooper b 1961, Angus Cooper b 1964); *Career* pilot on day fighters and trg sqdns RAF 1952-56, Empire Test Pilots Sch 1957, pilot Experimental Flying Dept RAE Farnborough 1958-60, RAF Staff Coll 1961, (Airline Tport Pilot's Licence Helicopters 1961; areoplanes 1972), Sqdn Cdr CFS Helicopter Wing 1962-64, HQ Flying Trg Cmd 1964-66, Def Ops Requirements Staff MOD 1966-70, ret 1960; Air Accidents Investigation Branch Dept of Tport (formerly Accidents Investigation Branch Dept of Trade): inspr of accidents 1970, chief inspr 1986; FRAeS 1984; *Recreations* amateur dramatics, dancing; *Style—* Wing Cdr Donald Cooper, AFC; 7 Lynch Rd, Farnham, Surrey GU9 8BZ (☎ 0252 715 519); Air Accidents Investigation Branch, Dept of Transport, RAE Farnborough, Hants GU14 6TD (☎ 0252 510 300, fax 0252 540 535, telex 858119 ACCINV G)

COOPER, Donald Frederick; OBE (1978); s of Henry John Neiles Cooper (d 1978), and Mabel, *née* Bartlett (d 1973); *b* 10 Nov 1920; *Educ* Itchen GS Southampton; *m* 7 March 1945, Robertha Margaret (Bobbie), da of James Peterson (d 1921); 1 s (John Neils b 1949), 1 da (Jacqueline Margaret b 1946); *Career* WWII RE: 4 Inf Div (wounded Dunkirk) 1939-41, 1 Airborne Div 1941-46, demob Warrant Offr Class 1; purchasing mangr: Trussed Concrete Steel Co Ltd 1946-56 (former purchasing offr), NCB E Mids area 7 1956-63, Southern Gas 1963-67; dir purchasing Br Gas Corpn 1967-80, fndr Coopers (Little Marlow) Ltd as advsr to govr and statutory auths Thailand, Hong Kong, Singapore, Ireland 1980-88; written various papers on energy 1970-80; FInstPS 1965 (memb 1947, pres 1972-73), memb Int Fedn Purchasing 1972 (pres 1979-81); Cdr Most Noble Order of Crown of Thailand 1983; *Recreations* spectator: cricket and music; *Clubs* MCC, RAC; *Style—* Donald Cooper, Esq, OBE; (fax 04946 71792, telex 837495 MEDBEC G)

COOPER, Dowager Lady; Dorothy Frances Hendrika; *née* Deen; da of late Emile Deen; *m* 1933, Sir Francis Ashmole Cooper, 4 Bt (d 1987); 1 s (Sir Richard Cooper, 5 Bt), 3 da (Elizabeth Sally Ann b 1936, Jacqueline Margaret b 1939, Dione Frances b 1944); *Style—* Dowager Lady Cooper; Mas Folie, 06490 Tourrettes sur Loup, France

COOPER, Evelyn Mary Jessamine; *née* Fox; da of late Edward Herbert Fox, and Alice, *née* Arbuthnot; *b* 7 April 1908; *m* 1, 1928 (m dis), Capt John Lionel Armytage (later Sir John Armytage, 8 Bt, d 1983); 1 s (Martin, 9 Bt, *qv*), 1 da (Ann); m 2, 1946 (m dis 1950), Capt John Samuel Pontifex Cooper; m 3, 1950, Lt-Col John Warwick Tainton Woodridge (decd); m 4, 1980 remarried John S P Cooper; *Career* garden designer; *Clubs* Sloane's; *Style—* Mrs Evelyn Cooper; Thompson's Hill, Sherston, Malmesbury, Wilts

COOPER, Rt Hon Sir Frank; GCB (1979), KCB (1974, CB 1970, CMG 1961, PC 1983); s of late Valentine H Cooper, of 37 The Square, Fairfield, Manchester; *b* 2 Dec 1922; *Educ* Manchester GS, Pembroke Coll Oxford (hon fellow 1976); *m* 1948, Peggie, da of F J Claxton; 2 s, 1 da; *Career* joined Civil Service 1948, dep under-sec of state Miny of Def 1968-70, dep sec CSD 1970-73, perm under-sec of state NI Off 1973-76, perm under-sec of state MOD 1976-82, ret 1982; dir: FKI Babcock 1983-, Morgan Crucible 1983-, N M Rothschild and Sons 1983-; chm: United Scientific Hldgs 1985, High Integrity Systems 1986-; memb cncl King's Coll London 1983- (fell 1987); chm: Kings Coll Med and Dental Sch 1984-, Imperial Coll 1983- (fell 1988); dep chm Cranbrook Sch 1982 (chm 1984); chm: Liddell Harbour Tstees 1986-, Inst of Contemperary Br History 1986-; vice-chm Army Records Soc 1986-88; memb Advsy Cncl on Public Records 1989-; *Clubs* Athenaeum, RAF; *Style—* The Rt Hon Sir Frank Cooper, GCB, CMG; Delafield, 34 Camden Park Rd, Chislehurst, Kent BR7 5HG

COOPER, George John; s of Sir Charles Cooper, 5 Bt (d 1984) by 2 wife - *see* Cooper, Lady (Mary Elisabeth); hp of bro, Sir William Cooper, 6 Bt, *qv*; *b* 28 June 1956; *Style—* George Cooper, Esq; 19 Norfolk Mansions, Prince of Wales Drive, London SW11, All Soul's Cottage, Eastleach, Cirencester, Glos

COOPER, Gen Sir George Leslie Conroy; GCB (1984, KCB 1979), MC (1953); s of Lt-Col G C Cooper (d 1978), of Bulmer Tye House, Sudbury, Suffolk, and Yvonne Victoria, *née* Hughes (d 1978); *b* 10 August 1925; *Educ* Downside, Trinity Coll Cambridge; *m* 1957, Cynthia Mary, da of Capt Trevor Hume, of Old Harlow, Essex; 1 s (Timothy b 1958), 1 da (Clare b 1961); *Career* Lt-Col RE 4 Div 1966-68 (Bengal Sappers and Miners 1945-48, Korea 1952-53; instructor Sandhurst, Staff Coll Camberley), Cmd 19 Airportable Inf Bde 1961-71, dir Army Staff Duties 1976-79, GOC SE Dist 1979-81 (SW Dist 1974-75), Gen 1981, Adj-Gen MOD 1981-84; Col Cmdt: RE 1980, Royal Pioneer Corps 1981-85; Col The Queen's Gurkha Engrs 1981-; ADC Gen to HM The Queen 1982-84, Chief Royal Engineer 1987-; memb GEC UK Bd of Mgmnt, dir GEC Mgmnt Devpt 1985-6, chm Infantile Hypercalcaemia Fndn 1981-; cncl memb Action Research for the Crippled Child 1983-; *Recreations* shooting, gardening; *Clubs* Army and Navy; *Style—* Gen Sir George Cooper, GCB, MC; c/o Barclays Bank Ltd, 3-5 King St, Reading, Berks

COOPER, Sir Gilbert Alexander; CBE (1964), ED (1943); s of Alexander Samuel and Laura Ann Cooper; *b* 31 July 1903; *Educ* Saltus GS Bermuda, McGill Univ Canada; *Career* memb House of Assembly Bermuda 1948-68, memb Legislative Assembly 1968-72, kt 1972; *Style—* Sir Gilbert Cooper, CBE, ED; Shoreland, Pembroke, Bermuda HM05 (☎ 295 4189)

COOPER, Gyles Penry; s of Penry Lowick Cooper, of London; *b* 8 Nov 1942; *Educ* Felsted Sch, St John's Coll Oxford (MA); *Career* CA 1968; dir: Aitken Hume Ltd 1982-84, Samuel Montagu & Co Ltd 1968-79, Société Générale Bank Ltd 1979-82, Chemical Bank Int Ltd 1984-85; non-exec dir Stagescreen Prodns Ltd 1984-, md First Austrian Int Ltd 1988-; chm Highgate Cemetery Ltd 1986-87, tstee The Highgate Cemetery Charity 1988-; Freeman City of London 1979, memb Worshipful Co of Chartered Accountants in England and Wales 1979; *Style—* Gyles Cooper, Esq; First Austrian International Ltd, Eldon House, 2 Eldon Street, London EC2M 7BX

COOPER, Hon Jason Charles Duff Bede; s and h of 2 Viscount Norwich; *b* 27 Oct 1959; *Educ* Eton, New Coll Oxford (BA), Oxford Poly (BA, Arch); *Career* architect, designer, journalist; *Recreations* piano, travel, skiing; *Style—* The Hon Jason Cooper; 24 Blomfield Rd, London W9

COOPER, John Edwyn; s of Reginald Vincent Cooper, MBE, and Mildred Anne, *née* Clayton; *b* 18 Sept 1949; *Educ* Kingsbury Co GS, Univ of Hull (BSc); *m* 1, 1972 (m dis 1988), Patricia Anne, da of Wing Cdr Gordon F Turner, of Watford, Herts; m 2, 19 May 1988, Penelope Freda, da of Douglas Keith Walters (d 1968), 1 s (James Alexander b 10 March 1988); *Career* asst master in mathematics Hymers Coll Hull 1971-72, exec offr in data processing Nat Data Processing Serv (Post Off) 1972-73, sr operational res programmer BA 1973-75, trg supervisor Digital Equipment Co 1976-81, UK trg mangr (previously commercial accounts mktg mangr) Wang UK 1981-86, dir of educn NCR 1986-88, mgmnt info servs dir Wang UK 1988-; memb bd of govrs and chm computing advsy panel Richmond-Upon-Thames Coll, co-opted memb Richmond-Upon-Thames educn ctee; Freeman City of London 1982, memb Worshipful Co of Plumbers 1982; *Recreations* golf, food and wine; *Clubs* Silvermere GC; *Style—* John Cooper, Esq; Appletree Cottage, 20B Langley Ave, Surbiton, Surrey; Wang House, 661 London Rd, Isleworth, Middx TWy 4EH (☎ 01 560 4151)

COOPER, Ven John Leslie; s of Leslie Cooper (d 1974), of East Molesey, Surrey, and Iris May, *née* Johnston; *b* 16 Dec 1933; *Educ* Tiffin Sch, Kingston Surrey, Kings Coll London Univ (BD, MPhil); *m* 19 Dec 1959, Gillian Mary, da of Eric Dodds (d 1986), of Esher, Surrey; 2 s (Jonathan b 1962, Philip Justin Michael b 1964), 1 da (Penelope Sue b 1963); *Career* Nat Service, RA Germany 2 Lt 1952-54; Gen Electric Co 1954-59; asst curate All Saints King's Heath Birmingham 1962-65, chaplain HM Prison Service 1965-72, research fell Queen's Coll Birmingham 1972-73, incumbent St Paul Balsall Heath Birmingham 1973-82, archdeacon of Aston and canon residentiary St Philip's Cathedral 1982-; *Recreations* photography, reading, music, carpentry, walking, swimming, travel; *Style—* The Ven the Archdeacon of Aston; 51 Moor Green Lane, Moseley, Birmingham B13 8NE (☎ 021 449 0766)

COOPER, Rear Admiral John Spencer; OBE (1974); s of Harold Spencer Cooper, of Hong Kong (d 1972), and Barbara, *née* Highet (d 1974); *b* 5 April 1933; *Educ* St

Edwards Sch Oxford, Clare Coll Cambridge (MA); *m* 13 Aug 1966, Jacqueline Street *née* Taylor; 2 da (Philippa b 1967, Lucy b 1970); *Career* chief strategic systems exec 1985-88; dir gen strategic weapon systems 1981-85; sr UK Polaris rep Washington 1978-80, dir Trials (Polaris) 1976-78, with Ferranti Int 1988-; *Recreations* sailing; *Style—* Rear Admiral J S Cooper, OBE; 3 Burlington Ave, Kew Gardens, Richmond, Surrey TW9 4DF (☎ 01 876 3675)

COOPER, Joseph Elliott Needham; OBE (1982); s of Wilfred Needham Cooper (d 1949), of Westbury-on-Trym, and Elsie Goodacre, *née* Elliott (d 1963); *b* 7 Oct 1912; *Educ* Clifton, Keble Coll Oxford (MA); *m* 1, 15 Nov 1947, (Marjorie) Jean (d 1973), da of Gp Capt Sir Louis Greig, KBE, CVO, DL (d 1953), of Thatched House Lodge, Richmond Pk; m 2, 4 July 1975, Carol Vivien Nelson, da of Charles John Nelson Borg (d 1986), of Brighton; *Career* WWII: 66 Searchlight Regt RA, cmmnd 2 Lt 1941, Capt 1943, WO Sch Aircraft Recognition 1944, served GHQ AA Troops (21 Army Gp Rear) Normandy 1944, demobed 1946; composer and arranger GPO Film Unit 1936-37, trained as concert pianist under Egon Petri, arrangement of Vaughan Williams Piano Concerto for 2 Pianos (with composer) 1946, debut Wigmore Hall 1947, concerto debut Philharmonia Orchestra 1950, debut BBC Promenade Concerts Royal Albert Hall 1953; tours: India 1953, extensively Br Isles and Continent; chm Face the Music BBC TV 1966-84; memb music panel Arts Cncl (chm piano sub-ctee) 1966-71, vice-pres SOS Soc (Old Peoples Homes) 1970-, tstee Countess of Munster Musical Tst 1975-80, vice-pres music cncl English Speaking Union 1985-, memb jury Anglo/French Music Scholarships 1985-, memb cncl Musicians Benevolent Fund 1987-; patron St Georges Music tst Bristol 1982-, pres Dorking Halls Concertgoers Soc 1985-, memb ctee for an organ St John's Smith Sq 1986-, govr Clifton Coll; former pres: Surrey Philharmonic Soc, Box Hill Musical Festival, Reigate Music Soc; various piano recordings incl The World of Joseph Cooper; Freeman City of London, Liveryman Worshipful Co Musicians 1963, ARCM; *Books* Hidden Melodies (1975), More Hidden Melodies (1976), Still More Hidden Melodies (1978), Facing the Music (Autobiog) (1979); *Recreations* countryside, animals, church architecture; *Clubs* Garrick; *Style—* Joseph Cooper, Esq, OBE; Octagon Lodge, Ranmore, Nr Dorking, Surrey RH5 6SX (☎ 04865 2658)

COOPER, Kenneth Reginald; s of Reginald Frederick Cooper, of Old Park Rd, Palmers Green, London, and Louisa May, *née* Turner (d 1962); *b* 28 June 1931; *Educ* Queen Elizabeth's GS Barnet, New Coll Oxford (MA); *m* 21 Dec 1955, Olga Ruth, da of Ernest Charles Harvey, MBE (d 1955); 2 s (Richard b 1960, Nicholas b 1961), 2 da (Sharon b 1959, Caroline b 1968); *Career* Nat Serv 2 Lt Royal Warwicks Regt 1949-51, Lt TA 1951-54; Miny Labour 1954-61, HM Treasy 1961-65, princ private sec to Min of Labour 1966-67, asst sec Insustl Trg 1967-70; chief exec: Employment Serv Agency 1970-74, Trg Servs Agency 1974-79; dir gen Building Employers Confedn 1979-84, chief exec Br Library 1984-; CBIM 1988, FIPM 1975; FITD 1980, Hon FIIS 1988; FRSA 1988; *Style—* Kenneth Cooper, Esq; 2 Sheraton St, London W1V 4BH (☎ 01 323 7273, fax 01 323 7039, car tel 0860 822 458)

COOPER, Lt Col (Leonard) Malcolm; TD (1945); s of Ernest Leonard Cooper (d 1940), of Great Brake, Otterey, St Mary, Devon, and Elspeth *née* Kellie Mac Allum (d 1966); *b* 11 August 1913; *Educ* Sherborne; *m* 7 Oct 1960, (Eleanora) Joan, da of Francis William Elcock Massey (d 1964), of Bembridge, IOW; *Career* cmmnd 4 Bn Devonshire Regt (TA) 1932, Staff Coll Camberley 1941, serv N Africa and Italy, Lt Col 1943 (despatches); slr 1936, ptnr Knapp-fishers until 1980, conslt Richards Butler; memb Law Soc 1936; *Recreations* foxhunting, deer stalking, horse racing; *Clubs* Boodles, Pratts, Jockey; *Style—* Lt Col Malcolm Cooper, TD; Mount Pleasant, Church St, Ropley, Hants SO24 0DR (☎ 0962 77 3361); 61 St Mary Axe, London EC3

COOPER, Lady; Mary Elisabeth; da of Capt John Eagles Henry Graham-Clarke, of Frocester Manor, Stonehouse, Gloucs, and Margaret, *née* Rouse; *b* 31 Oct 1917; *m* 1, (m dis), Robert Erland Nicholai d'Abo; 1 s (Robin); m 2, 17 Dec 1953, as his 2 wife, Sir Charles Eric Daniel Cooper, 5 Bt (d 1984); 2 s (William Daniel Charles, George John); *Style—* Elizabeth, Lady Cooper; Pudley Cottage, Castle St, Aldbourne, Wiltshire SN8 2DA (☎ 0672 40274)

COOPER, Lady Maureen Isabel; *née* Le Poer Trench; eldest da of late 6 Earl of Clancarty; *b* 20 Dec 1923; *m* 16 March 1949, Christopher Colin Cooper, o son of late Maj Colin Cooper, of Barnwell Castle, Northants; 1 s (Simon b 1956), 1 da (Claudia b 1952); *Style—* Lady Maureen Cooper; 542 Guadalmina Alta, San Pedro de Alcantara, Malaga, Spain

COOPER, Patrick Ernest; s of Stuart Ranson Cooper (d 1966), and Lila Flemmich Cooper (d 1954); *b* 27 Mar 1935; *Educ* Wellesley House Broadstairs, Rugby; *m* 1963, Katrina Farnham, da of Frederick Windisch (d 1979), of Connecticut, USA: 2 da (Alexandra b 1967, Lila b 1970); *Career* Coldstream Guards 1953-55, cmmnd W Yorkshire Regt and served Malaysia and NI, TA 1955-61, Capt, ret; CA; Cooper Bros audit mangr Lybrand Ross Bros and Montgomery 1961-62, dir Clive Discount and Co Ltd 1967, chief exec Clive Hldgs Gp 1971-72 (chm 1972), dir of financial servs Sime Darby Hldgs Ltd 1973, md Steel Bros and Co Ltd 1977 (dep chief exec and dep chm 1978), dep chm and chief exec Spinneys 1948 Ltd Jan 1980 (chm May 1980), chief exec Steel Bros Hldgs plc 1984; dir: Steel Bros Hldgs plc 1977-87, Steel Bros and Co Ltd 1977-87, Spinneys 1948 Ltd 1977-87; non-exec dir Mk Electric Gp 1983; Liveryman Vintners Co; *Recreations* golf, tennis, skiing, shooting, bridge, backgammon; *Clubs* Boodles, Royal Ashdown Forest Golf, Royal St Georges Golf; *Style—* Patrick Cooper, Esq; Glebe Ho, Fletching, Sussex, (☎ 082 572 2104)

COOPER, Philip John; s of Charles Cooper (d 1980), and Mildred Annie, *née* Marlow (d 1981); *b* 15 Sept 1929; *Educ* Deacons Sch Peterborough, Univ of Leicester (BSc); *m* 1, 1 Aug 1953, Dorothy Joan Chapman (d 1982), da of James Chapman of Rhos-on-Sea, N Wales (d 1970); 2 da (Vivien Anne b 1954, Valerie Joan b 1957); m 2, 8 Aug 1986, Pamela Mary Coad (d 1988), da of Henry John Pysden, of Durban, South Africa (d 1979); *Career* National Service 2 Lt Royal Signals 1953-55; dept of Govt chemist 1952, Dept of Sci and Industrl Res 1956-67, princ Miny of Technol 1967; PPS to Minister for Industrial Devpt 1972-73, assist sec 1973-79, under sec 1979-89 DOI and DTI; dir Warren Spring Lab DTI 1984-85, comptroller-general The Patent Office DTI 1986-89; *Books* various papers on analytical and chemical matters; *Style—* Philip Cooper, Esq; Abbottsmead, Sandy Lane, Kingswood, Surrey KT20 6ND (☎ 0737 833039)

COOPER, Richard John; s of William George Cooper (d 1979); *Educ* Slough GS; *m* 1950, Margaret Pauline, *née* Gould; 1 s, 1 da; *Career* former regional pres (Berks Bucks and Oxon region) Construction Surveyors Inst, dir Farrow Construction Ltd; *Recreations* deep sea fishing, golf, youth work; *Clubs* Eccentric; *Style—* Richard Cooper, Esq; Brantwood, 39 Littleton Rd, Harrow, Middlesex

COOPER, Sir Richard Powell; 5 Bt (UK 1905), of Shenstone Court, Shenstone, Co Stafford; s of Sir Francis Ashmole (Frank) Cooper, 4 Bt (d 1987), and Dorothy Francis Hendrika, *née* Deen; *b* 13 April 1934; *Educ* Marlborough; *m* 2 Oct 1957, Angela Marjorie, elder da of late Eric Wilson, of Stockton-on-Tees; 1 s (Richard Adrian b 1960), 2 da (Jane Alice b 1958, Belinda Gay b 1963); *Heir* s, Richard Adrian b 21 Aug 1960; *Recreations* foxhunting; *Clubs* Carlton, Bucks; *Style—* Sir Richard Cooper, Bt; Lower Farm, Chedington, Beaminster, Dorset DT8 3HY

COOPER, Robert; s of Alfred Cooper, of Marlborough, Wilts; *b* 18 Feb 1932; *Educ* Radley; *m* 1957 (m dis); 3 children; *Career* Capt TA; chm and chief exec: Coopers Hldgs Ltd, Coopers (Metals) Ltd (Queen's Award for Export 1982), Coopers (Swindon) Ltd; pres British Scrap Fedn 1984-1985; Queens Award for Export 1986; memb Worshipful Co of Butchers; *Recreations* country pursuits, tennis, gardens; *Clubs* Cavalry and Guards; *Style—* Robert Cooper, Esq; Ablington Manor, Bibury, Cirencester, Glos; Coopers (Holdings) Ltd, Bridge House, Gipsy Lane, Swindon, Wilts (☎ 0793 32111)

COOPER, Robert Douglas; s of Peter Cooper (d 1962), and Marguerite, *née* Slater; *b* 16 Mar 1939; *Educ* Daniel Stewart's Coll Edinburgh, Heriot-Watt Univ; *Career* Bass plc 1960, md Charrington Inns and Taverns Ltd; *Recreations* golf; *Clubs* Royal and Ancient, Royal Mid-Surrey; *Style—* Robert Cooper, Esq; Wildcroft Manor, Durney Heath, London SW15 3TS; Charrington & Co Ltd, North Woolwich Rd, London E16 2AD

COOPER, Maj-Gen Simon Christie; s of Maj-Gen Kenneth Christie Cooper, CB, DSO, OBE (d 1981), of Dorset, and Barbara Mary, *née* Harding-Newman (d 1988); *b* 5 Feb 1936; *Educ* Winchester, Hamburg Univ; *m* 1967, Juliet Elizabeth, da of Cdr Geoffrey Inderwick Palmer, of Somerset; 1 s (Jonathan Francis Christie b 1969), 1 da (Venetia Elizabeth Somerset b 1971); *Career* cmmnd Life Gds 1956, 1957-63 served Aden, London, BAOR; Capt, Adj Household Cavalry Regt 1963-65, ADC to CDS Earl Mountbatten of Burma 1965-66, Borneo, Malaya 1966-67, Staff Coll 1968, BAOR 1969-75, CO Life Gds 1974-76, GSOI Staff Coll 1976-78, OC Household Cav and Silver Stick in Waiting 1978-81, cdr RAC Centre 1981-82, Royal Coll of Def Studies 1983, dir RAC 1984-87, cmdt RMA Sandhurst 1987-89, Maj-Gen cmdg Household Div and Soc london Dist 1989-; Hon Col Westminster Dragoons and Hon Col Royal Yeo 1987-; *Recreations* tennis, cricket, sailing, shooting, skiing; *Clubs* MCC; *Style—* Maj-Gen Simon Cooper; c/o Royal Bank of Scotland, Holts, Lawrie House, Farnborough, Hants GU14 7PQ; Royal Military Academy Sandhurst, Camberley, Surrey (☎ 0276 63344 ext 2530)

COOPER, Dame Whina; DBE (1981), CBE (1974, MBE 1953, JP); da of Heremia Te Wake, JP, a chief of Ngati-Manowa Hapu of Te Rarawa tribe, and Kate Pouro; *b* 9 Dec 1895, in Panguru Hokianga; *Educ* St Joseph's Coll Green Meadows; *m* 1, 1916, Richard Gilbert (decd); 1 s (decd), 1 da; m 2, 1932, William Cooper, s of Robert Cooper; 2 s, 2 da; *Career* fndr and pres Te Roopu o te Matakite 1975-; *Style—* Dame Whina Cooper, DBE, JP; 4 McCulloch Rd, Panmure, Auckland, New Zealand

COOPER, Sir William Daniel Charles; 6 Bt (UK 1863) of Woollahra, New South Wales; s of Sir Charles Eric Daniel Cooper, 5 Bt (d 1984) by 2 wife - *see* Cooper, Lady (Mary Elisabeth); *b* 5 Mar 1955; *m* 22 Aug 1988, Julia Nicholson; *Heir* bro, George John Cooper, *qv*; *Career* dir: The Gdn Maintenance Serv, GMS Vehicles; *Style—* Sir William Cooper, Bt; 8 Yew Tree Close, East Oakley, Nr Basingstoke, Hants RG23 7HQ (☎ 0256 781814)

COOPER, Maj Gen William Frank; CBE (1972), MC (1945); s of Allan Cooper (d 1959), of Hazards, Shawford, Hants, and late Margaret Martha, *née* Pothelary; *b* 30 May 1921; *Educ* Sherborne; *m* 10 Aug 1945, Elizabeth Mary, da of George Finch (d 1918); 1 s (Allan George b 1950), 1 da (Gillian (Mrs Hewitt) b 1947); *Career* WWII cmmnd RE 1940, serv N Africa and Italy, Staff Coll 1951, Co Field sgdn RE Malayan Emergency, instr Staff Coll 1958-60, CRE 3 Div 1961-63, Lt-Col Staff HQ ME 1963-65, Brig Chief Engr 1968-70, Maj- Gen 1973-76; mil advsr GKN Gp 1976-83, dir Gn Rectifiers and Distillers Assoc and Vodka Trade Assoc 1976-88; *Recreations* fly-fishing, bird watching, reading; *Clubs* Army and Navy; *Style—* Maj Gen William Cooper CBE, MC; Neals, Aldbourne, Marlborough, Wilts SN8 2DW (☎ 0672 407 16); 110 Kensington Park Rd, London W11 2PJ (☎ 01 229 9222)

COOPER-HEYMAN, Hon Mrs - Hon Isobel; *née* Pargiter; da of Baron Pargiter, CBE (Life Peer); *b* 8 Sept 1931; *m* 26 June 1964, Ernest Cooper-Heyman, s of Harry Cooper Heyman; *Career* pharmaceutical chemist; *Recreations* opera, theatre, travel; *Style—* The Hon Mrs Cooper-Heyman; 34 Van Dyke Close, Redhill, Surrey RH1 2DS

COOPER-KEY, Hon Lady Lorna Peggy Vyvyan; *née* Harmsworth; da of 2 Viscount Rothermere (d 1979), by his 1 w Margaret; *b* 24 Oct 1920; *m* 11 Jan 1941, Sir Neill Cooper-Key (d 1981), er s of late Capt Edmund Moore Cooper-Key, CB, MVO, RN; 1 da (Emma b 1958, 1 da decd), 2 s; *Style—* The Hon Lady Cooper-Key; La Celinotte, Meribel les Allues, Savoie, France; Les Floralies, 1 ave de Grande Bretagne, Monte Carlo

COOTE, Rev Bernard Albert Ernest; s of Albert Coote (d 1988, age 100), of Steyning, Susex, and Emma Jane, *née* Tye (d 1957); *b* 11 August 1928; *Educ* Steyning GS, Univ of London (BD); *m* 17 Aug 1957, Ann, da of Donovan Hopper; 2 s (John b 1958, Michael b 1960); *Career* RAF 1946-49; vicar Sutton Valence and E Sutton 1963-76, dir Royal Sch for the Blind Leatherhead 1976-; chm Ctee on the Multihandcapped Blind 1984; *Recreations* cricket, walking, travel, music; *Style—* The Rev Bernard Coote; 2 Reigate Rd, Leather Head, Surrey (☎ 0372 376 395); 6 Coxham Lane, Steyning, W Sussex; Royal Sch for the Blind, Leatherhead, Surrey (☎ 0372 373 733)

COOTE, Sir Christopher John; 15 Bt (I 1621) of Castle Cuffe, Queen's County, Ireland; s of Rear-Adm Sir John Coote, 14 Bt, CB, CBE, DSC (d 1978); *b* 22 Sept 1928; *Educ* Winchester, Christ Church Coll Oxford (MA); *m* 23 Aug 1952, Anne Georgiana, yr da of Lt-Col Donald James Handford, RA (d 1980), of Guyers, Corsham, Wilts; 1 s, 1 d; *Heir* s, Nicholas Coote; *Career* late Lt 17/21 Lancers; coffee and tea merchant 1952-; *Style—* Sir Christopher Coote, Bt; Monkton House, Broughton Gifford, Melksham, Wilts SN12 8PA (☎ 0225 702286)

COOTE, Nicholas Patrick; s and h of Sir Christopher Coote, 15 Bt; *b* 28 July 1953; *Educ* Winchester; *m* 1980, Mona, da of late Moushegh Bedelian; 1 da; *Career* British Airways; *Style—* Nicolas Coote Esq

COOTE, Rt Rev Roderic Norman Coote; s of Cdr Bernard T Coote (d 1955), of

Woodham Park Way, W Byfleet, Surrey, and Grace Harriet, *née* Robinson; *b* 13 April 1915; *Educ* Woking Co Sch, Trinity Coll Dublin (DD); *m* 1964, Erica Lynette, da of late Rev Eric G Shrubbs, MBE, Rector of Lawshall, Suffolk; 1 s, 2 da; *Career* curate 1938-41, SPG missionary 1942-51, bishop of Gambia and the Rio Pongas 1951-57, suffragan Bishop of Fulham 1957-66, archdeacon of Colchester 1969-72, suffragan Bishop of Colchester 1966-87, asst Bishop in Diocese of London 1987-; *Style*— The Rt Rev Roderic Coote; 58 Broom Park, Teddington TW11 9RS (☎ 01 943 3648)

COPCUTT, Ronald William James; s of William Norton Copcutt (d 1948), of 18 Cecil Rd, Southgate, N14, and Hilda, *née* Hayward (d 1977), of Forest View, Fernside, Buckhurst Hill, Essex; *b* 2 Feb 1916; *Educ* Coopers' Company's Sch; *m* 1, Margaret (d 1966), da of Harold de la Mare (d 1949), of Greenwich, London; m 2, 3 Sept 1966, Vappu Hely, da of Väinö Nikolai Kunnas (d 1988), of Finland; 1 s (Nicholas William Väinö b 1971); *Career* WWII Civil Def Serv; sales rep Glovers Dyers & Cleaners Ltd 1932-44; dir: Copcutt Dobinson Ltd 1944-66, Frearsonia Ltd 1959-66, Keystone Cleaners Ltd 1948-68, BB&H Carpets Ltd 1960-66, Carpet Installations Ltd 1963-66; exec offr GLC 1967-81; chm: Miny Nat Insur and Pensions Local Advsy Ctee for NW Essex 1958-67 (memb 1949), Miny of Health and Soc Security Redbridge and Waltham Forest Local Advsy Ctee 1967-72, Dyehards Club 1950, Eltham Southend Res Assoc 1976-79, Eltham Assocs Ctee 1976-78; vice-chm Crown Woods Sch Assoc 1984-86; memb: Dept Health & Soc Security Local Appeals Tbnl 1950-88, Indust Injury Tbnl 1950-67, Miny of Lab & Nat Serv Mil Hardships & Reinstatement Ctee 1950-65, Coborn Estate Ctee 1959-71, Managing Ctee Nat Lib Club 1960-72, Lib Indust & Commercial Cncl 1961, Cncl of London & Southern Dyers & Cleaners 1948-53, Exec Cncl NALGO, Exec Ctee of Assoc of Voluntary Aided Secondary Schs 1981-88; former pres GLC; govr Stepney & Bow Educnl Fnd 1959-, pres Old Coopers Assoc 1967-68, tstee Gladstone Library 1964-78, specialist advsr to CAB on Tbnl Appeals 1988-; Freeman City of London 1952, Liveryman Worshipful Co of Coopers; *Clubs* Surrey CC; *Style*— Ronald Copcutt, Esq; 4 Enslin Rd, Eltham, London SE9 5BP (☎ 01 850 6401)

COPE, Rev Anthony William Groves; s of Charles Ernest Cope, and Jessie Groves, *née* Edwards; *b* 28 Dec 1908; *Educ* Sherborne Sch, Exeter Coll Oxford (MA); *m* 14 June 1939, Rosemary Averil, da of Sir Hamilton Asley Ballance, KBE, CB, MD, MS, FRCS; 1 s (Anthony), 2 da (Rosemary Anne, Penelope Madeleine); *Career* CF RAFVR 1940-45; curate Holy Trinity Tulse Hill 1934-36, priest i/c St Johns Putney 1936-39, rector and rural dean Feltwell 1939-56, rector of Upwell St Peter 1956-65, rector of Slingsby and vicar of Hovingham 1965-73; Master Haberdashers Co 1962-63; *Style*— Rev Anthony W G Cope; Great Durgates, Wadhurst, E Sussex TN5 6RT (☎ 089 288 2402)

COPE, David Robert; s of Dr Cuthbert Leslie Cope (d 1975), and Eileen Gertrude, *née* Putt (d 1987); *b* 24 Oct 1944; *Educ* Winchester, Clare Coll Cambridge (BA, MA); *m* 2 April 1966, Gillian Margaret, da of Richard Eyton Peck, of Wenhaston, Suffolk; 1 s (Damian b 1967), 2 da (Claire b 1968, Genevieve b 1974); *Career* asst master Eton 1965-67, asst Br Cncl rep cultural attaché Mexico City 1968-70, asst master Bryanston Sch 1970-73; headmaster: Dover Coll 1973-81, Br Sch of Paris 1981-86; master Marlborough 1986-; FRSA 1978; *Recreations* music, travel; *Clubs* Athenaeum; *Style*— David Cope, Esq; The Master's Lodge, Marlborough College, Wiltshire SN8 1PA (☎ 0672 52140)

COPE, David Robert; s of Lawrence William Cope, of Taunton, and Ethel Anne, *née* Harris (d 1980); *Educ* King's Coll Sch Wimbledon, Cambridge Univ (BA, MA), LSE (MSc); *m* 1 Sept 1973, Sharon Marie, da of J Edmund Kelly Jr, of Kenmore, NY, USA; *Career* res offr UCL 1968-70, lectr Univ of Nottingham 1970-81, environmental team ldr Int Energy Agency Coal Res 1981-86; dir UK Centre for Econ and Environmental Devpt 1986-; memb Inst of Energy; *Books* Energy Policy and Land-Use Planning - an International Perspective (with P Hills and P James, 1984); *Recreations* hill-walking, woodworking, classical music; *Clubs* Europe House; *Style*— David R Cope, Esq; The UK Centre for Economic and Environmental Development, 12 Upper Belgrave St, London SW1X 8BA (☎ 01 245 6440)

COPE, Lady; Eveline; da of late Alfred Eaton Bishop, of Gloucester; *m* 18 April 1936, as his 2 w, Sir Mordaunt Leckonby Cope, 16 Bt, MC (d 1972, when title became extinct); *Style*— Lady Cope; 5 Headbourne Worthy House, Winchester, Hants

COPE, John Ambrose; MP (C) Northavon 1983-; s of late George Arnold Cope, MC, FRIBA, of Leicester; *b* 13 May 1937; *Educ* Oakham Sch Rutland; *m* 1969, Djemila, da of Col P V Lovell Payne, of Martinstown, Dorset; 2 da; *Career* chartered accountant; personal asst to Chm Cons Party 1967-70, contested (C) Woolwich E 1970, special asst to Sec of State for Trade and Industry 1972-74; MP (C) South Glos 1974-83, govt whip 1979-87, a lord cmmnr of the Treasury 1981-83, dep chief whip and tres HM's Household 1983-87; minister of state Dept of Employment, minister for Small Firms 1987; FCA; *Style*— John Cope, Esq, MP; House of Commons, London SW1A 0AA

COPE, Samantha Mary; da of John Martin Brentnall Cope, and of Davina Rosemary Enid Nutting (resumed maiden name upon div 1969, and was *k* in a motor accident with her only son, Jonathan Edric 1976), only child of Edric Nutting (*ka* 1943, 2 s of Sir Harold Nutting, 2 Bt) by his w, Lady Rosemary Eliot (d 1963), elder da of 6 Earl of St Germans by his w, Lady Blanche Somerset, da of 9 Duke of Beaufort; co-heiress to baronies of Botetourt and Herbert which fell into abeyance upon the death of 10 Duke of Beaufort 1984; *b* 23 Sept 1963; *Style*— Miss Samantha Cope

COPE-STRACHAN, Lady; Joan Penelope; *née* Cope; da of Sir Denzil Cope, 14 Bt, (Cope of Hanwell, Oxfordshire); assumed surname Cope-Strachan by deed poll 1969; *b* 1 Jan 1926; *Educ* at home; *m* 1949, Sir Duncan Alexander Grant, 13 Bt (d 1961); 3 s, 2 da; *Heir* er s Sir Patrick Alexander Benedict Grant, 14 Bt, 2 The Crescent, Busty, Lanarkshire; *Career* nursed during WW II; writer; former co dir and rep in Ireland of the Société d'Etudes Techniques et Scientifiques of Avignon; *Books* Arabian Andalusian Casidas; *Recreations* piano, genealogy, conversation; *Style*— Lady Cope-Strachan; 34 Morehampton Rd, Ballsbridge, Dublin 4, Eire

COPELAND, Richard Spencer Charles; s of Richard Ronald John Copeland CBE, JP, DL of Kibblestone Hall, Stone, Staffs (d 1958), and Ida, *née* Fenzi (d 1964); *b* 18 Dec 1918; *Educ* St Peters Ct, Broadstairs Kent, Harrow, Alpine Coll Switzerland, Trinity Coll Cambridge (MA); *m* 1, 1940 (m dis), Sonia, da of late W J B Chambers of Hoylake; 1 s (David b 1943), 1 adopted da (Elizabeth b 1956); m 2, 1966, Jean, da of William Turner (d 1985), of Stoke on Trent; 1 s (William John Taylor b 1966); *Career* Lt RA LAA 1940-45; dir W T Copeland and Sons Ltd 1947, later Spode Ltd (md 1955-66, chm 1966-71), dir Caverswall China Co Ltd 1975-81; fndr and fell Inst of Ceramics 1955, pres Br Ceramic Soc 1959-60, vice-pres Assoc Euro de Ceramique 1960-62, pres Staffordshire Soc 1969-71, gen cmmr of Income Tax 1970-, memb cncl of Univ Coll North Staffordshire 1953 (now Univ of Keele); Hon MA Keele Univ 1987; Freeman City of London, Liveryman Goldsmiths Co; *Recreations* skiing, sailing; *Clubs* Royal Overseas League, Ski of GB, Royal Cwlth Yacht; *Style*— R Spencer C Copeland, Esq; Trelissick, Feock, Truro, Cornwall TR3 6QL (☎ 0872 862248)

COPEMAN, Dr Peter William Monckton; s of William Sydney Charles Copeman, CBE, TD, JP, FRCP (d 1970), and Helen, *née* Bourne (d 1980); *b* 9 April 1932; *Educ* Eton, CCC Cambridge (MA, MD), St Thomas's Hosp; *m* 19 May 1973, Lindsey Bridget, da of David Vaughan Brims, Heddon Hall, Heddon on the Wall, Northumberland; 1 s (Andrew b 1980), 3 da (Mary b 1975, Louisa b 1977, Caroline b 1980); *Career* conslt physician i/c dept of dermatology Westminster and Westminster Childrens Hosp, clinician and researcher; cncllr The Game Conservancy; patron of the living St James the Less Hadleigh Essex, patron tstee and churchwarden St Mary's Bourne St London; Liveryman Worshipful Co of Apothecaries; OSt J; FRCP 1975;; *Recreations* being head of Copeman family (formerly of Sparham Norfolk); *Clubs* Athenaeum; *Style*— Dr Peter Copeman; 20 Spencer Park, London SW18 (☎ 01 874 7549); 82 Sloane St, London SW1X 9PA (☎ 01 245 9333); Abshiel Farm, Morpeth, Northumberland

COPISAROW, Sir Alcon Charles; o s of late Dr Maurice Copisarow, of Manchester, and Eda Copisarow; *b* 25 June 1920; *Educ* Manchester Univ, Imperial Coll London, Sorbonne (DSc); *m* 1953, Diana Elissa, yr da of Major Ellis James Castello, MC, TD (d 1983); 2 s, 2 da; *Career* serv WWII Lt RN; HM cnsllr (scientific) Br Embassy Paris 1954-60, dir Dept of Scientific and Industl Res 1960-62, chief tech offr NEDC 1962-64, chief scientific offr Miny of Technol 1964-66; sr ptnr McKinsey and Co Inc 1966-76; formerly dir Br Leyland; memb: British National Oil Corpn, Press Cncl; dep chm of govrs English-Speaking Union, tstee Duke of Edinburgh's Award, govr Benenden Sch, chm exec ctee Trinity Coll of Music London; chm: Youth Business Initiative, The Prince's Youth Business Trust; memb Admin Council Royal Jubilee Trusts; currently chm gen commissioners for Income Tax; external memb Council of Lloyd's; dep chm Lloyds Tercentenary Fndn (formerly chm); dir: Widsor Festival, Touche Remnant Hldgs, TR Technol; chm APA Venture Capital Funds; kt 1988; *Clubs* Athenaeum, Beefsteak, MCC; *Style*— Sir Alcon Copisarow; 25 Launceston Place, London W8 5RN (telex LLOYDS G 987321)

COPLESTON, Michael Vernon Gordon; s of Edward Arthur Vernon Gordon Copleston (d 1968), of Wimbledon, and Rose, *née* Hunter (d 1974); *b* 11 Nov 1942; *Educ* Rutlish Sch Merton London; *m* 29 Sept 1971, Jill Irene, *née* Pinney, of Yeovil; 2 s (Simon b 4 May 1973, Eddie-G b 25 Aug 1977), 1 da (Philippa b 5 Dec 1974); *Career* Corpn of Lloyds 1960-64, broker Stewart Smith & Co 1964-68; Johnson Fry Ltd 1969- (pncpl, chm, md, currenlty jp owner); tres: local cons assoc, Area Guide Dogs for the Blind; memb: ctee Dorking Mini Rugger Club, Cranleigh Prep Sch Fin Ctee; youth cricket and rugger coach; ABIBA 1975, memb: Insur Brokers Registration Cncl 1981, RHS; *Recreations* cricket, tennis, coaching cricket and rugger; *Clubs* MCC, Surrey CCC; *Style*— Michael Copleston, Esq; Aldermoor Cottage, Holmbury St Mary, Surrey RH5 6NR (☎ 0306 730 439); Johnson Fry (Insurance Brokers) Ltd, Barrington Hse, Westcott, Surrey RH4 3NW (☎ 0306 887 941, fax 0306 740 360)

COPLESTONE-BOUGHEY, His Honour Judge; John Fenton; s of late Cdr A F Coplestone-Boughey, RN; *b* 5 Feb 1912; *Educ* Shrewsbury, BNC Oxford; *m* 1944, Gilian Beatrice, *née* Counsell; 1 s, 1 da; *Career* barr 1935, former dir Chester Chronicle and Associated Newspapers, a circuit judge 1969-85; *Clubs* Athenaeum; *Style*— His Honour Judge Coplestone-Boughey; 82 Oakley St, London SW3 5NP (☎ 01 352 6287)

COPNER, David John Templer; s of Capt Charles John Pomeroy Copner, MA (d 1976), of Braunton, Devon, and Beatrice, *née* Watters-Williams (d 1970); *b* 9 Feb 1920; *Educ* Bradfield; *m* 4 Nov 1950, Joy Elizabeth, da of Charles George Thimbleby Price (d 1965), of Hastings, Sussex; 1 s (Christopher b 1956), 1 da (Rosalie b 1953); *Career* Capt RA, serv WWII 1939-45 UK, N Africa, Sicily, Italy, Palestine 1945-46, ADC to GOC 1 Inf Div 1944-45; slr; sr ptnr Talbot Davies and Copner of Andover 1968-, local dir Sun Alliance Insur Gp 1971, underwriting memb of Lloyds 1974; Notary Public 1955; chm Goodworth Clatford Parish Cncl 1972-76, life govr Imperial Cancer Res Fund 1978; memb: Law Soc 1947, CLA Devon 1965; *Recreations* gardening, travel; *Style*— David Copner, Esq; Briar Hill, Goodworth Clatford, Andover, Hampshire SP11 7QX (☎ 0264 23250); c/o Talbot Davies and Copner, 16 Bridge St, Andover, Hampshire SP10 1BJ (☎ 0264 633 54, fax 0264 333 325)

COPPEL, Laurence Adrian; s of Henry Coppel, of Belfast (d 1979), and Anne (d 1964); *b* 15 May 1939; *Educ* Belfast Royal Acad, Queen's Univ of Belfast (BSc); *m* 28 Oct 1964, Geraldine Ann, da of David Morrison, of Natanya; 2 s (Kenton Andrew b 1968, Mark Hugo b 1972); *Career* exec dir: Singer and Friedlander Gp plc 1987, Singer and Friedlander Ltd 1971-; dir Nottingham Bldg Soc 1985-; dep chm Alida Hldgs plc 1985-; FCA; *Recreations* sailing, wines; *Clubs* Club Nautico Oliva; *Style*— Laurence Coppel, Esq; 206 Derby Rd, Nottingham (☎ 0602 419 721, fax 0602 417 992)

COPPEN, Dr Alec James; s of Herbert John Wardle Coppen (d 1974), of London, and Marguerite Mary Annie, *née* Henshaw (d 1971); *b* 29 Jan 1923; *Educ* Dulwich Coll, Bristol Univ (MB, ChB, MD, DSc), Maudsley Hosp, London Univ (DPM); *m* 9 Aug 1952, Gunhild Margareta, da of Albert Andersson, of Bastad, Sweden; 1 s (Michael Coppen b 1952); *Career* Br Army 1942-46; registrar then sr registrar Maudsley Hosp 1954-59, MRC neuropsychiatry res unit 1957-74, MRC external staff 1974-; conslt psychiatrist: St Ebba's Hosp 1959-64, West Park Hosp 1964-; hon conslt St George's Hosp 1965-70, head WHO designated Centre Biological Psychiatry UK 1974-, conslt WHO 1977-, examiner Royal Coll Psychiatry 1973-77, Andrew Woods visiting prof Iowa Univ 1981; lectr in: Europe, N and S America, Asia, Africa; memb cncl and chm res and clinical section RMPA 1965-70, chm biology psychiatry section World Psychiatric Assoc 1972, pres Br Assoc Psychopharmacology 1975; memb: Int Coll Neuropsychopharmacology 1960-(memb cncl 1979), RSM 1960-, Br Pharmocological Soc 1977-, special health authy Bethlem Royal and Maudsley Hosp 1982-; hon memb: Mexican Inst Culture; pres Collegium Internationale Neuro-Psychopharmacologicum; author numerous scientific papers on Mental Health; Freeman City of London 1980, Liveryman Soc Apothecaries 1985 (memb 1980); hon memb Swedish Psychiatric Assoc 1977, Corres Mem American Coll Neuropsychopharmacology 1977, distinguished fell APA 1981; MRCP 1975, FRCP 1980, FRCPsych 1971; *Books* Recent Developments in Schizophrenia (1967), Recent Developments in Affective Disorders (1968), Biological Psychiatry (1968), Psychopharmacology of Affective Disorders (1979), Depressive Illness: Biological and Psychopharmacological Issues (1981); *Recreations* golf, music, photography; *Clubs* Athenaeum, The Harveian Soc, RAC; *Style—* Dr Alec Coppen; 5 Walnut Close, Epsom, Surrey KT21 2SN (☎ 03727 20 800); MRC Neuropsychiatry Research Laboratory, West Park Hospital, Epsom, Surrey KT19 8PB (☎ 03727 26 459, fax 03727 42 602)

COPPER, Robert James; s of James Dale Copper (d 1954), and Daisy Louise, *née* Clark (d 1971); *b* 6 Jan 1915; *Educ* Rottingdean C of E Sch; *m* 10 May 1941, Marian Joan (d 1983), da of Albert Deal (d 1960), of Sussex; 1 s (John b 1949), 1 da (Jill b 1944); *Career* Trooper Life Guards 1933-35, det constable W Sussex Constabulary 1937-46; writer, broadcaster, traditional singer, author (in name of Bob Copper); *Books* A Song for Every Season (1971, Robert Pitman prize winner), Songs and Southern Breezes (1973), Early to Rise (1976); *Recreations* country walking, painting; *Style—* Robert J Copper, Esq; Broom Cottage, 73 Telscombe Road, Peacehaven, E Sussex BN10 7UB (☎ 0273 583549)

COPPLESON, Lady; Marjorie Florence; da of Stephen John Simpson; *m* 1972, as his 2 w, Sir Lionel Wolfe Coppleson (d 1981), sometime chm Custom Credit Corpn Gp in Australia; *Style—* Lady Coppleson; Addenbrooke, 21 Cranbrook Rd, Bellevue Hill, NSW 2023, Australia (☎ 36 6475)

COPPLESTONE, Frank Henry; 2 s of late Rev Frank T Copplestone; *b* 26 Feb 1925; *Educ* Truro Sch, Nottingham Univ; *m* 1, 1950, Margaret Mary, (d 1973), da of late Edward Walker; 3 s; m 2, 1977, Mrs Penelope Ann Labovitch, da of Ben Perrick; 1 s, 1 da (both step); *Career* dir: ITV News Ltd 1977-, ITV Publications Ltd 1976-; *Style—* Frank Copplestone, Esq; ITV News Ltd, 48 Wells St, W1

COPPOCK, David Arthur; QHDS (1985); s of Oswald John Coppock of Fordingbridge (d 1979), and Ada Katherine, *née* Bevin (d 1979); *b* 19 April 1931; *Educ* Bishop Wordsworth Sch Guys Hospital (BDS) George Washington Univ (MSc); *m* 31 May 1956, Maria Averil, *née* Ferreira (d 1985); 2 da (Phillipa (Mrs McIntyre) b 1957, Nicola (Mrs Tims) b 1959); *Career* Entered RN 1955; HM Ships: Eagle 1956, Tamar - Hong Kong 1959, Hermes 1963, Rookegibraltar 1965: US Navy Exchange Bethesda MD 1972, DEB-DIR Naval Dental Services 1980, cmd Dental Surgeon to c-in C Naval Home cmd 1983, Dir Naval Dental Services 1985; Director Defence Dental Services 1988-; *Recreations* fly fishing, tennis, golf; *Clubs* Royal Society of Medicine; *Style—* Surgn Rear Admiral David Coppock, QHDS; First Avenue House, High Holborn WC1 (☎ 01 430 5993)

COPPOCK, Lawrence Patrick; s of Eric Francis Coppock, of Harrogate, and Betty Winifred, *née* Wilson; *b* 27 Jan 1952; *Educ* Royal GS, King George V GS; *m* 1 May 1982, Gillian Mary, da of Richard Charles Darby, of Stratford-on-Avon; 2 da (Katherine b 1984, Victoria b 1987); *Career* CA; Coopers & Lybrand 1971-75, sr analyst BL Int 1976-78, fin controller Lex Serv plc 1978-83, gp fin dir Heron Motor Gp 1983-84, gp fin controller Heron Corpn plc 1985, fin and ops dir HP Bulmer Drinks Ltd 1986-88, fin dir B and Q plc 1988-; memb local Cons Pty, past tres Kyre Church Restoration; FCA 1980; *Recreations* skiing, walking; *Style—* Lawrence Coppock, Esq; The Close, Church Lane, Braishfield, Nr Romsey, Hants SO51 OQH (☎ 0794 08284); B and Q plc, Portswood House, 1 Hampshire Corporate Park, Chandlers Ford, Eastleigh, Hants SO5 3YX (☎ 0703 256004, fax 0703 256030, car 0836 708957, telex 47233)

COPPOCK, Prof (John) Terence; s of Capt Arthur Leslie Coppock (d 1962), and Valerie Margaret, *née* Phillips (d 1981); *b* 2 June 1921; *Educ* Penarth County School, Queens Col Cambridge (BA, MA), Univ of London (PhD); *m* 6 Aug 1953, Shiela Mary, da of Dr Gerard Burnett (d 1985); 1 s (John b 1960), 1 da (Helena b 1955); *Career* cmmnd Welch Regt 1941, serv ME 1942-46, Lt RA 1942; reader dept of geography UCL 1964 (asst lectr 1950, lectr 1952), prof of geography Univ of Edinburgh 1965 (prof emeritus 1986); sec and tres Carnegie Tst for Univs for Scot; visiting prof: tourism and leisure studies Loughborough Univ, geography Birkbeck Coll; fell UCL; vice pres: Scottish Recreational Land Assoc, Scottish Inland Waterways Assoc; chm exec ctee Sco Field Studies Assoc 1977-80, memb Sco Sport Cncl 1976-87, clerical offr Lord Cncllrs Dept 1938-46, exec offr Miny of Works 1946-47, offr Customs and Excise 1947; MIBG 1948- (pres 1973-74), FRSGS, FRGS 1950, FBA 1975, FRSE 1976, FTS 1980, FRSA 1981, FRSGS 1988; *Books* The Changing Use of Land in Britain (with R H Best 1962), An Agricultural Atlas of England and Wales (1964), An Agricultural Geography of Great Britain (1971), Recreation in the Countryside: a Spatial Analysis (with BS Duffield 1975), An Agricultural Atlas of Scotland (1976), Agriculture in Developed Countries (1984), Innovation in Water Management: The Scottish Experience (with WBD Sewell and A Pithethly 1986); *Recreations* badminton, walking, listening to music; *Style—* Prof Terence Coppock; 57 Braid Ave, Edinburgh EH10 6EB (☎ 031 447 3443); Carnegie Trust for the Universities of Scotland, 22 Hanover St, Edinburgh EH2 2EN (☎ 031 220 1217)

CORAL, Bernard; s of Joseph Coral, of 84 Dorset House, Gloucester Place, London NW1 5AF, and Dorothy Helen, *née* Precha; *b* 10 Jan 1929; *Educ* Dame Alice Owens; *m* 11 March 1953, Diane Jean, da of William Charles Cameron (d 1956); 1 s (Anthony Paul b 1955), 2 da (Joanna Marie b 1956, Michele Alexandra b 1965); *Career* Nat Serv 1947-49; dir Joe Coral Ltd (later Coral Leisure plc) 1944 -80; chm: Coral & Co 1981, Wig and Pen Club 1981-, Bud Flanagan Leukaemia Fund; *Recreations* golf; *Clubs* Porters Park GC, RAC; *Style—* Bernard Coral, Esq; 19E Grove End Rd, St Johns Wood, London NW8 9SD (☎ 01 289 9125); 229-230 Strand, London WC2 RIBA (☎ 01 583 7255, car tel 0860 370037)

CORBALLY STOURTON, Hon Mrs Edward; Beatrice Cicely; da of late Harold Ethelbert Page, of Wragby, Lincs and Titchwell, Norfolk; *m* 1934, Hon Edward Plantagenet Joseph Corbally Stourton, DSO (d 6 March 1966, having assumed in 1927, the additional name of Corbally), yst s of 23 Baron Mowbray, 24 Baron Segrave, and 20 Baron Stourton (d 1893); 1 s, 1 da; *Style—* The Hon Mrs Edward P J Corbally Stourton; Arlonstown Cottage, Dunsany, Co Meath, Eire (☎ 046 25290)

CORBEN, David Edward; s of Cyril Edward Corben, of Mayfield Cottage, Manor Road South, Elmbridge, Surrey, and Florence Ethel Jessie, *née* Lewthwaite; *b* 5 Mar 1945; *Educ* St Paul's; *m* 4 Jan 1969 (m dis), Fiona Elizabeth Macleod, da of Prof David Stern, of Teddington, Middx; 1 s (Mark b 1971), 1 da (Victoria b 1973); *Career* Lloyds Broker; dir: Jardine Thompson Graham 1971- (md 1976, chm 1986), Jardine Insur Brokers plc 1981-, Lloyd-Roberts Gilkes 1976-, Jardine Reinsurance Hldg 1983- (chm), Matheson and Co 1984-; memb Lloyds; *Recreations* skiing, golf, tennis, motor racing, riding; *Clubs* Gresham; *Style—* David Corben, Esq; 42 Roedean Crescent, Roehampton, London SW15 (☎ 01 876 1969); 19 Eastcheap, London EC3 (☎ 01 623 4611)

CORBET, Lt-Col Sir John Vincent; 7 Bt (UK 1808) of Moreton Corbet, Shropshire, MBE (1946), JP ((Salop 1957), DL 1961); s of Archer Henry Corbet (d 1950, ggs of 1 Bt), and Anne Maria (Anita), *née* Buxton (d 1951); suc kinsman Sir Gerald Vincent Corbet, 6 Bt 1955; *b* 27 Feb 1911; *Educ* Shrewsbury, RMA Woolwich, Magdalene Coll Cambridge; *m* 1, 1 Feb 1937 (m dis 1948), Elfrida Isobel, eldest da of A G Francis; m 2, 18 Oct 1948, Doreen Elizabeth Stewart (d 6 April 1964), da of Arthur William Gibbon Ritchie, and formerly w of Richard Gray; m 3, 4 Jan 1965, Annie Elizabeth, MBE, da of James Lorimer, of Christchurch, New Zealand; *Career* Royal Engineers, War Service India, Burma, Malaya 1942-46, (mentioned in despatches), ret 1955; High Sheriff of Shropshire 1966; co cncllr 1973-87; OStJ; *Recreations* sailing; *Clubs* Royal Thames Yacht; *Style—* Lt-Col Sir John Corbet, Bt, MBE, JP, DL; Acton Reynald, nr Shrewsbury, Shropshire (☎ 093 928 259)

CORBET, Air Vice-Marshal Lancelot Miller; CB (1958), CBE (1944); s of late John Miller Corbet, of Melbourne, Australia, and Ella Beatrice Corbet; *b* 19 April 1898,Brunswick Australia; *Educ* Melbourne HS, Scotch Coll Melbourne, Melbourne Univ; *m* 1924, Gwenllian Elizabeth, da of late Thomas Powell Bennett, of Claremont, W Australia; 1 s; *Career* RAF 1933, Dep Dir-Gen of Medical Services Air Miny 1956-58, ret; KStJ; *Style—* Air Vice-Marshal Lancelot Corbet, CB, CBE; 24 Hensman St, South Perth 6151, Western Australia (☎ 367 3025)

CORBET-MILWARD, Cdr (Neville) Roger; s of George Herbert Milward (d 1959), and Margaret Irene Louisa Corbet (d 1962); descended from pre-Norman Conquest family of Corbet; *b* 12 Jan 1915; *Educ* RNC Dartmouth; *m* 6 Jan 1945, Erna Julie (lady in waiting Queen Maud of Norway), da of Georges von Tangen (d 1941), of Norway; 1 s (John b 1946), 1 da (Kristin b 1949); *Career* Cdr RN, served Med, S Africa (despatches 1940), Pilot Fleet Air Arm; qualified Flying Instr, Fleet Aviation Offr (staff of C in C Home Fleet and C in C E Atlantic 1952-54); Naval Attaché Oslo 1957; *Recreations* gardening, cooking, writing, walking; *Style—* Cdr Roger Corbet-Milward; The Glebe House, Holdfast, Upton-on-Severn, Worcester

CORBETT, Hon Mrs (Catherine); *née* Lyon-Dalberg-Acton; 3 da of 3 Baron Acton, CMG, MBE, TD (d 1989); *b* 30 Sept 1939; *m* 20 Feb 1960, Hon Joseph Mervyn Corbett, 4 s (but 2 surviving) of 2 Baron Rowallan, KT, KBE, MC, TD; 1 s, 1 da; *Style—* The Hon Mrs Corbett; Chittlegrove, Rendcomb, nr Cirencester, Glos

CORBETT, Gerald Michael Nolan; s of John Michael Nolan Corbett (d 1982), of Old Horsmans, Sedlescombe, Sussex, and Pamela Muriel *née* Gay; *b* 7 Sept 1951; *Educ* Tonbridge, Pembroke Coll Cambridge (foundation scholar MA), London Business Sch (MSc), Harvard Business Sch (exchange scholarship); *m* 19 April 1976, Virginia Moore, da of Neill Newsum, of The Old Rectory, Hindolweston, Norfolk; 1 s (John b 20 Jan 1981), 3 da (Sarah b 4 June 1979, Olivia b 13 Nov 1982, Josephine b 5 Oct 1984); *Career* conslt and case leader Boston Consulting Gp 1976-82; Dixons Gp plc: gp fin controller 1982-85, corporate fin dir 1985-87; fin dir Redland plc 1987-; Freeman: City of London, Worshipful Co of Glaziers 1988; *Recreations* rugby, cricket, bridge, walking; *Style—* Gerald Corbett, Esq; Holtsmere End Farmhouse, Redbourn, Herts (☎ 058 285 2336); Redland plc, Redland House, Reigate, Surrey (☎ 07373 42488, car tel 0836 253136)

CORBETT, Hugh Askew; CBE (1968), DSO (1945, DSC 1943); s of Rev Frederick St John Corbett (d 1919), of St George-in-the-East, London and Elsie Washington (formerly Corbett), *née* Askew (d 1958); *b* 25 June 1916; *Educ* St Edmunds Sch Canterbury; *m* 1945, Patricia Nancy, da of Thomas Patrick Spens, OBE, MC, LLD (d 1980); 3 s (Patrick, Andrew, Henry); *Career* served RN 1933-69 (Capt), Capt HMS Fearless 1965-67, ret; warden Cambridge Univ Centre 1969-83; *Clubs* MCC; *Style—* Capt Hugh Corbett, CBE, DSO, DSC, RN (retd); 3 Clare Rd, Cambridge CB3 9HN

CORBETT, Hon John Polson Cameron; s and h of 3 Baron Rowallan and his 1 w Eleanor; *b* 8 Mar 1947; *Educ* Eton, RAC Cirencester; *m* 1, 1971 (m dis 1983), (Susan) Jane Diane, da of James Green, of S Linden, Northumberland; 1 s (Jason b 1972), 1 da (Joanna b 1974); m 2, 17 April 1984, Sandrew Filomena, da of William Bryson, of Holland Green, Kilmaurs, Ayrshire; 1 s (Cameron b 1985), 1 da (Soay b 1988); *Career* estate agent; chm Heritage Circle 1980-; organiser: 2 horse trials at Rowallan (affiliated to BHS), show jumping festival at Rowallan (affiliated to BSJA); ARICS; landowner (1000 acres); *Recreations* skiing, riding, commentator; *Style—* The Hon John Corbett; Rowallan Castle, Kilmarnock, Ayrshire (☎ 0563 38254)

CORBETT, Hon Joseph Mervyn; 4 s but 2 surviving of 2 Baron Rowallan, KT, KBE, MC, TD, DL (d 1977); *b* 22 April 1929; *Educ* Eton, Corpus Christi Coll Cambridge; *m* 20 Feb 1960, Hon Catherine Lyon-Dalberg-Acton, da of 3 Baron Acton, CMG, MBE, TD; 1 s (Sebastian b 1963), 1 da (Victoria (Mrs Merrill) b 1961); *Style—* The Hon Joseph Corbett; Chittlegrove, Rendcomb, nr Cirencester, Glos

CORBETT, Hon Mrs (Melanie June); *née* Moynihan; da of 2 Baron Moynihan (d 1965), and his 2 w June Elizabeth, *née* Hopkins; *b* 19 August 1957; *m* 30 July 1983, Peter-John Stuart Corbett, s of late John M N Corbett, of Sedlescombe, Sussex; 2 da (Poppy Ann b 18 Aug 1986, Daisy Angelica Jak b 10 Dec 1988); *Style—* The Hon Mrs Corbett

CORBETT, (Richard) Panton; s of Richard William Corbett (d 1987), and Doris Vaughan, *née* Kimber; *b* 17 Feb 1938; *Educ* Eton, Aix en Provence Univ; *m* 1, 28 April 1962 (m dis 1972), Leila Francis, *née* Wolsten-Croft; 1 s (Oliver b 1965); m 2, 11 July 1974, Antoinette Sibley, CBE, *qv*, da of E G Sibley, of Birchington on Sea; 1 s (Isambard b 1980), 1 da (Eloise b 1975); *Career* 2 Lt Welsh Gds 1957; md Singer and Friedlander Hldgs plc 1973-; dir: Saxon Oil plc 1980-86, First British American Corpn Ltd 1976, Interfinance and Investment Corpn 1974-80, Tex Hldgs 1987; tstee Royal Ballet Benevolent Fund, memb exec and fin ctee Royal Acad of Dancing; Freeman City of Shrewsbury 1979; *Recreations* tennis, shooting, opera, skiing, fishing; *Clubs* Boodle's, Queens; *Style—* Panton Corbett, Esq; 24 Chapel St, London SW1X 7BY (☎ 01 235 4506); Grove Farm, Longnor, nr Shrewsbury; 21 New Street, Bishopsgate, London EC2M 4HR (☎ 01 623 3000, fax 01 623 2122, telex 886977)

CORBETT, Peter Richard; s of John Lionel Garton Corbett, of Hampshire and Isle of Mull, and Susan Irene Sybil, *née* Wykham; *b* 25 Feb 1968; *Educ* Radley; *m* 23 March 1968, Margaret Catherine, da of Richard Holiday Pott, OBE (d 1968); 2 s (Richard b 1972, Charles b 1976), 1 da (Catherine b 1969); *Career* ptnr Pearsons 1974-86, dir Agric Div of Prudential Property Services; FRICS; *Recreations* shooting, dorset horn sheep; *Style—* Peter R Corbett, Esq; Dene House, Binley, St Mary Bourne,

Hampshire (☎ 0264 73 315); Agriculture House, Stockbridge, Hamps (☎ 0264 210702, car phone 0836 522181)

CORBETT, Hon Robert Cameron; s of 2 Baron Rowallan, KT, KBE, MC, TD, DL; *b* 29 Nov 1940; *Educ* Eton, Ch Ch Oxford; *Clubs* White's, Beefsteak, Turf, Puffin's (Edinburgh); *Style*— The Hon Robert Corbett; Conkerton, Stewarton, Kilmarnock, Ayrshire (☎ 0560 82963)

CORBETT, Maj-Gen Robert John Swan; s of Robert Hush Swan Corbett (d 1988), of Boughton Monchelsea, and Yalding Hill, Kent, and Patricia Elizabeth Cavan-Lambart (d 1988); *b* 16 May 1940; *Educ* Shrewsbury; *m* 23 Sept 1966, Susan Margaret Anne, da of Brig Michael James Palmer O'Clock, CBE, MC, of Kington Langley, Wilts; 3 s (Tom b 6 Dec 1967, Jonathan b 30 May 1969, Michael b 7 June 1973); *Career* cmmnd 1959, Staff Coll Camberley 1972-73, cdr Gds' Independent Parachute Co 1973-75, Adj Sandhurst 1975-78, 2 i/c 1 Bn Irish Gds 1978-79, US Armed Forces Staff Coll 1979-80, Bde Maj (Lt Col) Household Div 1980-81, Co 1 Bn Irish Gds 1981-84, chief of Staff Br Forces Falkland Islands 1984-85, cdr 5 Airborne bde 1985-87, Royal Coll of Def Studies 1987, dir def programme MOD 1987-88, cmdt Br Sector Berlin, Regtl Lt Col Irish Gds 1988; Freeman City of London 1961, Liveryman Worshipful Co of Vintners 1975; MBIM; *Recreations* reading, travel, english parish church, architecture; *Clubs* Army and Navy, Pratts; *Style*— Maj-Gen Robert Corbett; c/o HQ British Sector, Berlin BFPO 45

CORBETT, Robin; MP (Lab) Birmingham Erdington 1983-; s of Thomas Corbett, of West Bromwich, Staffs, and Margaret Adele Mainwaring; *b* 22 Dec 1933,Freemantle, Australia,; *Educ* Holly Lodge GS Smethwick; *m* 1970, Val Hudson (asst editor Farmers Weekly 1965-69); 1 da; *Career* NUJ, sr Lab advsr IPC Magazines Ltd 1969-74, contested (Lab): Hemel Hempstead 1966, Feb 1974, West Derby (by-election) 1967; MP (Lab) Hemel Hempstead Oct 1974-1979; communications consultant 1979-83; chm PLP Home Affairs Gp 1983-85; jt-sec Australia and New Zealand Parly Gp 1983; West Midlands Labour Whip 1984-85; memb Select Ctee on Home Affairs 1983-85; front bench spokesman Home Affairs 1985-, vice-chm: all-party motor industry gp 1987-, Friends of Cyprus 1987-; *Recreations* walking, collecting bric-à-brac; *Style*— Robin Corbett, Esq, MP; House of Commons, London SW1A 0AA

CORBETT, (Timothy) William Edward; er s of Richard William Corbett, TD (d 1987), of Grove Farm House, Longnor, nr Shrewsbury, and Doris Vaughan, *née* Kimber; descended from the Ven Joseph Plymley, Archdeacon of Shropshire (d 1830), who assumed the surname and arms of Corbett by Royal Licence 1804 on s to the Longnor estates which had been in possession of a cadet branch of the Corbets of Caus Castle since early in the 17th cent (*see*) Burke's Landed Gentry, 18 edn, vol II, 1969); *b* 6 Nov 1935; *Educ* Eton, Univ of Aix-en-Provence, RAC Cirencester; *m* 27 Feb 1965, (Iza) Priscilla, 2 da of Lt-Col Stephen S Murcott, of The Old Rectory, Neenton, Bridgnorth, Shropshire; 2 s (James Edward Isham b 14 Aug 1971, Thomas Alexander Caradoc b 23 July 1983), 2 da (Sophie Louisa b 10 June 1966, Isabelle Sarah b 1 Feb 1968); *Career* farmer; chm Shropshire branch Nat Farmers' Union 1979; memb Shropshire CC 1981-85; *Recreations* skiing, shooting, windsurfing, bridge, humorous conversation; *Style*— William Galleway, Esq; Dower House, Longnor, nr Shrewsbury, Shropshire (☎ 074373 628)

CORBETT-WINDER, Col John Lyon; OBE (1949), MC (1942, JP (Montgomeryshire 1959)); o s of Maj William John Corbett-Winder (d 1950, Lord-Lt Montgomeryshire 1944-50), of Vaynor Park, Berriew, Welshpool, Powys, and Margery Sophia Bardwell (d 1968); *b* 15 July 1911; *Educ* Eton, RMC Sandhurst; *m* 1944, (Margaret) Ailsa Ramsay, da of Lt-Col Joseph Ramsay Tainsh, CBE, VD (d 1954); 1 s, 2 da; *Career* 2 Lt 60 Rifles 1931, Lt-Col 1942, served 1940-43, Cdr 44 Reconnaissance Regt and 1 Bn 60 Rifles (Western Desert and N Africa, despatches 2), Cdr 2 Bn 60 Rifles 1947-48 (Palestine, despatches), AAG HQ Southern Cmd 1949-51, GSO 1 53 Welsh Inf Div (TA) 1952-54, Col GS SHAPE Mission to Royal Netherlands Army 1955, Dep Mil Sec BAOR 1957, ret 1958 (RARO); memb Parly Boundary Cmmn for Wales 1963-79, pres TA and VR Assoc for Wales 1976-81; KStJ, Cdr of Order of Nassau (Netherlands) 1958; Lord-Lieut Montgomeryshire/Powys 1960-86; *Recreations* gardening, forestry; *Style*— Col John Lyon Corbett-Winder, OBE, MC, JP; Vaynor Park, Berriew, Welshpool, Powys SY21 8QE (☎ 0686 640204)

CORBY, (Frederick) Brian; s of Charles Walter Corby (d 1984), of Raunds, Northants, and Millicent, *née* Pentelow; *b* 10 May 1929; *Educ* Kimbolton Sch, St John's Coll Cambridge (MA); *m* 1 Aug 1952, Elizabeth Mairi, da of Dr Archibald McInnes (d 1973); 1 s (Nicholas b 1960), 2 da (Fiona b 1955, Jane b 1957); *Career* gp chief exec Prudential Corpn plc 1982-; chm: Prudential Assur Co Ltd 1982-, Mercantile and General Reinsurance Co plc 1985-; dir Bank of England 1985-; FIA 1955; *Recreations* golf, gardening, reading; *Style*— Brian Corby, Esq; Prudential Corporation plc, 142 Holborn Bars, London EC1N 2NH (☎ 01 405 9222, fax 01 936 8822)

CORBY, Peter John Siddons; s of John Siddons Corby (d 1955), and Helen Anna, *née* Ratray (d 1974); *b* 8 July 1924; *Educ* Taplow GS; *m* 1, 16 Dec 1950 (m dis 1959), Gail Susan Clifford-Marshall; 1 s (Michael b 1951), 1 adopted s (Mark b 1950); m 2, 2 April 1960, Ines Rosemary, da of Dr George Anderson Mandow, of The Sloop, 89 High St, Cowes, IOW; 1 s (John b 1962); *Career* RAFVR 1942-48, war serv Aircrew 4 Gp Bomber Cmd, transferred Class E Reserve RAFVRT 1948, resigned 1951; regained original family business Corbys Ltd and John Corby Ltd Windsor, created manufactured and marketed many products incl The Corby Electric Trouser Press (1961); dir numerous cos 1950-89: Thomas Jourdon plc, Colour Centre Ltd, Savetower Ltd; non-exec dir various cos incl Tormend Ltd, Tyremasters Ltd; port offr (Cowes) Ocean Cruising Club, ctee memb Royal London YC; Freeman City of London 1977, Liveryman Worshipful Co of Marketors 1978 (guild memb); FIOD 1955, memb Lloyds 1974; *Recreations* sailing, bridge; *Clubs* Royal London YC, Oriental, Ocean Cruising; *Style*— Peter Corby, Esq; The Sloop, 89 High St, Cowes, Isle of Wight PO31 7AW (☎ 0983 292188)

CORBYN, Jeremy Bernard; MP (Lab) Islington North 1983-; s of David Benjamin Corbyn; *b* 26 May 1949; *Educ* Adams GS Newport Shropshire; *m* issue; *Career* memb Haringey Boro Cncl 1974-83, NUPE area offr until 1983; *Recreations* running, gardening, keeps chickens, a dog, cats and terapins; *Style*— Jeremy Corbyn, Esq, MP; House of Commons, London SW1A 0AA

CORCUERA, Lady Mary Virginia Shirley; *née* Acheson; 3 and yst da of Lt-Col 5 Earl of Gosford, DL, MC (d 1954), by his 1 w; *b* 1919; *m* 12 Dec 1941, Fernando Corcuera (d 1978), s of Pedro L Corcuera y Palomar, of Mexico City; 2 s, 3 da; *Style*— Lady Mary Corcuera; Hidalgo 14, San Angel, Mexico City 01000, Mexico (☎ 5 48 95 33/34)

CORDIAL, Ian Fergusson; s of late John Cordial; *b* 14 Nov 1926; *Educ* Kilmarnock Acad, Edinburgh Univ (MA); *m* 1953, Anna Hall Scobbie, *née* Hood; 1 s, 2 da; *Career* dir Patons and Baldwins Ltd, chm British Hand Knitting Assoc; rugby internationalist; *Style*— Ian Cordial, Esq; The Ashes, Barton, Richmond, N Yorks (☎ Barton 232)

CORDINGLEY, Lady Emma Geraldine Anne; *née* Wallop; da of Viscount Lymington (d 1984), and sis of 10 Earl of Portsmouth; *b* 1958; *m* 1981, Gerald Thomas Cordingley, s of late Thomas Cordingley of Bridlington, Yorks; 2 da (Katie Madelaine b 1983, Venetia Ruth b 1985); *Style*— Lady Emma Cordingley; Cheesecombe Farm, Hawkley, Liss

CORDINGLEY, Maj-Gen John Edward; OBE (1959); s of Air Vice Marshal Sir John Walter Cordingley, KCB, KCVO, CBE (d 1977), and Elizabeth Ruth, *née* Carpenter (d 1938); *b* 1 Sept 1916; *Educ* Sherborne, RMA Woolwich; *m* 1, 8 Feb 1940 (m dis 1961), Ruth Pamela, yr da of Maj Sydney Alexander Boddam-Whetham, DSO, MC, RA (d 1925); 2 s (Michael, Patrick); m 2, 1961, Audrey Helen Anne, da of Maj-Gen Frederick George Beaumont-Nesbitt, CVO, CBE, MC (d 1971), and formerly w of Maj Gordon Rennie (d 1984); 2 step-da; *Career* cmmnd 2 Lt RA 1936, served WW II Europe and Far East, Bde Cdr 1961-62, IDC 1963, Dir Work Study MOD 1964-66, Dep Dir RA 1967-68, Maj-Gen RA BAOR 1968-71, ret; bursar Sherborne Sch 1971-73; Col Cmdt RA 1973-81, regimental comptroller RA 1975-82 and 1984-85; dir J W Carpenter 1977- (chm 1984-87); FInstWSP, MBIM, FInstD; *Recreations* golf, gardening; *Clubs* Army and Navy, Senior Golfers; *Style*— Maj-Gen John Cordingley, OBE; Church Farm House, Rotherwick, Nr Basingstoke, Hants RG27 9BG (☎ 025 672 2734)

CORDINGLY, Dr David Michael Bradley; s of Rt Rev Eric William Bradley Cordingly, MBE (d 1976), and Mary Eileen, *née* Mathews; *b* 5 Dec 1938; *Educ* Christ's Hosp, Oriel Coll Oxford (MA), Sussex Univ (DPhil); *m* 8 May 1971, Shirley Elizabeth, da of Ian Gibson Robin; 1 s (Matthew), 1 da (Rebecca); *Career* graphic designer with various design gps and publishers 1960-68, exhibition designer Br Museum 1968-71, keeper of Art Gallery and Museum The Royal Pavilion and Museums Brighton 1971-78, asst dir The Museum of London 1978-80, keeper of pictures Nat Maritime Museum 1986- (asst keeper 1980-86); FRSA 1974; Order of the White Rose, Finland 1986; *Books* Marine Painting in England (1974), Painters of the Sea (1979), The Art of the Van de Veldes (1982), Nicholas Pocock (1986), Captain James Cook, Navigator (ed 1988), contrib also articles Burlington Magazine, The Connoisseur, Apollo Magazine; *Style*— Dr David Cordingly; 2 Vine Place, Brighton, Sussex BN1 3HE; The National Maritime Museum, Greenwich, London SE10 9NF (☎ 01 858 4422)

CORDLE, John Howard; s of Earnest William Cordle (d 1967); *b* 11 Oct 1912; *Educ* City of London Sch; *m* m 1, 9 Aug 1938 (m dis 1956), Grace Lucy, da of Air Cdre the Rev James Rowland Walkey, CBE; 3 s (Anthony John b 29 July 1939, Paul Howard b 29 Jan 1941, Charles Henry b 1 Sept 1945), 1 da (Rosanne b 6 April 1948 d 1970); m 2, 1957 (m dis 1966) Venetia, da of Col Alistair Maynard, OBE; 1 s (Rupert b 14 May 1959), 3 da (Sophie b 9 Feb 1958, Marina b 6 May 1960, Rachel b 3 Aug 1963); m 3, 7 Feb 1976, Terttu Maija, da of Herra Mikko Ilmari Heikura (d 1951), of Nurmes, Finland; 2 s (John-William b 17 Feb 1981, Howard b 29 June 1983); *Career* RAF (cmmnd) 1940-45; chm EW Cordle & Son Ltd 1957 (dir 1946, md 1954), owner C of E Newspaper 1959-64; dir: Church soc 1951, Amalgamated Developers 1970; memb Lloyds 1952; chm Wessex Aid to Drug Addicts 1986-, princ Cordle Tst (for speech impared children); MP (Bournmouth and Christchurch 1959-77); life govr St Pauls and St Marys Coll Cheltenham, Freeman: City of London, Worshipful Co of Founders 1957 (under warden 1988); memb: UK delegation to Cncl of Europe 1974-77, Western Euro Union Paris 1974-77, Nat Church Assembly 1946-53; chm Oxford Tst of Churches Patronage Bd 1955-; Grand Band Order of the Star of Africa (Liberia); *Recreations* shooting, golf, tennis, gardening; *Clubs* Carlton, National, Royal Cwlth - ESU; *Style*— John Cordle, Esq; Malmesbury House, The Close, Salisbury, Wilts (☎ 0722 27027)

CORDREY, Peter Graham; s of Wg-Cdr Percival William George Cordrey, and Marjorie Joan, *née* Strickland; *b* 1 June 1947; *Educ* Wellingborough Sch Wellingborough, City Univ (MSc); *m* 1972, Carol Anne, da of Peter Lawrence Ashworth; 2 da (Joanne b 1979, Rowena b 1982); *Career* merchant banker and chartered accountant; head banking at Singer & Friedlander Ltd (dir Bank in 1982); dir: First Br American Corpn Ltd, Singer and Friedlander Leasing Ltd, City & Provincial Home Loans Ltd; *Recreations* tennis, golf, swimming; *Clubs* St George's Hill Tennis; *Style*— Peter Cordrey, Esq; Ockham End, Old Lane, Cobham, Surrey KT11 1NF (☎ 0932 67997); Singer & Friedlander Ltd, 21 New St, Bishopsgate, London EC2 (☎ 01 623 3000)

COREN, Alan; s of Samuel and Martha Coren; *b* 27 June 1938; *Educ* East Barnet GS, Wadham Oxford, Yale, Univ of California at Berkeley; *m* 14 Oct 1963, Anne, da of Michael Kasriel (d 1981), of London; 1 s (Giles b 1969), 1 da (Victoria b 1972); *Career* joined Punch 1963, asst ed 1963-66, literary ed 1966-68, dep ed 1968-78, editor 1978-87, ed The Listener 1988-, tv critic The Times 1971-78; columnist: Daily Mail 1972-76, and Mail on Sunday 1984-, The Times 1971-; contributor to Sunday Times, TLS, etc; rector St Andrew's Univ 1973-76; *Books* The Dog It Was That Died (1965), All Except the Bastard (1969), The Sanity Inspector (1974), The Bulletins of Idi Amin (1974), Golfing for Cats (1974), The Further Bulletins of Idi Amin (1975), The Lady From Stalingrad Mansions (1977), The Peanut Papers (1977), The Rhinestone as Big as the Ritz (1979), Tissues for Men (1980), The Best of Alan Coren (1980), The Cricklewood Diet (1982), Present Laughter (1982), (ed) The Penguin Book of Modern Humour (1983), Bumf (1984), Something for the Weekend (1986), Bin Ends (1987), (ed) The Pick of Punch (annual) 1979-, (ed) The Punch Book of Short Stories, Book 1 (1979), Book 2 (1980), Book 3 (1981), etc; tv series The Losers (1978); *Recreations* broadcasting, riding, bridge; *Style*— Alan Coren, Esq; Wit's End, Godshill Wood, Fordingbridge, Hants; The Listener, 199 Old Marylebone Road, London NW1 (☎ 01 258 3581)

CORFE, Harold Martin; s of Ernest William Corfe, LDS, RCS (d 1964), and Ethel, *née* Smith (d 1951); served S Africa 1900-01 as one of first 4 dental surgeons attached Br Army; *b* 13 July 1922; *Educ* Highgate Sch; *m* 17 June 1960, Elizabeth Rosaleen Mary, step-da of Lt-Col Stanley Middleton, OBE (d 1986); 3 s (Nicholas b 1962, Patrick b 1964, Crispin b 1966); *Career* Sgt Royal Tank Regt 1942-46, served: N Africa, Italy; sr ptnr Greene and Co 1973-86, chm Discretionary Unit Fund Mangrs

Ltd, dir Rights and Issues Investmt Tst plc; memb Int Stock Exchange; *Recreations* golf, tennis, gardening, swimming; *Clubs* Inst of Directors; *Style—* H M Corfe, Esq; Faircrouch, Wadhurst, E Sussex TN5 6PS (☎ 089 288 2358); 66 Wilson St, London EC2A 2BL (☎ 01 247 0007)

CORFIELD, Rt Hon Sir Frederick Vernon; PC (1970), QC (1972); o s of late Brig Frederick Alleyne Corfield, DSO, OBE, IA (d 1939), of Chatwall Hall, Leebotwood, Shrops, and Mary Graham, *née* Vernon (d 1968); *b* 1 June 1915; *Educ* Cheltenham, RMA Woolwich; *m* 1945, Elizabeth Mary Ruth, yr da of Edmund Coston Taylor, JP, of Arden, Church Stretton, Shrops; *Career* WWII served RA (POW); called to the Bar 1945, bencher of the Middle Temple; MP (Cons) S Glos 1955-Feb 1974, min Aerospace DTI 1971-72, min Aviation Supply 1970-71, min state BOT June-Oct 1970, jt parly sec Miny Housing and Local Govt 1962-64), rec Crown Ct 1979-87; vice chm Br Waterways Bd 1980-83 (memb 1974-83)' dir Mid-Kent Water Co, chm LAPDA 1975-; kt 1972; *Clubs* Army and Navy; *Style—* The Rt Hon Sir Frederick Corfield, QC; Wordings Orchard, Sheepscombe, nr Stroud, Glos

CORFIELD, Kenneth Frederick; s of Frederick William Corfield, of Dalecroft, Sandford, Somerset, and Lillian Mary, Corfield; *b* 11 Mar 1902; *Educ* Bromsgrove, Birmingham Univ (BSc); *m* 12 Sept 1930, (Constance) Betty, da of Lt-Col GHA Barron, of Havencliff, Seaton, Devon; 1 s (Peter John b June 1936), 1 da ((Elizabeth) Anne b April 1933); *Career* dist engr Sudan Govt Railways 1924-30, sr engr Miny of Tport; AMICE 1930, MICE 1960; *Style—* Kenneth Corfield, Esq; Collabridge, Dunsford, Devon (☎ 064 724 230)

CORFIELD, Sir Kenneth George; s of Stanley Corfield, and Dorothy Elizaeth, *née* Mason; *b* 27 Jan 1924; *Educ* Wolverhampton Polytechnic; *m* 1960; 1 da; *Career* formerly with ICI Metals, md K G Corfield 1950-60; formerly: exec dir Parkinson Cowan, dep chm STC, dir Midland Bank 1979-, tstee of Science Museum 1975-, pres Telecommunications Engrg Mfrs' Assoc 1974-80, vice pres Engrg Employers' Fedn 1979-85; former memb cncl: CBI, IOD; vice pres BIM 1978, first chm Br Engrg Cncl 1982-84, chm Standard Telephones and Cables plc 1979-85 (dir 1969-85), vice pres ITT Europe Inc 1967-85, sr offr International Telephone and Telegraph Corpn (UK) 1974-85, memb Advisory Council for Applied Res and Devpt 1981-84, dir Britoil Ltd 1982-, dir Octagon Group 1987-, dir Distributed Information Processing Ltd 1987-, memb Mgmnt Cncl Templeton College (Oxford Centre for Mgmnt Studies), DUniv Surrey 1976, Hon DSc: City 1981, Bath 1982, London 1982, Aston 1985; Hon Degree Strathclyde 1982, Hon DEng Bradford 1983, Hon Degree Open Univ 1985, Hon DSc Technology Loughborough 1983; Freeman City of London, Liveryman of Worshipful Co of Engrs and Co of Scientific Instrument Makers; past pres Inst of Dirs; CE, FEng, FIMechE, CBIM, CompIEE, kt 1980; *Recreations* photography, music; *Clubs* Carlton; *Style—* Sir Kenneth Corfield; 49 Whitehall, London SW1A 2BX

CORK, Sir Kenneth Russell; GBE (1978); s of late William Henry Cork, of Hatch End, Middx, and Maud Alice, *née* Nunn; *b* 21 August 1913; *Educ* Berkhamsted; *m* 1937, Nina, da of late Ernest Alfred Lippold; 1 s, 1 da; *Career* served WW II Lt-Col Italy and M East; sr ptnr WH Cork Gully and Co 1946-83; common councilman Ward of Billingsgate 1950-70, alderman Tower Ward 1970-83, alderman sheriff City of London 1975-76, lord mayor of London 1978-79, one of HM Lts for City of London 1980; sr ptnr W H Cork Gully and Co 1946-83; dir: Advent Eurofund Ltd, Advent Capital Ltd, Advent Mgmnt Ltd, Aitken Hume Int plc, Aitken Hume Ltd, Brent Walker Hldgs plc, Grimms Dyke (Liberty) Estates Ltd, Inst of Credit Mgmnt Ltd, Ladbroke Gp plc (vice chm), Richmount Enterprise Zone Mangrs Ltd, Royal Shakespeare Enterprises Ltd, Royal Shakespeare Theatre (pres), Testaferrata Moroni Viani (Hldgs) Ltd; Liveryman: Worshipful Co of Horners, Worshipful Co of Chartered Accountants in Eng and Wales; Hon Freeman Inst of Chartered Secs and Administrators; pres City Branch IOD, Vity Branch BIM; Cdr de l'Ordre du Mérite (France), Order of Rio Branco (Brazil) 1976, Grand Oficiàl da Ordem Militaire de Cristo (Portugal), Order of Diplomatic Service Merit Gwanghwa Medal (Korea) 1979; Hon DLitt; FCA, FRSA, FCIS, FBIM; KStJ 1979; *Books* Cork on Cork (1988); *Recreations* sailing, photography, painting; *Clubs* Royal Thames Yacht, City Livery, Little Ship, Bosham Sailing; *Style—* Sir Kenneth Cork, GBE; Cherry Trees, Grimms Hill, Great Missenden, Bucks (☎ 02406 2628)

CORK, Major Norman Barrington; s of William Henry Cork (d 1940), of Hatch End, Middx, and Maud Alice, *née* Nunn (d 1964); *b* 08 Nov 1910; *Educ* Berhamsted Sch; *m* 1, 15 June 1935, Beryl May (d 1966), da of Herbert Ancell (d 1959), of Moor Park, Herts; 1 s (Michael b 26 Oct 1938), 1 da (Patricia b 28 Aug 1942); m 2, 22 March 1967, Pauline May, da of Charles Chamount (d 1948); *Career* serv Queen's Own Oxfordshire Hussars, WO section RA 2B and MI (L), later i/c Op Snowflake, seconded to Swedish Army onLiaison upon cessation of Hostilities, then to Swiss Army on Liaison, ret 1946; 1946- rejointed family firm of CAs in City of London; former dir and chm of various companies (now retired); memb exec ctee of cncl of mgmnt White Ensign Assoc HMS Belfast (London, SE1), gen cmmr of income tax (hon) in City of London; former chm Cons Assoc of Latimer and Ley Hill; Ordre Souverain De Saint-Jean De Jerusalem, Hon Maj Swiss Army 1946; *Recreations* shooting, golf; *Clubs* Royal Cinque Ports GC (Kent), Denham (Bucks); *Style—* Major Norman Cork; The Home Farm, Latimer, Bucks HP5 1TZ (☎ 024 04 2475); 10 Lowndes St, London SW1X 9EU (☎ 01 235 4516, car tel 0836 220505)

CORK, Roger William; s of Sir Kenneth Russell Cork, GBE, of Great Missenden, *qv*, and Lady Nina, *née* Lippold; *b* 31 Mar 1947; *Educ* St Martins Sch Northwood, Uppingham; *m* 9 May 1970, Barbara Anita Pauline, da of Reginald Harper, of Herne Bay; 1 s (Christopher b 1971), 2 da (Melissa b 1973, Georgina b 1974); *Career* CA: articled Moore Stephens & Co 1965-69, ptnr W H Cork Gully 1970- (joined 1969, W H Cork Gully changed to Cork Gully 1980 and associated with Coopers & Lybrand 1980); ptnr: Cork Gully 1980-, Coopers & Lybrand 1980-; memb: exec ctee Bucks Assoc of Youth Clubs, PCC St Mary at Hill, PCC and church warden St Olaves; church warden St Andrew Hubbard; govr St Dunstan's Coll Educnl Fndn, tstee Tower Hill Tst, hon memb Ct HAC, memb City of London Archaeological Tst, magistrate alderman Ward of Tower City of London 1983- (common councilman 1978-83), fndr memb Tower Ward Club (pres 1984-), master Billingsgate Ward Club 1980-81; Freeman City of London; memb: Co of Bowyers (renter warden 1988), Co of Butchers, Co of CAs, Guild of World Traders; fndr pres Fedn of Euro Credit Mgmnt Assocs; IOD (chm London Branch); past chm inst of Credit Mgmnt; FCA, FIPA, FICM; *Recreations* sailing, photography, DIY; *Clubs* Livery, Hardway Sailing, RYA; *Style—* Alderman Roger Cork, Esq; Rabbs, The Lee, Great Missenden, Bucks HP16 9NX (☎ 024, 020 296); Cork Gully, Shelley House, 3 Noble St, London EC2V 7DQ (☎ 01 606 7700, fax 01 606 9887, car tel 0860 311610, telex 884 730 CORKY G)

CORK AND ORRERY, 13th Earl of (I 1620); Patrick Reginald Boyle; also (sits as) Baron Boyle of Marston (GB 1711), Baron Boyle of Youghal (I 1616), Viscount Dungarvan (I 1620), Viscount Boyle of Kinalmeaky, Baron of Bandon Bridge and Baron Boyle of Broghill (I 1628), Earl of Orrery (I 1660); s of Major the Hon Reginald Courtenay Boyle, MBE, MC (d 1946); suc unc, 12 Earl 1967 (whose ancestor, 5 Earl, gave his name to the astronomical instrument known as an Orrery); *b* 7 Feb 1910; *Educ* Harrow, Sandhurst; *m* 1, 1952, Dorothy Kate (d 1978), da of Robert Ramsden and formerly w of (1) Marchese Demetrio Imperiali di Francavilla and (2) G F Scelsi; m 2, 1978, Mary Gabrielle, da of late Louis Ginnett and widow of Kenneth McFarlane Walker; *Heir* bro, Hon John Boyle, DSC; *Career* serv Burma Rifles SE Asia 1941-45, Maj Cameronians Scottish Rifles (severely wounded); sits as Cons in House of Lords; dep speaker and dep chm of ctees House of Lords 1973-78, memb of Cncl Cancer Res Campaign, hereditary life govr and exec chm Christian Faith Soc; vice-pres St Christophers Hospice Sydenham; FRSA; *Style—* The Rt Hon the Earl of Cork and Orrery; Flint House, Heyshott, Midhurst, W Sussex

CORKE, Martin Dewe; JP, DL; s of Lt Col Francis St Claire Corke (d 1971), and Aileen Joyce, *née* Lake (d 1989); *b* 8 June 1923; *Educ* Radley; *m* 1, 1948, Jean Violet Burton Denholm, da of George Denholm Armour (d 1949); 2 s (Piers, Nicholas), 2 da (Penelope, Juliet); m 2, 1984, France Margrete, da of Harold Marks, of London; *Career* WWII Capt India 1942-45; chm: West Suffolk Health Authy 1982, Theatre Royal Bury St Edmunds 1980; brewery dir; md Greene King and Sons plc 1983, Suffolk Gp Radio 1981; Capt Suffolk CCC 1946-65, played hockey for Berks and Cambs; *Recreations* foxhunting; *Clubs* MCC; *Style—* Martin Corke, Esq, JP, DL; Old Rectory, Gt Whelnetham, Bury St Edmunds (☎ 028 486 233)

CORKE, Hon Mrs (Shirley Frances); *née* Bridges; da of 1 Baron Bridges, KG, GCB, GCVO, MC, FRS (d 1969), and Hon Katharine, da of 2 Baron Farrer; *b* 23 Oct 1924; *m* 15 June 1957, Hilary Topham Corke, s of Alfred Topham Corke (d 1935), of Malvern, Worcs; 1 s, 3 da; *Style—* The Hon Mrs Corke; Eversheds, Abinger Hammer, Surrey

CORKE, Trafford Willoughby; s of Dr Antony Trafford Kernot Corke, of Lymington, Hampshire, and Marjorie, *née* Bassett; *b* 9 Feb 1948; *Educ* Clifton Coll Bristol; *m* 26 July 1976, Avril Bevan, da of William Davies, of Milford-on-Sea, Hampshire; 1 s (Peter Trafford Michael b 22 March 1978), 1 da (Helen Charlotte Avril b 4 April 1980), 1 step s (Mathew Mansell Walker b 28 March 1972); *Career* press and agency appts 1966-78, chm Willoughby Stewart Assocs Ltd 1978-, dir Sadler Int Ltd 1988-; MInstM 1977-; *Recreations* skiing, yachting, croquet, lawn mowing; *Clubs* Empress Garden, Berkeley Street; *Style—* Trafford W Corke, Esq; 50 Christchurch Rd, Ringwood, Hampshire BH24 1DW (☎ 0425 478 001, fax 0425 479 988, car tel 0836 291 262, telex 418428 WSAWSA G)

CORKERY, Michael; QC (1981); s of Charles Timothy Corkery (d 1968), of London, and Nellie Marie, *née* Royal; *b* 20 May 1926; *Educ* Kings Sch Canterbury; *m* 29 July 1967, Juliet Shore, da of Harold Glyn Foulkes (d 1966), of Shrewsbury; 1 s (Nicholas b 8 June 1968), 1 da (Charlotte b 29 May 1970); *Career* Lt Welsh Guards 1944-48; barr Lincoln's Inn 1949; jr Treasury Counsel 1959-70, sr Treasury Counsel 1970, 1 sr treasury counsel at Central Criminal Ct 1979-81; bencher Lincoln's Inn 1973; *Recreations* fishing, shooting, sailing, music, gardening; *Clubs* Cavalry and Guards', Hurlingham, Itchenor Sailing, Guards' Polo, Friends of Arundel Cricket; *Style—* Michael Corkery, Esq, QC; 5 Paper Buildings, Temple, London EC4 (☎ 01 583 6117)

CORLETT, Clive William; s of Frederick William Corlett (d 1973), of Bebington, Wirral, and Hanna Corlett; *b* 14 June 1938; *Educ* Birkenhead Sch, Brasenose Coll Oxford (BA); *m* 15 Feb 1964, Margaret Catherine, da of John Mathew Jones (d 1977), of Moelfre, Anglesey; 1 s (Stephen b 1975); *Career* joined Inland Revenue 1960; seconded to: Civil Serv Selection Bd 1970, HM Treasy 1972-74 (as private sec to Chllr Exchequer) and 1979-81; under sec Bd of Inland Revenue 1985-; *Recreations* walking; *Style—* Clive W Corlett, Esq; Somerset House, Strand, London, WC2

CORLETT, Dr Ewan Christian Brew; OBE; s of Malcolm James John Corlett (d 1956), and Catherine Ann, *née* Brew (d 1964); *b* 11 Feb 1923; *Educ* King William's Coll IOM, Oxford (MA), Durham Univ (Phd); *m* 1945, Edna Lilian, da of Arthur James Buggs, of Bromley, Kent; 3 s (Nigel, Brian, Malcolm); *Career* Naval Architect; chm and md Burness Corlett and Ptnrs 1952- (naval architects and marine conslts); Naval Architect to GB Project; tstee Nat Maritime Museum Greenwich; warden of Worshipful Co of Shipwrights; *Recreations* yachting (Stronnag), model shipbuilding; *Clubs* Manx Sailing and Cruising, Astronomy; *Style—* Dr Ewan Corlett, OBE; Cottimans, Port-e-Vullen, Ramsey IOM (☎ Ramsey 814009); Burness, Corlett and Ptnrs, Shipdesine House, Ramsey, IOM (☎ (0624) 813210)

CORLETT, Gerald Lingham; s of late Alfred Lingham Corlett; *b* 8 May 1925; *Educ* Rossall, Aberdeen Univ; *m* 1957, Helen, *née* Williamson; 3 s, 1 da; *Career* Lt Royal Indian Artillery; chm: Higsons Brewery plc 1982-88 (dir 1955-88), Radio City (Sound of Merseyside) plc 1985-88; dir Westminster Tst (Liverpool); tstee: AC Morrell Settlement, Bluecoat Soc Liverpool, S Sefton Laser Tst; cncl memb Rosall Sch; *Style—* Gerald Corlett, Esq; Kirk House, 4 Abbey Rd, W Kirby, Merseyside L48 7EW (☎ 051 625 5425)

CORLEY, Sir Kenneth Sholl Ferrand; s of late Sidney Walter Corley, of London, and late A L Corley; *b* 3 Nov 1908; *Educ* St Bees Cumberland; *m* 1937, Olwen Mary, da of Maurice Hart Yeoman, of London; 1 s, 1 da; *Career* chm and chief exec Joseph Lucas (Industries) Ltd 1969-73 (joined 1927); Chevalier de la Legion D'Honneur; kt 1972; *Clubs* Royal Automobile; *Style—* Sir Kenneth Corley; 34 Dingle Lane, Solihull, W Midlands (☎ 021 705 1597); Yewtree, Wasdale, Cumbria (☎ Wasdale 285)

CORLEY, His Honour; Michael Early Ferrand; s of Ferrand Edward and Elsie Maria Corley; *b* 11 Oct 1909; *Educ* Marlborough, Oriel Coll Oxford; *Career* barr 1934, circuit judge 1967-82 (ret); *Style—* His Honour Michael Corley; The Old Rectory, Rectory Road, Broome, Norfolk NR35 2HU

CORLEY, Paul John; s of Robert Charles Corley, MM, of Glebe Rd, Weston Super Mare, and Margaret Dorothy, *née* Hyde; *b* 23 Dec 1950; *Educ* Bablake Sch Coventry, Worcester Coll Oxford (BA); *m* 1973 (m dis 1978) ; *Style—* Paul Corley, Esq; Low Town Farm, Farlam, Brompton, Cumbria; Border TV, Carlisle, Cumbria (☎ 0228 25101)

CORLEY, Peter Maurice Sinclair; s of James Maurice Corley (d 1975), and Barbara Shearer, *née* Sinclair; *b* 15 June 1933; *Educ* Marlborough, Kings Coll Cambridge (MA);

m 11 March 1961, Dr Marjorie Constance Corley, MA, MB, BChir, da of William John Doddridge (d 1982); 2 da (Carolyn b 1963, Rosalind b 1968); *Career* entered civil serv 1957, commercial sec Brussels 1969-71, dir gen Economic Cooperation Off Riyadh 1976-78, under sec DTI 1981-; *Recreations* bookbinding; *Clubs* Oxford and Cambridge; *Style—* Peter Corley, Esq; c/o Dept of Trade and Industry, 1 Victoria St, London SW1H 0ET

CORLEY SMITH, Gerard Thomas; CMG (1952); s of Thomas Smith (d 1961), and Nina Alice, *née* Brown (d 1932); *b* 30 July 1909; *Educ* Bolton Sch, Emmanuel CollCambridge (BA); *m* 1937, Joan Marcia Geraldine (d 1984), da of Sir Godfrey Digby Napier Haggard; 1 s (Peter), 3 da (Gillian, Clare, Nicola); *Career* HM Diplomatic Service, various consular posts 1931-45, labour attaché Brussels 1945-48; cllr UK Delgn to UNO and alternate rep on UN Econ and Social Cncl 1949-52; press cnsllr Brit Embassy Paris 1952-54, labour cllr Br Embassy Madrid 1954-59; ambass: Haiti 1960-62, Ecuador 1962-67; sec gen Charles Darwin Fndn for the Galapagos Islands 1972-82; Grand Offr of the Order of Merit (Ecuador) 1980; *Recreations* music, mountains, birds; *Clubs* Travellers; *Style—* G T Corley Smith, Esq, CMG; Greensted Hall, Ongar, Essex CM5 9LD (☎ 0277 362031)

CORMACK, Ian Donald; s of Andrew Gray Cormack, of Falmouth, Cornwall, and Eliza Cormack; *b* 12 Nov 1947; *Educ* Falmouth GS, Pembroke Coll Oxford (BA); *m* 14 Sept 1968, (Elizabeth) Susan, da of Mark Tallack (d 1976), of Penryn, Cornwall; 1 s (James Mark Ian (Jamie) b 1975), 1 da (Sally Elizabeth b 1979); *Career* Citicorp: joined Citibank 1969-, dir SCAM 1976-78, dir Euro Trg Centre 1979, personnel dir N Europe 1980-84, head fin insts gp 1984-; chm: Citicorp UK Pension Fund 1980-, Citicorp Tstee Co 1987-, Infocast Ltd 1988-; memb: cncl of Assoc of Payment Clearing Systems, bd Cedel SA Luxembourg, chm Woolnoth Soc of City of London; *Recreations* soccer, golf, fly fishing, theatre; *Clubs* RAC; *Style—* Ian Cormack, Esq; Holly Lodge, Lammas Lane, Esher, Surrey KT10 8PA (☎ 0372 67730); Citibank NA, 336 Strand, London (☎ 01 438 1157, fax 01 836 5180)

CORMACK, Hon Mrs (Gwendoline Rita) Jean; *née* Davies; yr da of 1 Baron Davies of Plas Dinam, Llandinam, Montgomeryshire (d 1944), and Henrietta Margaret, *née* Fergusson (d.1948); *b* 1929,May; *Educ* Havergal Coll Toronto Canada, Downe House, House of Citizenship; *m* 1950 (m dis), John McRae Cormack, AFC, MA, s of Lt-Col H S Cormack of Mossgiel, Culver Road, Felpham, Sussex (d 1952); 1 s (Michael d 1980), 3 da (Shara, Amanda, Teresa); *Career* memb gen cncl and ctee of mgmnt Atlantic Salmon Tst; *Recreations* fishing; *Style—* The Hon Mrs Jean Cormack

CORMACK, Sir Magnus Cameron; KBE (1970); s of William Petrie Cormack and Violet McDonald Cameron; *b* 12 Feb 1906; *Educ* St Peter's Sch Adelaide S Australia; *m* 1935, Mary Gordon, *née* Macmeiken; 1 s, 3 da; *Career* farmer, pres Liberal Pty Organisation 1947-49, senator Victoria 1951-53 and 1962-78, pres of Senate 1971-74; *Style—* Sir Magnus Cormack, KBE; 7 Market Court, Portland, Vic 3305, Australia

CORMACK, Lady Miranda Maxwell; *née* Fyfe; da of 1 and last Earl of Kilmuir, PC, GCVO (d 1967); *b* 13 Dec 1938; *m* 2 April 1960, Michael Ormiston Cormack, er s of late H M Cormack, of Bookham, Newton Valence, Hants; 2 s, 1 da; *Career* teacher; *Style—* Lady Miranda Cormack; 31 White Hart Wood, Sevenoaks, Kent (☎ 0732 457230)

CORMACK, Patrick Thomas; MP (C) S Staffs 1983-; s of Thomas Charles Cormack, of Grimsby, and Kathleen Mary Cormack; *b* 18 May 1939; *Educ* St James' Choir Sch, Havelock Sch (both Grimsby), Univ of Hull; *m* 1967, Kathleen Mary, da of William Eric McDonald, of Aberdeen; 2 s; *Career* second master St James' Choir Sch Grimsby 1961-66, former english master and asst housemaster at Wrekin Coll, head of history dept Brewood GS Stafford; MP (C): Cannock 1970-74, Staffs SW 1974-83; pps to jt parly secs DHSS 1970-73; chm: All-Party Ctee Widows and One Parent Families 1974, Cons Pty Arts and Heritage Ctee 1979-83, All-Party Heritage Ctee 1979-; memb: select ctee Educ Science and Arts 1979-83, Speaker's Panel of Chairmen in the House 1983-, Faculty Jurisdiction Cmmn, Royal Cmmn on Historical Manuscripts 1981-, Historic Buildings Cncl 1979-85, Cncl for Br Archaeology; tstee Historic Churches Preservation Tst; vice-chm Heritage in Danger; cncl of Winston Churchill Memorial Trust 1983-; Honorary Citizen of Texas; FSA; *Books* Heritage in Danger (1976), Right Turn (1978), Westminster Palace and Parliament (1981), Castles of Britain (1982), Wilberforce the Nation's Conscience (1983), English Cathedrals (1984); *Recreations* visiting old churches, fighting philistines, not sitting on fences; *Clubs* Athenaeum, Brooks's; *Style—* Patrick Cormack, Esq, MP; House of Commons, London SW1A 0AA (☎ 01 219 5019/5514)

CORNER, John Michael; s of Thomas Matthias Corner, of Bishop Auckland, Co Durham, and Winifred, *née* Bell; *b* 2 Oct 1939; *Educ* King James I GS Bishop Auckland, Manchester Univ; *m* 3 Sept 1963, Gwendoline, da of Robert William Cook, of Bishop Auckland, Co Durham; 1 s (Adam b 1966); *Career* reporter The Northern Echo Darlington 1960-64, chief reporter The Northern Echo Darlington 1964-66, news ed The Northern Echo Darlington 1966-68, night news ed Morning Telegraph Sheffield 1968-73 (asst ed 1973-78), asst ed The Star Sheffield 1978-82, ed Sheffield Weekly Gazette 1982-83, ed The Star Sheffield 1983-, dir Sheffield Newspapers 1983-; memb: Br Section of Int Press Inst, Cncl of Cwlth Press Union, BBC NE Advsy Cncl, Cncl of Sheffield Chamber of Commerce, Sheffield Indust Year Ctee and Indust Matters Ctee, Sheffield Image Ctee, Sheffield Univ Chllr's Ctee on Br Assoc; tstee: Northern Radio, Five Weirs Walk, The Star Old Folk's Fund; govr Tapton Sch Sheffield; winner Cwlth Press Scholarship 1975; chm Parly and Legal Ctee Guild of Br Newspaper Eds 1984-; memb Guild of Br Newspaper Eds 1982; *Recreations* squash, gardening, snooker; *Style—* Michael Corner, Esq; 11 Winchester Crescent, Sheffield S10 4ED; The Star, York Street, Sheffield S1 1PU (☎ 0742 767676, fax 0742 753551, telex 265863)

CORNES, David Langford; s of Alan Howard Cornes (d 1974), of Endon, Staffs, and Joyce, *née* Phillipson; *b* 31 August 1944; *Educ* Rydal Sch, King's Coll London (BSc); *m* 27 July 1978, Katrina Penelope Darking, da of Kenneth John Smith, of Sherborne, Dorset; 2 s (Oliver William b 1972, Edward Fergus b 1982), 1 da (Charlotte Lucy b 1970); *Career* slr, sr ptnr Winward Fearon & Co; MICE, CEng, AKC; *Recreations* gardening, walking; *Style—* David Cornes, Esq; Manor Cottage, The Manor Hse, Little Gaddesden, Berkhamsted, Herts HP4 1PL (☎ 044 284 3336); Winward Fearon & Co, 35 Bow St, London WC2E 7AU (☎ 01 836 9081, fax 01 836 8382, telex 267651 WEWIN)

CORNES, John Addis; s of John Frederick Cornes; *b* 16 August 1944; *Educ* Eton, Oxford Univ; *m* 1971, Veronica Mary Alicia; 2 children; *Career* dir: West Downs Sch Ltd, Langton Investmt Services, Framlington Unit Mgmnt Ltd, Framlington Pensions Ltd; *Recreations* walking, watching sport; *Style—* John Cornes, Esq; Woodgates Farm, East Bergholt, Colchester, Essex

CORNESS, Sir Colin Ross; s of late Thomas Corness and Mary Evlyne, *née* Lovelace; *b* 9 Oct 1931; *Educ* Uppingham, Magdalene Cambridge (BA, MA), Harvard; *Career* Lt 3 Carabiniers (Prince of Wales) Dragoons Gds; barr 1956; chm Redland plc 1977- (md 1967-82); dir: W H Smith and Son plc 1980-87, Chubb and Son plc 1974-84, Nat Westminster Bank (SE regional bd) 1982-86, Courtaulds plc 1986-, Gordon Russell plc 1985-, S G Warburg Gp plc 1987-, Unitech plc 1987-; memb: Nat Econ Devpt Ctee for Building 1980-84, Indust Devpt Advsy Bd 1982-84; pres Nat cncl of Building Material Prods 1985, dir Bank of England 1987-, memb Advsy Bd Br-American C of C 1987-; kt 1986; *Recreations* squash rackets, music, travel; *Clubs* White's, Cavalry and Guards, Australian (Sydney); *Style—* Sir Colin Corness; 14 Alexander Sq, London SW3 (☎ 01 584 5986); Redland plc, Redland House, Reigate, Surrey RH2 0SJ (☎ 073 72 42488, telex 28626)

CORNFORD, Sir (Edward) Clifford; KCB (1977), CB (1966); s of John Herbert Cornford, of E Grinstead; *b* 6 Feb 1918; *Educ* Kimbolton Sch, Jesus Coll Cambridge; *m* 1945, Catherine, da of Frank Muir; 3 s, 3 da; *Career* Royal Aircraft Establishment 1938; chief exec and perm under-sec of state MOD (Procurement Exec) 1975-77, chief of Defence Procurement 1977-80; FRAeS, FEng; *Style—* Sir Clifford Cornford, KCB, CB; Beechurst, Shaftesbury Rd, Woking, Surrey (☎ 04862 68919)

CORNFORD, Geoffrey Arthur; TD (1945); s of the late Arthur Corniford, and Alice Camfield; *b* 25 April 1920; *Educ* Lewes County; *m* 25 Jan 1947, Lois Louise, da of Gerald Owen Quekett; 1 s (Simon Geoffrey), 2 da (Anstice Louise, Gillian Lois); *Career* WWII 1939-45; jnd as Sapper (RE) 1939, evacuated Dunkirk, cmmnd 1942, served Greece (acting Lt-Col), N Africa, Sicily, Italy and Austria with 13 Corps and Popskis Pte Army; articled T Burdett engr Uckfield RDG, asst engr Godstone RDC, town planning offr Uckfield RDC and Hailsham RDC, mangr (E Sussex), A C Draycott; ptnr Cornford Scott Robins, Tunbridge Wells; past chm and md: White Chalk Investments, Chalk Blue Estates, Gustaways Properties, Beauford Homes; chm: Ultramark Ltd, Mistywell Ltd; memb: Crowborough CC (past hon sec, chmn and Capt), Eastbourne CC (past Capt), Sussex RFC (past pres and 52 years on ctee), Sussex CCC (vice chm 1966-68); Freeman City of London (1966), Liveryman Gold and Silver Wyre Drawers Co (1966); *Clubs* MCC; *Style—* G A Cornford, Esq, TD; Little Swaines, 173 Turkey Rd, Bexhill (☎ 04243 6139); Enterprise Centre, Station Parade, Eastbourne (☎ 0323 639 504)

CORNISH, Alan Stewart; s of Alfred Stewart Cornish (d 1980), of Orpington Kent, and Ann Selina Westgate; *b* 27 April 1944; *Educ* Beckenham & Penge Co; *m* 8 March 1969, Daphne Elisabeth, da of Charles Gordon Saunders; 3 s (Nigel b 1972, Graham b 1975, Iain b 1982); *Career* gp fin controller assoc communications corpn plc 1975-82, vp Euro regnl off RCA records 1982-84, gp chief exec Good Relations Gp plc 1984-86, gp md Lowe Bell communications Ltd 1986-; cc fndr memb Orpington Dist Guide Dogs for the Blind assoc; London Borough of Bromley: cncllr 1974-80, dep ldr 1976-78, dep mayor 1978-79; ACMA 1971, FBIM 1978, FInst D 1986, FCMA 1976; *Recreations* sport; *Clubs* local cc, local badminton; *Style—* Alan Cornish, Esq; 7 Hertford St, London W1Y 7DY (☎ 01 495 4044, fax 629 1279, car tel 0836 279308)

CORNISH, (Robert) Francis; LVO (1978); s of C D Cornish; *b* 18 May 1942; *Educ* Charterhouse, RMA Sandhurst; *m* 1964, Alison Jane Dundas; 3 da; *Career* cmmnd 14/20 King's Hussars 1962; entered FCO 1968, Kuala Lumpur 1970, Jakarta 1971, first sec FCO 1973, Bonn 1976-80; asst private sec to HRH The Prince of Wales 1980-83; high cmmr Brunei 1983-1986, cnsllr (info), Washington and head of Br Info Servs, New York 1986-; *Clubs* Cavalry and Guards; *Style—* Francis Cornish, Esq, LVO; c/o Foreign and Cwlth Office, King Charles St, London SW1; British Embassy, 3100 Massachusetts Ave NW, Washington DC 20008, USA

CORNISH, James Easton; s of Eric Easton Cornish, of Scotland, and Ivie Hedworth, *née* McCulloch; *b* 5 August 1939; *Educ* Eton, Wadham Coll Oxford; *m* 1968, Ursula, da of Prof H R Pink, of German Federal Republic; 1 s (Toby b 1972); *Career* HM Dip Serv 1961-85; HM Embassy Bonn, BMG Berlin, HM Embassy Washington, Central Policy Review Staff; asst dir Phillips and Drew 1985-87, County Nat West Securities 1987, market Strategist 1988; *Recreations* reading; *Style—* James Cornish, Esq; Drapers Gardens, 12 Throgmorton Avenue, London EC2N 2ES

CORNISH, Prof William Rodolph; s of Jack Rodolph Cornish (d 1978), and Elizabeth Ellen, *née* Reid; *b* 9 August 1937; *Educ* St Peter's Coll Adelaide, Adelaide Univ (LLB), Oxford Univ (BCL); *m* 25 July 1964, Lovedy Elizabeth, da of Edward Christopher Moule (d 1942), 1 s (Peter b 1968) 2 da (Anna b 1970, Cecilia b 1972); *Career* lectr in law LSE 1962-68, reader QMC Coll London 1969-70, prof english law LSE 1970-; FBA 1984; *Books* The Jury (second edn 1970), Intellectual Property: Patents, Copy, Trade Marks and Allied Rights (1, 2 edn 1989), Law and Society in England 1750-1950 (1989); *Style—* Prof William Cornish; 74 Palace Rd, London, SW2, (☎ 01 405 7686)

CORNOCK, Maj-Gen Charles Gordon; CB (1988), MBE (1974); s of Gordon Wallace Cornock (d 1978), of Warwicks, and Edith Mary, *née* Keeley; *b* 25 April 1935; *Educ* King Alfred Sch, RMA Sandhurst; *m* 1962, Kay, da of Cyril John Sidney Smith (d 1987), of Jersey; 2 s (Ian b 1963, James b 1966); *Career* cmmnd RA 1956, CO 7 Para RHA 1974-76 (despatches 1975), cdr RA 3 Armd Div 1979-81, student Royal Coll of Def Studies 1982, dep cmdt Army Staff Coll Camberley, dir RA 1984-86, chief of Staff Live Oak 1986-; mangr England Jrs Hockey Team 1978-79; pres Army and Combined Serv Hockey 1985-87; FBIM; *Recreations* hockey, tennis, golf, skiing, water skiing; *Clubs* La Moye GC, Royal Hainaut GC, Special Forces; *Style—* Maj-Gen Charles Cornock, CB, MBE; Orchard House, Studley Park, Studley, Warwicks

CORNOCK, Maj-Gen (Archibald) Rae; CB (1975), OBE (1968); s of Matthew Cornock (d 1968), and Mary Munro, *née* MacRae; *b* 4 May 1920; *Educ* Coatbridge; *m* 1951, Dorothy Margaret Cecilia, *née* Plant; 2 da (Fiona, Mhoira); *Career* served WW II NW Frontier 1940-42, Burma 1942-46, CO 16 Bn RAOC 1961-63, Defence and Mil Attaché Budapest 1965-67, DDOS Strategic Cmd 1967-68, Brig Q (Maint) MOD 1969-72, Maj-Gen 1973, Dir Army Quartering 1973-75; Col Cmdt RAOC 1976-80; chm: Army Athletic Assoc 1968-75, London Electricity Consultative Cncl 1980-81; cncl memb Back Pain Assoc Charity 1980-; *Recreations* golf, opera, sailing; *Clubs* Lloyds Yacht, Highland Brigade; *Style—* Maj-Gen Rae Cornock, CB, OBE; 20 Claremont, 14 St John's Ave, Putney Hill, London SW15

CORNTHWAITE, Dr Derek; s of Harold Cornthwaite, of 51 Crimicar Lane, Sheffield, and Florence, *née* Jubb; *b* 5 Dec 1938; *Educ* The Leys Sch Cambridge, Sheffield Univ (BSc, PhD), Columbia Univ NY; *m* 28 Jan 1965, Pamela Mary, da of Rev Canon James

Brown (Canon of Sheffield Cathedral), of Hooton Pagnell Hall, Hooton Pagnell, Yorks (d 1983); 1 s (Mark b 1968), 1 da (Sarah b 1974); *Career* chm: ICI (China) Ltd, Hong Kong 1976-79, ICI Zeltia SA Spain 1980-88, Sopra SA France 1979-86, Solplant Spa Italy 1979-85, Br Agrochemicals Assoc 1983-84, Sincair McGill Ltd UK 1980-88, Société European de Semance SA Belgium 1987; dir: Plant Protection Div, ICI plc UK 1979-, Garst Co USA 1985-; pres: Agric Products Gp, ICI Americas Inc 1987-; vice-pres ICI Americas Inc USA 1987-; co-winner of the MacRobert Award 1978; *Recreations* sailing, squash, music, opera; *Clubs* Farmers; *Style*— Dr Derek Cornthwaite; ICI Agrochemicals, ICI plc, Fernhurst, Haslemere, Surrey (☎ 0428 55131); ICI Americas Inc, Concord Pike, Wilmington, Delaware, USA

CORNWALL; see Marshall-Cornwall

CORNWALL, Roger Eliot; *Career* chm Louis Dreyfus and Co 1982-; *Style*— R E Cornwall Esq; c/o Louis Dreyfus and Co Ltd, City Gate House, Finsbury Sq, EC2 (☎ 01 628 9600)

CORNWALL-JONES, Mark Ralph; s of Brig Arthur Thomas Cornwall-Jones, CMG, CBE (d 1980), and Marie Joan Evelyn, *née* Hammersley-Smith; *b* 14 Feb 1933; *Educ* Glenalmond Coll, Jesus Coll Cambridge (MA); *m* 1959, Priscilla, da of Col Harold E Yeo (d 1957); 3 s (Adam b 1964, Matthew b 1967, Jason b 1969), 1 da (Kate b 1961); *Career* investmt mangr: The Debenture Corp 1959-67, John Govett and Co Ltd 1967- (investmt dir 1983-88); dir: John Govett and Co Ltd 1968-, Halifax Building Soc Ecclesiastical Insur Gp, Century Oils Gp, Govett Oriental Investmt Tst, Updown Investmt Co, Trades Union Unit Tst; *Recreations* books, stalking, gardening, sailing, carpentry; *Clubs* Boodles; *Style*— Mark Cornwall-Jones, Esq; Erin House, 3 Albert Bridge Rd, Battersea SW11 4PX; Shackleton House, 4 Battle Bridge Lane, London SE1

CORNWALL-LEGH, Charles Legh Shuldham; CBE (1977), OBE (1971, AE 1946, DL (Cheshire 1949)); s of Charles Henry George Cornwall-Legh (d 1934, sixth in descent from 16 and last Baron of Burford, so styled although the Barons were never summoned to Parliament; the 16 Baron was himself sixteenth in descent from Richard King of the Romans, Earl of Cornwall and Provence, and Count of Poitou, 2 s of King John); *b* 10 Feb 1903; *Educ* King's Sch Bruton, Hertford Coll Oxford; *m* 1930, Dorothy Catherine Whitson, er da of late J W Scott, of Seal, Sevenoaks, Kent; 1 s, 2 da; *Career* Flight Lt AAF and RAF 1939-45, High Sheriff Cheshire 1939, JP 1938-74, co cllr 1949-77, chm: New Cheshire CC 1974-76, Cheshire Police Authy 1957-74; co-heir to Baronies of Grey of Codnor, abeyant since 1495 (*see also* 18 Baron Zouche) Basset of Sapcote, abeyant since 1378 and Mortimer of Richards Castle; *Clubs* Carlton, MCC; *Style*— Charles Cornwall-Legh, Esq, CBE, OBE, AE, DL; High Legh House, Knutsford, Cheshire WA16 0QR (☎ 092 575 3168)

CORNWALLIS, Hon (Patrick Wykeham) David; 2 s (but only s by 2 w) of 3 Baron Cornwallis, OBE, DL; *b* 28 May 1952; *Educ* Lancing, Aiglon Coll Switzerland; *m* 1977, Susannah, da of William Edward Guest, of Rufford Abbey, Notts, and widow of Stephen Thursfield; 3 s (Patrick Wykeham James b 1977, Thomas Wykeham Charles b 1980, William Wykeham George b 1982); *Style*— The Hon David Cornwallis; Hamnish Court, Hamnish, Leominster, Herefordshire

CORNWALLIS, 3 Baron (UK 1927); Fiennes Neil Wykeham Cornwallis; OBE (1963), DL (Kent 1976); only s of 2 Baron Cornwallis, KBE, KCVO, MC, JP, DL (d 1982) by his 1 w, Cecily (d 1943), da of Sir James Heron Walker, 3 Bt; *b* 29 June 1921; *Educ* Eton; *m* 1, 17 Oct 1942 (m dis 1948), Judith, o da of Lt-Col Geoffrey Lacy Scott, TD; 1 s, 1 da (decd); m 2, 1 June 1951, Agnes Jean, yr da of Capt Henderson Russell Landale; 1 s, 3 da; *Heir* s (by 1 w), Hon Jeremy Cornwallis, *qv*; *Career* serv WWII Lt Coldstream Gds (1941-44, then invalided); farmer; pres: Br Agric Contractors Assoc 1952-54, Nat Assoc Agric Contractors 1957-63 and 1986-; dir: Checkers Ltd, Planet Bldg Soc 1968- (chm 1971-75); chm: Magnet and Planet Building Soc 1975-77, Town and Country Building Soc 1977-81 (dir 1975-), CBI Smaller Firms Cncl 1974-82 (chm 1979-82), memb Bd of Tstees Chevening Estate 1979-; pro grand master (freemasons) United Grand Lodge 1982- (prev dep grand master); rep of Horticultural Co-operatives in EEC 1975-86, vice pres Fedn of Agric Co-operatives 1984-86; chm: FAC Fruit Forum 1972-89, Kingdom Quality Assur Scheme 1986-; FIHort; *Recreations* fishing; *Clubs* Brooks's, Farmers', Pratt's; *Style*— The Rt Hon the Lord Cornwallis, OBE, DL; Ruck Farm, Horsmonden, Tonbridge, Kent TN12 8DT (☎ 089 272 2267); Dundurn House, St Fillans, Crieff, Perthshire (☎ 076 485 252); 25B Queens' Gate Mews, London SW7 5QL (☎ 01 589 1167)

CORNWALLIS, Hon (Fiennes Wykeham) Jeremy; er s (but sole surviving child by 1 w) of 3 Baron Cornwallis, OBE, DL; *b* 25 May 1946; *Educ* Eton, RAC Cirencester; *m* 29 March 1969, Sara Gray de Neufville, da of Lt-Col Nigel Stockwell, of Benenden, Kent; 1 s (Fiennes Alexander Wykeham Martin b 1987), 2 da (Anna Julia Gray b 1971, Charlotte Louise b 1972); *Style*— The Hon Jeremy Cornwallis; 15 Mablethorpe Road, London SW6 6AQ (☎ 01 381 5307)

CORNWELL, (Stanley) Vyvyan Parry; MC (1946); s of Stanley William Cornwell (d 1958), and Catherine Nellie Dora, *née* Parry (desc from Harry Court, sometime High Sheriff of Worcestershire and cdr of Royalist Forces 1640s and 1650s); *b* 13 Oct 1914; *Educ* Clifton, Oxford Univ (MA); *m* 12 Dec 1942, Doreen Mabel, da of Andrew Grieve (d 1970); 3 da (Joanne b 1944, Carolyn b 1947, Felicity b 1952); *Career* WWII Lt-Col RA NW Europe 1939-45; formerly ptnr Coopers Lybrand; dir Bristol Utd Press 1961-, Bristol Evening Post 1978-; occasional broadcaster on agricultural accounting topics, former pres Bristol Chamber of Commerce and Indust; *Books* Management Accounting for Agriculture; *Recreations* walking, bridge; *Style*— Vyvyan Cornwell, Esq, MC; 9 Marklands, Julian Rd, Sneyd Park, Bristol (☎ 0272 687 248)

CORRAN, Hon Mrs; Miranda Amadea; *née* Chaplin; er da of 3 and last Viscount Chaplin (d 1981), by his 2 w, Hon Rosemary Lyttelton, da of 1 Viscount Chandos; *b* 3 Jan 1956; *m* 1980, Brian Corran; 1 s (Hereward b 1981); *Style*— Hon Mrs Corran; Wadstray House, Blackawton, Totnes, S Devon

CORRE, John Howard Abraham; s of Eric Albert Abraham Corre, of London, and Rosalind Freda, *née* Brookman; *b* 29 August 1944; *Educ* Marylebone GS; *m* 25 May 1969, Tabby, da of Maurice Silas, of London; 1 s (David Abraham b 14 Jan 1974), 2 da (Lisa Danielle b 22 June 1970, Joanne Deborah b 14 Feb 1972); *Career* ptnr Auerbach Hope CA 1971-, non-exec dir Intereuropean Property Hldgs Ltd 1976-79, non exec dir Frank usher Hldgs plc 1986-; memb Rhodes Boyson Parly Club, govr JFS Sch; FCA; *Recreations* soccer, tennis, theatre, jogging; *Style*— John Corre, Esq; Auerbach Hope, 58-60 Berners St, London WIP 4JS, (☎ 01 637 4121, car tel 0836 597 242, fax 01 636 5330, telex AUERBA 25894)

CORRIE, John Alexander; s of John Corrie (d 1965), of Kirkcudbright, and Helen Brown; *b* 29 July 1935; *Educ* Kirkcudbright Acad, George Watson's Coll, Lincoln Agric Coll NZ; *m* 1965, (Jean) Sandra Hardie; 1 s, 2 da; *Career* farmer Scotland (also NZ), national sheepshearing champion 1959; lectr: British Wool Marketing Bd 1967-74, Agric Training Bd 1969-74; parly candidate (Cons): N Lanark 1964, Central Ayr 1966; MP (Cons): Bute and N Ayr 1974-83, Cunninghame North 1983-87; opn whip 1975-76 (resigned over devolution), PPS to Geroge Younger as Sec of State Scotland 1979-81, sec All-Party British-Turkish Ctee 1979-87, memb select ctee Scottish Affairs 1981-83, chm Scottish Cons Backbench Ctee 1981-83, ldr Cons Gp on Scottish Affrs 1982-87, sec Cons Backbench Fish-farming Ctee 1982-87, sec Cons Backbench Forestry Ctee 1982-85; MEP 1975-76 and 1977-79; memb Cncl of Europe and Western European Union 1983-87; memb cncl National Cattle Breeders Assoc; chm Tport Users Consultative Ctee (Scotland) 1989-, memb Central Tport Consultative Ctee (London) 1989-; given Wilberforce Award for humane work on abortion reform 1981; *Books* Forestry in Europe, The Importance of Forestry in the World Economy, Fish Farming in Europe; *Recreations* shooting, fishing, tennis, car racing, hang gliding; *Style*— John Corrie, Esq; Park of Tongland, Kirkcudbright DG6 4NE (☎ 055 722 232)

CORRIGAN, Thomas Stephen; s of Thomas Corrigan and Renée Victorine, *née* Chaborel; *b* 2 July 1932; *Educ* Beulah Hill; *m* 1963, Sally Margaret, da of George Ernest Everitt (d 1980); 2 da; *Career* CA; chm: Inveresk Gp Ltd 1974-83 (md 1971-83), Havelock Europa plc 1983-, Post Off Users' Nat Cncl 1984-, Rex Stewart Gp Ltd 1987-; pres Br Paper and Board Industry Fedn 1975-77; Master Worshipful Co of Makers of Playing Cards 1978-79; *Recreations* golf, tennis, bridge; *Clubs* MCC; *Style*— Thomas Corrigan, Esq; Woodend, The Chase, Kingswood, Surrey KT20 6HZ (☎ 0737 832709); office: 46 Grosvenor Gardens, London SW1W 0EB (☎ 01 823 6633)

CORRIN, John Bowes; OBE (1983); s of Harold Rodolph Corrin (d 1957), of Castletown, IOM, and Mabel Florence, *née* Dorman (d 1970); *b* 26 Oct 1922; *Educ* Berkhamsted; *m* 1948, José Marion, da of Herbert Arthur Sharman (d 1949), of Northampton; 1 s (Peter), 1 da (Alexandra); *Career* CA, dir Nationwide Anglia Bldg Soc 1964 (chm 1981-85), former sr ptnr Grant Thornton; mayor Northampton 1964-65; pres Leics and Northants Soc of CA's 1959; Hon Freeman Northampton; FCA; *Recreations* golf, bridge; *Clubs* Northampton and County, Northamptonshire County Golf; *Style*— J B Corrin, Esq, OBE; Tynwald, Sandy Lane, Church Brampton, Northampton NN6 8AX (☎ 0604 845301)

CORRIN, His Hon Deemster; John William; s of Evan Cain Corrin (d 1967), of Isle of Man, and Dorothy Mildred, *née* Teare; *b* 6 Jan 1932; *Educ* Murrays Road Primary Sch, King William's Coll; *m* 1961, Dorothy Patricia, da of John Stanley Lace (d 1964), of Isle of Man; 1 da (Jane b 1965); *Career* HM first deemster, Clerk of the Rolls 1988-; HM attorney gen for Isle of Man 1974-80; HM second deemster 1980-88; dep govr Isle of Man 1988-; *Recreations* music, bridge, gardening; *Clubs* Ellan Vannin (Isle of Man); *Style*— His Hon Deemster Corrin; 28 Devonshire Road, Douglas, Isle of Man (☎ 0624 21806); Rolls Office, Douglas, IOM (☎ 0624 73358)

CORRY, Cynthia, Lady; Cynthia Marjorie Patricia; da of late Capt Frederick Henry Mahony; *m* 1, Capt David Polson (decd); m 2, 29 Jan 1946, as his 2 w, Sir James Corry, 3 Bt (d 1987); 1 da (Amanda Jane); *Style*— Cynthia, Lady Corry; Dunraven, Fauvic, Jersey, CI (☎ 0534 51565)

CORRY, James Michael; s and h of Lt-Cdr Sir William Corry, 4 Bt; *b* 3 Oct 1946; *Educ* Downside; *m* 1973, Sheridan Lorraine, da of Arthur Peter Ashbourne, of Crowland, Peterborough; 3 s (William James Alexander b 1981, Robert Philip John b 1984, Christopher Myles Anthony b 1987); *Career* various appts in Shell-Mex and BP 1966-75 and BP 1975-; currently in Int Trading Div BP Oil Int (London); *Style*— James Corry, Esq; 24 Ligo Ave, Stoke Mandeville, Aylesbury, Bucks HP22 5TX

CORRY, Viscount; John Armar Galbraith Lowry-Corry; s and h of 8 Earl of Belmore; *b* 2 Nov 1985; *Style*— Viscount Corry

CORRY, (Thornton) Roger; s of Wing Cdr Brian George Corry, OBE, DFC, AE (d 1973), of Ardvara, Cultra, Holywood, Co Down, and Nora St Clair, *née* Boyd (d 1988); *b* 22 Feb 1943; *Educ* Campbell Coll Belfast; *m* 24 March 1972, Carol Elizabeth, da of Howard Kent Finlay (d 1973), of Church Rd, Helens Bay, Co Down; 2 s (Simon b 16 Feb 1873, James b 28 Jan 1976), 1 da (Victoria b 26 May 1980); *Career* dir James P Corry & Co Ltd 1974- (chm 1985-), chm James P Corry Hldgs Ltd 1985-; memb Dept of Manpower Servs Mgmnt Advsy Ctee 1975-78, Belfast Harbour Cmmr 1985-; FBIM, FInstD; *Recreations* flying, tennis, squash, golf, boating, vintage cars; *Clubs* Royal Belfast Golf, MG Car, Ulster Vintage Car, Royal North of Ireland Yacht, Ulster Flying, Ulster Reform; *Style*— T Roger Corry, Esq; Ardvara, Cultra, Holywood, Co Down BT18 0AX (☎ 023 17 2020); Springfield Rd, Belfast BT12 7EH (☎ 0232 243 661, fax 0232 232 123)

CORRY, Lt-Cdr Sir William James; 4 Bt (UK 1885), of Dunraven, Co Antrim; s (by 1 m) of Sir James Corry, 3 Bt (d 1987); *b* 1 August 1924; *m* 8 Dec 1945, Diana Pamela Mary, da of Lt-Col James Burne Lapsley, MC, IMS; 4 s, 2 da; *Heir* s, James Michael Corry b 1946; *Career* Lt-Cdr RN (ret); *Style*— Lt-Cdr Sir William Corry, Bt; Easts Hillerton House, Hillerton Cross, Bow, Crediton, Devon EX17 5AD (☎ 03633 407)

CORSAR, Col Charles Herbert Kenneth; LVO (1989), OBE (1981, TD 1960, DL (Midlothian 1975)); s of Capt Kenneth Charles Corsar (d 1967), of Midlothian, and Winifred Paton, *née* Herdman; *b* 13 May 1926; *Educ* Merchiston Castle Sch, King's Coll Cambridge (MA); *m* 25 April 1953, Mary Drummond Buchanan-Smith, da of Rt Hon Lord Balerno of Currie (see Peerage and Baronetage); 2 s (George b 1954, David b 1957), 3 da (Kathleen b 1960, d 1960, Katharine b 1961, Mary b 1965); *Career* TA Col 1972-75, Hon ADC HM The Queen 1977-81, Hon Col 1/52 Lowland Volunteers 1975-87, chm Lowland TAVRA 1984-87; DL Midlothian 1975, cncllr for Midlothian 1958-67, JP 1965, zone cmmr Home Def E Scotland 1972-75, pres Edinburgh Bn Boys' Bde 1969-87 (vice pres UK 1970), chm Scottish Standing Conf of Voluntary Youth Organisations 1973-78, memb Scottish Sports Cncl 1972-75, chm Earl Haig Fund Scotland 1984; govr: Merchiston Castle Sch 1975, Clifton Hall Sch 1965; sec Royal Jubilee and Prince's Tsts (Lothians and Borders) 1977, sec for Scotland Duke of Edinburgh's Award 1966-87; *Recreations* shooting, gardening, bee-keeping; *Clubs* New (Edinburgh); *Style*— Col Charles H K Corsar, LVO, OBE, TD, DL; Burg, Torloisk, Ulva Ferry, Isle of Mull (☎ 068 85 289); 11 Ainslie Place, Edinburgh EN3 6AS (☎ 031 225 6318)

CORSAR, Hon Mrs (Mary Drummond); *née* Buchanan-Smith; o da of Brig Baron Balerno, CBE, TD (Life Peer, d 1984), and Mary Kathleen, *née* Smith of Pittodrie (d

1947); *b* 8 July 1927; *Educ* Westbourne St Denis, Edinburgh Univ (MA 1949); *m* 25 April 1953, Col Charles Herbert Kenneth Corsar, LVO, OBE, TD, JP, DL, The Royal Scots, s of Kenneth Charles Corsar (d 1968), of Cairniehill; 2 s (George b 1954, David b 1957), 2 da (Katharine b 1961, Mary b 1965), and 1 da d in infancy (1960); *Career* dep chief cmmr Girl Guides Scotland 1972-77, chm WRVS Scotland 1982-88; memb Parole Bd for Scotland 1982-, vice-chm WRVS 1984-88, (chm 1988-), govr Fettes Coll 1982-; hon pres Scottish Women's Amateur Athletic Assoc 1973-; visiting ctee Glenochil Young Offenders Inst 1972-; memb convocation Heriot Watt Univ 1986-; *Recreations* hill walking, embroidery; *Clubs* New (Edinburgh), Lansdowne, Scottish Ladies Climbing; *Style*— The Hon Mrs Corsar; Burg; Torloisk, Ulva Ferry, Isle of Mull (☎ 068 85 289)

CORTAZZI, Sir (Henry Arthur) Hugh; GCMG (1984), KCMG (1980, CMG 1969); s of Frederick Edward Mervyn Cortazzi, of Sedbergh, Yorks; *b* 2 May 1924; *Educ* Sedbergh Sch, St Andrews Univ, London Univ; *m* 1956, Elizabeth Esther, da of George Henry Simon Montagu, of London; 1 s, 2 da; *Career* Foreign Office 1949, former cnsllr (Commercial) Tokyo, RCDS 1971-72, minister (Commercial) Washington 1972-75, dep under-sec of state FCO 1975-80, ambass to Japan 1980-1984 dir: Hill Samuel and Co Ltd, F and C Investmt Tst, G T Japan Investmt Tst Thornton Pacific Investmt Tst; memb Econ and Social Research Cncl; *Books* Translations from Japanese: Genji Keita: The Ogre and other stories of Japanese Salarymen (1972), The Guardian God of Golf and other humorous stories (1972), both reprinted as The Lucky One (1980), ed, Mary Crawford Fraser: A Diplomat's Wife in Japan: Sketches at the turn of the Century (1982), Isles of Gold: Antique maps of Japan (1983), Higashi no Shimaguni, Nishi no Shimaguni (1984) Zoku Higashi no Shimaguni Nishi no Shimaguni (collections of articles and speeches in Japanese, 1987), Thoughts from a Sussex Garden (1984), Second Thoughts (1985), Japanese Encounter (1987, essays for Japanese students of English), Dr Willis in Japan: British medical pioneer 1862-1877 (1985), Japanese translation: Aru Eijin Ishi no Bakumatsu Ishin (1986), ed, Mitford's Japan: The Memoirs and Recollections of the First Lord Redesdale; Japanese translation: Aru Eikoku Gaikokan no Meiji Ishin (1985), Victorians in Japan: In and around the Treaty Ports (1987); Articles on Japanese themes in English and Japanese publications; *Clubs* RAF; *Style*— Sir Hugh Cortazzi, GCMG; c/o Hill Samuel and Co Ltd, 100 Wood St, London EC2P 2AJ

CORVEDALE, Viscount; Benedict Alexander Stanley Baldwin; s and h of 4 Earl Baldwin of Bewdley; *b* 28 Dec 1973; *Style*— Viscount Corvedale

CORY, Charles (Raymond); CBE (1982); s of Charles Kingsley Cory (d 1967), and Ethel Muriel, *née* Cottam (d 1975); *b* 20 Oct 1922; *Educ* Harrow, Ch Ch Oxford; *m* 19 Oct 1946, Vivienne Mary (d 1988), da of Maj John Fenn Roberts, MC (d 1971) of Kelowna BC Canada; 3 da (Elizabeth b 1948, Rosemary b 1950, Charlotte b 1953); *Career* served WW II Lt RNVR N Atlantic, Channel, North Sea; CinC commendation 1944; chm: John Cory and Sons Ltd 1965-, Mountstuart Dry Docks 1962-66, vice-chm: Br Transport Docks Bd 1970-80 (memb 1966), AB Electronic Products GR Ltd 1978-; chm: South Glamorgan Health Authy 1974-84, Milford Haven Conservancy Bd 1982-; memb mgmnt ctee RNLI 1954- (vice-pres 1969 dep chm 1985-), chm Finance Ctee Church in Wales 1975-88, dep chm Rep Body 1985 (hon tres 1988); chm: Welsh Cncl Mission to Seamen 1984-, Cncl Univ of Wales Coll of Med 1988; *Recreations* skiing, countryside; *Clubs* CArdiff and Country; *Style*— Raymond Cory, Esq, CBE; The Coach House, Llanblethian, Cowbridge, South Glamorgan, (☎ 044 63 2251); The Ridge, Wotton-U-Edge, Glos; office: Mount Stuart House, Cardiff (☎ 0222 488321, telex 498350)

CORY, Sir Clinton James Donald; 4 Bt (UK 1919), of Coryton, Whitchurch, Glamorgan; 2 s of Sir Donald Cory, 2 Bt (d 1935); suc bro 1941; *b* 1 Mar 1909; *Educ* Brighton Coll and abroad; *m* 14 Sept 1935, Mary, da of Arthur Douglas Hunt, MD, ChB; 1 s; *Heir* s, Clinton Charles Donald Cory; *Career* Sqdn Ldr RAFVR; *Style*— Sir Clinton Cory, Bt; 18 Cloisters Rd, Letchworth Garden City, Herts (☎ 0462 677206)

CORY, (Clinton Charles) Donald; s and h of Sir Clinton Cory, 4 Bt; *b* 13 Sept 1937; *Educ* Brighton Coll and abroad; *Recreations* collecting Greek and Roman antiquities, student of classical studies; *Style*— Donald Cory, Esq; (☎ 0462 677206)

CORY, John; JP (Glam 1961), DL (Glam 1968); er s of John Herbert Cory (d 1939), of The Grange, St Brides-super-Ely, Glam; *b* 30 June 1928; *Educ* Eton, Trinity Coll Cambridge; *m* 1965, Sarah Christine, er da of John Meade, JP, DL, of The Willows Farm, St Brides-Super-Ely, S Glam; 2 da; *Career* dir John Cory and Sons Ltd, former chm Cardiff RDC; jt MFH Glamorgan 1962-67, KStJ; *Clubs* Cardiff and Country; *Style*— John Cory, Esq, JP, DL; The Grange, St Brides-super-Ely, Cardiff (☎ 0446 760211)

CORY-WRIGHT, Elizabeth; OBE, DL (Herts 1982); yr da of James Archibald Morrison, DSO (unc of 1 Baron Margadale) by his 1 w Hon Mary Hill-Trevor (6 da of 1 Baron Trevor); *b* 5 July 1909; *m* 1, 1930 (m dis 1940), Nigel Gunnis, yst s of Francis Gunnis, of Hamsell Manor, Eridge, Sussex; 2 da (Lady Farnham, Gillian); m 2, 1940, as his 2 w, Eric Martin-Smith, sometime MP Grantham; 2 da (Joanna b 1942, Lucinda b 1948); m 3, Michael Cory-Wright, 2 s of Sir Geoffrey Cory-Wright, 3 Bt, by his w Felicity, da of Sir Herbert Beerbohm-Tree, the actor-manager; *Style*— Mrs Michael Cory-Wright, OBE, DL; Codicote Lodge, Hitchin, Herts

CORY-WRIGHT, Francis Newman; s of Ronald Cory-Wright, MC (d 1932), of Wicken Bonhunt, Essex, and Geraldine Mary, *née* Villiers-Stuard of Dromana (d 1976); *b* 21 July 1925; *Educ* Eton, Merton Coll Oxford (MA); *Career* WWII offr 15/19 Kings Royal Hussars (wounded in action in Germany); memb: exec ctee Utd Dominions Tst Ltd 1959-63, Lloyds 1964-; conslt Gt Bernera Industs Ltd Western Isles Scotland; dir Herts Archaeological Tst, hon sec Luton and Dist Assoc for the Control of Aircraft Noise, memb Herts Co Assoc of Change-Ringers; Queens Foreign Service Messenger 1964-82; fell London Zoological Soc; *Recreations* shooting, stalking, angling; *Clubs* City Univ; *Style*— Francis Cory-Wright, Esq; Oakridge, Little Gaddesden, Herts (☎ 044284 3485); 36 Highdown Rd, Hove, Sussex

CORY-WRIGHT, Lady Jane Katherine; *née* Douglas; da of 11 Marquess of Queensberry (d 1954), and his 2 w Cathleen Sabine, *née* Mann (d 1959); *b* 18 Dec 1926; *m* 25 Aug 1949 (m dis 1983), David Arthur Cory-Wright, 3 s of Maj Sir Geoffrey Cory-Wright, 3 Bt (d 1969); 3 s; *Style*— Lady Jane Cory-Wright; 11 Stowe Rd, London W12 8BQ

CORY-WRIGHT, Sir Richard Michael; 4 Bt (UK 1903), of Caen Wood Towers, Highgate, St Pancras, Co London and Hornsey, Middx; s of Capt (Anthony John) Julian Cory-Wright (ka 1944), and gs of Capt Sir Geoffrey Cory-Wright, 3 Bt (d 1969); *b* 17 Jan 1944; *Educ* Eton, Birmingham Univ; *m* 1976, Veronica Mary, o da of James Harold Lucas Bolton; 3 s; *Heir* s, Roland Anthony Cory-Wright b 11 March 1979; *Career* patron of one living; *Style*— Sir Richard Cory-Wright, Bt; Cox's Farm, Winterbrook Lane, Wallingford, Oxon OX10 9RE

CORYTON, Lady; Philippa Dorothea; el da of Daniel Hanbury, of Castle Malwood, Lyndhurst (himself s of Sir Thomas Hanbury, of La Mortola, Italy); *m* 1925, Air Chief Marshal Sir (William) Alec Coryton, KCB, KBE, MVO, DFC (d 1981), sometime chief exec Guided Weapons Miny of Supply and chm and md Bristol Aero-Engines; 3 da (one of whom, Angela Loveday Hanbury, m Sir Michael Nall, 2 Bt; another m Michael Clarke, *qv*); *Style*— Lady Coryton; Two Leas, Langton Matravers, Swanage, Dorset BH19 3EU (☎ 0929 422009)

COSEDGE, Andrew John; s of David Ernest Cosedge, of Bexleyheath, Kent, and Edna Amy Mary, *née* Cull; *b* 13 Jan 1949; *Educ* Christ's Hosp, Univ of Exeter (LLB); *m* 14 June 1986, Denise Hazel, da of Anthony Raymond Teasdale, of Sutton Coldfield; *Career* barr Inner Temple 1972; chm Old Blues RFC; *Recreations* rugby; *Clubs* Old Blues RFC; *Style*— Andrew Cosedge, Esq; 17 Sevenoaks Rd, Borough Green, Kent TN15 8AX (☎ 0732 884456); 3 Stone Bldgs, Lincoln's Inn, London WC2A 3XL (☎ 01 242 4937, fax 01 405 3896)

COSGRAVE, Lady Louisa; er da of 6 Earl Cathcart, CB, DSO, MC, *qv*; *b* 27 April 1948; *m* 1975, Norman Kirkpatrick Cosgrave; *Style*— Lady Louisa Cosgrave; Totterdown Lodge, Inkpen, nr Hungerford, Berks

COSH, Dr John Arthur; s of Arthur L S Cosh (d 1952), and Ellen Janisch (d 1931); *b* 17 June 1915; *Educ* Bristol GS, St Johns Coll Cambridge (MA), St Thomas' Hosp London (MD); *m* 23 March 1940, Kate, da of Percy Jackson (d 1958), of Bingley; 2 s (Nicholas b 1946, Ian b 1950), 1 da (Claire b 1942); *Career* Surgn Lt RNVR 1942-46 (despatches); lectr in medicine Univ of Bristol 1951-57, conslt physician Bath Health Dist 1957-79; memb bd of dirs Cancer Help Centre Bristol; author of various pubns in rheumatology and cardiology incl Rheumatic Diseases and the Heart (with J Lever, 1988); FRCP, FRSM; *Recreations* music, piano, garden; *Style*— Dr John A Cosh; Mead Ct, Maudlin Rd, Totnes, Devon TQ9 5EX (☎ 0803 863939)

COSH, (Ethel Eleanor) Mary; da of Arthur Lionel Strode Cosh (d 1952), of Bristol, and Ellen, *née* Janisch (d 1931); *Educ* Clifton HS Bristol, St Anne's Coll Oxford (BA, MA); *Career* freelance writer, historian, architecutral historian and lectr; contrib to: The Times, TLS, Glasgow Herald, Country Life, Spectator; memb all nat conservation orgns, former ctee memb Soc of Architectural Historians of GB, vice chm Islington Soc, ctee memb and former chm of Islington Archaeology and History Soc; FSA 1987; *Books* The Real World (1961), Inveraray and the Dukes of Argyll (with late Ian Lindsay, 1973, paperback edn 1988), A Historical Walk through Clerkenwell (second edn 1987), With Gurdjieff in St Petersburg and Paris (with late Anna Butkovsky, 1980), A Historical Walk through Barnsbury (1981), The New River (second edn 1988), The Squares of Islington (1989); *Recreations* opera, reading, historical research; *Style*— Mary Cosh; 10 Albion Mews, London N1 1JX (☎ 01 607 9305); 32 India St, Edinburgh

COSH, Nicholas John; s of John Henry Cosh; *b* 6 August 1946; *Educ* Dulwich Coll, Queens' Cambridge; *m* 1973, Anne Rosemary, da of Lewis Nickolls, CBE (d 1970); 2 s; *Career* professional cricketer Surrey CCC 1968-70, chartered accountant merchant banker, dir Charterhouse Japhet Ltd 1978 (joined 1972-); FCA; *Recreations* cricket (Blue 1966-68), golf, bridge, opera, rugby (blue 1966); *Clubs* MCC (ctee memb), Hawks; *Style*— Nicholas Cosh, Esq; 1 Paternoster Row, St Paul's, EC4 (☎ 01 248 3999)

COSLETT, Air Marshal Sir (Thomas) Norman; KCB (1963), CB (1960, OBE 1942); s of late Evan Coslett; *b* 8 Nov 1909; *Educ* Barry GS, RAF Halton and Cranwell; *m* 1938, Audrey, da of F N Garrett; *Career* Air Vice-Marshal 1962, Air Marshal 1963, AOCIC Maintenance Command 1963-66, ret; dir Flight Refuelling (Hldgs) Ltd 1966-; CEng, FIMechE; *Style*— Air Marshal Sir Norman Coslett, KCB; c/o Barclays Bank, Sandton City, Sandton, 2196, S Africa

COSSENS, Richard John; s of Col John Bisp Cossens, MBE (d 1975), Margaret, *née* Hunt; *b* 15 Oct 1938; *Educ* Taunton Sch, RAF Coll Cranwell; *m* 23 May 1964, Geraldine Ann, da of Bryan Lewis (d 1969); 1 s (Benjamin Mathew John), 1 da (Philippa Sarah Jean); *Career* md Forenede Papir (UK) Ltd 1971-; Freeman City of London, Liveryman Worshipful Co of Stationers and Newspapermakers; *Recreations* golf, cricket, claret; *Clubs* MCC, Royal Ashdown Forest GC; *Style*— Richard Cossens, Esq; The Old House, Funnells Farm, Nutley, Sussex (☎ 082 571 2509); Herontye House, Stuart Way, East Grinstead, West Sussex (☎ 0342 327944, fax 0342 328378, car tel 0860 611935, telex 95636)

COSSEY, Errol Paul; s of Frederack John Cossey, and Patricia Alexander, *née* Mcormick; *b* 18 May 1943; *Educ* Wentworth HS; *m* 10 Sept 1966, Sandra Marjorie Rose, da of Leonard William Francis Tatton-Bennett; 1 s (Adam b 6 July 1972), 1 da (Fiona b 4 Sept 1974); *Career* commerical dir Dan Air Servs 1973-78, founding dir and md Air Europe Ltd 1979-85, founding dir and chief exec Air 2000 Ltd 1985-, chm Aerospace Mgmnt 1985-; *Style*— Errol Paul Cossey, Esq; Oakdale, Broadfield Park, Crawley, W Sussex (☎ 0293 518966, fax 0293 22927, car tel 0836 519471)

COSSHAM, Christopher Hugh; CB (1989); s of William Lorimer Cossham (d 1954), of Bristol, and Gwendolin Ebba, *née* Ramsden (d 1972); *b* 12 April 1929; *Educ* Monkton Coombe Sch Bristol; *m* 1 Feb 1958, Joanna, da of Capt Maurice Henry Howard-Smith (d 1967), of Houghton Regis, Beds; 1 s (Nigel b 1962), 1 da (Jenny b 1963); *Career* barr 1958, legal asst BOT 1958, sr legal asst Dir of Public Prosecutions 1964, sr asst dir of Public Prosecutions (NI) 1972-; Dep Met Stipendiary Magistrate 1983-; *Recreations* cycling, listening to Wagner; *Clubs* Civil Service; *Style*— Christopher H Cossham, Esq, CB; Royal Courts of Justice, Belfast (☎ 0232 235 111 x 250)

COSSINS, John Brown; s of Albert Joseph Cossins, of Fairway, North Rd, Havering-Atte-Bower, Romford, Essex, and Elizabeth Henrietta, *née* Brown; *b* 15 Nov 1939; *Educ* Clark's Sch for boys Ilford Essex, NE London Poly; *m* 9 March 1968, Christine Millicent, da of Henry George Avis, of Romford, Essex; 2 s (Alexander b 1969, Jonathan b 1971); *Career* Thomas Saunders Partnership 1962-: assoc 1968-74, ptnr 1974-88, jt managing ptnr 1988-; ARIBA 1966, FCSD 1985; *Recreations* golf, gardening, shooting; *Style*— John B Cossins, Esq; 168 High St, Ingatestone, Essex CM4 9EZ (☎ 0277 353263); The Thomas Saunders Partnership, 15 Old Ford Rd, London E2 9PJ (☎ 01 980 4400, fax 01 981 6417, telex 897590)

COSSONS, Neil; OBE (1982); s of Arthur Cossons, of Beeston Notts (d 1963), and

Evelyn Edith, *née* Bettle (d 1986); *b* 15 Jan 1939; *Educ* Henry Mellish G S Nottingham, Univ of Liverpool (BA, MA); *m* 7 Aug 1965, Veronica, da of Henry Edwards, of Liverpool (d 1986), 2 s (Nigel b 1966, Malcolm b 1972), 1 da (Elisabeth b 1967); *Career* dep dir City of Liverpool Museums 1969-71; dir: Ironbridge Gorge Museum Tst 1971-83, Nat Maritime Museum 1983-86, Science Museum 1986-; BBC Gen Advsy Ctte 1987, Ancient Monuments Advsy Ctee for England 1984-; tstee: Mary Rose Tst 1983-, Ironbridge Gorge Museum Tst 1987-, HMS Warrior Tst 1988-; pres: Museums Assoc 1981-82, Asoc of Independent Museums 1983-; Freeman City of London 1983; Hon DSocSc Birmingham Univ 1979, DUniv Open Univ 1984, Hon Fell RCA 1987; FSA 1968, FMA 1970, FRSA 1988; *Books* Industrial Archaeology of the Bristol Region (with RA Buchanan 1968), Industrial Archaeology (1975 and 1987) Ironbridge: Landscape of Industry (with H Sowden 1977) The Iron Bridge: Symbol of the Industrial Revolution (with B S Trinder 1979); *Clubs* Athenaeum; *Style—* Neil Cossons, Esq; Science Museum, London, SW7 2DD, (☎ 01 938 8003 fax 01 938 8118)

COSTAR, Sir Norman Edgar; KCMG (1963), CMG (1953); *b* 18 May 1909; *Educ* Battersea GS, Jesus Coll Cambridge; *Career* Colonial Office 1932, Dominions Office 1935; UK High Cmmr's Office: Canberra 1937-39, Wellington NZ 1945-47; dep UK high cmmr: Ceylon 1953-57, Australia 1960-62; British high cmmr: Trinidad and Tobago 1962-66, Cyprus 1967-69; Immigration Appeals adjudicator 1970-81; *Clubs* United Oxford and Cambridge; *Style—* Sir Norman Costar, KCMG

COSTER, Peter Lloyd; JP (Middx 1978-); s of Charles Edward Coster, and Maude, *née* Wearing; *b* 19 Jan 1934; *Educ* East Barnet GS; *m* 8 May 1955, Sylvia Iris, da of Frederick Gordon Hills, of Enfield, Middx; 3 da (Tracey Susan (Mrs Perkins) b 22 July 1957, Sharon Elizabeth (Mrs Crofton-Diggens) b 18 April 1960, Sarah Jane (Mrs Dowling) b 23 July 1963); *Career* Midland Bank 1952; The Scottish Life Assur Co 1955: southern mangr 1979, devpt mangr 1983, asst gen mangr 1987; dir: Guardian Building Soc 1983-, Team Agencies plc 1986-87; Freeman City of London 1982, Liveryman Worshipful Co of Insurers 1983; memb Magistrates Assoc; MInstM 1978; *Recreations* golf, painting, gardening; *Clubs* Caledonian, Wig & Pen; *Style—* Peter L Coster, Esq, JP; 53 Old Park View, Enfield, Middx EN2 7EQ; Coastguard Cottage, Bacton, Norfolk; 33 London Rd, Enfield, Middx EN2 6DR (☎ 01 367 8595, fax 01 363 7509)

COTES, Peter; s of Walter Arthur Boulting, impresario and entrepreneur (d 1957), and Rose, *née* Bennett (d 1981); *b* 19 Mar 1912; *Educ* Merton House Prep Sch Latymer and privately educated, Italia Conti; *m* 1, 1937, Myfanwy, da of Taliasin Jones; m 2, 19 May 1948, da of Wallace Miller; *Career* theatrical and film producer and dir, theatre owner and company dir: Live Theatre, Peter Cotes Productions Ltd, Cotes Logan Productions, Brompton Theatre Co etc Military service in Queens Westminster RAF, ENSA, Army Kinematograph Service, Home Guard, made theatrical debut in arms of Vesta Tilley, Portsmouth Hippodrome 1916, and at age of 10 as page to Robert Loraine's Henry V at Theatre Royal Drury Lane (King George's Fund for Actors 1924,) before playing at same theatre in *Cavalcade* by Noel Coward, West End productions include: Pick Up Girl 1946, The Master Builder 1948, Miss Julie 1949, Come Back, Little Sheba 1951, The Mousetrap 1952, Happy Holiday 1954, The Rope Dancers 1959, Paint Myself Black 1965, Look, No Hands! 1971; films: The Right Person, Jane Clegg, Waterfront; sr drama dir AR-TV 1955-58, supervising prod Drama Channel 7 Melbourne 1961, play prod Anglia TV 1964; FRSA, Knight of Mark Twain; *Books* No Star Nonsense (1949), The Little Fellow (1951), George Robey (1972), Circus (1976), The Barbirollis (A Musical Marriage) (1983); *Clubs* Savage, Medical Legal Society, Our Society, Wine Society, TMA, Actors Equity, ACTT; *Style—* Peter Cotes, Esq; 7 Hill Lawn Ct, Chipping Norton, Oxon OX7 5NF (☎ 0608 41208)

COTMAN, (Harold) Peter; s of Dr Harold Herbert Cotman (d 1930), of Chatham, and Mary, *née* Knowles (d 1976); *b* 5 Nov 1929; *Educ* Epsom Coll; *m* 20 Sept 1956 (m dis 1988), Merrill Doris Eleda, da of Charles William Akerman (d 1976); 1 s (John b 1959), 3 da (Rebecca (Mrs Ward)b 1960, Helen b 1962, Hilary b 1965); *Career* slr; Freeman Worshipful Co of Vintners; *Recreations* snorkelling, history, genealogy; *Style—* Peter Cotman, Esq; 3 Bull Farm Mews, Bull Lane, Matlock, Derbyshire DE4 5NB (☎ 0629 55466)

COTRAN, Dr Eugene; s of Michael Cotran (d 1985), Chief Justice Cameroon, and Hassiba, *née* Khouri; *b* 6 August 1938; *Educ* Victoria Coll Alexandria Egypt, Univ of Leeds (LLM), Trinity Hall Cambridge (Dip Int Law, LLD); *m* 6 Oct 1963, Christiane, da of Homer Avierino (d 1972); 3 s (Marc b 1964, Patrick b 1966, Paul b 1972), 1 da (Layla b 1980); *Career* called to Bar Lincoln's Inn; lectr Sch of Oriental and African Studies Univ of London 1962-77, High Ct Judge Kenya 1977-82, practice in African and Cwlth bars; vis prof in law (with ref to Africa and M East) Sch of Oriental and African Studies 1988-89; rec of the Crown Ct, Int Arbitrator; FCIArb; *Books* Re-statement of African Law (Kenya 1963), Case Book on Kenya Customary Law (1987); *Recreations* racing, swimming, bridge; *Clubs* Garrick; *Style—* Dr Eugene Cotran; 16 Hart Grove, London W5 3NB (☎ 01 994 0432); 2 Paper Buildings, Temple, London EC4Y 7ET (☎ 01 353 9119, fax 01 583 3423)

COTRUBAS, Ileana; da of Vasile and Maria Cotrubas; *b* 9 June 1939, in Romania; *Educ* Scuola Speciala de Musica, Bucharest Conservatory, Vienna Academy; *m* 1972, Manfred Ramin; *Career* opera singer; debut at Opera Romana as Ynoild 1964, Frankfurt Opera 1967-70; has performed: Salzburg Festival, Glyndebourne Festival, Florence Festival, Royal Opera House Covent Garden, Wiener Staatsoper, La Scala Milan, Metropolitan Opera New York; main repertorie includes; Mimi, Susanna, Pamina, Amina, Norina, Adina, Gilda, Violetta, Micaela, Antonia, Tatyana, Melisande; recordings include: Bach cantatas, Mozart masses, Brahms requiem, and complete opera performances of: Rinaldo, Cosi fan Tutte, Le Nozze di Figaro, Die Zauberflöte, La Traviata, Rigoletto, Carmen, Manon, L'Elisir d'Amore; made Austrian Kammersängerin 1981; *Style—* Miss Ileana Cotrubas; c/o Royal Opera House, Covent Garden, London WC2

COTTAM, Brig (Henry William) Donald; OBE (1966); s of Philip Ashley Joy Cottam, of Herts, and Margaret Smith, *née* Richardson (d 1972); *b* 11 May 1919; *Educ* Dumfries Acad, RMA Woolich, Staff Coll Camberley, Nato Def Coll Paris; *m* 24 July 1946, Joan Diana Tregear, da of Brig Mervyn Vincent Smelt (d 1985); 2 s (Philip b 1948, Nicholas b 1951); *Career* cmmnd July 1939; WW II: RA and RHA, Normandy, NW Europe 1944-45 (despatches); Lt Col GSOI joint plans HQ NE Land Forces 1959-61, cmd 1961-64; chm defence movements planning staff MOD 1969-71, asst mil ctee rep to NATO (Col) Paris 1966-67, Brig Asst Chief of Staff HQ Allied Forces C Europe 1971-74; ret; *Recreations* golf, fishing; *Clubs* Army and Navy, Hankley Common GC; *Style—* Brig Donald Cottam, OBE; Little Acre, Douglas Grove, Farnham, Surrey

COTTAM, James Barrie; s of James Cottam, of Maryland, 59 The Common, W Wratting, Cambridge, and Agnes, *née* Stokes; *b* 3 June 1947; *Educ* North Kesteven GS, Leicester Poly (Dip Quantity Surveying); *m* 20 May 1972, Angela Helen, da of Alistair Charles Mirren Scott, of Dunsdale Lodge, Westerham, Kent; 1 da (Sophie Clare Louise b 1980); *Career* ptnr John Leonard Partnership 1974-87, formed James Cottam & Co Ltd 1974-87; pcc memb St Mary with St Peter London, ctee memb Earls Ct Gdns Residents Ctee; Freeman City of London, memb Worshipful Co of Farriers 1979; assoc RICS; *Clubs* Carlton; *Style—* James Cottam, Esq; 2 Earls Ct Gdns, London SW5 OTD (☎ 01 373 7530); 102 Dean St, London W1V 5RA (☎ 01 437 2914, fax 01 437 3064, car 0860 390634)

COTTAM, Robert Gwynne; s of Maj Gen The Rev A E Cottam, CB, CBE, MC (d 1964), of Bodiam Rectory, Robertsbridge, Sussex, and Margaret Eileen, *née* Haselden; *b* 5 June 1934; *Educ* Marlborough; *m* 7 Oct 1967, Morella Cumberland, da of Lt-Col Anthony Gerald Bartholmew Walker, of Chattis Hill House, Stoorbridge, Hants; 2 s (Charles b 1969, Henry b 1973), 1 da (Rosemary b 1971); *Career* Nat Serv 2nd Lt E Surrey Regt 1953-54; with Grieveson Grant & Co Stockbrokers 1959-64; ptnr: W I Carr Sons & Co 1979-82, Grieveson Grant & Co 1982-86; dir Kleinwort Benson Securities 1987-; *Recreations* golf, tennis; *Clubs* MCC, City of London, Gresham; *Style—* Robert Cottam, Esq; 7 Stanford Road, London W8 5PP; Kleinwort Benson Securities Ltd, 20 Fenchurch Street, London EC3P 3DB (☎ 01 937 2308)

COTTEE, David; s of William Victor Cottee, of Essex, and Eileen May, *née* Bray; *b* 9 April 1948; *Educ* Maldon GS, Kingston-upon-Thames Sch of Architecture (DArch, Architect RIBA); *m* 1985, Sylvia Mary, da of Dr Peter Ambrose Walford, of Essex; 1 s (Julian b 1985), 1 step da (Louise b 1976); *Career* architect; a fndr ptnr The Architects Gp Partnership 1983-; *Recreations* skiing, watersports; *Style—* David Cottee, Esq; 3 Geoffrey Bishop Ave, Fulbourn, Cambridge (☎ 0223 880616); Maris Lane, Trumpington, Cambridge (☎ 0223 843511)

COTTENHAM, 8 Earl of (UK 1850); Sir Kenelm Charles Everard Digby Pepys; 11 and 10 Bt (GB 1784 and UK 1801); also Baron Cottenham (UK 1836) and Viscount Crowhurst (UK 1850); s of 7 Earl (d 1968, 2 cous 7 times removed of Samuel Pepys, the diarist); *b* 27 Nov 1948; *Educ* Eton; *m* 1975, Sarah, yr da of Capt Samuel Richard Le Hunte Lombard-Hobson, CVO, OBE, RN; 2 s (Viscount Crowhurst, Hon Sam Richard b 26 April 1986), 1 da (Lady Georgina Marye b 9 Oct 1981); *Heir* s, Mark John Henry, Viscount Crowhurst b 11 Oct 1983; *Style—* The Rt Hon the Earl of Cottenham; Priory Manor, Kington St Michael, Chippenham, Wilts SN14 6JR (☎ 024 975 262)

COTTER, Sir Delaval James Alfred; 6 Bt (I 1763) of Rockforest, Cork, DSO (1944); s of Sir James Cotter, 5 Bt (d 1924); *b* 29 April 1911; *Educ* Malvern, RMC Sandhurst; *m* 1, 29 Sept 1943 (m dis 1949), Roma, o da of Adrian Rome, of Dalswinton Lodge, Salisbury, S Rhodesia and widow of Sqdn Ldr Kenneth A Kerr MacEwen; 2 da; m 2, 9 Dec 1952, Eveline Mary, eldest da of late Evelyn John Mardon and widow of Lt-Col John Frederick Paterson, OBE; RHA; *Heir* n, Patrick Cotter; *Career* late 13/18 Royal Hussars, NW Europe 1944-45; JP Wilts 1962-63; *Clubs* Army and Navy; *Style—* Sir Delaval Cotter, Bt, DSO; Green Lines, Iwerne Courtney, Blandford Forum, Dorset

COTTER, Patrick Laurence Delaval; s of Laurence Stopford Llewelyn Cotter (ka 1943), yr s of 5 Bt, and Grace Mary, *née* Downing; hp of unc, Sir Delaval Cotter, 6 Bt; *b* 21 Nov 1941; *Educ* Blundell's, RAC Cirencester; *m* 1967, Janet, da of George Potter, of Goldthorne, Barnstaple, N Devon; 1 s, 2 da; *Career* antique dealer; *Style—* Patrick Cotter, Esq; Lower Winsham Farm, Knowle, Braunton

COTTERELL, Alan Geoffrey; s of Graham Cotterell (d 1967), and Millicent Louise Crews (d 1982); *b* 24 Nov 1919; *Educ* Bishop's Stortford Coll; *Career* served WW II RA 1940-46; author; *BooksPublications* Then a Soldier (1944), This is the Way (1947), Randle in Springtime (1949), Strait and Narrow (1950), Westward the Sun (1952), The Strange Enchantment (1956), Tea at Shadow Creek (1958), Tiara Tahiti (1960), Go Said the Bird (1966), Bowers of Innocence (1970), Amsterdam the Life of a City (1972); *Recreations* golf; *Clubs* Royal Auto, Cooden Beach Golf; *Style—* Geoffrey Cotterell, Esq; 2 Fulbourne House, Blackwater Rd, Eastbourne BN20 7DN (☎ 29477)

COTTERELL, Christopher Sturge; s of Richard Archbold Cotterell; *b* 1 Oct 1932; *Educ* Beaumont Coll; *m* 1960, Angela Mary, da of late Leslie Cheshire, OBE; 2 s; *Career* 2 Lt King's Shropshire LI Korea, Capt 4 Bn (TA); co dir 1961-82; chm Fibre Building Board Fedn 1972-75, jt md Machin and Kingsley Ltd 1979-82, pres Timber Trade Fedn 1981-82; princ Chris Cotterell and Assocs 1982-; *Recreations* cricket, yeast (bread and beer making), travel by train in Eastern Europe, horology; *Style—* Christopher Cotterell, Esq; Chris Cotterell and Associates, 166 Cambridge St, London SW1V 4QE (☎ 01 821 7828)

COTTERELL, Hon Mrs (Harriet Pauline Sophia); *née* Stonor; yst da of 6 Baron Camoys (d 1976); *b* 6 Jan 1943; *m* 24 July 1965, Jonathan Julian Cotterell, o son of Maj Leonard Evelyn Cotterell; 2 s, 1 da; *Style—* The Hon Mrs Cotterell; Steeple Manor, Steeple, nr Wareham, Dorset

COTTERELL, Henry Richard Geers; s and h of Sir John Cotterell, 6 Bt; *b* 22 August 1961; *m* 5 July 1986, Carolyn Suzanne, elder da of John Moore Beckwith-Smith, of Maybanks Manor, Rudgwick, Sussex; *Career* cmmnd Blues and Royals 1981; *Style—* Henry Cotterell, Esq

COTTERELL, Sir John Henry Geers; 6 Bt (UK 1805) of Garnons, Herefordshire; DL (Hereford and Worcester); s of Lt-Col Sir Richard Cotterell, 5 Bt, CBE (d 1978), and 1 w, Lady Lettice, *née* Lygon (d 1973, da of 7 Earl Beauchamp, KG, KCMG, TD, PC, and Lady Lettice Grosvenor, da of late Earl Grosvenor, s of 1 Duke of Westminster); *b* 8 May 1935; *Educ* Eton, Sandhurst; *m* 7 Oct 1959, Vanda Alexandra Clare, da of Maj Philip Alexander Clement Bridgewater; 3 s, 1 da; *Heir* s, Henry Cotterell, *qv*; *Career* offr Royal Horse Gds 1955-61; chm Hereford and Worcs CC 1977-81; chm Radio Wyvern; memb Welsh Water Authority; pres Nat Fedn of Young Farmers Clubs; *Style—* Sir John Cotterell, Bt, DL; Garnons, nr Hereford HR4 7JU (☎ 098 122 232)

COTTERELL, Hon Lady; Hon Molly Patricia; *née* Berry; da of late 1 Viscount Camrose; *b* 1915; *m* 1, 19 May 1936, Capt Roger Charles George Chetwode (d 14 Aug 1940), o s of Field Marshal 1 Baron Chetwode, GCB, OM, GCSI, KCMG, DSO;

2 s; m 2, 23 March 1942 (m dis 1948), 1 Baron Sherwood; m 3, 21 July 1958, as his 2 w, Sir Richard Charles Geers Cotterell, 5 Bt, CBE, TD (d 1978); *Style*— The Hon Lady Cotterell; Flat 1, 4 Eaton Place, London SW1

COTTESLOE, 4 Baron (UK 1874); Sir John Walgrave Halford Fremantle; 4 Bt (UK 1821), GBE (1960), TD; Baron of the Austrian Empire (1816); s of 3 Baron Cottesloe, CB (d 1956), and Florence (d 1956), da of Thomas Tapling; *b* 2 Mar 1900; *Educ* Eton, Trinity Coll Cambridge; *m* 1, 16 Feb 1926 (m dis 1945), Lady Elizabeth Harris, da of 5 Earl of Malmesbury, and Hon Dorothy, CBE, da of 6 Baron Calthorpe; 1 s, 1 da; m 2, 26 March 1959, Gloria Jean Irene Dunn, adopted da of late W E Hill, of Barnstaple, N Devon; 1 s, 2 da; *Heir* s, Hon John Fremantle, *qv*; *Career* sits as Conservative in House of Lords; former chm: British Postgraduate Med Fedn, Royal Postgraduate Med Sch, Hammersmith Hosp; chm: NW Met Regnl Hosp Bd 1953-60, Tate Gallery 1959-60, South Bank Theatre Bd 1962-77, Arts Cncl 1960-65, Heritage in Danger 1973-; former vice-chm Port of London Authy Thomas Tapling and Co Ltd, The Dogs Home Battersea 1970-82; dep pres National Rifle Assoc (and former chm); pres The Royal Russell Sch, former pres Leander Club, govr King Edward VII's Hosp Fund 1973-83, former hon sec Amateur Rowing Assoc, steward Henley Royal Regatta; former memb: Hampstead Borough Cncl, London Co Cncl; former DL Co London; fell Royal Postgraduate Med Sch, hon fell Westfield Coll London Univ; *Recreations* rowed in winning Cambridge crew 1921 and 1922 Boat Races; several times Match Rifle Champion at Bisley and member English Team in long range match for Elche Shield on 54 occasions; *Clubs* Travellers'; *Style*— The Rt Hon the Lord Cottesloe, GBE, TD

COTTIER, Timothy Robin; s of Gordon Stephen Cottier, of Conway, Wales and Alice, *née* Floyd; *b* 27 Dec 1953; *Educ* Merchant Taylors Sch; *m* 1980, Helen Adele, da of Douglas Constantine, of St Clements Jersey; 2 da (Sophia b 1983, Claudia b 1985); *Career* CA 1977; Price Waterhouse and Co Bahamas 1978-80, established corporate financial servs cos 1981-; chm: Leeds Tst plc 1982-, Nuwara Eliya Tea Plantations plc 1982-, Rini Tea Co plc 1980-, Transmeridian Offshore Oil plc 1984-, Antonia and Charlotte Interior Designs plc 1985-, Amanda Hall Fashions Ltd 1984-, Sunwest Airlines Inc 1982-, Lakeview Bank of The Bahamas 1979-82, Highlands Rubber and Coffee Ltd 1984-, Swan Valley Minerals Pty 1983-, Western Reef Gold Mining Pty 1985-, Charles Graham Textiles Ltd 1984-; Grosvenor Finance and Credit Services Ltd, Larchfield Corpn Plc, Larchfield Racing Syndicate Ltd, Yacht Holidays plc; Audiotext plc, Olicana Securities plc, Leeds Securities Ltd; FCA 1982; *Recreations* shooting, sailing, rugby football, golf, tennis; *Clubs* Leeds, RAC, Public Schs, Nassam YC, Jersey Port Drinkers Assoc, Cayman YC, Harrogate; *Style*— Timothy Cottier, Esq; Larchfield, Kent Rd, Harrogate, N Yorks (☎ 0423 524655); t Andrews House, Burley St, Leeds (☎ 0423 524655)

COTTINGHAM, Barrie; s of John Cottingham of Sheffield, and Eleanor *née* Price; *b* 5 Oct 1933; *Educ* Carfield Sch Sheffield; *m* 5 Oct 1957, Kathleen, da of John Ernest Morton (d 1945) of Sheffield; 1 s (Nigel David b 13 Dec 1964), 1 da (Michelle Jayne b 5 Aug 1962); *Career* served RAF 1955-57, cmmnd Pilot Offr 1956; ptnr Coopers & Lybrand 1964, memb UK mgmnt ctee 1974-, ptnr in charge of regnl practice, memb governing bd; pres Sheffield and Dist Soc of Chartered Accountants 1964, memb of liason ctee on mgmnt and econ studies Sheffield Univ, hon auditor Sheffield c of c; FCA 1955, ATII 1965; *Recreations* squash, golf, watching rugby and cricket, oil painting, opera; *Clubs* Naval and Military, Sheffield; *Style*— Barrie Cottingham, Esq; Coopers & Lybrand, Albion Ct, 5 Albion Place, Leeds, LS1 6JP (☎ 0532 431343, fax GPS 2/3 Auto 0532 424009, telex 556230 Answerback 556230 COLYLD G)

COTTLE, Gerry; s of Reginald Brookes Cottle (d 1975), of Highbury, London, and Joan Miriam, *née* Ward, of Streatham, London; *b* 7 April 1945; *Educ* Rutlish Sch London Wimbledon; *m* 7 Dec 1968, Betty, da of James Fossett (d 1972), of Henley-In-Arden; 1 s (Gerry b 1981), 3 da (Sarah b 1970, April b 1973, Juliette b 1976); *Career* ran away from school and joined a small circus becoming juggler and equestrian 1961, formed Gerry Cottle's Circus 1974, flew complete circus to Oman for Sultan's birthday 1976; subsequent overseas tours 1981-84: Bahrain, Iran, Shajah, Iceland, Hong Kong, Macau, Singapore, Malaysia; currently world's most travelled circus touring two units 46 weeks a year; memb: Variety Club of GB, Circus Properties Assoc 1973-; *Recreations* horse-riding, collecting show business memorabilia; *Style*— Gerry Cottle, Esq; Woburn Park Farm, Addlestone Moor, Weybridge, Surrey KT15 2QE (☎ 0932 857 779); Gerry Cottle's Circus Ltd, Addlestone Moor, Weybridge, Surrey KT15 2QE (☎ 0932 857 779, fax 0932 859 902, car tel 0836 691 111)

COTTON, Dr Bernard Edward; CBE (1976); s of Hugh Harry Cotton (d 1963), and Alice Cotton; *b* 8 Oct 1920; *Educ* Sheffield City GS, Sheffield Univ; *m* 1944, Stephanie Anne, da of Rev Arthur Evelyn Furnival (d 1960); 3 s; *Career* served WWII, Lt Worcs Yeo 6 Airborne Div France and Normandy, Ardennes Rhine Airborne Landing; pres Samuel Osborn and Co Ltd 1978-79 (chm and chief exec 1969-78), dir Renold plc 1979-84, dep chm Baker Perkins plc 1982-86, John Mountford Co Ltd Manchester 1984-87; chm Yorkshire and Humberside Economic Planning Cncl 1970-79, pres Yorkshire and Humberside Devpt Assoc 1973-84; memb: Br Rail (eastern regn) 1976-85, Health Serv Supply Cncl 1980-85, South Yorkshire Residuary Body 1985-; pro-chllr Sheffield Univ 1983; Master Co of Cutlers in Hallamshire 1979; hon fell Sheffield City Poly 1980, hon LLD (Sheffield); *Recreations* gardening, quiet pursuits; *Style*— Dr Bernard Cotton, CBE; Stubbin House, Carsick Hill, Sheffield S10 3LU (☎ 0742 303082)

COTTON, Diana Rosemary; QC (1983); s of Arthur Frank Edward Cotton, of Herts, and Muriel, *née* John; *b* 30 Nov 1941; *Educ* Berkhamsted Sch for Girls, Lady Margaret Hall Oxford (exhibitioner, MA); *m* 1966, Richard Bellerby Allan, s of John Bellerby Allan (d 1985), of Oxon; 2 s (Jonathan b 1972, Jeremy b 1974), 1 da (Joanna b 1977); *Career* barr, recorder 1982; *Recreations* my family, sport; *Style*— Miss Diana Cotton, QC; Devereux Chambers, Devereux Court, Temple, London WC2 (☎ 01 353 7534)

COTTON, Lt Cdr George Lennox; DSC (1942), DL; s of Thomas Dawson Cotton (d 1970), and May Cotton, *née* Lennox (d 1976); *b* 25 Oct 1915; *Educ* Castle Park Dublin, Wrekin Coll Shropshire; *m* 1939, Eileen Geraldine, da of Maj Gerald William Ewart; 3 da (Caroline, Elizabeth, Kathleen); *Career* Ulster Div RNVR 1936; HMS Hermes 1939-40, Motor Torpedo Boats including CO 50 MTB Flotilla 1940-44, HMS Mull of Galloway 1945; slr, dir: Adria Ltd, Blakiston Houston Estate Co, Caledon Estate Co; *Recreations* shooting, golf, riding, racing; *Clubs* Ulster Reform (Belfast), Royal Co Down GC; *Style*— Lt Cdr Lennox Cotton, DSC, DL; Clontagh Lodge, Crossgar, Co Down, N Ireland (☎ 0396 831077); 7/11 Linenhall Street, Belfast (☎ 0232 322204)

COTTON, His Hon Judge; John Anthony; s of Frederick Thomas Hooley Cotton, of Harrogate, and Catherine Mary Cotton; *b* 6 Mar 1926; *Educ* Stonyhurst, Lincoln Coll Oxford; *m* 1960, Johanna Aritia, da of Johan Adriaan van Lookeren Campagne, of Holland; 3 s, 2 da; *Career* barr 1949, dep chm W Riding of Yorks Quarter Sessions 1967-71, recorder of Halifax 1971, recorder of Crown Court 1972, circuit judge 1973-; *Style*— His Hon Judge Cotton; 81 Lyndhurst Rd, Sheffield

COTTON, Sir John Richard; KCMG (1969), CMG (1959, OBE 1947, MBE 1944); s of Julian James Cotton, ICS (d 1927), and Sophia Raffaela, *née* Ricciardi-Arlotta (d 1958); *b* 22 Jan 1909; *Educ* Wellington, RMC Sandhurst; *m* 1937, Mary Bridget, da of Nicholas Connors, of Stradbally, Co Waterford; 3 s (David, John, Brian); *Career* 8 Light Cavalry IA 1929-37 Maj; Indian Political Serv 1934-47, Aden 1934-35, HM Legation Addis Ababa 1935, Persian Gulf 1937-38, Rajputana 1939-41, Hyderabad 1941-44, Kathiawar 1944-46, political dept Delhi 1946-47; HM Foreign Serv 1947-69, Foreign Off 1948-51, cnsllr Madrid 1951-54, consul-gen Leopoldville 1954-57, cnsllr Brussels 1957-62, consul-gen Sao Paolo 1962-65, ambass Kinshasa 1965-69; adjudicator Immigration Tribunals 1970-81; *Recreations* golf, photography; *Clubs* Army and Navy; *Style*— Sir John Cotton, KCMG, OBE; Lansing House, Hartley Wintney, Hants (☎ 0251 26 2681)

COTTON, Leonard Thomas; s of Edward George Cotton (d 1973), and Elizabeth Minnie Cotton; *b* 5 Dec 1922; *Educ* King's Coll Sch Wimbledon, Oriel Coll Oxford, King's Coll Hosp (MA, BM, BCh, MRCS, LRCP, MRCS, LRCP); *m* 20 Aug 1946, Frances Joan, *née* Bryan; 1 s(Thomas Edward Guy b 3 Aug 1950), 2 da (Ruth Frances b 16 Feb 1955, Elizabeth Mary b 30 Sept 1960); *Career* Nat Serv Maj RAMC (Surgical Div Tidworth Mil Hosp 1949-51); conslt surgn KCH 1957-88, dean and vice dean KCH Med Sch 1976-83, dean Kings Coll Sch of Med & Dentistry 1983-88, dir dept of med engrg & physics KCSMD 1967-88; FRCS (Eng); *Books* Short Textbook of Surgery (with Selwyn Taylor 1967), Surgical Catechism (1986); *Recreations* walking, travelling; *Clubs* Garrick; *Style*— Leonard Cotton, Esq; 3 Dome Hill Park, London SE26 6SP (☎ 01 778 8047);H Private Patients Wing (☎ 01 274 8570)

COTTON, Hon Sir Robert Carrington; KCMG (1978); s of H L Carrington Cotton; *b* 29 Nov 1915; *Educ* St Peter's Coll Adelaide; *m* 1937, Eve Elizabeth Macdougall; 1 s, 2 da; *Career* former pres of Liberal Pty (NSW), memb Senate 1965, Min Industry and Commerce 1975-77, consul-gen New York 1978-81, Australian ambass to the United States 1982-85; *see Debrett's Handbook of Australia and New Zealand for further details*; FASA; *Recreations* photograhy, writing, swimming, golf; *Clubs* Australian, The Brook (New York); *Style*— The Hon Sir Robert Cotton, KCMG; 75 Pacific Road, Palm Beach, NSW 2108, Australia (☎ 919 5456)

COTTON, Thomas; s of Lt Col B H C Cotton, OBE, RE (d 1970), of Blackheath, London, and Susanna, *née* Corner (d 1981); *b* 6 Jan 1936; *Educ* Cheltenham, Pembroke Coll Cambridge (Mech Sci), Cranfield Coll of Aeronautics (Dip OR); *m* 3 Apr 1964, Amanda Mary, da of Dr H P Mutchinson; 3 s (Benjamin b 1964, Christopher b 1966, Daniel b 1968); *Career* Nat Serv, Field Trp Cdr RE BAOR 1954-56, PO RAFVR 1956-58; Rootes Gp Ltd 1958-68, gen mangr Lancer Boss Gp 1968, sr exec Indust Reorganisation Corpn 1968-70, exec dir IC Gas 1970-85, mgmnt conslt 1985-86; dir planning and admin IMRO 1986-; involved local vol work and charities; memb IOD; *Recreations* family; *Clubs* IOD; *Style*— T Cotton, Esq; IMRO Ltd, Centre Point, 103 New Oxford Street, London WC1A 1PT (☎ 01 379 0601)

COTTON, William Frederick (Bill); OBE (1976), JP (Richmond 1976); s of Billy (William Edward) Cotton and Mabel Hope; *b* 23 April 1928; *Educ* Ardingly; *m* 1, 1950, Bernadine Maud Sinclair; 3 da; m 2, 1965, Ann Corfield, *née* Bucknall, 1 step-da; *Career* former jt md Michael Reine Music Co; head variety BBC TV 1967-70, head light entertainment 1970-77 (producer 1956-62, asst head 1962-67), controller BBC 1 1977-81, dep md BBC TV 1981-82, chm BBC Enterprises, memb of Bd of Management and first dir devpt and programmes BBC TV 1982-, md BBC DBS 1982-; *Style*— Bill Cotton, Esq, OBE, JP; BBC TV, Centre, London W12 7RJ (☎ 01 743 8000)

COTTRELL, Sir Alan Howard; s of Albert Cottrell and Elizabeth Cottrell, of Birmingham; *b* 17 July 1919; *Educ* Moseley GS, Birmingham Univ; *m* 1944, Jean Elizabeth, da of Ernest William Harber; 1 s; *Career* former lectr and prof of physical metallurgy Birmingham Univ, chief scientific advsr HM Govt 1971-74 (formerly dep chief); former vice pres Royal Soc, master Jesus Coll Cambridge 1974-86, vice-chllr Cambridge Univ 1977-79; memb Security Cmmn 1981-; Hon DSc: Oxford 1979, Birmingham 1983; FRS; kt 1971; *Style*— Sir Alan Cottrell; 40 Maids Causeway, Cambridge CB5 8DD (☎ 0223 63806)

COTTRELL, Bryce Arthur Murray; s of Brig Arthur Foulkes Baglietto Cottrell, DSO, OBE (d 1962), of Boughton Lees, Ashford, Kent, and Mary Barbara, *née* Nicoll (d 1986); *b* 16 Sept 1931; *Educ* Charterhouse, CCC Oxford (MA); *m* 1955, Jeane Dolores, da of R P Monk (d 1942), of Coventry; 2 s, 2 da; *Career* memb Stock Exchange 1958, chm Phillips and Drew Stockbrokers 1985-88 (ptnr 1963-85); govr Combe Bank Sch, and St Leonards Mayfield Sch; CBIM; *Recreations* railways, spectator sports, paintings; *Clubs* Guard's Polo, City of London; *Style*— Bryce Cottrell, Esq; Boscobel House, Bourne Lane, Tonbridge, Kent TN9 1LG (☎ 0732 353 959)

COTTRELL, David Vernon Swinfen; s of George Swinton Cottrell (d 1960), of the Manor House, Bredon, Hereford and Worcester, and Dorothy Mary Catherine, *née* Liddell (d 1957); *b* 15 Nov 1923; *Educ* Eton, Windsor, Trinity Coll Cambridge; *m* 6 June 1950, Leontine Mariette (Marylena), da of Capt James Allan Dyson Perrins, MC (d 1974), of Waresley House, Hartlebury, Worcs; 1 s (Mark b 1955), 1 da (Sarah (Mrs Macinnes) b 1955), 1 step s (Rupert b 1945), 1 step da (Rozanna (Mrs Hammond) b 1946); *Career* RNVR 1942-46; slr 1951, conslt practising Birmingham; chm and dir: S J Bishop & Son Ltd IOW 1955-63, Waterloo House (Birmingham) Ltd 1957 Temple St (Birmingham) Ltd 1957-88; dir Dares Brewery Ltd Birmingham 1960-63, fndr and life dir Newater Investmts Ltd Birmingham 1963-, chm and md Tewkesbury Marina Ltd 1969-; memb cncl Assoc Brokers & Yacht Agents 1970-, vice-chm Nat Yacht Harbour Assoc 1984- (memb cncl) 1972-, vice-pres 1974-76, pres and chm 1979-82, chm Midlands regn Br Marine Indust Fedn 1988-; High Sheriff Hereford and Worcs; memb cncl Lower Avon Navigation Tst 1951-, pres Gloucs branch Inland Waterways Assoc 1976- (chm 1974-76); memb Law Soc 1951; memb Yacht Brokers Designers and Surveyors Assoc 1975; *Recreations* yachting, shooting; *Clubs* Royal Yacht sqdn (Cowes LOW), Royal Solent YC; *Style*— David Cottrell, Esq; The Tewkesbury Marina Ltd, Bredon Rd, Tewkesbury Gloucestershire (☎ 0684 293 737)

COTTRELL, Hon Mrs (Fiona Caroline Mary); *née* Watson; 2 da of 3 Baron Manton; *b* 26 Sept 1953; *m* 1978, Mark Swinfen Cottrell, s of D V S Cottrell; 1 da (b 30 June 1988); *Style—* The Hon Mrs Cottrell; Masue Hall, Sancton, York

COTTRELL, Henry Claude; s of Henry Cottrell (d 1953); *b* 13 June 1921; *Educ* Lawrence Sheriff Sch Rugby; *m* 1949, Audrey, da of Thomas Hannah (d 1936); 1 s; *Career* served WWII, RAF; actuary; sr ptnr Phillips and Drew stockbrokers 1972-78; dir: AMEV Ltd, Caffyns plc; chm Watts Blake Bearne and Co plc; Liveryman Worshipful Co of Glass Sellers (Master 1977-78), Worshipful Co of Actuaries (Master 1981-82); receiver-gen Order of St John 1981-86, OStJ 1979, KStJ 1981; *Recreations* fly fishing; *Clubs* City Livery; *Style—* Henry Cottrell, Esq; Whitecraigs, Parkfield, Sevenoaks, Kent TN15 0HX (☎ 0732 61228)

COTTRELL, James Swinfen; s of Cdr Vincent Swinfen Cottrell (d 1956); *b* 10 Sept 1932; *Educ* Pangbourne Coll; *Career* shipbroker; dir: Eskglen Shipping Co Ltd, Howe Robinson and Co Ltd, Howe Matheson and Co Ltd, Howe Robinson (Hldgs) Ltd, Matheson Chartering Ltd; MICS; *Recreations* sailing; *Clubs* Royal Solent Yacht, Brooks's, City of London; *Style—* James Cottrell, Esq; 41 Queensdale Rd, Holland Park, London W11 (☎ 01 488 3444)

COTTRELL, Lawrence Charles Thomas; s of Charles George Vincent Cottrell (d 1965), and Nellie Elizabeth, *née* Eaton (d 1983); *b* 5 Feb 1919; *Educ* Hendon GS; *m* 26 Oct 1941, Joyce Angela, da of Sydney Giddings (d 1981); 2 da (Angela b 1945, Virginia b 1946); *Career* WWII RA, Maj 1943 (Jr Staff Coll, Camberley, WO); Sun Life Assur Soc plc: investmt mangr 1963, sec 1968, dir 1971, gen mangr 1975, ret 1976; dir Nat Employers Mutual Gen Insur Co Ltd 1976-80; md: Estates Property Investmt Co plc 1980-88 (chm 1981-88), Nat Employers Life Assur Co Ltd 1976-80; FCIS, ACII; *Recreations* bowls, golf, gardening, world wide travel; *Style—* Lawrence Cottrell, Esq; Sheriffmuir, The Highlands, East Horsley, Leatherhead, Surrey KT24 5BQ (☎ 048 65 2844)

COTTRELL, Richard John; MEP (EDG) Bristol 1979-; s of John Charles Cottrell and Winifred, *née* Barter; *b* 11 July 1943; *Educ* Court Fields Sch Wellington Somerset; *m* 1965, Dinah Louise, da of Leonard David; 2 da; *Career* journalist; formerly with Bristol Evening Post and Harlech TV; *Recreations* travel; *Style—* Richard Cottrell, Esq, MEP; Dean House, Bower Ashton, Bristol

COTTRELL, (Patrick) Rupert; s of Patrick Nelson Hickman, of Hants, and Leontrine Mariette (Marylena), *née* Dyson-Perrins; gs of Sir Alfred Hickman 2 Bt (see Peerage and Baronetage); assumed by Deed Poll 1953 the surname of Cottrell in lieu of his Patronymic; *b* 14 June 1945; *Educ* Gordonstoun; *m* 19 Oct 1968, Claire, da of Lt Col J G Round, OBE, DL, JP, of Essex; 1 s (Nicholas Rupert b 1970), 1 da (Jessica Victoria b 1974); *Career* dir: Macnicol and Co 1964-65, Montagu Loebl Stanley 1965-68, Cazenove & Co 1968-80, ptnr Bird Farms 1975, dir Maronhart Ltd 1978, proprietor Salamander Restorations 1980; exec dir: Buzzacott Investmt Mgmnt Ltd, Buzzacott Nominees Ltd 1985; Project 84 (Chelmsford) Ltd 1986; cncl memb FIMBRA 1986 (memb of membership sub ctee 1987); chm Essex Assoc of Boys Clubs 1985 (vice-chm 1983), cncl memb Nat Assoc of Boys Clubs 1985; *Recreations* sailing, shooting, hunting, fishing, racing, reading, writing; *Clubs* Boodles, Jockey, Club Rooms, Royal Yacht Sqdn, Royal London Yacht, Beefsteak, Essex, Hellens, Hardy's; *Style—* Rupert Cottrell, Esq; Green Birch, Colchester, Essex; 4 Wood St, London EC2

COTTRILL, Major (Geoffrey) Michael Cameron; MBE (1977); s of Charles Rushleigh Stanhope Cottrill (d 1949), and Elsie, *née* Wright (d 1976); *b* 11 June 1929; *Educ* Repton, Sandhurst; *Career* soldier; Hong Kong 1950-52, Korea 1954, ADC GOC Singapore 1955-56, Instr Eaton Hall OCS 1958-59, Staff Coll 1962, Sultan's Armed Forces Muscat and Oman 1963, HQ Farelf Singapore 1964-66 and 1968-70, asst mil attaché Australia and N Zealand 1970-72, Abu Dhabi Defence Force 1973-74, MS CBF Hong Kong 1974-77, Sec Allied Staff Berlin 1977-79, Co-ordinator Royal Sch of Artillery 1979-81, ret; *Recreations* polo, shooting, chorister, travel; *Clubs* Army and Navy, Victoria (Jersey); *Style—* Major Michael Cottrill, MBE; 52 High Street, Codford St Mary, Warminster, Wilts BA12 0NB (☎ 0985 50507); HQ Director Army Air Corps, Middle Wallop, Stockbridge, Hants

COTTS, Richard Crichton Mitchell; s and h of Sir (Robert) Crichton Mitchell Cotts, 3 Bt; *b* 26 July 1946; *Educ* Oratory Sch; *Style—* Richard Cotts, Esq

COUCHMAN, Ernest Henry; s of Henry Ernest Couchman, of Grays, Essex, and Eliza Gladys, *née* Glasson (d 1974); *b* 6 Mar 1939; *Educ* Wm Palmer Endowed Sch for Boys; *m* 14 Sept 1963, Patricia, da of Keith Robinson (d 1978); 1 s (James b 1968), 2 da (Caroline b 1972, Judith b 1978); *Career* CA, chief accountant Baird and Tatlock (London) Ltd 1965-68, head of business and professional studies Redditch Coll 1980-86, Chart Foulks Lynch plc 1989-; head of professional accounting studies SW London Coll 1986-; lay pastor Studley Baptist Church 1978-84; FCA; *Recreations* music; *Style—* Ernest H Couchman, Esq; 4 Stapleton Rd, Studley, Warwickshire (☎ 0527 85 2101); 35 Livery St, Birmingham (☎ 021 233 4045 35 Livery St, Birmingham (☎ 21 233 4045)

COUCHMAN, James Randall; MP (Cons) Gillingham 1983-; s of Stanley Randall Couchman and Alison Margaret Couchman; *b* 11 Feb 1942; *Educ* Cranleigh Sch, King's Coll Newcastle upon Tyne; *m* 1967, Barbara Jean, da of Max Heilbrun (d 1956); 1 s, 1 da; *Career* dir Chiswick Caterers Ltd 1980-; Paly candidate (Cons) Chester-Le-Street 1979, memb Bexley Borough Cncl 1974-82; chm: Bexley Social Servs 1975-78 and 1980-82, Bexley Health Authy 1981-83, PPS to Chllr Duchy of Lancaster (formerly Min for Health) 1984-; *Style—* James Couchman, Esq, MP; House of Commons, London SW1

COUCHMAN, Martin; s of Frederick Alfred James Couchman (d 1970), of Halstead, Kent, and Mary, *née* Argent; *b* 28 Sept 1947; *Educ* Sutton Valence Sch, Exeter Coll Oxford (BA); *m* 29 Oct 1983, Carolyn Mary Constance, da of Victor Frow Roberts, of Childer Thornton, Cheshire (d 1987); 2 s (Edmund b 1985, William b 1987); *Career* bldg indust 1970-77; Nat Economic Devpt Off: indust advsr 1977-84, head of admin 1984-87, on secondment as UK dir of European Year of the Environment 1987-88, sec to Nat Economic Devpt Cncl 1988-; *Recreations* amateur dramatics; Anglo-Saxon history, armchair archaelogy; *Style—* Martin Couchman, Esq; The Old Rectory, Halstead, Sevenoaks, Kent TN14 THG (☎ 0958 32253)

COUHOUN, Prof John; s of James Colhoun (d 1935), of Castlederg, Co Tyrone, and Rebecca, *née* Lecky (d 1963); *b* 15 May 1913; *Educ* Edwards Sch Castlederg Co Tyrone, The Queen's Univ Belfast (BSc, B Agr, M Agr), Imperial Coll of Sci London (DIC), University of London (PhD, DSc), Univ of Manchester (MSc, ex-officio degree); *m* 29 July 1949, Margaret Waterhouse, da of Prof Gilbert Waterhouse, of Belfast; 3 da (Lucy (Mrs Loerzer) b1950, Georgiana (Mrs Golub) b 1956, Jacqueline (Mrs Chaddock) b 1959)

COULL, Prof Alexander; s of William Coull (d 1964), of Peterhead, and Jane Ritchie, *née* Reid (d 1969); *b* 20 June 1931; *Educ* Peterhead Acad, Aberdeen Univ (BSc Eng, PhD, DSc), Cranfield Inst of Technol (MSc); *m* 27 Dec 1962, Frances Bruce, da of Francis T C Moir (d 1988), of Aberdeen; 1 s (Gavin b 1967), 2 da (Alison b 1964, Moyra b 1969); *Career* res asst MIT (USA) 1955, structural engr Eng Electric Co Ltd 1955-57; lectr: engrg Univ of Aberdeen 1957, civil engrg Univ of Southampton 1962-66; prof of structural engrg Univ of Strathclyde 1967-76 (dean 1969-72), regius prof of civil engrg Univ of Glasgow 1977- (dean of engrg 1981-84); chm Clyde Estuary Amenity Cncl 1981-86, govr Glasgow Coll 1987-, past memb of ctee Inst of Structural Engrs (Scottish Branch); chm: Ctee on Tall Concrete and Masonry Bldgs, Cncl on Tall Bldgs and Urban Habitat 1984-; FICE 1973, FIStructE 1973, FRSE 1971; *Books* ed: Tall Buildings (1967), Fundamentals of Structural Theory (1972); *Recreations* golf, skiing, hill-walking; *Clubs* Buchanan Castle Golf ; *Style—* Prof Alex Coull; 11 Blackwood Rd, Milngavie, Glasgow G62 7LB (☎ 041 956 1655); Department of Civil Engineering, University of Glasgow, Glasgow G12 8QQ (041 339 8855 ext 5200, fax 041 330 4808, telex 777 070)

COULMAN, Michael Raymound; s of Col Edward Raymond Coulman, OBE, TD (d 1956), of Bracken Cottage, Newtown, Newbury, Berks, and Margaret Annie, *née* Stow (d 1984); *b* 28 Oct 1932; *Educ* Winchester Coll, Trinity Coll, Oxford (BA, MA); *m* 1, 23 July 1969, Jacqueline (d 1980), da of Anthony Cuthbert Morris Marsham (d 1975), of West Malling, Kent; 1 s (Robert b 1975), 1 da (Camilla b 1977); m 2, 9 April 1981, Patricia Margaret, da of the Hon Edward Carson (d 1987), of Hastings, Sussex; 3 step da (Lucy Fife Jamieson b 1972, Georgina b 1976, Sophie b 1976); *Career* 2 Lt KRRC 1951-53; stockbroker Anglo American Corpn S Africa 1957-62, ptnr Sheppards 1968-85 (then taken over by BAII); *Recreations* golf; *Clubs* MCC, I Zingari, Tennis and Racquets Assoc, Rye GC; *Style—* Michael Coulman, Esq; Bainden Farmhouse, Horsmonden, Tonbridge, Kent (☎ 089 272 2528); Sheppards, No 1 London Bridge, SE1 (☎ 01 378 7000)

COULSHED, Brig Dame (Mary) Frances; DBE (1953, CBE 1949), TD (1951); da of Wilfred Coulshed and Maud, *née* Mullin; *b* 10 Nov 1904; *Educ* Parkfields Cedars Derby, Convent of the Sacred Heart Kensington; *Career* ATS 1938-49, subsequently WRAC 1949-54; served WW II, NW Europe Campaign (despatches), dep dir Anti-Aircraft Cmd 1946-50, dep dir War Office 1950, Dir WRAC 1951-54, Brig, ret; ADC to HM The King 1951, ADC to HM The Queen 1952-54; Order of Leopold I of Belgium with Palm, Croix de Guerre with Palm 1946; *Style—* Brig Dame Frances Coulshed, DBE, TD; 815 Endsleigh Court, Upper Woburn Place, London WC1

COULSON, Cdr Alexander Frederick William (Jim); *b* 28 Feb 1909; *Educ* Luton Modern Sch, London Univ, MIT Boston USA, Harvard USA; *m* 1937, Joan Milner, *née* Cowburm; 3 s, 1 da; *Career* WWII RN 1940-47, dir Admty R & D India 1944-47, Cdr RNVR 1947; dir (later md) R Greg & Co Ltd 1936-74; dir: Armitage & Rigby Ltd, Lee Bank Mill Co, John A Gilmour & Co Ltd and other textile cos; chm Quarry Bank Mill Tst Ltd 1978-85 (vice pres 1988), fndr memb and tres Derbyshire and Peak Dist Appeal Nat Tst; hon life memb Textile Inst; vice-pres Royal Foxhound Show Soc 1986; memb: CLA, CGA, Manchester Statistical Soc (hon life memb), Manchester Literary and Philosophical Soc; *Books* A study of the Cotton Textile Industry of the USA (1935) ; *Recreations* beagling, Nat Tst; *Style—* Cdr Alexander Coulson, RNVR; Sunart, Whaley Bridge SK12 7EW (☎ 066 33 2227)

COULSON, Ann Margaret; da of Sidney Herbert Wood (d 1972), and Ada, *née* Mills (d 1969); *b* 11 Mar 1935; *Educ* Chippenham GS, UCL (BSc), Univ of Manchester (Dip Soc Admin); *m* 19 Aug 1958, Peter James Coulson, s of Leslie Gerald Bell Coulson (d 1970) of Albury, Surrey; 2 s (Jeremy Richard b 12 April 1964, Michael Hugh b 5 May 1966), 1 da (Nancy Margaret b 19 Dec 1962); *Career* lectr then sr lectr Bromsgrove Coll 1968-76, asst dir N Worcs Coll 1976-80; dir of planning W Midlands RHA 1988- (service/capital planning 1980-88); memb: bd of dirs BRMB (local radio stn) 1982-, IBA 1976-80, Birmingham Voluntary Serv Cncl 1975-81, cllr City of Birmingham 1973-79; *Recreations* sailing, cooking; *Style—* Mrs Ann Coulson; Rowans, Leamington Hastings Nr Rugby, Warwickshire CV23 8DY (☎ 0926 633 264); 240 The Fairway, Kings Norton, Birmingham B38 8YN (☎ 021 458 1670); West Midlands RHA, Arthur Thomson House, 146 Hagley Rd, Edgbaston, Birmingham B16 9PA (☎ 021 456 1444, ext 1501, fax 021 454 4406)

COULSON, Hon Mrs (Elizabeth Anne); eldest da of Baron Crowther-Hunt (Life Peer); *b* 1947; *m* 1976, Peter John Coulson; children; *Style—* The Hon Mrs Coulson; 37 Deodar Rd, Putney, SW15

COULSON, Sir John Eltringham; KCMG (1957, CMG 1946); er s of Henry John Coulson (d 1959), of Bickley, Kent; *b* 13 Sept 1909; *Educ* Rugby, CCC Cambridge (hon fellow 1975); *m* 1944, Mavis Ninette, da of late Edwin Beazley, of Coleman's Hatch, Sussex; 2 s; *Career* Diplomatic Service: dep UK rep to UN NY 1950-52, asst under-sec of state FO 1952-55, min Washington 1955-57, seconded to Paymaster-Gen's Office 1957, ambassador to Sweden 1960-63, dep under sec of state FO 1963-65, chief Diplomatic Serv Admin 1965, sec-gen EFTA 1965-72; pres Hants BRCS 1972-79; *Style—* Sir John Coulson, KCMG; The Old Mill, Selborne, Hants (☎ 042 050 288)

COULSON, His Honour Judge; (James) Michael; s of William Coulson, of Wold Newton Hall, nr Driffield, E Yorks (d 1979), and Kathleen, *née* Abbott (d 1984); *b* 23 Nov 1927; *Educ* Fulneck Sch Yorkshire, Merton Coll Oxford, RAC Cirencester; *m* 1, 1 May 1955, Dilys, da of David Adair Jones of Knapton Hall, Merton, Yorkshire; 1 s (David James Ivo b 1963); m 2, Jan 1976, Barbara Elizabeth Islay, da of Dr Roland Moncrieff Chambers, of 37 Beaconsfield Road, London, 1 s (Timothy James Edward b 1978), 1 da (Sarah Elizabeth Rosamond b 1984); *Career* Major East Riding Yeomanry, ret; barr Middle Temple 1951, dep chm North Riding Quarter Sessions, asst recorder to Sheffield; MP (C) Kingston upon Hull North 1959-64, PPS to Slr Gen 1962-64; circuit judge Midlands and Oxford 1983, dep chm Northern Agricultural Land Tribunal 1967-72, regional chm of Indust Tribunals 1972-83; *Recreations* hunting, reading, gardening, country life; *Clubs* Cavalry and Guards until 1980 when resigned on increase of subscriptions; *Style—* His Hon Judge Coulson; The Tithe Barn, Wymondham, Melton Mowbray, Leicestershire

COULSON, (Bevis) Michael Leigh; s of Capt Thomas William Bevis Coulson (d 1944), of Coulsdon, Surrey, and Vera, *née* Leigh; *b* 18 May 1945; *Educ* Charterhouse, Liverpool Univ, City of London Coll (BSc), Drew Univ Madison New Jersey USA,

American Univ Washington DC USA; *m* 2 Oct 1971, Hilary Ann, da of Dr William Henry Cotton Croft; 3 da (Alice b 1978, Mary b 1981, Lisa b 1981); *Career* stockbroking investmt analysis 1970-; head mining res Phillips & Drew 1982-86, dir and head mining dept Kitcat & Aitken; Freeman City of London 1985, memb Worshipful Co of Weavers 1985; memb Soc of Investmt Analysts 1975; *Recreations* cricket, football, horticulture; *Style—* Michael Coulson, Esq; 9 Brodrick Rd, London SW17 7DZ (☎ 01 767 1608); Kitcat & Aitken, 71 Queen Victoria St, London EC4 (☎ 01 489 1966)

COULTASS, (George Thomas) Clive; *b* 5 July 1931; *Educ* Tadcaster GS Yorkshire, Univ of Sheffield (BA), King's Coll London (Educn Cert); *m* 17 Sept 1962, Norma Morris; *Career* teacher various schools in London 1956-62, lectr and sr lectr in history James Graham Coll Leeds 1962-69; Imp War Museum 1969-: keeper of film programming 1969-70, keeper of dept of film 1970-84, keeper of AV records 1984-; author of several articles in historical journals and organiser of various film historical confs; vice pres Int Assoc for AV Media in Historical Res and Educn 1978-85; *Recreations* music, travel, reading; *Style—* Clive Coultass, Esq; 39 Fairfield Grove, London SE7 8UA; Imperial War Museum, Lambeth Rd, London SE1 6HZ (☎ 01 735 8922)

COULTER, Michael Daley; s of Thomas Coulter (d 1976), and Elizabeth, *née* Daley; *b* 29 August 1952; *Educ* Holy Cross HS Hamilton; *m* 1 March 1976, Louise, da of William Brogan, of Glasgow; 2 s (Luke b 1981, Eliot b 1987), 2 da (Ruth b 1983, Sophie b 1985); *Career* dir of photography; films incl: No Surrender, Heavenly Pursuits,The Good Father, Housekeeping, The Dressmaker, Breaking In, Diamond Skull; memb Br Soc of Cinematographers; *Recreations* music (playing and listening); *Clubs* Leander; *Style—* Michael Coulter, Esq; 4 Turnberry Ave, Glasgow G11 5AG (☎ 041 339 0378)

COULTER, Roger Frederick; s of Thomas Coulter, of Thurgarton, and Freda Lucy, *née* Shaw; *b* 1 Oct 1946; *Educ* Kings Sch Worcester; *m* 12 June 1971, Caroline Rosemary, da of James Whitehead MC (d 1982); 2 da (Victoria b 1974, Diana b 1977); *Career* chm Shaw & Lyddon Ltd Nottingham, non exec dir Ernest Clark Ltd Nottingham; *Recreations* shooting, motoring in France; *Style—* Roger F Coulter, Esq; Elmcote, Whatton, Nottinghamshire (☎ 0949 50265, 0602 475130); 20-22 Broad St, Nottingham NG1 3AL

COULTHARD, Air Vice-Marshal Colin Weall; CB (1975), AFC (1953 and bar 1958); s of Wing Cdr George Robert Coulthard (d 1977), and Cicely Eva, *née* Minns (d 1953); *b* 27 Feb 1921; *Educ* Watford GS, De Havilland Aeronautical Tech Sch; *m* 1, 1941 (m dis), Norah Ellen Creighton; 1 s, 2 da; m 2, 1957, Eileen Pamela, da of late Frederick Barber; 1 s; *Career* RAF 1941, Day Fighter Pilot 1942-45 (despatches), OC No 266 (Rhodesia) Sqdn 1952-54, OC Air Fighting Devpt Sqdn 1957-59, Station Cdr RAF Gütersloh 1961-64, Dir Operational Requirements 1 (RAF) MOD 1967-69, Air Cdre 1967, Air Attaché Washington 1970-72, Air Vice-Marshal 1972, Mil Dep Defence Sales MOD 1973-75, ret; govr Truro Sch 1982-; FRAeS; *Recreations* walking, shooting, motor sport; *Clubs* RAF; *Style—* Air Vice-Marshal Colin Coulthard, CB, AFC; Fiddlers, Old Truro Rd, Goonhavern, Truro, Cornwall (☎ 087 254 312)

COUNSELL, Her Honour Judge Hazel Rosemary; da of Arthur Henry and Elsie Winifred Counsell; *b* 7 Jan 1931; *Educ* Clifton HS, La Châtellanie Switzerland, Bristol Univ; *m* 1980, Judge Peter Fallon, QC, *qv*; *Career* barr 1956, legal dept Min of Labour 1959-62, recorder Crown Court 1976-77, circuit judge 1978-; memb Matrimonial Causes Ctee 1983-; *Style—* Her Hon Judge Hazel Counsell; Crown Court, Guildhall, Bristol

COUNSELL, His Honour Judge; Paul Hayward; s of Frederick Charles and Edna Counsell; *b* 13 Nov 1926; *Educ* Colston Sch Bristol, Queen's Oxford; *m* 1959, Joan Agnes Strachan; 1 s, 2 da; *Career* slr 1951, barr 1962, slr-gen Rhodesia 1963-64, Zambia 1964, circuit judge 1973-; *Style—* His Hon Judge Counsell; c/o Hitchin County Court, Station House, Nightingale Rd, Hitchin, Herts (☎ 0462 50011)

COUPE, Barry Desmond; s of Harold Demons Coupe, of Dorincourt, Rothesay Rd, Talbot Woods, Bournemouth, Dorset, and Alice, *née* Roberts; *b* 4 June 1951; *Educ* Lawrence House, St Annes on Sea, Canford Sch, Leeds Poly (BA, DipArch, RIBA); *m* 6 May 1978, Shăn Patricia, da of J N R Wilson, of 21 Pinewood Ave, Bournemouth; 2 s (Matthew William b 1981, Benjamin James b 1984); *Career* architect; sr ptnr Forum Architects Cambridge; works include: Nobelight Bldg 1983, Leisure Complex Whittaker House 1984, Offrs Club RAF Milden Hall 1986, Beehive Shopping Centre Cambridge 1987, Headquarters Bldg Domino plc Cambridge 1987; *Recreations* motor car, historic collections, round table, photography; *Clubs* Ferrari Owners, Alfa Romeo Owners, Round Table, Farmers (Cambridge); *Style—* Barry Coupe, Esq; Reeves Croft, Reeves Pightle, Gt Chishill, Royston, Herts (☎ 0763 838048); Forum Architects, Elmhurst, Brooklands Ave, Cambridge (☎ 0223 838048, fax 0223 666714, car ☎ 0836 270213)

COUPE, Barry Desmond; s of Harold Desmond Coupe of Dorincourt, 2 Rothesay Rd, Talbot Woods, Bournemouth, and Alice, *née* Roberts; *b* 4 June 1951; *Educ* Canford Sch, Leeds Sch of Architecture (BA, Dip Arch); *m* 6 May 1928, Shân Patricia da of James Ninian Reid Wilson, Friston Cottage, Northbourne, Bournemouth; 2 s (Matthew b 6 Sept 1981, Benjamin b 11 Feb 1985); *Career* with Fitzroy Robinson & Ptnrs 1977-80, fndr ptnr Forum Architects 1980-; Usafe Design Award 1986,1987,1988; Usaf World Wide Award 1986, Civic Tst Award, Commendation 1987, Winner Domino plc comp for new HQ 1987; memb Cambridge Round Table, tstee Cambridge Children's Hospice, RIBA 1979; *Recreations* classic cars, motor sport, photography, round table; *Style—* Barry Coupe, Esq; The Old Rectory, Ashley, Newmarket, Suffolk CB8 9DU, (☎ 0638 730751), Forum Architects, Elmhurst, Brooklands Ave, Cambridge, (☎ 0223 66616, fax 0223 66714, car tel 0836 270213)

COUPER, Heather Anita; da of George Couper Elder Couper, of Bexhill-on-Sea, E Sussex, and Anita, *née* Taylor (d 1984); *b* 2 June 1949; *Educ* St Mary's GS, Univ of Leicester (BSc), Univ of Oxford ; *Career* mgmnt trainee Peter Robinson Ltd 1967-69, res asst Cambridge Observatories 1969-70, lectr Greenwich Planetarium 1977-83, broadcaster and writer on astronomy and sci 1983, pres Br Astronomical Assoc 1984-86, pres Jr Astronomical Soc 1987-89, tv presenter The Planets Channel 4 1985, The Stars (Channel 4 1988); astronomy columnist The Independent, presenter and contrib for many radio programmes; FRAS 1970, FRSA 1985; *Books* twenty pubns incl: The Space Scientist series, The Universe, The Restless Universe, The Stars, The Planets; *Recreations* travel, the English countryside, wine, food, London; *Style—* Miss Heather Couper

COUPER, Sir (Robert) Nicholas Oliver; 6 Bt (UK 1841); s of Maj Sir George Rupert Cecil Couper, 5 Bt (d 1975), and Margaret Grace, *née* Thomas (d 1984); *b* 9 Oct 1945; *Educ* Eton, RMA Sandhurst; *m* 1972 (m dis), Curzon Henrietta, da of Maj George Burrell MacKean, JP, DL (d 1983); 1 s, 1 da (Caroline b 1979); *Heir* s, James George Couper b 27 Oct 1977; *Career* Acting Maj Blues and Royals (ret); estate agent, ptnr Savills, dir Aylesfords and Co; *Style—* Sir Nicholas Couper, Bt; 55 Bassein Park Road, London W12 9RW (☎ 01 749 5489); Aylesfords, 103 Kensington Church St, London W8 (☎ 01 727 6663)

COUPLAND, Prof Rex Ernest; s of Ernest Coupland (d 1978), of Mirfield Yorks, and Doris, *née* Threadgold; *b* 30 Jan 1924; *m* 14 July 1947, (Lucy) Eileen, da of William Sargent (d 1950), of Smallrice, Sandon, Staffs; 1 s (Michael Adam b 22 July 1953), 1 da (Lesley Diana Eileen b 11 Feb 1950); *Career* Nat Serv MD RAF 1948-50; house surgn Leeds Gen Infirmary 1947, lectr Univ of Leeds 1950-58, asst prof Univ of Minnesota 1955-56, Cox prof of Anatomy Univ of St Andrews 1958-68, Fndn prof of Human Morphology Univ of Nottingham 1968- (Dean Faculty of Med 1981-87); contributor numerous articles in learned journals; memb: Derbyshire AHA 1978-81, Trent RHA 1981-88, Central Notts DHA 1988- (GMC 1981-88); chm MRC non-ionizing Radiation Ctee 1970-89; memb: MRC Biological Res Bd 1964-70, Med Advsy Bd Crippling Diseases 1971-75; pres: Anatomical Soc GBI 1976-78, Br Assoc ch Clinical Anatomists 1977-82; FRS (E) 1970; *Books* The Natural History of the Chromaffin Cell, (co-ed T Fujita Chromaffin 1965), Enterochromaffin and Related Cells (ed with T Fujita 1976), Peripheral Neuroendocrine Interaction (ed with WG Forssman 1978); *Recreations* gardening, shooting; *Clubs* RSM; *Style—* Prof Rex Coupland; Foxhollow, Quaker Lane, Farnsfield, Notts NG22 8EE (☎ 0623 882 028); The Medical School, Queens Medical Centre, Nottingham NG22 8EE (☎ 0602 422 227)

COURT, Hon Sir Charles Walter Michael; KCMG (1979), OBE (1946), MLA (Lib) Nedlands 1953-; s of late W J Court of Perth, Western Australia; *b* 29 Sept 1911,Crawley, England; *Educ* Leederville State Sch, Rosalie State Sch, Perth Boys' Sch; *m* 1936, Rita M, da of L R Steffanoni; 5 s; *Career* chartered accountant, practised to 1970; MLA WA (Lib) Nedlands 1953-82, former leader of opposition W Australia (dep ldr 1957-59 and 1971-72); min: W A for Indust Development and the NW 1959-71, for Railways 1959-67, for Transport 1965-66; premier of W Australia 1974-82, min co-ordinating Economic and Regional Devpt and Treasurer 1974-82 (ret); First Class Order of the Sacred Treasure; Inst CA of Australia, ASA; kt 1972; *Books* numerous technical papers; *Clubs* WELD, CTA, WA; *Style—* Hon Sir Charles Court, KCMG, OBE, AK, MLA; 46 Waratah Av, Nedlands, WA 6009, Australia

COURT, Dr Glyn; s of William George Court (d 1953), of Roadwater, and Ada, *née* Palser (d 1967); *b* 13 May 1924; *Educ* Taunton Sch, Univ Coll Exeter, Univ of London (BA, PhD), Univ of Paris (Br Inst), Univ of Grenoble; *m* 23 Sept 1950, Clare Ann, da of Maj G E Carpenter, MC, of Budleigh Salterton, Devon; 1 s (Mark), 3 da (Alison, Joy, Philippa); *Career* Queen's Royal Regt (TA Res) 1942, incorporated 1944, Fourteenth Army 1944-45; head modern languages depts 1959-74; Lib Party: branch, area and div chm Torrington N Devon and Bridgwater 1958-71, Parly candidate Westbury 1974 (twice) and N Dorset 1979, Euro Parly candidate Midlands West 1979; winner Brain of Britain 1973; memb Ilfracombe UDC 1964-67, Old Cleeve PC 1968-, Somerset CC 1973-77 and 1985-, (vice chm 1987-); chm: libraries and museums, highways, Dillington Coll Adult Educn, Quantock Hills Jt Liaison Gp: ACC nat parks and recreations ctees; Methodist local preacher 1958-, fndr memb and sec Burma Star Assoc W Somerset 1985-; AMA 1959-77; *Books* West Somerset in Times Past (1981), Somerset Carols (1983), Exmoor National Park (1987); *Recreations* travel, exploring countryside, local history (chm), European languages, genealogy, music; *Clubs* Liberal, Bridgewater; *Style—* Dr Glyn Court; Sunbeam House, Roadwater, W Somerset; County Hall, Taunton TA1 4DY (☎ 0823 333451)

COURTAULD, Samuel; s of Major George Courtauld (d 1980), of Essex, and Claudine Suzanne, *née* Booth (d 1983); The Courtaulds were a Huguenot family from Ile d'Olevon near La Rochelle, came to England in 1680's, 3 generations were practicing goldsmiths in London and subsequent predecessors become involved in weaving business and Founded Courtaulds Ltd; *b* 14 Mar 1940; *Educ* Gordonstoun, Magill Univ (Canada) Sorbonne; *m* 2 April 1963, Annette Susan, da of Major Chandos Ormisby Jodrell Godwin-Williams (d 1985), of Kent; 1 s (Samuel b 1969), 3 da (Serena b 1964, Melissa b 1965, Lucinda b 1968 (d 1968)); *Career* late 2 Lt Grenadier Gds; investmt advsr; Freeman City of London, Liveryman of the Worshipful Co of Goldsmiths; *Recreations* shooting, fencing, gardening, campanology; *Clubs* First Guards, Special Forces; *Style—* Samuel Courtauld, Esq; Don Johns Farm, Earls Colne, Colchester, Essex (☎ 07875 2627); 55N Hans Road, SW3 (☎ 01 589 6042); Greenwell Montague, 114 Old Broad Street, London (☎ 01 588 8817)

COURTENAY, Lady (Camilla) Gabrielle; da of late 16 Earl of Devon; *b* 8 April 1913; *Educ* The Maynard Exeter; *Style—* Lady Gabrielle Courtenay; The Briary, Exton, Exeter, Devon

COURTENAY, Lord; Hugh Rupert Courtenay; s and h of 17 Earl of Devon; *b* 5 May 1942; *Educ* Winchester, Magdalene Coll Cambridge; *m* 9 Sept 1967, Dianna Frances, elder da of Jack Watherston, of Menslaws, Jedburgh, Roxburghshire; 1 s, 3 da (Hon Rebecca Eildon b 1969, Hon Eleonora Venetia b 1971, Hon Camilla Mary b 1974); *Heir* s, Hon Charles Peregrine Courtenay b 14 Aug 1975; *Career* chartered surveyor Messrs Stratton and Holborow; *Style—* Lord Courtenay; Powderham Castle, nr Exeter, Devon EX6 8JQ (☎ 0626 890252)

COURTENAY, Lady Mary Elizabeth; 2 da of 16 Earl of Devon (d 1935); *b* 15 Jan 1910; *Career* State Registered Nurse, State Cert Midwife, Badge of Honour (Red Cross); *Recreations* gardening; *Style—* Lady Mary Courtenay; The Briary, Exton, Exeter, Devon

COURTICE, Lt-Col Robert Sandeman; s of Col George Courtice, DSO (d 1939), and Olive, *née* Sandeman (d 1962); *b* 11 Feb 1917; *Educ* Cheltenham Coll, RMA Woolwich, Clare Coll Camb (MA); *m* 9 Aug 1950, Janet Nesta, da of Edgar Moorsom (d 1933), of Baylham, Suffolk; 3 s (Mark b 1951, Giles b 1953, Richard b 1968); *Career* RE 1937-64, Lt-Col, France 1939-40, Far East 1942-45, Cabinet Off 1946-49; sch master Framlingham Coll 1968-82; *Recreations* ocean racing; *Clubs* Royal Ocean Racing; *Style—* Lt-Col Robert Courtice; White House, Bruisyard, Saxmundham, Suffolk (☎ 072 875 2870)

COURTIS, John; s of Flt Lt Thomas Courtis (d 1976), of Stock, Ingatestone, Essex, and Marjorie May, *née* Dodson (m 2 Massey); *b* 14 July 1937; *Educ* Westminster; *m* 15 Jan 1966, da of William McCall-Smith (d 1970), of Weavers, Stradishall, Suffolk; 1 s

(Neil Thomas b 1970), 1 da (Claudia Janet b 1969); *Career* FCA 1959; RAF 1960-63, Pilot Offr 1960-61 served Saxa Vord, Shetland; Flying Offr 1961-63, fin analyst Ford Motor Co 1963-67; dir: Reed Executive 1967-71, Executive Appointments Ltd 1971-74; chm: John Courtis & Ptnrs Ltd 1974-, DEEKO plc 1981-88, FRES 1985-88; dir Recruitment Soc, 1986-; memb ctee friends of New Shakespeare Co 1988-; *Books* Communicating for Results (1974), Money Matters for Managers (1976), Cost Effective Recruitment (1985), Selling Yourself in the Management Market (1986), Managing by Mistake (1987), Marketing Services (1987), Interviews: Skills and Strategy (1988), Bluffers Guide to Mgmnt 1986 (Accountancy 1987, Photography 1988); *Recreations* writing, cooking; *Clubs* Savile, RAF; *Style—* John Courtis, Esq; 31 Longmoore St, London SW1V 1JQ (☎ 01 834 5592); 104 Marylebone Lane, London W1M 5FU (☎ 01 486 6849, fax 01 487 4600)

COURTNEY, Cdr Anthony Tosswill; OBE (1947); s of Basil Tosswill Courtney (d 1933), of Ben Rhydding, Yorks, and Frances Elizabeth, *née* Rankin (d 1961); *b* 16 May 1908; *Educ* Edinburgh House Sch, RNC Dartmouth, RNC Greenwich; *m* 1, 1938, Elisabeth Mary, CStJ (d 1961), da of Rev Henry Cortlandt Stokes, of Sandown, IOW; m 2, 1962 (m dis 1966), Elizabeth, yr da of Charles Edward Churchill, of Ashton Keynes, Wilts, and widow of 1 Baron Trefgarne; m 3, 1971, Mrs Angela Bigland Bradford, da of Lloyd Fox, OBE; *Career* midshipman HMS Ramillies 1925, qualified as interpreter in Russian 1934, served WW II, dep head Naval Mission in Russia 1941-42, Intelligence Div Naval Staff Admiralty 1946-48, CSO (Intelligence) Germany 1949-51, qualified as interpreter in German, Intelligence Div Naval Staff Admty 1952-53, ret 1953 with rank of Cdr; export conslt ETG Consultancy Servs to 1965; contested (C) Hayes and Harlington 1955, MP (C) Harrow East 1959-66; princ New Eng Typewriting Sch 1969-; chm of govrs Urchfont Sch 1982-87; *Books* Sailor in a Russian Frame (1968); *Recreations* shooting, music, fishing; *Clubs* White's; *Style—* Cdr Anthony Courtney, OBE; Mulberry House, Urchfont, Devizes, Wilts (☎ 038 084 357)

COURTNEY, Nicholas Piers; s of Capt Frederick Harold Deming Courtney (d 1980), and Hazel, *née* Leigh-Pemberton (d 1972); *b* 20 Dec 1944; *Educ* The Nautical Coll Pangbourne, Royal Agric Coll Cirencester (Estate Mgmnt); *m* 30 Oct 1980, Vanessa Sylvia, da of John Bishop Hardwicke; *Career* land agent Greville Haggate & Co 1966-69, gen mangr The Mustique Co Mustique St Vincent West Indies 1970-74; author; ARICS 1967; *Books* The Tiger (1980), The Very Best of British (1986), In Society (1987); plus numerous works on the Royal Family including: Royal Children (1982), Sporting Royals (1983), Sisters-In-Law (1988); biographies of: The Princess of Wales, The Princess Royal, The Duke of York, Queen Elizabeth the Queen Mother; *Recreations* all field sports, gardening; *Clubs* Brooks's, Pen; *Style—* Nicholas P Courtney, Esq; 9 Kempson Rd, London SW6 4PX

COURTNEY, Rohan Richard; s of Arthur Richard Courtney, of Chingford, London, and Cecelia, *née* Harrington; *b* 28 Jan 1948; *Educ* William Morris GS London; *m* 12 Jan 1974, Marilyn, da of Ernest Arthur Charles Goward (d 1972), of Waltham Cross, Herts; 1 s (Liam b 1975), 1 da (Siân b 1977); *Career* banker; Nat Prov Bank London 1965-68; mangr: Rothschild Intercontinental Bank Ltd London 1968-75, AmEx Bank Ltd, London 1975-76, asst dir AmEx Bancom Ltd Hong Kong 1976-80; md European Asian Finance (UK) Ltd Hong Kong 1978-80; sr mangr Creditanstalt Bankverein London 1980-82, asst gen mangr and chief mangr State Bank of New South Wales, London 1982-; *Recreations* country pursuits; *Clubs* Royal Cwlth Soc, Overseas Bankers, Hong Kong CC; *Style—* Rohan Courtney, Esq; Old Hill, Radwinter, Saffron Walden, Essex CB10 2TL (☎ 079987 674); State Bank of New South Wales, 110-112 Fenchurch Street, London EC3M 5DR (☎ 01 481 8000, telex 8952331, fax 01 265 0740)

COURTOWN, 9 Earl of (I 1762); James Patrick Montagu Burgoyne Winthrop Stopford; also (sits as) Baron Saltersford (GB 1796), Baron Courtown (I 1758), Viscount Stopford (I 1762); s of 8 Earl of Courtown, OBE, TD, DL (d 1975); *b* 19 Mar 1954; *Educ* Eton, Berkshire Agric Coll, RAC Cirencester; *m* 6 July 1985, Elisabeth Dorothy, yr da of Ian Rodger Dunnett, of Pinders, Broad Campden, Glos; 1 s, 1 da (Lady Rosanna Elisabeth Alice b 13 Sept 1986); *Heir* s, James Richard Ian Montagu, Viscount Stopford b 30 March 1988; *Career* land agent; *Style—* The Rt Hon the Earl of Courtown; Pear Tree House, Broadway, Worcs

COURTOWN, Patricia, Countess of; Patricia; 3 da of late Capt Harry Stephen Winthrop of Auckland, New Zealand; *b* 25 Feb 1917; *m* 23 Feb 1951, as his 2 w, 8 Earl of Courtown (d 1975); 2 s, 1 da; *Style—* Rt Hon Patricia, Countess of Courtown; Threeways, Seer Green Lane, Jordans, Bucks

COUSE, Philip Edward; s of Oliver Couse (d 1969), of Birmingham, and Marion Couse (d 1968); *b* 24 Mar 1936; *Educ* Uppingham, Hackey Sch USA; *m* 1, May 1962 (m dis 1973), Jane Diana, da of Vernon Nicholson (d 1968); 2 s (James b 1963, Anthony b 1965), 1 da (Amanda b 1969); m 2, 13 April 1978, Carol Ann Pruitt, da of Ralph Johannessen (d 1985); 1 step da (Delaine Pruitt b 1969); *Career* CA; ptnr Coopers & Lybrand 1966-; dep pres ICAEW 1988- (memb cncl 1978-, vice pres 1987-88), pres: Birmingham CAs' Students Soc 1971-78, Birmingham and W Midlands Soc of CAs; dir Hillstone Sch Tst Ltd Malvern 1971-86, pres Birmingham and Edgbaston Debating Soc 1977-78, chm Edgbaston C of E Coll for Girls Ltd 1982-88; tres: Bishop of Worcester's Miny Fund, CAs' Dining Club, Birmingham Eye Fndn (tstee); memb: Arthritis and Rheumatism Cncl W Midlands, Queen Elizabeth Hosp Birmingham Jubilee Appeal Ctee; memb Ct Worshipful Co of CAs in England and Wales 1987 (Liveryman); FCA 1961; *Recreations* music, woodwork, watching rugby football; *Clubs* RAC; *Style—* Philip Couse, Esq; 15 Chad Road, Edgbaston, Birmingham B15 3ER; Coopers & Lybrand, 43 Temple Row, Birmingham B2 5JT (☎ 021 233 1100, fax 021 200 4040, telex 337892)

COUSENS, Lt-Col Richard Paul; s of Maj J R Cousens, MBE (d 1975), and Jean, *née* Montegomerie-Fleming Balfour Paul; *b* 13 Jan 1949; *Educ* Marlborough, RMA Sandhurst, Staff Coll Camberley, Jt Serv Def Coll Greenwich; *m* 1 Jan 1972, Avril Eva Margot, da of Maj John Bailey, MBE, of Little Stowe, Mark Way, Godalming; 2 s (Rupert b 1973, Edward b 1983), 3 da (Polly b 1975, Lucy b 1978, Sophie b 1980); *Career* cmd 2 Bn LI 1969, served in Malaysia, N Ireland & Cyprus 1969-71, Platoon Cdr LI Depot 1971-73, Co Cdr 1/2 Gurkha Rifles Brunei 1973-76, Adj 2 LI 1976-78, instr Sch of Inf 1978-80, Staff Coll 1980-81, Co-Cdr 2 LI 1982-84 (despatches 1982), Dep COS 12 Armoured Bde 1984-86, Co-Cdr Light Div Depot 1986-87, Jt Serv Def Coll 1987-88, CO 2 LI 1988-; MBIM 1989; *Recreations* offshore sailing, destructive gardening; *Clubs* Naval; *Style—* Lt-Col Richard Cousens; Second Bn LI, Tidworth (☎ 0980 46221)

COUSINS, Capt Jack; s of Herbert Sidney Cousins (d 1954), of Leigh on Sea, Essex, and Mabel Irene Hilda, *née* Andrews (d 1968); *b* 2 Feb 1920; *Educ* Storrington Coll, Alleyn Ct Sch, Highfield Coll, Chalkwell Hall Sch, Westcliff HS, TS Mercury , Sir John Cass Coll London Univ (Master Mariner Foreign Going); *m* 26 June 1948, Joyce Patricia (d 1969), da of Stanley Hennessy (d 1965), of Broomfield, Essex; 4 s (David b 1950, Roger b 1954, Simon b 1955, Andrew b 1958); *Career* Merchant Aircraft Carrier Amastra: 4 offr 1940, 3 offr 1941, 2 offr 1942, 1 offr 1943, Marine Offr/Master Basra Port Directorate Iraq 1948, with Marine Supts Dept Shaw Savill Line 1950; Royal Docks 1951-: harbour inspr asst dockmaster sr asst dockmaster dep dockmaster; traffic co-ordinator/asst harbour master Port of London Authy, marine conslt 1981; int sports corr 1981; Port of London rep to Perm Int Assoc of Navigation Congresses 1957- (individual memb 1980-); memb tech ctee Hon Co of Master Mariners 1965-; London Maritime Assoc: hon sec 1956-69, vice chm 1969, vice chm and hon tres 1980; memb Nat Union of Marine Aviation and Shipping Tport Offrs 1956 (liaison offr 1956), former pres 1987 and PR offr Essex Co Amateur Swimming Assoc; hon facilities sec Southern Cos Amateur Swimming Assoc 1976 (memb 1976), vice pres and life memb Southend-on-Sea Swimming Club (chm multi nat ctee), patron Little Theatre Club; life memb: Old Westcliffians Assoc RFC, Southend Airport Club, LSO Club, Les Amis d'Edith Piaf Paris, Nat Film Theatre Club, Br Film Inst, The Folio Soc; publicity offr TS Mercury Old Boys Assoc, memb: nat Swimming pool strategy working pty Sports Cncl 1976, Swimming Liaison gp Eastern Sports Cncl 1976, Br Swimming Coaches Assoc 1980; memb Hon Co of Master Mariners 1959; Freeman City of London 1969, Liveryman Honourable Co of Master Mariners; *Recreations* swimming, skiing, theatre (shareholder: really useful group ltd), philately, music, travel; *Style—* Capt Jack Cousins; Villa Valeta, 208 Carlton Ave, Westcliff-on-Sea, Essex SS0 0QD, (☎ 0702 343779); Piz D'Err, Dischmastrasse 20, 7260 Davos Dorf, Switzerland

COUSINS, John Stewart; s of Leslie Raymond Cousins (d 1976), of Ferndown, Dorset, and Margaret Betty Kate, *née* Fry; *b* 31 July 1940; *Educ* Brentwood Sch, Britannia RNC Dartmouth, Jesus Coll Cambridge (MA); *m* 1, 26 Oct 1970 (m dis 1979), Anne Elizabeth, da of Patrick O'Leary (d 1976), of Llanishen, Glamorgan; 1 da (Charlotte b 1973); m 2, 28 Dec 1979, Geraldine Anne, da of Col Thomas Ivan Bowers, CBE, DSO, MC (d 1980), of Yateley, Hants; *Career* RN 1958-62, cmmnd Sub Lt 1960, served Far East in HMS Belfast and HMS Maryton; md Kleinwort Benson Ltd Hong Kong 1973-78 (joined 1966, Far East rep Tokyo 1970-73), fin advsr to chm Porodisa Gp Indonesia 1979-80, ptnr de Zoete and Bevan 1980-85, dir Barclays de Zoete Wedd Securities 1985-, md Barclays de Zoete Wedd Equities Ltd; memb Panel on Takeovers and Mergers Hong Kong 1976-78; AMSIA 1968, memb Stock Exchange 1982; *Recreations* racing, rugby, cricket, field sports; *Clubs* Brooks's, Caledonian; *Style—* John Cousins, Esq; 73 Redcliffe Gardens, London SW10 (☎ 01 373 1919); Barclays de Zoete Wedd, Ebbgate House, 2 Swan Lane, London EC4 (☎ 01 623 2323, fax 01 623 6075, telex 01 888 221)

COUSINS, Raymond John Randal; s of Henry George Cousins (d 1983), and Freda Isabella *née* Roberts; *b* 14 July 1938; *Educ* Dulwich Coll Prep Sch, Alleyns Sch, Kings Coll Univ of London (BSc); *m* 28 Dec 1963, Ruth Imogen, da of William Charles Vigurs; 2 da (Fiona b 1967, Kirstie b 1969); *Career* ptnr Cyril Blumfield and Ptnrs 1973-; govr Alleyns Sch, church warden St Stephens S Dulwich; chm BSI Ctee; Liveryman: Worshipful Co of Woolman 1973 (clerk 1975-87), Worshipful Co of Engineers 1983 (asst clerk 1983-); FICE, FIStructE, MConsE; *Recreations* golf; *Clubs* Athenaeum, City Livery, Dulwich and Sydenham Hill Golf; *Style—* Raymond J R Cousins, Esq; 33 Hitherwood Drive, London, SE19 1XA (☎ 01 670 4673); Cyril Blumfield and Partners, 192-198 Vauxhall Bridge Road, London, SW1V 1DX (☎ 01 834 3631, fax 01 630 9632)

COUSSENS, Philip Arthur; s of Arthur George Coussens, and Ivy May Coussens; *b* 17 Jan 1945; *Educ* Portsmouth Southern GS; *m* 1 April 1967, Valerie Margaret (d 1986), da of George Boniface; 2 s (Nigel b 8 April 1986, Stephen (twin); m 2, 25 March 1989, Colette Suzanne, da of Jules Promme; *Career* vice-pres Tiger Int 1975-76, chm IBL plc 1977-87, pres Small Business Bureau (SBB) 1985-89; *Recreations* sailing, gardening; *Style—* Philip A Coussens, Esq; Purley Hall, Pangbourne, Berks; Watership Down Estates, Hants

COUTANCHE, Jurat the Hon John Alexander Gore; s of Baron Coutanche (Life Peer, d 1973); *b* 25 May 1925; *Educ* Sherborne; *m* 1, 1 Sept 1949, Jean Veronica (d 1977), da of late Alexander Thomson Dawson, of Portelet House, Jersey; 1 s, 2 da; m 2, 1978, Gillian Margaret, da of late Brig John Douglas Fellowes Fisher, CBE; *Career* Lt-Cdr RNR; Jurat of Royal Court of Jersey and Lt Bailiff; *Clubs* Royal Channel Islands YC; *Style—* Jurat the Hon John Coutanche; Clos des Tours, St Aubin, Jersey, CI

COUTTS, Alan; s of Stanley Coutts, of 4 Rossdale Road, Putney, London, and Eva Betty, *née* Gregory; *b* 6 Oct 1947; *Educ* Wandsworth Sch; *m* 8 Oct 1976, Philomena Margaret, da of Thomas Joseph Walsh, of 3 Collingwood Place, Walton on Thames, Surrey; 4 s (Mark b 1977, Stuart b 1978, Daniel b 1981, Thomas b 1983); *Career* dir Robert Fraser and Ptnrs Ltd 1979-88, Regentcrest plc 1987-; memb Inst of Taxation; *Recreations* tennis, watersports, theatre; *Style—* Alan Coutts, Esq; 7 Conduit Street, London W1R 9TG (☎ 01 408 1485)

COUTTS, (Thomas) Gordon; QC (1973); s of Thomas Coutts (d 1976), and Evelyn Gordon Coutts; *b* 5 July 1933; *Educ* Aberdeen GS, Aberdeen Univ (MA, LLB); *m* 1 Aug 1959, Winifred Katherine, da of William Alexander Scott (d 1982); 1 s (Julian b 1962), 1 da (Charlotte b 1964); *Career* passed Advocate 1959, standing Junior Counsel Dept, Agric and Fisheries (ScSt) 1965-73; chm: Industl Tbnls 1972, Med Appeal Tbnls 1984; *Recreations* golf, stamp collecting; *Clubs* New Edinburgh, Bruntsfield Links GC (Edinburgh); *Style—* T Gordon Coutts, Esq, QC; 6 Heriot Row, Edinburgh, EH3 6HU (☎ 031 556 3042)

COUTTS, Herbert; s of the late Herbert Coutts, and the late Agnes, *née* Boyle; *b* 9 Mar 1944; *Educ* Morgan Acad Dundee; *m* 24 Dec 1970, Angela Elizabeth Mason, da of late Henry Smith; 1 s (Christopher b 10 Feb 1976), 3 da (Antonia b 17 Nov 1971, Naomi b 12 April 1977, Lydia b 31 Dec 1980); *Career* keeper of Antiquities and Bygones Dundee Museum 1968-71 (asst keeper 1965-68), supt of Edinburgh City Museum 1971-73, city curator Edinburgh City Museums and Galleries 1973-; princ pubns: Ancient Monuments of Tayside (1970), Tayside Before History (1971), Edinburgh: An Illustrated History (1975), Huntly House (1980), Lady Stair's House (1980); exhibition catalogues incl Edinburgh Crafts (with R A Hill 1973), Aince a Bailie Aye a Bailie (1974), Gold of The Pharaohs (ed 1988), The People's Story Museum

(1989); maj projects: City of Edinburgh Art Centre (1980), Museum of Childhood Extension (1986); vice pres Museum Assts Gp 1967-70; memb: Govt Ctee on Future of Scotlands Museums and Galleries 1978-80 (report published 1981), Cncl of Museums Assoc 1977-78 and 1986-88, Bd of Scottish Museums Cncl 1971-74 and 1986-88; museums advsr to Convention of Scottish Local Authys 1986-, tstee Paxton House 1988-; contested S Angus (Lab) 1970; SBS&J 1977, AMA 1970, FMA 1976, FSAScot 1965; *Recreations* gardening, swimming, music, family; *Style—* Herbert Coutts, Esq; Kirkhill House, Queen's Rd, Dunbar, East Lothian, EH42 1LN (☎ 0368 63113); Huntly House Museum, 142 Canongate, Edinburgh, EH1 8DD (☎ 031 225 2424 ext 6607)

COUTTS DONALD, William Frederick James; s of late William Coutts Donald; *b* 27 Sept 1940; *Educ* Westminster Sch, Edinburgh Univ; *m* 1980, Priscilla Mary, *née* Aldington; 1 da; *Career* chartered accountant, dir Horne Bros Ltd 1974-; *Style—* William Coutts Donald, Esq; 47 Rosebank, 47 Holyport Rd, SW6 (☎ 01 381 3616)

COUVE DE MURVILLE, Most Rev Maurice Noël Léon; *see*: Birmingham, Archbishop of (RC)

COUZENS, Sir Kenneth Edward; KCB (1979, CB 1976); s of Albert Edward Couzens (d 1968), and May Phoebe, *née* Biddlecombe (d 1973); *b* 29 May 1925; *Educ* Portsmouth GS, Caius Coll Cambridge (BA), London Univ (BA); *m* 1947, Muriel Eileen, da of Albert Fey (d 1943); 1 s, 1 da; *Career* dep sec HM Treasy (joined 1951) Incomes Policy and Pub Finance 1973-77, second perm sec Overseas Finance 1977-82, perm sec Dept of Energy 1982-85; dep chm British Coal Corporation 1985-88, chm Coal Production Ltd 1988-; *Recreations* gardening, reading, travelling; *Clubs* Reform; *Style—* Sir Kenneth Couzens, KCB; Coverts Edge, Woodsway, Oxshott, Surrey (☎ 037 284 3207)

COVEN, Edwina Olwyn; CBE (1988) JP (1965) DL (1987); da of Sir Samuel Instone, CL, and Lady (Alice) Instone; *b* 23 Oct 1921; *Educ* St Winifred's Ramsgate, Queen's Coll London, Lycée Victor Duruy Paris, Marlborough Gate Secretarial Coll London; *m* 1951, Frank Coven; *Career* WRAC Maj, Army Interpreter (French), serv UK and overseas incl: staff appts, Plans and Policy Div, Western Union Def Organisation, NATO; directorate manpower planning WO 1942-56; 1959: children's writer Fleetway Publications, gen features writer Nat Magazine Co, BBC Woman's Hour reporter, performer and advsr children's and teenage ITV; memb advsy cncl Radio London (BBC) 1978-81; chm Davbro Chemists 1967-71, stores conslt on promotion and fashion 1960-77, memb advsy ctee (clothing and footwear sub ctee) BSI 1971-73, dir TV-am 1985-; JP Inner London N Westminster 1965-72 (dep chm 71-72), JP City of London for Cmmn 1969-88 (dep chm 1971-88), rep DL Greater London 1988 (DL 1987), memb Ctee 1971-77, chm City of London Police Ctee 1984-87 (dep chm 1983-84), memb Police Ctee AMA 1984-, memb jt ctee of mgmnt London Ct of Int Arbitration 1983-89; Dowgate Ward City of London: memb ct of common cncl 1972-, elected Alderman 1973 and 1974, dep 1975-; Chief Commoner City of London 1987-88; chm WRAC Assoc 1989- (memb cncl 1973-, vice pres 1984-88, vice-chm 1985-89), memb: TAVRA City of London 1979-86, Assoc Speakers 1975-, London Home Safety Cncl 1980-84; vice chm Cities of London and Westminster Home Safety Cncl 1984-, vice-pres Nat Orgn for Women's Mgmnt Educn 1983-, chm ctee 800 anniversary for Mayoralty and Corpn of London 1988-, memb bd of govrs City of London Sch 1972-77, chm bd of govrs City of London Sch for Girls 1978-81, memb Royal Soc of St George 1972, chm Vintry and Downgate Wards Club 1977, Hon Capt of Police Salt Lake City 1986, OStJ 1987; *Books* Tales of Oaktree Kitchen (second edn 1960); *Recreations* homemaking generally, lawn tennis, watching a variety of spectator sports; *Clubs* Queen's Hurlingham, Devonshire (Eastbourne); *Style—* Mrs Edwina Coven, CBE, JP, DC; 22 Cadogan Ct, Draycott Ave SW3 3BX (☎ 01 589 8286

COVENEY, Gerald Boore; s of Major Ronald Leslie Coveney, RE (d 1980), of Deepcut, Camberley, Surrey, and Hilary Elsie Boore; *b* 7 July 1938; *Educ* Farnham GS; *m* 1 Nov 1969, Shirley Rosemary Ann, da of Ronald Edmund Messenger, of Sussex; 2 s (Scott b 1971, Laurence b 1973); *Career* Coldstream Guards, Lt-Sgt Platoon Instructor; chm and md Gerry Coveney and Assoc (Ad Agency) 1984-, asst dir JWT 1969-74; md: BMDC 1972-74, Lansdowne Marketing 1974-81, Lansdowne Euro 1981-84; cncl memb IGD (Inst of Grocery Distribution); assoc memb: FDF (Food and Drink Fedn), CIES (Int Chain Stores Assoc); former chm Strangers Gallery; memb Marketing Ctee Lords Taverners; ctee memb Local C Assoc (former chm, former cllr (C)); *Recreations* home and family, swimming; *Clubs* Strangers Gallery; *Style—* Gerald B Coveney, Esq, MIGD; Minden Lodge, Deepcut, Camberley, Surrey; Cavendish House, 51-55 Mortimer Street, London W1 (☎ 01 631 0016, fax 01 255 2003, car ☎ 0836 219096)

COVENEY, John Michael; s of Dr William Finbarr Coveney (d 1976), of Northampton, and Angela Elizabeth, *née* Godber; *b* 20 Sept 1951; *Educ* Franciscan Coll Buckingham, Northampton GS, King's Coll London (LLB); *m* 6 July 1974, Sarah Ann Mary, da of Dr Robert Arthur Sladden; 2 s (James Robert Finbarr b 1983, Nicholas Michael Julius b 1986); *Career* called to the Bar Middle Temple 1974-; memb: Hon Soc of Middle Temple, Criminal Bar Assoc, Br Horse Soc, Br Showjumping Assoc; *Recreations* riding, music, reading, travel; *Style—* John Coveney, Esq; Rothwell, Northamptonshire; 3 Temple Gardens, London EC4 (☎ 01 583 1155)

COVENTRY, Lady Anne Donne; eldest da of 10 Earl of Coventry (d 1940), and Hon Nesta Donne Philipps, da of 1 Baron Kylsant; *b* 17 June 1922; *Educ* Open Univ (BA); *Style—* Lady Anne Coventry; Inverearn, Abernethy, Perthshire

COVENTRY, 11 Earl of (E 1697); George William Coventry; Viscount Deerhurst (I 1697); s of 10 Earl (ka 1940), and Hon Nesta Donne Philipps (who m 2, 1953, Maj Terence Fisher-Hoch), da of 1 and last Baron Kylsant; *b* 25 Jan 1934; *Educ* Eton, RMA Sandhurst; *m* 1, 22 March 1955 (m dis 1963), Marie Farquhar-Médard, da of William S Médard, of St Louis, USA; 1 s; m 2, 1969 (m dis 1975), Ann, da of Frederick William James Cripps; m 3, 1980, Valerie Birch; *Heir* s, Viscount Deerhurst, *qv*; *Career* late 2 Lt Gren Gds; *Style—* The Rt Hon The Earl of Coventry; Earls Croome Court, Earls Croome, Worcester

COVENTRY, Lady Maria Alice; resumed maiden name Coventry 1968; yst da of 10 Earl of Coventry (d 1940), and Hon Nesta Donne Philipps, da of 1 Baron Kylsant; *b* 2 Oct 1931; *m* 6 May 1954 (m dis 1968), John Richard Lewes, er s of late Capt John Hugh Lewes, CBE, DSC, RN (ret), of White Willows, Yelverton, Devon; *Style—* Lady Maria Coventry; Levant Lodge, Earls Croome, Worcester

COVENTRY, Bishop of 1985-; Rt Rev Simon Barrington-Ward; s of Robert McGowan Barrington-Ward, DSO, MC (d 1948), of London, and Margaret Adele Barrington-Ward (d 1975); *b* 27 May 1930; *Educ* Eton, Magdalene Coll Cambridge, (BA, MA), Westcott House Cambridge; *m* 13 Sept 1963, Jean Caverhill, da of Dr Hugh William Young Taylor, of Edinburgh; 2 s (Mary Caverhill b 1969, Helen McGowan b 1971); *Career* Nat Serv RAF 1949-50, PO 1949; lektor Free Univ Berlin 1953-54, chaplain Magdalene Coll Cambridge 1956; ordained: deacon 1956, priest 1957; lectr Univ of Ibadan Nigeria 1960-63, fell and dean Magdalene Coll Cambridge 1963-70, princ Crowther Hall Coll and Selly Oak Coll 1970-75, gen sec Church Missionary Soc 1975-85; chm Ptnrship for World Mission Int Affairs and Devpt Ctee; Chaplain to HM the Queen 1984-85; Prelate Order of St Michael and St George 1989-; Hon DD Wycliffe Hall Toronto 1983; FRAI; *Books* Love Will Out (1988); *Recreations* walking, bicycling; *Style—* The Rt Rev the Bishop of Coventry; Bishop's House, Davenport Rd, Coventry CV5 6PW (☎ 0203 72244)

COVERDALE, Lt Col Terence Gilbert; MBE (1945); s of Gilbert Coverdale (d 1947), of N Yorks, and Grace, *née* Weatherill (d 1956); *b* 25 Oct 1917; *Educ* Aysgarth Sch , Loretto Sch, RMC Sandhurst; *m* 4 Feb 1941, Nancy Margaret, da of Sir John Loudon (d 1948); 2 s (Andrew Terence Loudon b 1943, Jonathan Gilbert b 1947); *Career* cmmnd Kings own Scottish Borderers 1938, NW Europe 1939-40, directing staff Staff Coll 1943-44, Normandy 1944; mil asst to: Field Marshal Viscount Montgomery 1945-46, Sir Sholto Douglas 1946, Gen Sir Brian Robertson C-in-C and Mil Govr Germany 1948-50, Gen Sir Brian Robertson C-in-C Middle East Land Forces 1950-51; OC Regtl Depot KOSB 1951-54, ret 1954; mangr J W Cameron and Co (Brewers) 1954-61, md Winterschladen and Co (wine merchants) 1976-82, ret; *Recreations* shooting, golf, gardening; *Clubs* Naval and Military; *Style—* Lt Col Terence G Coverdale, MBE; Old Hall, Knayton, Thirsk, North Yorkshire (☎ 0845 537332)

COVILL, Richard Vernon; s of Frederick Charles Covill and Gladys Bertha Covill; *b* 23 July 1934; *Educ* Shrewsbury Sch, Pembroke Coll Oxford; *m* 1958, Sian Mary, da of David Thomas Prichard (d 1943); 1 s (Charles b 1969), 2 da (Sarah b 1965, Harriet b 1971); *Career* barr at law; md The Head Wrightson Machine Co Ltd (part of Davy Corpn, mfr of equipment for the metal industries) 1975-82; Queen's Award for Export 1982, dir Davy McKee (Poole) Ltd; *Clubs* Cavalry and Guards; *Style—* Richard Covill, Esq; 51 Elgin Road, Talbot Woods, Bournemouth (☎ 0202 52931); Davy McKee (Poole) Ltd, Wallisdown Road, Poole, Dorset (☎ 0202 537000)

COWAN, Brigadier (James) Alan Comrie; MBE (1956); s of Alexander Comrie Cowan, MC (d 1937), and Helen May Isobel, *née* Finlayson (d 1988); *b* 20 Sept 1923; *Educ* Rugby; *m* 2 Dec 1948, Jennifer Evelyn, da of Roland Evelyn Bland (d 1974); 2 s (Anthony b 28 March 1953, Adrian b 16 Jan 1955), 1 da (Varian b 18 Oct 1950); *Career* cmmnd Rifle Bde 1942, served in UK, Egypt and Italy 1942-45, regtl and staff appts in Egypt, Oxford Univ, BAOR, Army Staff Coll, WO, Kenya, Malaya 1945-60, DS Army Staff Coll Camberley 1961-63, CO 4 Royal Anglian (formerly 1 Royal Leicesters) in UK, Aden and Malta 1964-66, GSO 1 17 Div Malaysia 1966-67, Col GS MOD London 1967-69, Cmd 8 Inf Bde NI 1970-71, DAG HQ UK Land Forces Wiltshire 1972-75; NI Off London 1975-80: princ for Industl Econ and Social Affairs 1975-78, asst Sec 1978; sec Govt Hospitality Fund 1980-; Freeman of City of London 1985; *Recreations* current affairs, music, theatre, countryside; *Clubs* Army and Navy, MCC; *Style—* Brig Alan Cowan, MBE; c/o Hoare & Co, 37 Fleet Street, London EC4P 4DQ; Government Hospitality Fund, 8 Cleveland Row, St James's London SW1A 1DH (☎ 01 210 4280, fax 01 930 1148)

COWAN, Brig Colin Hunter; CBE (1984), DL (Dunbartonshire 1974); s of Lt Col Samuel Hunter Cowan, DSO (d 1953), and Jean Mildred, *née* Hore (d 1967); *b* 16 Oct 1920; *Educ* Wellington, RMA Woolwich, Trinity Coll Cambridge (MA); *m* 1, 17 Sept 1949, Elizabeth (d 1985), da of Stephen Williamson, MC (d 1986); 2 s (Michael b 1951, Simon b 1954), 1 da (Elizabeth b 1956); m 2, Janet, wid of A H Burnett (d 1979), da of Capt John Mackay (d 1975); *Career* cmmnd RE 1940, Royal Bombay Sappers and Miners 1942-46, WO (AG's Dept) 1952-54, cmd Malta Forces Sqdn RE 1954-56, WO (MO Directorate) 1957-60, cmd Engr Regt BAOR 1960-63, def advsr UK Mission to UN NY 1964-66, MOD (Army, SD Directorate) 1966-68 (Brig Engr Plans 1969-70); chief exec Cumbernauld Devpt Corpn 1970-85; MICE 1967, FRSA 1984; *Recreations* walking, music, photography; *Clubs* New (Edinburgh); *Style—* Brig Colin Cowan, CBE, DL; 12B Greenhill Gardens, Edinburgh EH10 4BW (☎ 031 447 9768)

COWAN, David Neville; s of Roy Neville Cowan (d 1987), of Heyshott, W Sussex, and Dorne Margaret, *née* Burgoyne-Johnson; *b* 21 May 1950; *Educ* Marlborough, Bath Univ (BSc, BArch); *m* 23 Aug 1975, Gillian Judith, da of David Hay Davidson, OBE (d 1983), of Lymington, Hants; 2 s (Jonathan b 1979, Christopher b 1988); *Career* architect 1975; formed David Cowan Associates 1983; dir: Cowan Thomson Associates 1987, Charterfield Gp of Cos 1985; RIBA 1976; *Recreations* skiing, badminton, riding; *Style—* David N Cowan, Esq; Oak Tree Cottage, Nursery Lane, Maresfield, E Sussex (☎ 0825 2751); Cowan Thomson Associates Ltd, Greenstede House, Station Road, East Grinstead, W Sussex (☎ 0342 410 242)

COWAN, (Harold) Derrick; s of Samuel David Cowan (d 1979); *b* 19 June 1923; *Educ* University Coll Sch; *m* 1948, June Beryl; 2 children; *Career* served with RAF in M East; chm Cowan de Groot plc 1978-88; *Recreations* golf, bridge, walking; *Clubs* Casanova; *Style—* Derrick Cowan, Esq; 47 Springfield Road, London NW8 0QJ (☎ 01 624 6244)

COWAN, Henry (Harry); s of Thomas Cowan, of Coatbridge, Lanarkshire, Scotland, and Annie Divens McKenzie, *née* Gregor; *b* 23 Sept 1947; *Educ* St Patricks Sch Coatbridge, Strathclyde Univ Glasgow (BSc); *m* 12 April 1971, Alice, da of Patrick Smith (1969); 1 s (Martin b 16 Aug 1973), 1 da (Debbie b 15 April 1976); *Career* mangr regnl customer support Sperry Univac 1977-74, commercial mangr WM Press Gp 1979-84, mangr corpn info systems Amersham Int 1984, ops dir Aetna Int 1984-88; dir: Pugh Carmichael Conslts 1988-, Gp Alpha 1988-, Apollo Gp of Co's 1988-; *Books* State of the Art Report (1986); *Recreations* rugby referee (London Soc), photography, squash; *Style—* Harry Cowan, Esq; 14 Lytton Rd, Hatch End, Middlesex, HA5 4RH; Pugh Carmichael Consultants Ltd, 250 Kings Rd, London, SW3 5UE (☎ 01 351 7655, fax 01 351 0034, car tel 0836 268 584)

COWAN, Prof Ian Borthwick; s of William Macaulay Cowan (d 1963), of Norgate, Rotchell Road, Dumfries, and Annie, *née* Borthwick (d 1982); *b* 16 April 1932; *Educ* Dumfries Acad, Univ of Edinburgh (MA, PhD); *m* 16 July 1954, Anna Little, da of Alexander Telford (d 1969), Balgownie, Langholm, Dumfriesshire; 3 da (Gilliam b 8 Dec 1957, Susan b 7 March 1961, Ingrid b 23 March 1965); *Career* PO RAF (Educn Branch) 1954-55, Flying Offr RAF (Educn Branch) 1955-56; asst lectr dept of scottish hist Univ of Edinburgh 1956-59, lectr in hist Newbattle Abbey Coll 1959-62, prof in scottish hist Univ of Glasgow 1983-(lectr dept of scottish hist 1962-70, sr lectr 1970-77, reader 1977-83); former pres Scottish Church Hist Soc; hon tres: Scottish Hist Soc, Scottish Historical Conf Tst; cncl memb Scottish Record Soc, vice pres Historical Assoc; winner Scottish Arts Cncl Literary Award 1982; FRHistS 1969, FSAScot 1977; *Books* The Parishes of Medieval Scotland (1967), The Enigma of Mary Stuart (1971), The Scottish Covenanters (1976), The Scottish Reformation (1982), Ayrshire Abbeys: Crossraguel and Kilwinning (1986), Mary Queen of Scots (1987); jtly: Medieval Religious Houses - Scotland (1976), The Reformation and Renaissance in Scotland (1983), The Knights of St John of Jerusalem (1983); *Recreations* travel; *Style—* Prof Ian Cowan; 119 Balshagray Ave, Glasgow G11 7EG (☎ 041 954 8494); Flat 16, 4 St Patrick Sq, Edinburgh EH8; Dept of Scottish History, University of Glasgow, Gilmorehill, Glasgow G12 8QQ (☎ 041 339 8855 ext 4148)

COWAN, Major Kenneth McCrea; s of Col William McCrea Cleeve Cowan (d 1967), of Shropshire, and Ethel Mary Glynn, *née* Begbie (d 1949); *b* 6 Dec 1920; *Educ* Shrewsbury Sch, RMA Woolwich, RMC of Science; Harvard Graduate Sch of Business 1968; *m* 18 Nov 1950, Penelope Ruth, da of Capt Edson Crawford Sherwood, RCN (d 1968), of Ottawa, Canada; 1 s (Peter b 1958), 3 da (Jane b 1952, Susan b 1954, Sally b 1957); *Career* Maj RA served in: France 1940, M East 1941-43, Italy 1944-45; army tech staff (UK and M East) 1948-54; div md Vickers Armstrong Engrg Gp (ret 1980); FRSA; *Recreations* croquet, tennis, golf, music; *Style—* Maj Kenneth Cowan; Argos Hill Lodge, Rotherfield, Sussex (☎ 089 285 2532)

COWAN, Michael John Julian; s of Kenneth Christopher Armstrong Cowan (d 1955), and Flora Muriel, *née* Stewart; *b* 24 June 1952; *Educ* Midhurst GS Sussex, Churchill Coll Cambridge (MA); *m* 26 Sept 1981, Hilary Jane Cowan, da of Albert Edward Slade (d 1987); 2 da (Eleanor Josephine, Philippa Rose); *Career* investmt advsr NM Rothschild & Sons Ltd 1973-78, investmt dir Lazard Bros & Co Ltd 1979-87, vice pres Morgan Stanley Int 1987-; *Recreations* golf, bridge, DIY; *Style—* Michael Cowan, Esq; Ranmoor, 5 Fairmile Ave, Cobham, Surrey KT11 2JA (☎ 0932 65400); PO Box 132, 1 Undershaft, London EC3P 3HP (☎ 01 280 8171, fax 01 283 4455, telex 917141)

COWAN, Sir Robert; s of Dr John McQueen Cowan and May Cowan; *b* 27 July 1932; *Educ* Edinburgh Acad, Edinburgh Univ (MA); *m* 1959, Margaret Morton, *née* Dewar; 2 da (Frances, Katherine); *Career* RAF Educ Branch 1955-58; Fisons Ltd 1958-62, asst to Sales Dir Wolsey Ltd 1962-64; mktg conslt PA Mgmnt Conslts Ltd, overseas assignments in Iran and Yugoslavia; dir of consulting servs PA Hong Kong 1975-52, incl assignments in USA, Japan, Thailand, Singapore, The Philippines and Indonesia; chm Highlands and Islands Devpt Bd 1982-; bd memb Scottish Devpt Agency 1982-; hon LLD Aberdeen Univ 1987; kt 1988; *Clubs* New (Edinburgh), Royal Scottish Automobile (Glasgow), Hong Kong (Hong Kong); *Style—* Sir Robert Cowan; The Old Manse Farr, Farr (☎ 08083 209); Highlands and Islands Dvpt Bd, Bridge House, Bank Street, Inverness (☎ 0463 234171, telex 75267)

COWARD, Clive Alan; s of Charles Richard Coward, and Catherine Ellen Elizabeth, *née* Summersbee; *b* 30 August 1945; *Educ* Kings Coll Sch Wimbledon, Pembroke Coll Cambridge (MA); *m* 6 July 1968, (Mary) Frances, da of Edward Vernon Geden (d 1981); 2 s (James b 1971, Giles b 1973), 1 da (Tammy b 1974); *Career* S G Whitaker Ltd: non exec dir 1968, exec dir 1970, md 1973; jt md London Shop plc 1986-89; pres Capel and Dist Horticulture Soc, vice pres Caper Cricket Club; memb govt Ctee of Inquiry into Mgmnt of Flats (NUGEE Ctee); Freeman City of London, Freeman Worshipful Co of Fletchers (Master 1988-89), Freeman Worshipful Co of Chartered Surveyors; FRICS; *Recreations* skiing, tennis, windsurfing, running; *Clubs* City Livery; *Style—* Clive Coward, Esq; Hope Hse, Great Peter St, London SW1P 3LT (☎ 01 222 2837)

COWARD, David John; CMG (1965), OBE (1962); s of Robert James Coward (d 1962), of Exmouth, and Beatrice, *née* Masters (d 1961); *b* 21 March 1917; *Educ* Exmouth GS, Sch of Law; *m* 25 Sept 1954, Joan Margaret, da of Reginald Frank (d 1959), of Doncaster, Yorks; 3 da (Susan (Mrs Fischel) b 1957, Ruth b 1960, Vivienne b 1967); *Career* WWII RN 1939-47, served HMS King George V 1941-43, HMS Benbow sec to SBNO Trinidad 1943-46, ADC to Govr of Trinidad 1947, demob Lt Cdr RNVR; admitted slr 1938; Colonial Legal Serv Kenya: asst registrar general 1948, dep registrar general 1952, registrar general public tstee and official receiver 1955-82 (permanent sec Miny of Justice and Constitutional Affrs kenya 1963-64); Kenya Police Reserve 1949-63 (latterly as supt i/c Nairobi Area); chm Working Pty on the Future of the Company Secretarial Profession in Kenya 1979-80, memb Accountants Registration Bd 1978-82, tstee Nat Museums of Kenya 1979-82; awarded Silver Medal of the Int Olympic Ctee 1981 (for servs to the Int Olympic Movement); Freeman City of London 1984, memb Worshipful Co of Chartered Secretaries and Administrators 1985; FCIS 1961, ACIArb 1984; *Recreations* golf; *Clubs* Nairobi and Limuru (Kenya), West Sussex GC; *Style—* D J Coward, Esq, CMG, OBE; North Perretts, Spinney Lane, West Chiltington, W Sussex RH20 2NX (☎ 090 66 2521)

COWARD, (John) Stephen; QC (1984); s of Frank Coward (d 1980), of Huddersfield, and Kathleen, *née* Bell; *b* 15 Nov 1937; *Educ* King James GS Huddersfield, Univ Coll London (LLB); *m* 4 March 1967, Ann Lesley, da of Frederick Leslie Pye; 4 da (Victoria b 1969, Sarah b 1971, Laura b 1974, Sophie b 1976); *Career* served RAF 1957-59; lectr in law and constitutional history UCL and Police Coll Bramshill 1962-64, barr Inner Temple 1964, recorder of Crown Ct 1980; chm Scaldwell Educnl Charity, memb Scaldwell Chamber Choir; *Recreations* singing, wine, gardening; *Clubs* Northampton and County, Scaldwell; *Style—* Stephen Coward, Esq, QC; The Grange, Scaldwell, Northampton NN6 9JP (☎ 0604 880255); 2 Crown Office Row, Temple, London EC4Y 7HJ (☎ 01 353 1365)

COWBURN, Dr Philip Musgrave; s of Arthur Basil Cowburn, MC, TD (d 1966), and Margaret Alice Cowburn (d 1973); *b* 10 Feb 1917; *Educ* Shrewsbury Sch, Lincoln Coll Oxford (MA), Univ of NSW (PhD); *m* 28 Dec 1957, Catherine, da of Sir Richard Denman, MP, Bt (d 1957); 1 s (Stephen b 1959), 1 da (Anne b 1961); *Career* served WW II Maj Welsh Div Reconnaisance Corps RAC 1939-46; lectr RN Coll Greenwich 1948-64; sr lectr/assoc prof Univ NSW Sydney 1965-75; tutor Warnborough Coll Oxford 1976-84; *Books* Welsh Spearhead (1946), A Salopian Anthology (ed 1956), The Warship in History (1966); *Style—* Dr Philip M Cowburn; Cherwell House, Old Kidlington, Oxon OX5 2EG (☎ 08675 5000)

COWDEROY, Norman Derrick; s of Frank Cecil Cowderoy (d 1957), of Esher, Surrey, and Celia Winifred Cowderoy (d 1988); *b* 11 June 1928; *Educ* Kingston GS, Balliol Coll Oxford (BA); *m* 20 Aug 1955, Jennifer Margaret Veryan, da of Cyril Hadlow Colton, CBE (d 1988), of Cobham, Surrey; 3 s (Adrian, James, David); *Career* army 1946-48, 2 Lt 1947, RHA Palestine 1947-48; shipbroker; joined H Clarkson and Co Ltd 1949 (dir 1966-74, sr exec dir 1974-86); shipping conslt 1987; viticulturalist, started Rock Lodge Vineyard Sussex 1965, fndr memb English Vineyards Assoc, fndr Weald and Downlands Vineyard Assoc; Freeman of City of London 1952, Liveryman of Worshipful Co of Shipwrights 1974; *Recreations* listening to music; *Style—* Norman Cowderoy, Esq; Rock Lodge, Scaynes Hill, West Sussex (☎ 0444 86224); Rock Lodge Vineyard, Scaynes Hill, West Sussex (☎ 0444 86567, fax 0444 86541, telex 878189)

COWDRAY, Lady Anne Pamela; *née* Bridgeman; da of 5 Earl of Bradford (d 1957); *b* 12 June 1913; *m* 19 July 1939 (m dis 1950), 3 Viscount Cowdray, TD, DL; 1 s, 2 da; *Style—* Lady Anne Cowdray; Broadleas, Devizes, Wilts

COWDRAY, 3 Viscount (UK 1917); Sir Weetman John Churchill Pearson; 3 Bt (UK 1894), TD; also Baron Cowdray (UK 1910); s (twin) of 2 Viscount (d 1933), and late Agnes Beryl (d 1948), da of Lord Edward Spencer-Churchill (5 s of 6 Duke of Marlborough); bro of late Hon Mrs Campbell-Preston, late Lady McCorquodale, of Newton, and Nancy, Viscountess Blakenham, Hon Mrs Hugh Carter and Hon Mrs John Lakin; *b* 27 Feb 1910; *Educ* Eton, Christ Church Coll Oxford; *m* 1, 19 July 1939 (m dis 1950), Lady Anne Bridgeman, da of 5 Earl of Bradford; 1 s, 2 da; m 2, 4 March 1953, Elizabeth Georgiana Mather, da of late Sir Anthony Mather-Jackson, 6 Bt; 1 s, 2 da; *Heir* s, Hon Michael Pearson; *Career* Capt Sussex Yeomanry; PPS to Under-Sec of State for Air 1941-42; chm S Pearson and Son Ltd 1954-77, pres Pearson plc; *Clubs* White's, Cavalry and Guards; *Style—* The Rt Hon Viscount Cowdray, TD; Cowdray Park, Midhurst, W Sussex (☎ 073 081 2461); Dunecht, Skene, Aberdeenshire (☎ 033 06 244); 17 Floor, Millbank Tower, Millbank, London SW1P 4QZ

COWDREY, (Michael) Colin; CBE (1972); s of late Ernest Arthur Cowdrey, of Bangalore, India, and Kathleen Mary, *née* Taylor; *b* 24 Dec 1932; *Educ* Tonbridge, BNC Oxford; *m* 1, 1956 (m dis), Penelope Susan, da of late Stuart Chiesman, of Chislehurst, Kent; 3 s, 1 da; m 2, 1985, Lady Herries of Terregles, *qv*; *Career* cricketer, capt Kent CCC 1957-71, 112 appearances for England, capt 23 times, conslt Barclays Bank plc, conslt Barclays Bank plc South East Region; Master Worshipful Co of Skinners' 1986; pres MCC 1987; *Recreations* golf; *Clubs* Boodle's, MCC; *Style—* Colin Cowdrey, Esq, CBE; Barclays Bank plc, 54 Lombard St, London EC3

COWDY, Anthony Dallimore; TD; s of Anthony Cowdy (d 1952), of Ireland, and Edith Muriel, *née* Dallimore (d 1976); *b* 18 Dec 1910; *Educ* Clifton, Jesus Coll Cambrige (BA); *m* 6 Sept 1939, Phyllis Armitage, da of Alwyn Ernest Holt (d 1936); 1 s (Michael Anthony); *Career* served WW II London Irish Rifles and Royal Iniskilling Fusiliers, Maj, Atlantic Convoys; with Lloyds of London 1937-74; dir: Philip N Christe and Co Ltd Underwriting Agents of Lloyds (chm and md 1962), Greemount and Boyne Linen Co, Walter Runciman and Co; JP (E Sussex) 1949; *Recreations* shooting, swimming; *Clubs* Hawks, Army and Navy; *Style—* Anthony D Cowdy, Esq, TD; Stonewall, Eridge Green, Tunbridge Wells TN3 9HX (☎ 089 275 265)

COWDY, Hon Mrs (Haidee Marylyn Antonina); *née* Rawlinson; da of Baron Rawlinson of Ewell, PC, QC (Life Peer), *qv*, by his 1 w Mrs Haidee Turner; *b* 9 May 1948; *m* 1, 1968 (William) Richard Annesley yr son of Gerald Annesley, *qv* by his 2 w Mary, *née* MacDonald; 1 s, 1 da; m 2 1965 Maj Ralf Edward Cope Cowdy DL, elder s of Robert McKean Cowdy; *Recreations* riding; *Style—* The Hon Mrs Cowdy; Summer Island, Loughall, Co Armargh, N Ireland

COWDY, Susan; MBE (1981); da of Capt Ivor Stewart-Liberty (d 1953), of Bucks, and Evelyn Katherine *née* Phipps (d 1966); *b* 6 August 1914; *Educ* Common Lane House Sch Letchmore Heath Herts, Bishops Tatchbrook Finishing Sch Warwicks; *m* 31 Aug 1935, late John Bernard Cowdy, s of Edward Cowdy, DL (d 1934), of N Ireland; 1 s (Michael b 1936), 2 da (Fenella b 1936, Evelyn b 1938); *Career* amateur natural historian and wildlife conservationist; pres: Bucks Bird Club, Chesham and District Natural History Soc; vice pres: Bardsey Island Tst, Bucks Archaeological Soc, The Berks Buckinghamshire and Oxfordshire Tst for Naturalists' Tst; cncl memb CPRE (Bucks); cncl memb RSPB, hon sec and vice pres Br tst for Ornithology; *Recreations* study of flora and fauna in British Isles; *Style—* Mrs Susan Cowdy, MBE; Rushmere, The Lee, Great Missenden, Bucks (☎ 024 020 341)

COWELL, Alan Christopher; MC (1944); s of Edmund Frederick Cowell (d 1928); *b* 4 Feb 1920; *Educ* St Christopher Sch Letchworth; *m* 1949, Muriel Dorothy, da of Ben Marsden (d 1953), of Ahmedabad, India; 2 s, 1 da; *Career* Maj Indian Army, Assam and Burma; dir: Electronic Rentals Gp and subsidiary cos 1947-85, Byrne Davy (UK) Ltd, Holbrook Estates Ltd; *Recreations* racing, rowing, rugby, wrestling; *Clubs* Army and Navy; *Style—* Alan Cowell, Esq, MC; Old Park, Rusper, Horsham, Sussex RH12 4QT (☎ 029 384 452)

COWELL, Peter Reginald; s of Reginald Ernest Cowell, CBE (d 1982) of Lowmoor, Craddock, Cullompton, Devon, and Philippa Eleanor Frances Anne *née* Prettejohn; *b* 9 Mar 1942; *Educ* Bedford Sch, Gonville and Caius Coll Cambridge (MA); *m* 4 Aug 1975, Penelope Jane, da of Andrew John Presgrave Bowring (d 1987), of New Romney, Kent; 2 s (Nicholas b 1976, William b 1980) 1 da (Sarah b 1980); *Career* called to the Bar Middle Temple 1964, asst recorder 1985-; memb Senate Inns of Court 1975-78; occasional ctee memb: Thames Hare and Hounds Club, The Old Stagers; *Books* Cowell, A Genealogy (1986); *Recreations* running, acting, genealogy; *Style—* Peter R Cowell, Esq; 141 Palewell Park, East Sheen, London, SW14 (☎ 01 878 2434); 3 New Square, Lincoln's Inn, London, WC2A 3RS (☎ 01 405 5577)

COWELL, Robert Douglas; s of Douglas Walter Cowell, of Newport, Gwent, and Gladys, *née* Williams; *b* 9 Feb 1947; *Educ* Newport GS Gwent, Balliol Coll Oxford (BA, MA, PhD); *m* 1, 18 Oct 1969 (m dis 3 Feb 1984), Janice Carol; 2 da (Elizabeth Sarah b 1978, Julia Mary b 1980); m 2, 24 July 1986, Elizabeth Henrietta, da of Timothy Patrick Neligan, of Esher, Surrey; *Career* night shift foreman Turner & Newall Ltd 1972, investment analyst Hoare Govett Ltd 1972-77, UK corporate devpt mangr Hanson Tst plc 1977-80, md Hoare Govett Securities (Hoare Govett) 1980-, chm Quoted UK Ltd 1982-; *Recreations* horse racing, golf; *Style—* Robert Cowell, Esq; Hoare Govett Securities Ltd, 4 Broadgate, London, EC2 (☎ 01 601 0101, fax 01 374 4440)

COWELL, Roger Housden; s of Ernest Frederick Cowell; *b* 3 Sept 1939; *Educ* King's Sch Rochester; *m* 1963, Margaret Anne, *née* Hillier; 1 s, 1 da; *Career* md Ace Filtration Ltd, dir Climavent SA Paris; CEng; *Recreations* squash, gardening, horology;

Clubs Rumford; *Style*— Roger Cowell, Esq; Rooks Drift, Southfleet, Kent (☎ 047 483 2660); Airflow Works, Seymour Rd, Northfleet, Kent DA11 7BW (☎ 0474 325666)

COWEN, John Rutland; s of late John William Cowen; *b* 18 Oct 1931; *Educ* Aldenham; *m* 1, 1955 (m dis 1979), Jennifer Alice; m 2, 1980 (m dis 1987), Marie Victoria Gwendolyn; 2 da; m 3, 1988, Suzanne Frances; *Career* chm: Utd Industs plc, March Gp plc, Amicus Investmts Ltd, Automotive Springs Ltd, J Day & Co Ltd, Linvar Ltd, Marwin Ltd, Marwin Cutting Tools Ltd, Materic Mgmnt Servs Ltd, Ratcliffe Properties Ltd, Ratcliffe Springs Ltd, Gladding Estates & Devpt plc; FInstM, FInstD, FBIM; *Clubs* City Livery; *Style*— John Cowen, Esq; 36 Iverna Gardens, London W8 6TW (☎ 01 937 7625)

COWEN, Hon Mrs (Shelagh Mary); yr da of 1 and last Baron Rank, JP (d 1972), and Hon Laura Ellen Marshall (er da of 1 and last Baron Marshall of Chipstead); *b* 14 Mar 1923; *m* 1, 22 Aug 1945 (m dis 1955), Fred Morris Packard, s of late Morris Packard, of Los Angeles; 1 s, 1 da; m 2, 23 Jan 1957, Major Rosslyn Fairfax Huxley Cowen, MBE, s of Edward George Huxley Cowen, MRCP (d 1962), of 42 Upper Brook St, W1; 2 s; *Style*— The Hon Mrs Cowen; Shawdon, Glanton, Northumberland

COWEN, Rt Hon Sir Zelman; AK (1977), GCMG (1977, CMG 1968), GCVO (1980), PC (1981), QC (1972); s of Bernard Cowen (d 1975), and Sara, *née* Granat; *b* 7 Oct 1919; *Educ* Scotch Coll Melbourne, Melbourne Univ, New and Oriel Colls Oxford (BCL, MA, DCL); *m* 1945, Anna, da of Hyman Joseph Wittner, (d 1974), of Melbourne; 3 s, 1 da; *Career* barr Gray's Inn 1947 (hon bencher 1978), barr Victoria 1951, Queensland (Aust) 1971; prof of public law and dean of faculty of law Melbourne Univ 1951-66, vice-chllr Univ of New England NSW 1967-70, Univ of Queensland 1970-77; govr-gen of Australia 1977-82, chm Press Cncl (UK) 1983-88, provost Oriel Coll Oxford 1982-, pro-vice chllr Univ of Oxford 1988, KStJ 1977; kt 1976; *for further details see Debrett's Handbook of Australia and New Zealand*; *Style*— The Rt Hon Sir Zelman Cowen, AK, GCMG, GCVO, QC; Provost's Lodgings, Oriel College, Oxford OX1 4EW (☎ 0865 722630, 276533)

COWEY, Brig Bernard Turing Vionnée (Bun); DSO (1945), OBE (1976), DL (Notts 1973); s of Lt-Col Reginald Vionneé Cowey, DSO, RAMC (d 1955), of Jersey CI, and Bernardine Augusta Blancke, *née* Hilversum (d 1921); *b* 20 Nov 1911; *Educ* Wellington Coll, RMC Sandhurst; *m* 1947, Margaret Heath Dean, da of H A Godwin, of Hucclecote, Glos; *Career* cmmnd The Welch Regt 1931, served WW II Egypt, Crete, Western Desert, India, Burma; CO 2 Y and L 1944, CO 2 Welch 1945-47, Co Cdr RMAS 1947-49, Chief Instr Staff Coll Quetta 1952-53, CO 1 Welch 1953-56, Cdr 9 Independent Armd Bde TA 1956, Cdr 148 Infantry Bde TA 1956-58, Dep Cdr Singapore Base Dist 1959-61, Inspr Intelligence 1961-63, ret 1963; sec Notts TA Assoc 1965-67, sec TA Cncl 1973-75 (dep sec 1967-72), E Mids regnl organiser Army Benevolent 1975-; played rugby for Wales Barbarians Army 1934-35, chm Army Rugby Union Referee Soc 1963-73; hon dir Arab Horse Show 1968-81; E Mids regnl sec Br Field Sports Soc 1975-83; *Recreations* racing home-bred thoroughbreds, watching rugby; *Clubs* Army and Navy, Br Sportsman's; *Style*— Brig Bernard Cowey, DSO, OBE, DL; Trent Hills Farm, Flintham, Newark, Notts NG23 4LL (☎ 0636 525274); Army Benevolent Fund, TA Centre, Sherwood Ave, Newark, Notts NG24 1QQ (☎ 0636 76995)

COWGILL, Brig Anthony Wilson; MBE (1945); s of Harold Wilson Cowgill (d 1965), and Hilda, *née* Garrett (d 1933); *b* 7 Nov 1915; *Educ* Manchester GS, Birmingham Univ (BSc), RCMS; *m* 2 April 1949, Joan Noel Mary, da of Peter James Stewart (d 1960); 1 s (Andrew Anthony b 1957), 1 da (Patricia Anne b 1951); *Career* cmmnd 1939, Def HQ Ottawa 1943-44, NW Europe 1944-45, GHQ India 1947, AHQ Pakistan 1948, Cwlth Div Korea 1953-54, MOD 1962-65 and 1966-69, ret as Brig 1969; chief indust engr Rolls Royce Ltd 1969-77, dir Br Mgmnt Data Fndn 1981-, headed Br Mgmnt Advanced Tech study teams to US, Japan and Eur 1980-87; chm Klagenfurt Conspiracy inquiry which cleared Harold Macmillan (later Lord Stockton) of War crimes charges 1986-89; FIMechE, FIERE, FMS, int fell American Soc for Advancement of Engrg, Int Technol Transfer Award 1987; *Books* Energy Management (1980), Management of Automation (1982); *Recreations* golf; *Clubs* Army and Navy, RAC; *Style*— Brig Anthony Cowgill, MBE; Highfield, Longridge, Sheepscombe, Stroud, Glos GL6 7QU (☎ 0452 813211); Melrose House, 4-6 Savile Row, London W1X 1AF (☎ 01 839 2798)

COWGILL, Bryan; *b* 27 May 1927; *Educ* Clitheroe GS; *m* 1966, Jennifer E Baker, 2 s; *Career* Lt 3 Royal Marine Commando Bde 1943-47; former head of BBC Sport and BBC TV Outside Broadcasts Gp, later controller BBC 1, md Thames TV 1977-, dir ITV, chm UPITN 1983-; *Style*— Bryan Cowgill, Esq; Thames Television House, 306-316 Euston Rd, London NW1 3BB (☎ 01 387 9494)

COWHAM, David Francis; s of Francis Ronald Cowham, of Gt Rossington, Glos, and Patricia, *née* Warwick; *b* 10 June 1940; *Educ* Owens Sch; *m* 2 June 1962, Kay Miriam, da of Charles Ward, of Histon, Cambs; 1 s (David b 1967), 1 da (Alison b 1965); *Career* banker, dir First Nat Fin Corpn plc 1985-, asst md First Nat Securities Ltd 1972-; *Recreations* theatre, literature, horseracing; *Clubs* Newmarket Race; *Style*— David F Cowham, Esq; Temple Close, Watford, Herts (☎ 0923 228161); First National House, Harrow, Middx (☎ 01 861 1313, car ☎ 0836 295 834)

COWIE, Rev Dr Leonard Wallace; s of Rev Reginald George Cowie (d 1952), of Lincolnshire, and Ella Constance, *née* Peerless; *b* 10 May 1919; *Educ* Royal GS Newcastle-on-Tyne, Oxford Univ (MA), London Univ (MA, PhD); *m* 9 Aug 1949, Evelyn Elizabeth, Robert Trafford (d 1948), of Peterborough; 1 s (Alan b 1955); *Career* clerk in Holy Orders; lectr: St Mark and St John's Coll Chelsea 1945-68, Roehampton Inst of Higher Educn 1969-82; *Books* Henry Newman 1708-43 (1956), The March of the Cross (1962), Eighteenth-Century Europe (1963), Martin Luther (1969), The Reformation (1974), The French Revolution (1987); *Recreations* gardening, town walking; *Clubs* Athenaeum; *Style*— Rev Dr Leonard W Cowie; 38 Stratton Road, Merton Park, London SW11 3JG

COWIE, (John) Michael; s of Stanley Reader Cowie, of 57 Mains Loan, Dundee and Janetta Brand, *née* Ramsay; *b* 2 Dec 1948; *Educ* Dundee HS; *m* 26 March 1976, Helen Boswell (known as Eilidh gaelic for Helen), da of James John MacAskill, of Drynoch, Carbost, Isle of Skye; 2 s (Stephen Alasdair b 1978, James Alexander b 1981), 1 da (Susan Victoria b 1983); *Career* chartered accountant admitted to Scottish Institute 1973, Thomson McLintock (Edinburgh) 1973-76, Ben Line (Edinburgh) 1977-79, Seaforth Maritime Ltd (Aberdeen) 1980-87; Belhaven plc (Perth) 1987-, dir: Seaforth Maritime Ltd and subsidiaries 1986-87, The National Hyperbaric Centre Ltd 1986-87, Belhaven plc 1987-; *Recreations* rugby (ret), squash, water skiing, music, reading (railways), wine; *Style*— Michael Cowie, Esq; 123 Glasgow Road, Perth PH2 0LU (☎ 0738 22039); Belhave plc, Belhaven House, Marshall Place, Perth PH2 8BE (☎ 0738 32926, fax 0738 35090, telex 76564 BELHAV)

COWIE, Thomas; OBE (1982); s of Thomas Stephenson Knowles Cowie (d 1960), and Florence, *née* Russell (d 1984); *b* 9 Sept 1922; *Educ* Bede GS Sunderland; *m* 1, 1948, Lillas Roberts, *née* Hunnam; 1 s (Thomas Andrew b 1950, *qv*), 4 da (Elizabeth b 1951, Susan b 1953, Sarah b 1959, Emma b 1962); m 2, 1975, Mrs Diana Carole Wentworth Evans; 3 da (Alexandra b 1975, Charlotte b 1978, Victoria b 1982), 1 step s (Steven b 1964), 1 step da (Catherine b 1965); *Career* chm and md T Cowie plc (motor distributor, agric, coach and travel, finance, contract hire and leasing co), landowner (1620 acres) ; *Recreations* shooting, walking; *Style*— Thomas Cowie, Esq, OBE; Broadwood Hall, Lanchester, Co Durham (☎ 0207 520 464); T Cowie plc, Millfield House, Hylton Rd, Sunderland SR4 7BA (☎ 091 514 4122 telex 537065)

COWIE, Thomas Andrew; s of Thomas Cowie of Broadwood Hall, Lanchester, Co Durham, *qv*; *b* 17 Feb 1950; *Educ* Rugby, Magdalene Coll Cambridge; *Career* dir T Cowie Ltd; *Recreations* golf, squash; *Clubs* Hawks, Jesters; *Style*— Thomas Cowie Esq; Millfield House, Hylton Rd, Sunderland, Tyne and Wear (☎ Sunderland 44122)

COWIE, Hon Lord; William Lorn Kerr Cowie; QC (Scot 1967); s of late Charles Rennie Cowie, MBE, and Norah Slimmon Kerr; *b* 1 June 1926; *Educ* Fettes Coll, Clare Coll Cambridge, Glasgow Univ; *m* 1958, Camilla Henrietta Grizel, da of Randall Colvin Hoyle; 2 s, 2 da; *Career* Sub Lt RNVR 1944-47, advocate Scotland 1952, appointed a senator of the coll of justice in Scotland with title of Lord Cowie 1977; *Clubs* New (Edinburgh), RSAC Glasgow; *Style*— The Hon Lord Cowie; 20 Blacket Place, Edinburgh 9 (☎ 031 667 8238)

COWLEY, Elsie, Countess; (Mary) Elsie; *née* May; *m* 1, Joseph Torbet Himes (decd); m 2, 1933, as his 2 w, 4 Earl Cowley (d 1962); 2 s (7 Earl and Hon Brian Timothy Wellesley); *Style*— The Rt Hon Elsie, Countess Cowley; 4900 Plumas St, Reno, Nevada 89509, USA

COWLEY, 7 Earl (UK 1857); Garret Graham Wellesley; also Baron Cowley of Wellesley (UK 1828), Viscount Dangan (UK 1857); s of 4 Earl Cowley (d 1962), by his 2 w, Mary Elsie May; suc half n, 6 Earl, 1975; *b* 30 July 1934; *Educ* S California Univ (BS), Harvard Univ (MBA); *m* 1, 1961 (m dis 1966), Elizabeth Susanne, da of late Hayes Lennon; 1 s, 1 da; m 2, 1968, Isabelle O'Bready; m 3 1981, Paige Deming; *Heir* s, Viscount Dangan, *qv*; *Career* gp vice pres Bank of America NT and SA London; International Investment Management Service 1980-85, dir Bank of America Int (London) 1978-85, chm Cowley and Co financial and business conslts 1985, dir of various Bank of America Trust Cos; *Style*— The Rt Hon the Earl Cowley; 4 Douro Place, London W8 5PH

COWLEY, Lt-Gen Sir John Guise; GC (AM 1935), KBE (1958, CBE 1946, OBE 1943), CB (1954); s of Rev Henry Guise Beatson Cowley (d 1938), of Fourgates, Dorchester, Dorset; *b* 20 August 1905; *Educ* Wellington, RMA Woolwich; *m* 1941, Irene Sybil, da of Percy Dreuille Millen, of Berkhamsted, Herts; 1 s, 3 da; *Career* 2 Lt RE 1925, Lt-Gen 1957, Controller of munitions Min of Supply 1957-60, Master-Gen of the Ordnance (War Office) 1960-62, ret; chm: Bowmaker Ltd 1962-71, Keith and Henderson Ltd 1973-76, Polamco Engrg 1976; former dir: C T Bowring and Co Ltd, Alastair Watson Ltd, Br Oxygen Ltd; chm of govrs: Wellington Coll 1969-76, vice pres 1969, Brockenhurst Coll 1969-83; FRSA; *Style*— Lt-Gen Sir John Cowley, GC, KBE, CB; Whitemoor, Sandy Down, Boldre, Lymington, Hants (☎ 0590 23369)

COWLEY, John Henry Stewart; s of Kenneth Cyril Cowley (d 1983), of Douglas, IOM, and Daphne, *née* Leake; *b* 20 Feb 1947; *Educ* King Wiliam's Coll; *m* 1, 12 May 1971, Mary, da of late Geoffrey Whitehead, of Manchester; 1 s (George Edward Douglas b 1976), 1 da (Joanne Jane Caroline b 1973); m 2, 20 March 1986, Carolyn, da of Barry Walter Golding Thompson, of Tunbridge Wells; 1 s (Daniel Kenneth Gordon b 1986); *Career* brewer, dir: Heron and Brearley Ltd (now Isle of Man Breweries Ltd) 1972, Okell and Son Ltd (brewers) 1972, Warburg Investmt Management (IOM) Ltd 1980, Bowring Tyson (IOM) Ltd 1984, Castletown Brewery Ltd 1986; chm and md IOM Breweries Ltd 1983; cncl memb IOM Chamber of Commerce 1985 (chm 1981-83, pres 1983-85); *Recreations* game shooting, sailing; *Clubs* Manx Automobile, Ellan Vannin; *Style*— John Cowley, Esq; Rock Villa, Strathallan Road, Onchan, IOM (☎ 0624 75478); Isle of Man Breweries Ltd, 25 Drumgold Street, Douglas, IOM (☎ 0624 74611, telex, 629781 BREWMN G)

COWLEY, Kenneth Martin; CMG (1963), OBE (1956); s of Robert Martin Cowley, OBE (d 1955), of IOM, and Mabel Priscilla, *née* Lee (d 1962); *b* 15 May 1912; *Educ* Merchant Taylors Crosby, Exeter Coll Oxford (BA); *m* 1948, Barbara, da of Arthur Walter Alfred Claude Tannahill, OBE (d 1945); 1 s (Robin), 1 step s (Christopher); *Career* dist offr (cadet) Colonial Admin Serv Kenya 1935, asst sec Secretariat Nairobi 1944, dist cmmr 1946, attorney general native courts offr 1949; sec for African Affrs 1953, provincial cmmr Southern Province Kenya 1956-63 (despatches 1957), sec Kenya Boundaries and Constituencies Cmmns 1962; sr admin mangr Express Tport Co Ltd Kenya 1963-70, sec Overseas Serv Pensioners Assoc 1971-79; ret 1979; *Recreations* natural history, reading; *Clubs* Nairobi (Kenya); *Style*— Kenneth Cowley, Esq, CMG, OBE; Oakview Cottage, Cricket Green, Hartley Wintney, Basingstoke, Hants. RG27 8PZ (☎ 025 126 4210)

COWLEY, Patrick Martin; s of Denis Martin Cowley, QC (d 1985), and Margaret Hazel, *née* Teare, of Ellan Vannin, The Quay, Castletown, IOM; *b* 18 August 1941; *Educ* Radley; *m* 1 Oct 1966, Alison Mary, da of Archibald Robert Alexander Marshall (d 1963); 1 s (Philip b 1970), 2 da (Penelope b 1967, Alexander b 1980); *Career* conlst Cowley Groves Co Ltd 1986, dir: Mercury Fund Mangrs (DOM), Ltd 1980, Douglas Gas Light Co 1985; vice-chm Isle of Man Childrens Home; *Recreations* motor racing, reading, shooting; *Clubs* Ellan Vannin, Executive; *Style*— Patrick Cowley, Esq; Sherdley, Princes Road, Douglas, IOM (☎ 0624 20060); Cowley Groves Co Ltd., 43 Athol Street, Douglas, IOM

COWLEY, Prof Roger Arthur; s of Cecil Arthur Cowley (d 1964), of Romford, Essex, and Mildred Sarah, *née* Nash; *b* 24 Feb 1939; *Educ* Brentwood Sch, Cambridge Univ (BA, PhD); *m* 4 April 1964, Sheila Joyce, da of Charles Wells (d 1970), of Romford, Essex; 1 s (Kevin David b 1969), 1 da (Sandra Elizabeth b 1966); *Career* res fell Trinity Hall Cambridge 1963-64, res offr Atomic Energy Canada Ltd 1964-70, prof of physics Univ of Edinburgh 1970-88, prof of experimental philosophy Univ of Oxford 1988-; FRSE 1971, FRS 1978; *Books* Structural Phase Transitions (1981); *Style*— Prof Roger Cowley; Tredinnock, Harcourt Hill, Oxford OX2 9AS (☎ 0865 247 570); Clarendon Laboratory, Parks Road, Oxford OX1 3P4 (☎ 0865 272 224)

COWLEY, Simon Charles; s of Charles Woods Cowley (d 1987), and Ruth Heloise, *née* Portch; *b* 30 August 1949; *Educ* Malvern Coll Worcs; *m* Annette Maria, da of Frank George Bevis (d 1986); 2 da (Georgina b 1984, Samantha b 1988); *Career* dir: Streets Fin Ltd 1979-86, AIM Technology Ltd 1987, AIM Cambridge Ltd 1987, dir: Prime Mgmnt Ltd 1988-, Porchester Properties Ltd 1989-, Melmun Ltd 1989-; memb IPA; FCA; *Books* Practice Development, A Guide to Marketing Technique for Accountants; *Recreations* squash, cooking; *Style*— Simon C Cowley, Esq; 9 Studdridge St, London SW6

COWLEY, Col Victor Charles Vereker; TD (1950), JP (1962), DL (1975); s of Lt Victor Travers Cowley, KSOB Baghdad (ka 1918 France) (bro of Lt-Cdr Charles Henry Cowley, VC, RNVR (ka while trying to convey supplies to the beleagured garrison of Kut-el-Amara 1916), by his w Marie Caroline, *née* Scandrett (d 1961); *b* 4 April 1918; *Educ* Merchiston Castle Edinburgh; *m* 6 July 1951, Moyra Mitchell, da of Hugh Walpole McClure (d 1940), of Glasgow; 1 s (Mark b 1952), 2 da (Jane b 1955, Wendy b 1961); *Career* cmmnd RA TA 1939, France 1940 (Air Op 1942), N Africa, Sicily, Italy, Burma, Indo-China (despatches 1944), piloted HM King George VI (Italy 1944), Col depute CRA 51 Highland Div 1957; farmer and master printer (ret); Vice-Convener E Lothian CC 1973, memb Regnl Cncl Lothian 1975, Cmmr of Income Tax E Lothian 1965-87; *Recreations* golf, shooting; *Clubs* Hon Co of Edinburgh Golfers, Royal Overseas League; *Style*— Col Victor Cowley, TD, JP, DL; Crowhill, Innerwick, Dunbar, E Lothian EH42 1QT (☎ 036 84 279)

COWLEY, William; s of Ralph Smith Cowley (d 1949), and Dora, *née* Munns (d 1982); *b* 27 July 1925; *Educ* John Clare Sch Northampton, Northampton Coll of Technol; *m* 6 Sept 1945, Marjorie Barbara, da of Walter James Humphries, MBE (d 1974); 1 s (Martyn Barry Cowley b 1948); *Career* md Airflow Steamlines plc; chm: Pegasus Phosprime Ltd, S Whiteley & Sons Ltd; *Recreations* golf, gardening; *Clubs* Northants County GC, IOD; *Style*— William Cowley, Esq; 67 Abington Park Crescent, Northampton (☎ 0604 406994); Airflow Streamlines plc, Main Road, Far Cotton, Northampton (☎ 0604 762261, fax 0604 701405)

COWPER, Barry William Meadows; s of William Coburn Cowper (d 1986), of Angmering on Sea, Sussex, and Gertrude Botterill, *née* Rolls; *b* 13 July 1933; *Educ* Aldenham Sch, Trinity Hall Cambridge (MA); *m* 9 March 1968, Brenda Mary, da of William Wallace Pelham, of Auckland, NZ; 2 s (Andrew b 1973, Timothy b 1974), 1 da (Philippa b 1970); *Career* ptnr George Henderson & Co Stockbrokers (later Henderson Crosthwaite & Co 1974) 1970-86, dir Henderson Crosthwaite Ltd 1987-; *Clubs* Leander, City Univ; *Style*— Barry W M Cowper, Esq; PO box 442, 32 St Mary At Hill, London, EC3P 3AJ (☎ 01 283 8577, fax 01 623 1997, telex 884035)

COWPER, Sir Norman Lethbridge; CBE (1958); yr s of Cecil Spencer de Grey Cowper (d 1919), and Alice Mary, *née* Dodd (d 1958); *b* 15 Sept 1896; *Educ* Sydney GS, Sydney Univ; *m* 1925, Dorothea Huntly, da of Hugh Raymond McCrae, of Sydney, NSW; 3 da; *Career* slr NSW 1923, ptnr Allen Allen and Hemsley 1924-70, former dir Australian Inst of Political Science; kt 1967; *see Debrett's Handbook of Australia and New Zealand for further details*; *Style*— Sir Norman Cowper, CBE; Wivenhoe, Millewa Ave, Wahroonga, Sydney, Australia (☎ 48 2336)

COWPERTHWAITE, Sir John James; KBE (1968) CMG (1964, OBE 1960); s of late John James Cowperthwaite of Edinburgh, and Jessie Wemyss Barron, *née* Jarvis; *b* 25 April 1915; *Educ* Merchiston Castle Sch, St Andrews Univ, Christ's Coll Camb; *m* 1941, Sheila Mary, da of Alexander Thomson, of Aberdeen; 1 s; *Career* colonial admin service Hong Kong 1941, Sierra Leone 1942-45, fin sec Hong Kong 1961-71, int advr Jardine Fleming and Co Ltd 1972-82; *Clubs* Royal Hong Kong Jockey, Royal Hong Kong Golf, Royal and Ancient Golf; *Style*— Sir John Cowperthwaite, KBE, CMG; 25 South St, St Andrews, Fife (☎ 0334 74759)

COWTAN, Maj-Gen Frank Willoughby John; CBE (1970, MBE 1947), MC and Bar (1942-45); s of Air Vice-Marshal Frank Cuninghame, CB, CBE, KHS (d 1950), of Surrey, and Nora Alice Cowtan, *née* Kennedy (d 1967); *b* 10 Feb 1920; *Educ* Wellington Coll, RMA Woolwich, Staff Coll, Nat Defence Coll Canada; *m* 1949, Rose Isabel, da of Herbert Vallack Cope (d 1970), of Devon; 1 s (Peter), 1 da (Jane); *Career* cmmnd RE 1939, served WW II: France, N Africa, Italy, NW Europe, Palestine, E Africa, ME and Germany 1945-58; Liaison Offr to US Corps of Engrs 1958-60; Cdr Parachute Engr Regt 1960-62 Victory Coll RMA Sandhurst 1962-65, Engr Bde BAOR 1965-67, dir of Quartering 1968-70, DQMG 1970-71, Cmdt RMC of Science 1971-75; ret Maj Gen 1975; Hon Col Parachute Engr and Commando Engrs 1975-80, Col Cmdt RE 1977-82; Country Landowners Game Fair 1978-86; *Recreations* shooting, wildfowling, golf, sailing, travel, languages; *Clubs* Army and Navy, RN Devon Golf; *Style*— Maj Gen John Cowtan, CBE, MC; Rectory Cottage, Coleshill, Swindon, Wilts SN6 7PR (☎ 0793 762653)

COX; *see*: Roxbee Cox

COX, His Honour Judge Anthony; (James) Anthony; s of Herbert Sidney Cox (d 1972), and Gwendolin Margaret Cox (d 1973); *b* 21 April 1924; *Educ* Cotham Sch Bristol, Bristol Univ (LLB); *m* 1950, Doris Margaret, da of Vincent Percy Fretwell (d 1933); 3 s, 1 da; *Career* barr 1949, recorder of the Crown Court 1972-76, circuit judge 1976; *Recreations* cricket, golf, sailing, the arts; *Clubs* MCC, Royal Western Yacht; *Style*— His Hon Judge Anthony Cox; c/o The Courts Administrator, The Castle, Exeter, Devon

COX, Sir Anthony Wakefield; CBE (1972); s of William Edward Cox, CBE (d 1960), of Teddington, and Elsie Gertrude, *née* Wakefield (d 1967); bro of Oliver Cox, *qv*; *b* 18 July 1915; *Educ* Mill Hill, Architectural Assoc Sch of Architecture; *m* 1943, Susan Babington, da of Sir Henry Babington Smith, GBE (d 1923); 2 da; *Career* WWII, Capt RE; ptnr Architects' Co-Partnership 1939-80;pres Architectural Assoc 1962-63; memb Royal Fine Art Cmmn 1970-85; FRIBA, FRSA; kt 1983; *Style*— Sir Anthony Cox, CBE; 5 Bacon's Lane, Highgate, London N6 (☎ 01 340 2543)

COX, Bradley Richard; s of Leslie Charles Cox (d 1978); *b* 12 Dec 1936; *Educ* Greenmore Coll; *m* Patricia; 1 da; *Career* Nat Serv RAF; dir: TFL Group Hldgs Ltd, Dean & Bowes Gp plc; Queen's Award for Export 1979; memb Lloyds, FInstD; *Recreations* sailing, tennis, shooting; *Clubs* Sporting, Diners; *Style*— Bradley Cox, Esq

COX, Baroness (Life Peer UK 1982), of Queensbury in Greater London; Caroline Anne; da of Robert John McNeill Love, MS, FRCS (d 1974), of Brickendon, Herts, and Dorothy Ida, *née* Borland; *b* 7 July 1937; *Educ* Channing Sch Highgate, London Univ (BSc, MSc Econ); *m* 1959, Murray Newell Cox, s of Rev Roland Lee Cox, of London; 2 s, 1 da; *Career* sits as Cons Peer in House of Lords; head Dept of Sociology N London Poly 1974-77; dir Nursing Education Research Chelsea Coll London Univ 1977-83; baroness-in-waiting and govt Whip 1985; *Books* The Right to Learn (co-author with Dr John Marks); Sociology: An Introduction for Nurses, Midwives and Health Visitors; *Recreations* squash, campanology, hill walking; *Clubs* Royal Cwlth Soc; *Style*— The Rt Hon Lady Cox; 1 Arnellan House, 144-146 Slough Lane, Kingsbury, London NW9 8XJ (☎ 01 204 2321); The White House, Wyke Hall, Gillingham, Dorset SP8 4WS (☎ Gillingham 3436)

COX, Charles; s of Harry Cox, of London, and Myra Emily, *née* Brooking; *b* 25 Sept 1949; *Educ* Stratford GS London; *m* 12 April 1975, Sandra Carol, da of Victor Anthony Willis Taylor (d 1974); 1 s (Peter b 1978), 1 da (Helen b 1976); *Career* CA; with Turquands Barton Mayhew 1968-79; ptnr Pannell Kerr Forster 1984- (joined 1979); memb PCC St Andrew's Church Hornchurch; FCA 1972; *Recreations* jogging, reading, running a youth club; *Style*— Charles Cox, Esq; Pannell Kerr Forster, New Garden House, 78 Hatton Garden, London EC1N 8JA (☎ 01 831 7393, fax 01 405 6736, telex 295 928)

COX, Brig Charles Francis; OBE (1945); s of Maj William Stanley Ramsay Cox (d 1954), of Ashe Leigh, Ross, Herefords, and Margaret Emma, *née* Whinfield (d 1968); see Burke's Landed Gentry 1952, Kennedy-Cox; *b* 28 April 1907; *Educ* Wellington, RMC Sandhurst; *m* 22 Nov 1955, Susan, da of Lt-Col J F Colvin, OBE, MC, JP, DL (d 1984), of Woldringfold, Horsham, Sussex; see Burkes Landed Gentry, 18 edn Vol 1 1965, Calvin of Monkhams Hall; 1 s (Christopher b 13 March 1957), 2 da (Camilla Rosemary b 20 Oct 1958, Serena Mary (Mrs Merton) b 1 May 1962); *Career* 1 Bn S Wales Borderers 1926 served: UK, Egypt, Palestine, Hong Kong; Gold Coast Regt: RWA FF 1932-38, Staff Capt HQ Br Forces Palestine and TransJordan 1938-39, 2 Bn SW Borderers Norway 1940, 2 Bn Gold Coast Regt RWAFF Gambia 1940-42; OC 5 Bn Gold Coast Regt: Gold Coast, India, Nigeria 1942-43, Burma 1943-44; OC 2 Bn E Surrey Regt 1945, OC 1 Bn S Wales Borderers Palestine and Cyprus 1945-48, dep pres Regular Cmmns Bd 1948-50, OC 1 Bn S Wales Borderers Eritrea and BAOR 1951-53, cmdt All Arms Trg Centre Sennelager BAOR 1953-54, cmd 133 Inf Bde UK 1954-57; asst cmmr-in-chief St John Ambulance Bde 1960-66; OStJ 1960; *Clubs* Naval & Military; *Style*— Brig Charles Cox, OBE; Broadwell House, Broadwell, Lechlade, Glos GL7 3QS (☎ 036 786 230)

COX, Dr Christopher Barry; s of Herbert Ernest Cox (d 1983), and May, *née* Bell; *b* 29 July 1931; *Educ* St Paul's, Balliol Coll Oxford (BA, MA), St John's Coll Cambridge (PhD), Univ of London (DSc); *m* 6 April 1961, Sheila, da of William Edward Morgan, (d 1978); 2 s (Timothy b 1962, Justin b 1970), 1 da (Sally b 1964); *Career* lectr zoology King's Coll London: asst lectr 1956-59, lectr 1959-66, lectr 1966-69, reader 1969-76, prof 1976-82, head of dept zoology 1982-85, head dept of biology 1985-88, prof div biosphere scis 1988-; Harkness fell Cwlth Fund Harvard; former chm: Woodcote Residents Assoc, Action Ctee for Epsom, Epsom Protection Soc; Freeman City of London 1983; memb Palaeontological Assoc 1960 (vice pres 1980-81); *Books* Prehistoric World (1975), Biogeography an Ecological & Historical Approach (fourth edn 1985), Atlas of the Living World 1989; *Recreations* tennis, gardening; *Style*— Dr Barry Cox; Conifers, Grange Rd, Leatherhead, Surrey KT22 7JS (☎ 0372 273 167); Div of Biosphere Sciences, King's Coll, Campden Hill Rd, London W8 7AH (☎ 01 937 5411)

COX, His Honour Judge Edward; (Albert) Edward; s of Frederick Stringer Cox; *b* 26 Sept 1916; *m* 1962, Alwyne Winifred Cox, JP; *Career* slr 1938, princ ptnr Claude Hornby and Cox 1946-76, recorder 1972-77, circuit judge 1977; memb Parole Bd 1970-74, chm The London (Metropolis) Licensing Planning Ctee 1979; pres Br Acad of Forensic Science 1978; *Style*— His Hon Judge Edward Cox; 38 Carlton Hill, London NW8; Petit Bois, Teilhet, Arrìège, France

COX, Lady; Elizabeth Anne Priestley; *née* Marten; *m* 1948, Sir (William) Robert Cox, KCB, sometime chief exec PSA (d 28 June 1981); 1 s, 1 da; *Style*— Lady Cox; 2 Marsham St, SW1

COX, Rev Canon Eric William; s of Sydney Eric Cox (d 1979), of Beeston, Nottingham, and Maude Marie Cox; *b* 17 July 1930; *Educ* Henry Mellish GS Bulwell Notts, Bede Coll Durham Univ (BA), Wells Theol Coll; *m* 7 Jan 1959, Jennifer Anne, da of Lt-Col The Rev Maurice James Fraser Wilson (d 1985), of Baschurch, Shropshire; 4 s (Peter b 1959, Timothy b 1960, Paul b 1963, Andrew b 1968), 1 da (Joanna b 1966); *Career* RAF 1949-51; ordained: deacon 1956, priest 1957; asst curate St Mary Magdalene Sutton-in-Ashfield 1956-59, asst chaplain Utd Anglican Church Brussels Belgium 1959-62; vicar: St Lukes Winnington Northwich Cheshire 1962-71, St Michael and All Angels Middlewich Cheshire 1971-; rector St John Evangelist Byley-cum-Leese Cheshire 1973-, rural dean Middlewich 1980-, hon canon Chester Cath 1984-; chm: govrs Sir John Deane's Coll Northwich, Middlewich and Dist Community Asoc; govr Middlewich HS, memb Rotary Club Northwich (past pres); *Style*— The Rev Canon Eric Cox; The Vicarage, 37 Queen St, Middlewich, Cheshire CW10 9AR (☎ 060 684 3124)

COX, Sir Geoffrey Sandford; CBE (1959, MBE 1945); s of (Charles William) Sandford Cox, of Wellington, NZ, and Mary, *née* MacGregor; *b* 7 April 1910; *Educ* Southland HS NZ, Otago Univ NZ, Oriel Coll Oxford; *m* 1935, Cecily Barbara Talbot, da of Alexander Turner, of Fernhurst, Sussex; 2 s, 2 da; *Career* WWII served NZ Army in Med; journalist (formerly reporter with *News Chronicle*, *Daily Express*); ed and chief exec ITN (fndr *News at Ten*) 1956-68, dep chm Yorkshire TV 1968-71, chm Tyne Tees TV 1972-74, chm UPITN Inc (USA) 1975-81, London Broadcasting Co 1977-81, ind dir *The Observer* 1981-; kt 1966; *Books* Defence of Madrid (1937), The Red Army Moves (1941), Road to Trieste (1947), Race for Trieste (1978), See It Happen (1983), A Tale of Two Battles (1987), Countdown to War (1989); *Recreations* fishing, tracing Roman roads; *Clubs* Garrick; *Style*— Sir Geoffrey Cox, CBE

COX, Sir (Ernest) Gordon; KBE (1964), TD; s of Ernest Henry Cox, (d 1987), of Bath, and Rosina, *née* Ring (d 1931); *b* 24 April 1906; *Educ* City of Bath Boys' Sch, Bristol Univ (DSc); *m* 1, 1929, Lucie Grace (d 1962), da of Charles Baker (d 1949); 1 s (Keith), 1 da (Patricia); m 2, 1968, Prof Mary Rosaleen Truter, da of Dr Douglas Norman Jackman (d 1976), of Battersea; *Career* served WWII Lt-Col NW Europe; reader in chemical crystallography Birmingham Univ 1940, prof of inorganic and structural chemistry Leeds Univ 1945-60, sec Agric Res Cncl 1960-71; FInstP, FIBiol, hon CChem, hon assoc RCVS; Hon LLD Bristol, Hon DSc Birmingham, Newcastle, E Anglia, Bath; FRS; *Clubs* Athenaeum, Lansdowne, English-Speaking Union; *Style*— Sir Gordon Cox, KBE, TD; 117 Hampstead Way, London NW11 7JN (☎ 01 455 2618)

COX, Harry Bernard; CBE (1956); s of Rev Charles Henry Cox, BSc (d 1964), and Ethel, *née* Wright (d 1963); *b* 29 Nov 1906; *Educ* Upholland GS, Keble Coll Oxford

(BA); *m* 1955, Joan, da of Percival Munn, of Burgess Hill; 1 s (Edward), 1 da (Janet); *Career* HM Overseas Serv; administration offr Nigeria 1930, dir of Commerce and Industs Nigeria 1949, A G devpt sec Nigeria 1954, cmmr for Nigeria in UK 1955, chm John Holt (Nigeria) Ltd 1958, dep chm Thomas Wyatt (Nigeria) Ltd, conslt Knight Frank and Rutley 1968; *Clubs* Oriental; *Style—* H B Cox, Esq, CBE; 5 Arundel House, 22 The Drive, Hoke BN3 3JD (☎ 0273 738798)

COX, Ian Herbert; CBE (1952); eldest s of Herbert Stanley Cox (d 1932), and Elizabeth Jessie, *née* Dalgarno (d 1967); *b* 20 Feb 1910; *Educ* Oundle, Magdalene Coll Cambridge (MA); *m* 1, 1932 (dis 1938), Katherine Alice, eldest da of late Charles Frederick Burton; 1 s; m 2, 1945, Suzanne Mary (d 1983), eldest da of late Norman Fowler Snelling, and wid of Flt Lt David Septimus Low; 1s, 1 da, 1 step da; *Career* WWII 1939-45, Cdr RNVR; geologist Oxford Univ Hudson Straits Expdn 1931, res dept of geology Cambridge 1932-36; BBC: 1936-39, 1946; sci corr London Press Serv 1947-48, dir of sci Festival of Britain Off 1948-51, Shell Int Petroleum Co 1952-70 (head sci and devpt TR div, convener grants ctee); memb cncl Chelsea Coll London 1968-74; mgmnt ctee Scott Polar Res Inst 1955-57; vice-pres Geological Soc 1966-68; memb bd of govrs and vice-pres exec ctee Euro Cultural Fndn 1971-84; corr memb Agric Typology Cmmn, Int Geographical Union; memb ct RCA; memb cncl: RGS 1953-57, 1959-62, Overseas Devpt Inst 1966-74, Br Assoc for Advancement of Science (gen tres 1965-70); conslt OECD 1971-; *Books* author of papers on geology and palaeontology of the Arctic; ed The Queens Beasts (1953), The Scallop (1957), monographs in World Land Use Survey; *Recreations* gardening, working in wood and stone; *Clubs* Athenaeum, Arctic; *Style—* Ian Cox, Esq, CBE; The Old Post Office, School Hill, Seale, Farnham, Surrey, GU10 1HY

COX, John; s of Frank Beddoe Cox; *b* 26 Nov 1946; *Educ* Queen Mary's GS Walsall; *m* 1971, Rosemary Anne, *née* Chisholm; 2 da (Deborah b 1974, Sarah b 1976); *Career* dir: E Walters (Ludlow) Ltd 1979, Heaps of Nantwich Ltd 1977, Tillies-Paveley Ltd 1978, E Walters (Brownhills) Ltd 1988; FCA; *Clubs* Ludlow Golf; *Style—* John Cox, Esq; The Forge, Orleton, nr Ludlow, Shropshire SY8 4HR (☎ 056 885 373); E Walters (Ludlow) Ltd, Old Street, Ludlow, Shropshire SY8 1NR (☎ 0584 3221)

COX, John; s of Leonard John Cox (d 1984), of Bristol, and Ethel Minnie May, *née* McGill (d 1980); *b* 12 Mar 1935; *Educ* Queen Elizabeth's Hosp Bristol, St Edmund Hall Oxford (BA); *Career* Nat Serv RN 1953-55; freelance dir theatre, TV, Opera, 1959-, dir of prodn Glyndebourne Fest Opera 1971-81, gen admin and artistic dir Scottish Opera 1982-86, prodn dir Royal Opera 1988-, prodns for: La Scala Milan, Metropolitan NY, Munich Frankfurt Cologne Stockholm, Brussels, Amsterdam, San Francisco, Sydney; maj interpreter: R Strauss, Stravinsky Mozart; fndr dir of Music Theatre Ensemble, world premiers of: Goehr, Birtwistle; UK premiers: Ravel, L'Enfant Et Les Sortileges, Stravinsky, Oedipus Rex; bd memb: Greenwich Theatre, Third Eye Glasgow; *Recreations* horticulture, fine art; *Clubs* Garrick; *Style—* John Cox, Esq; Royal Opera House, Covent Garden

COX, (Edward) John Machell; s of Sqdn Ldr Edward Machell Cox, and Joan Edith, *née* Hewlett; *b* 18 Sept 1934; *Educ* Charterhouse, St Peters Hall Oxford (MA); *m* 29 May 1965, Elizabeth Jean, da of Maj Anthony Frederick Halliday Godfrey (ka France 1939); 1 s (Charles Mark), 1 da (Victoria); *Career* Nat Serv Lt RASC 1953-55; CA, ptnr: Brown Peet & Tilly 1969-71, Howard Tilly 1971-88, Baker Tilly 1988-; Mayor Royal Borough of Kensington and Chelsea 1986-87 (cncllr 1974); memb: mgmnt ctee Octavia Hill & Rowe Housing Assoc, Br Museum (Nat Hist) Devpt Tst, ctee Brighter Kensington & Chelsea Soc; judge London in Bloom competitions; Freeman City of London, memb Worshipful Co of Fruiterers; FCA; *Clubs* Hurlingham; *Style—* E J M Cox, Esq; 13 St Ann's Villas, Royal Crescent, London W11 4RT (☎ 01 603 9828); Baker Tilly, Commonwealth House, 1 New Oxford St, London WC1A 1PF (☎ 01 404 5541, fax 01 405 2836, telex 21595)

COX, Vice Adm Sir John Michael Holland; KCB (1982); s of late Thomas Cox, MBE, and Daisy Anne Cox; *b* 27 Oct 1928,Peking,; *Educ* Hilton Coll Natal SA, RNC Dartmouth; *m* 1962, Anne Garden Farquharson, da of Donald Farquharson Seth Smith, MC, and formerly wife of Jacob, Viscount Folkestone (now 8 Earl of Radnor); 1 s, 1 da; *Career* HMS Britannia RNC 1946, ADC to Gen Sir Robert Mansergh C-in-C Allied Forces N Europe 1952 and to govr of Victoria 1955, Cdr 1962, Capt 1968, naval attaché Bonn 1969, Cdr guided missile destroyer HMS Norfolk 1972, dir Naval Ops and Trade 1973-75, Cdre NATO Standing Naval Force Atlantic 1976-77, Rear Adm 1977, COS to C-in-C Naval Home Cmd 1977-79, Cdr Anti-Submarine Gp 2 and flag offr Third Flotilla 1979-82, Vice Adm 1981, flag offr Naval Air Cmd 1982-83, ret; dir: Spastics Soc 1984-88, Soundalive 1988-; *Recreations* gardening, all sport; *Style—* Vice-Adm Sir John Cox, KCB; Rake, Liss, Hants; c/o MOD Personnel Records, Whitehall, SW1

COX, John Stanley; s of Stanley William Cox; *b* 21 May 1938; *Educ* St Dunstans Coll Catford; *m* 1962 (m dis), Irene; 1 s, 1 da; *Career* chartered accountant; sr ptnr Edward Moore and Son 1975; formerly in partnership with father (now retired); *Recreations* Rugby football, cricket, squash; *Clubs* Shirley Wanderers RFC, Purley Cricket; *Style—* John Cox, Esq; 5 Brambledown Rd, Wallington, Surrey

COX, Sir John William; CBE (1946); s of Henry James Cox (d 1948), and Ellen Augusta Cox; *b* 29 April 1900; *Educ* Saltus GS Bermuda; *m* 1, 1926, Dorothy Carlyle (d 1982), da of Joseph Downing Carlyle Darrell (d 1940); 3 s; *Career* merchant; memb House of Assembly of Bermuda 1930-68, speaker 1948-68; kt 1951; *Clubs* Royal Bermuda Yacht, RAC; *Style—* Sir John Cox, CBE; The Grove, Devonshire Parish, Bermuda (☎ (809) 29) home (2) 0303, work (5) 3232); Bank of Bermuda Ltd, Hamilton, Bermuda

COX, Neil Derek; s of Clifford Walter Earnest, and Meryl Rita, *née* Holland; *b* 1 August 1955; *Educ* King Edward VI GS, Glasgow Dept of Optometry (BSc); *m* 23 March 1981, Averin Moira, da of Philip Anthony Donovan; 1 s (Andrew b 1986), 1 da (Katy b 1984); *Career* sr optometrist King's Coll Hosp London, private contact lens practice London, cncl memb Int Glaucoma Assoc, lectured widely and published papers on clinical applications contact lenses; Liveryman Worshipful Co of Spetaclemakers; FBCO 1978; *Recreations* wine, food, photography; *Style—* Neil D Cox, Esq; 28 Weymouth St, London W1N 3FA (☎ 01 631 1046)

COX, Nicholas Anthony David; s of David Cox (d 1979), and Margaret Eva, *née* McClean; *b* 9 August 1942; *Educ* Nautical Coll, Pangbourne (RNSchol); *m* 1, 21 March 1964 (m dis 1972), (Barbara) Jennifer Downing-Smith; 1 s (James b 13 April 1970); m 2, 4 Oct 1972, (Angela) Wendy Robinson, da of Dr Robert Mason Bolam, of Ferndown, Dorset; 3 step s (Simon Robinson b 24 June 1963, Timothy Robinson b 8 Dec 1964, Matthew Robinson b 8 April 1967); *Career* navigation offr P&O 1958-61, broker and underwriter Lloyds 1961-68; yacht designer and boatbuilder: dir Impact Boats Ltd 1970-; ACII; *Recreations* shooting, sailing, golf, gardening; *Style—* N A D Cox, Esq; Top Hall, Lyndon, Rutland; Impact Boats Ltd, Edithweston, Rutland (☎ 0780 721 556)

COX, Norman Arthur; s of John Charles Cox (d 1966), and Florence *née* Walton (d 1966); *b* 19 Oct 1927; *Educ* Ilford HS, Coll of Law; *m* 26 July 1952, Pamela Mary, da of Arthur Cook (d 1930), of Barking, Essex; 2 s (Nigel Paul b 1953, Nicholas John b 1968), 1 da (Glenda Mary b 1957); *Career* slr, sr ptnr Kenwright-Cox 1971-, pres W Essex Law Soc 1973-74, tres London Slr's Litigation Assoc 1987-; memb Law Soc; *Recreations* walking, gardening, concert-going; *Style—* Norman Cox, Esq ; 38 Chancery Lane, London WC2A 1EL (☎ 01 242 0672, fax 01 831 9477, telex 21 855)

COX, Norman Ernest; CMG (1973); s of late Ernest William Cox and Daisy Beatrice, *née* Edmonds; *b* 28 August 1921; *Educ* Lycée Français Madrid, King's Coll, Univ Coll, LSE, London (MA); *m* 1945, Maruja Margarita, *née* Cruz; 1 s, 1 da; *Career* Intelligence Corps 1941-45; Diplomatic Service 1945, cnsllr (commercial) Moscow 1969-72, Inst Latin American Studies London Univ 1972-73, inspr 1973-74; ambass to: Ecuador 1974-77, Mexico 1977-81, ret; vice-chm Br-Mexican Soc 1981-82 (chm 1982-84, vice-pres 1984-); patron Lancaster Sch Mexico City; *Books* Politics in Mexico (joint author, 1985); *Recreations* walking, swimming, linguistic and politico-historical research; *Clubs* RAC; *Style—* Norman Cox, Esq, CMG; 36 Meadow Rd, Malvern Link, Worcs

COX, Oliver Jasper; CBE (1981); s of William Edward Cox, CBE (d 1960), of Teddington, and Elsie Gertrude Wakefield (d 1967); bro of Sir Anthony Wakefield Cox, *qv*; *b* 20 April 1920; *Educ* Mill Hill Sch, Architectural Assoc Sch of Architecture (AA Dip); *m* 1953, Jeanne Denise, da of Denis Cooper (d 1964), of Cambridge; 1 s (Paul), 2 da (Lucy, Jane); *Career* architect, painter, draughtsman, New Schs Div Herts CC Architects Dept 1948-49; Architects Dept Housing div LCC 1950-59, dep chief architect and ldr R and D Gp MOHLG 1960-64, sr ptnr Shankland Cox, Architects and Planners 1965-85; *Recreations* painting, drawing, print making; *Style—* Oliver Cox Esq, CBE; 22 Grove Terrace, London NW5 1PL (☎ 01 485 6929)

COX, Patrick Lathbridge; s of Terry Brian Cox, of Victoria, Br Columbia, Canada, and Maureen Patricia, *née* Clarke; *b* 19 Mar 1963; *Educ* Cordwainer's Coll Hackney (DATech 1985); *Career* footwear designer, work included in collections of Vivienne Westwood John Galliano, Alistair Blair, John Flett London and Paris 1985-87, exhibited in Aust Nat Galery, V and A; *Style—* Patrick Cox, Esq; 38D Georgiana St, London SW1 OEB (☎ 01 284 0641, fax 01 267 5470)

COX, Peter Donald; s of Edward Donald Cox (d 1980); *b* 19 August 1928; *Educ* RNC Dartmouth; *m* 1953, Philippa Belle, da of Philip Brandon, of Wellington, NZ; 1 s, 2 da; *Career* Lt Cdr RN, ret 1958; dir Bridport-Gundry plc 1964; exec dir James Pearsall & Co Ltd 1961-78, md Crewkerne Textiles Ltd 1978-83 (all subsids of Bridport-Gundry Hldgs), dir Crewkerne Textiles 1983; md Redport Net Co Ltd 1983-; *Recreations* golf, tennis, bridge, philately; *Clubs* Naval; *Style—* Peter Cox, Esq; Mayfield, West Monkton, Taunton, Somerset (☎ 0823 412382); Redport Net Co Ltd, 94 East St, Bridport, Dorset

COX, Peter Richmond; CB (1971); s of Richard Rendell Cox (d 1966), and Nellie Dorothy Richmond (d 1981); *b* 3 Sept 1914; *Educ* Kings Coll Sch; *m* 1971, Faith Blake, da of Harold Garnett Schenk (d 1961); *Career* actuary, dep govt actuary 1963-74, vice pres Inst of Actuaries 1966-68 (hon sec 1962-64), pres Eugenics Soc 1970-72, chm Civil Serv Insur Soc 1973-78; silver medal Inst of Actuaries 1975; FIA; *Books* Demography (1950), Surplus in British Life Assurance (1962); jt ed: Population and Pollution (1972), Resources and Population (1973), Population and the New Biology (1974), Equalities and Inequalities in Education (1975); various papers on statistical and financial subjects; *Recreations* music, painting, gardening, conservation; *Clubs* actuaries; *Style—* Peter Cox, Esq; The Level House, Mayfield, E Sussex TN20 6BW (☎ 0435 872217)

COX, Stephen Joseph; s of Levard John Cox (d 1984), of Bristol, and Ethel Mini May McGille (d 1980); *Educ* St Mary Redcliff Sch Bristol, Central Sch of Art and Design; *m* 1 June 1970, Judith, da of John Douglas Atkins, of Well Court Farm, Tyler Hill, nr Canterbury, Kent; 1 s (Pelé Delaney), 1 da (Georgia); *Career* sculptor, Br rep Indian Triennale 1986, exhibited Cairo Opera Hs 1988, Tate Gallery 1986; *Recreations* cricket, golf; *Clubs* Chelsea Arts; *Style—* Stephen Cox, Esq; 154 Barnsbury Rd, London N1 OER

COX, Thomas Michael; MP (Lab) Tooting 1983; *b* 1930; *Educ* LSE; *Career* MP (Lab): Wandsworth Central 1970-74, Wandsworth Tooting 1974-1983; former asst govt Whip, Lord Cmmr of the Treasury 1977-79; *Style—* Thomas Cox, Esq, MP; House of Commons, SW1

COX, Timothy John Lomas; TD (1971); s of Arthur Cox (d 1979), of Lower Willingdon, Sussex, and Winifred Mabel, *née* Lomas-Smith (d 1975); *b* 9 Mar 1939; *Educ* King's Sch Rochester; *m* 5 Sept 1970, Julia Rosemary, da of Henry Francis Workman (d 1988), of Grantown-on-Spey, Morayshire; 1 s (Adrian b 1974), 1 da (Rosemary b 1976); *Career* cmmnd 2 Lt RA TA 1959, (Actg Maj 1970-), Central Volunteer HQ RA 1973- (Maj 1975-); slr 1962, ptnr Oswald Hickson Collier & Co 1966-; Freeman City of London 1983; memb: various professional and military assocs; *Recreations* photography, scuba diving, country pursuits; *Style—* Timothy Cox, Esq, TD; Messrs Oswald Hickson Collier & Co, Essex Hse, Essex St, Strand, London, WC2R 3AQ (☎ 01 836 8333, fax 01 240 2236)

COX, Sir Trenchard; CBE (1954); s of late William Pallett Cox, of London, and Marion Beverley; *b* 31 July 1905; *Educ* Eton, King's Coll Cambridge; *m* 1935, Mary Désirée (d 1973), da of Sir Hugh Anderson (d 1928), Master of Gonville and Caius Coll Cambridge; *Career* former vice pres RSA, dir Birmingham Museum and Art Gallery, dir and sec V and A Museum 1956-66; author of gallery guides and books on art; Chev of the Légion d'Honneur; FRSA, FSA, FMA; kt 1961; *Style—* Sir Trenchard Cox, CBE; 33 Queen's Gate Gdns, London SW7 (☎ 01 584 0231)

COXEN, Lady; Kathleen Alice; da of late Edward Doncaster, of Snettisham, Norfolk and Sleaford, Lincs; *m* 1912, Maj Sir William George Coxen, 1 Bt (lord mayor of London 1939-40, d 1946 when title became extinct); *Style—* Lady Coxen; 8a Wellswood Park, Torquay, Devon

COXWELL-ROGERS, Col Richard Annesley; s of Maj-Gen Norman Annesley Coxwell-Rogers, CB, CBE, DSO (d 1985), of Cheltenham, and Diana Mary, *née* Coston; *b* 26 April 1932; *Educ* Eton, Sandhurst; *m* 21 Sept 1965, Martha Felicity, da of Col G T Hurrell, OBE; 2 s (James b 1969, Edward b 1973); *Career* serv 15/19 The Kings Royal Hussars 1952-82 (CO Regt 1973-75) Malaya, Germany, UK; appointed Col 15/19 Hussars 1988; area appeals organiser Avon, Glos and Wilts Cancer Research Campaign; *Recreations* hunting, shooting; *Clubs* Cavalry and Guards; *Style*— Col Richard A Coxwell-Rogers; Rossley Manor, Cheltenham, Glos GL54 4HG (☎ Cheltenham 820417)

COZENS, Air Cdre Henry Iliffe; CB (1946), AFC (1939); s of Samuel George Cozens (d 1940); *b* 13 Mar 1904; *Educ* St Dunstans Coll, Downing Coll Cambridge; *m* 1956, Gillian Mary, da of Wing-Cdr Owen Rupert Pigott (d 1965), of Wokingham, Berks; 1 s, 2 da; *Career* Air Cdre RAF 1949, dir of plans Air Miny 1949-1951, SHAPE 1951-54, Air Offr Admin Home Cmmd 1954, ret 1956; bursar Ashorne Hill Coll Br Steel Fedn 1957-70; vice pres Br Schools Exploring Soc; *Recreations* music, current affairs; *Clubs* RAF; *Style*— Air Cdre Henry Cozens, CB, AFC; Horley Manor, Banbury, Oxon (☎ 0295 730 256)

COZENS-HARDY, Hon Beryl Gladys; OBE (1971), JP (Norfolk); da of 3 Baron Cozens-Hardy (d 1956); *b* 30 Nov 1911; *Career* chm world ctee World Assoc of Girl Guides and Girl Scouts 1972-75; *Style*— The Hon Beryl Cozens-Hardy, OBE, JP; The Glebe, Letheringsett, Holt, Norfolk

CRABTREE, Maj-Gen Derek Thomas; CB (1983); s of late William Edward Crabtree, and Winifred Hilda Burton; *b* 21 Jan 1930; *Educ* St Brendan's Coll Bristol; *m* 1960, Daphne Christine, *née* Mason, 1 s, 1 da; *Career* Dir-Gen of Weapons (Army) MOD 1980-84 Col Duke of Edinburgh's Royal Regt (Berks and Wilts) 1982-87; gen mangr Regular Forces Employment Assoc 1987-; *Clubs* Army and Navy; *Style*— Maj-Gen Derek Crabtree, CB; 53 High St, Shrivenham, Swindon, Wilts SN6 8AW

CRABTREE, His Hon Judge; Jonathan; s of Charles Harold Crabtree (d 1982), of Stansfield Hall, Todmorden, Lancs, and Elsie Marion Gaukroger; *b* 17 April 1934; *Educ* Bootham, St John's Coll Camb (MA, LLM); *m* 1, 1957 (m dis 1976), Caroline Ruth Keigwin, da of Alan Edward Oliver (d 1983), of Lewes; 2 s (Daniel Edward b 1965 (decd), Abraham John b 1963), 3 da (Harriet Mary b 1958, Rose Charity b 1961, Alice Ann b 1964); m 2, 1980, Wendy Elizabeth, da of Douglas Robert Ward (d 1956); *Career* HM inspr of factories 1958-60; barr Grays Inn 1960-86, rec 1974-86, circuit judge 1986-; *Recreations* history and archaeology, cricket, cooking; *Style*— His Hon Judge Crabtree; 204 Mount Vale, York YO2 2DL (☎ 0904 646609); Courts Administrator, 10 Floor, Pennine Centre, 2022 Hawley St, Sheffield S1 2EA (☎ 0742 755866)

CRABTREE, Prof Lewis Frederick; s of Lewis Crabtree (d 1963), and Susan, *née* Wilson (d 1962); *b* 16 Nov 1924; *Educ* Leeds Univ (BSc), Imperial Coll (DIC), Cornell Univ (PhD); *m* 16 March 1955, Averil Joan, da of Henry J Escott (d 1973); 1 s (Richard Gareth Lewis b 1961), 1 da (Elizabeth Clare b 1958); *Career* air engr offr RNVR 1945-46; graduate apprentice Saunders Roe Ltd 1947-50, ECA fell Cornell Univ 1950-52, aerodynamics dept RAE 1953-73, Sir George White prof of aeronautical engrg Bristol Univ 1973-85 (now emeritus), visiting prof Cornell Univ 1957; FRAeS (pres 1978-79), FAIAA; *Books* incl: Elements of Hypersonic Aerodynamics (1960), contributions to Incompressible Aerodynamics (1960), Laminar Boundary Layers (1963); *Recreations* nature conservation, walking, gardening; *Style*— Prof Lewis Crabtree; Dan-y-Coity, Talybont-on-Usk, Brecon, Powys LD3 7YN (☎ (087487)

CRABTREE, (John) Raymond; s of late Harold Crabtree; *b* 1 May 1925; *Educ* Emanuel Sch, Christ's Coll Cambridge; *m* 1959, Evelyn Mary, da of Capt Charles Benstead, MC, RN (d 1980); 1 s, 2 da; *Career* chartered civil engr, dir PA Management Consultants Ltd 1973-84 (joined 1955), chm Pyrok Hldgs Ltd 1984-85, dir LAST (Metals) Ltd 1987-; *Clubs* Naval; *Style*— Raymond Crabtree, Esq; Bank House, Tanworth-in-Arden, Solihull, W Mids (☎ 056 44 2291)

CRABTREE TAYLOR, Neil Barry; s of Barry Joseph Crabtree Taylor, of 54 Bute Gdns, London, and Mary Ellesmore, *née* Millbourn; *b* 19 Feb 1961; *Educ* Seaford Coll; *Career* md: Crabtree Taylor Int 1983- (dir 1981-), Formech Ltd 1984-; pres Formech Inc USA 1987, chm Formech Int 1988; *Recreations* boating, water skiing; *Style*— Neil Crabtree Taylor, Esq; Formech, 6 McKay Place, 248/300 Kensal Rd, London W10 5BN (☎ 01 969 6955, fax 01 969 8071, car 0836 210365, telex 291759 SEUTOY)

CRACE, Andrew Laurence Spencer; s of Harold Clarence Crace (d 1971), of Much Hadham, Herts, and Gladys Caroline, *née* Wise (d 1977); descendant of Edward Crace, coach designer and appointed keeper of pictures to the Royal Palaces 1790; John and Frederick Crace furniture/wallpaper designers and manufacturers concerned with the interior decoration of the Royal Opera House, Carlton House, The Royal Pavilion Brighton, the Palace of Westminster; *b* 28 May 1953; *Educ* Coll of Estate Mgmnt, Univ of Reading; *Career* designer and retailer predominantly of furniture, garden products and buildings; proprietor: Alitag Plant Labels 1980) Andrew Crace Designs 1983; ARICS 1980; *Recreations* travel, photography, sculpture, opera music, gardening, bricklaying; *Style*— Andrew L S Crace, Esq; Harefield House, Much Hadam, Herts SG10 6ER; Bourne Lane, Much Hadham, Herts SG10 6ER (☎ 027 984 2685, fax 027 984 3645)

CRACKNELL, (William) Martin; s of John Sidney Cracknell (d 1975), of Exeter, and Sybil Marian, *née* Wood (d 1976); *b* 24 June 1929; *Educ* St Edward's Sch Oxford, RMA Sandhurst; *m* 1962, Gillian, da of Gp Capt Claude Frederick Goatcher (d 1981), of Gt Missenden, Bucks; 2 s (Charles b 1963, James b 1968), 2 da (Katherine b 1964, Emma b 1966); *Career* Royal Green Jackets 1947-69, Major; active service: Cyprus, Egypt, Borneo; Br Printing Industries Fedn 1969-76; chief exec Glenrothes Devpt Corpn 1976; dir: Glenrothes Enterprise Tst, New Enterprise Devpt Ltd; memb exec Scottish Cncl Devpt and Industry; chm Scottish Ctee, German Chamber of Industry and Commerce in the UK; FIOD; *Recreations* gardening, shooting, walking; *Clubs* Royal Green Jackets; *Style*— Martin Cracknell, Esq; Alburne Knowe, Orchard Drive, Glenrothes, Fife KY7 5RG (☎ 0592 752413); Glenrothes Development Corpn, Unicorn House, Glenrothes, Fife KY7 5PD (☎ 0592 754343)

CRACROFT, Air Vice-Marshal Peter Dicken; CB (1954), AFC (1932); s of late Lt-Col Hugh Cracroft, DSO (d 1923), of The Garth, Combe Down, Bath, and Georgina Montagu, *née* Stevenson (d 1937); *b* 29 Nov 1907; *Educ* Monkton Combe Sch Bath; *m* 27 April 1932, Margaret Eliza Sugden, da of late George Sugden Patchett, of Wellington, Shropshire; 2 s; *Career* cmmnd RAF 1927; Flying Instr RAF Leuchers 1932-35, Oxford Univ Air Sqdn 1937-39; RAF Mountbatten 1939-40, HQ Coast Cmd Air Staff 1940-41, OC RAF Chivenor 1941-43, SASO 19 Gp Plymouth 1943, SASO 17 Gp Edinburgh 1943-44, Dep SASO Air Cmd SE Asia Ceylon 1945, Mil Govr Penang 1945, AOC Bombay 1946, RAF Dir and OC Jt Anti-Sub Unit Londonderry 1946-48, Sr Air Liason 2nd Air Advsr SA 1950-52, ACC 66 Gp Edinburgh 1952-53, SASO HQ Coastal Cmd 1953-55, AOC 18 Gp Scotland and NI 1955-58; ret 1959; *Recreations* fishing, gardening; *Clubs* RAF; *Style*— Air Vice-Marshal Peter Cracroft, CB, AFC; Alderney House, Burton Bradstock, Bridport, Dorset DT6 4NQ

CRACROFT-ELEY, Bridget Katharine; da of Lt-Col Sir Weston Cracroft-Amcotts, MC, DL (d 1975), of Hackthorn Hall, Lincoln, and Rhona, *née* Clifton-Brown, DL; *b* 29 Oct 1933; *Educ* Lincoln Girls' HS, Crofton Grange Sch Buntingford Herts; *m* 31 Oct 1959, Robert (Robin) Peel Charles Cracroft-Eley (who assumed the additional surname of Cracroft), s of Charles Ryves Maxwell Eley, OBE (d 1982), of East Bergholt Place, Suffolk; 1 s (William b 1963), 1 da (Annabel b 1961); *Career* local organiser WRVS, pres Lincoln North Girl Guides, parish cncllr; *Recreations* gardening, upholstery, training dogs; *Style*— Mrs Cracroft-Eley; Hackthorn Hall, Lincoln

CRACROFT-ELEY, (Robert) Robin Peel Charles; er s of (Charles Ryves) Maxwell Eley, OBE (d 1983), of East Bergholt Place, Suffolk, and his 1 w, Violet Eva, yr da of Col Herbert Haworth Peel, CBE, of Highlands, East Bergholt; assumed the additional surname of Cracroft by Deed Poll 1988; *b* 23 Jan 1931; *Educ* Eton; *m* 31 Oct 1959, Bridget Katharine, 3 da of Lt-Col Sir Weston Cracroft- Amcotts, MC, JP, DL (d 1975), of Hackthorn Hall, Lincoln; 1 s ((Charles) William Amcotts b 8 March 1963), 1 da (Annabel Louise Cracroft b 15 Jan 1961); *Career* Nat Serv cmmn 8 Royal Tank Regt 1950; farmer, ptnr R P C & B K Eley, Hackthorn Hall, Lincoln; chm: East Bergholt Estate Co Ltd, Bromhead Nursing Home Tst Ltd, Eley Enterprises Ltd; memb: Cncl Lincs Agric Soc, Lincs CC 1984- (chm property management ctee 1986-); govr: Lincs Coll of Agric and Horticulture 1984-, William Farr (C of E) Comprehensive Sch 1987-; Freeman of City of London and memb Worshipful Co of Farmers 1988; *Recreations* country sports, tennis, sailing, travel; *Style*— Robin Cracroft-Eley, Esq; Hackthorn Hall, Lincoln LN2 3PQ (☎ 0673 60212); Estate Office (☎ 0673 60423)

CRADDOCK, (William) Aleck; LVO (1981); *b* 1924; *Educ* City of London Sch; *m* 1947, Olive Mary Brown; 1 s, 1 da; *Career* dir House of Fraser plc, Harrods Tst Ltd, Harrods Estate Office Ltd, Cartier Ltd; *Style*— Aleck Craddock, Esq, LVO

CRADDOCK, Nigel Christopher; s of William Alfred Craddock (d 1976), of 20 St Ronans Rd, Harrogate, N Yorks, and Louisa Maud, *née* Edmanson (d 1974); *b* 30 August 1937; *Educ* Harrogate GS; *m* 24 Sept 1966, Penelope Jane, da of Laurence Sydney Stevens (d 1987), of Landamere, Ampney Crucis, Cirencester, Glos; 3 s (Alexander, James, Daniel); *Career* Nat Serv RAF 1956-58; dir: Hogg Robinson (UK) Ltd 1965-78, Barclay Insur Servs Co Ltd 1978-; sales dir Barclays Unit Tsts and Insurance 1985-86, md Barclays Insurance Brokers Int Ltd 1986-; memb: Berkhamsted Cons Party, Worshipful Co of Insurers; FCII 1969; *Recreations* golf, rugby, cricket, reading, walking; *Style*— Nigel Craddock, Esq; Barclays Insurance Brokers Int Ltd, Capital Hse, 42 Weston St, London SE1 3QA (☎ 01 378 6410)

CRADOCK, Sir Percy; GCMG (1983), KCMG (1980, CMG 1968); *b* 26 Oct 1923; *Educ* St John's Coll Camb; *m* 1953, Birthe Marie Dyrlund; *Career* HM Dip Serv: joined FO 1954, first sec Kuala Lumpur 1957-61, Hong Kong 1961, first sec Peking 1962, FO 1963-66, cnsllr and head of chancery Peking 1966-68, charge d'affaires Peking 1968-69, head of planning staff FCO 1969-71, under-sec Cabinet Off 1971-75, leader UK delegn Geneva Test Ban Discussions 1977-78, ambass E Germany 1976-78, ambass People's Republic of China 1978-83, continuing responsibility for negotiations over future of Hong Kong 1983-84, foreign policy advsr to the Prime Minister 1984-; hon fell St John's Coll Cambridge 1982; *Style*— Sir Percy Cradock, GCMG; c/o 10 Downing St, London SW1

CRADOCK-HARTOPP, Sir John Edmund; 9 Bt (GB 1796), of Freathby, Leics, TD; s of Francis Gerald Cradock-Hartopp (d 1946, s of late Col Edmund Charles Cradock-Hartopp, 2 s of 3 Bt); suc kinsman, Sir George Francis Fleetwood Cradock-Hartopp, 8 Bt, 1949; *b* 8 April 1912; *Educ* Uppingham; *m* 29 April 1953, Prudence, 2 da of Sir Frederick William Leith-Ross, GCMG, KCB; 3 da; *Heir* cous, Lt-Cdr Kenneth Alston Cradock-Hartopp, MBE, DSC, RN; *Career* 1939-45 War as Major RE (despatches twice), dir Firth Brown Tools Ltd 1961-76; *Recreations* golf (semi-finalist English Golf Champ 1935, first reserve Eng v France 1935), cricket, tennis, motoring; *Clubs* East India, Devonshire, Sports and Public Schools, MCC, Royal and Ancient (St Andrews); *Style*— Sir John Cradock-Hartopp, Bt, TD; The Cottage, 27 Wool Rd, Wimbledon Common, SW20

CRADOCK-HARTOPP, Lt Cdr Kenneth Alston; MBE (1946), DSC (1952); s of Maj Louis Montague Cradock-Hartopp (d 1957), and Marjorie Somerville, *née* Watson (d 1971); hp of cous, Sir John Edmund Cradock-Hartopp, 9 Bt; *b* 26 Feb 1918; *m* 18 June 1942, Gwendolyn Amy Lilian, da of late Capt Victor Crowther Upton; 1 da; *Career* Lt-Cdr (ret) RN; served WW II and Korea (cmd HMNZ frigate Taupo 1951-52); chm Royal Naval Amateur Radio Soc 1984-87; FRGS 1949; Legion of Merit (USA) 1953; *Style*— Lt-Cdr Kenneth Cradock-Hartopp, MBE, DSC; Keepers, Yeovilton, Yeovil, Somerset BA22 8EX (☎ 0935 840240)

CRAFT, Prof Ian Logan; s of Reginald Thomas Craft, of St John's, Thorrington Rd, Great Bentley, Essex, and Mary Lois, *née* Logan; *b* 11 July 1937; *Educ* Owen Sch London, Univ of London, Westminster Hosp Med Sch (MB, BS); *m* 19 Dec 1959, Jacqueline Rivers, s of John James Symmons (d 1985), of 9 Merricks Ct, Temple Sheen, London; 2 s (Simon b 4 Sept 1964, Adrian b 1 Sept 1968); *Career* house offr radiotherapy dept and dept of obstetrics and gynaecology Westminster Hosp 1961-62, sr house offr (later house surgn and house physician) St James Hosp Balham 1962-63, house surgn Hammersmith Hosp 1965s, sr house offr (later surgical registrar) professional unit Westminster Hosp 1965-66, res med offr Queen Charlotte's Hosp London 1967, gynaecological registrar (later res registrar inst of obstetrics and gynaecology) Chelsea Hosp for Women 1968-69, res med offr Gen Lying-In Hosp London 1969, registrar Queen Mary's Hosp Roehampton 1970, sr registrar Westminster Hosp London 1970, rotational sr registrar Kingston Hosp Surrey 1971-72, sr lectr and hon conslt Queen Charlotte's Hosp and Chelsea Hosp for Women 1972-76, dir of gynaecology Cromwell Hosp London 1982-85, dir of fertility and obstetrics studies Humana Hosp Wellington London 1985; visiting prof UCL; frequent lectr and prolific contrib to medical literature; life memb: Zoological Soc, Nat Tst, RNLI, Friends of St Paul's Cathedral, Turner Soc, Walpole Soc; FRCS 1966, MRCOG 1970, FRCOG 1986; memb: RSM, Blair Bell Res Soc, Br Fertility Soc, Harveian Soc (London); *Recreations* art, ceramics, sculpture, music, opera, theatre, most sports, antiquities; *Clubs* Heritage, Natural Pursuits, Ornithology; *Style*— Prof Ian Craft; 10 Park St James, Prince Albert Road, London NW8 (☎ 01 586 6001), Humana Hospital Wellington, Wellington Place, London NW8 9LE (☎ 01 586 8861, 01 586 5959, fax 01

586 3869, telex 25184)

CRAFT, Prof Maurice; s of Jack Craft (d 1952), of London, and Polly, *née* Lewis (d 1973); *b* 4 May 1932; *Educ* Colfe's GS, LSE (BSc), Sch of Educ Univ of Dublin (HDipEd), Inst of Educn Univ of London (AcadDipEd), Univ of Liverpool (PhD); *m* 19 May 1957, Alma, da of Ellis Sampson (d 1975), of Dublin; 2 da (Anna b 1961, Naomi b 1964); *Career* Nat Serv 1953-55, cmmnd 2 Lt RAOC served Suez Canal Zone, appointed acting Capt; head dept of sociology Edge Hill Coll of Educn 1960-67, sr lectr Exeter Univ 1967-74, prof of educn La Trobe Univ Melbourne 1974-76, Goldsmith's prof of educn London Univ 1976-80, prof of educn Nottingham Univ 1980- (pro-vice-chllr 1983-87, former dean of faculty and chm of Sch Of Educn); UK del to UNESCO, Cncl of Europe and EEC Confs; vice chm CVU; author numerous learned books, monographs and papers; memb: exec ctee UCET, CNAA; *Books* Change in Teacher Education (1984), Education and Cultural Pluralism (1984), Teaching in a Multicultural Society (1981), Family, Class and Education (1970); *Recreations* music, walking; *Style*— Prof Maurice Craft; University of Nottingham, Nottingham NG7 2RD (☎ 0602 484848)

CRAIB, Douglas Duncan Simpson; CBE (1974), DL (Moray 1974); s of Peter Barton Salsbury Simpson (d 1916) and Helen Duncan; changed name by deed poll 1930; *b* 5 April 1914; *Educ* Aberdeen GS, Dundee HS; *m* 1939, Moyra Louise, da of late Alex Ewan Booth; 1 s, 1 da; *Career* Capt 7 Bn Seaforth Highlanders 1939-42; farmer 1937-83; dir: Cromar Nominees Ltd, D and M Craib Ltd, NALCO Ltd; memb: Potato Marketing Bd of GB 1968, Bd of N Scotland Coll of Agric 1970, Bd Rowett Res Inst 1970; tstee The MacRobert Trusts Scotland 1970, former chm of dirs Royal Highland and Agric Soc of Scotland, former bd memb N of Scotland Hydro-Electric Bd, former chm Electricity Consultative Cncl N Scotland Area; FRAgS; *Clubs* Farmers (London), Elgin (Moray); *Style*— Douglas Craib, Esq, CBE, DL; The Old School, Mosstodloch, Fochabers, Morayshire IV32 7LL

CRAIG, (Hildreth) Charles; *b* 4 Oct 1923; *Educ* Pimms Acad; *m* 20 June 1945, Audrey Doris, *née* Wells; 2 s (Michael b 20 July 1946, Nigel b 6 June 1948), 1 da (Alison b 15 Dec 1958); *Career* Civil Def 1940-42, RCS 1942, 52 Lowland Div UK & BLA, cmmnd Highland LI 1945, seconded to the Royal West African Frontier Force, demobbed 1948; Adams & Son (Printers) Rye 1937-40, Sweet & Maxwell Law Publishers 1937-40, mangr wine and spirit dept Woodheads Brewery 1947-52, Taplow & co 1952-67, prodn dir Bass Charrington Vintners 1962-67, chm Invergordon Distillers (Hldgs) 1983- (md 1967-83); The Scotch Whisky Assoc: lectr 1958-75, memb public affairs ctee 1975-77, memb cncl 1977-, hon tres 1978-; *Books* Glenpatrick The Story of an Unsuccessful Distillery (1982); *Clubs* Caledonian; *Style*— Charles Craig, Esq; The Cummins, Aldham, Colchester CO6 3PN (☎ 0206 242230); 9-21 Salamander Place, Leith, Edinburgh EH6 7JL (☎ 031 554 4404, fax 031 554 1531, telex 72624)

CRAIG, Charles James; s of James Craig (d 1928), and Anna Rosina Craig (d 1921); *b* 3 Dec 1919; *m* 1946, Dorothy, da of Victor Wilson (d 1953); 1 s (Stephen), 1 da (Gilda); *Career* operatic tenor; has performed in all major opera houses of the world, specializing in the role of Othello, and all other dramatic tenor roles (esp those of Verdi, Puccini, Wagner); *Recreations* motoring, gardening, cooking; *Style*— Charles Craig Esq; Whitfield Stone Haze House, Nr Brackley, Northants (☎ 02805 268)

CRAIG, Colin Fetherston; s of Rev Cuthbert Leslie Craig (d 1982), of Weardale, and Muriel, *née* Cole; *b* 29 August 1947; *Educ* Kent Coll Canterbury, Kingston Coll of Art; *Career* creative dir: Cogent Elliott Ltd 1975-78, Doyle Dane Bernbach Ltd 1978-79, Grierson Cockman Craig & Druiff Ltd 1979-86, Grey Ltd 1986-87, Holmes Knight Ritchie/WRG Ltd 1987-; writer of music for TV and radio 1968-, lectr in TV technique, writer of screenplays for TV and cinema, winner of over 50 nat and int TV awards, multi-instrumentalist, singer, conductor; memb: D & AD 1969, Songwriters Guild 1978, PRS 1977; *Recreations* yoga, horticulture, cinema, church, dalmatians; *Clubs* Lansdowne; *Style*— Colin Craig, Esq; Holmes Knight Ritchie/WRG Ltd, 43-45 Dorset St, London W1H 4AB (☎ 01 935 4411, fax 01 487 3694, telex 264002)

CRAIG, Air Chief Marshal Sir David Brownrigg; GCB (1984), (KCB 1980, CB 1978, OBE 1967); s of Maj Francis Brownrigg Craig (d 1943) and Olive Craig (d 1958); *b* 17 Sept 1929; *Educ* Radley, Lincoln Coll Oxford; *m* 1955, Elisabeth June, da of Charles James Derenburg (d 1976); 1 s, 1 da; *Career* cmmnd RAF 1951, AOC No 1 Gp RAF Strike Cmd 1978-80, vice-chief of Air Staff 1980-82, AOC-in-C Strike Cmd and C-in-C UKAF 1982-85, Chief of Air Staff 1985-, Air Chief Marshal 1983; *Clubs* RAF; *Style*— Air Chief Marshal Sir David Craig, GCB, OBE; c/o Royal Bank of Scotland, 9 Pall Mall, London SW1Y 5LX

CRAIG, Dr Donald Gwynvor; s of Donald Craig (d 1964), of Sheffield, Yorks, and Elizabeth May, *née* Williams (d 1980); *b* 19 August 1929; *Educ* King Edward VII Sch Sheffield, Balliol Coll Univ of Oxford (MA, BM, BCh), St Thomas Hosp London (DRCOG, DMJ, DVSA); *m* 3 July 1954, (Dorothy) Jill, da of Rt Hon E L Burgin (d 1945), of Harpenden; 4 da (Meredith Ann b 1955, Corinna b 1956, Lucinda Mary b 1959, Annabel Clare b 1962); *Career* Capt RAMC (regimental MO 1 Bn WG) 1955-57; sr lectr dept gen practice Guy's Hosp Med Sch 1975, sr ptnr Thamesmead Med Assocs 1975, sr forensic med examiner Met Police 1980, clinical asst dept genito-urinary medicine Greenwich Dist Hsop 1988; Freeman City of London 1970, Liveryman Worshipful Soc Apothecaries 1974 (memb Livery Ctee 1982-86); FRCGP 1985; memb: Med Offrs of Schs Assoc, Assoc Police Surgns, Soc Occupational Medicine, Royal Soc Medicine Assur Med Soc, Med Soc Study of Venerial Diseases; *Recreations* sailing, big projects, cornwall; *Clubs* Litte Ship; *Style*— Dr Donald Craig; 42 Dartmouth Row, London SE10 8AW (☎ 01 692 3061); 2 The Quarry, Portscatho, Truro, Cornwall TR2 5HP (☎ 087 258 670); Gallions Reach Health Centre, Thamesmead, London SE28 8BE (☎ 01 311 1010)

CRAIG, George Charles Graham; s of George Craig (d 1970), and Elizabeth Stachan, *née* Milne; *b* 8 May 1946; *Educ* Nottingham Univ (BA); *m* 9 March 1968, (Ethne) Marian, da of Herbert Henry Asquith Gallagher (d 1989); 2 s (Andrew b 9 June 1971, Robert b 13 July 1974), 1 da (Emily b 5 June 1978); *Career* asst princ Min of Tport 1967, private sec Min of State Welsh Off 1971, princ Welsh Off 1973, princ private sec Sec of State for Wales 1978, under sec Welsh Off 1986- (asst sec 1980); Methodist local preacher; *Style*— George Craig, Esq; Welsh Office, Cathays Park, Cardiff, CF1 3NQ (☎ 0222 823307)

CRAIG, Sir (Albert) James Macqueen; GCMG (1984), KCMG (1981, CMG 1975); s of James Craig (d 1954), of Scone by Perth, and Florence, *née* Morris; *b* 13 July 1924; *Educ* Liverpool Inst HS, Queen's Coll Oxford, Magdalen Coll Oxford; *m* 1952, Margaret Hutchinson; 3 s, 1 da; *Career* former lectr in Arabic Durham Univ; Foreign Service 1956, fell St Antony's Coll Oxford 1970-71; ambassador: Syria 1976-79, Saudi Arabia 1979-84; visiting prof in Arabic Oxford 1985-; dir-gen Middle East Assoc 1985-; dir: Saudi-Br Bank 1985-, Hong Kong Egyptian Bank 1987; advsr Hong Kong and Shanghai Bank 1985-; chm Roxby Engrg Int Ltd; hon fell Centre for Middle Eastern and Islamic Studies Durham Univ 1986; pres British Soc for Middle East Studies 1987; OStJ 1984 (memb cncl); *Clubs* Travellers'; *Style*— Sir James Craig, GCMG; 33 Bury St, London SW1

CRAIG, John Edgar; OBE (Mil 1967); *b* 25 August 1925; *Educ* Rossall, Worcester Coll Oxford (MA); *Career* WWII Black Watch attached 4 PWO Gurkha Rifles Burma 1945; Capt CCF 1951-82, hon Lt-Col (A/Lt Col 1965); schoolmaster (VI form English), Ardingly Coll 1951-85, housemaster 1953-77ol 1965); *Recreations* reading, bird-watching, sea-fishing, music; *Style*— John Craig, OBE; c/o Nat Westminster Bank plc, 1 Muster Green, Haywards Heath, W Sussex RH16 4AR

CRAIG, John Egwin; s of Thomas Joseph Alexander Craig, CIE (d 1969), and Mabel Frances, *née* Quinnell (d 1979); *b* 16 August 1932; *Educ* Charterhouse; *m* 27 June 1959, Patricia, da of Exmo Senor Joao Costa Lopes (d 1980), of Sintra, Portugal; 3 s (Colin b 5 Dec 1960, Andrew b 15 June 1962, James b 12 Oct 1968); *Career* cmmnd Royal Irish Fusilliers 1950; Cooper Bros 1958-61, The Stock Exchange 1961-64, md NM Rothschild & SM Ltd 1981-88 (joined 1964, dir 1970), Jupiter Tarbutt Ltd, United Dutch Hldgs NV; chm exec ctee Br Bankers' Assocm, memb Deposit Protection Bd; govr Abingdon Sch, tstee Purcell Sch; FCA, FRSA; *Clubs* Brook's; *Style*— John Craig, Esq; Saxonbury House, Frant, Nr Tunbridge Wells, Kent TN3 9HJ (☎ 0892 75 644); New Ct, St Swithin's Lane, London EC4P 4DU (☎ 01 280 5000, fax 01 929 1643)

CRAIG, Col John Mirrlees; TD (1970), DL (Gtr London 1970); s of Col Hugh Craig, OBE, TD, DL, Woodlands, Tudor Close, Woodford Green, Essex, and Elsie Evelyn, *née* Mallender; *b* 28 May 1936; *Educ* Chigwell Sch; *m* 5 Sept 1960, Susan, da of Maurice Carter (d 1988), of Romsey, Hants; 2 s (Stephen George b 1 March 1964, Giles Hugh Mirrlees b 1 May 1967); *Career* Nat Serv cmmnd 10 Royal Hussars 1956-58; TA: City of London Yeo 1958-60, Inns of Ct & City Yeo 1960-67, Royal Yeo 1967-69, 71 Yeo Signal Regt 1969-78, HQ London Dist 1979-81, Col TA; chm and md: Scrolapoint Ltd, Scrolapoint Devpt Co Ltd, JMC Investmnts Ltd, George M Craig & Sons Ltd, Aldwych Investmnts Ltd, Market Investmnts Ltd, IJB ptnrs Ltd, Town Houses (Woodbridge) Ltd, WCA (Sudbury) Investmts Ltd, JMC Overseas Ltd, dir Caird Gp 1987-88, memb Lloyds 1986; ADC to HM The Queen 1980-84, memb of HM Cmmn of Lieutenancy for the City of London; rep DL for London Borough of Islington, memb: cncl Union Jack Club, HAC, cncl Reserve Forces Assoc, ctee Yeo Benevolent Fund; vice chm Greater London TA 7 Vol Res Assoc, life managing govr Royal Scottish Corpn; Freeman City of London, Liveryman of the Worshipful Co of Fan Makers, memb Guild of Freemen; FInstD; *Recreations* sailing, skiing; *Clubs* Cavalry & Guards, City Livery; *Style*— Col John Craig, TD, DL; 15 Union Sq, London N1 7DH (☎ 01 704 9555); Old Estuary Ho, 83 Castle St, Woodbridge, Suffolk; Scrolapoint Ltd, 10 Benezet St, Ipswich, Suffolk (☎ 0473 211918/9, 0473 254630, fax 0473 250052, car tel 0860 629633)

CRAIG, Very Rev Prof Robert; CBE (1981); s of John Craig (stone mason, d 1972), and Anne Peggie Craig (linen weaver, d 1924); *b* 22 Mar 1917; *Educ* Fife CCncl Schs, St Andrews Univ (MA, BD, PhD), Union Theological Seminary NY USA (STM); *m* 1950, Olga Wanda, da of Michael Strzelec (d 1941); 1 s (John Michael Robert b 1961), 1 da (Anna Helena b 1956); *Career* Chaplain (4 class) Br Army: UK, NW Europe, Egypt, Palestine 1942-47, mentioned in despatches Normandy 1944; min of the Church of Scotland, moderator of the Gen Assembly of the Church of Scotland 1986-87, min of St Andrew's Scots Memorial Church Jerusalem 1980-85; Univ of Zimbabwe: prof of theology 1963-80, prof, principal and vice chllr 1969-80, now prof emeritus; prof of religion Smith Coll Northampton Mass USA 1957-63, prof of divinity Univ of Natal SA 1950-57; Hon CF 1947, Hon DD St Andrews Univ 1967; Hon LLD: Witwatersrand Univ 1979, Birmingham Univ 1980, Natal Univ 1981; Hon DLitt Zimbabwe Univ 1981; hon fell Zimbabwe Inst of Engrs 1976; City of Jerusalem Medal 1985, memb Jerusalem Ctee 1989-, Golden Jubilee Medal Witwatersrand Univ 1977; *Books* Social Concern in the Thought of William Temple (1963); *Recreations* listening and talking to people, comtemporary and recent history, light classical music; *Clubs* Kate Kennedy, University Staff, Students' Union (St Andrews), YMCA (Jerusalem); *Style*— The Very Rev Prof Robert Craig, CBE; West Port, Falkland, Fife KY7 7BL (☎ 0337 57238)

CRAIG, Hon Mrs (Roxane); *née* Balfour; o da of 2 Baron Balfour of Inchrye, *qv*; *b* 8 Sept 1955; *m* 1978, Adrian Laird Craig; 1 s (Robert Joseph b 1982), 2 da (Mary Ann Josephine b 1984, Alethea Katharine b 1986); *Style*— The Hon Roxane Craig; Libberton House, Libberton, nr Carnwath, Lanarkshire

CRAIG, Stuart Bowen; s of Alexander Craig and Maureen Lydia Frances, *née* Frost, of Swanage, Dorset; *b* 15 August 1943; *Educ* Kingston GS, Southampton Univ (LLB); *m* 1967, Lynnard Graham, da of Flying Offr Geoffrey Clay Whitehurst (d 1944); 1 s (Nolan b 1969), 1 da (Natasha b 1971); *Career* investment management; dir: Kleinwort Benson Investment Management Ltd 1978-86, Kleinwort Grieveson Investment Management Ltd 1986-87, Fraser Green Ltd 1987-; govr Kingston GS 1978-; tstee Charinco/Charishare 1978-; FCA; assoc memb Soc of Investment Analysts; *Recreations* rowing, sailing, swimming, food and wine; *Clubs* Weybridge Rowing, Leander, S Caernarvonshire Yacht, Abersoch Powerboat, Cannons Sports, Tramp; *Style*— S B Craig, Esq; Little Spinney, Caenshill Road, Weybridge, Surrey KT13 0SW (☎ Weybridge 848539); Fraser Green Ltd, 2 Friars Lane, Richmond, Surrey TW9 1NL (☎ 01 948 0164, telex 9413827, fax 01 948 4275)

CRAIG, (Anne Gwendoline) Wendy; da of George Dixon Craig (d 1968) and Anne Lindsay; *b* 20 June 1934; *Educ* Durham HS for Girls, Darlington HS, Yarm GS, Central Sch of Speech Training and Dramatic Art; *m* 30 Sept 1955, John Alexander (Jack), s of John Bentley (d 1944); 2 s (Alastair b 5 April 1957, Ross b 10 Nov 1961); *Career* actress; Ipswich Repertory Theatre 1953, Epitaph For George Dillon Royal Court 1957, and Broadway, The Wrong Side of the Park 1960, The Gingerman, Ride A Cock Horse, I Love You Mrs Patterson, Finishing Touches, Peter Pan 1968, Breezeblock Park 1975, Beyond Reasonable Doubt Queen's Theatre 1987; TV series: Not In Front Of The Children, And Mother Makes Three, And Mother Makes Five, Nanny, Butterflies, Laura and Disorder; Films: The Mindbenders, The Servant (British Academy nomination), The Nanny 1966, Just Like A Woman, I'll Never Forget What's-Is-Name, Joseph Andrews; LP recordings: Tales of Beatrix Potter (Gold disc), Show Me The Way 1988; BAFTA Award Best Actress 1968, BBC Personality of the Year 1969 (ITV 1973); *Books* Happy Endings (1972), The Busy Mums Cook Book

(1983), Busy Mums Baking Book (1986), Kid's Stuff (1988); *Recreations* walking, gardening; *Style*— Miss Wendy Craig; c/o Hatton and Baker, 18 Jermyn St, London SW1

CRAIG, Rt Hon William; PC (NI 1963); s of late John Craig, of Milecross, Newtownards, Co Down, and Mary Kathleen, *née* Lamont; *b* 2 Dec 1924; *Educ* Dungannon Royal Sch, Larne GS, Queen's Univ Belfast; *m* 1960, Doris, da of Ewald Hilgendorff, of Hamburg; 2 s; *Career* slr 1952, MP (U) Larne Div Antrim NI Parly 1960-73, MP (UU) Belfast E 1974-79, min of Devpt 1965-66, fndr and former ldr Ulster Vanguard and Vanguard Unionist Parties; *Style*— The Rt Hon William Craig; c/o N Ireland Privy Council Office, Whitehall SW1 1A2 AT

CRAIG HARVEY, Lady Julia Helen; *née* Percy; 3 da of 10 Duke of Northumberland, KG, GCVO, TD, PC (d 1988); *b* 12 Nov 1950; *m* 11 June 1983, Nicholas Robert Craig Harvey, er s of Andrew John Craig Harvey, of Lainston House, Sparshott, Hants; 1 s (Christopher Hugh b 4 Oct 1988), 1 da (Georgina Elizabeth b 29 May 1986); *Career* art dealer; *Style*— Lady Julia Craig Harvey; 7 Sibella Road, London SW4

CRAIG WALLER, Patrick Arthur Beaufort; s of Vice Adm Arthur William Craig Waller, CB (d 1943), of Co Meath, Eire, and Ella Mary, *née* Beaufort (d 1973); who was descended from Adm Sir Francis Beaufort KCB, FRS (1774-1857), Hydrographer of the Admiralty 1829-55, inventor of the Beaufort Wind Scale; *b* 5 Jan 1915; *Educ* Repton Sch; *m* 29 Oct 1943, Prudence Mary, da of Lt Col Francis Alfred Tighe, RA (d 1938), of Portchester, Hants; 5 s (Brian Hugh Digby b 1947, d 1966, Desmond Sean b 1949, Terence Patrick b 1950, Gregory Mark b 1953, Jonathan Paul b 1963); *Career* Lt RNVR 1939-46 home waters and Pacific; exec British Iron and Steel Fedn 1947-66, Br Nat Export Cncl 1966-72; *Clubs* MCC; *Style*— Patrick A B Craig Waller, Esq; Bowness, Church Hill, Horsell, Woking, Surrey GU21 4QE (☎ Woking 72841)

CRAIG-COOPER, (Frederick Howard) Michael; CBE (1982), TD (3 bars); s of Frederick William Valentine Craig-Cooper (d 1975), and Elizabeth Oliver-Thompson, *née* Macdonald; *b* 28 Jan 1936; *Educ* Horris Hill, Stowe; *m* 8 March 1968, Elizabeth, MVO, da of Leonard William Snagge (d 1971); 1 s (Peter b 3 March 1972); *Career* Nat Serv RA serv Combined operations UK Malta Cyprus 1954-56, TA 1956-88 cmd NGLO unit 29 Commando Regt RA 1972-75; Dep Lt Greater London 1986-, rep Lt Kensington and Chelsea 1987-; articled slr (to Sir Arthur Driver) Jaques & Co 1956-61, slr Allen & Overy 1962-64; Inco Ltd 1964-85: dir of Cos (UK, Europe, Africa, M East, India) 1972-84, conslt and non-exec dir Uk and M East 1984-85; dir: Craig Lloyd Ltd 1968-, Paul Ray Int 1984-, Carré Orban & Ptnrs Ltd 1989-; former tstee Cooper Devpt Tst Fund 1974-85, memb cncl Mining Assoc of UK 1977-82; 1966 and 1970 Parly Candidate (Cons) Houghton-Le-Spring; memb cncl Royal Borough of Kensington and Chelsea 1968-78 (cllr 1968-74, chief whip 1971-74, chm fin ctee 1972-74, memb investmt panel 1973-, alderman 1974-78), chm Chelsea Cons Assoc 1974-77 (pres 1983-), Nat Union of Cons and Unionist Assocs 1975- (tres Gtr London 1975-84), chm Cons Nat Property Advsy Ctee 1987-; chm Employers Support Ctee TAVRA Greater London; Freeman City of London 1964, Liveryman Worshipful Co of Drapers 1970 (jr warden 1987-88, Ct of Assistants 1987-); OStJ 1974; memb: Law Soc 1962, Inst of Arbitrators; Offr Order Merit with Swords of Sovereign Mil Order of Malta (1986); *Recreations* encouraging wife's gardening; *Clubs* Pratts, Whites; *Style*— Michael Craig-Cooper, Esq, CBE, TD; Paul Ray and Carré Orban Int, 7 Curzon St, London W1Y 7FL (☎ 01 491 1266, fax 01 491 4609, telex 296932 RAYLON G)

CRAIG-MCFEELY, Cmdt WRNS (ret) Elizabeth Sarah Anne; CB (1982); da of late Lt-Col Cecil Michael Craig McFeely, DSO, OBE, MC (d 1948), and Nancy Sarah, *née* Mann; *b* 28 April 1927; *Educ* St Rose's Convent Stroud, Anstey Coll of PE; *Career* joined WRNS 1952, naval memb Bd of Mgmnt NAAFI 1977-79, Hon ADC to HM The Queen 1979-, dir WRNS 1979-82, ret; *Recreations* gardening, country pursuits; *Style*— Cmdt Elizabeth Craig-McFeely, CB; Moonrakers, Mockbeggar Lane, Biddenden, Ashford, Kent

CRAIG-McFEELY, Lt Cdr Gerald Martin; s of Lt Col Cecil Michael Craig-McFeely, DSO, MBE, MC (d 1948), and Nancy Elton, *née* Mann (d 1981); *b* 5 April 1932; *Educ* Downside; *m* 12 April 1958, Joanna Mary Moubray, da of Douglas Jenkins; 2 s (Simon b 1959, Peter b 1971), 2 da (Julia b 1962, Mary b 1967); *Career* RN 1950-69, long TAs HMS Vernon 1957, HMS Defender 1958-61, 1 Submarine Sqdn 1961-63, staff offr ops 26 Escort Sqdn Far East 1963-65, HMS Vernon 1965-66, Naval Intelligence 1967-69, ret Lt-Cdr 1969; Lazard Bros and Co Ltd 1974- (personnel dir 1987-); ACIS 1970; *Recreations* fly fishing, shooting, painting; *Style*— Lt Cdr Gerald Craig-McFeely; Tintern, Hill Brow, Liss, Hants GU33 7QI (☎ 0730 89 2138); Lazard Brothers and Co Ltd, 21 Moorfields, London EC2P 2HT (☎ 01 588 2721)

CRAIGAVON, Viscountess; (Angela) Fiona; *née* Tatchell; yr da of late Percy Tatchell, MRCS, LRCP (d 1948), of 29 Barkston Gdns, SW; *m* 22 Nov 1939, 2 Viscount Craigavon (d 1974); 1 s (3 Viscount), 2 da (Hon Mrs MacInnes, Hon Mrs MacDonald); *Style*— The Rt Hon the Viscountess Craigavon; 27 Launceston Pla, W8

CRAIGAVON, 3 Viscount (UK 1927); Sir Janric Fraser Craig; 3 Bt (UK 1918); s of 2 Viscount Craigavon (d 1974); *b* 9 June 1944; *Educ* Eton, London Univ (BA, BSc); *Heir* none; *Career* FCA; *Style*— The Rt Hon The Viscount Craigavon; 17 Launceston Place, London W8

CRAIGEN, Desmond Seaward; s of John Craigen, of London (d 1934), and Anne Amelia (d 1958); *b* 31 July 1916; *Educ* Holloway Sch, Kings Coll London (BA); *m* 24 Feb 1961, Elena Ines, da of Norman de Launay Oldham (d 1975); 1 s (Jeremy John b 1963), 1 da (Barbara Claire b 1957); *Career* served as Maj 53 Reconnaissance Regt NW Europe 1944-46 (despatches); Prudential Assurance Co 1934-81: India 1950-57, dep gen mangr 1968, gen mangr 1969-78, chief gen mangr 1979-81, dir Prudential Corpn 1982-89; chm Vanburgh Life Assurance Co 1982-87, dir Pioneer Concrete (Hldgs) Co 1982-89; *Recreations* music, reading; *Style*— Desmond Craigen, Esq; 44 Crondace Road, London SW6 4BT

CRAIGEN, James Mark (Jim); JP; eldest s of late James Craigen, of Glasgow, and late Isabel Craigen; *b* 2 August 1938; *Educ* Shawlands Acad Glasgow, Strathclyde Univ, Heriot-Watt Univ (M Litt); *m* 20 March 1971, Sheena, da of late James Millar, of Linlithgow; *Career* compositor 1954-61, industl rels asst Scottish Gas 1963-64, asst sec Scottish TUC 1964-68, asst sec Scottish Business Educn Cncl 1968-74; MP (Lab and Co-op) Glasgow Maryhill 1974-87); pps to sec state Scotland 1974-76, memb UK delgn Cncl of Europe 1976-80, memb select ctee Employment 1979-83 (chm 1982-83), oppn front bench spokesman Scotland 1983-85; dir and sec Scottish Fedn of Housing Assocs 1988-; tstee Nat Museums of Scotland 1985-; CBIM; *Style*— Jim Craigen, Esq, JP; SFHA, 40 Castle Street North, Edinburgh EH2 3BN

CRAIGIE, Colin; s of James Patrick Craigie, of Glasgow (d 1924), and Isabella Baird, *née* Weir, of Glasgow (d 1952); *b* 28 Sept 1923; *Educ* London Univ (BSc Econ); *m* 23 March 1956, Catherine Boyd, da of Daniel Alexander Mackay (d 1951); 1 s (Colin Russell b 1958), 1 da (Gail Roger b 1960); *Career* financial controller Consolidated Gold Fields plc 1966-70; finance dir: Lines Bros Ltd 1971, STC (SA) Ltd 1971-73, Meyer Int plc 1982-88, Int Timber Corpn plc 1973-82; ACMA; MCT; *Recreations* cricket, marriage, philosophy; *Clubs* MCC; *Style*— Colin Craigie, Esq; 23A Barkston Gardens, London SW5 0ER (☎ 01 373 3781)

CRAIGMYLE, 3 Baron (UK 1929); Thomas Donald Mackay Shaw; s of 2 Baron Craigmyle (d 1944), and Lady Margaret Cargill Mackay (d 1958), da of 1 Earl of Inchcape; *b* 17 Nov 1923; *Educ* Eton, Trinity Coll Oxford (MA); *m* 22 Sept 1955, Anthea Esther Christine Theresa, da of late Edward Charles Rich, of 31 Yeomans Row, London SW3; 3 s (Thomas, Justin, Joseph), 3 da (Alison, Catriona, Madeleine), (and 1 s decd); *Heir* s, Hon Thomas Columba Shaw, *qv*; *Career* chm: Craigmyle and Co Ltd, Claridge Mills Ltd (Queen's Award for Export 1982 and 1987); vice-pres: Br Assoc SMO Malta Catholic Union of GB; FRSA; CStJ; *Clubs* Royal Thames Yacht, Caledonian; *Style*— The Rt Hon the Lord Craigmyle; 18 The Boltons, London SW10 9SY (☎ 01 373 3533/5157); Scottas, Knoydart, Invernes-shire PH41 4PL

CRAIGTON, Baron (Life Peer UK 1959); Jack Nixon Browne; CBE (1944), PC (1961); s of Edwin Gilbert Izod, of Rugby and Johannesburg, and Kathleen Roie, *née* Duke; assumed stepfather's surname Browne in lieu of patronymic 1920; *b* 3 Sept 1904; *Educ* Cheltenham Coll; *m* 1, 1936 (m dis 1949), Helen Anne, da of late G J Inglis, of Glasgow; 1 s (John Nixon, decd); m 2, 1950, Eileen Humphrey, da of Henry Whitford Nolan, of London; *Career* sits as (C) Peer in House of Lords; served WW II Actg Gp Capt RAF Balloon Cmd 1939-45; contested (C) Govan Glasgow 1945, MP (C) Govan 1950-55, MP Craigton Glasgow 1955-Sept 1959, PPS to sec of state for Scotland 1952-55, parly under-sec Scottish Office 1955-59, min of state 1959-64; chm All-Pty Conservation Group of Both Houses 1972-, United Biscuits (Hldgs) Ltd 1967-72; pres City of Westminster C of C 1966-83 (chm 1954); chm: Cncl for Environmental Conservation 1972-83, Fedn of Zoological Gardens 1975-81; vice pres World Wildlife Fund 1979 (memb cncl 1962-), chm Fauna and Flora Preservation Soc 1983 (memb cncl 1960-); memb cncl RSA 1975-80; *Recreations* gardening, small boats; *Clubs* Buck's; *Style*— The Rt Hon The Lord Craigton, CBE, PC; Friary House, Friary Island, Wraysbury, nr Staines, Middx (☎ 078 481 2213)

CRAIK, (Joseph) Ian; s of John Norman Craik (d 1961), late and Susan Beatrice Craik, *née* Bainbridge; *b* 21 April 1927; *Educ* Luton Modern Sch, Dept of Navigation - Southampton Univ; *m* 29 Dec 1953, Yvonne Barbara, Thomas Isaac Heeks, of Southampton; 2 s (Joseph Douglas b 1957, Norman Andrew b 1961); *Career* deck offr (late capt) Shell Tankers 1945-56, joined Gulf Oil 1957 and appointed tport mangr for Fare East 1962 (Tokyo), marine co-orindator (Pittsburgh Head Office) 1967; chm and md Stewart and Craik Technology Co (Scots) 1984-86; master mariner; MRIN; *Recreations* yachting (cruising); *Clubs* Tollesbury Cruising; *Style*— Master Mariner Ian Craik; "Marlside", Boreland, Lockerbie, Dumfries DG11 2LU (☎ 054 16 298); operate from home consultancy in Marine Oil Business

CRAIK, Maj Robert Rainey; OBE, (TD, JP, DL (Lancs 1983)); s of G B Craik of Tannadice, Angus; *b* 25 Mar 1925; *Educ* Forfar Acad; *m* 1957, Sybil M Carr; 1 s, 1 da; *Career* land surveyor and co dir, chm NW of England TAVRA 1987; *Recreations* shooting, skiing; *Clubs* Army and Navy; *Style*— Maj Robert Craik, OBE, TD, JP, DL; The Old Rectory, Mawdesley, Ormskirk, Lancs L40 3TD (☎ 0704 822787)

CRAINER, George Scott; s of George William Crainer; *b* 29 April 1936; *Educ* Greenock HS; *m* 1959, Isobel, da of David Webster (d 1967); 2 children; *Career* CA; md Bury and Masco (Hldgs) Ltd 1975-79, dir and div chief exec Scapa Gp plc 1978-87, chm Seamark Systems Ltd and major shareholder 1987-; FCMA; *Recreations* golf, music; *Style*— George Crainer Esq; 6 Johnsburn Park, Balerno, Midlothian EH14 7NA

CRAM, Lady Jeanne Louise; *née* Campbell; only da of 11 Duke of Argyll, TD (d 1973), by his 1 w, Hon Janet Aitken (now Hon Mrs Kidd, *qv*), only da of 1 Baron Beaverbrook; *b* 10 Dec 1928; *m* 1, 1962 (m dis 1963), as his 3 wife, Norman Mailer, the writer, s of Isaac Barnett Mailer; 1 da; m 2, March 1964, John Sergeant Cram, s of Henry Sergeant Cram, of Bluffton, S Carolina, USA; 1 da; *Style*— Lady Jeanne Cram; Foot Point Plantation, Bluffton, S Carolina, USA

CRAM, Stephen; MBE (1986); s of William Frank Cram, and Maria Helene, *née* Korte; *b* 14 Oct 1960; *Educ* Jarrow GS, Newcastle Poly (BA); *m* 17 Dec 1983, Karen Ann, da of John Andrew Waters; *Career* middle-distance runner; Cwlth Games: Gold Medallist 1500m 1982, Gold Medallist 800m and 1500m 1986; World Champs Gold Medallist 1500m 1983; Euro Champs Gold Medallist 1500m 1982, Gold Medallist 1500m and Bronze Medallist 800m 1986; Olympic Games Silver Medallist 1984, Br Olympic Squad 1988; world record holder the mile, (formerly 1500 m and 2000,) fndr Sunderland AFC Supporters Assoc; Hon Fell Sunderland Poly; *Recreations* golf, snooker; *Clubs* Jarrow and Hebburn AC, Sunderland AFC; *Style*— Stephen Cram, Esq, MBE; c/o John Hockey Associates, 106-110 Brompton Rd, London SW3 1JJ (☎ 01 581 5522)

CRAMER, Hon Sir John Oscar; s of J N Cramer, of Quirindi, NSW; *b* 18 Feb 1897; *Educ* State Public Schs; *m* 1921, Dame Mary Cramer, DBE, da of William M Earls; 2 s, 2 da; *Career* md Higgins (Bldgs) Ltd, former Mayor of N Sydney, sr ptnr Cramer Bros Real Estate Auctioneers, MHR (Lib) Bennelong NSW 1949-74, QRV, FREI; kt 1964; *see Debrett's Handbook of Australia and New Zealand for further details*; *Style*— The Hon Sir John Cramer; Unit 7, 47a Shirley Rd, Wollstonecraft, NSW 2065, Australia

CRAMOND, Ronald Duncan; CBE (1987); s of Adam Cramond, of Edinburgh (d 1974), and Margaret Weir, *née* McAulay (d 1978); late wife, Connie MacGregor direct descendant of John MacGregor, personal attendant and piper to Prince Charles Edward Stuart; *b* 22 Mar 1927; *Educ* George Heriot's Sch, Edinburgh Univ (MA); *m* 18 March 1954, Constance Margaret (d 1985), da of John MacGregor, of Auchterarder (d 1964); 1 s (Kenneth b 1959), 1 da (Fiona b 1957); *Career* Royal Scots, Europe 1949-51; private sec to Parly Under Sec Scottish Office 1956-7; post-grad fellow applied economics Glasgow Univ 1963; Haldane Medallist Royal Inst of Pub Admin 1964; under-sec Scottish Office 1971-83; dep chm Highlands and Islands Development Bd 1983-; memb Scottish Tourist Bd 1985-88, cmmr Countryside Comm for Scotland 1988-, tstee Royal Museum of Scotland 1985-; FBIM; FSA(S) cncl memb; *Books* Housing Policy in Scotland; *Recreations* golf, hill walking; *Clubs* Highland (Inverness), Scottish Arts (Edinburgh); *Style*— Ronald D Cramond, Esq, CBE; Countryside

Commision for Scotland, Battleby, Redgorton, Perth

CRAMP, Prof Rosemary Jean; CBE; da of Robert Raymond Kingston Cramp, of Conduit House, Hallaton, Leics, and Vera Grace, *née* Ractliffe (d 1965); *b* 6 May 1929; *Educ* Market Harborough GS, St Anne's Coll Oxford (MA, B Litt); *Career* lectr St Anne's Coll Oxford 1950-55; Univ of Durham: lectr 1955-60, sr lectr 1966-71, 1971-; prof archaeological advsr Durham Cathedral, tstee Br Museum, vice pres Cncl Br Achaeology, former pres Cumberland and Westmorland Antiquarian and Archaeological Soc, memb Redundant Churches Advsy Bd FSA; *Books* Corpus of Anglo Saxon Stone Sculpture (vol 1, 1984, vol 2 with RN Bailey, 1988); *Recreations* cooking, walking, reading; *Clubs* United Oxford & Cambridge Univ; *Style—* Prof Rosemary Cramp, CBE; Department of Archaeology, Durham University, (☎ 091 874 3620)

CRAMPTON, (Arthur Edward) Seán; MC (1943), GM (1944, TD 1946); eldest s of Joshua Crampton (d 1979), and Ethel Mary, *née* Dyas (d 1979); *b* 15 Mar 1918; *Educ* St Joseph DeCluny Prep Sch, Vittoria Junior Sch of Art, Birmingham Central Coll of Art; *m* 1959, Patricia Elizabeth Cardew, eldest da of Col Leslie John Cardew Wood; 1 s (Daniel), 4 da (Bridget, Katinka, Nicolette, Harriet); *Career* WW II; Capt London Irish Rifles: Western Desert, Sicily (MC), Italy (GM), wounded; sculptor FRBS (pres 1965-70); memb Art Workers Guild (master 1979); chair of Govrs Camberwell Sch of Art 1983-; govr London Inst 1986-; innumerable works throughout UK and USA; *Books* Humans, Beasts, Birds; *Clubs* Athenaeum, Chelsea Arts; *Style—* Seán Crampton Esq, MC, GM, TD; Rookery Farmhouse, Calne, Wilts SN11 0LH (☎ 0249 814068)

CRAMSIE, Lt-Col Alexander James; DL; s of Col Alexander James Henry Cramsie, OBE, DL, JP (d 1987), of O'Harabrook, Ballymoney, Co Antrim, NI, and Gabrielle Patricia, *née* Hornby; *b* 31 May 1941; *Educ* Wellington, RMA Sandhurst; *m* 11 Sept 1965, Bridget, da of Lt-Col Walter Derek Hamilton Duke, MC (Gordon Highlanders), of Langord Cottage, Fivehead, Somerset; 2 s (Rupert b 1966, Alexander b 1969); *Career* Lt Col (ret) Queen's Royal Irish Hussars 1961-81, cmd Queen's Own Yeomanry 1981-84, served Aden, Malaya, Borneo and NI; steward INHS ctee, regnl organiser Army Benevolent Fnd NI; won Grand Mil Gold Cup 1976 and 1983; landowner; *Recreations* hunting, racing, shooting, tennis; *Style—* Lt-Col Alexander Cramsie, Esq, DL; O'Harabrook, Ballynoney, Co Antrim, N Ireland (☎ 02656 66273)

CRAMSIE, Marcus James Lendrum; s of Arthur Vacquerie Cramsie, of Co Fermanagh, N I, and Susan Doreen, *née* Lendrum; *b* 24 April 1950; *Educ* Charterhouse, Trinity Hall Cambridge (BA); *m* 19 March 1983, Carol Lesley; 2 da (Camilla b 1984, Louise b 1986); *Career* Price Waterhouse 1972-76, Kleinwort Benson Ltd 1976-86 (dir 1986-); FCA; *Recreations* golf, shooting, tennis; *Style—* Marcus Cramsie, Esq; 20 Lyford Rd, London SW18; Kleinwort Benson Ltd 20 Fenchurch St, London EC3 (☎ 01 623 8000)

CRAN, James Douglas; MP (Cons) (Beverley 1987-); s of James Cran, of Aberdeen, and Jane McDonald Cran (d 1986); *b* 28 Jan 1944; *Educ* Ruthrieston Sch Aberdeen, Aberdeen Coll of Commerce, Kings Coll Univ of Aberdeen (MA); *m* 1973, Penelope Barbara, da of Richard Thomas Parker Wilson, of Bristol; 1 da (Alexandra Penelope b 1981); *Career* researcher (C) Research Dept 1970-71; sec and chief exec Nat Assoc of Pension Funds 1971-79; Northern dir CBI 1979-84, W Midlands dir CBI 1984-87, memb House of Commons Select ctee on Trade and Indust 1987-; *Recreations* travelling, reading biographies and autobiographies; *Style—* James Cran, MP; House of Commons, London SW1A 0AA (☎ 01 219 4445)

CRAN, Mark Dyson Gordon; QC (1988); s of Gordon Cran (d 1972), and Diana, *née* Mallinson; *b* 18 May 1948; *Educ* Gordonstoun, Millfield, Bristol Univ (LLB); *m* 29 July 1983 (m dis 1986), Prudence Elizabeth, *née* Hayles; *Career* barr Grays Inn 1973, practices NE circuit; *Recreations* country sports, convivial disputation, English language, theatre; *Style—* Mark Cran, Esq, QC; 1 Brick Court, Temple, London EC4Y 9BY (☎ 01 583 0777, fax 01 583 9401, telex 892687 IBRICK G)

CRANBORNE, Viscount; Robert Michael James (Gascoyne) Cecil; DL (Dorset 1988), MP (C) Dorset S 1979-; s and h of 6 Marquess of Salisbury; *b* 30 Sept 1946; *Educ* Eton, Oxford; *m* 1970, Hannah Ann, da of Lt-Col William Joseph Stirling of Keir, gs of Sir William Stirling-Maxwell, 9 Bt, (a Baronetcy dormant since 1956); 2 s (Hon Robert b 1970, Hon James Richard b 1973), 3 da (Hon Elizabeth Ann b 1972, Hon Georgiana b 1977, Hon Katherine b (twin) 1977); *Career* chm Afghanistan Support Ctee; PPS to Cranley Onslow as Min State FCO April-May 1982 when resigned to be free to criticise Govt's Ulster devolution plans; fndr memb Blue Chip Tory dining club; *Style—* Viscount Cranborne, DL, MP; The Lodge House, Hatfield Park, Herts; Tregonwell Lodge, Cranbourne, Wimborne, Dorset

CRANBROOK, Dowager Countess of; Fidelity; OBE; o da of Hugh Exton Seebohm, JP (d 1946), of Poynder's End, Hitchin, and his 1 wife Leslie, *née* Gribble (d 1913); sister of Baron Seebohm (Life Peer); *b* 1912; *m* 26 July 1932, as his 2 w, 4 Earl of Cranbrook, CBE (d 1978); 2 s, 3 da; *Career* JP; *Style—* The Rt Hon The Dowager Countess of; Red House Farm, Great Glemham, Saxmundham, Suffolk

CRANBROOK, 5 Earl of (UK 1892); Gathorne Gathorne-Hardy; also Viscount Cranbrook (UK 1878), Baron Medway (UK 1892); s of 4 Earl, CBE (d 1978) by his 2 w, Dowager Countess Cranbrook, OBE, JP, *qv*; *b* 20 June 1933; *Educ* Eton, Corpus Christi Coll Cambridge (MA), Univ of Birmingham (PhD); *m* 9 May 1967, Caroline, o da of Col Ralph George Edward Jarvis, of Doddington Hall, Lincoln, by his w Antonia Meade (*see* Peerage Earl of Clanwilliam); 2 s (J Jason Lord Medway b 1968, Hon Argus Edward b 1973), 1 da (Lady Flora b 1971); *Career* sr lectr zoology Univ of Malaya 1961-70, ed Ibis 1973-80; chm sub-ctee 'F' (Environment) Select Ctee on Euro Communities House of Lords; memb: Royal Cmmn on Environmental Pollution 1981-, Natural Environment Res Cncl 1982-88; pt time bd memb Anglian Water Authy 1987-; Skinner and Freeman of City of London; FLS, FZS, FRGS; OStJ, DL; *Books* Mammals of Malasia, Mammals of Borneo, Mammals of South East Asia; *Style—* The Rt Hon The Earl of Cranbrook; c/o National Westminster Bank, St James's Sq, London SW1 4JX

CRANCH, (Arthur) Graeme; s of Arthur Lakeman Cranch (d 1942), of 119 Cambridge Rd, Wimbledon, and Jessie Cowie, *née* Murdoch (d 1952); *b* 10 Aug 1910; *Educ* King's Coll Sch; *m* 10 Aug 1940, Molly Pernelle, da of Alfred Heath Pryce; 2 da (Carol b 1942, Alison b 1947); *Career* TA 1938; Cmmnd RA 1940, Capt 1942, Adj 1942, served Air Def of GB; mgmnt trainee (later maktg exec) Rowntree & Co York 1929, res exec London Pres Exchange Ltd 1936; Mather & Crowther Ltd (later Ogilvy & Mather Ltd): res dir 1946, appointed to bd and dir of subsid cos 1954; fndr and past pres Market Res Soc, past chm Int Mktg Fedn, ctee Chm Int C of C Paris, cncl memb Incorporated Practitioners in Advtg, mktg conslt UN/FAO Rome; govr King's Coll Sch; Liverman Worshipful Co of Carmen 1956; FIPA; *Books* The First 150 Years (history of King's Coll Sch, jtly), One Hundred Years Not Out (history of Old King's Club); *Recreations* antiques, watching cricket, gardening, foreign travel; *Clubs* East India, MCC; *Style—* Graeme Cranch, Esq; Summerlea, Beverley Lane, Kingston upon Thames, Surrey KT2 7EE (☎ 01 942 5250)

CRANE, Edwin Arthur; s of Charles Edmund Crane (d 1966), of Thrope House, Moira Rd, Ashby-de-la-Zouch Leics, and Lilian Elizabeth Crane, *née* Bartlett (d 1956); *b* 11 June 1918; *Educ* Repton Sch, Clare Coll Cambridge (BA); *m* 1 Sept 1943, Joan Ellen, da of Harold Langrish Esq (d 1969), of 76 Chichester Rd, Bognor Regis, Sussex; 2 s (David b 1950, John b 1953), 2 da (Mary b 1944, Frances b 1947); *Career* Major Royal Army Service Corps:UK and W Europe 1941-46; slr sr ptnr Crane and Walton Asby-de-la-Zouch Coalville and Leicester; pres Leicester Law Soc 1972, chm Breedon plc 1987, memb Leics CC 1977-85; dir Breedon plc 1970-; tstee: Leicester Tstee Savings Bank 1957-74, Tstee Savings Bank of Leicester and Nottingham 1978-80; dir and vice chm Coalville Permanent Building Soc 1957-76; *Recreations* local history, walking; *Style—* E A Crane, Esq; 11 Church Street, Swepstone, Leics LE6 1SA (☎ 0530 70639); South St, Ashby-de-la-Zouch, Leics Le6 5BT (☎ 0530 414111)

CRANE, Geoffrey David; s of Frederick David Crane (d 1982), and Marion Doris, *née* Gorman (d 1973); *b* 13 Oct 1934; *Educ* City of London Sch, Trinity Hall Cambridge (MA); *m* 1962, Gillian Margaret, da of Harry Thomas Austin (d 1979); 1 da (Jessica b 1968); *Career* RAF Flying Offr 1956-58; asst private sec to Min of Works 1961-62; sec: Historic Bldgs Cncl for Scotland, Ancient Monuments Bd for Scotland 1962-66; private sec to Min of Public Bldg and Works 1968-69, head of machinery of govt div CS Dept 1970-72, dep dir central unit on environment pollution DOE 1972-75, dir of res ops DOE and Tport 1978-80, of personnel mgmnt and trg DOE and Tport 1981-85, regl dir Eastern region DOE and Tport 1985-89, head freight directorate Dept of Tport 1989-; *Recreations* classical music, industrial archaeology, mathematics; *Clubs* RAF, Civil Service; *Style—* Geoffrey Crane Esq; 2 Marsham St, London SW1P 3EB (☎ 01 276 4919)

CRANE, Sir James William Donald; CBE (1977); s of William James and Ivy Winifred Crane; *b* 1 Jan 1921; *m* 1942, Patricia Elizabeth Hodge; 1 s, 1 da; *Career* joined Metropolitan Police 1946, chief inspector of Constabulary 1979-82 (formerly inspector); memb Parole Bd 1983-; kt 1980; *Style—* Sir James Crane, CBE; Home Office, 50 Queen Anne's Gate, London SW1

CRANE, John Lawrence Beale; s of late Walter Fred Crane; *b* 15 April 1921; *Educ* Bedford Sch, St Catharine's Coll Cambridge (MA); *m* 1960, Dorothy Jean, *née* Wiseman; 1 step da; *Career* chartered mechanical engr; dir Crane Fruehauf Ltd 1960-82; pres Commercial Trailer Assoc 1980-82, ret; *Style—* John Crane, Esq; Meadowcroft, Washbridge, Dereham, Norfolk (☎ 0362 697413)

CRANE, His Hon Judge; Peter Francis; s of Francis Roger Crane, of Northants, and Jean Berenice, *née* Hadfield (d 1987); *b* 14 Jan 1987; *Educ* Nottingham HS, Highgate Sch, Gonville and Caius Coll Cambridge (MA, LLM), Tulane Univ USA (LLM); *m* 1967, Elizabeth Mary, da of Noel Bawtry Pittman, of Northants; 4 da (Anna b 1968, Catherine b 1969, Rebecca b 1972, Lucy b 1974); *Career* barr MO circuit 1964-87, rec 1982-87; memb: Senate of the Inns of Court and the Bar 1983-86, Professional Conduct Ctee 1984-86, Bar Ctee 1985-86; circuit Judge 1987-; *Recreations* reading, walking, gardening, wine; *Clubs* Northampton and County; *Style—* His Hon Judge Crane; The Glebe House, Pytchley, Kettering, Northants NN14 1EW

CRANE, Robert Coutts; s of William Crane (d 1980), of Stirlingshire, and Mary Shearer, *née* Coutts; *b* 16 May 1935; *Educ* Denny HS, Inst of Chartered Accountants of Scotland (1957); *m* 1960, Anna Katerine, da of Capt John Arthur Jephson-Jones (d 1964), of Fife; 1 s (John b 1961), 1 da (Sheenagh b 1963); *Career* RN Sub Lt 1958-59, Capt UDR 1971-73; dep accountant BP Refinery Grangemouth 1960-63, (ch accountant, dep gen mangr 1963-67), md Belfast Telegraph Newspapers Ltd 1979-(accountant 1967, dep production mangr 1969, production mangr 1971, gen mangr Weekly Newspapers 1971, asst md 1976); *Recreations* trout fishing, photography; *Style—* Robert Crane, Esq; Logwood Mill, Logwood Road, Ballyclare, Co Antrim BT39 9LR; Belfast Telegraph Newapapers Ltd, Royal Avenue, Belfast BT1 1EB (☎ 0232 221242, fax 0232-)

CRANE, (Thomas Peter) Robin; s of Thomas Taversham Crane (d 1987), and Lilian Crane; *b* 8 Nov 1931; *Educ* Christ's Hosp; *m* 15 Aug 1955, Wendy Elisabeth, da of Lt-Col Frederick Skipwith (d 1960); 2 da (Jenni b 1958, Caroline b 1969); *Career* reg cmmn RASC 1950-57; resign as Capt; maltster; Arthur Guinness & Co 1957-59, Sandars & Co 1959-67; film dir and prodr World About Us BBC (Majorca observed, The Other Iceland, Rabbits - Wanted Dead of Alive?, Butterflies); Br Sponsored Film Festivals Gold Awards for: Event Horse 1975, The Colourmen 1984, Heritage of the Forest 1984; New York Film & TV Festival Silver Award for Mirror to the Fun 1984; chm Sussex Wildlife Tst (memb cncl 1969-); FRES 1979; *Recreations* nature conservation, music, golf; *Clubs* British Acad of Film and TV Arts; *Style—* Robin Crane, Esq; The Mead, Carron Lane, Midhurst, West Sussex GU29 9LD

CRANFIELD, Richard William Lionel; s of Lionel Sydney William Cranfield (d 1965), of Tewin, Herts, and Audrey Cecil Martin, *née* Pank; *b* 19 Jan 1956; *Educ* Winchester, Fitzwilliam Coll Cambridge (MA); *m* 26 Sept 1981, Gillian Isabel, da of Archibald Spence Fleming (d 1979), of Graden, Kelso, Roxburghshire; 1 s (Edward), 1 da (Sophie); *Career* Lt HAC 1979-86; slr; ptnr Allen & Overy; Freeman City of London 1985, Merchant Taylors; memb Law Soc; *Recreations* golf, field sports; *Style—* Richard Cranfield, Esq; Water House Farm, Layham Hadleigh, Suffolk IP7 5RA (☎ 0473 827 596); 9 Cheapside, London EC2V 6AD (☎ 01 248 9898, fax 01 236 2192)

CRANLEY, Viscount; Rupert Charles William Bullard Onslow; s and h of 7 Earl of Onslow; *b* 16 June 1967; *Educ* Eton; *Recreations* country sports; *Style—* Viscount Cranley; Temple Court, Clandon Park, Guildford, Surrey

CRANMER, Dr Philip; s of Arthur Henry Cranmer (d 1954), and Lilian Phillips (d 1972); *b* 1 April 1918; *Educ* Wellington Coll, Christ Church Oxford (MA); *m* 1939, Ruth, da of Ven H C Loasby; 1 s (Damian), 3 da (Gabrielle, Philippa, Eleanor); *Career* musician; Hamilton Harty prof of music Queens Univ Belfast 1954-70, prof of music Manchester Univ 1970-74; sec the Assoc Bd of the Royal Schs of Music 1974-83, pres The Incorp Soc of Musicians 1970, chm The Musicians Benevolent Fund 1980-87; hon tres The Royal Coll of Organists 1985-87; FRCO, FRCM, FRNCM, hon RAM; Chev of the Order of Leopold II Belgian Croix de Guerre 1946, Hon DMus Belfast 1985; *Style—* Dr Philip Cranmer; Quince Cottage, Underhill Lane, Clayton, Hassocks, W

Sussex BN6 9PJ (☎ 07918 3155)

CRANMER-BYNG, John Launcelot; MC (1944); s of Capt Launcelot Alfred Cranmer-Byng (d 1945), and his 2 wife Daisy Elaine, *née* Beach (d 1981); hp of kinsman, 11 Viscount Torrington; *b* 18 Mar 1919; *Educ* Haileybury, King's Coll Cambridge (MA 1944); *m* 19 Jan 1955, Margaret Ellen, o da of Reginald Herbert Hardy, of Sevenoaks, Kent; 1 s, 2 da; *Career* served 1939-45 war as Maj Airborne Forces; lectr in history Hong Kong Univ 1956-64, prof of history Univ of Toronto 1964-84; *Recreations* ornithology; *Style—* John Cranmer-Byng, Esq, MC; 27 Idleswift Drive, Thornhill, Ontario, Canada

CRANSTON, Prof Maurice William; s of William Cranston, (d 1944), of Edinburgh, and Catherine, *née* Harris (d 1932); *b* 8 May 1920; *Educ* St Catherine's Coll Oxford (MA, BLitt); *m* 11 Nov 1958, Baroness Maximiliana, da of Baron Theodor von und zu Fraunberg (d 1948), of Florence, Italy; 2 s (Nicholas b 1960, Stephen b 1962); *Career* Civil Def London 1939-45; Univ of London: social philosophy 1950-59, lectr in political sci 1959-64 (reader 1964-69), prof of political sci LSE 1969-85; literary advsr Methuen & Co 1959-69; visiting prof: Harvard Univ 1965-66, Dartmouth Coll USA 1970-71, Univ of Br Columbia 1973, Ecole des Hautes Etudes Paris 1977, Fndn Thiers Paris 1982, Univ of California at San Diego 1986-89; vice pres Alliance Francaise en Angleterre 1964-, registrar Royal Literary Fund 1973-79, pres Institut Internationale de Philosophie Politique 1978-81; FRSL 1958; Commandeur de l'Ordre des Palmes Academiques France 1987; *Books* Freedom (1953), John Locke (1957), Sartre (1964), What are Human Rights (1963), Political Dialogues (1968), Language and Philosophy (1969), The Mask of Politics (1973), Jean-Jacques; The Early Life of J J Rousseau (1983), Philosophers and Pamphleteers (1984); *Recreations* walking; *Clubs* Garrick; *Style—* Prof Maurice Cranston; 1A Kent Terr, Regents Park, London NW1 4RP (☎ 01 262 2698); London School of Economics, London WC2A 2AE (☎ 01 405 7686, fax 01 242 0392)

CRANWORTH, 3 Baron (UK 1899); Philip Bertram Gurdon; s of Hon Robin Gurdon (ka 1942, s of late 2 Baron, KG, MC who d 1964), and late Hon Yoskyl Pearson, da of 2 Viscount Cowdray (who m 2, Lt-Col Alistair Gibb, and m 3, 1 Baron McCorquodale of Newton, KCVO, PC); *b* 24 May 1940; *Educ* Eton, Magdalene Coll Cambridge; *m* 18 Jan 1968, Frances Henrietta, da of late Lord William Walter Montagu Douglas Scott, MC (s of 7 Duke of Buccleuch), and Lady Rachel Douglas-Home (da of 13 Earl of Home); 2 s (Hon Sacha William Robin b 1970, Hon Brampton Charles b 1975) 1 da (Hon Louisa-Jane b 1969); *Career* late Lt Royal Wilts Yeo; *Style—* The Rt Hon The Lord Cranworth; Grundisburgh Hall, Woodbridge, Suffolk

CRAPP, Leslie Rufus; s of Edward Crapp of Jersey, and Lilian Annie, *née* Horn; *b* 20 May 1935; *Educ* Victoria Coll Jersey; *m* 16 Aug 1962, Annette Desirée, da of Albert Charles Le Cuirot (d 1976); 2 s (Nicholas b 1963, Jonathan b 1973), 1 da (Vanessa b 1967); *Career* CA; sr ptnr Coopers and Lybrand, Channel Islands; hon chm Jersey Family Nursing Servs; hon tres Jersey Branch Save the Children; *Recreations* gardening, walking, French cuisine art and antique collecting; *Style—* Leslie R Crapp, Esq; La Botellerie, Rue de la Botellerie, St Ouens, Jersey (☎ 0534 83855); La Motte Chambers, St Helier, Jersey (☎ 0534 76777)

CRATES, (Cecil) Ralph (Stuart); s of Cecil James Gildroy Crates, of Kingswood, nr Bristol, and Hilda Clara Diana, *née* Randall (d 1958); *b* 4 Sept 1927; *Educ* Cannings Coll Bristol, Kingswood GS, W of Eng Coll of Art Loughborough; *m* 26 July 1952, Rosemary Maud, da of George Killingback Sprugeon Edgley, of Bristol; *Career* teacher of handcrafts and music Filton and Wellington Schs 1947-57, apptd by Colonial Off as educn offr, posted to N region Nigeria 1957-87, served in craft schs Mashi and Idah; princ of Teacher Trg Colls: Mubi, Gombe, Toro, Borno; state planning offr and dir of educn Min of Educn Govt of Borno State, currently ind conslt in technical, design, communication and further educn; *Style—* Ralph Crates, Esq; 35 Buckwell, Wellington, Somerset (☎ 082 347 2770)

CRATHORNE, 2 Baron (UK 1959); Sir Charles James Dugdale; 2 Bt (UK 1945), DL (Cleveland 1983); s of 1 Baron, TD, PC (d 1977), and Nancy, OBE (d 1969), da of Sir Charles Tennant, 1 Bt; *b* 12 Sept 1939; *Educ* Eton, Trinity Coll Cambridge; *m* 1970, Sylvia Mary, da of Brig Arthur Montgomery, OBE, TD; 1 s Hon Thomas Arthur John Dugdale b 1977), 2 da (Hon Charlotte b 1972, Hon Katharine b 1980); *Career* with Sotheby and Co 1963-66, asst to pres Parke-Bernet NY 1966-69, James Dugdale and Assocs London (Ind Fine Art Consultancy Service) 1969-; fine art lectr; dir Cliveden Hotel, Woodhouse Securities Ltd 1989; tstee Captain Cook Tst; memb exec ctee of the Georgian Gp 1985, Ct of the Univ of Leeds 1985, Yarm Civic Soc 1987; ctee Pevsner Meml Tst (1986), Works of Art sub ctee Westminster 1983; ed bd House Magazine 1983, Cons advsy gp on the Arts and Heritage 1988-, Yorks regnl ctee Nat Tst 1974-84 and 1988-; vice chm All Pty Photography Gp 1988, hon sec: All Party Parliamentary Arts and Heritage Gp (1981), pres Cleveland Family History Soc 1988, Cleveland Sea Cadets 1988, Hambledon Dist CPRE 1988, Cleveland Assoc of Nat Tst 1982; govr Queen Margarets Sch York 1986-; FRSA (memb cncl RSA 1983); *Books* co author 'Tennants Stalk' (1973); 'Edouard Vuillard' (1967); contribs Appollo and The Connoisseur; *Recreations* photography, travel, shooting, fishing; *Style—* The Rt Hon the Lord Crathorne, DL; 52 Lower Sloane Street, London SW1W 8BS (☎ 01 730 9131); Crathorne House, Yarm, Cleveland TS15 0AT (☎ (0642) 700431)

CRAUFORD, Peter Lane; s of William Harold Lane Crauford (d 1954), and Phyllis Maud Crauford; *b* 3 June 1917; *Educ* Highgate Sch, Peterhouse Cambridge (MA, LLM); *m* 14 Aug 1954, Aileen Veronica, da of Thomas McCabe (d 1983); 2 da (Patricia Lane b 1956, Nicola Lane b 1957); *Career* Maj Royal Signals 1939-46, served: M East, Ceylon, India, Burma; slr 1948-, sr ptnr Chambers, Rutland & Crauford; *Recreations* golf, theatre, gardening; *Clubs* MCC, Hawks (Cambridge); *Style—* Peter L Crauford, Esq; Greenfields, Waggon Rd, Hadley Wood, Herts; 351 Regents Park Rd, London N3 1DJ (☎ 01 346 8333)

CRAUFURD; *see*: Houison Craufurd

CRAUFURD, Sir Robert James; 9 Bt (GB 1781), of Kilbirney, N Britain; s of Sir James Craufurd, 8 Bt (d 1970); *b* 18 Mar 1937; *Educ* Harrow, Univ Coll Oxford (MA); *m* 1 1964, (m dis 1987) Catherine Penelope, yr da of late Capt Horatio Westmacott, RN, of Torquay, Devon; 3 da (Caroline b 1965, Penelope b 1967, Veronica b 1969); 2 Georgina Anne, da of late John Russell of Lymington Hants; *Career* memb London Stock Exchange 1969; *Style—* Sir Robert Craufurd, Bt; 7 Waldemar Avenue, London SW6 5LB

CRAUFURD, Ruth, Lady; Ruth Marjorie; da of Frederic Corder, linendraper, of Ipswich; *b* 9 Oct 1899; *Educ* Ipswich Girls' HS, Girton Coll Cambridge (BA); *m* 11 April 1931, Sir James Gregan Craufurd, 8 Bt (d 1970); 1 s, 2 da; *Career* formerly private sec to: Charles Williams, MP for Torquay, Dartmouth and Paignton, Maj-Gen Sir Reginald Hoskins, CB, CMG, DSO; tstee of Aldbury Memorial Almshouses; *Recreations* writing poems, operettas and stories, some of which have been published; *Clubs* United Oxford and Cambridge; *Style—* Ruth, Lady Craufurd; Brightwood, Aldbury, Tring, Herts HP23 5SF (☎ 044 285 262)

CRAVEN, Gemma; da of Gabriel Bernard Craven of Leigh-on-Sea, Essex (formerly Dublin), and Lillian Elizabeth Josephine, *née* Byrne; *b* 1 June 1950; *Educ* Loretto Coll Dublin, St Bernard's Convent Westcliff-on-Sea, Bush Davies Sch; *m* 10 June 1988, David Beamish, s of Phillip Beamish of Grensby, Wirral; *Career* actress; stage debut Let's Get a Divorce Palace Theatre Westcliff 1968, West End debut Anya in Fiddler on the Roof 1970, Audrey! 1971, Trelawney 1972; Chichester Festival Theatre 1974: R Loves J, Dandy Dick, The Confederacy, A Month in the Country; The Bristol Old Vic: The Threpenny Opera 1975; West End performances incl: Songbook 1979, They're Playing Our Song 1980-81 (SWET award Best Actress in a Musical), Song and Dance 1982, Loot 1984 (City Limits' Best Comedy Actress); NT 1985-87: A Chorus of Disapproval, Jacobowsky and the Colonel,The Magistrate, Three Men on a Horse; Nellie Forbush in South Pacific 1988-89 Prince of Wales Theatre London; Films incl: The Slipper and the Rose 1976 (Variety Club's Film Actress of the Year), Why Not Stay For Breakfast?, Wagner: TV incl: Pennies from Heaven 1977, Emily, East Lynne, She Loves me; *Recreations* cooking; *Style—* Miss Gemma Craven; c/o Stella Richards Mgmnt, 42 Hazlebury Rd, London SW6 (☎ 01 736 7786)

CRAVEN, John Anthony; s of William Herbert Craven (d 1984), of London, and Hilda Lucy, *née* Magness (d 1982), of London; *b* 23 Oct 1940; *Educ* Michaelhouse Natal SA, Jesus Coll Cambridge (BA), Inst of CA's of Ontario and Canada (CA); *m* 1, 1961 (m dis 1969), Gillian Margaret, *née* Murray; 1 s (Richard b 1963), 1 da (Nicola b 1963); m 2, 22 Nov 1970, Jane Frances, da of Richard Alfred Styles-Allen; 3 s (James b 1972, Benjamin b 1973, Thomas b 1984); *Career* dir SG Warburg and Co Ltd 1969-73, chief exec Credit Suisue First Boston Ltd (formerly White Weld and Co Ltd 1973-78, vice chm SG Warburg and Co Ltd 1979, fndr chm Phoenix Securities Ltd 1980-, chm Tootal Gp plc 1985-, chief exec Morgan Grenfell gp plc 1987-; FInst CA of Ontario and Canada; *Recreations* hunting, skiing, shooting, marathon running; *Clubs* Links (New York), City of London; *Style—* John Craven, Esq

CRAVEN, Lady; Marjorie Kathleen Wallis; da of late Alfred Henry Hopkins; *m* 1945, as his 2 w, Sir Derek Worthington Clunes Craven, 2 Bt (d 1946, when title became extinct); *Style—* Lady Craven; Aberfeldie, Peckon's Hill, Ludwell, Shaftesbury, Dorset

CRAVEN, Air Marshal Sir Robert Edward; KBE (1970, OBE 1954), CB (1966), DFC (1940); s of Gerald Craven of Port Elizabeth, SA, and Edith Craven; *b* 16 Jan 1916; *Educ* Scarborough Coll; *m* 1940, Joan, da of Capt E S Peters; 1 s, 1 da; *Career* joined RAF 1937, Air Vice-Marshal 1965, SASO Flying Training Cmd 1967, SASO Training Cmd 1968-69, Cdr Maritime Air Forces (AOC 18 Gp) 1969-72, Air Marshal 1970, ret 1972; Order of Menelik (Ethiopia) 1955; *Clubs* RAF; *Style—* Air Marshal Sir Robert Craven, KBE, CB, DFC; Letcombe House, Letcombe Regis, Oxon

CRAVEN, Rupert José Evelyn; s of Maj Hon Rupert Cecil Craven, OBE (d 1959, 2 s of 3 Earl of Craven) by 2 w, Josephine Marguerite (d 1971), da of José Reixach; hp of kinsman, 8 Earl of Craven; *b* 22 Mar 1926; *m* 22 Oct 1955, Margaret Campbell (d 1985), da of Alexander Smith, MBE, of Glasgow and Alness; *Career* Lt Cdr RN; *Style—* Rupert Craven, Esq; Swordly, Bettyhill, by Thurso, Caithness

CRAVEN, 8 Earl of (GB 1801); Simon George Craven; also Baron Craven (E 1665), Viscount Uffington (GB 1801); s (by 2 m) of late 6 Earl of Craven; suc bro, 7 Earl, who d 1983; *b* 16 Sept 1961; *Heir* kinsman, Rupert José Evelyn Craven, *qv*; *Style—* The Rt Hon the Earl of Craven; Peelings Manor, nr Pevensey, E Sussex

CRAVEN-SMITH-MILNES, Richard Assheton; s of Ralph Assheton Craven-Smith-Milnes, and Elizabeth Josephine Anne, *née* Topham; *b* 27 July 1935; *Educ* Eton, Trinity Coll Cambridge (MA); *m* 25 May 1963, Jane Alexandra, da of The Hon Alexander Valentine Rutherford Abbott (d 1978), of Perth, WA; 1 s (Charles b 1968), 2 da (Anna b 1964, Clare b 1967); *Career* Nat Serv 17-21 Lancers 2 Lt 1953-55, Sherwood Rangers Yeomanry 1955-64; Lloyds insur broker 1962-72, chm and md Red Griffin Ltd 1973-; *Clubs* White's; *Style—* Richard Craven-Smith-Milnes, Esq; Winkburn Hall, nr Newark, Notts; Middleham House, Middleham, Leyburn N Yorks (☎ 0636 86465)

CRAWFORD, Daniel Frank; s of Frank Lewis Crawford, and Edna, *née* Partington; *b* 11 Dec 1945; *m* 19 May 1985, Stephany, da of Lt Cdr, Howard Weiss USN (ret) Chicago, USA; 1 step da (Katey); *Career* fndr mangr and artistic dir King's Head Theatre; West End producer/co-producer: Kennedy's Children (Arts Theatre 1975), Spokesong (Vaudeville Theatre,1977), Fearless Frank (Princess Theatre Broadway, 1980), Mr Cinders (Fortune Theatre, 1983), Wonderful Town (Queen's Theatre, 1986), Easy Virtue (Garrick Theatre, 1988), Artist Descending a Staircase, (1988), panel memb Vivian Ellis Prize for New Musical Writing, memb Islington Theatre Assoc; *Recreations* survival courses; *Clubs* Savage, Grouchos; *Style—* Daniel Crawford, Esq; King's Head, 115 Upper St, Islington, London N1 (☎ 01 226 8561, 01 226 1916, 01 226 0364

CRAWFORD, Dennis Bryon; OBE (1984); s of Albert Edward Crawford (d 1964), of Hull, Yorks, and Lily, *née* Jubb (d 1968); *b* 8 Nov 1923; *Educ* Benmore Forest Sch, Hull Coll of Commerce; *m* 2 April 1955, Stella Fraser, da of William Thomson (d 1978), of Dumfries; 1 s (Mark b 1957), 1 da (Carol); *Career* Forestry Cmmn: 1945-54, Regional Tech Offr Co-op Forestry Soc 1954-57, Regional Man Scottish Woodland Owners Assoc 1957-67, md Scottish Woodland Owners Assoc Commercial Ltd 1967-83; chartered forestry conslt (part-time); chm Timber Growers UK Tech Ctee; memb: Gov Cncl, Forestry Cmmn S Scotland Regional Advsy Bd, Home Grown Timber Advsy Ctee Tech Ctee, HGTAC Supply and Demand Ctee, Forestry Cmmn Gt Spruce Bark Beetle Control Gp; FICFor, FArborA, FBIM, FRSA;; *Recreations* botany, photography, scottish pottery, music; *Clubs* Caledonian Edinburgh; *Style—* Dennis B Crawford, OBE; Craiglatch, Clovenfords, Border, Scotland (☎ 089 685624)

CRAWFORD, Eric Oliver; s of John Wilson Crawford of Dundee; *b* 18 May 1933; *Educ* Glasgow Acad; *m* 1963 (m dis 1978), Rosalind Jill, da of Reginald Herbert Diaper Ellwood; 3 da; *Career* CA; dir: Garthmore Investment Ltd 1970-, London and Lomond Investment Tst Ltd 1980-; chm Anglo-Scottish Investment Tst Ltd 1968-, Scan Data Int Ltd 1971-; *Clubs* City of London, Caledonian; *Style—* Eric Crawford, Esq; Sundial House, Maddox Lane, Bookham, Surrey

CRAWFORD, Prof Sir Frederick William; s of Wiliam Crawford (d 1955), and Victoria Maud, *née* Careless (d 1988); *b* 28 July 1931; *Educ* George Dixon GS Birmingham, London Univ (BSc, MSc, DSc), Liverpool Univ (PhD, DipEd, DEng); *m* 21 Oct 1963, Béatrice Madeleine Jacqueline, da of Roger Hutter, of Paris; 1 s (Eric b 1968), 1 da (Isabelle b 1965); *Career* scientist NCB mining res estab Middx 1956-57, sr lectr in electrical engrg Coll of Advanced Technol Birmingham 1958-59; Stanford Univ California 1959-82: prof of electrical engrg 1969-82, chm inst for plasma res 1973-80; vice-chllr Aston Univ 1980-; non-exec dir: Legal & Gen Gp 1988-, Bowater Industs 1989-; Freeman City of London 1986, Liveryman Worshipful Co of Engrs 1987; FEng 1985, FIEE 1965, FIEEE 1972, FInstP 1964, FAPS 1965, FIMA 1978, CBIM 1986, Kt 1986; *Clubs* Athenaeum; *Style—* Prof Sir Frederick Crawford; Aston House, 1 Arthur Rd, Edgbaston, Birmingham B15 2UW, (☎ 021 454 7545); Aston University, Aston Triangle, Birmingham B4 7ET, (☎ 021 359 3611, fax 021 359 7358, telex 336997 UNIAST G)

CRAWFORD, Maj-Gen George Oswald; CB (1956), CBE (1944); s of Arthur Gosset Crawford, of Nailsworth, Glos; *b* 1902; *Educ* Bradfield, RMC; *m* 1, Sophie Cecilia (d 1974), da of J C Yorke; 2 s, 1 da; m 2, 1974, Ella Brown of Shalford, Surrey; *Career* 2 Lt Glos Regt 1922, RAOC 1928, Maj-Gen 1955, ADC to HM the Queen 1954-55, Dir of Ordnance Services WO 1958-61; *Style—* Maj-Gen George Crawford, CB, CBE; Gwyers, Dinton, Wilts

CRAWFORD, Brig Henry Nevay; MBE (1941), JP (1965) DL (1960); s of Charles John Crawford (d 1940), of Wayside, St Andrews, Fife and Ella Francis Olive, *née* Anson (d 1954); 'Arms' (matriculated 1981) are quartered with those of Anson; *b* 23 May 1907; *Educ* Rugby Sch, RMA; *m* 29 Dec 1942, Philippa Marie, da of Col Hereward Sadler, OBE, DL (d 1947) assumed surname of Sprot by Deed Poll 1930, of St John's Wolsingham Co Durham; 2 s (James b 1946, Alexander b 1948), 1 da (Ann b 1944); *Career* RCS 1927, 4 Div Signals 1929-30; Adj 7 Mobile/Armd Div Signals Egypt 1939-40, CO 7 Armd Div Signals, A/Lt Col W Desert 1941-42, (despatch twice) CO T/Lt Col Gds Armd Div Signals UK 1943, A/Brig, posted as chief signal offr HQ 30 Corps for planning and subsequent ops N W Europe 1944; Br Army Staff Washington DC, chm Cwlth Jt Communications Ctee 1945-46, chief signal offr HQ London Dist T/Lt Col 1946-47 ret, Reg Army rank of Brig 1949 CO 2 Fife St Andrews Bn HG 1952-56, chm Fife T and AFA 1962-68; factor and mangr Naughton Estate Wormit Fife 1963-83; exec dir Tay Seafoods Ltd 1963-79; memb Fife CC 1955-64, chm Cupar local ctee Fife CC 1963-75; pres Fife Agric Assoc 1961; vice-chm Tay River Purification Bd 1970-75; chm E Fife sub-ctee Agric exec ctee 1970-72; dir Royal Highland and Agric Soc of Scotland 1960-66 (vice pres 1980); matriculated arms (Scotland) 5 Feb 1981; CStJ; CEng MIEE, FID 1977, C of St J; *Recreations* athletics, rugby, hockey, shooting, hunting, racing (ret); *Clubs* Naval and Mil, Royal and Ancient Golf; *Style—* Brigadier Henry Crawford, MBE, DL, JP; Nether Kirkton Farmhouse, Kirkton of Balmerino, Newport on Tay, Fife DD6 8SA (☎ 082 624733)

CRAWFORD, Brigadier Ian Campbell; CBE (1982); *b* 17 June 1932; *Educ* Dumfries Acad, Edinburgh Univ (MB, ChB); *m* 4 April 1959, Phyllis Mary; 1 s (Niall b 1967), 1 da (Fiona b 1960); *Career* conslt physician (Cardiology) Queen Elizabeth Mil Hosp Woolwich 1977-83 and 1985-; FRCPEd (1972), FRCP (1986); *Style—* Brig Ian C Crawford, CBE; The Arbour, Bobbing, Kent (☎ 0795 842292); Queen Elizabeth Mil Hosp, Woolwich SE18 (☎ 01 856 5533)

CRAWFORD, Major John Middleton; MC (1941); s of Maj-Gen John Scott Crawford, CB, CBE (d 1979), and Amy Middleton, *née* Andrews; *b* 26 Jan 1921; *Educ* Liverpool Coll, Royal Mil Coll; *m* 30 March 1946, Suzanne Euphrosine, da of Cyril banner (d 1964); *Career* enlisted Inns of Ct Regt, cmmnd RASC 1939, serv Western Desert 1941- 42, captured Tobruk 1942, escaped Bolzano 1943 on fall of Italy, recaptured 1944, released 1945, asst Mil attache Washington, served Malya 1947-51, ret; Samuel Banner & Co Ltd 1953-57, fndr own laundry and dry cleaning business 1957-80; memb: Surrey CC 1969-70, Surrey Health Borough Cncl 1987-; various offs local Cons branch 1967-; Freeman City of London, Worshipful Co of Carmen; Peter Beigel's Racing Pictures by Michael Joseph (ed, photographer and commentator, 1984); *Recreations* water colour painting, walking, horses and dogs; *Style—* Maj John Crawford, MC; Forge Cottage, School Road, Windleswham, Surrey (☎ 0276 72101)

CRAWFORD, Lyle David; JP (1986); s of Robert Lyle Crawford (d 1971), of N Berwick, and Nanny Hutchison, *née* Duncan; *b* 26 May 1946; *Educ* N Berwick HS (CA, ATII); *m* 1 July 1971, Margaret Ann, da of Robert Sinclair Anderson (d 1979); 2 da (Catriona b 1973, Mairi b 1975); *Career* CA 1969; princ of Lyle Crawford and Co; dir D C Watson and Sons (Fenton Barns) Ltd and subsids 1971- ATII 1968; *Recreations* North Berwick Pipe Band; *Clubs* N Berwick Burns; *Style—* Lyle D Crawford, Esq; Atholl Lodge, 13 East Road, N Berwick, E Lothian (☎ 0620 3484); 25 Westgate, N Berwick, E Lothian (☎ 0620 2171)

CRAWFORD, (George) Michael Warren Brown; s of Surgn Capt Thomas George Brown Crawford, RN (d 1988), and Eleanor Mary, *née* Warren; *b* 11 Jan 1942; *Educ* Rugby; *m* 8 Jan 1972, Jane Elizabeth, da of Capt Alastair James Petrie-Hay, RN; 2 s (Freddy b 8 Aug 1973, Thomas b 7 Nov 1975), 1 da (Victoria b 22 Oct 1979); *Career* Bank of England 1960-63, Buckmaster & Moore 1963-65 and 1970-86 (ptnr 1984-86), IBM Aust Ltd 1966-70; memb Int Stock Exchange 1983; dir: Citymax Intergrated Info Systems Ltd 1984, Credit Suisse Buckmaster & Moore Ltd 1986-;; *Recreations* shooting, sailing; *Clubs* Little Ship; *Style—* Michael Crawford, Esq; Mount Cross, The Quag, Minsted, Midhurst, Sussex (☎ 073 081 4284); Credit Suisse Buckmaster & Moore Ltd, The Stock Exchange, London EC2P 2JT (☎ 01 588 2868, fax 01 588 2660)

CRAWFORD, (Robert) Norman; CBE (1973); s of William Crawford (d 1944), of Londonderry, and Annie Catherine, *née* Rexter (d 1942); *b* 14 June 1923; *Educ* Foyle Coll Londonderry, Queen's Univ Belfast (B Com Sc); *m* 1948, Jean Marie Patricia, da of Hugh Carson (d 1954), of Portrush; 1 s (David), 5 da (Jennifer, Catherine, Mary, Zelda, Emma); *Career* CA; md The McNeill Gp (NI) Ltd 1960-68, chm: Nature Reserves Ctee 1966-85, NI Transport Hldg Co 1968-75; dir and chief exec William Clark and Sons Ltd 1983-87; pres: NI Outward Bound Assoc 1975-, NI C of C and Indust 1967-, Belfast Branch British Inst of Mgmnt 1972-; vice-pres S Belfast Scout Cncl 1984-; chm R N Crawford and Co Business Advisory 1968-, Regional Cncl British Inst of Management 1968-, NI Wildlife Campaign; memb: Senate of Queen's Univ Belfast 1; *Clubs* Ulster Reform; *Style—* R Norman Crawford, Esq, CBE; 4 Fort Rd, Helens Bay, Bangor, Co Down

CRAWFORD, Robert Gammie; s of William Crawford (d 1980), of Aberdeen, and Janet Beveridge, *née* Gammie (d 1974); *b* 20 Mar 1924; *Educ* Robert Gordon's Coll Aberdeen; *m* 4 Sept 1947, Rita, da of August Daniel Veiss (d 1975) of Latvia; 1 da (Fiona b 1959); *Career* Flt Lt navigator RAF 1942-47; slr ptnr Ince and Co 1950-73; (int shipping lawyers); chm Silver Navigation Ltd, Silver Line Ltd and subsidiaries 1974-, Highland and Island Airports Ltd 1986-; UK Protection and Indemnity Club 1983-; UK War Risk Club 1982-, UK Freight Defence and Demurrage Club 1987-; vice-chm Port of London Authy 1985-; memb bd Civil Aviation Authy 1984-, Lloyds Register of Shipping 1982-; dir: AVDEL plc 1983-; Donner Underwriting Hldgs Ltd and subsidiaries 1976-; Sterling Underwriting Agencies Ltd 1988-; memb Lloyds 1975-; govr Robert Gordon's Coll Aberdeen; *Recreations* shooting, golf, reading, conversation; *Clubs* Carlton; *Style—* Robert G Crawford, Esq; 9 London House, Avenue Rd, London NW8 7PX (☎ 01 483 2754); West Mains of Auchenhove, Lumphanan, Aberdeenshire AB3 4QT (☎ 033 983 208 or 667); CAA, Rm T 1410, CAA House, Kemble Street, London WC1 (☎ 01 832 5754)

CRAWFORD, Robert William Kenneth; s of Hugh Merrall Crawford (d 1982), of West Bergholt, Colchester, Essex, and Mary, *née* Percival; *b* 3 July 1945; *Educ* Culford Sch, Pembroke Coll Oxford (BA); *m* 9 Dec 1975, Vivienne Sylvia Crawford, da of Boghdan Andre Polakowski; 1 s (Alistair b 1987), 1 da (Helen b 1984); *Career* Imperial War Museum: Lead res and info office 1971-, keeper dept of photographs 1975-83, asst dir 1979-82, dep dir gen 1982-; *Style—* RWK Crawford, Esq; Imperial War Museum, Lambeth Rd, London SE1 6HZ (☎ 01 735 8922)

CRAWFORD, Stephany Light Smith; da of Lt Cmdr Howard Allen Weiss, of Chicago, Illinois, and Joan, *née* Light Smith; *b* 28 Feb 1954; *Educ* Univ of Milwaukee Wisconsin, Instituto de Allende San Miguel De Allende Mexico, Chicago Art Inst, California Coll of Art; *m* 1, 11 July 1980 (m dis 1984), Matthew Eliot Kastin; 1 da (Katherine); m 2, 10 May 1985, Daniel Frank Crawford; *Career* artist and poet; exhibitions New York, San Francisco, London, artist in residence New York Experimental Glass Workshop 1980, fndr Archangel Exhibitions 1988; curator and co-organises: The London Influence Slaughterhouse Gallery 1988, Americans Abroad Smiths Gallery and King's Head Theatre 1989; memb bd dir King's Head Theatre 1986-, originator Islington Theatre Assoc 1986; *Publications* Stonehouse I & Stonehouse II; *Recreations* dreaming up new projects, dining, museums, galleries, film theatres, being with husband and child; *Clubs* Groucho; *Style—* Ms Stephany Light Smith Crawford; The Kings Head Theatre, 115 Upper St, London N1; 22 Crooked Well, Kington, Hereford

CRAWFORD, Sir (Robert) Stewart; GCMG (1973, KCMG 1966, CMG 1951), CVO (1955); s of late Sir William Crawford, KBE (d 1950), and Marion Stewart, *née* Whitelaw; *b* 27 August 1913; *Educ* Gresham's Sch Holt, Oriel Coll Oxford; *m* 1938, Mary Katharine, da of late Eric Corbett, of Gorse Hill, Witley, Surrey; 3 s (and 1 s decd), 1 da; *Career* Air Miny 1936; FO 1947, political resident Persian Gulf 1966-70, dep under-sec FCO 1970-73; chm: Ctee of Broadcasting Coverage 1973-74, BBC Gen Advsy Cncl 1975-84, Broadcasters Audience Research Bd 1980-88; *Clubs* Utd Oxford and Cambridge, Phyllis Court; *Style—* Sir Stewart Crawford, GCMG, CVO; 19 Adam Court, Bell St, Henley-on-Thames, Oxon (☎ 0491 574 702)

CRAWFORD, Lady Susanna; *née* Montgomerie; eld da of late 17 Earl of Eglinton and Winton and Ursula, da of Hon Ronald Watson (s of late Baron Watson, Life Peer); *b* 19 Oct 1941; *m* 25 May 1963, Capt David Dundas Euing Crawford, late Royal Scots Greys, o son of Brig Alastair Wordrop Euing Crawford, JP, DL, of Auchentroig, Buchlyrie, Stirlingshire; 2 s (twins); 1 da; *Style—* Lady Susanna Crawford

CRAWFORD, Sir Theo(dore); s of Theodore Crawford (d 1925), and Sarah, *née* Mansfield (d 1958); *b* 23 Dec 1911; *Educ* St Peter's Sch York, Glasgow Acad, Glasgow Univ (BSc, MB, ChB, MD); *m* 1, 1938, Margaret Donald, MD (d 1973), da of Dr George Green, DSC; 2 s, 3 da; m 2, 1974, Priscilla Leathley, da of Guy Leathley Chater (d 1974); *Career* served RAMC 1941-45, UK, France, Belgium and Germany, Maj; dir of Pathological Services St George's Hosp and Medical Sch 1946-77, Prof of Pathology London Univ 1948-77, now Emeritus; pres Royal Coll of Pathologists 1969-72; Hon LLD Glasgow Univ 1979; FRCP; (Glasgow 1962), FRCPath 1963, FRC (London 1964); kt 1973; *Books* Modern Trends in Pathology (ed 1967), The Pathology of Ischaerric Heart Disease (1977); *Recreations* gardening, music, walking; *Clubs* Sloane; *Style—* Sir Theo Crawford; 9 Asher Reeds, Langton Green, Tunbridge Wells, Kent TN3 0AL (☎ 089 286 3341)

CRAWFORD, Vice Adm Sir William Godfrey; KBE (1961), CB (1958), DSC (1941); s of Henry Edward Venner Crawford, JP (d 1937), of Wyld Court, Axminster, Devon; *b* 14 Sept 1907; *Educ* RNC Dartmouth; *m* 29 April 1939, Mary Felicity Rosa, 2 da of Sir Philip Williams, 2 Bt (d 1958); 3 s, 1 da; *Career* Lt RN 1929, Rear Adm 1956, Imperial Def Coll 1956-58, flag offr Sea Training 1958-60, Vice Adm 1959, cdr Br Navy Staff and naval attaché Washington 1960-62, ret 1963; dir Overseas Offices BTA 1964-72; *Clubs* Naval and Military, Royal Cruising; *Style—* Vice Adm Sir William Crawford, KBE, CB, DSC; Broadlands, Whitchurch Canonicorum, Bridport, Dorset DT6 6RJ (☎ 0297 89591)

CRAWFORD, His Hon Judge William Hamilton Raymund; QC (1980); s of Col Mervyn Crawford, DSO, JP, DL (d 1977), of Dunscore, Dumfriesshire, and Martha Hamilton, *née* Walker; *b* 10 Nov 1936; *Educ* Winchester, Emmanuel Coll Cambridge; *m* 1965, Marilyn Jean, da of John Millar Colville; 1 s, 2 da; *Heir* Alexander Mervyn Colville Crawford; *Career* barr 1964, dep chm Agric Land Tbnl 1978, rec Crown Ct 1979-, circuit judge 1986; *Recreations* fishing, shooting, hill farming; *Clubs* Naval and Military, Northern Counties; *Style—* His Hon Judge William Crawford, QC; c/o The Crown Ct, Newcastle upon Tyne

CRAWFORD AND BALCARRES, Mary, Countess of; Mary Katherine; *née* Cavendish; da of late Col the Rt Hon Lord Richard Cavendish, CB, CMG, PC (gs of 7 Duke of Devonshire), and Lady Moyra de Vere Beauclerk (da of 10 Duke of St Albans); *b* 20 July 1903; *m* 9 Dec 1925, 28 (and 11) Earl (d 1975); 3 s (29 Earl, Hon Patrick Lindsay, Hon Thomas Lindsay); *Style—* The Rt Hon Mary, Countess of Crawford and Balcarres; Garden Flat, Balcarres, Colinsburgh, Fife (☎ 033 334 520)

CRAWFORD AND BALCARRES, 29 (and 12) Earl of (S 1398, 1651 respectively); Robert Alexander Lindsay; DL (Fife), PC (1972); also Lord Lindsay (of Crawford; *ante* 1143), Lord Lindsay of Balcarres (S 1633), Lord Lindsay and Balniel (S 1651), Baron Wigan of Haigh Hall (UK 1826), Baron Balniel (Life Peer UK 1974); Premier Earl of Scotland in precedence; maintains private officer-of-arms (Endure Pursuivant); s of 28 Earl, KT, GBE, FSA (d 1975), and Mary, da of late Col the Rt Hon Lord Richard Cavendish, CB, CMG, PC (gs of 7 Duke of Devonshire); *b* 5

Mar 1927; *Educ* Eton, Trinity Coll Cambridge; *m* 27 Dec 1949, Ruth Beatrice, da of Leo Meyer-Bechtler, of Zürich; 2 s, 2 da; *Heir* s, Lord Balniel; *Career* Grenadiers Gds 1945-49; MP (C): Hertford 1955-74, Welwyn and Hatfield Feb-Sept 1974; pps to: fin sec of Treasy 1955-57, min Housing and Local Govt 1957-60; memb Shadow Cabinet (Health and Social Security) 1967-70, min of state Def 1970-72, min of state Foreign and Cwlth Affrs 1972-74, chm Lombard N Central Bank 1976-80; vice-chm Sun Alliance Insur Gp 1975-; dir: Nat Westminster Bank 1975-88, Scottish American Investmt Tst 1978-88; first Crown Estate cmmr and chm 1980-1985; pres RDCs Assoc 1959-65; chm: Nat Assoc for Mental Health 1963-70, chm Historic Buildings Cncl for Scotland 1976-83, chm: Royal Cmmn on the Ancient and Historical Monuments for Scotland 1985-; *Style*— The Rt Hon the Earl of Crawford and Balcarres, DL, PC; House of Lords, London SW1

CRAWFURD, Dr (Anthony) Raymond; s of Kenneth Crawfurd, of Rogers Lane, Stoke Poges, Bucks, and Mary Isabel, *née* Jarrett; *b* 14 Jan 1942; *Educ* Winchester, Magdalen Coll Oxford (MA, BM, BCh), King's Coll Hosp Med Sch; *m* 4 Oct 1969, Dr Dorothy Mair Crawfurd, da of Rev David Charles Elijah Rowlands (d 1975), of Treorchy; 1 s (James b 1974), 1 da (Kate b 1971); *Career* jr hosp posts 1967-70: King's Coll Hosp, Royal Liverpool Childrens Hosp, Alder Hey Hosp, Kent and Canterbury Hosp; princ in gen prac 1971-, sr ptnr Dr Crawfurd and Ptnrs 1989; memb med sub ctee Br Olympic Assoc, corresponding memb med cmmn Fed Internationale D'Escrime; chm Tenterden Day Centre, govr Tenterden Infants Sch, chm Kent Co Amateur Fencing Assoc, hon med offr Amateur Fencing Assoc; Freeman City of London 1967, Liveryman Worshipful Soc of Apothecaries 1967; LMSSA 1966, MRCP 1974; *Recreations* fencing, heraldry, skiing; *Style*— Dr Raymond Crawfurd; Seymour House, Shoreham Lane, St Michaels, Tenterden, Kent (☎ 05806 2967); Ivy Ct, Tenterden, Kent TN30 6RB (☎ 05806 3666)

CRAWLEY, Aidan Merivale; MBE (1946); 2 s of Rev Arthur Stafford Crawley, MC (d 1948), Canon of Windsor, Chaplain to George VI, and Anjtice Katherine, *née* Gibbs; *b* 10 April 1908; *Educ* Harrow, Trinity Coll Oxford; *m* 1945, Virginia, OBE (d 1983), da of Dr Edward Spencer Cowles by his w Florence Wolcott Jaquith; 2 s (Andrew b 1947, m 1986, Sarah, da of Murray Lawrence, d 1988; Randall b 1950, m 1982, Marita, 3 da of Lt -Col Harold Phillips and sis of Duchesses of Abercorn and Westminster, *see* respective Dukes, d 1988); 1 da (Harriet b 1948); *Career* served Aux Air Force 1936-39, RAF 1939-47, asst air attaché Balkans 1940, cmd 73 Sqdn 1941 (shot down over N Africa; POW 1941-45); journalist 1930-36, educnl film producer 1936-39; MP (Labour) Buckingham 1945-51 (PPS to Colonial Sec 1945 and 1946-47, Parly under-sec Air 1950-51, resigned from Lab Pty 1957); editor-in-chief ITN 1955-56, TV documentarist for BBC 1956-60; MP (C) W Derbys 1962-68; chm LWT 1967-71 (pres 1971-73); pres MCC 1973; *Publications include* Escape from Germany (1956), De Gaulle: A Biography (1969), The Rise of Western Germany 1945-72 (1973), Dial 200-200 (1980), Escape from Germany (unexpurgated 1985); Leap Before You Look (reminiscences 1987); *Clubs* Queen's, MCC, Clermont, Vanderbilt; *Style*— Aidan Crawley, Esq, MBE; Oak Cottage, Queen Street, Farthinghoe, nr Brackley, Northants (☎ 0295 710 419)

CRAWLEY, Charles Aidan Stafford; s of Maj Kenneth Arnold Gibbs Crawley (d 1988), of The Livery, West Winterslow, Salisbury, Wiltshire, and Pamela Mary, *née* Vickers (d 1962); *b* 26 Dec 1945; *Educ* Harrow; *m* 8 July 1971, Nicola d'Anyers, da of Guy Russell d'Anyers Willis; 1 s Thomas Antony Kenneth b 17 Oct 1974), 1 da (Rosanna Clare Pamela b 19 May 1977); *Career* short service cmmn Coldstream Guards 1965-68; Coutts and Co 1968-77, dir Stenhouse Reed Shaw (MA) Ltd 1979; dir 1981: Harman Hedley Agencies Ltd, Hedley and Redgrove Agenices Ltd, Redgrove and Everington Ltd, Harman Gardner Roberts Ltd; dir 1982: Stenhouse Harman (MA) Ltd, Stenhouse Epps (MA) Ltd, Stenhouse Patrick (MA) Ltd; dir 1985: Bankside Membs Agency, Bankside Syndicates Ltd; *Recreations* golf, skiing, gardening; *Clubs* Whites, Pratts, City, Vanderbilt Raquet; *Style*— Charles Crawley, Esq; 15 Albert Sq, London SW8 1BS (☎ 01 582 9377); Bankside Members Agency Ltd, c/o Lloyd's (☎ 01 481 0888, fax 01 702 1920, telex 8814440)

CRAWLEY, Frederick William; s of William Clement Crawley (d 1962), and Elsie Florence, *née* Valentine (d 1984); *b* 10 June 1926; *m* 1951, Ruth Eva, da of Dr Hans Jungmann (d 1970); 2 da (Nicola, Fiona); *Career* dep chief gen mangr Lloyds Bank Int 1978 (exec dir 1975, asst chief gen mangr 1977), chief gen mangr Lloyds Bank California 1984, (vice chm chief exec offr 1982, dep chief gen 1984), dep chief exec Lloyds Bank plc 1985-87 (jt gen mangr 1975, dir 1985-88) dir Lloyds Devpt Capital Ltd, Alliance & Leicester Building Soc, Barratt Devpt plc, F S Assur Ltd; hon tres RAF Benevolent Fund; FCIB, CBIM; *Recreations* aviation, shooting, photography; *Clubs* Overseas Bankers; *Style*— Frederick Crawley Esq; 4 The Hexagon, Fitzroy Park, London N6 6HR (☎ 01 341 2279);

CRAWLEY, Thomas Henry Raymond; s of Charles William Crawley, of Cambridge, and Kathleen Elizabeth, *née* Leahy (d 1982); *b* 17 May 1936; *Educ* Rugby, Trinity Coll Cambridge (MA); *m* 22 April 1961, Felicity Merville, da of Gerald Ashworth Bateman (ret RN Cdr); 1 s (Charles b 1965), 2 da (Alice b 1967, Tessa b 1969); *Career* Martin's Bank Ltd 1959-61, slr 1965; awarded City of London Slrs Co prize and Charles Steele prize 1964, ptnr Turner Kenneth Brown 1967-, slr Hong Kong 1986, sr res ptnr Turner Kenneth Brown Hong Kong 1988-; Freeman City of London 1985, Liveryman Worshipful Co of Slrs 1987; memb: Law Soc, Law Soc Hong Kong; *Clubs* Travellers', Pacific, Aberdeen Boat; *Style*— T H R Crawley, Esq; 22 Watford Road, The Peak, Hong Kong (☎ 5 849 7824); 38 Wilmington Ave, London W43 3HA; Plas Hendy, Bryngwyn, nr Raglan, Gwent; 100 Fetter Lane, London ED4A 1DD; 19 Floor, Worldwide House, 19 Des Voeux Rd Central, Hong Kong (☎ 852 5 8105081, fax 852 5 8101295, telex 80468 HKTKB HX)

CRAWLEY-BOEVEY, Thomas Hyde Crawley-Boevey; s and h of Sir Thomas Crawley-Boevey, 8 Bt; *b* 26 June 1958; *Style*— Thomas Crawley-Boevey, Esq

CRAWLEY-BOEVEY, Sir Thomas Michael Blake; 8 Bt (GB 1784) of Highgrove, Glos; s of Sir Launcelot Valentine Hyde Crawley-Boevey, 7 Bt (d 1968), and Elizabeth Goodeth, da of Herbert d'Auvergne Innes; *b* 29 Sept 1928; *Educ* Wellington, St John's Coll Cambridge; *m* 16 Feb 1957, Laura (d 1979), da of late Jan Pouwels Coelingh, of Wassenaar, Netherlands; 2 s; *Heir* s, Thomas Crawley-Boevey; *Career* former shipping agent; editor Money Which? 1968-76, editor Which? 1976-80, editor-in-chief 1980-82; *Style*— Sir Thomas Crawley-Boevey, Bt; Trebanau, Cilycwm, Llandovery, Dyfed SA20 OHP (☎ 0550 20496)

CRAWSHAW, Sir Edward (Daniel) Weston; QC (Aden 1949); s of Godfrey Edward Crawshaw (d 1938), of Yorks; *b* 10 Sept 1903; *Educ* St Bees Sch, Selwyn Coll Cambridge; *m* 1942, Rosemary, da of Roger Carpenter Treffry, of Cornwall; 1 s (and 1 decd), 2 da; *Career* slr 1929, barr 1946, attorney-gen Aden 1947-52; Puisne judge Tanganyika 1952-60, justice of appeal Ct of Appeal for E Africa 1960-65, cmmr Foreign Compensation Cmmn 1965-75; kt 1964; *Style*— Sir Daniel Crawshaw, QC; 1 Fort Rd, Guildford, Surrey (☎ 576883)

CRAWSHAW, 4 Baron (UK 1892); Sir William Michael Clifton Brooks; 4 Bt (UK 1891); s of 3 Baron (d 1946), and Sheila, da of late Lt-Col P R Clifton, CMG, DSO; *b* 25 Mar 1933; *Educ* Eton, Christ Church Oxford; *Heir* bro, Hon David Brooks; *Career* sits as (C) in House of Lords; lord of the manor of Long Whatton, patron of the Living of Shepshed; Treasurer Loughborough Conservative Assoc 1954-58; co cmmr Leics Boy Scouts 1958-; *Style*— The Rt Hon The Lord Crawshaw; Whatton, Loughborough, Leics (☎ Hathern 225)

CRAWSHAY, Walter Brian Julian; s of Capt Walter Stanley Cubitt Crawshay (d 1955), of The Old Rectory, Carlton Forehoe, nr Norwich, and Elaine Grace (Betty), *née* Osborne (d 1978); *b* 28 Dec 1922; *Educ* Eton; *m* 6 Aug 1954, Ann Euphane, da of Arthur Woodman Blair, of Clint Stenton, by Dunbar, East Lothian; 1 s (William b 1960), 2 da (Emma b 1955, Louisa (Mrs Barrie) b 1958); *Career* WWII Cyrencacia, Tunisia, Italy, XII Royal Lancers 1941 (despatches 1944), Staff Coll Camberley 1952, HQ1 Br Corps 1953, retired Maj 1955; dir: Youngs Crawshay & Youngs Ltd 1955, Bullard & Sons Ltd 1956, Watney Combe Reid Ltd London 1966, Watney Mann Ltd and subsids 1970, assoc cos 1978; tres Tasburgh PCC, memb Depwade Rural Dist Cncl 1960-63; *Recreations* fishing, shooting, gardening, ballet; *Clubs* New (Edinburgh); *Style*— Julian Crawshay, Esq; Tasburgh Grange, Norwich NR15 1AR (☎ 0508 470 634)

CRAWSHAY, Col Sir William Robert; DSO (1945), ERD, TD; s of Capt Jack William Leslie Crawshay, MC (d 1950; whose mother Mary was da of Sir John Leslie, 1 Bt), sometime of Caversham Park, Oxon, by his w Claire, *née* Stickelbaut (who m subsequently Hon George Egerton, 2 s of 5 Earl of Wilton); *b* 27 May 1920; *Educ* Eton; *m* 1950, Elisabeth Mary Boyd Reynolds, da of Lt-Col Guy Franklin Reynolds, MC (d 1950); *Career* cmmnd (SR) 1 Royal Welch Fusiliers 1939, SOE France 1944-45, served WWII (despatches twice); Parachute Regt (TA) 1947-60, ADC to HM The Queen 1966-71, Hon Col 3 Royal Regt of Wales (Volunteer) Bn 1970-82; Vice-Lord Lt of Gwent 1979- (DL Glam 1964, Monmouthshire 1970, Gwent 1974); served Arts Cncl of GB 1962-74, chm Welsh Arts Cncl 1968-74, pres: National Museum of Wales 1977-82, Royal Br Legion Wales Area 1974-88; chm Univ Coll Cardiff Cncl 1966-87; Chev Légion d'Honneur 1945, Croix de Guerre 1945; KStJ 1969; kt 1972; *Clubs* White's, Cardiff and Co; *Style*— Col Sir William Crawshay, DSO, ERD, TD, DL, HM Vice Lord-Lt for Gwent; Llanfair Court, Abergavenny, Gwent (☎ 087 384 0215)

CREAGH, Giles Peter Vandeleur; TD (1967); s of Lt Cdr Giles Desmond Vandeleur Creagh, RNVR (d 1963), of Blo' Norton, Norfolk, and Olga Creagh, *née* Beckwith (d 1983); *b* 21 Nov 1927; *Educ* Marlborough, Clare Coll Cambridge (MA); *m* 1 Sept 1962, Jean Margaret Heather, da of Godfrey George Hoole (d 1980), of Krugersdorp, SA; 2 s (Desmond Giles Vandeleur b 1963, Henry Giles Vandeleur b 1965); *Career* Maj (TA) Suffolk Regt JRRU, 23 SAS Int Corps slr; dir Bury St Edmund's Bldg soc 1969-88, local dir Cheltenham & Gloucester Bldg Soc 1989-; registrar and legal sec Diocese of St Edmundsbury and Ipswich 1956-75, pres chm Social Security Appeal Tbnls 1984-; *Clubs* Carlton, United Oxford and Cambridge, Special Forces; *Style*— Giles P V Creagh, Esq, TD; The Old Rectory, Market Weston, Diss, Norfolk IP22 2PE; Greene and Greene, 80 Guildhall Street, Bury St Edmunds, Suffolk IP33 1QB (☎ 0284 62211, fax 0284 705739)

CREASE, David Plaistow; s of Gilbert Crease, of Beckenham, Kent (d 1971), and Margaret Frances Plaistow (d 1981); *b* 22 July 1928; *Educ* Christ's Hosp, Gonville and Caius Coll Cambridge (MA), Edinburgh Coll of Art (Diploma); *m* 15 Aug 1969, Jane Rosemary, da of Harold Leonard Goodey, of Reading; 1 da (Hermione b 1970); *Career* architect Public Works Dept, Hong Kong, 1955-59, practised in Brasilia, Brazil 1960-63, chief architect York Univ Design Unit 1966-81: (works include housing at Heslington, York and elsewhere in Yorkshire); ptnr own practice 1981, principal current work Bishops Wharf York); ARIBA; *Recreations* hunting the clean boot (human scent) with bloodhounds; *Style*— David P Crease, Esq; Old Carlton Farm, Warthill, York YO3 9XS (☎ 0904 400315); Crease, Edmonds, Strickland, Architects, Bishopgate House, Skeldergate Bridge, York YO2 1JH (☎ 0904 641289)

CREASEY, David Somersall; s of David Edward Creasey (d 1954), of Leeds, and Margaret Agnes, *née* Eve (d 1960); *b* 28 Feb 1924; *Educ* Leeds GS, Leeds Univ (LLB); *m* 6 Jan 1951, Lois Barbara, da of William Morris Morden Dorset (d 1953); 2 s (Andrew b 1956, Julian b 1952), 2 da (Caroline b 1960, Philippa b 1953); *Career* war serv RAF bomber cmd nav; slr; dir and sec Leeds Abbeyfield Soc; memb Law Soc Area Ctee; *Recreations* golf, bridge; *Clubs* Leeds, Skrack Lions (former pres); *Style*— David S Creasey, Esq; The Spinney, 142 Adel Lane, Leeds (☎ 679288); Harrison Jobbings, 31/32 Park Row, Leeds (☎ 433311); Jobbings Creasey, New Roadside, Horsforth

CREE, Brig Gerald Hilary; CBE (1946), DSO (1945); yr s of Maj-Gen Gerald Cree, CB, CMG (d 1932), of Heathcote, Purbrook, Hants, and Isabella, *née* Smith (d 1965); *b* 23 June 1905; *Educ* Kelly Coll, RMC Sandhurst; *m* 1945, Joan Agnes, da of Lt Col William Rushbrooke Eden, CMG, DSO, RA (d 1920), Glos; 1 da (Henrietta); *Career* Lt-Col 2nd Bn W Yorks Regt, served in Middle East and Burma 1942-45, Brig 25 (E African) Inf Bde, Burma and India 1944-45; Lt Col 1st Bn W Yorks Regt Austria 1946-48; Brig 127 Indian Bde (TA) Manchester 1953-56; Col PWO 1960-70; *Clubs* Naval and Miltary; *Style*— Brig Cree, CBE, DSO; Laurels, Sharpham Drive, Totnes, Devon (☎ 0803 862902)

CREED, Peter Howard; s of Sidney Howard Creed (d 1971), of Wolverhampton, and Gladys Marguerite, *née* Shaw (d 1977); *b* 27 June 1931; *Educ* Tettenhall Coll Wolverhampton; *m* 1956, Joan, da of Henry Francis (d 1986), of Wolverhampton; 2 s (Michael b 1958, Charles b 1962); *Career* sr air-craftsman RAF 1954-56; joined Express and Star; advertisement rep 1957, advertisement mangr: Shropshire Star 1964, dir (1968-73, Express and Star 1973; gp advertisement dir The Midlands News Assoc Ltd incl dir of Express and Star, Shropshire Star and Shropshire Weekly Newspapers 1980-; dir Precision Colour Printing Ltd Telford 1981-84; chm Newspaper sec Advertising Conference Ctee 1977-83 (memb main Advertising Ctee 1975-); Newspaper Soc rep on Code of Advertising Practice Ctee for Advertising Standards Authy 1985-; govr Tettenhall Coll 1978-; *Recreations* cricket, golf and ardent Wolves

Football Club supporter; *Clubs* Penn Cricket Wolverhampton, Wrekin Golf; *Style*— Peter Creed, Esq; 218 Henwood Road, Tettenhall, Wolverhampton, West Midlands WV6 8NZ (☎ 0902 752653); The Midland News Association Ltd, Queen Street, Wolverhampton, West Midlands WV1 3BU (☎ 0902 313131, fax 0902 21467, gp 2 and 3)

CREEK, Malcolm Lars; LVO (1980), OBE (1985); s of Edgar Creek (d 1977), and Lily, *née* Robertshaw (d 1950); *b* 2 April 1931; *Educ* Belle Vue Sch Bradford, London Univ (BA); *m* 1, (m dis 1970), Moira; 1 s (Jeremy b 1960), 1 da (Helen b 1955); m 2, 17 July 1970, Gillian Mary, da of Arthur Ridley Bell, of 27 Bertram Drive North, Meols, Wirral; 1 s (Richard b 1975), 2 da (Alison b 1973, Sarah b 1974); *Career* Nat Serv 1950-52; FO 1950 and 1952-56, vice-consul Mogadishiu and Harar 1956-58, FO 1958-59, 2 sec Mexico City 1959-62 (Abidjan 1962-64, Santiago 1964-68), 1 sec and head of chancery San Jose 1968-71 (Havana 1972-74), FO 1974-77, 1 sec Tunis 1978-81 (Lima 1981-85), high cmmr Vila Vanuatu 1985-88, consul gen Auckland 1988_; *Recreations* cricket, tennis; *Clubs* Yorks CCC; *Style*— Malcolm Creek, Esq, LVO, OBE; 17 Bertram Drive North, Meols, Wirral, Ches (☎ 051 632 5820); c/o FCO, King Charles St, SW1; c/o FCO, Auckland, NZ (☎ 9 329 52)

CREESE, Prof Richard; TD (1965); s of Leonard Creese (d 1947), of Clifton, Bristol, and Nellie Hawkesford, *née* James (d 1983); *b* 4 Dec 1919; *Educ* Clifton, King's Coll London, Westminster Med Sch, Univ of London (MB BS, PhD); *m* 8 May 1943, Louise May, da of Leon Jean Doumeyrou (d 1956), of Paris; 2 s (Anthony b 1949, Martin b 1950), 1 da (Claire b 1958); *Career* RMo The Queen's Bays RAMC 1946-47, RAMC (TA) 1948-81, Col L/RAMC (V) 1976; demonstrator, lectr and sr lectr London Hosp Med Coll 1950-60, visiting asst prof Univ of California Los Angeles 1955-56, reader St Marys Hosp Med Sch 1961-82 (prof physiology 1968-) govr Henry Compton Sch Fulham 1972-75; Mickle fell Univ of London 1959; Freeman City of London 1968, Liveryman Worshipful Soc of Apothecaries 1966; FRSM 1952, memb Physiology Soc 1953; *Books* Recent Advances in Physiology (ed 1963); *Recreations* travel, history, drama, running; *Clubs* Garrick; *Style*— Prof Richard Creese, TD; 93 Lonsdale Rd, London SW13 9DA (☎ 01 748 7002)

CREGGY, Stuart; JP (Westminster 1979); s of Leslie Creggy (d 1972), and Fay, *née* Schneider; *b* 27 May 1939; *Educ* Western Univ USA (MA), Law Soc Sch of Law; *Career* slr 1963, cmmr for oaths 1969, currently sr ptnr Talbot Creggy & Co; chm Juvenile Diabetes Fndn, Sussex Co Freeholds plc; memb Variety Club of GB; memb Law Soc, FBIM, FFA, ACIArb; *Recreations* swimming, philately; *Clubs* RAC; *Style*— Stuart Creggy, Esq, JP; 58 Viceroy Ct, Prince Albert Rd, St Johns Wood, London NW8 7PS (☎ 01 586 4465); 38 Queen Anne St, London W1M 9LB (☎ 01 637 8865, fax 01 637 2630, car tel 0836 234 008, 0836 234 009, telex 8954619)

CREIGHTON, Alan Joseph; s of Joseph Kenneth Creighton (d 1975), and Iris Mary, *née* McShea (d 1978); *b* 21 Nov 1936; *Educ* Gillingham Co GS, RNEC Manadon Plymouth, Royal Naval Coll Greenwich; *m* 25 July 1959, Judith, da of Jack Bayford of West Littleton; 2 da (Helen b 4 June 1962, Hannah b 13 April 1965); *Career* chief constructor MOD (N) 1974-80 (asst constructor 1961-65, constructor 1965-74), Royal Coll of Def Studies 1980-81, seconded tech dir Yarrow Shipbuilders 1981-84, dir-gen MOD (PE) 1986- (dir 1984-86); FRINA 1981; *Recreations* music, cabinet making, sailing, swimming, DIY; *Style*— Alan Creighton, Esq; Home Farm Cottage, West Littleton, Marshfield, Chippenham SN 14 8JE (☎ 0225 891 021); Ministry of Defence (PE), Foxhill, Bath (☎ 0225 883 635)

CREIGHTON, Harold Digby Fitzgerald; s of late Rev Digby Robert Creighton, and Amy Frances Rohde; *b* 11 Sept 1927; *Educ* Haileybury; *m* 1964, Harriet Mary Falconer, da of late A L P F Wallace of Candacraig (memb Queen's Body Guard for Scotland); 4 da; *Career* Nat Serv Army, Lt, served in India and ME 1945-48; Consolidated Tim Smelters Penang 1950-52; dir machine tool cos London 1952-63; chm Scottish Machine Tool Corpn Ltd Glasgow 1963-68; dep chm and chief exec Farmer Stedall plc; ed The Spectator 1973-75 (chm 1967-75); *Clubs* Beefsteak; *Style*— Harold Creighton, Esq; 5 Upper Brook St, London W1

CRESSMAN, Harry Gordon; s of Harry Edwin Cressman (d 1965); *b* 10 Jan 1927; *Educ* Black-Foxe Mil Inst Los Angeles California; *m* 1948, Barbara Ann, *née* Brodine, 2 s, 1 da; *Career* Tech Sgt US Army Coast Artillery; joined Bristol St Motors Ltd 1948 (dir 1949, md 1951), md chm and chief exec BSC Int 1967-80, dir: Heron Motor Gp Ltd 1980 (md 1981), Heron Corpn Ltd 1981-; dir-gen American Chamber of Commerce (UK) 1982; *Recreations* travel, racing, football, boats; *Clubs* American, Carlton, Lyford Cay (Nassau), Port La Galère (France), Ends of the Earth; *Style*— Harry Cressman Esq; 34 Petersham Place, S Kensington, London SW7 (☎ 01 584 2731); Eastcote Paddocks, Hampton-in-Arden, Solihull, W Midlands (☎ 067 55 2168); 1 Ave de l'Astrolabe, Port La Galère, Theoule, Alpes Maritimes, France (☎ 93 90 32 26)

CRESSWELL; *see*: Baker-Cresswell

CRESSWELL, Amos Samuel; s of Amos Cresswell (d 1978), of Walsall Wood, Staffs, and Jane, *née* Marriott (d 1972); *b* 21 April 1926; *Educ* Queen Mary's GS Walsall, Durham Univ (BA), Wesley House and Fitzwilliam Coll Cambridge (BA, MA), Theological Seminary Bethel bei Bielefield Westphalia Germany; *m* 11 Feb 1956, Evelyn Rosemary, da of Walter Marchbanks (d 1980), of Barnes, London; 2 s (Stephen Amos, Martin James), 1 da (Jane); *Career* teacher of english and latin HS for Boys Colchester 1947-49, methodist minister Clitheroe 1949-50, asst tutor in New Testament Richmond Methodist Coll London Univ 1953-56, Methodist minister Darlaston 1956-61, New Testament tutor Cliff Coll Calver Derbyshire 1961-66, editor Advance (a weekly journal) 1961-63, minister Bramhall Circuit Cheadle Hulme 1966-73, supt minister Welwyn Herts 1973-78, chm Plymouth and Exeter Methodist Dist 1976-, pres Methodist Conf of UK and Ireland 1983-84; memb Rotary Club: Darlaston 1957-61, Cheadle Cheshire 1968-73, Welwyn Garden City 1973-76; fndr Darlaston Fellowship for the Disabled 1960, pres Devonshire Assoc (for the Advancement of Sci Literature and Art) 1985-86; *Books* The Story of Cliff - History of Cliff Coll (2 edn 1983), The Story They Told - a Study of the Passion and Resurrection (1966), Life Power and Hope - a Study of the Holy Spirit (1971); *Style*— The Rev Amos Cresswell; 18 Velwell Rd, Exeter, Devon EC4 4LE (☎ 0392 72541)

CRESSWELL, Donald Rosslyn; s of George Cresswell (d 1949), and Gertie (d 1953); *b* 10 Oct 1928; *Educ* Loscoe Rd Sch; *m* April 1959, Margaret, da of Daniel Fletcher, of Bunny, Notts; 2 s (Stephen b 1960, Robert b 1961), 1 da (Anne b 1962); *Career* chm Robinsons Pickles, Derby; chm and md: Deredon Ltd, Inland Cash and Carry Ltd; *Recreations* cricket; *Clubs* Derbyshire, Heanor Town; *Style*— Donald Cresswell, Esq; The Gables, High St, Kimberley, Notts (☎ 0602 326986); Inland Cash and Carry Ltd, Abbey St, Ilkeston, Derbys

CRESSWELL, Peter John; QC (1983); s of Rev Canon JJ Cresswell, of 12 Eastleach, Glos, and Madeleine, *née* Foley; *b* 24 April 1944; *Educ* St John's Sch Leatherhead, Queens' Coll Cambridge (MA, LLM); *m* 29 April 1972, Caroline, da of Maj Gen Sir Philip Ward, KCVO, CBE, DL, of The Old Rectory, Patching, Sussex; 2 s (Oliver b 11 Nov 1973, d 1988, Mark b 25 Sept 1975); *Career* called to the Bar Gray's Inn 1966, rec 1986, chm London Common Law and Commercial Bar Assoc 1985-87; memb: Senate of Inns of Court and Bar 1981-86, Gen Cncl of the Bar 1987-89 (vice-chm 1989), cncl Cystic Fibrosis Res Tst (exec ctee); *Books* Encyclopaedia of Banking Law (1982-89); *Recreations* fly-fishing, river management; *Clubs* Athenaeum, Flyfisher's; *Style*— Peter Cresswell, Esq, QC; 25 Victoria Square, London, SW1 W0RB (☎ 01 834 2684); 3 Gray's Inn Place, Gray's Inn, London WC1 5EA (☎ 01 831 8441, fax 01 831 8479, telex 295119 LEXCOL G)

CRETNEY, Prof Stephen Michael; s of Fred Cretney (d 1980), and Winifred Mary Valentine, *née* Rowlands (d 1982); *Educ* The Manchester Warehousemen and Clerks Orphan Schs Cheshire, Magdalen Coll Oxford (DCL, MA); *m* 7 July 1973, Antonia Lois, da of Cdr Anthony George Glanusk Vanrenen, RN, of Fordingbridge, Hants; 2 s (Matthew b 1975, Edward b 1979); *Career* Nat Serv 1954-56; slr 1962, ptnr Macfarlanes 1964-65: Kenya Sch of Law Nairobi 1966-67, Southampton Univ 1967-68, fell Exeter Coll Oxford 1968-78, law cmmr 1978-83, prof of law Bristol Univ 1983- (dean of Faculty 1984-88); chm pt/t Social Security Appeals Tbnls 1984-; memb: ctee on Prison Disciplinary System, Judicial Studies Bd Civil and Family Ctee; chm Ctee of Heads Univ Law Schs; FBA 1985; *Books* Principles of Family Law (fourth edn 1984); *Recreations* scholarships; *Clubs* Utd Oxford and Cambridge; *Style*— Prof Stephen Cretney; 15 Canynge Sq, Clifton, Bristol BS8 3LA (☎ 0272 732983, 0272 303371)

CRETTON, Hon Mrs; Hon Catherine Anne; *née* Vesey; 2 da of 6 Viscount de Vesci (d 1983), and Susan Anne, *née* Armstrong-Jones (d 1986), sis of 1 Earl of Snowdon, *qv*; *b* 19 May 1953; *m* June 1984, Bruno Cretton; 2 s (Matthew, Alexis) 1 da (Ceeily); *Style*— The Hon Mrs Cretton; 121 Chemin de La Moraine, 74400 Argentière, France

CREW, Air Vice-Marshal Edward Dixon; CB (1973), DSO (1944, and bar 1950), DFC (1941 and bar 1942); er s of F Denys Crew (d 1936), of Higham Ferrers, Northants ; *b* 24 Dec 1917; *Educ* Felsted, Downing Coll Cambridge; *m* 1945, Virginia, da of Milton Martin, of Toronto; 1 s; *Career* RAFVR 1939, Cdr Air Forces Borneo 1965-66, AOC Central Reconnaissance Establishment 1968-69, Dep Controller Nat Air Traffic Servs 1969-73, Air Vice-Marshal 1969, ret 1973; DOE Planning Inspectorate 1973-87; *Recreations* golf; *Clubs* RAF; *Style*— Air Vice-Marshal Edward Crew, CB, DSO, DFC; 13 Silver St, Tetbury, Glos; c/o National Westminster Bank Ltd, 10 Benet St, Cambridge

CREWDSON, John Francis; s of Maj Eric Crewdson, MC, DL (d 1969), and Mary Stuart, *née* Fyers (d 1961); *b* 27 Nov 1923; *Educ* Dragoon Sch Oxford, Shrewsbury, Jesus Coll Cambridge (BA, MB, BChir); *m* 1, 1946, Gillian Dallas, da of Arthur Dallas Lawton Harington (d 1980); 2 da (Jacqueline b 1948, Ingrid Gillian b 1952); m 2, 1959, Patricia Marie, da of Dr William King Carew (d 1956); 1 s (Charles Willian Nepean b 1964); *Career* WWII Lt RNVR served motor torpedo boats N Sea; opthalmologist St Thomas's Hosp 1950-81 (cnslt 1974-81), cnslt French Hosp 1973-81, chief clinic asst Moorfields Eye Hosp 1958-81; vice-chm NW Sea Cadet Corps 1987-; *Clubs* Naval; *Style*— John F Crewdson, Esq; Winster House, Winster, Windermere, Cumbria LA23 3NU (☎ Windermere 2680)

CREWDSON, Hon Mrs (Lucy Clara); *née* Beckett; only da of Lt-Col 3 Baron Grimthorpe, DL (d 1963), by his 1 w; *b* 5 Sept 1926; *m* 12 July 1957, Wilson Peregrine Nicholas Crewdson, s of Brig Wilson Theodore Oliver Crewdson, CBE; 1 s, 3 da (1 decd); *Style*— Hon Mrs Crewdson; Oak House, Otley, nr Ipswich, Suffolk

CREWE, Prof Ivor Martin; s of Francis Crewe, of 10 Spath Rd, West Didsbury, Manchester, and Lilly Edith, *née* Neustadtl; *b* 15 Oct 1945; *Educ* Manchester GS, Exeter Coll Oxford (MA), LSE (MSc); *m* 3 July 1968, Jill Barbara, da of Dr Theo Gadian, 1 Park Lodge, 30 Park Street, Salford; 2 s (Ben b 1974, Daniel b 1977), 1 da (Deborah b 1972); *Career* asst lectr dept of politics Lancaster Univ 1967-69, jr res fell Nuffield Coll Oxford 1969-71, lectr Univ of Essex 1971 (sr lectr 1974, prof 1982-); dir ESRC data archive Univ of Essex 1974-82; co-dir Br Election Study 1977-82, ed Br Journal of Political Science 1977-82 and 1984-88; commentator on elections and public opinion BBC TV, Guardian; memb: Political Studies Assoc, American Political Studies Assoc; *Books* A social survey of higher Civil Service (1969), Decade of Dealignment (1983), British Parliamentary Constituencies (1984); *Recreations* Opera; *Style*— Prof I M Crewe; Dept of Government, Univ of Essex, Colchester, Essex CO4 3SQ (☎ 0206 872129 fax 0206 873598)

CREWE, Quentin Hugh; s of Maj Hugh Dodds Crewe, CMG, TD, of HM Consular Serv (né Dodds but changed name by deed poll 1945) and Lady Annabel, da of 1 and last Marquess of Crewe, KG, PC, JP; *b* 14 Nov 1926; *Educ* Eton, Trinity Coll Cambridge; *m* 1, 1956, Martha Sharp; 1 s (Sebastian b 1958), 1 da (Sabrina b 1959); m 2, 1961, Angela Huth; 1 da (Candida) (and 1 s decd); m 3, 1970, Susan, da of Capt Richard Cavendish, JP, DL (s of Col Rt Hon Lord Richard Cavendish, CB, CMG, yr bro of 9 Duke of Devonshire, by Lord Richard's w Lady Moyra Beauclerk, da of 10 Duke of St Albans); 1 s (Nathaniel b 1971), 1 da (Charity b 1972); *Career* journalist (of articles particularly on food) and author; has written for Queen, Vogue, Daily Mail, Sunday Times, Sunday Mirror, Sunday Telegraph, Spectator; *Books* A Curse of Blossom 1960, Frontiers of Privilege 1961, Great Chefs of France 1979, International Pocket Food Book 1980, In Search of the Sahara 1983, The Last Maharaja 1985, Touch the Happy Isles 1987; *Recreations* travel; *Clubs* Tarporley Hunt; *Style*— Quentin Crewe, Esq; 52 Beauchamp Place, London SW3

CREWE-READ, Hon Mrs (Diana Mary Wroughton); *née* Robins; da of 1 and last Baron Robins, KBE, DSO, ED (d 1962); *b* 11 Nov 1920; *Educ* St Mary's Wantage; *m* 1940, Col John Crewe-Read, OBE; 2 s, 1 da; *Style*— The Hon Mrs Crewe-Read; Croft House, Aston Tirrold, Didcot, Oxon (☎ Blewbury 850318)

CREWS, Hon Mrs; Anne Pauline; *née* Irby; da of 9 Baron Boston (d 1978), by his 1 w; *b* 28 Feb 1927; *Educ* Seaford Ladies Coll, Central and Camberwell Schs of Art and Craft; *m* 1951, Prof Sydney James Crews, s of Sydney Kirby Crews (d 1977); 1 s (Francis b 1953), 2 da (Emma b 1956, Bridget b 1963); *Career* artist, ceramic sculpture, water colours, print maker; art teacher and lecturer for 20 years in Birmingham; *Books* (illustrator) Solid Citizens - a study of sculpture in Birmingham; *Recreations* swimming, architectural walks; *Style*— The Hon Mrs Crews; 77 Wellington

Rd, Edgbaston, Birmingham B15 2ET (☎ 021 440 3459)

CRIBB, Evelyn Francis Theodore; s of Canon Charles Theodore Cribb (d 1976); descended from John Evelyn (b 1620), the diarist, one of the original fellows of the Royal Soc; *b* 24 June 1929; *Educ* Marlborough, Christs Coll Cambridge; *m* 1956 (m dis 1987), Jane Howard, da of Ronald Le Grice Eyre (d 1940); 1 s, 2 da; *Career* barr 1954, various appointments General Motors, GEC, BOC; dir: Freemans plc 1977- (co sec 1971-), Brixton Information Technology Centre, Direct Mail Services Standards Bd; chm: Peckham Settlement, cncl BASSAC 1983-85; memb Fulham Cncl (Cons ldr) 1959-62; CBI cncl; dir Commercial Union local bd; Business in the Community Cncl; chm Mailing Preference Service; memb European Cmmn's advisory Ctee on Commerce and Distribution; *Style—* Evelyn Cribb, Esq; The Squirrels, Fox Corner, Worplesdon, Guildford, Surrey GU3 3PP (☎ Worplesdon 236278)

CRIBB, Graham Thame Stanley; OBE (1985); s of John Stanley Cribb (d 1970), of St Margarets, E Twickenham, and Florence Winifred Constance, *née* Thame (d 1969); *b* 7 Nov 1924; *Educ* Isleworth County GS, Downing Coll Cambridge (BA, MA) Imperial Coll of Sci & Technol (DIC), Princeton Univ NJ; *m* 29 July 1950, Stella Rosemary, da of Joseph Charles Templeman, (d 1958), of Hounslow; 2 s (Christopher Joseph Stanley b 5 Jan 1956, Richard Graham Stanley b 26 June 1959); *Career* RE 1943-46, cmmnd 2 Lt 1944, Lt 1945, Capt 1945, serv: NW Europe 1945, India, Malaysia and Singapore 1945-46; Br Gas Plc: res chemist Fulham res Laboratory N Thames Gas 1949, section ldr Chemical Engrg Gp 1955, tech offr devpt and planning section Gas Cncl 1961, devpt engr prodn and supply div 1966, dir London res station Br Gas Corpn 1975, ret 1988; hon sec Inst of Gas Engr 1987- (pres 1985-86); correspondent sch govrs Goring C of E Primary Sch; memb: Goring and Streatley Probus; memb Guild of Servers Church of St Thomas of Canterbury Goring on Thames; Freeman city of London 1984, memb Worshipful Co of Engrs 1984, CEng, FIGasE 1969, FIChemE 1984, FRSA 1988; *Recreations* DIY, gardening, rowing, swimming, narrowboat owner; *Clubs* Leander, Twickenham Rowing, Wallingford Rowing; *Style—* Graham Cribb, Esq; 11 Holmlea Rd, Goring on Thames, Reading, Berks RG8 9EX (☎ 0491 872202)

CRIBBINS, Bernard; s of John Edward Cribbins (d 1964), and Ethel, *née* Clarkson; *b* 29 Dec 1928; *Educ* St Annes Elementary Sch Oldham Lancs; *m* 27 Aug 1955, Gillian Isabella, da of Maj Donald Victor Charles McBarnet (ka 1943); *Career* Nat Serv 1947-49: Parachute Regt, serv 3 Bn (later 2/3 Bn) Palestine 1947-48, 16 Div HQ Germany; asst stage mangr student Oldham Repertory Theatre (aged 14); Repertory, Hornchurch, Liverpool, Manchester, Weston-Super-Mare; first West End appearance Comedy of Errors Arts Theatre 1956: London theatre incl: Harmony Close, Lady at the Wheel, New Cranks, And and other thing, The Big Tickle, Hook Line and Sinker, Not Now Darling, There Goes The Bride, Run for Your Wife, Guys and Dolls; own TV series: Cribbins, Cuffy, Langley Bottom; TV: title role in Dangerous Davies, Good Old Days, Shillingbury Tales, High and Dry, Fawlty Towers, Call My Bluff; voices for The Wombles and Buzby; films incl: The Railway Children 1971, Casino Royale, Two Way Stretch, Wrong Arm of the Law, She, Carry On Jack, Carry On Spying, The Water Babies; recorded hit records incl: Right Said Fred, Hole in the Ground, Gossip Calypso; memb cncl Action Res for the Crippled Child, vice-pres SPARKS; *Recreations* fishing, shooting, golf; *Style—* Bernard Cribbins, Esq; c/o Crouch Assoc, 59 Frith St, London W1

CRICHTON, Sir Andrew Maitland-Makgill-; s of Lt-Col David Edward Maitland-Makgill-Crichton, Cameron Highlanders (d 1952), and Phyllis, *née* Cuthbert (d 1982); *b* 28 Dec 1910; *Educ* Wellington ; *m* 1948, Isabel, da of Andrew McGill, of Sydney, NSW, Australia, and widow of John Eric Bain; *Career* co dir; former vice-chairman Port of London Authority; kt 1963; *Style—* Sir Andrew Maitland-Makgill-Crichton; 55 Hans Place, Knightsbridge, London SW1 (☎ 01 584 1209)

CRICHTON, Charles Ainslie; s of John Douglas Crichton (d 1963), of Wallasey, and Hester Wingate *née* Ainslie (d 1959); *b* 6 August 1910; *Educ* Oundle, New Coll Oxford (BA); *m* 1, Dec 1936 (m dis), Pearl Allan; 2 s (David b 1938, Nicholas b 1943); m 2, Nadine Charlotte Haze; *Career* film dir; co-directed Dead of Night 1947; directed: Hue and Cry 1947, Against the Wind, Another Shore, Dance Hall, The Lavender Hill Mob 1951, The Titfield Thunderbolt 1953, The Love Lottery, The Divided Heart, Law and Disorder, Floods of Fear, Battle of the Sexes 1959, Boy Who Stole a Million 1960, The Third Secret 1963, He Who Rides a Tiger 1965, A Fish Called Wanda 1987; numerons TV credits incl: Danger Man, The Avengers, Block Beauty, Space 1999; *Recreations* fishing, photography; *Style—* Charles Crichton, Esq; 1 Southwell Gardens, London (☎ 01 373 6546)

CRICHTON, Lady Cleone Lucinda; eldest da of 6 Earl of Erne; *b* 27 August 1959; *Style—* Lady Cleone Crichton

CRICHTON, Lady Davina Jane; 2 da of 6 Earl of Erne; *b* 25 June 1961; *Style—* Lady Davina Crichton

CRICHTON, Viscount; John Henry Michael Ninian Crichton; s and h of 6 Earl of Erne; *b* 19 June 1971; *Style—* Viscount Crichton

CRICHTON, Lady Katherine Patricia; 3 da of 6 Earl of Erne; *b* 4 Nov 1962; *Style—* Lady Katherine Crichton

CRICHTON, Lady (Margaret Vanderlip); da of Col Livingston Watrous, of Washington, DC and Nantucket, Mass, USA; *m* 1944, Sir (John) Robertson (Dunn) Crichton (judge of Crown Ct and judge of High Ct Queen's Bench Div; d 1985); 2 s, 1 da; *Style—* Lady Crichton; Bell House, 22 Albert Square, Bowden, Altrincham, Cheshire WA14 2NO 4SG

CRICHTON, Maurice; s of Maurice Crichton (d 1957), of Glasgow; *b* 4 June 1928; *Educ* Kelvinside Acad, Cargilfield, Sedbergh; *m* 1959, Diana Russell, da of John Russell Lang, CBE; 3 s, 1 da; *Career* chartered accountant, former ptnr Touche Ross and Co; dir Woolwich Equitable Bldg Soc; memb E Kilbride Dvpt Corpn Bd; dir Macphie of Glenbervie Ltd; *Recreations* golf, shooting, music; *Clubs* Caledonian, Western Glasgow; *Style—* Maurice Crichton, Esq; Hall of Caldwell, Uplawmoor, Glasgow (☎ 050 585 248)

CRICHTON, Commander (Francis) Michael; s of Capt Reginald Louis Crichton, RN (d 1928), of Bedhampton, Hants, and Hester Beatrix, *née* White (d 1959); *b* 19 Oct 1909; *Educ* RNC Dartmouth, RNC Greenwich; *Career* served in Med 1927-30, E Indies 1931-34 in HMS Enterprise with HRH Don Juan, China in HMS Eagle and HMS Ladybird in Yangtse Flotilla 1937-39, E Coast Convoys HMS Raleigh, HMS Anson and 1 Lt HMS Illustrious 1939-45, Cmndr RN, CO HMS Rotherham, HMS Ranpura 1947-51; reserve fleet Londonderry 1952-54, Royal Sailingmaster 1948-51; land agent Cron Castle Estate 1954-57; *Recreations* sailing; *Clubs* Royal Cmwlth Soc, Royal Cruising, RN Sailing Assoc, Royal Norfolk and Suffolk Yacht, Lough Erne Yacht; *Style—* Cmndr Michael Crichton; Commander's, Lisbellaw, Enniskillen, N Ireland (☎ 0365 87 273)

CRICHTON, Nicholas; s of Charles Ainslie Crichton, and Vera Pearl McCallum, *née* Harman-Mills; *b* 23 Oct 1943; *Educ* Haileybury, Queen's Univ Belfast (LLB); *m* 29 March 1973, Ann Valerie, da of Col John Eliot Jackson, of Lopcombe Corner, Nr Salisbury, Wilts; 2 s (Simon b 25 Feb 1975, Ian b 12 Jan 1977); *Career* slr 1970; asst slr Currey & Co 1970-71 (articled 1968-70), ptnr Nicholls Christie & Crocker 1974-86 (asst slr 1972 -74); met stipendiary magistrate 1987-; *Recreations* cricket, golf, watching rugby, gardening, birdwatching, walking; *Style—* Nicholas Crichton, Esq; c/o Wells Street, Magistrates Court, 59 Wells St, London W1

CRICHTON, Patrick Henry Douglas; TD (1946); s of Col Hon Sir George Arthur Charles Crichton GCVO (d 1952 s of 4 Earl of Erne), of Queen's Acre, Windsor, Berks, and Lady Mary Augusta, *née* Dawson (d 1961 da of 2 Earl of Dartrey (extinct 1933)); *b* 16 August 1919; *Educ* Eton, Oxford Univ; *m* 1 Oct 1948, Gillian Moyra, da of Right Hon Sir Alexander George Montagu Cadogan OM, GCMG, KCB (d 1968); 2 s (Hugh b 1949 (twin), Desmond b 1953); 1 da (Jane b 1949 (twin); *Career* Maj R A 1939-46, serv: Europe, Malaya, Indonesia; co dir; deputy chm Foreign and Colonial Investment Tst and other Tsts; chm Queen Elizabeths Fndn for the Disabled; *Clubs* Boodle's, MCC; *Style—* Patrick H D Crichton, Esq, TD; West Field Cottage, Upton Grey, Basingstoke, Hampshire (☎ 0256 862230); 1 Laurence Pountney Hill, London EC4R 0BA (☎ 01 623 4680)

CRICHTON, Patrick Henry Douglas; TD (1946); s of Col the Hon Sir George Crichton, GCVO (d 1952), of Queen's Acre, Windsor, Berks, and Lady Mary, *née* Dawson (d 1961), yr da of 2 Earl of Dartrey; *b* 16 Aug 1919; *Educ* Eton, Oxford Univ; *m* 1 Oct 1948, Gilliam Moyra, s of Rt Hon Sir Alexander Codogan, OM, GCMG, KCB (d 1968), of Westminster Gdns; 2 s (Hugh b 1949, Desmond b 1953), 1 da (Jane (twin) b 1949); *Career* WWII 1939-46 served: UK, NW Europe, Malaya, Indonesia; dir Duncan Gilmour & Co Brewers (Sheffield) 1946-51, ptnr Buckmaster & Moore (stockbrokers) 1951-60, Foreign & Colonial Investmt Tst plc (investmt mangrs) 1961-; *Clubs* Boodle's; *Style—* Patrick Crichton, Esq, TD; West Field Cottage, Upton Grey, Basingstoke, Hants (☎ 0526 862 230); 1 Laurence Pountney Hill, London EC4R 0BA (☎ 01 423 4680)

CRICHTON, Col Richard John Vesey; CVO (1986), MC (1940); s of Col Hon Sir George Crichton, GCVO (d 1952, s of 4 Earl of Erne), br Patrick Crichton *qv*; *b* 2 Nov 1916; *Educ* Eton, RMC Sandhurst; *m* 1948, Yvonne Avril Catherine, da of Dr Harry Worthington of Kent; 3 s (Vesey, Adrian, Simon); *Career* cmmnd 2 Lt Coldstream Gds 1936, served WWII Belgium 1940, Italy 1943-44; (twice wounded, despatches); Cmd: 1st Bn Coldstream Gds 1954-57, Coldstream Gds 1958-61, ret 1961; comptroller Union Jack Servs Clubs 1964-66; memb: Hampshire CC 1964-67, HM Bodyguard Hon Corps of Gentlemen at Arms 1966-86; clerk of the Cheque 1979-81; Lt 1981-86; *Books* The Coldstream Guards 1946-70; *Clubs* Cavalry and Guards; *Style—* Col Richard Crichton, CVO, MC; Eglinton Lodge, Hartley Wintney, Hampshire (☎ 025 126 2440)

CRICHTON, Lady Tara Guinevere; yst da of 6 Earl of Erne

CRICHTON-BROWN, Sir Robert; KCMG (1980), CBE (1970), TD (1974); s of late Leslie Crichton-Brown, of Sydney, and Kathleen Mendel, *née* Senior; *b* 23 August 1919; *Educ* Sydney GS; *m* 1941, Norah Isabelle, da of late Albert Edward Turnbull, of Manchester; 1 s, 1 da; *Career* underwriting memb Lloyds 1946, co-ordinator HRH the Duke of Edinburgh's Award Scheme (Australia); company chm and dir, vice-chm Rothmans of Pall Mall Australia Ltd, chm and md Security and General Insurance Co Ltd; kt 1972; *see Debrett's Handbook of Australia and New Zealand for further details*; *Style—* Sir Robert Crichton-Brown, KCMG, CBE, TD; 11 Castlereagh St, Sydney, NSW 2000, Australia

CRICHTON-STUART, Lady James; Anna Rose; da of late Maj Henry McClintock Bunbury Bramwell, 2 Baron Rathdonnell), sometime master Duhallow Hunt, of The White House, Mallow, Co Cork, and Philippa (yst da of Thomas Joseph Carroll-Leahy, JP, sometime master The Woodfort Harriers); *b* 30 May 1940; *Educ* Newhall Sch, Chelmsford Essex; *m* 1970, as his 2 w, Lord James Charles Crichton-Stuart (d 1982), 3 but yr surviving s of 5 Marquess of Bute; 3 s (William b 1971, Hugh b 1973, Alexander b 1982); *Style—* Lady James Crichton-Stuart; Upton Grey House, Upton Grey, Basingstoke, Hants RG25 2RE

CRICHTON-STUART, Lord Anthony; 2 s of 6 Marquess of Bute, JP; *b* 14 May 1961; *Educ* Ampleforth; *Career* art expert; *Style—* Lord Anthony Crichton-Stuart; 15 Fabian Road, London SW6

CRICHTON-STUART, Lady David; Helen; da of William Kerr McColl; *m* 1972, Lord David Ogden Crichton-Stuart (d 1977), s of 5 Marquess of Bute; 1 s, 1 da; *Style—* Lady David Crichton-Stuart; Kames Court, Cronkbourne, Braddan, Isle of Man

CRICHTON-STUART, Lady Janet Egidia; *née* Montgomerie; 2 da of late 16 Earl of Eglinton and Winton by 1 w, Lady Beatrice Dalrymple, da of 11 Earl of Stair; *b* 3 May 1911; *m* 18 April 1934, Capt Lord Robert Crichton-Stuart, Scots Gds (d 1976), s of 4 Marquess of Bute; 2 s; *Style—* Lady Janet Crichton-Stuart; Wards Cottage, Gartocharn, Dunbarton (☎ 038 983 461)

CRICK, Alan John Pitts; OBE (1956); s of Owen John Pitts Crick (d 1972), of Minehead, Somerset, and Margaret, *née* Daw (d 1971); *b* 14 May 1913; *Educ* Latymer Upper Sch, King's Coll London (MA), Heidelberg Univ (DPhil); *m* 1941, Norah, *née* Atkins (d 1984); 2 da; *Career* served Army WWII 1939-46: Egypt, Libya, NW Europe (despatches), Maj; civil servant; joined MOD (Jt Intelligence Bureau) 1946, JSSC 1948, Br Jt Services Mission Washington 1953-56, asst dir Jt Intelligence Bureau MOD 1957-63, IDC 1960, cnsllr Br Embassy Washington 1963-65, asst sec Cabinet Office 1965-68, Defence Intelligence Staff MOD 1968-73, dir Econ Intelligence MOD 1970-73, ret; advsr Commercial Union Assur Gp 1973-78; *Recreations* travel, books, conversation; *Clubs* Naval and Military, Dormy House (Rye); *Style—* Alan Crick, Esq, OBE; 16 Church Sq, Rye, East Sussex (☎ 0797 222050)

CRICK, Charles Anthony; s of Maurice Arthur Crick, TD (d 1979), of 42 Westwood Park Road, Peterborough, and Margaret Matilda, *née* Edney; *b* 7 May 1949; *Educ* Oundle, UCL (LLB); *Career* admitted slr 1974, articled clerk and asst slr Allen and Overy 1972-80, asst slr Middleton Potts and Co 1980-81, ptnr D J Freeman and Co 1981-; Freeman City of London Slrs Co 1986; memb Law Soc; *Recreations* golf, music, painting; *Clubs* Hunstanton Golf ; *Style—* Charles Crick, Esq

CRICK, Richard William; s of Cyril Albert Edden Crick, of 'Jhansi', Rectory Road,

Easton-in-Gordano, Avon, and Blanche Helen, *née* Prewett; *b* 7 June 1946; *Educ* Clifton, Brasenose Coll Oxford (MA); *m* 17 July 1971 (sep), Judith Margaret, da of Huw Jackson (d 1982), of Gateshead; 1 s (James b 1974), 1 da (Sally b 1977); *Career* banker: Hill Samuel and Co Ltd 1972-, (dir 1981-); md Hill Samuel Merchant Bank (SA) Ltd 1981-85; chartered accountant Deloitte, Haskins and Sells 1967-71; *Recreations* golf, skiing, sailing, travel, wine; *Clubs* St Enodol Golf; *Style—* Richard W Crick, Esq; The Granary, Alton Priors, Nr Marlborough, Wiltshire (☎ 0672 85663); Hill Samuel and Co Ltd, 100 Wood Street, London EC2 (☎ 01 628 8011, fax 01 588 5292)

CRICK, Ronald Pitts; s of Owen John Pitts Crick (d 1972), of Minehead, Somerset, and Margaret, *née* Daw (d 1970); *b* 5 Feb 1917; *Educ* Latymer Upper Sch London, King's Coll Hosp Med Sch; *m* 22 March 1941, Jocelyn Mary Grenfell, da of Leonard Adolph Charles Robins (d 1968), of Hendon; 4 s (Martin b 1942, Jonathan b 1948, Adrian b 1950, Humprey b 1957), 1 da (Gillian b 1944); *Career* surgn South America route MN 1939-40, surgn Lt Fleet Air Arm Atlantic, Indian Ocean, Pacific theatres RNVR 1940-46; Kings Coll Hosp: ophthalmic registrar 1946-50, conslt ophthalmic surgn 1950-82; hon conslt ophthalmic surgn 1982-; Royal Eye Hosp: ophthalmic reistrar 1946-50, conslt surgn 1950-69; conslt ophthalmic surgn Belgrave Hosp for Children 1950-66, examiner RCS 1961-68; King's Coll Med Sch: teacher ophthalmology 1960-82, lectr emeritus ophthalmology 1982-; memb ophthalmic speciality ctee SE Thames Regnl Hosp Bd 1970-82, chm: ophthalmic trg ctee SE Thames RHA 1973-82; chm Int Glaucoma Assoc 1974-, Duke-Elder Award Glaucoma American Soc Contemporary Ophthalmology Miami 1985; LRCP 1939, memb Oxford Ophthalmology Congress 1943, DOMS (RCS) 1946, FRCS 1950, FRSM 1950, charter memb int congress American Soc Contemporary Ophthalmology 1977, MRCS; *Books* contributed chapter: The Computerised Monitoring of Glaucoma in Glaucoma-Contemporary International Concepts (J Bellows 1979), The Diagnosis of Chronic Simple Glaucoma in Glaucoma (J Cairns 1985), All About Glaucoma (1981), A Textbook of Clinical Ophthalmology (1987); *Recreations* motoring, sailing, swimming; *Clubs* RAC, Royal Motor Yacht; *Style—* Ronald Crick, Esq; Sandbanks House, Panorama Rd, Sandbanks, Poole, Dorset, BH13 7RD (☎ 0202 707 560); Kings Coll Hosp, Denmark Hill, London, SE5 9RS (☎ 01 274 6222)

CRICKHOWELL, Baron cr 1987 (Life Peer) Roger Nicholas Edwards; PC (1979); s of (H C) Ralph Edwards, CBE, FSA, and Marjorie Ingham Brooke; *b* 25 Feb 1934; *Educ* Westminster, Trinity Coll Cambridge (BA, MA); *m* 1963, Ankaret Healing; 1s, 2 da; *Career* Royal Welsh Fusiliers 1952-54, 2 Lt; employed at Lloyds by Wm Brandt's Ltd 1957-76, chief exec Insur Gp, dir Wm Brandt's 1974-76; dir R W Sturge (Hldgs) Ltd 1970-76, PA Int and Sturge Underwriting Agency Ltd 1977-79; memb Lloyds 1968-; dir Globtik Tankers Ltd 1976-79; MP (Cons) for Pembroke 1970-87 (ret), memb Shadow Cabinet and Cons Front Bench spokesman on Welsh Affairs 1974-79, sec of State for Wales 1979-87; dir Assoc Br Ports Hldgs plc 1987-, dep chm Anglesey Mining plc 1988-, dir HTV Gp plc and chm of its subsidiary Frost & Reed (Hldgs) 1987-, dir Ryan Int plc 1987- and chm of its subsidiary Ryan Keltecs Ltd 1988-, Ctty The Automobile Assoc; pres: Univ of Wales Coll of Cardif 1988-, Contemporary Art Soc for Wales 1988-, South East Wales Arts Assoc 1987-, memb cncl Welsh Nat Opera; *Recreations* fishing, gardening, collecting drawings & watercolours; *Clubs* Carlton, Cardiff and County; *Style—* The Rt Hon Lord Crickhowell; Pont Esgob Mill, Fforest Coal Pit, Abergavenny, Gwent N57 7LS; 4 Henning St, London SW11 3DR

CRICKMAY, John Rackstrow; s of John Edward Crickmay (d 1931), of Weybridge, and Constance May, *née* Bowyer (d 1968); *b* 16 May 1914; *Educ* Brighton Coll; *m* 31 Oct 1939, Peggy Margaret Hilda, *née* Rainer; 1 s (Michael b 1947); *Career* Artists Rifles 1936, Royal Regt of Artillery 1939-46, served in Far East (POW 1942-45); Legal and Gen Assur Soc: surveyor 1936-46, chief estates surveyor 1946-74; conslt to property interests 1974-; pres: Br Chapter Real Estate Property Fedn 1966, Chartered Auctioneers and Estate Agents Inst 1968; hon tres RICS 1980-85 (memb cncl 1972-85), dir Ecclesiastical Insur Off 1980-84, chm Percy Bilton plc 1984-89 (dir 1980-89); govr Royal Star & Garter Richmond 1975-, almoner Christ's Hosp 1977 (dep chm 1984); Freeman City of London 1956, Master Worshipful Co of Ironmongers 1976 (yeoman 1956), hon fell Coll of Estate Mgmnt 1988; FRICS, Medal of Int Real Estate Fedn 1974; *Recreations* cricket, golf; *Clubs* Oriental, MCC, W Sussex GC; *Style—* John Crickmay, Esq; Old Walls, Rectory Lane, Philborough, W Sussex RH20 2AF (☎ 079 82 2336)

CRIGHTON, Prof David George; s of George Wolfe Johnston Crighton (d 1976), and Violet Grace, *née* Garrison; *b* 15 Nov 1942; *Educ* Watford Boys GS, St John's Coll Cambridge (BA, MA), Imperial Coll London (PhD); *m* 1, 2 March 1969 (m dis 1986), Mary Christine, da of Stanley James West, of Tamworth; 1 s (Benjamin b 23 April 1970), 1 da (Beth b 3 Oct 1971); m 2, 6 Sept 1986, Johanna Veronica, *née* Hol; *Career* Prof applied mathematics Leeds Univ 1974-85; Cambridge Univ: prof applied mathematics 1986-, professorial fell St John's Coll 1986-; various scientific papers in jls and conf proceedings in fields of fluid mechanics, acoustics, wave theory and applied mathematics; chm: Joint Mathematical Cncl of UK, Euro Mechanics Ctee; FRAeS 1982, FIMA 1986, FIOA 1988; *Recreations* music, opera; *Style—* Prof David G Crighton; The Laurels, 58 Girton Rd, Cambridge CB3 0LN (☎ 0223 277 100); Cambridge Univ, DAMTP, Silver St, Cambridge CB3 9EW (☎ 0223 337 860, fax 0223 337 918, telex 81240 CAMPSL G)

CRILL, Sir Peter Leslie; CBE (1980); s of Sydney George Crill (d 1959), of Jersey, Connetable of St Clement 1916-58, and Olive, *née* Le Gros (d 1978); family were boatbuilders who came to Jersey from Mannheim in 1785; *b* 1 Feb 1925; *Educ* Victoria Coll Jersey, Exeter Coll Oxford (MA); *m* 1953, Abigail Florence Rosaline (MB), da of Albert Ernest Dodd, JP (d 1949), of Dromara, NI; 3 da (Joanna b 1954, Anthea b 1956, Helena b 1958); *Career* barr Middle Temple 1949, Jersey Bar 1949, States of Jersey Dep for St Clement 1951-58, States of Jersey Senator 1960-62, slr gen Jersey 1962-69, attorney gen Jersey 1969-75, dep bailiff 1975-86, bailiff 1986-; kt 1987; *Recreations* riding, sailing; *Clubs* United Oxford and Cambridge, Royal Yacht Sqdn; *Style—* Sir Peter Crill, CBE; Beechfield House, Trinity, Jersey; Bailiff's Chambers, Royal Court House, Jersey (0534 77111)

CRIPP, Robin Douglas; s of Reginald Henry John Cripp (d 1988), of 10 Leonards Rd, Frimley, Surrey, and Edith May, *née* Tilby; *b* 8 August 1944; *Educ* Wandsworth Comprehensive Sch; *m* 1 June 1968, Cheryl Francis, da of Alfred Lawrence Du Preez, of Southampton; 1 s (Peter Howard b 25 Aug 1969), 1 da (Katie Helen b 25 June 1975); *Career* Redfearn and Redfearn Estate Agents (office boy to mangr) 1960-71, conslt and dir various property cos 1972-74, negotiator and Willmotts of London 1974-79, formed Barnard Marcus & Co (estate agents) 1979; *Recreations* golf, travel; *Clubs* Coombe Hill Golf, RAC, Annabels, The Clermont; *Style—* Robin Cripp, Esq; 28 South St, Mayfair, London W1Y 5PJ (☎ 01 493 8889, car tel 0860 223 793, fax 01 491 3956, telex 269595 BARMAR G)

CRIPPIN, Harry Trevor; s of Harry Crippin and Mary Elizabeth, *née* Settle; *b* 14 May 1929; *Educ* Leigh GS Lancashire; *m* 19 Sept 1959, Hilda Green, JP; 1 s (Paul b 1966), 1 da (Hilary b 1960); *Career* LAC RAF 1947-49, asst Town Clerk Manchester 1970-74, dep dir admin Manchester 1974, city sec Cardiff City Cncl 1974-79, chief exec and town clerk Cardiff City Cncl 1979-88, OStJ, FCIS, FBIM, DMA; *Style—* Harry Crippin, Esq; 37 Ely Rd, Llandaff, Cardiff CF5 2JF (☎ 0222 564103)

CRIPPS, (Matthew) Anthony Leonard; CBE (1971), DSO (1943), TD (1947), QC (1958); s of Maj Hon Leonard Harrison Cripps, CBE (d 1959; 3 s of 1 Baron Parmoor), and Miriam Barbara, *née* Joyce (d 1961); hp of cousin, 4 Baron Parmoor; *b* 30 Dec 1913; *Educ* Eton, Christ Church Oxford (MA); *m* 21 June 1941, Dorothea Margaret, da of George Johnson-Scott (d 1964), of Hill House, Ashby-de-la-Zouch; 3 s (Seddon b 1942, Jeremy b 1943, James b 1956); *Career* Royal Leics Regt 1933-45, Lt-Col; barr: Middle Temple 1938 (bencher 1965, dep tres 1982, tres 1983), Inner Temple 1961, Hong Kong 1974, Singapore 1987; rec: Nottingham 1961-71, Crown Ct 1972-77; judge Ct of Arches 1969-80, dep sr judge Br Sovereign Bases Area Cyprus 1978-; memb: Senate Four Inns of Court 1967-71 and 1982-83, Bar Cncl 1967-69 and 1970-74; chm: disciplinary ctee Milk Mktg Bd 1956-, IOM Agric Mktg Cmmn 1961-62, Home Sec's Advsy Ctee on Serv Candidates 1966-, Nat Panel Approved Coal Merchants Scheme 1972-, legal advsy ctee RSPCA 1977-; memb Agric Wages Bd 1964-73, memb Miny of Agric Ctees of Inquiry: Foot and Mouth Disease 1968-69, Export of Live Animals for Slaughter 1973-74; chm: Reigate Cons Assoc 1961-64, Res Ctee Soc of Cons Lawyers 1963-67, Cons Pty Res Ctee of Inquiry into Discrimination against Women in Law and Admin 1968-69; memb exec ctee Nat Union of Cons Assocs 1964-72, cmmr Local Govt Election Petitions 1978-82; pres Coal Trade Benevolent Assoc 1983, Jr Warden of the Fullers' Co 1988; *Books* Agriculture Act (1947), Agricultural Holdings Act (1948), Cripps on Compensation (nineteenth edn); *Recreations* family life; *Clubs* Brooks's, Lansdowne; *Style—* Anthony Cripps, Esq, CBE, DSO, TD, QC; Woodhurst, McCrae's Walk, Wargrave, Berks RG10 8LN (☎ 073523 3449); 3 Middle Temple Lane, Temple, London EC4Y 9DA; chambers: 1 Harcourt Buildings, Temple, London EC4Y 9DA (☎ 01 353 9421, telex 8956718)

CRIPPS, Brian Edward; s of Henry George Cripps (d 1961), and Winifred Ena, *née* Perkins; *b* 19 August 1932; *Educ* Belmont Newbury; *m* 1, 3 June 1961 (m dis 1969), Jean Patricia Harvey; 1 s (Anthony b 1966), 2 da (Victoria b 1962, Rebecca b 1965); m 2, 23 May 1969, Caroline Ann Hardman, da of Sir Richard Ian Samuel Bayliss, KCVO, of London SW7; 1 step s (Peter b 1965), 1 da (Charlotte b 1970); *Career* CA; ptnr Cripps Weston; FCA; *Recreations* golf, foreign travel; *Clubs* Roehampton; *Style—* Brian Cripps, Esq; 2 Burdenshott Ave, Richmond, Surrey TW10 5ED; 206 Upper Richmond Rd, West London SW14 8AH

CRIPPS, Sir (Cyril) Humphrey; DL (Northants 1985); s of Sir Cyril Thomas Cripps, MBE (d 1979), and Amy Elizabeth, *née* Humphrey (d 1984); *b* 2 Oct 1915; *Educ* Northampton GS, St John's Coll Cambridge (MA); *m* 1942, Dorothea Casson, da of Reginald Percy Cook (d 1968); 3 s (Robert, John, Edward), 1 da (Eleanor); *Career* md Pianoforte Supplies Ltd 1960- (chm 1979-); chm: Air BVI 1971-86, Velcro Indust NV 1973-, Cripps Fndn 1979-; memb: Northants CC 1963-74 (ldr Independents), New CC 1973-81; bd memb Northampton Devpt Corpn 1968-85; life memb of ct Nottingham Univ 1953-; fndn govr Bilton Grange Prep Sch 1957-80; govr: Northampton GS 1963-74, Northampton Sch for Boys 1977-81 (vice-chm Fndn tst 1970-81 and 1986-88, chm 1988-), Northampton HS for Girls 1972-84 (chm); tstee Cripps Postgrad Med Centre at Northampton Gen Hosp 1969-; memb Tsts for Fabric of Peterborough Cathedral 1975-; hon fell: Cripps Hall Univ of Nottingham 1959, St John's Coll Cambridge 1966, Magdalene Coll Cambridge 1971, Selwyn Coll Cambridge 1971, Queens' Coll Cambridge 1979, pres Johnian Soc 1966; Hon DSc Nottingham 1975, Hon LLD Cantab 1976; Liveryman: Worshipful Co of Wheelwrights 1957 (memb ct 1970, Master 1982), Worshipful Co of Tallow Chandlers 1983; Freeman City of London 1957; High Sheriff Northamptonshire 1985-86; FCS, FRIC, CChem, FRSC; kt 1989; *Recreations* travel, photography, natural history (entomology-rhopalocera) philately; *Style—* Sir Humprey Cripps, DL; Bull's Head Farm, Eakley Lanes, Stoke Goldington, Newport Pagnell, Bucks MK16 8LP (☎ 0908 55223); Simplex Works, Road, Northampton NN7 2LG (☎ 0604 862441)

CRIPPS, Sir John Stafford; CBE (1968); s of Rt Hon Sir Stafford Cripps, CH, FRS, QC, sometime Chllr Exchequer (himself yst s of 1 Baron Parmoor), and Dame Isobel Cripps, GBE, *née* Swithinbank; *b* 10 May 1912; *Educ* Winchester, Balliol Oxford; *m* 1, 29 Dec 1936 (m dis 1971), Ursula, da of Arthur Cedric Davy, of Whirlow Court, Sheffield; 4 s, 2 da; m 2, 1971, Ann Elizabeth, da of Edwin G K Farwell, of Swanage; *Career* ed The Countryman 1947-71; chm: RDCs Assoc 1967-70 (memb Witney RDC 1946-74), Countryside Cmmn 1970-77, Rural Ctee Nat Cncl Soc Serv; memb: exec ctee CPRE 1963-69, South East Economic Planning Cncl 1966-73, Nature Conservancy 1970-73, Defence Lands Ctee 1971-73, Water Space Amenity Cmmn 1977-80, Devpt Cmmn 1978-82; pres Camping and Caravanning Club of GB and Ireland 1981-; kt 1978; *Recreations* walking, gardening, photography; *Clubs* Farmer's; *Style—* Sir John Cripps, CBE; Fox House, Filkins, Lechlade, Glos GL7 3JQ (☎ 036 786 209)

CRIPPS, Michael Frederick; s of Maj Charles Philip Cripps, TD, of Sussex, and Betty Christine, *née* Flinn; *b* 22 Oct 1947; *Educ* Felsted Sch Essex, Medway Coll (HNC); *m* 23 April 1982, Carolyn Louise, da of Elie Gabriel Farah; 2 s (Nicholas Frederick b 1985, Christopher Philip b 1988), 1 step s (Alexander Timothy James b 1974); *Career* dist mangr Johnson Gp 1969-72, branch mangr Drake Conslts 1972-73, chm and md Cripps Sears & Ptnrs Ltd (formerly Cripps Sears & Assocs) 1982- (ptnr 1973-78, owner/chief exec 1978-82); corporate MIPM, FInstD 1985; *Recreations* sport generally - active Rugby Football player & supporter, people, travel, contemporary & classical live music; *Clubs* Far Eastern Societies, City of London, MCC; *Style—* Michael Cripps, Esq; Cripps, Sears & Partners, International Buildings, 71 Kingsway, London, WC2B 6ST; (☎ 01 404 5701, fax 01 242 0515, telex 893 155)

CRIPPS, Philip Charles; s of Alan Derek Cripps (d 1958), and Winifred Mary Cripps (d 1958); *b* 29 Dec 1945; *Educ* Royal Pinner Sch Harrow, Aston Univ Birmingham

(BA); *m* 24 June 1967, Jayne, da of Stanley Roney; 2 da (Michelle b 21 Jan 1971, Cara b 7 Jan 1975); *Career* md Thameside Ltd Int Mgmnt Consultants 1977-; non exec dir various companies 1979-; pop single The Joker charted 1983; lectr UK, USA, Europe; *Recreations* squash, water skiing; *Clubs* East Berks Squash, Maidenhead, Westhorpe Water Ski Marlow; *Style*— Philip C Cripps, Esq; Thameside Ltd, International Management Consultants, Thameside House, Lower Rd, Chinnor, Oxon (car tel 0836 581744)

CRIPWELL, Peter; s of Felix John Cripwell, and Barbara Bamford, *née* Mayall; *b* 3 August 1932; *Educ* The Old Hall Shropshire, Repton Sch, RWA Sch of Architecture Bristol; *m* Elizabeth Marcia, da of Marcus Reginald Cholmondeley Overton (d 1940); 4 s (Andrew b 1962, Charles b 1963, Angus b 1965, Crispin b 1966), 1 da (Charlotte b 1970); *Career* chartered architect in private practice in Hereford 1961-; *Recreations* watercolour painting, walking, sailing, skiing, shooting; *Style*— Peter Cripwell, Esq; Lower Upcott, Almeley, Herefordshire HR3 6LA; 3 St Nicholas Street, Hereford, HR4 0BG (☎ 0432 266578)

CRISFORD, John Northcote; s of George Northcote Crisford, CBE, and Effie Mary, *née* Saul; *b* 27 Sept 1915; *Educ* Brighton Coll; *m* 28 June 1947, Prunella Beatrice Evelyn, da of John Ridout-Evans (d 1971); 1 s (Timothy b 1951), 2 da (Mary b 1949, Felicity b 1959); *Career* WWII served RASC, Lancs Fusiliers, Intelligence Corps (India), Capt 1939-45; Advertising, Unilever Ltd, Lintas Ltd 1932-39; dep chief Regnl Offr Central Off of Info Cambridge 1947-48, UK Info Offr Sydney 1949-51, dep publicity mangr The Metal Box Co Ltd 1957-62; associate dir Planned PR (subsidiary of Young and Rubicam Ltd) 1963-66; head of Public Relations, Br Transport Docks Bd 1966-77; chm Winsford Parish Cncl 1980-87; memb: cncl Inst of PR 1959-61, 1963-65 and 1966-72, IPR Examinations Bd 1962-67; FIPR 1969 (pres 1970-71); govr of Communication, Advertising and Mkting Educn Fndn 1969-72 (CAM Dip in PR); memb PR Inst of Australia 1950-53; FRSA 1954; visiting lectr Br Transport Docks Bd Staff Coll 1968-77; lectrs on poetry to clubs, schools, etc 1984 to date; memb PRInst Australia, FRSA 1954; *Publications* Public Relations Advances (1973), Management Guide to Corporate Identity (contrib, ed John Blake, Cncl of Industl Design 1971), The Role of PR in Management (contrib, author Sam Black, 1972), established Nettier House 1981 (publishing own poetry and local guide and history books by Douglas Stevens) publications incl: A Poet's Gift (1981), Were I a Giant (1983), Lot 201 (1984), A Gloria for Special Occasions (1988); *Recreations* reading, walking, writing and producing village amateur dramatics; *Style*— John Crisford, Esq; Nether Halse, Winsford, Minehead, Somerset TA24 7JE (☎ 064 385 314); Nether Halse Books, Winsford, Minehead, Somerset TA24 7JE (☎ 064 385 314)

CRISP, Bernard David James; s of Bertie Bela Crisp (d 1968); *b* 11 June 1926; *Educ* Whitgift, Liverpool Univ; *m* 1947, Lorna Jean, da of Sydney James Clarke (d 1971); 1 s, 1 da; *Career* Lt RNVR; md Cunard Travel Ltd; UK dir Cunard Line Ltd, dir Cunard Cruise Ships Ltd dir Cunard Hotels Ltd; pres SSAFA (Lon); OStJ; FInstM; *Style*— Bernard Crisp, Esq; 2 Norfolk Ave, Sanderstead, Surrey; Cunard Line Ltd, 30/35 Pall Mall, London SW1Y 5LS (☎ 01 930 4321 telex 295483

CRISP, John Charles; s and h of Sir (John) Peter Crisp, 4 Bt; *b* 10 Dec 1955; *Style*— John Crisp, Esq

CRISP, John William Maxwell; s of John Francis Crisp (d 1949), of Berkshire, and Lady Dora Scott, *née* Fox; *b* 10 Nov 1929; *Educ* Eton; *m* 1956, Elizabeth Frances Mary, da of Capt H B Barclay, OBE, MC, of Kenya; 2 s (Hugh b 1958, William b 1960); *Career* 2 Lt Kings Royal Rifle Corps 1949-50, Capt (TA) Westminster Rifles; chm: London Section Inst of Brewing 1951-56, Allied Brewing Trades Assoc 1970, Maltsters Assoc of GB 1973-74, Crisp Malting Ltd 1962-, Anglia Maltings Hldgs Ltd 1982-; chm Pony Club Polo Ctee, fell Inst of Brewing, FRSA; *Recreations* shooting, sailing, walking, tennis; *Clubs* Lansdowne, Green Jackets; *Style*— John Crisp, Esq; Winterlake, Kirtlington, Oxford OX5 3HG (☎ 0869 50384); Anglia Maltings Ltd, Gt Ryburgh, Fakenham, Norfolk NR21 7AS (☎ 0328 78391)

CRISP, Sir (John) Peter; 4 Bt (UK 1913) of Bungay, Suffolk; s of Sir John Wilson Crisp, 3 Bt (d 1950), and Marjorie, *née* Shriver (d 1977); *b* 19 May 1925; *Educ* Westminster; *m* 5 June 1954, Judith Mary, yst da of Herbert Edward Gillett, FRICS (d 1953), of Marlborough, Wilts, and niece of Sir Harold Gillett, Bt; 3 s, 1 da; *Heir* s, John Crisp; *Career* slr (ret) Ashurst Morris Crisp and Co; *Style*— Sir Peter Crisp, Bt; Crabtree Cottage, Drungewick Lane, Loxwood, W Sussex (☎ 752374)

CRISP, Major (John) Simon; s of Maj R J S Crisp (d 1966), of Kirby Cane Hall, Bungay, Suffolk, and Barbara Alexandra, *née* Gooch (d 1986); *b* 19 Jan 1937; *Educ* Eton, RMA Sandhurst; *m* 7 Nov 1975, Christine, Grote da of Count Freidrich-Franz Grote (d 1942), of Schloss Varchentin, Mecklenburg, Germany; 1 s (Edward b 12 Aug 1976); *Career* cmmnd RHG (The Blues) 1956, retd 1976; memb: St John Ambalance (Norfolk), Diocesan Synod; jt master Waveney Harriers 1978-81; Order of Storr (N Class) Afkanistan 1971; *Recreations* hunting, shooting, racing; *Clubs* White, Pratts; *Style*— Maj Simon Crisp; Kirby Cane Hall, Bungay, Suffolk (☎ 050 845 232)

CRISPIN, Nicholas Geoffrey; JP; s of Geoffrey Hollis Crispin, QC (d 1976), of Chipperfield, Herts, and Winifred, *née* Baldwin; *b* 20 Feb 1944; *Educ* Shrewsbury, Pembroke Coll Oxford; *Career* broker at Lloyd's 1966-69, schoolmaster in Uganda, Ascension Island and UK 1970-; memb Lloyd's 1982-; Freeman City of London, Liveryman Worshipful Co of Fan Makers (1968); *Recreations* walking, African affairs; *Style*— Nicholas Crispin, Esq, JP; 36 Little Gaddesden, Berkhamsted, Herts; Longdean School, Hemel Hempstead, Herts

CRITCHELL, Martin Thomas; s of Lionel James Critchell (d 1971), and Irene Florence, *née* Thomas; *b* 24 Sept 1942; *Educ* Betteshanger Sch Kent, Felsted, Oxford Sch of Architecture; *m* 26 Sept 1970, Jillian Ann, da of Francis Edward Coombe, of Cornwall; 2 s (Andrew b 14 June 1971, Alistair b 14 June 1971), 1 da (Kate b 26 Oct 1975); *Career* CA; co-founder and dir Critchell Harrington and Ptnrs Ltd, architects and town planners, ARIBA, FIAA; *Recreations* rifle shooting, skiing; *Clubs* National Rifle Assoc (life memb); *Style*— Martin Critchell, Esq; Cowdry Barn, Birdham, Chichester, W Sussex PO20 7BX (☎ 0245 511031); 44A North Street, Chichester, W Sussex PO19 1NF (☎ 0243 780351, fax 0243 782917)

CRITCHETT, Sir Ian George Lorraine; 3 Bt (UK 1908) of Harley St, Boro' of St Marylebone; s of Sir Montague Critchett, 2 Bt (d 1941), and Innes, *née* Wiehe (d 1982); *b* 9 Dec 1920; *Educ* Harrow, Clare Coll Cambridge (BA); *m* 1, 9 Oct 1948, Paulette Mary Lorraine (d 4 May 1962), eld da of late Col Henry Brabazon Humfrey; m 2, 10 Feb 1964, Jocelyn Daphne Margret, eldest da of Cdr Christopher Mildmay Hall, of Higher Boswarva, Penzance, Cornwall; 1 s, 1 da; *Heir* s, Charles George Montague Critchett; *Career* RAFVR 1942-1946; FO 1948, 3 sec Vienna 1950, 2 sec Bucharest 1951, 2 sec Cairo 1956, 1 sec and later cnsllr FCO 1962, ret 1980; *Clubs* Travellers', MCC; *Style*— Sir Ian Critchett, Bt; Uplands Lodge, Pains Hill, Limpsfield, Oxted, Surrey (☎ 0883 72 2371)

CRITCHLEY, Julian Michael Gordon; MP (C) Aldershot 1970-; s of Dr Macdonald Critchley, CBE, and his 1 wife Edna Auldeth, *née* Morris; *b* 8 Dec 1930; *Educ* Shrewsbury, Sorbonne, Pembroke Coll Oxford (MA); *m* 1, 1955, Paula Joan Baron; 2 da; m 2, 1965, Mrs Heather Goodrick, da of Charlie Moores (d 1947); 1 s, 1 da; *Career* writer, journalist; MP (C) Rochester and Chatham 1959-64; chm Bow Gp 1966-67; *Recreations* Staffordshire pottery, watching boxing, military history; *Style*— Julian Critchley Esq, MP; The Brewer's House, 18 Bridge Sq, Farnham, Surrey (☎ 0252 722075)

CRITCHLEY, (Cyril Fletcher) Peter; TD (1946); s of James Henry Critchley (d 1963), and Margaret Celia Fletcher; *b* 7 July 1909; *Educ* Dulwich Coll, London Univ (MS); *m* 15 March 1940, Dorothy Sinclair, da of Seymour Fell Law (d 1970), of Crediton, Devon; 1 s (John b 1942), 1 da (Ann b 1945); *Career* Lt-Col RAMC France 1939, 14 Army 1942-45; Hon Lt-Col 1946, gen surgn South East and South West Metropolitan Regnl Hosp Bds, now hon surgeon FRCS; *Recreations* hill walking, photography; *Clubs* Army and Navy; *Style*— Peter Critchley, Esq; Henley Old Farm, Buckland Newton, Dorset (☎ 030 05 210)

CRITCHLEY, Philip; s of Henry Stephen Critchley (d 1980), of Cumbria, and Edith Adela, *née* Currie (d 1980); *b* 31 Jan 1931; *Educ* Manchester GS, Balliol Coll Oxford (MA); *m* 1962, Stella Ann, da of Frederick John Barnes, of Kent; 2 s (Conrad b 1965, Brian b 1966), 1 da (Rachel b 1971); *Career* Nat Serv Intelligence Corps 1953-55, Corpl BAOR; civil servant; under sec DOE, dir Contracts Highways Admin and Maintenance Dept of Tport; *Recreations* cycling, walking, writing poetry; *Clubs* Blackheath Harriers, Oxford Union; *Style*— Philip Critchley, Esq; Redstone House, Maidstone Road, Ashford, Kent TN25 4NP (☎ 0233 621037); US/DHCAM, Dept of Tport, 2 Monck St, London SW1P 3EB (☎ 01 276 2830)

CRITCHLEY, Thomas Alan (Tom); yst s of Thomas Critchley (d 1963), of Middx, and Annie Louisa Darvell (d 1956); *b* 11 Mar 1919; *Educ* Queen Elizabeth's Sch Barnet; *m* 1942, Margaret Carol, da of Walter Harold Robinson (d 1954), of Barnet; 1 s (Alan), 2 da (Carol, Barbara); *Career* Lt RAOC 1945-46, Egypt; asst under sec of state Home Off 1971-76; Coronation Medal 1953; *Books* Civil Service Today (1959), A History of Police (1967), The Conquest of Violence (with P D James, 1970), The Maul and the Pear Tree (1971); *Recreations* gardening, reading, walking; *Clubs* Reform, Civil Serv; *Style*— Tom Critchley, Esq; 26 Temple Fortune Lane, London NW11 7UD

CRITCHLEY, Tom; s of Leonard Critchley (d 1986), and Jessie, *née* Turner (d 1988); *b* 17 August 1928; *Educ* Sheffield Coll of Technol; *m* 15 Dec 1951, Margaret, da of Frederick Bland (d 1934); 1 s (Andrew b 1959); *Career* Davy-Ashmore Gp 1951-66, Cammell Laird and Upper Clyde Gps 1966-69, JCB Gp 1969-70, EMI Gp 1970-80, head Investmt Casting Missen to Canada; UN advsr: Tanzanian Govt, High Cmmn for Refugees; sr ptnr Int Consultancy Practice 1980-85, memb bd Nat Inst of Govt Purchasing USA 1977-78, UK del Int Fedn of Purchasing and Materials Mgmnt 1978-82, dir Int Mgmnt Inst 1984-88, faculty memb Mgmnt Centre Europe 1980-86 fell Inst of Purchasing and Supply 1967 (chm of cncl 1974-75, pres 1977-78, chm External Affrs 1978-82 memb Int Cncl 1979-82); under sec Dept of Health 1986-, memb NHS Mgmnt Bd for Procurement and Distribution 1987-; *Recreations* competitive sports, live theatre, north American history; *Style*— Tom Critchley, Esq; NHS Procurement Directorate, 14 Russell Square, London WC1B 5EP (☎ 01 636 6811, fax 01 637 8990)

CRITCHLOW, Keith Barry; s of Michael Bernard Critchlow (d 1972), of London, and Rozalind Ruby, *née* Weston-Mann (d 1983); *b* 16 Mar 1933; *Educ* Summerhill Sch, St Martins Sch of Art London (Inter NDD), RCA (ARCA); *m* Gail Susan, da of Geoffrey W Henebery; 1 s (Matthew Alexander), 4 da (Louise Penelope, Amanda Jane, Amelia Poppy, Dawn Kathy); *Career* Nat Serv RAF 1951-53; lectr at most Art & Architecture Schools in the UK; teaching appts at: Harrow, Sir John Cass, Hornsey, Architectural Assoc Sch Watford, Wimbledon, The Slade, The Royal Coll; appts abroad in: Ghana, Kuwait, Sweden, Aust, India, USA, Canada, Jordan, Iran, Saudi Arabia; former; tutor and res dir The Architectural Assoc, tutor in painting Sch of the Royal Coll of Art, tutor Slade Sch, dir Visual Islamic Arts Course Royal Coll of Art; fndr own architectural design off; buildings designed in: USA, Kuwait, Saudi Arabia, Iran, Krishnamurti Study Centre in UK; FRCA 1986, FIMD (USA) 1987; *Books* Order in Space (1969), Chartres Maze a model of the Universe?, Islamic Pattern a cosmological approach, The Sphere Soul & Androgyne, Into the Hidden Environment; *Recreations* painting, writing, geometry, walking, photography, meditation; *Style*— Keith Critchlow, Esq; VIA Royal Coll of Art, Exhibition Rd, London SW7 2EU (☎ 01 504 5020, ext 294, 01 627 4326)

CROASDAILE, John Trench; s of John Ernest Croasdaile (d 1954), of Co Antrim (*see* Burke's Irish Family Records 1976), and Una Mary Fetherstonhaugh, *née* Barker (d 1960); *b* 14 Mar 1911; *Educ* Repton, Trinity Coll Dublin (BA, LLB); *Career* slr; *Recreations* gardening; *Style*— John T Croasdaile, Esq; 16 Ballywillan Road, Portrush, Co Antrim (☎ 0265 823229); 23 New Row, Coleraine, Co Londonderry (☎ 0265 2007, 0265 2970)

CROCKATT, Lt Cdr (Douglas) Allan; OBE (1981, MBE 1971), RD (1978), JP (WR Yorks 1956), DL (1971); s of Douglas Crockatt JP, (d 1980), of Wetherby, W Yorks, and Ella, *née* Lethem (d 1981); *b* 31 Jan 1923; *Educ* Bootham Sch York, Trinity Hall Cambridge, Southampton Univ; *m* 10 Aug 1946, Helen Townley (d 1985), da of Capt Thomas Arthur Tatton, MC (d 1968), of Cuerden Hall, Lancs; 1 da; *Career* WWII RNVR, Western Approaches and N Russia 1941-46; RNVSR 1946-64, RNR active list 1964-82; dir: Johnson Gp Cleaners 1961-84 (dep chm 1976-84), Johnson Gp Inc (USA) until 1984; memb: Multiple Shops' Fedn Cncl 1972-77, CC West Riding Yorks 1953-58; W Yorks Branch Magistrates' Assoc: hon sec 1958-72, chm 1975-77, pres 1977-79, life vice-pres 1980-; memb: Magistrates' Assoc Cncl 1959-80 (chm trg ctee 1974-80), Lord Chllr's Advsy Ctee for Trg of Magistrates 1964-79, Lord Chllr's Magistrates' Cts Rule Ctee 1979-81; local dir Martins and Barclays Banks W Yorks bd 1964-84; Freeman City of London 1958--, memb Worshipful Co of Dyers Vice Lord-Lt of West Yorks 1985-; *Recreations* cricket, sailing (yacht 'Union Jack'), fishing; *Clubs* Army and Navy, RNSA, Driffield Anglers; *Style*— Lt Cdr Allan Crockatt, OBE, RD, JP, DL; Paddock House, Sicklinghall, Wetherby, W Yorks LS22 4BJ (☎ 0937 62844)

CROCKATT, John Lethem; s of Douglas Crockatt, JP, LLD (d 1980), of Wetherby, W Yorks, and Ella, *née* Lethem (d 1981); *b* 7 June 1920; *Educ* Bootham Sch York,

Trinity Hall Cambridge (educ interrupted by WWII), London Univ (LLB); *m* 1941, Josephine Rose, *née* Dickenson; 5 s, 1 da; *Career* WWII Merchant Navy 1939-45 (inc 1 year seamanship instr at first Outward Bound Sch); chm Johnson Gp Cleaners 1975-85, chm American Cos 1985-87 (joined as trainee 1946), dir Univs Superannuation Scheme Ltd; pres Merseyside Pre-Retirement Assoc, vice-pres Merseyside and Deeside Outward Bound Assoc, memb Ct of Worshipful Co of Dryer (formerly Prime Warden); JP, FRSA; *Recreations* sailing, reading, music; *Clubs* Army and Navy, Royal Overseas, Holyhead Sailing, Cruising Assoc; *Style—* John L Crockatt, Esq; Rosemount, 112 Victoria Road, Formby, Liverpool L37 1LP, Merseyside

CROCKATT, Maj Richard Meredith; s of Brig Norman Richard Crockatt, CBE, DSO, MC (d 1956), of Ulverscroft, Virginia Water, Surrey, and Sidney Alice Rose *née* Tweedy (d 1962); *b* 27 Nov 1921; *Educ* Rugby; *m* 6 Dec 1947, Elizabeth, da of André Falck (d 1958), of Southampton; *Career* regular offr The Royal Scots 1941-56, India and Burma (despatches) 1942-45, Capt 1944, Malaya 1945, Maj 1951, Staff Coll 1951 (psc); Korea, Egypt, Cyprus 1954-56; memb London Stock Exchange 1956; ptnr: Earnshaw Haes and Sons 1956-76, James Capel and Co 1976-87; chm James Capel and Co (CI) 1985-87, chm CI Portfolio Mangrs 1988); *Recreations* golf; *Clubs* White's, City of London, Swinley Forest Golf, Victoria (Jersey); *Style—* Maj Richard M Crockatt; La Petite Lande, Corbière, Jersey, Channel Islands (☎ 0534 42864)

CROCKER, James William Tailby; s of Sir William Charles Crocker (d 1973), and Mary Madeline, *née* Tailby (d 1953); *b* 10 July 1925; *Educ* Marlborough, Clare Coll Cambridge (MA); *m* 26 July 1948, Barbara, da of Harold Riversdale Morgan (d 1950); 1 s (Simon b 1948); *Career* Lt RNVR 1944-46; admitted slr 1952, dir United Services Auto Assoc Ltd 1952-, sr ptnr Messrs William Charles Crocker; *Recreations* vintage cars and motor cycles, music; *Clubs* Arts; *Style—* James W T Crocker, Esq; 15 Graham Terrace, London SW1; Messrs William Charles Crocker, New Mercury House, 81-82 Farringdon St, London EC4A 4BT (☎ 01 353 0311, telex 883430, fax 01 583 1417)

CROCKER, Trevor James Codrington; s of Henry Ernest Crocker (d 1966), and Lily Lavinia, *née* Davis (d 1969); *b* 14 Mar 1925; *Educ* Reigate GS, London Univ (BSc), City Univ (MPhil), RCM; *m* 20 March 1954, Sylvia, da of Frederick George Hill; 3 da (Diana, b 1955, Pamela b 1958, Susan b 1961); *Career* co fndr and chm: Engrg Surveys Ltd 1960-70, Trevor Crocker & Ptnrs Int Consulting Engrs 1960-88, (fndr conslt 1988-); non-exec dir Allied Partnership Gp plc 1986, arbitrator numerous engrg disputes; City Univ: memb Ct 1972-, chm convocation 1982-86 (dep chm 1980-82); memb London Ctee Glastonbury Abbey Devpt Tst; Freeman City of London, Master Worshipful Co of Glaziers and Painters of Glass 1987- 88, co-fndr Worshipful co of Engrs (jr and sr warden), Liveryman Worshipful co of Fan Makers; FICE 1965, FIMechE 1968, FIE Aust 1968, FCIArb 1972, ARCM 1970; *Recreations* offshore sailing, music-making; *Clubs* City Livery, Carlton; *Style—* Trevor Crocker, Esq; 4 Ormsby, Grange Rd, Sutton Surrey; Freshwinds, Spinney Lane, Itchenor, Chichester, West Sussex (☎ 01 643 3056); Allied Partnership Group plc, Ryedale House, Piccadilly, York (☎ 0904 646891)

CROCKER, Sir Walter Russell; KBE (1976, CBE 1957); s of Robert Crocker (d 1957), of Parnaroo, S Australia, and Alma Eliza, *née* Bray (d 1949); *b* 25 Mar 1902; *Educ* Peterborough Sch, Adelaide Univ (BA), Balliol Coll Oxford (BA, MA), Stanford Univ USA; *m* 1951 (m dis 1968), Claire, da of Frederick J Ward, OBE (d 1958), and wid of Dr John Gooden; 2 s; *Career* served Br Colonial Serv (Nigeria) and Br Army UK, Africa, India 1940-46 (Croix de Guerre avec Palme 1945, Ordre Royal du Lion Belgium 1945), Lt-Col 1945; Australian dip ret 1970, Lt-Govr of S Australia 1973-82; Knight of Italy 1970, Grand Officer Order of Malta 1972; *see Debrett's Handbook of Australia and New Zealand for further details*; *Recreations* walking, gardening, music; *Style—* Sir Walter Crocker, KBE; 256 East Terrace, Adelaide, S Australia 5000

CROCKETT, Clifden Robert; s of Leonard Marhsall Crockett, OBE (d 1951), of Northampton, and Eleanor Carol Crockett, *née* Baker; gf Sir James Henry Clifden Crockett (d 1931), of Northampton; *b* 27 May 1922; *Educ* Charterhouse, Trinity Hall Cambridge; *m* 3 April 1948, Winifred Muriel, da of Norman Henry Mohun, (d 1977), of Kettering; 2 s (John b 1951, Nigel b 1954); *Career* Lt Royal Signals 1941-46, Italy, Palestine; slr to Duchy of Lancaster 1966-73, with treasury slr 1974-84 (ed of Statutory Publications 1982-85); *Recreations* photography, music, Open Univ; *Style—* Clifden R Crockett, Esq; 19 The Avenue, Dallington, Northampton (☎ 0604 51813)

CROCKFORD, Maj Kenneth Harold; MC (1946); *b* 16 July 1923; *Career* cmmnd KSLI 1943, served Herefordshire Regt UK and NW Europe 1944-46, Devon Regt Germany 1946, ADC to GOC 5 Div Germany 1947, SO Germany 1948-49, Instr Army Mechanical Tport Sch 1949-53, co cdr and SO Egypt 1953-56, Adj 3 Divnl Column 1957, student Long Tport Course 1958, cdr Jr Leader Unit RASC 1959-60, OC tport co Kenya 1961-62; SO2: HQ Maritime Gp 1963-65, Gurkha Bde Borneo 1966, HQ FARELF Singapore 1967-68; Save the Children Fund: supplies offr 1971-77, UK controller 1978-82, vehicle/insur mangr 1983-87; ret 1987; Chevalier de l'Ordre de Leopold II (avec Palme 1946); Croix de Guerre 1940 avec Palme 1946; *Recreations* country walking, photography, philately, gardening, travel; *Style—* Maj Kenneth Crockford, MC; 21 Home Farm Rd, Godalming, Surrey GU7 1TX

CROCKFORD, Philip David Vyvyan; s of Philip Theodore Clive Crockford (d 1950), and Muriel Mary, *née* Moorhouse (d 1988); *b* 21 Nov 1930; *Educ* Merchant Taylors', RMA Sandhurst; *m* 11 July 1953, Margaret Kathleen, da of Maj Charles Deane Cowper; 1 s (Adrian Robert Vyvyan b 27 April 1956), 2 da (Sarah Claire d'Ambrumenil 25 Aug 1954, Charlotte Kathleen Winifred b 2 March 1962); *Career* cmmnd RA 1951-55; sales mktg IBM (UK) Ltd, PA Mgmnt Conslts Ltd; dir: Willws Faber Dumas Ltd, Alexander Howden Underwriting Ltd; md Crockford Devitt Underwriting Agencies Ltd; memb Lloyds; *Recreations* foxhunting, collecting antiquarian books; *Clubs* City University; *Style—* David Crockford, Esq; 16 Byward St, London EC3

CROFT, Col (Noel) Andrew Cotton; DSO (1945), OBE (1970); s of Rev Canon Robert William Croft (d 1947), of Kelvedon Vicarage, Essex, and Lottie Alice Bland, *née* Clayton (d 1962); *b* 30 Nov 1906; *Educ* Lancing, Stowe, Christ Church Oxford (MA), Sch of Technol Manchester; *m* 24 July 1952, Rosalind, da of Cdr AH de Kantzow, DSO, RN (d 1928); 3 da (Clare b 1953, Corinna b 1955, Julia b 1957); *Career* under mangr cotton trade Manchester 1929-32, Br Trans-Greenland expdn (Guiness Book of Records longest self-supporting dog-sledge journey) 1933-34, ADC to Maharajah of Cooch Behar India 1934-35, 2 i/c Oxford Univ Artic Expdn to Swedish Lpland 1937-38, res Cambridge Univ 1938-39; WWII: serv capt 1939, cmd WO mission to Russo-Finnish war 1939-40, Bde Intellingence Offr Ind Companies Norwegian Campaign 1940, advsr Admty Combined Ops 1940-41, maj 1941, asst mil attaché Stockholm 1941-42, OC sear or parachute ops (Norway, Corsica, Italy, France, Denmark), Lt-Col 1945; asst dir of sci res WO 1945-48, WO rep Canadian Artic Exercise Musk-Ox 1945-46, sr observer NW Frontier Trials India 1946-47, attached Canadian Army 1947-48, GSOI WO 1948-51, Br Jt Servs Mission USA 1952-54, sr liason offr HQ Contnental Armies, OC Inf Jr Ldrs BN Plymouth 1954-57; cmdt: Army Apprentices Sch Harrogate 1957-60, Met Police Cadet Corps 1960-71; fell RGS (BACK award 1945 and 46, hon sec 1951, memb cncl 1949-51), corresponding fell Artic Inst of N America, memb ctees Scott Polar Res Inst 1946-, life memb RIIA; Polar Medal (1945 Clasp Arctic 1936); *Books* Polar Exploration (1939, seconded 1947), Under The Pole Star (with AR Glen 1937); *Recreations* sailing, skiing, mountaineering, photography; *Clubs* Alpine, Special Forces (tstee), Arctic (member and former sec); *Style—* Col Andrew Croft, DSO, OBE; The River House, 42 Strand-on-the-Green, London W4 3PD (☎ 01 994 6359)

CROFT, Hon Bernard William Henry Page; s and h of 2 Baron Croft by his w, Lady Antoinette Fredericka Hersey Cecilia Conyngham (d 1959), da of 6 Marquess Conyngham; *b* 28 August 1949; *Educ* Stowe, Wales Univ (BSc); *Style—* The Hon Bernard Croft

CROFT, Charles Beresford; s of Arthur James Croft (d 1979), and Margaret Bays Conyers, *née* Wright; *b* 14 Jan 1943; *Educ* Worksop Coll; Leeds Univ Medical Sch (MB, ChB); *m* 23 March 1968, Hilary Louise Whitaker, da of Ronald Whitaker (d 1968); 1 da (Emma Louise b 1972); *Career* conslt surgn and assoc prof Albert Einstein Sch of Med NY 1974-79; conslt surgn: The Royal Nat Throat Nose and Ear Hosp London, The Nat Heart and Chest Hosp London 1979-; civil conslt Laryngology RAF 1983-; FRCS Eng (1970), FRCS Edinburgh (1972); *Recreations* golf, tennis, sailing; *Clubs* Moor Park Golf, Royal Soc of Medicine; *Style—* Charles B Croft, Esq; 91 Copsewood Way, Northwood, Middx (☎ Northwood 23793); 55 Harley St, London W1N 1DD (☎ 01 580 242)

CROFT, David; OBE; s of Reginald Sharland (d 1944), of Hollywood, and Anne, *née* Croft (d 1960); *b* 7 Sept 1922; *Educ* Rugby; *m* 2 June 1952, Ann Callender, da of Reginald Coupland (d 1983), 4 s (Nicholas b 26 March 1953, John b 11 May 1964, Richard b 18 Nov 1969, Tim b 10 Sept 1973); 3 da (Penelope b 10 April 1954, Jane b 16 July 1960, Rebecca b 23 Jan 1962); *Career* WWII RA 1942, Dorset Regt 1944; served: N Africa, India, Malaya, WO; final rank Maj; actor 1946, BBC writer 1951-, script ed Rediffusion 1955, writer dir Tyne Tees 1960-61, writer dir BBC 1962; co-writer, prod and dir: Dad's Army, It Ain't 'Alf Hot Mum, Are You Being Served, Hi De Hi, Allo Allo; memb BAFTA; *Style—* David Croft, Esq, OBE; BBC TV, Television Centre, Shepherds Bush, London

CROFT, His Hon Judge; David Legh; QC (1982); s of Alan Croft (d 1965), of Dore, Sheffield, and Doreen Mary Mitchell; *b* 14 August 1937; *Educ* Haileybury, Nottingham Univ (LLB); *m* 1963, Susan Mary, da of George Richard Winnington Bagnall (d 1982), 2 s (Rupert b 1966, Jocelyn 1968); *Career* called to bar 1960, QC 1982, circuit judge 1987-; *Style—* His Hon Judge Croft, QC

CROFT, Maj Sir John Archibald Radcliffe; 5 Bt (UK 1818), of Cowling Hall, Yorks; s of Tom Radcliffe Croft, OBE (d 1964, s of 2 Bt); suc cous 1979; *b* 27 Mar 1910; *Educ* King's Sch Canterbury; *m* 26 Sept 1953, Lucy Elizabeth, da of late Maj William Dallas Loney Jupp, OBE; 1 s; *Heir* s, Thomas Croft; *Career* Maj W Yorks Regt (ret); *Recreations* shooting, fishing, golf; *Clubs* Army and Navy; *Style—* Maj Sir John Croft, Bt; The Barn House, Rayham Farm, Whitstable, Kent (☎ 0227 277816)

CROFT, Maj The Rev John Armentières; MC (1944); s of late Brig Gen WD Croft, CB, CMG, DSO (d 1968), of The Anchorage, Mawnan, Falmouth, and Esme Sutton (d 1977); *b* 1 Jan 1915; *Educ* Stowe, RMC Sandhurst, Staff Coll Guetta, Salisbury Theological Coll; *m* 19 Dec 1948, Sheila Kathleen, da of James Arthur Ford (Maj TA, d 1951), of Pengreep, Ponsanooth, nr Truro, Cornwall; 1 s (Hugh b 1954), 1 da (Patricia Lucy (Mrs Rowe) b 1951); *Career* cmmnd 1934, attached Duke of Wellington serv NW Frontier 1935 (despatches), serv 20 Lancers Royal Deccan Horse 1935-43, transferred 1/16 Punjab Regt in Imphal 1943, wounded 1944, staff coll transferred RA, staff appts HG AA Gp and W Africa, ret 1953; asst curate of Madron The Old Parish Church of Penzance, vicar og Gwinear Cornwall 1960-70, help as ret vicar South Devon (now Dorset/Wilts); hon chaplain Penzance Sea Cadets 1961-70; *Recreations* riding, rambling; *Clubs* Army and Navy; *Style—* Maj The Rev John Croft, MC; Vine House, The Common, Wincanton, Somerset (☎ 0963 32253)

CROFT, (Ivor) John; s of Oswald Hamilton Croft (d 1980), and Augusta Doris, *née* Phillips (d 1985); *b* 6 Jan 1923; *Career* temp jr admin offr FO 1942-45, asst teacher London CC 1949-51; Home Off: inspr childrens' dept 1952-66, sr res offr 1966-72, head of res unit 1972-81, head of res and planning unit 1981-83; chm criminological scientific cncl Euro ctee on crime problems Cncl of Europe 1981-83 (memb 1978-83); various one-man shows as a painter 1958-; memb exec ctee English Assoc, chm Pembridge Assoc; various publications on crime published by the Home Off and Cons Study Gp on Crime; *Clubs* Reform; *Style—* John Croft, Esq; 30 Stanley Rd, Peel, Isle of Man (☎ 0624 84 3707)

CROFT, June Alexandra; da of Derek Croft, of Wigan Lancashire, and Rita, *née* Kay; *b* 17 June 1963; *Educ* Cansfield HS; *Career* silver medallist 4 x100 medley relay Moscow 1980 olympics, 3 Gold Medals (100 freestyle and 200 freestyle and 4 x 100 freestyle relay) Brisbane 1982 Cwlth Games, Bronze medallist 400 mtr freestyle, Los Angeles 1984 Olympics, ret 1984-86, swam 1988 Seoul Olympics; *Recreations* swimming; *Clubs* Wigan Wasps Swimming; *Style—* Miss June Croft; 43 Upper Dicconson St, Wigan, Lancs (☎ 0942 41329)

CROFT, (Herbert) Kemble; s of (Herbert) William Croft (d 1964), and Marjory Kemble Howden (d 1951); *b* 20 July 1930; *Educ* Downside, Royal W of England Acad, Sch of Arch; *m* 9 May 1964, Juliet Sara, da of late Dr Robin Williamson; 2 s (John b 1965, Thomas b 1970), 1 da (Kate b 1966); *Career* Nat Serv cmmnd 2 Lt RA; regnl architect NW Thames RHA, md First Hosp Architecture 1986-; *Recreations* theatre, history of art, sport (esp cricket); *Style—* Kemble Croft, Esq; 2 Hillyard Barns, Sutton Courtenay, Oxon OX14 4BJ (☎ 0235 847439); First Hosp Architecture, 12-18 Grosvenor Gardens, London SW1 W0DH (☎ 01 824 8215, fax 01 730 4816)

CROFT, 2 Baron (UK 1940); Sir Michael Henry Glendower Page Croft; 2 Bt (UK 1924); s of 1 Baron, CMG, TD, PC (d 1947), and Hon Nancy Beatrice Borwick, da of 1 Baron Borwick; *b* 20 August 1916; *Educ* Eton, Trinity Hall Cambridge; *m* 1948, Lady Antoinette Conyngham (d 1959), da of 6 Marquess Conyngham; 1 s, 1 da; *Heir* s, Hon Bernard Croft; *Career* barr 1952; former dir Henry Page and Co and

Ware Properties Ltd; underwriting memb Lloyd's 1971-; FRSA; OStJ; *Style*— The Rt Hon the Lord Croft; Croft Castle, nr Leominster, Herefordshire

CROFT, Sir Owen Glendower; 14 Bt (E 1671) of Croft Castle, Herefordshire; s of Sir Bernard Croft, 13 Bt (d 1984), and Helen, Lady Croft, *qv*; *b* 26 April 1932; *m* 1959, Sally, da of Dr Thomas Montagu Mansfield of Brisbane, Australia; 1 s, (Thomas), 2 da (Patricia b 1960, Georgiana b 1964); *Heir* s, Thomas Jasper, *qv*; *Style*— Sir Owen Croft, Bt; Salisbury Court, Uralla, NSW 2358, Australia

CROFT, Thomas Jasper; s and h of Sir Owen Glendower Croft, 14 Bt, *qv*, and Sally, da of Dr Thomas Montagu Mansfield; *b* 3 Nov 1962; *Style*— Thomas Jasper, Esq; c/o Salisbury Court, Uralla 2358, NSW, Australia

CROFT, Thomas Stephen Hutton; s and h of Major Sir John Croft, 5 Bt, and Lady (Lucy) Croft; *b* 12 June 1959; *Educ* King's Sch Canterbury, UCL (BSc), RCA (MA); *Career* architect, Br Inst prize for Architecture, 1984; *Clubs* Groucho; *Style*— Thomas Croft, Esq; 53 Leinster Sq, London W2 4PV (☎ 01 229 6547)

CROFT-SMITH, Graham; s of Thomas John Winter Smith (d 1975); *b* 3 Oct 1951; *Educ* Highgate Wood Comprehensive, Haringay N London; *m* 29 Sept 1973, Josephine, da of Francois Mangion; 1 s (Steven b 22 March 1984), 1 da (Jane b 17 March 1980); *Career* dir Alexanders Rouse Ltd; *Recreations* golf, light music (not classical); *Style*— Graham Croft-Smith, Esq; Alexanders Rouse Ltd, 1 St Katherines Way, London E1 9UN (☎ 01 481 0283, car ☎ 0034 217 897)

CROFTON, 6 Baron (I 1797); Sir Charles Edward Piers Crofton; 9 Bt (I 1758); s of 5 Baron (d 1974), and Ann, da of Gp Capt Charles Tighe; *b* 27 April 1949; *m* 1976, Maureen Jacqueline, da of S Bray, of Taunton; 1 da; *Heir* bro, Hon Guy Crofton; *Career* with Buries Markes (Ship Mgmnt) Ltd; (Cert of Competancy as Master Mariner 5 July 1978), promoted to Master with Buries Markes (S.M) Ltd 1979; *Style*— The Rt Hon the Lord Crofton

CROFTON, Derek Fergus Regan; s of late William Crofton; *b* 15 Feb 1934; *Educ* Rockwell Coll, Univ Coll Dublin; *m* 1959, Marian Emily, *née* Lindsay; 2 s, 1 da; *Career* CA 1958, fin dir and co sec Shell Chemicals UK Ltd 1974-, chm Vencel Resil Ltd 1974-, dir Ward Blenkinsop Ltd; *Style*— Derek Crofton, Esq; The Red Lodge, North Rd, Hale, Cheshire (☎ 061 980 8280)

CROFTON, Hon Guy Patrick Gilbert; s of 5 Baron Crofton (d 1974), and hp of bro, 6 Baron; *b* 17 June 1951; *m* 1985, Gillian S B, only da of Harry Godfrey Mitchell Bass, CMG, of Reepham, Norfolk; 2 s (twins b 1988); *Career* Maj 9/12 R Lancers (POW); *Clubs* Cavalry and Guards'; *Style*— The Hon Guy Crofton; c/o Royal Bank of Scotland, Holts Branch, 22 Whitehall, London SW1

CROFTON, Sir John Wenman; er s of Dr William Mervyn Crofton; *b* 1912; *Educ* Tonbridge, Sidney Sussex Coll Cambrdge (BA, MA, MD), St Thomas's Hosp (MB BCh); *m* 1945, Eileen Chris Mercer, MBE (1984); *Career* prof of respiratory diseases and tuberculosis Edinburgh Univ 1952-77 (former sr lectr in medicine Postgraduate Medical Sch of London 1947-51), dean Faculty of Medicine 1963-66, vice principal 1970-71; pres Royal Coll of Physicians Edinburgh 1973-76; Hon FRACP; MRCS, LRCP, MRCP, FRCP, FRCPE, FACP, FRCPI, FFCM; kt 1977; *Style*— Sir John Crofton; 13 Spylaw Bank Rd, Edinburgh EH13 OJW (☎ 031 441 3730)

CROFTON, Hon Mrs Marcus; Madeleine Barbara (Pratt); da of late William, Heath, of Surrey; *m* Oct 1951, as his 4 w, Hon (Arthur) Marcus Lowther Crofton, s of 4 Baron Crofton (d 23 May 1962), late Maj Irish Gds; *Style*— The Hon Mrs Marcus Crofton; 401, 1430 Newport Ave, Victoria, Br Columbia, Canada

CROFTON, Sir Malby Sturges; 5 Bt (UK 1838), of Longford House, Sligo (but name does not, at time of going to press, appear on the Official Roll of Baronets); s of Sir Malby Richard Henry Crofton, 4 Bt, DSO and Bar (d 1962); *b* 11 Jan 1923; *Educ* Eton, Trinty Cambridge; *m* 14 Jan 1961 (m dis 1966), Elizabeth Madeline Nina, da of late Maj Rhys Clavell Mansel, of Ropley Manor, Alresford, Hants; *Heir* kinsman, (Henry Edward) Melville Crofton; *Career* Mayor Kensington and Chelsea 1978- (Leader Kensington Boro Cncl 1968-77), ptnr Messrs Fenn and Crosthwaite, memb London Stock Exchange 1957-75, memb GLC 1970-73 and (N Ealing) 1977; *Style*— Sir Malby Crofton, Bt; Longford House, Co Sligo, Eire; 17 Launceston Pla, W8

CROFTON, Margaret, Lady; Margaret Amelia; *née* Dallett; da of Judge Morris Dallett (d 1917), of Philadelphia, USA; *b* 1 April 1907; *m* 20 June 1933, as his 3 w, Lt-Col Sir Morgan George Crofton, 6 Bt, DSO (d 8 Dec 1958); 2 s (Hugh Denis b 1937, Edward Morgan b 1945); *Style*— Margaret, Lady Crofton; Woodbridge, Brockenhurst, Hants (☎ 0590 22139)

CROFTON, Mary, Baroness; Mary Irvine; *née* Friend; eldest da of Maj James Irvine Hatfield Friend, OBE, MC, DL (d 1955), and Louie Gertrude, *née* Cowley (d 1963); *b* 24 Sept 1920; *m* 1 (m dis), Robert W Flach, LLB; 2 s; m 2, 19 Dec 1964, as his 2 w, 5 Baron Crofton (d 1974); *Style*— The Rt Hon Mary, Lady Crofton; Flat 1, 123 Gloucester Terrace, London W2 (☎ 01 402 5015)

CROFTON, (Henry Edward) Melville; MBE (1970); s of Brig Roger Crofton, CIE, MC (d 1972), by 2 w Dorothy Frances (d 1953), da of Col Henry Melville Hatchell, DSO; hp of kinsman, Sir Malby Crofton, 5 Bt; *b* 15 August 1931; *Educ* Hilton Coll Natal, Trinity Coll Cambridge; *m* 10 Dec 1955, Mary Brigid, twin da of late Gerald K Riddle, of Buttercombe, Ogwell, Newton Abbot, Devon; 2 s (Julian b 1958, Nigel b 1964), 1 da (Nicola b 1961); *Career* former principal admin offr MHOCS; conslt in industl dvpt trg 1978-; *Style*— Melville Crofton Esq, MBE; Haldon, St Giles Hill, Winchester, Hants

CROFTS-GREENE, Dr Basil Wilson Harvey; only s of William Granville Greene (d 1919), of Fitzwilliam Sq, Dublin, and Charlotte Elizabeth Wilson, *née* Harvey (d 1972), g niece of Prof W Nesbitt, of Queen's Univ, and sis of Canon W Nesbitt Harvey, DD, BLitt (d 1981); assumed by deed poll 1948 additional name of Crofts; *b* 27 Mar 1918; *Educ* St Andrew's Coll, Dublin Univ, King's Inns Dublin, Univ de la Romande, Switzld, (MA, PhD); *m* 1946, Rosamund Patricia Nason, of Ballyhoura Lodge, Co Cork, only child of Christopher Nason Crofts (d 1947; tenth in descent from Thomas Croftes who d 1612, of West Stow and Sexham Parva, Suffolk, by his w Susan, maternal gda of 1 Baron Wentworth); 1 s (Nigel Harvey Nason b 1948); *Career* landowner, dir Pet Fair Ltd, Cork City; *Recreations* German shepherd dog judge and breeder, study of alternative medicine, genealogy; *Clubs* Royal Irish Automobile; *Style*— Dr Basil Crofts-Greene; Strancally Castle, Knockanore, Co Waterford, Eire (☎ 024 97164)

CROFTS-GREENE, Nigel Harvey Nason; s of Basil Crofts-Greene, and Rosamund Patricia Nason, *née* Crofts; *b* 9 Feb 1948; *Educ* Kingstown Sch, RAC Cirencester; *Career* farmer, md Pet Fair Ltd Cork City; *Recreations* militaria, water skiing, wind surfing; *Style*— N H N Crofts-Greene, Esq; Strancally Castle, Knockanore, Co Waterford, Ireland (☎ 024 97164)

CROHAM, Baron (Life Peer UK 1977); Sir Douglas Albert Vivian Allen; GCB (1973, KCB 1967, CB 1963); s of Albert John Allen (ka 1918), of Croydon, Surrey; *b* 15 Dec 1917; *Educ* Wallington GS, LSE; *m* 1941, Sybil Eileen, da of John Marco Allegro (d 1964), of Carshalton, Surrey; 2 s, 1 da; *Career* former civil servant; perm sec: Treasy 1968-74, CSD 1974-77; chm Br Nat Oil Corpn 1982-86 (dep chm 1978-82); dir Pilkington Bros Ltd 1978-; chm: Guinness Peat Gp 1983-87, Trinity Insur Ltd 1988-; industl advsr to govr of Bank of England 1978-83; chm: Anglo-German Fndn 1981-, Review of Univ Grants Ctee 1985-87; *Recreations* tennis, woodwork; *Clubs* Reform, Civil Service; *Style*— The Rt Hon The Lord Croham, GCB; 9 Manor Way, South Croydon, Surrey (☎ 01 688 0496); Guinness Mahon Holdings Gp plc, 32 St Mary at Hill, London EC3P 3AJ (☎ 01 623 6222, telex 893065)

CROISDALE-APPLEBY, Dr David; s of Mark Appleby (d 1967), of Belford, Northumberland, and Florence Isabel, *née* White; *b* 6 Feb 1946; *Educ* Royal GS Newcastle upon Tyne, London Univ (MA), Newcastle Univ (BSc), Brunel Univ (MSc), Lancaster Univ (PhD); *m* 3 Aug 1968, Carolynn Elizabeth, da of Maj Alan Cuthbert Croisdale, MBE (d 1974); 3 s (Mycroft b 1971, Lindsay b 1973, Merton b 1976), 1 da (Catriona b 1984); *Career* chief exec Allen Brady & Marsh Ltd 1979-82, worldwide ops dir SSC & B Lintas Ltd 1982-84; chm: Creative Synergy Ltd 1984-, The DCA Co Ltd 1985-, Retail Trading Devpts Ltd 1986-, Marylebone Railway World Ltd 1986-, Salmon Ventures Ltd 1987-; churchwarden St Michael's & All The Angels Amersham Bucks; FRSA 1988; *Recreations* motor racing, Lutyens, Aston Martins; *Style*— Dr David Croisdale-Appleby; Abbotsholme, Hervines Rd, Amersham, Bucks (☎ 0494 725 194); DCA House, 3 Warren Mews, London W1 (☎ 01 383 5566, fax 01 383 5950)

CROKER, Arthur Raymond; s of Edward Croker (d 1951), and Phylis Helen Savage (d 1978); ggs of Frederick James Savage personal detective to Queen Victoria 1885-93; *b* 16 August 1939; *Educ* Bristol Pro Cathedral Sch; *m* 29 Sept 1962, Mary Elizabeth Clarke, da of Capt John Patrick (d 1987), of Dublin Eire; 3 s (Damian b 1963, Mark b 1964, John b 1978); *Career* fin accountant in private practice; ptnr Yewtrees Int, dist cncllr 1968-72; ACEA, AIIA; *Recreations* squash, golf; *Clubs* Cadbury Country, Lions (Nailsea); *Style*— Arthur R Croker, Esq; Yew Trees Beckets Lane, Nailsea, Avon BS19 2LY (☎ 0272 856376); Croker Robb & Co, The Old Post Office, Station Road, Congresbury, Avon (☎ 0934 835485); 10 Church St, Tetbury, Glocestershire, Arthur Croker & Co, (☎ 0666 53484)

CROKER, Edgar Alfred (Ted); s of Harry Croker (d 1954), and Winifred, *née* Coton (d 1950); *b* 13 Feb 1924; *Educ* Kingston Tech Coll; *m* 1952, Kathleen Grace, da of Cornelius Mullins (d 1950); 1 s (Andrew), 2 da (Alison, Louise); *Career* served WW II, Flt Lt RAF 1942-46, Flt Lt RAFVR 1947-55; prof footballer: Charlton Athletic 1947-51, Headinton Utd 1951-56; sales dir Douglas Equipment 1956-61, chm and md Liner-Croker Ltd 1961-73, chm Liner Concrete Machinery Co Ltd 1971-73, chm Harrington Kilbride Ltd; gen sec and chief exec The Football Assoc 1973-89; *Books* autobiography 'The Next Voice You Hear Will Be'; *Recreations* golf, tennis, bridge; *Clubs* Sportsman, RAF, New Club Cheltenham; *Style*— Ted Croker, Esq; 'South Court', 45 The Park, Cheltenham, Glos (☎ 0242 224970)

CROLL, Walter William; s of Walter Alfred (d 1971), of 5 Marchwood Rd, Southampton, Hants, and Nellie Alice, *née* Meager (d 1954); *b* 26 Feb 1915; *Educ* C of E Freemantle Southampton; *m* 8 April 1939, Sarah Millicent, da of Oliver Phillips; 3 s (David, Colin, Edward); *Career* trained Harland Wolfe Southampton (shipping furnishings and renovation), founded Millbrook Furnishing 1946 (now managed by sons); memb Ramsay Cons Assoc; Freeman City of London, memb Worshipful Co of Furniture Makers 1980; *Recreations* field sports, game shooting, fly fishing, boating; *Clubs* Royal Southampton Yacht ; *Style*— Walter Croll, Esq; Berry Wood, Mile Hill, Romsey, Hants SO5 8NL (☎ 0794 512 253); Millbrook Furnishing Industries Ltd, S Hampshire Industrial Park, Totton, Southampton SO4 3RY (☎ 0703 865 744, fax 0703 869 565, telex 477122 MBFI G)

CROLLA, Hon Mrs; (Susan Patricia) Rose; *née* Cornwallis; 3 da of 3 Baron Cornwallis, OBE, DL (by his 2 w); *b* 30 Mar 1963; *m* 4 July 1986, Scott Simon Crolla, s of Romano Crolla, of Albert Court, London; *Style*— Hon Mrs Crolla; Ruck Farm, Horsmonden, Tonbridge, Kent TN12 8DT

CROMARTIE, 4 Earl of (UK 1861); Roderick Grant Francis Mackenzie; MC (1940), TD (1964), JP (Ross and Cromarty 1937), DL (1976); also Viscount Tarbat (UK 1861), Baron Castlehaven (UK 1861), Baron MacLeod of Castle Leod (UK 1861); the granting of these titles was in fact a restoration, with the Cromartie title, to the Earl's ggm, by HM Queen Victoria; chief of the Clan Mackenzie; s of Countess of Cromartie (d 1962, 3 holder of title) and Col Edward Walter Blunt (d 1949), who assumed additional surname Mackenzie 1905; present Peer discontinued surname of Blunt for himself and son; *b* 24 Oct 1904; *Educ* Charterhouse, RMC Sandhurst; *m* 1, 11 March 1933 (m dis 1945), Dorothy, da of Grant Butler Downing, of Kentucky, USA; 2 da; m 2, 30 Jan 1947 (m dis 1962), Olga, da of late Stuart Laurance of Paris; 1 s; m 3, 1 Dec 1962, Lilias Janet Garvie, MB, ChB, da of Prof (James) Walter MacLeod, OBE, FRS, FRSE; *Heir* s, Viscount Tarbat, *qv*; *Career* Maj Seaforth Highlanders (ret); convener: CC Ross and Cromarty 1963-77, Dist Cncl 1975-77; Freeman 1977, Hon Sheriff; FSAS; *Clubs* Pratt's, Army and Navy; *Style*— The Rt Hon the Earl of Cromartie, MC, TD, JP, DL; Castle Leod, Strathpeffer, Ross and Cromarty

CROMBIE, Alastair Charles MacDonald; s of Alistair Cameron Crombie of Oxford and Nancy *née* Hey; *b* 14 July 1947; *Educ* Downside, St Andrews Univ (MA); *Career* journalist: Investors Chronicle 1977-79, Investors in Industry 1979-81; corporate fin dept Guinness Mahon & Co Ltd 1982-85; ptnr Robson Rhodes 1985-; *Recreations* music, tennis, skiing, travel; *Style*— Charles Crombie, Esq; 186, City Road, London, EC1V 2NY, (☎ 01 251 1644 fax 01 250 0801)

CROMBIE, Alexander Llewellyn Wallace; s of James Wallace Crombie (d 1947), and Sarah Emily, *née* Morris; *b* 19 July 1943; *Educ* Ellesmere Coll, Worcester Coll For The Blind, Nottingham Univ (LLB); *m* 8 April 1972, Caroline Cawood, da of David John Laurance; 2 s (Duncan b 1975, Hamish b 1978), 1 da (Sarah b 1973); *Career* admitted slr 1955, sr ptnr Crombie Collins & Haddon-Grant 1971-88;ptnr Ironsides Ray & Vials 1988-, chm: Consumer Cncl for Visually Handicapped Leics 1982-89, Nat Library for the Blind 1982-87, Braille Chess Assoc 1987-89; memb Law Soc; *Style*— Alexander Crombie, Esq; Elwyn House, Market Place, Uppingham Leics, fax 0572 821502

CROME, David Robert; s of Robert Crome (d 1962), and Margaret, *née* Williamson; *b*

23 Nov 1937; *Educ* William Hulme's GS Manchester; *m* 28 Sept 1963, Sandra Joan, da of Albert Storrs, of Lowestoft; 3 da (Ruth Margaret b 1964, Helen Jayne (Mrs Hardy) b 1965, Wendy May b 1970); *Career* slr (hons) 1960; mangr ptnr of the firm now known as Bailey Crome with Gerard Dunne, notary public, 1977- (sr ptnr 1964); princ magistrate (becoming ch magistrate and acting ch justice) Solomon Islands 1980-82; chm (pt/time): Industl Tribunals (Bury St Edmunds regn) 1987, med Appeal Tribunals (N London regn) 1987; area cmmr St John Ambulance (Waveney) 1983-87, parly candidate (Lib) Lowestift (now Waveney) div 1966 and 1970, liveryman Worshipful Co of Arbitrators, FCI Arb 1973; *Recreations* sailing, singing (tenor), cycling; *Clubs* Royal Norfolk and Suffolk Yacht, Norfolk, Wig and Pen; *Style—* David Crome, Esq; Underhill, Poughfer's Pightle, Puddingmoor, Beccles, Suffolk; 17/21 Clapham Road, Lowestoft, Suffolk NR32 1PG (☎ 0502 573307, fax 0502 500614)

CROMER, 3 Earl of (UK 1901); George Rowland Stanley Baring; KG (1977), GCMG (1974, KCMG 1971), MBE (mil 1945), PC (1966); also Baron Cromer (UK 1892), Viscount Cromer (UK 1899), Viscount Errington (UK 1901); s of 2 Earl, GCB, GCIE, GCVO, PC (d 1953), and Lady Ruby Elliot, 2 da of 4 Earl of Minto, KG, GCSI, GCMG; *b* 28 July 1918, HM King George V stood sponsor; *Educ* Eton, Trinity Coll Cambridge; *m* 10 Jan 1942, Hon Esmé Mary Gabrielle Harmsworth, CVO, da of 2 Viscount Rothermere; 2 s, 1 da (decd); *Heir* s, Viscount Errington; *Career* served WWII, NW Europe (despatches) Lt-Col Gren Gds; page of honour to HM King George V 1933-35, to Queen Mary at Coronation 1937; econ min HM Embassy Washington, head of Treasury Delgn and UK exec dir IMF, IBRD, IFC 1959-61, govr Bank of England 1961-66, govr IBRD and dir Bank of Int Settlements Basle 1961-66, dir Compagnie Financière de Suez 1967-82; chm: London Multinational Bank Ltd 1967-70, IBM (UK) Ltd 1967-70 and 1974-79; dir: Daily Mail and General Tst Co Ltd 1974- (and 1949-61, 1966-70), Imperial Gp Ltd 1974-80, P and O 1974-80, Shell Tport and Trading Co Ltd 1974-, Robeco Gp of Investmt Tsts Rotterdam 1977-88, IBM World Trade Corpn NY 1977-83, Barfield Tst Co Ltd Guernsey 1979-, Baring Henderson Gilt Fund 1979-; memb advsy cncl IBM Corpn NY 1967-88; advsr Baring Bros and Co Ltd 1974- (md 1948-61, sr ptnr and md 1966-70); chm int advsy cncl Morgan Guaranty Tst Co of NY 1977-88; int advsr Marsh and McLennan Cos NY; HM ambass Washington 1971-74; HM Lt City of London 1961-; DL Kent 1968-79; chm Churchill Memorial Tst 1979; Hon LLD New York 1966; *Clubs* Brooks's, Beefsteak, White's; *Style—* The Rt Hon The Earl of Cromer, KG, GCMG, MBE, PC; Beaufield House, St Saviour, Jersey, Channel Islands (☎ 0534 61671); Morgan Guaranty Tst Co of New York, Queensway House, Queen St, St Helier, Jersey, Channel Islands (☎ 0534 71566, telex 4192358, 4192359)

CROMIE, Stephen John Henry; s of Dr Brian William Cromie, of 14 Park St, Kings Cliffe, N Hants, and Heather Anne Howie, *née* Wood; *b* 13 Jan 1957; *Educ* Abingdon Sch, Downing Coll Cambridge (MA); *m* 28 Aug 1982, Marianne Frances, da of John Edward Burton, of 14 Beverly Close, East Ewell, Surrey; *Career* slr 1981; ptnr Linklaters & Paines 1987- (joined 1981); memb: Law Soc, City of London Slr's Co; *Recreations* wine, cooking, cycling; *Style—* S J H Cromie, Esq; 4 Huntingdon St, London N1 1BU; Barrington House, 59/67 Gresham St, London EC2V 7JA (☎ 01 606 7080, fax 01 606 5113, telex 884349)

CROMPTON, DR Gareth; QHP 1984-87; s of Edward Drefach-Felindre Crompton, (d 1986) of Dyfed and Annie Jane, *née* Jones; *b* 9 Jan 1937; *Educ* Llandysul GS, Univ of Wales Coll of Med (MB, BCH); *m* 12 June 1965, Valmai Gloria, da of Reginald Thomas Lalande (d 1969) of Barry, S Glamorgan; 1 da (Elspeth b 1974); *Career* chief med offr Welsh Off 1978-, area med offr Gwynedd Area Health Authy 1974-77; Anglesey CC 1966-73 (county med offr, county welfare offr, prin schs med offr), specialty advsr Health Serv cmmr for Eng and Wales 1974-77, advsr in Wales of Faculty of Community Med of RCP 1974-77, chm Anglesey Disablement Advsy ctee 1969-77, sec Fluoridation study gp of Sec Med Offrs of Health 1969-73; memb: General Med Cncl 1981-83 and 1987-, Med Advsy Ctee to Registrar Gen 1988-; QHP 1984-87; DPH 1964, DRCOG 1962, FRCP 1986, FFCM 1976; *Recreations* bowls, gardening, golf, watching rugby football; *Clubs* Cardiff Athletic; *Style—* Dr Gareth Crompton; Welsh Office, Cathays Park, Cardiff, CF1 3NQ, (☎ 0222 823911 fax GP2 0222 823204, GP3 0222 823036 telex 498228

CROMPTON, Air Cdre Roy Hartley; OBE (1962); s of Francis John Crompton (d 1970), of Bedford, and Harriet Ann, *née* Hartley (d 1973); *b* 24 April 1921; *Educ* Bedford Sch, UCL (BA); *m* 1 (m dis 1961), m 2, 1961, Rita Mabel, da of late Robert Leslie of Dumfries, Scot; 1 da (Sheena Patricia b 1963); *Career* WWII and immediate post-war flying and staff appts 1942-55, Personal SO to AOC in C Fighter Cmd 1956-59, OC Flying RAF Oakington 1959-62, Chiefs of Staff Secretariat 1962-64, Station Cdr RAF Linton-on-Ouse 1965-67, Defence Policy Staff MOD London 1968-69, Gp Dir RAF Staff Coll Bracknell 1970, Project offr for establishing Nat Def Coll Latimer 1970-71, AOC and Cmdt Central Flying Sch Little Rissington 1972-74, Gp dir HO CD Coll Easingwold 1974-85, re-employed to head a Nat CD project 1987-88; played cricket: Derbyshire II 1938, Beds 1946-47, Capt Easingwold GC 1985-86, co helper RAF Benevolent Fund, vice pres York Branch RAF Assoc, chm Newton & Dist Branch Roy Br Legion, memb Assoc of Voluntary Guides City of York, dep pres Soc of Indust Emergency Servs Offrs; FBIM; *Books* co-author Guide to Emergency Planning (1986); *Recreations* golf, horticulture, music; *Clubs* RAF; *Style—* Air Cdre Roy Crompton, OBE; Sharnford Lodge, Huby, York YO6 1HT

CROMPTON, (Hon) Mrs Virginia Mary Clementine; da of 2 Baron Keyes; *b* 20 Mar 1950; *m* 1972, Rev (Roger) Martyn Francis Crompton; 4 da (Heather b 1976, Bryony b 1978, Rowan b 1981, Holly b 1983); *Style—* Mrs R M F Crompton; 8 Firs Walk, Woodford Green, Essex IG8 OTD

CROMPTON-INGLEFIELD, Col Sir John Frederick; TD, DL (Derbys 1953); er s of Adm Sir Frederick Samuel Inglefield, KCB (d 1921), and Cecil, *née* Crompton; assumed additional surname of Crompton by deed poll 1930; *b* 1 August 1904; *Educ* RNC Osborne, RNC Dartmouth; *m* 1, 1926, Rosemary (d 1978), da of Adm Sir Percy Scott, 1 Bt, KCB, KCVO (d 1924); 3 da; m 2, 1979, (Madeline) Rose, widow of W E Dodds, and da of late Col Conyers Alston, of Seven Rivers, Cape Province, S Africa; *Career* ret from RN 1926, served WWII Derbyshire Imperial Yeo 6 Armd Div, 1 Army N Africa, 79 Armoured Div (despatches), Lt-Col cmdg Derbys Yeo 1950-53, Bt Col 1954, Hon Col Leics and Derbys 1962-70; chm TA Derbyshire 1964-69 (vice-chm 1957-64), vice-chm TAVR Assoc E Midlands 1968-69; chm W Derbys Unionist and Cons Assoc 1951-65; Derbys CC 1932-55, JP 1933, High Sheriff 1938; OStJ 1970; kt 1963; *Recreations* study of Dutch and English sea paintings, reading Naval history; *Style—* Col Sir John Crompton-Inglefield, TD, DL; 73 Oakwood Court, Addison Rd, London W14 (☎ 01 602 1979)

CROMWELL, Baroness; Doris Vivian; yst da of Hugh de Lisle Penfold, of IOM; *m* 16 Jan 1954, 6 Baron Cromwell (d 1982); 2 s (7 Baron, Hon Thomas Bewicke-Copley), 2 da (Hon Anne Bewicke-Copley, Hon Davina Bewicke-Copley); *Style—* The Rt Hon The Lady Cromwell

CROMWELL, 7 Baron (E 1375); Godfrey John; s of 6 Baron Cromwell (d 1982; Barony abeyant 1497 to 1923, when abeyance terminated in favour of present Baron's gf, 5 Baron); *b* 4 Mar 1960; *Heir* yr bro, Hon Thomas Bewicke-Copley; *Style—* The Rt Hon The Lord Cromwell

CRONIN, Gerald Francis; s of William Francis Cronin (d 1948); *b* 28 Jan 1927; *Educ* Highgate, Oxford Univ (MA); *m* 1952, Margaret Patricia, da of Patrick John McNamara (d 1950); 2 s, 1 da; *Career* md Grosvenor Gp plc 1968-87; FCA; *Recreations* cricket, theatre; *Clubs* MCC, IOD; *Style—* Gerald Cronin, Esq; Sandown, 16 Chalfont Drive, Hove, East Sussex BN3 6QR (☎ 0273 540677)

CRONIN, John Walton; s of John Cronin (d 1952), and Alice Cronin (d 1944); *b* 14 Oct 1915; *Educ* Xaverian Coll Manchester, Manchester Univ, Cadet Coll Bangalore; *m* 1947, Mrs Eileen Veronica Bale, da of Michael Roy Rector (d 1959); 1 da (Sheelagh), 1 step-s (Peter Bale); *Career* WWII 1940-46, Maj Indian Army DAQMG; res magistrate and Acting High Court Judge, advsy cmmr to govr on detained persons N Rhodesia 1955-65, stipendiary and circuit magistrate Grand Bahama 1965-71, chm Industl Tribunals 1972-88; co dir Kent St John Ambulance 1974-78; OStJ 1977; *Clubs* Royal Cwlth Soc; *Style—* John Cronin, Esq; 6 Chelsea Court, Hythe, Kent (☎ 0303 67879); Industl Tribunals, Tufton House, Ashford, Kent (☎ 0233 21346)

CRONIN, Tacey Marguerite (Mrs David Bain); da of Flt Lt Anthony Arthur Cronin (d 1972), and Margaret Elizabeth, *née* Roberts; *b* 28 June 1959; *Educ* Stamford HS, Bristol Univ (LLB); *m* 3 Jan 1987, David Ian Bain, s of Capt David Walter Bain (d 1975); *Career* called to the Bar Middle Temple; memb: Bar Cncl 1985-86, Gen Bar Cncl; *Recreations* theatre, golf, motor racing, travel; *Style—* Ms Tacey Cronin; Albion Chambers East, Broad Street, Bristol BS1 1DR (☎ 0212 272 144, fax 262569)

CRONIN, Vincent Archibald Patrick; s of Archibald Joseph Cronin (d 1981), of Vevey, Switz, and Agnes Mary, *née* Gibson (d 1981); *b* 24 May 1924; *Educ* Ampleforth, Trinity Coll Oxford (BA); *m* 25 Aug 1949, Chantal, da of Comte Jean De Rolland (d 1985), of Manoir De Brion, Dragey Par, Sartilly 50530, France; 2 s (James b 1956, Luan b 1959), 3 da (Sulvilie b 1951, Dauphine b 1962, Natalie b 1967); *Career* author; memb cncl RSL 1976-86; *Books* incl: The Golden Honeycombe (1954), The Wire Man From the West (1955), A Pearl to India (1959), Louis XIV (1964), Napoleon (1964), The Florentine Renaissance (1967), The View From Planet Earth (1981); *Recreations* swimmng, tennis; *Style—* Vincent Cronin, Esq; Manoir De Brion, Dragey Par, Sartilly 50530, France; c/o Collins, 8 Grafton St, London W1X 3LA

CRONK, Anthony; s of Capt William Douglas Cronk (d 1947), and Evelyn Joyce, *née* Hanson-Dodwell; *b* 24 July 1917; *Educ* Tonbridge, Wye Coll London; *m* 26 Feb 1949, Margaret, da of Capt E C J Spencer (d 1975); 2 s (Paul Ricard b 1951, Quentin Charles Bargrave b 1959), 1 da (Felicity Mary b 1949); *Career* served WWII Maj RA; Lloyd's underwriter 1960-84; farmer (now ret); vice-pres Kent Co Agric Soc 1968- (fin chm 1964-74), memb Hops Marketing Bd 1955-65, tstee Marshall's Charity 1975-; author of books on local history and vernacular buildings; FSA 1978, FRSA 1973; *Clubs* Farmers', Castle (Rochester); *Style—* Anthony Cronk, Esq; c/o The Royal Bank of Scotland, 67 Lombard Street, London EC3P 3DL

CROOK, Anthony Donald (Tony); s of Thomas Roland (d 1926), of Woodland Grange, Hoghton, nr Preston, Lancs, and Emily, *née* Allsup; *b* 16 Feb 1923; *Educ* Clifton, Sidney Sussex Coll Cambridge; *m* 28 June 1943, Dianne Ada, da of William Smith (d 1958), of Lincoln; 1 da (Carole Anne); *Career* RAF 1939-46 (despatches twice), demob Flt Lt 1946; formed racing car partnership with Raymond Mays 1945, won first post-war motor race to be held in Britain 1946, raced and distributed Bristol Cars made by Bristol Aeroplane Co (over 400 races incl: formula one and two speed hill climbs and Grand Prix 1946-55; bought, (with the late Sir George White), Bristol Cars 1960 (by 1973 sole owner, md and chm); *Clubs* Br Racing Drivers; *Style—* Tony Crook, Esq; Bristol Cars Ltd, Head Office, 368-370 Kensington High St, London W14 8NL (☎ 01 603 0366)

CROOK, Clive Walter Levers; s of Frank Harefield Crook, and May, *née* Williams; *b* 29 July 1936; *Educ* Southall Tech Coll Southall Middx; *m* 10 Sept 1960, Jill Marion, da of J R Metson; 1 da (Helen Alison b 17 April 1965); *Career* dir: Kleinworth Benson Lonsdale plc 1988, Kleinwort Benson Ltd 1974, Banque Kleinwort Benson SA of Geneva 1978, Sharps Pixley Ltd London 1971; chm: Kleinwort Grievson Charlesworth Ltd London 1987 Kleinwort Benson Govt Securities Inc Chicago 1985, Virginia Trading Corp Chicago 1985; dep-chm Kleinwort Benson Securities Ltd London 1987, ret Kleinworts 1988; *Recreations* golf, music; *Clubs* Moor Park GC; *Style—* Clive W L Crook, Esq; 43 Highview, Pinner, Middx HA5 3PE (☎ 01 868 7610); Kleinwort Benson Ltd, 20 Fenchurch Street, London EC3P 3DB (☎ 01 623 8000)

CROOK, Colin; s of Richard Crook (d 1970), and Ruth Crook (d 1971); *b* 1 June 1942; *Educ* Harris Coll Preston, Liverpool Poly; *m* 1965, Dorothy Jean, da of Alfred Edward Taylor, of Wallasey; 2 da; *Career* Motorola (USA) 1969-79, dir advanced systems gp ops MGR Microcomputers 1975-78; md: Zunar Hldgs BV, Rank Precision Industs 1978-80, Br Telecom Enterprises; chm: HBS Ltd (UK) 1980-83, Nestar Systems (USA) 1980-83; main bd memb BT 1983-1984, sr vice-pres Data General Corpn 1984-; FEng, MIEE, MIERE (MIEEE, MACM-USA); *Recreations* photography, sailing, reading, travel; *Style—* Colin Crook, Esq; The Old School House, Harvest Hill, Hedsor, Bourne End, Bucks SL8 5JJ (☎ 062 8527479)

CROOK, 2 Baron (UK 1947), of Carshalton, Co Surrey; Douglas Edwin Crook; o s of 1 Baron Crook (d 1989), and Ida Gertrude Catherine, *née* Haddon (d 1985); *b* 19 Nov 1926; *Educ* Whitgift Sch Croydon, Imperial Coll London (BSc, DIC); *m* 15 Feb 1954, Ellenor, da of Robert Rouse (d 1962), of Sunderland; 1 s (Hon Robert Douglas Edwin b 29 May 1955), 1 da (Hon Catherine Hilary (Hon Mrs (Christopher John) Ramsdale) b 1960); *Heir* s, Hon Robert Douglas Edwin Crook b 1955; *Career* MICE; ACGI; *Style—* The Rt Hon Lord Crook; Ridge Hill Barn, Etchinghill, Folkestone, Kent CT18 8BP (☎ 0303 863353)

CROOK, Frances Rachel; da of Maurice Crook (d 1977), of London, and Sheila, *née* Sibson-Turnbull; *b* 18 Dec 1952; *Educ* Camden Sch London, Liverpool Univ (BA), Lancaster Univ (PGCE); 1 da (Sarah Rose Eleanor b 27 May 1988); *Career* Campaign Organiser Amnesty Int 1980-85, dir Howard League for Penal Reform 1985-; cncllr

Barnet Borough 1982-, memb: Lab Party, CND, TGWU; *Style*— Miss Frances Crook; The Howard League, 322 Kensington Park Rd, London SE11 4PP (☎ 01 735 3317)

CROOK, Prof (Joseph) Mordaunt; s of Austin Mordaunt Crook (d 1967), and Florence Irene, *née* Woolfendon (d 1986); *b* 27 Feb 1937; *Educ* Wimbledon Coll, Brasenose Coll Oxford (MA, DPhil); *m* 1, 4 Jul 1964, Margaret Constance, da of James Mulholland (d 1974); m 2, 9 July 1975, Susan, da of Frederick Hoyland Mayor (d 1972); *Career* lectr Bedford Coll London 1965-75, res fell Warburg Inst 1970-71, reader in architectural history Univ of London 1975-81, Slade prof of fine art Univ of Oxford 1979-80, visiting fell Brasenose Coll Oxford 1979-80, prof architectural history Univ of London 1981-, visiting fell and Waynflete lectr Magdalen Coll Oxford 1985, visiting fell Gonville and Caius Coll Cambridge 1986; public orator Univ of London 1988-; memb Historic Bldgs Cncl for Eng 1974-84, pres soc of Architectural Historians (GB); Freeman Goldsmiths co 1978 (Liveryman 1984); FSA, FBA; *Books* The British Museum (1972), The Greek Revival (1972), William Burges and the High Victorian Dream (1981), The Dilemna of Style: Architectural Ideas from the Picturesque to the post-modern (1987); *Recreations* strolling; *Clubs* Athenaeum, Brooks's; *Style*— Prof J Mordaunt Crook; 55 Gloucester Ave, London NW1 7BA (☎ 01 485 8280); Royal Holloway and Bedford New Coll, Egham, Surrey (☎ 0784 34455)

CROOK, Paul; s of William Giles Crook, of Poole, Dorset, and Helen Margaret, *née* Swales; *b* 6 Mar 1952; *Educ* Ruzawi Sch Zimbabwe, Peterhouse Sch Zimbabwe, Jesus Coll Cambridge (MA, LLB); *m* 11 Sept 1976, Dr Susan Jill, da of Dr Andrew Ernest Dossetor, of Newmarket, Suffolk; 1 s (John b 1988), 1 da (Anne b 1986); *Career* admitted slr 1978, ptnr Allen & Overy 1984-; Freeman City of London Slrs Co 1984; memb Law Soc; *Recreations* golf, hockey, skiing, squash, tennis; *Style*— Paul Crook, Esq; Allen & Overy, 9 Cheapside, London EC2V 6AD (☎ 01 248 9898, fax 01 236 2192, telex 881 2801)

CROOK, Brig Paul Edwin; CBE (1965, OBE 1946), DSO (1957); s of (Edwin) Herbert Frederick Crook (d 1966), of Lyme Regis, and Christine Elisabeth Beaumont (d 1972); *b* 19 April 1915; *Educ* Uppingham, Emmanuel Coll Cambridge (BA, MA); *m* 1, 1944 (m dis 1967), (Valentine) Joan, da of late William Lewis; 1 da; m2, 1967, Betty Lown, da of Lt-Col John William Wyles (d 1964); *Career* cmmnd Queen's own Royal West Kent Regt 1935, served WWII: Africa, NW Europe, SE Asia (despatches); cmd Army Airborne Training and Deppt Centre 1959-62, COS Jamaica Defence Force 1962-65, security ops advsr to High Cmmr for Aden and S Arabia 1965-67, Cdr Rhine Area 1969-71, ret 1971; ADC to HM The Queen 1965; Hon Col 16 Lincoln Co Para Regt (VR) 1974-79, Dep Hon Col 15 (Scottish) Bn The Para Regt (TAVR) 1979-84; chm Lincs County Scouts 1974-88, dep Hon Col 4 (V) Bn The Para Regt 1984-85; Bronze Star (US) 1945; *Recreations* cricket, golf, jazz; *Clubs* Naval and Military, MCC, Jamaica (Kingston); *Style*— Brig Paul Crook, CBE, DSO; Frieston House, Frieston, Grantham, Lincs NG32 3DA (☎ 0400 72 060)

CROOKENDEN, Lt-Gen Sir Napier; KCB (1970, CB 1966), DSO (1945), OBE (1954), DL (Kent 1979); 2 s of Col Arthur Crookenden, CBE, DSO (d 1962), and Dorothy, *née* Rowlandson; *b* 31 August 1915; *Educ* Wellington, RMC Sandhurst; *m* 3 Aug 1948, Hon Patricia Nassau, da of 2 Baron Kindersley, CBE, MC; 2 s, 2 da; *Career* Cheshire Regt 1935, comd 9 Para Bir 1944-46 and 16 Para Bde 1960-61, dir Land/Air Warfare 1964-66, Comdt Royal Mil Coll of Science 1958-59, GOCIC Western Cmd 1969-72; Col The Cheshire Regt 1969-71, Col Cmdt Prince of Wales Div 1971-74; tstee Imperial War Museum 1973-83; chm SSAFA 1974-85; Lt HM Tower of London 1975-81; dir: Lloyds Bank Ltd SE Regnl Bd 1973-86, Flextech Ltd 1973-86; *Books* Drop Zone Normandy (1976), Airborne at War (1978), Battle of the Bulge 1944 (1980); *Clubs* Army and Navy; *Style*— Lt-Gen Sir Napier Crookenden, KCB, DSO, OBE, DL; Twin Firs, Four Elms, Edenbridge, Kent TN8 6PL (☎ 073 270 229)

CROOKENDEN, Hon Lady; Hon Patricia Nassau; *née* Kindersley; er da of 2 Baron Kindersley, CBE, MC (d 1976); *b* 5 August 1922; *m* 3 Aug 1948, Lt-Gen Sir Napier Crookenden, KCB, DSO, OBE, DL, *qv*; 2 s, 2 da; *Style*— The Hon Lady Crookenden; Twin Firs, Mapleton Lane, Four Elms, Edenbridge, Kent TN8 6PL

CROOKENDEN, Simon Robert; s of Spencer Crookenden, CBE, MC, Maj Reston Hall, Staveley, Kendal, Cumbria, and late Jean, *née* Dewing; *b* 27 Sept 1946; *Educ* Winchester, Corpus Christi Coll Cambridge (MA); *m* 20 Aug 1983, Sarah Anne Georgina Margaret, da of George Leonard Pragnell, of 2 Paragon Terr, Bath Rd, Cheltenham; 1 s (Thomas Henry b 19 Sept 1987), 1 da (Rebecca Jean b 9 Nov 1985); *Career* called to the Bar Gray's Inn 1974; *Recreations* rowing; *Clubs* London Rowing; *Style*— Simon Crookenden, Esq; 4 Essex Court, Temple, London EC4 (☎ 01 583 9191)

CROOKS, John Leslie; s of Henry Leslie Crooks (d 1976), of Scarborough, and Elizabeth Ellen, *née* Johnson (d 1987); *b* 5 May 1928; *Educ* Uppingham Sch, London Univ (MRCVS); *m* 10 May 1952, Dorothy Heather, da of Thomas Reginald Brompton (d 1967), of Driffield; 1 s (James b 1956), 2 da (Annette b 1954, Elizabeth b 1960); *Career* veterinary surgeon; dir Veterinary Drug Co plc 1958 (chm 1982); pres Br Veterinary Assoc 1983-84; *Recreations* shooting, fishing, gardening, cooking; *Clubs* Royal Soc of Medicine London; *Style*— John L Crooks, Esq; Westwood Mill, Beverley HU17 8RG (☎ 0482 881296); Veterinary Drug Co plc, Common Road, Dunnington, York YO1 5RU (☎ 0904 48844, telex 57588 VETDRUG)

CROOKS, Very Rev John Robert Megaw; s of Canon the Rev Louis Warden Crooks, OBE (d 1958), and Maria Kathleen, *née* Megaw (d 1961); *b* 9 July 1914; *Educ* Campbell Coll Belfast, Trinity Coll Dublin (MA, Divinity Testmonium); *m* 2 Jan 1941, Elizabeth Catherine, da of John Charles Hill Vance (d 1954); 2 s (Tony b 1942, Michael b 1943); *Career* asst curate St Peter's Dublin 1938-43, hon vicar choral St Patrick's Cathedral Dublin 1939-43, catechist The High Sch Dublin 1939-43, asst curate Leighlin Cathedral 1943-44, incumbent Killylea Armagh 1956-73, diocesan sec Armagh 1963-79, clerical sec Gen Synod C of I 1970-, archdeacon of Armagh 1973-79, dean of Armagh 1979-; vice chm Govrs of Royal Sch Armagh, keeper Public Library Armagh; *Clubs* Kildare and Univ (Dublin); *Style*— The Very Rev the Dean of Armagh; 44 Abbey St, Armagh, Ireland (☎ 0861 523 142, 0861 522 540)

CROOKSHANK, John Kennedy; s of Lt-Col C K Crookshank; *b* 15 August 1932; *Educ* Repton, Sandhurst; *m* 1974, Diana Lesley, da of Cdr Brookes; 1 s, 1 da, 4 step children; *Career* Capt 5 Royal Inniskilling Dragoon Gds; ADC to Govr of Gibraltar 1958-60; publishing dir Reed Business Publishing 1972-; *Recreations* sailing, skiing, ornithology, archaeology, travel, book collecting; *Clubs* Royal London Yacht, RAC, Emsworth Sailing; *Style*— John Kennedy Crookshank, Esq; Ivy House, Westbourne, Emsworth, Hants

CROOM, Lady Endi Valerie; *née* Samuel; da of Dr David Samuel, JP; *m* 1940, Sir John Halliday Croom, TD (d 1986); 1 s, 1 da; *Career* actress known as Valerie Tudor; *Style*— Lady Croom; 27 Learmonth Terrace, Edinburgh EH4 1NZ (☎ 031 332 5933)

CROOM-JOHNSON, Rt Hon Lord Justice David Powell; PC (1984), DSC (1944), VRD (1953); 3 s of late Hon Sir Reginald Powell Croom-Johnson (d 1957), sometime a Judge of the High Court, and Ruby Ernestine, *née* Hobbs (d 1961); *b* 28 Nov 1914; *Educ* Stowe, Trinity Hall Cambridge (hon fell 1985); *m* 1940, Barbara Douglas da of Erskine Douglas Warren, of Toronto, Canada; 1 da; *Career* barr 1938, QC 1958, rec Winchester 1962-71, judge of Courts of Appeal Jersey and Guernsey 1966-71, High Court judge (Queen's Bench Div) 1971-84, Lord Justice of Appeal 1984-; kt 1971; *Clubs* Garrick; *Style*— The Rt Hon Lord Justice Croom-Johnson, DSC, VRD; Royal Courts of Justice, Strand, London WC2

CROOM-JOHNSON, Henry Powell; CMG (1964), CBE (1954, OBE Mil 1944), TD (1948); eldest s of Hon Sir Reginald Powell Croom-Johnson (d 1957), and Ruby Ernestine, *née* Hobbs (d 1961); bro of Sir David Powell Croom-Johnson, *qv*; *b* 15 Dec 1910; *Educ* Stowe, Trinity Hall Cambridge (MA); *m* 1947, Jane, da of Archibald George Mandry (d 1960); 2 s (Oliver, William); *Career* served with Queen's Westminsters and King's Royal Rifle Corps 1939-46 (staff Sicily, Italy, Greece) Lt-Col; asst master Bedford Sch 1932-34, offr of the Br Cncl 1935-73, controller: Finance Div 1951-56, Euro Div 1956-57; rep India 1957-64; controller Overseas Div B 1964-66, asst dir-gen 1966-72; ret 1973; *Recreations* music, climbing, books, TA (ret); *Clubs* Savile; *Style*— Henry Croom-Johnson Esq, CMG, CBE, TD; 3A Ravenscourt Square, London W6 0TW (☎ 01 748 3677)

CROPPER, Hilary Mary; da of Arnold Trueman, of Cheshire, and Madeline Emily, *née* Sutton; *b* 9 Jan 1941; *Educ* Convent, Univ of Salford (BSc); *m* 16 Sept 1963, Peter John Cropper, s of Samuel Cropper; 1 s (Carl St John b 1971), 2 da (Elizabeth b 1969, Charlotte b 1973); *Career* various sr mgmnt positions ICL 1970-85, chief exec FI Group plc 1985-, non-exec dir TSB plc 1987-; Freeman: City of London 1987, Worshipful Co of Information Technologists 1987; FBIM 1988; *Style*— Mrs Hilary Cropper; Woodlands, Pink Rd, Parslows Hillock, Lacey Gn, Nr Aylesbury, Bucks (☎ 024 028 227); F I Gp plc, Chesham House, Church Lane, Berks, Herts HP4 2HA (☎ 0442 875051, fax 0442 862903, car 0836 720308)

CROPPER, James Anthony; DL (1986 Cumbria); s of Anthony Charles Cropper (d 1967), of Tolson Hall, Kendal, and Philippa Mary Gloria, *née* Clutterbuck; *b* 22 Dec 1938; *Educ* Eton, Magdalene Coll Cambridge (BA); *m* 30 June 1967, Susan Rosemary, da of Col F J N Davis (d 1988), of Northwood, Middlesex; 2 s (Charles Michael Anthony b 1969 d 1974, Mark b 1974), 1 da (Sarah b 1972); *Career* dir James Cropper plc (papermakers) 1966- (chm 1971-); dir E Lancs Paper Gp plc 1982-84; memb: NW Water Authority 1973-80 and 1987-, Lancs River Authority 1968-74, S Westmorland RDC 1967-74, S Lakeland Dist Cncl 1974-77; pres British Paper and Board Industry Fedn 1987-; dir Cumbria Rural Enterprise Agency 1987-; chm govrs of Abbot Hall Art Gallery and Museum 1983-88; High Sheriff of Westmorland 1971; FCA; *Recreations* shooting, skiing, windsurfing; *Clubs* Brooks's; *Style*— James Cropper, Esq, DL; Tolson Hall, Kendal, Cumbria (☎ 0539 22011); James Cropper plc, Burneside Mills, Kendal, Cumbria (☎ 0539 22002)

CROPPER, Ralph; s of Charles William Cropper, and Florence, *née* Betts; *b* 6 June 1913; *Educ* LSE (BA, MSc); *m* 25 May 1935, Irene Amy; 4 children; *Career* sr exec offr Road Haulage Assoc up to 1949, independent tport conslt in rd tport 1949-; md: Conquers Tport Ltd 1952-82, Tport Counsellors Ltd 1956-80; former vice-pres Deptford Cons Assoc; chm: Movement for London 1982-, Copers Cope Residents Assoc; memb SE Gas Consultative Ctee for 25 years (chm of some of its ctees), memb indust tribunals for 15 years; Freeman City of London, Liveryman Worshipful Co of Carmen; FCIT, FREconS; *Clubs* City Livery; *Style*— Ralph Cropper, ESq; Dunbar, Beckenham Place Pk, Beckenham, Kent (☎ 01 650 1546)

CROPPER, Hon Mrs (Rosalind Evelyn); *née* Younger; da of 3 Viscount Younger of Leckie, OBE, TD; *b* 12 Oct 1937; *m* 14 May 1960, Thomas Ross Charles Cropper, s of Cecil Howe Cropper, DSO, MC, of Sydney; 2 s, 2 da; *Style*— The Hon Mrs Cropper; Greenhills, Willow Tree, NSW, Australia

CROSBIE, William; s of Archibald Shearer Crosbie (d 1961), of Faucheong, Hankow, Huphe, China, and Mary Nicol, *née* Nicoledgar (d 1948); *b* 31 Jan 1915; *Educ* Glasgow Acad, Glasgow Sch of Art/Univ (BA), Paris, Studio of Fernand Leger, Academy De La Grande Chaumiere; *m* 1 2 Oct 1944 (d 1973), Mary Grace McPhail; 2 da (Mary Pauline Elizabeth b 7 July 1947, Michel Louise b 6 April 1951 d 24 April 1951); *Career* conscipt MN 1942-45; artist studies in schs and studios in Paris, Brussels, Athens, Istanbul, Cairo, Rome, Florence; has exhibited on average every 2 years 1946-; principally one man exhibitions: Glasgow, Edinburgh, London, USA, Brussels, Hamburg; has works in: Kelvingrove Galleries Glasgow, Arts Cncl, Scottish provincial galleries, Edinburgh City Arts Centre (mural) 1980, Scottish Gallery of Modern Art 1980, Sydney State Gallery Aust, Wellington NZ, Royal Collection UK, Refectory Fruit Market Gallery Edinburgh 1980, nat Library of Scotland 1986; works in many private collections; govr: Edinburgh Coll of art 1972-75, Glasgow Sch of Art 1975-81, keeper RSA 1977-85; RGI 1975, RSA 1967 (hon prof); *Recreations* sailing, history (art & medieval); *Clubs* RNCYC, LSC, GAC; *Style*— William Crosbie, Esq; Rushes House, 10 Winchester Road, Peterfield, Hants, GU32 3BY (☎ 0730 66899)

CROSET, Paul John Francis; OBE (1967); s of Louis Paul Croset (d 1982), and May Eveline, *née* Garrett; *b* 15 Mar 1919; *Educ* Rishworth Sch, Stamford Sch; *m* 26 Aug 1944 (m dis 1985), (Margaret) Vivien, da of William Suckling, Radlett, Herts; 3 da (Jacqueline b 1946, Jane b 1948, Louise b 1956); *Career* served WWII Maj RE with BEF, BNAF, CMF; engr; chm and fndr Holset Engrg Co Ltd 1952-, md BHD Engrs 1959-73, underwriting memb Lloyd's 1968-, dep chm Readicut Int plc 1984- (dir 1969-, chm 1977-84)), local dir Barclay Bank plc Leeds 1977-84, dir: Cummins Engine Co Ltd 1981-84, Hepworth Ceramic Hldgs plc 1985-; Freeman of City of London 1972, Liveryman of Worshipful Co of Founders 1973; FRSA, CBIM 1980; *Recreations* fishing, shooting, horology; *Clubs* Army and Navy, RAC; *Style*— Paul Croset, Esq, OBE; Summer Court, 1a Otley Road, Harrogate, N Yorkshire HG2 ODJ (☎ 0423 68216); Clifton Mills, Brighouse, W Yorkshire HD6 4ET (☎ 0484 721223)

CROSFIELD, The Very Rev George Philip Chorley; s of James Chorley Crosfield (d 1951), and Marjorie Louise, *née* Morris (d 1976); *b* 9 Sept 1924; *Educ* George Watson's Coll Edinburgh, Coates Hall Edinburgh, Selwyn Coll Cambridge (MA); *m* 1956, Susan Mary Jullion, da of Geoffrey Noel Martin (d 1984), of Dorset; 1 s (Paul b 1966), 2 da (Fiona b 1957, Margaret b 1961); *Career* Capt RA 1942-46; ordained priest 1952; asst curate St David's Edinburgh 1951-53, St Andrew's 1953-55; rector St Cuthbert's 1955-60; chaplain Gordonstoun Sch 1960-68; vice-provost St Mary's Cathedral Edinburgh 1968-70; provost St Mary's Cathedral Edinburgh 1970; *Style*— The Very Rev George Crosfield; 8 Lansdowne Crescent, Edinburgh EH12 5EQ (☎ 031 225 2978); St Mary's Cathedral, Palmerston Place, Edinburgh EH12 5AW (☎ 031 225 6293)

CROSLAND, John David; s of Harold Leslie Crosland (d 1942), Margaret Jarratt; *b* 17 Oct 1936; *Educ* Silcoates Sch, St Catharine's Coll Cambridge (MA); *m* 31 March 1967, Susan Jane Frances, da of Wilfrid Francis Anthony Meynell; 1 s (Timothy John Edward b 1970), 1 da (Jane Ellen Lucy b 1972); *Career* merchant banker; dir Robert Fleming Hldgs Ltd 1973; non exec dir: Bankers Investment Tst plc, Bryant Gp plc, Concentric plc, Fleming Japanese Investment Tst plc, Hunting Gp plc, Wade Potteries plc; *Style*— John D Crosland, Esq; 17 Gerard Rd, Barnes SW13 9RQ (☎ 748 1663); Stone Cottage, Marehill, Pulborough, W Sussex; Robert Fleming Holdings Ltd, 25 Copthall Avenue, EC2

CROSS, Prof Anthony Glenn; s of Walter Sidney Cross (d 1941), and Ada *née* Lawson; *b* 21 Oct 1936; *Educ* High Pavement Sch Nottingham, Trinity Hall Cambridge (MA, PhD), Harvard (AM), Univ of E Anglia (D Litt); *m* 11 Aug 1960, Margaret, da of Eric Arthur Elson (d 1986); 2 da (Jane b 1964, Serena b 1967); *Career* Nat Serv 1955-57; Frank Knox Memorial Fell Harvard 1960-61, reader Univ of E Anglia 1972-81 (lectr 1964-69, sr lectr 1969-72); visiting fell: Centre for Advanced Study Univ of Illinois 1968-69, All Souls Coll Oxford 1977-78; Roberts prof of russian Leeds Univ 1981-85, prof of slavonic studies Cambridge Univ 1985-; Br Univs Assoc of Slavists (pres 1982-84); *Books* N M Karamzin (1971), Russia Under Western Eyes (1971), Anglo-Russian Revelations in the Eighteenth Century (1977), By the Banks of The Thames, Russians in Eighteenth Century Britain (1980), The Russian Those in Eng Literature (1985); *Recreations* collecting books, watching cricket; *Style*— Prof Anthony Cross; Dept of Slavonic Studies, Univ of Cambridge, Sidgwick Ave, Cambridge, CB2 9DA (☎ 0223 335007)

CROSS, 3 Viscount (UK 1886); Assheton Henry Cross; s of 2 Viscount (d 1932), and Maud, da of late Maj-Gen Inigo Richmond Jones, CVO, CB (Maud's maternal gf was Hon Richard Charteris, 2 s of 9 Earl of Wemyss and March); *b* 7 May 1920; *Educ* Shrewsbury, Magdalene Coll Cambridge; *m* 1, 12 Jan 1952 (m dis 1957), Patricia Mary, da of Edward Pearson Hewetson, of Windermere; 2 da (Hon Venetia Clare b 1953, Hon Nicola b 1954); m 2, 1972 (m dis 1977), Mrs Victoria Webb; m 3, 1983, (m dis 1987), Mrs Patricia J Rossiter; *Heir* none; *Career* sits as Cons Peer in House of Lords; formerly Capt Scots Gds; *Clubs* Cavalry and Guards; *Style*— The Rt Hon The Viscount Cross; Delph Cottage, Itchenor, Sussex

CROSS, Beverley; s of George Cross, theatrical mgr, and Eileen Williams, actress; *b* 13 April 1931; *Educ* Pangbourne, Balliol Coll Oxford; *m* 1975, Maggie Smith, CBE, the actress, *qv*; *Career* playwright, screenwriter and Librettist; One More River, Boeing Boeing, Half a Sixpence, The Mines of Sulphur, Hans Anderson, The Great Society, Jorrocks, The Scarlet Pimpernel, The Rising of the Moon, Miranda; *Clubs* Garrick; *Style*— Beverley Cross, Esq; Curtis Brown Ltd, 162 Regent St, London W1R 5TA (☎ 01 437 9700)

CROSS, Clifford Thomas; CB (1977); s of Arthur William Cross (d 1950), and Helena May Cross, *née* Stevens (d 1958); *b* 1 April 1920; *Educ* Latymer Upper Sch Hammersmith, Univ of London (LLB); *m* 21 Feb, Ida Adelaide, da of Hector Charles Barker (d 1981); 1 s (Michael b 1952), 2 da (Jean b 1947, Jaqueline b 1950); *Career* CS; Inland Revenue 1939; HM Customs and Excise 1946-79: asst sec 1959, cmmnr 1970, ret 1979; *Recreations* squash, chess, reading, watching television; *Style*— Clifford T Cross, Esq, CB; 'Longacre', 101 Histon Rd, Cottenham, Cambs (☎ 0954 50757)

CROSS, Denis Charles; s of late Lt Charles Cross, RN; *b* 13 May 1938; *Educ* Downside, Balliol Oxford; *m* 1963, Margaret McAdam, *née* Black; 2 s, 3 da; *Career* dir Hambros Bank Ltd 1971-; *Style*— Denis Cross Esq; 18 Bolingbroke Grove, London SW11 (☎ 01 673 8187)

CROSS, Rev Hugh Geoffrey; s of Rev Arthur James Cross (d 1945), and Frieda Annie, *née* Stern (d 1981); *b* 1 June 1930; *Educ* Bulawayo Tech Sch, Bristol Baptist Coll; *m* 10 July 1954, Doreen Barbara, da of Oliver Cecil Lay (d 1979); 2 s (Allan b 1959, Graham b 1957), 2 da (Janet b 1955, Kathleen b 1962); *Career* Baptist min: Swallownest and Treeton 1954-61, Morice Baptist Church Plymouth 1961-65; missionary bookseller 1965-68, minister Grove Hill Ecumenical Project Hemel Hempstead 1969-79, ecumenical offr Br Cncl of Churches 1979-; *Recreations* dinghy sailing; *Style*— The Rev Hugh G Cross; 23 Saturn Way, Hemel Hempstead, Herts HP2 5NY (☎ 0442 55023), Inter-Church House, 35-41 Lower Marsh, London SE1 7RL (☎ 01 620 4444)

CROSS, (William Richard) Jason Blount; s of Richard Blount Cross, of Chichester, and Margaret Marmion, *née* Crocker; *b* 15 Nov 1945; *Educ* Downside; *m* 13 Sept 1969, Frances Catherine Dawes, da of Dr John Fletcher Ramsden (d 1955); 2 s (Mark b 1973, Ivan b 1973), 1 da (Tanya b 1971); *Career* ptnr Josolyne Layton-Bennet & Co 1972-77; ICFC Bristol 1977-80; local dir 3i London 1980-86; ptnr, UK hd of Corporate Fin, Grant Thornton 1987-; ACA 1970, FCA 1977; *Recreations* history, wine, sailing, armchair sport; *Clubs* Army and Navy, Chichester Yacht; *Style*— Jason Cross, Esq; Grant Thornton, Grant Thornton House, Melton Street, Euston Square, London NW1 2EP (☎ 01 383 5100, fax 01 383 4715, telex 28984)

CROSS, Joan; CBE; *b* 7 Sept 1900; *Educ* St Paul's; *Career* joined Old Vic 1924 progressed from small singing roles to princ roles; dir Sadlers Well's Opera Co 1940-45, fndr memb English Opera Co 1945, created Ellen Orford (Peter Grimes), Female Chorus (Rape of Lucretia), Lady Billows (Albert Herring), Queen Elizabeth (Glorianna), Mrs Grose (The Turn of the Screw); *Recreations* gardening, collector of books, pictures; *Style*— Miss Joan Cross, CBE; Garrett House, Park Rd, Aldeburgh, Suffolk

CROSS, Air Chief Marshal Sir Kenneth Bryan Boyd; KCB (1959, CB 1954), CBE (1945), DSO (1943) DFC (1940); s of Pembroke H C Cross, of Eastoke Lodge Hayling Island, and Jean, *née* Boyd; *b* 4 Oct 1911; *Educ* Kingswood Sch Bath; *m* 15 Jan 1945, Brenda Megan, da of Wing Cdr Frank James Bickley Powell, of Hinton Cottage, Hinton, nr Melkesham, Wilts; 2 s, 1 da; *Career* RAF 1930, AOCIC Bomber Cmd 1959-63, Air Chief Marshal 1965, AOCIC Transport Cmd 1963-66, ret 1967; dir Red Cross (London Branch), ret 1981; *Clubs* RAF; *Style*— Air Chief Marshal Sir Kenneth Cross; 12 Callow St, London SW3

CROSS, Robert Kingsley; s of Dr John Cross, of Bingley, W Yorks; *b* 19 August 1942; *Educ* Bradford GS; *m* 1967, Angela Mary, da of Sydney Seymour, of Bradford; 2 da; *Career* dir/sec Heydemann Shaw Ltd (subsid of Coats Viyella plc) 1974-; FCA; *Recreations* travel, sailing, gardening; *Style*— Robert Cross, Esq; Little Oaks, Ridgeway, Tranmere Park, Guiseley, W Yorks LS20 8JA (☎ 0943 77152; office: 0274 874361)

CROSS, Lady; Sheila; da of late Gilbert Moffit, of Gwalia, W Australia; *m* 1939, Sir William Coats Cross, 2 Bt (d 1947, Btcy became extinct 1962); *Style*— Lady Cross; 16a Richardson Av, Claremont, Perth, W Australia

CROSS, (Harold) William; RNVR (pilot Fleet Air Arm) 1941-46; Colonial Serv E Africa 1947-53, fin controller Tunnel Portland Cement Co Ltd 1954-60, chm and chief exec Brent Chemicals Int plc 1970-85, chm Elswick plc 1985-; chm: Mission Aviation Fellowship, UK Evangelisation Tst; former chm Covenanters Youth Movement, churchwarden and lay reader C of E; FICA 1953; s of Cross, John Edward (d 1953), of Doncaster, Yorks, and Bertha Lillian, *née* Lake (d 1965); *b* 17 April 1922; *Educ* Doncaster GS; *m* 26 April 1947, Olive Mary Cross, (d 1988), da of Eric Hubert Swinstead (d 1956), of Buckhurst Hill, Essex; 2 s (David Andrew b 1951, Stephen John b 1953); *Recreations* sailing, windsurfing, fell walking, music, reading, theology; *Clubs* RAC, Phyllis Court (Henley); *Style*— William Cross, Esq; Kinwarton House, Alcester, Warwicks (☎ 0789 400532); Cinco Arcos, Pollensa, Mallorca, Spain; Elswick plc, Alcester, Warwicks (☎ 0789 400333, fax 0789 400794, car 0836 286848)

CROSS BROWN, Tom; s of Christopher James Cross Brown, and Georgina, *née* Forrester; *b* 22 Dec 1947; *Educ* Uppingham, Brasenose Coll Oxford (MA), Insead (MBA); *m* 1972, Susan Rosemary, da of Col Mansell Halkett Jackson (d 1967); 1 s (Nicol b 1975), 3 da (Gemma b 1977, Amelia b 1982, Claire twin b 1982); *Career* dir Lazard Bros and Co Ltd 1985-; non exec dir Whitegate Leisure plc; *Style*— Tom Cross Brown, Esq; Shipton Old Farm, Winslow, Buckingham MK18 3JL; 21 Moorfields, London EC2P 2HT

CROSS OF CHELSEA, Baron (Life Peer UK 1971); Sir (Arthur) Geoffrey (Neale) Cross; PC (1969); eldest s of late Arthur George Cross and Mary Elizabeth Dalton; *b* 1 Dec 1904; *Educ* Westminster, Trinity Coll Cambridge; *m* 1952, Mildred Joan, da of late Lt-Col Theodore Eardley-Wilmot, DSO (gn of Sir John Eardley Wilmot, 2 Bt), and widow of Thomas Walton Davies; 1 da; *Career* barr 1930, KC 1949, bencher 1959, judge of the High Court Chancery Div 1960-69, Lord Justice of Appeal 1969-71, a Lord of Appeal in Ordinary 1971-75, chm Takeover Panel Appeals Ctee 1976-81; chllr of Co Palatine of Durham 1959; kt 1960; *Style*— The Rt Hon Lord Cross of Chelsea, PC; The Bridge House, Leintwardine, Craven Arms, Shropshire (☎ 054 73 205)

CROSSE, John Ernest; s of Ernest Crosse (d 1972); *b* 11 Jan 1926; *Educ* Sebright Sch nr Kidderminster; *m* 1, 1952, Evelyn; m 2, 1981, Janet; 2 s, 2 da; *Career* SEAC 1945-47; md: Solartron Engineering Ltd 1952-58, Solartron (Farnborough) Ltd 1958-63; chm Plasmec Ltd 1963-; CBIM; *Style*— John Crosse Esq; The Mill House, Frensham, Farnham, Surrey (☎ 0251 25 2979); Plasmec Ltd, Weydon Lane, Farnham, Surrey (☎ 0252 721 236)

CROSSLAND, Prof Bernard; CBE (1980); s of Reginald Francis Crossland (d 1976), and Kathleen Mary, *née* Rudduck (d 1950); *b* 20 Oct 1923; *Educ* Simon Langton GS Canterbury, Derby Regnl Tech Coll, Univ Coll Nottingham (BSc, MSc, PhD, DSc); *m* 25 July 1946, Audrey, da of Frank Elliott Birks (d 1961), 2 d (Jennifer b 1948, Mary Anne b 1952); *Career* tech asst Rolls Royce Ltd 1943-45 (apprentice 1940-44), lectr Luton Tech Coll 1945-46, sr lectr mechanical engrg (formerly asst lectr and lectr) Univ of Bristol 1946-59; Queen's Univ of Belfast: prof and head of dept of mechanical and industl engrg 1959-84, dean engrg faculty, pro vice-chllr 1978-82; pres Inst of Mech Engrs 1986-87, vice-pres Royal Soc 1984-86, assessor King's Cross Underground Fire Investigation 1988; chm: Youth Careers Guidance Cmmn 1975-81, NI Manpower Cncl 1981-86; memb: NI Trg Cncl 1964-81, NI Econ Cncl 1981-85, AFRC 1981-87, NI Ind Devpt Bd 1982-87; Freeman City of London 1987, memb Worshipful Co of Engrs 1988; Hon DSc, Univ of Ireland 1984, Univ of Dublin 1985, Univ of Edinburgh 1987, The Queen's Univ Belfast 1988, Univ of Aston 1988, Cranfield Inst of Technol; FIMechE, FIW, Hon MASME, MRIA, FEng, FRS; *Recreations* walking, music, travel; *Clubs* Athenaeum; *Style*— Prof Bernard Crossland, CBE; 16 Malone Ct, Belfast BT9 6PA (☎ 0232 67 495); The Queens University, Belfast BT7 1NN (☎ 0232 247 303, fax 0232 247 895, telex 74487)

CROSSLAND, Sir Leonard; s of Joseph William Crossland (d 1962), of Stocksbridge, Sheffield, and Frances Crossland; *b* 2 Mar 1914; *m* 1964, Joan, da of Stanley Percival Brewer, of Bath; *Career* served WWII Europe; chm and dir Ford Motor Co Ltd 1968-72; chm: Eaton Ltd 1974-, Energy Research and Development Ltd 1974-; farmer (700 acres); kt 1969; *Recreations* shooting, fishing, golf; *Clubs* RAC, American, City Livery, BRDC; *Style*— Sir Leonard Crossland; Abbotts Hall, Great Wigborough, Colchester, Essex CO5 7RZ (☎ 020 635 456/301)

CROSSLAND, Prof Ronald Arthur; s of Ralph Crossland (d 1972), of Nottingham and Ethel, *née* Scattergood (d 1974); *b* 31 August 1920; *Educ* Nottingham HS, King's Coll Cambridge; *Career* served RA 1941-45, Lt 19 Field Regt RA (1st Div); service in GB, Tunisia and Italy; Henry Fell Yale Univ 1946-48; sr Student Ctee for Studentships in Oriental Languages and Literatures (Hittite philology) 1948-51; hon asst lectr Ancient History Birmingham Univ 1950-51; lectr in Ancient History King's Coll, Univs of Durham and Newcastle-upon-Tyne 1951-58, Harris Fell King's Coll Cambridge 1952-56, prof Greek Sheffield Univ 1958-82; British Cncl visiting lectr in Czechoslovakia 1961; visiting prof of Linguistics Texas Univ (Austin) 1962, Collitz visiting prof of Linguistics Michigan Univ 1967; dean of the faculty of arts Sheffield Univ 1973-75; visiting fell in classics Victoria Univ of Wellington 1979; Emeritus prof of greek Sheffield Univ 1982-; FSA; *Publications* Immigrants from the North, (Cambridge Ancient History, revised edition, 1/2, Chapter XXVII 1971), Linguistic problems of the Balkan area (Cambridge Ancient History, revised edition, Chapter 20c 1982), Bronze Age migrations in the Aegean (with Ann Birchall, 1973), Early Greek migrations (in M Grant, editor), Civilization of the ancient Mediterranean (1987); *Recreations* travel, music; *Style*— Ronald Crossland; 59 Sherlock Close, Cambridge CB3 0HP (☎ 0223 358085); University of Sheffield, Sheffield S10 2TN (☎ 0742 768555, ext 4603)

CROSSLEY, Sir Christopher John; 3 Bt (UK 1909) of Glenfield, Dunham Massey, Co Chester; s of late Lt Cdr Nigel Crossley, RN, s of late Eric Crossley, OBE (s of 1 Bt); suc great-unc, Sir Kenneth Irwin Crossley, 2 Bt, 1957; *b* 25 Sept 1931; *Educ* Canford; *m* 1, 28 Nov 1959 (m dis 1969), Carolyne Louise, Grey, da of late Leslie

Grey Sykes, of Sandbanks, Dorset; 2 s; m 2, 1977, Lesley A, da of late Dr K A J Chamberlain; *Heir* s, Nicholas Crossley; *Career* Lt Cdr RN (ret); *Style—* Sir Christopher Crossley, Bt; PO Box 100, Heliopolis, Egypt

CROSSLEY, Lady Elizabeth Joyce; da of late Enoch Shenton, of Boxmoor, Herts; *m* 16 Dec 1954, as his 2 w, Sir Kenneth Irwin Crossley, 2 Bt (d 22 Nov 1957); *Style—* Elizabeth, Lady Crossley; The Old Bakery, Milton Lilbourne, Pewsey, Wilts SN9 5LQ

CROSSLEY, Nicholas John; s (by 1 m) and h of Sir Christopher Crossley, 3 Bt; *b* 10 Dec 1962; *Style—* Nicholas Crossley, Esq

CROSSLEY, Hon (Richard) Nicholas; TD (1974), DL (N Yorks 1988); s of 2 Baron Somerleyton, MC (d 1959), and Bridget, *née* Hoare; *b* 24 Dec 1932; *Educ* Eton, Sandhurst; *m* 30 April 1958, Alexandra Ann Maitland, da of Wing Cdr Charles Donald Graham Welch, of Perrot Farm, Graffham, Sussex; 1 s, 2 da; *Career* farmer 1963-89, MFH 1969; Capt 9 Queen's Royal Lancers (ret), Maj Queen's Own Yeo (TA), CO Queen's Own Yeo 1973-76, Bt-Col 1977, Col TA NE Dist 1978-81, ADC (TAVR) to HM The Queen 1980-; memb HM Body Guard of Hon Corps of Gentlemen at Arms 1982-; area gov Ocean Youth Club 1985-; *Recreations* hunting, shooting, stalking, sailing; *Clubs* Cavalry and Guards', Pratt's; *Style—* Col The Hon Nicholas Crossley, TD, DL; Westfield Farm, Norton, Malton, N Yorks YO17 9PL

CROSSLEY, Maj-Gen Ralph John; CB (1987), CBE (1981); s of Edward Crossley (d 1978), of Sussex, and Eva Mary, *née* Farnworth (d 1965); *b* 11 Oct 1933; *Educ* Felsted; *m* 1957, Marion Hilary, da of Herbert Wilfred Bacon (d 1975), of Salisbury; 1 s (Robin), 1 da (Amanda); *Career* Army Offr; Dep Cmdt RMC of Science 1982, Dir Gen Weapons (Army 1984), ret 1986; dir defence policy Avon Rubber plc 1987; *Recreations* golf, gardening, walking; *Clubs* Nat Tst; *Style—* Maj-Gen Ralph Crossley, CB, CBE; Avon Rubber plc, Bradford-on-Avon, Wilts BA15 1AA (☎ 02216 3911)

CROSSLEY, Robert Alan; MC (1945), TD (1946); s of Lt Alan Hastings Crossley, of Letton Ct, Hereford; *b* 27 Mar 1912; *Educ* Wellington, Clare Coll Cambridge (BA); *m* 1938, Gabrielle Mary, da of Sir Robert Abraham Burrows, KBE (d 1964); 2 s; *Career* Maj RA, France 1940, ME, Italy; dep and later md Pillar-Wedge 1971-75, dir Br Moulded Fibre 1958-80; MIMechE; *Recreations* stalking, tennis, rowing, shooting; *Style—* Robert Crossley, Esq, MC, TD; Castrum, Elmdon, Saffron Walden CB11 4NG (☎ 0763 838134)

CROSSLEY-HOLLAND, Kevin John William; s of Peter Charles Crossley-Holland of Llangeler, Llandysul, Dyfed, and Joan Mary *née* Cowper, MBE; *b* 7 Feb 1941; *Educ* Bryanston, St Edmund Hall Oxford (BA); *m* 1, 6 Jul 1963 (m dis 1972), Caroline Fendall, da of Prof Leonard M Thompson of Connecticut USA; 2 s (Kieran b 1963, Dominic b 1967); m 2, 23 Sept 1972 (m dis 1978), Ruth, da of John Marris of Swanage; m 3, 26 March 1982, Gillian Paula, da of Peter Cook of Eaton Bank, Derbyshire; 2 da (Oenone b 1982, Eleanor b 1986); *Career* ed Macmillan & Co 1962-69, Gregory fell in poetry Univ of Leeds 1969-71, talks producer BBC 1972, ed dir Victor Gollancz 1972-77, lectr in English, Tufts in London program 1969-78, lektor Regensburg Univ 1979-80, Arts Cncl fellow in writing Winchester Sch of Art 1983 and 1984, vis prof St Olaf Coll Minnesota 1987, 1988, 1989; ed cnslt Boydell and Brewer 1983-; memb Walsham-le-Willows PCC, chm E Arts Assoc Literature panel; tstee and chm Friends of Wingfield Coll; *poetry*: 5 vols inc Waterslain (1986), The Painting-Room (1988); for children: The Green Children (1966, Arts Cncl award), The Storm (1985, Carnegie medal), British Folk Tales (1987); Wulf (1988), Sleeping Nanna (1989); translations from Old English: Beowulf (1968 jtly); The Norse Myths (1981), Pieces of Land (1972); edited: The Anglo-Saxon World (1982), Folk-Tales of The British Isles (1985), The Oxford Book of Travel Verse (1986); *Recreations* music, tennis, archaeology, travel; *Style—* Kevin Crossley-Holland, Esq; The Old Vicarage, Walsham-le-Willows, Bury St Edmunds, Suffolk (☎ 03598 287 8876)

CROSSMAN, Lady Rose Maureen; *née* Alexander; o da of Field Marshal 1 Earl Alexander of Tunis, KG, OM, GCB, GCMG, CSI, DSO, MC, PC (d 1969); *b* 28 Oct 1932; *m* 20 Jan 1956, Lt-Col Humphrey Crossman, JP, DL, s of Maj-Gen Francis Lindisfarne Morley Crossman, CB, DSO, MC (d 1947), of Cheswick House, Berwick-upon-Tweed; 1 s, 1 da; *Style—* Lady Rose Crossman; Cheswick House, Berwick upon Tweed, Northumberland TD15 2RL

CROSSWELL, Michael Stephen; s of Charles Henry Crosswell (d 1976), and Cecilia Margaret, *née* Jones; *b* 23 Jan 1943; *Educ* Stawley GS, S London; *m* 14 June 1980, da of George Marvin of Milton Keynes, Bucks; *Career* dir Blue Arrow plc (chief exec MAIN division, employment group); vice-chm Federation of Recruitment and Employment Services (FRES) (chm 1988-); *Recreations* golf; *Clubs* Woburn Golf; *Style—* Michael S Crosswell, Esq; 'Plovers', Hatching Green, Harpenden, Hertfordshire (☎ 05827 64269); Iviercury House, Triton Cdourt, Finsbury Square, London EC2 (☎ 01 256 5011)

CROSTHWAITE, Charles Doveton; s of John Graham Crosthwaite (d 1905), and Jean Stuart Menteith Hutchinson (d 1916); *b* 8 Nov 1902; *Educ* Wellington, City and Guilds Engineering Coll, London Univ; *m* 21 June 1936, Edith Mary, da of Gen Hutchinson; 3 s (John Murray b 1937, Christopher David b 1941, Charles Murray b 1952), 1 da (Brigid Jane b 1946); *Career* ret consulting engineer Freeman Fox and Partners; numerous papers on dams, bridges, demography, overseas aid; memb Am Soc CE, InstHE, Inst of Tport; *Recreations* skiing, mountaineering, farming; *Clubs* St Stephens Constitutional; *Style—* Charles D Crosthwaite, Esq

CROSTHWAITE, Sir (Ponsonby) Moore; KCMG (1960, CMG 1951); o s of late Ponsonby Moore Crosthwaite, MICE, and Agnes Alice, *née* Aitken; *b* 13 August 1907; *Educ* Rugby, Corpus Christi Coll Oxford; *Career* entered Diplomatic Service 1932: ambass Lebanon 1958-63, Sweden 1963-66; *Clubs* Athenaeum; *Style—* Sir Moore Crosthwaite, KCMG; 17 Crescent Grove, London SW4 (☎ 01 622 8842)

CROUCH, Dr Colin John; s of Charles John Crouch, of Charlbury, Oxon, and Doris Beatrice, *née* Baker; *b* 1 Mar 1944; *Educ* Latymer Upper Sch Hammersmith, LSE (BA), Univ of Oxford (DPhil); *m* 10 June 1970, Joan Ann, da of David Freedman (d 1972), of London E1; 2 s (Daniel b 1974, Ben b 1978); *Career* lectr sociology: LSE 1969-70, Univ of Bath 1972-73; reader LSE 1980-85 (lectr 1973-79, sr lectr 1979-80), fell and tutor in politics Trinity Coll and faculty lectr sociology Univ of Oxford 1985-, chm sub-faculty of sociology 1987-89, res interests the comparative study of industl relations systems in Western Europe; ed: Stress and Contradiction in Modern Capitalism (with Lindberg et al, 1975), Br Political Sociology Yearbook Vol III Participation in Politics (1977), The Resurgence of Class Conflict in Western Europe since 1968, vol I Nat Studies vol II comparative Analyses (with A Pizzorno, 1978), State and Econ in Contemporary Capitalism (1979), Int Yearbook of Organizations Democracy vol I Organizational Democracy and Political Processes (with F Heller, 1983) Corporatism and Accountability Organised Interests in Br Public Life (with R P Dore, 1989), European Industrial Relations: the Challenge of Flexibility (with G Baglioni, 1989); memb Oxford West and Abingdon Lab Pty, referee class 3 Oxfordshire Football Assoc; memb standing ctee of Ct of Govrs LSE 1980-84, jt ed The Political Quarterly 1985-86, chm Fabian Soc 1976 (memb exec ctee 1969-78); *Books* The Student Revolt (1970), Class Conflict and the Industrial Relations Crisis (1977), The Politics of Industrial Relations (2 edn 1982), Trade Unions the Logic of Collective Action (1982); *Recreations* playing violin, listening to music, gardening; *Style—* Dr Colin Crouch; 109 Southmoor Rd, Oxford OX2 6RE (☎ 0865 54688); Trinity Coll, Oxford OX1 3BH (☎ 0865 279 879, 279 900)

CROUCH, Sir David Lance; s of Charles Littler Stanley Crouch (d 1966), of Northwood, Middx, and Rosalie Kate, *née* Croom (d 1972); *b* 23 June 1919; *Educ* Univ Coll Sch; *m* 5 July 1947, Margaret Maplesden, da of Maj Sydney Maplesden Noakes, DSO, of Shorne, Kent; 1 s (Patrick b 19 May 1954), 1 da (Vanessa b 11 Oct 1951); *Career* served in RA 1939-46, Maj, attached RAF 1944-45; serv: N Africa, Europe, Burma; dir: David Crouch and Co Ltd, Lance Publishing Ltd; contested (C) W Leeds 1959; chm The Theatres Tst 1987-; MP (C) Canterbury 1966-87; pres The Kent Soc 1987-, govr Kent Inst of Art And Design 1988-; Hon DCL (Univ of Kent at Canterbury) 1987; FRSA; kt 1987; *Books* A Canterbury Tale (1987); *Recreations* golf, painting; *Clubs* Athenaeum, MCC; *Style—* Sir David Crouch; The Oast House, Fisher St, Badlesmere, Faversham, Kent (☎ 0227 730528)

CROUCH, Derek Charles Howard; s of Harry Oswald Crouch (d 1964); *b* 31 May 1921; *Educ* Oundle; *m* 1954, Pamela Martha Elizabeth, da of Frank Moore Odam (d 1952); 2 children; *Career* chm Derek Crouch plc (fndr Derek Crouch 1938); dir: Power Inc (USA) 1978-, Norwich Union Insurance Gp 1981-; memb Br Rail Property Bd 1982- (part-time memb Eastern Region BR Bd 1970-74, vice-chm Northern Region BR Bd 1975-77); *Recreations* shooting, skiing; *Style—* Derek Crouch, Esq; c/o Derek Crouch plc, Eye, Peterborough PE6 7UW (☎ 0733 222341)

CROUCHER, Norman Colville; s of Wilfred Gladston Croucher, MBE, and Mary Kate, *née* Bennett; *b* 17 May 1915; *Educ* Bristol GS, Monkton Coomb Sch; *m* 1, 18 Nov 1939, Mary Millicent (d 1987), da of the late C M Lane, of Bristol; 2 s (Richard Colville b 1944, Brian Robert b 1946); m 2, Oct 1988, June Cleverley; *Career* tech/liaison engr Harland Engrg Co Ltd Alloa 1937-46, chief M & E asst engr J Taylor & Sons London 1958-61, tech/works dir KSB Mfrg Co Ltd 1961-75, conslt engr 1975-83; life vice-pres Br Pump Mfrs Assoc 1983- (memb 1964-83, chm tech ctee 1971-83); chm: BSI ME/29 ctee 1972-83, ISO TC/115 ctee 1972-83; chief scrutineer motor sport div RAC 1957-85, former cncl memb BARC; Freeman City of London, Liveryman Worshipful Co of Blacksmiths 1964; *Recreations* motor sport; *Clubs* RAC; *Style—* Norman Croucher, Esq; 7 Vacasour House, North Embankment, Dartmouth, Devon TQ6 9PW (☎ 08043 4053)

CROWDEN, James Gee Pascoe; JP (Wisbech 1969), DL (Cambridge 1971); yr s of Lt-Col R J C Crowden, MC, of Peterborough; *b* 14 Nov 1927; *Educ* Bedford Sch, Pembroke Coll Cambridge (MA); *m* 1955, Kathleen Mary, wid of Capt F A Grounds, and da of late J W Loughlin, of Upwell; 1 s (decd); *Career* cmmnd Royal Lincs Regt 1947; chartered surveyor; rowed in Oxford and Cambridge Boat Race 1951 and 1952 (pres 1952), Capt GB VIII Euro Championships Macon 1951 (Gold Medallists), rowed 1950 Euro Championships and 1952 Olympics, coached 20 Cambridge crews, steward and memb Ctee of Mgmnt Henley Royal Regatta, memb cncl Amateur Rowing Soc 1957-77, sr ptnr Grounds & Co 1974-88, chm Cambridgeshire Olympic Appeal 1984-88; vice-pres British Olympic Assoc 1988; chm Appeals Exec Ctee Peterborough Cathedral 1979, govr: King's Sch Peterborough, St Hugh's Sch Woodhall Spa; High Sheriff Cambs and Isle of Ely 1970, Vice Lord Lieut Cambs 1985; junior warden Co of Watermen and Lightermen of the River Thames; *Recreations* rowing, shooting; *Clubs* East India, Devonshire, Sports and Public Schs, Hawks', Univ Pitt, Cambridge County, Leander, Sette of Odd Volumes; *Style—* J G P Crowden, Esq, JP, DL; 19 North Brink, Wisbech, Cambs PE13 1JR (☎ 0945 583320)

CROWDER, Frederick Petre; QC (1964); s of Sir John Ellenborough Crowder (d 1961), and Florence Gertrude Petre (d 1980); *b* 18 July 1919; *Educ* Eton, Christ Church, Oxford; *m* 12 July 1948, Hon Patricia Winifred Mary, da of 25 Baron Mowbray, MC (d 1965) (also 26 Baron Segrave and 22 Baron Stourton); 2 s (Richard b 1950, John b 1954); *Career* serv WWII Maj Coldm Gds (N Africa, Italy, and Burma); barr Inner Temple 1948, master of the Bench 1971; SE Circuit, rec Gravesend 1960-67; Herts QS, dep chm 1963-71; contested (C) N Tottenham 1945, MP (C): Ruislip-Northwood 1950-74, Hillingdon, Ruislip-Northwood 1974-79; pps to: Slr-Gen 1952-54, attorney-gen 1954-62; recorder (formerly of Colchester) 1967-; *Clubs* Pratt's; *Style—* Frederick P Crowder, Esq, QC; 8 Quarrendon St, SW6 3SU (☎ 01 731 6342); 2 Harcourt Bldgs, Temple EC4 (☎ 01 353 2112)

CROWDER, John Fairfax; s of Charles Fairfax Crowder (d 1951), and Theodora (d 1951), da of Robert Harding Milward; *b* 7 July 1902; *Educ* Lancing, King's Coll Cambridge (MA, LLM); *m* 1931, Ursula Reynolds, da of Benjamin John Fletcher, OBE (d 1951); 2 da; *Career* slr; dep div food offr (Midlands) 1942-45; pres Birmingham Law Soc 1948-49; memb bd of govrs United Birmingham Hosps 1947-57; govr: Queen's Coll Birmingham 1951-78, City of Birmingham Coll of Commerce 1962-65, Sch of Music 1968-70; hon consul of Austria (Midlands) 1961-82; Knight's Cross (1 class, Austria) 1975; *Recreations* singing, travelling; *Clubs* United Oxford and Cambridge; *Style—* John Crowder, Esq; 24 Harborne Rd, Birmingham B15 3AD (☎ 021 456 4477, telex 339130)

CROWDER, Ven Norman Harry; s of Laurence Smethurst Crowder (d 1977), and Frances Annie, *née* Hicks; *b* 20 Oct 1926; *Educ* Nottingham HS, St John's Coll Cambridge (MA), Westcott House Theo Coll Cambridge; *m* 16 Dec 1971, Pauleen Florence Alison, *née* Styles; 1 s (Richard b 1973); *Career* curate St Mary's Radcliffe-on-Trent 1952-55, residential chaplain to Bishop of Portsmouth 1955-59, asst chaplain Canford Sch 1959-64 chaplain 1964-72, vicar of St John's Oakfield Ryde IOW 1972-75, dir of religious educn Portsmouth Diocese and residentiary canon of Portsmouth Cathedral 1972-85, archdeacon of Portsmouth 1985-; *Recreations* water colour, travel; *Clubs* MCC; *Style—* The Ven the Archdeacon of Portsmouth; Victoria Lodge, 36 Osborn Road, Fareham, Hants PO16 7DS (☎ 0329 280101)

CROWDER, Hon Mrs (Patricia Winifred Mary); *née* Stourton; da of 25 Baron Mowbray, 26 Segrave and 22 Stourton, MC (d 1965); *b* 2 Nov 1924; *m* 12 July 1948, Frederick Petre Crowder, QC, MP, *qv*; 2 s (Richard John b 1950; John George b

1954); *Career* Foreign Office; *Style—* The Hon Mrs Crowder; 8 Quarrendon St, London SW6 3SU (☎ 01 731 6342)

CROWDY, Edmund Porter; VRD; s of Lt-Col Charles R Crowdy (d 1938), and Kate, *née* Porter; bro of Maj-Gen Joseph Crowdy, *qv*; *b* 13 Mar 1925; *Educ* Gresham's Sch Hall, Sidney Sussex Coll Cambridge; *m* 1958, Sheila Mary, *née* Davison; 2 s (Nicholas, Charles), 2 da (Sarah b 1962, Philippa b 1967); *Career* Cdr RNVR; engineer; md: Hawthorn Leslie (Engineers) Ltd 1972-78, Clark-Hawthorn Ltd 1978-80, Doxford Engines Ltd 1980-, Br Shipbuilders (Engrg and Tech Services) Ltd 1981-1984, ret; FEng; *Recreations* campanology, golf; *Style—* Edmund Crowdy, Esq, VRD; 18 Manor Rd, Benton, Newcastle upon Tyne (☎ 091 2666418)

CROWDY, Maj-Gen Joseph Porter; CB (1984), QHP (1981); s of Lt-Col Charles R Crowdy (d 1938), and Kate, *née* Porter; bro of Edmund Crowdy, *qv*; *b* 19 Nov 1923; *Educ* Gresham's Sch Holt, Edinburgh Univ (MB, ChB, DTM and H); *m* 1948, Beryl Elisabeth Sapsford; 4 da; *Career* house surgeon Norfolk and Norwich Hosp 1947-48, joined RAMC 1949, former Cmdt and postgraduate dean RAMC; FFCM, MFOM; *Style—* Maj-Gen Joseph Crowdy, CB, QHP; 5 Atterbury St, London SW1P 4RQ (☎ 01 821 7086)

CROWE, Brian Lee; CMG (1985); s of Eric Eyre Crowe (d 1952) and Virginia Bolling *née* Teusler (d 1981); *b* 5 Jan 1938; *Educ* Sherbourne, Magdallen Coll Oxford; *m* 19 Jan 1969, Virginia da of Col George Willis, MC OBE (d 1980); 2 s (Alexander b 1972, Charles b 1975); *Career* FO 1961, Br Embassy Moscow 1962-64, FCO London 1965-68, Br Embassy: Washington 1968-73, Bonn 1973-76, head policy planning staff FCO London 1976-78, head of chancery UK Perm Rep to EEc Brussels 1979-81, head of Euro Community Dept FCO London 1982-84, min commercial Br Embassy Washington 1985-; *Recreations* tennis, squash, winter sports; *Style—* Brian Crowe, Esq, CMG; c/o FCO, King Charles Street, London, SW1

CROWE, Sir Colin Tradescant; GCMG (1973, KCMG 1963, CMG 1956); s of Sir Edward Thomas Frederick Crowe, KCMG (d 1960), and Eleanor, *née* Lay (d 1947); *b* 7 Sept 1913; *Educ* Stowe, Oriel Coll Oxford; *m* 1938, Bettina, da of Burt and Bertha Lum, of Iowa USA; *Career* Foreign Office 1935, served Peking, Shanghai, Washington; Br chargé d'affaires Cairo 1959-61, dep UK rep to UN New York 1961-63, ambass to Saudi Arabia 1963-64, Supernumerary fellow St Antony's Coll Oxford 1964-65, chief of admin Diplomatic Service 1965-68, Br high cmmr in Canada 1968-70, Br perm rep to UN 1970-73, ret 1973; chm: Marshall Aid Commemoration Cmmn, Cheltenham Ladies Coll; vice-chm UCL Council; *Style—* Sir Colin Crowe, GCMG; Pigeon House, Bibury, Glos

CROWE, David Edward Aubrey; s of Norman Ronald Aubrey Crowe (d 1983) and Barbara Lythgoe, *née* Jones; *b* 31 August 1939; *Educ* Cranleigh Sch Surrey, Christ Church Oxford (MA); *m* 8 June 1963, Helen Margaret, da of George Denis Dale (d 1983); 2 da (Sarah b 1967, Lucy b 1971); *Career* solr 1964, ptnr: HA Crowe and Co 1964-68, Gouldens 1968-; Lib party candidate: Bromley 1970, Ravensbourne 1974, ldr Lib Gp Bromley Cncl 1974-78, vice chm London Lib Pty 1975, chm Bromley Consumer Gp 1978- 79, chm Beckenham and Bromley Nat Tst 1975-79 (hon sec 1979-88): memb Law Soc; *Recreations* opera going, gardening; *Clubs* Oxford and Cambridge, National Liberal; 22 Tudor Street, London EC4Y OJJ (☎ 01 583 7777, fax 01 583 3051)

CROWE, Dame Sylvia; DBE (1973, CBE 1967); da of Eyre Crowe; *b* 1901; *Educ* Berkhamsted, Swanley Hort Coll; *Career* served FANY and ATS 1939-45; designed gardens 1927-39, landscape architect in private practice 1945-; work as consult incl: Harlow and Basildon New Town Cororations, CEGB for Trawsfynydd and Wylfa Nuc Power Stations, Forestry Cmmn, reclamation of land after 1952 floods, gdns for Oxford Univ and Cwlth Inst London; resevoirs Bewl Bridge Wimleball and Rutland Water; sec Int Fed Landscape Architecture 1948-59, (vice-pres 1964); pres Inst Landscape Architects 1957-59, hon fell Aust Inst of Landscape Architects, chm Tree Cncl 1974-76, hon FRIBA 1969, hon fellow Royal Town Planning Inst 1970, Hon DLitt Newcastle 1975, Hon LLD Sussex 1978, Hon DLitt Heriott Watt Univ Edinburgh; hon fell Inst of Foresters, hon FRIBA 1969; *Books Incl:* Tomorrow's Landscape (1956), Garden Design (1958, 2nd edn 1981), Landscape Power, Landscape Roads, Pattern of Landscape; *Recreations* gardening, walking, countryside; *Style—* Dame Sylvia Crowe, DBE; 59 Ladbroke Grove, London W11 3AT (☎ 01 727 7794)

CROWLEY-BAINTON, Dr Theresa; da of Joseph Crowley, of Bucks, and Margaret Mary, *née* Heaton; *b* 4 Nov 1953; *Educ* Notre Dame London, Bedford Coll, Univ of London (BSc), UCL (PhD); *m* 18 Aug 1979, Christopher Stephen Bainton, s of David Bainton, of Dorset; *Career* psychologist: Austin Knight Ltd 1974-75, Kiernan and Co (UK) Ltd 1978-83, Manpower Services Cmmn 1983-85 (1975-77), Cabinet Off 1985-86, HM Tresay 1988-, Policy Studies Inst 1988-, Industl Soc 1988-; *Books* Redundancy (1985), many papers on employment and unemployment; *Recreations* riding, archaeology, the Western Mystery tradition; *Clubs* Nat Lib; *Style—* Dr Theresa Crowley-Bainton; Raven Cottage, 2 Ravensborne Gdns, Ealing, London W13 8EW; The Industl Soc, 48 Bryanston Sq, London W1

CROWLEY-MILLING, Air Marshal Sir Denis; KCB (1973), CBE (1963), DSO (1943), DFC (1941 and Bar 1942); s of Thomas William Crowley-Milling (d 1954), of Colwyn Bay, N Wales, and Gillian May, *née* Chinnery (d 1942); *b* 22 Mar 1919; *Educ* Malvern; *m* 1943, Lorna Jean Jeboult, da of H J Stuttard, of Park Lodge, Deganwy, N Wales; 1 s decd, 2 da; *Career* Roll Royce apprentice and RAFVR 1937-39, Sqdns 615,242,610 and 181 1939-44; AOC No 38 Gp RAF Odiham 1970-72, AOC 46 Gp RAF Upavon 1973, UK rep Perm Mil Deputies Gp CENTO 1974-75, controller RAF Benevolent Fund 1975-81; Gentleman Usher of the Scarlet Rod to the Order of the Bath 1979-85, registrar and secretary 1985-; *Style—* Air Marshal Sir Denis Crowley-Milling, KCB, CBE, DSO, DFC; Church Cottages, North Creake, Fakenham, Norfolk NR21 9JJ

CROWLEY-MILLING, Michael Crowley; CMG (1982); s of Thomas William Crowley-Milling (d 1954), of Colwyn Bay, N Wales and Gillian May, *née* Chinnery (d 1942); *b* 7 May 1917; *Educ* Radley, St John's Coll Cambridge (MA); *m* 1957, Gee, da of William Gray Dickson (d 1983), of West Ferry, Dundee; *Career* electrical engr, Metropolitan-Vickers Electric Co Ltd 1938-63; devpt of radar 1938-46, design and dvpt of electron linear accelerators for physics med and irradiation purposes 1946-63; Daresbury Nuclear Physics Lab 1963-71; Euro Orgn for Nuclear Res (CERN) Geneva 1971-83, responsible for control system for Super Proton Synchrotron (SPS) 1971-76, dir Acceleration Program 1981-83, conslt 1983-85, SLAC Stanford Univ (USA), conslt Los Alamos Nat Lab USA 1985-, dir Crowley Conslts 1984-; CEng, FIEE; *Recreations* vintage cars, sailing (yacht 'SPS'); *Clubs* VSCC, LPYC; *Style—* Michael Crowley-Milling, CMG; c/o Barclays Bank plc, 40 Conway Rd, Colwyn Bay, Clwyd LL29 7HU

CROWSON, Richard Borman; CMG (1986); s of Clarence Borman Crowson (d 1980), of Gainsborough, and Cecilia May, *née* Ramsden (d 1973); *b* 12 July 1929; *Educ* Queen Elizabeth's GS Gainsborough, Downing Coll Cambridge (MA); *m* 1, 29 Feb 1960 (m dis 1974), Sylvia, *née* Caralier; 1 s (Anthony b 26 Feb 1961), 1 da (Hilary b 3 March 1964); m 2, 21 May 1963, Judith Elaine, da of Marion Earl Clark, of Lincoln, Nebraska, USA; *Career* HM Colonial Serv Uganda 1955-62, FO 1962-63, 1 Sec (Commercial) Br Embassy Tokoyo 1963-68, dep high cmmr Barbados 1968-70, FCO 1970-74, cnsllr (Commercial & Aid) Br Embassy Jakarta 1975-77, cnsllr (Hong Kong Affairs) Br Embassy Washington (also accredited in Ottawa) 1977-82, cnsllr Br Embassy Berne 1983-85, Br high cmmr Mauritius and concurrently HM Ambass Fed Islamic Repub of the Comoros 1985-; FCIS 1962; *Recreations* music, theatre; *Clubs* Royal Cwlth Soc; *Style—* Richard Crowson, Esq, CMG; Westminster Ho, Floreal, Mautitius (☎ Mauritius 865 872); British High Commission, Floreal, Mauritius (☎ Mauritius 865 795, telex 4266 UKREP IW)

CROWTHER, Hon Charles Worth; s of Baron Crowther (Life Peer, d 1972); *b* 31 Jan 1939; *Educ* Winchester, Harvard (AB 1960), Corpus Christi Coll Cambridge (BA); *m* 20 July 1963, Barbara Sylvia, yr da of Prof Norman Merrett Hancox, MD, of Moorside House, Neston, Cheshire; 1 s, 1 da; *Style—* The Hon Charles Crowther; Bourne Bank, Bourne End, Bucks

CROWTHER, Hon David Richard Geoffrey; 2 s of Baron Crowther (Life Peer, d 1972); *b* 19 August 1943; *Educ* Eton, King's Coll Cambridge (BA); *m* 1974, Martina, *née* Menn-Fink; *Style—* The Hon David Crowther

CROWTHER, Eric John Ronald; OBE (1977); s of Stephen Charles Crowther (d 1943), and Olive Beatrix, *née* Selby (d 1951); *b* 4 August 1924; *m* 1959, Elke Auguste Ottilie, da of Ludwig Winkelmann (d 1976), of Germany; 1 s (Edward b 1963), 1 da (Evelyn b 1961); *Career* WWII RN (Mediterranean) 1943-47; Winner Inns of Court Contest in Advocacy 1951; barr Lincoln's Inn 1951-68; Metropolitan Stipendary Magistrate 1968-; Recorder Inner London Crown Courts 1983-; lectr in english Br Cncl 1951-81, lectr on evidence to RN 1968-; hon offr Int Students House 1981-; lectr on Elocution and Advocacy Cncl of Legal Educn 1955-; chm Training Sub Ctee Inner London Magistrates 1981-; ed Cwlth Judicial Journal 1973-77; *Books* Advocacy for the Advocate (1984), Last in the List (1988); *Style—* Eric J R Crowther, Esq, OBE; 21 Old Buildings, Lincoln's Inn WC2; Horseferry Road Magistrates Court, London SW1

CROWTHER, Hon Felicity Margaret; 3 da of Baron Crowther (Life Peer, d 1972); *b* 14 Jan 1947; *Style—* The Hon Felicity Crowther

CROWTHER, Hon Nicola Mary; yst da of Baron Crowther (Life Peer, d 1972); *b* 27 Jan 1950; *Style—* The Hon Nicola Crowther

CROWTHER, Peter Hayden; s of Charles William Crowther (d 1970), of S Glam, and Gwendoline Gladys, *née* Matthews (d 1965); *b* 1 June 1926; *Educ* Barry Boys' Sch, Manchester Coll of Technology; *m* 12 March 1955, Anne Marie, da of Sir Richard Rylandes Costain, CBE (d 1966), of Surrey; 1 s (Hugh b 1958), 1 da (Penelope b 1960); *Career* Lt RE 1945-48 BAOR;chartered engr, joined Babcock and Wilcox Ltd 1948, md Bailey Meters and Controls Ltd 1963-74, dir Babcock and Wilcox (UK Investmts) Ltd 1968-72, chm Digimatics Ltd 1971-74, dir Babcock and Wilcox (Mgmnt) Ltd 1972-74; joined Vickers plc 1975, chm local bd Vickers Engrg Gp Newcastle 1975-80, dir Vickers Engrg Gp 1975-80, chm and md B A J Vickers Ltd 1984-85, chm and md B A J Ltd 1985-86, dep chm B A J Hldgs 1985-87 (non-exec dir 1987), memb: Northern Industl Devpt Bd 1978-80, Herefordshire Dist Health Authy 1988-; ret; CEng, MInstE, FBIM, FRSA; *Recreations* reading, playing at farming; *Clubs* Army and Navy; *Style—* Peter Crowther, Esq; Highbridge Farm, Ledbury, Herefordshire HR8 2HT (☎ 0531 2798)

CROWTHER, Ronald David; s of Harry Crowther; *b* 30 Oct 1928; *Educ* Cockburn HS Leeds; *m* 1961, Audrey, *née* Ramsden; *Career* fin dir Barr and Wallace Arnold Trust plc 1973-; dir: BCB Motor Factors Ltd, Scottish Transit Tst Ltd, Skellys (Dumbarton) Ltd, Trust Motors (Bradford, Edinburgh, Leeds, York, Glasgow, Motherwell and Nottingham) Ltd, WASS (Leeds) Ltd, Trust Motors Leasing Ltd, Wallace Arnold Fuels Ltd, Wallace Arnold Tours Ltd, Wayahead Fuel Services Ltd, Wilks and Mead Ltd, BWAT Properties Ltd; FCA; *Recreations* golf, gardening; *Style—* Ronald Crowther, Esq; 104 Main St, Shadwell, Leeds LS17 8HN (☎ office: 0532 436041, home 737085)

CROWTHER, (Joseph) Stanley; MP (Lab) Rotherham 1976-; s of Cyril Joseph Crowther (d 1970), of Rotherham and Florence Mildred, *née* Beckett; *b* 30 May 1925; *Educ* Rotherham GS, Rotherham Coll of Technol; *m* 1948, Margaret, da of Llewellyn Royston (d 1956), of Huddersfield; 2 s; *Career* journalist formerly with Yorkshire Evening Post; Mayor of Rotherham 1971-72 and 1975-76; *Style—* Stanley Crowther Esq, MP; 15 Clifton Cres South, Rotherham (☎ 0709 64559)

CROWTHER, His Hon Judge Thomas Rowland; QC (1981); s of Dr Kenneth Vincent Crowther, of Gwent, and Winifred Anita, *née* Rowland; *b* 11 Sept 1937; *Educ* Newport HS, Keble Coll Oxford (MA); *m* 1969, Gillian Jane, da of William Leslie Prince (d 1978); 1 s (Thomas b 1970), 1 da (Lucy b 1971); *Career* barr, practising Oxford Circuit 1960-69, practising Wales and Chester Circuit 1970-84, jr of Wales and Chester Circuit 1974, rec Crown Ct 1980-84, Crown Ct judge 1985, dir Gwent Area Broadcasting Ltd 1982-84; *Recreations* garden, trout fishing, golf; *Clubs* Cardiff and County, Newport Golf; *Style—* His Hon Judge Crowther, QC; 'Lansor', nr Caerleon, Gwent NP6 1LS (☎ Tredunnock 224)

CROWTHER-HUNT, Hon Elizabeth Anne; da of Baron Crowther-Hunt (Life Peer d 1987); *b* 1947; *Style—* The Hon Elizabeth Crowther-Hunt

CROWTHER-HUNT, Baroness; Joyce; *née* Stackhouse; da of late Rev Joseph Stackhouse, of Walsall Wood, Staffs; *m* 1944, Baron Crowther-Hunt (Life Peer d 1987); 3 da; *Style—* The Rt Hon Lady Crowther-Hunt; 14 Apsley Road, Oxford (☎ 0865 58342)

CROXON, Derrick Gwynn; s of Charles William Croxon (d 1968) of Maidstone, Kent (d 1968); *b* 10 Jan 1923; *Educ* King's Sch Rochester, UCL; *m* 1947, Rachel Ann, da of late William Griffith Thomas; 2 da; *Career* Capt RE, Maj RASC Italy; chemical engineer/gen mgmnt trainee Reed Int 1949; works dir Kimberly-Clark Ltd 1954; md Kimberly-Clark Ltd 1961-83, ret as conslt; *Recreations* tennis, sailing, beekeeping; *Clubs* Medway Yacht; *Style—* Derrick Croxon, Esq; Somerfield Rd, Maidstone, Kent (☎ 0622 58161)

CROZIER, Francis Rawdon; s of Rev Edward Travers Crozier (MA), (d 1940), and

Eleanor Dorothea, *née* Thomas (d 1952); ggnephew of Capt Francis Rawdon Moira Crozier RN, arctic explorer and 2 i/c of the Franklin expdn of 1845 to discover the NW Passage; *b* 19 July 1922; *Educ* Lancing, St Edmund Hall Oxford (MA); *m* 14 Aug 1948, Frances Aline Margaret, da of Rev John Harris Davies (d 1937); 4 da (Susan b 1949, Caroline b 1952, Josephine b 1954, Sally b 1962); *Career* RN 1941-46 Lt RNVR, served Russian Convoy, invasion of N Africa, invasion of Sicily, D-Day buildup; Legal and General Assur Soc Ltd 1952-77: joined 1952, area mangr Cheltenham, Guildford, Croydon finally Ipswich; FCII; *Recreations* gardening, bridge, photography, carpentry; *Clubs* Ipswich and Suffolk; *Style—* Rawdon Crozier, Esq; Thorpell House, Wickham Market, Woodbridge, Suffolk IP13 0JL (☎ Wickham Market 746386)

CROZIER, William Frederick Grenfell; s of Frederick Crozier (d 1973), and Millicent, *née* Grenfell; *b* 25 July 1917; *Educ* Stockport GS, Manchester Univ (BSc, MSc); *m* 4 Oct 1941, Esme Augusta, da of Frederick Stokes (d 1951), of Blankney, Lincoln; 1 s (Peter Michael Anthony b 4 Nov 1943), 1 da (Rosemary b 31 Oct 1947); *Career* RE 1940-46, ret Acting Maj 612 Field Sqdn RE; jr engr 1939-40, chief structural engr George Wimpey & Co 1946-58, chief engr GKN Reinforcements (London) 1958-61; ptnr: Frederick J Brand & Ptnrs 1961-64, Brill & Crozier 1964-71, sr ptnr Crozier, Haskell-Thomas & Ptnrs 1971-83; Technl Sec and Publications Offr Féderation Internationale de la Précontrainte 1967 (Hon memb 1986); Liveryman the Worshipful of Co of Plaisterers 1977; MICE 1948, FICE 1956; *Recreations* Bridge; *Clubs* Hillingdon AC (Hon life memb), Northwood GC (former Capt); *Style—* William Crozier, Esq; 85 Hoylake Crescent, Ickenham, Middlesex UB10 8JG (☎ 0895 633626

CRUICKSHANK, Alexander Andrew Campbell; s of Alexander Cruickshank, MA, MB, CHB, FRCS (d 1980), and Eileen Bertha, *née* Coleman; *b* 30 Nov 1945; *Educ* Haileybury and ISC, Peterhouse Camb (MA); *m* 19 May 1973, Susan Mary, da of Alan Pearce Greenaway, Esq, JP, of Flat 18, Grand Avenue Mansions, Grand Avenue, Hove, E Sussex; 2 s (David b 1976, Benjamin b 1982), 1 da (Sarah b 1974); *Career* ESSO Petroleum Co, Refinery and Distribution Planning 1967-72; Automated Real-Time Investments Exchange Ltd 1973-78; Orion Royal Bank Ltd 1979 (dir 1985-88); sr dir Continental Bank NA 1988-; Liveryman Worshipful Co of Gardeners; *Recreations* golf, reading, gardening; *Clubs* St George's Hill Golf, City Livery, United Wards, City Pickwick (hon sec); *Style—* A A C Cruickshank, Esq; The Doone, Byfleet Rd, Cobham, Surrey KT11 1EA (☎ 0932 64714); 162 Queen Victoria Street, London EC4V 4BS (☎ 01 236 1015)

CRUICKSHANK, Alistair Ronald; s of Francis John Cruickshank, (d 1969), of Aberdeen, and Kate Cameron, *née* Brittain; *b* 2 Oct 1944; *Educ* Aberdeen GS, Univ of Aberdeen (MA); *m* 29 March 1967, (Alexandra) Sandra (Mary), da of John Noble, of Aberdeen; 3 da (Jennifer b 1970, Caroline b 1973, Diana b 1975); *Career* MAFF: joined as asst princ 1966, asst private sec to min 1969-70 (princ 1970), head Eggs and Poultry Branch 1970-74, head Milk Div Branch 1974-78 (asst sec 1978), head Mktg Policy and Potatoes div 1978-81, head Meat Hygiene Div 1982-84, head Milk Div 1984-86 (under sec 1986), hd Animal Health Gp; *Recreations* visiting old buildings, growing vegetables; *Style—* Alistair Cruickshank, Esq; Ministry of Agriculture, Fisheries and Food, 3-8 Whitehall Pl, London SW1A 2HH

CRUICKSHANK, Dr Charles Greig; s of George Leslie Cruickshank (d 1937), of Fyvie, Aberdeenshire, and Annie, *née* Duncan (d 1950); *b* 10 June 1914; *Educ* Aberdeen GS, Aberdeen Univ (MA), Hertford Coll Oxford (DPhil), Edinburgh Univ; *m* 16 June 1943, Maire Roisin, da of Matthew Kissane (d 1960), of Manchester; 3 s (Christopher b 1944, Charles b 1946, Matthew b 1952); *Career* Miny of supply 1940-46, Bd of Trade 1946-51; trade cmmr: Ceylon 1951-55, Canada 1955-58; sr trade cmmr NZ 1958-63, sec cwlth Econ Ctee 1964-66, dir Commodities Dir Cwlth Secretariat 1967-68 (regnl export dir London & SE 1969-71), inspr FCO 1971-72, CAA 1972-73, DTI 1973, author 1966-; FRHistS 1970; *Books* Elizabeth's Army (1966), Army Royal (1969), The English Occupation of Tournai (1971), A Guide to the Sources of British Military History (jtly 1971), The German Occupation of the Channel Islands (1975), Greece 1940-41 (1976), The Fourth Arm, Psychologoical Warfare 1938-45 (1977), Deception in World War 11 (1979), SOE in the Far East (1983), SOE in Scandanavia (1986), History of Royal Wimbledon Golf Club (1986); novels: The V-Mann Papers (1976), The Tang Murders (1976), The Ebony Version (1977), The Deceivers (1977), Kew for Murder (1984), Scotch Murder (1985); *Recreations* golf; *Clubs* Royal Wimbledon GC; *Style—* Dr Charles Cruickshank; 15 McKay Rd, Wimbledon Common, London, SW20 0HT (☎ 01 947 1074)

CRUICKSHANK, Donald Gordon; s of Donald Campbell Cruickshank, of Ingleholm, Fochabers, Moray, Scotland, and Margaret Buchan *née* Morrison; *b* 17 Sept 1942; *Educ* Fordyce Acad, Univ of Aberdeen (MA), Manchester Business Sch (MBA); *m* 17 Oct 1964, Elizabeth Buchan, da of Alexander Watt Taylor, of Fraserburgh, Aberdeenshire, Scotland; 1 s (Stewart b 1965), 1 da (Karen b 1969); *Career* CA; McKingsey and Co Inc 1972-77; dir and gen mangr Sunday Times, Times Newspapers Ltd 1977-80; dir Pearson Longman Ltd 1980-84; md Virgin Gp plc 1984-; chm Wandsworth District Health Authority 1986-; CA; *Recreations* opera, theatre, golf, sport; *Style—* Donald G Cruickshank, Esq; 95-99 Ladbroke Gove, London W11 1PG (☎ 01 229 1282, fax 727 8200)

CRUICKSHANK, George; s of George Cruickshank; *b* 13 July 1936; *Educ* Melville Coll, Heriot Watt Univ Edinburgh; *m* Catherine, *née* Macdonald; 1 s, 1 da; *Career* dir: Scottish Discount Co Ltd, Lloyds Bowmaker Gp of Cos, RIGP Fin; *Recreations* golf, curling, rugby, skiing, bridge; *Clubs* Royal Burgess Golf (Edinburgh), Curling, Caermount Golf; Stewart Melville: FP, FP Rugby, FP Curling; *Style—* George Cruickshank, Esq; 28 Inveralmond Drive, Edinburgh EH4 6J (☎ 031 336 4481); Lloyds Bowmaker Fin Gp, Fin House, Orchard Brae, Edinburgh EH4 1PF (☎ 031 332 2451)

CRUICKSHANK, Prof John; s of Arthur Cruickshank (d 1957), of Belfast, and Eva, *née* Shummacher (d 1974); *b* 18 July 1924; *Educ* Royal Belfast Academical Inst, Trinity Coll Dublin (BA, MA, PhD, LittD), École Normale Supérieure Paris; *m* 1, 3 May 1949 (m dis 1972), Kathleen Mary, da of late Arthur Gutteridge; 1 s (Michael John b 4 Nov 1957); m 2, 1 Sept 1972, Maguerite Doreen Penny, da of Harold Whaley (d 1982); *Career* WWII cryptographer Mil Intelligence 1943-45; lectr (later sr lectr) in french Univ of Southampton 1949-62, prof of French Univ of Sussex 1962-89; memb UGC 1970-77 (chm arts sub-ctee 1974-77), pres Soc for French Studies 1980-82, memb Modern Humanities Res Assoc; *Books* Albert Camus and the Literature of Revolt (1959), Montherlant (1964), French Literature and its Background (ed 6 vols 1968-70), Benjamin Constant (1974), Variations on Catastrophe: Some French Responses to the Great War (1982), Pascal: Pensées (1983); *Recreations* walking, birdwatching; *Style—* Prof John Cruickshank; Woodpeckers, East Hoathly, Lewes, E Sussex BN8 6QL (☎ 082584 364); Univ of Sussex, Falmer, Brighton BN1 9QN (☎ 0273 606755)

CRUICKSHANK, Dr Roger John; s of (John) Norman Cruickshank MC, MD, DSC, FRCP (d 1986), of Brill, Bucks, and (Helen) May Elizabeth, *née* Slimlmon; *b* 8 Feb 1926; *Educ* Gresham's Sch Holt, Glasgow Univ (MB, ChB); *m* 1, 23 Feb 1952, Joane Eluned; 3 s (Matthew b 1953, Adam b 1956, Benjamin b 1957), 1 da (Emma b 1955); m 2, 17 July 1986, Mary Glenallan Kathleen, da of Lester Dan Bray, of Salisbury, Wilts; *Career* Admiralty Ferry Service 1944-46; Surg Lt RNVR 1949-51; General Practitioner 1952-73; clinical asst (psychiatry) St Bernard's Hosp 1977-80; medical offr HM Prison Grendon 1980-; *Recreations* trout fishing, travel, ornithology; *Style—* Dr Roger Cruickshank, Esq; Corner House, the Green, Brill, Aylesbury, Bucks (☎ 0844 237811); HMP Grendon, Grendon Underwood Alesbury, Bucks (☎ 029 677 301)

CRUICKSHANK, Hon Mrs; (Victoria Elizabeth); *née* Mills; el da of 4 Baron Hillingdon (d 1978); *b* 23 July 1948; *m* 1, 1971 (m dis 1979), Anthony Roff; 2 da; m 2, 1981, D G R Cruickshank; 1 da; *Style—* The Hon Mrs Cruickshank; Elder St, Spitalfields, London E1

CRUICKSHANK OF AUCHREOCH, Martin Melvin; s of Brig Martin Melvin Cruickshank, CIE (d 1964), and Florence Watson Cruickshank (d 1976); *b* 17 Sept 1933; *Educ* Rugby, Eaton Hall, Corpus Christi Coll Cambridge; *m* 1 March 1958, Rona, da of Mary Fenella Paton of Grandhome (d 1949), of Grandhome House, Aberdeen; 3 s (Martin b 1960, Nicholas b 1961-73, Paul b 1963), 1 da (Fenella b 1959); *Career* cmmd Gordon Highlanders 1952, served Malaya 1952-53 (despatches), Cyprus 1955-56, Germany 1960-61, Congo 1962 (Co Cmd), Nigeria 1962-64 (Chief instr, Offr Cadet Sch, Bde Maj, Dep Cmdt, Nigerian Military Coll), ret 1967; landowner; dir Blairmore Soc Ltd (chm 1979-85); KStJ; FRGS, FSAS, MBIM; *Recreations* travel (particularly deserts), bird watching, golf, music, oenology; *Clubs* Army and Navy; *Style—* M M Cruickshank of Auchreoch; Auchreoch, Crianlarich, Perthshire (☎ 08384 218)

CRUM EWING, Humphry John Frederick; s of Humphry William Erskine Crum Ewing (d 1985) (and gggs of Humphry Ewing Crum Ewing, of Strathleven, Dunbartonshire, MP for Paisley 1857-74), and Winifred Mary, *née* Kyle (d 1988); *b* 11 May 1934; *Educ* Marlborough, Christ Church Oxford (MA); *m* 1, 30 April 1964, Carolyn Joan Maule, da of Lt-Col Ian Burn-Murdoch, OBE, IA (d 1963), and formerly w of 3 Baron Wrenbury; 1 s (Alexander b 1966), 1 da (Arabella b 1967), and 1 da (Nicola b and d 1969); m 2, 14 Feb 1980, Mrs Janet Angela Tomlinson, da of Leonard Bates (d 1965), of Leicester; *Career* public and int affairs conslt, pres Oxford Univ Cons Assoc 1956, contested (C) Swansea East Constituency 1959; chm Ingersoll Gp 1966-69, Rajawella Cos 1976-79, advsr to Shadow Foreign Sec 1977-79, min for Consumer Affairs 1981-83 and to Min for Higher Educn and Sci 1987-; *Recreations* bridge, cooking, travelling collecting; *Style—* Humphry Crum Ewing, Esq; 63 Baker St, Reading RG1 7XY (☎ 0734 585096)

CRUMPTON, Dr Michael Joseph; s of Charles Crumpton, and Edith Crumpton; *b* 7 June 1929; *Educ* Poole GS, University Coll Southampton; *m* 1960, Janet Elizabeth, *née* Dean; 1 s (Andrew), 2 da (Jenny, Caroline); *Career* head Biochemistry Div Nat Inst for Med Res Mill Hill 1966-79, dep dir of Imperial Cancer Research Fund 1979-; FRS 1979; *Recreations* gardening, reading; *Style—* Dr Michael Crumpton; 33 Homefield Road, Radlett, Herts WD7 8PX (☎ 092385 4675); Imperial Cancer Research Fund, P.O. Box 123, Lincoln's Inn Fields, London WC2A 3PX (☎ 01 242 0200, fax 01 405 1556, telex 265107 ICRF G)

CRUSH, Harvey Michael; s of George Stanley Crush (d 1970), of Chislehurst, Kent, and Alison Isabel, *née* Lang; *b* 12 April 1939; *Educ* Chigwell Sch Essex; *m* 1, 21 Aug 1965(m dis 1982), Diana, da of Frederick Joseph Bassett (d 1965), of Coulsdon, Surrey; 1 s (Nicholas b 1 Dec 1967), 1 da (Emily b 21 may 1971); m 2, 9 Dec 1982, Margaret (Maggie) Rose, da of Nicholas Dixson (d 1986); *Career* slr 1963; ptnr Norton Rose 1968-, dir TOSG Tst Fund Ltd 1970-; memb Supreme Ct Rule Ctee 1984-88; Liveryman: Worshipful Co of Slrs 1982 (vice-pres (chm) 1989-), Worshipful Co of Farriers 1984, (memb Ct of Assistants 1987-); MRAeS 1980; memb: Assoc of Br Aviation Conslts, Law Soc, American Bar Assoc, Int Bar Assoc; *Recreations* travel, flying, motor sport; *Style—* Harvey Crush, Esq; Alice Dene, Beechenlea Lane, Swanley Village, Kent (☎ 0322 664420); Sa Figuera, Porto Petro, Santanyi, Mallorca, Baleares, Spain; Norton Rose, Kempson House, Camomile St, London EC3A 7AN (☎ 01 283 2434, fax 01 588 1181)

CRUTCH, Frank Peter Garth; s of Frank Crutch, of 14 Highway Road, Thurmaston, Leicester, and Mary Annie Voce; gf Albert Crutch (decd), Master of Hounds Quorn Hunt; *b* 22 Mar 1940; *Educ* Humphrey Perkins Sch, Leicester Coll of Art (Nat Dip design), RCA (Dip Des RCA); *m* 28 March 1964, Mo Ashley; 2 da (Sarah Louise b 1970, Emma Lucy Jane b 1972); *Career* designer; worked with: Sir Basil Spence on the New Sussex Univ 1962-65, Sir Terence Conran, major project The Establishment of Habitat and its products 1965-70; founder memb and bd dir Fitch and Co Design Consultants plc 1970-87 (major project design of all public spaces at Terminal 4 Heathrow); freelance consultnt 1987; built collection of 50s, 60s, 70s historic Italian sports racing cars, established own consultancy 'Peter C' Design and established own racing team 'Scuderia Britalia' 1987; *Recreations* classic motor racing; *Clubs* 96, Ferrari Owners, Scuderia Del Portello; *Style—* F P G Crutch, Esq; 182 London Road, Twickenham, Middlesex TW1 1EX (☎ 892 8234); Flanders House, Crackington, Haven, Cornwall

CRUTHERS, Sir James Winter; s of James William Cruthers and Kate Cruthers (d 1950); *b* 20 Dec 1924; *Educ* Perth Tech Coll; *m* 1950, Alwyn Sheila, da of late Jack Della; 1 s, 1 da; *Career* magazines editor W Australian Newspapers Ltd 1953, chm and md TVW Enterprises Ltd 1975-81, chm Australian Film Cmmn 1981, dir News Corpn Ltd; vice-chm: News America Publishing Inc 1984-, Sky Television plc 1988-; Queen's Jubilee Medal 1977, W Australian Citizen of the Year 1980; kt 1980; *see Debrett's Handbook of Australia and New Zealand for further details*; *Style—* Sir James Cruthers; c/o News America Publishing Inc, 1211 Avenue of the Americas, New York, NY 10036, USA

CRYER, (George) Bob; MP (L): Keighley Feb 1974-83, Bradford South 87-; *b* 3 Dec 1934; *Educ* Salt HS Shipley, Hull Univ; *m* 1963, Ann, *née* Place; 1 s, 1 da; *Career* convener Campaign Gp of Labour MPs 1982-83; contested Darwen Lancs 1964, memb Keighley Boro Cncl 1971-74, Parly under-sec of state Dept of Industry 1976-78. chm joint and commons select ctees statutory instruments 1979-83 and 1987-; chair

Parliamentary Labour Party Employment ctee 1987-; *Style*— Robert Cryer, Esq, MP; 6 Ashfield Avenue, Shipley, W.Yorks BD18 3AL (☎ Bradford 584701)

CRYMBLE, Bernard; s of Clarence Frederick Crymble (d 1950), of Newcastle Upon Tyne, and Martha, *née* Gell (d 1976); *b* 6 May 1928; *Educ* Univ of Durham (MB BS); *m* 1, 4 July 1951, Elizabeth Anne (d 1967), da of John Robert Barnett (d 1965), of Middlesborough; 1 s (Gavin Vaughan b 1958), 1 da (Jane b 1954); m 2, 12 Nov 1967, Patricia (d 1984), da of John Riddel (d 1980), of Gosforth, Northumberland; m 3, 31 Aug 1984, Elaine, da of Robert Duncan of Helensborough, Scotland; *Career* Nat Serv Maj RAMC 1952-54; sr lectr neurosurgery Univ of London 1967-69, conslt neurosurgeon E & W Sussex 1969-88, conslt neurosurgeon emeritus 1988-, dep coroner E Sussex 1988-; memb Coroners Soc 1989, pres Brighton & Sussex Med-Chi Soc 1985; Freeman City of London 1976, Liveryman Worshipful Co of Apothecaries 1976; FRCS 1959, SBNS 1965, FRSM 1970; *Books* Intensive Care (contrib second edn 1984); *Recreations* romano-british archaeology, walking, golf; *Clubs* Athenaeum, Army and Navy; *Style*— Bernard Crymble, Esq; Westwood, North Common Rd, Wivelsfield Green, Haywards Heath, W Sussex RH17 7RJ (☎ 0444 84 607); 25 Westbourne Villas, Hove, E Sussex BN3 4GF (☎ 0273 720 217)

CRYSTAL, Prof David; s of Samuel Cyril Crystal, of London, and Mary Agnes, *née* Morris; *b* 6 July 1941; *Educ* St Mary's Coll Liverpool, UCL (BA), Univ of London (PhD); *m* 1, 1 April 1964, Molly Irene (d 1976), da of Capt Robert Stack (d 1965); 2 s (Steven David b 1964, Timothy Joseph b 1969, d 1972), 2 da (Susan Mary b 1966, Lucy Alexandra b 1973); m 2, Hilary Frances, da of Capt Kenneth Norman of Cuffley, Herts; 1 s (Benjamin Peter b 1977); *Career* res asst Survey of English Usage UCL 1962-63, asst lectr linguistics Univ Coll of North Wales 1965-69; Univ of Reading: lectr 1965-69, reader 1969-75, prof of linguistics 1975-85; hon prof of linguistics Univ of North Wales (Bangor) 1985-; ed: Journal of Child Language 1974-85, The Language Library 1978-, Applied Language Studies 1980-84, Child Language Teaching and Therapy 1985-, Linguistics Abstracts 1985-; assoc ed Journal of Linguistics 1970-73, co-ed Studies in Language Disability 1974-, consulting ed English Today 1984-, usage ed Great Illustrated Dictionary (Readers Digest, 1984); author of numerous pubns connected with English language and linguistics; fell Coll of Speech Therapists 1983, FRSA 1983; *Books* incl The Cambridge Encyclopedia of Language (CUP 1987); ed Cambridge General Encyclopedia (CUP 1990); *Recreations* cinema, music, bibliophily; *Style*— Prof David Crystal; Akaroa, Gors Ave, Holyhead, Gwynedd LL65 1PB (☎0407 2764); PO Box 5, Holyhead, Gwynedd LL65 1RG (telex 937400 ONECOM G; 40012001)

CRYSTAL, Jonathan; s of Samuel Cyril Crystal, OBE, of London, and Rachel Ethel, *née* Trewish; *b* 20 Dec 1949; *Educ* Leeds GS, QMC London (LLB); *m* 13 Jul 1987, Ashley Drew, da of Harry Copeland; *Career* called to the Bar Middle Temple 1972; memb Hon Soc of Middle Temple; *Recreations* sports, travel; *Style*— J Crystal, Esq; 2 Harcourt Bldgs, Temple, London EC4 (☎ 01 353 2622, fax 01 353 5405)

CRYSTAL, Peter Maurice; s of Boris Leonard Crystal, of Leeds, and Pauline Mary, *née* Fox; *b* 7 Jan 1948; *Educ* Leeds GS, St Edmund Hall Oxford (MA), McGill Univ (LLM); *m* 2 July 1978, Lena Elisabeth, da of Bror Olsson (d 1972), of Karlstad Sweden; 2 da (Emma, Anna); *Career* sr ptnr Memery Crystal, slrs; Parlimentary Candidate for Leeds NE (SDP) 1983, 1987; memb Law Soc; *Recreations* tennis, all sports, travel; *Clubs* Reform; *Style*— Peter Crystal, Esq; 31 Southampton Row, London WC1B 5HT (☎ 01 242 5905, fax 242 2058, telex 298957)

CUBBON, Sir Brian Crossland; GCB (1984, KCB 1977, CB 1974); *b* 9 April 1928; *Educ* Bury GS, Trinity Coll Cambridge; *m* 1956, Elizabeth Lorin Richardson; 3 s, 1 da; *Career* Home Office 1951; perm under-sec of state N Ireland Office 1976-79; perm under-sec of state Home Office 1979-; *Style*— Sir Brian Cubbon, GCB; Home Office, Queen Anne's Gate, London SW1H 9AT

CUBITT, Sir Hugh Guy; CBE (1977), JP (Surrey 1964, DL Gtr London 1978); s of Col Hon (Charles) Guy Cubitt, CBE, DSO, TD, DL (d 1979, 6 s of 2 Baron Ashcombe), and Rosamond Mary Edith, *née* Cholmeley (d 1984); *b* 2 July 1928; *Educ* RNC Dartmouth; *m* 26 June 1958, Linda Ishbel, da of Hon Angus Campbell, CBE, JP (d 1967), yr s of 1 Baron Colgrain; 1 s (Jonathan Guy b 1962), 2 da (Joanna Mary (Mrs Smyth-Osbourne) b 1960, Victoria Jane (Mrs Harding-Rolls) b 1964); *Career* Lt RN Korea 1949-50; Cubitt and West 1962-79; dir : Property Security Investmt Tst 1962-, Nat Westminster Bank 1977- (chm Outer London Regn 1977-78); memb Westminster City Cncl 1963-77 (alderman 1974, ldr cncl 1972-77), lord mayor 1977-78; chm: Housing Corpn 1980-, Lombard North Central 1980-; cmmr English Heritage 1988-, pres London C of C 1988-; High Sheriff of Surrey 1983; FRICS; Kt 1983; *Recreations* travel, photography, country sports; *Clubs* Boodle's; *Style*— Sir Hugh Cubitt, CBE, JP, DL; Chapel House, West Humble, Dorking, Surrey RH5 6AY (☎ 0306 882 994); 147 Tottenham Court Road, London W1

CUBITT, (Mark) Robin; s of late Maj the Hon Archibald Edward Cubitt (5 s of 2 Baron Ashcombe), by 2 w, Sibell, da of Ronald Collet Norman; bro of Countess of Harrington (*see* Harrington, Earl of); hp of 4 Baron Ashcombe, *qv*; *b* 13 June 1936; *Educ* Gordonstoun; *m* 21 July 1962, Juliet Perpetua, da of late Edward Corbet Woodall, OBE, of The Red House, Clifton Hampden, Abingdon, Berks; 3 s (Mark b 1964, David b 1966, Hugo b 1967); *Style*— Robin Cubitt, Esq; Annagh, Coolbawn, Nenagh, Co Tipperary

CUCKNEY, Sir John Graham; s of Air Vice-Marshal Ernest John Cuckney, CB, CBE, DSC (d 1965), and Lilian, *née* Williams; *b* 12 July 1925; *Educ* Shrewsbury, Univ of St Andrews ; *m* 1; m 2, 1960, Muriel, da of late Walter Scott Boyd; *Career* dir: Er Bro Trin Ho 1980-, Laxard Bros, Brixton Estates plc 1985-; dep chm TI Gp plc 1985-; chm: Royal Insur Hldgs plc 1985- (dir 1979-, dep chm 1983-85), 3i Gp plc 1987-; former chm: Westland Gp plc, The Thomas Cook Gp Ltd; John Brown plc, Brooke Bond Gp plc, Int Mil Servs Ltd, PLA, Standard Industl Tst, former dir J Biddy and Sons; kt 1978; *Style*— Sir John Cuckney; 3i Gp plc, 91 Waterloo Rd, London SE1 8XP

CUDDEFORD, Norman Allan; s of Charles Leonard Allan Cuddeford (d 1986), of Leigh-on-Sea, and Gwendoline May, *née* Hockley (d 1985); *b* 8 Jan 1933; *Educ* Felsted; *m* 1, 1963 (m dis 1975), Penelope Alexandra Cuddeford; 1 s (Alastair b 1964); m 2, 12 April 1975, Maria Concepcion del Carmen, da of Dr Erasmo Hoyo Hernandez, of Mexico City; 1 da (Vanessa b 1980), and 1 step da (Ana Gabriela b 1971); *Career* Nat Serv RAF 1952-54, cmmnd 1953, later CO RAF Sennen (at that time the youngest CO in RAF); associated with Lloyds of London since 1955; dir Howson F Devitt & Sons Ltd 1988-; also freelance sports commentator (covering athletics, cricket, tennis) BBC radio 1965-; memb of Rottingdean Preservation Soc; Freeman City of London 1956, Liverman Worshipful Co of Glass Sellers; *Recreations* travel, good company and convivial conversation, cricket; *Clubs* RAF, MCC, Lloyds Motor; *Style*— Norman Cuddeford, Esq; Point Clear, Lustrells Rd, Rottingdean, Sussex (☎ 0273 304 943); 6 Kinburn St, London SE 16; Howson F Devitt & Sons Ltd, 100 Whitechapel Rd, London E1 (☎ 01 247 8888)

CUDLIPP, Baron (Life Peer UK 1974); Hugh Kinsman Cudlipp; OBE (1945); s of William Cudlipp, of Cardiff; *b* 28 August 1913; *Educ* Howard Gdns Sch Cardiff; *m* 1; m 2, 1945, Eileen Ascroft (d 1962); m 3, 1963, Jodi, da of late John L Hyland, of Palm Beach, Fla, USA; *Career* took Lab Whip in Lords till Nov 1981 when resigned it and joined SDP; journalist; chm IPC Ltd 1968-73 (formerly dep chm), dep chm Reed Int Bd 1970-73, former dir Associated Television Ltd, chm: IPC Newspaper Div 1970-73, Mirror Newspapers Ltd 1963-68, advsr to PM on counter-inflation policies 1976; kt 1973; *Books* Publish and Be Damned! (1955), At Your Peril (1962), Walking on the Water (1976), The Prerogative of the Harlot (1980); *Style*— The Rt Hon The Lord Cudlipp, OBE

CUENE-GRANDIDIER, Richard John Davis; s of Jean Alphonse Cuene-Grandidier, of Les Alluets-le-Roi, 78580 Maule, France, and Paula Susan Davis of Orvault, Nantes, France; *b* 13 Sept 1955; *Educ* Downside; *m* 1, 13 June 1982 (m dis); 1 da (Sophie b 1985); *Career* various appointments Nat Westminster Bank plc 1976-83, PA to Mgmnt in Bordeaux (France) branch of Int Westminster Bank plc 1983-86; account mangr Société Générale, London Branch 1989- (deputy 1981-84); *Recreations* officiating at motor sport events, riding, shooting; *Clubs* Lansdowne, British Racing and Sport Car, British Motor Racing Marshals; *Style*— Richard Cuene-Grandidier, Esq; 10 Ingham Rd, London NW6 1DE (☎ 01 435 5893); Société Generale, 60 Gracechurch St, PO Box 513, London EC3V 0HD (☎ 01 626 5400, telex 886611, fax 623 7761)

CUEVAS-CANCINO, HE Señor Francisco; s of José Luis Cuevas, architect (d 1952), and Sofia Cancino; *b* 7 May 1921; *Educ* Free Faculty of Law Mexico City, McGill Univ Montreal (MCL); *m* 1, 1946, Ana Hilditch, 2 s, 1 da; m 2, 1968, Esmeralda, da of Fernando Arboleda (d 1954); *Career* joined Mexican Foreign Service 1946, ambassador 1965-, Mexican ambassador to UK and to Republic of Ireland 1983-; Foreign Service Decoration (Mexico) 1972; Order of the Liberator 1970 and Order of Andrés Bello (Venezuela) 1973; *Recreations* icons; *Clubs* Travellers', Garrick; *Style*— HE Señor Francisco Cuevas-Cancino; Mexican Embassy, 48 Belgrave Sq, London SW1 8QY

CUFFLIN, Michael John; OBE (1984); s of Harry Bradshaw Cufflin (d 1983), of 70 Shanklin Drive, Leicester, and Annie Elizabeth, *née* Palmer (d 1985); *b* 21 August 1932; *Educ* Wyggeston Boys' GS Leicester, Worcester Coll Oxford (MA); *m* 23 April 1960, Susan Jenifer, da of William Pollard (d 1949), of Four Oaks, Sutton Coldfield; 2 s (Oliver b 1 March 1962, Edward b 1 Dec 1967), 2 da (Joanna b 27 Jan 1961, Lucy b 26 June 1963); *Career* stockbroker; P N Kemp-Gee and Co 1954-59, Wilshire Baldwin and Co 1959-, chm; 1986-; chm Leicester Gs Tst since fndn of school in 1981, dir Leicester Action for Youth Tst Leicester YMCA, chm Br Aust Soc (Leics Branch), Hon Tres Leics Co Nursing Assoc, Vice chm Leicester Twinning Assoc, pres Leicester Cons Euro Cncl; memb: Leicester CC 1967-, Lord Mayor of Leicester 1984-85; memb: TSA; *Recreations* gardening; *Clubs* The Leicestershire, Leicester Rotary; *Style*— Michael Cufflin, Esq, OBE; 10 Southernhay Road, Leicester LE2 3TJ (☎ 0533 703063); Wilshere Baldwin and Co, 19 The Crescent, King Street, Leicester LE1 6RX (☎ 0533 541344, fax 0533 550969)

CULE, Dr John Hedley; s of Walter Edwards Cule (d 1942), of Glamorgan, and Annie, *née* Russ (d 1940); *b* 7 Feb 1920; *Educ* Porth County Sch, Kingswood Sch Bath, Trinity Hall Cambridge (MA, MB, BChir, MD), King's Coll Hosp (MRCS, LRCP); *m* 23 March 1944, Joyce Leslie, da of Henry Phillips Bonser (d 1962); 2 s (Simon b 1949, Peter b 1951), 1 da (Myfanwy b 1955); *Career* WWII Capt RAMC served Italy (despatches) 1943-46; surgical registrar Addenbrooke's Hosp 1947, med registrar KCH 1948, princ NHS GP ptnrship Camberley 1948-71, psychiatrist St Davids Hosp Carmarthen and psychiatric unit W Wales Gen Hosp 1972-86; Lectr (hist of medcine) Iniv of Wales Coll of Medcine Cardiff 1972-, pres Br Soc for History of Medicine 1985-87 (vice pres 1984, treas 1972-82); memb Cncl Harveian Soc 1964; tstee Sanders Watney Tst (Driving for the Disabled) 1986-; High Sheriff Co of Dyfed 1985-86; pres: Osler Club London 1972-74 (ass sec 1966-68, sec 1969-71), pres: History of Medicine Soc of Wales 1978-80; memb American Osler Soc Inc 1974-, chm Welsh Branch Br Driving Soc; liveryman Worshipful Soc of Apothecaries; Fell Faculty of Hist and Philospophy of Medcine, Worshipful Soc of Apothecaries 1979; FRCGP; *Books* Wreath on the Crown (1967), A Doctor for the People (1980), Child Care through the Centuries (1986 jt ed); *Recreations* horse carriage driving trials, fly fishing; *Clubs* Royal Society of Medicine; *Style*— Dr John H Cule; Abereinon, Capel Dewi, Llandysul, Dyfed, SA44 4PP (☎ 055 932 2229)

CULLEARN, David Beverley; s of Jack Cullearn (d 1944), of Bradford, and Gladys Irene, *née* Earnshaw; *b* 22 April 1941; *Educ* Grange GS Bradford, Leeds Sch of Archictecture (Dip Arch); *m* 12 June 1962, Suzanne Mary, da of Arthur Joseph Sherry; 2 s (Dominic b 1 Feb 1964, Patrick b 10 March 1968), 1 da (Odette b 1 Feb 1963); *Career* architect; in practice: Cullearn & Phillips Manchester and London; Globe Park Marlow: Structural Steel Design Award 1987, Malcolm Dean Design Award 1987, Off of the Year Award 1987-88; Queen Street Thorne: Civic Tst Commendation 1987, Met Borough of Doncaster Commendation 1988; exhibition sec Soc of Architect Artists; memb ARIBA; *Style*— David Cullearn, Esq; High Royd, Northgate, Honley, Huddersfield HD7 2QL (☎ 0484 663 663); 8 King St, Manchester M2 6AQ (☎ 061 832 3667, fax 061 832 3795, car tel 0836 268 277); 50 Lisson St, London (☎ 01 724 4430, fax 01 724 9844)

CULLEN, Prof Alexander Lamb; OBE (1960); s of Richard Henry Cullen, of Lincoln and Jessie, *née* Lamb; *b* 30 April 1920; *Educ* Lincoln Sch, Imperial Coll London, (BSc, PhD, DSc); *m* 24 Aug 1920, Margaret da of Andrew Lamb, OBE of Southgate, N London; 2 s (Michael b 1941, David b 1942) 1 da (Isobel b 1946); *Career* scientist Royal Aircraft Estab 1940-46; lectr and reader Univ Coll London 1945-55, prof and head Dept of Elec Engrg Univ of Sheffield, Pender prof elec engrg and head of dept UCL 1967-80, (sr fell SERC at UCL 1980-83, hon res associate 1983), hon prof NW Poly Univ Xian China; DSc Chinese Univ of Hong Kong (1983), Deng Sheffield Univ (1985), DSc Univ of Kent at Canterbury, (1986); FIEE, FIEEE (1967), FCGI (1964), F Eng (1977), FRS (1977), Hon FIERE (1987); *Books* Microwave Measurement (with H M Barlow) 1950; *Recreations* music; *Clubs* English speaking Union; *Style*— Prof A L Cullen, OBE; Univ Coll London, Torrington Place, London WC1E 7JE (☎ 01 387

7050)

CULLEN, Alma Valeria; *née* Fitzpatrick; da of Frank Fitzpatrick, and Elsie, *née* Harrison; *Educ* Childwall Valley High Sch Liverpool, Univ of Liverpool (MA); *m* James Cullen; 1 s, 1 da; *Career* radio and TV playwright 1979-; twelve plays for BBC radio; TV works incl: The Caledonian Cascade (Granada) 1979, Northern Lights (STV) 1984, Winter Sunlight (Limehouse for Channel 4), Intimate Contact (Central 1987, episodes of Inspector Morse (Central 1989; *Recreations* reading, walking, theatre, cinema; *Clubs* Univ (Edinburgh; *Style*— Ms Alma Cullen; c/o Lemon and Durbridge Ltd, 24 Pottery Lane, London W11 4 LZ (☎ 1 229 9216

CULLEN, Hon Lord Cullen (William) Douglas; QC (1973); s of Sheriff Kenneth Douglas Cullen (d 1956), and Gladys Margaret, *née* Douglas-Wilson; *b* 18 Nov 1935; *Educ* Dundee HS, Univ of St Andrews (MA), Univ of Edinburgh (LLB); *m* 1961, Rosamond Mary, da of William Henry Nassau Downer, OBE, of NI; 2 s, (Christopher, Adrian), 2 da (Sophia, Felicity); *Career* advocate 1960; standing jr counsel to HM Customs and Excise 1970-73, chm Med Appeal Tbnl 1977-86, advocate-deput 1978-81, chm of cncl The Cockburn Assoc (Edinburgh Civic Tst) 1984-86, Senator of the College of Justice in Scotland 1986; memb: Royal Cmmn on Ancient and Historical Monuments of Scotland 1987-, Ct of Inquiry into Piper Alpha Disaster 1988-; *Recreations* gardening, natural history; *Clubs* New (Edinburgh); *Style*— Hon Lord Cullen; 62 Fountainhall Rd, Edinburgh (☎ 031 667 6949)

CULLEN, Hon Mrs (Harriet Mary Margaret); *née* Berry; da of Baron Hartwell, MBE, TD (Life Peer); *b* 8 Nov 1944; *m* 1981, Don Martín Cullen, er s of Don Martín Cullen and Doña Mercedes Artayeta Uriburu, of Buenos Aires; 2 s (Miguel b 1982, Domingo b 1983); *Style*— The Hon Mrs Cullen; 117 Cheyne Walk, London SW10

CULLEN, Dr (Edward) John; s of William Henry Pearson Cullen and Ellen Emma Cullen; *b* 19 Oct 1926; *Educ* Cambridge Univ (MA, PhD), Texas Univ (MS); *m* 1954, Betty Davall Hopkins; 2 s, 2 da; *Career* dep chm Rohm and Haas (UK) Ltd to 1983; chm Health and Safety Cmmn 1983-, pres Inst of Chem Engrs 1988-89; *Recreations* gardening, swimming, reading, walking; *Clubs* IOD; *Style*— Dr John Cullen; Health and Safety Commission, Baynards House, 1 Chepstow Place, London W2 4TF (☎ 01 229 3456 telex: 25683)

CULLEN, John Gavin; s of Gavin Hunter Cullen (d 1964), and Alice Mary, *née* Grieve (d 1966); *b* 30 April 1936; *Educ* Robert Gordons Coll Aberdeen, RCM, Christ's Coll Cambridge (MA, organ scholar); *m* 9 April 1966, Mary Elaine, da of The Ven Thomas Berkeley Randolph (Archdeacon of Hereford and Canon of Hereford Cathedral, d 1987); 2 s (Christopher b 1967, Jonathan b 1974), 1 da (Alison b 1969); *Career* Organist and Master of choristers St Andrew's Cathedral Oxford 1961-63, dir of music Abingdon Sch Oxford 1964-67, dir of music and organist Tonbridge Sch Kent 1967-, conductor and musical dir Tonbridge Philharmonic Soc 1967-; chm educn section ISM 1979-80, chm Public and Preparatory Schs Music Ctee 1980-85, vice-pres The Curwen Inst; FRCO, ARCM, memb Incorp Soc of Musicians; *Books* several compositions for choir & organ; *Recreations* smallholding: golf; *Style*— John Cullen, Esq; The Old Farm House, Golden Green, Tonbridge, Kent (☎ 0732 850 739); Tonbridge Sch, Kent (☎ 0732 365555)

CULLEN, Col (Charles) Nigel; OBE (1987), TD (1976, and Bar 1982); s of Peter Carver Cullen, of Mapperley Park, Nottingham, and Dorothy, *née* Woodward; *b* 26 Sept 1944; *Educ* Trent Coll; *m* 15 April 1981, Brenda Suzanne, da of Flt Offr Franklin Paul Bowen, US Army, of Oklahoma, USA; 1 s (Stephen James b 1971), 1 da (Emily Josephine b 1979); *Career* TA: cmmnd 1964, platoon cdr 5/8 Bn Sherwood Foresters 1964-67, platoon cdr Mercian Vols 1967-72, co cdr 3 WFR 1972-78, GSO 2 V Nottingham 1978-81, 2 i/c 3 WFR 1981-83, SO 2 G3 V 54 Inf Bde 1984, CO 3 WFR 1984-87, SO 1 G3 V E Dist 1987-88, dep cdr 54 Inf Bde 1988-; admitted slr 1970, ptnr Dowson Wadsworth and Sellers, NP; cncl memb Notts Chamber of Commerce and Indust, sr vice pres Nottingham City Business Club, hon slr City of Nottingham Scouts; memb: Law Soc, Notts Law Soc, The Notaries Soc; *Recreations* jogging, bridge, theatre, photography; *Clubs* Notts, Athletic; *Style*— Nigel Cullen, OBE, TD; 10 Sefton Dr, Mapperley Pk, Notts NG3 5ER (☎ 0602 606906); Dowson Wadsworth and Sellers, 13 Weekday Cross, Notts NG1 2GG (☎ 0602 501087, fax 0602 588379, car 0860 385115)

CULLEN, Peter; DSC (1944); s of late Walter Cullen; *b* 22 August 1920; *Educ* Rugby, Oxford Univ; *m* 1941, Jane Primrose, *née* Greener; 4 s, 2 da; *Career* Lt RN; chm Cullens Stores plc 1980-85 (md 1978-85); *Recreations* hunting, stalking, walking; *Style*— Peter Cullen, Esq, DSC; The Old Rectory, Winkfield, Windsor, Berks (☎ 0344 882623);

CULLEN OF ASHBOURNE, 2 Baron (UK 1920); Charles Borlase Marsham Cokayne; MBE (1945); s of 1 Baron Cullen of Ashbourne, KBE (d 1932, whose f was the celebrated G(eorge) E(dward) C(okayne, Clarenceux King of Arms and editor of The Complete Peerage); *b* 6 Oct 1912; *Educ* Eton; *m* 1, 2 July 1942 (m dis 1947), Valerie Catherine Mary, da of late William Henry Collbran; 1 da (Hon Mrs Costa Sanseverino, *qv*); m 2, 21 June 1948, Patricia Mary, er da of Col S Clulow-Gray; *Heir* bro, Hon Edmund Cokayne; *Career* one of HM Lts City of London 1976, a Lord in Waiting to HM (Govt Whip) 1979-82, Maj Royal Corps of Signals (TA), serv WWII; amateur tennis champion 1947 and 1952; *Clubs* MCC, Swanlea Forest Golf ; *Style*— The Rt Hon the Lord Cullen of Ashbourne, MBE; 75 Cadogan Gdns, SW3 2RB (☎ 01 589 1981)

CULLIMORE, Colin Stuart; CBE (1978); s of Reginald Victor Cullimore (d 1960), and May Maria, *née* Jay; *b* 13 July 1931; *Educ* Westminster, Nat Coll of Food Technol; *m* 1952, Kathleen Anyta, da of Edgar Lamming (d 1951); 1 s (Jeremy Stuart b 1953); *Career* cmmnd Royal Scots Fus, seconded Parachute Regt 1951, served Cyprus, Egypt, Maj 1956, 10 Bn Parachute Regt (TA) 1960; gen mangr: Payne & Son Ltd 1960-65, J H Dewhurst Ltd 1969; md J H Dewhurst Ltd 1976-; dir: Albion Insur Co Ltd, Vestey Gp Cos; chm: Retail Consortium Food Ctee 1973-74, Multiple Shops Fedn 1977-85; dep chm: Meat Promotion Exec 1975-78, Inst of Meat 1982-83; vice-pres Br Retailers Assoc 1979-84, pres 1984-; dir NAAFI 1984-; pres Br Retailers Assoc 1984-89; vice-chm: Retail Consortium 1985-88, Coll Distributive Trades 1976-79: vice-pres: Confedn of Euro Retailers 1982-88, memb advsy bd Food from Br ctee for Commerce and Distribution of EEC 1984-, govr London Ist 1989-; Tstee Airborne Assault Normandy Tst; Freeman of City of London 1972, Liveryman of Worshipful Co of Butchers; Gold Medal of Inst of Meat 1956, Butchers' Co Gold Medal 1956; CBIM 1984, FInstD 1973, MRSH 1983, MInstM 1956; *Clubs* Naval and Military, Farmers'; *Style*— Colin Cullimore, Esq, CBE; 143 Whitehall Court, Westminster SW1A 2EP (☎ 01 839 3761); Palazzo Gianbatista, Zurrieq, Malta; 14-16 St John's Lane, London EC1M 4DU (☎ 01 248 1212. fax 01 251 3592); car ☎ 0836 210241

CULLIMORE, William Rae; s of William Cullimore (d 1949), of Christleton House, Chester; *b* 28 Nov 1918; *Educ* Shrewsbury, Gonville and Caius Coll Cambridge (MA); *m* 1948, Stella Mabel Florence, da of James Douglas Russell, CBE, (d 1964), of Hinderton Croft, Neston, Wirral; 1 s, 1 da; *Career* slr; clerk, dean and chapter Chester Cathedral; chm: Chester Waterworks Co,; *Recreations* gardening; *Clubs* Farmers'; *Style*— William Rae Cullimore, Esq; Faulkners Lodge, Christleton, Chester; Manor Farm, Morton, Thornbury, Avon

CULLINAN, Hon Mrs (Dorothea Joy); da of 1 Baron Horder, GCVO, MD (d 1955); *b* 1905; *m* 17 Sept 1930, Edward Revill Cullinan, CBE, MD, FRCP (d 16 March 1965), s of late Dr Edward Cullinan; 3 s, 1 da; *Style*— The Hon Mrs Cullinan; 10 Camden Mews, NW1

CULLINAN, Edward Horder; CBE (1987); s of Brig-Gen Edward Revill Cullinan, CBE (d 1965), of 10 Park Sq, West London NW1, and Dorothea Joy, *née* Horder ; *b* 17 July 1931; *Educ* Ampleforth, Cambridge Univ, Architectural Assoc (AA Dip), Univ of California at Berkeley; *m* Rosalind Sylvia *née* Yeates; 1 s (Thomas Edward b 1965), 2 da (Emma Louise b 1962, Kate 1963); *Career* Nat Serv Lt RE 1949-51; architect; in practice London 1959, fndr Edward Cullinan Architects 1968-; second year master Cambridge Univ Dept of Architecture 1968-73, Bannister Fletcher prof London Univ 1978-79; visiting critic 1973-85: Toronto, Cincinatti, MIT; Graham Willis prof Sheffield Univ 1985-87, George Simpson prof Edinburgh Univ 1987-89; sponsor: Architects For Peace, UK Architects Against Apartheid, Freeze; architect memb Duchy of Cornwall Wildlife and Environment Gp; FRSA 1981; *Books* Edward Cullinan Architects (1984); *Recreations* building, horticulture, silviculture, skiing, surfing; *Style*— Edward Cullinan, Esq, CBE; Gib Tor, Quarnford, Buxton, Derbyshire; 57D Jamestown Rd, London SW1 (☎ 01 485 2267, fax 01 267 2385)

CULLINGFORD, Eric Coome Maynard; CMG (1963); s of Francis James Cullingford (d 1944), and Lilian Mabel *née* Dunstan (d 1942); *b* 15 Mar 1910; *Educ* City of London Sch, St Catharine's Coll Cambridge (MA); *m* 1936, Friedel, da of Karl Fuchs; 2 s (Martin, Cedric), 1 da (Christine); *Career* Manpower Div of Control Cmmn for Germany 1951, labour attache Br Embassy Bonn 1961-65 and 1968-72, asst sec Min of Labour, ret 1972; *Books* Trade Unions in West Germany; The Pirates of Shearwater Island; *Style*— Eric Cullingford Esq, CMG; Flat 1, 25 Avenue Road, Malvern, Worcs

CULLIS, Prof Charles Fowler; s of Prof Charles Gilbert Cullis (d 1941), of Wimbledon London SW19, and Winifred Jefford, *née* Fowler (d 1976); *b* 31 August 1922; *Educ* Stowe, Trinity Coll Oxford (BA, BSc, Dphil, MA, DSC, DSc); *m* 3 Sept 1958, (Marjorie) Elizabeth, da of Sir Austin Innes Anderson (d 1973), of Clandon Surrey; 2 s (Jonathan b 1961, Philip b 1967), 2 da (Jane b 1963, Eleanor b 1965); *Career* res fell ICI Oxford Univ 1947-50, lectr in physical chemistry Imperial Coll London 1950-59 (sr lectr chemical engrg 1959-64), reader in combustion chemistry Univ of London 1964-66, prof physical chemistry City Univ 1967-84 (head chemistry dept 1973-84, pro vice-chllr 1980-84, Saddlers res prof 1984-87), emeritus res fell Leverhulme 1987-; visiting prof Univ of California Berkeley 1966, visiting scientist CSIRO Sydney 1970, academic visitor NSW Inst of Technol Ltd 1974; cncllr Mid Sussex 1986-; dir City Technol Ltd (Queen's Award for Technol 1982 and 1985, and for Export 1988), cncllr Mid Sussex 1986-; chm Safety in Mines Res Advsy Bd 1980-88, govr: City of London Poly 1982-84, Haywards Heath Coll 1986-, Oathall Community Coll 1986-; Liveryman Worshipful Co of Bakers 1983-; FRSC 1958, FRSA 1983; *Books* The Combustion of Organic Polymers (1981), The Detection and Measurement of Hazardous Gases (1981), author numerous original scientific papers; *Recreations* music, theatre, travel, golf; *Clubs* Athenaeum; *Style*— Prof Charles Cullis; City Univ, Northampton Sq, London EC1V OHB (☎ 01 253 4399, ext 01 250 0837)

CULLIS, Jeffrey; s of Donald Oscar Cullis (d 1974), of Nottingham, and Ada Elizabeth, *née* Fleet; *b* 9 August 1934,; *Educ* The Becket Sch Nottingham; *m* 29 May 1965, Petrina Joan (d 1982), da of Alan Barker, of Nottingham; 2 s (James b 1967, Mark b 1972), 1 da (Sarah b 1969); *Career* Mil Serv 1952-54; RAMC 1952-53, Corporal 1 BN N Staffs Korea 1953-54; sales dir Pressac Hldgs plc 1976-; dir: Pressac Ltd 1971-, Pressaco SRL (Milan), Pressac Inc (Detroit USA); *Recreations* hill walking, golf, sailing; *Clubs* Rushcliffe Golf (Notts), Rutland Sailing; *Style*— Jeffrey Cullis, Esq; 18 Groveside Crescent, Clifton Village, Nottingham NG11 8NT (☎ 0602 216317); Pressac Holdings plc, Acton Grove, Long Eaton, Nottingham NG10 1FW (☎ 0602 720141, fax 730358)

CULLIS, Michael Fowler; CVO (1955); s of Emeritus Prof Charles Gilbert Cullis (d 1941), of London, and Winifred Jefford Fowler (d 1976); *b* 22 Oct 1914; *Educ* Wellington, Brasenose Coll Oxford (MA); *m* 1968, Catherine Cameron, da of Alexander Cook Robertson, of Scotland; *Career* military intelligence Gibraltar 1939-40, min of Economic Warfare London 1940-44, dip serv 1945-58; FO responsible for Austria 1945-50; regnl information cllr Oslo and Copenhagen 1951-58; advsr to Govr of Malta 1959-61; sr res fell Atlantic Inst Paris 1962-65, dip serv, dir of Arms Control and Disarmament 1967-74, conslt Non-Governmental Bodies 1975-79; dir European Cultural Fndn Amsterdam; writer and broadcaster; *Clubs* Athenaeum (London); *Style*— Michael Cullis, Esq, CVO; County End, Bushey Heath, Herts WD2 1NY (☎ 01 950 1057)

CULLUM, Simon Edward; s of Denis John Cullum (d 1976), and Phylis Ethel, *née* Hoare; *b* 11 Jan 1943; *Educ* Brighton Hove and E Sussex GS; *m* 1, 8 Aug 1963 (m dis 1978), Janet Claire, da of Thomas Watkins (d 1977); 2 s (Benedict Simon b 1964, Damian Sebastian b 1969), 1 da (Rebecca Jane b 1966); 20 Sept 1982, Carolyn Margaret, da of David Gover, of Long Ashton, Avon; 2 s (Barnaby David Owain b 1983, Joshua John b 1985), 1 da (Kimberley Nastasha (twin) b 1985); *Career* Chartered Bank 1961-64, Charles Barker City Ltd 1964-79, Response Advertising Ltd 1979-83, St James Alliance Ltd 1983-; MIPA 1973; *Recreations* swimming, reading, gardening; *Style*— Simon Cullum, Esq; 18 Valley Rd, Rickmansworth, Herts WD3 4DS (☎ 0923 771 033); St James Alliance Ltd, 4 Red Lion Ct, Fleet St, London EC4A 3EB (☎ 01 583 2525, fax 01 583 3948, telex 883934)

CULME-SEYMOUR, Maj Mark Charles; s of Capt George Culme-Seymour (himself 3 s of Adm Sir Michael Culme-Seymour, GCB, GCVO, C-in-C at Portsmouth 1897-1900, the Admiral's w being Mary, gda in the male line of 2 Baron Sondes) by the Captain's w Janet, da of Charles Orr Ewing, sometime MP, himself 5 s of Sir Archibald Orr Ewing, 1 Bt of the 1886 cr; *see also* John Churchill (whose former 1 w is Maj Culme-Seymour's sis); Major C-S is hp to Btcy of his cousin, Cdr Sir Michael Culme-

Seymour, 5 Bt; *b* 20 Dec 1910; *Educ* Wellington, New Coll Oxford Univ; *m* 1, 26 June 1935 (m dis 1938), Babette, da of David Llewelyn Patric-Jones; m 2, 5 April 1941 (m dis 1949), Princesse Hélène Marie de la Trémoïlle, 3 da of Prince Louis Charles Marie, 12 Duc de Thouars, Prince and 11 Duc de la Trémoïlle, Premier Duc de France, 12 Prince de Tarante and 16 Prince de Talmond, and formerly w of Sir Campbell Mitchell-Cotts, 2 Bt; m 3, 6 Oct 1956 (m dis 1967), Patricia June, da of late Charles Reid-Graham and widow of Geoffrey Edward Ansell; 1 s, 2 da; m 4, 1973, Mary Darrall, da of Leander Armistead Riely, of Oklahoma City, and widow of Philip Kidd; *Career* served WWII Maj Rifle Bde M East and Italy; *Style*— Maj Mark Culme-Seymour; Vinas Viejas, Rancho Domingo, 29639 Benalmadena, Malaga, Spain

CULME-SEYMOUR, Cdr Sir Michael; 5 Bt (UK 1809), of Highmount, and Friery Park, Devonshire, RN; s of Vice Adm Sir Michael Culme-Seymour, 4 Bt, KCB, MVO (d 1925); *b* 26 April 1909; *m* 18 March 1948, Lady (Mary) Faith (d 1983), da of 9 Earl of Sandwich, and formerly wife of late Philip Booth Nesbitt; (2 s decd), 1 step da; *Heir* cous, Mark Culme-Seymour; *Career* farmer and landowner, ADC to Gov-Gen of Canada 1933-35, former CC Northants, RN ret 1947, DL Northants 1958-71, high sheriff Northants 1966; *Style*— Cdr Sir Michael Culme-Seymour, Bt, RN; Wytherston, Powerstock, Bridport, Dorset (☎ Powerstock 211)

CULVERHOUSE, Barbara Mary; da of Cyril Russell Dashwood, CBE (d 1962), and Laura Louise, *née* Steward (d 1959); *b* 16 April 1921; *Educ* Roedean; *m* 8 Feb 1947, Percival Emerson Culverhouse (d 1968), s of Percival Emerson Culverhouse (d 1953); 2 s (Ian b 1950, Hugh b 1951), 1 da (Lynette b 1948); *Career* CA in sole practice 1966-, dir Harthall Securities Ltd, and Ian Culverhouse & Co Ltd; memb ICAEW 1944- (memb of Cncl 1981-87), tstee Old Rhodeanian Assoc, memb Ct of Assts Worshipful Co of CAs; FCA; *Recreations* music, walking, travelling; *Style*— Mrs Barbara M Culverhouse; Wayside, Penn, High Wycombe, Bucks HP10 8LY (☎ 049481 2120)

CULVERHOUSE, Lt-Col (Arthur) Graham (Hewitt); MBE, TD; s of Herbert Sydney Culverhouse, and Lillian Augusta Hewitt; *b* 30 Dec 1907; *Educ* Victoria Coll Jersey; *m* 15 April 1931, Joyce, da of Clifton C Crowther (d 1946), of Oxshott, Surrey; 2 da (Elizabeth Ann Hewitt, Sally Rosina Hewitt); *Career* pre war was Audit Clerk; Sgt Artillery Co; Army Offr The East Surrey Regt Lt-Col; served Dunkirk, Italy, Greece; post war Aldershot (Mons OCTU) Nigeria; Southern Comnd Germany); dir Dawcul Ltd 1960-; *Recreations* hockey, squash; *Style*— Lt-Col Graham Culverhouse, MBE, TD; White Gates, Snowhill, Dinton; Dawcul House, 42 West Street, Marlow

CULYER, Prof Anthony John; s of Thomas Reginald Culyer (d 1979), and Betty Ely *née* Headland; *b* 1 July 1942; *Educ* Sir William Borlase's Sch Marlow, King's Sch Worcester, Exeter Univ (BA), Univ of California Los Angeles; *m* 26 Aug 1966, Sieglinde Birgit, da of Kurt Kraut (d 1947); 1 s, 1 da; *Career* Univ of York 1969-: lectr, sr lectr, reader, prof of economics; visiting prof: Queens Univ Canada 1976, Trent Univ Canada 1985-86; William Evans visiting Prof Otago Univ NZ 1979, co ed Jl of Health Economics 1982-, author pubns incl: Health Economics (1973), Economics of Social Policy (1973), Benhams Economics (1973), Economic Policies and Social Goals (1974), Need and the National Health Service (1976), Annotated Bibliography of Health Economics (1977), Human Resources and Public Finance (1977), Economic Aspects of Health Services (1978), Measuring Health (1978), Political Economy of Social Policy (1980), Economic and Medical Evaluation of Health Care Technologies (1983), Health Indicators (1983), Economics (1985), Public Finance and Social Policy (1985), International Bibliography of Health Economics (1986), Public and Private Health Services (1986) Health Care Expenditures in Canada (1988); church organist and choir master; chm York Dist of Royal Sch of Church Music; memb: N Allerton Health Authy, Full Sutton Prison Local Review Ctee; professional conslt to: UK Dept of Health, OECD, EEC, WHO, Govt of Canada, Govt of NZ; hon advsr Off of Health Economics, memb educn ctee Kings Fund Coll London; *Recreations* music; *Style*— Prof Anthony Culyer; The Laurels, Barmby Moor, York, YO4 5EJ (☎ 0759 302639); Dept of Economics and Related Studies, University of York, Heslington, York, YO1 5DD (☎ 0904 433762/433789, fax 0904 433433, telex 57933 YORKUL)

CUMBER, Sir John Alfred; CMG (1966), MBE (1953, TD 1946); s of Alfred Joseph Cumber, ARIBA, AMICE (d 1964) and Alexandra Irene, *née* Elliot (d 1956); *b* 30 Sept 1920; *Educ* Richmond (Surrey) Co Sch, Richmond Art Sch, LSE; *m* 1945, Margaret Anne, da of Martin Tripp (d 1960); 2 s (Mervyn, Nigel); *Career* WWII 1939-46 with 9 Bn Royal Fus and 2 Bn 2 Punjab Regt in New Guinea and Burma, ret as Maj; HM Colonial Serv Kenya 1947-63, ret as sr dist cmmr; administrator Cayman Islands, HM cmmr Anguilla 1964-69; dir-gen Save the Children Fund 1971-85; kt 1985; *Recreations* art, music, gardening, travel; *Clubs* Royal Cwlth Soc; *Style*— Sir John Cumber, CMG, MBE, TD; Barton Cottage, Throwleigh, Devon EX20 2HS (☎ 064 723 519)

CUMBERLEGE, Julia Frances; CBE (1985), DL (East Sussex 1986); da of Dr Lambert Ulrich Camm, of Redferns, Lewes, Sussex, and Mary Geraldine Gertrude, *née* Russell (d 1962); *b* 27 Jan 1943; *Educ* Convent of the Sacred Heart Kent; *m* 14 Jan 1961, Patrick Francis Howard Cumberlege, s of Geoffrey Fenwick Jocelyn Cumberlege DSO, MC (d 1979); 3 s (Mark b 1961, Justin b 1964, Oliver b 1968); *Career* memb: Lewes Dist Cncl 1966-79 (ldr 1977-78), E Sussex CC 1974-85 (chm Social Services Ctee 1979-82); JP 1973-85; memb E Sussex Health Authy 1977-81; chm: Brighton Health Authy 1981-88, Nat Assoc Health Authys, SW Thames Regnl Health Authy; memb Press Cncl 1977-83, Appts Cmmn 1984-, chm Review of Community Nursing for Eng 1985, vice-pres Royal Coll of Nursing 1988; govr several schs, memb of cncl Brighton Poly 1987- (Formation Ctee 1988-); *Clubs* RSM, New Cavendish; *Style*— Julia Cumberlege, CBE, DL; Vuggles Farm, Newick, Lewes, Sussex BN8 4RU (☎ 0273 400 453, fax 0273 401 084); South West Thames Regional Health Authority, 40 Eastbourne Terrace, London W2 3QR (☎ 262 8011, fax 258 3908)

CUMING, Hon Mrs (Christine Veronica Helen); *née* Robertson; da of 1 Baron Robertson of Oakridge, GCB, GBE, KCMG, KCVO, DSO, MC, DL; *b* 3 August 1927; *m* 13 Aug 1949, Col (Robert) Hugh Cuming, MBE, JP, DL, The Royal Scots Greys, er s of late Hugh Philip Cuming, of Doms, Stansted Mountfitchet, Essex; 2 s, 1 da; *Style*— The Hon Mrs Cuming; Hill Farm, Bragenham, Beds LU7 0EE

CUMING, Col (Robert) Hugh; MBE (1960), JP (1972), DL (Bucks 1976); er s of Hugh Philip Cuming (d 1959), of Doms, Stansted Mountfitchet, Essex and Monica Mary Josephine, *née* MacIntyre (d 1975); *b* 10 Sept 1920; *Educ* The Oratory, Army Staff Coll Camberley; *m* 13 Aug 1949, Hon Christine Veronica Helen, da of Gen Robertson, of Oakridge, GCB, GBE, KCMG, KCVO, DSO, MC, DL; 2 s, 1 da; *Career* cmmnd 1940 Seaforth Highlanders, served N Africa with Phantom, then Sicily and NW Europe, transferred Royal Scots Greys 1949, ret 1962, Col 1976; chm: Quarantine Kennels Assoc 1969-, Bucks Cncl of Voluntary Youth Serv 1975-77, Milton Keynes bench 1980-84, Bucks County Courts Ctee 1982-84; memb: exec cncl ACFA 1976-85, Thames Valley Police Authority 1979-82; *Recreations* shooting, fishing; *Clubs* Cavalry and Guards', Kennel; *Style*— Col Hugh Cuming, MBE, JP, DL; Hill Farm, Bragenham, Leighton Buzzard, Beds (☎ 052 527 257)

CUMMING; *see*: Gordon-Cumming

CUMMING, (John) Alan; CBE (1983); s of John Cumming; *b* 6 Mar 1932; *Educ* George Watson's Coll Edinburgh; *m* 1958, Isobel Beaumont, *née* Sked; 3 s; *Career* Woolwich Equitable Building Soc: chief exec 1969-86, exec vice-chm 1986-, dir 1978-; chm Building Soc Assoc 1981-83, Cavendish Wates First Assured plc, Woolwich Homes (1987) Ltd; pres Euro Community Mortgage Fedn 1984-87; chm Utd Reformed Church Tst, dir: Value and Income Tst plc; dir: Nat Kidney Res Fnd; *Recreations* bridge, golf; *Clubs* Caledonian; *Style*— Alan Cumming, Esq, CBE; 8 Prince Consort Drive, Chislehurst, Kent (☎ 01 467 8382); Woolwich Equitable Building Society, Equitable House, Woolwich, London SE18 6AB (☎ 01 854 2400)

CUMMING, John Stuart; s of Stuart F M Cumming, MC, FFA (d 1961); *b* 18 Mar 1928; *Educ* Marlborough, Corpus Christi Coll Cambridge; *m* 1956, Iseult Margaret, da of late Carl W Mercer; 1 s, 3 da; *Career* Lt RAOC; memb Inst of Chartered Accountants of Scotland, dir Hambros Bank Ltd 1977-88, dir Br Merchant banking and Securities Houses Assoc 1989-; *Recreations* travel, gardening, music; *Clubs* Sloane; *Style*— John Cumming, Esq; Cheyne House, Langton Green, Tunbridge Wells, Kent TN3 0HP (☎ Langton 862066, office ☎ 01 796 3606)

CUMMING-BRUCE, Hon Alec (Alexander) Pascoe Hovell-Thurlow; OBE (1960); yst s of 6 Baron Thurlow (d 1952); *b* 26 Oct 1917; *Educ* Shrewsbury, Trinity Coll Cambridge (BA, MA); *m* 21 Feb 1942, Catherine Agnes, da of Rev Hamilton Blackwood, of Scalby, Yorks; 2 s, 1 da; *Career* Colonial Admin Serv 1941-60, Home Civil Serv 1961-78; *Style*— Hon Alec Cumming-Bruce, OBE; Leazes Cottage, Leazes Place, Durham City

CUMMING-BRUCE, Rt Hon Lord Justice; Rt Hon Sir (James) Roualeyn Hovell-Thurlow-; PC (1977); 3 s (twin) of late 6 Baron Thurlow; *b* 9 Mar 1912; *Educ* Shrewsbury, Magdalene Coll Cambridge (BA); *m* 4 Aug 1955, Lady (Anne) Sarah Alethea Marjorie Savile, *qv*; 2 s, 1 da; *Career* barr Middle Temple 1937, judge of High Court Family Div 1964-77, presiding judge NE Circuit 1971-74, a Lord Justice of Appeal 1977-; kt 1964; *Clubs* Pratt's, United Oxford and Cambridge; *Style*— The Rt Hon Lord Justice Cumming-Bruce; 1 Mulberry Walk, London SW3 (☎ 01 352 5754)

CUMMING-BRUCE, Lady (Anne) Sarah Alethea Marjorie; *née* Savile; yst da of 6 Earl of Mexborough (d 1945) and Hon Margaret Eve de Burgh Knatchbull-Hugessen, da of 2 Baron Brabourne; *b* 17 Sept 1919; *m* 4 Aug 1955, Rt Hon Lord Justice Cumming-Bruce (Hon Sir James Roualeyn Hovell-Thurlow-Cumming-Bruce) *qv*; 2 s, 1 da; *Style*— Lady Sarah Cumming-Bruce; 1 Mulberry Walk, London SW3

CUMMINGS, John Scott; MP (Lab) Easington 1987-; s of George, ret coal miner, and Mary, *née* Cain; *b* 6 July 1943; *Educ* Murton Council Infant, Junior and Senior Sch; *Career* Colliery Electrician, Murton Colliery 1958-87, secretary Murton Colliery Mechanics 1967-87, memb Easington Rural and District Cncls (leader 1979-87), memb of Northumbrian Water Authy 1977-83, Peterlee and Aycliffe Devpt Corpn 1980-87; vice-chm Coalfield Community Campaign 1984-87; *Recreations* jack russell terriers, walking, travel; *Clubs* Murton Victoria, Murton Demmi, Murton Ex-Servicemans, Thornley Catholic, Peterlee Labour; *Style*— John Cummings, Esq; 76 Toft Crescent, Murton, Seaham, Co Durham (☎ 091 526 1142); House of Commons, London SW1A 0AA

CUNDALE, Ronald Herbert; s of Harry William Cundale (d 1964), of Tottenham, London, and Edith Margaret, *née* Tate (d 1965); *b* 29 Oct 1930; *Educ* Tottenham GS; *m* June Anne, da of Alfred Clarance Martin (d 1956), of Chadwell Heath, Essex; *Career* co chm: Sutch and Searle Shipping Ltd 1975- (md 1968), Sutch and Searle Shipping Nederland BV 1975-; chm Sutch and Searle (Ship Mgmnt) Ltd 1975-; dir Sutch and Searle Ltd 1975-; chm Essex Co Cricket Benefit Assoc 1987-88; life vice-pres and exec ctee memb Essex Co CC; *Recreations* cricket, charity work, reading, bowls; *Clubs* IOD; *Style*— Ronald H Cundale, Esq; 6 Green Mead, S Woodham Ferrers, Essex CM3 5NL (☎ 0245 320519); 17-23 Knighton Lane, Buckhurst Hill, Essex IG9 5HJ (☎ 01 505 3366,896955, fax 01 505 8329)

CUNDALL, Geoffrey Percival; s of William Percival Cundall (d 1967), of York, and Dorothy Mary, *née* Barker (d 1985); *b* 14 Oct 1924; *Educ* Bootham Sch York, Leeds Univ (BSc); *m* 16 Jun 1950, Rachel, da of Edward Holmes Horner (d 1960), of Settle Yorks; 3 da (Ruth b 1953, Heather b 1956, Joanna b 1959); *Career* former lectr: Manchester Univ of Sci and Tech, Sheffield Univ; fndr ptnr Cundall Johnston & Ptnrs; author of numerous papers particularly on energy; registering offr Newcastle monthly meeting Religious Soc of Friends 1977-, chm Newcastle Cncl for Vol Service 1987-; FIEE, FIMechE, FCIBSE, FRSA, MConsE; *Recreations* fell walking, skiing, photography; *Style*— Geoffrey Cundall, Esq; Cundall, Johnston & Partners, Horsley House, Regent Centre, Gosforth, Newcastle Upon Tyne NE3 3LU, (☎ 091 213 1515 fax 091 213 1701)

CUNDY, Clifford Benjamin; s of Walter Augustus Cundy (d 1956), of Immingham, Lincs, and Esme Miriam, *née* Spiers (d 1970); *b* 19 Dec 1927; *Educ* Humberstone Fndn Sch, Clee, Magdalen Coll Oxford; *m* 23 Dec 1950, Hazel Patricia, da of Benjamin Hazelwood (d 1946), of Rangoon, Burma; *Career* sculptor and painter; since 1973 has regularly exhibited his work at galleries incl: Upper Street Gallery Islington, Wills Lane Gallery St Ives, Alwin Gallery London, Armstrong Davis Gallery Arundel, Arts Centre Hong Kong, Caldwell Gallery Belfast and Dublin, Bath Arts Festival, Chapman Gallery London, Avivson Gallery Milwaukee; memb Nat Soc of Painters; *Clubs* Sketch; *Style*— Clifford Cundy, Esq; 32 Cambrian Rd, Richmond, Surrey TW10 6JQ (☎ 01 940 8494)

CUNDY, Wing Cdr Peter John; DSO (1943), DFC (1942), AFC (1945), TD (1945); s of Wright Cundy (d 1968), of Thorpeness, Suffolk, and Emma Louise Cundy, *née* Neary; *b* 3 Oct 1916; *Educ* Eastbourne Coll; *m* 8 Dec 1945, Sheila Mary, da of Lt Col Geoffrey Meadows Frost (d 1962); 3 s (Michael b 1947, Nigel b 1949, Simon b 1952), 1 da (Hazel b 1953); *Career* cmmnd Middlesex Regt (TA) 1937, transferred RAF 1940; active serv inc operational tours with 53 Sqdn (Blenheims) 1940-41, 120 Sqdn 1941-42 and 224 Sqdn (Liberators) 1942-43; Rhodesian Air Training Gp Kumalo Bulawayo 1947-50; JSSC 1951-52; sr Air Staff Offr RAF Gibraltar 1952-55, MOD

1955-57, Exchange Appt with US Navy San Diego California 1957-58, RAF Liaison Offr C-in-C Home Fleet 1959-61, Air Miny 1961-63 (ret); admin exec AGB Research Ltd 1964-69; surveyor mgmnt dept Folkhard and Hayward; *Recreations* golf, shooting, sailing; *Style—* Wing Cdr Peter J Cundy, DSO, DFC, AFC, TD; Cherry House, Alburgh, nr Harleston, Norfolk IP20 0BX (☎ Homersfield 640)

CUNEO, Terence Tenison (Terry); OBE (1987); s of Cyrus Cincinnata Cuneo (d 1916) and Nell Marian Tenison (d 1953); *b* 1 Nov 1907; *Educ* Sutton Valence; *m* 1934, Catherine Mayfield (d 1979), yr da of Maj Edwin George Monro, CBE; 2 da (Linda, Carole); *Career* portrait and figure painter, ceremonial, military and engrg subjects; served WWII RE and as war artist; has painted extensively in N Africa, S Africa, Rhodesia, Canada, USA, Ethiopia, Far East; one-man exhibitions: RWS Galleries London 1954 and 1958, Sladmore Gallery 1971, 1972, 1974; *Major works include* Coronation of HM The Queen Westminster Abbey (Royal Collection 1953), equestrian portrait of HM The Queen as Col-in-Chief Gren Gds (cmmnd by HM 1963), Garter Ceremony St George's Chapel Windsor (cmmnd by HM 1964), Sir Winston Churchill's Lying in State (1965), Rt Hon Edward Heath (1971), Field Marshal Viscount Montgomery of Alamein (1972), Duke of Beaufort (commemorating 40 years as Master of the Horse), King Hussein of Jordan (1980), Col H Jones, VC (1984), Fortieth Anniversary of D-Day (1984); *Books* The Mouse and his Master (autobiog 1977), The Railway Painting of Terence Cuneo (1980); *Recreations* travel, riding, writing; *Style—* Terence Cuneo, Esq, OBE; Fresh Fields, 201 Ember Lane, East Molesey, Surrey (☎ 01 398 1986/7981)

CUNINGHAME; *see*: Montgomery Cuninghame

CUNINGHAME; *see*: Fairlie-Cuninghame

CUNINGHAME; *see*: FERGUSSON-CUNINGHAME OF CAPRINGTON

CUNINGHAME, Lady (Marjorie) Joan Mary; *née* Wentworth-Fitzwilliam; 2 da of Lt-Col 7 Earl Fitzwilliam, KCVO, CBE, DSO, JP, DL (d 1943); *b* 19 Oct 1900; *m* 1, 4 Nov 1925 (m dis 1949), Maj Grismond Picton Philipps, CVO (Knt 1953), Gren Gds (d 1967); 1 s; 1 da; m 2, 6 Oct 1949, Lt-Col William Wallace Smith Cuninghame, DSO, JP, DL, late Life Gds, 16 Laird of Caprington (d 1959); *Style—* Lady Joan Cuninghame; Homestead, Vallee des Vaux, St Helier, Jersey CI

CUNINGHAME, William Alistair Fergusson; s of Capt Robert Wallace Fergusson-Cuninghame of Caprington, DL, O Caprington Castle, Kilmarnock, Ayrshire, and Rosemary Elizabeth Euing, *née* Crawford; *b* 23 Nov 1960; *Career* farmer and landowner; *Recreations* flying, shooting, arboriculture; *Clubs* New Club (Edinburgh), Lansdowne; *Style—* William Cuninghame, Esq, Yr of Caprington; Gatehouse of Caprington, Kilmarnock, Ayrshire KA2 9AA (☎ 0563 240 12)

CUNLIFFE, Andrew Mark; s of Sir Cyril Cunliffe, 8 Bt (d 1969); hp of bro, Sir David Cunliffe, 9 Bt; *b* 17 April 1959; *Educ* St Albans GS for Boys; *m* 1980, Janice Elizabeth, da of Ronald William Kyle; 1 s (Mark Ellis b 1982); *Career* postal exec Postal HQ London; *Recreations* sport, foreign cuisine, music, literature; *Clubs* Barnet Conservative; *Style—* Andrew Cunliffe, Esq; 37 Redbridge, Stantonbury, Milton Keynes, Bucks MK14 6BD (☎ 0908 310239)

CUNLIFFE, Hon Mrs Geoffrey; Barbara (Waring); da of late Dr J A Gibb, of Maidstone; *m* 1 (m dis), Laurence A Evans; m 2, 1947, as his 3 w, Hon Geoffrey Cunliffe (d 1982), s of 1 Baron Cunliffe, GBE (d 1920); *Style—* The Hon Mrs Geoffrey Cunliffe; c/o The Rt Hon the Lord Cunliffe, The Broadhurst, Brandeston, Woodbridge, Suffolk IP13 7AG

CUNLIFFE, Sir David Ellis; 9 Bt (GB 1759), of Liverpool, Lancashire; s of Sir Cyril Henley Cunliffe, 8 Bt (d 1969); *b* 29 Oct 1957; *Educ* St Alban's GS for Boys; *m* 1983, Linda Carol, da of John Sidney Batchelor, of Harpenden; 1 da (Emma Mary b 1986); *Heir* bro, Andrew Cunliffe; *Career* sales representative; *Style—* Sir David Cunliffe, Bt; Sunnyside, Burnthouse Lane, Needham, nr Harleston, Norfolk IP20 9LN (☎ 0379 853866)

CUNLIFFE, Hon Henry; s and h of 3 Baron Cunliffe; *b* 9 Mar 1962; *Educ* Eton; *Style—* The Hon Henry Cunliffe

CUNLIFFE, Kathleen, Lady; Kathleen Elsie; da of Ernest Brownfield Pope, of Wargrave, Berks; *m* 1, 1940, Capt Philip Robinson, RAMC (ka 1944); m 2, 24 Dec 1952, as his 2 w, 2 Baron Cunliffe (d 24 Nov 1963); *Style—* The Rt Hon Kathleen, Lady Cunliffe; Virginia Cottage, Dorchester-on-Thames, Oxford

CUNLIFFE, Lawrence Francis; MP (Lab) Leigh 1979-; *b* 25 Mar 1929; *Educ* St Edmund's RC Sch Worsley Manchester; *m* 1950, Winifred, da of William Haslem; 3 s, 2 da; *Style—* Lawrence Cunliffe, Esq, MP; House of Commons, London SW1

CUNLIFFE, Hon Luke; yr s of 3 Baron Cunliffe; *b* 29 June 1965; *Educ* Eton, Bransons Coll; *Style—* The Hon Luke Cunliffe

CUNLIFFE, Hon Merlin; yr s of late 2 Baron Cunliffe; *b* 29 April 1935; *Educ* Eton; *m* 1, 23 April 1960 (m dis), Deborah Rutherford, yst da of Harold Thornton Grimwade, MBE, of Urara, Lismore, Victoria, Australia; 1 da (and 1 da decd); m 2, 1978, Mrs Amanda June Foster, da of Samuel Rogers; *Style—* The Hon Merlin Cunliffe; Wills Rd, Dixon's Creek, Vic 3775, Australia

CUNLIFFE, 3 Baron (UK 1914); Roger Cunliffe; s of 2 Baron Cunliffe (d 1963), and his 1 w, Joan Catherine, da of late Cecil Lubbock (n of 1 Baron Avebury); *b* 12 Jan 1932; *Educ* Eton, Trinity Coll Cambridge (BA, MA), Architectural Assoc (AADipl), Open Univ; *m* 27 April 1957, Clemency Ann, da of late Maj Geoffrey Benyon Hoare, of Clover House, Aldeburgh, Suffolk; 2 s, 1 da; *Heir* s, Hon Henry Cunliffe; *Career* consulting architect, dir Exhibition Conslts Ltd, Reiach and Hall Consits Ltd; vice-chm Br Consits Bureau; Asst Worshipful Co of Goldsmiths; *Books* (with Leonard Manasseh) Office Buildings (1962); *Recreations* making bread, planting trees, cycling; *Style—* The Rt Hon Lord Cunliffe; The Broadhurst, Brandeston, Woodbridge, Suffolk IP13 7AG (☎ 072 882 751)

CUNLIFFE CAVE, Lt-Col Robert John; s of Wilfred Cunliffe Cave, of Cairo Mounted Police (assas 1922), and Winifred O'Connor (d 1954); *b* 15 Nov 1911; *Educ* Wellington, RMC Sandhurst, Br Staff Coll, Fr Ecole de Guerre (Paris); *m* 2 July 1955, Moira, da of Maj Gordon Utley (d 1978); *Career* cmmnd 2 Lt RSF 1932; French Language student Paris and attached 2 Hussards French Army 1934, GHQ staff Cairo and Palestine 1936-37, Italian language student Florence and attended HQ IV Corps Trento Italian Army 1938, GHQ Staff BEF Fr 1940, HQ Scot Cmd 1941, Bde Major 146 Bde Iceland 1942, GSO2 Accra 1943, AFHQ Staff Algiers and Italy, GSO1 SHAEF (US Bronze star) (despatches 1945), Mil Govt Staff Ger 1944-46, HQ Control Cmmn Ger 1948-49, Ecole de Guerre Paris 1952-53, Germany 1953-, sec to fr C in C Allied Forces Central Euro 1953-56 War Office, PR (Exhibitions) 1957; ret 1958; ed Br Army Review, MOD 1964-76; *Recreations* historical research, horses and riding; *Style—* Lt-Col Robert Cunliffe Cave; Trout Brook, Gussage all Saints, nr Wimborne, Dorset (☎ 0258 840308)

CUNLIFFE-LISTER, Hon Nicholas John; s of late Maj the Hon John Yarburgh Cunliffe-Lister, eld s of 1 Earl of Swinton, GBE, CH, MC, MP; raised to the rank of an Earl's son 1974; hp of bro, 2 Earl; *b* 4 Sept 1939; *Educ* Winchester, Worcester Coll Oxford; *m* 19 Feb 1966, Hon (Elizabeth) Susan, da of 1 Viscount Whitelaw, CH, MC, PC, *qqv*; 2 s, 1 da; *Career* late 2 Lt WG; slr 1966; *Style—* Hon Nicholas Cunliffe-Lister; Glebe House, Masham, Ripon, Yorks

CUNLIFFE-LISTER, Hon Mrs Nicholas; (Elizabeth) Susan; *née* Whitelaw; eldest da of 1 Viscount Whitelaw, *qv*; *b* 2 Nov 1944; *m* 19 Feb 1966, Hon Nicholas John Cunliffe-Lister, *qv*; 2 s, 1 da; *Style—* The Hon Susan Cunliffe-Lister; Glebe House, Masham, Ripon, Yorkshire

CUNNINGHAM, Sir Charles Craik; GCB (1974, KCB 1961, CB 1946), KBE (1952), CVO (1941); s of late Richard Yule Cunningham, of Abergeldie, Kirriemuir, Angus, and Isabella, *née* Craik; *b* 7 May 1906; *Educ* Harris Academy Dundee, Univ of St Andrews (MA, BLitt, LLD); *m* 1934, Edith Louisa, da of late Frank Coutts Webster, OBE; 2 da; *Career* joined Scottish Off 1929, priv sec to Sec State Scotland 1935-39, Scottish Home Dept 1939-57, (sec 1948-57); Perm under-sec Home Off 1957-66, dep chm UKAEA 1966-71, chm: Radiochemical Centre Ltd 1971-74, Uganda Resettlement Bd 1972-74; dir Securicor 1971-81; *Clubs* Reform, New (Edinburgh); *Style—* Sir Charles Cunningham, GCB, KBE, CVO; Bankside, Peaslake, Surrey GU5 9RL (☎ 0306 730402)

CUNNINGHAM, David; CB (1983); s of Robert Cunningham, of 15 Buchanan Drive, Bearsden, Dunbartonshire (d 1956) and Elizabeth *née* Shields (d 1983); *b* 26 Feb 1924; *Educ* High Sch of Glasgow, Univ of Glasgow (MA LLB); *m* 26 Aug 1955, Ruth Branwell, da of Rev Thomas James Campbell Crawford, MA (d 1955), of Barony Manse, West Kilbride, Ayrshire; 1 s (Robert Campbell (Keith) b 1956), 2 da (Isobel (Sharon) b 1958, Aileen Shields Branwell b 1962); *Career* capt Cameronians (seconded Intelligence Corps and Control Commn Germany) 1942-47); deputy slr to Sec of State for Scotland 1978-80, slr to Sec of State for Scotland 1980-84; *Recreations* hill walking, reading, motor cars, theatre; *Style—* David Cunningham Esq, CB; The Green Gates, Innerleithen, Peeblesshire EH44 6NH (☎ 0896 830436)

CUNNINGHAM, Hon Mrs (Edith Louise); *née* MacDermott; da of Baron MacDermott, MC, PC, (Life Peer) (d 1979); *b* 12 Jan 1930; *Educ* Wycombe Abbey, Queen's Univ Belfast (MB, BCh); *m* 30 April 1955, Samuel Barbour Cunningham, er s of Col James Glencairn Cunningham, OBE, DL, of Ballytrim, Co Down; 2 s (James, Samuel), 2 da (Anna, Rachel); *Career* general practitioner; MRCGP; *Recreations* gardening; *Style—* The Hon Mrs Cunningham,; Ballytrim House, 10 Ballytrim Road, Killyleagh Downpatrick, Co Down BT30 9TH

CUNNINGHAM, George; *b* 10 June 1931; *Educ* Manchester and London Univs; *m* 1957, Mavis Walton; 1 s, 1 da; *Career* with CRO 1956-63, cwlth offr Labour Party 1963-66, with Miny Overseas Dvpt 1966-69; contested Henley 1966, MP SW Islington 1970-74, MP Islington S and Finsbury 1974-83, MEP 1978-79; (Lab to Dec 1981, Ind 1981-82, SDP from 1982) oppn front bench spokesman Home Affrs 1979-81; chief exec The Library Assoc; *Books* Management of Aid Agencies (1974), Careers in Politics (1984); *Style—* George Cunningham, Esq; 28 Manor Gdns, Hampton, Middx (☎ 01 979 6221)

CUNNINGHAM, Lt-Gen Sir Hugh Patrick; KBE (1975, OBE 1966); s of Sir Charles Banks Cunningham, CSI (d 1967), of Campbelltown, Argyll and Grace, *née* Macnish; *b* 4 Nov 1921; *Educ* Charterhouse; *m* 1955, Jill, da of J S Jeffrey (d 1978), of E Knoyle, Wilts; 2 s, 2 da; *Career* 2 Lt RE 1942, GOC SW Dist 1971-74, ACGS (OR) MOD 1974-75, Lt-Gen 1975, Dep Chief of Def Staff (OR) 1976-78, ret; Col Cmdt RE 1976-81, Col Queen's Gurkha Engrs 1976-81, Col Bristol Univ OTC 1977-87; HM Lt of the Tower of London 1983-86; dir: Fairey Hldgs 1978-87, Fairey Engrg 1981-86, MEL 1982-89, Trend Communications Ltd 1983-86; chm: LL Consits 1983-; The Trend Group 1986-, Master Worshipful Co of Glass Sellers 1980-81; pres Old Carthusian Soc 1982-87; *Clubs* Army and Navy, MCC; *Style—* Lt-Gen Sir Hugh Cunningham, KBE; Brick Yard Farm, East Knoyle, Salisbury, Wilts SP3 6BP (☎ 074 783 281); 607 Howard House, Dolphin Sq, London SW1 (☎ 01 821 7960); Trend Group, High Wycombe, Bucks (☎ 06285 24977)

CUNNINGHAM, Gp Capt John; CBE (1963), DSO (1941), Bar to DSO (1942, 1944), DFC (1941), Bar to DFC (1941), AE (1941), DL (1948); s of Arthur Gillespie Cunningham (d 1930), of Croydon, Surrey, and Evelyn Mary, *née* Spencer (d 1968); *b* 27 July 1917; *Educ* Whitgift and De Havilland Tech Sch; *Career* joined 604 Sqdn Auxiliary Air Force 1935; CO: 604 Sqdn 1941-42, 85 Sqdn 1943-44, night fighting UK; Gp Capt; test pilot De Havilland Aircraft Co 1938-39; WWII mobilised 1939-45; chief test pilot De Havilland Engine Co 1945-46, chief test pilot De Havilland Aircraft Co 1946-61; dir: De Havilland Aircraft Co 1958-61, Hawker Siddeley Aviation 1961-77, Hawker Siddeley Aviation (Hatfield) 1961-77, Br Aerospace (Hatfield) 1977-80; Russian Order of Patriotic War (1st cl) 1944, USA Silver Star 1945-; *Recreations* gardening; *Clubs* RAF; *Style—* John Cunningham, Esq, CBE, DSO, DFC, AE, DL; Canley, Kinsbourne Green, Harpenden, Herts (☎ 058 27 2525)

CUNNINGHAM, Dr John Anderson; MP (Lab) Copeland 1983-; s of Andrew Cunningham; *b* 4 August 1939; *Educ* Jarrow GS, Bede Coll Durham Univ; *m* 1964, Maureen; 1 s, 2 da; *Career* former research chemist Durham (PhD 1966), then schoolmaster and Trades Union official; MP (Lab) Whitehaven, Cumbria 1970-1983, pps to James Callaghan when PM 1974-76, Parly under-sec of state Dept of Energy 1976-79, front bench oppn spokesman: Industry 1979-Nov 1983, Environment and memb Shadow Cabinet Nov 1983-; *Style—* Dr John Cunningham, MP; House of Commons, London SW1

CUNNINGHAM, John Roderick; s of John Cunningham (d 1952), of Kent, and Millicent, *née* Seal (d 1929); *b* 13 May 1926; *Educ* Beckenham Sch Kent, Queen's Univ Belfast (BSc); *m* 1964, Monica Rachel, da of Cedric Robert Seymour George (d 1964), of Horley, Surrey; 1 s (Roderick b 1965), 2 da (Meryl b 1955 (from previous marriage), Clare b 1970); *Career* dir Coutts and Co 1980-87, chm Nikko Bank plc 1987-; memb bd of Mgmnt of Cordwainers Coll, Master Worshipful Co of Loriners 1984; FCIB, FRSA; *Recreations* gardening in Southern Spain, City of London activities; *Clubs* IOD, Overseas Bankers, City Livery; *Style—* John R Cunningham, Esq; Oak Lodge, 126 Pembury Road, Tonbridge, Kent TN9 2JJ; The Nikko Bank (UK) plc, 17 Godliman St, London EC4V 5BD (☎ 01 528 7070)

CUNNINGHAM, Lady; Margery Agnes; da of Samuel Henry Slater, CMG, CIE, ICS (d 1965), and his 1 wife Muriel Agnes, *née* Streatfield; *b* 14 July 1905; *m* 1, 1927 (m dis 1938), Christopher Tancred; 1 s; m 2, 1943, Sir Harold Snagge, KBE (d 1949); m 3, 1951, Gen Sir Alan Gordon Cunningham, GCMG, KCB, DSO, MC (d 1983, GOCIC Eastern Command 1944-45, Cmmr and CIC Palestine 1945-48, Cmdt RA), s of Prof Daniel John Cunningham, FRS; *Style*— Lady Cunningham; Salters Cross, Yalding, Kent (☎ 0622 814368); c/o Lloyds Bank, 6 Pall Mall, London SW1

CUNNINGHAM, Samuel Barbour; DL (Co Down); s of Col James G Cunningham, OBE, of Glencairn Lodge, Tullykinlough RD, Killyleagh, Co Down, and Mollie Barbour, *née* Pears; *b* 7 Dec 1929; *Educ* Stowe; *m* Hon Edith Louise, da of Baron McDermott (Lord Chief Judice of N Ireland), of Glenburn, Cairnburn Rd, Belfast (d 1979); 2 s (James MacDermott b 16 Oct 1957, Samuel Clarke b 5 May 1962), 2 da (Anna Louise b 16 April 1956, Rachel Edith b 19 March 1964); *Career* aen mangr Dalgety Agriculture Ltd N Ireland;; *Recreations* county pursuits; *Clubs* Ulster Reform (Belfast); *Style*— Samuel Cunningham, Esq, DL; 10 Ballytrim Rd, Killlyleagh, Downpatrick, Co Down BT30 9th (☎ 0396 828 057); Dalgety Agriculture Ltd, 102 Corporation St, Belfast, BT1 3DX (☎ 0203 233 791)

CUNYNGHAME; *see*: Blair-Cunynghame

CUNYNGHAME, Sir Andrew David Francis; 12 Bt (NS 1702) of Milncraig, Ayrshire; s of Sir (Henry) David St Leger Brooke Selwyn Cunynghame, 11 Bt (d 1978) and Hon Lady (Pamela) Cunynghame, da of late 5 Baron Stanley of Alderley; *b* 25 Dec 1942; *Educ* Eton; *m* 1972, Harriet Ann Marie, da of Charles Thomas Dupont, of Montreal, Canada; 2 da (Ann b 1978, Tania b 1983); *Heir* bro, John Cunynghame; *Career* former chm City Vintagers Ltd; senior ptnr Chipchase Cunynghame; FCA; *Clubs* Brooks's; *Style*— Sir Andrew Cunynghame, Bt; 69 Hillgate Place, W8; Chipchase Cunynghame, 54-58 Caledonian Road, London N1 9RN (☎ 01 278 7992)

CUNYNGHAME, John Philip Henry Michael Selwyn; s of late Sir (Henry) David St Leger Brooke Selwyn Cunynghame, 11 Bt; hp of bro, Sir Andrew Cunynghame, 12 Bt; *b* 9 Sept 1944; *Educ* Eton; *m* 1981, Marjatta, da of Martti Markus, of Muhos, Finland; 1 s (Alexander b 1985), 1 da (Niina b 1983; *Career* dir GB Vintagers; *Style*— John Cunynghame, Esq; GB Vintagers, 430 High Road, London NW10 2HA (☎ 01 459 8011, telex: 923 540)

CUNYNGHAME, Hon Lady; Hon Pamela Margaret; 2 da of 5 Baron Stanley of Alderley, KCMG (d 1931); *b* 6 Sept 1909; *m* 7 Oct 1941, Sqdn Ldr Sir (Henry) David St Leger Brooke Selwyn Cunynghame, 11 Bt, RAFVR (d 1978); 3 s; *Career* actress; *Style*— The Hon Lady Cunynghame; 83 Clarendon Street, Leamington Spa, Warwickshire

CURL, Prof James Stevens; s of George Stevens Curl (d 1974), of Hillhall, Co Down, and Sarah, *née* McKinney; *b* 26 Mar 1937; *Educ* Campbell Coll, Queen's Univ, Belfast Coll of Art, Oxford Sch of Architecture, UCL; *m* 1 Jan 1960 (m dis 1986), Eileen Elizabeth, da of John Blackstock (d 1984), of Glendale Park, Belfast; 2 da (Astrid b 1962, Ingrid b 1964); *Career* architect, town planner, antiquarian, architectural historian; architectural editor Survey of London 1970-73; conslt architect to Scottish Ctee for European Architectural Heritage Year 1975, 1973-75; currently dir of Historical Architecture Res Unit sch of Architecture Leicester; Liveryman Worshipful Co of Chartered Architects; PhD, Dipl Arch, DipTP, FSA, RIBA, MRTPI, ARIAS, FSAScot; *Books* The Londonderry Plantation 1609-1914 (1986), English Architecture (1987), The Life and Work of Henry Roberts 1803-76 (1983), The Egyptian Revival (1982), A Celebration of Death (1980), The Erosion of Oxford (1977), Victorian Architecture (1973), The Victorian Celebration of Death (1972); author num articles and reviews; *Recreations* music, opera, travel, literature, food, wine, poetry, painting; *Clubs* Reform, Art Workers Guild; *Style*— Prof James Stevens Curl; 2 The Coach House, Burley-on-the-Hill, Oakham, Rutland, Leics LE15 7SJ (☎ 0572 755880); School of Architecture, PO Box 143, Leicester LE1 9BH (☎ 0533 551551, ext 2350)

CURLE, Sir John Noel Ormiston; KCVO (1975, CVO 1956), CMG 1966; s of Maj William Sidney Noel Curle, MC (d of wounds 1918), of Melrose; *b* 12 Dec 1915; *Educ* Marlborough, New Coll Oxford; *m* 1, 1940 (m dis 1948), Diana, da of Cdr Ralph H Deane, RN; 1 s, 1 da; m 2, 1948, Pauline, da of Hylton Welford, of Hylton, Co Durham, and wid of Capt David Roberts; 1 step-s, 2 step-da; *Career* served WWII Irish Gds Capt 1941; entered Dip Serv 1939; ambass to Liberia 1967-70, Guinea 1968-70, the Philippines 1970-72, Vice-Marshal of the Dip Corps 1972-75, ret; dir of Protocol Hong Kong 1976-85; advsr for Coronation of the King of Swaziland 1986; *Recreations* skiing; *Clubs* Cavalry and Guards, Beefsteak; *Style*— Sir John Curle, KCVO, CMG; Appletree House, nr Aston-le-Walls, Daventry, Northants NN11 6UG (☎ 029 586 211)

CURLING, David Richard Michael; s of Lt-Col Richard Robinson Curling, DSO (d 1953), and Victoria Margaret (d 1965), 2 da of Sir William Michael Curtis, 4 Bt; *b* 9 May 1923; *Educ* Gordonstoun; *m* 1954, Olive Marigold, da of Douglas Cory-Wright, CBE, and gda of Sir Arthur Cory-Wright, 2 Bt; 1 s, 2 da; *Career* Midshipman RNR Atlantic, Indian Ocean; advertiser, dir J Walter Thompson Co Ltd, High Sheriff of Bucks 1980/81; memb Automobile Association Ctee; *Recreations* sailing, shooting; *Clubs* Royal Yacht Squadron, Boodle's, Garrick, Royal Ocean Racing; *Style*— David R M Curling, Esq; The Rosary, Coleshill, nr Amersham, Bucks (☎ 0494 726431)

CURLING, Hon Mrs (Melissa); *née* Llewelyn-Davies; da of Baron Llewelyn-Davies (Life Peer); *b* 1 June 1945; *m* 1974, Christopher Desmond Curling, 2 s of Bryan William Richard Curling, VRD, of Conford Park, Liphook, Hants, and Elizabeth Mary, o da of Sir Eric Henry Bonham, 3 Bt; 1 s (Richard b 1983), 1 da (Rosa b 1979); *Style*— The Hon Mrs Curling; 3 Richmond Crescent, London N1

CURRAN, Sir Samuel Crowe; s of John Hamilton Curran (d 1959); *b* 23 May 1912; *Educ* Glasgow Univ (MA, BSc, PhD, DSc), Cambridge Univ (PhD); *m* 1940, Joan Elizabeth, da of Charles Millington Strothers (d 1975); 4 children; *Career* scientist and educationalist; former chief scientific advsr to Sec of State for Scotland, chief scientist UKAEA 1955-59; princ: Royal Coll of Sci and Technol 1959-64, Strathclyde Univ 1964-80, visiting prof in energy studies Univ of Glasgow 1980-; Cdr Order of St Olav Norway 1965, Cdr Polonia Restituta Poland 1970; FRS, FRSE, FEng; kt 1970; *Recreations* golf, horology; *Clubs* Caledonian; *Style*— Sir Samuel Curran; 93 Kelvin Court, Glasgow G12 0AH (☎ 01 334 8329)

CURRAN, Stephen William; s of Dr Richard Desmond Curran, CBE (d 1985, Capt RNVR), and Marguerite Claire, *née* Gothard; *b* 9 Mar 1943; *Educ* Marlborough, Wellington, RMA Sandhurst; *m* 21 June 1969, Anne Beatrice, da of Harry Grumbar, of Rats Castle, Roughway, nr Tonbridge, Kent; 1 s (Charles b 1972), 1 da (Louise b 1979); *Career* Lt 1 The Queens Dragoon Gds 1963-66; Permutit Co Ltd 1966-67, Bowater Co Ltd 1967-71, analyst Grumbar and Sec 1971-75, managing conslt Coopers and Lybrand Assocs 1975-79, project fin mangr NCB Pension Funds 1979-81, dep chief exec Candover Investmts plc 1981-; FCCA 1973; *Recreations* skiing, swimming, tennis, running; *Clubs* Cavalry and Guards', Hurlingham; *Style*— Stephen Curran, Esq; 25 Ongar Rd, London SW6 1RL (☎ 01 385 2747); Watcombe, Horseshoe Lane, Beckley, Rye, E Sussex TW31 6RX; Cedric House, 8-9 East Harding St, London EC4A 3AS (☎ 01 583 5090, fax 01 583 0717, telex 928035)

CURREY, Hon Mrs Heather Mary; *née* Drummond of Megginch; 2 da of 15 Baron Strange (d 1982), and Margaret Violet Florence (d 1975), da of Sir Robert William Buchanan Jardine, 2 Bt; was co-heiress with her sisters to the Barony of Strange (*see* Baroness Strange); *b* 9 Nov 1931; *Educ* Hatherop Castle; *m* 11 Aug 1954, Lt Cdr Andrew Christian Currey, RN, o s of Rear Adm Philip Currey, CB, OBE (d 1979), of Pond Cottage, Newton Valence, Hants; 2 s (Robert James Drummond b 1955, John Andrew Fairbridge b 1959), 1 da (Arabella Mary Christian b 1958); *Clubs* Army and Navy; *Style*— The Hon Mrs Currey; The Mill House, Santon, Isle of Man (☎ 0624 824053)

CURREY, Rear Adm (Edmund) Neville Vincent; CB (1960), DSO (1944, DSC 1940); s of Dr Edmund Francis Neville Currey, of Lismore, Co Waterford, Ireland (d 1953), and Constance Murray, *née* Binny (d 1960); *b* 1 Oct 1906; *Educ* RNC Osbsorne and Dartmouth; *m* 19 Feb 1941, Rosemary, da of William Lowry Craig Knight, CMG; 1 da (Frances b 1944); *Career* joined RN 1919, served 1929-45 in Destroyers and Assault Forces (S), Capt 1949, Rear Adm 1958, Chief of Staff to C in C Portsmouth 1958, ADC to HM Queen 1958, ret 1961; *Recreations* golf; *Style*— Rear Adm Neville Currey, CB, DSO, DSC; 75 Great Pulteney St, Bath (☎ 0225 63743)

CURRIE, Prof Sir Alastair Robert; s of John Currie (d 1948), of Isle of Islay, and Maggie Mactaggart; *b* 8 Oct 1921; *Educ* Glasgow HS, Glasgow Univ (BSc, MB); *m* 1949, Jeanne Marion MB, ChB, da of Edward Colin Clarke (d 1954), of Bournemouth; 3 s, 2 da; *Career* pathologist; Regius prof of Pathology Aberdeen Univ 1962-72; prof emeritus of pathology Edinburgh Univ 1972-86; Hon DSc (Birmingham) 1983; Hon DSc (Aberdeen) 1985; Hon LLD (Glasgow) 1987; FRCP (Lond, Edin, Glas), FRCSE, FRCPath, FRSE; kt 1979; *Clubs* New (Edinburgh); *Style*— Prof Sir Alastair Currie; 42 Murrayfield Ave, Edinburgh EH12 6AY (☎ 031 337 3100); Grianan, Strathlachlan, Argyll (☎ 036 986 769)

CURRIE, Brian Murdoch; s of William Murdoch Currie (d 1984), and Dorothy, *née* Holloway; *b* 20 Dec 1934; *Educ* Blundells, Oriel Coll Oxford (MA); *m* 21 Oct 1961, Patricia Maria, da of Capt Frederick Eaton-Farr (d 1945); 3 s (Murdoch b 1964, Lachlan b 1967, Gregor b 1975), 1 da (Lucinda b 1966); *Career* Subaltern BAOR RTR 1957-59; CA 1962, ptnr Arthur Andersen & Co 1970, fin memb HMSO Bd 1972-74, managing ptnr Arthur Andersen and Co London 1977-82; Inspr Dept of Trade 1978-81, memb restrictive Practices Ct, memb cncl and chm Parly and Law Ctee Inst of CAS, chm Public Sector Liaison Gp of Accounting Standards Ctee 1984-86; tstee Oriel Coll Devpt Tst 1980, fell Br Prod and Inventory Control Soc (memb of Nat Cmc; 1970-73); MIMC; *Recreations* natural history; *Clubs* Reform; *Style*— Brian Currie, Esq; Westbrook House, Bampton, Devon EX16 9HU (☎ 0398 31418); 1 Surrey St, London WC2R 2PS (☎ 01 438 3562, fax 01 831 1133, telex 8812711)

CURRIE, Brian Murdock; s of William Murdock Currie (d 1985), of N Devon, and Dorothy, *née* Holloway; *b* 20 Dec 1934; *Educ* Blundells, Oriel Coll Oxford (MA); *m* 21 Oct 1961, Patricia Maria, da of Capt Frederick Eaton-Farr (d 1945); 3 s (Murdoch b 1964, Lachlan b 1967, Gregor b 1975), 1 da (Lucinda b 1966); *Career* Royal Tank Regt Subaltern BAOR b 1957-59; CA 1962, ptnr Arthur Andersen and Co 1970, financial memb HMSO Bd 1972-74, mangr ptnr Arthur Andersen and Co London 1977-82 (dep mangr 1975); dept of Trade Inspector 1978-81, vice chm Parly and Law Ctee, Inst of Chartered Accountants 1985, chm Public Sector Liaison Gp of Accountants Standards Ctee 1984-86, tstee Oriel Coll Dvpt Tst 1980, fell British Product and Inventory Control Soc (memb of Nat Cncl 1970-73), MIMIC; *Recreations* natural history; *Clubs* Reform; *Style*— Brian M Currie, Esq; Witton Lodge, nr Blofield, Norwich NR13 5AS; 1 Surrey Street, London WC2 (☎ 01 438 3562)

CURRIE, Sir Donald Scott; 7 Bt (UK 1947); s of George Donald Currie (d 1980), and Janet, *née* Scott; suc unc, Sir Alick Bradley Currie, 6 Bt (d 1987); *b* 16 Jan 1930; *m* 1, 1948 (m dis 1951), Charlotte, da of Charles Johnstone, of Mesa, Arizona, USA; 1 s, 2 da (twins); m 2, 30 April 1952, Barbara Lee, da of A P Garnier, of California; 1 s, 2 da; *Heir* s, Donald Mark Currie, b 1949; *Career* US Dept of the Interior; US National Park Service; *Style*— Sir Donald Currie, Bt

CURRIE, Edwina; MP (C) South Derbyshire 1983-; *b* 13 Oct 1946; *Educ* Liverpool Inst, St Anne's Coll Oxford (MA), LSE (MSc); *m* 1972, Raymond Frank Currie; 2 da; *Career* teacher and lectr 1972-81, head Dept (Business Studies) Bromsgrove Sch 1978-81; city cllr Birmingham 1975-86, memb Birmingham AHA 1975-82, chm Central Birmingham Health Authority 1981-83; memb Birmingham Community Relns Cncl 1979-83, chm Birmingham Social Servs Ctee 1979-80, Housing Ctee 1982-83; memb Select Ctee on Social Servs 1983-86, vice-pres Fedn Cons Students 1984-85, BBC Gen Advsy Cncl 1985-6; Parly private sec to Sir Keith Joseph; Sec of State for Educn 1986; Parly undersec DHSS, Min for Women's Health 1986-; *Recreations* family, swimming, arts, domestic arts; *Clubs* Swadlincote Cons (Derbys); *Style*— Mrs Edwina Currie, MP; House of Commons, London SW1A 0AA

CURRIE, Ian Hamilton; s of John Currie (d 1984), and Vera Matilda Currie, *née* Lea; *b* 9 Mar 1948; *Educ* Portsmouth Northern GS; *m* 22 Feb 1972, Catherine Helen, da of Ernest William Pink (d 1983); 2 da (Victoria Catherine b 1979, Jacqueline Neoma b 1983); *Career* financial dir Grieves Gp plc; dir Bookpoint Ltd; chm Roundabout Garages Ltd; FICA (England and Wales) 1970; *Recreations* cruiser sailing; *Clubs* Portchestre Sailing; *Style*— Ian Currie, Esq, FCA; 22 The Hard, Portsmouth (☎ 0605 821351, fax 0705 826648, car tel 0836 270166)

CURRIE, James McGill; s of late David Currie, of Kilmarnock (Scotland), and Mary, *née* Smith; *b* 17 Nov 1941; *Educ* St Joseph's Sch Kilmarnock, Blair's Coll Aberdeen, Royal Scots Coll, Valladolid (Spain), Glasgow Univ (MA); *m* 27 June 1968, Evelyn Barbara, da of Alexander Malcolm Macintyre, of Glasgow; 1 s (Alister John b 1971), 1 da (Jennifer b 1973); *Career* civil servant, asst princ, Scottish Home and Health Dept 1968-72, Scottish Education Dept 1972-75; asst sec (Transport Policy) 1977-80, (Industrial Devpt) 1981-82; cnsllr for Social Affairs and Tport at UK Permanent Representation to EEC in Brussels 1982-86; dir European Regnl Devpt Fund in Regnl Policy Directorate of Euro Cmmn (Brussels) 1987-89, chef de cabinet to Sir Leon

Brittan, *qv* 1989-; *Recreations* guitar, tennis, good food; *Style—* James M Currie, Esq; Leeuwerikendreef 6, Overijse, Belgium; EEC Commission, 200 Rue De La Loi, 1040 Brussels, Belgium (☎ (010 322) 236 0125)

CURRIE, Joseph Austin; s of John Currie (d 1979), of Mullaghmarget, Dungannon, Co Tyrone, and Mary Currie, *née* O'Donnell (d 1984); *b* 11 Oct 1939; *Educ* Edendork PES; St Patrick's Acad, Dungannon; Queen's Univ, Belfast BA (jnt Hons Politics and History); *m* 13 Jan 1968, Annita, *née* Lynch; 2 s (Dualta b 1971, Austin b 1974), 3 da (Estella b 1968, Emer b 1979, Caitriona b 1970); *Career* lectr, conslt, writer, broadcaster; MP N Ireland 1964-72, memb N Ireland Assembly 1973-75, min of Hous Local Govt and Planning 1974; memb: N Ireland Constitutional Convention 1975-76, N Ireland Assembly 1980-84; *Recreations* golf, snooker, gaelic, football; *Style—* J A Currie, Esq; 35 Tullycurrion Rd, Tullydraw, Donachmore, Dungannon, Co Tyrone

CURRIE, Sir Neil Smith; CBE (1977, OBE 1972); s of Sir George Alexander Currie (d 1984), of Canberra, ACT, Australia and Margaret, *née* Smith (Lady Currie, *qv*); Sir George Currie was vice-chancellor of University of Western Australia; *b* 20 August 1926; *Educ* Wesley Coll Perth, Univ of WA (BA); *m* 1951, Geraldine Evelyn, da of Rev Walter Ernest Dexter, DSO, MC, DCM (d 1950); 2 s (Keith, Bruce, twins b 1953), 2 da (Deborah b 1952, Janet b 1959); *Career* RAAF 1945; sec: Dept of Mfrg Indust 1974-76, Dept of Indust and Commerce 1976-82, Aust ambass to Japan 1982-86; sec Dept of Supply 1971-74; dep sec DTI 1968-71; Dept of External Affrs (now Foreign Affrs) Tokyo, New York, Geneva 1948-59; DTI 1959-71;m: Aust Dairy Corpn 1986-, Howard Smith Ltd 1988-, Coal & Allied Industs Ltd 1988-; dir Westpac Banking Corpn 1987, memb Aust/Japan Fndn 1986-, exec memb Aust/Japan Business Coop Ctee 1988; Aust Eisenhower fell 1967; kt 1982; *see Debrett's Handbook of Australia and New Zealand for further details*; *Recreations* tennis, golf; *Clubs* Commonwealth (Canberra); Catalina Country; *Style—* Sir Neil Currie, CBE; 4/28 Wycombe Rd, Neutral Bay, NSW 2089, Australia

CURRIE, Rear Adm Robert Alexander; CB (1957), DSC (1944 and Bar 1945), DL (Suffolk 1968); 5 s of late John Currie, of Glasgow, and Rachel Thomson; *b* 29 April 1905; *Educ* RNC: Osborne, Dartmouth; *m* 1944, Edith Margaret (d 1985), da of Frank Agnew, of Eccles Hall, Norfolk, and widow of Cdr Sir Thomas Lubbock Beevor, 6 Bt, RN; *Career* staff offr Battle Cruiser Sqdn 1939, Admty Plans 12941, Convoy escort cmdr 1943, Capt. RN 1945, Assault Gp cmdr FE 1945, Capt, D 5 Destroyer Flotilla 1948, dir RN Staff College 1951, Rear Adm 1954, Br Jt Servs Mission Washington DC 1954, (ret 1957); memb W Suffolk CC 1962; *Style—* Rear Adm Robert Currie, CB, DSC; Saffron Pane, Hall Road, Lavenham, Suffolk CO10 9QU (☎ 0787 247409)

CURRIE, Prof Ronald Ian; CBE (1977); s of Ronald Wavell Currie, and Elizabeth, *née* Paterson; *b* 10 Oct 1928; *Educ* Univ of Glasgow (BSc), Univ of Copenhagen; *m* 10 July 1956, Cecilia, da of William A de Garis, of Le Grand Douit, St Saviours, Guernsey; 1 s (Crawford b 1960), 1 da (Susan b 1957); *Career* RN Scientific Serv 1949, William Scoresby Expedition to S Atlantic Ocean 1950, Discovery II Expedition to Antarctic 1951; head of biology dept Nat Inst of Oceanography 1961 (worked in N Atlantic 1953-62), chm biological planning Int Indian Ocean Expedition 1960, sec and dir Scottish Marine Biology Assoc 1966-87, professorial fell Univ of Edinburgh 1988-; hon sec Challenger Soc 1956-88, chm Kilmore Community Cncl; FRSE 1969, FIBiol 1967; *Books* The Benguela Current (1960), Antarctic Oceanography (1968); *Recreations* gardening, cooking, oil painting; *Clubs* Royal Overseas, Trout; *Style—* Prof Ronald Currie, CBE; Kilmore House, Kilmore by Oban, Argyll PA34 4XT (☎ 063 177 248); Grant Institute of Geology, University of Edinburgh EH9 3SW (☎ 031 667 1081)

CURRIE OF BALILONE, William McMurdo; Feudal Baron of Balilone; s of John Currie of Balilone (d 1943), and Helen Dick, *née* McMurdo (d 1955); *b* 28 Nov 1916; *Educ* Hyndland Sch, Royal Coll of Sci and Technol (BSc); *m* 23 Oct 1954, Irene Frances, da of Robert Hugh Semple Brierton (d 1970); *Career* WWII Br Special Servs 1939-45; conslt Br Cellophane Ltd 1951-53, textile conslt to Br jute trade 1953-68, cultural and diplomatic advsr to US Navy, 14 Submarine Sqdn, Holy Loch, Scotland, ambassador-at-large for free Polish govt in exile; FSAScot; memb Royal Archaeological Inst; Order of Virtuti Militari (Poland) 1943, Cross of Valour (Poland) 1944, Cdr (with star) Order of Polonia Restituta 1981, Polish Cross of Merit with Crossed Swords 1945, Belgian Médaille d'Honneur (silver) 1944, Croix Alliés 1946, Companion Mil Order of the Loyal Legion of USA 1977, awarded right to wear gold dolphins of US submarine force 1977; *Books* A History of the Curries of Cowal (1973), With Sword and Harp (1977), An Historical Description of Loch Lomond and District (1979); *Recreations* music, reading, fishing, hill-walking; *Clubs* Carrick, Glasgow Highland Officers'; *Style—* Baron Currie of Balilone; 78 Highburgh Road, Glasgow G12 9EN (☎ 041 339 8901)

CURRIE-CATHEY, (Vernon Howard) Peter; s of Edward Stanley Currie-Cathey, and Eileen Peggy, *née* Fryer; *b* 21 Aug 1941; *Educ* Sloane GS; *m* 2 Feb 1963, Jean Sylvia, *née* Rice; 2 s (James Vernon b 24 April 1967, Stuart Alex b 25 Sept 1969); *Career* ptnr Nigel Rose & Ptnrs (chartered wuantity surveyors); dept co cmmr Bucks Scout Assoc; Freeman City of London, memb Worshipful Co of Arbitrators; FRICS 1964, FCIArb 1973; *Recreations* badminton; *Style—* Peter Currie-Cathey, Esq; 6 Broad St, Workingham, Berks RG11 1AM (☎ 0734 774702, fax 0734 774829, car tel 0836 210276)

CURRIMBHOY EBRAHIM, Sir Zulfiqar Ali; 5 Bt (1913); s of Sir Mohammed Currimbhoy Ebrahim, 4 Bt and Dur-e-Mariam, da of Minuchehir Ahmud Ghulamaly Nana; *b* 5 August 1960; *Educ* Habib Public Sch, DJ Science Coll; *m* 1984, Adila, da of Akhtar Halipota; 1 s (Mustafa b 1985); *Heir* s, Mustafa b 22 Sept 1985; *Career* aeronautical engr 1982-; *Recreations* swimming, athletics; *Style—* Sir Zulfriqar Ali Currimbhoy Ebrahim, Bt; F-6511, Block 4, Clifton, Karachi, Pakistan (☎ Karachi 536429)

CURRY, David Maurice; MP Skipton and Ripon (Con) 1987, MEP (EDG) NE Essex 1979-; s of Thomas Harold Curry and Florence Joan, *née* Tyerman; *b* 13 June 1944; *Educ* Ripon GS, Corpus Christi Coll Oxford, Harvard (Kennedy Sch of Govt on Kennedy Scholarship); *m* 1971, Anne Helene Maud Roullet (has a PhD in Egyptology from Oxford); 1 s, 2 da; *Career* reporter: Newcastle Journal 1967-70, Financial Times (trade editor, international companies editor, Brussels correspondent, Paris correspondent, European news editor) 1970-79; sec Anglo-American Press Assoc of Paris 1978-; fndr Paris Cons Assoc 1977; chm Agric Ctee 1982-84 (yst ctee chm in European Parl's history); Conservative spokesman Budget Ctee 1984-; Rapporteur Gen EEC Budget 1987; *Books* The Food War: the EEC-US Conflict in Food Trade (1982); *Recreations* digging, wind-surfing; *Style—* David Curry, Esq, MP MEP; Newland End, Arkesden, Essex CB11 4HF (☎ (079 985) 368); constituency office: The Old Armoury, Saffron Walden, Essex CB10 1JN (☎ (0799) 22349); Constituency office: 19 Otley St, Skipton, N Yorks BD19 1DY (☎ Skipton 2092)

CURRY, John Arthur Hugh; s of Col Alfred Curry (d 1975); *b* 7 June 1938; *Educ* King's Coll Sch Wimbledon, St Edmund Hall Oxford (MA), Harvard Grad Sch of Business Admin (MBA); *m* 1962, Anne Rosemary, *née* Lewis; 3 s, 1 da; *Career* chm ACAL plc, non exec dir Unitech plc; FCA; *Recreations* tennis, rugby, travel; *Clubs* All England Lawn Tennis and Croquet, Int Lawn Tennis Club of GB; *Style—* John Curry, Esq; New Place, The Ridges, Finchampstead, Berks

CURRY, (Thomas) Peter (Ellison); s of Maj FRP Curry, RA (d 1955), and Sybil, *née* Woods; *b* 22 July 1921; *Educ* Tonbridge, Oriel Coll Oxford (MA); *m* 30 March 1950, Pamela Joyce, da of Gp Capt AJ Holmes, AFC (d 1950); 2 s (Guy b 1952, Iain b 1953), 2 da (Fleur b 1956, Jilly b 1959); *Career* WW II, enlisted 1939, offr Cadet 1940, OCTU Bangalore and Deolali India 1941; 1941-44: 1 Indian Field Regt, Indian Artillery (India, North West Frontier, Burma, Assam); air training course Peshawar 1944, Capt Air Force Devpt Centre Amesbury 1944, air directorate War Office GSO 3 1945-46; called to Bar Middle Temple 1953, QC 1966 (resigned 1967) slr Freshfields 1967, returned to Bar 1970, QC 1973, pres Aircraft and Shipbuilding Industries Arbitration Tribunal 1978-80; running Olympic Games 1948, Br 3000m steeplechase champion 1948, winner Oxford and Cambridge Cross Country 1947 and 1948; squash: represented Army, Oxford Univ, Sussex; asst scoutmaster Stepney Sea Scouts 1946; chm: Walson House Boys and Girls club 1954; Cobham Cons Assoc 1958; tres Barristers Benevolant Assoc 1964-71 and 1984-, chm Chancery Bar Assoc 1980-85, Trustee Stable Lads Welfare Tst 1986-; bencher Middle Temple 1979; *Recreations* lawn tennis, gardening, farming; *Clubs* Army and Navy; *Style—* Peter Curry, Esq; Hurlands, Dunsfold, Surrey (☎ 356 727 5730); 5 Victoria Grove Mews W8; 4 Stone Buildings, Lincolns Inn, WC2 (☎ 01 242 5524, fax 01 831 9152/Dunsfold 356, telex 892300)

CURRY-TOWNELEY-O'HAGAN, Hon Mrs (Helen Frances Alice Towneley); *née* O'Hagan; da of 3 Baron O'Hagan (d 1961); *b* 3 Mar 1912; *m* 23 May 1940, Capt Ian Desmond Curry, RA, who assumed by deed poll 1942 the surname of Curry-Towneley-O'Hagan (d 3 July 1969), 2 s of Thomas David Curry, of Upminster, Essex; 1 s; *Style—* The Hon Mrs Curry-Towneley-O'Hagan; 24 Burgh St, Islington, N1

CURTEIS, Ian Bayley; s of John Richard Jones, of Lydd, Kent, and Edith Marion Pomfret Cook, *née* Bayley; *b* 1 May 1935; *Educ* Slough GS, London Univ; *m* 1, 8 July 1964 (m dis 1985), Mrs Joan MacDonald; 2 s (Tobit b 1966, Michael b 1968); m2, 12 April 1985, Joanna (aka the novelist Joanna Trollope), da of AGC Trollope, of Overton Hants; 2 step da (Louise b 1969, Antonia b 1972); *Career* TV playwright, dir, actor and BBC TV script reader 1956-63, staff dir (drama) BBC and ATV; dir plays by: John Betjeman, John Hopkins, William Trevor 1963-67, chm Ctee on Censorship Writers Guild of GB 1981-; tv plays incl: Beethoven, Sir Alexander Fleming (BBC entry at Prague Fest 1973), Mr Rolls and Mr Royce, Long Voyage out of War (triology), The Folly, The Haunting, Second Time Round, A Distinct Chill, The Portland Millions, Philby, Burgess and Maclean (Br entry Monte Carlo Fest 1978), Hess, The Atom Spies, Churchill and the Generals (BAFTA nomination Best Play 1980), Suez 1956 (BAFTA nomination), Miss Morrisons Ghosts (Br entry Monte Carlo Festival), The Mitford Girls; film screenplays incl: Andre Malraux's La Condition Humaine (1982), Graham Greenes The Man Within (1983), Tom Paine (for Sir Richard Attenborough 1983), Eureka, The Nightmare Years, Cecil Rhodes; published plays: A Personal Affair, Long Voyage out of War (1971), Churchill and the Generals (1979), Suez 1956 (1980); FRSA 1984; *Recreations* avoiding television; *Clubs* Garrick, Beefsteak; *Style—* Ian Curteis, Esq; The Mill House, Coln St Aldwyns, Cirencester, Gloucestershire (fax 028 575 551)

CURTIS, Andrew Grant; s of Brigadier Francis Cockburn Curtis (d 1986), of 16 Marlborough Ct, Grange Rd, Cambridge, and Dorothy Joan Curtis, *née* Grant; *b* 1 August 1939; *Educ* Wellington, Trinity Hall Cambridge (MA); *m* 17 Oct 1964, Theresa Loraine, da of Theodore D Shephard, of Rocks Cottage, Uredale Rd, Oxted, Surrey; 1 s (Nicholas Simon b 1966), 2 da (Johanna Loraine b 1969, Jessica Martha b 1972); *Career* exec local dir Barclays Bank Plc: Bristol 1969, Darlington 1973, Manchester 1978, retail dir 1989; *Recreations* sailing, squash, tennis; *Clubs* Orford Sailing; *Style—* Andrew G Curtis, Esq; Tanyard Farm, Pickmere, Knutsford, Cheshire WA16 0JP (☎ 0565 893219); Barclays Bank plc, Regional Office, 17 York Street, Manchester M60 2AU (☎ 061 832 6717)

CURTIS, Anthony Samuel; s of Emanuel Curtis (d 1979), of London, and Eileen, *née* Freedman; *b* 12 Mar 1926; *Educ* Midhurst GS, Merton Coll Oxford (BA, MA); *m* 3 Oct 1960, Sarah, da of Dr Carl Myers, MB, Ch B; 3 s (Job b 1961, Charles b 1963, Quentin b 1965); *Career* served RAF 1945-48, lectr Br Inst of Sorbonne 1950-51, freelance journalist and critic (The Times, New Statesman, BBC) 1952-55, staff Times Educnl Supplement then asst ed Times Literary Supplement 1955-58, Hawkness Fell in journalism at Yale and elsewhere USA 1958-59, literary ed Sunday Telegraph 1960; Financial Times: arts & literary ed 1970-72, literary ed and book critic 1972-; numerous broadcasts on radio 3 and 4, author features & radio plays, reg appearances Critics Forum, Br Cncl lectr France & India; memb: Soc of Authors (tstee pension fund), Roy Lit Fund (tres); *Recreations* correspondence chess, backgammon, draughts ; *Clubs* Garrick, Travellers', Beefsteak; *Style—* Anthony Curtis, Esq; The Financial Times, Number One, Southwark Bridge, London SE1 9HL (☎ 01 873 3000, fax 01 236 9764)

CURTIS, Christopher Irvin (Chris); s of Harold George Curtis, of Norwich, and Gwendoline Lillian, *née* Ireland; *b* 24 Feb 1948; *Educ* Thorpe GS, Thorpe St Andrews Norwich; *m* 1, 30 April 1968 (m dis 1979), Wendy Diane, *née* Simmonds; 2 s (Simon b 1968, Patrick b 1970); m 2, 18 Aug 1979, Janet Elizabeth, *née* Gregory; *Career* order clerk Jarrold & Sons Ltd Norwich 1969-73, estimating and costing exec, Creaseys of Hertford 1973-74, political agent to John Pardoe MP 1974, print estimator Chapel River Press Andover 1975-77, sr prodn controller Macmillan Publishers Basingstoke 1977-83, self-employed print prodn conslt trading as CIC Print Tadley 1984-88, in partnership with Valerie A Shepard Prima Partnership (editorial servs and print prodn conslt) 1988-; Hants CC: memb 1981-, ldr Lib/Alliance/Social and Lib Democrat Gp 1983-; chm Tadley Town Cncl 1984-86 and 87- (memb 1983-); memb: ACC 1985-, Local Govt Int Bureau Policy Bd 1988-, rep body Cmmn Local Admin England (Local Ombudsman); sch govr: Burnham Copse Co Infant and Jr Schs 1981-88, Hurst Community Sch 1985-, Tadley Co Primary Sch 1988-; Tadley and Dist Community

Assoc 1982 (chm 1986 and 1987, pres 1988-); Tadley and District Citizens Advice Bureau Mngmnt ctee 1985-; *Recreations* reading, walking; *Style*— Chris Curtis, Esq; 38 Franklin Ave, Tadley, Basingstoke, Hants RG26 6ET (☎ 073 56 5682, fax 073 56 5682)

CURTIS, Maj Edward Philip; s of late Maj Gerald Edward Curtis, of Cwmbach Lodge, Glasbury-on-Wye, via Hereford; hp of kinsman, Sir William Curtis, 7 Bt; *b* 25 June 1940; *Educ* Bradfield, RMA Sandhurst; *m* 1978, Catherine Mary, da of Henry Armstrong, of Christchurch, NZ; 2 s (George b 1980, Patrick b 1986), 2 da (Henrietta, Clementine); *Career* Maj 16/5 The Queen's Royal Lancers, served Germany BAOR, Far East, Mid E, UK; Staff Offr 7 Armd Bde 1968-70, Adj 16/5 Lancers 1971, Sqn Ldr 16/5 Lancers 1971-73, Co Cdr RMA Sandhurst 1973-75, Staff Offr HQ 38 Gp RAF 1976-77, ret 1977; stockbroker Harris Allday Lea and Brooks; *Recreations* shooting, fishing, cricket, squash, philately, bridge; *Clubs* MCC, Free Foresters, I Zingari, Salmon and Trout; *Style*— Maj Edward Curtis; Lower Court, Bitterley, Ludlow, Shropshire SY8 3HP (☎ 0584 891052); office (☎ 0584 2391)

CURTIS, Most Rev (Ernest) Edwin; CBE (1976); s of Ernest John Curtis (d 1937), of Stalbridge, Dorset, and Zoe, *née* Tite (d 1927); *b* 24 Dec 1906; *Educ* Foster's Sch Sherborne, Univ of London, Royal Coll of Science (BSc, Dip Ed), Wells Theol Coll; *m* 1, 24 Dec 1937, Dorothy Anne (d 1965), da of John Hill; 1 s (Robert b 17 April 1940), 1 da (Audrey (Mrs Buckingham) b 16 Dec 1938); m 2, 7 Feb 1970, Evelyn Mary, da of Herbert Josling; *Career* sr maths master Lindisfarne Coll Westcliff-on-Sea 1928-31, civil chaplain and princ St Paul's Theol Coll Mauritius 1937-45; vicar: All Saints Portsea 1947-55, St John's Lockheath 1955-66; rural dean Alverstoke Portsmouth 1965-66; bishop: Mauritius and Seychelles 1966-73, Mauritius 1973-76; archbishop of Anglican Province of Indian Ocean 1973-76; *Style*— The Most Rev Archbishop Curtis, CBE; 5 Elizabeth Gardens, Havenstreet, Ryde, Isle of Wight PO33 4DU (☎ 0983 883049)

CURTIS, Lady; Joan Margaret; *née* Nicholson; o da of Reginald Nicholson, TD, JP (d 1952), and Lady Laura Margaret (d 1959), yr da of 9 Earl Waldegrave; *b* 19 May 1912; *m* 7 July 1934, Sir Peter Curtis, 6 Bt (d 1976); 1 s, 2 da; *Style*— Lady Curtis; Oak Lodge, Bank St, Bishops Waltham, Hants

CURTIS, John Gilbert; s of late Col A G Curtis; *b* 2 Oct 1932; *Educ* Charterhouse, Worcester Coll Oxford; *m* 1963, Susan Judith, *née* Whitefield; 2 s; *Career* Lt Royal Green Jackets; dir: Matheson and Co Ltd 1967-, Jamesons Chocolates 1980-; *Clubs* Gresham, Oriental; *Style*— John Curtis, Esq; Clayhurst, Odiham, Hants; Matheson and Co Ltd, 3 Lombard St, London EC3V 9AQ (☎ 01 480 6633)

CURTIS, Ken E; s of James Curtis (d 1932), and Rosina, *née* Hartley-Benton (d 1975); *b* 8 May 1919; *Educ* Eldon Sch, Hornsey Sch of Art, Instituto del Arte Florence Italy; *m* 21 June 1947, Anne, da of James Scully (d 1966); 1 s (Glenn b 14 Feb 1953), 1 da (Kim b 6 Oct 1956); *Career* WWII RCSTA Royal Mountain Regt and Med Regts 1939-46, mentioned in despatches Italy 1944; advertising agent Dorland Advertising (subsid) 1933-39, gen mangr Scientific Publicity 1946-48, md Skingle of the Strand We Design It Ltd 1948-68; dir: (jt) SF Ptnrs 1968-80, (account) Smedley McAlpine 1980-87, Lebeil Advertising 1987-; memb RA Comrades Assoc; Freeman City of London 1961, Liveryman Worshipful Co of Carmen 1961; MIPA; Polish Order of Merit (War Serv Polish Army in Italy 1944); *Recreations* wildlife, horticulture; *Clubs* City Livery, World Trade Centre; *Style*— Ken Curtis, Esq; 35 Brabourne Rise, Park Lanley, Beckenham BR3 2SQ; Lebeil Advertising, Crown House, 143-147 Regent St, London W1 (☎ 01 734 4521)

CURTIS, Lawrence Wesley; DFC (1943) and bar (1944); s of Alfred Curtis (d 1973), and Elizabeth Curtis *née* Powell; *b* 10 May 1921; *m* 11 May 1945, Barbara Mary, da of late Alfred Craven; 3 s (Ian b 1950, Martin b 1953, Simon b 1955); *Career* mil serv Sqdn Ldr RAF 1939-46, bomber cmd (UK), RAF serv flew with various Bomber Cmd Sqdns, inc 617 Sqdn (The Dam Busters); chm and md Curtis (Wool) Hldgs Ltd 1979- (dir 1958-), dir Curtis (Wool) Hldgs Ltd, Gore, NZ 1988, winner Queen's Award for Export Achievement; *Recreations* golf; *Clubs* RAF; *Style*— Lawrence Curtis, Esq, DFC; 'Greaghlone', East Morton, W Yorkshire; Curtis (Wool) Holdings Ltd, Auckland House, Bailey Hills Rd, Bingley, W Yorkshire (☎ Bradford 561317)

CURTIS, Sir (Edward) Leo; *b* 13 Jan 1907; *Educ* St Edmund's Coll Herts, St Patrick's Coll Goulburn NSW; *m* 1938, Elvira Lillian, da of Axel Prahl; 1 s, 3 da; *Career* Lord Mayor of Melbourne 1963-64 and 1964-65; chm Melbourne City Cncl; former state dep pres Winston Churchill Memorial Trust; kt 1965; *see Debrett's Handbook of Australia and New Zealand for further details*; *Recreations* golf, fishing, farming; *Style*— Sir Leo Curtis; 4 Armadalk St, Armadalk 3143, Victoria, Australia (☎ 509-4134)

CURTIS, Dr Leonard Frank; OBE (1989); s of Richard Herbert Curtis (d 1927), and Sarah Ann Maud *née* Miller (d 1969); *b* 2 Sept 1923; *Educ* Crypt Sch Gloucs, Univ of Southampton, Univ of Bristol (BSc, PhD); *m* 29 dec 1953, Diana Elizabeth Dorothy, da of Charles Thomas Oxenham (d 1968); 2 da (Sarah Curtis b 31 Oct 1954, Ruth Curtis b 14 Aug 1961); *Career* RAF 1942-46, cmmnd Navigator Flying Branch 1943, 89 Sqdn 1944-46, (sr India, Burma, Malaya); sr sci offr Soil Survey of England and Wales 1951-56, reader in geography and head of jt sch botany and geography Univ of Bristol 1956-78, chief offr Exmoor Nat Park 1978-88; vice-chm European Assoc of Remote Sensing laboratories 1987- (sec gen 1985-87); memb: Remote sensing soc, Br Soil Sci Soc; Hon sr res fell Univ of Bristol 1979; FRGS; *Books* Introduction to Environmental Remote Sensing (with E C Barrot (second edn 1982), Soils in the British Isles (1976), Environmental Remote Sensing (1974 and 1977); *Recreations* gardening, walking; *Clubs* Rotary (Exmoor); *Style*— Dr Leonard Curtis, OBE; Ley Croft, Bossington Lane, Porlock, Somerset TA 24 8HD

CURTIS, Richard Alexander John; s of Dato Richard John Froude Curtis (d 1987), and Marjorie, nee Snow; *b* 20 Nov 1951; *Educ* King's Sch Canterbury, Bristol Univ (LLB), London Business Sch; *Career* slr: Norton Rose Botterell & Roche London 1976-79, Jardine Matheson & Co Hong Kong 1979-83, dir Jardine Offshore Gp Singapore 1983-86, md Vase Ltd; memb: ctee Jermyn St Assoc, Law Soc; *Recreations* squash, tennis, golf, ceramics, water skiing; *Clubs* Oriental, RAC; *Style*— Richard Curtis, Esq; Vase Limited, 10 Clifton Road, London W9 1SS (☎ 01 286 2535, fax 01 266 3166)

CURTIS, Richard Herbert; s of Norman James Curtis, JP, (d 1983), and Dorothy Mary Curtis, *née* Willison; *b* 24 May 1933; *Educ* Shrewsbury, Oxford Univ (MA); *m* 1958, Gillian Morton, da of John Morton Cave (d 1969); 4 s (Rupert, Alexander, Jonathan, Benedict); *Career* barr Inner Temple 1958, rec Crown Ct 1974-, Queens Counsel 1977 hon rec City of Hereford 1981, bencher Inner Temple 1985; a pres Mental Health Review Tribunals 1983 formerly Lt The Sherwood Foresters (ME); *Recreations* viticulture, golf; *Style*— Richard Curtis, QC; 1 Kings Bench Walk, Temple, London EC4 (☎ 01 353 8436)

CURTIS, Very Rev Wilfred Frank; s of Wilfrid Arnold Curtis, MC (d 1984), and Flora May, *née* Burbidge (d 1980); *b* 24 Feb 1923; *Educ* Bishop Wordsworths Sch Salisbury, King's Coll London (AKC); *m* 1951, Muriel, da of Henry William Dover (d 1974); 2 s (Ian, Michael), 2 da (Hazel, Christine); *Career* Army 1941-47, Maj RA, India 1943-46; ordained 1952; area sec Church Missionary Soc, advsr in rural work 1955-65, home sec Church Missionary Soc 1965-74, provost of Sheffield 1974-88, provost emeritus 1988-; hon fell Sheffield City Poly 1980, hon canon Butere Cath Kenya 1982-; *Recreations* walking, natural history, photography; *Style*— The Very Rev Frank Curtis; Ashplant's Fingle Cottage, Drewsteighton, Exeter, Devon EX6 6QX (☎ 0647 21253)

CURTIS, Sir William Peter; 7 Bt (UK 1802), of Cullands Grove, Middlesex; s of Sir Peter Curtis, 6 Bt (d 1976); *b* 9 April 1935; *Educ* Winchester, Trinity Coll Oxford, RAC Cirencester; *Heir* kinsman, Maj Edward Curtis; *Career* late 16/5 Lancers; *Style*— Sir William Curtis, Bt; Oak Lodge, Bank St, Bishop's Waltham, Hants

CURTISS, Air Marshal Sir John Bagot; KCB (1980, CB 1979), KBE (1982); s of Maj E F B Curtiss, RFC; *b* 6 Dec 1924; *Educ* Radley, Wanganui Collegiate Sch NZ, Worcester Coll Oxford; *m* 1946, Peggy Drughorn, da of Edward Bowie; 3 s, 1 da; *Career* dir-gen orgn RAF 1975-77, Cmdt Staff Coll 1977-80, AOC No 18 Gp 1980-83; dir and chief exec Soc of Br Aerospace Cos 1984-, memb exec ctee Air League 1985-, pres Aircrew Assoc 1986-; FRSA; *Clubs* RAF, MCC, Pilgrims, Royal Lymington Yacht, Air League, RYS; *Style*— Air Marshal Sir John Curtiss, KCB, KBE; c/o Coutts and Co, 1 Old Park Lane, London W1Y 4BS

CURWEN, David Christian; s of John Ernest Curwen (d 1942), of Kent, and Blanche Lydia, *née* Whittaker (d 1972); *b* 30 Nov 1913; *Educ* Kings Sch Canterbury; *m* 1, 29 Jan 1944 (m dis 1949), Margaret Forsyth; 1 s adopted (Christopher b 1941); m 2, 23 Sept 1950, Helen Barbara Anne, da of Kyrle W Willans (d 1973); *Career* engr; with Short Bros Rochester 1938-39; fndr: David Curwen Ltd 1946, Curwen and Newbery Ltd 1952, conslt engr 1965-; *Recreations* fly fishing, building steam engines; *Style*— David C Curwen, Esq; The Cottage, Rectory Lane, All Cannings, nr Devizes, Wilts (☎ 038 086 204)

CURWEN, (David) Niel; s of Brian Murray Curwan (d 1954), and Dorothy, *née* Powell (d 1943); *b* 22 Jan 1930; *Educ* Rugby Sch, Gloucs Coll of Agric; *Career* Nat Serv Rifle Bde 1948-50; farmer; chm NFU Glos 1971, NFU rep jt advsy ctee Cotswold Area of Outstanding Nat Beauty 1972-, chm Area Trg Ctee Gloucs and North Avon 1974-, memb Bristol Avon Local Land Drainage Ctee Wessex Water Authy 1974-, memb cncl Gloucs Tst for Nature Conservation 1976-, govr Gloucs Coll of Agric 1978-, chm Nat Tst Local Ctee of Mgmnt for Minchinhampton Commons 1980-, pres Gloucs Farming and Wildlife Advsy Gp 1985- (chm 1980-85); dir: Three Avons Region Gp Traders' Assoc Ltd 1970-87, Brown's Estate Ltd 1981- (alternate dir 1964-81), chm 1988-; *Recreations* squash; *Style*— Niel Curwen, Esq; Yew Tree Cottage, Boundary Court, Woodchester, Stroud, Glos GL5 5PL (☎ 045 387 3580)

CURZON, Hon (Christian) Avril; da of Hon Francis Nathaniel Curzon (3 s of 4 Baron Scarsdale and yr bro of 1 and last Marquess Curzon of Kedleston, who was also cr Viscount Scarsdale) by his w Winifred Phyllis, da of Capt Christian and Lady Jane Combe (da of 3 Marquess Conyngham); yr sis of 3 Viscount Scarsdale; raised to rank title and precedence of Viscount's da 1980; *b* 24 April 1923; *Educ* Downham, Hatfield Heath Herts; *Career* pathology Dept Royal Northern Infirmary Inverness 1942-45; The British Racehorse 1949-57; E D O'Brien Organisation (Public Relations) 1961-77; *Recreations* photography, racing, gardening; *Style*— The Hon Avril Curzon; The House of the Pines, Virginia Avenue, Virginia Water, Surrey (☎ 099 04 3151)

CURZON, Hon David James Nathaniel; s (by 1 m) of 3 Viscount Scarsdale; *b* 3 Feb 1958; *Educ* Stowe; *m* 1981, Ruth, da of John Ernest Linton (d 1966), of Wavertree, Liverpool; 1 s (Andrew b 1986), 1 da (Emma b 1983); *Career* dir David Curzon Ltd; *Recreations* the Arts, golf, tennis; *Clubs* Lansdowne; *Style*— The Hon David Curzon; Chilton House, Lingfield Road, Wimbledon Village, London SW19 4PZ

CURZON, Hon Diana Geraline; da of late 2 Viscount Scarsdale; *b* 1934; *Style*— The Hon Diana Curzon; Cruz 47, Atico, Barcelona, Spain

CURZON, Lady Emma Charlotte; sister of 7 Earl Howe; *b* 10 Feb 1953; *Educ* Lawnside Great Malvern Worcs; *Career* SRN; *Style*— Lady Emma Curzon; Windsor Croft, Windsor Lane, Great Missenden, Bucks HP16 0DL

CURZON, Hon James Fergus Nathaniel; s (by 2 m) of 3 Viscount Scarsdale; *b* 12 Sept 1970; *Educ* Eton; *Style*— The Hon James Curzon; Kedleston Hall, Derby

CURZON, (Enid) Jane Victoria; *née* Fergusson; da of late Malcolm Mackenzie Fergusson, of Toronto Canada, and Enid Marie, *née* Forsythe (d 1953); *m* 1950 (m dis 1965), as his 2 w, Cdr (Chambré) George William Penn Curzon, RN (d 1976), s of Hon Frederick Graham Curzon (2 s of 3 Earl Howe); 1 s (7 Earl Howe), 1 da (Emma); *Career* serv WRNS 1943-45; radio actress; businesswoman; *Style*— Mrs Jane Curzon; Windsor Croft, Windsor Lane, Great Missenden, Bucks

CURZON, Hon Peter Ghislain Nathaniel; s (by 1 m) and h of 3 Viscount Scarsdale; *b* 6 Mar 1949; *Educ* Ampleforth ; *m* 1983, Mrs Karen Lynne Osbourne, *née* Jackson; 1 da (Danielle b 1983); *Career* landowner (50 acres); *Recreations* The Cresta Run, skiing, golf; *Style*— The Hon Peter Curzon; Battle Barn Stud Farm, Sedlescombe, E Sussex

CURZON, Hon Richard Francis Nathaniel; s (by 2 m) of 3 Viscount Scarsdale; *b* 30 Jan 1969; *Educ* Shiplake; *Style*— The Hon Richard Curzon; Kedleston Hall, Derby

CUSACK, Henry Vernon; CMG (1955), CBE (1947); s of Henry Edward Cusack, of Co Dublin (d 1954), chief mech engr Midland Gt Western Rlwy of Ireland, designed Royal Train for visit of TM King Edward VII and Queen Alexandra to Ireland 1903; ggs of Dr James William Cusack, Pres RCS (Ireland), Surg-in-Ordinary to HM Queen Victoria in Ireland (d 1863); mother, Constance Louisa (d 1932), eldest da of Col Edward Vernon, DL, of Clontarf Castle, co Dublin; *b* 26 June 1895; *Educ* Aravon Sch; *Career* Capt RASC attached RGA in France 1914-18 War, Belgium and N Russia: Colonial Audit Serv (later Overseas Audit Serv): entered 1920, Sierra Leone 1920-22, Nigeria 1922-28, Nyasaland 1928-33, asst dir in London 1933-37, dir of audit Gold Coast Colony (now Ghana) 1937-46, dep dir-gen of Overseas Audit Serv 1946-55; govr King's Hosp Sch Dublin (chm 1964-69); FRGS; Coronation Medal 1953; *Clubs* Naval and Military, Royal St George Yacht; *Style*— Henry Cusack, CMG, CBE; Our Lady's Manor, Bulloch Castle, Dalkey, Co Dublin

CUSACK, Mark Paul John; s of Capt Robert Joseph Cusack, of Dublin, and Olive Mary, *née* Byrne; *b* 28 Feb 1958; *Educ* St Paul's Sch Dublin, Trinity Coll Dublin (BBS); *Career* CA: Arthur Andersen & Co 1979-83; dir and head UK res Hoare Govett Securities 1988- (conglomerates analyst 1985-88, construction analyst 1983-85); *Recreations* squash, tennis; *Clubs* Queens, Fitzwilliam (Dublin); *Style*— Mark P Cusack, Esq; 4 Broadgate, London EC2M 7LE (☎ 01 601 0101, fax 01 256 8500, telex 297801)

CUSHING, Peter Wilton; OBE (1989); s of George Edward Cushing (d 1956) and Nellie Marian, *née* King (d 1961); *b* 26 May 1913; *Educ* Shoreham GS Sussex, Purley County Secondary Sch Surrey; *m* 10 May 1943, Violet Helene (Helen, d 1971), da of Ernest Beck (d 1951); *Career* actor; in repertory 1936, Hollywood 1939-41, toured Forces camps with ENSA 1942-44, Old Vic tour of Australasia with Sir Laurence Oliver 1948 (Richard III, The Skin of Our Teeth, The School for Scandal) and Oliver's Festival Season 1951 (Caesar and Cleopatra, Anthony and Cleopatra); TV incl: Nineteen Eighty Four (1954), "Sherlock Holmes" series 1969; Films incl: Chumps at Oxford (1939) H Hamlet 1948, Star Wars 1977, Top Secret 1982; Hammer Films 1957-73 incl: Curse of Frankenstein 1957, Dracula 1958, Hound of the Baskervilles 1959, Frankenstein Must Be Destroyed 1969, The Satanic Rites of Dracula 1973; *Books* Peter Cushing, An Autobiography (1986), Past Forgetting - Memoirs of the Hammer Years (1988); *Recreations* painting, reading; *Style*— Peter Cushing, Esq, OBE; Whitstable, Kent; C/O John Redway & Assoc, 16 Berners St, London W1P 3DD

CUSHING, Robert; JP (W Sussex 1959); s of Arthur Robert Cushing (d 1956), of Silverdale, Rowlands Road, Worthing, and Ethel Florence, *née* Jarvis (d 1976); *b* 19 July 1918; *Educ* Hardenwick Sch Harpenden Herts, Wykeham House Sch Worthing, Brighton Coll; *Career* admitted slr Supreme Court of Judicature 1946, sr ptnr Dixon Holmes & Cushing Slrs 1959- (joined as articled clerk 1936); Worthing & Dist Cncl of Social Serv (now Worthing Area Guild for Voluntary Servs): hon slr 1946-, chm 1964-75, vice-pres 1975; govr and tstee Queen Alexandra Hosp Home for Disabled Ex-Servicemen (hon slr to tstees); elected chm of Bench Worthing Petty Sessional Div 1985-88 (formerly asst chm, dep chm); memb: Law Soc, Sussex Law Soc, Worthing Law Soc (pres 1958-59); hon life vice pres Lawn Tennis Assoc 1988, pres Sussex Co Lawn Tennis Assoc; *Recreations* lawn tennis; *Clubs* West Worthing (pres); *Style*— Robert Cushing, Esq, JP; 31 Balcombe Ct, W Parade, Worthing, Sussex BN11 3PL (☎ 0903 206557); Dixon Holmes & Cushing, 12 Liverpool Gdns, Worthing, Sussex BN11 1RY (☎ 0903 38273, fax 0903 823014)

CUSSINS, Peter Ian; s of Philip Cussins (d 1976), of Newcastle upon Tyne, and Doreen Cussins; *b* 18 Mar 1949; *Educ* Bootham Sch York, London Univ (BSc); *m* 18 Sept 1973, Vandra Jean, da of Maynard Stubley, of Alnmouth, Northumberland; 1 s (Jabin b 1980), 3 da (Abigail b 1976, Alexandra b 1978, Lydia b 1983); *Career* chm: Lemmington Estates Ltd 1973-, Cussins Investmt Properties Ltd 1981-, Cussins Commercial Devpts Ltd 1981-, Cussins Green plc 1986, chm Cussins Property Gp plc 1981-; *Recreations* golf, fishing; *Style*— Peter I Cussins, Esq; Morwick Hall, Acklington, Morpeth, Northumberland NE65 9DG; 27 Egerton Terre, London SW3; Cussins Property Group plc, 1/2 Rutland Gardens, London SW1 (☎ 01 584 1424)

CUSSONS, Jeremy Alexander; s of Alexander Stockton Cussons (d 1986), and Wendy Grace Cussons; *b* 2 Sept 1950; *Educ* Marlborough; *m* 1, 5 Feb 1970, Renee Elizabeth, da of Arnold Hossman (d 1974); 1 s (Leo b 1971), 1 da (Angela b 1973); m 2, 4 Sept 1982, Rebecca Ann, da of Reginald Mercado, OBE (d 1985); 1 s (Sebastian b 1983); *Career* farmer; estate mangr; *Recreations* reading, tennis, charity fundraising; *Style*— Jeremy Cussons, Esq; Ballacotch Manor, Crosby, IOM (☎ 0624 851712)

CUST, Hon Peregrine Edward Quintin; s and h of 7 Baron Brownlow; *b* 9 July 1974; *Style*— The Hon Peregrine Cust

CUSTIS, Patrick James; CBE (1981); er s of Alfred William Custis (d 1945), of Dublin, and Any Custis; *b* 19 Mar 1921; *Educ* The High School Dublin; *m* 1954, Rita, yr da of Percy William Rayner (d 1968), of Bognor Regis; 1 s; *Career* accountant with Josolyne Miles Co CAs 1946-51, RTZ 1951-55, Glynwed Int 1956-67; joined Guest Keen and Nettlefolds (GKN) 1967, fin dir of worldwide gp 1974-81, ret; dir: New Court Property Fund Mngrs (Rothchilds Co) 1978-, Lloyds Bank (Birmingham and W Midlands Regnl Bd) 1979-, Assoc Heat Servs 1981-, Wolseley 1982-, Leigh Interests (dep chm) 1982-, Birmingham Technology 1983-, MCD Gp (chm) 1983-86, Wyko Gp plc 1985-, Benford Concrete Machinery plc 1985-86, dir Prisons Bd (Home Office) 1980-85; co-opted memb Cncl ICAEW 1979-85, chm Midlands Indust Gp of Fin Dirs 1977-80; part-time memb Monopolies and Mergers Cmmn 1981-82; liveryman Worshipful Co of Chartered Accountants in England and Wales; FCA, FCMA, FCIS, JDipMA, FRSA; *Recreations* gardening, walking, reading; *Clubs* Royal Overseas League, Lansdowne; *Style*— Patrick Custis, Esq, CBE; West Barn, Westmancote, Tewkesbury, Gloustershire GL20 7ES (☎ 0684 72865)

CUSWORTH, (George Robert) Neville; s of George Ernest Cusworth (d 1966), of Bad Homburg, Germany, and Violet Helene, *née* Cross (d 1969); *b* 14 Oct 1938; *Educ* St Paul's, Keble Coll Oxford (BA, MA), Courtauld Inst of Art History (Cert in Euro Art), Stanford Univ California USA; *m* 6 Sept 1963, (Vivien) Susan, da of Philip Glynn Grylls, of Worthing, Sussex; 1 s (Nicholas b 20 March 1964), 1 da (Juliet b 30 Jan 1966); *Career* chm Butterworth Law Publishers Ltd 1986- (md 1982-86), chief exec Butterworth Gp 1987; dir int Electronic Publishing Res Centre 1985-88, cncl memb Publishers Assoc 1988-, chm of bd Book House Trg Centre 1989-; tstee Camden Festival Tst 1986-; Freeman City of London 1982, Liveryman Worshipful Co Stationers and Newspapers 1984; FInstD; *Books* Halsbury's Laws of England (published edn 4 1980-86); *Recreations* theatre, heraldry, church crawling, walking; *Clubs* Garrick; *Style*— Neville Cusworth, Esq; 4 Old Close Dock, Kew Green, Richmond, Surrey TW9 3BL; Butterworths, Borough Green, Sevenoaks, Kent TN15 8PH (☎ 0732 884 567)

CUTFORTH, John Ashlin; s of Edwin Henry (d 1950), and Cecilia, *née* King (d 1957); *b* 8 May 1911; *Educ* Ashby de la Zouch GS, UCL (BA); *m* Isabel Laura, da of May Thomas Eacott (d 1934); *Career* Coldstream Gds 1939-41: Staff Capt Intelligence Corps 1941-49; Eng Sch Château d'Oex Switzerland sch master: St Cyprian's Eastbourne 1935-39, Worksop Coll 1948-49; HM inspr of Schs 1949-51, memb bd dirs Basil Blackwell Publishers Oxford 1954-81 (joined 1951); external examiner of English Colls of Educn Univ of Bristol 1960-70, memb Oxford's educnl ctee 1980-85; reader C of E 1967, chm govrs Cooper Sch Bicester 1982-; *Books* English in The Primary School (1952, 1959), Mystery Magic and Adventure (1956), Children and Books (with SH Battersby 1962), Light and Shadow (ed with H R Thomas and N Thomson 1968, 1970, 1975); *Clubs* Greyhound, Marsh Gibbon; *Style*— John Cutforth, Esq; Home Close, Townsend, Marsh Gibbon, Bicester OX6 0EY (☎ 086 97 292)

CUTHBERT, Barry Gordon; *Career* CA; co sec Grange Motors (Brentwood) Ltd 1980, dir 1981; AICA, FICA; *Style*— Barry G Cuthbert, Esq; The Glen, Warley Road, Great Warley, Brentwood, Essex CM13 3HT; Grange Motors (Brentwood) Ltd, Brook Street, Brentwood, Essex (☎ 0277 216161, fax 0277 220187)

CUTHBERT, Mark William Harcourt; s of Nicholas Harcourt Cuthbert, of Dorking, Surrey, and Pauline Barbara, *née* Pledge (d 1984); *b* 14 August 1954; *Educ* City of London Freemen's Sch, Kingston Poly Sch of Architecture (BA, Dip Arch); *m* 10 May 1986, Moya Christine, da of John Patrick Grey Walsh (d 1986); *Career* architect and designer; dir Domus Design Ltd; *Recreations* musician (classical guitar), painter; *Style*— Mark W H Cuthbert, Esq; Studio 3, Mandeville Courtyard, 142 Battersea Park Rd, London SW11 (☎ 01 627 4017)

CUTHBERT, Stephen Colin; s of Colin Samuel Cuthbert (d 1975), formerly of Sanderstead, Surrey, and Helen Mary Cuthbert, *née* Scott (d 1986); *b* 27 Oct 1942; *Educ* Trinity Sch of John Whitgift, Bristol Univ (BSc); *m* 1, 22 Feb 1969, Jane Elizabeth (m diss 1986), da of David Bluett (decd), of Sydney Australia); 2 s (Simon b 1974, Ian b 1974), 1 da (Nicola b 1971); m 2, 27 Oct 1987, Susan Melanie, da of Kenneth Gray, of Brighton; stepchildren 1 s (Christopher b 1982), 2 da (Joanna b 1971, Nicola b 1974); *Career* md Brent Chemicals International plc, appointed to present position 1980 (dir 1976); *Recreations* cruising, sailing, family interests; *Style*— Stephen Cuthbert, Esq; Ridgeway, Iver, Bicks SL0 9JJ (☎ 0753 651812, fax 0753 652460)

CUTHBERT, Lady Victoria Lucy Diana; *née* Percy; 2 da of 10 Duke of Northumberland, KG, GCVO, TD, PC (d 1988); *b* 19 April 1949; *m* 1975, (John) Aidan Cuthbert; 1 s (David Hugh b 1987), 3 da (Alice Rose b 1978, Lucy Caroline b 1982, Mary Belinda b 1984); *Style*— Lady Victoria Cuthbert; Beaufront Castle, Hexham, Northumberland

CUTHBERT, William Moncrieff; DL (Stirling and Falkirk 1984); s of Alan Dalrymple Cuthbert and Elspeth Moncrieff, *née* Mitchell; *b* 22 June 1936; *Educ* Shrewsbury; *m* 1960, Caroline Jean Balfrur Mitchell; 2 s, 1 da; *Career* md Clyde Shipping Co Ltd; dir: The Murray Johnstone Investmt Tsts, Scottish Amicable Life Assur Soc; chm exec ctee Nat Tst for Scotland 1984-; mem Royal Co of Archers (Queen's Body Guard for Scotland); *Style*— William Cuthbert Esq, DL; Clyde Shipping Co Ltd, 78 Carlton Place, Glasgow G5 (☎ (041 429) 2181, telex 777923)

CUTHBERTSON, Eric Ian; s of Ranald Ker Cuthbertson (d 1983), of Ravelston Brae, Ravelston Dykes Rd, Edinburgh, and Agnes Thomson, *née* Mitchell (d 1967); *b* 17 Nov 1934; *Educ* Edinburgh Acad; Sedbergh; Edinburgh Univ; *m* 17 Nov 1962, Shona Campbell Aitken, da of Francis Aitken Wright (d 1959); 1 da (Fiona b 1967); *Career* writer to the Signet and Slr 1963-;dir: Scottish Equitable Life Assurance Soc , Scottish Bldg Soc (chm), Invertiviot Properties (Edinburgh) Ltd ; *Recreations* shooting, fishing, mountain walking, gardening; *Clubs* Bruntsfield Links Golf, Royal Scottish Automobile; *Style*— Eric I Cuthbertson, Esq; 102 Ravelston Dykes, Edinburgh (☎ 031 337 7629); 21 Melville St, Lane, Edinburgh EH3 7QB (☎ 031 225 7500, telex 727149)

CUTHBERTSON, Sir Harold Alexander; s of Thomas Alexander Cuthbertson and Vera Rose Cuthbertson; *b* 16 Nov 1911; *Educ* Hutchins Sch Hobart; *m* 1937, Jean Westbrook; 2 da; *Career* md Blundstone Pty Ltd 1957-, pres Savings Bank of Tasmania; pres Tas Chamber of Manufrs 1964-67, vice-pres Assoc of Aust chambers of Manufrs 1966-67; memb Cwlth Immigration Planning Cncl 1968-75; warden Marine Bd of Hobart 1963-75; dir Tasman Devpt Authy; kt 1983; *Recreations* bowls, fishing; *Style*— Sir Harold Cuthbertson; 3 David Avenue, Sandy Bay, Tas 7005, Australia (☎ 002 251619)

CUTLER, Hon Sir Charles Benjamin; KBE (1973) ED (1960); s of George Hamilton Cutler, of Orange NSW (d 1971, family arrived 1836), and Elizabeth Cutler (d 1977, family arrived 1817); *b* 20 April 1918; *Educ* Orange Public Schs; *m* 1943, Dorothy Stella, OBE (1976), da of Joseph Pascoe (d 1941); 3 s, 1 da; *Career* dep premier and min for Education and Science (NSW) 1965-72, dep premier and min for Local Govt and Highways 1972-75, min for Tourism 1974-75; *see Debrett's Handbook of Australia and New Zealand for further details*; *Style*— Sir Charles Cutler, KBE ED; 52 Kite St, Orange, NSW 2800, Australia (☎ 62 6418 or Sydney 20 577)

CUTLER, Lady Helen Gray Annetta; AC (1980); da of David Eric Morris, of Bellevue Hill, Sydney (d 1969), and Elsie Veronica, *née* Clare (d 1981); ggda of David Morris (b Wales 1813), who arrived Sydney 1849; *b* 5 May 1923; *Educ* Sydney C of E Girls' GS; *m* 1946, Sir (Arthur) Roden Cutler, VC, AK, KCMG, KCVO, CBE, *qv*; 4 s; *Career* Lt AWAS WWII 1944, Hon Col WRAAC 1967-85; formerly pres: Aust Red Cross Soc NSW Divn 1966-81, vice-pres Girl Guides Assoc NSW; pres Save the Children Fund (NSW) Div; DStJ (1977, CStJ 1965); *Recreations* tennis, swimming, reading, gardening; *Clubs* Queen's (Sydney); *Style*— Lady Cutler, AC; 22 Ginahgulla Rd, Bellevue Hill, NSW 2023, Australia (☎ 326 1233)

CUTLER, Sir Horace Walter; OBE (1963), DL (Gtr London 1981); eldest s of Albert Benjamin Cutler and Mary Ann Cutler; *b* 28 July 1912; *Educ* Harrow GS; *m* 1957, Christiane, da of Dr Klaus Muthesius; 1 s, 3 da (and 1 s of previous m); *Career* former Mayor of Harrow, ldr of Oppn GLC 1974-77 (dep ldr 1964-67 and 1973-74), memb Harrow West 1964-, ldr: GLC 1977-81, Oppn 1981-82, contested (C) Willesden East 1970; kt 1979; *Books* The Cutler Files (autobiog, 1982); *Style*— Sir Horace Cutler, OBE, DL; Hawkswood, Hawkswood Lane, Gerrards Cross, Bucks (☎ 3182)

CUTLER, Keith Charles; s of Henry Walter Cutler, of Woburn Sands, Bucks, and Evelyn Constance, *née* Butcher; *b* 14 August 1950; *Educ* Rickmansworth GS, Cedars Sch, Bristol Univ (LLB); *m* 30 Aug 1975, Judith Mary, da of Ronald Philip Haddy (d 1974); 1 s (James b 1982), 1 da (Anna b 1985); *Career* barr; called to Bar 1972; memb: Hon Soc Lincoln's Inn; FSJ; *Clubs* RAC; *Style*— Keith Cutler, Esq; 3 Pump Ct, Temple, London EC4Y 2AJ (☎ 01 353 0711, fax 01 353 3319)

CUTLER, Sir (Arthur) Roden; VC (1941), AK (1981), KCMG (1965), KCVO (1970), CBE (1957); s of Arthur William Cutler, of Bathurst and Sydney (d 1935, family arrived as free settlers in 1833), and Ruby Daphne, *née* Pope (d 1974); *b* 24 May 1916,, in Manly NSW; *Educ* Sydney HS, Univ of Sydney (BEcon); *m* 1946, Helen Gray Annetta, AC, *qv*; 4 s (David, Anthony, Richard, Mark); *Career* Lt AIF 1939-45 Syria, (lost leg (VC)); Hon Air Cdre: 22 Sqdn (ret 1981) RAAF; Public Tst Off NSW 1935-42, state sec RSS and AILA NSW (now RSL) 1942-43 (state pres ACT 1958), asst dep dir of Security Serv NSW 1943, asst cmmr for Cwlth (Repatriation Dept)

1943-46; Aust high cmmr: NZ 1946-52, Ceylon 1952-55; HM's Aust Min to Egypt 1955-56, Sec-Gen SEATO Cncl and Mil Advsrs' Meeting Canberra 1957, chief of protocol Dept of External Affairs Canberra 1957-58, Aust high cmmr Pakistan 1959-61, Aust rep to Somali Republic Ind Celebrations 1960, Aust consul-gen NY 1961-65, Aust delegate to UN Gen Assembly 1963 and 1964, Aust rep on Fifth Ctee UN 1963-65, Aust ambass Netherlands 1965-66, govr of NSW 1966-81 (longest term), memb bd Rothmans Hldgs Ltd (Australia) Ltd 1981-, memb bd of NSW Permanent Tstee Co 1981-; chm: Air NSW 1981-, of the State (formerly Rural) Bank 1981-86; patron and life memb of numerous societies, clubs and orgns; Hon LLD (Sydney), Hon DSc (NSW), Hon DSC (Newcastle), Hon D Lit (U of New England), Hon D Lit Wollongong, Hon FCA; KStJ 1965, Knight of Justice 1967; *Recreations* swimming, fly fishing; *Style—* Sir Roden Cutler, VC, AK, KCMG, KCVO, CBE; 22 Ginahgulla Rd, Bellevue Hill, NSW 2023, Australia (☎ 326 1233)

CUTTLE, Geoffrey; s of Ralph Cuttle (d 1972), of Essex, and Ethel Maud Piper (d 1988); *b* 16 Oct 1933; *Educ* Malvern Coll, Downing, Cambridge (MA); *m* 30 Sept 1961, Elizabeth Mary, da of Thomas James Copeland, of Essex; 1 s (Edward William John b 1967), 2 da (Mary Linsdell b 1964, Elizabeth Ann b 1966); *Career* mangr dvpt performance, ICL 1984-; held various mgmnt positions with ICL 1956-, FBCS, FIQA, CEng, MBIM; published Executive Programs and Operating Systems (1970); *Recreations* croquet, wine, collecting; *Clubs* Royal Inst of GB, Ski (GB); *Style—* Geoffrey Cuttle, Esq; Lynwood, 35 Mount Hermon Rd, Woking, Surrey GU22 7UN (☎ Woking 04862 62808); ICL, Lovelace Road, Bracknell, Berks RG12 4SN (☎ 0344 424842)

CUTTS, Katherine; *b* 30 Oct 1942; *m* 23 March 1963, (George) Nigel Cutts; 3 da (Sara Christabel b 14 Feb 1964, Louise Victoria b 8 Jan 1966, Charlotte Emma b 31 Aug 1968); *Career* chm and co sec Clower Properties 1985-; memb Indus Tbnl Panel 1986; memb: Quorn Hunt Pony Club (local orgnsr), Notts Bldg Preservation Tst Ltd, Parish cncl 1972-79, Rushcliffe BC 1979-89; Candidate Notts CC 1989; *Recreations* hunting, conservation, politics; *Style—* Mrs Katherine Cutts; Normanton House, Old Melton Rd, Nomanton-on-the-Wolds, nr Plumtree, Notts NG12 5NN (☎ 0602 2495); Castle House, 74 St James's St, Nottingham NG1 6FJ

CYPRUS AND THE GULF, Bishop of 1987-; Rt Rev John Edward Brown; s of Edward Brown and Muriel Brown; *b* 13 July 1930; *Educ* Wintringham GS Grimsby, Kelham Theol Coll (BD); *m* 1956, Rosemary, *née* Wood; 1 s ; *Career* ordained: deacon 1955, priest; master St George's Sch Jerusalem, curate St George's Cath Jerusalem, chaplain Amman Jordan 1954-57, curate i/c All Saints Reading 1957-60, missionary and chaplain All Saints Cath Khartoum Sudan 1960-64; vicar: Stewkley Buckingham 1964-69, St Luke's Maidenhead 1969-73, Bracknell Berks 1973-77; rural dena Sonning 1974-77, archdeacon of Berks 1978-86, episcopal canon St George's Cath Jerusalem 1987-; *Recreations* walking, Middle East and African studies; *Style—* The Rt Rev the Bishop of Cyprus and the Gulf; P O Box 2075, Nicosia, Cyprus

CZERNIN, Hon Mrs; Hon (Mary) Hazel Caridwen; *née* Scott-Ellis; da of 9 Baron Howard de Walden and 5 Baron Seaford and Lady Howard de Walden, *née* Countess Irene Harrach (d 1975); *b* 12 August 1935; *m* 20 Nov 1957, Joseph Czernin, s of late Count Franz Josef Czernin (of the family granted title of Count (*Reichsgraf*) of the Holy Roman Empire by the Emperor Ferdinand III 1652 with the predicate 'Hoch und Wohlgeboren (High and well-born)'); 1 s, 5 da; *Career* co-heiress to Barony of Howard de Walden; *Style—* The Hon Mrs Czernin; White Oak House, Highclere, Newbury, Berks RG15 9RJ

CZERNIN, Maud, Countess; Maud Sarah; da of Ronald Hamilton, OBE (d 1958; s of Rt Hon Lord George Hamilton, GCSI, JP, 3 s of 1 Duke of Abercorn, KG, PC; Lord George Hamilton m Lady Maud Lascelles, CI, da of 3 Earl of Harewood), and Florence Marguerite (the actress 'Sarah Brooke'; d 1959), da of Maj John Hannah; *b* 4 April 1917; *m* 4 Nov 1939 (m dis 1947), Count Manfred Maria Edmund Czernin, DSO, MC, DFC (d 1962), yst s of Count Otto Czernin; 1 s, 1 da; *Style—* Maud, Countess Czernin; 1 Egerton Gdns, SW3

CZIRJAK, Gyula; s of Gyula Czirják (d 1975), and Etelka, *née* Ruber (d 1982); *b* 7 Jan 1929; *Educ* Piarist GS Budapest, Univ of Econs Budapest; *m* 19 March 1955, Marta, da of Ferenc Voros (d 1971); *Career* asst to prof Univ of Econs Budapest 1951-54, various posts Nat Bank of Hungary Budapest 1954- (latterly gen mangr), dep chm Hungarian Int Bank Ltd London 1973-77 and 1983-; memb Foreign Banks Assoc London; *Recreations* photography, gardening, reading; *Clubs* RAC; *Style—* Gyula Czirják, Esq; Princes house, 95 Gresham St, London EC2V 7LU (☎ 01 606 5371, fax 01 606 8565, telex 887206)

D

D'ABO, Lady Ursula Isabel; *née* Manners; da of 9 Duke of Rutland (d 1940); *b* 8 Nov 1916; *m* 1, 25 July 1943 (m dis 1948), Anthony Freire Marreco, late Lt RNVR; m 2, 22 Nov 1951, Robert Erland Nicolai d'Abo (d 1970); 2 s, 1 da; *Career* a train bearer to HM The Queen (now Queen Elizabeth the Queen Mother) at the Coronation of HM King George VI 1937; Coronation Medal 1937; *Style*— Lady Ursula d'Abo; 29 Kensington Sq, London W8; West Wratting Park, Cambs

D'AETH, Prof Richard; s of Walter D'Aeth and Marion Edith Turnbull; *b* 3 June 1912; *Educ* Bedford Sch, Emmanuel Coll Cambridge (PhD), Harvard Univ (AM); *m* 1943, Pamela Straker; 2 da; *Career* prof of educn Univ Coll of West Indies 1952-58, Univ of Exeter 1958-77; pres Hughes Hall Cambridge 1978-84; *Style*— Prof Richard D'Aeth; Hughes Hall, Cambridge CB1 2EW (☎ 0223 352866)

D'ALBIAC, James Charles Robert; s of Air Marshal Sir John D'Albiac, KCVO, KBE, CB, DSO (d 1963), and Lady Sibyl Mary, *née* Owen; *b* 14 Oct 1935; *Educ* Winchester, Magdalen Coll Oxford (BA); *m* 2 May 1964, Carole Ann, da of Robert Percy Garner (d 1988); 1 da (Jane Sibyl b 22 Sept 1966); *Career* Nat Serv 2 Lt Lincolnshires serv Malaya 1954-56; stockbroker, ptnr Rowe & Pitman stockbrokers London 1968-86, dir Mercury Asset Mgmnt 1986-; memb Int Stock Exchange, AMSIA; *Recreations* golf, chess; *Clubs* Berkshire Golf, United Oxford & Cambridge Univ; *Style*— James D'Albiac, Esq; 65 Pont Street, London SW1; Mercury Asset Management, 33 King William Street, London EC4 (☎ 01 280 2197, 0844 278 961, fax 0844 279 106, car tel 0836 242 306)

D'AMBRUMENIL, Christopher Hugh; s of Lewis d'Ambrumenil (d 1968); *b* 17 Jan 1926; *Educ* Wellington; *m* 1962, Cathleen Marion, *née* Speight; *Career* WWII Capt Coldstream Gds; memb Hexham RDC 1964-74, chm gen purposes ctee Northumberland CC 1971-81, hon alderman Northumberland CC 1981, memb Northern RHA 1979-83, chm Pyman Bell & Co 1980-86; *Clubs* Cavalry and Guards', Norfolk (Norwich); *Style*— Christopher d'Ambrumenil, Esq; Church Court, Kettlestone, Norfolk NR21 0AU (☎ 032 877 783)

D'AMBRUMENIL, David Philip; s of Sir Philip d'Ambrumenil (d 1974), and late Gertrude Merriel, da of C H Bailey, of Newport, Mon; *b* 1 August 1930; *Educ* Rugby, New Coll Oxford; *m* 1983, Sarah Caroline, er da of Alan Hodson and Rita, *née* Ropner; 1 da (Sophie b 1985); *Career* joined Gardner Mountain and d'Ambrumenil 1952 (dir 1956); following merger of Gardner Mountain and Hogg Robinson joined bd of Staplegreen and Hogg Robinson Gardner Mountain, resigned 1969, formed Seascope Hldgs 1970 (dep chm Seascope Hldgs), chm Seascope Insur Servs, following merger of Seascope Hldgs and Henry Ansbacher joined bd of Henry Ansbacher 1983, resigned from Henry Ansbacher and Seascope Insur Servs and formed ABC Insur Servs Ltd 1985, acquired control of J Besso & Co Ltd and apptd chm; resigned from ABC Insur Serv Ltd and J Besso and Co Ltd and formed Lionspring Enterprises Ltd 1986; *Recreations* skiing, shooting; *Clubs* Turf, Buck's, Corviglia, Travellers; *Style*— David d'Ambrumenil, Esq; 24 Milner St, London SW3; Lionspring Enterprises Ltd, 81 Piccadilly, London W1 (☎ 01 491 1270, telex 291860, fax 01 493 6091)

D'AVIGDOR-GOLDSMID, Lady; Rosemary Margaret; eldest da of Lt-Col Rice Iltyd Charles Nicholl, TD (d 1950); *b* 22 July 1910; *m* 1, 29 Oct 1931 (m dis 1934), Sir Peter Horlick, 3 Bt (d 1958); m 2, 23 Feb 1940, Maj Sir Henry Joseph d'Avigdor-Goldsmid, 2 Bt, DSO, MC, TD, MP (C) Walsall S 1955-74 (d 1976); 2 da (1 decd); *Recreations* racing (horses: Emrys, Tebbitto); *Style*— Lady d'Avigdor-Goldsmid; The Old Laundry, Tudeley, nr Tonbridge, Kent (☎ 0732 352314); 2 Eaton Mansions, Cliveden Place, London SW1 (☎ 01 730 3034)

D'ERLANGER, Lady Caroline Mary; *née* Cholmondeley; 3 and yst da of 6 Marquess of Cholmondeley, GCVO, MC, *qv*; *b* 10 April 1952; *m* 1982, Rodolphe d'Erlanger, s of late Leo Frederic Alfred d'Erlanger (d 1978); 2 s (Leo Frederic Hugh b 1983, Robert b 1987); *Style*— Lady Caroline d'Erlanger

D'ERLANGER, Hon Mrs; Hon (Mary) Elizabeth Josephine; *née* Pellew; da of Viscount Exmouth (d 1970), and his wife Maria-Luisa (Marquesa de Olias in Spain), widow of Don Gonzalo Alvarez Builla y Alvera, and da of late Luis de Urquijo, Marques de Amurrio, and of the Marquesa de Zarreal, of Madrid; *b* 16 Mar 1947; *m* 4 Jan 1969, Robin Gerard d'Erlanger, only s of Sir Gerard John Regis Leo d'Erlanger, CBE (d 1962); 2 s (Gerard b 1970, Hugh b 1976), 3 da (Josephine b 1972, Marietta b 1974, Emilia b 1982); *Recreations* sailing (yacht 'Five Fishes'); *Clubs* Buck's; *Style*— The Hon Mrs d'Erlanger; Manor Farm House, Compton Valence, Dorchester, Dorset (☎ 03083 462)

D'EYNCOURT; see Tennyson d'Eyncourt

D'JANOEFF, Alexander Constantine Basil; s of Constantine V D'Janoeff (d 1986), of Windsor, and Margarita A, *née* Rotinoff; *b* 27 March 1952; *Educ* Eton, Strasbourg Univ France, Oxford Poly ; *Career* qualified CA 1977; Coopers & Lybrand: joined 1972, Paris 1977-80, London 1980-85 (seconded Schroder Ventures (mgmnt buy out fund) 1985-), corporate fin dept 1986-, ptnr 19860, dir mergers and acquisitions Europe 1989-; FCA, FRSA; *Recreations* mountain walking in Switzerland; *Clubs* Brooks's, Annabel's, Guards Polo; *Style*— Alexander D'Janoeff, Esq; Coopers & Lybrand, Plumtree Ct, London EC4 (☎ 01 822 4696, fax 01 822 4631)

D'OYLY, Hadley Gregory; s and h of Sir Nigel D'Oyly, 14 Bt; *b* 1956; *m* 28 Oct 1978 (m dis 1982), Margaret Mary, *née* Dent; *Style*— Hadley D'Oyly, Esq; Flat B, 37 New North Rd, London N1 6JB

D'OYLY, Sir Nigel Hadley Miller; 14 Bt (E 1663) of Shottisham, Norfolk; s of Sir Hastings D'Oyly, 11 Bt (d 1950), and his 2 w Evelyn; suc half bro Sir John Rochfort D'Oyly, 13 Bt (d 1986); *b* 6 July 1914; *Educ* Radley, Sandhurst; *m* 27 Oct 1939, Dolores (d 1971), da of Robert Gregory, of New Lodge, Crowhurst, Sussex; 1 s (Hadley b 1956), 2 da (Carol b 1942, Sherry b 1946); *Heir* s, Hadley Gregory, *qv*; *Career* served WWII, Maj, The Royal Scots, Hong Kong, France, War Office; civil engr, md OPS (London) & Co; *Recreations* rugby, tennis, swimming, photography; *Clubs* SCGB, Knights'; *Style*— Sir Nigel D'Oyly, Bt; Woodcote, Crowhurst, nr Battle, E Sussex TN33 9AB (☎ 042 483 489)

DA SILVA, John Burke; CMG (1969); s of John Christian da Silva (d 1965); *b* 30 August 1918; *Educ* Stowe, Trinity Coll Cambridge; *m* 1, 1940, Janice Margaret (d 1963), da of Royal Mayor, of Bermuda; 1 da; m 2, 1963, Jennifer Jane, da of Capt Hon Trevor Tempest Parker, DSC, RN (d 1973); 1 s, 2 da; *Career* Intelligence Corps 1940-46, Maj (despatches); with Control Cmmn Germany 1946-48; HM Diplomatic Service 1948-73, served Germany, Rome, Hamburg, Bahrein, Aden; cnsllr Washington 1966; FCO 1969-73; conslt Commercial Union Assurance Co Ltd 1973-85; *Recreations* oriental art; *Clubs* Travellers'; *Style*— John da Silva Esq, CMG; Copse Close, Virginia Water, Surrey (☎ 099 04 2342)

DABORN, Alan Francis; OBE (1966), TD (1963), JP (1970), DL (1971); s of Alwyne Victor Daborn (d 1969); *b* 20 Feb 1923; *Educ* Kings Coll Sch Wimbledon; *m* 1949, Thelma Elizabeth, da of Samuel Greenwood (d 1948); 2 s; *Career* served WWII Para Regt, TA with 4 Bn KSLI and Bde HQ Col; chartered surveyor; ptnr Alwyn Daborn & Son amalgamated 1970 to ptnr John German; *Recreations* golf; *Clubs* Naval and Military; *Style*— Alan Daborn, Esq, OBE, TD, JP, DL; 15 Dogpole, Shrewsbury, Shropshire SY1 1EN (☎ 0743 56176)

DACEY, Lionel Ivor Herbert (Lyn); s of John William Archer Dacey (d 1966), and Esther Ann Rees (d 1982); *b* 9 Sept 1932; *Educ* Newport HS; *m* 9 Dec 1959, Patricia Ann, da of Leonard George Kinsey Black (d 1984); 1 s (Paul, b 1971); *Career* gp planning exec Dobson Park Industs plc; md Markon Engrg Co Ltd; dir Dobson Park Industs plc 1984; chm and chief exec Kango Wolf Power Tools Ltd Jan 1984; chm and dir: Kango Wolf Power Tools Ltd UK, Kango Wolf Int Inc Canada, Kango Wolf Power Tools Pty Ltd Australia, Kango Wolf Tools Inc USA; dir Ralliwolf Ltd India; *Recreations* golf, shooting; *Style*— Lionel Dacey, Esq; Toll Bar House, Burley, Oakham LE15 7TA (☎ 0572 55606); Flat 5, Marcourt Lawns, Hillcrest Rd, London W5 1HN (☎ 01 998 6751); Kango Wolf Power Tools Ltd, Hanger Lane, London W5 1DX (☎ 01 998 2911, fax 01 997 5708)

DACIE, Sir John Vivian; s of John Charles Dacie; *b* 20 July 1912; *Educ* King's Coll London, King's Coll Hosp (MD); *m* 1938, Margaret Kathleen Victoria, *née* Thynne; 3 s, 2 da; *Career* sr lectr Br Postgraduate Medical Sch 1946-57; prof of haematology London Univ, 1957-77; author; FRS 1967, Hon FRSM 1984; kt 1976; *Books* Haemolytic Anaemias, Practical Haematology; *Recreations* entomology, music; *Style*— Sir John Dacie; 10 Alan Rd, Wimbledon, London SW19 (☎ 01 946 6086)

DACRE, Baroness (E 1321); Hon Rachel Leila; *née* Brand; da of 4 Viscount Hampden, who was also 26 Baron Dacre, following whose death (1965) the Viscountcy passed to his bro while the Barony fell into abeyance between the two surviving daughters, till terminated in favour of Rachel, the elder, 1970; *b* 24 Oct 1929; *m* 26 July 1951, Hon William Douglas-Home, *qv*; 1 s, 3 da; *Heir* s, Hon James Thomas Archibald Douglas-Home b 16 May 1952; *Style*— The Rt Hon Lady Dacre; Kilmeston, Alresford, Hants

DACRE LACY, Alastair de Saumarez; s of Edward Dacre Lacy (d 1969); *b* 29 Nov 1928; *Educ* Bradfield; *m* 1960, Avril, da of Edward Frederick Ranger (d 1982); 2 da; *Career* chm and md Technicare Int Newbury 1972- (Queens's Award for Export 1979, 1983); chm and md Thor Engrg Services Ltd Poole, dir: Turriff Corpn plc, Value Engrg Australasia Pty Ltd (Perth Australia), Technicare Private Ltd (State of Brunei), Technicare 1983, Sendirian Berhad (Kuala Lumpur), Dacre Lacy and Assocs Ltd, Technicare Australasia Pty Ltd (Australia), ADL Technicare Ltd, Bellman Computing Ltd, Kuwait British Technical Services Ltd, Nesco Int Computer Personnel Ltd, Technicare Gp Ltd, Technicare Private Ltd Singapore, Technicare Documentation Systems Ltd, Waleed Technical Services (LLC) Oman; *Clubs* Royal Thames Yacht, Oil Industries; *Style*— Alastair Dacre Lacy', Esq; Coombe Lodge, Farnborough, nr Wantage, Oxon OX12 8NP

DACRE OF GLANTON, Baroness - Lady Alexandra Henrietta Louisa; *née* Haig; *m* 1, 10 June 1941 (m dis 1954), Rear Adm Clarence Dinsmore Howard-Johnston, CB, DSO, DSC; 2 s, 1 da; m 2, 4 Oct 1954, Hugh Trevor-Roper, *see* Dacre of Glanton, Baron; *Career* chm Music Therapy Charity 1969-82, Edinburgh Festival Guild 1960-80, Border Regn; organiser Oxford Subscription Concerts 1962-80; patron Cambridge Univ Opera Society; *Recreations* music, painting, interior decoration, gardening; *Style*— The Rt Hon Lady Dacre of Glanton; The Old Rectory, Didcot, Oxon

DACRE OF GLANTON, Baron (Life Peer UK 1979); Hugh Redwald Trevor-Roper; s of Dr Bertie William Edward Trevor-Roper; *b* 15 Jan 1914; *Educ* Charterhouse, Ch Ch Oxford; *m* 4 Oct 1954, Lady Alexandra Haig, da of Field Marshal 1 Earl Haig, the WW I General; *Career* sits as Conservative in House of Lords; former tutor Ch Ch Oxford, regius prof modern history Oxford 1957-80; master Peterhouse Cambridge 1980-87; nat dir Times Newspapers 1974; *Clubs* Athenaeum, Beefsteak, Savile; *Style*— The Rt Hon Lord Dacre of Glanton; The Old Rectory, Didcot, Oxon OX11 7EB

DADA, Feroze Ahmad; s of Ahmad Valimohamed Dada, of Pakistan, and Halima; *b* 21 April 1952; *Educ* St Patrick's Sch (Karachi), Univ of Karachi (BCom); *m* 4 Feb 1984, Farida, da of U HLA Maung, of Burma; 1 da (Sumaya b 1986); *Career* chartered accountant, ptnr Freeman & Partners 1981-; dir: Reyker Securities Ltd 1984-, FSI

Group Plc 1986-, FSI Hotels 1988-; FCA, ATII; *Books* Interest Relief for Companies (1981) ; *Recreations* cricket; *Style*— F A Dada, Esq; 25 Coppice Walk, Totteridge, London N20 8DA (☎ 01 446 7846); 30 St James's St, London SW1A 1HB (☎ 01 925 0770, fax 01 925 0726)

DAFFERN, Antony Richard; s of late Edward William Daffern; *b* 14 May 1934; *Educ* King Edward VI Sch Nuneaton, Manchester Univ; *m* 1959, Freda, *née* Appleby; 2 da; *Career* co dir; asst md Telefusion plc 1978-83, dep chm 1983-; memb NTRA Cncl 1978-; *Style*— Antony Daffern, Esq; 27 Rowland Lane, Cleveleys, Blackpool FY5 2QX (☎ 0253 854562)

DAFTER, Raymond Maurice (Ray); s of Maurice Henry Dafter, of Swindon, Wilts, and Dorothy Joan, *née* Vincent; *b* 22 April 1944; *Educ* Marlborough GS, The Coll Swindon, Harvard Univ; *m* 25 Sept 1965, Christine, da of William Charles Richard Franklin (d 1976), of Swindon, Wilts; 2 da (Ynonne Louise b 5 May 1968, Claire Rachel b 13 Dec 1970); *Career* journalist: Evening Advertiser Swindon 1961-64, Evening Post Bristol 1964-70, Financial Times London 1970-83; central dir public and overseas relations Electricity Cncl London 1983-88, exec dir and head of PR Valin Pollen Ltd 1988-, cncl memb Br Inst of Energy Econ, memb professional standards ctee PR Conslts Assoc; FInstPet 1978, MIRR 1988; *Books* Running Out of Fuel (1978), Scraping the Barrel (1980), Winning More Oil (1982); *Recreations* sailing, music, flying, walking; *Clubs* Rochester Aviation; *Style*— Ray Dafter, Esq; Wolsey Oast, Claygate Rd, Laddingford, Kent (☎ 089 273 376); Valin Pollen, 18 Grosvenor Gardens, London SW1 (☎ 01 730 3456)

DAGGER, John Frederick Hannay; s of Richard Leslie Dagger, MD (d 1973), of Newcastle-upon-Tyne, and Iris, *née* Hannay (d 1973); *b* 13 July 1927; *Educ* Uppingham; *m* 19 June 1948, Patricia Anne, da of Charles Edward Thompson (d 1979), of Sheffield; 1 s (Richard b 1950), 1 da (Sarah b 1953); *Career* Capt Coldstream Gds 1945-52, Malaya 1948-50, tea planter S India 1952-56, Hopfactors (UK) Ltd 1957 (dir 1963-86); genealogist, memb AGRA 1984; *Recreations* walking, looking up old relatives; *Style*— John Dagger, Esq; Oak House, Horsmonden, Tonbridge, Kent TN12 8LP (☎ 0892 722272)

DAGWORTHY PREW, Wendy Ann; da of Arthur Sidney Dagworthy (d 1972), of Gravesend Kent, and Jean Annie, *née* Stubbs; *b* 4 Mar 1950; *Educ* Northfleet Secdy Sch for Girls, Medway Coll of Design, Hornsey Coll of Art (BA); *m* 4 Aug 1973, Jonathan William, s of Capt William Sidney Augustus Prew (d 1961), of Somerset and Africa; 1 s (Augustus b 1987); *Career* designer/dir Wendy Dagworthy Ltd 1972-, lectr various colls, coll external assessor BA Hons degree fashion and textiles; current assessor: St Martins Sch of Art, Trent Poly, Leicester Poly, Squire Coll, Hong Kong Poly; dir London Designer Collections 1982, conslt CIYAA Fashion/Textiles Bd 1982-, judge Art and Design Projects various mfrs, memb RSA Bd; participating designer: Fashion Aid, Albert Hall; exhibitor VRA: seasonal exhibitor: London, Milan, NY, Paris; various TV appearances; Fil D'Or Int Linen Award; memb Br Fashion Cncl; *Recreations* dining out, theatre, horse racing, reading, painting, cooking; *Clubs* Chelsea Arts, Groucho; *Style*— Ms Wendy Dagworthy Prew; 18 Melrose Terrace, London W6 (☎ 01 602 6676); 15 Poland Street, London W1 (☎ 01 437 6105)

DAHL, Roald; s of Harald Dahl (d 1920); *b* 13 Sept 1916; *Educ* Repton; *m* 1, 1953 (m dis 1983), Patricia Neal, actress; 1 s (Theo b 1960), 4 da (Olivia b 1955, d 1962, Tessa b 1957, m James Kelly; Ophelia b 1964, Lucy b 1965); m 2, 1983 Felicity Ann, 2 da of Alphonsus Liguori D'Abreu, CBE; *Career* joined RAF 1939, 80 Sqdn Western Desert 1940 (wounded), Greece, Syria, asst Air Attaché Washington 1942-43, Wing Cdr 1943, memb bd security co-ordination Washington 1943-45; Shell Co Eastern Staff Shell Co 1939-40; contrib various pubns: Edgar Allen Book Award Mystery Writers of America 1954-59; *Books Incl:* : *Novels* Sometime Never (1948), My Uncle Oswald (1979); *short stories* Over to You (1945), Someone Like You (1953), Kiss Kiss (1960), Switch Bitch (1974), Tales of the Unexpected (1979), More Tales of the Unexpected (1980), The Best of Roald Dahl (1983), Roald Dahl's Book of Ghost Stories (1983); *children's books* The Gremlins (1943), James and the Giant Peach (1962), Charlie and the Chocolate Factory (1964), The Magic Finger (1966), Fantastic Mr Fox (1970), Charlie and the Great Glass Elevator (1972), Danny, the Champion of the World (1975), The Wonderful Story of Henry Sugar (1977), The Enormous Crocodile (1978), The Twits (1980), George's Marvellous Medicine (1981), Revolting Rhymer (1982), The BFG (1982), Dirty Beasts (1983), The Witches (1983, Whitbread Award), Boy Tales from Childhood (1984), The Giraffe and The Pelly and Me (1985), Going Solo (1986), Matilda (1988); *play* The Honeys (1955); *screenplays* Chitty Chitty Bang Bang (1968), Willy Wonka and the Chocolate Factory (1971); *tv* Tales of the Unexpected (1979); *Recreations* mushrooming; *Style*— Roald Dahl, Esq; Gipsy House, Great Missenden, Bucks

DAHRENDORF, Sir Ralf; KBE (1982); s of Gustav Dahrendorf (d 1954), and Lina, *née* Witt (d 1980); *b* 1 May 1929,Hamburg; *Educ* Hamburg Univ (DPhil), LSE (PhD); *m* 1980, Ellen Joan; *Career* lectr Saarbrücken 1957; prof sociology: Hamburg 1958-60, Tübingen 1960-64, Konstanz 1966-69 (vice-chm founding ctee Konstanz Univ 1964-66); parly sec of state W German FO 1979-70, memb EEC Brussels 1970-74, dir LSE 1974-84 warden St Antony's Coll Oxford 1987-; memb: Hansard Soc Cmmn on Electoral Reform 1975-76, Royal Cmmn on Legal Servs 1976-79; tstee Ford Fndn 1976-88; FBA, FRSA, hon MRIA; hon fell: Imp Coll, LSE; Hon DLitt: Reading, Dublin; Hon LLD: Manchester, Wagner Coll NY, York (Ontario); Hon DHL: Kalamazoo Coll, John Hopkins Univ Baltimore; Hon DSc: Ulster, Bath; Hon DUniv: Oxford, Maryland, Surrey; Hon Dr: Université Catholique de Louvain; Gr Cross de l'Ordre du Mérite (Sénégal) 1971, Gr Bundesverdienstkreuz mit Stern und Schulterband (FDR) 1974, Gr Croix de l'Ordre du Mérite (Luxembourg) 1974, gr goldenes Ehrenzeichen am Bande für Verdienste (Austria) 1975, Gr Croix de l'Ordre de Léopold II (Belgium) 1975; *Clubs* Reform, Garrick; *Style*— Sir Ralf Dahrendorf, KBE; St Antony's College, Oxford OX2 6JF

DAICHES, Lionel Henry; QC (Scotland 1956); s of Rev Dr Salis Daiches (d 1945), of Edinburgh, and Flora Levin (d 1983); *b* 8 Mar 1911; *Educ* Geo Watson's Coll Edinburgh, Edinburgh Univ (MA, LLB); *m* 1947 (m dis 1973), Dorothy Bernstein; 2 s (Michael, Nicholas); *Career* N Staffs Regt 1940-46, Maj J A G Staff, 1 Army N Africa, Italy (including Anzio Beachhead); admitted to faculty of advocates 1946, standing jr counsel Bd of Control Scotland 1950-56; fell Int Acad of Trial Lawyers 1976; *Books* Russians at Law (1960); *Recreations* talking, globe trotting; *Clubs* New, Scottish Arts, RNVR (Glasgow), Puffins (Edinburgh); *Style*— Lionel Daiches, Esq, QC; 10 Heriot Row, Edinburgh EH3 6HE (☎ 031 5564144); Parliament Hse, Parliament Sq, Edinburgh EH1 1RF (☎ 031 2262881)

DAIN, David John Michael; s of John Gordon Dain, of Oakford, Devonshire, and Gladys Ellen, *née* Connop; *b* 30 Oct 1940; *Educ* Merchant Taylors, St John's Coll Oxford (MA); *m* 29 June 1969, Susan Kathleen, da of J Richard F Moss, OBE, of Stapleford, Cambridge; 1 s (Christopher b 1977), 4 da (Sarah b 1974, Penelope b 1979, Tessa b 1981 Sophie (twin) b 1981; *Career* HM Diplomatic Serv 1963-: Sch of Oriental and African Studies (Persian Studies) Br Embassy Tehran 1964, Oriental sec Kabul 1965-68, Cabinet Office 1969-72, Bonn 1972-75, FCO 1975-78, head of chancery Athens 1978-81, dep head cmmr Nicosia 1981-85, head Western European dept FCO 1985-89; fell Inst of Linguists; memb Frant Church Ctee Royal Order of Merit Norway 1988; *Recreations* tennis, bridge, walking, natural history, fishing; *Clubs* United Oxford and Cambridge Univ, Oxford Union; *Style*— David Dain, Esq; Foreign and Commonwealth Office, Whitehall, London SW1

DAINTON, Baron (Life Peer UK 1986); Frederick Sydney Dainton; s of George Whalley Dainton; *b* 11 Nov 1914; *Educ* Central Sch Sheffield, St John's Coll Oxford (MA, BSc, PhD, ScD, hon fell); *m* 1942, Barbara Hazlitt, JP (1968) Nottingham, Oxford, *née* Wright; 1 s, 2 da; *Career* fell and praelector St Catharine's Coll Cambridge 1945-50, H O Jones lectr in physical chemistry Cambridge Univ 1947-50, prof of physical chemistry Leeds Univ 1950-65, vice-chllr Nottingham Univ and hon dir Cookridge High Energy Radiation Research Centre Leeds Univ 1965-70, Dr Lee's prof of chemistry Oxford Univ 1970-73, chllr Sheffield Univ 1979-; chm: Univ Grants Ctee 1973-78, Nat Libraries Ctee 1969-70, Cncl Scientific Policy, Advsy Bd for the Research Cncls 1969-73, Harkness Fellowship UK Selection Ctee 1974-81, Nat Radiological Protection Bd 1978-85, Br Library Bd 1978-85, Royal Postgraduate Medical Sch 1979-, Edward Boyle Meml Tst 1982-; govr: Henley Admin Staff Coll 1974-, LSE 1980-; tstee: Br Museum (natural history) 1976-, Wolfson Fndn 1979-; prime warden Goldsmiths Co 1982-83; cmmr Museums & Galleries; hon fell: St Catharine's Coll, Royal Coll Physicians, Royal Coll Rad, Br Inst Rad; recipient of many honorary doctorates from Br and overseas univs; FRS 1957 (Davy Medal 1969), FSC 1938; *Books* Chain Reactions (1956, 1966, in Polish and Chinese translations), Photochemistry and reaction Kinetics (1967, jt ed and contributor), Choosing a British University (1980), Universities and the National Health Service (1983); *Recreations* walking, colour photography; *Clubs* Athenaeum; *Style*— The Rt Hon Lord Dainton; Fieldside, Water Eaton Lane, Oxford OX5 2PR (☎ 08675 5132)

DAINTY, Hon Mrs (Priscilla); *née* Wolfenden; da of Baron Wolfenden, CBE (d 1985); *b* 1937; *m* 1959, Col F L Dainty; *Style*— The Hon Mrs Dainty; Thump Head Cottage, 22 Boobery, Sampford Peverell, Devon

DAKERS, Dr Lionel Frederick; CBE (1983); s of Lewis Dakers (d 1978), and Eleanor, *née* Hooper (d 1976); *b* 24 Feb 1924; *Educ* Rochester Cathedral Choir Sch, Pupil of Sir Edward Bairstow (organist of York Minster), Royal Acad of Music; *m* 21 April 1951, Mary Elisabeth, da of Rev Claude Williams (d 1963); 4 da (Rachel, Mary, Juliet, Felicity); *Career* WWII, served RAEC 1942-47; asst organist St George's Chapel Windsor 1950-54, asst music master Eton 1952-54; organist: Ripon Cathedral 1954-57, Exeter Cathedral 1957-72; dir Royal Sch of Church Music 1972-89; DMus Lambeth 1979; FRCO 1945, FRAM 1962, FRCM 1980; *Books* Church Music at the Crossroads (1970), A Handbook of Parish Music (1979), Making Church Music Work (1978), Music and the Alternative Service Book (ed 1980), The Chorister's Companion (ed 1980), The Psalms - Their Use and Performance Today (1980); The Church Musician as Conductor (1982), Church Music in a Changing World (1984), Choosing - and using - Hymns (1985); *Recreations* book collecting, gardening, continental food, travel; *Clubs* Athenaeum; *Style*— Dr Lionel Dakers, CBE; 6 Harcourt Terrace, Salisbury, Wiltshire SP2 7SA (☎ 0722 24880)

DAKIN, Christopher John; s of George Frederick Dakin, CBE (d 1969), and Helena May, *née* Samuels (d 1973); *b* 20 August 1931; *Educ* Haileybury, Gonville and Caius Coll Cambridge (MA); *m* 1956, Maureen, da of Albert George Seymour (d 1977); 2 s (Gervase, Simon), 1 da (Samantha); *Career* dir: Plessey Res (Caswell) Ltd 1982-85, Stromberg-Carlson Corpn USA 1984-85, Plessey Major Systems Ltd 1985-86; chief exec and dir Plessey Public Networks Ltd 1984-85; BICC Cables Ltd 1987; FIEE; *Recreations* bricklaying; *Style*— C John Dakin, Esq; Stack Polly, Woodbank Lane, Chester CH1 6JD (☎ 0244 880035); BICC Cables Ltd, Helsby, Warrington, Cheshire, WA6 0DJ; (☎ 09282 5375, telex 628811)

DAKIN, Dorothy Danvers; OBE (1982), JP (1976); da of Edwin Lionel Vivian Dakin (d 1972), of London, and Mary Danvers, *née* Walker (d 1965); *b* 22 Oct 1919; *Educ* Sherborne Sch for Girls, Newnham Coll Cambridge (MA); *Career* WRNS 1943-50; housemistress Wycombe Abbey Sch 1950-60, headmistress Red Maids Sch Bristol 1961-81; reader Bristol Diocese C of E 1982-, asst chaplain Pucklechurch Remand Centre and Prison 1984-87; memb steering ctee to found Boarding Schs Assoc; pres: W of Eng Branch of the Assoc of Headmistresses 1967-71, Assoc of Heads of Girls Boarding Schs 1971-73; fndr pres Girls Schs Assoc (Independant and Direct Grant) 1973-75; memb: Direct Grant Schs Jt Ctee 1973-80, Independant Schs Jt Cncl 1975-80; chm: Independant Schs Info Serv 1976-80, ISIS Assoc 1980-82; vice chm Independant Schs Action Ctee 1980-82; govr: St George's Sch Ascot, Loddeage Comprehensive Sch, Notton House Special Sch; Bath HS, Winterbourne Collegiate Sch, Embleden Rd Infants Sch, Buster Cathedral Sch, Monds Park Comprehensive Sch; pres Bristol Soroptimist Club 1967; chm trg ctee Bristol Girl Guides 1962-73; memb: Bristol Silver Jubilee Ctee 1976-77, Parish Cncl St Peters Church Henleaze 1973-82, ctee Bristol VSO Assoc, Bristol Outward Bound Assoc; *Recreations* embroidery, fencing, painting; *Style*— Miss Dorothy Dakin, OBE, JP; 41 Park Grove, Henleaze, Bristol (☎ 0272 628309/623985)

DAKIN, Robert Baxter; s of John Dakin (d 1975), and Gladys Ivy, *née* Reakes (d 1972); *b* 6 Oct 1934; *Educ* Monkton Combe Sch; *m* 28 May 1960, Dieuwertje Matthea Johanna, da of Jan Hendrik Berkhout, Beverwyk, Holland; 2 s (Mark b 1962, John b 1973), 1 da (Joanna b 1961); *Career* mil serv 2 Lt Somerset LI and W India Regt in Jamaica 1957-60; CA 1957; Price Waterhouse & Co 1964-67, now in private practice in Cambridge; lectr in taxation; played hockey for Jamaica; lay reader C of E 1965-; FCA; *Recreations* golf, hockey; *Style*— Robert Dakin, Esq; 48 Lantree Crescent, Trumpington, Cambridge (☎ 0223 840040)

DALAL, Maneck Ardeshir Sohrab; s of Khan Bahadur Ardeshir Sohrab Dalal, OBE (d 1958), and Amy Nanavutty (d 1940); *b* 24 Dec 1918; *Educ* Barnes HS Deolali India, Trinity Hall Cambridge; *m* 1947, Kathleen Gertrude, da of Frank Richardson (d 1971); 3 da (Christina, Susan, Caroline); *Career* barr Middle Temple 1945; pres: Indian

Chamber of Commerce in GB 1959-62, Indian Mgmnt Assoc of UK 1960-63; regional dir Air India London 1959-77; chm: Foreign Airlines Assoc of UK 1965-67, Indian YMCA in London 1972-, Bharatiya Vidya London 1975-; min for tourism of Civil Aviation High Cmmn of India 1973-77, md Tata Ltd London 1978-, gp dir Tata Industs Bombay 1980-; vice-pres Friends of Vellore 1979-, vice-chm Festival of India GB 1980-81, dep-chm Royal Overseas League 1981-, (chm 1985); memb: Inst of Travel of Tourism, Br Cncl of Churches, LCCI London and Regional Affairs Ctee, Int Bd of Utd World Colleges; FCIT, FBIM; *Recreations* tennis, squash rackets (captained Cambridge Univ in both games); *Clubs* Royal Overseas League, Hurlingham; *Style—* M A S Dalal, Esq; Tall Trees, Marlborough Rd, Hampton, Middlesex (☎ 01 979 2065); Tata Ltd, 18 Grosvenor Place, London SW1X 7HS (☎ 01 235 8281, telex 21501 or 917422)

DALBY, Thomas; s of William Dalby (d 1958), and Kate, *née* Boag (d 1942); *b* 28 Dec 1921; *Educ* Quarry Mount Sch, Leeds Coll of Printing; *m* 27 April 1946, Nancy Lawrence; 1 s (Richard b 1949); *Career* Field Artillery Regt 1939-46, served Iraq, N Africa, Italy, Normandy; publishing mangr Fountain Press London 1946-59, ed mangr mgmnt and tech div Hutchinson Publishing Gp 1959-70, publishing dir Associated Business Programmes Ltd 1970-76, publishing mangr Pergamon Press Ltd 1976-81, publishing conslt mgmnt industl and professional books 1981; *Recreations* photography; *Style—* Thomas Dalby, Esq; 4 Westbourne Park, Scarborough, North Yorkshire (☎ 0723 377049)

DALE, Antony; OBE (1973); s of Maj Claude Henry Dale, CMG, OBE (d 1946), and Dorothy, *née* Liddell (d 1974); *b* 12 July 1912; *Educ* Brighton Coll, Oriel Coll Oxford (BA, BLitt, MA); *m* 10 May 1941, Yvonne Chevallier, da of Douglas Arthur Macfie; 1 da (Madeline Heather (Mrs Rijndorf); *Career* admitted slr 1938; chief investigator of historic bldgs DOE 1961-76 (investigator 1946-61); hon sec Regency Soc of Brighton and Hove 1945-, pres Sussex Archaeological Soc 1979-80; fell Soc of Antiquaries 1953; *Books* Fashionable Brighton (1946), The History and Architecture of Brighton (1948), About Brighton (1951), Brighton Old and New (1953), James Wyatt (1956), Brighton Town and Brighton People (1976), The Theatre Royal Brighton (1980), The Wagners of Brighton (with Sir Anthony Wagner, 1982), Brighton Churches (1989); *Clubs* Athenaeum; *Style—* Antony Dale, Esq, OBE; 38 Prince Regent's Close, Brighton BN2 5JP

DALE, David Kenneth Hay; CBE (1976); s of Kenneth Hay Dale, and Francesca Susanna Hoffman; *b* 27 Jan 1927; *Educ* Dorchester GS; *m* 1956, Hanna Szydlowska; 1 s; *Career* dep govr Seychelles 1975; sec to Cabinet, Republic of Seychelles 1976; FCO 1977-80; govr Montserrat 1980-85; *Style—* David Dale, Esq, CBE; Chatley Cottage, Batcombe, Nr Shepton Mallet, Somerset BA4 6AF

DALE, Iain Leonard; OBE (1989); s of Leonard H Dale, CBE, DL (d 1986), and Doris Anne Smithson (d 1984); fndr Dale Electric Int plc Gp 1935; *b* 9 June 1940; *Educ* Scarborough Coll Yorkshire; *m* Maria, da of Josef Lanmuller (d 1973), of Pottendorf-Landegg, Lower Austria, Austria; 3 s (Jonathan Iain b 1963, Paul Josef b 1967, David Leonard b 1969); *Career* creative dir Streets Advertising 1969-71; md: Hicks Oubridge Public Affairs 1971-74, Dale Electric Int plc 1971; dir: Dale Electric of GB Ltd, Comptoir General Impex (France), Ottomotores Dale Sa De Cv (Mexico), Dale Electric Power Systems Ltd (Thailand), Erskine Systems Ltd (UK), Houchin Ltd (UK); chm Assoc of Br Generating Set Manufacturers (ABGSM) 1984-85, SE Asia Trade Advsy Gp; Nat Cncl of Confederation Br Industries (CBI) 1984-, NEDO Generating Set Sub Gp 1982-87, memb Latin American Trade Advsy Gp; *Recreations* walking; *Clubs* Royal Overseas League; *Style—* Iain L Dale, Esq, OBE; Grove House, Low Marishes, Malton, N Yorks YO17 0RQ (☎ 065 386 223); Dale Electric International plc, Electricity Buildings, Filey, Yorkshire (☎ 0723 514141)

DALE, John Howard; s of Rev David Howard Dale, of St Ives Huntingdonshire, and Elizabeth Margarite (Betty), *née* Rosser; *b* 18 July 1951; *Educ* King Henry VIII GS for Boys, Bretton Hall Coll Leeds Univ (Cert Ed); *m* 25 Aug 1979, Mary Elizabeth, da of Joseph Frank Waterhouse, of Birmingham; 1 s (Joseph), 1 da (Charlotte); *Career* actor 1971-73: Hull, Sheffield, Brighton; artistic dir Community Arts Centre Brighton 1973-75, asst dir Royal Ct Theatre London 1975-77, writer and dir BBC TV Childrens Dept 1977-80, conslt Industl Personnel Depts 1981-82, exec prodr childrens and young people's dept TVS 1983-86; devised Sat ITV formats: Number 73, Motormouth; head of late evening progs TVS, devised POV 1986-87; prodr and dir: 6 hrs network adult drama, 27 hrs childrens drama incl Knights of God (ITV); freelance writer, and dir and prodr in TV and theatre; memb bd Artswork Ltd, dir J & M Prodns; *Recreations* children, pubs, writing; *Style—* John Dale, Esq; J & M Productions, 32 Court Road, London SE9 5NU,

DALE, Thomas Edward (Tom); s of Leonard George Dale (d 1964), of The Warren, St Osyth, Essex, and Sybil Eileen Mary, *née* Stevenson (d 1988); *b* 14 Mar 1931; *Educ* Gosfield Sch Halstead, LSE (BSc), Univ of London Inst of Educ (PGCE); *Career* Nat Serv RA 1950-52; Warden Cambridge Int Centre 1960-66, organising sec Lib Int (Br Gp) 1967-, PA to Ldr of Lib Pty 1967-76, int offr Lib Pty 1977-85, dir TEAM Promotions Ltd 1986-, Lib Pty candidate Harwich 1959, 1964, 1966, Alliance Pty candidate Centl Suffolk 1987, pres Harwich Lib Assoc (now SLD), former chm E Regnl Lib Pty, former memb ELDR Brussels, pres London Univ Union 1957-58, sec LSE SU 1955-56, govr LSE 1981-87, memb Essex CC 1965-67 and 1973-77, dep ldr SLD Gp, rep Brightlingsea Div 1981-, spokesman highways and agric estates, memb Tending DC 1979-, chm ACC Consumer Affrs Ctee 1986-87 and 1988-; govr: Gasfield Sch (former chm), Colchester Inst; sec: Hampden Educnl Tst, Herbert Samuel Fndn; *Recreations* theatre, films, travel; *Clubs* Nat Lib; *Style—* Tom Dale, Esq; Flat 1, 2 Barking Road, London, E6 3BP, (☎ 01 470 8640, telex 8956 551); The Warren, St Osyth, Clacton-on-Sea, Essex CO16 8EH (☎ 0255 820 236)

DALE, Sir William Leonard; KCMG (1965); s of late Rev William Dale; *b* 1906; *Educ* Hymers Coll Hull; *m* 1, 1948 (m dis 1953), Elizabeth Romeyn, da of Prof Adolph Elwyn, of NY; m 2, 1966, Mrs Gloria Finn, *née* Spellman; 1 da; *Career* barr 1931; entered Colonial Off 1935; legal advsr: Govt of Libya 1951-53, Miny of Educn 1954, Sec of State for Cwlth Rels 1961-66; int legal conslt; *Books* Law of the Parish Church, Legislative Drafting:A New Approach, The Modern Commonwealth; *Clubs* Travellers'; *Style—* Sir William Dale, KCMG; 20 Old Buildings, Lincoln's Inn, WC2A 3UP (☎ 01 242 9365)

DALE, William Paterson; s of John Robert Dale (d 1969), of Auldhame, N Berwick, E Lothian, and Mary Waugh, *née* Paterson (d 1980); *b* 2 Mar 1923; *Educ* Sedbergh Sch; *m* 1, 5 March 1947, Kathleen Ann (d 1977), da of William David Simpson of Highfield, N Berwick, E Lothian; 2 s (Robert b 1956, Alec b 1958), 3 da (Anne b 1948, Mary b 1959, Cynthia b 1953); m 2, Rosemary Joy, widow of Arthur Harrison and da of Stewart Paton, of Templeton Burn, Kilmarnock; *Career* WWII served HG and Coast Guard 1939-45; farmer: Lochhouses, Dunbar 1944-84, Myreton Aberlady 1966-79, Setonmains Longniddry 1966-84, The Holmes, St Boswells and Hoebbidge, Melrose 1979-; dir: Myreton Motor Museum Aberlady 1966-, Melrose Motor Museum 1983-; elder Church of Scotland; *Recreations* Vintage car rallies; *Clubs* Bentley Drivers Bullnose Morris; *Style—* William P Dale, Esq; The Holmes, St Boswells, Melrose, Roxburghshire TD6 OEL (☎ 0835 22356)

DALES, Richard Nigel; s of Kenneth Richard Frank Dales, TD, of Southwold, Suffolk, and Olwen Mary, *née* Preedy; *b* 26 August 1942; *Educ* Chigwell Sch, St Catharines Coll Cambridge (MA); *m* 10 Sept 1966, Elizabeth Margaret, da of Edward Owen Martin (d 1966), of Loughton, Essex; 1 s (Jeremy b 1973), 1 da (Eleanor b 1976); *Career* entered FO 1964, third sec Yaoundé, Cameroon 1965-67, FCO 1968-70, second sec 1969, second (later first) sec Copenhagen 1970-73, asst private sec to Sec of State for Foreign and Commonwealth Affairs 1974-77, first sec Hd of Chancery and HM Consul Sofia 1977-81, asst S Asian Dept FCO 1981-82, cnsllr Copenhagen 1982-86, dep high cmmr Harare 1986-89; head of South African dept FCO 1989-; *Recreations* music, walking; *Style—* Richard Dales, Esq; c/o Foreign and Commonwealth Office, King Charles St, London SW1A 2AH

DALEY, Michael John William; s of Desmond William Daley, of Cockfosters, Herts, and Alma Joan, *née* Ellen; *b* 23 Sept 1953; *Educ* Hatfield Sch; *Career* S G Warburg & Co Ltd 1973-77, Credit Suisse First Boston Ltd 1977-86 (asst mangr 1979, mangr 1982); dir Credit Suisse First Boston Asset Mgmnt Ltd 1985, vice-pres and head Fixed Income Gp Morgan Stanley Int 1986-, exec dir Morgan Stanley Asset Mgmnt Ltd 1986-88; MBIM 1986, FInstD 1984; *Recreations* golf, skiing, mountaineering, motoring; *Clubs* RAC, Annabel's; *Style—* Michael Daley, Esq; Morgan Stanley Int, Kingsley House, Wimpole St, London W1 (☎ 01 280 8120, car tel 0836 608 105)

DALGARNO, Frederick George Scott; s of Frederick Dalgarno; *b* 17 June 1943; *Educ* Robert Gordon's Coll Aberdeen, Aberdeen Univ, Strathclyde Univ; *m* 1969, Moyra, da of William Ellis; 1 s, 2 da; *Career* dir: Murray Johnstone Ltd 1986-, Richards plc 1984-, Lasalle Ltd; *Recreations* golf, soccer, swimming; *Clubs* Royal Northern and Univ (Aberdeen), Royal Aberdeen GC; *Style—* Fred Dalgarno, Esq; 14 Westfield Terr, Aberdeen (☎ 0224 642470)

DALGETY, Hugh Barkly Gonnerman; Lord of the Manors and patron of the livings of Lockerley and E Tytherley; s of Arthur William Hugh Dalgety (d 1972), and Wanzie, *née* Rodgers, of Lockerley Hall; ggs of Frederick G Dalgety the fndr of Dalgety plc; *b* 16 August 1943; *Educ* Milton Abbey, RAC Circencester; *m* 1976, Margaret Anne, da of Desmond Charles Nigel Baring, of Ardington, Oxon; 2 s (Richard b 1977, Thomas b 1984), 1 da (Katherine b 1979); *Career* MFH Tedworth 1964-65, Hursley 1975-78, Portman 1978-82, S & W Wilts 1986-88; *Recreations* field sports, travel; *Clubs* White's; *Style—* Hugh Dalgety, Esq; Millards Hill Home, Trudexhill, Frome, Somerset BA11 5DW (☎ 037384 229)

DALGETY, Ramsay Robertson; QC (Scotland, 1986); s of James Robertson Dalgety, of Dundee, and Georgia Alexandra, *née* Whyte; *b* 2 July 1945; *Educ* Dundee HS, Univ of St Andrews (LLB); *m* 13 Nov 1971, Mary Margaret, da of Rev Neil Cameron Bernard, of Edinburgh; 1 s (Neil b 1975), 1 da (Caroline b 1974); *Career* advocate at the Scottish Bar 1972-85; dir and chm Archer Transport Ltd and Archer Transport (London) Ltd 1982-98, dir and chm Venture Shipping Ltd 1983-88; dir Scottish Opera Glasgow 1980-, dep chm and tstee Opera Singers' Pension Fund London 1983-, dir Scottish Opera Theatre Tst Ltd Glasgow 1987-; cncllr City of Edinburgh DC 1974-80; Temp Sheriff 1987-; dep traffic cmmr for Scotland 1988-; memb: Faculty of Advocates 1972, Inst of Dirs 1982; *Recreations* boating, golf, opera, travel; *Clubs* Wellington; *Style—* Ramsay R Dalgety, Esq, QC; 196 Craigleith Rd, Edinburgh EH4 2EE (☎ 031 332 1417); Faculty of Advocates, Advocates Library, Parliment House, Edinburgh EH1 1RF (☎ 031 226 5071, 226 2881, fax 031 225 3642, telex 727856 FACADV G)

DALGLISH, Capt James Stephen; CVO (1955), CBE (1963); s of Rear Adm Robin Campsie Dalglish, CB (d 1934), and Dulcie, da of late Maj James Y Stephen, of Amersham, Bucks; *b* 1 Oct 1913; *Educ* RNC Dartmouth; *m* 1939, Evelyn Mary, da of Rev Arthur Llewellyn Meyricke (d 1950); 1 s, 1 da; *Career* joined RN 1927, served WWII Atlantic, Med and Pacific; Cdr 1948, Cmd HMS Aisne and HM Yacht Britannia (as actg Capt - unique appt normally held by an Adm), Capt 1954, Cmd: HMS Woodbridge Haven and the inshore flotilla, HMS Excellent and HMS Bulwark; ret Capt 1963; welfare offr Met Police 1963-73; *Recreations* gardening, painting; *Style—* Capt James Dalglish, CVO, CBE, RN; Park Hall, Aislaby, Whitby, N Yorks YO21 1SW (☎ 0947 810213)

DALHOUSIE, 16 Earl of (S 1633); Simon Ramsay; KT (1971), GCVO (1979), GBE (1957), MC (1944); also Lord Ramsay of Dalhousie (S precedence of 1618), Lord Ramsay and Keringtoun (S 1633) and Baron Ramsay of Glenmark (UK 1875); s of 14 Earl of Dalhousie (d 1928), and Lady Mary Heathcote- Drummond-Willoughby (d 1960), da of 1 Earl of Ancaster; suc bro, 15 Earl of Dalhousie 1950 ; *b* 17 Oct 1914; *Educ* Eton, Ch Ch Oxford; *m* 26 June 1940, Margaret, CStJ, da of Brig-Gen Archibald Stirling of Keir, JP, DL, MP (d 1931); 3 s, 2 da; *Heir* s, Lord Ramsay, *qv*; *Career* 4/5 Bn Black Watch, Maj 1942; Ensign Royal Co of Archers (Queen's Body Guard for Scotland) 1956; MP (C) Angus 1945-50, Cons whip 1946-48, DL (1951), JP (1967) Angus, Ld-Lt 1967-; govr-gen Fedn of Rhodesia and Nyasaland 1957-63; lord chamberlain to HM Queen Elizabeth The Queen Mother 1965-; chllr Dundee Univ 1977-; *Recreations* gardening, shooting, fishing; *Clubs* White's; *Style—* The Rt Hon the Earl of Dalhousie, KT, GCVO, GBE, MC; 5 Margaretta Terrace, London SW3 (☎ 01 352 6477); Brechin Castle, Brechin, Angus (☎ (035 62) 2176)

DALITZ, Prof Richard Henry; s of Frederick William Dalitz (d 1959), of Melbourne, Aust, and Hazel Blanche, *née* Drummond (d 1970); *b* 28 Feb 1925; *Educ* Scotch Coll Melbourne (BA, BSc), Trinity Coll Cambridge (PhD); *m* 8 Sept 1946, Valda, da of William Victor Giffen Suiter (d 1970), of Melbourne, Aust; 1 s (Rodric b 10 Nov 1947), 3 da (Katrine b 4 Aug 1950, Heather b 22 March 1960, Ellyn b 24 March 1964); *Career* res asst in physics Univ of Bristol 1948-49, reader in mathematical physics Univ of Birmingham 1955-56 (lectr 1949-55), prof of physics Enrico Fermi Inst for Nuclear Studies Univ of Chicago 1956-66, Royal Soc res prof Oxford Univ 1963-; fell All Souls Coll Oxford 1964-; fell American Physical Soc 1959, FRS 1960, corr memb Australia Acad Sci 1978, foreign memb Polish Acad Sci 1980; *Books* K Mesons and Hyperons: Reports on Progress in Physics (1957), Strange Particles and Strong

Interactions (1962), Nuclear Interactions of the Hyperons (1965), Quark Models for the Elementary Particle: High Energy Physics (1966), Nuclear Energy Today and Tomorrow (contrib 1971); *Recreations* biographical researches, study of Sorbian (Wendish) language, history and emigration, travelling hopefully; *Style*— Prof Richard Dalitz; 28 Jack Straws Lane, Oxford, Oxon OX3 0DW (☎ 0865 62531); Dept of Theoretical Physics, 1 Keble Road, Oxford OX1 3NP (☎ 0865 273967, fax 0865 273418, telex 83295 NUCLOX G)

DALKEITH, Countess of; Lady Elizabeth Marian Frances; *née* Kerr; 4 da of 12 Marquess of Lothian, KCVO, *qv*; *b* 8 June 1954; *Educ* London Sch of Economics (BSc); *m* 31 Oct 1981, Earl of Dalkeith, *qv*; 2 s, 1 da; *Career* radio journalist BBC; *Recreations* music, reading, theatre, television; *Style*— Countess of Dalkeith; Dabton, Thornhill, Dumfriesshire; 24 Lansdowne Road, London W11

DALKEITH, Earl of; Richard Walter John Montagu Douglas Scott; s and h of 9 and 11 Duke of Buccleuch and Queensberry, KT, VRD, JP, *qv*; *b* 14 Feb 1954; *Educ* Eton, Christ Church Oxford; *m* 31 Oct 1981, Lady Elizabeth Marian Frances Kerr, 4 da of 12 Marquess of Lothian; 2 s, (Lord Eskdaill, Hon Charles David Peter b 1987), 1 da (Lady Louisa b 1982); *Heir* s, Walter John Francis Montagu Douglas Scott (Lord Eskdaill) b 2 Aug 1984; *Career* page of honour to HM Queen Elizabeth The Queen Mother 1967-69; BBC External Serv; *Style*— Earl of Dalkeith; 1 Pembridge Crescent, London W11 (☎ 01 221 7322); Dabton, Thornhill, Dumfries (☎ 0848 30467)

DALLAS, John Eastwood; s of Sidney John Dalls (d 1979), of Rodhuish, Somerset, and Joan Constance Evelyn, *née* Griffiths; *b* 21 Nov 1942; *Educ* Winchester, New Coll Oxford (MA); *m* 3 April 1985, Vivette, da of Isak Francko (d 1984), of Geneva, Switzerland; *Career* co dir: Security Tag Systems Inc 1983, Fountmill Ltd 1986; *Recreations* travel, walking, theatre; *Style*— John E Dallas, Esq; Fountmill Ltd, 27 Sloane Ave, London SW3 3JB (☎ 01 589 1582)

DALLMEYER, Hon Mrs (Ursula Nina); *née* Balfour; da of 2 Baron Kinross (d 1939), and Caroline Elsie (d 1969), da of Arthur M Johnstone-Douglas, DL; *b* 12 Mar 1914; *m* 14 Sept 1939, Col Christopher James York Dallmeyer, DSO and bar, WS; 3 s, 1 da; *Style*— The Hon Mrs Dallmeyer; Green Corner, Tyninghame, Dunbar, E Lothian EH42 1XL (☎ 0620 860394)

DALLY, Brian John Michael; RD; s of David Charles Dally (d 1971), and Eileen, *née* Oates (d 1936); *b* 11 Oct 1930; *Educ* Univ Coll Sch Hampstead, Silcoates Sch Wakefield; *m* 21 Sept 1957, Philida Susan, da of Lt Cdr Kenneth McIver Woods, RN (ka 1940); 2 s (David b 1960, Jonathan b 1962); *Career* Lt Cdr RNR 1952-76; slr of Supreme Ct, ptnr Taylor Garrett, advocate and slr of High Cts of Singapore and Malaysia, ptnr Donaldson and Burkinshaw Singapore 1961-66, dir Rutland Tst plc; hereditary Freeman Borough of Pembroke 1963, Freeman City of London; *Recreations* sailing, skiing, squash, opera; *Clubs* Royal Lymington Yacht, Tanglin (Singapore); *Style*— Brian J M Dally, Esq, RD; 20 St Mary's Road, Wimbledon, London SW19 (☎ 01 946 0408); 180 Fleet Street, London EC4 (☎ 01 430 1122)

DALLY, Harold Roy; s of William Dally (d 1941), and Sarah, *née* Carver (d 1966); *b* 1 Nov 1928; *Educ* Midsomer Norton, Kent Hort Inst, Royal Botanic Gdns Kew; *m* 4 Sept 1954, Sybil Efan, da of William John (d 1970); 1 da (Rohan b 1956); *Career* horticulturist; botany dept Univ Coll Cardiff 1953-57, Fisons Ltd 1957-63, States of Guernsey 1963-68, now md Kenilworth Vineries Ltd Guernsey; dir: Leale Ltd, Les Nicolles Vineries Ltd; chm Guernsey Grower Co-operative Ltd; *Recreations* gardening, carving, photography; *Style*— Harold Dally, Esq; Val au Vallee, La Rue de la Falaise, Guernsey (☎ 0481 38139); Kenilworth Vineries Ltd, Route Militaire, Vale, Guernsey (☎ 0481 44774, telex 4191317 KENING)

DALMENY, Lord; Harry Ronald Neil Primrose; s and h of 7 Earl of Rosebery; *b* 20 Nov 1967; *Style*— Lord Dalmeny

DALRYMPLE; *see*: Hamilton-Dalrymple

DALRYMPLE, Lady Antonia Marian Amy Isabel; *née* Stewart; only da of Lt-Col 12 Earl of Galloway (d 1978); *b* 3 Dec 1925; *m* 5 April 1946, Sir (Charles) Mark Dalrymple, 3 Bt, who d 1971, when the title became ext; *Style*— Lady Antonia Dalrymple; Newhailes, Musselburgh, Midlothian

DALRYMPLE, Hon Colin James; JP, DL (Midlothian); 4 and yst s of Lt-Col 12 Earl of Stair, KT, DSO, JP, DL (d 1961); *b* 19 Feb 1920; *Educ* Eton, Trin Coll Cambridge; *m* 1, 25 Aug 1945 (m dis 1954), Pamela Mary, only da of Maj Lamplugh Wickham, CVO; 1 da; m 2, 12 March 1956, Fiona Jane, only da of late Adm Sir Ralph Alan Bevan Edwards, KCB, CBE; 1 s, 2 da; *Career* served WWII, Italy, Scots Gds, ret Maj, vice pres Scottish Landowners Fedn; memb Queen's Body Guard for Scotland (Royal Co of Archers); *Recreations* landowning and farming; *Clubs* New (Edinburgh); *Style*— Hon Colin Dalrymple, JP, DL; Oxenfoord Mains, Dalkeith, Midlothian, Scotland

DALRYMPLE, Hon David Hew; 2 s of 13 Earl of Stair; *b* 30 Mar 1963; *Style*— The Hon David Dalrymple

DALRYMPLE, Hon Hew North; TD, DL (Ayrshire); s of 12 Earl of Stair (d 1961); bro of 13 Earl of Stair, *qv*; *b* 27 April 1910; *Educ* Eton; *m* 1, 20 June 1938, Mildred Helen (d 1980), da of Hon Thomas Henry Frederick Egerton (d 1953), 3 s of 3 Earl of Ellesmere (5 Earl became 6 Duke of Sutherland); 1 s; m 2, 20 Jan 1983, Helen M W Phillips; *Career* formerly Capt 2 Bn Black Watch (TA), served N Africa and Burma (twice wounded); memb Queen's Body Guard for Scotland (Royal Co of Archers); *Style*— The Hon Hew Dalrymple, TD, DL; Castlehill, Ballantrae, Ayrshire KA26 0LA

DALRYMPLE, Viscount; John David James Dalrymple; s and h of 13 Earl of Stair, KCVO, MBE; *b* 4 Sept 1961; *Career* short serv commission with Scots Gds 1982-; *Style*— Viscount Dalrymple

DALRYMPLE, Hon Michael Colin; yst s of 13 Earl of Stair; *b* 1 April 1965; *Style*— The Hon Michael Dalrymple

DALRYMPLE-CHAMPNEYS, Lady Norma Hull; da of late Col Richard Hull Lewis and wid of A S Russell, MC,; *Educ* Oxford Univ (MA); *m* 1974, as his 2 w, Capt Sir Weldon Dalrymple-Champneys, 2 Bt, CB (d 14 Dec 1980, when title became extinct); *Career* hon res fell (formerly fell and librarian) Somerville Coll hon fell Oriel Coll, Oxford; *Books* The Notebook of Thomas Bennet (1956), Bibliography of William Cowper (1963), Poems of William Cowper (1967), The Complete Poetical Works of George Crabbe, 3 vols (1987).; *Style*— Lady Dalrymple-Champneys

DALRYMPLE-HAMILTON, Christian Margaret; DL (District of Wigtown 1982); er da of Adm Sir Frederick Hew George Dalrymple-Hamilton, of Bargany, KCB (whose f, Col Hon North D-H, MVO, was 2 s of 10 Earl of Stair, KT, JP, DL), by his w Gwendolen, 3 da of Sir Cuthbert Peek, 2 Bt; *b* 20 Sept 1919; *Style*— Miss Christian Dalrymple-Hamilton, DL; Cladyhouse, Cairnryan, Stranraer, Wigtownshire

DALRYMPLE-HAMILTON OF BARGANY, Capt North Edward Frederick; CVO (1961, MVO 1954), MBE (1953), DSC (1943), JP (1980), DL (Ayrshire 1973); s of Adm Sir Frederick Hew George Dalrymple-Hamilton of Bargany, KCB (d 1974, gs of 10 Earl of Stair, KT, JP, DL) by his w Gwendolen, 3 da of Sir Cuthbert Peek, 2 Bt; *b* 17 Feb 1922; *Educ* Eton; *m* 1, 23 July 1949, Hon Mary Helen (d 1981), da of Rt Hon David John Colville, GCIE, TD, PC, 1 Baron Clydesmuir (d 1954); 2 s (North John Frederick b 1950, James Hew Ronald b 1955); m 2, 9 April 1983, Geraldine Inez Antoinette (who m 1, 1955, Maj Rowland Beech (d 1972); 2 da), da of late Maj Frank Harding; *Career* entered RN 1940, served WWII and Korea, Cdr 1954, cmdg HMS Scarborough 1958, exec offr HM Yacht Britannia 1959-60, Capt 1960, Capt (F) 17 Frigate Sqdn 1963, dir Naval Signals MOD 1965, Capt Adm Surface Weapons Estab 1967, ret 1970; ensign Queen's Bodyguard for Scotland (Royal Co of Archers); *Clubs* New (Edinburgh), Pratt's, MCC; *Style*— Capt North Dalrymple-Hamilton of Bargany, CVO, MBE, DSC, JP, DL, RN; Lovestone House, Bargany, Girvan, Ayrshire KA26 9RF (☎ 046 587 227)

DALRYMPLE-HAY, Sir James Brian; 6 Bt (GB 1798) of Park Place, Wigtownshire; s of Lt-Col Brian George Rowland Dalrymple-Hay (d 1943); suc cous, 5 Bt (d 1952); *b* 19 Jan 1928; *Educ* Blundells; *m* 12 April 1958, Helen Sylvia, da of late Stephen Herbert Card, of Reigate, Surrey; 3 da (Fiona, Charlotte, Lucie); *Heir* bro, John Hugh Dalrymple-Hay; *Career* Lt RM 1948; ptnr in firm of Estate Agents 1968-85; *Style*— Sir James Dalrymple-Hay, Bt; The Red House, Church St, Warnham, nr Horsham, W Sussex

DALRYMPLE-HAY, John Hugh; s of Lt-Col Brian Dalrymple-Hay (d 1943); hp of bro Sir James Dalrymple-Hay, 6 Bt; *b* 16 Dec 1929; *Educ* Blundell's Sch; *m* 6 Oct 1962, Jennifer Phyllis Roberta, da of Brig Robert Johnston, of 44 Exeter House, Putney Heath, SW15; 1 s; *Career* late Capt Royal Scots Fusiliers; *Recreations* golf, squash, sailing; *Style*— John Dalrymple-Hay, Esq; Little Meadow, Forty Green Rd, Knotty Green, Beaconsfield, Bucks HP9 1XL

DALRYMPLE-WHITE, Sir Henry Arthur Dalrymple; 2 Bt (UK 1926) of High Mark, Co Wigtown; DFC (1941) and bar (1942); s of Lt-Col Sir Godfrey Dalrymple Dalrymple-White, 1 Bt (d 1954, s of Gen Sir Henry Dalrymple White, KCB, who cmd 6 Inniskilling Dragoons throughout Crimean War and was maternal gs of Sir Hew Dalrymple, 1 Bt), by his w Hon Catherine Mary, da of 12 Viscount Falkland; *b* 5 Nov 1917; *Educ* Eton, Magdalene Cambridge, London Univ; *m* 17 Sept 1948 (m dis 1956), Mary, only da of Capt Robert Henry Cuncliffe Thomas, 8 Royal Hussars, by his wife Cynthia, 2 da of Capt Francis Sandford; 1 s; *Heir* s, Jan Hew Dalrymple-White; *Career* Wing-Cdr RAFVR, served WW II; *Style*— Sir Henry Dalrymple-White, Bt, DFC; c/o Aero Club of East Africa, PO Box 40813, Nairobi, Kenya

DALRYMPLE-WHITE, Jan Hew; s and h of Sir Henry Arthur Dalrymple Dalrymple-White, 2 Bt; *b* 26 Nov 1950; *Educ* Stowe, Huddersfield Polytechnic, Univ of Stirling; *Style*— Jan Dalrymple-White Esq

DALTON, Sir Alan Nugent Goring; CBE (1969), DL (Cornwall 1982); s of Harold Goring Dalton and Phyllis Marguerite, *née* Ash; *b* 26 Nov 1923; *Educ* King Edward VI Sch Southampton; *Career* md English Clays, Lovering and Pochin and Co Ltd 1961-84; dep chm Eng China Clays plc 1968-84 (chm 1984); dir: Sun Alliance and London Assur Gp 1976-, (Western regnl bd) Nat Westminster Bank Ltd 1977-; chm BR (Western) Bd 1978-; dir Westland plc 1980-85; CBIM, FRSA; kt 1977; *Recreations* sailing, painting, reading; *Clubs* Royal Yacht Squadron, Royal Western Yacht England; *Style*— Sir Alan Dalton, CBE, DL; English China Clays plc, John Keay House, St Austell, Cornwall

DALTON, Vice Adm Sir Geoffrey Thomas James Oliver; KCB (1986); s of Jack Roland Thomas Dalton (d 1981), of Epsom, Surrey, and Margaret Kathleen, *née* Oliver (d 1978); *b* 14 April 1931; *Educ* Reigate GS, RNC Dartmouth; *m* 30 March 1957, Jane Hamilton, da of Colin Hamilton Baynes (d 1976), of Suffolk; 4 s (Alastair b 1964, David b 1966, Richard b 1970, Antony b 1971); *Career* joined RN 1949; cmd: HMS Maryton 1958-60, HMS Relentless 1966-67, HMS Nubian 1969-70, HMS Jupiter and Seventh Frigate Sqdn 1977-79; HMS Dryad (Sch of Maritime Ops) 1979-81, asst Chief of Naval Staff (Policy) 1918-84, Dep Supreme Allied Cdr Atlantic 1984-87, Cdr 1966, Capt 1972, Rear Adm 1981, Vice Adm 1984; Sec Gen MENCAP 1987-; Freeman of City of London 1953, Liveryman of Drapers' Company 1957; FBIM 1987; *Recreations* tennis, gardening, walking; *Clubs* Royal Overseas League; *Style*— Vice Adm Sir Geoffrey Dalton, KCB; Farm Cottage, Catherington, Hants PO8 OTD (☎ 0705 592369); MENCAP National Centre, 123 Golden Lan, London EC1Y ORT (☎ 01 253 9433)

DALTON, Vice-Adm Sir Norman Eric; KCB (1959, CB 1956), OBE 1944; s of late William John Henry Dalton; *b* 1 Feb 1904; *Educ* RNCs Osborne and Dartmouth; *m* 1927, Teresa (Terry) Elizabeth (d 1982), da of late Richard James Jenkins; 1 s (David), 1 da (Celia); *Career* RN 1917; served Admiralty, E Indies and Pacific WWII, Capt 1946, on staff C-in-C Portsmouth 1954, Rear-Adm 1954, dep engr-in-chief Admiralty 1955-57, Engr-in-Chief of the Fleet 1957-60 and dir Training 1959-60, Vice-Adm 1957, ret 1960; *Style*— Vice-Adm Sir Norman Dalton, KCB, OBE; New Lodge, Peppard Lane, Henley-on-Thames, Oxon (☎ 0491 575552)

DALTON, Patrick Michael; s of Jack Rowland Thomas Dalton (d 1984), and Kathleen Margaret, *née* Oliver (d 1978); *b* 4 Oct 1941; *Educ* Whitgift Sch; *m* 7 June 1967, (Elizabeth) Gillian Vera, da of Charles Claude Allan, of Shawburn, by Selkirk, Scotland; 2 s (Barnaby John Allan b 10 April 1971, Nicko Alexander Neale b 17 Nov 1972); *Career* BRNC Dartmouth, gen serv HMS Kemerton, HMS Wakeful 1960-65, Fleet Air Arm 1965-73; Mullens & Co 1973-78; ptnr: Capel-Cure Myers 1978-88, ANZ McCaughan 1988-; memb Small Farms Orgn; Freeman City of London, Liveryman Worshipful Co of Drapers; FCIS; *Recreations* farming, skiing, tennis, sailing; *Clubs* Western (Glasgow); *Style*— Patrick Dalton, Esq; Millwood Farm, Hartfield, East Sussex (☎ 089 277 619); ANZ- McCaughan, 65 Holborn Viaduct, London EC1 (☎ 01 236 5101)

DALTON, Peter Gerald Fox; CMG (1958); s of Sir Robert William Dalton (d 1961), and Louise Bonney (d 1971), da of late A L Bamberger, of NY; *b* 12 Dec 1914; *Educ* Uppingham, Oriel Coll Oxford (BA); *m* 1944, Josephine Anne, da of Percivale Helyar (d 1928); 1 s (Michael), 1 da (Patricia); *Career* HM Dip Serv 1937-69, political advsr Hong Kong 1953-56, head of Far Eastern dept FO 1957-60, cncllr Warsaw 1960-63; conslt-gen Los Angeles San Francisco 1964-67, min Moscow 1967-69; *Style*— Peter Dalton, Esq, CMG

DALTON, Robin Ann; da of Dr Robert Agnew Eakin (d 1965), of Sydney, Aust, and Lyndall Everad, *née* Solomon (d 1950); *b* 22 Dec 1920; *Educ* Frensham NSW Aust,

SOAS London Univ; *m* 1, 8 Oct 1940 (m dis 1942), Ian (John) Gordon Spencer, of Queensland, Aust; m 2, 1 May 1953, Emmet Michael Dalton (d 1957), s of Maj-Gen James Emmet Dalton, MC (d 1978), of Dublin; 1 s (Seamus Emmet b 1956), 1 da (Lisa Maria b 1954); *Career* special advsr and press offr Thai govt 1953-58, literary agent Robin Dalton Assocs Ltd 1965-87, dir Int Famous Agency (now ICM) 1972-75, entered film indust 1984, project developer Nineteen Eighty-Four 1984, exec prodr Emma's War 1985, prodr Madame Sousatzka 1988; life memb Anglo-Thai Soc, memb BAFTA; *Books* Aunts up the Cross (as Robin Eakin 1963, reprinted 1980), Australia Fair? (chapter in anthology, 1984), numerous magazine and newspaper articles; *Style—* Mrs Robin Dalton; 127 Hamilton Terrace, London NW1 9QR (☎ 01 328 6169)

DALY, Barbara Susan (Mrs Laurence Tarlo); da of Philip Daly (d 1985), and Eva, *née* Sapherson (d 1971); *b* 24 Mar 1944; *Educ* Leeds Coll of Art; *m* 16 March 1982, Laurence Joel Frederic Tarlo, s of William Tarlo, of Long Island, New York; *Career* make-up artist; BBC 1964-68, freelance 1968-86, md Colourings Ltd 1986-; films incl: A Clockwork Orange; make-up conslt to HRH The Princess of Wales; patron Skin Treatment and Res Trust Westminster Hosp, ctee memb Orgn for Trg, patron Nat Assoc Drama for Visually Handicapped; memb BAFTA 1987; *Books* Daly Beauty, Make-up Made Easy, New Looks From Barbara Daly; *Recreations* eastern philosophy, swimming; *Clubs* RAC; *Style—* Ms Barbara Daly; Colourings Ltd, 4 Albion Place, Galena Rd, London W6 OLT (☎ 01 741 8090, fax 741 2951, telex 263440)

DALY, Most Rev Cahal Brendan; *see*: Down and Connor, Bishop of

DALY, Lt-Col Denis James; s of Maj Denis Bowes Daly, MC (d 1984), of The Glen House, Ballingarry, Co Limerick, Eire, and Diana, *née* Lascelles (d 1971); *b* 23 May 1930; *Educ* Eton; *m* 20 Feb 1954, Valerie Margaret, da of Maj Rae Crawford Stirling-Stuart (d 1977), of Cowbridge Lodge, Malmesbury, Wilts; 2 s (Anthony b 1959 d 1982, Christopher b 1964), 1 da (Phillipa Jane b 1957); *Career* cmmnd RHG 1949, cmd household Cav Regt 1969-72, def advsr Br High Cmmn Malawi 1973-75, cmd Driving and Maintenance Sch RAC Centre 1978-80, ret 1983; COI 1983-85, Capt of Invalids Royal Hosp Chelsea 1986-; *Recreations* field sports; *Clubs* Cavalry and Gds, Royal Cwlth Soc; *Style—* Lt-Col Denis Daly; 41B Warwick Gdns, London W14 8PL; Royal Hosp, Chelsea, London SW3 4SR (☎ 01 730 0161)

DALY, Francis D; s of Edward M Daly, of Montenotte, Cork (d 1983), and Clare, *née* Egan (d 1987); *b* 16 Sept 1943; *Educ* Glenstal Abbey, Univ Coll Cork (BCL); *m* 21 February 1970, Patricia Mary, da of the late H P O'Connor, of Cork; 2 s (Teddy b 14 Nov 1970, Ken b 23 Apr 1971), 2 da (Aiveen b 14 Nov 1973, Alex b 6 Oct 1976); *Career* admitted slr 1966, ptnr Ronan Daly Jermyn & Co 1970- (joined 1966); chm: Allied Metropole Hotel plc, Cork Charitable Coal Fund; memb Cncl Inc Law Soc (chm fin ctee); *Recreations* golf, sailing; *Clubs* Cork Golf, Cork & County, Schull Sailing; *Style—* Francis D Daly, Esq; Cleveland, Blackroad Rd, Cork; Corthna, Schull, Co Cork (☎ 021 294 279); 12 South Mall, Cork (☎ 021 272 333, fax 021 273 521, telex 76165)

DALY, Margaret Elizabeth; MEP Somerset Dorset West 1984-; da of Robert Bell (d 1978), of Belfast, and Evelyn Elizabeth, *née* McKenna; *b* 26 Jan 1938; *Educ* Methodist Coll Belfast; *m* 1964, Kenneth Anthony Edward Daly, s of Edward Joseph Daly (d 1983), of Ireland; 1 da (Denise b 1971); *Career* Trade Union official ASTMS 1959-70, conslt Cons Central Off 1976-79, dir Cons TU Orgn 1979-84; *Style—* Mrs Margaret Daly, MEP; The Old School House, Aisholt, Bridgwater, Somerset; European Parliament Strasbourg (☎ 027 867 688)

DALY, Prof Michael de Burgh; s of Dr Ivan de Burgh Daly, CBE (d 1974), of Long Crendon, Bucks, and Beatrice Mary, *née* Leetham (d 1976); *b* 7 May 1922; *Educ* Loretto, Gonville and Caius Coll Cambridge (MA, MD, ScD), St Bartholomews Hosp London; *m* 4 Sept 1948, Beryl Esmé, da of Wing Cdr Alfred James Nightingale (d 1948), of London; 2 s (Colin de Burgh b 10 Sept 1950, Nigel de Burgh b 20 March 1954); *Career* house physician St Bartholomews Hosp London 1947-48, lectr in physiology UCL 1948-54, pt/t extramural contract Miny of Supply (now MOD) Porton Wilts 1949-51, Rockefeller Fndn travelling fell in med Univ of Pennsylvania USA 1952-53, Locke res fell Royal Soc at Dept of Physiology UCL 1955-58, chair of physiology Univ of London at St Bartholomews Hosp Med Sch London 1958-84; visiting prof: physiology Univ of NSW Aust 1966, Ethel Mary Bailleu fell Baker Med Res Inst Melbourne 1976, distinguished visitor in physiology Royal Free Hosp Sch of Med 1984-; many pubns in sci jls, film William Harvey and the Circulation of the Blood (awarded Gold Medal of BMA); tres St Bartholomews Hosp Med Sch 1983-84, ed Jl of Physiology 1956-63 and 1984-89i, chm monographs bd of Physiological Soc 1981-87 (memb 1979-87); awarded: Schafer Prize in Physiology UCL 1953, Thruston Medal Gonville and Caius Coll Cambridge 1958, Sir Lionel Whitby Medal Cambridge Univ 1963; memb: Physiological Soc 1951-86 (hon memb 1986-), Soc of Experimental Biology 1965-, Undersea and Hyperbaric Med Soc 1972-88, Euro Undersea Biomed Soc 1972-, Br Heart Fndn Res Fund Ctee 1982-85; FRSM 1958-; *Recreations* model engineering; *Clubs* Royal Soc of Med; *Style—* Prof Michael Daly; 7 Hall Drive, Sydenham, London SE26 6XL (☎ 01 788 8773); Dept of Physiology, Royal Free Hosp Sch of Med, Rowland Hill St, London NW3 2PF (☎ 01 794 0500)

DALY, Michael Francis; **CMG**; s of late William Thomas Daly, and Hilda Frances Daly; *b* 7 April 1931; *Educ* Downside, Gonville and Caius Coll Cambridge; *m* 1, 1963, Sally Malcolm Angwin (d 1966); 1 da; m 2, 1971, Juliet Mary Siragusa, *née* Arning; 1 step da; *Career* Transreef Industrial & Investment Co 1955-66, General Electric Co London 1966; HM Diplomatic Service: first sec FCO 1967, first sec (Commercial) Rio de Janeiro 1969, first sec (info) and head of chancery Dublin 1973, asst head Cultural Relations Dept FCO 1976, cnsllr consul-gen and head of chancery Brasilia 1977-78, ambass Ivory Coast Upper Volta and Niger 1978-83, head W African Dept FCO and non-resident ambass Chad 1983-86, ambass Costa Rica and non-resident ambass to Nicaragua 1986-; *Style—* Michael Daly, Esq, CMG; Foreign and Commonwealth Office, King Charles St, London SW1 (☎ 01 233 4576)

DALY, Lt-Gen Sir Thomas Joseph; KBE (1965, CBE 1953, OBE 1944), CB (1965), DSO (1945); s of Lt-Col Thomas Joseph Daly, DSO, VD, of Melbourne (d 1968, family arrived 1878) and Eileen Mary Daly (d 1948, family arrived 1853); *b* 19 Mar 1913; *Educ* St Patrick's Coll Sale Vic, Xavier Coll Kew Vic, RMC Duntroon (Sword of Honour), Staff Coll Camberley UK (psc), Joint Services Staff Coll Latimer UK (jssc), Imperial Def Coll London (idc); *m* 1946, Heather Ada, da of James Patrick Fitzgerald (d 1965); 3 da; *Career* served WWII 1941-45 (despatches twice), cmd 2/10 Aust MF Battalion 1944-45, Middle East and SW Pacific, cmd 28 Br Cwlth Bde Korea 1952-53, Vietnam, US Legion of Merit 1953, dir ps and plans AHQ 1952-53, GOC Northern Cmd Aust 1957-60, GOC Eastern Cmd Aust 1963-66, Chief of Gen Staff 1966-71, ret 1971; Col Cmdt RAR and Hon Col Pacific Is Regt 1971-75, cncllr Royal Agric Soc of NSW 1972-85; (hon cncllr 1985-); dir: Jennings Industs 1973-85, Fruehauf Gp of Cos 1973-88, chm Cncl of Aust Nat War Meml 1974-82; *see Debrett's Handbook of Australia and New Zealand for further details*; *Recreations* golf, cricket, skiing, gardening; *Clubs* Australian, Sydney, Royal Sydney GC, Melbourne Cricket, Ski Club of Aust; *Style—* Lt-Gen Sir Thomas Daly, KBE, CB, DSO; 16 Victoria Rd, Bellevue Hill, NSW 2023, Australia (☎ 327 7627)

DALYELL, Hon Mrs (Kathleen Mary Agnes); *née* Wheatley; da of Baron Wheatley (Life Baron) (d 1988); *b* 17 Nov 1937; *Educ* Convent of Sacred Heart, Queens Con, Aberdeen, Edinburgh Univ; *m* 26 Dec 1963, Tam Dalyell, MP, *qv*; 1 s, 1 da; *Career* teacher of history; memb Historic Buildings Cncl of Scotland; *Recreations* reading, travel, hill walking; *Style—* The Hon Mrs Dalyell; The Binns, Linlithgow EH49 7NA

DALYELL, Tam; MP; s of Lt-Col Gordon Dalyell, CIE, and Eleanor; *b* 9 August 1932; *Educ* Eton, King's Coll Cambridge, Moray House, Edinburgh Univ; *m* 26 Dec 1963, Kathleen Mary Agnes, da of Baron Wheatley, QC, *qv*; 1 s (Gordon b 26 Sept 1965), 1 da (Noira b 25 May 1968); *Career* Nat Serv Royal Scots Greys 1950-52; MP (Lab) for Linlithgow 1962-; memb: Public Accounts Ctee, Select Ctee on Sci and Tech 1965-68, Nat Exec Ctee of Lab Pty 1986-87; weekly columnist New Scientist 1967-; memb: Educn Inst of Scot, NUR; *Books* Case for Ship Schools (1960), Ship School Duneva (1962), Devolution: the End of Britain ? (1978), One Man's Falklands (1983), A Science Policy for Britain (1983), Misrule How Mrs Thatcher Misled Parliament (1987); *Style—* Tam Dalyell, Esq, MP; Binns, Linlithgow, Scotland

DALZEL-JOB, Lt Cdr Patrick; DL (1979); s of Capt Ernest Dalzel Job (ka 1916), and Ethel, *née* Griffiths (d 1970); *b* 1 June 1913; *Educ* Berkhamsted Sch, Switzerland; *m* 26 June 1945, Bjorg (d 1986), da of Erling Bangsund (d 1977), of Tromso, Norway; 1 s (Iain b 1946); *Career* naval offr and writer; Lt Cdr, ret 1956, youth organiser Duke of Edinburgh's Award adventure Schooners; Kt (1 class) Royal Norwegian Order of St Olav; *Recreations* sailing, skiing; *Clubs* Special Forces; *Style—* Lt Cdr Patrick Dalzel-Job, DL; Nead-an-Eoin, by Plockton, Ross-shire, Scotland (☎ 059984 244)

DALZELL, Ian Robert; s of Thomas Leon Dalzell (d 1958), and Barbara, *née*, Curnock; *b* 22 Nov 1949; *Educ* The Heath Sch, Univ of Lancaster (MA); *m* 13 Dec 1974, Susan Amy, da of Percy Phillips (d 1971); 2 s (Ross b 1981, James b 1984); *Career* CA 1971; res offr Int Centre for Res in Accounting 1972-76, princ lectr Lancashire Poly 1976-87, ptnr Ross Dalzell Grange-over-Sands 1987-, dir Grange Investment Servs 1987; pres NW Soc of CA 1982-83; *Recreations* swimming, fell-walking, bird watching; *Style—* Ian Dalzell, Esq; Badger's Sett, Windermere Rd, Grange-over-Sands, Cumbria; Ross Dalzell, Main St, Grange-over-Sands, Cumbria

DALZELL, Lady Muriel Marjorie; *née* Dalzell; da of late 13 Earl of Carnwath; *b* 22 Sept 1903; *m* 18 Jan 1927, Lt-Col John Norton Taylor, who assumed, by Royal Licence, surname and arms of Dalzell on marriage; only son of late James Taylor, Lisnamallard, to Tyrone; 1 s; *Style—* Lady Muriel Dalzell; Sand House, Wedmore, Somerset (☎ 0934 712224)

DALZIEL, Ian Martin; s of John Calvin Dalziel (d 1983), and Elizabeth Roy, *née* Bain; *b* 21 June 1947; *Educ* Daniel Stewart's Coll Edinburgh, St John's Coll Cambridge, Université Libre de Bruxelles; *m* 1972, Nadia Maria Iacovazzi; 4 s; *Career* Mullens & Co 1970-72 (Mfrs Hanover Ltd (London and NY) 1972-83); co-fndr and dep md Adam & Co plc 1983-; memb Richmond upon Thames Cncl 1978-79; MEP (EDG) Lothians 1979-84; *Recreations* golf, shooting; *Clubs* New (Edinburgh); *Style—* Ian Dalziel, Esq; Adam & Co plc, 22 Charlotte Sq, Edinburgh EH2 4DF (☎ 031 225 8484); Callands House, West Linton, Peebleshire EH46 7DE (☎ 0721 52209)

DALZIEL, Malcolm Stuart; CBE (1984); s of Robert Henderson Dalziel (d 1979), and Susan Aileen, *née* Robertson (d 1981); *b* 18 Sept 1936; *Educ* Banbury GS, St Catherine's Coll Oxford (MA); *m* 1961, Elizabeth Anne, da of Major Philip Collins Harvey (d 1977); 1 s (Rory b 1974), 2 da (Caroline, Annabel); *Career* Nat Serv 1955-57, Lt The Northamptonshire Regt; The British Cncl: educn offr Lahore Pakistan 1961-63, regnl dir Penang Malaysia 1963-67, regnl rep Lahore Pakistan 1967-70, rep Sudan 1970-74, dir mgmnt serv dept and dep controller estabs div 1974-79, controller higher educn div 1983-87; cncllr cultural affairs The British Embassy Cairo 1979-83, sec Int Univ and Poly Cncl 1983-87; memb exec ctee Cncl for Educn in the Cwlth 1983-88, affiliate Queen Elizabeth House Int Devpt Centre Oxford Univ, assoc conslt CERES (Conslts in Econ Regeneration in Europe Servs) 1988-; memb exec ctee Council for Education in the Commonwealth 1983-; memb Court Univ of Essex 1983-; *Recreations* theatre, ballet, rugby football, walking; *Clubs* United Oxford and Cambridge; *Style—* Malcolm Dalziel Esq, CBE; 368 Woodstock Rd, Oxford OX2 8AE (☎ 0865 58969)

DAMANT, David Cyril; s of William Alexander Arthur Damant (d 1983), and Mary Edith Damant; *b* 15 Mar 1937; *Educ* Queens' Coll Cambridge; *Career* former ptnr Investmt Res Cambridge; pres Euro Fedn of Fin Analysts Socs 1974-76, chm Soc of Investmt Analysts 1980-82 (fellow 1986, former ptnr, Quilter Goodison Co 1982-86, md Paribas Asst Mgmnt (UK) Ltd 1987-; bd memb Int Accounting Standards Ctee 1986-, memb UK Accounting Standards Ctee 1987-; *Recreations* travelling; *Clubs* Beefsteak, Garrick, City of London; *Style—* David Damant, Esq; Agar House, 12 Agar St, London WC2 (☎ 01 379 6926); 16 Orchard St, Cambridge (☎ 0223 357768); Paribas Asset Management (UK) Ltd, 68 Lombard St, London EC3V 9LJ (☎ 01 621 1161, fax 621 9108, telex 886055)

DAMANT, Maj John Louis; s of Cdr Eric Louis Baxter Damant (d 1964), and Sybil Alice, *née* Joy; *b* 13 April 1930; *Educ* Cheltenham, RMA Sandhurst; *m* 8 Oct 1960 (m dis 1974), Gillian, da of John Harvey; 2 s (Patrick John Charles, Charles Francis), 1 da (Louisa Jane); m 2, 8 Feb 1979, Jane Garrett; *Career* cmmnd 7 (QO) Hussars 1950: Korea 1952 (ADC Gen Mike West), Hong Kong and Malaya 1954-56, UN Cyprus 1964, withdrawal Aden 1967, ret 1968; set up Food for Thought restaurant in Covent Garden London 1977, ret to France in 1983 (leaving restaurant under charge of step-da) to continue painting, studied in Paris Atêlier Goetz 8 Cours De Ville Montparnasse 1974; *Recreations* racing, roulette, art exhibitions; *Clubs* Lansdowne, Charlie Chesters; *Style—* Maj John Damant; La Vernelle, Monsaguel, Issigeac 24560, France (☎ 53 58 71 48)

DAMERELL, Derek Vivian; s of Lt-Col William James Damerell and Zoe Damerell; *b* 4 August 1921; *Educ* Imperial Serv Coll, Edinburgh Univ, Harvard Business Sch; *Career* memb parent bd BPB Industs 1953-64, regnl dir Int Wool Secretariat 1965-73, dir The Medical Centre, chm and fndr Ind Hosp Gp Cncl, govr and chief exec BUPA 1974-84, dep chm 1984-88; *Style—* Derek Damerell, Esq; The Miller's House,

Houghton, Cambs PE17 2BQ (☎ 0480 63285)

DAMERELL, Lady Mary Barbara; *née* Carnegie; yr da of 13 Earl of Northesk, *qv*; *b* 10 Feb 1953; *Educ* Oak Hall Haslemere, Heathfield Ascot; *m* 1977, William Patrick Sterling Damerell; 3 s (Charles b 1980, Thomas b 1982, Robert b 1985); *Style*— Lady Mary Damerell; 2 Kempson Road, Fulham, London SW6 4PV

DAMPNEY, Major Theo Douglas; TD (1960), JP (Dorset 1964); s of Douglas Reeks Dampney (d 1974), and Kathleen Mary, *née* Hall (d 1972); *b* 4 Mar 1922; *Educ* Blundells; *m* 4 Sept 1957, Joan Elizabeth Mary, da of Roy Dry of Dorset; 3 s (Trelawney b 1958, Tristram b 1960, Piers b 1962), 1 da (Alexandra b 1964); *Career* Royal Wilts Yeo 1939, cmmnd Sandhurst 1942, 3 Hussars ME and Italy 1942-46, Royal Wilts Yeo 1948-60, ret Maj; memb cncl RASE 1976, (dep chm and chm Hants exec ctee 1964-73), memb cncl NFU 1961-79 (chm Hants 1957); *Recreations* sailing, shooting; *Clubs* Cavalry and Guards, Farmers; *Style*— Maj Theo Dampney; Parley Court, Hurn, Christ Church, Dorset BH23 6BB (☎ 0202 573361)

DANCE, Brian David; s of Leonard Harold Dance (d 1964), of E Molesey, and Marjorie Greenfield (d 1978), (later Mrs Swain), *née* Shrivelle; *b* 22 Nov 1929; *Educ* Kingston GS, Wadham Coll Oxford (BA, MA), London Univ; *m* 17 Aug 1955, Chloe Elizabeth, da of John Frederic Allan Baker, CB, (d 1987); 2 s (David b 1956, Richard b 1959), 2 da (Amanda b 1962, Sarah b 1964); *Career* Nat Serv 1948-49, Flt Lt RAFVR (T) 1954-61; asst master Kingston GS 1953-59; sr history master: Faversham GS 1959-62, Westminster City Sch 1962-65, headmaster Cirencester GS 1965-66, princ Luton Sixth Form Coll 1966-73, headmaster St Dunstans Coll Catford 1973-; memb Cambridge Local Examinations Syndicate 1968-73, fndr chm Lewisham Environmental Tst 1987-88, govr Bromley HS 1983-; memb HMC 1973, SHA (formerly Headmasters Assoc 1965-, cncl memb 1968-76, nat exec ctee 1972-76); *Books* Articles for Times Educational Supplement and Headmasters' Association Review; *Recreations* theatre, music, watching but no longer playing ball games; *Clubs* East India, Devonshire, Sports and Public Sch; *Style*— Brian Dance, Esq; The Headmaster's House, St Dunstan's College, London SE6 4TY (☎ 01 690 1277); St Dunstan's College, Stanstead Road, Catford, London SE6 4TY (☎ 01 690 1274/7)

DANCE, Charles Walter; s of Walter Dance (d 1950), of Birmingham, and Eleanor,*née* Perks (d 1985) ; *b* 10 Oct 1946; *Educ* Widey Tech Sch Plymouth, Plymouth Sch of Art, Leicester Coll of Art and Design; *m* 18 July 1970, Joanna Elizabeth Nicola Daryl, da of Francis Harold Haythorn, of Plymstock, Devon; 1 s (Oliver b 1974), 1 da (Rebecca b 1980); *Career* actor 1970-; seasons at repertory theatres: Leeds, Oxford, Windsor, Swindon, Chichester, Greenwich; memb New Shakespeare Co, joined RSC 1975 roles incl: Catesby in Richard III, Oliver in As You Like It, Lancaster in Henry IV, title role in Henry V, Aufidius and title role in Coriolanus; television: Seigfried Sasson in The Fatal Spring, Truman in Rainy Day Women, Harry Maxim in The Secret Servant, Guy Perron in The Jewel in the Crown (nomination for Best Actor); films: Plenty, The Macguffin, The Golden Child, Good Morning Babylon, Hidden City, White Mischief, Pascali's Island; *Style*— C W Dance, Esq; c/o Caroline Dawson Associates, 47 Courtfield Rd, London SW7 (☎ 01 370 0708)

DANDO, John Penstone; s of Lionel Victor Dando (d 1935), and Winifred Kate, *née* Penstone (d 1970); *b* 17 Feb 1935; *Educ* Wembley County Sch; *m* 18 April 1960, Patricia Ann, da of Henry Gammel Lee (d 1977); 1 s (Gavin b 1967), 2 da (Stella b 1963, Karen b 1964); *Career* dir: F Bolton & Co (Aviation) Ltd 1967-84, F Bolton & Co (Foreign) Ltd, Matheson Bolton & Co Ltd, F Bolton and Co (Hldgs) Ltd 1975; md: F Bolton Int Ltd 1975-84, Frizzell D E P Ltd 1983; *Recreations* trombone, wildlife, reading, walking, boating, wine; *Style*— John P Dando, Esq; College Farm House, Ferry Road, South Stoke, Reading RG8 0JP; Frizzell D E P Ltd, 14-22 Elder Street, London E1 (☎ 01 247 6595)

DANDY, Robert Michael; s of John Dandy, DL, of Bedford, and Mary Dandy, *née* Simkins (d 1978); *b* 11 May 1954; *Educ* Wellingborough Sch, Coll of Law Guildford; *m* 12 April 1980, Eithne Bridget, da of Dr J J Holloway, of Northampton (d 1967); 1 s (Peter John b 1982), 1 da (Eleanor Mary b 1984; *Career* slr Messrs C C Bell and Son Bedford 1980-87; company sec Gibbs and Dandy plc 1980-86 (dir 1984), md 1986); dir: Bedford Bldg Soc Bedford 1982-, Assoc Heating Equipment Distributors Ltd, Gibbs and Dandy Pension Tstees Ltd, Luton 1986-; *Recreations* cricket, soccer; *Clubs* Bedford, MCC; *Style*— Michael Dandy, Esq; Gibbs and Dandy plc, PO Box 17, Gidan House, chapel Street, Luton LU1 2SF (☎ 0582 21233)

DANGAN, Elizabeth, Viscountess; Elizabeth Anne; da of late Lt-Col Pelham Rawstorn Papillon (d 1940), DSO, of Crowhurst Park, Sussex; *b* 14 May 1920; *m* 1, 16 July 1938, Flt Lt Stephen Avers Hankey, RAF (ka 1943); m 2 da (Stephanie b 1939, Mrs Roger Parkman Griswold; Caroline b posthumously 1944, Mrs Robert Fitz Randolph Ballard); 2, 17 Nov 1944 (m dis 1950), Denis Arthur, Viscount Dangan (later 5 Earl Cowley, d 1968); 1 s (Richard Francis, 6 Earl Cowley b 1946, d 1975); 2, 11 Dec 1953, Freeman Winslow Hill, of Bermuda; 1 da; *Style*— Elizabeth, Viscountess Dangan; PO Box 285, Paget, Bermuda

DANGAN, Viscount; Garrett Graham Wellesley; s (by 1 m) and h of 7 Earl Cowley; *b* 30 Mar 1965; *Career* Traded Options, Hoare Govett Ltd; *Clubs* 151 Club, Brooks's; *Style*— Viscount Dangan

DANIEL, David Albiston; JP (Cheshire 1960); s of Norman Albiston Daniel (d 1965), of Gandria, Congleton, Cheshire, and Evelyn Mary *née* Congdon (d 1987); *b* 16 Dec 1928; *Educ* Trent Coll; *m* 17 Sept 1955, Joyce, da of George Beach Aylett (d 1964), of Bodelwyddan, Clwyd; 1 s (Julian Albiston b 1963), 1 da (Sara Caroline Bostock b 1957); *Career* slr; dep coroner Ches 1960-74, chm SE Ches Petty Sessional Div 1967-74, pres N Staffs Law Soc 1987-88; *Style*— David Daniel, Esq; Copperfields, Peel Lane, Astbury, Congleton, Ches CW12 4RE (☎ 0260 273180); 8/10 West St, Congleton, Ches CW12 1JS (☎ 0260 272777, telex 667111 LEX G, fax 0260 274243)

DANIEL, Gerald Ernest; s of Ernest Daniel, and Beata May Daniel; *b* 7 Dec 1919; *Educ* Huish's GS Taunton; *m* 1942, Ecila Roslyn Dillow; 1 s, 1 da; *Career* appts in borough tres' depts 1935-68, city tres Nottingham 1968-74, county tres Nottinghamshire 1974-84; dir: Horizon Travel plc 1975-85; public sector advsr Pannell Kerr Forster CAs 1984-; memb IPFA 1949- (pres 1983-84), FCA, FRVA, SAT, FRSA; *Clubs* Royal Overseas League; *Style*— Gerald Daniel Esq; Brookvale, Star Lane, Blackboys, Uckfield, East Sussex TN22 5LD (☎ 082 582712); New Garden House, 78 Hatton Garden, London EC1N 8JA (☎ 01 831 7393, telex 295928 panker)

DANIEL, Sir Goronwy Hopkin; KCVO (1969), CB (1962); s of David Daniel; *b* 21 Mar 1914; *Educ* Pontardawe Secdy Sch, Amman Valley County Sch, Univ Coll of Wales Aberystwyth, Jesus Coll Oxford; *m* 28 March 1940, Lady Valerie Lloyd-George *qv*; 1 s, 2 da; *Career* lectr dept of econs Bristol Univ 1940-41, clerk House of Commons (attached to select ctee Nat Expenditure) 1941-43, Miny of Town & Country Planning 1943-47, chief statistician Miny of Fuel and Power 1947, under sec 1955-64, perm under sec of state Welsh Off 1964-69; prince Univ Coll of Wales Aberystwyth 1969-79, vice chllr Univ of Wales 1977-79; dep chm Commercial Bank of Wales 1984- (dir 1972-); HM Lieutenant for Dyfed 1979-; former chm HGTAC; former memb: gen advsy cncl BBC, Welsh Language Cncl, SSRC; chm Welsh Fourth TV Channel Authy 1981-86; dep chm Prince of Wales Ctee 1980-86; Hon Freeman City of London; hon fell: Jesus Coll Oxford, Univ of Wales; Hon LLD Wales; *Clubs* Travellers'; *Style*— Sir Goronwy Daniel, KCVO, CB; Ridge Farm, Letterston, Dyfed (☎ 0348 840586); 4 Deans Close, Llandaf, Cardiff (☎ 0222 553150)

DANIEL, His Hon Judge Gruffydd Huw Morgan; second s of Professor John Edward Daniel (d 1962), and Catherine Megan Parry, *née* Hughes (d 1972); *b* 16 April 1939; *Educ* Ampleforth, Univ Coll of Wales (LLB), Inns of Court Sch of Law; *m* 10 Aug 1968, Phyllis Margaret Bermingham, da of Walter Ambrose Bermingham Esq, of Clifden, Connemara, Eire (d 1988); 1 da (Antonia Siwan Bermingham); *Career* CJ 1986-; Nat Service 1958-60 (volunteered) served 24 Foot, the South Wales Borderers, cmmnd 2 Lt 23 Foot the Royal Welch Fusiliers, Capt 67 RWF 1965, served MELF (Cyprus) and UK; barr Gray's Inn 1967-86 (rec 1980-86), in practice Wales and Chester circuit, circuit jr 1975, asst parly boundary cmmr for Wales 1981-82 (Gwynedd Enquiry) and in 1985, liaison judge for Gwynedd 1988- (dep liaison judge 1984-88); *Recreations* shooting, sailing, gardening; *Clubs* Reform, Royal Anglesey Yacht ; *Style*— His Hon Judge Gruffydd Daniel; Rhiw Goch, Halfway Bridge, Bangor, Gwynedd; The Castle, Chester

DANIEL, (Reginald) Jack; OBE (1958); s of Reginald Daniel Daniel and Florence Emily, *née* Woods; *b* 27 Feb 1920; *Educ* Royal Naval Engrg Coll Keyham, RNC Greenwich; *Career* warship and submarine designer; dir Submarine Design and Prodn 1970-74, dir gen Ships and head of RCNC and MOD 1974-79, bd memb Br Shipbuilders and dir of technol warships 1979-84, conslt and Canadian project dir VSEL plc 1984-; FEng, FRINA, FIMarE, RCNC; *Style*— R Jack Daniel, Esq, OBE; Meadowland, Cleveland Walk, Bath; VSEL Upper Borough Walls, Bath BA1 1RG (☎ 0225 61 177)

DANIEL, James Wallace (Jim); JP (W London 1981-83); s of James Warren Daniel, of St Ives, Cornwall, and Isabella Fullarton, *née* Robb; *b* 7 Dec 1941; *Educ* Truro Sch, Brasenose Coll Oxford (MA), Leeds Univ (DipTESL); *m* 14 Aug 1965, Jennifer Ruth, da of Albert George Hamer, MBE, of Shaftesbury; 1 s (James), 1 da (Tamsin); *Career* Br Cncl 1964-, cultural attaché Br Embassy Washington DC USA 1987-; Freeman City of London 1982, Liveryman Painter-Stainers 1982; FBIM 1980; *Books* Topo (trans 1989); *Recreations* travel, reading, listening to music; *Clubs* Oriental; *Style*— Jim Daniel, Esq, JP; c/o Foreign and Commonwealth Office, King Charles St, London SW1A 2AH

DANIEL, Norman Alexander; CBE (1974, OBE 1968); s of George Frederick Daniel (d 1945); *b* 8 May 1919; *Educ* Frensham Heights Sch, Queen's Coll Oxford (BA), Edinburgh Univ (PhD); *m* 1941, Marion Ruth (d 1981), da of Harold Wadham Pethybridge; 1 s (decd); *Career* Br Cncl rep Sudan 1962, dir visitors dept Br Cncl London 1970, cultural attaché Cairo 1971, Br Cncl rep and cultural cnsllr Br Embassy Cairo 1973-79, ret 1979; author on history of Arab-Euro relations; Egyptian Order of Merit 1977; *Books* Islam and the West (1962, 1964, 1966, 1980), Islam Europe and Empire (1966), The Cultural Barrier (1975), Arabs and Medieval Europe (1975, 1979, Lao Silesu prize 1981 for Italian edition), Heroes and Saracens (1984); *Style*— Norman Daniel, Esq, CBE; Institut d'Etudes Orientales, 1 rue Masna al Tarabich, Abbasiah, Cairo, Egypt (☎ 825509); Rés le Grammont, St Gingolph, 74500 Evian, France (☎ (50) 76 72 62)

DANIEL, Peter; s of Lt-Col H O Daniel (d 1953), and Margery, *née* Thomas (d 1974); *b* 6 Nov 1924; *Educ* St Paul's Sch London, King Williams Coll IOM, Liverpool Univ (B ARch, MCD); *m* 6 Sept 1951 (m dis 1971), Helen, da of C W Cockrell (d 1977), of Liverpool; 1 s (William b 1954), 2 da (Sarah b 1958, Tacye (adopted) b 1956); *Career* RN 1943-46 Sub Lt RNVR served Russian Convoys and Far East Fleet; former dep chief architect Peterlee Newtown 1960, chief architect and planner Livingston New Town 1962, private practice as conslt landscape architect and planner 1965-; *Recreations* art, music, gardening; *Clubs* Edinburgh Univ Staff; *Style*— Peter Daniel, Esq; Church House, Foulden, by Berwick upon Tweed TD15 1UH (☎ 0289 86307, fax 041 332 7520)

DANIEL, Philip Louis; 2 s of Oscar Louis Wood Moore (d 1931), and Louisa Ann, *née* à Court (d 1919); name changed by Deed Poll from à Court Moore 1945; *b* 23 June 1919; *Educ* Cardinal Vaughan Meml Sch Kensington, LSE (BA); *Career* cadet OTC (RA) Univ of London 1937-39, cmmnd RA 1940, Capt 1942, served Burma and India 1942-45, Maj 1944, SO HQ SEAC 1944-45 (Supreme Allied Cdr's Commendation 1945); Maj RARO 1945-69; asst princ Civil Serv; Miny of Food: joined 1948, served Overseas Food Corpn Tanganyika, priv sec to Sir Laurence Helsby 1950, Sir Frank Lee 1951 and Sir Henry Hancock 1952; Air Miny 1953, asst sec Dept Econ Affrs 1965, dep chm SE Econ Planning Bd 1968; DOE: head London geographical planning div 1972-78, new towns div 1978-79, memb planning inspectorate 1980-89; chm int ctee Newman Assoc GB 1960-84 (pres 1969-71), chm issues ctee Catholic Union GB 1980-, memb cncl Town and Country Planning Assoc 1982-; tres Reigate and Banstead Heritage Tst 1980-, memb cncl Reigate Soc; hon memb Phi Kappa Theta Fraternity Fairfield Conn USA 1971; Freeman City of London 1972 (memb Guild of Freeman 1974), Liveryman Worshipful Co of Scriveners 1978; FBIM 1980; KSG (HH Pope Paul VI) 1975, Kt Order of Holy Sepulchre of Jerusalem 1980 (cdre 1985); *Books* articles incl: Can World Poverty Be Abolished (World Justice Vol XII), A Nation's Shame, Three Decades of London Housing (East London Papers Vol 13, 1971); reports incl: South East Joint Planning Study (1970), London Manpower Study (1976); *Recreations* motoring, fencing, theatre, historical and economic writing; *Clubs* Army and Navy, Players' Theatre; *Style*— Philip Daniel, Esq; Meadhouse, 37 Somerset Rd, Redhill, Surrey RH1 6LT; Rendel Planning, 61 Southwark St, London SE1 1SA (☎ 01 620 1481)

DANIEL, Ruth; da of Rev Richard William Bailey Langhorne (d 1944); whose forebears incl Daniel Langhorne the antiquary (d 1681), Richard Langhorne a victim of Titus Oates (executed 1679) and among American cousins Lady (Nancy) Astor, *née* Langhorne; da of Victoria Winifred Helen, *née* Poole (d 1968); *b* 5 July 1915; *Educ* Maynard Sch Exeter, St Anne's Coll, Oxford Univ (MA); *m* 12 Sept 1946, Glyn

Edmund Daniel (d 1986), s of John Daniel (d 1948), of Glamorgan; *Career* served WW II in photographic intelligence, Flight Offr WRAF 1941-46; production ed Antiquity (a review of archaeology) 1956-86; *Recreations* music; *Clubs* United Oxford & Cambridge Univ Club (Lady Associate Memb); *Style*— Mrs Glyn Daniel; The Flying Stag, 70 Bridge Street, Cambridge CB2 1UR

DANIEL, Lady Valerie Davidia; *née* Lloyd George; da of 2 Earl Lloyd-George of Dwyfor; *b* 14 Feb 1918; *m* 28 March 1940, Sir Goronwy Daniel, KCVO, CB, *qv*; 1 s, 2 da; *Style*— Lady Valerie Daniel; Ridge Farm, Letterston, Dyfed (☎ (0348) 840586); 4 Deans Close, Llandaf, Cardiff (☎ (0222) 535150)

DANIELL, Antony Piers de Tabley; OBE (1960), MC (1944), TD (1945); s of Henry Thesiger Whiteman Daniell (d 1935), of Pencraig, Llangefni, Anglesey, and Maud Edith Thesiger, *née* Phibbs (d 1953); *b* 19 June 1913; *Educ* Greshams, Trinity Coll Cambridge (MA); *m* 30 Sept 1947, Noreen Mary Alison, da of Col Alexander John Cruickshank, DSO (d 1978), of Innage House, Shifnal, Salop; 1 s (John b 1950); *Career* TA RE 1937, enlisted 1939, Capt 1940, Maj 1942; OC 59 Fd Co RE in 4 Br Div: N Africa 1 Army 1943, Italy 1944, RE Newark 1944, demob 1945, rejoined TA Lt-Col 1947, Col 1956; civil engrg contractor; dir Wilson Lovatt & Sons Ltd 1955-71 (joined 1935); chm The Network 1982-89; memb: Ironbridge Gorge Devpt Tst 1971-78, Shropshire Conservation Devpt Tst 1981-; DL: Staffs 1962. Shropshire 1974; FICE 1960 (memb 1939); *Recreations* walking, bird watching, gardening; *Clubs* Naval and Military; *Style*— Col Antony Daniell, OBE, MC, TD; Cottage Farm House, Frodesley, Shrewsbury SY5 7HD (☎ 06944 626)

DANIELL, Col Erroll Bampfylde; OBE (1945); s of Harold Bampfylde Daniell (d 1955), of Ceylon, and Hariet Agnes, *née* Woodward; *b* 31 Mar 1905; *Educ* Sherborne Sch Cirencester, Agriculture Coll (Dip Agric); *m* 15 Feb 1936, Beatrice Jenny, da of Major John William Oldfield (d 1955); 1 s (Anthony b 1939); *Career* served WW II; Capt RA 1939-40, provost marshal Gen Slim's HQ, Burma Campaign (despatches), OBE for Kohima Siege; tea planter 1923-39; Ceylon Garrison Artillery 1925; adc to HE Govrs of Ceylon 1932-37; military police 1940-; Col; ret; *Clubs* Army and Navy; *Style*— Col Erroll B Daniell, OBE; Flat G2, Marine Gate, Marine Drive, Brighton BN2 5JQ (☎ 693066)

DANIELL, Brig Kenneth Francis; CBE (1963, OBE 1955); s of Lt-Col Francis Edward Lloyd Daniell, DSO (ka 1916), by his w Maud Esmie Duperier (d 1913); *b* 22 Oct 1910; *Educ* Malvern, RMA Woolwich, Cambridge Univ; *m* 1935, Doreen Norah, da of Canon A E P French (d 1943); 3 s, 1 da; *Career* Brig (Malta, India, Burma, Middle East, BAOR) ret as chief engr Western Cmd 1963; dir of works Commonwealth War Graves Cmmn 1963-71; *Style*— Brig Kenneth Daniell, CBE; Higher Chalk, Iwerne Minster, Blandford, Dorset (☎ Fontmell Magna 811787)

DANIELL, Hon Mrs (Mary Elizabeth Jill Rodd); da of 2 Baron Rennell (d 1978); *b* 1932; *m* 1, 13 Nov 1954, Michael Langan Dunne; 2 s (John b 1957, Stephen b 1961), 3 da (Mary Jemima b 1955, Teresa b 1962, Miranda b 1966); m 2, 7 March 1985, Christopher Bridges Daniell; *Style*— The Hon Mrs Daniell; 7 Elvaston Mews, London SW7; Ashley Farm, Stansbatch, Pembridge, Herefordshire

DANIELL, Sir Peter Averell; TD (1950), DL (Surrey 1976); s of late Roger Henry Averell Daniell; *b* 8 Dec 1909; *Educ* Eton, Trinity Coll Oxford (MA); *m* 18 July 1935, Leonie Mayne, da of late Henry Beauchamp Harrison; 2 s (Roger b 1939, James b 1949), 1 da (Celia (Mrs Prideaux) b 1936); *Career* KRRC 1939-45; sr ptnr Mullens and Co, ret 1973; sr govt broker 1963-73; kt 1971; *Clubs* Brooks's, Alpine; *Style*— Sir Peter Daniell, TD, DL; Glebe House, Buckland, Surrey (☎ 073 784 2320)

DANIELLS-SMITH, Roger Charles; s of Charles Frederick Daniells-Smith, of Harlow, Essex, and Marie, *née* Daniells; *b* 26 August 1952; *Educ* Newport GS, King's Coll London Univ (LLB); *m* 26 May 1979, Annette Louise, da of Stefan Kazimiercz Wacnik, DSO (d 1986); 2 da (Helena Elizabeth b 1981, Sophie Anne b 1983); *Career* barr Middle Temple 1974; *Recreations* gardening, motoring, watersports, antiques; *Style*— Roger Daniells-Smith, Esq; 92 Devenay Rd, Stratford, London E15 (☎ 01 555 5792); 8 King's Bench Walk, Temple, London EC4 (☎ 01 353 7851)

DANIELS, (David) Donald; s of Leon Daniels (d 1964), of London, and Anna, *née* Kettelapper (d 1964); *b* 27 Jan 1911; *Educ* Holborn GS, London Poly; *m* 1, 1937 (m dis 1947), Elizabeth Phillips; 1 s (Paul b 22 Feb 1943); m 2, 8 Aug 1950, Miriam (Mimi), da of Morris Aarons (d 1965), of London; 1 da (Linda b 6 June 1952); *Career* Royal Armed Corps 1941, Intelligence Corps (counter espionage interrogator in Europe languages) 1944, demobbed 1946; dep chm S Daniels Co Ltd London 1973 (co-fndr 1946), underwriting memb at Lloyds London; memb: cncl London C of C, nat exec ctee BACFID (Br Assoc of Food Importers ad Distributors); past chm Trades Advsy Cncl, past vice chm ROSPA Advanced Drivers Assoc, former memb Grocers Inst, past pres Portsoken Ward Club; Freeman: City of London 1950, Worshipful Co of Basket Makers; *Recreations* golf, bird breeding, music, travelling; *Clubs* Verulam GC, St Albans City Livery, memb Governing Body Utd Wards Club City of London ; *Style*— Donald Daniels, Esq; Wilec House, 82/100 City Rd, London EC1 (☎ 01 253 9013, fax 01 251 8828, telex 28837 DANOXA)

DANIELS, George; MBE (1982); s of George Daniels and Beatrice, *née* Cadou; *b* 19 August 1926; *m* 1964, Juliet Anne, *née* Marryat; 1 da; *Career* served 2 Bn E Yorks Regt 1944-47; author, watchmaker, horological consultant; began professional horology 1947-, restoration of historical watches 1956-, hand watch-making to own designs 1969-; Master Worshipful Co of Clockmakers 1980, Victor Kullberg Medal Stockholm Watch Guild 1977, Gold Medal Br Horological Inst 1981, Tompion Gold Medal 1981; *Books* English and American Watches (1965), The Art of Breguet (1975, 2nd edition 1978), Watchmaking (1981), Sir David Salomons Collection (1981); *Recreations* vintage cars, fast motorcycles, opera, Scotch whisky; *Style*— George Daniels, Esq, MBE; 34 New Bond St, London W1A 2AA

DANIELS, Karl; s of Harold George Daniels of Ipswich (d 1965); *b* 1 Dec 1935; *Educ* Ipswich Sch; *m* 1960, Janice Margaret, da of Vernon Billing; 2 s; *Career* pension scheme consultant; md Noble Lowndes Pensions Ltd 1979-, Lowndes Associated Pensions Ltd, English Pension Tstees Ltd, Lowndes Mgmnt Incentives Ltd, dir Scottish Pension Tstees Ltd 1976-; *Clubs* RAC; *Style*— Karl Daniels Esq; Church Cottage, Church Rd, Lingfield, Surrey (☎ 832023)

DANIELS, Laurence John; CB (1979), OBE (1970); s of Leslie Daniels and Margaret, *née* Bradley; *b* 11 August 1916; *Educ* Rostrevor Coll S Australia, Sydney Univ; *m* 1943, Joyce Carey; 2 s, 8 da; *Career* AASA 1939, Cwlth (Australian) Taxation Off 1934-53, Cwlth Dept of Health 1953-72; dir-gen Dept of Social Security 1973-77, sec Dept of Capital Territory (Australia) 1977-81; *Style*— Laurence Daniels, Esq, CB, OBE; 5 Nares Crest, Forrest, ACT 2603, Australia (☎ (062) 95 1896)

DANIELS, Newton Edward (Paul Daniels); s of Handel Newton Daniels and Nancy, *née* Lloyd; *b* 06 April 1938; *Educ* Sir William Turner's GS Coatham Redcar; *m* 1, 26 March 1960 (m dis 1975); 3 s (Paul b 9 Sept 1960, Martin b 19 Aug 1963, Gary b 15 March 1969); m 2, 2 April 1988, Debbie, *née* McGee; *Career* Nat Serv Green Howards 1957-59 served Hong Kong; magician and entertainer; clerk (later internal auditor) local govt, mobile grocery business (later shop owner), turned professional 1969, TV debut Opportunity Knocks 1970; subsequent TV series incl: The Paul Daniels Magic Show, Odd One Out, Ever Second Counts, Wizbit (children's series); theatre: It's Magic (Prince of Wales) 1980-82, An Evening with Paul Daniels (Prince of Wales) 1983; summer seasons: Great Yarmouth 1979, Bournemouth 1980, Blackpool 1983; appeared in 5 Royal Variety Shows; winner: Magician of the Year award Hollywood's Acad of Magical Arts 1983, Golden Rose of Montreux trophy 1985 (for Paul Daniels' Easter Magic Show BBC); memb Inner Magic Circle; *Books* Paul Daniels Magic Bok (1980), More Magic (1981), Paul Daniels Magic Annual (1983), 77 Popular Card Games and Tricks (1985); *Recreations* photography, golf, tennis; *Clubs* The Magic Circle; *Style*— Paul Daniels, Esq; PO Box 250, Uxbridge, Middlesex UB9 5DX (☎ 0302 321 233, fax 0895 834 891)

DANIELS, Raymond Alfred; MC (1946); s of late Alfred Daniels; *b* 15 July 1923; *Educ* Bedford Modern Sch; *m* 1954, Helen, nee Clark; 3 s; *Career* md William Press & Son 1975-; *Style*— Raymond Daniels Esq, MC; Greystock, 64 Merrybent, Darlington, Co Durham (☎ (0325) 74 238)

DANIELS, Robert George Reginald; CBE (1984) JP (Essex 1969), DL (Essex 1980); s of Robert Henry Daniels and Edith *née* Brignall; *b* 17 Nov 1916; *Educ* private and state; *m* 26 Oct 1940, Hancock; 1 da (Patricia Ann b 1942); *Career* despatches (twice); insur rep with Prudential Assur 1938-76 ret; dir: Essex Export Agency 1987, gen cmmr of Income Tax Epping Div 1970, Theydon bois Roy Be Legion 1985-, memb Essex CC 1965- (chm planning ctee) ; *Recreations* reading; *Clubs* Essex; *Style*— Robert Daniels Esq, CBE, JP, DL; Essex County Council, County Hall, Chelmsford, Essex

DANILOVICH, Hon Mrs (Irene); *née* Forte; 3 da of Baron Forte (Life Peer), *qv*; *b* 15 Dec 1956; *m* 19 March 1977, John J Danilovich; 1 s (John Charles Amadeus b 14 Sept 1981), 1 da (Alice Irene Angelica b 4 Jan 1985); *Style*— The Hon Mrs Danilovich; 37 Carlyle Square, London SW3 6HA

DANIN, Clement Paul; s of Dr Adolph Danin, FFARCS, of Brighton, and Irene Danin, *née* Stone (d 1986); *b* 22 April 1937; *Educ* Westminster Sch; *m* 3 Ma;rch 1962, Bridget Mary, da of Kenneth Augustus Mason (d 1948); 1 s (Timothy b 1965), 2 da (Joanna b 1963, Kate b 1948); *Career* Nat Serv, RA 1956-58, RA TA 1958-62 (Lt RA); Metal Broker, dir Boustead David (metal brokers) Ltd 1975-86; md Charles David (metal brokers) Ltd 1986-; memb Ctee of London Metal Exchange 1984- (vice chm 1986), chm London Metal Exchange 1986; *Recreations* music, art, golf, theatre; *Style*— Clement P Danin, Esq; Braeside House, High Street, Cranbrook, Kent TN17 3EN (☎ (0580) 713271); Charles David (metal brokers) Ltd, 9-13 Fenchurch Buildings, London Ec3M 5HR (☎ 01 626 3538, telex 883928, fax 01 626 0316)

DANKS, Arthur Reginald; MBE (1976), TD (1945); s of Arthur Benjamin Danks (d 1925), and Christian Marianne, *née* Snow (d 1958); *b* 12 April 1906; *Educ* Malvern; *m* 1951, Hon Serena Mary, *qv*, da of late 4 Baron Gifford; 1 s (John b 1954), 1 da (Fenella b 1952, m 1981 Hon John Best, *qv*); *Career* HAC RHA 1926-39, Capt 1939, 2 Regt RHA 1940 1 Armd Bde Greece 1941; Bank of Eng 1924-1945; chm Glos Old People's Welfare Ctee 1960-78, memb governing body nat OPW Cncl, Age Concern 1968-80, memb Glos Diocesan Bd of Fin 1961-76; hon tres Glos Community Cncl 1968-78 (memb ctee 1960-), gen cmmr for Income Tax Gloucester Area 1967-81, memb social servs ctee Glos CC 1974-81; *Style*— Arthur Danks Esq, MBE, TD; Loscombe, Sydling St Nicholas, Dorchester, Dorset DT2 9PD

DANKS, Hon Mrs (Serena Mary); *née* Gifford; da of 4 Baron Gifford (d 29 Jan 1937), and Anne Maud, da of Bt Col William Aitchison, JP, DL, of Drumore; *b* 30 Sept 1919; *m* 1, 28 Sept 1940 (m dis 1945), Patrick de Gruchy Vignoles Crawshay Warren; 1 s; m 2, 17 Oct 1951, Arthur Reginald Danks, MBE, TD, *qv*; 1 s, 1 da; *Style*— The Hon Mrs Danks; Loscombe, Sydling St. Nicholas, Dorchester, Dorset, DT2 9PD

DANKWORTH, John Philip William; CBE (1974); *b* 20 Sept 1927; *Educ* Monoux GS, Royal Acad of Music, Berklee Coll; *m* 1958, Cleo Laine; 2 s (Stuart, Alex), 1 da (Jackie); *Career* musician, closely involved with post war devpt of Br jazz 1947-60; cmmnd compositions incl: Improvisations (with Matyas Seiber) 1959, Escapade (Northern Sinfonia Orchestra) 1967, Tom Sawyers Saturday (Farnham) 1967, String Quartet 1971, Piano Concerto (Westminster Fest) 1972, Lady in Waiting (Houston Ballet), Man of Mode (RSC), Edward II (Nat Theatre); film scores incl: We Are the Lambeth Boys, The Criminal, Saturday Night Sunday Morning 1964, Darling, The Servant 1965, Modesty Blaise, Sands of Kalahari, Morgan, Return From the Ashes (Academy Award nomination) 1966, Accident 1969, Salt and Pepper 1969, Fathom 1969, 10 Rillington Place 1971, The Last Grenade 1971; musical theatre incl: Boots with Strawberry Jam (with Benny Green) 1968, Colette (starring Cleo Laine) 1979, TV theme for the Avengers series; Hon MA Open Univ; ARAM 1969; *Recreations* driving, household maintenance; *Style*— John Dankworth, Esq, CBE; c/o Laurie Mansfield, Int Artistes, 235 Regent St, London W1

DANN, Clifford Thomas; s of George Dann (d 1971), of Hellingly, Sussex, and Grace Sophia, *née* Hook (d 1970); *b* 17 July 1927; *Educ* Hailsham Co Sch, London Univ (BSc); *m* 1, 14 Aug 1948 (m dis 1988), Bronwen Annie, da of the late Gordon Gauld, of Coventry; 1 s (Vyvian b 1959), 1 da (Angela b 1951); m 2, 21 Nov 1988, Patricia Anne Purdon, da of The Very Rev Ivan Delacherois Neill, CB, OBE; *Career* chartered surveyor; RICS: chm jr orgn 1957-58, cncl 1958-61, 1973-87 chm Sussex branch 1973-74, chm public affairs ctee 1975-80, chm policy Review Ctee 1980-82, pres 1983-84; Int Fedn of Surveyors: UK delegate 1958-82, memb London Congress ctee 1967-70, chm Town Planning Cmmn 1974-75; lectr on arbitration practice; fndr and sr ptnr Clifford Dann & Ptnrs 1956; dir: Individual Life Insur Co 1972-76, Network Date Ltd 1981-83; chm: Lewes Round Table 1958, Sussex Area World of Property Housing Tst 1965-72, League of Friends of Chailey Heritage 1978; vice-chm Chailey Heritage Sch Govrs 1985-; memb: The Speaker's Appeal for St Margarets Westminster Ctee, Friends of Lewes Ctee 1957-63, Lewes Old Peoples' Welfare Ctee 1962-68, govr Lewes Tech Coll 1967-73 (vice-chm 1971-73), pres Lewes C of C 1965 memb Surrey and Sussex Rent Assessment Panel 1965-72, govr Brighton Poly 1989-; Freeman City of London 1979, Liveryman Worshipful Co of Chartered Surveyor; memb FIABCI

1960-85, ARICS 1949, FRICS 1957; *Books* author of numerous articles in professional journals including Economic Factors in Urban Devpt in 13 Countries (1962), Community Land Scheme (1971-75); *Recreations* music, organist, choirmaster, gardening, DIY, travelling abroad; *Style—* Clifford Dann, Esq; The Old Jewellers, 176 High St, Uckfield, Sussex; Albion House, Lewes, Sussex (☎ 0273 477022)

DANSON, Hon Barnett Jerome; PC (Canada); s of Joseph B Danson and Saidie W Danson (both decd); *b* 8 Feb 1921; *Educ* Toronto Public Sch, Toronto HS; *m* 1943, Isobel, da of J Robert Bull of London; 4 s; *Career* served WW II, Queen's Own Rifles of Canada (wounded Normandy 1944, ret as Lt, appointed Hon Lt-Col 1974); consulgen for Canada in Boston 1944-46; fndr and pres Danson Corpn Ltd (Scarborough) 1953-74; MP (Lib) York North 1968-79, parly sec to PM Trudeau 1970-72, min of State Urban Affairs 1974-76, min of Nat Defence 1976-79; chm of bd de Havilland Aircraft of Canada Ltd 1982-84; dir Ballet Opera House Corpn, dir: ameritus Canadian Cncl for Native Business, Algoma Central Railway, Gen Steelwares Ltd, Scintrex Ltd; chm Inst for Political Involvement; *Recreations* fishing, skiing, music; *Clubs* Donalda (Toronto); *Style—* The Hon Barnett Danson; 1106-561 Avenue Road, Toronto M4V 2J8, Canada (☎ 416 323 3274)

DANTER, Maj John Trevor; s of William Herbert Danter (d 1955), of Gloucester, and Kathrine Louise, *née* Rudge; *b* 30 July 1930; *Educ* The Crypt Sch Gloucester, RMA Sandhurst, RAC Cirencester; *m* 12 April 1955, Heather Maud, da of Richard Judd (d 1984), of Cambridgeshire; 1 s (Alistair b 1957); *Career* cmmnd South Staffs Regt 1951-68; served: N Ireland, Cyprus, Germany, Aden, Kenya, UK; ret Maj; agent to Trinity Coll managing The Trimley Estate Felixstowe Suffolk 1970-87; ptnr Bidwells Chartered Surveyors 1980, md Bidwells and King Perth 1987; chm Suffolk Coastal Cons Assoc 1985-87; *Recreations* fly-fishing, horse racing, walking, music, reading; *Clubs* Army & Navy; *Style—* Major John Danter; Annfield Cottage, Glenalmond, Perthshire, PH1 3SE (☎ 073 888 267); Bidwells & King, 5 Atholl Place, Perth (☎ 0738 26 178)

DANTZIC, Roy Matthew; s of David A Dantzic, of Whitecraigs, Glasgow, and Renee, *née* Cohen; *b* 4 July 1944; *Educ* Brighton Coll Sussex; *m* 3 June 1969, Diane, da of Abraham Clapham (d 1984), of Whitecraigs, Glasgow; 1 s (Toby Alexander b 15 Feb 1975), 1 da (Emma Lucy b 23 Sept 1973); *Career* with: Coopers & Lybrand 1962-69, Kleinwort Benson Ltd 1970-72, Drayton Corpn Ltd 1972-73, Samuel Montagu & Co Ltd 1974-80 (dir 1975); fin dir Br Nat Oil Corpn (now Britoil plc) 1980-84; dir: Pallas Gp SA 1984-85, Moor Dark (1958) Ltd; exec dir County Natwest Wood Mackenzie & Co Ltd 1985-, non-exec dir Br Nuclear Fuels plc 1987-; pt/t memb CEGB 1984-87; FICAS 1969; *Recreations* golf, theatre, sitting in the shade; *Clubs* MCC, Moor Park Golf; *Style—* Roy Dantzic, Esq; Moor Park, Northwood, Middlesex; Drapers Gardens, 12 Throgmorton Ave, London, EC2P 2ES (☎ 01 382 1000)

DANVILLE, Comte Norbert Leon; s of Comte André Danville, (d 1986), of Paris, and Valentine, *née* de Topolsky (d 1979); *b* 26 Nov 1947; *Educ* Ecole Alsacienne Paris, Law Sch (Paris Panthéon), Sciences PO Paris; *m* 1 (m dis 1988), Annick Jousset; m 2, 24 Oct 1988, Madame Ines Voute, da of Jean Sapinno, of Geneva, Switzerland; 1 step da (Melissende Voute b 1980); *Career* 19 Sqdn Cavalry Regt at Les Invalides, Paris 1973-74; with Compagnie Finangère Edmond de Rothschild, Paris 1974-78; Barclays Bank SL France 1978-82; dir: BAII Leasing Ltd, BAII Equipment Ltd; cncllr Franco-British Chamber of Commerce; memb: Franco-Swiss Chamber Geneva, The French Benevolent Soc London; FIOD; *Clubs* Overseas Bankers', RAC; c/o BAII, 1 London Bridge, London SE1 9QN; BAII, 2 rue Thalberg, 1208 Geneva, Switzerland

DARANYI-FORBES-SEMPILL, Hon Mrs (Kirstine Elizabeth); *née* Forbes-Sempill; changed names by deed pool 1986 to Daryani-Forbes-Sempill; da of 19 Lord Sempill (d 1965) by 2 w, Cecilia, *née* Dunbar-Kilburn; half-sis of Lady Sempill, *qv*; *b* 9 August 1944, ; *m* 1 June 1968 (m dis 1985), John Michael Forbes-Cable (who assumed by deed poll 1968 the additional name of Forbes), second s of late Richard Cable, of Woodhill Compton, Wolverhampton, Staffs; 2 s (William Richard Craigievar b 1970, Malcolm Dunbar Craigievar b 1972); *Style—* The Hon Mrs Daranyi-Forbes-Sempill; Wingham Barton Manor, Westmarsh, Nr Canterbury, Kent (☎ 0304 812355)

DARBOURNE, John William Charles; CBE (1977); s of late William Leslie Darbourne, and Violet Yorke; *b* 11 Jan 1935; *Educ* Battersea GS, UCL, Harvard; *m* 1960, Noreen Fifield (d 1988); 1 s, 3 da; *Career* ptnr Darbourne & Ptnrs (architects, landscape architects and planners) RIBA, assoc Inst of Landscape Architects; *Style—* John Darbourne Esq, CBE; 6 The Green, Richmond, Surrey (☎ 01 940 7182)

DARBY, Prof (Henry) Clifford; CBE (1978, OBE 1946); s of Evan Darby (d 1955); *b* 7 Feb 1909; *Educ* Neath Co Sch, St Catharine's Coll Cambridge (MA, PhD, LittD); *m* 1941, Eva Constance, da of William Thomson (d 1935); 2 da; *Career* Intelligence Div Admty 1941-45; lectr in geography Cambridge Univ 1931-45; prof of geography: Liverpool Univ 1945-49, UCL 1949-66, Cambridge Univ 1966-76, (emeritus 1976-); visiting prof: Chicago Univ 1952, Harvard Univ 1959 and 1964-65, Washington Univ Seattle 1963; author geographical and historical pubns; fell King's Coll Cambridge (hon fell 1983), hon fell St Catharine's Coll Cambridge; Hon Doctorates: Chicago, Liverpool, Durham, Hull, Ulster, Wales, London; FBA; kt 1988; *Style—* Prof Sir Clifford Darby, CBE; 60 Storey's Way, Cambridge CB3 0DX (☎ (0223) 354745)

DARBY, (Elizabeth Anne) Foxy; *née* Foxon; da of Lt-Col Arthur Denham Foxon VSO, TD, of Orford, Suffolk and Vera Mae, *née* Newsome; *b* 02 Feb 1952; *Educ* Westonbirt Sch, Kingston Coll of Art (Dip, AD), RCA (MA); *m* 1 Oct 1983, Keith Harry Darby, s of Harry Darby (d 1970), of Hagley Works; 2 s (Harry b 1986, Randel b 1987); *Career* personal design asst to John Stefanidis 1977-79, dir: Fanny Foxon Ltd (interior design) 1979-83, Country Fittings Ltd 1983-89; conslt Triumph Hldgs Ltd 1986-89; ctee memb: Winged Tst (Cumbria Appeal), Wishing Well (Cumbria Appeal); *Recreations* Jack Russell Terriers, horse riding, designing. reading books on architecture, houses and gardens; *Style—* Mrs Keith Darby; Warnell Hall, Sebergham, Cumbria; 8 Gerald Rd, London SW1 (fax 0768 67941)

DARBY, Dr Francis John; TD (1964); s of late Col John Francis Darby, TD, CBE, and Georgina Alice; *b* 24 Feb 1920; *Educ* Nottingham HS, Edinburgh Acad, Edinburgh Univ (MB, ChB); *m* 1969, Pamela Elizabeth, da of Sidney Hill (d 1970); 3 s; *Career* served 1939-46 Capt Royal Signals (despatches); DHSS 1964-82: dep chief med advsr Social Security 1978-80, chief med advsr 1980-82; chief med offr and conslt physician Cayman Islands 1983-85, hon physician to HM The Queen 1980-84; memb Worshipful Soc of Apothecaries of London 1978, Freeman City of London 1979; MFOM, MRCGP, DIH, DMJ, FRSM; *Recreations* sailing, swimming; *Clubs* Army & Navy, Royal Lymington Yacht, Royal Signals Yacht; *Style—* Dr Francis Darby, TD; Ruardean, Captains Row, Lymington, Hants SO41 9RP (☎ 0590 77119)

DARBY, The Rt Rev Harold Richard; *see*: Sherwood, Bishop of

DARBY, Hon Mrs; Meriel Kathleen; *née* Douglas-Home; da of Baron Home of the Hirsel; *b* 27 Nov 1939; *m* 30 March 1964, Adrian Marten George Darby; 1 s, 1 da; *Style—* The Hon Mrs Darby; 12 Park Town, Oxford

DARBY, Dr Michael Douglas; s of Arthur Douglas Darby, of The Old Rectory, Ilketshall St Margaret, Nr Bungay, Suffolk, and Ilene Doris, *née* Eatwell (d 1986); *b* 2 Sept 1944; *Educ* Rugby, Reading Univ (PhD); *m* 26 Aug 1977, Elisabeth Susan, da of Lesley Robert Done; *Career* asst to Barbara Jones 1963; head of pubns, exhibitions and design V & A 1988- (textiles dept 1964-72, prints and drawings 1973-76, exhibitions offr 1977-83, dep dir 1984-87); memb: Crafts Cncl 1984-87, IOW advsy ctee English Heritage 1986-; FRES 1977, FRGS 1984; *Books* Stevengraphs (jtly 1968), Marble Halls (jtly 1973), Early Railway Prints Victoria and Albert Museum (1974, 1979), The Islamic Perspective (1983), British Art in the V and A (1983), John Pollard Seddon (1983) and writer of numerous articles in popular and learned jls; *Recreations* books, beetles, drawing; *Style—* Dr Michael Darby; Victoria and Albert Museum, London SW7 2RL (☎ 01 938 8502)

DARBY, Sir Peter Howard; CBE (1973), QFSM (1970); s of the late William Cyril Darby, and Beatrice, *née* Colin; *b* 8 July 1924; *Educ* Coll of Advanced Technol Birmingham; *m* 1948, Ellen Josephine, *née* Glynn; 1 s, 1 da; *Career* chief offr London Fire Brigade 1977-80; HM's chief inspr of Fire Servs 1980-87, dir Argus Alarms; chm: Certifire, FS Nat Examinations Bd, govrs of St James Secdy Modern Sch Barnet; Freeman City of London, Liveryman Worshipful Co of Basketmakers; CStJ 1982, FIFireE 1968, CBIM 1983, kt 1985; *Recreations* golf, fishing, sailing; *Clubs* Livery, Candlewick Ward, City of London; *Style—* Sir Peter Darby, CBE, QFSM; 10 Moor Lane, Rickmansworth, Herts WD3 1LG

DARBYSHIRE, David Glen; s of Thomas Leslie Darbyshire (d 1979), and Alice, *née* Moss; *b* 20 May 1944; *Educ* Wigan GS, Liverpool Coll of Art, Univ of Newcastle upon Tyne (BA, BArch); *m* 7 July 1973 (sep 1987), Jane Helen; 1 da (Kate); *Career* architect Ryder and Yates Ptnrs 1972-75, princ architect Washington Devpt Corpn 1975-79, ptnr Jane and David Darbyshire 1979-87; Civic Tst Award for Dukes Cottages Backworth; Civic Tst Commendation for: Church St Cramlington, St Johns Green Percy Main; winner of: St Oswald's Hospice Special Category Regnl Ltd Competition and Civic Tst Award, The Times/RIBA Community Enterprise Scheme Commendation; princ Darbyshire Architects 1987-; memb RIBA; *Recreations* music, mechanical engineering, fine art; *Clubs* Bristol Owners; *Style—* David Darbyshire, Esq; 10 Lily Crescent, Jesmond, Newcastle upon Tyne (☎ 091 281 0501); Hawthorn Cottage, Hawthorn Rd, Gosforth, Newcastle upon Tyne NE3 4DE (☎ 091 284 2813)

DARBYSHIRE, David Stewart; s of Wing Cdr Rupert Stanley Darbyshire (ka 1941), and Ann, *née* Todd; *b* 14 Nov 1940; *Educ* Radley, Oriel Coll Oxford (MA); *m* 24 Jan 1970, Elizabeth, da of Eric Watts; 1 s (Rupert b 1975), 2 da (Sophie b 1973, Alice b 1978); *Career* Capt SAS AVR 1964-70; barr 1965-66; Arthur Anderson & Co: London 1966-72, Paris 1972-79, ptnr 1976, Leeds 1979-85, London 1985-; FCA 1970, ATII 1971, memb Ordre des Experts Comptables and Compagnie des Commissaires aux Comptes 1977; *Recreations* sailing, hill walking; *Clubs* Special Forces, Sea View Yacht; *Style—* David Darbyshire, Esq; 11 Warwick Sq, London SW1V 2AA; Hutton Mount, Ripon, N Yorks HG4 5DR; Arthur Anderien & Co, 1 Surrey St, London WC1R 2PS (☎ 01 438 3731, fax 01 831 1133, telex 8812711)

DARBYSHIRE, Jane Helen; *née* Wroe; da of Gordon Desmond Wroe, of Brixham, S Devon, Patricia, *née* Keough; *b* 5 June 1948; *Educ* Dorking GS, Newcastle Univ (BA, BArch); *m* 7 July 1987 (m dis), David Glen, s of Thomas Darbyshire (d 1980), of Wigan, Lancs; 1 da (Kate b 1979); *Career* chartered architect; in private practice, sr ptnr David Glen 1979-87, princ Jane Darbyshire & Assocs 1987-; works: exhibitor at RIBA 'women in architecture' 1983, winner of St Oswalds Hospice Design Competition 1981, exhibitor DLI Museum Durham 1981; Civic Tst: Award for restoration 1982, commendation for Cramlington Housing 1983, commendation flat refurbishment Percy Main 1986, Award St Oswalds Hospice Gosforth Newcastle upon Tyne 1987; Award for Housing Design, Morper 1988, Nat RIBA Award 1988; features: Channel 4 'Design Matters', BBC 'Townscape'; Civic Tst Assessor 1984-; *Recreations* music, art, history of architecture; *Style—* Ms Jane Darbyshire; 4 Laurel Walk, Gosforth, Newcastle upon Tyne; Jane Darbyshire Assocs, Milburn House, Side, Newcastle upon Tyne NE1 1LE

DARCY DE KNAYTH, Baroness (18 in line, E 1332); Davina Marcia Ingrams; *née* Herbert; da of 17 Baron Darcy de Knayth (*née* Hon Mervyn Herbert, 2 s of 4 Earl of Powis by his w (Violet) Countess of Powis, in whose favour the abeyance existing in the Barony of Darcy de Knayth was terminated in 1903) and Vida, da of late Capt James Harold Cuthbert, DSO; *b* 10 July 1938; *m* 1 March 1960, Rupert George Ingrams (k in a motor acc 28 Feb 1964), s of Leonard St Clair Ingrams, OBE, and bro of Richard Ingrams, *qv*; 1 s, 2 da; *Heir* s, Hon Caspar Ingrams; *Career* sits as Independent peeress in House of Lords; *Style—* The Rt Hon Lady Darcy de Knayth; Camley Corner, Stubbings, Maidenhead, Berks (☎ Littlewick Green 2935)

DARE, Barry Stanton; s of Clifford Stanton Dare (d 1985), and Doris Muriel, *née* Geeson (d 1988); *b* 29 July 1936; *Educ* St Paul's Sch, UCL (BSc-Econ); *m* 16 June 1962, Wendy Angela Vivien, da of Fl/Lt Walter Wilkins (d 1986); 2 s (Clifford Stanton b 1967, Jocelyn Stanton b 1970); *Career* sr acct Tansley Witt 1958-62, co sec predecessor to AFA Minerva 1962-65, mgmnt cnslt (eventually ptnr) John Tyzack & Ptnrs 1965-69, gp chief exec Conduit Hldgs 1969-71, diversified interests inc mgmnt conslty and specialised accountancy practice 1971-, dir sev cos and md Unsins Seeds Ltd; FCA, FBIM; *Recreations* cricket, fishing, dry stone walling; *Clubs* The Carlton; *Style—* Barry S Dare, Esq; 61 Kingston Lane, Teddington, Middx; Old Mill Dene, Blockley, Moreton in Marsh, Gloucester; 23 Regatta Ct, Oyster Row, Cambridge; Unwins Seeds Ltd, Histon, Cambridge

DARE, Hon Mrs (Phyllida Anne); da of Baron Benson (Life Peer), GBE; *b* 1943; *m* 1967, Simon John Dare; *Style—* The Hon Mrs Dare; 10 Bowerdean St, SW6

DARE, Wendy Angela Vivien; da of Walter Wilkins (d 1985), of Teddington, Middx, and Majorie Vivien, *née* Williams (d 1974); *b* 10 Feb 1942; *Educ* Twickenham County GS, Kingston Poly (BA); *m* 16 June 1962, Barry Stanton Dare, s of Clifford Stanton Dare (d 1986), of Teddington, Middx; 2 s (Clifford Roderick b 1967, Jocelyn David b 1970); *Career* recruitment specialist, Dare recruitment; raising children; chm Teddington Soc, memb Richmond and Kingston Young Enterprise Bd; *Recreations* gardening, looking at gardens, reading about gardens; *Clubs* Univ Women's, Network, WIM; *Style—* Mrs Wendy Dare; 61 Kingston Lane, Teddington, Middx (☎ 01 977

2502); Old Mill Dene, Blockley, Moreton-in-Marsh, Glos (☎ 0386 700 457)

DARELL, Guy Jeffrey Adair; s and h of Sir Jeffrey Lionel Darell, 8 Bt, MC; *b* 8 June 1961; *Educ* Eton, RMC Sandhurst; *Career* cmmnd Coldstream Guards 1981; insur broker with Minets London Lloyds 1984-; *Style*— Guy Darell Esq; 23 Coleford Rd, London SW18 (☎ 01 874 8432); Denton Lodge, Harleston, Norfolk (☎ Homersfield (098 686) 206)

DARELL, Brig Sir Jeffrey Lionel; 8 Bt (GB 1795), of Richmond Hill, Surrey, MC (1945); s of Col Guy Marsland Darell, MC (d 15 April 1947), 3 s of 5 Bt; suc cous, Sir William Darell, 7 Bt (d 10 Feb 1959); *b* 2 Oct 1919; *Educ* Eton, RMC Sandhurst; *m* 30 June 1953, Bridget Mary, da of Maj-Gen Sir Allan Adair, 6 Bt, GCVO, CB, DSO, MC; 1 s, 2 da; *Heir* s, Guy Jeffrey Adair Darell (*qv*); *Career* Brig (ret) Coldstream Guards, served in 1939-45 War, Lt-Col 1957, cmd 1 Bn Coldstream Guards 1957-59, AAG War Office 1959-61, Cdr RMA Sandhurst 1961-64, regimental Lt-Col cmdg Coldstream Guards 1964, vice pres Regular Commissions Bd 1968, Cmdt Mons Officer Cadet Sch 1970-72; tstee and memb London Law Trust 1981-; High Sheriff of Norfolk 1985-86; *Clubs* Cavalry and Guards'; *Style*— Brig Sir Jeffrey Darell, Bt, MC; Denton Lodge, Harleston, Norfolk (☎ 098 686 206); 55 Green St, London W1 (☎ 01 629 3860)

DARELL-BROWN, Hon Mrs; Christina Louise; *née* Vanneck; da of 6 Baron Huntingfield; *b* 26 Jan 1946; *m* 8 July 1967, Anthony Darell-Brown, s of late Col Mark Darell-Brown, DSO, of 10 Queen's Elm Sq, SW3; 2 s, 1 da; *Style*— The Hon Mrs Darell-Brown; The Old Rectory, Witnesham, Ipswich, Suffolk

DARESBURY, 2 Baron (UK 1927), of Walton, Co Chester; Sir Edward Greenall; 3 Bt (UK 1876), JP (Cheshire 1945); yr (but only surv) s of 1 Baron Daresbury, CVO (d 1938), by his w, late Frances Eliza, OBE (d 1953), *née* Wynne-Griffith; *b* 12 Oct 1902; *Educ* Eton; *m* 1, 11 Aug 1925, Joan Madeline (d 15 March 1926), da of Capt Robert Thomas Oliver Sheriffe; m 2, 12 Sept 1927, Josephine (d 13 Nov 1958), da of Brig-Gen Sir Joseph Laycock, KCMG, DSO, TD; 1 s; m 3, 16 June 1966, Lady Helena Albreda Marie Gabriella (d 1970), da of late 7 Earl Fitzwilliam and formerly w of Maj Chetwode Charles Hamilton Hilton-Green; *Heir* s, Hon Edward Greenall; *Career* late 2 Lt 1 Life Gds, jt master Belvoir Foxhounds 1934-77, MFH Co Limerick 1947-89; *Style*— The Rt Hon Lord Daresbury, JP; Altavilla, Askeaton, Co Limerick, Eire (☎ Limerick 64281)

DARGAN, Dr Michael Joseph; *b* 14 Sept 1918; *Educ* Patrician Brothers Ballyfin Co Meath, Trinity Coll Dublin; *m* m Catherine (Blanche) O'Rourke; 2s, 3da; *Career* former: chm and chief exec Aer Lingus: chm: CRH plc, Bank of Ireland Fin Ltd, Intercontinental Hotels (Ireland) Ltd, dir Bank of Ireland, Burlington Industs Inc (USA); chm: Robert J Goff plc, Int Bloodstock Holdings, Klopman Int, Atlantic Mills; dir CRH plc; memb Post Off Review Gp 1978; life fell Int Acad of Mgmnt, sr steward Irish Turf Club; *Clubs* Irish Turf, Links (NY); *Style*— Dr Michael Dargan; c/o CRH plc, 19 Lower Pembroke St, Dublin 2, Eire (☎ (0001) 76 58 51)

DARGIE, Sir William Alexander; CBE (1969, OBE 1960),; s of Andrew and Adelaide Dargie; *b* 4 June 1912; *Educ* Melbourne; *m* 1937, Kathleen, da of late G Howitt; 1 s, 1 da; *Career* served AIF, Capt RAAF and RAN, Mid E, New Guinea, India and Burma as official war artist; artist/portraitist; former head Vic Nat Gallery Art School, chm Cwlth Art Advsy Bd 1969-73; numerous awards for Art; FRSA 1951; kt 1970; *Recreations* books, chess; *Clubs* Melbourne, Naval and Military; *Style*— Sir William Dargie, CBE; 19 Irilbarra Rd, Canterbury, Vic 3126, Australia (☎ (836) 3396)

DARKAZALLY, Mamoun; s of Abdul Hadi (d 1986), and Farizeh Arabi; *b* 9 Oct 1942; *Educ* New York Graduate Sch of Business (MBA), New York Univ (BS); *m* 2 June 1971, Vivian, da of William Ram (d 1968); 1 s (Anwar b 1973); *Career* with Chase Manhattan Bank: NY 1973-74, Beirut 1974-75; Commercial Bank of Qatar 1975-79; dep gen regnl mangr Al Saudi Banque London 1981- (Paris 1979-81); memb IOD, BIM, Arab Bankers Assoc; *Style*— Mamoun Darkazally Esq; 7A Inverness Gardens, London W8 (☎ 01 221 1874); 31 Berkeley Square, London W1 (☎ 01 493 8942, fax 01 493 7193, car tel 0860 326 210, telex 23875)

DARKE, Geoffrey James; s of Harry James Darke (d 1983), and, Edith Annie Darke (d 1973); *b* 1 Sept 1929; *Educ* Prince Henry's GS Worcs, Birmingham Sch of Architecture (Dip Arch); *m* 1959, Jean Yvonne, ARCM, da of Edwin Rose (d 1971); 1 s (Christopher), 2 da (Elizabeth, Sarah); *Career* cmmnd RE 1954-56, Malaya; sr architect Stevenage New Town Dvpt Corpn 1952-58, private practice 1958-61, ptnr Darbourne & Darke, Architects and Landscape Planners 1961-, work incl several large cmmns, particularly public housing (also commerical and civic bldgs); success in nat and int competitions incl: Stuttgart 1977, Hanover 1979, Bolzano 1980, Hanover (Misburg) 1982; fndr Geoffrey Darke Assoc 1987; memb RIBA Cncl 1977-83, chm RIBA Competitions Working Gp 1979-84; memb Aldebrugh Festival Snape Maltings Fndn 1979-; ARIBA, FRSA; numerous medals and awards for architectural work; co-recipient (with John Darbourne) Fritz Schumacher Award, Hamburg 1978, for Services to architecture and town planning; *Recreations* music; *Clubs* Reform; *Style*— Geoffrey Darke Esq; Geoffrey Darke Assoc, EBC House, Kew Rd, Richmond, Surrey TW9 2NA (☎ 01 332 1551, telex 268821 EBC GD, fax 01 948 6004)

DARLING, Hon Sir Clifford; MP (Bahamas); s of Charles and Aremelia Darling; *b* 6 Feb 1922; *Educ* Acklins Public Sch; several public schs in Nassau; *Career* senator 1964-67; dep speaker House of Assembly 1967-69; min of State 1969; min of Labour and Welfare 1971; present Min of Labour and National Insurance; kt 1977; *Style*— The Hon Sir Clifford Darling, MP; C H Bain Building, POB 1525, Nassau, Bahamas

DARLING, Lt-Cdr Gerald Ralph Auchinleck; RD (1968), QC (1967, Hong Kong 1968); s of Lt-Col Ralph Reginald Auchinleck Darling (d 1958), of N Ireland, and Moira Freda Bessie, *née* Moriarty (d 1983); *b* 8 Dec 1921; *Educ* Harrow, Hertford Coll Oxford (MA); *m* 1954, Susan Ann, da of Brig Mervyn Hobbs, OBE, MC of W Australia; 1 s (Patrick), 1 da (Fiona, Mrs Torrens-Spence); *Career* served RNVR 1940-46, Fleet Fighter Pilot, Mediterranean, Test Pilot Eastern Fleet, Chief Test Pilot Br Pacific Fleet; served with RNR to 1968; barr Middle Temple 1950, bencher 1970; Lloyd's appeal arbitrator 1978, judge of Admiralty Ct of Cinque Ports 1978-; wreck cmmr; freeman City of London; tstee Royal Naval Museum Portsmouth 1985; landowner (242 acres); *Recreations* fly fishing, shooting; *Clubs* Naval and Military, Tyrone County; *Style*— Lt-Cdr Gerald Darling, RD, QC; Crevenagh House, Omagh, Co Tyrone, N Ireland BT79 0EH (☎ (0662) 42138); Queen Elizabeth Building, Temple, London EC4Y 9BS (☎ 01 353 9153, telex 262762 INREM G)

DARLING, Dr Henry Shillington; CBE (1967); s of John Singleton Darling, MD, FRCS (d 1927), and Marjorie, *née* Shillington (d 1964); *b* 22 June 1914; *Educ* Watts Endowed Sch Lurgan, Greenmount Agric Coll N Ireland, Queen's Univ Belfast (BSc, MAgr), Imperial Coll of Tropical Agric Trinidad (AICTA), London Univ (PhD), Ahmadu Bello Univ Nigeria; *m* 8 Aug 1940, Vera Thompson, da of Thomas George Chapman, of Belfast; 1 s (Owen Henry Shillington), 2 da (Ruth Marjorie (Mrs Triffitt), Susan Chapman (Mrs Chester)); *Career* research cadet British Colonial Agric Service 1940-42; British Middle East Anti-Locust Unit 1942-44; research divn Dept of Agric: Uganda 1944-47, Sudan 1947-49; faculty agric Univ Coll Khartoum 1949-52; head of hop research dept Wye Coll London Univ 1954-62; prof of agric and dir of Inst for Agric Research Ahmadu Bello Univ Nigeria 1962-68; dep vice-chancellor Ahmadu Bello Univ 1967-68; princ Wye Coll London Univ 1968-77; dir-gen Int Centre for Agric Research in Dry Areas (ICARDA) 1977-81; Fell of Wye Coll London Univ 1982, Hon DSc Ahmadu Bello Univ Nigeria 1968, Hon DSc Queen's Univ Belfast 1984; FRES, MBiol; Order of the Hop (Belgium) 1959; *Recreations* reading, walking, Christian dialogue; *Clubs* Farmers', Samaru (Nigeria); *Style*— Dr H S Darling, CBE; 1A Jemmett Road, Ashford, Kent TN23 2QA (☎ 0233 32982)

DARLING, Hon Isabel; da of Baron Darling of Hillsborough (Life Peer) (d 1985); *b* 1948; *Style*— The Hon Isabel Darling

DARLING, Sir James Ralph; CMG (1958), OBE (1953); s of Augustine Major Darling (d 1937), and Jane Baird, *née* Nimmo (d 1957); *b* 18 June 1899; *Educ* Repton, Oriel Coll Oxford (MA), Melbourne Univ (MA); *m* 1935, Margaret Dunlop, da of John Dewar Campbell (d 1931); 1 s, 3 da; *Career* pres: Australian Coll of Education 1959-63, Australian Elizabethan Theatre Trust 1962-78; chm: Immigration Publicity Cncl (memb 1962-71), Aust Broadcasting Control Bd 1955-61, ABC 1961-67, Aust Road Safety Cncl 1961-70, Aust Frontier Cmmn 1962-71; Hon fell Oriel Coll Oxford 1986, kt 1968; *see Debrett's Handbook of Australia and New Zealand for further details*; *Style*— Sir James Darling, CMG, OBE; 3 Myamyn St, Armadale, Vic 3143, Australia (☎ (20) 6262)

DARLING, Hon (Robert) Julian (Henry); s and h of 2 Baron Darling; *b* 29 April 1944; *Educ* Wellington Coll, RAC Cirencester; *m* 1970, Janet Rachel, da of J Mallinson; 2 s, 1 da; *Career* farmer; FRICS; *Recreations* fishing; *Clubs* Norfolk; *Style*— The Hon Julian Darling; The White House, Intwood, Norwich (☎ (0603) 51548)

DARLING, Gen Sir Kenneth Thomas; GBE (1969, CBE 1957), KCB (1963, CB 1957), DSO (1945); eld s of (George) Kenneth Darling, CIE (d 1964), of Dial House, Aldeburgh; *b* 17 Sept 1909; *Educ* Eton, RMC; *m* 1941, Pamela Beatrice Rose, eld da of Maj Henry Denison-Pender, DSO, OBE, MC (d 1967), of Hook, Hants; *Career* 2 Lt 7 Royal Fus 1929, served WW II, 6 Airborne Div NW Europe (wounded), cmdg 5 Parachute Bde Java 1946, cmdg Airborne Forces Depot 1948, cmdg 16 Independent Parachute Bde 1950, COS 1 Corps 1955, COS 2 Corps 1956, Dep Dir of Staff Duties WO 1957, Maj-Gen 1958, Dir of Ops Cyprus 1958-60, Dir of Inf WO 1960-62, Lt-Gen 1962, GOC 1 Corps 1962-63, GOC-in-C Southern Cmd 1964-66, Gen 1967, C-in-C Allied Forces N Europe 1967-69, Col Royal Fus 1963-68, Col Royal Regt of Fus 1968-74, Col Cmdt Para Regt 1965-67, ADC (Gen) to HM The Queen 1968-69; *Recreations* riding, hunting; *Clubs* Army & Navy; *Style*— Gen Sir Kenneth Darling, GBE, KCB, DSO; Vicarage Farmhouse, Chesterton, Bicester, Oxon OX6 8UQ (☎ 0869 252092)

DARLING, Hon Peter George; s of Baron Darling of Hillsborough (Life Peer) (d 1985); *b* 1950; *Style*— The Hon Peter Darling

DARLING, 2 Baron (UK 1924); Robert Charles Henry Darling; DL (Somerset 1972, Avon 1974); s of Maj Hon John Darling, DSO (s of 1 Baron); suc gf 1936; *b* 15 May 1919; *Educ* Wellington, Sandhurst; *m* 15 Aug 1942, Bridget Rosemary Whishaw, da of Rev Francis Cyprian Dickson; 1 s, 2 da; *Heir* s, Hon Julian Darling, FRICS; *Career* served WW II, Italy, Maj; chief exec Royal Bath & West & South Counties Soc 1961-79; dir Bristol Waterworks 1978-; regnl dir Lloyds Bank 1979-; *Recreations* fishing, gardening; *Style*— The Rt Hon Lord Darling, DL; Puckpits, Limpley Stoke, Bath, Avon (☎ (022 122) 2146)

DARLING, Vera Hannah; OBE (1985); da of Leonard William Henry Darling, of Surrey, and Rosy Louise Darling, *née* Whybrow; *b* 18 July 1929; *Educ* Varndean Sch for Girls Brighton, Brunel Univ; *Career* inspr Nurse Trg Sch The Gen Nursing Cncl for Eng and Wales 1968-73 (examinations offr 1973-78); princ offr the joint bd of Clinical Nursing Studies 1978-83; prof offr Educn and Trg, The Eng Nat Bd for Nursing Midwifery and Health Visiting 1984; dir The Lisa Sainsbury Fndn 1985-; SRN, RNT, OND, BTAC; *Books* Research for Practising Nurses (with Vera Darling/Rogers Jill, Themes in Nursing Series 1986), Ophthalmic Nursing (Vera Darling/Margaret Thorpe, Special Interest Text, Bailliere Tindall, 2nd Ed 1981); *Style*— Miss Vera H Darling, OBE; The Lisa Sainsbury Foundation, 8-10 Crown Hill, Croydon, Surrey CR0 1RY (☎ 01 686 8808)

DARLINGTON, Rear Adm Sir Charles Roy; KBE (1965); s of Charles Arthur Darlington (d 1962), of Stoke-on-Trent, and Alice, *née* Edwards, of Prestatyn (d 1919); *b* 2 Mar 1910; *Educ* Orme Sch Newcastle-under-Lyme, Manchester Univ (BSc); *m* 1935, Nora Dennison, da of James Wright, of Maulds Meaburn, Westmorland; 1 s, 1 da; *Career* joined RN 1941, served WW II, HMS Valiant in Med and E Indies; HMS Excellent; Instr Capt 1956, Instr Rear Adm 1960, dir Naval Educ Serv 1960-65, ret; memb staff of Haileybury 1965-75; *Recreations* maths, cricket, hill walking; *Style*— Rear Adm Sir Charles Darlington, KBE; 11 Freestone Rd, Southsea, Hants (☎ 0705 825974)

DARLINGTON, Frank Thomas; s of Frank Cecil Henry Darlington (d 1963), Naval Rating (1 WW), of London, and Ellen Florence Darlington, *née* Wood (d 1985); *b* 1 Sept 1928; *Educ* Drayton Manor GS, Ealing, Middlesex; *m* 20 June 1953, Irene Gladys, da of Edward John Richardson (d 1945); *Career* actuary (FIA 1958); princ appts: insur offr, NALGO 1963-70; chief exec Teachers Assurance Co 1970-; dirships: Coverquote (Motor & General Insurance Services) Ltd 1984, Public Offrs Assurance (services) Co Ltd 1985, Sovereign Unit Tst Mangrs Ltd 1986, Soverign Unit Tst Services Ltd 1986, Sovereign Life (Marketing) Ltd 1986; *Recreations* chess; *Style*— Frank T Darlington, Esq; Teachers Assurance Co Ltd, 12 Christchurch Road, Bournemouth, BH1 3LW (☎ (0202) 291111)

DARLINGTON, Gavin Leslie Brook; s of Arthur Brook Darlington, and Pamela Leslie, *née* Roberts; *b* 27 June 1949; *Educ* Rugby, Downing Coll Cambridge (LLB); *m* 11 April 1977, Pavla Ann, da of Karel Kucek; 1 s (Nicholas James b 7 Jan 1986); *Career* ptnr Freshfields 1980- (articled clerk 1972-74, asst slr 1974-80); memb: Law Soc, Int Bar Assoc; *Recreations* gardening, golf, swimming, theatre, cinema; *Style*— Gavin Darlington, Esq; 28 Lancaster Rd, Wimbledon, London SW19 5DD; Grindall House, 25 Newgate St, London EC1A 7LH

DARLOW, Paul Manning; s of Brig Eric William Townsend Darlow, OBE, of New Inn Cottage, E End, Witney, Oxon, and Joan Elsie, *née* Ring, JP; *b* 7 Feb 1951; *Educ* (LLB); *Career* barr Middle Temple 1973, Western Circuit; *Style*— Paul Darlow, Esq; St John's Chambers, Small Street, Bristol BS1 1DW (☎ 0272 213456, fax 0272 294821)

DARNLEY, 11 Earl of (I 1725); Adam Ivo Stuart Bligh; sits as Baron Clifton of Leighton (E 1608); also Baron Clifton of Rathmore (I 1721), Viscount Darnley (I 1723); s of 9 Earl (d 1955), by his 3 w, Rosemary, da of late Basil Potter; suc half-bro, 10 Earl, 1980. Lord Darnley's gf, the 8 Earl, when still the Hon Ivo Bligh, captained the English cricket XI in their 1882-83 tour of Australia and gave currency to the term 'The Ashes' (originally coined by *The Sporting Times* when speaking of the cremated body of English cricket). It is said that, after Bligh had won two matches in Australia to the natives' one, some Melbourne ladies burned a bail or bails and presented him with the ashes. Attempts since to analyse the ashes to determine their exact composition (a matter of controversy) were allegedly frustrated by a conscientious housemaid who long ago cleaned out the urn containing them, whereupon a butler refilled the urn with wood ash. Lord Darnley's paternal grandmother was Dame Florence Morphy, DBE, niece of the celebrated chess player; *b* 8 Nov 1941; *Educ* Harrow, Ch Ch Oxford; *m* 14 Oct 1965, Susan Elaine, JP, da of Sir Donald Forsyth Anderson (d 1973), by his w and Margaret, sis of Sir Harry Llewellyn, 3 Bt, CBE (*qv*); 1 s, 1 da (Lady Katherine Amanda b 1971); *Heir* s, Lord Clifton of Rathmore; *Style*— The Rt Hon Earl of Darnley; Netherwood Manor, Tenbury Wells, Worcestershire (☎ (08854) 221)

DARROCH, Donald Ewen Dugald MacInnes; s of Donald Darroch, of Feolin Ferry, Isle of Jura, and Isabella, *née* MacInnes; *b* 10 June 1956; *Educ* Craighouse Secdy Jura; *m* 24 Feb 1984, Dorothy Jill, da of Thomas Rankin Kimble, of Clarkston, Glasgow; 1 da (Dawn b 1 June 1987); *Career* mangr/advsr to Sir William Lithgows Estates Jura 1980, proprietor Darroch: Farming 1983-, Property & Shipping 1983-, Cosmetics 1987-, Mktg 1988-; ptnr Darroch Crafts 1988-; *Recreations* fishing, stalking, shooting, skiing, reading; *Clubs* CGA; *Style*— Donald Darroch, Esq; Inver Lodge, Craighouse, Isle of Jura, Argyll, Scotland PA60 7XX (☎ 049682 223); PO Box 1, Craighouse, Isle of Jura, Argyll, Scotland PA60 7XX (☎ 049682 223, fax 049682 223, telex 934999 TXLINK G/MBX 049682223)

DARROCH OF GOUROCK, Captain Duncan; 7 of Gourock, Lord of the Barony of Gourock (Renfrewshire), Chief of the name of Darroch; er s of Lt-Col Duncan Darroch, 6 of Gourock, Lord of the Barony of Gourock (d 1960), and Rose Mary Lillian Helena, *née* Henderson (d 1989); descended from Duncan Darroch (d 1823), who purchased the estate and barony of Gourock 1784; each successive head has borne the name of Duncan and, with one exception, served in the army (*see* Burke's Landed Gentry, 18 edn, vol 1, 1965); *b* 12 Oct 1931; *Educ* Harrow, RMA Sandhurst; *m* 24 March 1956, Nicola Jeanne, o da of Robert George Seidl, of Zürich, Switzerland; 7 da (Claire Nicola (Mrs Darroch-Thompson) b 1956, Laura Jenny (Mrs Gilbert) b 1959, Louise Rosemary (Mrs Burk) b 1959 (twin), Melanie Jeanne (Mrs Knight) b 1960, Melissa Carolyn (Baroness Bernard de Haldevang) b 1963, Christine Joanna b 1965, Alexandra Marguerite b and d 1967); *Career* cmmnd The Argyll and Sutherland Highlanders 1952, ADC 1955-56, Capt 1957, ret 1958; memb Lloyd's; FLIA 1964; *Recreations* swimming, windsurfing; *Clubs* Army and Navy; *Style*— Duncan Darroch of Gourock; The Red House, Branksome Park Road, Camberley, Surrey (☎ 0276 23053); office, 76-78 Red Lion Street, London WC1R 4NA (☎ 01 404 4599; fax, 01 831 1775)

DARTMOUTH, 9 Earl of (GB 1711); Gerald Humphry Legge; also Baron Dartmouth (E 1682) and Viscount Lewisham (GB 1711); s of 8 Earl, CVO, DSO, RN (d 1962), and Roma, Countess of Dartmouth, *qv*; *b* 26 April 1924; *Educ* Eton; *m* 1, 21 July 1948 (m dis 1976), Raine, da of Alexander George McCorquodale (d 1964), and who m 2, 1976, 8 Earl Spencer, LVO, *qv*; 3 s, 1 da; m 2, 1980, Mrs Gwendoline May Seguin, da of late Charles René Seguin; *Heir* s, Viscount Lewisham; *Career* served WW II, Capt Coldstream Guards (despatches); chm: Ocean Wilsons Hldgs plc, Scottish Cities Investmt Tst plc, Lancashire & London Investmt Tst plc, Anglo-Brazilian Soc, Royal Choral Soc; Hon Dr of Law Dartmouth Coll USA; FCA; *Clubs* Buck's, Naval and Military; *Style*— The Rt Hon Earl of Dartmouth; The Manor House, Chipperfield, King's Langley, Herts (☎ 09277 64498)

DARTMOUTH, Roma, Countess of; Roma Ernestine; da of Sir Ernest Burford Horlick, 2 Bt (d 1934), by his 1 w Jane Shillaber (who m 2, 1931, Sir Francis Oppenheimer, KCMG, who d 1961), da of Col Cunliffe Martin, CB, Bengal Cav; *b* 25 Nov 1903; *m* 10 April 1923, Humphry, 8 Earl of Dartmouth (d 1962); 1 s (9 Earl, Gerald Humphry), 1 da (Lady Heather Mary Margaret, Baroness Herschell, w of 3 Baron); *Style*— The Rt Hon Roma, Countess of Dartmouth; 15b Bedford Towers, Brighton, Sussex

DARWEN, 2 Baron (UK 1946) of Heys-in-Bowland; Cedric Percival Davies; s of 1 Baron Darwen (d 1950); *b* 18 Feb 1915; *Educ* Sidcot Sch, Manchester Univ (BA); *m* 14 July 1934, Kathleen Dora, da of the late George Sharples Walker, of Pendleton, Manchester; 3 s, 1 da; *Heir* s, Hon Roger Michael Davies; *Career* sat as Lab peer in House of Lords until 1982 when he joined Lib Pty; chm and md Darwen Finlayson Ltd 1954-73, pres Independent Publishers' Guild 1973-87; former schoolmaster; *Style*— The Rt Hon Lord Darwen; White Lodge, Sandelswood End, Beaconsfield, Bucks (☎ (049 46) 3355)

DARWENT, Rt Rev Frederick Charles; *see*: Aberdeen and Orkney, Bishop of

DARWIN, George Erasmus; s of William Robert Darwin (d 1970; gs of Charles Darwin); *b* 11 Feb 1927; *Educ* Winchester, Trinity Coll Cambridge (MA); *m* 5 Oct 1956, Shuna Mary, da of George Ronald Service, of Kinfauns House, by Perth (d 1961); 2 s, 1 da; *Career* Babcock & Wilcox Ltd 1957-78; chief exec Richardsons Westgarth Gp 1978-82; chm Home Grown Produce (Hldgs) 1979-; *Recreations* sailing, bridge; *Clubs* Savile; *Style*— George Darwin, Esq; 3A Pembroke Gdns, London W8 (☎ 01 602 6474); Home Grown Produce (Hldgs) Ltd, Greenhill House 90/93 Cowcross St, London EC1M 6BH (☎ 01 251 1089, telex 27737)

DARWIN, Henry Galton; CMG 1977; s of Sir Charles Galton Darwin KBE, FRS, of Newnham Grange, Cambridge, and Katharine Darwin, *née* Pember; *b* 6 Nov 1929; *Educ* Marlborough, Trinity Coll Cambridge (MA); *m* 5 July 1958, Jane Sophia, da of John Traill Christie (d 1980), Princ of Jesus Coll Oxford; 3 da (Sophia b 1961, Emma b 1964, Carola b 1967); *Career* second legal advsr, Foreign and Cwlth Off 1984, called to the Bar Lincoln's Inn 1953, asst legal advsr and later legal cnsllr and depty legal advsr 1954-60, 1963-67, 1970-73 and 1976-84, legal advsr Br Embassy Bonn and UK Mission to the UN 1960-63 and 1967-70, dir gen, legal serv, cncl secretariat EC Brussels 1973-76; contributions to books on peaceful settlement of int disputes and int settlement of frontier disputes; *Clubs* Athenaeum; *Style*— Henry G Darwin, Esq, CMG; 30 Hereford Square, London SW7 4NB (☎ 01 373 1140)

DARWIN, Philip Waring; s of William Robert Darwin (d 1971), and Sarah Monica, *née* Slingsby (d 1987); *b* 23 Oct 1929; *Educ* Winchester, Trinity Coll Cambridge (BA); *Career* Nat Serv 2 Lt 3 The Kings Own Hussars 1948-49; CA 1955; Moores Carson & Watson 1952-55, Schweppes Ltd 1955-57, Schweppes (USA) Ltd 1957-60 (vice pres 1958-60); Laurence Prust & Co: ptnr 1962-83, sr ptnr 1974-83, dir 1986-; memb The Cable Authy; Freeman Worshipful Co of Drapers; *Clubs* Savile; *Style*— P W Darwin, Esq; 4 Gore St, London SW7 5PT (☎ 01 584 8842); Laurence Prust & Co Ltd, 27 Finsbury Square, London EC2A 1LP (☎ 01 628 1111, fax 01 638 7660)

DARYNGTON, 2 Baron (UK 1923); Jocelyn Arthur Pike Pease; s of 1 Baron Daryngton, PC (d 1949); *b* 30 May 1906; *Educ* Eton, Trinity Coll Cambridge; *Heir* none; *Career* memb Inner Temple 1932; asst master: Doone House and Stone House Prep Schs Thanet; *Style*— The Rt Hon the Lord Daryngton

DAS NEVES, Hon Mrs (Amanda Mary Alnwick); *née* Grey; only da of Baron Grey of Naunton; *b* 23 Jan 1951; *Educ* St Mary's Sch Calne, Bedford Coll, Univ of London; *m* 1975, Jose das Neves; *Style*— The Hon Mrs das Neves; 18 Wakehurst Rd, London SW11

DASHWOOD, Cyril Francis; s of Cyril Russell Dashwood, CBE (d 1962), of Slough, and Laura Louise, *née* Steward (d 1959); *b* 15 Mar 1925; *Educ* Cranleigh Sch; *m* 20 Sept 1958, Prudence Elizabeth, da of Arnold George Oliver Williams, of Amersham; 2 s (Richard b 1961, William b 1968), 1 da (Joanna b 1964); *Career* Flt Lt RAF 1943-47; CA; sr ptnr Moores Rowland; vice pres Hockey Assoc 1988- (hon tres 1983-), cncl memb English Sinfonia Orchestra 1982-, chm Amersham and Chesham Bois Choral Soc, former chm Broad St Ward Club; Freeman: City of London 1985, Worshipful Co of CAs 1986; FCA 1950; *Recreations* music, sport, gardening; *Clubs* Carlton, Wig and Pen, MCC; *Style*— Cyril Dashwood, Esq; Ruthwell, Oakway, Chesham Bois, Bucks HP6 5PQ, (☎ 0494 725103); Cliffords Inn, Fetter Lane, London EC4A 1AS. (☎ 01 831 2345 fax 01 831 6123 telex 886504 MARCA)

DASHWOOD, Edward John Francis; s (by 1 m) and h of Sir Francis John Vernon Hereward Dashwood, 11 Bt, *qv*, by his 1st w; *b* 25 Sept 1964; *Educ* Eton Coll, Reading Univ (BSc); *Career* land agent, landowner; *Recreations* shooting, fishing, tennis; *Style*— Edward Dashwood Esq; West Wycombe Park, Bucks (☎ (0494) 24411)

DASHWOOD, Sir Francis John Vernon Hereward; 11 Bt (Premier Bt of GB, cr 1707), of West Wycombe, Buckinghamshire; s of Sir John Dashwood, 10 Bt, CVO (d 1966); *b* 7 August 1925; *Educ* Eton, Ch Ch Oxford, Harvard Business Sch; *m* 1, 3 May 1957, Victoria Ann Elizabeth Gwynne (d 1976), da of Maj John Frederick Foley, Baron de Rutzen (d 1944) (whose ancestor Augustus, Col in the Army of the Grand Duchy of Lithuania, obtained an acknowledgement of nobility from King Wladislaw IV of Poland *ante* 1677), of Slebech Park, Pembrokeshire, by his w Sheila Victoria Katrin (now Lady Dunsany), da of Sir Henry Philipps, Bt, of Picton Castle; 1 s, 3 da (Emily b 1958, m 1981 Charles Naper; Georgina b 1960; Caroline b 1962); m 2, 1977, Marcella Teresa Guglielmina Maria, formerly w of Giuseppe Sportoletti Baduel, widow of Jack Frye, CBE, and da of Marcellino Scarafia; 1 stepson (Marco Sportoletti Baduel b 1966); *Heir* s, Edward John Francis; *Career* landowner and farmer; Lloyd's underwriting agent and memb; contested (C) W Bromwich 1955 and Gloucester 1957; High Sheriff Bucks 1976; chm Bucks Branch CLA 1980; *Books* The Dashwoods of West Wycombe; *Recreations* shooting, windsurfing; *Clubs* White's; *Style*— Sir Francis Dashwood, Bt; West Wycombe Park, High Wycombe, Bucks HP14 3AJ (☎ 0494 23720); office: Knollys House, 47 Mark Lane, London EC3 (☎ 01 929 0811)

DASHWOOD, Dowager Lady; Helen Moira; da of late Lt-Col Vernon Eaton, Royal Canadian House Artillery; *m* 20 Dec 1922, Sir John Lindsay Dashwood, 10 Bt, CVO (d 1966); 2 s (Sir Francis, 11 and present Bt; John b 1929), 1 da (Sarah b 1924, Lady Aberdare); *Style*— Dowager Lady Dashwood; 10 Cumberland House, Kensington High St, W8 (☎ 01 937 7314)

DASHWOOD, Sir Richard James; 9 Bt (E 1684), of Kirtlington Park, Oxfordshire, TD (1987); s of Sir Henry Dashwood, 8 Bt (d 1972), by his w, Susan Mary (d 1985), da of late Maj Victor Robert Montgomerie-Charrington; *b* 14 Feb 1950; *Educ* Eton; *m* 1984, Kathryn Ann, er da of Frank Mahon, of Berkshire; 1 s (b 1988); *Career* Lt 14/20 King's Hussars 1969, TA & VR 1973 (Brevet Major 1987); *Clubs* Cavalry and Guards'; *Style*— Sir Richard Dashwood, Bt; Ledwell Cottage, Sandford St Martin, Oxon OX5 4AN (☎ (060 883) 267)

DAUBENY, (Charles) Niel; s of Richard Louis Daubeny (d 1968) of Miri Sarawak, and Madeleine Florence *née* Marsh; *b* 4 August 1937; *Educ* Wellington; *m* 23 Sept 1967, Mary Rose, da of Sir Alan Cumbrae Rose McLeod, KCVO (d 1981), of London; 1 s (Richard b 1977), 2 da (Victoria b 1969, Louise b 1972); *Career* Nat Serv RN 1958-60, TA 21 SAS 1960-63; Price Waterhouse & Co 1960- 66, dep gp chief accountant Mercantile and Gen Reinsurance Co 1970- 74, gp fin controller Bank of America Int Ltd 1974-78, dir and gp dir fin Scandinavian Bank Gp plc 1978-; FCA 1974; *Recreations* squash, gardening; *Clubs* IOD; *Style*— Niel Daubeny, Esq; Halnacker Hill, Bowlhead Green, Godalming, Surrey GU8 6NN (☎ 042 879 2170); Scandinavian Bank Group plc, 2-6 Cannon St, London EC4 6XX (☎ 01 236 6090)

DAUKES, Lt-Col John Clendon; s of Lt Col Sir Clendon Turberville Daukes, CIE (d 1947), of Sevenoaks, and Lady Dorothy Maynard, *née* Lavington Evans (d 1968); *b* 20 Nov 1916; *Educ* Charterhouse, RMA Woolwich; *m* 2 Sept 1944, Elizabeth, da of Capt Cosmo Alec Onslow Douglas, DSO (d 1971), of Berks; 2 s (Clendon Douglas b 1945, David Jeremy Gordon), 1 da (Jennifer Ann); *Career* Lt Col RA, cmmnd 1937, Brevet Lt Col 1955, Dunkirk evacuation 1940, Normandy landing D-Day, (despatches); Staff Coll Camberley 1942, instr 1944-45, RN Staff Coll Greenwich 1951, ret 1958; gen asst Int Pipeline Agency Paris (CEOA) 1958 (exec asst 1962), personnel mangr Dep Dir Admin, Int Staff NATO Paris & late Brussels 1967, bursar Charterhouse and clerk to the Governing Body 1969, chm Schs Bursars Assoc 1975-78, ret 1981; memb Ct of Assts of Sons of the Clergy Corpn 1975; tstee Carthusian Tst 1979-, memb Ctee of the Clergy Orphan Corpn 1980-; memb governing body: St Margaret's Bushey 1980-, St Edmund's Canterbury 1980-, Farlington Horsham 1980-86, Tormead Guildford 1980-86; memb Governing Bodies Assoc Exec Ctee 1982-84; *Recreations* skiing & many games; *Style*— Lt-Col John C Daukes; Chaucers, Seale, Farnham, Surrey GU10 1HP (☎ 02518 2096);

DAULTRY, Joseph George; s of Joseph Daultry (d 1954), of St Georges Rd, London SE11, and Gladys Mary, *née* Dudley (d 1968); *b* 24 August 1916; *Educ* Archbishop Temples Central Sch, Gibson & Weldon Sch of Law; *m* 24 March 1941, Lily, da of John Benjamin Butterfield (d 1962), of Dewsbury Rd, Leeds; 2 da (Jennifer Linda (Mrs Roberts) b 1948, Susan Josephine (Mrs Simpson) b 1952); *Career* WWII Flt Sgt RAF 1940-46; slr 1949, practised in London (ret 1983); vice pres RAF Assoc; appointed by Lord Chllr as pres Mental Health Review Tribunal (NE Thames Area) 1979-88; Freeman City of London 1961, Freeman Worshipful Co of Butchers 1961; memb Law Soc 1949; *Recreations* bowls; *Clubs* Seldorne and Bounds Green, Bowls and GC; *Style—* Joseph Daultry, Esq; 33 Eversley Crescent, Winchmore Hill, London N21 1EL (☎ 01 360 1730); 109-111 Cecil Rd, Enfield, Middx EN2 6TN (☎ 01 366 6387)

DAUNCEY, Brig Michael Donald Keen; DSO (1945), DL (Gloucester 1983); s of Thomas Gough Dauncey (d 1965), of Crowthorne, Berks, and Alice, *née* Keen (d 1988); the name Dauncey was first recorded in Uley, Glos, c1200s; *b* 11 May 1920; *Educ* King Edward's Sch Birmingham; *m* 1945, Marjorie Kathleen, da of Hubert William Neep (d 1967); 1 s (John), 2 da (Gillian, Margaret); *Career* cmmnd 22 Cheshire Regt 1941, seconded to Glider Pilot Regt 1943, Arnhem 1944 (wounded, taken prisoner, later escaped), MA to GOC-in-C Greece 1946-47, seconded to Para Regt 1947-49, Staff Coll 1950, instr RMA Sandhurst 1957-58, CO 1 Bn 22 Ches Regt 1963-66 (BAOR and UN Peace-keeping Force Cyprus), DS Plans JSSC 1966-68, Cmdt Jungle Warfare Sch 1968-69, Cmdt Support Weapons Wing Sch of Inf Netheravon 1969-72, Brig 1973, def and mi attaché Br Embassy Madrid 1973-75, ret from Army 1976; Col 22 Ches Regt 1978-85, Hon Col 1 Cadet Bn Glos Regt (ACF) 1981-; *Recreations* rough shooting, travelling, tennis, under-gardener; *Clubs* Army & Navy; *Style—* Brig Michael Dauncey, DSO, DL; Uley Lodge, Uley, Nr Dursley, Glos GL11 5SN (☎ 0453 860216)

DAUNCEY, Roger Martyn; s of Arnold Falconer Dauncey (d 1967), and Maud Mary, *née* Penney (d 1972); *b* 7 Mar 1923; *Educ* Bromsgrove Sch, Birmingham Univ; *m* 25 Aug 1951, Rosamond Lavinia, da of Lt Col Preston Dennis, OBE (d 1972); 4 s (Mark b 1952, Peter b 1953, Stephen b 1956, Timothy b 1958); *Career* civil servant prison serv; govr: Usk Borstal and Detention Centre 1965-70, Feltham Borstal 1970-75; dep regnl dir N Region Prison Serv 1975-83; ret 1983; chm parish cncl; *Style—* Roger Dauncey, Esq; Craycroft, The Street, Minsterworth, Gloucester (☎ 0452 754 372)

DAUNT, Maj-Gen Brian; CB (1956), CBE (1953), DSO (1943); s of Dr William Daunt (d 1920), of Parade House, Hastings, and Sarah Jeannie, *née* Gould (d 1962) ; *b* 16 Mar 1900; *Educ* Tonbridge, RMA Woolwich; *m* 8 Dec 1938, (Millicent) Margaret, da of Capt Alfred Stephen Balfour (d 1946); 1 s (Barry Balfour b 1947, d 1952), 2 da (Miranda, Nicola); *Career* RA 1920-65, Brig 1944, Maj-Gen 1954, Col-Cmdt RA 1960-65, controller Home Dept BRCS 1957-66; CStJ; *Recreations* the arts, gardening; *Clubs* Army and Navy; *Style—* Maj-Gen Brian Daunt, CB, CBE, DSO; 10 Church Lane, Wallingford, Oxon 0X10 0DX (☎ 0491 38111)

DAUNT, Patrick Eldon; s of Dr Francis Eldon Daunt (d 1953), of Hastings, and Winifred Doggett, *née* Wells; descendant of Daunt family of Owlpen Manor Gloucs, and Kilkascan Castle, Co Cork; *b* 19 Feb 1925; *Educ* Rugby, Wadham Coll Oxford (BA, MA); *m* 1958, Jean Patricia, da of Lt Col Percy Wentworth Hargreaves (d 1983), of Herts; 3 s (William, Thomas, Francis), 1 da (Caroline); *Career* housemaster Christ's Hosp 1961 headmaster Thomas Bennett Comprehensive Sch Crawley 1965-73, princ admin educn dept Cmmn of Euro Communities 1974-82, head of bureau for action in favour of disabled people Cmmn of Euro Communities 1982-87, visiting fell London Inst of Educn 1988-89; *Books* Comprehensive Values (1974); *Recreations* botanizing, books; *Clubs* Utd Oxford and Cambridge; *Style—* Patrick Daunt, Esq; 4 Bourn Bridge Rd, Abington, Cambridge (☎ 0223 891485)

DAVE, Dr Narendra Pranlal Girdharlal; s of Pranlal Girdharlal Dave (d 1968), of Nairobi, Kenya, and Yasumati, *née* Vyas; *b* 2 Nov 1951; *Educ* HH The Aga Khan Sch Mombasa Kenya, Middlesex Hosp Med Sch, Univ of London (MB, BS, DRCOG); *m* 10 April 1978, Bhavna, da of Jagdish Natwarlal Bhatt (d 1984), of London; 1 da (Punita b 1983); *Career* Capt RAMC (TA) 1981, transferred RARO (cl II) 1985; physician; Cleveland Vocational Trg Scheme for Gen Practice (Univ of Newcastle upon Tyne) 1979-82; med offr: Govt of Tristan Da Cunha 1982-84, Yorkshire Clinic Bingley 1984-85, Govt of Anguilla W Indies 1985-88, Fulford Grange Hosp Rawdon 1988-; FRSM, FRIPH, Fell Soc of Community Medicine; memb: Biochemical Soc, Royal Soc of Health; *Recreations* golf; *Style—* Dr Narendra P G Dave; 27 Stoneway, Hartwell, Northampton, NN7 2JY (☎ 0604 863005); office (☎ 0532 502909)

DAVENPORT; *see*: Bromley-Davenport

DAVENPORT, Brian John; QC (1980); s of Robert Cecil Davenport, FRCS; *b* 17 Mar 1936; *Educ* Bryanston Sch, Worcester Coll Oxford; *m* 1969, Erica Tickell, yr da of Prof E N Willmer; 2 s, 1 da; *Career* called to the Bar (Grays Inn) 1960; jr counsel to: Dept of Employment 1972-74, Bd of Inland Revenue 1974-80; law cmmr 1981-88; joined Inner Temple (ad eundem) 1978, bencher of Grays Inn 1984; *Style—* Brian Davenport Esq, QC; 43 Downshire Hill, London NW3 1NU (☎ 01 435 3332)

DAVENPORT, Maj David John Cecil; DL (Hereford and Worcester 1974); Lord of the Manors of Mansel Lacy, Wormsley, Yazor and Bishopstone; e s of Maj John Lewes Davenport, TD, JP, DL (d 1964), and Louise Aline (d 1987), only surviving child of Col Cecil John Herbert Spence-Colby, CMG, DSO, TD, of Donnington Hall, Ledbury; *b* 28 Oct 1934; *Educ* Eton, RMA Sandhurst, RAC Cirencester; *m* 1, 1959 (m dis 1970), Jennifer, *née* Burness, 2 da; m 2, 1971, Lindy, *née* Baker; 1 s; *Career* Grenadier Gds 1954-67, ret Maj; chm Leominster DC 1975-76; memb Forestry Cmmn Nat Advsy Ctee for Eng 1974-87; chm COSIRA 1982-88 (rural devpt cmmr 1982-, dep chm 1988), pres Herefordshire Branch CCA 1986-; *Clubs* Boodle's, MCC; *Style—* Maj David Davenport, DL; Mansel House, Mansel Lacy, Hereford HR4 7HQ (☎ 098 122 224)

DAVENPORT, Rear Adm Dudley Leslie; CB (1969), OBE (1954); s of Vice Adm Robert Clutterbuck Davenport (d 1965), of Hants, and Gwladwys Mabel, *née* Gwatkin-Williams (d 1973); *b* 17 August 1919; *Educ* RNC Dartmouth; *m* 1950, Joan Winifred Morris, da of Surgeon Cmdr Henry Burns (d 1955), of Warwicks; 2 s (James Dudley b 1952, Robert Charles b 1955); *Career* Capt Inshore Flotilla (Far East) 1960-62; dir Naval Offrs Appointments (Seaman Offrs) 1962-64; CO HMS Victorious 1964-66, Flag offr Malta 1967-69; ret 1969; *Clubs* Army & Navy; *Style—* Rear Adm Dudley Davenport, CB, OBE; 2 Anchor Mews, Lymington, Hampshire SO41 9EY (☎ (0590) 78166)

DAVENPORT, John Martin; s of Eric Davenport, of Ridge Acre, Hook Heath, Woking (d 1961), and Winifred Mary, *née* Elder; *b* 16 Oct 1931; *Educ* Uppingham, Oriel Coll Oxford (MA); *m* 14 Sept 1957, Wendy Angela, da of Claude Wyatt, of 8 Milner Rd, West Overcliff Dr, Bournemouth; 2 s (Philip b 1961, Peter b 1966); *Career* exec dep chm F & C Pacific Investmt Tst plc 1966-; exec dir Foreign & Colonial Mgmnt Ltd; investmt mangr; dir Community Hosps plc 1981-; FCA; *Recreations* railways, gardening; *Clubs* Gresham; *Style—* John Davenport, Esq; 1 Laurence Pountney Hill, London EC4R 0BA (☎ 01 623 4680)

DAVENPORT, Martyn Herbert; s of Horace Devenport (d 1944), and Marjorie Violet, *née* Fergusson (d 1973); *b* 11 Jan 1931; *Educ* Maidstone GS, Gonville and Caius Coll Cambridge (MA); *m* 1957, Mary Margaret, da of Percy Vincent Lord (d 1984); 3 s (Andrew, William, Edward), 1 da (Kate); *Career* asst master Eton Coll 1957-67, headmaster Victoria Coll 1967-; memb Headmasters' Conference 1967-; pres: Jersey Festival Choir 1983-, Jersey Assoc of Headteachers 1988-89;; *Recreations* sailing (yacht 'Con Brio'), photography; *Clubs* Public Schs; *Style—* Martyn Herbert Davenport, Esq; Sans Souci, Faldouet, Gorey, Jersey C1,(☎ 0534 52795); Victoria College, Jersey C1 (☎ 0534 37591)

DAVENPORT, Montague; CBE (1972, OBE 1959); s of Hayward Montague Davenport (d 1959); *b* 26 May 1916; *Educ* Sherborne, Pharmaceutical Soc Coll (PhC); *m* 1952, Olive Margaret, da of Donald Frank Brabner (d 1948); 2 s; *Career* WWII Lt-Cdr RNVR; FCO 1946- (asst sec 1971-78); govr dir J T Davenport Ltd 1959-80; *Style—* Montague Davenport, Esq, CBE; Chalcots, Orchard Way, Esher, Surrey (☎ 0732 62384)

DAVENPORT, (Arthur) Nigel; s of Maj Arthur Davenport, MC, of Sidney Sussex Coll, Cambridge; *b* 23 May 1928; *Educ* Cheltenham, Trinity Coll Oxford; *m* 1, 1951 (m dis 1962) Helena (d 1978); 1 s (Hugo), 1 da (Laura); m 2, 1972 (m dis 1980; she m 1, 1968, Richard Durden-Smith), Maria Penelope Katharine (b 1945), da of Sir William Aitken, KBE, MP (d 1964, n of 1 Baron Beaverbrook), and sis of Jonathan Aitken, MP; 1 s (Jack); *Career* served RASC and with Br Forces Network in Germany 1946-48; late memb OUDS; actor 1951-; co dir; vice pres Equity 1978-81, pres 1987-; *Recreations* gardening, travel; *Clubs* Garrick; *Style—* Nigel Davenport Esq; c/o Leading Artists, 60 St James's St, London SW1

DAVENPORT, Robert Simpson; s of Richard Simpson Davenport, and Dorothy Mary, *née* Evans; *b* 7 Jan 1941; *Educ* Canford; *m* 1970, Patricia, *née* Temple; 2 s; *Career* Singlton Fabian & Co (later merged with Binder Hamlyn) 1958-62, Peat Marwick Mitchell & Co (later Peat Marwick McLintock & Co) 1963-67, S G Warburg & Co Ltd 1968-88 (exec dir 1988-), exec dir Hill Samuel Bank 1988-; govr Elliott Sch Putney 1982-88; *Clubs* Hurlingham; *Style—* Robert Davenport, Esq; 1 Genoa Ave, London SW15 6DY; 2 Eaton Cottage, Dolmans Hill, Lytchett Matravers, Nr Poole, Dorset BH16 8HP

DAVENPORT-HANDLEY, Sir David John; OBE (1962), JP (Rutland 1948), DL (Leics 1974); s of John Davenport-Handley (d 1943); *b* 2 Sept 1919; *Educ* RNC Dartmouth; *m* 1943, Leslie Mary, da of Wing Cdr Sydney Mansfield Goldsmith, RAF; 1 s, 1 da; *Career* Lt RN, ret 1947; chm: Clipsham Quarry Co Ltd 1947-, Rutland and Stamford Cons Assoc 1952-65; Rutland Petty Sessional Div 1957-84, E Mids Area Cons Assoc 1971-77 (tres 1965-71), Nat Union of Cons and Unionist Assocs 1979-80 (vice chm 1977-79); Vice Lt Rutland 1972 (High Sheriff 1954, DL 1962); tstee Oakham Sch 1970-86; memb Parole Bd 1981-84; pres E Mids Area Cons Cncl 1987-; chm Rutland Historic Churches Preservation Tst 1987-; kt 1980; *Recreations* gardening, music; *Clubs* English Speaking Union; *Style—* Sir David Davenport-Handley, OBE, JP, DL; Clipsham Hall, Oakham, Rutland, Leics (☎ 078 081 204)

DAVENTRY, 3 Viscount (UK 1943); Francis Humphrey Maurice FitzRoy Newdegate; JP (Warwickshire 1960), DL (1970); father assumed by Royal Licence the additional surname of Newdegate 1936; s of Cdr the Hon John Maurice FitzRoy Newdegate, RN (d 1976), s of 1 Viscountess Daventry (d 1962), and Hon Mrs John FitzRoy Newdegate, *qv*; *b* 17 Dec 1921; *Educ* Eton; *m* 1959, Hon Rosemary, *qv*, da of Lt-Gen 1 Baron Norrie, GCMG, GCVO, CB, DSO (d 1977); 2 s, 1 da;; *Heir* Hon James Edward Fitzroy Newdegate; *Career* Capt Coldstream Gds 1943, ADC to Viceroy of India 1946-48; High Sheriff Warwicks 1970 (Vice Lord-Lieut 1974); *Clubs* Boodle's; *Style—* The Rt Hon the Viscount Daventry, JP, DL; Temple House, Arbury, Nuneaton, Warwickshire CV10 7PT (☎ 0203 383514)

DAVENTRY, Viscountess; Rosemary; *née* Norrie; da of late 1 Baron Norrie, GCMG, GCVO, CB, DSO, MC; *b* 1926; *m* 1959, 3 Viscount Daventry, JP, DL, *qv*; 2 s, 1 da; *Style—* The Rt Hon' the Viscountess Daventry; Temple House, Arbury, Nuneaton, Warwicks

DAVEY, Francis; s of Wilfred Henry Davey (d 1971); *b* 23 Mar 1932; *Educ* Plymouth Coll, New Coll Oxford (MA), CCC Cambridge; *m* 1960, Margaret Filby, da of Harold Charles Lake, MusDoc, FRCO (d 1961); 1 s, 1 da; *Career* asst master Dulwich Coll 1955-60, head classics dept Warwick Sch 1960-66, headmaster: Dr Morgan's GS Bridgwater 1966-73, Merchant Taylors' Sch 1974-82; *Recreations* rugby football, gardening, travel, naval history; *Clubs* Union (Oxford), East India Sports & Public Schools; *Style—* Francis Davey Esq; Crossings Cottage, Dousland, Yelverton, S Devon PL20 6LU (☎ (0822) 853928)

DAVEY, Hon Mrs (Heather Mary); *née* Grasmere; only da of Baron Morris of Grasmere; *b* 17 August 1925; *m* 1, 1946 (m dis 1972) Tom Berry Caldwell, son of William Caldwell, of Wigan, Lancs; 1 s, 2 da (m dis); m 2, 1972, Alfred G Davey; *Style—* The Hon Mrs Davey; Coach House, Kirk Hammerton, York

DAVEY, Jon Colin; s of Frederick John Davey, and Dorothy Mary, *née* Key (d 1969); *b* 16 June 1938; *Educ* Raynes Park GS; *m* 1962, Ann Patricia, da of Maj Stanley Arthur Streames (d 1977); 2 s (Simon b 1964, Jonathan b 1967), 1 da (Jennifer b 1972); *Career* asst sec Broadcasting Dept HO 1981-85; dir gen Cable Authy 1985-; other HO appointments - asst sec of Franks Ctee on Official Secrets 1971-72, sec of Williams Ctee on Obscenity and Film Censorship 1977-79, sec of Hunt Inquiry into Cable Expansion and Broadcasting Policy 1982; *Recreations* music, lawn-making, English countryside; *Style—* Jon Davey, Esq; 71 Hare Lane, Claygate, Esher, Surrey KT10 0QX (☎ (0372) 62078); Cable Authority, Gillingham House, 38-44 Gillingham Street, London SW1V 1HU (☎ 01 821 6161)

DAVEY, Hon Mrs (Margaret Wilmett); only da of Baron Helsby (Life Peer d 1978), by his w Wilmett *see* Baroness Helsby; *b* 6 Nov 1939; *m* 1, 1960, (John Frederick) Keith St Pier, eldest son of Norman Frederick St Pier, of Purley, Surrey; m 2, 1976, Brian Davey; *Style—* The Hon Mrs Davey; 7 Holmlea Court, Chatsworth Road, East Croydon CRO 1HA

DAVEY, Norman Thomas; s of Edward Thomas Davey (d 1979), of Torquay, Devon, and Kathleen Taylor, *née* Griffiths; *b* 28 Sept 1925; *Educ* Homelands Cent Sch, Torquay, Torquay Sch of Art, S Devon Tech Coll, Oxford Sch of Arch (Dip Arch); *m* 11 Feb 1962, Anne Felicity, da of Rev Arthur Douglas Young (d 1965); 3 s (Geoffrey b 1963, Benedict b 1965, Clement b 1968); *Career* RN 1943-47: AB, radar, gunnery; architect, private practice, (chiefly concerned with church architecture) 1964, memb Guildford diocesan advsy ctee for Care of Churches and Churchyards, tstee Soc for the Maintenance of the Faith, co-opted memb governing cncl of Chichester Theol Coll; RIBA 1953; *Recreations* reading, musical appreciation, countryside, villages, pubs, churches, naval history, current naval affairs; *Style—* Norman Davey, Esq; The Cottage, 2 Heatherley Rd, Camberley, Surrey GU15 3LW (☎ 0276 64615)

DAVEY, Peter John; s of John Davey (d 1981), and Mary Roberts; *b* 28 Feb 1940; *Educ* Oundle Sch, Edinburgh Univ (BArch); *m* 1968, Carolyn Frances, da of Francis St George Pulford (d 1978); 2 s (Pelham b 1977, Meredith b 1979); *Career* architect; ed architectural review 1981-; RIBA; *Books* Arts and Crafts Architecture (1982); *Recreations* fishing, mushroom hunting, cooking; *Style—* Peter Davey Esq; Architectural Review, 9 Queen Anne's Gate, London SW1 (☎ 01 222 4333)

DAVEY, (Margaret) Rowena; *née* Davies; da of Edward Smith Thomas Davies (d 1938), of Easton, Dunmow, Essex, and Muriel Davies, *née* Gaunt (d 1938); *b* 14 Nov 1917; *Educ* Cheltenham Ladies, Queen's Coll Harley St; *m* 19 Oct 1940, late Norris Gerald Davey, MC, TD, s of Edward Octavius Davey (d 1937), of Tower House, Dunmow; 1 s (John Edward Norris b 1946), 1 da (Mary Rubina b 1943); *Career* chm: housing Dunmow RDC (memb 1956-74), health and childrens ctees Essex CC (memb 1961-82), Uttlesford DC 1974-76 (currently memb), East Anglian Children's Regnl Planning Ctee 1969-79, West Essex Health Authy 1982-86, Uttlesford Cncl for Voluntary Serv; pres: Dunmow and Dist Over-60s Welfare Assoc, Dunmow Blind and Housebound Club, Dunmow Physically Handicapped Assoc, Greville Theatre Club; memb: Ctee of Inquiry into the Care and Supervision Provided in Relation to Maria Colwell 1973, Harlow Hosp Mgmnt Ctee 1963-73, NE Thames RHA 1974-82; hon vice pres Essex branch Br Red Cross Soc, hon life vice-pres Saffron Walden Cons constituency assoc (also Dunmow and Barnston branch); *Recreations* statring things and watchin them grow, reading, sewing, being at home; *Style—* Mrs Rowena Davey; Tower House, Dunmow, Essex CM6 3BA (☎ 0371 2162)

DAVEY, William; CBE (1978); *b* 15 June 1917; *Educ* Univ Coll Nottingham, Techn Coll Huddersfield; *m* 1941, Eunice Battye; 2 s; *Career* head of dept Chemistry and Biology London Poly 1953-59, princ Portsmouth Coll of Technol 1960-69, pres Portsmouth Poly 1969-82; FRSA, FRSC, CBIM; *Style—* William Davey Esq, CBE; 67 Ferndale, Waterlooville, Portsmouth, Hants (☎ 070 14 263014)

DAVID, Brian Rhodri; TD (and three bars); s of Herbert Cyril David (d 1978), and Enid Mary, *née* Reese (d 1968); *b* 20 Sept 1917; *Educ* Mill Hill Sch; *m* 30 Dec 1939, Joan Margarer (Peggy), da of HG Kemp (d 1938); 1 s (Nicholas Brian b 27 March 1942), 1 da (Sally Margaret b 30 Sept 1944); *Career* cmmnd RA TA 1937, Capt 1940, Maj July 1941, 2 i/c HAA Regt, ret 1953; Robinson David & Co Ltd: joined 1936, dir 1941, asst md 1949, resigned 1968; dir: Burts & Renton Ltd 1968-74, Principality Bldg Soc 1958-(dep chm 1976-81, chm 1981-); memb Indust Tbnl 1978-87, gen cmmr for Income Tax 1979-; *Recreations* watching rugby football; *Clubs* Cardiff and Co, Glamorgan Wanderers RFC; *Style—* Brian David, Esq, TD; 20 Mill Rd, Llanishen, Cardiff CF4 5XB (☎ 0222 752 514); PO Box 89, Principality Bldgs, Queen St, Cardiff CF1 1UA (☎ 0222 344 188, fax 0222 314 567)

DAVID, David Michael; s of Ronald Alexander Davis, and Elizabeth *née* Brown; *b* 23 Dec 1948; *Educ* Bec GS, Warwick Univ (BSc), London Business Sch (MSc), Harvard (AMP); *m* 28 July 1973, Doreen Marjery, da of Alfred John Cook; 2 da (Rebecca b 1974, Sarah b 1977); *Career* dir Tate & Lyle plc 1987; *Recreations* flying, mountaineering, writing; *Clubs* Reform; *Style—* D M David, Esq; House of Commons, Westminster, London SW1

DAVID, Elizabeth; *née* Gwynne; CBE (1986, OBE 1976); 2 da of Rupert Sackville Gwynne, MP (d 1924), and Hon Stella Ridley (who m 2, 1933, Capt John Hamilton, Extra ADC to Gov of Jamaica, and d 1973), 2 da of 1 Viscount Ridley (d 1904); *b* 1913; *m* 30 Aug 1944 (m dis 1960), Lt-Col Ivor Anthony David, IA; *Career* author of numerous cookery books; FRSL 1982; DUniv (Essex) 1980; Chev du Mérite Agricole (Fr) 1977; *Books* A Book of Mediterranean Food (1950), French Country Cooking (1951), Italian Food (1954), Summer Cooking (1955), French Provincial Cooking (1960), English Cooking, Ancient and Modern; vol I, Spices, Salts and Aromatics in the English Kitchen (1970), English Bread and Yeast Cookery (1977) An Omelette and a Glass of Wine (1984); *Style—* Mrs Elizabeth David, CBE; c/o Penguin Books, Harmondsworth, Middx

DAVID, Joanna; da of Maj John Almond Hacking, and Davida Elizabeth, *née* Nesbitt; *b* 17 Jan 1947; *Educ* Altrincham GS, Elmhurst Ballet Sch, Royal Acad of Dancing, Webber Douglas Acad of Dramatic Art; *m* Edward Charles Morice Fox, s of Robin Fox (d 1970); 1 da (Emilia Rose Elizabeth b 31 July 1974); *Career* actress; Chichester Festival Theatre 1971, Family Reunion 1973 and Uncle Banya 1977 Royal Exchange Manchester, Cherry Orchard 1983 and Breaking the Code 1986, Theatre Royal Haymarket; TV appearances incl: War and Peace, Sense and Sensibility, Last of the Mohicans, Duchess of Duke Street, Rebecca, Carrington and Strachey, Fame is the First Among Equals, Paying Guests, Unexplained Laughter, Hannay; memb ctee: Ladies Theatrical Guild, Unicorn Theatre for Children; *Style—* Miss Joanna David; c/o Peter Browne Management, Pebro House, 13 St Martins Road, London SW9 (☎ 01 737 3444)

DAVID, Joseph; OBE (1983); s of Morris David (d 1955), of Glamorgan, and Goldie Freedman; *b* 22 Mar 1928; *Educ* Pontypridd Boys Sch, Manchester Univ (BSc Tech); *m* 1959, Shirley, da of Hyman Selbey, of London; 1 s (Alun b 1964), 2 da (Keren b 1963, Deborah b 1968); *Career* chartered textile technologist; co dir 1968, chm and md Catomance Ltd 1977-; pres: Br Pest Control Assoc 1976-78, Br Wood Preserving Assoc 1986-; FTI; *Recreations* conservation and restoration, theatre, reading; *Style—* Joseph David, Esq, OBE; 1 Coneydale, Welwyn Garden City, Herts AL8 7RX (☎ (0707) 326625); Catonance Ltd, 96 Bridge Road, East Welwyn, Garden City, Herts AL7 1JW (☎ (0707) 324373, telex 267418, fax (0707) 372191)

DAVID, Hon Nicholas Christopher; er s of Richard William David and Baroness David (Life Peer), *qv*; *b* 1937; *m* 1, 1962 (m dis 1975), Hilke Hennig; m 2, 1977 (m dis 1982), Iva Williams; m 3, Judy Sterner; *Style—* The Hon Nicholas David; Dept of Archaeology, Univ of Ibadan, Nigeria

DAVID, Baroness (Life Peer UK 1978); Nora Ratcliff David; JP (Cambridge City 1965); da of George Blockley Blakesley, JP (d 1934); *b* 23 Sept 1913; *Educ* Ashby-de-la-Zouch Girls' GS, St Felix Southwold, Newnham Coll Cambridge (MA); *m* 1935, Richard William David, s of late Rev Ferdinand Paul David; 2 s, 2 da; *Career* sits as Labour Peer in House of Lords, dep chief oppn whip 1983-87 and oppn spokesman for environment/local govt in Lords 1983-86, oppn spokesman for educn 1986-; former Cambridge city cllr, Cambs co cllr 1974-79; memb Bd Peterborough Devpt Corpn 1976-78; Baroness-in-Waiting to HM The Queen 1978-79; Hon Fell Newnham Coll Cambridge 1986; *Recreations* swimming, theatre, reading; *Style—* The Rt Hon Lady David, JP; 50 Highsett, Cambridge CB2 1NZ (☎ 0223 350376); Cove, New Polzeath, nr Wadebridge, Cornwall (☎ 020 886 3310); House of Lords, London SW1 (☎ 01 219 3159)

DAVID, Hon Richard Sebastian David; s of Richard William David, CBE, and Baroness David, *qqv*; *b* 1940; *Educ* MB, BChir, MA; *m* 1963, Eva Ross; *Career* surgn, gen practitioner Fort Macleod Alberta 1975-; FRCS; *Style—* The Hon Richard David; Box 820, Fort Macleod, Alberta, Canada

DAVID, Richard William; CBE (1967); s of Rev F P David (d 1955), and Mary W David; *b* 28 Jan 1912; *Educ* Winchester Coll, CCC Cambridge (MA); *m* 1935, Nora (Baroness David, *qv*); 2 s, 2 da; *Career* publisher 1936-74; London mangr Cambridge Univ Press 1948-63, sec to the Syndics 1963-70, univ publisher 1970-74; pres Botanical Soc of the Br Isles 1979-81; *Books* The Janus of Poets (1935), Love's Labour Lost (Arden Shakespeare edition 1951), Shakespeare in the Theatre (1978); pt-author: Review of the Cornish Flora (1981), Sedges of the Br Isles (1982); *Clubs* Garrick; *Style—* Richard David Esq, CBE; 50 Highsett, Cambridge CB2 1NZ (☎ (0223) 350376); Cove, New Polzeath, nr Wadebridge, Cornwall PL27 6UF (☎ (020 886) 3310)

DAVID, Tudor; s of Thomas David (d 1941) of Barry, Wales and Blodwen *née* Jones (d 1988); *b* 25 April 1921; *Educ* Barry GS, Univ of Manchester (BA), Univ of Oxford; *m* 1, Jan 1943 (d 1984) Nancy, da of Robert Ramsay (d 1948), of Crook, Co Durham; 1 s (Martyn b 1946), 1 da (Glenwyn b 1947); m 2, 21 Feb 1987, Margaret, da of Glyndwr Dix (d 1978), of Glynneath, Glamorgan; *Career* cmmd tech branch RAF 1942, staff offr Flying Trg Cmd 1943-45, Sqdn Ldr Air HQ India 1945-46; extra mural lectr Univ of Newcastle 1946-48, local govt offr Lincolnshire, 1949-53; asst ed Education 1953-74, ed: The Teacher 1974-79, Education 1979-86, Journal of Oil and Gas Accountancy 1986-; freelance journalist 1986-; cncl memb Hon Soc of Cymmrodorion, memb Welsh Acad; FCP, FRSA; *Books* Perspectives in Geographical Education (1973), Education: The Wasted Years? (1988); *Recreations* opera, rugby; *Style—* Tudor David, Esq; 21 Pointers Close, Isle of Dogs, London E14 9AP (☎ 01 987 8631)

DAVIDGE, Christopher Guy Vere; OBE (1982); s of (Cecil) Vere Davidge (d 1981), of Little Houghton, Northants, and his 1 w, (Ursula) Catherine (d 1948), yr da and co-heir of Christopher Smyth, JP, DL (d 1934); *see* Burke's Landed Gentry, 18 edn, vol II, 1969; *b* 5 Nov 1929; *Educ* Eton, Trinity Coll Oxford (MA); *m* 1 Feb 1963, Winifred Marian, da of John Stanley Crome, ARIBA; *Career* dir Mixconcrete (Holdings) plc 1964-82 (md 1964-69); chm various private cos 1960-; memb Cncl of Lloyds 1982-; dir Lloyds of London Press Ltd 1985- (chm 1989-); chm of govrs and tstee: Three Shires Hosp Northampton 1981-, Maidwell Hall Sch Northampton 1979-; govr St Andrews Hosp Northampton 1969-; High Sheriff of Northants 1988- 89; Freeman of City of London, memb Worshipful Co of Watermen; rowed for Great Britain 1952-63, Steward Henley Royal Regatta 1967-, chm Leander Club 1968-78; pres Amateur Rowing Assoc 1977-85, Hon Tres Commonwealth Games Cncl 1969-74 (vice-chm 1974-), vice-chm British Olympic Assoc 1972-76, chef de mission GB Team Olympic Games 1976, vice-pres British Olympic Assoc 1976-, cncl memb FISA (int rowing fedn), chm Regattas Cmmn of FISA; *Recreations* rowing, gardening, restoration of old houses; *Clubs* Leander, Vincents; Little Houghton House, Northampton (☎ 0604 890234); 33 John's Mews, London WC1N 2NS (☎ 01 242 6644)

DAVIDSON, Alan Stuart Birks; TD; s of Albert Davidson, CBE (d 1932), and Emma, *née* Birks (d 1956); *b* 27 Sept 1909; *Educ* Bradfield, Balliol Coll Oxford; *m* 1937, Frances (d 1982), da of Dennis McDonald; 3 s (John, Paul, Nicholas), 1 da (Anne); *Career* served WW II RA, Maj (despatches 1945); Oxford & Cambridge delgn to Argentina 1931, trainee with Rowntree & Co York 1932-35, export mangr Yorkshire Copper Works Leeds 1935-39; chm Hattersley & Davidson Ltd Sheffield and assoc cos 1955; ret; *Recreations* sailing, shooting, golf; *Style—* Stuart Davidson Esq, TD; 1 Orchard Court, Grindleford, Sheffield S3O 1JH

DAVIDSON, Andrew Scott Rutherford; s of Andrew Rutherford Davidson of Edinburgh (d 1967), and Jean, *née* McKenzie (d 1983); *b* 18 Nov 1929; *Educ* Merchiston Castle Sch, Edinburgh; *m* 2 Sept 1960, Dorothy Mowat Proudfoot, da of Dr Charles Crighton Robson, MC (d 1958); 1 s (Charles b 1966), 2 da (Katharine b 1962, Sarah b 1964); *Career* Capt the Royal Scots 1950; joined Bank of Scotland 1951, gen mangr (England) 1971-; non exec dir: The Br Linen Bank Ltd 1978-, Capital Export Servs Ltd 1980, Kellock Ltd 1981-; chm Bankers Benevolent Fund; memb: ESU, Canada - UK C of C, The Lombard Assoc, London C of C & Indust, Br Nat Ctee of int C of C, Bank assoc memb American C of C, Freeman City of London 1978, FIB (Scotland); *Recreations* golf, fishing, watching, rugby, football; *Clubs* City of London, MCC, Walton Heath Golf; *Style—* Andrew Davidson, Esq; 38 Threadneedle Street, London EC2P 2EH (☎ 01 601 6555, fax 01 601 6526)

DAVIDSON, Anthony Beverley; s of Dr Ronald Beverley Davidson, MB ChB (d 1972), and Edna Robina Elizabeth, *née* Cowan; *b* 25 Dec 1947; *Educ* Morgan Acad Dundee, St Andrews Univ (MA); *m* 21 Dec 1971, Avril Rose, da of John Pearson Duncan of 10 Barnes Ave, Dundee; 2 s (Ronald b 1975, Duncan b 1982), 2 da (Amanda b 1977, Laura b 1979); *Career* CA 1974; mangr Deloitte Haskins and Sells (Edinburgh) 1970-75, sr mangr Whitelaw Wells and Co 1975-76, chief accountant highways dept Lothian Regnl Cncl 1976-77, chief inspr TSB (Tayside and Central Scotland) 1977-79, head inspection divn TSB Gp 1979-82, gen mangr TSB (Tayside and Cntl Scotland) 1982-83; sr exec dir TSB Scotland plc 1987- (gen mangr 1983-87); memb Co of Merchants of City of Edinburgh 1986; FCMA 1984, FIB (Scot) 1987; *Recreations* golf, photography, skiing; *Clubs* Wentworth and Gullane GC; *Style—* Anthony Davidson, Esq; Ingleton, Whim Road, Gullane, East Lothian EH31 2BD (☎ 0620 842146); TSB Scotland plc, Henry Duncan House, 120 George Street, Edinburgh EH2 4TS (☎ 031 225 4555, fax 031 220 0240, car 0836 713888, telex 727512)

DAVIDSON, Arthur; QC (1978); *b* 7 Nov 1928; *Educ* Liverpool Coll, King George V Sch Southport, Trinity Cambridge; *Career* MP (Lab) Accrington 1966-83; principal oppn front bench spokesman Legal Affrs 1982-83 (Dep Oppn Spokesman Legal Affrs 1981-82); pps to Slr-Gen 1968-70, fought Blackpool S 1955, Preston N 1959, Parly Sec Law Offrs Dept 1974-79; memb Nat Exec of Fabian Soc; former: chm PLP Home Affrs Gp, memb Consumers' Assoc Cncl; Home Affrs Select Ctee 1980-; *Style*— Arthur Davidson Esq, QC; 11 South Sq, Gray's Inn, London WC1R 5EU

DAVIDSON, Brian; CBE (1965); s of Edward Fitzwilliam Davidson (d 1953), and late Esther, *née* Schofield; *b* 14 Sept 1909; *Educ* Winchester, New Coll Oxford; *m* 1935, Priscilla Margaret (d 1981), da of late Arthur Farquhar Chilver; 2 s (1 d 1970), 1 da; *Career* barr 1933, slr 1939; Air Miny and Miny of Aircraft Prodn 1940-43, Bristol Aeroplane Co 1943-68; slr Br Gas Corpn 1969-75, Monopolies Cmmn 1956-68; *Style*— Brian Davidson, Esq, CBE; Sands Court, Dodington, Avon BS17 6SE (☎ 0454 313077)

DAVIDSON, Hon Lord; Charles Kemp Davidson; s of Rev Donald Davidson, DD (d 1970), of Edinburgh, and Charlotte Davidson; *b* 13 April 1929; *Educ* Fettes, Oxford Univ (MA), Edinburgh Univ (LLB); *m* 1960, Mary, da of Charles Mactaggart, MC (d 1984), of Argyll; 1 s (Donald), 2 da (Caroline, Louise); *Career* 2 Lt Argyll & Sutherland Highlanders (Nat Serv) 1953-55; admitted to Faculty of Advocates 1956; QC (Scotland) 1969; keeper Advocates Library 1972-76; vice-dean 1977-79; dean 1979-83; procurator to Gen Assembly of the Church of Scotland 1972-83; senator of the Coll of Justice 1983-; dep chm Boundary Cmmn for Scotland 1985; chm Scottish Law Cmmn 1988-; FRSE; *Style*— Hon Lord Davidson; 22 Dublin Street, Edinburgh 1 (☎ (031) 556 2168)

DAVIDSON, Charles Peter Morton; s of Dr William Philip Morton Davidson (d 1978), of Northumberland, da of Muriel Maud Davidson, *née* Alderson (d 1987); *b* 29 July 1938; *Educ* Harrow, Trinity Coll Dublin (MA, LLB); *m* 15 Sept 1966, Pamela Louise, da of Harry Campbell-Rose, of Natal; *Career* barr Inner Temple 1963; contested (C) N Battersea Gen Election 1966, chm London Rent Assessment Panel 1973-84, pt/t Immigration appeals adjudicator 1976-84; London Borough cncl: Wandsworth 1964-68, Merton 1968-71; met stipendiary magistrate 1984-; *Recreations* music, travel; *Style*— Peter Davidson, Esq; Horseferry Rd, Magistrate Ct, 70 Horseferry Rd, London SW1P 2AX

DAVIDSON, Christopher William Sherwood (Bill); s of Thomas Leigh Davidson, of Iddesleigh, Queens Road, Ilkley, W Yorks, and Donaldine, *née* Brown (d 1982); *b* 29 July 1940; *Educ* Uppingham, Nottingham Univ (BA); *Career* articles with R K Denby (later Sir Richard Denby) 1962-65, slr 1966; asst slr: Winkworth & Pemberton Westminster 1966-67, Coward Chance 1968-70; ptnr Ashton Hill & Co Nottingham 1971-75, gp slr and co sec NUS Servs Ltd 1975-77; co sec: Endsleigh Insur Servs Ltd 1968- (legal advsr 1966-), NUS Servs Ltd 1984-; fndr (later sr ptnr) Christopher Davidson & Co 1977-; memb Law Soc; *Recreations* socialising and reading humorous/ crime fiction; *Clubs* Constitutional, Cheltenham; *Style*— Bill Davidson, Esq; The Old Rectory Kemerton Nr Tewkesbury Gloucestershire GL20 7HY (☎ 0242 9689 244); 2/3 Oriel Terr Oriel Rd Cheltenham Gloucestershire GL20 7HY (☎ 0242 581 481, fax 0242 221 210)

DAVIDSON, Hon Mrs (Elizabeth Maud); *née* Younger; da of 2 Viscount Younger of Leckie (d 1946), and Maud (d 1957), er da of Sir John Gilmour, 1 Bt; *b* 22 May 1913; *m* 13 March 1937, Lt-Col Kenneth Bulstrode Lloyd Davidson, only s of late Col Charles Lloyd Davidson, DSO, of The Manor House, Eglinton; 4 s, 1 da; *Style*— The Hon Mrs Davidson; The Manor House, Eglinton, Co Londonderry, N Ireland (☎ (0504) 222)

DAVIDSON, Howard William; CMG (1961), MBE (1942); s of late Joseph Christopher Davidson (d 1932), of Johannesburg S Africa and Helen, *née* Forbis (d 1948); *b* 30 July 1911; *Educ* King Edward VII Sch Johannesburg, Witwatersrand Univ, Oriel Coll Oxford, (BA, MA); *m* 1, 1941 (m dis 1955), Anne Elizabeth, da of late Capt R C Power, of Johannesburg; 1 da (Elizabeth-Anne), m 2, 1956 (m dis 1972), Dorothy Janet, da of late Sir William Polson, KCMG (d 1960), of Wanganui, NZ; *Career* Colonial Admin Serv 1935-63; Sierra Leone, Fiji, N Borneo; min of fin Sabah Malaysia 1963-64, fin advsr 1964-65; SPDK Sabah State Honours List (1964); *Recreations* cricket, croquet, learning; *Clubs* E India Sports & Public Schs, Cowdray Park Polo, Sussex County Croquet; *Style*— Howard Davidson, Esq, CMG, MBE

DAVIDSON, Ian Douglas; CBE (1957); s of Rev John Davidson, JP, and Elizabeth Helen, *née* Whyte; *b* 27 Oct 1901; *Educ* King William's Coll; *m* 1, 1936, Claire Louise (d 1937), da of E S Gempp, of St Louis, USA; 1 da; m 2, 1938, Eugenia, da of late Marques de Mohernando, and Lorenza, Marquesa de Mohernando; 1 da; *Career* pres: Mexican Eagle Oil Co 1936-47, Cia Shell de Venezuela 1953-57, Canadian Shell Ltd 1957-61; *Style*— Ian Davidson Esq, CBE; 1 Benevenuto Place, Apt 105, Toronto, Ontario M4V 2L1, Canada

DAVIDSON, Judge Ian Thomas Rollo; QC (1977); s of Dr Robert Davidson (d 1970), and Margaret Miller Davidson (d 1980); *b* 3 August 1925; *Educ* Fettes Coll, Corpus Christi Coll Oxford (BA); *m* 1, 1954, Gyöngyi (m dis 1982), da of Prof Csaba Anghi; 1 s (Stuart), 1 da (Amanda); m 2, 1984, Barbara Ann, da of Jack Watts; 1 s (Alasdair); *Career* RAC 1943-47, Lt Derbyshire Yeo; barr Gray's Inn 1955, asst lectr UCL 1959-60, dep rec Nottingham 1971, rec of the Crown Ct 1974, circuit judge 1984-; *Recreations* music, golf, photography; *Clubs* Forty, Notts Servs, Muswell Hill Golf, Notts Golf; *Style*— His Hon Judge Ian Davidson, QC; 15 Park Valley, The Park, Nottingham NG7 1BS (☎ 0602 470 672)

DAVIDSON, James Patton; CBE (1980); s of Richard Davidson (d 1971), and Elizabeth Ferguson, *née* Carnichan; *b* 23 Mar 1928; *Educ* Rutherglen Acad, Glasgow Univ (BL); *m* 1, 1953, Jean Stevenson Ferguson, da of John B Anderson (d 1979); 2 s (Euan b 1958, Hamish b 1963); m 2, 1981, Esmé Evelyn, da of Robert Ruben Ancill, JP (d 1966); *Career* Lt RASC 1948-50; md Clydeport Authy 1966 (chm 1980-83); chm: Ardrossan Harbour Co 1976-83, Clydeport Stevedoring Servs 1977-83, Rhu Marina 1976-80; chm Nat Assoc of Port Employers 1974-79, memb Br Ports Assoc 1980-82, chm Pilotage Cmmn 1983-; FRSA, FCIT, CBIM; *Recreations* sailing, golf, reading, music; *Clubs* Oriental, Royal Troon GC, Cambuslang GC; *Style*— James Davidson, Esq, CBE; 44 Guthrie Ct, Gleneagles, Perthshire PH3 1SD; Pilotage Commission, 8 Great James St, London

DAVIDSON, 2 Viscount (UK 1937); John Andrew Davidson; s of 1 Viscount Davidson, GCVO, CH, CB, PC (d 1970), and Hon Dame Frances, DBE (Baroness Northchurch, d 1985); *b* 22 Dec 1928; *Educ* Westminster, Pembroke Coll Cambridge; *m* 1, 30 June 1956 (m dis 1974), Margaret Birgitta (who m 2, 1974, as his 2 w, 4 Viscount Colville of Culross), da of Maj-Gen Cyril Henry Norton, CB, CBE, DSO; 4 da (including Hon Mrs Oldfield and Lady Edward Somerset, *qqv*); m 2, 1975, Mrs Pamela Joy Dobb, da of John Vergette; *Heir* bro, Hon Malcolm Davidson; *Career* served with Black Watch and 5 Bn King's African Rifles 1947-49; Lord in Waiting 1985-86; Capt Queen's Body Guard of the Yeomen of the Guard (Dep Chief Whip in House of Lords) 1986-; dir Strutt & Parker (Farms) Ltd 1960-75; memb Cncl CLA 1965-75; RASE 1973-75; *Style*— The Rt Hon Viscount Davidson; House of Lords, London SW1A 9PW

DAVIDSON, Dr (William) Keith Davidson; CBE (1982); s of James Fisher Keith Davidson (d 1978), Bearsden, Glasgow, and Martha Anderson, *née* Milloy (d 1956); *b* 20 Nov 1926; *Educ* Coatbridge Secdy Sch, Glasgow Univ; *m* 6 Feb 1952, Dr Mary Waddell Aitken, da of Dr George Jamieson (d 1967), Chryston; 1 s (Keith b 1954), 1 da (Mhairi b 1956); *Career* Med Offr 1 Bn RSF 1950, Maj 2 i/c 14 Field Ambulance 1950-51, Med OIC Holland and Belgium 1952; chm: Glasgow Local Med Ctee 1971-75, Scottish Gen Med Servs Ctee 1972-75-, dep chm Gen Med Servs ctee (UK) 1975-79; memb: Scottish Med Practices ctee 1968-80, Scottish Health Serv Policy Bd 1985-; chm Scottish Health Serv Planning Cncl 1984-; BMA: memb cncl 1972-81, fell 1975, chm scottish cncl 1978-81, vice pres 1983-; hon pres Glasgow Eastern Med Soc 1984-85, pres Scottish Midland and Western Med Soc 1985-86; JP (Glasgow) 1962, SBSTJ 1976; elder Church of Scotland 1956-, session clerk Stepps Parish Church 1983-; memb Bonnet Makers and Dyers Craft 1964; BMA 1949, DPA 1967, FRCGP 1980, RSM 1988; *Recreations* gardening, caravanning; *Clubs* RSAC; *Style*— Dr Keith Davidson, CBE; Dunvegan, Stepps, Glasgow G33 6DE (☎ 041 774 2103); 67 Gilbertfield Street, Ruchazie, Glasgow G33 3TU (☎ 041 774 5987, car tel 0035 240 221)

DAVIDSON, Hon Kristina Louise; da (twin) of 2 Viscount Davidson by 1 w; *b* 17 Feb 1963; *Style*— The Hon Kristina Davidson

DAVIDSON, Malcolm Alexander; s of Robert Stanley Davidson (d 1987), and Hilda, *née* Capewell (d 1975); *b* 30 Nov 1933; *Educ* Prescot GS; *m* 31 July 1958, Patricia Edna, da of Raymond Parker Lenton (d 1982); 1 s (Alasdair Malcolm b 1965), 1 da (Fiona Sarah b 1967); *Career* Nat Serv Queen's Own Cameron Highlanders 1952-54; md Littlewoods Pools 1987-, dir The Littlewoods Orgn 1987-; *Recreations* shooting, tennis, swimming, music; *Style*— Malcolm A Davidson, Esq; Littlewoods Pools, Walton Hall Ave, Liverpool L67 1AA (☎ 051 525 3677, 051 342 3920)

DAVIDSON, Hon Malcolm William Mackenzie; s of 1 Viscount Davidson; *b* 28 August 1934; *Educ* Westminster, Pembroke Cambridge; *m* 1970, Mrs Evelyn Ann Carew Perfect, da of William Blackmore Storey; 1 s (John b 1971), 1 da (Sophie b 1973); *Clubs* Travellers', Pratt's; *Style*— The Hon Malcolm Davidson; Widden Hill House, Horton, Chipping Sodbury, Bristol

DAVIDSON, Maj Philip Lowthian; JP (1950), DL (Cumbria 1972); s of William Davidson (d 1937); *b* 4 June 1902; *Educ* Queen Elizabeth GS Penrith; *m* 1, 1934, Isabel Agnes, *née* Brodie (d 1938); m 2 1949, Barbara Margery, *née* Keay (d 1976); *Career* Maj RE (UK, India), chartered architect RTBA in private practice, ret 1977; *Recreations* foxhunting - (MFH Blencathra Hunt), watching Rugby Union, cricket; *Clubs* English Speaking Union; *Style*— Maj Philip Davidson, JP, DL; 38 St John St, Keswick, Cumbria CA12 5AG (☎ (0596) 72922)

DAVIDSON, Roderick Macdonald; JP (1976); s of Dr Stephen Moriarty Davidson, of Bristol, and Kathleen Flora, *née* Macdonald; *b* 2 Jan 1938; *Educ* Clifton Coll, St John's Coll Cambridge; *m* 17 June 1961, Jane Margaret da of Dr Basil Stanley Kent of Kingsclere; 1 s (Michael b 1965), 2 da (Emma b 1963, Juliet b 1969); *Career* Nat Serv RM 1956-58, cmmnd 1957; md Stock Beech and Co Ltd 1986: (stockbroker, ptnr 1965); Bristol city cncllr 1969-74; memb cncl: Clifton Coll, St Peters Hospice, Bristol, and Clifton Zoo, Clifton HS for Girls; membership sec Antient of St Stephens Ringers Dolphin Canynges; tax cmmr 1978, High Sherriff of Avon 1981-82; memb: Worshipful Co of Curriers, The Securities Assoc; *Recreations* golf, fishing, music; *Clubs* MCC, Clifton, Thurlestone Golf; *Style*— Roderick Davidson, Esq, JP; Stock Beech & Co Ltd, The Bristol & West Building, Broad Quay, Bristol, BS1 4DD (☎ 0272 260051)

DAVIDSON, Hon Mrs (Sheila Anne); yr da of 2 Baron Greenhill; *b* 1951; *m* 1979, Robert Davidson, of Edmonton; *Style*— The Hon Mrs Davidson; c/o Rt Hon Lord Greenhill, 10223, 137th St, Edmonton, Alberta, Canada

DAVIDSON, Air Vice-Marshal Rev Sinclair Melville; CBE (1968); s of James Stewart Davidson (d 1961), and Anne Sinclair Davidson, *née* Cowan (d 1938); *b* 1 Nov 1922; *Educ* Bousfield Sch Kensington, RAF Cranwell, RAF Tech Coll, Chichester Theological Coll; *m* 1944, Jean Irene, *née* Flay; 1 s (and 1 s decd); *Career* served WW II, RAF (despatches), psa 1956, air staff Air Miny 1957-60, jssc 1960, Asst Cmdt RAF Locking 1963-64, chm Jt Signal Bd (Middle East) 1965, idc 1968, dir Signals (Air) MOD 1969-71, Air Offr Wales and Station Cdr RAF St Athan 1972-74, asst chief Defence Staff (Signals) 1974-75; sec Inst of Electronic and Radio Engineers 1977-82; ordained 1982, priest-in-charge Parish of Holy Trinity (High Hurstwood) 1983-; *Recreations* parish affairs, maintenance of home and garden; *Clubs* RAF; *Style*— Air Vice Marshal Rev Sinclair Davidson, CBE; Trinity Cottage, High Hurstwood, Uckfield, East Sussex (☎ (0825) 812151)

DAVIDSON, William Bird; s of John Noble Davidson (d 1976), and Martha, *née* Scott (d 1956); *b* 18 May 1912; *Educ* Penrith Queen Elizabeth GS; *m* 1941, da of Ben Ireton (d 1923); 2 s (John, Edward); *Career* TA 1938, War Serv 1939-45, UK ME & Italy, Capt RA; banker, entered Nat Provincial Bank 1929, (jt gen mangr 1961, chief gen mangr 1967), chief exec Nat Westminster Bank 1970-72 (dep chm 1973-76), dir Allied London Properties plc 1976-84; *Recreations* golf; *Style*— William Davidson, Esq; Rose Cottage, 9 Starrock Road, Coulsdon, Surrey CR3 2EH (☎ 073 75 53687)

DAVIDSON KELLY, Charles (Norman); s of Frederick Nevil Davidson Kelly (d 1976), of Edinburgh, and Mary Lyon Campbell, *née* MacLeod; *b* 2 June 1945; *Educ* Edinburgh Acad, Oxford Univ (BA), Edinburgh Univ (LLB); *m* 2 Sept 1972, Annabella Daphne Pitt, da of Herbert Alasdair Pitt Graham, of the Bahamas; 1 s (John b 1977), 1 da (Suzanna b 1979); *Career* slr with Ivory & Sime Edinburgh; co sec Oil Exploration (Hldgs) Ltd 1974-79, corporate devpt dir LASMO plc 1986-; *Recreations* sheepbreeding; *Clubs* Puffins; *Style*— Norman Davidson Kelly, Esq; Little Boarhunt, Liphook, Hants GU30 7EE; 140 London Wall, London EC2Y 4ON (☎ 01 600 8021)

DAVIDSON-HOUSTON, Maj Aubrey Claud; s of Lt-Col Wilfred Bennett Davidson-Houston, CMG (d 1960), and Annie Henrietta, *née* Hunt (d 1941); *b* 2 Feb 1906; *Educ* St Edward's Sch Oxford, RMA Sandhurst, Slade Sch of Fine Art; *m* 29 Sept 1938, Georgina (Nina) Louie Ethel (d 1961), da of Capt Harold Dobson (ka 1915); 1 da (Sarah (Madame Jacques Arragon) b 1941); *Career* served WW II Europe and post-war

Germany, Maj, ret 1949; portrait painter 1952-; royal portraits include: HM The Queen (for RWF), The Duke of Edinburgh (for 8 King's Royal Irish Hussars, Duke of Edinburgh's RR, House of Lords, Oxford and Cambridge Univ Club), Queen Elizabeth the Queen Mother (for Black Watch of Canada), The Prince of Wales (twice for Royal Regt of Wales), Mary Princess Royal (for WRAC), Henry Duke of Gloucester (for Royal Inniskilling Fusiliers, Scots Gds, Trinity House), Duchess of Kent (for Army Catering Corps); other portraits for regiments, city livery cos, Oxford and Cambridge Univs; *Recreations* painting; *Clubs* Buck's, MCC, Naval and Military; *Style—* Maj Aubrey Davidson-Houston; Hillview, 42 West End Lane, Esher, Surrey KT10 8LA (☎ 0372 64769); 4 Chelsea Studios, 412 Fulham Rd, London SW6 1EB (☎ 01 385 2569)

DAVIE; *see*: Ferguson Davie

DAVIE, Alan; CBE (1972); *b* 28 Sept 1920; *Educ* Edinburgh Coll of Art (DA); *m* 1947, Janet Gaul, 1 da; *Career* painter, poet, musician, silversmith and jeweller; many one man and mixed exhibitions world-wide 1946-, incl London, Edinburgh, New York, Paris, Florida, Perth, Japan; work included in Br Painting 1700-1960 Moscow, Br Painting and Sculpture 1960-70 Washington, Br Paintings 1974 Hayward Gallery, and 25 years of Br Art RA London 1977; many works in public collections world-wide; external assessor Art Degrees 1967-; music concerts and bdcasts with Tony Oxley Sextet 1974-75; Gregory Fell Leeds Univ; voted Best Foreign Painter, VII Bienal de Sao Paulo 1963; Saltire Award 1977; FRSA; Order of the Southern Cross Brazil 1987; *Books* Alan Davie (edited by Alan Bowness, Lund Humphries 1967); *Recreations* sailing, underwater swimming, music; *Style—* Alan Davie, Esq, CBE; Gamels Studio, Rush Green, Hertford

DAVIE, Belinda Mary; da of Wing Cdr Minden Vaughan Blake, DSO DFC, (d 1981) of Virginia Water, Surrey, and Mary Jessie Blake; *b* 18 June 1951; *Educ* St Margarets Sch Bushey Herts, Bristol Univ (BSC), Insead Fontainebleau France (MBA); *m* 13 Sept 1986, Jonathan Richard Davie, s of Richard Davie of Wimbledon London; *Career* with Hill Samuel Investmt Mgmnt Ltd 1972-79, INSEAD France 1979-80, dir Warburg Investmt Mgmnt Int Ltd 1984- (joined 1980); *Recreations* golf, tennis, skiing; *Clubs* Berkshire GC, Royal Wimbledon GC; *Style—* Belinda Mary Davie

DAVIE, Sir Paul Christopher; s of Charles Christopher Davie, JP (d 1939); *b* 30 Sept 1901; *Educ* Winchester, New Coll Oxford (BA); *m* 1938, Betty Muriel, da of Capt Robert Ronald Henderson, MP (d 1932); 1 s, 1 da; *Career* barr Lincoln's Inn 1925; asst legal advsr Home Office 1936-53, remembrancer City of London 1953-67; chm National Deaf Children's Soc 1970-74; kt 1967; *Recreations* history, gardening; *Clubs* Travellers'; *Style—* Sir Paul Davie; The Old Rectory, Bentley, Hants, (☎ 0420 23128)

DAVIE-THORNHILL, Capt Humphrey Bache Christopher; JP (1954), DL (Derbys 1981); Lord of the Manor of Stanton-in-Peak and patron of 2 livings; s of Lt-Col Bertie George Davie (d on active service 1917), by his w Flora Helen Frances, Lady of the Manor of Stanton-in-Peak (d 1958), only da and heiress of Maj Michael M'Creagh (who assumed by Royal Lic 1882, addl surname of and arms of Thornhill on the s of his wife to the Stanton-in-Peak estate); *b* 5 Feb 1905; *Educ* Eton, Trinity Hall Cambridge; *m* 12 Nov 1930, Anna Elizabeth (d 1976), da of Sir John Barlow, 1 Bt, JP (d 1932); 2 s, 1 da; *Career* served 1939-45, RA Armaments Inspection Dept, Capt 1942; High Sheriff Derbys 1955; Freeman of Barnstaple; AIMechE; *Clubs* Naval & Military; *Style—* Humphrey Davie-Thornhill Esq, JP, DL; Stanton Hall, Matlock, Derbys (☎ Youlgrave 216)

DAVIES, Hon Mr Justice Mervyn; Hon Sir (David) (Herbert) Mervyn Davies; MC (1944), TD (1946); s of Herbert Bowen and Esther Davies; *b* 17 Jan 1918; *Educ* Swansea GS; *m* 1951, Zita Yollanne Angelique Blanche Antoinette, z da of Rev E A Phillips, of Bale, Norfolk; *Career* served WW II 18 Bn Welch Regt, 2 London Irish Rifles in Africa & Europe; slr 1939, barr Lincoln's Inn 1947, QC 1967, circuit judge 1978-82, high court judge chancery 1982-; kt 1982; *Style—* The Hon Mr Justice Mervyn Davies, MC, TD; 7 Stone Buildings, Lincoln's Inn, WC2 (☎ 01 242 8061); The White House, Great Snoring, Norfolk (☎ Walsingham 575)

DAVIES, Cdre Alan; s of Maj David Robert Davies, MBE, RA (d 1973), of Northumberland, and Olive, *née* English; *b* 23 Feb 1922; *Educ* Dame Allens Sch Newcastle on Tyne, Sir John Cass Coll London; *m* 14 Dec 1948, (Mary) Joyce, da of Ernest Bowes (d 1979), of Consett; 2 s ((Alan) Martin b 28 May 1950, Richard Michael b 17 Aug 1953), 1 da (Alison Joyce b 4 Sept 1951); *Career* Br Tanker Co: apprentice 1937, cdr 1951, Cdre 1973, ret 1978; churchwarden St Barts Whittingham, lay reader, sec Cons Assoc branch; Royal Inst Navigation (life memb); *Recreations* gardening, winemaking; *Style—* Cdre Alan Davies; Lime Trees Cottage, Whittingham, Alnwick, Northumberland NE66 4RA (☎ 066 574 615)

DAVIES, Air Marshal Sir Alan Cyril; KCB (1979, CB 1974), CBE 1967; s of Richard Davies, of Maidstone; *b* 31 Mar 1924; *m* 1949 Julia Elizabeth Ghislaine, da of James Russell, of Forres; 2 s (and 1 s decd); *Career* joined RAF 1941, cmmnd 1943, cmd Jt Anti-Submarine Sch Flight 1952-54, cmd Air Sea Warfare Devpt Unit 1958-59, Air Warfare Coll 1962, dep DOR MOD 1964-66, cmd RAF Stradishall Suffolk 1967-68, dir Air Plans MOD 1969-72, MOD 1972-74, dep COS HQ Allied Air Forces Central Europe 1974-77, dep C-in-C RAF Strike Command 1977, dir Int Mil Staff NATO Brussels 1978-81, hd RAF Support Area Economy Review Team 1981-83; co-ordinator Anglo/American Relations, MOD 1984; *Clubs* RAF; *Style—* Air Marshal Sir Alan Davies, KCB, CBE; 10 Crispin Close, Caversham Heights, Reading, Berks RG4 7JS (☎ 0734 470765)

DAVIES, Alun Grier; CBE (1980); s of Thomas Davies (d 1957), of Beth-Horon, Penygroes, Llanelli, and Sarah Ann *née* Edwards (d 1978); *b* 16 Sept 1914; *Educ* Amman Valley GS, Univ Coll of Wales Aberystwyth (BA); *m* 29 June 1940, Claudia Eleanor, da of John Evans (d 1948), of Penygraig, Aberdovey, Gwynedd; 1 s (Gareth); *Career* barr Gray's Inn, HM inspr of taxes Inland Revenue 1936-47, taxation controller Consolidated Zinc Corpn 1947-65, exec dir RTZ Corpn plc 1965-79, int conslt 1979-87; hon tres Univ Coll of Wales 1980- (memb of ct 1973-), memb of Central Fin Bd Methodist Church 1960-88; pres: Christian Assoc of Business Execs 1977-82, Int Fiscal Assoc 1979-83; cncl memb: Inst of Directors 1966-84, Confedr of Br Indust 1970-73; chm of tax ctees: IOD 1965-78, CBI 1970-73; Freeman City of London 1975, Worshipful Co of Loriners 1975; fell: IOD, Inst of Taxation; *Books* Man the World Over (1947), Render unto Caesar (1966); *Recreations* wine tasting, freelance journalism; *Clubs* Caledonian, RAC; *Style—* Alun Davies, Esq, CBE; 7 Craigleith, Grove Road, Beaconsfield HP8 1PT (☎ 0494 671 601); The Toft, Aberdovey, Gwynedd, Wales

DAVIES, Very Rev Alun Radcliffe; *see*: Llandaff, Dean of

DAVIES, Very Rev Alun Radcliffe; s of Rev Rhys Davies and Jane Davies; *b* 6 May 1923; *Educ* Cowbridge GS, Univ Coll Cardiff (BA), Keble Coll Oxford (MA), St Michael's Coll Llandaff; *m* 1952, Winifred Margaret Pullen; 2 s, 1 da; *Career* archdeacon of Llandaff 1971-77, residentiary canon of Llandaff Cathedral, dean of Llandaff 1977; *Style—* The Very Rev the Dean of Llandaff; The Deanery, The Cathedral Green, Llandaff, Cardiff (☎ 0222 561 545)

DAVIES, Sir Alun Talfan; QC (1961); s of Rev William Talfan Davies, of Gorseinon, Swansea; *b* 22 July 1913; *Educ* Gowerton GS, University Coll of Wales Aberystwyth (LLB), Gonville and Caius Coll Cambridge (MA, LLB); *m* 1942, Eiluned Christopher, da of Humphrey R Williams, of Stanmore Middx; 1 s, 3 da; *Career* barr Gray's Inn 1939, bencher 1969; recorder of: Merthyr Tydfl 1963-68, Swansea 1968-69, Cardiff 1969-71; a recorder of the Crown Court 1972-86, hon recorder of Cardiff 1972-86, judge of Court of Appeal Jersey and Guernsey 1969-83; memb Criminal Injuries Compensation Bd 1976-85, pres Royal National Eisteddford of Wales 1979-82, pres Court Welsh National Opera 1978-1981, dep chm Commercial Bank of Wales 1973- (dir 1971-); former v-chm HTV (Gp) Ltd and chm Welsh bd, chm of tstees Aberfan Fund; hon prof fellow Univ Coll Wales Aberystwyth 1971; Hon LLD Wales (Aberystwyth) 1973, pres Welsh Centre of Int Affairs; kt 1976; *Style—* Sir Alun Davies, QC; 10 Park Rd, Penarth, S Glam (☎ (0222) 701341); 34 Park Place, Cardiff (☎ (0222) 22454)

DAVIES, Rear Adm Anthony; CB (1964), CVO (1972); s of James Arthur Davies (d 1939), and Margaret Davies (d 1971); *b* 13 June 1912; *Educ* RNC Dartmouth, Open Univ (BA); *m* 1940, Lilian Hilda Margaret (d 1980), da of Sir Harold Martin Burrough, GCB, KBE, DSO (d 1977); 2 s, 2 da; *Career* joined RN 1926, dep dir RN Staff Coll 1956-57, Far East Fleet Staff 1957-59, dep dir Naval Intelligence 1959-62, head Br Defence Liaison Staff Canberra Australia 1963-65; warden St George's House, Windsor Castle 1966-72; *Style—* Rear Adm Anthony Davies, CB, CVO; 11A South St, Aldbourne, Marlborough, Wilts (☎ 0672 40418)

DAVIES, Anthony Roger; s of Richard George Davies (d 1968), of Brockenhurst, Bridgend, Glamorgan, and Megan Davies, *née* Matthews; *b* 1 Sept 1940; *Educ* Bridgent GS; King's Coll London (LLB, AKC); *m* 23 Sept 1967, Clare, da of Cdr W A Walters RN, of Woking, Surrey; 2 s (George and Hugo b 1974 (twins)), 1 da (Antonia b 1972); *Career* barr Grays Inn 1965, practice 1965-85, metropolitan stipendiary magistrate 1985-; *Recreations* reading (history, biography); opera; gardening, family life; *Style—* Roger Davies, Esq

DAVIES, Sir (David) Arthur; KBE (1980); *b* 11 Nov 1913; *Educ* Barry GS, Univ of Wales (MSc); *m* 1938, Mary, *née* Shapland; 1 s, 2 da; *Career* RAFO 1937-39, served WW II, BEF France 1939-40, NWEF Narvik 1940, Coastal Cmd 1940-42, Iceland 1942-43 (despatches), HQ Transport Cmd 1943-46, Yalta Conference 1945, RAF Staff Coll psa 1946; princ scientific offr Air Miny 1946-49; dir E African Meteorological Dept Nairobi 1949-55; sec-gen World Meteorological Orgn Geneva 1955-79 (sec-gen emeritus 1980-); vice pres and hon conslt Welsh Centre for Int Affairs 1983-; Hon DSc (Wales), fellow Univ Coll Cardiff; numerous other honorary doctorates and scientific awards; *Recreations* music, reading; *Clubs* Royal Cwlth Society (London), Anglo-Belgian (London), Explorers' (New York); *Style—* Sir Arthur Davies, KBE; 2 Ashley Close, Patcham, Brighton, E Sussex BN1 8YT (☎ (0273) 509437)

DAVIES, Barbara; da of Mr W Jennings, of 35 Hyptio Rd, Stourton, Stourbridge, W Midlands, and Ruby Annie Jennings; *b* 22 June 1947; *Educ* Haden Hill Sch Old Hill, Dudity Girls HS; *m* 2 Aug 1968, John Herbert Simeon, s of Mr A C Davies (d 1967); 2 s (Chris b 1970, Mile b 1973); *Career* dir and co sec: BSC (contracts) Ltd, Bloomfield Steel Construction Co Ltd; *Recreations* golf, skiing; *Clubs* Enville GC; *Style—* Mrs Barbara Davies; Kloomfield Rd, Tipton, West Midlands DY4 9HB

DAVIES, Betty Alicia; JP (1971); da of Charles William Pearl (d 1975), of Nottingham, and Alice *née* Stevenson; *b* 13 April 1934; *Educ* Haywood Sch Nottingham, London Guildhall Sch of Music and Drama (LGSM); *m* 3 April 1954, Barry Douglass Davies, s of Cecil Vivien Davies (d 1972), Bidston, Cheshire; *Career* chm md Campus Clothes Ltd 1966-, chm design dir Betty Davies Academy Collection 1966-, princ Crusade PR 1966-; JP (Nottingham 1971-), memb of ct Nottingham Univ, public memb Press Cncl 1983-89, memb bd of govrs Nottingham Girls H S 1987-; first chm Nottingham Cncl for Voluntary Serv 1981-84, dir Royal Scottish Acad Edinburgh MBIM 1982; *Recreations* musical, theatrical, collects paintings of contemporary woman artists, seal watching; *Style—* Mrs Betty Davies, JP; Baileys's Garden, Nottingham NG3 5BW (☎ 0602 621 555/285 219) 28 North Bridge, Edinburgh (☎ 021 225 635, fax 0602 506 023, car telephone 0836 722 479)

DAVIES, (James) Brian Meredith; s of late Dr G Meredith Davies, and Caroline Meredith Davies; *b* 27 Jan 1920; *Educ* Bedford Sch, Med Sch St Mary's Hosp, London Univ (MD, FFCM DPH); *m* 1944, Charlotte, *née* Pillar; 3 s; *Career* hon lectr in (Preventive) Paediatrics Univ of Liverpool 1964-84; dir Social Services City of Liverpool 1971-82; MFCM, FFCM; *Books* Community Health Preventive Medicine and Social Services (5 ed 1983), Community Health and Social Services (4 ed 1984), The Disabled Child and Adult (1982); *Recreations* skiing, fishing, golf; *Style—* Brian Meredith Davies, Esq; Tree Tops, Church Rd, Thornton Hough, Wirral, Merseyside (☎ (051) 336 3435)

DAVIES, Christopher Henry; s of William Henry Davies (d 1976); *b* 6 Nov 1939; *Educ* Wolverhampton GS, Durham Univ (BA); *m* 1968, Elisabeth, da of Leo Thalmann (d 1947); 2 children; *Career* md Forbo-Nairn Ltd 1983-87; chief exec Sea Fish Indust Authy 1988-; *Style—* Christopher Davies Esq; 7 West Carnethy Ave, Colinton, Edinburgh EH13 0ED; Nairn Floors Ltd, PO Box 1, Kirkcaldy KY1 2SB (☎ 0592 261111); Sea Fish Indust Authy, 10 Young St, Edinburgh EH2 4JQ (☎ 031 225 2515)

DAVIES, Cyril James; CBE; s of James Davies (d 1967), of Newcastle upon Tyne, and Frances Charlotte *née* Baker (d 1960); *b* 24 August 1923; *Educ* Heaton GS Newcastle-upon-Tyne; *m* Elizabeth Hay Leggett, da of James William Hay (d 1954), of Newcastle; 2 s (Nigel b 1950, Chistopher b 1954), 2 da (Elizabeth b 1952, Julia b 1953); *Career* WW11 Lieut (A) RNVR Fleet Air RN 1942-46; city tres: Newcastle-upon- Tyne 1969-74, Tyne and Wear 1974-80; chief exec Newcastle-upon-Tyne 1980-86;memb: Newcastle Univ Cncl, Arts Cncl Touring Bd; dir: N Housing Assoc, Theatre Royal Tst, Tyne Theatre Tst, Northern Art; ts tee: William Leech Charity, Rothley Charity, Newcastle Cathedral Tst; *Recreations* gardening, music, theatre, walking; *Clubs* Naval; *Style—* Cyril Davies, Esq, CBE; 36 Lindisfarne Close, Jesmond, Newcastle-upon-Tyne NE2 2HT (☎ 091 281 5402

DAVIES, David Cyril; s of D T Davies, and Mrs G Davies, JP; *b* 7 Oct 1925; *Educ* Lewis Sch Pengam, UCW Aberystwyth (LLB); *m* 1952, Joan Rogers; 2 children;

Career headmaster Crown Woods Sch 1971-84; *Style*— David Davies, Esq; 9 Plaxtol Close, Bromley, Kent (☎ 01 464 4187)

DAVIES, Hon David Daniel; yr s of Baron Davies of Penrhys (Life Peer), *qv*; *b* 1944; *m* 1969, Cheryl, da of Thomas Herbert, of Tylorstown, Rhondda; 1s; *Style*— The Hon David Davies

DAVIES, 3 Baron (UK 1932), of Llandinam, Co Montgomery; David Davies; s of 2 Baron Davies (ka 1944), by his w, Ruth Eldrydd (d 1966), da of Maj W M Dugdale, CB, DSO, of Glanyrafon Hall, Llanyblodwell, Shropshire; *b* 2 Oct 1940; *Educ* Eton, King's Coll Cambridge; *m* 1972, Beryl, da of W J Oliver; 2 s (Hon David Daniel, Hon Benjamin Michael Graham b 7 July 1985), 2 da (Hon Eldrydd Jane b 1973, Hon Lucy b 1978); *Heir* s, Hon David Daniel Davies b 23 Oct 1975; *Career* chm Welsh National Opera Co 1975-; CEng, MICE; *Style*— The Rt Hon Lord Davies; Plas Dinam, Llandinam, Powys

DAVIES, David Evan Naunton; CBE (1986); s of David Evan Davies (d 1935), and Sarah, *née* Samuel (d 1982); *b* 28 Oct 1935; *Educ* West Monmouth Sch, University of Birmingham (MSc, PhD, DSc); *m* 21 July 1962, Enid, da of James Edwin Patilla; 2 s (Christoper James b 1965, Michael Evan b 1967); *Career* lectr and sr lectr Univ of Birmingham 1961-67, hon sr princ sci off Royal Radar Estab Malvern 1966-67, asst dir res dept BR Derby 1967-71, vice Provost UCL 1986-88 (prof of electrical engrg 1971-86), vice-chllr Loughborough Univ 1988-; Rank Prize for optoelectronics 1984, Callendar Medal (Inst Measurement and Control) 1984, Centenial Medal (Inst of Electrical and Electronic Engrs USA) 1984, Faraday Medal (IEE) 1987; memb and chm of numerous ctees of: MOD, DES, Cabinet Off; FIEE (1967), F Eng, FRS 1984; *Books* over 150 publications mainly concerned with radar and fibre optics; *Style*— Prof David Davies; Tall Trees, The Ridgeway, Rothley, Leicestershire LE7 7LE and 5 Prince Regent Mews, Netley St, London NW1; Vice Chancellor, Loughborough University, Loughborough, Leicestershire (☎ 0509 222 000, fax 0509 610 723)

DAVIES, Sir David Henry; s of David Henry Davies; *b* 2 Dec 1909; *Educ* Brierley Hill Sch Ebbw Vale; *m* 1934, Elsie May, da of Joseph Battrick; 1 s, . da (and 1 da decd); *Career* asst gen sec Iron and Steel Trades Confedn 1953-66, gen sec 1967-75; hon sec Br Section Int Metalworkers Fedn 1960-; chm Br Lab Party 1963 (hon tres 1965-67); vice-chm Nat Dock Labour Bd 1966-68; chm Euro Coal and Steel Community Consultative Ctee 1973; memb: gen cncl TUC 1967-75, English Industl Estates Corpn 1971-75, Industl Arbitration Bd 1974; first chm Welsh Devpt Agency 1976-79; kt 1973; *Style*— Sir David Davies; 82 New House Park, St Albans, Herts (☎ St Albans 56513)

DAVIES, David Levric; CB (1982), OBE (1962); s of Benjamin Davies (d 1955), and Elizabeth, *née* Jones (d 1985); *b* 11 May 1925; *Educ* Llanrwst GS, Univ of Wales Aberystwyth (LLB Hons); *m* 1955, Beryl Justine, da of Charles Clifton Newman, of Dorset; *Career* Sub Lt RNVR served in France, Belgium, Holland, Iceland 1943-46; barr Middle Temple 1949, colonial legal service 1950-64: Aden 1950-56 (crown counsel) Tanganyika 1956-64; asst to Law offrs 1956, parly draftsman 1958, slr gen 1961 Home Civil Service 1964-82; sr legal asst parly counsel office 1964-72, seconded Jamaica as sr parly counsel 1965-69, seconded Seychelles as attorney gen 1970-72; HM treasy slrs Office, asst Treasy Slr 1973, under sec (legal) head of advsy div 1977-; *Style*— David Davies, Esq, CB, OBE; Greystones, Breach Lane, Shaftesbury, Dorset (☎ 0747 51224)

DAVIES, David Yorwerth; s of Hywell Morris Davies (d 1985), and Marjory Winnifred Davies (d 1970); *b* 24 Feb 1939; *Educ* Grove Park GS Wrexham, Univ of Durham (Dip Arch); *m* 31 May 1969, Angela, da of Jack Theed (d 1966); 2 s (Andrew b 1970, Gareth b 1972); *Career* fndr DY Davies Assoc Chartered Architects 1969, exec chm DY Davies plc 1986-; cmmnd bldgs incl Heathrow Terminal 3, Blue Circle Industs HQ Aldermaston; dir Docklands Devpt Corpn 1988; Freeman Worshipful Co of Blacksmiths 1975; CIArb, RIBA (vice pres 1987); *Recreations* gold, food, wine; *Clubs* RAC, City Livery, Sunningdale Golf; *Style*— David Davies, Esq; 36 Paradise Road, Richmond, Surrey, TW9 1SE (☎ 01 948 5544)

DAVIES, Rt Hon (David John) Denzil; PC (1978), MP (Lab) Llanelli 1970-; s of G Davies; *b* 9 Oct 1938; *Educ* Queen Elizabeth GS Carmarthen, Pembroke Oxford; *m* 1963, Mary Ann Finlay, of Illinois, USA; 1 s, 1 da; *Career* barrister Gray's Inn 1964; taught Chicago Univ 1963, law lecturer Leeds Univ 1964; memb Public Accounts Ctee 1974-, pps to Sec of State Wales 1974-76, min of state Treasury 1976-79; oppn front bench spokesman: treasury matters 1979-81, defence and disarmamemt 1981-88; shadow Welsh sec 1983; chief opposition spokesman on defence 1985-; *Style*— The Rt Hon Denzil Davies, MP; House of Commons, London SW1A 0AA (☎ 01 219 5197)

DAVIES, Derek Lewis; s of Glyndwr Lewis, and Lily May, *née* Jones; *b* 28 Sept 1933; *Educ* Birmingham Central Coll of Tech; *m* 4 Oct 1954, Barbara Joy, da of Charles Barwick; 2 s (Jeremy b 1960, Robert b 1966); *Career* Lt Royal Mil Police 1954-56; GEC: student apprentice Birmingham 1950-54, chief engr Pakistan 1958-62, dir Overseas Servs 1973-81, dir Electrical Projects 1981-86; sales mangr Foster Transformers Ltd 1962-67, sales dir Otternill Switchgear 1967-73, chm Drake & Scull Hldgs plc 1986-, dir Simon Engrg plc 1987-; memb NEDO Airports Ctee 1985, chm UK Airports Gp 1984-86; memb Worshipful Co of Feltmakers; FRSA, Assoc RAcS; *Recreations* rugby, golf; *Clubs* Athenaeum; *Style*— Derek Davies, Esq; Simon House, PO Box 31, Stockport, Cheshire (☎ 061 428 3600); Hamlyn House, Highgate Hill, London N19 5PS (☎ 01 272 0233, fax 01 272 1807

DAVIES, Donald; CBE (1978, OBE 1973); s of Wilfred Lawson Davies (d 1972), and Alwyne Davies; *b* 13 Feb 1924; *Educ* Ebbw Vale GS, Univ Coll Cardiff (BSc); *m* 1948, Mabel, da of John Henry Hellyar (d 1960); 2 da; *Career* civil engr; memb National Coal Bd 1973-84 (area dir 1967-73); chm: NCB Opencast Exec 1973-83, NCB Ancillaries 1979-87; conslt mining engineer; FIMinE; *Recreations* golf, fishing; *Clubs* RAC; *Style*— Donald Davies, Esq, CBE; Wendy Cottage, Dukes Wood Ave, Gerrard's Cross, Bucks (☎ (0753) 885083; business: 01 235 2020)

DAVIES, Douglas Arthur Douglas A; s of Joseph Davies (d 1932), and Ellen Dewhurst, *née* Penswick (d 1975); *b* 16 Sept 1927; *Educ* Waterloo GS; *m* 1953, Jean, da of Walter Marsh (d 1978); 2 s (Alan Robert and Duncan James b 1962 (twins)), 1 da (Ruth Louise b 1965); *Career* dir: Royal Life Hldgs Ltd, RL Insurance Ltd, R L Estates Ltd, Royal Heritage Life Assurance Ltd, RL Diret Marketing Ltd, Royal Insurance Property Mgmnt Ltd, RL Insurance Ireland Ltd, VNG GP, National Investmt Hldgs Ltd, Royal Insurance Leasing Ltd, Riverside Ct Mgmnt Chester Ltd; *Recreations* travel, boating, antique glass; *Style*— Douglas A Davies, Esq; The Old House, Checkley, Hereford HR1 4ND; Royal Insurance plc, New Hall Place, Liverpool L69 3HS (☎ (051) 224 3303)

DAVIES, (Gwilym) Ednyfed Hudson; MP Caerphilly 1979-; s of Rev E Curig Davies by his w Enid, *née* Hughes; *b* 4 Dec 1929; *Educ* Friars Sch Bangor, Dynevor GS Swansea, Univ Coll Swansea, Balliol Oxford; *m* 1972, Amanda, da of Peter Barker-Mill; 2 da; *Career* barr 1975; MP (L) Conway 1966-70, memb Select Ctee Energy, All-Party Tourism Ctee; chm Welsh Tourist Bd 1976-78; joined SDP 1981; former TV & radio interviewer, presenter & commentator for BBC, also lecturer in political thought; *Style*— Ednyfed Davies, Esq, MP; House of Commons, London, SW1

DAVIES, Hon Edward David Grant; 2 s of 1 Baron Davies (but er s by his 2 w); *b* 30 Jan 1925; *Educ* Gordonstoun, King's Cambridge; *m* 1, 1949, Patricia, yr da of Clifford Roberts Musto, of Salisbury, Rhodesia; 1 s, 3 da; m 2, 1975, Shirley, da of Le Grew Harrison and former w of Johnny Gaze; *Career* chm London Tst; dir Globe Investment Tst; *Style*— The Hon Edward Davies; 30 Southacre, Hyde Park Crescent, London W2; Ingestone, Foy, Ross-on-Wye, Herefordshire

DAVIES, Elidir (Leslie Wish); s of late Rev Thomas John Landy Davies, and Hetty Boucher, *née* Wish; *b* 3 Jan 1907; *Educ* Colchester Sch, Bartlett Sch of Architecture, London Univ; *m* 1, Vera, *née* Goodwin (d 1974); m 2, 1976, Kathleen Burke-Collis; *Career* chartered architect Elidir L W Davies and Ptnrs; FRIBA, FRSA; *Clubs* Garrick; *Style*— Elidir Davies Esq; Burnswood, Groombridge, Kent

DAVIES, Emrys Thomas; s of Evan William Davies (d 1954), and Dinah, *née* Jones; *b* 8 Oct 1934; *Educ* Parmiters Fndn Sch London, Sch of Slavonic Studies Camb, Sch of Oriental & African Studies London; *m* 1960, Angela Audrey, da of Paul Robert Buchan May ICS (d 1952); 1 s (Robert), 2 da (Victoria, Elizabeth); *Career* RAF 1953-1955, served Peking and Shanghai 1956-59, FO 1959-60, Political Residence Bahrain 1960-62, UN Gen Assembly NY 1962, FO 1962-63, asst political advsr to Hong Kong Govt 1963-68, Br High Cmmn Ottawa 1968-71, FCO 1972-76, commercial cnsllr HM Embassy Peking 1976-78; (charge 1976 and 1978), Oxford Univ Business Summer Sch 1977; NATO Defense Coll Rome 1979, dep high cmmr Ottawa 1979-82; Diplomatic Serv Overseas inspr 1982-83, dep perm rep to OECD Paris 1984-87, HM ambass Hanoi Vietnam 1987; *Books* "Albigensians and Cathars" (transl.); *Recreations* tennis, walking; *Clubs* Royal Cwlth Soc; *Style*— Emrys Davies, Esq; His Excellency, British Embassy, 16 Pho Ly Thuong Kiet, Hanoi, Vietnam

DAVIES, Hon Francis William Harding; s of Rt Hon John Emerson Harding Harding-Davies, who was nominated a Life Peer 16 June 1979, but who d 4 July 1979 before the Peerage was cr; raised to rank of a Baron's s 1980; *b* 22 Nov 1946; *Educ* Windlesham House Sch, The Nautical Coll Pangbourne, Strasbourg Univ; *m* 1972, Lynda Margaret Mae, *née* Squires; 3 children; *Career* asst mangr int EMI Records 1966-68, int export mangr Liberty Records 1968-70; pres: Love Productions Ltd 1970-78, Partisan Music Productions Inc 1978-82, ATV Music Gp Canada 1982-85, exec vice pres Thompson Music Publishing 1986; *Recreations* photography, music; *Style*— The Hon Francis Davies; PO Box 615, Don Mills, Ontario M3C 2T6, Canada

DAVIES, Frank John; s of Lt Col F H Davies, of Lincoln, and Veronica Josephine Davies (d 1943); *b* 24 Sept 1931; *Educ* Monmouth Sch, Manchester UC of Technol; *m* 1956, Sheila Margaret, da of Geoffrey Bailey (d 1938); 3 s (James, Stephen, Jonathan); *Career* chief exec and md Rockware Gp plc, chm Rockware Glass Ltd, dir Ir Glass plc, pres Glass Mfrs Fedn 1986 and 1987; memb; Oxon Health Authy 1983, cncl CBI 1986-; OstJ 1979; Freeman: City of London, Basketmakers, CBIM, FRSA; *Recreations* gardening, music, theatre; *Clubs* Carlton; *Style*— Frank Davies, Esq; Stonewalls, Castle Street, Deddington, Oxon OX5 4TE (☎ 0869 38131); Cliftonville House, Bedford Road, Northampton NN4 0PX, (☎ 0609 26931, telex 317490)

DAVIES, Gareth; s of Lewis Davies (d 1985), of S Devon, and Margaret Ann, *née* Jones; *b* 13 Feb 1930; *Educ* King Edward's GS Aston Birmingham; *m* 12 Sept 1953, Joan Patricia, da of Edmond Charles Prosser (d 1986), of NZ; 1 s (Mark b 1959); *Career* chm and gp chief exec Glynwed Int plc and subsidiary co's 1986- (joined 1969); dir Raglan Property Tst plc 1985-, The BTS Gp plc 1987-; FCA, CBIM; *Recreations* music, opera; *Style*— Gareth Davies, Esq; 4 Beech Gate, Roman Road, Little Aston, W Midlands; Headland House, 54 New Coventry Road, Sheldon, Birmingham B26 3AZ (☎ 021 742 2366, telex 336608, fax 021 742 0403)

DAVIES, (David) Gareth Griffiths; s of Tudor Griffiths Davies, of Preston, and Dilys Katherine, *née* Davies; *b* 29 Oct 1951; *Educ* Winchester, Downing Coll Cambridge (BA, MA); *m* 30 July 1977, Daphne Sarah, da of Edward Chambre Dickson, TD, DL; 1 s (Nicholas b 1981), 1 da (Philippa b 1984); *Style*— Gareth Davies, Esq; Green House, Balderstone, nr Blackburn, Lancashire BB2 7LL (☎ 0254 812 334); 7 Station Rd, Hesketh Bank, Preston PR4 6SN (☎ 0772 814 921, fax 0772 815 008)

DAVIES, (David) Garfield; s of David John Davies (d 1976), of Glamorgan, and Lizzie Ann Davies, *née* Evans; *b* 24 June 1935; *Educ* Heolgam Secondary Modern Bridgend, Bridgend Tech Coll, Port Talbot Sch of Further Educn; *m* 1960, Marian, da of Raymond Jones Trelewis; 4 da (Helen, Susan, Karen, Rachel); *Career* Nat Serivce, RAF, Sr Aircraftsman; electrician 1958-69; JP (Ipswich) 1972-79; gen sec Union of Shop Distributive and Allied Workers; *Style*— Garfield Davies Esq; 64 Dairyground Road, Bramhall, Stockport, Cheshire (☎ (061) 439 9548); Union of Shop, Distributive & Allied Workers, 188 Wilmslow Road, Fallowfield, Manchester M14 6LJ (☎ (061) 224 2804)

DAVIES, Gavyn; s of W J F Davies, of Southampton, and M G Watkins; *b* 27 Nov 1950; *Educ* Taunton's Sch Southampton, St John's Coll Cambridge (BA), Balliol Coll Oxford; *Career* econ advsr Policy Unit 10 Downing St 1974-79, UK economist Phillips and Drew 1979-81, chief UK economist: Simon and Coates 1981-86, Goldman Sachs 1986-; visting prof LSE 1988; *Recreations* sport; *Style*— Gavyn Davies, Esq; 5 Old Bailey, London EC3M 7AH (☎ 01 248 6464, fax 01 489 2968)

DAVIES, Captain Geoffrey Franklin; TD (1964); s of Franklyn George Davies (d 1952), of Kidderminster, Worcs, and Doris, *née* Thatcher (d 1987); *b* 13 Jan 1930; *Educ* King Charles I Sch Kidderminster, King Edward VI Sch Stourbridge, Univ of Birmingham (LLB); *m* 1, 19 June 1954 (m dis 1970), Barbara Mary, da of Maj William Horace Cooper (d 1965), of The Old Rectory, Hagley, W Midlands; 1 s (Nigel William b 16 Nov 1956), 1 da (Jayne Elizabeth b 1 Sept 1958); m 2, 31 Oct 1970 (m dis 1972), Barbara Jean, da of James Skillen, of USA; 1 s (James Skillen b 12 Aug 1971); m 3, 30 July 1977, Barbara (Bobby) Joyce, da of Harold Williams (d 1959), of Chaddesley, Corbett, Worcs; *Career* cmmnd 2 Lt RASC 1953, Capt RASC later RCT 1956, served with 110 Tport Column until 1964; slr 1952; ptnr: Thursfield Adams Westons 1956-, Desmond & Holder Worcester 1987-; former chm WM Cooper & Sons (Bldrs), sec John Brecknell Charity 1956-, cases sec and/or chm NW and SE Shropshire branch

NSPCC 1956-, memb Kidderminster BC (chm 2 ctees) 1970-76, chm Kidderminster Cons 200 club 1970-83, vice pres Stourport Boat Club, former prov Jr Grand Warden Worcs; past Provincial Aide de Campe Knights Templar (Worcs) memb Law Soc (1952); *Recreations* rowing, golf; *Clubs* Leander, Worcester Rowing, Kidderminster GC; *Style—* Capt Geoffrey F Davies; Drayton Lodge, Drayton, Belbroughton, nr Stourbridge, W Midlands (☎ 0562 730 240); 14 Church St, Kidderminster, Worcestershire (☎ 0562 820 575, fax 0562 66 783, telex 337 837 THURSF G)

DAVIES, George Raymond (Gerry); OBE (1977); s of George John Davies (d 1935); *b* 3 Oct 1916; *Educ* E Ham GS; *m* 1945, Sylvia, *née* Newling; 1 s, 1 da; *Career* dep city librarian Cambridge 1953-55; gen sec The Booksellers Assoc of GB & Ireland 1955-64, md Bowker Publishing Co Ltd 1966-69; dep ed The Bookseller 1969-70, pres: Int Booksellers Fedn 1978-81 (hon memb 1988), Book Trade Benevolent Soc 1974; chm BA Serv House Ltd 1977-82; dir The Booksellers Assoc of GB and Ireland 1964-66 and 1970-81 (hon life memb 1981); ed Booksellers Int 1981-87; fell Library Assoc (life memb 1981), jt ed: 'Books are Different', 'A Mortal Craft', 'Book and their prices'; *Recreations* workds, music, estate management; *Clubs* Savile; *Style—* Gerry Davies Esq, OBE; Crotchets, Mayfield, E Sussex (☎ 872356)

DAVIES, George William; s of George Davies (d 1987), of Formby, Lancs, and Mary, *née* Wright; *b* 29 Oct 1941; *Educ* Bootle GS, Birmingham Univ; *m* 1, 25 Sept 1965 (m dis 1985), Anne Margaret, da of Maj Donald Dyson Allan, of Hants; 3 da (Melanie b 8 Aug 1966, Emma b 23 Sept 1968, Alexandra b 7 Sept 1973); *m* 2, 7 Dec 1985, Mrs Elzbieta (Liz) Krystyna Devereux-Batchelor, da of Stanislaw Ryszard Szadbey; 1 da (Lucia b 22 May 1988); *Career* stock controller/merchandise Littlewoods Stores 1967-72; School Care (own business) 1972-75; party plan/lingerie Pippadee 1975-81; joined J Hepworth & Son 1981-; responsible for launch of Next Feb 1982; jt gp md J Hepworth & Son 1984, chief exec 1985, chm and ch exec 1987-; memb Court of Leics Univ 1988-; FRSA 1987, Sr Fell RCA 1988; *Recreations* golf, tennis, squash; *Clubs* Formby Golf, Rothley (Leicester) Golf, Leicester Squash; *Style—* George Davies Esq; Next plc, Desford Road, Enderby, Leicester LE9 5AT (☎ 0533 866411, fax 0533 848998, telex 34415 HEPNEX G)

DAVIES, Geraint Talfan; s of Aneirin Talfan Davies OBE (d 1980), of Cardiff and Mary Anne, *née* Evans (d 1971); *b* 30 Dec 1943; *Educ* Cardiff HS For Boys, Jesus Coll Oxford (MA); *m* 9 Sept 1967, Elizabeth Shan, da of Thomas Vaughan Yorath, of Cardiff; 3 s (Matthew b 1969, Rhodri b 1971, Edward b 1974); *Career* asst ed Western Mail 1974-78, head of news and current affairs HTV Wales 1978-82, asst controller of programmes HTV Wales 1982-87, dir of programmes Tyne Tees TV 1987; chm Newydd Housing Assoc 1975-78; tstee: Tenovus Cancer Appeal 1984-87, Br Bone Marrow Donor Appeal 1987-; memb: mgmnt ctee Northern Sinfonia 1989-, Cncl of Inst of Welsh Affairs 1988-; *Style—* Geraint Davies, Esq; 25 West Ave, Gosforth, Newcastle-upon-Tyne NE3 4ES; Tyne Tees Television Ltd; City Rd, Newcastle-upon-Tyne NE1 2AL (☎ 091 261 0180, fax 091 261 2302, telex 53279)

DAVIES, (Edward) Glyn; s of Thomas Davies (d 1976); *b* 16 Feb 1944; *Educ* LLanfair Caereinion HS; *m* 26 July 1969, Bobbie, da of Austen Rboerts, of Welshpool; 3 s (Edward b 1970, Patrick b 1973, Tim b 1980), 1 da (Sally b 1976); *Career* farmer; dist cncllr The Montgomeryshire Cncl 1976-88 (cncl chm 1985-88), chm Devpt Bd for rural Wales 1989-; *Recreations* squash, running; *Style—* Glyn Davies, Esq; Cil Farm, Berriew, Montgomeryshire, Mid-Wales (☎ 068685 247); Chairman's Office, Development Board for Rural Wales, Ladywell House, Newton, Montgomeryshire (☎ 0686 626965)

DAVIES, Gp Capt (Hubert) Gordon; CBE (1965), AE (1946); s of Hubert Offen Davies (d 1948); *b* 25 July 1919; *Educ* Purley GS, Regent St Polytechnic; *m* 1941, Alice Rhoda, da of late Philip Lawrence; 1 s, 1 da; *Career* CO Hull Univ Air Sqdn 1950-53, asst Air Force advsr UK, high cmmr Ottawa 1954-56, chief instr No 2 Flying Sch Syerston Notts 1958-60, Gp Capt orgn and plans HQ NEAF Cyprus 1962-65, dir Mgmnt and Staff Training MOD 1965-67, CO RAF Tern Hill Shropshire 1967-70, dep dir War Coll Greenwich 1972-74; sr mgmnt devpt advsr HCITB Wembley 1974-77, regnl mangr S and E HCITB 1977-83, asst head of training HCITB 1983-84; *Recreations* travel; *Clubs* RAF; *Style—* Gp Capt H Gordon Davies, CBE, AE; Pantiles, 18 Garnet Drive, Ratton, Eastbourne, E Sussex BN20 9AE (☎ (0323) 507207); Apt 201 Gommar, Puerto Pollensa, Mallorca

DAVIES, Graham Penry; s of Alcwyn Penry Davies (d 1958); *b* 16 Sept 1925; *Educ* City of London Sch, Peterhouse, Camb; *m* 1953, Rosemary Graham, *née* Down; 1 s, 2 da; *Career* Sub-Lt (A) (AE) RNVR; chm and md Erith plc 1972; pres Soc of Builders Merchants 1978-80, cncl RNVR Offrs Assoc 1976; memb Inst of Management Consultants; *Recreations* golf, yacht racing (yacht 'Fleur Vigueur II'); *Clubs* Naval, Parkstone Yacht, Parkstone Golf; *Style—* Graham Davies Esq; 66 Anthonys Ave, Poole, Dorset (☎ Canford Cliffs 707 298)

DAVIES, Gwilym Prys; s of William and Mary Matilda Davies; *b* 8 Dec 1923; *Educ* Towyn Sch, Univ Coll Wales Aberystwyth; *m* 1951, Llinos Evans; 3 da; *Career* ptnr Morgan Bruce and Nicholas Slrs Cardiff Pontypridd and Porth 1957; *Style—* Gwilym Davies Esq; Lluest, 78 Church Rd, Tonteg, Pontypridd, Mid Glam (☎ Newton Llantwit 2462)

DAVIES, Hon Gwynfor; er s of Baron Davies of Penrhys; *b* 1942; *m* 1969, Linda, da of late Anthony Henry, of Port Talbot, Glam; *Style—* The Hon Gwynfor Davies

DAVIES, Handel; CB (1961); s of Henry John Davies (d 1960), of Llwydcoed, Aberdare, Mid Glamorgan, and Elizabeth, *née* Howells (d 1968); *b* 2 June 1912; *Educ* Aberdare GS, Univ Coll Cardiff, Univ of Wales (BSc, MSc); *m* 28 March 1942, Mary Graham, da of Prof R G Harris (d 1964), of Manor Rd, Farnborough; *Career* sr princ sci offr Royal Aircraft Estab Farnborough 1948-51, chief supt Aeroplane and Armanent Experimental Estab 1952-55, sci advsr Air Miny 1955-56, dir gen sci res (air) Miny of Supply 1956-59, dep dir Royal Aircraft Estab 1959-63, dep controller R & D (Air) Miny of Tech 1963-69, gp tech dir BAC 1969-78, chm standing conf on Sch's of Sci and Tech 1978-81; govr Woking Sixth Form Coll; pres Royal Aeronautical Soc 1976-77; FAIAA 1960, Hon FAAeS 1980, FEng 1981; *Recreations* sailing, skiing; *Clubs* RAF Yacht; *Style—* Handel Davies, Esq, CB; Keel Cottage, Woodham Rd, Horsell, Woking, Surrey GU21 4DL (☎ 048 62 4192)

DAVIES, Hereward Scott; s of George Frederick Davies (d 1986), of Aldeburgh, Suffolk, and Florence, *née* Scott (d 1987); *b* 1 August 1935; *Educ* Berkhamsted Sch; *m* 7 June 1958 (m dis 1988), Sarah Brigid, da of Cdr William John Adlam Willis, CGM, MVO, QPM, RN (d 1984), of Dovercourt; 1 s (Simon b 1959), 1 da (Claire b 1961); *Career* Nat Serv RAF 1958-60; ptnr Hereward Scott Davies CA 1960-; former chm N London CA Gp; FCA 1958; *Recreations* nat hunt horse racing, good food and wine; *Clubs* Rotary Club (Friern Barnet & Whetstone); *Style—* Hereward Davies, Esq; Alice Ct, Station Rd, Finchley, London N3 2SQ (☎ 01 346 7282); Hillside House, 2/6 Friern Park, London N12 9BY (☎ 01 446 4371, fax 01 446 7606)

DAVIES, Howard John; s of Leslie Powell Davies, of Rochdale, Lancs, and Marjorie, *née* Magowan; *b* 12 Feb 1951; *Educ* Manchester GS, Memorial Univ of Newfoundland, Merton Coll Oxford (MA), Stanford Univ Calif (MS Mgmnt Sci); *m* 30 June 1984, Prudence Mary, da of Eric Phillipps Keely, CBE (d 1988), of Findon; 2 s (George b 1984, Archibald b 1987); *Career* FO 1973-74, private sec to HM Ambass Paris 1974-76, HM Tresy 1976-82, McKinsey and Co 1982-85, special advsr to Chllr of the Exchequer 1985-86, McKinsey and Co 1986-87, controller of audit The Audit Cmmn 1987-; *Recreations* cricket, writing; *Clubs* Barnes Common Cricket; *Style—* Howard Davies, Esq; 1 Vincent Sq, London SW1 (☎ 01 828 1212, car tel 0836 282797)

DAVIES, Brig (David) Hugh; MC (1944); s of David John Davies, JP (d 1938), of Carmarthen, Dyfed, Wales, and Catherine Jane, *née* Philipps (d 1963); *b* 17 August 1918; *Educ* Cathedral Sch Hereford, RMC Sandhurst; *m* 20 March 1943, Audrey, da of Jesse James Smith (d 1954), of Tenterden, Kent; 1 da (Jane Caroline (Mrs Cookson) b 15 Nov 1945); *Career* cmmnd KORR 1938, active serv Palestine 1938-39 (wounded), WWII serv 107 Regt RAC (Adj, Sqdn Ldr, Actg CO), Holland (wounded 1944), Staff Coll Haifa Palestine 1945, GS02 1 Div and Actg GS01 Palestine 1946-48, transferred 7 QOH, Adj 1948-49 (despatches 1949), DAAG AG 17 WO 1949-51, Sqdn Ldr and 2 i/c 7 Hussars 1951-53, instr Staff Coll Camberley 1956-58, Co 1058-61 asst dir plans Jt Planning Staff MOD 1961-63, Cdr 5 Inf Bde Gp 1963-65, Col QOH 1964-72, Brig RAC HQ Western Cmd 1966-68; chm Rose Smith & Co (Fuel) Ltd 1978-84 (non exec dir 1968-75); chm: Kent Royal Br Legion, Rolvenden branch Royal Br Legion; pres Ashford Valley Foxhounds, tres Rolvenden Cons Assoc; Hon Freeman Carmarthen 1950; *Recreations* hunting, fishing; *Clubs* Cavalry and Guards, Army and Navy; *Style—* Brig Hugh Davies, MC; Barton Wood, Rolveden, Cranbrook, Kent (☎ 0580 241 294)

DAVIES, Hugh Llewelyn; s of Vincent Ellis Davies, OBE, of 12 St Swithuns Close, East Grinstead, Sussex, and Rose Trench, *née* Temple; *b* 8 Nov 1941; *Educ* Rugby, Churchill Coll Cambridge (BA); *m* 21 Sept 1968, Virginia Ann, da of Hugh Lucius; 1 s (Jonathan b 1973), 1 da (Charlotte b 1970); *Career* dip serv FO 1965, Chinese Language studies Hong Kong 1966-68, second sec and HM consul Peking 1969-71, China Desk FCO 1971-74, first econ sec Br Embassy Bonn 1974-77, head of chancery Br High Cmmn Singapore 1977-79, asst head Far Eastern Dept FCO 1979-82, secondment Barclays Bank Int 1982-83, commercial cnsllr Br Embassy Peking 1984-87, dep permanent Br rep OECD Paris 1987-; *Recreations* sports, art, gardens; *Style—* Hugh Davies, Esq; c/o FCO (OECD Paris), King Charles Street, London, SW1A 2AH

DAVIES, (Edward) Hunter; s of late John Davies, and Marion, née Brechin; *b* 7 Jan 1936; *Educ* Creighton Sch Carlisle, Carlisle GS, Univ of Durham; *m* 1960, Margaret Forster, *qv*; 1 s, 2 da; *Career* author of over 30 books; journalist Sunday Times 1960-84, ed Sunday Times Magazine 1975-77, columnist Punch 1979-89, presenter BBC Radio Four's Bookshelf 1983-86; *Books Incl:* Here We Go Round the Mulberry Bush (1965), The Good Guide to the Lakes (publisher 1984); *Style—* Hunter Davies, Esq; 11 Boscastle Rd, London NW5 (☎ 01 485 3785); Grasmoor House, Loweswater, Cockermouth, Cumbria

DAVIES, His Hon Judge Ian Hewitt; TD; s of Rev John Robert Davies (d 1968), and Gwendoline Gertrude *née* Garling; *b* 13 May 1931; *Educ* Kingswood sch, St John's coll, Cambridge (MA); *m* 31 July 1962, Molly Cecilia Vaughan da of Brig Charles Hilary Vaughan Vaughan, DSO (d 1978); *Career* nat serv 1950-51, cmmnd KOYLI serv with 3Bn Parachute Regt, TA 1951-71, Lt Col; barr Inner Temple 1958, circuit judge 1986; *Recreations* lawn tennis, sailing; *Clubs* Boodles, MCC, Hurlingham; *Style—* His Hon Judge Davies, TD; c/o Middlesex Crown Court, Parliament Square, London

DAVIES, Hon Islwyn Edmund Evan; CBE (1986), JP (Powys), DL (Powys 1983); s of 1 Baron Davies; *b* 10 Dec 1926; *Educ* Gordonstoun; *m* 1959, Camilla Anne, elder da of Col Lawrence William Coulden, of Hadley Wood, Herts; 3 s; *Career* FRAgS; Hon LLD (Wales); *Style—* The Hon Islwyn Davies, CBE, JP, DL; Perthybu, Sarn, Newtown, Powys (☎ (068) 688 620)

DAVIES, Jack Gale Wilmot; OBE (1946); s of Langford George Davies, and Lily Barnes Davies; *b* 10 Sept 1911; *Educ* Tonbridge Sch, St John's Coll Cambridge; *m* 1949, Georgette O'Dell, *née* Vanson; 1 s; *Career* formerly exec dir Bank of England; dir Portals Water Treatment Ltd; *Style—* Jack Davies, Esq, OBE; 31 Wingate Way, Cambridge (☎ 0223 841284)

DAVIES, Rev Jacob Arthur Christian; s of Jacob S and Christiana Davies; *b* 24 May 1925; *Educ* Univ of Reading (BSc), Selwyn Coll Cambridge, Imperial Coll of Tropical Agric; *m* Sylvia Onikeh Cole; 2 s, 2 da; *Career* high cmmr for Sierra Leone in London 1972-74; non-resident ambass to Denmark, Sweden and Norway 1972-74; dir Personnel Div FAO 1976- (formerly dep dir Agric Operations Div); *Style—* The Rev Jacob Davies; Agricultural Operations Division, FAO, Viale Delle Terme di Caracolla, Rome, Italy

DAVIES, (David) John; s of J N J Davies (d 1978), of Epsom, and P, *née* Williams (d 1983); *b* 17 Mar 1933; *Educ* Christ's Coll Cambridge (MA); *m* 29 Oct 1960, Pauline Margot, s of E R Owen (d 1955), of Ashtead; 2 s (Gordon Howard b 1964, Richard James b 1967, d 1988); *Career* analyst Cazenove and Co 1968-71, Quilter Goodison Co 1971-86 (ptnr 1973-, managing ptnr and md 1981-86), dep md Banque Paribas Capital Mkts Ltd 1987-; Freeman City of London, memb Worshipful Co of Upholders; memb Stock Exchange 1973, MBIM, FRSA, fell IOD; *Recreations* water sports; *Clubs* Carlton; *Style—* John Davies, Esq; Paddock Cottage, Downsway, Tadworth, Surrey KT20 5DH (☎ 073 781 3226); Banque Paribas Capital Markets Ltd, 33 Wigmore St, London W1H OBN (☎ 01 355 2000, fax 01 355 2080)

DAVIES, Prof John Duncan; OBE (1984); s of Ioan and Gertrude Davies; *b* 19 Mar 1929; *Educ* Pontardwe Sch, Treforest Sch of Mines, London Univ (PhD, DSc); *m* 1949, Barbara, *née* Morgan; 3 da; *Career* formerly prof of civil engrg and dean Univ Coll Swansea, princ W Glam Inst of Higher Educn 1976-77, dir Poly of Wales 1978; memb: OU Delegacy 1978-83 (Visiting Ctee 1986-89), MSC Ctee Wales 1979-83, Wales Advsy Body for HE 1982-88, Cncl for Nat Academic Awards (CNAA) 1985-; *Style—* Prof John Davies, OBE; Polytechnic of Wales, Treforest, Pontypridd, Mid Glam, Wales (☎ 0443 405133)

DAVIES, John Howard; CBE (1984), DL (Clwyd 1986); s of Rev William Hugh Davies (d 1981), of Cardiff, and Mary Eunice, *née* Thomas (d 1971); *b* 6 May 1926; *Educ* Holyhead Co Sch, UCW, Poitiers Univ France (BA, DipEd); *m* 5 Oct 1954, Elizabeth, da of James Jenkins JP (d 1965), of Carmarthen; 3 s (Jonathan b 1956, Mark b 1958, Timothy b 1960); *Career* Capt Royal Welch Fusiliers 1944-48, cmmnd Indian Mil Acad; served: India, Burma, Malaya, Sumatra; Colonial Educn Serv North Nigeria 1952-56, dist educn offr Notts 1957-58; dep dir of educn: Montgomeryshire 1958-66, Flintshire 1966-70; dir of educn Flintshire 1970-74, Clwyd 1974-85; chm Welsh Fourth Channel Authy (S4C) 1986; chm cncl UCW Bangor; memb: cncl and ct UCW, cncl UCW (Coll of Med), cncl and ct Nat Library of Wales, N Wales Arts Cncl; chm Clwyd Appeal Fund for Hosp scanner equipment; hon memb Gorsedd of Bards 1985; FRSA 1980; *Recreations* golf, gardening; *Style*— John Howard Davies, Esq, CBE, DL; Staddle Stones, Hendy Rd, Mold, Clwyd, (☎ 0352 700110); S4C, Sophia Close, Cardiff, (☎ 0222 343421, fax 0222 341643, telex 9401 7032 SIAN G)

DAVIES, John Kenyon; s of Harold Edward Davies, of Liverpool, and Clarice Theresa, *née* Woodburn; *b* 19 Sept 1937; *Educ* Manchester GS, Wadham Coll Oxford (BA), Merton Coll Oxford (MA), Balliol Coll Oxford (DPhil); *m* 1, 8 Sept 1962 (m dis 1978), Anna Elbina Laura Margherita, da of Morpurgo (d 1939), of Rome; m 2, 5 Aug 1978, Nicola Jane, da of Dr R M S Perrin; 1 s (Martin b 1979), 1 da (Penelope b 1981); *Career* Harmsworth scholar Merton Coll Oxford 1960-63, jr fell Centre for Hellenic Studies Washington DC 1961-62, Dyson jr fell Balliol Coll 1963-65, lectr in ancient history Oriel Coll Oxford 1968-77, Rathbone prof of ancient history and classical archaeology Univ of Liverpool 1977-, pro vice-chllr Univ of Liverpool 1986-89; ed: Jl of Hellenic Studies 1973-77, Archaeological Reports 1972-74; chm: St Patrick's Isle (IOM) Archaeological Tst 1982-85, NW Archaeological Tst 1982-; FBA 1985, FSA 1986, FRSA 1988; *Books* Athenian Propertied Families 600-300BC (1971), Democracy and Classical Greece (1978), Wealth and the Power of Wealth in Classical Athens (1981), The Trojan War: its historicity and context (jt ed with L Foxhall, 1984); *Recreations* choral singing; *Style*— Prof John Davies; 20 North Rd, Grassendale Park, Liverpool L19 0LR (☎ 051 427 2126); Dept of Classics and Archaeology, University of Liverpool, Abercromby Square PO Box 147, Liverpool L69 3BX (☎ 051 794 2400, fax 051 708 6502, telex 027 095 UNILPL G)

DAVIES, Hon Jonathan Hugh; s of 2 Baron Davies; *b* 25 Jan 1944; *Educ* Eton, UC Oxford; *m* 15 Oct 1966, (Mary) Veronica, da of Sir (William) Godfrey Agnew, KCVO; 2s, 4 da; *Career* memb Museums and Galleries Cmmn 1985-; *Style*— The Hon Jonathan Davies; Stonehill House, Abingdon, Berks

DAVIES, Keith Laurence Maitland; s of Wyndham Matabele Davies, QC (d 1972) and Enid Maud Davies (d 1971); *b* 3 Feb 1938; *Educ* Winchester, ChCh Oxford (MA); *m* 20 June 1964, Angela Mary, da of C.D. Fraser Jenkins; 1 s (Julian b 1973), 2 da (Claire b 1967, Annabel b 1968); *Career* barr Inner Temple 1962, private practice 1962-84, met stipendiary magistrate 1984-; *Style*— Keith Davies, Esq; c/o 1 Paper Buildings, London EC4

DAVIES, Kenneth Seymour; s of George Seymour, of Eastcote, Middx, and (Isobel) Dorothy, *née* Corfield; *b* 11 Feb 1948; *Educ* St Nicholas GS Northwood; *m* 15 May 1971, Brenda Margaret, da of William George Cannon (d 1987), of Ruislip, Midd; 4 s (Mark b 1972, Peter b 1974, Robert b 1976, Trevor b 1982), 1 da (Kirsty b 1980); *Career* CA 1970; ptnr Pannell Kerr Forster 1974-; hon tres Willing Wheels Club (Cancer Charity); FCA; *Recreations* gardening, walking; *Style*— Kenneth Davies, Esq; Braunston, 15 Berks Hill, Chorleywood, Herts WD3 5AG (☎ 09278 2156); Pannell Kerr Forster, 78 Hatton Garden, London EC1N 8JA (☎ 01 831 7393, fax 01 405 6737, telex 295928)

DAVIES, Col Lucy Myfanwy; *née* Anwyl-Passingham; CBE (1968, OBE 1962); da of Col Augustus Mervyn Owen Anwyl-Passingham, CBE, DL, JP, of Bala, Merioneth (d 1955), and late Margaret, *née* Radclyffe; *b* 8 April 1913; *Educ* Francis Holland Sch; *m* 1955, Maj D W Davies, TD, RAMC (d 1959); *Career* driver FANY 1939, Dep Dir WRAC 1964-68, Dep Controller Cmdt WRAC 1967-77, ret 1968; underwriting memb of Lloyds 1971; OStJ 1938; *Recreations* horse racing, travel; *Style*— Col Lucy Davies, CBE; 6 Elm Place, London SW7 (☎ 01 373 5731)

DAVIES, Mark Edward Trehearne; s of Denis Norman Davies of Slinfold, Sussex, and Patricia Helen, *née* Trehearne; *b* 20 May 1948; *Educ* Stowe; *m* 1, June 8 1974 (m dis 1984), Serena Barbara, *née* Palmer; m 2, 20 Nov 1987, Antonia Catherine, da of Jeremy Barrow Chittenden, of Lytes Cary Manor, Som; 1 da (Sophia b 13 May 1988); *Career* commodity broker Ralli Int 1969, fndr Inter Commodities 1972 (awarded Queens Award for Export Achievement 1981), md GNI Ltd (formerly Inter Commodities Ltd) 1972; dir: GNI Hldgs Ltd 1976, Inter Commodities Trading Ltd 1976, Tweseldown Racecourse Ltd 1979; chm GNI Freight Futures Ltd 1981; dir: ICV Info Systems Ltd 1981, Inter Commodities Ltd 1982, Gerrard and Nat Hldgs plc 1985, dir: Guy Morrison Ltd 1986, GH Asset Mgmnt Ltd 1988; chm GNI Wallace Ltd 1986; memb London Metal Exchange; *Books* Trading in Commodities (co-author 1974); *Recreations* hunting, racing; *Clubs* Lansdowne; *Style*— Mark Davies, Esq; 25 Mulberry Walk, London SW3; Colechurch House, 1 London Bridge Walk, London SE1 2SX (☎ 01 378 7171, fax 01 407 3848, car 0860 519 400)

DAVIES, Lady (Mary Bailey); *née* Liptrot; da of Henry Liptrot, of Aberstwyth; *m* 1933, Rt Hon Sir (William) Arthian Davies, (d 1979); 1 da; *Style*— Lady Davies; Ballinger Lodge, Great Missenden, Bucks

DAVIES, (Albert) Meredith; CBE (1982); s of Rev E A Davies; *b* 30 July 1922; *Educ* Royal Coll of Music, Stationers Co's Sch, Keble Oxford, Accademia di St Cecilia Rome; *m* 1949, Betty Hazel, *née* Bates; 3 s, 1 da; *Career* princ Trinity Coll of Music 1979, conductor: Royal Choral Soc 1972-85, Leeds Philharmonic Soc 1975-83; *Style*— Meredith Davies, Esq, CBE; c/o Trinity Coll of Music, Mandeville Place, London W1

DAVIES, Hon Mr Justice Michael; Sir (Alfred William) Michael; s of Alfred Edward Davies (d 1958), of Stourbridge, Worcs; *b* 29 July 1921; *Educ* King Edward's Sch Birmingham, Birmingham Univ; *m* 1947, Margaret, da of Robert Ernest Jackson, of Sheffield; 1 s, 3 da; *Career* barrister Lincoln's Inn 1948, QC 1964, leader Midland Circuit 1968, dep chm Northants Quarter Sessions 1963-71; recorder: Grantham 1963-65, Derby 1965-71, Crown Ct 1972; judge of the High Ct of Justice (Queen's Bench Div) 1973; chm Mental Health Review Tribunal for Birmingham Area 1965-71, chllr Diocese of Derby 1971-73, chm Hospital Complaints Procedure Ctee 1971-73; kt 1973; *Style*— The Hon Mr Justice Davies; Royal Courts of Justice, London WC2

DAVIES, (Angie) Michael; *b* 23 June 1934; *Educ* Shrewsbury, Queens' Coll Cambridge (MA); *m* 1960, Jane Priscilla; 2 children; *Career* FCA; former chm and chief exec Imperial Foods and dir Imperial Gp (to May 1982); non-exec dir: Donner Underwriting Agencies 1975, CD Underwriting Agencies 1983, Littlewoods Orgn 1982, Alexander Syndicate Mgmnt 1982, Tozer Kemsley and Millburn (Hldgs) 1982-86 (chm 1985-86), Newman Industs 1983, TV AM 1983, Br Airways 1983, TI Gp 1984, Alva Investmt Tst 1984, (chm 1986), CC Conversions 1984; Bredero Properties (chm 1986), Calor Gp 1987, James Wilkes 1987, John Perkins Meats (chm 1987); Blue Arrow 1987; FCA; *Style*— A Michael Davies Esq; Little Woolpit, Ewhurst, Cranleigh, Surrey (☎ (0483) 277344); 1 Cheyne Place, London SW3 (☎ 01 352 2012)

DAVIES, (John) Michael; s of Vincent Ellis Davies, OBE, of Bentley Lodge, E Grinstead, Sussex and Rose Trench, *née* Temple; *b* 2 August 1940; *Educ* King's Sch Canterbury, Peterhouse Cambridge (BA); *m* 1971, Amanda, da of Hedley Wilton Atkinson, of Shaldon, Devon; 2 s (William b 1976, Harry b 1982), 1 da (Anna b 1973); *Career* private sec to ldr of House of Lords and chief whip 1971-74, princ clerk Overseas and Euro Off 1983-85, clerk of private bills House of Lords 1985; sec Soc of Clerks-at-the-Table in Cwlth Parls (jt ed of The Table) 1967-83, sec of Statute Law Ctee 1974-83; *Recreations* cricket, France; *Style*— Michael Davies Esq; 26 Northchurch Terrace, London N1 4EG; House of Lords, London SW1 (☎ 01 219 3233)

DAVIES, Col Norman Thomas; MBE (1970), JP (Hants 1984); s of Edward Ernest Davies (d 1937), and Elsie, *née* Scott; *b* 2 May 1933; *Educ* Holywell, RMA Sandhurst, Open Univ (BA); *m* 1961, Penelope Mary, da of Peter Graeme Agnew, of Cornwall; 1 s (Peter), 1 da (Clare); *Career* cmmnd RA 1954, served in Malaya, Germany and UK 1954-64; mil asst to COS Northern Army Gp 1968-69; cmd C Battery RHA; 2 i/c 3 Regt RHA 1970-72; GSO I (DS) Staff Coll Camberley and Canadian Land Forces Cmd and Staff Coll 1972-74; cmd 4 Field Regt RA 1975-77, mil dir of Studies RMC of Science Shrivenham 1977-80, Col 1977; registrar gen Dental Cncl 1981; memb EEC advsy ctee on the Trg of Dental Practitioners 1983; *Recreations* golf, gardening, wine, household maintenance; *Style*— Norman Davies, Esq, MBE, JP; Lowfields Cottage, London Road, Hartley Wintney, Hamps (☎ Hartley Wintney 3303); General Dental Council, 37 Wimpole Street, London W1M 8DQ

DAVIES, Sir Oswald; CBE (1973), DCM (1944), JP (1969); s of George Warham Davies and Margaret, *née* Hinton; *b* 23 June 1920; *Educ* Central Schs Sale, Manchester Coll of Technol; *m* 1942, Joyce, da of Thomas Henry Eaton; 1 s, 1 da; *Career* dir Fairclough Construction Group (chief exec 1965-78, chm 1965-83), chm Amec plc 1983-85, dir 1985; CBIM, FIHT, FCIOB, FFB, FRGS, FRSA; kt 1984; *Style*— Sir Oswald Davies, CBE, DCM, JP; c/o Amec plc, Sandiway House, Northwich, Cheshire CW8 2YA (☎ (0606) 883885)

DAVIES, Patrick Taylor; CMG (1978), OBE (1967); s of Andrew Taylor Davies (d 1983), and Olive Kathleen Mary, *née* Hobson (d 1972); *b* 10 August 1927; *Educ* Shrewsbury, St John's Coll Cambridge (BA), Trinity Coll Oxford; *m* 1959, Marjorie Eileen, da of late Arthur Wilkinson; 2 da (Jennifer, Susan); *Career* entered HM Colonial Admin Serv Nigeria 1952, perm sec Kano State 1970-79, chief inspr Area Cts 1972-79; *Style*— Patrick Davies, Esq, CMG, OBE; Rose Cottage, Childs Ercall, Salop TF9 2DB (☎ 095 278 255)

DAVIES, Peter Douglas Royston; s of Douglas Frederick Davies, of Christchurch, Dorset, and Edna Matilda, *née* Dingle; *b* 29 Nov 1936; *Educ* Brockenhurst Co HS Hants, LSE (BSc); *m* 28 Jan 1967, Elizabeth Mary Lovett, da of Dr Leslie Williams (d 1956); 1 s (Simon Leslie Peter b 1968), 2 da (Eleanor Catherine b 1971, Jane Olivia b 1974); *Career* FCO: FO 1964-66, 2 sec Nicosia 1966-67, FO 1967-68, 1 sec Budapest 1968-71, FCO 1971-74, consul Rio de Janiero 1974-78, cnsllr The Hague 1978-82, dep high cmmr Kuala Lumpur 1982-86, RCDS 1986-87, head cmmr Kuala Lumpur 1982-86, RCDS 1986-87, head of arms control and disarmament dept FCO 1987-; *Recreations* reading, walking; *Style*— Peter Davies, Esq; FCO, King Charles St, London SW1A 2AH (☎ 01 270 2242)

DAVIES, (Roger) Peter Havard; OBE (1978); s of Arthur William Davies (d 1926), of Berkswell and Edith Mary, *née* Mealand (d 1966); *b* 4 Oct 1919; *Educ* Bromsgrove Sch, St Edmund Hall Oxford (MA); *m* 1956, Ferelith Mary Helen, da of Maj John McLaughlin Short (d 1969); 2 s (Mark, Simon), 2 da (Jessica, Lucy); *Career* served WW II, Capt RA (AOP); Br Cncl offr 1949-80: served in Hungary, Israel, Sarawak, Finland, Chile and India, dir Drama and Music Dept 1965-69, Info 1974-75; dir Anti-Slavery Soc 1980; chm Exec Cncl of Int Service for Human Rights Geneva; chm Human Rights Sub-Ctee, UN Assoc; *Recreations* music, golf, walking, family life; *Clubs* Royal Cwlth Soc, Union (Oxford), Bengal (Calcutta); *Style*— Peter Davies Esq, OBE; Ley Cottage, Elmore Rd, Chipstead, Surrey CR3 3SG (☎ Downland 53905); The Anti-Slavery Society, 180 Brixton Rd, London SW9 6AT (☎ 01 582 4040)

DAVIES, Peter Lewis Morgan; OBE 1978; s of David Morgan Davies (d 1962), and Annie Lee, *née* Jones (d 1983); *b* 15 Feb 1927; *Educ* Fishguard Co Sch; *m* 23 May 1953, Gwenith, da of Thomas Devonald Thomas Cilgerran, (d 1969), of Cilgerran; *Career* Lt Welch Regt and Royal Welch Fusiliers 1944-48; Midland Bank plc 1943-51; Barclays Bank Int Ltd: Bahamas 1952-55, Nigeria 1955-67, Libya 1968-70, Zambia 1970-79, mangr Kaunda Square Kitwe (northern area mangr), alternate dir Barclays Zambia Ltd; team ldr World Bank Mission to Indonesia 1979-80, Br Exec Serv Overseas Turks and Caicos Islands 1982-83, md Pembrokeshire Business Initiative 1983-86, business cnslr Welsh Devpt Agency 1986-; memb TAVRA: W Wales regnl ctee and assoc, nat Employers liason ctee Wales; county tres Royal Br Legion Pembrokeshire, govr Fishguard Secondary Sch, hon patron 4 Bn Royal Regt of Wales, bd memb Fishguard Music Festival; FBIM 1973; *Recreations* photography, philately; *Style*— Peter L M Davies, Esq, OBE; Court House, Tower Hill, Fishguard, Pembrokeshire, SA65 9LA (☎ 0348 873 793)

DAVIES, Sir Peter Maxwell; CBE (1981); s of Thomas Davies and Hilda Davies; *b* 8 Sept 1934; *Educ* Leigh GS, Manchester Univ (MusB 1956), Royal Manchester Coll of Music; *Career* composer; studied with Goffredo Petrassi in Rome 1957, dir of music Cirencester GS 1959-62, fndr and co-dir (with Harrison Birtwistle) The Pierrot Players 1967-70, fndr and artistic dir Fires of London 1971, fndr and dir St Magnus Festival Orkney Islands 1977, dir of music Dartington Hall Summer Sch of Music 1980; pres School's Music Assoc 1983; works incl operas: Taverner (1970), The Martyrdom of St Magnus (1976), The Two Fiddlers (1978, opera for children), The Lighthouse (1979), chamber opera), Cinderalla (1980, opera for children); ballet Salome; two orchestral symphonies (1976 and 1980); FRNCM 1978, Hon RAM 1978; Hon DMus Edinburgh 1979, Manchester 1983, Bristol 1984, Open Univ 1986; Hon LLD: Aberdeen 1981, Warwick 1986; kt 1987;; *Works include* operas: Taverner (1970), The Martyrdom of St Magnus (1976); The Two Fiddlers (1978, opera for children), The Lighthouse

(1979, chamber opera), Cinderella (1980, opera for children); ballet Salome; two orchestral symphonies (1976, 1980); *Style*— Sir Peter Maxwell Davies, CBE; c/o Mrs Judy Arnold, Flat 3, 50 Hogarth Rd, London SW5 (☎ 01 370 1477, telex 8951859 BASIL G)

DAVIES, Ven Philip Bertram; s of Rev Bertram Davies, MA (d 1970), and Nancy Jonsson, *née* Nicol (d 1978); *b* 13 July 1933; *Educ* Lancing Coll, Cuddesdon Theol Coll; *m* 29 June 1963, (Elizabeth) Jane, da of The Ven John Farquhar Richardson, *qv*; 2 s (Simon Philip b 1964, Matthew James b 1968), 2 da (Sarah Jane b 1966, d 1973, Eleanor Mary b 1974); *Career* asst supt Travancore Tea Estates Co S India 1954 (supt 1957-58), asst sales mangr Lewis's Ltd Manchester 1959-61; asst curate St John the Baptist Atherton Lancs 1963-66, vicar St Mary Magdalene Winton Eccles 1966-71, rector St Philip with St Stephen Salford 1971-76, vicar Christ Church Radlett Herts 1976-87, rural dean Aldenham 1979-87, archdeacon of St Albans 1987; *Recreations* fishing, gardening, bridge; *Style*— The Ven the Archdeacon of St Albans; 6 Sopwell Lane, St Albans, Herts AL1 1RR (☎ 0727 57973)

DAVIES, Hon Philip Cedric Mark; s of 2 Baron Darwen; *b* 2 Oct 1951; *Educ* Sybford Sch; *Style*— The Hon Philip Davies

DAVIES, Maj-Gen Philip Middleton; OBE (1974); s of Hugh Davies (d 1942); *b* 27 Oct 1932; *Educ* Charterhouse; *m* 1956, Mona, da of Richard Wallace (d 1980); 2 children; *Career* CO 1 Bn The Royal Scots 1973-76, Cdr 19 Airportable Bde and 7 Field Force 1977-79, Cdr Land Forces Cyprus 1981-83, Maj-Gen 1983, GOC NW District 1983-, ret April 1986, md Utd Aircraft Industs Ltd 1986-88; *Recreations* flyfishing, tennis, gardening; *Clubs* Army and Navy; *Style*— Maj-Gen Philip Davies, OBE; c/o National Westminster Bank, Warminster, Wilts

DAVIES, Quentin; MP (C) Stamford and Spalding 1987; s of Dr Michael Ivor, and Thelma Davies; *b* 29 May 1944; *Educ* Dragon Sch Oxford, Leighton Park, Gonville and Caius Coll Cambridge (BA)Harvard Univ (Frank Knox Fell); *m* 1983, Chantal, da of Lt Col R L C Tamplin, of Lincs; 1 s (Alexander); *Career* HM Dip Serv 1967-79 (3 sec FCO 1969-72, 2 sec Moscow 1973-74 1 sec FCO); Morgan Grenfell & Co Ltd (mangr, asst dir 1974-78), rep France, dir gen & pres 1978-81 ; *Recreations* reading, walking, riding, skiing, travel; *Clubs* Beefsteek (London), Travellers (London), Constitutional (Spalding), S Lincs Cons (Bourne), Travellers (Paris); *Style*— Quentin Davies, Esq, MP; c/o House of Commons, London SW1

DAVIES, Prof (Robert) Rees; s of William Edward Davies (d 1967), of Corwen, Clwyd, and Sarah Margaret, *née* Williams (d 1986); *b* 6 August 1938; *Educ* Ysgol Y Berwyn Bala, UCL (BA), Merton Coll Oxford (D Phil); *m* 29 July 1966, Carys, da of Ifor Lloyd Wynne (d 1970), of Wrexham, Clwyd; 1 s (Prys b 1972), 1 da (Manon b 1968); *Career* lectr: Univ Coll Swansea 1961-63, UCL 1963-76; prof and head of Dept of History Univ Coll of Wales Aberystwyth 1976- (vice princ 1988-); asst and review ed History 1963-73, James Ford special lectr Univ of Oxford 1988, Wiles lectr Queen's Univ Belfast 1988; memb: Ancient Monuments Bd for Wales 1978, Cncl Nat Museum of Wales 1987-; winner (jt) Wolfson Literary Award for History 1987; FRHistS (vice pres 1989-); FBA; *Books* Lordship and Society in the March of Wales 1282-1400 (1978), Conquest, Coexistence and Change Wales 1063-1415 (1987), The British Isles 1100-1500 (1988); *Recreations* walking, music; *Style*— Prof Rees Davies; Dept of History, Univ College of Wales, Aberystwyth, Dyfred (☎ (0970) 623 111 ext 3515)

DAVIES, Prof (Eurfil) Rhys; s of Daniel Haydn Davies (d 1957), and Mary, *née* Jenkins (d 1961); *b* 18 April 1929; *Educ* Rhondda GS, Llandovery Coll, Clare Coll Cambridge (BA, MA, MB, BChir), St Mary's Hosp London; *m* 15 Dec 1962, Zoë Doreen, da of Stanley Ivan Victor Chamberlain (d 1984); 3 s (Matthew b 1966, Huw b 1968, Timothy (twin) b 1968); *Career* Nat Serv Capt RAMC 1954-56, regtl MO 24 Regt 1955-56; conslt radiologist Utd Bristol Hosps 1966-81, prof of radiodiagnosis Univ of Bristol 1981-; pres Br Nuclear Med Soc 1972-74; memb: Admin of Radioactive Substances Advsy Ctee, Bristol and Weston Dist Health Authy 1984-86; Royal College of Radiologists: registrar 1976-81, warden 1984-86, pres 1986-89; Hon Fell Faculty of Radiologists RCSI 1976; fell: RSM, Faculty of Radiologists 1964, Royal Coll of Radiologists 1976, RCP(Ed) 1972, Fell Faculty of Dental Surgns RCS 1989, civilian conslt in radiodiagnosis to the RN 1988-; memb: BMA, Br Inst of Radiology Gen Med Cncl 1989-; *Books* Radionuclides in Radiodiagnosis (jty, 1974), Nuclear Medicine: Applications in Surgery (ed with G Thomas 1988); *Recreations* walking, theatre, wine; *Style*— Prof Rhys Davies; 19 Hyland Grove, Westbury on Trym, Bristol BS9 3NR (☎ 0272 501532)

DAVIES, Sir Richard Harries; KCVO (1984, CVO 1982), CBE (1962); s of Thomas Henry Davies (d 1964) and Minnie Oakley, *née* Morgan (d 1964); *b* 29 June 1916; *Educ* Porth Co Sch, Cardiff Tech Coll (BSc); *m* 1, 15 April 1944, Hon Annie (Nan) Butcher (d 24 Sept 1976), er da of 1 Baron Macpherson of Drumochter (d 1965); 2 s, 2 da; m 2, 1979, Mrs Patricia P Ogier; *Career* scientist: Civil Serv 1939-46, Br Air Cmmn Washington DC 1941-45; vice pres Ferranti Electric Inc NY 1959-63, dir Ferranti Ltd 1970-76; pres Br American C of C NY 1959-62, vice pres Manchester C of C 1976; HRH Duke of Edinburgh's Household: asst private sec 1977-82, tres 1982-84, extra equerry 1984; Pres Radio Soc of GB 1988; FIEE; *Recreations* gardening, sailing, amateur radio; *Clubs* Athenaeum, Pratt's; *Style*— Sir Richard Davies, KCVO, CBE; Haven House, Thorpeness, Leiston, Suffolk IP16 4NR

DAVIES, Richard James Guy; s of George Glyn Davies MBE, of Frinton-On-Sea Essex, and Cynthia Joan, *née* Franklin; *b* 7 Dec 1953; *Educ* Felsted Sch Essex, St Catharine's Coll Cambridge (MA); *m* 19 July 1980, Michele Clarke, da of Michael C Lipscomb (d 1981); 2 s (Michael b 1985, Christopher b 1987); *Career* dir Lazard Bros & Co Ltd 1986 (joined 1976), 1986 seconded to Korea Merchant Banking Corpn Seoul Korea 1978-80; *Recreations* sailing, music, literature; *Clubs* Royal Burnham YC; *Style*— Richard Davies, Esq; 262 Trinity Rd, London SW18 (☎ 01 874 1442); lazard Brothers & Co Ltd, 21 Moorfields, London EC2P 2HT (☎ 01 588 2721, fax 01 628 2485, telex 886438)

DAVIES, Robert John; s of William Edward Davies (d 1956), of Wimbledon, and Esther Emily, *née* Weeks (d 1982); *b* 28 May 1926; *m* 24 Aug 1957, Pamela Margaret, da of Hugh Hume Dixon, CBE, of Majorca; 2 s (Stephen b 1959, Martin b 1960), 1 da (Alison b 1966); *Career* coastal cmd air sea rescue servs RAFVR 1943-47; American Express Bank: vice-pres and gen mangr India and Pakistan 1967-73, vice-pres and gen mangr Greece 1973-76, md Italy (SPA) 1976-80, vice-pres and gen mangr UK (Ltd) 1981-84, vice-pres gen mangr and head military banking div for UK Iceland (Ltd) 1985-; memb nat ctee 85 Anniversary Appeal St Elizabeths Much Hadham Herts; FCIB 1970, FCIS 1972; Cavaliere Ufficiale of the Order Al Merito Della Republica Italiana 1980; *Recreations* golf, cycling, reading; *Clubs* Oriental; *Style*— Robert Davies, Esq; American Express Bank Ltd, Military Banking HQ, PO Box 102, High Wycombe, Bucks (☎ 0494 20904, fax 0494 447649, car 0836 376082, telex 838839)

DAVIES, Robert Stephen; s of Richard George Davies (d 1968), and Megan, *née* Matthews; *b* 23 Feb 1945; *Educ* Bridgend GS; *m* 25 July 1970, Philippa Mary, da of Herbert Woodley (d 1971); 2 s (Charles b 1972, Nicholas b 1975), 2 da (Lucy b 1982, Katy b 1982); *Career* articled clerk Mann Judd 1965-69 (audit mangr 1969-71), mgmnt conslt 1971-72, supervisor budgets and planning Gulf Oil Int London 1974-76 (sr fin analyst 1972-74), mangr fin and servs Gulf Oil Refining Ltd 1976-78, fin dir Gulf Oil Switzerland AG 1978-80, fin dir Gulf Oil (GB) Ltd 1980-; fndr memb Jaguar Car Club, corporate memb governing body Cheltenham Ladies Coll; FCA 1969; *Recreations* music, antique collecting, vintage cars, tennis; *Clubs* Bentley Drivers; *Style*— Robert Davies, Esq; The Quadrangle, Imperial Sq, Cheltenham, Glos (☎ 0242 225 302, fax 0242 573 059); Tewkesbury, Glos

DAVIES, (Anthony) Roger; s of (Richard) George Davies of Brockenhurst, Bridgend, Glam (d 1968), and Megan, *née* Matthews; *b* 1 Sept 1940; *Educ* King's Coll London Univ (LLB, AKC); *m* 23 Sept 1967, Clare, da of Cdr William Arthur Walters (RN); 2 s (George, Hugo (twins) b 1974), 1 da (Antonia b 1972); *Career* barr, called to Bar Gray's Inn 1965, metropolitan stipendiary magistrate Feb 1985, Lord Justice Holker Sr Scholar; *Recreations* music, history, reading; *Style*— Roger Davies, Esq; c/o Bow Street Magistrates Court, London

DAVIES, Ronald; MP (Lab) Caerphilly 1983-; s of late Ronald Davies; *b* 6 August 1946; *Educ* Bassaleg GS, Portsmouth Polytechnic, Univ Coll of Wales Cardiff; *m* 1981, Christina Elizabeth Rees; *Career* former tutor and organiser WEA, sponsored by NUPE, memb Rhymney Valley District Cncl 1969, Mid-Glamorgan CC educn offr; *Style*— Ronald Davies Esq, MP; House of Commons, London SW1

DAVIES, Hon (Francis) Ronald; s of 1 Baron Darwen; *b* 29 Mar 1920; *Educ* Bootham Sch; *m* 1942, Margaret Phyllis, da of John George Cockworth; 2 s, 1 da; *Career* barr Gray's Inn 1948; *Style*— The Hon Ronald Davies; 39 Parkside, Mill Hill, NW7

DAVIES, Ronald George; s of Alfred Davies (d 1952), of Bunger Lane, Blackburn, and Mary Ellen Davies (d 1954); *b* 22 August 1916; *Educ* Queen Elizabeth GS Blackburn; *m* 24 Dec 1940, Gladys, da of Peter Haworth, of Blackburn, Lancs; 3 s (Bryan b 1942, Michael b 1945, Ronald b 1946), 1 da (Elizabeth b 1947); *Career* Sgt Irish Guards 1940-42, Maj E Yorks Regt and RA 1942-46; md Containerway and Roadferry Ltd 1947-76; chm (non exec) Russell Davies Ltd 1948-87; Silver Jubilee Medal 1977; *Recreations* cricket; *Clubs* East Lancs; *Style*— Ronald G Davies, Esq; Kingsfield, Himtlesham, Ipswich, Suffolk (☎ Himtlesham 580)

DAVIES, Ryland; s of Gethin and Joan Davies; *b* 9 Feb 1943; *Educ* Royal Manchester Coll of Music; *m* 1, 1966 (m dis 1981), Anne Elizabeth Howells; m 2, 1983, Deborah Rees; 1 da (Emily); *Career* Int opera singer (tenor); performed at Int Opera houses throught the world including: Convent Garden, Glyndebourne, NY Met, Milan, Paris, Vienna, Bonn, etc; also many recordings, radio, TV and film; fell Royal Manchester Coll of Music; *Style*— Ryland Davies Esq; Milestone, Broom Close, Esher, Surrey

DAVIES, Sharron Elizabeth; da of Terry Davies, and Sheila, *née* Conybeare; *b* 1 Nov 1962; *Educ* Kelly Coll Devon; *Career* memb Br Olympic Team 1976 (youngest memb), and 1980 (Silver Medallist); Cwlth Record Holder and double champion 1978; Sportswoman of the Year 1978/80; TV Personality; *Style*— Sharron Davies

DAVIES, (John) Simon; s of Arthur Rees Davies (d 1982), of Newcastle Emlym, Dyfed, and Catherine Elizabeth, *née* Jones; *b* 12 Mar 1937; *Educ* Cardigan GS, Coll of Estate Mgmnt (pres SU); *m* 24 Oct 1959, Anja Ilse, da of Gerhard Körner (d 1965), of Munich; 1 s (Michael Stephen b 1 April 1960, d 1978), 1 da (Kathleen Anja b 1 June 1964); *Career* princ and sr ptnr Kemp and Hawley CS's; former chm London Welsh assoc; former pres: London Cardiganshire Soc, Newcastle Emlyn Agric Show, Newcastle Emlyn RFC, Cardigan Eisteddfod; hon memb Gorsedd of Bards; pres Voyagers Club; Freeman City of London; FRICS; *Recreations* rugby, opera; *Style*— Simon Davies, Esq; 47 Upper Montagu St, London W1H 1FQ (☎ 01 262 4305); 13 Monmouth St, London WC2H 9DA (☎ 01 405 8161, fax 01 836 2214)

DAVIES, Stanley Mason (Sam); CMG (1971); s of Charles Davies, MBE (d 1948), of Liverpool, and Constance Evelyn, *née* Mason (d 1973); *b* 7 Feb 1919; *Educ* Bootle GS, Sch of Mil Engrg; *m* 1943, Diana Joan, da of Herbert G Lowe, of Southampton; 3 da (Ilsa, Prudence, Charlotte); *Career* served WW II, Europe, Capt RE; civil servant 1936-76, under-sec DHSS 1975-76 (asst sec 1969-75); dir: Simonsen & Weels Ltd (Denmark) 1978, Alliance Cap Mgmnt Inc; memb NY Acad of Sci; FSA (Edin); Croix de Guerre (Fr) 1944; *Recreations* philately, ornithology, archaeology; *Clubs* Savile; *Style*— Stanley Davies, Esq, CMG; 31 Leverstock Green Rd, Hemel Hempstead, Herts (☎ 0442 54312)

DAVIES, Hon Stephen Humphrey; s of 2 Baron Darwen; *b* 3 Oct 1945; *Educ* Royal GS, High Wycombe; *m* 1968, Kathleen Prestwood; 2 s (Timothy b 1970, Peter b 1980), 2 da (Ruth b 1972, Rachel b 1976); *Style*— The Hon Stephen Humphrey; c/o Rt Hon Lord Darwen, White Lodge, Sandelswood End, Baconsfield, Bucks

DAVIES, Hon Mrs; Teresa Katherine; *née* David; da of Richard William David, CBE, and Baroness David (*qqv*); *b* 1944; *m* 1967, Llewlyn Anthony Davies; *Style*— The Hon Mrs Davies; 50 Clarence Rd, Birmingham 13

DAVIES, Hon Thomas Barratt; 2 s of 1 Baron Darwen (d 1950); *b* 4 June 1916; *Educ* Bootham Sch, Coll of Art Liverpool; *m* 8 March 1941, Doreen, da of Arthur James Allen, of Portsmouth; 1 s (Alan (twin) b 1949), 3 da (Barbara b 1944, Frances b 1947, Judith (twin) b 1949); *Career* lectr in art education Reading Univ 1948-65; *Style*— The Hon T. Barry Davies; 56 Old Street, Upton-upon-Severn, Worcs, WR8 0HW (☎ 06846 3088)

DAVIES, Tudor Griffith; s of Griffith Davies, of Barry, Glamorgan, and Rhiannon, *née* Martin; *b* 2 Dec 1951; *Educ* Barry Boys GS, Manchester Univ (BSc); *m* 26 July 1980, Julia Alison, da of John William Harvey, of Trentham, Staffs; 3 s (William, Gwyn, Rhodri), 1 da (Sally); *Career* dir: Thurman Publishing Gp 1978-80, CBS Architectural Ironmongery 1980-84; corporate recovery ptnr Arthur Young CAs 1984-88; ACA; *Recreations* fishing, shooting, rugby football, walking; *Clubs* United Service (Cardiff); *Style*— Tudor Davies, Esq; Netherton Hse, Fintry, Stirlingshire, Scotland G63 0YH (☎ 036086 242); 173 City Rd, Cardiff, S Glam (☎ 0222 497 138, car tel 0836 702 357)

DAVIES, Lady Venetia Constance Kathleen Luz; *née* Hay; da of 14 Earl of Kinnoull; *b* 1929; *m* 1953, Maj Joseph Trevor Davies; 2 da (Nicola b 1957, Sally b

1960); *Style*— Lady Venetia Davies; 14 Old School Court, Grimston Gardens, Folkestone, Kent CT20 2UA

DAVIES OF PENRHYS, Baron (Life Peer UK 1974); Gwilym Elfed Davies; s of David Davies (d 1942); *b* 9 Oct 1913; *m* 1940, Gwyneth, da of Daniel Rees, of Trealaw, Rhondda; 2 s, 1 da; *Career* memb St John Ambulance Bde 1926-46; CC (1954) Glamorgan, chm Local Govt Ctee 1959-61, MP (L) Rhondda (E) 1959-74; PPS: Min of Labour 1964-68, Min of Power 1968; *Style*— The Rt Hon the Lord Davies of Penrhys; Maes-y-Ffrwd, Ferndale Rd, Tylorstown, Ferndale, Rhondda, Glamorgan (☎ Ferndale 730 254)

DAVIES-COOKE, Capt Philip Peter; s of Col Philip Ralph Davies-Cooke, CB (d 1974), of Gwysaney Hall, Mold, Clwyd, and Kathleen Mabel Davies-Cooke, OBE; *b* 4 July 1925; *Educ* Eton; *m* 1, 6 July 1957, Jane (d 1981), da of Edmund George Coryton (d 1981), of Linkincom, Yelverton, Devon; 3 s (Richard b 1 July 1960, Paul b 30 March 1962, Michael b 2 Nov 1965); m 2, 24 Sept 1985, Zinnia Mary Arfwedson; da of late Col Reggie Hodgkinson; *Career* 1 Royal Dragoons 1945-54; landowner; memb: BFFS, BASC, TRBL; *Recreations* fishing, shooting; *Clubs* Cavalry and Guards; *Style*— Capt Peter Davies-Cooke; Gwysaney Hall, Mold, Clwyd

DAVIES-SCOURFIELD, Col David Gwyn; MC (1944); s of Henry Gwyn Saunders-Davies-Scourfield (d 1934), and Helen, *née* Newton (d 1974); *b* 9 July 1911; *Educ* Winchester, RMC Sandhurst; *m* 25 Sept 1935, Elizabeth Emily Prudence, da of John Charles Close-Brooks (ka 1915), of Birtles Macclesfield; 1 s (Charles b 1940), 1 da (Precelly b 1937); *Career* Regular Soldier Welsh Gds 1932-58, Col N Africa and Italy (wounded 1945); *Clubs* Naval and Military; *Style*— Col David Davies-Scourfield, MC; Eversley Cross House, Eversley, Basingstoke, Hants (☎ 0734 732210)

DAVIES-SCOURFIELD, Brig Edward Grismond Beaumont; CBE (1966, MBE 1951), MC (1945), DL (1984); s of Henry Gwyn Davies-Scourfield (d 1934), of Sussex, and Helen Mary, *née* Newton (d 1973); *b* 2 August 1918; *Educ* Winchester Coll, RMC Sandhurst; *m* 24 Nov 1945, Diana Lilias, da of Sir Nigel Davidson, CBE (d 1961), of Sussex; 1 s (Nigel b 1959), 1 da (Susan b 1948); *Career* army offr, ret 1973; cmmnd 2 Lt KRRC 1938, CO 1 Bn Rifle Bde 1960 (Lt-Col), Bde Col Royal Green Jackets 1962, Brig Cdr Br Jt Servs Trg Team (Ghana) 1964; Dep Cdr Nearelf 1966, cmd Salisbury Plain Area 1970; gen sec Nat Assoc of Boys Clubs (vice pres) 1973-82, memb CPRE chm Hants Army Benevolant Fund, church warden 1975-88, tstee regtl funds; *Recreations* riding, shooting, tennis, walking; *Clubs* Army and Navy, Mounted Infantry; *Style*— Brig Edward Davies-Scourfield, CBE, MC, DL; Old Rectory Cottage, Medstead, Alton, Hants GU34 5LX (☎ 0420 62133)

DAVIS; *see*: Lovell-Davis

DAVIS; *see*: Hart-Davis

DAVIS, Albert Edward; s of Albert Ellerd Davis (d 1954), of 27 Church Street, Luton, Beds, and Kate Elizabeth, *née* Sell (d 1962); *b* 15 July 1928; *Educ* Luton GS; *m* 1 March 1952, Rhona, da of Walter Maurice Temple-Smith (d 1980), of 21 Park Mount, Harpenden, Herts; 1 s (Andrew Albert b 1956); *Career* sr ptnr Davis & Co certified accountants 1964- (joined 1945, jr ptnr 1950-64); memb: City of London Branch Royal Soc of St George, Utd Wards Club of the City of London; Freeman City of London 1984, Liveryman Worshipful Co of Arbitrators 1984; FTII 1951, FCCA 1952, FCIArb 1968; *Recreations* music, walking, travel, horticulture; *Clubs* City Livery; *Style*— Albert Davis, Esq; Hamilton House, 1 Temple Ave, Temple, London EC4Y 0HA (☎ 01 353 4212, fax 01 353 3325)

DAVIS, Lady Alison Elizabeth; yst da of 1 Earl Attlee (d 1967); *b* 14 April 1930; *m* 8 March 1952, Richard Lionel Lance Davis, son of late Maj Arthur Owen Lance Davis, of Hinckley, Leics; 3 da (Jennifer (Mrs Lochen) b 1953, Tessa (Dr Dormon) b 1955, Belinda (Mrs Johnston) b 1957); *Style*— Lady Alison Davis; Westcott, Beacon Rise, Sevenoaks, Kent TN13 2NJ

DAVIS, Sir (William) Allan; GBE (1985); s of Wilfred Egwin Davis (d 1953), and Annie Ellen, *née* Fraser (d 1978); *b* 19 June 1921; *Educ* Cardinal Vaughan Sch Kensington; *m* 1944, Audrey Pamela, da of Lionel Arthur Louch (d 1966); 2 s (Michael, Paul), 1 da (Jane); *Career* served WWII pilot RNVR 1940-44; joined Barclays Bank 1939; apprentice Dunn Wylie & Co 1944 (ptnr 1952, sr ptnr 1972-76); sr ptnr Armitage & Norton London 1979-87 (ptnr 1976); dir: Catholic Herald Ltd, Crowning Tea Co Ltd, Dunkelman & Son Ltd, Fiat Auto UK Ltd, Internatio-Muller UK Ltd and UK subsids NRG Hldgs Ltd; common councilman ward of Queenhithe 1971-76; ald Ward of Cripplegate 1976, Sheriff City of London 1982-83, Lord Mayor of London 1985-86; chm: Port and City of London helath ctee and social servs ctee 1974-77; mgmnt ctee London Homes for the Elderly 1975-88; memb Court HAC 1976; chm City of London Centre St John's Ambulance Assoc 1987 (hon tres 1979-82 and 1983-84, vice pres 1985); govr: Bridewell Royal Hosp 1976, Cripplegate Fndn 1976 (chm 1981), Cardinal Vaughan Meml Sch 1968-81 and 1985-88, Lady Eleanor Holles Sch 1979; tstee: Sir John Soane's Museum 1979, Morden Coll 1982; chm govrs Research into Ageing 1987, chm tstees Winged Fellowship 1987, dep pres Publicity Club of London; cncl memb: Young Enterprise, Order of St John for London 1986-, City Univ London 1986-; Liveryman Worshipful Co of Painter Stainers 1959 (hon tres 1962, memb ct 1962-); Hon Liveryman: Worshipful Co of CA's, Worshipful Co of Launderers; KCSG 1979; MICAS, FRSA, FTII, memb ICEAW; Order of Merit Qatar (Class 1) 1985, Cdr Isabel the Catholic 1986, Cdr Order of Merit FRG 1986; *Clubs* City Livery and Oriental; *Style*— Sir Allan Davis, GBE; 168 Defoe House, Barbican EC2Y 8DN (☎ 01 638 5354)

DAVIS, Col Anthony Wilmer; MBE (1972); s of Brig Thomas William Davis, OBE (d 1982), of Sea Point, South Africa, and Margot Caddy, *née* Mackie (d 1983); *b* 11 August 1930; *Educ* Bryanston; *m* 28 June 1957, Susan Ward, da of Stephen Edgar Hames (d 1985), of Prestbury, Cheshire; 1 s (Simon b 1959), 1 da (Fiona b 1961); *Career* RMA Sandhurst 1949-51, cmmnd Manchester Regt 1951, Staff Coll Camberley 1961, Armed Forces Staff Coll Norfolk, Virginia, USA 1968, Bde Maj Berlin Inf Bde 1969-71, CO 1 Bn King's Regt 1972-74, Directing Staff Nat Def Coll Latimer 1975-77, Col GS Staff Coll Camberley 1978-81; Comptroller and Sec Forces Help Soc and Lord Roberts Workshops 1982-; FBIM 1976; *Recreations* golf, classical music; *Style*— Col AW Davis, MBE, FBIM; c/o Midland Bank plc, Knightsbridge Branch, London SW1X 9RG

DAVIS, Hon Mrs (Beatrice Margaret); da of 1 Viscount Mills (d 1968), and Winifred Mary (d 1974), da of George Conaty, of Birmingham; *b* 21 July 1916; *Educ* Edgbaston C of E Coll for Girls Birmingham; *m* 20 Dec 1941, Walter Goodwin Davis (d 1973), s of Goodwin Julian Davis (d 1940); 2 s (Patrick b 1947, Andrew b 1950), 1 da (Jane b 1957); *Career* antique dealer; *Style*— The Hon Mrs Davis; Chantry House, Sheep Street, Stow-on-the-Wold, Glos G54 1AA (☎ 0451 30450)

DAVIS, Maj-Gen Brian William; CB (1985), CBE (1980, OBE 1974); s of late Edward William Davis, MBE, and Louise Jane, *née* Webber; *b* 28 August 1930; *Educ* Weston-super-Mare GS, Mons Offr Cadet Sch Aldershot; *m* 1954, Margaret Isobel Jenkins; 1 s, 1 da; *Career* cmmnd RA 1949, Lt Col Staff Coll Camberley 1969-71, CO 32 Light Regt RA serving in BAOR NI and UK 1971-74, Col logistic plans and ops HQ BAOR 1975, Brig 1975, Cdr RA 3 Div 1976-77, RCDS 1978, COS NI 1979-80, C-in-C Mission to Soviet Forces Germany 1981-82, Maj-Gen 1982, COS Logistic Exec (Army) MOD 1982-83, Vice QMG 1983-85, ret 1985; Head of Public Affairs RO plc 1985-; *Recreations* rugby, cricket, fishing; *Clubs* Army & Navy, Special Forces, HAC, MCC, Somerset CCC, Piscatorial Soc; *Style*— Maj-Gen Brian Davis, CB, CBE; c/o Williams and Glyn's Bank, Laurie House, Victoria Rd, Farnborough, Hants

DAVIS, Calum; s of Roy Albert George, of Pigeon House Corner, Rockford, Ringwood, Hants, and Catherine Jessie; *b* 18 June 1951; *Educ* Taunton Sch, Canterbury Sch of Architecture (Dip Arch); *m* 20 Aug 1977, Joan Anne, da of John alfred Stevens; 1 s (Jamie b 1981), 1 da (Josie b 1984); *Career* architect; princ and fndr Architon Gp Practice, CA, Planning Consultants; dir: Cabvesquare Ltd 1984, Architon Services Ltd 1986, Mainstreet Designs Ltd 1986, Architects Registration Cncl UK 1979; England trialist U19 Rugby 1969, RIBA, Dip in Architecture 1976; *Recreations* golf, skiing, windsurfing, conservation of historic buildings; *Style*— Calum Davis, Esq; Cotmandene House, Dene St, Dorking, Surrey RH4 2BZ; Architon Gp Practice, 525 London Rd, N Cheam, Surrey SM3 8JR (☎ 01 330 6069, fax 01 330 7374, car ☎ 0860 331349)

DAVIS, Sir Charles Sigmund; CB (1960); s of Maurice Davis (d 1943); *b* 22 Jan 1909; *Educ* Trinity Coll Cambridge; *m* 1940, Pamela Mary, da of Kenneth Dawson, OBE (d 1957); 2 da (Caroline, Elizabeth); *Career* HG 1940-45; barr Inner Temple 1930, legal advsr to MAFF and The Forestry Cmmn 1957-74, counsel to the Speaker House of Commons 1974-83; chm of cncl Nat Soc for Cancer Relief 1983-85, (tstee 1985); LRAM, ARCM; kt 1965; *Recreations* music; *Style*— Sir Charles Davis, CB; The Little House, 43 Wolsey Rd, E Molesey, Surrey KT8 9EW (☎ 01 979 6617)

DAVIS, Chloë Marion; *née* Pound; OBE (1975); da of Richard Henry Pound; *b* 15 Feb 1909; *m* 1928, Edward Thomas Davis; 1 s; *Career* memb Consumer Consultative Ctee EEC 1973-76, Cncl on Tribunals 1970-79, Consumer Standards Advsy Ctee of Br Standards Inst 1965-78 (chm 1970-73); chm Consumer Affrs Gp of Nat Organisations 1973-; *Style*— Mrs Edward Davis OBE; Auberville Cottage, 246 Dover Rd, Walmer, Kent

DAVIS, Sir Colin Rex; CBE (1965); s of Reginald George Davis (d 1944), of Weybridge, Surrey, by his w Lillian; *b* 25 Sept 1927; *Educ* Christ's Hosp, Royal Coll of Music; *m* 1, 1948 (m dis 1964), April Cantelo; 1 s, 1 da; m 2, 1964, Ashraf Naini, da of Abeolvahab Naini Assar (d 1978); 3 s, 2 da; *Career* formerly conductor BBC Scottish Orch, Sadler's Wells (musical dir 1961-65), chief conductor BBC Symphony Orch 1967-71, conducted Bayreuth 1977, musical dir Royal Opera House Covent Garden 1971- 1986, princ guest conductor Boston Symphony Orch 1972, London Symphony Orchestra 1974-, music dir Bayerischer Rundfunk Orch Munich since 1983; Commendatore of Repub of Italy 1976, Chev de la Legion d'Honneur 1982, Cdr's Cross of the Order of Merit of Fed Republic of Germany 1987; kt 1980; *Recreations* reading, gardening; *Clubs* Athenaeum; *Style*— Sir Colin Davis, CBE; c/o 7A Fitzroy Park, London N6 6HS; c/o Columbia Artists Mgmnt Inc., 165 W. 57th St, New York, NY 10019, USA

DAVIS, David William; s of George Henry Davis, of Beaconsfield, and Lucy Ada,*née* Tylee (d 1959); *b* 29 Oct 1942; *Educ* Emanuel School; *m* 25 Nov 1967, Jennifer, da of Wilfred Snell; 1 s (Kenneth b 28 May 1971), 1 da (Jacqueline 25 Feb 1970); *Career* CA 1966, ptnr Fryer Sutton Morris & Co 1967-, ptnr Fryer Whitehill & Co 1971-, ptnr Clark Whitehill 1982-; FCA 1975, MBIM 1975; *Recreations* badminton, bridge; *Style*— David Davis, Esq; Elm End House, Henton, Oxon OX9 4AH (☎ 0844 521 64); Clark Whitehill, 25 New Street sq, London EC4A 3LN (☎ 01 353 1577, fax 01 583 1720, car tel 0860 632 382, telex 887 422)

DAVIS, Donald Conway; s of George Davis (d 1981), of Liverpool, and Edna Ruth, *née* Conway; *b* 19 Mar 1932; *Educ* Quarry Bank HS; *m* 1965, Edwina Margaret Lawson, da of Edwin Lawson Spence (d 1955), of Lancs; 1 s (Simon b 1971), 3 da (Alexandra b 1966, Lucinda b 1968, Emily b 1986); *Career* army (2 Lt) 1955-57; CA; gp dir: Liverpool Daily Post & Echo Ltd (publishing and printing) 1962-69, Harrison & Son Ltd (printing) 1969-73; gp md Pitman plc (publishing and printing) 1973-82, md HunterPrint Gp plc; exec chm: Security Hldgs Ltd (printing) 1983-86; Metcalfe Cooper Ltd, HunterPrint Corporate & Financial Ltd; FCA; *Recreations* sailing, golf, shooting, cricket and rugby, reading, photography; *Clubs* Hon Artillery Co, Beaconsfield Golf, Royal Southampton Yacht Upper Thames Sailing, N London Rifle, Wasps Rugby Football, Lancashire County Cricket, Royal Soc of Artspy Worshipful Co of Stationers & Newspaper Makers; *Style*— Donald Davis, Esq; "Austenwood", Austenwood Common, Gerrards Cross, Buckinghamshire SL9 8NL; Metcalfe Cooper Ltd, New Roman House, 10 East Rd, London N1 6AJ (☎ 01 253 5010)

DAVIS, Frank; JP; s of Julius Davis (d 1970), of Hampstead Garden Suburb, and Dinah, *née* Benjamin; *b* 8 June 1920; *Educ* London Poly, Inns of Ct Sch of Law; *m* 4 Jan 1945, Irene, da of Isaac Lipman (d 1964); 2 s (Malcolm, Richard); *Career* Special Servs; memb Lloyds of London 1979, md various companies; cncllr Finchley BC 1956-65, ldr Finchley Cncl, cncllr London Borough of Barnet 1964-71; parly candidate Finchley 1966, Acton 1968; chm Wingate Charity Tst, fndr Wingate FC, govr Tel Aviv Univ, vice-pres Maccabi Assoc, memb Trades Advsy Cncl 1951-87; magistrate for Inner London 1963- (dep chm), memb appeals tribunals Dept of Social Servs, Dept of Employment, lay judge of Crown Ct (appeals), Mayor of Finchley 1963-64; memb The Hon Soc of Grays Inn 1953, Order of Independance Uganda 1964; *Recreations* travel, horticulture, avoiding public speaking; *Clubs* Rotary Int; *Style*— Frank Davis, Esq, JP

DAVIS, Grahame Watson; s of William Henry, of Chatham, Kent (d 1944), and Georgina, *née* Watson (d 1985); *b* 9 Sept 1934; *Educ* King's Sch Rochester; *m* 29 Aug 1963, Wendy Lovelace Davis, JP, da of Antony Lovelace Wagon, of Rochester (d 1978); 1 s (Piers b 1971), 1 da (Helena b 1966); *Career* slr; sr ptnr Hextall Erskine Co of London; dir: Complete Security Serv Ltd, Elmswood Commercial Conslts Ltd, Ashley Communications UK Ltd, Cheapside Conslts Ltd, Retail Discount Vouchers Ltd; memb The Law Soc; *Recreations* golf, cricket; *Clubs* Wig and Pen, Castle; *Style*— Grahame W Davis, Esq; 79 Eccleston Square, London SW1V 1PW (☎ 01 828 7011);

52-54 Leadenhall St, London EC3A 2AP (☎ 01 488 1424, fax 01 828 8341, car ☎ 0860 351311)

DAVIS, Herbert Edmund (Bert); s of Edmund Christopher Davis (d 1936), of Woodford Green, Essex, and Emily Maud, *née* Gurran (d 1949); *Educ* Business Coll; *m* 5 June 1937, (Lydia) Mary Elizabeth, da of Frank Henry Sturges (d 1942), of Surbiton, Surrey; 2 s (John Anthony b 30 Sept 1947, Charles Edmund b 29 Dec 1949), 1 da (Jane Ellen b 20 Aug 1938); *Career* served HG until 1941; RAOC: Lt 1941, Capt 1943, served 51 Div 1943-46, Maj 1945, demobbed 1946; chm Esher Laundry Ltd 1988-(md 1942-88), vice-pres Inst Br Launderers 1961-62; Freeman City of London 1978, fndr memb Worshipful Co Launderers 1960; Knight of the Order Orange Nassau with Swords Holland 1946; *Recreations* golf; *Clubs* Coombe Wood GC (former Capt 1973); *Style—* Bert Davis, Esq; 14 Berystede, Kingston upon Thames, Surrey KT1 7PQ (☎ 01 549 8631); Esher Laundry Ltd, Kingston upon Thames, Surrey KT1 3DT (☎01 546 6266)

DAVIS, Sir (Ernest) Howard; CMG (1969), OBE (1960); s of Edwin Howard Davis; *b* 22 April 1918; *Educ* Christian Bros Sch Gibraltar, Coll of St Joseph Blackpool, London Univ; *m* 1948, Marie, da of Gustave Bellotti; 2 s; *Career* dep govr Gibraltar 1971-78; kt 1978; *Style—* Sir Howard Davis, CMG, OBE; 36 South Barrack Rd, Gibraltar (☎ A 70358)

DAVIS, Ivor John Guest; CB (1983); s of Thomas Henry Davis (d 1963); *b* 11 Dec 1925; *Educ* Devonport HS, London Univ (external BSc); *m* 1954, Mary Eleanor, da of Robert Porter Thompson (d 1974); 2 children; *Career* govt service; comptroller-gen (patents, trade marks and designs) Patent Office 1978; pres admin cncl European Patent Office 1981; Govt Service Comptroller-Gen (Patents, Trade Marks and Designs) Patent Office 1978-85; pres Admin Cncl European Patent Office 1981-84; dir Common Law Inst of Intellectual Property 1986; *Recreations* music, gardening; *Style—* Ivor Davis, Esq, CB; 5 Birch Close, Eynsford, Dartford, Kent (☎ 0322 862725);

DAVIS, James Gresham; CBE (1988); s of Col Robert Davis, OBE, JP (d 1963), and Josephine Rebecca, *née* Edwards (d 1976); *b* 20 July 1928; *Educ* Bradfield, Clare Coll Cambridge (MA); *m* 24 Nov 1973, Adriana Johanna (Hanny), da of Evert Verhoef (d 1977), of Rhoon, Holland; 3 da (Mariske b 1974, Katrina b 1978, Charlotte b 1980); *Career* RN 1946-49; P & OSN Co 1952-72: Calcutta 1953-54, Kobe (Japan) 1954-56, Hong Kong 1956-57; dir: P & O Lines 1967-72, Kleinwort Benson Ltd 1973-88; chm: DFDS Ltd 1985-, Bromley Shipping plc 1989-; dir: Pearl Cruises of Scandinavia Inc 1982-86, Rodskog Shipbrokers (Hong Kong) Ltd 1983-88, Assoc Br Port Hldgs plc 1983-, Tport Devpt Gp plc 1984-, TIP Europe plc 1987-, Sedgwick Marine & Cargo Ltd 1988-; advsr Tjaereborg UK Ltd 1985-87; memb advsy bd: J Lauritjen A/S Copenhagen 1981-85, DFDS A/S Copenhagen 1981-85; pres: CIT 1981-82, World Ship Soc 1969 (1971, 1984, 1985, 1986), Inst of Freight Forwarders Ltd 1984-86, Harwich Lifeboat, Nat Waterways Tport Assoc 1986-; vice-pres: Br Maritime League 1984, Inst of Chartered Shipbrokers 1988; chm: Int Maritime Industs Forum 1981-, DRDS Ltd 1984-, Friends of the World Maritime Univ 1985-, Marine Soc 1987-, Simplification of Int Trade Procedures Bd 1987-, Br Rail Anglian Bd 1988-; cncl memb Missions to Seamen 1981-; memb: Baltic Exchange 1973, Greenwich Forum 1982; pres RNLI (Harwich) 1985-; chm Marine Soc; Freeman City of London 1986, Liveryman Worshipful Co of Shipwrights 1982, Asst to the Ct 1989; FCIT 1969, FNI 1985, FInstFF 1986, FRSA 1986, FCIS 1988; *Recreations* golf, family, ships; *Clubs* Hurlingham, Golfers, Harwich and Dovercourt Golf, Royal Calcutta Golf; *Style—* James Davis, Esq, CBE; Summer Lawn, Dovercourt, Harwich, Essex (☎ 0255 502981); 115 Woodsford Sq, Addison Rd, London W14 8DT (☎ 01 602 0675); 15a Hanover Street, London W1R 9HG (☎ 01 493 4559, fax 01 493 4668)

DAVIS, John Burton; s of Percy Oliver Davis (d 1980); *b* 20 Oct 1922; *Educ* Trinity Sch of John Whitgift, Croydon; Queen Mary Coll London Univ (BSc); *m* 1944, Irene Margaret, da of late William Victor Reid; 1 s, 1 da; *Career* Lt REME; sr exec Lead Industries Gp Ltd; dir: Assoc Lead Mfrs Ltd, Assoc Lead Mfrs (Pty) Ltd SA, Frys Metals (Pty) Ltd SA, Waldies Ltd Calcutta India, Tewin Wood Roads Ltd; *Style—* John Davies Esq; 5 Bishops Rd, Tewin Wood, Welwyn, Herts (☎ 043 879 597)

DAVIS, Sir John Gilbert; 3 Bt (UK 1946); s of Sir Gilbert Davis, 2 Bt (d 1973); *b* 17 August 1936; *Educ* Oundle, RNC Dartmouth; *m* 16 Jan 1960, Elizabeth Margaret, da of Robert Smith Turnbull, of Falkirk; 1 s (Richard b 1970), 2 da (Wendy, Linda); *Career* gp vice-pres Abitibi Price Inc (Toronto); chm Abitibi Price Sales Corpn (NY); *Recreations* squash, golf, reading, piano; *Clubs* Toronto, Rosedale Golf, Donalda; *Style—* Sir John Davis, Bt; 5 York Ridge Road, Willowdale, Ontario M2P 1R8, Canada

DAVIS, Sir John Henry Harris; CVO (1985); s of Sydney Myering Davis, of London, and Emily, *née* Harris; *b* 10 Nov 1906; *Educ* City of London Sch; *m* 1, 1926, Joan Buckingham; 1 s; m 2, 1947, Marion Gavid; 2 da; m 3, 1954 (m dis 1965), Dinah Sheridan; m 4, 1976, Mrs Felicity Rutland; *Career* Br Thomson Houston Gp 1931-38; joined Odeon Theatres Ltd (later The Rank Orgn) 1938, pres The Rank Orgn 1977-83 (chief exec 1962-74, chm 1962-77); dir Eagle Star Insur Co Ltd 1948-82, chm Southern TV Ltd 1968-76, jt pres Rank Xerox 1972-83, chm Nat Centre of Films for Children 1951-80; dir The Rank Fndn 1953; chm and tstee The Rank Prize Funds 1972; Hon DTech Loughborough 1975; Commandeur de l'Ordre de la Couronne (Belgium), KStJ; kt 1971; *Recreations* gardening, reading, travel, music; *Clubs* RAC; *Style—* Sir John Davis, CVO; 4 Selwood Terrace, London SW7; business: Suite 11/12 (2nd Floor), 25 Victoria St, London SW1H 0EX (☎ 01 222 4808)

DAVIS, John Patrick; s of Ralph Patrick Davis, of The Beacon, Pilgrims Way, Chaldon, Surrey, and Vivian Hilda, *née* Braund; *b* 12 June 1944; *Educ* Tonbridge Sch, Univ of Nottingham (BSc); *m* 5 Aug 1972, Fenella Irene, da of Guy Charles Madoc, CBE, KPM, of Close Foillan, Ramsey, Isle of Man; 1 s (Michael b 23 June 1975), 1 da (Rosemary b 11 June 1976); *Career* gen mangr mech engrg Redpath Dorman Long Ltd 1979-83; chief exec and gp md Aerospace Engrg plc 1985-; churchwarden; memb: CEng 1971, FIEE 1986, MIWeldE 1983; *Recreations* mountain walking, bee keeping; *Style—* John Davis, Esq; The Old Vicarage, Bourton, Swindon, Wiltshire SN6 8HZ (☎ 0793 782344); Aerospace Engineering plc, PO Box 25, South Marston Industrial Estate, Swindon, Wiltshire SN3 4TR (☎ 0793 827000, fax 0793 827578, car 0836 762669, telex 44317 VFPBEN G)

DAVIS, Jonathan Lewis; s of Cyril Harris Davis, BEM, of London, and Caroline, *née* Rubens; *b* 11 Nov 1948; *Educ* Clifton, City Univ (BSc), Cranfield Sch of Mgmnt (MBA); *m* 23 July 1972, Elizabeth, da of late Louis Natali; 2 s (Neil Louis b 1976, Andrew Henry b 1978), 1 da (Emma Rachel b 1983); *Career* production engr Reliance Cords and Cables 1972-74 (production mangr 1974-77, dir 1978-81), independent conslt 1981-82, joined The Guidehouse Gp plc 1982 (dir 1984-), md Guidehouse Ltd 1985-; Freeman of City of London, Liveryman of Worshipful Co of Musicians; MIProdE, MBIM; *Recreations* walking, scuba diving, reading, music; *Clubs* RAC; *Style—* Jonathan Davis, Esq; The Guidehouse Group plc, Vestry House, Greyfriars Passage, Newgate St, London EC1A 7BA (☎ 01 606 6321, fax 01 606 5722)

DAVIS, Kenneth John; s of Kenneth John Davis, of Marine Drive, Saltdean, Sussex, and Ethel Viola, *née* Miller; *b* 10 Mar 1943; *Educ* Addey and Stanhope GS; *m* 18 Feb 1967, Janette Doreen, da of John Henry Lighton; 1 s (Anthony Lee b 1971), 1 da (Elizabeth Ann b 1974); *Career* Alexander Stenhouse Ltd: regnl dir 1982-85, mktg dir 1985-86, chief operating offr (all UK and Eire branches) 1986-87, chief exec offr 1988-; dir Cawick Hall Insur Servs 1983-; FCII; *Books* Marketing Insurance a Practical Guide (jtly 1986); *Recreations* sailing; *Clubs* Little Ship; *Style—* Kenneth Davis, Esq; Alexander Stenhouse Ltd, 10 Devonshire Sq, London EC2M 4LE (☎ 01 621 9990, fax 01 621 9950, telex 920368 ASLDN G)

DAVIS, Lucinda Jane; s of Dennis Michael Davis, of W Sussex, and Wendy Francis, *née* Odgear; *b* 22 Mar 1958; *Educ* Haywards Heath GS, Kings Coll London Univ (LLB); *Career* called to the Bar Grays Inn 1981, SE Circuit; memb Hon Soc Grays Inn 1980; *Style—* Ms Lucinda Jane; Chichester Chambers 3 East Pallant Chichester W Sussex PO19 1TR (☎ 0243 784 538)

DAVIS, Prof Mark Herbert Ainsworth; s of Christopher Ainsworth Davis (d 1951), and Frances Emily *née* Marsden JP, of Loughborough, Leics; *b* 1 May 1945; *Educ* Oundle, Clare Coll Cambridge (BA, MA, ScD), Univ of California Berkeley (MS, PhD); *m* 15 Oct 1988, Jessica Isabella Caroline, da of Robert Sinclair Smith, of Broadstairs Kent; *Career* res asst electronics res lab Univ of California Berkeley 1969-71; Imperial Coll Univ of London: lectr 1971-79, reader 1979-84, prof system theory 1984-; visiting prof: Harvard Univ, MIT; FSS 1985; *Books* Linear Estimation and Stochastic Control (1977), Stochastic Modelling and Control (1985); *Recreations* classical music (violin and viola); *Style—* Prof Mark Davis; 11 Chartfield Ave, London SW15 6DT (☎ 01 789 7677); Dept of Electrical Engrg, Imperial Coll, London SW7 2BT (☎ 01 589 511, ext 5200)

DAVIS, Martin Mitchell; s of Kenneth Bertram Davis (d 1983), of Alcester, Warwickshire, and Emily Mary Tillett, MBE, *née* Gateley; *b* 30 May 1943; *Educ* Ampleforth, Univ Coll Oxford (MA); *m* 21 June 1975, Caroline Ann, da of John James Yorke Scarlett (d 1984), of Kingsbridge, S Devon; 3 s (Edmund b 1976, Leo b 1977, Thomas b 1979), 1 da (Agnes b 1982); *Career* slr; ptnr Wiggin & Co Cheltenham 1974-77, fndr Davis & Co; pres Cheltenham Legal Assoc 1987-88, chm Cheltenham Cncl of Churches 1977-78, ctee memb Glos & Wilts Law Soc; *Recreations* gardening, walking, photography, listening to music, cycling, recycling; *Clubs* Pax Christi, Newman Assoc; *Style—* Martin Davis, Esq; Syreford, Nr Andoversford, Cheltenham, Glos (☎ 0242 820474); 25 Rodney Rd, Cheltenham (☎ 0242 235202, fax 0242 224716, telex 437244 MINTL/G)

DAVIS, Sir Maurice Herbert; OBE (1953), QC (1965); *b* 30 April 1912,St Kitts,; *m* Kathleen; 1 s, 5 da; *Career* memb Exec Cncl St Kitts, dep pres Gen Legve Cncl and memb Fed Exec Cncl, chief justice W Indies Assoc States Supreme Ct and Supreme Ct of Grenada 1975-80; kt 1975; *Style—* Hon Sir Maurice Davis, OBE, QC; PO Box 31, Basseterre, St Kitts, W Indies

DAVIS, Dr Michael; s of William James Davis (d 1955); *b* 9 June 1923; *Educ* Exeter Univ (BSc), London Univ (BSc), Bristol Univ (PhD), Toronto Univ; *m* 1951, Helena Hobbs, *née* Campbell; *Career* served 1943-46, Lt RNVR, 4 Cruiser Sqdn Br Pacific Fleet (despatches); UK Atomic Energy Authority (commercial dir, technical advsr) 1956-73; dir: EEC Cmmn Brussels, Nuclear Energy and Electricity 1973-81, Energy Saving, Alternative Energy Sources, Electricity and Heat 1981; FInstP FIMM, CPhys, CEng; *Recreations* sculpture; *Clubs* Utd Oxford and Cambridge; *Style—* Dr Michael Davis

DAVIS, Norman Harold; s of Tobias Davis, of Edgware, Middlesex, and Sybil, *née* Bernstein (d 1984); *b* 16 July 1931; *Educ* Strodes Foundation Egham Surrey; *m* 10 June 1956, Evelyn, da of Harry Lester (d 1954), of Finchley, London; 1 s (Robin b 1961); *Career* CA, sr ptnr Lane Heywood Davis 1955; dir: Yale and Valor Fin 1969, Dixon Strand plc (chm 1978); vice-chm Jewish Blind Soc; *Clubs* Oriental; *Style—* Norman H Davis, Esq; 30 Church Mount, Hampstead Garden Suburb, London N2 ORP (☎ 01 455 8977); Lane Heywood Davis, 47 Queen Anne Street, London W1M ODN (☎ 01 486 5001, fax 01 935 0453, telex 892596; car ☎ 0836 596 614)

DAVIS, Penelope Jane; da of Anthony John Davis, of Cambridge, and Jean Margaret, *née* Stone; *b* 25 July 1960; *Educ* Cambridgeshire HS For Girls, Cambridge Coll Arts and Tech, Univ of Lancaster (BA Hons); *Career* mangr Siggi Hats 1984, weekly columnist Fashion Weekly 1988-, md Davis & Hesbacher Ltd; *Recreations* riding, cooking, reading, cinema; *Style—* Miss Penelope Davis; 7 Racton Rd, Fulham, London SW6 1LW (☎ 01 323 1292)

DAVIS, Peter John; s of John Stephen Davis, and Adriantie, *née* de Baat; *b* 23 Dec 1941; *Educ* Shrewsbury Sch; *Career* mgmnt trainee and salesman Ditchburn Orgn 1959-65, mkt and sales Gen Foods Ltd 1965-72, Fitch Lovell Ltd 1973-76, mktg dir Key Markets 1973-76, dir and asst md J Sainsbury plc 1976-86; chief exec Reed Int plc 1986-; dir Granada gp 1987-, dep chm fin dvpt bd NSPCC, govr Duncombe Sch Hertford;; *Recreations* sailig, swimming, opera, ballet, wine; *Clubs* Carlton, Trearddur Bay Sailing (Cdre 1982-84); *Style—* Peter Davis, Esq; Reed House, 83 Piccadilly, London W1A 1EJ (☎ 01 491 8279)

DAVIS, Peter Kerrich Byng; s of Frank C Davis, MC (d 1979), and Barbara, *née* Hartshorne; *b* 4 May 1933; *Educ* Felsted, London Univ, St Thomas' Hosp Med Sch (MB BS); *m* 24 April 1965, Jennifer Anne, da of Brig-Gen (Creemer) Paul Clarke (d 1971); 1 s (Paul b 14 Aug 1966), 1 da (Emma b 9 Aug 1968); *Career* sr registrar in plastic surgery Churchill Hosp Oxford 1968-71; conslt plastic surgn (1971-): St Thomas' Hosp London, Queen Marys' Hosp Roehampton, Kingston Hosp, St Stephen's Hosp London; Br Assoc of Aesthetic Plastic Surgns: memb 1977-, vice pres 1981, pres 1982-84, hon sec 1988-; memb: BMA 1959, BAPS 1971, RSM 1971, ICPRS 1971, ISAPS 1979; *Books* contrib: Operative Surgery (1982), Maxillo - Facial Injuries (1985); *Recreations* fishing; *Style—* Peter Davis, Esq; Woodley End, Coombe Park, Kingston-on-Thames, Surrey (☎ 01 549 2691); 97 Harley St, London W1 (☎ 01 486 4976, car tel 0860 333 472)

DAVIS, Philip; s of David Davis (d 1949), of Forest Gate, and Amelia, *née* Rees (d 1949); *b* 14 Dec 1919; *Educ* Clarkes Coll; *m* 19 Aug 1968, Barbara Edith, da of Alfred Millward, of Kidderminster; *Career* RSC TA 1938, mobilised BEF 1939, evacuated from Dunkirk 1940, Home Serv WO Signals 1941, demobbed 1946; md own company controlling chain of retail fish and poultry shops, chm London Fish and Poultry Retailers Assoc 1968, pres Nat Fedn Fishmongers 1973, buyer and mangr fish dept Barkers of Kensington 1977, fish conslt J Sainsbury 1982-89; town cncllr Staines 1956-57, chm numerous ctees, Staines CC; Freeman City of London 1956, Liveryman Worshipful Co Fishmongers 1959; *Recreations* chess; *Style—* Philip Davis, Esq; 15 Matlock Ct, Kensington Park Rd, London W11 3BS

DAVIS, Hon Mr Justice; Sir (Dermot) Renn; OBE (1971); s of Capt Eric Renn Davis, OBE (d 1945), of Highlands Hotel, Molo, Kenya, and Norah Alexandrina, *née* Bingham (d 1967); *b* 20 Nov 1928; *Educ* Prince of Wales Sch Nairobi, Oxford (BA); *m* 1984, Mary Helen Farquharson, da of Brig Thomas Farquharson Ker Howard, DSO (d 1963), of Goldenhayes, Woodlands, Hants, and wid of William James Pearce; *Career* barr; crown counsel Kenya 1956-62, attorney-gen Solomon Islands and legal advsr to high cmmr for Western Pacific 1962-73, Br Judge Anglo-French Condominium of the New Hebrides 1973-76; chief justice: Solomon Islands and Tuvalu 1976-80, Gilbraltar 1980-86, Falkland Islands 1987; kt 1981; *Clubs* Utd Oxford and Cambridge, Muthaiga Country (Nairobi); *Style—* The Hon Mr Justice Davis, OBE; Ivy House, Shalbourne, nr Malrborough, Wilts SN8 3QH; Supreme Ct, Stanley, Falkland Islands

DAVIS, Air Vice-Marshal Robert Leslie; CB (1984); s of Sidney Davis; *b* 22 Mar 1930; *Educ* Woolsingham GS, Bede Sch Collegiate, Sunderland Co Durham; *m* 1956, Diana, *née* Bryant; 1 s, 1 da; *Career* Cdr RAF staff and air attaché, Br Defence Staff Washington DC 1977-80, admin of the Sovereign Base Areas and Cdr Br Forces and Air Officer Cmdg Cyprus 1980-83, ret 1983; *Clubs* RAF; *Style—* Air Vice-Marshal Robert Davis, CB; High Garth Farm, Witton-le-Wear, Co Durham

DAVIS, Robert Michael Pennick; *b* 26 July 1942; *Educ* Brighton Coll; *m* 11 March 1973, Suzanne Margaret; 2 s (Steven David Pennick b 2 Aug 1974, Mark Richard b 5 Aug 1976); *Career* Smith New Ct plc (formerly Smith Bros) 1960-73 (dir 1973-); membership sec Totteridge Manor Assoc; memb Stock Exchange 1965; *Recreations* golf, cricket; *Clubs* MCC, Gresham; *Style—* Robert Davis, Esq; Smith New Ct plc, 24 Chetwynd House St Swithins Lane, London EC4N 2AE (☎ 01 283 0151, fax 01 623 3947, car telephone 0836 234 658)

DAVIS, Rodney Colin; s of (Arthur) Cyril Gordon Davis of 13 Glenleigh Park, Warblington, Havant, Hants, and Phyllis Eleanor Margaret Griffiths, *née* Roberts (d 1977); *b* 9 July 1940; *Educ* Churcher's Coll Petersfield, King's Coll Univ of London (LLB), Tulane Univ New Orleans USA (LLM); *m* 4 Sept 1965, Elizabeth Jeanne, da of Arthur William Richards of Englefield, Sturminster Newton, Dorset; 1 s (Ian b 1968), 1 da (Sarah b 1970); *Career* asst slr Durham CC 1965-70, asst clerk Berks CC 1970-74, ptnr Coward Chance 1979-87 (asst slr 1974-79); ptnr Clifford Chance 1987-; memb: City of London Slr Co; *Recreations* gardening; *Style—* Rodney Davis, Esq; Bridge House, Thames Road, Goring, Reading RG8 9AY (☎ 0491 872207); Blackfriars House, 19 New Bridge St, London EC4 (☎ 01 353 0211, fax 01 489 0046)

DAVIS, (Richard) Simon; s of Peter Richard Davis, DSC, of Busby Lodge, Chartridge Lane, Chesham, Bucks, and Evelyn Janet Hill *née* Richmond; *b* 29 July 1956; *Educ* Wellington Sch Somerset, Leicester Univ (LLB); *m* 26 July 1980, Caroline Jane, da of Hugh Robert Neal, of Bucks; 1 s (Toby, b 1987); *Career* barr 1978; *Recreations* rugby, squash, swimming, tennis; *Style—* Simon Davis, Esq; 3 Temple Gardens, Temple, London (☎ 01 353 3533, fax 01 353 8504)

DAVIS, Stanley Clinton; s of Sidney Davis; *b* 6 Dec 1928; *Educ* Hackney Downs Sch, Mercers Sch, King's Coll London; *m* 1954, Frances Jane, *née* Lucas; 1 s, 3 da; *Career* MP (Lab) Hackney Central 1970-83, parly under-sec Trade 1974-79, oppn front bench spokesman Trade 1979-81, Foreign and Cwlth Affrs 1981-83; fought Portsmouth Langstone 1955, Yarmouth 1959 & 1964; memb APEX & Hackney Rotary Club, pres Br Multiple Sclerosis Soc (Hackney Branch), cllr (Hackney) 1959-71, mayor Hackney 1968-69; slr 1953-84; memb Cmmn of European Communities (responsible for transport, environmental and nuclear safety) 1985; *Books* joint author Report of a Br Parliamentary Delegation (1982); *Recreations* reading political biographies, golf, watching assoc football; *Style—* Clinton Davis, Esq; Commission of the European Communities, rue de la Loi 200, 1049 Brussels

DAVIS, Prof Stanley Stewart; s of William Stanley Davis, of Warwick, and Joan, *née* Lawson; *b* 17 Dec 1942; *Educ* Warwick Sch, London Univ (BPharm, PhD, DSc); *m* 24 Nov 1984, Lisbeth, da of Erik Illum (d 1986), of Denmark; 3 s (Benjamin b 1970, Nathaniel b 1974, Daniel b 1984); *Career* lectr London Univ 1967-70, sr lectr Aston Univ 1970-75, Lord Trent prof of pharmacy Nottingham Univ 1975-; FRSC, fell Royal Pharmacaeutical Soc; *Books* Imaging in Drug Research (1982), Microspheres in Drug Therapy (1984), Delivery Systems for Peptides (1987), Site Specific Drug Delivery (1986), Polymers for Controlled Drug Delivery (1987); *Recreations* skiing, tennis, painting; *Style—* Prof Stanley Davis; 19 Cavendish Crescent North, The Park, Nottingham NG7 1BA; Department of Pharmaceutical Sciences, Nottingham University, University Park, Nottingham (☎ 0602 484848 ext 3217)

DAVIS, Steven Ilsley; s of Lt-Col George Ilsley Davis, of Tinmouth, Vermouth, USA, and Marion Brown Davis; *b* 6 Nov 1934; *Educ* Phillips Acad Mass USA, Amherst Coll Mass USA (BA), Harvard Business Sch (MBA); *m* 27 Feb 1960, Joyce Ann, *née* Hirtz, da of Theodore S Hirtz (d 1962), of NY; 2 s (Andrew Tinmouth b 1962, Christopher Stamer b 1963), 1 da (Stephanie b 1975); *Career* private USA Army Reserve 1958; asst vice pres JP Morgan & Co 1959-66, US Agency for Int Devpt 1966-68, first vice pres Bankers Trust Co 1968-72, md First Int Bankshares Ltd 1972-79, md Davis Int Banking Conslts 1979-; asst dir US govt Agency for Int Devpt 1966-68; Hon Phi Beta Kappa Amherst Coll; *Books* The Eurobank (1975), The Management of Int Banks (1979), Excellence in Banking (1985), Managing Change in the Excellent Banks (1989); *Recreations* skiing, tennis, hiking; *Clubs* Roehampton; *Style—* Steven Davis, Esq; 66 South Edwardes Sq, London W8 (☎ 01 602 6348); 15 King St, London SW1 (☎ 01 839 9255, fax 01 839 9250)

DAVIS, Mrs André; Sue; *see*: Thomson, Sue

DAVIS, Terence (Terry) Anthony Gordon; MP (Lab) Birmingham, Hodge Hill 1983-; s of Gordon Davis; *b* 5 Jan 1938; *Educ* King Edward VI GS Stourbridge, UCL, Univ of Michigan; *m* 1963, Anne, *née* Cooper; 1 s, 1 da; *Career* contested (Lab): Stechford March 1977 (by-election), Bromsgrove 1970, 1971, 1974 (twice); MP Bromsgrove 1971- 1974, MP (Lab) Stechford 1979-1983; oppn front bench spokesman: health serv 1981-83, Tresy and econ affrs 1983-86, indust 1987-; memb Public Accounts Ctee 1987-; memb MSF, former memb Yeovil RDC, business exec (MBA) and motor indust mangr; *Style—* Terry Davis, Esq, MP; c/o House of Commons, London SW1

DAVIS, Sir Thomas Robert Alexander Harries; KBE (1980); s of Sidney Thomas Davis; *b* 11 June 1917; *Educ* King's Coll Auckland, Otago Univ Med Sch (MB, ChB 1945), Sch of Tropical Medicine Sydney Univ; Harvard Sch of Public Health (Master of Public Health); *m* 1, 1940, Myra Lydia Henderson, 3 s; m 2, 1979 Pa Tepaeru Aviki; *Career* MO and surg specialist Cook Islands Med Serv 1945-52 (chief MO 1948); dept nutrition Harvard Sch 1952-55, chief dept environmental Med Fairbanks 1955-56; dir: Environmental Med Fort Knox 1956-61, Natick 1961-63; res exec Arthur D Little Inc 1963-71; formed Democratic Party of Cook Islands 1981; patron: Cook Islands Sports Assoc (men's Olympic Ctee), Boxing Assoc; vis dir Bishop Museum Hawaii; Pa Tu Te Rangi Ariki 1979; Prime Minister Cook Islands 1978; FRSTM and H , FRSH; memb Royal Soc Med (1960); Silver Jubilee Medal; Order of Merit Fed Repub of Germany 1978; *Books* Doctor to the Islands (1954), Makutu (1956), numerous scientific pubns; *Clubs* Avatiu Sports (Patron), Lions (pres), Rarotonga Yacht (Patron), Avatiu Cricket (Patron), Wellington Club (NZ), Harvard (Boston USA); *Style—* Sir Thomas Robert Davis, KBE; Aremangoi, Rarotonga, Cook Islands

DAVIS, William; *b* 6 Mar 1933; *Educ* City of London Coll; *m* 1967, Sylvette Jouclas; *Career* former financial ed: Evening Standard, Sunday Express, The Guardian; presenter BBC TV's Money Programme 1967-69, ed Punch 1969-79, ed High Life (BA in-flight magazine) 1973, dir Fleet Hldgs and Morgan Grampian 1979-81, ed-in-ch Financial Weekly 1980-81, chm and editorial dir Headway Publications, dir Maxwell Communications (USA), dir Thomas Cook; broadcaster, columnist, author; *Books* Three Years Hard Labour, Merger Money Talks, Have Expenses Will Travel, It's No Sin to be Rich, The Best of Everything (ed), Money in the 1980's: How to make it, how to keep it, The Rich, Fantasy, The Corporate Infighters Handbook, The Supersalesman's Handbook, The Innovators; *Style—* William Davis, Esq

DAVIS, Hon William Grenville; QC (Can); s of Albert Grenville; *b* 30 July 1929; *Educ* Brampton HS, Univ Coll, Univ of Toronto, Osgoode Hall Law Sch; *m* 1, 1953, Helen, *née* Macphee (d 1962); m 2, 1963, Kathleen Louise, *née* Mackay; 2 s, 3 da; *Career* called to Bar of Ontario 1955; memb (C) Provincial Parliament; min of education 1962-71, min of univ affairs 1964-71; premier of Ontario and pres of the Council Ontario 1971; leader Progressive (C) Party of Ontario; *Style—* The Hon William Davis, QC; Office of the Premier of Ontario, Parliament Buildings, Toronto, Ontario, Canada; 61 Main St South, Brampton, Ontario, Canada

DAVIS, William Herbert; s of William Davis (d 1972); *b* 27 July 1919; *Educ* Waverley GS, Birmingham Coll of Technol, Univ of Aston (BSc); *m* 1945, Barbara Mary Joan, da of W Summerfield (d 1963); 1 da; *Career* serv WWII S/Sgt Army: France, Belgium, M East and Italy; engr; dep md BMC 1961-68; md Triumph and Rover Triumph 1968-73; dir of manufacture Br Leyland 1973-75; conslt engr BL (UK) 1975-83 (ret); FIMechE, FIIM,, SME(USA); *Recreations* photography, gardening, travel; *Clubs* Austin Ex-Apprentices, Aston Graduates; *Style—* William Davis Esq, Esq; Arosa, The Holloway, Alvechurch, Worcs B48 7QA (☎ 0527 66187)

DAVIS-GOFF, Sir Robert William; 4 Bt (UK 1905); s of Sir Ernest Davis-Goff, 3 Bt (d 1980); *b* 12 Sept 1955; *Educ* Cheltenham; *m* 1978, Nathalie Sheelagh, da of Terence Chadwick, of Lissen Hall, Swords, Co Dublin; 2 s (William b 1980, Henry b 1986), 1 da (Sarah b 1982); *Career* picture dealer, property mgmnt.; *Recreations* shooting; *Clubs* Kildare Street & University; *Style—* Sir Robert Davis-Goff, Bt; office: 17 Duke Street, Dublin 2, Repub of Ireland

DAVISON; *see*: Biggs-Davison

DAVISON, Prof Alan Nelson; s of Alfred Nelson Davison (d 1950), of Leigh-On-Sea, Essex, and Ada Elizabeth, *née* Dahl (d 1985); *b* 6 June 1925; *Educ* Westcliff HS, Univ Coll Nottingham (B Pharm), Birkbeck Coll London (BSc); *m* 3 July 1948, Patricia Joyce, da of Ernest Frederick Pickering (d 1932); 1 s (Andrew Nelson b 1957), 2 da (Heather Jane (Mrs Gilbert) b 1952, Ann Catherine (Mrs Jenkins) b 1954); *Career* MRC toxicology unit 1950-54, MRC exchange fell Sorbonne Paris 1954- 55, Roche Prods Welwyn Gdn City 1955-57, res fell dept of Pathology Guy's Hospital Med Sch 1957-60, prof of biochemistry Charing Cross Hosp Med Sch 1965-71; Inst of Neurology prof of neurochemistry and chemical pathology 1971-82, former sec Biochemical Soc, chief ed of Neurochemistry, memb editorial bd of several learned jls; Freeman City of London 1988, Worshipful Co of Pewterers 1988; church Warden C of E; FRC Path; memb: Biochemical Soc, Euro and Int Neurochemical Soc; *Books* Biochemistry of Neurological Diseases (1976), Myelination (1970), Biochemical Correlates of Brain Structure and Function (1977), Applied Neurochemistry (1968); *Recreations* choral singing, painting; *Style—* Prof Alan Davison; Drivers, 54 High St, Stock, Ingatestone, Essex CM4 9BW (☎ 0277 840 362); Dept Neurochemistry, Inst of Neurology, Queen Square, London WC1N 3BG (☎ 01 829 8722, fax 01 278 5069)

DAVISON, Arthur Clifford Percival; CBE (1974); s of Aurthur MacKay Davison, (d 1970), of Montreal, Canada, and Hazel Edith, *née* Smith, (d 1978); *b* 25 Sept 1918; *Educ* McGill Music Conservatory Montreal, Conservataire de Musique Montreal, RAM; *m* 1, 1950 (m dis 1977) Barbara June, *née* Hildred; 1 s (Darrell Richard), 2 da (Beverley Ann Mildred, Lynne Barbara); m 2, 2 March 1978, Elizabeth, da of Richard Blanche; *Career* dir and dep leader London Philharmonic Orch 1957-65, asst conductor Bournemouth Symphony Orch 1965-66; musical dir and conductor: Little Symphony of London 1964-, Virtuosi of England 1970-; guest conductor of orchs 1964-: London Philharmonic, London Symphony, Philharmonia, Royal Philharmonic, BBC Orchs, Birmingham Symphony, Bournemouth Symphony and Sinfonietta, Ulster, Royal Liverpool Philharmonic, New York City Ballet, CBC Radio and Television Orchs, Royal Danish Ballet; dir and conductor Nat Youth Orch of Wales 1966-, fndr Authur Davison Concerts for Children 1966, conductor and Lectr Goldsmith's Coll London Univ 1971-, govr and guest lectr Welsh Coll of Music and Drama 1973-, EMI/CFP award for sale of half a million classical records 1973, Gold Disc for sale of one million classical records 1977, European tour recorded for BBC TV; articles in various musical jls; Mus M Wales Univ 1974; FRAM 1966, FRSA 1977; *Style—* Arthur Davison, Esq, CBE; Glencairn, Shepherd's Hill, Merstham, Surrey RH1 3AD (☎ 07374 2206 & 4434)

DAVISON, Barry George; s of William Davison; *b* 12 Dec 1935; *m* 1960, Jean Doreen; 3 da (Tracy b 1962, Katharine b 1964, Joanne b 1970); *Career* 2 Lt RA; chm and md Foster Bros Clothing plc 1978-85; chm Non Foods Policy Ctee Retail Consortium 1981-85; dir chm Crossland Lighting plc 1987, chm John Partridge Sales Ltd 1986; dir: Neville Industrial Securities Ltd 1986, MV Imports and Exports Ltd 1987, Midlands Residential Corpn plc 1988; FCA; *Recreations* golf; *Clubs* Blackwell GC, Thurlestone GC; *Style—* Barry Davison, Esq; The Firs, Lovelace Avenue,

Solihull, West Midlands (☎ 021 705 2850); 7 Links Court, Thurlestone, Devon (☎ 054 857 770)

DAVISON, Clive Phillip; s of Maj Laurence Napier Davison (d 1966), and Rosa Rachel Louisa, *née* Parker; *b* 14 Mar 1944; *Educ* Grange Sch, Christchurch, Dorset, Poly of the Bank and Thames Poly; *m* 30 March 1968 (m dis 1982) Sandra, da of Thomas Keith Lord of Billericay Essex; ptnr, Jane Elise, da of Roger Howorth, of Shooters Hill, London; 1 s (Alexander Napier); *Career* chartered architect, assoc Trehearne & Norman Preston & Ptnrs 1974-77, ptnr Trehearnes 1977-79, co sec and dir I M Coleridge Ltd 1987, design and site supervisor of Min of P T T Riyadh 1977-83, princ Davison Assoc, RIBA; *Recreations* squash, guitar, reading, skiing; *Clubs* CGA, Christchurch and Kingston Rowing, Sandown Park; *Style—* Clive Davison, Esq; 3 Croft Rd, Christchurch, Dorset BH23 3QQ (☎ 0202 479341); 'Priory Chambers', 6 Church St, Christchurch, Dorset (☎ 0202 470176)

DAVISON, Derek Harold; CBE (1985); s of John George Davison (d 1959), and Lillian, *née* Riley (d 1966); *b* 26 July 1923; *Educ* Queen Elizabeth GS, Southampton Univ; *m* 1, 1946, Germaine, da of Emile Riffard (d 1970), of Egypt; 2 s (John b 1947, Guy b 1949); m 2, 1979, Lavinia, da of Roland Wellicome (d 1960), of Bournemouth; *Career* RAF 1941-46, pilot bomber cmd and pathfinder sqdn M East, Italy; M East communication sqdn Heliopolis Egypt; Br S American Airways Corpn-BOAC 1947-53, Pakistan Int Airlines 1953-57, El Al 1957-62; chief pilot Britannia Airways 1962, ops dir and chief pilot 1965, asst md and chief pilot 1973, md 1976, chm and chief exec 1982, ret 1988; dir Thomson Travel Ltd 1976; Britannia & European Independent Airlines formed Assoc des Compagnies Aériennes de la Communauté Européenne (ACE), pres ACE 1980 and 1981, Nat dir ACE UK 1982-88; chm Emeritus memb Airworthiness Requirements Bd 1985; pres Int Air Carrier Assoc (IACA); chm Br Air Tport Assoc; Queen's Commendation for Valuable Servs in the Air 1977; *Recreations* private flying, sailing, skiing, swimming; *Clubs* RAF; *Style—* Derek Davison; British Air Transport Association, 5/6 Pall Mall East, London SW1 (☎ 01 930 0036/01 930 5746, telex 925967 BATRAN G)

DAVISON, Hon Mrs; Elizabeth Slater; da of Baron Slater, BEM (Life Peer d 1977); *b* 1934; *m* 1955, Frank Davison; *Style—* The Hon Mrs Davison; 1 Seymour Grove, Eaglescliffe, Co Durham

DAVISON, (George) Gordon; s of George Robert Davison (d 1984), and Winifred Margaret, *née* Collie (d 1982); *b* 30 Nov 1934; *Educ* Kings Sch Tynemouth, Kings Coll, Univ of Durham (BSc); *m* 1, 30 Dec 1961, Anne; 1 da (Susan b 1970), 1 s (Peter b 1974); m 2, 4 July 1969, Judith Agnes; *Career* chm Berghaus Ltd 1966-; *Recreations* climbing, skiing, windsurfing, diving, squash; *Style—* Gordon Davison, Esq; 1 Dene Grange, 23 Lindisfarne Rd, Jesmond, Newcastle upon Tyne NE2 2HE (☎ 091 281 4151); 34 Dean St, Newcastle upon Tyne NE1 1PG (☎ 091 232 3561, fax 091 216 0922, telex 537728 BGHAUS G)

DAVISON, Hon (William) Kensington; DSO, DFC; yr s of 1 Baron Broughshane, KBE (d 1953); *b* 1914; *Educ* Shrewsbury Sch, Magdalen Coll Oxford; *Career* barr Inner Temple; served in World War II as w/Cdr RAFVR; *Clubs* Carrick; *Style—* The Hon Kensington Davison DSO, DFC; 3 Godfrey St, London SW3 3TA (☎ 01 352 7826)

DAVISON, Rt Hon Sir Ronald Keith; GBE (1978), CMG (1975), PC (1978); s of Joseph James Davison; *b* 16 Nov 1920; *Educ* Auckland Univ (LLB); *m* 1948, Jacqueline May, da of the late Charles Edward Carr; 2 s (1 decd), 1 da; *Career* barrister and slr 1948, QC NZ 1965; memb NZ Law Soc Cncl 1964-66; pres Auckland District Law Soc 1965-66 (memb cncl 1959); chm Montana Wines Ltd 1971-78; memb: Legal Aid Bd 1968-78, Aircrew Industl Tribunal 1971-78, Environmental Cncl 1969-74; dir NZ Insurance Co Ltd 1975-78; chief justice of NZ 1978-89; *Recreations* golf, fishing; *Clubs* Northern (Auckland), Wellington; *Style—* The Rt Hon Chief Justice Sir Ronald Davison, GBE, CMG; 68 Rama Cres, Khandallan, Wellington, New Zealand

DAVSON; *see*: Glyn, Bt, Sir Anthony

DAVSON, Christopher Michael Edward; s of Sir Edward Davson, 1 Bt, KCMG (d 1937); hp to bro Sir Anthony Glyn, 2 Bt, *qv*; *b* 26 May 1927; *Educ* Eton; *m* 1, 2 June 1962 (m dis 1972), Evelyn (*née* Wardrop); 1 s (George Trenchard Simon b 1964); m 2, 1975, Kate, da of Ludo Foster, of Greatham Manor, Pulborough, Sussex; *Career* Capt, formerly Welsh Guards; formerly finance dir of cos in the Booker McConnell Gp; dir Kate Foster Ltd; Liveryman Worshipful Co of Musicians FCA; *Recreations* Archaeocology; *Style—* Christopher Davson Esq; 5 Market Rd, Rye, Sussex

DAVY; *see*: Arthington-Davy

DAVY, Horace George; MBE (1970); s of Charles Horace (d 1972), and Florence Maude, *née* Weedon (d 1960); *b* 25 Feb 1927; *Educ* Sir John Cass Fndn Sch, Alleyn's Coll, City of London Coll; *m* 2 July 1955, Gabrielle Mary, da of Thomas Joseph Reginald Scotman (d 1971); 1 s (Christopher b 1957), 1 da (Kim b 1959); *Career* RAFVR 1944-45, RNVR 1945, RASC 1946-48, Warrant Offr (M East) City of London Yeo (Rough Riders) TA 1950-53; joined UK Chamber of Shipping 1941 (asst sec 1960, sec 1963, asst gen mangr 1966, gen mangr 1969); dep dir Gen Cncl Br Shipping 1975 (dir 1980, dep dir-gen 1987); sec Br Shipping Fedn 1987; gen mangr Br Motor Ship Owners Assoc 1981-86; dir BOSVA 1985; organiser first Tanker Safety Conf 1967; *Books* author articles on Merchant Shipping and Def Including Brassey's Guide; *Recreations* Abbotsbury Shetland Pony Stud; *Clubs* Baltic Exchange, The Anchorites; *Style—* Horace Davy, MBE; Highcroft Paddocks, Hempstead Rd, Bovingdon, Herts HP3 0HE (☎ (0442) 832653); Gen Cncl of Br Shipping, 30-32 St Mary Axe, London EC3A 8ET (☎ 01 283 2922)

DAVY, Patricia Mary; da of Col Sir John Dick-Lauder, 11 Bt, DL (d 1958), and Phyllis Mary, *née* Iggulden (d 1976); *b* 29 April 1920; *Educ* Oxenfoord Castle, Abbots Hill, Brillantmont (Lausanne); *m* 11 June 1940, Major Ian Alastair George, s of A J G Davy (d 1985), of Inverness-shire; 1 s (Alastair b 1944), 4 da (Charlotte b 1942, Jean b 1947, Lila b 1950, Alice b 1961); *Career* FANY 1939-41; exec J Walter Thompson (Lexington) 1968-82; *Recreations* gardening, fishing; *Style—* Mrs Patricia M Davy,; Chilton Brook House, 24 Callis Street, Clare, Suffolk (☎ 0787 277273)

DAWBARN, Sir Simon Yelverton; KCVO (1980), CMG (1976); s of Frederic Dawbarn, and Maud Louise, *née* Mansell; *b* 16 Sept 1923; *Educ* Oundle, CCC Cambridge; *m* 1948, Shelby Montgomery,*née* Parker; 1 s, 2 da; *Career* WWII Reconaissance Corps; FCO 1949-53 and 1961-71; served: Brussels, Prague, Tehran, Algiers, Athens; FCO 1971-75, head of W African Dept and non-resident ambass to Chad 1973-75, consul-gen Montreal 1975-78, ambass to Morocco 1978-82; *Style—* Sir Simon Dawbarn, KCVO, CMG

DAWE, Roger James; CB (1988), OBE (1970); s of Harry James, and Edith Mary, *née* Heard; *b* 26 Feb 1941; *Educ* Hardye's Sch Dorchester, Fitzwilliam House Cambridge; *m* 1965, Ruth Day, da of Frederic Jolliffe; 1 s (Mark b 1968), 1 da (Caroline b 1971); *Career* joined Miny of Lab 1962, private sec to: PM 1966-70, Secs of State for Employment 1972-74; under sec Manpower Servs Cmmn 1981-84, dep sec Dept of Employment 1985-88, dir gen Trg Agency 1988-; *Recreations* tennis, soccer, theatre, music; *Style—* Roger Dawe, Esq, CB, OBE; Dept of Employment, Caxton House, Tothill St, London SW1 (☎ 01 213 3900)

DAWES, Prof Edwin Alfred; s of Harold Dawes (d 1939), of Goole, Yorks, and Maude, *née* Barker (d 1967); *b* 6 July 1925; *Educ* Goole GS, Leeds Univ (BSc, PhD, DSc); *m* 18 Dec 1950, Amy, da of Robert Dunn Rogerson (d 1980), of Gateshead; 2 s (Michael b 1955, Adrian b 1963); *Career* lectr in Biochemistry Leeds Univ 1950 (asst lectr 1947-50), sr lectr in Biochemistry Glasgow Univ 1961-63 (lectr 1951-61); Hull Univ: Reckitt Prof of Biochemistry 1963-, dean of Sci 1968-70, pro vice-chllr 1977-80, dir Biomedical Res Unit 1981-; ed Biochemical Jl 1958-65, ed-in-chief Jl Gen Microbiology 1976-81, Pubns Mangr Fedn of Euro Microbiological Socs 1982- (ed-in-chief FEMS Microbiology Letters), chm sci advsy ctee Yorks Cancer Res Campaign 1978- (Campaign dep chm 1987-), hon vice pres The Magic Circle London (memb 1959-, historian 1987-), hon life pres Scottish Conjurers Assoc 1973-, pres Br Ring Int Brotherhood of Magicians 1972-73, pres Hull Lit and Philosophical Soc 1976-77 (cncl memb 1973-), visiting lectr Biochemical Soc Australia and NZ, American Medical Alumni lect St Andrews Univ 1980-81; memb: FRSC 1956, FIBiol 1964; *Books* Quantitative Problems in Biochemistry (sixth edn 1980), Microbiol Energetics (1986), Biochemistry of Bacterial Growth (jtly third edn 1982), The Biochemist in a Microbial Wonderland (1982), The Great Illusionists (1979), Isaac Fawkes: Fame and Fable (1979), Vonetta (1982), The Barrister in The Circle (1983), The Book of Magic (1986), The Wizard Exposed (1987), Philip Larkin: the Man and His Work (contrib 1989); *Recreations* conjuring, book-collecting; *Clubs* Savage; *Style—* Prof Edwin Dawes; Dane Hill, 393 Beverley Road, Anlaby, N Humberside HU10 7BQ (☎ 0482 657998); Department of Applied Biology, University of Hull, Hull, N Humberside HU6 7RX (☎ 0482 465316, fax 0482 466205, telex 592592 KHMAIL G, f a o HULIB 375)

DAWES, Ewan David; JP (1975 Northumberland); s of Joseph Dawes (d 1965), of Ashington, Northumberland, and Florence, *née* Woodgate (d 1982); *b* 6 Nov 1937; *Educ* King Edward VI GS Morpeth, Univ of Manchester (Dip Arch 1960); *m* 8 Aug 1963, Joan Elizabeth, da of James Bland Tomlin (d 1978), of Ashington Northumberland; 2 da (Jan b 1966, Lyn b 1967); *Career* ptnr in sundry private practices 1960; memb Jt Technical Ctee Working Gp on Design and Build Tendering Procedures 1981-82; ARIBA 1963, memb Univ of Science and Technology Manchester 1960, memb Architects in Industry and Commerce 1972; FRSA 1983, FBIM 1983; *Recreations* rotary, golf; *Style—* Ewan D Dawes, Esq; Millard Design Partnership, Ilex House, 7 Holly Avenue West, Newcastle-upon-Tyne NE2 2AR (☎ 091 281 5297, fax 091 281 4286)

DAWES, Prof Geoffrey Sharman; CBE (1980); s of Rev W Dawes; *b* 21 Jan 1918; *Educ* Repton, New Coll Oxford (BA, BSc, BM, BCh, DM), Rockerfeller travelling fell 1946; *m* 1941, Margaret Monk; 2 s, 2 da; *Career* dir Nuffield Inst for Medical Res Oxford 1948-85; chm Physiological Systems and Disorders Bd MRC 1978-80 chm Lister Inst of Preventive Med 1988; govr of Repton, 1959-87 (chm 1971-84), vice pres Royal Soc 1977 and 1979; memb MRC 1978-82; Max Weinstein Award 1963, Gairdner Fndn Award 1966, Maternité Award of European Assoc Perinatal Medicine 1976, Virginia Apgar Award, American Acad of Pediatrics 1980; FRCOG, FRCP, hon FACOG; *Books* Foetal and Neonatal Physiology (1968), numerous scientific pubs; *Style—* Prof Geoffrey Dawes; 8 Belbroughton Rd, Oxford (☎ 0865 58131)

DAWES, Howard Anthony Leigh; s of George Roland Dawes (d 1965), of Weatheroak Hall, nr Alvechurch, Worcs, and (Phyllis) Kathleen, *née* Reeves; *b* 4 August 1936; *Educ* Uppingham; *m* 13 July 1962, (Yvonne) Anne, da of Baron Rex Joseph (d 1987); 1 s (Christopher b 1965), 3 da (Catherine b 1967, Domini b 1970, Imogen b 1972); *Career* chm and chief exec: Dawes Tst Ltd 1965-, Neville Industl Securities 1965-88, dir Velcourt Gp plc 1968-; chm: Epag Int Ltd 1976-, LAC Edgbaston Nuffield Hosp 1984-, past chm Ctee of Friends of Birmingham Museums and Galleries, hon tres Birmingham Cons Assoc 1968-76, memb Midland Industl Cncl 1977-, hon sec Scientific Instrument Soc 1984-; Freeman City of London, Liveryman Worshipful Co of Glaziers; FCA, FRAS 1960, FRSA 1975; *Recreations* history of science; *Clubs* Kildare Street (Dublin); *Style—* Howard Dawes, Esq; Craycombe House, nr Fladbury, Worcestershire WR10 2QS (☎ 0386 860 692); P O Box 15, Pershore, Worcestershire WR10 2RD (☎ 0386 860 075, fax 0386 861 074)

DAWICK, Viscount; Alexander Douglas Derrick Haig; s and h of 2 Earl Haig, OBE; *b* 30 June 1961; *Educ* Stowe, Cirencester; *Style—* Viscount Dawick; The Third, Melrose, Roxburghshire TD6 9DR (☎ 057 36287)

DAWKINS, (Arthur Francis) Bill; s of Clinton George Evelyn Dawkins (d 1964), and Francis Enid, *née* Smythies (d 1982); *b* 26 Oct 1916; *Educ* Marlborough, Balliol Coll Oxford (BA); *m* 18 May 1946, Diana Constance, da of Alan Wilfred Ladner, of Cornwall; 1 s (Thomas b 1949), 1 step da (Penelope b 1942); *Career* RE (TA) 1939, Essex Regt 1940, 1 Sierra Leone Regt 1940-45 (Maj 1943), Burma Campaigns 1943-45, (despatches twice); Colonial Admin Serv 1945-62, admin Montserrat (W Indies) 1956-60; asst master Brentwood Sch 1962-74; JP 1963-74; *Recreations* knitting, gardening; *Style—* Bill Dawkins, Esq; Newlands, Dalwood, Axminster, Devon (☎ 040 488485)

DAWKINS, Cecil Leslie; s of George Dawkins, of Cardiff, and Gladys, *née* Shaughnessy (d 1962); *b* 10 Jan 1933; *Educ* St Julians HS Gwent; *m* 9 June 1956, Beryl Elaine, da of Charles William Lippiatt (d 1952); 1 da (Karen Lesley b 1961); *Career* md: Power Deisels and Electrical Ltd 1972-79, MWG Agriplant Ltd 1979; dir: Ben Turner Hldgs Ltd 1972-79, American OEM Automotive Components (UK) Ltd 1982, Export Industl Services 1986; fin dir MWG Gp of Cos 1980; ctee memb Aid Funded Business Advsy Service, European Dvpt Fund World Bank; FInstD, AIAA, AIPM; *Recreations* rugby, referee, hockey umpire, writing; *Clubs* Sussex Soc, RFU Referees, Country Gentlemans Assoc; *Style—* Cecil L Dawkins, Esq; M W G House, Hanworth Lane, Chertsey, Surrey

DAWKINS, Simon John Robert; s of Col William John Dawkins, and Mary, *née* King; *b* 09 July 1945; *Educ* Solihull Sch, Nottingham Univ (BA), Queens Coll Cambridge (PGCE), Birbeck Coll London (MA); *m* 25 July 1968, Janet Mary, da of Gordon Harold Stevens; 1 s (Thomas Peter James b Nov 1974), 1 da (Sarah Mary Louise b Oct

1972); *Career* head of econs and housemaster Dulwich Coll, headmaster Merchant Taylors' Sch Crosby Liverpool; *Recreations* sport, gardening; *Clubs* East India; *Style*— Simon Dawkins, Esq; Brackenwood, St George's Rd, Hightown, Liverpool (☎ 051 929 3546; Merchant Taylors' Sch, Crooby, Liverpool L23 (☎ 051 928 3308)

DAWNAY, Lady Angela Christine Rose; *née* Montagu Douglas Scott; 5 da of 7 Duke of Buccleuch and Queensberry, KT, GCVO (d 1935), and sis of HRH Princess Alice, Duchess of Gloucester; *b* 26 Dec 1906; *m* 28 April 1936, Vice Adm Sir Peter Dawnay, KCVO, CB, DSC, *qv*; 1 s, 1 da; *Style*— Lady Angela Dawnay; The Old Post Cottage, Wield, Alresford, Hants (☎ 0420 63041)

DAWNAY, Hon George William folkes; MC (1945), DL (Norfolk); yr s of Lt-Col 9 Viscount Downe, CMG, DSO, JP, DL (d 1931); *b* 20 April 1909; *Educ* Eton; *m* 23 July 1945, Rosemary Helen (d 19 Sept 1969), yr da of Lord Edward Arthur Grosvenor (d 1929), s of 1 Duke of Westminster; 2 s (Valentine b 1948, Edward b 1950), 2 da (Elizabeth b 1946, Mrs Victor Cazalet b 1955); *Career* served WW II, Maj Coldstream Gds; dir Barclays Bank ret 1979; *Style*— Maj the Hon George Dawnay, MC, DL; Hillington Hall, King's Lynn, Norfolk (☎ 0485 600304)

DAWNAY, Hon Mrs Iris Irene Adele; *née* Peake; LVO (1959); da of 1 Viscount Ingleby (d 1966), and Lady Joan, *née* Capell, Vicountess Ingleby (d 1979); *b* 23 July 1923; *m* 25 March 1963, as his 2 w, Oliver Payan Dawnay, CVO (d 1988), s of Maj-Gen Guy Dawnay, CB, CMG, DSO, MVO (d 1952), of Longparish House, Hants, *see* Viscount Downe; 1 da (Emma b 1964); *Career* lady-in-waiting to HRH The Princess Margaret 1952-62; *Style*— The Hon Mrs Dawnay, LVO; Wexcombe House, Marlborough, Wilts (☎ 026 489 229); Flat 5, 32 Onslow Sq, London SW7 (☎ 01 584 3963)

DAWNAY, (Charles) James Payan; s of Capt Oliver Payan Dawnay, CVO (d 1988), and Lady Margaret Stirling Aird, *née* Boyle; *b* 7 Nov 1946; *Educ* Eton, Trinity Hall Cambridge (MA); *m* 10 June 1978, Sarah, da of Edgar David Stogdon, MBE, of Little Mead, Witchampton, Wimborne, Dorset; 1 s (David b 1985), 3 da (Alice b 1979, Olivia b 1981, Fenella b 1988); *Career* dir Mercury Asset Mgmnt Gp plc 1987-, chm Mercury Fund Managers Ltd 1987-; *Recreations* fishing, collecting; *Clubs* Brooks, Pratts; *Style*— C J P Dawnay, Esq; 85 Eglin Crescent, London W11 (☎ 01 229 5940); 33 King William St, London EC4 (☎ 01 280 2800)

DAWNAY, Hon James Richard; s of 10 Viscount Downe; *b* 8 Sept 1937; *m* 1976, Gillian, yst da of Major James Dance, MP (d 1971), of Moreton Morrell, Warwicks, and formerly w of Capt Simon George Melville Portal, *see* Baronetage, Portal; 1 s (Thomas b 1978); *Style*— The Hon James Dawnay; 31 Eaton Mansions, SW1 (☎ 730 2471)

DAWNAY, Lady Katharine Nora de la Poer; *née* Beresford; 2 da of 6 Marquess of Waterford; *b* 23 Dec 1899; *m* 14 Oct 1926, Maj-Gen Sir David Dawnay, KCVO, CB, DSO (d 1971), *see* Peerage Viscount Downe; 2 s (Hugh b 1932, Peter (twin) b 1932), 2 da (Blanche b 1928, d in a motor acc at Copenhagen 1953, Rachel b 1929 d 1983); *Style*— Lady Katharine Dawnay; Whitfield Court, Waterford, Eire

DAWNAY, Vice Adm Sir Peter; KCVO (1961, MVO 1939), CB 1958, DSC (1944), DL (Hants 1975); s of Maj the Hon Hugh Dawnay, DSO (ka 1914), 2 s of 8 Viscount Downe), and Lady Susan, *née* de la Poer Beresford (d 1947, da of 5 Marquess of Waterford), and bro of late Maj-Gen Sir David Dawnay, KCVO, CB, DSO; *b* 14 August 1904; *Educ* RNCs Osborne and Dartmouth; *m* 28 April 1936, Lady Angela Christine Rose Montagu-Douglas-Scott, 5 da of 7 Duke of Buccleuch and Queensberry, KT, GCVO; 1 s (Charles b 1938), 1 da (Mrs Timothy de Zoete b 1946); *Career* RN 1918, Lt-Cdr 1935, Cdr 1940, Capt 1946, dep controller of the Admty 1956, Rear-Adm 1956, Flag Offr Royal Yachts 1958-62, Vice-Adm 1959, ret 1962; an extra equerry to HM The Queen 1958-; High Sheriff Hants 1973-74; OStJ; Offr of Legion of Merit (USA); pres London Assoc for the Blind 1966; *Style*— Vice-Adm Sir Peter Dawnay, KCVO, CB, DSC, DL; The Old Post Cottage, Wield, Alresford, Hants SO24 9RS (☎ 0420 63041)

DAWOOD, Nessim Joseph; s of late Yousef Dawood and Muzli, *née* Toweg; *b* 27 August 1927; *Educ* Exeter Univ, London Univ; *m* 1949, Juliet, *née* Abraham; 3 s; *Career* Arabist; md The Arabic Advertising and Publishing Co Ltd London 1958, dir Contemporary Translations Ltd (London) 1962, ME conslt; fell Inst of Linguists; *Book Translations* The Muqaddimah of Ibn Khaldun (1967), The Thousand and One Nights (1954) The Koran (1956, 33 edn 1988), Aladdin and Other Tales (1957), Tales from the Thousand and One Nights (1973, 15 edn 1988), Arabian Nights (illustrated children's edn 1978); *Recreations* theatre; *Clubs* Hurlingham; *Style*— Nessim Dawood, Esq; Berkeley Sq House, Berkeley Sq, London W1X 5LE (☎ 01 409 0953)

DAWS, Andrew Michael Bennett; s of Victor Sidney Daws (d 1976), and Doris Jane Daws; *b* 11 Mar 1943; *Educ* King's Sch Grantham, Univ of Exeter (LLB), Coll of Law; *m* 1, 1969 (m dis 1979), Edit, *née* Puskas; m 2, 27 Aug 1981, Phoebe, da of Clifford Hughes (d 1955); 1 s (Harry Arthur Victor Bennett b 1986), 1 da (Constance Clemency Jane Bennett b 1984); *Career* slr 1967, ptnr Denton Hall Burgin and Warrens 1975-; *Recreations* golf, squash; *Clubs* Royal Mid-Surrey GC, Roehampton; *Style*— Andrew M B Daws, Esq; 5 Chancery La, London, WC1A 1LF (☎ 01 242 1212, fax 01 404 0087, telex 263567 BURGIN G)

DAWS, Dame Joyce Margaretta; DBE (1975); da of Frederick William Daws, of Hounslow (d 1960), and Daisy Ethel Daws; *b* 21 July 1925; *Educ* Royal Sch for Naval and Marine Officers' Daughters, St Paul's Girls' Sch, Royal Free Hosp London Univ; *Career* surgn Queen Vic Memorial Hosp Melbourne 1958-85, thoracic surgn Prince Henry's Hosp Melbourne 1975 (formerly assist thoracic surgn); pres Vic Branch Aust Medical Assoc Cncl 1976, Bd of Management After-Care Hosp Melbourne 1980-85; FRCS, FRACS (*see* Debrett's Handbook of Australia and New Zealand for further details; *Recreations* opera, ballet, desert travel, protea grower; *Clubs* Lyceum, Soroptimist Int (Melbourne); *Style*— Dame Joyce Daws, DBE; 26 Edwin St, Heidelberg West, Vic 3081, Australia (☎ 425 579)

DAWSON, Anthony Michael; s of Leslie Joseph Dawson, and Mable Annie, *née* Jayes; bro of J L Dawson, *qv*; *m* 1956, Barbara Anne Baron, da of late Thomas Forsyth, MD, ChB; 2 da; *Career* MD, physician: St Bartholomew's Hosp, King Edward VII Hosp for Officers, King Edward VII Hosp Convalescent Home for Officers, Osborne; physician to HM The Queen 1982- (formerly to the Royal Household); FRCP; *Style*— Anthony Dawson, Esq; 35 Meadowbank, Primrose Hill Rd, London NW3 3AY

DAWSON, Bruce Amager; *b* 17 Dec 1928; *Educ* Univ of Edinburgh (MA); *Career* fndr memb Kuwait Investmt Off London 1963-; chm: Hays Gp, London Sinfonietta, vice-chm Torras Hostench SA; dir: Autobar Industries, Ercros SA, Matrix Investmts, Sassoon Hldgs, Granfel plc, St Martins Investmts, Prima Inmobiliaria SA; *Recreations* arts, sport; *Clubs* Hon Co of Edinburgh, Sunningdale, Valderrama (Spain); *Style*— Bruce Dawson, Esq; c/o St Vedast House, 150 Cheapside, London

DAWSON, Lady; Caroline Jane; only child of William Anthony Acton, of La Foscarina, Komeno, Gouvia, Corfu; *b* 12 May 1933; *m* 7 July 1955, Sir (Hugh Halliday) Dawson, 3 Bt (d 14 Feb 1983); 2 s (*see* Dawson, Sir Hugh M T, Bt); *Style*— Lady Dawson

DAWSON, Hon Justice; Hon Sir Daryl Michael Dawson; AC (1988), KBE (1982), CB (1980); s of Claude Charles Dawson and Elizabeth May Dawson; *b* 12 Dec 1933; *Educ* Canberra HS, Melbourne Univ (LLB), Yale Univ (LLM); *m* 1971, Marylou, da of Dr Thomas; *Career* QC 1971, Vic slr-gen 1974-82, justice of the High Court of Australia 1982; *see Debrett's Handbook of Australia and New Zealand for further details*; *Recreations* squash; *Style*— The Hon Justice Dawson, AC, KBE, CB; High Court of Australia, Canberra, ACT, Australia

DAWSON, (James) Gordon; CBE (1980); s of late James Dawson and Helen Mitchell, *née* Tawse; *b* 3 Feb 1916; *Educ* Aberdeen GS, Aberdeen Univ; *m* 1941, Doris Irene, *née* Rowe (d 1982); 1 s, 1 da; *Career* tech dir Perkins Engines 1955-66; dir Dowty Gp Ltd 1966-69, chm Zenith Carburettor Co Ltd 1969-81 (formerly md); pres IMechE 1979-80; FEng, Hon FIMechE 1986; Hon FI Mech E 1986; *Clubs* Caledonian; *Style*— Gordon Dawson Esq, CBE; Mildmay House, Apethorpe, Peterborough, Cambs PE8 5DP (☎ 078 087 348)

DAWSON, Lt-Col Herbrand Vavasour; DL (N Yorks 1988); Lt Col; s of Maj John Vavasour Dawson (d 1935), and Charlotte Gerda, *née* Romilly (d 1980); *b* 13 June 1918; *Educ* Winchester, RMA Sandhurst; *m* 19 Dec 1942, Grizelda Louise, da of Maj George Mitchell Richmond (d 1957), of Kincairney, Murthly, Perthshire; 1 s (Christopher b 1943), 1 da (Catherine b 1944) ; *Career* cmmnd Queens Own Cameron Highlanders 1938; served: France 1939-40, Sicily 1943, Holland & Germany 1944-45, GSO III HQ BAOR 1946-48, student Staff Coll 1950, Bde-Maj 155 Inf Bde 1951-53, DAAG HQ Scottish Cmd 1957-60, cmd 4/5 Bn Queens Own Cameron Highlanders 1960-62, AAG HQ Northern Cmd, ret Lt-Col 1968; elected N Yorks CC 1973 (vice chm 1985), chm Public Protection Ctee 1981; *Recreations* skiing; *Style*— Lt-Col Herbrand Dawson, DL; Weston Hall, Otley, Yorks (☎ 0943 462430)

DAWSON, Sir Hugh Michael Trevor; 4 Bt (UK 1920), of Edgwarebury, Co Middlesex; s of Sir (Hugh Halliday) Trevor Dawson, 3 Bt (d 1983), and Lady Dawson, *qv*; *b* 28 Mar 1956; *Educ* at home; *Heir* bro, Nicholas Dawson, *qv*; *Style*— Sir Hugh Dawson, Bt; 11 Burton Court, Franklin's Row, London SW3

DAWSON, John Leonard; s of late Leslie Joseph Dawson, and Mabel Annie Jayes; *b* 30 Sept 1932; *Educ* King's Coll Hosp London (MB, MS); *m* 1958, Rosemary Brundle; 2s, 1 da; *Career* surgn: Bromley Hosp, King Edward VII Hosp for Offrs, King's Coll Hosp, to HM's Royal Household 1975-83, to HM 1983-; dean faculty of clinical med Kings Coll Sch of Med and Dentistry; FRCS; *Style*— John Dawson, Esq; 107 Burbage Rd, Dulwich, London SE21 7AF

DAWSON, Mark Patrick; s of Douglas George Damer Dawson; *b* 19 Oct 1941; *Educ* Wellington; *m* 1, 1970 (m dis 1983), Carol Anne, da of John Dudley Groves; 2 s; m 2, 1987 (Constance) Clare Power, *née* Mumford; *Career* Lt Essex Yeo; former chm and md Pickford Dawson & Holland Ltd; md: Jardine Matheson Insur Brokers UK Ltd 1978-79, Jardine Matheson Underwriting Agencies Ltd 1979, Jardine Glanvill Underwriting Agencies Ltd (re-named Jardine (Lloyd's Underwriting Agents) Ltd); *Clubs* Boodle's, City of London; *Style*— Mark Dawson, Esq; Cooks Green, Lamarsh, Bures, Suffolk (☎ 01 736 0768)

DAWSON, Nicholas Antony Trevor; s of Sir (Hugh Halliday) Trevor Dawson, 3 Bt (d 1983); hp of bro, Sir Hugh Dawson, *qv*; *b* 17 August 1957; *Style*— Nicholas Dawson Esq

DAWSON, Rev Peter; OBE (1986); s of Richard Dawson (d 1963), of London, and Henrietta Kate, *née* Trueman (d 1984); *b* 19 May 1933; *Educ* Beckenham Tech Sch, Beckenham GS, LSE (BSc), Westminster Coll (PGCE); *m* 20 July 1957, Shirley Margaret Pentland, da of William James Johnson (d 1983); 2 da (Miriam b 6 June 1959, Paula b 24 May 1961); *Career* RAF Nat Serv 1951-53, Mauripur Pakistan; schoolmaster fell commoner: Keble Coll Oxford 1969, Corpus Christi Coll Cambridge 1979; schoolmaster London and Liverpool 1957-70, headmaster Eltham Green Sch London 1970-80, gen sec Professional Assoc of Teachers 1980-; ordained Methodist Minister 1985; *Books* Making a Comprehensive Work (1981), Teachers and Teaching (1984); *Recreations* reading, golf, family activities; *Clubs* Carlton; *Style*— The Rev Peter Dawson, OBE; 3 Lawns Heads Ave, Littleover, Derby DE3 6DR (☎ 0332 367 615); Professonal Association of Teachers, St James Court, 77 Friar Gate, Derby DE1 1EZ (☎ 0332 372 337, fax 0332 290 310/292 7431)

DAWSON, Ven Peter; s of late Leonard Smith Dawson and Cicely Alice Dawson; *b* 31 Mar 1929; *Educ* Manchester GS, Keble Oxford, Ridley Hall Cambridge; *m* 1955, Kathleen Mary Sansome; 1 s, 3 da; *Career* rector of Morden (diocese of Southwark) 1968-77, rural dean of Merton 1975-77, archdeacon of Norfolk 1977; *Style*— The Ven the Archdeacon of Norfolk; Intwood Rectory, Norwich, Norfolk (☎ 0603 51946)

DAWSON, (Joseph) Peter; s of Joseph Glyn Dawson (d 1980), and Winifred Olwen, *née* Martin (d 1957); *b* 18 Mar 1940; *Educ* Bishop Gore GS Swansea, UC of Swansea (BSc); *m* 1964, Yvonne Anne Charlton, da of Charlton Smith (d 1974), of London; 1 s (Alex b 1972), 1 da (Jo-anne b 1969); *Career* TU official; negotiating sec: Assoc of Teachers in Tech Insts (ATTI) 1974-75, Nat Assoc of Teachers in Further and Higher Educn (NATFHE) 1976-79 (gen sec 1979); hon Fell Coll of Preceptors 1984; *Recreations* church activities, cricket, tennis, assoc football; *Clubs* Surrey CCC; *Style*— Peter Dawson, Esq; 27, Britannia Street, London WC1X 9JP (☎ 01 837 3636)

DAWSON, Robin Peter; s of Harry (Henry) Leonard Dawson, of 14 Woodhurst South, Maidenhead, Berks, and Marian, *née* Crosland; *b* 11 Mar 1947; *Educ* Slough GS, Univ of Bradford (BTech), S Bank Poly (BSc hons); *m* 15 Aug 1969, Gillian Mary, da of John Rhodes Aspden (d 1975); 2 s (Paul Derek b 1972, Martin Stuart b 1975); *Career* engr trg with Rolls Royce Ltd, UKAEA and C&CA; ptnr H L Dawson and Ptnrs 1970-; consultancy retains cmmns for engrg design in Royal and other palaces, castles, nat museums, art galleries and gen industl projects; Freeman City of London, Liveryman Co of Engineers; CEng, Eur Ing, FIMechE, FIEE, FCIBSE, MIM, FIHospE, MIES (NA), FRSA; *Recreations* aeronautical history, industl and other archaeology; *Clubs* City Livery, Royal Overseas; *Style*— Robin Dawson, Esq; Waylands, Kings Oak Cl, Monks Risborough, Aylesbury, Bucks HP17 9LB (☎ 08444

6534); H L Dawson and Partners, 5 Queen Victoria Rd, High Wycombe, Bucks HP11 1BA (☎ 0494 34646, fax 0494 465032)

DAWSON, Sandra June Noble; da of Wilfred Denyer, of Corton Denham, Sherborne, Dorset, and Joy Victoria Jeanne, *née* Noble; *b* 04 June 1946; *m* 23 Aug 1969, Henry Richards Currey Dawson, s of Horace Dawson (d 1952), of Sotik, Kenya; 1 s (Tom Stephen John b 1983), 2 da (Hannah Louise Joy b 1976, Rebecca Annie Brenda b 1978); *Career* Imperial Coll London; res offr industl sociology unit 1969-70, sr lectr dept of social and econ studies 1980 (lectr 1973), dep dir the mgmnt sch Imperial Coll 1988; memb issues gp Diocesan Bd of Social Responsibility, policy devpt ctee Inst of Occupationsl Health, Br Sociological Assoc 1970-;; *Books* Analysing Organisations (1986), MacMillan, Safety at Work: the Limits of Self Regulations (1988); *Recreations* music, walking; *Style—* Mrs Sandra Dawson; The Management Sch, Imperial College, 53 Princess Gate, Exhibition Rd, London SW7 2PG (☎ 01 589 5111 ext 7015)

DAWSON, Air Chief Marshal Sir Walter Lloyd; KCB (1954, CB 1945), CBE (1943), DSO (1948); s of Walter James Dawson, of Sunderland; *b* 6 May 1902; *Educ* privately, RAF Cranwell; *m* 1927, ELizabeth Leslie (d 1975), da of late D V McIntyre, of Cotherstone; 1 s, 1 da; *Career* enlisted in RAF as boy mechanic 1919, cmmnd from Cranwell 1922, Wing Cdr 1939, served WW II Coastal Cmd and Air Miny as dir Anti-U-Boat Ops and dir Plans, Gp Capt 1944, Air Cdre 1946, AOC Levant 1946-48, Air Vice-Marshal 1948, Cmdt Sch of Land-Air Warfare 1948-50, dir IDC 1950-52, dep COS SHAPE 1953-56, Air Marshal 1953, Inspr Gen RAF 1956, Air Chief Marshal 1956, air memb Supply and Orgn Air Miny 1958-60, ret 1960; chm Handley Page Ltd 1966-69, dir Southern Electricity Bd 1961-72; *Clubs* RAF; *Style—* Air Chief Marshal Sir Walter Dawson, KCB, CBE, DSO; Woodlands, Heathfield Ave, Sunninghill, Berks

DAWSON-DAMER, Hon Lionel John Charles Seymour; yr s of George Lionel Seymour, Viscount Carlow (ka 1944, s and h of 6 Earl of Portarlington), and Peggy, *née* Cambie (d 1963); *b* 12 Oct 1940; *Educ* Eton; *m* 10 Dec 1965 (m dis 1975), Rosemary Ashley Morrett (who m 1977 (m dis 1983), as his 3 w, 7 Marquess of Northampton), da of P G M Hancock; m 2, 1982, Ashley Judith, da of Gp Capt W Mann, of Perth, W Australia; *Style—* The Hon John Dawson-Damer; Oran Park, Narellan, NSW 2567, Australia

DAWSON-GOWAR, Hon Mrs; Hon Judith Margaret; *née* Gordon Walker; er da of Baron Gordon-Walker, CH, PC (Life Peer, d 1980); *b* 1936; *Educ* N London Collegiate Sch, Lady Margaret Hall Oxford (MA), Univ Coll London (BA, PhD); *m* 1, 1957 (m dis 1975), Graham Carleton Greene, *qv*, s of Sir Hugh Carleton Greene, KCMG, OBE; m 2, 1981, Prof Norman William Dawson-Gowar, s of Harold James Dawson-Gowar; 1 step s, 1 step da; *Career* lectr in psychology Birkbeck Coll London Univ 1966-76, prof of psychology Open Univ 1976; *Publications* (under name Judith Greene) Psycholinguistics: Chomsky and Psychology (1972), Thinking and Language (1975), Learning to use Statistical Tests in Psychology (with M d'Oliveira 1982), Basic Cognitive Processes (with Carolyn Hicks, 1984), Language Understanding (1986); *Style—* Prof the Hon Judith Dawson-Gowar; The Homestead, Cuddington, Bucks

DAWTRY, Sir Alan; CBE (1968, Mil MBE 1945), TD (1948); s of Melancthon Dawtry, of Sheffield; *b* 8 April 1915; *Educ* King Edward VII Sch Sheffield, Sheffield Univ; *Career* served WWII, France, N Africa and Italy (despatches twice), Lt-Col; slr 1938, asst slr Sheffield 1938-48; dep town clerk: Bolton 1948-52, Leicester 1952-54; town clerk: Wolverhampton 1954-56, Westminster 1956-77; memb Metrication Bd 1969-74, Clean Air Cncl 1960-75; chm Sperry RAND Ltd 1977-86, Sperry RAND (Ireland) Ltd 1977-86, pres London Rent Assessment Panel 1979-86; FBIM, FRSA; has been awarded numerous for decorations; kt 1974; *Style—* Sir Alan Dawtry, CBE, TD; 901 Grenville House, Dolphin Square, London SW1 (☎ 01 798 8100)

DAY, Bernard Maurice; CB (1987); s of Maurice James Day (d 1959), of Chingford, Essex, and May Helen, *née* Spicer (d 1972); *b* 7 May 1928; *Educ* Bancroft's Woodford Green Essex, LSE (BSc); *m* 11 Feb 1956, (Ruth Elizabeth) Betty, da of Richard Stansfield (d 1957), of Walton-on-Thames; 2 s (Keith b 1961, Geoffrey b 1965), 1 da (Christine b 1959); *Career* Intelligence Corps and RA 1946-48, cmmnd RA 1948; cabinet secretariat central staffs and air force 1959-61, sec Meteorological Off 1965-70, estab offr Cabinet Off 1970-72; MOD: head air staff secretariat 1972-74, under sec appts 1974-84, under sec fleet support 1985-88, ret 1988; Civil Serv Selection Bd: res chm 1984-85, panel chm 1988-; churchwarden and parish church cncllr St Mary Oatlands; *Recreations* swimming, change ringing; *Clubs* Cwlth Trust; *Style—* Bernard Day, Esq, CB; 2 Farmleigh Grove, Walton-on-Thames, Surrey KT12 5BU (☎ 0932 227416)

DAY, Sir Derek Malcolm; KCMG (1984, CMG 1973); s of Alan W Day (d 1968), and Gladys Day, *née* Portlock (d 1974); *b* 29 Nov 1927; *Educ* Hurstpierpoint Coll, St Catharine's Coll Cambridge (MA); *m* 1955, Sheila, da of George Nott (d 1955), of Newnhan Bridge, Worcs; 3 s (William, Richard, Nicholas), 1 da (Katharine); *Career* HM For Serv 1951: 3 sec Br Embasssy Tel Aviv 1953-56, private sec to ambass Rome 1956-59, 2 then 1 sec FO 1959-62, 1 sec HM Embassy Washington 1962-66, 1 sec FO 1966-67, asst private sec to Sec of State for For Affairs 1967-68, head of personnel ops dept FCO 1969-72, cnsllr Br High Cmmn Nicosia 1972-75, HM ambass to Ethiopia 1975-78, asst under-sec FCO 1979, dep under-sec of state FCO 1980, chief clerk 1982-84, Br high cmmr Ottawa 1984; dir Monence Ltd Montreal; cmmr Cwlth War Graves Cmmn, vice chm BRCS, chm and govr Hurstpierpoint Coll, govr Bethany Sch; *Clubs* Hawks (Cambridge), Utd Oxford & Cambridge; *Style—* Sir Derek Day, KCMG; Etchinghill, Goudhurst, Kent

DAY, John Eddy; s of Charles William Day (d 1965), of Exeter, and Elizabeth Jane, *née* Williams (d 1956); *b* 1 Mar 1922; *Educ* Exeter Sch; *m* 30 Aug 1946, Pamela Winifred, da of Douglas Hamilton Beckett (d 1956), of Dolgelley; *Career* RM 1940-51: cmmnd Probationary 2 Lt 1940, 1 Bn 1941-42, HMS Howe 1942-43 served Artic and Med, 45 RM Commando 1944-45 served France Holland Germany (wounded twice, despatches 1945), Br Mil Mission France 1946-47, instr French Commando Sch Algeria, HQ Plymouth Gp 1947-48, Instr Offrs Sch 1948-51; Malayan Civil Serv 1951-58: cadet Telok Anson Perak 1951, sec to Br advsr Perak 1951-52, asst dist offr Kroh Perak 1952-53, asst sec def dept Kuala Lumpur 1953-54, dist offr Pekan Pahang 1955-58; UK Security Serv 1958-82; French Croix de Guerre 1944; *Books* The Story of 45 RM Commando (1948); *Recreations* reading, walking my dogs; *Clubs* Naval & Military; *Style—* J E Day, Esq

DAY, Lance Reginald; s of Reginald Day (d 1974), of Welwyn Garden City, Herts, and Eileen, *née* McKeone; *b* 2 Nov 1927; *Educ* Sherrardswood Sch Welwyn Garden City, Alleyne's GS Stevenage, Northern Poly, London Univ, UCL (BSc, MSc); *m* 3 Jan 1959, Mary Ann, da of late John Sheahan, of Dublin; 1 s (Nicholas b 1960), 2 da (Anneliese b 1959, Caroline b 1972); *Career* Science Museum: Library keeper 1976-87 (res asst 1951-62, sr res asst 1962-64, asst keeper 1964-69), asst keeper dept of chemistry 1970-74, keeper dept of electrical engrg and communications 1974- 76; sec Nat Railway Museum Ctee 1973-75, hon sec Newcomen Soc for the Study of the History of Engrg and Technol 1973-82, hon organiser RNIB Welwyn Garden City 1968-86; *Books* Broad Gauge (1985); *Style—* Lance Day, Esq; 12 Rhinefield Close, Brockenhurst, Hants SO42 7SU (☎ 0590 22079)

DAY, Margaret Lucy; da of Robert Manley Day (d 1968), of The Grange, Great Brington, Northampton, and Mary Elizabeth, *née* Evans (d 1986); *b* 12 Dec 1941; *Educ* E Haddon Hall and Mon Fertile Switzerland; *Career* farmer; *Recreations* hunting, racing, country persuits; *Style—* Miss Margaret Day; Mill House, East Haddon, Northampton NN5 8DV (☎ 0604 770243)

DAY, Martin James; s of Flt Lt Clifford Day, RAFVR (d 1961), and Molly, *née* Dale; *b* 12 April 1944; *Educ* City of London Sch, Univ of Durham (BA), Christ's Coll Cambridge (LLM); *m* 1, 1970 (m dis 1976), Elizabeth Mary, da of Sqdn Ldr Thomas H Sykes; m 2, Loraine Frances, da of Frank Leslie Hodkinson (d 1984), of Langton Green, Tunbridge Wells, Kent; 1 s (James b 1978), 1 da (Philippa b 1983); *Career* articled clerk Austin Wright & Co 1966-68, ptnr Linklaters & Paines 1976- (asst slr 1969-76); chm: Tstees of the Hampton Arts Tst and Hampton Music Festival 1969-72, Thameside Arts Tst 1973, Westminster Children's Charitable Fndn 1976-; memb: Ct of Common Cncl (Ward of Aldersgate) 1977-79; Liveryman City of London Slrs Co 1976; dir Slrs Benevolent Assoc 1988; memb: Law Soc, American Bar Assoc; FRGS (1965); *Books* Unit Trusts: The Law and Practice (with P I Harris 1974); *Recreations* collecting contemporary art and furniture; *Clubs* Carlton; *Style—* Martin J Day, Esq; Barrington House, 59-67 Gresham St, London, EC2V 7JA (☎ 01 606 7080, fax 01 606 5113, telex 884349 and 888167)

DAY, Robin; OBE; s of Arthur Day (d 1956), of High Wycombe, Buckinghamshire, and Mary, *née* Shersby (d 1956); *b* 25 May 1915; *Educ* High Wycombe Sch of Art, RCA; *m* 5 Sept 1942, Lucienne, da of Felix Conradi (d 1957), of Croydon, Surrey; 1 da (Paula Day b 1954); *Career* princ of own design practise 1940-; seating design: Royal Festival Hall 1951, Shakespeare Meml Theatre, Barbican Arts Centre and other major bldgs; interior design Super VC10 aircraft, Royal Designers for Ind 1959; Gold Medal for Design Triennale Exhibition 1951, Siad Design Medal 1957, design centre awards 1957, 1961, 1965, 1966; served on juries of nat and int design competitions; design colls: lectr and assessor diploma work; ARCA; *Recreations* walking, mountaineering, ski touring; *Clubs* Alpine; *Style—* Robin Day, Esq, OBE; 49 Cheyne Walk, London SW3 5LP (☎ 01 352 1455)

DAY, Sir Robin; s of late William Day; *b* 24 Oct 1923; *Educ* Bembridge Sch, St Edmund Hall Oxford; *m* 1965 (m dis 1986), Katherine Mary, da of R I Ainslie, CBE, DSO, QC, of Perth, W Australia; 2 s; *Career* called to the Bar 1952; TV broadcaster and journalist; presenter: Panorama BBC 1967-72, World at One BBC Radio 4, Question Time BBC TV; chm Hansard Soc for Parly Govt 1981-83; kt 1981; *Clubs* Garrick, Athenaeum; *Style—* Sir Robin Day; c/o BBC TV Studios, Lime Grove, London W12

DAY, Stephen Peter CMG (1989); s of Frank Day; *b* 19 Jan 1938; *Educ* Bancroft's Sch, CCC Cambridge; *m* 1965, Angela, *née* Waudby; 1 s, 2 da; *Career* HMOCS 1961-65; FO 1965-: Singapore, UK mission NY, Beirut, consul-gen Edmonton 1979-81, head of FCO ME Dept, ambass Qatar 1981-84, Tunis 1987-; *Style—* Stephen Day, Esq, CMG; c/o Foreign and Commonwealth Office, King Charles St, London SW1;

DAY, Stephen Richard; MP (Cons Cheadle 1987); s of late Francis Day, and Annie, *née* Webb; *b* 30 Oct 1948; *Educ* Otley Secdy Mod Sch, Park Lane Coll of Further Educ, Leeds Poly; *m* 2, 25 Nov 1982, Frances, da of late James Raywood Booth, of 7 Upper Green Lane, Hove Edge, Nr Brighouse, W Yorks; 1 s (Alexander (by previous marriage) b 1973); *Career* sales clerk William Sinclair & Sons 1965-70 (asst sales mangr 1970-77); sales rep: Larkfield Printing Co 1977-80, A H Leach & Co 1980-84; sales exec: PPI Chromacopy 1984-86, Chromagene Ltd 1986-87; conslt Chromagene Photo Labs 1987; memb: Otley Town Cncl, Leeds City Cncl; parly candidate (Cons) Bradford gen election 1983; successfully sponsored Motor Vehicles - Wearing of Seat Belts by Children Act 1988; *Recreations* music, films, Roman history; *Clubs* Royal Wharfedale, Cheadle and Gatley Cons, Cheadle Hulme Cons; *Style—* Stephen Day Esq, MP; Flat 2, 73 Woodford Rd, Bramhall, Cheshire (☎ 061 428 6349; ☎ 01 219 6200)

DAY, William Arthur; MBE (1986); s of Arthur Day (d 1946), and Bessie Ann, *née* Dando (d 1934); *b* 30 Jan 1911; *Educ* Southend HS; *m* 1, 30 May 1941, Winifred Mabel, da of Winston Griffin (d 1937), of Westcliff-on-Sea; 1 da (Pauline b 1946); m 2, 2 April 1958, Margaret Jean, da of Edward Horace Chaplin (d 1926), of N Finchley; *Career* WWII RAFVR (Sergeant medical) served G13, India, Burma, NW Europe (despatches 1944) 1940-46; clerk in rubber co 1927-37, rep Crosse & Blackwell 1937-40; Burderop Park Trg Coll 1947-48; teacher: Bournville Junior Sch 1948-55 (introduced special educn for retarded children), Sandhill Park Residential Special Sch 1956-62; dep Headmaster Monkton Priors Special Sch 1962-64, headmaster Fairmead Special Sch 1964-71; fndr memb Radio Camelot, former vice-chm Weston-super-Mare Football League, circuit youth sec of 18 Methodist Churches; written plays and sketches and composed many hymns for children; *Recreations* athletics, soccer, photography; *Style—* William Day, Esq, MBE; 11 Hayes End Manor, South Petherton, Somerset TA13 5AG

DAY-LEWIS, Sean Francis; s of Cecil Day-Lewis (Poet Laureate 1967-72 (d 1972), of London, and Constance Mary, *née* King (d 1975); *b* 3 August 1931; *Educ* Allhallows Sch Devon; *m* 1960, Gloria Ann (Anna), da of James Henry Mott (d 1980); 1 s (Finian b 1966), 1 da (Keelin b 1963); *Career* Nat Serv RAF 1949-51; ed: Bridport News 1952-53, Southern Times Weymouth 1953-54, Herts Advertiser St Albans 1954-56, Express and Star Wolverhampton 1956-60; arts ed Socialist Commentary 1966-71, TV and radio ed Daily Telegraph 1970-86 (ed 1960), TV ed London Daily News 1986-87, freelance writer and commentator on broadcasting matters 1987; *Books* Bulleid, Last Giant of Steam (1964), An English Literary Life (1980); *Recreations* music, ball games, country life; *Style—* Mr Sean Day-Lewis; 52 Masbro Rd, London W14 0LT (☎ 01 602 3221); Restorick Row, Rosemary Lane, Colyton, Devon (☎ 0297 53039)

DAYKIN, Christopher David; s of John Francis (d 1983), and Mona, *née* Carey; *b* 18 July 1948; *Educ* Merchant Taylors' Sch Northwood, Pembroke Coll Cambridge, (BA 1970, MA 1973); *m* 1977, Kathryn Ruth, da of Harold William Tingey, of Hamps; 2 s

(Jonathan b 1982, Jeremy b 1984), 1 da (Rachel b 1981); *Career* Govt Actuary's Dept 1970, 1972-78, 1980 (principal actuary 1982-84), directing actuary 1985; VSO Brunei 1971, princ (Health and Soc Services) HM Treasy 1978-80, FIA; *Recreations* travel, photography, language; *Style*— Christopher Daykin, Esq; Government Actuary's Dept, 22 Kingsway, London WC2B 6LE (☎ 01 242 6828)

de BLOCQ van KUFFELER, John Philip; s of Capt F de Blocq van Kuffeler of Royal Netherlands Navy, and Stella *née* Hall; *b* 09 April 1949; *Educ* Atlantic Coll, Clare Coll Cambridge (MA); *m* 3 April 1971, Lesley, da of Dr E M Callendar; 2 s (Hugo b 1974, Alexander b 1979), 1 da (Venetia b 1977); *Career* CA 1973, Peat M arwick Mitchell & Co 1970-77 (assignments UK, Holland, Germany, Egypt) head of corporate fin Grindlay Brandts Ltd 1980-82 (mangr 1977-80); Brown Shipley 7 Co Ltd: dir 1983-, head of corporate fin 1983-, memb exec ctee 1985-, head investmt banking UK and USA 1986-; currently gp chief exec of Brown Shipley Hldgs plc, dir numerous public cos incl: Campbell and Armstrong plc, St Paul's fin and Investmt Ltd, Lease Management Servs Ltd; memb ctee Issuing Houses Assoc 1984-88; FCA; *Recreations* fishing, shooting, tennis; *Clubs* Newmarket; *Style*— John de Blocq van Kuffeler, Esq; Founders Court, Lothbury, London EC2R 7HE (☎ 01 606 9833, fax 01 606 9833 x 4128, car tel 0860 525 290, telex 886704)

DE BOINVILLE, Simon Murdoch Chastel; s of Charles Alfred Chastel de Boinville (d 1985), of Stobo Hill, Lower Bourne, Farnham, Surrey, and Frances Anne, *née* Morrison (d 1984); *b* 16 Mar 1955; *Educ* Dragon Sch Oxford, Radley, Royal Agric Coll Cirencester; *m* 4 Oct 1980, Shaunagh Elisabeth, da of Dermott Bibby Magill, of Mulberry Hill, Baughurst, Basingstoke, Hants; 1 s (Reuben b 1986, d 1988), 1 da (Cordelice); *Career* chartered surveyor with Cluttons 1979; *Recreations* gardening, reading, tennis, fishing; *Clubs* Farmers; *Style*— Simon de Boinville, Esq; Grantham Farm, Baughurst, Basingstoke, Hants (☎ 07356 5821); Cluttons, 127 Mount St, London W1Y 5HA (☎ 01 499 4155, fax 01 409 1983)

DE BONO, Edward Francis Charles Publius; s of late Prof Joseph Edward de Bono, CBE, of St Julian's Bay, Malta, and Josephine, *née* Burns; *b* 19 May 1933; *Educ* St Edward's Coll Malta, Royal Univ of Malta (BSc, MD), Ch Ch Oxford (Rhodes Scholar) (D Phil Oxon, PhD); *m* 1971, Josephine Hall-White; 2 s; *Career* asst dir research Dept of Investigative Medicine Cambridge Univ 1963-76, lectr in Medicine 1976-83; dir Cognitive Research Tst Cambridge 1971-83; *Books* The Use of Lateral Thinking (1967), Lateral Thinking; a text book of creativity (1970), Wordpower (1977), de Bono's Thinking Course (1982); *Style*— Dr Edward de Bono; Cranmer Hall, Fakenham, Norfolk

DE BUNSEN, Hon Mrs; Alexandra; *née* Carrington; da of 6 Baron Carrington; *b* 11 April 1943; *m* 8 Sept 1965, Maj Peter Noel de Busen, Coldstream Guards (ret), eldest s of Charles de Bunsen, of Fincastle, Pitlochry, Perth (gs Sir Fowell Buxton 3rd Bt, GCMG) 2 s (Charles b 1970, Peter b 1973), 1 da (Victoria b 1968); *Style*— The Hon Mrs de Bunsen; Court Lodge, Harrietsham, Maidstone, Kent

DE BUNSEN, Sir Bernard; CMG (1957); s of Lothar Henry George de Bunsen (d 1950), and Victoria Alexandina (d 1953), 4 da of Sir (Thomas) Fowell Buxton, 3 Bt, GCMG, DL, JP; *b* 24 July 1907; *Educ* Leighton Park Sch Reading, Balliol Coll Oxford; *m* 1975, Joan Harmston, MBE; *Career* teacher Liverpool elementary schs 1931-34, asst dir of educn Wilts 1934-38, HM inspr of schs Miny of Educn 1938-46, dir of educn Palestine 1946-48, prof of educn Makerere Univ Coll E Africa 1948, (princ 1950-64, hon fell 1968, vice chllr 1963-65), princ Chester Coll 1966-71; chm: Africa Educnl Tst 1967-, Cncl for Aid to African Students 1976, Noel Buxton Tst 1975-83; vice pres: Anti-Slavery Soc, Royal African Soc; kt 1962; *Style*— Sir Bernard de Bunsen, CMG; 3 Prince Arthur Rd, London NW3 (☎ 01 435 3521)

DE BUNSEN, Ronald Lothar; s of Lothar Henry George De Bunsen (d 1950), and Victoria Alexandrina (d 1953), da of Sir (Thomas) Fowell Buxton, 3 Bt, GCMG; *b* 19 Feb 1910; *Educ* Westminster Sch, Trinity Coll Cambridge (BA, MA); *m* 29 Nov 1941, Margaret Forester, da of Cdr Morris Edward Cochrane, DSO, RN; 3 da (Margaret b 1943, Emma b 1947, Helen b 1949); *Career* WWII Flying Offr RAFVR; bank offr Barclays Bank Ltd; *Clubs* Travellers, Pall Mall; *Style*— Ronald L De Bunsen, Esq; Burgess Farm, Upshire, Waltham Abbey, Essex EN9 3TG

DE BUTLER, Norman Frank Paul; s of Paul Butler (d 1981), of Tipperary and Oak Brook, Illinois USA, and Adèle Josephine Rooney (d 1975); *b* 2 Dec 1918; *Educ* Hodder, Stonyhurst, Downside, Oxford Univ, Colombia Univ Graduate Sch of Law USA; *m* 1, 28 Oct 1948 (m dis 1958), Pauline Catherine (d 1983), da of Hon Charles Winn (s of 2 Baron St Oswald) and former w of Hon Edward Ward (twin s of 2 Earl of Dudley); 2 da (Mrs Timothy Heise b 1949, Baroness Ernest von Wedel b 1953); m 2, 1959, (m dis 1978) Hon Penelope Cynthia, da of 3 Baron Forteviot; 2 s (Paul b 1960, Sean b 1963), 1 da (Tracey b 1961); m 3, 1981, Baroness Gabriella Gröger von Sontag, of Cracow, Poland; 1 s (Patrick); *Career* served WW II, US Marines (inventor of radar life raft); dir and vice pres Butler Co Illinois; fndr and chm Butler Co SA; fndr Old Oak Brook and Kilboy Estates Stud Farms Ireland; breeder and owner (horses include: Pabui, Kilboy, Pidget); Air Medal, Presidential Citation 1945; *Recreations* gardening, polo, sailing, surfing, breeding horses and Irish Wolf Hounds; *Clubs* Union, Buck's, Oxford & Cambridge, Boojums, Oak Brook Polo, Butler Int Golf, River (NY), Bath & Tennis, Everglades, Seminole Polo (Palm Beach), Lansdowne, Union League, Chicago, Arts (Dublin); *Style*— Norman de Butler Esq; Barclays Bank, Monte Carlo; 1637 Charmey, Switzerland; Glen Mawnan, Mawnan Smith, Cornwall TR11 5LL

DE BUTTS, Brig Frederick Manus; CMG (1967), OBE (1961, MBE 1942), DL (Herts) 1975; s of Brig Frederick Cromie De Butts, CB, DSO, MC (d 1977), of Coolnakilly House, Glenealy, Co Wicklow, by his 1 w Kathleen Primrose Manus (d 1916), da of Octavius O'Donnell, of Hyntle Place, Hintlesham, Suffolk; *b* 17 April 1916; *Educ* Wellington Coll, Oriel Coll Oxford; *m* 8 July 1944, Evelyn Cecilia, da of Sir Walter Halsey, 2 Bt, OBE (d 1950); 1 s (David b 1950), 1 da (Mrs Anthony Bond b 1952); *Career* cmmnd Somerset Light Inf 1937, served WWII in M East (Western Desert and 8 Army), Italy and NW Europe, Staff Coll 1944, Jt Servs Staff Coll 1954, CO 3rd Bn Aden Protectorate Levies 1958-60, Bde Col Light Inf 1961-64, Cmd Trucial Oman Scouts 1964-67, Defence Attaché Cairo 1968-71; ret 1971; chief of staff MOD Utd Arab Emirates 1971-73, Hon Brig 1973; hon dir Herts Soc 1981-; *Recreations* tennis, hill-walking; *Style*— Brig Frederick De Butts CMG, OBE, DL; The Old Vicarage, Great Gaddesden, Hemel Hempstead, Herts (☎ 0442 62129)

DE CABARRUS, Lady Caroline Mary; *née* Percy; eldest da of 10 Duke of Northumberland, KG, GCVO, TD, PC, JP (d 1988); *b* 3 May 1947; *m* 1973, Count Pierre de Cabarrus; 2 da (Chiara b 1974, Diana b 1977); *Style*— Lady Caroline de Cabarrus; Syon House, Brentford, Middlesex TW8 8JF

DE CAICEDO, Marquesa; Hon Camilla Edith Mairi Elizabeth; *née* Jessel; elder and only surv da of 2 Baron Jessel (by 1 m); *b* 17 April 1940; *m* 1 Nov 1960, Don Juan Carlos del Prado y Ruspoli, 11 Marquès de Caicedo (cr Spain 1712); b 30 June 1934, succession to title recognised 28 Sept 1966; 2 s (Miguel b 1961, Alfonso b 1966); *Style*— Marquesa de Caicedo; C Alonso Cano 43, Madrid, Spain

DE CHAIR, Hon Mrs (Alexandra Mary); *née* Foley; da (by 1 m) of 8 Baron Foley; *b* 3 April 1960; *m* 25 July 1987, (Somerset) Carlo de Chair, s of Capt Somerset Struben de Chair, and his 2 w, June, *née* Appleton; *Career* arms and armour cataloguer Sotheby's; *Style*— The Hon Mrs de Chair; 36 Rosary Gardens, London SW7

DE CHAIR, Lady (Anne) Juliet Dorothea Maud; *née* Wentworth-Fitzwilliam; only child of 8 Earl Fitzwilliam (k in a flying acc in France 1948); *b* 24 Jan 1935; *Educ* St Hilda's Oxford; *m* 1, 23 April 1960 (m dis 1972), as his 2 w, 6 Marquess of Bristol (d 1985); 1 s (Lord Nicholas Hervey b 1961); m 2, 1974, as his 4 w, Capt Somerset Struben de Chair, s of Adm Sir Dudley de Chair KCB, KCMG, MVO; 1 da (Helena b 1977); *Style*— Lady Juliet de Chair; St Osyth's Priory, St Osyth, Essex

de CHAZAL, Paul André; s of Claude and Simone de Chazal; *b* 25 Sept 1942; *Educ* Downside, Sidney Sussex Coll Cambridge (BA); *m* 1978, Donatienne, da of Jean Louis Dierckx de Casterle; 2 da (Mélusine b 1979, Julie b 1982); *Career* slr; ptnr Messrs Simmons and Simmons; dir: Br American Insur Co Ltd 1972-88, Windsor Life Assur & Co Ltd 1978-88, Windsor Gr Ltd 1987-88, Hamilton Life Assur Co Ltd, Hamilton Insur Co Ltd; hon gen sec of Belgo-Luxembourg C of C; *Style*— Paul de Chazal, Esq; 15 Patten Rd, London SW18 3RH (☎ 01 874 5003, office 01 628 2020)

DE CLIFFORD, 27 Baron (E 1299); John Edward Southwell Russell; er s of 26 Baron de Clifford, OBE, TD (d 1982), by his 1 w, Dorothy Evelyn, da of Ferdinand Meyrick, MD, of Kensington Court, W8 and Kate Meyrick the nightclub owner; *b* 8 June 1928; *Educ* Eton, RAC Cirencester; *m* 27 June 1959, Bridget Jennifer, yst da of Duncan Robertson, of Llantysilio Hall, Llangollen, by his w Joyce (sis of Sir Watkin Williams-Wynn, 10th Bt, CBE, *qv*); *Heir* bro, Hon William Russell; *Career* farmer; *Clubs* Naval & Military; *Style*— The Rt Hon Lord de Clifford; Cliff House, Sheepy, Atherstone, Warwicks CV9 3RQ (☎ (0827) 880280)

DE COURCY, Hon Diana Ruth; da of 34(29) Baron Kingsale (d 1969), by 2 w Ruth, *née* Holmes; *b* 17 August 1951; *Style*— The Hon Diana de Courcy; c/o Cavalry and Guards, 127 Piccadilly, London W1

DE COURCY, Nevinson Russell; s of Nevinson William de Courcy (d 1919), and Grace, *née* Russell (d 1967); ggs of Adm Hon Michael de Courcy, 3 s of 25(20) Baron Kingsale); hp to kinsman, 30 Baron, Premier Baron of Ireland; *b* 21 July 1920, (posthumously); *m* 23 July 1954, Nora Lydia, da of James Plint, of Great Cosby, Lancs; 1 s (Nevinson Mark, b 11 May 1958), 1 da (Katherine Grace, b 26 April 1955); *Career* MA, MICE, MNZIE; *Style*— Nevinson de Courcy Esq; 15 Market Rd, Remuera, Auckland 5, NZ

DE COURCY HUGHES, Rosemary Margaret; da of Col Edward Guy Lethbridge Thurlow (d 1966), and Margaret Merry, *née* Vaughan (d 1952); *b* 19 June 1919; *Educ* Royal Sch Bath; *m* 1, 14 Feb 1947, Jasper John Ogilvie; 2 s (Philip b 1948, David b 1952); m 2, James Henry de Courcy Hughes; *Career* offr ATS 1943-47; Territorial Efficiency Medal; *Recreations* gardening, travelling; *Clubs* Army & Navy; *Style*— Mrs Rosemary de Courcy Hughes; The Old Rectory, Hinton St George, Somerset (☎ 0460 73031)

DE COURCY LING, John; MEP (EDG) Midlands Central 1979; s of late Arthur Norman Ling and Veronica, *née* de Courcy; *b* 14 Oct 1933; *Educ* King Edward's Sch Edgbaston, Clare Coll Cambridge; *m* 1959, Jennifer, *née* Haynes; 1 s, 3 da; *Career* served FO 1959-78; cnsllr HM Embassy Paris 1974-77; farmer 1977, chm Euro Parly Delgn to Israeli Knesset 1979-81, chief whip Euro Democratic (C) Gp MEPs to 1983; vice-chm Development Aid Ctee 1984, underwriting memb of Lloyd's 1969-; *Style*— John de Courcy Ling Esq; 4 Rothwell Street, Regent's Park, London NW1 (☎ 01 722 4279); Old Chalford House, Chipping Norton, Oxon, OX7 5QW

DE FALBE, Christian Vigant William; s of Brig-Gen Vigant William de Falbe, CMG, DSO, DL, JP (d 1940), of Whittington House, nr Lichfield, and Amy Rhona, *née* Hanbury (d 1947); *see* Burke's Landed Gentry, 18 edn, vol III, 1972; *b* 1 Jan 1923; *Educ* Eton; *m* 12 June 1954, Jane, da of Maj Rowland Arthur Marriott, OBE, of Cotesbach Hall, Lutterworth, Leics; 3 s ((Charles) Christian b 1957, John b 1963, (William) Frederick b 1966), 3 da ((Emma) Rose b 1955, Sophia (Mrs Thomas Newton) b 1959, Clarissa (Mrs Julian Coles) b 1961); *Career* served KRRC 1941-46, wounded N Africa 1942, Major; dir H Clarkson and Co (Insurance) Ltd 1953-73; underwriting memb Lloyds 1953-88; *Clubs* Cavalry and Guards'; *Style*— Christian V W de Falbe, Esq; Saffins, Bicknoller, nr Taunton, Somerset

DE FERRANTI, Sebastian Basil Joseph Ziani; s of Sir Vincent de Ferranti, MC; bro of Basil, *qv*; *b* 5 Oct 1927; *Educ* Ampleforth; *m* 1, 9 April 1953, Mona Helen, o da of T E Cunningham, of Broomfield Cottage, Sunningdale, Berks; 1 s, 2 da; m 2, 1983, Naomi Angela Rae; *Career* chm Ferranti plc 1963-82 (md 1958-75, dir 1954); dir: GEC plc 1982-, Nat Nuclear Corp 1984-88; Br Airways Helicopters 1982-84; pres Electrical Research Assoc 1968-69, BEAMA 1969-70, Centre for Educn in Science Educn and Technology Manchester and region 1972; chm Int Elec Assoc 1970-72, Civic Tst NW 1978; memb Nat Defence Industries Cncl 1969-77, cncl IEE 1970-73; vice pres RSA 1980; Tstee Tate Gallery 1971-78; High Sheriff of Cheshire 1988-89; Hon DSc Salford Univ 1967; Cranfeld Inst of Technol; *Clubs* Cavalry and Guards, Pratts'; *Style*— Sebastian de Ferranti Esq; Henbury Hall, Macclesfield, Cheshire (☎ 0625 22101)

DE FONBLANQUE, John Robert; s of Maj-Gen Edward Barrington de Fonblanque, (d 1982), of The Cottage, Bank, Lyndhurst, Hants, and Elizabeth Flora Lutley, *née* Sclater; *b* 20 Dec 1943; *Educ* Ampleforth, King's Coll Cambridge (MA), LSE (MSc); *m* 24 March 1984, Margaret, da of Harry Prest, of 158 Cannock Rd, Stafford; 1 s (Thomas b 1985); *Career* HM Diplomatic Service since 1968: 2 sec Jakarta 1969-71, 1 sec UK rep to EC 1971-77, principal HM Treasury 1977-79, FCO 1979-83, asst sec Cabinet Off 1983-85, cnsllr Delhi 1986-87, UK rep to Euro Community 1988-; *Recreations* mountain walking; *Style*— John R de Fonblanque, Esq; UK Representation to the EC, Brussels

DE FREITAS, Lady; Helen Graham; da of Laird Bell, Hon KBE, Hon LLD Harvard, of Chicago; *m* 1938, Rt Hon Sir Geoffrey de Freitas, KCMG (d 1982, MP Central Nottingham, Lincoln and Kettering, parly under-sec Air and Home Office, high cmmr Ghana 1961-63, Kenya 1964; 3 s, 1 da; *Style*— Lady de Freitas; 34 Tufton Court, Tufton St, London SW1 (☎ 01 799 3770)

DE FRESNES, Lady Fiona, Baroness; Fiona Huddleston; *née* Abney-Hastings; da of 13 Countess of Loudoun; co-heiress to Baronies of Botreaux, Stanley and Hastings (cr 1461) in abeyance since 1960; *b* 26 Feb 1923; *m* 27 Sept 1940, Capt Robert Conroy-Robertson, 12 Baron de Fresnes, *qv*; 4 s (and 1 decd), 1 da; *Style*— Lady Fiona de Fresnes; Cessnock Castle, Galston, Ayrshire, Scotland

DE FRESNES, (Christopher) Ian; eldest s of 12 Baron de Fresnes (French title), *qv*; *b* 8 May 1942; *Educ* Ampleforth, Glasgow Sch of Art; *m* 1, 1969 (m dis 1971) Elvira Maria, da of Wing Cdr Marcel Pustelniak; 1 s (Robert b 1970); m 2 1973 Angela da of Lt-Col Denys Ainsworth Yates; 1 s (Rawdon b 1974), 1 da (Nicola b 1975); *Style*— Ian de Fresnes Esq; Elm Tree House, High Halden, Ashford, Kent

DE FRESNES, 12 Baron (Fr 1642); Capt Robert (Conray-Robertson); assumed by deed poll 1944 surname de Fresnes on succeeding maternal gf as Baron de Fresnes; *b* 1908; *Educ* St Egmont's Sch France, Schs of Art Glasgow, London, Paris and Milan; *m* 1940, Lady Fiona, *née* Abney-Hastings, *qv*; 4 s (1 decd) (Christopher b 1942, *qv*, Nigel b 1944, Paulyn b 1949, Vivian b 1960), 1 da (Nicole b 1957); *Career* joined RA 1940, War Office 1945, hon patron Galston Branch Br Legion (Scotland), art critic, journalist and conslt in interior design; artist and portrait painter; Assoc of Interior Decorators and Design Assoc; *Clubs* County (Ayr); *Style*— Baron de Fresnes; Cessnock Castle, Galston, Ayrshire (☎ Galston 314)

DE FREYNE, 7 Baron (UK 1851); KM Francis Arthur John French; s of 6 Baron, JP, DL (d 1935), by Victoria, da of Sir John Arnott, 2 Bt; *b* 3 Sept 1927; *m* 1, 30 Jan 1954 (m dis 1978), Shirley Ann, da of late Douglas Rudolph Pobjoy; 2 s (Hon Fulke, Hon Patrick b 1969), 1 da (Hon Vanessa b 1958); m 2, 1978, Sheelin Deirdre, da of Col Henry O'Kelly, DSO, of Co Wicklow, and widow of William Walker Stevenson; *Heir* s, Hon Fulke Charles Arthur John French, *qv*; *Style*— The Rt Hon Lord De Freyne; c/o The House of Lords, Westminster, London

DE GELSEY, William Henry Marie; s of Baron Henry de Gelsey (d 1963), formerly of Hungary, and Marguerite, *née* Lieser (d 1965); *b* 17 Dec 1921; *Educ* Roman Catholic Univ Public Sch Budapest, Trinity Coll Cambridge (MA); *Career* investment banker; exec dir Hill Samuel and Co Ltd 1959-71, md Orion Bank Ltd 1971-80, dep chm Orion Royal Bank Ltd 1980-; *Recreations* travelling; *Clubs* Annabel's, Mark's, Harry's Bar; *Style*— William de Gelsey, Esq; Orion Royal Bank Ltd, Hibiya Kokusai Building, 2-3 Uchisaiwaicho 2-Chome, Tokyo 100, Japan (☎ 3 501 6431, fax 3 501 7833)

DE GERLACHE DE GOMERY, Baron (Belgium 1924, by King Albert I); Philippe; LVO (1963); s of Baron de Gerlache de Gomery (cr Baron 1924, Polar explorer, the first to winter in the Antarctic, d 1934), gn of Baron (Etienne Constantin) de Gerlache (cr 1844), who was Pres of the Belgian Congress and led the Delegation that offered the Belgian crown to Prince Leopold of Saxe-Saalfeld-Coburg; a second Barony (cr 1885, the first having become extinct 1883) is held by a senior branch of the family; a common ancestor of both lines was Jean Louis de Gerlache, Seigneur de Gomery, who received a confirmation of nobility from the Empress Maria Theresa 1751; *b* 12 Nov 1906; *Educ* Bedales, Decroly (Brussels), Univ of Antwerp; *m* 1937, Yvonne, da of Maurice Verhoustraeten; 1 s; *Heir* s, Baron Jean de Gerlache de Gomery b 20 Dec 1952; *Career* Capt Cdr Belgian Artillery 1940; head Belgian Econ Mission London 1946-47, special cnsllr Belgian Embassy London 1948-73, sec Anglo-Belgian Club 1974, exec chm 1982; *Recreations* painting, walking, reading; *Clubs* Anglo-Belgian; *Style*— Baron de Gerlache de Gomery, LVO; 3 Upper Cheyne Row, SW3 5JW (☎ 01 352 3343)

DE GREY, Hon Mrs Amanda Lucy; *née* Annan; elder da of Baron Annan (Life Peer); *b* 13 June 1952; *m* 1977, Spencer Thomas de Grey, s of Roger de Grey, PRA; 1 da (Georgia Catherine b 1988); *Style*— The Hon Mrs de Grey; 56 Clapham Manor St, London SW4

DE GREY, Hon Mrs Richard; Dorothy; da of late Thomas Knight, of Sidcup; *m* 11 Jan 1969, as his 2 w, Hon Richard Patrick de Grey, TD (d 1984), s of 7 Baron Walsingham (d 1929); *Style*— The Hon Mrs Richard de Grey; Hassocks, Merton, Thetford, Norfolk (☎ Watton 881325)

DE GUINGAND, Anthony Paul; s of Paul Emile De Guingand (d 1976), and Olwyn Doreen, *née* Witts; *b* 7 August 1947; *Educ* Ampleforth; *m* 24 Nov 1973, Diana Mary, da of John Harrington Parr; 2 s (Marcus b 1977, Peter b 1982), 1 da (Emily b 1979); *Career* exec dir Int Commodities Clearing House Ltd 1973-86; dir: London Traded Options Mkt, Int Stock Exchange 1986-; memb ctee London Soc of CAs (chm City Gp); *Recreations* rugby, golf; *Style*— The International Stock Exchange, London EC2N 1HP (☎ 01 588 2355, fax 01 374 0451); The Int Stock Exchange, London EC2N 1HP (☎ 01 588 2355, fax 01 374 0451)

DE HAAS, Margaret Ruth; da of Joseph de Haas, of 1 Grove Pk, Wanstead, London E11, and Lisalotte Herte, *née* Meyer; *b* 21 May 1954; *Educ* Townsend Girls Sch Bulawayo Zimbabwe, Univ of Bristol (LLB); *m* 18 May 1980, Iain Saville Goldrein, s of Neville Clive Golrein, of Torreno, 18 St Andrews' Rd, Blundellsands, Crosby, Liverpool; 1 s (Alastair Philip b 1 Oct 1982), 1 da (Alexandra Ann b 22 Feb 1985); *Career* barr Middle Temple 1977, practising N circuit; memb Family Law Bar Assoc; *Books* Property Distribution on Divorce (second edn with Iain S Goldrein, 1985), Personal Injury Litegation (with I Goldrein 1985), Domestic Injuctions (1987), Butterworths Personal Injury Litigation Service (second edn with Iain S Goldrein, 1988); *Recreations* family, swimming, law, theatre; *Style*— Miss Margaret de Haas; 4 Linden Ave, Blundellsands, Crosby, Liverpool L23 8UL (☎ 051 924 2610); 48 Castle St, Liverpool L2 7LQ (☎ 051 227 5009, fax 051 227 5488, car 0836 583 257)

DE HALPERT, Cdr Simon David; s of Lt Cdr Michael Francis de Halpert, DSC, RN, of Petersfield, Hants, and (Eleanor) Anne Love, *née* White; *b* 27 Dec 1946; *Educ* Lanford, BRNC Dartmouth; *m* 19 Dec 1970, Katherine Marie Lafferty, da of James Daly, of Hayant, Hants; 2 s (Michael b 1974, Christopher b 1975), 1 da (Natasha b 1972); *Career* Midshipman HMS Highburton 1965, Midshipman and Sub Lt HMS Tiger 1966, Sub Lt HMS Llandaff 1966-67, Sub Lt and Lt HMS Mohawk 1968-70, Lt HMS Upton, HMS Brighton 1972-73, Warfare Course HMS Dryad 1973-74, HMS Charybois 1974-75, Advanced ASW Course HMS Vernon 1976, seconded US Navy 1976-78 (Lt and Lt Cdr), Lt Cdr HMS Lowestoft 1979-80, HMS Diomede 1980, HMS Dryad 1981-82, HMS Cleopatra 1983-84, Cdr and OC HMS Argonaut 1985-86, Cdr HMS Dryad 1987-89; *Recreations* squash, real tennis, cricket, gardening, music; *Style*— Cdr Simon de Halpert

DE HAVILLAND, John Anthony; s of Maj-Gen Peter Hugh de Havilland, CBE, DL, *qv*, of Horkesley Hall, Colchester and Helen Elizabeth Wrey, (d 1976), only da of William Whitmore Otter-Barry, of Horkesley Hall; *b* 14 April 1938; *Educ* Eton, Trinity Coll Cambridge; *m* 1964, Hilary Anne, da of Robert Ewen MacKenzie of Ulceby, Lincs; 1 s (Piers b 1970), 2 da (Lucinda b 1964, Victoria b 1968); *Career* joined J Henry Schroder Wagg & Co Ltd 1959, (md 1971-89); *Recreations* shooting and rifle shooting (for England 1961-88, Capt English VIII 1979-89), winner Match Rifle Championship nine times between 1963-87; *Clubs* Army and Navy; *Style*— John de Havilland, Esq; Shimpling Hall, Bury St Edmunds, Suffolk; J Henry Schroder Wagg & Co Ltd, 120 Cheapside, London EC2V 6DS (☎ 01 382 6475)

DE HAVILLAND, Maj-Gen Peter Hugh; CBE (1945, OBE 1940), DL (Essex 1962); s of Hugh de Beauvoir de Havilland, JP (d 1952), of The Manor House, Great Horkesley, Colchester; *b* 29 July 1904; *Educ* Eton, RMA Woolwich; *m* 1, 9 July 1930, Helen Elizabeth Wrey (d 1976), da of William Whitmore Otter-Barry, of Horkesley Hall, Colchester (d 1976); 2 s; m 2, 1981, Angela, da of R Franklin; *Career* 2 Lt RA 1925, served WW II France and Belgium 1939-40 and 1944-45, M East 1942, N Africa 1943, dep land cmmr Schleswig Holstein 1948-49, Col 1949, Maj-Gen 1954, UK mil rep to Supreme HQ Europe 1951-53, COS Northern Cmd 1953-55, ret 1955; dir Steel Works Plant Assoc 1958-77; *Recreations* shooting, flying; *Clubs* Army & Navy; *Style*— Maj-Gen Peter de Havilland, CBE, DL; Horkesley Hall, Colchester, Essex (☎ 0206 271 259)

DE HOGHTON, Sir (Richard) Bernard Cuthbert; 14 Bt (E 1611); s of Sir Cuthbert de Hoghton, 12 Bt (d 1958), and half-brother of Sir (Henry Philip) Anthony (Mary) de Hoghton, 13 Bt (d 1978); *b* 26 Jan 1945; *Educ* Ampleforth, McGill Univ Montreal, Birmingham Univ (BA, MA); *m* 1974, Rosanna Stella Virginia, da of Terzo Buratti, of Florence; 1 s, 1 da; *Heir* s, Thomas de Hoghton (b 1980); *Career* landowner; stockbroker with BZW Securities Ltd 1977-; kt of Malta; *Recreations* shooting, tennis, skiing; *Clubs* Royal Overseas League; *Style*— Sir Bernard de Hoghton, Bt; Hoghton Tower, Hoghton, Preston, Lancs (☎ 025 485 2986)

DE JONG, Maj Nicholas Charles Callard; s of David de Jong (d 1919); *b* 15 Oct 1911; *Educ* Queen Elizabeth's Crediton, Technological Coll Cardiff, Univ of S Wales, London Univ (BSc), Open U (BA); *m* 1937, Olwen May, da of Henry James East (d 1960); 1 da; *Career* Maj BEF, served N W Europe, France, Belgium, Holland and Germany; telephone manager Preston 1953-57, controller NI 1957-61, dep engr-in-ch PO HQ 1961-66; dir: Postal Mechanisation 1966-73, Pitney Bowes Ltd 1973-83; Offr of Order of Orange Nassau 1945, American Bronze Star 1946; *Recreations* golf, walking, boating, art; *Style*— Maj Nicholas de Jong

DE KLEE, Col Murray Peter; OBE (1974); s of Lt-Col Frederick Bertram de Klee (d 1963), and Violet Virginia, *née* Guthrie (d 1988); *b* 3 Jan 1928; *Educ* Wellington; *m* 6 July 1955, Angela Moira Jean, da of Patrick Stormonth-Darling (d 1960); 3 s (Rupert b 1956, Hugo b 1957, Richard b 1960), 1 da (Nichola b 1959); *Career* Scots Gds 1945-83, regimental duty incl tours with the Parachute Regt and SAS Regt interspersed with staff appointments, Malaya 1948, Near East 1956, Cyprus 1956, Borneo 1965, S Arabia 1968, Malay Peninsula 1969, NI 1970 Lt Col Cmdg Scots Gds 1975; despatches 1950, 1956; Croix de Guerre 1958; *Recreations* stalking, skiing; *Style*— Col Murray P de Klee; Auchnacraig, Isle of Mull, Argyll

DE L'ISLE, 1 Viscount (UK 1956); Sir William Philip Sidney; 9 Bt (UK 1806 & 1818), of Castle Goring, Sussex, and 7 Bt of Penshurst Place, Kent, respectively, VC (1944), KG (1968), GCMG (1961), GCVO (1963), PC (1951); also Baron De L'Isle and Dudley (UK 1835); s of 5 Baron De L'Isle and Dudley, JP (d 1945), and Winifred (d 1959), da of Roland Yorke Bevan and Hon Agneta, da of 10 Lord Kinnaird; *b* 23 May 1909; *Educ* Eton, Magdalene Coll Cambridge; *m* 1, 8 June 1940, Hon Jacqueline Corinne Yvonne Vereker (d 1962), o da of Field Marshal 6 Viscount Gort (I) and 1 Viscount Gort of Hamsterley (UK 1946), VC, GCB, CBE, DSO, MVO, MC (d 1946); 1 s, 4 da (Hon Mrs Rattray b 1941, Hon Mrs Villiers b 1942, Hon Mrs Harries b 1947, Hon Mrs Middleton b 1953; m 2, 24 March 1966, Margaret, da of Maj-Gen Thomas Shoubridge, CB, CMG, DSO, and wid of 3 Baron Glanusk, DSO; *Heir* s, Maj the Hon Philip John Algernon Sidney, MBE b 21 April 1945; *Career* served Grenadier Guards Reserve 1929 and WW II; sits as Conservative peer in House of Lords; MP (C) Chelsea 1944-45; parly sec Miny of Pensions 1945; sec of state for air 1951-55; govr-gen of Australia 1961- 65; chm Freedom Assoc 1975-84 (pres 1984-); chm Churchill Memorial Tst; dep pres Victoria Cross and George Cross Assoc; pres SE of England Tourist Bd; former tstee: British Museum, Nat Portrait Gallery, RAF Museum, Royal Armouries Museum; hon bencher Gray's Inn 1982; hon memb Grocers' Co 1987; Hon LLD Sydney Univ and Hampden Sydney Coll Virginia; hon fell Magdalene Coll Cambridge; hon FRIBA; hon fell Australian Inst of Architecture; FCA; KStJ; *Clubs* White's; *Style*— The Rt Hon Viscount De L'Isle, VC,; Penshurst Place, Tonbridge, Kent (☎ 0892 870223); Glanusk Park, Crickhowell, Brecon

DE L'ISLE BUSH, Lt-Cdr (Christopher) Godfrey; s of Lt Hugh Godfrey de L'Isle Bush, MC, Glous Regt (d 1918); *b* 10 Dec 1916; *Educ* Abberley Hall, RNC Dartmouth; *m* 1950, Christine, da of Clifford Exell, of Little Court, Hardenhuish, Chippenham, Wilts; 4 children; 9 gchildren; *Career* Lt Cdr RN, cmd HM Destroyers Leamington, Newmarket, Farndale and Hambledon WW II; chm: Reytex Oil and Gas Inc, Explaura Gold plc, Texican Oil plc; dir Grand Central Investment Holdings plc and subids; *Recreations* salmon fishing, picture restoration; *Style*— Lt-Cdr Godfrey de L'Isle Bush; Frampton Lodge, Frampton-on-Severn, Gloucester GL2 7EX (☎ Gloucester 740 246)

DE LA BARRE DE NANTEUIL, HE Luc; s of Jean De La Barre de Nanteuil (d 1937), and Marguerite, *née* De Beauchamp (d 1971); *b* 21 Sept 1925; *Educ* Licence or Letters, Dip d'Etudes Superieures de Droit, Ancien Elève de l'Ecole Nationale d'Administration; *m* 1, Philippa MacDonald; 1 s (Charles-Edouard b 1963); m 2, 1973, Hedwige, Frèrejean de Chavagneux; 1 s (François b 1982), 1 s decd (Jean b 1976, d 1980), 1 da (Sophie b 1978); *Career* secrétariat gen 1951-52, Pacts Service 1952-53, Econ Affairs Dept 1954-59, first sec London 1959-64, asst dir African and M East Affairs Dept 1964-70, Min Plen 1969, Head of Economic Co-operation Service Directorate of Econ Affairs 1970-76, Ambassador to Netherlands 1976-77, French Permanent Rep to EEC Brussels 1977-81 and to Security Cncl to NY and Head of French Permanent Mission to UN NY 1981-84, French Permanent Rep to EEC Brussels 1984-86, Diplomatic Advsr 1986, Ambassador to UK 1986; Offr of the Legion of Honour, Cdr of the Order of Merit; *Books* Jacques-Louis David; *Recreations* economics and the arts; *Clubs* Traveller's, White's; *Style*— HE The French Ambassador; The French Embassy, 58 Knightsbridge, London SW1

DE LA BEDOYERE, Comtesse Michael; Charlotte; *née* Halbik; *b* 24 Nov 1931;

Educ The Old Palace Mayfield Sussex; *m* 1961, as his 2 w, Comte Michael de la Bédoyère, sometime ed Catholic Herald and gs through his f of Alexis Huchet, Marquis de la Bédoyère (who m 1869 Hon Mildred Greville-Nugent, da of 1 Baron Greville); Charles Huchet de la Bédoyère was cr Comte 1710 and was Procureur-Général of the Bretagne Parlement, while another Huchet was cr Comte 1815 by Napoleon; Bertrand Huchet, Seigneur de la Huchetais and Sec of State to Jean V, Duke of Brittany, m c 1420 Jeanne de la Bédoyère, Dame de la Bédoyère; Comte Michael was gs through his mother of Dr A Thorold, sometime Bishop of Winchester; 2 children; *Career* md Search Press Ltd, Burns & Oates Ltd (publishers to the Holy See 1842-); *Recreations* gardening, swimming, photography; *Clubs* Hurlingham; *Style*— Comtesse Michael de la Bédoyere; Spey House, Mayfield, E Sussex

DE LA BERE, Adrian; s of Sir Rupert De la Bère, 1 Bt (d 1978); hp of bro, Sir Cameron De la Bère, 2 Bt, *qv*; *b* 17 Sept 1939; *Style*— Adrian De la Bère Esq

DE LA BERE, Sir Cameron; 2 Bt (UK 1953); s of Sir Rupert De la Bère, 1 Bt, KCVO (d 1978), Lord Mayor of London 1952-53 by Marguerite (d 1969) el da Lt Col Sir John Humphrey of Surrey; *b* 12 Feb 1933; *Educ* Tonbridge and abroad; *m* 20 June 1964, Clairemonde, only da of Casimir Kaufmann, of Geneva; 1 da (Rejane b 1965); *Heir* bro, Adrian De la Bère; *Career* jeweller; Liveryman Skinner's Co; *Clubs* Société Litéraire (Geneva), Hurlingham; *Style*— Sir Cameron De la Bère Bt; 1 Avenue Theodore Flournoy, 1207 Geneva, Switzerland (☎ 86 00 15)

DE LA MARE, Prof Albinia Catherine; da of Richard Herbert Ingpen de la Mare (d 1986), and Amy Catherine, *née* Donaldson (d 1968); *b* 2 June 1932; *Educ* Queens Coll Harley St London, Lady Margaret Hall Oxford (BA, MA), Warburg Inst Univ of London (PhD); *Career* asst librarian Bodleian Library Oxford 1964-88 (temp cataloguer 1962-64), prof of palaeography King's Coll London 1989-, Civil Def Corps 1965-68, memb Nat Voluntary Civil Aid Oxford 1968; memb Comité International de Paléographie Latine 1986, FRHistS, FBA 1987; *Books* Catalogue of the Italian Manuscripts of Major J R Abbey (with J Alexander, 1969), Catalogue of the Lyell Manuscripts Bodleian Library Oxford (1971), Handwriting of Italian Humanists (1973), Miniatura Fiorentina del Rinascimento (contrib, 1985); *Recreations* gardening, listening to music, travel; *Clubs* Univ Women's; *Style*— Professor Albinia de la Mare; Department of Palaeography, King's Coll, London

DE LA MARE, Sir Arthur James; KCMG (1968, CMG 1957), KCVO (1972); s of Walter de la Mare, of Jersey; *b* 15 Feb 1914; *Educ* Victoria Coll Jersey, Pembroke Coll Cambridge; *m* 1940, Katherine Sherwood; 3 da; *Career* FO 1936, served Tokyo, San Francisco, Seoul; head Security Dept 1953-56, cnsllr Washington 1956-60, head Far Eastern Dept FO 1960-63; ambass: Afghanistan 1963-65, Thailand 1970-73, asst under-sec FO 1965-67, high cmmr Singapore 1968-70; chm: Anglo-Thai Soc 1976-82, Royal Soc Asian Affairs 1978-84, Jersey Soc in London 1980-85; *Style*— Sir Arthur de la Mare, KCMG, KCVO; 66 Sylvan Road, Exeter, Devon EX4 6HA

DE LA RUE, Sir Eric Vincent; 3 Bt (UK 1898); s of Sir Evelyn Andros de la Rue, *qv*, 2 Bt, JP (d 1950); *b* 5 August 1906; *Educ* Oundle; *m* 1, 5 June 1945, Cecilia (d 17 March 1963), da of Maj Walter Waring, DL, MP (d 1930); 2 s; m 2, 13 Feb 1964 Christine, da of Kurt Schellin, MD, of Connecticut, USA; 1 s; *Heir* s, Andrew George Ilay de la Rue b 3 Feb 1946; *Career* Capt Notts Yeo 1942-45; *Style*— Sir Eric de la Rue, Bt; Caldra, Duns, Berwickshire (☎ 0361 3294)

DE LA TOUR, Ms Frances; da of Charles De La Tour (d 1983), and Moyra Silberman, *née* Fessas; family of the painter Georges Fautin De La Tour (d 1652); *b* 30 July 1945; *Educ* Lycée Francais De Londres, Drama Centre London; *m* 1 s (Josh Kempinski b 7 Feb 1977), 1 da (Tamasin Kempinski b 12 Nov 1973); *Career* actress: Standard Award for Best Actress 1980 for 'Duet for One', Critics Award Best Actress 1980, SWET Award Best Actress in a new Play 1980 for 'Duet for One', SWET Award for Best Actress in a Revival 1983 for 'Moon for the Misbegotten'; nominated for BAFTA award Best Actress 1985 for 'Duet for One'; *Style*— Ms Frances De La Tour

DE LA WARR, Anne, Countess; Anne Rachel; *née* Devas; o da of late Capt Geoffrey Charles Devas, MC, of Hunton Court, Maidstone, Kent, and Joan, *née* Campbell-Bannerman; *m* 18 May 1946, 10 Earl De La Warr, DL (d 1988); 2 s (11 Earl, Hon Thomas Sackville), 1 da (Lady Arabella); 93 Eaton Place, London SW1 (☎ 01 235 7990)

DE LA WARR, Sylvia, Countess; Sylvia Margaret; DBE (1957); da of William Reginald Harrison, of Liverpool, and sister of Rex Harrison, actor; *m* 1, 15 April 1925, first and last Earl of Kilmuir, PC, GCVO (d 1967); 2 da (Lady Pamela Blackmore, Lady Miranda Cormack and Lalage b 1926 d 1944); m 2, 1 March 1968 as his 2 w, 9 Earl De La Warr, PC, GBE (d 1976); *Style*— The Rt Hon Sylvia, Countess De La Warr, DBE; Ludshott Manor, Bramshott, Hants GU30 7RD (☎ 0428 724668)

DE LA WARR, 11 Earl (GB 1761); William Herbrand Sackville; also Baron De La Warr (E 1299 and 1570), Viscount Cantelupe (GB 1761), and Baron Buckhurst (UK 1864); er s of 10 Earl De La Warr, DL (d 1988); *b* 10 April 1948; *Educ* Eton; *m* 1978, Anne, *née* Leveson, former w of Earl of Hopetoun (s of 3 Marq of Linlithgow); 2 s (Lord Buckhurst, Hon Edward b 1980); *Heir* s, William Herbrand Thomas, Lord Buckhurst b 13 June 1979; *Career* stockbroker, Mullens & Co; *Style*— Lord Buckhurst; 49 Smith St, London SW3 (☎ 01 352 1317); Buckhurst Park, Withyam, E Sussex (☎ 089 277 346)

DE LASZLO, Damon Patrick; only s of Patrick David de Laszlo (d 1980), and Deborah, *née* Greenwood, da 1 viscount Greenwood PC, KC, and gs of Philip de Laszlo (d 1937), the portrait painter; *b* 8 Oct 1942; *Educ* Gordonstoun; *m* 1972, Hon Sandra Daphne, da of 2 Baron Hacking (d 1971); 2 s (Robert b 1977), 1 da (Lucy b 1975); *Career* memb Lloyds; co dir; chm Economic Research Cncl 1980-; *Recreations* shooting, scuba diving, economics; *Clubs* Boodle's, Carlton, City of London,; *Style*— Damon De Laszlo, Esq; A2 Albany, Piccadilly, London W1V 9RD (☎ 01 437 1982); Southfield Farm, Chawton, nr Alton, Hants (☎ 0420 83318)

DE LISLE, Hon Mrs Mary Rose; *née* Peake; da of 1 Viscount Ingleby (d 1966), and Lady Joan Rachel de Vere, *née* Capell (d 1979), da of 7 Earl of Essex; *b* 23 April 1940; *Educ* Queens Coll London; *m* 2 April 1959, Everard John Robert March Phillipps de Lisle, DL (Leics 1980) RHG (ret), el s of Major John de Lisle DL (d 1961), of Stockerston Hall, Uppingham, Leics; 2 s (Charles b 1960, Timothy b 1962), 1 da (Mary Rosanna b 1968); *Career* churchwarden of St Peter's, Stockerston; *Recreations* tennis, reading, family history; *Style*— The Hon Mrs de Lisle; Stockerston Hall, Uppingham, Leics (☎ Uppingham 0572 822404); Hereford Mansions, Hereford Rd, London W2 (☎ 01 229 4120)

DE LONGUEMAR, Vicomte Pierre; s of Col Vicomte de Longuemar and Odette, *née* Cesbron Lavau; *b* 9 May 1929; *Educ* Ecole des Hautes Etudes Commerciales Paris; *m* 7 Feb 1955, Armelle, da of Comte Michel de Beaumont; 2 s (Thierry b 1955, Geoffroy b 1957), 1 da (Diane-Marie b 1961); *Career* int dept Banque Paribas (Paris) 1954-66, Int Finance Corp Washington 1966-69, sous-directeur Banque Paribas (Paris) 1969 (directeur adjoint 1977, directeur 1984), md Banque Paribas London 1987-; non-exec dir: Banque Paribas Capital Markets 1987, Banque Franco-Yougoslave, Société Nouvelle de Banque Europe; *Clubs* Overseas Bankers', Jockey (Paris); *Style*— Vicomte Pierre de Longuemar; Banque Paribas, 68 Lombard Street, London EC3V 9EH (☎ 01 929 4545, fax 01 726 6761, telex 886055)

DE LONGUEUIL, 11 Baron (sole title in Peerage of Canada, cr 1700); Raymond David Grant; s of 10 Baron (d 1959, whose half unc, 7 Baron, received recognition of cr of Louis XIV by Queen Victoria in 1880 under terms of Treaty of Quebec which ceded sovereignty of Canada from Fr to GB) and Ernestine (d 1981), da of Hon Ernest Bowes-Lyon, 3 s of 13 Earl of Strathmore, formerly wife of Francis Winstone Scott; *b* 3 Sept 1921; *m* 1946, Anne, da of late Patrick Brough Maltby; 1 s; *Heir* s, Michael Charles b 1947; *Style*— Baron de Longueuil; 64190 Navarrenx, France

DE LOS ANGELES, Victoria; *b* 1 Nov 1923; *Educ* Escoles Milá i Fontanals de la Generlitat de Catalumya Barcelona Conservatorio de Liceo Barcelona (hons grad completed the 6 year course in 3 years); *m* 1948, Enrique Magriná (dec'd); 2 s; *Career* lyric-soprano, opera 2 concert arisite; concert debut de la Musica Catalana Barcelona 1944, opera debut Gran Teztro del Liceo Barcelona 1945, Concert and opera tours of Europe, N Central and S America, S Africa, the Middle and Far East, Australia, N-Z, Thailand, Korea, Philippines, Singapore, Hong Kong and most Eastern European countries 1945-; her repertoire of German lieder, French art songs and Spanish songs exceeds 1000; operatic repertoire incl: Marriage of Figero, Lohengrin, Tannhouser, Meistersinger, Trautatz, Cavelleriz Rusticana, I Pagliecci, La Boheme, Madame Butterfly, Manon; I prize concoud Int Geneva 1947, gold medal Barcelona 1958, medal premio Roma 1969 and many French, Italian and Dutch awards; gold disc for 5 million records sold FB; hon Doctorate Univ of Barcelona; cross of Lazo de Dama Spain, Condecoracion Bancla de la order Civil de Alfubiox Spain; *Style*— Miss V De Los Angeles; Avenide de Pedralbos 57, 08034 Barcelona, Spain; Basil Douglas Artists Management, 8 St George's Terrace, London NW1 8XJ (☎ 01 722 7142, fax 01 722 1841)

DE LOTBINIERE *see also*: Joly de Lotbinière

DE MARÉ, Eric Samuel; s of Bror August Erik de Maré (d 1948), timber broker of London, and Ingrid Inga-Brita, *née* Tellander (d 1964); genealogy traced to first Crusade from France; Jean de Maré, Huguenot, assassinated the Duc de Guise; Jacques Le Bel de Maré, refugee, taught the King of Sweden how to wield the epée; gf, govr of Dalarna Province, Sweden; cous, Rolf de Maré, founder of Swedish Ballet Company and Museum of Dance, Stockholm; br Dr Patrick de Maré, pioneer of Group Psychotherapy; *b* 10 Sept 1910; *Educ* St Paul's, Architectural Assoc Sch of Architecture London; *m* 1, 1936, Vanessa Burrage (d 1972); 2, 1974, Enid Verity, artist and colour conslt, da of Edward Hill (d 1970), of London; *Career* freelance architectural writer and photographer, ed Architects Journal 1943-46, hon tres Social Credit Pty 1938-46; *Books* incl: Canals of England, Bridges of Britain, Time on the Thames, Scandinavia, London's Riverside, London 1851, Wren's London, Architecture and Photography, Victorian Woodblock Illustrators (Yorks Post Award 1980), Swedish Crosscut: The Story of the Göta Canal, A Matter of Life or Debt (The Douglas Creed), in the light of the Micro-Chip Revolution; *Recreations* philosophising with friends, bashing the Money Mafia; *Style*— Eric de Maré Esq; The Old Chapel, Tunley, nr Sapperton, Cirencester, Glos GL7 6ZW (☎ 028 576 382)

DE MARFFY VON VERSEGH, Hon Mrs; Pelline Margot; *née* Lyon-Dalberg-Acton; da of 3 Baron Acton; *b* 24 Dec 1932; *m* 30 June 1953, Lazlo de Marffy von Versegh; 7 s (1 decd) (Denis b 1954, Miklos b 1956, Joseph b 1957, Paul b 1958, Robert b 1962, Stephen b 1965), 1 da (Gabriella b 1960); *Style*— Hon Mrs de Marffy von Versegh; Ealing Farm, PO Box 29, Umvukwes, Zimbabwe

DE MAULEY, 6 Baron (UK 1838); Gerald John Ponsonby; s of 5 Baron de Mauley (d 1962); *b* 19 Dec 1921; *Educ* Eton, Ch Ch Oxford (BA, MA); *m* 1954, Helen, widow of Lt-Col Brian Abdy Collins, OBE, MC, and da of Hon Charles Sholto Douglas (d 1960, 2 s of 19 Earl of Morton); *Heir* bro, Hon Thomas Maurice Ponsonby, *qv*; *Career* Lt Leics Yeo, Capt RA, served 1939-45 (France), barr Middle Temple; *Style*— The Rt Hon Lord de Mauley; Langford House, Little Faringdon, Lechlade, Glos

DE MEO, Justin Reny; s of Italo Renato de Meo (d 1973), and Pamela, *née* Winnick; *b* 17 May 1950; *Educ* Ardingley; *m* 21 June 1975, Anne Elizabeth, da of John Dennis Robbins, OBE, TD, FCA (d 1986), of Orpens Hill House, Birch, Essex; 2 s (Simon b 1979, William b 1982); *Career* property developer; co dir 1985; *Recreations* golf, fly fishing, travel; *Clubs* Roehampton; *Style*— Justin de Meo, Esq; c/o Barclays Bank plc, 25 Charing Cross Rd, London WC2

DE MEYER, Lady Susan Ankaret; *née* Howard; da of 11 Earl of Carlisle (d 1963), of Naworth Castle, Carlisle and his 2 w Esmé Mary Shrubb, Countess of Carlisle, *née* Iredell; *b* 13 Nov 1948; *Educ* Benenden; *m* 1, 9 Sept 1967 (m dis 1978), Charles James Buchanan-Jardine, s of Capt Sir John William Buchanan-Jardine, 3 Bt (d 1969); 1 da (Flora b 1971); m 2, 1978, Count Hubert Charles Guillaume de Meyer, s of Count Hervé Marie de Meyer, of Fribroug, Switzerland; 1 s (Alexander b 1978); *Style*— Lady Susan de Meyer; 37 Lennox Gardens, London SW3 (☎ 01 584 9474); Little Fosse Farm, Nettleton, nr Chippenham, Wilts, Castlecombe (☎ 0249 782315) Oxford OX5 3PG (☎ Steeple Aston 40239)

DE MILLE, Noel James; s of Frank Wilfred de Mille (d 1917), of Canada, and Cecilia, *née* Humphrys (d 1974); *b* 20 Nov 1909; *Educ* King George HS Vancouver Canada; *m* 9 April 1938, Ailsa Christine, da of Lt Col Sholto Stuart Ogilvie, DSO, and 2 bars (d 1961), of Ness House, Sizewell, Leiston, Suffolk; 2 s (Peter Noel b 1944, Andrew Stuart b 1947), 1 da (Christina Mary b 1940); *Career* served WWII; with Boeing Aircraft Co of Canada Ltd until 1930; worked gold mines Br Columbia, chief surveyor and assayor Relief Arlington Mine 1934; came to England 1935, with Saunders Roe Ltd IOW, jt md Sargrove Electronics Research 1946, fndr Noel de Mille and Co Ltd 1951; won Olympic Bronze Medal 1932 in Double Sculls with C E Pratt in Canadian Olympic Team, winner many other Sculling Championships; FRSA; *Recreations* sculling, sailing, music, painting; *Clubs* Vancouver Rowing (hon life memb), Leander, London Rowing, Aldeburgh Yacht; *Style*— Noel de Mille, Esq; Alexander House,

Thorpeness, Leiston, Suffolk IP16 4NB (☎ 072 885 3496)

DE MONTMORENCY, Sir Arnold Geoffroy; 19 Bt (I 1631), of Knockagh, Co Tipperary; s of James Edward Geoffrey de Montmorency (d 1934); suc cous, Sir Reginald d'Alton Lodge de Montmorency, 18 Bt, 1979; *b* 27 July 1908; *Educ* Westminster, Peterhouse Cambridge; *m* 20 April 1949 (m annulled 1953) and remarried, 1972, Nettie Hay, da of William Anderson of Morayshire; *Heir* none; *Career* serv war, Maj RASC 1939-45; barr Middle Temple 1932, chm (pt/t) industl tbnls 1975-81, chm Contemporary Review Cmmn 1962; parly candidate (Lib) contested: Cambridge 1959, Cirencester and Tewkesbury 1964; fndr and pres Friends of Peterhouse; *Books* Integration of Industrial Legislation (1984); *Clubs* Nat Liberal; *Style*— Sir Arnold de Montmorency Bt; 2 Garden Ct, Temple, London EC4

dE NAHLIK, Wing Commander Andrew John Julius Adolph; s of Wiktor Nahlik (d 1963), and Marja, *née* Rucker; *b* 27 Feb 1920; *Educ* Tech Univ of Lwow Poland (BEng), Univ of Bath (dip industl admin); *m* 8 July 1943, Anne Ella Renee, da of Maj H Milton (d 1969); 2 s (Christopher Andrew Victor b 28 June 1945, Philip Adam Charles b 1 June 1950); *Career* Polish Air Force serv: France 1940, UK 1940-47 (interpreter, fighter pilot, flying instr, staff offr); RAF 1947-68: RAF Eastleigh, Nairobi 1961-65, dir of studies Cmd and Staff Sch RAF Ternhill 1965-67, dir Sr Offrs Mgmnt Courses RAF Upavon, ret Wing Cdr 1968; personnel devpt mangr Satchwell Controls (GEC) 1969-72, Manpower devpt mangr Bristol Myers Co 1973-83; head Br Deer Soc Ctee developing a syllabus of deer mgmnt studies for Univs and Colls 1986-89; MBIM, MPIM; Cross of Merit with Swords (Poland) 1942; *Books* Wild Deer (1958), Deer Management (1978), Revised Wild Deer (1987) ; *Recreations* deer stalking, game shooting, fly fishing, photography; *Clubs* Royal Air Force; *Style*— Wing Commander Andrew de Nahlik; 5 Burdock Close, Goodworth Clatford, Andover, Hants SP11 7RS (☎ 0264 58383)

DE NORMANN, John Anthony; s of Sir Eric de Normann, KBE, CB (d 1982), of Surrey, and Winifred Scott, *née* Leigh (d 1968); *b* 25 Jan 1923; *Educ* Westminster Sch, Ch Ch Oxford (MA); *m* 1959, Diana, da of Charles Phipps (d 1960), of Wilts; 2 s (Roderick b 1959, Anthony b 1961); *Career* Capt RA Far East 1942-45; Imperial Chemical Industries 1947-80, chm Farrow Gp 1970-80; cncllr: Economic and Social Consultative Assembly, European Community Brussels 1982-; dir: British Standards Inst, Nat Cncl of Building Material Producers; *Recreations* book collecting, gardening, travel, motoring; *Clubs* Whites; *Style*— John A de Normann, Esq; Lower Leaze, Box, nr Corsham, Wilts (☎ 0225 742 786); Rue Ravenstein 2, 1000 Brussels (☎ 519 90 11, telex 25 983 CESEUR)

DE PELLEGRINO FARRUGIA, Dr Joseph Francis; s of Don Romeo Farrugia (d 1951), and Donna Angela dei Nobili Pellegrino (d 1975); *b* 21 Mar 1924; *Educ* Lyceum, St Andrews Univ (MB, ChB); *m* 2 June 1966, Margaret Constance, da of Johan Arvid North (formerly von Johannson), of Null and Turku; 2 s (Adrian b 1967, Guy b 1969), 1 da (Giuliana-Augusta b 1974); *Career* cmmnd 1941, Weapon Trg Offr 1942, Maj 1943-48, dir PW Intelligence Bureau E A Cmd; RAMC 1956, RARO 1966; specialist in psychiatry, rotating interships W Cornwall Hosps 1956-58, MO Menston Psychiatric Hosp 1968-83, princ in family med 1963-86, dir surgery and sr examiner St John's Ambulance Bde 1965-80, MO Nat Blood Transfusion Serv 1987; *Recreations* architecture, books, wine, opera; *Clubs* The Challoner (found memb); *Style*— Dr Joseph De Pellegrino Farrugia; Primrose House, Broughton, Skipton, N Yorks BD23 3AM (☎ Skipton 69585); Coutts & Co, Hanover St, Branch; Lindley House Nursing Home, Otley Rd, Shipley, W Yorks (☎ 0274 580502)

DE PEYER, Gervase; *b* 11 April 1926; *Educ* King Alfred's London, Bedales, Royal Coll of Music; *m* 1, 1950 (m dis 1971), Sylvia Southcombe; 1 s, 2 da; m 2, 1971 (m dis 1979), Susan Rosalind Daniel; m 3, 1980, Katia Perret Aubry; *Career* dir London Symphony Wind Ensemble, fndr and conductor Melos Sinfonia fndr memb Melos Ensemble of London, solo clarinettist Chamber Music Soc of Lincoln Center NY 1969; gold medal Worshipful Co of Musicians 1948; ARCM, Hon ARAM; *Style*— Gervase de Peyer Esq; Porto-Vecchio 1250, SO Washington St, Alexandria, Virginia 22314 USA

DE PIRO, His Hon Judge; Baron Alan Caesar Haselden de Piro; QC (1965); s of Joseph William de Piro (killed 1942), of Singapore; *b* 31 August 1919; *Educ* Repton, Trinity Hall Cambridge (MA); *m* 1, 1947, Mary Elliot (decd); 2 s; m 2, 1964, Mona Addington; 1 step s, 1 step da; *Career* Capt, served W Africa; barrister 1947, dep chm Warwicks QS and Bedford QS 1967-72, master of the bench Middle Temple 1971-, recorder 1972-82, circuit judge 1983-; vice pres Union Internationale des Avocats 1969-71, cncl memb Int Bar Assoc 1967-86; *Recreations* canals, gardening, conversation; *Clubs* Hawks (Cambridge); *Style*— His Hon Judge de Piro, QC; Toll House, Bascote Locks, Leamington Spa, Warwicks; 3 Temple Gdns, London EC4; 23 Brimingham Road, Stoneleigh, Warwicks

DE RAMSEY, 3 Baron (UK 1887); Ailwyn Edward Fellowes; KBE (1974), TD, DL (1973 Huntingdon and Peterborough, 1974 Cambs); s of Capt Hon Coulson Churchill Fellowes (d 1915, s of 2 Baron and Lady Rosamond, *née* Spencer-Churchill, sis of 8 Duke of Marlborough; suc gf, 2 Baron, 1925; *b* 16 Mar 1910; *Educ* Oundle; *m* 27 July 1937, Lilah Helen Suzanne (d 1987), da of late Francis Anthony Labouchere, of 15 Draycott Av, SW3, by his w Evelyn Mary, da of Sir Walter Stirling, 3 Bt (ret 1934); 2 s, 2 da; *Heir* s, Hon John Ailwyn Fellowes; *Career* Capt (135 Fd Regt) Herts Yeo RA (TA) 1939; patron of four livings; Ld-Lt of Huntingdonshire 1947-65, of Huntingdon and Peterborough 1965-68; pres Country Landowners' Assoc 1963-65; *Style*— Rt Hon Lord De Ramsey, KBE, TD, DL; Abbots Ripton Hall, Huntingdon (☎ Abbots Ripton 234)

DE RENUSSON D'HAUTEVILLE, Comtesse Gérard; Hon Joanna Phoebe; *née* Rodd; er da of 2 Baron Rennell, KBE, CB (d 1978); *b* 4 July 1929; *Educ* Westonbirt Sch for Girls; *m* 2 July 1966, Comte Gérard de Renusson d'Hauteville, Offr de la Légion d'Honneur, Croix de Guerre, s of Marquis de Renusson d'Hauteville (d 1949), of Croissy-sur-Seine, France; *Career* bookseller; *Recreations* reading, riding, showing dogs; *Clubs* Ebury Court, Société Canine de Monaco; *Style*— Comtesse Gérard de Renusson d'Hauteville; 10 Rue Francois Mouthon, 75015 Paris; 9 Rue Puget, 06100 Nice Alpes, Maritimes, France

DE ROS, 28 Baron (E 1264); Peter Trevor Maxwell; Premier Baron of England; s of 27 Baroness de Ros (d 1983), and Cdr David Maxwell, RN, *qv*; gs of Hon Mrs (Angela) Horn (*qv*); *b* 23 Dec 1958; *Educ* Headfort Sch Kells, Stowe, and Down HS Downpatrick; *m* 5 Sept 1987, Angela Siân Ross; 1 s (Hon Finbar James b 14 Dec 1988); *Heir* s, Hon Finbar James Maxwell b 14 Nov 1988; *Style*— Rt Hon Lord de Ros; Old Court, Strangford, Co Down, N Ireland (☎ 039686 318)

DE ROSNAY, Baroness Joël; Hon Stella Candida; *née* Jebb; yr da of 1 Baron Gladwyn, GCMG, GCVO, CB; *b* 7 Dec 1933; *m* 12 Dec 1959, Baron Joël de Rosnay, 1 s (Alexis b 1967), 2 da (Tatiana b 1961, Cecilia b 1963); *Style*— Baroness Joël de Rosnay; 146 rue de l'Universite, Paris VII, France

DE ROTHSCHILD; *see*: Rothschild

DE ROTHSCHILD, Edmund Leopold; TD; s of Maj Lionel Nathan de Rothschild, OBE, JP (d 1942), of Exbury House, Exbury, nr Southampton, and Marie Louise, *née* Beer; *b* 2 Jan 1916; *Educ* Harrow, Trinity Coll Cambridge; *m* 1, June 1948, Elizabeth (d 1980), da of Marcel Lentner, of Vienna; 2 s (Nicholas, Lionel), 2 da (Katherine, Charlotte (twin with Lionel)); m 2, 26 April 1982, Anne Evelyn, JP, widow of J Malcolm Harrison, CBE; *Career* Maj RA (TA) WW II, BEF, BNAF, CMF; merchant banker; dir N M Rothschild & Sons 1975- (ptnr 1946-, sr ptnr 1960-70, chm 1970-75); chm: AUR Hydropower Ltd, Straflo Ltd; pres Assoc of Jewish Ex-Service Men and Women, British Fndn for Age Res; Hon LLD Memorial Univ Newfoundland 1961, Hon DSc Salford 1983; Order of the Sacred Treasure (1 class) Japan 1973; *Books* Window on the World (1949); *Recreations* gardening, fishing, cine-photography, hunting butterflies; *Clubs* White's, Portland, Mount Royal (Montreal); *Style*— Edmund de Rothschild, Esq, TD; New Court, St Swithin's Lane, EC4P 4DU (☎ 01 280 5000, fax 01 929 1643, telex 888031); c/o Exbury Estate Office, Exbury, Southampton SO4 1AZ (☎ 0703 897131)

DE ROTHSCHILD, Sir Evelyn Robert Adrian; s of Anthony de Rothschild, DL (d 1961 3 s of Leopold de Rothschild, CVO, JP, 1 cousin Edmund de Rothschild *qv*) and Yvonne da late Robert Cahen d'Anvers of Paris; *b* 29 August 1931; *Educ* Harrow, Trinity Coll Cambridge; *m* 1, 1966 (m dis 1971), Jeanette (d 1981), da of Ernest Bishop; m 2, 1973, Victoria, da of Lewis Schott; 2 s (Anthony b 1977, David b 1978), 1 da (Jessica b 1974); *Career* chm: N M Rothschild & Sons, Economist Newspaper 1972-, United Racecourses Ltd 1977-; kt 1989; *Style*— Evelyn de Rothschild Esq; Ascott, Wing, Leighton Buzzard, Beds; N M Rothschild & Sons, New Court St, St Swithin's Lane, London EC4P 4DU (☎ 01 280 5000)

DE SALABERRY, Count Pascal; s of Comte de Salaberry, of Le Bailly, Nemours, France, and Comtesse de Salaberry, *née* Burrus; *b* 15 Nov 1941; *Educ* Univ of Paris, Univ of Geneva; *Career* Banque Transatlantique Paris 1969-77, Ivory and Sime plc Edinburgh 1978-; chm Ivory and Sime: Zurich 1983, Int 1987; non exec dir: Facom SA France 1981, Personal Assets Tst plc 1983, Euro Priva Tt 1987; *Recreations* sports, bridge, backgammon, antiques; *Clubs* Dean Tennis Edinburgh; *Style*— Count Pascal de Salaberry; 8 Great Stuart St, Edinburgh EH3 7TN (☎ 031 225 5060); One Charlotte Sq, Edinburgh EH2 4DZ (☎ 031 225 1357, fax 031 225 2375, telex 727242)

DE SALIS, 9 Count (Holy Roman Empire 1748, cr by Francis I); John Bernard Philip Humbert de Salis; also Hereditary Knight of the Golden Spur (1571); s of 8 Count de Salis (Lt-Col Irish Gds), of Lough Gur, Co Limerick (d 1949, descended from Peter 1 Count de Salis-Soglio, Envoy of the Grisons Republic to Queen Anne at the time of the Treaty of Utrecht; Jerome, 2 Count de Salis, was naturalised Br by Act of Parliament 1731 following his marriage to Mary, da and co-heiress of the last Viscount Fane); an earlier member of the family, Feldzeugmeister Rudolph von Salis, was cr a Baron of the HRE by the Emperor Rudolf II in 1582 for gallantry against the Turks; through Sophia, da of Adm Francis William Drake, w of Jerome, 4 Count de Salis, the family is heir-gen of the great Sir Francis; the 8 Count's mother was Princess Hélène de Riquet, da of Prince Eugène de Caraman-Chimay (Prince of Chimay 1527 HRE by Maximilian I, Belgium 1889 by Leopold II), a descendant of Jean de Croy killed at Agincourt 1415, and gs of Therese de Cabarrus (Madame Tallien); *b* 16 Nov 1947; *Educ* Downside, CCC Cambridge; *m* 1, 1973 (m dis and annulled), Contessa Samaritana, da of Conte di Serego della Scala, of Verona; m 2, Marie-Claude, 3 da of Col René-Henri Wüst, Swiss Army, of Zürich and Geneva; 1 s (Count John-Maximilian Henry b 3 Nov 1986); *Heir* s, Count John-Maximilian Henry de Salis b 3 Nov 1986; *Career* late Capt 9/12 Royal Lancers (Prince of Wales's); barrister Gray's Inn; delegate Int Ctee Red Cross (missions in: M East, Africa, Asia, Iraq, Thailand), special envoy in Lebanon 1982; memb bd of Mgmnt Hosp of St John and St Elizabeth, memb Cncl Br Assoc Order of Malta; Kt of Honour and Devotion Sov Mil Order Malta 1974, Kt of Justice Order of Constantinian St George; *Recreations* melancholia; *Clubs* Cavalry & Guards, Travellers', Beefsteak, Royal Bangkok Sports Club; *Style*— Count de Salis; Maison du Bailli, CH-1422 Grandson, Switzerland (☎ 024 241466); office: 20 rue du Conseil-Général, C.P. 231 - 1211 Geneva 11 Switzerland (☎ 022 288488)

DE SALIS, Timothy Stephen (Fane); s of Rev Andrew Augustine Fane De Salis (d 1962), of Honiton, Devon, and Violet Eileen Charlotte, *née* Higgens; *b* 2 Sept 1936; *Educ* Allhallows Sch Devon; *m* 11 June 1966, Penelope Elisabeth, da of the Very Rev Michael John Nott, of Southsea, Hants; 2 s (Mark b 1967, Jonathan b 1971), 1 da (Nicola b 1969); *Career* dir: CGA Insur Brokers Ltd 1978 (md 1986), County Gentlemens Assoc plc 1986, CGA Financial Servs Ltd 1987; *Recreations* reading, walking; *Style*— Timothy S De Salis, Esq; 21 Broadwater Avenue, Letchworth, Herts SG6 3HF (☎ 0462 684182); Country Gentlemens Assoc plc, Icknield Way West, Letchworth, Herts SG6 4AP (☎ 0462 480011, fax 0462 481407)

DE SAUMAREZ, 6 Baron (UK 1831); James Victor Broke Saumarez; yr but only surv s of 5 Baron de Saumarez (d 1969); *b* 28 April 1924; *Educ* Eton, Millfield, Magdalene Coll Cambridge; *m* 28 April 1953, Joan (Julia) Beryl, da of Douglas Raymond Charlton; 2 s ((twins) Hon Eric and Hon Victor b 1956), 1 da (Hon Mrs MacGregor); *Career* serv Life Gds BAOR; farmer; dir Shrubland Health Clinic Ltd; *Style*— The Rt Hon the Lord de Saumarez; Shrubland Vista, Coddenham, Ipswich, Suffolk (☎ 830220)

DE SAVARY, Peter John; *Educ* Charterhouse; *m* 1 (m dis), Marcia; 2 da; m 2, 1985 (m dis 1986), Alice, *née* Simms; m 3 1986, Lucille Lana, *née* Paton; 1 da; *Career* America's Cup Challenger 1983; dir of various int co's; *Style*— Peter de Savary Esq; Littlecote House, Hungerford, Berks

DE SILVA, (George) Desmond Lorenz; QC (1984); s of Edmund Frederick Lorenz de Silva, MBE, of Kandy, Sri Lanka, and Esme Norah Gregg, *née* Nathanielsz (d 1982); *b* 13 Dec 1939; *Educ* Trinity Coll Kandy Sri Lanka; *m* 5 Dec 1987, HRH Princess Katarina of Yugoslavia, o da of HRH Prince Tomislav of Yugoslavia, *qv*; *Career* barr: Middle Temple 1964, Sierra Leone 1968, Gambia 1981; memb home affrs standing ctee Bow Gp 1982, editorial advsy bd Crossbow; vice- pres St John Ambulance London (Prince of Wales Dist) 1984; Cnclman City of London (ward of Faringdon Without); landowner (Taprobane Island in the Indian Ocean); Freeman of the City of London, memb Worshipful Co of Fletchers; CStJ 1985 (OStJ 1980);

Recreations politics, shooting, travel; *Clubs* Carlton, City Livery, Orient (Colombo); *Style*— Desmond de Silva Esq, QC; 28 Sydney Street, London SW3; Villa Taprobane, Taprobane Island, off Sri Lanka; 2 Paper Buildings, Temple, London EC4Y 7ET (☎ 01 353 9119)

DE SPON, Baron (Holy Roman Empire and Bavaria, cr by Charles VII, with appellation *Wohlgeboren*, **1742); John Seymour**; also Noble of the HRE (Matthias, 1612), Baron of France (Louis XV 1743); s of John Baron de Spon (d 1966, ggs of François Nicolas Baron de Spon, premier président du Conseil Souverain d'Alsace 1776-90, who emigrated to England 1792 s in his turn of Jean François Baron de Spon, Comte zu Forbach was Imperial and Bavarian ambass to Frederick the Great 1743-47); *b* 28 Dec 1913; *Educ* Lower Sch of John Lyon Harrow, King's Coll London; *m* 1 May 1948 (m dis 1953), Florence, *née* Ashe; *Career* ret journalist, with Western Morning News, Rand Daily Mail, Daily Mirror, News of the World, Sunday Times, Daily Telegraph, Sunday Telegraph; ed Burke's Peerage and Burke's Landed Gentry 1941-46; contested (Lib) N Kensington 1935 and W Islington for LCC 1937; patron L'Orchestre du Monde; Freeman City of London 1963, Liveryman Worshipful Co of Stationers 1985 (Freeman 1982); FRGS 1963; Kt of Sacred Military Order of Constantine of St George (conferred by HRH Prince Ferdinand de Bourbon Deux-Siciles 1981); *Recreations* shooting, book collecting; *Clubs* Travellers'; *Style*— Baron de Spon; 17 Goodwood Court, Devonshire St, London W1 (☎ 01 636 2649)

DE STACPOOLE, 6 Duke (Papal title, conferred 1831 by Gregory XVI); George Geoffrey Robert Edward de Stacpoole; also Count Stacpoole (French cr of Louis XVIII 1818) and Marquis de Stacpoole (Papal title conferred by Leo XII 1826); s of 5 Duke, JP (d 1965). The Stacpooles have resided in Ireland from the twelfth century, the family name is taken from a feudal lordship in Pembrokeshire; *b* 21 June 1917; *Educ* Downside; *m* 15 July 1947, Dorothy Anne, o da of late Richard Edmund Dease, RAFVR, of Rath House, Co Leix; 2 s (George b 1948, David b 1951), 1 da (Mrs Jeremy Richardson b 1950); *Career* Maj late Royal Ulster Rifles; served WW II; *Style*— Major the Duke de Stacpoole; Hemstead Corner Cottage, Bevenden, Cranbrook, Kent TN17 4ET;

DE TRAFFORD, Sir Dermot Humphrey; 6 Bt (UK 1841), of Trafford Park, Lancs; VRD; o s of Sir Rudolph de Trafford, 5 Bt, OBE (d 1983), by his 1 w, June Isabel, MBE (d 1977), only da of Lt-Col Reginald Chaplin; *b* 19 Jan 1925; *Educ* Harrow, Christ Church Coll Oxford (MA); *m* 1, 26 June 1948 (m dis 1973), Patricia Mary, o da of late Francis Mycroft Beeley, of Long Crumples, nr Alton, Hants; 3 s, 6 da; m 2, 1974, Xandra Carandini, da of Lt-Col Geoffrey Trollope Lee and former w of Roderick Walter; *Heir* s, John Humphrey de Trafford; *Career* Lt Cdr RNR E Mediterranean; md GHP Gp Ltd 1961 (chm 1966-77); dep chm Imperial Continental Gas Assoc 1972-87 (dir 1963-87); chm: Low & Bonar plc 1982- (dep chm 1980); CBIM, IOD, FRSA; *Recreations* gardening, golf; *Clubs* White's, Royal Ocean Racing; *Style*— Sir Dermot de Trafford, Bt, VRD; 59 Onslow Sq, London SW7 (☎ 01 589 2826); The Old Vicarage, Appleshaw, nr Andover, Hants (Weyhill 2357); Flat 15, 1 Mount St, London W1Y 5AA

DE TRAFFORD, John Humphrey; elder s, and h, of Sir Dermot de Trafford, 6 Bt, VRD, *qv*, and his 1 w, Patricia; *b* 12 Sept 1950; *Educ* Ampleforth, Bristol U (BSc); *m* 1975, Anne, da of Jacques Faure de Pebeyre; 1 s (Alexander Humphrey b 1978), 1 da (Isabel b 1980); *Career* Vice Pres American Express Europe Ltd 1987-; *Clubs* Royal Ocean Racing Club; *Style*— John de Trafford, Esq; 12 Burlington Gdns, Chiswick, London W4 4LT

DE TRAFFORD, Katherine, Lady; Katherine; eldest da of William Walter Balke, of Cincinnati, USA; *m* 1, Sebastiano Lo Savio; m 2, 2 Feb 1939, m his 2 w, Sir Rudolph Edgar Francis de Trafford, 5 Bt, OBE (d 1983); *Style*— Katherine, Lady de Trafford; 70 Eaton Sq, London SW1

DE VALOIS, Dame Ninette (Edris); CH (1980), DBE (1951, CBE 1947); 2 da of Lt-Col Thomas Robert Alexander Stannus, DSO, JP (d of wounds 1917) (Anglo-Irish Protestant family settled in Ireland c 1618), and Elizabeth Graydon *née* Smith (d 1961); *b* 6 June 1898; *m* 5 July 1935, Dr Arthur Blackall Connell; *Career* fndr dir Royal Ballet 1931-63 (previously Sadlers Wells Ballet), fndr Royal Ballet Sch; pres London Ballet Circle to 1981; former prima ballerina Covent Garden Royal Opera Season 1919-1928, with Diaghilev's *Ballet Russes* 1923-26; choreographer: *Rake's Progress*, *Checkmate*, *Don Quixote*; Chev of the Legion of Honour (France) 1950; Royal Albert Medal 1963, Erasmus Prize Foundation Award 1974; *Books* Invitation to the Ballet (1937), Come Dance With Me (1957), Step By Step (1977); *Style*— Dame Ninette de Valois, CH, DBE; c/o Royal Ballet School, 153 Talgarth Rd, W14 (☎ 01 748 6335/3123)

DE VESCI, 7 Viscount (I 1776); Thomas Eustace Vesey; 9 Bt (I 1698); also Baron Knapton (I 1750); s of 6 Viscount de Vesci (d 1983), by his w Susan Ann (d 1986), da of late Ronald Owen Lloyd Armstrong-Jones, MBE (and sister of Earl of Snowdon, *qv*); *b* 8 Oct 1955; *Educ* Eton, Oxford Univ; *m* 5 Sept 1987, Sita-Maria Arabella, o da of Brian de Breffny (d 1989), of Castletown Cox, Co Kilkenny and Maharaj Kumari Jyotsna Dutt, da of late Maharajadhiraj Bahadur Uday Chand Mahtab of Burdwan, KCIE; 1 s (Damian Brian John Vesey b 1985), 1 da (Cosima b 1988); *Career* bloodstock agent, stud farmer; *Recreations* reading, fishing; *Clubs* Whites; *Style*— The Rt Hon the Viscount de Vesci; Abbey Leix, Co Leix, Ireland (☎ 0502 31101/31162)

DE VIBRAYE, Comtesse Honor Cecilia; *née* Paget; da of Adm Sir Alfred Paget, KCB, KCMG, DSO (2 s of Gen Lord Alfred Paget, CB, MP, 5 s of 1 Marquess of Anglesey), and Viti, da of Rt Hon Sir William Macgregor, GCMG, CB, PC; *b* 18 June 1907; *m* 1, 25 April 1928 (m dis 1930), Lt-Cdr Vivian Russell Salvia Bowlby, RN (ret), s of Col Robert Bowlby; m 2, 15 April 1936 (m dis 1946), Ralph Gledhill, of Portland Oregon; m 3, 11 Nov 1952 (m dis 1957), Comte François Hurault de Vibraye (presumably a collateral of the Huraults, anciently (c 1479) Seigneurs of, among other fiefs, Cheverny (Loir-et-Cher), la Grange, and Vibraye, and descended from a Seigneur of St Denis-sur-Loire c 1340, a member of this family being cr Marquis by Louis XIII 1625, while the 6 Marquis had conferred on him again the title of Marquis (having already been cr a *Pair de France* (Peer) 1815) by Louis XVIII 1817); *Style*— Comtesse Honor de Vibraye

DE VIGIER, William Alphonse; Hon CBE (1978); s of late Dr Wilhelm de Vigier; *b* 22 Jan 1912; *Educ* La Chataigneraie Coppet Switzerland; *m* 1939, Betty Kendall; 2 da; *Career* formerly chm and fndr Acrow plc; Acrow Corpn of America, Acrow Canada, Acrow Misr Egypt, SOFIM Switzerland; dir: Vigier Cement SA Switzerland, Acrow Australia Ltd, Acrow Peru SA, Acrow India, Acrow Richmond Canada, Acrow-Carpenter New Zealand, Acrow Zimbabwe, Poenamo Ltd Australia; memb BA Bd 1973-78; kt Star of the North (Sweden), GC Order of Star of Africa; *Clubs* East India, Devonshire, The Metropolitan NY; *Style*— William de Vigier, Esq, CBE; Suite 4, 5 Carlton Gardens, London SW1Y 5AD; Sommerhaus, Soleure, Switzerland

DE VILLIERS, Hon Alexander Charles; s and h of 3 Baron de Villiers; *b* 29 Dec 1940; *m* 1966; *Style*— The Hon Alexander de Villiers

DE VILLIERS, 3 Baron (UK 1910); Arthur Percy de Villiers; s of 2 Baron de Villiers (d 1934); *b* 17 Dec 1911; *Educ* Diocesan Coll S A, Magdalen Coll Oxford; *m* 9 Nov 1939 (m dis 1958), Edna Alexis Lovett, da of Dr A D MacKinnon, of Wilham Lake, BC, Canada; 1 s, 2 da; *Heir* s, Hon Alexander Charles de Villiers; *Career* barr Inner Temple 1938; Auckland Supreme Ct 1949; farmer, ret; *Style*— The Rt the Hon Lord de Villiers; PO Box 66, Kumeu, Auckland, NZ (☎ 411 8173)

DE VINK, Peter Henry John; s of Dr Ludovicus Petrus Hendricus Josephus De Vink (d 1987), and Catharina Louisa Maria Van Iersel; *b* 9 Oct 1940; *Educ* Edinburgh Univ (BCOMM); *m* 27 May 1967, Jenipher Jean, da of Ranald Malcolm Murray-Lyon, MD, FRCPE (d 1969); 1 s (Patrick b 1971), 1 da (Natalie b 1970); *Career* Nat Serv 1961-63, cmmnd Dutch Army; Ivory & Sime 1966 (ptnr 1969, dir 1975); fndr Edinburgh Fin & General Hldgs Ltd 1978; dir: Viking Resources Oil & Gas Ltd 1972, Viking Resources Tst plc 1972, Benline Offshire Contractors Ltd 1974, Wereldhave NV 1973, Edinburgh Fin & General Hldgs Ltd 1978, Albany Oil & Gas Ltd 1987, memb Exec Scottish Cncl (Devpt and Ind); *Recreations* shooting, golf, fishing; *Clubs* New (Edinburgh); *Style*— Peter H J De Vink, Esq; Cotswold, 46 Barnton Ave, Edinburgh EH4 6JL (☎ 031 336 2004); Edinburgh Financial & General Holdings Ltd, 7 Howe St, Edinburgh EH3 6TE (☎ 031 225 6661, fax 031 556 6651, car tel 0836 700 956, portable 0836 702 335)

de VOGÜÉ, Count Ghislain Alain Marie Melchior; s of Comte Robert Jean de Vogüé, and Anne, *née* d'Eudeville; *b* 11 Aug 1933; *Educ* Univ in le Havre; *m* 1 July 1960, Catherine Marie Monique, *née* Fragonard; 1 s (Marc b 14 Dec 1979), 1 da (Laurence b 1 Feb 1976); *Career* mgmnt attaché Banque de L'Union Europeenne 1959-64, md Moët & Chandon Epernay 1969-75 (joined 1965), vice chm of bd Moët-Hennessy Paris 1988- (dir 1976-); chm: Moët & Chandon (London) Ltd, Ditta Claretta Torino (Italy); bd memb: Moët & Chandon (Fance), Jas Hennessy (France), Moët-Hennessy Distribution (France), Imprimerie FPGV (France), Proviar Buenos Aires (Argentina), Provifin Sao Paolo (Brazil) ; *Recreations* music, tennis, skiing, golf, sailing; *Style*— Count Ghislain de Vogüé; 174 Boulevard St Germain, 75006 Paris; 13 Grosvenor Crescent, London SW1X 7EE

DE VOIL, Paul Walter; s of late Pfarrer Paul Vogel, and late Maria Christine, *née* Hurfeld; adopted s of late Very Rev Walter Harry de Voil, of Carnoustie; *b* 29 Sept 1929; *Educ* Fettes, Hertford Coll Oxford; *m* 26 July 1952, Shelia, da of late William George Danks, of Elsecar; 1 s (Nicholas b 1962), 1 da (Sally b 1960); *Career* Flying Offr RAF 1950-53; taxation conslt: Inland Revenue 1953-60, Ford Motor Co 1960-63, Herbert Smith & Co 1964-69, Baker Sutton & Co 1969-78, Lonrho plc 1978-87, Arthur Young 1987-; churchwarden and reader; Freeman: City of London 1969, City Slrs Co 1969; memb: (cncl) FTII 1964, Law Soc 1967; *Books* de Voil on Tax Appeals (1969), de Voil on Value Added Tax (1972); *Recreations* wine, music, statues, bright-eyed love; *Clubs* Royal Air Force; *Style*— Paul de Voil, Esq; Water Lane Barn, Denston, Newmarket, Suffolk (☎ 0440 820 181); Arthur Young, Compass House, 80 Newmarket Rd, Cambridge (☎ 0223 461 200, fax 0223 324 609, telex 81771)

DE WAAL, Constant Hendrik; CB (1977); 3 s of late Hendrik de Waal; *b* 1 May 1931; *Educ* Tonbridge, Pembroke Coll Cambridge; *m* 1964, Julia Jessel; 2 s; *Career* called to the Bar Lincoln's Inn 1953, Law Cmmn 1969-71, parly counsel 1971-81, second parly counsel 1981-; *Style*— Constant de Waal Esq; 62 Sussex St, London SW1

de WAAL, Rev Canon Hugo Ferdinand; s of Bernard Hendrik de Waal, of 4 Sherford Court, Taunton, and Albertine Felice, *née* Castens; *b* 16 Mar 1935; *Educ* Tonbridge, Pembroke Coll Cambridge (MA), Munster Univ Germany, Ridley Hall Cambridge; *m* 4 April 1961, Brigit Elizabeth Townsend, da of Rev John Massingberd-Mundy, of 79 Wolverton Rd, Newport Pagnell; 1 s (Bernard b 1967), 3 da (Katharine b 1962, Joanna b 1964, Penelope b 1966); *Career* curate St Martins-in-the Bull Ring Birmingham 1960, chaplain Pembroke Coll Cambridge 1964, priest i/c Dry Drayton Diocese of Ely (rector 1967), anglican minister Ecumenical Church Bar Hill Cambs, vicar Blackpool Parish Church 1974, princ Ridley Hall 1978-, hon canon Ely Cathedral 1985; *Recreations* music, squash, fly-fishing, walking; *Style*— The Rev Canon Hugo de Waal; The Principal's Lodge, Ridley Hall, Cambridge (☎ 0223 353 040)

DE WEND FENTON, (Michael Richard) West; o s of Maj William Ross de Wend Fenton, TD (d 1951), of Underbank Hall and Ebberston Hall, Yorkshire, and Margaret Constance Millicent, *née* Dunn (d 1965); descended from William Fenton (d 1743), who acquired Underbank by his marriage to Frances, o da and heiress of Capt Richard West, whose ancestors had held it since early 16 century, and whose descendant another William Fenton was murdered by robbers in Spain 1855, leaving the life interest of his estate to his four sisters, of whom the third, Jessey, m Maj James Douglas de Wend and conveyed the estate to her descendants (*see* Burke's Landed Gentry, 18 edn, vol III, 1972); *b* 2 Feb 1927; *Educ* Eton, RAC Cirencester; *m* 23 April 1955, Margaret Annora Mary, eldest da of Reginald Arthur Lygon (d 1976), of 3 Embankment Gardens, London SW3; 2 s (Jonathan Lygon West b 28 July 1958, Ross Matthew Mark b 9 July 1960), 2 da (Rosalie Marye Margaret b 21 June 1957, Clarissa Emily b 4 Sept 1962); *Career* served in Scots Guards, KSLI and French Foreign Legion; farmer; pioneered minibus tours of Russia and Eastern Europe; memb Ebberston Church and Parish Cncls; *Recreations* shooting, travelling, teasing; *Style*— West de Wend Fenton, Esq; Ebberston Hall, Scarborough, N Yorkshire (☎ 0723 85516)

DE WICHFIELD, Lady Maryel - Lady Angela Alice Maryel; *née* Drummond; da of 16 Earl of Perth (d 1951); *b* 5 Mar 1912; *m* 1, 14 June 1937 (m dis 1959), Count Alessandro Augusto Giovanni Giacinto Barnaba Manassei di Collestatte (d 1962); 2 s (John b 1937, Michael b 1947), 1 da (Mrs Francesco Montesi Righetti); m 2, 26 Sept 1960, Viggo Dmitri de Wichfeld; *Style*— Lady Maryel de Wichfeld; 41 Lennox Gdns, SW3

DE WOLF, Vice-Adm Harry George; CBE (1946), DSO (1944), DSC (1944), CD; s of late Henry George De Wolf, of Bedford, Nova Scotia, Canada; *b* 1903; *Educ* Royal Coll of Canada, RN Staff Coll Greenwich; *m* 1931, Gwendolen Fowle, da of Thomas St George Gilbert, of Somerset, Bermuda; 1 s, 1 da (d 1986); *Career* served War 1939-45; vice-chief of Naval Staff 1950-52; chm Canadian Jt Staff Washington 1953-55; chief of Naval Staff Canada 1956-60, ret; DSc (Mil, hc): RMC Kingston 1966, Royal Roads

Mil Coll 1980; *Recreations* golf; *Clubs* Royal Ottawa GC, Ribbell's Bay, G&CC Bermuda; *Style*— Vice-Adm Harry De Wolf, CBE, DSO, DSC, CD; (winter) Old Post Office, Somerset, Bermuda; (summer) 200 Rideau Terrace, Ottawa, Ontario, Canada (summer)

DE ZULUETA, Hon Lady (Marie-Louise); *née* Hennessy; eldest da of 2 Baron Windlesham (d 1962); *b* 9 Mar 1930; *m* 14 Sept 1955, Sir Philip de Zulueta (d 1989), *qv*; 1 s (Francis b 1959), 1 da (Louise b 1956); *Style*— The Hon Lady de Zulueta; 3 Westminster Gdns, Marsham St, London SW1P 4JA; Eastergate House, Eastergate, nr Chichester, Sussex

DE ZULUETA, Capt Paul Gerald; *see*: Torre Diaz, Count of

DEACON, Hon Mrs; (Elizabeth Anne); *née* Vane; 2 da of 11 Baron Barnard, TD, JP, by his w, Lady Davina, *née* Cecil, da of 6 Marquess of Exeter; *b* 17 May 1956; *m* 1982, Glyn Deacon, eldest s of late A Deacon; 2 da (Jerrica Anne b 1982, Laura Sophie b 1984); *Style*— The Hon Mrs Deacon; 91 The Green, Headcam, Gainford, Darlington, Co Durham DL2 3HA

DEACON ELLIOTT, Air Vice-Marshal Robert; CB (1967), OBE (1954), DFC (1941), AE (1944, two mentions); s of Frank Deacon Elliott (d 1966), and Alice Mary, *née* Bird (d 1969); *b* 20 Nov 1914; *Educ* Northampton Sch, PSC; *m* 1948, Grace Joan, da of late William Willes, of Newbold Comyn, Leamington Spa (d 1955, his mother was Alice, da of Rev Sir William Cope, 12 Bt); 2 s, 1 da; *Career* joined RAF 1937, serv WWII (Dunkirk, Battle of Britain), Gp Capt 1956, CO RAF Leconfield and Driffield 1956-58, Air Univ (USAF) 1958-61, Air Cdre 1962, Cmdt Offrs and Aircrew Selection Centre Biggin Hill 1962-65, AOC RAF Gibraltar and Cdr Maritime Air (NATO) 1965-66, AOC RAF Malta 1966-68, Dep C-in-C (Air) Allied Forces Med (NATO) 1966-67, ret 1968 with rank of Air Vice-Marshal; bursar Civil Serv Coll Sunningdale 1969-79; *Recreations* fishing, shooting, photography; *Clubs* RAF; *Style*— Air Vice-Marshal Robert Deacon Elliott, CB, OBE, DFC, AE; Thor House, Old Roar Rd, St Leonards-on-Sea, E Sussex TN37 7HH (☎ 0424 752699)

DEADMAN, Henry; CBE (1966); s of James Henry Gordon Deadman (d 1964); *b* 5 August 1908; *Educ* N W London Polytechnic; *m* 1936, Winifred Margery, da of Percy Edward Elmer; 2 da; *Career* regional dir N Midland Region of Miny of Fuel and Power 1952-54, London Gp 1954-59, head of Branch Gas Div Miny of Power 1959-61, asst sec and sr offr for Wales 1961-69; sec Welsh Ctee Countryside Cmmn 1969-73; memb rep and governing body of the Church in Wales and chm Reconstruction Ctee 1968-74; *Style*— Henry Deadman, Esq, CBE; Meadowcroft, Whitegate Rd, Minehead, Somerset TA24 5SS (☎ 0643 4553)

DEAKIN, Maj-Gen Cecil Martin Fothergill; CB (1961), CBE (1956); s of William R Deakin; *b* 20 Dec 1910; *Educ* Winchester; *m* 1934, Evelyn Mary Frances (d 1984), da of Sir Arthur Grant, 10 Bt of Monymusk, CBE, DSO (d 1931); 1 s, 1 da; *Career* cmmd Grenadier Gds 1931, serv WWII; Cdr: 2 bn Grenadier Gds 1945-46, 1 bn 1947-50, 32 Gds Bde 1953-55, 29 Inf Bde 1955-57, Suez Expedition (despatches 1956) BGS 1957-59, dir of Mil Trg 1959, GOC 56 London div (TA) 1960, dir TA 1960-62, Cmdt Jt Servs Staff Coll 1962-65, ret 1965; dir Mental Health Fndn 1966-, pres Grenadier Gds' Assoc 1966-82; *Clubs* Royal Yacht Sqdn; *Style*— Maj-Gen Cecil Deakin, CB, CBE; Stocks Farm House, Beenham, Berks

DEAKIN, Hon Mrs; (Rose Albinia); *née* Donaldson; da of Baron Donaldson of Kingsbridge (Life Peer); *b* 4 Nov 1937; *m* 16 Dec 1961, Nicholas Deakin, s of Sir William Deakin, DSO, *qv*; 1 s and 1 da; *Style*— The Hon Mrs Deakin; 126 Leighton Rd, London NW5

DEAKIN, Sir (Frederick) William (Dampier); DSO (1943); s of Albert Witney Deakin, of Aldbury, Tring, Herts; *b* 3 July 1913; *Educ* Westminster Sch, Ch Ch Oxford; *m* 1, 1935 (m dis 1940), Margaret Ogilvy, da of Sir Nicholas Beatson Bell, KCSI, KCIE (d 1936); 2 s; m 2, 1943, Livia Stela, da of Liviu Nasta, of Bucharest; *Career* fellow and tutor Wadham Coll Oxford 1936-49, first sec HM Embassy Belgrade 1945-46, research fellow Wadham 1949, warden of St Antony's Coll Oxford 1950-68, ret; hon fellow Wadham 1961, St Antony's 1969, hon student Ch Ch Oxford 1979; Grosse Verdienstkreuz 1958, Chev de la Légion d'Honneur 1953; Hon FBA 1981; kt 1975; *Clubs* White's, Brooks's; *Style*— Sir William Deakin, DSO; 83330 Le Beausset, Le Castellet, Var, France

DEAKINS, Eric Petro; s of Edward Deakins (d 1970) of 19 Strode Rd, London, and Gladys Frances, *née* Townsend (d 1964); *b* 7 Oct 1932; *Educ* Tottenham GS, LSE (BA); *Career* Nat Serv 2 Lt RASC 1953-55; divnl gen mangr FMC Ltd 1969-70 (exec 1959-69), political conslt 1987-, dir Consumer Watch 1988-; cncl memb: World Devpt Movement 1980-, Population Concern 1983-; memb Tottenham B C 1958-61, 1962-63; MP (Lab): West Walthamstow 1970-74, Walthamstow 1974-87; Parly under sec: Trade 1974-76, Health & Social Security 1976-79; *Books* A Faith to Fight For (1964), You and Your MP (1987), What Future for Labour? (1988); *Recreations* writing, cinema, squash, football; *Style*— Eric Deakins, Esq; 36 Murray Mews, London NW1 9RJ (☎ 01 267 6196)

DEAKINS, Peter John; s of William Amos Deakins (d 1955), and Ethel Sarah, *née* Pigeon (d 1975); *b* 15 Mar 1934; *Educ* Torquay GS; *m* 3 June 1966, Wendy Patricia, da of Henry Martin Finn (d 1946); 3 s (Sasha b 1967 d 1969, St John b 1968, Guy b 1970); *Career* memb Cons and Preservation Gp for: Albert Bridge 1968, Addington Sq 1968, Battersea Sq 1970, Clapham Junction 1971; fndr memb Intentionally Moderate Size Housing Assoc 1968, memb of Bd of S London Family Housing Assoc 1978-; RIBA; *Books* South London Parks, Gardens and Open Spaces; *Recreations* sailing, walking, travel; *Style*— Peter J Deakins, Esq; 34 Albany Mansions, Albert Brige Rd, London SW11 4PG (☎ 01 223 5999); Studio 57, 140 Battersea Park Rd, London SW11 (☎ 01 223 5999)

DEAL, John Leonard; s of late Isaac and Frances Deal; *b* 30 Mar 1922; *Educ* Devonport HS, Exeter Coll Oxford; *m* 1946, Brenda Frances, *née* Joiner; 2 s, 1 da; *Career* ret oil co exec; dir: Irish Refining Co 1968-79, The Assoc Octel Co Ltd 1974-82, Mainline Pipeline Ltd 1978-82, UK Oil Pipeline 1979-82; *Style*— John Deal, Esq; Hill Farm Barn, Westcott Heath, Dorking, Surrey (☎ 0306 887178)

DEALTRY, Thomas Richard; s of George Raymond Dealtry, and Edith, *née* Gardner; *b* 24 Nov 1936; *Educ* Cranfield Inst of Advanced Technol; *m* 1962 (m dis 1982), Pauline, *née* Sedgwick; 1 s, 1 da; *Career* dir Gulf region planning Gulf Orgn for Industrial Consulting, 1978-82; md RBA Mgmnt Servs (London & Kuwait) 1982-; MIMechE, MInstM; *Style*— Thomas Dealtry Esq

DEAN, Lady; Anne; *née* Gibson; da of William Farquhar Gibson, of Summerau, Pencisely Rd, Cardiff; *m* 1943, Sir Maurice Joseph Dean, KCB (d 1978); 1 s (John b 1946), 1 da (Sarah b 1943); *Style*— Lady Dean; 27, Bathgate Rd, SW19

DEAN, Barbara Florence; da of Albert Sidney Dean and Helen Catherine Dean; *b* 1 Sept 1924; *Educ* N London Collegiate Sch, Girton Coll Cambridge, London Inst of Educn; *Career* headmistress Godolphin and Latymer School Hammersmith 1974-85 (formerly dep); *Style*— Miss Barbara Dean; 9 Stuart Ave, Ealing, London W5 (☎ 01 992 8324)

DEAN, Brenda; da of Hugh Dean, of 35 Consett Ave, Thornton, Cleveleys, Lancs; *b* 29 April 1945; *Educ* St Andrews, Eccles, Stretford GS; *Career* Manchester Branch Sogat: admin sec 1959-71, asst branch sec 1971, sec 1976; SOGAT: pres 1983, gen sec 1985; memb: Womens Nat Cmmn (co-chm 1975-78), Nat Econ Devpt Cncl 1985-, BBC gen advsy cncl 1985-, TUC gen cncl 1985-, TUC econ ctee 1987-; hon MA Salford Univ 1986; *Recreations* reading, cooking, sailing; *Style*— Ms Brenda Dean; SOGAT House, 274-288 London Road, Hadleigh, Benfleet, Essex SS7 2DE (☎ 0702 554111)

DEAN, Frederick Harold; CB (1976), QC (1979); s of Frederick Richard Dean (d 1955), of Lancs, and Alice, *née* Baron (d 1969); *b* 5 Nov 1908; *Educ* Manchester GS, Manchester Univ (LLB, LLM); *m* 1, 1939 (m dis 1966), Gwendoline Mary Eayrs Williams (d 1975); m 2, 1978, Mary Rose, da of Cdr Frank Louis Merriman, RN; 1 s (Richard), 1 da (Ruth); *Career* 1945-50; RAF (emergency cmmn) 1940-46; Sqdn Ldr served in UK, Iraq, Egypt, E Africa; barr Middle Temple 1933, practice Northern Circuit 1934-50, asst J A G 1950-68 (UK, Egypt, Far East, Cyprus, Germany), vice judge advocate gen 1968-72; judge advocate gen 1972-79; cmmr Duke of York's Royal Mil Sch 1972-79; chm Inst of Chartered Accountants Appeal Ctee 1980-87; *Books* Bibliography of British Military Law (2 edn), Royal Forces in Halsbury's Laws of England (4 edn collaboration); *Recreations* walking, watching cricket, music, theatre; *Clubs* Athenaeum; *Style*— Harold Dean, Esq, CB, QC; The Old Farmhouse, Lower St Quainton, Aylesbury, Bucks HP22 4BL (☎ Quainton 263)

DEAN, Ian Hall; s of George William Dean (d 1972) and Irene Violet Alice *née* Hall; *b* 19 Sept 1944; *Educ* Kilburn GS, Eastbourne GS; *m* 1, 3 Sept 1966, Jacqueline Mary, da of Alan Maurice Rayne, of 3 Spencer Rd, Eastbourne E Sussex; 2 da (Carole b 1969, Catherine b 1971); m 2, 2 Sept 1976, Diane, da of Leslie Ambrose Nicol of 192 Seven Sisters Road, Eastbourne, E Sussex; 1 s (Richard b 1978); *Career* deputy underwriter SC Lloyd Haine & Co 1974 (joined 1963, claims settler 1970), dep chm and dir of reinsurance Excess Insurance Gp 1980-81 (dir of underwriting 1979, dep 1977, mngr 1974, underwriter 1974); chm Sphere Drake Insurance Group plc 1982-; dir: Arpel Trimark Agencies Ltd, Dai Tokyo Insur (UK) Ltd, Sphere Drake Insurance plc and subsidiaries; *Recreations* walking, tennis, reading; *Style*— Ian H Dean, Esq; Winster House, Forest Rd, Forest Row, East Sussex RH18 5NA (☎ 034282 2472); Sphere Drake Insurance Group plc, 52-54 Leadenhall St, London EC3A 2BJ (☎ 01 480 7340, telex: 935015, fax: 01 481 3828, car: 0860 712530)

DEAN, Hon Mrs; Jenefer; *née* Mills; da of 5 Baron Hillingdon (by 1 m); *b* 6 April 1935; *m* 7 April 1962, His Honour Judge Joseph Jolyon Dean *qv*, s of Basil Dean, CBE (d 1978); 1 s (Ptolemy Hugo b 1967), 2 da (Antigone b 1963, Tacita b 1965); *Style*— The Hon Mrs Dean; The Hall, West Brabourne, Ashford, Kent

DEAN, His Hon Joseph Jolyon; s of Basil Dean, CBE (d 1978), and Esther Bagger, *née* Van Gruisen, formerly Dean (d 1983); *b* 26 April 1921; *Educ* Harrow, Oxford (MA); *m* 7 April 1962, Hon Jenefer, *née* Mills, *qv*, da of 5 Baron Hillingdon MC (d 1982), of the Tod House, Seal, Kent; 1 s, 2 da; *Career* Military Service, Royal Artillery 1941-46, Capt 51 Highland Div, Western Desert Sicily, Normandy, Holland, Germany; barrister 1947, bencher Middle Temple 1972, Circuit Judge 1976 (ret 1987); *Books* Hatred Ridicule or Contempt, A Book of Libel Cases (1953); *Clubs* Army and Navy; *Style*— His Honour Joseph Dean,; The Hall, West Brabourne, Ashford, Kent

DEAN, (Wilfred) Martin (Vernon); s of Basil Dean, CBE (d 1978), of London and Esther Van Gruisen (d 1983); *b* 18 March 1920; *Educ* Harrow, Brasenose Coll Oxford (MA); *m* 20 April 1949, Nancy Clare, da of Joseph Victor Lynch, OBE (d 1962); 3 s (Anthony b 1955, d 1955, Christopher b 1957, d 1957, John b 1963), 4 da (Patricia b 1950, Rosemary b 1952, d 1956, Theresa b 1954, Mia b 1958); *Career* RE 1940-45, cmmnd 1941, Capt 1944, attached KGV'sO Benghal Sappers & Miners 1942-45; admitted slr 1948, conslt Blount Petre & Co (slrs) 1988- (ptnr 1951-87); memb Law Soc 1948; *Recreations* gardening, photography, bridge; *Clubs* Garrick; *Style*— Martin Dean, Esq; 23 St Petersburgh Place, London W2 4LA (☎ 01 229 5505)

DEAN, Sir Patrick Henry; GCMG (1963, KCMG 1957, CMG 1947); s of Prof Henry Roy Dean (d 1961); *b* 16 Mar 1909; *Educ* Rugby, Gonville and Caius Cambridge; *m* 1947, Patricia Wallace, da of T Frame Jackson; 2 s; *Career* barr 1934; asst legal advsr FO 1939-45, head German Political Dept FO 1946-50, min Rome 1950-51, sr civilian instr IDC 1952-53, asst under-sec FO 1953-56, dep under-sec 1956-60, perm UK rep to UN 1960-64, ambassador Washington 1965-69, memb dept ctee to examine operation Section 2 Official Secrets Act 1971; chm Cambridge Petroleum Royalties 1975-82; dir: Taylor Woodrow 1969-84 (conslt 1986-), Ingersoll-Rand Hldgs 1971-81, Amex Bank 1976-81 (int advsr American Express 1969-); chm Governing Body Rugby Sch 1972-84; vice pres English-Speaking Union 1983- (chm 1973-83); hon fell: Gonville and Caius Cambridge, Clare Coll Cambridge (fell 1932-35); hon bencher Lincoln's Inn 1965, hon LLD: Columbia Univ, William and Mary Coll and additional US Univs; KStJ; *Recreations* walking; *Clubs* Brooks's; *Style*— Sir Patrick Dean, GCMG; 5 Bentinck Mansions, Bentinck St, London W1 (☎ 01 935 0881)

DEAN, Sir (Arthur) Paul; MP (Cons Woodspring 1983-); s of Arthur Dean; *b* 14 Sept 1924; *Educ* Ellesmere Coll, Exeter Coll Oxford (MA, BLitt); *m* 1, 1957, Doris (d 1979), da of Frank Webb, of Sussex; m 2, 1980, Peggy, *née* Parker; *Career* serv WWII Capt Welsh Gds ADC to Cdr 1 Corps BAOR; former farmer; CRD 1957, resident tutor Swinton Cons Coll 1958-62, asst dir CRD 1962-64, Parly candidate (Cons) Pontefract 1962, MP (Cons) N Somerset 1964-83, front bench oppn spokesman Health and Social Security 1969-70, Parly under-sec DHSS 1970-74, chm Cons Health and Social Security Ctee 1979-82; memb: Commons Servs Select Ctee 1979-82, exec ctee Cwlth Parly Assoc UK branch 1975-, Commons Chm's Panel 1979-82; second dep chm House of Commons and dep chm Ways and Means 1982-87, first dep chm Ways and Means and dep speaker; formerly: memb Church in Wales Governing Body, govr BUPA, chm Cons Watch-Dog Gp for Self-Employed; dir: Charterhouse Pensions, Watney Mann and Truman Hldgs; govr Cwlth Inst 1981-; pres Oxford Univ Cons Assoc; kt 1985; *Clubs* Oxford Carlton (pres); *Style*— Sir Paul Dean, MP; House of Commons, London SW1A 0AA

DEAN, Peter Henry; s of Alan Walduck Dean, and Gertrude, *née* Bürger; *b* 24 July

1939; *Educ* Rugby, London Univ (LLB); *m* 31 July 1965, Linda Louise, da of The Rev William Edward Keating; 1 da (Amanda b 1967); *Career* slr 1962; dir RTZ Corp Plc 1974-85 (sec 1972-74, joined 1966), freelance business cnslt 1985-; non exec dir: Assoc Br Ports Hldgs plc 1980-, Liberty Life Assur Co Ltd 1986-; memb: Monopolies and Mergers Cmmnn 1982-, cncl of mgmnt Highgate Counselling Centre 1985-; chm English Baroque Choir 1985-; memb Law Society; *Recreations* music, especially choral singing, skiing; *Clubs* Ski Club of Great Britain, Kandahar; *Style*— Peter Dean, Esq; 52 Lanchester Road, Highgate, London N6 4TA (☎ 01 883 5417)

DEAN, (Cecil) Roy; s of Arthur Dean, and Flora Clare Dean, of Herts (d 1980); *b* 18 Feb 1927; *Educ* Watford GS, London Coll of Printing and Graphic Arts (dip), Coll for the Distributive Trades (MIPR); *m* 1954, Heather, da of Sydney Sturtridge (d 1981); 3 s (Jonathan, Nicholas, Charles); *Career* RAF 1945-48 (India and Pakistan), COI 1948-58;HM Dipl Serv: Colombo 1958-62, Vancouver 1962-64, Lagos 1964-68, FCO 1968-71, Houston 1971-73, FCO 1973-76, dir of Arts Control and Disarmament Res Unit 1976-83, dep Br high cmmnr Accra Ghana 1983-86, ret ; UN Sec-Gen's expert group on disarmament insts 1980-81, tstee of Urbanaid 1986; writer and broadcater, author of numerous pamphlets and articles on int affrs, BBC radio series The Poetry of Popular Song; *Recreations* crosswords (Times Nat Champion 1970 and 1979), light verse; *Clubs* Royal Cwlth Soc, Royal Utd Servs Inst; *Style*— Roy Dean, Esq; 14 Blyth Rd, Bromley, Kent BR1 3RX (☎ 01 460 8159);

DEAN, Hon Mrs; (Thalia Mary); *née* Shaw; da of late 2 Baron Craigmyle; *b* 7 August 1918; *m* 4 Sept 1939, Winton Basil Dean, s of Basil Dean, CBE (d 1978); 1 s and 2 da (both decd); *Style*— The Hon Mrs Dean; Hambledon Hurst, Godalming, Surrey

DEAN, Winton Basil; s of Basil Herbert Dean, CBE (d 1978), of London, formerly of Little Easton Manor, Dunmow, Essex, and Esther, *née* van Gruisen (d 1983); *b* 18 Mar 1916; *Educ* Harrow, King's Coll Cambridge (MA); *m* 4 Sept 1939, Hon Thalia Mary Shaw, da of 2 Baron Craigmyle (d 1944); 1 s (Stephen b 1946), 2 da (Brigid b 1943 d 1945, Diana b and d 1948), 1 adopted da (Diana b 1955); *Career* Admiralty (Naval Intelligence) 1944-45; memb: music panel Arts Cncl 1957-60, ctee Handel Opera Soc 1955-60, cncl Royal Musical Assoc 1965- (vice-pres 1970-); Ernest Bloch Prof of Music 1965-66, Regent's Lecturer 1977, Univ of California (Berkeley), Matthew Vassar Lecturer Vassar Coll Poughkeepsie NY 1979; memb mgmnt ctee Halle Handel Soc 1979-; Kuratorium, Göttingen Handel Festival 1981-; translated libretto of Weber's opera Abu Hassan (performed Cambridge Arts Theatre 1938), ed (with Sarah Fuller) Handel's opera Julius Caesar (performed Birmingham 1977); Hon RAM 1971; FBA 1975; *Books* The Frogs of Aristophanes (translation of songs and choruses to music by Walter Leigh) (1937), Bizet (1948, 3rd revised edn 1975), Shakespeare and Opera (in Shakespeare and Music 1964), Handel and The Opera Seria (1969), Beethoven and Opera (in The Beethoven Companion 1971), Handel, Three Ornamented Arias (ed 1976), The Rise of Romantic Opera (jt ed E J Dent 1976), The New Grove Handel (1982), Handel's Operas 1704-1726 (with J M Knapp 1987), Essays on Opera (1989), French Opera, Halieu Opera and German Opera in the Age of Beethoven 1790-1830 (in the New Oxford History of Music vol VIII 1982); *Recreations* shooting, naval history; *Clubs* English Speaking Union; *Style*— Winton Dean, Esq; Hambledon Hurst, Godalming, Surrey GU8 4HF (☎ 042879 2644)

DEAN OF BESWICK, Baron (Life Peer UK 1983), of West Leeds in the Co of West Yorks; Joseph Jabez Dean; s of John Dean, of Manchester; *b* 3 June 1922; *m* 1945, Helen, da of Charles Hill; *Career* MP (Lab) Leeds W 1974-83; *Style*— The Rt Hon Lord Dean of Beswick; House of Lords, London SW1

DEANE, John Woodforde; s of Lt Col Michael Wallace Blencowe Deane (d 1973), and Eileen Haslewood McNish, *née* Porter (d 1968); *b* 2 August 1929; *Educ* Winchester; *m* 8 Jan 1966, Gillian Merriman, da of Humphrey Morgan Hughes (d 1965); 2 s (Nicholas b 1967, Michael b 1972), 2 da (Lucy b 1968, Rebecca b 1969); *Career* RMC Sandhurst 1947-48, Lancs Fusiliers and Royal Regt Fusiliers 1949-71; sr princ DOE 1981-85 (princ 1971-81), asst sec head of industl personnel Property Servs Agency, memb mgmnt ctee Civil Servs Benevolent Fund 1988; chm Ripe and Chalvington Flower Show Ctee; memb: New Sussex Opera, E Sussex Chorale; *Recreations* gardening, cycling, bellringing, choral singing; *Clubs* Army and Navy; *Style*— John Deane, Esq; Lovers Farmhouse, Chalvington, Nr Hailsham, (☎ 032 183 207); Room A602, Whitgift Centre, Croydon (☎ 01 760 4410)

DEANE, Hon Robert Fitzmaurice; s and h of 8 Baron Muskerry; *b* 26 Mar 1948; *Educ* Sandford Park Sch Dublin, Trinity Coll Dublin; *Style*— The Hon Robert Deane; 15 Glenroy Rd, Manor Gardens, 4001 Durban, S Africa

DEANE-DRUMMOND, Anthony John; CB (1971), DSO (1960), MC (1942) and Bar (1945); s of Col John Drummond Deane-Drummond (d 1969), and Marie Lily (d 1966), da of Martano de Cuadra, of 47 Castellana, Madrid; *b* 23 June 1917; *Educ* Marlborough, RMA Woolwich; *m* 1944, Mary Evangeline, da of S Boyd, MRCS (d 1970), of Hampstead; 4 da (Shirley, Angela, Anna, Celia); *Career* Cmmnd RS 1938, Regular Army 1938-71, Italy 1941-42 POW, escaped), Holland 1944 (escaped); Bde Maj 3 Para Bde 1945-46, Cdr 22 SAS Regt Malaya & Oman 1957-60, Asst Cmdt RMA Sandhurst, GOC 3rd Div 1966-68; MOD 1968-71; chief exec Paper Bd 1971-79; dir 3 Counties Woodburning Centre 1980-83; *Books* Return Ticket (1955, total sales all editions & translations approx 250,000), Riot Control (1973); *Recreations* cabinet making, antique restoration, gliding (Br Gliding Champion 1957, memb of Br team competing internationally in Poland 1958, Argentina 1960, W Germany 1962, UK 1964); *Clubs* Special Forces; *Style*— Anthony Deane-Drummond, Esq, CB, DSO, MC; Old Manor House, Halford, Shipston on Stour, Warwickshire CV36 5BT

DEANS, Rodger William; CB (1977); s of Andrew and Elizabeth Deans; *b* 21 Dec 1917; *Educ* Perth Acad, Edinburgh Univ; *m* 1943, Joan Radley; 1 s, 1 da; *Career* WWII Maj RA and REME, mil prosecutor Palestine 1945-46; slr to sec of state for Scotland and to HM Treasy 1971-80 (legal asst 1947-50, sr legal asst Scottish Off 1951-62, asst slr 1962-71), conslt ed Green & Son Edinburgh 1981-82, sr chm Supplementary Benefit Appeal Tbnls 1982-84; regnl chm (Scotland) Social Security Appeal Tribunals and Medical Appeal Tbnls; *Recreations* hill-walking, gardening; *Clubs* Scottish Arts (Edinburgh), Caledonian (Edinburgh), Royal Cwlth Inst; *Style*— Rodger Deans, Esq, CB; 25 Grange Rd, Edinburgh 9 (☎ 031 667 1893, office 031 225 1440)

DEAR, Geoffrey James; QPM (1982), DL (1985); s of Cecil William, and Violet Mildred Dear, *née* Mackney; *b* 20 Sept 1937; *Educ* Fletton GS, UC London (LLB); *m* 1958, Judith Ann, da of J W Stocker (d 1972), of Peterborough; 1 s (Simon b 1963), 2 da (Kate b 1961, Fiona b 1966); *Career* joined Peterborough combined Police after cadet service 1956, inspector to superintendent Mid-Anglia constabulary 1965-72, asst chief constable Nottinghamshire constabulary 1972, dep asst cmmnr Metropolitan Police 1980-81, asst cmmnr Metropolitan Police 1981-85, chief constable West Midlands Police 1985-; *Recreations* field sports, rugby football, fell-walking, music, reading; *Clubs* Naval and Military; *Style*— Geoffrey Dear, Esq, QPM, DL; West Midlands Police, Lloyd House, Colmore Circus, Queensway, Birmingham B4 6NQ (☎ 021 236 5000)

DEARDEN, Neville; s of Maj Issac Samuel Dearden (d 1979), and Lilian Anne, *née* Claxton (d 1983); *b* 1 Mar 1940; *Educ* Rowlinson Technical Sch Sheffield, King Alfred Coll Winchester, Univ of Southampton; *m* 1, 4 April 1963, Jean Rosemary, da of Walter Francis Garratt, of Sheffield; 2 s (Adrian b 1968, David b 1970), 1 da (Karen b 1966); m 2, 3 May 1980, Eileen Bernadette, da of Dr William John Sheehan; 3 s (Michael b 1981, Patrick b 1984, Ciaran b 1987); *Career* head of science dept Lafford Sch Lincolnshire 1961-67; md: W Garratt & Son Ltd 1972-78, M & H Fabrications Ltd 1972-77; chief exec S W Fabrications Ltd 1980-84, md Sheffield Brick Gp plc 1982-87, chief exec Pan Computer Systems Ltd 1982-85; chm: Parker Winder and Achurch Ltd 1983-85, C H Wood Security Ltd 1983-, Smith Widdowson Eadem Ltd 1983- (md 1986-), md F G Machin Ltd 1983-; FBIM, FIIM, FICE; *Recreations* game and sea fishing, boating, practical craft work; *Clubs* Birmingham Press, De La Salle Association, Royal Yachting Association; *Style*— Neville Dearden, Esq; Smith Widdowson and Eadem Ltd, 296 Penistone Rd, Sheffield S6 2FT (☎ 0742 852201, telex: 547545, fax: 0742 852531)

DEARE, Ronald Frank Robert; CMG (1988); s of late Albert Victor Deare, and Lilian Deare; *b* 9 Oct 1927; *Educ* Wellington; *m* 1952, Iris Mann; 1 s; *Career* Colonial Office 1948; private sec to Min Overseas Devpt 1971, cnsllr (Overseas Devpt) Washington; alternate exec dir World Bank 1976-79; head: WI & Atlantic Dept FCO 1980-81, Central & S Africa Dept ODA 1981-82 Bilateral Coordination Dept ODA 1983-84 min Br Embassy Rome: perm rep to UN Food and Agric Orgn 1985-88; conslt UN/FAO World Food Programme 1989; *Style*— Ronald Deare, Esq, CMG; Conifers, Oakhurst, Haywards Heath, W Sussex RH16 1PD (☎ 0444 450590)

DEARING, (Ian) Barry; s of Ernest Dearing, of Read, and Winifred Mary, *née* Roberts; Lord of the Manor of Balderstone; *b* 24 July 1947; *Educ* Burnley GS (Edward Livesey Scholar), Leeds Univ (LLB); *m* 11 Sept 1974, Jennifer, da of John Harrison Woodward, MBE, of Glengarry, Lytham; 3 s (Richard b 1978, Peter b 1981, Edward b 1984); *Career* slr 1971; notary public 1987; *Recreations* fishing, books; *Clubs* Law Soc; *Style*— Barry Dearing, Esq; Brookside, Read, Lancs (☎ (025482 2295); Stanley House, Clitheroe, Lancs (☎ (0200 26811, telex 635170, fax 0200 28223)

DEARING, Sir Ronald Ernest; CB (1979); s of Ernest Henry Ashford Dearing (d 1941), and M T Dearing; *b* 27 July 1930; *Educ* Doncaster GS , Hull Univ (BSc Econ), London Business Sch; *m* 1954, Margaret Patricia Riley; 2 da; *Career* regional dir N Region DTI 1972-74, under-sec DTI/Dept of Industry 1972-76, dep-sec Dept of Industry 1976-80, chm Post Office 1981-87 (dep chm 1980); gp chm Nationalized Industries Chairmen's Gp 1983-84; non exec dir Whitbread Co plc 1987-, chm cncl for National Academic Awards 1987-; kt 1984; *Recreations* music and gardening; *Clubs* City Livery; *Style*— Sir Ronald Dearing, CB; 28 Westhawe, Bretton, Peterborough PE3 8BA

DEARNLEY, Christopher Hugh; s of Rev Charles Dearnley; *b* 11 Feb 1930; *Educ* Cranleigh, Worcester Coll Oxford (organ scholar, MA, DMus); *m* 1957, Bridget, *née* Wateridge; 3 s, 1 da; *Career* organist and master of the choristers Salisbury Cathedral 1957-68, organist and dir of music St Pauls Cathedral 1968-, chm Friends of Cathedral Music 1971-; FRCO; *Books* The Treasury of English Choral Music Vol III (1965), English Church Music 1650-1750 (1970); *Style*— Christopher Dearnley, Esq; 8b Amen Court, London EC4M 7BU (☎ 01 248 3314)

DEAS, Roger Stewart; s of George Stewart (d 1983), of Motherwell, and Winifred Mary, *née* Ogden; *b* 1 August 1943; *Educ* The HS of Glasgow, Univ of Glasgow (BSc); *m* 27 June 1970, Carole, da of Percy Woodward, of Nottingham; 2 da (Angela Elizabeth b 1972, Wendy Jane b 1974); *Career* fin dir Brown Bros Ltd 1974-81, gp fin dir Currys Gp plc 1981-84, fin dir Heron Corpn plc 1984-86, nat fin ptnr Deloitte Haskins & Sells 1986-; ACMA 1974, FCMA 1986; *Recreations* sailing; *Clubs* New Haven YC; *Style*— Roger Deas, Esq; Fairways, Park Rd, Farnham Royal, Bucks SL2 3BQ (☎ 02814 2377); Deloitte Haskins & Sells, 128 Queen Victoria St, London EC4P 4JX (☎ 01 248 3913, telex 894941)

DEATH, Basil; s of Charles Death (d 1943), of Herts, and Carrie Helena, *née* Piper (d 1961); *b* 18 Jan 1916; *Educ* Downside, Pembroke Coll Cambridge; *Career* Major Irish Bds 1939-45, served NW Europe; dir R K Harrison & Co Ltd 1947-57; memb Lloyds; pres Int Gundog League (Retriever Soc), chm The Labrador Club; *Recreations* stalking, shooting, fishing, gardening; *Clubs* Brooks's, Kennel; *Style*— Basil Death, Esq; Dunellan House, Strathtay, Perthshire PH9 0PJ (☎ Strathtay 221)

DEAVE, John James; s of Charles John Deave (d 1970), of London, and Gertrude Debrit, *née* Hunt (d 1972); *b* 1 April 1928; *Educ* Charterhouse, Pembroke Coll Oxford (MA); *m* 16 Aug 1958, Gillian Mary, now Rev GM Deave (Deacon 1987), da of Admiral Sir Manley Power, KCB CBE DSO, of Norton Cottage, Yarmouth, IOW (d 1981); 1 s (Jonathan b 1959), 1 da (Victoria b 1961); *Career* barr Gray's Inn 1952, recorder, chm of Med Appeal Tbnl; *Recreations* gardening, history; *Clubs* Notts United Services; *Style*— John Deave, Esq; Greensmith Cottage, Stathern, Melton Mowbray, Leics (☎ 0949 603 40); 24 The Ropewalk, Nottingham (☎ 0602 472581)

DEAVILLE, Timothy John Norfolk; s of Rev Robert Deaville (d 1972), and Phyllis Eleanor, *née* Laycock; *b* 3 August 1933; *Educ* Marlborough, Christ's Coll Cambridge Univ (MA); *m* 26 Aug 1961, Jette, da of Dr Odont Frode Hilming, of Copenhagen, Denmark; 2 da (Caroline b 1965, Georgina b 1971); *Career* Nat Serv 2 Lt REME 1955-57, TA Lt Staffs Yeomanry 1957-63; devpt engr Rolls Royce Ltd 1957-59, project engr Ind Coope Ltd 1959-62, mgmnt conslt P-E Consulting Gp Ltd 1962-64, md Troman Bros Ltd and two other subsidiaries of Cope Allman Internat Ltd 1944-66, divnl mangr Mobbs Miller Ltd 1969-71, owner and ptnr Hatchers Poultry 1971-; *Recreations* sailing, opera; *Clubs* Royal Southern Yacht, Royal Yachting Assoc; *Style*— Timothy Deaville, Esq; Hatchers Farm, Farley, Salisbury, Wilts SP5 1AQ (☎ 072 272 356, telex 94070345 HATC G); Casa Congilio, Sao Clemente, Vale Formoso, Almansil, 8100 Loulé, Portugal

DEAVIN, Stanley Gwynne; CBE (1971, OBE, 1958); s of Percy John and Annie Deavin; *b* 8 August 1905; *Educ* Hymer's Coll Hull; *m* 1, 1934, Louise Faviell (d 1982); 1 s, 1 da; m 2, 1982, Mrs Hilda Jenkins; *Career* formerly chm North Eastern Gas Bd, ret; FCA; OStJ; *Style*— Stanley G Deavin, Esq, CBE; 50 Hookstone Drive,

Harrogate, North Yorks (☎ 0423 884301)

DEAYTON, Cdr Roger Davall; VRD (1961 and bar 1971); s of Edward Lewis Deayton (d 1961), and Phyllis Mabel, *née* Davall (d 1968); *b* 12 Oct 1917; *Educ* Caterham; *m* 1 March 1949, Susan Agnes, da of Baille William Weir (d 1948); 3 s (Alan b 1950, William b 1953, Angus b 1956); *Career* joined RNVR as Ord Seaman 1938 and ret as Cdr 1972 with continuous service inc WW II, overseas mangr Prudential Assurance 1970-80; chm Bd of Govrs Caterham Sch 1979-89, sec and chm Caterham Dist Scout Cncl, ACIS; *Recreations* travel, bird watching, hill walking, genealogy; *Clubs* Royal Overseas League; *Style*— Commander Roger D Deayton, VRD; 15 Loxford Way, Caterham, Surrey (☎ 0883 46005); Knoll Cottage, Burnham Market, Kings Lynn, Norfolk (☎ 0328 738857)

DEBARGE, Hon Mrs (Robina Jane); *née* Cayzer; da of 2 Baron Rotherwick; *b* 24 Jan 1953; *Educ* St George's Switzerland; *m* 4 July 1981, Olivier Debarge, MA, PhD, s of Albert Emile Joseph Debarge (d 1972), of Paris; 2 da; *Career* chm Robina Cayzer Ltd; *Recreations* skiing; *Style*— The Hon Mrs Debarge; 3 Redesdale St, London SW3 4BL (☎ 01 352 6955)

DEBENHAM, Hon Mrs; Daphne Joan; *née* Godber; da of 1 and last Baron Godber (d 1976); *b* 17 August 1923; *m* 20 June 1942, Archibald Ian Scott Debenham, DFC, AE; 2 s, 2 da; *Style*— The Hon Mrs Debenham; Bowerland Farm, Bowerland Lane, Lingfield, Surrey RH7 6DF (☎ 0342 832878)

DEBENHAM, George Andrew; s and h of Sir Gilbert Ridley Debenham, 3 Bt; *b* 10 April 1938; *Educ* Bryanston, Trinity Cambridge; *m* 1969, Penelope Jane, da of John David Armishaw Carter; 1 s, 1 da; *Style*— George Debenham, Esq

DEBENHAM, Sir Gilbert Ridley; 3 Bt (UK 1931) of Bladen, Co Dorset; s of Sir Ernest Ridley Debenham, 1 Bt, JP (d 1952); suc bro, Sir Piers Kenrick Debenham, 2 Bt, 1964; *b* 28 June 1906; *Educ* Eton, Trinity Coll Cambridge; *m* 1 April 1935, Violet Mary, da of His Honour Judge (George Herbert) Higgins (d 1937); 3 s, 1 da; *Heir* s, George Andrew Debenham; *Career* consultant psychiatrist NHS 1949-; farmer; ret; *Style*— Sir Gilbert Debenham, Bt; Tonerspuddle Farm, Dorchester, Dorset (☎ Bere Regis 471 245)

DEBENHAM, Michael George Scott; s of Archibald Ian Scott Debenham DFC of Bowerland Farm, Bowerland Lane, Lingfield, Surrey, and Daphne Joan, *née* Godber; *b* 12 Oct 1943; *Educ* Haileybury and ISC, St Andrews Univ (BSc); *m* July 1966 (m dis 1980), Janine Elizabeth, da of Anthony Davies, of Crockham Hill, Edenbridge, Kent; 3 da (Sarah b 14 April 1968, Anna b 27 March 1970, Tessa b 11 April 1974); m 2, 6 March 1981, Roberta, da of Luigi Courir, of Genova, Italy; *Career* Br Inspecting Engr Ltd: dir (Material Control Ltd) 1971, dir 1976, dir (Internat Ltd) 1976, dir (Pipelines Ltd) 1982, md 1987, dir (Hldgs Uk Ltd) 1987; memb Tandridge PCC 1976-77; Liveryman Worhsipful Co of Taylors; MIHT 1968, MICE 1971, CEng 1971, AWeldI 1985, FIQA 1986; *Recreations* tennis, squash, gardening; *Style*— Michael Debenham, Esq; British Inspecting Engineers Ltd, Bank of America House, Elmfield Rd, Bromley, Kent (☎ 01 464 3434, fax 01 290 0701, telex 919 572)

DEBENHAM, Maj (Alfred) Thomas Keeys; MBE; s of Alfred Edward Debenham (d 1944), of 20 Harns Court, London SW1, and May, *née* Penson (d 1940); *b* 6 Mar 1910; *Educ* Marlborough; *m* 30 Aug 1935, Mary Elizabeth, da of Arthur Raymond Lound (d 1947), of Croydon; 1 s (John Keeys b 1944), 1 da (Mary Anne b 1955); *Career* pre-war RA TA WWII served: ME 1941, Egypt, Cyprus, Palestine, staff offr SORA 1943, staff offr Eastern Cmd RA, Maj TA 1948; former oil co exec; rifle shooting: England int, shot for GB against Australia, NZ and Canada; pre war racing driver at Brooklands; memb Royal Br Legion; *Recreations* rifle shooting, ocean racing; *Clubs* Royal Ocean Racing; *Style*— Maj Thomas Debenham, MBE

DEBENHAM TAYLOR, John; CMG (1967), OBE (1959), TD (1967); s of John Francis Taylor (d 1941), and Harriett Beatrice, *née* Williams (d 1973); *b* 25 April 1920; *Educ* Whitgift, Aldenham; *m* 1966, Gillian May, da of Cyril Bernard James (d 1981), of Sussex; 1 da (Catherine Jessica b 1972); *Career* Maj RA (TA) Finland, Middle East and SE Asia 1939-45; FO 1946, control cmmn Germany 1947-49, second sec Bangkok 1950, acting consul Songhkla 1951-52, vice-consul Hanoi 1952-53, FO 1953-54, first sec Bangkok 1954-56, FO 1956-58, Singapore 1958-59, FO 1960-64, cnsllr Kuala Lumpur 1964-66, FO 1966-69, cnsllr Washington 1969-72 and Paris 1972-73, For and Cwlth Off 1973-77, ret 1977; industl consIt 1978-87; *Recreations* walking, reading, history; *Clubs* Naval and Military; *Style*— John Debenham Taylor, Esq, CMG, OBE, TD; c/o Lloyds Bank, 1 Butler Place, London SW1H 0PR

DEBY, John Bedford; QC (1980); s of late Reginald Bedford Deby and late Irene, *née* Slater; *b* 19 Dec 1931; *Educ* Winchester, Trinity Coll Cambridge (MA); *Career* barr Inner Temple 1954, rec Crown Ct 1977-, bencher Inner Temple 1986; *Style*— John Deby, Esq, QC; 11 Britannia Rd, London SW6 2 HJ (☎ 01 736 4976)

DECIES, 6 Baron (I 1812); Arthur George Marcus Douglas de la Poer Beresford; only s of 5 Baron Decies, DSO, PC (d 1944; ggs of 1 Baron Decies who was bro of 1 Marquess of Waterford), by his 1 w, Vivien (d 1931), da of George Jay Gould, of New York, USA; *b* 24 April 1915; *Educ* Bryanston, Bonn Univ; *m* 1, 21 Oct 1937, Ann (d 28 March 1945), da of late Sidney Walter Trevor, of Camperdown, Victoria, Australia; m 2, 12 Sept 1945, Diana, widow of Maj D W A Galsworthy, Royal Fus, and da of Wing-Cdr G Turner-Cain; 1 s, 2 da; *Heir* s, Hon Marcus Hugh Tristam de la Poer Beresford; *Career* served 1939-45 as Flying Offr RAFVR; DFC (USA); *Style*— The Rt Hon The Lord Decies; c/o Coutts and Co, 1 Park Lane, London W1

DEEDES, Maj-Gen Charles Julius (John); CB (1968), OBE (1953), MC (1944); s of Gen Sir Charles Deedes, KCB, CMG, DSO (d 1968), of Budleigh Salterton, Devon, and Eve Mary, *née* Dean-Pitt; *b* 18 Oct 1913; *Educ* Oratery Sch, RMC Sandhurst; *m* 4 Sept 1939, Beatrice Elaine (Betty), da of HM Murgatroyd (d 1961), of Brockfield Hall, York; 3 s (Charles (Michael) Julius b 1941, Christopher b 1944, Jeremy b 1955); *Career* cmmnd KOYLI 1933, regtl appts 1939-44, serv NW Europe, Italy, Caribbean, Italy (wounded), Bde Cdr 1946, asst mil sec GHQ Middle East 1946-48, CO Glider Pilot Regt 1949-50, GSO 1 WO 1951-54, CO 1 Bn KOYLI 1954-56, serv Kenya, Aden, Cyprus, Col Gen Staff WO 1957-59, Bde Cdr 150 Inf Bdes Ta 1959-62, dep dir staffs duties MOD 1963-65, chief of staff HQ Eastern Cmd 1965-68, Col KOYLI 1966-70, COS HQ Southern Cnd 1968, Dep Col (Yorks) LI 1970-72; tres: Thirsk and Malton Cons Assoc, Ryedale Cons Assoc; FBIM 1968; Norwegian Military Cross 1940; *Recreations* foxhunting, horticulture, tennis; *Style*— Maj-Gen John Deedes, CB, OBE, MC; Lea Close, Brandsby, York YO6 4RW (☎ 034 75 239)

DEEDES, Baron (Life Peer UK 1986) William Francis; MC (1944), PC (1962), DL (Kent 1962); s of Herbert William Deedes, JP, of Saltwood Castle (which was sold 1925) and Sandling Park (which was sold 1897), and Melesina Gladys, JP, 2 da of Philip Chenevix Trench, gs of Richard Chenevix Trench, yr bro of 1 Baron Ashtown; *b* 1 June 1913; *Educ* Harrow; *m* 1942, Evelyn Hilary, da of Clive Branfoot, of Stonegrave, Yorks; 1 s (Jeremy b 1943) & 1 s decd, 3 da (Juliet b 1948, Victoria b 1950, Lucy b 1955); *Career* served WW II Maj KRRC (TA); ed The Daily Telegraph 1974-85; memb Historic Bldgs Cncl England 1958-62, MP (C) Ashford 1950-74, min without portfolio 1962-64, parly under-sec Home Office 1955-57, parly sec Miny Housing and Local Govt 1954-55; *Clubs* Carlton, Beefsteak, Royal and Ancient; *Style*— The Rt Hon Lord Deedes, MC, DL, PC; New Hayters, Aldington, Kent (☎ 023 372 269)

DEELEY, Michael; s of John Hamilton-Deeley (d 1979), and Josephine Frances Anne, *née* Deacon; *b* 6 August 1932; *Educ* Stowe; *m* 1, 1955 (m dis 1967), Teresa Harrison, 1 s (Manuel b 4 Jan 1964), 2 da ((Catherine) Anne b 26 Aug 1956, Isobel b 16 July 1957); m 2, 16 Jan 1970, Ruth Vivienne Emilie, da of Vivian George Stone-Spencer of Brighton, Sussex; *Career* Nat Serv 1950-52, 2 Lt IRWK served Malaya 1951-52; film prodr; md: Br Lion Films 1972-76, EMI Films Ltd 1976-79; pres EMI Films Inc (USA) 1977-79, chm and chief exec offr Consolidated Entertainment Inc 1984-; prodr more than thirty motion pictures incl: The Deer Hunter (Best Film Oscar 1978), The Italian Job, Convoy, Murphy's War, The Man Who Fell to Earth, Blade Runner, Robbery; NAACP Image Award for 'A Gathering of Old Men'; dep chm Br Screen Advsy Cncl, fndr memb: PM's Working Party on the Film Indust (1974), Interim Action Ctee on the Film Indust; memb Motion Picture Acad Arts & Sciences (US), ACTT; *Recreations* sailing; *Clubs* Garrick, Wianno YC; *Style*— Michael Deeley, Esq; Little Island, Osterville, Mass 02655, USA; 9000 Sunset Boulevard, 415, Los Angeles, CA 90069, USA (☎ 213 275 5719, fax 213 275 5786)

DEELEY, Patricia Anne; *née* Jones; da of Walter Edgar Jones (d 1983), of Stoneymoor, Wood Farm, Nr Kenilworth, and Ellen Elizabeth, *née* Goddard; *b* 30 Sept 1944; *Educ* St Joseph's Convent Kenilworth, Bristol Univ (LLB); *m* 9 July 1966, Peter Anthony William Deeley, s of George William Deeley (d 1985), of Meeting House Lane, Balsall Common Warwicks; 3 da (Eleanor b 28 Sept 1976, Anna b 10 Aug 1982, Rosemary b 27 Nov 1984); *Career* barr Lincoln's Inn 1970, Midlands and Oxford circuit; memb of res and ethical ctee for Coventry and dist; govr St Joseph's Convent Sch; memb Hon Soc of Lincoln's Inn; *Recreations* music, cats, embroidery; *Style*— Mrs Patricia Deeley; Icarus, Vicarage Road, Stoneleigh, Warwickshire (☎ 0203 414436); Shorestones, Pier Road, Sea View, Isle of Wight; 2 Fountain Ct, Steelhouse Lane, Birmingham B4 6DR (☎ 021 236 3882)

DEER, Sir (Arthur) Frederick; CMG (1973); s of Andrew and Maude Deer; *b* 15 June 1910; *Educ* Sydney Boy's HS, Sydney Univ (BA, LLB); *m* 1936, Elizabeth Christine, da of George Charles Whitney; 1 s, 3 da; *Career* barr 1934, dir The Mutual Life and Citizens' Assurance Co Ltd 1956-83; chm Expo Oil NL 1980; kt 1979; *see Debrett's Handbook of Australia and New Zealand for further details*; *Style*— Sir Frederick Deer, CMG; 1179 Pacific Highway, Turramurra, NSW 2074, Australia (☎ (44) 2912)

DEERHURST, Viscount; Edward George William Omar Coventry; s (by 1 m) and h of 11 Earl of Coventry; *b* 24 Sept 1957; *Style*— Viscount Deerhurst; 18 Tanjenong Place, Burleigh Heads, Qld 4220, Australia

DEERING, Peter Henry; s of William John Deering (d 1962), and Margaret Florence Deering; *b* 25 Feb 1931; *Educ* Tottenham Poly Sch of Bldg, N London Poly Sch of Architecture; *m* 9 Aug 1952, Fay Constance, da of Walter Frederick Sermons (d 1984); *Career* Nat Serv 1955-56; architect, assoc Martin Hutchinson 1962-67 (asst 1949-67), self employed conslt 1967-73, ptnr David Hogg and Ptnrs (architects) 1973-, past (fndr) chm of Forty Hill (Enfield) conservation area study gp, memb Enfield Preservation Soc, pres Myddelton House (Enfield) Cricket Club; magistrate Haringey Div, memb Bd of Visitors Pentonville Prison; *Recreations* cricket, bowls; *Clubs* Marylebrie CC, Cricketers Club of London; *Style*— Peter Deering, Esq; 11 Lambroune Gardens, Enfield, Middx EN1 3AD (☎ 01 363 4093); David Hogg and Ptnrs, 20 Crawford Place, London W1H 1JE (☎ 01 724 5720)

DEHN, Conrad Francis; QC (1968); s of Curt Gustav Dehn (d 1948), of London, and Cynthia Doris, *née* Fuller (d 1987); *b* 24 Nov 1926; *Educ* Charterhouse, ChCh Oxford (BA, MA); *m* 1, 1954, Sheila, da of William Kilmurray Magan (d 1967), of London; 2 s (Hugh b 1956, Guy b 1957), 1 da (Katharine b 1959); m 2, 1978, Marilyn, da of Peter Collyer (d 1979), of Oxon; *Career* RA 1945-48, best cadet Mons OCTU 1946, 2 Lt 1947; called to the Bar Gray's Inn 1952, rec 1974, bencher 1977; Dir Bar Mutual Insur Fund 1988; *Recreations* theatre, travel, walking; *Clubs* Reform; *Style*— Conrad F Dehn, Esq, QC; Fountain Ct, Temple, London EC4Y 9DH (☎ 01 583 3335, telex 8813408 FONLEG G, fax 01 353 0329)

DEHN, Thomas Clark Bruce; s of Harold Bruce Dehn and Jean Margaret Henderson, *née* Ewing; *b* 6 Mar 1949; *Educ* Harrow, St Bartholomew's Hosp Med Coll London (MB BS, MS) LRCP); *m* 15 Sept 1984, (Dorothea) Lorraine, da of Gilbert Maurice Baird; 2 da (Henrietta b 1986, Emily b 1988); *Career* general surgeon; clinical lectr in surgery Nuffield Dept of Surgery, John Radcliffe Hosp Oxford 1984-88; lectr in surgery St Bartholomew's Hosp Med Coll 1980-84; memb Hosp Jnr Staff Ctee 1987-88; FRCS, LRCP; Freeman of City of London, Liveryman Worshipful Co of Distillers; *Recreations* flying; *Style*— Thomas Dehn, Esq; c/o Nuffield Dept of Surgery, John Radcliffe Hospital, Oxford

DEIGHTON, Robert John Greenway; s of Col John Harold Greenway Deighton, OBE, MC, of Ennis, Co Clare, and Maureen Hunt, of Co Limerick; *b* 5 Sept 1948; *Educ* Wellington Coll, Durham Univ (BA); *m* 1 May 1971, Olivia Jane Nikola, da of Lt-Col Leslie Garrick Young (d 1984); 2 s (Jamie b 1976, Harry b 1980), 1 da (Clare b 1974); *Career* dir Doyle Dane Bernbach 1976-80, dep md Foote Cone Belding 1980-83, chm and chief exec Kirkwoods 1983-86, chm Deighton & Mullen 1987-; *Recreations* cricket, squash, shooting; *Clubs* MCC, Naval and Military; *Style*— Robert J G Deighton, Esq; Deighton & Mullen, 41 Gt Pulteney Street, London W1R 3DE (☎ 01 434 0040, telex 8955246, fax 01 439 1590)

DEITH, Geoffrey Wilson; s of Leslie Herbert Deith (d 1973), and Mary Elizabeth May, *née* Holt; *b* 15 Jan 1935; *Educ* Stand GS Whitefield Lancs, Royal Tech Coll Salford (HNC); *m* 15 Aug 1959 (legally separated), Mavis Ann, da of James Payne, of Mudeford, Bournemouth; 2 s (Christopher b 1960, Ivan b 1965), 1 da (Gillian b 1962); *Career* Nat Serv Army 1951-53; process and devpt engr Unilever, Birds Eye Foods 1959-63; md: RE Ingham & Co 1963-80, Rank Orgn int indust div, Toshiba Corpn, Rank Toshiba TV Manufacture 1980-84; bd dir Waterford Glass Gp plc; dir Waterford

Crystal Inc; chm Waterford-Aynsley (UK) Ltd 1984-87; chm Aynsley Group plc; dir: Concepts Devpt Ltd, COAB Ltd; *Recreations* skiing, horse riding; *Style*— Geoffrey Deith, Esq; Coachman's Cottage, Coach House Mews, Blithfield, Rugeley, Staffs WS15 3NL (☎ 088921 439); Waterford-Aynsley (UK) Ltd, Portland Works, Longton, Stoke-on-Trent, Staffs ST3 1HS (☎ 0782 319216, fax 0783 343100, telex 36423)

DEITH, Raymond Cecil; s of William and Edith Deith; *b* 8 Nov 1905; *Educ* Ipswich GS; *m* 30 April 1938, Mary, da of James Ernest and Beatrice Ramsey; 1 s (Richard Ramsey), 2 da (Rosemary Ann, Valerie Patricia); *Career* CA; master of Worshipful Co of Fletchers 1945 and 1956; served on City of London Ct of Common Cncl 1944-87 (father of the Ct for many years); Freeman of the City of London 1932; dep Alderman for Farringdon within (Northside) Ward; *Recreations* chess, golf, City of London; *Clubs* Farringdon Ward, City Livery; *Style*— Raymond Deith, Esq; 3 Hillcrest Gardens, Hinchley Wood, Esher, Surrey KT10 0BT

DEL MAR, Norman René; CBE (1975); s of M Del Mar, of 12 Kidderpore Gdns, NW3; *b* 31 July 1919; *Educ* Marlborough, Royal Coll of Music; *m* 1947, Pauline Joy, da of G C Mann, of Chigwell; 2 s (Jonathan, Robin); *Career* conductor; asst to Sir Thomas Beecham 1947, princ conductor English Opera Gp 1949-55, prof of conducting Guildhall Sch of Music 1953-60; conductor: Yorks Symphony Orch 1955-56, BBC Scottish Orch 1960-65; princ guest conductor Gothenburg Symphony Orch 1969-73, conductor Royal Acad of Music 1973-77, princ conductor Acad of the BBC Bristol 1974-77, conductor and prof of conducting Royal Coll of Music 1972-, artistic dir Norfolk and Norwich Triennial Festival 1979-82, princ guest conductor Bournemouth Sinfonietta 1982-85, artistic dir and princ conductor Aarhus Symphony Orch 1985-88, freelance conductor in UK and abroad; FRCM, FGSM; *Books* Richard Strauss (3 vols) 1962-72, Mahler's Sixth Symphony A Study (1980), Orchestral Variations (1981), Anatomy of the Orchestra (1981), Companion to the Orchestra (1987); *Style*— Norman Del Mar, Esq, CBE; Witchings, Hadley Common, Barnet, Herts

DELACOMBE, Maj-Gen Sir Rohan; KCMG (1964), KCVO (1970, KBE 1961, CB 1957, CBE 1951, DSO 1944, MBE 1939), DSO (1944); s of Lt-Col Addis Delacombe, DSO (d 1941), of Shrewton Manor, nr Salisbury, Wilts; *b* 25 Oct 1906; *Educ* Harrow, RMC and Staff Coll Camberley; *m* 15 Feb 1941, Eleanor Joyce, CStJ, da of Robert Lionel Foster, JP (d 1952), of Egton Manor, York; 1 s, 1 da; *Career* 2 Lt Royal Scots 1926, served Egypt, N China and India, served France, Norway, Normandy and Italy WW II, active serv 1937-39 (Palestine, despatches), Lt-Col cmdg 2 and 8 Bns Royal Scots 1943-45, GSO (1) 2 Inf Div S E Asia 1945-47, Col (GS) HQ BAOR 1949-50, cmd 5 Inf Bde 1950-53, dep mil sec War Off 1953-55, GOC 52 (Lowland) Div and Lowland Dist 1955-58, Maj-Gen 1956, GOC Berlin (Brit Sector) 1959-62, Col Royal Scots 1956-64, Hon Col 1 Armoured Regt to 1974, Hon Air Cdre RAAF; govr of Victoria, Australia 1963-74, Hon Freeman City of Melbourne, Hon LLD Melbourne and Monash, administrator of the Cwlth of Australia on four occasions 1971-72 and 1973; memb Royal Co of Archers (Queen's Body Guard for Scotland), pres Royal Br Legion (Wilts); FRAIA, KStJ; *Style*— Maj-Gen Sir Rohan Delacombe, KCMG, KCVO, KBE, CB, CBE, DSO, MBE; Shrewton Manor, nr Salisbury, Wilts SP3 4DB (☎ 0980 620253)

DELACOURT-SMITH, Hon Lesley Clare; da of Baron Delacourt-Smith (Life Peer) (d 1972); *b* 28 Sept 1948; *Educ* Frensham Heights, Sussex Univ; *Style*— The Hon Lesley Delacourt-Smith

DELACOURT-SMITH, Hon Stephen; s of Baron Delacourt-Smith (Life Peer) (d 1972); *b* 16 July 1946; *Educ* Windsor GS, West London Coll; *Style*— The Hon Stephen Delacourt-Smith; 4 Weech Hall, Fortune Green Rd, NW6 (☎ 794 6111)

DELACOURT-SMITH OF ALTERYN, Baroness (Life Peeress UK 1974); Margaret Rosalind; da of F J Hando; *b* 5 April 1916; *Educ* Newport High Sch, St Anne's Coll Oxford; *m* 1939, Lord Delacourt-Smith, PC (Life Peer) (d 1972); 1 s, 2 da; m 2, 1978, Prof Charles Blackton; *Career* cncllr of Royal Borough of New Windsor 1962-65, JP 1962-67; *Style*— The Rt Hon The Lady Delacourt-Smith of Alteryn; 56 Aberdare Gdns, NW6 (☎ 01 624 1728)

DELAHUNT, Anthony Henry; s of Henry John Delahunt (d 1962), of London, and Mary Lanegan; *b* 2 Sept 1940; *Educ* St Ignatius Coll; *m* 1967, Veronica, da of Brian Farrell, of Ireland; 3 s (Ian b 1968, Graham b 1970, Stephen b 1972); *Career* financial dir Noble Lowndes & Ptnrs Ltd 1985; FCA; *Recreations* cricket, reading, theatre; *Clubs* Royal Automobile, Catenian Assoc; *Style*— Anthony Delahunt, Esq; Wembury, 4A Green Lane, Purley, Surrey CR2 3PG (☎ 01 660 2190); Noble Lowndes & Ptnrs Ltd, PO Box 144, Norfolk House, Wellesley Road, Croydon CR9 3EB (☎ 01 686 2466, fax 01 680 7998)

DELAMAIN, Capt Nicholas Sinclair; o s of Lt-Col Walter Thomas Delamain (d 1976), of Trevellyan Cottage, Barrington, nr Ilminster, Som, and Philippa Anne, *née* Clifford (d 1966); *b* 24 Nov 1931; *Educ* Rugby and RMA Sandhurst; *m* 1, 30 May 1959 (m dis 1965), Juliet, da of Capt Charles Kendall, of Kent; 2 s (Rupert b 1959, Charles b 1960); m 2, 16 Dec 1968 (m dis 1975), Alix, da of Col Harold Brigham, of Cork; 1 s (Julian b 1972), 1 da (Georgina b 1969); m 3, 31 Aug 1985, Juliet Flora, da of Capt Alan J M Richardson, of Southrop Manor, Southrop, Lechlade, Glos (d 1965); *Career* commnd 10 Royal Hus (PWO) 1952-60, served Germany, Jordan and Australia (ADC to Govr of W Australia), served Royal Wilts Yeo 1960-64; jt md Hill & Delamain Ltd, Shipping Agents, 1966-84; md Pelican Airways Ltd, Freight Airline 1980-84; jt md H & D Walford Ltd, Forwarding Agents 1984-86; md Sinclair Marine Ltd Confirming House; *Recreations* racing, hunting; *Clubs* Turf, Cavalry and Guards, MCC; *Style*— Capt Nicholas Delamain; Gove Farm House, Cold Aston, nr Cheltenham, Glos GL54 3BN (☎ 0451 20651, work ☎ 0451 21967, telex 427214)

DELAMERE, 5 Baron (UK 1821); Hugh George Cholmondeley; s of 4 Baron Delamere (d 1978, whose gf 2 Baron was fifth cous of 1 Marquess of Cholmondeley) and his 1 w, Phyllis, da of Lord George Montagu Douglas Scott (3 s of 6 Duke of Buccleuch); *b* 18 Jan 1934; *Educ* Eton, Magdalene Coll Cambridge (MA Agric); *m* 1964, Ann Willoughby, da of Sir Patrick Renison, GCMG, and formerly w of Michael Tinné; 1 s; *Heir* s, Hon Thomas Patrick Gilbert Cholmondeley b 19 June 1968; *Career* farmer; sr settlement officer Kinangop 1962-63; landowner (57,000 acres); *Recreations* racing, shooting, flying; *Clubs* Pitt, Muthaiga Country, Jockey (Kenya); *Style*— Lord Delamere; Soysambu, Elmenteita, Kenya; Delamere Estates Ltd, Private Bag, Nakuru, Kenya (☎ Elmenteita 28)

DELANEY, Francis (Frank) James Joseph; 5 s of Edward Joseph Delaney (d 1968), of Ireland, and Elizabeth Josephine O'Sullivan; *b* 24 Oct 1942; *Educ* Abbey Schs Tipperary, Rosse Coll Dublin; *m* 1966 (m dis 1980), Eilish, *née* Kelliher; 3 s (Edward b 1968, Bryan b 1971, Owen b 1976); m 2 1988, Susan, *née* Collier; *Career* writer, broadcaster, TV, Radio, Journalism; chm Nat Book League 1984-86; *Books* James Joyce's Odyssey (1981), Betjeman Country (1983), The Celts (1986), A Walk in the Dark Ages (1988), My Dark Rosaleen (novella 1989); *Clubs* Athenaeum; *Style*— Frank Delaney, Esq; 43 Old Town, London SW4

DELANEY, Gerald Palmer; JP (Northumberland 1981); s of Francis Harold Delaney (d 1961), of Moncton, Canada, and Ruth Amanda McKenzie (d 1980); *b* 2 July 1925; *Educ* Moncton HS; *m* 26 March 1947, Cecily Patricia, da of Albert Edward Murrell, MBE; 2 s (Patrick b 1951, Stephen b 1953); 2 da (Geraldine b 1950, Marion b 1957); *Career* Canadian Army 1941-45, Corpl France, Belgium, Holland, Germany; Health Serv Admin; gp sec St George's Hosp Morpeth 1968-73, area admin N Tyneside Health Authy 1973-80; AHSM; *Style*— Gerald Delaney, Esq, JP; Hillside, Burnhouse Rd, Wooler, Northumberland (☎ 0668 81237)

DELAP, Hon Mrs; Anastasia Diana; *née* Noble; 3 da of Baron Glenkinglas (Life Peer, d 1984), and Baroness Glenkinglas, *qv*; *b* 17 Jan 1948; *m* 7 Oct 1967, Jonathan Sinclair Delap, s of William Frederick Delap, of Kalou, Kenya; 2 s; *Style*— The Hon Mrs Delap; Little Armsworth, Alresford, Hants

DELBRIDGE, Richard; s of Tom Delbridge, and Vera, *née* Lancashire; *b* 21 May 1942; *Educ* LSE (BSc), Univ of California Berkeley (MBA); *m* 19 Mar 1966, Diana Genevra Rose, da of H W Bowers-Broadbent; 1 s (Mark b 1973), 2 da (Roseanna b 1970, Cressida b 1982); *Career* articled clerk Arthur Andersen and Co 1963-66, qual chartered accountant 1966, ptnr Arthur Andersen and Co 1974-76 (mgmnt cnslt 1968-); sr vice-pres and gen mangr London office Morgan Guaranty Tst Co of New York 1987- (int operations 1976-79, comptroller 1979-85, asst gen mangr 1985-87); bd memb The Securities Accoc; ACA (1966), FCA (1972); *Recreations* walking, reading; *Style*— Richard Delbridge, Esq; 48 Downshire Hill, London NW3 1NX; Morgan Guaranty Tst Co, 1 Angel Ct, London EC2

DELDERFIELD, Antony D; s of Stanley William Delderfield, of Bromley; *b* 10 May 1925; *Educ* Quernmoore Coll; *m* 1948, Hella Marie Anna; 3 children; *Career* Lloyd's broker, Lloyd's Underwriting memb; chm Wigham Poland Marine Far East Ltd 1981-; dir Wigham Poland Holdings Ltd 1981-; *Recreations* sailing, music; *Clubs* Lloyds Yacht; *Style*— A D Delderfield Esq; 10 Burnsall St, Chelsea, London SW3 (☎ 01 481 0505); Wigham Poland Holdings, 24 Minories, London EC3 (☎ 01 481 0505)

DELEVINGNE, Hon Mrs (Angela Margo Hamar); *née* Greenwood; da of 1 Viscount Greenwood, KC, PC, and Margery, DBE (d 1968), da of Rev Walter Spencer (d 1948); *b* 8 July 1912; *m* 1937, (Edward) Dudley Delevingne (d 1974), s of late Edward Charles Delevingne; 2 s (Edward Hamar, Charles Hamar), 2 da (Venetia (d 1988), Caroline); *Style*— The Hon Mrs Delevingne; 22 Ovington St, London SW3

DELEVINGNE, Charles Hamar; s of (Edward) Dudley Delevingne (d 1974), and Hon Angela Margo Hamar, *née* Greenwood, *qv*; *b* 25 June 1949; *Educ* Embley Park; *m* 18 June 1983, Pandora Anne, da of Jocelyn Greville Stevens, *qv*, of Testbourne, Hampshire; 2 da (Chloe b 1984, Poppy b 1986); *Career* chm of Property Investmt Co; *Recreations* shooting, fishing; *Clubs* Buck's; *Style*— Charles Delevingne, Esq; 95 Albert Bridge Road, London SW11 (☎ 01 585 0301); Testbourne Lodge, Hampshire (☎ Longparish 569); Kimbolton Lodge, Fulham Road, SW3 (☎ 01 589 1126)

DELFONT, Baron (Life Peer UK 1976); Bernard Delfont; s of Isaac Winogradsky (d 1936), of Odessa, Russia; *b* 5 Sept 1909, Tokmak, Russia; *Educ* Rochelle St Sch London; *m* 1946, Helen Violet Carolyn (formerly an actress under the name Carole Lynne), da of Victor Cecil Haymen, and formerly w of late Derek Farr; 1 s (Hon David, *qv*), 2 da (Hon Mrs Meddings, Hon Mrs Morse, *qqv*); *Career* chm and chief exec: EMI Film and Theatre Corpn 1969-80 (later chief exec EMI), Trusthouse Forte Leisure 1981-82, First Leisure Corpn 1983-; director of various companies; life pres Entertainment Artists Benevolent Fund, pres Entertainment Charities Fund, former pres Printer's Charitable Corpn, former chm Barker Variety Club of Gt Britain; Companion Rat Grand Order of Water Rats; kt 1974; *Style*— The Rt Hon Lord Delfont; House of Lords, London SW1

DELFONT, Hon David Stephen; only s of Baron Delfont (Life Peer); *b* 1953; *m* 1982, Sarah Louise, da of Peter Edgington; 2 s (Joseph b 1983, Alexander b 1985); *Style*— The Hon David Delfont

DELL, David Michael; CB (1986); s of Montague Roger Dell (d 1980), and Aimée Gabrielle, *née* Gould (d 1964); *b* 30 April 1931; *Educ* Rugby, Balliol Coll Oxford (MA); *Career* 2 Lt Royal Signals, serv Egypt and Cyprus 1954-55; Admty 1955-60, MOD 1960-65, Miny of Technol 1965-70; DTI 1970-; dir: Industl Devpt Unit 1984-87, Euro Investmt Bank 1984-87; chief exec Br Overseas Trade Bd 1987; *Clubs* St Stephen's Constitutional (Leeds); *Style*— David M Dell, Esq, CB; 1 Victoria St, London SW1

DELL, Rt Hon Edmund Emanuel; PC (1970); s of Reuben and Frances Dell; *b* 15 August 1921; *Educ* Owen's Sch London, Queen's Coll Oxford (MA); *m* 1963, Susanne Gottschalk; *Career* Lt RA served Europe 1944-45; memb Manchester City Cncl 1953-60, pres Manchester and Salford Trades Cncl 1958-61, MP (Lab) Birkenhead 1964-79, parly sec Miny of Technol 1966-67, parly under-sec of state Dept of Econ Affrs 1967-68; min of state: BOT 1968-69, Dept of Employment and Productivity 1968-70; chm Commons Pub Accounts Ctee 1973-74 (acting chm 1972-73), paymaster-gen 1974-76, sec of state Trade and pres BOT 1976-78, memb ctee Three Wise Men appointed by Euro Cncl to review procedures of EEC 1978-79; chm: Hansard Soc Cmmn on Paying for Politics 1979-80, Ctee on Int Business Taxation 1982, Working Pty on Co Political Donations 1985 (Hansard Soc and Const Reform Centre); chm and chief exec Guinness Peat Gp 1979-82, chm Channel Four TV Co Ltd 1980-87, dir Shell Tport and Trading Co plc, dep chm London C of C and Indust; chm: Pub Fin Fndn 1984, Prison Reform Tst 1988; dep chm govrs Imperial Coll 1988; hon fell Fitzwilliam Coll Cambridge 1986; *Publications* The Good Old Cause (ed with J E C Hill, 1949), Brazil: The Dilemma of Reform (Fabian pamphlet, 1964), Political Responsibility and Industry (1973), Report on European Institutions (with B Biesheuvel and R Marjolin, 1979), The Politics of Economic Independence (1987); articles in learned journals; *Recreations* listening to music; *Style*— The Rt Hon Edmund Dell; 4 Reynolds Close, NW11 7EA (☎ 01 455 7197)

DELL, Dame Miriam Patricia; DBE (1980, CBE 1975), JP (1975); Wilfred Matthews (d 1940, family arrived NZ 1824) and Ruby Miriam, *né* 1948); *b* 14 June 1924; *Educ* Epsom Girls' GS, Auckland Univ (B Teachers' Training Coll (Teaching Cert); *m* 1946, Dr Richard Kenneth da; *Career* teacher 1945-47, 1957-58 and 1961-71; nat chm Young Wi memb: exec Cncl for Equal Pay and Opportunity 1966-76, various sub-cte

Assoc 1967-70, Joint Ctee on Womens Employment, Nat Devpt Cncl 1969-74, convener tutor trg Hutt Valley Marriage Guidance Cncl 1971 (tutor 1964-70), memb: exec Environment and Conservation Organisation 1971-78, chm Environment & Conservation Organisation 19880, Ctee of Inquiry into Equal Pay 1971-72, nat exec Nat Marriage Guidance Cncl 1972-76, fndn memb Hutt Valley Branch Fedn Univ Women, chairwoman Ctee on Women 1974-81, memb Nat Cmmn for UNESCO 1974-85, memb Nat Cncl Urban Devpt Assoc 1975-78, memb Steering Ctee and conslt Nat Cmmn for IYC 1977-79, memb Security Appeal Authority 1974-, pres Inter-Church Cncl of Public Affairs 1982- (vice-pres 1979-82), memb Nat Cncl of Women of NZ, rep for Mothers' Union Wellington branch 1957, fndn memb Hutt Valley branch 1958 (pres 1966-68), vice-pres Bd of Offrs 1967-70, Nat Pres 1970-74, convener Physical Environment Standing Ctee 1974-78, convener Status of Women Standing Ctee 1978-79, co-opted memb Parly Watch Ctee 1974-, vice-convener Standing Ctee on Physical Environment Int Cncl of Women 1973-76, pres Int Council of Women 1979-86 (vice-pres 1976-79) memb: Social Responsibility Cmmn Anglican Church NZ 1988-, project devpt bd Museum of NZ 1988-; pres: lut Cncl of Women 1979-86, (hon pres 1986-88), co-ordinator ICW Devpt Programme 1988-; has organised numerous workshops, leadership training courses and seminars and has represented NZ at many overseas conferences; Adele Ristori Prize 1976, Queen's Silver Jubilee Medal 1977; *Recreations* gardening, handcraft; *Style—* Dame Miriam Dell, DBE, JP; 98 Waerenga Rd, Otaki, New Zealand (☎ 069 97267), 24 Townsend Rd, Wellington, New Zealand (☎ 04 888-726)

DELL, Archdeacon of, 1973-; Ven Robert Sydney; s of Sydney Edward Dell (d 1957); *b* 20 May 1922; *Educ* Harrow County Sch, Emmanuel Coll Cambridge, Ridley Hall; *m* 1953, Doreen Molly, da of William Layton (d 1957); 1 s, 1 da; *Career* ordained 1948, vice-princ Ridley Hall Cambridge 1957-65, archdeacon of Derby 1973-. vicar of Chesterton Cambridge 1966-73, hon canon of Derby Cathedral and examining chaplain to Bishop of Derby 1973-, canon residentiary of Derby Cathedral 1981-; memb of the Gen Synod of the Church of Eng 1978-85; *Clubs* Royal Cwlth Soc; *Style—* The Ven the Archdeacon of Derby; 72 Pastures Hill, Littleover, Derby, DE3 7BB (☎ 0332 512700); Derby Church House, Full St, Derby DE1 3DR (☎ 0332 382233)

DELLA GRAZIA, Duchessa; Lady Hermione Gwladys; *née* Herbert; only da of 4 Earl of Powis (d 1974), and Hon Violet Ida Eveline (Baroness Darcy de Knayth in her own right); *b* 17 Sept 1900; *m* 6 Nov 1924, Conte Roberto Lucchesi Palli, 11 Duca della Grazia, and 13 Principe di Campofranco (recognised by King Umberto I 1891), who d 1979; 1 da; *Style—* Duchessa della Grazia; Hotel Beaurivage, 1006 Lausanne, Switzerland

DELLBORG, Rolf Gudmund; s of J George DellBorg (d 1961), and D Harriett, *née* Kjeallman (d 1948); *b* 20 August 1929; *Educ* Univ of Upsala (LLB); *m* 20 Oct 1949, Elison Mary Christine; 1 s (Richard b 1954); *Career* 2 Lt Swedish Army; banker, advocate/fin conslt; md Hambros Bank 1966-79 (ret); dir: Hambros Bank Ltd, Nat Bank of Sharjah Sharjah UAE, BT Rolatruc Sweden; chm Wesley Investmts Ltd; *Recreations* fishing, golf, shooting; *Clubs* Royal Batchelors Gothenburg, Addington Golf Surrey; *Style—* Rolf G DellBorg, Esq; Flat 15, 22 St James's Square, London SW1Y 4JH

DELLIERE, John Peter; s of Robert Fernand George Dellière, of The Sands, NR, Farnham, Surrey, and Elaine Gorton, *née* Hobbs; *b* 6 August 1944; *Educ* Whitgift Sch; *m* 28 June 1969, Elizabeth Joan, da of Gordon Keith Harman, of Lower Kingswood, Surrey; 3 s (Christian John b 10 Jan 1972, James Peter 26 Aug 1976, Michael Robert Gordon b 2 Oct 1979); *Career* Mellors Basden & Co (City Accountants) 1963-68, Arthur Andersen & Co 1968-70, dir The White House (Linen Specialists) Ltd 1970, jt md The White House Ltd & Subsidiary Cos 1982 (dir 1980), md The White House Ltd and Subsidiaries 1985; ACA 1967, FCA 1979, ATII 1967; *Recreations* golf, tennis; *Clubs* RAC, St James's; *Style—* John Dellière; Silverwood, Fairacres, Cobham, Surrey KT11 2JN (☎ 0932 63390); The White House Ltd, 51 New Bond St, London W1Y 0BY (☎ 01 629 3521, fax 01 629 8269, car telephone 0836 206 362, telex 299 815 WYTOWZ G)

DELMAR-MORGAN, Michael Walter; s of Curtis Delmar Morgan (d 1987), and Susan Henrietta Hargreaves Brown; *b* 1 Mar 1936; *Educ* Eton; *m* 17 Feb 1962, Mardie, da of John Kennedy Logan (d 1984); 1 s (Ben b 1966), 2 da (Katherine b 1968, Alexandra b 1971); *Career* banker; dir Brown Shipley & Co Ltd 1966-88; *Recreations* sailing; *Clubs* Royal Yacht Sqdn; *Style—* Michael W Delmar-Morgan, Esq; Swaynes, Rudgwick, nr Horsham, Sussex RH12 3JD

DELVE, Sir Frederick William; CBE (1942); s of Frederick John Delve, of Brighton, and Eleanor Maria, *née* Brown; *b* 28 Oct 1902; *Educ* Brighton; *m* 9 Feb 1924, Ethel Lillian Morden (d 1980); *Career* RN 1918-23; joined Fire Service 1923, chief offr Croydon Fire Bde 1934-41, dep inspr-in-chief NFS 1941-43, chief regnl fire offr London Reg NFS 1943-48, chief offr London Fire Bde 1948-62; hon pres Securicor Ltd; KPFSM 1940; kt 1962; *Style—* Sir Frederick Delve, CBE; 53 Ashley Court, Grand Avenue, Hove, E Sussex (☎ 0273 774605)

DELVIN, Dr David George; *b* 28 Jan 1939; *Educ* St Dunstan's Coll, King's Coll Hosp Univ of London; *Career* TV doctor and writer; memb Gen Med Cncl, med conslt to FPA, conslt ed of Gen Practitioner, vice-chm Med Journalist Assoc, winner Best Book Award of American Med Writers' Assoc; LRCP, MRCS, DRCOG, Consumer Columnist of the Year and MRCGP, Médaille de la Ville de Paris; *Recreations* scuba, running, opera; *Clubs* Royal Soc of Medicine; *Style—* Dr David Delvin; c/o Coutts & Co, 440 Strand, London WC2

DELVIN, Lord; Sean Charles Weston Nugent; s and h of 13 Earl of Westmeath; *b* 16 Feb 1965; *Educ* Ampleforth; *Style—* Lord Delvin

DEMERY, Edward Peter; s of Peter Demery and Cecilia Gwyneth Nepean, *née* Clifford-Smith; *b* 12 Dec 1946; *Educ* Bradfield; *m* 16 Jan 1971, Alexandra, da of Harold Paillet Rodier of Overdale, St Nicholas Hill, Leatherhead, Surrey; 1 s (Rupert b 1972), 1 da (Miranda b 1973); *Career* dir Clifford-Smith (underwriting agencies) Ltd 1976-85, joined Justerini & Brooks Ltd, wine merchants 1967 (dir 1977, sales dir 1986-); memb Worshipful Co of Vintners; *Recreations* golf, cricket, tennis; *Clubs* Izingari, Band of Brothers, Royal and Ancient GC, Royal St George's GC; *Style—* Edward Demery, Esq; 72 Vineyard Hill Rd, Wimbledon, London SW19 7JJ (☎ 01 946 7056); 61 St James's St, London SW1A 1LZ (☎ 01 493 8721, telex 264 470 WINEJB G)

DEMPSTER, Lady Camilla Dorothy Godolphin; *née* Osborne; da of 11 Duke of Leeds (d 1963); *b* 14 August 1950; *m* 1, 1971 (m dis 1976), Robert Julian Brownlow Harris; 1 da; m 2, 1977, as his 2nd w, Nigel Richard Patton Dempster, the columnist; 1 da; *Style—* Lady Camilla Dempster; 11 Neville Terrace, London SW7

DEMPSTER, Ian Tom; s of Tom Roberts Dempster (d 1972), of Broxbourne, Herts, and Mary, *née* Parry (d 1984); *b* 2 April 1934; *Educ* Charterhouse; *m* 1, 7 Feb 1967, Judith Clare (d 1971), da of Kenneth Bernard Pearce, of Hertford; 2 da (Ellen b 1967, Victoria b 1969); m 2, 2 Jan 1978, Elizabeth Mary, da of Robert Muir Meek (d 1960), of Girvan, Ayrshire; 1 da (Clare b 1979); *Career* Pilot Offr RAF (pilot GD Branch) 1957-58; CA Chalmers Impey and Co 1952-63, chm Sign and Metal Industs plc 1964-, dir Cheshunt Bldg Soc 1979-; fin offr London N Euro Constituency Cons Cncl; chm Enfield Dist Mfrs Assoc 1973 (dir 1988-), pres Electric Sign Mfrs Assoc 1975; cncl dir Br Sign Assoc Ltd 1988-; FCA; *Recreations* hockey, gardening; *Clubs* October; *Style—* Ian Dempster, Esq; The White House, Greyhound Lane, South Mimms, Potters Bar, Herts EN6 3NX (☎ 0707 43 183); Sign and Metal Industries plc, Sewardstone Rd, Waltham Abbey, Essex (☎ 0992 719 662, fax 0992 710 101; telex 267444)

DEMPSTER, John William Scott; s of Dr David Dempster (d 1981), of Plymouth, and Mary Constance, *née* Simpson (d 1985); *b* 10 May 1938; *Educ* Plymouth Coll, Oriel Coll Oxford; *Career* civil servant; under sec Dept of Tport, princ private sec to the Sec of State for the Environment 1976-77, finance offr Dept of Tport 1977-81, princ est & finance offr Lord Chancellor's Dept 1981-84, head of marine directorate Dept of Tport 1984-; *Recreations* mountaineering, sailing (part owner of yacht Carolina); *Clubs* Royal Southampton Yacht, Swiss Alpine; *Style—* John Dempster, Esq; Dept of Tport, Sunley House, 90/93 High Holborn, London WC1V 6LP (☎ 01 405 6911)

DEN BRINKER, Carl Siegmund; s of Hermanus Maria den Brinker (d 1975); *b* 29 Mar 1930; *Educ* St Franciscus Coll Rotterdam, Bath Univ (MSc); *m* 1965, Margaret, da of Frank Todd; 1 s, 3 da; *Career* physicist Texas Instruments Ltd 1961-75, dir Mackintosh Conslts 1976-78, tech dir Redifon Ltd 1978-; memb cncl Nat Academic Awards 1978-84, Defence Scientific Advsy Cncl (Comm Tech Cmtee) 1984-, vice-pres IERE 1984-87, dir Rediffusion Business Electronics 1985-; Freeman City of London, asst Worshipful Co of Scientific Instrument Makers; CEng, FIERE, SenMIEEE, FIOD; author 16 scientific papers and 28 patents; *Clubs* IOD; *Style—* Carl den Brinker Esq; 55 Underhill Rd, London SE22 0QR (☎ 01 693 5970); Redifon Ltd, Newton Rd, Crawley, Sussex RH10 2PY (☎ 0293 518855, telex 877131)

DENBIGH AND DESMOND, Betty, Countess of; Verena Barbara; da of William Edward Price (d 1966), of Hallgates, Cropston, nr Leicester; *b* 1 Mar 1904; *m* 1 1923, Lt-Col Thomas Paget Fielding Johnson (decd); 1 da; m 2, 17 May 1940, 10 Earl of Denbigh and Desmond (d 1966); 1 s (11 Earl), 1 da (Lady Clare Simonian); *Style—* The Rt Hon Betty, Countess of Denbigh and Desmond; Newnham Paddox, nr Rugby, Warwicks (☎ 0788 832236)

DENBIGH AND DESMOND, 11 and 10 Earl of (E 1622 and I 1622); William Rudolph Michael Feilding; also Baron Feilding, Viscount Feilding (both E 1620), Baron Feilding, Viscount Callan (both I 1622), and Baron St Liz (E 1663); s of 10 and 9 Earl of Denbigh and Desmond (d 1966; 2 cousin seven times removed of Henry Feilding the novelist and magistrate); *b* 2 August 1943; *Educ* Eton; *m* 2 Sept 1965, Caroline Judith Vivienne, da of Lt-Col Geoffrey Cooke; 1 s, 2 da (Lady Samantha b 1966, Lady Louisa b 1969); *Heir* s, Viscount Feilding, *qv*; *Career* sits as Liberal peer in House of Lords; *Style—* The Rt Hon Earl of Denbigh and Desmond; 21 Moore Park Rd, SW6 (☎ 01 736 0460); Pailton House, Newnham Paddox, Rugby, Warwicks (☎ 832176)

DENBY, Patrick Morris Coventry; CMG (1982); s of Robert Coventry Denby and Phyllis, *née* Dacre; *b* 28 Sept 1920; *Educ* Bradford GS, and CCC Oxford (MA); *m* 1950, Margaret Joy, da of Lt-Col C L Boyle; 2 da and 1 da decd; *Career* asst dir-gen (tres and financial comptroller) Int Labour Office Geneva 1976-81 (joined ILO 1951); *Clubs* United Oxford and Cambridge Univ,; *Style—* Patrick Denby Esq, CMG; Fern Side, Fern Lane, Marlow, Bucks SL7 3SD

DENCER, Geoffrey Hargreaves; s of late Charles Dencer; *b* 20 Sept 1928; *Educ* Stockport GS, Manchester Univ (BSc); *m* 1981, Patricia, *née* Crocome; children by previous m; *Career* chartered civil engineer, construction dir IDC Construction Ltd Stratford 1970- (formerly with Charles Tennet & Son Stockton on Tees); *Style—* Geoffrey Dencer, Esq; 138 Bridgetown Rd, Stratford-upon-Avon, Warwickshire CU37 7JH

DENCH, Dame Judi(th) Olivia (Dame Judi Williams); *née* Dench; DBE (1988, OBE 1970); da of Reginald Arthur and Eleanora Olave Dench; *b* 9 Dec 1934; *Educ* The Mount Sch York, Central Sch of Speech and Drama; *m* 1971, Michael Williams, actor; 1 da (Tara b 1972); *Career* associate memb Royal Shakespeare Co 1969-; numerous performances for RSC, The Old Vic Company, Nat Theatre, and in West End, also films and television; pres Festival of Br Theatre 1983-; received SWET Best Actress of the Year Award 1977, 1980 and 1984, Variety Club Actress of the Year Award 1982, Broadcasting Press Guild TV and Radio Award for Best Actress, and *Standard* Best Actress Award 1983; Hon DLitt: Univ of York 1978, Warwick Univ 1980; SWET Best Actress Award 1984; BAFTA Best Supporting Actress Award 1987; *Style—* Dame Judi Dench, DBE, OBE

DENHAM, 2 Baron (UK 1937); Sir Bertram Stanley Mitford Bowyer; 10 Bt (E 1660), of Denham, and 2 Bt (UK 1933), of Weston Underwood; PC (1981); s of 1 Baron Denham (d 1948), and Hon Daphne Freeman-Mitford, da of 1 Baron Redesdale; suc to Btcy of Denham on death of kinsman 1950; *b* 3 Oct 1927; *Educ* Eton, King's Coll Cambridge; *m* 14 Feb 1956, Jean, da of Kenneth McCorquodale, MC, TD; 3 s, 1 da; *Heir* s, Hon Richard Grenville George Bowyer; *Career* late Lt Oxford and Bucks LI; a lord in waiting to HM The Queen 1961-64 and 1970-71, Capt of Yeomen of the Gd (dep chief whip in House of Lords) 1971-74, Capt Hon Corps Gentlemen-at-Arms 1979- (govt chief whip House of Lords), oppn dep chief whip 1974-78 and oppn chief whip 1978-79; *Books* The Man Who Lost His Shadow (1979), Two Thyrdes (1983), Foxhunt (1988); *Clubs* White's, Pratt's, Buck's, Carlton; *Style—* The Rt Hon the Lord Denham, PC; The Laundry Cottage, Weston Underwood, Olney, Bucks (☎ 0234 711535)

DENHAM, Dowager Baroness Hon Daphne; *née* Freeman-Mitford; da of late 1 Baron Redesdale, GCVO, KCB; *b* 3 Sept 1895; *m* 27 Feb 1919, 1 Baron Denham, MC (d 1948); 2s (1 ka), 1 da; *Style—* The Hon Dowager Lady Denham; Dunsland, Shrublands Rd, Berkhamsted, Herts HP4

DENINGTON, Baroness (Life Peeress UK 1978), of Stevenage, co Herts; Dame Evelyn Joyce Denington; DBE (1974, CBE 1966); da of Philip Bursill, of Woolwich; *b* 9 August 1907; *Educ* Blackheath HS, Bedford Coll London Univ; *m* 1935,

Cecil Dallas Denington, s of Richard Denington, of Wanstead; *Career* journalist 1927-31, teacher 1933-50; gen sec Nat Assoc Lab Teachers 1937-47; memb: St Pancras Borough Cncl 1945-59 (chm Staff Ctee, Planning Ctee and General Purposes Ctee), LCC 1946-65 (vice-chm housing ctee 1949-60, chm dvpt & mgmt sub-ctees 1949-60, chm new & expanding towns ctee 1960-65), GLC 1964-77 (chm of council 1975-76, dep ldr opposition 1967-73, chm housing ctee 1964-67, chm tport ctee 1973-75), Stevenage Dvpt Corpn 1950-80 (chm 1965-80), Ministers' Central Housing Advsy Ctee 1955-73 (memb sub-ctee producing Parker Morris Report and chm sub-ctee producing Our Older Homes Report), SE economic planning ctee 1966-79; memb and chm of various bds of mgmt and gov of schos in St Pancras and Islington 1945-73, chm London Coll for the Garment Trades (Coll of Fashion), memb and chm of govs Ardale Sr Boys' Approved Sch, chm Hornchurch Childrens' Home; memb: Sutton Dwellings Housing Tst 1976-82, Shackleton Housing Assocn 1976-82, N Br Housing Assoc 1976-78, St Pancras Housing Assoc 1977-78, Gtr London Secdy Housing Assoc 1978-83, Sutton (Hastoe) Housing Assoc 1981-87, St Edward's Housing Assoc 1983-87; memb and vice-chm Town & Country Planning Assoc; Freeman City of London; Hon FRIBA, Hon MRTPI; *Style—* The Rt Hon Lady Denington, DBE; Flat 3, 29 Brunswick Sq, Hove, E Sussex

DENISON, (Alan) David; s of Wing Cdr Alan Amos Denison MBE, MC (d 1977), and Mary Myfanwy Blakeman, *née* Roberts of Sidmouth, Devon; *b* 4 May 1945; *Educ* William Ellis Sch Highgate, RAF Cranwell; *m* 9 Sept 1972, Virginia Jane, da of Reinhold Anton Wassman (d 1971) of Br Columbia, Canada; 3 s (Nicholas, Mungo, Barnaby); *Career* PO RAF 1964-67; chartered accountant; Coopers & Lybrand 1967-72, Baring Bros & Co Ltd 1972-82; md BASF Int Hldgs plc 1984-; *Recreations* flying, collecting first editions; *Clubs* RAF Club; *Style—* David Denison, Esq; Midsummer House, Midsummer Boulevard, Central Milton Keynes, MK9 3BN (☎ 0908 664 315, fax 0908 665 312, car tel 0836 625 318, telex 265871 MONREF G)

DENISON, Dulcie Winifred Catherine; CBE (1983); da of Arnold Savage-Bailey, CBE (d 1935), Judge in Jahore, and Kate Edith Clulow (k by Japanese while trying to escape to England on the Roosboom (ship) 1942); *b* 20 Nov 1920; *m* 1939, (John) Michael Terence Wellesley Denison, actor, *qv*, s of Gilbert Dixon Denison (d 1959); *Career* actress and writer (as Dulcie Gray); 106 plays (40 in London), 14 films (starred in 10), numerous television plays, currently playing Kate Harvey in Howards' Way (BBC) innumerable radio plays; Queen's Jubilee Medal 1977; FRSA, FLS; *Books* Butterflies on my Mind, 18 crime novels, one book of short stories; novels incl: The Glanville Women, Anna Starr, Mirror Image; *Style—* Miss Dulcie Gray, CBE; Shardeloes, Amersham, Buckinghamshire

DENISON, Edward Allan Kitson; OBE (1986), TD and clasp; s of W Cdr Amos Allan Denison MBE, MC (d 1976), of Devon, and Margery, *née* Morton (d 1975); *b* 13 Sept 1928; *Educ* St Peter's York, Brasenose Coll Oxford (MA, BCL); *m* 18 May 1957, Mary Hey, da of William Peacock, of Esersykes, Malton, N Yorks; 1 s (Mark b 1960) 1 da (Clare b 1962); *Career* cmmnd W Yorks Regt 1947, served occupation of Austria, TA 1948-67, Lt-Col 3 Prince of Wales Own, Yorks and Humberside TA and AVR Assoc; slr and sr ptnr in private practice; formerly head of legal dept to Shepherd Bldg Gp and first chm legal gp to Bldg Employers Fedn; chm and pres: Thirsk and Malton Cons Assoc, Ryedale Cons Assoc; chm London York Fund Mngrs Ltd, Intelligence Technol Hldgs Ltd; non-exec dir: Ben Johnson & Co Ltd 1978-85, Equity & Gen plc 1984-86, University of Leeds Fndn and many private cos; public appts: N Riding CC 1970-74, N Yorks CC 1973-81 (ldr 1977-81), ACC Fin Ctee 1977-81, Yorks & Humberside Econ Planning Cncl, Yorks, Humberside & E Midlands Industl Devpt Bd; pres York Euro Cons Assoc; boxed for Oxford Univ 1950-51; memb Headingley RUFC 1950-56; *Recreations* shooting, skiing, tennis, travel; *Clubs* Army and Navy, Yorkshire, Vincents; *Style—* Edward A K Denison, Esq, OBE, TD; The Old Vicarage, Bossall, York; Chancery House, 141-143 Holgate Rd, York (☎ 0904 610820), telex 57939, fax (0904 656972)

DENISON, John Law; CBE (1960, MBE Mil 1945); s of Rev Herbert Bouchier Wiggins Denison (d 1968), of Bexhill, Sussex; *b* 21 Jan 1911; *Educ* Brighton Coll, Royal Coll of Music, St George's Sch Windsor Castle; *m* 1, 1936 (m dis 1946), Anne Claudia Russell, da of late Col Claude Russell Brown, CB, DSO (d 1939); m 2, 1947, Evelyn Donald (d 1958), da of John Moir; 1 da; m 3, 1960 Audrey Grace Burnaby (d 1970), da of Brig-Gen Frederick Gilbert Bowles, RE (d 1947); m 4, 1972, Françoise Henriette Mitchell (d 1985), da of Maître Garrigues; *Career* served 1939-45 War (despatches); music dir Arts Cncl of GB 1948-65, dir South Bank Concert Halls 1965-76; chm Cultural Programme, London Celebrations, Queen's Silver Jubilee 1977; hon tres Royal Philharmonic Soc 1976-89; chm: Royal Concert (in aid of musical charities) 1976-87, Arts Educ Schs; memb of Cncl Royal Coll of Music; FRCM, Hon RAM, Hon GSM; Cdr Order of Lion (Finland), Chev dans l'Ordre des Arts et des Lettres (France); *Clubs* Garrick; *Style—* John Denison, Esq, CBE; 22 Empire House, Thurloe Place, London SW7 2RU

DENISON, (John) Michael Terence Wellesley; CBE (1983); s of Gilbert Dixon (d 1959), and Marie Louise Denison, *née* Bain (d 1915); maternal gf A W Bain on Kimberley diamond rush 1871, founded A W Bain & Sons Insur Brokers Leeds 1874 (now Bain-Dawes), Lord Mayor of Leeds 1913; *b* 1 Nov 1915; *Educ* Wellesley House Broadstairs, Harrow (Entrance Exhibitioner), Magdalen Coll Oxford (BA); *m* 1939, Dulcie Winifred Catherine (Dulcie Gray, *qv*), da of Arnold Savage-Bailey, CBE (d 1935); *Career* Army 1940-46; Capt Intelligence Corps: NI, ME, Greece, UK; actor; equity cncllr 1949-77 (vice-pres 1952, 1961-63, 1974); dir: Allied Theatre Prodns 1966-75; Play Co of London 1970-74, New Shakespeare Co 1971-; 108 theatrical prodns of which 50 in London; 15 films; innumerable radio and TV plays (including 80 as Boyd QC); Queen's Jubilee Medal 1977; *Books* The Actor and His World (1964), Overture and Beginners (1973), Double Act (1985); articles for the Dictionary of National Biography on Sir Noël Coward, Sir Peter Daubeny and Peter Bridge (1985-86); *Recreations* painting, golf, travel; *Clubs* MCC; *Style—* Michael Denison, Esq, CBE; Shardeloes, Amersham, Buckinghamshire

DENISON-PENDER, Hon Emma Charlotte; elder da of 3 Baron Pender; *b* 1 Feb 1964; *Style—* The Hon Emma Denison-Pender

DENISON-PENDER, Hon Mary Anne Louise; yr da of 3 Baron Pender; *b* 17 Nov 1965; *Style—* The Hon Mary Denison-Pender

DENISON-PENDER, Hon Robin Charles; yr s of 2 Baron Pender, CBE (d 1965) and bro of 3 Baron; *b* 7 Sept 1935; *Educ* Eton; *m* 7 May 1966, Clare Nell, only da of Lt-Col James Currie Thomson, MBE, TD, JP, DL, of Stable Court, Walkern, Herts; 2 s, 1 da; *Career* late 2 Lt 11 Hussars 1954-56; memb of London Stock Exchange, vice-pres Royal Albert Hall 1970-83; *Recreations* golf, gardening, tennis; *Clubs* White's; *Style—* The Hon Robin Denison-Pender; Jessups, Mark Beech, Edenbridge, Kent TN8 5NR (☎ 034 286 684)

DENMAN, 5 Baron (UK 1834); Sir Charles Spencer Denman; 2 Bt (UK 1945), of Staffield, Co Cumberland; CBE (1976), MC (1942), TD; s of Hon Sir Richard Denman, 1 Bt (d 1957); suc cous, 4 Baron, 1971; *b* 7 July 1916; *Educ* Shrewsbury; *m* 11 Sept 1943, Sheila Anne (d 1987), da of Lt-Col Algernon Bingham Anstruther Stewart, DSO; 3 s, 1 da; *Heir* s, Hon Richard Thomas Stewart Denman; *Career* served WW II Duke of Cornwall's LI (TA), Maj 1943, served India, M East, Mediterranean; contested Leeds Central (C) 1945; chm Marine and General Mutual Life Assurance Soc; formerly dir Consolidated Gold Fields and other cos; vice pres Middle East Assoc; memb: Ctee of Middle East Trade, Ctee on Invisible Exports; tstee: Kitchener Memorial Fund, Arab Br Charitable Fndn; govr Windlesham House School; now chm Arundell House plc and dir Close Bros Gp British Wastewater Ltd; chm Saudi British Soc, pres Royal Soc for Asia Affairs, cncl memb Inst for Study of Conflict; *Clubs* Brooks's; *Style—* The Rt Hon Lord Denman, CBE, MC TD

DENMAN, Hon Christopher John; s of 5 Baron Denman, MC; *b* 5 Sept 1955; *Educ* Millfield, The Mill Littlehampton; *m* 1984, Jenny B, only da of Rupert Allen, of Willaston in Wirral, Cheshire; 1 s (Alexander b and d 1987); *Style—* The Hon John Denman

DENMAN, Prof Donald Robert; s of Robert Martyn Denman (d 1915), of Belfast, and Letitia Kate, *née* Barnes (d 1968); *b* 7 April 1911; *Educ* Christ's Coll Finchley, London Univ (BSc, MSc, PhD), Cambridge Univ (MA); *m* 12 April 1941, (Jessie) Hope, da of Richard Henry Prior (d 1919); 2 s (Jonathon b 1949, Richard b 1951); *Career* WWII serv Air Miny RAF (Civil) 1939-41, dep exec Cumberland War Agric Ctee 1941-46; chartered surveyor in private practice 1937-39; Cambridge Univ: land agent 1946-48, lectr 1948-68, head dept land economy 1962-78, prof land economy 1968-78, fell Pembroke Coll 1962-78, emeritus prof and fell 1978-; established land econ tripos and dept at Cambridge Univ, undertook similar pioneering work in other univs UK and overseas; patron Small Farmers' Assoc; memb: cncl Land Decade Educnl Cncl, ctees RICS, ctees Cwlth Assoc of Surveying and Land Econ; chm Cwlth Human Ecology Cncl, memb advsy panel Aims of Indust, fndr Human Ecology Fndn, advsr Govt of Iran 1968-74; memb: Agric Improvement Cncl, Cncl Nat Academic Awards, Nat Cmmn UNESCO, Ecology Cmmn, Int Union for Conservation of Nature; memb Ely Church Assembly; Hon DSc Univ of Kumasi 1979, Hon fell Royal Swedish Acad of Forestry and Agric 1971, Hon fell Ghana Inst of Surveyors 1970: FRICS (gold medallist); Distinguished Order of Hamayoun, Imperial Court of Persia 1974; *Books* over 40 publications incl: Origins of Ownership (1958), Land use and the Constitution of Property 1969, Land Use: an Introduction to Proprietary Land Use Analysis (1971), The Place of Propeorty (1978), Land in a Free Society 1980, Markets Under the Sea 1983, After Government Failure 1987; *Recreations* travel; *Clubs* Carlton, Farmers; *Style—* Prof Donald Denman; 12 Chaucer Road, Cambridge CB2 2EB (☎ 0223 357 725)

DENMAN, Lady Frances Esmé; *née* Curzon; 2 da of 5 Earl Howe (d 1964), by his 2 w, Joyce Mary McLean, da of Charles McLean Jack, of Johannesburg, S Africa; *b* 1939; *m* 1, 1962, Derek Alan Whiting, yr s of William Thomas Whiting, of Beckenham, Kent; 2 s; m 2, 1976, Harold Denman, yr bro of 5 Baron Denman; 1 s; *Style—* Lady Frances Denman; Wybarnes, Ticehurst, E Sussex

DENMAN, Harold; s of Hon Sir Richard Denman, 1 Bt (d 1957); *b* 26 Jan 1922; *Educ* Repton, Balliol Oxford; *m* 1976, Lady Frances Esmé Curzon, da of 5 Earl Howe; 1 s; *Career* Capt RA 1939-45; dir Tennant Budd Ltd 1959; *Style—* Harold Denman Esq; Wybarnes, Ticehurst, E Sussex (☎ 200332)

DENMAN, Hon James Stewart; s of 5 Baron Denman, MC; *b* 7 August 1954; *Educ* Stowe, The Mill Littlehampton; *Style—* The Hon James Denman

DENMAN, Hon Richard Thomas Stewart; s and h of 5 Baron Denman, MC; *b* 4 Oct 1946; *Educ* Milton Abbey; *m* 18 April 1984, (Lesley) Jane, da of John Stevens, of 2 Shakespear Drive, Hinckley, Leics; 2 da (Natasha Anne b 1986); *Career* ACA; articled to Deloitte 1966; *Clubs* Brooks's; *Style—* The Hon Richard Denman

DENMAN, Sir (George) Roy; KCB (1977, CB 1972), CMG (1968); s of Albert Denman, of 20 River Park, Marlborough, Wilts; *b* 12 June 1924; *Educ* Harrow, St John's Coll Cambridge; *m* 1966, Moya, da of John M Lade; 1 s, 1 da; *Career* served WW II as Maj Royal Signals, BOT 1948, served in HM Embassies Bonn and UK delgn to Geneva 1957-61 and 1965-67, under-sec BOT 1967-70; memb: negotiating delgn EEC 1970-72, BOTB 1972-75; dep sec: DTI 1970-74, Dept of Trade 1974-75; second perm sec Cabinet Off 1975-77, dir-gen External Affairs EEC 1977-82, head of delegation cmmn of EC to US 1982-; *Style—* Sir Roy Denman, KCB, CMG; 2100 M Street, NW (Suite 707), Washington DC, 20037 USA (☎ 010 1 202 862 9500)

DENNES, John Mathieson; s of Norman Dennes, BSc (d 1964), formerly of Middle Green, Poulshot, Devizes, Wilts, and Muriel Evelyn Thomas (d 1985); *b* 19 May 1926; *Educ* Rugby, Christ's Coll Cambridge (MA); *m* 5 April 1961, Verity Ann Mary, da of Lt-Col Leslie Rushworth Ward MC, RA (ret), Freeman of the City of London (d 1977), formerly of Caltofts, Harleston, Norfolk; 4 s (Jonathan b 1962, Thomas b 1963, Adam b 1964, William b 1966); *Career* Military Service 1944-47, Intelligence Corps (Far East); slr sr ptnr Waltons & Morse; dir: Waltons & Morse Nominees (app 1977), Malayan Insurance Co (UK) Ltd (app 1984), Great Western Soc Ltd (vice-chm 1970-75); *Recreations* choral music, industrial archaeology, driving, good food and wine; *Style—* John M Dennes, Esq; Mill House, Felsted, Dunmow, Essex CM6 3HQ; Plantation House, 31-35 Fenchurch Street, London EC3 (☎ 01 623 4255, telex 884209 WALTON G, fax 01 626 4153)

DENNETT, Angelina Brunhilde; da of Leonard Arthur Dennett (d 1978), and Antonia Augustine Elizabeth Dennett; *b* 11 June 1956; *Educ* Ridgeway Secdy Sch, West Kent Coll, City of London Poly (BA), Univ of London (LLM); *Career* called to the Bar Middle Temple 1980; awards incl: Middle Temple Blackstone Pupillage Award 1981, Malcolm Wright Pupillage Award 1981; memb Family Law Bar Assoc; *Style—* Ms Angelina Dennett; Conavon Court Barristers Chambers, 12 Blackfriars St, Salford, Manchester M3 5BQ (☎ 061 834 7007, fax 031 834 8462)

DENNING, Baron (Life Peer UK 1957); Alfred Thompson Denning; PC (1948), DL (Hants 1978); s of Charles Denning (d 1941), of Whitchurch, Hants, and Clara, *née* Thompson; *b* 23 Jan 1899; *Educ* Andover GS, Magdalen Coll Oxford; *m* 1, 28 Dec 1932, Hilda Mary Josephine (d 22 Nov 1941), da of late Rev Frank Northam Harvey; 1

s; m 2, 27 Dec 1945, Joan Daria, da of John Vinings Elliott-Taylor, and widow of John Matthew Blackwood Stuart, CIE; *Career* barr Lincoln's Inn 1923, KC 1938, bencher 1944; chllr: Diocese of Southwark 1937-44, London 1942-44; recorder of Plymouth 1944, judge of the High Ct of Justice 1944-48, lord justice of appeal 1948-57, lord of appeal in ordinary 1957-62, Master of the Rolls 1962-82, ret; hon master of the bench: Middle Temple 1972, Gray's Inn 1979, Inner Temple 1982; chm Roy Cmmn on Historical Manuscripts to 1982, pres Nat Marriage Guidance Cncl to 1983; conducted Profumo Inquiry 1963; tres Lincoln's Inn 1964; hon fell: Magdalen Coll Oxford, Univ Coll London; author, broadcaster; kt 1944; *Publications* Smith's Leading Cases (joint ed, 1929), Bullen and Leake's Precedents (1935), Freedom under the Law (Hamlyn Lectures, 1949), The Changing Law (1953), The Road to Justice (1955), The Discipline of Law (1979), The Due Process of Law (1980), The Family Story (1981), What Next in the Law (1982), The Closing Chapter (1983); Landmarks in the Law (1984) Leaves from my Library (1988); *Clubs* Athenaeum; *Style—* The Rt Hon Lord Denning, PC, DL; The Lawn, Whitchurch, Hants (☎ 025 689 2144)

DENNING, (Michael) John; s of Frederick Edward Denning (d 1985), of Bath, and Linda Agnes Albertine, *née* Young (d 1953); *b* 29 Nov 1934; *Educ* Benedicts; *m* 12 March 1966, Elizabeth Anne, da of Ralph William Beresford, of High Clere, Ben Rhydding, Ilkley, Yorks; 1 s (Simon b 1969), 2 da (Jacqueline b 1968, Nicola b 1972); *Career* owner of historic 13 century Burghope Manor; fndr The Heritage Circle of Historic Country Houses, lectr and after dinner speaker on the Stately Homes of GB; organiser of tours for overseas gps to visit and stay in Stately Homes; *Recreations* shooting, travel; *Style—* Michael Denning, Esq; Burghope Manor, Winsley, Bradford-on-Avon, Wiltshire BA15 2LA (☎022 122 223557, 022 122 222695)

DENNING, Lt-Gen Sir Reginald Francis Stewart; KCVO (1975), KBE (1946), CB (1944), DL; s of Charles Denning (d 1941), of Whitchurch, Hants, and Clara, *née* Thompson (d 1948); bro of Lord Denning (*qv*); descended from Newdigate Poyntz (fl 1686); *b* 12 June 1894; *Educ* privately, Staff Coll Camberley; *m* 5 July 1927, Eileen Violet, OBE (1969), OStJ (1961), da of late Henry Wilford Currie (d 1942), of 17 Westbourne Terr, W2; 2 s (Jack Reginald Newdigate Poyntz b 1929, Charles Henry David b 1933), 1 da (Dianna Anne b 1937); *Career* served WW I Bedfordshire Regt (wounded, despatches), 2 Lt 1915, Adj 1 & 2 Bns Bedfs & Herts, Bt Maj 1934, Maj 1938, Bt Lt-Col 1939, Brig 1941, Subst Col 1942, Maj-Gen 1943, princ admin offr to The Supreme Allied Cdr SE Asia 1944-46, COS Eastern Commd 1947-49, GOC NI 1949-52; Col Bedfordshire and Hertfordshire Regts 1948-58, Col E Anglian Regt 16/44 Foot 1958-64, Col Roy Anglian Regt 1964-66; chm SSAFA 1953-74; DL Essex 1959-68; vice pres Liverpool Sch Tropical Medicine 1967-77; CStJ 1946; Cdr Legion of Merit (USA); *Clubs* Army and Navy, MCC; *Style—* Lt-Gen Sir Reginald Denning, KCVO, KBE, CB, DL; Delmonden Grange, Hawkhurst, Cranbrook, Kent (☎ 058 05 2286)

DENNING, Dr the Hon Robert Gordon; only child of Baron Denning, PC; *b* 3 August 1938; *Educ* Winchester, Magdalen Coll Oxford (MA, PhD); *m* 30 Dec 1967, Elizabeth Carlyle Margaret, da of E R Chilton, of Oxford, 2 children; *Career* 2 Lt KRRC 1957-58; fell and tutor in Inorganic Chemistry, Magdalen Coll Oxford 1968-; *Style—* Dr the Hon Robert Denning; Magdalen College, Oxford OX1 4AU

DENNINGTON, Dudley; s of John Dennington (d 1962), and Beryl, *née* Hagon (d 1944); *b* 21 April 1927; *Educ* Clifton, Imperial Coll London (BSc); *m* 1951, Margaret Patricia, da of Andrew Mackenzie Stewart (d 1976); 2 da; *Career* 2 Lt RE; mangr George Wimpey 1959-65, chief engr GLC 1965-70, traffic cmmr and dir of devpt GLC 1970-72, ptnr Bullen & Ptnrs 1972-; visiting prof King's Coll London Univ 1978-80; FCGI, FEng, FICE, FIStructE, FHKIE; *Recreations* painting; *Clubs* Reform; *Style—* Dudley Dennington, Esq; 25 Corkran Rd, Surbiton, Surrey (☎ 01 399 2977); Bullen and Partners, 188 London Road, Croydon (☎ 01 686 2622, telex 8811965)

DENNIS, Maj-Gen Alastair Wesley; CB (1985), OBE (1973); s of Ralph Dennis and Helen, *née* Henderson; *b* 30 August 1931; *Educ* Malvern, RMA Sandhurst; *m* 1957, Susan Lindy Elgar; 1 s, 2 da; *Career* Col GS Cabinet Off 1974-75, Cdr 20 Armd Bde 1976-77, Dep Cmdt Staff Coll 1978-80, dir Defence Policy (B) MOD 1980-82; dir Military Assistance Overseas MOD 1982-85; sec Imperial Cancer Research Fund 1985-; chm Assoc Med Res Charity 1987-; Sench 88 Cancer Tst 1987-, memb cncl and govr Malvern Coll 1987-; *Recreations* golf, gardening, bees; *Style—* Maj-Gen Alastair Dennis, CB, OBE; c/o Barclays Bank, 2 Market Place, Wallingford, Oxon OX10 0EJ

DENNIS, Lt-Col Delwyn Distin; OBE (1943); s of Claude Distin Dennis (d 1968), of Weston-super-Mare, and Annie Gertrude Dennis; *b* 11 Jan 1914; *Educ* Bristol GS; *m* 26 Feb 1938, Madge Josephine, da of John Nelson Phillips (d 1930), of Weston-super-Mare; 1 s (Barrie Distin George b 1945 (decd)); *Career* Mil Serv: France 1939-40, N Africa 1942-44, Lt-Col Normandy-Germany (despatches) 1944-45; sr vice pres and gen mangr (UK and Ireland) Canada Life Assurance Co 1962-79 (hon vice pres and non exec dir 1979-); dir: Canada Life Assurance Co of GB Ltd, Canada Life Unit Tst Mangrs Ltd, Low Bell Financial Ltd, Trinity Estates plc (chm); Freeman : Worshipful Co of Blacksmiths, Worshipful Co of Marketers; *Recreations* golf, skiing; *Clubs* RAC, Burhill GC, City Livery; *Style—* Lt-Col Delwyn Dennis, OBE; Shelmerdene, 27 Ashley Drive, Walton-on-Thames, Surrey KT12 1JT (☎ 0932 227 590); 97-101 Cannon St, London BC4N 5AD (☎ 01 283 9871)

DENNIS, Rt Rev John; *see*: St Edmundsbury and Ipswich, Bishop of

DENNIS, Raymond Andrew; s of Sir Raymond Dennis, KBE (d 1939), of Grafham Grange, Bramley, Surrey, and Sybil Margaret, eldest da of Sir Leonard Wilkinson Llewelyn, KBE, JP (d 1924), controller Munitions Supply WWI; *b* 30 Nov 1936; *Educ* Down House; *m* 1968, Penelope Anne, da of Col John Lugard (d 1969), and cous of Baron Lugard, GCMG, CB, DSO, PC (extinct 1945), of Priory Court, Duns Tew, Oxon; 1 s, 1 da; *Career* underwriting agent and farmer; memb Lloyd's 1961-, dir R L Glover & Co underwriting agents Ltd 1970-; Freeman City of London; *Recreations* fishing, painting; *Clubs* City of London (life memb Guild of Freemen of City of London); *Style—* Raymond Dennis, Esq; 8 Canning Place, London W8 (☎ 01 584 8636, office 01 623 9104); Berry House, Shillingford, Tiverton, Devon (☎ 039 86 275)

DENNISON, Mervyn William; CBE (1967), MC (1944, DL 1972); s of Rev W Telford Dennison (d 1959); *b* 13 July 1914; *Educ* Methodist Coll Belfast, Queen's Univ of Belfast (BA); *m* 1944, Helen Maud, da of Claud George Spiller (d 1958); 1 s, 1 da; *Career* served 1939-45 War; called to the Bar of NI 1945, Middle Temple 1964, crown counsel N Rhodesia 1947, sr crown counsel and parly draftsman Fed Govt of Rhodesia and Nyasaland 1953, QC N Rhodesia 1960, high ct judge N Rhodesia/Zambia 1961-66, sec Fermanagh CC 1966-73, chief cmmr Planning and Water Appeals Cmmns for NI 1973-80, chm Indust Tribunals NI 1980-83; KStJ 1978 (CStJ 1964); *Style—* Mervyn Dennison, Esq, CBE, MC, DL; Creevyloughgare, Saintfield, Co Down, N Ireland (☎ 0238 510397)

DENNISON, Stanley Raymond; CBE (1946); s of Stanley Dennison (d 1943), of N Shields, and Florence Ann Dennison (d 1984); *b* 15 June 1912; *Educ* Secdy Sch, Univ of Durham (MA), Trinity Coll Cambridge (MA); *Career* lectr Manchester Univ 1935-39, prof of economics Univ Coll of Swansea 1939-46, chief econ asst War Cabinet Off 1940-46, lectr econs and fell Gonville and Caius Coll Cambridge 1946-58; prof of econs: Queen's Univ of Belfast 1958-61, Univ of Newcastle-upon-Tyne 1962-72 (pro-vice-chllr 1966-72); vice-chllr Univ of Hull 1972-79 (hon prof 1974-79, emeritus 1979); vice-chm Ctee of Vice-Chancellors and Principals of the UK 1977-79; Hon LLD Hull 1980; *Recreations* music; *Clubs* Reform; *Style—* Stanley Dennison, Esq, CBE; 22 Percy Gardens, Tynemouth, Tyne and Wear NE30 4HQ

DENNISS, Gordon Kenneth; CBE (1979); eldest s of Harold William Denniss (d 1972), of Worthing, Sussex, and Sybil Marie, *née* Thoburn (d 1980); *b* 29 April 1915; *Educ* Dulwich Coll, Coll of Estate Mgmnt; *m* 1939, Violet Lilia Fiedler, of Montreal, Canada; 1 s (Bruce), 2 da (Georgina, Helen); *Career* consult Eastman & Denniss 1945-82; crown estate cmmnr 1965-71, memb Lib Pty Agric Parly Panel; chartered surveyor; farmer and landowner (1850 acres) E Sussex and Kent; FRICS, MRSH; *Recreations* golf, watching cricket, reading; *Clubs* Farmers', MCC, Surrey CC; *Style—* Gordon Denniss, Esq, CBE; 6 Belgrave Place, London SW1 (☎ 01 235 4858); Evans Leap, Withyham, Hartfield, E Sussex (☎ 089 277 720)

DENNISTON, Rev Robin Alastair; s of late Alexander Guthrie Denniston, CMG, CBE; *b* 25 Dec 1926; *Educ* Westminster, Ch Ch Oxford (BA); *m* 1, 1950, Anne Alice Kyffin (d 1985), da of Dr A Geoffrey Evans (d 1951); 1 s, 2 da; m 2, 1987, Rosa Susan Penelope Beddington; *Career* 2 Lt 66 Airborne Light Regt, RA, served UK; md Hodder & Stoughton Ltd 1968-72 (previously promotion mangr, editorial dir), dep chm George Weidenfeld & Nicolson 1973; non-exec chm A R Mowbray & Co 1974-; chm: Sphere Books 1975-76, Thomas Nelson & Sons 1975-78, Michael Joseph 1975-78, George Rainbird Ltd 1975-78; dir Thomson Pubns Ltd and Hamish Hamilton Ltd 1975-78; ordained: deacon 1978, priest 1979; acad publisher 1978; *Books* Partly Living (1967); *Recreations* farming, music; *Clubs* Oxford and Cambridge; *Style—* The Rev Robin Denniston; Great Tew Vicarage, Great Tew, Oxfordshire OX7 4AG (☎ 060883 293)

DENNY, Sir Alistair Maurice Archibald; 3 Bt (UK 1913), of Dumbarton, Co Dunbarton; s of Sir Maurice Edward Denny, 2 Bt, KBE (d 1955); *b* 11 Sept 1922; *Educ* Marlborough; *m* 18 April 1949, Elizabeth, da of Maj Sir (Ernest) Guy Richard Lloyd, 1 Bt, DSO (d 1987); Argyll; 2 s (and 1 s decd); *Heir* s, Charles Alistair Maurice Denny; *Career* served with Fleet Air Arm 1944-46; *Recreations* golf, music, photography, gardening; *Clubs* Royal and Ancient Golf; *Style—* Sir Alistair Denny, Bt; Crombie Cottage, Abercrombie, Anstruther, Fife KY10 2DE (☎ 033 37 631)

DENNY, Sir Anthony Coningham de Waltham; 8 Bt (I 1782), of Castle Moyle, Kerry; s of Rev Sir Henry Lyttelton Lyster Denny, 7 Bt (d 1953); *b* 22 April 1925; *Educ* Clayesmore, Anglo-French Art Centre, Regent St Polytech Sch of Architecture; *m* 1 Sept 1949, Anne Catherine, er da of late Samuel Beverley, FRIBA; 2 s, 1 adopted da; *Heir* s, Piers Anthony de Waltham Denny b 14 March 1954; *Career* serv RAF (air crew) 1943-47; designer; ptnr in Verity and Beverley, Architects and Designs, with offices inLondon, Tetbury,Gloucestershire and Lisbon, Portugal; Hereditary Freeman of Cork; MCSD, FRSA, MCSD. FRSA; *Style—* Sir Anthony Denny, Bt; Daneway House, Sapperton, nr Cirencester, Glos (☎ 028 576 232)

DENNY, Capt Anthony Miles; only child of Sir (Jonathan) Lionel (Percy) Denny, MC, Lord Mayor of London 1965-66 (d 1985), and Doris (d 1985), da of Robert George Bare, FSI, of Putney; *b* 14 Dec 1925; *m* 28 June 1952 (m dis 1969), Pamela Diana, only child of late Capt Thomas Hamilton Dennys, MBE, IA (d 1959), a collateral of the Denny of Castle Moyle barts; 1 s, 1 da; HM Lt for City of London 1980-; *Style—* Capt Anthony Denny, Esq

DENNY, Charles Alistair Maurice; s and h of Sir Alistair Denny, 3 Bt; *b* 7 Oct 1950; *Educ* Wellington, Edinburgh Univ; *m* 1981, Belinda (Linda), yr da of J P McDonald, of Dublin; 1 s (Patrick Charles Alistair b 1985); *Recreations* golf, gardening; *Clubs* Royal and Ancient Golf, St Andrews; *Style—* Charles Denny, Esq

DENNY, James Frederick Lowndes; yr s of late John Anthony Denny (d 1943), and Eileen Alice Maud, da of Col Meyrick Edward Selby-Lowndes, of Mursley Grange, Bucks; *b* 1925; *Educ* Hawtreys, Eton; *m* 1 April 1950, Mary Clare, only da of late Col Francis William Wilson-FitzGerald, DSO, MC, of Purton House, Wilts; 1 s (John William b 27 Oct 1958), 2 da (Sarah Elizabeth b 10 Feb 1953, Lucinda Clare b 4 April 1954); *Career* chm: E M Denny (Hldgs) Ltd, Denny Meat Trading Ltd and E M Denny & Co Ltd; dir Coey Ltd and the Ulster Farmers' Ltd, ret; conslt UK Provision Trade Fedn.; *Recreations* painting; *Clubs* Boodle's, RAC; *Style—* James Denny, Esq; The Old Farm House, Goring-on-Thames, Reading, Berks RG8 9HD (☎ 0491 872323)

DENNY, Linda May; *née* Magnun; da of Maximilian Magnun, of Calcutta, India, and Suzi Kathleen, *née* Allen; *b* 22 Feb 1950; *Educ* Bath Acad of Art; *m* 1, 19 Aug 1968, William Jones; 1 s (Stephen William Magnun b 1967); m 2, 24 Aug 1984, Richard William Geoffrey Denny, *qv*, s of Rev Sir Henry Littleton Lyster Denny, 7 Bt (d 1952), of Tralee Castle, Co Kerry; *Career* mangr: Mgmnt Publishing Ltd, Mgmnt Ltd, Results Trg Ltd; horse breeder, commenced breeding Irish Draught (endangered breed) 1987, and British Sport Horse; *Recreations* skiing, painting, farm interest, conservation, hunting with Royal Artillery; *Clubs* Sloane; *Style—* Mrs Richard Denny; Coldicote Farm, Moreton in Marsh, Gloucs (☎ 0680 50515); 85 Pursewardens Close, Culmington Rd, Ealing W13; Mgmnt House, 20 Northgate St, Devizes, Wilts SN10 1JT (☎ 0380 5514, car phone 0836 508024)

DENNY, Piers Anthony de Waltham; er s and h of Sir Anthony Denny, 8 Bt; *b* 14 Mar 1954; *Educ* King Alfred Sch, Westfield Coll London Univ; *Style—* Piers Denny, Esq

DENNY, Richard William Geoffrey; s of Rev Sir Henry Lyttelton Lyster Denny, 7 Bt (d 1952), of Co Kerry, and Joan Dorothy Lucy, *née* Denny (d 1976); bro Sir Anthony Denny, 8 Bt, *qv*, architect to Royal Household, and Robyn Denny, distinguished modern painter; *b* 4 Feb 1940; *Educ* Royal Masonic Sch Bushey Herts, Plumpton Coll of Agric Sussex; *m* 1, 24 Feb 1961 (m dis 1978), Andrée Suzanne Louise, eldest da of Marcel Louis Parrot; 4 s (Lyster b 1961, Walter b 1963, Giles b 1964, Julius b 1966); m 2, 24 Aug 1984, Linda May, *qv*, da of Maximilian Magnun, of

Calcutta, India; *Career* int conference speaker on motivation, md Denny Farms Ltd 1967-, co-fndr and dir Leadership Devpt Ltd 1974, lectured round the world on selling, motivation and people mgmnt 1974-79; fndr, md and chm Results Trg Ltd, Man Mgmnt Publishing Ltd, Man Mgmnt Ltd 1979-; writer and presenter World's first video sales course on professional selling 1983, toured Australia and NZ 1985, recorded 'Dare to be Great' 1986, writer and presenter 'The Professional Manager' World's largest video mgmnt course; author Selling to Win (1988); *Recreations* sheep-breeding, farming, sailing, squash, hunting, photography, skiing; *Clubs* Sloane; *Style*— Richard Denny, Esq; Coldicote Farm, Moreton in Marsh, Gloucestershire; Man Mgmnt Ltd, Mgmnt Huose, 20 Northgate St, Devises, Wilts (☎ 0380 77555, car phone 0836 508024)

DENNY, Ronald Mackinnon; s of Frank Herbert Denny (d 1947), of Enfield, Middx, and Gladys Amy, *née* Mackinnon (d 1966); *b* 23 Dec 1920; *Educ* Edmonton GS, RAF Coll, London Univ (Dip TS), Kent Univ (MA), Birmingham Univ; *m* 14 Feb 1945, Gwenllian Audrey Caroline, da of Brinley Richard Cound (d 1948), of Burryfort, S Wales; 2 da (Diane Meryl b 1948, Sally Sian b 1953); *Career* RAFVR 1939, commnd Pilot Offr Tech Radar Branch 1943, Offr i/c Flt/Lt Airborne Radar Honiley 1944-46, demob 1946 Flt/Lt; asst airport mangr Heathrow Airport 1953-56, dist & supt Mercantile Marine Serv Newcastle 1956-58; seconded to: NATO Paris 1958-60, Chateauroux France 1960-64; controller Eastern Rd Construction Unit 1968-73, Asst Sec Dept of Transport 1974-80, Dep Dir-Gen Br Property Fedn 1981-87, mgmnt conslt 1988-; AAA Champion 120 yards high hurdles Middx and Southern Counties 1939; FBIM 1971, FIHT 1980, MCIT 1981, Hon Fell Architectural Assoc 1981; *Recreations* travel, gardening; *Clubs* RAF; *Style*— Ronald Denny, Esq; Maplescombe Oasts, Farningham, Kent DA4 0JY (☎ 0322 864 363); 35 Catherine Place, London SW1E 6DY (☎ 01 828 0111, fax 01 834 3442)

DENNY, Ronald Maurice; s of Maurice Ellis Louis Denny (d 1981) and Ada Beatrice, *née* Bradley; *b* 11 Jan 1927; *Educ* Gosport County Sch; *m* 7 Nov 1952, Dorothy, da of William Hamilton (d 1933); 1 s (Andrew b 1964), 2 da (Jane b 1957, Elizabeth b 1958); *Career* chartered engineer, chief exec Rediffusion plc 1979 (chm 1985), dir: Bet plc 1982, Thames Television 1980, Electrocomponents plc 1984, memb Philharmonia Orchestra Tst 1984, FIERE 1975 FRSA 1985, Hon RCM 1984; *Recreations* music, reading; *Clubs* Athenaeum, Arts; *Style*— Ronald Denny, Esq; 19 Nichols Green, London W5 2QU (☎ 01 998 3765); Rediffusion plc, Buchanan House, 3 St James's Square, London SW1 4LS (☎ 01 925 0550, telex: 919673, fax: (GR3) 01 8397135)

DENNYS, Hon Mrs (Lavinia Mary Yolande); *née* Lyttelton; yst da of 9 Viscount Cobham (d 1949); *b* 21 August 1921; *m* 1, 15 Feb 1945, Capt Cecil Francis Burney Rolt, 23 Hussars (ka 6 April 1945); m 2, 12 Dec 1949, Maj John Edward Dennys MC (d 1973); 1 s; *Career* Subaltern ATS 1941-45; *Style*— The Hon Mrs Dennys; Cannon Cottage, Fore St, Budleigh Salterton, Devon (☎ 039 54 3100)

DENNYS, Rodney Onslow; CVO (1981, MVO 1969), OBE (1943); s of Frederic Onslow Brooke Dennys, and Florence Claire, da of Rudolph Hermann Wolfgang Leopold de Paula; *b* 16 July 1911; *Educ* Canford, LSE; *m* 12 Jan 1944, Elisabeth Katharine, da of Charles Henry Greene and sister of Graham Greene, the novelist, *qv*; 1 s, 2 da; *Career* served WW II Intelligence Corps (Lt-Col 1944), RARO 1946; served FO 1937-41 and 1947-57 (The Hague, Egypt, Turkey, Paris); asst to Garter King of Arms 1958-61, Rouge Croix Pursuivant 1961-67, Somerset Herald of Arms 1967-82 (served on Earl Marshal's Staff for State Funeral of Sir Winston Churchill 1965, and Investiture of HRH Prince of Wales 1969), dep dir Heralds' Museum 1978- (dir 1983), Arundel Herald of Arms Extraordinary 1982-; dir Arundel Castle Trustees Ltd 1977-87; memb CPRE 1972-: memb nat exec 1973-78, chm Sussex branch 1972-77 (vice-pres 1977); chm cncl Harleian Soc 1977-83; High Sheriff of E Sussex 1983 and 84; Freeman City of London, Liveryman and Freeman Scriveners' Co; FSA, FRSA, FSG; *Books* The Heraldic Imagination (1975), Heraldry and the Heralds (1982); *Recreations* ornithology, heraldry; *Clubs* Garrick, Sussex, City Livery; *Style*— Rodney Dennys, Esq, CVO, OBE, Arundel Herald of Arms Extraordinary; Heaslands, Steep, nr Crowborough, Sussex (☎ 089 26 61328); College of Arms, Queen Victoria St, London EC4

DENOON DUNCAN, Russell Euan; s of Douglas Denoon Duncan (d 1955), of Johannesburg, and Ray, *née* Reynolds (d 1981); *b* 11 Mar 1926; *Educ* Michaelhouse Natal S Africa; *m* 28 Jan 1956, Caroline Jane Lloyd, da of Noel Wynne Spencer Lewin (d 1980), of London; 2 s (James b 1957, Angus b 1960); *Career* SA Artillery 1943-45; serv: Egypt, Italy; slr 1961, ptnr Webber Wentzel and Co Johannesburg 1952-61, sr ptnr Cameron Markby (formerly Markbys) 1987- (ptnr 1963-); Freeman Worshipful Co of Slrs 1987; *Recreations* mountain walking, tennis, painting; *Clubs* City of London, Royal Tennis Ct, Rand; *Style*— Russell Denoon Duncan, Esq; Rose Cottage, Watts Road, Thames Ditton, Surrey KT7 OBX (☎ 01 398 5193); Cameron Markby, Sceptre Court, 40 Tower Hill, London EC3N 4BB (☎ 01 702 2345, fax 01 702 2303, telex 925779 CAMLAW G)

DENSON, John Boyd; CMG (1972), OBE (1965); s of George Denson (d 1965), of Cambridge, and Alice, *née* Boyd; *b* 13 August 1926; *Educ* Perse Sch Cambridge, St John's Coll Cambridge (BA, MA); *m* 1957, Joyce Myra, da of Charles Henry Symondson (d 1973), of Bucks; *Career* Capt Intelligence Corps RA, Malaya 1944-47; Dip Serv 1951-83: chargé d'affaires Peking 1969-71, RCDS 1972, cncllr Athens 1973-77, ambass Kathmandu 1977-83, ret; memb Universities' China Ctee 1987-; Gorkha Dakshina Bahu First Class (Nepal) 1980; *Recreations* wine, theatre, pictures; *Clubs* Royal Overseas League, Achilles; *Style*— John Denson, Esq, CMG, OBE; Little Hermitage, Pensile Road, Nailsworth, Stroud, Glos GL6 0AL (☎ 045 383 3829)

DENT, Hon Mrs (Ann Camilla); *née* Denison-Pender; da of 2 Baron Pender, CBE (d 1965); *b* 18 June 1931; *m* 2 Oct 1952, Robin John Dent, *qv*; 2 da (Annabel Jane b 1954, m 1981 James Meade, Jennifer Ann b 1957, m 1982 Andrew Everard Martin Smith); *Style*— The Hon Mrs Dent; 44 Smith St, London SW3 (☎ 01 352 1234)

DENT, Hon Mrs (Anne Elizabeth); *née* Taylor; da of Baron Ingrow, OBE, TD (Life Baron 1982); *b* 1951; *m* 1975, Charles Jonathan Dent, elder s of John Harker Dent; 1 s (James Geoffrey b 1980), 1 da (Sarah Louise b 1984); *Style*— Hon Mrs Dent; Ribston Hall, Wetherby, Yorks

DENT, Hon Mrs (Diana Mary); *née* Taylor; da of Baron Ingrow, OBE, TD (Life Baron 1982); *b* 1953; *Educ* Benenden; *m* 1979, John Patrick Dent, yr s of John Harker Dent; 1 s (b 1984), 1 da (b 1986); *Style*— Hon Mrs Dent; Clock Farm, Hunsingore, Wetherby, Yorks

DENT, Evelyn Robert Wilkinson; s of Sir Robert Annesley Wilkinson Dent, CB (d 1983), of Maulds Meaburn, Penrith, Cumbria (High Sheriff of Westmorland 1959), and Elspeth Muriel, *née* Tritton (d 1988); *b* 16 May 1934; *Educ* Eton, Trinity Coll Camb (MA); *m* 15 June 1963, (Celia) Margaret, da of Douglas Hazard Harris, of Steep, Petersfield, Hants; 2 s (Julian b 1964, Nicholas b 1970), 1 da (Caroline b 1966); *Career* admitted slr 1960; pres W Surrey Law Soc 1973-74; ret from practice 1984; chm Rent Assessment Ctee (SE area) 1984-; Freeman of the City of London 1955, Liveryman of the Grocers' Co 1964; *Style*— Evelyn Dent, Esq; Meaburn Edge, Petworth Road, Haslemere, Surrey

DENT, Sir John; CBE (1976, OBE 1968); s of Harry F Dent; *b* 5 Oct 1923; *Educ* King's Coll, London Univ (BSc); *m* 1954, Pamela Ann, da of Frederick G Bailey; 1 s; *Career* FEng; CEng; chm CAA 1982-6; dir: Engineering Gp Dunlop Ltd Coventry 1968-76; Dunlop Holdings Ltd 1970-82; md Dunlop 1978-82; dir Industrie Pirelli Spa 1978-81; Dunlop AG 1979-82; kt 1986; *Style*— Sir John Dent, CBE; Hellidon Grange, Hellidon, Daventry, Northants (☎ Byfield 60589)

DENT, Maj-Gen Jonathan Hugh Baillie; CB (1984), OBE (1974); s of Lt-Col Joseph Alan Guthrie Dent (d 1986), of North Houghton Manor, Stockbridge, Hants, and Hilda Ina, *née* Baillie (d 1976); *b* 19 July 1930; *Educ* Winchester; *m* 1 June 1957, Anne Veronica, only da of Maj Harold John Inglis, DSO, MC (d 1967), of Llansantffraed House, Bwlch, Powys; 1 s (Christopher b 1966), 3 da (Juliet b 1958, Susan b 1960, Victoria b 1962); *Career* Army Offr, cmmnd Queens Bays 1949, Adj 1958, 1 The Queen's Dragoon Gds 1959, RMCS Shrivenham 1962-63, Staff Coll Camberley 1964, RCDS 1977; serv BAOR, Jordan, Libya 1949-56, Borneo 1965-66, MOD 1967-70 and 1971-77, dir Munitions BDS Washington 1978-81; dir-gen fighting vehicles and engr equipment MOD (Maj-Gen) 1981-85 ret; *Recreations* shooting, fishing, bird watching, classical music; *Style*— Maj-Gen Jonathan Dent, CB, OBE; c/o Lloyds Bank, 6 Pall Mall, London SW1Y 5NH

DENT, Robin John; s of Rear Adm John Dent, CB, OBE (d 1973); *b* 25 June 1929; *Educ* Marlborough; *m* 1952, Hon Ann Denison-Pender, *qv*; 2 da; *Career* md Baring Bros & Co Ltd 1967-86; dir TR City of London Tst plc 1977-; dir Barings plc 1985-, chm Barfield Bank & Tst Co Ltd Guernsey 1987-, chm Mase Westpac Ltd 1989-; memb Deposit Protection Bd 1982-85, dep chm Export Guaranty Advsy Cncl 1983-85, chm exec ctee Br Bankers Assoc 1984-85, dep chm Public Works Loan Bd 1988-, memb bd Cancer Res Campaign 1967-; tres King Edward's Hosp Fund for London 1974-, Special tstee St Thomas Hosp 1988-; *Clubs* White's; *Style*— Robin Dent, Esq; 44 Smith St, London SW3 (☎ 01 352 1234)

DENT, Ronald Henry; s of Henry Francis Dent, (d 1975), and Emma, *née* Bradley (d 1978); *b* 9 Feb 1913; *Educ* Portsmouth GS; *m* 1939, Olive May, da of Alfred Wilby (d 1980), of Minehead; 1 s (Nicholas), 1 da (Hilary); *Career* served WWII Maj, UK, France, India 1939-45; chartered accountant; chm: Cape Industs plc 1962-79; dir: Charter Consolidated 1969-79, Eng China Clays 1975-85, Powell Duffryn 1975-83 and other cos; FCA; *Recreations* gardening; *Style*— Ronald Dent, Esq

DENT, Hon Rosamond Mary (Sister Ancilla, OSB); da of William Herbert Shelley Dent, MC, and 19 Baroness Furnivall (d 1969, when the Barony became abeyant between Sister Ancilla and Hon Mrs Bence, *qv*); co-heiress to Barony, renounced right in favour of sister; *b* 3 June 1933; *Educ* Holy Child Convent Mayfield; *Style*— Sister Ancilla, OSB; Minster Abbey, Minster, nr Ramsgate, Kent

DENT, Lady Rosanagh Elizabeth Angela Mary; *née* Taylour; elder da of 6 Marquess of Headfort, by his 1 w (*see* Hon Mrs Knight); *b* 20 Jan 1961; *Educ* St Mary's Convent Ascot, Oxford Poly (BA); *m* 30 July 1983, Andrew Congreve Dent, eldest s of Robin Dent, of Olivers, Painswick, Glos; *Career* dir DMD Ltd 1987-; *Recreations* polo; *Style*— Lady Rosanagh Dent; Shipton Glebe, Woodstock, Oxon

DENT, Hon Mrs (Sarah); *née* Douglas-Home; eldest da of Baroness Dacre and Hon William Douglas-Home; *b* 4 July 1954; *m* Dec 1978, Nicholas Charles Dent, yst s of Maj T C Dent, of 51 Addison Rd, W14; 1 da; *Style*— The Hon Mrs Dent; Derry House, Kilmeston, Alresford, Hants

DENT, Hon Mrs (Tatiana Ines Alexandra); *née* Wilson; 2 da of 4 Baron Nunburnholme; *b* 17 Sept 1960; *m* 5 March 1988, Nigel L Dent; *Style*— The Hon Tatiana Wilson

DENTON, Charles Henry; s of Alan Denton; *b* 20 Dec 1937; *Educ* Reading Sch, Bristol Univ (BA); *m* 1961, Eleanor Mary, *née* Player; 1 s, 2 da; *Career* director of programmes ATV; md Black Lion Films; *Style*— Charles Denton, Esq; Manor Farm, Wolverton, Stratford-on-Avon, Warwicks

DENTON, Prof Sir Eric James; CBE (1974); s of George Denton; *b* 30 Sept 1923; *Educ* Doncaster GS, St John's Coll Cambridge (ScD), Univ Coll London; *m* 1946, Nancy Emily, da of Charles Wright; 2 s, 1 da; *Career* lectr physiology Univ of Aberdeen 1948-56, physiologist Marine Biological Assoc Laboratory Plymouth 1956-74 (dir 1974-87), Royal Soc res prof Univ of Bristol 1964-74; FRS; kt 1987; *Style*— Prof Sir Eric Denton, CBE; Fairfield House, St Germans, Saltash, Cornwall PL12 5LS (☎ 0503 30204); The Laboratory, Citadel Hill, Plymouth, Devon PL1 2PB (☎ 0752 222772)

DENTON, Kenneth Raymond; s of Stanley Charles Denton (d 1957), of Rochester, and Lottie Bertha Rhoda, *née* Dorrington (d 1972); *b* 20 August 1932; *Educ* Rochester Tech and Sch of Art, Medway Coll of Art and Design; *m* 5 Oct 1957, Margaret, da of Thomas Nesbitt (d 1969), of Crossnenagh, Keady, Co Armagh, N Ireland; 3 s (Colin b 1959, Martin b 1960, Nigel b 1961); *Career* Nat Serv RASC, transferred to REME 1952-54; freelance designer and decorative artist 1954-63; designs incl: domestic interiors and furniture, interiors and inn-signs for major brewing Cos, boardroom for Grants of St James; lectr 1963-67: Royal Sch Mil Engrg, Maidstone Coll of Art, Medway Coll of Design, Erith Coll of Art; landscape and marine artist 1967-; exhibitions in UK, Europe, Canada, USA; 27 one-man shows; Two-man exhibitions with: Patrick Hall, Leslie Moore, Enzo Plazzotta; work in many private and public collections, numerous TV and radio appearances; FBID (1963), RSMA (1976), FCSD (1987); *Recreations* classical music, piano-playing; *Clubs* Rotary; *Style*— Kenneth Denton, Esq; Priory Farm Lodge, Sporle, Kings Lynn, Norfolk PE32 2DS (☎ 0760 22084)

DENTON-CLARK, Jeremy; s of Bryan Sandford Clark, of Geneva Switzerland, and Janet Lambie, *née* Neil (d 1971); *b* 7 Sept 1944; *Educ* Cheltenham; *m* 30 Oct 1971, Catherine Enrich, da of Timothy James O'Leary; 2 s (James Anthony b 2 Nov 1974, Nicholas Edward b 28 June 1977); *Career* dir London Interstate Bank Ltd 1984-86, md City Merchants Bank Ltd 1986-; *Style*— Jeremy Denton-Clark, Esq; City Merchants Bank Ltd, 13 Austin Friar, London EC2N 2AJ (☎ 01 638 3511, fax 01 638 2187, telex

886 532)

DENYER, Stephen Robert Noble; s of Wilfred Denyer, of Sherborne, Dorset, and Joy Victoria Jeanne, *née* Noble; *b* 27 Dec 1955; *Educ* Fosters GS Sherborne, Durham Univ (BA); *m* 3 Sept 1988, Monika Maria Wolf, da of Heinrich Christoph Wolf, of Lübeck, W Germany; *Career* slr; ptnr Allen & Overy (specialising in corporate finance work) 1986-; memb: City of London Slrs Co 1986, Law Soc 1980; *Recreations* walking, travel, gardening; *Style*— Stephen R N Denyer, Esq; Allen & Overy, 9 Cheapside, London EC2V 6AD (☎ 01 248 9898, fax 01 236 2192, telex 8812801)

DENZA, Eileen; CMG (1984); da of Alexander Young, of Aberdeen, and Ellen Duffy (d 1981); *b* 23 July 1937; *Educ* Aberdeen Univ (MA), Oxford Univ (MA), Harvard Univ (LLM); *m* 1966, John Denza, s of Luigi Carlo Denza; 2 s (Mark b 1969, Paul b 1971), 1 da (Antonia b 1967); *Career* asst lectr in law Bristol Univ 1961-63, barr Lincoln's Inn 1963, asst legal advsr FCO 1963-74, legal cncllr FCO 1974-86, legal advsr to UK Representation to Euro Community 1980-83, pupillage and practice at Bar 1986-87, second counsel to the Chm of Ctees, counsel to European Communities Ctee House of Lords 1987-; *Books* Diplomatic Law (1976); contributor to: Satow, Diplomatic Practice, and to Essays in Air Law; *Recreations* music; *Style*— Mrs Eileen Denza, CMG

DERAMORE, 6 Baron (UK 1885); Sir Richard Arthur de Yarburgh-Bateson; 7 Bt (UK 1818); yr s of 4 Baron Deramore (d 1943), and bro of 5 Baron (d 1964); *b* 9 April 1911; *Educ* Harrow, St John's Coll Cambridge (MA); *m* 28 Aug 1948, Janet Mary, da of John Ware; 1 da; *Heir* none; *Career* serv 1940-45, Fl-Lt, RAFVR; chartered architect; memb Cncl Architectural Assoc 1951-54; ARIBA; ptnr Cherry and Deramore 1965-70; practised as Arthur Deramore in Bucks, then Yorks 1970-82; *Recreations* water-colour painting, cycling, golf, motoring, writing; *Clubs* RAF, RAC; *Style*— Rt Hon Lord Deramore; Heslington House, Aislaby, Pickering, N Yorks (☎ 73195)

DERBY, Archdeacon of; *see*: Dell, Ven Robert Sydney

DERBY, 18 Earl of (E 1485); Edward John Stanley; 12 Bt (E 1627), MC (1944), DL (Lancs 1946); also Baron Stanley of Bickerstaffe (UK 1832) and Baron Stanley of Preston (UK 1886); s of Capt Rt Hon Lord Stanley (as he was styled), PC, MC (d 1938), and gs of 17 Earl, KG, PC, GCB, GCVO (d 1948, himself gs of 14 Earl, Conservative PM); *b* 21 April 1918; *Educ* Eton, Magdalen Coll Oxford; *m* 22 July 1948, Lady Isabel, JP, da of Hon Henry Augustus Milles-Lade, JP (d 1937), and sis of 4 Earl Sondes; *Heir* nephew, Edward Richard William Stanley, *qv*; *Career* chm Aintree Tst 1982-; pres Caravan Club; CO 5 Bn King's Regiment TA 1947-51; chm NW Area TA Assoc 1979-83; pres: Rugby Football League 1948-, Professional Golfers' Assoc 1964-; late Maj Gren Gds (Res); Hon Col Liverpool Scottish 1964-67; Hon Col 5/8 Bn King's Regt 1975-88; (Cmdg) 5 Bn 1947-51 (Hon Col 1951-67), Hon Col 4(V)Bn The Queens Lancashire Regt 1975-; TA&VR Hon Col 1 and 2 Bns Lancastrian Vols 1967-75; Hon Capt Mersey Div RNR 1952-; Hon LLD Liverpool and Lancaster, pres of Merseyside Chamber of Commerce 1972-; Ld-Lt of Co Lancaster 1951-68; pro-chllr of Univ of Lancaster 1964-71; constable of Lancaster Castle 1972-; *Clubs* White's, Jockey; *Style*— The Rt Hon the Earl of Derby, MC, DL; Knowsley, Prescot, Merseyside (☎ 051 489 6147); Stanley House, Newmarket, Suffolk (☎ 3011)

DERBY, Countess of; Lady Isabel; *née* Milles-Lade; da of Henry Augustus Milles-Lade (d 1937), yst s of 1 Earl Sondes, DL; raised to the rank of an Earl's da 1942; *b* 1920; *m* 22 July 1948, 18 Earl of Derby, *qv*; *Style*— The Rt Hon the Countess of Derby; Stanley House, Newmarket; Knowsley Hall, Prescot, Lancs

DERBY, Peter Jared; s of Samuel Jonathan James Derby, of 22 Harberton Drive, Belfast (d 1974), and Frances Emma, *née* Leckie; *b* 21 Feb 1940; *Educ* Inchmarlo Sch, Royal Belfast Academical Inst, Queens Univ Belfast (BSc); *m* 3 Aug 1968, Rosemary Jane, da of Charles Euan Chalmers Guthrie (d 1985), of Swanston Cottage, 36 Gamekeepers Road, Edinburgh; 1 s (Andrew b 1971), 2 da (Lucy b 1969, Polly b 1973); *Career* jt asst actuary Scottish Widows Fund 1965-67 (joined 1961), ptnr Wood Mackenzie and Co 1970-86 (joined 1967), dir Hill Samuel and Co Ltd 1986-88; dir Ashton Tod McLaren 1988-; sidesman Christ Ch Shamley Green; memb Guildry of Brechin, Angus 1973, Freeman City of London and Co of Actuaries 1979-; FFA (1965), AIA (1968), memb Stock Exchange (1970); *Recreations* golf, tennis, squash, skiing, music; *Clubs* Travellers, New (Edinburgh), Woking Golf; *Style*— Peter J Derby, Esq; Haldish Farm, Shamley Green, Guildford GU5 0RD (☎ 0483 898 461); Ashton Tod McLaren, 3 St James's Square, London SW1Y 4JU (☎ 01 925 2727, fax 01 930 7820)

DERBY, Bishop of 1988-; Rt Rev Peter Spencer Dawes; s of late Jason Spencer Dawes, and late Janet, *née* Blane ; *b* 5 Feb 1928; *Educ* Aldenham, Hatfield Coll Durham (BA); *m* 4 Dec 1954, Ethel; 2 s (Michael b 1959, Daniel b 1964), 2 da (Janet b 1956, Mary b 1968); *Career* ordained: deacon 1954, priest 1955; curate: St Andrew Islington, St Ebbes Oxford 1954-60; tutor Clifton Theological Coll 1960-65, vicar Good Shephard Romford 1965-80, examining chaplain to Bishop of Chelmsford 1970, archdeacon of West Ham 1980-88; memb: Gen Synod 1970, Standing Ctee 1985; *Style*— The Venerable Peter S Dawes; 6 King Street, Duffield, Derby DE6 4EU

DERBY, Richard Outram Walker; s of Maj John Derby, TD (d 1964), and Marie Enid Derby (d 1982); *b* 27 April 1940; *Educ* Harrow; *m* 1, 20 July 1963, Sarah Mary, only da of late Lt-Col Peter John Luard, DSO, OBE; 1 s (Edward), 2 da (Amanda, Henrietta); m 2, 1979, Anthea Mary Boyd, da of Lt-Col J R Roberts, RA, of Wincanton, Somerset; *Career* sr ptnr Godfray, Derby & Co (stockbrokers); dir Nat Investmt Gp plc; memb Cncl of the Int Stock Exchange; *Recreations* fox hunting, shooting; *Style*— Richard Derby, Esq; College Green Manor, East Pennard, Somerset (☎ 0458 50240); Godfray, Derby & Co, Penniless Porch, Market Place, Wells, Somerset BA5 1DJ (☎ 0749 76373)

DERBYSHIRE, Sir Andrew George; s of late Samuel Reginald Derbyshire; *b* 7 Oct 1923; *Educ* Chesterfield GS, Queen's Coll Cambridge, Architectural Assoc; *m* Lily Rhodes, *née* Binns, widow of Norman Rhodes; 3 s, 1 da; *Career* architect; chm: RMJM Ltd, CHMN (and ptnr), Robert Matthew, Johnson-Marshall & Partners; MA, D Univ (York), AADip, FRIBA, FSIA; FRSA; kt 1986; *Style*— Sir Andrew Derbyshire; 42 Weymouth St, London W1A 2BG (☎ 01 486 4222); 4 Sunnyfield, Hatfield, Herts AL9 5DX (☎ 65903)

DERHAM, Sir Peter John; s of J W and Mary Derham; *b* 21 August 1925; *Educ* C of E GS Melbourne, Melbourne Univ (BSc); *m* 1950, Averil, *née* Wigan; 2 s, 1 da; *Career* dir Moulded Plastics Ltd (Australasia) 1953 (later Nylex Corpn Ltd), sales dir 1960, gen mangr 1967, md 1972; chm Armstrong Nylex Pty Ltd, fed pres Aust Inst of Dirs, chm advsy bd Cwlth Scientific and Industrial Research Org 1981-; yachtsman, challenger Advance Australia Cup Port Phillip Bay 1983; kt 1980; *Style*— Sir Peter Derham; 12 Glenbervie Rd, Toorak, Vic 3142, Australia

DERING, Lady (Betty Bridgett); *née* Powys Druce; only da of late Lt-Col Vere Powys Druce, of Charminster, Dorset; *b* 15 May 1916; *Educ* Beaufront, Camberley Surrey; *m* 17 April 1940, Lt-Col Sir Rupert Anthony Yea Dering, 12 Bt (d 1975, when the title became extinct); 1 da; *Recreations* croquet, horse racing, travel; *Style*— Lady Dering; Bellings, Midhurst, Sussex

DERMOTT, William; CB (1984); s of William and Mary Dermott; *b* 27 Mar 1924; *Educ* Univ of Durham (MSc); *m* 1946, Winifred Joan Tinney; 1 s, 1 da; *Career* agric scientist Univ of Durham and Wye Coll Univ of London 1943-46, sr sci specialist and dep chief sci specialist MAFF 1971-76; head of Agric Science Service, Agric Devpt and Advsy Service, Miny of Agric Fisheries & Food 1976-; *Style*— William Dermott, Esq, CB; 22 Chequers Park, Wye, Ashford, Kent (☎ 0233 812694)

DERRINGTON, John Anthony; CBE; s of late John Derrington; *b* 24 Dec 1921; *Educ* Battersea Polytechnic (BSc), Imperial Coll London (DIC); *m* 1971, Beryl June, *née* Kimber; 1 s, 3 da; *Career* chartered civil engineer conslt; formerly dir Sir Robert McAlpine & Sons; *Recreations* gardening, travel, reading; *Style*— John Derrington, Esq; 3 Gorham Ave., Rottingdean, Sussex

DERRY, Anthony Edward; s of Wilfred Francis Derry (d 1976); *b* 18 April 1933; *Educ* Hereford GS; *m* 1951, Marie Elaine, da of Reginald Edwards (d 1981); 3 children; *Career* chm and md Long John Scotch Whisky 1982- (previously sales dir Arthur Bell & Sons, int sales dir Whyte & Mackay); *Recreations* private flying, rugby; *Style*— Tony Derry, Esq; c/o Long John International plc, 20 Queen Anne's Gate, London SW1 (☎ 01 222 7060); 3 Laleham Abbey, Laleham Park, nr Staines, Middx (☎ 0784 63244)

DERVAIRD, Hon Lord; John Murray; QC (Scotland 1974); s of John Hyslop Murray (d 1984), of Beoch, Stranraer, and Mary, *née* Scott; *b* 8 July 1935; *Educ* Cairnryan Sch, Edinburgh Acad, CCC Oxford (MA), Edinburgh Univ (LLB); *m* 30 July 1960, Bridget Jane, 2 da of Sir William Maurice Godfrey, 7 Bt (d 1974); 3 s (Alexander Godfrey b 12 Feb 1964, William John b 21 Oct 1965, David Gordon b 4 June 1968); *Career* Lt Royal Signals 1954-56; advocate 1962; memb Scottish Law Cmmn 1979-88; chm: Agric Law Assoc 1981-85 (vice pres 1985-), Scottish Cncl of Law Reporting 1978-88, Scottish Lawyers Euro Gp 1978-82, Med Appeal Tribunals 1978-79 and 1985-88; chm Scottish ctee on Arbitration 1986-, Lord of Session (Senator of the Col of Justice) 1988-; hon pres Advocates Business Law Gp 1988-; chm Scottish Ensemble (formerly Scottish Baroque Ensemble); *Books* Stair Encyclopedia of Scots Law - Title 'Agriculture' (1987); *Recreations* music, farming, gardening, birdwatching; *Clubs* New (Edinburgh), Puffins (Edinburgh); *Style*— The Hon Lord Dervaird; 4 Moray Place, Edinburgh EH3 6DS (☎ 031 225 1881); Fell Cottage, Craigcaffie, Stranraer DG9 8QS (☎ 0776 3356); Wood of Dervaird Fann, Glenluce, Wigtownshire (☎ 05813 222)

DERVISH, Djemal; s of Dervish Djemal (d 1979), of Harrow, Middx, and Nazire, *née* Abdullah; *b* 21 Oct 1944; *Educ* Lymington Sch Hampstead, Univ of London (BSc); *m* 16 Sept 1972, Meral, da of Mehmet Selcuk, of Cyprus; 2 s (Serkan b 1974, Tarhan b 1985); *Career* sci res asst 1969-70, admitted slr of the supreme ct 1974, sr ptnr Fletcher Dervish & Co 1979, memb Slrs Complaints Negligence Panel 1986, chm Trainee Slrs Monitoring Panel 1987, pres N Middx Law Soc 1988; hon legal advsr CAB: Tottenham, Wood Green, Edmonton, Hornsey; hon legal advsr Religious Charity; memb: Law Soc 1972, N Middx Law Soc 1977; *Recreations* gardening, reading, walking; *Clubs* The Portman, The Belfry; *Style*— Djemal Dervish, Esq; 389 Cockfosters Rd, Hadley Wood, Herts (☎ 01 449 7573); Principal Office, 582/4 Green Lanes, Harringey, London N8 ORP (☎ 01 800 4615, fax 01 802 2273 or 808 1504, car phone 0836 776 201)

DERWENT, 5 Baron UK (1881); Sir Robin Evelyn Leo Vanden-Bempde-Johnstone; 7 Bt (GB 1796), LVO (1957); s of 4 Baron Derwent, CBE (d 1986), and Marie Louise, *née* Picard (d 1985); *b* 30 Oct 1930; *Educ* Winchester, Clare Coll Cambridge (MA); *m* 12 Jan 1957, Sybille Marie Louise Marcelle, da of Vicomte de Simard de Pitray (d 1979); 1 s (Hon Francis Patrick Harcourtb 1965), 3 da (Hon Emmeline Veronica Louise (Hon Mrs Winterbotham) b 1958, Hon Joanna Louise Claudia b 1962, Hon Isabelle Catherine Sophie b 1968); *Heir* s, Hon Francis Patrick Harcourt b 1965; *Career* 2 Lt Kings Royal Rifle Corps, Lt Queen Victoria's Rifles (TA Reserve); second sec FO 1954-55, private sec to Br Ambass Paris 1955-58; second sec: FO 1958-61, Mexico City 1961-65; first sec Washington 1965-68; FO 1968-69; N M Rothschild & Sons Ltd 1969-85, md Hutchison Whampoa (Europe) Ltd; dir: Metallurgie Hoboken-Overpelt, Genfin Ltd, Tanks Consolidated Investments plc Guidehouse Gp plc; Chev Legion of Honour 1957, Officier de l'Ordre Nationale du Mérite (France) 1978; *Recreations* fishing, shooting; *Clubs* Beefsteak, Boodle's; *Style*— The Rt Hon Lord Derwent, LVO; Hackness Hall, Scarborough, N Yorks; 30 Kelso Place, London W8 5QG (☎ 01 937 2826)

DESCH, Stephen Conway; QC (1980); s of Dr Harold Ernest Desch, DPhil Oxon (d 1978); *b* 17 Nov 1939; *Educ* Dauntsey's Sch, Magdalen Coll Oxford (MA, BCL), Northwestern Univ Chicago; *m* 1973, Julia Beatrice, da of John Geoffrey Little, OBE, RN ret (d 1975); 2 da; *Career* Gray's Inn 1962, lectr in law Magdalen Coll Oxford 1963-65, joined Midland Circuit 1964, recorder of the Crown Court 1979-; *Style*— Stephen Desch, Esq, QC; 2 Crown Office Row, Temple, London EC4Y 7HJ (☎ 01 353 9337)

DESMOND, Denis Fitzgerald; CBE (1989); s of Maj James Fitzgerald Desmond, DL JP, of Ballyarton House, Killaloo, Londonderry, and Harriet Ivy, *née* Evans (d 1972); *b* 11 May 1943; *Educ* Castle Park Dublin, Trinity Coll Glenalmond Perthshire; *m* 25 July 1965, Annick Marie Marguerite Francoise, da of M Jean Faussemagne, of Nancy France; 1 da (Stephanie b 1970); *Career* RCT (TA) 1964-69: 2 Lt, Lt; chm and md Desmond & Sons Ltd Londonderry 1970- (dir 1966-70), chm Adria Ltd Strabane 1976-81, dir Ulster Devpt Capital Ltd Belfast 1985-, regnl dir Nationwide Anglia Building Soc 1986-; High Sheriff Co Londonderry 1974, ADC to Govr NI 1967-69; Hon DSc Queen's Univ of Belfast 1987; *Recreations* fishing, tennis; *Style*— Denis Desmond, Esq, CBE; Desmond & Sons Ltd, Drumahoe, Londonderry BT47 3SD (☎ 0504 44901, fax 0504 48447/47331, car 0860 747839, telex 74402)

DETSINY, (Anthony) Michael; s of Rudolph Detsiny, JP (d 1987), and Edith, *née* Scheff; *b* 25 July 1941; *Educ* Highgate; *m* 2 Dec 1967, Angela Hazel, da of Francis Charles Cornell (d 1977); 2 s (Warren Rodney b 1969, Stephen Charles b 1978), 1 da (Hazel Karen b 1972); *Career* dir: Cadbury Ltd 1977-83, Allied Breweries 1983-86 Creative Business Communications plc 1986-; md The Creative Business Ltd;

Recreations gardening, reading; *Clubs* RAC; *Style*— Michael Detsiny, Esq; The Willows, Moor End Common, Frieth, nr Henley-on-Thames, Oxon (☎ 0494 881176); The Creative Business Ltd, 37 Dean Street, London W1V 5AP (☎ 01 434 2631, telex 8952165, fax 01 437 0194)

DEUTSCH, André; s of late Bruno Deutsch, and Maris, *née* Havas; *b* 15 Nov 1917; *Career* set up André Deutsch Ltd 1951 (joint chm and joint md); founder African Universities Press Lagos and E Africa Publishing House Kenya; *Style*— André Deutsch, Esq; 5 Selwood Terrace, London SW7

DEUTSCH, Renee; da of Maurice Deutsch, and Matilda Deutsch; *b* 2 August 1944; *Educ* Hendon Co GS, Northern Poly Sch of Architecture; *m* divorced; *Career* architecture and design for 10 years, mgmnt consultancy for 6 years; appeals co-ordinator (3 years): Almeida Theatre, Half Moon Theatre, London Contemporary Dance; head of consumer PR Dennis Davidson Assocs, md consumer products UK Walt Disney Co Ltd (formerly mktg dir); *Recreations* performing arts, visual, arts, reading, spectator tennis, conversations; *Clubs* Groucho, YMCA; *Style*— Miss Renee Deutsch; The Walt Disney Co, 31-32 Soho Sq, London W1V 6AP (☎ 01 734 8111, 01 586 3504, fax 01 439 8741, telex 21532)

DEVAS, Michael Campbell; MC (1945); only s of Geoffrey Charles Devas, MC (d 1971; whose mother was Edith, da of Lt-Col Hon Walter Campbell, 3 s of 1 Earl Cawdor), by his w Joan (d 1975), great niece of Rt Hon Sir Henry Campbell-Bannerman, the Liberal PM (1906-08); *b* 6 June 1924; *Educ* Eton; *m* 1, 28 June 1952 (m dis 1966), Patience Merryday, da of late Sir Albert Gerald Stern, KBE, CMG (d 1966); 1 s, 1 da; m 2, 12 Oct 1967, Gillian Barbara, da of late Col H M P Hewett, of The Court House, Chipping Warden, nr Banbury, and formerly w of Charles Arthur Smith-Bingham; 1 s; *Career* banker; chm Colonial Mutual Life Assurance (London Bd) 1982-, joined M Samuel & Co Ltd 1947, dir 1960; dir Kleinwort Benson Ltd 1965-86, chm Kleinwort Charter Investmt Tst plc, dir Dover Corpn (USA); *Recreations* sailing, skiing; *Clubs* White's, Royal Yacht Squadron; *Style*— Michael Devas, Esq, MC; Hunton Court, Maidstone, Kent (☎ 06272 307); work: 24 Lugdate Hill London EC4P 4BD

DEVAS, Gp Capt William George; CBE (1959), DFC (1944), AFC (1943); s of late Ambrose Joseph Devas, of Gaston, Kilmeston, Hants, and Corina Mary (d 1978), da of George Andrew Batchelor; *b* 17 Dec 1912; *Educ* Beaumont Coll; *m* 14 Nov 1939, Monica Mary Cecil, da of late Henry Francis Hobart Kerr (d 1972) ggs of 6 Marquess of Lothian; 2 s (Christopher b 1944, John b 1947); *Career* RAF: served No 29 (Fighter) Sqdn 1933-35, India 1935-37, S Africa 1941-43, Bomber Command 1944, RAF Staff Coll 1948-50, Hong Kong 1950-52, Cyprus 1956-58, Thorney Island 1958-60, Norway 1960-62, MOD 1962-68; ADC to HM The Queen 1965-68, ret 1968; *Style*— Gp Capt William Devas, CBE, DFC, AFC; Brick Kiln Farmhouse, Chilgrove, Chichester, W Sussex PO18 9HS (☎ E Marden (0243 59) 240)

DEVERELL, Sir Colville Montgomery; GBE (1963, OBE 1946), KCMG (1957, CMG 1955), CVO (1953); s of George Robert Deverell, of Kilencoole, Castle Bellingham, Co Louth, and Maud, *née* Cooke; *b* 21 Feb 1907; *Educ* Portora Sch Enniskillen Ulster Trinity Coll Dublin (LLB), Trinity Coll Cambridge; *m* 5 Oct 1935, Helen Margaret, da of Dallas A Wynne Willson, of St Mary's Lodge, Kidlington, Oxford; 3 s; *Career* entered Colonial Admin Serv 1931, asst dir civil affrs branch E Africa Cmd HQ 1941-46, memb Earl de la Warr's delegation to Ethiopia 1944, sec devpt and reconstruction authy Kenya 1946-49, admin sec Kenya 1949-52, colonial sec Jamaica 1952-55 govr the Windward Islands 1955-59, govr and C-in-C of Mauritius 1959-62, sec-gen Int Planned Parenthood Fedn 1964-69; KStJ; *Style*— Sir Colville Deverell, GBE, KCMG, CVO; 123 Greys Rd, Henley-on-Thames, Oxon

DEVERELL, Brig (John Freegard) Jack; OBE (1987, MBE 1979); s of Harold James Frank Deverell (d 1986), of Bath, and Joan Beatrice, *née* Carter; *b* 27 April 1945; *Educ* King Edwards Sch Bath, RMA Sandhurst, Royal Naval Coll Greenwich; *m* 15 Dec 1973, Jane Ellen, da of Gerald Tankerville Norris Solomon, of Hindon, Wilts; 1 s (Simon b 21 Oct 1978), 1 da (Emma b 23 Nov 1976); *Career* RMA Sandhurst 1964-65; cmmnd Somerset and Cornwall Light Infantry 1965, cmd 3 Bn Light Infantry 1984-86, dir Staff Royal Mil Coll of Sci 1986-88, Cdr UK Mobile Force 1988; *Recreations* cricket, rugby, golf, rackets, riding; *Clubs* Army and Navy, 1 Zingari, Free Foresters, Mounted Infantry; *Style*— Brig Jack Deverell, OBE, MBE

DEVEREUX, Alan Robert; CBE (1980), DL; s of Donald Charles, and Doris Louie Devereux; *b* 18 April 1933; *Educ* Colchester Sch, Clacton County HS, Mid-Essex Technical Coll; *m* 1, 1959, Gloria Alma, *née* Hair (d 1985); 1 s (Iain b 1964); m 2, 1987, Elizabeth; *Career* dir Scottish Mutual Assur Soc 1972-, chm CBI (Scot) 1977-79; dir: Walter Alexander plc 1980-, Solsgirth Investmt Tst Ltd 1981-, Scottish Mutual Assurance Soc 1972-, Hambros Scotland Ltd 1984-; chm Hambro Legal Protection (Scotland) Ltd 1985-; chm Scottish Tourist Bd 1980-, memb Br Tourist Authy 1980-; CBIM; *Recreations* reading, work, running for aeroplanes; *Clubs* E India, Devonshire, Sports and Public Schools; *Style*— Alan Devereux, Esq, CBE, DL; Viewfield, 293 Fenwick Rd, Glasgow G46 6UH; Scottish Tourist Bd, 23 Ravelston Terrace, Edinburgh EH4 3EU (☎ 031 332 2433, fax 031 343 1513)

DEVEREUX, Robert Charles Debohun; s of Herbert Morris Devereux (d 1949), and Fanny Rosemary Devereux (d 1980); *b* 15 Dec 1928; *Educ* Repton, Cambridge Univ (MA); *m* 23 Oct 1954, Anna-Mary, da of Henry Edmund Theoderic Vale (d 1969); 1 s (Charles b 3 June 1956), 2 da (Christina b 13 April 1958, Jane b 12 June 1961); *Career* Nat Serv RE 1947-49, Actg Capt Egypt; Heinz Corpn 1952-53; Wellcome plc 1953-: chief engr 1958, gen prodn mangr 1964-69, chm Calmic Aust 1969-72-; memb Chem Industs Assoc Trade Affrs Bd 1959-69, pres NW Kent Post Grad Med Centre 1972-77; CEng, MIMechE, FBIM; *Recreations* reading, gardening; *Clubs* RAC; *Style*— Robert Devereux, Esq; Wellcome plc, Temple Hill, Dartford, Kent DA1 5AH (☎ 0322 23488, fax 0322 28564, car tel 0836 243465, tlx 896758)

DEVESI, Sir Baddeley; GCMG (1980); s of Mostyn Tagabasoe Norua and Laisa Otu; *b* 16 Oct 1941; *Educ* St Stephen's Sch Auckland NZ, Ardmore Teachers' Coll Auckland; *m* 1969, June Marie Barley; 3 s, 2 da; *Career* govr-gen Solomon Islands 1978-, chllr Univ of S Pacific 1980-, dep chm Solomon Islands B'dcasting Corpn 1976; KStJ; *Style*— Sir Baddeley Devesi, GCMG; Government House, Honiara, Solomon Islands

DEVEY, John Michael; s of William James Devey (d 1966), of Wolverhampton, and Ada Florence, *née* Lawson; *b* 19 Feb 1938; *Educ* St Peter's Collegiate Sch Wolverhampton; *m* 25 Oct 1962, Brenda, da of John Arthur Whitehead (d 1977), of Wolverhampton; 1 s (Paul), 1 da (Jacqueline); *Career* CA; ptnr Campbell & Co Wolverhampton; former chm Wolverhampton Lawn Tennis and Squash Club; FCA 1961; *Recreations* golf, squash, tennis; *Clubs* South Staffs GC; *Style*— John Devey, Esq; Deepdale Cottage, Stratford Brook, Hilton, Bridgnorth, Shrops (☎ 074 64 588); Campbell & Co, 87 Tettenhall Rd, Wolverhampton (☎ 0902 21441)

DeVILLE, Harold Godfrey (Oscar); CBE (1979); s of Harold DeVille (d 1980); *b* 11 April 1925; *Educ* Burton-on-Trent GS, Trinity Coll Cambridge (MA); *m* 1947, Pamela Fay, da of late Capt Rowland Ellis; 1 s; *Career* Lt RNVR 1943-46; personnel mangr Ford Motor Co 1949-65, exec dep chm BICC Ltd 1980-84 (gen mangr central personnel rels 1965-70, dir 1971, exec vice-chm 1978-80), chm Meyer Int plc 1987- (dir 1984); memb: Cmmn on Industl Rels 1971-74, Central Arbitration Ctee 1976-77, cncl ACAS 1976-, cncl CBI 1977-85; memb cncl and fell: Inst Manpower Studies 1971-, Indust Soc 1977-84; Iron and Steel Econ Devpt ctee 1984-86, Govt Review of Vocational Qualifications 1985-86, Br Bd 1985-; memb cncl reading Univ 1985-, chm Nat Cncl for Vocational Qualifications 1986-; CBIM, FIPM; *Recreations* genealogy, fell-walking; *Style*— Oscar DeVille, Esq, CBE; Bexton Cottage, 18 Pound Lane, Sonning on Thames, Berks; Meyer Int, Villiers House, 41-47 Strand, London WC2N 5JG

DEVINE, (John) Hunter; s of John Hunter Devine (d 1982), of Lenzie, Scotland, and Joan Margaret, *née* Hislop; *b* 1 Dec 1935; *Educ* Lenzie Acad, Dux of School; *m* 25 Jan 1964 (m dis 1989), Gillian, da of Edwin John Locke (d 1982), of Chester; 2 s (Oliver John Hunter b 1968, Gavin Richard b 1970); *Career* pensions sales mangr Scottish Amicable 1971-75 (actuarial trainee Scottish Amicable Life Assur Soc 1953-64, London sec 1964-70); dir Leslie & Godwin (Life and Pensions) Ltd 1975-78; md Godwins Ltd 1987-; md subsidiaries: Godwins Central Servs Ltd 1978-81, Godwins Central Ltd 1982-86; Freeman City of London 1983, memb Worshipful Co of Actuaries 1982; FFA 1964, FPMI 1977, ASA 1980, FIOD 1988; *Recreations* football, golf, squash, theatre, travel; *Clubs* Queens Park FC, Hindhead GC; *Style*— Hunter Devine, Esq; Godwins Ltd, Briarcliff House, Kingsmead, Farnborough, Hants GU14 7TE (☎ 0252 544 484, fax 0252 522 206, car tel 0836 211 735, telex 858241)

DEVITT, Wing Cdr Howson Charles; OBE (1941); yr s of Howson Foulger Devitt (d 1949, 2 s of Sir Thomas Lane Devitt, 1 Bt), and Winifred Lina, *née* Woollcombe (d 1972); *b* 30 Jan 1909; *Educ* Sherborne, Trin Hall Camb (MA); *m* 2 Sept 1939, Elizabeth Carola, yr da of Edward George Fairholme, OBE, of Burke's Corner, Beaconsfield, Bucks; 1 s (Richard Howson b 1940), 1 da (Carola Waveney b 1942); *Career* Wing-Cdr RAFO, served WWII; underwriting memb of Lloyd's; chm: Howson F Devitt & Sons Ltd, Howson Devitt (Agents) Ltd, Douglas, Cox, Tyler & Co Ltd; dir: Devitt, Langton and Downay Day Ltd, Devitt (DA Insurance) Ltd, AA Insurance Services Ltd; govr Pangbourne Nautical Coll; *Clubs* City of London, Royal Cruising, Royal Ocean Racing; *Style*— Wing-Cdr H C Devitt, OBE; Gat-e-Whing, Andreas, Isle of Man

DEVITT, James Hugh Thomas; s (by 3 m) and h of Sir Thomas G Devitt, 2 Bt, of 49 Lexden Rd, Colchester, Essex, and his 3 w (Janet Lilian, da of late Col Hugh Sidney Ellis, CBE, MC; *b* 18 Sept 1956; *Educ* Sherborne Sch, CCC Cambridge (MA); *m* 20 April 1985, Susan Carol, da of Dr (Adrian) Michael (Campbell) Duffus of Woodhouse Farm, Thelbridge, Crediton, Devon; 1 s (Jack b 1988), 1 da (Gemma Florence b 1987); *Career* chartered surveyor; estates devpt mangr Greene King and Sons plc; ARICS; *Clubs* Ipswich Town Football; *Style*— James Devitt, Esq; 2 Brookside, Dalham, Newmarket, Suffolk; Greene King and Sons plc, Westgate Brewery, Bury St Edmunds, Suffolk

DEVITT, Wing Cdr Peter Kenneth; AE (1950); s of Howson Foulger Devitt (d 1949); *b* 4 June 1911; *Educ* Sherborne; *m* 1, 12 Sept 1935 (m dis 1950), Eunice Stephanie, yst da of Sir Charles Sheriton Swan (d 1944); 1 s, 3 da; m 2, 20 Jan 1950 (m dis 1953), Joan Elizabeth, da of late T Forbes Robertson, of Santa Barbara, Calif; m 3, 1953 (m dis 1965), Eunice Stephanie, his former w; *Career* served 1939-45 War with RAuxAF (Battle of Britain, despatches Burma), Actg Gp Capt, Wing Cdr 1944; Lloyd's broker and underwriting memb; govr Royal Merchant Navy Sch 1946 (chm 1956-62), vice pres 1967-80, vice-patron 1980; former company director; former vice-chm Surrey Territorial and Air Force Assoc; Master Worshipful Co of Skinners 1962-63; former DL Surrey; *Recreations* golf, croquet, shooting, painting; *Clubs* RAF; *Style*— Wing Cdr Peter Devitt, AE; Upper Sherbrook, Sherbrook Hill, Budleigh Salterton, E Devon

DEVITT, Richard Howson; s of Howson Devitt, OBE, of Andreas, Isle of Man, and Elisabeth Carola, *née* Fairholme; *b* 12 August 1940; *Educ* Pangbourne Nautical Coll, Trinity Hall Cambridge (MA); *Career* memb Lloyds 1964; dir: Howson F Devitt and Sons Ltd Lloyds Broker 1967, Devitt Langton and Dawnay Day Ltd 1971, Devitt and Moore Nautical College Ltd 1974, Devitt Gp Ltd 1980; govr Pangbourne Coll; Freeman City of London 1964, Liveryman Worshipful Co of Skinners 1969; ACII 1967, FIIBA 1967; *Recreations* sailing, skiing; *Clubs* City of London, Royal Ocean Racing, Royal Yacht Squadron, Royal Cruising; *Style*— Richard Devitt, Esq; 100 Whitechapel Rd, London E1 1JG (☎ 01 247 8888)

DEVITT, Lt-Col Sir Thomas Gordon; 2 Bt (UK 1916), of Chelsea, Co London; s of Arthur Devitt (d 1921), s of 1 Bt; suc gf, Sir Thomas Lane Devitt, 1 Bt, 1923; *b* 27 Dec 1902; *Educ* Sherborne, Corpus Christi Coll Cambridge; *m* 1, 21 June 1930 (m dis 1936), Joan Mary, 2 da of late Charles Reginald Freemantle; m 2, 25 Jan 1937 (m dis 1953), Lydia Mary, da of late Edward Milligen Beloe; 2 da; m 3, 12 Dec 1953, Janet Lilian, da of late Col Hugh Sidney Ellis, CBE, MC; 1 s, 1 da; *Heir* s, James Hugh Thomas Devitt; *Career* Regular Army 1926-30; ptnr Devitt and Moore; former chm Sharmans Garages Ltd, Macers Ltd, govrs Nautical Coll Pangbourne; govr of Sherborne; chm Nat Serv for Seafarers; *Clubs* MCC; *Style*— Lt-Col Sir Thomas Devitt, Bt; 5 Rembrandt Close, Holbein Place, London SW1W 8HS; 49 Lexden Rd, Colchester, Essex CO3 3PY (☎ 0206 577958)

DEVLIN, Lt-Col Brian; OBE (1963, MBE 1959); s of Dr Francis Joseph Devlin (d 1965), of Liverpool, and Selina Mary, *née* Allan (d 1973); *b* 30 June 1919; *Educ* St Francis Xavier Coll Liverpool, Stonyhurst Coll, Univ of Liverpool (MB, ChB, DPH); *m* 1 Jan 1948, Dr Esther Margaret, da of Michael Joseph Carr (d 1948), of Dundalk, Co Louth; 3 s (Hugh b 1951, Mark b 1955, Patrick b 1965), 1 da (Fiona b 1949); *Career* RAMC: Lt 1942, Capt 1943, Maj 1946, Lt-Col 1959; 1 Airborne Div (served N Africa, Italy, Holland, Norway) 1943-45, SMO Br Mil Mission to Saudi Arabia 1946-49, DADAH Singapore 1952-55, WO 1955-58, PMO MOD Malaya 1958-62; RAMC (TA) 1966-72; MO MPNI, MSS DHSS 1963-71; adjudicating med practitioner DHSS 1984-89 (SMO 1971-84); memb Somerset CC 1985-; *Recreations* golf, bridge, fishing;

Clubs RAMC HQ Officers Mess; *Style*— Lt-Col Brian Devlin, OBE, MBE; Rectory Stables, Mells, Frome, Somerset BA11 3PT (☎ 0373 812 951)

DEVLIN, Hon Dominick; s of Baron Devlin PC (Life Peer); *b* 2 Dec 1942; *Educ* Winchester, UCL; *m* 27 May 1967, Carla, da of Lamberto Fulloni, of Rome; 2 s (Daniel b 1968, Christopher b 1972), 1 da (Maddalena b 1969); *Style*— The Hon Dominick Devlin; 4 Chemin de Chaumont, 1232 Confignon, Switzerland

DEVLIN, Hon Gilpatrick; s of Baron Devlin PC (Life Peer); *b* 26 Dec 1938; *Educ* Winchester; *m* 28 Feb 1967, Glenna, da of John Parry-Evans, MRCS, of Colwyn Bay, Denbighshire; 1 s (Benedict b 1967); *Style*— The Hon Gilpatrick Devlin; 19, 1 Ave East, Johannesburg, S Africa

DEVLIN, James Alexander (Jim); s of James Alexander Devlin (d 1971), of Prince Albert Drive, Glasgow, and Eleanor, *née* Porter; *b* 1 May 1934; *Educ* Possil Sch, FCIS; *m* 2 May 1964, Caroline Ann Whitaker, da of Bernard John Austin; 1 s (David James b 1966, Ann Fiona b 1968); *Career* directorships 1984-87 (ret): Shell Overseas Services Ltd, Shell Co of Turkey Ltd, Shell Co of Qatar Ltd, Shell Mkts (ME) Ltd, Shell Trading (ME) Ltd, Shell Oman Trading Co Ltd; *Recreations* golf, sailing, travel; *Style*— James A Devlin, Esq; Chapel Rossan, Ardwell, Stranraer, Galloway DG9 9NA (☎ 077 686 208)

DEVLIN, His Hon Judge Keith Michael; s of Francis Michael Devlin and Norah; *b* 21 Oct 1933; *Educ* Price's Sch, London Univ (LLB, MPhil, PhD); *m* 12 July 1958, Pamela Gwendoline, da of Francis James Phillips (d 1984), of Inverkeithing, Fife, Scotland; 2 s (Stephen b 1964, Philip b 1966), 1 da (Susan b 1968); *Career* cmmnd Nat Serv 1953-55, barr Gray's Inn 1964; deputy chief clerk, Met Magistrates Cts Serv 1964-66; various appts as a dep met stipendiary magistrate 1975-79; asst recorder 1980-83; recorder 1983-84; circuit judge 1984; lectr in law Brunel Univ 1966-71, reader in law 1971-84, assoc prof of law 1984-, memb of Univ Court 1984-88; fell Netherlands Inst for Advanced Study in the Humanities and Social Sciences, Wassenaar 1975-76; memb Consumer Protection Advsy Ctee 1976-81; Magistrates' Assoc (memb of legal ctee 1974-88, vice-chm 1984-88, co-opted memb of cncl 1980-88); JP Inner London (Juvenile Ct Panel) 1968-84, chm 1973-84; jt fndr and ed Anglo-American Law Review 1972-84; *Publications* Sentencing Offenders in Magistrates' Courts (1970), (with Eric Stockdale) Sentencing the Criminal Law Library No5 (1987), articles in legal journals; *Recreations* Roman Britain, watching cricket, fly fishing; *Clubs* Athenaeum, MCC, Hampshire CC; *Style*— His Hon Judge Keith Devlin; Crown Court, St Albans, Hertfordshire AL1 3XE (☎ 0727 24481)

DEVLIN, Hon Matthew; s of Baron Devlin PC (Life Peer); *b* 8 June 1946; *Educ* Winchester, New Coll Oxford; *m* 25 July 1969, Rosemary Joan Boutcher, 3 da of Lt Col E C Van der Kirte, of The Old Rectory, Durrington, Wilts; 2 s (William b 17 March 1972, Edward b 21 April 1975), 2 da (Beatrice b 16 May 1970, Mary b 10 Jan 1977); *Career* banker Citibank NA; *Style*— The Hon Matthew Devlin; Ruffway, Platt Common, St Mary's Platt, Sevenoaks, Kent TN7 8JX (☎ 0732 885380)

DEVLIN, Baron (Life Peer UK 1961); Patrick Arthur Devlin; PC (1960); s of William J Devlin; *b* 25 Nov 1905; *Educ* Stonyhurst, Christ's Coll Cambridge; *m* 12 Feb 1932, Madeleine, da of Sir Bernard Oppenheimer, 1 Bt; 4 s, 2 da; *Career* barr Gray's Inn 1929, bencher 1947, tres 1963; KC 1945; justice of the High Court (Queen's Bench divn) 1948-60, lord justice of Appeal 1960-61, lord of Appeal in Ordinary 1961-64; chm Bedford Coll for Women 1953-59; chm Ctee of Inquiry into Dock Labour Scheme 1955-56; chm Nyasaland Cmmn of Inquiry 1959; chm Press Cncl 1964-69; high steward of Cambridge Univ 1966-, kt 1948; *Style*— Rt Hon Lord Devlin, PC; West Wick House, Pewsey, Wilts (☎ 3458)

DEVLIN, Roger William; s of William Devlin, of Lancs, and Edna, *née* Cross; *b* 22 August 1957; *Educ* Manchester GS, Wadham Coll, Oxford, (MA); *m* 1983, Louise Alice Temlett, da of John Frost Tucker, of Som; *Career* merchant banking; dir Hill Samuel & Co Ltd 1986-; *Recreations* golf, horseracing, travelling; *Clubs* Worplesdon, Royal St George's Golf; *Style*— Roger Devlin, Esq; 87 Portland Road, Holland Park, London W11 (☎ 01 243 1916); Hill Samuel & Co Ltd, 100 Wood Street, London EC2P (☎ 01 628 8011)

DEVLIN, Stuart Leslie; AO (1988), CMG (1980); *b* 9 Oct 1931; *Educ* Gordon Inst of Technol Geelong, Royal Melbourne Inst of Technol, Royal Coll of Art; *m* 1986, Carole Hedley-Saunders; *Career* goldsmith, silversmith and designer; Royal Warrant as Goldsmith Jeweller to HM The Queen 1982; Freeman City of London 1966, Liveryman Worshipful Co of Goldsmiths' 1986, DesRCA (Silversmith), DesRCA (Industl Design-Engrg); *Style*— Stuart Devlin, Esq, AO, CMG; 90 St John St, London EC1 (☎ 01 253 5471)

DEVLIN, Hon Timothy; 3 s of Baron Devlin, PC (Life Peer), *qv*; *b* 28 July 1944; *Educ* Winchester, Univ Coll Oxford; *m* 31 Jan 1967, Angela, elr da of A J G Laramy; 2 s, 2 da; *Career* journalist, former news ed TES, reporter The Times 1971-73, educ corr 1973-77, nat dir ISIS 1977-84, public relations dir Inst of Dirs 1984-86, assoc dir Charles Barker Traverse-Healy; *Style*— The Hon Timothy Devlin; Ramsons, Maidstone Rd, Staplehurst, Kent TN12 0RD

DEVLIN, Timothy Robert (Tim); s of H Brendan Devlin, and Ann Elizabeth Devlin, MB, BCh, *née* Heatley; gf Dr J J Devlin, OBE; *b* 13 June 1959; *m* 1987, Jacqueline, da of George Bonner; *Career* memb of the Cons Research Dept 1981; accountant 1981-84; barr Lincoln's Inn 1985; former chm LSE Cons, sec Islington North Cons Assoc 1985; chm Islington North Cons Assoc 1986; memb: of Stockton-on-Tees Cons Assoc, Soc of Cons Lawyers; ctee memb Foreign Affairs Forum; memb: Franco-Br Parly Gp, All-Pty Disablement Gp, IPU, Br-American Parly Gp, All-Pty Arts and Heritage Gp, All-Pty Clubs Gp; *Style*— Tim Devlin, Esq; 2 Russell St, Stockton-on-Tees, Cleveland TS18 1NS (☎ 0642 603035)

DEVNEY, (Constance) Marie; CBE (1978, OBE 1973); da of Dr Richard Swanton Abraham; *b* 1 April 1934; *Educ* Pendleton HS, Bedford Coll London Univ; *m* 1960 (m dis 1976), Thomas Michael Valentine Patterson; m 2, 1984, Barrie Spencer Devney; *Career* nat woman officer TGWU 1963-76, nat officer 1976-84, chm Gen Council of TUC 1974-75 and 1977 (memb 1963-84), pt-time memb Equal Opportunities Cmmn 1976-84; dir Remploy 1968-; memb Hotel and Catering Training Bd 1966-; *Style*— Mrs Marie Devney, CBE; 15 Mackeson Rd, London NW3 (☎ 01 267 1820)

DEVON, 17 Earl of (E 1553); Sir Charles Christopher Courtenay; 13 Bt (I 1644), JP (Devon 1950); patron of four livings; s of Rev the 16 Earl of Devon, MA (d 1935); *b* 13 July 1916; *Educ* Winchester, RMC; *m* 29 July 1939, Sybil Venetia, da of Capt John Vickris Taylor, JP (d 1956), and formerly wife of 6 Earl of Cottenham; 1 s, 1 da; *Heir* s, Lord Courtenay, *qv*; *Career* Capt Coldstream Gds (RARO), WWII 1939-43 (wounded, despatches), Actg Maj 1942; *Style*— The Rt Hon the Earl of Devon, JP; Powderham Castle, Exeter EX6 8JQ (☎ 0626 890253)

DEVONALD, Hon Mrs (Charlotte Elizabeth Ann); da of 2 Baron Croft, *qv*; *b* 1952; *Educ* Benenden; *m* 4 June 1975, Emrys Thomas Devonald; 1 s (James b 1979), 1 da (Jennifer b 1977); *Style*— The Hon Mrs Devonald; Enderley, Stony Lane, Little Kingshill, Great Missenden, Bucks

DEVONPORT, Viscountess; Sheila Isabel; da of Col Charles Hope-Murray (d 1938), of Morishill, Beith, Ayrshire; *Educ* St Leonards, and St Andrews Univ; *m* 12 March 1938, 2 Viscount Devonport (d 1973); 1 s (3 Viscount), 1 da; *Style*— The Rt Hon The Viscountess Devonport; The Old Vicarage, Peasmarsh Place, nr Rye, E Sussex TN31 6XB

DEVONPORT, 3 Viscount (UK 1917); Sir Terence Kearley; 3 Bt (UK 1908); also Baron Devonport (UK 1910); s of 2 Viscount Devonport (d 1973); *b* 29 August 1944; *Educ* Aiglon Coll Switzerland, Selwyn Coll Cambridge (BA, DipArch, MA), Univ of Newcastle (BPhil); *m* 7 Dec 1968 (m dis 1979), Elizabeth Rosemary, 2 da of late John G Hopton, of Chute Manor, Andover; 2 da (Hon Velvet b 1975, Hon Idonia b 1977); *Heir* kinsman, Chester Dagley Hugh Kearley; *Career* architect: David Brody NY USA 1967-68, London Borough of Lambeth 1971-72, Barnett Winskill Newcastle-upon-Tyne 1972-75; landscape architect Ralph Erskine Newcastle 1977-78, in private practice 1979-; forestry manager 1973-, farmer 1978-; dir various companies 1984-; ARIBA, ALI; *Recreations* skiing, travel, good food, country sports; *Clubs* Beefsteak, Farmers', RAC, MCC, Northern Counties (Newcastle); *Style*— The Rt Hon the Viscount Devonport; Ray Demesne, Kirkwhelpington, Newcastle-upon-Tyne, Northumberland NE19 2RG

DEVONSHIRE, 11 Duke of (E 1694); Andrew Robert Buxton Cavendish; MC (1944), PC (1964); also Baron Cavendish of Hardwicke (E 1605), Earl of Devonshire (E 1618), Marquess of Hartington (E 1694), Earl of Burlington and Baron Cavendish of Keighley (both UK 1831); s of 10 Duke of Devonshire, KG, MBE, TD (d 1950) and Lady Mary Gascoyne-Cecil, GCVO, CBE (d 1988), da of 4 Marquess of Salisbury, KG, PC; *b* 2 Jan 1920; *Educ* Eton, Trinity Coll Cambridge; *m* 19 April 1941, Hon Deborah Mitford (*see* Devonshire, Duchess of); 1 s, 2 da (Lady Emma Tennant, Lady Sophia Morrison, *qqv*); *Heir* s, Marquess of Hartington; *Career* served WW II as Capt Coldstream Gds; contested Chesterfield (C) 1945 and 1950 (pres Chesterfield Cons Assoc 1982); parly under-sec of state for Cwlth Rels 1960-62, min of state Cwlth Rels Off 1962-1964, min of state Colonial Affrs 1963-64; former exec steward Jockey Club, memb Horserace Totalisator Bd 1977-86; vice-lord-lieut Derbys 1957-87; chllr Univ of Manchester 1965-86; chm Grand Cncl Br Empire Cancer Campaign 1956-81; pres: Royal Hosp and Home for Incurables, National Assoc for Deaf Children; former pres Lawn Tennis Assoc, former nat pres Cons Friends of Israel; KStJ; *Books* Parktop A Romance of the Turf (1976); *Clubs* Brooks's, White's, Pratt's; *Style*— His Grace The Duke of Devonshire, PC, MC; Chatsworth, Bakewell, Derbyshire (☎ 024 688 2204); 4 Chesterfield St, London W1 (☎ 01 499 5803)

DEVONSHIRE, Duchess of; Hon Deborah Vivien; *née* Mitford; 6 da of 2 Baron Redesdale (d 1958), and sister of Nancy, Pamela, Unity and Jessica Mitford (*see* Treuhaft, Hon Mrs), also of Hon Lady Mosley, *qv*; *b* 1920; *Educ* privately; *m* 1941, 11 Duke of Devonshire, *qv*; 1 s, 2 da; *Career* dir: Chatsworth House Tst, Cavendish Hotel Bastow, Devonshire Arms Hotel Bolton Abbey; non exec dir: Tarmac plc, W & FC Bonhams Ltd; chm Chatsworth Food Ltd, ptnr Chatsworth Carpenters; pres: Rare Breeds Survival Tst, Derbyshire Historic Bldgs Tst; *Books* The House: A Portrait of Chatsworth (1982); *Style*— Her Grace The Duchess of Devonshire; Chatsworth, Bakewell, Derbyshire

DEVONSHIRE, John Warrick; VRD (1956); s of Ernest Warrick Devonshire (d 1954), and Mabel Cecily Woods (d 1982); gggs of Adm Sir John Ferris Devonshire, KCH (d 1839) one of Lord Nelson's Captains; *b* 21 Dec 1912; *Educ* Sutton Valence Sch Kent; *m* 28 July 1949, Elizabeth, da of Col Frederick George Glanville Weare (d 1975); 2 da (Sally b 1953, Penelope b 1955); *Career* WWII Cdr RNVR served Atlantic convoys, Narvik, Mediterranean, Indian Ocean (last convoy to Singapore), staff of Adm Sir Philip Vian, mentioned in despatches 1944 and 1946; banker, regnl dir Lloyds Bank 1975-81 (regnl gen mangr 1970-74, joined 1931); *Recreations* cricket, golf, gardening, tracing ancestry; *Clubs* MCC, The Naval, The County Guildford; *Style*— John W Devonshire, Esq, VRD; Langhurst Place, Chiddingfold, Surrey GU8 4XP (☎ 042879 4572)

DEVONSHIRE, Michael Norman; TD (1969); s of Maj Norman George Devonshire (d 1983), of Tunbridge Wells, and Edith, *née* Skinner (d 1965); *b* 23 May 1930; *Educ* The Kings Sch Canterbury; *m* 31 March 1962, Jessie Margaret, da of Meirion Roberts (d 1974), of Tywyn Merioneth; *Career* 2 Lt RA 1953-55; TA 1956-69: Queen's Own Royal West Kent Regt, Queen's Regt; slr 1953, Master of Supreme Ct (Taxing Office) 1979, rec of Crown Ct 1987; pres London Slrs Litigation Assoc 1974-76, memb Cncl RYA 1978-; *Books* Taxation of Contentious Costs (1979); *Recreations* sailing; *Style*— Michael Devonshire, Esq; 17 Chestnut Avenue, Southborough, Tunbridge Wells, Kent TN4 OBS (☎ 0892 28672); Royal Courts of Justice, Strand, London WC2 (☎ 01 936 6000)

DEWAR; *see*: Beauclerk-Dewar

DEWAR, Albert Duncan (Bill); s of Alexander Dewar (d 1947), of Smeaton, Midlothian & Dover, Kent, and Bertha Jane, *née* Mortby (d 1962); *b* 30 Mar 1915; *Educ* Dover GS, Univ of London (BSc, PhD); *m* 16 July 1955, Ann Vallack, da of Dr Clive Vallack Single, DSO (d 1931), of Sydney, Australia; *Career* WWII Civil Defence London 1939-45; physiology dept Br Drug Hosp London 1937-45, demonstrator physiology Univ of Liverpool 1945-48, sr lectr physiology Univ of Edinburgh 1945-82 (hon fell 1982-85), res publications on physiology of reproduction, developer The Edinburgh Masker Anti-Stammering Device; restorer: Old Kirk of Weem Perthshire (Heritage Year Award 1975), Castle Menzies Weem; ed Clan Menzies Magazine; memb: Physiological Soc, Soc for Endocinology; *Recreations* scottish architectural history and restoration work; *Style*— Dr A D Dwar; 1 Belford Place, Edinburgh (☎ 031 332 3607) and Smithy Cottage, Camserney, By Aberfeldy, Perthshire

DEWAR, Donald Campbell; MP (Lab) Glasgow Garscadden 1978-; s of Dr Alasdair Dewar, of Glasgow; *b* 21 August 1937; *Educ* Glasgow Acad, Glasgow Univ; *m* 1964 (m dis 1973), Alison Mary, da of Dr James S McNair, of Glasgow; 1 s, 1 da; *Career* MP (Lab) Aberdeen South 1966-70, pps to Pres BOT 1967, front bench oppn spokesman Scottish Affrs 1981- (chm Commons Select Ctee Scottish Affrs 1979-81), re-elected to Shadow Cabinet Nov 1983; *Style*— Donald Dewar Esq, MP; 23 Cleveden

Rd, Glasgow G12 0PQ (☎ (041) 334 2374)

DEWAR, Lady Elisabeth Jeronima; *née* Waldegrave; 3 da of 12 Earl Waldegrave; *b* 4 April 1936; *m* 17 Oct 1963, Hon John Dewar, s of 3 Baron Forteviot; 1 s, 3 da; *Style*— Lady Elisabeth Dewar; Aberdalgie House, Perth

DEWAR, Hamish Richard John; s of Richard John Gresley Dewar, of Hay Hedge, Bisley Nr Stroud, Glos, and Andrena Victoria Dewar; *b* 15 Jan 1956; *Educ* Sherborne, Downing Cambridge Univ (MA); *m* 21 May 1983, Anna Maria, da of Patrick Cloonan of Sawbridgeworth, Herts; 1 s (Lachlan b 18 July 1987), 1 da (India b 3 Jan 1989); *Career* specialist in conservation and restoration of painting; studied under Richard Maelzer at Edward Speelman Ltd 1977-81; own practise 1982-; main restoration works incl: David with Head of Goliath by Guido Reni, Seed of David (alter piece from Llandaff Cathedral) by Rossetti, Hope by G F Watts, Bubbles by Sir John Everett Millais; *Recreations* golf, racing; *Clubs* Sunningdale Golf; *Style*— Hamish Dewar, Esq; 23 Clapham Manor St, London SW4 6DN (☎ 01 622 0309); 9 Old Bond St, London W1X 3TA (☎ 01 629 0317, car tel 0860 622 537)

DEWAR, Ian Peter Furze; s of late John Thompson Dewar, and Joan Eileen, *née* Knott; *b* 2 Mar 1947; *Educ* Eltham GS, Coll for Distributive Trades (Dip M); *m* 1 Feb 1975, Wendy Jane, da of Brian Palmer; 2 s (Oliver John b 1985, Francis James b 1987); *Career* Brunnings Yorks 1979-82, dir THB & W 1982-84, dir O & M Direct 1984-85, fndr Dewar Coyle Maclean 1985-; MInstM 1970; *Recreations* food and drink; *Clubs* Pinball Owners Assoc; *Style*— Ian Peter Furze, Esq; 48 Palace Rd, East Molsey, Hampton Ct, Surrey KT8 9DW ; 147-148 Wardour St, London W1V 3TB (☎ 01 287 2343, fax 01 494 3502)

DEWAR, Ian Stewart; s of William Stewart Dewar, of Penarth (d 1955); *b* 29 Jan 1929; *Educ* Penarth County Sch, UC Cardiff, Jesus Coll Oxford (MA); *m* 1968, Nora Stephanie, da of Stephen House (d 1970), of Kettering; 1 s, 1 da; *Career* civil servant 1953-83: private sec to min of Labour 1956-58, asst civil service cmmr 1961-62, dir Manpower Res Unit 1965-66, under-sec Welsh Off 1973-83, planning inspr 1983-85; Glamorgan ccllr 1985-; JP Glamorgan 1985-; memb Governing Bodies: Univ of Wales, Nat Museum of Wales; *Recreations* hill-walking, historical research, book collecting; *Clubs* Civil Service, United Services Mess (Cardiff); *Style*— Ian Dewar, Esq, JP; 59 Stanwell Rd, Penarth, South Glamorgan CF6 2LR (☎ 0222 703255)

DEWAR, Hon John James Evelyn; s and h of 3 Baron Forteviot, MBE; *b* 5 April 1938; *Educ* Eton; *m* 17 Oct 1963, Lady Elisabeth Jeronima, 3 da of 12 Earl Waldegrave, KG; 1 s, 3 da; *Style*— The Hon John Dewar; Aberdalgie House, Perth

DEWAR, Robert James; CMG (1969), CBE (1964); s of Dr Robert Scott Dewar (d 1939); *b* 1923; *Educ* Glasgow HS, Edinburgh Univ, Wadham Oxford; *m* 1947, Christina Marianne, da of Olaf August Ljungberger of Stockholm (decd); 2 s, 1 da; *Career* chief conservator of Forests 1960-64, perm sec Natural Resources Malawi 1964-69; staff memb World Bank 1969-84, chief of agric div Regional Mission for Eastern Africa 1974-84; conslt to the World Bank 1984-86; *Recreations* golf, angling; *Clubs* Royal Cwlth Soc; *Style*— Robert Dewar Esq, CMG, CBE; 18 Middle Bourne Lane, Farnham, Surrey Guioznh (☎ 0252 713690); Dunsloy, 20 Birch Grove, Inverness-shire (☎ 295 047983)

DEWAR, Hon Simon Thomas; s of 3 Baron Forteviot, MBE, and Cynthia Monica Starkie; *b* 11 Feb 1941; *Educ* Bradfield; *m* 1970 (m dis 1973), Helen Bassett; m 2, 1979, Jennifer Alexandra, da of John Edward St John Hedge (d 1982), of Avoca, NSW; 3 da (Fiona b 1980, Alexandra b 1982, Mary b 1984); *Career* landowner (16,000 acres); *Recreations* game fishing, Yacht 'Samantha D'; *Clubs* Union, Imperial Services (Sydney); *Style*— The Hon Simon Dewar; Terling Pk, Moree, NSW 2400, Australia, (☎ 067 548 620)

DEWAR DURIE, Miss Christian Frances; da of Lt Col Raymond Varley Dewar Durie of Durie, Pewsey, Wilts *qv*, and Frances, *née* St John Maule; *b* 6 Aug 1945; *Educ* Downe House Newbury, Belfast Coll of Art, St Martin's Sch of Art (DipAD); *Career* asst designer H & M Rayne 1966-70, gp Designer Euromanik Ltd 1970-73, fashion co-ordinator AndréPeters-Louis Ferraud 1974-75, fashion dir Nigel French Enterprises Ltd 1975-78, managing ed Prism Fashion Publications 1978-81; owner and dir Parasol Assocs 1981-; Winston Churchill Memorial Tst Travel Fellowship 1969; crusader for better public servs and a cleaner Britain; FRSA 1967; *Recreations* skiing, travel, theatre, literature, art; *Style*— Miss Christian Dewar Durie; Parasol Associates, 3 King's House, 400 King's Road, London SW10 0LL (☎ 01 351 3236, telex 8951182 GECOMS G)

DEWAR-DURIE, Andrew Maule; s of Lt-Col Raymond Varley Durie of Durie, of Court House, Pewsey, Wiltshire, and Wendy, *née* Frances St John Maule; *b* 13 Nov 1939; *Educ* Cheam Sch Berks, Wellington ; *m* 25 Aug 1972, Marguerite Jamila, da of Graf Kunata Kottulinsky, of Vienna, Austria; 2 s (James Alexander b 26 April 1978, Philip Antony b 29 Aug 1986), 1 da (Nicola Louise b 19 Sept 1974); *Career* cmmnd Argyll & Sutherland Highlanders 1958-68, served: UK, BAOR, SE Asia, Aden; ret Capt 1968; White Horse Distillers 1968- 83: dir 1973-82, sr export dir 1982-83; int sales dir Long John Int (Whitbread & Co plc) 1983-88; James Burrough Distillers: Euro sales dir 1988, dep md 1988-89, md 1989-; Liveryman Worshipful Co of Distillers 1986; *Recreations* sailing, tennis, rough shooting, skiing; *Clubs* Army & Navy, The Cresta, Woodroffes; *Style*— Andrew Dewar-Durie, Esq; Woolfield Farm, Froxfield, nr Petersfield, Hants GU32 1DF (☎ 0730 88 201); James Burrough Distillers, 60 Montford Placek, Kennington Lane, London SG11 5DF (☎ 01 735 8131, fax 01 793 0228 telex 262 647)

DEWE, Roderick Gorrie; s of Douglas Percy Dewe (d 1978), and Rosanna Clements Gorrie (d 1971); *b* 17 Oct 1935; *Educ* abroad, Univ Coll Oxford (BA); *m* 1964, Carol Anne, da of Michael Beach Thomas (d 1941), of Herts; 1 s (Jonathan 1967), 1 da (Sarah b 1965); *Career* chm Dewe Rogerson Gp Ltd; *Recreations* golf, travel; *Clubs* City of London; *Style*— Roderick Dewe, Esq; 55 Duncan Terrace, London N1 (☎ 01 359 7318); Booking Hall, Southill Station, nr Biggleswade, Beds (☎ 0462 811 274); 3 1/2 London Wall Buildings, London Wall, EC2M 5SY (☎ 01 638 9571, fax 01 628 3444, telex 883610)

DEWE MATHEWS, Bernard Piers; TD (1965); s of Denys Cosmo Dewe Mathews (d 1985), of 1 Park Village West, Regents Park, London, and Elizabeth Jane, *née* Davies (d 1937); *b* 28 Mar 1937; *Educ* Ampleforth, Harvard Business Sch; *m* 10 Feb 1977, Catherine Ellen, da of Senator John Ignatius Armstrong (d 1977) of NSW Aust; 1 s (Charles-Frederick (Freddie) b 1985), 3 da (Jacqueline b 1978, Laura b 1979, Chloe b 1982); *Career* Nat Serv 2 Lt served Malaya 1956-57, TA Major 21 SAS Regt 1957-67; Edward Moore & Sons CAs 1957-62, BP Co Ltd 1962-65, Coopers & Lybrand & Assocs 1965-69, J Henry Schroder Wagg & Co Ltd 1969- (dir hd of project fin 1978-), dir Thames Power Ltd 1988-; govr St Paul's Girls' Prep Sch, cncl memb London C of C 1986-; memb SEATAG, ACA 1962, FCA 1972; *Recreations* music, opera, skiing, landscape gardening; *Clubs* Roehampton; *Style*— Bernard Dewe Mathews, Esq, TD; 112 Castelnau, Barnes, London SW13 9EU (☎ 01 741 2592); J Henry Schroder Wagg & Co Ltd, 120 Cheapside, London EC2V 6DS (☎ 01 382 6682, fax 01 382 3950, telex 885029)

DEWEY, Sir Anthony Hugh; 3 Bt (UK 1917) of South Hill Wood, Bromley, Kent; JP (1961); s of Maj Hugh Grahame Dewey, MC (d 1936) and gs of 2 Bt (d 1948); *b* 31 July 1921; *Educ* Wellington, RAC Cirencester; *m* 22 April 1949, Sylvia, da of late Dr Ross MacMahon; 2 s, 3 da; *Heir* s, Rupert Grahame Dewey; *Career* serv 1940-46 (NW Europe) Capt RA; farmer Somerset; *Clubs* Army & Navy; *Style*— Sir Anthony Dewey, Bt, JP; The Rag, Galhampton, Yeovil, Somerset (☎ 096340213)

DEWEY, Prof John Frederick; s of John Edward Dewey (d 1982), of London, and Florence Nellie Mary, *née* Davies; *b* 22 May 1937; *Educ* Bancrofts Sch, Univ of London (BSc, DIC, PhD), Univ of Cambrid (MA, ScD), Univ of Oxford (MA, DSc); *m* 4 July 1961, Frances Mary, da of William Blackhurst (d 1971), of Wistow, Cambs; 1 s (Jonathan Peter 1965), 1 da (Ann Penelope b 1963); *Career* lectr: Univ of Manchester 1960-64, Univ of Cambridge 1964-70; prof: Univ Albany New York 1970-82, Univ of Durham 1982-86, Univ of Oxford 1986-; FGS 1960, FRAS 1983, FRS 1985; *Recreations* water colour painting, model railways, tennis, skiing, cricket; *Clubs* Athenaeum; *Style*— Prof John Dewey; Sherwood Lodge, 93 Bagley Wood Rd, Kennington, Oxford OX1 5NA (☎ 0865 735525); Dept Earth Sciences, Parks Rd, Oxford OX1 3PR (☎ 0865 272021)

DEWEY, Rupert Grahame; s and h of Sir Anthony Dewey, 3 Bt; *b* 29 Mar 1953; *m* 23 Oct 1978, Suzanne Rosemary, da of late Andrew Lusk, of Fordie Comrie, Perthshire; 2 s (Thomas Andrew b 27 Jan 1982, Oliver Nicholas b 1984), 1 da (Laura Kate b 1988); *Career* slr Wood & Andry Chippenham; *Style*— Rupert Dewey, Esq; Church Farm House, Wellow, Bath BA2 8QS

DEWHIRST, Alistair Jowitt; CBE (1987); s of Capt Stanley Dewhirst (d 1955); *b* 23 Nov 1921; *Educ* Worksop Coll; *m* 1948, Hazel Eleanor, da of Ernest Reed (d 1979); 3 children; *Career* Maj 14 Army Burma (despatches 1945); chm I J Dewhirst Hldgs plc (clothing manufacturers); *Recreations* sailing, golf; *Clubs* Army and Navy, Royal Ocean Racing, Royal Yorks Yacht, Royal London Yacht, Ganton Golf, The Leeds; *Style*— Alistair Dewhirst, Esq, CBE; Nafferton Grange, Driffield, E Yorks; c/o I J Dewhirst Holdings plc, Duwear House, Westgate, Driffield, N Humberside (☎ 0377 42561)

DEWHIRST, Timothy Charles; s of Alistair Jowitt Dewhirst, CBE, of Driffield, N Humberside, and Hazel Eleanor, *née* Reed; *b* 19 August 1953; *Educ* Worksop Coll; *m* 15 July 1978, Prudence Rosalind, da of Frank Geoffrey Horsell, of Knaresborough, N Yorks; 1 s (Charles Alistair Geoffrey b 4 June 1980), 1 da (Samantha Prudence b 26 June 1983); *Career* chief exec I J Dewhirst Hldgs plc (clothing and toiletry manufacturers) 1986-; *Recreations* hockey, shooting; *Clubs* Annabel's, York Gimcrack; *Style*— Timothy C Dewhirst, Esq; Nafferton Heights, Nafferton, Nr Driffield, N Humberside YO25 0LD; I J Dewhirst Ltd, Duwear House, Westgate, Driffield, N Humberside YO25 7TH (☎ 0377 42561, telex 527530, fax 0377 43814, car ☎ 0836 620832)

DEWHURST, Prof Sir (Christopher) John; s of late John Dewhurst; *b* 2 July 1920; *Educ* St Joseph's Coll Dumfries, Victoria Univ Manchester; *m* 1952, Hazel Mary Atkin; 2 s, 1 da; *Career* formerly prof of obstetrics and gynaecology London Univ at Queen Charlotte's Hospital for Women, dean Inst of Obstetrics and Gynaecology 1979-85; Hon FACOG, Hon FRCSI, Hon FCOG (SA), Hon FRACOG, Hon DSc Sheffield, Hon MD Uruguay; FRCOG, FRCSE; kt 1977; *Style*— Prof Sir John Dewhurst; 21 Jack's Lane, Harefield, Middx UB9 6HE (☎ 089 582 5403)

DEWHURST, William; s of William Dewhurst (d 1967); *b* 12 Jan 1921; *Educ* Bolton Polytechnic; *m* 1940, Emily, da of Thomas Edward Horridge; 2 s; *Career* chartered engineer; Br Reinforced Concrete Engrg Co Ltd Stafford: joined 1949, works dir 1969, dir subsid Spencer Mesh Ltd (Wakefield) 1972-; MIMechE; *Recreations* golf; *Clubs* Wolstanton (Newcastle-under-Lyme), Brocton Hall Golf (Stafford); *Style*— William Dewhurst, Esq; Evesham, Old Coach Lane, Brocton, Stafford Ex. D.

DEWS, Peter; s of John Dews (d 1961), and Edna, *née* Bloomfield (d 1976); *b* 26 Sept 1929; *Educ* Queen Elizabeth GS Wakefield, Univ Coll Oxford (BA, MA); *m* 1960, Ann, da of Arthur Stanley Rhodes (d 1982); *Career* schoolmaster 1952-54; BBC dir sound and TV 1954-64; dir: Ravinia Festival Chicago 1964 and 1971, Birmingham Rep Theatre 1966-72, Hadrian VII Birmingham 1967 (London 1968, NY 1969), Chichester Festival Theatre 1978-80, Stratford Ontario 1973, 1981, 1984; Antoinette Perry (Tony) Award Broadway 1969, Guild of TV Drama Prodrs and Dirs award for Best Drama Prodn An Age of Kings 1960; Hon D Litt Bradford Univ; *Style*— Peter Dews, Esq; 29 Water Street, Deal, Kent CT14 6DJ (☎ 0304 368937)

DEXTER, Bunny Katharine Weston; da of M W Dexter, and H L Taylor Dexter; *Educ* Walnut Hill, Bryn Mawr Coll (BA), NYU Film Sch; *Career* journalist (science, political, travel), writer of numerous film scripts incl Flora (best short subject film Chicago Film Festival); dir European Games Agency 1988, invented board game SHRINK 1988; mangr political campaign New York State Senator election; sec Ambrose Tst; memb BAFTA; *Clubs* Chelsea Arts; *Style*— Ms Bunny Dexter; 37 Lennox Gardens, London SW1 (☎ 01 581 0196)

DEXTER, Edward Ralph; s of Ralph Marshall Dexter (d 1974), and Elise Genevieve, *née* Dartnall (d 1974); *b* 15 May 1935; *Educ* Radley, Jesus Coll Cambridge; *m* 1963, Susan Georgina, da of Thomas Cuthbert Longfield; 1 s (Thomas), 1 da (Genevieve); *Career* Nat Serv, 2 Lt 11 Hussars Malaya; dir Edward & Susan Dexter Ltd (P/R); cricket Capt Cambridge, Sussex and England 1960-65; contested (C) Cardiff 1965; Sunday Mirror cricket contributor, BBC/TV commentator; Malaya Campaign Medal; *Recreations* golf; *Clubs* Sunningdale Golf, Royal & Ancient Golf; *Style*— Ted Dexter, Esq; 20a Woodville Gardens, E··ling, London W5 2LQ (☎ 01 998 6863)

DHERSE, Jean-Loup Marie; s of Louis Charles Dherse, of Paris; *b* 17 Jan 1933; *Educ* Ecole St Louis de Gonzague Pris, William Penn Charter Sch Philadelphia, Ecole Polytechnique, Ecole des Mines de Paris; *m* 1958, Néia Marie Hedwige, da of Baron René de Cassin de Kainlis (d 1970); 2 da; *Career* with French Govt (Algeria, then Dept of Industry), Ciments Lafarge 1964-68, Pechiney Ugine Kuhlmann 1968-74; dir Rio Tinto Zinc Corpn Ltd 1974-83; vice pres World Bank Washington 1983-; Ordre du Mérite (Fr) 1979; *Recreations* Skiing; *Style*— Jean-Loup Dherse, Esq; 5116 Lowell Lane, NW Washington, DC 20016, USA

DHILLON, Tarlochan Singh; s of Darshan Singh Dhillon, of W Midlands, and Parkash Kaur Dhillon, *née* Uppal; *b* 27 Nov 1949; *Educ* King Edward VI GS Birmingham; *m* 17 July 1971, Ravinderjit Kaur, da of Bakshish Singh Randhawa, of India; 1 s (Bal Navjot Singh b 1983), 4 da (Tribhavanjit b 1977, Inderpreet b 1977, Gurmeet b 1980, Harjeet b 1981); *Career* CA; Russell Durie Kerr Watson & Co (later, Spicer & Pegler), audit supervisor Price Waterhouse & Co CAs 1974-78; divnl mgmnt accountant: Truflo Ltd 1978-79, Durapipe Ltd 1980-84; in practice on own account as Dhillon & Co; memb of social, cultural and charitables societies: Sandwell Community Relations Cncl 1982-84, tres Sandwell Cncl for Voluntary Service; fell of Inst of Chartered Accountants England & Wales, memb British Inst of Mgmnt 1968-74; *Recreations* reading, chess; *Style—* Tarlochan S Dhillon, Esq; 15 Arden Grove, Langley, Oldbury, Warley, W Midlands B69 4SU (☎ 021 544 6426); 33 Broad St, Wolverhampton, W Midlands WV1 1HZ

DHRANGADHARA, Maharaja Sriraj of Makharan-; His Highness Mahamandlesvar Maharana Sriraj Meghrajji III Jhaladhipati; 45th Regnant and Head of the Jhalla-Makhavan Clan and of the Shaktimant Order, &c; s of HH M Sriraj Ghanashyamsinhji, GCIE, KCSI, and suc 4 February and enthroned 15 February 1942; *b* 3 Mar 1923; *Educ* Local Rajput Hostel, Dhrangadhara Rajdham Shala (Palace School) which was moved to UK and became Millfield Somerset, Heath Mount and Haileybury Herts, St Joseph's Acad, Dehra Dun, Sivaji Mil School Poona, Christ Church, Ruskin School of Drawing, Institute of Social Anthropology Oxford (Dip and BLitt).; *m* 1943, Princess Brijrajkunvarba, da of HH the Maharaja of Marwar-Jodhpur; 3 s; *Heir* s, Yuvaraj of Dhrangadhara, Jhalavrit Maharajkumar Shri Sodhsalji; *Career* governed 1942-48; agrarian, social and constitutional reformer; acceded to India 9 August 1947; ceded powers to Saurashtra 1948; Upa-Rajpramukh and Acting Rajpramukh of Saurashtra 1948-52; Oxford 1952-58: elected to Gujarat Legve Assembly and from Jhalavad (Gujarat) to Parliament (Lok Sabha) 1967; promoter and intendant gen Consultation of Rulers of Indian States in Concord for India 1967. KCSI, FRAS, FRAI, ARHistS; *Recreations* research in sociology, social history, ethnography; *Style—* His Highness Maharaja Sriraj of Dhrangadhara; 108 Malcha Marg, New Delhi-110021

DIAMAND, Peter; CBE (1972); *b* 1913; *Educ* Schiller-Realgymnasium Berlin, Berlin Univ; *m* 1, 1948 (m dis 1971), Maria Curcio; m 2, (m dis 1979) Sylvia Rosenberg; 1 s; *Career* dir: Holland Festival 1948-65, Edinburgh Int Festival 1965-78; conslt: Orchestre de Paris 1976-, Teatro alla Scala (Milan) 1977-78, dir and gen mangr Royal Philharmonic Orch 1978-81, dir Mozart Festival Paris 1981- ; Hon LLD Edinburgh; Offr des Arts et des Lettres France 1985; *Style—* Peter Diamand, Esq, CBE; 28 Eton Court, Eton Ave, London NW3 (☎ 01 586 1203)

DIAMOND, Prof Aubrey Lionel; s of Alfred Diamond (d 1951), of London, and Millie, *née* Solomons (d 1963); *b* 28 Dec 1923; *Educ* Central Foundation Sch London, LSE (LLM); *m* 26 Nov 1955, Eva Marianne, da of Dr Adolf Bobasch (d 1976), of London; 1 s (Paul b 1960), 1 da (Nicola b 1958); *Career* RAF 1943-47; law dept LSE 1957-66, ptnr Lawford & Co 1959-71 (consult 1987-), law prof QMC 1966-71, law cmmr 1971-76, dir Inst Advanced Legal Studies 1976-86; hon fell LSE 1984, fell QMC 1984, law prof Notre Dame Univ (USA) 1987-, co dir London law centre 1987-; visiting prof: Stanford Univ, Virginia Univ, Tulane Univ, Melbourne Univ, Univ of East Africa; memb Latey ctee on Age of Majority 1965- 67, vice pres Inst Trading Standards Admin 1975-, chm Hamlyn Tst 1977-88, adviser on Security interests DTI 1986-88 (cncl memb 1976); *Books* The Consumer, Society and the Law (with Sir Gordon Borrie, 1963), Introduction To Hire-Purchase Law (1967), Commercial and Consumer Credit (1982); *Style—* Prof Aubrey Diamond; University of Notre Dame, London Law Centre, 7 Albemarle St, London (☎ 01 493 9002, fax 01 408 4465)

DIAMOND, Dennis Oscar; s of Capt Sidney Diamond, DCM (d 1951), of Colwyn Bay, and Sarah, *née* Cooper (d 1968); *b* 5 August 1931; *Educ* Rydal Sch, Clare Coll Cambridge (MA); *m* 1, June 1957 (m dis 1969), Elizabeth Mary June, da of Ambrose Davies (d 1969), of Cambridge; 3 da (Kerry Ann b 4 May 1958, Lesley Jane b 30 Sept 1959, Shirley Ruth b 10 April 1963); m 2, 17 April 1970, Josephine; *Career* Nat Serv 1950-52, cmmnd Welch Regt 1951; slr 1957, asst rec 1984, sr ptnr Walker Smith & Way Chester; memb Rugby Football Union Ctee for Cheshire 1984-; Parly candidate (Lib) East Flintshire 1963-65; memb Law Soc; *Recreations* rugby, reading, WWI; *Clubs* East India; *Style—* Dennis Diamond, Esq; 2 Cedar Park, Vicars Cross, Chester (☎ 0244 311208); Walker Smith & Way, 26 Nicholas Street, Chester CH1 2PQ (☎ 0244 321111, fax 0244 327080, telex 61150 WAYLEX)

DIAMOND, Hon Derek; s of Baron Diamond PC (Life Peer); *b* 1933; *Style—* The Hon Derek Diamond; c/o Aynhoe, Doggetts Wood Lane, Chalfont-St-Giles, Bucks HP8 4TH

DIAMOND, Col (Clifford) Hugh; s of George Clifford Diamond, OBE (d 1985), of The Cathedral Green, Llandaff, Cardiff, and Beryl, *née* Jones (d 1984); *b* 1 Jan 1934; *Educ* Cardiff HS, RMA Sandhurst, Nat Def Coll; *m* Feb 1960, Susan Jane Mayo, da of Gerald Mayo Meates (d 1944); 1 s (Jonathan b 1963); *Career* cmmnd The Welch Regt 1954 (amalgamated into Royal Regt of Wales 1969), seconded to 2 KEO Gurkha Rifles 1962-65, served BAOR, Middle East, Far East, Australia, Turkey, Africa, UK, final appt def and mil attaché Khartoum and Mogadishu; OstJ 1973; *Recreations* shooting, social tennis, gardening under command of wife, reading, music; *Clubs* Naval and Military, MCC; *Style—* Col Hugh Diamond; Moor Farm Cottage, Bodenham Moor, Herefordshire (☎ 056 884 398)

DIAMOND, Hon Joan; da of Baron Diamond PC (Life Peer); *b* 1949; *Style—* The Hon Joan Diamond; c/o Aynhoe, Doggetts Wood Lane, Chalfont St Giles, Bucks

DIAMOND, Baron (Life Peer UK 1970); John Diamond; PC (1965); s of late Rev S Diamond, of Leeds; *b* 30 April 1907; *Educ* Leeds GS; *m* 1, 1932 (m dis 1947); 2 s, 1 da; m 2, 1948, Julie; 1 da; *Career* former dir: Sadlers Wells Trust Ltd, London Opera Centre; MP (Lab) Manchester 1945-51, Gloucester 1957-70; chief sec to the Treasury 1964-70 (memb of Cabinet 1968-70); dep chm of ctees House of Lords 1974; chm: Royal Cmmn on the Distribution of Income and Wealth 1974-79, Indust and Parliament Tst 1976-; tstee Cncl for Social Democracy 1981-; hon tres Fabian Soc; elected SDP Leader in House of Lords 1982; *Style—* Rt Hon Lord Diamond, PC; Aynhoe, Doggetts Wood Lane, Chalfont St Giles, Bucks

DIAMOND, Hon Martin; s of Baron Diamond PC (Life Peer); *b* 1935; *Style—* The Hon Martin Diamond; c/o Aynhoe, Doggetts Wood Lane, Chalfont St Giles, Bucks

DIAMOND, Peter Michael; s of William Howard Diamond (d 1979), and Dorothy Gladys, *née* Powell (d 1961); *b* 5 August 1942; *Educ* Bristol GS, Queens' Coll Cambridge (MA); *m* 1968, Anne Marie; 1 s (Benjamin b 1969), 1 da (Candida b 1972); *Career* chief arts & museums offr Bradford 1976-80, chm Yorkshire Sculpture Park 1978-81, dir Birmingham Museums & Art Gallery 1980-; memb cncl Aston Univ 1983-, memb Craft Cncl 1981-84; *Style—* Michael Diamond, Esq; 40 Jordan Rd, Four Oaks, Sutton Coldfield, W Midlands B75 5AB (☎ 021 308 3287); City Museum & Art Gallery, Chamberlain Square, Birmingham B3 3DH (☎ 021 235 2833)

DIBBEN, Capt George Walter; OBE; s of Harry Herbert Dibben (d 1924), of Gosport, Hants, and Clara Mary Ann, *née* Battey (d 1970); *b* 4 July 1913; *Educ* Gosport Secdy Sch; *m* 16 Dec 1944, Barbara Mary, da of Sidney Hodgson (d 1973), of Bickley, Kent; 2 s (Robert b 1945, Nigel b 1950), 1 da (Bridget b 1947); *Career* RN Engine Room Artificer Apprentice 1929; attained cmmnd rank 1936 as Sub Lt (E), RNC Greenwich 1936-37, HMS Argus 1937-39, early pt of war in cruisers HMS Aurora and Emerald in Far East, apptd trg offr at RN Apprentice Trg Establishment Newcastle under Lyme Staffs transfd to FAA 1944, RN Air Station Abbotsinch Renfrewshire as Lt Cdr (E) RN Air Station Halfar Malta, returned to UK to take up appt in Admiralty with Dir Aircraft Maintenance and Repair, reverted to Marine Engrg appt to HMS Newfoundland as Engr Offr with rank of Cmdr (E) serving in Middle East incl Suez Crisis, as Marine Engr Overseer North West area for RN, dep Supt N Ireland (Belfast) aircraft repair yard, Capt 1960, apptd to staff of Flag Offr Trg with responsibilities for air engrg matters in Air Stations in FOFT's cmd, returned Belfast as Supt, RNARY, Sydenham, i/c Civilian Manned Establishment 1966-68, ret; *Style—* Capt George Dibben, Esq, OBE

DIBBEN, Kenneth Francis; s of Stanley Cyril Dibben (d 1978), and Edna Florence, *née* Hobbs (d 1977); *b* 13 Feb 1929; *Educ* King Edward VI Sch Southampton, Worcester Royal GS, Southampton Univ (BCom); *m* 1962, Dora Mary Bower, *née* Tunbridge; 1 s (Gye b 1975); *Career* former dir Hambros Bank Ltd, former Cons pty candidate; dir: Kalamazoo, Chilworth Centre, Univs Superannuation Scheme, Great American Software Inc; memb Univs Authties Panel, tres Southampton Univ, hon tres Wider Shareownership Cncl and Fountain Soc; Freeman City of London, memb Worshipful Co of CAs; FCA; CBIM, FCT; *Clubs* Carlton, Hong Kong (HK); *Style—* Kenneth Dibben, Esq; 3 Marsham Ct, Marsham St, London SW1P 4JY (☎ 01 821 9153); Naish Priory, East Coker, Somerset BA22 9HQ (☎ 093 586 2201)

DIBBLE, Robert Kenneth; s of Herbert William Dibble (d 1973), and Irene Caroline Dibble; *b* 28 Dec 1938; *Educ* Westcliff HS for Boys; *m* 26 Aug 1972, Teresa Frances, da of James Vincent MacDonnell; 4 s (William b 5 July 1973, Thomas b 12 April 1975, Edward b 7 Feb 1979, Matthew b 31 Dec 1980); *Career* RNC Dartmouth 1955-58, HMS Belton 1958-59, Lt HMS Britannia 1959- 60, HMS Caesar 1961-62, Russian interpreter's course 1962-64, mixed manned ship USS Claude V Ricketts 1964-65, long communications course 1965-66, Sqdn Communications Offr HMS Ajax 1966-67, Lt Cdr HMS Hamshire 1967-68, head of electronic warfare HMS Mercury 1968- 70, def fell Kings Coll London 1970-71, Staff Ops Offr to Sr Naval Offr W Indies 1971-72, Cdr naval staff MOD 1972-75, i/c HMS Eskimo 1975-76, directing staff Maritime Tactical Sch 1976-77; articled clerk then slr Linklaters and Paines 1978-81, ptnr Wilde Sapte 1982; Freeman City of London; memb: City of London Solicitors Co, Worshipful Co of Shipwrights; *Recreations* family, tennis, music, reading, languages; *Style—* Robert Dibble, Esq; Wilde Sapte, Queensbridge House, 60 Upper Thames St, London EC4V 3BD (☎ 01 236 3050, fax 01 236 9624, telex 887793 WILDES G)

DIBELA, Sir Kingsford; GCMG (1983, CMG 1978); s of Norman Dibela and Edna Dalauna; *b* 16 March 1932; *m* 1952, Winifred Tomolaria; 2 s, 4 da; *Career* MP Papua New Guinea 1975-82, former speaker National Parl; govr-gen Papua New Guinea 1983-; *Style—* Sir Kingsford Dibela, GCMG; Government House, Port Moresby, Papua New Guinea

DICE, Brian Charles; s of Frederic Dice, MC, of Minehead, Somerset (d 1979); *b* 2 Sept 1936; *Educ* Clare Coll Cambridge (MA); *m* 22 May 1965, Wendy, da of De Warrenne Harrison (d 1983); 2 da (Nicola b 1968, Melissa b 1971); *Career* Cadbury Schweppes plc 1960-86 (dir 1979-86), chief exec Br Waterways Bd 1986-; *Style—* Brian Dice, Esq; Stratton Wood, Beaconsfield, Bucks HP91HS

DICK, (John) Antony; s of Cdre John Mathew Dick, CB, CBE (d 1981), and Anne Moir, *née* Stewart; *b* 23 March 1934; *Educ* Trinity Coll Glenalmond, Worcester Coll Oxford (BA); *m* 15 May 1967, Marigold Sylvia, da of Rev Cecil B Verity; 1 s (Crispin b 1971), 2 da (Amy-Clare b 1972, Jasmine b 1974); *Career* RN 1952-54; qualified CA 1956; investment mangr: Iraq Petroleum Co Ltd 1961-67, J Henry Schroder Wagg and Co Ltd 1967-68; md Kingsdrive Investmt Mgmnt Ltd 1969-70; dir GT Mgmnt plc 1970-, non exec dir: USDC Investmt Tst 1987, Nordic Investmnt Tst 1985, GT Investmt Fund SA 1980; memb Advsy Ctee to Local Authy Mutual Investmt Tst; *Recreations* sailing, psychological astrology; *Style—* Antony Dick, Esq; 26 Chalcot Square, London NW1 8YA (☎ 01 722 5126); GT Management plc, 8 Devonshire Square, London EC2M 4YJ (☎ 01 283 2575, fax 01 626 6176, telex 886100)

DICK, Brian Booth; s of James Dick, and Doris Ethel, *née* Booth; *b* 20 Dec 1943; *Educ* Kilmarnock Acad; *m* 19 Oct 1966, Caryl Anne, da of James McClure; 1 s (Alistair b 25 Oct 1972), 2 da (Laura b 26 Oct 1967, Susanna b 19 May 1969); *Career* sec: Crown Continental Merchant Bank Jamaica 1971-74, Caribbean Bank 1974-76; fin dir and sec: Lyle Shipping plc 1980-83, Noble Grossart Ltd 1983-; involved with: Stewart Melville Coll hockey, Holy Corner Church Centre, Eric Liddell Centre; MICAS; *Recreations* hockey, golf, curling, refereeing sport; *Style—* Brian Dick, Esq; 2 Ravelston House Rd, Edinburgh EH4 3LW (☎ 031 332 1120); Noble Grossart Ltd, 48 Queen St, Edinburgh EH2 3NR (☎ 031 226 7011, fax 031 226 6032)

DICK, Gavin Colquhoun; s of John Dick (d 1949), of Motherwell, Lanarkshire, and Catherina MacAuslan, *née* Henderson (d 1983); *b* 6 Sept 1928; *Educ* Hamilton Acad, Glasgow Univ (MA), Balliol Coll Oxford (MA), SOAS; *m* 20 Dec 1952, Elizabeth Frances, da of Jonathan Hutchinson (d 1972), of Haslemere, Surrey; 2 da (Helen b 1953, Catherine b 1956); *Career* Lt RTR 1952-54; Civil Serv DTI (formerly Bd of Trade): asst princ 1954-58, princ 1958-67, UK trade cmmr Wellington NZ 1961-64, asst sec 1967-75, jt sec Review Ctee on Overseas Representation 1968-69, under-sec 1975-84, govr Coll of Air Trg Hamble 1975-80, bd memb English Estates 1982-84, conslt Off of Telecommunications 1984-87, conslt radio communications div 1987; *Recreations* linguistics, bird-watching; *Clubs* United Oxford and Cambridge; *Style—* Gavin Dick, Esq; Fell Cottage, Bayley's Hill, Sevenoaks, Kent TN14 6HS (☎ 0732 453704); Waterloo Bridge House, Waterloo Road, London SE1 8UA (☎ 01 215 2068, 01 215 7877, fax 01 928 5746, telex 2152158)

DICK, Prof George Williamson Auchinvole; s of Rev David A Dick (d 1965), of Ramsay Gardens, Edinburgh, and Blanche, *née* Spence (d 1945); *b* 14 August 1914;

Educ Royal HS Edinburgh, Edinburgh Univ, John Hopkins Univ Baltimore USA; *m* 6 June 1941, Brenda Marian, da of Samuel Cook; 2 s (Bruce b 3 Feb 1948, John-Mark b 24 Aug 1953), 2 da (Alison b 18 Jun 1950, Caroline b 14 April 1952); *Career* WW II Lt RAMC 1940, Capt RAMC graded specialist 1941, East Africa Cmd 1942-46 (Maj, specialist pathology, OC Mobile Lab BR and Italian Somaliland and reserved areas, mobile res unit), Lt Col OC Med Div No IEA gen hosp; pathologist Colonial Med Res Serv 1946-51; fell 1947-48: Rockefeller Fndn, John Hopkins Univ (res fell 1948-49); scientific staff MRC 1951-54, prof microbiology Queen's Univ Belfast 1955-65, dir Bland-Sutton Inst 1966-73, Bland-Sutton prof pathology Middlesex Hosp Med Sch London Univ 1966-73; 1973-81: asst dir Br Postgrad Med Fedn, postgrad dean SW Thames RHA, prof pathology London Univ, hon lectr and hon conslt Inst Child Health; chm MARC Ltd, pres Inst Med Laboratory Technol 1966-76, tres RCPath 1973-78, pres Rowhook Med Soc 1975-; memb: Mid Downs Health Authy W Sussex 1981-84, Jt Bd Clinical Nursing Studies 1982-85; chm DHSS/Regnl Librarians ctee 1982-; examiner Med Schs (in UK, Dublin, Nairobi, Kampala, Riyadh, Jeddah), assessor HNS and CMS S London Coll; Liveryman Worshipful Co Apothecaries; memb RSM, BMA, Int Epidemiol Soc, Path Soc GB (and Ireland); *Books* Immunisation (1978, re-issued as Practical Immunisation 1986), Immunilogy of Infectious Diseases (ed 1979), Health on Holiday and other Travels (1982); over 200 scientific papers on yellowfever, arbor viruses, polio, hepatitis, multiple sclerosis and others; *Recreations* epidemiology of infectious diseases and prevention, travel, gardening, natural history; *Style*— Professor George Dick

DICK, John Alexander; MC (1944), QC (Scotland 1963); yr s of Rev David Auchinvole Dick, and Blanche Hay Spence; *b* 1 Jan 1920; *Educ* Maid Academy Anstruther, Univ of Edinburgh; *m* 1951, Rosemary Benzie, *née* Sutherland; *Career* cmmnd Royal Scots 1942, served Italy 1944, Palestine 1945-46; called to Scots Bar 1949, lectr in public law Univ of Edinburgh 1953-60, jr counsel in Scotland to HM Commissioners of Customs and Excise 1956-63; cmmr under Terrorism (N Ireland) Order 1972-73; Sheriff of the Lothians and Borders at Edinburgh 1968-78, Sheriff Princ of N Strathclyde 1978-82, Sheriff Princ of Glasgow and Strathkelvin 1980-86; *Recreations* hillwalking; *Clubs* Royal Scots (Edinburgh); *Style*— Sir John Alexander Dick, MC, QC; 66 Northumberland Street, Edinburgh EH3 6JE (☎ 031 556 6081)

DICK, John Kenneth; CBE; s of late John Dick, and Beatrice May, *née* Chitty; *b* 5 April 1913; *Educ* Sedbergh; *m* 1942, Pamela Madge *née* Salmon; 3 s (1 decd); *Career* CA Mann Judd & Co Chartered Accountants 1936 (ptnr 1947); Mitchell Cotts Gp Ltd: jt md 1957, md 1959, dep chm 1964, chm 1966-78; memb: Cwlth Devpt Corpn 1967-80, Br Nat Export Ctee 1968-71, chm ctee for ME trade 1968-71, pres ME Assoc 1971-81 (vice-pres 1970); chm: Hume Hldgs Ltd 1975-80, NM Rothschild (Leasing) Ltd 1978-; dir: NM Rothschild and Sons Ltd 1978-, Esperanza Ltd 1978-80, Sinclair Res Ltd 1983-; memb Covent Gdn Market Authy 1976-82; FCA, FRSA; *Recreations* golf; *Style*— John Dick, Esq, CBE; Overbye, 18 Church St, Cobham, Surrey, (☎ 01 280 5000)

DICK, Rear-Adm Royer Mylius; CB (1951), CBE (1943), DSC (1918); s of Louis Henry Mylius Dick (d 1928), and Edith Alice, *née* Guy (d 1945); *b* 14 Oct 1897; *Educ* RNC Osborne, RNC Dartmouth; *m* 1, 1928, Agnes Mary, da of late H D Harben; 1 s (ka Cyprus, RM 1956), 1 da (d 1985); m 2, 1955, Vera Sadie, da of Sir John Henry (d 1930), and widow of Col Bertram Pott; *Career* midshipman 1914; at sea 1914-18 Falklands, Jutland, N Russia; Lt 1918, Cdr 1933, Capt 1940, Cdre 1942, Rear-Adm 1949; DCS Med Station 1940-42 (Matapan), Br Admty Delgn to Washington 1942, COS to C-in-C Mediterranean Station Adm Sir Andrew Cunningham 1942-44 (despatches twice) , HMS Belfast 1944-46, dir Tactical and Staff Duties (Admiralty) 1947-48, COS to Flag Offr W Europe 1948-50, naval ADC to HM The King 1949, Flag Offr Trg Sqdn 1951-52, Standing Gp liaison offr to N Atlantic Cncl 1952-55, Vice Adm (Actg) 1953, ret 1955; cmmr-in-chief St John Ambulance Bde (dep C-in-C 1957-62, C-in-C 1962-67); dep chm Horticultural Marketing Cncl 1960-63, chm Royal Utd Service Inst 1965-67, a vice-pres Royal UK Beneficent Assoc 1979; chm St John Cncl for London 1971-75; KStJ 1961, Bailiff Grand Cross Order of St John 1967; Offr Legion of Merit (USA) 1943, Offr Legion of Honour 1943, Croix de Guerre (avec palme) 1946; *Clubs* Army & Navy, RAC; *Style*— Rear-Adm Royer Dick, CB, CBE, DSC; 15 Dorchester Court, Sloane St, London SW1X 9SE (☎ 01 235 8171)

DICK-LAUDER, Lady; Hester Marguerite; da of Lt-Col George Cecil Minett Sorell-Cameron, CBE (d 1947), by his w Marguerite Emily (d 1968), elder da of Hon Hamilton James Tollemache; *b* 1920; *m* 13 Nov 1945, Maj Sir George Andrew Dick-Lauder, 12 Bt (d 1981); 2 s, 2 da; *Style*— Lady Dick-Lauder; Firth Mill House, by Auchendinny, Roslin, Midlothian

DICK-LAUDER, Mark Andrew; s of Sir George Dick-Lauder, 12 Bt (d 1981); bro and hp of Sir Piers Dick-Lauder, 13 Bt; *b* 3 May 1951; *m* 1970 (m dis 1982), Jeanne, *née* Mullineaux, of Bolton; 1 s (Martin b 1976); *Style*— Mark Dick-Lauder, Esq

DICKENS, Prof (Arthur) Geoffrey; CMG (1974); s of Arthur James Dickens (d 1957), of Hull, and Gertrude Helen, *née* Grasby (d 1979); *b* 6 July 1910; *Educ* Hymers Coll Hull, Magdalen Coll Oxford (BA, MA), Univ of London (D Lit); *m* 1 Aug 1936, Molly (d 1978), da of Capt Walter Bygott, RE (d 1959); 2 s (Peter Geoffrey b 1940, Paul Jonathan b 1945); *Career* served RA 1940-45, 2 Lt 1941, Lt 1942, Capt 1943; fell of Keble Coll Oxford 1933-49; prof of history: Univ of Hull 1949-62 (pro-vice-chllr 1959-62), King's Coll London 1962-67 (FKC 1967), Univ of London 1967-77; dir Inst of Historical Research 1967-77; foreign sec Br Acad 1968-78; pres: Central London Branch Historical Assoc 1980-, Hornsey Historical Soc 1982-, German History Soc 1980-89; hon vice-pres: Royal Historical Soc 1977-, The Historical Assoc 1978-; Hon D Litt 1977: Kent, Sheffield, Leicester, Liverpool, Hull; FBA 1966, FSA 1963, FRHistS 1947; Order of Merit (Cdr's Class) of Federal Republic of Germany 1980; *Books* 17 books and numerous articles on the Renaissance and Reformation period and local history, mainly Yorkshire; *Recreations* studying modern British painting (ca 1900-50); *Clubs* Athenaeum; *Style*— Prof A G Dickens, CMG, FBA; Institute of Historical Research, Senate House, London WC1E 7HU (☎ 01 636 0272)

DICKENS, Geoffrey Kenneth; JP (St Albans, Barnsley then Oldham 1968), MP (C) Littleborough and Saddleworth 1983-; s of John Wilfred Dickens (d 1979); *b* 26 August 1931; *Educ* E Lane Sch Wembley, Harrow Tech Coll Acton Tech Coll; *m* 1956, Norma Evelyn Boothby; 2 s; *Career* Nat Serv RAF; chm Cleveland Octanes Ltd; chm: Sandridge Parish Cncl 1968-69 (memb 1960-73), St Albans Rural Dist Cncl 1970-71 (memb 1967-74); memb Herts CC 1970-75; hon alderman City and Dist of St Albans 1976; MP (C) Huddersfield West 1979-83; Royal Humane Soc Testimonial on Vellum for Bravery Saving Lives; vice-chm Assoc of Cons Clubs, member Parly Select Ctee on Energy, contested Teeside Middlesbrough Feb 1974; contested Ealing North Oct 1974; vice pres Lancashire Fed of Conservative Clubs; *Clubs* Conservative; *Style*— Geoffrey Dickens, Esq, JP, MP; The Sycamores, Greenfield, Oldham, Lancs OL3 7PB (☎ 045 77 71191)

DICKENS, Air Cdre Sir Louis Walter; DFC (1940, AFC 1938), DL (Berks 1966); s of C H Dickens; *b* 28 Sept 1903; *Educ* Clongowes Wood Sch, Cranwell Cadet Coll; *m* 1939, Ena Alice (d 1971), da of F J Bastable; 1 s, 1 da; *Career* RAF Bomber Cmd 1940 and 1943-44, Flying Instr Canada 1941-42, SHAEF France 1944-45, ret 1947; chm Berks CC 1965-68 (memb 1952-74, Alderman 1959-73); kt 1968; *Style*— Air Cdre Sir Louis Dickens, DFC, DL; Wayford, Bolney Ave, Shiplake, Henley, Oxon

DICKENS, Monica Enid (Mrs R O Stratton); MBE (1981); da of late Henry Charles Dickens; *b* 10 May 1915; *Educ* St Paul's Girls' Sch Hammersmith; *m* 1951, Cdr Royal Olin Stratton, US Navy; 2 da; *Career* writer; fndr of US Samaritans; *Books* One Pair of Hands, Mariana, One Pair of Feet, The Fancy, Thursday Afternoon, The Happy Prisoner, Joy and Josephine, Flowers on the Grass, My Turn to Make the Tea, No More Meadows, The Winds of Heaven, The Angel in the Corner, Man Overboard, The Heart of London, Cobbler's Dream, Kate and Emma, The Room Upstairs, The Landlord's Daughter, The Listeners, The House at World's End, Summer at World's End, Follyfoot, World's End in Winter, Dora at Follyfoot, Spring Comes to World's End, Talking of Horses, Last Year When I was Young, The Horse at Follyfoot, Stranger at Follyfoot, An Open Book (autobiography), The Messenger, Ballad of Favour, The Haunting of Bellamy 4, Cry of a Seagull, Miracles of Courage, Dear Doctor Lily (1988), Enchantment (1989); *Style*— Miss Monica Dickens, MBE; Lavender Cottage, Brightwalton, Berks RG16 OBY (☎ 048 82 302)

DICKENS, Olive Kate; da of George Rogers (d 1960), of Ivy House, Cyfarthfa, Merthyr Tydfil, and Florence Kate, *née* Davies (d 1961); *b* 28 July 1902; *Educ* Manor House Sch Cambridge, Cours Monceau Paris; *m* 24 July 1929, Capt William Samuel Dickens, OBE, KPM, s of Capt William Dickens (ka); *Career* Capt Womens Section Mauritius Police Force Colonial Serv 1939-41, first chief supervisor Jewish detainment camp Mauritius, quartermaster Red Cross Beau Bassin Div Mauritius, cmmr (B Co) Girl Guides 1942, prison active welfare Mauritius; film censor Mauritius 1940-44; *Recreations* music, painting, bridge; *Clubs* CGH; *Style*— Mrs Olive Dickens; 6 Kings Gate, 111 The Drive, Hove, East Sussex BN3 6EK (☎ 0273 21 781)

DICKENSON, Lt-Col Charles Royal; CMG (1965); s of Charles Roland and Gertrude Dickenson; *b* 17 June 1907; *Educ* Shaftesbury GS Dorset; *m* 1950, Hendrika Jacoba Margaretha Schippers; 2 da; *Career* serv WWII Royal Signals 1939-45 Lt-Col; engrg apprentice Br PO 1923, Br PO HQ 1932-39; asst controller Telecommunications 1945-47, BPO HQ London 1947-50, loaned to S Rhodesia Govt 1950-54, controller of Telecommunications Miny of Post Fedn of Rhodesia and Nyasaland 1954-57, regnl controller N Rhodesia Fedn of Rhodesia and Nyasaland 1957-61, dep postmaster-gen Rhodesia and Nyasaland 1961-62, postmaster-gen 1962-63, postmaster-gen of Rhodesia 1964-68, ret; hon memb S Africa Inst of Electronic and Radio Engrs 1966; Independence Commemorative Decoration, Offr Legion of Merit (both Rhodesia); *Recreations* growing orchids, photography; *Style*— Lt-Col Charles Dickenson, CMG; 4600 Gatlin Oaks Lane, Orlando, Florida 32806, USA (☎ 407 859 5433)

DICKER, Col Geoffrey Seymour Hamilton; CBE (1965), TD (1953), DL (1963), DCL (1985); s of Capt Arthur Seymour Hamilton Dicker, MBE (d 1974), of Oakley House, Acle, Norfolk, and Margaret Kathleen, *née* Walley (d 1971); *b* 20 July 1920; *Educ* Haileybury, King's Coll Cambridge; *m* 1942, Josephine Helen, da of F G Penman (d 1963), of Inwood, Bushey, Herts; 1 s, 2 da (1 decd); *Career* joined Royal Signals 1940, Adj 6 Armoured Divisional Signals 1943-45, GSO (2) AFHQ Caserta 1945-46 (MBE, despatches), cmmnd TA 1948, Hon Col 54 (E Anglian) Signal Regt (TA) 1960-67, Hon Col 36 (E) Signal Regt (V) 1979-85, ADC (TA) to HM The Queen 1965-70, vice chm Cncl of TA and VR Assocs 1975-80, Hon Col Cmdt Royal Corps of Signals 1970-80, chm Reserve Forces Assoc 1976-83, vice pres (UK) Inter-Allied Confederation of Reserve Offrs 1976-83; CA 1950; tres Univ of East Anglia 1973-85, pro-chllr and chm of Council 1985-, chm Eastern Region Board Eagle Star Insurance Co 1969-86, pres Great Yarmouth Conservative Assoc 1969-86, ptnr Lovewell Blake and Co Gt Yarmouth, Lowestoft, Norwich and Thetford (ret 1983); tres Scientific Exploration Soc 1987; *Recreations* golf, sailing (yachts 'Skall III', 'Camberwell Beauty', motor cruiser 'Leomina'); *Clubs* Norfolk, Army and Navy, Royal Norfolk and Suffolk Yacht (Cdre 1978-80), Norfolk Broads Yacht (Cdre 1959-62); *Style*— Col Geoffrey Dicker, CBE, TD, DL; The Hollies, Strumpshaw, Norwich NR13 4NS (☎ 0603 712357)

DICKIE, Brian James; s of Robert Kelso Dickie and Harriet Elizabeth, *née* Riddell (d 1969); *b* 23 July 1941; *Educ* Haileybury, Trinity Coll Dublin; *m* 1968, Victoria Teresa Sheldon, da of Edward Christopher Sheldon Price, of Glos; 2 s (Patrick b 1969, Edward b 1974), 1 da (Eliza b 1970); *Career* artistic dir Wexford Festival 1967-73, administrator Glyndebourne Touring Opera 1967-81, gen administrator Glyndebourne 1981-; *Clubs* Garrick; *Style*— Brian Dickie Esq,; c/o The Canadian Opera Co, 227 Front St East, Toronto, Ontario M5A 1E8, Canada

DICKIE, Colonel Charles George; TD (1975); s of Rev Robert Pittendreigh Dickie (d 1934), of The Manse, Longriggend, Lanarks, and Margaret, *née* Brock (d 1964); *b* 21 Jan 1932; *Educ* Uddington GS; *m* 5 Oct 1956, Sheena Mitchell, da of William Marshall (d 1971); 1 s (Stuart b 28 Feb 1963), 2 da (Dianne b 8 May 1961, Susan b 6 Feb 1965); *Career* Nat Serv RA 1950-52; TA 1952-56 and 1963-82, RARO 1983-; RASC to 1965, then RCT, then staff appts SOI Liaison, US Logistics Tport Branch NW Dist Col (TA) Non-infantry HQ NW Dist, ADC (TA) to HM The Queen 1980-83; co sec Liverpool Bldg Soc 1972-82; (now Birmingham Midshires Bldg Soc) 1982-; dir Kolkaas and Hayward Services Ltd; Mersey Synod tres Utd Reform Church 1980-84; pres CBSI 1989- (dep pres 1988-89, and memb 1980-), civil rep W Midlands Reg Forces Employment Assoc, vice-chm TA & VRA NW Eng; DL Merseyside 1983-88; FCBSI, AIBScot; *Clubs* Army & Navy, Inst of the RCT ; *Style*— Colonel CG Dickie, TD; The Malthouse, Folley Rd, Ackleton, Shropshire, WJ6 7JL (☎ 07465 420); Birmingham Midshires Building Society, PO Box 81, 35/49 Lichfield St, Wolverhampton WV1 IEL (☎ 0902 710710, fax 0902 28849, car tel 0836 732663)

DICKIE, Rev Prof Edgar Primrose; MC; s of William Dickie; *b* 12 August 1897; *Educ* Dumfries Acad, Edinburgh Univ, Ch Ch Oxford, New Coll Edinburgh, Marburgh Tubingen; *m* 1927, Ishbel Graham Holmes; *Career* emeritus professor of divinity St Mary's Coll St Andrews Univ 1967- (Prof 1935-67); extra chaplain to the Queen in

Scotland 1967- (chaplain 1956-67); *Style*— The Rev Prof Edgar Dickie; Surma, Hepburn Gdns, St Andrews, Fife (73617)

DICKIN, Malcolm Donald; s of Donald Arthur Swingler Dickin (d 1981), and Ethel Ada, *née* Bennett (d 1965); *b* 5 May 1939; *Educ* William Hulme's GS Manchester; *m* 1 s (Andrew Malcolm b 1969), 1 da (Sally Nicola b 1972); *Career* solicitor; *Style*— Malcolm D Dickin, Esq; 18 Coppice Close, Woodley, Stockport SK6 1JH (☎ 061 494 9812); 1 Market St, Denton, Manchester M34 3BX (☎ 061 336 5031)

DICKINS, Basil Gordon; CBE (1952, OBE 1945); s of late Basil Dickins; *b* 1 July 1908; *Educ* private schs, Imperial Coll of Science and Technology (BSc, ARCS, DIC, PhD); *m* 1, 1935, Molly Aileen (d 1969), da of late Horace Walters Reburn; m 2, 1971, Edith, widow of Warren Parkinson; *Career* head Operational Research HQ Bomber Command RAF 1941-45; asst scientific advsr Air Miny 1945, dir of Technical Personnel Admin 1948, dep scientific advsr to Air Miny 1952, dir of Guided Weapons Research and Devpt Miny of Supply 1956, dir-gen: Atomic Weapons Miny of Supply 1959, Guided Weapons Miny of Technology 1962; dep controller Guided Weapons Miny of Aviation 1966-68; *Style*— Dr Basil Dickins, CBE; 5 Batisse de la Mielle, Route de la Haule, St Brelade, Jersey, C I

DICKINSON, (Vivienne) Anne (Mrs David Phillips); da of Oswald Edward (d 1956), of Mapperley Park, Nottingham, and Ida Ismay Harris (d 1984); *b* 27 Sept 1931; *Educ* Nottingham Girls HS; *m* 1, 15 March 1951 (m dis 1961), John Kerr Large, s of Maj Thomas Large (d 1959), of Cotgrave, Notts; m 2, 22 June 1979, David Hermas Phillips; *Career* exec Crawford 1960-64; promotions ed: Good Housekeeping 1964-65, Harpers Bazaar 1965-67; dir: Nat Magazine Co 1967-68, Benson PR Ltd 1968-70 (md 1970-71); bought Kingsway PR Ltd (formerly Benson PR) 1971 (sold to Saatchi & Saatchi 1985), chm chief ed Saatchi & Saatchi 1988; chm Woman of the Year Lunch 1983-85 (vice chm 1987-88), vice chm PRCA 1978-82, PR Professional of the Year 1988; FIPR 1986, CBIM 1986, M Inst M 1979; *Recreations* riding; *Clubs* Civil Service Riding; *Style*— Miss Anne Dickinson; 26 Bedford Gardens, Kensington, London W8; Kingsway Rowland Ltd, 67-69 Whitfield Street, London W1 (☎ 01 436 4060)

DICKINSON, Antony Havergal; s of Adolphus Havergal Dickinson (d 1946), of Gosforth, Newcastle upon Tyne, and Sophia Hamilton, *née* Woods (d 1947); *b* 27 Nov 1901; *Educ* Loretto Sch Musselburgh Scotland, Pembroke Coll Cambridge (MA); *m* 16 Sept 1930, Eunice Louisa, da of Thomas George Mylchreest, of Eltofts Thorner, nr Leeds, Yorks; 1 da (Catherine Elisabeth (Mrs Pestell) b 1934); *Career* CD Controller Tyne & Wear Sub-Region Area West; admitted slr 1927, former sr ptnr Ingledew Mather and Dickinson (formerly Mather and Dickinson) slrs and notaries Newcastle; vice pres Nat Hist Soc of Northumbria, vice pres Ponteland CC Northumberland; memb: Law Soc, Soc of NP's, Newcastle upon Tyne Law Soc, Slrs Benevolent Soc; *Recreations* fishing, squash racquets; *Clubs* Northern Counties, hon memb Northumberland GC; *Style*— Antony Dickinson, Esq; Riftswood, Woolsington Bridge, Newcastle upon Tyne NE13 8BL (☎ 091 2869186); Ingledew Botterell, Milburn House, Dean St, Newcastle upon Tyne NE1 1NP (☎ 091 2611661, telex 53598 INGLAW)

DICKINSON, Bruce Bradbury; s of Harold Raymond Dickinson, of Australia, and Isobel Flora Dickinson, *née* Bremner; *b* 2 July 1934; *Educ* Manly Boys High, Queensland Univ; *m* 1961, Dorothy Yvonne, da of Gerald George Carpenter, of Swansea; 1 s (Mark b 1969), 2 da (Fiona b 1963, Claire b 1965); *Career* banker, sr gen mangr Australia & New Zealand Banking Gp; md Grindlays Bank plc; *Recreations* golf; *Clubs* Union, Royal Sydney Yacht Sqdn, Metropolitan Golf, Royal Blackheath Golf; *Style*— Bruce Dickinson; 4 Woodhall Avenue, Dulwich, London SE21 (☎ 01 693 6636); PO Box 7, Montague Close, London SE1

DICKINSON, Clive Havelock Maplesden; s of Richard Havelock Dickinson, of Oxfordshire, and Betty Evelyn, *née* Maplesden; *b* 1 Oct 1953; *Educ* Lord Williams GS Thame, Wadham Coll Oxford (MA); *m* 30 Aug 1980, Claire Marguerite Amey, da of Edward Algernon Richardson (d 1970); 1 s (Ralph b 1986); *Career* writer in best sellers listing (under various names) 1980, 1986, 1987; co-fndr Travellers Press 1988; FRGS; *Recreations* architectural restoration, skiing; *Clubs* Vincent's (Oxford); *Style*— Clive H M Dickinson, Esq; Wootton Farm, Checkley, Herefordshire HR1 4NA (☎ 043 279 422)

DICKINSON, Hon David Christopher; 4 s of Hon Richard Sebastian Willoughby Dickinson, DSO (d 1935, only s of 1 Baron Dickinson), of Washwell House, Painswick, Gloucs; granted 1944 title, rank and precedence of the son of a baron, which would have been his had his father survived to succeed to the title; *b* 29 Jan 1935; *Educ* Eton, Trinity Coll Oxford; *m* 1970, Caroline Mary, da of late Arthur Denton Toosey, and formerly w of late Peter Yeoward; *Style*— The Hon David Dickinson; Nanneys Bridge, Church Minshull, Nantwich, Cheshire

DICKINSON, Sir Harold Herbert; s of late William James Dickinson and Barwon Venus Clarke; *b* 27 Feb 1912; *Educ* Singleton Public Sch, Tamworth HS, Wollongong HS, Sydney Univ (LLB); *m* 1946, Elsie May Smith; 2 da; *Career* chm: NSW Pub Service Bd 1971-79, Prince Henry Hosp and Prince of Wales Hosp 1975-; dir: Devpt Finance Corpn Ltd 1979-, Aust Fixed Trusts Ltd 1979-; chm AFT Property Co Ltd 1980-; kt 1975; *Recreations* sailing; *Style*— Sir Harold Dickinson; 649 Old South Head Rd, Rose Bay North, NSW 2030, Australia (☎ 371 7475)

DICKINSON, Prof Harry Thomas; s of Joseph Dickinson (d 1979), and Elizabeth Stearman, *née* Warriner (d 1979); *b* 9 Mar 1939; *Educ* Gateshead GS, Durham Univ (BA, DipEd, MA), Newcastle Univ (PhD), Edinburgh Univ (DLitt); *m* 26 Aug 1961, Jennifer Elizabeth, da of Albert Galtry, of Kilham, E Yorks; 1 s (Mark James b 1967), 1 da (Anna Elizabeth b 1972); *Career* Earl Grey fell Newcastle Univ 1964-66; Edinburgh Univ: asst lectr 1966-68, lectr 1968-73, reader 1973-80, prof of British history 1980-; concurrent prof of history Nanjing Univ China 1987-; author of many historical essays and articles; FRHistS; *Books* Bolingbroke (1970), Walpole and the Whig Supremacy (1973), Politics and Literature in the Eighteenth Century (1974), Liberty and Property (1977), Political Works of Thomas Spence (1982), British Radicalism and the French Revolution (1985), Caricatures and the Constitution (1986), Britain and the French Revolution (1989); *Style*— Prof Harry Dickinson; 44 Viewforth Terr, Edinburgh EH10 4LJ (☎ 031 229 1379); History Department, Univ of Edinburgh, Edinburgh EH8 9JY (☎ 031 667 1011 ext 6556)

DICKINSON, Very Rev the Hon Hugh Geoffrey; s of Hon Richard Sebastian Willoughby Dickinson, DSO (d 1935), of Washwell House, Painswick, Glos; raised to the rank of a baron's son, which would have been his had his father survived to succeed to the title, 1944; *b* 17 Nov 1929; *Educ* Westminster, Trinity Coll Oxford, Cuddeston Theol Coll; *m* 29 June 1963, Jean Marjorie, da of Arthur Storey, of Leeds; 2 s, 1 da; *Career* ordained 1956; chaplain: Trinity Coll Cambridge 1958-63, Winchester Coll 1963-69; bishop's advsr for Adult Education Coventry Diocese 1969-77; Vicar St Michael's St Albans 1977-86, Dean of Salisbury 1986-; *Style*— The Very Rev the Hon Hugh Dickinson; The Deanery, 7 The Close, Salisbury, Wilts SP1 2EF (☎ 0722 22457)

DICKINSON, Hon Mrs (Jessica Rosetta); *née* Mancroft; da of 2 Baron Mancroft, KBE, TD; *b* 10 May 1954; *m* 15 Oct 1983, Simon C Dickinson, eld s of Peter Dickinson, of Newbrough, Northumberland; 2 da (Phoebe Victoria b 1984, Octavia Jessica b 1986); *Style*— The Hon Mrs Dickinson; Wortley House, Wotten-under-Edge, Gloucs (☎ 0453 843174)

DICKINSON, Prof (Christopher) John; s of Reginald Ernest Dickinson (d 1978), of London, and Margaret, *née* Petty (d 1983); *b* 1 Feb 1927; *Educ* Berkhamsted Sch, Oxford Univ (BA, BSc, MA, BM, BCh, DM); *m* 26 June 1953, Elizabeth Patricia, da of William Patrick Farrell (d 1982), of London; 2 s (Mark John b 1956, Paul Tabois b 1964), 2 da (Emma Elizabeth b 1954, Caroline Margaret b 1957); *Career* Capt RAMC jr med specialist 1955-56; jr staff appts UCH 1953-54; Middx Hosp: registrar 1957-58, res fell 1959-60; Rockefeller fell Cleveland Clinic USA 1960-61; UCH 1961-75: lectr, sr lectr, conslt; prof medicine St Bartholemew's Hosp Med Coll 1975-; memb: Med Res Cncl, Assoc of Physicians; former chm: Med Res Soc, Assoc Clinical Profs of Med; former vice pres RCP; former sec: Harveian Soc, Euro Soc Clinical Investigation; MRCP 1956, FRCP 1965; *Books* Eelctrophysiological Technique (1950), Clinical Pathology Data (1952), Clinical Physiology (1960), Neurogenic Hypertension (1965), Computer Model of Human Respiration (1975), Software for Educational Computing (1980); *Recreations* theatre, opera, playing the organ; *Clubs* Garrick; *Style*— Prof John Dickinson; Griffin Cottage, 57 Belsize Lane, London NW3 5AU (☎ 01 431 1845) St Bartholomew's Hospital, London EC1A 7BE (☎ 01 601 7531)

DICKINSON, Hon Martin Hyett; er s and h of 2 Baron Dickinson; *b* 30 Jan 1961; *Style*— The Hon Martin Dickinson

DICKINSON, Hon Mrs Richard; May Southey; *née* Lovemore; *m* 15 May 1924, Hon Richard Sebastian Willoughby Dickinson, DSO (d 1935), only s of 1 Baron Dickinson; 1 s (present peer); *Career* JP; *Style*— The Hon Mrs Richard Dickinson; The Poultry Court, Painswick, Glos

DICKINSON, Patric Laurence; s of John Laurence Dickinson, and April Katherine, *née* Forgan, of Stroud, Glos; *b* 24 Nov 1950; *Educ* Marling Sch, Exeter Coll Oxford (MA); *Career* res asst College of Arms 1968-78, Rouge Dragon Pursuivant of Arms 1978-89, Richmond Herald 1989-; barr Middle Temple 1979; hon tres: English Genealogical Congress 1975-, Bar Theatrical Soc 1978-; hon sec and registrar Br Record Soc 1979-; *Recreations* music, cycling, swimming, walking, talking, attending memorial services; *Style*— Patric Dickinson, Esq; College of Arms, Queen Victoria St, London EC4V 4BT (☎ 01 236 9612)

DICKINSON, Hon Peter Malcolm de Brissac; s of Hon Richard Sebastian Willoughby Dickinson, DSO (s of 1 Baron Dickinson); raised to the rank of a Baron's s 1944; *b* 16 Dec 1927; *Educ* Eton, King's Coll Cambridge; *m* 25 April 1953, Mary Rose, er da of Vice Adm Sir Geoffrey Barnard, KCB, CBE, DSO (d 1988), of Bramdean, Alresford, Hants; 2 s (John Geoffrey Hyett b 1962, James Christopher Meade b 1963), 2 da (Philippa Lucy Ann b 1955, Dorothy Louise b 1956); *Career* author; asst editor Punch 1952-69; chm mgmnt ctee Society of Authors 1978-80; has published numerous children's books and detective novels; *Style*— The Hon Peter Dickinson; 61a Ormiston Grove, London W12

DICKINSON, 2 Baron (UK 1930); Richard Clavering Hyett Dickinson; s of Hon Richard Sebastian Willoughby Dickinson, DSO (d 1935) and gs of 1 Baron (d 1943); *b* 2 Mar 1926; *Educ* Eton, Trinity Coll Oxford; *m* 1, 1957 (m dis), (Margaret) Ann, da of late Brig Gilbert R McMeekan, CB, DSO, OBE, JP; 2 s; m 2, 1980, Rita Doreen Moir; *Heir* s, Hon Martin Hyett Dickinson; *Style*— Rt Hon Lord Dickinson; The Stables, Painswick House, Painswick, Stroud, Glos (☎ Painswick 813204)

DICKINSON, Sir Samuel Benson; s of S R Dickinson and Margaret, *née* Clemes; *b* 1 Feb 1912; *Educ* St Andrew's Coll NZ, Haileybury Coll Melbourne, Melbourne Univ (MSc); *m* 1960, Dorothy Joan Weidenhofer; 3 s, 1 da; *Career* mining advsr to South Australian Govt 1975-84; chm: SA Govt Uranium Enrichment Ctee, Burmine Ltd; kt 1980; *see Debrett's Handbook of Australia and New Zealand for further details*; *Recreations* golf, bowls; *Style*— Sir Samuel Dickinson; PO Box 269, Stirling, S Australia 5152 (☎ 80 339 5135)

DICKINSON, Stephen; s of Rev Arthur Edward Dickinson, of 48 Cliff Parade, Hunstanton, Norfolk, and Ada Violet, *née* Hickey; *b* 12 Oct 1934; *Educ* St Edwards Sch Oxford, Kings Coll Newcastle, Univ of Durham (BA); *m* 23 March 1968, Mary Elisabeth, da of Maj Richard Quintin Gurney (d 1980) of Bawdeswell Hall, East Dereham, Norfolk; 2 s (Michael Edward b July 1969, James Stephen b May 1971); *Career* Nat Serv Flying Offr RAF 1957-59; CA Br Virgin Islands 1963-74, md Grainger Tst plc (Newcastle upon Tyne); FCA 1962; *Recreations* field sports, farming; *Clubs* Whites, Northern Counties, RAF; *Style*— Stephen Dickinson, Esq; Crow Hall, Bardon Mill, Hexham, Northumberland (☎ 0434 344495); Grainger Trust plc Chaucer Buildings, 57 Grainger St, Newcastle upon Tyne (☎ 091 261 1819, fax 091 232 7874)

DICKINSON, Capt Trevor Gledhill; s of Percy Parkin Dickinson (d 1972), and Winifred Jane, *née* Gledhill (d 1985); *b* 29 August 1924; *Educ* Bradford GS, Kings Coll Cambridge; *m* 18 Dec 1954, Pauline, da of Archie Seymore Pearce; 2 da (Penelope b 1956, Jane b 1962); *Career* served WW II UK & E Africa, Capt RA (awarded Sword of Honour on being cmd 1945) and RE 1943-47; slr sr ptnr Geoffrey Parker & Bourne Leamington Spa; a dep County Ct & High Ct registrar (Midland & Oxford circuit) 1984-; chm Coventry Insur Appeal Panel Tribunal 1972; part time immigration adjudicator for Immigration Appeals 1987-; *Recreations* music, Rotary international; *Clubs* Army & Navy, St James'; *Style*— Captain Trevor G Dickinson; 5 Elliotts Orchard, Barford, Warwick CV35 8EH (☎ 0926 624565); Geoffrey Parker & Bourne, 9 Euston Place, Leamington Spa CV32 4LP (☎ 0926 27211), telex 317148 DATAS G)

DICKS, Terence Patrick; MP (C) Hayes and Harlington 1983-; s of Frank and Winifred Dicks; *b* 17 Mar 1937; *Educ* LSE, Oxford Univ; *m* (m dis); 1 s, 2 da; *Career* Min of Labour 1959-66; *Style*— Terence Dicks Esq, MP; House of Commons, London SW1

DICKSON, Alec (Alexander) Graeme; CBE (1967, MBE 1945); s of late Norman Bonnington Dickson, of Struan, Wimbledon Park, and late Anne, *née* Higgins; *b* 23

May 1914; *Educ* Rugby, New Coll Oxford; *m* 1951, Mora Agnes, da of Laurence Hope Robertson; *Career* founder and first dir VSO, 1958-62; founder Community Service Volunteers 1962 (hon dir 1962-); consultant to Cwlth Secretariat 1974-77; *Style*— Alec Dickson, Esq, CBE; 19 Blenheim Rd, London W4 (01 994 7437)

DICKSON, Jennifer Joan; da of late John Liston Dickson; *b* 17 Sept 1936; *Educ* Goldsmiths' Coll Sch of Art London Univ, S W Hayter's Atelier 17 Paris; *m* 1961, Ronald Andrew Sweetman; 1 s; *Career* emigrated to Canada 1969 and became a citizen 1974; artist and photographer; public collections include works in: Nat Gallery of Canada Ottawa, Canada Cncl Art Bank Ottawa, Musée d'Art Contemporain Montreal, Montreal Museum of Fine Arts, Met Museum New York, Nat Gallery Melbourne, Nat Gallery of Art Wellington (NZ), Victoria and Albert Museum, Br Museum; winner of many awards; memb RA 1976 (and the first Canadian to be so honoured), fell Royal Soc of Painter-Etchers and Engravers; Hon LLD Univ of Alberta Edmonton; *Recreations* documenting European gardens; *Style*— Miss Jennifer Dickson; 227 Bank St, Ottawa, Ontario K2P 1W9, Canada (☎ (613) 233 2315); 20 Osborne St, Ottawa, Ontario K15 429 Canada (☎ 613 236 5602)

DICKSON, Jeremy David Fane; s of Lt Col J D L Dickson, MC (d 1959), and Elizabeth Daphne, *née* Fane; *b* 23 June 1941; *Educ* Marlborough, Emmanuel Coll Cambridge (MA); *m* 9 Oct 1965, Patricia, da of Laurence Cleveland Martin (d 1980); 1 s (James David Laurence b 30 Jan 1970), 1 da (Lucy Camilla b 25 June 1971); *Career* ptnr Deloitte Haskins and Sells 1977, chm Deloitte Haskins and Sells UK and Int Insur Gps; memb: Insur Ctee, Fedn des Experts Comptames Euro Gp Assur; FCA; *Recreations* golf, cricket, shooting, philately; *Clubs* MCC, Royal Wimbledon GC; *Style*— Jeremy Dickson, Esq; 8 Alan Rd, Wimbledon, London SW19 7PT (☎ 01 946 5854); PO Box 20 7, 128 Queen Victoria St, London EC4 4JX (☎ 01 248 3913, fax 01 248 3623)

DICKSON, John Abernethy; CB (1970); s of John Dickson (d 1918); *b* 19 Sept 1915; *Educ* Robert Gordons Coll Aberdeen, Aberdeen Univ; *m* 1942, Helen Drummond, da of Peter Drummond Jardine (d 1974); 2 da; *Career* joined Forestry Cmmn 1938 (head of Harvesting and Marketing 1965-68, dir-gen and dep chm 1968-76), chm Cwlth Forestry Assoc 1972-75, dir Economic Forestry (Scotland) Ltd 1977-84, chm Forest Thinnings Ltd 1981-86 (dir 1978-86); *Style*— John Dickson Esq, CB; 56 Oxgangs Rd, Edinburgh (☎ 031 445 1067);

DICKSON, Lt-Col Leonard Elliot; CBE (1972), MC (1944), TD (1950), DL (Glasgow, 1963); s of Rev Robert Marcus Dickson (d 1967), of Hope Bank, Lanark; *b* 17 Mar 1915; *Educ* Uppingham, Magdalene Coll Cambridge (LLB); *m* 1950, Mary Elisabeth, da of late Lt-Col L A Cuthbertson; 1 s, 1 da; *Career* served 1939-45 War with 1 Glasgow Highlanders in NW Europe, Lt-Col 1952; former sr ptnr Dickson Haddow & Co slrs Glasgow, ret; *Clubs* Royal Scottish Automobile (Glasgow); *Style*— Lt-Col Leonard Dickson, CBE, MC, TD, DL; Bridge End, Gartmore by Stirling, FK8 3RR (☎ 087 72 220)

DICKSON, Hon Mrs (Lynda Mary Kathleen); *née* Aitken; da (by 2 w) of Sir Max Aitken, Bt (d 1985; 2 Baron Beaverbrook, who disclaimed his peerage 1964); *b* 1948; *m* 1, 1969 (m dis 1974), Nicolas Saxton, s of Robert Saxton, of La Jolla, Calif; m 2, 1977, Jonathan James Dickson; 2 s (Joshua James b 1977, Leo Casper b 1981); *Style*— The Hon Mrs Dickson; 45 Broomwood Road, London SW11

DICKSON, Murray Graeme; CMG (1961); s of late Norman Bonnington Dickson, OBE, and late Anne, *née* Higgins; bro of Alec Dickson (*qv*); *b* 19 July 1911; *Educ* Rugby, New Coll Oxford (MA), Univ of London (Dip Ed); *Career* Ordinary Seaman MN 1934-35, War Serv with Force 136 SE Asia; Maj; Prison Serv (Borstals) 1935-40; joined Educn Dept Govt of Sarawak 1947, dir of educn Sarawak 1955-66; UNESCO advsr on educn to Govt of Lesotho 1967-68; *Books* A Sarawak Anthology, Understanding Kant's Critique of Pure Reason (1986); *Clubs* Royal Cwlth Soc; *Style*— M G Dickson, Esq, CMG; 1 Hauteville Court Gardens, Stamford Brook Ave, London W6 0YF

DICKSON, Ruth Marjorie; MBE, JP; da of Col Randolf Nelson Greenwood, MC, JP (d 1977), and Beatrice Marion, *née* Montfort-Bebb (d 1949); *b* 9 Feb 1923; *Educ* St Margarets Welwyn Herts, Eastbourne Coll (Dip Domestic Econ); *m* 12 May 1944, Col David D Livingstone Dickson, TD, DL (d 1984), s of Frederick Livingstone Dickson (d 1960); 2 s (Duncan Charles Livingstone b 1945, Malcolm James Livingstone b 1949); *Career* ATS 1940, cmmnd 1941, discharged 1943; fndr Ruth Dickson Tst for Disabled 1974-; pres: Stone Handicapped Club, Stafford Multiple Sclerosis Club; former memb and chm Stone RDC (joined 1958), memb Stafford Borough Cncl 1973- (Mayor 1974-75); *Recreations* gardening, gundogs; *Style*— Mrs Ruth Dickson; Hill Cottage, Barlaston, Stoke on Trent (☎ 078 139 2434)

DICKSON, Col Seton Graeme; JP (1967), DL (1965); s of Norman Bonnington Dickson, OBE (d 1944), of Struan, Wimbledon Park, and Agnes Anne Edith, *née* Higgins (d 1952); *b* 11 Nov 1909; *Educ* Rugby, Sandhurst; *m* 22 Feb 1941, Ellison, da of Col William Pollok-Morris, CMG, DSO, DL (d 1936); 2 s (David b 1950, William b 1955), 3 da (Jane Anne b 1947, Susan b 1948, Catherine b 1953); *Career* cmmnd The Royal Scots 1930, India and UK 1931-39, served BEF Middle East, Italy, Burma 1939-43, GSO II 56 (London) Div, Instr ME Staff Coll Haifa 1944-45, cmd IR Scots 1947-48, 5 Malay Regt 1951-53; memb Queen's Bodyguard for Scotland Royal Co of Archers, Hon Col Ayrshire ACF 1965; *Clubs* New (Edinburgh); *Style*— Col Seton Dickson, JP, DL; Field House, Symington, Kilmarnock, Ayrshire (☎ 0563 830323)

DICKSON, Dame Violet Penelope; DBE (1976, CBE 1964, MBE 1942); 2 da of Neville Lucas-Calcraft, of Moat House, Gautby, Lincs, by his w Emily Delmar, 3 da of Robert Lindley; *b* 3 Sept 1896; *Educ* Miss Lunn's Sch Woodhall Spa, Les Charmettes Vevey Switzerland; *m* 1920, Harold Richard Patrick Dickson, CIE (d 1959), s of John Dickson (d 1908); 1 s, 1 da; *Career* memb Royal Central Asian Soc; Lawrence of Arabia Medal; FRZS; *Books* Wild Flowers of Kuwait and Bahrain, Forty Years in Kuwait; *Style*— Dame Violet Dickson, DBE; Seef, Kuwait, Arabia (☎ 432310)

DIEHL, John Bertram Stuart; QC 1987; s of Ernest Henry Stuart Diehl, of Swansea, and Caroline Pentreath, *née* Lumsdaine; *b* 18 April 1944; *Educ* Bishop Gore Sch Swansea, Univ Coll of Wales Aberystwyth (LLB); *m* 29 July 1967, Patricia; 2 s (Robert b 1973, Stephen b 1975); *Career* asst lecr, Univ of Sheffield 1965-69; barr Lincoln's Inn 1968, recorder 1984; *Recreations* squash, sailing; *Clubs* Bristol Channel Yacht; *Style*— JBS Diehl, Esq, QC; 4 Grange Road, West Cross, Swansea SA3 5ES; Angel Chambers, 94 Walter Road, Swansea SA1 5QA (☎ 0792 464623)

DIEHL, Hon Mrs (Sybil Diana); 3 da (only child by 2 m) of 3 Baron Tollemache (d 1955); *b* 1 May 1930; *m* 24 Nov 1966, Harold Diehl; *Style*— The Hon Mrs Diehl

DIERDEN, Kenneth Norman (Ken); s of Norman William Dierden (d 1984), of Havant, and Marjorie Harvey, *née* Nicholas; *b* 26 Feb 1952; *Educ* Bancrofts Sch Woodford Green, Southampton Univ (BA); *m* 28 Aug 1976, Margaret Ann, da of Walter Roland Charles Hayward, of Stoke-on-Trent; 1 da (Isabella b 1988); *Career* Freshfields Slrs 1980- (ptnr 1987-); memb Worshipful Co of Solicitors; memb Law Soc, ATII; *Recreations* hockey, squash; *Style*— Ken Dierden, Esq; Freshfields, Grindall House, 25 Newgate Street, London EC1A 7LH (☎ 01 606 6677, fax 01 248 3487/8/9, telex 889292)

DIGBY, 12 Baron (I 1620 and GB 1765); Edward Henry Kenelm Digby; JP (1959); s of 11 Baron, KG, DSO, MC (d 1964), and Hon Pamela, *née* Bruce (d 1978), da of 2 Baron Aberdare; bro-in-law of late Averell Harriman; *b* 24 July 1924; *Educ* Eton, Trinity Coll Oxford, RMC; *m* 18 Dec 1952, Dione Marian, DL, yr da of Rear Adm Robert St Vincent Sherbrooke, VC, CB, DSO; 2 s, 1 da; *Heir* s, Hon Henry Noel Kenelm Digby, *qv*; *Career* Capt Coldstream Gds 1947, ADC to C-in-C Far E Land Forces 1950-51; memb Dorchester RDC 1962; memb Dorset CC 1966-81 (vice-chm 74-81); Lord-Lt for Dorset 1984- (DL 1957, vice Lord-Lt 1965-84); dep chm SW Econ Planning Cncl, pres Council of St John for Dorset 1984, pres Royal Bath and West Soc 1976, chm RAS of the Cwlth 1967-79, dir C H Beazer (Hldgs) plc, pres Wessex Branch Inst of Dirs; dir: Gifford-Hill Inc, (Dallas) Kier Int Ltd; churchwarden St Andrews Minterne Magna; KStJ 1984; *Recreations* skiing, tennis; *Clubs* Pratt's; *Style*— The Rt Hon the Lord Digby, JP; Minterne, Dorchester, Dorset DT2 7AU (☎ 030 03 370)

DIGBY, Hon Henry Noel Kenelm; s and h of 12 Baron Digby; *b* 6 Jan 1954; *Educ* Eton; *m* 12 July 1980, Susan E, er da of Peter Watts, of 6 Albert Terrace Mews, SW1; 1 s (Edward St Vincent Kenelm b 5 Sept 1985), 1 da (Alexandra Jane Kira b 13 March 1987); *Career* gp fin controller Jardine Davies (Manila) 1980-81, asst tres Jardine Matheson & Co Ltd 1981-84, dir Jardine Fleming Investmt Mgmnt Ltd Hong Kong 1984-; ACA; *Recreations* skiing, tennis; *Style*— The Hon Henry Digby; Minterne, Dorchester, Dorset; office: Jardine Fleming Hldgs Ltd, 47th Floor, Connaught Centre, Hong Kong

DIGBY, Hon Rupert Simon; yr s of 12 Baron Digby; *b* 21 August 1956; *Educ* Eton, Southampton Univ (BSc); *m* 2 Aug 1986, Charlotte Fleury, yr da of late Robert Hirst, of Alderton House, Hurstbourne Tarrant, Hants; *Career* electronic design engineer; *Style*— The Hon Rupert Digby; Rookwood Farm House, Stockcross, Newbury, Berks

DIGBY, Hon Zara Jane; only da of 12 Baron Digby; *b* 27 May 1958; *Educ* Cobham Hall, Le Vieux Chalet Chateau d'Oex Switzerland; *Career* dress designer; *Recreations* skiing, tennis, cooking, sailing, the arts; *Style*— The Hon Zara Digby; 82 Horder Rd, London SW6 5EE (☎ 01 736 2872)

DIGGENS, Ronald William; OBE (1945); s of Frederick William Diggens (d 1932); *b* 26 Nov 1911; *Educ* Haberdashers' Aske's; *Career* served NW Europe Lt-Col; chm: Allnatt London Properties Ltd 1962-78, Guildhall Property Co Ltd 1963-78; dir Slough Estates Ltd 1956-85.; *Recreations* sailing, flying; *Clubs* Royal Thames Yacht; *Style*— Ronald Diggens, Esq, OBE; Sedgley, 14 Russell Rd, Moor Park, Northwood, Middx; Polridmouth Cottage, Menabilly, nr Par, Cornwall

DIGGLE, Maj James; TD; s of James Stanley Diggle (d 1973), and Dorothy Mary Mellalieu (d 1961); *b* 20 August 1915; *Educ* Canford, St Johns Coll Cambridge (MA); *m* 1 Oct 1938, Margaret, da of Henry Hood (d 1941); 2 s (Richard James b 1947, Peter Hood b 1950), 2 da (Julia b 1940, Lorna b 1944); *Career* WWII served 42 Dir RASC as Maj; memb Manchester Stock Exchange 1937; sr ptnr Charlton Seal Dimmock 1981, now conslt Charlton Seal Ltd; *Recreations* golf, fishing, gardening, masonry; *Clubs* Prestbury Golf; *Style*— Maj James Diggle, TD; White Cottage, 33 Castle Hill, Prestbury, Cheshire SK10 4AS (☎ 0625 829328)

DIGGLE, Maj Peter John; s of Lt-Col Wadham Heathcote Diggle, DSO, OBE, MC (d 1958), of Eden House, Malton, Yorks, and Nancy Diggle (d 1958), da of Henry Conran, of Coorabelle, Westgate-on-Sea, Kent; *b* 17 July 1921; *Educ* Stowe, Trinity Coll Cambridge; *m* 17 Sept 1959, Anna Sylvia, da of Freiherr von der Lancken-Wakenitz (d 1956), of Seidlitzhof, Krefeld; 2 s (Richard b 1961, William b 1962); *Career* Maj Gren Gds 1940-52, serv NW Europe and Malaya; dir: J M Potter Ltd 1953-62, R C Carr Ltd, J Senior Ltd and J Haig Ltd 1962-66, City Jewellers Ltd 1965-66; fndr Diamond Investmt Concept 1968, dir Inter Diamond Brokers SA 1972-76; chm Amalgamated Diamond Brokers 1976-86, dir Pub Servants Housing Fin Assoc Homeownership Club 1984-, controller Minibars (UK) Ltd 1986-; patron Harrogate Abbeyfield Soc, pres Household Div Assoc Yorks Branch, chm Sydney Smith Appeal; *Recreations* tennis, shooting, equitation; *Clubs* Army and Navy, Shikar, White's; *Style*— Maj Peter Diggle; The Old Brewery, Thornton le Clay, York YO6 7TE (☎ 065381 334); 100 Park Lane, London W1Y 4AR (☎ 01 408 0534, fax 01 491 2483)

DIGNAN, Maj-Gen Albert Patrick; CB (1978), MBE (1952); s of Joseph William Dignan (d 1964), and Rosetta Weir (d 1978); *b* 25 July 1920; *Educ* Christian Brothers Sch Dublin, Trinity Coll Dublin (MA, MD); *m* 1952, Eileen, da of James John White (d 1956); 2 s, 1 da; *Career* Brig and consulting surgeon FARELF 1969-71, sr consultant surgeon and asst prof of military surgery Queen Alexandra Military Hosp Millbank 1972-73, dir Army Surgery and consulting surgeon to the Army 1973-78, QHS 1974-78, hon consultant surgeon Royal Hosp Chelsea, hon consultant oncology and radiotherapy Westminster Hosp 1975-78, consultant in accident and emergency medicine Ealing Hosp 1978-79; fell Assoc of Surgns of GB and Ireland, FRCS, FRCSI, FRSM; *Recreations* gardening, golf; *Style*— Maj-Gen Albert Dignan, CB, MBE; 37 Queens Rd, Beckenham, Kent (☎ 01 658 7690)

DILHORNE, 2 Viscount (UK 1964); Sir John Mervyn Manningham-Buller; 5 Bt (UK 1866); also Baron Dilhorne (UK 1962); s of 1 Viscount Dilhorne, sometime Lord High Chllr and Lord of Appeal in Ordinary (d 1980, ggs of Sir Edward M-B, 1 Bt, who was bro of 1 Baron Churston) by his w Lady Mary Lindsay (4 da of 27 Earl of Crawford and Balcarres); *b* 28 Feb 1932; *Educ* Eton, RMA Sandhurst; *m* 1, 8 Oct 1955 (m dis 1973), Gillian Evelyn, elder da of Col George Cochrane Stockwell, JP; 2 s, 1 da (Hon Mary b 1970); m 2, 1981, Mrs Susannah Jane Gilchrist, da of late Cdr W C Eykyn, RN; *Heir* s, Capt Hon James Edward Manningham-Buller; *Career* Lt Coldstream Gds 1952-57, served Egypt, Germany, Canal Zone; CCllr Wilts 1964-66; barrister 1979; md Stewart Smith (LP&M) Ltd 1970-74; memb Jt Parly Ctee on Statutory Tribunals 1981-; fellow Inst of Taxation (memb cncl 1969-82); *Recreations* skiing, opera singer (bass), shooting; *Clubs* Buck's, Pratt's, Royal St George's, Swinley Forest Golf; *Style*— Rt Hon Viscount Dilhorne; 164 Ebury St, London SW1 W8UP

DILHORNE, Dowager Viscountess; Lady Mary Lilian; *née* Lindsay; 4 da of 27 Earl of Crawford and Balcarres (d 1940); *b* 27 Sept 1910; *m* 18 Dec 1930, 1 Viscount Dilhorne (d 1980); 1 s (present peer); 3 da; *Style*— Rt Hon Dowager Viscountess Dilhorne; 134 Cranmer Court, Whiteheads Grove, London SW3

DILKE, Sir John Fisher Wentworth; 5 Bt (UK 1862) of Sloane Street, Chelsea; s of Sir Fisher Wentworth Dilke, 4 Bt, Major (TA), Lloyd's underwriter (d 1944), of Lepe Point, Exbury, Hants, and Ethel Lucy (d 1959), e da of W K Clifford; *b* 8 May 1906; *Educ* Winchester, New Coll Oxford; *m* 1, 15 Sept 1934 (m dis 1949), Sheila, o da of Sir William Seeds, KCMG (d 1973), sometime ambass to Brazil and Russia; 2 s; m 2, 28 Dec 1951, Iris Evelyn, only child of late Ernest Clark, of 99 Torrington Park, NI2; *Heir* s, Rev Charles John Wentworth Dilke; *Career* HM Foreign Service 1929-32, sub-editor and foreign correspondent for The Times 1936-39, rejoined Foreign Service 1939, head Br Official Wireless News 1942, political correspondent COI 1945, BBC External Dept 1950; Lloyd's underwriter 1944-; *Clubs* Royal Thames Yacht; *Style*— Sir John Dilke, Bt; Ludpits, Etchingham, E Sussex (☎ 058 081 383)

DILKES, Frank Pool; OBE (1989); s of Frank Pool Dilkes (d 1926), and Bridget, *née* Ryan (d 1961); *b* 30 April 1918; *Educ* High Pavement Secondary Sch Nottingham, London Univ (LLB); *m* 13 Aug 1955, Audrey Helen, da of Donald Leslie Tyler (d 1957); 3 s (Paul b 1957, David b 1961, Simon b 1963), 1 da (Teresa b 1959); *Career* RAOC, REME India and Burma, 1 year attached to IA (despatches); asst sec Dewsbury and W Riding Building Soc 1957; asst mangr W Bromwich Building Soc 1958 (gen mangr 1961, md 1965-83, chm 1983-); tres Midland Assoc of Building Socs 1961-69 (chm 1970-71, vice-pres 1984-); nat pres The Chartered Building Socs Inst 1972-73; pres The Sandwell Assoc of Industry and Commerce 1979-80; FCIS 1949, FCBSI 1949, FRSA 1980, CBIM 1970, FID 1970; *Recreations* reading, music, walking; *Style*— Frank P Dilkes, Esq, OBE; 282 Broadway North, Walsall, W Midlands WS1 2PT (☎ 0922 23924); 374 High Street, West Bromwich, West Midlands B70 8LR (☎ 021 525 7070)

DILKS, Prof David Neville; s of Neville Ernest Dilks, of Worcester, and Phyllis, *née* Follows; *b* 17 Mar 1938; *Educ* Worcester Royal GS, Hertford Coll Oxford (BA), St Antony's Coll Oxford; *m* 15 Aug 1963, Jill, da of John Henry Medlicott (d 1971), of Shrewsbury; 1 s (Richard b 1979); *Career* asst lectr (later lectr) LSE 1962-70; res asst: Sir Anthony Eden (later Earl of Avon) 1960-62, Marshal of the RAF Lord Tedder 1963-65, Rt Hon Harold Macmillan (later Earl of Stockton) 1964-67; Univ of Leeds: prof of int history 1970-, chm sch of history 1974-79, dean of the faculty of arts 1975-77, dir master's course in modern int studies 1988; memb Univs Funding Cncl 1988-; tstee: Imperial War Museum, Edward Boyle Memorial Tst, Heskel and May Nathaniel Tst, Lennox-Boyd Memorial Tst; Freeman City of London 1979, Liveryman Worshipful Co of Goldsmiths 1983; FRHistS, FRSL; *Books* Curzon in India (vol 1 1969, vol 2 1970), The Diaries of Sir Alexander Cadogan (ed 1971), The Conservatives (contrib, 1977), Neville Chamberlain (vol 1, 1984); *Clubs* Brooks's, Royal Cwlth Soc; *Style*— Prof David Dilks; Wits End, Long Causeway, Leeds LS16 8EX (☎ 0532 673466); School of History, The University, Leeds LS2 9JT (☎ 0532 333584/5/6)

DILL, Sir (Nicholas) Bayard; CBE (1951), JP; s of late Col Thomas Melville Dill, of Devonshire, Bermuda, and Ruth Rapalje Neilson Dill; *b* 28 Dec 1905; *Educ* Saltus GS Bermuda, Trinity Hall Cambridge; *m* 1930, Lucy Clare, da of late Sir Henry William Watlington, OBE, of Bermuda; 2 s; *Career* memb Colonial Parl Bermuda (Devonshire Parish) 1938-68, memb HM Exec Cncl 1944-54; former chm (Bermuda): Bd of Trade, Bd of Educn, Bd of Works, Bd of Civil Aviation, Bermuda Trade Devpt Bd; memb Legve Cncl Bermuda 1968-73; sr ptnr Conyers Dill & Pearman Barristers-at-Law 1928-; chllr Anglican Church 1951-84; kt 1955; *Clubs* Royal Bermuda Yacht, Royal Thames Yacht, Royal Amateur Dinghy, Canadian and Met (New York); *Style*— Sir Bayard Dill, CBE, JP; Newbold Place, Devonshire, Bermuda (292-4463); office (☎ 295-1422, telex 3213)

DILLON, Rt Hon Lord Justice; Sir (George) Brian Hugh Dillon; PC (1982); s of Capt George Crozier Dillon, RN (d 1946); *b* 2 Oct 1925; *Educ* Winchester, New Coll Oxford; *m* 1954, Alisoun Janetta Drummond, da of Hubert Samuel Lane, MC (d 1962); 2 s, 2 da; *Career* barr Lincoln's Inn 1948, QC 1965, bencher Lincoln's Inn 1973, high court judge (Chancery) 1979-82, Lord Justice of Appeal 1982-, memb Supreme Ct Rule Ctee 1986-; *Style*— Rt Hon Lord Justice Dillon; Bridge Farm House, Grundisburgh, Woodbridge; Royal Courts of Justice, WC2

DILLON, Hon Mrs (Erica Helen Susan); *née* Rollo; only da of 13 Baron Rollo; *b* 12 Dec 1939; *m* 1970, Valentine Edward Dillon; *Style*— The Hon Mrs Dillon; 45 Sandford Rd, Dublin

DILLON, 22 Viscount (I 1622); Henry Benedict Charles Dillon; also Count Dillon (Fr cr of Louis XIV 1711 for Hon Arthur Dillon, 3 s of 7 Viscount and father of 10 and 11 Viscounts, who was Col proprietor of the Dillon Regt, promoted to Lt-Gen in the Fr service, govr of Toulon, and cr titular Earl Dillon 1721/22 by the Chevalier de St Georges, otherwise known as the Old Pretender or, to his supporters, James III); s of 21 Viscount Dillon (d 1982); *b* 6 Jan 1973; *Heir* unc, Hon Richard Dillon, *qv*; *Style*— Rt Hon the Viscount Dillon; 83 Talfourd Rd, London SE15 (☎ 01 701 5931)

DILLON, Hon Ines Marie Jeanne; 2 da of 20 Viscount Dillon; *b* 1 Jan 1952; *Style*— The Hon Ines Dillon

DILLON, Irène, Viscountess; Irène Marie France; *née* Merandon du Plessis; da of René Merandon du Plessis, of Whitehall, Mauritius and Jeanne Cecile, *née* de Bricqueville; *Educ* Queen's Coll; *m* 4 Dec 1939, 20 Viscount Dillon (d 1979); 4 s (21 Viscount (d 1982), Richard, Patrick, Michael), 4 da (Hon Isabelle (Hon Mrs Cobbe) b 1942, Hon Ines b 1952, Hon Rosaleen b 1953, d 1960; Hon Magdalen b 1957); *Career* painter; *Style*— Rt Hon Irène, Viscountess Dillon; 14 St Mary's Cottages, Drogheda, Co Louth, Ireland

DILLON, Viscountess; (Mary) Jane; da of late John Young, of Castle Hill House, Birtle, Lancs; *m* 1972, 21 Viscount Dillon (d 1982); 1 s (Henry, 22 Viscount Dillon, *qv*), 1 da (Beatrice Ines Renee b 28 Dec 1978); *Career* designer; *Style*— Rt Hon Viscountess Dillon; 28 Canning Cross, London SE5 8BH

DILLON, Sir John Vincent; CMG (1974); s of Roger Dillon and Ellen, *née* Egan; *b* 6 August 1908; *Educ* Christian Brothers Coll Melbourne; *m* 1935, Sheila Lorraine D'Arcy; 3 s, 1 da; *Career* chm Medical Salaries Ctee 1959-62; under-sec Chief Sec's Dept Vic 1961-73; chm Racecourses Licences Bd 1961-73; ombudsman for Victoria (cmmr for Administrative Investigations) 1973-80; memb State Public Service Board 1941-54; stipendiary magistrate 1947-61; Hon LLD Melbourne; AASA; kt 1980; *Recreations* racing, golf, reading; *Clubs* Athenaeum, Metropolitan; *Style*— Sir John Dillon, CMG; 25 Kelvin Grove, Armadale, Vic 3143, Australia

DILLON, Sir Max; s of Cyril and Phoebe Dillon; *b* 30 June 1913; *Educ* Wesley Coll Melbourne, Melbourne Univ; *m* 1940, Estelle Mary Jones; 1 s, 1 da; *Career* gen mangr Cable Makers Australia Pty Ltd 1957-70, dep md Metal Manufacturers Ltd Group 1970-75; pres Confedn of Aust Industry 1977-80; memb Exec Ctee Aust Manufacturing Cncl 1978-80; Queen's Jubilee Medal 1977, John Allison Award 1981; kt 1979; *Recreations* golf, swimming; *Clubs* Australian, Elanora County; *Style*— Sir Max Dillon; 33 Church St, Pymble, NSW 2073, Australia (02 44 3160)

DILLON, Hon Michael Edmund; 4 s (twin) of 20 Viscount Dillon; *b* 29 Oct 1957; *Educ* Glenstal Abbey Sch Co Limerick, Hampshire Coll of Agric Sparsholt; *m* 1 Oct 1983, Henrietta Catherine Elwell, yr da of Charles Elwell, of Bottrells Close, Chalfont St Giles; 1 s (Charles b 1985); *Style*— The Hon Michael Dillon

DILLON, Hon Mrs; Priscilla Frances; yr da of 2 Baron Hazlerigg; *b* 30 July 1952; *m* 1975, Hon Richard Dillon, 2 s of 20 Viscount Dillon; *Style*— The Hon Mrs Dillon; 5 Edith Grove, London SW10

DILLON, Hon Richard Arthur Louis; 2 s of 20 Viscount Dillon; hp to n, 22 Viscount Dillon; *b* 23 Oct 1948; *Educ* Downside, RAC Cirencester; *m* 1975, Hon Priscilla (Scilla) Frances, da of 2 Baron Hazlerigg; 1 s (Thomas Arthur Lee b 1 Oct 1983), 1 da (Charlotte Frances b 1978); *Career* served RHG 1966-69; *Style*— The Hon Richard Dillon

DILLON, Lady; (Elia) Synolda Augusta; *née* Cholmondeley Clarke; o da of Cecil Butler Cholmondeley Clarke (d 1924), of The Hermitage, Holycross, Co Tipperery and Fanny Ethel (d 1971), er da of Maj Edward Augustus Carter, of Theakston Hall Yorks; *b* 19 Mar 1916; *Educ* Alexandra Coll Dublin; *m* 11 Feb 1947, Sir Robert William Charlier Dillon, 8 Bt (d 1982, when the title became extinct, also Baron Holy Roman Empire cr 1782) s of Robert Arthur Dillon, of Folkstone; *Style*— Lady Dillon, Lismullen, 174 Glebemount, Wicklow, Co Wichlow, Ireland

DILLON, Terence John; *b* 16 July 1939; *Educ* St Joseph's Coll Upper Norwood; *m* 10 Aug 1968, Claire; 2 da (Jennifer Joan b 1973, Susan Jane b 1975); *Career* fin & planning BP 1963- (Investmt Dept 1973-); FCA 1961; *Recreations* tennis, chess lepidoptera, antiquarian books; *Style*— Terence Dillon, Esq; British Petroleum Pension Trust, Britannic House, Moore Lane, London EC2Y 9BU (☎ 01 920 4279)

DILLOWAY, Clifford Charles; *b* 22 April 1926; *Educ* Wanstead Co HS; *m* Ada Lilian; 1 s (Graham b 1953), 1 da (Hilary b 1957); *Career* Sgt Air Gunner RAF; arbitrator and expert witness in computer disputes, ed of Software World Series; dir: Dilloway and Son Ltd, Endispute Ltd; dir and gen mangr Package Programs Ltd; Computer Centre mangr, Ford Motor Co Ltd; memb: copyright ctee Br Computer Soc, Br Copyright Cncl; FCMA, FBCS, JDipMA, FCIArb, MIDPM; *Recreations* assisting in his wife's bed and breakfast business; *Style*— Clifford Dilloway, Esq; Highcroft, Gunhouse Lane Stroud, Glos GL5 2DB (☎ 04536 3387)

DILLWYN-VENABLES-LLEWELYN *see also*: Venables-Llewelyn

DILLWYN-VENABLES-LLEWELYN, Lady Delia Mary; da of Capt Michael Hugh Hicks-Beach, MP (Viscount Quenington, s of 1 Earl St Aldwyn, and who was ka 1916, vp); raised to the rank of an Earl's da 1920; *b* 2 August 1910; *m* 3 Dec 1934, Brig Sir (Charles) Michael Dillwyn-Venables-Llewelyn, 3 Bt, MVO, (d 1976); 1 s, 1 da; *Style*— Lady Delia Dillwyn-Venables-Llewelyn; Llysdinam, Newbridge-on-Wye, Llandrindod Wells, Powys (☎ 059 789 200)

DILNOT, Mary; OBE (1981); da of George Dilnot; *b* 23 Jan 1921; *Educ* St Mary's Coll Hampton; *m* 1974, Thomas William Ruffle; *Career* ed Woman's Weekly 1971-81, dir IPC Women's Magazines Gp 1976-81, ret; *Recreations* travel, cooking, golf, reading tapestry work; *Style*— Mrs Thomas Ruffle, OBE; 28 Manor Rd South, Hinchley Wood, Esher, Surrey KT10 0QL (☎ 01 398 5796)

DILWORTH, Stephen Patrick Dominic; s of Patrick Dilworth, of London, and Ida Dilworth; *b* 20 Oct 1951; *Educ* St Josephs Acad Blackheath, Open Univ (BA); *m* 12 April 1975, Susan Carolyn, da of Patrick Joseph Stopps, of Herts; 1 s (Nicholas b 1981), 1 da (Laura b 1982); *Career* regnl mangr Leeds Perm Bldg Soc: Thames Valley 1982-86, London 1986-88; asst gen mangr mktg Town and Country Bldg Soc 1988-; dir Soho Ltd; ctee memb Soho Housing Assoc, assoc memb Borehamwood Operatic Soc; FCBSI 1977; *Books* More Than A Building Society (1987); *Recreations* squash golf, films, football, history, economics; *Clubs* RAC; *Style*— Stephen Dilworth, Esq 215 The Strand, London WC2 (☎ 01 353 1399, fax 01 353 1398)

DIMBLEBY, David; s of Richard Dimbleby, CBE (d 1966), and Dilys, da of late A A Thomas; *b* 28 Oct 1938; *Educ* Charterhouse, Christ Church Oxford, Paris Univ Perugia Univ; *m* 1967, Josceline Rose, da of Thomas Gaskell; 1 s, 2 da; *Career* freelance broadcaster, newspaper proprietor; news reporter BBC Bristol 1960-61, presenter and interviewer on network programmes on (amongst others): religion (Quest), science for children (What's New?), politics (In My Opinion), Top of the Form 1961-63, reporter BBC2 (Enquiry) dir of films including Ku-Klux-Klan, The Forgotten Million, Cyprus: The Thin Blue Line 1964-65; special correspondent CBS News New York, documentary film (Texas-England) and film reports for '60 minutes' 1966-, commentator Current Events 1969, presenter BBC1 24 Hours 1969-72, chm The Dimbleby Talk-In 1971-74, films for Reporter at Large 1973, Election Campaign Report 1974, BBC Election and Results programmes 1979, film series The White Tribe of Africa 1979 (Royal TV Soc Supreme Documentary Award); md Wandsworth Borough News Ltd 1979-86 (chm 1986); presenter: Panorama BBC1 1974-77, 1980-82 (reporter 1967-69), People and Power 1983, General Election Results programmes 1983-87, This Week Next Week 1984-86; md family firm Dimbleby & Sons Ltd 1966-86 (chm 1986-); *Books* An Ocean Apart 1988; *Style*— David Dimbleby, Esq; 14 King St, Richmond, Surrey TW9 1NF

DIMBLEBY, Jonathan; s of Richard Dimbleby, CBE (d 1966), and Dilys, da of A A Thomas; *b* 31 July 1944; *Educ* UCL; *m* 1968, Bel Mooney; 1 s, 1 da; *Career* broadcaster and freelance journalist; television and radio reporter BBC Bristol 1969, with: World at One 1970-71, Thames TV's This Week 1972-78, TV Eye to 1979; prodr and presenter Jonathan Dimbleby in South America 1979 Thames TV; Yorkshire TV (Jonathan Dimbleby in Evidence) 1979-82: The Police 1980, The Bomb 1980, The Eagle and the Bear 1981, The Cold War Game 1982; presenter and ed 1983 series First Tuesday, In Search of the American Dream 1986-88, presenter and interviewer This Week 1987-88 (Thames TV), presenter On The Record 1988- (BBC), chm Any Answers (Radio 4); Soc of Film and TV Arts Richard Dimbleby Award for most outstanding contrib to factual TV 1974; *Books* Richard Dimbleby (1975), The

Palestinians (1979); *Recreations* music, sailing, tennis, walking; *Style—* Jonathan Dimbleby, Esq; c/o David Higham Associates Ltd, 5 Lower John St, London W1

DIMES, Francis Gordon; s of John Francis Arthur Dimes, OBE (d 1966), of New Malden, Surrey, and Elizabeth, *née* Larkey; *b* 17 June 1920; *Educ* Tiffin Sch, Chelsea Coll Univ of London (BSc), Kingston Poly (NCAA, MSc); *m* 8 Sept 1945, Ellen Margaret, *née* Archibald; 3 da (Susan b 1946, Gina b 1948, Jane b 1949); *Career* WWII conscripted 1942, Bombardier signal trg RA 1943, 2 Oban (Air landing) Anti-Tank Regt RA 1 Airborne Divn 1945, Army Educn Corps 1946, WO II 1946, discharged 1947; curator of bldg and decorative stone collections Dept of Palaeontology Geological Survey and Museum 1939-81; vice pres Palaentographical Soc (former sec), chm Friends of the Orton Tst, Freeman City of London, Liveryman Worshipful Co of Masons; memb Palaeontological Assoc; FGS; *Books* Stone in Building (with John Ashurst, 1977), Fossil Collecting (with Richard V Melville, 1979), Conservation of Building and Decorative Stone (with John Ashurst and David Honeyborne, 1988); *Clubs* City Livery, Tetrapods; *Style—* Francis G Dimes, Esq; 31 Bowness Cres, Kingston Vale, London SW15 3QN (☎ 01 546 2079)

DIMMICK, Alexander Mark; s of Roland George Alexander Dimmick (d 1980), late of Bilton Rugby, and Margaret Jayne, *née* Lodge; *b* 17 Oct 1939; *Educ* Rugby Sch, St John's Coll Cambridge (MA); *m* 15 Oct 1962, Josephine Mary, da of Neville Holmes, of Spa Ct, Ripon, N Yorks; 1 s (Alexander b 1970); *Career* chemical engr (chartered); sr ptnr Amplan Mgmnt Systems-Information Tech in Agric, Trade Assoc AEA; ICI Wilton 1968-81, Kimberly Clark Ltd Maidstone 1962-68; *Recreations* antique collecting, music; *Clubs* Inst of Chem Engrs, Br Computer Soc, Nat Art Collections Fund, Old Rugbean Soc, CGA; *Style—* Mark Dimmick, Esq; Whitestone Lodge, Thirlby, Thirsk, Yorks YO7 2DJ (☎ 0845 597330)

DIMMOCK, Rear Adm Roger Charles; s of Frank Charles Dimmock, and Ivy Annie, *née* May; *b* 27 May 1935; *Educ* Price's Sch; *m* 1958, Lesley Patricia Reid; 3 da (Sandra b 1959, Jacqueline b 1960, Nicola b 1963); *Career* entered RN 1953, pilot's wings FAA 1954, USN 1955, qualified Flying Instructor 1959, Master Mariner Foreign Going Cert of Service 1979; served RN Air Sqdns and HM Ships Bulwark, Albion, Ark Royal, Eagle, Hermes, Anzio, Messina, Murray, Berwick (i/c), Naiad (i/c), to 1978; CSO to FO Carriers and Amphibious Ships 1978-80; cmd RNAS: Culdrose 1980-82, HMS Hermes 1982-83; dir Naval Air Warfare MOD 1983-84, Naval Sec 1985-87, Flag Offr Naval Air Cmd 1987, Fleet Air Arm Museum 1987-; chm United Services Hockey Club Portsmouth 1983-87; pres: RN Hockey Assoc 1985-, Combined Services Hockey Assoc 1987-, Denmead-Hambledon Branch RNLI 1981-; memb Ctee of Mgmnt RNLI 1987-; *Recreations* hockey umpire, cricket, squash, golf, family and friends; *Clubs* Royal Cwlth, RN; *Style—* Rear Adm Roger Dimmock; c/o Naval Air Command HQ, RNAS, Yeovilton, Somerset

DIMSON, Dr Elroy; s of David Dimson, of London, and Phyllis, *née* Heilpern; *b* 17 Jan 1947; *Educ* Univ of Newcastle upon Tyne (BA), Univ of Birmingham (MCom), London Univ (PhD); *m* 1 July 1969, Dr Helen Patricia, da of Max Sonn, of Whitley Bay; 3 s (Jonathan Ashley b 1971, Benjamin Simon b 1979, Daniel Marc b 1986), 1 da (Susanna Rachel b 1973); *Career* Tube Investmts 1969-70, Unilever Ltd 1970-72, London Business Sch 1972- (dir MBA Prog 1986-); dir: Mobil Tstee Co, London Univ Pension Fund, Elroy Dimson Assocs; bd memb: Journal of Banking and Fin, Investmt Mgmnt Review; visiting prof: Chicago Univ, Berkeley Univ, Hawaii Univ and Euro Inst Brussels; advsr: SIB, Int Stock Exchange; *Books* Cases in Corporate Finance (with Paul Marsh, 1988), Stock Market Anomalies (1988), Risk Measurement Service (with Paul Marsh, 1979-89); *Style—* Dr Elroy Dimson; London Business Sch, Sussex Place, Regents Park, London NW1 4SA (☎ 01 262 5050, fax 01 724 7875, telex 27461)

DIMSON, Gladys Felicia; CBE (1976); da of late I Sieve; *Educ* Laurel Bank Sch Glasgow, Glasgow Univ, LSE; *m* Dr S B Dimson; 1 da; *Career* memb GLC for Battersea North 1973-85 (former chm GLC Housing Ctee); memb Inner London Education Authority 1970-85; chm: Toynbee Housing Assoc 1976-, East London Housing Assoc 1979-; tstee: Sutton Housing Trust 1982-, SHAC (Shelter Housing Aid Centre); board memb Shelter; memb Council of Toynbee Hall 1983-; *Style—* Mrs Gladys Dimson, CBE

DIN, Russhied Ali; s of Matab Ali Din, of Rawalpindi, Pakistan, and Hilda Rose, *née* Dring (d 1985); *b* 8 April 1956; *Educ* Ordsall Secdy Mod, Salford Coll Technol, Birmingham Poly (BA); *Career* designer: City Industl Shopfitters 1978, Fitch and Co 1979, Italy Studies Giardi Rome 1980, Thomas Saunders Architects 1981, Peter Glynn Smith Assoc 1982-84 (BAA Gatwick refurbishment 1983), Allied Int Designers 1984-86; formed Din Assoc 1986 (became Ltd Co 1988), appt design conslt to Next Retail plc 1987, top office exhibition 1988, dept X concept completed Oxford St 1988, designed theatre set and costumes for Leicester Haymarket Theatre 1989; MCSD; *Recreations* equestrian pursuits, tennis; *Style—* Russhied Din, Esq; Bushell Rd, Balham, London (☎ 01 673 0276); 6 South Lambeth Pl, Vauxhall, London SW8 (☎ 01 582 0777, Fax 01 582 3080)

DINAN, Lady Charlotte Elizabeth Anne; *née* Curzon; da of 6 Earl Howe, CBE; *b* 5 July 1948; *m* March 1988, Barry Dermot Dinan; 1 s (Richard); *Style—* Lady Charlotte Dinan; Chalkpit House, Knotty Green, Beaconsfield, Bucks

DINARDO, Carlo; s of Nicandro Dinardo, and Rosaria, *née* Iannacone; *b* 5 July 1939; *Educ* St Patrick's High Coatbridge Scotland, Paddington Tech Coll, Tech Coll Coatbridge Scotland, Univ of Strathclyde; *m* 30 Aug 1962, Irene Rutherford, da of William James Niven (d 1977), of Helensburgh; 1 s (Mark b 27 April 1967), 2 da (Karen b 24 Oct 1965, Lorraine b 7 Aug 1973); *Career* fndr ptnr Roxburgh Dinardo & Ptnrs consulting engrs 1969, princ Dinardo & Ptnrs 1978-; dir: Scottish Conslts Int 1987-, Dinardo Properties Ltd 1988-; paper published for Inst of Petroleum 1977; Inst of Structural Engrs: paper published on educn 1987, and on structural repairs at Uniroyal 1988, ctee memb of educn task gp 1987-; ctee memb of Industl Trg Advsy Bd at Paisley Coll of Technol; memb bd of govrs Westbourne Sch for Girls Glasgow 1984-; C Eng 1965, MIStructE 1965, MICE 1967, FIStrucE 1976, FICE 1976, MIHT 1979, FInstPet 1979, ACIArb 1980, FGS 1982, FIHT 1982, MConsE 1984, FEANI; *Recreations* golf, skiing, fishing, rugby, curling, historical travels; *Clubs* Royal Northern & Univ (Aberdeen), Buchanan Castle GC (Drymen), Glasgow GC, Royal Aberdeen GC; *Style—* Carlo Dinardo, Esq; Tighness, Main St, Killearn G63 9NB (☎ 0360 50298); Dinardo and Partners, Mirren Court, 119 Renfrew Rd, Paisley, Renfrewshire PA3 4EA (☎ 041 889 1212, fax 041 889 5446, car tel 0860 836 757, telex 265871 84 DAPOO1)

DINGEMANS, Rear Admiral Peter George Valentin; DSO; s of Dr George Albert Dingemans, of Grenofen, Steyning, Sussex, and Marjorie Irene, *née* Spong; *b* 31 July 1935; *Educ* Brighton Coll; *m* 25 March 1961, Faith Vivien, da of Percy Michael Bristow (d 1986); 3 s (Timothy George b 1962, James Michael b 1964, Piers Anthony b 1966); *Career* entered RN 1953, jr offr Vanguard, Superb, Ark Royal 1953-58, 1 Lt Woolaston 1958-60, torpedo anti-sub offr HMS Yarmouth 1963, OIC Leading Rating's Leadership Course 1964, CO HMS Maxton 1965-67, RAF staff course Bracknell 1968, 1 Lt HMS Torquay 1969-70, staff of Flag Offr 2 i/c Far East Fleet, MOD Directorate of Naval Plans 1971-3, cdr: HMS Berwick 1973-74, MOD staff asst COS (policy) 1974-76, Capt Fishery Protection, Mine Counter Measure 1976-78, Royal Coll of Def Studies 1979, i/c HMS Intrepid Falkland Islands Conflict 1980-82, Cdre Amphibious Warfare, Rear Adm 1985, Flag Offr Gibralter 1985-87, COS to C in C Fleet 1987-; Freeman City of London, Liveryman Worshipful Co of Coachmakers and Coach Harnessmakers; *Recreations* family and friends, shooting, tennis; *Clubs* Naval and Military, City Livery; *Style—* Rear Admiral Peter Dingemans, DSO; c/o Lloyds Bank Ltd, Steyning, Sussex

DINGLEY, Gerald Albert; s of Albert Dingley, and Cecilia, *née* Frost; *Educ* Henry Compton Sch for Boys, LSE; *m* 1957, Christine, da of Alexander Wait; 1 s (Mark), 1 da (Tina); *Career* RAF; md Pentax UK Ltd until 1979, pres dir-gen Pentax France SA until 1982; *Style—* Gerald Dingley, Esq; c/o Pentax UK Ltd, Pentax House, South Hill Ave, South Harrow, Middx (☎ 01 864 4422)

DINGWALL, Lady; *see:* Lucas of Crudwell, Baroness

DINGWALL-FORDYCE, Andrew; s of James Alexander Dingwall-Fordyce, TD (d 1988), and Edith Mary, *née* Leather; *b* 22 Feb 1957; *Educ* Rugby, North of Scotland Coll of Agric (OND), Webber Douglas Acad of Dramatic Art; *m* 28 June 1986, Lucinda Mary-Jane, da of Col Francis John Kevin Williams, CBE, TD, DL, of Brimstage, Merseyside; *Career* actor 1976-78, farmer and landowner, sporting agent; vice chm East Aberdeenshire Cons, regnl sec Game Conservancy 1983-, chm North East Region Scottish Landowners Fedn 1989-, memb Club of Deir Aberdeenshire, proess New Deer Agric Assoc Aberdeenshire, pres Highland Gundog Club; *Recreations* shooting, golf, skiing, theatre, bridge, drink, squash; *Clubs* Royal Northern and Univ (Aberdeen); *Style—* Andrew Dingwell-Fordyce of Brucklay; Brucklay Hse, Maud, Peterhead, Aberdeenshire (☎ 07714 253); Brucklay Estate Office, Shevado, Maud, Peterhead, Aberdeenshire

DINKEL, Emmy Gerarda Mary; da of John Jacob Keet (d 1937), of Orsett, Grays, Essex, and Mary, *née* Hartoch (d 1951); *b* 5 Sept 1908; *Educ* Palmer's Coll Grays Essex, Southend on Sea Coll of Art, Royal Coll of Art London; *m* 25 Oct 1941, Prof Ernest Michael Dinkel (d 1983), s of Charles Dinkel (d 1944), of Huddersfield, Yorks; 2 s (John Michael Antony b 9 Oct 1942, Philip Charles Christian b 3 Oct 1946); *Career* teacher of embroidery and design to Evening Insts London 1932-34, arts and crafts teacher Sherborne Sch for Girls 1934-37, freelance illustrator and designer 1937-39, sr instr Coll of Art Gr Malvern 1939-41, supply teacher Edinburgh 1957-61; princ works incl: Dream Children, Funeral of Mozart, Babe Eternal, Jane Eyre, Hungarian Peasant Women, Precious Bane, Flight to Freedom and Peace, The Dream Cloud, Aconites in Duntisbourne; exhibitions incl; RA, RSA, RWA and other galleries; memb Cirencester Civic Soc; RWA 1987, ARCA 1933; *Style—* Mrs Michael Dinkel; 1 The Mead, Cirencester, Glos GL7 2BB (☎ 0285 65 3682)

DINKIN, Anthony David; s of Hyman Dinkin, of London, and Mary, *née* Hine; *b* 2 August 1944; *Educ* Henry Thornton GS Clapham, Coll of Estate Mgmnt London Univ (BSc); *m* 20 Oct 1968, Derina Tanya, da of Benjamin Green, of Surbiton, Surrey; *Career* called to Bar 1968, examiner in law Univ of Reading 1985, rec 1989; Anglo-American Real Property Inst; govr Ripley First Sch; *Recreations* gardening, theatre, music, travel,; *Clubs* Players; *Style—* Anthony Dinkin, Esq; 8 New Sq, Lincolns Inn, London WC2 (☎ 01 242 4986, fax 01 405 1166)

DINWIDDIE, Ian Maitland; s of Lauderdale Maitland Dinwiddie (d 1978), and Frances Lilian Pedrick; *b* 8 Feb 1952; *Educ* Sherborne Sch Dorset, Exeter Univ (BA); *m* 1978, Sally Jane, da of Leslie Ronald Croydon; 1 s (Andrew b 1984), 1 da (Laura b 1981); *Career* audit mangr Arthur Young & Co 1972-82; fin controller Arbuthnot Savory Milln Hldgs Ltd 1982-86, gen mangr Savory Milln Ltd 1986, finance dir Arbuthnot Latham Bank Ltd 1987; *Recreations* sailing; *Style—* Ian Dinwiddie, Esq; Arbuthnot Latham Bank Ltd, 131 Finsbury Pavement, Moorgate, London EC2A 1AY (☎ 01 628 9876, fax 01 638 1545, telex 885970)

DIRKSE-VAN-SCHALKWYK, Hon Mrs ((Lilian) Anne Grenville); da of Rev Hon Louis Chandos Francis Temple Morgan-Grenville, Master of Kinloss (d 1944) and yr sis of Lady Kinloss, *qv*; raised to the rank of a Baron's da 1947); *b* 8 June 1924; *m* 1, 25 Jan 1951, Ernest Frederick Harris, CBE (d 1965); m 2, 10 June 1965, Maurice Emile Deen (d 1971); m 3, 1973, Willem Dirkse-van-Schalkwyk (late S African ambass to Ottawa, Paris and Rome); *Style—* The Hon Mrs Dirkse-van-Schalkwyk; 26 Boulevard des Moulins, Monte Carlo, MC 98000, Monaco

DISBREY, Air Vice-Marshal William Daniel; CB (1966), CBE (1945), AFC (1939); s of Horace William Disbrey (d 1965), and Florence Thornell (d 1923); *b* 23 August 1912; *Educ* Minchenden Secdy Sch, RAF Coll Cranwell; *m* 1939, Doreen Alice, da of William Ivory, of Herts; 2 da (Sally, Patricia); *Career* RAF pilot and engr, dir gen engr RAF, Air Vice-Marshal 1964-67, dir res & dept Bomber Aircraft, Air Cdre 1958-61, Air Off Engrg Strike Cmd (Air Vice-Marshal) 1967-1970; CEng, FIMechE, FRAeS; *Recreations* golf, squash, sailing; *Clubs* RAF; *Style—* Air Vice-Marshal William Disbrey, CB, CBE, AFC; Old Heatherwode, Buxted, E Sussex (☎ 082 581 2104)

DISLEY, John Ivor; CBE (1979); s of Harold Disley and Marie Hughes; *b* 20 Nov 1928; *Educ* Oswestry HS, Loughborough Coll; *m* 1958, Sylvia Cheeseman; 2 da; *Career* former Br steeplechase record holder and former Welsh mile record holder; Bronze Medal winner Helsinki Olympics 1952, Sportsman of the Year 1955; vice-chm Sports Cncl 1974-82; dir: London Marathon Ltd, Fleetfoot Ltd, Silva UK Ltd; memb Royal Cmmn on Gambling.; *Books* Tackle Climbing, Orienteering, Expedition Guide, Yourway with Map & Compass; *Recreations* mountaineering, running; *Clubs* Climbers, Ranelagh Harriers; *Style—* John Disley, Esq, CBE; Hampton House, Upper Sunbury Rd, Hampton, Middlesex (☎ 01 979 1707)

DISS, Eileen (Mrs Raymond Everett); da of Thomas Alexander Diss, and Winifred, *née* Irvine; *b* 13 May 1931; *Educ* Ilford Co HS, Centl Sch of Art and Design; *m* 18 Sept 1953, Raymond Terence Everett, s of Elmon Terence Everett; 2 s (Timothy Patrick b 1959, Matthew Simon Thomas b 1964), 1 da (Danielle Claire b 1956); *Career* BBC TV designer 1952-59, freelance designer 1959-; TV designs for BBC incl: Maigret, Cider with Rosie; for ITV incl: The Prime of Miss Jean Brodie, Porterhouse

Blue; theatre designs for Nat Theatre and West End Theatres; feature films: A Doll's House, Betrayal, 84 Charing Cross Road, A Handful of Dust; BAFTA awards: 1961, 1965, 1974; RDI, FRSA; *Style*— Miss Eileen Diss; 4 Gloucester Walk, London W8 4HZ (☎ 01 937 8794)

DIVER, Hon Sir Leslie Charles; s of J W Diver; *b* 4 Nov 1899; *Educ* Univ Coll Nottingham; *m* 1, 1922, Emma, *née* Blakiston; 1 s, 2 da; m 2, 1971, Mrs Thelma Evans; *Career* farmer and grazier; memb Legislative Cncl WA (County Party) for Central Province 1952-74, pres Legislative Cncl WA 1960-74; kt 1975; *Recreations* bowls; *Clubs* Manning Memorial Bowling; *Style*— The Hon Sir Leslie Diver; 48 Sulman Ave, Salter Point, Como, WA 6152, Australia

DIX, Alan Michael; OBE (1985); s of late Cdr Charles Cabry Dix, CMG, DSO, RN, and Ebba Sievers; *b* 29 June 1922; *Educ* Stenhus Kostskole Denmark; *m* 1955, Helen Catherine McLaren; 1 s, 1 da; *Career* escaped from Nazi occupied Denmark to Scotland 1943; cmmnd RAF 1944; pres Capitol Car Distributors Inc USA 1958-67, gp vice pres Volkswagen of America 1967-68, md Volkswagen (GB) Ltd 1968-72, pres Mid-Atlantic Toyota Inc USA 1972-73, dir of marketing BL Int 1973-74, proprietor Alan M Dix Assocs 1974-76, chm Motor Agents Pensions Administrators Ltd 1976-85, dir Hire Purchase Information Ltd 1977-85, dir-gen The Motor Agents Assoc Ltd London 1976-85; contributor to automotive trade journals; King Christian X War Medal 1947; Freeman and Liveryman Worshipful Co of Coachmakers' and Coach Harness Makers' 1980; FMI, FInstM, FIMH, FBIM; *Recreations* yachting, photography, study of professional mgmnt (int speaker on mgmnt and orgn); *Clubs* Danish, RAF, Burkes, RAF Yacht (Hamble); *Style*— Alan Dix, Esq, OBE; "Tigh Na Failte", Fir Hill, Letham Grange, Near Arbroath, Angus, Scotland (☎ 0241 89421)

DIX, Anthony Arthur William; JP (Wimbledon 1981); s of Lt-Col Harold Arthur George Dix (d 1961), of Charlwood, Surrey, and Olga Antonia Jane Dix; *b* 5 Nov 1930; *Educ* Tonbridge, Univ of London (BSc), Brunel Univ (MA); *m* 18 July 1959, Ellen Maria Helene, da of late Karl Keuneke, of Lübeck; 3 da (Angela Helene Antonia b 1960, Bettina Jane Maria b 1961, Catherine Elizabeth b 1964); *Career* 2 Lt Middx Regt serv KAR 1950; barr Lincoln's Inn 1956, memb Stock Exchange 1962, memb cncl Howard League memb Merton Borough Cncl 1971-74; Parly candidate: (Lib) South Kensington 1964, (Lab) Bridlington 1974; *Recreations* sailing; *Style*— Anthony Dix, Esq JP; 9 Margin Drive, Wimbledon, London SW19 5HA (☎ 01 946 1479); Keith Bayley Rogers & Co, 93-95 Borough High St, London SE1 1NL (☎ 01 378 0657)

DIX, Prof Gerald Bennett; s of Cyril Dix (d 1984), and Mabel Winifred, *née* Bennett (d 1970); *b* 12 Jan 1926; *Educ* Altrincham GS, Univ of Manchester (BA, Dip TP), Harvard (Master Landscape Architecture); *m* 1956 (m dis); 2 s (Stephen b 1957, Graham b 1959); m 2, 1963, Lois, da of John Noel Nichols (d 1966); 1 da (Kate b 1964); *Career* RAF 1944-47; studio asst in architecture Manchester Univ 1950-51 (asst lectr 1951-53), chief asst to Sir Patrick Abercrombie and city planning offr Addis Ababa 1954-56, sr planning offr Singapore 1957-59, acting planning advsr Singapore 1959, sr res fell Ghana 1959-63, sr planner BRS/ODA UK Govt 1963-68, lectr then sr lectr Nottingham Univ 1966-70 (prof of planning 1970-75); Liverpool Univ: Lever prof 1978-80, pro vice-chllr 1984-87, hon sr fell 1988-; memb: E Midlands Econ Planning Cncl 1973-75, Historic Areas Advsy Ctee English Heritage 1986-88; pres World Soc for Ekistics 1987-89; ARIBA 1950-87, FRTPI; *Books* Ecology and Ekistics (ed 1977), Third World Planning Review (fndr ed 1978-); *Recreations* travel, photography; *Clubs* Athenaeum; *Style*— Prof Gerald Dix; 13 Friars Quay, Norwich NR3 1ET (☎ 0603 632 433); Dept of Civic Design, Univ of Liverpool, P O Box 147, Liverpool L69 3BX (☎ 051 794 3121, fax 051 708 6502, telex 627095 UNIL PLG)

DIX, Wing Cdr Kenneth John Weeks; OBE (1975), AFC (1958), QC (1967); s of Eric John Dix (d 1982), of Dorset, and Kate, *née* Weeks; *b* 12 Sept 1930; *Educ* HMC Canford Dorset (PSC, AWC); *m* 1, 1963 (m dis 1966); 19 July 1969, Susan Mary, da of Lt Cdr C Sharp (d 1954); 1 s (Michael b 1956), 1 da (Linda b 1954); *Career* RAF 1948-83, ret Wing Cdr, served Europe, ME, Far East; business devpt mangr electronic def systems Marconi Def Systems Ltd; dir Electric Def Assoc; Queens Commendation 1967; MRAeS, MBIM, MIEE; *Recreations* fly fishing, horse riding, shooting, study of antiques; *Clubs* RAF; *Style*— Wing Cdr Kenneth J W Dix, OBE, AFC; 41 Lincoln Park, Amersham, Bucks (☎ 0494 725562); Marconi Def Systems, The Grove, Warren Lane, Stanmore, Middx (☎ 01 954 2311)

DIXEY, Paul Arthur Groser; s of Charles Neville Douglas Dixey, JP (d 1947), of Little Berkhampstead, nr Hertford, and Marguerite Isabel, *née* Groser (d 1973); *b* 13 April 1915; *Educ* Stowe, Trinity Coll Cambridge (BA); *m* 23 Sept 1939, Mary Margaret Baring, JP, da of Herbert Geoffrey Garrod (d 1974); 4 s (Michael b 1942, Charles b 1944, James b 1947, Benjamin b 1953), 1 da (Elizabeth b 1950); *Career* WWII Gunner RA 1939-45; underwriter Lloyds 1938, chm PIERI Underwriting Agencies Ltd 1982-88, memb Lloyds Underwriters Assoc 1962-74; elected ctee memb Salvage Assoc 1962-74, (chm 1964 and 1965), memb gen ctee Lloyds Register of Shipping 1964-, ctee memb Lloyds 1964-70 and 1972-75 (dep chm 1967, 1969 and 1972, chm 1973 and 1974); memb cncl Morley Coll 1952-62, chm govrs Vinehall Sch 1966-76, memb London Insur Mkt Delgn to Indonesia 1958; chm Essex Hunt 1980-,; *Recreations* fishing, fox hunting; *Style*— Paul A G Dixey, Esq; Little Easton Spring, Dunmow, Essex (☎ 0371 2840)

DIXIE, Lady (Dorothy Penelope); da of E King-Kirkman; *m* 7 Dec 1950, as his 2 wife, Sir (Alexander Archibald Douglas) Wolstan Dixie, 13 Bt (d 1975, when title became dormant); 2 da (Eleanor b 1952, Caroline b 1960); *Style*— Lady Dixie; Bosworth Park, Leics

DIXON, Dr Bernard; s of Ronald Dixon (d 1962) and Grace Pierson; *b* 17 July 1938; *Educ* Queen Elizabeth GS Darlington, King's Coll Univ of Durham (BSc), Univ of Newcastle upon Tyne (PhD); *m* 1963 (m dis 1987), Margaret Helena Charlton; 2 s, 1 da; *Career* formerly res fell Univ of Newcastle, dep ed World Medicine 1966-68; ed New Scientist 1969-79 (dep ed 68-69); European ed: The Sciences 1980-85, Science 1980-86, The Scientist 1986-; columnist Br Med Journal, Biol Technology (USA), Biotec (Italy), Tiede (Finland); conslt ed Scientific Research in Europe project; memb bd Speculations in Sci and Technology Mircen Journal; vice pres Section Br Assoc for Advancement of Sci, exec memb Cncl for Sci and Soc; memb cncl: Palos Inst London, European Environmental Res Organisation; CSS 1982; FIBiol 1982 CBiol 1984; *Books* What is Science For (1973), Beyond the Magic Bullet (1978), Invisible Allies (1976), Health and the Human Body (1986), Ideas of Science (1984), How Science Works (1989), From Creation to Chaos (1989); *Style*— Dr Bernard Dixon; 139 Cornwall Rd, Ruislip Manor, Middlesex HA4 6AW (☎ 0895 632 390)

DIXON, Bernard Tunbridge; s of Archibald Tunbridge Dixon; *b* 1928; *Educ* Owen's Sch, UCL (LLB); *m* 1962, Jessie Netta Watson, *née* Hastie; 1 s, 3 da; *Career* slr 1952, former ptnr Dixon & Co, sr legal asst with charity cmmrs 1970-74, dep charity cmmr 1975-81, charity cmmr 1981-84; *Style*— Bernard Dixon, Esq; T J Smith & Son, 14 Castle St, Liverpool L2 0SG

DIXON, Brian Ringrose; s of Reginald Ernest Dixon (d 1978), of Market Weighton, and Marianne, *née* Ringrose; *b* 4 Jan 1938; *Educ* Pocklington Sch; *m* 8 Oct 1966, Mary Annette, s of Sidney Robertson (d 1982), of Hawick; 2 s (James b 1971, John b 1973); *Career* Barclays Bank plc: asst mangr Scarborough 1971-73, asst mangr Grimsby 1973-76, asst dist mangr (staff) York dist 1976-79, mangr Berwick upon Tweed 1979-83, regnl dir Scotland 1983-; cncl memb Scottish Enterprise Fndn; memb: governing cncl Scottish Business in the Community, Royal Highland and Agric Soc of Scotland; ACIB; *Recreations* rugby, cricket; *Style*— Brian Dixon, Esq; 90 St Vincent St, Glasgow G2 5UQ (☎ 041 221 9585, fax 041 221 1714, telex 777286)

DIXON, Christopher John Arnold; TD; s of Hubert John Dixon, MC (d 1972), of Wimbledon, and Mary Frances (d 1958); *b* 17 August 1928; *Educ* Rugby; *m* 8 Oct 1955, Ethelwyn Ada, da of Lt-Col J H Mousley, DSO, TD (d 1959), of Middleton Tyas, Yorks; 3 s (Anthony b 1958, Timothy b 1962, Michael b 1963), 1 da (Phyllida b 1960); *Career* Nat Serv and Short Serv Cmmn 2 Lt RA 1947-50, Maj TA 1951-60; Norton Rose 1951-88: ptnr 1960-81, dep sr ptnr 1981-; memb Law Soc 1955; *Recreations* sailing; *Clubs* City Univ, RA YC; *Style*— Christopher Dixon, Esq; Norton Rose, Kempson House, Camomile St, London EC3A 7AN (☎ 01 283 2434, fax 01 588 1181, telex 883652)

DIXON, Colin Steele; s of Oliver Colin Dixon, MBE, TD, of The Four Winds, Thorsway, Caldy, Wirral, and Kathleen Mary, da of Peter Gray; ggf founded paper firm of L S Dixon & Co Ltd 1876; *b* 3 May 1952; *Educ* Ampleforth; *m* 16 Aug 1975, Penelope Jane, da of Wing-Cdr James Eric Storrar, DFC, AFC, AE, of 14 The Tower House, Curzon Park North, Chester; 1 s (Charles Lanty b 1985), 2 da (Rozanne b 1980, Laura (twin) b 1980); *Career* md L S Dixon Gp Ltd 1987; chm Walter Scott Motors; dir: Slater Harrison 7 Co Ltd, Dean Valley Ltd; *Recreations* racing, shooting, tennis; *Clubs* Turf; *Style*— Colin Dixon, Esq; The Old Post House, Woodmancott, nr Winchester, Hants SO21 3BL (☎ 025 675 541)

DIXON, Hon Mrs (Daphne Cecil Rosemary); da of 1 Baron Harmsworth (d 1948); *b* 1901; *m* 1, 14 March 1928 (m dis 1937), Capt Colin David Brodie; m 2, 12 May 1938, Lt-Col Harold Macneile Dixon, RASC; 2 da; *Style*— The Hon Mrs Dixon; Lagham Manor, South Godstone, Surrey

DIXON, David Michael; s of Rev James Eric Dixon, MC (d 1955), of Surrey, and Florence, *née* Pye (d 1980); *b* 1 May 1926; *Educ* Whitgift Sch, Oxford Univ (MA), Harvard Univ Law Sch, Cwlth Fund Fellow (LLM); *m* 1953, Alison Mary, da of Sir Leonard Sinclair (d 1984), of Surrey; 2 s, 1 da; *Career* chm ELF UK plc; slr; ptnr Withers 1957- (sr ptnr 1982-86), hon legal advsr Br Olympic Assoc 1977-; hon sec Cwlth Games Fedn 1982-; RAFVR 1944-47; parachute jumping instructor; Oxford Univ athletics blue; pres OUAC 1950; *Recreations* sport, travel; *Clubs* Brooks's, Hurlingham, Achilles, Vincent's; *Style*— David Dixon, Esq; 10 Peek Crescent, London SW19 5ER (☎ 01 946 4125); Mains of Panholes, Blackford, Perthshire (☎ 076 482 351); 197 Knightsbridge, London SW7 1RZ (☎ 01 225 5555, telex 919156, fax 01 225 5197)

DIXON, Donald; MP (Lab) Jarrow 1979-; s of late Christopher Albert and Jane Dixon; *b* 6 March 1929; *Educ* Ellison Street Elementary Sch Jarrow; *m* Doreen Morad; 1 s, 1 da; *Career* shipyard worker 1947-74; branch sec GMWU 1974-79; cllr Sth Tyneside MDC 1963-; *Style*— Don Dixon, Esq, MP; 1 Hillcrest, Jarrow, Tyne and Wear NE32 4DP (☎ 091 897635)

DIXON, Guy Holford; s of late Montague Dixon, and late Edith Goward, *née* Holford; *b* 20 March 1902; *Educ* Abbotsholme Sch Derbys, Repton, Univ Coll Oxford (BA); *Career* called to the Bar Inner Temple 1929, rec of Newark on Trent 1965-71 (hon rec 1972-); dep chm: Leics QS 1960-71; Northamptons QS 1966-71, rec of Crown Ct 1972-75; lay cannon Leics Cathedral 1962-84 (lay cannon emeritus 1984-); *Recreations* collecting and looking at paintings, icons and antiques, gardening; *Clubs* Reform; *Style*— Guy Dixon, Esq; The Old Rectory, Brampton Ash, Market Harborough, Leicester (☎ 085885 200); Barristers Chambers, 2 New St, Leicester (☎ 0533 25906)

DIXON, Ian Leonard; s of late Leonard Frank Dixon; *b* 3 Nov 1938; *Educ* S W Essex Co Tech Sch, Harvard Business Sch; *m* 1961, Valerie Diana, da of late Alexander Barclay; 2 s, 1 da; *Career* chartered builder; jt chm and chief exec Willmott Dixon Hldgs Ltd 1971-, ccncllr Beds 1977-85, tstee The Bedford Charity 1977-86; chm Herts Health Authy 1984-87, CBJ Eastern Region; FCIOB (pres elect), CBIM, FRSA; *Recreations* shooting, philately; *Style*— Ian Dixon, Esq; 19 Albany St, Regents Park, London, NW1 4DX (☎ 01 4867237)

DIXON, James Wolryche; s of Michael Wolryche Dixon, of Withy Fold, Cook's Corner, Crowborough, Sussex, and Barbara Mary, *née* Eccles; *b* 20 Feb 1948; *Educ* Lancing, Corpus Christi Coll Oxford (MA); *Career* RAFVR actg PO Oxford Univ Air Sqdn 1966-69; articled with Barton Mayhew & Co 1969, ptnr Ernst & Whinney 1984-; FCA 1972, FRSA 1988; *Books* Vat Guide and Casebook (conslt ed, first edn), Tax Case Analysis (contrib), Vat Planning (contrib); *Recreations* cycling, photography, bridge, cooking; *Clubs* United Oxford and Cambridge Univ; *Style*— James Dixon, Esq; 48 Lytton Grove, Putney, London SW15 2HE (☎ 01 788 6717); Ernst & Whinney, Becket Ho, 1 Lambeth Palace Rd, London SE1 7EU (☎ 01 928 2000, fax 01 928 1345)

DIXON, Capt Sir John George; 3 Bt (UK 1919) of Astle, Chelford, co Palatine of Chester; s of Sir John Dixon, 2 Bt (d 1976), and Gwendolen Anne (d 1974), da of Sir Joseph Layton Elmes Spearman, 2 Bt; *b* 17 Sept 1911; *Educ* Cranleigh; *m* 1 May 1947, Caroline, da of late Charles Theodore Hiltermann; 1 da; *Heir* nephew, Jonathan Mark Dixon; *Clubs* Cavalry; *Style*— Capt Sir John Dixon, Bt; c/o Miss Beryl Dixon, 96 East St, Corfe Castle, Dorset

DIXON, Jonathan Mark; s of Capt Nigel Dixon, OBE, RN (d 1978), and Margaret, da of late Maurice John Collett; hp of unc, Sir John Dixon, 3 Bt; *b* 1 Sept 1949; *Educ* Winchester, Oxford Univ (BA); *m* 1978, Patricia Margaret, da of James Baird Smith; 2 s, 1 da; *Recreations* fishing; *Style*— Jonathan Dixon Esq; 19 Clyde Road, Bristol BS6 6RJ

DIXON, Kenneth Herbert Morley; s of Arnold Morley Dixon (d 1975); *b* 19 August 1929; *Educ* Cranbrook Sch Sydney Aust, Manchester Univ; *m* 1955, Patricia Oldbury, *née* Whalley; 2 s (Michael, Giles b 1969); *Career* Lt Royal Signals BAOR Cyprus; chm Rowntree Mackintosh Ltd 1981- (dep chm 1978-81); dir: Rowntree and Co Ltd, Rowntree Mackintosh (Ingredients) Ltd; chm Fox's Glacier Mints Ltd, dir Fox's Hldgs (Leicester) Ltd and others; *Recreations* reading, music, fell walking; *Style*— Kenneth Dixon, Esq; Rowntree Mackintosh Ltd, Wigginton Rd, York (☎ 0904 53071)

DIXON, Oliver Colin; MBE (1945), TD (1950); s of Herbert Lancelot Dixon (d 1969), of Little Stanney, nr Chester, and Kathline May, *née* Carrigan (d 1973); gs of Lancelot Steele Dixon, who founded Paper Firm of L S Dixon & Co Ltd 1876; *b* 1 Sept 1918; *Educ* Uppingham; *m* 1943, Kathleen Mary, da of Peter Gray (d 1964), of Wirral; 1 s (Colin), 1 da (Gillian); *Career* 2 Cheshire Fd Sqn RE, 7 and 10 Armd Divs in Western Desert 1940-43 (despatches), SHAEF G-2 Div 1943-46 Maj (despatches); pres: L S Dixon Gp Ltd 1945, Slater Harrison & Co Ltd 1947, Dean Valley Ltd 1947, Hurcott Paper Mills Ltd 1946; dir Walter Scott Motors Ltd 1977; US Bronze Star 1946; *Recreations* gardening; *Clubs* Army & Navy, Liverpool Racquet; *Style*— Oliver Dixon, Esq, MBE, TD; The Four Winds, Thorsway, Caldy, Wirral (☎ 051 625 9469); L S Dixon Gp Ltd, Richmond House, Rumford Place, Liverpool (☎ 051 236 3060, telex 668861)

DIXON, Hon Peter Herbert; s of 2 Baron Glentoran; *b* 15 May 1948; *Educ* Eton, Grenoble U; *m* 1975, Jane Blanch, da of Eric Cutler; 2 da (Louise Vyvyan Mary b 1977, Rose Clare b 1980); *Career* chartered accountant; *Recreations* tennis, shooting; *Clubs* Boodle's; *Style*— The Hon Peter Dixon; The Old Rectory, Yattendon, Newbury, Berks

DIXON, Peter Richard Hamilton; ERD (1963); s of Arthur Frederick William Dixon, CSI, CIE (d 1947), of Church Crookham, Hants, and Gwendolen Mary, *née* Hamilton (d 1952); *b* 3 Oct 1931; *Educ* Shrewsbury, Christs Coll Cambridge (MA, LLB); *m* 17 Dec 1966, Christine Mary, da of Alderman Edward Francis Gethin (d 1959), of Shrewsbury; 1 s (John Peter Christian b 25 Jan 1970); *Career* Nat Serv RCS 1950-52, army emergency res RCS 1952-70, 81 Signal Sqdn OC (V) 1967-70 (Hon Col (V) 1981-87); slr 1959; sr ptnr Radcliffes & Co 1981-(ptnr 1961-); Liveryman Worshipful Co of Makers of Playing Cards; memb Soc of Knights of the Round Table; memb Law Soc 1959; *Recreations* rowing, travel; *Clubs* East India, Leander; *Style*— Peter Dixon, Esq, ERD; 25 Victoria Grove, London W8 5RW (☎ 01 584 7954); Flat C2, The Court, St Mary's Place, Shrewsbury; 10 Little College St, Westminster, London SW1P 3SJ (☎ 01 222 7040)

DIXON, Peter Vibart; s of Meredith Vibart Dixon (d 1967), of Surrey, and Phyllis Joan, *née* Hemingway (d 1982); *b* 16 July 1932; *Educ* Radley, King's Coll Cambridge (MA); *m* 1955, Elizabeth Anne Howie, da of Dr Max Davison (d 1970), of Surrey; 3 s (Patrick, Henry, Nigel); *Career* Nat Serv RA 1950-51; various posts in: HM Treasy, Off of the Lord Privy Seal, Colonial Off, Civil Serv Cmmn; economic cncllr Br Embassy Washington 1972-75, press sec and head of information div HM Treasy 1975-78, under sec (industl policy) HM Treasy 1978-82, Sec to Nat Economic Devpt Cncl 1982-87; dir of planning and admin Turner Kenneth Brown (slrs) 1987-; memb Royal Institute of Public Admin; FRSA, FBIM; *Clubs* United Oxford & Cambridge Univ; *Style*— Peter Dixon, Esq; 17 Lauriston Road, Wimbledon, London SW19 4TJ (☎ 01 946 8931); Nat Economic Devpt Off, Millbank Tower, Millbank, London SW1P 4QX (☎ 01 211 4148)

DIXON, Piers; s of Sir Pierson Dixon (d 1965), by his w (Alexandra) Ismène (d 1987); *b* 20 Dec 1928; *Educ* Eton, Magdalene Coll Cambridge (MA), Harvard Business Sch; *m* 1, 1960 (m dis 1973), Edwina, da of Lord Duncan-Sandys; 2 s (Mark, Hugo); m 2, 1976 (m dis 1981), Janet, wid of 5th Earl Cowley and da of Ramiah Doraswamy Aiya, of Wales; m 3, 1984, Anne, da of John Cronin; 1 s (Piers b 1981); *Career* 2 Lt Grenadier Gds 1948-49; merchant banking London and NY 1954-64, ptnr Sheppards and Chase (stockbrokers) 1964-81, MP (C) Truro 1970-74, sec Cons Backbenchers' Finance Ctee 1970-71 (vice-chm 1972-74); sponsor Rehabilitation of Offenders Act 1974; *Books* Double Diploma (1968), Cornish Names (1973); *Recreations* tennis, modern history; *Clubs* Beefsteak, Brooks's, Pratt's; *Style*— Piers Dixon, Esq; 22 Ponsonby Terrace, London SW1 (☎ 01 821 6166, telex 895 1859 BASIL G)

DIXON, Prof Richard Newland; s of Robert Thomas Dixon (d 1985), of Borough Green, Kent, and Lilian, *née* Newland (d 1973); *b* 25 Dec 1930; *Educ* Judd Sch Kent, Kings Coll London Univ (BSc), St Catharines Coll Cambridge Univ (PhD, DSc); *m* 18 Sept 1954, Alison Mary, da of Gilbert Arnold Birks (d 1966), of Horsforth, Leeds; 1 s (Paul b 1959), 2 da (Joan b 1961, Sheila b 1962); *Career* post doctoral fell Nat Res Cncl of Canada 1957-59, ICI fell lectr in chem Sheffield Univ 1959-69, Sorby res FRS Sheffield Univ 1964-69, prof of chem Univ of Bristol 1969- (dean of sci 1979-82), visiting scholar Stanford Univ USA 1982-83; memb: Faraday Cncl of Royal Soc of Chem (vice-pres 1989-), SERC ctees; C Chem 1976, FRSC 1976, FRS 1986; *Books* Spectroscopy and Structure (1965), Theoretical Chemistry (Vol 1 1971, Vol 2 1973, Vol 3 1975); *Recreations* mountain walking, travel, theatre, concerts, photography; *Style*— Prof Richard Dixon; 22 Westbury Lane, Bristol BS9 2PE (☎ 0272 681691); School of Chemistry, University of Bristol, Cantock's Close, Bristol BS8 1TS 1TS (☎ 0272 303030 ex 4270)

DIXON, Hon (Thomas) Robin Valerian; MBE (1969), DL (1979); er s of 2 Baron Glentoran, KBE, PC, *qv*, and Lady Diana Wellesley, da of 3 Earl Cowley; *b* 21 April 1935; *Educ* Eton; *m* 1, 12 Jan 1959 (m dis 1975), Rona, da of Capt George C Colville, of Bishop' Waltham; 3 s; m 2, 1979, Alwyn Gillian, da of Hubert A Mason, of Donaghadee Co Down; *Career* 2 Lt Grenadier Gds 1954, Capt 1958, Maj 1966; md Redland of N Ireland 1972-; *Recreations* sailing (yacht 'Lazy Life'), squash, skiing; *Clubs* Kildare St Univ (Dublin); *Style*— The Hon Robin Dixon, MBE, DL; Drumadarragh House, Ballyclare, Co Antrim, N Ireland; c/o Redland of N Ireland Ltd, 61 Largy Rd, Crumlin, Co Antrim, N Ireland BT29 4RR (0843 94 22791)

DIXON, Roy; s of Tom Dixon (d 1972), and Gladys, *née* Walsh (d 1988); *b* 9 Feb 1938; *Educ* King William's Coll IOM; *m* 25 March 1961, Shirley; 1 s (Andrew b 1964), 1 da (Amanda b 1962); *Career* slr, md Poco Properties Ltd 1972-86, dir McArd Hldgs Ltd 1986-; *Recreations* motor sport, skiing; *Style*— Roy Dixon, Esq; Newhaven Shore Rd, Port St Mary, IOM (☎ 0624 832233); Church Rd, Port Erin, IOM (fax 0624 833011); car phone 0860 640 014)

DIXON, Stanley; s of Sidney Dixon (d 1962), of Walsall, Staffs, and Rose, *née* Forrester (d 1975); *b* 19 May 1927; *Educ* Queen Marys GS Walsall, Univ of Birmingham (BSc, PhD); *m* 12 July 1951, Diana Joyce, da of Alfred Kendrick; 2 da (Wendy b 1955, Valerie b 1959); *Career* res scientist and supervisor Ei Du Pont Inc 1951-61; Du Pont UK Ltd: lab dir 1963-68, sales mangr 1968-71; div dir Geneva Du Pont Int 1971-83, md Benzole Producers Ltd 1983-; memb SIGMA X1; *Recreations* golf; *Clubs* Sandy Lodge, Oriental; *Style*— Dr Stanley Dixon; Nantucket, Violet Way, Loudwater, Rickmansworth, Herts WD3 4JP (☎ 0923 776139); 44 Lowndes St, London SW1X 9BB (☎ 01 235 6895, fax 01 245 6796, telex 21574 BRCL G)

DIXON SMITH, Robert William (Bill); DL 1986; s of Mr Dixon Smith, of Lascelles, Thistley Green Rd, Bocking, Braintree, Essex, and Alice Winifred Smith (d 1976); *b* 30 Sept 1934; *Educ* Oundle, Writtle Agric Coll; *m* 13 Feb 1960, Georgina Janet, da of George Cook, of Firview, Tidings Hill, Walstead, Essex; 1 s (Adam William George b 11 Jan 1962), 1 da (Sarah Jane b 16 Dec 1960); *Career* Nat Serv 2Lt King's Dragoon Guards 1955-57; farmer; chm Essex CC 1986-(memb 1965-); Freeman Worshipful Co of Farmers 1988; *Style*— Bill Dixon Smith, Esq, DL; Houchins, Coggeshall, Essex CO6 !RT (☎ 0336 61448); c/o County Hall, Chelmsford, Essex

DIXON-GREEN, Anthony Joseph; s of Joseph Dixon Green, MBE (d 1963), and Lilian May Dixon (d 1972); *b* 12 Sept 1926; *Educ* Stowe; *m* 1, 6 Oct 1955, Angela Dawn Holley, da of Major Kenneth Herbert Holley, of Herts; 1 s (Simon Anthony), 1 da (Melanie Clare); m 2, 11 July 1981, da of Susan Faulkener, of Hants; *Career* Capt Royal Hampshire Regt (Palestine 1946-47); chm LS Dixon Gp Ltd 1987, dir: Walter Scott Motors Ltd 1977, Dean Valley Ltd 1952, Hurcott Paper Mills Ltd 1952, Walter Scott Motors (London) 1978; memb of Ct Worshipful Co of Stationars and Newspaper Makers 1983;; *Recreations* sailing, hunting, skiing; *Clubs* Royal Yacht Sqdn, Royal Ocean Racing; *Style*— Anthony Dixon-Green, Esq; Sunbeam Cottage, Church Oakley, Basingstoke, Hants; L S Dixon Gp Ltd, Octagon House, Rectory Road, Oakley, Hants RG23 7LJ (☎ 0256 782106)

DOBB, Erlam Stanley; CB (1963), TD; s of Arthur Erlam Dobb (d 1957); *b* 16 August 1910; *Educ* Ruthin, Univ Coll of N Wales; *m* 1937, Margaret, da of Percy Williams (d 1955), of Colwyn Bay; *Career* asst and land cmmr Miny of Agric Fish and Food 1935-47, Agric Land Serv 1947-71 (dir 1959-70), dir-gen ADAS 1973-75; govr Royal Agric Coll 1960-75, chm Thomas Phillips Price Trustees 1971-83 (trustee and memb 1984); memb Agric Res Cncl 1973-75; *Clubs* Farmers'; *Style*— Erlam Dobb, Esq, CB, TD; Churchgate, Westerham, Kent (☎ 0959 62294)

DOBBS, Joseph Alfred; CMG (1972), OBE (1957, MBE 1945), TD (1945); s of John Large, of Ireland, and Ruby Adelaide, *née* Gillespie; *b* 22 Dec 1914; *Educ* Worksop Coll, Trinity Hall Cambridge (MA);; *m* 1949, Marie Joan, da of Reginald Francis Catton, of Aust; 4 s (Michael, Geoffrey, Peter, Christopher); *Career* serv WWII Maj RA (despatches); HM Dip Serv; FO 1946, serv Moscow 1947-51, 1954-57 and 1965-68, FO 1951-54, Delhi 1957-61, Warsaw 1961-64, Rome 1964-65, consul gen Zagreb 1969-70, min Moscow 1971-74; *Recreations* reading, riding, gardening; *Style*— Joseph Dobbs, Esq, CMG, OBE, TD; The Coach House, Charlton Musgrove, Wincanton, Somerset (☎ 0963 33356)

DOBBS, Richard Arthur Frederick; JP (1956 Co Antrim), DL (1957 Co Antrim); o s of Maj Arthur Frederick Dobbs, JP, DL (d 1955), of Castle Dobbs, memb Senate of N Ireland 1923-33 and 1937-55, and Hylda Louisa, *née* Higginson (d 1957); descended from Robert Dobbs, of Batley, Yorkshire, whose gs John Dobbs went to Ireland in 1596 (*see* Burke's Irish Family Records); *b* 2 April 1919; *Educ* Eton, Magdalene Coll Camb (BA, MA); *m* 28 Aug 1953, Carola Day, da of Gp Capt Christopher Clarkson, of Old Lyme, Connecticut, USA; 4 s ((Richard Francis) Andrew b 28 May 1955, Nigel Christopher b 19 March 1957, Matthew Frederick b 5 July 1959, Nicholas Arthur Montagu b 12 Feb 1973), 1 da (Sophia Carola b 27 Aug 1965); *Career* T/Capt Irish Guards (Supplementary Reserve), served WW II; barr Lincoln's Inn 1947, memb Midland circuit 1951-55; HM Lt for Co Antrim 1959-75 (Lord Lt 1975-); *Clubs* Cavalry and Guards'; Castle Dobbs, Carrickfergus, Co Antrim, Northern Ireland (☎ 0960372238)

DOBBS, Prof (Edwin) Roland; s of Albert Edwin Dobbs (d 1961), and Harriet, *née* Wright; *b* 2 Dec 1924; *Educ* Ilford County HS, Queen Elizabeth's GS Barnet, UCL (BSc, PhD, DSc); *m* 7 April 1947, Dorothy Helena, da of the late Alderman A F T Jeeves of Stamford, Lincs; 2 s (Richard b 1952, Jeremy b 1964) 1 da (Jane b 1949); *Career* radar res offr Admty 1943-46, lectr in physics Queen Mary Coll Univ of London 1949-58, assoc prof physics Brown Univ USA 1959-60 (res assoc applied maths 1958-59), AEI fell Cavendish Lab Univ of Cambridge 1960-64, prof of physics and head of dept of physics Univ of Lancaster 1964-73; Hildred Carlile: prof of physics Bedford Coll London 1973-85, prof and head of dept of physics RHBNC Univ of London 1985-, dean faculty of sci Univ of London 1988- (vice dean 1986-88); visiting prof: Brown Univ 1966, Wayne State Univ 1969, Univ of Tokyo 1977, Univ of Delhi 1983, Cornell Univ USA 1984, Univ of Florida 1989; memb: Physics Ctee SRC 1970-73, Nuclear Physics Bd SRC 1974-77; chm Solid State Physics Sub Ctee Sci and Engrg Res Cncl 1983-86; FInst P 1964 (hon sec 1976-84), FIOA 1977 (pres 1976-78); *Books* Electricity and Magnetism (1984), Electromagnetic Waves (1985); *Recreations* travel, gardening, music; *Clubs* Athenaeum; *Style*— Prof Roland Dobbs; Royal Holloway and Bedford New College, Egham Hill, Egham, Surrey TW20 0EX (☎ 0784 34455, fax 0784 37520, telex 935504)

DOBBY, David Lloyd; s of William Lloyd Dobby, of Walmer, Deal, Kent, and Susan Kathleen, *née* Jobson (d 1986); *b* 6 April 1936; *Educ* St Dunstan's Coll Catford, Regent St Poly (Dip Arch); *m* 17 March 1967, Lesley Madeline, da of Frederick William Herron, of Walmer, Deal, Kent; 2 da (Anna b 19 March 1969, Liz b 27 July 1971); *Career* architect 1965; CWS 1957-59, Ronald Ward & Partnership 1959-61, Raymond Spratley & Ptnrs 1961-63, Douglas Marriott & Ptnrs 1963-65, James Munce Ptnrship 1965-68, Rush & Tompkins Gp Architects 1968-73; ptnr private practice 1973-86: John Floydd Ptnrship, Dobby Foard & Ptnrs, DY Davies Dobby Foard; dir practice DY Davies plc 1986-88, md Sargent & Potiriadis 1988-; House of the Year Design Award 1970 and 1972; designs incl: first Bush Bank West Africa, theme park Florida, new railway village Ashford Kent, Rush & Tompkins HQ offs Sidcup Chatham House, Duke of York St, St James parish cncllr 1978-86; tres local ballet sch 1980-85, memb Dover Girls GS PTA 1980-86, former master and tres City Lodge; Freeman City of London 1981, Liveryman Worshipful Co of Joiners and Ceilers 1981; RIBA 1965; *Recreations* golf, reading; *Clubs* Royal Cinque Ports, East India, Folio Soc; *Style*— David Dobby, Esq; 10 Jarvist Place, Kingsdown, nr Deal, Kent CT14 8AL (☎ 0304 373331); Sargent & Potiriadis, 3-5 Charing Cross Rd, London WC2H OHA (☎ 01 930 9010, fax 01 925 0219)

DOBELL, Anthony Russell; s of Thomas Russell Dobell, MBE, TD, of Cheshire, and Fiona Helen, *née* Barrett (d 1974); *b* 15 Sept 1948; *Educ* Rugby; *m* 15 April 1983, Hilary, da of Ronald Shaw, of Cheshire; 2 s (Richard b 1985, Myles b 1987); *Career*

CA 1971, ptnr Robson Rhodes Manchester 1978-88, AR Dobell & Co 1988-, AR Dobell & Co 1988-; hon sec Manchester Soc of CA 1986-; memb Over Peover Parish Cncl 1985-; hon sec Friends of Manchester Northern Hosp 1975-; FCA; *Recreations* family, gardening, walking, most sports; *Clubs* St James's Manchester, Knutsford Golf, Alderley Edge Tennis and Squash; *Style*— Anthony R Dobell, Esq; Pear Tree Farm, Peover Heath, Cheshire, Chelford (☎ 0625 861454); 13 Hyde Road, Denton (☎ 061 320 4111)

DOBIE, Brig Joseph Leo; CBE (1969); s of David Walter Dobie (d 1943); *b* 26 Sept 1914; *Educ* Tynemouth HS, Univ of Durham (BSc), Mil Coll of Sci; *m* 1940, Joan Clare, da of Frank Watson (d 1982); 1 s, 3 da; *Career* 2 Lt RE (TA) 1937, Tyne Electrical Engrs RE (TA), Lt RAOC 1938, REME 1942, serv WWII; Cmdt Army Apprentices' Sch Aborfield 1962-65 (Col), DDEME 1 Br Corps Germany 1965-66 (Brig), inspr of REME MOD 1966-69 (Brig); exec external Rels and mktg ERA 1970-74; dir: external activities and exec special projects IEE London 1974-82, Michael Shortland Assocs (consits in computer aided engrg) 1982-87; CEng, FIEE; *Recreations* golf, gardening; *Clubs* Liphook Golf; *Style*— Brig Joseph Dobie, CBE; Findings, Tower Rd, Hindhead, Surrey GU26 6ST (☎ 042 873 5469)

DOBKIN, Ronald; s of Morris Dobkin (d 1940), of Bethnal Green, London, and Anne *née* Goodman; *b* 15 Feb 1909; *Educ* Davenant Fndn GS Whitechapel E London; *m* 1 2 Nov 1958 (m dis 1983), Marian *née* Green; 1 s (Jonathan Michael b 3 March 1964) 1 da (Elaine b 25 Nov 1965); m2 13 Dec 1986, Marion Joan (Lee), da of Arthur Roland Shutler, of Hythe, Southampton; *Career* CA, trainee Viney Price & Goodyear 1956-62, gen mangr Craven House Securities 1963-67, chief accountant Macmillans 1967-72, princ Ronald Dobkin & Co 1973-76; ptnr: Dobkin Smallman & Co 1976-80, Dobkin Northover & Co 1980-; tres Winchester RFC 1969-80, The Lords Taverners Hants Region 1986-, The Bollinger Boys Luncheon Club 1984-; FCA 1962; *Recreations* bridge, chess, rugby football; *Clubs* Winchester; *Style*— Ronald Dobkin, Esq; Saxon House, 36/40 St George's Street, Winchester SO23 8BE (☎ 0962 841616, fax 0962 841611)

DOBLE, Denis Henry; s of Percy Claud Doble, of Canterbury, and Dorothy Grace, *née* Petley; *b* 2 Oct 1936; *Educ* Dover GS, New Coll Oxford (MA); *m* 18 July 1975, Patricia Ann, da of Peter Robinson (d 1985), 1 s (Robin b 1981), 1 da (Katie b 1979); *Career* colonial off 1960-65; HM Dip Serv 1965-: second sec Br Embassy Brussels 1966-68, first sec (devpt) Br High Commn Lagos 1968-72, S Asian Dept FCO 1972-75, first sec (econ) Br Embassy Islamabad 1975-78, first sec Br Embassy Lima 1978-82, E African Dept FCO 1982-83, actg dep high cmmr Bombay 1985, dep high cmmr calcutta 1985-87, dep high cmmr Kingston 1987-, SBStJ 1972; *Recreations* tennis, cricket; *Clubs* MCC; *Style*— Denis Doble, Esq; 22 Hitherwood Drive, London SE19; Foreign and Commonwealth Office, King Charles St, London SW1A 2AH

DOBREE, John Hatherley; er s of Hatherley Moor Dobrée, OBE (d 1956), and Muriel (d 1960), da of George Fountaine Ware Hope, of Stanford-le-Hope, Essex; *b* 25 April 1914; *Educ* St Barts Hosp, Univ of London (MS); *m* 16 Sept 1941, Evelyn Maud, da of Thomas Francis Smyth (d 1950), of Dublin; 2 s (Charles b 1947, Robert b 1950); *Career* Capt RAMC, MEF 1942-46; ophthalmic surgn; conslt: St Barts Hosp London, N Middx Hosp London; vice-pres Ophthalmic Soc UK, dep master Oxford Ophthalmic Contress, hon sec Sect of Ophthalmic RSM; FRCS ; *Books* The Retina, Blindness; *Style*— John Dobree, Esq

DOBREE BELL, Hon Mrs; Astrid Signe; *née* Williamson; da of 3 Baron Forres (d 1978), and Gillian Ann Maclean, (now Mrs Miles H de Zoete), da of late Maj John M Grant, RA; *b* 20 Dec 1951; *m* 1976, Peter Karl Dobree Bell, 1 s (Hugh John b 1982), 1 da (Lucy Claire b 1984); *Style*— The Hon Mrs Dobree Bell; Conifer Cottage, Aldermaston, nr Reading, Berks RG7 4LF

DOBSON; *see*: Howard-Dobson

DOBSON, Hon Mrs (Anne Mary); *née* Hope; only da of 3 Baron Rankeillour (d 1967); *b* 20 Dec 1936; *m* 5 July 1958, John Stephen Dobson, JP (*qv*); 1 s, 2 da; *Style*— The Hon Mrs Dobson; Papplewick Lodge, Notts

DOBSON, Christopher Selby Austin; CBE (1976); s of Alban Tabor Austin Dobson, CB, CVO, CBE (d 1962), of Walsham-le-Willows, Suffolk (s of Austin Dobson, LLD, the poet and writer) and 1 w Katharine Jean Selby (d 1936), da of Maj Robert Grey Donaldson-Selby, of Holy Is, Northumberland; *b* 25 August 1916; *Educ* Clifton, Emmanuel Coll Cambridge; *m* 1941, Helen Broughton (d 1984), da of Capt E B Turner (d 1941), of Holyhead; 1 s (decd), 1 da; *Career* Lt Middx Regt 1940-46; asst Nat Cncl of Social Serv 1938-39, temp asst princ Miny of Educn 1946-47, asst librarian House of Lords 1947-56 (librarian 1956-77) ret 1977; *Recreations* book-collecting, philately; *Clubs* Roxburghe (hon sec); *Style*— Christopher Dobson, Esq, CBE; Swan House, Symonds Lane, Linton, Cambridge CB1 6HY

DOBSON, Sir Denis William; KCB (1969, CB 1959), OBE (1945), QC (1971); s of William Gordon Dobson, of Newcastle upon Tyne; *b* 17 Oct 1908; *Educ* Charterhouse, Trinity Coll Cambridge; *m* 1, 1934 (m dis 1947), Thelma, da of Charles Swinburne, of Newcastle upon Tyne; 1 s, 1 da; m 2, 1948, Mary Elizabeth, da of Capt J A Allen, of Haywards Heath; 2 s, 1 da; *Career* serv WWII with RAF (UK, W Desert, Italy), Wing Cdr 1944; slr 1933, barr Middle Temple 1951, bencher 1968, dep clerk of the Crown in Chancery Lord Chllr's Office 1954-68, clerk of the Crown in Chancery and perm sec to Lord Chllr 1968-77; *Clubs* Athenaeum; *Style*— Sir Denis Dobson, KCB, OBE, QC; 50 Egerton Crescent, London SW3 (☎ 01 589 7990)

DOBSON, Frank Gordon; MP (Lab) Holborn and St Pancras 1983-; s of James William Dobson, and Irene Shortland, *née* Laley; *b* 15 Mar 1940; *Educ* Archbishop Holgate's GS York, LSE; *m* 1967, Janet Mary, da of Henry Alker; 3 children; *Career* former administrator CEGB and Electricity Cncl; asst sec Cmmn for Local Admin 1975-79; memb exec Chile Solidarity Campaign 1979-, NUR sponsored MP (Lab) Holborn and St Pancras South 1979-1983, oppn front bench spokesman: Educn 1981-83, Shadow Health Minister 1983-87, Shadow Leader of the House and campaign co-ordinator 1987-; *Style*— Frank Dobson, Esq, MP; 22 Great Russell Mansions, Great Russell Street, London WC1

DOBSON, John Stephen; JP (1962); elder s of John Dobson (d 1960), of The Old Vicarage, Farnsfield, Notts; *b* 19 July 1932; *Educ* Ampleforth; *m* 5 July 1958, Hon Anne Mary, *née* Hope, da of 3 Baron Rankeillour (d 1967); 1 s, 2 da; *Career* textile mfr chm 1964-; dist cllr 1974-; High Sheriff Notts 1975-76; pres: Ashfold Cons Assoc, Dist Scouts; *Recreations* hunting, sailing, skiing, tennis; *Clubs* Army and Navy, Aldeburgh Yacht, Royal Thames Yacht; *Style*— John Dobson, Esq, JP; Papplewick Lodge, Notts (☎ 0602 632975); 14 Fawcett Rd, Aldeburgh, Suffolk (☎ 072 885 3485); 209 Lillie Rd, London SW6 (☎ 01 385 4872)

DOBSON, Michael William Romsey; s of Sir Denis Dobson, KCB, OBE, QC, of 50 Egerton Crescent, London SW3 *qv*, and Lady Mary Elizabeth, *née* Allen; *b* 13 May 1952; *Educ* Eton, Trinity Coll Cambridge (MA); *Career* Morgan Grenfell 1973-: NY 1978-80, dir Investmt Servs London 1980-84, md NY 1984-88, head of int investment London 1985-86, md Asset Mgmnt 1987-, chm Asset Mgmnt 1988-; dep gp chief exec Morgan Grenfell Gp plc; dir: Anglo and Overseas Tst plc 1987-, The Overseas Investment Tst plc 1987-; *Recreations* tennis, golf; *Clubs* Brooks', Turf, Queens, Hurlingham, New York Racquet & Tennis; *Style*— M W R Dobson, Esq; 61 Onslow Sq, London SW3 (☎ 01 584 1956); 23 Great Winchester St, London EC2 (☎ 01 588 4545, fax 01 588 5598, telex 8953511)

DOBSON, Sir Richard (Portway); s of Prof John Frederic Dobson (d 1948); *b* 11 Feb 1914; *Educ* Clifton, King's Coll Cambridge; *m* 1946, Mrs Emily Margaret Carver, da of J R Herridge; 1 step da; *Career* served in China 1936-40, Flt Lt RAF 1941-45 (pilot); with Br-American Tobacco Co Ltd in China, Rhodesia and London 1946 (dir 1955, chm 1970-76, pres 1976-79); dir: Exxon Corpn, Davy Int 1975, Lloyds Bank Int 1976; non-exec chm BL 1976-77; kt 1976; *Clubs* United Oxford and Cambridge; *Style*— Sir Richard Dobson; 16 Marchmont Rd, Richmond upon Thames, Surrey (☎ 940 1504)

DOBSON, Susan Angela (Sue); da of Arthur George Henshaw and Nellie *née* Flower (d 1978); *b* 31 Jan 1946; *Educ* Holy Family Convent, Assumption Convent, Ursuline Convent, NE London Poly (BA, Dip HE); *m* 1966 (m dis 1974), Michael Dobson; *Career* fashion, cookery and beauty; ed Femina 1965-69, contributing ed Fair Lady 1969-71; ed: SA Inst of Race Rels 1972, Wedding Day and First Home 1978-81, Successful Slimming 1981, Woman & Home 1982-; *Books* The Wedding Day Book (1981-89); *Recreations* travel, books, photography, theatre, music; *Style*— Ms Sue Dobson; IPC Magazines, Kings Reach Tower, Stamford St, London SE1 9LS (☎ 01 261 5423)

DOCHERTY, Peter Thomas Christopher; s of Dr Joseph Francis Docherty (d 1975), and Sylvia, *née* Kinnamont; *b* 1 Sept 1939; *m* 6 Aug 1966, Eleanor, da of Brian Bolgar, of Ireland; 4 s (Ian b 1967, Bruce b 1972, Duncan b 1971, Brian b 1977); *Career* conslt Ophthalmic Surgeon Derbyshire Royal Infirmary; designer of a cannula used worldwide for cataract surgery; author of many articles in medical journals; FRCS; FRCSI; LRCPI & LM; DO; DOMS RCPST; *Recreations* golf, scuba diving; *Clubs* Irish Graduates Soc, Mickleover Golf; *Style*— Peter Docherty, Esq; "Shamrock Lodge", 9 Farley Road, Derby DE3 6BY; Derbyshire Royal Infirmary, London Road, Derby DE1 2QY (☎ 0332 47141, ext.328)

DOCKER, Rt Rev Ivor Colin; *see*: Horsham, Bishop of

DOCKERTY, John Samuel; s of Edgar Samuel Dockerty (d 1973), of Berkswell, Nr Coventry, and Olive Irene, *née* Manger (d 1982); *b* 2 Nov 1929; *Educ* King Henry VIII Coventry; *m* 17 March 1956, Jean Ann, da of William Arthur James Brick (d 1975), of Stamford, Lincs; 2 s (Christopher b 1960, Andrew b 1967), 2 da (Deborah b 1957, Nicola b 1963); *Career* co dir: Timber Importer, J O Walker & Co plc 1960 (dep chm 1973), Wisbech Stevedores Ltd 1967-; chm E Anglian Timber Trade Assoc 1986-88; *Recreations* cricket, gardening, travelling abroad; *Style*— John Dockerty, Esq; Broadlawns, Barton Rd, Wisbech, Cambs (☎ 0945 583614); J O Walker & Co plc, Nene Quay, Wisbech (☎ 0945 582215)

DOCKRAY, Brian; s of George Arthur Dockray, of Kendal, Cumbria, and Dorothy Mary, *née* Mason (d 1985); *b* 18 Oct 1930; *Educ* Leeds Sch of Architecture; *m* 21 July 1956, Edith Emilie, da of Olaf Friestad (d 1987), of Kristiansand, Norway; 1 s (David Olaf b 1964); *Career* cmmnd RE Chatham 1954, Capt RE TA; sr ptnr: Gill Dockray and Ptnrs Chartered Architects Kendal, Kirkby Lonsdale and Ambleside 1961-, won over 30 Civic Tst Awards and 4 Euro Heritage Awards; represented Br Army in cross country and athletic events 1954-56 and Yorkshire 1955-57; FRIBA; *Recreations* golf, walking lakeland hills, water colours; *Clubs* Ulverston Golf, Kendal Golf; *Style*— Brian Dockray, Esq; Skewbarrow Top, High Tenterfell, Kendal, Cumbria LA9 4PQ (☎ 0539 21684); 45 Highgate, Kendal, Cumbria LA9 4EE (☎ 22656)

DODD, Denis Featherstone; TD and Bar (1946); s of Ralph Harry Dodd (d 1962), of Sutton Coldfield, and Marian Edith, *née* Featherstone (d 1959); *b* 27 July 1914; *Educ* St Peters Sch York; *m* 1943, Emily Lavington, *née* Lindsay (d 1984), da of Hugh Lindsay, of Edinburgh (d 1917); 1 s (Ian), 2 da (Margaret, Rosemary); *Career* Royal Warwickshire Regt Capt acting Maj France and Belgium; CA, ptnr Wenham Major & Co 1946-68; former chm: Concentric Ltd, Br Rollmakers Corpn, Samuel Groves & Co Ltd, Thomas Walker & Sons Ltd; former dir Johnson & Firth Brown Ltd, Leys Foundries & Engrg Ltd; Teaching Hosps Assoc 1972-75, bd of govrs Utd Birmingham Hosps 1968-74; dep-pro-chllr Univ of Birmingham 1985-87 (Hon MA); *Recreations* rugby; *Style*— Denis Dodd, Esq, TD; 2 Morningside, Sutton Coldfield, W Mids B73 6BL (☎ 021 354 3548); Braeside, Elgol, Broadford, Isle of Skye

DODD, Air Vice-Marshal Frank Leslie; CBE (1968), DSO (1944), DFC (1944), AFC (1943, and bars 1955 and 1959), AE (1945); s of Frank Herbert Dodd (d 1944), of Dunston, Staffs; *b* 5 Mar 1919; *Educ* King Edward VI Sch Stafford, Reading Univ; *m* 1942, Joyce Lilian, da of George Claxton Banyard (d 1957), of Thetford, Norfolk; 1 s, 3 da; *Career* joined RAFVR 1938, photo-recce Mosquitos 1944-45, station cdr RAF Coningsby 1961-63, cmdt Central Flying Sch 1965-68, Air Cdre 1966, dir RAF Estabs 1968-70, dir-gen Special Air Def Project 1970-74, Air Vice-Marshal 1970, ret 1974; admin MacRobert Tst 1974-85, LRPS (1987); *Recreations* golf, photography; *Clubs* RAF; *Style*— Air Vice-Marshal Frank Dodd, CBE, DSO, DFC, AFC, AE; Frilford, Abingdon, Oxon OX13 5NX 304)

DODD, Ian Wilfred; s of William Ogilvy Dodd, of 9 Whitethorn Dr, Brighton, and Margery Lillian Dodd, *née* Harper (d 1942); *b* 14 July 1942; *Educ* Brighton Coll, RNC Dartmouth; *m* 1, 25 Sept 1965 (m dis 1979), Marilyn Grace, da of Jack Smith, of Brighton; 3 s (Andrew Ogilvy b 1967, Alexander Mark b 1969, Alistair Ian Paul b 1974); m 2, 20 Dec 1986, Patricia Marian, *née* Keeling; *Career* slr Eastbourne Borough Cncl 1966-67, ptnr then sr ptnr Griffith Smith Dodd & Riley Slrs 1967-; scout cmmr Brighton (ret), hon slr Brighton Hove & Dist Samaritans, vice pres Mencap (Brighton Hove & Dist), fndr pres Rotary Club of Brighton & Hove Soiree, vice chm Rotary Dist 125, hon sec and tstee Muttinat ctee of Polioplus; govr: Brighton Coll, Queens Park Co Primary Sch; memb Law Soc; *Recreations* reading, music, gardening, walking, sailing and skiing, dining well; *Style*— Ian Dodd, Esq; 47 Old Steyne, Brighton BN1 1NW (☎ 0273 24041, fax 0273 203796, telex 878112)

DODD, John; s of Albert Victor Jack Dodd (d 1971), and Marjorie Violet, *née*

Lowenhoff; *b* 3 June 1934; *Educ* Lawrenceville Sch New Jersey USA, Chiswick Poly, Coll Of Law (slrs Hons), London Univ (LLB); *m* 1, 24 June 1961 (m dis 1985), Wendy Patricia, da of Patrick George Channell (d 1987); 4 s (Paul b 3 May 1963, Benjamin b 19 Dec 1969, Jamie b 7 April 1972, Timothy b 2 July 1975), 1 da (Samantha b 21 Feb 1965); m 2, 30 Nov 1985, Yvonne Myvanwy, da of Albert John Thomas Purdue; 2 step s (Graeme b 21 March 1987, Neil b 2 March 1980), 1 step da (Caroline b 3 Oct 1973); *Career* Nat Serv RA: England, Korea, Hong Kong; admitted slr 1961; ptnr: Hair & Co 1963-77, Young Jones Hair & Co 1977-79, Devonshires 1980-; memb: adoption panel LDS Social Servs Adoption Agency 1984-88, advsy bd LDS Social Servs; area counsel Church of Jesus Christ of the Latter-Day Saints 1987- (regnl ldr 1965-); memb Law Soc Admission Panel; Freeman City of London, Liveryman City of London Slrs Co; *Recreations* skiing, swimming, water sports; *Style—* John Dodd, Esq; Devonshires, Salisbury House, London Wall, London EC2M 5QY (☎ 01 628 7576, fax 01 256 7318)

DODD, Ken - Kenneth Arthur; OBE (1982); s of Arthur Dodd, by his w Sarah; *b* 1931; *Educ* Holt HS Liverpool; *Career* singer, comedian, actor, entertainer; *Style—* Kenneth Dodd Esq, OBE; 76 Thomas La, Knotty Ash, Liverpool

DODD, Col Norman Lavington; s of Ralph Harry Dodd (d 1962), of Moorcroft, Beaconsfield Rd, Four Oaks, Sutton, Coldfield, and Marion Edith Dodd (d 1959); *b* 23 June 1917; *Educ* St Peters York, RMA Woolwich; *m* 18 Sept 1942, Eileen Charlotte, da of Maj George Gibbs (d 1940), of Wellington, NZ; 1 da (Maureen (Mrs Judge) b 16 Oct 1946); *Career* cmmnd RA 1937, 1 Field Regt RA India 1937-39, 4 RHA Egypt 1940, Capt Surrey Yeo 1940, SO RA Nigeria 1941, Maj OC 3 Light Batty W African Artillery Nigeria and Burma 1941-45, 2 i/c 101 Lt Regt 1945, 2 i/c and co Lt-Col Dorset Yeo 1945, Staff Coll 1945, DAAG 4 Armd Bde 1946, BM 69 AA Bde 1947-49, Batty cmd and staff Nigeria 1949-52, Batty Cmd locating batty 1953-56, NATO HQ Fontainbleu 1956-58, CO 280 (City of Glasgow) Field Regt RA TA 1958-60, Lt Col SBLO USA REUR Heidelberg 1960-62, staff AFNORTH Oslo 1962-64, Col Head Br Def Intelligence Liaison Staff Washington USA 1964-67, Chief of PR AFCENT Holland 1967-70, ret 1970; def corr in numerous int def jls 1970-89; pres Sidmouth Branch Royal Br Legion 1980-(Callompton branch 1971-80), memb Burma Star Assoc, co sec Devon Scouts, contrib to Scouting Magazine; memb: Inst of Journalists 1969-88, RUSI until 1989; *Recreations* shooting, travel, riding, painting, skiing; *Style—* Col Norman L Dodd; Byways, 23 Cotlands, Cotmaton Rd, Sidmouth, Devon EX10 8SP (☎ 0395 514 693)

DODD, William Atherton; CMG (1983); s of Frederick Dodd (d 1979), of Mayfield, Newton Lane, Chester, and Sarah, *née* Atherton (d 1976); *b* 5 Feb 1923; *Educ* City GS Chester, Christs Coll Cambridge (MA, Cert Ed); *m* 10 Aug 1949, Marjorie, da of Maj Reginald Charles Penfold, MC (d 1970), of Reckerby, Queens Park, Chester; 2 da (Patricia b 1954, Janet b 1957); *Career* WW11 Capt 8 Gurkha Rifles 1942-45; sr history master Ipswich Sch 1947-52, educn offr Miny of Educn Tanganyika/Tanzania 1952-65, under sec ODM 1980-83 (chief educn advsr 1978-83, advsr 1970-77); cnslt Univ of London Inst of Educn 1983- (lectr 1965-70); chm Sir Christopher Cox Memorial Fund, UK rep UNESCO Exec Bd 1983-85; *Books* Primary School Inspection in New Countries (1968), Society Schools and Progress in Tanzania (with J Cameron 1970), Teacher at Work (1970); *Recreations* walking, music, watching cricket; *Clubs* MCC, Kent CR, Sevenoaks Vine; *Style—* William Dodd, Esq, CMG; 20 Bayham Rd, Sevenoaks, Kent TN13 3XD (☎ (0732) 454238; Inst of Education, Univ of London, 20 Bedford Way, London WC1H 0AL (☎ 01 636 1500 (ext 734)

DODDS, (George) Christopher Buchanan; CMG (1977); s of George Hepple Dodds (d 1955), of Newcastle-upon-Tyne, and Gladys Marion, *née* Ferguson (d 1963); *b* 8 Oct 1916; *Educ* Rugby, Gonville and Caius Coll Cambridge (BA); *m* 28 Oct 1944, Olive Florence Wilmot, da of Oliver John Ling of Elmer's End, Kent; *Career* asst princ Admty 1939, Lt Royal Marines W Africa 1940-41, private sec to the Sec of Admty 1941-43, princ 1943, 1944 asst private sec (temp) to PM (asst sec 1951), Imperial Def Coll 1959, under sec MOD 1963, civilian dep to the head of def sales 1966-69, ret as asst under sec of state (int & industl policy) 1976; represented England vs Scotland in Boys' Golf Int 1934, played golf twice for Northumberland; *Recreations* golf, bird-watching, walking, bridge; *Clubs* Royal Mid-Surrey Golf; *Style—* Christopher Dodds, Esq, CMG; 5 Bryanston Square, London W1H 7FE (☎ 01 262 2852)

DCDDS, Denis George; CBE (1977); s of Herbert Yeaman Dodds (d 1941), of Newcastle upon Tyne, and Violet Katherine Dodds (d 1928); *b* 25 May 1913; *Educ* Rutherford Coll Newcastle upon Tyne, Armstrong Coll Durham Univ, London Univ (LLB); *m* 27 Feb 1937, Muriel Reynolds (Pearly), da of Edward Smith (d 1950), of Durham; 2 s (Michael Edward b 9 Sept 1937, Gareth Yeaman b 26 June 1943), 3 da (Philippa Helen b 30 Aug 1944, Jaqueline Eira b 4 March 1947, Stephanie Eileen b 20 Feb 1951); *Career* Lt RNVR 1940-46 serv: destroyers, light coastal forces, naval trg; slr 1936; dep town clerk Cardiff 1946-48, sec and slr S Wales Electricity Bd 1948-57, industl relations advsr Electricity Cncl 1957-60, chm Merseyside and N Wales Electricity Bd 1962-77 (dep chm 1960-62); memb Electricity Cncl 1961-77: chm nat jt ctee for managerial pay and conditions, vice chm nat jt industl cncl for pay and conditions of manual employees; chm: Port of Preston advsy bd 1977-79, Br Approval Serv for Electric Cables Ltd 1981-, Merseyside C of C and Indust 1976-78; memb: CBI Cncl Wales 1962-78, NW Econ Planning Cncl 1971-79, Nat Advsy Cncl for Employment of Disabled People 1981-; cmmr for Boy Scouts Penarth S Wales 1950-57, gen sec Bristol Free Churches Housing Assoc 1983-, memb Westbury-on-Trym PCC 1984-87; CIEE 1960-, FBIM 1960-77; *Recreations* music, gardening; *Clubs* Cwlth Soc; *Style—* Denis Dodds, Esq, CBE; Corners, 28 Grange Park, Westbury-on-Trym, Bristol BS9M 4BP (☎ 0272 621440)

DODDS, Sir Ralph Jordan; 2 Bt (UK 1964) of W Chiltington, co Sussex; s of Sir (Edward) Charles Dodds, 1 Bt, MVO, (d 1973); *b* 25 Mar 1928; *Educ* Winchester, RMA Sandhurst; *m* 9 Oct 1954, Marion, da of Sir Daniel Thomas Davies, KCVO (d 1966), of 36 Wimpole St, W1; 2 da; *Career* Capt 13/18 Royal Hussars; underwriting memb of Lloyd's 1964; insur broker: Bray Gibb & Co (later Stewart Wrightson (UK) Ltd 1958-83), with Willis Faber & Dumas 1983-; *Clubs* Cavalry and Guards', Hurlingham; *Style—* Sir Ralph Dodds, Bt; Picton House, Thames Ditton, Surrey

DODDS-PARKER, Sir (Arthur) Douglas; only s of Arthur Percy Dodds-Parker FRCS (d 1940); sr rep of jr line of Parker of Little Norton, Co Derby (the Parkers became ironmasters and made much of the cannon used against the Americans and Napoleon, William Parker being master cutler 1761); assumed additional surname and arms of Dodds by Royal Licence 1908; the name Dodds comes from Sir Douglas' father's godfather, Ralph Dodds, sometime Lord Mayor of Newcastle; has inherited through maternal gf (Wise) the feudal right to collect dung from the streets of Dundee; by his w Mary (d 1934), da of Joseph Alexis Patrick Wise, JP, of Belleville Park, Cappoquin, Co Waterford; *b* 5 July 1909; *Educ* Winchester, Magdalen Coll Oxford (MA); *m* 6 April 1946, Aileen Beckett, only da of Norman Beckett Coster (d 1929), of Paris, and wid of Capt Ellison Murray Wood, IG; 1 s; *Career* served WWII Gren Gds (despatches), special ops 1940-45, with Sudan Political Serv 1930-1939; co dir 1946-; MP (C) Oxfordshire (Banbury Div) 1945-59, MP (C) Cheltenham 1964-74; under-sec of state for Foreign and Cwlth Affrs 1953-57, chm Cons Parly Foreign and Cwlth Ctee 1970-73, UK memb of Euro Parl Strasbourg 1973-74; Légion d'Honneur (Fr), Croix de Guerre avec Palme (Fr); kt 1973; *Recreations* fishing, walking; *Clubs* Carlton, Leander, Vincents, Special Forces (chm and pres 1975-81); *Style—* Sir Douglas Dodds-Parker; 9 North Court, Great Peter St, London SW1; The Lighthouse, Westport, New York, NY 12993, USA

DODGEON, David Charles; s of Walter Dodgeon (d 1968), of Singapore, and Anne Elizabeth, *née* Mills; *b* 21 Nov 1952; *Educ* King's Sch Bruton, Chelmer Inst of Higher Educ (HND); *m* 28 Feb 1976, Yvonne Christine, da of Anthony Vernon Hollington, of Clacton-on-Sea; *Career* accountant P&O steam Navigation Co Ltd 1976-78, co sec Hedger Mitchell Stark 1978-81, gp fin controller Grandfield Rork Collins Ltd 1981-86, fin dir Granard Rowland Communications Ltd 1986-88; ICSA 1976, MBIM 1978; *Recreations* sport including golf, squash,photography; *Clubs* RAC, Pall Mall; *Style—* David Dodgeon, Esq; Great Braxted Hall Barn, Great Braxted, Essex CM8 3EN (☎ 0621 892999), Blacklands Terrace, London SW3 HUD (☎ 01 225 0076, fax 01 225 3409)

DODMAN, Alan Victor; s of C V Dodman (d 1949), of Byfleet, Surrey, and A M Dodman, *née* Matcham (d 1985); *b* 12 July 1924; *Educ* Woking GS for Boys Surrey; *m* 17 Sept 1949, Hazel, da of Alfred Reeves (d 1937); 3 s (Eric Alan b 13 Jan 1952, John Richard b 17 Nov 1961, Philip Andrew b 18 Sept 1964); *Career* serv WWII RAF Warrant Offr-Pilot; sales dir TF Firth & Sons Ltd 1963-67; md Firth Carpets Ltd 1977-83; exec dep chm Readicut Int plc 1988- (md 1983-88), dir/chm of various Readicut Subsidiary Cos 1983-; *Recreations* Cricket and interest in most other sports; *Clubs* Yorkshire CCC; *Style—* Alan Dodman, Esq; Peper Harow, 113 Pannal Ash Rd, Harrogate, N Yorks HG2 9JL; Readicut International plc, Clifton Mills, Brighouse, Yorks HD6 4ET (☎ 0484 721223, fax 0484 716135, telex 517457)

DODSON, Hon Christopher Mark; s and h of 3 Baron Monk Bretton, *qv*; *b* 2 August 1958; *Educ* Univ of S Calif (MBA); *Style—* The Hon Christopher Dodson

DODSON, Sir Derek Sherborne Lindsell; KCMG (1975, CMG 1953), MC (1945), DL (Lincoln 1987);; s of Charles Sherborne Dodson, MD (d 1957); *b* 20 Jan 1920; *Educ* Stowe, RMC Sandhurst; *m* 1952, Julie Maynard, only child of Hon Maynard Bertram Barnes (d 1970), of St Richard's Manor, Maryland, USA; 1 s, 1 da; *Career* served 1939-48 in RSF, mil asst to Br Cmmr Allied Control Cmmn for Bulgaria 1945-46; private sec to Min of State FO 1955-58, consul Elisabethville 1962-63, cnsllr and consul-gen Athens 1966-69; ambass: Hungary 1970-73, Brazil 1973-77, Turkey 1977-80; special rep to Sec of State for Foreign and Cwlth Affairs 1980-; chm Anglo Turkish Soc 1982-, Beaver Guarantee Ltd 1984-86, dir Benguela Rlwy Co 1984-; *Clubs* Boodle's, Travellers'; *Style—* Sir Derek Dodson, KCMG, MC, DL; 47 Ovington St, London SW3 (☎ 01 589 5055); Gable House, Leadenham, Lincoln (☎ Loveden 0400 72212)

DODSON, Hon Henry George Murray; s of 3 Baron Monk Bretton; *b* 11 Feb 1960; *Style—* The Hon Henry Dodson

DODSON, Jane Leila; da of Maj Michael Bedell Dodson, of Northington Down, nr Alresford, Hants, and Leila Mary, *née* Downer; *b* 20 Feb 1950; *Educ* Sorbonne, Birkbeck Coll London (BA); *m* 4 Oct 1986, Mervyn Peter Michael Walker, s of Dr Richard Hillier Walker, of The Old Parsonage, Galmpton, nr Kingsbridge, South Devon; 1 s (Alexander Michael Luke Wolfe b 24 Feb 1988); *Career* dir and shareholder Benjamin Benjamin Assocs 1976-82, dir and owner The Kinnerton Street Design Co Ltd 1980 (Interior designers and decorators); memb Save the Rhino Appeal; *Recreations* theatre, music, reading, art, languages, antiques, sculpture, skiing, tennis, swimming, sailing, cooking, entertaining, gardening; *Style—* Miss Jane Dodson; 29 Ballingdon Rd, Clapham Common, West Side, London SW11 6AJ; 45 Wilton Crescent, London SW1; (☎ 01 223 3863; The Kinnerton St Design Co Ltd, 36 Kinnerton St, Knightsbridge, London SW1X 8ES (☎ 01 235 9315, fax 01 823 1595, car phone 0836 213839)

DODSWORTH; *see*: Smith-Dodsworth

DODSWORTH, Geoffrey Hugh; JP (York 1961, later Herts); s of late Walter J J Dodsworth and Doris *née* Baxter; *b* 7 June 1928; *Educ* St Peter's Sch York; *m* 1, 1949, Isabel Neale (decd); 1 da (Helen b 1958); m 2, 1971, Elizabeth Ann, da of Dr Alan W Beeston, of Cumbria; 1 s (Simon b 1972), 1 da (Mary b 1974); *Career* dir Grindlays Bank Ltd 1976-80, chief exec Grindlay Brandts Ltd 1977-80, Oceanic Fin Servs 1980-85, pres and chief exec Oceanic Fin Corpn 1980-85, pres Jorvik Fin Corpn Ltd 1986-, dir County Properties Gp plc 1987-88, curr chm Dodsworth & Co Ltd (formed 1988); memb York City Cncl 1959-65, MP (Cons) Herts SW 1974-79; FCA; *Recreations* riding; *Clubs* Carlton; *Style—* Geoffrey Dodsworth, Esq, JP; Well Hall, Well, Bedale, N Yorks DL8 2PX (☎ 0677 70223); 78, Cliffords Inn, Fetter Lane, London EC4A 1BX (☎ 01 831 8926)

DODSWORTH, Robert Leslie; s of Harold Dodsworth; *b* 7 Sept 1936; *Educ* Barnard Castle Sch, Durham Univ; *m* 1964, Hazel Joan, *née* Moyse; 2 s; *Career* CA; gp chief exec Ransomes Sims & Jefferies plc (engrs) Ipswich 1977-; *Recreations* golf, squash; *Clubs* Ipswich & Suffolk Golf, Woodbridge Golf; *Style—* Robert Dodsworth, Esq; 223 Rushmere Rd, Ipswich, Suffolk (☎ 0473 724974); Ransomes Sims & Jefferies plc, Ipswich (☎ 0473 270000)

DODWELL, Prof (Charles) Reginald; S of William Henry Walter (d 1969), of Cheltenham, and Blanche, *née* Mudway (d 1965); *b* 3 Feb 1922; *Educ* Pates Sch Cheltenham, Gonville and Caius Coll Cambridge (MA, PhD, LIHD); *m* 5 Dec 1942, Sheila Juliet, da of James Henry Fletcher (d 1981), of Cheshire; 1 s (David b 8 July 1955), 1 da (Jane b 5 Dec 1951); *Career* Lt RNVR 1941-45; fell Gonville and Caius Coll Cambridge 1950-81, sr fell Warburg Inst 1950-53, librarian Lambeth Palace 1953-58; Trinity Coll Cambridge fell, lectr and librarian Trinity Coll Cambridge 1958-66; Pilkington prof history of art dir Whitworth Art Gallery 1966-89; memb Br Acad 1960; *Books* Canterbury School of Illumination (1954), Theophilus De Diversis Artibus (1961), Reichenau Reconsidered (1965), Painting in Europe 800-1200 (1971), Anglo-

Saxon Art (1982); *Recreations* opera, Shakespeare, badminton; *Style*— Prof Reginald Dodwell; The Old House, 12 Park Rd, Cheadle Hulme, Cheshire, SK8 7DA (☎ 061 485 3923); Univ of Manchester, Oxford Rd, Manchester M13 9PL (☎ 061 275 3311)

DOEGAR, Rakesh Chandar; s of Hans Raj Doegar, of New Delhi, India, and Kamla Sood (d 1946); *b* 10 Jan 1945; *Educ* Dehra Sch, Queens Coll, Punja State Univ, (BA); *m* 31 July 1971, Anne Marilyn, da of James William Herbert, of Moonrakers, Elveley Drive, W Ella, Hull, E Yorks; 1 s (Chand-Edward b 1982), 2 da (Hemione b 1973, Evemala b 1978); *Career* CA; sr ptnr R C Doegar & Co 1985, sr ptnr Jackson Taylor 1986, chm: M E I Engrg plc 1985, Sheppee Engrg Ltd 1986, Wiltex Ltd 1987; FICA; *Recreations* swimming, moor and fell walking, landscape gardening; *Clubs* Groucho; *Style*— Rakesh Doegar, Esq; Walton House, Walton on the Hill, Tadworth, Surrey KT20 7UJ; 159 Putney High St, London SW15 1RT

DOGGART, Anthony Hamilton (Tony); s of James Hamilton Doggart, of Albury Park, Albury, Nr Guildford, Surrey GU5 9BB, and Leonora Margaret, *née* Sharpley; *b* 4 May 1940; *Educ* Eton, King's Coll Cambridge (MA); *m* 1 May 1964, Caroline Elizabeth, da of Nicholas Gerard Voute, of Flat 2, Huize Boschzicht, Neuhuyskade 2, 2596 XL The Hague; 1 s (Sebastian Hamilton b 6 April 1970), 1 da (Nike Henrietta b 16 March 1972); *Career* head of special business dept Save & Prosper Gp 1970-74, pres First Investmt Annuity Co of America 1974-78, int exec vice-pres Insur Co of N America 1978-80, fin dir Save & Prosper Gp 1986- (sales dir 1980-86); barr Middle Temple 1962 (memb Lincoln's Inn); chm tax ctee Unit Trust Assoc, ctee memb Iris Fund for the Prevention of Blindness, involved with Waterboatmen Ltd; *Books* Tax Havens and Offshore Funds (Economist Intelligence Report 1972); *Recreations* skiing, water skiing, wild mushrooms, oak furniture; *Clubs* Garrick, Brooks's, City of London, Hurlingham; *Style*— Tony Doggart, Esq; 23 Ovington Gardens, London SW3 1LE (☎ 01 584 7620); Save & Prosper Gp Ltd, 1 Finsbury Ave, London EC2M 2QY (☎ 01 588 1717, fax 01 247 5006/01 377 5213, telex 883838)

DOLE, John Anthony; s of Thomas Stephen Dole (d 1974), and Winifred Muriel, *née* Henderson; *b* 14 Oct 1929; *Educ* Berkhamsted Sch; *m* 1952, Patricia Ivy, da of Victor Clements, of Kent; 2 s (Nicholas, Marcus); *Career* admin The Sports Cncl 1972-75, dir Sr Staff Mgmnt DOE and Tport 1978-82, under sec Controller of the Crown Suppliers 1982-86, Controller and Chief Exec HM Stationery Office 1987-89; *Recreations* writing, philately; *Clubs* Gresham

DOLL, Prof Sir (William) Richard (Shaboe); OBE (1956); s of Henry William Doll, and Amy Kathleen Shaboe; *b* 28 Oct 1912; *Educ* Westminster, St Thomas's Hosp (DM, MD, DSc); *m* 1949, Joan Mary Faulkner, da of Charles William Duncan Blatchford; 1 s, 1 da; *Career* serv WWII RAMC; dir Statistical Research Unit MRC 1961-69; Regius prof of Med Oxford 1969-79; first warden Green Coll Oxford 1979-83; chm: adverse reaction sub-ctee Ctee Safety of Medicines 1970-77, UK co-ordinating ctee Cancer Research 1972-77; vice-pres Royal Society 1970-71; memb: MRC 1970-74, Royal Cmmn on Environmental Pollution 1973-79, standing cmmn Energy and Environment 1978-82; RCP lectr: Milroy lecturer 1953, Marc Daniels 1969; orator Harveian 1982; hon fell: London Sch Hygiene and Tropical Medicine 1982-, Royal Soc Medicine 1982-; Hon DSc: Reading, Newcastle, Newfoundland, Belfast; Hon DM Tasmania; Royal Soc's Buchanan Medal, Royal Soc's Royal Medal 1986, RIPH&H Gold Medal, BMA Gold Medal 1983; FRCP, FRCGP; kt 1971; *Style*— Prof Sir Richard Doll, OBE, FRS; 12 Rawlinson Rd, Oxford (☎ 0865 58887)

DOLLEY, Christopher; s of late Dr Leslie George Francis Dolley; *b* 11 Oct 1931; *Educ* Bancrofts Sch, Corpus Christi Coll Cambridge; *m* 1966, Christine Elizabeth Cooper, 3 s; *Career* chm Penguin Books 1971-73 (former export mangr, dir, md); dir book devpt IPC 1973-77; chm Damis Group Ltd 1971-; *Style*— Christopher Dolley, Esq; Elm Place, 54 St Leonards Rd, Windsor, Berks (☎ 66961)

DOLLING, Frank - Francis Robert; s of Frederick Dolling; *b* 21 Jan 1923; *Educ* Tottenham County Sch; *m* 1949, Maisie Noquet; 2 da; *Career* served WW II RAF; joined Barclay's Bank Int 1947; chm: Barclays Merchant Bank 1980-, Barclays Bank Int 1983-; dep-chm Barclays Bank 1983-; *Style*— Frank Dolling Esq; Rowan Cottage, The Ridgway, Pyrford, Surrey (☎ Byfleet 43362); Barclay's Bank International Ltd, 54 Lombard St, London EC3P 3AH (☎ 01 283 8989)

DOLLOND, Steven; s of Charles Dollond; *b* 28 Nov 1943; *Educ* Quintin Sch, Lincoln Coll Oxford (MA), Harvard Business Sch (MBA); *Career* barr Middle Temple; private off of Ldr of the Opposition 1968-70, contested (C) Eton and Slough Feb and Oct 1974; mgmnt conslt Arthur D Little 1972-77 mktg dir; Br Technol Gp 1977-86, md Strategy Int 1988-; *Recreations* exotic travel; *Clubs* Carlton; *Style*— Steven Dollond, Esq; 804 Grenville House, Dolphin Sq, London SW1V 3LR (☎ 01 798 8089)

DOLMAN, James William; s of Victor William Dolman, of Ilminster, Somerset, and Dorothy Edith, *née* Angell (d 1973), of Calne Wiltshire; *b* 26 April 1934; *Educ* Ilminster GS, St John's Coll Cambridge (MA, LLM); *m* 28 Dec 1957, Jean, da of Harry Angles (d 1966), of Ipswich; 1 s (Edward James b 1960), 3 da (Elizabeth (Mrs Page) b 1961, Katherine b 1963, Emily b 1966); *Career* Nat Serv cmmnd RAF 1952; sr ptnr Bircham & Co, hon slr King Edward VII's Hosp for Offrs; hon fell Purcell Sch of music, chm Samuel Gardner Meml Tst; memb: Law Soc 1960, City of Westminster Law Soc; *Recreations* arts, cycling, rough sports; *Style*— James Dolman, Esq; 15 Spencer Walk, Putney, London SW15; 1 Dean Farrar St, Westminster, London SW1 (☎ 01 222 8044)

DOLMAN, Julian Henry; s of Arthur Frederick Dolman (d 1976), of Newport, Monmouthshire, and Margaret Mary, *née* McKinnon; *b* 16 Sept 1939; *Educ* Sherborne, St Catherine's Coll Cambridge (MA); *m* 1, 29 Nov 1962 (m dis 1974), Juliet, da of James White, of Charmouth; 2 da (Catherine b 1964, Sarah b 1966); m 2, 21 Sept 1974, Susan Jennifer, da of Roy Frederick Palmer, of Little Aston, Sutton Coldfield; 2 s (Charles b 1975, Edward b 1976); *Career* admitted slr 1966, ptnr Wall James and Davies; author of numerous articles on town planning law; Freeman City of London 1979; memb Law Soc 1966; *Recreations* Africana 1840-52, history, gardening; *Style*— Julian Dolman, Esq; Forge Mill Farm, Shelsley Beauchamp, Worcs WR6 6RR; Wall James and Davies, 19 Hagley Road, Stourbridge, W Mids DY8 1QW (☎ 0384 371 622, fax 0384 374 057)

DOLMETSCH, Carl Frederick; CBE; s of Arnold Dolmetsch, and Mabel *née* Johnston; *b* 23 August 1911; *m* (m dis); 2 s (1 decd), 2 da; *Career* musician; first public concert at 7 and first tour at 8; tours incl: Alaska, Austria, Belgium, Canada, Columbia, Denmark, France, Germany, Italy, Japan, Netherlands, NZ, Sweden, Switzerland, USA; dir: Soc of Recorder Players 1937-, Haslemere Festival of Early Music and Instruments 1940-; Dolmetsch Int Summer Sch 1971-, md Arnold Dolmetsch Ltd 1940-76 (chm 1963-78), chm Dolmetsch Musical Instruments 1982-; memb Art Workers Guild, hon fell Trinity Col of Music; Hon Dlitt Univ of Exeter Univ; ISM; *Books* author of many edns of Music, and books on recorder playing (1957, 1962, 1970, 1977); *Recreations* ornithology, natural history; *Style*— Carl Dolmetsch, Esq, CBE; Jesses, Haslemere, Surrey GU27 2BS (☎ 0428 3818)

DOLMETSCH, Mary Douglas; *née* Ferguson; da of James Alexander Ferguson (d 1963), of Dumfriesshire, and Janet Weir (d 1964); *b* 16 Feb 1916; *Educ* Dumfries Acad, Abbots Hill Hemel Hempstead, Glasgow Coll of Domestic Sci; *m* 24 Feb 1937, Carl Frederick, s of Eugene Arnold Dolmetsch (d 1940), of Haslemere, Surrey; 2 s (François b 1940, Richard b 1945 decd), 2 da (Jeanne b 1942, Marguerite (twin) b 1942); *Career* dir Arnold Dolmetsch Ltd Early Musical Instruments 1938-81; life memb Dolmetsch Fndn, hon organising sec 1947-61; Br Red Cross Peeblesshire 1966-73; Nat Dip Housewifery, ret; *Recreations* gardening, reading, travel, music, theatre; *Clubs* The Caledonian, Edinburgh; *Style*— Mrs Mary D Dolmetsch; Greybield, Peebles, Scotland EH45 9JB

DOLTON, David John William; s of Walter William Dolton (d 1969), and Marie Frances Duval, *née* Rice; *b* 15 Sept 1928; *Educ* St Lawrence Coll Kent; *m* 1, 1959, Patricia Helen, da of late Maj Ernest G Crowe; 1 s (Kevin b 1964), 1 da (Catherine b 1961); m 2, 1986, Rosalind Jennifer, da of Harold Victor Chivers, of Bath, Avon; *Career* Delta Metal Gp 1950-76, commercial dir Extrusion Div, dir of Admin and Personnel, Rod Div 1967-76 (and various non-executive directorships); chief exec Equal Opportunities Cmmn 1976-78; asst gen mangr UK Nat Employers Mutual General Insur Ltd 1979-89; dir and asst gen mangr NEM Business Services Ltd 1980-89; Mgmnt Conslt 1989-; Reader: Diocese of Gloucester; Liveryman Worshipful Co of Gold and Silver Wyre Drawers; FCIS, FBIM, FIPM; *Recreations* music, reading, hill walking, swimming, travel; *Style*— David Dolton, Esq; 85 Corinium Gate, Cirencester, Glos GL7 2PX (☎ Cirencester 657739)

DOLTON, Nigel Timothy; s of Robert Hugh Dolton, of Walton-on-Thames, Surrey, and Vera Florence, *née* Hemming; *b* 21 Feb 1944; *Educ* Bradfield Coll; *m* 17 May 1969, Jutta, da of Herr Roderich Hans Emil Dittmar; 1 s (Timothy b 1974), 1 da (Sally b 1976); *Career* advertising exec; dir Saward Advertising Ltd 1980-; *Recreations* golf, theatre; *Clubs* Burhill Golf; *Style*— Nigel T Dolton, Esq; Balaton, Oatlands Close, Weybridge, Surrey; 178-202 Great Portland Street, London W1N 6AR (☎ 01 631 4474, fax 01 631 1402)

DOMINGO, Rashid; MBE (1987); s of late Achmat Domingo, and Rukea Domingo, of Cape Town; *b* 24 June 1937; *Educ* Trafalgar HS Cape Town, Univ of Cape Town (BSc); *m* 1962, Moreeda, *née* Maureen Virginia Sheffers; 1 s, 1 da; *Career* prodn mangr: Seravac Laboratories 1961-67, Miles Seravac Laboratories 1967-71; md Biozyme Laboratories Ltd 1971-; FBS, MIBiol, CChem, FRCS, CGIA, FInstD, FInstM; *Style*— Rashid Domingo, Esq; The Beeches, Pen-y-Pound, Abergavenny, Gwent (☎ 0873 4652; work: 0495 790678)

DOMINIAN, Dr (Jacob) Jack; s of Charles Joseph Dominian, and Mary,*née* Scarlatou; *b* 25 August 1929; *Educ* Lycee Leonin Athens, St Mary's HS Bombay, Stamford GS, Fitzwilliam House Cambridge (MA, MB, BChir), Exeter Coll Oxford (MA); *m* 23 Jun 1955, Edith Mary, da of John Smith (d 1961), of 5 Brighton Grove, N Shields; 4 da (Suzanne Mary b 1957, Louise Regina b 1958, Elise Aline (Mrs Milne) b 1961, Catherine Rene b 1964); *Career* Nat Serv RAOC 1948-49; conslt physician then sr house offr Radcliffe Infirmary 1957-58, sr registrar Maudsley Hosp 1958-64, conslt physician Central Middlesex Hosp 1965-88; dir Marriage Res Centre 1971-; memb: Catholic Marriage Advsy Cncl, Church of England's Cmmn on Marriage; Hon DSc Univ of Lancaster 1976; memb: BMA, RSM; FRCPEd, FRC Psych; *Books* Christian Marriage (1967), Marital Breakdown (1968), The Church and the Sexual Revolution (1971), Cycles of Affirmation (1975), Authority (1975), Proposals for a New Sexual Ethic (1977), Marriage Faith Love (1981), The Capacity to Love (1985), Sexual Integrity (1987); *Recreations* writing, music, theatre; *Style*— Dr Jack Dominian; Pefka, The Green, Croxley Green, Rickmansworth, Herts (☎ 0923 720 972); 2 Devonshire Place, London W1

DOMVILE, Denys Barry; s of Charles Barry Domvile (d 1936), of Loughlinstown Ho, Co Dublin, and Hon Ada Kate Bellew; *b* 19 Mar 1921; *Educ* Eton, Trinity Coll Oxford; *m* 8 April 1958, Mary Elise, da of Lt-Col, Roland Morrow Byers, of Birchwood, Virginia Water, Surrey; 1 s (Rowland Barry b 1960), 2 da (Katherine b 1959, Rosamund Lucy b 1965); *Career* Maj Life Gds and Inns of Court Regt (TA), W Desert, Italy, NW Europe; *Clubs* Cavalry and Guards'; *Style*— Denys Domvile, Esq; Brook House, Sutton Courtenay, Oxon OX14 4AH (☎ (0235) 848238)

DON, Andrew George; s of Air Vice-Marshal Francis Percival Don, OBE (d 1964), of Elmham House, East Dereham, Norfolk, and Angela Jane, *née* Birkbeck; *b* 23 August 1934; *Educ* Eton, Trinity Coll Cambridge (MA); *m* 30 May 1974, Diana Susan, da of John Edward Dykes, of 48 Chesil Court, London SW3 and Haverthwaite, Cumbria;; *Career* barr Inner Temple 1960; local chm Social Security Appeal Tbnls 1984, dep chm Agri Land Tbnl 1986; memb Norfolk CC 1969-77; steward Gt Yarmouth and Fakenham Racecourses, church warden Little Dunham; *Recreations* fishing, shooting, racing, travel; *Clubs* Cavalry and Guards, Norfolk (Norwich) ; *Style*— Andrew Don, Esq; The Old Rectory, Little Dunham, Kings Lynn, Norfolk PE32 2DG (☎ 0760 22584); 48 Chesil Court, London SW3; Octagon House, 19 Colegate, Norwich (☎ 0603 623186)

DON, Robert Seymour; s of Air Vice-Marshal Francis Percival Don, OBE, DL (d 1964), of Elmham House, North Elmham, Norfolk and Angela Jane, *née* Birkeck; *b* 5 April 1932; *Educ* Eton, Trinity Coll Cambridge, (MA); *m* 2 July 1955, Judith Henrietta, da of Geoffrey Nicholas Holmes, of the Old Rectory, Shotesham All Saints, Norfolk; 4 da (Charlotte b 1956, Joanna b 1958, Fiona b 1962, Henrietta b 1965); *Career* Nat Serv 1 The Royal Dragoons 1950-52, TA Fife & Forfar Yeomanry 1953-54; John Harvey & Sons Ltd 1957-65, RS Don Ltd/Hicks & Don Ltd Wine Merchants (chm 1966), owner Elmham Park Vineyard & Winery 1970-; memb bd English Vineyards Assoc, former chm Norfolk Fruit Growers Assoc; Master of Wine; *Books* Teach Yourself Wine (1968), Off the Shelf (1967); *Recreations* shooting, fishing, deer stalking, skiing, photography; *Clubs* The Cavalry & Guards; *Style*— Robert Don, Esq; Elmham House, Park Hose, North Elmham, Dereham, Norfolk, NR20 5JY (☎ 036 281 363)

DON, Stuart Warren; s of Stuart M Don (d 1931); *b* 14 Sept 1914; *Educ* Hotchkiss Sch, Princeton Univ USA (BA); *m* 1, 1938, Elsie Burke (d 1983), da of Herbert H Foster (d 1962); 3 da; m 2, 1984, Ann, da of Lt-Col R G Barlow, and widow of Roger Thornycroft, DSC; *Career* Lt-Col US Army; exec recruitment John Courtis and Ptnrs

1976-, vice-pres Chemical Bank NY Tst 1959-69, Chase Manhattan Bank 1954-59, dir American Chamber of Commerce (UK) 1958- (pres 1967-69), US/UK Educnl Cmmn 1968-, tstee American Sch in London 1969-, exec cmmr Br-American Associates 1970-; Bronze Star 1945, Croix de Guerre 1945; *Recreations* foxhunting; *Clubs* Boodle's, City of London, Buck's, American, Monday Luncheon (co-chm 1972-); *Style*— Stuart Don, Esq; The Green, Kingham, Oxon; 5 Orchard Court, Portman Sq, London W1H 9PA (☎ 01 935 6704)

DON-WAUCHOPE, Sir Patrick George; 10 Bt (NS 1667), of Newton; s of Patrick Hamilton Don-Wauchope, WS (d 1939), 3 s of 8 Bt; suc unc, Sir John Douglas Don-Wauchope, 9 Bt, 1951; *b* 7 May 1898; *Educ* Edinburgh Acad; *m* 15 Aug 1936 (m dis 1947), Ismay Lilian Ursula, da of Sidney Richard Hodges, of Edendale, Natal, S Africa; 2 s; *Heir* s, Roger Hamilton Don-Wauchope; *Career* served 1914-18 with RFA (France and Belgium, wounded, two medals), 1939-46 (Egypt and Italy); horticulturist (ret); *Style*— Sir Patrick Don-Wauchope, Bt; Private Bag 729, Margate, 4275 Natal, S Africa

DON-WAUCHOPE, Roger Hamilton; elder s and h of Sir Patrick Don-Wauchope, 10 Bt; *b* 16 Oct 1938; *Educ* Hilton Coll Natal; *m* 14 Dec 1963, Sallee, yr da of Lt-Col Harold Mill-Colman, OBE, of Durban; 2 s, 1 da; *Career* CA; *Style*— Roger Don-Wauchope, Esq; Festival, 54 Haygarth Rd, K100f 3600 Natal, S Africa

DONALD, Dr Alastair Geoffrey; OBE (1982); s of Dr Pollok Donald (d 1955), of Whitehouse Rd, Edinburgh, and Henrietta Mary, *née* Laidlaw (d 1975); *b* 24 Nov 1926; *Educ* Edinburgh Acad, Corpus Christi Coll Cambridge (MA), Edinburgh Univ (MB, ChB); *m* 3 April 1952, (Edna) Patricia, da of Richard Morrison Iceland WS (d 1944), of 12 Mortonhall Rd, Edinburgh; 2 s (Ian Pollok b 1955, William b 1960), 1 da (Patricia Mary b 1953); *Career* Sqdn Ldr med branch RAF 1952-54; GP Edinburgh 1954-; lectr dept gen practice Univ of Edinbrugh 1960-70; RCGP: vice-chm of cncl 1976-77 (chm 1979-82), chm bd of censors 1979-80, chm int ctee 1987-; former chm and provost SE Scotland faculty, radio doctor BBC Scotland 1976-78, chm UK Conf of Postgrad Advrs in Gen Practice 1978-80, chm jt ctee on Postgrad Trg for Gen Practice 1982-85, specialist advsr to House of Commons Social Servs Ctee 1986-87; chm: Armed Servs Gen Practice Approval Bd 1986-, Scottish ctee Action on Smoking and Health 1986-, med advsy gp BBC Scotland 1988-; James MacKenzie Medal RCP Edinburgh 1983, James MacKenzie lectr RCGP 1985, Bruce Meml Lectr 1987; pres Rotary Club Leith 1957-58, chm ct of dirs The Edinburgh Acad 1978-85 (dir 1957-85), pres Edinburgh Academical Club 1978-81, FRCGP 1971, FRCPE 1981; *Recreations* golf; *Clubs* Hawks (Cambridge), Univ of Edinburgh Staff; *Style*— Dr Alastair Donald, OBE; 30 Cramond Rd North, Edinburgh EH4 6JE (☎ 031 336 3824); Leith Mount, 46 Ferry Rd, Edinburgh EH6 4AE (☎ 031 554 0558)

DONALD, Hon Mrs (Angela Caroline); da of Baron McFadzean, KT (Life Peer); *b* 5 Dec 1942; *Educ* Benenden; *m* 21 Sept 1963, Robin Vyvyan Carter Donald, s of Norman Donald, of Newbury, Berks; 3 children; *Recreations* reading, tennis; *Style*— The Hon Mrs Donald; Osborne House, Bathampton, Bath, Avon BA2 6SW (☎ 0225 64212)

DONALD, Craig Reid Cantlie; CMG (1963), OBE (1959); s of Rev Francis Cantlie Donald (d 1974), of Lumphanan, Aberdeenshire, and Mary, *née* Reid (d 1945); *b* 8 Sept 1914; *Educ* Fettes, Emmanuel Coll Cambridge (BA, MA); *m* 2 June 1945, Mary Isabel, da of John Speid (d 1912), of Sidpore Tea Estate, India; 1 da (Rosemary Ann (Mrs John) b 1946); *Career* WWII Lt-Col MEF and CMF 1940-46; admin offr Cyprus 1937, cmmr Famagusta 1948, registrar Co-op Socs 1951, dep fin sec Uganda 1951, sec to the Treasy 1956-63 (memb legislative Cncl 1954-62); Bursar Malvern Coll 1964-79; govr Ellerslie and Downs Colwall Schs; *Recreations* gardening; *Clubs* Traveller's; *Style*— Craig Donald, Esq, CMG, OBE; 55 Geraldine Rd, Malvern, Worcs WR14 3NU (☎ 0684 561446)

DONALD, David Mitchell Cooke; WS; *b* 29 Sept 1914; *Educ* Aberdeen GS, Aberdeen Univ (LLB); *m* 1941, Mary Catherine; *Career* served 21 Army Gp, Maj, DAAG; merchant banker 1960; chm: Fleming Claverhouse Investmt Tst plc, Fleming Fledgeling Investmt Tst plc, Fleming Universal Investmt Tst plc, Mercantile and General Reinsurance Co plc; non-exec dir: Robert Fleming Hldgs Ltd, Prudential Corpn plc; *Recreations* gardening; *Clubs* Carlton; *Style*— David Donald Esq, WS; Downs House, Plumpton, Sussex BN7 3DH (☎ 0273 890465); Robert Fleming Holdings Ltd, 8 Crosby Sq, London EC3A 6AN (☎ 01 638 5858)

DONALD, Ian Francis; s of Harold Gordon Donald (d 1975), of Capetown, SA, and Jean Dorian, *née* Graham (d 1947); *b* 20 August 1928; *Educ* St Peters Coll Adelaide S Aust; *m* 20 Nov 1958, Sonia Evelyn, da of James Bruce Leask, CBE (d 1980), of Pangbourne, Berks; 1 s (Adrian Francis b 1963), 1 da (Caroline Bruce b 1968); *Career* jt md Firth Cleveland Ltd 1960-72, dep chm Guest Keen & Nettlefolds plc (now GKN plc) 1972-88; chm: Utd Engrg Steels Ltd 1986-, Allenwest Ltd Ayr 1985-, Llanelli Radiator (Hldgs) Ltd 1988-; dir Hall Engrg (Hldgs) plc 1987-; dep chm Hayward Fndn, chm Charles Hayward Tst; FIOD; *Recreations* shooting, fishing, sailing; *Clubs* Royal Thames YC, RAC; *Style*— Ian Donald, Esq; Rockfield Farm, Monmouth NP5 4NH, (☎ 0600 3217, fax 0600 4715)

DONALD, William Sainsbury; *b* 30 May 1933; *Educ* Aberdeen GS, Aberdeen Coll of Agric; *m* 1956, Bertha Mary; 2 children; *Career* md Donald-Russell Ltd; former pres Scottish Assoc of Wholesale Meat Salesmen; *Recreations* shooting, fishing, squash; *Clubs* Farmers', Directors'; *Style*— William Donald, Esq; Binghill House, Milltimber, Aberdeen (☎ 0224 732554); Donald-Russell, Inverurie, Aberdeenshire (☎ 0467 22601)

DONALDSON, David Abercrombie; s of Robert Donaldson, and Margaret, *née* Cranston; *b* 29 June 1916; *Educ* Coatbridge Secdy Sch, Glasgow Sch of Art; *m* 1, 1942 (m dis 1947) Kathleen Boyd Maxwell; 1 s (David Lennox b 15 July 1943); m 2, Marysia, da of Maj Leon Mora-Szorcy (d 1984) of Carcavelos, Portugal; 2 da (Sally Mora b 23 Nov 1950, Caroline Mary b 14 Sept 1956); *Career* head of drawing and painting Glasgow Sch of Art 1967-81 (lectr 1944-67), Cargill Award 1969, appointed HM The Queen's Painter and Limner in Scotland 1977, fndr RGI 1977, paintings in public and private collections throughout world; LLD Strathclyde Vniv 1971, D Litt Glasgow Univ 1988; ARSA 1951, RSA 1962, RSPP 1969; *Recreations* cooking, music; *Clubs* Glasgow Art; *Style*— David Donaldson, Esq; 5 Cleveden Dr, Glasgow G12 OSB (☎ 041 334 1029); 7 Chelsea Manor Studios Flood St, London SW3 (☎ 01 352 1932); St Roman de Malegarde, Vaucluse 8490, France

DONALDSON, David Torrance; QC 1984; s of Alexander Walls Donaldson, of Glasgow, and Margaret Merry, *née* Bryce; *b* 30 Sept 1943; *Educ* Glasgow Acad, Gonville and Caius Coll Cambridge (MA), Univ of Freiburg (DrJur); *m* 31 Dec 1985, Therese Marie Madeleine, da of Pierre Arminjon; *Career* fell Gonville and Caius Coll Cambridge 1965-1969, called to Bar Gray's Inn 1968; *Style*— David Donaldson, Esq QC; 2 Hare Court, Temple, London EC4Y 7BH (☎ 01 583 1770, fax 01 583 9269, telex 27139

DONALDSON, Air Cdre Edward Mortlock; CB (1960), CBE (1954), DSO (1940), AFC 1941 and Bar (1947); s of Charles Edgerton Donaldson (d 1918), of Federated Malay States CS, and Gwendoline Mary Macdonald; *b* 22 Feb 1912; *Educ* Kings Sch Rochester, Christs Hosp, McGill Univ Montreal Canada; *m* 1, 1936 (m dis 1944), Winifred Constant; 2 da (Susan, Sarah); m 2, 1944 (m dis 1956), Estellee, da of Emmett Leon Holland, of Arizona, USA; 1 s (David); m 3, 1957 (m dis 1982), Anne Sofie Stapleton; *Career* RAF Station Colerne 1944-45; CO: 151 Sqdn 1938 to end of Battle of Britain, RAF Station Fassberg Germany 1952-54, Millfield Rocket Firing Tning; Air Commodore 1955, CO RAF Arabian Penninsular 1958-1960; won World Speed record 1946; air corr The Daily Telegraph 1960-79; US Legion of Merit; *Recreations* saling (yacht 'Ariadne'); *Clubs* RAF, Island Sailing (Cowes); *Style*— Air Cdre Edward Donaldson, CB, CBE, DSO, AFC; 3 Fair Oak Court, Alverstoke, PO12 2TX; Suite Royale, El Palma, Spain

DONALDSON, Hamish; s of James Donaldson (d 1983), of Ferring, Sussex, and Marie Christine Cormack, *née* Smith; *b* 13 June 1936; *Educ* Oundle, Christ's Coll Cambridge (MA); *m* 18 Dec 1965, Linda, da of Dr Leslie Challis Bousfield (d 1980), of Billingshurst, Sussex; 3 da (Fiona b 1968, Sally b 1969, Catherine b 1973); *Career* dir Hill Samuel & Co Ltd 1978-85, md Hill Samuel Merchant Bank (SA) 1985-86, chief exec Hill Samuel Bank Ltd 1987-; memb Company of Information Technologists 1988; Freeman City of London 1988; *Books* A Guide to the Successful Management of Computer Projects (1978), Designing a Distributed Processing System (1979); *Recreations* amateur operatics, golf; *Style*— Hamish Donaldson, Esq; Edgecombe, Hill Road, Haslemere, Surrey GU27 2JN (☎ 0428 4473)

DONALDSON, Prof John Dallas; s of John Donaldson (d 1988), of Elgin, and Alexandrina Murray Ross, *née* Dallas (d 1985); *b* 11 Nov 1935; *Educ* Elgin Acad, Univ of Aberdeen (BSc, PhD), Univ of London (DSc); *m* 22 March 1961, Elisabeth Ann, da of George Edmond Forrest, of Easbourne; 1 s (Richard b 1969), 2 da (Claire b 1962, Sarah b 1965); *Career* asst lectr Univ of Aberdeen 1958-61, chemistry lectr Chelsea Coll London 1961-72, reader inorganic chemistry Univ of London 1972-80; The City Univ: prof indust chemistry 1980-, dir Indust & Biological Chemistry Res Centre 1988-; chm J D Donaldson Res Ltd 1984-, memb Nat Ctee for Chemistry 1985-; tstee Zimbabwe Tech Mgmnt Trg Tst 1983-, memb chemistry ctee Int Tin Res Inst; Freeman City of London 1982, Liveryman Worshipful Co of Pewterers 1983 (Freeman 1981); FRSC 1959, CChem, FRSA 1986, fell Soc of Indust Chemistry; *Books* Symmentry & Sterochemistry (with S D Ross 1972), Cobalt in Chemicals (with S J Clarke and S M Grimes 1986), Cobalt in Medicine Agriculture and the Enviroment (with S J Clarke & S M Grimes 1986), Cobalt in Electronic Technology (with S J Clarke & S M Grimes 1988); *Style*— Prof John Donaldson; 21 Orchard Rise, Richmond, Surrey TW10 5BX (☎ 01 876 6534); Dept of Chemistry, The City, Univ Northampton Sq, London EC1V 0HB (☎ 01 253 4399, fax 01 250 0837)

DONALDSON, Dame (Dorothy) Mary; GBE (1983), JP (Inner London 1960); da of Reginald George Gale Warwick (d 1956), and Dorothy Alice Warwick (d 1979); *b* 29 August 1921; *Educ* Portsmouth HS for Girls (GPDST), Wingfield Morris Orthopaedic Hosp, Middx Hosp (SRN); *m* 1945, Rt Hon Lord Donaldson of Lymington, *qv*; 1 s, 2 da; *Career* chm Women's Nat Cancer Control Campaign 1967-69; vice pres: Br Cancer Cncl 1970, Counsel and Care for the Elderly 1980-; memb: NE Met Regnl Hosp Bd 1970-74, NE Thames RHA 1976-81, Cities of London and Westminster Disablement Advsy Ctee 1974-, ILEA 1968-71, City Parochial Fndn 1969-75; govr: London Hosp 1971-74, Great Ormond Hosp for Sick Children 1978-80, City of London Sch for Girls 1971-, Berkhampsted Schs 1976-80; chm: cncl Banking Ombudsman 19854, Voluntary Licensing Authy In Vitro Fertilisation and Human Embryology 1985; memb: Automobile Assoc Ctee 1985, governing body Charterhouse Sch 1980-84, Inner London Juvenile Ct Panel 1960-65, Ct of Common Cncl 1966-75; Alderman City of London (Coleman Street Ward) 1975-, Sheriff City of London 1981-82, Lord Mayor of London 1983-84; Liveryman Worshipful Co of Gardeners, memb Guild of Freemen City of London; Freeman City of Winnipeg; hon memb CIArb; Order of Oman 1981; hon fell Girton Coll Cambridge 1983; Inst of Pub Rels President's Medal 1984; Hon DSc City Univ 1983; Grand Officier de L'Ordre National du Mérite 1984; Hon Freeman Worshipful Co of Shipwrights 1985, Hon Liveryman Worshipful Co of Fruiterers 1985; DStJ 1983; *Recreations* sailing (yacht 'Rogger'), ski-ing, gardening; *Clubs* Royal Cruising, Royal Lymington Yacht, Bar Yacht; *Style*— Dame Mary Donaldson, GBE, JP; c/o The Guildhall, PO Box 270, London EC2P 2QJ (☎ 01 588 6610)

DONALDSON, Hon Michael John Francis; o s of Baron Donaldson of Lymington, PC (Life Peer), *qv*; *b* 16 Nov 1950; *Educ* Stanbridge Earls; *m* 11 Nov 1972, Judith Margaret, SRN, da of Edgar William Somerville, FRCS, *qv* of Stone House, Garsington, Oxford; 2 s (William Michael Somerville b 29 Aug 1977, James John Francis b (twin) 29 Aug 1977); *Career* negotiator with Knight, Frank & Rutley, London 1969-71; dir: Edwood Property Co Ltd 1972-75, Nab Properties Ltd 1972-80; md and chm Marquis & Co, commercial property surveyors and valuers 1975-; chm SW London branch Incorporated Soc of Valuers and Auctioneers 1982-85; memb Nat Cncl of Incorporated Soc of Valuers and Auctioneers 1985-; memb Professional Practice Ctee 1985-; Freeman City of London, Liveryman Worshipful Co of Cutlers; ASVA, ARVA, ACIArb 1973, FSVA, FRVA 1981; *Recreations* sailing, skiing, walking; *Clubs* Royal Southampton Yacht, Guildford Coastal Cruising; *Style*— The Hon Michael Donaldson; The Old Coach House, Westwood Rd, Windlesham, Surrey GU20 6LT (☎ 0990 26909); office, 61 Richmond Road, Twickenham, Middx TW1 3AW (☎ 01 891 0222; fax 01 891 1767)

DONALDSON, Dr (James) Roy; s of James Donaldson (d 1979), and Ellen Hill, *née* Burnside; *b* 24 Dec 1927; *Educ* Bearsden Acad Dunbartonshire, West of Scotland Agric Coll (Nat and Coll Dip in Dairying), Glasgow Univ (B Chir), Royal Coll of Pathologists (Dip memb), London Univ Sch of Tropical Med and Hygiene (Dip in Bacteriology); *m* 25 July 1956, Flora, da of John MacDonald (d 1968); 1 s ((James) Graham), 1 da (Lynne Marie); *Career* Maj RAMC 1965, 2 i/c 24 Field Ambulance Aden 1965-67; pathologist David Bruce Laboratories Wilts 1967-68, Br Mil Hosp Minister BAOR 1968-70, Herbert Hosp Woolwich 1970-71; clinical pathologist: US Army Med Res Unit, Inst of Med Res Kuala Lumpur 1971-74; Lt-Col 1972, pathologist Cambridge

Mil Hosp Aldershot 1974-76, conslt pathologist and co offr David Bruce Laboratories Wilts 1976-81, awarded The Herbert Parkes & Tulloch Medals for First in Order of Merit, Army Health & Pathology 1965, Tri-Serv Alexander Gold Medal for Res 1974, Gen Serv Medal South Arabia 1967, Silver Jubilee Medal Queen Elizabeth II 1977; dairy bacteriologist 1948-50, surgical med and obstetric house offr 1957-59; princ gen med practice: Birmingham (partnership) 1959-61, Scotland 1961-65; conslt microbiologist: Greater Glasgow Bd, The Bacteriology & Serology of Gen Practice, Obstetric & Neonatal Paediatric Patients, The Bacteriology of Public Health and the Environment; memb: Scottish Food Coordination Ctee, Greater Glasgow Environmental Health Sub-Ctee; hon clinical lectr Glasgow Univ; memb Royal Coll of Pathologists 1975 (fell 1987), Hosp Infection Soc, Br Soc for Study of Infection; *Recreations* trout fishing, occasional golf, gardening, the philosophy of man's inhumanity; *Style*— Dr Roy Donaldson; Bacteriology Laboratory, Wolfson Centre (Level 5), Taylor St, Glasgow G4 0NA (☎ 041 552 1991)

DONALDSON, Hon Thomas Hay; s of Baron Donaldson of Kingsbridge, OBE (Life Peer) and Lady Donaldson of Kingsbridge, *qqv*; *b* 1 June 1936; *Educ* Eton, Cincinnati Univ USA, Trinity Coll Cambridge (BA); *m* 1962, Natalie, da of Basil Wadovsky, of Miami Beach; 2 s, 4 da; *Career* with Empire Trust Co NY 1958-62, W E Hutton and Co NY 1962-63, Morgan Guaranty Trust Co of NY London Office 1963- (vice pres 1972-, Euro credit offr 1982-); FIB; *Books* Lending International Commercial Banking, The Medium Term Loan Market (with J A Donaldson), Understanding Corporate Credit, How to Handle Problem Loans, Thining About Credit; *Recreations* bridge, reading, writing; *Clubs* Brooks's; *Style*— The Hon Thomas Donaldson; Brambles, Nairdwood Land, Great Missenden, Bucks (☎ 02406 2179)

DONALDSON, Rear Adm Vernon D'Arcy; s of Adm Leonard Andrew Boyd Donaldson, CB, CMG (d 1956), and Mary Mitchell Thompson (d 1944); *b* 1 Feb 1906; *Educ* RNC Osborne, RNC Dartmouth; *m* 27 July 1946, Joan Cranfield Monypenny of Pitmilly (holder of feudal barony of Pitmilly, recognised by Lord Lyon), who d 1986, da of James Egerton Howard Monypenny (d 1931); *Career* joined RN 1919, weapon specialist China and Mediterranean Stns, Cdr 1939, serv WWII, Capt 1944, Naval Staff Admty, Naval Attaché China 1948-50, ADC to HM The Queen 1954, ret list 1954, recalled as dir Supplies and Tport 1954, actg Rear Adm 1955, ret 1957 with hon rank Rear Adm; various posts in ind 1958-72; *Clubs* Naval and Military, Caledonian Club (Edinburgh); *Style*— Rear Adm Vernon Donaldson; 36 Knox Court, Knox Place, Haddington, East Lothian EH41 4EB (☎ 062 082 5428)

DONALDSON, Mr (Charles) William; s of Charles Glen Donaldson (d 1957), of Sunningdale, Berks, and Elizabeth Jane Stockley (d 1955); *b* 4 Jan 1935; *Educ* Winchester, Magdalene Coll Cambridge (BA); *m* 1, 1958, Sonia Iris, da of Edward Avory; 1 s (Charles b 1960); m 2, 1967 (m dis 1975), Claire Evelyn Gordon; m 3, 1986, Cherry Jane Hatrick; *Career* author: Nat Serv RN 1953-55, cmmnd as Sub Lt, served in 5 Submarine Sqdn; theatrical producer 1958-70; shows incl: The Ginger Man, Beyond the Fringe, The Bedsitting Room; books incl: The Henry Root Letters, The English Way of Doing Things, Is This Allowed?; *Recreations* watching television, reading Martin Amis; *Style*— William Donaldson, Esq; 139 Elm Park Mansions, Park Walk, London SW10 (☎ 01 352 9689)

DONALDSON OF KINGSBRIDGE, Baroness; Frances Annesley; da of Frederick Lonsdale (d 1954), the playwright, and Leslie Brooke, *née* Hoggan; *b* 13 Jan 1907; *m* 20 Feb 1935, Baron Donaldson of Kingsbridge, *qv*; 1 s, 2 da; *Career* author; *Books* Approach to Farming (1941), Four Years Harvest (1945), Milk Without Tears (1955), Freddy Lonsdale (1957), Child of the Twenties (1959), The Marconi Scandal (1962), Evelyn Waugh: Portrait of a Country Neighbour (1967), Edward VIII (1974, Wolfson History Award 1975), King George VI and Queen Elizabeth (1977), Edward VIII: the Road to Abdication (1978), P G Wodehouse: a Biography (1982), The British Council: the first fifty years (1984), The Royal Opera House In The Twentieth Century (1988); *Style*— Rt Hon Lady Donaldson of Kingsbridge; 17 Edna Street, Battersea, London SW11 3DP (☎ 01 223 0259)

DONALDSON OF KINGSBRIDGE, Baron (Life Peer UK 1967); John George Stuart Donaldson; OBE (1944); s of Rev Stuart Alexander Donaldson (d 1915), master of Magdalene Coll Cambridge, by his wife Lady Albinia Frederica Hobart-Hampden (d 1932), sis of 7 Earl of Buckinghamshire; *b* 9 Oct 1907; *Educ* Eton, Trinity Coll Cambridge; *m* 20 Feb 1935, Frances Annesley Lonsdale, *qv*; 1 s, 2 da; *Career* takes SDP Whip (1981-) in House of Lords; Parly under-sec of state (Lab) N Ireland 1974-76, min of state Dept of Educn and Sci (Master of the Arts) 1976-79; dir: Royal Opera House, Covent Gdn 1958-74, Sadler's Wells Opera 1962-74; chm: Nat Cncl for the Care and Resettlement of Offenders 1965-74, Fedn of Zoos 1971-74; chm: Hotels Catering NEDO 1972-74, Confedn of Art & Design Instns 1982-84; *Clubs* Brooks's, Garrick; *Style*— Rt Hon Lord Donaldson of Kingsbridge, OBE; 17 Edna Street, Battersea, London SW11 3DP (☎ 01 223 0259)

DONALDSON OF LYMINGTON, Baron (Life Peer UK 1988), of Lymington in the County of Hampshire; John Francis Donaldson; PC (1979), QC (1961); s of Malcolm Donaldson (d 1973), by his 1 w, Evelyn Helen Marguerite, eldest da of late Maj Alistair Gilroy, 11 Hussars; *b* 6 Oct 1920; *Educ* Charterhouse, Trinity Coll Cambridge (MA); *m* 1945, (Dorothy) Mary (*see* Donaldson, Dame Mary); 1 s (Michael b 1950), 2 da (Margaret-Ann b 1946, Jennifer b 1948); *Career* serv WWII Royal Signals and Gds Armd Div Signals; barr Middle Temple 1946, High Ct judge (Queen's Bench) 1966-79, lord justice of appeal 1979-82, master of the rolls and chm Ld Chllr's advsy cncl on Public Records 1982-; pres Br Maritime Law Assoc 1979-; govr Sutton's Hosp in Charterhouse 1981-85; visitor: Nuffield Coll Oxford and UCL 1982-; London Business Sch 1987-; former memb Gen Cncl Bar, dep chm Hants QS, memb Cncl on Tbnls and pres Nat Industl Rels Court; FCIArb, pres Chartered Inst of Arbitrators 1980-83; Hon DUniv (Essex) 1983; Hon LLD (Sheffield) 1984, hon fell Trinity Coll Cambridge; kt 1966; *Style*— The Rt Hon Lord Donaldson of Lymington, PC; Royal Courts of Justice, Strand, London WC2 (☎ 01 936 6002, home 588 6610)

DONCASTER, Archdeacon of; see: Carnelley, The Ven Desmond

DONCASTER, Bishop of, 1982-; Rt Rev William Michael Dermot Persson; s of Leslie Charles Granville Alan Persson (d 1948), and Elizabeth Mercer, *née* Chambers; *b* 27 Sept 1927; *Educ* Monkton Combe Sch, Oriel Coll Oxford (MA); *m* 27 April 1957, Ann, da of Reginald Charles Ward Davey (d 1983), of Heronsgate; 2 s (Matthew b 1960, Adam b 1966), 1 da (Rachel b 1958, m Lt Charles Anthony Johnstone-Burt); *Career* Royal Signals 1948-51, served in Germany, cmmnd 2 Lt; deacon 1953, priest 1954, vicar Christ Church Barnet 1958-67, rector of Bebington 1967-79, vicar of Knutsford 1979-82, bishop of Doncaster 1982-; proctor in Convocation 1975-82; examining chaplain to Bishop of London 1981-82, delegate to WCC Vancouver Assembly 1983; memb: BCC Assembly 1977-80 and 1984-; *Clubs* Nat Lib; *Style*— Rt Rev the Bishop of Doncaster; Bishop's Lodge, Hooton Roberts, Rotherham, S Yorkshire S65 4PF (☎ 0709 853370)

DONEGALL, 7 Marquess of (I 1791); Dermot Richard Claud Chichester; LVO; sits as Baron Fisherwick (GB 1790); also Viscount Chichester of Carrickfergus and Baron Chichester of Belfast (I 1625), Earl of Donegall (I 1647), Earl of Belfast (I 1791), Baron Templemore (UK 1831); Hereditary Lord High Admiral of Lough Neagh and Govr of Carrickfergus Castle; s of 4 Baron Templemore, KCVO, DSO, OBE, PC, JP, DL (d 1953), and Hon Clare Meriel Wingfield (d 1969), da of 7 Viscount Powerscourt; suc kinsman, 6 Marquess of Donegall 1975, having suc as 5 Baron Templemore 1953; *b* 18 April 1916; *Educ* Harrow, RMC; *m* 16 Setp 1946, Lady Josceline Gabrielle Legge, *qv*, da of 7 Earl of Dartmouth, GCVO, TD (d 1958); 1 s, 2 da; *Heir* s, Earl of Belfast; *Career* 2 Lt 7 Hussars 1936, (POW 1941-44), Maj 1944, served in Egypt, Libya, Italy; one of HM Bodyguard, Hon Corps of Gentlemen at Arms 1966; grand master Masonic Order Ireland, sr grand warden England, grand warden United Grand Lodge (Masonic) 1982-, Standard Bearer HM Body Guard of Hon Corps of Gentleman at Arms 1984-86; *Recreations* shooting, fishing; *Clubs* Cavalry and Guards', Kildare St (Dublin); *Style*— Most Hon Marquess of Donegall LVO; Dunbrody Park, Arthurstown, Co Wexford, Eire (☎ Waterford 89104)

DONEGALL, Marchioness of; Lady Josceline Gabrielle; *née* Legge; 5 and yst da of 7 Earl of Dartmouth, GCVO, TD (d 1958), and Lady Ruperta Wynn-Carrington (d 1963) (da of 1 and last Marquess of Lincolnshire), whereby Lady Donegall is 1 cous once removed to Lord Carrington; *b* 22 May 1918; *m* 16 Sept 1946, 7 Marquess of Donegall; 1 s, 2 da; *Career* First Aid Nursing Yeo; *Style*— The Most Hon the Marchioness of Donegall; Dunbrody Park, Arthurstown, Co Wexford, Eire

DONEGALL, Maureen, Marchioness of; Maureen; da of Maj Geoffrey C Scholfield, MC, of Birkdale, Lancs; *m* 1, Douglas McKenzie; m 2, 17 Aug 1968, as his 2 w, 6 Marquess of Donegall (d 1975); *Career* served in WRNS, SEAC; *Style*— The Most Hon Maureen, Marchioness of Donegall; 5 Lake View Court, Wimbledon Park Road, London SW19

DONERAILE, Melva, Viscountess; Melva Jean; *née* Clifton; da of George W Clifton, of St Louis, MO, USA; *m* 1945, 9 Viscount Doneraile (d 1983); 3 s, 2 da; *Style*— Rt Hon Melva, Viscountess Doneraile; 405 Eve Circle, Placentia, California 92670, USA

DONERAILE, 10 Viscount (I 1785); Richard Allen St Leger; also Baron Doneraile (in the process of establishing right to the Peerages at time of going to press); s of 9 Viscount Doneraile (d 1983), and Melva, Viscountess Doneraile, *qv*; *b* 17 August 1946; *Educ* Orange Coast Coll California; *m* 1969, Kathleen Mary, da of Nathaniel Simcox; 1 s, 1 da (Hon Maeve b 1974); *Heir* s, Hon Nathaniel St Leger b 13 Sept 1971; *Career* air traffic control specialist Missippi Univ; *Style*— Rt Hon Viscount Doneraile; 405 Eve Circle, Placentia, California 92670, USA

DONGER, Alan David; s of William James Donger (d 1957), of Courtenay Road Winchester and Hilda Marion, *née* Markham (d 1954); *b* 21 Oct 1919; *Educ* Charterhouse; *m* 9 Sept 1949, Annette Strathern da of Air Chief Marshal Sir Douglas CS Evill GBE, KCB, AFC (d 1971); 1 s (William Alan b 1953), 1 da (Alison Sophie b 1951); *Career* joined TA Hamps Carabiniers Yeo 1938, mobilised Munich Crisis 1938; serv WWII: N Africa, Italy, (despatches) 1945, mil govt Austria 1945-46, Lt Col, cdr Hamps Carabiniers Yeo 1952-55, 295 HAA Regt RATA; chartered surveyor 1948, sr ptnr Pink & Arnold later Pink Donger & Lowry 1977-84, conslt Dreweatt Neate 1984-; JP (Winchester) 1951-89; memb Lord Chllrs Panel of Agric Arbitrators 1967-86, mangr Home Off Approved Sch 1952-72, memb advsy ctee local authy community home 1972-79, conslt valuer to Dean and Chapter of Winchester 1975-84, receiver to Hosp of St Cross and Almhouse of Noble Poverty 1975-84; ARICS 1948, FRICS 1954; *Recreations* gardening; *Style*— Alan Donger, Esq, TD

DONKIN, Air Cdre Peter Langloh; CBE (19 48), DSO (1944); s of Frederick Langloh Donkin (d 1925), of Woodbury, NZ, and Phyllis Donkin (d 1952); *b* 19 June 1913; *Educ* Sherborne, RAF Coll Cranwell; *m* 1941, Elizabeth Marjorie, da of J Cecil Cox (d 1968), of The Cottage, Knott Park, Oxslott; 2 da (Elizabeth, Petronella); *Career* RAF 16 Sqdn 1933-38, Mission to Poland 1939, CO: 225 Sqdn 1940, 239 Sqdn 1941-42, 35 Wing 1943-44; Sch of Land Air Warfare 1945, HQ Levant 1945, RCAF Staff Coll 1948-49, exchange USA 1950, CO RAF Chivenor 1951-53, Air Attache Moscow 1954-55, HQ Allied Air Forces Central Europe 1957-58, IDC 1959, AOC Hong Kong 1960-62; *Recreations* shooting, yachting; *Clubs* Carlton; *Style*— Air Cdre Peter Donkin, CBE, DSO; Coombecross Cottage, Templecombe, Somerset

DONKIN, Dr Robert Arthur; s of Arthur Donkin (d 1967), of Loansdean, Morpeth, Northumberland, and Elisabeth Jane, *née* Kirkup (d 1969); *b* 28 Oct 1928; *Educ* Univ of Durham (BA, PhD), Univ of Cambridge (MA); *m* 13 Sept 1970, Jennifer, da of Joseph Edward Kennedy (d 1968), of Michael's Fold, Grasmere, Westmorland; 1 da (Lucy b 1977); *Career* Nat Serv Lt RA 1953-55; King George VI Meml fell Univ of California (Berkeley) 1955-56, asst lectr dept of geography Univ of Edinburgh 1956-58, lectr dept of geography Univ of Birmingham 1958-70, Leverhulme res fell 1966, visiting prof of geography Univ of Toronto 1969; Cambridge Univ: lectr geography of Latin America 1971-, fell Jesus Coll 1972-, tutor Jesus Coll 1975-85; memb Hakluyt Soc 1967; FBA 1985, FRGS 1975, FRAI 1969; *Books* The Cistercian Order in Europe: a bibliography of printed sources (1969), Spanish Red: an ethnogeographical study of cochineal and the Opuntia cactus (1977), The Cistercians: studies in the geography of medieval England and Wales (1978), Agricultural Terracing in the Aboriginal New World (1979), Manna: an historical geography (1980), The Peccary: with observations on the introduction of pigs to the New World (1985); The Muscovy Duck Carina moschata domestica (1989); *Style*— Dr Robin Donkin; 13 Roman Hill, Barton, Cambridge (☎ 0223 262 572); Jesus College, Cambridge

DONNE, David Lucas; s of late Dr Cecil Lucas Donne, of Wellington, NZ, by his w Marjorie Nicholls Donne; *b* 17 August 1925; *Educ* Stowe, Chrust Church Oxford, Syracuse Univ; *m* 1, 1957, Jennifer Margaret Duncan (d 1975); 2 s, 1 da; m 2, 1978, Clare, da of Maj F J Yates; *Career* barr Middle Temple 1949; chm Dalgety 1977- (dep chm 1975-77), chm: Crest Nicholson 1973-, Steetley 1983- (dep chm 1979-83); chm ASDA-MFI plc 1986-; dir: Assoc Dairies, Royal Tst Bank; *Style*— David Donne, Esq; 21 Hertford Street London W1Y 7DA

DONNE, Sir Gaven (John); KBE (1979); s of Jack Alfred and Mary Elizabeth Donne;

b 8 May 1914; *Educ* Palmerston North Boys' HS, Hastings HS, Victoria Univ Wellington NZ Auckland Univ NZ; *m* 1946, Isabel Fenwick, da of John Edwin Hall; 2 s, 2 da; *Career* barr and slr 1938, stipendiary magistrate 1958-75, Puisne Judge Supreme Court of Western Samoa 1970-71, chief justice Western Samoa 1972-75, memb Court of Appeal of Western Samoa 1975-82, chief justice of: Niue 1974-82, the Cook Islands 1975-82; rep of HM The Queen in the Cook Islands 1975-84; chief justice: Nauru 1985-, Tuvalu 1985-; ct of appeal of Kiribati 1986-; *Style—* Sir Gaven Donne, KBE; Supreme Ct Navru; Otaramarre, RD4, Rotorua, NZ

DONNE, Sir John Christopher; s of Leslie Victor Donne (d 1960), of Hove, by his w Mabel Laetitia Richards, *née* Pike; *b* 19 August 1921; *Educ* Charterhouse; *m* 1945, Mary Stuart, da of George Stuart Seaton (d 1938); 3 da; *Career* slr 1949, notary public; conslt Donne Mileham & Haddock; pres Sussex Law Soc 1969-70; chm: SE Regnl Hosp Bd 1971-74, SE Thames RHA 1973-83, NHS Trg Authy (for England and Wales) 1983-86; govr: Guy's Hosp 1971-74, Guy's Hosp Med Sch 1974-83; governing tstee Nuffield Provincial Hosp Tst 1975-; memb: mgmnt ctee King Edward Hosp Fund for London 1982-84, ct Sussex Univ 1979-87, memb ct of Assts Worshipful Co of Broderers Co (Master 1983-84); FRSA, FRSocM; kt 1976; *Recreations* music, photography, gardening; *Clubs* Pilgrims, MCC, Army and Navy, Butterflies; *Style—* Sir John Donne; The Old School House, Acton Burnell, Shrewsbury, Shropshire SY5 7PG (☎ 06944 647)

DONNELLAN, Declan Michael Dominic Martin; s of Thomas Patrick John Donnellan, of Ballinlough, Co Roscommon, Eire, and Margaret Josephine, *née* Donnellan; *b* 4 August 1953; *Educ* St Benedicts Ealing, Queen's Coll Cambridge (MA); *Career* barr Middle Temple 1976-; artistic dir Cheek By Jowl Theatre Co 1980-: touring incl Wallsall to Rio, Cairo to Kathmandu; Br premiéres incl The CID by Corneille, Andromache by Racine, A Family Affair by Ostrowski; Macbeth and Philoctetes Finnish Nat Theatre, Fuente Ovejuna Br Nat Theatre, Drama and Olivier awards (best dir of year); *Style—* Declan Donnellan, Esq; Cheek By Jowl, Alford Ho, Avelinest, London SE1 (☎ 01 793 0153, 01 793 0154, fax 01 735 1031, telex 8951182 GECOMS G)

DONNELLY, John; s of Thomas Donnelly, of Elgin St, Bolton, and Mary Elizabeth, *née* Prescott; *b* 20 Dec 1934; *Educ* Thornleigh Salesian Coll Bolton; *m* 22 May 1961, Jean, da of James Mullineux; 3 s (Robert b 17 Feb 1962, Julian b 30 Oct 1963, Andrew b 16 Feb 1970), 1 da (Kathryn b 18 May 1966), 1 adopted s ((Robert) Paul b 18 May 1966); *Career* Nat Serv RAF 1958-60; articled clerk Cooper and Cooper CAs, off mangr Greenhalgh Son and Dutton CAs 1960-62, Co Sec WHS Taylor & Co Ltd 1962-74, fndr and now sr ptnr J F Donnelly CAs 1974-; dir: Hartnell and Rose Ltd, Melrose Projects Ltd, Heath Moss Ltd; govr: Broadfield Special Sch Lancs, St Johns Primary Sch Bolton; interview chm for NW Eng Project Tst, chm mgmnt ctee Barl Youth Club Lancs CC; FCA; *Recreations* cycling, walking, swimming, interest in all sports; *Style—* John Donnelly, Esq; 9 Greenacres, Turton, Bolton BL7 0QG (☎ 0204 852127); J & F Donnelly, Peel House, 2 Chorley Old Road, Bolton BL1 3AA (☎ 0204 381712)

DONNELLY, Maurice John; s of James Heenan Donnelly (d 1965), and Mary Agnes Donnelly (d 1985); *b* 31 May 1933; *Educ* Stonyhurst, Durham Univ (BSc); *m* 1980, June, da of F W Donohue (d 1967; sr research engr and memb of research team on The Davis Escape; decorated by HM King George VI for work on poisonous gases), of Morecambe; 3 da (Nicola, Caroline, Linsey), 1 step s (Michael J Steward), 1 step da (Mrs Gail Prill); *Career* cmmnd HM RM 1955, Nat Serv; chief exec Lunesdale Farmers Ltd 1966-74; joined Tube Investmts 1975 (sales dir 1980, business devpt dir 1983); *Recreations* golf, squash; *Clubs* Morecambe Golf, Vale of Lune Rugby; *Style—* Maurice Donnelly, Esq; Eden Vale, 338 Marine Rd, Morecambe, Lancs LA4 5AB (☎ 0524 415544)

DONNER, John Melville; s of Gerald Melville Donner (d 1964), and Pearl, only da of Sir Frank Bernard Sanderson, 1 Bt (d 1965); *b* 18 July 1930; *Educ* Stowe, RMA Sandhurst; *m* 1952, Patricia Mary, da of Barnet Thomas Jenkins (d 1941); 1 s (Rupert b 1955), 1 da (Annabel b 1958); *Career* Coldstream Gds 1948-53 and 1966 (Suez), T/ Capt; entered Lloyds 1955 (Arbon Langrish), elected memb 1964, dir Fenchurch Insur Holding 1969, (md 1969-74); chm: Donner Underwriting Agencies Ltd 1976 (Queen's Award for Export 1983 and 1988), JD Underwriting Agencies Ltd 1979, RD Underwriting Agencies 1980, CD Underwriting Agencies Ltd 1983; dir Alexander Syndicate Mgmnt Ltd 1982-; chm Western Bloodstock Ltd; chm bd of govrs St Michael's Sch Tawstock; Freeman City of London 1977, Liveryman Worshipful Co of Plaisterers; *Recreations* old vehicles, gardening, travel, food and wine; *Clubs* Carlton, Boodle's, Adelaide (Australia), Bentley Drivers, Rolls Royce Enthusiasts; *Style—* John Donner, Esq; 39 Bramerton St, London SW3 (☎ 01 352 9964); Quarkhill, Crowcombe, Taunton, Somerset TA4 4BJ (☎ 098 48 651)

DONNET, Hon Gavin Alexander; s of Baron Donnet of Balgay (Life Peer; d 1985); *b* 2 Oct 1950; *Educ* Hyndland Secdy Sch Glasgow; *m* 1976, Margaret Louise, *née* Scott; 2 children; *Style—* The Hon Gavin Donnet; 9 Scotscraig, Broughty Ferry, Dundee DD5 3SU

DONNET, Hon Stephen Christopher; s of Baron Donnet of Balgay (Life Peer; d 1985); *b* 31 Dec 1960; *Educ* Jordanhill Coll Sch, Strathclyde Univ; *Style—* The Hon Stephen Donnet

DONNET OF BALGAY, Baroness; Mary; da of Gavin Mitchell Black; *m* 1945, Baron Donnet of Balgay (Life Peer; sometime pres Scottish TUC; d 1985); 2 s, 1 da; *Style—* Rt Hon Lady Donnet of Balgay; 8 Jordanhill Drive, Glasgow G13 (☎ 041 954 8188)

DONOHOE, Peter Howard; s of Harold Steven Donohoe (d 1974), and Marjorie, *née* Travis; *b* 18 June 1953; *Educ* Chetham's Sch, Leeds Univ (BA), Royal Northern Coll of Music (B Mus), Paris Conservatoire of Music, Tchaikowsky Conservatory of Music Moscow; *m* 23 Oct 1980, Elaine, da of William Geoffrey Burns; 1 da (Jessica b 21 April 1986); *Career* Int Concert Pianist; London debut 1979, US debut 1983, recording debut 1982; appearances in major festivals and with major orchs incl annual visits to Henry Wood Promenade Concerts London 1979-; winner seventh int Tschaikovsky Competition Moscow 1982; recordings for EMI/Angel label incl Tschaikovsky piano concerto number 2 (winner Concerto Record of the Year Award 1988); hon fell Royal Northern Coll Music 1983; *Style—* Peter Donohoe, Esq; Saint Just, 82 Hampton Lane, Solihull, West Midlands B91 2RS (☎ 021 704 4450); c/o Harold Holt Ltd, 31 Sinclair Rd, London W14 0NS (☎ 01 603 4600/5148, fax 01 603 0019, telex 22 339 Hunter)

DONOUGHMORE, Jean, Countess of; (Dorothy) Jean; MBE (1947); eldest da of John Beaumont Hotham (d 1924), Clerk of the Senate and Assist Clerk oif the Parliament of N Ireland; *b* 12 August 1906; *m* 27 July 1925, 7 Earl of Donoughmore (d 1981); 2 s (8 Earl, Hon Mark Hely-Hutchinson), 1 da (Lady Sara Collins); *Career* SSStJ; *Style—* Rt Hon Jean, Countess of Donoughm; High Coodham, Symington, Ayrshire, Scotland KA1 5SJ (☎ Symington 830253 13 01)

DONOUGHMORE, 8 Earl of (I 1800); Richard Michael John Hely-Hutchinson; sits as Viscount Hutchinson of Knocklofty (UK 1821); also Baron Donoughmore of Knocklofty (I 1783) and Viscount Donoughmore of Knocklofty (I 1797); s of Col 7 Earl of Donoughmore (d 1981), and Jean, Countess of Donoughmore, MBE, *qv*; *b* 8 August 1927; *Educ* Winchester, New Coll Oxford (BM, BCh); *m* 1 Nov 1951, Sheila, da of late Frank Frederick Parsons and Mrs Roy Smith-Woodward; 4 s; *Heir* s, Viscount Suirdale; *Career* Capt RAMC; fin conslt, co dir; chm Headline Book Publishing plc; *Recreations* fishing, shooting, racing (Paris); *Clubs* Kildare Street, Interallié, Jockey (Paris); *Style—* Rt Hon Earl of Donoughmore; The Manor House, Bampton, Oxon OX8 2LQ

DONOUGHUE, Baron (Life Peer UK 1985), of Ashton, Co Northants; Bernard Donoughue; s of Thomas Joseph Donoughue and Maud Violet, *née* Andrews; *b* 8 Sept 1934; *Educ* Northampton GS, Lincoln Coll Oxford, Nuffield Coll Oxford (MA, DPhil); *m* 1959, Carol Ruth, da of late Abraham Goodman; 2 s, 2 da; *Career* lectr, sr lectr, reader LSE 1963-74, sr policy advsr to PM 1974-79, devpt dir Economist Intelligence Unit 1979-81, asst ed The Times 1981-82, head of Res and Investmt Policy Grieveson Grant & Co 1984-86 (ptnr 1983), dir Kleinwort Benson Bank 1986-88; exec vice-chm London & Bishopsgate Int Investmt Hldgs 1988-; memb: advsy bd Wissenschaftzentrum Berlin 1978, cncl LSE; assoc memb Nuffield Coll Oxford, hon fell Lincoln Coll Oxford, chm Exec London Symphony Orch; *Books* Trade Unions in a Changing Society (1963), British Politics and the American Revolution (with W T Rodgers 1964), The People into Parliament (with G W Jones 1966), Herbert Morrison: portrait of a politician (1973), Prime Minister (1987); *Style—* Rt Hon Lord Donoughue; 1 Sloane Square, London SW1

DONOVAN, Wing Cdr Edmund; OBE (1958), DFC (1943); s of Richard John Donovan (ka 1917), and Evelyn McIlvenna (d 1986); *b* 23 August 1916; *Educ* Ratcliffe Coll, RAF Staff Coll (psa); *m* 17 Dec 1951, Ann Rosemary, da of James Gresher Blackedge, OBE, JP (d 1976); 2 da (Jane Mary, Ann Catherine); *Career* Wing Cdr RAF invalided 1962, served Western Desert NATO; Freeman City of London, fndr memb Worshipful Co of Marketers; FInstM; *Recreations* military history, gardening, poetry; *Style—* Wing Cdr Edmund Donovan, OBE, DFC; East End House, Watlington, Oxon OX9 5BT (☎ 049 1612520)

DONOVAN, Hon Hugh Desmond; s of Baron Donovan, PC (Life Peer, d 1971); *b* 23 Feb 1934; *Educ* Harrow, New Coll Oxford; *m* 26 July 1968, Margaret, da of Hugh Forbes Arbuthnott (gs of 8 Viscount of Arbuthnott); 1 s (Charles Edward b. 1974); *Career* served RN as Midshipman; barr; *Recreations* golf, photography; *Clubs* Royal Wimbledon Golf; *Style—* The Hon Hugh Donovan; 40 Felden St, SW6 (☎ 01 731 4001)

DONOVAN, Ian Edward; s of John Walter Donovan (d 1986), and Ethel Molyneux Studdy Hooper; *b* 2 Mar 1940; *Educ* Leighton Park Sch Reading; *m* 26 July 1969, Susan Betty da of William Harris, of Abbotbury, Dorset; 2 s (Christopher George b 1971, James William b 1974); *Career* finance dir: Lucan Girling Koblenz 1978-81, Lucan Electrical 1982- 84; gp dir Finance and Central Servs CAA 1985-88, memb for finance CAA 1986-88; dir and gp controller Smiths Industs Aerospace & Def Systems Ltd 1988-; FCMA; *Recreations* sailing, music; *Style—* Ian Donovan, Esq; Lawn Farm, Church Lane, Tibberton, Droitwich; 35 Carillon Ct, Oxford Rd, Ealing, London

DONOVAN, John Edward; s of late Leslie Donovan, Maj RE; *b* 24 Sept 1930; *Educ* Wimbledon Coll; *m* 1957, Margaret Bridget, *née* O'Brien; 1 s (twin); 2 da; *Career* Flying Offr RAF Nat Serv; gp chief accountant London Weekend Television Ltd; fin dir Lovelace Investmt Ltd; hon tres: Handicapped Childrens' Pilgrimage Tst, Hosanna House Tst; FCA, ATII; *Recreations* music, reading, jogging; *Style—* John Donovan, Esq; St Josephs, 56 Molesey Park Rd, East Molesey, Surrey KT8 0JZ

DONOVAN, Judith; da of Ernest Nicholson, of Bradford, and Joyce, *née* Finding; *b* 5 July 1951; *Educ* St Josephs Coll Bradford, Woking Girls GS, Univ of Hull (BA); *m* 12 Nov 1977, John Patrick Donovan, s of William Donovan, of Darlington; *Career* mktg trainee Ford Motor Co 1973-75, account mangr J Walter Thomson 1976, advertising mangr Gratton 1977-82, md Judith Donovan Assocs 1982; former pres Bradford Jr C of C (cncl memb), govr Friends of Bradford Art Galleries & Museums; dir: Bradford Bounce Ltd, Bradford Ptnrship; former chm Bradford Business Club; MInstM 1977, MBIM 1978, MCAM 1979, memb IOD 1983; *Recreations* reading, collecting books and paintings, pets; *Style—* Mrs Judith Donovan; 42 HEaton Grove, Bradford, W Yorks BD9 4EB (☎ 0274 543 966); Judith Donovan Assocs Ltd, 288 Harrogate Rd, Bradford BD2 3SP (☎ 0274 641 333, fax 0274 641 350, car phone 0836 610 683)

DOOTSON, Thomas; s of Samuel Dootson (d 1970), of Fulham, London, and Ethel, *née* Boardman (d 1946); *b* 16 July 1941; *Educ* Blackburn Tech HS, Sir Christopher Wren Sch of Bldg & Art, London; *m* 7 Dec 1963, Margaret Katherine May, da of William Windsor Connell (d 1964), of Thornton Heath; 1 s (Alistair William Samuel b 8 Nov 1971), 2 da (Sarah Louise b 13 April 1970, Charlotte Elizabeth b 14 March 1973); *Career* dir: Abbeygate Securities Ltd 1979-86, Connell-Menzies Ptnrships 1979-86, Peel Hlds plc 1983-86, TAM Hldgs IOM Ltd 1987, Peregrine Int Ltd 1987, Cresta Hldgs Ltd 1988 (listed LSE); chm Cresta Properties 1988; *Recreations* sailing, diving, golf; *Style—* Thomas Dootson, Esq; Winterbourne, Hillberry Green, Douglas, IOM; Peregrine House, Peel Rd, Douglas, IOM (☎ 0624 73800, fax 0624 73827, car ☎ 0860 640020)

DORAN, Dr Derek Malise Leslie; s of Joseph Leslie Doran (d 1947), of Glasgow, and Edith Mary, *née* Herbertson (d 1948); *b* 14 Dec 1914; *Educ* Glenalmond, Pembroke Coll Oxford, (MA) St Thomas's Hosp (BM, BCh); *m* 4 Nov 1941, Joan Alice, da of Alec Charles Hayley (d 1936), of Ceylon; 3 s (Peter b 1942, Robert b 1948, Christopher b 1953), 1 da (June b 1951); *Career* served WW II Surgn Lt RNVR 1941-46 on HMS Southdown (North Sea Convoys), HMS Verstaile (Atlantic); conslt physician and dir dept of rheumatology and rehabilitation W Middx Univ Hosp Isleworth 1948-79, examiner for Chartered Soc of Physiotherapy 1963-79; (past pres section of Rheumatology); FRCP, FRM; *Books* Manipulation of Joints of Extremitires (Physical Medicine Library vol 5, 1960); *Recreations* fishing, sailing, skiing; *Clubs* Vincents, Royal Southern Yacht, Ski (GB), Little Ship; *Style—* Dr Derek Doran; Dell Farm, Vicarage Lane, Copythorne, Southampton SO4 2PA (☎ 0703 812502)

DORCHESTER, Bishop of 1988; Rt Rev Dr Anthony John Russell; *née* s of

Michael John William Russell and Beryl Margaret Russell; *b* 25 Jan 1943; *Educ* Uppingham, Univ of Durham (BA), Univ of Oxford (DPhil), Cuddesdon Theol Coll; *m* 1967, Sheila Alexandra, da of Alexander Scott; 2 s (Jonathan b 1971, Timothy b 1981), 2 da (Alexandra b 1969, Serena b 1975); *Career* dir Arthur Rank Centre; canon theologian of Coventry Cathedral; examining chaplain to Bishop of Hereford; chaplain: Royal Agric Soc of England, Royal Agric Benevolent Inst; chaplain to HM the Queen; *Books* Groups and Teams in the Countryside (1975), The Clerical Profession (1980), The Country Parish (1986); *Style*— The Rt Rev the Bishop of Dorchester; The Rectory, Whitchurch, Stratford-on-Avon, Warwickshire CV37 8NS (☎ 078 987 225)

DORE, Brian James; s of Albert Dore (d 1979), of Oxford, and Cissie, *née* Barratt; *b* 16 Mar 1935; *Educ* City of Oxford HS for Boys; *m* 14 June 1958, Mary Roberta, da of Henry Hansford (d 1977), of Oxford; 2 s (Andrew Michael b 1961, Trevor John b 1965); *Career* accountant: sr ptnr Weller Messenger & Kirkman Oxford (ret); memb: Chartered Assoc of Certified Accountants and Taxation; ICAEW; *Recreations* ornithology, travel; *Clubs* Clarendon; *Style*— Brian J Dore, Esq; c/o National Westminster Bank, Comlomberle, Jersey; Weller Messenger & Kirkman, 8 King Edward St, Oxford OX1 4HL (☎ 0865 723131)

DOREY, Geoffrey Richard; s of Conseiller John Dorey (d 1984), and Blanche Flere, *née* Bichard; *b* 28 August 1944; *Educ* Elizabeth Coll Guernsey, City of London Coll Moorgate; *m* 1969, Evelyne Genevieve, da of Col Renaud Sabattier, of France; 2 s (Olivier b 1972, Pascal b 1976), 1 da (Sophie b 1974); *Career* dir: Fruit Export Gp 1972 (md 1978-; Islands Insur Co Ltd 1978-), Channel TV 1985-; Douzainier de la Paroisse du Castel 1987, Sénéchal Fief Le Comte 1987; *Recreations* period cars, wine, vernacular architecture, badminton; *Clubs* United, Guernsey; *Style*— Geoffrey Dorey, Esq; Les Queux, Castel, Guernsey; Fruit Export Co Ltd, PO Box 350 , St Peter Port, Guernsey (☎ 0481 23881, telex 4131616)

DORIN, Geoffrey Stephen Neilson; s of Stephen Dorin (d 1972), and Lily, *née* Miller (d 1988); *b* 21 Dec 1925; *Educ* Whitley Bay HS, Kings Coll Univ of Durham, Open Univ (BA); *m* 2 April 1955, Patricia Margaret, da of James Norman Adamson (d 1966); 1 s (Andrew James Neilson b 1961), 1 da (Julia Ruth b 1963); *Career* mil serv 1946 RAPC (Capt); former md: Smith & Barnes Ltd, John W & S Dorin Ltd; dir Gramvole Ltd; admin dir St Oswals's Hospice Newcastle-on-Tyne 1982-; *Recreations* country pursuits, travel, gardening; *Style*— Geoffrey S N Dorin, Esq; Oak Tree Cottage, West Rainton, Houghton-le-Spring, Wearside (☎ 091 584 9070); Silverdale Cottage, Snitter, Rothbury (☎ 0669 21084); St Oswalds Hospice, Regent Avenue, Newcastle upon Tyne NE3 1EE (☎ 091 285 0063)

DORJI, Hon Mrs (Manjula); *née* Sinha; er da of 3 Baron Sinha, *qv*; *b* 1947; *m* (m dis), Tobgye Dorji, s of late Jigme Dorji, PM of Bhutan; 1 s (Jigme); *Style*— Hon Mrs Dorji; 7 Lord Sinha Rd, Calcutta

DORKING, Bishop of 1986-; Rt Rev David Peter Wilcox; s of John Wilcox (d 1961), and Stella May, *née* Bower (d 1977); *b* 29 June 1930; *Educ* Northampton GS, St John's Coll Oxford (MA), Lincoln Theological Coll; *m* 11 Aug 1956, Pamela Ann, da of Herbert Leslie Hedges, of 27 The Drive, Hailsham, Sussex; 2 s (Peter b 1961, Christopher b 1968), 2 da (Sara b 1957, Frances b 1959); *Career* asst curate St Helier Morden Southwark 1954-56, staff sec Student Christian Movement and asst curate Univ Church Oxford 1956-59; Theological Coll posts: Lincoln 1959-64, Bangalore S India 1964-70; vicar Gt Gransden and rector Lt Gransden Ely 1970-72, canon Derby Cathedral and warden E Midlands Jt Ordination Scheme 1972-77, princ Ripon Coll Cuddesdon and vicar Cuddesdon 1977-86; *Recreations* walking, music, art, theatre; *Style*— The Rt Rev the Bishop of Dorking; Dayspring, 13 Pilgrims Way, Guildford, Surrey GU4 8AD (☎ 0483 570829)

DORMAN, Lt-Col Sir Charles Geoffrey; 3 Bt (UK 1923), of Nunthorpe, York, MC (1942); o child of Sir Bedford Lockwood Dorman, 2 Bt, CBE (d 1956); *b* 18 Sept 1920; *Educ* Rugby, Brasenose Coll Oxford; *m* 22 Dec 1954 (m dis 1972), Elizabeth Ann (CStJ), only da of late George Gilmour Gilmour-White, OBE, JP; 1 da; *Heir* kinsman, Philip Dorman; *Career* served 3 Kings Own Hussars 1941-47, Capt 1942, Maj 1954, Lt-Col 1961, GSO (1) (ADSR) AORE 1961-64, GSOI (W), IFVME 1964, ret 1970; *Recreations* gliding; *Style*— Lt-Col Sir Charles Dorman, Bt, MC; Hutton Grange Cottage, Gt Rollright, Chipping Norton, Oxon (☎ Hook Norton 737535)

DORMAN, Sir Maurice Henry; GCMG (1961, KCMG 1957, CMG 1955), GCVO (1961), DL (Wilts 1978); s of John Ehrenfried Dorman (d 1957), of 77 Eastgate, Stafford, and Madeleine Louise, *née* Bostock (d 1978); *b* 7 August 1912; *Educ* Sedbergh, Magdalene Coll Cambridge (MA); *m* 4 Dec 1937, (Florence) Monica Churchward, DStJ, da of Montague George Smith (d 1947), of Torquay, Devon; 1 s (John b 1939), 3 da (Joanna (Mrs Oswin) b 1941, Elisabeth (Mrs Latham) b 1943, Sibella (Mrs Laing) b 1949); *Career* admin offr Tanganyika Territory 1935, clerk cncls Tanganyika 1940-45, asst to lt-govr Malta 1945, princ asst sec Palestine 1947, seconded to Colonial Service 1948, dir Social Welfare and Community Devpt Gold Coast 1950, colonial sec Trinidad and Tobago 1952-56 (acting govr Trinidad 1954-55), govr-gen Sierra Leone 1961-62 (govr, C-in-C and Vice Adm 1956-61 independence), govr-gen Malta 1964-71 (govr and C-in-C 1962-64 independence); dep chm Pearce Cmmn on Rhodesian Opinion 1971-72, chm Br Observer Gp at Zimbabwe Independence Elections 1980; chm Swindon Health Authority 1981-88 (chm Wilts Area Health Authority 1974-80, Swindon Hosp Mgmnt Ctee 1972-74); chm West of England (previously Ramsbury) Building Soc 1983-87 (dir 1972-83); tstee Imperial War Museum 1972-85; lord prior Ven Order St John 1980-85 (chief cdr St John Ambulance 1975-80, almoner Order St John 1972-75), GCStJ 1978 (KStJ 1957); hon DCL (Durham) 1962, hon LLD (Malta) 1964; *Recreations* golf, gardening, grandchildren; *Clubs* Athenaeum, Casino Maltese (Valletta); *Style*— Sir Maurice Dorman, GCMG, GCVO, DL; The Old Manor, Overton, nr Marlborough, Wilts SN8 4ER (☎ 067 286 600 8698)

DORMAN, Philip Henry Keppel; s of Richard Dorman (d 1976), gs of 1 Bt; hp of kinsman, Sir Charles Dorman, 3 Bt, MC; *b* 19 May 1954; *Educ* Marlborough, St Andrews Univ; *m* 12 April 1982, Myriam Jeanne Georgette, da of late René Bay and of Royan, France; 1 da (Megan Bay Keppel b 1984); *Career* tax conslt; *Recreations* golf; *Clubs* MCC, Waterhall Golf (Brighton); *Style*— Philip Dorman, Esq

DORMAN, Richard Bostock; CBE (1984); s of John Ehrenfried Dorman (d 1957), of Stafford, and Madeleine Louise Bostock (d 1975); *b* 8 August 1925; *Educ* Sedbergh Sch, St John's Coll Cambridge (BA); *m* 1950, Anna, da of Maj Frank Illingworth (d 1977), of Surrey; 1 s (Paul b 1963), 2 da (Julia b 1953, Deborah b 1959); *Career* HM diplomatic service (ret); first sec Nicosia 1960-64; dep high cmmnr Freetown 1964-66; NATO Defense Coll Rome 1968-69; cnsllr Addis Ababa 1969-73; commercial cnsllr Bucharest 1974-77; cnsllr South Africa 1977-82; high cmmr Port Vila 1982-85; *Recreations* coordinator, Bristish Friends of Vanuatu; *Clubs* Royal Cwlth Soc; *Style*— Richard Dorman, Esq, CBE; 67 Beresford Rd, Cheam, Surrey SM2 6ER (☎ 01 642 9625)

DORMAND OF EASINGTON, Baron (Life Peer UK 1987), of Easington, Co Durham John Donkin; s of Bernard & Mary Dormand; *b* 27 August 1919; *Educ* Bede Coll Durham, Loughborough Coll, Oxford, Harvard; *m* 1963, Doris Robinson; 1 step s, 1 step da; *Career* chm PLP 1981-87; formerly teacher, educn advsr & district educn offr; assst govt whip 1974, lord cmmr of Treasury 1974-79; memb: Peterlee Lab Club, Easington Workingmens Club; MP (Lab) Easington 1970-87; *Style*— The Rt Hon the Lord Dormand of Easington; House of Lords, London SW1A 0PW

DORMER, 16 Baron (E 1615); Sir Joseph Spencer Philip Dormer; 16 Bt (E 1615); s of Capt 14 Baron Dormer, CBE, JP, DL, RN (d 1922); suc bro, 15 Baron Dormer, 1975; *b* 4 Sept 1914; *Educ* Ampleforth, Christ Church Oxford; *Heir* cous, Lt Cdr Geoffrey Henry Dormer, RN; *Career* served WW II, Capt Scots Gds, NW Europe; sits as cons peer in the House of Lords; pres Warwick and Leamington Cons Assoc 1983; hon vice pres Worcestershire branch Grenadier Guards Assoc; landowner and farmer; *Recreations* shooting, fishing, gardening; *Clubs* Cavalry & Guards; *Style*— Rt Hon Lord Dormer; Grove Park, Warwick CV35 8RF (☎ 0926 498838)

DORMER, Michael Henry Stanhope; o child of Robert Stanhope Dormer (d 1960)), and Ebba (d 1961), widow of Sir Everard Hambro, KCVO and da of Charles Cecil Beresford Whyte, JP, DL, of Hatley Manor, co Leitrim; he is descended through the Counts Buttlar from the 'Blood-Countess' Elisabeth Báthory (walled-up alive and d 1614); *b* 8 Dec 1930; *m* 21 Jan 1959, Daphne Margaret, elder da and co-heiress of Capt Oswald James Battine (d 1938), and his w Gwendoline who was eldest da and co-heiress of Col Sir Colin MacRae of Feoirlinn (d 1952), by his w Lady Margaret (d 1954), da of 3 Marquess of Bute; 1 s, 2 da; *Career* Kt of Honour and Devotion SMO Malta, Kt of Justice of the Constantinian Order of St George; *Recreations* gardening, genealogy, painting; *Clubs* Turf; *Style*— Michael Dormer, Esq; Bowdown House, Greenham, Newbury, Berks (☎ 0635 43311)

DORMER, Robin James; s of Dudley James Dormer (d 1983), and Jean Mary, *née* Brimacombe; *b* 30 May 1951; *Educ* Int Sch of Geneva, Switz, Univ Coll of Wales Aberystwyth (LL B) ; *Career* Coward Chance 1976-80 slr 1980, mem of legal staff Law Cmmn 1980-87, asst Parly counsel Off of the Parly Counsel 1987-; memb Law Soc; *Style*— Robin Dormer, Esq; 36 Whitehall, london, SW1A 2AY (☎ 01 210 3000, fax 01 210 6632)

DORMER, Hon Rosamund Jane; JP (Warwicks 1948); yst da of 14 Baron Dormer, CBE (d 1922); *b* 15 April 1911; *Career* Jr Cdr ATS 1942; *Style*— The Hon Rosamund Dormer, JP; School House, Spetchley, Worcs

DORR, HE Noel; s of John (d 1958); *b* 1 Nov 1933; *Educ* Nat Univ of Ireland, UC Galway (BA B Comm, HDip in Ed), Georgetown Univ Washington DC (MA); *m* 1983, Caitriona; *Career* asst sec Dept of For Affrs Dublin 1974-77, dep sec 1977-80); perm rep of Ireland to the UN NY 1980-1983, Irish ambass to the Ct of St James's 1983-,; *Clubs* Garrick, Athenaeum, RAC; *Style*— HE the Irish Ambassador; Irish Embassy, 17 Grosvenor Place, London SW1X 7HR (☎ 01 235 2171)

DORREEN, Dr James M; s of late Ernest James Dorreen, civil engr, and late Margaret Dorothy Dorreen; *b* 11 Jan 1916; *Educ* Univ of New Zealand (MSc), Imperial Coll London (PhD); *m* Ruth Sinclair; 3 s (Peter James, Mark Sinclair, Adrian Luke); *Career* Capt NZ Engrs 2 NZEF 1939-45; Int oil conslt; formerly with Exxon in Australasia, S America, Far East, Europe and N Africa; ret as pres and md Esso Morocco, Exploration & Production Inc; dir: Texas Pacific Oil, Premier Consolidated Oilfields, Falcon Resources.; *Books* papers in scientific journals; *Recreations* geology; *Clubs* American (London), Royal Overseas League; *Style*— Dr James Dorreen; The Woodlands, Cavendish Road, St George's Hill, Weybridge, Surrey KT13 0JY

DORRELL, Stephen James; MP (C) Loughborough 1979-; s of Philip Dorrell; *b* 25 Mar 1952; *Educ* Uppingham, Brasenose Coll Oxford; *m* 1980, Penelope Anne Wears, da of James Taylor, of Windsor; *Career* PA to Rt Hon Peter Walker MP 1974, export dir family clothing firm, contested (C) Kingston-upon-Hull E Oct 1974; PPS to Rt Hon Peter Walker MP, sec of state Energy 1983-, asst govt whip June 1987; *Recreations* walking, flying; *Style*— S J Dorrell, Esq, MP; House of Commons, London SW1

DORRIEN-SMITH, Lady Emma; *née* Windsor-Clive; da of 3 Earl of Plymouth; *b* 13 Feb 1954; *m* 1975, Robert Arthur (Smith-)Dorrien-Smith, eldest s of late Lt Cdr Thomas Mervyn Smith-Dorrien-Smith, RN, of Tresco, Isles of Scilly, and Tamara, Lady O'Hagan; 2 s (Adam b 1978, Michael b 1987), 1 da (Frances b 1980); *Style*— Lady Emma Dorrien-Smith; Tresco Abbey, Isles of Scilly

DORSET, Archdeacon of; *see*: Walton, Ven Geoffrey Elmer

DOSSOR, Rear Adm Frederick; CBE (1959), CB (1963); s of John Malcolm Dossor (d 1940), of Hull, and Edith Kate Brittain (d 1938); *b* 12 Mar 1913; *Educ* Hymers Coll Hull, Loughborough Coll London (BSc, DLC); *m* 1951, Pamela Anne, da of Ralph Huxley Newton (d 1960), of Southbourne; 2 da (Penelope, Caroline); *Career* Dept Electric Engrs Admiralty 1939-50, Electrical Branch RN 1950-65, Polaris project offr Miny of Aviation 1963-68, dir Hovercraft Dept of Trade & Indust 1968-71, conslt Utd Builders Merchants 1971-78; *Recreations* travel, gardening; *Clubs* Royal Cwlth Soc; *Style*— Rear Adm Frederick Dossor; 1A Lynch Road, Farnham, Surrey (☎ 0242 721931)

DOTRICE, Roy; s of Louis Dotrice and Neva, *née* Wilton; *b* 26 May 1925; *Educ* Dayton Acad, Intermediate Sch Guernsey, Elizabeth Coll; *m* 1946, Kay Newman; 3 da (Michèle m 1987, Edward Woodward, the actor, Karen m 1986, Alex Hyde White, actor s of Wilfrid Hyde White, Yvette m 1985, John E R Lumley); *Career* actor; 9 years with Royal Shakespeare Co; over 30 West End performances; 6 Broadway appearances including 2 one-man shows *viz* Abraham Lincoln and Brief Lives, Emmy Award the latter in Guinness Book of World Records as longest running solo performance (1,700); best actor award TV England 1969 (Brief Lives), America 1966 (The Caretaker); Tony nomination as best Broadway actor 1981; latest films Amadeus, Corsican Brothers, The Eliminators; Latest American TV, A Team, The Wizard, Magnum PI, Beauty and the Beast; *Recreations* fishing, riding, golf; *Clubs* Garrick, Players; *Style*— Roy Dotrice, Esq; c/o Bernard Hunter, Leading Players, 31, Kings Road, London SW3

DOUBLE, Michael Stockwell; s of Cyril William Stockwell Double (d 1942), and Alice Elizabeth Ellen, *née* Smith; *b* 3 Mar 1935; *Educ* Christ's Hosp and Pembroke Coll,

Cambridge (MA); *m* 26 Feb 1966, Julia, da of Harold Ashwell Westrope (d 1961); 2 da (Lucy b 1967, Clare b 1970); *Career* Nat Serv Royal Corps of Signals; CA; dir: Madame Tussaud's Ltd 1981-; Warwick Castle Ltd 1987-, Chessington World of Adventures 1987-, Wookey Hole Caves Ltd 1987-; FCA; *Recreations* sailing, theatre, walking; *Clubs* Island Cruising; *Style*— Michael Double, Esq; Madame Tussaud's Ltd, Marylebone Rd, London NW1 5LR (☎ 01 935 6861, fax 935-8906)

DOUBLEDAY, Lt-Col Garth Leslie; TD (1950), JP (Kent 1956), DL (1965); s of Sir Leslie Doubleday (d 1975), by his w Nora, da of William Foster, of Tunbridge Wells; *b* 13 July 1913; *Educ* Charterhouse, Clare Coll Cambridge; *m* 1946, May Alison, da of Frank Hann; 3 s, 3 da; *Career* serv WWII with RA, Middle East, Cdr 516 LAA regt (TA) 1949-52; High Sheriff 1976-77; Master Worshipful Co of Fruiterers 1968; gen cmmr of Income Tax 1970; *Clubs* Farmers', MCC; *Style*— Lt-Col Garth Doubleday, TD, JP, DL; Rodmersham House, Rodmersham, Sittingbourne, Kent (☎ 0795 23545)

DOUBLEDAY, John Vincent; s of Gordon Vincent Doubleday, of Essex, and Margaret Elsa Verder, *née* Harris; *b* 19 Oct 1947; *Educ* Stowe, Goldsmith's Coll Sch of Art; *m* 1969, Isobel Jean Campbell, da of Maj Frederick Robert Edwin Durie, of Argyll; 3 s (Robert b 1974, Edwin b 1977, James b 1979); *Career* exhibitions incl: Waterhouse Gallery 1968-69 and 1970-71, Richard Demarco Gallery Edinburgh 1973, Laing Art Gallery Newcastle, Bowes Barnard Castle 1974, Pandion Gallery NY Aldeborough Festival 1983; Portraits incl: Baron Ramsey of Canterbury 1974, King Olav of Norway 1975, Prince Philip Duke of Edinburgh, Earl Mountbatten, Golda Meir 1976, Ratu Sukuna 1977, Regeneration 1978, Maurice Bowra 1979, Charlie Chaplin (Leicester Square), Lord Olivier, Mary and Child Christ (Rochester Cathedral), Caduceus (Harvard Mass), Isambard Kingdom Brunel (two works Paddington and Bristol), Charlie Chaplin (Vevey 1982, and London), Beatles (Liverpool), Dylan Thomas (Swansea 1984 and Phoenix 1985); Commando Memorial 1986, Sherlock Holmes (Town Square Meiringen) 1988; works in public collections: Ashmolean, Brit Museum, Herbert F Johnson NY, Tate Gallery, V & A, National Museum of Wales; *Recreations* cross-country skiing; *Style*— John Doubleday Esq; Lodge Cottage, Goat Lodge Rd, Gt Totham, Maldon, Essex (☎ 0621 892085); Torrdarroch, Ardrishaig, Argyll, Scotland

DOUBLEDAY, (Richard) Noel; s of John Frederick Doubleday, and Ivy Muriel Mitchell (d 1957); gs of pioneer of Public Library System; *b* 27 May 1930; *Educ* Rossall Sch, King Edward's Edgbaston Birmingham, Downing Coll Cambridge (MA); *m* 1, 27 Sept 1958, Hilary Estcourt Jackson; m 2, 13 April 1982, Catherine Mary, da of The Ven Philip L C Price (d 1983); *Career* former dir of devpt Keston Coll; dir: Open Doors (UK), Living Bibles Int (UK); freelance prodr and contributor to BBC; *Recreations* swimming, walking, dining out, classical music; *Clubs* Athenaeum; *Style*— Noel Doubleday, Esq; 22 Forest Road, Bordon, Hampshire GU35 0BH (☎ 04203 7668)

DOUEK, Ellis Elliot; s of Cesar Douek, of London, and Nelly, *née* Sassoon; *b* 25 April 1934; *Educ* English Sch Cairo Egypt, Westminster Med Sch (MRCS, LRCP); *m* 22 March 1964, Nicole Iris, da of Robert Galante (d 1984); 2 s (Daniel b 1965, Joel b 1967); *Career* Capt RAMC 1960-62; registrar ENT Royal Free Hosp 1965, sr registrar Kings Coll Hosp 1968, conslt otologist Guys Hosp 1970; FRCS 1967, RSM, BAO; *Books* Sense of Smell and It's Abnormalities (1974), contrib chapters in: Textbook of Otology and Laryngology 1988, Robbs Surgery 1976; *Recreations* painting; *Clubs* Athenaeum; *Style*— Ellis Douek, Esq; 1-24 Reynolds Close, London NW11 (☎ 01 455 6047); 2 Silerchie, Camaiore, Italy; 97 Harley St, London W1 (☎ 01 935 7828, 01 487 4695)

DOUGHERTY, Maj-Gen Sir Ivan Noel; CBE (1946), DSO (1941, and bar 1943), ED; *b* 6 April 1907; *Educ* Mudgee HS, Sydney Teachers' Coll, Univ of Sydney; *m* 1936, Emily Phyllis, *née* Lofts; 2 s, 2 da (and 1 c decd); *Career* Brig AIF 1939-45 (North Africa, Greece, Crete, Southwest Pacific), and 1948-52, Maj-Gen 1952-57, Aust Mil Forces (AMF); educationist with New South Wales Dept of Education 1928-55 (inc headmaster 1946-47, insp of schools 1948-53, staff insp 1953-55), dir of Civil Defense for NSW 1955-73; kt 1968; *see Debrett's Handbook of Australia and New Zealand for further details*; *Clubs* Royal Automobile (Sydney, Australia); *Style*— Maj-Gen Sir Ivan Dougherty, CBE, DSO and Bar, ED; 4 Leumeah St, Cronulla, New South Wales 2230, Australia (☎ 02 523 5465)

DOUGHTY, Dr Andrew Gerard; s of Samuel Henry Doughty (d 1963), and Ella Cadman, *née* Scott (d 1970); *b* 2 Sept 1916; *Educ* Beaumont Coll Berks, St Thomas's Hosp Med Sch Univ of London (MB, BS); *m* 8 Oct 1949, Peggy, da of Frank Harvey Giles (d 1979); 1 s (Gerard Francis Peter b 1955), 1 da (Catherine Mary b 1952); *Career* Lt RAMC 1942, transferred IMS 1942; serv: India, Burma, Borneo; demobilised Maj specialist in anaesthetics 1946; conslt anaesthetist: Kingston Hosp Surrey 1950-80, St Teresa's Maternity Hosp Wimbledon 1951-82; estab course of practical instruction in epidural analgesia in childbirth Kingston Hosp; FRSM (pres anaesthetic section 1977), FFARCS, pres Obstetric Anaesthetists Assoc 1979-81, FRCOG (ad eundem); *Books* Symposium on Epidural Analgesia in Obstetrics (1972), Epidural Analgesia in Obstetrics (a second symposium 1980); *Recreations* music ensemble and solo singing; *Clubs* RSM; *Style*— Dr Andrew Doughty; 10 River Ave, Thames Ditton, Surrey KT7 ORS (☎ 01 398 3408)

DOUGLAS, Prof Alexander Shafto (Sandy); CBE (1985); s of Maj Quentin Douglas, RE (d 1974), of Kensington, London, and Edith Dorothy, *née* Ingram (d 1965); *b* 21 May 1921; *Educ* Marlborough, Coll of Estate Mgmnt (BSc), Trinity Coll Cambridge (BA, MA, PhD); *m* 16 Dec 1945, Audrey Mary Brasnett, da of Reginald George Parker (d 1983), of Mildenhall, Suffolk; 1 s (Malcolm b 1956), 1 da (Shirley (Mrs Mauger) b 1953); *Career* WWII Royal Signals: Signalman 1941, offr cadet 1942, 2 Lt India 1943, Lt 1943 (served 2 Div Kohima), released 1946; visiting prof Univ of Illinois USA 1953-57, fell and jr bursar Trinity Coll Cambridge 1954-55, dir Univ of Leeds Computing Laboratory 1957-60, tech dir CEIR UK Ltd (now SD - SCICON) 1960-68, chm Leasco Systems and Res Ltd 1968-69, prof LSE 1969-84 (emeritus prof 1984-), chm Buxton Douglas & Ptnrs Ltd (consulting and litigation support) 1971-, non-exec dir The Monotype Corpn 1973-78, pt/t visiting prof Middx Business Sch Middx Poly 1987-; vice pres Int Cncl for Computers and Communications 1981-, dir UK Cncl for Computers for Devpt 1987-, advsr sci and technol parliamentary ctees 1970-76; memb Def Sci Advsy Cncl 1971-88, sci advsy ctee Br Cncl 1978-88; Freeman City of London 1965, Liveryman Worshipful Co of Wheelwrights 1965, memb Worshipful Co of Info Technologists 1986; FBCS (fndr memb 1956, pres 1972), FIMA 1964, ACIArb 1986, FRSA 1983; *Books* Second Report of the Secretary General on the Application of Computers to Development (jtly 1973); *Recreations* tennis, bridge, philately; *Clubs* City Livery, Athenaeum; *Style*— Prof Alexander Douglas, CBE; 9 Woodside Ave, Walton-on-Thames, Surrey KT12 5LQ (☎ 0932 224 923); The Buxton Douglas Partnership, 116 Temple Chambers, Temple Ave, London EC4Y 0DT (☎ 01 583 1379)

DOUGLAS, Arthur John Alexander; CMG (1965), OBE (1962); s of late Alexander Douglas, of Torkatrine, Dalbeattie, Kirkcudbrightshire, by his w Eileen; *b* 31 May 1920; *Educ* Dumfries Academy, Edinburgh Univ; *m* 1948, Christine Scott, da of late Dr K H Dyke; 2 da; *Career* serv RN WWII; HM Overseas Serv, Basutoland, 1946 Colonial Off 1957; Bechuanaland: administration sec 1959, govt sec and chief secretary 1962-65, dep cmmr 1965-66; Overseas Devpt Miny 1967-80, asst sec Overseas Devpt Admin FCO 1975-80; *Style*— Arthur Douglas Esq, CMG, OBE; 13 Pickers Green, Lindfield, W Sussex

DOUGLAS, Hon Charles James Sholto; yr s of 21 Earl of Morton; *b* 14 Oct 1954; *m* 1981, Anne, da of late William Gordon Morgan, of Waikato, New Zealand; 1 s (James William Sholto b 1984), 2 da (Rebecca Katherine b 1982, Jilian Rosamund Florence b 1986); *Career* ptnr Dalmahoy Farms; *Style*— Hon Charles Douglas; Dalmahoy, Kirknewton, Midlothian

DOUGLAS, Sir Donald MacLeod; MBE (1943); s of William Douglas; *b* 28 June 1911; *Educ* Madras Coll, St Andrews Univ (ChM), Minnesota Univ (MS Minn); *m* 1945, Margaret Diana Whitley; 2 s, 2 da; *Career* asst surgn Edinburgh Municipal Hosps 1945, reader in experimental surgery Univ of Edinburgh 1945-51; surgn Ninewells Hosp Dundee 1951-76, prof of surgery Univ of Dundee (formerly Queen's Coll) 1951-76, emeritus 1977, dean of faculty of medicine Univ of Dundee 1969-70; pres: RCSE 1971-73, Assoc of Surgns of GB and Ireland 1964; surgn to HM The Queen in Scotland 1965-76, extra surgn to HM The Queen in Scotland 1977-; FRCSE, FRCS, FRSE, Hon FACS, Hon FRCS (SA), Hon FRCSI, Hon DSc St Andrews; kt 1972; *Style*— Sir Donald Douglas, MBE; The Whitehouse of Nevay, Newtyle, Angus (☎ 022 85 315)

DOUGLAS, Gavin Stuart; RD (1970), QC (Scot 1971); s of late Gilbert Georgeson Douglas and Rosena Campbell Douglas; *b* 12 June 1932; *Educ* South Morningside Sch, George Heriot's Sch, Edinburgh Univ (MA, LLB); *Career* qualified as slr 1955; Nat Ser RNVR; admitted Faculty of Advocates 1958, sub-ed (pt-time) The Scotsman 1957-61; memb Lord Advocate's Dept London (Parly draftsman) 1961-64; resumed practice at Scots Bar 1964; jr counsel to BOT 1965, counsel to Scottish Law Cmmn 1965-; Hon Sheriff in various sheriffdoms 1965-71; chm Industl Tbnls 1966-78; counsel to sec of state for Scotland under Private Legislation Procedure (Scotland) Act 1936 1969-75 (sr counsel under that Act 1975-); editor Sessions Cases (7 volumes) 1976-82; *Recreations* skiing, golf; *Clubs* University Staff (Edinburgh); *Style*— Gavin Douglas, Esq, RD, QC; Parliament House, Parliament Sq, Edinburgh 1 (☎ 031 226 5071)

DOUGLAS, Lord Gawain Archibald Francis; s of 11 Marquess of Queensberry (d 1954), by his 3 w (*qv* Mimi, Marchioness of Queensberry); *b* 23 May 1948; *Educ* Downside, Royal Acad of Music (LRAM); *m* 1971, Nicolette, da of Col Frank Eustace (d 1976), of Hong Kong; 1 s (Jamie b 1975), 5 da (Dalziel b 1971, Elizabeth b 1974, Natasha b 1976, Margarita b 1978, Mary-Anne b 1981); *Career* former prof of pianoforte Blackheath Conservatoire of Music, music prof Kent Rural Music Sch Canterbury, concert recitalist, accompanist & duettist in company with Lady Nicolette (wife); *Recreations* tennis, swimming, books; *Clubs* Polish Hearth; *Style*— Lord Gawain Douglas; 2 Archery Sq, Walmer, Deal, Kent (☎ 030 45 5813)

DOUGLAS, Henry (Russell); s of Russell Douglas (d 1975), and Jeannie Douglas, *née* Drysdale (d 1977); *b* 11 Feb 1925; *Educ* Lincoln Coll Oxford (MA); *m* 1951, Elizabeth Mary, da of Ralph MacHattie Nowell, CB (d 1973), of Wimbledon; 2 s (James, Alexander), 3 da (Jane, Catherine, Dominica); *Career* Lt RNVR (submarines) 1943-46; journalist; features ed, ldr write and dep ed Liverpool Daily Post 1950-69, ldr writer The Sun 1969-76, legal mangr News Gp 1976-89; fell Inst of Journalists (pres 1972); *Recreations* chess, motoring; *Clubs* Utd Oxford and Cambridge; *Style*— Henry Douglas Esq; Austen Croft, Austen Rd, Guildford, Surrey GU1 3NP (☎ 0483 576960)

DOUGLAS, James Murray; CBE 1985; s of Herbert Douglas (d 1968), and Amy Crawford Murray (d 1976); *b* 26 Sept 1925; *Educ* Morrisons Acad Crieff, Aberdeen Univ (MA), Balliol Coll, Oxford (BA) ; *m* 1950, Julie, da of Hermann Kemmner (d 1969); 1 s (Michael b 1952), 1 da (Kathleen b 1954); *Career* entered CS 1950, Treasy 1960-63, asst sec Miny Housing and Local Govt 1964, sec Royal Cmmn on Local Govt 1966-69, dir-gen CLA 1970; vice-pres Confedn of Euro Agric 1971-88, chm Environment Ctee 1988-; memb: Econ Devpt Ctee for Agric 1972, cncl CBI 1986-; sec Euro Landowning Orgns Gp 1972-87; *Publications* various articles on local govt and landowning; *Recreations* golf, music, reading, films, theatre; *Clubs* Utd Oxford and Cambridge; *Style*— James Douglas, Esq, CBE; 1 Oldfield Close, Bickley, Kent (☎ 01 467 3213); 16 Belgrave Square, London SW1 (☎ 01 235 0511)

DOUGLAS, John Robert Tomkys; s of Sir Robert McCallum Douglas, OBE, and Millicent Irene Tomkys, *née* Morgan (d 1980); *b* 24 July 1930; *Educ* Oundle, Univ of Birmingham (BSc); *m* 12 Oct 1957, Sheila Margaret, da of Miles Varey (d 1963), of Ruthin, N Wales; 2 s (Philip b 1960, Jonathan b 1962), 1 da (Alison b 1958); *Career* Nat Serv RE 1953-55, 2 Lt 1954; civil engr; dir various cos in Douglas Gp 1953-, md Robert M Douglas Hldgs plc 1976-87 (chm 1978-); ldr Sutton Coldfield Crusaders 1956-81, gen cmmr for income tax 1968-, memb ct of govrs Univ. of Birmingham 1972-, cncl memb Birmingham Chamber of Industry and Commerce 1981-, tstee TSB Fndn for England and Wales 1986-; dir Birmingham Heartlands Ltd 1987-; pres Fedn of Civil Engrg Contractors 1987-; Freeman Worshipful Co of Paviors; FIHT (MIHT 1967), FCIOB 1973, FRSA 1982, CBIM 1983,; *Recreations* music, theatre, sailing; *Clubs* Caledonian, Royal Engineer Yacht; *Style*— John Douglas, Esq; Robert M Douglas Hldgs plc, 395 George Rd, Birmingham B23 7RZ (☎ 021 344 4888, fax 021 344 4801, telex 338399 RMDBHM G)

DOUGLAS, Keith Humphrey; s of Arthur Ernest (d 1977), and Gladys Kitty, *née* Dyson (d 1926); *b* 11 May 1923; *Educ* Claremont, Leamington Tech Coll; *m* 1944, Joan Lilian, da of Henry Sheasby (d 1976), of Leamington Spa; 2 s (Russell b 1948, Alistair b 1957); *Career* dir GKN Gp 1966-85, chm and md Keith Douglas (Motor Sport) 1964-, ptnr Keith Douglas Associates 1985-, advsr to the bd Guthrie Douglas Ltd; resident commentator Silverstone 1962-, commentator ITV 1964-66; dir RAC Motor Sports Assoc 1975-, vice chm RAC Motorsports Cncl 1975-, vice pres Br Motor Racing Marshals Club 1975-, chm RAC MSC Race Ctee 1980-, tstee RAC ACU Motor Sports Trg Tst; pres Nottingham Sports Car Club 1966-71; *Recreations* motor sport commentating, game fishing, music, charity work for motor industry fund (BEN); *Clubs* RAC, BRDC, JDC, JCC, Guild of Motoring Writers, Thursday (organiser); *Style*— Keith Douglas, Esq; 281 Four Ashes Road, Dorridge, Solihull, W Midlands (☎ 0564 773203); GKN Technology Ltd, Birmingham New Road, Wolverhampton (fax 0902 334778)

DOUGLAS, Kenneth; s of John Carr Douglas (d 1948), and Margaret Victoria, *née* Allen (d 1980); *b* 28 Oct 1920; *Educ* Sunderland Tech Coll, (Dip Naval Arch, 1 cl); *m* 1942, Doris, da of Thomas Henry Southern Lewer (d 1958); 1 s (Colin), 2 da (Gloria, Sally); *Career* tech asst, Ship Division, NPL 1945-46; mangr Vickers Armstrong Naval Yard 1946-53, dir & gen mangr William Gray & Co 1953-58; md: Austin & Pickersgill 1958-69 & 1979-83, Upper Clyde Shipbuilders 1969-73; chm: Simons Lobnitz, UCS Training Co; dep chm Govan Shipbuilders 1971-73; chm Douglas (Kilbride) Ltd 1972-77; chm and md Steel Structures Ltd 1974-76, ship repair mktg dir Br Shipbuilders 1978-79, md Austin and Pickersgill Ltd 1979-83, chm Kenton Shipping Services Darlington 1968-77; chm of govrs Sunderland Poly 1982-, memb of Tyne & Wear Residuary Bd 1985-88, fell Sunderland Poly 1980-; FRSA 1987; *Clubs* Sunderland, Ashbrooke; *Style*— Kenneth Douglas, Esq; 7 Birchfield Rd, Sunderland, Tyne and Wear SR2 7QQ; Monks Cottage, Romaldkirk, Barnard Castle, Co Durham

DOUGLAS, Richard Giles; MP (Lab) Dunfermline West 1983-; *b* 4 Jan 1932; *Educ* Govan HS, Cooperative Coll Stanford Hall Loughborough, Strathclyde Univ, and LSE; *m* 1954, Jean Gray, da of Andrew Arnott; 2 da; *Career* Co-op Pty sponsored, AEU, econ conslt, contested (Lab): S Angus 1964, Edinburgh W 1966, Glasgow Pollok (by-election) 1967; MP (Lab): Stirlingshire E and Clackmannan 1970-Feb 1974 (contested same in Oct 1974), Dunfermline 1979-1983; memb: Def Select Ctee, 1983-87; *Style*— Richard Douglas, Esq, MP; Braehead House, High Street, Auchtermuchty, Fife

DOUGLAS, Rodney Hugh Rovery; s of Hugh Rovery Douglas, of Egham, Surrey and Florence Alice, *née* Haggerty; *b* 18 Nov 1933; *Educ* Willesden Co GS, Univ Coll of London (BSc); *m* 4 June 1960, Elise Margaret, da of Capt Bertram Vautier, (d 1970), of Egham; 2 s (Graham b 1962, Adrian b 1964), 1 da (Heather b 1970); *Career* cmmn RAF 1956-59, Flt Lt (airfield construction); served 5001 sqdn: Malta, Libya, Cyprus, Aden; cmmnd Maj RE (Ta, Engr and Staff Corps) 1985; with Mersey River Bd 1954-56, ptnr responsible for airport highway and public health projects Sir Frederick Snow & Ptnrs (conslt engrs) 1959-; former pres Woking and dist Scot Soc; C Eng (civil); FICE, F Inst HT, M Cons E; *Recreations* yacht cruising, scottish dancing; *Clubs* RAF, Cruising Assoc; *Style*— Rodney Douglas, Esq; Saltwood, Onslow Crescent, Woking, Surrey GU22 7AU (☎ 048 62 72637); Sir Frederick Snow and Partners, Ross House, 144 Southwark Street, London SE1 OSZ (☎ 01 928 5688, fax 01 928 1774, telex 917478 Snowmen London)

DOUGLAS, Rt Hon Sir William Randolph; KCMG (1983), PC (1977); s of William P Douglas; *b* 24 Sept 1921; *Educ* Bannatyne Sch, Verdun HS Quebec, McGill Univ (BA), LSE (LLB); *m* 1951, Thelma Ruth, da of Ernest Gershon Gilkes; 1 s, 1 da; *Career* barrister Middle Temple 1947, slr-gen Jamaica 1962 (formerly asst attorney-gen), Puisne Judge (Jamaica) 1962, chief justice (Barbados) 1965-; kt 1969; *Style*— The Rt Hon Sir William Douglas, KCMG; Leland, Pine Gdns, St Michael, Barbados (☎ 429 2030); Chief Justice's Chambers, Supreme Court, Coleridge St, Bridgetown, Barbados (☎ 426 3461)

DOUGLAS AND CLYDESDALE, Marquess of; Alexander Douglas Douglas-Hamilton; s and h of 15 Duke of Hamilton and (12 of) Brandon; *b* 31 Mar 1978; *Style*— Marquess of Douglas and Clydesdale

DOUGLAS MILLER, Robert Alexander Gavin; s of Francis Gavin Douglas Miller (d 1950), and Mary Morrison, *née* Kennedy; *b* 11 Feb 1937; *Educ* Harrow, Oxford Univ (MA); *m* 9 March 1963, Judith Madeleine, da of Richard Michael Desmond Dunstan, OBE, of Pear Tree Cottage, Firbeck, nr Worksop, Notts; 3 s (Andrew b 30 Sept 1963, Robert b 8 Jan 1965, Edward b 20 May 1966), 1 da (Emma b 8 Jan 1969); *Career* served in 9 Lancers 1955-57; joined Jenners Edinburgh 1962, md 1972, chm and md 1982-; dir: Kennington Leasing Ltd, Bain Clarkson Ltd, Chamber Developments Ltd; former pres Edinburgh C of C 1985-87; tres Royal Co of Archers (Queen's Body Guard for Scotland); landowner (5850 acres); *Recreations* shooting, fishing; *Clubs* New (Edinburgh); *Style*— Robert Douglas Miller, Esq; Bavelaw Castle, Balerno, Midlothian (☎ 031 449 3972); Jenners, 48 Princes Street, Edinburgh EH2 2YJ (☎ 031 225 2442)

DOUGLAS OF BARLOCH, Baroness; Adela Elizabeth; da of George Derbridge, DD; *m* 1, Capt George La Croix Baudains, DSO, MC (decd); m 2, 1971, as his 2 w, 1 Baron Douglas of Barloch, KCMG (d 1980, when title became extinct); *Style*— Rt Hon Lady Douglas of Barloch; 73 Cambridge Mansions, Battersea, London SW11; Maxfield Manor, Three Oaks, Hastings, Sussex

DOUGLAS OF KIRTLESIDE, Baroness; Hazel; 2 da of late George Eric Maas Walker, of Mill Hill, NW, and widow of Capt W E R Walker; *m* 2, 28 Feb 1955, as his 3 wife, 1 Baron Douglas of Kirtleside (d 1969, when title became extinct); 1 da (Hon Katharine Douglas); *Style*— Rt Hon Lady Douglas of Kirtleside,; Misbourne Cottage, Denham Village, Bucks

DOUGLAS PENNANT, Lady Janet Marcia Rose; *née* Pelham; only da of 6 Earl of Yarborough (d 1966), and Hon Pamela Douglas Pennant (d 1968), 2 da of 3 Baron Penrhyn; *b* 17 Oct 1923; *m* 20 March 1948, John Charles Harper (s of Sir Charles Henry Harper, KBE, CMG), who assumed by Royal Licence the surname Douglas Pennant in lieu of his patronymic 1950; 2 s (Richard b 1955, Edmond b 1960); *Style*— Lady Janet Douglas Pennant; Penrhyn, Bangor, Gwynedd (☎ 0248 353286)

DOUGLAS-HAMILTON, Lord David Stephen; 5 and yst s of 14 Duke of Hamilton and (11 of) Brandon, KT, GCVO, AFC, PC (d 1973); *b* 26 Dec 1952; *Educ* Eton; *Style*— Lord David Douglas-Hamilton

DOUGLAS-HAMILTON, Lord Hugh Malcolm; 3 s of 14 Duke of Hamilton and (11 of) Brandon, KT, GCVO, AFC, PC (d 1973); *b* 22 Dec 1946; *Educ* Eton; *m* 1971, June Mary Curtis; 1 s, 1 da; *Clubs* Scottish Arts; *Style*— Lord Hugh Douglas-Hamilton; Begbie Farmhouse, Haddington, E Lothian (☎ Haddington 3141)

DOUGLAS-HAMILTON, Lord James Alexander; MP (C) Edinburgh W, Oct 1974-; 2 s of 14 Duke of Hamilton and Brandon, KT, GCVO, AFC, PC (d 1973); *b* 31 July 1942; *Educ* Eton, Balliol Coll Oxford (MA), Edinburgh Univ (LLB); *m* 1974, Hon (Priscilla) Susan (Susie), *née* Buchan, *qv*, da of 2 Baron Tweedsmuir; 4 s (John Andrew b 1978, Charles Douglas b 1979, James Robert b 1981 and Harry Alexander (twin) b 1981); *Career* offr TA 6/7 Bn Cameronians Scottish Rifles 1961-66, TAVR 1971-73, Capt 2 Bn Lowland Volunteers; Parly Under Sec of State for Home Affrs and Environment for Scottish Off 1987-; advocate (Scots) 1968-74; contested (C) Hamilton Feb 1974; Scottish Cons whip 1977, Scots govt whip and lord cmmr Treasy 1979-81, memb Scottish select ctee Scottish Affrs 1981-; hon sec: Cons Parly Constitutional Ctee, Cons Parly Aviation Ctee 1983-; chm Scottish Parly All-Pty Penal Affrs Ctee 1983, PPS to Malcolm Rifkind, MP, jr min Scottish Off, min FO 1983-; hon pres Scottish Amateur Boxing Assoc 1975-; Oxford Boxing Blue 1961, pres Oxford Union Soc 1964; pres Royal Cwlth Soc (Scotland) 1979-87, Scottish Nat Cncl UN Assoc 1981-87; life memb Nat Tst for Scotland (cncl memb 1977-82); *Books* Motive for a Mission: The Story Behind Hess's Flight to Britain (1971), The Air Battle for Malta: the Diaries of a Fighter Pilot (1981), Roof of the World: Man's First Flight over Everest (1983); *Recreations* golf, forestry, debating, history, boxing; *Style*— Lord James Douglas-Hamilton, MP; 12 Quality Street Lane, Davidsons Mains, Edinburgh (☎ 031 336 4213)

DOUGLAS-HAMILTON, Lady Malcolm; Natalie Wales; CBE; da of Maj Nathaniel Brackett Wales, and the late Mrs Charles E Greenough of NY; *b* 8 Aug 1909; *Educ* private schools, New York City; *m* 1, Kanelm Winslow (decd), 2 da (Natalie Wales Winslow Burnett (decd), Mrs Mary-Chilton Winslow Mead); m 2 Edward Latham (decd); m 3 Edward Bragg Paine (decd), m 4 as his 2 w, Lord Malcolm Douglas-Hamilton, OBE, DFC, MP Inverness, k in air crash 1964; (He was 3 s of 13 Duke of Hamilton); *Career* fndr and pres: Bundles for Britain Inc, The Commitee to Unite America Inc, The American-Scottish Fndn Inc; *Style*— Lady Malcolm Douglas-Hamilton, CBE; Apt 10-E, 174 E 74th St, New York, NY 10021, USA; The American-Scottish Foundation Inc, PO Box 537, Lenox Hill Station, New York City, NY 10021, USA (☎ 212 249 5556)

DOUGLAS-HAMILTON, Lord Patrick George; 4 s of 14 Duke of Hamilton and (11 of) Brandon, KT, GCVO, AFC, PC (d 1973); *b* 2 August 1950; *Educ* Eton; *Style*— Lord Patrick Douglas-Hamilton; Flat 3, 136 Ebury St, SW1 (☎ 01 730 3760); Lennoxlove, Haddington, E Lothian (☎ 062 082 2156)

DOUGLAS-HAMILTON, Lady James; Hon (Priscilla) Susan; *née* Buchan; o child of 2 Baron Tweedsmuir, CBE, CD, and Baroness Tweedsmuir of Belhelvie (cr Life Peeress 1970, d 1978); *b* 22 August 1949; *Educ* St Margaret's Sch Aberdeen, Hatherop Castle Glos; *m* 1974, Lord James Alexander Douglas-Hamilton, MP, *qv*; 4 s (including twins); *Style*— Lady James Douglas-Hamilton; Ryvra, 3 Fidra Rd, North Berwick, East Lothian EH39 4LY (☎ 0620 2918); 12 Quality Street Lane, Davidsons Mains, Edinburgh (☎ 031 336 4213)

DOUGLAS-HOME, Hon (Lavinia) Caroline; DL (Berwicks 1983); eldest da of Baron Home of the Hirsel, KT, PC; *b* 11 Oct 1937; *Career* woman of the bedchamber (temp) to HM Queen Elizabeth The Queen Mother 1963-65, lady-in-waiting (temp) to HRH The Duchess of Kent 1966-67; tstee Nat Museum of Antiquities of Scotland 1982-85; ; Dep Lt for Berwickshire 1983-; FSAS; *Recreations* antiquities, fishing s; *Style*— The Hon Caroline Douglas-Home, DL; Dove Cottage, The Hirsel, Coldstream, Berwickshire TD12 4LP (☎ 0890 2834)

DOUGLAS-HOME, Hon David Alexander Cospatrick; only s of Baron Home of the Hirsel and h to Earldom of Home (disclaimed by his father 1963, from 1951 to which date Hon David D-H was known as Lord Dunglass); *b* 20 Nov 1943; *Educ* Eton, Christ Church Oxford; *m* 1972, Jane Margaret (b 20 Feb 1949), yr da of Col John Williams-Wynne, *qv*; 1 s (Michael David Alexander b 1987), 2 da (Iona Katherine b 1980, Mary Elizabeth b 1982); *Career* dir: Morgan Grenfell & Co Ltd 1974-, Morgan Grenfell (Scotland) 1978-, Economic Forestry Gp 1981-, Agricultural Mortgage Corpn 1979-; chm: Morgan Grenfell Int Ltd 1987, Morgan Grenfell (Scotland) Ltd 1986 and Ctee for Middle East Trade 1986; The Ditchley Fndn: govr and memb cncl of mgmnt 1976-; ECGD: export guarantee advsy cncl memb and memb country and fin ctee 1988-; govr Cwlth Inst 1988-; *Recreations* outdoor sports; *Clubs* Turf; *Style*— The Hon David Douglas-Home; 99 Dovehouse St, London SW3

DOUGLAS-HOME, Hon Edward Charles; s of 14 Earl of Home, KT, TD (d 1951); *b* 1 Mar 1920; *Educ* Eton; *m* 24 July 1946, Nancy Rose, da of Sir Thomas Dalrymple Straker-Smith (d 1970), of Carham Hall, Cornhill-on-Tweed, Northumberland; 3 s; *Career* 2 Lt 155 Field Regt RA; *Style*— The Hon Edward Douglas-Home; Westnewton, Kirknewton, Wooler, Northumberland

DOUGLAS-HOME, Hon Mrs Henry; Felicity Betty; da of late Maj Aubrey Thomas Jonsson, RIR, of Cranford, Winterskloof, Natal, S Africa; *m* 1, 28 July 1948 (m dis 1962), the Hon (Victor) Patrick Hamilton Wills; 2 s, 1 da; m 2, 16 Feb 1966, as his 3 w, Maj the Hon Henry Montagu Douglas-Home, MBE (d 1980), 2 s of 13 Earl of Home, KT, TD; 1 s; *Style*— Hon Mrs Henry Douglas-Home; Old Greenlaw, Berwickshire, Scotland

DOUGLAS-HOME, Hon James Thomas Archibald; only s of Hon William Douglas-Home and Baroness Dacre; h to the Barony of Dacre; *b* 16 May 1952; *m* 1979, Christine, da of William Stephenson, of The Ridings, Royston, Herts; 1 da (Emily b 1983); *Style*— The Hon James Douglas-Home; c/o Rt Hon Baroness Dacre, Derry House, Kilmeston, nr Alresford, Hants

DOUGLAS-HOME, Lady (Alexandra) Margaret Elizabeth; da of 6 Earl Spencer (d 1922); *b* 4 July 1906; *m* 7 July 1931 (m dis 1947), Maj Hon Henry Montagu Douglas-Home (d 1980); 2 s (both decd), 1 da; *Style*— Lady Margaret Douglas-Home; Trimmers, Burnham Market, King's Lynn, Norfolk (☎ Burnham Market 243)

DOUGLAS-HOME, Hon William; 3 s of 13 Earl of Home, KT, TD (d 1951); *b* 3 June 1912; *Educ* Eton, New Coll Oxford; *m* 26 July 1951, Baroness Dacre, *qv*; 1 s, 3 da; *Career* 2 Lt The Buffs 1941, Capt 1943; author and playwright; *Style*— The Hon William Douglas-Home; Derry House, Kilmeston, nr Alresford, Hants

DOUGLAS-JONES, Neville; TD; s of Harry Douglas-Jones (d 1964), of Swansea, and Agnes Ellen Cecilia, *née* Harries; *b* 13 Mar 1915; *Educ* Mill Hill; *m* 8 Dec 1945, Rachel, da of Charles Worrall Morris (d 1969); 3 s (Peter b 1947, Timothy b 1949, Jeremy b 1951); *Career* cmmnd RASC (TA) 1938, WW II served BEF, MEF (A/Maj) 1939-45; slr and NP, sr ptnr Douglas-Jones and Mercer (ret 1988); elected Lloyds underwriter 1977; past pres: Swansea and Dist Law Soc, Royal Inst of S Wales (currently memb cncl), Mumbles Chamber of Tde; co-fndr and past pres: Gower Ornithological Soc, Glamorgan Wildlife Tst; former dir: Swansea Albion and Gower Bldg Soc, Swansea Porcelain Ltd; memb bd of mgmnt Swansea and Dist Deaf Mission; *Style*— Neville Douglas-Jones, TD, Esq; Winterstoke House, Groves Avenue, Langland Bay, Swansea SA3 4QF (☎ 0792 366220)

DOUGLAS-MANN, Bruce Leslie Home; s of Leslie Douglas-Mann, MC (decd), of Torquay, and Alice Home Douglas-Mann; *b* 23 June 1927; *Educ* Upper Canada Coll

Toronto, Jesus Coll Oxford; *m* 1955, Helen, da of Edwin and Ellen Tucker (decd), of Dulwich; 1 s, 1 da; *Career* slr 1954; MP (Lab) Kensington North 1970-74, Merton, Mitcham & Morden 1974-82, MP (Lab to Dec 1981, when resigned from Labour Party; subsequently joined SDP, but was refused party whip in House of Commons and sat as Independent Social Democrat, resigned seat May 1982 and refought on SDP ticket June 1982, June 1983, June 1987) Chm Parly select ctee Environment 1979-82; chm PLP Housing & Construction Gp 1974-79, PLP Environment Gp 1979-81 (vice-chm 1972-79); pres or vice pres Socialist Environment & Resources Assoc 1973-80; vice pres Building Socs Assoc 1973-; memb bd Shelter 1974 (chm Exec Cttee 1987-); chm Soc of Labour Lawyers 1974-80; former memb Kensington & Chelsea Cncl; chm Arts Council Tst for Special Funds; *Style—* Bruce Douglas-Mann, Esq; 33 Furnival St, London EC4A 1JQ (☎ 01 405 7216)

DOUGLAS-PENNANT, Hon Gillian Frances; elder da of 6 Baron Penrhyn; *b* 2 Sept 1955; *Style—* The Hon Gillian Douglas-Pennant

DOUGLAS-PENNANT, Hon Nigel; yr s of 5 Baron Penrhyn (d 1967), by his 2 w, and hp of bro, 6 Baron Penrhyn, DSO, MBE; *b* 22 Dec 1909; *Educ* Eton, Clare Coll Cambridge; *m* 1, 6 Sept 1935, Margaret Dorothy (d 1938), da of Thomas George Kirkham; 1 s; m 2, 20 July 1940, Eleanor Stewart (d 1987), eldest da of late Very Rev Herbert Newcome Craig, Dean of Kildare; 1 s, 1 da; *Career* formerly Maj RM; *Style—* The Hon Nigel Douglas-Pennant; Brook House, Glemsford, Sudbury, Suffolk

DOUGLAS-PENNANT, Hon Susan Victoria; 3 and yst da of 5 Baron Penrhyn (only da by 2 w); *b* 24 May 1918; *Educ* Owlstone Croft, Cambridge, St Bartholomew's Hosp, London,; *Career* SRN, SCM; *Style—* The Hon Susan Douglas-Pennant; Adam's Cottage, Horningsham, Warminster, Wilts

DOUGLAS-SCOTT-MONTAGU, Hon Mary Rachel; da of 3 Baron Montagu of Beaulieu by 1 wife; *b* 16 Nov 1964; *Educ* Central Sch of Art and Design (BA); *Career* theatrical designer; *Style—* The Hon Mary Douglas-Scott-Montagu

DOUGLAS-SCOTT-MONTAGU, Hon Ralph; s (by 1 m) and h of 3 Baron Lord Montagu of Beaulieu by 1 wife; *b* 13 Mar 1961; *Educ* Millfield, Brockenhurst Sixth Form Coll, Central Sch of Art and Design; *Career* graphics designer; *Books* The Producers Guide to Graphics (book and video) (1986); *Clubs* BBC; *Style—* The Hon Ralph Douglas-Scott-Montagu; Palace House, Beaulieu, Brockenhurst, Hants SO42 7ZN

DOUGLAS-WITHERS, Maj-Gen John Keppel Ingold; CBE (1969), MC (1943); s of Lt-Col H H Douglas-Withers, OBE, MC, FSA (d 1948), of Manorbier, and Vera Guy, *née* Everett (d 1978); *b* 11 Dec 1919; *Educ* Shrewsbury, Christ Church Oxford, Univ of Poitiers (diploma in French); *m* 1945, Sylvia Beatrice, da of Arthur Dean (d 1956), of Norbury; 1 s (Mark Guy b 1945), 1 da (Sally Julia b 1948); *Career* cmmnd RA 1940; serv WWII UK, Iraq, Western Desert, N Africa, Italy; gunnery instr School of Artillery 1945-47, served with 1 RHA Canal Zone 1948-49, WO 1951-53, King's Troop RHA 1954-55, instr staff Coll Camberley 1956-58, Asst Mil Sec MoD 1961-62; commanded: G Battery (Mercer's Troop) RHA BAOR 1959-60, 49th Field Regt BAOR and Hong Kong 1962-64, 6 Infantry Brigade 1966-67 BAOR; Imperial Def Coll Hong Kong 1965; COS 1 Br Corps 1966-67, BAOR GOC SW District UK 1970-71, asst chief Personnel & Logistics Central Staff MoD 1972-74, ret 1974; asst dir and gp personnel mangr Jardine Matheson & Co Ltd Hong Kong 1974-80; *Recreations* gardening, golf, military history, military music; *Clubs* East India, Hong Kong, MCC; *Style—* Maj-Gen John Douglas-Withers, CBE, MC; Lloyds Bank, Shipston-on-Stour, Warwickshire CV36 4AJ

DOUGLASS OF CLEVELAND, Baroness; Edith; da of Charles Amer; *m* 1926, Baron Douglass of Cleveland (Life Peer, d 1978); 1 da (Hon Mrs Long); *Style—* Rt Hon Lady Douglass of Cleveland; 5 The Chase, Stanmore, Middx HA7 3RX (☎ 01 954 2101)

DOULTON, Alfred John Farre; CBE (1973, OBE (Mil) 1946), TD (1954); s of Hubert Victor Doulton (d 1942), of Dulwich, and Constance Jessie Farre (d 1965); *b* 9 July 1911; *Educ* Dulwich, Brasenose Coll Oxford (MA); *m* 14 June 1940, Vera Daphne, da of Ronald Angus Wheatley (d 1973), of Esher; 4 s (John b 1942, Angus and Peter (twins) b 1944, Roger b 1947), 1 da (Valerie b 1947); *Career* serv WWII 1940-46, active serv: Burma, Malaya, Java (despatches twice) AAQMG (Lt Col) 23 Indian Div; schoolmaster, asst master Uppingham Sch 1934-40, housemaster Uppingham Sch 1946-54, headmaster Highgate Sch 1955-74; statistician Ind Schools Information Service 1974-80; alderman and vice-chm Educn Ctee Haringey Cncl 1968-71; *Recreations* music, cricket, reading, dinghy sailing, ornithology, gardening; *Clubs* Athenaeum, MCC; *Style—* Alfred J F Doulton, CBE, TD; Field Cottage, Beadon Lane, Salcombe, Devon TQ8 8JS (☎ 054 884 2316)

DOULTON, Roger Stewart; s of Lt Col Alfred John Farre Doulton, CBE, TD, of Salcombe, Devon, and Daphne Vera, *née* Wheatley; *b* 28 Mar 1949; *Educ* Rugby, Oxford Univ (MA); *m* June 1978 (m dis 1988), Shonni Doulton; 2 s (Ben b 30 Dec 1979, Jem b 25 April 1983); *Career* asst slr: Herbert Smith & Co 1976-81, Davies Arnold and Cooper 1981-84; ptnr Winward Fearon and Co 1986-; ctee memb and legal corr Br Insur Law Assoc; *Recreations* french horn playing; *Clubs* Wig and Pen, Salcombe Yacht ; *Style—* Roger Doulton, Esq; Winward Fearon, 35 Bow Street, London WC2E 7AU (☎ 01 836 9081)

DOUNE, Lord; John Douglas Stuart; s and h of 20 Earl of Moray; *b* 29 August 1966; *Style—* Lord Doune

DOURO, Marquess of; Arthur Charles Valerian Wellesley; MEP (C) Surrey 1979-; s and h of 8 Duke of Wellington; *b* 19 August 1945; *Educ* Eton, Christ Church Oxford; *m* 3 Feb 1977, Antonia (chm Guinness Trust, tstee Getty Nat Gallery Endowment Fund, gov London Festival Ballet), da of HRH Prince Frederick von Preussen (d 1966, s of HIH Crown Prince Wilhelm, s and h of Kaiser Wilhelm II), and Lady Brigid Ness, *qv*; 1 s, 2 da (Lady Honor b 25 Oct 1979, Lady Mary b 16 Dec 1986); *Heir* s, Earl of Mornington b 31 Jan 1978; *Career* chm Deltec Securities (UK) Ltd; dir: Eucalyptus Pulp Mills 1979-88, Transatlantic Hldgs, Sun Life Assur Soc plc; dep chm: Thames Valley Broadcasting 1975-84, Guiness Mahon Hldgs plc; contested Islington N (C) 1974; dep chm Deltec Panamerica SA; dir: Continental & Industrial Tst plc, Global Asset Mgmnt Worldwide Inc; *Style—* Marquess of Douro, MEP; The Old Rectory, Stratfield Saye, Reading; Apsley House, Piccadilly, London W1

DOUSE, Raymond Andrew; s of Reginald Conrad Raymond Douse, of Eastbourne, and Patricia Heatherley; *b* 10 May 1947; *Educ* Downside, New Coll Oxford (BA); *m* 2 Nov 1974, Christine Lesley, da of Maurice Hayes, of Melbourne, Australia; 2 s (Nicholas b 1977, Christopher b 1986), 1 da (Olivia b 1980); *Career* investment banker; md MMG Patricof & Co Ltd, dir Hill Samuel & Co Ltd 1980-85; *Recreations* music, horse racing; *Style—* Raymond A Douse, Esq; 94 Arthur Road, Wimbledon, SW19; 24 Upper Brook Street, London W1Y 1PD (☎ 01 409 2339)

DOUTHWAITE, Charles Philip; s fo Alfred George Douthwaite, of Saffron Walden, Essex, and Margaret, *née* Rose; *b* 23 Mar 1949; *Educ* Kingswood Sch, Jesus Coll Cambridge (MA); *m* 14 Feb 1976, Margaret Ann, da of Derek Linford. MBE (d 1975), of Stanford-Le-Hope, Essex; 1 s (Henry b 1980), 1 da (Harriet b 1982); *Career* called to Bar Gray's Inn 1977; *Style—* Charles Douthwaite, Esq; Field Cottages, Chishall Grange, Heydon, Royston, Herts SG8 7NT (☎ 0763 838 061); 2 Crown Office Row, Temple, London EC4Y 7HJ (☎ 01 583 8755, fax 01 583 1205)

DOUTY, Hugh Harrington Cazalet; CBE (1973), DL (Warwicks 1982); s of Dr Robert Cazalet Douty, FRCS, MRCP (d 1956); *b* 1912; *Educ* Epsom; *m* 1936, Winifred Lilly Sanzen (d 1984), da of John William Colman; 2 s; *Career* territorial army 1930-37, serv WWII Capt Rifle Bde N Africa (POW 1941-45); CC and County Alderman Warwicks 1955-74, CC 1977-85, chm Planning Ctee 1981-85, dep chm Educn (secondary and further) Ctee 1981-85 (chm Warwicks Educn Ctee 1967-74), vice pres Assoc Educn Ctees 1970-72 (pres 1972-74); sr asst organiser London Youth Orgns Ctee 1936-39, Midlands devpt offr Nat Assoc Boys' Clubs 1945-47, Midlands regnl offr 1947-64, sr field sec 1964-77; chm of govrs Dunsmore Schs Rugby 1974-85 and Ashlawn Sch Rugby 1985-57; hon MA (Warwick); *Recreations* reading, rugby football; *Style—* Hugh Douty, CBE, DL; 24 Southam Road, Dunchurch, Rugby, Warwicks CV22 6NL (☎ 0788 810351)

DOVE, Hon Mrs - Hon Elizabeth; *née* Carington; only da of 5 Baron Carrington (d 1938); *b* 4 June 1917; *m* 13 Nov 1943, Capt William Lionel Dove, MB, ChB, MRCS, LRCP, RAMC, s of late Edward William Dove; 2 s; *Style—* The Hon Mrs Dove; 6 Woolton Hill Rd, Liverpool L25 6HX

DOVE, Jack Richard; s of William Jack Dove (d 1978), and Hannah Elizabeth Dove (d 1973); *b* 16 June 1934; *Educ* Berkhamsted Sch; *m* 18 Dec 1958, Janet Yvonne, da of Melville Clarke (d 1985), of Kingsthorpe, Northampton; 1 s (Ian William b 31 Dec 1963; *Career* CA; Nat Serv RAF 1956-58; fndr Dove Naish & Ptnrs, chm Northamptonshire Business Ctee of Rural Devpt Cmmn; tstee: Lamport Hall Preservation Tst, Northampton Football Club (The Saints); FCA 1956, ATII 1957; *Recreations* music, gardening, rugby football, country pursuits; *Clubs* Cheyne Walk Northampton, Northampton Cons; *Style—* Jack R Dove, Esq; 29 Abington Park Crescent, Northampton NN3 3AD (☎ 0604 36918) Eagle House 28 Billing Rd, Northampton NN1 5AJ

DOVE, John Edward; JP (Cheshire 1975, currently Hampshire); s of Rev Frederick John Dove (d 1976), and Lesley, *née* Robson (d 1981); *b* 1 Mar 1922; *Educ* Owen's Sch London, Northern Poly London; *m* 28 June 1952, Ann Nomori, da of John Ireson (d 1968); 2 s (Robert b 1953, Martin b 1959), 1 da (Sally (Mrs Grunwell) b 1956); *Career* teacher of music and maths Akeley Wood Sch Buckingham 1940-45, surveyor (later dir) Dove Bros Ltd (builders) 1948-62, regnl mangr H Fairweather & Co Ltd 1963-67, mktg mangr Taylor Woodrow Construction Midlands ltd 1967-70, dir John Finlan Ltd; (property developers) 1970-73; md: Jartay Devpts Ltd 1973-80, Ward Dove Ltd 1981-; Royal Cwlth Soc: joined 1940, cncl memb 1954-, vice pres 1986; ctee memb Emsworth Ratepayers Assoc; memb: Langstone Cons Club, Probus; Freeman City of London 1949; Liveryman: Worshipful Co of Tylers and Bricklayers 1949 (Master 1977-78), Worshipful Co of Leathersellers 1951; FCIOB; *Recreations* music, lawn tennis, public speaking; *Clubs* City Livery, Emsworth Sail; *Style—* John Dove, Esq, JP; Tadworth Lodge, 25 Park Cres, Emsworth, Hants PO10 7NT (☎ 0243 373520)

DOVE, Leonard Ernest; CBE (1969); s of Alfred Dove (d 1955); *b* 10 Feb 1913; *Educ* Wilson's GS Camberwell; *m* 1938, Florence May, da of William Humphrey Shipley (d 1942); 1 s (and 1 s decd), 2 da; *Career* accountant and comptroller Gen Bd of Customs and Excise 1963-73; hon tres Methodist Church (overseas div) 1972-84; *Style—* Leonard Dove, Esq, CBE; 23 Stambourne Way, West Wickham, Kent BR4 9NE (☎ 01 777 5213)

DOVE, Martin David John; s of John Edward Dove, and Ann Nomori, *née* Ireson; *b* 29 April 1959; *Educ* Helsby GS, Adams GS, King's Coll London (BA, AKC); *m* 11 April 1987, Sharon Rose Elizabeth, da of Roy William Rogers Edmonds; *Career* Coopers and Lybrand London 1980-86, Cwlth Devpt Corpn London 1986-89 Industl Venture Co Ltd Thailand 1989-; memb Woodmansterne Baptist Church; Freeman City of London, Liveryman Worshipful Co of Leathersellers; ICAEW 1983; *Recreations* squash, hockey; *Style—* Martin Dove, Esq; Industrial Venture Co Ltd, 67/11 Saisuan Plu, South Sathorn Rd, Bangkok 10120 Thailand (☎ 213 1254/5, fax 213 1163. telex 20606 IDEA TH)

DOVER, Den; MP (C) Chorley 1979-; s of Albert Dover (d 1971), and Emmie, *née* Kirk (d 1971); *b* 4 April 1938; *Educ* Manchester GS, Manchester Univ (BSc); *m* 1959, Anne Marina, da of Jeffrey Wright (d 1952); 1 s, 1 da; *Career* civil engr; chief exec National Building Agency 1971-72; projects dir Capital and Counties Property plc 1972-75; contracts mangr Wimpey Laing Iran 1975-77, dir of Housing Construction GLC 1977-79; *Recreations* cricket, hockey, golf; *Style—* Den Dover, Esq, MP; 30 Countess Way, Euxton, Chorley, Lancs; 166 Furzehill Rd, Boreham Wood, Herts (☎ 01 953 5945)

DOVER, Sir Kenneth James; s of Percy Henry James Dover (d 1978) and Dorothy Valerie Anne Healey (d 1973); *b* 11 Mar 1920; *Educ* St Paul's, Balliol Coll Oxford (MA, DLitt), Merton Coll Oxford; *m* 1947, Audrey Ruth, da of Walter Latimer (d 1931); 1 s, 1 da; *Career* serv WWII RA; fell Balliol Coll Oxford 1948-55 (hon fell 1977), prof of greek St Andrews Univ 1955-76, dean faculty of arts 1960-63 and 1973-75, chllr 1981-; pres: Corpus Christi Coll, Oxford 1976-1986 (hon fell 1986), Soc for Promotion of Hellenic Studies 1971-74, Classical Association 1975, Br Academy 1978-81, FRSE, FBA; Hon LLD: Birmingham 1979, St Andrews 1981; Hon DLitt: Bristol, London 1980, St Andrews 1981, Liverpool 1983, Durham 1984; Hon DHL Oglethorpe 1984; hon fell Merton Coll Oxford; Sather visiting prof Univ of California 1967-; prof-at-large Cornell Univ 1983-89; kt 1977; *Books* Greek Word Order (1960), Greek Popular Morality in the time of Plato & Aristotle (1974), Commentaries on various classical Greek Literature, Greek Homosexuality (1978); papers: learned journals; *Recreations* historical linguistics; *Clubs* Athenaeum; *Style—* Sir Kenneth Dover; 49 Hepburn Gdns, St Andrews, Fife KY16 9LS (☎ 0334 73589)

DOVER, Michael Grehan; s of Maj E J Dover (d 1983), of Ireland, and Ida, *née* Grehan; *b* 22 Oct 1948; *Educ* King's Sch Canterbury, Trinity Coll Dublin (BA); *m*

1972, Ruth, da of Capt T A Pearson (d 1972), of Ireland; 2 s (Alexander b 1975, Linden b 1983), 1 da (Katherine b 1979); *Career* ed dir Weidenfeld Publishers Ltd 1982, publisher Weidenfed Publishers Ltd 1987; *Recreations* boating; *Clubs* Chelsea Arts, Hurlingham Yacht; *Style*— Michael Dover, Esq; 11 Oxford Road, London SW15 2LG (☎ 01 788 1474); Weidenfeld & Nicolson, 91 Clapham High St, London SW4 7TA (☎ 01 622 9933)

DOW, (John) Christopher Roderick; s of Warrender Begernie Dow (d 1950), of Shoreham-by-Sea; *b* 25 Feb 1916; *Educ* Bootham Sch York, Brighton, Hove, Sussex GS, Univ Coll London; *m* 1960, Clare Mary Keegan; 1 s, 3 da; *Career* economist; econ advsr, HM Treasy 1945-54, dep dir Nat Inst of Econ and Social Research 1954-62, sr econ advsr HM Treasy 1962-63, asst sec-gen Orgn for Econ Co-operation and Devpt 1963-73, dir Bank of England 1973-81, advsr to govr of Bank of England 1981-84; three year study on Br economy Nat Inst of Econ and Social Res 1984-; *Clubs* Reform; *Style*— Christopher Dow, Esq; c/o Reform Club, 104 Pall Mall, London SW1

DOW, Hon Mrs (Jessica Catherine); 3 and yst da of 2 Baron Stamp (d 1941, as result of enemy action during European War); *b* 21 Sept 1936; *Educ* London Univ (BA); *m* 9 Sept 1961, John Edward Chalmers Dow; 2 da (Charlotte b 1963, Juliette b 1966); *Style*— The Hon Mrs Dow; 30 Norfolk Farm Rd, Pyrford, Woking, Surrey GU22 8LH (☎ 04862 22710); Great Missenden, Bucks HP16 9BX

DOWDEN, Richard George; s of Peter John Dowden, of Fairford, Glouces, and Eleanor Isabella, *née* Hepple; *b* 20 Mar 1949; *Educ* St Georges Coll Bedford Coll, London (BA); *m* 3 July 1976, (Mary Catherine) Penny, da of Stanley William Mansfield (d 1977); 2 da (Isabella Catherine b 1981, Sophie Elizabeth b 1983); *Career* sec Cmmn for Int Justice and Peace RC Bishops Conf 1972-75, ed Cattolic Herald 1976-79, journalist The Times 1980-86, Africa ed The Independent 1986-; *Style*— Richard Dowden, Esq; 7 Highbury Grange, London N5 (☎ 01 359 0456); 40 City Rd, London EC1Y 2DB (☎ 01 253 1222)

DOWDESWELL, Lt-Col (John) Windsor; MC (1943), TD (1947), JP, DL (1976); s of Maj Thomas Reginald Dowdeswell (d 1967), and Nancy Olivia, *née* Pitt (d 1966); *b* 11 June 1920; *Educ* Malvern; *m* 1948, Phyllis Audrey, da of Donald Gomersal Horsfield (d 1972); 1 s (Patrick), 1 da (Bridget); *Career* serv WWII RA 50 Div: France and Belgium 1940, Middle E 1941-43, Sicily 1943, NW Europe 1944-46; Lt Col cmdg 272 (N) Fd Regt RA(TA) 1963-66, Hon Col 101 (N) Field Regt RA (V) 1981-86; md Engineering Co 1960-63 ; magistrate Gateshead 1955-; chm Gateshead Health Authority 1984-; Vice Lord-Lt Tyne and Wear 1987-; *Clubs* Northern Counties, Newcastle; *Style*— Lt-Col Windsor Dowdeswell, MC, TD, JP, DL; 40 Oakfield Rd, Gosforth, Newcastle NE3 4HS (☎ 091 2852196)

DOWDING, Cecil John; s of Walter Charles Dowding (d 1951), of Hill Farm, Shepton Montague, and Annie Mullins, *née* Sims; *b* 1 Sept 1905; *Educ* Sexey's Sch Bruton; *m* 12 Oct 1955, Ruth Mary, da of Maj Arnold William Reginald Brevet, of Nethercott, Iddesleigh, Devon, Devon; 3 s (Oliver b 1957, Charles b 1959, Fergus b 1960), 3 da (Margaret, Nancy, Ruth); *Career* dir: Shepton Farms Ltd, W of England Farmers Ltd 1934-77; pres Wincanton RDC; chm govrs Sexey's Sch Bruton; *Recreations* formerly: hockey, tennis, shooting, archaeology; *Style*— Cecil Dowding, Esq; Orchard House, Shepton Montague, Wincanton, Somerset (☎ 0749 813319)

DOWDING, Baron (Life Peer UK 1943); Wing Cdr Derek Hugh Tremenheere Dowding; only s of Air Chief Marshal of the RAF 1 Baron Dowding, GCB, GCVO, CMG (d 1970); *b* 9 Jan 1919; *Educ* Winchester, Cranwell; *m* 1, 17 Feb 1940 (m dis 1946), Joan Myrle, da of Donald James Stuart, of Nairn; m 2, 7 May 1947 (m dis 1960), Alison Margaret, da of James Bannerman, LRCP, LRCS, of Norwich, and widow of Maj R W H Peebles, BCS; 2 s; m 3, 17 Dec 1961, Mrs Odette L M S Hughes, da of Louis Joseph Houles; *Heir* s, Hon Piers Dowding; *Career* Pilot Offr 1939 74 (F) Sqdn, UK Mid East WWII, Co No 49 (B) Sqdn 1950, Wing Cdr 1951; *Style*— Rt Hon The Lord Dowding; 501 Gilbert House, Barbican, EC2 (☎ 01 628 8547)

DOWDING, Fergus James Edward; s of Cecil John Dowding (d 1988), and Ruth Mary, *née* Arnold; *b* 10 Oct 1960; *Educ* Sherborne, Seale-Hayne Agric Coll; *Career* farmer 1982-85, dir Shepton Farms Ltd, antique furniture dealer Pelham Galleries Chelsea London 1985-; *Recreations* calligraphy, genealogy, palaentology, architecture; *Style*— Fergus Dowding, Esq; Orchard House, Shepton Montague, Wincanton, Somerset (☎ 0749 813319); 17 Glenfield Rd, London SW12 (☎ 01 673 7180)

DOWDING, Hon Mark Denis James; yr s of 2 Baron Dowding by 2 wife; *b* 11 July 1949; *Educ* Wymondham Sch; *Style*— The Hon Mark Dowding

DOWDING, Michael Frederick; CBE (1973); s of Guy Francis Dowding (d 1947), Frances Constance, *née* Bragger (d 1963); *b* 19 Nov 1918; *Educ* Westminster, Magdalene Coll Cambridge; *m* 1947, Rosemary, da of Somerville Hastings, MS, FRCS (d 1967); 1 s, 2 da; *Career* serv WWII, Maj RA, NW Europe (despatches); independent consulting engineer; with Davy Corpn 1947-70 (engrg and sales dir Davy United Eng Co Ltd 1951-59, md 1961-64); chm: Davy International, Michael Dowding Associates Ltd (consulting engineers) 1972-, Rautaruukki UK Ltd 1982-86; pres Metals Society 1979; cdr Order of the Finnish Lion 1969; *Recreations* field sports, painting; *Clubs* Brooks's, MCC; *Style*— Michael Dowding, Esq, CBE; Lowlands, Bath Rd, Marlborough, Wiltshire SN8 1NR (☎ 0672 53278)

DOWDING, Muriel, Baroness; Muriel; da of late John Albino; *Educ* Walthamstow Hall Sevenoaks, Convent of the Holy Child Sussex; *m* 1, 1935, June Maxwell Whiting, RAF (ka 1944); 1 s; m 2, 25 Sept 1951, as his 2 w, Air Chief Marshal 1 Baron Dowding, GCB, GCVO, CMG (d 1970); *Career* vice-pres RSPCA to 1981-83; pres Nat Anti-Vivisection Soc, trustee of Ferne Animal Sanctuary, pres Nat Animal Rescue Kennels, hon tres Int Assoc Against Painful Experiments on Animals, founder and chm Beauty Without Cruelty 1959, resigned 1981; *Books* Beauty not the Beast (1980); *Recreations* theosophy, spiritualism, astrology, all occult subjects; *Style*— Rt Hon Muriel, Lady Dowding; Ashurst Lodge, Speldhust Rd, Langton Green, Tunbridge Wells, Kent TH3 0JF

DOWDING, Hon Piers Hugh Tremenheere; s and h of 2 Baron Dowding by 2 wife; *b* 18 Feb 1948; *Educ* Fettes; *Style*— The Hon Piers Dowding

DOWELL, Anthony James; CBE (1973); s of Arthur Henry Dowell (d 1976), and Catherine Ethel, *née* Raynes (d 1974); *b* 16 Feb 1943; *Educ* Hants Sch, Royal Ballet Sch; *Career* princ dancer Royal Ballet, assoc dir Royal Ballet, dir Roy Ballet 1986-; *Clubs* Marks; *Style*— Anthony Dowell, Esq, CBE; The Royal Opera House, Covent Garden, London, WC2E 7QA (☎ 01 240 1200)

DOWELL, Richard Gough; s of Richard Stanley Dowell (d 1943), and Dorothy Gough (d 1919); *b* 5 Jan 1915; *Educ* Rugby, Magdalene Coll Cambridge (MA); *m* 9 May 1942, Diana Vera, da of John Percy Tilley (d 1951), of Ranworth Oxshott, Surrey; 4 da (Susan b 1943, Carolyn b 1945, Wendy b 1947, Jane b 1950); *Career* wartime RAF VR Pilot Flt Lt UK, Europe; co dir of 8 private cos 1945 down to 3 in 1987; JP for Surrey 1964-81; GCIT for Surrey 1968-81; FZS since 1945; *Recreations* real tennis, other sports; *Clubs* Royal Tennis Court Hampton Court Palace, RAF, Piccadilly, MCC; *Style*— Richard Dowell, Esq; The Gables, South Walk, Middleton-on-Sea, Sussex (☎Middleton-on-Sea 4107)

DOWER, Robert (Robin) Charles Philips; s of John Gordon Dower (d 1947), and Pauline, *née*Trevelyan, CBE, JP; *b* 27 Oct 1938; *Educ* The Leys Sch Cambridge, St John's Coll Cambridge (MA), Univ of Edinburgh (BArch), Univ of Newcastle (DipLD); *m* 4 Nov 1967, Frances Helen, da of Henry Edmeades Baker, of Owletts, Cobham, Kent; 1 s (Thomas b 1971), 2 da (Beatrice b 1974, Caroline b 1976); *Career* architect, landscape designer; Yorke Rosenberg Mardall London 1964-71, in private practice as princ, Spence & Dower (chartered architects) Newcastle-upon-Tyne 1974-; memb: Cncl for Protection of Rural England, Northumberland and Newcastle Soc 1971, Nothern Cncl for Sport and Recreation 1976-86, Countryside Cmmn for England and Wales 1982; minister's nominee to Northumberland Nat Park 1978-81; ARIBA 1965; *Recreations* wood engraving, lettering inscriptions, walking, gardening; *Style*— Robin Dower, Esq; Cambo House, Cambo, Morpeth, Northumberland NE61 4AY (☎ 067 074 297); c/o Spence & Dower, 1 Osborne Road, Newcastle-upon-Tyne NE2 2AA (☎ 091 281 5318)

DOWLING, Kenneth; CB (1985); s of Alfred Morris Dowling (d 1963), and Maria Theresa Dowling, *née* Berry (d 1952); *b* 30 Dec 1933; *Educ* King George V GS Lancs; *m* 1957, Margaret Frances, da of Alfred Cyril Bingham (d 1974); 2 da (Angela, Catherine); *Career* barr Gray's Inn 1960; asst dir Public Prosecutions 1972, 1978 and 1982-85; *Recreations* golf, reading; *Clubs* Wyke Green Golf (Middlesex); *Style*— Kenneth Dowling, Esq, CB; 4-12 Queen Anne's Gate, London SW1H 9AZ (☎ 01 213 6026)

DOWLING, Prof Patrick Joseph; s of John Dowling (d 1951), of Dublin, and Margaret, *née* McKittrick; *b* 23 Mar 1939; *Educ* Christian Brothers Sch Dublin, Univ Coll Dublin (BE), Imperial Coll London (DIC, PhD); *m* 14 May 1966, Dr Grace Carmine Victoria, da of Palladius Mariano Agapitus Lobo, of Zanzibar; 1 s (Tiernan b 7 Feb 1968), 1 da (Rachel b 8 March 1967); *Career* bridge engr Br Constructional Steelwork Assoc; Imperial Coll London: res fell 1966-74, reader 1974-79, BSC 1979-; fndr ptnr Chapman & Dowling 1981, hd Civil Engrg Dept Imp Coll 1985-, memb exec ctee & cncl Steel Construction Inst 1985-, conslt KML Conslt Engrs 1988-; Gustave Trasenster Medal, Assoc des Ingénieurs Sortis de L'Université de Liege; FIStructE 1978, FICE 1979, FEng 1981, FRINA 1985; *Books* ed: Journal of Constructional Steel Research, Steel Plated Structures (1977), Buckling of Shells in Offshore Stuctures (1982), Design of Steel Structures (1988); *Recreations* reading, travelling, sailing; *Clubs* Athenaeum, Chelsea Arts; *Style*— Prof Patrick Dowling; Imperial Coll, Civil Engineering Dept, London SW7 2BU (☎ 01 589 5111, ext 4709, fax 01 584 7596, telex 918351)

DOWN, Sir Alastair (Frederick); OBE (1944, MBE 1942), MC (1940), TD (1951); s of Capt Frederick Edward Down (d 1959); *b* 23 July 1914; *Educ* Marlborough; *m* 1947, Bunny (Maysie Hilda), da of Capt Vernon Mellon; 2 s, 2 da; *Career* serv WWII (despatches twice), with 8 Army and 1 Canadian Army as Lt-Col and Col; CA 1938, dep chm and md BP Co Ltd 1962-75, pres BP Gp in Canada 1957-62, chm and chief exec Burmah Oil Co Ltd 1975-83; kt 1978; *Recreations* shooting, golf, fishing; *Style*— Sir Alastair Down, OBE, MC, TD; Brieryhill, Hawick, Roxburghshire TD9 7LL Scotland

DOWN, Peter Ashford; s of Ernest Augustus Down, of 47 Boscombe Overcliff Dr, Bournemouth, and (Dorothy Irene) Audrey, *née* Sparkes; *b* 12 Sept 1928; *Educ* Clayesmore Sch Blandford Dorset, Queens' Coll Cambridge (MA); *m* 24 June 1954, Ann, da of late John Cater Crawshaw; 1 s (Andrew John b 1963), 2 da (Sally Ann b 1957, Frances Elizabeth b 1960); *Career* works servs RE 1947-49; architect; ptnr E A Down & Son 1957-60, Jackson Greenen Down & Ptnrs 1960-87; dir Jackson Greenen Down 1987 (div of of D Y Davies plc); former chm: Hants & Isle of Wight Architectural Assoc, local RIBA branch; former pres Bournemouth 41 Club, memb Bournemouth Rotary; FRIBA 1957; *Books* Environment and the Industrial Society (jtly, 1976); *Recreations* travel, painting, photography; *Style*— Peter Down, Esq; Jackson Greenen Down & Partners Ltd, Hinton Offices, Hinton Rd, Bournemouth BH1 2DZ (☎ 0202 26266, fax 0202 26057)

DOWN, Rev Canon William John Denbigh; s of William Leonard Frederick Down (Flying Offr, RAFVR), of 10 Haldon Avenue, Teignmouth, Devon, and Beryl Mary, *née* Collett; *b* 15 July 1934; *Educ* Farnham GS, St John's Coll Cambridge (BA, MA), Ridley Hall Theol Coll Cambridge; *m* 29 July 1960, Sylvia Mary, da of Martin John Aves (d 1986); 2 s (Andrew b 1962, Timothy b 1975), 2 da (Helen (Mrs Burn) b 1964, Julia b 1968); *Career* chaplain: RANR 1972-74, HMAS Leeuwin Fremantle W Aust 1972-74; ordained: deacon 1959, priest 1960; asst curate St Paul's Church Fisherton Anger Salisbury, asst chaplain The Missions to Seamen S Shields 1963-64 (sr chaplain 1964-65), port chaplain The Missions to Seamen Hull 1965-71, sr chaplain The Missions to Seamen Fremantle W Aust 1971-74, dep gen sec The Missions to Seamen London 1975 (gen sec 1975-), chaplain St Michael Paternoster Royal City of London 1976-; Hon Canon: Holy Trinity Cath Gibraltar 1985, St Michael's Cath Kobe Japan 1987; memb: cncl Merchant Navy Welfare Bd, Marine Soc, Partnership for World Mission, The Oxford Mission, Int Christian Maritime Assoc (chm 1981-85); Freeman City of London 1981; Hon Chaplain: Worshipful Co of Carmen 1978 (Hon Liveryman 1981), Worshipful Co of Farriers 1983 (Hon Liveryman 1986), Worshipful Co of Innholders 1983; *Recreations* golf, watching cricket, ships and seafaring, walking; *Clubs* Royal Commonweath Soc; *Style*— The Rev Canon William Down; 6 Hartsbourne Avenue, Bushey Heath, Watford, Herts WD2 1JL (☎ 01 950 3178); The Missions To Seamen, St Michael Paternoster Royal, College Hill, London EC4R 2RL (☎ 01 248 5202, 01 248 7442, fax 01 248 4761)

DOWN AND CONNOR, Bishop (RC) of (1982-); Most Rev Cahal Brendan Daly; s of Charles Daly (d 1939), of Loughguile, Co Antrim, and Susan Daly (d 1974); *b* 1 Oct 1917; *Educ* St Malachy's Coll Belfast, Queen's Univ Belfast (MA), St Patrick's Coll Maynooth (DD), Institut Catholique Paris (LPh); *Career* ordained 1941, classics master St Malachy's Coll Belfast 1945-46, lectr in scholastic philosophy Queen's Univ Belfast 1946-63 (reader 1963-67); consecrated Bishop 1967, Bishop of Ardagh and

Clonmacnois 1967-82; *Books* Morals, Law and Life (1962), Natural Law Morality Today (1965), Violence in Ireland and Christian Conscience (1973), Peace, the Work of Justice (1979); *Recreations* reading, writing; *Style*— The Most Rev Cahal Daly, Bishop of Down and Connor; Lisbreen, 73 Somerton Rd, Belfast BT15 4DJ, N Ireland (☎ 0232 776185)

DOWN AND DROMORE, 96 Bishop of 1986-; Rt Rev Gordon McMullan; s of Samuel McMullan (d 1952, professional footballer); *b* 31 Jan 1934; *Educ* Queen's Univ Belfast (BSc, PhD), Ridley Hall Cambridge (Dip Relig Studies, ThD); *m* 1957, Kathleen, da of Edward Davidson (d 1965); 2 s; *Career* ordained 1962, archdeacon of Down 1979-80, bishop of Clogher 1980-86; chm BBC Religious Advisy Ctee (N Ireland), memb Central Religious Advsy Cncl for Bdcasting (BBC/IBA); *Books* A Cross and Beyond (1976), We Are Called... (1977), Everyday Discipleship (1979), Reflections on St Mark's Gospel (1984); *Recreations* association football, rugby football, cricket; *Style*— The Rt Rev the Bishop of Down and Dromore; The See House, 32, Knockdene Park South, Belfast BT5 7AB, N Ireland (☎ 0232 471973)

DOWNE, 11 Viscount (I 1681); John Christian George Dawnay; sits as Baron Dawnay of Danby (UK 1897); er s of 10 Viscount Downe, OBE, JP, DL (d 1965); *b* 18 Jan 1935; *Educ* Eton, Christ Church Oxford; *m* 16 Sept 1965, Alison Diana, da of Ian Francis Henry Sconce, OBE, TD, of Brasted Chart, Kent; 1 s, 1 da (Hon Sarah Frances b 2 April 1970); *Heir* s, Hon Richard Henry Dawnay b 9 April 1967; *Career* served as Lt Gren Gds 1954; Vice Lord-Lt N Yorks 1982-; industl mangr electronics indust; *Recreations* analogue circuit design and railways (selectively); *Clubs* Pratt's; *Style*— The Rt Hon the Viscount Downe; Wykeham Abbey, Scarborough, N Yorks (☎ 862404); 5 Douro Place, W8 (☎ 01 937 9449)

DOWNER, Dr Martin Craig; s of Dr Reginald Lionel Ernest Downer (d 1937), of Shrewsbury, and Eileen Maud Downer, *née* Craig (d 1962); *b* 9 Mar 1931; *Educ* Shrewsbury, Liverpool Univ (LDS, RCS), London Univ (DDPH, RCS), Manchester Univ (PhD); *m* 1961, Anne Catherine, da of R W Evans, of Cheshire; 4 da (Stephanie b 1962, Caroline b 1965, Diana b 1968, Gabrielle b 1972); *Career* area dental offr Salford 1974-79, chief dental offr: Scottish Home and Health Dept 1979-83, DHSS 1983-; hon sr lectr Univs of Edinburgh and Dundee 1979-83; mem: WHO, Expert Panel on Oral Health; *Books* contributor: Cariology Today (Basel 1984), Strategy for Dental Caries Prevention in European countries (Oxford 1987); *Style*— Dr Martin Downer; Dept of Health, Richmond House, 79 Whitehall, London SW1A 2NS

DOWNES, George Robert; CB (1967); s of Philip George Downes (d 1919), of Burnham on Crouch, and Isabella, *née* Webster (d 1967); *b* 25 May 1911; *Educ* King Edward's GS Birmingham, Grocers' London; *m* 24 May 1947, Edna Katherine, da of William Longair Millar (d 1969), of Ringwood; 2 da (Alison b 1948, Marianne b 1951); *Career* RNVR in destroyers 1942-45 (Lt 1943); GPO: asst surveyor 1937, asst princ 1939, princ 1946; princ private sec Lord Pres of Cncl 1948-50 (Lord Privy Seal 1951, asst sec 1951), Imperial Def Coll 1952; GPO: dep regnl dir London 1955, dir London postal region 1960, dir postal servs 1965, dir ops and oversea 1967-71; dir of studies Royal Inst of Public Admin 1973-, vice-chm Gtr London Regn Abbeyfield Soc 1978, chm Abbeyfield N London Ex Care Soc 1977-; *Recreations* music, gardening; *Style*— George Downes, Esq, CB; Orchard Cottage, Frithsden, Berkhamstead, Herts HP4 1NW (☎ 0442 866620)

DOWNES, George Stretton; CBE (1976); s of late George Stretton Downes and late Rosalind, *née* Ward; *b* 2 Mar 1914; *Educ* Cardinal Vaughan Sch Kensington; *m* 1939, Sheilah Gavigan (d 1986); 2 s, 2 da; *Career* joined Met Police Off 1934, sec 1969, dep receiver Met Police Dist 1973-76, ret; *Recreations* golf, gardening; *Clubs* RAC; *Style*— George Downes, Esq, CBE; 9 Browning Rd, Leatherhead, Surrey (0372 58735)

DOWNES, Justin Alasdair; s of Patrick Thomas Downes (d 1978), and Eileen Marie, *née* Mackie; *b* 25 Sept 1950; *Educ* The Oratory; *Career* dir: Fin Strategy 1980-85, Street Fin Strategy 1985-86; md Fin Dynamics Ltd 1986-; memb Somerset CC 1976-; *Style*— Justin Downes, Esq; Sentinel House No 2 Eyre St Hill, London EC1

DOWNES, Prof (John) Kerry; s of Ralph William Downes, and Agnes Mary, *née* Rix (d 1980); *b* 8 Dec 1930; *Educ* St Benedict's Ealing, Courtauld Inst of Art (BA, PhD); *m* 1962, Margaret, da of John William Walton (d 1963); *Career* Librarian: Barber Inst of Fine Arts, Univ of Birmingham 1958-66; lectr Univ of Reading 1966 (reader 1971, prof of history of art 1978-); memb Royal Cmmn on Historical Monuments of England 1981-; FSA 1962; *Books* Hawksmoor (1959,1969), Vanbrugh (1977,1987), Wren (1971, 1982), Rubens (1980), English Baroque Architecture (1966);; *Recreations* music, drawing, microchips, contemplation; *Style*— Prof Kerry Downes; Dept of History of Art, Univ of Reading, Reading, RG1 5AQ, (☎ 0734 318891)

DOWNES, Ralph (William); CBE (1969); s of late James William Downes; *b* 16 August 1904; *Educ* Derby Municipal Secdy Sch, RCM London, Keble Coll Oxford, (MA, BMus); *m* 1929, Agnes Mary, nee Rix (d 1980); 1 s (Kerry); *Career* asst organist Southwark Cathedral 1924, dir chapel music and lectr Princeton Univ USA 1928-35, organist Brompton Oratory 1936-78 (now emeritus) curator-organist Royal Festival Hall 1954-, organ prof RCM 1954-75 organ curator LCC 1949; organ designer and supervisor: Royal Festival Hall 1952, Brompton Oratory 1954, St John's Co-Cathedral Valletta Malta 1961, St Albans Cathedral 1963, Paisley Abbey 1968, Gloucester Cathedral 1971, St Davids Hall Cardiff 1983; Hon RAM 1965, Hon FRCO 1966, FRCM 1969; KSG (Papal) 1970; *Books* Baroque Tricks: Adventures with the Organbuilders (1983); *Style*— Ralph Downes, Esq, CBE; c/o The Oratory, London SW7

DOWNEY, Sir Gordon Stanley; KCB (1984, CB 1980); s of Capt Stanley William Downey (d 1940), of London, and Winifred, *née* Dick (d 1970); *b* 26 April 1928; *Educ* Tiffin's Sch, LSE (BSc); *m* 7 Aug 1952, Jacqueline Norma, da of Samuel Goldsmith (d 1972), of London; 2 da (Alison b 1960, Erica b 1963); *Career* 2 Lt RA 1946-48; Miny of Works 1951-52, Miny of Health 1961-62, Treasury 1952-78; dep head of Central Policy Review Staff 1978-81; Comptroller and Auditor Gen 1981-87; special advsr to Ernst & Whinney 1988-; Complaints Cmmr for Securities Assoc 1989-; CIPFA 1982; *Recreations* reading, visual arts, tennis; *Clubs* Army and Navy; *Style*— Sir Gordon Downey, KCB; Chinley Cottage, 1 Eaton Park Road, Cobham, Surrey KT11 2JG (☎ 0932 67878)

DOWNEY, Air Vice-Marshal John Chegwyn Thomas; CB (1975), DFC (1945, AFC 1950); s of Thomas Cecil Downey (d 1961), of Croydon, and Mary Evelyn, *née* Van Dulken (d 1954); the Downeys came from Lindisfarne in early c19 and became Thames Master Lightermen; the Van Dulkens were Dutch immigrants late c19; *b* 26 Nov 1920; *Educ* Whitgift Sch; *m* 1941, (Ilma) Diana, da of Maj Louis E White, of London; 1 s (Nicholas), 2 da (Judith, Patricia); *Career* RAF Offr 1939, wartime serv as Pilot Coastal Cmd, post war serv trg R & D Bomber & Coastal Cmds 1973-75; dep controller Aircraft R&D, MOD, Air Vice Marshal; *Books* Management in the Armed Forces: An Anatomy of the Military Profession 1977; *Recreations* sailing (yacht 'Quadrille'), writing, skiing; *Clubs* RAF; *Style*— Air Vice-Marshal John Downey, CB, DFC, AFC; Windmill House, Windmill Field, Bosham, Sussex PO18 8LH (☎ 0243 572723)

DOWNEY, Maurice Edmund; s of late Edmund Downey, author (as F M Allen) (d 1937); *b* 2 April 1930; *Educ* Waterpark Coll; *m* 1956, Marie, da of late Timothy Flynn; 5 children; *Career* chartered accountant; ptnr Reynolds Cooper McCarron (CA) 1973-, dir Irish Lee Assurance Co 1978-, chm Waterford Harbour Commissioners 1976-, mayor of Waterford 1970-71, former cncl memb Inst of Chartered Accountants in Ireland; *Recreations* rugby, walking, travel; *Style*— Maurice Edmund Esq; Milltown Grove, Milltown, Dublin (☎ 01 697236); Fairview, Newtown, Waterford, Eire (☎ 051 74191)

DOWNIE, Prof Robert Silcock; s of Capt Robert Mackie Downie (d 1980), Glasgow, and Margaret Barlas, *née* Brown (d 1974); *b* 19 April 1933; *Educ* HS of Glasgow, Glasgow Univ (MA), Queen's Coll Oxford (BPhil); *m* 15 Sept 1958, Eileen Dorothea, da of Capt Wilson Ashley Flynn (d 1942), of Glasgow; 3 da (Alison, Catherine, Barbara); *Career* Russian linguist Intelligence Corps 1955-57, lectr in philosophy Glasgow Univ 1959-69, visiting prof of philosophy Syracuse NY USA 1963-64, prof of moral philosophy Glasgow Univ 1969-, Stevenson lectr in medical ethics 1986-88; FRSE; *Books* Government Action and Morality (1964), Respect for Persons (1969), Roles and Values (1971), Education and Personal Relationships (1974), Caring and Caring (1980), Healthy Respect (1987), Health Promotion (1990); *Recreations* music; *Style*— Prof Robert Downie; 17 Hamilton Drive, Glasgow G12 8DH; Kilnaish, By Tarbert, Argyll (☎ 041 339 1345); Dept of Philosophy, Glasgow Univ, Glasgow G12 8QQ (☎ 041 339 8855 ext 4273)

DOWNING, Dr Anthony Leighton; s of Sydney Arthur Downing and Frances Dorothy Downing; *b* 27 Mar 1926; *Educ* Arnold Sch Blackpool, Cambridge Univ, London Univ; *m* 1952, Kathleen Margaret Frost; 1 da; *Career* dir Water Pollution Research Laboratory 1966-73; ptnr Binnie & Partners Consulting Engineers 1974-86; self-employed consultant 1986-; FIChemE; FIBiol, Hon FIWEM; FRSA; *Recreations* golf; *Clubs* Knebworth Golf, United Oxford and Cambridge; *Style*— Dr Anthony Downing; 2 Tewin Close, Tewin Wood, Welwyn, Herts (☎ 043 879 474)

DOWNING, Dr David Francis; s of Alfred William Downing (d 1963), and Violet Winifred, *née* Wakeford; *b* 4 August 1926; *Educ* Bristol GS, Univ of Bristol (BSc, PhD), Univ of California Los Angeles; *m* 1948, Margaret, da of Raymond Llewellyn (d 1958); 1 s (Jonathan b 1962), 1 da (Anna b 1961); *Career* army Lt Royal Welch Fusiliers 1944-48; Univ of Bristol (undergraduate & postgraduate) 1948-55, fell Univ of California Los Angeles 1955-57, lectr Dept of Agriculture and Horticulture Univ of Bristol 1957-58, Chemical Def Estab MOD 1958-63 and 1966-68; scientific liason offr Br Embassy Washington DC USA 1963-66, cnsllr (scientific) Br High Cmmn Ottawa Canada 1968-73, asst dir Royal Armaments R & D Estab MOD 1973-78, cnsllr (scientific) Br Embassy Moscow USSR 1978-81, asst dir resources and programmes MOD 1981-83, attaché (Def R & D) Br Embassy Washington DC USA 1983-87, p/t chm Civil Serv Commn Recruitment Bds; FRSA; *Recreations* cross country skiing, arctic art, bird watching; *Clubs* Army & Navy; *Style*— Dr David Downing; 13 The Close, Salisbury, Wilts SP1 2EB

DOWNING, John Cottrill Ralph; DL (1981); s of Dr Charles Cottrill Ralph Downing (d 1962), of Cardiff, and Ruby, *née* Elliot (d 1980); *b* 22 May 1931; *Educ* Felsted, Pembroke Coll Cambridge (MA); *m* 1959, Muriel Maureen, da of Leslie Webb (d 1983), of Cardiff; 2 da (Caroline b 1961, Nicola b 1963); *Career* sr dir Lyddon Stockbrokers; dir Nat Investmt Gp Plc; memb of the Stock Exchange; *Recreations* golf, collecting watercolours, stage musicals; *Clubs* Brooks's, Constitutional, Windsor, Cardiff and County, Royal Porthcawl; *Style*— John Downing, Esq, DL; North Lodge, Court Colman, Pen-y-fai, nr Bridgend, Mid Glamorgan LF31 4NG (☎ 0656 721208); National Westminster Bank Building, 113 Bute Street, Cardiff CF1 1QS (☎ 0222 473111)

DOWNING, Paul Nicholas; s of Sydney Edward Downing (d 1982), of Berkhamsted, and Glady *née* Miles; *b* 9 Mar 1947; *Educ* Berkhamsted Sch, Univ of Essex; *m* 19 June 1971, Suzanne Mary, da of Dr Howel Norman Rees (d 1983), of Port Talbot, S Wales; 1 da (Charlotte); *Career* slr; ptnr with Clifford Chance; memb Law Soc; *Recreations* riding, scuba diving, skiing; *Clubs* Ski Club of GB, Br Sub-Acqua; *Style*— Paul Downing, Esq; 22 Parkside Gardens, Wimbledon, London SW19 5EU (☎ 01 946 7331); Blackfriars House, 19 New Bridge Street, London EC4V 6BY (☎ 01 353 0211, fax 01 489 0046, telex 887847 LEGIS G)

DOWNS, Barry; s of Samuel Downs (d 1964), of Stockport, and Hilda, *née* Barlow (d 1947); *b* 6 Sept 1931; *Educ* Dial Stone Sch, Henton Mour Coll; *m* 20 July 1957, Kay, da of Frank Etchells, of Bramway High Lane, Stockport; 1 s (Simon Paul b 1960), 1 da (Philippa Anne b 1963); *Career* CA; 1957 practiced B Downs & Co 1969; sec S Casket plc 1960-64; lectr Textile Cncl Productivity Centre 1964-69; dir: Jones Travel (Lirmston) Ltd 1969, Sun Island Holidays Ltd 1975, Happiday Travel Ltd 1984, Royal Exchange Theatre Catering Ltd 1981; chm Governors Offerton High Sch; *Recreations* cricket, golf, politics, theatre; *Clubs* Grange, Bramhall Golf; *Style*— Barry Downs, Esq; The Old Vicarage, 5 Egerton Rd, Davenport, Stockport (☎ 061 483 4617); B Downs & Co, 67 Wellington Rd, S Stockport (☎ 061 480 0845)

DOWNS, Sir Diarmuid; CBE (1979); s of John Downs, by his w Ellen McMahon; *b* 23 April 1922; *Educ* Gunnersbury Catholic GS, City Univ London; *m* 1951, Mary Carmel, *née* Chillman; 1 s, 3 da; *Career* chm and md Ricardo Consulting Engineers plc 1976-87; dir Universe Publications Ltd; kt 1985-; *Recreations* theatre, literature, music; *Clubs* St Stephen's (London), Hove (Hove); *Style*— Sir Diarmuid Downs, CBE; The Downs, 143 New Church Rd, Hove, E Sussex BN3 4DB (☎ 0273 419 357); Ricardo Consulting Engineers plc, Bridge Works, Shoreham Rd, Shoreham-by-Sea, Sussex (☎ 0273 455 611, telex 87 383)

DOWNS, Maj Eric John; ERD (1961), TD (1950, clasp 1954); s of Eli Downs (d 1938), and Hannah Mary Smith (d 1952); *b* 10 April 1904; *Educ* Merchant Taylors' Sch Crosby Lancs; *m* 3 Oct 1945, Margaret Evelyne, da of Major Henry Wadams (d 1964); 1 step s (Peter b 1938), 3 da (Penelope b 1946, Joan b 1946, Mary b 1946), 1 step da (Jane b 1940); *Career* cmmnd E Lancs Regt (SR) 1934, RA (SR) 1935, 106 Lancs Yeo Regt RHA (TA) 1939, served Palestine 1940-41, DRO Haifa and Galilee and Libyan Campaigns 1941-42, Tobruk (POW 1942-45), Maj (AER) 1952-64; memb W Lancs TA 1963-64; bank official 1921-64 (sr inspr 1955-64); pres Southport Organists Assoc 1934, chm Southport Arts Club 1937, memb Southport Borough Cncl 1963-74 (chm tport ctee 1965-67, vice-chm educn ctee 1969-73), memb Sefton Borough Cncl 1973-76 (chm planning ctee 1973-76), Town Mayor of Southport 1974; chm Knowsley St Helens & Sefton War Pensions Ctee 1981-87; memb Liverpool Diocesan Synod 1973-76; schs govr; ATCL, ARCO, ACIB; *Recreations* rugby football, tennis, swimming, riding, music, philately, photography; *Clubs* Naval and Military, Lancs RFU, Rugby, Cricket, Arts (Southport), Dramatic; *Style*— Maj Eric J Downs, ERD, TD; Barclays Bank plc, 4 Water Street, Liverpool L69 2DU

DOWNS, Richard Hudson; s of Arthur Stanley Downs (d 1931); *b* 19 July 1920; *Educ* West Leeds HS, London Poly, Bradford Tech; *m* 1942, Mary; 1 s; *Career* Flt Lt UK and India; chm: Cindex Ltd 1976-82, Cindico plc 1982-84, Medop Ltd 1982-88, Infojet Ltd; *Recreations* aviation; *Style*— Richard Downs Esq; Point Neptune, Fort George, Guernsey, CI (☎ 0481 26525, fax 0481 26528)

DOWNTON, Dr Christine Veronica; da of Henry Devereux Downton (d 1962), and Christina Vera, *née* Threadgold; *b* 21 Oct 1941; *Educ* Caerphilly GS Glamorgan, LSE (BSc, PhD); *m* 1981, Joseph Chubb, s of Percy Chubb II (d 1983), of New Jersey; *Career* investmt banker: exec Co Nat-West Investmt Mgmnt, sr conslt to the pres Fed Res Bank of NY), asst dir N M Rothschild, asst advsr Bank of England; *Recreations* reading, walking; *Style*— Dr Christine V Downton; 21 Belgrave Mews South, London SW1; 110 Riverside Drive, NY, USA; Fenchurch Exchange, London EC3

DOWNWARD, Maj-Gen Peter Aldcroft; CB (1979), DSO (1967), DFC (1952); s of Aldcroft Leonard Downward (d 1969), Mary Rigby Downward *née* Halton (d 1978); *b* 10 April 1924; *Educ* King William's Coll IOM; *m* 1, 1953, Hilda Hinckley Wood (d 1976); 2 s (Jeremy, Julian); m 2, 1980, Mrs Mary Boykett Procter (*née* Allwork); *Career* enlisted 1942 (The Rifle Bde), cmmnd S Lancs Regt (PWV) 1943, seconded Parachute Regt, NW Europe 1944-45, India and SE Asia 1945-46, Palestine 1946, Berlin Airlift 1948-49, Korea 1951-53 as Army pilot, Cdr 1 Bn The Lancs Regt (PWV) South Arabia 1966-67, Cdr Berlin Inf Bde 1971-74, Cdr Sch of Infantry 1974-76, GOC W Midland Dist 1976-78; Col The Queen's Lancashire Regt 1978-83, Col Cmdt The King's Div 1979-83; Hon Col Liverpool U OTC 1979-; Lt-Govr Royal Hosp Chelsea 1979-84; Dir Oxley Devpt Coy 1984-; chm Museum of Army Flying 1984-; pres Br Korean Veteran's Assoc 1987; pres Assoc of Service Newspapers 1987-; *Recreations* sailing, shooting, skiing; *Clubs* Army and Navy; *Style*— Maj-Gen Peter Downward, CB, DSO, DFC; c/o Lloyds Bank, Warminster, Wilts; Oxley Developments Coy Ltd, Ulverston, Cumbria LA12 9QG (☎ 0229 52621)

DOWNWARD, Sir William Atkinson; JP (1973), DL (1971); s of George Thomas Downward (d 1915); *b* 5 Dec 1912; *Educ* Manchester HS, Manchester Coll of Technol; *m* 1946, Enid, da of late Alderman Charles Wood; *Career* memb Manchester City Cncl 1946, lord mayor of Manchester 1970-71, alderman Manchester 1971-74, Lord Lt Greater Manchester 1974-77 (DL 1971 Lancs); memb ct of govrs Manchester Univ 1969, chm Manchester Overseas Students Welfare Conference 1972-87, dir Manchester Royal Exchange Theatre Co 1976-89; pres Greater Manchester Fedn of Boys Club 1978-; hon LLD Manchester 1977; kt (1977); *Style*— Sir William Downward, JP, DL; 23 Kenmore Rd, Northenden, Manchester M22 4AE (☎ 061 998 4742); Greater Manchester Lieutenancy Office, Byron House, Quay St, Manchester M3 3JD (☎ 061 834 0490)

DOWSE-BRENAN, Lt Col Anthony Edward Francis; JP (1972); s of Maj Frederick Esmonde Dowse-Brenan, OBE (d 1955), of Longdown Lodge, Sandhurst, Berks, and Frances Sarah, *née* Crecy (d 1965); *b* 24 April 1923; *Educ* Winchester, King's Coll Durham Univ; *m* 13 April 1952, Elizabeth, da of George Chartis Wood Homer (d 1953), of Bardolf Manor, Dorchester, Dorset; 2 da (Frances Elizabeth Christine b 5 Nov 1955, Annette Caroline (Mrs Davies) b 21 April 1959); *Career* cmmnd Royal Regt of Artillery 1942, HQ 6 Armd Div N Africa 1943-44, 52 Field Regt (Ayreshire Yeo) Italy and Austria 1944-45,Capt 1 RHA ACD to Gen Sir Charles Loewen Italy and Palestine, instr RAC Bovington 1949-51, Adj 81 HAA Regt 1952-53, instr RMA Sandhurst 1953, student Staff Coll Camberley 1954, WO 1955-56, Maj 18 Medium Regt 1957-58, Bde Maj RA 43 Div 1959-60, battery cdr 3 RHA 1961-, 255 Medium Regt, Lt-Col Somerset Yeo and LI 1967-68; headmaster St Martins Sch Crewkerne 1966-84; chm: Cncl Colleges of Further and Higher Educn 1983-84, chm cncl Educational Fndn For Visual Aids 1986-87; vice-chm cncl Appaloosa Horse Soc 1988-89; dep ldr and chm educn Somerset CC 1977-81, chm Crekerne Town Cncl 1984-87; pres Crewkerne ctees: civic, twinning, Conservative; govr and vice chm Yeovil Coll; memb Royal Inst of Int Affrs 1955-82; *Recreations* athletics, breeding Appaloosa horses; *Clubs* Farmers; *Style*— Lt-Col Anthony Dowse-Brenan; Moor Lands House, Merriott, Somerset; Old Manor Farm. (Alder Stud) Buckland St Mary, Somerset, (☎ 0460 72442); Tollraine Services, Oxen Rd, Crewkerne, Somerset, (☎ 0460 74111, fax 0460 77101)

DOWSETT, Prof Charles James Frank; s of Charles Aspinall Dowsett (d 1957), and Louise, *née* Stokes (d 1983); *b* 02 Jan 1924; *Educ* Owen's Sch Islington, St Catherine's Soc Oxford, Peterhouse Cambridge (MA, PhD), Ecole Nationale des Langues Orientales Vivantes Pris, Institut Catholique Paris; *m* 19 Sept 1949, Friedel (d 1984), da of Friedrich Lapuner (d 1958), of Kalweitschen, East Prussia; *Career* reader in armenian SOAS London 1965 (lectr 1954-65), Cabuste Gulbenkian prof of armenian studies Univ of Oxford and fell Pembroke Coll 1965-; visiting prof Univ of Chicago 1976; cncl memb: Royal Asiatic Soc 1972-76, Philological Soc 1973-77; bd memb: Marjary Wardrop Fund for Georgian Studies; contrib of various articles to specialist and learned pubns; FBA 1978; *Books* The History of the Caucasian Albanians by Movses Daskhurantzi (1962), The Penitential of David of Gandjak (1962), Kutahya tiles and pottery from the Armenian Cathedral of St James Jerusalem Vol 1 (with John Carswell, 1972); *Style*— Prof Charles Dowsett; 21 Hurst Rise Rd, Cumnor Hill, Oxford OX2 9HE

DOWSING, Douglas Robert Frederick; JP (1960); s of Douglas Lemuel Dowsing (d 1938), civil servant HM Prison Cmmn Home Off, and Annie Florence Thorp (d 1969); *b* 24 Oct 1916; *Educ* Portsmouth Munic Coll (now Polytechnic), AMIEE; *Career* Lt RNVR 1943-46; electrical engrg PO Telephones 1938, inspector 1946, asst engr 1966, exec engr ret 1976; appointed JP for Hampshire 1960; chm of Havant PSD Bench 1980-85; chm and dir Abbeyfield Havant Soc 1969; *Recreations* hockey, cricket, philately, ornithology, wild life preservation; *Clubs* Marylebone Cricket, Hampshire CCC, The Naval, Friends of Arundel Castle CC; *Style*— Douglas Dowsing, JP; Eastwold, 25 Bellair Rd, Havant, Hampshire PO9 2RG (☎ 0705 484550)

DOWSON, Prof Duncan; s of Wilfrid Dowson (d 1970), of Kirkymoorside, Yorks, and Hannah, *née* Crosier (d 1987); *b* 31 August 1928; *Educ* Lady Lumley's GS Pickering Yorks, Univ of Leeds (BSc, PhD, DSc); *m* 15 Dec 1951, Mabel, da of Herbert Strickland (d 1961), of Kirkbymoorside, Yorks; 2 s (David Guy b 1953, Stephen Paul b 1956, d 1968); *Career* Sir W G Armstrong Whitworth Aircraft Co 1952-54; dept mechanical engrg Univ of Leeds 1954-: lectr 1954-63, sr lectr 1963-65, reader 1965-66, prof of fluid mechanics and tribology 1966-, dir inst of tribology 1967-86, head of dept 1967-, pro vice-chllr 1983-85, dean for int relations 1988-; visiting prof Univ of NSW Sydney 1975; memb: Educn and Sci Working Pty on Lubrication Educn and Res 1972-76, orthopaedic implant ctee DHSS 1974-77, regnl sci ctee YRHA 1977-80, res ctee Arthritis and Rheumatism Cncl 1977-85, SERC ctees 1987-; Hon DTech Chalmers Univ of Technol Göteborg Sweden 1979; FIMechE 1973, FEng 1982, FRS 1987, FRSA; Fell: ASME, ASLE; memb Royal Swedish Acad of Engrg Sci 1986; *Books* Elastohydrodynamic Lubrication (second edn, 1977), History of Tribology (1979), Biomechanics of Joints and Joint Replacements (1981), Ball Bearing Lubrication (1981); *Recreations* walking; *Style*— Prof Duncan Dowson; Ryedale, 23 Church Lane, Adel, Leeds LS16 8DQ (☎ 0532 678933); Dept of Mechanical Engineering, The University of Leeds, Leeds LS2 9JT (☎ 0532 332153, fax 0532 424611, telex 556473 UNILDS G)

DOWSON, Graham Randall; s of late Cyril James Dowson, by his w late Dorothy Celia (*née* Foster); *b* 13 Jan 1923; *Educ* Alleyn Court Sch, City of London Sch, Ecole Alpina Switzerland; *m* 1, 1954 (m dis 1974), Fay Weston; 2 da; m 2, 1975, Denise, da of Sydney Shurman; *Career* served WW II Sqdn Ldr pilot Coastal Cmd; dir: A C Neilsen Co Oxford 1953-58, Southern Television 1958-75; chief exec Rank Orgn Ltd ; 1972-74 (dep 1960-72); chm Erskine Ho Investmts 1975-83; dir: Carron Co (Hldgs) Ltd 1976-82, Carron Investmts Ltd 1976-82, Cambridge Communications Ltd 1978-79, R C D Holdings Ltd 1979-; dep chm: Nimslo Int Ltd, Nimslo Ltd, Nimslo Euro Hldgs and Nimslo Corpn 1978-; chm: Pincus Vidler Arthur Fitzgerald (advertising agency) 1979-84, chm Marinex Petroleum Ltd, Marinex Petroleum USA Inc and Marinex Petroleum Petroleum Hldgs 1980-84; pres Euro League for Econ Co-operation (Br Section) 1983- (chm 1972-83); dep chm Nat Playing Fields Assoc; chm: Migraine Tst, Teltech plc 1984-85; dir Filmbond 1985-1987; chm Graham Dowson Associates 1975-; chm Dowson-Salisbury Ass 1987-, chm Premier Speakers 1988-; dep chm Paravision (UK) 1988-; *Recreations* sailing; *Clubs* Royal London Yacht (Cdre 1978-79), Royal Southern Yacht, RAF, Distillers Livery, Carlton; *Style*— Graham Dowson, Esq; 193 Cromwell Tower, Barbican, London EC2

DOWSON, Sir Philip Manning; CBE (1969); s of Robert Manning Dowson, of Geldeston, Norfolk; *b* 16 August 1924; *Educ* Gresham's Sch Holt, Univ Coll Oxford, Clare Coll Cambridge (MA); *m* 1950, Sarah Albinia, da of Brig Wilson Theodore Oliver Crewdson, CBE (d 1961), by his w Albinia Joane, 2 da of Sir Nicholas Henry Bacon, 12 Bt, of London; 1 s, 2 da; *Career* Sub Lt RNVR; architect; Ove Arup and Ptnrs 1953, Arup Assocs, Architects and Engrs (fndr ptnr) 1963; memb Royal Fine Art Cmmn 1970-, tstee The Thomas Cubitt Tst 1978-, bd of tstees Royal Botanic Gdns Kew 1983-, tstee The Armouries 1984-; Royal Gold Medal for Architecture 1981, AA Opl, ARIBA, FSIAD; assoc Royal Acad of Arts (1979), appointed to cncl 1981; kt 1980; *Style*— Sir Philip Dowson, CBE, RA; 2 Dean Street, London W1V 6QB (☎ 01 734 8494); 1 Pembroke Studios, Pembroke Gdns, London W8

DOYE, Paul Frederick; s of Herbert Walter Charles Doye (d 1946), and Hilda Katie Louise Edwards; *b* 6 July 1940; *Educ* Hassenbrook Sch Essex; *m* 15 Sept 1962, Brenda Marion Kelway, da of Henry Tongeman (d 1975), of Stanford-le-Hope, Essex; 3 s (Stephen b 1964, Philip b 1967, Jonathan b 1971), 1 da (Ruth b 1966); *Career* dir: Keyser Ullmann Ltd 1969-81, Petrocon Gp plc 1972-88, Lonrho plc 1979-83, Charterhouse Bank Ltd 1980-; *Recreations* reading, walking, family; *Style*— Paul F Doye, Esq; 22 Monkhams Drive, Woodford Green, Essex (☎ 01 505 1418); Charterhouse Bank Ltd, 1 Paternoster Row, London EC4 (☎ 01 248 4000)

DOYLE, (Frederick) Bernard; s of James Hopkinson Doyle, and Hilda Mary nee Spotsworth; *b* 17 July 1940; *Educ* Manchester Univ, Harvard Business Sch (MBA); *m* Ann, *née* Weston; 2 s (Stephen Francis, Andrew John), 1 da (Elizabeth Ann); *Career* chartered engr; former mgmnt conslt: London, Brussels, USA; with Booker McConnell 1973-81 (dir 1979, chm engrg div to 1981); chief exec SDP 1981-83; chief exec Welsh Water Authy 1983-87; ops-dir FJC Lilley plc 1987, dir public sector ops MSL Int (UK) Ltd 1988-; CBIM, FICE, FIWES, FRSA; *Recreations* reading, theatre, walking, sailing; *Style*— Bernard Doyle, Esq; 15 Oldfield Place, Hotwells, Bristol B58 4QJ

DOYLE, Hon Mrs (Katharine Alexandra); *née* McClintock-Bunbury; eldest da of 4 Baron Rathdonnell (d 1959), and Pamela, *née* Drew; *b* 19 Feb 1940; *m* 1960, James Joseph Doyle, s of Timothy Doyle, of Tobinstown, Co Carlow; *Style*— The Hon Mrs Doyle; Coole Stables, Rathvilly, Co Carlow

DOYLE, Prof William; s of Stanley Joseph Doyle (d 1973), of Scarborough, Yorks, and Mary ALice, *née* Bielby; *b* 4 Mar 1942; *Educ* Bridlington Sch, Oriel Coll Oxford (BA, MA, DPhil); *m* 2 Aug 1968, Christine, da of William Joseph Thomas (d 1969), of Aberdare, Glam; *Career* sr lectr in history Univ of York 1978-81 (asst lectr 1967-69, lectr 1969-78), prof mod history Univ of Nottingham 1981-85, prof of history Univ of Bristol 1986-; visiting prof: Columbia S Carolina 1969-70, Bordeaux 1976, Paris 1988; Doctor Honoris Causa Universite de Bordeaux III France; FRHistS; *Books* The Parlement of Bordeaux and the End of the Old Regime 1771-90 (1974), The Old European Order 1660-1800 (1978), Origins of the French Revolution (1980), The Ancien Regime (1986), The Oxford History of the French Revolution (1989); *Recreations* books, decorating, travelling about; *Clubs* Athenaeum, United Oxford and Cambridge; *Style*— Prof W Doyle; 2 Beaufort East, Bath, Avon BA1 6QD (☎ 0225 314341); Dept of Hist, Univ of Bristol, 13 Woodland Rd, Bristol BS8 1TB (☎ 0272 303429)

DOYLE, Dr William P (Bill); s of James Wendal Doyle (d 1967), and Lillian Irene, (*née* Kime); *b* 15 Feb 1932; *Educ* Seattle Univ (BSc), Oregon State Univ (PhD); *m* 1957, Judith Ann, da of William Gosha (d 1943); 2 s (Paul, Loren), 1 da (Nora); *Career* md Texaco Ltd 1981-, pres: Texaco N Sea UK Co, UK Offshore Operators Assoc 1985; *Recreations* music, walking; *Style*— Dr Bill Doyle; 1 Knightsbridge Green, London SW1 (☎ 01 584 5000, telex 916921)

DOYNE, Capt Patrick Robert; s of Col Robert Harry Doyne (d 1965), of Somerset, and Verena Mary Doyne, *née* Seymour (d 1979); *b* 9 Oct 1936; *Educ* Eton; *m* 7 Dec 1963, Sarah Caroline, da of Brig James Erskine Stirling, DSO, DL (d 1968), of Inverness-shire; 1 s (Timothy b 1966), 1 da (Lucinda b 1964); *Career* Capt Royal Green Jackets 1965-69, served in Kenya, Malaya, Germany, Cyprus, USA; broker Lloyds 1969-74; food indust 1974-83; sec Ski Club of GB 1983-86; Lloyds underwriter 1968-; High Sheriff Warwickshire 1987; *Recreations* country sports, cricket; *Clubs* Boodle's, Pratt's, MCC; *Style—* Capt P R Doyne, Esq; Woodlands, Idlicote, Shipston-on-Stour, Warwickshire CV36 5DT (☎ 0608 61594)

DRABBLE, Margaret; da of His Honour John Frederick Drabble, QC (d 1982), by his w Kathleen Bloor; *b* 5 June 1939; *Educ* The Mount Sch York, Newnham Coll Cambridge; *m* 1, 1960 (m dis 1975), Clive Walter Swift; 2 s, 1 da; m 2, 1982, Michael Holroyd, CBE (*qv*); *Career* author of many books; dep chm National Book League; Hon DLitt Sheffield; *Style—* Ms Margaret Drabble; c/o A D Peters, 10 Buckingham St, London WC2

DRABBLE, Phil Percey Cooper; s of Dr Edward Percy Drabble, and Madeline Ursula, *née* Steele; *b* 14 May 1914; *Educ* Bromsgrove, London Univ; *m* 6 Sept 1939, Jessie Constance, da of George Thomas; *Career* engrg indust 1958-61, dir George Salter & Co Ltd (spring balance makers); author and broadcaster 1961-; best known for One Man and His Dog 1975-; contrib: Country Times, Country, Derbyshire Life, Trust, Birmingham Evening Mail; lectr Foyles Lecture Agency 1964-; professional naturalisst managing a wildlife reserve of 90 acres (specialising in badgers and herons); author of over 20 books on rural and naturalist topics; *Recreations* natural history; *Style—* Phil Drabble, Esq; Goat Lodge, Abbots Bromley, Rugeley WS15 3EP Staffs (☎ 0283 840 345)

DRACUP, Michael Henry Empsall; s of George Robinson Dracup, of Ilkley; *b* 9 Oct 1930; *Educ* Denston Coll; *m* 1957, Jean Shirley, da of Albert Knight (d 1974); 3 children; *Career* dir: Robinson & Peel Ltd 1957-77, Colonial Combing Co (Lana) Ltd 1961-77, Sir James Hill & Son Ltd 1967-77 (md 1968-77), Woolcombers Mutual (vice-chm 1972-77), Hallcroft Estate Co 1971-; dir and chief exec Lister & Co plc 1977-; chm: Woolcombers Employers' Fedn 1969-71, Br Wool Confedn 1973-75; *Recreations* golf; *Clubs* Bradford Golf, Otley RUFC; *Style—* Michael Dracup, Esq; Beech House, 78 Cleasby Rd, Menston, nr Ilkley (☎ 0943 72552); Lister & Co plc, Manningham Mills, Bradford, Yorks

DRAIN, Geoffrey Ayrton; CBE (1981), JP (1966); s of Charles Henry Herbert Drain, MBE, of Lee-on-Solent, Hants; *b* 26 Nov 1918; *Educ* Skipton GS, QMC London (BA, LLB); *m* 1950 (m dis 1959), Dredagh Joan Rafferty; 1 s; *Career* served as Staff Capt Paiforce and India; gen sec NALGO 1973-83 (dep gen sec 1958-73); dir: The Bank of England 1978-86; Collins-Wilde plc 1985; chm Home Bridging plc 1986-, visiting prof Imperial Coll London 1983-88, dep chm Euro Movement 1982- memb: Employment Appeal Tbnl 1982-, Engrg Cncl 1982-84; tres Vol Centre 1983-; tstee Community Projects Fndn 1974-; fell and govr QMC London 1980-; *Recreations* cricket, football, walking, birdwatching, bridge; *Clubs* Reform, MCC; *Style—* Geoffrey Drain, Esq, CBE, JP; Flat 3, Centre Heights, Swiss Cottage, London NW3 6JG (☎ 01 722 2081)

DRAKE; *see*: Rivett-Drake

DRAKE, Sir (Arthur) Eric (Courtney); CBE (1952), DL (Hants 1983); s of Dr (Arthur William) Courtney Drake (d 1964); *b* 29 Nov 1910; *Educ* Shrewsbury, Pembroke Coll Cambridge (hon fell); *m* 1, 1935, Rosemary, da of late P L Moore, of Swansea; 2 da; m 2, 1950, Margaret Elizabeth, da of late Ralph Goodbarne Wilson, of Walford Court, Ross-on-Wye, Herefordshire; 2 s; *Career* md Br Petroleum Co Ltd 1958 (chm 1969-75), dep chm P & O 1976-81, pres cncl Chamber of Shipping in UK 1964; life memb of court City Univ 1969; hon petroleum advsr Br Army 1971-; elder brother Trinity House 1975-; chm Mary Rose Trust 1979-83; one of HM Lieutenants for City of London; Hon DSc Cranfield 1971; kt 1970; *Recreations* sailing (owner ketch 'Shimran'), shooting; *Clubs* Royal Yacht Sqdn, Leander; *Style—* Sir Eric Drake, CBE, DL; The Old Rectory, Cheriton, nr Alresford, Hants (☎ 096 279 334)

DRAKE, Fabia; OBE (1987); da of late Francis Drake McGlinchy, of Cavendish Rd, Herne Bay, Kent, and Annie, *née* Dalton (d 1939); *b* 20 Jan 1904; *Educ* St Martin-in-the-Fields HS London, Camposenea Finishing Sch Fleury Meudon France, ADA (currently RADA) London; *m* 14 Dec 1938, Judge Maxwell Turner (d 1960), s of Augustus Turner; 1 da (Deirdre Hastings Fabia Gabrielle b 1940); *Career* Shakespearian actress Stratford-upon-Avon, Warwickwhire 1930-33; London performances incl plays by: John Galsworthy, Aldous Huxley, St John Ervine; film and TV appearances incl: The Jewel in the Crown (Mable Layton) 1984, A Room with a View (Catherine Alan) 1985, Valmont (Rosemonde) 1989; *Books* Blind Fortune - (autobiography, forward by Sir Laurence Olivier); *Style—* Miss Fabia Drake, OBE; 103 Cranmer Court, Chelsea, London SW3 3HJ (☎ 01 581 1798); c/o Julian Belfrage Associates, 68 St. James Street, London SW1 (☎ 01 491 4400)

DRAKE, (John) Gair; s of John Nutter Drake (d 1980), and Anne, *née* Waddington (d 1988); *b* 11 July 1930; *Educ* Univ Coll Sch, The Queen's Coll Oxford (MA); *m* 1957, Jean Pamela, da of William George Bishop, of Sussex; 1 s (Paul), 1 da (Susan); *Career* chief registrar and chief accountant Bank of England 1983; *Recreations* sport, family; *Clubs* Chaldon CC; *Style—* Gair Drake, Esq; Bank of England, New Change, London EC4M 9AA (☎ 01 601 4444)

DRAKE, Sir James; CBE (1962); s of James Drake (d 1945), of Altham, Lancs and Ellen, *née* Hague; *b* 27 July 1907; *Educ* Accrington GS, Manchester Univ (BSc); *m* 1937, Kathleen Shaw, da of late Richard S Crossley, JP, of Accrington; 2 da; *Career* borough engr and surveyor Blackpool Co Borough 1938-45, county surveyor and bridgemaster Lancs CC 1945-72; dir Leonard Fairclough Ltd (now AMEC) 1972-77; Hon DSC, FEng, FICE, PPInstHTE; kt 1973; *Recreations* golf; *Clubs* Royal Lytham and St Anne's Golf; *Style—* Sir James Drake, CBE; 11 Clifton Court, 297 Clifton Drive South, St Annes-on-Sea, Lancs (☎ 0253 721635)

DRAKE, Hon Mr Justice; Hon Sir (Frederick) Maurice Drake; DFC (1944); s of Walter Charles Drake (d 1980), of Harpenden; *b* 15 Feb 1923; *Educ* St George's Sch Harpenden, Exeter Coll Oxford; *m* 1954, Alison May, da of William Duncan Waterfall, CB (d 1970), of Harpenden; 2 s, 3 da; *Career* served WWII, Flt Lt RAF; barr Lincoln's Inn 1950, bencher 1976, QC 1968, dep chm Beds QS 1966-71, rec Crown Ct 1972-78, standing sr counsel to Royal Coll of Physicians 1972-78, judge of the High Court (Queen's Bench Div) 1978-, presiding judge Midland and Oxford Circuit 1979-83; memb of Parole Board 1984-6, vice-chm 1985-6; hon alderman St Albans Dist Council; kt 1978; *Recreations* music, opera, gardening; *Style—* The Hon Mr Justice Drake, DFC; Royal Courts of Justice, Strand, London WC2; The White House, West Common Way, Harpenden, Herts (☎ 058 27 2329)

DRAKE, Hon Mrs Rosemary Etheldreda; *née* Adderley; eldest da of 6 Baron Norton (d 1961 as a result of a fall from his horse), and Elizabeth, *née* Birkbeck (d 1952); *b* 17 Oct 1913; *m* 29 Sept 1949, Rev John Paul Drake, s of Canon Frederick William Drake (d 1930), of Eastchurch Rectory, Isle of Sheppey; 1 s (Simon b 1956), 1 da (Catherine b 1950); *Career* in charge of physiotherapy dept Westminster Hosp 1947-50; memb Chartered Soc Physiotherapy; *Style—* The Hon Mrs Drake; 3 The Cloisters, Welwyn Garden City, Herts AL8 6DU (☎ 0707 325379)

DRAKE-BROCKMAN, Hon Sir Thomas Charles; DFC (1944); s of Robert J Drake-Brockman; *b* 15 May 1919; *Educ* Guildford GS; *m* 1, May 1942 (m dis), Edith Sykes; 1 s, 4 da; m 2, 1972, Mary McGinnity; *Career* 10 Light Horse Regt (CMF) 1938-40; RAF 1941-45 serv Aust Europe MEast Malta; farmer 1938-40, exec memb Farmers Union of W Aust 1952-58 (wool section pres 1955-58), vice-pres Aust Wool and Meat Prodrs Fedn 1957-58; former Aust min for Air, min for Admin Servs and min for Aboriginal Affrs; former dep pres of Senate; senator (Country Pty) for W Aust 1958-78, ldr Nat Country Pty in Senate 1969-75, actg ldr of govt in Senate on several occasions; gen pres Nat Country Party (WA) Inc 1978-81, fed pres Nat Country Party of Aust 1978-81; state pres Australia-Britain Soc 1982-; kt 1979; *Style—* The Hon Sir Thomas Drake-Brockman, DFC; 80 Basildon Rd, Lesmurdie, WA 6076, Australia

DRAPER, Alan Gregory; s of William Gregory Draper (d 1973), of Leeds, Yorkshire, and Ada Gertrude Davies (d 1982); *b* 11 June 1926; *Educ* Leeds GS, The Queen's Coll Oxford (MA); *m* 1, 1953 (m dis), Muriel, da of Arthur Tremlett Cuss (d 1974); 3 s (Nicholas b 1955, Timothy b 1957, Jeremy b 1961), 1 da (Pascale b 1966); m 2, 1977, Jacqueline, da of Leandre Gubel; *Career* Sub Lt RNVR 1945-47, civil servant 1950-85; first sec UK Delegation to NATO 1964-66, asst sec 1966-84 (counsellor 1974-77), chm NATO budget ctees 1977-81; dir gen Personnel Royal Ordnance 1982-84, training 1985; hon sr lecturer RMCS Shrivenham; *Recreations* reading, music, amateur dramatics, travel, golf; *Style—* Alan Draper, Esq; c/o RMCS Shrivenham (☎ 0973 782551, ext 2492 or 2555)

DRAPER, Donald Alfred James; DFC (1944), AE (1952), JP (1953), DL (1967); s of Alfred Burns Draper (d 1973), and Janet Meikle, *née* Fairley (d 1971); *b* 10 April 1919; *Educ* Uppingham; *m* 1939, Eglantine Mary, da of John Drummond Walker, OBE (d 1952); 2 s (John, Graeme), 2 da (Priscilla, Elizabeth); *Career* TA 1937-40; RAF 1940-61 served: Norway, France, Belgium, Holland, Germany; consult in insolvency; mayor of Lewisham 1953-54; memb ct of common cncl City of London 1955-58; chm Ranyard Home 1960-81; pres Lewisham Branch RAFA; Liveryman Co of Carmen; FCA, ACIS, FIPA; *Recreations* travel; *Clubs* City Livery, RAF; *Style—* Donald Draper, Esq, DFC, AE, JP, DL; 52 Belmont Hill, London SE13 5DN (☎ 01 852 4160);

DRAPER, Gerald Carter; OBE (1974); s of Alfred Henderson Draper (d 1962), and Mona Violanta, *née* Johnson (d 1982); *b* 24 Nov 1926; *Educ* Avoca Sch, Trinity Coll Dublin (MA); *m* 1951, Winifred Lilian, *née* Howe; 1 s (Alan), 3 da (Valerie, Hilary, Shirley); *Career* dir commercial ops Br Airways 1978-82, md BA Intercontinental Servs Div May-Aug 1982; dir: Br Airways Associated Cos 1972-82, Br Intercontinental Hotels Ltd 1976-82; chm Br Airtours Ltd 1978-82; ret from BA bd 1982; chm Silver Wing Surface Arrangements Ltd 1971-82; dep chm Tst Houses Forte Travel Ltd 1974-82; ALTA Ltd 1977-82; chm: govt advsy ctee on Advertising 1978-83, Draper Assocs Ltd 1983-87; govr Coll of Air Training 1983-84; memb bd Communications Strategy Ltd 1983-86; memb: Marketors Livery Co, bd AGB (TRI) Ltd 1983-85, Hoverspeed UK Ltd 1984-86; Centre for Airline and Travel Marketing Ltd; chm Outdoor Advertising Assoc of Gt Britain 1985-; Sr Warden Worshipful Co of Marketors; FInstM, FRSA; *Recreations* shooting, golf, fishing; *Clubs* Burhill Golf, City Livery; *Style—* Gerald Draper, Esq, OBE; Old Chestnut, Onslow Rd, Burwood Park, Walton-on-Thames, Surrey (☎ 0932 228612; office: 01 935 4426); 13B La Frenaie, Cogolin, Var, France

DRAPER, Prof Col Gerald Irving Anthony Dare; OBE (1965); s of Harold Irving Draper (d 1930); *b* 30 May 1914; *Educ* privately, King's Coll London (LLB, LLM); *m* 1951, Julia Jean, da of Capt Gordon Reinhold Bald, RN (d 1956); *Career* slr 1936-41; served Irish Gds 1941-44, N Africa and NW Europe; office of the Judge Advocate Gen 1944-48, mil prosecutor (War Crimes Tribunals) Germany 1945-49, barr Inner Temple 1946, directorate of Army Legal Staff 1948-56, ret as Col 1956; lectr and reader in Law: London Univ 1956-67, Sussex Univ 1967-79 (prof of law 1976-79, emeritus 1980-); titular prof Inst of Int Humanitarian Law San Remo Italy; memb: faculty of Judge Advocate Gen Mil Law Sch of the US Army 1968, Medical-Juridical Cmmn of Monaco; chm Industl Tribunals 1966-86; memb editorial bd Br Year Book of Int Law 1980; fell NATO 1958; *Recreations* the study of human endeavour; *Clubs* Beefsteak; *Style—* Prof Col Gerald Draper, OBE; 2 Hare Court, Temple, London EC4 (☎ 01 583 1770); 16 Southover High St, Lewes, Sussex (☎ 0273 2387)

DRAPER, Richard Donald; s of Richard Jack, of Trefeinon Farm, Talgarth, Brecon, Powys, and Margaret Alice, *née* Snook; *b* 14 Sept 1934; *Educ* Sherborne ; *m* 23 April 1959, Nicole, da of Prof Lucien Lefort (d 1979), of Cours Vitton, Lyons, France; 1 s (Nicolas b 1960), 1 da (Frances b 1962); *Career* chm and md R J Draper and Co Ltd Glastonbury Somerset; *Recreations* golf, cricket, rugby football; *Style—* Richard Draper, Esq; The Manor House, E Horrington, Wells, Somerset BA5 3EA (☎ 0749 72512); R J Draper & Co Ltd, PO Box 3, Chilkwell St, Glastonbury, Somerset BA6 8YA (☎ 0458 31420, telex 449427)

DRAPER, Prof Ronald Philip; s of Albert William Draper, and Elsie, *née* Carlton; *b* 3 Oct 1928; *Educ* Nottingham Boys HS, Nottingham Univ (BA, PhD); *m* 19 June 1950, Irene Margaret; 3 da (Anne Elizabeth b 1957, Isobel Frances b 1959, Sophia Mildred b 1964); *Career* Pilot Officer/Flying Offr RAF 1953-55; lectr in english Adelaide Univ 1955-56; Leicester Univ: asst lectr 1968-73, lectr 1958-68, sr lectr 1968-73; Aberdeen Univ: prof of english 1973-, reguis Chalmers prof of english 1987-; *Books* DH Lawrence (1964), DH Lawrence The Critical Heritage (ed 1970), Hardy the Tragic Novels (ed 1975) George Eliot 'The Mill on the Floss' and 'Silas Marner' (ed 1978), Tragedy Developments in Criticism (ed 1980), Lyric Tragedy (1985), Shakespeare: 'The Winter's Tale' Text and Performance (1985), DH Lawrence 'Sons and Lovers' (1986), Shakespeare's Twelfth Night (1988), The Literature of Region and Nation (ed 1988); *dramatic scripts* The Canker and the Rose (with PAW Collins, Mermaid theatre, 1964), DHL A Portrait of DH Lawrence (with Richard Hoggart, Nottingham Playhouse 1967, New End Theatre, Hampstead 1978, BBC2 TV, 1980); *Recreations* reading, walking, listening to music; *Style—* Prof Ronald Draper; 50 Queen's Road, Aberdeen

AB1 6YE (☎ 0224 318 735; University of Aberdeen, Taylor Building, King's college, Old Aberdeen AB9 2UB (☎ 0224 272 625)

DRAYCOTT, Douglas Patrick; QC (1965); s of George Draycott, and Mary Ann, *née* Burke; *b* 28 August 1918; *Educ* Wolstanton GS, Oriel Coll Oxford (MA) ; *m* 1, (m dis 1974), Elizabeth Victoria, da of F H Hall; 2 s (Philip b 1947, Simon b 1950), 3 da (Julia b 1954, Charlotte b 1957, Emma b 1961); m 2, 2 March 1979, Margaret Jean Brunton, da of Andrew Watson Speed; *Career* Royal Tank Regt Europe 1939-46; Liaison Offr to War Cabinet (Historical Section); barr Middle Temple 1950, Master of the Bench 1972, leader Midland and Oxford circuit 1979-83; *Recreations* inland waterways narrow boats; *Style—* Douglas P Draycott, Esq, QC; 11 Sir Harry's Rd, Edgbaston, Birmingham B15 2UY (☎ 021 440 1050); 4 Kings Bench Walk, London EC4Y 7DL (☎ 01 353 3581); 5 Fountain Court, Birmingham B4 6DR (☎ 021 236 5771)

DRAYCOTT, Gerald Arthur; s of late Arthur Henry Seely Draycott, and late Maud Mary Draycott; *b* 25 Oct 1911; *Educ* King Edwards Sch Stratford-on-Avon; *m* 1, Phyllis Moyra, da of late Ralph Evans, of Norfolk; 2 s (Richard, Hugh), 1 da (Lucy); *Career* Sqdn Ldr RAF 1939-46, (despatches); barr Middle Temple, practiced SE Circuit, dep rec of Bury St Edmunds 1966, rec Crown Ct 1972-86; chm: Local Appeal Tbnl, Med Appeal Tbnl, Vaccine Damage Tbnl, Rent Assessment & Nat Insur ctees; *Recreations* gardening; *Clubs* Norfolk Co; *Style—* Gerald A Draycott; Nethergate House, Saxlingham Nethergate, Norwich NR15 1PB (☎ 0603 623186); Octagon House, Colegate, Norwich

DRAYSON, Brig Harold Percy; CBE (1958); s of Col Alfred Percy Drayson (d 1953), OBE, TD, DL; *b* 19 Mar 1905; *Educ* Wellington, RMA Woolwich, St John's Coll Cambridge; *m* 1945, Renée Lucie Jeanne, da of Robert Lecoq capitaine de Vaisseau French Navy (d 1963); 1 step s; *Career* 2 Lt RE 1925, served 1939-45 War (NW Europe), Lt-Col 1949, dir RE Equipment Miny of Supply 1953-56, Brig 1956, dir of engineer stores war office 1956-58, ret 1958; *Recreations* photography, gardening; *Clubs* Royal Torbay Yacht, Army and Navy; *Style—* Brig Harold Drayson, CBE; 7 Wellswood Park, Torquay, Devon TQ1 2QB (☎ 0803 212855)

DRAYSON, Robert Quested; DSC (1943); s of Frederick Louis Drayson (d 1963), of Kent, and Elsie Mabel Drayson, *née* West (d 1971); *b* 5 June 1919; *Educ* St Lawrence Coll Ramsgate, Downing Coll Cambridge (BA, MA); *m* 1943, Rachel, da of Stephen Spencer Jenkyns (d 1956); 1 s (Nicholas), 2 da (Gillian, Elizabeth); *Career* RNVR 1939-46; Lt in cmd HM Motor Torpedo Boats; asst master & housemaster St Lawrence Coll 1947-50, asst master Felsted Sch 1950-55; headmaster: Reed's Sch Cobham 1955-63, Stowe Sch 1964-79; res lay chaplain to Bishop of Norwich 1979-84; memb HMC Ctee 1973-75; chm of Govrs Riddlesworth Hall Sch 1980-84, govr: Parkside 1958-63, Bilton Grange 1966-79, Beachborough 1965-79, Beechwood Park 1967-79, Monkton Combe Sch 1976-85, Felixstowe Coll 1981-84, St Lawrence Coll 1976-; memb: gen cncl S American Missionary Soc (chm selection Ctee 1980-), Allied Schs Cncl 1980-, cncl McAlpine Educn Endowments Ltd 1982-, cncl Martyrs' Meml C of E Tst 1983-; FRSA; *Recreations* hockey (Cambridge Blue 1946-47), Kent XI (capt 1947-56, Final Eng trial 1950), golf, walking; *Style—* Robert Drayson Esq; Three Gables, Linkhill, Sandhurst, Cranbrook, Kent TN18 5PQ (☎ Sandhurst 447)

DRAYSON, Hon Mrs Shirley Joan Bailey; granted title, rank and precedence of a Baron's da; 2 da of Hon Herbert Crawshay Bailey, JP (d 1936); sis of 4 Baron Glanusk; *b* 28 April 1912; *m* 31 Jan 1946, George Dupin Drayson (d 1969); 1 s (Charles b 1947); *Style—* The Hon Mrs Drayson; Rectory Cottage, Rectory Lane, Ashington, W Sussex

DREVERMAN, Hon Mrs; Sarah Jane Moira; *née* Nivison; yr da of 3 Baron Glendyne; *b* 1 May 1957; *m* 21 April 1979, Ian Dreverman, eldest s of A H Dreverman, of Gordon, NSW, Australia; *Style—* Hon Mrs Dreverman; Hurdcott, Barford St Martin, Salisbury, Wilts

DREW, Sir Arthur Charles Walter; KCB (1964), (CB 1958, JP (Richmond 1963 & 1973-82)) 1986; er s of Arthur Drew (d 1920), of Mexico City, by his w Louisa, da of Carl Schulte Uemmingen, of Bochum, Germany; *b* 2 Sept 1912; *Educ* Christ's Hosp, King's Coll Cambridge; *m* 9 Jan 1943, Rachel Anna, er da of Guy William Lambert, CB, sometime asst under-sec state War; 1 s, 3 da; *Career* private under-sec: WO 1963-64, Army; MOD 1964-68; memb Admty, Army and Air Force Bds 1968-72; tstee: Natural History Museum 1972-82, Br Museum 1973-85; chm: Standing Cmmn Museums and Galleries 1978-85 (memb 1973-85), Ancient Monuments Bd England 1978-86, QMC London 1982-; memb: cncl Nat Tst 1974-84, Historic Bldgs Cncl 1982-84; tstee: Imperial War Museum 1973-84, RAF Museum 1976, Nat Army Museum 1981-; pres Museums Assoc 1984, re-elected 1985, chm Cncl of Voluntary Welfare Work 1979; Master Drapers Co 1977-78; FMA (hon) 1986; *Style—* Sir Arthur Drew, KCB, JP; 2 Branstone Rd, Kew, Surrey TW9 3LB (☎ 01 940 1210)

DREW, Dan Hamilton; s of Daniel Edward Drew (d 1974), of Petworth, Sussex, and Rena Frayer, *née* Hamilton; *b* 31 Jan 1938; *Educ* Stubbington House Tonbridge; *m* 1, 1963, Carol Ann (m dis), da of Dr Robert Gibson Miller, of Helston, Cornwall; 1 s (Angus b 1967), 1 da (Xanthe b 1966); m 2, 1976, Beverley, da of Alan Lestor Roberts (d 1981), of Graffham, Sussex; 1 da (Frances b 1979); *Career* CA; gp fin dir Interlink Express plc 1982-; *Recreations* shooting, fishing; *Style—* Dan H Drew, Esq; Lower Poswick, Whitbourne, Worcester WR6 5SS (☎ 0886 21275); Unit 21, Hartlebury Trading Estate, Kidderminster DY10 4JB (☎ 0299 250697, fax 0299 251174; car telephone 0836 516146)

DREW, Dorothy Joan; da of Francis Marshall Gant (d 1956), of Reading, Berkshire, and Wilhelmina Frederica, *née* Dunster (d 1982); *b* 31 Mar 1938; *Educ* The Sch of St Helen and St Katharine, London Univ (External Student, LLB); *m* 12 Dec 1959, Patrick Keith, s of Alec Charles Drew (d 1967), of Reading, Berks; 2 s (Dean Patrick b 1961, Jon Philip Francis b 1967), 1 da (Jane Caroline b 1964); *Career* called to the Bar Grays Inn 1981, tutor Cncl of Legal Educn 1982-1985, chm Social Security Appeal Tribunals sitting at Central London 1986-; magristrate Reading Bench 1975, memb Kensington Social Security Appeal Tribunal 1984-86; memb: Gray's Inn 1979; *Recreations* music, theatre, gardening, tennis; *Style—* Mrs Dorothy Drew; Handpost, Swallowfield, Reading, Berks RG7 1QY; 13 Draycott Ave, London SW3

DREW, Jane Beverly; *b* 24 Mar 1911; *Educ* Croydon; *m* 1; 2 da; m 2, 1942, Edwin Maxwell Fry; *Career* architect; ptnr Fry Drew & Ptnrs 1946-; author; FRIBA; *Style—* Ms Jane Drew; West Lodge, Cotherstone, Barnard Castle, Co Durham DH12 9PF (☎ Teesdale 50217)

DREW, Peter Leonard; s of Leonard George Drew (d 1942); *b* 28 Feb 1943; *Educ* Kings Coll Wimbledon; *m* 1972, Angela Margaret, *née* Naylor; 2 da (Anneli b 1976, Tamsin b 1979); *Career* md Centurion Leisure Ltd trading as Select Holidays (part of International Leisure Group plc); chm OSL Channel Islands Travel Service Ltd; *Recreations* golf; *Style—* Peter Drew, Esq; Barwick House, Barwick, nr Ware, Herts; Centurion House, Bircherley Street, Hertford SG14 1BH (☎ 0992 57311, telex 817848)

DREW, Lt-Gen Sir (William) Robert (Macfarlane); KCB (1965, CB 1962), CBE (1952, OBE 1940); s of William Hughes Drew of NSW Australia (d 1936); *b* 4 Oct 1907; *Educ* Sydney GS, Sydney Univ; *m* 1934, Dorothy Merle, da of Alfred Edwin Dakingsmith, of NSW Australia; 1 s, 1 da (decd); *Career* Lt-Gen, Medical Offr 1931-69, Cmdt Royal Army Medical Coll 1960-63, dir Medical Servs BOAR 1963-65, dir-gen Medical Servs 1965-69, dep dir Br Postgraduate Medical Fedn London Univ 1970-78; company dir; chllr Royal Blind Soc of NSW; KStJ (1978, CStJ 1965); Commander Order of Al-Rafidain (Iraq) 1952; *see Debrett's Handbook of Australia and New Zealand for further details*; *Recreations* swimming, travel; *Clubs* Army and Navy, Australian (Sydney), Royal Sydney Golf; *Style—* Lt-Gen Sir Robert Drew, KCB, CBE; 5b and 5c Wakefield Apartments, 26-28 Etham Avenue, Darling Point 2027, Australia (☎ 02 328 1964)

DREWE, (Adrian) Francis; JP (1953); s of Sir Cedric Drewe, KCVO (1953), MP (1924) (d 1971), of Honiton, Devon, and Beatrice Foster Newington (d 1982); *b* 11 August 1919; *Educ* Eton, Trinity Cambridge; *m* 27 Mar 1942, Joan Elizabeth, da of Paul Ernest Negretti (d 1953), of Lodsworth, Sussex; 1 s (Adrian b 1945), 3 da (Valerie b 1943, Mary-Anne b 1948, Diana b 1952); *Career* serv WWII Capt 1940-46, Royal Engineers Bomb Disposal UK; ret Civil Engineer, JP 1953, formerly dir of various companies; *Recreations* sailing, genealogy; *Clubs* Cruising Association; *Style—* Francis Drewe, Esq; Oakover, Ticehurst, East Sussex TN5 7DL (☎ 0580 200 240)

DREWITT, Brian; s of Albert Edward Drewitt, and Dorothy Aida Tyler, *née* Cullum; *b* 9 Dec 1940; *Educ* St Olaves GS London, Gonville and Caius Coll Cambridge (MA); *m* 8 Feb 1964, (m dis 1984); 2 da (Alison Sarah b 1965, Emma Louise b 1967); *Career* cmmd RAF 1962-81, diverse appts incl operational helicopter pilot Malaya 1965-68 engrg mgnt project offr (avionics) for Tornado aircraft in MOD (procurement exec) 1972-76, NATO MRCA mgnt agency Munich 1976-80; ret Sqdn Ldr 1981; Messerschmitt-Bölkow-Blohm GmbH (MBB) Munich (currently sales mangr helicopter Division); MRAeS; CEng; *Recreations* squash, skiing, music; *Clubs* RAF; *Style—* Brian Drewitt, Esq; MBB Helicopter Group, PO Box 801140, D-8000 Munich, West Germany (fax 010 4989 6000 8720)

DREWITT, Timothy Paul Geoffrey; s of Lt-Col Geoffrey Bernard Drewitt, TD, DL, FRIBA, AA Dip (d 1987), and Elma Alberta Joan, *née* Thomas; *b* 16 May 1943; *Educ* Blundells Sch Devon, The Architectural Assoc, Sch of Architecture (AA Dip); *m* 19 Dec 1970, Marie Josée (architect), da of Dr Campbell Davoine (d 1964), of Mauritius; 1 s (Campbell b 21 May 1973), 1 da (Zoe b 27 April 1972); *Career* architect: principal in own practice with wife 1967-; former projects incl: Burne House Telephone Exchange Marylebone 1970, The Round House Chalk Farm 1985-87; present projects: New archive and reading room GT Smith St Library Westminster 1987-, restoration of Prideaux Place (the house dates from Elizabeth I) Padstow Cornwall 1987-; *Recreations* shooting, sailing, music; *Clubs* Royal Ocean Racing, St James's Place; *Style—* Timothy Drewitt, Esq; 28 Upper Park Rd, London NW3 (☎ 01 586 0671)

DREWRY, Dr David John; s of Norman Tidman Drewry (d 1984), of Grimsby Lincs, and Mary Edwina, *née* Wray; *b* 22 Sept 1947; *Educ* Havelock Sch Grimsby, QMC London (BSc), Emmanuel Coll Cambridge (PhD); *m* 10 July 1972, Gillian Elizabeth, da of Clifford Francis Holbrook (d 1978); *Career* Cambridge Univ: Sir Henry Strakosh fell 1972, sr asst in res 1978-83, asst dir of res 1983, dir Scott Polar Res Inst, dir Br Antartic Survey 1987-; Polar Medal 1986; memb Inst Glaciological Soc 1969, FRGS 1972; US Antarctic Serv Medal 1979; *Books* Antarctica: Glaciological and Geophysical Folio (1983), Glacial Geologic Processes; *Recreations* music, walking, gastronomy; *Style—* Dr David Drewry; British Antarctic Survey, High Cross, Madingley Rd, Cambridge CB3 0ET (☎ 0223 61188, fax 0223 62616)

DREXEL, Hon Mrs (Mildred Sophia) Noreen Stonor; yr da of 5 Baron Camoys (d 1968), by his w Mildred (d 1961), da of late William Watts Sherman, of New York and Rhode Is; *b* 1922; *m* 3 Feb 1941, John R Drexel III, only s of late John R Drexel, of New York and Philadelphia; 1 s, 2 da; *Style—* The Hon Mrs Drexel; Stonor Lodge, Bellevue Ave, Newport, Rhode Island, USA

DREYER, Cdr Christopher William Stuart; DSO (1943), DSC (1940); s of Maj-Gen John Tuthill Dreyer, CB, DSO (d 1959), of Orchard Hill, Liss, Hampshire, and Penelope Aylmer, *née* Holme (d 1973); gf Dr John L E Dreyer who was pres Royal Astronomical Soc, PhD (Copenhagen), DSc (Belfast), MA (Oxon), dir Armagh Observatory 1878-1916; *b* 18 June 1918; *Educ* RNC Dartmouth; *m* 31 July 1940, Olivia Constance Isabel (JP Faringdon 1962, chm Wantage and Faringdon Magistrates 1983-86), da of Sir Leo Francis Page, of Newton House, Faringdon, Berks; 1 s (William b 1947), 5 da (Veronica b 1942, Jane b 1943, Rachel b 1949, Belinda b 1955, Emma b 1959; *Career* Naval Offr, served mainly in motor torpedo boats, torpedo specialist 1942, Cdr 1950, cdr HMS Ark Royal 1953-55, invalided from RN 1955, joined Vosper Ltd Warshipbuilders Portsmouth 1956 (dir 1961), chm Vosper Thornycroft Singapore 1966-71 (ret 1976); pres Coastal Forces Veterans Assoc 1987; Chev Order of the Sword (Sweden) 1954; *Recreations* cricket, natural history; *Style—* Cdr Christopher Dreyer, DSO, DSC; Newton Lodge, Faringdon, Oxfordshire (☎ 036 787 204)

DREYER, Adm Sir Desmond Parry; GCB (1967, KCB 1963, CB 1960), CBE (1957), DSC (1940), JP (Hants 1968), DL (Hants 1985); s of Adm Sir Frederic Charles Dreyer, GBE, KCB (d 1956), of Winchester, by his w Una Maria, da of Rev J T Hallett; *b* 6 April 1910; *Educ* RNC Dartmouth; *m* 1, 1934, Elisabeth (d 1958), da of Sir Henry Getty Chilton, GCMG (d 1954); 1 s, 1 da (and 1 son decd); m 2, 12 Dec 1959, Marjorie Gordon (widow of Hon Ronald George Whiteley, OBE, yr s of 1 Baron Marchamley), da of Ernest Jukes, of Rickmansworth; *Career* RN 1924, served HMSS Ajax, Coventry, Cairo and Duke of York and at Admty WWII, Capt 1948, COS to C-in-C Med 1955-57, Rear-Adm 1958, ACNS 1958-59, Flag Offr (Flotillas) Mediterranean 1960-61, Vice-Adm 1961 Flag Offr Air (Home) 1961-62, Cdr Far East Fleet 1962-65, Adm 1965, Second Sea Lord and chief Naval Personnel 1965-67, chief advsr (personnel and logistics) to Sec of State for Def 1967, ret 1968; first and princ Naval ADC to HM The Queen 1965-68; memb: Nat Bd for Prices and Incomes 1968-71, Armed Forces Pay Review Body 1971-79; pres RN Benevolent Tst 1970-78; Not Forgotten Assoc 1973-, Regular Forces Employment Assoc. 1978-82; Offrs' Pension Soc 1978-84; Gentleman Usher to the Sword of State 1973-80; High Sheriff Hants

1977; *Recreations* dry fly fishing, golf; *Clubs* Army and Navy; *Style*— Adm Sir Desmond Dreyer, GCB, CBE, DSC, JP, DL; Brook Cottage, Cheriton, Nr Alresford, Hants (☎ 096 279 215)

DREYER, Capt Jeremy Chilton; s of Adm Sir Desmond Dreyer, GCB, CBE, DSC, DL, of Brook Cottage, Cheriton, Alresford, Hants, and Elisabeth, *née* Chilton (d 1958); *b* 24 May 1935; *Educ* Winchester; *m* 6 Aug 1960, Antoinette Marion (Toni), da of William Cornwall Stevens (d 1983), of Trevessa, Princes Risborough, Bucks; 2 s (Michael b 20 March 1963, Benjamin b 13 July 1967), 2 da (Katherine b 9 Nov 1961, d 1980, Sophie b 3 May 1970); *Career* RN 1953, qualified Signal Communications 1963; cmd: HMS Falmouth 1970-72, HMS Exeter 1980-82; Cdre Dep Chief Allied Staff to C-in-C Eastern Atlantic 1982-85, ret 1985; asst clerk of course Ascot Racecourse 1985-; *Recreations* shooting, fishing, golf, tennis, skiing; *Style*— Capt Jeremy Dreyer, RN; Old Mill Cottage, Droxford, Hants SO3 1QS (☎ 0489 877208); Ascot Racecourse, Ascot, Berks SL5 7JN (☎ 0990 22211)

DRIBBELL, Jack Lodewyk Charles; s of the late Alexander Dribbell; *b* 30 July 1922; *Educ* Westminster (BA); *m* 1945, Rinalda, da of late Vittorio Duranti of Ravenna, Italy; 2 s; *Career* wine merchant; md Findlater, Mackie Todd & Co Ltd 1970-1981; mayor of Westminster 1961-62; FCIS; OStJ; *Recreations* painting, golf; *Style*— Jack Dribbell, Esq; Dalkeith, Chester Ave, Richmond, Surrey (☎ 01 940 2732)

DRING, Lt-Col Sir (Arthur) John; KBE (1952), CIE (1943, JP Hants 1954, DL 1972); s of Sir William Arthur Dring, KCIE, VD (d 1912), by his w Jane Reid Greenshields, widow of W L Alston; *b* 4 Nov 1902; *Educ* Winchester, RMC Sandhurst; *m* 1, 13 Oct 1934, Marjorie Wadham (d 1943), da of late J C Wadham, of Green Orchard, Lindfield, Sussex; 2 da; m 2, 20 March 1946, Alice Deborah, wid of Maj-Gen John Stuart Marshall, CB, DSO, OBE, and only da of Maj-Gen Gerald Cree, CB, CMG (d 1932); *Career* joined Guides Cavalry IA 1923, Maj 1939, transferred Political Serv 1927, dep sec Viceroy's exec cncl 1936, sec to govr NWFP 1937-40, political agent S Waziristan 1940 (despatches), dir of Civil Supplies NWFP 1943-47, chief sec 1947; prime minister to Nawab of Bahawalpur 1948-52; advsr on plebiscites to Govrs and Govrs-Gen of Gold Coast (1955-56), Nigeria (1959); *Recreations* gardening, riding; *Style*— Lt-Col Sir John Dring, KBE, CIE, JP, DL; Ava Cottage, Purbrook, Porsmouth, Hants PO7 5RX (☎ 070 14 263000)

DRINKWATER, Sir John Muir; s of John Drinkwater OBE, cdr RN (d 1971), and Edith Constance St Clair Drinkwater, *née* Muir (d 1978); *b* 16 Mar 1925; *Educ* RNC Dartmouth; *m* 10 Oct 1952, Jennifer Marion Drinkwater, da of Edward Fitzwalter Wright (d 1956), of Morley Manor, Derby; 1 s (Jonathan Dominick St Clair b 1956); 4 da (Jane Fairrie b 1954, Joanna Elizabeth b 1958, Juliet Caroline Leslie b 1961, Jessanda Katharine Jemima b 1964); *Career* 1943-47 HM Submarines, Flag Lt to Cinc Portsmorth and first Sea Lord 1947-50, Lt Cdr 1952, invalided 1953; barr Inner Temple 1957, rec Crown Ct 1972, memb Parly Boundary Cmmn for England 1975-79, Income Tax cmmnr; dir BAA plc; kt 1988; *Clubs* Garrick, Pratts; *Style*— Sir John Drinkwater, QC; Meysey Hampton Manor, Cirencester, Gloucestershire; 27 Kilmaine Rd, London SW6; Le Moulin De Lohitzun, 64120 St Palais, France; 2 Harcourt Bldgs, Temple, London EC4 (☎ 01 353 8415)

DRINKWATER, (Collingwood) Peter; s of Roddam Collingwood Drinkwater (d 1965), of Kirby, Isle of Man, and Dorothy Mary Adeney; *b* 2 Sept 1931; *Educ* Eton, Sandhurst; *m* 22 June 1956, Belinda Rennie, da of Albert Cyril Sharwood (d 1976), of Ballater, Aberdeenshire; 2 s (James b 1963, Richard b 1965), 2 da (Carolyn b 1958, Nicola b 1960); *Career* served Coldstream Gds 1949-58, Capt; chm E Austin plc and Gp Cos 1959-86; *Recreations* shooting; *Style*— Peter Drinkwater, Esq; Kirby, Isle of Man (☎ 0624 75411, work: 0624 20333)

DRISCOLL, James Patrick; s of Henry James Driscoll (d 1965); *b* 24 April 1925; *Educ* Coleg Sant Illtyd Cardiff, Univ Coll Cardiff; *m* 1955, Jeanne Lawrence, *née* Williams; 1 s, 1 da; *Career* asst lectr Univ Coll Cardiff 1951-53, Br Iron & Steel Fedn 1953-67 latterly as exec dir), md corporate strategy Br Steel Corpn 1967-80, dir Nationalised Industs' Chairmen's Gp 1975-, chm and md Woodcote Conslts Ltd 1980 Parly candidate (Cons) Rhondda West 1950; nat dep chm Young Cons 1950, dep chm Cons Fedn 1949-50, dep chm Nat Union of Students 1951-53; res fell Cncl of Europe 1953; univ fell univ Coll Cardiff; memb court of govrs Univ Coll Cardiff 1970-; memb CBI cncl 1970-; observer NEDC 1975-; chm: Econ Ctee, Int Iron & Steel Inst 1972-74; FREconS, FRSA; *Recreations* travel, reading; *Style*— James Driscoll, Esq; Foxley Hatch, Birch Lane, Purley, Surrey (☎ 01 668 4081); Nationalised Industries' Chairmen's Group, Hobart House, Grosvenor Place, London SW1X 7AE (☎ 01 235 2020)

DRIVER, Sir Arthur John; s of Percy John Driver (d 1924), of E Sheen, Surrey; *b* 20 Mar 1900; *m* 1937, Margaret Jessie Isobel, da of Hugh Semple McMeekin (d 1941), of Carmoney, N Ireland; 1 s, 1 da; *Career* served in RAF 1918-19; slr; conslt with Jaques & Lewis; pres Law Soc 1961-62, JP (SW London) supp list; hon LLD Buckingham 1983, and hon deputy Knight Princ of The Imperial Soc of Knights Bachelor; kt 1962; *Recreations* local affairs, gardening; *Clubs* Reform; *Style*— Sir Arthur Driver; Frogmore Cottage, Ripley Rd, East Clandon, nr Guildford, Surrey GU4 7SE (☎ 0483 222355); Jaques & Lewis, 2 South Square, Gray's Inn, London WC1R 5HR (☎ 01 242 9755);

DRIVER, Charles Jonathan (Jonty); s of Rev Kingsley Ernest Driver (d 1964), and Mrs Phyllis Edith Mary Baines, *née* Gould; *b* 19 August 1939; *Educ* St Andrews Grahamstown, Univ of Cape Town (BA, BEd), Trinity Coll Oxford (MPhil); *m* 1967, Ann Elizabeth, da of Dr Bernard Albert Hoogewerf, of Chislehurst (d 1958); 2 s (Dominic b 1968, Thackwray b 1969), 1 da (Tamlyn b 1972); *Career* pres Nat Union of S African Students 1963-64; housemaster Int Sixth Form Centre Sevenoaks Sch 1968-73, dir Sixth Form Studies Matthew Humberstone Sch 1973-78, princ Island Sch Hong Kong 1978-83, headmaster Berkhamsted Sch 1983-89; FRSA; *Books* Elegy for a Revolutionary (1968), Send War in Our Time, O Lord (1969), Death of Fathers (1971), A Messiah of the Last Days (1973); poetry: I Live Here Now (1973), Occasional Light (with Jack Cope, 1980); biography: Patrick Duncan, S African and Pan-African (1980), Hong Kong Portraits (1986); *Recreations* long-distance running, rugby, reading; *Style*— Jonty Driver, Esq; Wilson House, Berkhamsted Sch, HP4 2BE

DRIVER, Christopher Prout; s of late Dr Arthur Driver; *b* 1 Dec 1932; *Educ* Rugby, Christ Church Oxford; *m* 1958, Margaret Elizabeth, *née* Perfect; 3 da; *Career* writer and ed; Guardian staff 1960-68, ed The Good Food Guide 1969-82; Guardian food and drink ed 1984-88, obituaries ed 1988-; Jubilee Medal 1977; *Books* A Future for the Free Churches? (1962), The Disarmers (1964), The Exploding University (1971), The British at Table 1940-80 (1983), Pepys at Table (1984), Twelve Poems (1985); *Style*— Christopher Driver, Esq; 6 Church Rd, Highgate, London N6 4QT (☎ 01 340 5445); The Book In Hand, Bell St, Shaftesbury, Dorset

DRIVER, (James) Donald; s of John Driver (d 1970), of Lancs, and Dorothea (Leslie) (d 1987); *b* 20 Dec 1924; *Educ* Clitheroe Royal GS, Manchester Univ; *m* 1948, Delia Jean, da of James Wilkinson, of Clitheroe; 1 s (John b 1952), 2 da (Susan b 1950, Joanna b 1957); *Career* Lt HM Royal Marines 1942-46; admitted slr 1948, private practice until 1970; gp legal advsr Investors in Industry plc (3i) 1973-85; dir: Meggitt Hldgs plc (chm 1985-), Kall-Kwik Printing (UK) Ltd, Dollar Air Services Ltd; *Recreations* sailing, cycling; *Style*— Donald Driver, Esq; Littlefield, Dedswell Drive, West Clandon, Guildford, Surrey GU4 7TA (☎ 0483 222 518, fax 0483 225 313)

DRIVER, Sir Eric William; s of William Weale and Sarah Ann Driver; *b* 19 Jan 1911; *Educ* Strand Sch London, King's Coll London; *m* 1, 1938, Winifred Bane; 2 da; m 2, 1972, Sheila Mary Johnson; *Career* civil engr, ICI Ltd 1938-; chief civil engr Mond Div to 1973; chm Mersey Regnl Health Auth 1973-82: kt 1979; *Style*— Sir Eric Driver; Chapel House, Crowley, Northwich, Cheshire (☎ 056 585 361)

DRIVER, Mrs John Michael; Olga Lindholm; *see*: Aikin, Olga Lindholm

DROGHEDA, 11 Earl of (I 1661); Charles Garrett Ponsonby Moore; KG (1972), KBE (1964, OBE 1964); also Baron Moore (I 1616 and UK 1954, the latter being title by which he sits in House of Lords) and Viscount Moore (I 1621); s of 10 Earl of Drogheda, KCMG, PC (d 1957), by his 1 w, Kathleen, CBE (d 1966), da of Charles Pelham Burn; *b* 23 April 1910; *Educ* Eton, Trinity Coll Cambridge; *m* 16 May 1935, Joan Eleanor, da of late William Carr; 1 s; *Heir* s, Viscount Moore; *Career* chm: Royal Ballet Sch 1978-82, Henry Sotheran 1977-, Clifton Nurseries 1979-86, P & D Colnaghi 1980-83; dir: Times Newspapers Hldgs 1981- (independent nat dir 1983-), Earls Court & Olympia Ltd 1976-; late chm Financial Times (md 1945-70); chm: Royal Opera House Covent Gdn 1958-74, London Celebrations Ctee Queen's Silver Jubilee; late tstee Br Museum, jt-chm (with Sir Robert Mayer) Youth & Music to 1981, vice pres Robert Mayer Tst for Youth & Music 1981-; Hon DCL Durham 1982; *Books* Double Harness (memoirs, 1978), Covent Garden Album (co-author, 1981); *Clubs* White's, Army and Navy; *Style*— Rt Hon Earl of Drogheda, KG; Parkside House, Wick Lane, Englefield Green, Surrey TW20 0XA (☎ Egham 0784 32800)

DROMGOOLE, Jolyon; s of Nicholas Arthur Dromgoole, of 68 Meopham Rd, Mitcham, Surrey, and Violet Alice Georgina Brookes (d 1959); *b* 27 Mar 1926; *Educ* Christ Hosp, Dulwich, Univ Coll Oxford (MA); *m* 10 March 1956, Anthea, da of Sir Antony Bowlby, 2 Bt, of The Old Rectory, Ozleworth, nr Wootton-under-Edge, Glos; 5 da (Emma b 1957, Julia b 1961, Rose, Susanna, Belinda (identical triplets) b 1964); *Career* dir: (cncl secrétariat) ICE 1985; deputy under sec of state (Army) 1984, MOD, entered HM Forces 1944; cmmnd 14/20 King's Hussars 1946; Univ Coll 1948-50; entered administrative Cl Civil Service; assigned to War Off 1950; priv sec to Permanent Under-Sec 1953, princ 1955, priv sec to Sec of State 1964-65, asst sec 1965, cmmnd sec HQ FARELF Singapore 1968-71, Royal Coll of Defence Studies 1972, under-sec Broadcasting Dept Home Off 1973-76, asst under-sec of State Gen Staff 1976-79, personnel and logistics 1979-84 MOD; *Recreations* polo, literature; *Clubs* Athenaeum, Royal Commonwealth, Tidworth Polo; *Style*— Jolyon Dromgoole, Esq; 13 Gladstone St, London SE1 6EY (☎ 01 928 2162); Montreal House, Barnsley, Glos (☎ 028 574 331); Institution of Civil Engineers, Great George St, London SW1P 3AA (☎ 01 222 7722, fax 222 7500)

DROMGOOLE, Patrick Shirley Brookes Fleming; s of Nicholas Arthur Humphrey and Violet Dromgoole; *b* 30 August 1930; *Educ* Dulwich, Univ Oxford (MA); *m* 1960, Jennifer Veronica Jill, da of S O Davis of Weymouth; 2 s (Sean, Dominic), 1 da (Jessica); *Career* actor and variously employed, London and Paris 1947-51; BBC drama producer/dir 1954-63; freelance theatre, film and tv dir 1963-69; programme controller HTV Ltd 1969, asst md 1981. md 1987, ch exec HTV Gp plc 1988; dir: Bristol Hippodrome Tst, English Shakespeare Co; FRTS; *Recreations* travel, breeding dexter cattle, swimming; *Clubs* Savile, Clifton (Bristol), Lotos (New York), Castel's (Paris); *Style*— Patrick Dromgoole, Esq; 38 Petersham Place, London SW7 51U (☎ 01 584 2237); 99 Baker Street, London W1M 2AJ (☎ 01 486 4311 ext 275; fax, 01 935 6724; car ☎ 0836 217044; telex, 264357)

DRON, Melville James; s of James Tod Dron (d 1950), and Jean Paterson, *née* McIntyre; *b* 1 Dec 1934; *Educ* Hutchesons Boys GS Glasgow; *m* 5 April 1963, Hazel Mary, da of Thomas Evelyn Caldecott of Malpas Ches; 3 s (James Melville Thomas, Andrew Donald McIntyre, Angus Richard Tod); *Career* Nat Serv Coldstream Guards 1953-55; ptnr Peat Marwick McLintock 1969-; FCA, FCCA, ACMA; *Recreations* golf, gardening, piping; *Clubs* Caledonian; *Style*— Melville Dron, Esq; Backfield House, Wotton Rd,Iron Acton, Bristol BS17 1XD (☎ 045422 509); 40 Andrewes House, The Barbican, London EC2Y 8AX (☎ 01 638 3144); 1 Puddle Dock, Blackfriars, London EC4V 3PD (☎ 01 236 8000, fax 01 248 6552, telex 8811541 PMMLO4 G)

DRUMLANRIG, Viscount; Sholto Francis Guy Douglas; s and h of 12 Marquess of Queensberry; *b* 1 June 1967; *Style*— Viscount Drumlanrig

DRUMM, David Andrew Francis; s of Owen Eugene Drumm, and Kathleen Mary Drumm (d 1986); *b* 18 Feb 1949; *Educ* Univ Sussex (BA); *m* 6 Sept 1975, Veronica Kaye, da of Arthur Aubrey; 1 s (Simon b 1980), 1 da (Jacqueline Jane b 1983); *Career* Lazard Brothers & Co Ltd 1971-78, Gulf Int Bank Bahrain 1979-86, branch mangr Gulf Int Bank London 1987-; *Recreations* tennis, photography; *Style*— David Drumm, Esq; Rays Court Hall, Friary Rd, South Ascot, Berks SL5 9HD (☎ 0990 26028); Gulf Int Bank, 2/6 Cannon St, London EC4M 6XP (☎ 01 248 6411, fax 01 248 6411 Ext. 281, telex 8812889)

DRUMM, Liam Joseph; s of Christopher Austin Drumm, of Belfast, NI, and Josephine, *née* Ormsby; *b* 23 August 1951; *Educ* St Marys GS Belfast N Ireland; *m* 29 Aug 1974, Kathleen, da of Thomas Rooney (d 1979) of Belfast; 1 s (Cathal Liam Austin), 1 da (Ciara Theresa Josephine); *Career* accountant, fin controller Elders Grain Europe; dir: Elders Grain Europe Ltd, Elders Malt Ltd; *Recreations* theatre, music, parachute jumping, mountaineering, golf; *Clubs* City and Counties, Peterborough, Rumpole's; *Style*— Liam Drumm, Esq; 6 Curlew Walk, Deeping St James, Peterborough (☎ 0778 346683); Peterscourt, City Road, Peterborough (☎ (0733) 310880)

DRUMMOND, Lady Elizabeth Helen; *née* Kennedy; only da of 7 Marquess of Ailsa, OBE, *qv*; *b* 23 Feb 1955; *m* 1976, Rev Norman Walker Drummond, MA, BD; 2 s (Andrew b 1977, Christian b 1986), 2 da (Margaret b 1980, Marie Clare b 1981); *Style*— Lady Elizabeth Drummond; Headmasters' House, Loretto, Musselburgh,

Midlothian EH21 7RA

DRUMMOND, Guy Malcolm Dixon; OBE (1982); s of Bernard Gilbert Drummond (d 1957), of Stowmarket, and Olive, *née* Dixon (d 1954); *b* 9 Sept 1914; *Educ* Ipswich Sch; *m* 1942, Daphne, da of Neville George Flawn (d 1957); 1 s (Robert), 2 da (Elizabeth, Margaret); *Career* dir James Crosby & Sons Ltd 1957-86, local dir Barclays Bank Ltd 1965-83; chm: Trind Ltd 1963-84, Buckwood Gp Ltd 1959-86; FCA; *Recreations* golf, bridge; *Clubs* St James (Manchester); *Style—* Guy Drummond, Esq, OBE; Woodpeckers, York Drive, Bowdon, Cheshire (☎ 061 928 6906 9516)

DRUMMOND, Hon James David; s and h of Viscount Strathallan; *b* 24 Oct 1965; *Style—* The Hon James Drummond

DRUMMOND, Hon James Reginald; yr s of 17 Earl of Perth, PC; *b* 28 July 1938; *Educ* Downside, Trinity Coll Cambridge; *m* 24 July 1961 (m dis 1985), Marybelle, da of late Capt Charles Gordon, of Park Hill, Aberdeen, half-sister of Lady (Lukyn) Coats; *Style—* The Hon James Drummond; 76 Holland Park, London W11 3SL W2

DRUMMOND, John Richard Gray; s of late Capt A R G Drummond, by his w Esther (*née* Pickering), of Perth, w Australia; *b* 25 Nov 1934; *Educ* Canford, Trinity Coll Cambridge; *Career* joined BBC 1958; former asst head Music and Arts; dir Edinburgh Int Festival 1978-83; vice-chm Br Arts Festival Assoc 1981; FRSA; *Style—* John Drummond, Esq; 61c Campden Hill Court, London W8 7HL (☎ 01 937 2257)

DRUMMOND, Maldwin Andrew Cyril; JP (1963), DL (Hampshire 1976-); s of Maj Cyril Augustus Drummond JP, DL (d 1945), of Cadland House, and Mildred Joan, *née* Humphrys (d 1976); *b* 30 April 1932; *Educ* Eton, RAC Cirencester, Univ of Southampton; *m* 1, 1955 (m dis 1977), Susan, da of Sir Kenelm Cayley; 2 d(Frederica a (Mrs Templer) b 1957, Annabella (Mrs Robinson) b 1959); m 2, 1 Jan 1978, Gillian Vera (Gilly), da of Gavin Clark, of Menton, S France; 1 s (Aldred b 1978);; *Career* Nat Serv The Rifle Bde 1950-52; Capt Queen Victoria's Rifles TA 1952-65; farmer and owner Manor of Cadland; dir: Newtown Oyster Co 1960-85, Rothesay Seafoods 1968-, Southampton Harbour Bd and Br Tports Docks Bd 1965-75, Southern Water Authy 1983-86; chm: bldg ctee STS Sir Winston Churchill 1964-66, Sail Trg Assoc 1967-72, Maritime Tst 1980-, boat ctee RNLI 1984-, New Forest Ninth Centenary Tst 1987-; pres: Hampshire Field Club and Archaeological Soc, Shellfish Assoc of GB and NI 1987-; tstee: Mary Rose Tst 1976-, Royal Naval Museum 1986-; memb ctee of mgmnt RNLI 1971-; memb: New Forest DC 1957-65, Hampshire CC 1965-75; verderer of the New Forest 1961-, Countryside cmmr 1980-86, High Sheriff of Hampshire 1980-81; City of London 1986, Memb of Ct Worshipful Co of Fishmongers 1986; FRGS, FRSA; *Books* Conflicts in an Estuary (1973), Secrets of George Smith Fisherman (ed and illustrator 1973), Tall Ships (1976), Salt-Water Palaces (1979), The Yachtsman's Naturalist (with Paul Rodhouse, 1980), The New Forest (with Philip Allison 1980), The Riddle (1985); *Recreations* sailing; *Clubs* Royal Yacht Squadron, Royal Cruising, Whites, Pratts, Leander Rowing; *Style—* Maldwin Drummond, Esq, JP, DL; Cadland House, Fawley, Southammpton (☎ 0703 891 543); Manor of Cadland, Cadland House, Fawley, Southampton SO4 1AA (☎ 0703 892 039); Wester Kames Castle, Isle of Bute (☎ 0700 3983)

DRUMMOND, Rev Norman Walker; s of Edwin Payne Drummond, of Renfrewshire (d 1971), and Jean Drummond, *née* Walker; *b* 1 April 1952; *Educ* Crawfordton House Moniaive, Merchiston Castle Edinburgh, Fitzwilliam Coll Cambridge (MA), New Coll Edinburgh (BD); *m* 1976, Lady Elizabeth Helen Kennedy, da of 7 Marquess of Ailsa; 2 s (Andrew b 1977, Christian b 1986), 2 da (Margaret b 1980, Marie Clare b 1981); *Career* ordained as minister of the Church of Scotland, cmmnd to serve as Chaplain to HM Servs Army 1976; chaplain: Depot Parachute Regt and Airborne Forces 1977-78, 1 Bn The Black Watch (Royal Highland Regt) 1978-82, Fettes Coll 1982-84; moderator of Gen Assembly of Church of Scotland 1980, headmaster Loretto Sch 1984-88,; memb ct Heriot Watt Univ; chm: Musselburgh and District Cncl of Social Service, Ronald Selby Wright Christian Leadership Tst; memb Scottish Ctee Duke of Edinburgh Award Scheme; *Books* The First 25 Years - the official History of the Kirk Session of The Black Watch (Royal Highland Regiment); *Recreations* rugby football, cricket, golf, curling, traditional jazz Isle of Skye; *Clubs* MCC, Free Foresters, New (Edinburgh), Hawks (Cambridge); *Style—* The Rev Norman Drummond; Pinkie House, Loretto Sch, Musselburgh, East Lothian, Scotland (☎ 031 665 3108)

DRUMMOND, Patrick Thomas; s of Thomas John Drummond, MM; *b* 11 May 1937; *m* 1961 (m dis); 2 children; *Career* dir Associated Asphalt Co Ltd, London Roadstone Ltd; *Recreations* golf; *Style—* Patrick Drummond, Esq

DRUMMOND, Robert Malcolm; so of Guy Malcolm Dixon Drummond, OBE, of Cheshire, and Daphne, *née* Flawn; *b* 3 June 1945; *Educ* Rugby, St Andrews Univ, Manchester Business Sch; *m* 1970, Brenda (m dis); 1 da (Alison b 1975); m 2, 1981, Lorraine, da of Thomas Kitchiner Aymes; *Career* regnl dir/asst gen mangr ICFC later Investors In Industry (3i's) Leeds and London 1972-84; Alta Berkeley Assocs ptnr of venture capital partnership 1984-85; md County NatWest Ventures Ltd (Venture and dvpt capital) 1985-89; vice-chm Electra Mgmt Tst plc, non-exec dir Southnews plc (newspaper publisher) 1986; non-exec chm Aqualisa Products (shower mfg) 1987; FCA, LLB, MBA; *Recreations* golf, skiing; *Style—* Robert Drummond, Esq; 14 Avenfield House, 118-127 Park Lane, London W1Y 3AS (☎ 01 491 4156); The School House, The Common, Henfield, W Sussex BN5 9RS (☎ 0273 493195); Electra Management Services Ltd, 65 Kingsway, London WC2B 6QT (☎ 01 831 6464, telex 265525, fax 01 404 5388)

DRUMMOND, Capt Spencer Heneage; DSC (1943); s of Algernon Cecil Heneage Drummon (d 1975), and Janetta Vandfleur (d 1958); *b* 2 June 1922; *Educ* RNC Dartmouth, Southampton Univ (MPhil); *m* 17 Dec 1949, Miss Keane, da of Col Michael Keane, OBE, of Ireland; 2 s (Crispin b 1955, Hereward b 1959), 3 da (Deirdre b 1953, Ianthe b 1960, Helena b 1963); *Career* RN serv WWII Med; (ret) as Dep Chief of Allied Staff to NATO C in C with rank of Cdre; memb: RORC, Sail Trg Assoc; *Recreations* yacht racing; *Clubs* Nat Lib; *Style—* Capt Spencer Drummond, DSC; Keepers Cottage, Petersfield, Hampshire

DRUMMOND, Hon Mrs (Theodosia Beatrix Catherine Mary Meade); only child of Richard Charles (Meade), Lord Gillford (d 1905), s of 4 Earl of Clanwilliam; *b* 1 Feb 1898; *m* 11 Nov 1961, Angus Julian Drummond; *Style—* The Hon Mrs Drummond; 62 Ashley Gdns, London SW1

DRUMMOND LAMBERT, Eric Thomas; CMG (1969), OBE (1946), KPM (1943); s of late Septimus Drummond Lambert, of Dublin Ireland; *b* 3 Nov 1909; *Educ* Royal Sch Dungannon; *Career* Indian Police, Indian NE Frontier Administrator 1929-46, temp Maj-Gen Chinese Armed Forces (Distinguished Service Order China) 1942, chief civil liaison offr XIV Army India, Burma 1945, Foreign and Cwlth Off 1947-68; tstee Nat Library of Ireland, pres Burma Star Assoc Republic, cncl memb Military History Soc of Ireland; Cruz Militar Venezuela 1983; Police Medal Ecuador 1962; *Recreations* golf; *Clubs* Stephen's Green (Dublin); *Style—* Eric Drummond Lambert, Esq, CMG, OBE, KPM; Drumkeen, Glenamuck, Carrickmines, Dublin 18, Ireland (☎ Dublin 893169)

DRUMMOND OF MEGGINCH, Hon Adam Humphrey; eldest s and h of Lady Strange, *qv*, and Capt Humphrey Drummond of Megginch, MC, *qv*; *b* 20 April 1953; *Educ* Eton; *m* 14 May 1988, Mary Emma Jeronima, eldest da of Hon John James Evelyn Dewar (s and h of 3 Baron Forteviot); *Career* Maj Gren Guards; *Style—* Maj the Hon Adam Drummond of Megginch

DRUMMOND OF MEGGINCH, Capt Humphrey; MC (1945); formerly Humphrey ap Evans, changed name by decree of Court of Lord Lyon 1966; s of Maj James John Pugh Evans, MBE, MC (d 1974), of Lovesgrove, Aberystwyth; *b* 18 Sept 1922; *Educ* Eton, Trinity Coll Cambridge; *m* 2 June 1952, Cherry Drummond, Lady Strange (16th holder of the peerage); 3 s, 3 da; *Career* served 1940-45 with 1 Mountain Regt; Indian Political Serv 1947; gen sec Cncl for Preservation of Rural Wales 1947-51; Welsh rep of Nat Tst 1949-54; Gold Staff offr coronation of HM Queen Elizabeth II; author and farmer; chm Soc of Authors (Scot) 1975-81; *Books* Our Man in Scotland, The Queen's Man, The King's Enemy, Falconry, Falconry For You, Falconry in the East; *Clubs* Garrick; *Style—* Capt Humphrey Drummond of Megginch, MC; Tresco, 160 Kennington Rd, London SE11; Megginch Castle, Errol, Perths (☎ 08212 222)

DRUMMOND-HAY, Lady Bettina Mary; *née* Lindsay; elder da of 29 Earl of Crawford and (12 of) Balcarres; *b* 26 June 1950; *Educ* Camden Sch for Girls, Goldsmith's Coll London; *m* 1975, Peter Charles, s of John Hay-Drummond-Hay, gs of Sir Robert Drummond-Hay, CMG, who added the first 'Hay' to his name; 3 da; *Career* school teacher; *Style—* Lady Bettina Drummond-Hay; Balcarres, Colinsburgh, Leven, Fife

DRUMMOND-HAY, Lady Margaret; *née* Douglas-Hamilton; 2 da of 13 Duke of Hamilton and (10 of) Brandon (1940); *b* 13 Oct 1907; *m* 1 Feb 1930, Maj James Drummond-Hay (d 1981); 2 s, 4 da; *Style—* Lady Margaret Drummond-Hay; PO Box 114, Ramsgate, S Africa

DRUMMOND-MORAY OF ABERCAIRNY, William George Stirling Home; Laird of Abercairny from time immemorial, since the lands came to the Morays as dowry with a daughter of the Earls of Strathearn 'by the Indulgence of God' (who, alone among the Counts in Christendom, nominated their own bishops), successors to the ancient Kings of Strathearn; 2 (but eldest surviving) s of Maj James Drummond-Moray, twenty-first of Abercairny, and of Ardoch, Perthshire, JP, DL, by his w Jeanetta (twin da of Lt-Col Lord George Scott, OBE, JP, DL, 3 s of 6 Duke of Buccleuch & (8 of) Queensberry); *b* 22 August 1940; *Educ* Eton, RAC Cirencester; *m* 7 Jan 1969, (Angela) Jane, da of Lt Cdr Michael Baring, RN (d 1954); 3 da (Anne b 1971, Frances b 1974, Georgia b 1979); *Career* estate mangr; *Recreations* shooting, polo; *Style—* William Drummond-Moray of Abercairny; Abercairny, Crieff, Perthshire (☎ 0764 3114)

DRUMMOND-MURRAY OF MASTRICK, Hon Mrs (Barbara Mary Hope); 4 and yst da of 2 Baron Rankeillour, GCIE, MC (d 1958); *b* 21 Feb 1930; *Educ* private; *m* 12 June 1954, (William Edward) Peter Louis Drummond-Murray of Mastrick, *qv*; 4 s, 1 da; *Style—* The Hon Mrs Drummond-Murray of Mastrick; 67 Dublin Street, Edinburgh, EH3 6NS (☎ 031 556 2913)

DRUMMOND-MURRAY OF MASTRICK, (William Edward) Peter Louis; s of Edward John Drummond-Murray of Mastrick (d 1976), and Eulalia Ildefonsa Wilhelmina Heaven (d 1988); *b* 24 Nov 1929; *Educ* Beaumont Coll; *m* 1954, Hon Barbara Mary, *qv*; 4 s, 1 da; *Career* dir Utd and Gen Tst and other cos; chief exec Hosp of St John and St Elizabeth London 1978-82; Slains Pursuivant of Arms to the Lord High Constable of Scotland the Earl of Erroll 1981-; Kt of Honour and Devotion SMOM 1971, Grand Cross of Obedience 1984; Chllr Br Assoc SMOM 1977-; Grand Cross of Justice Constantinian Order of St George 1982; CStJ 1977, KStJ 1988; *Recreations* archaeology, genealogy, heraldry, baking, brewing; bookbinding; *Clubs* Beefsteak, New (Edinburgh), Puffin's (Edinburgh); *Style—* Peter Drummond-Murray of Mastrick; 67 Dublin Street, Edinburgh, EH3 6NS (☎ 031 556 2913)

DRURY, Rev John Henry; s of Henry and Barbara Drury; *b* 23 May 1936; *Educ* Bradfield, Trinity Hall Cambridge (MA), Westcott House Cambridge; *m* 1972, (Frances) Clare, da of Rev Prof Dennis Eric Nineham, DD, of Bristol; 2 da; *Career* resident canon of Norwich Cathedral and examining chaplain to Bishop of Norwich 1973, vice-dean of Norwich 1978, lectr in religious studies Univ of Sussex 1979-82; dean of chapel King's Coll Cambridge 1983-; *Books* Tradition and Design in Luke's Gospel (1976), The Parables in the Gospels (1985); *Recreations* music, drawing; *Style—* The Rev John Drury; King's Coll, Cambridge (☎ 0223 350411)

DRURY, Martin Dru; s of Walter Neville Dru Drury, TD, of Little Brookstreet, Edenbridge, Kent, and Rae, *née* Sandiland; *b* 22 April 1938; *Educ* Rugby; *m* 5 Jan 1971, Elizabeth Caroline, da of The Hon Sir Maurice Bridgeman, KBE (d 1980), of The Glebe House, Selham, Sussex; 2 s (Matthew b 8 Aug 1972, Joseph b 18 June 1977), 1 da (Daisy b 6 Sept 1974); *Career* 2 Lt 3 The King's Own Hussars 1957, Lt The Queen's Own Hussars 1958, Capt Army Emergency Reserve 1966; broker at Lloyds 1959-65, assoc dir Mallett & Son (Antiques) Ltd 1965-73; The Nat Tst: historic buildings rep and advsr on furniture 1973-81, historic buildings sec 1981-; vice-chm Attingham Summer Sch, memb exec ctee The Georgian Gp, former memb cncl Furniture History Soc; dir: Landmark Tst, Arundel Castle Tst Ltd; Liveryman Worshipful Co of Goldsmiths; *Recreations* walking, travel, gardening; *Clubs* Brooks's, Pratt's; *Style—* Martin Drury, Esq; 3 Victoria Rise, London SW4 0PB (☎ 01 622 1411); 18 The Street, Stedham, Sussex; The National Trust, 36 Queen Anne's Gate, London SW1 (☎ 01 222 9251, telex 8950997 NTRUST G)

DRURY, Prof (Victor William) Michael; OBE (1978); s of George Leslie Drury (d 1936), of Bromsgrove, and Trixie, *née* Maddox; *b* 5 August 1926; *Educ* Bromsgrove Sch, Birmingham Univ (MB, ChB, MRCS, LRCP); *m* 7 Oct 1950, Joan, da of Joseph Williamson, of Winsford, Cheshire; 3 s (Mark b 9 May 1952, Simon b 17 March 1958, James b 27 July 1960), 1 da (Linda b 19 July 1954); *Career* Capt (surgical specialist) RAMC 1951-53, civilian conslt to Army 1985-; travelling fell Nuffield 1965, GP Bromsgrove 1953-, sr clinical tutor Dept of Med Univ of Birmingham 1973-80, prof general practice Univ of Birmingham 1980, visiting prof Canterbury NZ 1984, Jeffcote Professorship Westminster and Charing Cross 1989-, pres RCGP; FRCP 1988, FRCGP 1970, FRACGP 1988; *Books* Medical Secretary's Handbook (5 edn 1986),

Introduction to General Practice (1979), Treatment, A Handbook of Drug Therapy (37 instalments 1978-88), The Receptionist (1987), Treatment & Prognosis (1989); *Recreations* gardening, bridge, talking; *Style*— Prof Michael Drury, OBE; Rossall Cottage, Church Hill, Bolbroughton, nr Stourbridge, W Midlands DY9 ODT (☎ 0562 730229); The Medical School, University of Birmingham, Birmingham (☎ 021 414 3758)

DRURY, Ruth Elizabeth; da of Lt-Col George Richard Johnston, RA (d 1974), of Wood Corner, Lank Hills Rd, Winchester, Hants, and Unity Ussher, *née* Quicke (d 1980); *b* 19 June 1927; *Educ* privately; *m* 11 Dec 1948, Denis Gordon de Courcy Drury, s of Gordon de Courcy Drury, MC (d 1947), of Kenya and London; 2 s (Robert b 20 Feb 1950, Gordon b 13 Nov 1951), 2 da (Caroline b 12 March 1954, Rosemary b 7 March 1957); *Career* fashion photogrpahy; memb: Central London branch Parkinson's Disease Soc, cncl White Lion Soc Royal Coll of Arms, exec ctee Soc for Individual Freedom, ctee Poppy Ball in aid of Royal Br Legion; Freeman City of London 1989; *Clubs* St Stephens Constitutional; *Style*— Mrs Denis Drury; 8 Evelyn Mansions, Carlisle Place, Westminster, London SW1P 1NH (☎ 01 828 0665)

DRURY-LOWE, Capt Patrick John Boteler; s of Lt-Col John Drury Boteler Packe-Drury-Lowe (d 1960), of Prestwold Hall, Loughborough, Leicestershire, and Lady Rosemary Brinckman, *née* Hope-Vere; *b* 9 August 1931; *Educ* Eton; *m* 1, 12 Oct 1959 (m dis 1968), Belinda Mary, da of Sir Hardman A Mort Earle Bt (d 1979), of Kensington Sq, London; 2 da (Lucy b 1961, Candida b 1963); m 2, 2 Nov 1968 (m dis 1972), Mrs Pamela Estelle Cayzer; *Career* serv Scots Guard 1949-58, ADC to Govr S Australia 1955-58; cdr and cmmr St John Ambulance Brig Derbyshire 1971-72 (cmmr 1963), vice-pres St John Cncl of Derbyshire (former vice chm); county cncllr Derbyshire 1961-64; jt master Meynell and S Staffs Hunt 1970-75; KStJ; *Recreations* shooting; *Clubs* White's, Pratt's; *Style*— Capt Patrick Drury-Lowe; Locko Park, Derby, DE2 7BW (☎ 0322 673 517); Estate Office, Locko Park, Derby, DE2 7BW (☎ 0332 662 785)

DRYDEN, Sir John Stephen Gyles; 11 Bt (GB 1733) of Ambrosden, Oxfordshire and 8 Bt (GB 1795) of Canons-Ashby, Northamptonshire; s of Sir Noel Percy Hugh Dryden, 10 Bt (d 1970); 6 in descent from Sir Erasmus Dryden, 6 Bt, bro of the poet John Dryden); *b* 26 Sept 1943; *Educ* The Oratory; *m* 1970, Diana Constance, da of Cyril Tomlinson, of New Zealand; 1 s, 1 da; *Heir* s, John Frederick Simon Dryden b 26 May 1976; *Style*— Sir John Dryden, Bt; Spinners, Fairwarp, Uckfield, Sussex

DRYDEN, Rosamund, Lady Rosamund Mary; *née* Scrope; eldest da of Stephen Francis Eustace Scrope (d 1936), and Ethelburga Mary Magdalen Pega, yst da of Edmund Waterton, JP, DL, of Deeping Waterton, Lincs, Privy Chamberlain to HH Pope Pius IX; *b* 13 July 1915; *m* 22 Aug 1941, Sir Noel Percy Hugh Dryden, 10 Bt (d 1970); 1 s (Sir John Dryden, 11 and present Bt); *Style*— Rosamund, Lady Dryden; Spinners Cottage, Fairward, Uckfield, E Sussex

DRYHURST, Michael John; s of Edward Dryhurst, 0-9, Northwood Lane, Highgate, London, and Lilian Mae, *née* Roberts (d 1956); *b* 22 Mar 1938; *Educ* Brighton Coll; *m* 2 Nov 1975, Anna Dryhurst, da of Thomas Manscier (d 1940); 3 da (Lorraine Horder, Deborah Cottrell, Samantha Lester); *Career* camera asst Pinewood Studios 1955-60; asst dir: Aspect Prodns Ltd (tv commercials) 1960-64, Shepperton Studios (over 40 films) 1964-73; moved to Hollywood 1973, prodn assoc The Stone Killer for Dino de Laurentiis, assoc (line) prodr The Terminal Man for Warner Bros; recent films incl: Excalibur, Amityrille II, Superman III, Never say Never Again, The Emerald Forest, Harem (mini-series), Hope and Glory (5 Oscar Nominations 1988); completed screenplay Redmayne West 1988; memb: BFI, ACTT ; *Books* London Bus and Tram Album (1963, 67, 79), The London Trolleybus (1987); *Recreations* reading, cinema, photography, music, driving old double decker buses; *Clubs* Groucho; *Style*— Michael Dryhurst, Esq; Orchard Bay House, St Lawerence PO38 1UN, Isle of Wight (☎ 0983 852 038); 502 San Vincente Boulevard £202, Santa Monica, CA 90402, USA (☎ 010 1 213 395 0462); Michael Dryhurst Productions Ltd, 9056 Santa Monica Boulevard, Suite 307, Los Angeles, California 90069, USA

DRYLAND, Michael Hubert; s of Maj Hubert Dryland, MBE, and Eva May, *née* Farrant, JP; *b* 24 Jan 1927; *Educ* Worksop Coll Notts, Exeter Coll Oxford (MA); *m* 17 April 1954, Wendy, da of Neville Gilbert Sparkes (d 1988); 2s (Timothy Michael b 31 Aug 1956, Jonathan Charles b 28 Sept 1959); *Career* RN 1945-48; slr; sr ptnr Ware & Peters of York; chm Yorkshire Rent Assessment Panels and Rent Tbnls; former Master Worshipful Co of Merchant (York); memb Law Soc 1952; *Recreations* music, tennis, walking; *Style*— Michael Dryland, Esq; Linden Cottage, Huntington, York; Ware & Peters, 9 New Street, York Y01 2RQ

DRYSDALE, Andrew Watt; s of Sir Matthew Drysdale (d 1963), of 46 Onslow Square SW3, and Nesta, *née* Lewis (d 1964); *b* 15 Feb 1932; *Educ* Eton, Magdalene Coll Cambridge (LLB); *m* 3 Jan 1956, Merida, da of Maj-Gen Sir Julian Gascoigne, KCMG, KCVO, CB, DSO; 3 da (Laura b 28 April 1958, Helena b 6 May 1960, Alexandra b 26 Sept 1962); *Career* Nat Serv 2 Lt 60 Rifles 1950-52, TA Queens Westminster Rifles, Capt Queens Royal Rifles, ret 1962; Lincolns Inn, underwriter Lloyds 1956-; jt master Coakham Bloodhounds Hunt; memb Worshipful Co of Merchant Taylors; *Recreations* hunting, fishing, sailing; *Clubs* Boodles', City of London; *Style*— Andrew Drysdale, Esq; Ferriers Grange, Hookwood, Horley, Surrey (☎ 0293 783 218); Andrew Drysdale Underwriting Ltd, Jamacia Bldgs, St Michaels Alley, London EC3 (☎ 01 626 2324)

DRYSDALE, Lady; Maisie Joyce; *née* Purves-Smith; *m* 1964, as his 2 w, Sir (George) Russell Drysdale, AC, the Australian artist (d 1981); *Style*— Lady Drysdale; Bouddi Farm, Kilcare Heights, Hardy's Bay, NSW 2256, Australia

DRYSDALE, Neil; s of Stuart Drysdale, of Crieff, and Sigrid Drysdale, *née* Waldmann; *b* 4 Sept 1955; *Educ* Morrison's Acad Crieff, Aberdeen Univ (LLB); *m* 28 Feb 1980, Miriam Clare, da of Rev James Ekron Little, of Perthshire; 2 s (Anthony Lewis b 1980, Mark b 1983); *Career* sr ptnr Colville & Drysdale W S 1979-; dir: Grampian Light Industries Ltd 1980, Crieff Visitors Centre Ltd 1985, Perthshire Paperweights Ltd 1986; *Recreations* tennis, golf, gardening; *Style*— Neil Drysdale, Esq; Newmilne, Fowlis Wester, by Crieff, Perthshire (☎ 0764 83 362, fax 0764 2903, car 0860 410 830

DRYSDALE WILSON, John Veitch; s of Alexander Drysdale Wilson (d 1949), and Winifred Rose, *née* Frazier (d 1972); *b* 8 April 1929; *Educ* Solihull Sch, Guildford Tech Coll; *m* 27 March 1954, Joan Lily, da of John Cooke, of Selsey, Sussex; 1 s (Alexander B 30 June 1958), 1 da (Jane b 7 July 1962); *Career* Nat Serv Capt on staff of CREME 6 Armd Div; Dennis Bros Ltd Guildford: apprentice engr 1946-50, MIRA res trainee 1949-50, jr designer 1950-51; mgmnt trainee BET Fedn Ltd 1953-55, Esso Petroleum Co Ltd: tech sales engr 1955-59, head of mechanical laboratories 1959-66; Edwin Cooper Ltd (prev Burmah Oil Trading Ltd, formerly Castrol Ltd): Chief engr R & D 1966-77; projects and res offr 1977-79, dep sec 1979-; dir Mechanical Engrg Pubns Ltd 1979-; author of numerous papers on engine lubrication; Freeman City of London, Liveryman: Worshipful Co of Engrs, Worshipful Co of Arbitrators; CEng, FIMechE, FCIArb, FInstPet, MSAE, MBIM; *Recreations* travel; *Clubs* East India, Caravan; *Style*— John Drysdale Wilson, Esq; Inst of Mechanical Engrs, 1 Birdcage Walk, London SW1H 9JJ (☎ 01 222 7899, fax 01 222 4557, telex 917944)

DU BREUIL, Lady Joanna Edwina Doreen; *née* Knatchbull; elder da of 7 Baron Brabourne and Countess Mountbatten of Burma, *qqv*; *b* 5 Mar 1955; *Educ* Atlantic Coll, Kent Univ, Columbia Univ USA; *m* 3 Nov 1984, Baron Hubert Henry François du Breuil, yr s of Baron and Baronne du Breuil of Paris; 1 da (Eleuthera b 1986); *Style*— Lady Joanna du Breuil; 16 Bishop's Rd, London SW6 (☎ 01 385 3684)

DU CANE, John Peter; OBE (1964); 4 s of Charles Henry Copley Du Cane (d 1938), late of Braxted Park, Essex, and his 2 wife Mathilde (d 1961), da of Henri Allain, of Dinard, France; *b* 16 April 1921; *Educ* Canford; *m* 12 Nov 1945, Patricia Wallace, da of James Desmond, of Townsville, Qld, Aust; 2 s; *Career* serv WWII, RN Air Arm; chm: Selection Tst Ltd 1978-81 (dir 1966-81, md 1975-81), Seltrust Hldgs (Aust) 1978-81, Selco Mining Corpn (Canada) 1978-81, Consolidated African Selection Tst 1978-81; dir: Amax Inc 1966-, BP Int 1980-81 (chief exec BP Minerals Int 1980-81), Aust Consolidated Minerals 1981-85 (dep chm 1983-85), Ultramar plc 1983-87; FRSA; *Recreations* sailing, fishing, photography; *Clubs* Royal Naval Sailing Assoc, The Mining Club (New York); *Style*— John Du Cane, Esq, OBE; 20 Jameson St, London W8 7SH (☎ 01 727 1974)

DU CANN, Charlotte Jane Lott; da of Richard Dillon Lott Du cann, QC, and Charlotte Mary *née* Sawtell; *b* 20 June 1956; *Educ* Felixstowe Coll, Birmingham Univ (BA); *Career* shopping ed Vogue 1979-81; freelance writer 1981-84-, The Observer, Sunday Express mag, Time Out, Harpers & Queen; features writer The World of Interiors 1984, style ed The Magazine 1984-85, shopping and beauty ed Tatler 1986-87, contributing ed Elle 1987-88, fashion ed Independent 1988-; *Books* Offal and The New Brutalism (1984), Vogue Modern Style (1988); *Recreations* poetry and cooking; *Style*— Charlotte Du cann; The Independent, 40 City Rd, London, EC1, (☎ 01 253 1222, fax 01 608 1149)

DU CANN, Rt Hon Sir Edward Dillon Lott; KBE (1985), PC (1964); er s of Charles Garfield Lott du Cann, (d 1983); er bro of Richard du Cann, QC, *qv*; *b* 28 May 1924; *Educ* Colet Court, Woodbridge Sch, St John's Coll Oxford; *m* 1962, Sally Innes, da of James Henry Murchie (d 1967), of Ainways, Caldie, Cheshire; 1 s, 2 da; *Career* contested (C): W Walthamstow 1951, Barrow in Furness 1955; MP (C) Taunton Div of Somerset Feb 1956-1987, econ sec Treasy 1962-63, min state BOT 1963-64; chm 1922 Ctee 1972-, liaison ctee Select Ctee Chm 1974-83; chm select ctee: Public Expenditure 1971-73, Public Accts 1974-79, Treasury & Civil Service Affrs 1979-83; memb select ctee: House of Lords Reform 1962, Privilege 1972-87; former chm: Cons Pty Orgn, Burke Club; former memb Ld Chllr's Advsy Ctee Public Records; former jt hon sec: UN Parly Gp, Cons Parly Fin Gp; pres: Anglo-Polish Cons Soc 1972-74, Nat Union Cons and Unionist Assocs 1981-82; vice-chm Br American Parly Gp 1978-81; fndr Unicorn Gp Unit Tsts 1957; chm: Unicorn Gp 1957-62 and 1964-72, Assoc Unit Tst Mangrs 1961, Keyser Ullman 1972-75, Cannon Assur 1972-80; Lonrho: dir 1972-, dep chm 1983-84, chm 1984-; dep chm Family Planning Int Ctee 1971; vice-chm Wider Share Ownership Ctee 1970-; vice pres Br Insur Brokers 1978-; dir Bow Gp Pubns; chm All-Pty Maritime Affrs Gp visiting fell Lancaster Univ Business Sch 1970-82; Freeman Taunton Deane Borough; Hon Col 155 Wessex Regt RCT (Volunteers) 1972-82, retains hon rank of Col, hon life memb Inst of RCT 1983 ; *Clubs* Carlton, Pratt's, Royal Thames Yacht, House of Commons Yacht (cdre 1962, adm 1974), Somerset Co; *Style*— Rt Hon Sir Edward du Cann, KBE; 9 Tufton Court, Tufton St, London SW1 (☎ 01 222 1922); Lonrho Plc, Cheapside House, London EC2V 6BL (☎ 01 606 9898)

DU CANN, Richard Dillon Lott; QC (1975); yr s of Charles Du Cann (d 1983), and bro of Edward du Cann, *qv*; *b* 27 Jan 1929; *Educ* Steyning GS, Clare Coll Cambridge; *m* 1955, Charlotte Mary Sawtell; 2 s, 2 da; *Career* barr Gray's Inn 1953 (bencher 1980), treasy counsel Inner London QS 1966-70, treasy counsel Centl Criminal Court 1970-75, chm Criminal Bar Assoc 1977-80, chm Bar of England and Wales 1980/81, rec S E Circuit 1982-; *Style*— Richard du Cann, Esq, QC; 29 Newton Rd, W2 (☎ 01 229 3859)

DU CROS, Sir Claude Philip Arthur Mallet; 3th Bt (UK 1916) of Canons, Middx; s of Sir Philip Harvey du Cros, 2nd Bt (d 1975); *b* 22 Dec 1922; *m* 1, 1953 (m dis 1974), Mrs Christine Nancy Tordoff (d 1988), da of F E Bennett; 1 s; m 2, 1974, Margaret Roy, da of late Roland James Frater; *Heir* s, Julian Claude Arthur Mallet du Cros; *Career* farmer; *Style*— Sir Claude du Cros, Bt; Longmeadow, Ballaugh, Glen, Ramsey, Isle of Man

DU CROS, Julian Claude Arthur Mallet; s and h of Sir Claude Mallet, 3 Bt; *b* 23 April 1955; *Educ* Eton; *Style*— Julian du Cros, Esq

DU CROS, Rosemary, Lady - Rosemary Theresa; MBE (1945); only da of Sir John David Rees, 1 Bt, KCIE, CVO, MP (d 1922); *b* 23 Sept 1901; *m* 3 Nov 1950, as his 2 w, Capt Sir Philip Harvey du Cros, 2 Bt (d 1975); *Career* Capt ATA; dame pres Cons Assoc (Torrington parly constituency), patron Cons Assoc (Torridge and W Devon parly constituency); *Books* ATA Girl, Memoirs of a Wartime Ferry Pilot, contributions to The Aeroplane and Flight; *Clubs* Naval & Military; *Style*— Rosemary, Lady du Cros, MBE; Bocombe, Parkham, Bideford, N Devon

DU PARCQ, Hon John Renouf; s of Baron du Parcq (Life Peer, d 1949); *b* 9 June 1917; *Educ* Rugby, Exeter Coll Oxford (MA); *m* 16 Nov 1940, Elizabeth, da of Evan Skull Poole; 1 s (Richard 6 1943), 1 da (Elizabeth b 1947); *Career* chartered electrical engr, ret 1972; MIEE; *Recreations* joinery; *Style*— The Hon John du Parcq; 10 Anchor Quay, Norwich NR3 3PR (☎ 0603 667782)

DU PREEZ, Hon Mrs (Carina Gillian); *née* Hacking; da of 2 Baron Hacking (d 1971); *b* 28 May 1956; *Educ* Benenden; *m* 1981, Jac Jacobus du Preez; *Recreations* swimming, tennis, walking; *Style*— The Hon Mrs du Preez; 8 Winters Wynd, Newlands 7700, Cape Province, S Africa (☎ 010 27 21 619324)

DU SAUTOY, Peter Francis; CBE (1971), OBE (1964); s of Col E F du Sautoy, OBE, TD, DL (d 1964), and Mabel, *née* Howse (d 1973), descended from Pierre François du Sautoy, a French officer (a supporter of the Young Pretender) who while a

POW on parole in England married Mary Abbot in 1758 and founded the English branch of the family; *b* 19 Feb 1912; *Educ* Uppingham, Wadham Coll Oxford (MA); *m* 1937, Phyllis Mary (Mollie), da of Sir Francis Floud, KCB, KCSI, KCMG (d 1965); 2 s (Bernard, Stephen); *Career* asst educn offr City of Oxford 1937-40, served with RAF 1940-45 (Sqdn Ldr, Air Miny); pres Publishers Assoc 1967-69, dir Faber and Faber Ltd 1946-77 (chm 1971-77), dir Faber Music Ltd 1965-87 (chm 1971-76); vice-pres Aldeburgh Festival Fndn 1988- (dep chm 1982-87); *Clubs* Garrick; *Style*— Peter du Sautoy, Esq, CBE; 31 Lee Rd, Aldeburgh, Suffolk IP15 5EY (☎ 072 885 2838)

DU VIVIER, Dr Anthony Wilfred Paul; s of Major Paul Edward du Vivier (d 1967), and Joan Beryl, *née* Swann; *b* 16 June 1944; *Educ* Ampleforth, St Bartholomew's Hosp Medical Sch, London Univ (MD); *m* 13 Aug 1977, Judith Vivienne, da of Cmdr Reginald Sidney Brett, RN (ret); *Career* consultant dermatologist, King's Coll Hosp, London 1978-; FRCP; *Clubs* RSM; *Style*— Dr Anthony W P du Vivier; 115a Harley Street, London W1N 1DG (☎ 01 935 6465)

DU VIVIER, Richard Adolphe Charles; CBE (1973, MBE 1945); s of James du Vivier, of Belgium; *b* 27 Dec 1911; *Educ* Malvern, King's Coll Cambridge; *m* 1936, Margaret, da of Sir Robert Aske, 1 Bt; 2 s, 2 da; *Career* Maj WW II serv: N Africa, Italy, NW Europe); ret schoolmaster, Br Cncl Rep Uruguay & Mexico 1951-55 & 1970-73; *Recreations* tennis, golf; *Clubs* Hurlingham, Sudbury Golf; *Style*— Richard du Vivier, Esq, CBE; 45 Chatsworth Rd, W5

DUBOWITZ, Prof Victor; s of Charley Dubowitz, and Olga, *née* Schattel; *b* 6 August 1931; *Educ* Beaufort W Central HS S Africa, Univ of Cape Town (BSc, MB, ChB, MD), Univ of Sheffield (PhD); *m* 10 July 1960, Lilly Magdalena Suzanne, *née* Sebok; 4 s (David b 1963, Michael b 1964, Gerald b 1965, Daniel b 1969); *Career* res assoc histochemistry Royal Postgrad Med Sch 1958-60, clinical asst Queen Mary's Hosp for Children Carshalton 1958-60, lectr clinical pathology Nat Hosp for Nervous Diseases 1960-61, lectr child health Univ of Sheffield 1961-65 (sr lectr 1965-67); reader child health and developmental neurology Univ of Sheffield 1967-72; 1972-: prof of paediatrics Univ of London, hon conslt paediatrician Hammersmith Hosp, dir Jerry Lewis Muscle Res Centre; FRCP 1972; Cdr Order Constantine the Great 1980, Arvo Ylppo Gold Medal Finland 1982; *Books* Developing and Diseased Muscle A Histochemical Study (1968), The Floppy Infant (2nd edn 1980), Muscle Biopsy: A Modern Approach (2nd edn 1985), Gestational Age of the Newborn: A Clinical Manual (1977), Muscle Disorders in Childhood (1978), Neurological Assessment of the Preterm and Full-term infant (1981), A Colour Atlas & Muscle Disorders in Childhood (1989); *Recreations* sculpting, hiking; *Style*— Prof Victor Dubowitz; Dept of Paediatrics, Royal Postgrad Med Sch, Ducane Rd, London W12 (☎ 01 740 3295)

DUBRAS, Bernard Louis; s of Leon Dubras, and Binda Blampied ; *b* 10 Jan 1926; *Educ* De La Salle Coll Jersey; *m* 19 Sept 1957, Molly, da of Samuel James Baughen; 2 da (Louise Adele b 9 Dec 1960, Charlotte Mary b 29 Feb 1964); *Career* Lloyds Bank plc 1940-47, CH Dubras Ltd 1947-52, chm Dubras Hldgs Ltd, md Chandis Ltd, non exec dir Jersey Electricity Co Ltd, non exec dir S G Warburg (Jersey) Ltd, dir CH Dubras Ltd, St John's Pharmacy Ltd; chm Jersey Cheshire Home Fndn, Procureur du Bien Public (tstee) Municipality of St Helier, chm Care ctee Parish of St Helier, memb Jersey Circle - Catenian Assoc; past pres Jersey C of C and Indust; former chm Jersey Cncl for Safety and Health at Work, Advsy cncl BBC Local Radio; former cncl memb Jersey Milk Mktg Bd; FIOD; *Recreations* boating, gardening; *Style*— Bernard Dubras, Esq; Clos Des Chênes, Route De La Vallee, St Peter, Jersey (☎ 0534 81 871); 5 Great Union Rd, St Helier, Jersey (☎ 0534 36 401, fax 0534 68 442)

DUCAT-AMOS, Air Cmdt Barbara Mary; CB (1974), RRC (1 Class, 1971); da of Capt George William Ducat-Amos (d 1942), master mariner, and Mary, *née* Cuthbert (d 1974); *b* 9 Feb 1921; *Educ* The Abbey Sch Reading, Nightingale Training Sch, St Thomas's; *Career* trained SRN and CMB (pt 1) St Thomas's Hosp, dep matron RAF Hosp Nocton Hall 1967-68, sr matron RAF Hosp Changi Singapore 1968-70, princ matron MOD (RAF) 1970-72 Queens Hon Nursing Sister 1972-78, matron-in-chief Princess Mary's RAF Nursing Serv and dir RAF Nursing Services 1972-78; nursing offr (sister) Cable and Wireless plc 1978-85; nat chm Girls Venture Corps 1982-; CStJ 1975; Queen's Hon Nursing Sister 1972-78; *Recreations* music, theatre, travel; *Clubs* RAF; *Style*— Air Cmdt Barbara Ducat-Amos, CB, RRC; c/o Barclays Bank, Wimbledon Common, Wimbledon High St, SW19

DUCE, Edward Harold; s of Nathan Duce (d 1960), and Ellen, *née* Picton; *b* 14 April 1911; *Educ* Reading Sch; *m* 25 Aug 1973, Sheila Grace Ellen, da of Arthur Edward Paine (d 1986); *Career* RNVR 1943-46, Lt (S) 1944; slr 1936; ptnr: Ratcliffe & Duce Reading 1940-57, Ratcliffe Duce & Gammer 1957-76; pres: Berks Bucks & Oxon Incorp Law Soc 1960-61 (sec 1949-75), Mental Health Review Tbnls 1960-73; first chm Legal Aid Area Ctee (S Area) 1950-53; sec: Southern Area Assoc of Law Socs 1950-75, Jt Ctee with the Bar 1970- 75, chm Assoc Prov Law Socs; memb Reading C of C; tres: Maidenhead Civic Soc, Thames Reach Residents Assoc; memb Berks Playing Fields Assoc; memb Law Soc 1936-; Freeman: City of London 1966, Worshipful Co of Upholders 1966;; *Books* History of Berks Bucks & Oxon Law Soc (1989); *Recreations* music, model railway; *Style*— Harold Duce, Esq; The Lodge, 2(B) College Avenue, Maidenhead, Berks SL6 6AJ; Eastgate House, 1 & 2 High St, Wallingford, Oxon OX10 OBJ (☎ 0491 34400, fax 0491 33740)

DUCHESNE, Brigadier (Peter) Robin; OBE (1978); s of Herbert Walter Duchesne (d 1978), of Dyffryn, Conway Rd, Mochdre, Clwyd, and Irene, *née* Cox (d 1979); *b* 25 Sept 1936; *Educ* Colwyn Bay GS, RMA Sandhurst, RMC of Science, Royal Navy Staff Coll; *m* 30 Mar 1968, Jennifer MacLean, da of Brian Elphinstone Gouldsbury, of 1 Whites Close, Piddlehinton, Dorset; 1 s (Charles b 7 Apr 1974), 1 da (Emma b 1 Oct 1977); *Career* cmmnd RA 1956, 4 Regt RHA Germany, 7 Parachute Regt RHA 1961-72, Capt instr RMA Sandhurst 1965-67, Co 49 Field Regt RA 1975-77, dir Staff Army Staff Coll Camberley 1977-79, Cdr with Mil Advsy Team Ghana 1979-81, Cdr 1 Armd Div RA Brig 1981-83, D/Cdr and Cos UN force Cyprus 1984-86; memb: UN Assoc, local church chour; vice chm sailing ctee Sail Trg Assoc Cncl; sec gen RYA 1986-, skipper jt serv entry Whitbread Round the World Race 1978; chm: RMAS, RFC, UN RFC Cyprus (former memb Army RFU); FBIM 1987; *Recreations* water sports, walking; *Clubs* RORC; *Style*— Brig Robin Duchesne, Lake Lodge, Churt, Farnham, Surrey GU10 2QB (☎ 025 125 3901); Royal Yachting Association, Romsey Rd, Eastleigh, Hamps (☎ 0703 629 962, fax 0703 629 924, telex 47393 BOATIN G)

DUCIE, 6 Earl of (UK 1837); Basil Howard Moreton; also Baron Ducie (GB 1763) and Baron Moreton (UK 1837); s of Hon Algernon Howard Moreton (d 1951), 2 s of 4 Earl of Ducie; suc unc 1952; *b* 15 Nov 1917; *Educ* C of E GS Brisbane Queensland; *m* 15 April 1950, Alison May, da of Leslie Atkins Bates, of Brisbane, Queensland; 3 s, 1 da; *Heir* s, Lord Moreton; *Career* patron of 2 livings; served 1941-45 with 62 A I Bn and 2/3 A I Bn New Guinea and Islands; *Style*— Rt Hon Earl of Ducie; Tortworth House, Tortworth, Wotton-under-Edge, Glos

DUCKER, Bernard John; s of Arthur John Ducker (d 1972), of Blackheath, and Ella Maud, *née* Jermy (d 1953); *b* 26 July 1922; *Educ* Roan Sch; *m* 7 May 1949, Dr Daphne Mary, da of Edward Harry Norris Dowlen (d 1977); 3 s (Adrian John b 11 June 1951, Gerard Bernard b 28 Feb 1954, Roderick Edward John b 2 Aug 1956); *Career* WWII Flt Lt RAF 1942-46; qualified CA 1949; ptnr: E C Brown & Batts 1949-81, Callingham Crane 1981-87; dir: Nicholas Reinsurance Ltd, Dukes Gp plc 1988, Pillinger Air Ltd; memb Worshipful Co of Scriveners; *Recreations* sailing, vintage and veteran vehicles; *Clubs* RAF; *Style*— Bernard Ducker, Esq; Merrileas, Leatherhead Rd, Oxshott, Surrey KT22 0EZ; 526 Purley Way, Croydon, Surrey (☎ 01 680 7770, fax 01 680 2345, telex 291312 PILAIR)

DUCKWORTH, Anthony John Stanhope; 3 and yst s of Sir George Herbert Duckworth, CB (d 1934), of Dalingridge Pl, Sharpthorne, Sussex, half-bro of Virginia Woolf; *b* 2 Oct 1913; *Educ* Eton, Trinity Cambridge; *m* 23 April 1941, Audrey Diana, da of Johannes Nicolaas Tollenaar, of 74 Chester Sq, SW1; 2 s, 1 da; *Career* sr ptnr Fielding Newson-Smith Stockbrokers 1970-77, dir Eagle Star Trust Co Ltd (former chm), Moet & Chandon (London) Ltd, Parfums Christian Dior (UK) Ltd; *Recreations* shooting, golf; *Clubs* Bucks; *Style*— Anthony Duckworth, Esq; 2 Eaton Place, SW1 (☎ 01 235 4776); Southacre House, Southacre, nr Kings Lynn, Norfolk (☎ Castleacre 272)

DUCKWORTH, His Hon Judge; Brian Roy; s of Eric Roy Duckworth (d 1972); *b* 26 July 1934; *Educ* Sedbergh, Oxford Univ (MA); *m* 1964, Nancy Carolyn, da of Christopher Holden (d 1972); 3 s, 1da; *Career* barr 1958, rec Crown Court 1972-83, Circuit judge (Northern Circuit) 1983-; *Recreations* golf, sailing, gardening; *Clubs* St James's (Manchester), Pleasington Golf ; *Style*— His Hon Judge Duckworth; c/o The Crown Court, Lancaster Road, Preston, Lancs

DUCKWORTH, Edward Richard Dyce; s and h of Sir Richard Duckworth, 3 Bt; *b* 13 July 1943; *Educ* Marlborough, Cranfield; *m* 1976, Patricia, only da of Thomas Cahill, of Eton, Berks; 1 s, 1 da; *Career* eng and mgmnt conslt; *Recreations* tennis, fishing; *Style*— Edward Duckworth, Esq

DUCKWORTH, Dr (Walter) Eric; s of Albert Duckworth (d 1947), and Rosamund Duckworth, *née* Biddle (d 1978); *b* 2 August 1925; *Educ* Waterloo GS, Queens' Coll Cambridge (MA, PhD); *m* 1949, Emma, da of Thomas Cowan (d 1980); *Career* md Fulmer Ltd 1969-, chm Yarsley Technical Centre Ltd 1977-87; dir: Ricardo Consulting Engrs plc 1978-85, Fleming Technol Investmt Tst 1984-; *Style*— Dr Eric Duckworth; Fulmer Ltd, Holly Bush Hill, Stoke Poges, Bucks SL2 4QD (☎ 02816 2181, telex 849374)

DUCKWORTH, Brig Geoffrey Loraine Dyce; CBE (1978); s of Capt Arthur Dyce Duckworth, RN (d 1973), of Aldershaw House, Southborough, Kent, and Grace Ella Mary, *née* Pontifex; *b* 24 May 1930; *Educ* Stowe; *m* 16 Dec 1961, Philippa Ann, da of Sir Percy Rugg, JP, DL (d 1986); 1 s (Jeremy b 1963), 1 da (Juliet b 1964); *Career* cmmnd RTR 1950, Staff Coll Camberley 1961, Lt-Col 1968, GSO1 directing staff Aust Staff Coll 1968-70, CO 2 RTR 1970-72, COS 2 Armd Div 1973-75, Cdr Br Army Trg Unit Suffield Canada 1975-77, Regtl Col RTR 1978-80, Brig 1980, Dep Fortress Cdr Gibraltar 1980-83, vice pres Regular Cmmns Bd 1983-85; ADC to HM The Queen 1982-85; admin mangr Quilter Goodison Stockbrokers London 1986, head of admin The Game Conservancy Fordingbridge 1987; memb: local PCC, Salisbury Music Soc; pres Army Cadet League Battersea; Freeman City of London 1957, memb Ct Asst Worshipful Co of Armourers and Brasiers 1988; Kt of the Hon Soc of Knights of The Round Table 1988; *Recreations* fly fishing, gardening, making music; *Style*— Brig Geoffrey Duckworth, CBE; Weir Cottage, Bickton, Fordingbridge, Hants SP6 2HA; (☎ 0425 55813); The Game Conservancy, Fordingbridge, Hants SP6 1EF (☎ 0425 52381)

DUCKWORTH, John Clifford; s of late Harold Duckworth, by his wife Mrs A H Duckworth, *née* Woods; *b* 27 Dec 1916; *Educ* KCS Wimbledon, Oxford U; *m* 1942, Dorothy Nancy, *née* Wills; 3 s; *Career* md National Research Devpt Corpn 1959-1970; chm: Lintott Contral Equipment Ltd, BVT Ltd, Focom Ltd; dir: Rank Organisation plc; Science Museum Trustee; *Style*— John Duckworth, Esq; Suite 33, 140 Park Lane, London W1 (☎ 01 499 0355, telex 27314)

DUCKWORTH, Hon Mrs; Hon (Mary) Katharine Medina; *née* Chatfield; OBE (1946); da of Adm of the Fleet 1 Baron Chatfield, GCB, OM, KCMG, CVO, PC (d 1967), and Lilian Emma, CStJ, *née* Matthews (d 1977); *b* 1911; *m* 22 Sept 1947, Henry George Austen de L'Etang Herbert Duckworth, RA, s of late Sir George and Lady Margaret Duckworth; 2 da; *Career* WVS 1939-46; *Style*— The Hon Mrs Duckworth, OBE; Dalingridge Place, Sharpthorne, Sussex (☎ 0342 810411)

DUCKWORTH, Maj Peter Alexander; s of Evelyn Poole Duckworth (d 1930), of Darjeeling, India, and Muriel Bowen, *née* Dobbie (d 1979); *b* 16 July 1923; *Educ* Royal Masonic Sch; *m* 30 Sept 1950, Ann, da of Lt Cdr George Cuthbert Irwin Ferguson (d 1941), of Copythorne, nr Southampton; 3 s (Luke b 1954, Rollo b 1957, Rufus b 1961), 1 da (Georgia b 1966); *Career* served 5 Royal Inniskilling Dragoon Gds: France, Germany BLA 1944-45, Korea 1951, Egypt 1953; Br Modern Pentathlon Champion 1949 and 1951, army epee champion 1951, introduced orienteering to Br Army as a sport and methods of training, Br Olympic Modern Pentathlon team mangr 1960; chm hart Dist Cncl 1983-85, rep of Hants Dist Cncls on Serplan, chm Hants Banch Assoc of Dist Cncls; head gardener Bramshot House Fleet; *Recreations* swimmig, gardening; *Clubs* Epee; *Style*— Maj Peter A Duckworth; Bramshot House, Fleet, Hants (☎ 0252 617304)

DUCKWORTH, Sir Richard Dyce; 3 Bt (UK 1909), of Grosvenor Place, City of Westminster; s of Sir Edward Dyce Duckworth, 2 Bt (d 1945); *b* 30 Sept 1918; *Educ* Marlborough; *m* 5 Sept 1942, Violet Alison, da of Lt-Col George Boothby Wauchope, DSO (d 1952), of Highclere, Newbury, by his wife Violet Adelaide, widow of Capt Merveyn Crawshay (ka 1914), da of Capt Edward von Mumm; 2 s; *Heir* s, Edward Duckworth; *Career* Retired East India merchant; *Style*— Sir Richard Duckworth, Bt; Dunwood Cottage, Shootash, Romsey, Hants

DUCKWORTH, Roger Peter Terence; s of Ronald Duckworth (d 1966), of Blackburn, Lancs, and Bessie, *née* Smith (d 1980); *b* 16 Jan 1943; *Educ* Accrington GS; *m* 12 June 1965, Marion, da of William Henry Holden (d 1981), of Blackburn, Lancs; 1 s (Myles b 1972), 1 da (Laurel b 1970); *Career* chm and chief exec offr

Netlon Ltd and the Netlon Gp of Cos; ACIMA; *Recreations* music, fellwalking, theatre; *Clubs* Farmers; *Style*— Roger Duckworth, Esq; Netlon Ltd, Blackburn, Lancs (☎ 0254 62431, telex 63313, fax 0254 680008)

DUCKWORTH-CHAD, Anthony Nicholas George; s of A J S Duckworth of Southacre Hse, King's Lynn, Norfolk; *b* 20 Nov 1942; *Educ* Eton, RAC Cirenuester; *m* 6 May 1970, Elizabeth Sarah da of Capt C B H Wake-Walker of East Bergholt Lodge, Suffolk, 2 s (James b 1972, William b 1975) 1 da (Davina b 1978); *Career* farmer & landowner; memb: Walsingham RDC 1963-74, North Norfolk DC 1974-; (chm 1987-); chm Norfolk branch country landowners assoc 1977-78; govr Greshams, sch 1974-; Liveryman Worshipful Co of Fishmongers; *Recreations* country, sports; *Clubs* Whites, Pratts; *Style*— Anthony Duckworth-Chad, Esq; 5 Cumberland Street, London, SW1V 4LS; Pynkney Hall, East Rudham, King's Lynn, Norfolk

DUCKWORTH-KING, Lady; Alice Patricia; da of Thomas Rutledge, of Fugar House, Ravensworth, co Durham; *m* 29 July 1943, as his 2 wife, Sir John Richard Duckworth-King, 7 Bt (d 1972, when the title became extinct); *Style*— Lady Duckworth-King; 47 Avenue de Hassan, 11 Tangier, Morocco

DUDBRIDGE, Bryan James; CMG (1961); s of Walter Dudbridge, OBE, and Anne Jane, *née* Baker; *b* 2 April 1912; *Educ* King's College Sch Winbledon, Selwyn Coll Cambridge; *m* 29 Oct 1943, (Audrey) Mary, da of W B Heywood; 2 s (John b 1945, Simon b 1953), 1 da (Josephine b 1949); *Career* Colonial Admin Serv: cadet Tanganylka Territory 1935 (sundry sub dists and dist 1939-52), sec lane utilization ctee Southern Highland Province 1952; actg provincial cmmr: i/c Southern Province 1953 (sr dist offr 1953), local govt in secretariat 1955; prov cmmr i/c Western Province 1957, min for prvincial affrs 1959-60, ret 1961; Christian Aid (overseas charity arm of Br Cncl of Churches): assoc dir 1963, later dep dir, actg dir 1970, ret 1972; parish cncllr High Halden; memb: CAB Ashford, Wye Coll Beagles, Stoke Hill Beagles; *Clubs* Royal Cwlth Soc; *Style*— Bryan Dudbridge, Esq, CMG; Red Rock Bungalow, Elm Grove Rd, Topsham, Exeter EX3 OEJ (☎ 0392 874 468)

DUDBRIDGE, Glen; s of George Victor Dudbridge, and Edna Kathleen, *née* Cockle; *b* 2 July 1938; *Educ* Bristol GS, Magdalene Coll Cambridge: (BA, MA, PhD), New Asia Inst of Advanced Chinese Studies Hong Kong; *m* 16 Sept 1965, Sylvia Lo Fung-Young, da of Lo Tak-Tsuen (d 1981); 1 s (Frank b 1967), 1 da (Laura b 1968); *Career* Nat Serv RAF 1957-59; jr res fell Magdalene Coll Cambridge 1965, lectr modern chinese Oxford Univ 1965-85 fell Wolfson Coll Oxford 1966-85, (emeritus fell 1985), visiting assoc prof: Yale Univ 1972-73, Univ of California at Berkeley 1980, prof chinese Cambridge Univ 1985-89, prof chinese Oxford Univ 1989-, fell Univ. Coll Oxford 1989-; fell Magdalene Coll Cambridge 1985-89; FBA 1984; *Books* The Hsi-yu chi: a study of antecedents to the 16th century Chinese novel (1970), The legend of Miao-shan (1978), The Tale of Li Wa: study and critical ed of a Chinese story from the 9th century (1983); *Style*— Prof Glen Dudbridge; Oriental Inst, Pusey Lane, Oxford, OX1 2LE (☎ 0865 278200, fax 0865 270708)

DUDDERIDGE, John Webster; OBE (1962); s of William George Dudderidge (d 1945), of Cheddon Fitzpaine, Somerset, and Mary Ethel, *née* Webster (d 1962); *b* 24 August 1906; *Educ* Magnus GS Newark-on-Trent, University Coll Nottingham (BSc); *m* 25 July 1936, (Gertrude Louisa) Evelyn, da of Rev Frederick S Hughes, of N China Mission, Peking, China; 2 s (John b 1937, Philip b 1949), 2 da (Ruth b 1938, Hilary b 1944); *Career* asst master Manor House Sch London 1929-31, housemaster Haberdashers' Aske's Sch 1931-69 (asst master); memb: of Cambridge Wildlife Tst, Cncl for the Protection of Rural Eng, Nat Tst; Br Olympic Assoc: cncl 1949-69, exec ctee 1969-73, dep chm 1973-77, vice-pres 1977-; Br Canoe Union: fndr memb 1936, sec for racing 1936-49, gen sec 1939-59, pres 1959-77, hon life pres 1977-. award of Honour 1961; Int Canoe Fedn: memb bd 1938-80, vice pres 1946-48, hon memb 1980-; award of honour 1962, Gold Medal 1980; sec/tres Cwlth Canoeing Fedn 1968-84; memb cncl for Eng Cwlth Ganes Fedn 1976-83, memb ctee of advsrs Sports Aid Fndn 1976-80; memb Br Olympic Canoe Team 1936, mangr Br Canoe Racing Team 1938-58, int official 1948-81; *Books* author of numerous articles on canoes and canoeing, for magazines, jls, almanacks and encyclopaedias (1974); *Recreations* canoeing, walking, gardening, reading; *Clubs* Royal Canoe, Canoe Camping; *Style*— John Dudderidge, Esq, OBE; Tyros, 15 Lacks Close, Cottenham, Cambridge, CB4 4TZ (☎ 0954 51752)

DUDDERIDGE, Philip Stephen; s of John Webster Dudderidge, OBE, of North Leigh, Oxon, and Gertrude Louisa Evelyn, *née* Hughes; *b* 6 Feb 1949; *Educ* Haberdashers' Aske's; *m* 1973, Jennifer Anne, da of Terence W Hayes; 5 s, 1 da; *Career* sound engr and artistes' mangr; fndr, chm and md Soundcraft Electronics Ltd 1973- (Queen's Award for Export 1979 and 1985); *Recreations* flying; *Style*— Philip Dudderidge, Esq; Chilterns, Grimms Hill, Great Missenden, Bucks; Soundcraft Electronics Ltd,Borehamwood Industrial Park, Rowley Lane, Borchamwood, Herts WD6 5PZ (☎ 01 207 5050)

DUDGEON, Air Vice-Marshal Antony Greville; CBE (1955), DFC (1941); s of Prof Herbert William Dudgeon (d 1935); *b* 6 Feb 1916; *Educ* Eton, RAF Cranwell, RAF Staff Coll, RAF Flying Coll, Mgmnt Systems Course USA; *m* 1942, Phyllis Margaret, da of late Gp Capt John McFarlane, OBE, MC, AFC, of Lowestoft, Suffolk; 1 s, 1 da; *Career* joined RAF 1933, cmmnd 1935; serv WWII: Far East, ME, Europe, UK; Cmdt ATC 1960-62, dir Flight Safety MOD (RAF) 1963-65, Air Vice-Marshal 1965, COS to Head Br Defence Staff NATO, Washington and Belgium 1965-68, 3500 hours as pilot, ret 1968; mangr Professional Staff Servs and Recruiting McKinsey & Co Paris, 1968-78, rep France Grangersol Ltd 1978-81; *Books* all autobiographical: A Flying Command (as Tom Dagger 1962), The Luck of the Devil (1985), Wings over North Africa (1987); *Recreations* writing, photography, swimming, languages (French, Egyptian); *Clubs* RAF; *Style*— Air Vice-Marshal Antony Dudgeon, CBE, DFC; 43 Winchendon Rd, London SW6 5DH (☎ 01 731 0718)

DUDLEY, Bishop of 1977-; Rt Rev Anthony (Tony) Charles Dumper; s of Lt Charles Frederick Dumper, MC (d 1965), and Edith Mary, *née* Ribbins (d 1966); *b* 4 Oct 1923; *Educ* Surbiton GS, Christ's Coll Cambridge (BA, MA), Westcott House Cambridge; *m* 5 June 1948, Sibylle Anna Emilie, da of Paul Hellwig (d 1945), of Germany; 2 s (Peter Nicholas b 1951, Michael Richard Thomas b 1956), 1 da (Hildegard Sarah Sibylle b 1954); *Career* ordained 1947, archdeacon N Malaya 1955-64, dean of Singapore 1964-70, rural dean Stockton on Tees 1970-77; memb: CND, Dudley Borough Educn Ctee; *Books* Vortex of the East (1962); *Recreations* walking, gardening, reading; *Style*— The Rt Rev the Bishop of Dudley; 366 Halesowen Rd, Cradley Heath, W Midlands (☎ 021 550 3407)

DUDLEY, Baroness (14 in line, E 1439); Barbara Amy Felicity Wallace; *née* Lea-Smith; da of 12 Baron Dudley (d 1936); suc bro, 13 Baron, 1972; *b* 23 April 1907; *m* 1929, Guy Raymond Hill Wallace (d 1967); 3 s, 1 da; *Heir* s, Hon Jim Wallace; *Style*— The Rt Hon the Lady Dudley; Hill House, Napleton Lane, Kempsey, Worcs (☎ 0905 820253)

DUDLEY, Hon Mrs (Betty); *née* Montague; da of 1 Baron Amwell (d 1966); *b* 15 Oct 1920; *m* 1941, John Forbes Dudley; 1 da; *Style*— The Hon Mrs Dudley; 76 Eastcourt Rd, Burbage, Wilts

DUDLEY, Charles Edward Steele; s of Col Stewart Dudley, MC (d 1977), of Tiverton, Devon, and Gertrude Alexandra, da of Maj-Gen Sir SB Steele, KCMG, CB, MVO and ggggda of the Marquis de Lothinére; *b* 4 Sept 1935; *Educ* St Andrews Coll Grahamstown, RMA Sandhurst; *m* 29 Mar 1965, Marianne, da of Douglas Sandford Kemp, of Belize and Brazil; 2 da (Charlotte Elaine b 1969, Lucie Elizabeth b 1973); *Career* cmmnd KSLI 1956; Sultans Armed Forces Oman 1965; farming and business 1971; fndr memb of The Free Angola Campaign, a UK Gp supporting the Nat Union for the Total Independance of Angola, chm 1987-; resided and travelled extensively throughout Africa and the Middle East; *Recreations* long distance riding, Elizabethan history, freelance writing, port wines; *Style*— Charles Dudley, Esq; The Free Angola Campaign, PO Box 380, Reading, Berkshire RG3 6GR (☎ 0734 410998, fax 07354 4339)

DUDLEY, Grace, Countess of; Grace Maria Kolin; *m* 1, Prince Stanislas Radziwill; 2, 1961, as his 3 w, 3 Earl of Dudley (d 1969); *Style*— The Rt Hon Grace, Countess of Dudley; Greycliff, Nassau, Bahamas

DUDLEY, Prof Hugh Arnold Freeman; CBE (1988); s of Walter Lionel Dudley (d 1944), and Ethel Marion, *née* Smith (d 1938); *b* 1 July 1925; *Educ* Heath GS Halifax, Edinburgh Univ (MBChB, ChM); *m* 17 July 1947, Jean Bruce Lindsay, da of James Johnston (d 1966), of Keltneyburn, Aberfeldy, Perthshire; 2 s (Raymond James Desomeri b 1948, Nigel Hugh Desomeri b 1951), 1 da (Iona Mary Bruce Lindsay); *Career* Lt and Col RAMC 1948-50, Maj (Actg Lt Col) RAAMC 1968-72; lectr Edinburgh Univ 1954-58, sr lectr Aberdeen Univ 1958-62, fndn prof Monash Univ 1962-72, prof St Mary's Hosp London 1972-88; pres: Surgical Res Soc of Australia, Surgical Res Soc of GB and Ireland, Biological Engrg Soc of GB; chm Br Journal of Surgery Soc; hon fell SA Coll of Surgns; Medal of Merit S Vietnam 1971; FRCSE 1951, FRACS 1964, FRCS 1974; *Recreations* shooting; *Style*— Prof Hugh Dudley, CBE; Broombrae, Glenbuchat, Strathdon, Aberdeenshire AB3 8UE (☎ 097 5641341); Room 3/124, Queen Elizabeth The Queen Mother Wing, St Marys Hospital, London W2 1NY (☎ 01 725 6246)

DUDLEY, Maurice; s of Samuel Geoffrey Dudley (d 1933) and Evelyn Horton (d 1986); *b* 19 Jan 1925; *Educ* secdy sch, night sch, correspondence coll; *m* 17 Dec 1949, Rose Eileen Esther, da of James Sidney Massey (d 1978); 2 s (Paul Maurice b 1955, Mark Ian b 1958); *Career* WWII RAF aircrew with 2 Tactical Airforce; CA; md: Dismantling & Engrg Gp Ltd; dir: Dismantling & Engrg Ltd, Kidderminster Steel Ltd, Deks Clear Ltd; past pres: Nat Fdn of Demolition Contractors; former chm: Demolition Industry Register, memb: Drafting Ctee for code of practise for Demolition & Dismantling Br Standards Inst, past pre Euro Demolition Assoc; *Recreations* golf, swimming; *Clubs* Sutton Coldfield Golf (former capt); *Style*— Maurice Dudley, Esq; Grey Gables, 16A Le More, Four Oaks, Sutton Coldfield, West Midlands (☎ 021 308 4351); Lion House, Mucklow Hill, Halesowen, West Midlands (☎ 021 550 9041, telex: 338063, fax: 021 501 3023, car ☎ 0836 590330)

DUDLEY, Prof Norman Alfred; CBE (1977); s of Alfred Dudley (d 1949), of Selly Oak, Birmingham, and Alice Maud Dudley, *née* Bolstridge (d 1959); descended from the Dudleys of Davenham, Cheshire, and the Bolstridges of Bedworth, a branch of the Bulstrode family of Bucks circa 1300; *b* 29 Feb 1916; *Educ* Kings Norton GS, Univ of London (BSc), Univ of Birmingham (PhD); *m* 1940, Hilda Florence, da of John Miles (d 1968); 1 s (John Miles), 2 da (Ann, Jane); *Career* head Dept of Engrg Prod and dir Univ Inst for Engrg Prod 1956-80, Lucas Prof of Engrg Prod Birmingham Univ 1959-80 (emeritus 1981-); ed Int Journal of Prod Research 1961-80; memb: W Midlands economic Planning cncl 1970-78, W Midlands Cncl Advsy Ctee on Economic Devpt 1975-77, SRC Manufacturing Technol and Teaching Co Mgmnt Ctees 1977-80; FEng, Hon FIProdE, FBIM; Hon DTech (Loughborough); memb UK delgn to UNCSAT Geneva 1963; emeritus memb CIRP 1981; hon memb Int Fndn for Prod Res 1982; *Recreations* gardening, genealogy; *Style*— Prof Norman Dudley, CBE; 37 Abbots Close, Knowle, Solihull, W Midlands B93 9PP (☎ 0564 775976)

DUDLEY, 4 Earl of (UK 1860); William Humble David Ward; also Baron Ward of Birmingham (E 1664) and Viscount Ednam (UK 1860); s of 3 Earl of Dudley, MC (d 1969), by his 1 w, Lady Rosemary, *née* Sutherland-Leveson-Gower, RRC (d 1930), da of 4 Duke of Sutherland; *b* 5 Jan 1920; *Educ* Eton, Christ Church Oxford; *m* 1, 1946 (m dis 1961), Stella, da of Miguel Carcano, KCMG, KBE, sometime Argentinian Ambass to UK; 1 s, 2 da (twins); m 2, 1961, Maureen Swanson; 1 s, 5 da; *Heir* s, Viscount Ednam; *Career* sits as Cons in House of Lords; 2 Lt 10 Hussars 1941, Capt 1945; ADC to the Viceroy of India 1942-3; dir: Baggeridge Brick Co Ltd, Tribune Investmt Tst Ltd; *Clubs* White's, Pratt's, Royal Yacht Sqdn; *Style*— The Rt Hon The Earl of Dudley; Vention House, Putsborough, Georgeham, N Devon (☎ 0271 890631/ 890632); 6 Cottesmore Gdns, W8 (☎ 01 937 5671)

DUDLEY, William Stuart; s of William Stuart Dudley, and Dorothy Irene, *née* Stacey; *b* 4 Mar 1947; *Educ* Highbury GS, St Martins Sch Art (BA), Slade Sch of Art UCL (Post Grad Dip Fine Art); *Career* res stage designer Nat Theatre 1970-; prodns incl: The Mysteries, Lark Rise, Undiscovered Country, The Critic, Cat on a Hot Tin Roof, The Shaughraun, The Changeling; stage designs RSC incl: Richard III, A Midsummer Night's Dream; stage designs Royal Opera House incl: Don Giovanni, Tales of Hoffman, Der Rosen Kavalier; designer of The Ring at Bayreuth 1983; fndr memb folk band Morris Minor and the Austin Seven 1980, hon pres Tower Theatre 1988, hon dir Irish Theatre Comp London; memb Soc Br Theatre Designers; *Recreations* playing the concertina and the cajun accordian; *Style*— William Dudley, Esq; 30 Crooms Hill, Greenwich, London SE10 (☎ 01 858 8711)

DUDLEY EDWARDS, Ruth; da of Robert Walter Dudley Edwards (d 1988), and Sheila, *née* O'Sullivan (d 1985); *b* 24 May 1944; *Educ* Sacred Heart Convent Dublin, Sandymount HS Dublin, Univ Coll Dublin (BA, MA), Girton and Univ Colls Cambridge, City of London Poly (dip Business Studies); *m* 1, 31 July 1965 (m dis 1975), Patrick John Cosgrave, s of Patrick Joseph Cosgrave (d 1952); m 2, Jan 1976, John Robert Matlock, s of John Leonard Matlock (d 1986); *Career* principal DOI 1975-79, freelance writer 1979-, company historian The Economist 1982-; memb Exec Ctee Br Irish Assoc 1981-, chm Br Assoc for Irish Studies 1986-; *Books* An Atlas of Irish History (1973, Patrick Pearse: the triumph of failure (1977), James Connolly (1981), Corridors of Death (1981), Harold MacMillan: a life in pictures (1983), The Saint Valentine's Day Murderers (1984), Victor Gollancz: a biography; *Recreations* friends, reading, conversation, laughter, walking around big cities; *Clubs* Reform; *Style—* Miss Ruth Dudley Edwards; 40 Pope's Lane, Ealing, London W5 4NU (☎ 01 579 1041)

DUDLEY-SMITH, Rt Rev Timothy; *see*: Thetford, Bishop of

DUDLEY-WILLIAMS, Sir Alastair Edgcumbe James; 2 Bt (UK 1964), of City and Co of the City of Exeter; s of Sir Rolf Dudley Dudley-Williams, 1 Bt (d 1987); *b* 26 Nov 1943; *Educ* Pangbourne Nautical Coll; *m* 1972, Diana Elizabeth Jane, twin da of Robert Henry Clare Duncan, of Haslemere, Surrey; 3 da (Marina Elizabeth Catherine b 1974, Lorna Caroline Rachel b 1977, Eleanor Patricia Rosemary b 1979); *Heir* bro, Malcolm Philip Edgcumbe Dudley-Williams, *qv*; *Career* field salesman Hughes Tool Co Texas 1962-64, oil well driller Bay Drilling Corpn (Louisiana) 1964-65; driller: Bristol Siddeley Whittle Tools Ltd 1965-67, driller Santafe Drilling Co (North Sea and Libya) 1967-72, Incape plc 1972-86, Wildcat Conslts 1986-; *Recreations* gardening, fishing, shooting; *Clubs* Port Pendennis YC; *Style—* Sir Alastair Dudley-Williams, Bt; The Corner Cottage, Brook, Godalming, Surrey

DUDLEY-WILLIAMS, Helen, Lady; (Margaret) Helen; *née* Robinson; er da of late Frederick Eaton Robinson, OBE, AMICE, AMIMechE, of Enfield, Middx; *m* 25 May 1940, Sir Rolf Dudley Dudley-Williams, 1 Bt (d 1987); 2 s; *Style—* Helen, Lady Dudley-Williams; The Old Manse, S Petherton, Somerset TA13 5DB

DUDLEY-WILLIAMS, Malcolm Philip Edgcumbe; yr s of Sir Rolf Dudley Dudley-Williams, 1 Bt (d 1987); bro and hp of Sir Alastair Edgcumbe James Dudley-Williams, 2 Bt, *qv*; *b* 10 August 1947; *Educ* Pangbourne Nautical Coll; *m* 1973, Caroline Anne Colina, twin da of Robert Henry Clare Duncan, of The Wall House, High Street, Haslemere, Surrey; 2 s (Nicholas Mark Edgcumbe b 1975, Patrick Guy Edgcumbe b 1978), 1 da (Clare Helen Colina b 1982); *Style—* Malcolm Dudley-Williams, Esq

DUDMAN, George Edward; CB (1973); s of William James Dudman (d 1940); *b* 2 Dec 1916; *Educ* Merchant Taylors', St John's Coll Oxford, Churchill Coll Cambridge ; *m* 1955, Joan Doris, da of Frederick John Eaton (d 1956); 1 s, 1 da; *Career* HM Forces 1940-46, FO (Control Cmmn Germany) 1946-49, called to the bar 1950, Law Offrs' Dept 1951-65 (legal sec 1958-65), legal advsr Dept of Educn and Science 1965-77, ed Statutes in Force 1977-81; *Recreations* chess, painting, cooking, gardening, studying philosophy; *Style—* George Dudman Esq, CB; 10 Viga Rd, Grange Park, London N21 1HJ

DUFF, Alistair David Buchanan; s of Maj David Keer Duff (d 1963), of Tighnabruaich House, Argyll and Muriel Kerr, *née* Cavaghan; *b* 19 July 1928; *Educ* George Watson's Edinburgh, Edinburgh Univ; *m* 1 Feb 1958, Cynthia Mary, da of Maurice Stork Hardy (d 1974), of Cleughhead, Annan, Dumfriesshire; 1 s (Roderick b Oct 1963), 1 da (Carolyn b Aug 1962); *Career* Nat Serv RA Malaya 1947-49; vice chm Cavaghan & Gray Ltd Carlisle 1967-88 (dir 1957-63 and 1963-77); chm: Br Bacon Curers Fedn 1975-76, TSB Lancs and Cumbria 1976-83 (tstee Eng and Wales 1983, dep chm NW regnl bd 1984-, memb central bd 1976-86); dir Carlisle Race Course Co 1978-; govr local sch; *Recreations* shooting, horse racing, sailing; *Clubs* Farmers, Border and County; *Style—* Alistair Duff, Esq; Monkcastle, Southwaite, Carlisle, Cumbria CA4 OPZ (☎ 069 74 73 273)

DUFF, Rt Hon Sir (Arthur) Antony; GCMG (1980, KCMG 1973, CMG 1964), CVO (1972), DSO (1944), DSC (1943), PC (1980); yr s of Adm Sir Arthur Allan Morison Duff, KCB, JP, DL (d 1952, ggs of Robert Duff, whose mother was Lady Helen Duff, da of 1 Earl of Fife, ancestor of Dukes of Fife. Robert's f was Vice Adm Robert Duff of Logie and Fetteresso, one of twenty-three children of Patrick Duff of Craigston); *b* 25 Feb 1920; *Educ* RNC Dartmouth; *m* 1944, Pauline Marion, da of Capt R H Bevan, RN, and widow of Flt Lt J A Sword; 1 s, 1 step s, 2 da; *Career* served RN 1937-46; entered Foreign Service 1946, first sec Foreign Office 1952, first sec Paris 1954, counsellor Bonn 1962-64, ambass to Nepal 1964-65, Commonwealth Office 1965-68, dep high cmmr Kuala Lumpur 1969-72, high cmmr Kenya 1972-75, dep under-sec of State FCO 1975-80, dep to Permanent Under-Sec of State 1977-80; dep govr Southern Rhodesia 1979-80, dep sec Cabinet Office 1980-; *Clubs* Army and Navy; *Style—* The Rt Hon Sir Antony Duff, GCMG, CVO; c/o National Westminster Bank, 17 The Hard, Portsea, Hants

DUFF, Gordon Ray; s of Maj David Kerr Duff (d 1963), of Tighnabruaich House, Argyll, and Muriel, *née* Cavaghan (d 1988); *b* 17 Mar 1930; *Educ* George Watsons Coll Edinburgh, Open Univ (BA); *m* 23 May 1959, Wilda Mary, da of James Glover (d 1967), of Arinagour, Isle of Coll, Argyll; 4 s (David, Ian, Ranald, Alistair); *Career* enlisted RE 1949, cmmnd 1950, Capt 1953, 4 Bn Border Regt (TA) on transfer to RARO 1961; regnl dir Scottish subsids of Cavaghan of Gray Gp 1959-69, mgmnt conslt 1969-88 (Cumbria & Inverness-shire), currently conslt Crown Estates Cmmrs Scotland; memb: Lochaber Presbytery, bd of stewardship and fin Church of Scotland, cncl BIM; vice-chm Scottish ctee BIM; MMS 1986, FIMC 1986, FBIM 1980; *Recreations* shooting, fishing; *Clubs* Highland; *Style—* Gordon Duff, Esq; Highbridge, Spean Bridge, Inverness-shire PH34 4EX (☎ 0397 81 391); 101 High Street, Fort William, Inverness-shire PH33 6DG (☎ 0397 5924, fax 0397 5030)

DUFF, Timothy Cameron; s of Timothy Duff, (d 1974) of Tynemouth, and Marjory Magdalene, *née* Cameron; *b* 2 Feb 1940; *Educ* Royal GS Newcastle upon Tyne, Caius Coll Cambridge (MA, LLM); *m* 23 June 1966, Patricia, da of John Munby Walker Capt DLI, d 1955), of N Shields; 2 s (John b 1968, James b 1970), 1 da (Emma b 1973); *Career* admitted slr 1965; sr ptnr Hadaway and Hadaway of N Shields and Whitley Bay 1988-(ptnr since 1968); dir Tynemouth Bldg Soc 1985, sec and clerk to tstee Tyne Mariners Benevolent Inst 1984; held office in num local orgns inc: Tynemouth Rowing Club, Percy Park RFC, Holy Saviours Church; Law Soc (1966), Ecclesiastical Law Soc (1988); *Recreations* sailing, piping, reading, hunting, camping, walking; *Clubs* Green Wyvern Yacht; *Style—* Timothy C Duff, Esq; 26 The Drive, Tynemouth, Tyne & Wear (☎ 091 257 1463); Hadaway and Hadaway, 58 Howard Street, North Shields, Tyne & Wear, NE30 1AL (☎ 091 253 0382), fax 091 296 1904

DUFF GORDON, Sir Andrew Cosmo Lewis; 8 Bt (UK 1813), of Halkin, Ayrshire; s of Sir Douglas Frederick Duff-Gordon, 7 Bt (d 1964, whose ggf, Sir William Duff Gordon, 2 Bt, was paternal gs of 2 Earl of Aberdeen); *b* 17 Oct 1933; *m* 1, 1967 (m dis 1975), Grania Mary, da of Fitzgerald Villiers-Stuart, of Dromana, Villerstown, Co Waterford; 1 s; m 2, 1975, Eveline (Evie) Virginia, da of Samuel Soames, of Boxford House, Newbury; 3 s; *Heir* s, Cosmo Henry Villiers Duff-Gordon b 18 June 1968; *Career* dir Nelson Yorst-Mersy Agencies Ltd; *Style—* Sir Andrew Duff Gordon, Bt; 27 Cathcart, London SW10; Downton House, Walton, Presteigne, Powys (☎ 054 421 223)

DUFF OF MELDRUM, Robin (Robert) Beauchamp; MBE (1985); er (but only surviving) s of Douglas Garden Duff, OBE (himself 1 cous of Sir Garden Beauchamp Duff, 1 and last Bt, of Hatton, and seventh in descent from Patrick Duff (d 1731), whose er bro William was f of 1 Earl of Fife and ancestor of the Dukes of Fife), and Margaret Crawley, *née* Vincent (d 1971); *b* 27 Feb 1915; *Educ* Winchester, Trinity Coll Cambridge (MA); *Career* dep chm Air Transport Users Ctee to 1984 (chm 1985); pres The Scottish Ballet; former memb Scottish Housing Advsy Ctee & Scottish Hygiene Advsy Ctee, chm Health & Welfare Ctee Aberdeen CC; former war correspondent BBC and foreign correspondent Daily Express; personal advsr HH Maharaja of Bundi 1947-54; *Clubs* Garrick; *Style—* Robin Duff of Meldrum, MBE; Meldrum House, Old Meldrum, Aberdeenshire (☎ 065 12 2294); 48 Swan Court, London SW3

DUFF-ASSHETON-SMITH, Hon Lady (Millicent) Joan Marjoribanks; da of 3 Baron Tweedmouth (decd); *b* 1906; *m* 1935 (m dis 1937) Sir Charles Michael Robert Vivian Duff-Assheton-Smith, Bt (d 1980); *Style—* The Hon Lady Duff-Assheton-Smith; 45 Westminster Gdns, London, SW1

DUFFELL, Michael Royson; s of Roy John Duffell (d 1979); *b* 19 June 1939; *Educ* Dulwich Coll; *m* 1964, Gisela, *née* Rothkehl; 1 s (Christian Royson b 1964), 1 da (Julie Royson b 1969); *Career* reception mangr Hyde Park Hotel 1966-69, gen mangr Grosvenor Hotel Chester 1969-76, controller of the Household to HM King Hussein of Jordan 1976-80, dir and gen mangr The Ritz 1980-84; md: Cunard Hotels and The Ritz 1984-88, Hotel Atop the Bellevue Philadelphia USA 1988; *Recreations* sports; *Style—* Michael Duffell, Esq; 26 Brechin Place, London SW7 4QA (☎ 01 373 2213); Hotel Atop the Bellevue, 1145 Chancellor St, Philadelphia, PA 19102 (☎ 215 893 1776)

DUFFELL, Brig Peter Royson; CBE (1988, OBE 1981), MC (1966); s of Roy John Duffell (d 1979), of Lenham, Kent, and Ruth Doris, *née* Gustaffson; *b* 19 June 1939; *Educ* Dulwich Coll; *m* 9 Oct 1982, Ann Murray, da of Col Basil Bethune Neville Woodd (d 1975), of Rolvenden, Kent; 1 s (Charles Basil Royson b 20 Oct 1986), 1 da (Rachel Leonie Sylvia b 9 April 1985); *Career* cmmnd 2 KEO Gurkha Rifles 1960, attended Staff Coll Camberley 1971, Brigade Maj 5 Brigade 1972-74, MA to CinC UKLF 1976-78, Cmdt 1 Bn 2 KEO Gurkha Rifles 1978-81, Col GS MOD 1981-83, Cdr Gurkha Field Force 1984-5; CoS 1 (BR) Corps 1986-87, RCDS 1988; FRGS 1975; *Recreations* golf, reading, writing, travel; *Clubs* Travellers'; *Style—* Brigadier Peter Duffell, CBE MC; c/o Drummonds, 49 Charing Cross, London SW1A 2DX

DUFFERIN AND AVA, Marchioness of; Lindy - Serena Belinda Rosemary; *née* Guinness; da of Gp Capt Loel Guinness, OBE (d 1988), and his 2 w, Lady Isabel Manners, yr da of 9 Duke of Rutland; *b* 25 Mar 1941; *m* 21 Oct 1964, 5 and last Marquess of Dufferin and Ava (d 1988); *Career* writer and artist; *Recreations* gardening and nature conservation; Clandeboye, Co Down, Northern Ireland; 4 Holland Villas Rd, W14

DUFFERIN AND CLANDEBOYE, 10 Baron (I 1800); Francis George Blackwood; 7 Bt (UK 1814); also 11 Bt (I 1763) of Ballyleidy, and 7 Bt (UK 1814); s of late Capt Maurice Baldwin Raymond Blackwood, DSO, RN (d on active serv 1941) and Dorothea (d 1967), da of late Hon G Bertrand Edwards, of Huon Park, Sydney, NSW; suc to cousin's baronetcy 1979; suc to barony of Dufferin and Clandeboye and baronetcy of Ballyleidy 1988 on death of 5 and last Marquess of Dufferin and Ava; *b* 20 May 1916; *Educ* Knox GS Wahroonga, Sydney Technical Coll; *m* 1941, Margaret, da of Hector Kirkpatrick, of Lindfield, NSW, Aust; 2 s, 1 da; *Heir* s, Hon John Francis Blackwood, *qv*; *Career* former chemical engr, now consulting engr in private practice; FIEAust, ARACI; *Style—* Sir Francis Blackwood, Bt; Uambi, 408 Bobbin Head Rd, N Turramurra, NSW 2074 Australia

DUFFETT, Christopher Charles Biddulph; s of Capt Charles Henry Duffett, CBE, DSO (d 1981), Leonora Biddulph; *b* 23 August 1943; *Educ* Bryanston, Peterhouse Cambridge (MA), Wharton Sch Univ of Pennsylvania (MBA); *m* 1973, Jennifer Edwards; 2 s (Samuel Owen Salisbury b 1975, Daniel Charles William Biddulph b 1977); *Career* asst economist Nat Devpt Off 1965-67, exec banking dept S G Warburg and Co Ltd 1969-71, area fin mangr Inco Ltd NY 1971-74, tres Inco Europe Ltd 1974-77, gp tres Rank Orgn Ltd 1977-79, gp fin dir The Economist Newspaper Ltd 1979-, md The Law Debenture Corpn plc; FCT; *Recreations* gardening, sailing, walking; *Clubs* Royal Oak Racing; *Style—* Christopher Duffett, Esq; 25 St James St, London SW1 (☎ 01 839 7000)

DUFFUS, Sir Herbert George Holwell; s of William Alexander Duffus, JP (d 1963), and Emily Henrietta Mary, *née* Holwell (d 1961), a direct descendant of John Zephaniah Holwell, HEICS, one of the 23 survivors of the Black Hole of Calcutta; *b* 30 August 1908; *Educ* Cornwall Coll Jamaica; *m* 1939, Elsie Mary, da of Richard Leslie Hollinsed, JP (d 1950), of Barbados; *Career* Capt Jamaica Local Forces 1940-46; slr Supreme Ct: of Jamaica 1930-55, of England 1948-55; barr Lincoln's Inn 1956, Puisne judge Jamaica 1958-62, judge of appeal Jamaica 1962-64, pres Ct of Appeal Jamaica 1964-68, chief justice of Jamaica 1968-73, actg govr-gen Jamaica 1973, chllr of the Church (Anglican) in Jamaica 1973-76; chm cmmn: Enquiry into Prisons in Jamaica 1954, Operations of Private Land Developers in Jamaica 1975-76, Police Brutality and The Admin of Justice in Grenada 1973-74, Barbados Govt's Private Enterprises 1977-78, Local Govt Elections in Jamaica 1986; kt 1966; *Recreations* chm of several charitable instns and fndns; *Style—* Sir Herbert Duffus; 6 Braywick Rd, PO Box 243, Kingston 6, Jamaica (☎ 809 92 70171); 119 Main St, Witchford, nr Ely, Cambs (☎ 0353 3281)

DUFFUS OF DALCLAVERHOUSE, James Coutts; s of James Montague Coutts Duffus of Dalclaverhouse and of the Mansion of Claverhouse, by Dundee, Angus (d 1947); *b* 3 June 1919; *Educ* Arnhall Coll Sch Dundee; *Career* Corps of RE (TA) (despatches) WWII; holder in life-rent of the superiority of the lands, estate and feudal fief of Dalclaverhouse, Co Angus; recognised in present name and style by Lord Lyon King of Arms 1955; archivist; FRSA, FSA Scot; *Style—* James Duffus of Dalclaverhouse; 68 New Cavendish St, W1 (☎ 01 580 5152)

DUFFY, Bryan Scott Alan; s of Francis Duffy (d 1966); *b* 21 Mar 1943; *Educ* Hull Univ (BSc Econ); *m* 1968, Krystyna Elizabeth Maria, da of Bohden Bitner, of Cracow, Poland; 2 children; *Career* chm Brown & Jackson plc 1977-; tstee The Marriage & Family Trust; chm of appeals Nat Marriage Guidance Cncl; FCA; *Recreations* tennis, golf, opera; *Clubs* Vanderbilt; *Style—* Bryan Duffy, Esq; Dane End House, Dane End,

Herts SG12 0LR; Brown & Jackson plc, Battle Bridge House, 300 Gray's Inn Rd, London WC1 (☎ 01 278 9635)

DUFFY, Dr Francis Cuthbert; s of John Austin Duffy (d 1944), and Annie Margaret Duffy, *née* Reed; *b* 3 Sept 1940; *Educ* St Cuthberts GS, Newcastle upon Tyne Architectural Assoc Sch, London (AADip), Univ of California (MArch), Princeton Univ (MA, PhD); *m* 4 Sept 1965, Jessica Mary, da of Phillip Bear, of Chiddingstone, Kent; 3 da (Sibylla b 1966, Eleanor b 1969, Katya b 1970); *Career* asst architect Nat Bldg Agency 1964-67, Harkness fellow of the Cwlth Fund 1967-70 (in USA), est and head London Off of JFN Assoc 1971-74, fndr and chm Bldg Use Studies 1980-88, fndr and chief ed Facilities (newsletter) 1984-, chm Bulstrode Press 1985-; est and fndr ptnr Duffy Eley Giffone Worthington (DEGW) architects 1974-; conslt on the working environment to many cos and insts incl: Corpn of Lloyds, Stock Exchange, Lloyds Bank, IBM, Stanhope Properties plc, Rosehaugh plc; ARIBA; *Books* Planning Office Space (jtly 1976), The Orbit Study (1984), Orbit 2 (jtly 1985), The Changing City (jtly 1989); *Clubs* Princeton, New York, Architectural Assoc, London; *Style—* Dr Francis Duffy; 195 Liverpool Rd, London N1 0RF (☎ 01 837 3064); 3 The Terrace, Walberswick, Suffolk (☎ 0502 723814); 8-9 Bulstrode Place, Marlebone Lane, London W1 (☎ 01 486 6090)

DUFFY, Capt Harold Thomas; MBE, VRD, DL (Lancs 1968, Merseyside 1974); s of William J Duffy; *b* 22 Dec 1914; *Educ* Granby St Sch Liverpool; *m* 1941, Grace, da of William T Watling; 3 da; *Career* served WWII RN, sr offr Wireless Dists 1963 RNR, CO Mersey Div RNR 1966; memb Liverpool Stock Exchange 1952; St John Ambulance County Cmmr (Merseyside) 1975 and 1981; CStJ 1982; *Clubs* Naval (London); *Style—* Capt Harold Duffy, MBE, VRD, DL; 22 Montclair Drive, Liverpool LI8 0HA

DUFFY, John Rutherford; s of Thomas Leo Duffy (d 1972), of Rugby, and Mary Agnes, *née* Collins; *b* 16 August 1932; *Educ* Lawrence Sheriff Sch Rugby, Rugby Sch; *m* 23 June 1959, Muriel Hamilton, da of John Birkett (d 1966), of Rugby; *Career* slr, sr ptnr Bretherton Turpin & Pell Rugby; chm Social Security Appeal Tribunal Coventry 1985-; govr Lawrence Sheriff Sch Rugby 1970- (chm 1985-); chm: Rugby Round Table 1967-68, chm Area 45 Round Table 1969-70; *Recreations* golf, fishing; *Clubs* Northamptonshire County Golf (capt), The Rugby, The Rotary (Rugby); *Style—* John R Duffy, Esq; 19 Hillmorton Road, Rugby (☎ Rugby 565260); 16 Church Street, Rugby (☎ Rugby 73431)

DUFFY, Mark Peter; s of Arthur Peter Duffy, and Mary Louise Duffy; *b* 8 Nov 1956; *Educ* Liverpool Inst, Peterhouse Cambridge (MA); *Career* investmt analyst W Greenwell and Co 1980-85; asst dir S G Warburg Securities 1985-; *Publications* Rothmans International (1984), Bat and Financial Services (1985), RJR Nabisco - Profile of a New Group (1986), Tobacco Stocks and Diversification (1988), Bat the Dollar and Farmers Group (1988); *Style—* Mark Duffy, Esq; S G Warburg Securities, 1 Finsbury Ave, London EC2M 2PA (☎ 382 4383, fax 382 4292)

DUFFY, Maureen Patricia; da of Grace Wright; *b* 1933; *Educ* Trowbridge HS, Sarah Bonnell HS for Girls, King's Coll London (BA); *Career* author playwright and poet; co-fndr Writers' Action Gp; jt chm Writers' Guild of GB 1977-78; vice pres Beauty Without Cruelty; *Style—* Ms Maureen Duffy; 14A Richmond Mansions, Old Brompton Rd, London SW5 (☎ 01 373 1020)

DUFFY, (Albert Edward) Patrick; MP (Lab) Sheffield Attercliffe 1970-; s of James Duffy (d 1973); *b* 17 June 1920; *Educ* LSE (BSc Econ, PhD), Columbia Univ NY (PhD); *Career* served 1940-46 RN, Lt, Fleet Air Arm; economist; lectr Leeds Univ; MP (Lab) Colne Valley Yorks 1963-66, parly under-sec of state for defence (Navy) 1976-79, former chm Lab Parly Econ Affairs Fin Gp; oppn spokesman: Defence 1979-80 and 1983-, Disarmament 1983-; memb North Atlantic Assembly 1979- (vice-pres 1987); *Clubs* Trades & Labour (Doncaster), Naval; *Style—* Patrick Duffy, Esq, MP; 153 Bennetthorpe, Doncaster; House of Commons, London SW1A 0AA

DUFTY, Arthur Richard; CBE (1971); s of Thomas Ernest Dufty (d 1915); *b* 23 June 1911; *Educ* Rugby, Liverpool Sch of Architecture, DLit 1988; *m* 1937, Kate Brazley, da of Charles Ainsworth (d 1928); 3 children; *Career* served WWII, Lt RNVR, North Sea; sec and gen ed to Royal Cmmn on Historical Monuments (E) 1962-72, Master of the Armouries in HM Tower of London 1963-76, pres Soc of Antiquaries 1978-81, vice-chm Cathedrals Advsy Cmmn 1981-87, chm Wells Cathedral West Front Conservation Ctee 1974-86, tstee College of Arms Tst 1978-; recipient London Conservation Award (silver Medal) 1984; *Books* W Morris's Cupid and Psyche; *Recreations* appreciation of architecture, William Morris and the Arts and Crafts Movement, gardens and music; *Clubs* Athenaeum, Arts, Naval; *Style—* Richard Dufty, Esq, CBE; Kelmscott Manor, Oxfordshire; 46 Trafalgar Court, Farnham, Surrey

DUGDALE, Hon David John; s of 1 Baron Crathorne, PC, TD (d 1977); *b* 4 May 1942; *Educ* Eton, Trinity Coll Cambridge; *m* 1972, Susan Louise, da of Maj L A Powell (d 1972); 1 s, 1 da; *Career* farmer and engr; *Recreations* building, photography, shooting; *Style—* The Hon David Dugdale; Park House, Crathorne, Yarm, Cleveland (☎ 0642 700225; work: 700295)

DUGDALE, Dennis (Tim); Rev Canon; OBE (1978); s of Brian Dugdale (d 1955), of Wetherby, Yorks, and Beatrice Mary, *née* Mountain (d 1922); *b* 22 Mar 1919; *Educ* King James' GS Knaresborough Yorks, Worcester ordination Coll; *m* 15 Sept 1945, (Angel) Honor, da of Capt James Alexander Pollard Blackburn, DSC (d 1979), of Eastbourne; *Career* Midshipman RNR 1938, Sub Lt 1940, Lt 1942, Lt Cdr 1950, survivor of HMS Rawalpindie 1939, POW in Germany 1939-45, resigned Cmmn 1955; cadet Clan Line Steamer's Ltd 1935-35, second offr Trg Ship Arethusa 1946-48, marketing exec Massey-Harris-Ferguson Ltd 1949-64; Ordination Coll 1965-68, Ordained Guilford Cathedral: deacon 1968, priest 1969; curate St Mary the Virgin Shalford Surrey 1968-71, rector Sandon Wallington and Rushden Herts 1971-74, anglican chaplin Ghent and Ypres Belgium 1974-84, canon pro-Cathedral Brussels 1982; *Recreations* walking and countryside pursuits; *Style—* The Rev Canon Tim Dugdale, OBE; 12 High Trees, Carew Road, Eastbourne BN21 2JB (☎ 0323 26661)

DUGDALE, John Robert Stratford; s of Sir William Francis Stratford Dugdale, 1 Bt (d 1965); bro of Sir William Dugdale, 2 Bt, *qv*; *b* 10 May 1923; *Educ* Eton, Ch Ch Oxford; *m* 1956, Kathryn Edith Helen, DCVO, JP, *qv*; 2 s, 2 da; *Career* CC Salop 1969-81, Lord-Lieut 1975-; chm Telford Devpt Corpn 1971-75; KStJ; *Clubs* Brooks's, White's; *Style—* John Dugdale, Esq,; Tickwood Hall, Much Wenlock, Salop TF13 6NZ (☎ 0952 882644)

DUGDALE, Dame Kathryn Edith Helen; DCVO (1984, CVO 1973), JP (Salop 1964); da of Col Rt Hon Oliver Frederick George Stanley, MC, PC, MP (d 1950), and Lady Maureen Vane Tempest Stewart (see Londonderry); gda of 17 Earl of Derby; and Lady Alice Montagu, da of Duke of Manchester; *b* 4 Nov 1923; *m* 1956, John Robert Stratford Dugdale, *qv*; 2 s, 2 da; *Career* woman of the bedchamber to HM The Queen 1955- (temporary extra 1961-71); *Style—* Dame Kathryn Dugdale, DCVO, JP; Tickwood Hall, Much Wenlock, Salop TF13 6NZ (☎ 0952 882644)

DUGDALE, Peter Robin; CBE (1987); s of Dr James Norman Dugdale, and Lilian, *née* Dolman; *b* 12 Feb 1928; *Educ* Canford, Magdalen Coll Oxford (MA); *m* 1957, (Esme) Cyraine, da of Norwood Brown; 3 s (Mark b 1958, Luke b 1961, Paul b 1967); *Career* md: Guardian Royal Exchange Assurance plc 1978, Guardian Royal Exchange plc 1984; dir Aviation and Gen Insur Co Ltd (chm 1982-84), chm Trade Indemnity plc; dep chm Br Insur Assoc 1979 -; (chm 1981-82), chm Assoc of Br Insurers 1987-; sr warden Worshipful Co of Insurers 1988; CBIM; *Recreations* flat coated retrievers; *Clubs* Oriental; *Style—* Peter Douglas, Esq, CBE; Cherry Copse, Broad Lane, Hambledon, Hants PO7 6QS (☎ 070 132 462); Royal Exchange, London EC3V 3LS (☎ 01 283 7101, fax 01 623 3587, telex 883232)

DUGDALE, William Matthew Stratford; s and h of Sir William Stratford Dugdale, 2 Bt; *b* 22 Feb 1959; *Style—* William Dugdale, Esq

DUGDALE, Sir William Stratford; 2 Bt (UK 1936) of Merevale and Blyth, Co Warwick; CBE (1982), MC (1943), JP (Warwicks 1951), DL (1955); s of Sir William Francis Stratford Dugdale, 1 Bt (d 1965), and bro of John R S Dugdale, *qv*; *b* 29 Mar 1922; *Educ* Eton, Balliol Coll Oxford; *m* 1, 13 Dec 1952, Lady Belinda Pleydell-Bouverie (d 1961), da of 7 Earl of Radnor, KG, KCVO; 1 s, 3 da; m 2, 17 Oct 1967, Cecilia Mary, da of Lt-Col Sir William Mount, 2 Bt, ED, DL; 1 s, 1 da; *Heir* s William Matthew Stratford Dugdale; *Career* Capt Grenadier Gds 1944, served in Africa and Italy (despatches); slr 1949; chm: Trent River Authy 1965-73, Severn Trent Water Authy 1974-84, Nat Water Cncl 1982-84; dir Phoenix Assur 1985 and other cos; High Sheriff Warwicks 1971-72; High Steward of Stratford-upon-Avon 1976-; *Clubs* Brooks's, White's, MCC, Jockey; *Style—* Sir William Dugdale, Bt, CBE, MC, JP, DL; Blyth Hall, Coleshill, Birmingham B46 2AD (☎ 0675 62203); Merevale Hall, Atherstone, Warwicks (☎ 082 770 3143); 24 Bryanston Mews West, London W1 (☎ 01 262 2510)

DUGDALE SYKES, Hon Mrs; Hon Betty Charlotte; *née* Deane; o da of 8 Baron Muskerry, *qv*; *b* 3 July 1951; *Educ* Alexandra Coll Dublin, Trinity Coll Dublin (BA); *m* 1974, Jonathan Martin Dugdale Sykes, s of Martin Colin Dugdale Sykes, of 1 Churchill Close, W Coker, Yeovil, Somerset; 1 s (Daniel b 1980), 1 da (Karen b 1985); *Career* business woman; *Recreations* tennis, gardening; *Style—* The Hon Mrs Dugdale Sykes; The Kennels, Springfield, Dromcollogher, Co Limerick, Eire

DUGGAN, Shaun Walker; s of Francis Rupert Duggan, MD (d 1959), and Mary Elinor, *née* Walker (d 1981); *b* 30 Mar 1940; *Educ* Christ's Hosp; *m* 19 June 1940, Lavinia Debonnaire Hope, da of Maj Ian McIntyre Stevens (d 1964); 1 s (Charles b 1966), 2 da (Emma b 1968, Victoria b 1972); *Career* CA 1964; stockbroker: Laing & Cruickshank 1967-84 (ptnr 1972) with Capel-Cure Myers 1987-; memb Stock Exchange 1971; *Recreations* skiing, the Times crossword; *Clubs* Bucks, City of London; *Style—* Shaun W Duggan, Esq; The Grove, Turners Hill, West Sussex RH10 4SF (☎ Copthorne 716146); 65 Holborn Viaduct, London EC1A 2EU (☎ 01 236 5080)

DUGMORE, Rev Prof Clifford William; s of Rev Canon William Ernest Dugmore, MA, RD (d 1953); *b* 9 May 1909; *Educ* King Edward VI Sch Birmingham, Exeter Coll Oxford (MA, DD), Queens' Coll Cambridge (MA); *m* 1, 1938, Ruth Mabel Archbould (d 1977), da of George Prangley (d 1941), of Formby, Lancs; 1 da; m 2, 1979, Kathleen Mary, da of Frank Whiteley (d 1949), of Manchester; *Career* clerk in Holy Orders; sub-warden St Deiniol's Library 1937-38, rector Ingestre-with-Tixall and chaplain to Earl of Shrewsbury 1938-43, chaplain Alleyn's Coll of God's Gift Dulwich 1943-44, sr lectr in ecclesiastical history Manchester Univ 1946-58, prof of ecclesiastical history King's Coll London 1958-76, emeritus 1976-; memb advsy editorial bd The Journal of Ecclesiastical History 1979- (editor 1950-78)); Br memb editorial bd Novum Testementum 1956; author; *Recreations* philately, reading; *Style—* Rev Prof Clifford Dugmore; Thame Cottage, The Street, Puttenham, Surrey (☎ (0483) 810460)

DUGUID, Ian McIver; s of John Duguid (d 1980), and Georgina, *née* McIver (d 1983); *b* 16 April 1926; *Educ* Aberdeen GS, Aberdeen Univ (MB, ChB, MD); Univ London (DO, PhD); *m* 16 Dec 1961, Yvonne Jean, da of William Michie (d 1959), of Aberdeen; 2 s (Graham b 1963, Stewart b 1967); *Career* sr ophthalmic surgn: Moorfields Eye Hosp London, Charing Cross and Westminster Hosps London; FRCS 1961, FCOpth 1988; Offr de L'Ordre National Du Merite (1986); *Recreations* rugby, cars; *Style—* Ian Duguid, Esq; 30 Chester Close North, London NW1 4JE; 73 Harley St, London W1N 1DE (☎ 01 935 5874)

DUGUID, Hon Mrs ((Sandra) Lillias); *née* Donnet; da of Baron Donnet of Balgay (Life Peer; d 1985); *b* 1947; *m* 1971, Dr Nigel Duguid; 2 s (Douglas, David), 1 da (Andrea); *Style—* The Hon Mrs Duguid; 8 Sackville Street, St John's, Newfoundland A1A 4R3, Canada

DUHIG, (Robert) Ian; s of Robert Augustine Duhig (d 1983), and Margaret Mary, *née* Torpey (d 1985); *b* 9 Feb 1954; *Educ* Cardinal Vaughan GS, Leeds Univ (BA, PGCE); *m* 12 June 1981, Jane, da of Derek Alfred Tony Vincent (d 1980); 1 s (Owen b 1986); *Career* Rehabilitation of Metropolitan Addicts (ROMA) 1977-79, Extern Belfast 1979-80, Short-stay Young Homeless Project 1980-81, Leeds Young Person's Housing Tst 1982-85, Leeds Housing Concern 1985-88, York City Cncl Housing Dept 1988-; poetry published in various national and local pubns incl TLS and Irish Review, winner 1987 Nat Poetry Competition; memb mgmnt ctee Leeds Federated Housing Assoc; ; *Style—* Ian Duhig, Esq; 16 Pasture Terrace, Leeds LS7 4QR (☎ 0532 696255); 1 Museum St, York (☎ 0904 613161)

DUKE, Hon Derek John Philip; s and h of 3 Baron Merrivale; *b* 16 Mar 1948; *Educ* Arcachon France, Lycée Français London, Lycée Janson de Sailly Paris; *Style—* The Hon Derek Duke; 15 Rue Raynouard, Paris XVI, France (☎ Auteuil 75 99)

DUKE, Maj-Gen Sir Gerald William; KBE (1966, CBE 1945), CB (1962), DSO (1945), DL (Kent 1970); s of late Lt-Col Arthur A G Duke, Indian Army; *b* 12 Nov 1910; *Educ* Dover Coll, RMA Woolwich, Jesus Coll Cambridge; *m* 1946, Mary Elizabeth, *née* Burn (d 1979); 1 s, 1 da; *Career* 2 Lt RE 1931, served with MEF 1936-44, Lt-Col 1942, Brig 1944, NW Europe 1944-45, SEAC 1945-46 (despatches 4), military attaché Cairo 1952-54, Maj-Gen 1959, engineer-in-chief War Office 1963, MOD (Army Dept) 1964-65, ret; Col Cmdt Military Provost Staff Corps 1961-67, Col Cmdt RE 1966-75; vice pres Hockey Assoc 1965-; chm SS & AFA Kent 1973-85; pres

Scout Assoc Kent 1974-85; govr Dover Coll 1961-; *Clubs* Royal Ocean Racing, Rye Golf; *Style—* Maj-Gen Sir Gerald Duke, KBE, CB, DSO; Little Barnfield, Hawkhurst, Kent (☎ 058 05 3214)

DUKE, Lawrence Kenneth; s of Dr Marvin L Duke, of Tokyo, Japan, and Judith Anne, *née* Jackoway; *b* 7 Mar 1956; *Educ* Monterey HS, Mass Inst of Technol (BS), NY State Univ (BS), Harvard Business Sch (MBA); *Career* US Navy Offr Nuclear Power Program and Civil Engr Corps 1978-82 (Navy Achievement Medal 1981); portfolio mangr Citibank NA treasy Dubai UAE, chief dealer futures and options gp treasy Midland Bank London 1986, dep gen mangr treasy Nomura Bank Int London 1986-; memb In Forex Assoc 1984; *Recreations* jogging, basketball; *Style—* Lawrence Duke, Esq; 30 Prospect Place, Wapping Wall, London E1 9SP (☎ 01 480 6786); 24 Monument St, Nomura House, London EC3R 8AJ (☎ 01 623 9553, fax 01 626 0851, telex 9413065, 94130660)

DUKE, Neville Frederick; DSO (1943), OBE (1953), DFC (1942) and two bars (1943, 1944), AFC (1948); s of Frederick Herbert Duke; *b* 11 Jan 1922; *Educ* Convent of St Mary and Judd Sch Tonbridge; *m* 1947, Gwendoline Dorothy, da of Sydney Fellows; *Career* RAF fighter pilot and test pilot 1940-48, served WWII (UK, W Desert, N Africa) CO 145 Sqdn Italy 1944, Sqdn Ldr, ret RAF 1948; CO 615 Sqdn RAuxAF 1950-51; chief test pilot Hawker Aircraft Ltd 1948-56, md Duke Aviation, mangr Dowty Gp Aircraft Operating Unit, technical advsr conslt and chief test pilot Miles Aviation Ltd; MC (Czech) 1946; Queen's Commendation 1955; *Recreations* flying, fishing, sailing; *Clubs* RAF, Royal Cruising, Royal Naval Sailing Assoc, Royal Lymington Yacht; *Style—* Neville Duke, Esq, DSO, OBE, DFC, AFC; 8 The Grange, Everton, Lymington, Hants

DUKE-WOOLLEY, Hon Mrs Elizabeth Alice Cecilia; *née* Jolliffe; da of 3 Baron Hylton (d 1945); *b* 1906; *m* 1, 1928 (m dis 1937), Lt-Col Edmond Joly de Lotbinière (kt 1964); 2 s; m 2, 1938 (m dis 1946), Hilary Beecham Duke-Woolley, DFC, RAF; *Style—* The Hon Mrs Elizabeth Duke-Woolley; Cedar Cottage, Alfriston, Polegate, E Sussex BN26 5XH

DULAKE, Thomas Anthony; s of Thomas Sowerby Dulake (d 1961), and Hilda Mary Anderson, *née* Crass (d 1984); *b* 9 July 1945; *Educ* Kings Sch Bruton; *m* 7 Oct 1978, (Linda) Robin, da of John Derek Willcox (d 1980); 4 s (Thomas b 1979, George b 1980, Edward b 1982, Bartholomew b 1985); *Career* md HMS Warrior 1860, chm Royal Stafford China Co Ltd; building advsr Landmark Tst, dep chm Warship Tst, dir Portsmouth Naval Heritage Tst; *Clubs* Reform; *Style—* Thomas Dulake, Esq; 7 Gayfere St, Westminster, London SW1

DULVERTON, 2 Baron (UK 1929); Sir Frederick Anthony Hamilton Wills; 3 Bt (UK 1897), CBE (1974), TD, DL (Glos 1979); s of 1 Baron Dulverton, OBE (d 1956), and Victoria, OBE, da of Rear-Adm Sir Edward Chichester, 9 Bt, CB, CMG; *b* 19 Dec 1915; *Educ* Eton, Magdalen Coll Oxford (MA); *m* 1, 1939 (m dis 1960), Judith Betty (d 1983), da of Lt-Col Hon Ian Leslie-Melville, TD, s of 11 Earl of Leven and (10 of) Melville; 2 s, 2 da; m 2, 1962, Ruth Violet Mary, da of Sir Walter Randolph Fitzroy Farquhar, 5 Bt, and formerly w of Maj R G Fanshawe; *Heir* s, Hon (Gilbert) Michael Hamilton Wills; *Career* sits as Conservative in House of Lords; jt master N Cotswold 1950-56, Heythrop 1967-70; 2 Lt Lovat Scouts 1936, Maj 1944; pres: Timber Growers' Orgn Ltd 1976-78, Bath and West and Southern Counties Agric Soc 1973, Three Counties Agric Soc 1975, Br Deer Soc (retd), Gloucestershire Trust for Nature Conservation; hon pres Timber Growers of UK ; former memb: Home Grown Timber Advsy Ctee, Scottish Advsy Ctee to Nature Conservancy Cncl; memb Red Deer Cmmn (retd); chm Dulverton Tst, former tstee World Wildlife Fund; hon life fellow The Wildfowl Trust, Waynflete fellow Magdalen Coll Oxford; filmaker on wildlife subjects; Gold Medal of Royal Forestry Soc of England, Wales and NI 1982; Cdr of the Order of the Golden Ark (Netherlands); *Style—* The Rt Hon the Lord Dulverton, CBE, TD, DL; Batsford Park, Moreton-in-Marsh, Glos (☎ 50303); Fassfern, Kinlocheil, Fort William, Inverness-shire (☎ Kinlocheil 232)

DULY, Surgn Rear Adm Philip Reginald John; CB (1982), OBE (1971); s of Reginald and Minnie Duly; *Educ* The London Hosp (LDSRCS 1947); *m* 1948, Mary Walker Smith; 2 s, 1 da; *Career* Surgn Lieut (D) RN 1948; dir Naval Dental Services 1980-83, QHDS 1978-83; *Style—* Surgn Rear-Adm Philip Duly, CB, OBE; 13 The Avenue, Alverstoke, Gosport, Hants PO12 2JS (☎ 01 726 5000)

DUMA, Alexander Agim; s of Dervish Duma, of West Horsley, Surrey, and Naftali, *née* Andoni (d 1966); *b* 30 Mar 1946; *Educ* UCL (LLB); *m* 1980 (m dis 1983), Mary Gertrude, da of Surgn-Col E W Hayward, of Oxon; *Career* barr Grays Inn 1969; Parly candidate (Cons) 1979, GLC candidate Bermondsey (Cons) 1977; dir: Blackfriars Settlement 1977-84 and 1986-, Barclays Merchant Bank Ltd 1983-87, Chase Investment Bank Ltd 1987-, Equity & Gen plc 1987-, Torday & Carlisle plc 1988-; cncl memb Newcomen Fndn 1977-, pres Bermondsey Cons Assoc 1979-83; *Recreations* Carlton; *Style—* Alexander Duma, Esq; 13 Coulson St, London SW3 (☎ 01 823 7422); Chase Investment Bank Ltd, Woolgate House, Coleman St, London EC2 (☎ 01 726 7245)

DUMAS, Maj Henry; CBE (1974), MC (1945); s of Henry Raymond McLeod Dumas (d 1971), of Hill Deverill Manor, Wilts, and Hilda Mary, *née* Reid (d 1982); *b* 31 May 1915; *Educ* Radley, New Coll Oxford; *m* 1, 12 Feb 1945, Hester Hermione, da of Brig Henry John Lenton (d 1953), of Capetown; 1 s (Henry Raymond b 1952), 2 da (Louise b 1946, Madeleine b 1948); m 2, 30 May 1985, Joanna Margaret, da of Roger Wyatt Roberts, of Dorsington; *Career* WW II Maj Royal Tank Regt N Africa, Burma, Italy; dir Willis Faber & Dumas 1950-71 (dep chm 1969-71), chm Lloyd Brokers Assoc 1960-61, memb Ctee of Lloyds 1962-65, hon marine insurance advsr to Dept of Trade 1962-79; High Sheriff of Surrey 1966-67; *Recreations* natural history, philately, shooting, fishing; *Clubs* Brooks; *Style—* Maj Henry Dumas, CBE, MC; The Old Rectory, Orcheston St Mary, Salisbury, Wilts SP3 4RP (☎ 0980 620477)

DUMAS, Henry Raymond; s of Henry Dumas, CBE, MC, of The Old Rectory, Orcheston St Mary, Wilts, and Hester, *née* Lenton; *b* 18 Sept 1952; *Educ* Radley Coll, Bristol Univ (BSc); *m* 21 Sept 1979, Marina Helene, da of Allan Hayman, QC, of Sidbourne Estate, Orford, Suffolk; 1 s (Henry Frederick b 1986), 2 da (Caroline Sophie b 1981, Lucy Emily b 1983); *Career* insurance broker Willis Faber & Dumas 1976-81, dir and active underwriter Wellington Underwriting Agencies 1986- (with co 1981-); *Style—* Raymond Dumas, Esq; Coldharbour Farm, Wick, Avon BS15 5RJ

DUMFRIES, Earl of; John Colum Crichton-Stuart; s and h of 6 Marquess of Bute, *qv*; *b* 26 April 1958; *Educ* Ampleforth; *m* 1984, Carolyn, da of Bryson Waddell (d 1975); 2 da (Lady Caroline b 1984, Lady Cathleen b 1986); *Career* motor racing driver as Johnny Dumfries 1980-; Br Formula Three champion, runner-up in FIA European Formula Three Championship 1984, contracted to Ferrari grand prix team as test driver 1985, number two driver for John Player Special Team Lotus 1986, selected IMSA races in America 1988; *Style—* Earl of Dumfries; Dumfries Racing Ltd, The Old Rectory, North Creake, Fakenham, Norfolk NR21 9JJ

DUMMETT, Prof Michael Anthony Eardley; s of George Herbert Dummett (d 1970), and Mabel Iris, *née* Eardley-Wilmot (d 1980); *b* 27 June 1925; *Educ* Sandroyd Sch, Winchester Coll, Ch Ch Oxford; *m* 1951, Ann Chesney; 3 s, 2 da (1 s, 1 da, decd); *Career* reader philosophy of mathematics Oxford Univ 1962-74, Wykeham prof of Logic Oxford Univ 1979-, fell All Souls Coll Oxford 1950-79 (sr research fell 1974-79); fell New Coll Oxford 1979-; author of books on philosophy and Tarot; FBA (1968); *Books Incl:* Truth and Other Enigmas (1978), The Game of Tarot (1980); *Recreations* playing exotic card games; *Style—* Prof Michael Dummett; 54 Park Town, Oxford (☎ 0865 58698); New College, Oxford (☎ 0865 248451)

DUMPER, Anthony Charles; *see*: Dudley, Bishop of

DUNALLEY, 6 Baron (I 1800); Henry Desmond Graham Prittie; s of 5 Baron Dunalley, DSO (d 1948); *b* 14 Oct 1912; *Educ* Stowe, RMC; *m* 23 April 1947, (Mary) Philippa, o da of Maj Hon Philip Plantagenet Cary (d 1968), s of 12 Viscount Falkland, JP, DL; 2 s, 1 da; *Heir* s, Hon Henry Francis Cornelius Prittie b 30 May 1948; *Career* 2 Lt Rifle Bde 1933, served E Africa, Mid East, Italy and SEAC 1939-46, attached 4 KAR 1937-41, instr Staff Coll 1943, 2 KRRC 1951-52, Lt-Col, ret 1953; *Recreations* fishing; *Clubs* Kildare Street and University, Greenjackets, Christchurch (NZ) (hon memb); *Style—* The Rt Hon the Lord Dunalley; Church End House, Swerford, Oxford OX7 4AX (☎ 0608 730005)

DUNBAR; *see*: Hope-Dunbar

DUNBAR, Sir Archibald Ranulph; 11 Bt (NS 1700), of Northfield, Moray; s of Maj Sir (Archibald) Edward Dunbar, 10 Bt, MC (d 1969); *b* 8 August 1927; *Educ* Wellington, Pembroke Coll Cambridge, Imperial Coll of Tropical Agric Trinidad; *m* 1974, Amelia Millar Sommerville, da of H C Davidson, of Currie, Midlothian; 1 s, 2 da; *Heir* s, Edward Horace Dunbar b 18 March 1977; *Career* entered Colonial Service 1953, agric offr Uganda, ret 1970; *Books* A History of Bunyoro-Kitara (1965), Omukama Chwa II Kabarega (1965), The Annual Crops of Uganda (1969).; *Recreations* cross-country running; model railway; *Clubs* New (Edinburgh); *Style—* Sir Archibald Dunbar, Bt; The Old Manse, Duffus, Elgin, Scotland IV30 2QD (☎ 0343 830270)

DUNBAR, Sir Drummond Cospatrick Ninian; 9 Bt (NS 1698) of Durn, Banffshire; MC (1943); s of Sir George Alexander Drummond, 8 Bt (d 1949); *b* 9 May 1917; *Educ* Radley, Worcester Coll Oxford; *m* 1957, Sheila Barbara Mary, da of John B de Fonblanque; 1 s; *Heir* s, Robert Drummond Cospatrick Dunbar; *Career* served European War 1939-45 in Middle E 1942-43, Sicily 1943, Normandy 1944 (twice wounded); Maj Black Watch, ret 1958; *Clubs* Naval and Military; *Style—* Sir Drummond Dunbar, Bt, MC; Town Hill, Westmount, Jersey, CI

DUNBAR, James Michael; s and h of Sir Jean Dunbar, 13 Bt; *b* 17 Jan 1950; *Career* Capt USAF; *Style—* James Dunbar, Esq

DUNBAR, Sir Jean Ivor; 13 Bt (NS 1694), of Mochrum, Wigtownshire; s of Sir Adrian Ivor Dunbar, 12 Bt (d 1977); *b* 4 April 1918; *m* 1944, Rose Jeanne Hertsch; 2 s, 1 da; *Career* late Sgt Mountain Engineers, USA Army; *Style—* Sir Jean Dunbar, Bt; 44/55 39th St, Long Island City, New York, USA

DUNBAR, John Greenwell; s of John Dunbar; *b* 1 Mar 1930; *Educ* UCS London, Balliol Oxford (MA); *m* 1974, Elizabeth Mill Blyth; *Career* sec Royal Cmmn on the Ancient and Historical Monuments of Scotland 1978-; memb Ancient Monuments Bd for Scotland 1978; FSA, FSA Scot, hon FRIAS; *Books* The Architecture of Scotland (revised edn 1978), Accounts of the Masters of Works vol 2 1616-1649; *Clubs* New (Edinburgh); *Style—* John Dunbar, Esq; Patie's Mill, Carlops, by Penicuik, Midlothian (☎ 0968 60250)

DUNBAR, Robert Drummond Cospatrick; s and h of Sir Drummond Dunbar, 9 Bt; *b* 17 June 1958; *Educ* Harrow, Ch Ch Oxford; *Career* investmt mangr; *Style—* Robert Dunbar, Esq

DUNBAR, William John; OBE (1986); s of Capt William George Dunbar (d 1980), and Margaret May, *née* Probin (d 1939); *b* 19 May 1931; *Educ* Prior Park Bath; *m* 8 Feb 1958, Maureen Ann, da of Col C Harris, OBE, MC (d 1966); 2 s (Simon b 1959, Richard b 1960), 2 da (Catherine b 1961 d 1983, Anna b 1964); *Career* Nat Serv 2 Lt Trieste Italy 1953-55; chief fin offr Olayan Saudi Hldgs 1978-80, chief exec BSC Ind Ltd 1980-85, gp md BETEC plc 1985, dir Clayhithe plc 1986-; FCMA, FBCS, FBIM; *Recreations* tennis, squash, skiing; *Clubs* IOD; *Style—* W J Dunbar, Esq, OBE; BETC plc, Mandeville Rd, Aylesbury, Bucks HP21 8AB (☎ 0296 395911, telex 83210, fax 0296 82424)

DUNBAR OF HEMPRIGGS, Dame Maureen Daisy Helen; Btss (NS 1706), of Hempriggs, Caithness-shire; da of Courtenay Edward Moore (decd), s of late Jessie Mona Duff (decd), (who m Rev Canon Courtenay Moore), da of de jure 5 Bt; suc kinsman, Sir George Cospatrick Duff-Sutherland-Dunbar, 7 Bt, 1963; assumed name of Dunbar 1963, and recognised in the name of Dunbar of Hempriggs by Lyon Court 1965; *b* 19 August 1906; *Educ* Headington Sch Oxford, RCM (LRAM); *m* 1940, Leonard James Blake, former dir of Music, Malvern Coll; 1 s, 1 da; *Heir* s, Richard Francis Dunbar of Hempriggs, yr; *Career* music teacher; *Style—* Dame Maureen Dunbar of Hempriggs, Btss; 51 Gloucester St, Winchcombe, Cheltenham, Glos (0242 602122)

DUNBOYNE, 28 Baron (18 by Patent) (I 1324 and 1541) Patrick Theobald Tower Butler; VRD; s of 27 Baron (d 1945), and Dora Isolde Butler (d 1977), da of Cdr F F Tower, OBE, RNVR; *b* 27 Jan 1917; *Educ* Winchester, Trinity Coll Cambridge (MA); *m* 29 July 1950, Anne Marie, o da of late Sir Victor Alexander Louis Mallet, GCMG, CVO; 1 s, 3 da; *Heir* s, Hon John Fitzwalter Butler; *Career* 2 Lt (Supp Reserve) Irish Gds 1939, Lt 1940-44 (POW 1940-43, Kings Badge); refugee dept For Off 1945-46; barr Middle Temple 1949, Inner Temple 1962, King's Inns Dublin 1966; practised from London 1949-71, rec Hastings 1961-71; dep chm: Kent QS 1963-71, Middx QS 1962-65, Inner London QS 1971; circuit judge 1972-86; Archbishop of Canterbury's commissary gen for Canterbury Diocese 1959-71; pres and fell Irish Genealogical Res Soc; *Books* The Trial of JG Haigh (Notable British Trials Series, 1953), Recollections of the Cambridge Union 1815-39 (jtly 1953), Butler Family History (1966, 5 edn 1982), Happy Families (1983) ; *Recreations* lawn tennis, Butler genealogies; *Clubs* International Lawn Tennis (pres 1973-83), 45 (pres 1974-), All England Lawn Tennis, Union (Cambridge, pres 1939), Pitt (Cambridge), Irish; *Style—*

His Hon The Rt Hon Lord Dunboyne, VRD; 36 Ormonde Gate, London SW3 4HA (☎ 01 352 1837)

DUNCAN, Alexander John (Alex); s of Alexander Gideon Duncan (d 1963), and Ada Emmie Jervis, of Newcastle, Staffs; *b* 5 Feb 1925; *Educ* Newcastle Under Lyme HS Staffs, Univ of Birmingham (BComm); *m* 29 Oct 1962, Elsie Jeannette, da of George William Pember (d 1969); *Career* tres Birmingham Univ Guild of Undergraduates Guild 1950-51; pres North Staffordshire Soc of CAs 1980-81; MICA England and Wales 1957; *Recreations* listening to jazz and other music, theatre; *Style—* Alex Duncan, Esq; Wychways, 28 Parkway, Trentham, Stoke-on-Trent (☎ 0782 657951), Alex G Duncan & Co, 31 Hartshill Rd, Stoke-on-Trent (☎ 0782 44808)

DUNCAN, Prof Archibald Sutherland; DSC (1943); s of Rev Henry Cecil Duncan, K-I-H (d 1963), of Darjeeling, India, and (Rose) Elsie, *née* Edwards (d 1958); *b* 17 July 1914; *Educ* Merchiston Castle Sch, Edinburgh Univ (MB, ChB); *m* 12 April 1939, Barbara, da of John Gibson Holliday, JP (d 1955), of Penrith, Cumbria; *Career* WWII Surgn Lt Cdr RNVR Med and UK; jr hosp appts in Royal Infirmary Edinburgh and Gt Ormond St London 1936-41, temp obstetrician and gynaecologist Inverness 1945-46, univ lectr and pt/t conslt obstetrician and gynaecologist Aberdeen 1946-50, sr lectr Univ of Edinburgh and conslt Western Gen Hosp Edinburgh 1950-53, prof of obstsetrics and gynaecology Univ of Wales 1953-66, conslt Utd Cardiff Hosps 1953-66, exec dean faculty of med and prof of med educn Univ of Edinburgh 1966-76; chm Scottish cncl on Disability 1977-80, vice pres Inst of Med Ethics 1985-, gen cncl assessor ct Edin Univ 1979-83; hon pres: Br Med Students Assoc 1965-66, Univ of Edinburgh Graduates' Assoc; memb: Lothian Health Bd 1977-83 (vice chm 1981- 83), James IV Assoc of Surgns, Gen Med Cncl 1974-78; hon memb Alpha Omega Alpha Honor Med Soc (USA); Hon MD Univ of Edinburgh 1984; memb: BMA, Assoc for Study of Med Educn; FRCS (Edinburgh) 1939, FRCOG 1955, FRCP (Edin) 1969; *Books* Dictionary of Medical Ethics (ed jtly, second edn 1981); *Recreations* photography, mountains; *Clubs* New (Edinburgh); *Style—* Prof Archibald Duncan, DSC; 1 Walker St, Edinburgh EH3 7JY (☎ 031 225 7657)

DUNCAN, Lady; Beatrice Mary Moore; da of Thomas O'Carroll and widow of Maj Philip Blair-Oliphant; *m* 1960, as his 2 w, Sir James Alexander Lawson Duncan, 1 Bt (d 1974); *Style—* Lady Duncan; Jordanston, by Alyth, Perthshire

DUNCAN, Rev Denis MacDonald; s of Reginald Duncan, BD, BLitt (d 1951), of Edinburgh, and Clarice Ethel, *née* Hodkinson (d 1967); *b* 10 Jan 1920; *Educ* George Watson's Coll Edinburgh, Univ of Edinburgh (MA, BD); *m* 21 March 1942, Henrietta Watson Mackenzie, da of Capt John Barclay Houston, RN (d 1940), of Edinburgh; 1 s (Raymond Denis b 1942), 1 da (Carol Louise Watson (Mrs Pyle) b 1945); *Career* minister: St Margaret's Juniper Green Edinburgh 1944-50, Trinity Ch Duke St Glasgow 1950-57; ed British Weekly 1958-70 (managing ed 1962-70); assoc dir and training supervisor Westminster Pastoral Fndn 1972-79; dir The Churches' Cncl for Health and Healing 1983-88; md Arthur James Ltd (Publishers) 1983-; chm World Assoc for Pastoral Care and Counselling 1977-79; writer and interviewer Scottish Television 1974-79; chm: Highgate Counselling Centre London 1970-, St Barnabas Ecumenical Centre for Christian Counselling and Healing Norwich; pres Green Pastures Home of Healing; memb Inst of Journalists; fell: Int Inst of Community Serv, Int Biographical Assoc; *Books* Creative Silence, A Day at a Time, Love, The Way of Love, Victorious Living, Here is my Hand!; editor of: Through the Year with William Barclay, Through the Year with JB Phillips, Everyday with William Barclay, Marching Orders, Marching On; *Clubs* Arts; *Style—* The Rev Denis Duncan; 1 Cranbourne Rd, London N10 2BT (☎ 01 883 1831, fax 01 883 8307); 4 Broadway Rd, Evesham, Worcs WR11 (☎ 0386 6566, fax 0386 6566)

DUNCAN, Derek Cecil; s of Joseph Hugh Duncan (d 1960), of Farnham, Surrey, and Hilda Madeleine, *née* Pickford; *b* 10 June 1932; *Educ* Rugby, Cambridge Univ (MA); *m* 17 Feb 1973, Yvonne Louise, da of Ernest Stanley Crisp (d 1981), of Rustington, Sussex; *Career* Lt 33 Parachute Fd Regt RA 1953; admitted slr 1960, asst sec Stock Exchange 1964, sr asst sec Law Soc 1976, area dir Southern Legal Aid 1980; memb Oxford and Cambridge Golf Soc 1963; Liveryman Worshipful Co of Grocers 1968; memb Law Soc 1960; *Books* In Alpine Pastures (1963); *Recreations* golf, judo, aikido, photography, sitting in the sun; *Style—* Derek Duncan, Esq; Heather Way, Lower Bourne, Farnham, Surrey (☎ 025 125 4291); Legal Aid Area Office, 80 Kings Rd, Reading RG1 4LT (☎ 0734 589696)

DUNCAN, Lady Eileen Elizabeth; *née* Hope Johnstone; da of Maj Percy Wentworth Hope Johnstone, RA (TA), *de jure* 10 Earl of Annandale and Hartfell (d 1983), by his 2 w, Margaret (*see* Dowager Countess of Annandale and Hartfell); *b* 3 Oct 1948; *m* 1969, Andrew Walter Bryce Duncan, son of Sir Arthur Bryce Duncan (d 1984); 3 s; *Style—* Lady Eileen Duncan; Newlands, Kirkmahoe, Dumfries-shire

DUNCAN, Lady - Etelka de Vangel; *m* 1958, Sir (Charles Edgar) Oliver Duncan, 3 and last Bt (d 1964); *Style—* Lady Duncan; Horsforth Hall, Guiseley, W Yorks

DUNCAN, George; s of William Duncan (d 1966), and Catherine Gray Duncan, *née* Murray; *b* 9 Nov 1933; *Educ* Holloway Co GS, LSE (BSc), Wharton Sch of Fin, Pennsylvania Univ (MBA); *m* 1965, Frauke Ulricke; 1 da (Fiona b 1969); *Career* chief exec Truman Habury Buxton Ltd 1967-71, chief exec Watney Mann Ltd 1971-72, vice-chm Int Distillers & Vintners Ltd 1972, chm Lloyds Bowmaker Ltd 1976-86 (dir 1973), chief exec Yule Catto & Co Ltd 1973-75; chm ASW Hldgs plc 1986-, HHC Gp plc 1986, Whessoe plc 1987-(dir 1986), Humberside Fin Gp Ltd 1987; dir: BET plc 1981-, Lloyds Bank 1982-87, Haden plc 1974-85 (dep chm 1984-85), TR City of London Tst plc 1977-, Assoc Br Ports Hldgs plc 1986-, Newspaper Publishing plc 1986-, Dewe Rogerson Gp Ltd 1987; chm CBI Cos Ctee 1980-83, memb CBI president's ctee 1980-83; Freeman City of London 1971; FCA, CBIM; *Recreations* tennis, skiing, opera; *Style—* George Duncan, Esq; c/o Granville House, 132 Sloane St, London SW1X 9AX (☎ 01 730 0491)

DUNCAN, Ian Alexander; s of late Kenneth George Duncan, and Peggy Pauline, *née* Stochbury; *b* 21 April 1946; *Educ* Central GS Birmingham; *m* Carol Hammond, da of William Wilford Smith, of Bucks; 2 s (Adam Harvey b 1966, Alexander James b 1975), 1 da (Tavira Caroline b 1975); *Career* certified accountant, founding fell Assoc of Corporate Treasurers, fin dir Tomkins (and subsidiaries and assocs) 1984-, formerly fin dir Pentos plc (resigned Pentos and all subsidiaries 1984); *Recreations* travel, DIY, gardening, music, reading; *Style—* Ian A Duncan, Esq; The Tudor House, Devonshire Ave, Amersham-on-the-Hill, Bucks HP6 5JF; East Putney House, 84 Upper Richmond Rd, London SW15 2ST (☎ 01 871 4544, fax 01 871 2928)

DUNCAN, Sir James Blair; s of John Duncan and Emily MacFarlane Duncan; *b* 24 August 1927; *Educ* Whitehall Sch Glasgow; *m* 1974, Betty Psaltis; *Career* chm Transport Devpt Gp Ltd 1975-; ; memb LTA (p/t) 1979-82; Scottish cncl memb 1976- (chm 1982-), vice pres London Exec Ctee 1983-, chm London Chamber of Commerce 1986-88; pres: Inst of Road Transport Engrs 1984-88, Chartered Inst of Transport 1980-1981; CA (Scotland), FCIT, CBIM, FRSA (1977); Kt 1981; *Books* Papers on Transport matters; *Recreations* travel, reading, walking, swimming, theatre; *Clubs* Caledonian; *Style—* Sir James Duncan; 17 Kingston House South, Ennismore Gdns, London, SW7

DUNCAN, John Spenser Ritchie (Jock); CMG (1967), MBE (1953); s of Rev John Henry Duncan (d 1951), and Sophia Playfair Duncan, *née* Ritchie (d 1985); *b* 26 July 1921; *Educ* Kilmarnock Acad, George Watson's, Glasgow Acad, Dundee HS, Edinburgh Univ (MA); *m* 1950, Sheila Grace Fullarton, da of the Rev Duncan Conacher (d 1962); 1 da (Kirsty); *Career* HM Forces 1941-43; Sudan Political Serv 1942-56; HM Diplomatic Serv 1956-81; minister (political) Canberra 1969-71, high cmmr Zambia 1971-75, ambass Rabat 1975-78, high cmmr Bahamas 1978-81; *Books* The Sudan: A Record of Achievement (1952), The Sudan's Path to Independence (1957); *Clubs* New (Edinburgh); *Style—* J S R Duncan, Esq, CMG, MBE; 9 Blackford Road, Edinburgh EH9 2DT (☎ 031 447 4340)

DUNCAN, Kathleen Nora; da of George James Denis Dale (d 1983), and Nellie Logan, *née* Jamieson; *b* 26 Sept 1946; *Educ* Christs Hosp, St Aidans Coll Durham (BA), Poly of Central London (Dip Arts Admin); *m* 11 Jan 1975 (m dis 1983), Neil Stuart Duncan; *Career* head of arts servs London Borough of Havering 1971-73, dep dir SE Arts 1974-76, chief exec Composers and Authors Soc of Hong Kong (CASH) 1977-79, gen mangr Archer Travel Hong Kong 1979-82, int mktg dir Boosey & Hawkes Music Publishers Ltd 1983-86, mktg dir Order of St John 1986-; almoner and govr Christs Hosp; MInstD, memb Inst of Charity Fundraising Mangrs; *Recreations* music, travel, walking; *Style—* Mrs Kathleen Duncan; 148 Cranmer Ct, London SW3 3HF (☎ 01 589 6777); The Order of St John, 1 Grosvenor Cres, London SW1X 7EF (☎ 01 235 5231, fax 01 235 0796)

DUNCAN, Dr Kenneth Playfair; CB (1985); s of Rev John Henry Duncan (d 1951), and Sophia, *née* Ritchie (d 1985); *b* 27 Sept 1924; *Educ* HS of Dundee, Univ of St Andrews (BSc, MB, ChB); *m* 1950, Gillian, da of Dr Douglas Arthur Crow (d 1944); 4 da (Janet, Sally, Mary, Lucy); *Career* chief MO UKAEA 1958-69; head of Health and Safety Br Steel 1969-75, visiting prof London Sch of Hygiene 1976-80, dep dir-gen HSE 1982-85 (dir med servs 1975-81), asst dir (bio-med) NRPB 1985-; FRCPE, FRCP; *Recreations* gardening, walking; *Style—* Dr Kenneth Duncan; Westfield, Steeple Aston, Oxon (☎ 0869 40277); NRPB (☎ 0235 831600)

DUNCAN, Kenneth Sandilands (Sandy); OBE; s of Dr William Arthur Duncan (d 1946), of 3 Wilmington Terrace, Eastbourne, Sussex, and Ethel Mary, *née* Edwards (d 1969); *b* 26 April 1912; *Educ* St Andrew's Eastbourne, Malvern Coll, New Coll Oxford (BA); *m* 1, 4 June 1941, Katharine Beatrice, *née* Darwall (d 1955); 1 s (Andrew Duncan b 1943); m 2 June 1957 (m dis 1966), Dorothy, *née* Wentworth; *Career* WWII 2 Lt 176 Field Battery RA 1940, lectr OCTU Ilkley Yorks 1942-44, Asst Staff Capt RA 1944-45 3 Br Inf Div, lectr WO Sch of Mil Admin No 1 Trg Wing, Maj (non substantive) reverting to Capt; master Bradfield 1935-38, gen sec Univs Athletics Union 1949-51, hon sec Achilles Club (Oxford and Cambridge Blues and half Blues) 1948-87, gen sec Cwlth Games Cncl for Eng 1948-72, hon sec Cwlth Games Fedn 1948-82, gen sec Br Olympic Assoc 1948-75 (conslt/librarian); Double Blue (Oxon) Athletics 1931, Soccer 1935, competed GB Int Athletics 1932-37; winner: Silver Medal 4 x 110 yds relay Cwlth Games 1938, Gold Medal 4 x 110 yds World Univ Games (Paris) 1937; Chef de Mission of 12 GB Olympic Teams (summer and winter) 1952-72; Olympic Order 1984, The White Rose and Lion of Finland 1952; *Books* The Oxford Book of Athletic Training (1957), Athletics - Do it This Way (1952); *Clubs* East India - Overseas League; *Style—* Sandy Duncan, Esq, OBE; Flat 1, 57 Gloucester Rd, South Kensington, London SW7 4QN (☎ 01 584 4012); The British Olympic Association, 1 Wandsworth Plain, London SW18 1EN (☎ 01 871 2677, fax 01 871 9104, telex 932312 BOA G)

DUNCAN, Michael Greig; s of Alec Greig Duncan (d 1979), and Betty, *née* Shaw; *b* 9 Sept 1957; *Educ* King Williams Coll IOM, Downing Coll Cambridge (BA); *m* 2 July 1983, Fiona Helen, da of Michael John Carlisle Glaze, CMG; 1 s (Rory b 8 March 1985), 1 da (Chloe b 14 Oct 1986); *Career* admitted slr 1981, ptnr Allen & Overy 1987- (asst slr 1981-86); memb City of London Law Soc; *Style—* Michael Duncan, Esq; 9 Cheapside, London EC2V 6AD (☎ 01 248 9898, fax 01 236 2192, telex 881 2801)

DUNCAN, Roderick; s of Kenneth George Duncan, DCM (d 1979), and Peggy Pauline, *née* Stutchbury; *b* 9 Feb 1949; *Educ* Central GS for Boys Birmingham, Birmingham Coll of Commerce; *m* 23 Sept 1972, Susan Deborah, da of Lionel William Lane, of Solihull; 2 s (Matthew James b 9 May 1978, Alistair Scott b 19 Nov 1980); *Career* sales dir Co Unit Tsts Ltd 1985-87, investmt sales dir Aetna Int (UK) Ltd 1987-, dir Aetna Unit Tsts Ltd 1987-; ACIS 1972; *Recreations* golf, militaria, golf memorabielia; *Style—* Roderick Duncan, Esq; Amberley, Orchard Rd, Shalford, Surrey GU4 8ET; Aetna Ho, 2-12 Pentonville Rd, London N1 9XG (☎ fax 01 837 2111, telex 27797)

DUNCAN, Stanley Frederick St Clare; CMG (1983); s of Stanley Gilbert Scott Duncan; *b* 13 Nov 1927; *Educ* Latymer Upper; *m* 1967, Jennifer Bennett; 2 da; *Career* India Office 1946; CRO 1947-67; Diplomatic Service 1967-, head Consular Dept FCO 1977-80, Canadian Nat Def Coll Kingston Ontario 1980-81, Br ambass Bolivia 1981-85; Br high cmmr Malta 1985-; *Style—* His Excellency Mr Stanley Duncan, CMG; 7 St Anne Street, Floriana, Valletta, Malta; c/o Foreign and Commonwealth Office, King Charles St, London SW1A 2AH

DUNCAN, Hon Mrs; (Doreen) Synolda Tower Butler; da of 27 Baron Dunboyne (decd); *b* 17 Feb 1918; *m* 1945, Maj Atholl Duncan, MC, RA (d 1983); 2 s, 2 da; *Style—* The Hon Mrs Duncan; 9 Marland House, 28 Sloane St, London SW1X 9NE

DUNCAN MILLAR, Ian Alastair; CBE (1978), MC (1945), JP (Perthshire 1952), DL (1963); s of late Sir James Duncan Millar; *b* 22 Nov 1914; *Educ* Gresham's, Trinity Coll Cambridge (MA); *m* 1945, Louise Reid, da of W McCosh (d 1937); 2 s, 2 da; *Career* WWII Maj RE 1940-45; dir Macdonald Fraser & Co Ltd Perth 1961-86, chm Utd Auctions (Scotland) 1967-74; chm: Inst of Fisheries Mgmnt (Scotland) 1980-83 (fell 1988-), Consultative Ctee on Freshwater Fisheries (Freshwater and Salmon Fisheries Scotland Act 1976) 1981-86; vice pres Scottish Landowners Fedn 1986, memb North of Scotland Hydro Electric Bd 1956-72 (dep chm 1970-72), govr Hill Farming Res Orgn 1966-67; memb Perth and Kinross CC 1945-74 (convenor 1970-74), reg cncllr and convenor Tayside Regnl Cncl 1974-78; Parly candidate (Lab): Banff 1945, Kinross and Perthshire 1949 and 1963; memb Royal Co of Archers (Queen's Body Guard for Scotland); *Style*— I A Duncan Millar, Esq, CBE, MC, JP, DL; Reynock, Remony, Aberfeldy, Perthshire (☎ 08873 400)

DUNCAN-SANDYS *see also*: Sandys

DUNCAN-SANDYS, Hon Laura Jane; 3 and yst da of Baron Duncan-Sandys, CH, PC (Life Peer d 1987), and only da by his 2 w Marie-Claire, *née* Schmitt; *b* 1964; *Educ* Queen's Coll Harley St; *Career* dir Newton Sandys Ltd (mktg consultancy), conslt to traders in Eastern Euro Block ; *Style*— The Hon Laura Duncan-Sandys; 28 Redcliffe Road, London SW10 (☎ 01 351 6511)

DUNCOMBE; *see*: Pauncefort-Duncombe

DUNCOMBE, (Nicholas) Guy; s of Roy Duncombe, and Joan Thornley Duncombe, *née* Pickering; *b* 1 Sept 1952; *Educ* Abbotsholme Derbyshire; *m* 1, 14 Jan 1973; 2 da (Kirsty Nicola b 1974, Zoe Louise b 1975); m 2, 16 Oct 1986, Sharon, da of Leonard Finch; *Career* CA; dir: Ferry Pickiering Gp plc, Finance & Equity Ltd, Finance & Equity Properties Ltd, Circletech Ltd; *Recreations* shooting, skiing; *Clubs* Naval and Military; *Style*— Guy Duncombe, Esq; Bramble Cottage, Osbaston, Nuneaton, Warks (☎ 0455 291007); Quarn House, 21 Station Road, Hinckley, Leics (☎ 0455 611044, car telephone 0836 514955)

DUNCOMBE, Roy; VRD (1957); *b* 7 June 1925; *Educ* Hinckley GS; *m* 6 May 1946, Joan Thornley; 1 s 2 da; *Career* Pilot Fleet Air Arm, Lt Cdr (A) RNR; chm Nationwide Anglia Bldg Soc (former dep chm), fin dir Ferry Pickering Gp plc 1943-87; *Recreations* walking, swimming, boating, ornithology; *Clubs* Naval and Military; *Style*— Roy Duncombe, Esq VRD; Westways, Barton Rd, Market Bosworth, Nr Nuneaton, Warwickshire CV13 0LQ (☎ 0455 291728), work (☎ 01 242 8822, car ☎ 0836 621167)

DUNCUMB, Dr Peter; s of late William Duncumb), and Hilda Grace, *née* Coleman; *b* 26 Jan 1931; *Educ* Oundle, Clare Coll Cambridge; *m* 1955, Anne Leslie Taylor; 2 s, 1 da; *Career* dir and gen mangr T1 Gp Res Laboratories 1979-87, dir res centre in superconductivity Univ of Cambridge 1988-; FRS; *Style*— Dr Peter Duncumb; 5 Woollards Lane, Great Shelford, Cambridge (☎ 0223 843064)

DUNDAS, (Robert) Alexander; Sixteenth Representative of the Robertsons of Auchleeks; s of Ralph Dundas (d 1982), of Airds, Appin, Argyll, and Margaret Beryl, *née* Maclean, *qv*; *b* 12 June 1947; *Educ* Harrow, Christ Church Oxford; *m* 9 July 1977, Sarah Rosalind, da of (William) Simon Wilson, of Ballochmorrie, Barrhill, By Girvan, Ayrshire; 1 s (Ralph b 1988), 1 da (Catriona b 1985); *Career* Grieveson, Grant and Co stockbrokers 1970-79 (portfolio mangr Far East 1974-79), dir and investmt mangr Japan G T Mgmnt Asia Ltd 1980-, dir GT Mgmnt plc 1984- (chm investmt ctee 1988-); *Recreations* scottish history, art objects, gastronomy, shooting, armchair cricket; *Clubs* Boodle's, Pratt's, Puffin's (Edinburgh), Royal Hong Kong Jockey; *Style*— Alexander Dundas, Esq; 6 Eldon Rd, London W8 5PU; G T Mgmnt plc, Eighth Floor, 8 Devonshire Sq, London EC2M 4YJ (☎ 01 283 2575, fax 01 626 6176, telex 886100 GTMLDN G)

DUNDAS, Lord (Richard) Bruce; s of 3 Marquess of Zetland; *b* 16 Jan 1951; *Educ* Harrow; *m* 1, Jane, da of E Wright; 1 s, 1 da; m 2, 1983, Sophie, only da of Henry Giles Francis Lascelles and Caroline, *née* Baring; 1 da (Flora b 1986); *Style*— Lord Bruce Dundas; 18 Wetherby Gdns, London SW5

DUNDAS, Lord David Paul Nicholas; s of 3 Marquess of Zetland; *b* 2 June 1945; *Educ* Harrow, Central Sch of Speech and Drama; *m* 1971, Corinna, da of Denys Scott, of Chelsea; 1 s, 1 da; *Career* song writer; *Style*— Lord David Dundas; Aske, Richmond, Yorkshire

DUNDAS, Hugh McKenzie; s of Hon Richard Serle Dundas (d 1968), (3 s of 6 Viscount Melville), and his 1 w, Lydia Catherine, *née* Mackenzie (d 1922); hp to Viscountcy of Melville; *b* 3 June 1910; *Educ* Saskatchewan Univ; *m* 29 Sept 1939, Catherine Sanderson, da of late John Wallace, of Edinburgh; 1 s (Robert b 1943), 1 da (Catherine b 1948); *Clubs* Toronto Royal Canadian Military Inst, Pembroke Golf and Country, Pembroke Curling; *Style*— Hugh Dundas, Esq; 298 Alfred St, Pembroke, Ontario K8A 3A6, Canada (☎ 613 home: 732 3116; work: 732 8581)

DUNDAS, Sir Hugh Spencer Lisle; CBE (1977), DSO (1944, and Bar 1945), DFC (1941), DL (Surrey 1969); 2 s of Frederick Dundas (himself s of Hon John Dundas, sometime MP for Richmond, and yr bro of 3 Earl and 1 Marquess of Zetland) and Sylvia, da of Hugh March Phillipps; *b* 22 July 1920; *Educ* Stowe; *m* 1950, Hon (Enid) Rosamond, *qv*; 1 s, 2 da; *Career* served RAF WWII UK fighter cmd and Mediterranean, ret 1947; chm: BET plc 1982- (md 1973-82, dep chm 1981-82), Thames TV 1981-87, Rediffusion 1978-85, Rediffusion TV 1978-85, BET Omnibus Services 1978-85, BET Investments 1978-85; formerly with Beaverbrook Newspapers Ltd; memb: Cncl Financial and Gen Purposes Ctee RAF Benevolent Fund 1976-; tstee: Nat Soc Cancer Relief 1976-, HFT Devpt Tst; chm The Prince's Youth Business Trust; kt 1987; *Clubs* White's, RAF; *Style*— Sir Hugh Dundas, CBE, DSO, DFC, DL; The Schoolroom, Dockenfield, Farnham, Surrey (☎ 025 125 2331); 55 Iverna Court, London W8 (☎ 01 937 0773)

DUNDAS, Lady; Isabel; da of Charles Goring; *m* 1933, Maj Sir Thomas Calderwood Dundas, 7 and last Bt, MBE (d 1970); *Style*— Lady Dundas; 6 The Green, Slaugham, Handcross, Sussex

DUNDAS, James Frederick Trevor; s of Hugh Dundas, CBE, DSO, DFC, *qv* , and Hon Lady Dundas; *b* 4 Nov 1950; *Educ* Eton, New Coll Oxford, Inns of Court Sch of Law; *m* 27 June 1979, Jennifer Ann, da of John Daukes; 2 da; *Career* barr Inner Temple 1972, dir Morgan Grenfall & Co Ltd 1981; *Style*— James Dundas, Esq; 23 Great Winchester St, London EC2P 2AX (☎ 01 588 4545)

DUNDAS, Margaret Beryl; *née* Maclean of Ardgour; da of Lt-Col Alexander John Hew Maclean of Ardgour, DL, JP (d 1930), of Ardgour, Argyllshire, and Hon Muriel Annette Burns, OBE, JP (d 1969), yr da of 3 Baron Inverclyde; *b* 20 Jul 1923; *Educ* Oxenfoord Castle; *m* 16 July 1946, Ralph Dundas (d 1982), s of Robert William Dundas, MC (d 1928); 2 s ((Robert) Alexander, *qv* b 1947, Hew Ralph b 1953); *Career* WWII ATS 1942-45; pres ARgyll Girl Guide Assoc (co cmmr 1960-82); Mrs Margaret Dundas; *Books* Airds, Appin, Argyll (☎ 063 173 224)

DUNDAS, Lord; Robin Lawrence Dundas; s and h of Earl of Ronaldshay and gs of 3 Marquess of Zetland, ED, DL; *b* 5 Mar 1965; *Educ* Harrow Sch, Royal Agric College Cirencester; *Career* dir The Catterick Racecourse Co Ltd; *Style*— Lord Dundas

DUNDAS, Hon Lady; (Enid) Rosamond; da of 3 Baron Trevethin and 1 Baron Oaksey (d 1971); sis of 2 Baron Oaksey, *qv*; *b* 1924; *m* 1950, Gp Capt Sir Hugh (Spencer Lisle) Dundas, *qv*; 1 s (James b 1950), 2 da (Sarah b 1953, Amanda b 1956); *Style*— The Hon Lady Dundas; The Schoolroom, Dockenfield, Farnham, Surrey; 55 Iverna Court, London W8 (☎ 01 937 0773)

DUNDEE, 12 Earl of (S 1660); Alexander Henry Scrymgeour of Dundee; also Viscount Dudhope (S 1641), Lord Scrymgeour (S 1641), Lord Inverkeithing (S 1660), Baron Glassary (UK 1954); Baron of Barony of Wedderburn; Hereditary Royal Standard Bearer for Scotland; s of 11 Earl of Dundee (d 1983), and Patricia, Countess of Dundee, *qv*; *b* 5 June 1949; *Educ* Eton, St Andrews Univ; *m* 1979, Siobhan Mary, da of David Llewellyn, of Sayers, Gt Somerford, Wilts; 1 s, 2 da (Lady Marina Patricia Siobhan b 21 Aug 1980, Lady Flora Hermione Vera b 30 Sept 1985, Lady Lavinia Rebecca Elizabeth b 5 Nov 1986); *Heir* s, Lord Scrymgeour, *qv*; *Career* contested (C) Hamilton by-election 1978; *Style*— The Rt Hon the Earl of Dundee; Farm Office, Birkhill, Cupar, Fife

DUNDEE, Patricia, Countess of; Patricia Katharine; da of Lt-Col Lord Herbert Andrew Montagu Douglas Scott, CMG, DSO (decd), (5 s of 6 Duke of Buccleuch and Queensberry); *m* 1, 1931, Lt-Col Walter Douglas Faulkner, MC, Irish Gds (ka 1940); 1 s 1 da (*see* Sir Iain Moncreiffe of that Ilk, Bt); *m* 2, 1940, Lt-Col Hon David Scrymgeour Wedderburn, DSO, Scots Gds (d 1944 of wounds received in action); 2 da; m 3, 1946, 11 Earl of Dundee (d 1983); 1 s, *qv* 12 Earl of Dundee; *Recreations* painting; *Clubs* Caledonian; *Style*— The Rt Hon Patricia, Countess of Dundee

DUNDERDALE, Cdr Wilfred Albert; CMG (1942), MBE (1920); s of Richard Albert Dunderdale (d 1945), and Sophie, *née* Urbanek (d 1955); *b* 24 Dec 1899; *Educ* Russia; *m* 1, 1952, Mrs Dorothy Mabel Brayshaw Hyde (d 1978), da of James Murray Crofts, DSC, CBE; m 2, 1980, Deborah Jackson McLeod, da of Eugene Bailey Jackson, of USA (d 1935); *Career* trained for naval architect 1914-17, served WW I, with Mediterranean Fleet 1918-22 (despatches), transferred to Br Embassy Constantinople 1922-26, Paris Embassy 1926-40, Cdr RNVR 1939, attached Foreign Serv London 1946-67; ret 1967; French Legion of Honour and Croix de Guerre with palm, US Legion of Merit, Polish Polonia Restituta; *Recreations* yachting; *Clubs* Boodle's, Royal Harwich Yacht, Knickerbocker (New York); *Style*— Cdr Wilfred Dunderdale, CMG, MBE; One East 66th St, New York City, NY 10021, USA

DUNDONALD, Dowager Countess of; Ann Margaret; *née* Harkness; da of late Sir Joseph Welsh Park Harkness, CMG, OBE; *b* 3 August 1924; *m* 1 (m dis), C F Edward Staib; 1 s (John, *see* STAIB, Hon Mrs); m 2, 1978, 14 Earl of Dundonald (d 1986); *Career* serv WVS 1942-43, WRNS 1943-46; *Recreations* travel, painting; *Clubs* Caledonian, Sloane; *Style*— The Rt Hon Dowager Countess of Dundonald; Beau Coin, La Haule, Jersey, Channel Islands

DUNDONALD, 15 Earl of (S 1669) Iain Alexander Douglas Blair; also Lord Cochrane of Dundonald (S 1669), Lord Cochrane of Paisley and Ochitree (S 1669), and Marquesate of Maranhao (Empire of Brazil 1823 by Dom Pedro I for 10 Earl); s (by 1 m) of 14 Earl of Dundonald (d 1986); *b* 17 Feb 1961; *Educ* Wellington, Royal Agric Coll (Dip Ag); *m* 4 July 1987, (M) Beatrice (L), da of Adolphus Russo, of Gibraltar; *Heir* Kinsman Lord Cochrane of Cutts; *Career* dir:Arthurstone Devpts plc, Duneth Securities Ltd, New Capital and Scottish Properties Ltd; *Recreations* skiing, sailing, shooting, fishing; *Style*— The Rt Hon the Earl of Dundonald; Lochnell Castle, Ledaig, Argyll

DUNFORD, Campbell Edward; s of Arthur Edward Dunford, and Margaret Muriel, *née* Trowbridge; *b* 24 Dec 1944; *Educ* Hove GS, St Edmund Hall Oxford (MA); *m* 18 Nov 1974, Karen Christian, da of Isaac Henry Thompson (d 1983), of Market Overton, Rutland, Leics; *Career* dir overseas investmt Aladdin Industs Ltd 1974-76, business devpt mangr Guthrie Int Ltd 1976-79, dir and gen mangr Guthrie Trading (UK) Ltd 1979-81, trade fin dir Midland Bank 1981-1988, gen mangr Moscow Narodny Bank Ltd 1988-; vice-pres Br Exporters Assoc, chm London C of C, Export Fin Ctee, memb LCCI cncl, chm Aid Funded Advsy Serv; *Recreations* squash, classical music, gardening; *Style*— Campbell Dunford, Esq; Great Down Farm, Marnhull, Dorset; 81 King William St, London EC4P 4JS (☎ 01 623 2066, fax 01 283 4840, telex 885401)

DUNFORD, Neil Roy; s of Charles Roy Dunford, and Joyce Ellen; *b* 16 Jan 1947; *Educ* Edinburgh Acad, Sedbergh Sch, St Andrews Univ (MA); *m* 24 Apr 1976, Gillian; *Career* Deloitte & Co 1968-7?, J Henry Schroder Wagg 1972-81, Scottish Widows Fund 1981-85, Morgan Grenfell Asset Mgmnt 1985-; *Style*— Neil Dunford, Esq; 21 Ashley Drive, Walton-on-Thames, Surrey KT12 1JL (☎ 0932 246 496); Morgan Grenfell Asset Mgmnt, 46 New Broad Street, London EC2M 1NB (☎ 01 256 7500, fax 01 826 0331, telex 920286 NGAM G)

DUNGEY, Roger Harvey (aka Roger Harvey); s of William Arthur Dungey (d 1978), and Norah Isabella *née* Harvey; *b* 27 Sept 1939; *Educ* Lingfield Co Secondary Sch Surrey, and Writtle Agric Coll, Essex; *m* 1, 30 Jan 1965, Kathleen Anne Bootherstone; 2 s (Graham b 1968, Stephen b 1971), 1 da (Suzanne Louise b 1973); m 2, 11 Sept 1982, Joanna Frances Pettit; *Career* dir Rochford House Plants 1965-76 and Roger Harvey Ltd 1976; Horticulturist; memb Inst of Horticulture; *Recreations* walking, gardening, travelling; *Style*— Roger Dungey, Esq; The Farm House, Bragbury Lane, Stevenage, Herts SG2 8TJ (☎ 0438 814979); Roger Harvey Garden Centre, Bragbury Lane, Stevenage, Herts SG2 8TJ (☎ 0438 811777); Mazoe, Main St, Walberswick, Suffolk (☎ 0502 722432)

DUNGLASS, Lord; *see*: Home of the Hirsel, Baron

DUNHAM, John Wilfred; s of William Henry Dunham (d 1953), of London, and Emma Eleanor, *née* Mack (d 1981); *b* 22 April 1923; *Educ* St Georges Coll, Hornsey Coll of Art; *m* 28 March 1945, Rosa Margaret, da of Gaetano d'Angela (d 1966); 1 s (Geoffrey Michael b 1964, d 1972); *Career* insur broker Lloyds of London 1939-; Freeman City of London, Liveryman Worshipful Co of Fruiterers 1979; *Clubs* Oriental, MCC, Wig and Pen; *Style*— John Dunham, Esq; Dunham Financial Servs Ltd, 54 London Fruit Exchange, Brushfield St, London E1 6EU (☎ 01 247 6751; 037 27 27959)

DUNHAM, Sir Kingsley Charles; s of Ernest Pedder Dunham, of Brancepeth, Co Durham (d 1947), and Edith Agnes, *née* Humphreys (d 1939); *b* 2 Jan 1910; *Educ* Durham Johnston Sch, Durham Univ (DSc, PhD), Harvard Univ (MS, SD); *m* 1936, Margaret, da of William Young, of Choppington, 1 s Northumberland; *Career* geologist with HM Geological Survey of Great Britain 1935-50, New Mexico Bureau of Mines 1939; prof of geology Durham Univ 1950-66; dir Institute of Geological Sciences 1967-75; consulting geologist 1976-; dir Weardale Minerals Ltd; foreign secretary The Royal Soc 1971-76; hon doctorates from 11 UK and US universities; FRS, FRSE, FEng; kt 1972; *Recreations* music, gardening; *Clubs* Geological Society's, formerly Athenaeum;

Style— Sir Kingsley Dunham; Charleycroft, Quarryheads Lane, Durham DH1 3DY (☎ 091 3848977)

DUNHILL, Richard; s of Vernon Dunhill (d 1938), and Helen, *née* Field Moser (d 1984); Co Alfred Dunhill formed by gf 1907; *b* 27 Oct 1926; *Educ* Beaumont Coll; *m* 5 April 1952, Patricia Susannah, da of Henry B Rump (d 1965); 3 s (Christopher John b 1954, (Alfred) Mark b 1961, Jonathan Henry b 1962), 1 da (Susan Mary b 1953); *Career* army conscript 1944-48; joined Alfred Dunhill Ltd 1948, dir 1961, dep chm 1967, chm 1977, chm Dunhill Holdings plc 1981; Barker Variety Club of GB; Master Worshipful Co of Pipemakers and Tobacco Blenders 1987-88; *Recreations* gardening, backgammon; *Clubs* RAC; *Style*— Richard Dunhill, Esq; 30 Duke Street, St James's, London SW1Y 6DL (☎ 01 499 9566, fax 01 499 6471)

DUNKELD, Bishop of, 1981-; Rt Rev Vincent Paul Logan; s of Joseph Logan (d 1975), and Elizabeth, *née* Flannigan; *b* 30 June 1941; *Educ* Balirs Coll Aberdeen, St Andrew's Coll Drygrange Melrose, Corpus Christi Coll London (DipRE); *Career* ordained priest Edinburgh 1964; asst priest: St Margaret's Davidsons Mains Edinburgh 1964-66, Corpus Christi Coll London 1966-67; Chaplain St Joseph's Hosp Rosewell Midlothian 1967-77, advsr in religious educn Archdiocese of St Andrews and Edinburgh 1967-77, parish priest St Mary's Ratho Midlothian 1977-81, episcopal vicar for educn Archdiocese of St Andrews and Edinburgh 1978-81; *Style*— The Rt Rev the Bishop of Dukeld; Bishop's House, 29 Roseangle, Dundee DD1 4LS (☎ 0382 24327)

DUNKLEY, Christopher; s of Robert Dunkley, and Joyce Mary Dunkley, *née* Turner; *b* 22 Jan 1944; *Educ* Haberdashers' Aske's; *m* 1967, Carolyn Elizabeth, s of Lt Col Arthur Philip Casey Lyons (d 1976), of Hampstead; 1 s (Damian b 1969), 1 da (Holly b 1971); *Career* journalist and broadcaster, feature writer and news ed UK Press Gazette 1965-68, reporter then specialist correspondent and critic The Times 1968-73, TV critic Financial Times 1973-; presenter of Feedback BBC Radio 4 1986-; winner Br Press Awards Critic of the year 1976 and 1986; *Books* "Television Today and Tomorrow: Wall to Wall Dallas?"; *Recreations* motorcycling, collecting, books, eating Italian food; *Style*— Christopher Dunkley; 38 Leverton Street, London NW5 2PG (☎ 01 485 7101)

DUNKLEY, Capt James Lewis; CBE (1970, OBE 1946), RD (1943); s of William Edward Dunkley (d 1911); *b* 13 Sept 1908; *Educ* Lawrence Sheriff, Rugby, Thames Nautical Training Coll HMS Worcester; *m* 1937, Phyllis Mary (d 1970), da of William John Cale; 1 da; *Career* served WW II in armed merchant cruisers; cadet Peninsular and Oriental Steam Navigation Co 1925, Cdre 1964-67, marine mangr P & O passenger div 1971-72; master Hon Co of Master Mariners 1970; *Clubs* City Livery; *Style*— Capt James Dunkley, CBE, RD; 1 Collindale Gdns, Clacton-on-Sea, Essex (☎ 0225 813950)

DUNLEATH, 4 Baron (UK 1892); Charles Edward Henry John Mulholland; TD, DL (Co Down 1964); s of 3 Baron Dunleath, CBE, DSO (d 1956), and Henrietta, da of Most Rev C F D'Arcy, Archbishop of Armagh; *b* 23 June 1933; *Educ* Eton, Cambridge Univ; *m* 1959, Dorinda Margery, da of late Lt-Gen Arthur Percival, CB, DSO, OBE, MC; *Heir* cous, Maj Sir Michael Mulholland, 2 Bt; *Career* 11 Hussars, cmd North Irish Horse, actg Lt-Col 1967-69, Capt Ulster Def Regt 1971-73; Hon Col North Irish Horse 1981-86; nat govr (N Ireland) BBC 1967-73; memb: NI Legislative Assembly and asst speaker 1973-75 and 1982-86, NI Constitutional Convention 1975-76, Ards Borough Cncl 1977-81; chm: Carreras Rothmans (N Ireland) Ltd 1974-84, N Ireland Independent TV Ltd, Dunleath Estates Ltd, Ulster & General Hldgs Ltd; dir Northern Bank Ltd; CBIM; *Style*— The Rt Hon The Lord Dunleath, TD, DL; Ballywalter Park, Newtownards, Co Down, N Ireland (☎ 024 77 58203)

DUNLOP, Rear Adm Colin Charles Harrison; CB (1972), CBE (1963), DL (Kent 1976-); s of Rear Adm Samuel Harrison Dunlop, CB (d 1950), of Surrey, and Hilda Dunlop, (d 1965); *b* 4 Mar 1918; *Educ* Marlborough; *m* 1941, Moyra Patricia O'Brien, da of John Albert Gorges (d 1968); 3 s (Angus, Robin, d 1946, Graham); *Career* RN 1935-74, serv WWII HMS: Kent, Valiant, Diadem, Orion, in Far East, Med and Atlantic; cmd HMS Pembroke 1964-66, dir Def Policy 1968-69, Rear Adm 1969, cmd Br Naval Staff Washington 1969-71, Flag Offr Medway 1971-74; dir gen Cable TV Assoc and Nat TV Rental Assoc 1974-83; *Recreations* cricket, country pursuits; *Clubs* Army and Navy, MCC, I Zingari, Free Foresters, Band of Bros; *Style*— Rear Adm C C H Dunlop, CB, CBE, DL; Chanceford Farm, Frittenden, nr Cranbrook, Kent (☎ 058 080 242)

DUNLOP, Sir (Ernest) Edward; CMG (1965), OBE (1947); s of James Henry Dunlop (d 1947), of Benalla, Australia and Alice Emily Maud, *née* Payne; *b* 12 July 1907; *Educ* Benalla HS, Melbourne Univ (MB BS, MS), Ormond Coll, Br Postgrad Med Sch Hammersmith; *m* 1945, Helen Leigh Raeburn, da of Mephan John Ferguson (d 1949); 2 s; *Career* surgn specialist EMS St Mary's Hosp Paddington 1939, Capt RAAMC 1935, medical liaison offr Br Troops Greece and Crete 1941, CO 1 Allied Gen Hosp Java 1942 (Col) cdr various prison camps and hospitals in Java, Malaya and Siam 1942-45, ADMS 'Blackforce' 1946 (despatches), Col RAAMC (ret); conslt surgn Royal Melbourne Hosp 1967-, hon surgn Royal Victorian Eye and Ear Hosp 1949-67, conslt surgn Peter Macallum Clinic for Cancer 1955-67, Colombo Plan advsr Thailand and Ceylon 1956, India 1960, Gordon Taylor Oration Malaysia 1978, pres Anti Cancer Cncl of Victoria 1980-; 'Australian of the Year' award 1977; Blues boxing and Rugby Union football, Australian caps Rugby Union 1932, 1934; ldr Surgical Team South Vietnam 1969; vice-pres Int Soc of Surgns 1982-83; pres Alcohol and Drug Fndn, Victoria 1970-82; landowner (100 acres); FRCS, FRACS, FACS, DSc (Hon) Punjabi; kt 1969; *Recreations* golf, travelling, farming; *Clubs* Melbourne Naval and Military, Melbourne Cricket and Br Barbarian; *Style*— Sir Edward Dunlop, CMG, OBE; 605 Toorak Rd, Toorak, Australia , 3142; 14 Parliament Pla, Melbourne, Vic 3002, Australia,

DUNLOP, Frank; CBE (1977); s of Charles Norman Dunlop and Mary, *née* Aarons; *b* 15 Feb 1927; *Educ* Kibworth Beauchamp GS, Univ Coll London (BA); *Career* theatre dir (Old Vic, Nat Theatre, RSC, Royal Court, amongst others), former ass dir and admin dir Nat Theatre; fndr The Young Vic 1969, dir 1969-83, conslt 1978-80; dir Edinburgh Int Festival 1984-; Hon Fell UCL 1979, Hon Doctorate Philadelphia Coll of Performing Arts 1978; Chev Order of Arts and Letters (France) 1987; *Style*— Frank Dunlop, Esq, CBE; Edinburgh Int Festival, 21 Market Street, Edinburgh EH1 1BW (☎ 031 226 4001, telex 728115 EDFEST)

DUNLOP, (Norman) Gordon (Edward); **CBE**; s of Ross Munn Dunlop (d 1947); *b* 16 April 1928; *Educ* Trinity Coll Glenalmond; *m* 1952, Jean, da of George Fyfe Taylor (d 1975); 1 s, 1 da; *Career* CA; former chief exec Commercial Union Assur Co Ltd, dir Inchcape Berhad Singapore 1979-83, chief fin offr Br Airways 1982-, memb bd Br Airways 1983-; *Recreations* skiing, fishing, gardening; *Clubs* Caledonian, Buck's; *Style*— Gordon Dunlop, Esq; 28 Brunswick Gardens, London W8 4AL (☎ 01 221 5059); Br Airways, PO Box 10, Hounslow, Middx (☎ 01 562 5691)

DUNLOP, Rev Ian Geoffrey David; s of Walter Nigel Usher Dunlop (d 1988), and Marguerite Irene, *née* Shakerley (d 1965); *b* 19 August 1925; *Educ* Winchester, New Coll Oxford (MA), Strasbourg Univ; *m* 2 Nov 1957, Deirdre Marcia, da of Archibald Marcus De La Maziere Jamieson (d 1981); 1 s (Robin Alastair b 6 July 1966), 1 da (Harriet Elizabeth b 28 Nov 1967); *Career* Lt Irish Gds 1944; vicar Bures Suffolk 1962-71, chllr Salisbury Cathedral 1971-; memb: Gen Synod 1975-85, Cathedral's Advsy Cmmn 1980-85; tstee Historic Churches Preservation Tst 1969; contributor to: The Connoisseur, Country Life, The Field, The Church Times; FSA 1965; *Books* Versailles (1956, 2 edn 1970), Palaces and Progresses of Elizabeth 1 (1962), Chateaux of the Loire (1969), Companion Guide to the Ile De France (1979), The Cathedrals Crusade (1982), Royal Palaces of France (1985), Thinking It Out (1986); *Recreations* birdwatching; *Clubs* Army and Navy; *Style*— The Rev Canon Ian Dunlop; 24 The Close, Salisbury, Wilts SP1 2EH (☎ 0722 336 809)

DUNLOP, John Leeper; s of Dr John Leeper Dunlop (d 1959), and Margaret Frances Mary, *née* Fiffett (d 1972); *b* 10 July 1939; *Educ* Marlborough; *m* 22 June 1965, Susan Jennifer, da of Gerard Thorpe Page (d 1985), of The Old Rectory, Harpole, Northants; 3 s (Timothy b 1966 d 1987, Edward b 1968, Harry b 1976); *Career* Nat Serv 2 Lt Royal Ulster Rifles 1959-61; racehorse trainer 1964- (trained Derby winner and 1600 other winners); memb-ctee: Nat Trainers Fedn, Stable Lads Welfare Tst, Br Racing Sch; *Recreations* coursing, breeding racehorses, owning show horses; *Clubs* Turf; *Style*— John Dunlop, Esq; House on the Hill, Arundel, Sussex (☎ 0903 882 106); Castle Stables, Arundel, Sussex (☎ 0903 882 194, fax 0903 884 173, car tel 0860 339 805, telex 87475 RACDEL)

DUNLOP, Robert Fergus; AE (1956); s of Maj A Fergus Dunlop OBE, TD, (d 1980) and Gwendolen Elizabeth *née* Coit; *b* 22 June 1929; *Educ* Marlborough, St John's Coll Cambridge, MIT; *m* 1966, Jane Clare, da of Lt-Col George Hervey McManus of Canada (d 1959); 1 s, 2 da; *Career* cmmd 2 Lt RA, later Flt Lt 501 (County of Gloucester) fighter sqdn RAuxAF; Sloan fell 1960; Bristol Aeroplane Co Ltd and subs Br Aircraft Corpn 1952-66, Westland Aircraft Ltd 1966-70; dir Lonrho plc 1972- (joined 1970); CEng, MRAeS; *Recreations* sailing, skiing; *Style*— Robert Dunlop Esq, AE; 42 Woodsford Square, London W14 8DP (☎ 01 602 2579)

DUNLOP, Thomas; s and h of Sir Thomas Dunlop, 3 Bt; *b* 22 April 1951; *Educ* Rugby, Aberdeen Univ (BSc); *m* 1984 Eileen, da of Alastair Stevenson; 1 da ; *Style*— Thomas Dunlop, Esq; Bredon Croft, Bredons Norton, Nr Tewkesbury, Glos

DUNLOP, Sir Thomas; 3 Bt (UK 1916) of Woodbourne, Co Renfrew; s of Sir Thomas Dunlop, 2 Bt (d 1963); *b* 11 April 1912; *Educ* Shrewsbury, St John's Coll Cambridge; *m* 1947, Adda Mary Alison, da of Thomas Arthur Smith (d 1952); 1 s, 1 da (and 1 da decd); *Heir* s, Thomas Dunlop; *Career* ptnr Thomas Dunlop and Sons, shipowners, late chm of Savings Bank of Glasgow, govr Hutchesons Sch 1957-80; CA; OStJ 1965; *Recreations* fishing, shooting and golf; *Clubs* Western Glasgow; *Style*— Sir Thomas Dunlop, Bt; The Corrie, Kilmacolm, Renfrewshire (☎ 0505 87 3239)

DUNLOP, Sir William (Norman Gough); s of Norman Matthew Dunlop; *b* 9 April 1914; *Educ* Waitiki Boys' HS; *m* 1940, Ruby Jean Archie; 3 s, 3 da; *Career* farmer; md Dunlop Farms Ltd, kt 1975; *Style*— Sir William Dunlop; 242 Main Rd, Monks Bay, Christchurch 8, New Zealand (☎ Christchurch 849056)

DUNLUCE, Viscount; *see*: Earl of Antrim

DUNMORE, Anne, Countess of; Anne Augusta; da of Thomas Clouston Wallace, of Holodyke, Dounby, Orkney; *b* 18 June 1943; *Educ* Downe House Newbury; *m* 1967, 9 Earl of Dunmore (d 1980); 2 da (Lady Kate b 1969, Lady Rebecca b 1970); *Style*— The Rt Hon Anne, Countess of Dunmore; 14 Regent Terrace, Edinburgh 7

DUNMORE, 11 Earl of (S 1686); Kenneth Randolph Murray; JP (Beaconsfield Municipality Tasmania 1962); also Viscount Fincastle, Lord Murray of Blair, Moulin and Tillimet (Tullimet; both S 1686); 2 s of Arthur Charles Murray (d 1964); suc er bro 1981; the Earls of Dunmore descend from the 2 s of 1 Marquess of Athole; *b* 6 June 1913; *m* 1938, Margaret Joy, da of P D Cousins (decd), of Burnie Tasmania; 2 s; *Heir* s, Viscount Fincastle; *Career* late Sgt 12/50 Bn Australian Inf; former Master Tamar Valley Masonic Lodge 42 Tasmanian Constitution 1957-58; patron: Exeter RSL Bowls Club, Combined Scottish Soc of NSW Australia; *Style*— The Rt Hon the Earl of Dunmore, JP; Gravelly Beach, 7251 W Tamar, Tasmania, Australia

DUNN, Angus Henry; s of Col Henry George Mountfort Dunn (d 1969), and Catherine Mary (d 1986); *b* 30 Dec 1944; *Educ* Marlborough, King's Coll Cambridge (MA), Pennsylvania Univ; *m* 1973, Carolyn Jane, da of Alan Bartlett, of The Oast, High Tilt, Cranbook, Kent; 2 s (Thomas b 1974, James b 1977), 1 da (Eliza b 1983); *Career* HM Diplomatic Service 1968-73; FCO, (Kuala Lumpur, Bonn); joined Morgan Grenfell & Co Ltd 1972-, dir 1978-, exec deputy chm Morgan Grenfell (Asia) Ltd Singapore 1983-85; dir Julianas Hldgs plc 1983-85; *Books* Export Finance (co-author, 1986); *Recreations* riding, sailing; *Clubs* Royal Thames Yacht; *Style*— Angus Dunn, Esq; Dower House, Oxon Hoath, Tonbridge, Kent

DUNN, Douglas Eaglesham; s of William Douglas Dunn (d 1980), and Margaret, *née* McGowan; *b* 23 Oct 1942; *Educ* Renfrew HS, Camphill Sch Paisley, Scottish Sch of Librarianship, Univ of Hull (BA); *m* 1, Lesley Balfour, *née* Wallace (d 1981); m 2, 10 Aug 1985, Lesley Jane, da of Robert Bathgate (d 1979); 1 s (William Robert Bathgate b 5 Jan 1987); *Career* writer: books of poetry incl: Terry Street (1969), The Happier Life (1972), Love or Nothing (1974), Barbarians (1979), St Kilda's Parliament (1982), Elegies (1985), Selected poems (1986), Northlight (1988); Short Stories Secret Villages (1985), Somerset Maugham Award 1972; Geoffrey Faber Meml Prize 1975, Hawthornden Prize 1982, Whitbread Book of the Year Award for 1985 (1986); hon LLD Dundee 1987, hon prof Univ of Dundee 1987, hon fell Humberside Coll; FRSL 1981; *Recreations* music, gardening; *Style*— Douglas E Dunn, Esq; c/o Faber & Faber Ltd, 3 Queen Square, London, WC1N 3AU

DUNN, Geoffrey Richard; s of Kenneth Grayson Dunn, of 7 Woodlands, Pound Hill, Crawley, Sussex, and Nila Jane, *née* Griffiths; *b* 10 July 1949; *Educ* Ifield GS, Manchester Univ (BSc, MSc), Manchester Business Sch (Dip); *m* 26 July 1973, Patricia Ann, da of John Thompson, of 8 Craiglands, Lightcliffe, nr Halifax, W Yorks; *Career* investmt controller ICFC Ltd 1975-78, corporate fin exec SG Warburg & Co Ltd 1978-80, asst gp tres GKN plc 1980-83, head of fin and planning Midland Bank plc 1984-87, gp fin dir Exco Int plc 1987-; memb: MCT 1982; *Recreations* mountaineering, skiing, opera and music; *Clubs* London Mountaineering; *Style*— Geoffrey Dunn, Esq; 5

Church Walk, Highgate, London N6 6QY (☎ 01 348 4893); EXCO Int plc, 80 Cannon St, London EC4N 6LJ (☎ 01 623 4040, fax 01 283 8450, telex 887198)

DUNN, (William) Hubert; QC (1982); s of William Patrick Millar Dunn (d 1964), of Tudor Hall, Holywood, Co Down, and Isobel, *née* Thompson (d 1954); *b* 8 July 1933; *Educ* Winchester, New Coll Oxford (BA); *m* 23 Sept 1971, Maria Henriquetta Theresa D'Arouje Perestrella, da of George Hoffacker de Moser, 3 son of Count de Moser in the nobility of Portugal; 1 s (Sebastian b 29 Aug 1973), 1 da (Eugenia b 27 May 1972); *Career* 2 Lt The Life Gds 1956-57, Household Cavalry Reserve of Offs 1957-64; barr Lincoln's Inn 1958; local govt cmmr 1963; rec Crown Ct 1980; chm City of London and Westminster South Lib Pty 1976-79; *Recreations* travel, literature; *Clubs* Boodle's; *Style—* Hubert Dunn, Esq, QC; 19 Clarendon Street, London SW1; 5 King's Bench Walk, Temple, London EC4 (☎ 01 353 4713)

DUNN, John Churchill; s of John Barrett Jackson Dunn (d 1984), and Dorothy Dunn, *née* Hiscox; *b* 4 Mar 1934; *Educ* Christ Church Cathedral Choir Sch, Oxford; The King's Sch, Canterbury; *m* 19 April 1958, Margaret, da of Stanley Farrand Jennison (d 1982); 2 da (Joanna b 1960, Emma b 1963); *Career* broadcaster BBC staff 1956-76; freelance radio 2, (programmes include: Breakfast Special, Late Night Extra and numerous others); currently hosts own show 1976-; *Recreations* working, skiing, sailing, wine; *Style—* John C Dunn, Esq

DUNN, Lydia Selina; DBE (1989, CBE 1983, OBE 1978), JP (1976), LLD (1984); da of Yenchuen Yeh Dunn (d 1965); *b* 29 Feb 1940; *Educ* St Paul's Convent Sch, Univ of California at Berkeley (BS); *Career* chm: Swire & Maclaine Ltd 1982- (exec trainee 1963, dir 1973, md 1976), Swire Loxley Ltd 1982-, Camberley Enterprises Ltd, Swire Mktg Ltd; dir: Swire Trading (Taiwan) Ltd 1969-, John Swire & Sons (HK) Ltd 1978-, Hongkong and Shanghai Banking Corpn 1981-, Cathay Pacific Airways Ltd; exec dir: Swire Pacific Ltd 1982; chm Hong Kong Trade Devpt Cncl 1983-, dep chm: Exec Ctee Commonwealth Parly Assoc (Hong Kong Branch); sr memb Exec Cncl Hong Kong 1988- (memb 1982-88), memb Legislative Cncl of the Asia Soc and Hong Kong Assoc; memb cncl: Chinese Univ 1978-, Trade Policy Res Centre London 1980-; cncl memb Volvo Int Advsy Bd 1984; *Recreations* collecting of antiques; *Clubs* Hong Kong, Hong Kong Country, World Trade Centre, The Royal Hong Kong Jockey; *Style—* The Hon Dame Lydia Dunn, DBE, JP; John Swire & Sons (HK) Ltd, 5th Floor, Swire House, 9 Connaught Rd, Central, Hong Kong (☎ 5 230011), John Swire & Sons Ltd, Swire House, 59 Buckingham Gate, London SW1E 6AJ (☎ 01 834 7717)

DUNN, Lady Mary Helen Alma Graham; da of 6 Duke of Montrose; *b* 11 April 1909; *m* 1, 21 April 1931, Maj John Percival Townshend Boscawen, MBE, Gren Gds (d 1972), s of Townshend Evelyn Boscawen; 2 s; m 2, 1975, Brig Leslie Dunn, TD, DL, s of William Lawrie Dunn, of Kilmacolm, Renfrewshire; *Style—* Lady Mary Dunn

DUNN, Lady Mary Sybil; *née* St Clair-Erskine; da of 5 Earl of Rosslyn; *b* 6 May 1912; *m* 1, 1933 (m dis 1944), Philip Gordon Dunn (afterwards 2 Bt); 2 da (*see* Dunn, Nell); m 2, 5 Oct 1946 (m dis 1959), as his 2 w, Robin Francis Campbell, CBE, DSO (d 1985); m 3, 5 Oct 1962 (m dis 1969), Charles Raymond McCabe; m 4, 1969, Sir Philip Gordon Dunn, 2 and last Bt (d 1976); *Style—* Lady Mary Dunn; Draycot Fitzpayne Manor, Marlborough, Wilts

DUNN, Neil; s of Robert Dunn (d 1980), and Jean Hendrie Dunn, *née* Ramage (d 1987); *b* 15 Dec 1949; *Educ* Leith Acad Sch, Heriot Watt Univ (BA); *m* 1970, Dianne Isabella Mary, da of Robert Gilchrist Burgess (d 1965); 2 da (Elissa Lucienne b 1974, Chrisanna Amy b 1976); *Career* dir: Ivory & Sime plc, Trenwick Inc, Nippon Assets Investmts SA, Foso Assets Investmets SA, Sumitomo Life Ivory Asset Mgmnt Ltd, Somitrust Ivory & Sime Ltd, Ivory & Sime (Far East), Ivory & Sime (Japan), Ivory & Sime (UK), Ivory & Sime (Bermuda), Ivory & Sime International Ltd, Ivory & Sime International Inc; *Recreations* reading, fishing, walking; *Clubs* Aberdeen Marina; *Style—* Neil Dunn, Esq; 35A Garden Terrace, Old Peak Road, Hong Kong (☎ 5 258505); St Johns, Temple, Midlothian; 2104, Two Exchange Square, Central, Hong Kong (☎ 4 215633)

DUNN, Nell Mary; yr da of Sir Philip Dunn, 2 Bt (d 1976), and Lady Mary Dunn, *qv*; *b* 9 June 1936; *m* 1957 (m dis 1979), Jeremy Christopher (writer), s of Christopher Sandford, of Eye Manor, Leominster; 3 s (Roc b 1957, Reuben b 1964, Jem b 1967); *Career* author; *Works include* Poor Cow, Up the Junction, Steaming (play); *Style—* Miss Nell Dunn

DUNN, Air Marshal Sir Patrick Hunter; KBE (1965, CBE 1950), CB (1956), DFC (1941); s of William Alexander Dunn (decd), of Ardentinny, Argyllshire; *b* 31 Dec 1912; *Educ* Glasgow Academy, Loretto, Glasgow Univ; *m* 1939, Diana Ledward Smith; 2 da (*see* Sir Nigel Marsden, Bt); *Career* cmmnd RAF 1933; serv WWII: Egypt, Libya, Sudan, Air Miny and Fighter Cmd; ADC to HM The Queen 1953-58; Cmdt RAF Flying Coll Manby 1956-58; Air Vice-Marshal 1959; AOC No 1 Gp Bomber Cmd 1961-64, AOC-in-C Flying Training Cmd 1964-66; Air Marshal 1965, ret 1967; dir Management Services Br Steel Corpn 1967-68; dep chm Br Eagle Int Airlines 1968, vice-pres UK NATO Defence Coll Assoc 1969, chm Eagle Aircraft Services Ltd 1969, dir Gloucester Cricklewood Kingston and Coventry Trading Estates Ltd 1969-81; trustee and govr Loretto Sch 1959-81, pres Fettesian Lorettonian Club 1972-75, pres Lorettonian Society 1980-81; memb: ctee Assoc of Governing Bodies of Public Schools 1976-79, Br Atlantic Ctee 1976-; FRAeS; *Style—* Air Marshal Sir Patrick Dunn,; Little Hillbark, Cookham Dean, Berks SL6 9UF (☎ Marlow 5625)

DUNN, Paula; da of Paul Kenneth Dunn, and Louise, *née* Brissett; *b* 3 Dec 1964; *Career* med clerical offr; UK's top female sprinter for the past 3 years; UK champion 100m and 200m: 1986, 1987, 1988; WAAA champion 100m and 200m: 1987, 1988; Cwlth Games 1986: Silver Medallist 100m, Gold Medallist 4 x 100m relay; Olympic Games 1988: quarter-finalist 100m, semi-finalist 200m, semi-finalist 4 x 100m relay; involved with local schs and sports clubs; *Recreations* athletics, reading; *Clubs* Stretford AC; *Style—* Miss Paula Dunn; 4 Salisbury Road, Chorlton-cum-Hardy, Manchester M21 1SL (☎ 061 881 6068); Manchester City Housing Dept, Medical Section, Town Hall Ext, Manchester M60 2JX (☎ 061 234 4736)

DUNN, Robert John; MP (C) Dartford 1979-; s of Robert Dunn (d 1986); *b* 14 July 1946; *Educ* State Schs; *m* 1976, Janet Elizabeth, da of Denis Wall (d 1983); 2 s; *Career* former sr buyer with Sainsbury's; contested (C) Eccles 1974 (vice-pres Eccles Cons Assoc 1974-); jt sec Cons Backbench Educn Ctee 1980-82, advsr to Professional Assoc of Teachers 1982-83; PPS: DES to 1982, Cecil Parkinson (chm Cons Party) 1982-83, under-sec of state DES 1983-88, chm Con Back Bench Social Security Ctee 1988-, memb 1922 Ctee 1988-; pres Dartford YCs 1976-; *Clubs* Carlton; *Style—* Robert Dunn, Esq, MP; House of Commons, SW1 (☎ 01 219 5209)

DUNN, Rt Hon Sir Robin Horace Walford; MC (1944), PC (1980); s of Brig Keith Frederick Wlliam Dunn, CBE, DL (d 1985), and his 1 w, Ava, *née* Kays; *b* 16 Jan 1918; *Educ* Wellington, RMA Woolwich; *m* 1941, Judith Allan, da of Sir Gonne St Clair Pilcher, MC (d 1966); 1 s, 1 da (and 1 da decd); *Career* cmmnd RA 1938, RHA 1941; serv WWII France, Belgium, Libya, Normandy, NW Europe (despatches 2), Staff Coll 1946, ret Hon Maj 1948; Hon Col Cmdt RA 1981-1984, Hon Col 1984; barr Inner Temple 1948, jr counsel Registrar of Restrictive Trading Agreements 1959-62, memb gen cncl Bar 1959-63 (tres 1967-69), QC 1962, bencher Inner Temple 1969, judge High Ct of Justice Family Div 1969-80, presiding judge Western circuit 1974-78, Lord Justice of Appeal 1980-84, ret; kt 1969; *Clubs* Cavalry and Guards'; *Style—* Rt Hon Sir Robin Dunn, MC; Lynch Mead, Allerford, Somerset TA24 8HJ (☎ 0643 862509)

DUNN, Dr Robin Martin Kenneth; s of Edward Bernard Dunn, MC (d 1973), and Dorothy, *née* Dymond (d 1972); *b* 10 August 1923; *Educ* Southampton GS, Liverpool Sch of Architecture (DipArch, Dip Civic Design), Aberdeen Univ (LLD); *m* 19 July 1952, Margery Ursula Powell, BArch, ARIBA, da of Maj G P Thomas (d 1944), of Bridgend; 1 s (David Bernard b 1958), 1 da (Nicola Sarah b 1956); *Career* 1942-46 Capt RE N Africa and Italy (despatches); qualified architect/town planner 1950, asst architect to Sir Hugh Casson, PPRA 1952-54, own practice Robin and Margery Dunn 1954-56, ptnr George/Trew/Dunn Architects 1956-83; Civic Tst Awards for Bowring Building London and London Univ Buildings Aberdeen; FRIBA;; *Recreations* sailing, walking; *Clubs* Lansdowne; *Style—* Dr Robin Dunn; Gold Court, Wareham, Dorset BH20 4LZ (☎ 092 95 3320)

DUNN, (George) Roger; s of George Dunn, and Marjorie Rose, *née* Brown; *b* 10 Jan 1936; *Educ* Tettenhall Coll, Univ of Bristol (BSc); *m* 22 Aug 1970, (Patricia) Jane, da of Frank J R Law (d 1972), of Churchill, Worcs; 3 da (Sarah b 1972, Claudia b 1975, Juliet b 1977); *Career* Tube Investmts 1958-67, AIC Ltd 1967-75, chm and md Arcontrol Ltd 1975-; memb: SE Regnl Cncl of CBI, Engrg Cncl Regnl Orgn, ct Bristol Univ; chm GAMBICA Ctee (for mfrg electrical Switchgear and centl gear assemblies); FIEE, MIMechE, FInstD; *Recreations* swimming, playing the flute, private flying; *Style—* Roger Dunn, Esq; Ancontrol Ltd, Borough Green, Kent TN15 8RD (☎ 0732 883151, fax 0732 885982, telex 95580)

DUNN, Lt-Col Sir (Francis) Vivian; KCVO (1969), OBE (1960), RM; s of Capt W J Dunn, MVO, MC, RHG; *b* 24 Dec 1908; *Educ* Peter Symonds Sch Winchester, Konservatorium der Musik Cologne, RAM; *m* 1938, Margery Kathleen Halliday; 1 s, 2 da; *Career* international conductor; principal dir of Music RM, ret 1968; Liveryman and Ct memb Worshipful Co of Musicans; ARAM, FRAM; *Style—* Lt-Col Sir Vivian Dunn, KCVO, OBE, RM; 16 W Common, Haywards Heath, Sussex (☎ 412987)

DUNN-MEYNELL, Hugo Arthur; s of Arthur James Dunn, of London (d 1959), and Mary Louise Maude, *née* Meynell (d 1945); *b* 4 April 1926; *Educ* John Fisher Sch Purley; *m* 1, 1952 (m dis 1980), Nadine Madeleine, da of late Percy Denson; 3 s, 1 da; m 2, 1980, Alice Wooledge, da of Dr Pierre Joseph Salmon, of Hillsborough, California; *Career* wine and food writer and consultant; pres Lonsdale Advertising Int 1978-, chm International Wine and Food Soc 1978-80 (dir-gen 1983-); Liveryman Worshipful Company of Inn Holders; Grand-Officer Les Chevaliers du Tastevin; FRGS, FIPA; *Recreations* wine and travel; *Clubs* Athenaeum; *Style—* Hugo Dunn-Meynell, Esq; 125 Mount St, London W1Y 5HA (☎ 01 629 2647); International Wine and Food Society, 108 Old Bromtpon Road, London SW7 3RA (☎ 01 370 0909)

DUNNE, Lady Miranda; *see*: Lowther

DUNNE, W Peter; s of William Joseph Dunne (d 1985), and Mary Anne, *née* Hynes (d 1958); *b* 6 Nov 1936; *Educ* Dublin; *m* 29 Nov 1969, Fionuala Anne, da of James Joseph Fox of Dublin; *Career* chief exec offr (confs and travel): cwlth econ ctee 1961-66, cwlth secretariat 1966-; *Recreations* antiquarian books, music, cricket; *Clubs* MCC, Royal Overseas League, RDS (Dublin); *Style—* W Peter Dunne, Esq; The Nuik, 55 Bodley Rd, New Malden, Surrey KT3 5QD, (☎ 01 942 1434); 11 Martello Mews, Dublin, 4; Commonwealth Secretariat, Marlborough House, Pall Mall, London SWIY 5HX (☎ 01 839 3411, fax 01 930 0827, tlx 27678)

DUNNETT, Dr Alastair MacTavish; s of David Sinclair Dunnett and Isabella Crawford MacTavish; *b* 26 Dec 1908; *Educ* Overnewton Sch, Hillhead HS; *m* 1946, Dorothy, da of Alexander Halliday; 2 s (Ninian, Mungo); *Career* Commercial Bank of Scotland Ltd 1925; co-fndr: The Claymore Press 1933-34, Glasgow Weekly Herald 1935-36, The Bulletin 1936-37, Daily Record 1937-40; chief press offr Sec of State for Scotland 1940-46, ed Daily Record 1946-55; Smith Mundt Scholarship to USA 1951; ed The Scotsman 1956-72; md, Scotsman Publications Ltd 1962-70, chm Scotsman Publications Ltd 1970-74; memb exec bd Thomson Organisation Ltd 1974-78, chm Thomson Scottish Petroleum Ltd 1972-79; dir 1979-87; dir Scottish Television Ltd 1975-79: memb Scottish Tourist Bd 1956-72, Press Cncl 1959-62, Cncl Nat Tst for Scotland 1962-69; memb exec bd Thomson Orgn 1974-78; chm Thomson Scottish Petroleum Ltd 1972-79 (dir 1979-87); dir Scottish Television Ltd 1975-79; md The Scotsman Pubns Ltd 1962-70 (chm 1970-74), memb: Edinburgh U Ct 1964-66, Cncl of Cwlth Press Union 1964-78, Edinburgh Festival Cncl 1967-80; govr Pitlochry Festival Theatre - 1984; hon LLD Strathclyde 1978; *Books* Treasure at Sonnach (1935), Heard Tell (1946), Quest by Canoe (1950, repr 1967), Highland and Islands of Scotland (1951), The Donaldson Line (1952), The Land of Scotch (1953), The Duke's Day (1970, as Alec Travis), Alistair Maclean Introduces Scotland (ed, 1972), No Thanks to the Duke (1978), Among Friends (autobiog, 1984); plays: The Original John Mackay (Glasgow Citizens 1956), Fit to Print (Duke of York's 1962); *Recreations* sailing, riding, walking; *Clubs* Caledonian, Scottish Arts, New (Edinburgh); *Style—* Dr Alastair Dunnett; 87 Colinton Road, Edinburgh EH10 5DF (☎ 031 337 2107)

DUNNETT, Lady; Clarisse; *b* 7 May 1924; *Educ* Budapest Hungary, Bristol; *m* 1, Grantley Loxton-Peacock (decd); 1 s, 1 da (*see* Osborne, Sir Peter, Bt); m 2, 1979, as his 2 w, Sir Anthony Grover, sometime chm Lloyds and Lloyds Register of Shipping (d 1981); m 3, 1983, Sir James Dunnett, GCB, CMG, *qv*; *Career* painter (twelve one-man exhibitions, London, New York, Düsseldorf); *Recreations* gardening; *Style—* Lady Dunnett; 85 Bedford Gdns, W8 (☎ 01 727 5286)

DUNNETT, Denzil Inglis; OBE (1962), CMG (1966); s of Sir James Dunnett, KCIE (d 1957), of Edinburgh, and Annie Sangster (d 1955); *b* 21 Oct 1917; *Educ* Edinburgh Acad, Oxford (MA) ; *m* 1946, Ruth (d 1973), da of Laurence Rawcliffe (d 1948), of Lancs; 2 s (Roderick b 1946, James b 1948), 1 da (Ursula b 1950); *Career* RA 1939-46 (Maj India, Germany); HM dip serv 1947-77; (ambass: Senegal, Mali, Mauretania, Guinea, Guinea-Bssau 1972-75; London representative of the Scottish Devpt Agency 1978-82; dir The Sea Vegetable Co 1985-; *Recreations* fountains, golf; *Clubs*

Caledonian; *Style*— Denzil Dunnett, OBE, CMG; 11 Victoria Grove, London W8 5RW (☎ 01 584 7523)

DUNNETT, (William Herbert) Derek; s of William Herbert Dunnett (d 1978), of Surrey, and Lilian Agnes, *née* Waugh (d 1968); *b* 9 Feb 1921; *Educ* Rugby; *m* 14 Dec 1950, Peggy Cummins; 1 s (William b 1954), 1 da (Margaret b 1962); *Career* dir Carters Tested Seeds Ltd 1946-62 (md 1962-67); md Raynes Park Securities Ltd 1969-; memb of Lloyds (external) 1978-; rackets champion: public schools (doubles 1939, singles 1938), services singles 1955, Open Invitation doubles 1951; FID; *Recreations* sport, racing, arts; *Clubs* Queens, MCC; *Style*— Derek Dunnett, Esq; 105 Comeragh Rd, West Kensington, London W14 9HS

DUNNETT, Dorothy; *née* Halliday; da of late Alexander Halliday, and Dorothy, *née* Millard; *b* 25 August 1923; *Educ* James Gillespie's HS for Girls Edinburgh; *m* 1946, Alastair Mactavish Dunnett; 2 s (Ninian, Mungo); *Career* civil servant 1940-55; portrait painter 1950-, novelist 1961-; tstee: Scottish Nat War Meml 1962-, tstee Nat Library of Scotland 1986-; dir Scottish TV plc 1979-; FRSA (1986); *Books* Game of Kings (1961), Queens' Play (1964), The Disorderly Knights (1966), Dolly and the Singing Bird (1968), Pawn in Frankincense (1969), Dolly and the Cookie Bird (1970), The Ringed Castle (1971), Dolly and the Doctor Bird (1971), Dolly and the Starry Bird (1973), Checkmate (1975, Scottish Arts Cncl Award 1976), Dolly and the Nanny Bird (1976), King Hereafter (1982), Dolly and the Bird of Paradise (1983); Niccolò Rising (1986), The Spring of the Ram (1987), The Highlands of Scotland (with A M Dunnett, 1988); *Recreations* travel, sailing, music, ballet, mediaeval history; *Clubs* New (Edinburgh), Caledonian (London); *Style*— Mrs Alastair Dunnett; 87 Colinton Rd, Edinburgh EH10 5DF (☎ 031 337 2107)

DUNNETT, Jack; *b* 24 June 1922; *Educ* Whitgift Middle Sch Croydon, Downing Coll Cambridge; *m* 1951, Pamela Lucille; 2 s, 3 da; *Career* serv WWII, Royal Fusiliers and Cheshire Regt (Capt); slr 1949; memb GLC 1964-67; MP (Lab) Nottingham Central 1964-74, Nottingham East 1974-83; PPS to: sec of state Defence and min of Defence (Army) 1964-66, min of Aviation 1966-67, min of Transport 1969-70; vice-pres Football Assoc 1981-, pres Football League 1981-; *Style*— Jack Dunnett, Esq; Whitehall Court, London SW1

DUNNETT, Sir (Ludovic) James; GCB (1969, KCB 1960, CB 1957), CMG (1948); s of Sir James Dunnett, KCIE (d 1953), bro of Sir George Sangster Dunnett; *b* 12 Feb 1914; *Educ* Edinburgh Acad, Univ Coll Oxford; *m* 1, 1944, Olga Adair (d 1980), m 2, 1983, Clarisse, Lady Grover; *Career* joined Air Miny 1936, transferred to Miny of Civil Aviation 1945 (asst sec 1945, under-sec 1948-51), under-sec (Air) Miny of Supply 1951-53 (dep sec 1953-58), dep sec Ministry of Transport 1958 (permanent sec 1959-62), permanent sec Ministry of Labour 1962-66, permanent under-sec of state MOD 1966-74; chm Int Maritime; Industs Forum 1974-79; pres Institute of Manpower Studies 1977-80, memb SSRC 1977-83; visiting fell Nuffield Coll Oxford 1960-68; *Clubs* Reform; *Style*— Sir James Dunnett, GCB, CMG; 85 Bedford Gardens, London W8

DUNNETT, Pamela Dawn Hamilton; *née* Johnson; da of Claude Hamilton (d 1967), and Elsie Muriel, *née* Street (d 1972); *b* 4 Nov 1925; *Educ* St Dominics Priory, Port Elizabeth SA; *m* 26 Oct 1946, Hanbury William Dunnett, s of Hanbury Dunnett (d 1961); 1 s (Geoffrey b 21 April 1950), 1 da (Gillian b 10 Nov 1947); *Career* WWII SAAF 1943-45; dir Dunnetts (Birmingham) Ltd 1971-; memb Cons Assoc, former ctee memb Sunshine Homes for Blind Children, former govr Knowle Hill Approved Sch Kenilworth; *Recreations* golf, bridge, painting; *Clubs* Coventry, Warwick Boat; *Style*— Mrs Pamela Dunnett; Barons Lodge, Hareway Lane, Barford, Warwicks (☎ 0926 624 034); Dunnetts (Birmingham) Ltd, Vanguard Works, Kings Rd, Tyseley, Birmingham (☎ 021 706 0271, fax 021 706 6169)

DUNNING, Prof John Harry; s of John Murray Dunning (d 1966), and Anne Florence, *née* Baker (d 1965); *b* 26 June 1927; *Educ* Lower Sch of John Lyons Harrow, City of Coll, UCL (BSc), Univ of Southampton (PhD); *m* (m dis 1975), 1 da Teresa; 1 s (Philip John b 1957); m2, 4 Aug 1975, Christine Mary, da of Ernest Stewart Brown; *Career* sub Lt RNVR 1945-48; lectr and sr lectr in econs Univ of Southampton 1952-64; Univ of Reading: fndn prof of econs 1964-75, Esmee Fairbairn prof of int investmt and business studies 1975-88, ICI res prof in int business 1988-, chm Econs Advsy Gp Ltd; conslt to UK Govt depts OECD, UN Centre on Transnat Corpns, Hon PhD Uppsala Univ Sweden 1975; memb Royal Econ Soc, Acad of Int Business pres AIB 1987-88; *Books* incl: American Investment in British Manufacturing Industry (1958), British Industry: Change and Development in the Twentieth Century (with C J Thomas, 2 edn 1963), The Economics of Advertising (with D Lees and others, 1967), An Economic Study of the City of London (with E V Morgan, 1971), Reading in International Investment (1972), Economic Analysis and the Multinational Enterprise (1974), The World's Largest Industrial Enterprises 1962-77 (1981), International Capital Movements (with John Black, 1982), Multinational Enterprises, Economic Structure and International Competitiveness (1985), Japanese Participation in British Industry (1986), Explaining International Production (1988); Multinationals, Technology and Competitiveness (1988); *Recreations* gardening, walking; *Clubs* Athenaeum; *Style*— Prof John H Dunning; Department of Economics, University of Reading, Whiteknights, Reading, Berkshire RG6 2AA (☎ 0734 318159)

DUNNING, Kathleen, Lady; Kathleen Lawrie Cuthbert; da of J Patrick Cuthbert, MC; *m* 1936, Sir William Leonard Dunning, 2 Bt (d 1961); *Style*— Kathleen, Lady Dunning; Barclayhills, Guildtown, Perth

DUNNING, Sir Simon William Patrick; 3 Bt (UK 1930) of Beedinglee, Lower Beeding, Sussex; s of Sir William Leonard Dunning, 2 Bt (d 1961); *b* 14 Dec 1939; *Educ* Eton; *m* 1975, Frances Deirdre Morton, da of Maj Patrick William Morton Lancaster; 1 da; *Heir* none; *Career* insurance broker and underwriting memb of Lloyd's; *Clubs* Turf, Western (Glasgow); *Style*— Sir Simon Dunning, Bt; Low Auchengillan, Blanefield, by Glasgow, G63 9AU (☎ Blanefield 70323)

DUNNINGTON-JEFFERSON, Isobel, Lady; (Frances) Isobel; da of Col Herbert Anderson Cape, DSO, of Thorganby, York; *m* 1938, Lt-Col Sir John Alexander Dunnington-Jefferson DSO, 1 Bt (d 1979); 1 s, 1 da; *Style*— Isobel, Lady Dunnington-Jefferson; Rectory Cottage, Escrick, York (☎ 090 487 686)

DUNNINGTON-JEFFERSON, Sir Mervyn Stewart; 2 Bt (UK 1958); s of Lt-Col Sir John Alexander Dunnington-Jefferson, 1 Bt, DSO (d 1979); *b* 5 August 1943; *Educ* Eton; *m* 1971, Caroline Anna, da of John Bayley, of Hillam Hall, Monk Fryston, Yorks; 1 s, 2 da; *Heir* s, John Alexander Dunnington-Jefferson b 23 March 1980; *Career* ptnr Marldon Construction; *Recreations* sport; *Clubs* MCC, Queens; *Style*— Sir Mervyn Dunnington-Jefferson, Bt; 7 Bolingbroke Grove, London SW11 (☎ 01 675 3395)

DUNPARK (Johnston), Alastair McPherson; TD; s of Rev Alexander McPherson Johnston (d 1957), of Stirling, and Eleanora Guthrie, *née* Wyllie (d 1966); *b* 15 Dec 1915; *Educ* Merchiston Castle Sch Edinburgh, Cambridge Univ (BA), Edinburgh Univ (LLB); *m* 1, 16 Dec 1939, Katharine Margaret, *née* Mitchell (d 1983); 3 s (Alan Charles Macpherson b 13 Jan 1942, (Alastair) Bryan Mitchell b 9 March 1948, Colin Lindsay Wyllie b 23 Oct 1952); m 2, 29 Sept 1984, Kathleen Elizabeth Sarah Welsh; *Career* advocate 1946, jr counsel Miny of Food and Miny of Tport, QC 1958, sheriff princ Dumfries and Galloway 1966-68, Scottish Law Cmmn 1968-71, senator Coll of Justice and Lord of Sessian Scotland 1971; pres: Lothian Marriage Counselling Serv 1974-87, Scottish Univ's Law Inst 1977-; chm: RA Assoc Scotland 1962-76, Cockburn Assoc (The Edinburhg Civic Tst) 1969-74, St George's Sch for Girls Edinburgh 1973-89, Edinburgh Legal Dispensary 1961; *Recreations* golf, fishing, walking; *Clubs* New (Edinburgh), Honourable Co of Edinburgh Golfers; *Style*— Hon Lord Dunpark, TD; 17 Heriot Row, Edinburgh EH3 6HP (☎ 031 556 1896); Parliament House, Edinburgh

DUNPHIE, Maj-Gen Sir Charles Anderson Lane; CB (1948), CBE (1942), DSO (1943); s of Sir Alfred Dunphie, KCVO; *b* 20 April 1902; *Educ* RNCs Osborne, RNC Dartmouth, RMA Woolwich; *m* 1, 1931, Eileen (d 1978), da of Lt-Gen Sir Walter Campbell, KCB, KCMG, DSO; 1 s, 1 da; m 2, 1981, Susan, widow of Col P L M Wright, of Roundhill, Wincanton; *Career* cmmnd RA 1921, Brig RAC 1941, Cdr 26 Armoured Bde 1942-43 (despatches), dep dir RAC WO 1943-45, dir gen Armoured Fighting Vehicles 1945-48, ret 1948; chm Vickers Ltd 1962-67; memb HM's Hon Corps Gentlemen-at-Arms 1952-62; cdr Legion of Merit (USA), Silver Star (USA); kt 1959; *Clubs* Army and Navy; *Style*— Maj-Gen Sir Charles Dunphie, CB, CBE, DSO; Roundhill, Wincanton, Somerset BA9 8HH (☎ 0963 33278)

DUNPHIE, Brig Christopher Campbell; MC (1972); s of Maj-Gen Sir Charles Anderson Lane Dunphie, CB, CBE, DSO, *qv*, of Roundhill, Wincanton, Somerset, and Lady Eileen Isabella, *née* Campbell (d 1978); *b* 29 Mar 1935; *Educ* Eton, RMA Sandhurst; *m* 28 Sept 1963, Sonia Diana, da of Brig Rudolph Charles Hogg Kirwan, DSO, OBE; 1 s (Charles b 1970); *Career* cmmnd Rifle Bde 1955 (later, Royal Green Jackets); Regtl Serv in: Kenya, Malaya, BAOR, Cyprus 1955-67, Staff Coll 1968, MA to CGS 1969-71 (Maj), Co Cmd 3 RGJ served UN Force Cyprus and NI 1971-73, instr Staff Coll 1973-76 (Lt Col), CO 3 RGJ Berlin, UK and NI 1976-78, asst dir of Def Policy MOD 1979-82 (Col), COS to LANDEP C in C Fleet (Op Corporate 1982, Cmdt, Tactics Wing Sch of Inf 1983-85, Div Brig Light Div 1985-87, ret 1988; memb Queens Bodyguard for Scotland, Roy Co of Archers; *Books* Brightly Shone the Dawn (with Garry Johnson 1980); *Recreations* cricket, skiing, field sports; *Clubs* I Zingari, Free Foresters, Perth; *Style*— Brig Christopher Dunphie, MC; Wester Cloquhat, Bridge of Cally, Blairgowrie, Perthshire PH10 7JP (☎ 025 086 320)

DUNRAVEN AND MOUNT-EARL, Nancy, Countess of;; da of Thomas Burks Yuille, of Halifax Co, Virginia, USA; *m* 1934, as his 2 w, 6 Earl of Dunraven and Mount-Earl, CB, CBE, MC (d 1965); 1 s (7 Earl), 2 da (Lady Melissa Brooke, w of Maj Sir George B, 3 Bt, MBE; Marchioness of Waterford, w of 8 Marquess); *Style*— The Rt Hon Nancy, Countess of Dunraven and Mount-Earl; Kilgobbin, Adare, Co Limerick

DUNRAVEN AND MOUNT-EARL, 7 Earl of (I 1822); Sir Thady Windham Thomas Wyndham-Quin; 7 Bt (GB 1781); also Baron Adare (I 1800), Viscount Mount-Earl (I 1816), Viscount Adare (I 1822); s of 6 Earl of Dunraven and Mount-Earl, CB, CBE, MC (d 1965; one of the small number of families of Celtic antecedents in the Irish peerage Lord Dunraven and Mount-Earl's ancestors were chiefs of a clan situated long before even the Norman invasions of Ireland in Co Clare and the O'Quins are the origin of the name of the Barony of Inchiquin); *b* 27 Oct 1939; *Educ* Ludgrove, Le Rosey Switzerland; *m* 1969, Geraldine, da of Air Cdre Gerard W McAleer, CBE; 1 da (Lady Ana b 1972); *Heir* none; *Career* Farming and Property Devpt; *Clubs* Kildare Street (Dublin); *Style*— The Rt Hon The Earl of Dunraven and Mount-Earl; Kilcurley House, Adare, Co Limerick, Ireland (☎ 061 86201)

DUNROSSIL, 2 Viscount (UK 1959); John William Morrison; CMG (1981); s of 1 Viscount, GCMG, MC, PC, QC (d 1961); *b* 22 May 1926; *Educ* Fettes, Oriel Oxford; *m* 1, 1951 (m dis 1969), Mavis da of A Llewellyn Spencer-Payne, LRCP, MRCS, LDS; 3 s, 1 da; m 2, 1969, Diana Mary Cunliffe, da of C M Vise; 2 da (Hon Joanna Catherine b 25 April 1971, Hon Mary Alison b 12 Dec 1972); *Heir* s, Hon Andrew William Reginald Morrison; *Career* served RAF 1945-48; CRO 1951, private sec to sec of state 1952-54, 2 sec Canberra Australia 1954-56, first sec and dep actg high cmmr E Pakistan 1958-60, first sec Pretoria Capetown 1961-64 (seconded to Foreign Service 1961), Diplomatic Service Admin Office 1965, on loan to Intergovernmental Maritime Consultative Orgn (IMCO) 1968-70, cnsllr and head of chancery Ottawa 1970-75, cnsllr Brussels 1975-78, high cmmr Fiji, Republic of Nauru, and Tuvalu 1978-82, high cmmr Barbados and (concurrently but non-resident) Antigua & Barbuda, St Vincent & The Grenadines, St Lucia, Cwlth of Dominica, Grenada and also Br Govt rep WI Assoc State of St Kitts-Nevis 1982-83, govr and C-in-C of Bermuda 1983-; KStJ 1983; *Style*— The Rt Hon the Viscount Dunrossil, CMG; c/o Foreign and Commonwealth Office, Downing Street, London SW1; Government House, Hamilton, Bermuda

DUNSANY, 19 Baron (I 1439); Lt-Col Randal Arthur Henry Plunkett; s of 18 Baron Dunsany, DL, LittD, the author (d 1957), and Lady Beatrice (d 1970), *née* Child-Villiers, da of 7 Earl of Jersey; hp to Barony of Killeen (*see* 12 Earl of Fingall); *b* 25 August 1906; *Educ* Eton; *m* 1, 1938 (m dis 1947), da of Senhor G De Sà Sottomaior, of São Paulo, Brazil; 1 s; m 2, 1947, Sheila Victoria Katrin, da of Sir Henry Philipps, 2 Bt, and widow of Maj John Frederick Foley, Baron de Rutzen, Welsh Gds; 1 da; *Heir* s, Hon Edward Plunkett; *Career* joined 16/5 Lancers (SR) 1926, transfd IA 1928, Guides Cavalry Indian Armoured Corps, ret 1947; *Style*— Lt-Col The Rt Hon The Lord Dunsany; Dunsany Castle, Co Meath, Ireland (☎ 046 25198)

DUNSDON, Graham Eric; s of Walter Eric Dunsdon (d 1985) of Horsham, West Sussex and Dorothy Edith *née* Hawkins (d 1975); *b* 13 Sept 1944; *Educ* Collyers GS, Horsham; *m* 18 Sept 1965, Mary, da of Joseph Nathaniel Bradley (d 1984); 1 s (Simon b 1967), 2 da (Helen b 1969, Lucy b 1973); *Career* insurance official ACII; assist general mngr TSB Trust Co Ltd 1975-82; dir: TSB Insurance Services Ltd 1981-82, Household International (UK) Ltd 1984-; md: FIMS Ltd 1982-83, Hamilton Insurance Co Ltd 1983-, Hamilton Life Assurance Co Ltd 1983-, chm: Hamilton Financial Planning Services Ltd 1986-; church warden St Mary's Church Abbotts Ann 1986-; *Recreations* church activities, clay pigeon shooting, family; *Style*— Graham Dunsdon,

Esq; Meadow View, Old Salisbury Road, Abbotts Ann, Andover, Hants (☎ 0264 710018); Hamilton Insurance Group, PO Box 60, Bracknell, Berkshire RG12 1HS (☎ 0344 489911, fax 0344 411115)

DUNSEATH, Robert William (Robin); s of William Hamilton Dunseath (d 1946), of Bangor, NI and Barbara, *née* Brown; *b* 14 June 1907; *Educ* Campbell Coll Belfast, Concord HS Massachussets USA, Queens Univ Belfast, Manchester Univ (BSc, Dip Tech Sci); *m* 19 May 1962, Hazel Mary, da of Peter Copsey, Peterborough, Eng; 1 s (Ashley b 1964), 1 da (Elizabeth b 1971); *Career* dir Royal Lyceum Theatre Edinburgh 1984-, world pres The World Haggis Hurling Soc 1978; FInstD; *Recreations* restoring old cottages, cars; *Style*— Robin Dunseath, Esq; 16 Maybury Road, Edinburgh; The Coach House, Dundonnachie, Dunkelp, Scotland; 5 Castle Terrace, Edinburgh, Scotland (☎ 031 228 6992, fax 031 228 6889, car ☎ 0860 326552)

DUNSEATH, Robin William; s of William Hamilton Dunseath (d 1946), and Barbara, *née* Brown; *b* 7 Jan 1938; *Educ* Campbell Coll Belfast, Queen's Univ Belfast, Manchester Univ (BSc, Dip Tech Sci); *m* 19 May 1962, Hazel Mary, da of Peter Copsey, of Peterborough; 1 s (Ashley b 1964), 1 da (Elizabeth b 1971); *Career* dir: Public Relations Consultancy, Royal Lyceum Theatre Edinburgh; World Pres Haggis Hurling for Charity Assoc; FID; *Recreations* theatre; *Style*— Robin W Dunseath, Esq; 16 Maybury Road, Edinburgh; Dunseath Stephen, 5 Castle Terrace, Edinburgh

DUNSIRE, Thomas; s of Thomas Dunsire (d 1976), of 30 Fairford Rd, Highbridge, Som, and Joan, *née* Duncan (d 1985); *b* 16 Nov 1926; *Educ* George Watson's Coll, Edinburgh; Morrison's Acad, Crieff; Edinburgh Univ (MA, LLB); *m* 17 Dec 1966, Jean Mary, da of John Bellwood Wright (d 1961), of Studley Rd, Middlesborough; *Career* War Serv 1944-47, Ordinary Seaman RN; slr 1950, memb of Soc of Writers to the Signet 1950; govr of Morrison's Acad 1972 (chm 1984); ptnr J & J Milligan WS 1951 (now Morton Fraser & Milligan, WS) sr ptnr 1983-88, ocnslt 1988; *Glubs* Royal Scots, Edinburgh; *Style*— Thomas Dunsire, Esq; 40 Liberton Brae, Edinburgh

DUNSTAN, HE (Lt-Gen) Sir Donald Beaumont; KBE (1979, CBE 1969, MBE 1954), CB (1972); s of Oscar Reginald Dunstan (d 1936), and Eileen Dunstan (d 1984); *b* 18 Feb 1923; *Educ* Prince Alfred Coll Adelaide, RMC Duntroon; *m* 1948, Beryl June, da of James Clyde Dunningham; 2 s; *Career* GOC Field Force Cmd 1974-77, Chief of Gen Staff 1977-82 (formerly Deputy Chief); govr South Australia 1982-; KStJ 1982; *see Debrett's Handbook of Australia and New Zealand for further details*; *Recreations* golf, trout fishing, cross-country skiing; *Clubs* Australian (NSW), Royal Sydney Golf ; *Style*— HE Sir Donald Dunstan, KBE, CB; Government House, North Terr, Adelaide, S Australia 5000 (☎ 223 6166)

DUNSTAN, Hon Maj Harry (Hal) Bernard; TD 1964; s of Bernard Mainwaring Dunstan (d 1946), of Warrington, Lancs, and Nellie Dunstan, *née* Sneyd (d 1956); *b* 21 July 1918; *Educ* Bolton Sch; *m* 10 April 1948, Dorothy Mary Johnston, da of John Gordon (d 1952), of Scotland; 2 s (Michael John b 1953, Peter Gordon b 1954), 1 da (Christine Mary b 1950); *Career* Duke of Lancasters Own Yeo TA 1939-40 and 1948-67, cmmd 40 Bn RTR 1941, HQ 8 Armd Div 1941-42, 3 Kings Own Hussars 1942-46; served: N Africa, Italy, Palestine; resigned cmmn TARD 1967 and granted hon rank of Maj; worked in Coal Indust 1934-82 (ret as mktg mangr NCB 1982); *Recreations* travel, gardening; *Clubs* Army and Navy; *Style*— Hon Maj Hal Dunstan, TD; Denstone House, Lincoln Road, Tuxford, Notts NG22 0HP (☎ 0777 870380)

DUNSTER, Francis Henry; s of Henry Frank Dunster (d 1960), and Elsie, *née* Whitehorn; *b* 24 August 1935; *Educ* Leighton Park Sch, Coll of Estate Mgmnt; *m* 19 Oct 1963, Maria Patricia, da of George Walsh (d 1983); 2 s (James b 1967, Charles b 1970), 1 da (Sarah b 1964); *Career* Healey & Baker: assoc ptnr 1965, equity ptnr 1969-, ptnr i/c Glasgow Off 1982-88; FRICS, ACIarb; *Recreations* tennis, golf, rugby; *Clubs* MCC, Royal Scottish Automobile Reading Rugby, Maidenhead Golf ; *Style*— Francis Dunster, Esq; 29 St George St, Havover Sq, London W1A 3BG (☎ 01 629 9292)

DUNSTER, (Herbert) John; CB (1978); s of Herbert Dunster (d 1980); *b* 27 July 1922; *Educ* UCS, Imperial Coll of Science and Technol; *m* 1945, Rosemary Elizabeth, nee Gallagher; 1 s, 3 da; *Career* scientist (radiology), Royal Naval Scientific Serv 1942, scientist UKAEA 1946-71, asst dir Nat Radiological Protection Bd 1971-76, dep dir-gen Health and Safety Exec 1976-; ARCS; *Recreations* music, photography, work; *Style*— John Dunster Esq, CB; Hill Cottage, 65 Castlebar Rd, W5 (☎ 01 997 0439)

DUNTHORNE, John William Bayne; s of Philip Bayne Dunthorne,of Alton, Hants, and Ruth Mabelle, *née* Sturch; *b* 26 August 1946; *Educ* Abingdon Sch, Oxford Sch of Architecture (Dip Arch); *m* 16 Aug 1974, Maggie Alice, da of John Edgar Taylor (d 1988), of Blofield, Norfolk; 1 s (Oliver b 1983), 1 da (Joanna b 1981); *Career* assoc ptnr Chapman Lisle Assoc 1972-74, jt sr ptnr Dunthorne Parker Architects & Designers 1978-88, dir DPSL 1985-88; RIBA, MCSD; *Books* An Airport Interface (with MP Parker, 1971); *Recreations* cricket, golf, snow skiing; *Clubs* MCC, Forty , Lord Gnome's CC; *Style*— J W B Dunthorne, Esq; 5 Aspley Rd, London SW18 2DB (☎ 01 874 4904); Dunthorne Parker, Architects & Designers, 8 Seymour Place, London W2H 5WF (☎ 01 258 0411)

DUNTZE, Nesta, Lady; Nesta; da of late T R P Herbert; *m* 1, Godfrey Ariel Evill; m 2, 1966, as his 2 w. Sir George Edwin Douglas Duntze, 6 Bt (d 1985); *Style*— Nesta, Lady Duntze; 25 Ennismore Gardens, London SW7

DUNWICH, The Bishop of 1980-, The Rt Rev Eric Nash Devenport; s of Joseph Samuel Devenport (d 1964), and Emma (d 1947); *b* 3 May 1926; *Educ* St Chad's Sch, private sch, Open Univ, Kelham Theol Coll; *m* 19 April 1954, Jean Margaret, da of Cliff Richardson (d 1985); 2 da (Rachel Mary b 1956, Clare Helen b 1962); *Career* curate St Mark Leicester 1951-54; St Matthew Barrow-in-Furness 1954-56; succentor Leicester Cathedral 1956-59; vicar: Shepshed 1959-64, Oadby 1964-73; leader of mission Leicester 1973-80; hon canon Leicester 1973-80; Bishop of Dunwich 1980-; chm Hospital Chaplaincies Cncl; diocesan communications offr; *Recreations* theatre, painting; *Clubs* Royal Cwlth Soc; *Style*— The Rt Rev the Bishop of Dunwich; 94 Henley Road, Ipswich IP1 4NJ (☎ 0473 58394)

DUNWICH, Viscount; Robert Keith Rous; s (by 1 m) and h of 6 Earl of Stradbroke, *qv*; *b* 17 Nov 1961; *Style*— Viscount Dunwich

DUNWOODY, Hon Mrs Gwyneth Patricia; MP (Lab) Crewe and Nantwich 1983-; da of Baroness Phillips (Life Peer) and Morgan Phillips (decd), sometime Gen Sec Labour Pty; *b* 12 Dec 1930; *Educ* Fulham County Secondary Sch, Convent of Notre Dame; *m* 1954 (m dis 1975), Dr John Elliot Orr Dunwoody; 2 s, 1 da; *Career* former journalist for Fulham local newspaper and writer for radio, also former memb Totnes Cncl; MP (Lab): Exeter 1966-70, Crewe 1974-1983; Parly sec Bd of Trade 1967-70, UK memb of European Parl 1975-79, memb Labour NEC 1981-, chm NEC Local Govt Sub-Committee Nov 1981-, oppn front bench spokesman Health Service 1981-, memb Labour Home Policy Ctee 1982-; dir Film Production Assoc of Gt Britain 1970-74; responsibility for co-ordinating Lab Party campaigns 1983-; *Style*— The Hon Mrs Gwyneth Dunwoody, MP; House of Commons, London SW1

DUNWOODY, (Thomas) Richard; s of George Rutherford Dunwoody, of Clanfield, Oxon, and Gillian Margaret, *née* Thrale; *b* 18 Jan 1964; *Educ* Rendcomb Coll; *m* 16 July 1988, Carol Ann, da of Robert Ronald George Abraham, of Wantage, Oxon; *Career* nat hunt jockey; Amateur Championship 1983-84 season (3 place), winner Grand Nat Aintree riding West tip 1985-86 season, Jockey's Championship 1986-87 season (3 place), winner Cheltenham Gold Cup riding Charter Party, Jockey's Championship 1987-88 season (3 place); subject of the BBC documentary Come the Spring; *Recreations* squash, golf, shooting; *Style*— Richard Dunwoody, Esq; 29 Calais Dene, Bampton, Oxon OX8 2NR (☎ 0993 851342, car tel 0836 502290)

DUPLESSIS, Hugo Jules; s of Capt gerald Duplessis (d 1949), of Newtown Park, Lymington, and Kathleen, *née* McCalmont 1971, gd of Baron of Kingsale); *b* 30 June 1923; *Educ* Beaumont Coll, Southampton Univ; *m* Oct 1952, Joyce (m dis 1979), da of Capt C Percy Keevil (d 1969), of Cockfosters, Herts; 1 s (Christopher b 1963), 1 da (Primrose b 1962); *Career* WWII Fleet Air Arm RN 1942-46; Admty scientific serv 1950-52, project ldr Decca Radar 1952-54; md: Newtown Industs 1954-, Fibreclad Ltd and Ropewalk Boatyard 1958-61; dir Koloplas Ltd 1962-71. Irish Atlantic charters 1977-; conslt on fibreglass boats, yacht surveyor and designer 1954- (semi-ret 1985); Irish del to EEC ctee on fibreglass boats 1982; memb: New Forest RDC 1963-71, Boldre Parish Cncl 1956-71, New Forest Assoc of Parish Cncls 1958-71 (chm 1964-67), Hants Assoc of Parish Cncls 1962-67; memb: RINA, Plastics and Rubber Inst, Irish Fedn of Marine Industs, Inst of Oceanography, Soc of Plastics Engrs, Irish Boat Rentals Assoc; *Books* Fibreglass Boats, Fibreglass Boats Fitting Out, Fibreglass Boats Maintenance and Repair, Fibreglass Boats Blistering, Money From Your Boat, Iniquity Joe, Harry Haywire, Tales of the Schooner Inn, Turtle Tales, Black Hugh's Castle, The Man Who Was Not There, Tidco, Pursuit of Heaven, Cat and Broomstick, The Sinking of the Mudlark; *author* of numerous tech papers and articles on nautical matters incl Fibreglass boats; *Recreations* cruising, country pursuits, saving the world from extermination;; *Clubs* Royal Cruising, Irish Cruising, Ocean Cruising, Bantry Bay SC (cdre 1975-78, vice-cdre 1984-88); *Style*— Hugo Duplessis, Esq; Ballylickey, Bantry, Co Cork, Ireland; Irish Atlantic Charters, Bentry Co Cork, Ireland

DUPPLIN, Viscount; Charles William Harley Hay; s and h of 15 Earl of Kinnoull, Arthur William George Patrick Hay, and Countess of Kinnoull, Gay Ann Hay, *née* Lowson; *b* 20 Dec 1962; *Educ* Eton, Christ Church Oxford (MA), City Univ; *Career* investmt banker with Credit Suisse First Boston Ltd 1985-88; *Recreations* skiing, squash, motor cars, racing; *Clubs* Turf, MCC, Lansdowne, Utd Oxford and Cambridge; *Style*— Viscount Dupplin; 59 Scarsdale Villar, London W8 (☎ 01 938 4265)

DUPRE, Sophie (Mrs Clive Farahar); *née* Dupré; da of Desmond John Dupré, lutenist (d 1974), and Catherine Lane, novelist, of Oxford; *b* 6 Jan 1955; *Educ* Convent of the Sacred Heart Tunbridge Wells; *m* 12 April 1980, Clive Robert Farahar, antiquarian bookseller; 1 s (Henry Robert b 1981) and 2 s decd (Frederick James b 1984 d 1985, Theodore Austen b and d 1987), 1 da (Emily Alexandra b 1979); *Career* specialist in autographed letters and mss, runs internat business supplying private collectors and institutes; *Recreations* travel; *Style*— Sophie Dupré; XIV The Green, Calne, Wilts SN11 8DQ (telex 449795 Islip)

DUPREE, Gordon John Felix; OBE (1978); s of Gordon Dupree (d 1950) and Rose Winifred Kate (d 1977); *b* 14 Oct 1929; *Educ* Lime Grove Sch of Building, Arts & Crafts; *m* 20 Oct 1951, Jeanette Gladys, da of Stanley Woodcock; 3 s (Kevin, Martin, Neil), 1 da (Susan Diane); *Career* chm & chief exec L.A. Rumbold Ltd; *Recreations* bowls, football, racing; *Clubs* Sutton Bowling and Bracknell; *Style*— Gordon Dupree, Esq, OBE; Stonesteep, 210 Upper Chobham Road, Camberley, Surrey (☎ Cam 28471); L A Rumbold Ltd, Doman Road, Camberley Surrey (☎ Cam 66456)

DUPREE, Harry William; s of Harry Dupree (d 1932), of Tunbridge Wells, and Kate Evelyn, *née* Gilliam (d 1967); *b* 20 Dec 1913; *Educ* Tonbridge Sch; *m* 30 Oct 1939, Joanne Gwendoline, da of Hugh Philip, Bishop (d 1986); 1 s (Michael b 1943), 2 da (Philippa b 1948, Lucy b 1954); *Career* WWII Sqdn Ldr RAF (airfield construction branch) 1944-47; sr engr Kuwait Oil Co 1947-49, chief engr Basildon Devpt Corp 1949-61; Sir Owen Williams and Ptnrs: ptnr 1961-77, conslt 1977-87; CEng, FICE, FIHT, MConsE; *Books* Urban Transportation: The New Town Solution (1987); *Clubs* RAF; *Style*— Harry Dupree, Esq; Broadway House, The Broadway, Amersham, Buckinghamshire (☎ 0494 726 464)

DUPREE, Sir Peter; 5 Bt (UK 1921); s of Sir Victor Dupree, 4 Bt (d 1976); *b* 20 Feb 1924; *m* 1947, Joan, da of Capt James Desborough Hunt (decd); *Heir* kinsman, Thomas William James David Dupree b 5 Feb 1930; *Style*— Sir Peter Dupree, Bt; 15 Hayes Close, Chelmsford, Essex CM2 0RN

DUPUCH, Hon Sir (Alfred) Etienne Jerome; OBE (1949); s of Leon Edward Hartman Dupuch (d 1914), fndr of The Tribune, Nassau Bahamas; *b* 16 Feb 1899; *Educ* Boys' Central Sch Nassau, St John's Univ Minnesota; *m* 1928, Marie Anne, da of Henry Plouse (d 1929), of Pennsylvania, and Frances, *née* Hoover, a relative of Herbert Hoover sometime USA Pres; 3 s, 3 da; *Career* serv WWI with BWI Regt on Eastern and Western Fronts; MHA Bahamas 1925-42 and 1949-56, MLC 1960-64, Senator 1964-68, memb Nat Advsy Bd American Security Cncl 1981; ed-in-chief and publisher The Tribune 1919-72, contrib editor 1972- (listed in Guiness Book of World Records as longest serving ed), KCSG 1963, Knight of Malta; Kt 1965; *Books* We Call Him Friend (tribute to Lord Beaverbrook), The Tribune Story (1967), Salute to Friend and Foe (1981); *Recreations* swimming, walking; *Clubs* Coral Gables Country, Rotary (E Nassau and Coral Gables), Lions (Pennsylvania); *Style*— Sir Etienne Dupuch, OBE; Camperdown Heights, PO Box N-3207, Nassau, Bahamas (☎ office: 22270; home: 41374); 700 Coral Way, Coral Gables, Florida, USA (☎ 442 1594)

DURACK, Dame Mary; DBE (1978, OBE 1966); da of Michael Patrick Durack and Bessie Ida Muriel, *née* Johnstone (d 1980); *b* 20 Feb 1913; *Educ* Loreto Convent Perth; *m* 1938, Horace Clive (d 1980), s of John Pettigrew Miller; 2 s, 2 da (and 2 da decd); *Career* author, playwright and historian; former memb of staff W Aust Newspapers Ltd; hon life memb Fellowship of Aust Writers (pres WA Branch 1958-63), hon life memb Int PEN Sydney Centre; memb: Aust Soc of Authors, Nat Trust, Royal Western Aust Historical Soc, former exec memb Aboriginal Cultural Fndn, dir

Aust Stockman's Hall of Fame and Outback Heritage Centre (patron WA Branch); hon life memb: fellowship of Aust Writers (pres WA Branch 1958-63), Int PEN Aust; memb: Aust Soc of Authors, Nat Tst, Roy WA Historical Soc, Aust Soc of Women Writers (presented with the Alice Award 1982), former exec memb Aboriginal Cultural Fndn; Cwlth Literary Grants 1973 and 1977, Aust Research Grant 1980 and 1984-85, Emeritus fellowship 1983-84 from Literature Bd of the Aust cncl; has written numerous scripts for ABC Drama Dept; Hon DLitt Univ of WA 1978; *Books* Keep Him My Country (1955), Kings in Grass Castles (1959), To Ride a Fine House (1963), Kookanoo & Kangaroo (1963), The Australian Settler (1963), The Courteous Savage (1964), The Rock and the Sand (1969), To Be Heirs Forever (1976), Sons in the Saddle (1983); *Plays include* The ship of Dreams (1968), Swan River Saga (1972); *Style*— Dame Mary Durack, DBE; 12 Bellevue Ave, Nedlands, W Australia 6009 (☎ 386 1117)

DURAND, Rev Sir (Henry Percy Mortimer) Dickon Evelyn Marion St George; 4 Bt (UK 1892); s of Lt Cdr Mortimer Henry Marion Durand, RN (d 1969), 4 s of 1 Bt; suc unc, Brig Sir Alan Algernon Marion Durand, 3 Bt, MC, 1971 descends from Ducal House of Northumberland; gggs of Bishop Heber famous hymn writer; The Durand line (border of India (now Pakistan), Afghanistan & Russia) was created by grandfather and great uncle, Sir Henry & Sir Mortimer Durand; Archbishop E W Benson (d 1896), originated Service of Nine Lessons with Carols, c 1880 one of the best loved Anglican services; *b* 19 June 1934; *Educ* Wellington, Sydney Univ (Aus), Salisbury Theological Coll; *m* 1971, Stella Evelyn, da of Capt Christopher L'Estrange, of Lisnalurg, Sligo (d 1984); 2 s (Edward b 1974, David b 1978), 2 da (Rachel b 1972, Madeleine b 1980); *Heir* s, Edward Alan Christopher Percy Durand b 21 Feb 1974; *Career* clergyman (Anglican) Church of Ireland; ordained 1969, priest-in-charge St Benedict's Ashford Common (dioc London) 1975-79, Bp's curate in charge Kilbixy Union of Parishes (dioc Meath) 1979-82, rector Youghal Union of Parishes (dioc Cork Cloyne & Ross); *Recreations* history, railways, heraldry, philately, militaria; *Style*— Rev Sir Dickon Durand, Bt; The Rectory, Youghal, Co Cork, Republic of Ireland

DURANT, (Robert) Anthony Bevis (Tony); MP (C) Reading West 1983-; s of Capt Robert Michael Durant (d 1962), of Woking, and Violet Dorothy, *née* Bevis; *b* 9 Jan 1928; *Educ* Bryanston; *m* 1958, Audrey Stoddart; 2 s, 1 da; *Career* agent Clapham Cons Off 1958-62, nat organiser Young Cons Movement, CCO 1962-67, dir Br Indust and Scientific Film Assoc 1967-70, dir AVCAS 1970-72, gen mangr and co sec Talking Pictures Ltd 1972-84, memb Woking Urban Cncl 1968-74 (chm educ ctee 1969-74 and memb Surrey), contested (C) Rother Valley 1970, MP (C) Reading North Feb 1974-1983, memb Parly Cmmn for Admin select ctee 1974-83, former vice-chm Parly Gp for World Govt, former chm All-Pty Ctees: Inland Waterways, Widows and Single-Parent Families; former conslt: Delta Electrical Ltd, Br Film Prod Assoc - GB; Asst Government Whip 1984-86, Lord Commissioner of the Treasury and Government Whip 1986-, Crown Estates Paving Cmmr 1987-, chm Cwlth Parly Assoc (UK Branch) 1987-; *Recreations* boating, golf; *Clubs* Golfers; *Style*— Tony Durant, Esq, MP; Hill House, Surley Row, Caversham, Reading, Berkshire

DURBAN, Donald Desmond; CBE (1986); s of Douglas Ernest Durban (d 1937); *b* 25 July 1924; *Educ* Roan GS; *m* 1948, Daphne Olliver, da of Eric May (d 1973), of Australia; 1 s (David), 1 da (Susan); *Career* serv WWII, Lt RN (Air Arm), pilot in FAA; dep chief exec (rtd) and gp co sec Trusthouse Forte (48 years with the co, apart from RN serv), ret from exec duties 1986; chm Nat Cncl British Hotels, Restaurants & Catering Assoc; dir Kids Leisure Corp plc; Freeman City London; memb of Court of Worshipful Company of Chartered Secretaries & Administrators; memb Hotel and Catering NEDO 1972-79 & chm of ctee on Hotel Prospects; *Recreations* golf, cricket, family; *Clubs* MCC, Royal Blackheath Golf (former capt), Caterpillar, (founder memb),; *Style*— Donald Durban, Esq, CBE,; 54 Foxes Dale, Blackheath, London SE3 (☎ 01 852 1907); Chalkstones, Park Lane Churchill, Wilts (☎ 0249 813 091)

DURBIN, Prof James; s of George William Durbin (d 1970), and Lucy Winifride, *née* Coffey (d 1948); *b* 3 June 1923; *Educ* Wade Deacon GS Widnes, St Johns Coll Cambridge (BA, MA); *m* 22 Mar 1958, Anne Dearnley, da of Philip Outhwaite (d 1984), of Spofforth; 2 s (Richard b 1960, Andrew b 1962), 1 da (Joanna b 1964); *Career* Army Operational Res Gp 1943-45, Boot and Shoe Trade Res Assoc 1945-47, Dept of Applied Econ Cambridge 1948-49, asst lectr then lectr LSE 1950-53, reader in statistics LSE 1953-61; prof of statistics LSE 1961-88; visiting prof: Univ of N Carolina 1959-60, Stanford Univ 1970-71, Univ of Calif Berkeley 1970, Univ of Capetown 1978, UCLA 1984; ISI (pres 1983-85), RSS (pres 1986-87); *Books* Distribution Theory for Tests Based on the Sample Distribution Function; *Recreations* skiing, mountain walking, travel, opera, theatre; *Style*— Prof J Durbin; 31 Southway, London NW11 6RX (☎ 01 458 3037)

DURBIN, Leslie Gordon James; CBE (1976), MVO (4 class, 1943); s of Harry Durbin (d 1918); *b* 21 Feb 1913; *Educ* Central Sch of Arts and Crafts; *m* 1940, Phyllis Ethel, da of Arthur James Ginger; 1 s, 1 da; *Career* served RAF 1940-45 (Allied Central Interpration Unit, making topographical target models), indefinite leave to make Stalingrad Sword (given by King George VI to Stalingrad) 1943; silversmith; apprenticed to Omar Ramsden 1929-38, travellng scholarship and full time scholarship awarded by Worshipful Co of Goldsmiths 1938-40, tutor Central Sch 1945-50, tutor Royal Coll of Art 1945-60, own workshop in partnership with Leonard Moss 1945-76, designed Silver Jubilee Hallmark; 50 Years Silversmith Retrospective Exhibition at Goldsmiths' Co 1982; Royal Mint accepted designs of four regions for new one pound coin 1983; Liveryman Worshipful Co of Goldsmiths, Hon LLD Cambridge; *Style*— Leslie Durbin, Esq, CBE, MVO; 298 Kew Rd, Richmond, Surrey TW9 3DU

DURBRIDGE, Francis Henry; s of Francis Durbridge; *b* 25 Nov 1912; *Educ* Bradford GS, Wylde Green Coll, Birmingham Univ; *m* 1940, Norah Elizabeth Lawley; 2 s; *Career* playwright, screen-writer, prod (TV and radio); *Style*— Francis Durbridge, Esq; c/o Harvey Unna and Stephen Durbridge Ltd, 24 Pottery Lane, Holland Park, London W11 4LZ

DURDEN-SMITH, Neil; s of Anthony James Durden-Smith (d 1963), of Middx, and Grace Elizabeth Neill (d 1938); *b* 18 August 1933; *Educ* Aldenham Sch, Royal Naval Coll; *m* 1964, Judith Rosemary Locke, da of David Norman Chalmers (d 1952), of Cheshire; 1 s (Mark b 1968), 1 da (Emma b 1967); *Career* RN 1952-63; prodr BBC Outside Broadcasts Dept (special responsibility 1966 World Cup) 1963-66; radio and tv broadcasting includes: Test Match and Country Cricket, Olympic Games 1968 and 1972, Trooping the Colour, Royal Tournament, Money Matters, Sports Special; dir The Anglo-American Sporting Clubs 1969-74; chm and md Durden-Smith Communications 1974-81; chm: Sport Sponsorship Int 1982-, The Altro Gp 1982-, Voyager Prodns 1982-, The Lord's Taverners 1980-82; Freeman City of London; memb Lloyd's 1983; vice-pres: Eng Schools Cricket Assoc, Eng Indoor Hockey Assoc; *Books* Forward for England (1967), World Cup '66 (1967); *Recreations* theatre, current affrs, cricket, golf, tennis, reading the newspapers; *Clubs* MCC, Lord's Taverners, I Zingari, Wig & Pen, Free Foresters, Lords and Commons CC, Eccentric; *Style*— Neil Durden-Smith, Esq; Sports Sponsorship International, 344 Kensington High St, London W14 8NS (☎ 01 602 6121, telex 267009)

DURHAM, Earldom of (UK 1833); *see*: Lambton, Lord (Anthony Claud Frederick)

DURHAM, Archdeacon of

DURHAM, Dean of; *see*: Arnold, Very Rev John Robert

DURHAM, Baron; Edward Richard Lambton; s and h of Lord Lambton, *qv*; *b* 19 Oct 1961; *m* 1983, Christabel Mary, yst da of Rory McEwen (decd), of Bardrochat; 1 s (b 23 Feb 1985); *Style*— (known as) Lord Durham

DURHAM, (James Coulton) Gordon; JP; s of Capt James Gordon Durham, MC (ka 1940), of East Boldon, Co Durham, and Vera Mary, *née* Hunter (d 1966); *b* 27 April 1933; *Educ* Canford, Gonville and Caius Coll Cambridge (MA); *m* 21 June 1958, Heather, da of John Booker Wilkinson (d 1975), of Swinton, Mexborough, Yorks; 2 s (Malcolm Gordon b 1961, David Roger b 1963); *Career* cmmnd RE 1952, ret Capt TA 1961; chm Gordon Durham & Co Ltd 1975, Hadrian Building Soc 1981-83; dep chm of Engl Bldg Soc 1988-, dir Federated Employers Press 1988-; cncllr Boldon UDC 1961-74, nat jr vice-pres Bldg Employers Confed 1988-89; pres (Northern Counties Region): NFBTE 1978-79, BEC 1987-88; memb Kirkby Malhamdale Parish Cncl 1986-; FCIOB 1975; *Recreations* sailing, shooting, walking; *Clubs* The Sunderland; *Style*— Gordon Durham, Esq, JP; The Mill House, Scalegill, Kirkby, Malham, nr Skipton, N Yorks BD23 4BN (☎ 07293 293); Gordon Durham & Co Ltd, East Boldon, Tyne & Wear NE36 0AG (☎ 0915 367 207, fax 07 293 293)

DURHAM, Countess of; Hermione; da of Sir George Bullough, 1 and last Bt; *m* 1931, as his 2 w, 5 Earl of Durham (d 1970); 1 s (Hon John Lambton); *Style*— The Rt Hon the Countess of Durham; West Marden Hall, Chichester, Sussex

DURHAM, Sir Kenneth; s of late George Durham, and Bertha, *née* Aspin; *b* 28 July 1924; *Educ* Queen Elizabeth GS Blackburn, Manchester Univ (BSc); *m* 1946, Irene Markham; 1 s, 1 da; *Career* serv WWII RAF; chm: BOCM Silcock 1971, Unilever 1982- (joined 1950, vice-chm Unilever Ltd 1978-82, dir Unilever NV and Unilever 1974-86), Woolworth Hldgs plc 1986-; dir: Br Aerospace 1980- (dep chm 1986), Delta Gp plc 1984, Morgan Grenfell Gp plc 1986; tstee Leverhulme Tst; kt 1985; *Style*— Sir Kenneth Durham; Woolworth Holdings plc, North West House, 119 Marylebone Rd, London NW1 5PX (☎ 01 724 7749, telex 267007)

DURHAM, 92 Bishop of (cr 635) 1984-; Rt Rev David Edward Jenkins; patron of 101 livings, the Archdeaconries of Durham and Auckland, and all the Canonries in his Cathedral (the see was first established at Holy Island 635, but on the invasion of the Danes removed to Chester-le-Street and finally to Durham); er s of Lionel Charles Jenkins and Dora Katherine, *née* Page; *b* 26 Jan 1925; *Educ* St Dunstan's Coll Catford London, Queen's Coll Oxford (MA); *m* 1949, Stella Mary, da of Henry Leonard Peet (d 1976); 2 s (Christopher, Timothy), 2 da (Deborah, Rebecca); *Career* temp cmmn RA 1943-47, Capt; priest 1954, succentor Birmingham Cathedral 1953-54, fell, chaplain and praelector in theology The Queen's Coll Oxford 1954-69, dir Humanum studies World Cncl of Churches Geneva 1969-73, dir William Temple Fndn Manchester 1979-, prof of theology Leeds Univ 1979-84; Hon DD Durham Univ 1987; *Books* Guide to the Debate about God (1966), The Glory of Man (1967, republished 1984), Living with Questions (1969), What is Man? (1970), The Contradiction of Christianity (1976, republished 1985) Man Fallen and Free (contrib, 1969), God, Miracles and the Church of England (1987), God, Politics and the Future (1988), God, Jesus and Life in the Spirit (1988); *Recreations* music (opera), walking, travel books; *Style*— The Right Rev the Bishop of Durham; Auckland Castle, Bishop Auckland, Co Durham DL14 7NR (☎ 0388 602576)

DURIE, Sir Alexander Charles; CBE (1973); s of Charles Durie (d 1948); *b* 15 July 1915; *Educ* Queen's Coll Taunton; *m* 1941, Joyce May, da of late Lionel Richard Hargreaves; 1 s, 1 da; *Career* serv WWII, Lt-Col; dir: Shell Co (Australia) Ltd 1954-56, Shell-Mex and BP Ltd 1962 (joined 1933, md 1963-64), Mercantile Credit 1973-80, Thomas Cook Gp 1974-79, Private Patients Plan Ltd 1977-87, H Clarkson Hldgs 1978-85, Chelsea Building Soc 1979-87; vice-pres: Br Assoc Industl Eds 1959-71, Alliance Int de Tourisme 1965-71 (pres 1971-77), Ind Schs Careers Orgn 1973- (chm 1969-73), AA 1977- (dir gen 1964-77), Br Road Fedn 1978 (memb 1962-), Ashridge Coll 1978- (govr 1963-78), Surrey CC 1980- (memb ctee 1970-80, pres 1984-85); memb govt inquiries into: Civilianisation of Armed Forces 1964, Cars for Cities 1964, Road Haulage Operators' Licencing 1978; memb: cncl Motor and Cycle Trades Benevolent Fund 1959-73, Nat Rd Safety Advsy Cncl 1965-68, advsy cncl on Rd Res 1965-68, mktg ctee BTA 1970-77, advsy cncl Traffic and Safety Tport and Rd Res Lab 1973-77, Int Road Fedn (London); gen cmmr Income Tax 1960-85; FCIT, Hon FInstHE, FBIM (memb cncl 1962-73, vice-chm 1962-67, chm exec ctee 1962-65, chm bd of fellows 1970-73); Freeman City of London; memb cncl Imperial Soc of Knights Batchelor 1978- (chm 1988); kt 1977; *Clubs* Carlton, Royal and Ancient Golf ; *Style*— Sir Alexander Durie, CBE; The Garden House, Windlesham, Surrey (☎ 0276 72035)

DURIE, Joanna (Jo) Mary; da of John Durie (d 1984) of Bristol, bank manager, and Diana Nell *née* Ford; *b* 27 July 1960; *Educ* Clifton HS; *Career* tennis player: winner under 12 and under 14 Nat Championships, won all three Nat Championships at age of 16, ranked 5 in the World 1984, ranked GB no 1 1983,1984,1985,1987; semi-finalist US open 1983, winner num tournaments worldwide; represented GB in Wightman Cup 1980 and Federation Cup 1981-; *Recreations* golf (handicap 20); *Style*— Miss Jo Durie; Winchmore Hill, London

DURIE OF DURIE, Lt Col Raymond Varley Dewar; MID (1943); s of Robert Nugent Dewar Durie, OBE, MC (d 1959), and Ida Pollexfen Varley (d 1972); illustrious forebear George Durie, last Abbot of Dunfermline 1480-1573, 2 cousin of W B Yeats; *b* 10 August 1905; *Educ* Blundells; *m* 1 1932, Joan (d 1934), da of R Dolbey (d 1933); m 2 1938, Frances, da of Col H N st J Maule, CMG, of Bath; 1 s (Andrew b 1939), 2 da (Diana b 1934, Christian b 1943); *Career* Regular Army Offr Argyll and Sutherland Highlanders, Lt Col China; *Recreations* cricket, hockey, tennis, shooting, polo; *Style*— Lt Col Raymond Durie of Durie, MID; Court House, Pewsey, Wiltshire SN9 5DL (☎ Marlborough 63452)

DURKIN, Air Marshal Sir Herbert; KBE (1976), CB (1973); s of Herbert Durkin (d

1968); *b* 31 Mar 1922; *Educ* Burnley GS, Emmanuel Coll Cambridge; *m* 1951, Dorothy Hope, da of Walter Taylor Johnson; 1 s, 2 da; *Career* joined RAF 1941, serv WWII in Europe and India, Gp Capt 1962, Air Cdre 1967, dir of Eng Policy (RAF) MOD 1967, Air Vice Marshal 1971, Air Marshal 1976, ret 1978; pres Inst of Electrical Engrs 1980-81, pres Assoc of Lancastrians in London 1988-89; *Recreations* golf; *Clubs* RAF; *Style—* Air Marshal Sir Herbert Durkin, KBE, CB; Willowbank, Drakes Drive, Northwood, Middx (☎ 092 74 23167)

DURLACHER, Nicholas John; s of John Sydney Durlacher MC; *b* 20 Mar 1946; *Educ* Stowe, Magdalene Coll Cambridge; *m* 1971, Mary Caroline, da of Maj G L I McLaren (d 1978); 1 s; *Career* memb London Stock Exchange, ptnr Wedd Durlacher Mordaunt & Co 1971-86, dir Barclays de Zoete Wedd Futures Ltd 1986-; *Recreations* skiing, tennis, golf, shooting; *Clubs* City of London; *Style—* Nicholas Durlacher, Esq; Archendines Fordham, nr Colchester, Essex (☎ Colchester 240 627)

DURRAN, Percy; CBE (1966); s of late Dr John George Durran (decd); *b* 26 Sept 1911; *Educ* Daniel Stewart's Coll Edinburgh, Edinburgh Univ; *m* 1969, Joanna Brenda, da of late C W Nash ; *Career* Sudan Vet Serv 1935-55, FAO of UN Ethiopa 1955-56, HMOS Nigeria 1956-57, vet and animal husbandry advsr Middle East Devpt Div Beirut 1957-71; *Style—* Percy Durran, Esq, CBE; Caledon, Gatehouse of Fleet, Kirkcudbrightshire (☎ 05574 521)

DURRANCE, Philip Walter; s of Arthur Durrance (d 1960), of Ilkley, Yorkshire, and Marguerite Grace, *née* Rotheray (d 1966); *b* 30 June 1941; *Educ* Harrow, Oriel Coll Oxford (MA); *m* 16 Sept 1966, Francoise Genevieve Jeanne, da of Marcel Tiller; 1 s (Christopher b 29 July 1967), 1 da (Genevieve b 8 Sept 1968); *Career* admitted slr June 1965, ptnr Withers Crossman Block 1968-; dir: F Bender, Henkel Chemicals, Leo Laboratories; FInstD, memb Law Soc; *Recreations* theatre, cinema, art, tennis, squash, cricket; *Style—* Philip Durrance, Esq; 5/14 Fairhazel Gdns, London NW6 (☎ 01 328 6590); 20 Essex St, London WC2 (☎ 01 836 8400, fax 240 2648, telex 24213)

DURRANT, Albert Arthur Molteno; CBE (1954); s of Sir Arthur Isaac Durrant, CBE, MVO (decd); *b* 11 Sept 1898; *Educ* Alleyn's Sch Dulwich; *m* 1922, Kathleen, da of A J Wright (decd); *Career* chief engr (buses and coaches) London Passenger Transport Bd 1935, chief mechanical engr (road servs) 1945-65; *Style—* Albert Durrant, Esq, CBE; 108 Chiltern Ct, Baker St, NW1

DURRANT, William Alexander Estridge; JP; s and h of Sir William Durrant, 7 Bt; *b* 26 Nov 1929; *m* 1953, Dorothy Croker; 1 s, 1 da; *Career* Capt 12/16 Hunter River Lancers; *Style—* William Durrant, Esq, JP; Spring Pk, Gaspard via Quirindi, NSW, Australia

DURRANT, Sir William Henry Estridge; 7 Bt (GB 1784), JP (NSW 1940); s of Sir William Henry Estridge Durrant, 6 Bt (d 1953); *b* 1 April 1901; *m* 1927, Georgina Beryl Gwendoline (d 1968), da of Alexander Purse; 1 s, 1 da; *Heir* s, William Alexander Estridge; *Career* serv WWII; CA; associated with the formation of the film indust in NSW 1930s and construction of film studios; former pres and life patron NSW Justices Assoc, memb: UN Orgn Aust, cncl Royal Cwlth Soc NSW; *Style—* Sir William Durrant, Bt, JP; 1634 Pacific Highway, Wahroonga, NSW, Australia

DURRELL, Lawrence George; s of Lawrence Samuel Durrell and Louisa Florence, *née* Dixie; *b* 27 Feb 1912; *Educ* Coll of St Joseph Darjeeling India, St Edmund's Sch Canterbury; *m* 1, 1937; m 2 1947; m 3, 1960; 2 da; *Career* novelist, playwright, poet; *Books Incl:* Bitter Lemons (1957), The Alexandria Quartet: Justine (1957), Balthazar (1958), Mountolive (1958), Clea (1960); Sebastian, or Ruling Passions (1983); *Style—* Lawrence Durrell Esq; c/o Grindlay's Bank, 13 St James's Sq, SW1

DURWARD, Alan (Scott); s of Archibald Durward (d 1964), and Dorothy, *née* Westlake (d 1978); *b* 30 August 1935; *Educ* St John's Coll Cambridge (MA); *m* 1962, Helen, da of Joseph Gourlay; 2 s (Giles b 1964, Hugo b 1966); *Career* chief gen mangr Alliance & Leicester Building Soc 1986-; formerly with Imperial Tobacco and Rowntree; *Style—* Scott Durward, Esq; Alliance & Leicester Building Society, 49 Park Lane, London W1Y 4EQ (☎ 01 629 6661); The Old House, Medbourne, Market Harborough, Leics LE16 8DX (☎ 085 883 207)

DUTFIELD, William Henry (Harry); s of John Hubert Dutfield, and Janie Scott, *née* Blair; *b* 12 Dec 1908; *Educ* King Charles I GS Kidderminster, Worcs; *m* 2 June 1938, Daisy Iris (Bobby), *née* Huxter; a s (Simon John b 1946), 1 da (Susan Jane (Mrs Standerwick) b 1944); *Career* carpet mfr in attic at home 1925-27, moved to new premises and formed Dutfield & Quayle 1928-37; started Axminster Carpets Ltd 1937- (ceased carpet mfr and produced air craft parts for Rolls Royce etc 1940-45); acquired woollen mill now Buckfast Spinning Co Ltd 1950, fndr Marlin Carpets Ltd Christchurch NZ 1960, pres and fndr Game Fishing Co of Fiji 1965, dir Fiji Resorts Ltd; first importer from NZ of Drysdale sheep (world's finest carpet wools); *Books* Harry Dutfield, Carpet Manufacturer & Fisherman (1974); *Recreations* big game fishing, golf, salmon fishing; *Style—* W H Dutfield, Esq; Little Cloakham, Axminster, Devon (☎ 0297 32158); Porthsawl, Portscatho, Nr Truro, Cornwall; Axminster Carpets Ltd, Axminster, Devon (☎ 0297 32244, fax 0297 35241, telex 42923)

DUTHIE, Sir Robin (Robert Grieve); CBE (1978); s of George Duthie; *b* 2 Oct 1928; *Educ* Greenock Acad; *m* 1955, Violetta Noel, da of late Harold MacLean; 2 s, 1 da; *Career* CA (apprentice with Thomson Jackson Gourlay & Taylor 1946-51), former chm Greenock Provident Bank; former chm: Bruntons (Musselburgh) plc 1984-86 Britoil plc 1988-; dir: Insight Gp plc (formerly Black & Edington (Hldgs) plc) 1983-; chm: Insight Int Tours Ltd 1983-; joined Blacks of Greenock 1952, appointed md 1962; chm Black & Edgington 1972-83; Scottish Devpt Agency 1979-; dir Greenock C of C 1967-68; tax liaison offr Scotland CBI 1976-79; dir: Carcio Engrg Gp plc 1986-, Sea Catch plc 1987-, Roy Bank of Scotland Ltd 1978-, Clyde Port Authy 1971-83 (chm 1977-80), Br Assets Tst plc 1977-, Edinburgh American Assets Tst plc 1977-88, Investors Capital Tst plc 1985-; pres Made Up Textiles Assoc of GB 1972; memb: Scottish Telecommunications Bd 1972-77, E Kilbride Devpt Corpn 1976-78, Scottish Econ Cncl 1980-; pres Inverkip Soc 1966, cmmr Queen Victoria Sch Dunblane 1972-88; memb cncl Inst of CAs of Scotland 1974-79, CBIM 1975; FRSA 1983, Hon LLD Strathclyde Univ 1984; kt 1987; *Recreations* curling memb cncl Royal Caledonian Curling Club 1984-88, golf; *Clubs* Greenock; *Style—* Sir Robin Duthie, CBE; Fairhaven, 181 Finnart St, Greenock PA16 8JA (☎ 0475 22642); Britoil plc, 301 St Vincent St, Glasgow (☎ 041 225 2525)

DUTHIE, Sir Robin Greive; CBE (1978); s of George Duthie, and Mary, *née* Lyle; *b* 2 Oct 1928; *Educ* Greenock Acad; *m* 5 April 1955, (Violetta) Noel, da of Harry Maclean; 2 s (David b 1956, Peter b 1959), 1 da (Susan b 1962); *Career* Nat Serv Army 1946-49; apprentice CA Thoson Jackson Gourlay & Taylor 1946-51, qualified CA 1952; chm: Black & Edgington plc 1972-83 (md 1962-80), Brutons (Musselburgh) plc 1984-86, Britoil plc 1988-, Capital House plc 1988-, Tay Residential Investments plc 1989-; dir: Insight Gp plc (formerly Black & Edgington), Br Asset Tst plc 1977-, Royal Bank of Scotland plc 1978-, Investors Capital Tst plc 1985-, Carclo Engrg Gp plc 1986-, Royal Bank of Scotland Gp plc 1986-, Sea Catch plc 1987-, Tay Residential Investments plc 1989-; tres Nelson St EU Congrational Church Greenock 1970-, cmmr Scottish Congregational Ministers Pension Fund-; memb: Scottish Econ Cncl 1980-, governingcncl Scottish Business in the Community 1987-, ct Strathclyde Univ 1988-; Hon LLD Strathclyde Univ 1984; CBIM 1975, FRSA 1983; Kt 1987; *Recreations* curling, golf; *Clubs* Greenock Imperial; *Style—* Sir Robin Duthie, CBE; Fairhaven, Finnart St, Greenock, (☎ 0475 22642); Britoil plc, 301 St Vincent St, Glasgow G2 5DD, (☎ 041 225 5143, 041 225 2263, telex 777633)

DUTT, Trevor Peter; s of Dr Bishnu Pada Dutt (d 1970), of Mitcham, Surrey, and Phyllis Ida, *née* Roche; *b* 14 Sept 1943; *Educ* St Barts Hosp Med Coll (MB BS), Dulwich Coll,; *m* 27 May 1986, Pauline Deirdre, da of Walter Edward Chapman, of Chigwell, Essex; 1 step s (Damien Nicholas Edward Caracatsanis b 2 May 1974); *Career* Surgn Lt Cdr RNR (London Div), Sr MO Royal Marines Res (London Div); jr med staff posts 1965-80: St Barts, Whipps Cross, Royal Northern, City of London Maternity and Charing Cross Hosps; conslt obstetrics and gynaecology Royal Northern and Whittington Hosps 1980; Freeman City of London 1967, Liveryman Worshipful Co of Apothecaries 1967; MRCS, LRCS, FRCOG 1988 (memb 1975); *Recreations* sailing, sub-aqua diving, horse riding; *Clubs* Athenaeum, Savage; *Style—* Trevor Dutt, Esq; 129 Mount View Rd, London N4 4JH (☎ 01 348 7054); 28 Weymouth St, London WIN 3FA (☎ 01 580 1723, car tel 0860 625 431)

DUTTON, Francis Moore; s of Thomas Moore Dutton, of Edgecroft, Rowton, Cheshire (d 1939); *b* 21 Dec 1899; *Educ* St Bees Sch Cumberland; *m* 1, 1932, Amy Louisa Huntly (d 1946), da of George Henderson, of Bonnington House, Midlothian; m 2, 1948, Margaret Marian, da of Samuel Worthington, (ka 1917); 1 s, 1 da; *Career* served WWI and WWII; High Sheriff Cheshire 1968; *Style—* Francis Moore Dutton, Esq; Tushingham Hall, Whitchurch, Shropshire (☎ 0948 2225)

DUTTON, Hon Mrs George; Pauline Stewart; s of Maj Stewart Robinson; *m* 1959, as his 2 w, Hon George Dutton (d 1981), yr s of 6 Baron Sherborne; *Style—* The Hon Mrs George Dutton; Westerley, Kingsthorne, Herefordshire (☎ 0981 540 309)

DUTTON, Richard Odard Astley (Dickie); s of William Astley Dutton (d 1959), of 73 Iverna Ct, London W8, and Alice Margaret, *née* Halls; *b* 9 Sept 1935; *Educ* Lancing, RMA Sandhurst; *m* 2 Dec 1961, Susan Kathleen, Major JR O'B Warde, TD JP, DL (d 1976), of Squerryes Ct, Westerham, Kent; 1 s (Rodney Henry Odard Ralph b 1967), s da (Sarah b 1965, Harriet b 1972); *Career* cmmnd KOYLI 1956: Capt and Adj 1 Bn 1962-63, Mons Offr Cadet Sch 1963-65; sales mangr Ross Foods 1965-66, classified ad mangr The Times 1967-70, vice-chm Marlar Int 1972-; dir Enterprise Ballet; *Recreations* long distance cycling, singing; *Clubs* Arts; *Style—* Dickie Dutton, Esq; 61 Ellerby St, London SW6 6EU (☎ 01 736 2899); 14 Grosvenor Pl, London SW1 X7HH (☎ 01 235 9614)

DUTTON, Robert William; s of Wilfred Harry (d 1982) and Florence Amy *née* Monk; *b* 17 Feb 1949; *Educ* Manchester Business Sch (MBA); *Career* CA; merchant banker: Hill Samuel & Co Ltd 1973-84; corporate fin dir County NatWest Ltd 1985-88 (previously County Bank); fin dir County NatWest Securities Ltd (incorporating Wood Mackenxie & Co Ltd) 1988-; FCA; *Recreations* music, theatre, skiing, mountain walking, travel; *Style—* Robert Dutton, Esq; Drapers Gardens, 12 Throgmorton Avenue, London EC2P 2ES (☎ 01 382 1000, telex: 916041, fax 01 638 2152)

DUVAL, Derrick Brian; s of Harold Smith (d 1985), and Florence Gertrude Smith, *née* Osborne (d 1960); *b* 1 Jan 1935; *Educ* Wednesbury Tech Coll, Birmingham and Portsmouth Schs of Architecture (Dipl Arch); *m* 20 Aug 1960, Pauline, da of Horace Cockley; 1 s (Spencer Gavin b 1970); *Career* nat serv with RA (air reconnaissance intelligence); architect, princ Duval Brownhill Ptnrship, architects to the Close in Lichfield and cnslts to English Heritage and num heritage orgns; dir property co; *Recreations* political work, elected cncllr; *Clubs* Rotary; *Style—* Derrick Duval, Esq; 23 Dam St, Lichfield, Staffs WS13 6AE (☎ 0543 264303); Georgian House, 24 Bird St, Lichfield, Staffs WS13 6PT (☎ 0543 254257)

DUVAL, Sir (Charles) Gaëtan; QC (1975); s of René Charles Duval, of Mauritius (d 1932); *b* 9 Oct 1930; *Educ* Royal Coll Curepipe, Univ of Paris Faculty of Law; *m* 1952 (m dis); 1 child; *Career* barr Lincoln's Inn; memb Town Cncl Curepipe 1960-63 (chm 1960-61); memb Legislative Cncl: min Housing and Lands 1963-65, min of External Affairs, Tourism and Emigration 1969, min of Foreign Affrs 1970-73 and 1983-; Cdr de la Légion d'Honneur (France) 1973; kt 1981; *Recreations* riding; *Style—* Sir Gaëtan Duval, QC; Melville, Grand Jaube, Mauritius

DUVOLLET, Hon Mrs (Sheila Helen Parnell); da of 6 Baron Congleton (decd); *b* 1923; *m* 1959, Roger Henry Duvollet; 1 da; *Style—* The Hon Mrs Duvollet; Burton Lodge, Burton Bradstock, Bridport, Dorset

DWEK, Joseph Claude; s of Victor Joseph Dwek; *b* 1 May 1940; *Educ* Carmel Coll, Manchester Univ (BSc, BA); married with 2 children; *Career* chm and md Bodycote Int plc and subsids; dir: KM Kledingbedrijven Ehco NV, Vetements Professionels France, Caledonian Property Gp Ltd, Panelflex Hldgs plc (and chm), Carmel Coll Ltd, memb: Ct of Univ of Manchester, Ct UMIST, pub purchasing ctee CBI, conslutative taxation ctee CBI, Dept of Ind NW Advsy Bd; cncl memb: Nat Inst for Fiscal Studies, govr and tres Carmel Coll; tstee and pres Dunham Forest Golf and Country Club Ltd FTI; AMCT; *Recreations* golf; *Style—* Joseph Dwek, Esq; The Coppins, Hill Top, Hale; Bodycote Int plc, 140 Kingsway, Manchester M19 1BA (☎ 061 257 2345, telex 667072, fax 257 2353)

DWORKIN, Prof Ronald Myles; s of David Dworkin; *b* 11 Dec 1931; *Educ* Harvard Coll, Oxford Univ, Harvard Law Sch; *m* 1958, Betsy Celia Ross; 1 s, 1 da; *Career* professor of jurisprudence Oxford Univ 1969, fell Univ Coll 1969-; FBA; *Style—* Prof Ronald Dworkin; University Coll, Oxford

DWYER, Air Vice-Marshal Michael Harington; *née* Emmett; CB (1961), CBE (1955); s of Lt Michael Herbert Dwyer, Royal Garrison Artillery, (d 1919), and Isabella Frances, *née* Harington, (d 1975); *b* 18 Sept 1912; *Educ* Oundle ; *m* 11 July 1936, Barbara Evelyn, da of Sterry Baines Freeman, CBE (d 1953); 1 s (Michael b 1940), 1 da (Georgina b 1942); *Career* entered RAF 5 Flying Trg Sch 1931, 16 (AC) Sqdn 1932, 31 (AC) Sqdn 1933, Air Armament Sch 1936, 5 Flying Trg Sch 1937, HQ Trg Cmd 1939. HQ 81 (F) Gp 1941, OC 456 (NF) Sqdn RAAF 1943, OC Central Gunnery Sch 1944, HQ Br Air Forces of Occupation Germany 1945, OC RAF Lubeck

1946, RAF Staff Coll 1947, Air Miny 1948, OC RAF FAYID 1949, Jt Serv Staff Coll 1951, SASO HQ 1 (B) Gp 1952, AOC 62 (Southern) Res Gp 1954, SASO HQ 3 (B) Gp 1955, IDC 1958, AOC 3 (B) Gp 1959, AOA HQ Bomber Cmd 1961 ret 1965; Regnl Dir Civil Def (NW Region) 1966-68; memb mgmnt Bd Princess Marina House, Rustington; *Style*— Air Vice-Marshal Michael H Dwyer, CB, CBE; Island House, Rambledown Lane, West Chiltington, Pulborough, Sussex (☎ 07983 2442)

DYAS, Anthony Rodney Joseph; s of Charles Joseph Henry Dyas, of Northolt, Middlesex, and Dorothy Ada, *née* Hutchinson; *b* 14 August 1940; *Educ* Greenford County GS; *m* 16 March 1963, Vivien Ann, da of William Alec George Herbert (d 1982); 3 da (Jennifer (Jenny) b 1966, Kristina (Tina) b 1968, Suzanne (Suzi) b 1970); *Career* certified accountant: Pearl Assurance Co Ltd 1957-59, Ass Br Foods Ltd 1959-69, Singer and Friedlander Ltd 1969- (dir 1974); FCCA 1964; *Recreations* running, motor cars; *Clubs* Ruislip 41; *Style*— Anthony Dyas, Esq; 18 the Avenue, Ickenham, Uxbridge UB10 8NP (☎ 0895 632343); 21 New St, Bishopsgate, London EC2M 4HR (☎ 01 623 3000, fax 01 623 2122, telex 886977)

DYAS, Patrick; OBE (1984); s of Samuel Robert Dyas (d 1942), and Helen Marion, *née* Wood (d 1949); ggf Harry Dyas was owner of stallion Man of War and Grand National winner Manifesto; *b* 30 April 1917; *Educ* Lancing, RMA Sandhurst; *m* 1953, Helen Margaret, da of Donald William Morphy (d 1975); 4 da (Hilary, Nicola, Mary-Ann, Dinah); *Career* serv WWII, Capt in 7 Armd Div, Africa and NW Europe (Normandy through to Germany); dir Robert Dyas Ltd 1946- (chm 1961-); chm cncl Royal Yachting Assoc 1980-85; winner Edinburgh Cup 1957 and 1968; landowner; Croix de Guerre (France) 1944; *Recreations* sailing (yacht 'Jerboa II'), skiing, golf; *Clubs* Royal Yacht Sqdn, Royal Thames Yacht, Royal Corinthian Yacht ; *Style*— Patrick Dyas, Esq; Broadbridge Farm, Horsham, Sussex RH12 3NA (☎ 0403 52805); Robert Dyas Ltd, 35 Imperial Way, Croydon, Surrey CR0 4RR (☎ 01 681 0311)

DYER, Lt Cdr Anthony Gascoyne (Tony); MBE (1983); s of Joseph Bernard Dyer (d 1983), of Tewkesbury, Glos, and Lymington, Hants, and Rosetta Elizabeth, *née* Brading (d 1966); *b* 19 Mar 1933; *Educ* Tewkesbury GS, Britannia RNC Dartmouth; *m* 19 March 1966, Sally Joan, da of William Metcalfe (d 1986), of Taunton, Somerset; 1 s (Richard b 24 Feb 1971), 1 da (Caroline b 29 Jan 1974); *Career* Cadet HMS Devonshire 1951-52, Midshipman HMS Newcastle served Korean War 1952-53, Sub Lt HMS Venus Dartmouth Sqdn 1954-55, Lt HMS Ulysses Med and Pacific 1956-57, HMS Dryad navigation course 1958, HMS Hartland Point Far East 1959-60, HMS Troubridge West Indies 1961-62, Lt Cdr staff of Flag Offr Middle East Aden 1963, HMS Sryad Advanced Navigation Course 1964, HMS Maidstone 3 Submarine Sqdn 1964-66, HMS Glamorgan Western Fleet 1966-68, HMS Jupiter West Indies 1968-71, staff of Flag Offr Submarines 1971-74, staff of Flag Offr Malta 1974-77, Asst Queen's Harbourmaster Plymouth 1977-83, Hydrographic Dept 1983-84, ret Lt Cdr 1983; Harbour Master Cattewater Harbour Cmmn Plymouth 1984-; sec Port of Plymouth Marine Liaison Ctee 1977-; ctee memb: Royal Western Yacht Club England, Trans-Altantic Race Ctee, Round Britain Race Ctee; fell Royal Inst of Navigation 1978 (cncl memb 1975-78 and 1982-83), fell Nautical Inst 1981 (cncl memb 1981-83), memb Soc for Nautical Res 1973; *Recreations* yacht racing and cruising, moor walking, gardening; *Clubs* Royal Western YC of England; *Style*— Lt Cdr Tony Dyer, MBE, RN; White Cottage, 119 Priory Rd, Lower Compton, Plymouth, Devon PL3 5EX; 2 The Barbican, Plymouth, Devon PL1 2LR (☎ 0752 669534, fax 0752 669691, telex 45225)

DYER, Barbara, Lady; Barbara; JP; da of Hereward Irenius Brackenbury, CBE, of Tweedhill, Berwick-on-Tweed; *b* 28 April 1905; *m* 1925, Sir Leonard Schroeder Swinnerton Dyer, 15 Bt (d 1975); 1 s, 1 da; *Career* chm National Fedn of Women's Institutes 1957-61; *Style*— Barbara, Lady Dyer, JP; Garden Cottage, Westhope, Craven Arms, Shropshire

DYER, Charles; s of James Dyer (d 1980), and Florence, *née* Stretton (d 1975); *b* 7 July 1928; *Educ* Highlands Cncl Sch Ilford, Queen Elizabeth's GS Barnet; *m* 1960, Fiona, da of Elizabeth Thomson; 3 s (John, Peter, Timothy); *Career* Flying Offr RAFVR, navigator 512 Sqdn Europe and 243 Sqdn Pacific, de-mobbed 1948; playwright, author, actor, director; has acted in 250 plays and films, has appeared at 120 theatres; made West End debut as Duke in Delderfield's Worm's Eye View (Whitehall Theatre 1948); has written plays for Royal Shakespeare Co; his works, mostly duologues, are in constant production; latest productions L'Escalier (Theatre de L'Oeuvre Paris 1985-86) and "Sottoscala" (SatiriTheatre Rome 1987-88), recent play Lovers Dancing (Albery Theatre London 1983-84); his Loneliness Trilogy (Rattle of a Simple Man, Staircase, Mother Adam) has been translated into most languages; *Style*— Charles Dyer, Esq; Old Wob, Gerrards Cross, Bucks SL9 8SF

DYER, Lois Edith; OBE (1984); da of Richard Morgan Dyer (d 1961), and Emmeline Agnes Dyer, *née* Wells (d 1976); *b* 18 Mar 1925; *Educ* Richmond County Sch, Middlesex Hosp Sch of Physiotherapy; *Career* physiotherapist Middlesex Hosp London 1945-47, sr physiotherapist Coronation Non-Euro Hosp Johannesburg SA 1948-51, supt physiotherapist Johannesburg Gp of Hosps 1951-56, Westminster Hosp London 1958-61, Roy Nat Orthopaedic Hosp Stanmore Middlesex 1963-72; physiotherapy offr DHSS London 1976-85; freelance Conslt Physiotherapist; MCSP 1945; co-ed Physiotherapy Practice, FCSP (1986); *Books* numerous publications in journals and books; *Recreations* country pursuits, music, bridge, animal welfare, conservation; *Style*— Miss Lois Dyer, OBE, FCSP; Garden Flat, 6 Belsize Grove, London NW3 4UN

DYER, Prof Sir (Henry) Peter Francis Swinnerton-; 16 Bt (E 1678), of Tottenham, Middx; KBE; s of Sir Leonard Schroeder Swinnerton Dyer, 15 Bt (d 1975), and Barbara, *née Brackenbury*; *b* 2 August 1927; *Educ* Eton, Trinity Coll Cambridge; *m* 25 May 1983, Dr Harriet Crawford, er da of Rt Hon Sir Patrick Browne, OBE, TD, *qv*; *Heir* kinsman, Richard Dyer-Bennet, *qv*; *Career* Cwlth Fund Fell Univ of Chicago 1954-55, res fell Trinity Cambridge 1950-54 (fell 1955-73, dean 1963-73); master St Catharine's Coll Cambridge 1973-83; prof of mathematics Cambridge Univ 1971-88 (lectr 1960-71, univ lectr Cambridge Mathematical Lab 1960-67); vice chllr Cambridge Univ 1979-81; visiting prof Harvard 1971; chm Ctee on Academic Orgn (London Univ) 1980-82; chm steering gp responsible for planning inst to replace New Univ of Ulster and Ulster Poly 1982-84; fellow Eton 1981-, dir Prutec 1981-86, chm Univ Grants Ctee 1983-89; chief exec Univs Funding Cncl 1989-, chm CODEST 1987- (memb 1984-); Hon DSc Bath 1981, hon fellow: Worcester Coll Oxford, Trinity Cambridge, St Catharine's Cambridge; FRS; *Recreations* destructive gardening; *Style*— Prof Sir Peter Dyer, Bt, KBE; The Dower House, Thriplow, Cambs (☎ 076 382 220); University Grants Committee, 14 Park Crescent, London W1 (☎ 01 636 7799)

DYER, Simon; s of Maj-Gen G M Dyer, CBE, DSO (d 1979), of Richmond, and Evelyn Mary, *née* List; *b* 19 Oct 1939; *Educ* Ampleforth, Univ of Paris, Oxford Univ (BA, MA); *m* 21 Jan 1967, (Louise) Gay, da of Anthony Lister Walsh, (d 1968), of Headley; 2 da (Jemima b 1970, Louise b 1973); *Career* AA: chief accountant 1967-72, dir 1972-, md 1982-87, dir-gen 1987-; Freeman City of London, Liveryman Worshipful Co of Coachmakers and Coach Harnessmakers (1984); FCA 1978; *Recreations* gardening, tennis, skiing; *Clubs* Cavalry and Guards, Hurlingham; *Style*— Simon Dyer, Esq; The Automobile Assoc, Fanum House, Basingstoke, Hants (☎ 0256 20123)

DYER-BENNET, Richard; s (by 1 w) of Maj Richard Stewart Dyer-Bennet, (d 1983, gggs of Sir Thomas Swinnerton Dyer, 9 Bt); hp of kinsman, Sir (Henry) Peter Francis Swinnerton-Dyer, 16 Bt, *qv*; *b* 1913; *m* 1, 1936 (m dis 1941), Elizabeth Hoar Pepper; 2 da; m 2, 1942, Melvene Ipcar; 2 da; *Career* musician; *Style*— Richard Dyer-Bennet Esq,; Star Route 62, Box 29, Great Barrington, Mass 01230, USA

DYER-SMITH, Rear Adm John Edward; CBE (1972); s of Harold Edward (d 1967), of Plymouth, and Emily Sutton (d 1946); *b* 17 August 1918; *Educ* Devonport HS, Roy Naval Engrg Coll, Imp Coll of Science; *m* 1940, Kathleen, da of Henry George Powell (d 1943), of Capetown SA; 4 s (Peter, Richard, Martyn, Christopher), 1 da (Vivien); *Career* serv WWII, Engr Offr HMS Prince of Wales 1940-41, Asst Fleet Engr Offr Eastern Fleet 1942-43, HMS Illustrious 1943, var appointments 1946-54, hd of Naval Air Dept Royal Aircraft Estab 1957-61, Dir of Naval Aircraft & Helicopters 1961-64; Defence Attaché Tokyo 1965-67; Supt Naval Air Yard Belfast 1968-70; Dir Gen Aircraft Navy Dept 1970-72; *Recreations* music, wood sculpture, golf; *Clubs* Stoneham Golf (Hants); *Style*— Rear Adm John Dyer-Smith, CBE; Casa Gomila, 31 Carrer Ample, Cala Alcaufar, Sant Lluis, Menorca, Baleares, Spain

DYKE; *see*: Hart Dyke

DYKE-COOMES, Martin; s of Ernest Thomas Dyke-Coomes, of 67 Furzefield, West Green, Crawley, Sussex, and Gladys Dorothy, *née* Bignell; *b* 14 August 1948; *Educ* Sarah Robinson Sec Modern, Ifield GS, Architectural Assoc; *m* 24 June 1978, Margaret, *qv*, da of George Herbert Pinhorn, of Woodside, Comp Lane, St Mary's Platt, nr Sevenoaks, Kent; 1 s (Ned Alexander b 1981), 1 da (Amy Elizabeth b 1983); 2 adopted s (Anthony b 1967, Claude b 1973); *Career* qualified architect ARCUK 1973; set up CGHP Architects in 1979; worked from 1976-79 in Covent Garden for the Community Assoc opposing and changing the GLC plans for the area; principle works: Hoxton St London N1 Regeneration (Times/RIBA award 1985), Jubilee Hall Redevelopment 1984-87 (Times/RIBA award 1988); Holland & Thurstan Dwellings 1982-86; participant in 1986 RIBA 40 under 40's exhibition; *Recreations* sleeping, dreaming, drinking, scheming, fishing; *Clubs* Manchester United, 7 Dials Social Centre; *Style*— Martin Dyke-Coomes, Esq; CGHP Architects, 41 Gt Windmill St, London W1V 7PA (☎ 01 439 0254)

DYKES, Andrew Christopher; s of John Christopher, Dykes (d 1981), of London, and Mollie Theresa, *née* Cheesman; *b* 7 June 1954; *Educ* Westminster, Trinity Coll Cambridge (MA); *m* 24 April 1982, Christina Anne, of Lt Col James Malcolm Harrison, OBE, TD (1979), of Bickerton, Cheshire; 2 s (Barnaby b 1987, Thomas (twin) b 1987); *Career* called to the Bar Inner Temple 1977, Thomas R Miller & Son 1977-87; dir: Thomas Miller P & I 1985-87, Int Tankers Owners Pollution Fedn Ltd 1986-87; Sloan fell London Business 1988; Freeman City of London 1977, Liveryman Worshipful Co of Coopers 1977; *Books* Limitation of Shipowners Liability: The New Law (jtly 1986); *Recreations* fishing, shooting, sailing; *Style*— Andrew Dykes, Esq; The Forge, Exbury, nr Southampton SO4 1AH (☎ 0703 894717; business 0703 899008, telex 931 2131 465 AD G)

DYKES, Hugh John; MP (C) Harrow East 1970-; s of Richard Dykes of Weston-super-Mare, Somerset; *b* 17 May 1939; *Educ* Weston-super-Mare GS, Pembroke Coll Cambridge; *m* 1965, Susan Margaret, da of Elwand Smith of Wakefield, Yorks; 3 s; *Career* investment analyst and stockbroker: ptnr Simon & Coates 1968-78, assoc memb Quilter Goodison & Co (formerly Quilter, Hilton, Goodison) 1978; contested (C) Tottenham 1966, research sec Bow Gp 1965-66, PPS to: Parly under-secs Defence 1970-, Parly under-sec Civil Service Dept, UK memb European Parl 1974-, chm Cons Parly European Ctee 1979-80 (former sec, vice-chm), vice pres Cons Gp for Europe 1982 (chm 1979-1980), dir Dixons plc Far Eastern Div; *Clubs* Beefsteak, Garrick, Carlton; *Style*— Hugh Dykes, Esq, MP; House of Commons, London SW1

DYKSTRA, Ronald Gerrit Malcolm (Ronnie); s of Cdr Gerrit Abe Dykstra (d 1978), of Wilmslow, and Margaret Kirk (d 1970); *b* 4 Mar 1934; *Educ* Edinburgh Acad; *m* 1, 28 April 1960 (m dis), Jennifer Mary, da of James Cramer (d 1964), of Manchester; 3 s (Peter b 1961, Richard b 1963, Paul b 1966); m2, 6 Sept 1986, Sonia, da of Arthur Hughes, of Hereford; *Career* slr 1957, sr ptnr Addleshaw Sons & Latham slrs Manchester 1987- (asst slr 1957-61, ptnr 1961-87); pres Wilmslow & Dist Amateur Swmming Club, hon slr Wilmslow Green Room Soc, memb ctee Soc of Construction Arbritrators; memb Law Soc (1961); *Recreations* swimming, walking, amateur drama; *Style*— Ronnie Dykstra, Esq; 7 Racecourse Rd, Wilmslow, Cheshire SK9 5LF (☎ 0625 525 856); Dennis house, Marsden St, Manchester M2 1JD (☎ 061 832 5994)

DYMOKE, Lt-Col John Lindley Marmion; MBE (1960), DL (Lincs 1976); thirty-fourth Queen's Champion (in full: The Honourable the Queen's Champion and Standard Bearer of England); s of Lionel Marmion Dymoke (d 1963), and Rachel Isabel (d 1989), da of Hon Lennox Lindley (3 s of 1 Baron Lindley); *b* 1 Sept 1926; *Educ* Christ's Hosp; *m* 1953, Susan Cicely, eldest da of Lt Francis Fane, RN (himself ggggs of 8th Earl of Westmorland), of The Manor, Fulbeck, Lincs; 3 s (Francis, m 1982, Rosalie, da of Maj Anthony Goldingham; Philip, m 1982, Arabella, da of Sir Ralph Dodds, 2 Bt; Charles); *Career* Lt-Col Royal Anglian Regt; served Royal Lincolnshire Regt; instr RMA Sandhurst 1962, commanded 3 Bn Royal Anglian Regt 1966-1969 ret 1972; landowner (3000 acres) and farmer; High Sheriff of Lincs 1979; chm Lincs branch CLA 1982-85; master of Worshipful Co of Grocers 1977; *Clubs* Army and Navy; *Style*— Lt-Col John Dymoke, MBE, DL; The Estate Office, Scrivelsby Court, Horncastle, Lincs (☎ 065 82 3325)

DYMOND, Charles Edward; CBE (1976); s of Charles George Dymond; *b* 15 Oct 1916; *Educ* Tiverton GS, Exeter Univ (BSc); *m* 1945, Dorothy Jean Peaker; 2 s, 2 da; *Career* Consul-Gen Perth 1973-76, ret; *Style*— Charles Dymond, Esq, CBE; PO Box 15, Sawyers Valley, 6074, W Australia

DYNES, John Brian; s of John Dynes; *b* 17 Oct 1933; *Educ* Portadown Tech Coll, Queen's Univ Belfast; *m* 1961, Alice Mary, *née* Graham; 1 s, 1 da; *Career* md Henry

Denny & Sons (Ulster) Ltd 1977-, dir Henry Denny & Sons Ltd 1978-, ACMA; *Recreations* golf, bridge, amateur radio; *Clubs* Farmers'; *Style—* John Dynes, Esq; 30 Breagh Rd, Portadown, Co Armagh, N Ireland (☎ 0762 338360); H Denny & Sons (Ulster) Ltd, Obins Street, Portadown, Co Armagh (☎ 0762 334914)

DYNEVOR, 9 Baron (GB 1780); Richard Charles Uryan Rhys; s of 8 Baron Dynevor, CBE, MC (d 1962, fifth in descent from Baroness Dynevor, herself da of 1 and last Earl Talbot, of the same family as the Earls of Shrewsbury); *b* 19 June 1935; *Educ* Eton, Magdalene Coll Cambridge; *m* 1959 (m dis 1978), Lucy Catherine King, da of Sir John Rothenstein, CBE; 1 s, 3 da; *Heir* s, Hon Hugo Griffith Uryan Rhys b 19 Nov 1966; *Style—* The Rt Hon the Lord Dynevor; Flat 2, 17 Sheffield Terrace, London W8

DYOTT, Richard Burnaby Kennedy; s of Maj William Boyd Kennedy Shaw (d 1979), and Eleanor, *née* Dyott (d 1982); *b* 6 Feb 1945; *Educ* Radley, RAC Cirencester (MRAC); *m* 1981, Sara Jane Modwena, da of Robert Westby Perceval, of Staffordshire; 1 s (William b 1987), 1 da (Caroline b 1985); *Career* chartered surveyor, High Sheriff of Staffordshire 1983; FRICS; *Recreations* forestry, shooting; *Clubs* Boodle's; *Style—* Richard Dyott, Esq; Freeford Manor, Lichfield, Staffs (☎ 0543 262300); Godfrey-Payton, Old Bablake, Hill St, Coventry (☎ 0203 26684)

DYSART, Countess of (eleventh holder of title, S 1643); Rosamund Agnes; also Lady Huntingtower (S 1643); da of Maj Owain Edward Whitehead Greaves, JP, DL (d 1941), and Countess of Dysart (tenth holder, d 1975); *b* 15 Feb 1914; *Heir* sister, Lady Katherine Grant, *qv*; *Style—* The Rt Hon the Countess of Dysart; Bryn Garth, Grosmont, Abergavenny, Gwent

DYSON, John Michael; s of Eric Dyson; *b* 9 Feb 1929; *Educ* Bradfield, Corpus Christi Coll Oxford; *Career* slr 1956; ptnr Field Roscoe & Co (subsequently Field Fisher & Co, then Field Fisher & Martineau) 1957-73; master of the Supreme Ct of Judicature (Chancery Div) 1973-; *Style—* J M Dyson, Esq; 20 Keats Grove, London NW3 2RS (☎ 01 794 3389)

DYSON, Prof Roger Franklin; s of John Franklin Dyson (d 1969), and Edith Mary Dyson, *née* Jobson (d 1981); *b* 30 Jan 1940; *Educ* Counthill GS Oldham, Univ of Keele (BA), Univ of Leeds (PhD); *m* 8 Aug 1964, Anne Elizabeth Greaves, da of Travis Edward Greaves (d 1983); 1 s (Mark Dyson b 1965), 1 da (Miranda b 1967); *Career* lectr econ and industl relations Univ of Leeds 1966-74 (asst lectr 1963-66), sr lectr industl relations and dep dir adult educn Univ of keele 1974-76; prof and dir adult educn Univ of Keele 1976-86, adult and continuing educn Univ of Keele 1986-; dir Mercia Pubns Ltd 1984-, ed Health Servs Manpower Review 1975-86; conslt advsr of state at DHSS 1979-81; chm North Staffs Health Authy 1982-86; RSM 1982 gardening and gastronomy; *Clubs* Carlton; *Style—* Prof Roger Dyson; Elendil, Newcastle Rd, Ashley Heath, Nr Market Drayton, Shropshire TF9 4PH, (☎ 063 087 2906); University of Keele, Department of Adult and Continuing Education, Keele, Staffordshire, (☎ 0782 625116, fax 0782 613847, telex 36113 UNKLIB G)

EADE, Robert Francis; s of Stanley Robert Eade, of Hulverstone, Isle of Wight; *Educ* Bromsgrove, London External (BSc); *m* 1965, Mary Lindsay, da of Sidney John Coulson, of Stratton-on-the-Fosse, Somerset; 3 children; *Career* dir: Commercial Technology 1983-85, md Internat THORN EMI plc 1985-, Metal Industries Ltd, James G. Biddle Co, Thorn Mod. Barbados Ltd, Evershed & Vignoles France, SA, INMOS Int plc, THORN EMI (USA) Inc, THORN EMI South Africa (Pty) Ltd, THORN EMI New Zealand Ltd, THORN EMI (Australia) Ltd, THORN EMI Licht Organschaft, THORN EMI AB; memb cncl British Electrical and Allied manufacturers' Assoc (BEAMA); pres Scientific Instrument Manufacturers' Assoc (SIMA, fed memb of BEAMA) 1981-82; pres GAMBICA (assoc for the instrumentation, control and automation industry) 1982-84; CEng, FIEE, FRS; *Style*— Robert Eade, Esq; Furnace Lodge, Furnace Farm Road, Felbridge, East Grinstead, W Sussex RH19 2PU; Thorn EMI House, Upper St Martin's Lane, London WC2H 9ED (☎ 01 836 2444)

EADIE, Alastair Gordon; s of Col James Alister Eadie, DSO, TD, DL (d 1961), of Vernons Oak, Sudbury, Derbyshire; *b* 25 June 1940; *Educ* Eton; *m* 14 April 1966, Hon Jaqueline, *qv*; 3 s (James b 1967, Christopher b 1969, Edward b 1972); *Career* dir International Distillers and Vintners (UK) Ltd, W & A Gilbey (Wine and Spirit Merchants) Ltd and Morgan Furze (Brick St) Ltd; *Recreations* shooting and stalking; *Clubs* Cavalry & Guards; *Style*— Alastair Eadie, Esq; Bourne Orchard, Brickendon, Hertford, SG13 8NU

EADIE, Alex(ander); BEM (1960), JP (Fife 1951), MP (Lab) Midlothian 1966-; s of Robert Eadie; *b* 23 June 1920; *Educ* Buckhaven Sr Secdy Sch; *m* 1941, Jemima, da of T Ritchie, of Wemyss; 1 s; *Career* former coal miner, chm Fife Housing Ctee; memb: Educn Ctee, Scottish Cncl Labour Party Exec Ctee, Scottish NUM; fought Ayr 1959 and 1964; former PPS to min for Social Security (Miss M Herbison), parly under-sec Energy 1974-79, oppn front bench spokesman Energy 1973-74, 1979-85 and 1986-87; chm PLP Power and Steel Gp, Miners' Parly Gp; vice-chm Parly Trade Union Gp; sec Miners' Parly Gp 1983-85 and 1986-87; *Style*— Alex Eadie, Esq, BEM, JP, MP; Balkerack, The Haugh, East Wemyss, Fife (☎ Buckhaven (0592) 71-3636)

EADIE, Hon Mrs (Jacqueline Noel); yr da of 5 Baron Ashtown, OBE (d 1979), by his wife Ellen Nancy, *née* Garton (d 1949); *b* 22 Dec 1940; *m* 14 April 1966, Alastair Gordon Eadie, *qv*; 3 s (James b 1967, Christopher b 1969, Edward b 1972); *Style*— The Hon Mrs Eadie; Bourne Orchard, Brickendon, Hertford SG13 8NU

EADIE, John Harold Ward; s of Harold George Eadie, CBE, and Marjorie Sanborn, *née* Ward; *b* 29 May 1909; *Educ* Cheltenham Coll; *m* 1946, Ellice Aylmer, CBE,*qv*; *Career* Maj RASC and Combined Operations, chm Gilbertson & Page Ltd and Gilbertson & Page (Can) Inc; *Recreations* cricket, golf; *Clubs* Royal and Ancient, MCC; *Style*— John Eadie, Esq; 74 Roebuck House, Palace St, SW1 (☎ 01 828 6158)

EADIE, Paul James McGregor; s of Hugh Russell McGregor Eadie (d 1960), and Helen, *née* Kondorgeorgeakis; *b* 18 Feb 1943; *Educ* Oundle, Geneva, Munich, Grenoble, Madrid, Perugia; *m* 1965, Victoria Cynthia, da of Frederick Gutwein (d 1969), of USA; 2 s (Russell Paul b 1967, James Cameron b 1969), 2 da (Holly Katherine b 1971, Charlotte Léonie b 1977); *Career* co dir, chm & ch exec Eadie Bros & Co Ltd 1982-; ch exec Eadie Hldgs Ltd 1982-85, dep chm Eadie Hldgs lc 1985-87; dir BRT Ltd, India 1979-; dir Manchester Chamber of Commerce, memb of exec Ctee of British Textile Machinery Assoc, also Latin American Trade Advsy Gp; AIL; *Recreations* theatre, cinema, reading; *Style*— Paul Eadie, Esq; The Pole Mews, Pole Lane, Antrobus, Cheshire CW9 6NN (☎ 0606 891522); Victoria Works, PO Box 22, Paisley PA1 1PD (☎ 041-889-4126); Ralli Courts, West Riverside, Salford (☎ 061-835-3333)

EADIE, Sam; s of late George Eadie; *b* 12 Mar 1935; *Educ* Trinity Coll Glenalmond, Exeter Coll Oxford; *m* 1958, Fiona Stewart; 1 s, 2 da; *Career* RNVR 1953-57; Royal Dutch Shell 1957-77; research consultant 1978-, dir Energy Advice Ltd 1987-; *Recreations* squash, skiing, music, travel, languages; *Style*— Sam Eadie, Esq; 4 Wotton Way, Cheam, Surrey (☎ 01 393 4230)

EADY, Anthony James; s of John James Eady, and Doris Amy, *née* Langley (d 1988); *b* 9 July 1939; *Educ* Harrow, Oxford Univ (MA); *m* 23 June 1973, Carole June, da of Cyril Albert James Langley (d 1957); 2 s (Jeremy b 1974, d 1975, Nigel b 1976), 1 da (Joanna b 1978); *Career* Theodore Goddard and Co 1962-66, admitted slr 1966, J Henry Schroder Wagg and Co Ltd 1966-79, sec Lazard Bros and Co Ltd 1979-; Liveryman Worshipful Co of Slrs 1979; *Recreations* Hertford Soc, road running; *Clubs* Thames Hare and Hounds; *Style*— Anthony Eady, Esq; Lazard Bros and Co Ltd, 21 Moorfields, London EC2P 2HT (☎ 01 588 2721, fax 01 628 2485)

EADY, David; QC (1983); s of Thomas William Eady (d 1978), and Kate, *née* Day; *b* 24 Mar 1943; *Educ* Brentwood Sch, Trinity Coll Cambridge (MA, LLB); *m* 1974, Catherine Hermione, yr da of Joseph Thomas Wiltshire, of The Red House, Wantage Rd, Streatley, Berks; 1 s (James b 1977), 1 da (Caroline b 1975); *Career* barr Middle Temple 1966; Recorder of the Crown Court 1986; *Books* The Law of Contempt (jtly with A J Arlidge QC); *Recreations* music; *Style*— David Eady, Esq, QC; Goodshill Ho, Tenterden, Kent TN30 6UN (☎ Tenterden (058 06) 3644); 1 Brick Ct, Temple, London EC4Y 9BY (☎ 01 353 8845)

EADY, Hon Georgina Mary Rose Swinfen; *née* Swinfen; da of 3 Baron Swinfen, JP; *b* 1 Feb 1964; *Educ* Christ's Hospital Girls' Sch, Simon Langton Girls' Sch; *Career* sec to Richard Wright (dir of admin) at the Royal Opera House, Covent Garden, WC2 1983-; *Recreations* opera, ballet, riding; *Style*— Hon Georgina Eady; Dene House, Wingham, Canterbury, Kent CT3 1NV; The Royal Opera House, Covent Garden, London WC2 (☎ 01 240 1200)

EADY, Hon (Hugh) Toby Swinfen; s of 2 Baron Swinfen; *b* 28 Feb 1941; *Educ* Bryanston, Wadham Coll Oxford; *Style*— Hon Toby Eady; 12 High St, SW1

EAGLE, Ronald Arthur; s of Charles Henry Eagle (d 1986), and Marjorie Isobel; *b* 8 Feb 1950; *Educ* Gravesend Technical High Sch; *m* 1, 12 April 1971, Pauline, da of Frederick Benton of Gravesend Kent; 1 s (Nicholas Reddick b 1974); m 2, 7 Sept 1978, Sandra, da of Kenneth Minchin of Peregrin Road Sunbury on Thames Middlesex; 1 s (Jonathan Charles b 1980), 1 da (Alexandra Katherine b 1982); *Career* statistics clerk Daily Mail 1966, media buyer Hobson Bates & Ptnrs 1966-68, media planner Ogilvy & Mather 1968-71, sales gp head Border TV Ltd 1971-76, sales controller HTV Ltd 1976-84; sales dir Tyne Tees TV 1984-; dir: Tyne Tees Hldgs plc, Tyne Tees TV Ltd, Tube Productions Ltd; *Recreations* reading, swimming, caravanning, travel; *Style*— Ron Eagle, Esq

EAGLES, Lt-Col (Charles Edward) James; LVO (1988); s of Maj Charles Edward Campbell Eagles, DSO, RMLI (ka 1918), and Esmé Beatrice, *née* Field (d 1965); *b* 14 May 1918; *Educ* Marlborough; *m* 1941, Priscilla May Nicolette, da of Brig Arthur Cottrell, DSO, OBE (d 1962), of Boughton Aluph Cottage, Ashford, Kent; 1 s (Anthony), 3 da (Susan, Jane, Mary); *Career* RM 1936-65; Civil Service, MOD 1965-83; HM Body Gd of Hon Corps of Gentlemen-at-Arms: memb 1967-, Harbinger 1981-86, Standard Bearer 1986-88; *Recreations* shooting; *Clubs* Army and Navy; *Style*— Lt-Col James Eagles, LVO, RM; Fallowfield, Westwell, Ashford, Kent (☎ 023 371 2552)

EARDLEY-WILMOT *see also*: Wilmot

EARDLEY-WILMOT, Sir John Assheton; 5 Bt (UK 1821) of Berkswell Hall, Warwickshire; LVO (1956), DSC (1943); s of Cdr Frederick Neville Eardley-Wilmot (d 1956), and n of Maj Sir John Eardley-Wilmot, 4 Bt (d 1970); *b* 2 Jan 1917; *Educ* Stubbington, RNC Dartmouth; *m* 23 June 1939, Diana Elizabeth, yr da of late Cdr Aubrey Moore, RN; 1 s, 1 da; *Heir* s, Michael John Assheton Eardley-Wilmot; *Career* Cdr (RN) ret 1967; on staff Monopolies Cmmn 1967-82; Liveryman Paviors' Co; FRSA (1970); *Recreations* fishing; *Clubs* Wig and Pen; *Style*— Sir John Eardley-Wilmot, Bt, LVO, DSC; 41 Margravine Gdns, London W6 8RN (☎ 01 748 3723)

EARL, Donald George Monk; s of Lt-Col Stanley Albert Earl (d 1955), and Elsie Earl, *née* Pitt (d 1979); *b* 10 August 1921; *Educ* Wolverhampton Sch, Wrexham GS, Norwich GS; *m* 10 July 1945, Patricia, da of Harold Williamson (d 1956); 1 s (Michael John b 1951); *Career* banker; pres Banking Insur Finance Union 1970-72 (vice pres 1970-72); memb: Industl Tnbls 1975-88, Business and Technicians Trg Cncl (GB & NI) 1979-82 and 1985-88; FCIB (cncl memb 1971-82); *Recreations* golf, gardening; *Style*— Donald Earl, Esq; 6 Arden Road, Dorridge, Solihull, W Midlands B93 8LG (☎ 0564 774229)

EARL, Hon Mrs; Hon Edith (Honor) Betty; *née* Maugham; 2 da of 1 Viscount Maugham (d 1958) (former Lord Chancellor), and Viscountess Maugham, *née* Helen Mary Romer (d 1950); *b* 24 Mar 1901; *m* 25 April 1925, Sebastian Earl (d 1983, Oxford Rowing Blue 1919-22 and sometime md Peter Jones and Selfridges), s of Alfred Earl, of Chepstow Villas, W4; 2 s (Julian, Stephen); *Career* portrait painter; *Style*— Hon Mrs Earl; Flat 6, 6 Onslow Square, London SW7 3NP (☎ 01 589 4758); The Flat Chilland Ford, Martyr Worthy, nr Winchester, Hants (☎0962 78329)

EARL, Kimble David; s of Leonard Arthur Earl, of Surrey, and Margaret Lucy, *née* Pulker; *b* 29 Nov 1951; *Educ* Caterham Sch Surrey; *Career* dep chief exec Argus Press Gp, chief exec newspaper div and consumer publishing div Argus Press Ltd; chm: Reading Newspaper Co Ltd, Windsor Newspaper Co Ltd, Surrey Herald Newspapers Ltd, London and West Surrey Newspapers Ltd, Surrey and South London Newspapers Ltd, South London Press Ltd, North London and Herts Newspapers Ltd, London and Essex Guardian Ltd, Argus Consumer Magazines Ltd, Argus Books, Argus Specialist Exhibitions, SM Distribution Ltd, Clareville Design, Programme Pubns Ltd; dir: Argus Press Hldgs Inc, Team Argus Inc, Argus Business Pubns Ltd, Great Western Newspapers Ltd; *Recreations* walking, motor coach driving, travel; *Style*— Kimble Earl, Esq; Argus Press Gp, PO Box 700, Yateley, Camberley, Surrey GU17 7UA (☎ 0252 875075)

EARL, Roger Lawrence; s of Lawrence William Earl, of 44 Ventnor Villas, Hove, Sussex, and Doris Florence, *née* Copelin; *b* 4 Oct 1940; *Educ* St Christophers Sch Kingswood Surrey, Hollingbury Court Brighton Sussex, St Pauls; *m* 22 July 1968, Lynda Marion, da of Harold Frederick Waldock, of 16 Tynemouth Drive, Enfield; 2 da (Meredith Louise b 12 June 1970, Alexandra Kirsten b 20 July 1972); *Career* jr broker Arbon Langrish & Co (Lloyds brokers) 1957-65; Bland Welch & Co/Bland Payne & Co (Lloyds brokers): asst dir 1966-70, exec dir 1970-73, bd dir and md North American div 1973-79; md and chief exec Fenchurch Gp (Lloyds brokers) 1979-, dir GPG plc 1987-; memb Lloyds 1970; memb Kew Soc; *Recreations* motor sport, swimming, scuba diving, tennis; *Clubs* Inst of Dirs, Hurlingham, Riverside, Ferrari Owners, Annabels; *Style*— Roger Earl, Esq; 4 Cumberland Road, Kew, Surrey TW9 3HQ (☎ 01 948 1714); 9E Barkston Gardens, SW5 (☎ 01 370 0387); Flouquet, Lacour de Visa, Tarn et Garonne, France; La Carabela, 46 Via Del Bosque, Canyamel, Mallorca, Spain; Fenchurch Insurance Holdings Ltd, 136 Minories, London EC3N 1QN (☎ 01 488 2388/01 481 3863, fax 01 481 9467, car tel 0836 232758, telex 8870047 LOQOTE G/884442 LOQOTE LONDON)

EARLAM, Peter Francis; s of Dr Francis Earlam (d 1960), of Liverpool 18, and Elspeth, *née* Skippers; *b* 16 Dec 1931; *Educ* Uppingham, St John's Coll Cambridge (MA); *m* 1957, Amanda Mary, da of Frederick Noel Hornsby (d 1974); 2 s (Nicholas, Johnathan), 2 da (Jennifer, Lucy); *Career* Lt RA TA; dir Elder Dempster Lines

Liverpool 1970-83, ch exec UK/West Africa Lines Liverpool 1974-83; chm Owners Cttee North Atlantic/European Canadian Conferences 1985-; dir Italian Gen Shipping London 1984-; *Recreations* sailing, tennis; *Clubs* Anglo-Belgian; *Style—* Peter Earlam, Esq; 29 Croome Drive, West Kirby, Wirral, Merseyside (☎ 051 625 7717); Lamare, Ravenspoint, Trearddur Bay, Anglesey (☎ 0407 860451); Canadian Atlantic Freight Secretariat Ltd, Stoner House, Kilmead, Crawley, West Sussex RH10 2BG (☎ 0293 540401, telex 878142)

EARLAM, Richard John; s of Francis Earlam, MD (d 1960), of Mossley Hill, Liverpool, and Elspeth Earlam *née* Skippers, of Brambridge House, Winchester; *b* 26 Mar 1934; *Educ* Liverpool Coll, Uppingham Sch, Trinity Hall Cambridge (Ma, MChir), Liverpool Univ; *m* 6 Sept 1969, Roswitha, da of Alfons Teuber, of Munich, Playwright (d 1971); 2 da (Melissa b 1976, Caroline b 1979); *Career* Capt RAMC 1960-62, surgical specialist Br Mil Hosp Hong Kong, TA MO Field Regt RA, examiner Royal Coll of Surgeons 1982-, conslt gen surgn The London Hosp 1972, Fulbright Scholar 1966, Alexander Von Humboldt Fellowship West Germany 1968, chm: NE Thames Regl Advsy Ctee in Gen Surgery, Med Res Cncl Sub Ctee on Oesophageal Cancer; memb: MRC Cancer Therapy Ctee, Manpower Ctee; examiner Royal Coll of Surgns 1982-86; res asst Mayo Clinic USA 1966-67, clinical asst Professor Zenker Munich; memb RSM 1968; FRCS; *Books* Clinical Tests of Oesophageal Function (1976), chapters and papers on abdominal surgery, oesophagus, stomach and gallbladder disease, epidemiology, surgical audit and coding; *Recreations* tennis, mountains summer and winter, beekeeping; *Clubs* Association of Surgeons Internationale Chirurgiae Digestivae, Furniture History Soc; *Style—* Richard John Earlam, Esq; 4 Pembroke Gardens, London W8 (☎ 01 602 5255); 55 Harley St, London W1 (☎ 01 637 4288)

EARLE, Air Chief Marshal Sir Alfred; GBE (1966, KBE 1961, CBE 1946), CB (1956); s of Henry Henwood Earle (d 1948), of Lovacott, Black Torrington, Beaworthy Devon, and Mary Winifred, *née* Rawle; *b* 11 Dec 1907; *Educ* Shebbear Coll, RAF Halton, RAF Coll Cranwell; *m* 1, 9 Aug 1934, Phyllis Beatrice (d 1960), o da of Walter James Rice, of Watford; 1 s, 1 da; m 2, 22 June 1961, Rosemary (d 1978), widow of Air Vice-Marshal Francis Joseph St George Braithwaite, CBE (d 1956), and o da of late George Grinling Harris, of Clifford's Inn, London EC4; m 3, 1979, Clare, widow of Rev Gp Capt Ivor Newell, and da of Thomas Yates, DD; *Career* joined RAF 1925, Sqdn Ldr 1938, served WWII (Air Miny, Bomber Cmmd, Offs of War Cabinet and MOD), AOC No 300 Gp Australia and No 232 Gp Far East 1945-46, Air Cdre 1952, Cmdt RAAF Staff Coll 1951-53, dir of policy (Air Staff) Air Miny 1954, Air Vice-Marshal 1955, Asst Ch of Air Staff (Policy) 1955-57, AOC 13 Gp 1957-60, dep CDS (Air Marshal) 1960-62, AOC-in-C Techl Trg Cmmd 1962-64, Air Chief Marshal 1964, vice-chief of Def Staff 1964-66, ret RAF 1966; dir-gen Intelligence MOD 1966-68; chm Waveney DC 1974-76; *Clubs* RAF; *Style—* Air Chief Marshal Sir Alfred Earle, GBE, CB; 3 Buttermere Gdns, Alresford, Hants

EARLE, Col David Eric Martin; OBE (1969); 2 s of Brig Eric Greville Earle, DSO (d 1965), of Bucks, and Noel, *née* Downes-Martin (d 1975; family originated from Stockton, Cheshire 15 century; gggf created a Bt 1869 (*see* Sir Hardman Earle, 6 Bt); *b* 14 August 1921; *Educ* Stowe, Ch Ch Oxford; *m* 8 April 1947, Betty Isabel, yst da of Lawford Shield (d 1964), of Glos; 2 s (Charles b 1951, George b 1953), 2 da (Victoria b 1952, Charlotte b 1959); *Career* RA 1944; WW II 1940-45 in UK, India, Ceylon and Malaya; instr in gunnery, airborne artillery, directing staff, Staff Coll Camberley, CO 32 Heavy Regt RA and Station Cmd Hildesheim; sec for studies, NATO Def Coll; Col GS MOD Offr Trg; ret 1974; entered Civil Serv by way of Principals Competition; DOE, served in directorates of social and res servs, def servs 1976, Civil Accommodation 1977 on Crown Cts and as regnl admin offr PSA Bristol 1979-82; chm: Bath Centre for Voluntary Serv 1986-87, Relate N and W Wilts Marraige Guidance, N Wilts Gp Cncl for Protection of Rural Eng; FBIM 1973; *Recreations* photography, archaeology; *Style—* Col David E M Earle, OBE; Shipways, Church Lane, Kington Langley, Chippenham, Wilts SN15 5NR (☎ 024975 274)

EARLE, Sir (Hardman) George Algernon; 6 Bt (UK 1869), of Allerton Tower, Woolton, Lancs; s of Sir Hardman Alexander Mort Earle, 5 Bt (d 1979), and Maie, Lady Earle, (d 1986); *b* 4 Feb 1932; *Educ* Eton; *m* 24 Jan 1967, Diana Gillian Bligh, da of Col Frederick Ferris Bligh St George, CVO (d 1970), ggs of Sir Richard Bligh St George, 2 Bt; 1 s, 1 da; *Heir* s, Robert George Bligh Earle, b 24 Jan 1970; *Career* Nat Serv Ensign in Grenadier Gds, memb of London Metal Exchange 1962-73; *Recreations* fox hunting, sailing; *Clubs* Roy Yacht Sqdn; *Style—* Sir George Earle, Bt; Abington, Murroe, Co Limerick, Eire (☎ 061 386108)

EARLE, Dr James Henry Oliver; s of John James Earle (d 1942), of Worcester Park, Surrey, and Constance Mary, *née* Gardner; *b* 5 June 1920; *Educ* Tiffin GS Kingston-upon-Thames, Kings Coll Univ of London, Westminster Med Sch (MD, BS); *m* 1, 26 Dec 1942, (m dis 1976), Jean Bessell, da of Edmund Bessell Whalley (d 1968), of Rogate, Sussex; 1 s (Nigel James b 1948), 1 da ((Mary) Jane b 1944); m 2, 7 Sept 1976, Lady Helen Norah, wid of Rt Hon Lord Runcord, TD (d 1968), da of Sir Crosland Graham (d 1946), of Clywd Hall, Ruthin, N Wales; *Career* lectr and sr lectr clinical pathology Westminster Med Sch 1949-53, asst conslt pathologist Royal Marsden Hosp 1953-56, conslt pathologist and dir laboratories Royal Masonic Hosp 1956-63, conslt pathologist teaching gp Westminster Hosp 1963-85; memb cncl and exec ctee Marie Curie Fndn (Cancer Care) 1953- (currently chm homes and nursing cmmn); memb: academic bd Westminster Med Sch (subsequently Charing Cross Med Sch) 1970-85, bd govrs Westminster Hosp 1972-74; rep Univ of London Kingston and Richmond Health Authy 1974-82 (vice-chm 1978-82), chm DMT and chm area scientific ctee Roehampton Health Dist 1974-82; Silver Jubilee Medal 1977; Freeman City of London 1978, Liveryman Worshipful Co Apothecaries 1977; FRSM, FRCPath, MRCS, LRCP; *Recreations* fishing, gardening, opera, photography; *Style—* Dr James Earle; 18 Hillside, Wimbledon SW19 4NL (☎ 01 946 3507)

EARLE, Joel Vincent (Joe); s of James Basil Foster Earle, of Kyle of Lochalsh, Ross-shire, and Mary Isabel Jessie, *née* Weeks; *b* 1 Sept 1952; *Educ* Westminster, New Coll Oxford (BA); *m* 10 May 1980, Sophia Charlotte, da of Oliver Arbuthnot Knox, of London; 2 s (Leo b 1981, Martin b 1984); *Career* V & A Museum: keeper far eastern dept 1983-87 (res asst 1974-77, asst keeper 1977-83), head of public servs 1987; maj exhibitions: Japan Style 1980, Great Japan Exhibition 1981, Toshiba Gallery of Japanese Art 1986; tstee: Chiddingstone Castle Kent, The Design Museum; memb ctee Japan Festival 1991; *Books* An Introduction to Netsuke (1980), An Introduction to Japanese Prints (1980), The Great Japan Exhibition (contrib 1981), The Japanese Sword (1983), Japanese Art and Design (ed 1987); *Style—* Joe Earle, Esq; 123 Middleton Rd, London E8 4LL; Victoria and Albert Museum, London SW7 2RL (☎ 01 938 8368/9, fax 01 938 8341, telex 268831 VICART G)

EARLE, Maie, Lady; Maie; da of John Drage, of The Red House, Chapel Brampton, Northampton; *m* 27 July 1931, Sir Hardman Alexander Mort Earle, 5 Bt, TD (d 1982); 1 s (Sir Geor ge Earle, 6 Bt, *qv*), 1 da (Mrs Anthony Forbes); *Style—* Maie, Lady Earle; 2 Cadogan Gdns, London SW3 (☎ 01 730 5683)

EARLE, Michael George; s of Henry George Earle (d 1984), of Hambleden, nr Henley-on-Thames, Oxon, and Elizabeth Mary, *née* Wheeler (d 1953); *b* 30 July 1944; *Educ* Sir William Borlase's Sch; *Career* dir: Keene Game Products (UK) Ltd 1978-, Keene Game Products (Overseas) Ltd 1978-, md & dir Br & Gen Tube Co Ltd, 1982-84; dir Globelion Ltd 1984-, md Barnham Press Ltd 1985-, dir Bancrofts Designprint (GMB) Ltd 1986-; *Recreations* shooting; *Style—* Michael Earle, Esq; 227 Marlow Bottom, Marlow, Bucks (☎ 062 84 71618, Barnham Press Ltd, Marlborough Trading Estate, High Wycombe, Bucks HP11 2LB (☎ 0494 450631)

EARLE, Col Peter Beaumont; MC (1945), DL (1967); s of Loftus Earle (d 1949); *b* 9 April 1917; *Educ* Eton, RMA Sandhurst; *m* 1, 1940, Ursula, da of late Maj F W Warre, OBE, MC; 1 s, 1 da; m 2, 1971, Judith, da of late Dr G T MacKinnell Childs; *Career* KRRC 1937-58, Col 1958, mil asst to CIGS War Off 1943-45; FO (PID) 1945-46, MOD (JIB) 1947-48, memb Def Res Bd Canada 1948-49, dir Henry Kendall and Sons Ltd 1959-; warden St George's Hanover Sq, London 1962-; Croix de Guerre (France) 1945; FRSA 1947; Cdr Order of Merit (Peru) 1964; *Clubs* Brooks's; *Style—* Col Peter Earle, MC, DL; King's Farm, Noar Hill, Selborne, Hants GU34 3LW (☎ 042 050 393)

EARLE, Peter Desmond Noel; s of late Brigadier E.G. Earle, DSO, of Walton Hall Bletchley, Bucks, and late Noel Fielding-Johnson *née* Downs-Martin; *b* 20 Nov 1923; *Educ* Wellington, Ch Ch Oxford; *m* 6 Sept 1953, Hope, da of Wallace Sinclair Macgregor of Vancouver BC; 1 s (Robert b 1959), 2 da (Heather b 1960, Melanie b 1964); *Career* company dir (currently chmn 1983) The Country Gentlemen's Associations plc (formerly chief exec 1972-86); editor CGA magazine and Guide to Country Living (Hutchinson & David & Charles); served RN 1942-47 home waters, South Atlantic, Indian Ocean and Pacific (Far East) Lt RNVR exec officer, navigator etc; *Recreations* gardening, writing, swimming, tennis, skiing, yachting; *Clubs* Naval, Dwits; *Style—* Peter Earle, Esq; Stow Bedon House, Attleborough, Norfolk (☎ Caston 284); CGA plc, Letchworth, Herts (☎ 0462 480011)

EARLE, Richard Greville; DL (1984); s of John Greville Earle, JP (d 1933), and Jacobina Reid, *née* Clark (d 1970); *b* 12 Nov 1925; *Educ* Winchester Trinity Coll, Cambridge (MA); *m* 19 Jan 1956, Joanna Mary, JP, da of Cdr Henry Kelsall Beckford Mitchell, RN, CBE, JP, DL, of Sherborne, Dorset; 2 da (Elizabeth b 1957, Susan b 1959); *Career* RNVR 1943-47, Sub Lieut (A); farmer and landowner; chm: Dorset NFU 1964, Standing Conf on Oil and Gas Exploration, English Channel 1980-84, Dorset Small Industs Ctee (COSIRA) 1972-81, Leonard Cheshire Fndn Appeal in W Dorset 1985-88, W Dorset Family Support Serv 1987-, Community Cncl of Dorset 1987-; memb: Dorset CC 1967-85, Cncl of Country Landowners Assoc 1985-; dir: Wessex Grain Ltd, Henstridge Grain Servs Ltd 1985-; High Sheriff 1983; *Recreations* countryside; *Clubs* Farmers; *Style—* Richard Earle, Esq, DL; Frankham Farm, Ryme Intrinseca, Sherborne DT9 6JT (☎ 0935 872304)

EARLES, Prof Stanley William Edward; s of William Edward Earles (d 1984), of Birmingham, and Winnifred Anne, *née* Cook (d 1959); *b* 18 Jan 1929; *Educ* King's Coll London (BSc, PhD, AKC), Univ of London (DSc); *m* 23 July 1955, Margaret Isabella, da of John Brown (d 1988), of Wormley, Hertfordshire; 2 da (Melaine Jane b 1962, Lucy Margaret b 1964); *Career* scientific offr Admiralty Engrg Laboratory 1953-55; at dept of mechanical engrg QMC: lectr 1955-69, reader 1969-75, prof 1975-76; prof of mechanical engrg and head of dept King's Coll London 1976-; dean of engineering Univ of London 1986-: govr: Goff's Sch Hertfordshire 1964-88, Turnford Sch Hertfordshire 1970-87; FI MechE 1976; *Recreations* real tennis, gardening; *Style—* Prof Stanley Earles; Woodbury, Church Lane, Wormley, Broxbourne, Herts EN10 7QF (☎ 0992 464 616); Department of Mechanical Engineering, King's Coll, Strand, London WC2R 2LS (☎ 01 836 5454, fax 01 836 1799)

EARNSHAW, (Thomas) Roy; CBE (1977, OBE 1971); s of Godfrey Earnshaw (d 1962), and Edith Annie, *née* Perry (d 1962); *b* 27 Feb 1917; *Educ* Marlborough Coll Liverpool; *m* 2 Sept 1953, Edith, da of Willie Rushworth (d 19760, of Rochdale; 2 da (Rachel Catherine (Mrs Tsirigotakis) b 17 Nov 1957, Hilary Jane (Mrs Jacobs) b 3 May 1960); *Career* Infantry 1940-46, rising to Maj and 2 i/c 1 Bn Lancs Fusiliers; shipping and shipbroking Liverpool 1933-39; various appts subsid cos of Turner & Newhall Ltd; export appts (latterly export sales mangr) Turner Brothers Asbestos Co Ltd 1939-40 and 1946-53, dir AM & FM Ltd Bombay 1954-59, export dir Ferodo Ltd 1959-66, dir and divnl gen mangr TBA Industl Products Ltd 1966-76, memb advsy cncl BOTB 1975-82 (Export Year and Export Utd advsr 1976-83); dir: Actair Int Ltd 1979-83, Act Hldgs Ltd 1979-83, Unico Fin Ltd 1979-81; London econ advsr to Merseyside CC 1980-82, visiting fell Henley Mgmnt Coll 1981-, conslt and lectr in int mgmnt 1982-; former pres Rochdale C of C, chm NW Region C of C, UK del Euro C of C; memb bd of mangrs Henley YMCA; MICS 1937, MIEx 1948, FRSA 1980; *Recreations* painting, sketching, music, walking; *Clubs* Leander; *Style—* Roy Earnshaw, Esq, CBE

EASON, His Honour Robert Kinley; 2 s of Henry Alexander Eason (d 1926), and Eleanor Jane, *née* Kinley; *b* 12 April 1908; *Educ* Douglas HS, King Williams Coll and Univ Coll London (LLB); *m* 1937, Nora Muriel, da of Robert Raisbeck Coffey (d 1956), of Douglas, Isle of Man; *Career* called to the Bar Gray's Inn 1929, advocate Manx Bar 1930, high bailiff and chief magistrate IOM 1961-69, a High Court judge (Deemster) IOM 1969, first Deemster, Clerk of the Rolls and dep govr IOM 1974-80; chm: Unit Tst Tbnl 1968-74, Criminal Injuries Compensation Tbnl IOM 1969-74, IOM Income Tax Appeal Cmmrs 1974-80, Tynwald Arrangements Ctee 1974-80; chm: tstees Cunningham House Scout and Guide HQ 1964-, Ellan Vannin Home 1981-; pres Ellynyn Ny Gael 1974-, IOM Anti-Cancer Assoc 1969-, Wireless Telegraphy Appeal Bd for IOM 1971-80, SSAFA (IOM branch) 1973-, King William's Coll Soc 1978-80; Queen's Silver Jubilee Medal 1977; *Recreations* organ music; *Clubs* Ellan Vannin, Manx Automobile; *Style—* His Honour Robert K Eason; Greenacres, Highfield Drive, Baldrine, Isle of Man (☎ 0624 781622)

EASSON, Malcolm Cameron Greig; s of Prof Eric Craig Easson (d 1983), of Cheshire, and Moira McKechnie, *née* Greig; *b* 7 April 1949; *Educ* Marple Hall GS, Univ of Manchester; *m* 6 July 1972, Gillian, da of Stanley Oakley, of Cheshire; 1 s

(James b 1979), 1 da (Helen b 1982); *Career* princ of firm of CAs specialising in taxation and finance for Doctors of Med, regular contrib of fin articles to medical jls; FICA; *Recreations* golf, gardening, reading, music; *Style—* Malcolm C G Easson, Esq; Frith Knoll, Eccles Road, Chapel-el-le-Frith, Derbyshire SK12 6RR; Rex Buildings, Wilmslow, Cheshire SK9 1HZ (☎ 0625 527351)

EAST, David Edward; s of Edward William East, of London, and Joan Lillian East; *b* 27 July 1959; *Educ* Hackney Downs Sch, Univ of East Anglia (BSc); *m* 1984, Jeanette Anne, da of Leonard Frank Smith (d 1985), of Loughton, Essex; 1 s (Matthew David b 1986); *Career* professional cricketer Essex CCC 1981-; *Style—* David East, Esq; c/o Essex CCC, Chelmsford, Essex (☎ 0245 354533)

EAST, Gerald Reginald Ricketts; s of Reginald Butterfill East (d 1960), of Littleton, Winchester, and Dora Harriet Kate, *née* Ricketts; *b* 17 Feb 1917; *Educ* Peter Symonds Sch, St Edmund Hall Oxford (MA);; *m* 7 June 1944, Anna Elder, da of Robert Smyth (d 1969), of Cullybackey, Co Antrim; 1 s (Gerald Robert), 1 da (Jane Elisabeth); *Career* enlisted RA 1939, cmmnd 1940, Maj 1944; served: UK, France and Germany; asst princ WO 1947, private sec Sec of State 1954-55, inspr of estabs 1958, princ estab offr 1970, Civil Serv cmmr 1974, ret 1977; chm Incorporated Froebel Educnl Inst and pres Froebel Assoc 1978-; *Recreations* travel; *Style—* Gerald East, Esq; 43 Manor Rd North, Esher, Surrey KT10 0AA (☎ 01 398 2446)

EAST, Grahame Richard; CMG (1961); 2 s of William Robert East (d 1938), and Eleanor Maude Beatrice East (d 1971); *b* 10 Feb 1908; *Educ* Bristol GS, Corpus Christi Coll Oxford (MA); *m* 1937, Cynthia Mildred, da of Adam Louis Beck, OBE (d 1964); 2 s (Richard, John), 2 da (Rosalind, Celia); *Career* asst master Roy Belfast Academical Instn 1929; civil serv 1930-, asst sec Bd of Inland Revenue 1941-, special cmmnr of Income Tax 1962-, ret 1973; *Style—* Grahame East, Esq, CMG; 44 Devonshire Rd, Sutton, Surrey SM2 5HH (☎ 01 642 0638)

EAST, John Richard Alan; s of Bertram David (Barry) East, of Eaton Square, London, and Gladys, *née* Stone (d 1957); *b* 14 May 1949; *Educ* Westminster; *m* 1, 14 May 1971 (m dis 1986), Judith Adrienne, da of Clive Hill, of Horshall, Surrey; 2 s (Robin b 1974, Christopher b 1978); m 2, 12 July 1986, Charlotte Sylvia, da of Lt-Cdr Peter Gordon Merriman, DSC, RN (d 1965); *Career* Speechly Bircham (Slrs) 1967-70, Mitton Butler Priest and Co Ltd 1971-73, Panmure Gordon and Co 1973-77; Margetts and Addenbrooke (formerly Margetts and Addenbrooke East Newton, prev Kent East Newton and Co) 1977-86: ptnr 1977-80, managing ptnr 1980-86, sr ptnr 1983-86; dir Nat Investmt Gp plc 1986-87, dir Guidehouse Gp plc 1987-, md Guidehouse Securities Ltd 1987-; memb exec ctee Putney Cons Assoc, chm Parkshide Ward; memb Stock Exchange 1974; *Recreations* music, the playing and recording of electronic musical instruments, travel; *Clubs* Carlton; *Style—* John East, Esq; Hermiston 110, Victoria Drive, Wimbledon, London SW19 6PS (☎ 01 789 4918); Vestry House, Greyfriars Passage, Newgate St, London EC1A 7BA (☎ 01 606 6321, fax 01 606 7002, car 0836 251555, telex 894011 GUIDE G)

EAST, Sir (Lewis) Ronald; CBE (1951); s of Lewis Findlay East, ISO (d 1948), of Melbourne, and Annie Eleanor, *née* Burchett; *b* 17 June 1899; *Educ* Scotch Coll Melbourne, Melbourne U; *m* 1927, Constance Lilias, MA, da of Alexander Keil, of Kilwinning, Ayrshire; 3 da; *Career* chm State Rivers and Water Supply Cmmn Vic 1936-65, pres Aust Inst of Engineers 1952, cmmr River Murray Cmmn 1936-65, memb Snowy Mountains Cncl 1953-65, vice-pres Int Cmmn on Irrigation and Drainage 1959-62; kt 1966; *Books* numerous publications incl: River Improvement, Land Drainage and Flood Protection (1952), The Kiel Family and related Scottish Pioneers (1974); *Style—* Sir Ronald East, CBE; 57 Waimarie Drive, Mt Waverley, Vic 3149, Australia (Melbourne 277 4315)

EAST, Stephen John; s of Charles William East, of Croydon, Surrey, and Olive Lillian, *née* East; *b* 3 Mar 1958; *Educ* Selhurst GS Croydon, Loughborough Univ of Technol (BSc); *Career* Binder Hamlyn Chartered Accountants 1979-83; Redland Plc: asst tres 1983-84, dep tres 1984-87, gp tres 1987-; memb programme ctee Assoc Corporate Tres, memb Croydon South Cons Assoc; ACA 1982, MCT 1986; *Style—* Stephen East, Esq; 34 Lower Barn Rd, Sanderstead, Surrey CR2 1HQ (☎ 01 660 1602); Redland House, Reigate, Surrey RH2 0SJ (☎ 0737 233 307, fax 0737 221 938, car tel 0836 290 180, telex 28626)

EASTAUGH, Rt Rev John Richard Gordon; *see*: Hereford, Bishop of

EASTHAM, Kenneth; MP (Lab) Manchester Blackley 1979-; s of late James Eastham; *b* 11 August 1927; *Educ* Openshaw Tech Coll; *m* 1951, Doris, da of Albert Howarth; *Career* former planning engr GEC Trafford Park, memb: NW Econ Planning Cncl 1975-79, Manchester City Cncl 1962-80 (sometime dep ldr, chm educ ctee), AUEW sponsored, memb employment select ctee; *Style—* Kenneth Eastham, Esq, MP; House of Commons, London SW1

EASTHAM, Hon Mr Justice; Hon Sir (Thomas) Michael; yst s of His Hon Sir Tom Eastham, QC, JP, DL (d 1967), and Margaret Ernestine, *née* Smith; *b* 26 June 1920; *Educ* Harrow, Trinity Hall Cambridge; *m* 1942, Mary Pamela, o da of late Dr H C Billings, of Shere, Surrey; 2 da (and 1 da decd); *Career* WWII Capt Queen's Roy Regt 1940-46; barr Lincoln's Inn 1947, QC 1964, rec of: Deal 1968-71, Cambridge 1971; hon rec Cambridge 1972, bencher Lincoln's Inn 1972, rec Crown Ct 1972-78, judge of the High Ct of Justice Family Division 1978-; kt 1978; *Style—* The Hon Mr Justice Eastham; 7a Porchester Terrace, London W2 (☎ 01 723 0770)

EASTICK, Barrington Richard; s of Douglas Martineau Eastick (d 1957), of Berkshire, and Sylvia, *née* Weddle (d 1934); *b* 17 July 1934; *Educ* St Andrew's Sch Eastbourne, Uppingham; *m* 15 Jan 1966, Madeleine Anne, da of John Nathaniel Preston (d 1982), of Co Meath; 2 s (James b 1966, Benjamin b 1971), 1 da (Tara b and d 1969); *Career* RAF F/O Middle East 1952-55; md Ragus Sugars and Associated Cos 1957-87, conslt and dir 1988-; motor racing driver 1952-77; reformed ERA Club 1958 (sec), ERA Team Mngr 1958-60; memb Bentley Drivers Club Ctee 1965-79, competitions ctee and WO Bentley Memorial Fund Co-ordinator; *Recreations* vintage and classic cars, military history, Switzerland; *Clubs* Leander, Henley Rowing, Bentley Drivers', ERA, Vintage Sports Car; *Style—* Barrington R Eastick, Esq; Fawley Lodge, Fawley, Henley-on-Thames, Oxfordshire RG9 3AJ (☎ 0491 571763); Ragus Sugars, Sugar Manufacturers, 193 Bedford Ave, Trading Estate, Slough, Berkshire SL1 4RT (☎ 0753 75353, telex 849156)

EASTICK, Bernard Charles Douglas; MBE (1945), TD (1950); s of Frederick Charles Eastick (d 1970), and Clarisse Elvira, *née* Smith (d 1916); *b* 1 Dec 1916; *Educ* Tonbridge, St John's Coll Cambridge; *m* 13 Dec 1941, Myra, da of Albert James Hall (d 1971); 1 s, 2 da; *Career* cmmnd Royal Berks Regt 1936, WWII 1939-46 Serv: France, N Africa, Italy (despatches 1945); sugar refiner; Freeman of City of London, Liveryman of the Grocers Co; sugar refiner; *Recreations* travel, skiing, gardening; *Clubs* Royal Channel Island's YC; *Style—* Bernard Eastick, Esq, MBE, TD; Cartref, Bon Air Lane, St Saviour, Jersey, CI

EASTMAN, The Venerable Derek Ian Tennent; MC (1945); s of late Archibald Tennent Eastman and Gertrude Towler, *née* Gambling; *b* 22 Jan 1919; *Educ* Winchester, Ch Ch Oxford, Cuddesdon Theol Coll Oxford; *m* 1949, Judith Mary, eldest da of Rev Canon Philip David Bevington Miller; 3 s, 1 da; *Career* Coldstream Gds 1940-46: Guards Armoured Div, Temp Major; clerk in Holy Orders; assist curate Brighouse 1948-51, priest-in-charge St Andrew's Caversham 1951-56, vicar of Headington Oxford 1956-64, vicar of Banbury 1964-70, archdeacon of Buckingham and vicar of Chilton and Dorton 1970-77, proctor in convocation for Dioc of Oxford 1964-70, memb Gen Synod 1975-77, canon of St George's Chapel Windsor 1977-85, archdeacon emeritus 1985; *Recreations* gardening, painting; *Style—* The Ven Derek Eastman, MC; Abbott's Corner, 43 Clay Lane, Beaminster, Dorset DT8 3BX (☎ 0308 862443)

EASTMAN, Lady Mary Agatha; *née* Campbell; yr da of 4 Earl Cawdor (d 1914); *b* 6 Jan 1905; *m* 5 Feb 1931, Brig Henry Claude Warrington Eastman, DSO, MVO, late RA (d 1975), s of Thomas Eastman, MA, of Northwood Park, Winchester; 1 s, 1 da; *Style—* Lady Mary Eastman; Pandy Newydd, Halfway Bridge, Bangor, Gwynedd

EASTMENT, Peter John; s of Alexander John Eastment, of Setters Glade, Holcombe, Bath, and Kathleen Mary, *née* Blackmore; *b* 26 April 1947; *Educ* Wells Cathedral Sch; *m* 6 Sept 1975, Linda Loraine, da of Patrick Gould (d 1987); 1 s (Mark b 1978), 1 da (Rebecca b 1980); *Career* Casswells Ltd: dir 1973, sec 1980, md 1986; former: vice chm Young Cons, govr Wrighlington Sch Avon; graduate Nat Inst Hardware 1968; *Recreations* travel, golf; *Clubs* Fosseway-Country; *Style—* Peter Eastment, Esq; Casswells Ltd, 6-9 High St, Midsomer Norton, Bath, Avon (☎ 0761 413 331)

EASTON, Hon Mrs (Caroline Ina Maud); *née* Hawke; eldest da of 9 Baron Hawke (d 1985); *b* 13 Feb 1937; *Educ* Hatherop Castle Glos; *m* 6 Aug 1960, John Francis Easton, o s of late Rev Cecil Gordon Easton, Vicar of Littlewick Green, Berks; 1 s, 1 da; *Career* barr Middle Temple 1959 (not practising now); *Recreations* music, sport; *Style—* The Hon Mrs Easton; The Old Hall, Barley, nr Royston, Herts (☎ 076 384 368)

EASTON, Dendy Bryan; s of Leslie Herbert Easton (d 1962), of Tadworth, Surrey, and Dora, *née* Napper (d 1969); *b* 13 Mar 1916; *Educ* Cranleigh Sch, Univ of Reading (Dip Hort); *m* 28 June 1941, Iris Joan, da of Albert Edward Keyser (d 1979), of Hove Sussex; 2 s (Timothy b 1943, Dendy b 1950), 2 da (Ann b 1942, Jane b 1947); *Career* mil serv: cmmnd 1939, BEF France 1939-40, UK and PAIFORCE 1944-45 RARO 1946, Capt and Adj 6 CRASC; nurseryman; chm and md Meare Close Nurseries Ltd (family business) 1938-; MI Hort; *Recreations* gardening, fly fishing, motoring, preservation of common land; *Clubs* Vintage Sports Car, Aston Martin Owners; *Style—* Dendy Easton, Esq; Hunters Hall, Tadworth, Surrey KT20 5SB; Meare Close Nurseries Ltd, Tadworth Street, Tadworth, Surrey KT20 5RQ (☎ 0737 812449)

EASTON, Adm Sir Ian; KCB (1975), DSC (1946); s of Walter Easton (d 1965), of West Mersea, Essex, and Janet Elizabeth Rickard; *b* 27 Nov 1917; *Educ* RNC Dartmouth; *m* 1, 1943 (m dis 1962), Shirley Townend White; 1 s, 1 da; m 2, 1962, Margharetta Elizabeth Martinette Van Duyn de Sparwoude; 1 da; *Career* entered RN 1931, qualified as pilot 1939, served WW II, Capt RN 1960, Rear-Adm 1969, assistant chief of Naval Staff (Policy) 1969-71, flag offr Admiralty Interview Bd 1971-73, V-Adm 1972, head of Br Defence Staff and Defence Attaché Washington 1973-76, Adm 1976, Cmdt Roy Coll of Defence Studies 1976-77, ret 1978; *Clubs* Royal Solent Yacht, Royal Thames; *Style—* Adm Sir Ian Easton, KCB, DSC; Causeway Cottage, Freshwater, IOW (☎ 0983 752775)

EASTON, Air Cdre Sir James Alfred; KCMG (1956), CB (1952), CBE (1945); s of late William Coryndon Easton of Winchester, and Alice Sophia, *née* Summers; *b* 11 Feb 1908; *Educ* Peter Symond's Sch Winchester, RAF Coll Cranwell; *m* 1, 29 April 1939, Anna Mary (d 1977), da of Lt-Col James Andrew McKenna, of Ottawa; 1 s, 1 da; m 2, 1980, Jane Walker, da of late Dr J S Leszynski and wid of William M Walker, Jr, of Detroit; *Career* joined RAF 1926, served WW II (despatches), Gp Capt 1941, Air Cdre 1943, ret 1949; HM Consul-Gen Detroit 1958-68; research consultant on Trade Development in Great Lakes Area USA 1968-71; dep chm Host Ctee for 1974 World Energy Conference 1972-75; Legion of Merit (USA); *Style—* Air Cdre Sir James Eaton, KCMG, CB, CBE; 71 Cornwall Gdns, London SW7 (☎ 01 937 0430); 390 Chalfonte Ave, Grosse Pointe Farms, Mich 48236, USA

EASTON, John Francis; s of Rev Cecil Gordon Easton (d 1959), of The Vicarage, Littlewick Green, Maidenhead, Berks, and Nora Gladys, *née* Hall; *b* 20 August 1928; *Educ* City of London Sch, Keble Coll Oxford (MA); *m* 6 Aug 1960, Hon Caroline Ina Maude, da of 9 Baron Hawke (d 1985), of Faygate Place, Faygate, Horsham, Sussex; 1 s (Nicholas John b 1961), 1 da (Ina Frances b 1964); *Career* Nat Serv RASC 1951-53; called to bar Middle Temple 1951, slr Inland Revenue's Off 1955-58, pt/t chm VAT Tbnls 1988; reader Diocese St Albans; *Recreations* languages, swimming; *Style—* John Easton, Esq; The Old Hall, Barley, Royston, Herts SG8 8JA (☎ 076 384 368)

EASTON, Dr (Alfred) Leonard Tytherleigh; s of Leonard Tytherleigh (d 1945), and Maria Adelaida Bertran de Lis (d 1973); *b* 11 July 1921; *Educ* Harrow, Pembroke Coll Cambridge (MD); *m* 29 July 1945, Mary Josephine, da of John Latham (d 1962); 1 s (Edward b 1949 d 1966), 1 da (Claire b 1946); *Career* Sqdn Ldr (Med) RAF ME 1947-49; surgeon, obstetrician and gynaecologist; cnslt London Hosp 1958-82, King George Hosp Ilford 1958-73, ret 1986, hon conslt surgeon London Hosp; FRCS, FRCOG; *Recreations* arts, theatre, opera, cricket; *Clubs* Garrick, MCC; *Style—* Dr Leonard Easton; 612 Gilbert House, Barbican, London EC2Y 8BD (☎ 01 638 0781)

EASTON, Timothy Nigel Dendy; s of Capt Dendy Bryan, and Iris Joan, *née* Keyser; *b* 26 August 1943; *Educ* Mowden Sch, Christ Coll Brecon, Kingston Coll of Art, Heatherley Sch of Art London (scholarship); *m* 5 April 1967, Christine Margaret, da of Flt Lt James William Darling (d 1984); 2 da (Lucy Kathryn Rebecca b 1969, Isabella b 1971); *Career* artist/sculptor; mural church of the Good Shepherd Tadworth 1969-71, mural Theological Coll Salisbury 1967-73, (drawings for Salisbury mural exhibited Chicago and Kansas USA 1968), first London exhibition 'Young Artists' Upper Grosvenor Gallery 1970, began exhibiting sculptures in bronze 1971; various exhibitions of paintings and sculptures since 1970 in: England, Germany, Luxembourg, America; Elizabeth Greensfields Meml Fndn Award Montreal Canada 1973; sec Debenham Local Hist Gp, lectr Cambridge Extra Mural Bd; *Books* An Historical Atlas of Suffolk (contributor, 1988); *Recreations* vernacular architecture in suffolk; *Style*— Timothy Easton, Esq; Bedfield Hall, Bedfield, Woodbridge, Suffolk IP13 7JJ (☎ 0728 76 380)

EASTWOOD, (Noel) Anthony Michael; s of Edward Norman Eastwood (d 1984), of Headingley, Yorkshire and Irene, *née* Dawson (d 1979); *b* 7 Dec 1932; *Educ* The Leys Sch Cambridge, Christ's Coll Cambridge (MA); *m* 1965, Elizabeth Tania Gresham, da of Cdr Thomas Wilson Boyd, CBE, DSO, DL; 3 s (Rupert b 1967, James b 1969, Alexander b 1972); *Career* Lt RA 1951-54, Pilot Ofr RAFVR 1954-56; De Havilland Aircraft Co 1956-60, RTZ Gp 1960-61, AEI Gp 1961-64; dir: Charterhouse Japhet Ltd 1964-79, Daniel Doncaster & Sons Ltd 1971-81, The Barden Corpn 1971-81, Hawk Publishing Co (UAE) 1981-86, Caribbean Publishing Co 1981-84, IDP Interdata (Aust) 1984-; chm Interdata Gp 1981-; pres Charterhouse Japhet Texas Inc 1974-77; sec Roy Aeronautical Soc 1982-83; London Ctee Yorkshire and Humberside Devpt Assoc 1975-; dir: Europa Associates Ltd 1988-, ERGO Communication Service Ltd 1987-, Spearhead Communications Ltd 1988-; *Recreations* skiing, sailing (Daydream), travel, family; *Clubs* Roy Thames Yacht; *Style*— Anthony Eastwood, Esq; Palace Ho, Much Hadham, Herts SG10 6HW (☎ 027984 2409)

EASTWOOD, (Herbert) David; CBE (1973), MC (1944); s of Rev Canon John Eastwood (d 1968); *b* 27 Jan 1919; *Educ* All Saints Sch Bloxham, St Edmund Hall Oxford; *m* 1948, Betty Ann Margaret, da of Walter Vivian Douglas Skrine (d 1964); 1 s; *Career* served 1939-45 War in Oxf and Bucks Lt Inf and Parachute Regt in Sicily, Italy and NW Europe, Malayan CS 1946-57, War Office 1957-79, ret; *Recreations* enjoying retirement in the countryside; *Clubs* Army and Navy; *Style*— David Eastwood, Esq, CBE, MC; Sandpitts, Gastard, Corsham, Wilts, SN13 9QW (☎ 0240 973 240)

EASTWOOD, (John) Hugo; s of John Francis Eastwood, OBE, KC (d 1952), of 5 Sloane Ct East, Lodon SW3, and Dorothea Constance Cecil, *née* Butler (d 1961); *b* 10 Dec 1935; *Educ* Eton; *m* 1, 15 Dec 1956 (m dis 1965), Susan Elizabeth, da of Cdr Peter Harry Cator (d 1979), of St Mary's Happisburgh, Norwich; 2 s (John Fabian b 20 Jan 1958, (Thomas) Edmund b 4 Dec 1960); m 2, 8 Feb 1966, Davina Naldera, da of Maj Edward Dudley Metcalfe, MVO, MC (d 1957), of London; 1 s (Philip Hugo b 17 Sept 1966), 1 da (Emma Alexandra b 12 Feb 1969); *Career* memb London Stock Exchange 1963-69, farmer 1970-; dir Anglers Co-op Assoc Tstee Co, John Eastwood Water-Protection Tst; memb cncl Anglers Co-op Assoc; *Recreations* fishing, shooting, growing rhododendrons; *Clubs* Brooks's, Fly Fishers; *Style*— Hugo Eastwood, Esq; The Pheasantry, Bramshill Park, Bramshill, Hants RG27 OJN (☎ 025 126 2343); 4 Lydon Rd, Clapham Old Town, London SW4

EASTWOOD, (William) James Michael; s of William Walter Rashleigh Eastwood (d 1941) and Mabel Caroline *née* Ellershaw (d 1959); *b* 13 June 1917; *Educ* Wellington; *m* 8 May 1954, (Katherine) Gillian, da of C Maurice Champness (d 1960), of Orchardleigh, Purley; 3 da (Diana (Mrs Kenchington), Miranda (Mrs Hilton), Annie (Mrs Dixon)); *Career* KRRC 1940-46; serv: India, Burma, China; with Dunlop Rubber Co 1935-39 and 1946, Beecham Gp 1953-58, C Shippam Ltd 1959-80; dir James Eastwood & Assocs 1980- (conslts in food industry Europe to Australasia), Veeraswamy's Food Products 1988-; chm: Chichester branch Euro Movement 1983-88, Food Mfrs Export Ctee 1969-73, Aust and NZ Trade Advsy Ctee 1969-; Liveryman Worshipful Co of Merchant Taylors 1946; *Recreations* cricket, gardening, travel; *Clubs* MCC, RAC, Aust; *Style*— James Eastwood, Esq, MBE; office: Little Mandage, Funtington, Chichester (☎ 0234 575 409, fax 0234 786 930, telex 86402)

EASTWOOD, Sir John Bealby; DL (Notts 1981); s of William Eastwood and Elizabeth Townroe, *née* Bealby; *b* 9 Jan 1909; *Educ* Queen Elizabeth's GS Mansfield; *m* 1, 1929, Constance Mary Tilley (d 1981); 2 da; m 2, 1983, Mrs Joan Mary McGowan, *née* Hayward (d 1986); *Career* chm Adam Eastwood & Sons (builders) 1946-; OStJ; kt 1985; *Style*— Sir John Eastwood, DL; Adam Eastwood & Sons, Burns Lane, Warsop, Mansfield, Notts

EASTWOOD, (Anne) Mairi; *née* Waddington; da of John Waddington (d 1979), and Helen Cowan, *née* MacPherson; *b* 11 July 1951; *Educ* St Leonards Sch, Imperial Coll London Univ (BSc, ARCS); *m* 10 Aug 1974 (m dis 1987), James William Eastwood, s of late Donald Smith Eastwood; 1 s (Donald James b 1983), 1 da (Joanna b 1980); *Career* Arthur Young articled 1973, qualified 1976, ptnr in charge of computer servs consultancy 1985-87, recruitment ptnr 1985-87, Nat Staff ptnr 1988-; memb alumni bd Imp Coll; ACA 1977, FCA 1982; *Clubs* IOD, Lansdowne; *Style*— Mrs Mairi Eastwood; Appledore Cottage, 4 Brewers Ct, Winsmore Lane, Abingdon, Oxon OX14 5BG; Arthur Young, Rolls House, Rolls Bldgs, Fetter Lane, London EC4A 1NH (☎ 01 831 7130)

EASTWOOD, (John) Stephen; s of Rev John Edgar Eastwood (d 1972), of Over Wallop, Hants, and Elfreda, *née* Behrendt (d 1962); *b* 27 May 1925; *Educ* Denstone Coll Staffs, Open Univ (BA); *m* 11 June 1949, Nancy, da of Samuel Charles Gretton (d 1988), of Felpham, Sussex; 1 s (David b 1955), 2 da (Elizabeth (Mrs Chamberlain) b 1954, Gillian (Mrs Wright) b 1957); *Career* WWII coder RN 1943-46; admitted slr 1949, asst slr Salop CC 1950-53 (Leics CC 1949-50), sr asst slr Northants CC 1953-58, ptnr Wilson and Wilson Kettering 1958-76, chm Industl Tbnls 1976-82, regnl chm Industl Tbnls Nottingham 1982-; asst rec 1981-87, rec 1987-; pres Northants Law Soc 1986-87; pres: Kettering Rotary 1973-74 (memb 1963-77), Kettering Huxbe Rotary 1983-84 (memb 1983-); chm Kettering Round Table 1963-64 (memb 1961-66), chm Abbeyfield (Kettering) Soc 1974-; memb Law Soc; *Recreations* painting, reading, music, walking, gardening; *Style*— Stephen Eastwood, Esq; 20 Gipsy Lane, Kettering, Northants NN16 8TY (☎ 0536 85612); Regional Office of the Industrial Tribunals, Birkbeck House, Trinity Sq, Nottingham (☎ 0602 475701)

EASTWOOD, Dr Wilfred; s of Wilfred Andrew Eastwood (d 1977), and Annice Gertrude, *née* Hartley (d 1985); *b* 15 August 1923; *Educ* Hemsworth GS, Sheffield Univ (BEng), Aberdeen Univ (PhD); *m* 1947, Dorothy Jean, da of Charles St George Gover, of 40 Grange Court, Totley, Sheffield 1 s (Richard), 1 da (Janet); *Career* conslt engr; sr ptnr Eastwood and Ptnrs 1972-; prof of civil engrg Univ of Sheffield 1964-70, pres Instn of Structural Engrs 1976-77; chm: Cncl of Engrg Insts 1983-84, Cwlth Engrg Cncl 1983-85; Hon DEng (Sheffield) 1984; FEng; *Recreations* watching cricket from third man and gardening; *Clubs* Yorks CC; *Style*— Dr Wilfred Eastwood; 45 Whirlow Park Rd, Sheffield S11 9NN (☎ 0742 364645); office: St Andrew's House, 23 Kingfield Rd, Sheffield S11 9AS (☎ 0742 583871, telex 547266)

EATES, Edward Caston; CMG (1968), LVO (1961), QPM (1961), CPM (1955); o s of Edward Eates (d 1953), and Elizabeth Lavinia Issac, *née* Caston (d 1965); *b* 8 April 1916; *Educ* Highgate, King's Coll London (LLB); *m* 30 Aug 1941, Maureen Teresa, da of Daniel McGee (d 1968); *Career* served WWII 1939-46, 22 (Cheshire) Regt and 2 Derbyshire Yeo, T/Maj 1944, Staff Coll Quetta 1945 (sc); entered Colonial Police Serv 1946; served in: Nigeria 1946-54, Sierra Leone 1954-57, The Gambia (Cmmr) 1957-63, Hong Kong 1963-69 (Cmmr 1967-69); FCO 1971-76; *Recreations* travel, history; *Clubs* Royal Commonwealth Soc, E India, Surrey County Cricket; *Style*— Edward Eates, Esq, CMG, LVO, QPM, CPM; 2 Riverside Ct, Colleton Cres, Exeter EX2 4BZ (☎ 0392 436434)

EATON, Arthur Raymond; s of Arthur Albert Eaton (d 1954), of Teddington, Middlesex, and Enid Bell (d 1973); *b* 13 Mar 1930; *Educ* Maiden Earleigh Berkshire, Ardingly Coll Haywards Heath Sussex; *m* 2 Nov 1973 (second m), Pamela Winifred, da of Richard Weston (d 1982), of The Bear, Stock, Essex; 2 s (Nicholas b 1958, Andrew b 1964), 2 da (Caron b 1956, Jacqueline b 1957), 1 stepda (Tracy b 1964); *Career* Nat Serv RHG, Festival of Br Staff Admin 1950-51; Ardath Tobacco Co 1951-68, licensee 1968; *Recreations* rowing, horse riding, music, theatre; *Style*— Arthur Eaton, Esq; 30 Mill Rd, Stock Ingatestone, Essex CM4 9LJ

EATON, Charles Le Gai; s of Charles Eaton (d 1921), and Ruth Frances Eaton, *née* Muddock (d 1973); *b* 1 Jan 1921; *Educ* Charterhouse, King's Coll Cambridge (MA); *m* 1, 1944, Katharine Mary, *née* Clayton; 1 s (Leo Francis b 1945); m 2, 1956, Corah Keturah, *née* Hamilton; 1 s (Maurice Le Gai b 1959), 2 da (Judith Layla Ruth b 1957, Corah Ann b 1961); *Career* journalist and lectr in West Indies and Egypt 1945-54; COI 1955-59; dir UK Info Servs: Jamaica 1959-64; Madras, 1964-66; grade 6 offr FCO 1967-69, 1 sec (Info), Br High Cmmn Trinidad 1969-73 Cwlth Coordination Dept 1973-76, ret 1977; conslt Islamic Cultural Centre London 1978-; author, broadcaster and lectr; *Books* The Richest Vein: Eastern Religions and Modern Thought (1950), King of the Castle: Choice and Responsibility in the Modern World (1977), Islam and the Destiny of Man (1985, German and French translations); *Recreations* photography, gardening; *Clubs* The Travellers; *Style*— Gai Eaton, Esq; 35 Riddlesdown Rd, Purley, Surrey CR2 1DJ (☎ 01 660 1252); Islamic Cultural Centre, Park Road NW8 7RG (☎ 01 724 3363)

EATON, Donald Stuart; s of Arthur Edward Eaton (d 1930), of Heaton Chapel, Cheshire, and Lillie, *née* Lord (d 1974); *b* 30 Mar 1923; *Educ* King Edward VII Sch Lytham Lancs; *m* 23 April 1949, Margaret Hibbert, da of Harold Slater (d 1937), of Lytham St Annes, Lancs; 1 s (David b 1959), 2 da (Hazel b 1953, Rachel b 1956); *Career* HG 1940-42; dep accountant Rank Orgn 1945-47, asst gen mangr Metro Goldwyn Mayer 1947-51; gp fin dir: Caxton Publishing Gp plc 1951-61, Pratt Standard Range plc 1961-66; fndr and sr ptnr Eaton & Ptnrs CAs 1966-81, ret; memb: ctee Assoc of Lancestrians in London 1961-81 (chm 1976), Freedom Assoc (chm Middx 1971-81); parental govr Richmond upon Thames Coll 1978-79; Freemen: City of London 1971, Worshipful Co of Plumbers 1971, Worshipful Co of Chartered Acountants 1978; FCA 1945, FTH (1945), MBIM 1967, FFB 1975; *Recreations* cricket, filming and video, photography, sailing; *Clubs* City Livery, United Wards; *Style*— Donald Eaton, Esq

EATON, Guy Ashley; s of Paul Eaton, of Maidenhead, Berks, and Elizabeth Ann (d 1971); *b* 27 April 1951; *Educ* Oundle Sch, Bristol Univ; *m* 21 Sept 1983, Ulker, da of Tarik Sagban, of Bursa, Turkey; 1 da (Natalia b 1987); *Career* CA; banker; FICA; *Recreations* music, photography; *Clubs* RAC; *Style*— Guy A Eaton, Esq; 129 Thomas More House, Barbican, London EC2 (☎ 01 588-6677); 140 Park Lane, London W1

EATON, Peter; *b* 24 Jan 1914; *Educ* Manchester; *m* 1, Ann Wilkinson; m 2, Valerie Carruthers; 2 s (Russell, Rupert); m 3, 1952, Margaret, da of Henry Gordon Taylor (d 1980); 2 da (Ruth, Diana); *Career* antiquarian bookseller, fndr and dir Peter Eaton (Booksellers) Ltd; artist; publisher and author of: A History of Lilies, Marie Stopes, A Preliminary Checklist of her Writings; Peter Eaton Library on Robert Owen & Co-op Movement, named after him now in Japanese Univ;; *Recreations* collecting works of pre-raphaelites, reading, music; *Clubs* Reform; *Style*— Peter Eaton, Esq; Lilies, Weedon, Aylesbury, Bucks HP22 4NS (☎ 0296 641393)

EATON, Philip Bromley; s of Percy Eaton, of N Wales, and Ethel Mary, *née* Swindell; *b* 3 June 1925; *Educ* Sir John Talbot's Sch, Liverpool Univ Sch of Architecture (BArch); *m* 3 April 1953, Joan, da of William Frederick Welch, MBE; 1 s (Mark b 1956); *Career* Capt KSLI served: Egypt, Palestine, Cyprus; fndr Eaton Manning Wilson architectural practice 1961; chm: Shrops Soc of Architects 1986-88, hon pres Ludlow Constituency Democrats 1982; ARIBA; *Recreations* travelling, gardening, music and the arts; *Style*— Philip B Eaton, Esq; Scotsmansfield, Burway, Church Stretton, Shrops; 6 High St, Shrewsbury (☎ 0743 67744)

EATON, Stuart John; JP; s of Leslie Yates Eaton (d 1970), and Beatrice Nancy, *née* Jevon (d 1983); *b* 26 Nov 1927; *Educ* Dudley GS, Dudley Tech Coll; *m* 29 May 1950, Doreen May, da of Horace Enoch Dickens (d 1969); 2 s (Robert, Christopher); *Career* writer RN 1945-47 served: Australia, Colombo, Hong Kong; Tipton & Coseley Building Soc: clerk/cashier 1941, chief clerk/cashier 1950, chief exec 1958-87, dir 1981-87, non exec dir 1987-; pres: Tipton Harriers, Tipton Scout Cncl; tres and tstee Tipton Med Tst; memb: ctee Tipton Cons and Unionist Club, Tipton Rotary Club (past pres), Fellowship Ltd Dudley Castle Mess (past chm); JP West Bromwich 1972; MBIM 1971, FBIM 1980; *Recreations* walking, jogging, choral singing; *Clubs* Tipton Cons; *Style*— Stuart Eaton, Esq, JP; 215 Northway, Sedgley, Dudley DY3 3RG (☎ 09073 3046)

EATON, Captain Thomas Christopher; OBE (1962), TD (1946), DL (1971); s of Frederic Ray Eaton (d 1962), of Norwich; *b* 13 Oct 1918; *Educ* Stowe; *m* 1958, Robin Elizabeth, da of Alexander Berry Austin (ka 1944); 1 s, 2 da; *Career* served 4 Bn Royal Norfolk Regt (TA) 1936-50, served in WWII (wounded, despatches, POW Singapore 1942-45); slr and Notary Public 1947, memb Norwich City Cncl 1949-74 (ldr 1969-70), lord mayor of Norwich 1957-58, parly candidate (C) Norwich North 1951 and 1955; tstee E Anglian Tstee Savings Bank 1957-80; govr Theatre Royal (Norwich) Tst Ltd 1972-85, chm Memorial Tst 2 Air Div USAAF 1975-; *Recreations* theatre and travel; *Clubs* Norfolk; *Style*— Capt Thomas Eaton, OBE, TD, DL; 3 Albemarle Rd, Norwich, Norfolk NR2 2DF (☎ 0603 53962)

EATWELL, Dr John Leonard; s of Harold Jack Eatwell, of Swindon, Wilts, and Mary, *née* Tucker (d 1987); *b* 2 Feb 1945; *Educ* Headlands GS Swindon, Queens' Coll Cambridge (BA, MA), Harvard Univ (AM, PhD); *m* 24 April 1970, Hélène, da of Georges Seppain, of Marly-le-Roi, France; 2 s (Nikolai b 1971, Vladimir b 1973), 1 da (Tatyana b 1978); *Career* teaching fell Harvard Univ 1968-69; Cambridge Univ: res fell Queens' Coll 1969-70, fell and dir of studies in econs Trinity Coll 1970-, univ lectr in econs 1977- (asst lectr 1975-77); visiting prof of econs New Sch for Social Res NY 1980-; econ advsr to Rt Hon Neil Kinnock, MP 1985-; memb Cambridge Constituency Lab Pty; memb: Royal Econ Soc, American Econ Assoc; *Books* An Introduction to Modern Economics (with Joan Robinson 1973), Keynes's Economics and the Theory of Value and Distribution (with Murray Milgate 1983), Whatever Happened to Britain? (1982), The New Palgrave A Dictionary of Economics (with Murray Milgate and Peter Newman 1987); *Recreations* watching rugby football; *Style*— Dr John Eatwell; Trinity Coll, Cambridge CB2 1TQ (☎ 0223 338406)

EAYRS, Gp Capt Douglas Joyce; CB (1955), CBE (1946), DFC (1944); s of William Henry Eayrs (d 1944), of Manton, Oakham, Rutland; *b* 13 July 1908; *Educ* Oakham Sch, RAF Coll Cranwell; *m* 1949, Doreen Arthy, da of late Felix Arthy Scriven, MBE, of Bradford; 2 s, 1 da; *Career* Gp Capt RAF 1944, Australia, Europe, Keyna, CO Central Flying Sch Australia 1941-43, Sr RAF Offr Kenya 1952-54; *Clubs* RAF; *Style*— Gp Capt Douglas Eayrs, CB, CBE, DFC; North Farmcote, Winchcombe, Glos

EBAN, Hon Mrs (Rosemary); *née* Inman; da of 1 and last Baron Inman, PC (d 1979); *b* 26 Feb 1933; *m* 1, 19 Feb 1955 (m dis), Nicholas Milton Kollitsis, MD, FRCS, s of Miltiades Kollitsis, of Kythrea, Cyprus; 1 s, 2 da; m 2, 1982, Dr Raphael Eban, FRCP, FRCR; *Style*— Hon Mrs Eban; Parsonage House, Goosey, Oxon SN7 8PA

EBBISHAM, 2 Baron (UK 1928); Sir Rowland Roberts Blades; 2 Bt (UK 1922), TD; s of 1 Baron Ebbisham, GBE (d 1953, sometime MP (C) Epsom, treasurer Conservative Party and Lord Mayor of London) and Margaret, MBE, OStJ, Officier de la Légion d'Honneur(d 1965), da of Arthur Reiner, of Sutton, Surrey; *b* 3 Sept 1912; *Educ* Winchester, Ch Ch Oxford; *m* 26 Oct 1949, Flavia Mary, yst da of Charles Francis Meade, JP (d 1975) (gs of 3 Earl of Clanwilliam), and Lady Aileen (d 1970), *née* Brodrick, da of 1 Earl of Midleton; 3 da; *Career* served WW II, Lt 98 Surrey & Sussex Yeo Field Regt RA, POW; common councilman City of London Candlewick Ward 1948-83, pres London C of C 1958-61, pres Assoc of Br Chambers of Commerce 1968-70, master Mercers' Co 1963-64, one of HM Lieuts for City of London, chm City Lands Ctee and chief commoner Corpn of London 1967-68; pres Br Importers' Confedn 1978-80; chm: Anglo-Dal plc; dir: Williams Lea plc, vice-pres London Record Soc; memb Euro Trade Ctee BOTB 1973-82; hon tres Br Printing Industs Fedn 1971-81; former Capt Surrey Second Eleven (cricket); Hon DSc The City Univ 1984 Order of Yugoslav Flag with Gold Wreath, Cdr Order of Orange Nassau;; *Style*— The Rt Hon Lord Ebbisham, TD; St Ann's, Church Street, Mere, Wilts BA12 6DS (☎ 0747 860376)

EBDON, Howard Tom; s of Tom Ebdon (d 1931), and Ellen Ebdon (d 1961); *b* 1 June 1919; *m* 22 Oct 1961, Grace, da of William Thomas Bond (d 1951), of Monmouthshire; *Career* with Miny of Agric, surveyor, lectr in valuations and law of dilapidations; memb Nat Art-Collection Fund; associate of Croquet Assoc London, sidesman St Woolos Cathedral Newport Gwent, friend of RA; *Recreations* arts; *Clubs* Royal Overseas, St James London; *Style*— Howard T Ebdon, Esq; Harlyn, 56 Bryngwyn Rd, Newport, Gwent NP9 4JT

EBDON, Thomas John; s of Thomas Dudley Ebdon, of Rustington, W Sussex, and Hilda Minnie Ebdon, *née* Hayward; *b* 3 April 1940; *Educ* Wallington GS, Brixton School of Building (HND); *m* 27 March 1965, Janet Wendy, da of Herbert Noel Cobley (d 1982); 1 s (Robert John b 1965), 1 da (Elizabeth Wendy b 1967); *Career* dep md James Longley & Co Ltd 1987 - (joined 1963, dir 1972), dir Heating & Ventilation Southern Ltd 1974, dir James Longley Hldgs Ltd 1989-; chm Pennthorpe Sch Tst Ltd 1979-, fndr memb St Catherine's Hospice Crawley 1979 (chm 1989-), churchwarden Horsham (Diocese of Chichester) 1974-79; Freeman City of London 1980 memb Worshipful Co of Paviors 1982; *Recreations* cricket, photography, philately, walking; *Clubs* MCC; *Style*— John Ebdon, Esq; James Longley & Co Ltd, East Park, Crawley, West Sussex RH13 6EU (☎ 0293 561212, fax 0293 564564)

EBERLE, Adm Sir James Henry Fuller; GCB (1981, KCB 1979); s of Victor Fuller Eberle (d 1974), of Bristol, and Joyce Mary Eberle; *b* 31 May 1927; *Educ* Clifton Coll, RNC Dartmouth; *m* 1950, Ann Patricia (d 1988), da of E Thompson, of Hong Kong; 1 s, 2 da; *Career* served RN 1941-83, served WW II, Capt 1965, Rear-Adm 1971, asst chief Fleet Support 1972-74, Flag Offr: Sea Training 1974-75, Aircraft Carriers and Amphibious Ships 1975-77; Chief of Fleet Support 1977-79, C-in-C Fleet and Allied C-in-C Channel and E Atlantic 1979-81, C-in-C Naval Home Cmd 1981-82, Flag ADC to HM The Queen 1981-82; dir Royal Inst of Int Affrs 1983-; *Clubs* Farmers'; *Style*— Adm Sir James Eberle, GCB; Roy Inst for International Affairs, Chatham House, 10 St James's Sq, London SW1 (☎ 01 930 2233)

EBERLIN, Richard Harold; s of Capt Albert Edgar Eberlin, MC (d 1977), and Edith Annie Eberlin (d 1965); *b* 15 August 1926; *Educ* Sedbergh, Univ of Nottingham (Dip Arch); *m* 10 May 1952, Christine Russell, da of Dr Edward Russell Trotman (d 1984), of Nottingham; 4 s (David Richard (decd), Jonathan Russell, Michael Anthony, Andrew William); *Career* RAF WWII; princ ptnr Eberlin and Ptnrs; flag offr Trent Valley Sailing Club 1963-65, memb Nottingham Derby and Lincoln Soc of Architects (pres 1967), fndr Royal Yachting Assoc E Mids regn (chm 1968); memb: water recreation ctee of the Sports Cncl (vice-chm 1969); Royal Yachting Assoc Cncl 1971-78; chm: Nat Facilities Ctee Royal Yachting Assoc for England and Wales, Bramcote Conservation Soc; pres Nottingham City Business Club 1972; memb: Nottingham Derby and Lincoln Jt Consultative Bd Craftsmanship Award panel 1972, Magistrates Courts Ctee 1979, Police Ctee 1983; JP 1970; Freeman City of London; ARIBA 1956, FRIBA 1964; *Recreations* sailing, bowls; *Clubs* Naval and Military, Nottingham and Notts United Servs, Trent Valley SC, ICC Salcombe YC, Queen Anne's Bowling; *Style*— Richard Eberlin, Esq; 3 Coll St, Notts

EBERSTEIN, Robert David; s of Douglas Eberstein, of Drill Hall Cottage, Southwold; *b* 12 Feb 1941; *Educ* Wellington; *m* 1968, Rosemary Margaret, da of Charles Capper Hemming, of Great Chesterford; 1 s, 2 da; *Career* fin dir Smith Kline & French Laboratories Ltd 1973-, regnl dir Smith Kline & French Int Co 1979, vice-pres 1980-; FCA; *Style*— Robert Eberstein Esq; Smith Kline & French International Co, Mundells, Welwyn Garden City, Herts (☎ 325111); Hyde House, Firs Drive, Gustardwood, Herts (☎ 0438 832909)

EBERT, Peter; s of Prof Carl Ebert, CBE (d 1980), of Calif, USA, and Lucie Oppenheim; *b* 6 April 1918; *Educ* Salem Sch Germany, Gordonstoun; *m* 1, 1944, Kathleen Havinden; 2 da; m 2, 1951, Silvia Ashmole; 5 s, 3 da; *Career* theatre dir; dir of productions Scottish Opera 1964-76, Opera Sch Toronto Univ 1967-68; intendant: theatres in Augsburg 1968-73, Bielefeld 1973-75, Wiesbaden 1975-77; gen admin Scottish Opera 1977-80; Hon Doctor of Music St Andrew's Univ 1979; *Style*— Peter Ebert, Esq; Ades House, Chailey, E Sussex, BN8 4HP (☎ 082 572 2441)

EBERTS, John David (Jake); s of Edmond Howard Eberts (d 1977), and Elizabeth Evelyn, *née* MacDougall; *b* 10 July 1941; *Educ* Bishops Coll Sch Quebec, McGill Univ (BChemE), Harvard Business Sch; *m* 1968, Fiona Louise, da of John Baillie Hamilton Leckie (d 1978); 2 s (Alexander b 1973, David b 1975), 1 da (Lindsay b 1979); *Career* film financier and prodr: Oppenheimer & Co Ltd 1972-76, Goldcrest Films Ltd 1976-83, Embassy Communications Ltd 1984-85, Goldcrest Films and TV Ltd 1985-87, Allied Film makers 1985-; *Recreations* tennis, ski-ing, photography; *Clubs* Queens; *Style*— Jake Eberts, Esq; 107 Oakwood Ct, London W14 (☎ 01 602 2919); Katevale Productions Ltd, 8 Queen St, London W1 (☎ 01 493 3362, fax 499 4120)

EBRAHIM, Sir (Mahomed) Currimbhoy; 4 Bt (UK 1910), of Bombay; s of Sir (Huseinali) Currimbhoy Ebrahim, 3 Bt (d 1952); *b* 24 June 1935; *m* 15 Nov 1958, Dur-e-Mariam, da of Minuchehir Ahmud Nurudin Ahmed Ghulam Ally Nana, of Karachi; 3 s, 1 da; *Heir* s, Zulfiqar Ali Currimbhoy Ebrahim; *Career* memb Standing Council of Baronetage; *Style*— Sir Currimbhoy Ebrahim, Bt; c/o Home Office, St Annes Gate, London SW1

EBRAHIM, Zulfiqar Ali Currimbhoy; s and h of Sir Currimbhoy Ebrahim, 4 Bt; *b* 5 August 1960; *Style*— Zulfiqar Currimbhoy Ebrahim, Esq

EBRINGTON, Viscount; Charles Hugh Richard Fortescue; s (by 1 m) and h of 7 Earl Fortescue; *b* 10 May 1951; *Educ* Eton; *m* 1974, Julia, er da of Air Cdre J A Sowrey; 3 da (Hon Alice Penelope b 8 June 1978, Hon Kate Eleanor b 25 Oct 1979, Hon Lucy Beatrice b 29 April 1983); *Style*— Viscount Ebrington; Ebrington Manor, Chipping Campden, Glos

EBSWORTH, Her Hon Judge; Ann Marian; da of Arthur Ebsworth, OBE, BEM, RM (ret), and late Hilda Mary Ebsworth; *b* 1937; *Educ* London Univ; *Career* barrister Gray's Inn 1962, Recorder Crown Court 1978-83, circuit judge (Northern Circuit) 1983-; *Style*— Her Hon Judge Ebsworth; 33 Warren Drive, Wallasey, Cheshire

EBURNE, Sir Sidney Alfred William; MC (1944); s of Alfred Edmund Eburne, and Ellen Francis Eburne; *b* 26 Nov 1918; *Educ* Downhills Sch; *m* 1942, Phoebe Freda, *née* Beeton Dilley; 1 s, 1 da; *Career* served WW II Capt RA; dir: Morgan Grenfell 1968-75 (joined 1946), Morgan Grenfell Hldgs 1971-75, Abbey Capital Hldgs Ltd; md Crown Agents 1976 (dir finance 1975), sr crown agent and chm Crown Agents for Overseas Govts and Administrations 1978-83; dir Peachey Property Corpn plc 1983-88; govr Peabody Tst 1983; kt 1982; *Clubs* Carlton; *Style*— Sir Sidney Eburne, MC; Notts Farm, Eridge, E Sussex TN3 9LJ

EBURY, Denise, Baroness; Hon Denise Margaret; *née* Yarde-Buller; 2 da of late 3 Baron Churston, MVO, OBE (d 1930); *b* 24 Oct 1916; *m* 21 Nov 1941 (m dis 1954), as his 2 w, 5 Baron Ebury (d 1957); 2 s (Hon William Grosvenor, Hon Richard Grosvenor), 2 da (Hon Mrs Cross, Hon Ms Vane Percy); *Style*— Denise, Lady Ebury; Barton's Lodge, Eversholt, Bletchley, Bucks

EBURY, 6 Baron (UK 1857); Francis Egerton Grosvenor; s of 5 Baron Ebury, DSO (d 1957, whose ggf, 1 Baron, was yr bro of 2 Marquess of Westminster and 2 Earl of Wilton; thus Lord Ebury is hp to 7 Earl of Wilton and ultimately, since Lord Wilton is himself hp to all the 6 Duke of Westminster's titles except the Dukedom, might inherit those honours too), by his 1 w, Anne, da of Herbert Acland-Troyte, MC (gn of Sir Thomas Acland, 10 Bt); *b* 8 Feb 1934; *Educ* Eton; *m* 1, 10 Dec 1957 (m dis 1962), Gillian Elfrida Astley, o da of Martin Soames and Myra Drummond, niece of 16 Earl of Perth; 1 s; m 2, 8 March 1963 (m dis 1973), Kyra, o da of L L Aslin; m 3, 1974, Suzanne, da of Graham Suckling, of NZ; 1 da (Hon Georgina Lucy b 1973); *Heir* s, Hon Julian Grosvenor; *Recreations* ornithology; *Clubs* Melbourne, Melbourne Savage; *Style*— The Rt Hon Lord Ebury; 8B Branksome Tower, 3 Tregunter Path, Hong Kong

EBURY, Dowager Baroness; Sheila Winifred; *née* Dashfield; da of Arthur Edward Dashfield, of Oxford; *b* 28 April 1925; *m* 1, - Anker; m 2, 12 Oct 1954, as his 3 w, 5 Baron Ebury (d 1957); *Style*— Rt Hon Dowager Lady Ebury; 37 Linkside Ave, Oxford OX2 8JE

ECCLES, Alexander Herbert Lindsey; s of Herbert Eccles, JP, FRS (d 1928); *b* 14 May 1908; *Educ* Repton; *m* 1965, Doris Ann, da of Edwin Albert Kitt, company director (d 1965); *Career* served WW II, Lt, Suffolk Yeomanry, served Normandy 1944; farmer; High Sheriff West Glamorgan 1981-82; *Recreations* shooting, fishing; *Clubs* Bristol Channel Yacht, British Racing Drivers' (drove Bugattis 1931-36); *Style*— Alexander Eccles, Esq; Bryn Cottage, Penmaen, Gower, Glamorgan SA3 2HQ (☎ 044 125 233)

ECCLES, 1 Viscount (UK 1964); David McAdam Eccles; CH (1984), KCVO (1953), PC (1951); also 1 Baron Eccles (UK 1962); s of William McAdam Eccles, FRCS (d 1946), and Anna Coralie, *née* Anstie (d 1930); *b* 18 Sept 1904; *Educ* Winchester, New Coll Oxford; *m* 1, 10 Oct 1928, Hon Sybil Frances Dawson (d 1977), eldest da of 1 & last Viscount Dawson of Penn, GCVO, KCB, KCMG, PC (d 1945); 2 s, 1 da; m 2, 26 Sept 1984, Mary, widow of Donald Hyde, of Four Oaks Farm, Somerville, NJ, USA; *Heir* s, Hon John Dawson Eccles CBE; *Career* sits as Conservative in House of Lords; MP (C) Chippenham Wilts 1943-62, Min of Works 1951-54, of Education 1954-57, pres Bd of Trade 1957-59, min of educn 1956-62, chm of Tstees Br Museum 1966-70; Paymaster Gen 1970-73, chm Br Library Bd 1973-78, pres World Crafts Cncl 1974-78; *Style*— The Rt Hon Viscount Eccles, CH, KCVO, PC; Dean Farm, Chute, nr Andover, Hants (☎ Chute Standen 026 470 210); 6 Barton St, SW1 (☎ 01 222 1387)

ECCLES, Jack Fleming; CBE (1980); s of Thomas Eccles (d 1962), of Manchester; *b* 9 Feb 1922; *Educ* Chorlton HS Manchester, Manchester Univ (BA) (COM); *m* 24 May 1952, Hon Milba Hartley, *qv*; 1 s, 1 da; *Career* served Burma in ranks 1944-45; ret trade union official 1948-86, GMBATU, chm and pres TUC 1984-85; dir Remploy Ltd,; memb Eng Industl Estates Corpn 1976-, chm Plastics Processing Indust Trg Bd 1982-88, non exec dir Br Steel Corpn (appointed for 3 years for 1986);; *Recreations* cine-photography; *Style*— Jack Eccles, Esq, CBE; Terange, 11 Sutton Rd, Alderley Edge, Ches SK9 7RB

ECCLES, Prof Sir John Carew; s of William James Eccles, of Melbourne, and Mary Eccles; *b* 27 Jan 1903; *Educ* Melbourne Univ, Magdalen Coll Oxford; *m* 1, 1928 (m dis 1968), Irene Frances, da of Herbert Miller, of Motueka, NZ; 4 s, 5 da; m 2, 1968, Helena Táboříková; *Career* dir Kanematsu Institute Sydney Hosp 1937-43, Prof of Physiology Otago U NZ 1944-51, prof of physiology ANU Canberra 1951-66, Chicago Research Institute 1966-68, prof of neurobiology State Univ Buffalo New York 1968-75, emeritus 1975-; Baly Medal RCP 1961, Royal Medal Royal Society 1962,

Cothenius Medal Deutsche Akademie der Naturforscher Leopoldina 1963, Nobel Prize for Medicine (jointly) 1963; FRS, FAA, FRACP; kt 1958; *Publications include* Physiology of Nerve Cells (1957), Physiology of Synapses (1964), The Inhibitory Pathways of the Central Nervous System (1969), Facing Reality (1970), The Understanding of the Brain (1973), The Self and its Brain (jt-author; 1977), The Human Mystery (1979), The Human Psyche (1980), The Wonder of Being Human (jt-author 1984), Evolution of the Brain: Creation of the Self (1989); *Style*— Prof Sir John Eccles; Ca' a la Gra', CH 6646 Contra (Locarno), Ticino, Switzerland (☎ 093 67 2931)

ECCLES, Hon John Dawson; CBE (1985); s and h of 1 Viscount Eccles, CH, KCVO, PC, and his 1 w Hon Sybil Frances Dawson (d 1977), da of 1 Viscount Dawson of Penn; *b* 20 April 1931; *Educ* Winchester, Magdalen Coll Oxford (BA); *m* 29 Jan 1955, Diana Catherine, 2 da of Raymond Wilson Sturge, of Ashmore, nr Salisbury; 1 s, 3 da; *Career* Capt TA; Head Wrightson & Co Ltd 1955-77; dir: Glynwed Int plc 1972-, Investors in Industry plc 1974-88, Davy Int plc 1977-81; chm Chamberlin & Hill plc 1982-; memb Monopolies & Mergers Cmmn 1976-85 (dep chm 1981-85); memb Cwlth Devpt Corpn 1982-85, gen mangr 1985-; chm Bd of Tstees Royal Botanic Gdns Kew 1983-; chm The Georgian Theatre Royal Richmond Yorks; *Recreations* gardening, theatre; *Clubs* Brooks's; *Style*— Hon John Eccles, CBE; Moulton Hall, Richmond, Yorks (☎ 0325 77 227); 6 Barton Street, London SW1P 3NG (☎ 01 222 7559)

ECCLES, Hon Mrs (Milba Hartley); da of Baron Williamson (Life Peer, d 1983), and Hilda, *née* Hartley (d 1988); *b* 19 June 1926; *m* 24 May 1952, Jack Fleming Eccles, CBE, *qv*; 1 s, 1 da; *Style*— The Hon Mrs Eccles; Terange, 11 Sutton Rd, Alderley Edge, Cheshire SK9 7RB

ECCLES, Brig Ronald; DSO (1972); s of Rowland Eccles (d 1976), and Penelope May Kerr Sinnatt, *née* Thom (d 1975); *b* 23 August 1928; *Educ* Barnard Castle Sch, RMA Sandhurst; *m* 25 July 1953, Glenys Mary Walker, da of Gareth Walton Budden (d 1959); 2 da (Sarah b 1955, Karen b 1957); *Career* York and Lancaster Regt 1948, seconded Parachute Regt 1952-54, cmd 1 Green Howards 1969-72, def advsr New Delhi 1980-82, Col York and Lancaster Regt 1979-87; Clerk to Worshipful Co of Fruiterers 1986-88; *Clubs* Army and Navy; *Style*— Brig Ronald Eccles, DSO

ECCLES, Hon Simon Dawson; yr s of 1 Viscount Eccles; *b* 11 Sept 1934; *Educ* Repton; *m* 17 Oct 1961 (m dis 1986), Sheelin Lorraine; 1 s, 1 da; *Career* Capt Royal Fusiliers, dir Kleinwort Benson Inc (London); *Recreations* tobogganing, music; *Style*— Hon Simon Eccles; 27 Chestnut Street, Boston, Massachusetts 02108, USA

ECCLES-WILLIAMS, Hilary a'Beckett; CBE (1970); s of The Rev Cyril Archibald Eccles-Williams (d 1952), of Summer Fields, nr Oxford, and Hermione a'Beckett, *née* Terrell (d 1984); *b* 5 Oct 1917; *Educ* Eton, Brasenose Coll Oxford (MA); *m* 21 Sept 1943, Jeanne Marjorie, da of W J Goodwin, of 36 St Bernard's Rd, Solihull, W Midlands; 2 s (Simon b 1955, Mark b 1959), 4 da (Virginia b 1946, Tamare b 1947, Sherry b 1949, Sophie b 1963); *Career* served WWII Maj RA 1939-45, served Dunkirk and Normandy; consul: Cuba 1953-61, Nicaragua 1951-59, Bolivia 1965-82, Costa Rica 1964-; chm and dir various cos; ldr govt trade missions Czechoslovakia and Canada 1965; chm: Br Export Houses Assoc 1958-60, Br Heart Fndn Midland Ctee 1973-76, Asian Christian Colls Assoc 1966-70, Guardians Birmingham Assay Off 1979-88, Birmingham Cons Assoc 1976-79 (pres 1979-84), W Midlands Met Ctee of Cons Party 1980-86, Latin American Forum Cons For and Overseas Cncl 1985-88, Golden Jubilee Appeal Ctee Queen Elizabeth Hosp Birmingham 1987-89; pres: Birmingham C of C 1965-66, Assoc of Br Cs of C 1970-72, Birmingham Consular Assoc 1973-74, Birmingham E Euro Constituency 1984-, Sparkbrook constituency Cons Assoc 1988-; vice pres W Midlands Cons Cncl 1985-, memb Nat Union Exec Ctee Cons Pty 1975-85, gen cmmr Income tax 1966-70, govr Birmingham Univ 1967-; Hon Capt Bolivian Navy 1964-; Freeman City of London; *Recreations* golf, walking; *Clubs* N Warwickshire GC; *Style*— Hilary Eccles-Williams, Esq, CBE; 36 St Bernard's Road, Solihull, W Midlands B92 7BB

ECCLESTON, Harry Norman; OBE (1979); s of Harry Norman Eccleston (d 1971), of Coseley Staffs, and Kate, *née* Pritchard (d 1978); *b* 21 Jan 1923; *Educ* Sch of Art Bilston, Coll of Art Birmingham (Dip Painting, Art Teachers Dip), RCA Engraving Sch; *m* 5 Aug 1948, Betty Doreen, da of Wilfrid Gripton (d 1954), of Bilston Staffs; 2 da (Judith Elizabeth, Jennifer Margaret); *Career* RN 1942-46, temp cmmn RNVR 1943; artist, lectr in illustration and printmaking SE Essex Tech Coll 1952-58, artist designer Bank of England Printing Works 1958-83 (designer of current series of banknotes with historical portraits £1 Newton, £5 Wellington, £10 Nightingale, £20 Shakespeare, £50 Wren), conslt bank of Eng Printing Works 1983-86; exhibited prints and watercolours home and abroad 1948-; ARE 1948, RE 1961 (pres 1975), RWS 1975, memb Art Workers Guild 1984, FRSA 1972; *Clubs* Arts; *Style*— Harry Eccleston, Esq, OBE; 110 Priory Rd, Harold Hill, Romford, Essex RM3 9AU (☎ 04023 40275)

ECCLESTON, Simon Antony Sudell; JP (1977); s of James Thomas Eccleston, of Shrops, and Kathleen Mary, *née* Cryer (d 1964); *b* 4 April 1944; *Educ* Denstone Coll Staffs; *m* 4 Oct 1967, Angela Penelope Gail, da of Noel Harrison (d 1988), of Wolverhampton; 2 s (Piers b 1971, Crispin b 1982), 2 da (Cressida b 1974, Candida b 1981); *Career* md Conveyer Systems Ltd; pres Walsall Chamber of Commerce & Indust 1986-87, exec memb Staf and Shrops Magistrates Assoc; memb Wolverhampton Health Authy 1987-, CBI Cncls (regnl and small firms); chm Cons Assoc branch 1971-79 and 1980; memb Staffs Shrops Euro Cons Exec, S Staffs Cons Assoc Exec 1972-, memb PCC; FInstD; *Recreations* trout fishing, shooting, riding, ocean sailing, landscape gardening, squash; *Style*— Simon Eccleston, Esq, JP; chatwell Ct, Great Chatwell, Shrops; Conveyor Systems Ltd, Kings Hill, Wednesbury, W Mids (☎ 021 526 4971)

ECHENIQUE, Dr Marcial Hernan; s of Marcial Echenique, of Santiago, Chile, and Rosa *née* Talavera; *b* 23 Feb 1943; *Educ* Catholic Univ Santiago Chile, Barcelona Univ Spain (Dip Arch, D Arch), Cambridge Univ (MA); *m* 23 Nov 1963, Maria Louisa, da of Ernesto Holzmann (d 1978), of Santiago, Chile; 2 s (Marcial Antonio b 16 July 1964, Martin Jose b 25 Nov 1965), 1 da (Alejandra b 1 Aug 1969); *Career* asst lectr in urbanism Univ of Barcelona Spain 1963-65, reader in architecture and urban studies Cambridge Univ 1980- (lectr in architecture 1970-80), md Marcial Echenique & ptnr Ltd (architectural and planning conslts) 1985-, memb bd Banco de Bilbao y Vizcaya Spain 1988; memb: Cinc Soc Huntingdon & Godmanchester 1979, RSA 1986; ARCUK 1988; *Books* Urban Development Models (jtly 1975), Modelos de la Estructura Espacial Urbana (1975), La Estructura Del Espacio Urbano (jtly 1975); *Recreations* music; *Style*— Dr Marcial Echenique; Farm Hall, Godmanchester, Cambs; 49-51 High St, Trumpington, Cambridge (☎ 0223 840 704, fax 0223 840 84, telex 817 977 MEPOLA G)

ECHLIN, Sir Norman David Fenton; 10 Bt (I 1721); s of Sir John Frederick, 9 Bt (d 1932); *b* 1 Dec 1925; *Educ* Masonic Boys' Sch Clonskeagh Co Dublin; *m* 8 Dec 1953, Mary Christine, o da of John Arthur, of Oswestry, Salop; *Style*— Sir Norman Echlin Bt; Nartopa, Marina Av, Appley, Ryde, Isle of Wight

ECKERSLEY, Sir Donald Payze; OBE (1977), JP (1982); s of Walter Roland Eckersley (d 1979), and Ada Gladys Moss; *b* 1 Nov 1922; *Educ* Muresk Agricultural Coll WA; *m* 1949, Marjorie Rae, da of Raymond Arthur Clarke (d 1959), of Roelands, WA; 1 s, 2 da; *Career* farmer; inaugural pres Nat Farmers' Fedn of Aust 1979-81, Man of the Year in Agriculture 1979, dir Chamberlain John Deere 1979-82, memb Univ Senate WA 1981-82, chm WA Artificial Breeding Bd 1982; kt 1981; *see Debrett's Handbook of Australia and New Zealand for further details*; *Recreations* golf, fishing; *Style*— Sir Donald Eckersley, OBE, JP; Korijedale, Harvey, WA 6220, Australia (☎ 097 291472)

ECKERSLEY, Tobias William Hammersley (Toby); MBE (1989); s of Timothy Huxley Eckersley (d 1980), and Penelope Anne, *née* Hammersley; *b* 22 July 1941; *Educ* Charterhouse, St John's Coll Oxford (MA), LSE (MSc); *Career* HM Foreign Serv 1964-67, with IMF 1967-71, Williams & Glyn's Bank 1971-75, ICI 1976-; fndr and sec London Assoc for Saving Homes 1974-77, parly candidate (C) Peckham 1983, chm Dulwich Cons Assoc 1988-, memb Cons Pty Policy Gp for London 1983-86; London Borough of Southwark: ldr of opposition 1979-85, cncllr 1977-86, memb ministerial advsy panel on Abolition of GLC and Met Counties 1984-86; *Recreations* tree cultivation; *Style*— Tobias Eckersley, Esq, MBE; Imperial Chemical Indust plc, Millbank, London SW1 (☎ 01 798 5118)

ECKERSLEY-MASLIN, Rear Adm David Michael; CB (1984); eldest s of Cdr C E Eckersley-Maslin, OBE, RN, of Tasmania, and Mrs L M Lightfoot, of Bedford; *b* 27 Sept 1929,Karachi;; *Educ* RNC Dartmouth; *m* 1955, Shirley Ann, da of late Capt H A Martin, DSC, RN; 1 s, 1 da; *Career* Capt: HMS Eastbourne 1966-68, HMS Euryalus 1971-72, HMS Fife 1975, HMS Blake 1976, RCDS 1977; dir Naval Operational Requirements 1978-80, flag offr Sea Trg 1980-82, asst chief Naval Staff (Falklands) April 1982, Def Staff (Signals) July 1982, Def Staff (CIS) 1983-84; asst dir: Cmd Control and Communications Systems, Int Mil Staff NATO HQ Brussels 1984-86; ret; dir gen NATO Communications and Informations Systems Agency Brussels 1986-; *Recreations* cricket, tennis, squash, golf; *Clubs* MCC, Royal Cwlth Soc, RN Cricket; *Style*— Rear Adm David Eckersley-Maslin, CB; Dunningwell Hall Court, Shedfield, Southampton, Hants (☎ 0329 832350, office Brussels 246 8267)

ECROYD, (Edward) Peter; s of William Edward Bedingfeld Ecroyd (d 1951) of Cumberland, and Iris Bloxsone, *née* Day; *b* 24 Nov 1932; *Educ* Harrow, Royal Agric Coll; *m* 25 April 1957, Felicity Anne Graham, da of Frederick Graham Roberts, OBE (d 1981); 1 s (Edward Charles b 1959), 2 da (Emma Lucinda b 1961, Susanna Victoria b 1963); *Career* landowner; High Sheriff of Cumbria 1984-85; memb Regnl Fisheries Ctee N W Water Authy 1974, chm: Eden & District Fisheries Ctee 1974-80, N Area Fisheries Ctee 1980-83, Eden and District Fisheries Assoc 1970-83, (pres 1984); vice chm Salmon and Trout Assoc 1988- (memb cncl 1970-), memb Salmon Advsy Ctee 1987-, fndr and chm Eden Owners Assoc 1986-, chm Cumberland branch County Landowners Assoc 1988-; *Recreations* fishing, shooting; *Style*— Peter Ecroyd, Esq; Low House, Armathwaite, Carlisle, Cumbria CA4 9ST (☎ 06992 242)

EDDEN, Alan John; CMG (1957); s of Thomas Frederick Edden (d 1953), of Edmonton, and Nellie, *née* Shipway; *b* 2 Dec 1912; *Educ* Latymer Sch Edmonton, Gonville and Caius Coll Cambridge; *m* 1939, Pauline Johanna Agnes, da of Lt-Col Johan W Klay (d 1942), of The Hague; 1 s; *Career* joined Consular Serv 1935-; cnsllr FO 1954-58, Beirut 1958-62, consul-gen Durban 1962-66; ambassador: Cameroon, Central African Republic, Gabon and Chad 1966-70, Equatorial Guinea 1969-70, Lebanon 1970-71; *Recreations* music; *Style*— Alan Edden, Esq, CMG; 4 Ridgewood, 328 Ridge Rd, Berea, 4001 Durban, S Africa

EDDEN, Vice Adm Sir (William) Kaye; KBE (1960, OBE 1944), CB (1956), DL (West Sussex 1977); s of Maj Harold William Edden (d 1927), of The Red House, Aldermaston, Berks, and Elizabeth Rodger Wilkes Neilson; *b* 27 Feb 1905; *Educ* RNC Osborne, RNC Dartmouth; *m* 17 April 1936, Isobel Sybil (d 1970), da of Alfred Pitman, and gda of Sir Isaac Pitman; 1 s; *Career* joined RN 1918, served WW II, Capt 1944, Cmdt Joint Services Staff Coll 1953-56, Rear Adm 1954, Flag Offr 2-in-C Far East Station 1956-57, Vice Adm 1957, Adm cmdg Reserves 1958-60, ret 1960; *Clubs* Army and Navy; *Style*— Vice Adm Sir Kaye Edden, KBE, CB, DL; Littlecroft, Old Bosham, Chichester, West Sussex PO18 8LR (☎ 0243 573119)

EDDISON, Roger Tatham; s of Edwin Eddison (d 1917), of Leeds, and Hilda Muriel, *née* Leadam (d 1963); *b* 16 Sept 1916; *Educ* Charterhouse, Cambridge Univ (MA); *m* 10 May 1941, Rosemary Christine, da of Cdr Charles B Land, RN (d 1947); 2 s (Charles b 1942, Hugh b 1949), 1 da (Sally b 1944); *Career* Maj RA 1939-46, Hd of Operational Res, BISRA 1948-55, NAAFI 1955-61; pres (fndr memb and Silver Medallist) of Operational Res Soc 1966-67; dir Science in General Mgmnt Ltd, Novy Eddison & Ptnrs 1970, M Harland & Son Ltd 1968-86; memb Cncl Metra Int Paris 1961-70, Tavistock Inst Human Relations; visiting prof Univ of Sussex 1968-74; *Clubs* Athenaeum; *Style*— Roger T Eddison, Esq; Horstedpond Farm, Uckfield TN22 5TR (☎ 0825 2636); Novy Eddison & Ptnrs, 1 Frayslea, Uxbridge UB8 2AT (☎ 0895 57791)

EDE, Jeffery Raymond; CB (1978); s of Richard Arthur Ede (d 1927), and Lily, *née* Jeffery (d 1963); *b* 10 Mar 1918; *Educ* Plymouth Coll, King's Coll Cambridge (MA); *m* 1944, Mercy, da of Arthur Radford Sholl (d 1956); 1 s (Martyn), 1 da (Katharine); *Career* served WWII Intelligence Corps in W Europe and ME (despatches), GSO 2 HQ 8 Corps Dist BAOR 1945-46; Pub Record Off: asst keeper 1947-59, princ asst keeper 1960-66, dep keeper 1966-69, keeper 1970-78; lectr Archives Admin Sch of Librarianship and Archives UC London 1956-61, UNESCO conslt Tanzania 1963-64; chm Br Academy Ctee on Oriental Documents 1972-76, vice pres Int Cncl on Archives 1976-78, pres Soc of Archivists 1974-77; Freeman: City of London, Worshipful Co of Goldsmiths'; Hon Memb L'Institut Grand Ducal de Luxembourg; FRHistS; *Recreations* horticulture, countryside; *Style*— Jeffery Ede, Esq, CB; Palfreys, Drayton, Langport, Somerset TA10 0J2 (☎ 0458 251314)

EDE, (Robert) John; s of Walter John Ede (d 1978), and Gladys Ellizabeth, *née* Barber (d 1987); *b* 8 Sept 1932; *Educ* Dorking GS, Open Univ (BA); *Career* dist cmmr Nat Savings Ctee 1967-77, chm Br Homeopathic Assoc 1975-; chm Surrey Co Assoc of Parish and Town Cncls 1984-87; Freeman City of London; *Recreations* bridge; *Clubs*

Royal Overseas League; *Style*— John Ede, Esq; Strood Copse, Capel, Dorking, Surrey RH5 5HE

EDELL, Stephen Bristow; s of Ivan James Edell (d 1958), and Hilda Pamela Edell (d 1976); *b* 1 Dec 1932; *Educ* Uppingham London (LLB); *m* 20 Sept 1958, Shirley, da of Leslie Ross Collins (d 1984); 2 s (Philip b 1969, Nicholas b 1973), 1 da (Theresa b 1964); *Career* Nat Serv RA (2nd Lieut) 1951-53; qual slr 1958, ptnr Knapp-Fishers 1959-73, Law Commnr 1975-83, ptnr Crossman Block & Keith 1984-87; Bldg Soc Ombudsman 1987-; *Books* Inside Information on The Family and The Law (1969), The Family's Guide To The Law (1974); *Recreations* family life, music, opera, theatre, golf, tennis; *Clubs* City Livery; *Style*— Stephen B Edell, Esq; Office of the Building Societies Ombudsman, Grosvenor Gardens House, 31-37 Grosvenor Gardens, London SW1X 7AW (☎ 01 931 0044)

EDELMAN, Colin Neil; s of Gerald Bertram Edelman (d 1955), and Lynn Queenie, *née* Tropp; *b* 2 Mar 1954; *Educ* Haberdashers' Aske's, Clare Coll Cambridge (MA); *m* 26 Oct 1978, Jacqueline Claire, da of Hardy Wolfgang Seidel, of London; 1 s (James Simon b 14 Jan 1983), 1 da (Rachel Laura b 17 Sept 1981); *Career* called to the Bar Middle Temple 1977, MO Circuit; *Recreations* badminton, skiing; *Style*— Colin Edelman, Esq; Devereux Chambers, Devereux Ct, London WC2R 3JJ (☎ 01 353 7534, fax 01 353 1724)

EDELMAN, David Laurence; s of Gerald Edelman (d 1954), and Lynn, *née* Tropp, JP; *b* 7 April 1948; *Educ* Haberdashers Askes, Leeds Univ (BCom); *m* 4 July 1971, Sandra Marice, da of Ephraim Freeman; 1 s (Jonathan b 1984), 2 da (Emma b 1976 (d 1979), Tanya b 1981); *Career* tax ptnr Edelman & Co (CAs) 1976-81, dir City Tst Ltd (bankers) 1981-86, jt md Moorfield Estates plc 1983-89; chm London Borough of Hillingdon Wishing Well Appeal for Great Ormond St Hosp 1987-89; FCA 1972; *Recreations* skiing, art, music; *Style*— David Edelman, Esq; 34 Links Way, Northwood, Middx HA6 2XB; Moorfield Estates plc, Moorfield House, The Avenue, Bushey, Herts WD2 2LL, (☎ 0923 227118, fax 0923 56230, car phone 0836 274964, telex 295030)

EDELMAN, Jack; CBE (1987); s of Samuel Edelman (d 1971), and Netta, *née* Smith; *b* 8 May 1927; *Educ* Sir George Monoux GS, Imperial Coll London (BSc), Univ of Sheffield (PhD), Univ of London (DSc); *m* 15 Aug 1958, Joyce Dorothy; 2 s (Alex b 1959, Daniel b 1961), 1 step s (Simon b 1954), 1 step da (Jane b 1950); *Career* reader in enzymology Imp Coll London 1956-64, prof of botany London Univ 1964-73, visiting prof Univs of Nottingham and London 1975-83; dir Ranks Hovis McDougall plc 1982-88, chm Marlow Foods; chm Br Industl Biological Res Assoc 1978-83, govr The Latymer Fndn 1983-, vice-pres Inst of Biology 1984-86 (chm nutrition ctee), tstee Rank Prize Funds 1984-; cncl memb: Queen Elizabeth Coll London 1979-85, industl consultative ctee on biotechnology DTI 1983-, Univ of Kent at Canterbury 1983, King's Coll London 1985-; memb of many industl and govt ctees; author of various text books and children's science books; *Clubs* Athenaeum; *Style*— Dr Jack Edelman, CBE; Marlow Foods, 9 Station Rd, Marlow, Bucks SL7 1NG (☎ 0628 890 850, fax 0628 890 549)

EDELMAN, Keith Graeme; *b* 10 June 1950; *Educ* Haberdashers Askes, Elstree, Inst of Sci and Technol Univ of Manchester (BSc); *m* 29 June 1974, Susan Margaret; 2 s (Daniel b 3 April 1978, Nicholas b 1 July 1980); *Career* dir Ladbroke Gp plc 1986-, chm Texas Homecare; *Recreations* skiing, tennis, collecting antiques, cooking; *Style*— Keith Edelman, Esq; 4 Heathside Close, Moor Park, Northwood, Middlesex HA6 2EQ; Ladbroke Group plc, 87 Wimpole St, London WIM 7DB (☎ 01 935 2853 fax 01 935 3520, telex 291 268)

EDELSHAIN, Martin Bernard; s of Norman Israel Edelshain, of Israel, and Monna Annette Carlish; *b* 18 Dec 1948; *Educ* Clifton Coll, Jesus Coll Cambridge (BA); *m* 1984, Yasuko Okada, da of Yukitane Okada, of Japan; 1 s (Benjamin b 1986), 1 da (Deborah b 1987); *Career* dir: S G Warburg & Co Ltd 1983-86, S G Warburg, Akroyd, Rowe & Pitman, Mullens Securities Ltd 1986-; *Recreations* cricket, skiing; *Clubs* MCC; *Style*— Martin B Edelshain, Esq; 8 Wellington Place, London NW8 9JA (☎ 01 289 8733); 1 Finsbury Avenue, London EC2M 2PA (☎ 01 280 2748, telex 937011)

EDEN, Hon Andrew Francis; s of 7 Baron Henley; *b* 4 Sept 1955; *Educ* Dragon Sch Oxford, Clifton Coll Bristol; *Style*— Hon Andrew Eden; Laundry Cottage, Watford, Northampton

EDEN, Hon Jack - John Edward Morton; s of Baron Eden of Winton (Life Peer); *b* 26 Jan 1966; *Style*— Hon Jack Eden

EDEN, John Forbes; s of late Thomas Eden, of 57 Hillpark Ave, Edinburgh, and Eleanor Dundas, *née* Harford; *b* 9 Mar 1929; *Educ* St Peter's Coll Adelaide Australia, St John's Coll Cambridge (MA); *m* 9 May 1959, Mary Caroline, da of Denis Piercy Prowse, of Portishead, Avon (d 1977); 1 s (Charles b 1963), 3 da (Caroline (Mrs Green) b 1960, Alison (Mrs Stacey) b 1962, Suzanne b 1965); *Career* 2Lt RA 1951-52, TA 1952-61, Maj OC Gloucester volunteer Artillery 1959-60; admitted slr 1956, sr ptnr Bevan Ashford Exeter; pres: Assoc SW Law Socs 1968-69, Devon and Exeter Incorporated Law Soc 1988-89; inspr DTI 1987-89; clerk Dean and Chapter Exeter 1966-, memb of Univ of Exeter 1968-, registrar Archdeaconry Exeter 1968-87, dep registrar High Ct and Co Ct 1977-, tstee Exeter Cathedral Preservation Tst 1988-; memb Law Soc 1956; *Recreations* music, badminton; *Style*— John Eden, Esq; 25 West Ave, Exeter, Devon EX4 4SD (☎ 0392 559 55); 21 Northernhay St, Exeter, Devon EX4 3ER (☎ 0392 411 111)

EDEN, Prof Richard John; OBE (1978); s of James Arthur Eden and Dora M Eden; *b* 2 July 1922; *Educ* Hertford GS, Peterhouse Cambridge; *m* 1949, Mrs Elsie Jane Greaves, da of late Herbert Edwards; 1 s, 1 da and 1 step da; *Career* served WW II, Capt REME Airborne Forces Europe and India; reader in Theoretical Physics 1964-; head Energy Research Group at Cavendish Lab Cambridge Univ; visiting prof/scientist at various universities in USA and Europe 1954-73; prof of energy Cambridge Univ 1983-; *Recreations* reading and painting; *Clubs* Army and Navy; *Style*— Prof Richard Eden, OBE; 6 Wootton Way, Cambridge, CB3 9LX

EDEN, Hon Robert Frederick Calvert; s (by 1 m) and h to baronetcies of Baron Eden of Winton, 9 and 7 Bt, PC; *b* 30 April 1964; *Style*— Hon Robert Eden

EDEN, Hon Robert Ian Burnard; s and h of 9 Baron Auckland; *b* 25 July 1962; *Educ* Blundells Sch Tiverton; *m* May 1986, Geraldine, of Dublin; *Style*— Hon Robert Eden; c/o Tudor Rose House, 30 Links Rd, Ashtead, Surrey KT21 2HF

EDEN, Hon Roger Quentin Eden; yr s of 6 Baron Henley (d 1962), and Lady Dorothy Georgiana Howard (d 1968), da of 9 Earl of Carlisle; *b* 18 June 1922; *Educ* Rugby; *m* 26 June 1946, Carys Wynne, da of Ifi Hywi Dyfed Davies (d 1973), of Camwy, Penrhyndeudraeth, Gwynedd; 2 s (Morton, Elvyn), 2 da (Carol, Jane); *Career* Flying Offr RAF 1944; Shell Int Petroleum 1950-81 (head of automotive fuels devpt 1975-80); CEng, MRAeS; *Style*— Hon Roger Eden; 29A Hamilton Terrace, St John's Wood, London NW8 9RE; Askerton Castle, Brampton, Cumbria

EDEN, Hon Ronald John; yr s of 8 Baron Auckland, MC (d 1957); *b* 5 Mar 1931; *Educ* Glenalmond, ChCh Oxford; *m* June 1957, Rosemary Dorothy Marion, yr da of Sir John Frederick Ellenborough Crowder (d 1961), of 116 Ashley Gdns SW1; 2 s; *Career* former stockbroker; *Books* Going to The Moors; *Recreations* reading, writing; *Style*— Hon Ronald Eden; Cromlix, Dunblane, Perthshire (☎ 0786 822125)

EDEN OF WINTON, Baron (Life Peer UK 1983), of Rushyford, Co Durham; Rt Hon Sir John Benedict Eden; 9 Bt (E 1672), of West Auckland, Durham, and 7 Bt (GB 1776), of Maryland, America, PC (1972); s of Sir Timothy Calvert Eden, 8 and 6 Bt (d 1963); *b* 15 Sept 1925; *Educ* Eton, St Paul's Sch USA; *m* 1, 28 Jan 1958 (m dis 1974), Belinda Jane, da of late Sir (Frederick) John Pascoe; 2 s, 2 da; m 2, 1977, Margaret Ann, da of late Robin Gordon, former w of Viscount Strathallan, *qv*; *Heir* (to baronetcies only) s, Hon Robert Frederick Calvert Eden; *Career* served WW II, Lt RB, 2 Gurkha Rifles 1943-47, Adj The Gilgit Scouts; MP (C) Bournemouth West Feb 1954-83; oppn front bench spokesman for Power 1968-70, min of state Miny of Technol June-Oct 1970, min for Indust 1970-72, min of Post and Telecommunications 1972-74; memb Trade and Indust sub-ctee of Commons Expenditure Ctee 1974-76; chm: select ctee European Legislation 1976-79, select ctee Home Affrs 1979-83; pres: Ind Schs Assoc 1969-71, Wessex Area of Nat Union of Cons and Unionist Assocs 1974-77; chm: Wonder World plc 1982-, Gamlestaden plc 1987-, bd of tstees Royal Armouries 1986-; *Recreations* gardening; *Clubs* Boodle's, Pratt's; *Style*— The Rt Hon Lord Eden of Winton, PC; 41 Victoria Rd, London W8; Knoyle Place, East Knoyle, Salisbury, Wilts

EDES, (John) Michael; CMG (1981); s of late Lt. Col N H Edes and Louise Edes; *b* 19 April 1930; *Educ* Blundell's Clare Coll Cambridge (BA), Yale Univ (MA); *m* 1978, Angela Mermagen; 2 s; *Career* ambass to Libya 1980-83; head UK delegation to conference on Security and Disarmament in Europe (Stockholm) 1983-86; visiting Fell Int Inst for Strategic Studies 1987; head UK delegation (with personal rank of ambass) to negotiations on Conventional Armed Forces in Europe and on Confidence-and-Security Building Measures, Vienna 1989; *Recreations* gardening, listening to music; *Clubs* Athenaeum, Hawk's, Cambridge; *Style*— Michael Edes, Esq, CMG; Foreign and Commonwealth Office, King Charles St, London SW1

EDEY, Russell Philip; s of Lt-Col Anthony Russell Edey, of S Africa, and Barbara Stephanie Ann, *née* Rees-Jones; *b* 2 August 1942; *Educ* St Andrew's Coll, Grahamstown S Africa; *m* 8 June 1968, Celia Ann Malcolm, da of James Bisdee Malcolm Green, surgn, of Colchester, Essex; 2 s (Philip b 1971, Anthony b 1975), 1 da (Kate b 1973); *Career* CA; dir: N M Rothschild & Sons Ltd 1981, FKI Babcock plc 1988, Northern Foods plc 1988, dir: Br Lung Fndn 1985, Friends of The Open Air Theatre 1984; *Recreations* tennis, theatre, current affairs, wine; *Clubs* Australian, Melbourne; *Style*— Russell Edey, Esq; Starling Leeze, Coggeshall, Essex, CO6 1SL; N M Rothschild & Sons Ltd, New Ct, St Swithins Lane, London EC4P 4DU

EDGCUMBE, Lady Alison Nicole; 5 and yst da of 8 Earl of Mount Edgcumbe; *b* 1971; *Style*— Lady Alison Edgcumbe

EDGCUMBE, Lady (Valerie) Denise; el da of 8 Earl of Mount Edgcumbe; *b* 1960; *Style*— Lady Valerie Edgcumbe

EDGCUMBE, Lady Megan Francis; 2 da of 8 Earl of Mount Edgcumbe; *b* 1962; *Career* gardener, bar assistant; *Recreations* travel; *Style*— Lady Megan Edgcumbe; Woodpark Cottages, Anderton, Millbrook, Torpoint, Cornwall

EDGCUMBE, Piers Valletort; 2 surving s of George Edgcumbe (d 1977), but er by his 2 w, Una Pamela, da of Edward Lewis George, of Perth, W Australia; hp to half-bro, 8 Earl of Mount Edgcumbe; *b* 23 Oct 1946; married and divorced; *Style*— Piers Edgcumbe Esq

EDGCUMBE, Lady Tracy Anne; 3 da of 8 Earl of Mount Edgcumbe; *b* 1966; *Style*— Lady Tracy Edgcumbe

EDGCUMBE, Lady Vanessa Erina Michelle; 4 da of 8 Earl of Mount Edgcumbe; *b* 24 Feb 1969; *Style*— Lady Vanessa Edgcumbe

EDGE, Geoffrey; s of John Edge (d 1977), of Tividale, Warley W Midlands, and Alice Edith, *née* Rimell (d 1986); *b* 26 May 1943; *Educ* Rowley Regis GS, LSE, Birmingham Univ (BA); *Career* asst lectr geography Leicester Univ 1967-70, lectr geography Open Univ 1970-74, res fell Birmingham Poly 1979-80, sr res fell Preston and Northeast London Polys 1980-84, New initiatives coordinator Copec Housing Tst 1984-87; sr assoc P-E Inbucon 1987-; chm planning ctee Bletchley UDC 1972-74, vice chm planning ctee Milton Keynes Borough's Cncl 1973-76, MP (Lab) Aldridge Brownhills 1974-79 (parly private secretary, dept Educn and Science privy and off), chm econ devpt ctee W Midlands CC 1981-86, chm W Midlands Enterprise Bd 1982- Leader Walsall Metropolitan Borough Cncl 1983- (and chm policy and resources ctee); memb: Town and Country planning Assoc, Regional Studies Assoc, Geographical Assoc, Assoc Univ Teachers 1967, Inst Br Geographers 1964; Regional Analysis & Devpt (jt ed, 1973); *Recreations* gardening, walking, travel, reading, listening to classical music; *Style*— Geoffrey Edge, Esq; 31 Doodley Rd West, Tividale, Warley, West Midlands; 18 Harringworth Court, Lichfield Rd, Shelfield, Walsall, West Midlands (☎ 021 557 3858); West Midlands Enterprise Board, Wellington House, 31/34 Waterloo St, Birmingham B2 5JT (☎ 021 236 8855, fax 021 233 3942 telex 021 233 3942)

EDGE, Capt Philip Malcolm; s of Stanley Weston Edge (d 1977), and Edith Harriet, *née* Liddell; *b* 15 July 1931; *Educ* Rock Ferry HS, HMS Conway, Liverpool Nautical Coll; *m* 18 Feb 1967, Kathleen Anne, da of Richard Nelson Alfred Greenwood (d 1986); 1 s (David b 1977), 1 da (Caroline b 1974); *Career* i/c Shipping subsidiary BP 1969 (apprentice 1949, jr Offr 1951); Corpn of Trinity House: elder bro and bd memb 1978-, dep master and bd chm 1988-; memb Port of London Authy 1980-, dir Standard Protection & Indemnity Assoc Ltd 1988-; Freeman City of London 1980, Freeman Hon Co of Master Mariners 1980, Freeman and Memb of Ct Watermans Co of River Thames 1983; FNI 1979; *Recreations* sailing, DIY; *Clubs* Royal Thames YC; *Style*— Capt Malcolm Edge; Hillside, Layters Way, Gerrards Cross, Bucks SL9 7QZ (☎ 0753 887937); Trinity House, Tower Hill, London (☎ 01 480 6601, fax 01 480 7662, telex 987526 NAVAID G)

EDGE, Maj-Gen Raymond Cyril Alexander; CB (1968), MBE (1945); s of Raymond Clive Edge (d 1951), of Cheltenham, and Mary, *néa* Masters (d 1945); *b* 21 July 1912; *Educ* Cheltenham Coll, Royal Mil Acad (Woolwich), Gonville and Caius Cambridge

(BA); *m* 1, 5 June 1939, Margaret Patricia (d 1982), da of William Wallace McKee (d 1921); 1 s (William b 1943), 1 da (Mary b 1940); m 2, 9 July 1983, Audrey Anne, da of Sir Lewis Richardson, 1 Bt, CBE (d 1934); *Career* Army Offr RE 1932; serv: UK, India, Far & Middle East, BAOR; War Serv: India, Burma (Despatches) Malaya; Survey of India and of Pakistan (Offg DG 1948); ret as Dir Gen Ordnance Survey (Major General) 1969; Colonel Cmdt RE 1970-75 (rep Col Cmdt 1974); chm: Geodesy sub-ctee Royal Soc 1968-75, assoc of Br Geodesists 1963-65, Field Survey Assoc 1968-70, Land Surveyors Cncl 1970-72; memb: various ctees & sub ctees Royal Society, Cncl RGS 1966-69, Cncl RICS 1966-72 (vice pres 1970-72), Sec of State's Panel of Independent Inspectors DOE 1971-82; pres Section E British Assoc 1969; *Recreations* listening to music; *Clubs* Army & Navy; *Style*— Maj-Gen Raymond Edge, CB, MBE; Brook Farm, North Curry, Taunton TA3 6DJ

EDGE, Stephen Martin; s of Harry Hurst Edge, of Bolton, Lancs, and Mary, *née* Rigg; *b* 29 Nov 1950; *Educ* Canon Slade GS Bolton, Exeter Univ (LLB); *m* 6 Sept 1975, Melanie, da of Eric Stanley Lawler, of Hassocks, Sussex; 2 da (Charlotte Louise b 1982, Katharine Sarah b 1987); *Career* slr, ptnr (specialising in corporate tax) Slaughter and May 1973-; various contributions to publications and articles on tax; *Clubs* MCC; *Style*— Stephen Edge, Esq; 35 Basinghall St, London EC2V 5DB (☎ 01 600 1200, 01 726 0038)

EDGE-PARTINGTON, Capt (Thomas) Keppel; RN; s of Thomas William Edge-Partington (d 1920, Br High Cmmr to Solomon Is), and Mary Mabel, *née* Sparkes (d 1971); *b* 31 August 1920; *Educ* RNC Dartmouth, JSSC Latimer, RN War Coll Greenwich; *m* 3 April 1948, Mary Rosamond, da of Lt-Col George Hilton Latham, RE (d 1969); 1 s (Peter b 1955), 3 da (Tamsin b 1950, Rosanne b 1951, Sandra b 1953); *Career* RN 1934, Capt 1961, Naval ADC to HM The Queen 1970-71 (ret 1971), exchange serv with US Navy as Instr at Fleet Sonar Sch San Diego Calif 1949-51, Fleet Torpedo Anti-Sub Offr on Staff of C-in-C Far East 1957-59, Staff TAS Offr to Flag Offr Submarines Gosport 1953-56; Naval Advsr to Br High Cmmr Pakistan 1962-64, asst dir Navy Plans MOD 1964-66, dir of Weapons Equip (underwater) 1966-68, i/c HMS Vernon 1969-70; admin exec Sir William Halcrow & Ptnrs (Consulting Civil Engrs) 1971-83; FBIM 1976 (MBIM 1971); *Recreations* golf, gardening; *Style*— Capt Keppel Edge-Partington, RN; Grove House, Daglingworth, Cirencester, Glos GL7 7AW (☎ 0285 654727)

EDGE-PARTINGTON, (James) Patrick Seymour; s of Rev Canon Ellis Foster Edge-Partington, MC, MA, Queen's Chaplain (d 1957), and Esther Muriel, *née* Seymour (d 1948); *b* 16 Mar 1926; *Educ* Marlbrough Coll; *m* 1951, Monica Madge, da of Howard Philip Smith (d 1964); 2 s (Julian, Simon), 1 da (Jane); *Career* Coldstream Gds 1944-47, T/Capt Palestine; CA 1951; chm Crown Ho plc 1963-, Tilbury Gp plc 1975-; FCA, CBIM; *Clubs* RAC; *Style*— Patrick Edge-Partington, Esq; c/o Crown House plc, 2 Lygon Place, SW1 (☎ 01 730 9287, telex 918602)

EDGLEY, Colin Ronald; s of Andrew Charles Edgley, and Doreen, *née* Major; *b* 18 Dec 1945; *Educ* Haberdasher's Askes' Sch; *m* 9 Aug 1969, Carole, da of Alexander Cornish (d 1981), of Wallington; 1 s (Simon Alexander Charles b 1972), 1 da (Alison Charlotte b 1975); *Career* var directorships Spillers Foods Ltd 1981-88 (chm 1982-84 and 1986-88): Gland Supplies Ltd, Manor Produce Ltd, Suir Endocrine Ltd, chm Castlefield Foods Ltd 1986-88, chief exec Homepride Foods Ltd 1988-; FCCA 1976; *Recreations* rugby, golf; *Style*— Colin Edgley, Esq; 14 Dudley Grove, Epsom, Surrey KT18 7NB (☎ 037 2723181); Compass House, 80 Newmarket Rd, Cambs (☎ 0223 461600, car 0860 725742, telex 818878)

EDGSON WRIGHT, Paul; s of Hugh Edgson Wright, MM (d 1979), of Folkestone, Kent, and Diana Christine, *née* Smith; *b* 3 Mar 1935; *Educ* Marlborough; *m* 11 June 1960, Gillian Elspeth, da of Sidney Leonard Shaw, of Santiago, Chile; 2 s (Mark b 1963, (Andrew) Peter b 1967), 1 da (Kathryn b 1961); *Career* articled Barton Mayhew & Co CA 1953-59; Riddell Stead Graham & Hutchinson CAs Montreal PQ Canada 1959-61; Stanhay (Ashford) Ltd Gp 1961-72, taken over by Hestair plc 1971, apptd fin dir and co sec 1970, chm Stanhay (Autos) Ltd 1972-76, gp chief accountant MacBlast Gp of cos 1976-77, Rothman Pantall & Co, CAs 1978-84, formed Shaws, CAs (insolvency practitioner) specialising in insolvency and investigations 1985; FCA; *Recreations* shooting, fishing, sailing, ornithology; *Style*— Paul Edgson Wright, Esq; Clareville House, 26/27 Oxendon St, London SW1Y 4EP (☎ 01 930-2217, telex 893715 ROTHCO G, fax 01 930-9849)

EDLMANN, Stephen Raphael Reynolds; s of Capt Raphael Francis Reynolds (d 1975), and Waltraud Helga Mathilde, *née* Sevecke (d 1984); *b* 13 Mar 1954; *Educ* Tonbridge, Trinity Hall Cambridge (MA); *m* 14 July 1979, Deborah Catherine, da of Roger John Nimmo Booth, Ireland; 4 s (Richard b 1980, Oliver b 1981, Nicholas b and d 1981, Lawrence b 1983); *Career* joined Linklaters and Paines slrs 1977 (ptnr 1985-); rugby blue 1974-75; memb Worshipful Co of Slrs 1985; memb: Law Soc 1979, Int Bar Assoc 1986; *Recreations* entertaining, racing, shooting, golf; *Clubs* Hawks, MCC, Roehampton, Harlequins; *Style*— Stephen Edlmann, Esq; Linklaters and Paines, Barrington House, 59-67 Gresham St, London EC2V 7JA (☎ 01 606 7080, fax 01 606 5113, telex 884349/888167)

EDMENSON, Sir Walter Alexander; CBE (1944); s of late Robert Robson Edmenson, of Monkseaton, Northumberland; *b* 2 Dec 1892; *m* 1918, Doris (d 1975), da of John Davidson; 1 s (ka 1940), 1 da (d 1975); *Career* served WWI with N Irish Horse and RFA (despatches), served WWII NI rep Miny of War Tport 1939-46; N Continual Shipping Co 1948-70, Ulster Tport Authy 1948-61, shipowner, Belfast Harbour Cmmr 1940-61, Clyde Shipping Co 1946, 1964; pres: The Ulster Steamship Co, G Heyn & Sons; dir various other shipping cos; dir: British European Airways 1946-63, Gallaher Ltd 1946-66, The Belfast Banking Co 1946-70, Belfast Bank Executor & Trust Co 1946-70, Commercial Insurance Co of Ireland 1964-72; chm N Ireland Civil Aviation Advsy Cncl 1946-61; memb Lloyd's Register of Shipping 1949-74; Council of Chamber of Shipping 1943-73; cmmr Irish Lights 1950-85; DL Belfast 1951-87; American Medal of Freedom with Palms 1945; kt 1958; *Style*— Sir Walter Edmenson, CBE; 101 Bryansford Rd, Newcastle, Co Down, N Ireland (☎ 09967 22769)

EDMISTON, Robert Norman; s of Vivian Randolph Edmiston and Norma Margaret Edmiston; *b* 6 Oct 1946; *Educ* Abbs Cross Tech, Barking Regnl Coll of Technol; *m* 1967, Patricia Ann, da of Alfred Edward Talbot (d 1962); 1 s (Andrew b 1969), 2 da (Deborah b 1971, Angela b 1975); *Career* fin analyst Ford Motor Co, capital planning mangr Chrysler (mangr fin analysis), fin dir Jensen Motor Co, chm and md Int Motors Ltd; *Recreations* church activities, swimming, windsurfing, flying, shooting; *Clubs* Windsurfing, Draycott, nr Rugby; *Style*— Robert Edmiston, Esq; The Woodlands, Spring Hill, Arley, nr Coventry, W Midlands (☎ 0676 40626); International Motors Ltd, Ryder Street, West Bromich, West Midlands (☎ 021 557 6200, telex 337554)

EDMONDS, David Albert; s of Albert Edmonds, of Kingsley Cheshire, and Gladys Edmonds; *b* 6 Mar 1944; *Educ* Helsby GS Cheshire, Univ of Keele (BA); *m* 1966, Ruth, da of Eric Beech, of Christleton Chester; 2 s (Jonathan, Benedict), 2 da (Jane, Elizabeth); *Career* asst princ Miny of Housing and Local Govt 1966-69, (private sec/parly sec 1969-71), princ DOE 1971-73, observer Civil Serv Selection Bd 1973-74, visiting fell Johns Hopkins Univ Baltimore USA 1974-75, private sec/permanent sec DOE 1975-77 (asst sec 1977-79), private sec to sec of state DOE 1979-83, under sec Inner Cities Directorate DOE 1983-84, chief exec The Housing Corpn 1984-, dep chm New Statesman and Society 1988-; pres Int New Towns Assoc 1988-; dir The Housing Fin Corpn 1988-; *Recreations* cricket, golf, walking, films; *Clubs* Wimbledon Park Golf, Wimbledon Wanderers CC; *Style*— David Edmonds, Esq; 61 Cottenham Park Rd, W Wimbledon, London SW20 0DR (☎ 01 946 3729); The Housing Corpn, 149 Tottenham Ct Rd, W1P 0BN (☎ 01 357 9466)

EDMONDS, Dr Herbert; s of Dr Arthur Edmonds; *b* 24 July 1930; *Educ* Mountain Ash County GS, Wales (Cardiff) and Leeds Univs; *m* 1960, Hannah, *née* Oppenheimer; 3 s, 1 da; *Career* chemistry; md Coutinho Caro & Co Ltd, past chm Int Steel Trade Assoc; FRSC; *Style*— Dr Herbert Edmonds; c/o Coutinho Caro & Co plc, Walker House, 87 Queen Victoria St, London EC4 (☎ 01 236 1505)

EDMONDS, Cdr John Christopher; CMG (1978), CVO (1971); s of Capt Archibald Charles Mackay Edmonds, OBE, RN (d 1961), of Bognor Regis, Sussex; *b* 23 June 1921; *Educ* Kelly Coll; *m* 1, 1948 (m dis 1965), Elena, da of Serge Tornow; 2 s; m 2, 1966, Armine, da of Clement Hilton Williams, MBE (d 1963), of Sonning, Berks; *Career* RN 1939-59, Cdr 1957; staff of: NATO Defence Coll 1953-55, C-in-C Home Fleet 1955-57, CDS 1958-59; Dip Serv 1959-, cnsllr British Embassy Ankara 1968-71, Paris 1972-74, head arms control and disarmament dept FCO 1974-77; leader UK del to comprehensive test ban treaty negotiations Geneva (with personal rank of ambassador), 1978-81; visiting fellow in internat relations Reading Univ 1981-; *Recreations* golf, gardening, travel; *Clubs* Army and Navy; *Style*— Cdr John Edmonds, CMG, CVO, RN; North Lodge, Sonning, Berkshire RG4 0ST (☎ 0734 690017)

EDMONDS, John Walter; s of Walter Edgar Edmonds (d 1986), and Maude Rose; *b* 28 Jan 1944; *Educ* Christ's Hosp, Oriel Coll Oxford (MA); *m* 30 Sept 1967, Janet Linden, da of Franklyn Arthur Callaby (d 1982); 2 da (Lucinda Jane b 1969, Nanette Sally b 1972); *Career* gen sec and tres General, Municipal, Boilermakers and Allied Trades Union 1986-; dir Unity Tst plc 1986-; visiting fell Nuffield Coll Oxford; gov London Sch of Economics and Political Science; *Recreations* cricket, cabinet making; *Style*— John W Edmonds, Esq; Mitcham; Thorne House, Ruxley Ridge, Claygate, Esher, Surrey (☎ 0372 62091, telex 27428, fax 0372 67164)

EDMONDS, Knowler Gilliam; s of Herbert Southgate Edmonds, (d 1950), of Chatham, Kent, and Dorothy Kate, *née* Dunkin (d 1973); *b* 27 July 1922; *Educ* Rochester Tech Coll, Medway Coll Art and Crafts (Dip); *m* 6 Oct 1945, Gretta Marjorie (d 1988), da of Herbert Lovelady, DFC (d 1976); 1 s (Richard b 1950 d 1967), 1 da (Christine b 1948); *Career* WWII Sgt RAF (Radar Service) 1942-46; printing estimator C Tinting Co Ltd 1948-50, printing prodn offr Automatic Telephone & Electric Co Ltd 1950-56, printing mangr Hazel Grove Printing & Boxmaking Co Ltd 1956-60, printing conslt and prodr Cross Courtenay Ltd 1960-67, gp publicity mangr A Monk & Co Ltd 1967-83; numerous awards in art, printing and typography: newspaper contrib under pseudonym Edmond Gill; *Recreations* books, photography, sketching, golf; *Clubs* former memb of Printing Historical Soc, and Br Assoc Indust Eds;; *Style*— Knowler Edmonds, Esq; Kensington, London Road North, Poynton, Cheshire SK12 1BX (☎ 0625 873603)

EDMONDS, Richard Edward Howard; JP; s of late Eric Edmonds; *b* 7 July 1925; *Educ* Wellington, Oriel Coll Oxford; *m* 1958, Sarah Anne, da of Hugh Merriman, DSO, MC, TD, DL; 1 s, 2 da; *Career* Lt Oxfordshire and Bucks LI, served Palestine 1945-47; chm: Clements (Watford) Ltd, Coln Gravel Ltd; co dir and farmer; *Recreations* shooting, fishing, skiing; *Style*— Richard Edmonds Esq, JP; Micklefield Hall, Rickmansworth, Herts WD3 6AQ (☎ 0923 774747, off 244222)

EDMONDS, Robert Humphrey Gordon; CMG (1969), MBE (1944); s of Air Vice-Marshal Charles Humphrey Kingsman Edmonds, CBE, DSO (d 1954), and Lorna Karim Chadwick, *née* Osborn (d 1954); *b* 5 Oct 1920; *Educ* Ampleforth Coll, Brasenose Coll Oxford (MA); *m* 1, 1951 (m dis 1975), Georgina, da of Cdr Anthony Boyce Combe, of Little Ferry House, Golspie, Sutherland; 4 s (Robert, James, Charles, Dominic); m 2, 1976, Enid Flora, widow of Dr Michael Balint; *Career* Army 1940-46, Maj, (despatches); HM Foreign (later Diplomatic) Serv 1946-78; advsr Kleinwort Benson Ltd 1978-83 (conslt 1984-86); ret; *Books* Soviet Foreign Policy - The Brezhnev Years (1983), Setting The Mould - The United States and Britain 1945-50 (1986); *Clubs* Turf; *Style*— Robin Edmonds Esq, CMG, MBE; 43 North Rd, London N6; Hill Cottage, Street, Somerset

EDMONDSON, Hon Anthony James Kinghorn; yr s of 1 Baron Sandford (d 1959), and Edith Elizabeth, *née* Freeman (d 1946); *b* 20 July 1924; *Educ* Eton, Harvard Univ; *m* 1, 26 April 1947 (m dis 1969), Olivia Charlotte, yst da of late Rev Oswald Andrew Hunt; 3 s, 1 da; m 2, 21 Aug 1969, Hilary Pauline, o child of Col E S Trusler, OBE; 1 s (d 1979); *Career* Capt Gren Gds (ret); *Style*— The Hon Anthony Edmondson; Upton Manor, East Knoyle, Salisbury, Wilts SP3 6BW (☎ 0747 83 270)

EDMONDSON, Hon James John Mowbray; s and h of 2 Baron Sandford, DSC, *qv*; *b* 1 July 1949; *Educ* Eton, York Univ; *m* 1973, Ellen Sarah, da of Jack Shapiro,of Toronto; 1 da; *Career* school teacher; *Style*— Hon James Edmondson; 103 North Warwick Ave, Burnaby, BC, Canada

EDMONDSON, Dr Philip Charles; s of Dr Reginald Edmondson (d 1964), of Dunchurch, Rugby, and Phyllis, *née* Elam; *b* 30 April 1938; *Educ* Uppingham, Christs Coll Univ of Cambridge (MA, MD, MB, B Chir), St Bart's Hosp London; *m* 7 Sept 1968, Margaret Lysbeth, da of Stanley Bayston, of Saxton, Tadcaster, Yorks; 3 da (Camilla b 25 April 1970, Claire b 12 May 1972, Cordelia b 5 Jan 1980); *Career* physician to Westminster Abbey 1979, conslt physician to many major industl co's; Freeman City of London, Liveryman Worshipful Co of Apothecaries; FRSM, MRCP, fell Med Soc of London; *Recreations* fishing, country pursuits; *Clubs* Boodles; *Style*— Dr Philip Edmondson; 18 Lennox Gdns, London SW1X 0DG (☎ 01 584 5194); Hornton Lodge, Vicarage Lane, Dunchurch, Rugby (☎ 0788 810 500); 99 Harley St, London W1N 1DF (☎ 01 935 7501)

EDMONDSON, Stephen John; s of George Edmondson, of Scunthorpe, Lincs, and Jean Mary, *née* Stanton; *b* 21 Aug 1950; *Educ* Scunthorpe GS, Middx Hosp Med Sch (BSc, MB BS); *m* 17 July 1976, Barbara Bridget Alison, da of Dr MNS Duncan, TD; 1 s (Adam George b 18 Jan 1984); *Career* conslt cardiothoracic surgn St Bartholomew's Hosp London 1984-, late sen registrar Dept Cardiothoracic Surgery Hammersmith Hosp London, registrar Dept Surgery Nat Heart Hosp London; FRCS 1979, MRCP 1980, memb Soc of Thoracic and Cardiovascular Surgeons 1982, memb British Cardiac Soc 1984; publications; papers on cardiac and thoracic surgery specialising in coronary artery surgery and cardiac arrythmias; *Recreations* sports; *Clubs* The Vanderbilt Racquet, Ealing GC; *Style—* Stephen Edmondson, Esq; 69 Harley St, London W1N 1DE (☎ 01 935 6375, fax 01 224 3823, car tel 0860 613 624)

EDMONSTONE, Hon Mrs (Alicia Evelyn); *née* Browne; o da of 5 Baron Kilmaine (d 1946) and Lady Aline Kennedy (d 1957), da of 3 Marquess of Ailsa; *b* 4 Feb 1909; *m* 30 Nov 1936, Cdr Edward St John Edmonstone, RN (d 1983), yr s of Sir Archibald Edmonstone, 5 Bt, CVO, (d 1954), 1 s (William), 1 da (Helen); *Style—* Hon Mrs Edmonstone; Barcombe Old Rectory, nr Lewes, Sussex BN8 5TN

EDMONSTONE, Sir Archibald Bruce Charles; 7 Bt (GB 1774), of Duntreath, Stirlingshire; s of Sir Archibald Charles Edmonstone, 6 Bt (d 1954), and Dowager Lady Edmonstone, *qv*; *b* 3 August 1934; *Educ* Stowe; *m* 1, 17 Jan 1957 (m dis 1967), Jane, er da of Maj-Gen Edward Charles Colville, CB, DSO (s of Adm Hon Sir Stanley Colville, GCB, GCMG, GCVO (2 s of 1 Viscount Colville of Culross) by his w Lady Adelaide Meade, da of 4 Earl of Clanwilliam); 2 s (Archibald Edward Charles, Nicholas William Mark b 16 April 1963), 1 da (Philippa Carolyn b 12 June 1959); m 2, 2 June 1969, Juliet Elizabeth, o da of Maj-Gen Cecil Martin Fothergill Deakin, CB, CBE; 1 s (Dru Benjamin Marshall b 26 Oct 1971), 1 da (Elyssa Elizabeth b 11 Sept 1973); *Heir* s, Archibald Edward Charles Edmonstone (*qv*); *Career* 2 Lt Royal Scots Greys 1954-56; *Recreations* shooting, fishing; *Clubs* White's; *Style—* Sir Archibald Edmonstone, Bt; Duntreath Castle, Blanefield, by Glasgow (☎ 0360 70215)

EDMONSTONE, Archibald Edward Charles; s (by 1 m) and h of Sir Archibald Edmonstone, 7 Bt; *b* 4 Feb 1961; *Educ* Stowe, RMA Sandhurst; *Career* commissioned as 2 Lt Scots Gds 1982; *Style—* Archibald Edmonstone, Esq

EDMONSTONE, Dowager Lady; Gwendolyn Mary; da of late Marshall Field, of Chicago; *m* 5 April 1923, Sir Archibald Charles Edmonstone, 6 Bt (d 1954); *Style—* Dowager Lady Edmonstone; Lettre Cottage, Killearn, Glasgow

EDMONTON, Bishop; Rt Rev Brian John Masters; s of Stanley William Masters (d 1965), and Grace Hannah, *née* Stevens; *b* 17 Oct 1932; *Educ* Collyers Sch Horsham, Queens' Coll Cambridge (MA); *Career* insurance broker Lloyds 1955-62; asst curate St Dunstan and All Saints Stepney 1964-69, vicar Holy Trinity Hoxton 1969-82, bishop of Fulham 1982-84; *Recreations* theatre, squash; *Clubs* United Oxford and Cambridge Univ; *Style—* The Rt Rev the Bishop of Edmonton; 13 North Audley St, London W1Y 1WF (☎ 01 629 3891)

EDMUND, John Humphrey; s of Charles Henry Humphrey Edmund, of Swansea, and Vera May Edmund, *née* Warmington; *b* 6 Mar 1935; *Educ* Swansea GS, Jesus Coll Oxford (MA); *m* 4 Sept 1965, (Elizabeth Ann) Myfanwy, da of William Lewis Williams, of Newport, Dyfed (d 1975); *Career* Nat Serv RN 1953-55; admitted slr 1961; ptnr Beor, Wilson & Lloyd, Swansea; Undersheriff W Glam 1983-, Clerk to Gen Cmmmrs of Taxes (Swansea Divn) 1986-; Law Soc 1962; *Clubs* Vincents (Oxford), Bristol Channel Yacht; *Style—* John Edmund, Esq; 84 Pennard Rd, Pennard, Swansea, West Glamorgan SA3 2AA (☎ 044128 2526); Calvert Hse, Calvert Tce, Swansea SA1 6AP (☎ 0792 655 178, fax 0792 467 002)

EDMUND-DAVIES, Baron (Life Peer UK 1974); Herbert Edmund Edmund-Davies; PC (1966); assumed additional name of Edmund to patronymic 1974; 3 s of Morgan John Davies, of Mountain Ash, Glam, and Elizabeth Maud Edmunds; *b* 15 July 1906; *Educ* Mountain Ash, King's Coll London, Exeter Coll Oxford; *m* 1935, Eurwen, da of late John Williams, JP, of Barry; 3 da; *Career* barrister 1929, bencher 1948, tres 1965 and 1966 Gray's Inn; former rec: Merthyr Tydfil, Swansea, Cardiff, High Court judge (Queen's Bench) 1958-66, Lord Justice of Appeal 1966-74, Lord of Appeal in Ordinary 1974-82; life govr and fellow King's Coll London, pro-chllr Univ of Wales 1974-85; chm Aberfan Inquiry Tribunal 1966; kt 1958; *Style—* The Rt Hon Lord Edmund-Davies, PC; 5 Gray's Inn Sq, London WC1

EDNAM, Viscount; William Humble David Jeremy Ward; s and h of 4 Earl of Dudley; *b* 27 Mar 1947; *Educ* Eton, Christ Church Oxford; *m* 1, 1972 (m dis 1976), Sarah, da of Sir Alastair Coats, 4 Bt; m 2, 1976 (m dis 1980), Debra Louise, da of George Robert Pinney; 1 da; *Style—* Viscount Ednam; Villa Montanet, Les Garrigues, 84220 Goult-Gordes, France

EDWARD, Prof David Alexander Ogilvy; CMG (1981), QC (Scot 1974); s of John Ogilvy Christie Edward (d 1960), of Perth, and Margaret Isabel, *née* MacArthur; *b* 14 Nov 1934; *Educ* Sedbergh, Univ Coll Oxford, Edinburgh Univ; *m* 1962, Elizabeth Young, da of Terence McSherry, of Edinburgh; 2 s (Giles b 1965, John b 1968), 2 da (Anne b 1964, Katherine b 1971); *Career* Nat Serv Sub Lt RNVR 1955-57; advocate 1962, clerk of the Faculty of Advocates 1967-70 (tres 1970-77); pres consultative ctee of the Bars and Law Socs of the European Community 1978-80; tstee Nat Library of Scotland 1966-; memb: law advsy ctee British Cncl 1976-88, panel of arbitrators Int Centre for Settlement of Investmt Disputes 1979-; chm Continental Assets Tst plc, Scottish Cncl for Arbitration, Hopetown House Preservation Tst; Adam & Co Gp plc, The Harris Tweed Assoc Ltd; Salvesen prof of European Inst Univ of Edinburgh 1985; *Clubs* Athenaeum, New (Edinburgh); *Style—* Prof David Edward, CMG, QC; 32 Heriot Row, Edinburgh (☎ 031 225 7153); Europa Institute, Old College, Edinburgh EH8 9YL (☎ 031 667 1011, ext 4215, telex 727442 (unived G))

EDWARD, Hon Mrs (Gillian Margaret); *née* Hunter; da of Baron Hunter of Newington, MBE (Life Peer); *b* 25 May 1948; *Educ* Dundee HS, St Leonards Sch; *m* 1973, Malcolm Greig Edward, s of Oswald Andrew Edward (d 1976); 1 s (Mark b 1979), 1 da (Marisa b 1974); *Career* RGN, SCM; no longer practising; *Style—* The Hon Mrs Edward; 82 Lordswood Rd, Harborne, Birmingham B17 9BY (☎ 021 427 2069)

EDWARDES, Hon Mrs David; Elizabeth; yst da of late Robert Alexander Longman Broadley, of Priest Hill, Limpsfield, Surrey; *m* 22 July 1939, Cdr Hon David Edwardes, DSC (d 1983), 3 s of late 6 Baron Kensington, CMG, DSO, TD, JP, DL; 3 da; *Style—* The Hon Mrs David Edwardes; Carpenter's Yard, Compton Pauncefoot, Yeovil, Somerset

EDWARDES, Leonard Edward (Len); s of Charles James Henry Edwardes (d 1973), of 4 Grove Cottages, High St, Horsell, Woking, Surrey, and Emily, *née* Brown (d 1965); *b* 9 Oct 1931; *Educ* Goldsworth Co Secdy Sch Surrey; *m* 7 June 1954, Sheena, da of Robert George Gray (d 1968); 2 s (Simon b 7 April 1963, Richard b 15 May 1965); *Career* Nat Serv RAF 1950-52; chief engr Debenhams Ltd 1967-75, ptnr Cranage & Perkins (consltg engrs) 1975-80; sr ptnr: Edwardes Friedlander 1980-82, Edwardes Whittle Partnership 1982-; chm and md Nationwide Maintenance Ltd; dir: Falcon Mechanical servs Ltd, E & C Engrg Servs Ltd, Docklands Maintenance Ltd, Falcon Bldg Maintenance Ltd; Freeman: City of London 1981, Worshipful Co of Fanmakers; FBIM 1986; *Recreations* swimming; *Clubs* Chris Lane; *Style—* Len Edwardes, Esq; Nationwide Maintenance Ltd, Falcon House, Catteshall Lane, Godalming, Surrey GU7 1JP, (☎ 04868 28674-04868 20556, fax 0483 426987)

EDWARDES, Sir Michael Owen; s of Denys Owen Edwardes, and Audrey Noel, *née* Copeland; *b* 11 Oct 1930; *Educ* St Andrew's Coll Grahamstown S Africa, Rhodes Univ (BA); *m* 1958, Mary Margaret, *née* Finlay; 3 da; *Career* chm and chief exec BL Ltd 1977-82; non-exec chm Chloride Gp plc 1982- (joined 1951, dir 1969-77, chief exec 1972-74, chm and ch exec 1974-77, non-exec dep chm 1977); non-exec chm Hill Samuel South Africa 1982- (non-exec dir Hill Samuel Gp 1980-, memb judging panel for Hill Samuel Business Awards 1982); first chm Mercury Communications 1982-1983; exec chm ICL plc 1984-; memb: CBI Cncl 1974-81, CBI President's Ctee 1981-, NEB 1975-77; CBIM (vice-chm 1977-80); non-exec dir IntMgmnt Dvpt Inst 1978-; dir A J Gooding Gp 1983-, exec chm Dunlop Hldgs 1984-; Hon FIMechE, Hon LLD Rhodes; kt 1979; *Books* Back From The Brink (1983); *Style—* Sir Michael Edwardes; ICL, Bridge House, Fulham, London SW6 (☎ 01 788 7272)

EDWARDES, Hon (William) Owen Alexander; s and h of 8 Baron Kensington; *b* 21 July 1964; *Style—* The Hon Owen Edwardes; Friar Tuck, Mt West, PO Box 549, Mooi River 3300, Natal, S Africa

EDWARDES, Hon Mrs Michael; Sylvia Inez Pakenham; *née* Johnstone; da of Col Hope Johnstone, CBE (d 1939), and Lilian Ada, *née* Stocker; *m* 1, 21 March 1926 (m dis 1946), Lt-Col Alfred Joseph Thorburn McGaw; 1 da; 2, 22 Aug 1946, Lt-Col Hon Michael George Edwardes, MBE (d 1985), yst s of 6 Baron Kensington; *Style—* Hon Mrs Michael Edwardes; The Stables, Barton Abbots, The Green, Tetbury, Glos GL8 8DN

EDWARDS, Alan Kenneth Warneford; s of late Trevor James Edwards; *b* 6 June 1927; *Educ* Birkenhead Sch; *m* 1952, Valerie Frances, *née* Burbridge; 3 s, 1 da; *Career* in practice 1954-1961; fin dir Lonsdale Universal Ltd 1962-69, md and dep chm 1969-83; chm Turner Whitehead Industries Ltd 1983-; FCA; *Recreations* cricket, motor racing, rugby; *Clubs* MCC; *Style—* Alan Edwards, Esq; Hill Close, Sandy Lane, Cobham, Surrey (☎ 0932 62068)

EDWARDS, Andrew John Cumming; s of John Edwards (d 1977), and Norah Hope, *née* Bevan; *b* 3 Nov 1940; *Educ* Fettes Coll Edinburgh, St John's Coll Oxford (MA), Harvard Univ (AM, MPA); *m* 11 Oct 1969 (m dis 1987), Charlotte Anne, da of Arthur L Chilcot, MBE (d 1981); 1 s (Angus b 1974), 2 da (Hermia b 1972, Madeline b 1978); *Career* asst master Malvern Coll 1962-63, asst princ HM Treasy 1963-67, private sec to Sir William Armstrong 1966-67, princ HM Treasy 1967-75, Harkness fell Cambridge Mass 1971-73, asst sec HM Treasy 1975-84, RCDS 1979, asst sec DES 1984-85, under sec HM Treasy 1985-; sec Bd of Royal Opera House 1988-; conductor: Treasy Singers 1968-84, Acad of St Mary's Wimbledon 1980-; govr Br Inst of Recorder Sound 1975-79; *Books* Nuclear Weapons, the balance of terror, the quest for peace (1986); *Recreations* music, writing, reading, walking; *Style—* Andrew Edwards, Esq; Treasury Chambers, Parliament St, London SW1P 3AG (☎ 01 270 4480)

EDWARDS, Hon Mrs (Ann Cecily Mary); *née* Talbot; da of 8 Baron Talbot de Malahide, MC (d 1975); *b* 22 Dec 1931; *m* 10 Oct 1955, Col Edward Reginald Edwards, s of Edward John Edwards, of Pontypridd, Glamorgan; 3 s; *Style—* Hon Mrs Edwards; Malahide, Whiteway, Litton Cheney, Dorchester, Dorset DT2 9AG

EDWARDS, Hon Mrs; Anna Elizabeth; *née* Turner; da of 2 Baron Netherthorpe; *b* 17 Dec 1961; *Educ* Abbot's Hill Sch; *m* 20 Dec 1986, Simon M Edwards, er s of late Roland Edwards; *Career* artist; *Style—* The Hon Mrs Edwards; 31 Sutherland Sq, London SE11

EDWARDS, (John) Basil; CBE (1972); s of Charles Edwards (d 1951), of 137 Bath Road, Worcester, and Susan, *née* Thomas (d 1923); *b* 15 Jan 1909; *Educ* King's Sch Worcester, Wadham Coll Oxford (MA); *m* 2 Aug 1935, Molly Patricia (d 1979), da of late James Philips; 1 s (Charles Marcus (*qv*) b 10 Aug 1937), 2 da (Caroline (Mrs Docker) b 15 May 1939, Patricia Susan (Hon Mrs Samuel Coleridge) b 17 March 1944); *Career* Mayor of Worcester 1947-49, chm Worcester City Justices 1951-79, hon tres Magistrates Assoc 1968-70 (dep chm 1970-76, chm 1976-79; memb James Ctee; chm Worcester Three Choirs Festival 1947-72; Liveryman: City of London, Worshipful Co of Haberdashers, Worshipful Co of Distillers; *Style—* Basil Edwards, Esq, CBE, JP; 21 Britannia Sq, Worcester WR1 3DH (☎ 0905 29933); 8 Sansome Walk, Worcester (☎ 0905 723561)

EDWARDS, Brian; CBE (1988); s of John Albert Edwards (d 1979), of Bebington, and (Ethel) Pat, *née* Davis (d 1980); *b* 19 Feb 1942; *Educ* Wirral GS; *m* 7 Nov 1964, Jean Edwards, da of William Cannon, of Neston; 2 s (Christopher b 28 April 1973, Jonathan (twin) b 28 April 1973, 2 da (Penny Adrienne b 27 May 1967, Paula Michelle b 14 Nov 1968); *Career* various hosp posts 1958-69, lectr in health serv studies Univ of Leeds 1969-71, dep gp sec Hull Hosp Mgmnt Ctee 1971-73, dist admin Leeds Dist Health Authy 1973-76, area admin Cheshire AHA 1976-81, regnl gen mangr Trent RHA 1984- (regnl admin 1981-83) visiting prof Univ of Keele 1989; pres Inst of Health Servs Mgmnt 1983; chm: manpower advsy gp NHS 1983-85, regnl gen mangrs gp England 1986; memb standing advsy ctee on audit RCP, conslt WHO, ed Health Servs Manpower Review; FHSM 1964, CBIM 1988; *Books* Si Vis Pacem (1973), Planning the Child Health Services (1975), Manager and Industrial Relations (1979), Merit Awards for Doctors (1987),; *Recreations* golf; *Clubs* Bakewell GC; *Style—* Brian Edwards, Esq, CBE; 3 Royal Croft Drive, Baslow, Derbyshire DE4 1SN (☎ 024 688 3459); Trent Regional Health Authority, Fulwood, Sheffield, S Yorks (☎ 0742 630 300)

EDWARDS, Hon Mrs (Catherine Gerran); *née* Lloyd; da of Baron Lloyd of Kilgerran, CBE, QC (Life Peer); *b* 1 Mar 1947; *Educ* Roedean; *m* 1972, Philip Gwynfryn Edwards; 4 c; *Recreations* tennis; *Clubs* Royal Cwlth Soc; *Style—* Hon Mrs Edwards; 13 Lancaster Ave, Hadley Wood, Herts (☎ 01 440 9503)

EDWARDS, (David) Cenwyn; s of Alwyn John Edwards (d 1986), of 15 Glasfryn, Pontarddulais, and Edwina Jane, *née* Thomas; *b* 27 Oct 1945; *Educ* Llanelli Boys GS,

Univ of N Wales Bangor (BA); *m* 17 April 1971, Margaret Eluned, da of Thomas Owen Davies (d 1977); 1 s (Gruffudd b 1979), 1 da (Lowri b 1977); *Career* joined HTV 1969; asst hd news and current affrs 1978-82, head of current affairs 1982-85, asst programme controller and N Wales Exec 1985-; controller Features and Religion; memb: Diplomatic and Cwlth Writers Assoc of Br, Nat Eisteddfod Ct; *Recreations* drama, rugby, cricket; *Clubs* Wil Bryan, Llaneli RFC; *Style*— Cenwyn Edwards, Esq; Arfryn, Heol Glyndwr, Gwernymynydd, Yr Wyddgrug, Clwyd (☎ 0532 2739); HTV, Civic Centre, Mold, Clwyd (☎ 0352 55331, fax 0352 55465)

EDWARDS, Sir Christopher John Churchill; 5 Bt (1866) of Pye Nest, Yorkshire; s of Sir (Henry) Charles (Serrell Priestly) Edwards, 4 Bt (d 1963), and Daphne, *née* Birt; *b* 16 August 1941; *Educ* Frensham Heights Sch, Loughborough Coll; *m* 1972, Gladys Irene Vogelgesang; 2 s; *Heir* s, David Charles Priestley Edwards b 22 Feb 1974; *Career* md Kelsar Corpn; *Style*— Sir Christopher Edwards, Bt; 11637 Country Club Drive, Westminster, Colorado 80234, USA (☎ 0101 30346 93156)

EDWARDS, Sir (John) Clive Leighton; 2 Bt (UK 1921), of Treforis, Co Glamorgan; s of Sir John Bryn Edwards, 1 Bt (d 1922), and Kathleen Ermyntrude, *née* Corfield (d 1975); *b* 11 Oct 1916; *Educ* Winchester; *Career* European War 1940-45 with RASC and as Capt Royal Pioneer Corps; *Style*— Sir Clive Edwards, Bt; Milntown, Lezayre, nr Ramsey, IOM

EDWARDS, (John) Colin; s of John Henry Edwards (d 1985), of Penzance, and Gwendoline Doris, *née* Sara; *b* 27 August 1936; *Educ* Clifton Coll, Lincoln Coll Oxford (MA); *m* 24 Aug 1967, (Daphne) Paulette, da of (Herbert) Peter Bayley, of New Jersey, USA; 1 s (Gavin Perran b 30 March 1973), 1 da (Rebecca b 20 April 1971); *Career* slr 1960; attorney at law Jamaica 1971, dep coroner Truro Dist 1975, chm Social Security Appeal Tbnl 1980-, dep registrar High and Co Ct Western Circuit 1985-; chm Jamaica Rugby Football Union 1972-74 (rep 28 times 1962-72), dep chm Truro Squash Club 1983-87 (Jamaican Champion 1962-72); memb: Law Soc 1960, Jamaica Law Reform Ctee; *Recreations* golf, jogging, squash, reading, gardening; *Clubs* Truro Golf, Truro Squash; *Style*— Colin Edwards, Esq; 15 Nansavallon Road, Truro, Cornwall (☎ 0872 77138); Carlyon & Son, 78 Lemon Street, Truro, Cornwall (☎ 0872 78641, fax 0872 72072)

EDWARDS, David Manning; s of Maj Eric Arthur James Edwards, MC, OBE (d 1983), of Godalming, Surrey, and Sybil Manning, *née* Fenton; *b* 28 April 1947; *Educ* Guilford Sch of Art (BA); *m* 4 May 1974, Linda Jane, da of Norman Arthur Robert Winton, of Clockhouse Mews, Huxley Close, Charterhouse, Godalming, Surrey; 2 s (Adam Harry b 30 Nov 1979, Guy b 30 July 1982); *Career* cartoon film dir and designer, BAFTA Best Animated Cartoon Film Superted 1986; *Recreations* motor racing; *Style*— David Edwards, Esq; Berrymeadow Moorlands, Cowbridge, South Glamorgan CF7 7RQ (☎ 044 634622)

EDWARDS, David Michael; s of Denis Arthur Edwards, of London, and Maude, *née* Cruse; *b* 4 Dec 1947; *Educ* Tulse Hill, London Coll of Printing; *m* 1968, and Christine Nancy, da of John Carzana, of Kent; 2 s (Justin b 1979, Julian b 1981); *Career* publishing Print Buying; chm Paperback Production Gp 1981-82; chm Book Production Gp 1986-87, dir Macdonald & Co Ltd 1981-82; dir (fndr) Century Publishing Co Ltd 1982-85; dir Century Hutchinson Publishing Gp Ltd 1985-; *Recreations* golf, tennis, photography; *Clubs* Played Soccer Corinthian Casuals AFC (1st team) 1966-68; *Style*— David Edwards; 50 Barnfield Wood Road, Beckenham, Kent BR3 2SU; Brookmount House, 62-65 Chandos Place, London WC2N 4NW (telex 261212 LIT LDNG, fax 01-836 1409)

EDWARDS, David St John; s of Capt Herbert Edwards (ka 1917); *b* 16 April 1917; *Educ* Wellington, St John's Coll Cambridge; *m* 1947, Kathleen Mary, da of Surgn Rear Adm Gilbert Syms; 1 s, 2 da; *Career* freight forwarder, dir LEP Transport & Associated Cos 1960-, chm Express Container Transport 1972-; *Recreations* sailing, bridge; *Style*— David Edwards, Esq; Shenley, The Drive, Woking, Surrey (☎ 61535)

EDWARDS, (Ronald) Derek Keep; JP (Hampshire) 1984; s of Wing Cdr Ronald Allan George Edwards (d 1981), of Hampshire, and Edith Vere, *née* Keep (d 1974); *b* 22 Nov 1934; *Educ* Winchester; *m* 1, 6 June 1958, (m dis 1984), Sally Anne Edwards, da of Patrick Boyle Lake Coghlan, of Fernhurst, West Sussex; 4 s (David b 1959, Simon b 1960, James b 1962, Charles b 1969); m 2, 3 March 1988, Julia Ann; *Career* Kings Dragoon Gds 1953-55, Inns of Ct Regt (TA) 1955-61; memb Stock Exchange 1959; ptnr: R Edwards Chandler & Co 1965-69, Brewin Dolphin & Co 1969-80, AH Cobbold & Co 1980-85 dir Cobbold Roach Ltd 1985; govr Amesbury Sch 1971-86, churchwarden St Mary Aldermary City 1958-80; ctee memb: Hampshire Hunt Club, Bassishaw Ward Club (chm 1971), memb Ct of Common Cncl 1978-; Freeman City of London 1971, Worshipful Co of Loriners; FBIM; *Recreations* field sports, riding, skiing; *Clubs* Cavalry and Guards', City Livery; *Style*— Derek Edwards, Esq; Coneycroft House, Selborne, Hampshire; 73 Cornhill, London EC3; 2 New Town, Chichester, West Sussex (☎ 01 626 1601/0243 775373)

EDWARDS, Dr (Iorwerth) Eiddon Stephen; CMG (1973), CBE (1968); s of Edward Edwards (d 1944), and Ellen Jane, *née* Higgs (d 1942); *b* 21 July 1909; *Educ* Merchant Taylors', Gonville and Caius Coll Cambridge (MA, LittD); *m* 1938, Annie Elizabeth, yst da of Charles Edwards Lisle (d 1945); 1 s (Philip d 1968), 1 da (Lucy); *Career* keeper of egyptian antiquities Br Museum 1955-74, jt ed Cambridge Ancient History (3 edn) Vols 1-III; FBA; for assoc memb of the Académie des Inscriptions et Belles-Lettres Paris, ordinary memb of the German Archaeological Inst corresponding memb of the Fondation Egyptologique Reine Elisabeth Brussels; *Books* several publications on Egyptian archaeology and language; *Recreations* gardening; *Clubs* Athenaeum; *Style*— Dr Eiddon Edwards, CMG, CBE; Dragon House, Deddington, Oxford OX5 4TT (☎ 0869 38481)

EDWARDS, Elton Percy (Bill); *b* 25 Mar 1929; *Educ* Hereford HS for Boys; *m* 3 Sept 1956, Monica Jill; 1 s (Mark William b 3 Aug 1961), 1 da (Elizabeth Jane b 10 June 1958); *Career* CA Thompson and Wood Hereford 1951 (articled 1945-50), co sec and accountant Russell Baldwin and Bright 1954, ptnr Little Co 1964-86, sr ptnr Edwards Little Co 1986-, established insolvency practice 1967; sec OFFA Gp 1988, bd memb Wales and Border Counties Div of TSB Eng and Wales plc 1988; former chm Hereford Round Table, vice pres City of Hereford Rotary Club;; *Recreations* golf, fishing, swimming, motor caravanning; *Clubs* Rotary (Hereford); *Style*— Bill Edwards, Esq; Casita, 7 Yew Tree Gardens, Kings Acre, Hereford (☎ 0432 263040)

EDWARDS, Frank Wallis; CBE (1984); s of Arthur Edwards (d 1962), of Ipswich, and Mabel Lily, *née* Hammond (d 1956); *b* 23 Dec 1922; *Educ* Royal Liberty Sch Essex, Bradford Univ; *m* 1959, Valerie Ann, da of Reginald Claude Hitch, of Balcombe; 2 da (Elena, Melinda); *Career* Capt REME 1944-47; Dorr-Oliver Co 1953-70; project and sales engr 1953-59, dir 1959-70, md Euro ops 1966-69, divnl vice-pres int divn 1969-70, md Eur ops 1966-69, divnl vice-pres int divn 1969-70; Humphreys & Glasgow Ltd UK 1970-: dir 1971, md 1974, dep chm 1978-; dir: Humphreys & Glasgow Int Ltd 1973-, Process & Energy Consits Ltd (chm) 1974-, MHG Int Ltd 1975-83, Hydreq Ltd 1976-83 (chm 1982-83), Humphreys & Glasgow (Atlantic) Ltd 1976-, Energy Industs Cncl 1976-88, Canatom Heavy Water Ltd 1978-, Humphreys & Glasgow Inc 1981-, Goldmace Ltd 1981-83, Project Evaluation & Implementation Ltd 1982-, INITEC 1982-86, Humphreys & Glasgow (Overseas) Ltd 1982-, Humphreys & Glasgow Pacific Pty Ltd 1984-, Ebasco Humphreys & Glasgow 1984-86; cncl memb: Br Chemical Engrg Contractors Assoc 1974-83 (chm 1982-83), process plant NEDO 1977-83, Latin America Trade Advsy Gp (BOTB) 1978-84 (chm 1982-84), Sino-Br Trade Cncl (BOTB) 1977- (vice-pres 1983-); CEng, FIMechE, MIMechE, FInstD, FRSA (1983); Ordre Du Mono, Rupublic of Togo 1978; *Recreations* gardening, walking, theatre, woodland conservation; *Clubs* Army & Navy, Reform; *Style*— Frank Edwards, Esq, CBE; Spinney Corner, Church Rd, Woldingham, Surrey CR3 7JH (☎ 088 385 3360); Humphreys & Glasgow Ltd, Enserch House, 8 St James Sq, London SW1Y 4JU (☎ 01 930 7586, telecopy 01 930 8651, telex 28105)

EDWARDS, Gareth Owen; s of Arthur Wyun Edwards (d 1974), and Mair Eluned Jones; *b* 26 Feb 1940; *Educ* Herbert Stratt GS Derbyshire, Oxford Univ (Ba, BCL); *m* 1967, Katharine Pek Har, da of Goh Keng Swee, of Kuala Lumpur, Malaysia; 2 s (David b 1970, John b 1974), 1 da (Kim b 1968); *Career* barr Inner Temple 1963; Capt Army Legal Service 1963-65, Germany; Asst Legal Advsr Cwlth Office 1965-67, practised Wales and Chester Circuit 1967-; QC 1985, rec Crown Ct 1978; Boundaries Asst Cmmnr 1975-80; *Recreations* chess, cricket, tennis, hill walking; *Clubs* Army and Navy; *Style*— Gareth Edwards, Esq; 58 Cache Lane, Chester (☎ 0244 677795); Goldsmith Building, Temple (☎ 01 353 7881)

EDWARDS, Maj Geoffrey Francis; CBE (1975), OBE (1968, MBE 1956, TD 1949); s of Oliver Edwards (d 1938), of Langley, Bucks, and Frances Margaret, *née* Baylis (d 1971); *b* 28 Sept 1917; *Educ* Brighton Coll; *m* 1, 1949, Joyce Black (d 1953); 1 da (Sarah b 1953); m 2, 1961, Johanna Elisabeth Franziska Taeger, da of Dr Werner Heinen (d 1976); *Career* Maj NW Europe 1939-45; former memb HM Diplomatic Serv, finance div Control Cmmn for Germany 1945-49, Br Mil Govt Berlin 1949-66, HM consul-gen Berlin 1966-75, ret 1975; awarded Ernst Reuter Silver Plaque for Services to Berlin 1975; *Recreations* gardening, fishing and golf; *Style*— Maj Geoffrey Edwards, CBE, OBE, MBE, TD; Am Kurgarten 105, 5485 Sinzig-Bad Bodendorf, Germany (☎ 02642 44821

EDWARDS, Sir George Robert; OM (1971), CBE (1952, MBE 1945), DL (Surrey 1981); s of late Edwin George Edwards, of Highams Park, Essex; *b* 9 July 1908; *Educ* SW Essex Tech, London Univ (BSc); *m* 1935, Marjorie Annie, da of John Lawrence Thurgood; 1 da; *Career* aeronautical engineer; joined design staff Vickers Aviation Ltd 1935, experimental mangr 1940, ch designer Weybridge Works 1945, dir Vickers Ltd 1955-67; chm British Aircraft Corpn 1963-75; pro-chllr Surrey Univ 1964-79 (emeritus 1979-); memb Royal Instn 1971-; FRS; kt 1957; *Style*— Sir George Edwards, OM, CBE, DL; Albury Heights, White Lane, Guildford, Surrey (☎ 0483 504488)

EDWARDS, Prof (James) Griffith; yr s of late Dr James Thomas Edwards, and Constance Amy, *née* McFadyean; *b* 3 Oct 1928; *Educ* Andover GS, Balliol Coll Oxford, St Bart's Hosp Med Sch; *m* 1, 1969 (m dis 1981), Evelyn Humphries Morrison; 1 s (Daniel b 1970), 1 da (Rose b 1973 and 1 da decd); m 2, 1981, Frances Susan, da of late Lt-Col F H A Stables; *Career* hon conslt psychiatrist Bethlem Royal and Maudsley Hosps 1967-; Inst of Psychiatry: dir addiction res unit 1970-, prof of addiction behaviours 1979-; ed Br Journal of Addiction 1978-; *Books* Unreason in an Age of Reason (1971), Opium and the People (with Virginia Berridge, 1981), Treatment of Drinking Problems (1982, 2nd ed 1987, translated into 5 languages); *Clubs* Athenaeum; *Style*— Prof Griffith Edwards; 32 Crooms Hill, London SE10 8ER

EDWARDS, Hilary Anne; *née* Skinner; da of Charles Stapleton Skinner (d 1974), of Chichester, Sussex, and Dorothy Stapleton, *née* Morton (d 1978); *b* 20 Feb 1923; *Educ* Sydenham HS and Bromley HS; *m* 24 May 1947, John May Edwards, s of William May Edwards (d 1961), of Hove, Sussex; 1 s (Simon b 1954), 1 da (Amanda b 1951); *Career* regnl offr UN Assoc 1968-88, vice -hm Women's Advsy Cncl of UN 1986- (and 1978-84), memb exec ctee Soc for Int Devpt 1974-, convener SID UK Chapter Women in Devpt Gp 1981-, Gilbert Murray Sr Award for work in Int Affairs; *Recreations* gardening, philosophy, visual arts, writing poetry, travelling; *Clubs* Penn; *Style*— Mrs Hilary Edwards; Assaye, 29 Wellington Road, Parkstone, Poole, Dorset BH14 9LF (☎ 0202 743968)

EDWARDS, Jack Trevor; CBE (1985); s of Col Cyril Ernest Edwards, DSO, MC, JP, DL (d 1953), of Bullwood Hse, Hockley, Essex, and Jessie Boyd; *b* 23 June 1920; *Educ* Felsted, Imperial Coll London (BSc); *m* 3 Jan 1959, Josephine (Sally), da of late S W Williams; 1 da (Susan Nicola b 1960); *Career* RAF: Armament Branch 1941-45, Airfield Construction Branch 1945-46, Sqdn-Ldr 1946; consulting engr James Williamson & Ptnrs 1946-50, sr ptnr Freeman Fox & Ptnrs 1980-86 (engr 1951-64, ptnr 1965-79), chm Halcrow Fox Assocs 1985-, pres Herongate and Ingrave Preservation Soc, hon sec Brentwood and Dist Branch RNLI; chm Br Conslts Bureau 1983; Liveryman Worhsipful Co of Painter-Stainers; memb ACE, Fell FCGI 1982, FICE 1963, FCIT 1976; *Recreations* sailing; *Clubs* St Stephens Constitutional, Royal Cruising, Royal Burnham Yacht; *Style*— Jack Edwards, Esq, CBE

EDWARDS, James Valentine; CVO (1978); yst s of Capt Alfred Harold Edwards, OBE (d 1964), and Eleanor, *née* Hayes; *b* 4 Feb 1925; *Educ* Radley, Magdalen Coll Oxford (MA); *m* 1965, Barbara, twin da of Sir John Coldbrook Hanbury-Williams, CVO (d 1965), and formerly wife of Prince Michael Cantacuzène, Count Speránsky; 2 da (1 step s and 1 step da); *Career* served RN, Atlantic 1943 and Pacific 1944-45, able seaman; headmaster Heatherdown Sch 1959-82; *Clubs* MCC, Free Foresters, Vincent's (Oxford); *Style*— James Edwards, Esq; Long Sutton House, Long Sutton, nr Langport, Somerset (☎ 045 824 284)

EDWARDS, John; s of late Arthur Leonard Edwards; *b* 2 Jan 1932; *Educ* Wolverhampton Municipal GS; *m* 1, 1954, Nancy Woodcock (d 1978); 1 s, 1 da; m 2, 1979, Brenda Rankin; 1 da; *Career* journalist; editor Yorkshire Post 1969- (joined paper 1961); *Style*— John Edwards Esq; 1 Edgerton Rd, West Park, Leeds LS16 5JD

EDWARDS, John; s of Joseph Edwards, CBE, and Lily, *née* Edelmann; *b* 6 Nov 1941; *Educ* Kantonsschule Zurich Switzerland, Trinity Coll Cambridge (BA, MA); *m* 5 June 1980, Annemarie Alice Jessica, da of Claude Arpels, Légion D'Honneuv, of Rye, New

York; 1 s (Luke b 21 Nov 1980), 1 da (Kate b 5 Feb 1984); *Career* admitted slr 1969, ptnr Linklaters and Paines; sr visiting fell QMC London; memb Law Soc, Int Bar Assoc; *Recreations* swimming, skiing, music, literature, pictures; *Clubs* Annabel's, Mark's, RAC; *Style*— John Edwards, Esq; 46 Chelsea Pk Gdns, London SW3 (☎ 01 352 5749); Barrington House, 59-67 Gresham St, London EC2V 7JA (☎ 01 606 7080)

EDWARDS, John Coates; s of Herbert John Edwards and Doris May Edwards; *b* 25 Nov 1934; *Educ* Skinners' Sch Tunbridge Wells, Brasenose Coll Oxford; *m* 1959, Mary, *née* Harris; 1 s, 1 da; *Career* HM Dip Serv; head British Dvpt Div in the Caribbean 1978-81; head West Indian and Atlantic Dept FCO 1981-84; dep high cmmr British High Cmm Nairobi Kenya 1984-; *Clubs* Royal Cwlth Soc, Multaiga Country Club (Nairobi); *Style*— John Edwards, Esq; Fairways, Ightham, Sevenoaks, Kent (☎ 0732 883556); Foreign and Commonwealth Office, King Charles St, London SW1

EDWARDS, John Daniel; s of David Daniel Edwards (d 1954), of London, and Margaret, *née* Jenkins (d 1964); *b* 23 June 1922; *Educ* Central Sch London, St Martins Sch of Art, Architectural Assoc; *m* 31 May 1969, Patricia Margaret, da of Randolph Gibson (d 1973), of Bradford; *Career* RAFVR 1941-46; asst publicity mangr Crittall MFG Co Ltd 1947-61, mktg srevs mangr Ingersoll-Rand Co Ltd 1962-72, psychologist private practice 1973-; memb exec ctee London Welsh Assoc; Freeman City of London 1976, Liveryman Worshipful Co of Marketors 1977; FInstM 1972, FNCP 1983; *Recreations* travel, photography, motoring, flying, swimming, walking; *Style*— John Edwards, Esq; Ridgedale, Allison Gdns, Purley on Thames, Reading, Berks RG8 8DF (☎ 0734 422955)

EDWARDS, Prof John Hilton; s of Harold Clifford Edwards, CBE, of Cambridge, and Ida Margaret, *née* Phillips (d 1981); *b* 26 Mar 1928; *Educ* Uppingham, Cambridge Univ (BA, MB, BChir, MRCP); *m* 18 July 1953, Felicity Clare, OBE, da of Dr Charles Hugh Christie Toussaint (d 1985), of E Harting or Norfolk; 2 s (Conrad b 1959, Matthew b 1965), 2 da (Vanessa b 1956, Penelope b 1962); *Career* geneticist: MRC unit of population genetics Oxford 1958-59, Children's Hosp Philadelphia 1960; dept human genetics Univ of Birmingham: lectr, sr lectr, reader and prof 1961-79; consult WHO 1972-, med genetics NHS Oxford Regnl 1979-; prof of genetics Univ of Oxford 1979-; memb Nat Radiological Protection Bd 1987-; involved with Oxford local gp Muscular Dystrophy Gp of GB; FRCP 1972, FRS 1979; *Books* An Outline of Human Genetics (1978); *Recreations* gliding, skiing; *Clubs* Athenaeum; *Style*— Prof John Edwards; 78 Old Rd, Headington, Oxford OX3 7LP (☎ 0865 60430); Genetics Laboratory, Dept of Biochemistry, Univ of Oxford, South Parks Rd, Oxford OX1 3QU (☎ 0865 275 317, fax 0865 275 259, telex 83681)

EDWARDS, John Revill; s of Revill Edwards; *b* 18 July 1947; *Educ* Oundle, Aston Univ, Wharton Graduate Sch of Finance Pennsylvania Univ; *m* 1970, Vienneta Diane, *née* Oxford; 3 s; *Career* marketing dir Edgar Vaughn & Co Ltd; md Evco Chemicals Ltd; dir Houghton Danmark (Denmark); *Style*— John Edwards Esq; Old Birchwood Farm, Hoar Cross, Burton-on-Trent, Staffs (☎ 028 375 381)

EDWARDS, Joseph Robert; CBE (1963), JP (Oxford 1964); yst s of Walter Smith Edwards; *b* 5 July 1908; *Educ* HS Gt Yarmouth; *m* 1, 1936, Frances Mabel Haddon Bourne (d 1975); 3 s, 1 da; m 2, 1976, Joan Constance Mary Tattersall; *Career* joined Austin Motor Co 1928; md Br Motor Corpn 1966-68; chm Harland & Wolff Ltd 1970; dep chm Associated Engrg 1969-78; chm Penta Motors Ltd Reading 1978-87; dep chm Martin Electrical Equipment (Theale) Ltd 1979- dir: Br Printing Corpn 1973-81, CSE Aviation 1973-87, chm: Canewdon Conslts plc 1985-, Creative Industries Gp Inc (USA) 1985-; *Style*— Joseph Edwards, Esq, CBE, JP; Flat 16, Shoreacres, Banks Rd, Sandbanks, nr Bournemouth, Dorset (☎ Canford Cliffs 709315)

EDWARDS, Keith Harrap; s of Sir Martin Llewllyn Edwards (d 1987), and Lady Dorothy Ward *née* Harrap; *b* 17 Oct 1940; *Educ* Uppingham; *m* 23 May 1964, Susan Eleanore, da of John Walker Clevedon; 3 da (Juliet b 1967, Elizabeth b 1968, Caroline b 1971); *Career* slr 1966, ptnr C and M Edwards Shepherd and Co 1968-78, admin ptnr Edwards Geldard and Shepherd 1979-84; managing ptnr Edwards Gerdard 1985-; (Edwards Geldard Soliciters with offices in Cardiff, London, Derby, Hereford and Monmouth); *Clubs* Cardiff and County, Cardiff Athletic; *Style*— Keith Edwards, Esq; Ivydene, Aberthin, Cowbridge, S Glamorgan (☎ (04463) 2788); 16 St Andrews Crescent, Cardiff, South Glamorgan CF1 3RD (☎ 0222 238239, fax 0222 237268, telex 497913)

EDWARDS, (Alfred) Kenneth; MBE (1963); s of Ernest Edwards (d 1959), of Carteret House, Westway, London, and Florence May Branch (d 1983); *b* 24 Mar 1926; *Educ* Latymer Upper Sch, Magdalene Coll Cambridge, Univ Coll London (BSc); *m* 17 Sept 1949, Jeannette Lilian, da of David Louis Speeks, MBE; 1 s (Vaughan b 1951), 2 da (Vivien b 1954, Deryn b 1960); *Career* Fl Offr RAF 1944-47 (RAF Coll Cranwell 1945); HM Overseas Civil Serv Nigeria 1952-63; gp mktg mangr Thorn Electrical Industs Ltd 1964, int dir Brookhirst Igranic Ltd (Thorn Gp) 1967, gp mktg dir Cutler Hammer Europa 1972, chief exec Br Electrical and Allied Manufacturers Assoc Ltd (BEAMA) 1976-82; CBI memb cncl 1974 and 1976-82, memb fin and gen purposes ctee 1977-82, vice-chm Eastern Regnl Cncl 1974, memb pres's ctee 1979-82, dep dir gen 1982-; memb: exec ctee Organisme de Liaison des Industries Metalliques Europeennes (ORGALIME) 1976-82, bd Br Standards Inst (BSI) 1978-82 and 1984-; chm Br Electrotechnical Ctee and Electrotechnical Divnl Cncl 1981-, memb Br Overseas Trade Bd (BOTB) 1982-, memb Salvation Army London Advisory Bd 1982-, dir Business and Technician Educ Cncl (B/TEC) 1983-, memb BBC Consultative Gp on Industrial and Business Affairs 1983-; pres: European Ctee for Electrotechnical Standardisation (CENELEC) 1977-79, (memb Exec Ctee 1982- chm, finance ctee 1983-86), Union des Industries de la Communaute Europeenne (UNICE); memb ct Cranfield Inst of Technol 1970-75; memb of Bd and exec ctee, Business in the Community 1987-; FRSA 1985; *Recreations* music, books; *Clubs* Athenaeum, RAC, RAF; *Style*— Kenneth Edwards, Esq; Centre Point, 103 New Oxford St, London WC1A 1DU (☎ 01 379 7400 ext 2153, fax 01 240 1578)

EDWARDS, Hon Sir Llewellyn Roy; s of Rev Roy Thomas Edwards, AC, of 35 Quarry Street, Ipswich, Queensland, Australia and Agnes Dulcie, *née* Llewellyn; *b* 2 August 1935; *Educ* Ipswich GS, Univ of Queensland (MB BS); *m* 1957, Late Leone Sylvia, da of Leo Burley; 2 s (Mark, David), 1 da (Louise); *Career* dep med superintendent Ipswich Hosp; private med practice Ipswich (6 yrs), elected State memb for Ipswich 1972; state Min for Health 1974; elected Dep Premier and Tres, and Liberal Pty Ldr 1978; ret Queensland Parl 1983; Chm Ansvar Australia Insurance Ltd; Chm: Ansvar Australia Insurance Ltd, Northern Securities Mgmt Ltd, World Expo 88 Authority, Brisbane 1983-; Dir Westpac Banking Corp; Memb Univ of Queensland Senate; hon LLD Queensland Univ; fell Royal Australia Coll of Med Administrators (FRACMA); companion of the Order of Australia (1989); kt 1984; *Recreations* tennis, walking, cricket, rugby union, swimming, reading; *Clubs* Ipswich, Brisbane, United Services, Queensland Cricketers; *Style*— The Hon Sir Llewellyn Edwards; 8 Ascot Street, Ascot, Brisbane, Qld 4006, Australia; World Expo 88 House, 234 Grey St, South Bank, South Brisbane, Qld 4101, Australia (☎ 844 2844, telex 141988)

EDWARDS, Malcolm John; CBE (1985); s of John James Edwards (d 1967), of London, and Edith Hannah, *née* Riley (d 1966); *b* 25 May 1934; *Educ* Alleyn's Sch Dulwich, Jesus Coll Cambridge (MA); *m* 2 Dec 1967, Yvonne Sylvia, da of JAW Daniels, of Port Lincoln, Australia; 2 s (Jonathan John b 1970, Mark b 1972); *Career* bd memb Br Coal 1986 (dir of mktg 1973, commercial dir 1985), memb fin and gen purpose ctee Southwark Diocesan Bd of Educ; Freeman City of London; CBIM 1988; *Recreations* music, gardening, design 1860-1914; *Style*— Malcolm Edwards, Esq, CBE; Lodge Farm, Mootlane, Downton, Salisbury, Wilts SP5 3LN (☎ 0725 21538); British Coal, Hobart House, Grosvenor Place, London SW1 (☎ 01 235 2020)

EDWARDS, His Hon Judge; (Charles) Marcus; s of (John) Basil Edwards, CBE, (*qv*), of Worcester, and Molly Patricia *née* Philips (d 1979); *b* 10 August 1937; *Educ* Dragon Sch, Rugby, Brasenose Coll Oxford (BA); *m* 1, 1963, Anne Louise (d 1970), da of Sir Edmund Stockdale, Hoddington Ho, nr Basingstoke; m 2, Sandra Wates, da of J Mouroutsos, of Mass, USA; 1 da (Alexandra b 1983); *Career* 2 Lt Intelligence Corps 1955-56; HM Dip Serv 1960-65, third sec: Spain, S Africa, Laos, Whitehall; called to the Bar 1962, practising 1965-86, circuit judge 1986-; chm Pavilion Opera 1986-; *Recreations* gardening, walking, travel; *Clubs* Beefsteak; *Style*— His Hon Judge Edwards; Melbourne House, S Parade, London W4 1JU (☎ 01 995 9146)

EDWARDS, (John) Michael; CBE (1986), QC (1981); er s of Dr James Thomas Edwards (d 1951), and Constance Amy (d 1985) yr da of Sir John McFadyean; bro of Prof James Griffith Edwards, *qv*; *b* 16 Oct 1925; *Educ* Andover GS, Univ Coll Oxford (BA, BCL, MA); *m* 1, 1952 (m dis), Morna Joyce, *née* Piper; 1 s (James b 1957), 1 da (Caroline b 1955); m 2, 3 March 1964, Rosemary Ann, da of Douglas Kinley Moore (d 1982); 2 s (Tom b 1967, Owen b 1969); *Career* barr Middle Temple 1949, practised 1950-55; asst Parly cnsl to the Treasury 1955-60; dep legal advsr and dir of certain subsid cos Courtaulds Ltd 1960-67; Steel Corpn: joined 1967, dir legal services 1967-81, md (Int) 1968-81 chm and md (Overseas Service) 1975-81; memb: E Euro Trade Cncl 1973-81, Overseas Project B 1973-81, student educn advsy gp Inst of CAS 1982-88, academic cncl Inst of Int Business Law and Practice of ICC (Paris) 1982-88, disciplinary appeal ctee, Chartered Inst of Certified Accountants 1983- (chm 1987-); provost City of London Poly 1981-88; dir: Regnl Opera Tst (Kent Opera) 1981-88 (chm 1983-86) Bell Gp Int Ltd (formerly Associated Communications Corpn) 1982-, (md 1988) TVW (UK) Ltd 1982-, Product Innovation Ltd 1983-, Bell Resources Ltd (Aust) 1984-88; dep chief exec Bond Corpn (UK) Ltd 1988-; memb: Bar Cncl 1971-79 and 1980-83, Senate of Inns of Court and the Bar 1974-79 and 1980-83 (memb fin and exec ctees), ctee memb Bar Assoc for Commerce fin and Industry 1967- (chm 1972-78, vice-pres 1980-82); chm: Eastman Dental Hosp 1983- Inst of Dental Surgery 1983-; govr Br Past-graduate Med Fedn 1987-; Freeman: City of London, memb Court Worshipful Co of Ironmongers; CBIM, FRSA, FCIA 1984; *Recreations* listening to music, vernacular architecture, local history; *Clubs* Garrick; *Style*— Michael Edwards, Esq, CBE, QC; Bond Corporation (UK) Ltd, 140 Piccadilly, London W1V 9FH (☎ 01 495 2820)

EDWARDS, Norman John; s of Ernest Edwards, MBE, and Maude Mary Edwards; *b* 18 Oct 1920; *Educ* Eltham Coll; *m* 14 June 1952, (Isabelle) Margaret Doff, da of Edmond Compton; 1 s (Andrew b 1956), 2 da (Rosalyn b 1954, Gay b 1958); *Career* RE 1940-46, Bengal Sappers and Miners Indian Army 1942-46; ptnr Bernerd Thorpe & Ptnrs 1958-85; govr Eltham Coll (chm Walthamstow Hall 1975-85); memb Worshipful Co of Paviors; memb RICS 1948; *Recreations* gardening, sailing; *Clubs* Oriental, City Livery; *Style*— Norman Edwards, Esq; Westfield, Holbrook Lane, Chislenvest, Kent (☎ 01 467 3458)

EDWARDS, Paul Spencer; s of Alfred Henry Edwards of 43 Southview Rd, Hornsey, London N8, and Margery Caroline Edwards (d 1979); *b* 11 Nov 1942; *Educ* Stationer's Company GS; *m* 7 Sept 1963, Maureen Patricia, da of George Gregory, of 45 Augustus Road, Wimbledon SW19; 2 da (Michelle Caroline b 1966, Colette Mary b 1969); *Career* co dir (finance); dir: Albacore Leasing Ltd, Bermuda 1986, Commercial Container Transport Ltd 1986, Dolton Shipping Ltd 1983, Furness Travel Ltd 1984, Golden Cross Line Ltd 1984, Johnston Warren Lines Ltd 1985, W. Kemp & Co Ltd 1983, Manchester Adamson Ltd 1984, Manchester Liners Ltd 1982, Pacific Steam Navigation Co 1986, Royal Mail Lines Ltd 1986, Shaw Savill & Albion Co Ltd 1982, Stevinson Hardy (Tankers) ltd 1986; *Recreations* reading, military modelling and DIY; *Style*— Paul Edwards, Esq; 4, Eversley Mount, Winchmore Hill, London N21 1JP; 53 Leadenhall Street, London EC3A 2BR (☎ 01 481 2020)

EDWARDS, Peter Guy; JP (Durham 1963); s of Brig Claud Taylor Edwards, CBE (d 1978), and Maud Harriet (d 1977), da of Charles Hornung, of Oaklands, Horley, Surrey; *b* 9 Feb 1924; *Educ* Clifton, Pembroke Coll Cambridge, Durham Univ (BSc); *m* 1959, Jill Mary, da of William Devas Everington, of Blakeney, Norfolk; 1 s (Giles b 1961), 2 da (Camilla b 1963, Nicola b 1969); *Career* RE served 1942-45, SEAC 1945-47, resigned Hon Capt 1948; dir Smiths Dock Co 1957-66, chm Tees Div 1965-66, memb Tees-side ctee N Regnl Bd for Indust 1959-65 (chm 1965); cncl memb Newcastle Univ 1963-67, dir Dunford & Elliott 1967-77, chm Brown Bayley Steels Ltd and Dunford Hadfields 1970-77, pres BISPA 1975-77; dir Hunting Petroleum Servs 1978-; chm Lake & Elliot Ltd 1979-84 (dir 1978-84); north regnl dir Granville & Co 1981-; High Sheriff Co Durham 1968-69; CEng, CBIM; *Recreations* shooting, fishing; *Clubs* Northern Counties; *Style*— Peter Edwards, Esq, JP; Low Walworth Hall, Darlington, Co Durham (☎ 0325 468004)

EDWARDS, Peter Robert; s of Robert Edwards of Worthing, West Sussex, and Doris Edith, *née* Cooper; *b* 30 Oct 1937; *Educ* Christ's Hosp; *m* 1967, Elizabeth Janet, da of Maitland Barrett; 1 s (Simon b 1970), 1 da (Sarah b 1971); *Career* Arthur Young 1955-(managing ptnr 1988-); Freeman City of London 1956, memb Worshipful Co of Merchant Taylor; ICAS 1960; *Recreations* ornithology; *Clubs* Caledonian; *Style*— Peter Edwards, Esq; Glebe Cottage, Church Lane, Bury, Pulborough, West Sussex RH20 1PB (☎ 0798831 774), Arthur Young, Rolls House, 7 Rolls Buildings, Fetter Lane, London EC4A 1NH (☎ 01 831 7130, fax 01 405 2147, telex 888604)

EDWARDS, Rear Adm (John) Phillip; CB (1984), LVO (1971); s of Robert Edwards (d 1981), of Llanbedr, Ruthin, and Dilys Myfanwy, *née* Phillips (d 1947); *b* 13 Feb 1927; *Educ* Brynhyfryd Sch Ruthin, HMS Conway, RNEC (MA); *m* 1951, Gwen, da of John Lloyd Bonner (d 1982), of Cefn, Llandyrnog, Denbigh, Clwyd; 3 da (Susan, Lynn, Siân); *Career* RN 1944-83; Rear Adm serving as dir gen Fleet Support 1980-83; currently fell and bursar Wadham Coll Oxford, memb Welsh Health Policy Bd, pres Midland Naval Offrs Assoc, vice pres Oxfordshire SSAFA, pres Oxford Branch RNA; FIMechE, FBIM; *Recreations* golf; *Clubs* Frilford Heath GC; *Style—* Rear Adm Phillip Edwards, CB, LVO; Wadham Coll, Oxford OX1 3PN (☎ 0865 277963)

EDWARDS, His Hon Judge Quentin Tytler; QC (1975); s of Herbert Jackson Edwards (d 1950), of Alexandria, Egypt and Burgess Hill, Sussex, and Juliet Hester, *née* Campbell (d 1940); *b* 16 Jan 1925; *Educ* Bradfield; *m* 18 Nov 1948, Barbara Marian, da of Lt Col Alec Guthrie (d 1952), of Hampstead; 2 s (Adam b 1951, Simon b 1954), 1 da (Charlotte b 1949); *Career* WWII RN 1943-46; called to the Bar Middle Temple 1948, bencher 1972, circuit judge 1982; chllr: diocese of Blackburn 1977, diocese of Chichester 1978; memb Diocese Cmmn Gen Synod 1978-, fndr memb Highgate Soc 1965-, vice chm Ecclesiastical Law Soc 1987-, pres Highgate Literary and Scientific Inst 1988; memb of the Bar Cncl 1958-60 and 1977-81, licensed as a reader in the diocese of London 1967-, memb Legal Advsy Cmmn of Gen Synod C of E 1971-, columnist Guardian Gazette 1975-82; Hon MA awarded by Archbishop of Canterbury 1961; *Books* Ecclesiastical Law, (Third Edn), Halsbury's Law of England (with K Macmorran et al 1952); *Recreations* the open air, architecture; *Clubs* Athenaeum; *Style—* His Hon Judge Quentin Edwards, QC; Bloomsbury County Ct, 7 Marylebone Rd, London NW1 5HY (☎ 01 637 8703)

EDWARDS, Robert John; CBE (1986); s of William Gordon Edwards (d 1938); *b* 26 Oct 1925; *Educ* Ranelagh Sch Bracknell; *m* 1, 1952 (m dis 1972), Laura Ellwood; 2 s, 2 da; m 2, 1977, Brigid O'Neil Forsyth, *née* Segrave; *Career* editor: Tribune 1951-54, Sunday Express 1957-59 (dep), Daily Express 1961 (managing editor 1959-61), Evening Citizen Glasgow 1962-63, Daily Express 1963-65, Sunday People 1966-72, Sunday Mirror 1972-85, dep chm Mirror Gp Newspapers 1985-86; *Books* Goodbye Fleet Street (1988); *Recreations* sailing; *Clubs* Kennel, Reform, Roy Southern Yacht, Variety Club of GB; *Style—* Robert Edwards, Esq; 74 Duns Tew, Oxford OX5 4JL

EDWARDS, Robert Wynnie (Bob); MBE (1986); s of late Edward Thomas Edwards, of Sycharth, Llangedwyn, nr Oswestry, and late Angelena Louise, *née* Morris; *b* 12 Sept 1917; *Educ* Oswestry Boys HS, Shrewsbury Tech Coll; *m* 4 Dec 1948, Joan, *née* Gretton; 1 s (Kenneth b 1951), 3 da (Mary b 1949, Janet b 1953, Jean b 1955); *Career* WWII serv 6 years: Vickers machine gunner trg CI, coastal def Kent and Sussex, Normandy landing; bank clerk 1936-47, currently farms 450 acres at Llangedwyn; Agric Trg Bd: chm Clwyd Trg Ctee 1978, former memb Welsh Conslt Ctee, pres Dyffryn Tanat Trg Gp 1987- (chm 1975-87); NFU: pres Oswestry Branch 1982-84 (chm 1968-70), former chm Educn and Trg Panel, former chm Land Use Panel; memb Welsh Jt Educn Ctee; chm: Clwyd Rural Enterprise Unit, bd govrs Llysfasi Coll, jt ctee Welsh Agric Coll; former chm bd govrs: Llfyllin HS, Dinas Bran Sch; memb: Regnl Land Drainage Ctee 1985-, Clwyd and Powys Area Manpower BD 1983-88; fndr memb and vice-chm: Clwyd Rural Devpt Panel (later Clwydfro), Antur Tanat Cain; Ceiriog DCllr 1968-74, Denbighshire cllr 1971-74, Clwyd cllr (ind memb) 1974-, vice-chm Clwyd CC 1987 (chm 1988), chm Clwyd SW Cons Assoc 1985-88; memb CLA, NFU; *Style—* Bob Edwards, Esq; Gartheys, Llangedwyn, Nr Oswestry SY10 9LQ (☎ 049 186 336)

EDWARDS, Hon Robin Ernest; o s of Baron Chelmer, MC, TD (Life Peer); *b* 23 Sept 1940; *Educ* privately; *m* 1967, Carol Mayes; 1 da (Charlotte b 1969); *Style—* Hon Robin Edwards; 14 Augustin Way, Bicknacre, Danbury Way, Essex (☎ 024 541 4321)

EDWARDS, Prof Ron Walter; s of Walter Henry Edwards (d 1975), of Birmingham, and Violet Ellen, *née* Groom; *b* 7 June 1930; *Educ* Solihull Sch, Univ of Birmingham (BSc, DSc); *Career* 2 Lt RAOC 1948-50; res scientist: Freshwater Biological Soc 1953-58, Water Pollution Res Laboratory 1958-68; prof and head dept Univ of Wales Inst Sci and Technol 1968-; memb Natural Environment Res Cncl 1970-73 and 1981-84, memb and dep chm Welsh Water Authy 1974-, memb Nat Rivers Authy Advsy Ctee 1988; memb: nat ctee Euro Year of Environment 1987-88 (chm Wales), Prince of Wales Ctee, cncl RSPB 1988-(chm Wales); FIBiol, FIWEM, FIFM; *Books* Ecology of the River Wye, Conservation and Productivity of Natural Waters, Pollution, Acid Waters; *Recreations* collecting 19 century staffordshire pottery; *Style—* Prof Ron Edwards; Talybont-on-Usk, Brecon, Powys; Hollybush Heights, Cyncoed, Cardiff, South Glam

EDWARDS, Prof Sir Samuel Frederick; s of Richard Edwards, of Swansea, and Mary Jane Edwards; *b* 1 Feb 1928; *Educ* Swansea GS, Gonville and Caius Coll Cambridge (MA, PhD, fell 1972), Harvard; *m* 1953, Merriell E M Bland; 1 s, 3 da; *Career* prof of theoretical physics Manchester Univ 1963-72, John Humphrey Plummer prof of physics Camb Univ 1972-84, Cavendish prof of physics Camb Univ 1984-; UK del to NATO Sci Ctee 1974-79; Inst of Mathematics and its Applications: memb of cncl 1976-, vice-pres 1979, pres 1980-81; Defence Scientific Advsry Cncl: memb 1973, chm 1977-80; memb advsy cncl on R & D, Dept of Energy, 1974-77, chm and chief scientific advsr 1983-88; memb Cncl Euro Res & Devpt (EEC) 1976-80; chm cncl BAAS 1977-82 (pres 1988-89); chm SRC 1973-77; non-exec dir: Lucas Indust 1981-, Steetley plc 1985-; FRS, Hon DSc (Bath, Birmingham, Edinburgh, Salford, Strasbourg and Wales), Hon D Tech (Loughborough), FInstP, FRSC, FIMA, kt 1975; *Books* Technological Risk (1980), Theory of Polymer Dynamics (1986); *Clubs* Athenaeum; *Style—* Prof Sir Sam Edwards; 7 Penarth Place, Cambridge CB3 9LU (☎ 0223 66610); Cavendish Laboratory, Cambridge (☎ 0223 337259)

EDWARDS, Sandra Mouroutsos; da of James Mouroutsos, of USA, and Joanna, *née* Felopulos; *b* 14 July 1941; *Educ* Bennington HS, Mount Holyoke Coll (BA); *m* 1, 10 Jan 1965 (m dis 1975), Christopher Stephen Wates; 3 da (Melina b 1966, Georgina b 1967, Joanna b 1970); m 2, 21 Nov 1975 (Charles) Marcus Edwards His Hon Judge, *qv*; 1 da (Alexandra b 1983); *Career* conslt Conspectus Project Mgmnt Conslts 1986-88 (ptnr 1988-); nat chm: Fair Play for Children 1972-77, Pre Sch Playgroups Assoc 1974-77; memb: Westminster City Cncl 1974-78, Ealing Borough Cncl 1978-82; Parly candidate Swansea East 1979; memb: NW Thames RHA 1980-84, Hammersmith and Queen Charlotte's Special Health Authy 1984- (dep chm 1986-); chm: Paddington Churches Housing Assoc 1977-, Sutherland Housing Assoc 1977-, memb Nat Fedn Housing Assocs Cncl 1978-81 and 1987- (dep chm 1989-), chm Knowles Tst 1980-; *Recreations* indoor gardening; *Style—* Mrs Sandra Edwards; Melbourne House, South Parade, London W4 1JU (☎ 01 995 9146)

EDWARDS, Sydney Clive; s of late Edward George Edwards; *b* 29 Oct 1935; *Educ* Newton-Le-Willows GS; *m* 1960, Marjorie Eleanor, da of Richard Bryce Fowler; 1 s, 1 da; *Career* CA with Price-Waterhouse (Holland) 1960-65; accountant and dir Alliance Wholesale Grocers/Food Securities 1965-75; fin dir: Mojo Carryway Ltd 1975-77, Lo-Cost Stores Ltd 1977-; FCA; *Recreations* local and family history, music, Welsh; *Style—* Sydney Edwards, Esq; 22 Woodlands Rd, Parkgate, South Wirral, Cheshire (☎ 051 336 1190)

EDWARDS, (Cecil Ralph) Timothy; s of (Herbert Cecil) Ralph Edwards, CBE (d 1978) and Grace Marjorie, *née* Brooke (d 1983); *b* 25 July 1928; *Educ* Westminster, Trinity Coll Cambridge (MA); *m* 1957, Brenda Mary, da of Joseph Henry Vaughan Gibbs; 3 s (Mark b 1957, Simon b 1959, Stephen b 1967), 2 da (Jane b 1961, Katharine b 1963); *Career* served Welsh Guards 1947-48, 2 Lt; ptnr Grieveson Grant & Co (stockbrokers); memb: Stock Exchange 1961, Cncl of Stock Exchange 1980-88, dir The Securities Assoc 1987; chm Kleinwort barrington Ltd dir: Kleinwort Smaller Companies Investment Tst plc, Balston Investment Tst plc; vice pres Nat Museum of Wales 1987-; *Clubs* Brooks's, Leander; *Style—* Timothy Edwards, Esq; Grendon Court, Upton Bishop, Ross-on-Wye H29 7QP

EDWARDS, Wilfred Thomas; s of Thomas Edwards (d 1965), of Caverswall, and Bessie Edith, *née* Rooke (d 1981); *b* 6 Jan 1926; *Educ* Newcastle HS, Univ of London (LLB, Dip HA); *Career* Nat Serv 1944-47; inspr of taxes HM Inland Revenue dept 1948-86 (univ recruitment liason regnl offr dist and head off), tax conslt 1986-; chm Art Club 1974-; memb bd dirs English Speaking Union Club 1979- (govr 1972-78), former chm cncl Staffordshire Soc, voluntary asst Westminster Abbey; Freeman City of London 1971, Liveryman Worshipful Co Loriners 1981; FGS, FRSA; *Recreations* painting, landscape and portrait; *Clubs* Athenaeum, Hurlingham; *Style—* Wilfred Edwards, Esq; Corner Cottage, Brancaster, Norfolk; Friarswood, The Park, Cheltenham, Glos; 18 North Lodge Close, London SW15 6QZ(☎ 01 789 3935)

EDWARDS, William Philip Neville; CBE (1949); s of Neville Perrin Edwards (d 1956), of Orford, Littlehampton, Sussex; *b* 5 August 1904; *Educ* Rugby, Corpus Christi Coll Cambridge, Princeton Univ USA; *m* 1, 8 April 1931, Hon Sheila Cary (d 1976), 2 da of 13 Viscount Falkland, OBE (d 1961); 2 s; m 2, 1976, Joan, da of Reginald Graham Barker, and widow of Norman Mullins; *Career* head industrial information div Miny of Production 1943-45; cnsllr Br Embassy Washington, in charge of Br Info Serv in USA 1946-49; dir Confedn of Br Ind 1949-66; md Br Overseas Fairs Ltd 1960-66, chm 1966-68; *Recreations* golf and gardening; *Clubs* Carlton; *Style—* William Edwards, Esq, CBE; Four Winds, Kithurst Lane, Storrington, W Sussex

EDWARDS, William Philip Neville (Bill); CBE (1949); s of Neville Perrin Edwards (d 1956), of Orford, Littlehampton, Sussex, and Margaret Alexandrina Eliza, *née* Connal (d 1960); *b* 4 August 1904; *Educ* Rugby, Corpus Christi Coll Cambridge (MA), Princeton Univ USA; *m* 1, 8 April 1931, Hon Sheila Cary (d 1976), da of 13 Viscount Falkland, OBE (d 1961); 2 s (Timothy b 1933, d 1987, Jeremy b 1937); m 2, 1976, Joan Ursula, wid of Norman Mullins, da of Capt Reginald Graham Barker; *Career* London Transport Bd (formerly Underground Electric gp of cos) 1927-41: sec to Lord Ashfield, asst outdoor supt of railways 1938, PR offr 1939; asst to chm of supply cncl Miny of Supply 1941-42, head of industl info div Miny of Prodn and dir of infor Br Supply Cncl N America 1943-45, dir overseas info div Bd of Trade 1945-46, head of Br Info Servs in USA (FO) 1946-49, dir CBI and md Br Overseas Fairs LTd 1949-66, chm Br Overseas Fairs Ltd 1966-68, UK assoc dir Business Int SA 1968-75, chm PR Indust Lt 1970-75; Chevalier first class of the Order of Dannebrog Denmark 1955, Cdr of the Order of Vasa Sweden 1962; *Recreations* golf, gardening; *Clubs* Carlton, Walton Heath GC, West Sussex GC; *Style—* Bill Edwards, Esq, CBE; Four Winds, Kithurst Lane, Storrington, Sussex RH20 4LP (☎ 09066 4507)

EDWARDS-JONES, Ian; QC (1967); s of Col Henry Vaughan Edwards Jones, MC, DL (d 1959), of Swansea, and Mary Catherine, *née* Bloomer (d 1976); *b* 17 April 1923; *Educ* Rugby, Trinity Coll Cambridge (BA); *m* 3 June 1950, Susan Vera Catharine, da of Col Edward Stanley McClintock (d 1975), of Wallingford, Berks; 3 s (Simon b 1952, Mark b 1955,Michael b 1957); *Career* war serv Field Artillery 1942-47 (ME, N Africa, Italy); barr Middle Temple and Lincoln's Inn 1948, practised at Chancery Bar 1949-79, bencher Lincoln's Inn 1975; social security cmmr 1979-85, The Banking Ombudsman 1985-88, fisheries memb Regnl Fisheries Advsy Ctee and other Ctees ot Welsh Water Authy 1982-; *Recreations* fishing, shooting, photography, wine growing; *Clubs* United Oxford and Cambridge; *Style—* Ian Edwards-Jones, Esq, QC; 7 Stone Bldgs, Lincoln's Inn, London WC2 (☎ 01 405 3886)

EDWARDS-MOSS, Sir David John; 5 Bt (UK 1868), of Roby Hall, Lancs; eldest s of Sir John Herbert Theodore Edwards-Moss, 4 Bt (d 1988); *b* 2 Feb 1955; *Educ* Cranleigh; *Heir* bro, Peter Michael Edwards-Moss b 26 Sept 1957; *Style—* David Edwards-Moss, Esq; Ruffold Farm, Cranleigh, Surrey

EDWARDS-MOSS, Lady; Jane Rebie; *née* Kempson; o da of Carteret John Kempson, of Four Corners, Ewhurst, Surrey; *m* 21 Nov 1951, Sir John Herbert Theodore Edwards-Moss, 4 Bt (d 1988); 5 s (Sir David John, 5 Bt, *qv*, Peter Michael b 26 Sept 1957, Paul Richard b 12 May 1960, Christopher James b 27 Jan 1963, Jonathan Francis William b 29 May 1967), 1 da (Penelope Anne b 3 Feb 1956); *Style—* Lady Jane Edwards-Moss; Ruffold Farm, Cranleigh, Surrey

EDYNBRY, Lance David; s of Ryes Edynbry (d 1960), of Sussex, and Kathleen Janet Whittle, *née* Kidman; *b* 21 April 1947; *Educ* Worthing Boys GS, Rose Bruford Coll of Speech & Drama (Dip Holder), Newcastle Univ (MEd); *m* 3 Sept 1977, Geneviève Marie-Louise Andrée, da of Jean-Joseph Cros, of France; 1 da (Anne-Claire b 1980); *Career* professional repertory actor 1969-70, i/c drama in Lower Sch Thomas Bennett 1970-71, head of drama & sixth form tutor Hayfield CS 1971-76, sr lectr in drama Charlotte Mason Coll of Educn 1976-85; export dir Vignobles Jean Cros France 1985; FRSA; *Recreations* riding, gardening; *Clubs* Farmers; *Style—* Lance Edynbry, Esq; La Jancade, Senouillac, 81160 Gaillac, France (☎ 63 41 51 16); Le Mas des Vignes, 81140 Cahuzac/Vere (☎ 63 33 92 62, telex 532 691 F)

EELEY, Nicholas John; s of Sqdn-Ldr (Thomas) Ian Samuel Eeley (d 1979), of Lindfield, Sussex, and Muriel Evelyn, *née* Hockley; *b* 16 April 1936; *Educ* Charterhouse; *m* 28 Sept 1963, Gillian Mary Francis, da of Cyril Joseph Cooke, of Upminster, Essex; 1 da (Harriet Amelia Catherine b 6 Feb 1967); *Career* Nat Serv pilot RAF 1953-55; NM Rothschild & Sons Ltd 1956-83; dir: NM Rothschild Asst Mgmnt Ltd 1973-83, Global Asset Mgmnt (UK) Ltd 1984-; Freeman City of Oxford 1960; *Recreations* farming, antique furniture; *Style—* Nicholas Eeley, Esq; 33 Chalcot Cres, London NW1 8YG (☎ 01 586 0366); Gam House, 12 St James's Place, London

SW1A 1NX (☎ 01 493 9990, fax 01 493 0715, telex 296099 GAMUK G)

EELLS, Hon Mrs (Harriet Elizabeth); *née* Bridges; o da of 2 Baron Bridges, GCMG, *qv*; *b* 28 Nov 1958; *m* 4 July 1981 (m dis), John Charles Eells, s of Prof James Eells, of Wellesbourne, Warwick; *Style*— Hon Mrs Eells

EFFINGHAM, 6 Earl of (UK 1837); Mowbray Henry Gordon Howard; also 16 Baron Howard of Effingham (E 1554); s of 5 Earl of Effingham (d 1946); *b* 29 Nov 1905; *Educ* Lancing; *m* 1, 28 Oct 1938 (m dis 1946), Maria Malvin Gertler; m 2, 12 Aug 1952 (m dis 1971), Gladys Irene Kerry; m 3, May 1972, (Mabel) Suzanne Mingay, da of late Maurice Jules-Marie Le Pen, of Paris, and widow of Wing Cdr Francis Talbot Cragg; *Heir* n, Cdr David Peter Mowbray Algernon Howard, RN; *Career* RA and 3 Maritime Regts WWII; *Recreations* shooting, fishing, philately; *Style*— The Rt Hon Earl of Effingham; House of Lords, London SW1 9DR

EGAN, Sir John Leopold; s of James Edward Egan (d 1982); *b* 7 Nov 1939; *Educ* Imperial Coll London (BSc), London Business Sch (MSc); *m* 1963, Julia Emily, da of George Treble, of Leamington Spa; 2 da; *Career* parts and service dir Leyland Cars 1971-76, corporate parts dir Massey Ferguson 1976-80, chm and chief exec Jaguar Cars Ltd 1980-; kt 1986; *Recreations* skiing, squash, walking, music; *Clubs* Warwick Boat; *Style*— Sir John Egan; Jaguar Cars Ltd, Browns Lane, Coventry CV5 9DR (☎ 0203 402121)

EGAN, Lt-Col Leonard John; DL; s of Leonard John Egan (d 1964), and Mary Elizabeth, *née* Donavon (d 1970); *b* 12 Mar 1924; *Educ* Downside; *m* 1 June 1948, Mina Patience Mary, da of Harry Hickley, of Rowford House, Cheddon Fitzpaine, Taunton Somerset; 1 s (Tom b 1949), 4 da (Harriet b 1950, Joanna b 1954, Mary-Anne b 1956, Naomi b 1962); *Career* cmmnd Royal Welch Fusiliers 1943; served: India, Burma, Japan, Malaya, Germany, W Indies, Malaya, Cyprus, Singapore, Germany, UNF Cyprus, Gulf States 1943-71; cmd 1 RWF 1966-69 (Lt-Col 1966), ret 1975; dep sec TAVR Assoc, Wales 1975-; memb St John Cncl for Clwyd 1975 (chm 1985), OStJ 1981, CStJ 1987; *Recreations* gardening; *Clubs* St John House, Eaton Place, London SW1; *Style*— Lt-Col Leonard Egan, DL; c/o Lloyds Bank, 6 Pall Mall, London SW1Y 5NH

EGAN, Patrick Valentine Martin; s of Eric Egan; *b* 17 July 1930; *Educ* Downside; *m* 1953, Mary Theresa, da of Frederick Hinds Coleman (d 1960); 3 da; *Career* Signals Instr Roy Artillery Far East 1949-50; exec dir Unilever plc and Unilever NV 1978-; *Recreations* riding, hunting, gardening; *Style*— Patrick Egan Esq; Whiteways, Sissinghurst, Cranbrook, Kent (☎ 0580 713201)

EGDELL, Dr (John) Duncan; s of John William Egdell, of Bristol, and Nellie; *b* 5 Mar 1938; *Educ* Clifton, Univ of Bristol (MB, CLB), Univ of Edinburgh (Dip Soc Med); *m* 9 Aug 1963, Dr Linda Mary, da of Edmund Harold Flint (d 1974), of Barnehurst, Kent; 2 s (Brian, Robin), 1 da (Ann); *Career* house physician and surgn Utd Bristol Hosps 1961-62, gen practice 1962-65, admin med offr Newcastle Regnl Hosp Bd 1966-67 (asst sr med offr 1968-69), asst sr med offr SW Region Hosp Bd 1969-72 (princ asst sr med offr 1972-74, regnl specialist in community med 1974-76), regnl med offr Mersey Regnl Authy 1977-86, community physician Clywd Health Authy 1986-; FFCM 1979; *Recreations* nature conservation, delving into the past; *Style*— Dr Duncan Egdell; Gelli Gynan Lodge, Llanarmon-yn-ial, Near Mold, Clywd CH7 4QX (☎ 08243 345); Clywd Health Authority, Preswylfa, Hendy Road, Mold, Clywd CH7 1PZ (☎ 0352 700227)

EGERTON; *see*: Grey Egerton

EGERTON, Brian Balguy Le Belward; bro and hp of Sir Philip Grey Egerton, 15 Bt, *qv*; *b* 5 Feb 1925; *Educ* Repton; *Style*— Brian Egerton Esq; Vinha Velha, Vale de Currais, 8400 Praia do Carvoeiro, Algarve, Portugal

EGERTON, Cyril Reginald; s of late Hon Francis William George Egerton (2 s of 3 Earl of Ellesmere); hp of 1 cous, 6 Duke of Sutherland; *b* 7 Sept 1905; *Educ* Lancing, Trinity Coll Cambridge; *m* 1, 8 Dec 1934, Mary (d 23 Sept 1949), da of Rt Hon Sir Ronald Hugh Campbell, GCMG; 1 s (Francis), 3 da (Mrs Michael (Lucy) Pelham, Mrs Frank (Katharine) Watts, Mrs Thomas (Alice) Fremantle); m 2, 29 Jan 1954, Mary Truda (d 1982), o da of late Sir (Thomas) Sydney Lea, 2 Bt; *Career* 1939-45 War as Capt Hampshire Regt, seconded to RIASC; memb London Stock Exchange 1931-83; prime warden of Dyers' Co 1953-54; *Style*— Cyril Egerton, Esq; Hall Farm, Newmarket, Suffolk (☎ 0638 662557)

EGERTON, Maj-Gen David Boswell; CB (1969), OBE (1956), MC (1940); s of Vice Adm Wion de Malpas Egerton, DSO (ka 1942), of Chilfrome, Dorset, and Anita Adolphine, *née* David (d 1972); *b* 24 July 1914; *Educ* Stowe, RMA Sandhurst, Army Staff Coll, RMC of Science, Imperial Def Coll; *m* 1946, Margaret Gillian, da of Rev Canon Charles Cuthbert Inge (d 1957); 1 s (William), 2 da (Charlotte, Caroline); *Career* offr RA 1934- served: India, France, Belgium, Egypt, Italy, USA, Col i/c ammunition design 1955-58, Brig Def Res Policy Staff 1959-62, Brig cmdg Artillery Trials Estab 1962-63, Maj-Gen Air Def Working Pty 1963-64, Dir Gen Artillery 1964-67, vice-pres Ordnance Bd 1967-69 (pres 1969-70); gen sec Assoc of Recognised Eng Language Schs 1971-79, memb cncl Gabbitas Thring Educnl Tst 1976-, vice-chm and tstee Dorset Assoc for the Disabled 1982; *Clubs* Army & Navy; *Style*— Maj Gen David Egerton, CB, OBE, MC

EGERTON, Francis Louis; MC; s of Louis Edwin Egerton (2 s of Sir Alfred Egerton, KCVO, CB, by his w Hon Mary Ormsby-Gore, er da of 2 Baron Harlech) and bro of Sir Alfred Egerton, who adopted Francis after his f's death in action 1917; Louis's w was Jane, da of Rev Lord Victor Seymour, 4 s of 5 Marquess of Hertford; *b* 14 Feb 1918; *Educ* Eton, Christ Church Oxford; *Career* Capt Welsh Guards; private sec to Sir Alexander Cadogan at Security Cncl New York 1946-47; chm Mallett & Son 1950-; *Recreations* travelling, gardening; *Clubs* White's; *Style*— Francis Egerton, Esq, MC; The Hermitage, Crichel, Wimborne, Dorset (☎ 0258 840 223)

EGERTON, Sir Jack (John Alfred Roy); s of J G Egerton; *b* 11 Mar 1918; *Educ* Rockhampton HS, Mt Morgan HS, Aust Admin Staff Coll; *m* 1940, Moya, da of W Jones; 1 s; *Career* former pres Qld Trades and Labour Cncl, dir Qantas Airways Ltd 1973-, chm Labour Enterprise Pty Ltd, chm Labour Broadcasting Pty Ltd; alderman and deputy mayor Gold Coast City Council; kt 1976; *Recreations* reading, Rugby League, golf; *Clubs* NSW and Queensland League; *Style*— Sir Jack Egerton; Gold Coast City Centre, Bundall Rd, Southport, Qld 4215, Australia

EGERTON, Sir Seymour John Louis; GCVO (1977, KCVO 1970); s of Capt Louis Edwin Egerton (2 s of Sir Alfred Egerton, KCVO, CB, himself sixth in descent from Hon Thomas Egerton, 3 s of 2 Earl of Bridgwater, of an illegitimate line from the ancestors of the Grey-Egerton Bts) and Jane, da of Rev Lord Victor Seymour, 4 s of 5 Marquess of Hertford; *b* 24 Sept 1915; *Educ* Eton; *Career* served WW II Capt Gren Gds; banker, chm Coutts & Co 1951-76; Sheriff Gtr London 1968; *Clubs* Boodle's, Beefsteak, Pratt's; *Style*— Sir Seymour Egerton, GCVO; Flat A, 51 Eaton Sq, London SW1 (☎ 01 235 2164)

EGERTON, Sir Stephen Loftus; KCMG (1988, CMG 1978); s of William le Belward Egerton, ICS (ggs of William Egerton, yr bro of Sir John and Rev Sir Philip Grey-Egerton, 8 and 9 Bts respectively) and Angela Doreen Loftus, *née* Bland; *b* 21 July 1932; *Educ* Eton, Trinity Coll Cambridge (MA); *m* 1958, Caroline, da of Maj Eustace Thomas Cary-Elwes, TD, of Laurel House, Bergh Apton, Norfolk; 1 s, 1 da; *Career* 2 Lt KRRC 1951-53; Dip Serv 1956-: consul-gen Rio de Janeiro 1977-80, ambass Iraq 1980-82, asst under-sec of state FCO 1982-5, ambass Saudi Arabia 1986-; Order of King Faisal Bin Abdul Aziz Class 1 (1987); *Clubs* Brooks's, Greenjackets, Eton Ramblers; *Style*— Sir Stephen Egerton, KCMG; c/o FCO (Riyadh), London SW1

EGERTON, Thomas Edward Sydney; s of Cdr Hugh Sydney Egerton (d 1969), of Sussex, and Muriel Georgina, *née* Beckwith-Smith (d 1969); *b* 13 Oct 1918; *Educ* Eton, Christ Church Oxford (MA); *m* 19 Dec 1962, Harriet Anne, da of Ralph Cobbold (d 1987), of Suffolk; 1 s (Charles b 1963), 2 da (Lucinda b 1965, Philippa b 1969); *Career* Capt Coldstream Gds 1940-46, (serv N Africa, Italy); farmer of 1000 acres Heads Farm and 650 acres Mountfield; chm Tattersalls Ctee, High Sheriff E Sussex 1975; memb: Berks CC 1954-64, E Sussex CC 1964-74; *Recreations* shooting, racing; *Clubs* White's, Turf, Pratt's, Jockey; *Style*— Thomas E S Egerton, Esq; Heads Farm Chaddleworth, Newbury (☎ 04882 255); Mountfield Court, Robertsbridge (☎ 0580 880442)

EGERTON-WARBURTON, Hon Mrs (Marya Anne); *née* Noble; da of Baron Glenkinglas (Life Peer, d 1984), and Baroness Glenkinglas, *qv*; *b* 10 Dec 1944; *m* 6 June 1969, as his 3 wife, Peter Egerton-Warburton, *qv*; 1 s, 1 da (twin); *Style*— Hon Mrs Egerton-Warburton; Mulberry House, Bentworth, Alton, Hants GU34 5RB (☎ 0420 62360); 54 Prince's Gate Mews, London SW7 2RB

EGERTON-WARBURTON, Peter; Lord of the Manor of Grafton, patron of the livings of Plemstall and Guilden Sutton; o s of Col Geoffrey Egerton-Warburton, DSO, TD, JP, DL (d 1961); ggs of Rowland Egerton, bro of Sir John Grey-Egerton, 8 Bt, and Rev Sir Philip Grey-Egerton, 9 Bt), and Hon Georgiana Mary Dormer, MBE (d 1955), eldest da of 14 Baron Dormer, CBE, DL; *b* 17 Jan 1933; *Educ* Eton, RMA Sandhurst; *m* 1, 29 Jan 1955 (m dis 1958), Belinda Vera, da of late James R A Young, of Cowdrays, East Hendred, Berks; m 2, 10 Nov 1960 (m dis 1967), Sarah Jessica, er da of Maj Willoughby Rollo Norman (2 s of Rt Hon Sir Henry Norman, 1 Bt); 2 s; m 3, 6 June 1969, Hon Marya Anne, *qv*, 2 da of Baron Glenkinglas, PC; 1 s, 1 da (twin); *Career* cmmnd Coldstream Gds 1953, ret 1962 with rank of Capt; Maj Cheshire Yeo 1963; ptnr John D Wood Estate Agents 1966-86; fndr and chm Egerton Ltd Estate Agents 1986-; landowner; *Clubs* White's, Pratt's, Beefsteak; *Style*— Peter Egerton-Warburton, Esq; 54 Prince's Gate Mews, London SW7 2PR (☎ 01 589 9254); Mulberry House, Bentworth, Alton, Hants GU34 5RB (☎ 0420 62360)

EGGAR, Hon Mrs (Angela Lilian); *née* Mackenzie; only da of 1 Baron Amulree, GBE, PC, KC (d 1942); *b* 16 Jan 1905; *m* 28 Nov 1931, Patrick James Eggar, eldest s of Robert Henry Eggar, of Bentley, Hants; *Style*— Hon Mrs Eggar; The Barton, Ditcheat, Somerset

EGGAR, Tim(othy) John Crommelin; MP (C) Enfield N 1979-; s of John Drennan Eggar (d 1983), and Pamela Rosemary Eggar; *b* 19 Dec 1951; *Educ* Winchester, Magdalene Coll Cambridge, London Coll of Law; *m* 1977, Charmian Diana, da of Peter William Vincent Minoprio, late Capt WG; 1 s, 1 da; *Career* barr; banker; PA to Rt Hon William Whitelaw 1974, pps to Min Overseas Devpt 1982-85, parly under-sec of state FCO 1985-; dir Charterhouse Petroleum 1983-85; *Style*— Tim Eggar, Esq, MP; House of Commons, London SW1 (☎ 01 735 0157)

EGGINGTON, Dr (William Robert) Owen; s of Alfred Thomas Eggington, MC (d 1980), and Phyllis *née* Wynne (d 1980); *b* 24 Feb 1932; *Educ* Kingswood Sch Bath, Guy's Hosp Med Sch (MB BS, DTM & H, DPH, DIH); *m* 20 Jan 1962, Patricia Mary Elizabeth, da of Maj Henry David Grant, MBE, MC (d 1980), of Cameronians & Palestine Police; 1 s (Patrick Thomas b Oct 1962), 1 da (Claire Mary Ruth b Jan 1964); *Career* RAMC, RMO 2 RHA 1957-60, sr specialist Army Health 1962-73, ret Lt-Col 1973; DHSS Norcross Blackpool: med offr 1973, sr med offr 1979, princ med offr 1984, chief med advsr Socl Security; MFCM 1970; *Recreations* Goss heraldic china, mil history, assoc football; *Style*— Dr Owen Eggington; 1 Steeple Ct, Coventry Road, London E1 5QZ (☎ 01 247 2455); Friars House, 157-168 Blackfriars Rd, London SE1 8EU (☎ 01 928 0850, fax 01 928 5162)

EGGINTON, Anthony Joseph; s of Arthur Reginald Egginton (d 1952), and Margaret Anne, *née* Emslie (d 1951); *b* 18 July 1930; *Educ* Selhurst GS, UCL (BSc); *m* 30 Nov 1957, Janet Leta, da of Albert Herring (d 1966); 2 da (Katharine b 1960, Sarah b 1962); *Career* dir programmes Sci and Engrg Res Cncl 1983-; res assoc: UCL 1951-56, AERE Harwell (Gen Physics Div) 1956-61; head: Beams Physics Gp, NIRNS Rutherford High Energy Laboratory 1961-65, Machine Gp, SRC Daresbury Nuclear Physics Laboratory 1965-72, Engrg Div 1972-74; dir: Engrg and Nuclear Physics 1974-78, Sci and Engrg 1978-83, Engrg 1983-88; *Books* papers and articles in journals and conference proceedings on particle accelerators; *Recreations* sport, cinema, music; *Clubs* Lansdowne; *Style*— Anthony Egginton, Esq; Witney House, West End, Witney OX8 6NQ (☎ 0993 3502); Science and Engineering Research Council, Polaris House, North Star Avenue, Swindon SN2 1ET (☎ 0793 26222 ext 2139, telex 449466, fax 0793 511181)

EGGLESTON, Hon Sir Richard Moulton; s of John Bakewell Eggleston (d 1932),and Elizabeth Bothwell, *née* McCutcheon (d 1912); *b* 8 August 1909; *Educ* Wesley Coll Melbourne, Queen's Coll Melbourne Univ (LLB); *m* 1934, Isabel Marjorie, da of Francis Edward Thom (d 1948); 1 s, 2 da (and 1 decd); *Career* judge Cwlth Industrial Ct and Supreme Ct ACT 1960-74, judge Supreme Ct Norfolk Is 1960-69, dir Barclays Australia 1974-80; Hon LLD (Melbourne 1973, Monash 1983); kt 1971; *see Debrett's Handbook of Australia and New Zealand for further details*; *Recreations* painting, golf, billiards; *Style*— Hon Sir Richard Eggleston; Willow St, Malvern, Vic 3144, Australia (☎ 20 5215)

EGGLESTON, Prof Samuel John; s of Edmund Eggleston (d 1959), and Josephine Eggleston (d 1985); *b* 11 Nov 1926; *Educ* Chippenham GS, London Univ (MA, BSc, DLitt); *m* 1957, Greta Margaret, da of James Patrick (d 1967), of Hereford; 2 s, 2 da; *Career* prof of educn Keele Univ 1967-84; prof and chm of educn Warwick Univ 1985-; dir of Res Multi Cultural Educn 1978-85; memb consultative ctee assessment of performance unit DES 1980-; memb trg ctee Arts Cncl 1983-87; chm educn ctee centl TV 1987-, chm of judges Young Electronics Designer Competition 1986-, judge Granada Power Game; academic advsr: Routledge and Kegan Paul 1977-, Trentham Books Books 1983-; ed: Sociological Review, Studies in Design Education; chm ed bd Euro Jl of Educn, Multi Cultural Teaching; lectr and examiner many home and overseas universities; FCP 1983; *Books Incl:* The Ecology of the School (1977), Work Experience in Schools (1982), Education for Some (1986); *Recreations* work in design and craft, skiing, riding, travel, gardening; *Style—* Prof Samuel Eggleston; Whitmore Heath, Newcastle-under-Lyme, Staffordshire (☎ 0782 680483); University of Warwick, Warwickshire (☎ 0203 253848)

EGLESTON, Lady Clarissa; *née* Windsor-Clive; da of 2 Earl of Plymouth (d 1943); *b* 15 Jan 1931; *m* 24 April 1953, Maj Keith Maclean Forbes Egleston, late Rifle Bde, yr s of late Maj Thomas Buchanan Maclean Egleston, MC, of White Hart Lodge, Limpsfield, Surrey; 1 s, 2 da; *Style—* Lady Clarissa Egleston; 7 Ernest Gdns, W4

EGLINGTON, Charles Richard John; s of Richard Eglington, and Treena Margaret Joyce Eglington; *b* 12 August 1938; *Educ* Sherborne; *Career* dir Akroyd & Smithers plc, jt dep chm Cncl of Stock Exchange 1981-84, chm Stock Exchange Property and Finance Ctee 1983-86; dir: S G Warburg, Akroyd, Rowe and Pitman, Mullens Securities Ltd; govr: Sherborne Sch, Twyford Sch; *Recreations* cricket, golf; *Clubs* MCC, Walton Heath, Rye, Royal & Ancient; *Style—* Charles Eglington, Esq; Warburg Securities, 1 Finsbury Avenue, London EC2M 2PA

EGLINTON AND WINTON, 18 Earl of (S 1507 and UK 1859); Archibald George Montgomerie; Lord Montgomerie (S 1449), Baron Seton and Tranent (UK 1859), Baron Ardrossan (UK 1806); Hereditary Sheriff of Renfrewshire; s of 17 Earl of Eglinton and Winton (d 1966), and Ursula (d 1987), da of Hon Ronald Bannatyne Watson, s of Baron Watson (Life Peer, d 1899); *b* 27 August 1939; *Educ* Eton; *m* 7 Feb 1964, Marion Carolina, da of John Henry Dunn-Yarker, of Le Château, La Tour de Peilz, Vaud, Switzerland; 4 s (Lord Montgomerie b 1966, Hon William b 1968, Hon James b 1972, Hon Robert b 1975); *Heir* s, Lord Montgomerie; *Career* dep chm Gerrard & Nat Hldgs plc; *Style—* The Rt Hon the Earl of Eglinton and Winton; The Dutch House, West Green, Hartley Wintney, Hants (☎ 3160); Gerrard and National Holdings plc, 33 Lombard St, London EC3V 9BQ (☎ 01 623 9981, telex 883589)

EGMONT, 11 Earl of (I 1733); Sir Frederick George Moore Perceval; 15 Bt (I 1661); also Baron Perceval (I 1715), Viscount Perceval (I 1722), Baron Lovell and Holland (GB 1762), Baron Arden (I 1770), Baron Arden (UK 1802); s of 10 Earl (d 1932 before establishing claim to Earldom), and Cecilia (d 1916), da of James Burns Moore; *b* 14 April 1914; *m* 31 Aug 1932, Ann Geraldine, da of Douglas Gerald Moodie, of Calgary, Alberta; 1 s (and 2 decd), 1 da; *Heir* s, Viscount Perceval; *Style—* The Rt Hon the Earl of Egmont; Two-dot Ranch, Nanton, Alberta, Canada

EGNER, William Edward; CBE (1974), JP (1968); s of George August Egner (d 1943); *b* 20 Feb 1911; *Educ* Jarrow Secondary Sch, Durham Univ (BSc), Cambridge Univ (BA); *m* 1939, Anne Muriel, da of John Davison Young (d 1968); 1 s, 2 da; *Career* sr scientific offr Fighter Cmd RAF, scientific advsr to C-in-C Flying Training Cmd RAF and head of Operational Research Section 1943-45; headmaster: Easingwold Grammar Sch 1939-46, Heanor G S Derbyshire 1946-50, Ormskirk G S Lancs 1950-55, Grammar Tech Sch for Boys S Shields 1955-74, Harton Comprehensive Sch S Shields 1974-76, ret 1976; memb Nat Cncl for Academic Awards 1968-74, fnd fellow Inst of Mathematics and Its Application, memb Nat Cncl for Audi Visual Aid Educn; former pres S Shields Rotary; author of articles in journals on operational research in educn, computer educn, application of computing; *Recreations* travel, painting in oils and music; *Clubs* Victory (London); *Style—* William Egner, Esq, CBE, JP

EGREMONT, 2 Baron (UK 1963) and 7 Baron Leconfield (UK 1859); (John) Max Henry Scawen Wyndham; s of 6 Baron Leconfield and 1 Baron Egremont, MBE (d 1972; as John Wyndham was priv sec to Rt Hon Harold Macmillan, when PM); *b* 21 April 1948; *Educ* Eton, Christ Church Oxford; *m* 15 April 1978, Caroline, da of Alexander Ronan Nelson and Hon Audrey Paget (da of 1 and last Baron Queenborough, s of Lord Alfred Paget, 5 s of 1 Marquess of Anglesey); 1 s (Hon George Ronan Valentine b 31 July 1983), 3 da (Hon Jessica Mary b 27 April 1979, Hon Constance Rose b 20 Dec 1980, Hon Mary Christian b 4 Oct 1985); *Heir* s, Hon George Wyndham; *Career* farmer and writer; chm The Friends of the Nat Libraries 1985-, tstee The Wallace Collection; memb Royal Cmmn on Historical MSS 1989; *Books* The Cousins (1977), Balfour (1980), The Ladies Man (1983), Dear Shadows (1986), Painted Live (1989); *Style—* The Rt Hon Lord Egremont; Petworth House, Petworth, W Sussex GU28 0AE (☎ 0798 42447)

EGREMONT, Dowager Baroness, and Leconfield; Pamela; da of Capt Hon Valentine Wyndham Quin (d 1983, 2 s of 5 Earl of Dunraven and Mount-Earl); sis of Lady Roderic Pratt and Marchioness of Salisbury; *b* 29 April 1925; *m* 24 July 1947, 1 Baron Egremont (and 6 Baron Leconfield), MBE (d 1972); 2 s (2 (& 7) Baron Egremont (and Leconfield), Hon Harry Wyndham), 1 da (Hon Mrs Chisholm); *Style—* The Rt Hon Dowager Lady Egremont; Cockermouth Castle, Cockermouth, Cumbria; 62 Chester Sq, London SW1 (☎ 01 730 2003)

EHRMAN, John Patrick William; s of Albert Ehrman (d 1969), and Rina, *née* Bendit; *b* 17 Mar 1920; *Educ* Charterhouse, Trinity Coll Cambridge (MA); *m* 1 July 1948, Elizabeth Susan Anne, da of Vice Adm Sir Geoffrey Blake, KCB, DSO (d 1968); 4 s (William b 1950, Hugh b 1952, Richard b 1956, Thomas b 1959); *Career* fell Trinity Coll Cambrdige, 1947-52; historian Cabinet Off 1948-56, Lee's Knowles lectr Cambridge Univ 1957-8, James Ford special lectr Oxford Univ 1976-77; hon tres Friends Nat Libraries 1960-77, vice-pres Navy Records Soc 1968-70 and 1974-76, memb reviewing ctee on Export of Works of Art 1970-76, tstee nat Portrait Gallery 1971-85, memb Royal Cmmn Historical Mss, chm advsy Br Library Reference Div 1975-84; FBA, FSA, FRHist S; *Books* The Navy in the War of William III (1953), Grand Strategy 1943-45 (1956), The British Government and Commercial Negotiations with Europe (1962), The Younger Pitt (vol 1 1969, vol 2 1983), Cabinet Government and War 1890-1940 (1988); *Clubs* Army and Navy, Beefsteak, Garrick; *Style—* John Ehrman, Esq; The Mead Barns, Taynton, Burford, Oxfordshire

EILLEDGE, Elwyn Owen Morris; s of Owen Eilledge, of Oswestry, Shropshire, and Mary Elizabeth Eilledge (d 1973); *b* 20 July 1935; *Educ* Oswestry Boys HS, Merton Coll Oxford (BA, MA); *m* 30 March 1962; 1 s (Julian Alexander Stephen b 15 June 1970), 1 da (Amanda Gail Caroline b 20 Nov 1968); *Career* qualified CA 1963, sr ptnr Ernst & Whinney (formerly Whimey Murray) 1986-88 (joined 1965, ptnr 1972-83, managing ptnr 1983-86), chm Ernst & Whimey Int 1988-; secondments: Govt of Liberia 1966-68, Hamburg 1968-71; memb Worshipful Co of CA's; FCA; *Recreations* gardening, snooker; *Clubs* Brooks's Gresham; *Style—* Elwyn Eilledge, Esq; Whitethorn Ho, Long Grove, Seer Green, Beaconsfield, Bucks (☎ 0494 676 600); Ernst & Whinney, Becket Ho, 1 Lambeth Palace Rd, London SE1 7EU (☎ 01 928 2000, fax 01 928 1345, telex 885234)

EILOART, Mildred Joy; da of George Maxwell Eiloart, DFC, RFC (despatches twice; his log book mentions flying gold out to Lawrence of Arabia), of Lyndhurst Gdns, Hampstead (d 1964), and Mildred Octavia, *née* Coles (d 1982); niece of Cyril Eiloart, Lt Ir Gds (ka 1918, France), Oswald Eiloart, Actg Capt 1 Bn London Regt (ka 1917, France), and Actg Maj Horace Eiloart, DSO, MC (d 1920 from wounds rec'd in France); gd of F E Eiloart; (sr ptnr Watney Eiloart, Inman and Nunn, City Estate Agents and Surveyors); *Career* sec/PA to: Dep Overseas Dir FBI 1958-63, Capt Jaspar Teale, RN, chief of the Navy Section, Ops Div, SHAPE, Paris; sec/asst librarian to Chief Economist at Rio-Tinto Zinc Corpn 1965-81; since when free-lance; *Recreations* theatre, ballet, art exhibitions, music, horse racing, reading, walking in the country, European travel; *Clubs* Theatregoers', European Assocn of Prof Secs, Nat Tst, Racegoers'; *Style—* Miss Mildred Eiloart; Flat 38, 7 Elm Park Gardens, London SW10 9QG (☎ 01 352 4222)

EILON, Prof Samuel; s of Abraham Joel (d 1974), and Rachel, *née* Deinard (d 1982); *b* 13 Oct 1923; *Educ* Reali Sch Haifa, Technion Haifa (BSc, DipIng), Imperial Coll London (PhD, DSc); *m* 8 Aug 1946, Hannah Ruth, da of Max Samuel; 2 s (Amir, Daniel), 2 da (Romit, Carmel); *Career* Maj Israel Defence Forces 1948-52; engr in indust 1945-48; Imperial Coll London: res asst/lectr 1952-57, reader 1959-63, prof of mgmnt sci 1963-89, head of section/dept 1963-87 sr res fell 1989-; assoc prof Technion Haifa 1957-59, conslt to indust 1957-; Silver Medal The Operational Res Soc 1982; hon FCGI 1978; FIMechE, FIProdE, CBIM, FEng; *Recreations* tennis, walking; *Clubs* Athenaeum; *Style—* Prof Samuel Eilon; Imperial Coll, Exhibition Rd, London, SW7 (☎ 01 589 5111 ext 7001)

EISLER, Hon Mrs (Jean Mary); 2 da of 1 Baron Layton, CH, CBE (d 1966), and Eleanor Dorothea, *née* Osmaston (d 1959); *b* 14 April 1916; *Educ* St Paul's Girls' Sch London, Royal Coll of Music (ARCM), Nordoff/Robbins Music Therapy Diploma; *m* 12 June 1944, Paul Eisler (d 15 Aug 1966), yr s of Ernst Eisler (d 1951), of Prague; 2 s (John b 1946, Ivan b 1948); *Career* music therapist; sr music therapist Goldie Leigh SE2 1976-, sr music therapist Queen Mary's Hosp for Children Carshalton 1984-, sr Music Therapist Nordoff/Robbins Music Therapy Centre London 1984-; fndn memb management ctee Nordoff/Robbins Music Therapy Centre; *Style—* Hon Mrs Eisler; Syskon Cottage, 2 Millfield Lane, London N6

EISNER, Hans - Gunter (Hans); s of Ludwig Eisner (d 1972), of 321 Wilbraham Road, Chorlton-cum- Hardy, Manchester, and Hertha, *née* Buckwitz (d 1976); *b* 4 July 1929; *Educ* Manchester Central High GS, Univ of Manchester Sch of Architecture (BArch); *m* 13 June 1953, (Doreen) Annette Elizabeth, da of Reginald Barker-Lambert, of Tree Tops, Marley Rd, Exmouth, Devon; 2 s (Christopher Paul David b 20 Nov 1954, Andrew James Stephen b 27 May 1961); *Career* architect in private practice 1983-; with Assoc Architects Fairhursts Manchester 1952-53, architect and gp leader Middlesbrough Educn Architects Dept 1954-56, architect i/c Drawing Office Borough of Watford 1956-57, sr assoc architect New School Section Derbyshire Co Architects Dept 1957-62, sr architect i/c R & D Gp Manchester City Housing Dept 1962-63, princ assoc architect SW Regnl Health Authy 1963-75, architect and area build- ing offr Devon Area Health Authy 1975-83; princ projects include: Ladgate Primary Sch Middlesbrough, Devpt Project for Infant Educn Sawley Infants Sch Long Eaton Derbys, Royal United Hosp Bath Phase I; memb: RIBA Cncl 1975-78, RIBA P/R TV and Bdcast Ctee 1965-69, RIBA Devon and Exeter Branch Exec 1984-, RIBA SW Regnl Cncl 1975- 78, Cncl Assoc of Official Architects 1959-85 (chm 1972-82), Rotary Club of Exeter (jr vice-pres), RIBA; *Recreations* walking, music, sketching, travel, gardening; *Clubs* Rotary; *Style—* Bickleigh House, Edginswell Lane, Kingskerswell, Devon TQ12 5LU (☎ 08047 3597, 008 047 3597, 0392 263 089)

EKINS, Eric Walker; s of Thomas Edward Ekins (d 1982), of Barrow-in-Furness, Cumbria, and Janet Walker, *née* Armstrong; *b* 16 June 1938; *Educ* Preston Catholic Coll Lancs; *m* 22 Sept 1962, Patricia Mary, da of Timothy Brendan Laffan, of Eastbourne, E Sussex; 1 da (Clare b 1975); *Career* sr ptnr Ekins and Co Chartered Accountants; FCA; *Recreations* walking, ornithology, music; *Clubs* North Wilts Rotary; *Style—* Eric Ekins, Esq; 3 Manor Close, Blunsdon, Swindon SN2 4BD (☎ 0793 721 292); Ekins & Co, 31 Victoria Rd, Swindon SN1 3AQ (☎ 0793 642 577)

ELAM, His Hon Judge Henry Havelock; o s of Thomas Henry Elam (d 1912), of 41 Holland Park, London, and Ethel Matilda, *née* Stanper (d 1955); *b* 29 Nov 1903; *Educ* Charterhouse, Lincoln Coll Oxford (MA); *m* 1, 1930, Eunice (d 1975), yr da of J G Matthews, of 41 Redington Rd, NW3; 1 da (Jane); m 2, 1975, Doris Annie, da of George Horsford (d 1968), of Burwash, E Sussex; *Career* Sqdn Ldr and Dep Judge Advocate RAF 1939-44; jr prosecuting cnsl for Crown 1937-53, rec: Poole 1941-48, Exeter 1948-53; a circuit judge (late dep chm ct Quarter Sessions, Inner London) 1953-76 ret; *Recreations* fly fishing; *Style—* His Hon Judge Elam; Clymshurst, Burwash Common, E Sussex (☎ 0435 883 335)

ELAM, (John) Nicholas; s of John Frederick Elam, OBE, and Joan Barrington, *née* Lloyd; *b* 2 July 1939; *Educ* Colchester Royal GS, New Coll Oxford, Frank Knox fell Harvard Univ; *m* 14 Oct 1967, (Florence) Helen, da of Pieter Lentz; 2 s (Peter, Michael), 1 da (Alexandra); *Career* entered HM Dip Serv 1962, FO 1962-64, served Pretoria and Capetown 1964-68, Treasy Centre Admin Studies 1968-69, FCO 1969-71, first sec Bahrain 1971, comm sec Brussels 1972-76, FCO 1976-79 (dep head News Dept 1978-79, cnsllr and Br Govt rep Salisbury 1979), dep high cmmr Salisbury (later Harare) 1980-83, consul gen Montreal 1984-87, head Cultural Relations Dept FCO 1987-; *Recreations* travel, the arts; *Style—* Nicholas Elam, Esq; Foreign and Commonwealth Office, King Charles St, London SW1A 2AH

ELBORNE, Robert Edward Monckton; s of Sidney Lipscomb Elborne, MBE, (d 1986), of Water Newton, nr Peterborough, and Cavil Grace Mary, *née* Monckton (d 1984); *b* 10 Nov 1926; *Educ* Eton, Trinity Coll Cambridge (MA); *m* 25 July 1953, (Leslie) Vivienne, da of Lt Gen Sir Ernest Wood, KCB, CIE, CB, MC (d 1972), of Foxton House, nr Cambridge; 2 s (Mark Edward Monckton b 1958, William Henry Alexander b 1966), 1 da (Charlotte Julia Mary Beare); *Career* Lt Life Gds 1945-47, Lt The Inns of Ct Regt TA 1950-56; called to the Bar Inner Temple Midland Circuit 1950-57, ptnr Waltons & Co 1958-67, sr ptnr Elborne Mitchell & Co 1968-82 (conslt 1982-87); non exec dir: Leicester Building Soc 1982-86, Alliance and Leicester

Building Soc 1986-, Chllr Insur Co Ltd 1988-; external memb Cncl of Lloyds 1983-87; Freeman City of London, Liveryman Worshipful Soc of Waterman and Lightermen; *Clubs* Boodle's, Beefsteak, City of London; *Style*— Robert Elborne, Esq; Seaton Old Rectory, Oakham, Leicestershire LE15 9HU (☎ 057 287 276)

ELCOAT, Rev Canon (George) Alastair; s of George Thomas Elcoat (d 1955), of 137 High View, Wallsend-on-Tyne, and Hilda Gertrude, *née* Bee (d 1962); *b* 4 June 1922; *Educ* Tynemouth Sch, The Queen's Coll Birmingham; *Career* RAF 1941-46; ordained deacon Newcastle 1951, priest 1952, asst curate Corbridge 1951-55, vicar: Spittal 1955-62, Chatton W Chillingham 1962-70, Sugley 1970-81, Tweedmouth 1981; rural dean: Newcastle West 1977-81, Norham 1982; chaplain HM The Queen 1982; *Recreations* fell walking, music, photography; *Style*— Rev Canon Alastair Elcoat; The Vicarage, 124 Main St, Tweedmouth, Berwick-on-Tweed TD15 2AW

ELDEN, Jeremy Mark; s of Reginald Elden, and Sheilagh, *née* Carter; *b* 21 June 1958; *Educ* Northgate GS Ipswich, Hertford Coll (BA), Univ of Strathclyde (MSc); *m* 19 Sept 1987, Victoria Mary, *née* Bone; *Career* field engr Schlumberger Overseas SA 1980-82, reservoir engr Britoil 1982-83, oil analyst Phillips & Drew 1984-; *Style*— Jeremy Elden, Esq ; 74 Andrewes House, Barbican, London EC2Y 8AY (☎ 01 588 2995); 120 Moorgate, London EC2M 6XP (☎ 01 628 4444, fax 01 628 6471)

ELDER, Prof Murdoch George; s of Archibald James Elder, of Biggar, Scotland, and Lotta Annie Catherine, *née* Craig; *b* 4 Jan 1938; *Educ* Edinburgh Acad, Edinburgh Univ (MB, ChB, MD); *m* 3 Oct 1964, Margaret Adelaide, da of Dr James McSuicker (d 1985), of Portrush, Co Antrim, Ireland; 2 s (James b 1968, Andrew b 1970); *Career* Nat Serv: Captain RAMC (TA and VR) 1964; lectr Univ of Malta 1969-71, sr lectr and reader Univ of London (Charing Cross Hosp Med Sch) 1971-75, WHO res fell 1976, RCOG travelling fell 1977; prof and head Dept of Obstetrics and Gynaecology Royal Postgraduate Med Sch Univ of London 1978-; dir WHO clinical res centre 1980-, memb Hammersmith and Queen Charlottes Special Authy 1982-, chm hosp med ctee 1980-85; examiner Univs of: London, Oxford, Edinburgh, Glasgow, Leeds, Liverpool, Birmingham, Bristol, Malaysia, Capetown; sec Assoc of Profs (O and G) 1984-86, memb WHO steering ctee on contraception 1980-86; FRCS (1968), FRCOG (1978), silver medal Hellenic Obstetrical Soc 1983; *Books* Current Fertility Control (1978), Pre Term Labour (1982), Reproduction, Obstetrics and Gynaecology (1988); *Recreations* golf, travel; *Clubs* Roehampton; *Style*— Prof Murdoch Elder; 4 Stonehill Road, London SW14 8RW (☎ 01 876 4332); Hammersmith Hospital, Du Cane Road, London W12 0HS (☎ 01 743 7171)

ELDER, Walter Brisbane; s of William Johnstone Elder, of Eildon, Strathaven, Lanarkshire, and Jane, *née* Young; *b* 18 Nov 1904; *Educ* Strathaven Acad Hindenburg Sch; *m* 28 March 1963 Christine Margaret Brisbane, da of William Stewart (1972), of Rio de Janeiro, Brazil; *Career* RASC 1944-46; ARP 1939-43 served in France and Germany, dir and chm Hamilton ACasFC 1956-70, chm Elder & Watson 1946-80; pres: Strathaven MIA 1946-56; Glasgow C of C 1946-80; *Recreations* gardening, conservation; *Clubs* Constitutional; *Style*— Walter Elder, Esq; The Spittal House & Lodge, Stonehouse, Lanarkshire (☎ 792224)

ELDERFIELD, Maurice; s of Henry Elderfield (d 1977), and Kathleen Maud, *née* James; *b* 10 April 1926; *Educ* Southgate Co GS; *m* 22 Aug 1953, Audrey June, da of Sydney James Knight (d 1981); 1 s (Christopher b 10 March 1956), 3 da (Sallie b 15 May 1958, Carol (twin), Jacqueline b 11 Oct 1961); *Career* WWII Fleet Air Adm RNVR 1944-47; memb bd and fin dir Segas 1960-73, fin dir SWA 1973-75, memb bd fin PO 1975-76, fin dir Ferranti Ltd 1977, memb bd fin Br Shipbuilders 1977-80; chm Throgmorton Tst 1972-84, Sheldon and Ptnrs Ltd, Sheldon Aviation Ltd, Saga Ltd, Midland Industl Leasing Ltd, Berfield Assocs Ltd; tstee East Grinstead Lawn Tennis and Squash Club, govr Forest Row Primary Sch; FCA 1949; *Recreations* golf, tennis; *Clubs* Les Ambassadeurs, Gravetye Manor; *Style*— Maurice Elderfield, Esq; Hadleigh, Cansiron Lane, Ashurst Wood, Sussex RH19 3SD (☎ 0342 822638); Sheldon and Ptnrs Ltd, 65 Buckingham Gate, London SW1E 6AT (☎ 01 404 4363, fax 01 222 4908, telex 261689)

ELDON, 5 Earl of (UK 1821); John Joseph Nicholas Scott; Baron Eldon (GB 1799), Viscount Encombe (UK 1821); s of 4 Earl of Eldon, GCVO (d 1976, fifth in descent from the 1 Earl), and Hon Margaret Fraser, OBE (d 1969), da of 16 Lord Lovat; *b* 24 April 1937; *Educ* Ampleforth, Trin Coll Oxford; *m* 1 July 1961, Countess Claudine, da of Count Franz von Montjoye-Vaufrey and de la Roche (originally a cr of Louis XV of France 1736, confirmed 1743 (also by Louis) and later by Emperor Franz Josef of Austria-Hungary 1888), of Vienna; 1 s, 2 da (Lady Tatiana b 1967, Lady Victoria b 1968); *Heir* s, Viscount Encombe; *Career* 2 Lt Scots Gds, Lt Army Emergency Reserve; *Style*— The Rt Hon The Earl of Eldon; 2 Coach House Lane, Wimbledon, SW19

ELDRED, Dr Vernon Walter; MBE (1970); s of Vernon Frank Eldred (d 1929), of Sutton, Coldfield, and Dorothy *née* Lyon (d 1968); *b* 14 Mar 1925; *Educ* Bishop Vesey's GS Sutton Coldfield, St Catharine's Coll Cambridge (MA, PhD); *m* 4 Aug 1952, Pamela Mary, da of Arthur Wood (d 1943), of Sutton Coldfield; 2 s (Andrew b 1952, John b 1958), 1 da (Sally b 1956); *Career* dept scientific and industl res Fuel Res Station Greenwich 1945-47, Atomic Energy Res Establishment Harwell 1947-48, dept Metallurgy Univ of Cambridge 1948-53, Nelson res Labs English Electrical Co Stafford 1953-55; Windscale laboratory UKAEA: sr scientific offr 1955-59, res mangr Metallurgy 1959-76, head of fuel examination div 1976-84, head fuel performance div and dep head lab 1984-87, head of lab 1987-; memb cncl inst Metallurgists 1966-69, chm ctee Nat Certificate and Dip in Metallurgy 1967-73, bd memb Br Nuclear Energy Soc 1974-77; fndr memb and first chm West Cumbria Metallurgic Soc; FIM 1968, FEng 1984; *Recreations* beekeeping, fell walking, genealogy, gardening, computers; *Clubs* United Oxford and Cambridge Univ; *Style*— Dr Vernon Eldred, MBE; Fell Gate, Santon Bridge, Holmrook, Cumbria CA19 14P (☎ 09406 275); Head of Laboratory, Northern Res Laboratories, Windscale, UKAEA, Seascale, Cumbria CA20 1PF (☎ 09467 71947, fax 09467 77616, telex 64140 ATOM WINDSCALE)

ELDRIDGE, David John; s of Frederick George Eldridge (Lt-Col ret), of Little Court, Pathfields Close, Haslemere, Surrey, and Irene Mary, *née* Buston; *b* 12 Jan 1935; *Educ* Kings Coll Sch Wimbledon; *m* 1, 14 May 1960, Diana Mary (d 1981), da of Eric Copp, 19 Oval Grange, Hartlepool, Cleveland; 1 s (Charles b 1961), 2 da (Catherine b 1964, Victoria b 1966); m 2, 15 Dec 1984, Anna Maria, da of Jerzy Kowalski, of Warsaw, Poland; *Career* slr 1956; ptnr: Stanley Attenborough & Co 1958-74, Martin & Nicholson 1975-77, Amhurst Brown Colombotti 1977-89; dir Equity & Gen plc; tstee (since inception 1974) Musuem of Islamic Art (Jerusalem); donation govr Christs Hosp Horsham; Freeman City of London, Liveryman and memb Ct Worshipful Co of Fletchers (Master 1984-86), memb Ct of Assts Guild of Freemen (Master 1983-84); memb Law Soc 1957; *Recreations* fine arts, sport; *Clubs* RAC, City Livery; *Style*— David Eldridge, Esq; The Coach house, 2c Woodborough Rd, Putney, London SW15 (☎ 01 789 7655); Amhurst Brown Colombotti, 2 Duke St, St James's, London SW1 (☎ 01 930 2366, fax 01 930 2250, telex 261857 Ambron)

ELDRIDGE, Eric William; CB (1965), OBE (1948); o s of William Eldridge (d 1954), of London; *b* 15 April 1906; *Educ* Millfields Central Sch, City of London Coll; *m* 1936, Doris Margaret, da of Peter Kerr (d 1964), of Edgeware; 1 s, 1 da; *Career* slr 1934, conslt with Lee and Pembertons Slrs 1971-1988, chief admin offr Public Tstee Off 1955-60 (asst public tstee 1960-63, public tstee 1963-71); *Recreations* foreign travel and gardening; *Style*— Eric Eldridge, Esq, CB, OBE; Old Stocks, Gorelands Lane, Chalfont St Giles, Bucks HP8 4HQ (☎ 024 07 2159); Gull Cottage, 249 High St, Aldeburgh, Suffolk

ELEGANT, Robert Sampson; s of Louis Elegant (d 1965), and Lillie Rebecca Sampson (d 1984); *b* 7 Mar 1928; *Educ* Univ of Pennsylvania 1946; Yale 1948, Columbia 1950 (MA, MS); *m* 16 April 1956, Moira Clarissa Brady; 1 s (Simon David Brady b 1960), 1 da (Victoria Ann b 1958); *Career* Far East correspondent Overseas News Agency 1951-52; war corres Korea 1952-53; corres in Singapore and SE Asia for Columbia Broadcasting Service, McGraw-Hill News Service, and North American Newspaper Alliance, 1954-55; South Asian Corres & chief New Delhi bureau Newsweek 1956-57; SE Asian corres & chief Hong Kong bureau Newsweek 1958-61; chief Central Euro bureau (Bonn-Berlin), Newsweek, 1962-64; chief, Hong Kong bureau, Los Angeles Times, 1965-69; foreign affairs columnist, Los Angeles Times/Washington Post News Service 1970-72, Hong Kong 1973-76; Visiting Prof Univ of South Carolina, Journalism and International Affairs, 1976; public lectr 1964; independent author and journalist 1977-; Pulitzer Travelling fell 1951-52, fell Ford Fndn 1954-55, Edgar Allen Poe Award Mystery Writers of America 1967, four Overseas Press Club Awards; *Books* China's Red Masters (1951), Maors Chiang: The Battle for China (1972), The Seeking (1969), Dynasty (1977), Manchu (1980), Mandarin (1983), White Sun, Red Star (1986); *Recreations* sailing, raising Shih Tzu dogs; *Clubs* Hong Kong Foreign Correspondents, Lansdowne; *Style*— Robert Elegant, Esq; The Manor House, Middle Green, Langley, Berks SL3 6BS (☎ 0753 20654)

ELEY, Sir Geoffrey Cecil Ryves; CBE (1947); s of Charles Cuthbert Eley, JP, VMH (d 1960), and Ethel Maxwell, *née* Ryves, of East Bergholt Place, Suffolk; *b* 18 July 1904; *Educ* Eton, Trinity Coll Cambridge (MA), Davison Scholar Harvard Univ; *m* 1937, Penelope Hughes, da of Adm Sir (William) Frederic Wake-Walker, KCB, CBE (d 1945); 2 s, 2 da; *Career* chm: Br Drug Houses Ltd 1948-65, Richard Crittall Hldgs Ltd 1948-68, Richard Thomas & Baldwins Ltd 1959-64, Thomas Tilling Ltd 1965-76 (dir 1959-76), Heinemann Gp of Publishers Ltd 1965-76; dir: Bank of England 1949-66, Equity and Law Life Assur Soc 1948-80; vice chm Br Bank of Middle East 1952-77 (dir 1950-77), BOC Int Ltd 1964-77 (dir 1959-77); vice pres Middle East Assoc 1962-85, memb ctee Royal UK Benevolent Assoc 1957-85; High Sheriff: Co of London 1954-55, Greater London 1966; kt 1964; *Recreations* gardening, the arts; *Style*— Sir Geoffrey Eley, CBE; The Change House, Great Yeldham, nr Halstead, Essex CO9 4PT (☎ 0787 237260)

ELEY, Piers David Christopher; s of Sir Geoffrrey Cecil Ryves Eley, CBE, *qv*; *b* 20 May 1941; *Educ* Eton, Trinity Coll Cambridge (MA), London Grad Sch of Business Studies (MSc); *m* 1 April 1967, Sarah Cloudesley, da of Lt Col David E Long-Price, OBE, of Fryerning, Ingatestone, Essex; 1 s (Damian Edward Piers b 24 Jan 1970), 1 da (Thalia Catherine b 9 Sept 1971); *Career* Norton Rose Boterelle & Roche 1964, Hambros Bank Ltd 1964-73, mangr/dir Nordic Bank plc 1973-84, dir Coopers & Lybrand 1984-; chm Friends of St Matthias Richmond 1986-, Guildsman of St Brides Fleet St, AMIOB 1967, London Business Sch Assoc 1969, Business Graduates Assoc 1969; *Recreations* painting, gardening, fishing, sailing, shooting, photography, music; *Clubs* Brooks's, Pitt, Fox, Omar Khayyam, St Mawes SC; *Style*— Piers D C Eley, Esq; 35 Montague Road, Richmond, Surrey TW10 6QJ (☎ 01 940 0788); Coopers & Lybrand, Plumtree Court, Farringdon Street, London EC4A 4HT (☎ 01 588 5000, fax 01 822 4652, telex 887470)

ELFORD, Colin David; s of Charles John Elford (d 1962), of Tavistock, Devon, and Enid Audrey, *née* Jope; *b* 3 August 1936; *Educ* Tavistock Sch; *m* 14 Oct 1966 (m dis 1974), Caroline Margaret, da of Julian Vann (d 1940); 2 s (Julian Charles Colin b 1968, Stuart Michael Paul b 1969); *Career* TA cmmnd 1954-60; ptnr: Mann & Co 1966-69, Hampton & Sons 1969-71; dir Shanning Homes Ltd 1971-77, self-employed 1977-80, dir Mortgage Systems Ltd 1981-86, md City & Provincial Home Loans Ltd 1986-; former cncllr Fleet Urban DC, chm and pres Fleet CC 1968-80, life vice-pres and fndr Fleet Hockey Club, chm Guildford & Godalming Athletic Club 1985-86; AVI 1962, FSVA 1977, FPCS 1981; *Recreations* shooting, angling, squash, cricket; *Clubs* Fleet CC, Fleet Hockey Club, Guildford & Godalming AC; *Style*— Colin Elford, Esq; Brecon House, Ganghill, Guildford, Surrey (☎ 0483 504521); Milton Ct, Dorking, Surrey (☎ 0306 887766, fax 0306 888664, car 0860 359329)

ELFORD, Hon Mrs; Hon Rowena (Frances); eldest da of 2 Viscount St Davids; *b* 7 August 1940; *m* 31 Oct 1959 (m dis 1977), David Elford, s of late Richard Elford, of Melbourne, Australia; 1 s, 3 da; *Style*— Hon Mrs Elford; 4 Holland Court, Oakleigh, 3166 Victoria, Australia

ELGIN AND KINCARDINE, 11 and 15 Earl of (S 1633 and 1647); Andrew Douglas Alexander Thomas Bruce; KT (1981), CD (1985) JP (Fife 1951), DL (1955),; also Lord Bruce of Kinloss (S 1604), Lord Bruce of Torry (S 1647), Baron Elgin (UK 1849); 37 Chief of the Name of Bruce; s of 10 Earl of Elgin, KT, CMG, TD (ggs of the 7 Earl who removed to safety the statuary known as The Elgin Marbles from the Parthenon in Athens) and Hon Dame Katherine Elizabeth Cochrane, DBE, da of 1 Baron Cochrane of Cults; *b* 17 Feb 1924; *Educ* Eton, Balliol Coll Oxford (MA); *m* 27 April 1959, Victoria Mary, o da of Dudley George Usher, MBE, TD, of Gallow Ridge Ho, Dunfermline; 3 s (Lord Bruce, Hon Adam Robert, Hon Alexander Victor b 1971), 2 da; *Heir* s, Lord Bruce; *Career* served WW II (wounded); chm Nat Savings Ctee Scotland 1972-78; dir: Scottish Amicable Life Assurance Soc (and pres), Roy Highland and Agric Soc 1973-76; pres: Roy Caledonian Curling Club 1968-69, Roy Scottish Automobile Club; Lord High Cmmr to Gen Assembly of Church of Scotland 1980-81; Grand Master Mason of Scotland 1961-65; Brig Roy Co of Archers (Queen's Body Guard for Scotland); Hon Col Elgin Regt of Canada (1969); Hon LLD Dundee 1977, Glasgow 1983, Hon DLitt St Mary's NS 1976; *Style*— The Rt Hon The Earl of

Elgin and Kincardine, KT, CD, JP, DL; Broomhall, Dunfermline KY11 3DU (☎ 0383 872222)

ELGIN AND KINCARDINE, Dowager Countess of; Hon Dame Katherine Elizabeth; *née* Cochrane; DBE (1938, MBE 1919); da of 1 Baron Cochrane of Cults (Hon Thomas Cochrane, yr s of 11 Earl of Dundonald), sometime MP Ayrshire N and under-sec Home Office, by his w Lady Gertrude Boyle, OBE (da of 6 Earl of Glasgow); *b* 1890; *m* 5 Jan 1921, 10 Earl of Elgin and Kincardine (d 1968); 3 s (including 11 Earl), 3 da (Lady Martha Bruce, Lady Jean Wemyss, Lady Alison Stewart-Patterson); *Career* Clerk Foreign Office 1916-19; Local Government, SWRI; 1921-40, Red Cross and WRVS; *Style—* The Rt Hon the Dowager Countess of Elgin and Kincardine, DBE; Broomhall, Dunfermline, Fife KY11 3DU

ELIAS-JONES, Peter John; s of William Peter Jones (d 1973), of Llangefni, Anglesey, and Margaret, *née* Elias; *b* 29 May 1943; *Educ* Llangefni Ysgol Gyfun, Univ of Leeds (BA), Univ of Manchester (Dip); *m* 10 April 1971, Elinor Mair, da of Cyril Owens (d 1988), of Ammanford, Dyfed; 2 da (Elen b 1973, Mari Wyn b 1976); *Career* teacher of music and drama Wallasey ches 1966, studio mangr TWW Ltd Cardiff 1967; HTV Ltd Cardiff: dir news 1968, prodr and dir children's progs 1971, head of children's progs 1974, asst prog controller 1981, prog controller entertainment 1988; author of four books for young people and numerous articles; *Style—* Peter Elias-Jones, Esq; HTV, TV Centre, Culverhouse Cross, Cardiff, S Glam CF5 6XJ (☎ 0222 590 590, fax 0222 597183, telex 497703)

ELIBANK, 14 Lord (S 1643); Sir Alan D'Ardis Erskine-Murray; 14 Bt (NS 1628); s of Maj Robert Alan Erskine-Murray, OBE(d 1939), unc of 13 Lord; suc cous 1973; *b* 31 Dec 1923, Wynberg, S Africa,; *Educ* Bedford, Peterhouse Cambridge; *m* 1962, Valerie Sylvia, o da of late Herbert William Dennis, of St Margaret's, Twickenham; 2 s; *Heir* s, Master of Elibank; *Career* barr 1949-55, personnel mangr Shell Int Petroleum Co 1955-77 (gen mangr and rep in Qatar 1977-80), personnel mangr Deminex Oil and Gas Ltd 1981-86; *Style—* The Rt Hon Lord Elibank; The Coach House, Charters Rd, Sunningdale, Ascot, Berks

ELIBANK, Master of; Hon Robert Francis Alan Erskine-Murray; s and h of 14 Lord Elibank; *b* 10 Oct 1964; *Educ* Harrow, Reading Univ; *Recreations* photography, soccer, swimming, judo; *Style—* The Master of Elibank

ELIOT, Lady Alethea Constance Dorothy Sydney; da of 1 and last Earl Buxton, GCMG, PC (d 1934, sometime Govr-Gen and C-in-C South Africa and gs of Sir Thomas Buxton, 1 Bt) by his 2 w, Dame Mildred Smith, GBE, JP, sister of 1 Baron Bicester; *b* 2 August 1910; *m* 12 July 1934, Canon Peter Charles Eliot, MBE, TD, *qv*; *Style—* Lady Alethea Eliot; The Old House, Kingsland, Leominster, Herefordshire (☎056 881 285)

ELIOT, Lord; Jago Nicholas Aldo Eliot; s and h of 10 Earl of St Germans; *b* 24 Mar 1966; *Educ* Millfield; *Style—* Lord Eliot

ELIOT, Ven Canon Peter Charles; MBE (1945), TD (1945); s of Hon Edward Granville Eliot (yst bro of 7 and 8 Earls of St Germans) by his w Clare (herself da of William Phelips, JP, DL, by his 2 w Constance, da of Hon Sir Spencer Ponsonby-Fane, GCB, PC, 6 s of 4 Earl of Bessborough); *b* 30 Oct 1910; *Educ* Wellington, Magdalene Coll Cambridge; *m* 12 July 1934, Lady Alethea, *qv*; *Career* Lt-Col Cmdg Kent Yeo RA (TA), served WWII BEF, M East and Italy; slr 1934-53; ordained 1954, rural dean 1960-61, archdeacon of Worcester 1961-75, residentiary canon of Worcester 1965-75; *Recreations* sightseeing, sketching, gardening, amateur theatricals; *Clubs* Travellers'; *Style—* The Ven Canon Peter Eliot, MBE, TD; The Old House, Kingsland, Leominster, Herefordshire (☎ Kingsland (056 881) 285)

ELIOT, Hon (Montagu) Robert Vere; s of 8 Earl of St Germans, KCVO, OBE (d 1960); *b* 28 Oct 1923; *Educ* Eton, Ch Ch Oxford; *m* 1983, Marie Frances Richmond Lusk, widow of A R Lusk, of Fordie, Comrie, Perthshire and da of late Geoffrey Mervyn Cooper, of Preston Candover, Hants (d 1984); *Career* a train bearer at Coronation of King George VI, a page of honour to HM 1937-40; served Gren Gds 1943-52, Capt (ret), NW Europe (wounded) 1944, Palestine (medal) 1945-48; retired company dir; memb: Westminster City Cncl 1952-61, Cornwall County Cncl 1977-; contested (C) Mansfield Notts 1959; provincial grand master for Cornwall, United Grand Lodge of England 1978-; pres Royal Inst of Cornwall 1983-84; chm Cornwall Heritage Tst 1984-89, pres Cornwall Family History Soc 1988-; Coronation Medal 1937; *Recreations* bridge, reading; *Clubs* Carlton; *Style—* Hon Robert Eliot; Lux Cross House, Pengover Rd, Liskeard, Cornwall PL14 3EL (☎ 0579 42755)

ELIOTT OF STOBS, Charles Joseph Alexander; 12 Bt (MS 1666), of Stobs, Roxburghshire; Chief of the Clan Eliott or Elliot; s of late Charles Rawdon Heathfield Eliott (himself s of half-bro of Sir Arthur Eliott of Stobs, 9 Bt); succ half second cousin, Sir Arthur Eliott of Stobs, 11 Bt (d 1989); *b* 9 Jan 1937; *Educ* St Joseph's Christian Bros, Rockhampton nr Brisbane; *m* 1959, Wendy Judith, da of Henry John Bailey, of Toowoomba, Queensland; 1 s (Rodney Gilbert Charles b 1966), and 1 s decd, 4 da (Elizabeth (Mrs Armanasco) b 1960, Jenny (Mrs Land) b 1961, Josephine (Mrs Grafski) b 1963, Clare Melinda b 1973); *Heir* s, Rodney Gilbert Charles Eliott b 1966; *Career* builder (C J & W J Eliott); *Style—* Sir Charles Eliott of Stobs, Bt; 27 Cohoe St, Toowoomba, Queensland 4350, Australia (☎ 32 7390)

ELKAN, Walter; s of Hans Septimus Elkan (d 1933), of Hamburg, and Maud Emily, *née* Barden (d 1957); *b* 1 Mar 1923; *Educ* Frensham Heights, LSE (BSc, PhD); *m* 28 Dec 1946 (m dis 1981), Susan Dorothea, da of Emanuel Jacobs (d 1965); 1 s (David b 1952), 2 da (Ruth b 1954, Jenny b 1955); *Career* served Pioneer Corps and RA 1942-47; sr res fell Makerere Inst Socl Res Uganda 1953-60, lectr Durham Univ 1960 (prof econs 1965-79), visiting res prof Nairobi Univ 1972-73, prof of econs Brunel Univ 1979- (Emeritus prof 1988); formerly: pres African Studies Assoc, memb Northern Econ Planning Cncl, bd memb School of Hygiene and Tropical Medicine, memb Cncl Royal Econ Soc; memb Cncl Overseas Devpt Inst, memb Econ and Soc Ctee for Overseas Res; *Books* An African Labour Force (1959), Economic Development of Uganda (1961), Migrants and Proletarians (1961), Introduction to Development Economics (1973); *Recreations* music, art; *Style—* Prof Walter Elkan; 98 Boundary Rd, London NW8 ORH (☎ 01 624 5102); Brunel University, Dept of Economics, Uxbridge, Middx (☎ 0895 56461 ext 282, telex 261173)

ELKIN, Alexander; CMG (1976); o s of Boris Elkin (d 1972), and Anna Elkin (d 1973); *b* 2 August 1909,St Petersburg; *Educ* Grunewald Gymnasium, Russian Academic Sch Berlin, Univs of Berlin, Kiel and London; *m* 1937, Muriel, da of Edwin M Solomons (d 1964), of Dublin; *Career* war time govt serv 1942-45 (BBC Monitoring Serv 1939-42); barr Middle Temple 1937; assoc chief Legal Serv UN Interim Secretariat 1945-46, asst dir UN Euro Off Geneva 1946-48, legal advsr to UNSCOB Salonica 1948, dep legal advsr and later legal advsr OEEC (OECD 1960-) 1949-61, UNECA legal conslt formation of African Devpt Bank 1962-64, acting gen counsel of ADB 1964-65, special advsr on Euro Communities Law FCO 1970-79, legal consultancies for : WHO 1948, IBRD 1966, UNDP 1967-68, W African Regnl Gp 1968, OECD 1975; lectured on Euro Payments System and OECD: Univ of the Saar 1957-60, Univ Inst of Euro Studies Turin 1957-65; on drafting of treaties UNITAR Seminars The Hague, Geneva and NY for legal advsrs and diplomatics 1967-84; on language and law: Univ of Bradford 1979-83, Univ of Bath 1979-; memb RIIA, Ford Fndn Leadership Grant 1960; *Books* contributions to European Yearbook, Journal du Droit International, Revue Générale du Droit International Public, Survey of International Affairs 1939-46, Travaux pratiques de L'Institut de Droit Comparé de la Faculté de Droit de Paris; *Recreations* reading, visiting art collections, travel; *Clubs* Travellers'; *Style—* Alexander Elkin, Esq, CMG; 70 Apsley House, Finchley Road, St John's Wood, London NW8 0NZ (☎ 01 483 2475)

ELKIN, Sonia Irene Linda; OBE (1981, MBE 1966); da of Godfrey Albert Elkin (d 1947), and Irene Jessamine Archibald (d 1968); *b* 15 May 1932; *Educ* Beresford Howe Sch Eastbourne; *Career* overseas sec Assoc of Br Chambers of Commerce 1956, overseas dept Lloyds Bank 1966, CBI 1967 (head of W Euro Dept 1967), head of Regnl and Small Firms Dept 1972 (dep dir 1973), dir for Smaller Firms 1979-83, cmmr Manpower Servs Cmmn 1981-85; dir: CBI's Regnl Orgn 1983, Regions & Smaller Firms 1985; *Books* What About Europe? (1967, updated with the co-op of Mr Angus Hislop and republished in 1971 under the title What About Europe Now?); *Recreations* music; *Clubs* United Oxford & Cambridge Univ (lady associate); *Style—* Miss Sonia Elkin, OBE; CBI, Centre Point, 103 New Oxford St, WC1A 1DU (☎ 01 379 7400, telex 21332)

ELKINGTON, Robert John; s of John David Rew Elkington, OBE; *b* 7 Oct 1949; *Educ* Eton, Exeter Univ (BA); *m* 1, 1974 (m dis 1983), Penelope Josephine, da of late Lt-Col Richard Ian Griffith Taylor, DSO; 1 s; m 2, 1984, Mary Patricia, da of late Maj Hon Antony John Ashley Cooper; 1 da; *Career* banker; md Gerrard and Nat Hldgs plc; *Recreations* tennis, shooting, golf; *Clubs* Boodle's, Pratt's; *Style—* Robert Elkington, Esq; Cranbourne Grange, Sutton Scotney, Winchester, Hants SO21 3NA (☎ 0962 760 494, office 01 623 9981)

ELLEN, Eric Frank; QPM (1980); s of Robert Frank Ellen (d 1969), and Jane Lydia Ellen (d 1982); *b* 30 August 1930; *Educ* Univ of London (LLB Hons); *m* 1949, Gwendoline Dorothy, da of John Thomas Perkins (d 1937); 1 s (Stephen), 1 da (Susan); *Career* Nat Serv; joined port of London Police 1950, chief constable 1975, Police Long Serv and Good Conduct Medal 1 class 1973, the Republic of China Police Medal 1 class 1979, Queen's Police Medal for Distinguished Police Serv 1980, ret from police service 1980; first dir of ICC: Int Maritime Bureau 1981, Counterfeiting Intelligence Bureau 1985 Corporate Security Servs 1988; conslt Commmercial Crime Unit; special advsr International Assoc of Ports and Harbours on port security matters and maritime crime; pres International Assoc of Airport and Seaport Police 1977-79, chm Euro Assoc of Airport and Seaport Police 1975-78 (now life memb, exec sec chm: Electronic Intelligence Ltd 1985-86, PEBs 1985; memb: Hon Soc of the Middle Temple, Br Acad of Forensic Sciences, Ctee of Cons Lawyers examining Maritime Fraud, Inst of Shipbrokers Ctee on Maritime Fraud; Freeman City of London; presented or chaired seminars on Int Commercial Fraud and product counterfeiting in over 50 countries, advised Barbados govt on formation of a new police force for the Barbados Port Authy 1983, reviewed security at ports of Jeddah and Dammam in Saudi Arabia; frequent television and radio appearances on the subject of marine fraud, terrorism, piracy and product counterfeiting; CBIM; *Books* Int Maritime Fraud (co-author), conslt ed Air and Seaport Security Int Reference Book (conslt ed 1987-89), published many articles on varied subjects including specialist policemen, marine sabotage, piracy and terrorism, product counterfeiting and fraud; Violence at Sea (ed 1987), Piracy at Sea (ed 1989); *Recreations* golf; *Clubs* Wig and Pen; *Style—* Eric Ellen, Esq, QPM; 41 Brookside, Emerson Park, Hornchurch, Essex; Int Maritime Bureau, Maritime Ho, 1 Linton Rd, Barking, Essex

ELLENBOROUGH, Dorothy, Baroness; (Helen) Dorothy; da of Harry William Lovatt, late of Co Down; *b* 1901; *m* 31 Jan 1923, 7 Baron Ellenborough MC, JP, DL (d 1945); 2 s (8 Baron, Hon Cecil Law); *Career* DGStJ; *Style—* The Rt Hon Dorothy, Lady Ellenborough, DGStJ; Little Park House, Brimpton, nr Reading, Berks

ELLENBOROUGH, 8 Baron (UK 1802); Richard Edward Cecil Law; s of 7 Baron (d 1945); *b* 14 Jan 1926; *Educ* Eton, Magdalene Coll Cambridge; *m* 9 Oct 1953, Rachel Mary (d 1986), da of late Maj Ivor Mathews Hedley, 17 Lancers; 3 s; *Heir* s, Hon Rupert Law; *Career* sits as Conservative Peer in House of Lords; stockbroker; dir Towry Law & Co; *Style—* The Rt Hon Lord Ellenborough; Withypool House, Observatory Close, Church Rd, Crowborough, East Sussex TN6 1BN (☎ (08926) 63139)

ELLERAY, Anthony John; s of Alexander John Elleray, of Waddington, Clitheroe, Lancs, and Sheila Mary, *née* Perkins; *b* 19 August 1954; *Educ* Bishops Stortford Coll, Trinity Coll Cambridge (MA); *m* 17 July 1982, Alison Elizabeth, da of William Goring Potter, DFC, of Twyford, Berks; 1 da (Harriet b 29 Aug 1985); *Career* barr Inner Temple 1977, chancery barr Northern Circuit, memb: Chancery Bar Assoc, Northern Chancery Bar Assoc; *Recreations* bridge, theatre, pictures, wine; *Clubs* Manchester Tennis and Racquets; *Style—* Anthony Elleray, Esq; 4 Amherst Rd, Fallowfield, Manchester M14 6UQ (☎ 061 225 5317); St James Chambers, 68 Quay St, Manchester M3 3EL (☎ 061 834 7000, fax 061 834 2341)

ELLERTON, Geoffrey James; CMG (1963), MBE (1956); er s of Sir (Frederick) Cecil Ellerton (d 1962), and Dorothy Catherine, *née* Green; *b* 25 April 1920; *Educ* Highgate Sch, Hertford Coll Oxford; *m* 1946, Peggy Eleanor, da of Frederick George Watson (d 1954); 3 s; *Career* Colonial Admin Serv Kenya 1945-63; sec to Cmmns on Mgmnt and Staffing in Local Govt 1964; chm Elder Dempster Lines 1972-74, exec dir Ocean Tport and Trading Ltd 1972-80, chm Electra Gp Servs 1980-83, dir Globe Investmt Tst 1982-86, chm Local Govt Boundary Cmmn for England 1983-; hon tres Hakluyt Soc 1986-; *Recreations* books and music; *Clubs* MCC, Brooks's, Beefsteak; *Style—* Geoffrey Ellerton, Esq, CMG, MBE; Briar Hill House, Broad Campden, Chipping Campden, Glos GL55 6XB (☎ 0386 841003)

ELLERY, Nina; *née* Petrova; da of Alexander Petrov (d 1968), of London, and Lubov Georgivna, *née* Nicholaeva (d 1978); *b* 9 June 1913; *Educ* St Dunstans Abbey Rd Sch, Plymouth Sch, Carlyle Sch; *m* 31 July 1937, Maj (John) Edgar (Eggi) Ellery, s of James

Ellery, OBE (d 1953); *Career* author (writes under name of Nina Petrova); sec BRCS, memb ctee Russian Refugee Relief Assoc (helped after war), sec local Leasehold Assoc 1970-71; memb Soc of Authors; *Books* Russian Cookery (1968), Best of Russian Cookery (1978), article for Taste Magazine (about Russian Easter); *Recreations* reading, making clothes, garden; *Clubs* GB USSR Assoc; *Style*— Mrs Edgar Ellery; 106 Edith Rd, London W14 9AP (☎ 01 603 5106)

ELLES, Baroness (Life Peeress UK 1972); Diana Louie Elles; MEP (EDG) Thames Valley 1979-; da of Col Stewart Francis Newcombe, DSO (d 1956), and Elizabeth Chaki; *b* 19 July 1921; *Educ* London Univ (BA); *m* 1945, Neil Patrick Moncrieff Elles, s of Edmund Hardie Elles, OBE; 1 s, 1 da; *Career* Flight Offr WAAF 1942-45; barr 1956, Care ctee worker Kennington 1956-72, UK delegate UN 1972, MEP 1973-75, memb UN Sub-Cmmn on Discrimination and Minorities 1974-75, oppn front bench spokesman on Foreign and European Affairs 1975-79, chm Cons Party Int Off 1973-78, vice-pres European Parl 1982-87; chm: Legal Affairs Ctee, European Parl 1987-; *Style*— The Rt Hon Lady Elles, MEP; 75 Ashley Gdns, London SW1 (☎ 01 828 0175)

ELLES, Hon James Edmund Moncrieff; MEP Oxford and Bucks 1984-; s of Neil Elles, of 75 Ashley Gardens, London SW1, and Baroness Elles, MEP (Life Peeress); *b* 3 Sept 1949; *Educ* Eton, Edinburgh Univ; *m* 1977, Françoise, da of François Le Bail; 1 s (Nicholas b 22 Aug 1982), 1 da (Victoria b 27 July 1980); *Career* admin External Relations EEC 1977-80, asst to dep dir-gen of Agric EEC 1980-84; memb Budget and Agric Ctees; *Recreations* skiing, golf, tennis; *Clubs* Royal and Ancient Golf (St Andrews), Carlton; *Style*— Hon James Elles; c/o Conservative Centre, Church St, Amersham, Bucks HP7 0BD (☎ Amersham 21577); 97-113 Rue Belliard, 1040 Bruxelles (☎ 234 2442)

ELLETSON, Lady Alexandra Susan; *née* Marquis; da of 2 Earl of Woolton (d 1969), and his 2 w (Cecily) Josephine (da of Sir Alexander Gordon-Cumming, MC, 5 Bt), now Countess Lloyd-George of Dwyfor; *b* 12 Jan 1961; *m* 27 April 1984, Philip Roger Chandos Elletson, s of Roger Chandos Elletson, *qv*; 2 da (Laura b 1985, Sophia b 1986); *Style*— Lady Alexandra Elletson; The Old Rectory, Huish, Marlborough, Wilts

ELLETSON, Roger Chandos; yr s of Harry Chandos Elletson (d 1928), of Parrox Hall, Preesall, Lancs, and Katherine Helen (d 1970), da of Rev Edward Philips, Rector of Hollington, Staffs; family owned large estates dating back to a gift of 'four oxgangs of land' by King John, ancestors include a Govr of Jamaica, and Dr ffyfe, Physician to King Charles II; *b* 4 June 1911; *Educ* Harrow; *m* 1, 18 Nov 1938 (m dis 1949), Simone, da of Joseph Boudard, of Morbihan, France; 1 s (Philip Roger b 23 Dec 1947, *see* Lady Alexandra Elletson), 1 da (Lorraine Joan b 11 March 1946); m 2, 20 Oct 1958, Pamela Mary, da of Leslie Brown, of The Cottage, Little Brington; 2 da (Anne b 31 July 1960, Hope b 13 Feb 1963), 1 adopted (step) s (Anthony Leslie b 26 Feb 1953); *Career* served Army M East, taken prisoner Battle of Crete; md Smith & Philips Witney 1937-39, founder R C Elletson & Co Ltd 1947; former chm textile companies and former dir Humphrey Lloyd & Sons Ltd; dir Parrox Investments Ltd and others; Lloyd's underwriter 1961-; part-time journalist; landowner; *Recreations* bridge, golf, skiing; *Clubs* Brooks's, Royal Lytham Golf; *Style*— Roger Elletson, Esq; Grey House, Forton, Preston, Lancs PR3 0AN (☎ 0524 791225)

ELLICOTT, (Mary) Elizabeth; da of John M Robbins (d 1977), and Elizabeth, *née* Rooney; *b* 15 Mar 1947; *Educ* Pembroke Sch Dublin, London Sch of Journalism; *m* 31 Dec 1976, (William) Drew, s of Lt Col C W Ellicott; *Career* asst ed journalist Creation Publications Dublin 1968-69 (trainee journalist 1964), co dir Robbins Assoc (prodn consits and actors agency) 1969-74, freelance prodr 1974-81, co dir DEE & Co Ltd (TV prog distributors) 1981-; *Recreations* t'ai chi chuan; *Clubs* London Sch of Wu Style T'ai Chi; *Style*— Mrs William Ellicott; 46 Potters Lane, Barnet, Herts EN5 5BE (☎ 01 441 3656); Suite 204, Canalot, 222 Kensal Rd, London W10 5BN (☎ 01 960 2712, fax 01 960 2728, telex 940 128 26 DECO G)

ELLINGTON, Marc Floyd; DL (1984 Aberdeenshire); Baron of Towie Barclay (Feudal Barony), Laird of Gardenstown and Crovie; s of Homer Frank Ellington (d 1984), of Memsie, Aberdeenshire, and Vancouver BC, and Harriette Hannah Kellas; *b* 16 Dec 1945; *m* 21 Dec 1967, Karen Leigh, da of Capt Warren Sydney Streater; 2 da (Iona Angeline Barclay of Gardenstown b 1979, Kirstie Naomi Barclay b 1983); *Career* memb: nat ctee Architectural Heritage Soc of Scotland, Historic House Assoc; vice-pres Buchan Heritage Soc; tstee Scottish Historic Building Tst; chm Heritage Press (Scot); dir: Aberdeen Univ Research Ltd, Gardenstown Estates Ltd, Soundcraft Audio; ptnr Heritage Sound Recordings; awarded Saltire Award 1973, Civic Tst Award 1975, European Architectural Heritage Award 1975; contributor to various architectural and historical jls and periodicals, composer and recording artiste, producer documentary films and television programmes; memb: performing Rights Soc, Historic Building Cncl for Scotland 1980-, convention of Baronage of Scotland; FSA; *Recreations* sailing, historic architecture, art collecting, music; *Style*— Marc Ellington of Towie Barclay, DL; Towie Barclay Castle, Auchterless, Turriff Aberdeenshire AB5 8EP (☎ 08884 347)

ELLINGWORTH, Lady Amanda Patricia Victoria; *née* Knatchbull; da of 7 Baron Brabourne and Countess Mountbatten of Burma, *qqv*; *b* 26 June 1957; *Educ* Gordonstoun, Kent Univ, Peking Univ, Goldsmith Coll London; *m* 31 Oct 1987, Charles V Ellingworth, er s of William Ellingworth, of Laughton, Leics; *Career* social worker; *Style*— Lady Amanda Ellingworth; Newhouse, Mersham, Ashford, Kent TN25 6NQ

ELLIOT, Alan Christopher; s of Ian Frederick Lettsom Elliot (d 1981), of 142 Pavilion Rd, London SW1, and Madeline Adelaide Mary, *née* Maclachlan (d 1977); *b* 9 Mar 1937; *Educ* Rugby, Ch Ch Oxford (MA); *m* 20 Jan 1967, Tara Louise Winifred, da of Sir Thomas Brian Weldon, 8 Bt (d 1979), of The Fighting Cocks, West Amesbury, Wilts; 1 s (Dominic b 1975), 3 da (Sacha b 1968, Larissa b 1970, Natalya b 1978); *Career* Nat Serv 1958-60: 2 Lt Welsh Guards cmmnd 1959, sr under offr Mons Off Cadet Sch; PA to md Metropole Industs 1960, md Dufay Ltd 1963 (dir 1962), chm Blick Time Recorders 1971- (organised mgmnt buyout from Dufay Ltd 1966), chm Blick plc 1986-; *Recreations* shooting, fishing, bridge, skiing; *Clubs* Whites, Portland; *Style*— Alan Elliot, Esq; The Old Rectory, Chilton Foliat, Hungerford, Berks RG17 OTF (☎ 0488 82423); 142 Pavilion Road, London SW1 (☎ 01 235 3382); Blick plc, Bramble Rd, Swindon, Wilts (☎ 0793 692 401, fax 0793 618147, car 0860 521087, telex 44332)

ELLIOT, Lady Ann; *née* Child-Villiers; yr da of 8 Earl of Jersey (d 1923); *b* 23 May 1916; *m* 8 June 1937, Maj Alexander Henry Elliot, late RA, s of Gilbert Compton Elliot (d 1931, he was gs of Hon Sir George Elliot, KCB, MP, 2 s of 1 Earl of Minto); 1 s, 2 da; *Style*— Lady Ann Elliot; Broadford, Chobham, Surrey (☎ 0276 7222)

ELLIOT, Hon (George Esmond) Dominic; yr s of 5 Earl of Minto (d 1975); *b* 13 Jan 1931; *Educ* Eton, Madrid Univ; *m* 1, 4 May 1962 (m dis 1970), Countess Marie-Anna (Marianne) Berta Felicie Johanna Ghislaine Theodora Huberta Georgina Helene Genoveva, da of Count (Maria) Thomas Paul Esterhazy; 1 s (Esmond b 1965), 1 s (Alexander b 1963 d 1985) m 2, 25 June 1983, Jane Caroline, da of Lawrence Reeve, of Sandridge Lodge, Bromham, Wilts; *Career* formerly Lt Scots Gds, served Malaya, London; company director; *Clubs* White's, New (Edinburgh); *Style*— Hon Dominic Elliot; 88 St James's St, London SW1A 1PW (☎ 01 839 5746); Minto, Hawick, Scotland

ELLIOT, Sir Gerald Henry; s of Surgn Capt John Stephen Elliot, RN (d 1972), and Magda Virginia, *née* Salvesen (d 1985); *b* 24 Dec 1923; *Educ* Marlborough, New Coll Oxford (BA); *m* 1950, Margaret Ruth, da of Rev John Stephen Whale; 2 s, 1 da; *Career* served Indian Army 1942-46, Capt; consul for Finland in Edinburgh and Leith 1957-, sec and chm Scottish branch Royal Inst of Int Affairs 1963-77; chm: Forth Ports Authority 1973-79, Scottish Arts Council 1980-86, Christian Salvesen plc 1981- (dep chm and md 1973-81), Scottish Provident Instn 1983-, Scottish Unit Managers Ltd 1984- BTL 1987-, chm of the Tstees of the David Hume Institute 1985-; Tstee National Musems of Scotland 1987-; Order of the White Rose of Finland, Kt of First Class 1975; kt 1986; *Style*— Sir Gerald Elliot; Christian Salvesen plc, 50 East Fettes Ave, Edinburgh EH4 1EQ

ELLIOT, Graeme Arthur; s of Ian Frederick Lettsom Elliot (d 1981), and Madeline Adelaide Mary Elliot, *née* Maclachlan (d 1977); *b* 28 August 1942; *Educ* Rugby, Magdalene Coll Cambridge (MA); *m* 1, 1966, Hermione, da of Lt-Col John Delano-Osborne, of Hants; 2 da (Alexandra b 1968, Victoria b 1971); m 2, 1983, Nicola Nella Simpson, da of Keith Alexander Taylor, of Queensland; *Career* CA; exec vice-chm Slough Estates plc 1986; dir: Bredero plc 1987, Landrover Investmts plc 1988; FCA; *Recreations* bridge, golf, tennis, skiing; *Clubs* Portland, Berkshire Golf, Royal Melbourne Golf, Sotogrande Golf; *Style*— Graeme Elliot, Esq; Slough Estates plc, 234 Bath Road, Slough, Berks SL1 4EE (☎ (O753) 37171)

ELLIOT, Prof Harry; CBE (1975); s of Thomas Elliot (d 1961), of Weary Hall Style, Mealsgate, Cumbria, and Hannah Elizabeth, *née* Littleton (d 1928); *b* 28 June 1920; *Educ* Allhallows Sch, Nelson Sch, Manchester Univ (BSc, MSc, Phd); *m* 27 May 1943, Betty, da of Henry Leyman (d 1974), of Doddiscombsleigh, Devon; 1 s (Brian b 1944), 1 da (Jean b 1948); *Career* WWI 1941-46; PO Tech (Sigs) RAFVR, served Coastal Cmd incl liason duties with USAAF and USN, demob FLt Lt 1946; lectr physics Univ of Manchester 1948-53; Imperial Coll 1953-: sr lectr 1953-60, prof 1960-80, sr res fell 1981-; Holweck Prize and Medal of Inst of Physics and French Physica Soc; memb Sci Res Cncl; chm: Astronomy Space and Radio Bd 1971-77, Cncl Royal Soc 1978, Euro Space Agency; numerous papers and articles published in learned jls; ARCS Imperial Coll 1961; FWAAS 1983, FRAS 1984, FRS 1973; *Recreations* painting, gardening, military history; *Style*— Prof Harry Elliot, CBE, FRS; Imperial Coll of Science, Technology and Medicine, Prince Consort Rd, London SW7 2BZ

ELLIOT OF HARWOOD, Baroness (Life Peeress UK 1958); Katharine; DBE (1958, CBE 1946), JP (Roxburghshire 1967); da of late Sir Charles Tennant, 1 Bt; *b* 15 Jan 1903; *Educ* Abbot's Hill; *m* 2 April 1934, as his 2 wife, Rt Hon Walter Elliot, CH, MC, PC, FRS, MP (d 1958); *Career* sits as Conservative Peeress in House of Lords; farmer; memb King George V Jubilee Tst 1936-68, ccncllr Roxburghshire 1945-75, contested (C) Kelvingrove Glasgow 1958; chm: Nat Union of Cons and Unionist Assocs 1957-58, Carnegie UK Tst 1965-86 (tstee 1940-86), Consumer Cncl 1963-68; UK delegate to UN Gen Assembly, New York 1954-56 and 1957; Hon LLD Glasgow 1959; Grand Silver Cross Austrian Order of Merit; FRSA; *Recreations* riding, music; *Style*— The Rt Hon Lady Elliot of Harwood; 17 Lord North St, London SW1 (☎ 01 222 3230); Harwood, Bonchester Bridge, Hawick, Roxburghshire TD9 9TL (☎ 045 086 235)

ELLIOTT, Anthony Charles Raynor; s of Charles Edward Murray Elliott (d 1987), of London, and Lucy Eleanor, *née* Arthur (d 1982); *b* 28 Jan 1937; *Educ* Radley, Trinity Coll Cambridge (MA); *m* 1960, Christina, da of Capt William Theobald Hindson, of Surrey; 2 s (Nicholas Charles Raynor b 1964, Paul William Anthony b 1967); *Career* 2 Lt East Surrey Regt 1955-57; slr 1963, Linklaters & Paines 1963-66; exec dir: RTZ Pillar Ltd (previously Pillar Hldgs Ltd 1966-76), S G Warburg & Co Ltd 1976-86; non-exec dir: Bridon plc, Norcros plc, S G Warburg & Co Ltd; governor St Mary's Hall Brighton 1967-; *Recreations* classical music, arts, walking, wine; *Style*— Anthony Elliott, Esq

ELLIOTT, Dr Arnold; OBE (1977); *b* 27 Jan 1921; *Educ* Royal Belfast Academical Inst, Queens Univ Belfast (MB BCh); *m* 8 June 1948, Lee; 2 s (Paul b 1955, Simon b 1957), 1 da (Louise b 1951); *Career* WWII Capt (later Actg Maj RAMC 1944-47; GP; MBMA 1948: memb gen med servs ctee 1952-, chm practise organization sub-ctee 1960-86, memb cncl 1982-, chm doctors and social work ctee, memb mental health ctee; Gen Med Cncl 1979-: memb exec, memb educn ctee, memb health ctee; pres Soc of Family Practitioner Ctees of England & Wales 1980, memb panel of assessors Dist Nurse Trg 1972-82, memb Central Cncl for Educn and Trg in Social Work 1974-84; memb: NHS Essex Exec Cncl until 1965-74, NHS Exec Cncl NE London 1965- (chm 1972-74), Redbridge and Waltham Forest Family Practitioner Ctee 1974- (chm 1974-77); sec Redbridge and Waltham Forest Local Med Ctee 1984-, fndr and organiser Ilford and Dist Vocational Tng Scheme for gen practice 1977-87, provost NE London faculty RCGP 1979-82; Freeman City of London 1971, Liveryman Worshipful Soc of Apothecaries 1968-; FRCGP 1976, FRSM; *Recreations* theatre, art, music; *Clubs* RSM; *Style*— Dr Arnold Elliott, OBE; Newbury Park Health Centre, Perrymans Farm Rd, Barkingside, Ilford, Essex IG2 7LE (☎ 01 554 9551)

ELLIOTT, Dr Charles Kennedy; s of Charles Harper Elliott (d 1948), of Ireland, and Martha, *née* Kennedy (d 1960); *b* 14 May 1919; *Educ* Campbell Coll Belfast, Trinity Coll Dublin (MA, MB, DLitt); *m* 1949, Elizabeth Margaret, da of John Andrew Kyle (d 1979), of Dublin; *Career* physician to HM The Queen 1980-86; pres Int Assoc of Agric Medicine and Rural Health 1972-78, sub dean Faculty of Homeopathy 1976-79; SBStJ; *Recreations* heraldry, silent cinema; *Clubs* RSM; *Style*— Dr Charles Elliott; Cashelbawn, W Walton, Wisbech, Cambs (☎ 0945 780269)

ELLIOTT, Rev Prof Charles Middleton; s of Joseph William Elliott (d 1982), and Mary Evelyn, *née* Jones (d 1958); *b* 9 Jan 1939; *Educ* Repton, Oxford (MA, DPhil); *m* 1962, Hilary Margaret, da of Harold Hambling, of Cockfosters, Barnet, Herts; 3 s

(Jonathan, Francis, Giles); *Career* asst lectr (later lectr) in pure econs Univ of Nottingham 1963-65, sr res fell UN Res Inst of Social Devpt Geneva 1964-65, reader in econ and head of dept Univ of Zambia 1965-69, asst sec Res Dir Sodepax Geneva 1969-72, sr res assoc Overseas Devpt Gp Univ of E Anglia 1972-75, sr lectr in econ Sch of Devpt Studies Univ of E Anglia 1975-77, dir ODG (md ODG Co Ltd) 1976-77, special advsr Parly Select Ctee on Overseas Aid and Devpt 1976-80, prof of devpt policy and planning Univ of Wales 1979-82, dir Centre for Devpt Studies UC Swansea 1979-82, dir Christian Aid 1982-84, GEM Scott fell Univ of Melbourne Australia 1984-85, Benjamin Meaker prof Univ of Bristol 1985-86, prebendary of Lichfield Cathedral 1987-, visiting Prof King's Coll London 1987-; *Books* Praying the Kingdom (Collins Religious Book Prize 1985), Comfortable Compassion 1987, Praying Through Paradox 1987; Sword and Spirit: Christianity in a Divided World (1989); *Recreations* fly fishing, hill walking, sailing; *Style—* The Rev Prof Charles Elliott; 119 Fentiman Rd, London SW8 1J2; c/o Cwmberwyn, Hundred House, Llandrindod Wells, Powys

ELLIOTT, Clive Christopher Hugh; s and h of Sir Hugh Elliott, 3 Bt, *qv*; *b* 12 August 1945; *Educ* Bryanston, Univ Coll Oxford; *m* 1975, Marie Thérèse, da of Johann Rüttimann, of Hohenrain, Switzerland; 2 s (Ivo Antony Moritz b 1978, Nicolas Johann Clive b 1980); *Career* ornithologist; research offr Cape Town Univ (PhD 1973) 1968-75; FAO/UN Regnl Quelea Project Tchad/Tanzania 1975-81, FAO project mangr: Arusha Tanzania 1982-86, Nairobi Kenya 1986-; *Recreations* tennis; *Style—* Clive Elliott, Esq; PO Box 24607, Nairobi (Karen), Kenya

ELLIOTT, Denholm Mitchell; CBE (1988); s of Myles Layman Farr Elliott, MBE (d 1933), and Nina, *née* Mitchell (d 1967); *b* 31 May 1922; *Educ* Malvern, RADA; *m* 1, 1954 (m dis 1957), Virginia McKenna (actress) *qv*; m 2, 15 June 1962, Susan Darby, da of Ted Robinson, Jr, of New York, USA; 1 s (Mark b 26 Jan 1967), 1 da (Jennifer b 8 June 1964); *Career* served WWII with RAF Bomber Cmd 1940-45 (prisoner in Germany 1942-45); actor stage and films; plays incl Ring Round the Moon New York 1950, Stratford on Avon Season 1960; The Seagull, The Crucible, Ring Round the Moon Nat Repertory Co NY 1963-64; has appeared in 85 films incl: King Rat 1964, Alfie 1966, Here We Go Round the Mulberry Bush 1967, The Seagull 1968, Bad Timing 1980, Brimstone and Treacle, Trading Places 1982, The Missionary 1983, A Private Function 1984; awards incl: BAFTA Best TV Actor, New Standard Best Film Actor 1981, BAFTA Best TV Actor, New Standard Best Film Actor 1981, BAFTA Best Supporting Film Actor 1984; *Recreations* gardening; *Clubs* Garrick; *Style—* Denholm Elliott, Esq, CBE; Can Peve y San Dic, Ibiza, Balearics, Spain; c/o London Management, 235 Regent Street, London W1 (☎ 01 493 1610)

ELLIOTT, Hon Mrs; Hon Elinor; *née* Spring Rice; eldest (twin) da of 6 Baron Monteagle of Brandon, *qv*; *b* 23 April 1950; *m* 1974, Myles Clare Elliott; 1 s (Thomas b 1977), 2 da (Nina b 1980, Emma b 1983); *Recreations* golf, tennis; *Clubs* Roehampton; *Style—* Hon Mrs Elliott; 41 Ravenscourt Rd, London W6

ELLIOTT, Geoffrey Charles; s of Alfred Stanley Elliott (d 1985), of Coventry, and Elsie, *née* Wilday; *b* 10 May 1945; *Educ* Bablake Sch Coventry; *m* 5 April 1969, Lynda Barbara, da of John Arthur Williams (d 1980), of Shipston-on-Stour, Warwicks; 1 s (Nicholas John b 1974), 1 da (Joanne Marie b 1971); *Career* Coventry Evening Telegraph: reporter, feature writer, chief feature writer 1962-72, dep ed 1973-79, ed 1981-; ed Kent Messenger 1979-80; Guild Br Newpaper Eds: chm Parly and Legal Ctee 1983-86, chm West Midlands 1987-88; memb Press Cncl; memb Round Table: Rugby Webb Ellis (chm 1977-78), Bearsted Kent, Coventry Mercia; *Recreations* sport, gardening, music; *Style—* Geoffrey Elliott, Esq; 119 Beechwood Avenue, Easrlsdon, Coventry (☎ 0203 76637); Coventry Newspapers Ltd, Corporation Street, Coventry CV1 1FP (☎ 0203 633633, fax 0203 631736)

ELLIOTT, Grahame Nicholas; s of Charles Morris William Elliott (d 1966); *b* 23 Dec 1938; *Educ* Mill Hill Sch; *m* 1968, Zita Catherine, *née* Jones; 2 s, 1 da; *Career* CA, sr ptnr Elliott Templeton Sankey and Stoy Hayward (Manchester); *Clubs* Turf, St James's (Manchester), Racquets (Manchester); *Style—* Grahame Elliott, Esq; Highbury, Harrop Rd, Hale, Ches (☎ 061 980 4857)

ELLIOTT, Sir Hugh Francis Ivo; 3 Bt (UK 1917) of Limpsfield, Surrey, OBE (1953); s of Sir Ivo D'Oyly Elliott, 2 Bt (d 1961); *b* 10 Mar 1913; *Educ* Dragon Sch Oxford, Eastbourne Coll, Univ Coll Oxford; *m* 12 Dec 1939, Elizabeth Margaret, da of Adolphus George Phillipson (d 1948), of North Finchley; 1 s, 2 da; *Heir* s, Clive Christopher Hugh Elliott; *Career* HM Overseas Civil Service (Tanganyika Administration 1937-61, seconded as Administrator Tristan da Cunha 1950-52, perm sec Miny of Natural Resources 1958-61); Int Union for Conservation of Nature and Natural Resources 1961-80 (sec-gen 1964-66), tstee Natural History Museum 1971-81; pres Br Ornithologist Union 1975-78; Netherlands Order of the Golden Ark (Ridder 1973, Cdr 1980); *Recreations* travel, natural history; *Style—* Sir Hugh Elliott, Bt, OBE; 173 Woodstock Rd, Oxford OX2 7NB (☎ 0865 515469)

ELLIOTT, Hugh Percival; CMG (1959); s of Percy William Elliott (d 1956), of 22 Museum Rd, Oxford, and Elspeth Lucy, *née* Macpherson; both sides of the family served in India in various branches of the Indian Civil Serv back to E India Co days; *b* 29 May 1911; *Educ* St Lawrence Coll Ramsgate, Hertford Coll Oxford; *m* 1951, Bridget Rosalie, da of Rev Adolf Peterson (d 1961), of 12 Eldon Ave, Shirley, Croydon; *Career* Colonial Admin Serv Nigeria 1934, asst district offr 1937-44, seconded Colonial Off 1946-50, supervisor Colonial Serv Training Courses London 1948-50, asst sec Cncl of Mins Lagos 1951-53, perm sec Eastern Nigeria 1954-58, chief sec Eastern Nigeria 1958-59, advsr to Govt of Eastern Nigeria 1960-67; CON 1964 (Cdr Order of the Niger, Nigeria); *Recreations* Africa, water colour painting; *Clubs* Royal Cwlth Soc; *Style—* Hugh Elliott, Esq, CMG; Flat 8, Rosewood Lodge, 79 Wickham Rd, Shirley, Croydon CR0 8TB

ELLIOTT, John Charles Kennedy; s of Charles Morris William Elliott (d 1967), of Altrincham, Cheshire, and Lesley Margaret, *née* Bush; *b* 13 Mar 1937; *Educ* Merton House Sch Penmaenmawr, Mill Hill Sch London, Victoria Univ of Manchester; *m* 28 July 1962, Angela Mary, da of Col Geoffrey William Noakes OBE, JP, DL; 3 s (Charles Geoffrey b 3 Nov 1963, William James b 10 April 1965, Thomas Richard b 11 May 1969), 1 da (Vanessa Jane b 9 Feb 1967); *Career* admitted slr 1961; articled to John Gorna & Co 1956-61, James Chapman & Co 1961-62, Fentons Stansfield & Elliott 1962-68, fndr and sr ptnr Elliott & Co 1968-; chm Shirt Manufacturing Co 1986-; dir: Northern Rock Building Soc (Northern Bd) 1988-,Hogg Robinson & Gardner Mountain plc; chm Young Slr's Gp of Law Soc 1973-74, pres Manchester Law Soc 1980; NSPCC: chm Manchester and Salford, vice chm Greater Manchester area ctee, Central Exec Ctee 1980-87; memb Law Soc; *Clubs* The St Jame's (Manchester); *Style—* John Elliott, Esq; Bradwall House, Bradwall Cheshire CQ11 9RB (☎ 0270 765 369); Centurion House, Deansgate, Manchester M3 3WT (☎ 061 834 9933, fax 061 832 3693, car telephone 0860 619346, telex 667252)

ELLIOTT, Michael Alwyn; s of William Alwyn Edwards and Mrs Jill Elliott, *née* Thornton; assumed stepfather's name; *b* 15 July 1936; *Educ* Raynes Park GS, Insead; *m* 1962, Caroline Margaret, da of John Edward McCarthy; 2 s (Gregory, Dominic), 1 da (Sophie); *Career* dir Kimberly Clark Ltd 1977-79; gen admin Nat Theatre 1979-85; dir admin Denton, Hall Burgin & Warrens (slrs) 1985-88; business conslt 1988-; *Recreations* theatre, golf; *Style—* Michael Elliott, Esq; 149 Forest Rd, Tunbridge Wells, Kent TN2 5EX

ELLIOTT, Sir Norman Randall; CBE (1957, OBE 1946); s of William Randall Elliott, of London, and Catherine Dunsmore; *b* 19 July 1903; *Educ* privately and St Catharine's Coll Cambridge; *m* 1963, late Mrs Phyllis Clarke, da of Mark Markham, of London; *Career* served 21 Army Gp, Col, dep dir of Works; barr 1932; subsequently with: London Passenger Tport Bd, London & Home Counties Jt Electricity Authy (as gen mangr and chief engr), Yorks Electric Power and (as dir) Isle of Thanet Electric Supply Co; chm: Howden Gp 1973- (engrg and air-handling, specialising in energy conservation), Electricity Cncl 1968-72; dir: Newarthill & McAlpine Gp 1972-, Schlumberger Ltd 1977-, James Howden & Co; kt 1967; *Style—* Sir Norman Elliott, CBE

ELLIOTT, Patrick James; s of Ernest George Elliott (d 1954), of Brighton, Sussex, and Mary, *née* Keywood (d 1967); *b* 19 Dec 1927; *Educ* Xaverian Coll Brighton; *m* 17 March 1953, Beryl Olivia Catherine (Kate), da of Major Henry Carroll (d 1983), of Brighton; 2 s (Christopher James b 1954, Martin John b 1955), 1 da (Jane Catharine b 1970); *Career* Royal Navy PO 1944-47; ARICS 1952; dir: Priest Marians Hldgs plc 1985-1988 Imry Property Holdings plc 1984; memb Mgmnt Ctee: Pan European Property Unit Tst 1979-87, North American Property Unit Tst 1981; memb Mgmnt Bd Griffin Housing Assoc Bd 1979-; memb General Practice Divisional Cncl and other Ctees RICS; FRICS; KSG 1982; *Recreations* hill walking, cricket, music; *Clubs* Carlton, MCC; *Style—* Patrick Elliott, Esq; 2 Blakesley Avenue, London W5 2DW (☎ 01 998 2266); 19 St James Square, London W1Y 4JT (☎ 01 321 0266)

ELLIOTT, Philip Nigel Westbrooke; s of John Stuart Westbrooke Elliott, of Huntmill Farm, Wootton Bassett, and Katherine Briar, *née* Smith; *b* 4 August 1958; *Educ* Wootton Bassett Sch; *m* 6 April 1984, Silvia Regina Cavalini, da of Pedro Palmieri, of Colina, S-P, Brazil; 1 da (Stephanie); *Career* polo player: Young Player of the Year 1980, England II 1982 and 1983, challenge Cup (twice), Warwickshire Cup, Br Open Championship, Queen's Cup (twice); rated: 5 handicap England, 6 Handicap Brazil; *Recreations* music, reading; *Clubs* Royal County of Berks Polo, Helvetia Polo & Country (Brazil); *Style—* Philip Elliott, Esq; Haras Taboro, Couna, Brazil, CEP 14770; Garswood, Bracknell, Berks, England

ELLIOTT, Sir Randal Forbes; KBE (1977, OBE 1975); s of Col Sir James Sands Elliott (d 1957), and Lady (Anne) Elliot, MBE, DStJ (d 1955), da of William Forbes, of Ross-shire; *b* 12 Oct 1922; *Educ* Hereworth Sch, Wanganui Coll Sch, Otago Univ New Zealand (MB, ChB (NZ) DO); *m* 1949, Pauline June, da of Col John George Young, CBE (d 1977); 1 s (John Randal), 6 da (Sally Ann, Mary Jane, Philippa Louise, Penelope Joan, Amanda Caroline); *Career* Gp Capt RNZAF Pacific 1941-45, Malaysia, Borneo, Vietnam; Ophthalmic Surgeon Wellington Hosp 1953-87; Ophthalmic Consultant NZ Armed Forces 1960-; pres NZ Medical Assoc 1976 (dep chm Medical Assoc (NZ) 1965-71, memb Medical Assoc 1972-74); past pres Ophthalmological Soc NZ; FRCS, FRACS, KStJ 1978, GCStJ 1987 *for further information see Debrett's Handbook of Australia and New Zealand*; *Recreations* skiing, mountaineering, sailing; *Clubs* Wellington; *Style—* Sir Randal Elliott, KBE; 186 The Terrace, Wellington, New Zealand (☎ 731 080); Wellington Club Plaza, 90 The Terrace, Wellington, New Zealand (☎ 721 375)

ELLIOTT, Prof Sir Roger James; s of James Elliott (d 1932), and Gladys, *née* Hill; *b* 8 Dec 1928; *Educ* Swanwick Hall Sch Derbys, New Coll Oxford (MA, DPhil); *m* 1952, Olga Lucy, da of Roy Atkinson (d 1940); 1 s (Martin James b 1962), 2 da (Jane Susan b 1955, Rosalind Kira b 1957); *Career* sr proctor Oxford Univ 1969-70, sec to delegates and chief exec OUP 1988- (delegate 1971-78), Wykeham prof of physics Oxford Univ 1974-88, chm computor bd for Univs and Res Cncls 1983-87, physical sec and vice pres Royal Soc 1984-88; Hon DSc Paris 1983; FRS 1976; kt 1987; *Clubs* Athenaeum; *Style—* Prof Sir Roger Elliott; 11 Crick Rd, Oxford OX2 6QL; Oxford University Press, Walton St, Oxford OX2 6DP (☎ 0865 56767)

ELLIOTT, Sir Ronald Stuart; s of Harold John William Elliott (d 1965), and Mercedes Emma Manning (d 1983); *b* 29 Jan 1918; *Educ* Ballarat C of E GS; *m* 1944, Isabella Mansbridge, da of William Nixon Boyd (d 1952); 1 s, 1 da; *Career* banker; md Cwlth Banking Corpn 1976-81; dir: Brambles Industs Ltd 1981-, Int Commodities Clearing House Ltd (Aust Bd) 1981-88, Int Bd Security Pacific Nat Bank USA 1983-, Security Pacific Australia Ltd 1985-, tres The Australian Opera 1982-87; ABIA; kt 1980; *Recreations* golf, opera; *Clubs* Aust Golf, Union (Sydney); *Style—* Sir Ronald Elliott; Glenhaven, PO Box 1401, Armidale NSW 2350, Australia (☎ 067 722387)

ELLIOTT, Hon Mrs; Hon Rosemary Aletta; *née* de Villiers; yr da of 3 Baron de Villiers; *b* 20 Mar 1946; *Educ* Rhodes Univ; *m* 1967, Robin Anderson Elliott, TD; 3 s; *Style—* Hon Mrs Elliott; 52 St John Rd, Houghton, Johannesburg, S Africa; Sangar Hill Farm, Magaliesburg, Transvaal

ELLIOTT, Hon Mrs (Sophia Anne); *née* Sackville-West; 3 da (by 1 m) of 6 Baron Sackville; *b* 19 July 1957; *m* 17 Dec 1988, Guy R Elliott, o s of Robert Elliott, of Little Ashley Farm, Bradford-on-Avon, Wilts; *Style—* The Hon Sophia Sackville-West; 11 Sinclair Gardens, London W14

ELLIOTT, Hon Lord; Walter Archibald; MC (1943), QC (1960); s of Prof Thomas Renton Elliott, CBE, DSO, FRS (d 1961), of Broughton Place, Broughton, Peebleshire, and Martha, *née* M'Cosh; *b* 6 Sept 1922; *Educ* Eton, Edinburgh Univ; *m* 1954, Susan Isobel, da of late Phillip Mackenzie Ross; 2 s; *Career* Capt Scots Gds Italy, NW Europe WW II; barr and advocate 1950, pres Lands Tribunal for Scotland 1971-, chm of Scottish Land Court with title Lord Elliott 1978-; Brig Queen's Body Guard for Scotland (Royal Co of Archers); *Books* Us and Them, A Study of Group Consciousness (1986); *Recreations* gardening, travel; *Clubs* New, Scottish Arts (both Edinburgh); *Style—* The Hon Lord Elliott, MC; Morton House, Fairmilehead, Edinburgh 10 (☎ 031 445 2548); office: 1 Grosvenor Crescent, Edinburgh (☎ 031 225 7595)

ELLIOTT, William Rowcliffe; CB (1969); s of Thomas Herbert Elliott of Ruislip,

Middx, and Ada, *née* Rowcliffe; *b* 10 April 1910; *Educ* St Paul's Sch, Queen's Coll Oxford (MA); *m* 1937, Karin Tess, da of Dr Ernest Classen, of 28 Esmond Gdns, Bedford Park, London W4; 1 s (Mark); *Career* schoolmaster 1933-36, HM inspr of schs 1936-44, staff inspr 1944-55, chief inspr 1955-66, dep sr chief inspr 1966-67, sr chief inspr 1968-72; memb Oxfam governing cncl 1974-80, pres Section L Br Assoc 1969, chm govrs Friend's Sch Saffron Walden 1982-84, govr The Retreat York 1984-; *Books* Monemvasia, The Gibraltar of Greece (1971); *Recreations* village life, gardening, photography; *Clubs* Overseas League; *Style*— William Elliott, Esq, CB; Malthus Close, Farthinghoe, Brackley, Northants NN13 5NY (☎ 0295 710388)

ELLIOTT OF MORPETH, Baron (Life Peer UK 1985); Sir (Robert) William Elliott; s of Richard Elliott (d 1957), of Low Heighley, Morpeth, Northumberland; *b* 11 Dec 1920; *Educ* King Edward GS Morpeth; *m* 1956, (Catherine) Jane, da of John Burton Morpeth, of Newcastle; 1 s, 4 da; *Career* farmer 1939-; chm, vice-pres and pres Northern Area Young Conservatives 1948-55; contested (C) Morpeth 1954 and 1955; MP (C) Newcastle-upon-Tyne N 1957-83; PPS to: jt Parly secs Miny of Transport and Civil Aviation 1958-59, Parly under-sec of state Home Office 1959-60, min of state Home Office 1960-61, min for Technical Co-operation 1961-63; asst govt whip 1963-64, opposition whip 1966-70; comptroller of HM Household June-Oct 1970; vice-chm Conservative Party Organisation 1970-74; chm Select Ctee on Agriculture, Fisheries and Food 1980-83; kt 1974; *Clubs* Northern Counties; *Style*— The Rt Hon Lord Elliott of Morpeth; Lipwood Hall, Haydon Bridge, Northumberland (☎ 043 484 777); 19 Laxford House, Cundy Street, London SW1 (☎ 01 730 7619)

ELLIOTT-BINNS, Edward Ussher Elliott; CB (1977); s of Rev Canon Leonard Elliott Elliott-Binns (d 1963), of Essex, and Anna Scott Kilner (d 1957); *b* 24 August 1918; *Educ* Harrow, King's Coll Cambridge (MA); *m* 1942, Katharine Mary Macleod, da of Dr John Morrison Caie, (d 1949); 1 da (Margaret b 1943); *Career* Leicestershire Regt & SOE (Maj); Civil Serv 1946-78 Scottish Off: asst sec Royal Cmmn on Capital Punishment 1949-53, private sec Min of State 1956-57, under sec in charge of hosp servs 1965-75, (emergency servs 1975-78); *Recreations* philately, classics, walking; *Clubs* Special Forces; *Style*— Edward Elliott-Binns, Esq, CB; 22 Wilton Road, Edinburgh EH16 5NX (☎ 031 667 2464)

ELLIOTT-MURRAY-KYNYNMOUND, Hon G E D; *see*: Elliot

ELLIS, Andrew Steven; OBE (1984); s of Peter Vernon Ellis, and Kathleen, *née* Dawe; *b* 19 May 1952; *Educ* St Dunstan's Coll Catford, Trinity Coll Cambridge (BA), Univ of Newcastle (MSc), Newcastle Poly (BA Law); *m* 13 Jul 1975(m dis 1987), Patricia Ann Stevens, da of William Skinner; *Career* propr Andrew Ellis (printing and duplicating services) 1973-81, election organiser 1981-85, sec gen Lib Pty 1985-86; chief exec SLD 1988-; vice chm Lib Pty 1980-86; contested (Lib) Newcastle upon Tyne Central (1974, 1976 by election, 1979), Boothberry (1983); ldr Lib gp Tyne and Wear CC 1977-81; *Books* Algebraic Structure (with Terence Treeby, 1971), Let Every Englishman's Home be his Castle (1978); *Clubs* Nat Liberal; *Style*— Andrew Ellis, Esq, OBE; 19 Hayle Road, Maidstone, Kent ME15 6PD (☎ 0622 678 443); Social and Liberal Democrats, 4 Cowley Street, London SW1 (☎ 01 222 7999, fax 01 799 2176)

ELLIS, Lady Angela Mary; *née* Shirley; eldest da of 13 Earl Ferrers; *b* 16 June 1954; *m* 1975, Jonathan Ellis, FCA; 1 s (Charles b 1979), 2 da (Louise b 1977, Georgina b 1981); *Style*— Lady Angela Ellis; The Old Rectory, Thurning, nr Dereham, Norfolk NR20 5QX (☎ Saxthorpe 861)

ELLIS, Carol Jacqueline; QC (1980); da of Ellis W Ellis (d 1974), of London, and Flora, *née* Bernstein; *b* 6 May 1929; *Educ* Abbey Sch Reading, Univ of Lausanne, UC London (LLB),; *m* 1957, Ralph Gilmore; 2 s (Jeremy, David); *Career* ed The Law Reports and Weekly Law Reports; *Style*— Miss Carol Ellis, QC; 11 Old Sq, Lincoln's Inn, London WC2

ELLIS, David Raymond; s of Raymond Ellis (d 1986), of Charney Bassett, Nr Wantage, Oxon, and Ethel, *née* Gordon; *b* 4 Sept 1946; *Educ* St Edward's Sch Oxford, Christ Church Coll Oxford (MA); *m* 18 December 1974, Cathleen Margaret, da of late Dr Albert Joseph Hawe, CBE, of Accra, Ghana; 1 s (Thomas b 1978), 1 da (Caroline b 1979); *Career* called to the Bar Inner Temple 1970, asst rec 1986; *Clubs* Leander; *Style*— David Ellis, Esq; Lamb Building, Temple, London EC4Y 7AS (☎ 01 353 6701)

ELLIS, Dr E(ric) Leslie; s of Charles Robert Ellis (d 1966), of Harrogate, and Ellen Elizabeth (d 1961); *b* 23 Nov 1914; *Educ* Rydal Sch, St Catharine's Coll Cambridge (MA), Leeds Univ; *m* 21 July 1947, Denise Gabrielle, da of Charles Jacot des Combes (d 1963), of Harrogate; 1 s (Charles b 1949), 1 da (Christiane b 1955); *Career* war service 1939-45: major RAMC, India, Malaya 1940-42 (POW Singapore, Indo-China, Thailand 1942-45); gen medical practitioner Titchfield 1947-84; cncllr Fareham UDC/BC 1954-76 (chm: housing, finance, policy and resources ctees); MRCS; LRCP; *Recreations* sailing, bridge; *Clubs* Achilles, Royal Southern YC; *Style*— Dr E Leslie Ellis; The Old Surgery, 2 Coach hill, Titchfield, Fareham, Hants PO14 4EE (☎ 0329 43570)

ELLIS, Geoffrey Albert; s of Albert Edward Ellis (d 1989), of Eaglescliffe, Cleveland, and Alice Isabel, *née* Bell; *b* 20 Sept 1937; *Educ* City of Leicester Boys Sch, Manchester Univ (Dip Architecture); *m* 8 March 1969, Annette Ray Ellis; 2 da (Vanessa Claire b 1975, Verity Fiona b 1981); *Career* architect; asst then sr architect W S Hattrell & Partnership Manchester 1961-66, sr architect R Seifert & Ptnrs Manchester 1966-68; ptnr: Gelling Ellis Lomas & Ptnrs Douglas IOM 1968-78, Ellis Brown Ptnrship Douglas IOM 1978-; life memb Douglas Rugby Club, memb IOM Soc of Architects and Surveyors; RIBA 1966, FFAS 1984, FFB 1971; *Recreations* swimming, touring, camping; *Style*— Geoffrey Ellis, Esq; Old School House, South Cape, Laxey, IOM (☎ 0624 781 682); Longlast, Selbourne Drive, Douglas, IOM; Ellis Brown, 5 Goldie Terr, Douglas, IOM (☎ 0624 21375/0624 22692, fax 0624 28465)

ELLIS, Geoffrey Gordon; *née* Anstice; s of Frederick Ellis (d 1966) of London and Vera, *née* Clark; *b* 25 July 1940; *Educ* Gravesend GS Isleworth; *m* 16 Sept 1961, Jean Heather, da of Ronald Coles (d 1978) of Bath; 1 da (Kate b 1971); *Career* journalist: Bath Evening Chronicle 1957-68, Thomson Regional 1968-71, The Guardian 1971-79, Now! Magazine 1979-81, The Times 1981-85; dir PR Broad Street Assoc 1985-; *Recreations* wine appreciation, aviation, jazz, books, cooking, France; *Style*— Geoffrey Ellis, Esq; 30 Furnival St, London, EC4A 1JE, (☎ 01 831 3113, fax 01 831 6044)

ELLIS, Prof Hadyn Douglas; s of Alfred Douglas Ellis, and Myrtle Lillian Ellis; *b* 22 Dec 1922; *Educ* Reading Univ (BA, PhD), Aberdeen Univ (DSc); *m* 17 Sept 1966, Diane Margaret, da of Denis Newton, of St Briavels, Glos; 3 s (Stephen David b 1967, Robert b 1980, Jack Richard b 1983); *Career* Univ of Aberdeen: lectr 1970-79, sr lectr 1979-86; prof applied psychology UWIST 1986-88, prof psychology UWCC 1988-; FBPS 1986; *Style*— Prof Haydn Ellis; The Homestead, Castleton, Cardiff CF3 8GN; School of Psychology, WWCC, Cardiff CF1 3YG (☎ 0222 874 000)

ELLIS, Prof Harold; CBE; s of Samuel and Ada Ellis; *b* 13 Jan 1926; *Educ* Univ of Oxford (BM, BCh, MC, DM); *m* 20 Apr 1958, Wendy, da of Henry Levine; 1 s (Jonathan b 1959), 1 da (Suzanne b 1962); *Career* Capt RAMC 1950-51; res surgical appts 1948-60, sr lectr Univ of London 1960-62, prof of surgery Univ of London at Westminster Hosp 1962-88; univ clinical anatomist Univ of Cambridge 1989-; former vice pres: RCS, RCM; pres Br Assoc of Surgical Oncology; FRCS, FRCOG; *Recreations* medical history; *Style*— Prof Harold Ellis, CBE; 16 Bancroft Avenue, London, N2 (☎ 01 348 2720); Dept of Anatomy, University of Cambridge, Tennis Court road, Cambridge

ELLIS, Dr (William) Herbert (Baxter); AFC (1954); s of William Baxter Ellis (d 1969), of Newcastle-upon-Tyne, and Georgina Isabella, *née* Waller (d 1963); *b* 2 July 1921; *Educ* Oundle, Durham Univ (MB BS, MD); *m* 1, 1948 (m dis), Margaret Mary, da of Frank Limb, OBE (d 1987), of Yorks; 1 s (Christopher b 1954), 1 da (Penny (Mrs Deakin) b 1952), m 2, Mollies Margurite, *née* Clarke; *Career* surgn Cdr RN 1945-59; qualified Naval Pilot appts incl: RN Hosp Malta 1945-47, RAF Inst of Aviation Med Farnborough 1950-56, US Navy Acceleration laboratory Johnsville USA 1956-58, RN Air Med Sch Gosport 1958-59; mktg dir Appleyard Gp 1959-64, vice pres Schweppes (USA) 1964-65, dir Bewac 1965-71, dir gen Dr Barnardos 1971-73; med conslt DHSS 1973-, Employment Med Advisory Serv 1973-81, med conslt Plesseys, St Johns Ambulance: co surgn 1979-87, co cdr 1989-; KstJ 1989 (OStJ 1979, C St J 1987); *Books* Hippocrates RN: Memoirs of a Naval Flying Doctor (1988); *Recreations* walking, mending fences; *Clubs* Army and Navy, Naval and Military, St John; *Style*— Dr Herbert Ellis, AFC; 7 Honeywood House, Alington Rd, Canford Cliffs, Poole, Dorset BH14 8LZ, (☎ 0202 700 421)

ELLIS, Dr (William) Herbert Baxter; AFC (1954); er s of William Baxter Ellis and Georgina Isabella, *née* Waller; *b* 2 July 1921; *Educ* Oundle Sch, Durham Univ; *m* 1, 1947 (m dis), Margaret Mary, *née* Limb; 1 s, 1 da; m 2, 1977, Mrs Mollie Marguerite Clarke, *née* Weller; 1 step da; *Career* served RN 1945-59, Surgn Cdr, Fleet Air Arm, pilot; motor industry 1960-71; dir-gen Dr Barnardo's 1971-73, Employment Medical Advsy Service 1973-81; conslt DHSS 1973-; Cdr St John Ambulance Gloucestershire; Chief Cdr St John Ambulance 1989-; CStJ; *Recreations* study of humanity; *Clubs* Army & Navy, Naval & Military; *Style*— Dr Herbert Ellis, AFC; The Manor House, Compton Abdale, nr Cheltenham, Glos

ELLIS, Humphry Francis; MBE (1945); s of Dr John Constable Ellis (d 1928), of Metheringham, Lincs, and Alice Marion, *née* Raven (d 1960); *b* 17 July 1907; *Educ* Tonbridge, Magdalen Coll Oxford (MA); *m* 1933, Barbara Pauline, da of late Wilfrid Hasseldine; 1 s, 1 da; *Career* WWII RA (AA Cmd) 1939-45, Maj 1944-45; writer and ed; former dep ed Punch; contributor New Yorker 1954-; *Books* A J Wentworth, BA (1949, 1980), RA Commemoration Book (co ed 1950), Manual of Rugby Union Football (ed 1952), Mediatrics (1961), A Bee in the Kitchen (1983); *Recreations* fishing, gardening, birds, watching rugby and cricket; *Clubs* Garrick and MCC; *Style*— Humphry Ellis, Esq, MBE; Hill Croft, Kingston St Mary, Taunton, Somerset (☎ 082345 264)

ELLIS, Sir John Rogers; MBE (1943); 3 s of late Frederick William Ellis, MD, FRCS; *b* 15 June 1916; *Educ* Oundle, Trinity Hall Cambridge, London Hosp (MA, MD, FRCP); *m* 1942, Joan, da of late C J C Davenport; 2 s, 2 da; *Career* dean London Hosp Med Coll 1968-81 (formerly sub-dean then vice-dean), physician to London Hosp 1951-81; pres Med Protection Soc, vice-pres Assoc for the study of Med Educn; kt 1980; *Recreations* painting, gardening; *Style*— Sir John Ellis, MBE; Little Monkhams, Monkhams Lane, Woodford Green, Essex (☎ 01 504 2292)

ELLIS, Dr Jonathan (John) Richard; s of Richard Ellis of 28 Heath Drive, Potters Bar, Herts, Eng 1EH, and Beryl Lilian, *née* Ranger (d 1985); *b* 1 July 1946; *Educ* Lochinver House Sch, Highgate Sch, King's Coll Cambridge Univ (BA, PhD); *m* 11 July 1985, Maria Mercedes, da of Alfonso Martinez Arizabeleta (d 1982), of Cali, Columbia, USA; 1 da (Jennifer b 17 Jan 1988); *Career* res assoc Stanford Linear Accelerator Centre 1971-72, Richard Chase Tolman Fell Calif Inst of Tech 1972-73; ldr Theoretical Studies Divn Euro Orgn for Nuclear Res (CERN) Geneva 1988-(staff memb since 1973); Miller Prof Univ of California Berkeley 1988; FRS (1984); *Recreations* reading, listening to music, hiking in mountains; *Style*— Dr John Ellis; 5 Chemin Du Ruisseau, Tannay, 1295 Mies, Switzerland (☎ 010 41 22 764 858); Theoretical Studies Division, Cern, 1211-Geneva 23, Switzerland (☎ 010 41 22 834 142, fax 010 41 22 833 914)

ELLIS, Laurence Edward; s of Dr Edward Alfred Ellis (d 1952), of Great Yarmouth, and the late Ida Ethel, *née* Dawson; *b* 21 April 1932; *Educ* Winchester, Trinity Coll Cambridge (BA,MA); *m* 5 April 1961, Elizabeth, da of Norman James Ogilvie, of Castle Cary; 2 s (Jonathan b 8 May 1962, Simon b 29 Sept 1971), 1 da (Mary b 23 May 1964); *Career* Rifle Bde 1950-52 (S/Lt KRRC 1951-52); housemaster Marborough Coll 1968-77 (asst master 1955-68), rector (headmaster) Edinburgh Acad 1977-; memb various ctees incl: Business Educn Review Gp 1986-87, MEG (GCSE) Cncl 1986-; AFIMA, FRSA; *Books* SMP Mathematics Course (jtly, 1964-76); *Recreations* music, crosswords, woodwork; *Style*— Laurence Ellis, Esq; 50 Inverleith Place, Edinburgh EH3 5QB; The Edinburgh Academy, Henderson Row, Edinburgh EH3 5BL (☎ 031 556 4603)

ELLIS, Mark; s of David Meurig Ellis (d 1960); *b* 27 Sept 1953; *Educ* Llandovery Coll Dyfed, St John's Coll Cambridge (MA, LLB); *Career* barr 1977; mangr corporate finance Arbuthnot Latham Bank 1978-83, jt md Polly Peck Int plc 1983-; *Recreations* tennis, squash, reading, travel, theatre, cinema; *Style*— Mark Ellis, Esq; Polly Peck Int plc

ELLIS, Nigel George; s of George Ellis, of Selsey, Sussex, and Ivy, *née* Howell; *b* 19 April 1939; *Educ* Farnborough GS; *m* 31 July 1965, Yvonne Meline Elizabeth, da of Norman Tracy (d 1976), of Crowborough, Sussex; 1 s (Timothy b 1971), 1 da (Victoria b 1968); *Career* co sec City of London Real Property Co 1967-74; dir: Holland America UK Ltd 1974-79, Hammerson Property Devpt and Investmt Corpn 1979-88, BAA plc 1988-; Freeman Worshipful Co of Fanmakers 1984, FCA 1963, FC CA 1985; *Recreations* philately, chess; *Style*— Nigel Ellis, Esq; Woodland Chase, Tennyson's Lane, Haslemere, Surrey (☎ 0428 2428) Fougeryat, Saussignac, 24240 Sigoules, France; BAA plc, 130 Wilton Rd, London SW1 (☎ 01 932 6657, fax 01 932 6734, car tel 0836 630 753, telex 919268 BAA PLC)

ELLIS, Dr Norman David; s of George Edward Ellis, (d 1968), of London, and Annie

Leslie, *née* Scarfe (d 1978); *b* 23 Nov 1943; *Educ* Minchenden Sch, Leeds Univ (BA), MA (Oxon), PhD; *m* 1966, Valerie Ann, da of Haddon Fenn, of East Sussex; 1 s (Mark b 1975); *Career* res fell Nuffield Coll Oxford 1971-74; gen sec Assoc First Div Civil Servants 1974-78; under sec British Medical Assoc 1978-; *Recreations* reading, railways, local community affairs; *Style—* Dr Norman Ellis; British Medical Association, BMA House, Tavistock Square, London WC1

ELLIS, Peter Johnson; s of Albert Goodall Ellis (d 1985), and Evelyn, *née* Johnson; *b* 24 Nov 1937; *Educ* Queen Elizabeth GS Wakefield, Trinity Coll Cambridge (MA); *m* 14 July 1960, Janet Margaret, da of Thomas Palmer, of Cambridge; 3 da (Jacqueline b 11 Oct 1961, Christine b 3 July 1964, Rosalind b 4 Jan 1967); *Career* RAF 1955-57; systems analyst IBM (UK) Ltd 1960-64, data processing mangr J&A Scrimgeour 1964-70, jt dep chief exec Grieveson Grant & Co 1982-86 (ptnr 1976-86), dep chm Kleinwort Benson Investmt Mgmnt 1988- (jt chief exec 1986-88); memb: Soc of Investmt Analysts 1970- (cncl memb 1976-84), Stock Exchange 1973-; *Recreations* theatre, reading, bridge; *Style—* Peter Ellis, Esq; La Barranca, Tyrrell's Wood, Leatherhead, Surrey (☎ 0372 372343); Kleinwort Benson Investment Management, 10 Fenchurch St, London EC3M 3LB (☎ 01 623 8000, 01 956 7260)

ELLIS, Peter Rowland; s of Capt Frederick Rowland Ellis, MBE (d 1942), Madge, *née* Wass (d 1988); *b* 4 April 1927; *Educ* Burton-on-Trent GS, Sidney Sussex Coll Camb (MA); *Career* flying offr RAF 1948-50; dir Yardley of London Ltd 1975-78, md Yardley Contracts Ltd 1978-82; md Peter Black Toiletries Ltd 1983-87, dir non-exec dir Peter Black Hldgs plc 1987-; *Style—* Peter Ellis, Esq; Rosevine, 391C Ham Green, Holt, Trowbridge, Wilts BA14 6PZ (☎ 0225 782462)

ELLIS, Raymond Joseph; MP (Lab) North-East Derbyshire 1979-; s of Harold and Ellen Ellis; *b* 17 Dec 1923; *Educ* Sheffield Univ, Ruskin Coll; *m* 1946, Cynthia, *née* Lax; 4 children; *Career* sponsored by NUM, former branch sec, pres Derbyshire NUM 1972; memb: S Yorkshire CC 1976-79, Select Ctee on Euro Legislation 1979-; *Style—* Raymond Ellis, Esq, MP; House of Commons, London SW1

ELLIS, Richard Tunstall; OBE (1970), DL (1967); s of Herbert Tunstall Ellis (d 1925), of Liverpool, and Mary Elizabeth Muriel, *née* Sellers (d 1929); *b* 6 Sept 1918; *Educ* Merchant Taylor's Crosby, Silcoates Sch Wakefield Yorkshire, Aberdeen Univ (MA, LLB); *m* 2 Jan 1946, Jean Bruce Maitland, da of Maj Richard Reginald Maitland Porter, MC (d 1979), of Aberdeen; 2 s (Keith b 1949, Andrew b 1960), 2 da (Janet (Mrs Baldwin) b 1947, Katharine (Mrs Parker) b 1956); *Career* Royal Signals 51 Div 2 Lt 1939 (POW Germany 1940-45) Lt 1942, Capt 1945; sr ptnr Paull & Williamsons Advocates Aberdeen 1970-83 (ptnr 1949-70); Trustee Savings Bank: chm Scotland 1983-86, Scotland plc 1986-89, dir Gp plc 1986-89; memb: Scottish Bd Norwich Union Insur Socs 1973-80, Aberdeen Bd Bank of Scotland 1972-82; memb Ct Univ of Aberdeen 1984, cncl memb Nat Tst for Scotland, chm Scottish div IOD 1988; memb: Law Soc of Scotland, Law Soc London; *Recreations* golf, hill walking, skiing; *Clubs* Royal Northern Aberdeen, New Edinburgh Army & Navy; *Style—* Richard Ellis, Esq, OBE, DL; 18 Rubislaw Den North, Aberdeen; (☎ 0224 316 680); TSB Scotland plc, Henry Duncan House, 120 George St, Edinburgh (☎ 031 225 4555)

ELLIS, Ven Robin Gareth; s of Rev Joseph Walter Ellis, BA, and Morva Phyllis Morgan-Jones; *b* 8 Dec 1935; *Educ* Oldham Hulme GS, Worksop Coll, Pembroke Coll Oxford (BCL, MA); *m* 1964, Anne, da of James Sydney Landers (d 1970); 3 s (Timothy b 1966, Simon b 1968, Dominic b 1971); *Career* asst curate St Peter's Swinton Manchester 1960-63, asst Chaplain Worksop Coll 1963-66; vicar: Swaffham Prior with Reach Cambs 1966-74, St Augustine's Wisbech 1974-82, Yelverton 1982-86; archdeacon of Plymouth 1982-; *Recreations* cricket, theatre, prison reform; *Style—* The Ven the Archdeacon of Plymouth; 33 Leat Walk, Roborough, Plymouth (☎ 0752 793397)

ELLIS, Roger Henry; e s of Francis Henry Ellis (d 1953), of Debdale Hall, Mansfield; *b* 9 June 1910; *Educ* Sedbergh, King's Coll Cambridge (MA); *m* 1939, (Audrey) Honor, o da of late Arthur Baker, JP, DL; 2 da; *Career* WWII Private 1939, Maj 5 Fusiliers 1944, serv Italy and Germany; Public Record Off: asst keeper 1934, princ asst keeper 1954, conslt ed Catalogue of Seals 1972-86; sec Royal Cmmn on Historical MSS 1957-72, lectr in archive studies UCL 1947-57, pres Soc of Archivists 1964-73 (vice pres Business Archives Cncl 1958-; memb and sec jt records ctee Royal Soc and Royal Cmmn on Historical MSS 1968-75, chm Br Standards ctee for drafting BS 5454 1967-72; memb: ICA ctee on sigillography 1962-77, advsy ctee on Export of Works of Art 1964-72, London Cncl Br Inst in Florence 1947-55; jt ed Rivista for Br Italian Soc 1946-49, memb exec ctee Friends of the Nat Libraries 1965-88 (hon tres 1977-79), vice pres Royal Inst 1975-76 (mangr 1973-76); corr memb Indian Historical Records Cmmn, FSA, FRHistS; *Publications* Ode on St Crispin's Day (1979), Walking Backwards (1986), Catalogue of Seals in the Public Record Office, Personal Seals I and II (1979-81) Monastic Seals I (1986); *Clubs* Athenaeum; *Style—* Roger Ellis, Esq; Cloth Hill, 6 The Mount, Hampstead, London NW3

ELLIS, Sir Ronald; s of William Ellis, and Besse Brownbill; *b* 12 August 1925; *Educ* Preston GS, Manchester Univ; *m* 1, 1956, Cherry Hazel Brown (d 1978); 1 s, 1 da; m 2, 1979 Myra Ann Royle; *Career* dir BL Motor Corpn 1970-76, chm Bus Mfrs Hldg Co 1972-76; head of Def Sales MOD 1976-81; dir Wilkinson Sword Gp 1981-86, Bull Thompson & Assocs Ltd; non-exec dir Yarrow 1981-86, non-exec dir Redman Heenan Int 1981-86, pres and md Allegheny Int (industl div) 1982-85; govr and memb cncl Univ of Manchester Inst of Sci & Technol 1970-, vice pres 1983-; chm EIDC Ltd; BScTEch, FEng, FIMechE, FCIT, CBIM, FRSA; kt 1978; *Recreations* fishing, sailing, reading; *Clubs* Turf, Royal Thames Yacht; *Style—* Sir Ronald Ellis; West Fleet House, Abbotsbury, Dorset DT3 4JF; Flat F, 20 Cornwall Gdns, London SW7

ELLIS, (Robert Thomas) Tom; s of Robert Ellis (d 1986), of Rhosllanerchrugog Clwyd, and Edith Ann, *née* Hughes; *b* 15 Mar 1924; *Educ* Ruabon GS, Univ of Wales Univ of Nottingham (BSc mining); *m* 22 Dec 1949, Williams, da of Vernon Harcourt Williams of Hendre Hall, Penrhyndeudraeth, Gwynedd; 3 s (Charles Thomas b 1953, Mark Alexander Harcourt b 1957, Graham Jonathan b 1960), 1 da (Susan Lucy b 1950); *Career* works chemist 1944-47, mining engnr 1954-70; MP (L) Wrexham 1970-81, (SDP) Wrexham 1981-83; *Recreations* golf, music; *Style—* Tom Ellis, Esq; 3 Old Vicarage, Ruabon, Clwyd (☎ 0978 821128)

ELLIS, Vivian; CBE (1984); s of Harry Ellis and Maud Isaacson; *Educ* Cheltenham Coll; *Career* RNVR 1939-46 (ret Lt Cdr); composer and author; pres Performing Right Society 1983-; has composed scores for numerous musicals incl: Mister Cinders (1929, revived 1983), Bless The Bride (1947 revived 1987); songs include: Spread A Little Happiness, Ma Belle Marguerite, This Is My Lovely Day, I'm On A See-Saw, Other People's Babies; Ivor Novello Award 1973 and 1983; Novels: Faint Harmony, Day Out, Chicanery, Goodbye Dolly, I'm on a Seesaw (autobiography); Humour: How to Make Your Fortune on The Stock Exchange, How to Enjoy Your Operation, How to Busy Yourself in the Country, How to be a Man About Town; *Recreations* gardening, painting; *Clubs* Garrick; *Style—* Vivian Ellis, Esq, CBE; c/o Performing Right Society, 29 Berners St, London W1

ELLIS, Col Wilfred Desmond; OBE (1952), TD (1944) and three bars, DL (1962); 2 s of V C Bertram Wyburne Ellis (d 1944), and Winifred Dora Ellis; *b* 7 Nov 1914; *Educ* Temple Grove, Canford Sch; *m* 1947, Effie Douglas, JP, da of Dr Alex Barr (d 1976), of Canonbie, Dumfries-shire; 1 s, 2 da; *Career* 8 Middx Regt (TA) 1937 (despatches 1944), Cdr 7 Middx 1950-56, Dep Cdr 47 (London) Inf Bde 1957-62 Cmdt Middx Army Cadet Force 1958-62; ADC to HM The Queen 1966-69; mangr Conversion and Customer Service, The Gas Cncl 1966-72; lay memb Press Cncl 1969-75; dep chm Greater London TA 2 VR Assoc 1968-70; *Recreations* shooting and local affairs; *Clubs* Naval & Military; *Style—* Col Wilfred Ellis, OBE, TD, DL; Lea Barn, Winter Hill, Cookham Dean, Berks (☎ 06284 4230)

ELLIS, William Henshaw; s of Alfred Ellis (1943), and Edna May, *née* Henshaw; *b* 7 August 1918; *Educ* RNC Dartmouth, HMS Dryad; *m* 15 June 1940, Margaret May, da of Capt Henry Paul, OBE (d 1967); 5 s (Paul b 1946, Robert b 1949, Martin b 1951, William b 1955, Charles b 1962), 1 da (Naiad b 1943); *Career* HMS Basilish Norway May-June sunk Dunkirk June 1940, HMS Douglas 1941, King George V, HMS Harrier 1943 (despatches), HMS Garth 1944, HMS Aurora Med 1945-46, ret 1946; dir: Starch Products Ltd 1946-68, Peacock Chads Ltd 1947-67, Stadex-Pirie Ltd 1959-63; underwriting memb of Lloyds 1966-, memb RDC cookham 1949-; *Books* The Knife Edge (UK 1972, Norway 1974 & 82, Germany 1975); *Recreations* sailing, writing, arborculture, travelling, walking; *Style—* William Ellis, Esq; Hannaford Barton, Kennford, Exeter, Devon EX6 7XZ (☎ 0392 832 185)

ELLISON, Prof Arthur James; s of Lawrence Joseph Ellison, of Birmingham (d 1978), and Elsie Beatrice Ellison; *b* 15 Jan 1920; *Educ* Solihull Sch, London Univ (BSc, DSc); *m* 1, 1952, Marjorie (d 1955), da of Walter Cresswell, of Sheffield; m 2, 1963, Marian Elizabeth, da of John Gordon Gumbrell, of London (d 1976); 1 s, 1 da; *Career* design engr Higgs Motors Ltd 1938-43, tech asst Royal Aircraft Estab 1943-46, design engr Br Thomson-Houston Co Ltd 1947-58 (graduate apprentice 1946); lectr and sr lectr Queen Mary Coll Univ of London 1958-72, hon prof Nat Univ of Engrg Lima, Peru 1968, fndr and chm Int Conf on Electrical Machines 1974-85 (pres of honour), pres Soc for Psychical Res 1976-79 and 1981-84; prof of electrical and electronic engrg and head of dept City Univ London 1972-85; prof emeritus 1985-; *Recreations* reading, meditation, parapsychology and travel; *Clubs* Athenaeum; *Style—* Prof Arthur Ellison; 10 Foxgrove Ave, Beckenham, Kent (☎ 01 650 3801); The City University, Northampton Sq, London EC1V 0HB (☎ 01 253 4399)

ELLISON, Donald Roy; s of Herbert James Ellison (d 1970), of New Milton, Hants, and Marguerite Evelyn, *née* Swapp (d 1976); *b* 20 Jan 1913; *Educ* Solihull Sch, Balliol Coll Oxford (MA); *m* 24 Aug 1954 (m dis 1976), Joan Audrey, da of Joseph Benn Anderson Baker (d 1967), of Cumbria; 1 s (Anthony b 1959), 1 da (Lucy b 1956); *Career* barr, called to Middle Temple 1940, dep circuit judge and asst rec 1976-83; *Books* Clinical Papers and Essays on Psycho-Analysis by Karl Abraham (jt ed, 1955), Rayden on Divorce (jt ed, 1960); *Recreations* listening to music, theatre going, walking, foreign travel, pursuing useless but interesting knowledge; *Style—* Donald R Ellison, Esq; 27 Wheatsheaf Lane, Fulham, London SW6 6LS (☎ 01 381 5817)

ELLISON, Rt Rev and Rt Hon Gerald Alexander; KCVO (1981), PC (1973); s of Rev Prebendary John Henry Joshua Ellison, CVO (d 1944, Chaplain in Ordinary to HM Queen Victoria), and Sara Dorothy Graham, *née* Crum; *b* 10 August 1910; *Educ* Westminster, New Coll Oxford; *m* 1947, Jane Elizabeth, da of Brig John Houghton Gibbon, DSO (d 1960); 1 s, 2 da; *Career* ordained 1935; curate Sherborne Abbey 1935-37; chaplain to Bishop of Winchester 1937-39; served chaplain RNVR 1939-43 (despatches); chaplain to Archbishop of York 1943-46, vicar St Marks, Portsea 1946-50; canon of Portsmouth 1950, bishop suffragan of Willesden (diocese of London) 1950-55, bishop of Chester 1955-73, bishop of London 1973-81; dean of the Chapels Royal 1973-81, vicar-gen diocese of Bermuda 1983-84; prelate: Order of the Br Empire 1973-81, Imperial Soc of Knights Bachelor 1973-; chaplain and sub-prelate Order of St John 1973-; episcopal canon of Jerusalem 1973-81; pres Actors' Church Union 1973-81; hon bencher Middle Temple 1976; pres Nat Fedn Housing Assocs 1981-; *Books* The Churchman's Duty (1957), The Anglican Communion (1960); *Clubs* Leander, Army and Navy; *Style—* Rt Rev and Rt Hon Gerald Ellison, KCVO; Billeys House, 16 Long St, Cerne Abbas, Dorset (☎ Cerne Abbas (030 03) 247)

ELLISON, Ian Keith Casey; CBE (1985); s of Alan Olaf Ellison, of Rugeley, and Joan (d 1965) *née* Heasman; *b* 12 May 1942; *Educ* Hurstpierpoint Coll, Keele Univ (BA), Reed Coll Portland Oregon USA; *m* 21 March 1970, Mary Joy, da of John East (d 1964); *Career* HM Dip Serv 1965-73 (asst to Dep Govr Gibraltar 1969-71), DTI 1973-75, OFT 1975-78, DOI 1978-79, Cabinet Off 1979, princ private sec to Sec of State (Sir K Joseph and Mr P Jenkin) 1979-82, asst sec Telecommunications Div 1982-85; dir Robert Fleming & Co 1985-; *Recreations* gardening, music, birds, cats; *Style—* Ian Ellison, Esq, CBE; Beedon Hill House, Beedon, Newbury; Robert Fleming & Co Ltd, 25 Copthall Avenue, London EC2 (☎ 01 638 5858)

ELLISON, Cncllr His Hon Judge John Harold; VRD (and clasp); s of Harold Thomas Ellison, MIMechE (d 1940), of Woodspeen Grange nr Newbury, and Frances Amy (who m 2ndly 1947, Crossley Swithinbank, and d 1972), da of Robert John Read of Norwich; *b* 20 Mar 1916; *Educ* Forres Sch Swanage, Uppingham, Kings Coll Cambridge (MA); *m* 1952, Margaret Dorothy Maud, da of Maynard Deedes McFarlane, of Sun City, Arizona, USA (d 1984); 3 s (John, Crispin, Francis), 1 da (Jane); *Career* Lt RE (49 W Riding Div TA) 1938-39, Offr RNVR 1939-51: 1940 HMS Lorna and HMS St Day, Gunnery Specialist HMS Excellent 1940, HMS Despatch 1940-42, Sqdn Gunnery Offr 8 Cruiser Sqdn 1942-44 Naval Staff, Trade Div, 1944-45 Staff Offr, Ops to Flag Offr Western Med, ret Lt-Cdr; barr Lincoln's Inn 1947, practised common law and criminal work Oxford Circuit 1947-71, circuit judge 1972-87, chllr dioceses of Salisbury and Norwich 1955-, pres SW London Branch of Magistrates Assoc 1974-87, govr Forres Sch Tst Swanage; FRAS; *Books* Halsbury's Law of England (3 Edn on Courts, 3 and 4 Edns on Allotments and Small Holdings); *Recreations* organs & music, sailing, shooting, skiing, fishing; *Clubs* Bar YC, Ski of GB, Kandahar Ski; *Style—* Chancellor His Honour John Ellison, VRD; Goose Green House, Egham, Surrey TW20 8PE

ELLISON, Mark Christopher; s of Anthony Ellison (d 1959), and Arlette Maguire, *née* Blundell; *b* 8 Oct 1957; *Educ* Pocklington Sch, Skinners Sch, Univ of Wales (LLB), Inns of Ct Sch of Law; *m* 21 Nov 1981, Kate Augusta, da of Michael Humphrey Middleton, CBE; 1 s, 2 da; *Career* called to Grays Inn 1979, SE Circuit, specialising in criminal law; *Style*— Mark Ellison, Esq; Queen Elizabeth Building, Temple, London EC4Y 9BS (☎ 01 583 5766)

ELLISON, William Eric; s of Albert Eric Ellison (d 1965), and Alice May, *née* Ineson; *b* 12 Oct 1929; *Educ* Ackworth and Leighton Park Sch, Univ of Leeds (BCom); *m* 1, 29 Aug 1953, Belinda, da of Robert William Theakston (d 1968); 1 s (David W b 1956), 1 da (M J Polly b 1958); m 2, 5 March 1982, Winifred Mary, da of John William Heaps (d 1965); *Career* sec Leeds, Bradford and District soc of CA (Ernst and Whinney) 1961-65, tres Yorkshire Assoc for Disabled 1982-(tres 1968-82); ptnr Ernst and Whinney (ret Dec 1987); govr Harrogate Int Festival 1975- (tres 1975-80); fin dir Northern Horticultural Soc 1988-; FICA; *Recreations* art, music, travel, computers, golf; *Clubs* The Leeds; *Style*— William E Ellison, Esq; Westfield, Pye Lane, Burnt Yates, Harrogate HG3 3EH (☎ 0423 770 029)

ELLS, Eric John; s of Eric Edwin Ells (d 1975); *b* 6 April 1929; *Educ* Blackfen Central; *m* 1952, Amelia Florence, *née* Baulch; 1 s, 2 da; *Career* dir: Beradin Hldgs plc, Beradin (UK) Ltd, Sungkas Hldgs (Australia) Ltd, DIMID Agencies Ltd, MP Evans & Co Ltd, MP Evans Secretarial Serv Ltd (chm), Jitra Rubber Plantations plc, Lloyds Ave Registrars Ltd (chm), Lloyds Ave Trading Co Ltd, The London Rubber Exchange Co Ltd, Padang Senang Hldgs plc, Padang Senang (UK) Ltd, Ragalla Tea Hldgs Ltd, Rowe Evans (Indonesia) Ltd, Rowe Evans Investments plc, RW Securities Ltd, The Singapore Para Rubber Estates plc, Sungkai Estates Ltd, Sungkai Hldgs Ltd; alternate: Bertam Hldgs plc, Dimbula Valley (Ceylon) Tea Co Ltd, General Ceylon Rubber & Tea Estates Ltd, Lendu Hldgs plc, Lendu (UK) Ltd, Rembia Rubber plc, Rowe White & Co Ltd, Supara Investments Ltd; *Recreations* travel; *Style*— Eric Ells, Esq; 10 Hurstwood Drive, Bickley, Bromley, Kent (☎ 01 467 6456)

ELLSWORTH, Robert Fred; s of Willoughby Fred Ellsworth (d 1964), and Lucile Rarig (d 1978); Moses Ellsworth (d 1802), was a major supplier to American Army during the American War of Independence; *b* 11 June 1926; *Educ* Univ of Kansas (BSME), Univ of Michigan (JD); *m* 1956, Vivian Esther, da of William A Sies (d 1985); 1 s (Robert), 1 da (Ann); *Career* WWII US Navy 1944-46 served Pacific, Lt Cdr US Navy 1950-53 served Atlantic and Med; venture capitalist; memb of Congress 1961-67, asst to Pres of US 1969, US ambass to NATO 1969-71, asst sec US Dept of Def 1974-75 (dep sec 1975-77), chm Howmet Corpn 1983-; dir: Andal Corpn 1978-, Price Communications Corpn 1982-, Corporate Property Investors 1985-; pres Robert Ellsworth & Co Inc 1977-; vice-chm of cncl Int Inst for Strategic Studies London, dir Atlantic Cncl of the US Washington DC, vice-chm American Cncl on Germany NYC; landowner; Nat Security Medal 1977, Medal for Distinghished Public Serv 1975; *Recreations* hiking, reading, writing, music; *Clubs* Brook (NYC), Army & Navy (Washington DC); *Style*— Robert F Ellsworth, Esq; 2001 L Street, NW, Washington DC 20006 (☎ 202 628 1144, fax 202 331 8735, telex 710 822 0020 RECO)

ELLWOOD, Air Marshal Sir Aubrey Beauclerk; KCB (1949, CB 1944), DSC (1918), DL (Somerset 1960); s of Rev Charles Edward Ellwood, of Cottesmore, Rutland; *b* 3 July 1897; *Educ* Cheam Sch, Marlborough; *m* 1920, Lesley Mary Joan (d 1982), da of late William Peter Matthews, of Walmer, Kent; 1 s, 1 da (and 1 s decd); *Career* with RN Air Service 1916, cmmnd RAF 1919, served India 1919-23 and 1931-36, with RAF Staff Coll, Air Miny and Army Co-operation Cmd during WW II, AOC 18 Gp RAF 1943-44, SASO HQ Coastal Cmd RAF 1944-45, dir-gen Personnel Air Miny 1945-47, Bomber Cmd 1947-50, Air Marshal 1949, AOC-in-C Transport Cmd 1950-52; *Style*— Air Marshal Sir Aubrey Ellwood, KCB, DSC, DL; The Old House, North Perrott, Crewkerne, Somerset

ELLWOOD, Peter Brian; s of Isaac Ellwood (d 1986), of Bristol, and Edith Trotter (d 1981); *b* 15 May 1943; *Educ* Kings Sch Macclesfield; *m* 14 Sept 1968, Judy Ann, da of Leonard George Windsor, of Bristol; 1 s (Richard b 23 Sept 1975), 2 da (Elizabeth b 21 April 1970, Rachel b 11 Jan 1973); *Career* Barclay's 1961-: Bristol, corporate banker and gen mangr's asst to sr gen mangr hd off London, controller Barclaycards ops 1983-, chief exec Barclaycard 1985- (previously dep chief exec); tstee Royal Theatre Northampton, govr Nene Coll Northampton; ACIB; *Recreations* theatre, music; *Style*— Peter Ellwood, Esq; Sunderland House, Great Brington, Northants; Barclaycard, Northampton NN1 1SG (☎ 0604 252 716, fax 060 4254 848, car tel 0860 520 187, telex 31210100)

ELLY, (Richard) Charles; s of Harold Elly, of Sherborne, Dorset, Dora Ellen, *née* Luing (d 1988); *b* 20 Mar 1942; *Educ* Sir William Borlase's Sch Marlow, Hertford Coll Oxford (MA); *m* 7 Oct 1967, Marion Rose, da of Bernard Walter Blackwell (d 1987); 1 s (Mark b 1972), 1 da (Frances b 1975); *Career* slr 1966, ptnr Reynolds Parry-Jones & Crawford 1968, sec Southern Area Assoc of Law Socs 1975-82, pres Berks Bucks & Oxon Law Soc 1988-89 (sec 1975-82); Law Soc: memb 1961- cncl memb 1981-, chm legal aid ctee 1984-87, chm standards and guidance ctee 1987-; chm Maidenhead Deanery Synod 1972-79, pres Cookham Soc 1987-, memb Berks CC 1980-82; *Recreations* ornithology, theatre, walking, gardening; *Clubs* Oxford & Cambridge, Sloane; *Style*— Charles Elly, Esq; Court Cottage, Dean Lane, Cookham Dean, Maidenhead, Berkshire SL6 9AF (☎ 06284 2637); 10 Easton Street, High Wycombe, Bucks HP11 1NP (☎ 0494 25941, fax 0494 30701)

ELMES, Dr Peter Cardwell; s of Capt Florence Romaine Elmes (d 1965), of Culmdavy House, Hemyock, Nr Cullompton, Devon, and Lilian Bryham (d 1950); *b* 12 Oct 1921; *Educ* Rugby, Christchurch Coll Oxford (MA, BSc, BM, BCh), Western Reserve Univ Cleveland USA (MD); *m* 19 Jan 1957, Dr Margaret Elizabeth Cardwell, da of Henry Sambell Staley (d 1960), of Jabalpur, India; 2 s (John Peter Henry b 1960, David Antony b 1964), 1 da (Ann Elizabeth b 1957); *Career* Capt RAMC 1946-49; registrar, sr registrar and tutor in medicine Hammersmith Hosp 1950-57; lectr, sr lectr, reader, prof Dept of Therapeutics Queens Univ Belfast 1958-76; dir MRC Pneumoconiosis Unit 1976-82, conslt in occupational pulmonary disease 1982-; memb Poisons Bd NI, former chm citizens advice bureaux NI, former memb Medicines Cmmn; chm Dinas Powys Civic Trust and Mabon Club; FRCP 1967, FFOM 1982; *Recreations* DIY, gardening; *Style*— Dr Peter Elmes; Dawros House, St Andrews Rd, Dinas Powys, S Glamorgan CF6 4HB (☎ 0222 512102, fax 0222 515975)

ELMHIRST, Lady; Marian Louisa; er da of Lt-Col Lord Herbert Andrew Montagu-Douglas-Scott, CMG, DSO, DL (d 1947; 5 s of 6 Duke of Buccleuch and (8 of) Queensberry) by his w Marie Josephine Agnes (d 1965), yr da of James Andrew Edwards; *b* 16 June 1908; *m* 1, 1 Nov 1927, Col Andrew Henry Ferguson, The Life Guards (d 4 Aug 1966; his mother was Hon Margaret Brand, eldest da of 2 Viscount Hampden and 24 Baron Dacre), of Polebrook Hall, Oundle; 2 s (John b 1929, d 1939; Ronald b 1931, father of HRH the Duchess of York, *see* Royal Family); m 2, 30 Oct 1968, Air Marshal Sir Thomas Walter Elmhirst, KBE, CB, AFC, DL (d 6 Nov 1982), 4 s of Rev William Elmhirst; *Style*— Lady Elmhirst; The Cottage, Dummer, Basingstoke, Hants

ELMHIRST, Roger Thomas; s of Air Marshal Sir Thomas Walter Elmhirst, KBE, CB, AFC (d 1982), and his 1 wife, Katharine Gordon, *née* Black (d 1965); *b* 3 Sept 1935; *Educ* Eton, Trinity Hall Cambridge (MA); *m* 1966, Celia Rozanne, da of Dr H M Jaques (d 1963); 4 children; *Career* Lt Nat Service; pres dir-gen: Charterhouse SA (France) 1978-84, Ermeto SA (France) 1986-; chm: Coloroll Ltd 1982-84, Bradley & Lomas (Electrical) Ltd 1987-; dep md Charterhouse Corporate Investments 1982-84; exec dir Paragon Gp Ltd 1984; *Clubs* Cavalry & Guards, Eton Ramblers, Fife Hunt, New Zealand GC; *Style*— Roger Elmhirst, Esq; c/o Paragon Group Ltd, 25 Gilbert Street, London W1Y 2EJ (☎ 01 493 6661,) 15 Ladbroke Grove, London W11 3BD (☎ 01 727 0336); Knowle Cottage, Beaminster, Dorset DT8 3BD (☎ (0308) 863038)

ELMSLIE, Kenward Gordon; s of Gordon Forbes Elmslie (d 1955), and Doris Julia, *née* Woollatt (d 1983); *b* 8 April 1927; *Educ* Cheltenham, Jesus Coll Cambridge (MA, LLM); *m* 6 Sept 1958, Jean Elsa, da of Arthur Pearson (d 1960); 2 s (Andrew Gordon b 15 Feb 1960, Ian Forbes b 15 July 1962); *Career* Lt RM 1945-48; barr Inner Temple 1951-55; Colonial Serv Nigeria 1953-55; slr 1956-; sr ptnr Richards Butler 1985-88 (ptnr 1960-85); memb cncl Cheltenham Coll 1983-85 and 1987-; *Recreations* opera, swimming; *Clubs* Royal Overseas League, Baltic Exchange; *Style*— Kenward Elmslie, Esq; Cedar Lodge, Lilley Drive, Kingswood, Surrey KT20 6JA (☎ 0737 832847); 61 St Mary Axe, London EC3A 8AA (☎ 01 621 1144, fax 01 929 1132, telex 949494 RBLAW G)

ELPHINSTON, Alexander; s and h of Sir John Elphinston of Glack, 11 Bt; *b* 6 June 1955; *Educ* Repton, St John's Coll Durham; *m* 1986, Ruth Mary Dunnett; *Career* slr; *Style*— Alexander Elphinston, Esq; Maybelle Cottage, Sandford, Crediton, Devon

ELPHINSTON OF GLACK, Sir John; 11 Bt (NS 1701), of Logie, Co Aberdeen; s of Thomas George Elphinston (d 1967; s of de jure 9 Bt), and Gladys Mary, *née Congdon (d 1973); suc unc, Sir Alexander Logie Elphinstone of Glack, 10 Bt (d 1970)*; *b* 12 August 1924; *Educ* Repton, Emmanuel Coll Cambridge (BA); *m* 29 May 1953, Margaret Doreen, da of Edric Tasker (d 1968), of Cheltenham; 4 s (Alexander b 1955, Charles b 1958, Andrew James b 1961, William Robert b 1963); *Heir* s, Alexander Elphinston, *qv*; *Career* Lt RM 1942-47; chm Lancs, Cheshire, IOM branch of Royal Inst of Chartered Surveyors, Agric Div 1975; pres Cheshire Agric Valuers' Assoc 1967; memb Lancashire River Authority 1969-74; school govr; estates mangr ICI, Mond Div; conslt land agent with Gandy & Son, Northwich, Cheshire 1983-88; FRICS, FAAV; *Recreations* church, shooting, ornithology, cricket; *Style*— Sir John Elphinston of Glack, Bt; Pilgrims, Churchfields, Northwich, Cheshire CW8 2JS (☎ 0606 883327)

ELPHINSTONE, Master of; Hon Alexander Mountstuart Elphinstone; s and h of 18 Lord Elphinstone; *b* 15 April 1980; *Style*— The Master of Elphinstone

ELPHINSTONE, Sir (Maurice) Douglas Warburton; 5 Bt (UK 1816) of Sowerby, Cumberland, TD; s of Rev Canon Maurice Curteis Elphinstone (d 1969), 4 s of 3 Bt; suc cous, Sir Howard Graham Elphinstone, 4 Bt, 1975; *b* 13 April 1909; *Educ* Loretto, Jesus Coll Cambridge (BA 1931, MA 1949); *m* 30 June 1943, Helen Barbara, da of late George Ramsay Main, of Houghton, Kilmacolm; 1 s, 1 da; *Heir* s, John Howard Main Elphinstone; *Career* served 1939-45 War as Maj London Scottish; FFA, FRSE; *Style*— Sir Douglas Elphinstone, Bt, TD; West Dene, 10 The Green, Houghton, Carlisle, Cumbria CA3 0LW (☎ 0228 23297)

ELPHINSTONE, 18 Lord (S 1509); James Alexander Elphinstone; also Baron Elphinstone (UK 1885); s of Rev Hon Andrew Charles Victor Elphinstone (d 1975; 2 s of 16 Lord and Lady Mary Bowes-Lyon, da of 14 Earl of Strathmore and sis of HM Queen Elizabeth The Queen Mother), and Jean Frances, CVO (who m 3, 1980, Lt-Col John Wilson Richard Woodroffe), da of late Capt Angus Valdimar Hambro, MP, and widow of Capt of Hon Vicary Paul Gibbs, Gren Gds; *b* 22 April 1953; *Educ* Eton, RAC Cirencester; *m* 1978, Willa Mary Gabriel, yr da of Maj (George) David Chetwode, MBE, Coldstream Gds; 3 s (Master of Elphinstone, Hon Angus John b 1982, Hon Fergus David b 1985); *Heir* s, Hon Alexander Mountstuart, Master of Elphinstone; *Career* ARICS; *Clubs* Turf; *Style*— The Rt Hon Lord Elphinstone; Drumkilbo, Meigle, Blairgowrie, Perths (☎ 082 84 216)

ELPHINSTONE, John Howard Main; s and h of Sir Douglas Elphinstone, 5 Bt, TD; *b* 25 Feb 1949; *Educ* Loretto; *Style*— John Elphinstone, Esq

ELPHINSTONE, Keith; MBE (1945); s of late Sydney Henry Elphinstone; *b* 6 April 1919; *Educ* Surbiton Co Sch, London Poly (City and Guilds London Nat Cert); *m* 1949, Frances Naomi, da of Frank William Mills (d 1940); 3 da; *Career* Maj REME, served France, N Africa, Italy 1943-46 (despatches 1944); Euro export mangr Marconi 1956-58, export mangr EMI Electronics 1958-62, md and dep chm Sale Tilney & Co (joined 1962); chm: Sale Tilney Technol plc, Badalex Ltd, Sale Tilney Int Ltd, Peabody Industrial Ltd (ret 1984); *Recreations* gardening; *Clubs* IOD; *Style*— Keith Elphinstone, Esq; Killaspy, North Rd, Chesham Bois, Amersham, Bucks HP6 5NA (☎ 0494 433780); Sale Tilney plc, 28 Queen Anne's Gate, London SW1H 9AB (☎ 01 222 1771)

ELRICK, Lady Patricia Ruth; *née* Fiennes-Clinton; o da of 18 Earl of Lincoln, *qv*; *b* 1 Feb 1941; *m* 27 Jan 1959 (m dis 1970), Alexander George Stuart Elrick, s of Francis Elrick; 3 s (Nicholas James b 24 Aug 1959, David Wayne b 29 June 1961, Warren Stuart b 4 Dec 1962); 73 Picton Road, Bunbury, W Australia 6230

ELRINGTON, Christopher Robin; s of Brig Maxwell Elrington, DSO, OBE (ka 1945), and Beryl Joan, *née* Ommanney; *b* 20 Jan 1930; *Educ* Wellington, Univ Coll Oxford (MA), Bedford Coll London (MA); *m* 1951, Jean Margaret, da of Col Robert Vernon Maynard Buchanan (d 1969), of Ferndown; 1 s (Giles), 1 da (Judy); *Career* ed Victoria History of the Counties of England 1977-; FSA, FRHistS; *Style*— Christopher Elrington, Esq; 34 Lloyd Baker St, London, WC1X 9AB (☎ 01 837 4971); Inst of Historical Res, Univ of London WC1E 7HU (☎ 01 636 0272)

ELSDON, Gp Capt Thomas Arthur Francis; OBE (1945), DFC (1940); s of Sqdn Ldr Thomas Wilfred Elsdon (d 1959), of Norfolk, and Winifred Beatrice, *née* Butler (d 1978); *b* 22 Jan 1917; *Educ* Forest Sch Essex; *m* 13 May 1950, Iris Jean, da of Lt-Col H Reginald W Dawson (d 1937); 1 s (Thomas Nigel Charles b 1951), 1 da (Rosemary Margaret b 1953); *Career* RAF 1938-59 Battle of Britain, Burma Campaign (wounded 1940 and 1941, despatches twice), OC 136 (F) Sqdn 1941-42, OC No 169 Wing 1942-

43, OC No 165 Wing 1943-44, ret RAF 1959; bursar: King's Sch Worcester 1960-71, St Anne's Sch Windermere 1972-74, ret 1975; *Recreations* RAF; *Clubs* RAF; *Style*— Gp Capt Thomas A F Elsdon, OBE, DFC

ELSON, Edward Elliott; s of Harry Elson (d 1979), and Esther, *née* Cohn; *b* 8 Mar 1934; *Educ* Phillips Acad Andover Massachusetts, Univ of Virginia (BA), Emory Univ Lamar School of Law (JD); *m* 24 Aug 1957, Suzanne, da of Charles Francis Goodman, of Memphis, Tennessee, USA; 3 s (Charles b 1959, Louis b 1962, Harry b 1965); *Career* chm: Atlanta News Agency Inc 1959-85, Elson's 1973-88, Bank of Gordon Co 1979-83, WH Smith & Sons Hldgs (USA) 1985, Majestic Wine Corpn 1988; dir: Citizens & Southern Georgia Corpn 1976-, WH SMith Gp plc 1985-, Atlantic American Corpn 1985-, Citizens & Southern Tst Co Inc 1986-, Genesco Inc 1987-; tstee (non profit orgns): Talledaga Coll 1973-, Univ of Mid-America 1979-81, Univ of Virginia 1984-, Brenau Coll 1985-, Hampton Inst 1985-, Univ of Virginia Med Soc 1986-, Brown Univ 1988-, Emory Univ Bd of Visitors 1986-; American Jewish Ctee (non-profit orgn): memb be govrs 1966-, tres and vice-pres 1984-85, chm bd tstees 1986-89; Jewish Historical Soc (non-profit orgn): tstee 1979-, memb exec ctee 1979-, vice-pres 1980-84; memb pres cncl Brandeis Univ 1967-, memb alumni cncl Phillips Acad 1975-, co-chm parents cncl Brown Univ 1986-88, memb bd mangrs alumni assoc Univ of Virginia 1982-, pres Jewish Pubn Soc 1987-, memb exec ctee Univ of Virgina Med Soc 1987-, vice-pres Muscular Dystrophy Assoc America; pres Lyndon B Johnson's Cmmn Obscenity and Pornography 1967-71, vice chm Atlanta-Fulton Co Recreation Authy 1972-80, 1 chm Nat Pub Radio 1976-79, chm Georgia Advsy Ctee to US Civil Rights Cmmn 1976-84; chm advsy bd Southeastern Centre Contemporary Art Winston-Salem North Caroline 1976-; chm bd visitors Emory Museum Art and Archeology Atlanta Georgia 1985-, bd Bayley Museum Charlottesville Virgina 1986-; tstee American Fedn Arts 1985-, memb resource planning ctee Nat Gallery Washington DC 1986-; Robert B Downs Award Univ of Illinois Graduate Sch Library Sci 1971, American Jewish Ctee's Distinguished Serv Award 1975, Nat Radio's Distinguished Serv Award 1979, Inst Human Relations Award 1982; *Clubs* University NY, Farmington Country Virginia, Buckhead Georgia; *Style*— Edward Elson, Esq; 65 Valley Road, NW, Atlanta, Georgia 30305 (☎ 404 261 4492); 475 Park Ave, New York NY 10022 (☎ 212 593 3963); 69 Eaton Place, London SW1 (☎ 01 235 8270)

ELSTEIN, David Keith; s of Albert Elstein (d 1983), and Millie Cohen (d 1985); *b* 14 Nov 1944; *Educ* Haberdasher's Aske's, Gonville and Caius Coll Cambridge (BA, MA); *m* 16 Jul 1978, Jenny, da of Alfred Conway; 1 s (Daniel b 1981) ; *Career* BBC: The Money Programme, Panorama, Cause for Concern, People in Conflict 1964-68; Thames TV: This Week, The Day Before Yesterday, The World at War 1968-72; London Weekend TV, Weekend World 1972-73; ed This Week, exec producer documentaries Thames TV 1973-82; md and exec producer: Brook Productions 1982-86 (Almonds and Raisins, Low), Primetime TV 1983-86 (Seal Morning, Return to Treasure Island, Deliberate Death of a Polish Priest, Double Image), exec producer Goldcrest TV 1982-83 (Concealed Enemies); dir of programmes Thames TV 1986-; *Recreations* cinema, theatre, bridge, reading; *Style*— D K Elstein, Esq; Thames Television, 306 Euston Rd, London NW1 (☎ 01 387 9494)

ELSTOB, Eric Carl; s of Capt Eric Bramley Elstob, OBE, RN, (d 1949), and Signe Mathilda, *née* Ohlsson (d 1968); *b* 5 April 1943; *Educ* Marlborough, Queen's Coll Oxford (MA); *Career* dir The Foreign and Colonial Investmt Tst plc (joint mangr 1973-); dir: F and C Pacific Investmt Tst plc 1984, dep chm F and C Eurotrust plc 1972, T R Tstees Corpn plc 1973, G T Japan Investmt Tst plc 1972; Child Health Res Investmt Tst plc 1980, chm Foreign and Colonial Reserve Fund; dir Foreign and Colonial Mgmnt Ltd 1969, chm Foreign and Colonial Portfolios Fund SIC AV, chm Foreign and Colonial Reserve Fund, Child Health Res Investmt Tst plc 1980, Bangkok Fnd Ltd 1986; tres Friends of Christ Church Spitalfields; *Books* Sweden, A Traveller's History (1978); *Recreations* fell walking, canoeing, architecture; *Clubs* Cercle Interalliée, Paris; *Style*— Eric Elstob, Esq; 14 Fournier Street, Spitalfields, London EC16QE (☎ 01 247 5942); Foreign and Colonial Management, 1 Laurence Poutney Hill, London EC4ROBA (☎ 01 623 4680, fax 626 4947)

ELSTOB, Peter Frederick Egerton; s of Frederick Charles Elstob (d 1974), and Lillian, *née* Page; *b* 22 Dec 1915; *Educ* Michigan Univ; *m* 1, 1937 (m dis 1953), Medora, da of Lionel Leigh-Smith (d 1942); 3 s (Blair b 1940, Michael b 1942; Harry b 1950), 2 da (Ann b 1937, Penelope b 1938, d 1982); m 2, 1953, Barbara, da of Chester Zacheisz (d 1936); 1 s (Mayo b 1951), 1 da (Sukey b 1957); *Career* served WW II RTR Troop Sergeant 1940-46 (despatches); author, novelist, military historian; sec-gen Int PEN 1974-82, vice-pres 1982-; md of cosmetic manufacturing business, Archive Press Ltd and other companies; Bulgarian Commemorative Medal 1982; *Books* Spanish Prisoner 1938 (based on his experiences when imprisoned as a suspected spy by the Communists, having volunteered to fly for Spanish Govt during Civil War), military histories and novels; *Recreations* travel, playing the stock exchange; *Clubs* Garrick, Savage; *Style*— Peter Elstob, Esq; Burley Lawn House, Burley Lawn, Hants BH24 4AR (☎ 04253 3406)

ELSTON, Christopher David; s of Herbert Cecil Elston (d 1962), and Ada Louva Elston, *née* Paige (d 1978); *b* 1 August 1938; *Educ* Univ Col Sch Hampstead, King's Coll Cambridge (BA), Yale Univ USA (MA); *m* 17 Oct 1964, Jennifer Isabel, da of Dr A E Rampling (d 1983); 1 s (Peter b 1966), 2 da (Lucinda b 1968, Elizabeth b 1975); *Career* with Bank of England 1960-, seconded to Bank for int settlements, Basle Switzerland 1969-71, private sec to govr Bank of England 1976-77, asst to chief cashier 1977-79, seconded HM Diplomatic Service as fin attaché Br Embassy, Tokyo 1973-83, advsr (Asia and Australia) Bank of England 1983-; *Recreations* music, photography, gardening, walking; *Style*— Christopher D Elston, Esq; Bank of England, Threadneedle Street, London EC2R 8AH (☎ 01 601 4265)

ELSTON, John David; s of Lt-Col John William Elston, and Alwyn, *née* Fawbert; *b* 2 August 1946; *Educ* Norwich Sch, Richmond Sch Yorks, Univ of Newcastle upon Tyne (BA); *m* 27 Sept 1980, Victoria Ann Harding (Vicky), da of Victor William Brown, of 41 Cherry Post Crescent, Etobicoke, Toronto, Canada; 2 s (James b 1982, Henry b 1988), 1 da (Georgina b 1986); *Career* James Capel & Co 1973- (sr exec 1985-); FCA 1979; *Recreations* squash, tennis, bridge; *Style*— John Elston, Esq; The Dene, 9 Kippington Road, Sevenoaks, Kent TN13 2LH (☎ 0732 457087); James Capel & Co, James Capel House, PO Box 551, 6 Bevis Marks, London EC3A 7TQ (☎ 01 621 0011, fax 01 621 0496, telex 888866 JC LDN G)

ELTIS, Walter Alfred; s of Rev Dr Martin Eltis (d 1968), and Mary, *née* Schnitzer (d 1977); *b* 23 May 1933; *Educ* Wycliffe Coll, Emmanuel Coll Cambridge (BA), Nuffield Coll Oxford (MA); *m* 5 Sept 1959, Shelagh Mary, da of Prebendary Douglas Aubrey Owen (d 1964); 1 s (David b 1963), 2 da (Sarah b 1966, Clare b 1968); *Career* PO navigator RAF 1951-53; fell and tutor in econs Exeter Coll Oxford 1963-88, visiting reader in econs Univ of W Aust 1970-71; visiting prof: Univ of Toronto 1976-77, Euro Univ Florence 1979; econ dir Nat Econ Devpt Off 1986-88 (dir gen 1988-), gen ed Oxford Econ Papers 1975-81, memb CNAA 1987- (chm social science ctee 1987-88); memb cncl of govrs Wycliffe Coll 1974-88; *Books* Economic Growth: Analysis and Policy (1965), Growth and Distribution (1973), Britain's Economic Problem: Too Few Producers (with Robert Bacon 1976), The Classical Theory of Economic Growth (1984); *Recreations* chess, music; *Clubs* Reform; *Style*— Walter Eltis, Esq; Danesway, Jarn Way, Boars Hill, Oxford, OX1 5JF (☎ 0865 735 440) National Economic Development Office, Millbank Tower, London SW1P 4QX (☎ 01 211 5386)

ELTON, Anne, Lady; Anne Frances; eldest da of late Brig Robert Adolphus George Tilney, DSO, TD, DL, and Frances Moore, *née* Barclay; *b* 18 Oct 1933; *m* 18 Sept 1958 (m dis 1979), as his 1 wife, 2 Baron Elton; 1 s, 3 da; *Style*— Anne, Lady Elton; The Hall, Sutton Bonington, Loughborough, Leics (☎ 050 97 2355); 70B Pavilion Rd, London SW1 (☎ 01 581 5967)

ELTON, Sir Arnold; CBE (1982); s of Max Elton (d 1953), and Ada, *née* Levy; *b* 14 Feb 1920; *Educ* UCL (MS); *m* 9 Nov 1952, Billie Pamela, da of John Nathan Briggs; 1 s (Michael Jonathan b 1953); *Career* formerly sr surgical registrar Charing Cross Hosp; house surgn, house physician and casualty offs UCH; conslt surg: Mt Vernon Hosp 1960-70, Harrow Hospital 1951-70; memb: ct of patrons RCS, Cons Cncl and Nat Exec Ctee, Br Assoc Surgical Oncology (fndr memb), govt ctee on screening for breast cancer, Hunterian Soc Assoc of Surgns; assoc fell Br Assoc of Urological Surgns, memb and chm Court of Examiners to RCS; previously examiner to Gen Nursing Cncl, surgical tutor RCS 1970-82, chm Cons Med Soc 1975-; Liveryman of the Apothecaries Co and Carmen Co; Jubilee Medal for Community Servs 1977; FRCS; kt 1987; *Books* various contributions to Medical Journals; *Recreations* tennis; *Clubs* Carlton, RAC, MCC; *Style*— Sir Arnold Elton, CBE; Carlton Club, 69 St James's Street, London W1; The Consulting Rooms, Wellington Hospital, Wellington Place, London NW8

ELTON, Sir Charles Abraham Grierson; 11 Bt (GB 1717), of Bristol; s of Sir Arthur Hallam Rice Elton, 10 Bt (d 1973), and Lady (Margaret) Elton, *qv*; *b* 23 May 1953; *Educ* Eton, Reading Univ; *Heir* kinsman, Charles Tierney Hallam Elton; *Career* with BBC Publications; *Style*— Sir Charles Elton, Bt; Clevedon Court, Clevedon, Somerset; 34 Pembridge Villas, London NW11

ELTON, Charles Tierney Hallam; s of late Charles Henry Elton (gs of 6 Bt), by 1 w, Edith, da of J F Ward; hp of kinsman, Sir Charles Elton, 11 Bt; *b* 1898; *m* 1924, Helen (d 1963), da of late Capt Frederick Waud; 1 da; *Style*— Charles Elton, Esq

ELTON, Prof Sir Geoffrey Rudolph; er s of late Prof Victor Leopold Ehrenberg, PhD, and Eva Dorothea, *née* Sommer; changed name 1944; *b* 1921; *Educ* Prague, Rydal Schs London (external BA), UCL; *m* 1952, Sheila Lambert; *Career* formerly history lectr Glasgow, then Cambridge Univ, fell Clare Coll Cambridge 1954-, prof of english constitutional history Cambridge 1967-83, regius prof of Modern History Cambridge 1983-88; author of books on Tudor England, the Reformation, the Renaissance; FBA; kt 1986; *Style*— Prof Sir Geoffrey Elton; Clare College, Cambridge (☎ 0223 333200); 30 Millington Rd, Cambridge (☎ 0223 352109)

ELTON, Prof George Alfred Hugh; CB (1983); s of Horace William Elton (d 1980), and Violet Elton; *b* 27 Feb 1925; *Educ* Sutton County Sch, London Univ; *m* 1951, Theodora Rose Edith, da of George Henry Theodore Kingham (d 1965); 2 da; *Career* chief scientist (Miny of Fisheries and Food) 1981-85 (dep chief scientist 1972, under-sec 1974); Hon DSc Reading 1984; vice chm EEC Scientific Ctee for Food 1985-; *Recreations* golf; *Clubs* Savage, MCC; *Style*— Prof George Elton, CB; Green Nook, Bridle Lane, Loudwater, Rickmansworth, Herts WD3 4JH

ELTON, Hon Jane; 2 da of 2 Baron Elton; *b* 15 Jan 1962; *Style*— Hon Jane Elton

ELTON, Hon Lucy; yr da of 2 Baron Elton; *b* 19 Dec 1963; *Educ* Central Sch of Art & Design; *Career* sculptress; *Style*— Hon Lucy Elton

ELTON, Michael Anthony; s of Francis Herbert Norris Elton (d 1976), and Margaret Helen *née* Gray; *b* 20 May 1932; *Educ* Peter Symonds Sch, Brasenose Coll Oxford (BA, BCL, MA); *m* 16 July 1955, Isabel Clare da of Thomas Gurney Ryott (d 1965); 2 s (Tim b 1965, Mark b 1970), 2 da (Caroline b 1960, Louise b 1969); *Career* articles 1954-57, admitted slr 1957; asst slr Cumberland CC 1958-61, Surrey CC 1961-65; asst clerk Bucks CC 1965-70, dep clerk of the Peace for Bucks 1967-70; chief exec ABTA 1970-86, dir gen Nat Assoc of Pension Funds 1987-, dir gen Euro Fedn for Retirement Provision 1987-; former Hants Co Squash player; memb: Winchester Music Club, Winchester Lawn Tennis Club; *Books* Future Perfect (with Gyles Brandreth 1988); *Recreations* music, tennis, bridge, gardening; *Clubs* Utd Oxford and Cambridge; *Style*— Michael Elton, Esq; 12-18 Grosvenor Gardens, London SW1W 0DH (☎ 01 730 0585, fax 01 730 2595)

ELTON, Michael John; s of John Thomas Humphrey Elton, and Kathleen Margaret, *née* Bird; *b* 20 Dec 1933; *Educ* SW Essex Tech Coll Royal Naval Electrical Sch; *m* 26 March 1965, Carole Elizabeth, da of William Saunby, of Kettering, Northants; 2 s (James Robert b 1967, Charles Lindsey b 1969); *Career* Sub Lt RNVR 1955-57 serv: 108 Minesweeping Sqdn Malta, base electrical offr Cyprus; Lt RNR 1958-; engrg and sales positions STC London 1957-63, staff of mktg dir ITT Europe Paris 1963-64, mktg mangr STC Data Systems London 1964-69; Control Data 1969-81: mangr int data servs Minneapolis 1969-70 and Brussels 1970-71, md Stockholm 1971-74, chm and md Helsinki 1973-74, gen mangr Brussels 1974-79, gen mangr London 1979-81; vice pres and gen mangr Technitron Int Inc 1981-86, md and chief exec Technitron plc 1986-; CEng, FIEE, FBCS, FBIM; *Recreations* swimming; *Clubs* Naval; *Style*— Michael Elton, Esq; Technitron plc, Silwood Park Ascot, Berks SL5 7TQ (☎ 0990 872 821, fax 0990 872 275, telex 848076)

ELTON, Miles Caversham; s of Leo Elton (d 1947), of London, and Minnie, *née* Fleischman (d 1974); *b* 22 Dec 1918; *Educ* St Pauls Sch London, Pembroke Coll Oxford (BA, MA), Poly of Central London (DipLaw), Central Cncl for Legal Educn; *m* 8 May 1947, (Evelyn) Marcia, da of Louis Curwen (d 1952), of Liverpool; 1 s (Lionel b 1949), 2 da (Elizabeth (Mrs Roche) b 1954, Caroline (Mrs Franklin) b 1957); *Career* cmmnd RA 1940, served Indian Artillery 1940-45, on secretariat of War Cabinet sub-ctee 1945-46, released from Military Serv 1946; chm and md Lead and Alloys Ltd 1955-74 (taken over by Chloride Gp plc 1974), chm Chloride Metals Ltd 1974-75; studied Law 1980-82, called to the Bar Gray's Inn 1982; memb Farriers Co; *Style*—

Miles Elton, Esq; 54 Eyre Court, Finchley Rd, London NW8 (☎ 01 586 1877); Rectory Cottage, Noke, Oxfordshire

ELTON, 2 Baron (UK 1934); Rodney; TD (1970); s of 1 Baron Elton (d 1973), and Dedi (d 1977), da of Gustav Hartmann, of Oslo, Norway; *b* 2 Mar 1930; *Educ* Eton, New Coll Oxford; *m* 1, 18 Sept 1958 (m dis 1979), Anne Frances, da of late Brig Robert Adolphus George Tilney, DSO, TD, DL; 1 s, 3 da; m 2, 24 Aug 1979, (Susan) Richenda, yst da of late Sir Hugh Gurney, KCMG, MVO; *Heir* s, Hon Edward Paget Elton b 28 May 1966; *Career* formerly: farmer, teacher and lectr; contested (C) Loughborough Leics 1966 and 1970; oppn spokesman Educn and Welsh Affrs 1974-79, dep sec Int Affrs Ctee of Gen Synod of C of E 1976-78, vice-chm Andry Montgomery Ltd 1977-79, memb Boyd cmmn (South Rhodesia elections 1979); parly under-sec state: NI Off 1979-81, DHSS 1981-82, Home Office 1982-84; min of state Home Off 1984-85, Dept of Environment 1985-86; chm Financial Intermediaries; mangrs & brokers Regulatory Assoc (FIMBRA) 1987-; cncl memb panel on takeovers and mergers, chm: Enquiry into Discipline in Schs 1988; *Clubs* Cavalry and Guards, Beefsteak, Pratts; *Style—* The Rt Hon Lord Elton, TD; House of Lords, London SW1

ELVEDEN, Viscount; Arthur Edward Rory Guinness; s and h of 3 Earl of Iveagh; *b* 10 August 1969; *Style—* Viscount Elveden

ELVIDGE, John Allan; s of Allan Elvidge (d 1970), and Edith, *née* Dallman; *b* 19 Mar 1946; *Educ* Kingston GS, Downing Coll Cambridge (MA, LLB); *Career* barr 1969-; ldr London Borough of Merton; fell Downing Coll Cambridge 1969-75; *Recreations* golf, tennis; *Style—* John Elvidge, Esq; 5 Kings's Bench Walk, Temple, London, EC4, (☎ 01 353 2882)

ELWES, Edward Hervey; s of Capt John Elwes, MC (ka 1942), of Farnborough, Hants, and Isabel Pamela Ivy Talbot, *née* Beckwith; *b* 21 Mar 1941; *Educ* Beaudesert Park, Eton ; *m* 18 June 1977, Margaret Frances, da of Dr Robert Joseph House, of Tewkesbury; 2 s (Nicholas b 1979, Toby b 1982); *Career* engr; cncllr Tewksbury Borough Cncl 1975-81, chm Bushley Parish Cncl 1983- (cncllr 1981-); md Lawrence Elwes Ltd 1974-; page to Duke of Northumberland at coronation of Queen Elizabeth II; AMBIM, memb Inst Agric Engrs, TEng; *Recreations* shooting, gardening, motor racing; *Clubs* Naval, Country Gentlemans Assoc; *Style—* Edward H Elwes, Esq; Yew Tree Cottage, Bushley Green, Tewkesbury, Glos GL20 6JB (☎ 0684-294316); Eurocap, High Street, Winchcombe, Cheltenham, Glos GL54 5LJ (☎ 0242-603344, telex 43670, fax 0242-603723)

ELWES, Henry William George; DL (Glos 1982); s of Maj John Hargreaves Elwes, MC, Scots Gds (ka N Africa 1943), and Isabel Pamela Ivy, *née* Beckwith, gda of 7 Duke of Richmond and Gordon; a distant cous of Capt Jeremy Elwes, *qv*; *b* 24 Oct 1935; *Educ* Eton, RAC Cirencester; *m* 8 Sept 1962, Carolyn Dawn, da of Joseph William Wykeham Cripps (d 1958), of Ampney Crucis, Cirencester (3 cous of the post war chllr Sir Stafford Cripps) and 1 cous of 6 Baron Cromwell, also 4 cous of 4 Baron Parmoor; 3 s (John b 1964, Frederick b 1966, George b 1971); *Career* late Lt Scots Gds; farmer and forester; chm Western Woodland Owners Ltd 1971-85, pres 1981-; regnl dir Lloyds Bank plc 1985-, dir Colebourne Estate Co; chm: Glos Heritage Tst, Royal Jubilee and Princes Tst (Glos); tstee dir: Cirencester Benefit Soc, Crickley Hill Tst; tstee: Glos Arthiritis Tst, Barnwood House Tst, Central Telethon Tst; memb: Cirencester Rural Dist Cncl 1959-74, Glos CC 1971- (vice chm 1976-83, chm 1983-85); High Sheriff Glos 1979-80 ; *Clubs* Confrerie des Chevaliers du Tastevin; *Style—* H W G Elwes, Esq, DL; Colesbourne Park, Cheltenham, Glos GL53 9NP (☎ 024287 262)

ELWES, Hugh Damian; s of Sir Richard Elwes (d 1967), and Lady (Freya) Elwes, eld da of Sir Mark Sykes, Bt, of Sledmere; *b* 27 Sept 1943; *Educ* Ampleforth; *m* 18 April 1973, Susan, da of W J Buchanan (d 1971), of Sydney, Australia; 3 da (Chloe b 1978, Flora b 1981, Sophie b 1984); *Career* publisher; chm Roxby & Lindsey Hldgs Ltd and its subsidiary co's; *Style—* Hugh Elwes, Esq; Elm Grove, Henstridge, Somerset BA8 0TQ; 82 Wakehurst Rd, London SW4; Roxby Press Ltd, 126 Victoria Rise, London SW4 0NW (☎ 01 720 8872, fax 01 622 9528)

ELWES, Lady Jean Evelyn; *née* Hope Johnstone; da of Evelyn Wentworth Hope Johnstone (*de jure* 9 Earl of Annandale and Hartfell; d 1964), and Marie (May) Eleanor (d 1969), da of Compton Charles Domvile; *b* 9 July 1917; *m* 4 April 1950, as his 2 wife, Maj Robert Philip Henry Elwes, MBE, MC (d 1976), eldest s of late Robert Hammond Arthur Elwes, JP, of Congham House, Norfolk; 1 da (Mrs Arthur Galbraith, b 1951); *Style—* Lady Jean Elwes; Flat 4, 24 Collingham Gardens, London SW5 0HL

ELWES, Jeremy Gervase Geoffrey Philip; DL (Lincs 1969, Humberside 1974); s of Lt-Col Rudolph Philip Elwes, OBE, MC (d 1962; whose mother was Lady Winefride Feilding, da of 8 Earl of Denbigh, while his f, Gervase Elwes, was Privy Chamberlain to the Pope, and a celebrated tenor), and Helen Hermione, *née* Wright (d 1956); *b* 1 Sept 1921; *Educ* Ampleforth, Sandhurst; *m* 9 July 1955, Clare Mary, er da of Maj Gen Arthur Joseph Beveridge, CB, OBE, MC; 4 s; *Career* served WW II Capt M East (despatches); farms 1000 acres in partnership in Lincs from 1949; pres Cncl Preservation Rural England (Lincs) 1957-; High Sheriff Lincs 1969; fndr Lincs and Humberside Arts Assoc; fndr/chm: Shrievalty Assoc 1971, Elwes Enterprises, Elsham Hall Country Park; vice Lord-Lt for Humberside 1983-; vice-chm Environmental Medicine Fndn 1987, co-fndr Scarbank tst for holidays for handicapped children; *Recreations* natural history, the Arts, handicapped people; *Clubs* Green Jackets, Royal Overseas; *Style—* Capt Jeremy Elwes, DL,; Elsham Hall, near Brigg, S Humberside DN20 0QZ (☎ 0652 688738)

ELWES, Jeremy Vernon; CBE (1984); s of Eric Vincent Elwes (d 1985), of Sevenoaks, Kent, and Dorothea, *née* Bilton; *b* 29 May 1937; *Educ* Wirral GS, Bromley GS, City of London Coll (ACIS); *m* 1963, Phyllis Marion, da of George Herbert Harding Relf, of Halstead, Sevenoaks, Kent; 1 s (Jonathan b 1969); *Career* chartered sec; dir Sevenoaks Constitutional Club Co Ltd 1977-; chm: Sutton Enterprise Agency Ltd 1986- SE Area Provincial Cncl 1986-, Cons Political Centre Nat Advsy Ctee 1981-84, personnel dir Reed Business Publishing Ltd 1982-; govr: Eltham Coll 1977-, Walthamstow Hall 1977- (chm 1984-), Wildernesse Sch for Boys 1977-88 (vice-chm 1982-88); memb: Cons Pty Nat Union Exec Ctee 1974-, Gen Cncl Cons Gp for Europe 1977- (Gp Ctee 1985-); memb and judge Int Wine & Spirit Competition Ltd 1983-; Chevalier Ordre des Chevaliers Bretvins (Baillage de GB, Maitre des Ceremonies 1984-88 (chanceller 1986-); *Recreations* wine, food, reading, golf; *Clubs* Carlton, St Stephen's Constitutional; *Style—* Jeremy Elwes, Esq, CBE; Crispian Cottage, Weald Rd, Sevenoaks, Kent TN13 1QQ (☎ 0732 454208); Reed Business Publishing Ltd, Quadrant Ho, The Quadrant, Sutton, Surrey SM2 5AS (☎ 01 661 3019, telex 892084 REEDBP G, fax 01 661 8948)

ELWES, Nigel Robert; s of late Capt Robert Philip Henry Elwes, of Athry House, Ballinafad, Co Galway, Eire, and his 1 wife, Mrs Vivien Elizabeth Fripp, *née* Martin-Smith; *b* 8 August 1941; *Educ* Eton; *m* 1965, Carolyn Peta, da of Sir Robin McAlpine, CBE of Aylesfield, Alton, Hampshire; 1 s (Andrew b 1969), 2 da (Serena b 1967, Melisa b 1973); *Career* CA, stockbroker, ptnr Rowe & Pitman; Stock Exchange: joined 1970, cncl memb 1983-86, cncl memb Inst Stock Exchange 1988-; fin dir S G Warburg Securities 1986-, chm Domestic Equity Mkt Ctee 1988-; FCA; *Recreations* hunting, racing; *Clubs* White's; *Style—* Nigel Elwes, Esq; 1 Finsbury Ave,. London EC2 (☎ 01 606 1066, telex 8952485)

ELWES, Peter John Gervase; s of Lt-Col Simon Edmund Vincent Paul Elwes, RA (d 1975), of Amberley, Sussex, and Hon Gloria Elinor, *née* Rodd (d 1975); *b* 17 Oct 1929; *Educ* Eton, Miles Aircraft Tech Coll, Kingston and Gateshead Coll of Advanced Technol; *m* 7 May 1960, Hon Rosalie Ann, da of Brig James Brian George Hennessy, 2 Baron Windlesham (d 1962), of Askefield, Bray, Ireland; 3 s (Luke b 26 July 1961, Benedict b 4 May 1963, Marcus b 27 Nov 1964), 1 da (Harriet b 3 Dec 1968); *Career* 2 Lt Royal Scots Greys BAOR Germany 1950-52, Lt Northumberland Hussars 1953-56; Vickers Armstrong Ltd Weybridge and Newcastle 1948-53, Ransomes & Rapier Ltd Ipswich 1953-56, Rio Tinto-Zinc Corpn Ltd 1956-73, md Hamilton Bros Oil and Gas Ltd 1973-77, dir Kleinwort Benson Ltd 1977-, chief exec Enterprise Oil plc 1983-84, md Renown Energy Ltd 1988-; FInstPet; *Recreations* painting, gardening, music; *Clubs* Cavalry and Guards; *Style—* Peter Elwes, Esq; 75 Murray Rd, Wimbledon, London SW19 4PF (☎ 01 946 6623); Renown Petroleum Ltd, 30 St James's St, London SW1A 1HB (☎ 01 925 1266, fax 01 925 0515, telex 918503)

ELWES, Hon Mrs (Rosalie Ann); *née* Hennessy; da of 2 Baron Windlesham; *b* 18 Feb 1934; *m* 7 May 1960, Peter John Gervase Elwes, eldest surv s of Simon Edmund Vincent Paul Elwes, RA, and Hon Gloria Elinor Rodd, yr da of 1 Baron Rennell, PC, GCB, GCVO, CMG; 3 s, 1 da; *Style—* Hon Mrs Elwes; 75 Murray Rd, Wimbledon, London SW19 4PF

ELWORTHY, Hon Anthony Arthur; s of Baron Elworthy, GCB, CBE, DSO, MVO, DFC, AFC (Life Peer); *b* 10 Mar 1940; *m* 1967, Penelope Joy Hendry; 1 s (Alexander b 1973), 1 da (Tracy b 1971); *Style—* Hon Anthony Elworthy; Box 782404, Sandton 2146, South Africa

ELWORTHY, Hon Christopher Ashton; s of Baron Elworthy, GCB, CBE, DSO, MVO, DFC, AFC (Life Peer); *b* 1946; *m* 1968, Anne, da of late Harry Bell Lewis Johnstone; *Style—* Hon Christopher Elworthy; Gordon's Valley Station, RD2, Timaru, NZ

ELWORTHY, John Henry; MBE (1987); s of Henry Elworthy (d 1982), and Hilda Jane, *née* Davey (d 1981); *b* 28 Oct 1923; *Educ* Watford Tech Coll; *m* 5 Jan 1946, Joan Donella Victoria, da of the late George Pierce; 2 s (Graham b 1949, Trevor b 1953), 1 da (Penelope b 1960); *Career* WWII Naval Air Arm (Petty Offr); served: E Africa, India, SEAC 1942-46; chm and md Protocol Ltd 1953-, Protocol Engrg plc 1972-, Protocol Corp (USA) 1984-, Protocol Scientific 1985-; pres IPEX 1984, memb Printing Machinery NEDO Sector working party; FIOP; *Recreations* golf, clay pigeon shooting; *Style—* John Elworthy, Esq, MBE; Old Thatch, The Green, Edlesborough, Nr Dunstable, Beds; Whaddon Hall, Whaddon, Bucks; Protocol Group of Companies, Northbridge Road, Berkhamsted, Herts (☎ 04427-71122, fax: 04427 72251, telex: 826205)

ELWORTHY, Baron (Life Peer UK 1972); Marshal of the RAF Samuel Charles Elworthy; KG (1977), GCB (1962, CBE 1946, DSO, LVO 1953, DFC, AFC); s of late Capt Percy Ashton Elworthy, late 1 Life Gds, and Bertha Victoria, *née* Julius, of Gordons Valley, Timaru, New Zealand; *b* 23 Mar 1911; *Educ* Marlborough, Trinity Coll Cambridge (MA); *m* 1936, Audrey (d 1986), da of late Arthur Joseph Hutchinson, OBE, of Auckland, New Zealand; 3 s (Timothy b 1938, Anthony b 1940, Christopher b 1946), 1 da (Clare b 1950); *Career* RAF 1935; barr 1935; Chief of Air Staff 1963-67, Chief of Defence Staff 1967-71, Marshal of RAF 1967; constable and govr of Windsor Castle 1971-78, lord lt Gtr London 1973-78; KStJ; *Recreations* fishing; *Clubs* RAF, Leander, Christchurch (NZ), South Canterbury (NZ); *Style—* Marshal of the RAF the Rt Hon Lord Elmworthy, KG, GCB, CBE, DSO, LVO, DFC, AFC; Gordon's Valley, RD2, Timaru, New Zealand (☎ Otipua 702)

ELWORTHY, Air Cdre the Hon Timothy Charles; CBE (1986); eldest s of Baron Elworthy, KG, GCB, CBE, DSO, LVO, DFC, AFC (Life Peer); *b* 27 Jan 1938; *Educ* Radley, RAF Coll Cranwell; *m* 1, 1961 (m dis), Victoria Ann, da of Lt-Col H C W Bowring; m 2, 1971, Anabel, da of late Reginald Ernest Harding, OBE; children; *Career* RAF, Air Cdre DOR (Air) 2 MOD; Capt of The Queen's Flight 1989; *Clubs* RAF, Boodle's; *Style—* Air Cdre the Hon Timothy Elworthy, CBE; c/o The Queen's Flight, RAF Benson, Oxon OX9 6AA

ELWYN-JONES, Baron (Life Peer UK 1974); (Frederick) Elwyn Jones; CH (1976), PC (1964); s of Frederick Jones, of Llanelli, Carmarthenshire, and Elizabeth Jones; *b* 24 Oct 1909; *Educ* Llanelli Co Intermediate Sch, Univ Coll of Wales Aberystwyth, Gonville and Caius Cambridge (MA, pres Union 1931); *m* 1937, Pearl, da of Morris Binder, of Fenton and Manchester; 1 s, 2 da; *Career* sits as Labour Peer in House of Lords; Maj RA (TA), served UK, N Africa, CMF; barr Gray's Inn 1935 (bencher 1960, tres 1980), rec 1949-64, QC 1953, QC NI 1958; MP (Lab): Plaistow W Ham 1945-50, W Ham S 1950-70, Newham S 1970-74; pps to attorney-gen 1946-51, attorney-gen 1964-70, lord chllr 1974-79, a lord of appeal 1979-, oppn spokesman (Lords) Legal Affrs 1983-, pres Univ Coll Cardiff 1971-88; pres Mental Health Fndn 1974-; author; kt 1964; *Books* Hitler's Drive to the East (1937), The Battle for Peace (1938), The Attack from Within (1939), In My Time (1983); *Recreations* walking, travelling; *Style—* The Rt Hon Lord Elwyn-Jones, CH, PC; House of Lords, London SW1 (☎ 01 219 5410)

ELY, 8 Marquess of (I 1801); Sir Charles John Tottenham; 9 Bt (I 1780); sits as Baron Loftus (UK 1801); also Baron Loftus (I 1785), Viscount Loftus (I 1789); s of George Leonard Tottenham (d 1928), and gggs of Rt Rev Lord Robert Ponsonby Tottenham, Bp of Clogher, 2 s of 1 Marquess; suc kinsman 1969; *b* 30 May 1913; *Educ* Queen's Univ Kingston Ontario; *m* 1, 23 June 1938, Katherine Elizabeth (d 1975), da of Lt-Col W H Craig, of Kingston, Ontario; 3 s, 1 da; m 2, 1978, Elspeth Ann, da of late P T Hay, of Highgate; *Heir* s, Viscount Loftus; *Career* headmaster Boulden House, Trinity Coll Sch, Port Hope, Ontario; *Style—* The Most Hon the Marquess of Ely; 20 Arundel Court, Jubilee Place, London SW3 (☎ 01 352 9172); Trinity Coll School, Port Hope, Ontario, Canada

ELY, Michael; s of Harold Ely, of Frinton, Essex and Violet Emily, *née* Bruce; *b* 23 April 1943; *Educ* Suttons Hornchurch Essex; *m* 1, 30 Aug 1965, Christine Mary; 1 s (Jonathan b 1975), 1 da (Jane b 1970); 2 m, 25 July 1986, Marion Patricia; *Career* Lloyds Insur broker, dir: Tennant Budd Ltd 1978-83, Tennant Insurance Services Ltd 1973-, Cayzer Steel Bowater International Ltd; md: Offshore Insurance (Services) Ltd; *Recreations* golf, sailing; *Style—* Michael Ely, Esq; Cayzer Steel Bowater International Ltd, 32/38 Dukes Place, London EC3R 7LX

ELY, 66 Bishop of 1977-; Rt Rev Peter Knight Walker; patron of 116 livings (15 alternately) 3 Canonries, 20 Hon Canonries and the Archdeaconries of Ely, Huntingdon and Wisbech; the Diocese, founded in 1109, now includes the major part of Cambridgeshire and 3 Rural Deaneries in West Norfolk; s of late George Walker, and Eva Muriel, *née* Knight; *b* 6 Dec 1919; *Educ* Leeds GS, Queen's Coll Oxford; *m* 1973, Mary Jean, JP, yr da of late Lt-Col J A Ferguson, OBE; *Career* RN 1940-45, Lt RNVR; asst master: King's Sch Peterborough 1947-50, Merchant Taylors' Sch 1950-56; ordained 1954, curate Hemel Hempstead 1956-58, fellow, dean of chapel and asst tutor Corpus Christi Coll Cambridge 1958-62, princ Westcott House Cambridge 1962-72, hon canon Ely Cathedral 1966-72, bishop of Dorchester (suffragan for Diocese of Oxford) 1972, canon Christ Church Oxford 1972-77; chm Hospital Chaplaincies Cncl 1982-86; Hon Fell CCC Cambridge, Queen's Coll Oxford; Hon DD Cambridge Univ 1977; *Books* The Anglican Church Today: Rediscovering The Middle Way (1988); *Clubs* Cambridge County; *Style—* The Rt Rev the Lord Bishop of Ely; The Bishop's House, Ely, Cambs CB7 4DW (☎ 0353 662749)

ELY, see The Ven Archdeacon of; see: The Ven David Walser

ELY, Thea, Marchioness of; Thea Margaret Gordon; da of Lars G Gronvöld (d 1954), and Amy Maria (who was sis of Olive Margaret Gordon, 4 of Craigie, and da of Huntley Gordon Murray of Craigie (d 1908, he was s of Thomas Hamilton Murray, of Castle Douglas, Stewartry of Kirkcudbright, himself only s by Maria Hamilton of John Murray of Auchinard) and Margaret (d 1920), da of Thomas Bushby, Lord of the Manor of West Preston, Sussex; *b* 2 May 1911; *m* 5 Sept 1928, 7 Marquess of Ely (d 31 May 1969); 1 da (Anne b and d 1933); *Style—* The Most Hon Thea, Marchioness of Ely; 19 North Pallant, Chichester, W Sussex

ELY, Vernon Newbury; CBE (1972); s of Bernard Ely (d 1947), of Wimbledon, and Anne Maud, *née* Buck (d 1968); *b* 14 Jan 1907; *Educ* King's Coll Sch Wimbledon, Berkhamstead Sch; *m* 1944, late Florence Maud, da of Walter Armstrong Higgins (d 1917); 1 s (James); *Career* WWII Wing Cdr RAF 1941-45; memb bd of mgmnt Drapers Inst and Cottage Homes 1938- (chm 1948-50 and 1959-67, tres 1952-59, tstee 1976-, chm tstees 1980-); chm: S London Amateur Athletic Assoc 1935-47 (pres 1947-55), Elys of Wimbledon 1947-; cncl memb Wimbledon C of C: cncl memb 1947-65, chm exec cncl 1952-54, vice pres 1954-86; govr King's Coll Sch 1949-55, memb bd of govrs Wimbledon Technical Coll 1948-65, ldr Retail Productivity Team to USA 1952, chm exec cncl Drapers Chamber of Trade 1955-56 (pres 1975-83), pres Surbiton Lawn Tennis and Squash Club 1968-88, memb Employers Side Retail Drapery and Outfitting Wages Negotiating Ctee 1960-69 (chm 1970-75), fndr and first chm Retail Watges Liaison Ctee 1960-72, memb Ctee of Inquiry on Decimal Currency 1962-63 (favoured ten shilling unit), chm Retails Decimal Ctee 1963-67; memb: retail Consortium (chm Retail Alliance) 1968-73, HO Ctee on Crime Prev ention 1971-72, memb of Unit for Retail Planning Info Working Pty and Cncl 1973-75, pres Assoc of Retail Distributors 1978-80; FRSA; *Books* Fifty Years Hard (autobiography, 1976); *Recreations* real tennis; *Clubs* Surrey CCC, MCC, Royal Tennis Ct; *Style—* Vernon Ely, Esq, CBE; Elys, Wimbledon, London SW19 (☎ 01 946 9191); 42 West Farm Ave, Ashtead, Surrey

ELYAN, David Asher Gremson; s of Max Elyan, of Castletown, IOM, and Freda, *née* Gremson; *b* 4 Oct 1940; *Educ* Cork GS, Trinity Coll Dublin (BA, BComm, MA); *Career* co sec Gordon & Gotch Hldgs plc 1970-74, assoc dir AGB Res plc 1980-87 (co sec 1974-87); dir: Attwood Res of Ireland Ltd 1981-, Irish TAM Ltd 1981-, Corporate Lease Mgmnt Ltd 1984-, Communication Investmts Ltd 1987-, Langton Videotex Ltd 1987-, Elyan Estates Ltd 1987-; hon tres Trinity Coll Dublin Dining Club 1968-; memb: of senate Dublin Univ 1966-, Corpn of Lloyds 1983, cncl for Br Trinity 400 1987; Freeman City of London, Liveryman Worshipful Co of Chartered Secs 1978; ACCS 1967, ACIS 1969, FCIS 1976, FRSA 1972; *Recreations* bridge, collecting first editions, tennis, squash, art, music; *Clubs* MCC, Kildare St (Dublin), E Gloucestershire (Cheltenham), Union (Malta); *Style—* David Elyan, Esq; 49 Chester Ct, Regent's Pk, London NW1 4BU; 3 Coates Mill, Winchcombe, Gloucestershire GL54 5NH; 8th Floor, Queen's House, Holly Rd, Twickenham, Middx TW1 4EG

ELYAN, Prof Sir (Isadore) Victor; s of Jacob Elyan, PC, JP, and Olga Elyan; *b* 5 Sept 1909; *Educ* St Stephen's Green, Trinity Coll Dublin; *m* 1, 1939, Ivy Ethel Mabel Stuart-Weir (d 1965); m 2, 1966, Rosaleen Jeanette, da of William Andrew O'Shea; *Career* served WWII, GSO (2) Mil Sec's Branch (DAMS), Maj IA; barr King's Inn 1949, Middle Temple 1952; judge of appeal Court of Appeal for Basutoland Bechuanaland Protectorate and Swaziland 1955-66, chief justice Swaziland 1965-70; prof of law and dean Faculty of Law Durban-Westville Univ 1973-77; kt 1970; *Style—* Prof Sir Victor Elyan; PO Box 3052, Durban, Natal, South Africa

ELYSTAN-MORGAN, Baron (Life Peer UK 1981); (Dafydd) Elystan; s of Dewi Morgan (d 1971), of Llandre, Aberystwyth, Cardiganshire, and Olwen Morgan; *b* 7 Dec 1932; *Educ* Ardwyn GS Aberystwyth, Univ Coll of Wales Aberystwyth; *m* 1959, Alwen, da of William E Roberts, of Carrog, Merioneth; 1 s, 1 da; *Career* sits as Lab Peer in House of Lords; MP (L) Cardiganshire 1966-74; parly under-sec of state Home Off 1968-70; pres Welsh Local Authorities Assoc 1967-73, chm Welsh Parly Party 1967-68; barr Gray's Inn 1971 (formerly a slr); rec Wales and Chester Circuit 1983-; *Style—* The Rt Hon Lord Elystan-Morgan; Carreg-Afon, Dolau, Bow Street, Dyfed (☎ 097 0828 408)

EMANUEL, Dr Richard Wolff; s of Prof Joseph George Emanuel (d 1958), of 10 Harborne Road, Edgbaston Birmingham, and Ethel Miriam Cecelia *née* Wolff; *b* 13 Jan 1923; *Educ* Bradfield Coll, Oriel Coll Oxford (BA, MA), Middx Hosp Med Sch (BM, BCh, DM); *m* 2 Nov 1950, Lavinia, da of George Albert Hoffman, of Fairhaven, Old Bosham, West Sussex; 3 s (Richard b 8 Nov 1951, Tom b 21 March 1956, Mark b 18 Oct 1961); *Career* Capt RAMC 1948-50; res fell in med Vanderbilt Univ 1956-57, physician National Heart Hosp 1963- (asst dir Inst of Cardiology and hon physician 1961-63), physician Middx Hosp 1963-87, advsr in cardiovascular disease to Govt of Sudan; chm Cardiology Ctee RCP 1979-85 (sec 1973-79), chm Med Ctee Nat Heart Hosp 1972-75, academic bd Middx Hosp Med Sch 1975-77, cncl memb Middx Hosp Med Sch 1976-77, chm Dist Hosp Med Ctee Middx Hosp 1976-77, sec Working Pty of the RCP to examine the problem of Cardiovasular Fitness of Airline Pilots 1977, sec Working Pty of the RCP and RCS to revise the 1967 Report on 'A Combined Medical and Surgical Unit for Cardiac Surgery' 1977, cncl memb: Chest, Heart and Stroke Assoc 1977-, Br Heart Foundaton 1979-; memb: jt Liaison ctee DHSS 1980-, Chairs and Res Gps Ctee Br Heart Fndn, Res Funds Ctee, Br Heart Fndn 1982-85; chm: Physicians Ctee, Nat Heart Hosp 1985-, Cardiac Care Ctee, Br Heart Fndn 1987-; tst Gordon Memorial Tst Fund 1987-; civillian cnslt in Cardiology to the RAF 1980-88, advsr in Cardiology to the CAA 1981-, contributed to over 80 publications on Cardiovasular disease; memb: Br Acad of Forensic Sci, 1960, Assoc of Physicians of GB and Ireland; sec Br Cardiac Soc 1968-70 (memb 1961, asst sec 1966-68, cncl memb 1981-85); hon memb: Assoc of Physicians of Sudan, Heart Assoc of Thailand; hon fell Phillippine Coll of Cardiology; *Recreations* fishing, 18 Century glass and ceramics; *Clubs* Oriental; *Style—* Dr Richard Emanuel; 6 Upper Wimpole St, London W1M 7TD (☎ 01 935 3243)

EMBIRICOS, Epaminondas George; s of George Epaminondas Embiricos (d 1980), of Athens, Greece, and Sophie, *née* Douma; *b* 15 July 1943; *Educ* Philips Exeter Acad New Hamps USA, MIT (BSc, MSc); *m* 19 March 1977, Angela, da of Nicholas Pittas, of London; 2 s (George Epaminondas b 8 May 1978, Nicholas Epaminondas b 8 June 1980); *Career* chm Embiricos Shipping Agency Ltd 1969-; dir: Liberian shipowners Cncl 1979-84, UK Freight Demurrage and Def Assoc 1984-, Baltic Exchange Ltd 1985-, Chartering Brokers Mutual Insur Assoc 1986-; vice chm: Greek Shipping Co-op Ctee 1986-, Greek Ctee Det Norske Veritas 1986-; Freeman City of London 1984, Worshipful Co of Shipwrights 1985; *Recreations* sailing, reading; *Clubs* Royal Thames YC, Royal YC of Greece, Royal London YC, Royal Corinthian YC, Island Sailing; *Style—* Epaminondas Embiricos, Esq; Commonwealth House, 1-19 New Oxford St, London WC1A 1NU (☎ 01 831 4388, fax 01 872 9385, telex 920688 Epembi G)

EMBLETON, Michael John; s of John James Andrew Embleton, and Georgina Emily Adie, *née* Evans (d 1973); *b* 20 June 1941; *Educ* Kingswood Sch; *m* 30 April 1966, (Leslie) Carol Alfreda, da of Thomas Charles Alan Scribbans (d 1953); 1 s (Philip (Raz)), 1 da (Georgina); *Career* slr, ptnr Pinsent & Co Birmingham and London; memb: The Law Soc, The Birmingham Law Soc; *Recreations* shooting, skiing, sailing; *Style—* Michael Embleton, Esq; Abnalls Cottage, Lichfield WS13 8BN; Pinsent & Co, Post and Mail Ho, Colmore Circus, Birmingham B4 6BH (☎ 021 200 1050, fax 021 200 1040, telex 335101 PINCOS)

EMBREY, Prof Derek Morris; OBE (1986); s of Frederick Embrey (d 1972), and Ethel May, *née* Morris; *b* 11 Mar 1928; *Educ* Wolverhampton Poly; *m* 1951, Frances Margaret, da of Arthur Ewart Stephens (d 1971); 1 s (Stephen Adrian), 1 da (Fiona Jacquiline); *Career* Flight Lt RAFVR; group tech dir: AB Electronics Group plc 1973-, AB Systems Ltd, AB Components Ltd, Voice Micro Systems Ltd; chm WAB 1987; visiting prof Univ of Technology Loughborough 1977-86; memb: Welsh Industries Bd 1982-85, Engrg Cncl 1982-86, Cncl of Uwist 1983-; NEC 1983-; CEng, FIEE, FIMechE, FIERE, MIGasE; *Recreations* music, archaeology, piloting and navigating aircraft; *Clubs* RAF London, Birmingham Electric; *Style—* Prof Derek Embrey, OBE; Maytrees, 102 Mill Rd, Lisvane, Cardiff CF4 5UG (☎ 0222 758473); AB Electronic Products Group Ltd, Ynysboeth, Abercynon, Mountain Ash, Mid-Glamorgan (☎ 0443 740331)

EMBUREY, John Ernest; s of John Alfred Emburey (d 1984), and Rose Alice, *née* Roff; *b* 20 August 1952; *Educ* Peckham Manor Sch; *m* 1, 22 Sept 1974 (m dis 1980), Sandra Ann, *née* Ball; m 2, 20 Sept 1980, Susan Elizabeth Ann, da of John Michael Booth, of Melbourne, Aust; 2 da (Clare Elizabeth b 1 March 1983, Chloe Louise b 31 Oct 1985); *Career* cricket, represented England in 57 test matches: toured 7 times, Capt to Sharjah 1987, capt in 2 tests vs W Indies 1988, vice capt 1986-, Middlesex vice capt 1983-: 5 county championships (1976, 1977, 1980, 1982 and 1985), county testimonical 1986; *Books* Emburey A Biography (1987); *Recreations* golf, squash; *Style—* John Emburey, Esq; Middlesex County Cricket Club, Lords Cricket Ground, London NW8 8QN (☎ 01 289 1300)

EMERSON, Michael Ronald; s of James Emerson, of Wilmslow, Cheshire, and Priscilla Emerson; *b* 12 May 1940; *Educ* Hurstpierpoint Coll and Balliol Coll Oxford; *m* 1966, Barbara Christine, da of late Harold Brierley; 1 s, 3 da; *Career* dir Macroeconomic Analyses and Policy, directorate-gen for Economic and Financial Affairs EEC Cmmn Brussels 1980- (former economic advsr to president Roy Jenkins); *Style—* Michael Emerson, Esq; 50 Rue Clement Delpierre, 1310 La Hulpe, Belgium (☎ 02 354 3730)

EMERSON, Dr Peter Albert; s of Albert Richard Emerson (d 1979), of Epsom, Surrey, and Gwendoline Doris, *née* Davy (d 1968); *b* 7 Feb 1923; *Educ* Leys Sch, Clare Coll Cambridge (MA, MD), St Georges Hosp Med Sch (MB, BChir); *m* 22 Nov 1947, Ceris Hood, da of John Frederick Price (d 1943), of Stone, Staff; 1 s (James Peter b 1949), 1 da (Sally (Mrs Stothard) b 1951); *Career* Sqdn Ldr med branch 1947-51; jr med posts 1947-48, registrar posts 1952-57, asst prof med State Univ NY 1957-58, conslt physician Westminster Hosp 1958-88, hon conslt physician King Edward VII Hosp Midhurst 1969-88, dean Westminster Med Sch 1981-84, vice pres and sr conslt Royal Coll Physicians 1985-86; currently: dir of outcare quality review Westminster Hosp, hon conslt physician Westminster Hosp, hon conslt physician diseases of the chest to RN; memb numerous med ctees; hon fell American Coll of Physicians; FRCP, memb BMA, memb Royal Coll of Physicians; *Books* Thoracic Medicine (1981); *Recreations* tennis, restoring old buildings; *Clubs* RAF; *Style—* Dr Peter Emerson; Kidlington Mill, Mill End, Kidlington, Oxon OX5 EG, (☎ 08675 2212); 3 Halkin St, Belgrave Sq, London SW1X 7DJ, (☎ 01 235 8529)

EMERSON, Ronald Victor; s of Albert Victor Emerson, and Doris, *née* Hird; *b* 22 Feb 1947; *Educ* W Hartlepool GS, Manchester Univ (BSc), Durham Univ (MSc); *m* 21 June 1969, Joan Margaret (d 1988), da of James Hubery Willis; 2 s (Christopher Mark b 28 May 1971, Simon Nicholas b 5 March 1975); *Career* De La Rue Gp 1970-75, commercial devpt controller Formica Int; Bank of America 1975-: hd of London Corporate off and UK Country mangr 1985-88, head payment servs and fin insts Europe Middle East and Africa; *Recreations* flying, sport, reading; *Clubs* Foxhills; *Style—* Ronald Emerson, Esq; 11 Luckley Wood, Wokingham, Berkshire; Bank of America, 25 Cannon St, London EC4P 4HN (☎ 01 634 4306)

EMERTON, Rev Prof John Adney; s of Adney Spencer Emerton (d 1969), of Southgate, and Helena Mary, *née* Quin (d 1964); *b* 5 June 1928; *Educ* Minchenden GS Southgate, Corpus Christi Coll Oxford, Wycliffe Hall Oxford (BA, MA), Cambridge

Univ (MA, BD, DD); *m* 14 Aug 1954, Norma Elizabeth, da of Norman Bennington (d 1986); 1 s (Mark Simon b 1961), 2 da (Caroline Mary b 1958, Lucy Anne b 1966); *Career* ordained: deacon 1952, priest 1953, curate Birmingham Cathedral 1953, asst lectr theology Univ of Birmingham 1952-53, lectr in hebrew and aramaic Univ of Durham 1953-55, univ lectr in divinity Cambridge 1955-62, visiting prof of old testament and near eastern studies Trinity Coll Toronto 1960, reader in semitic philology Univ of Oxford 1962-68, fell St Peter's Coll Oxford 1962-68, Regius prof of hebrew Univ of Cambridge 1968-, fell St John's Coll Cambridge 1970-, visiting fell Inst for Advanced Studies Hebrew Univ of Jerusalem 1983, visiting prof of old testament Utd Theol Coll Bangalore 1986; sec Int Orgn for the Study of the Old Testament 1971-; hon canon St George's Cathedral Jerusalem 1984-; editor Vetus Testamentum 1976-; Hon DD Univ of Edinburgh 1977, FBA 1979; *Books* The Peshitta of the Wisdom of Solomon (1959), The Old Testament in Syriac - the Song of Songs (1966); *Style*— The Rev Prof John Emerton; 34 Gough Way, Cambridge CB3 9LN; St John's College, Cambridge CB2 1TP

EMERTON, Philip John; s of Edward Alec Emerton (d 1987), of Springhill House, Goring-on-Thames, and Dorothy Evelyn, *née* East (d 1972); *b* 10 Feb 1935; *Educ* Abingdon Sch; *m* 25 July 1959, Mary Patricia, da of Harold Harvey Creedon (d 1970), of Petersfield; 2 s (Richard b 1960, Mark b 1963); *Career* served RA 1958-60, 2 Lt; ptnr Haines Watts Gp 1963- (sr ptnr 1973-); British Legion; FCA 1958, FACCA; *Recreations* fishing, skiing, wine buying; *Style*— Philip Emerton, Esq; Herons Creek, Wargrave (☎ Wargrave 2642); Leysin, Switzerland; Cagnes-Sur-Mer, France; 27 Couching St, Watlington, Oxon (☎ 049161 3611, fax 049161 3730)

EMERY, Prof Alan Eglin Heathcote; s of Harold Heathcote-Emery (d 1977), and Alice, *née* Eglin (d 1972); *b* 21 August 1928; *Educ* Manchester GS, Chester Coll, Manchester Univ (BSc, MSc, MB, ChB, MD, DSc), Johns Hopkins Univ USA (PhD); *m* 13 Oct 1988, Marcia Lynn, da of John Miller (d 1986), of Cleveland, USA; *Career* Nat Serv 14/20 Kings Hussars 1945-47; conslt physician 1966-, emeritus prof Univ of Edinburgh 1983-(prof of human genetics 1968-83); visiting fell Green Coll Oxford 1986-, hon res fell Royal Hosp of Sick Children Edinburgh 1988-; visiting prof univ: NY 1968, Heidelberg 1972, Hyderabad 1975, California (UCLA) 1980, Padua 1984, Med Coll Peking 1985, RPMS 1986, Duke Univ (MC, USA) 1986; ctee memb: ASH, res ctee RCP (London), scientific advsy ctee Brittle Bone Sec, Nat Assoc of Pagets Disease, scientific ctee Faculty of Community Med, Pres Br Clinical Genetics Soc 1980-83, hon fell Muscular Dystrophy Assoc of Brazil 1982; Nat Fndn (USA) Internat Award for Res 1980; FRCP (Ed) 1970, FRS (Ed) 1972, MFCM (1974), FLS (1985); *Books* Elements of Medical Genetics (seventh edn 1988), Modern Trends in Human Genetics (vol 1 1970, vol 2 1975), Antenatal Diagnosis of Genetic Disease (1973), Genetic Registers (1976), Psychological Aspects of Genetic Counselling (1984), Introduction to Recombinant DNA (1984), Methodology in Medical Genetics (second edn 1986), Duchenne Muscular Dystrophy (1987), Principles & Practise of Medical Genetics (second edn 1989); *Recreations* oil painting, marine biology; *Clubs* Scottish Arts (Edinburgh); *Style*— Prof Alan Emery; 1 Eton Terr, Edinburgh EH4 1QE (☎ 031 343 2262); Medical Sch, Edinburgh EH8 (☎ 031 667 1011 ext 2505)

EMERY, Anthony Hayward; s of Thomas Frederick Emery; *b* 10 July 1930; *Educ* Bablake Sch Coventry, Bristol Univ (BA), UCL; *Career* formerly chm: Reed Info Servs Ltd, dir Reed Business Publishing Gp; cmmr Historic Bldgs and Monuments for England, cncl memb Royal Archaeological Inst; *Recreations* architectural historian (author of *Dartington Hall* and papers on late medieval buildings), independent travel, fine arts, Nineteenth Century piano music; *Style*— Anthony Emery, Esq; Willow House, Biddestone, Wilts; Hightrees House, Nightingale Lane, London SW12

EMERY, Brian David; TD (1968, with 3 Bars); s of Alan Joseph Emery (d 1972), of Watford, Herts, and Winifred Houghton, *née* Wells (d 1982); *b* 9 April 1932; *Educ* Watford GS, Queens' Coll Cambridge (BA, MA); *m* 9 Sept 1961, (Margaret) Clare, da of Eric Hurndall (d 1970), of Bushey, Herts; 2 s (Patrick b 1962, Matthew b 1974), 1 da (Vivienne b 1964); *Career* Nat Serv RE 1951-53 (2 Lt 1952), Territorial Serv 1953-86, 122 Field Engr Regt (TA): Lt and Capt 249 FD Sqdn RE (TA) Luton 1953-60, Capt 2 i/c 248 FD Sqdn RE (TA) Bedford 1960-66 (Maj OC 1966-67); transferred Royal Corps of T'port under CVHQ RCT Bedford: Capt 2 i/c 270 Port Sqdn RCT (V) 1967-70, Maj OC 271 Port Sqdn RCT (V) 1970-74, DAQMG 2 TPT Gp RCT 1974-77; CVHQ RCT moved to Grantham becoming HQ RCT TA; Lt-Col CO 161 Ambulance Regt RCT (V) 1977-81, SO1 495 Movement Control Liaison Unit 1981-83, COL Cmd BRSC Liaison & Movements Staff (TA) 1983-86, ret 1986; Equity & Law Life Assur Soc plc 1956-: various appts London and High Wycombe 1956-78, chief accountant 1978-85, pensions mangr 1985-86; dir Equity & Law (Managed Funds) Ltd and Equity & Law (Tstees) Ltd 1985- asst gen mangr 1986-; half blues Water Polo 1955 and 1956, capt Old Fullerians RFC 1957-60; memb examiners ctee CII 1983-; FCII 1969, FCIS 1981; *Recreations* walking, swimming, reading; *Style*— Brian Emery, Esq, TD; 8 Stoneleigh Rd, Gibbet Hill, Coventry CV4 7AD (☎ 0203 417 663); Equity & Law Life Assur Soc plc, Equity & Law Ho, Corporation St, Coventry CV1 1GD (☎ 0203 555 424, fax 0203 227 734, telex 311439)

EMERY, David John; s of John Emery, of Tolworth, Surrey, and Joan, *née* Bellenie; *b* 13 Oct 1946; *Educ* Tiffin Sch Kingston; *m* 13 April 1974, Irene Thelma, da of George Board, of Ealing W13; 2 s (Matthew David b 1979, Samuel Jack b 1984), 2 da (Alexandra Lillian b 1976, Georgia Lauren b 1987); *Career* journalist: Surrey Comet 1964-69, Luton Evening News 1969-70, Daily Mail 1970-72, Daily Express 1972-78, Daily Star 1978-82, Daily Express 1982-; chief sports writer Daily Express 1983-87; sports ed Daily Express 1987; highly commended in Sports Cncl Awards for Journalism 1987; chm Sports Writers Assoc of GB 1986-, pres 26.2 Road Runners Club 1984; *Books* Lillian (1971), Waterskiing (with Paul Seaton 1976), Who's Who of the 1984 Olympics, World Sporting Records (1986); *Recreations* squash, marathon running, cricket, golf; *Clubs* Mid Surrey Squash, 26.2 Road Runners, Claygate CC, Surbiton Golf; *Style*— David Emery, Esq; Westwood, 39 Greenways, Hinchley Wood, Surrey KT10 0QH (☎ 01 398 1901); Daily Express, 245 Blackfriars Rd, London SE1 9UX (☎ 01 928 8000, fax 01 633 0244, telex 21841/21842)

EMERY, George Edward; CB (1980); s of Frederick Arthur Emery (d 1930), and Florence Emery; *b* 2 Mar 1920; *Educ* Bemrose Sch Derby; *m* 1946, Margaret, *née* Rice; 2 da; *Career* under sec MOD 1973; dir gen Defence Accounts (MOD) 1973-80; ret; *Recreations* gardening, amateur dramatics; *Style*— George Emery, Esq, CB; 3 The Orchard, Freshford, Bath (☎ 022 122 3561)

EMERY, Gordon Haig; CBE; s of Frank Milwain Emery (d 1947), of Stockport, Cheshire, and Alice, *née* Harrison (d 1919); *b* 11 Nov 1918; *Educ* Manchester Coll of Tech; *m* 1, 1947 (m dis); 2 da (Michelle b 1966, Louise b 1975), 1 adopted da (Joanne (Ms Aylmer) b 1965); m 2, 29 Aug 1980, Dr Josephine Angela, da of John Arthur Thomas (d 1974), of Prestbury, Cheshire; *Career* TA 1939, BEF France 1939-40 and Dunkirk 1940, 8 Army 42 Div 1942-47 in N Africa, Alamein, Tobruk and Tripoli; chm: Gordon Emery Gp (bldg contractors, devpt and resource mgmnt), Gordon Emery Ltd, Emery (estate agents) Ltd, Emery Farm Estates Ltd, D & G Emery Ltd, GHE Ltd, Fog Lane Properties Ltd, Hampson and Kemp Ltd, Gordon Emery Inc (USA), Kingfisher Oil Co Ltd, Gold Investmts (Yukon) Ltd; involved with: Stockport Lad's Club 1957 (vice chm 1980), Pendlebury Charitable Tst 1958, Centurion Lacross Club 1968, Outward Bound Assoc 1973, Churchill Club 1976, NW Industl Cncl 1979, Manchester Literary and Philosophical Soc 1979, Halle Soc (patron) 1984, NW Regnl Health Authy 1985, Fedn of Boys Clubs 1985, Manchester Young Con's (pres) 1985-87; Stockport Con Assoc: joined 1954, chm 1960-62, pres 1978-81, vice-chm 1985-; cncllr Stockport Borough Cncl 1957-63, govr Stockport Sch 1978-88; memb Manchester C of C 1975-, Aims of Indust 1976; FInstD 1979; *Recreations* tennis, swimming, golf; *Clubs* Carlton, St James's (Manchester); *Style*— Gordon Emery, Esq, CBE; 184 Heaton Moor Road, Heaton Moor, Stockport, Cheshire SK4 4DU (☎ 061 432 3460/1713, fax 061 431 0786, car tel 0860 815790, telex 666514)

EMERY, Sir Peter Frank Hannibal; MP (C) Honiton 1967-; s of Frank George Emery (d 1960), of Highgate; *b* 27 Feb 1926; *Educ* Scotch Plains N J USA, Oriel Coll Oxford; *m* 1, 1954 (m dis), Elizabeth, da of Philip Nicholson, of Dunsa House, Endsor, Derbys; 1 s, 1 da; m 2, 1972, Elizabeth, yst da of G J R Monnington, of Upper Stonham, Lewes, Sussex; 1 s, 1 da; *Career* MP (C) Reading 1959-66; PPS to successive Min State Foreign Affrs Rt Hon David Ormsby-Gore (later 5 Lord Harlech) 1960-61, and Rt Hon Joseph Godber (later Lord Godber of Willington) 1961-63 oppn front bench spokesman Treasy Economics and Trade 1964-66, parly under-sec DTI 1972-74, Energy 1974; jt fndr and first sec Bow Gp; chm select ctee procedure, memb select ctee Industry and Trade; chm: Shenley Tst Servs Ltd, Wingglaw Gp; delegate to Cncl of Europe & WEU 1964-66 and 1970-72, memb North Atlantic Assembly 1983-, chm science & technical ctee NAA 1986-; capt House of Commons Bridge Team; FInstPS; kt 1981; *Recreations* skiing, tennis, theatre, bridge, travel; *Clubs* Leander, Carlton, Turf, Portland; *Style*— Sir Peter Emery, MP; 15 Tufton Court, Tufton St, SW1 (☎ 01 222 6666); Tytherleigh Manor, nr Axminster, Devon EX13 7BD (☎ 0460 309); office: 40 Park St, London W1Y 3PF (fax 493-5096)

EMERY-WALLIS, Frederick Alfred John; DL; s of Frederick Henry Wallis (d 1949), and Lillian Grace Emery, *née* Coles (d 1963); *b* 11 May 1927; *Educ* Blake's Acad Portsmouth; *m* 22 Aug 1960, Solange, da of William Victor Randall (d 1957), of Mitcham, Surrey; 2 da (Selina b 4 April 1963, Jennette b 5 March 1971); *Career* SCU4 RCS Middle East Radio Security 1945-48; Portsmouth CC: cncllr 1961-74, lord mayor 1968-69, alderman 1969-74; Hampshire CC: cncllr 1973-, vice chm 1975-76, ldr 1976-; chm Southern Tourist Bd 1976-88, Assoc of CCs: memb exec ctee and policy ctee, chm ACC recreation ctee 1982-85; govr Portsmouth Poly; chm: Hampshire Archives Tst, New Theatre Royal Tst Portsmouth, govrs Portsmouth HS for Girls; tstee: Mary Rose Tst, RN Museum Portsmouth; memb Warrior Preservation Tst, chm Hampshire Sculpture Tst; FSA, Hon FRIBA; *Recreations* music, book collecting; *Style*— Frederick Emery-Wallis, Esq, DL; Froddington, Craneswater Park, Portsmouth, Hampshire PO4 0NR, (☎ 0705 731409); Hampshire County Council, The Castle, Winchester, Hampshire SO23 8UJ, (☎ 0962 847943, fax 0962 67273, telex 477729)

EMLEY, Miles Lovelace Brereton; s of Col Derek Brereton Emley, OBE, of Tenny's Court, Marnhull, Sturminster Newton, Dorset, and Mary Georgina, *née* Lovelace; *b* 23 July 1949; *Educ* St Edward's Sch Oxford, Balliol Coll Oxford (MA); *m* 26 June 1976, Tessa Marcia Radclyffe, da of Radclyffe Edward Crichton Powell, MBE (d 1985); 2 s (Oliver b 1978, Alexander b 1982), 1 da (Katherine b 1980); *Career* dir N M Rothschild & Sons Ltd 1982- (joined 1972), dir Virago Press Ltd 1988-; Liveryman Worshipful Co of Leathersellers 1979; *Style*— Miles Emley, Esq; Whitehall House, Ashford Hill, Newbury, Berks (☎ 0635 23 306); N M Rothschild & Sons Ltd, New Court, St Swithin's Lane, London EC4P 4DU (☎ 01 280 5000)

EMLY, John Richard Keith; s of Charles Richard Lewis Emly (d 1975), and Lillian Villette, *née* Jenner (d 1971); *b* 15 Sept 1941; *Educ* St Dunstans Coll Catford; *m* 26 July 1969, Maria Joan, da of Frederic Jozef Jan Gumosz, of Catford (d 1964); 2 s (Timothy b 1978, Benjamin b 1980), 2 da (Gillian b 1972, Sarah b 1974); *Career* jt investmt mangr The Law Debenture Corpn Ltd 1971-1975 (joined 1960), joined Robert Fleming Holdings Ltd 1975, main bd dir 1985-; dir: Robert Fleming Investmt Mgmnt Ltd 1978-88, Robert Fleming Asset Mgmnt Ltd 1988-; chm & chief exec Fleming Investmt Mgmnt Ltd 1988-; sch govr; memb FRICS 1972, AMSIA; *Recreations* family life; *Style*— John Emly, Esq; Robert Fleming Holdings Ltd, 25 Copthall Avenue, London EC2R 7DR (☎ 01 638 5858, fax 01 588 7219, telex 297451)

EMLYN, Viscount; Colin Robert Vaughan Campbell; s (by 1 m) and h of 6 Earl Cawdor; *b* 30 June 1962; *Educ* Eton, St Peter's Coll Oxford; *Style*— Viscount Emlyn; Cawdor Castle, Nairn, Scotland

EMLYN JONES, John Hubert; CBE (1986), MBE (1941); s of Ernest Pearson Jones (d 1959), of Llandudno, and Katherine Cole, *née* Nicholas (d 1962); *b* 6 August 1915; *Educ* Dulwich Coll; *m* 2 Oct 1954, Louise Anne Montague, da of Raymond Ralph Horwood Hazell (d 1965), of Great Missenden; 2 s (Thomas, William), 1 da (Eiluned); *Career* war serv RE 1939-46, Maj 1943, served in NW Europe; memb Lands Tribunal 1968-86, ptnr Rees-Reynolds & Hunt and Alfred Savill & Sons Chartered Surveyors 1950-68; pres: Rating Surveyors Assoc 1965-66 (hon memb 1968), Climbers Club 1966-69 (hon memb 1970), Alpine Club 1980-82; High Sheriff Bucks 1967-68, JP (Bucks 1968-85), Lord of the Manor of Ivinghoe; FRICS 1954; *Recreations* mountaineering, music; *Clubs* Alpine, Garrick; *Style*— J H Emlyn Jones, Esq, CBE; Ivinghoe Manor, Leighton Buzzard, Beds LU7 9EH (☎ 0296 668202)

EMMERSON, John Corti; s of Sir Harold Cort Emmerson, GCB, KCVO (d 1984), and Lady Lucy Kathleen, *née* Humphreys; *b* 10 Sept 1937; *Educ* Merchant Taylors' Sch Northwood, Magdalen Coll Oxford; *m* 30 Oct 1970, Pamela Anne, da of Lt Col James Shaw, TD (d 1970); 1 s (Dominic b 1973), 1 da (Kate b 1975); *Career* Nat Serv, 2/Lt 4 Royal Tank Regt 1956-58, asst princ Air Ministry 1961-63; slr, ptnr McKenna & Co; dir: William Evans Ltd, Woodard Schs (Southern Div) Ltd; *Recreations* fly fishing; *Clubs* Brooks's; *Style*— John C Emmerson, Esq; 30 Norland Square, London W11 4PU; McKenna & Co, Inveresk House, 1 Aldwych, London WC2 (☎ 01 836 2442)

EMMET, Hon Christopher Antony Robert; JP (W Sussex); eldest s of Baroness Emmet of Amberley (Life Peeress, d 1980), and Thomas Addis Emmet (d 1934); *b* 21 Nov 1925; *Educ* Ampleforth, Balliol Coll Oxford; *m* 22 July 1947, Lady Miranda, *qv*; 1 s, 3 da; *Career* W Sussex Co Cllr (Pulborough) 1952-62; Cdre Arun Yacht Club Littlehampton 1972-73, pres Houghton Bridge and Dist Angling Soc 1960; *Recreations* owner of 36 ft Halberdier Ketch 'Sarva of Beaulieu'; *Style*— The Hon Christopher Emmet, JP; Seabeach House, Selhurst Park, Halnaker, Chichester, Sussex (☎ 0243 773156)

EMMET, Hon David Alastair Rennell; 2 s of Baroness Emmet of Amberley (Life Peeress, d 1980), and Thomas Addis Emmet (d 1934); *b* 31 Jan 1928,; *Educ* Ampleforth, Worcester Coll Oxford; *m* 22 July 1967, Sylvia Delia, o da of late Willis Knowles, of Buenos Aires; 1 s, 1 da; *Career* memb Br Community Cncl Argentina 1964-68; FRGS; *Style*— Hon David Emmet; 2 Edificio Las Rocas, Calle 12, Punta del Este, Maldonado, Uruguay

EMMET, Hon Mrs; (Jocelyne); *née* Portman; yst da of 4 Viscount Portman (d 1929); *b* 27 May 1903; *m* 27 Nov 1923, Capt James Albert Garland Emmet LG (ret), eldest surv s of late Maj Robert Emmet, DSO; 2 s (and 1 s decd), 1 da; *Style*— Hon Mrs Emmet; 62 Centre Drive, Newmarket, Suffolk

EMMET, (Arthur) Maitland; MBE (1947), TD (1948); s of Rev C W Emmet (d 1923), of Univ Coll Oxford, and Gertrude Julia, *née* Weir (d 1972); *b* 15 July 1908; *Educ* Sherbourne, University Coll Oxford (MA); *m* 26 April 1972, Emilie Catherine (Katie), da of Alfred Gough (d 1917), of Saffron Walden; *Career* cmmn TA 1933, Capt 1938, Co Cdr 6 Bn Oxfordshire & Buckinghamshire Light Inf 1940-42, sr Liaison Offr (Maj) 25 Indian Div 1942-45, Co Lt-Col St Edward's Sch CCF 1947-56; housemaster St Edward's Sch 1949-56 (asst master 1931-56), pt/t headmaster RAF selection bd 1957-79, examiner english language London Univ Examinations Bd 1957-79; hon treas 25 Indian Div Offs' Dining Club 1984- (hon sec 1947-84); The Stamford Raffles Award (Zoological Soc of London, 1981); rowing: Oxford Univ Trial Eights 1929 and 1930; Royal Entomological Soc: memb 1969-, vice-pres 1980-81, hon fell 1984; memb: Linnean Soc, Br Entomological & Nat History Soc (pres 1971), Amateur Entomologists' Soc (pres 1975); *Books* The Arakan Campaign of the 25th Indian Div (1947), The Smaller Moths of Essex (1981), The larger Moths and Butterflies of Essex (with G A Pyman 1985), The Moths and Butterflies of Great Britain and Ireland (ed and contrib author 1976-); *Recreations* entomology; *Clubs* Leander; *Style*— Maitland Emmet, Esq, MBE, TD; Labrey Cottage, Victoria Gdns, Saffron Walden, Essex CB11 3AF (☎ 0799 23042)

EMMET, Lady Miranda Mary; *née* Fitzalan Howard; da of 3 Baron Howard of Glossop and sis of 17 Duke of Norfolk (raised to the rank of a Duke's da, 1975); *m* 22 July 1947, Hon Christopher Anthony Robert Emmet, *qv*; 1 s, 3 da; *Career* international judge of Arabian horses, past pres Arabian Horse Society; *Recreations* riding, long distance walking in the fells; *Style*— Lady Miranda Emmet; Seabeach House, Selhurst Park, Halnaker, nr Chichester, W Sussex PO18 0LX (☎ 0243 773156)

EMMETT, Bryan David; s of Lilian, *née* Emmott (d 1957); *b* 15 Feb 1941; *Educ* Portsmouth Northern, Chislehurst & Sidcup and Tadcaster GS's; *m* 25 Nov 1960, Moira, da of John Miller (d 1984), of Edinburgh; 1 s (Mark David b 1961); *Career* Miny of Labour and Nat Serv 1958-59, exec offr War Dept 1959-64, asst princ MOP 1965-69 (asst private sec 1968-69), princ Electricity Div DTI 1969-74; Dept of Energy: princ and private sec to Min of State 1974-75, asst sec and princ private sec to S of S 1975-76; asst sec Petroleum Engrg Div 1977-80, under sec and princ estab offr 1980-81, princ estab and finance offr 1981-82, chief exec Employment Div of MSC 1982-85, head of Energy Policy Div 1985- 86, head of Oil Div 1986-87; dir gen Energy Efficiency Off 1987-88, chief exec Educn Assets Bd 1988-; *Recreations* national hunt racing, hacking, snooker; *Clubs* Leeds; *Style*— Bryan Emmett, Esq; Hayside Farm, Low St, Sancton, E Yorkshire (☎ 0430 827552) Education Assets Board, Dudley House, Leeds LS2 8PN (☎ 0532 461221, fax 0532 460569)

EMMINS, Christopher John; s of Frederick William Emmins, and Vera Jennie, *née* Ferry; *b* 30 Jan 1948; *Educ* George Monoux GS, Worcester Coll Oxford (MA), Coll of Law; *Career* barr Middle Temple 1970, in practice 1973-76 and 1987-, lectr Inns of Ct Sch of Law 1976-87; active in local church gps; *Books* A Practical Approach to Criminal Procedure (4 edn 1987), A Guide to the Criminal Justice Act (1982), A Practical Approach to Sentencing (1984), A Guide to the Criminal Justice Act (1988); *Recreations* watching sport, reading, listening to music; *Style*— Christopher Emmins Esq; Howard Rd, Walthamstow, London E17 (☎ 01 520 7506)

EMMS, David Acfield; s of late Archibald George Emms, of Lowestoft, Suffolk, and Winifred Gladys, *née* Richards; *b* 16 Feb 1925; *Educ* Tonbridge, BNC Oxford (MA); *m* 8 Sept 1950, Pamela Baker, da of late Edwin Leslie Speed, of Ponteland, Northumberland; 3 s (John b 1952, Richard b 1959, Christopher b 1969), 1 da (Vicki b 1954); *Career* Capt Royal Indian Airborne Artillery; asst master Uppingham Sch 1951-60, headmaster Cranleigh Sch 1960-70, headmaster Sherborne Sch 1970-74, master Dulwich Coll 1975-86; chm Headmasters' Conference 1984, dir London House for Overseas Graduates 1987-, vice-pres Independent Sch Careers Orgn 1973-; dep chm ESU; govr: Bickley Park Sch 1978-81, St Felix Sch Southwold 1983-88, Feltonfleet Sch Cobham 1968-87, Tonbridge Sch (chm) 1988-, Brambletye Sch East Grinstead 1982-88, Portsmouth GS 1987-; dep pro-chancellor City Univ 1989-; Freeman of City London 1950, Master of the Skinners' Co 1987-88; FRSA 1988; *Books* HMC Schools and British Industry (1981); *Publications* HMC Schools and British Industry (1981); *Recreations* radical gardening; *Clubs* Vincent's (Oxford), East India Devonshire Sports and Public Schools, Itchenor Sailing; *Style*— David Emms, Esq; The Director's Flat, London House for Overseas Graduates, Mecklenburgh Square, London WC1N 2AB (☎ 01 837 8888); Seaforth, Spinney Lane, Itchenor, nr Chichester, West Sussex PO20 7DJ (☎ 0243 512585)

EMMS, Peter Anthony; s of Anthony Hubert Hamilton Emms, and Daphne Emms, *née* Cooper-Lake; *b* 29 June 1949; *Educ* Stoneham GS Reading, City of London Poly (BA); *m* 6 Nov 1981, Susan Gwendolen, da of Harold Kemp; 1 s (Ben b 1975), 1 da (Joanna b 1977); *Career* exec dir mktg Allied Dunbar Assurance plc 1985-; memb: FCII 1975; *Recreations* gardening, reading; *Style*— Peter Emms, Esq; 55 Ridgeway, Wargrave-on-Thames, Berkshire; Allied Dunbar Assurance plc, Allied Dunbar Centre, Swindon, Wilts SN1 1EL (☎ 0793 514514)

EMO CAPODILISTA MALDURA, Lady Arabella Avice Diana; *née* Sackville; da of 10 Earl De La Warr; *b* 20 June 1958; *m* 1981, Conte Giovanni Emo Capodilista Maldura, s of Conte Gabriele Emo Capodilista (Austrian cr of 1829, Italian of 1917), a Patrician of Venice; *Style*— Lady Arabella Emo Capodilista Maldura; 21 Pelham Place, London SW7 (☎ 01 589 3845)

EMPSON, Adm Sir (Leslie) Derek; GBE (1975), KCB (1973, CB 1969); s of Frank Harold Empson (d 1960), of Four Oaks, Warwickshire, and Madeleine Norah, *née* Burge; *b* 29 Oct 1918; *Educ* Eastbourne Coll, Clare Coll Cambridge; *m* 1958, Diana Elizabeth, da of P J Kelly, of London; 1 s, 1 da; *Career* joined RNVR 1940, served WW II Fleet Air Arm pilot, Cmdr 1952, Capt 1957, naval asst to First Sea Lord 1957-59, Rear Adm 1967, flag offr Aircraft Carriers 1967-68, asst ch of Naval Staff (Ops and Air) 1968-69, Cdr Far East Fleet 1969-70, Vice Adm 1969, Second Sea Lord and chief of Naval Personnel 1971-64, Adm 1972, C-in-C Naval Home Cmmd and flag offr Portsmouth Area 1974-75, Flag ADC to HM The Queen 1974-75, ret 1976; Rear Adm of UK 1985-; chm of govrs Eastbourne Coll 1972-; consultant Thorn EMI Ltd 1976-86; chm Federation Against Copyright Theft 1983-; *Style*— Adm Sir Derek Empson, GBE, KCB; Deepdale, Hambledon, Hants (☎ 070 132 451); c/o Roymark United, 36 Soho Square, London W1V 5DG (☎ 01 437 9121)

EMSALL, Keith Fletcher; s of Harold Emsall (d 1946), of Manchester, and Lily Fletcher (d 1956); *b* 23 Feb 1937; *Educ* Stand GS Manchester; *m* 5 Oct 1963, Carol Ann, da of Albert Lee, of Derbyshire; 2 da (Nicola b 1964, Claire b 1967); *Career* RAf 1955-57; involved in marketing Mobile Oil Co 1958-; memb: North Hertfordshire Dist Cncl 1978-86 and 1987- (chm 1984-85), mgmnt bd Motor and Cycle Trades Benevolent Fund 1983-; chm Benevolent Housing Assoc Ltd 1983-87; tstee Knebworth Tst 1984-85; *Recreations* golf, reading; *Style*— Keith F Emsall, Esq; 8 Field Lane, Letchworth, Herts SG6 3LE (☎ 674543); 54/60 Victoria Street, London SW1E 6QB (☎ 01 828 9777)

EMSDEN, Kenneth Edward Clare; s of Lt-Col Leslie George Emsden OBE, JP (d 1974), of Verandah House, Clare, Suffolk, and Emma Nora, *née* Metcalfe (d 1967); *b* 15 July 1929; *Educ* Wellington Coll, Trinity Hall Cambridge; *m* 25 Aug 1956, Diana Mabel, da of Maj Colin Edward Arthur Grayling; 1 s (Peter Clare b 1961), 2 da (Jennifer Mary b 1959, Gillian Sarah b 1965); *Career* mangr plastics div Shell Chemical (UK) Ltd, dir Vencel Resil; Liveryman Worshipful Co of Horners; *Recreations* walking, sailing, gardening; *Style*— Kenneth Emsden, Esq; Gleanings, Spinnet Lane, Rabley Heath, Welwyn, Herts AL6 9TF (☎ 0438 813391)

EMSLEY, Kenneth; s of Clifford Briggs Emsley, and Lily, *née* Goldsborough; *b* 7 Dec 1921; *Educ* Bingley GS, Loughborough Coll, St John's Coll Cambridge (MA) Univ of Newcastle-upon-Tyne (LLM); *m* 14 May 1959, Nancy Audrey, da of Alfred Ernest Slee; *Career* served WWII; chm Smith & Hardcastle Ltd 1955-65; painter of watercolour drawings and miniature paintings, author of books and articles, lectr in law, ret 1980; pres: The Br Watercolour Soc, The Soc of Miniaturists, The Bradford Arts Club (former chm) until 1985; memb cncl Yorks Archealogical Soc Leeds, hon sec Wakefield Manorial Ct Rolls Series; FRSA 1945, FCCS 1957, ACIS 1970, MSEng 1948, PBWS 1985, PSM 1985; *Books* Tyneside (with CM Fraser, 1973), Northumbria (with CM Fraser 1979), The Courts of the County Palatine of Durham (1984), Wakefield Manorial Court Rolls (with CM Fraser, vol 1 1979 and vol 5 1987); *Recreations* formerly: cricket, rugby, tennis, now bowls; *Clubs* The Bradford, Cambridge Union, Cambridge Univ Cricket; *Style*— Kenneth Emsley, Esq; 34 Nabwood Drive, Shipley, West Yorkshire BD18 4EL; The Yorkshire Archaeological Society, Claremont, Clarendon Rd, Leeds LS2 9NZ

EMSLIE, Hon Derek Robert Alexander; s of Baron Emslie, MBE, PC, QC (Life Peer); *b* 21 June 1949; *Educ* Edinburgh Acad, Trinity Coll Glenalmond, Gonville and Caius Coll Cambridge (BA), Edinburgh (LLB); *m* 1974, Elizabeth Jane Cameron, da of Andrew Maclaren Carstairs; 2 children; *Career* advocate; standing jr counsel DHSS 1979-; *Clubs* Hawks; *Style*— The Hon Derek Emslie; 35 Ann St, Edinburgh EH4 1PL (☎ 031 332 6648)

EMSLIE, Baron (Life Peer UK 1979); George Carlyle Emslie; MBE (1946), PC (1972); s of Alexander and Jessie Blair Emslie; *b* 6 Dec 1919; *Educ* The HS of Glasgow, Glasgow Univ (MA, LLB, Hon LLD); *m* 1942, Lilias Ann Mailer, da of Robert Hannington, of Glasgow; 3 s; *Career* advocate Scot 1948, QC Scot 1957, sheriff of Perth and Angus 1963-66, dean of Faculty of Advocates 1965-70, senator of the Coll of Justice, a lord of session with title Lord Emslie 1970, lord justice gen of Scotland and lord pres of the Court of Session 1972; FRSE; *Recreations* golf; *Clubs* New (Edinburgh), Caledonian (London); *Style*— The Rt Hon Lord Emslie, MBE, PC; 47 Heriot Row, Edinburgh (☎ 031 225 3657)

EMSLIE, Hon Richard Hannington; yst s of Baron Emslie, MBE, PC (Life Peer); *b* 28 July 1957; *Educ* Edinburgh Acad, Trinity Coll Glenalmond, Gonville and Caius Coll Cambridge (BA); *Career* wildlife biologist, researching for PhD Witwatersrand Univ Joburg, the applied grazing ecology of Umfolozi Game Reserve, Zululand; *Recreations* football, hockey, golf, skiing, squash, tennis, hypnosis, photography, bird-watching; *Clubs* Edinburgh Ski, Umfolozi Country; *Style*— Hon Richard Emslie; c/o Resource Ecology Gp, Botany Dept, Witwatersrand Univ, 1 Jan Smuts Ave, Jo'burg 2001, S Africa; 47 Heriot Row, Edinburgh EH3 6EX (☎ 031 225 3657)

EMSLIE-SMITH, Dr Donald; s of Lt Col Harry Emslie-Smith (d 1946), of Dunfermline, and Maribel, *née* Milne (d 1952); *b* 12 April 1922; *Educ* Trinity Coll, Glenalmond Univ of Aberdeen (MD, ChB); *m* 19 Sept 1959, Ann Elizabeth, da of Col Thomas Milne, CB, DSO, of Milford-on-Sea, Hants; 1 s (Alistair b 1960), 1 da (Sophie b 1963); *Career* physician; Fl/Lt (medical) RAF VR UK, Egypt, Sudan 1946-48; registrar in Cardiology Dundee Teaching Hosps 1953-54; E Wilson memorial research fell Baker Inst Melbourne 1955-56; tutor and sr registrar Royal Postgrad Med Sch and Hammersmith Hosp 1958-61; sr lecture in medicine Univ of: St Andrews 1961-67, Dundee 1967-71 (reader 1971-87); hon conslt cardiologist Tayside Health Bd 1961-87; sr memb Assoc of Physicians of GB and Ireland (exec ctee 1977-80); memb: Br Cardiac Soc (chm 1987), Scottish Soc of Physicians, Harveian Soc of Edinburgh (pres 1986-87 and Harveian Orator), many other prof socs; FRCP; FRCP (Edin); *Books* Text book of Physiology (8-11 edn, jt/ed), Accidental Hypothermia (1977), chapter in medical text books and papers in medical journals mainly on cardiac electrophysiology and hypothermia; *Recreations* music, fishing, sailing; *Clubs* Flyfishers, Royal Lymington Yacht; *Style*— Dr Donald Emslie-Smith; 48 Seafield Road, Broughty Ferry, Angus DD5 3AN; c/o Dept of Medicine, The University, Dundee DD1 4HN

EMSON, Colin Jack; s of Alfred Jack Emson, of Ashford, Kent, and Rose Florence Jobson (d 1987); *b* 25 July 1941; *Educ* Maidstone GS; *m* 14 Sept 1974, Jennifer Claire Lynch, da of Lt Col James Lynch, of Vancouver, Canada; 2 s (Alexander Chase b 1976, Henry James b 1980), 2 da (Annabel Christina b 1975, Camilla Rose b 1985);

Career md and princ shareholder Robert Frazer & Ptnrs Ltd 1979-; fndr ptnr Emson and Dudley 1966-79; *Recreations* polo, skiing, tennis; *Clubs* Turf, Naval and Military, Cowdray Park, Polo, St Moritz Tobogganing; *Style*— Colin J Emson, Esq; Shotters Farm, Newton Valence, nr Alton, Hampshire (☎ Tisted 222); Robert Fraser and Partners Ltd, 29 Albemarle Street, London W1 (☎ 01 493 3211, car telephone 0860 520 786)

EMSON, Air Marshal Sir Reginald Herbert Embleton; KBE (1966), CBE (1946, CB 1959, AFC 1941); s of Francis Reginald Emson, of Hitcham, Bucks; *b* 11 Jan 1912; *Educ* Christ's Hosp, RAF Coll Cranwell; *m* 1934, Doreen Marjory, da of Hugh Duke, of Holyport, Maidenhead, Berks 2 s, 2 da; *Career* joined RAF 1931, served WW II in Aeroplane Armament Experimental Establishment Gunnery Research Unit Exeter, Fighter Cmmd HQ, Centl Fighter Estab; Gp Capt 1943, dir Armament Research and Devpt (Air) Miny of Supply 1956-59; Air Cdre 1958, Cmdr RAF and Air Attaché Br Defence Staffs Washington 1961-63, Air Vice-Marshal 1962, Asst Chief of Air Staff (Operational Requirements) Air Miny 1963, MOD (RAF) 1964-66, Dep Chief of Air Staff 1966-67, Air Marshal 1966, Inspector-Gen RAF 1967-69, ret; *Clubs* RAF; *Style*— Air Marshal Sir Reginald Emson, KBE, CB, AFC; Vor Cottage, Holyport, Maidenhead, Berks (☎ 0628 21992)

ENCOMBE, Viscount; John Francis Thomas Marie Joseph Columba Fidelis Scott; s and h of 5 Earl of Eldon; *b* 9 July 1962; *Style*— Viscount Encombe

ENDACOTT, Colin William Gresham; OBE (1984); s of William Charles Endacott (d 1974), and Lily Alice,*née* Jeffs; *Educ* Shene Sch, Ashridge Mgmt Coll, Cranfield Sch of Mgmt; *m* 27 Nov 1965, Dianne Paula, da of Lemuel Eber Watkins, of NZ; 2 s (Chauncy, Romilly), 1 da (Tamsin); *Career* The Chartered Bank: overseas serv (India, Singapore, Thailand, Malaysia), chief mangr Singapore 1979-83; gen mangr standard chartered Bank London: former chm Singapore Int c of c ; *Recreations* golf, squash; *Clubs* Oriental, RAC; *Style*— Colin Endacott, Esq; 38 Bishopsgate, London EC2N 4DE (☎ 01 280 6700)

ENDACOTT, Patricia Ann (Pat); da of William Frederick Williams (d 1985), and Bertha Emma, *née* Sanderson; *b* 5 Mar 1946; *Educ* Newmarket GS, Univ of Sussex (BSc); *m* 17 June 1972 (m dis 1980), Michael John Endacott, s of Alfred John Endacott; *Career* programmer Pye of Cambridge Ltd 1968-71, programmer Standard Telephones and Cables Ltd 1971-72; Texas Instruments Ltd; customer serv (Croydon) 1972-76, mangr communications (ISD) 1976-80, mangr field serv (DSD) 1980-82; Prime Computer: dir customer serv (UK Ltd) 1982-85, mktg mangr products and systems (EMEA) 1985-86, dir UK software devpt (UK R&D Ltd) 1986-; MInstD 1988; *Recreations* running, reading, music; *Style*— Ms Pat Endacott; Prime Computer (R & D) Ltd, Willen Lake, Milton Keynes MK15 ODB (☎ 0908 666622, fax 0908 674406, car 0836 310626, telex 826157 PRMSMD G)

ENDERBY, (George Edward) Hale; s of George Alfred Enderby (d 1945) of Boston, Lincolnshire, and Gertrude, *née* Hale (d 1930); *b* 9 June 1915; *Educ* Kingswood Sch Bath, St John's Coll Cambridge (MA), Guy's Hosp London (MB BChi Cambridge); *m* 22 June 1940, Dorothy Frances, da of Arthur Watson Grocock (d 1957), of Boston, Lincolnshire; 1 s (David Hale b 1942), 2 da (Diana Frances b 1944, Angela Jane b 1946); *Career* conslt anaesthetist (then hon sr consultant); Maxillo-facial & jaw unit Rooksdown House, Basingstoke 1944-50; Metropolitan Ear, Nose & Throat Hosp 1948-50; Royal National Orthopaedic Hosp 1948-66; Queen Victoria Hosp E Grinstead 1950-80; fell and Board memb Faculty of anaesthetists RCS 1973-83 (examiner for fellowships 1975-82, faculty medal 1985); pres anaesthetics section RSM 1981-2; dir RCS 1979-; *Recreations* golf; *Clubs* Oxford and Cambridge, Royal Ashdown Forest Golf; *Style*— Hale Enderby, Esq; Furzefield Dormans Park, East Grinstead RH19 3NU (☎ 0342 87255); 149 Harley Street, London W1N 2DE (☎ 01 935 4444)

ENDERBY, Col Samuel; CVO (1977), DSO (1944, MC 1939); s of Col Samuel Herbert Enderby (d 1956), of The Halesend, by Malvern, Worcs, and Mary Cunninghame; *b* 15 Sept 1907; *Educ* Uppingham, RMC Sandhurst; *m* 1936, Pamela, eld da of Maj Charles Beck Hornby, DSO (d 1949), of Anick Cottage, Hexham, by his w Dorothy, da of C W Henderson; 2 s (Daniel, Charles), 1 da (Caroline); *Career* served as regular Royal Northumberland Fusiliers 1928-49 (WW II in N Africa & Italy), cmd 2/4 King's Own Yorks LI & 2/5 Leicester Regt during WW II, Cmdt Sch of Infantry Palestine; memb Corps of Gentlemen-at-Arms 1954-76, standard bearer 1975-76; High Sheriff Northumberland 1968; *Clubs* Army & Navy; *Style*— Col Samuel Enderby, CVO, DSO, MC; The Riding, Hexham, Northumberland (☎ 0434 602250)

ENERGLYN, Baroness; Jean Thompson; *née* Miller; da of John Miller, of Cardiff; *m* 15 March 1941, Baron Energlyn, DL (d 1985; Life Peer UK 1968); *Style*— The Rt Hon Lady Energlyn; The Dentons, Denton Road, Eastbourne, East Sussex BN20 7SW

ENFIELD, Viscount; William Robert Byng; s and h of 8 Earl of Strafford by his 1 wife, Jennifer Mary Denise, *née* May; *b* 10 May 1964; *Educ* Winchester, Durham Univ; *Style*— Viscount Enfield

ENGESET, Jetmund; s of Arne Kaare Engeset (d 1973), and Marta, *née* Birkeland; *b* 22 July 1938; *Educ* Slemdal and Ris Skoler Oslo Norway, Univ of Aberdeen (MB ChB, ChM); *m* 3 June 1966, Anne Graeme, da of Allan Graeme Robertson (d 1946); 2 da (Anne-Marie, Nina Katrine); *Career* sr lectr Univ of Aberdeen 1974-87, hon conslt surgn Grampian Health Bd 1974-87 (conslt surgn 1987-), surgn to HM The Queen in Scotland 1985-; FRCS(Ed) 1970, FRCS(Glas) 1982; *Recreations* skiing, squash, angling, gardening; *Style*— Jetmund Engeset, Esq; Pine Lodge, 315 North Deeside Rd, Milltimber, Aberdeen (☎ 0224 733753); Aberdeen Royal Infirmary, Foresterhill, Aberdeen (☎ 0224 681818)

ENGHOLM, Sir Basil Charles; KCB (1968), CB (1964); o s of Charles F G Engholm (d 1936), of London; *b* 2 August 1912; *Educ* Tonbridge, Sorbonne, Sidney Sussex Coll Cambridge; *m* 1936, Nancy, er da of Lifford Hewitt, of St Anthony, Rye, Sussex; 1 da; *Career* memb Gray's Inn; metal business New York 1933-34; joined Miny of Agric and Fisheries 1935, private sec to Min 1943-45, asst sec 1945, under-sec 1954, fisheries sec 1960-62, dep sec 1964-67, perm sec Miny Ag Fish and Food 1968-72; memb Landcape Advsy Ctee Dept of Transport 1973-84, dir Comfin Ltd 1973-84, chm BFI 1978-81, dir Sadler's Wells Theatre 1975-, tstee Theatres Tst 1977-84; *Style*— Sir Basil Engholm, KCB; 93 Meadway, London NW11 6QH (☎ 01 455 3975)

ENGLAND, Colin Philip; s of Harry Richard England, of Langton Green, Tunbridge Wells, Kent, and Edith Francis, *née* Martin; *b* 4 Feb 1937; *Educ* Open Univ (BA, Dip Municipal Admin), Associate Chartered Inst of Secretaries and Administrators; *m* 28 Sept 1963, Christine Elaine, da of Reginald George Henry Paskins Twitchen (d 1974), of Bexleyheath; 1 s (Neil David b 12 Nov 1966), 1 da (Joanne Caroline b 26 May 1975); *Career* chief exec (UK) Money Concepts 1988-; dir: Genesis (UK) Ltd Hldgs, Genesis (Fin Servs), Genesis (Recruitment Servs), Genesis (Business Servs); govr Ravensbourne Sch for Girls Bromley Kent; Freeman City of London, Liveryman Worshipful Co of Masons; ACISA 1984; *Style*— Colin England, Esq; 36 The Chase, Bromley, Kent BR1 3DF (☎ 01 464 0563); 37 Spring St, Londn W2 1JA (☎ 01 706 4084, fax 01 706 4083)

ENGLAND, Glyn; JP; *b* 19 April 1921; *Educ* Penarth Co Sch, Queen Mary Coll London Univ, LSE; *m* 1942, Tania, *née* Reichenbach; 2 da; *Career* served WW II 1942-47; Electricity Supply Ind 1974-, chief operations engr CEBG 1966-71, dir-gen SW Region 1971-73, chm SW Electricity Bd 1973-77, chm Centl Electricity Generating Bd 1977-82 (part-time memb 1975-77); non-exec dir: F H Lloyd Hldgs 1982-87, dir Triplex Lloyd plc 1987-; conslt to World Bank; chm: Cncl for Environmental Conservation 1983-, Dartington Institute 1985-; FEng, FIEE, FIMechE, CBIM; *Recreations* actively enjoying the countryside; *Style*— Glyn England, Esq, JP; Woodbridge Farm, Ubley, Bristol (☎ 0761 62479)

ENGLE, Sir George Lawrence Jose; KCB (1983), CB (1976, QC 1983); o s of late Lawrence Engle; *b* 13 Sept 1926; *Educ* Charterhouse, Ch Ch Oxford; *m* 1956, Irene, da of Heinz Lachmann (d 1971); 3 da; *Career* barr Lincoln's Inn 1953-57 (bencher 1984), entered Parly Counsel Off 1957, seconded as first parly counsel to Fed Govt of Nigeria 1965-67, parly counsel 1970-80, with Law Cmmn 1971-73, second parly counsel 1980-81, first parly counsel 1981-86, pres Cwlth Assoc of Legislative Cncl 1983-86; *Publications* Law for Landladies (1955), contributor to Ideas (1954), O Rare Hoffnung (1960), Oxford Companion to English Literature (1985), co-ed, Cross on Statutory Interpretation (2nd ed, 1987); *Style*— Sir George Engle, KCB, QC; 32 Wood Lane, Highgate, London N6 5UB (☎ 01 340 9750)

ENGLEDON, Geoffrey; MBE (1982); s of William Engledon, of Birmingham, and Barbara, *née* Wild; *b* 20 May 1936; *Educ* King Edwards Sch Birmingham, Aston Univ (BSc); *m* 12 Aug 1961, Anne Lettice Flora Louise, da of Harry Higton BEM, of Erdington, Birminghan; 1 s (Alex Harry); *Career* tech dir: Thermalite (Holdings) Ltd, Thermalite Ltd, Thermalite Scotland Ltd; dir: Thermalite Employee Shares (Trustee) Ltd; *Recreations* fly fishing, model making, reading, gardening; *Clubs* Sloane, Royal Overseas; *Style*— Geoffrey Engledon, Esq; 31 New Road, Water Orton, Birmingham B46 1QP; Thermalite Ltd, Station Road, Coleshill, Birmingham B46 1HP (telex 335969, fax 0675 65445)

ENGLEHART, Robert Michael; QC; s of G A F Englehart (d 1969), of London, and of Mrs P K Englehart, *née* Harvey (d 1973); *b* 1 Oct 1943; *Educ* St Edward's Sch Oxford, Trinity Coll Oxford (MA), Harvard Law Sch (LLM), Bologna Centre; *m* 2 Jan 1971, Rosalina Mary, da of L A Foster, of Greatham Manor, Sussex; 1 s (Oliver b 1982), 2 da (Alice b 1976, Lucinda b 1978); *Career* assistente Univ of Florence 1967-68; called to the Bar & practising barrister 1969-, QC (1986), rec of the Crown Ct 1987-; vice chm London Common Law and Commercial Bar Assoc 1988; *Books* Il Controllo Giudiziario: a Comparative Study in Civil Procedure (contrib 1968); *Recreations* shooting, cricket, windsurfing; *Clubs* MCC; *Style*— Robert Englehart, Esq, QC; 2 Hare Court, Temple, London EC4Y 7BH (☎ 01 583 1770, fax 01 583 9269, telex 27139 LINLAW)

ENGLEHEART, Henry Francis Arnold; DL (Suffolk, 1988); s of Francis Henry Arnold Engleheart (d 1963), of The Priory, Stoke by Nayland, Suffolk, and Filumena Mary, *née* Mayne (d 1983); *b* 18 Mar 1930; *Educ* Ampleforth Coll, Downing Coll Cambridge (MA); *m* 9 June 1979, Victoria, da of Maj Ian Maitland Pelham Burn (d 1985), of Elenge Plat, Colgate, Horsham, Sussex; 1 s (John b 22 Oct 1981), 2 da (Lucy b 8 May 1980, Mary b 28 April 1985); *Career* land agent and chartered surveyor 1955-62, farmer 1957-, chm Suffolk Preservation Soc 1969-72; memb: Melford RDC 1964-74, Babergh DC 1973- (chm 1979-82); High Sheriff of Suffolk 1986; RICS 1956; *Style*— Henry Engleheart, Esq, DL; The Priory, Stoke by Nayland, Suffolk CO6 4RL (☎ 0206 262 216)

ENGLISH, Cyril; s of Joseph English, and Mary Hannah English; *b* 18 Feb 1923; *Educ* Ashton-under-Lyne GS; *m* 1945, Mary Brockbank; 2 da; *Career* Nationwide Anglia Building Soc; asst sec 1961, asst gen mangr 1967, gen mangr 1971, dep chief gen mangr 1974, dir 1978, chief gen mangr 1981-85, dep chm 1989; chm Nationwide Housing Tst Ltd 1987-; *Recreations* golf, music; *Clubs* Calcot Park GC, Reading; *Style*— Cyril English, Esq; Ashton Grange, Cedar Drive, Flowers Hill, Pangbourne, Berks RG8 7BH (☎ 073 57 3841); Nationwide Anglia Building Society, Chesterfield Ho, Bloomsbury Way, London WC1V 6PW (☎ 01 242 8822)

ENGLISH, Sir Cyril Rupert; s of William James English; *b* 19 April 1913; *Educ* Northgate Sch Ipswich; *m* 1936, Eva Violet, da of George Alfred Moore; 2 s; *Career* served RN 1939-46; tech teacher 1935-39; HM Inspr of Schools: inspr 1946-55, staff inspr 1955-58, chief inspr 1948-65, sr chief inspr 1965-68; dir-gen City and Guilds of London Institute 1968-76; kt 1972; *Style*— Sir Cyril English; 12 Pineheath Rd, High Kelling, Holt, Norfolk

ENGLISH, Sir David; *b* 26 May 1931; *Educ* Bournemouth Sch; *m* 1954, Irene Mainwood; 1 s, 2 da; *Career* took over editorial responsibility for *Mail on Sunday* July-Nov 1982, ed *Daily Mail* 1971-, *Daily Sketch* 1969-71 (feature ed 1956-59), assoc ed *Daily Express* 1967-69 (foreign ed 1965-67, ch US correspondent 1963-65, Washington correspondent 1961-63, joined 1960), foreign correspondent *Sunday Dispatch* 1959-60, with *Daily Mirror* 1951-53; kt 1982; *Style*— Sir David English; c/o Daily Mail, Fleet St, London EC4Y 0JA (☎ 01 353 6000)

ENGLISH, Terence Alexander Hawthorne; s of Arthur Alexander English (d 1934), and Mavis Eleanor, *née* Lund (d 1959); *b* 3 Oct 1932; *Educ* Hilton Coll SA, Witwaterstrand Univ SA (BSc), Guy's Hosp Med Sch (MB, BS), Cambridge Univ (MA); *m* 23 Nov 1963, Ann Margaret, da of Mordaunt Dicey (d 1964); 2 s (Arthur Alexander b 1968, William Andrew b 1971) 2 da (Katharine Ann b 1967, Mary Eleanor b 1970); *Career* sr surgical registrar Brompton and Nat Heart Hosps 1968-72, conslt cardiothoracic Surgn Papworth and Addenbrookes Hosps 1973-, dir heart transplant res Unit Br Heart Fndn 1980-88, conslt cardiac advsr Wellington Hosp London 1982-88, pres Int Soc for Heart Transplantation 1984 and 1985; cncl memb: RCS 1981, GMC 1983-, FRCS 1967, FACC 1986, MRCP 1987; *Recreations* tennis, walking, reading; *Style*— Terence English, Esq; 19 Adams Rd, Cambridge CB3 9AD (☎ 0223 68744); Papworth Hosp, Cambs CB3 8RE

ENGLISH, Terence Michael; s of John Robert English, of Edmonton, London, and Elsie Letitia, *née* Edwards; *b* 3 Feb 1944; *Educ* St Ignatius Coll Stamford Hill London, London Univ (LLB ext); *m* 23 July 1966, Ivy Joan da of Charles William Weatherley (d

1959), of Wood Green, London, 1 s (Andrew b 1972), 1 da (Melanie b 1967); *Career* solicitor of Supreme Ct 1970; clerk to justices: Newbury Hungerford & Lambourn (now W Berks) 1977-85, Slough & Windsor 1985-86; met stipendiary magistrate 1986-, memb East Berk Family conciliation serv; *Recreations* golf, watching sport; *Style*— Terence English, Esq; Wells Street Magistrates Court, 59-65 Wells St, London W1A 3AE (☎ 01 436 8600)

ENNALS, Baron (Life Peer UK 1983), of Norwich, Co Norfolk; David Hedley Ennals; PC (1970); s of Capt Arthur Ford Ennals, MC (d 1977), and Jessie Edith, *née* Taylor; bro of John Arthur Ford Ennals, former dir UK Immigrants Advsy Service, and Martin Ennals,*qv*; *b* 19 August 1922; *Educ* Queen Mary's GS Walsall, Loomis Inst Connecticut; *m* 1, 1950 (m dis 1977), Eleanor Maud, da of Reginald Victor Caddick, of Bath; 3 s, 1 da; m 2, 1977, Mrs Katherine Tranoy; *Career* served WW II Capt RAC; sec UN Assoc 1952-57, overseas sec Labour Party 1957-64, MP (Lab) Dover 1964-70, Norwich North Feb 1974-83, Social Servs sec 1976-79, min state DHSS 1968-70 and FCO 1974-76, parly under-sec Home Off 1967-68 and Army 1966-67, PPS to min Overseas Dvpt 1964 and min Transport 1966; chm Cncl Ockenden Venture 1979-, memb Horn of Africa and Aden Cncl 1984-; *Style*— The Rt Hon Lord Ennals, PC; House of Lords, London SW1A 0AA

ENNALS, Hon John Richard; s of Baron Ennals, PC (Life Peer) by his first w; *b* 16 Sept 1951; *Style*— Hon John Ennals

ENNALS, Kenneth Frederick John; CB (1983); s of Ernest and Elsie Dorothy Ennals; *b* 10 Jan 1932; *Educ* Alleyn's Sch Dulwich, LSE; *m* 1958, Mavis Euphemia; 1 s, 2 da; *Career* dep sec Dept of the Environment 1980-87 (asst sec 1970, under-sec 1976-80); memb Local Govt Boundary Cmmr; *Clubs* Royal Cwlth Soc; *Style*— Kenneth Ennals, Esq, CB; Skitreadons, Petworth Road, Haslemere, Surrey (☎ Haslemere 2733)

ENNALS, Martin; s of Capt Arthur Ford Ennals, MC (d 1977), and Jessie Edith, *née* Taylor; bro of Baron Ennals, PC, *qv*; *b* 27 July 1927; *Educ* Queen Mary's Sch Walsall, LSE (BSc); *m* 1951, Jacqueline B Morris; 1 s, 1 da; *Career* int human rights campaigner and conslt UNESCO 1951-59; memb Nat Cncl for Civil Liberties 1959-66; Nat Ctee for Cwlth Immigrants 1966-68; Sec Gen Amnesty Int 1968-80; Conslt to: UNICEF, UNESCO, Cncl of Europe, United Nations and Greater London Cncl 1980-84; established 'Article 19' (Freedom of Info) 1985/6, sec gen of Int Alert concerned with internal conflict, human rights and development 1986-, first chair Euro Human Rights Fndn and of the int Human Rights Info and Documentation Systems (HURIDOCS), Chair UK Human Rights Network 1974-88; *Style*— Martin Ennals, Esq; 157 Southwood Lane, London N6 (☎ 01 340 8629)

ENNALS, Hon Paul Martin; s of Baron Ennals, PC (Life Peer) by his first w; *b* 7 Nov 1957; *Style*— Hon Paul Ennals

ENNALS, Hon Simon; s of Baron Ennals, PC (Life Peer) by his first w; *b* 14 Nov 1959; *Style*— Hon Simon Ennals

ENNALS, Hon Susan; da of Baron Ennals, PC (Life Peer) by his first w; *b* 26 Oct 1953; *Style*— Hon Susan Ennals

ENNISKILLEN, 6 Earl of (I 1789); David Lowry Cole; MBE (1954), JP (Co Fermanagh 1972); also Baron Mountflorence (I 1760), Viscount Enniskillen (I 1776) and Baron Grinstead (UK 1815); s of Hon Galbraith Lowry Egerton Cole (d 1929; 3 s of 4 Earl of Enniskillen), and Lady Eleanor Balfour (d 1979), da of 2 Earl of Balfour; suc unc 5 Earl 1963; *b* 10 Sept 1918; *Educ* Eton, Trinity Coll Cambridge (BA); *m* 1, 31 July 1940 (m dis 1955), Sonia Mary (d 1982), da of late Maj Thomas Syers by his w Mary (who, after the Maj's death, m, as his 2 w, the 5 Earl); 1 s, 1 da; m 2, 7 May 1955, Nancy Henderson, da of late Dr John Alexander MacLennan, of Bridgeport, Conn, USA; *Heir* s, Viscount Cole; *Career* serv WWII Capt Irish Gds; Cmdt Kenya Police Reserve 1950-55; Capt Ulster Def Regt 1971-73; agriculturist; former memb Kenya Meat Cmmn, exec KNFU, vice-chm Kenya Stockowners, memb exec Kenya Bd of Agric, memb Land and Agric Bank of Kenya, chm Solio Ranch Ltd, memb bd EA Diatomite Syndicate Ltd; memb: Kenya Legislative Cncl 1961-63, Fermanagh CC (Finance) 1963-69; DL Co Fermanagh 1963-76; memb Wright Int Bd of Economic & Investment Advisors 1987-; *Recreations* forestry, fishing, shooting, golf; *Clubs* Carlton, Turf, Muthaiga Country (Nairobi), New (Edinburgh), Royal Perth Golfing Society, Cavalry and Guards'; *Style*— The Rt Hon Earl of Enniskillen, MBE, JP; Kinloch House, Amulree, Dunkeld, Perthsire PH8 0EB

ENNISMORE, Viscount; Francis Michael Hare; s (by 3 m) and h of 5 Earl of Listowel, GCMG, PC; *b* 28 June 1964; *Style*— Viscount Ennismore

ENNOR, George Patrick Francis; s of Patrick George Albert Ennor, of Byfleet, Surrey, and Phyllis Mary Ennor, *née* Veitch; *b* 17 Dec 1940; *Educ* Malvern Coll; *m* 30 April 1966 (m dis), Martha Bridget Liddell, da of Lewis Civval (d 1973), of Ockley, Surrey; 2 s (Julian b 1970, Daniel b 1973), 1 da (Charlotte b 1968); *Career* racing journalist; The Sporting Life 1960-85 (sr correspondent 1984-85), chief reporter The Racing Post 1985-; pres Horserace Writers and Reporters Assoc 1974-; *Recreations* history, crime, politics, Portsmouth FC; *Style*— George P F Ennor, Esq; 59 Blenheim Rd, Horsham, Sussex (☎ 0403 60 821); The Racing Post, 120 Coombe Lane, London SW20 (☎ 01 879 3377)

ENRIGHT, Derek Anthony; s of Lawrence Enright (d 1962), and Helen Smith, *née* Burns; *b* 2 August 1935; *Educ* St Michael's Coll Leeds, Wadham Coll Oxford (BA Hons, DipEd); *m* 1963, Jane Maureen, da of late Geoffrey Simmons; 2 s (Duncan b 1964, Simon b 1969), 2 da (Amanda b 1965, Jacqueline b 1967); *Career* dep headmaster St Wilfrid's HS Featherstone 1970-79; MEP Leeds 1979-84; del of EEC to Guinea Bissau 1985-87; conslt EEC; Distinção de Merito da Republica da Guine Bissau; *Style*— Derek Enright, Esq; The Hollies, 112 Carleton Rd, Pontefract, W Yorks; Ave Emil Max 98, 1040 Brussels

ENSOM, Donald; s of Charles R A W Ensom (d 1953), and Edith, *née* Young (d 1942); *b* 8 April 1926; *Educ* Norbury Manor Sch Surrey; *m* 11 Sept 1951, Sonia Florence, da of John Brockington Sherrard, of Westcott, Surrey; 1 s (Paul Charles b 1952), 1 da (Jacqueline Elizabeth b 1955); *Career* Sgt RA Survey 1943-47, WOII Surrey Yeo 1949-53; ptnr Debenham Tewson & Chinnocks (formerly Nightingale Page & Bennett) 1958-86 (conslt 1986-); RICS: pres Building Surveyor's Div 1975-76, chm Professional Practice Ctee 1978-83, chm RICS Insur Servs Ltd 1981-83 Hon Sec 1983-, VP 1988-; chm Building Conservation Tst 1980-83; Freeman City of London, Livery Worshipful Co of Chartered Surveyors; ARICS 1951, FRICS 1958, FCI Arb 1970; *Recreations* opera, music, social and transport history, caravanning, canals; *Clubs* East India; *Style*— Donald Ensom, Esq; Saxons, Grange Rd, Cambridge, CB3 9AA (☎ 0223 329706)

ENSOR, (George) Anthony; s of George Ensor, of Maesgwyn, Ala Road, Pwllheli, Gwynedd, and Phyllis, *née* Harrison; *b* 4 Nov 1936; *Educ* Malvern Coll, Liverpool Univ (LLB); *m* 14 Sept 1968, Jennifer Margaret, *née* Caile; 2 da (Elizabeth b 1972, Jane b 1978); *Career* slr 1961; dep coroner (city of Liverpool) 1966-, pt/t chm Indust Tbnls 1975-, dep judge Crown Ct 1979-, Recorder of the Crown Ct 1983-; dir Liverpool FC 1985-, tstee Empire Theatre Liverpool 1986-, memb Judicial Studies Bd 1986-; pres: Artists Club Liverpool 1976, Liverpool Law Soc 1982; *Recreations* golf; *Clubs* Artists (Liverpool), Formby Golf, Waterloo Rugby; *Style*— Anthony Ensor, Esq; 23 Far Moss Road, Blundellsands, Liverpool L23 8TG (☎ 051 924 5937); Weightman Rutherfords, Richmond House, 1 Rumford Place, Liverpool L3 9QW (☎ 051 227 2601, fax 051 227 3223, telex 627538)

ENSOR, David; OBE; s of Rev William Walters Ensor (d 1967), and Constance Eva Ensor; *b* 2 April 1924; *Educ* Kingswood Sch Bath; *m* 1947, Gertrude Kathleen, da of Herbert Brown (d 1947); 2 s; *Career* WWII Royal Signals, ADC to GOC Bengal Dist SEAC; md: Knapp Drewett & Sons Ltd 1969-79, Croydon Advertiser Ltd 1979-85; vice-pres Methodist Conf 1981, vice chm Press Cncl 1987 (memb 1982-) ; *Style*— David Ensor, Esq, OBE; Milborne Lodge, Dinton Rd, Fovant, Salisbury, Wilts SP3 5JW (☎ 072 270 521)

ENSOR WALTERS, Peter Hugh Bennetts; OBE (1957); s of Rev Charles Ensor Walters (d 1938), of London, and Muriel Havergal, *née* Bennetts (d 1966); *b* 18 July 1912; *Educ* Manor House Sch, St Peter's Coll Univ Oxford; *m* 19 March 1936, (Ella) Marcia, da of Percival Burdle Hayter; *Career* vol enlistment Army 1940, cmmnd RAPC 1942, invalided out 1943; staff of late Rt Hon David Lloyd George 1935-39, nat agent Wales and W England 1939-40, gen sec Nat Liberal Orgn 1951-58 (nat organiser GB 1944-51),, PR conslt 1959-; pres Central Worthing Cons Assoc 1983-89; former MIPR, FInstD; *Recreations* travel; *Clubs* Union Soc Oxford; *Style*— Peter Ensor Walters, Esq, OBE; 2 Hopedene Ct, Wordsworth Rd, Worthing, W Sussex BN11 1TB (☎ 0903 205 678)

ENTICKNAP, Dr John Brandon; s of Walter John Enticknap (d 1971), and Dorothy Constance, *née* Silk (d 1972); *b* 28 Feb 1922; *Educ* King Edward VI Royal GS Guildford, Kings Coll London, Charing Cross and Guy's Hosp Med Sch; *m* 1, 27 May 1944, Winifred Mary Graham, da of Andrew Graham Grieve (d 1968); 3 s (Nicholas b 1947, Jonathan b 1948, Alasdair b 1950); m 2, 15 Dec 1972, Pauline Mavis, da of Samuel Tickle Meadow (d 1973); *Career* Capt RAMC served W Africa 1947-49; conslt chemical pathologist NW Thames RHB 1954-82, coroners pathologist Eastern District Greater London 1954-; MD London 1952, MB BS 1945, DCP 1946, FRC Path 1966; *Recreations* manual work; *Clubs* Athenaeum; *Style*— Dr John B Enticknap; Tinkers, Wesley End, Stambourne, Halstead, Essex CO9 4PG (☎ 044 085 316); 15 Guilford St, London WC1N 1DX (☎ 01 405 0839)

ENTRACT, Norman (Leslie); s of Charles Edward Entract (formerly Eintracht) (d 1960), and Edith Amy, *née* Furlong (d 1972); *b* 19 Mar 1918; *Educ* Hornsey Co Sch; *m* 22 July 1961, Dorothy Marjorie Evelyn, da of William Harold Simmons (d 1965); *Career* WW II (WO1) RAOC served 4 years India 1939-45; stamp dealer and dir leading London dealers assoc for 25 years; hon sec Kipling Soc; *Recreations* theatre, opera, reading, gardening; *Clubs* Travellers, Royal Cwlth Soc; *Style*— Norman L Entract, Esq; Fairfield, Three Oates Lane, Haslemere GU27 2LD (☎ 52709)

ENTWISTLE, John; DL (Lancs 1983); s of Herbert Entwistle (d 1980), and Clara Entwistle (d 1981); *b* 16 July 1932; *Educ* St Thomas Primary RC Sch, St Marys RC Cntl Sch Burnley Lancs; *m* 1962, Kathleen, da of Patrick Mooney (d 1963); 3 s, 1 da; *Career* Br Telecom engr; co cllr Lancashire; chm Police Authority; active trade unionist, branch sec National Communications Union; *Recreations* cycling (England team 1958), golf; *Style*— John Entwistle, Esq, DL; 47 Pritchard St, Burnley, Lancs BB11 4JT (☎ 0282 53480); c/o LN13 TEC, Centenery Way, Burnley, Lancs (☎ 0282 34876)

ENTWISTLE, Sir (John Nuttall) Maxwell; s of Isaac Entwistle (d 1954), of Formby, Liverpool, and Hannah Entwistle; *b* 8 Jan 1910; *Educ* Merchant Taylors' Sch Great Crosby; *m* 1940, Jean Cunliffe McAlpine, da of John Penman, MD ChB (d 1952); 2 s; *Career* served RN 1944-46; slr 1931, notary public 1955, conslt to Maxwell Entwistle & Byrne (slrs) Liverpool; City of Liverpool: cllr 1938-60, alderman 1960-64, ldr CC 1961-63 (when he initiated plans for redevpt of City Centre); underwriting memb of Lloyd's 1964-; pres Edge Hill Conservative Assoc 1965-70, pres Old Boys' Assoc 1969-70, govr Boys' and Girls' Schs 1970-75; chm Liverpool Abbeyfield Soc 1970-75; kt 1963; *Recreations* gardening, shooting; *Style*— Sir Maxwell Entwistle; Stone Hall, Sedbergh, Cumbria (☎ 0587 20700)

ENTWISTLE, Peter John; s of Herbert Entwistle (d 1988), of Bolton, Lancs, and Winifred Alice Lilian, *née* Fullex (d 1963); *b* 3 June 1933; *Educ* St John's Coll Johannesburg SA, Rhodes Univ Grahamstown SA (BSc), Lincoln Coll Oxford (BA); *m* 4 Jan 1958, Pamela, *née* Ashby; 1 s (Timothy b 1961), 1 da (Sarah-Jane b 1959); *Career* Barclays Bank DCO 1960-63, IBM (UK) Ltd 1963-71, Lloyds Bank 1972 (asst gen mangr 1984) dir BACS 1985; memb Diabetes and Related Diseases Res Assoc; ACIB 1962; *Recreations* gardening, furniture restoration; *Style*— Peter Entwistle, Esq; 1 De Crespigny Park, Camberwell, London SE5; Parc De La Croisette, Bvd Alexandre III, Cannes, France; Lloyds Bank plc, 71 Lombard St, London EC3

ENTWISTLE, Phillida Gail Sinclair; JP (Liverpool 1980); da of Geoffrey Burgess, CMG, CIE, OBE (d 1972), and Jillian Margaret Eskens, *née* Hope; *b* 7 Jan 1944; *Educ* Cheltenham Ladies' Coll, London Univ (BSc), Liverpool Univ (PhD); *m* 6 Sept 1968, John Nicholas McAlpine Entwistle, s of Sir (John Nuttall) Maxwell Entwistle, of Stone Hall, Sedbergh, Cumbria; 1 s (Nicholas b 1970), 1 da (Louise b 1971); *Career* gen cmmr of Inland Revenue 1985-; memb Mersey Regnl Health Authy 1987-; dir J Davey & Sons (Liverpool) Ltd 1983-; govr Liverpool Poly 1988-; FRSA; *Style*— Mrs Phillida Entwistle, JP; Gorstage Hall, Cuddington, Cheshire CW8 2SG (☎ 0606 888830)

EPPEL, Leonard Cedric; s of Dr David Eppel (d 1963), of Bickenhall Mansions, Baker St, London W1, and Vera, *née* Diamond (d 1973); *b* 24 June 1928; *Educ* Highgate Sch; *m* 15 July 1954, Barbara Priscilla, da of Robert Silk, of Dorset House, Gloucester Place, London W1; 1 s (Stuart Neil b 26 March 1959), 1 da (Rochelle Eleanor b 7 Oct 1956); *Career* md Silks Estates Investmts Ltd 1968 (dir 1954); chm: Arrowcroft Gp plc 1969, Albert Dock co Ltd 1983; vice pres British Red Cross Soc (Merseyside), dir Merseyside Tourist Bd Ltd 1986; dir Millwall FC 1971 (chm 1979-83); Freeman City of London, Freeman Worshipful Co of Fletchers 1984; FVI 1962, FSVA 1968, Fell IOD 1987; *Recreations* jogging, golf; *Clubs* Carlton; *Style*— Leonard

Eppel, Esq; 24 Hanover Square, London W1R 9DD (☎ 01 499 5432, fax 01 493 0323, car tel 0860 623 351)

EPPS, Hon Mrs (Pamela Anne); *née* Moncreiff; ya da of 4 Baron Moncreiff (d 1942); *b* 17 July 1927; *Educ* Dollar Acad, Edinburgh Univ (MB, ChB 1950); *m* 1, 24 Sept 1951 (m dis 1973), Edward James White, s of Henry Thomas White, of Edinburgh; 2 s, 2 da; m 2, 1979, Ernest Frederic Epps (d 1987), s of Reginald George Epps (d 1937); *Career* general medical practitioner under name of Dr White; *Style*— Hon Mrs Epps; 13 Barntongate Ave, Edinburgh EH4 8BQ (☎ 031 667 1577); Ardchoille, Eredine, by Dalmally, Argyll; office: 14 Rankeillor St, Edinburgh EH8 9HY (☎ 031 607 1577)

EPSTEIN, David Leslie; s of Samuel Epstein (d 1969), of London, and Bessie, *née* Silver; *b* 31 August 1938; *Educ* Tottenham GS; *m* 13 Dec 1964, Adele, da of Barnet Kosky (d 1985), of Leicester; 1 da (Amanda b 1966); *Career* Nat Serv SAC RAF; jt md Kuoni Travel Ltd 1969-81, dir gen Assoc of Br Travel Agents (ABTA) 1987-; FICA 1966, memb of Travel and Tourism 1987; *Recreations* amateur stage performing (drama and musical); *Style*— David L Epstein, Esq; Dalebrook, 5 Crooked Usage, Finchley, London N3 3HD (☎ 01 346 3244); 55-57 Newman Street, London W1P 4AH (01 637 2444)

EPSTEIN, Hon Mrs (Edwina Maureen); *née* Stanley; da of 6 Baron Stanley of Alderley; *b* 19 Jan 1933; *m* 1, 5 Jan 1953 (m dis 1966), John Dawnay Innes (d 17 July 1966), 2 s of Lt-Col James Archibald Innes, DSO, of Horringer Manor, Bury St Edmunds, Suffolk; 2 s, 1 da; m 2, 25 Oct 1968, Joshua Philip Epstein, s of Dr Samuel Hyman Epstein, of Boston Mass; *Style*— Hon Mrs Epstein; 22 Stevenage Rd, London SW6 (☎ 01 736 5034)

ERCOLANI, Lucian Brett; DSO, DFC; s of Lucian Randolph Ercolani, OBE (d 1976), and Eva May, *née* Brett; *b* 9 August 1917; *Educ* Oundle; *m* 16 June 1941, Cynthia Violet, da of Major James Douglas, MC (d 1938) 1 da (Jane (Mrs Reynolds) b 10 Aug 1950); *Career* RAF 1940-46, PO Flt Lt 214 Sqdn 1941, Sqdn Ldr 99 Sqdn 1942, Sqdn Ldr 355 Sqdn 1943, Wing Cdr OC 99 Sqdn 1944, Wing Cdr OC 159 Sqdn 1944-45; Ercol Furniture Ltd: joined 1934, jt md 1946, chm 1976-; govr Bucks Coll of Higher Educn, pres Radnage Branch Royal Br Legion; Freeman: City of London 1953, Worshipful Co of Furniture Makers 1953 (Master 1980-81), Worshipful Co of Turners 1959; *Recreations* sailing; *Clubs* RAF, Royal Southern YC Royal Cruising; *Style*— Lucian B Ercolani, Esq, DSO, DFC; Neighbours, Radnage, High Wycombe, Bucks HP14 4BY (☎ 024 026 2133); Ercol Furniture Ltd, London Rd, High Wycombe, Bucks HP13 7AE (☎ 0494 21261, fax 0494 462467, telex 83616)

ERDMAN, Edward Louis; s of Henry David Erdman (d 1945), and Pauline, *née* Jarvis (d 1950); *b* 4 July 1906; *Educ* Grocers' Company Sch; *m* 22 Dec 1949, Pamela, da of late John Howard Mason; 1 s (Timothy James b 1953); *Career* 1937 TA KRRC, Capt N Africa and Italy 1939-45; apprenticeship surveyors off 1923, fndr of Edward Erdman, surveyors 1934, ret, conslt 1974-; dir: Chesterfield Properties plc 1960 (chm 1979), Warnford Investments plc 1962; World of Property Housing Tst (now Sanctuary Housing) Assoc: memb central cncl 1974, chm 1978, pres 1987; memb Poperty Advsy Panel to Treasy 1975-77; FSVA, FRSA; *Books* People and Property (1982); *Recreations* football, farming, cycling, athletics; *Clubs* IOD, Annabels, Naval and Military; *Style*— Edward Erdman, Esq; Edward Erdman, Surveyors, 6 Grosvenor Street, London W1X 0AD (☎ 01 629 8191, fax: 01 409 2757)

EREAUT, Sir (Herbert) Frank (Cobbold); s of Herbert Parker Ereaut and May Julia, *née* Cobbold; *b* 6 May 1919; *Educ* Tormore Sch Upper Deal Kent, Cranleigh Sch Surrey, Exeter Coll Oxford; *m* 1942, Kathleen FitzGibbon; 1 da; *Career* served WW II RASC, N Africa, Italy, NW Europe; barr Inner Temple 1947; slr-gen Jersey 1958-62, attorney-gen 1962-69, dep bailiff of Jersey 1969-74, bailiff of Jersey 1975-85, judge of the Ct of Appeal in Guernsey 1976-; dir Standard Chartered Bank (CI) Ltd, chm TSB Fndn for the Channel Islands; KStJ 1983 (CStJ 1978); kt 1976; *Recreations* music, gardening, travel; *Style*— Sir Frank Ereaut; Les Cypres, St John, Jersey, CI (☎ 0534 22317)

EREMIN, Prof Oleg; s of Theodore Eremin, of Melbourne, Aust, and Maria, *née* Avramenko (d 1978); *b* 12 Nov 1938; *Educ* Christian Brothers Coll Melbourne Aust, Univ of Melbourne (MB, BS, MD); *m* 23 Feb 1968, Jennifer Mary, da of Ellis Charles Ching (d 1972), of Melbourne, Aust; 2 s (Andrew b 1972, Nicholas b 1973), 1 da (Katharine b 1968); *Career* asst surg Royal Melbourne Hosp Aust 1971-72 (formerly house offr, sr house offr and registrar 1965-71), sr registrar Combined Norwich Hosps 1972-74, sr res assoc in immunology Dept of Pathology Cambridge Univ 1977-80 (res asst 1974-77), sr lectr and conslt surgn Edinburgh Royal Infirmary 1981-85, prof surg and conslt surg Aberdeen Royal Infirmary; FRACS, FRCSE, Surgical Res Soc, Assoc of Surgs GB and I, James IV Assoc of Surgs; *Recreations* classical music, literature, sport; *Style*— Prof Oleg Eremin; 3 The Chanonry, Aberdeen AB2 1RP (☎ 0224 484065); Dept of Surgery, Univ Med Bldgs, Foresterhill, Aberdeen AB9 2ZD (☎ 0224 681818, ext 53004)

ERICKSON, Prof Charlotte Joanne; da of Knut Eric Erickson (d 1965), of Rock Island, Illinois, and Lael Alberta Regina, *née* Johnson (d 1983); *b* 22 Oct 1923; *Educ* Augustana Coll Rock Is Illinois (BA), Cornell Univ NY (MA, PhD); *m* 19 July 1952, (Glen) Louis Watt, s of Thomas Watt (d 1941), of Dover; 2 s (Thomas b 1956, David b 1958); *Career* instr Vassar Coll Poughkeepsie NY 1950-52, res fell NIESR London 1952-55; LSE 1955-83: asst lectr, lectr, sr lectr, reader, prof; Paul Mellen prof of american hist Cambridge Univ 1983-; FRHS 1970; *Books* American Industry and the European Immigrant (1957), British Industrialists, Steel and hosiery (1959), Invisible Immigrants (1974), Emigration from Europe, 1815-1914 (1976); *Recreations* music, gardening; *Clubs* CCC Cambridge; *Style*— Prof Charlotte Erickson; 8 High St, Chesterton, Cambridge CB4 1NG (☎ 0223 323 184); History Faculty, West Road, Cambridge CB3 9EF (☎ 0223 335 315)

ERICKSON, Raymond John; s of Lawrence Erickson (d 1968), of Penarth, and Olive Annie (d 1983); *b* 2 August 1926; *Educ* Penarth Co Sch; *m* 7 March 1964, Mary Frances, da of Thomas Brian (d 1981), of Barry; 1 da (Lisa b 1964); *Career* Nat Serv 1944-48, India, Burma, Malasia, Singapore, Japan; mgmnt accountant, chm John Curran Ltd, dir 1976-; *Style*— Raymond J Erickson, Esq; 5 Minehead Ave, Sully, Penarth CF6 2TH; John Curran Ltd, PO Box 72, Curran Road, Cardiff CF1 1TE

ERITH, Robert Felix; TD (1977); eld s of Felix Henry Erith, of Vinces Farm, Ardleigh, Colchester, Essex, and Barbara Penelope, *née* Hawken; *b* 8 August 1938; *Educ* Ipswich Sch, Writtle Agric Coll; *m* 7 May 1966, Sara Kingsford Joan, da of Dr Christopher Frederick James Muller; 3 s (Charles b 1967, James, Edward (twins) b 1970); *Career* 10 Hussars: 2 Lt Serv in Aqaba Jordan and Tidworth Hants 1957-58, AVR serv in Aden, Oman, Cyprus, Hong Kong, W Germany, Berlin, UK, 1962-79, Maj 1973; builders merchant salesman and mgmnt trainee 1960-64: GEO Wallis (London), Broad & Co (London), Hechinger Co (Washington DC) Simon Hardware Co (Oakland California), Bunnings Timber (Perth W Aust) SBCI Savory Milln Ltd; bldg specialist Milln & Robinson 1966-, (EB Savory Milln & Co 1967-), ptnr then sr ptnr EB Savory Milln & co 1983-, chm SBCI Savory Milln Ltd 1985-, Swiss Bank Corporation Stockbroking 1989; memb Stock Exchange 1969-; non exec dir: Erith plc (dep chm), Royal London Mutual Insur Soc Ltd, Cawberry Ltd; church warden Holy Innocents Church Lamarsh; memb: Dedham Vale Soc, Colne Stour Countryside Assoc; parly candidate (C) Ipswich 1976-79 memb NEDO Housing Ctee, Centre for Policy Studies; Liveryman Worshipful Co of Builders Merchants 1987, Freeman City of London 1987; AMSIA 1971, FID 1986; *Books* Britain into Europe (jtly 1962), Savory Milln's Building Book (Annual 1968-83); *Recreations* village cricket, tennis, skiing, stamp collecting, environmental pursuits; *Clubs* Cavalry & Guards, City of London, MCC, Royal Philatelic Soc; *Style*— Robert Erith, Esq, TD; Shrubs Farm, Lamarsh, Bures, Suffolk C08 5EA (☎ 0787 227520, fax 0787 227197); 38 Westminster Mansions, Great Smith St, London SW1P 3BP (☎ 01 222 1969); Swiss Bank Corporation Stockbroking, New City Court, 20 St Thomas St, London SE1 9RP (☎ 01 638 1212, fax 01 403 3370/3383, telex 887289)

ERNE, 6 Earl of (I 1798); Henry George Victor John Crichton; JP; sits as Baron Fermanagh (UK 1876); also Baron Erne (I 1768) and Viscount Erne (I 1781); s of 5 Earl (ka 1940), and Lady Davidema, da of 2 Earl of Lytton, KG, GCSI, GCIE, PC; *b* 9 July 1937; *Educ* Eton; *m* 1, 5 Nov 1958 (m dis 1980), Camilla Marguerite, da of late Wing Cdr Owen George Endicott Roberts; 1 s, 4 da; m 2, 1980, Mrs Anna Carin Hitchcock (*née* Bjorck); *Heir* s, Viscount Crichton; *Career* page of honour to HM King George VI 1952, to HM The Queen 1952-54; Lt N Irish Horse 1960-68; Lord Lt Co Fermanagh; *Clubs* Whites, Lough Erne Yacht; *Style*— The Rt Hon Earl of Erne, JP; 10 Kylestrome House, Cundy Street Flats, Ebury St, London SW1 (☎ 01-730 1700); Crom Castle, Newtown Butler, Co Fermanagh (☎ 036 573 208)

ERRINGTON, Viscount; Evelyn Rowland Esmond Baring; s and h of 3 Earl of Cromer, KG, GCMG, MBE, PC; *b* 3 June 1946; *Educ* Eton; *m* 1971, Plern, da of Dr Charanpat Isarangkul na Ayudhya (d 1978), of Thailand; *Career* md Inchcape (China) Ltd 1977-; *Recreations* boating (yacht 'MV Parika'), climbing; *Clubs* Turf, Oriental, Hong Kong, Royal Hong Kong Yacht; *Style*— Viscount Errington; 7B Bowen Rd, Hong Kong BCC (☎ 5 236426 and 5 229179; office: 5 8931066)

ERRINGTON, Col Sir Geoffrey Frederick; 2 Bt (UK 1963) of Ness, in Co Palatine of Chester; s of Sir Eric Errington, 1 Bt (d 1973), and Marjorie, *née* Grant-Bennett (d 1973); *b* 15 Feb 1926; *Educ* Rugby, New Coll Oxford; *m* 24 Sept 1955, Diana Kathleen Forbes, da of late Edward Barry Davenport, of Edgbaston; 3 s; *Heir* s, Robin Davenport Errington; *Career* GSO 3 (Int) HQ 11 Armd Div 1950-52, GSO 3 MI 3 (b) War Off 1955-57, Bde Maj 146 Inf Bde 1959-61, Co Cdr RMA Sandhurst 1963-65, mil asst to Adj-Gen 1965-67, CO 1 Bn King's Regt 1967-69, GSO 1 HQ 1 BR Corps 1969-71, Col GS HQ NW District 1971, AAG M1 (Army) MOD 1974-75, ret 1975; Col King's Regt 1975-86; dir personnel services Br Shipbuilders 1977-78, employer bd memb Shipbuilding ITB 1977-78; chm: EAL Int Ltd 1982- (dir 1979-), Guy Redmayne & Ptnrs Ltd 1982- (dir 1980-), Moore Wingate Ltd 1982-; Freeman City of London 1980, Liveryman Worshipful Co Coachmakers and Coach Harness Makers Co; *Recreations* travelling, gardening; *Clubs* Boodle's, Army & Navy, Woodroffe's (chm 1987-); *Style*— Col Sir Geoffrey Errington, Bt; 203a Gloucester Place, London NW1; Stone Hill Farm, Sellindge, Ashford, Kent; office: 18 Grosvenor St, London W1X 9FD (☎ 01 499 0513)

ERRINGTON, Sir Lancelot; KCB (1976), CB (1962); eld s of Maj Lancelot Errington (d 1965), of Beeslack, Milton Bridge, Midlothian; *b* 14 Jan 1917; *Educ* Wellington, Trinity Coll Cambridge; *m* 1939, Katharine Reine, o da of T C Macaulay, MC, of Painswick, Glos; 2 s, 2 da; *Career* served WW II RNVR; entered Home Off 1939, Miny of Nat Insur 1945, asst sec 1953, under-sec Miny of Pensions and Nat Insur 1957-65, seconded Cabinet Off 1965, Dept of Health and Social Security 1968, dep under-sec of State 1971-73, 2 perm sec DHSS 1973-76; *Style*— Sir Lancelot Errington, KCB; St Mary's, Fasnacloich, Appin, Argyll (☎ 063 173 331)

ERRINGTON, Richard Percy; CMG (1955); 2 s of Robert George Errington (d 1960), of King's Lynn Norfolk, and Edna Mary, *née* Warr (d 1970); *b* 17 May 1904; *Educ* Sidcot sch; *m* 1935, Ursula, da of Henry Joseph Laws Curtis (d 1920); 1 da (Ursula Jill); *Career* asst tres Nigeria Govt 1929-37, Colonial Admin Serv 1937-46, Nyasaland (now Malawi) 1946-48, financial sec to govt of Aden Colony (also memb of bd of Tstees of Port of Aden, exchange controller, comptroller of customs, controller of supplies) 1948-51, memb exec cncl Aden 1948-58, sr unofficial memb Aden Legislative Cncl 1951-60 (official memb 1948-51); chm: Aden Port Tst 1951-60, Aden Soc for the Blind 1951-60, Aden Labour Advsy Bd 1951-57; area cmmnr St John Ambulance Brigade West Norfolk 1963-71; SBStJ; FCA; *Recreations* walking; *Style*— Richard Errington Esq, CMG; Whitecliffs, Wodehouse, Rd, Old Hunstanton, Norfolk PE36 6JD (☎ 048 53 2356)

ERRINGTON, Robin Davenport; s and h of Col Sir Geoffrey Errington, 2 Bt; *b* 1 July 1957; *Educ* Eton; *Recreations* tennis, skiing, music; *Clubs* Boodle's; *Style*— Robin Errington, Esq; 17A Roland Gdns, London SW7

ERRINGTON, Roger; s of Roger Errington, CBE, MD (d 1960) of Gosforth, Newcastle upon Tyne, and Margaret Lilian, *née* Appleby (d 1964); *b* 7 April 1927; *Educ* Fettes Coll Edinburgh, King's Coll Newcastle upon Tyne; *m* 4 Feb 1956, Susan Margaret, da of George Robert Hodnett, CBE, TD, MA (d 1979); 2 s (Richard b 1957, Charles b 1959), 1 da (Claire b 1961); *Career* farmer 1951; dir: T Crossling & Co Ltd 1960 (chm 1974), J T Parrish plc 1978 (chm 1980-86), rural district cncllr 1954-74; Castle Morpeth district cncllr 1974-, dep Mayor 1988; *Recreations* sailing, shooting, flying; *Clubs* Northern Counties; *Style*— Roger Errington, Esq; Abbey House, Newminster, Morpeth, Northumberland NE61 2YJ (☎ 0670 514678); PO Box 5, Coast Rd, Newcastle upon Tyne NE6 5TP (☎ 091 2654266)

ERROLL, 24 Earl of (S 1452); Merlin Sereld Victor Gilbert Hay; 12 Bt (NS 1685), of Moncreiffe, Perthshire; also 28 Hereditary Lord High Constable of Scotland (conferred as Great Constable of Scotland *ante* 1309 and made hereditary by charter of Robert I 1314), Lord Hay (S 1429) and Lord Slains (S 1452); Chief of the Hays; as Lord High Constable, has precedence in Scotland before all other hereditary honours after the Blood Royal; also maintains private officer-at-arms (Slains Pursuivant); s of

Countess of Erroll (d 1978) by her 1 husb, Sir Iain Moncreiffe of that Ilk, 11 Bt (d 1985); his gggggf (the 18 Earl)'s w, Elizabeth FitzClarence natural da of King William IV, whose arms he quarters debruised by a baton sinister; *b* 20 April 1948; *Educ* Eton, Trin Cambridge; *m* 8 May 1982, Isabelle, o da of Thomas Sidney Astell Hohler, of Wolverton Park, Basingstoke; 1 s (Lord Hay), 2 da (Lady Amelia b 23 Nov 1986, Lady Laline Hay b 1987); *Heir* s, Harry Thomas William (Lord Hay), b 8 Aug 1984; *Career* computer conslt; memb Queen's Body Guard for Scotland (Royal Co of Archers); Lt Atholl Highlanders; OStJ; *Recreations* skiing, climbing, parachuting, territorials; *Clubs* Turf, White's, Pratt's, Puffin's; *Style*— The Rt Hon the Earl of Erroll; Wolverton Farm, Basingstoke, Hants (☎ 0635 298267); Old Slains, Collieston, Aberdeenshire

ERROLL OF HALE, 1 Baron (UK 1964); Frederick James Erroll; PC (1960), TD; s of George Murison Erroll (d 1926); s of Bergmans Theodor John, of Rotterdam, by his w Margaret Murison (d 1924); he assumed the surname Erroll by deed poll 1914), and Kathleen Donovan Edington (d 1952); *b* 27 May 1914; *Educ* Oundle, Trin Cambridge; *m* 19 Dec 1950, Elizabeth, da of R(ichard) Sowton Barrow, of Foxholes, Exmouth, Devon; *Career* MP (C) Altrincham and Sale 1945-64; parly sec Miny of Supply 1955-56, Bd of Trade 1956-58, economic sec to Treasury 1958-59, min of state Bd of Trade 1959-61 (pres 1961-63), min of Power 1963-64; memb NEDC 1962-63; chm: Bowater Corpn 1973-84, Consolidated Gold Fields 1976-83 (pres 1983-), Whessoe plc (engrg gp based in Darlington), Automobile Assoc 1973- (vice pres 1988-); *Style*— The Rt Hon Lord Erroll of Hale, PC, TD; House of Lords, London SW1A 0PW

ERSKINE, (Thomas) Adrian; s of Daniel Erskine, and Molly, *née* Balmer (d 1979); *b* 7 August 1934; *Educ* St Malachys Coll Belfast, Queen's Univ Belfast (BSc), Imperial Coll London Univ (DIC); *Career* civil engr dept of highways Ontario Canada 1957-59, structural engr Ove Arup and Ptnrs London 1960-62, head Ulster branch BRC Engrg Co Ltd 1964-69, assoc i/c civil and structural work Belfast off Building Design Partnership 1969-78, ptnr McGladdery & Ptnrs (consulting, civil and structural engrs) Belfast 1978-; CEng, MICE 1962; *Recreations* squash, golf, cricket; *Clubs* Belfast Boat, Belvoir GC, Woodvale CC; *Style*— Adrian Erskine, Esq; 24 Sandhurst Dr, Belfast BT9 5AY (☎ 0232 668706); McGladdery and Partners, 64 Malone Ave, Belfast BT9 6ER (☎ 0232 660682)

ERSKINE, Hon (Richard) Alastair; s of 6 Baron Erskine (d 1957), and bro of 16 Earl of Buchan; *b* 8 Jan 1901; *Educ* Charterhouse; *m* 23 Oct 1933, Patricia, da of late Major Paul FitzGerald Norbury, DSO; 2 s (1 decd), 1 adopted da; *Style*— Hon Alastair Erskine; Little Cheesecombe, Hawkley, Liss, Hants

ERSKINE, Hon Alexander David; 2 s of 13 Earl of Mar and 15 of Kellie; *b* 26 Oct 1952; *Educ* Eton, Pembroke Coll Cambridge; *m* 1977, Katherine Shawford, eld da of T C Capel, of Narrabri, NSW; 1 s (Alexander b 1979), 1 da (Isabel b 1982); *Career* economist Dept of PM and Cabinet Canberra Australia 1979-; *Recreations* hillwalking, outdoor sports; *Style*— Hon Alexander Erskine; 8 Robson St, Garran, ACT 2605, Australia (010 61 61 824121)

ERSKINE, Lady Arabella Fleur; yr da of 17 Earl of Buchan, JP; *b* 1969; *Style*— Lady Arabella Erskine

ERSKINE, Hon Mrs David; Caroline Mary; yr da of Sir Alan Frederick Lascelles, GCVO, KCB, CMG, MC, PC (d 1981); *b* 15 Feb 1927; *m* 1, 20 May 1949, 2 Viscount Chandos (d 1980); 2 s, 2 da; m 2, 3 May 1985, Hon David Hervey Erskine, *qv*; *Style*— Hon Mrs David Erskine; Felshm House, Felsham Bury, Bury St Edmunds, Suffolk

ERSKINE, Hon David Hervey; JP (Suffolk 1971-86), DL (Suffolk 1983); 3 s of John Francis Ashley, Lord Erskine, GCSI, GCIE (d 1953, himself s of 12 Earl of Mar and (14 Earl of) Kellie), and Lady Marjorie Harvey (d 1967), er da of 4 Marquess of Bristol; *b* 5 Nov 1924; *Educ* Eton, Trinity Coll Cambridge; *m* 1, 5 Dec 1953, Jean Violet (d 1983), da of Lt-Col Archibald Vivian Campbell Douglas of Mains; 3 da; m 2, 3 May 1985, Caroline Mary, widow of 2 Viscount Chandos (d 1980), and da of Rt Hon Sir Alan Lascelles, GCVO, KCB, CMG, MC (d 1981); *Career* Italy and Palestine 1944-47 (Italy star); barr, Inner Temple, 1950; late Capt Scots Gds; ccllr W Suffolk 1969-74 and Suffolk 1974-85; *Recreations* historical study, sightseeing; *Clubs* Brooks; *Style*— Hon David Erskine, JP, DL; Felsham House, Felsham, Bury St Edmunds, IP30 0QG (☎ Rattlesden 326); 17 Clareville Court, Clareville Grove, SW7 5AT (☎ 01 373 4734)

ERSKINE, Sir (Thomas) David; 5 Bt (UK 1821), of Cambo, Fife; JP (Fife 1951), DL (1955); s of Lt-Col Sir Thomas Wilfred Hargreaves John Erskine, 4 Bt, DSO, DL (d 1944, third in descent from Sir David Erskine, 1 Bt, natural gs of 9 Earl of Kellie) of Cambo, Kingsbarns, Fife, and Magdalen Janet, da of Sir Ralph Anstruther, 6 Bt of Balcaskie; *b* 31 July 1912; *Educ* Eton, Magdalene Coll Cambridge (BA); *m* 4 Oct 1947, Ann, da of Col Neil Fraser-Tytler, DSO, MC, TD, DL (d 1937), of Aldourie Castle, Inverness, and Mrs (C H) Fraser-Tytler, CBE *qv*; 2 s (Peter, William), 1 da (Caroline d 1976); *Heir* s, Thomas Peter Neil Erskine; *Career* served WW II, M East, India, Malaya as Maj Indian Corps Engrs; with Butterfield & Swire Hongkong & China 1935-41; landed proprietor (approx 1600 acres) & farmer 1946-; Fife ccllr 1953-74, chm Fife CC 1970-73 (vice-chm 1967-70), Fife regnl cllr 1974-82; vice-lieut Fife 1982-87; *Recreations* gardening, shooting, travel; *Clubs* New (Edinburgh); *Style*— Sir David Erskine, Bt, JP; Westnewhall, Kingsbarns, St Andrews, Fife (☎ 0333 50228)

ERSKINE, Donald Seymour; DL (Perth and Kinross 1969); s of Col Sir Arthur Edward Erskine, GCVO, DSO (d 1963), and Rosemary, *née* Baird; *b* 28 May 1925; *Educ* Wellington Coll; *m* 1963, Catharine Annandale, da of late Kenneth T McLelland; 1 s, 4 da; *Career* served 1943-47 as Capt RA (Europe and Palestine); chartered surveyor; factor for Country Gentlemen's Assoc 1950-55, ALPF Wallace of Candacraig 1955-61; factor and dep dir Nat Tst for Scotland 1961-; memb Queen's Body Guard for Scotland (Royal Co of Archers) 1958; *Recreations* shooting and singing; *Clubs* New (Edinburgh); *Style*— Donald Erskine, Esq, DL; Cleish House, Cleish, Kinross (☎ 057 75 232); Nat Tst for Scotland, 5 Charlotte Sq, Edinburgh (☎ 031 226 5922)

ERSKINE, Lord James Thorne Erskine; s and h of Major the 13 Earl of Mar (and 15 of) Kellie, JP, *qv*; *b* 10 Mar 1949; *Educ* Eton, Moray House Coll of Educn Edinburgh (Dip Social Work, Dip Youth & Community Work); *m* 1974, Mary Irene, da of Dougal McDougal Kirk, of 137 Easter Road, Edinburgh, and former w of Roderick Mooney; 5 step children; *Heir* bro, Hon Alexander David Erskine; *Career* page of honour to HM 1962-63; community service volunteer York 1967-68, youth and community worker Craig Millar 1971-73; social worker: Sheffield 1973-76, Elgin 1976-77, Forres 1977-78, Aviemore 1979, HM Prison Inverness 1979-81, Inverness West 1981, Merkinch 1982; supervisor Community Service by Offenders Inverness 1983-87; Flying Offr RAuxAF 1982-86 (2622 Highland Sqdn); assoc Abbey Life Assur Co Ltd 1983; *Recreations* RNXS, cycling, gardening, elder of Church of Scotland, railways; *Clubs* New; *Style*— Lord Erskine; Erskine House, Kirk Wynd, Clackmannan FK10 4JF (☎ 0259 212438)

ERSKINE, Rev the Hon Michael John; s of 13 Earl of Mar and 15 of Kellie; *b* 5 April 1956; *Educ* Eton, Edinburgh Univ; *m* 5 Sept 1987, Jill, er da of late Campbell S Westwood, of 11 Leighton Gdns, Ellon; *Recreations* hillwalking, travel, outdoor sports; *Clubs* New (Edinburgh); *Style*— Rev the Hon Michael Erskine; c/o Claremont House, Alloa, Clackmannanshire (☎ 0259 212020)

ERSKINE, Hon Montagu John; s of 17 Earl of Buchan, JP; *b* 17 Jan 1966; *Style*— Hon Montagu Erskine

ERSKINE, (Thomas) Peter Neil; s and h of Sir David Erskine, 5 Bt, JP, DL; *b* 28 Mar 1950; *Educ* Eton, Birmingham Univ; *m* 1972, Catherine, da of Col G H K Hewlett; 2 s (Thomas Struan b 1977, James Dunbar b 1979); 2 da (Gillian Christian b 1983, Mary Caroline b 1986); *Career* worked hotel indust Brazil, returned home to estate; opened visitor centre on one of the farms 1982; currently converting the estate to organic farming; professional photographer; *Style*— Peter Erskine, Esq

ERSKINE, Ralph; CB (1986); s of Robert Todd Erskine (d 1980), and Mary Elizabeth *née* Motherwell; *b* 14 Oct 1933; *Educ* Campbell Coll, Queen's Univ Belfast (LLB); *m* 30 April 1966, Joan, da of Thomas Henry Palmer (d 1957); 1 s (Paul), 1 da (Diane); *Career* called to the Bar Gray's Inn 1962; first legislative draftsman NI 1979-; *Recreations* skiing, cycling, modern naval history; *Style*— Ralph Erskine, Esq, CB; Office of the Legislative Draftsmen, Parliament Buildings, Stormont, Belfast BT4 3SW, (☎ 63210 ext 2253)

ERSKINE, Hon Robert William Hervey; yst s of late John Francis Achley, Lord Erskine, GCSI, GCIE (d 1953); *b* 13 Oct 1930; *Educ* Eton, King's Coll Cambridge; *m* 1, 21 May 1955 (m dis 1964), Jennifer Shirley, yr da of L J Cardew Wood, of Farnham Royal Bucks; m 2, Oct 1969 (m dis 1975), Annemarie Alvarez de Toledo, da of Jean Lattes, of Paris; 1 s (Alistair Robert); m 3, 1977, Belinda, da of Raymond Blackburn, of London; 2 s (Thomas Gerald, Felix Benjamin); late 2nd Lt, Scots Gds; *Style*— Robert Erskine, Esq; 100 Elgin Cres, London W11 (☎ 01 221 6229)

ERSKINE, Lady Seraphina Mary; er da of 17 Earl of Buchan, JP; *b* 14 July 1961; *Style*— Lady Seraphina Erskine

ERSKINE OF RERRICK, Henrietta, Baroness; Henrietta; da of late William Dunnett, of East Canisbay Caithness; *m* 15 Sept 1922, 1 Baron Erskine of Rerrick, GBE (d 1980); 1 s (2 Baron), 1 da (Hon Mrs Butler); *Career* CStJ; *Style*— The Rt Hon Henrietta, Lady Erskine of Rerrick; 8B Churchfields Avenue, Weybridge, Surrey

ERSKINE OF RERRICK, 2 Baron (UK 1964); Maj Sir Iain Maxwell Erskine; 2 Bt (UK 1961); s of 1 Baron (d 1980); *b* 22 Jan 1926; *Educ* Harrow; *m* 1, 20 July 1955 (m dis 1964), Marie Elisabeth Burton (now Elizabeth Countess of Caledon), da of late Maj Richard Burton Allen, 3 Dragoon Gds; m 2, 1974, Marie Josephine, da of Dr Josef Klupt; 3 da (Hon Henrietta b 1975, Hon Griselda b 1979, Hon Cora b 1981); *Career* WWII 1939-45, 2 Lt Grenadier Gds 1945, Regular Army 1943-65 (temp Lt-Col 1958), ADC RMA Sandhurst 1951-52, comptroller to Govr-Gen of NZ 1960-61, ret Maj 1963; PRO to Household Bde 1964-66; higher exec offr Civil Serv MOD 1965-67, advty and PR dir Saward Baker Ltd 1967-73, dir Wansdyke Security :td 1974-85, London mangr Marples Ridgway Construction Ltd 1974-85, md Lonrho Ltd Iran; dir: Ardil Ltd, Crighton Int Ltd 1984-; professional photographer; life memb: Nat Tst of Scotland, Royal Photographic Soc (and ctee memb), ctee memb and dir De Havilland Aircraft Museum (British Aerospace); qualified pilot; chm Guards Flying Club, Col Confederate States Air Force 1983, tstee RAF Museum (Bomber Cmd); OStJ; MIPR 1967-75, MInstM 1967-75, FIOD 1967-75; Chevalier Legion of Honor (France); *Recreations* fly fishing, photography, good food; *Clubs* Whites, Special Forces; *Style*— Maj The Rt Hon Lord Erskine of Rerrick; c/o House of Lords, London SW1

ERSKINE-HILL, Alexander Roger; s and h of Sir Robert Erskine-Hill, 2 Bt, and Christine Alison, *née* Johnstone; *b* 15 August 1949; *Educ* Eton, Aberdeen Univ (LLB); *m* 6 Oct 1984, Sarah Anne Sydenham, da of Dr Richard John Sydenham Clarke (d 1970); 1 s (b 1986) 1 da (Kirsty b 1985); *Career* dir: Salestrac Ltd, Map Mktg Ltd; *Style*— Roger Erskine-Hill, Esq; Great Coleford, Stoodleigh, Tiverton, Devon EX16 9QG; Salestrac Ltd, Cowley Bridge Rd, Exeter EX4 5HQ (☎ 0392 210631)

ERSKINE-HILL, Sir Robert; 2 Bt (UK 1945) of Quothquhan, Co Lanark; er s of Sir Alexander Galloway Erskine-Hill, 1 Bt, KC, DL (d 1947), and Christian Hendrie, *née* Colville, MBE (d 1947); *b* 6 Feb 1917; *Educ* Eton, Trinity Coll Cambridge (BA); *m* 7 Aug 1942, Christine Alison, o da of late Capt Henry James Johnstone, of Alva, RN; 2 s, 2 da (*see* Stormonth-Darling, R A); *Heir* s, Alexander Roger Erskine-Hill; *Career* served RNVR 1936-42; CA; ptnr Chiene and Tait 1946-80; chm Life Assoc of Scotland 1960-86 (dir 1951-87); memb Royal Co of Archers (Queen's Body Guard for Scotland); *Style*— Sir Robert Erskine-Hill, Bt; Quothquhan Lodge, Biggar, Lanarks (☎ 089 93 332)

ERSKINE-MURRAY, Arthur Sydney Elibank; o s of Lt-Col Arthur Erskine-Murray, CBE, DSO (d 1948), ggs of 7 Lord Elibank, and Ena Nelson, *née* Trestrail (d 1942); *b* 29 Mar 1909; *Educ* Bedford Sch, Birmingham Univ (BSc); *m* 29 June 1940, Florence Duncan, da of William Duncan Robertson; 2 da (Ann, Susan); *Career* management conslt then v-chm Inbucon Ltd 1944-69; dir Thomas Poole & Gladstone 1973-78; chm Churchill Guns Ltd 1974-76; dir: Grindley of Stoke Ltd 1974-78, Bentley Pianos Ltd 1974-78, S Newman Ltd 1973-78; MICE, MBIM; *Style*— Sydney Erskine-Murray Esq; Myrtle Bank, Great Amwell, Ware Herts (☎ Ware 870146)

ERSKINE-MURRAY, (Arthur) Sydney Elibauh; s of Lieut Col Arthur Erskine-Murray (d 1947), and Ena Nelson, *née* Trestrail; *see* Peerage and Baronetage (Lord Elibank); *b* 29 Mar 1909; *Educ* Bedford Sch, Birmingham Univ (BSc, CEng); *m* 29 June 1940, Florence Duncan, da of William Duncan Robertson (d 1983); *Career* dir: Assoc Industrial Consultants, Beatty Pianos Ltd 1971-76, A Clough Co Ltd 1971-76, Churchill Gdns Ltd, Thomas Poole Gladstone Ltd 1971-76; vice chm Jubaeon Ltd, md Mead Carvery & Co 1970-76; BSc Hons (Civil Eng); *Recreations* golf, skiing; *Style*— Sydney Erskine-Murray, Esq; Cautherly Lane, Great Amwell, Ware, Herts SG12 9SN (☎ 0920 870146)

ERSKINE-MURRAY, Hon Timothy Alexander Elibank; yr s of 14 Lord Elibank; *b* 6 May 1967; *Educ* Eton, Exeter Univ; *Recreations* rugby, golf, tennis, squash, sailing, fives; *Style*— Hon Timothy Erskine-Murray; The Coach House, Charters Rd,

Sunningdale, Ascot, Berks SL5 9QB (☎ 0990 22099)

ERSKINE-TULLOCH, Brig Rolland Padraig Stewart; CBE (1967); s of Capt Denis Rolland Diarmid Stewart Erskine-Tulloch (d 1943), of Barnwood Oxted, Surrey; *b* 1918; *Educ* Christ's Hosp, RMC; *m* 15 Aug 1940, Margaret Helen, o da of Capt Henry Winton Seton, late 9 Gurkhas; 2 da (Elspeth Jane b 1948, Charlotte Lucy b 1958); *Career* Brig late Northamptonshire and 2 E Anglian Regts; WW II 1939-45 in France, Madagascar, Middle East, Sicily and Italy; Palestine 1946-47; *Style—* Brigadier R P S Erskine-Tulloch, CBE; Mains of Corse, Lumphanan, Aberdeenshire (☎ 033983 224)

ERVIN, Wilson; CBE (1986); s of Robret John Ervin (d 1966), of 32 Lucerne Parade, Belfast, and Jane, *née* McVeigh (d 1983); *b* 13 Dec 1923; *Educ* Royal Belfast Academical Inst; *m* Joan Catherine, da of John Mercer, of 7 Broughton Park, Belfast; *Career* banker; dir (formerly chief exec) Northern Bank Ltd (ret from active banking 1985), non-exec dir Northern Bank Ltd; chm TBF Thompson (Garugh) Ltd and Jas Anderson Ltd; formerly pres Inst of Bankers in Ireland; fell Inst of Bankers; served in Fleet Air Arm RN (non cmmnd) in Home Waters, Far East, India, Bumra and Australia; *Clubs* Ulster Reform, Belvoir Park Golf; *Style—* Wilson Ervin, CBE; 29 Broomhill Park, Belfast BT9 5JB

ESAM, David Richard; s of Richard Terrell Esam, of Bath, Avon, and Hilda Margaret, *née* Caswell; *b* 29 Jan 1952; *Educ* Highgate Sch, Warwick Univ (BA), Coll of Law; *m* 21 June 1975, Drusilla Mary, da of James Beesley, of Burnham-on-Sea, Somerset; 1 s (Andrew David b 1987); *Career* slr; ptnr George Carter & Co London and Bristol (sr ptnr in Bristol); *Recreations* birdwatching; *Style—* David R Esam, Esq; 56 Kingsdown Parade, Kingsdown, Bristol B56 5UQ; George Carter & Co, 27 Orchards St, Bristol B51 5EH (☎ 0272 211895, fax 0272 211592)

ESCRITT, (Charles) Ewart; OBE (1970); s of Rev Charles Escritt (d 1949); *b* 26 August 1905; *Educ* Christ's Hosp, Keble Coll Oxford; *m* 1939, Ruth Mary, da of Thomas Chapman Metcalf (d 1962); 2 s, 1 da; *Career* served WW II Div RASC Capt 1940, POW Singapore and Thailand 1942-45; asst master Bromsgrove Sch 1928-29, gp training offr Tootal Broadhurst Lee Co Ltd 1933-47; sec Oxford Univ Appointments Ctee 1947-70, chm mgmnt advsy ctee Oxford Coll of Technology 1950-70; exec cncl BACIE 1948-70, HM advsy cncl on Relationship between Employment in the Servs and Civilian Life 1950-54, academic bd Cncl for Further Educn 1950-70 (chm advsy ctee for mgmnt); fellow Keble Coll Oxford 1965-70; *Recreations* Japanese studies; *Clubs* Oxford Union, Oxford Management (fndr memb, chm 1948), Oxford Japanese Soc (pres 1952); *Style—* Ewart Escritt, Esq, OBE; 32 Portland Rd, Summertown, Oxford OX2 7EY (☎ 0865 57072)

ESDAILE, (James) Edmund Kennedy; s of Arundell James Kennedy Esdaile, CBE (d 1956), and Katharine Ada, *née* McDowall (d 1950); *b* 21 Sept 1910; *Educ* Lancing, Pembroke Coll, Oxford (Res Sch); *m* 26 Aug 1939, Ellen Jane Sausmarez (d 1984), da of Rev Christopher Sausmarez Carey (d 1938); 2 da (Julia Susan Ianthe b 1941, Sarah Jane Philomena b 1946); *Career* announcer BBC 1935-38; schoolmaster and lecturer; insurance (Legal & General) (ret); asst to mother for her publications: The Stantons of Holborn (1929), Temple Church Monuments (1933), etc; contrib Thieme Becker's Allgemeines Künstler Lexikon (*ca* 1929-35), Country Life, etc; reviewer TLS, etc; author: Monuments in Ely Cathedral (1973); co-fndr Men of the Stones 1947, author of many articles on the history of cricket, edited and illustrated in pen and ink A Silver Shape by his ggf George Crawshay (1980); poet; *Recreations* cricket (when young), shooting (unambitiously); *Clubs* Arundel Park CC, Hertford; *Style—* Edmund Esdaile, Esq; 61 North Road, Hertford SG14 1N7

ESDALE, Gerald Paton Rivett; s of Charles James August Esdale (d 1949), of Sutton, Surrey, and Avice Mary, *née* Rivett (d 1963); *b* 21 Oct 1929; *Educ* Malvern, Cambridge (MA); *m* 6 May 1957, Patricia Joyce, da of Elliot David Lindop (d 1974); 1 s (Mark b 1958), 1 da (Patricia b 1963); *Career* Nat Serv 2 Lt WG 1948-50; dir WKD Ltd 1962; chm 1972: Thames Liquid Fuels Ltd (dir 1962), Thames Rico, Thames Petroleum Scotland; CEng, MInstMechE, MInstPel; *Clubs* MCC; *Style—* Gerald Esdale, Esq; 58 Wildwood, Rd, Hampstead, London NW11 6UP (☎ 01 455 5860); 11 Elvaston Pl, London SW7 (☎ 01 581 1729)

ESHER, 4 Viscount (UK 1897); Maj Lionel Gordon Baliol Brett; CBE (1970); also Baron Esher (UK 1885); s of 3 Viscount, GBE (d 1963); *b* 18 July 1913; *Educ* Eton, New Coll Oxford; *m* 22 Oct 1935, (Helena) Christian Olive, da of Ebenezer John Lecky Pike, CBE, MC, DL, of Ditcham Park, Petersfield, Hants; 5 s, 1 da; *Heir* s, Hon Christopher Brett; *Career* served WW II RA (despatches); architect and planner Hatfield New Town 1949-59; memb Royal Fine Art Cmmn 1951-69, pres Royal Inst of Br Architects 1965-67, memb advsy bd Victoria & Albert Museum 1967-72, govr London Museum 1970-77, rector and vice-provost Royal Coll of Art 1971-78; chm: Art Panel Arts Cncl of GB 1972-77, Advsy Bd for Redundant Churches to 1983; tstee Soane Museum 1976-, chm Northern Home Counties Nat Tst 1979-85; Hon DLitt Strathclyde 1967, Hon D Univ York 1970, Hon DSc Edinburgh 1981; *Books* (writes as Lionel Brett) Houses (1947), The World of Architecture (1963), Landscape in Distress (1965), York: a Study in Conservation (1969), Parameters and Images (1970), A Broken Wave: the Rebuilding of England 1940-80 (1981), The Continuing Heritage (1982), Our Selves Unknown (1984); *Clubs* Arts; *Style—* Maj The Rt Hon Viscount Esher, CBE; Christmas Common Tower, Watlington, Oxford

ESMONDE, Eithne, Lady - Eithne Moira Grattan; da of late Sir Thomas Henry Grattan Esmonde, 11 Bt; *b* 1902; *m* 9 June 1927, Sir Anthony Charles Esmonde, 15 Bt (d 1981); 3 s, 3 da; *Style—* Eithne, Lady Esmonde; Ballynastragh, Gorey, Co Wexford

ESMONDE, Sir Thomas Francis Grattan; 17 Bt (I 1962); s of His Honour Judge Sir John Esmonde, 16 Bt (d 1987); *b* 14 Oct 1960; *Educ* Sandford Park Sch, v of Dublin (MB, BCh, BAO); *m* 26 April 1986, Pauline Loretto, da of James Vincent Kearns; *Heir* s, Sean Vincent Grattan Esmonde, b 8 Jan 1989; *Career* MRCPI, MRCP; *Style—* Sir Thomas Esmonde, Bt; 6 Nutley Ave, Donnybrook, Dublin 4, Ireland

ESPLEN, Sir (William) Graham; 2 Bt (UK 1921) of Hardres Ct, Canterbury; s of Sir John Esplen, 1 Bt, KBE (d 1930), and Laura Louise, *née* Dickenson (d 1936); *b* 29 Dec 1899; *Educ* Harrow; *m* 11 Oct 1928 (m dis 1951), Aline Octavia, da of A Octavius Hedley (d 1926); 1 s; *Heir* s John Graham Esplen; *Style—* Sir Graham Esplen, Bt; c/o Alldens Cottage, Thorncombe Street, Bramley, Surrey

ESPLEN, John Graham; o s and h of Sir Graham Esplen, 2 Bt; *b* 4 August 1932; *Educ* Harrow, St Catharine's Coll Camb (BA); *m* 6 Oct 1956, Valerie Joan, yr da of Maj-Gen Albert Percy Lambooy, CB, OBE; 1 s, 3 da; *Style—* John Esplen, Esq; Alldens Cottage, Thorncombe St, nr Bramley, Surrey GU5 0NA

ESPLIN, Air Vice-Marshal Ian George; CB (1963), OBE (1946, DFC 1943); s of Donald Thomas Esplin (d 1962), of Sydney, NSW, Australia, and Emily Freame Esplin (d 1962); *b* 26 Feb 1914; *Educ* Sydney Univ (BEc), Oxford Univ (MA); *m* 1944, Patricia Kaleen, da of late C C Barlow, of London; 1 s, 1 da; *Career* Air Vice-Marshal RAF, served UK, Germany, India, USA; *Recreations* golf, tennis, swimming, photography; *Clubs* Vincents, Leander; *Style—* Air Vice-Marshal Ian Esplin, CB, OBE, DFC; c/o Nat West Bank Ltd, West End Office, 1 St James's Square, London SW1

ESSENHIGH, Bryan Geoffrey; s of Cdr Thomas Roland Essenhigh (d 1975), of Sevenoaks, Kent, and Winifred, *née* Fox (d 1957); *b* 22 Mar 1927; *Educ* Tonbridge Sch, Glasgow Univ; *m* 15 Nov 1952, Barbara Mary, da of Charles Stanley Murgatroyd (d 1962), of Otford, Kent; 1 s (Simon b 1955), 2 da (Susan b 1953, d 1954, Mary b 1958); *Career* Naval Airman 1945-47; estate mangr (finance) 1948-; dir: Brydon Finance Ltd 1970-, Oastbarn Ltd 1981-; Liveryman The Worshipful Co of Patternmakers 1981-; *Recreations* philately, usual country pursuits; *Style—* Bryan G Essenhigh, Esq; Knap Farm, Ridge, Chilmark, Salisbury, Wilts SP3 5BS (☎ 0747 870267); Morrison Estate Office, Fonthill Bishop, Salisbury,

ESSER, Robin Charles; s of Charles Esser (d 1982), and Winifred Eileen, (d 1972) ; *b* 6 May 1935; *Educ* Wheelwright GS Dewsbury, Wadham Coll Oxford (BA MA); *m* 1, 5 Jan 1959, Irene Shirley, *née* Clough (d 1973); 2 s (Daniel b 1962, Toby b 1963), 2 da (Sarah Jane b 1961, Rebecca b 1965); m 2, 30 May 1981, Tui, *née* France; 1 s (Jacob b 1986); *Career* cmmnd 2 Lt KOYLI 1955, transferred General Corps 1956, Capt acting ADPR BAOR 1957; freelance reporter 1956; Daily Express: staff reporter 1957-60, ed William Hickley Column 1960, features ed 1963, NY Bureau 1965, northern ed 1969, exec ed 1970; conslt ed Evening News 1977, exec ed Daily Express 1984-, ed Sunday Express 1986-; *Books* The Hot Potato (1969), The Paper Chase (1971); *Recreations* lunching, sailing, talking, reading; *Clubs* Kennel (Bucks); *Style—* Robin Esser, Esq; Express Newspapers plc, 121 Fleet St, London EC4P 4JT (☎ 01 353 8000, fax 01 583 3642)

ESSEX, Christine, Countess of; Christine Mary; da of late George Frederick Davis, of Handsworth Wood, Warwicks; *m* 1957, as his 4 w, 8 Earl of Essex (d 8 Dec 1966); *Style—* The Rt Hon Christine, Countess of Essex; 16 Ocean Dve, Merimbula, NSW 2548, Australia

ESSEX, David Anthony Dampier; s of Roland Reginald Essex, and Joan Herring Dampier, *née* Terry; *b* 10 May 1946; *Educ* Lancing Coll, City Univ Business Sch (MSc); *m* 29 April 1972, Virginia, da of Percy Kenneth Styles Wilkinson; 3 da (Harriet b 1974, Polly b 1976, Tiffany b 1979); *Career* CA: fin controller Br Aerospace 1982-85 (chief internal auditor 1979-82); ptnr (i/c services to mfrs) Ernst & Whinney 1987- (ptnr since 1985); FCA 1969; *Recreations* family, walking, gardening; *Style—* David Essex, Esq; 1 Lambeth Palace Road, London SE1 7EW (☎ 01 928 2000)

ESSEX, Francis; s of Harold Essex-Lopresti (d 1967), (5 in descent from Count Lopresti, of Sicily), and Beatrice Essex-Lopresti (d 1971); *b* 24 Mar 1929; *Educ* Cotton Coll, N Staffs; *m* 13 Aug 1956, Jeanne, da of John Shires (d 1982); 2 s (Martin, Stephen); *Career* author, composer, prodr, prodr BBC TV (Light entertainment) 1954-60, sr prodr ATV 1960-65, prog controller Scottish TV 1965-69, prodn controller ATV 1969-76 (dir 1974-, dir of prodns 1976-81); wrote and presented T Bells of St Martins 1953, directed Six of One (Adelphi theatre) 1964; film scripts: Shillingbury Tales, The Silent Scream, The Night Wind, Cuffy (series), Kimboy (series), The Shenaky, Waterways (series), Gabrielle and the Doddleman; music scores: Luke's Kingdom, The Seas must Live, The Lightning Tree, Maddie with Love, The Cedar Tree etc; writer: plays, songs; FRTS; Br Acad Light Entertainment Award 1964; Leonard Brett Award 1964, 1981; *Books* Shillingbury Tales (1983), Skerrymor Bay (1984); *Recreations* blue water sailing, gardening, tennis; *Style—* Francis Essex, Esq; 'Punta Vista', Aldea de las Cuevas, Benidoleig, Alicante, Spain

ESSEX, Nona, Countess of; Nona Isobel; da of David Wilson Miller, of Christchurch, NZ; *m* 1, Francis Sydney Smythe, of Sussex (decd); m 2, 6 Nov 1957, as his 2 w, 9 Earl of Essex, TD (d 1981); *Style—* Rt Hon Nona, Countess of Essex; Capell, 3 Leyburne Close, Ledburn, nr Leighton Buzzard, Beds

ESSEX, 10 Earl of (E 1661); Robert Edward de Vere Capell; also Baron Capell of Hadham (E 1641), and Viscount Malden (E 1661); s of Arthur Algernon de Vere Capell (d 1924; gs of Capt Hon Algernon Capell, RN, bro of 6 Earl of Essex), and Alice Mabel, *née* Currie (d 1951); suc kinsman, 9 Earl, 1981, but has not yet established his right to the Peerages; *b* 13 Jan 1920; *m* 3 Jan 1942, Doris Margaret, da of George Tomlinson; 1 s; *Heir* s, Viscount Malden; *Career* serv WWII, Flt Sgt RAF; *Style—* The Rt Hon Earl of Essex; 2 Novak Place, Torrisholme, Morecambe, Lancs

ESSEX, William Alexander Wells; s of Norman Arthur Essex, and Jane Rosemary Wells, *née* Tickler; *b* 13 August 1958; *Educ* Marlborough Univ of East Anglia; *m* 24 Sept 1988, Penelope Anne, da of Lt Cdr David McKerrow Baird; *Career* joined Fin Times Gp 1982, ed Resident Abroad Magazine 1985- ; *Style—* William Essex, Esq; Triad House, Forncett End, Norfolk (☎ 095 389 8114); 108 Clerkenwell Rd, EC1M 5SA (☎ 01 251 9321, fax 01 251 4686)

ESSINGTON-BOULTON, Hon Mrs; Hon Crystal; *née* Russell; da of 2 Baron Russell of Liverpool, CBE, MC, by his 2 w; *b* 4 Jan 1936; *m* 23 June 1955 (m dis 1969), John Mark Essington-Boulton, s of Maj Clive Essington-Boulton, of Turvey, Beds; 1 s, 1 da; *Career* restaurateur; ptnr in Edward's Poissonnerie, Wine Bar and Restaurant, Bath, Avon; *Recreations* clay-pigeon shooting, skiing, charity fund raising; *Style—* Hon Mrs Essington-Boulton; Ann Boleyn's Cottage, Grandmother's Rock Lane, Beach, Ditton, nr Bristol, Avon

ESSON-SCOTT, Hon Mrs (Rosemary Sylvia); da of 13 Viscount Falkland, OBE, and aunt of 15 Viscount; *b* 22 Feb 1910; *m* 1, 17 July 1928 (m dis 1936), John de Perigault Gurney Mayhew, er s of late Lt-Col Sir John Dixon Mayhew, TD, JP, DL; 1 s; m 2, 6 Jan 1937, Aubrey Esson-Scott, s of David Esson-Scott, of Ashley Croft, Walton-on-Thames; *Style—* Hon Mrs Esson-Scott; R2 Marine Gate, Brighton, Sussex

ESTEVE-COLL, Elizabeth Anne Loosemore; da of PW Kingdon and Nora Kingdon; *b* 14 Oct 1938; *Educ* Darlington Girls HS, Birkbeck Coll London Univ (BA); *m* 1960, Jose Alexander Timothy Esteve-Coll; *Career* head learning resources Kingston Poly 1977, univ librarian Univ of Surrey 1982, keeper Nat Art Library and A Museum 1985, dir and A Museum 1988-; *Recreations* reading, music, foreign travel; *Style—* Mrs Elizabeth Esteve-Coll; c/o Victoria & Albert Musueum, South Kensington, London, SW7 2RL, (☎ 01 938 8501)

ETHERIDGE, (Walter) William (Jacques); OBE (1968); s of Walter Etheridge (d

1928), of Croydon, and Lucy Mary Ducket (d 1928), of Croydon, and Lucy Mary, *née* Ducket (d 1986); *b* 20 Feb 1914; *Educ* John Ruskin Sch Croydon, London Univ (BA); *m* 14 Aug 1943, Dorothy Emily, da of James Harry Skelding (d 1927); 2 s (Anthony b 1944, Christopher b 1949); *Career* headmaster 1958-74, chm London Nat Savings Ctee; town cncllr (relinquished 1985) Ross-on-Wye, dist cncllr Herefordshire; *Recreations* travel; *Style*— William Etheridge, Esq, OBE; "Cressingham", Bridstow, Ross-on-Wye, Herefordshire (☎ Ross-on-Wye 64694)

ETHERTON, Ralph Humphrey; o s of Louis John Walpole Etherton (d 1943), and Bertha Mary, *née* Bagge; *b* 11 Feb 1904; *Educ* Charterhouse, Trinity Hall Cambridge; *m* 1944, Johanne Patricia, yst da of late Gerald Cloherty, of Galway; 1 s, 1 da; *Career* barr Inner Temple 1926; chm Coningsby Club 1933-34; MP (Nat C) Stretford Div of Lancs 1939-45; served in RAFVR as Fl-Lt 1940-42; memb Parly Delgn to Aust and NZ 1944; engaged in commerce 1945-73; *Recreations* riding, travel; *Clubs* Carlton, Pratt's; *Style*— Ralph Etherton, Esq; Greentree Hall, Balcombe, Sussex (☎ 044 483 319)

ETTRICK-WELFORD, George Henry; AE; s of George Henry Welford, OBE (d 1965), of North Court, Jubbulpur and Calcutta India, and Flora Swain (d 1948); *b* 4 Dec 1916; *Educ* Winton Sch Norwich, HMTS Worcester, Off Greenhythe Kent, Kings Coll Durham Univ (BSc); *m* 2 Nov 1940, Betty Elise, da of Sverre Hjersing (d 1956), of Newcastle upon Tyne and Moss, Norway; 4 s (Stuart Ettrick b 1942, Michael Sverre b 1945, Jonathan b 1953, Anthony Robert Hylton b 1957); *Career* flying trg 607 Sqdn Co Durham 1938, intermediate and advanced trg (Hurricanes) 1939, 607 (F) Sqdn Battle of Britain 1940, Central Flying Sch 1940-41, Flying Offr II EFTS Perth 1941, glider pilots and instr trg Cambridge 1943, Flt Lt AFU Ternhill and 570TU Eshott 1944, 222 Sqdn (Spitfires and Tempests) 1944, NW Europe 1945, demob 1945; designer and draughtsman marine engrg 1947, conslt engr PE Gp 1948, export mangr textiles co 1965 (prodn mangr 1951, internal conslt 1960), mangr and dir Gp Trg Scheme 1970-81; dep pres and chm local branch RNLI, former cncl memb Exeter Maritime Museum, govr Tiverton Sch 1978-84; FMIB 1975, MIPE, CEngr1975; *Recreations* sailing, cruising, painting; *Clubs* Royal Overseas League, RYA, RAFA; *Style*— George Henry Ettrick-Welford, Esq, AE; Shandon, Coreway, Sidford, Sidmouth, Devon EX10 9SD (☎ 0395 512858)

EUGSTER, Christopher Anthony Alwyn Patrick; s of Gen Sir Basil Eugster, KCB, KCVO, CBE, DSO, MC and Bar, DL (d 1984), and Marcia Elaine Smyth-Osbourne (d 1983); *b* 17 Mar 1941; *Educ* Downside; *m* 12 Nov 1965, Carole Jane, da of Sqdn Ldr John Bouwens, (ka 1941); 2 s (John b 1967, Rupert b 1969); *Career* dir Kleinwort Benson Ltd 1976-; *Recreations* shooting, fishing; *Clubs* White's, Pratt's; *Style*— Christopher Eugster, Esq

EUSTACE, Hon Mrs (Dorothy Anne); yr da of 1 and last Baron Percy of Newcastle (d 1958), and Stella Katherine, *née* Drummond; *b* 21 Sept 1926; *Educ* Durham Univ (MB, BS); *m* 23 March 1957, Maj Thomas Robert Hales Eustace, Royal Irish Fusiliers, o s of late Louis Charles Moss Eustace, of The Cliff, Mousehole, Penzance, Cornwall; 1 s (James b 1960), 2 da (Alicia b 1958, Katherine b 1965); *Style*— Hon Mrs Eustace; Glebe House, Boughton Aluph, Ashford, Kent

EUSTACE, Dudley Graham; s of Albert Eustace, MBE, of Bristol, and Mary *née* Manning; *b* 3 July 1936; *Educ* The Cathedral Sch Bristol, Univ of Bristol (BA); *m* 30 May 1964, Diane, da of Karl Zakrajsek (d 1974), of Nova Racek, Yugoslavia; 2 da (Gabriella b 1965, Chantal b 1967); *Career* Actg PO RAFVR 1955-58; CA 1962; appts Alcan Aluminium Ltd of Canada in: Canada, Argentina, Brazil, Spain, UK (tres in Canada, dir of fin UK); dir of fin Br Aerospace plc; memb: Beaconsfield Cons Assoc, advsy cnsl ECGD, 100 Gp; FCA; *Recreations* philately, gardening, reading; *Clubs* University Club of Montreal Canada; *Style*— Dudley G Eustace, Esq; St Anthony's Cottage, Tylers Green, Penn, Bucks, HP10 8EQ (☎ 049 481 2627); 3540 Ave Du Musée, Montreal, Quebec, Canada; 11 Strand, London, WC2N 5JT (☎ 01 389 3933, fax 3983, car tel 0860 303 272, telex 919 221)

EUSTACE, Gillian Rosemary; da of John William Seeds, of Cheshire, and Ethel; *b* 3 Feb 1946; *Educ* Loreto Sch Cheshire; *m* 28 Feb 1970, John Malcolm, s of Malcolm Edmund Fawcett Eustace (d 1982); 2 da (Emma b 1970, Zoe b 1972); *Career* co-fndr and dir Crombre Eustace Ltd 1980-, dir Storeforce Ltd 1979-; *Recreations* theatre, tapestry, Georgian restoration, logic puzzles; *Clubs* Network, IOD, Women of the Year Assoc; *Style*— Mrs Gillian R Eustace; 63 St John St, Oxford OX1 2LG (☎ 0865 56528); Wallingford House, Wallingford on Thames, Oxon (☎ 0491 33333)

EUSTON, Earl of; James Oliver Charles FitzRoy; s and h of 11 Duke of Grafton, KG; *b* 13 Dec 1947; *Educ* Eton, Magdalene Coll Cambridge (MA); *m* 1972, Lady Clare Annabel Margaret Kerr (appeal pres Elizabeth FitzRoy Homes), da of 12 Marquess of Lothian; 1 s (Henry Oliver Charles, Viscount Ipswich, b 1978), 4 da (Lady Louise Helen Mary b 1973, Lady Emily Clare b 1974, Lady Charlotte Rose b 1983, Lady Isobel Anne b 1985); *Heir* s, Viscount Ipswich; *Career* page of honour to HM The Queen 1962-63; asst dir J Henry Schroder Wagg & Co 1973-82, exec dir Enskilda Securities 1982-87; dir: Jamestown Investments Ltd 1987-, Central Capital Holdings 1988-, Capel-Cure Myers Capital Management 1988-; FCA; *Style*— Earl of Euston; 6 Vicarage Gdns, London W8

EVAN-COOK, John Edward (Jack); JP (City of London 1950); s of Evan Cook (d 1947), Mayor of Camberwell 1918, and Ada, *née* Young (d 1950); *b* 25 Oct 1902; *Educ* Westminster City Sch, Goldsmiths Coll (Eng), Leyland Motors (apprentice); *m* 14 July 1928, Winifred Elizabeth (d 1985), da of Joseph Samuel Pointon; *Career* Maj RAOC 1940-46; advsr on packaging War Office 1940-46, chm Bd of Visitors HM Prison Brixton 1967-73, late chm Visiting Ctee Brixton Prison; Evan-Cook Gp (ret); Nat chm Inst of Packaging, pres 1954-57; Sheriff of London 1958-59, common councilman 1960-66 and 1968-73; Order of Homauyorn, 3rd Clan (Iran) Grand Cross of Merit, Order of Merit (Fed Rep of Germany), Paul Harris fellowship (Rotary) 1986; Chief Scout's; Medal of Merit 1962, Silver Acorn 1968; past Master Worshipful Co of Paviors; *Style*— John Evan-Cook, Esq; Deaks Manor, Deaks Lane, Cuckfield, W Sussex RH17 5JA

EVANS *see also*: Gwynne-Evans, Havard-Evans, Tudor Evans

EVANS, (Laurence) Adrian Waring; s of Laurence Ansdell Evans, of Chesworth House, Horsham, Sussex, and Barbara Alice Waring Blount, *née* Gibb; *b* 29 June 1941; *Educ* Stowe, Trinity Coll Cambridge (BA); *m* 1, 18 Aug 1962 (m dis 1981), Caroline Velleman, da of Antony Ireland Baron von Simunich; 1 s (Dominic b 11 Sept 1968), 2 da (Kate b 26 Oct 1965, Laura b 23 July 1971); m 2, 25 Nov 1983, Ingela Brita Byng, da of Axel Berglund, of Stockholm; *Career* vice pres Citibank NA NY 1963-71, dir First Nat Finance Corpn Ltd 1971-76, md Grindlays Bank plc 1976-85, GAP md Benchmark Gp plc 1986-, dir TSB Commercial plc 1986-; chm cncl of mgmnt gp Activity Projects; *Clubs* Brooks's; *Style*— Adrian Evans, Esq; 17 Elm Park Rd, Loncon SW3 (☎ 01 351 9342); Henrietta Ho, 9 Henrietta Place, London W1 (☎ 01 631 3313)

EVANS, Sir Anthony Adney; 2 Bt (UK 1920); s of Sir Walter Harry Evans, 1 Bt (d 1922), and Margaret Mary, *née* Dickens (d 1969); *b* 5 August 1922; *Educ* Shrewsbury, Merton Coll Oxford; *m* 1, 1 May 1948 (m dis 1957), Rita Beatrice, da of late Alfred David Kettle, of Souldern, Oxon, and formerly w of Larry Rupert Kirsch; 2 s, 1 da; m 2, 1958, Sylvia Jean; *Style*— Sir Anthony Evans, Bt; Almer Manor, Blandford, Dorset

EVANS, Anthony David; s of Capt William Price Evans, of Swansea, and Joan Furze, *née* Pitchford; *b* 14 Dec 1946; *Educ* Grove Park Sch Wrexham, Univ Coll Wales Aberystwyth (LLB); *m* 10 Jan 1987, Diane Janet, da of Bernard Pauls, of Leamington, Ontario, Canada; *Career* ptnr MacFarlanes Slrs 1982-; dep chm Swansea W Cons Assoc 1070, chm Lion Boys' Club Hoxton London 1985-; Liveryman Worshipful Co of Coopers 1975, Freeman Worshipful Co of Solicitors 1978; memb Law Soc 1971; *Recreations* sailing, climbing; *Style*— Anthony Evans, Esq; 1 Grove Park, London SE5 8LT; Macfarlanes, 10 Norwich St, London EC4A 1BD (☎ 01 831 9222, fax 01 831 9607, telex 296381 MACFAR G)

EVANS, Prof Anthony John; s of William John Evans (d 1965), and Marion Audrey, *née* Young (d 1988); *b* 1 April 1930; *Educ* Queen Elizabeth's Hosp Bristol, Sch of Pharmacy London Univ (BPharm, PhD), Univ Coll London (PG Dipl Librarianship); *m* 21 Aug 1954, Anne, da of John Horwell (d 1960), of Grimsby; 2 da (Jane b 1957, Susan b 1960); *Career* lectr in pharmaceutical engrg sci, Sch of Pharmacy Univ of London 1954-57; librarian: Sch of Pharmacy Univ of London 1958-63, Loughborough Univ of Technol 1964-; dean of the School of Educnl Studies Loughborough Univ 1973-76; memb exec bd Int Fedn Library Assocs and Insts (IFLA) 1983-88 (tres 1985-88); hon life memb Int Assoc of Technol Univ Libraries (treasurer 1968-70, pres 1970-75); vice-pres Assoc for Info Mgmnt (ASLIB) 1985-87; conslt Br Cncl, UNESCO, UNIDO, World Bank in some 11 countries particularly Mexico and China; FLA 1969; *Recreations* travel, sport, model railways; *Clubs* Royal Cwlth Soc; *Style*— Professor Anthony Evans; 78 Valley Rd, Loughborough, Leicestershire LE11 3QA (☎ 0509 215670); Pilkington Library, University of Technology, Loughborough, Leicestershire LE11 3TU (☎ 0509 222340, fax 0509 234806, telex 34319 UNITEC G)

EVANS, Sir Athol Donald; KBE (1963), CBE (1954, MBE 1939); s of Henry Alfred Evans, of Indive, S Africa, and Rhoda May, *née* Greenlees; *b* 16 Dec 1904; *Educ* Graeme Coll, Rhodes Univ S Africa (BA, LLB); *m* 12 Sept 1931, Catherine Millar, da of William M Greig of East London, Cape Province, S Africa; 1 s, 2 da; *Career* joined S Rhodesia Public Service 1928, law offr, legal advsr, memb Public Service Bd, sec for Int Affairs, sec for Home Affrs (Fedn of Rhodesia and Nyasaland); chm: Bd of Tstees Rhodes Nat Gallery, Zimbabwe Nat Tst, Nat Cncl for Care of the Aged; Gold Cross of St Mark (Greece) 1962; *Style*— Sir Athol Evans, KBE; 8 Harvey Brown Ave, Harare, Zimbabwe (☎ 25164)

EVANS, Hon Mrs (Audrey Mary); o da of 1 Viscount Leathers, CH, PC (d 1965); *b* 21 Dec 1915; *Educ* Benenden, St Andrews Univ; *m* 7 July 1938, Edward Noel Evans (d 1964), s of Edward William Evans; 2 s, 1 da; *Career* publisher; *Recreations* travel; *Style*— Hon Mrs Evans; Flat 5, 28 Hyde Park Gdns, London W2 (☎ 01 723 2909)

EVANS, The Hon Benedict Blackstone; o s of Thomas Charles Evans (d 1985), ex-dir of King's Fund Coll, and Baroness Blackstone, *qv*; *b* 6 Sept 1963; *Educ* William Ellis Sch for Boys, Manchester Polytechnic (BA Hons), Royal Coll of Art (MA); *Recreations* skiing; *Clubs* WAG, Zanzibar (London), Paradise Garage (N York); *Style*— The Hon Benedict Evans; 17 Fournier St, Spitalfields, London E1; Royal Coll of Art, Kensington Gore, London SW7 (☎ 01 584 5020)

EVANS, Sir (Robert) Charles; o s of late Robert Charles Evans, of Wrexham; *b* 19 Oct 1918; *Educ* Shrewsbury Sch, Univ Coll Oxford (BM, BCh, MA); *m* 1957, Denise Nea, da of Jean-Antoine Morin, of Paris; 3 s; *Career* served W II RAMC SE Asia (despatches); surgical registrar United Liverpool Hosps and Liverpool Regnl Hosps 1947-57, Hunterian prof Royal Coll of Surgeons Eng 1953, princ Univ Coll of North Wales Bangor 1958-84, v-chllr Univ of Wales 1965-67 and 1971-73; dep ldr Everest Expedition 1953, ldr Kangchenjunga Expedition 1955; FRCS; kt 1969; *Books* Eye on Everest (1955), On Climbing (1956), Kangchenjunga - The Untrodden Peak (1956); *Clubs* Alpine (pres 1967-70); *Style*— Sir Charles Evans; Ardincaple, Capel Curig, N Wales

EVANS, Charles Wackett; s of David Richard Evans (d 1970), of Essex, and Emily Alice, *née* Wackett (d 1974); *b* 14 May 1914; *Educ* Burlington Coll; *m* 28 Dec 1951, Hazel Baldam, da of George Baldam (d 1985), of Dorset; 1s (Christoper Charles b 13 Aug 1954), 1 da (Hilary Jane B 20 Dec 1952); *Career* Air Miny Aeronautical Inspection Directorate 1940-42, special duties TaTa Aircraft Ltd Bombay 1942-46; tech mangr Air Tport Charter Ltd Jersey 1947-52, chm and fndr Aviation Jersey Ltd 1953-; FRGS 1953; *Recreations* gardening, travel; *Clubs* Special Forces; *Style*— Charles Evans, Esq; Champ Des Fleurs, Le Hurel, St Ouem, Jersey, Channel Islands (☎ 0534 43 535); Aviation Jersey Ltd, Rue Des Pres, St Savior, Jersey (☎ 0534 25 301, fax 0534 59 449, telex 419 2161 AVIOJY G)

EVANS, Hon Mrs; Cicili Carol; *née* Paget; yst da of 1 and last Baron Queenborough, GBE (d 1949) (by 2 w), gs of 1 Marquess of Anglesey; *b* 18 April 1928; *m* 10 Dec 1949, Capt Robert Victor John Evans, Welsh Guards, s of late Brig John Meredith Jones Evans, CBE, MC, of Wishanger, Churt, Farnham, Surrey; 2 s, 1 da; *Style*— Hon Mrs Evans; Gainsford House, Cowden, Kent

EVANS, Clifford John; s of Wallace Evans (d 1971), and Elsie Evans (d 1975); *b* 9 Oct 1928; *Educ* Cardiff HS, Gonville and Caius Coll Cambridge; *m* 4 April 1953, Sheila Margaret (Molly), da of James Walker, of Abergavenny, South Wales; 2 s (Christopher b 23 May 1957, Robert b 16 Sept 1959); *Career* chief engr Caribbean Construction Co Ltd Jamaica 1954-61, sr ptnr Wallace Evans and Ptnrs and ptnr of associated partnerships in Hong Kong and the Caribbean 1971- (ptnr 1962-); memb: Penarth Rotary Club 1966-, Penarth RNLI Ctee 1986-; attache Welsh team Cwlth Games Jamaica 1966-; pres IStructE 1982-83, fell Fellowship of Engrg; memb: Cncl CIArb, Panel of Arbitrators of ICE and CIArb, Standing Ctee for Structural Safety 1983-, Cncl ICE 1984-87, Cncl ACE 1980-83, Ct of Univ of Wales, Coll of Cardiff; convenor President's Ctee for Urban Environment 1987-; Freeman of London; Liveryman: Worshipful Co of Engineers, Worshipful Co of Arbitrators (1985), Co of Constructors; FIStructE, FEng, FCIArb, FICE, FIHT, FIWEM, FASCE, MCONSE; *Recreations* sailing, offshore yacht racing, skiing, swimming; *Clubs* Royal Thames YC, Royal Ocean Racing, Royal Corinthian YC, Royal Jamaica YC, Hawks, Cardiff and County, Livery; *Style—* Clifford Evans, Esq; Mariner's Way, Marine Parade, Penarth, South Glamorgan CF6 2BE (☎ 0222 705577); Wallace Evans and Partners, Plymouth House, Penarth, South Glamorgan CF6 2YF (☎ 0222 705577, fax 0222 709793, car 0860 719740, telex 497338 WEPCON G)

EVANS, David John; MP (C) Welwyn Hatfield 1987-; *b* 23 April 1935; *m* Janice Hazel *née* Masters; 2 s, 1 da; *Style—* David Evans, Esq, MP; House of Commons, London SW1A 0AA

EVANS, David Marshall; QC (1981), Circuit Judge (1987); s of Robert Trevor Evans and Bessie Estelle, *née* Thompson; *b* 21 July 1937; *Educ* Liverpool Coll, Trinity Hall Cambridge (MA, LLM), Univ of Chicago (JD); *m* 1961, (Alice) Joyce, da of Ernest Rogers (d 1961); 2 s (Richard b 1967, James b 1969); *Career* teaching fell Stanford Univ Palo Alto California 1961-62, asst prof Univ of Chicago Illinois 1962-63, lectr UC of Wales Aberystwyth 1963-65; barr Grays Inn 1964, Northern circuit, recorder of Crown Ct 1984; circuit judge 1987-; *Recreations* walking, photography, visual arts, motorsport; *Clubs* Athenaeum, Liverpool; *Style—* His Hon Judge D Marshall Evans, QC; Queen Elizabeth II Law Courts, Derby Square, Liverpoll L2 1XA (☎ 051 236 4555)

EVANS, Hon David Robert Cynlais; s of Baron Evans of Claughton (Life Peer); *b* 1964; *Educ* Birkenhead Sch, UCL (LLB); *Recreations* hockey, rugby, golf, squash, cars, literature; *Style—* Hon David Evans

EVANS, David Vernon; s of Walter Evans (d 1976), of Osmotherley, N Yorks, and Florence Ethel, *née* Vernon; *b* 8 Mar 1935; *Educ* Durham Sch, St Catharine Coll Cambridge Univ (MA, LLM); *m* 5 May 1962, Sonia, *née* Pyle; 1 s (Andrew b 1963), 2 da (Rachel b 1966, Judith b 1967); *Career* slr Crombie Wilkinson & Robinson York 1959-61, managing ptnr Simpson Curtis Leeds 1982- (ptnr 1963, joined 1961); govr Leeds GS, church warden Leeds Parish Church (tstee appeal fund), memb ctee St Catharine's Soc (chm Yorks branch); past chm Leeds Round Table; memb Law Soc; *Recreations* music, tennis, bee-keeping; *Clubs* Leeds,; *Style—* David Evans, Esq; Thorner Lodge, Thorner, Leeds LS14 3DE (☎ 0532 892 517); 41 Park Square, Leeds LS1 2NS (☎ 0532 433 433, fax 0532 445598, car tel 0860 227 383, telex 55376)

EVANS, David Wyke; s of Mervyn Evans (d 1987), and Phyllis Evans; *b* 13 Mar 1934; *Educ* Prince Alfred Coll Adelaide S Australia, Univ of Adelaide (BEc), Univ of Oxford (MA); *m* 3 Oct 1959, Pamela Rubina, da of Peter McKenzie Strang (d 1945); 2 s, (Kym b 1961, Peter b 1967), 1 da (Nicola b 1964); *Career* Aust: Dip Serv 1959-: second sec Jakarta 1962-65 (later third sec), political affairs UN Branch Dept of Foreign Affairs 1965-68; first sec UN New York 1968-70, cnsllr Belgrade 1970-72, dir organisation staffing and trg 1972-74, high cmmr Accra 1974-77 (Ambassador to Senegal 1974-77 and Ivory Coast 1975-77), asst sec info branch 1977-79, hd Europe Americans and NZ div 1980, Aust Nat Observer Gp Zimbabwe elections 1981, ambassador Moscow and Mongolia 1981-84, high cmmr Kuala Lumpur 1984-87, dep high cmmr London 1987-; Freedom City of London 1987; S Australian Rhodes Scholar 1957; *Style—* David Evans, Esq; Australian High Commission, Strand, London WC2B 4LA (☎ 01 438 8211)

EVANS, Prof Dennis Frederick; s of George Frederick Evans (dec), and Gladys Martha (dec); *b* 27 Mar 1928; *Educ* Nottingham HS, Lincoln Coll Oxford (MA, DPhil); *Career* res fell ICI Oxford 1952-83 and 1954-56, res assoc Univ of Chicago 1953-54; Dept of Chemistry Imperial Coll Sci: lectr 1956-, sr lectr 1963, reader 1964, prof of chemistry 1981; FRS 1981; *Recreations* wine, travel; *Clubs* Chelsea Arts; *Style—* Prof Dennis Evans; 64a Cathcart Rd, London, SW10 9JQ (☎ 01 352 6540); Dept of Chemistry, Imperial Coll of Science, London, SW7 2AY (☎ 01 589 5111 ext 4579)

EVANS, Hon Edward Broke; VRD; yr s of 1 Baron Mountevans (d 1958), and his 2 wife Elsa, *née* Andvord (d 1963); *b* 21 August 1924; *Educ* Wellington; *m* 15 July 1947, Elaine Elisabeth, da of late Capt (S) William Wilson Cove, RN (ret), of The Clock House, Bodenham, Wilts; 2 s, 1 da; *Career* Cdr (E) RNR (ret), employed ICI Ltd; *Style—* Hon Edward Evans, VRD; 15 York Mansions, Prince of Wales Drive, London SW11

EVANS, Edward Somers Fleming; s of late Capt E F H Evans, JP; *b* 26 April 1910; *Educ* Cheltenham Coll, CCC Oxford (MA); *m* 1947, Erica Grace, da of late Col W D Conner; 2 s (Edward William b 1948, Christopher Frank b 1950); *Career* vol serv with the Oxford Gp (Moral Re-armament) in Europe and America 1933-38, served with 1 Bn Worc Regt in Middle East 1940-41, staff Capt HQ Western Cmd 1942-45; farmer and landowner; High Sheriff Herefordshire 1964; chm: Hill Evans & Co Ltd Worcester 1961-67, Herefordshire CLA 1971-74, western region Timber Growers Orgn 1975-78; since 1965 visited every continent to explore the rôle of agric in world devpt; *Recreations* shooting, fishing; *Clubs* Royal Cwlth Soc; *Style—* Edward Evans, Esq; Dial House, Whitbourne, nr Worcester WR6 5SG (☎ 0886 21223)

EVANS, Lady; Elizabeth; da of William Jaffray, of Aberdeen; *m* 8 Sept 1945, Sir (Sidney) Harold Evans, 1 and last Bt, CMG, OBE (d 1983); 1 da, and 1 s decd; *Style—* Lady Evans; 1 Kipling Court, St Aubyns Mead, Rottingdean, Sussex

EVANS, Hon Elizabeth Ann Cynlais; da of Baron Evans of Claughton (Life Peer); *b* 1957; *Educ* BEd; *Style—* Hon Elizabeth Evans

EVANS, Prof (David) Ellis; yr s of David Evans (d 1948), and Sarah Jane, *née* Lewis; *b* 23 Sept 1930; *Educ* Llandeilo GS, Univ Coll of Wales Aberystwyth, Univ Coll of Swansea, Jesus Coll Oxford; *m* 1957, Sheila Mary, er da of David Thomas Jeremy, of Swansea, Wales; 2 da; *Career* former lectr, reader and prof of welsh language and literature, Univ Coll Swansea; Jesus prof of celtic, Oxford and fell of Jesus Coll 1978-; FBA; hon fell Univ Coll Swansea 1985-; *Recreations* music, walking; *Style—* Prof Ellis Evans; Jesus College, Oxford (☎ Oxford 0865 279700/279739)

EVANS, Col (James) Ellis; CBE (1973), (OBE 1952, TD 1947, JP (Flintshire 1951)); s of James William Evans (d 1970), and Eleanor Evans, MBE, JP; *b* 6 August 1910; *Educ* Epworth Coll Rhyl; *Career* served 1939-45 with RA (France, N Africa and Italy), Lt-Col 1944, Cdr 384 Light Regt RA (RWF) TA 1947-52, Col 1952, Cdr RA 53 (Welsh) Div 1953-57; chm Denbighshire and Flintshire T and AF Assoc 1961-68 and N Wales Sub-Assoc of Wales and Monmouthshire TA and VR Assoc 1968-71; chartered accountant 1927-, memb Prestatyn UDC 1939-74, chm 1947; chm N Wales Police Authority 1976; DL Flintshire 1953, vice-lieut 1970-74, vice lord-lieut 1977-79, HM Lord-Lieut 1979-85; CStJ 1982; *Recreations* lawn tennis (played for Lancs and Wales); *Clubs* E India, Devonshire, Sports and Public Schs, and City (Chester); *Style—* Col Ellis Evans, CBE, TD; Trafford Mount, Gronant Rd, Prestatyn, Clwyd (☎ 074 56 4119)

EVANS, Very Rev (Thomas) Eric; s of Eric John Rhys Evans and Florence May Rogers; *b* 1 Feb 1928; *Educ* St David's Coll, St Catherines's Coll Oxford; *m* 1957, Linda Kathleen, *née* Budge; 2 da; *Career* ordained Canterbury Cath: deacon 1954, priest 1955; curate st John Margate 1954-58, first dir Bournemouth Samaritans and diocesan youth chaplain Dio of Gloucester 1962-69, canon missioner Gloucester Cathedral 1969-75, archdeacon of Cheltenham 1975-88, dean of St Paul's 1988-; memb bd of govrs Church Cmmrs (Assets Ctee) 1978-88, dir Ecclesiastical Insurance Office 1978-, chm Cncl for Care of Churches 1981-88, memb of Standing Ctee of Gen Synod 1981-88, chm Glos Assoc of Mental Health 1983-85, govr Cheltenham Ladies' Coll 1983-, chm Glos Diocesan Advsy Cmmn 1984-88; dean: Order of the Br Empire, Order of St Michael and St George; *Recreations* travel (especially Middle East); *Clubs* Carlton, The Downhill Only (Wengen, Switzerland); *Style—* The Very Rev the Dean of St Paul's; The Deanery, 9 Amen Court, London EC4M 7BU (☎ 01 236 2827)

EVANS, Evelyn Jane Alice; CBE (1960), MBE (1955); da of Charles Evans (d 1971),of Hollycroft, Fife Rd, Coventry, and Edith Florence, *née* Wilkinson (d 1961); *b* 22 Mar 1910; *Educ* Barr's Hill GS Coventry; *Career* chartered librarian; dep city librarian York 1941-45, Br Cncl librarian Gold Coast 1945-50, dir of library servs Gold Coast/Ghana 1950-65, UNESCO library conslt Sri Lanka 1967-70; conslt Ranfurly Library Serv 1975-; govr Cwlth Inst 1966-67; FLA; *Recreations* reading, walking, dogs; *Style—* Miss Evelyn Evans, CBE; 8 Park Close, Bladon, Oxford OX7 1RN (☎ 0993 811 359)

EVANS, Frederick Anthony; CVO (1973); s of Herbert Anthony Evans, and Pauline, *née* Allen; *b* 17 Nov 1907; *Educ* Charterhouse, Corpus Christi Coll Cambridge (MA); *m* 1934, Nancy, da of H Meakin; 2 s (Peter, Richard), 1 da (Suzanne); *Career* HM Colonial Serv 1935-57, colonial sec and acting govr Bahamas 1947-51, perm sec Ghana 1951-57; gen sec Duke of Edinburgh's Award 1959-72; *Books* (nom de plume Deric) The State Apartments at Buckingham Palace - a Souvenir (1985); *Style—* Frederick Evans, Esq, CVO; Bamber Cottage, Saintbury Hill, Froyle, nr Alton, Hants; Adviser for the Handicapped, Duke of Edinburgh's Award, 5 Prince of Wales Terrace, London W8

EVANS, Geoffrey Clifford; s of Ralph Clifford Evans (d 1967), of Carisbrooke, Isle of Wight, and Florence Grace, *née* Grimshaw (d 1973); *b* 18 Sept 1921; *Educ* King James I Sch Newport IOW; *m* 24 Sept 1949, (Mina Betty) June, da of Bertram Downer (d 1953), of Freshwater, IOW; 1 da (Caroline b 1955); *Career* jt gen mangr Lloyds Bank 1975-81, regnl dir 1982-84; dir: C E Heath plc 1982-87, Hunting Gp plc 1981-, Trade Indemnity plc 1982-, Greyhound Bank Ltd 1982-87, Pitman plc 1982-85; FCIB 1975; *Recreations* golf, sailing, gardening, painting; *Style—* Geoffrey Evans, Esq; Lymore Gate, Lymington Road, Milford-on-Sea SO41 0QN (☎ 0590 42044)

EVANS, George Harold; s of George John Evans (d 1988), of London, and May,*née* Frazer; *b* 20 Oct 1920; *Educ* Quinton Sch, King's Coll London (BSc), Imperial Coll London (DIC); *m* 14 March 1946, Hazel Evelyn, da of Frederick Charles Brett (d 1958), of London; 1 s (Michael Andrew b 1948), 1 da (Lesley Ann b 1953); *Career* WW11 Flying Offr RAF 1939-45; sr engr Holst & Co Ltd 1948-58, sr ptnr Alan Marshall & Ptnrs 1958-82; memb Worshipful Co of Paviors; FICOB 1939, FIStructE 1950; *Recreations* golf, swimming, bridge; *Clubs* RAC; *Style—* George Evans, Esq; 7 Broom Park, Teddington, Middx TW11 9RN (☎ 01 977 5591)

EVANS, Sir Geraint Llewellyn; CBE (1959); s of William John Evans; *b* 16 Feb 1922; *Educ* Guildhall Sch of Music and Drama; *m* 1948, Brenda Evans Davies; 2 s; *Career* opera singer; principal baritone Covent Garden; pres Guild for the Promotion of Welsh Music; dir: Harlech TV, Buxton Festival; appearances at Covent Garden, Glyndebourne, Vienna Staatsoper, La Scala, The Metropolitan, San Francisco, Lyric Chicago, Salzburg, Edinburgh Festival, Paris Opéra, Colon Buenos Aires, Berlin, Scottish Opera; Harriet Cohen Int Museum Award 1967, Fidelio Medal Int Assoc Opera Dirs 1980, San Francisco Opera Medal 1980, patron Churchill Theatre Bromley, memb Gorsedd of Bards Roy Nat Eisteddfod of Wales, vice-pres Kidney Research Unit for Wales Fndn; Worshipful Co Musicians Sir Charles Santley Memorial Award 1963; fellow: Univ Coll Cardiff, Jesus Coll Oxford 1979; FGSM, FRNCM, FRCM, FRSA, hon Freeman City of London 1984; Hon DMus: Wales 1965, Leicester 1969, London 1982, Coll of Nat Academic Awards 1982, Oxford 1985; Hon RAM 1969; kt 1969; *Books* Sir Geraint Evans: a Knight at the Opera (with Noel Goodwin 1984); *Style—* Sir Geraint Evans, CBE; Trelawney, Aberaeron, Dyfed, Wales

EVANS, Harold Matthew; s of late Frederick and Mary Evans, of Prestatyn, N Wales; *b* 28 June 1928; *Educ* St Mary's Rd Central Sch Manchester, Durham Univ (MA); *m* 1, 1953 (m dis 1978), Enid, da of late John Parker; 1 s, 2 da; m 2, 1981, Cristina Hambley-Brown (Tina Brown, *qv*), da of George H Brown, of San Pedro de Alcántara, Spain; *Career* with Reporter Newspaper (Ashton-under-Lyme) 1944-46 and 1949; joined Manchester Evening News 1952, asst editor 1958-61; editor: Northern Echo 1961-66 (ed-in-chief North of England Newspaper Co 1963-66), Sunday Times 1967-81 (chief asst to ed 1966, managing ed 1966, dir 1968), The Times 1981-82 (dir Times Newspapers Ltd 1978); dir Goldcrest Films and Television 1982- (makers of Chariots of Fire and Gandhi); memb exec bd Int Press Inst 1974-80; FSIAD, fellow Inst of Journalists (gold medal award 1979); hon visiting prof of journalism City Univ 1978-80; awards: hon medal Roy Photographic Soc, Editor of the Year 1975, Editor of the Year 1982 (Granada TV's What the Papers Say); Hon Doctorate Stirling Univ 1982, Poynter fellow Yale Univ, visiting prof Duke Univ North Carolina; *Books* The Active Newsroom, Editing and Design (five vols), We Learned to Ski (1974), The Story of Thalidomide (1978), Good Times, Bad Times (1983); *Clubs* Garrick, RAC; *Style—* Harold Evans, Esq; Goldcrest Films and Television Ltd, 51 Holland St, London W8 7JB (☎ 01 937 8022; telex 267458 GOLDCR)

EVANS, Hubert John Filmer; CMG (1958); yst s of Harry Evans (d 1914), and Edith Gwendoline, *née* Rees (d 1936); *b* 21 Nov 1904; *Educ* City of London Sch, Jesus Coll Oxford (MA, LLD); *m* 1948, Marjory Maureen Filmer, da of Howard Filmer Carrick (d 1954), and widow of Col R A M Tweedy; *Career* Indian Civil Serv: dep cmmr of Delhi 1938-42, pres Delhi Municipal Cncl, sec Delhi Provincial Admin 1942-45; HM Diplomatic Serv: financial advsr Persian Gulf 1950-51, ambass Managua 1952-54 (Korea 1957-61, Central Asian Res Centre 1964-69); chm Ed Bd Asian Affairs 1965-70; *Books* Islam in Iran (1985), Looking Back on India (1988); *Recreations* oriental studies; *Clubs* Athenaeum; *Style—* Hubert Evans, Esq, CMG; Manoir D'Arlette, Fatouville, 27210 Beuzeville, France

EVANS, Huw Prideaux; s of Richard Hubert Evans (d 1963), and Kathleen Annie, *née*

Collins; *b* 21 August 1941; *Educ* Cardiff HS; King's Coll Cambridge (MA), London Sch of Economics (MSC); *m* 1 April 1966, Anne, (head of English, Walthamstow Hall, Sevenoaks, da of Prof Percival Thomas Bray (d 1988), of Cyncoed, Cardiff; 2 s (Richard b 1969, Lewis b 1971); *Career* under sec HM Treasy Internat Fin Gp 1986) (Econ Assessment Gp 1980-86; *Style*— Huw P Evans, Esq; HM Treasury, Parliament St, London SW1 (☎ 01 270 4430)

EVANS, James; s of Rex Powis Evans and Louise Evans; *b* 27 Nov 1932; *Educ* Aldenham, St Catharine's Coll Camb (MA); *m* 1961, Jette Holmboe; 2 da; *Career* md and chief exec Int Thomson Orgn plc 1985-; dir: Reuters Hldgs plc 1984-, The Press Assoc Ltd 1983-; *Style*— James Evans, Esq; First Floor, The Quadrangle, PO Box 4YG, 180 Wardour Street, London W1A (☎ 01 437 9787, telex 261349)

EVANS, James Donald; yr s of Arthur Evans and Isabella McKinnon Evans; *b* 12 Nov 1926; *Educ* Royal GS High Wycombe; *m* 1946, Freda, *née* Bristow; 2 s, 3 da; *Career* editor the Northern Echo 1966-82; dir North of England Newspapers 1973-82 (editor-in-chief 1966-82); special correspondent for all Westminster Press daily newspapers 1983-86 (ret 1986); *Recreations* reading, driving, travel; *Clubs* Nat Liberal; *Style*— James Evans, Esq; 11 Onslow Road, Newent, Gloucestershire GL18 1TL (☎ 0531 822001)

EVANS, Hon Jane Lucy Cynlais; da of Baron Evans of Claughton (Life Peer); *b* 1968; *Style*— Hon Jane Evans

EVANS, Hon Jeffrey Richard; s of 2 Baron Mountevans (d 1974), and hp of bro, 3 Baron; *b* 13 May 1948; *Educ* Nautical Coll Pangbourne, Pembroke Coll Cambridge; *m* 1972, Hon Juliet, *qv*, da of 2 Baron Moran, KCMG; 2 s (Alexander b 1975, Julian b 1977); *Career* shipbroker; with H Clarkson & Co; Liveryman Worshipful Co of Shipwrights; *Recreations* cross-country skiing, fishing, reading; *Style*— Hon Jeffrey Evans; 42 Gloucester Walk, London W8 4HU

EVANS, John; MP (Lab) St Helens North 1983-; s of James Evans (d 1937), and Margaret, *née* Robson (d 1987); *b* 19 Oct 1930; *Educ* Jarrow Central Sch; *m* 1959, Joan, da of Thomas Slater; 2 s, 1 da; *Career* former marine fitter and engr, memb Hebburn UDC 1962-74 (chm 1972-73, ldr 1969-74), memb S Tyneside Met Dist Cncl 1973-74, MP (Lab) Newton Feb 1974-1983, memb Euro Parl 1975-79 (chm regnl policy and tport ctee 1976-79), asst govt whip 1979, pps to Rt Hon Michael Foot as ldr of oppn 1980-1983, NEC 1982-, oppn front bench spokesman Employment 1983-87; *Style*— John Evans, Esq, MP; House of Commons, London SW1

EVANS, John Alexander Llewellyn; s of Alan Lile Llewellyn Evans (d 1982), and Charlotte Mary, *née* Alexander; *b* 30 Nov 1942; *Educ* Rugby, Univ of Southampton (BSc); *m* 19 March 1983, (Carol) Ann, da of John Cornelius Ferris (d 1988) ; *Career* CAP Ltd 1976-80, Bos Software Ltd 1981-84, dir Vamp Health 1985-; Liveryman Worshipful Co Cutlers; CEng; *Recreations* fishing; *Clubs* Hurlingham; *Style*— John Evans, Esq; 16 Langthorne St, London SW6 6JY (☎ 01 385 9809); Pool Cottage, Newcastle, Monmouth, Gwent; Vamp Health, 39 East Hill, London SW18 (☎ 01 871 2866)

EVANS, Doctor (Noel) John Bebbington; CB (1980); s of William John Evans and Gladys Ellen, *née* Bebbington; *b* 26 Dec 1933; *Educ* Hymers Coll Hull, Christ's Coll Cambridge (MA, MB, BChir), London Univ (DPH); FRCP; FFCM; *m* 1, 1960 (m dis), Elizabeth Mary Garbut; 2 s (David, Hugh), 1 da (Sarah); m 2, 1974, Eileen Jane, *née* McMullan; *Career* barr Gray's Inn; dep chief medical offr DHSS 1977-83, dep sec DHSS 1977-84, proprietor John Evans Photographic Grosmont, conslt in Pub Health and Health Service Mgmnt; *Style*— John Evans, Esq, CB; Athelstan, Grosmont, Abergavenny, Gwent NP7 8LW (☎ 0981 240616)

EVANS, His Honour Judge; John Field; QC (1972); 2 s of John David Evans (d 1950), of Llandaff, Cardiff, and Lucy May, *née* Field (d 1975); *b* 27 Sept 1928; *Educ* Cardiff HS, Exeter Coll Oxford (MA); *Career* RAF 1947-49, pilot offr 1948; barr Inner Temple 1953, dep chm Worcs QS 1964-71, rec Crown Ct 1972-78, circuit judge Midland and Oxford 1978-; *Recreations* golf; *Clubs* Vincent's (Oxford), R St David's Golf; *Style*— His Hon Judge Evans, QC; 1 Fountain Court, Birmingham B4 6DR; Dudley Crown Court, Dudley, West Midlands

EVANS, Prof (Henry) John; s of David Evans, DCM (d 1963), and Gladys May, *née* Jones; *b* 24 Dec 1930; *Educ* Llanelli GS, Univ Coll of Wales Aberystwyth (BSc, PhD); *m* 1, 1 June 1957, Gwenda Roslind, *née* Thomas (d 1974); 4 s (Paul b 16 Dec 1958, Hugh b 1 April 1960, John b 28 Oct 1961, Owen b 24 July 1963); m 2, 9 June 1976, Dr Roslyn Rose, da of Dr Leigh Angell, of Canberra, Australia; *Career* res scientist MRC radiobiological res unit Harwell 1955-64, prof genetics Univ of Aberdeen 1964-69, dir MRC Human Genetic Unit Edinburgh 1969-; Hon Prof Univ of Edinburgh 1970; FRSE 1971, FIBiol 1980, FRCP Ed 1989; *Books* Human Radiation Cytogenetics (1967), Mutagen-Induced chromosome Damage in Man (1978); *Recreations* golf, music; *Clubs* Royal Cwlth; *Style*— Prof John Evans; 45 Lauder Rd, Edinburgh EH9 1UE (☎ 031 667 2437); MRC Human Genetics Unit, Western Gen Hosp, Edinburgh (☎ 031 332 2471, fax 031 343 2620)

EVANS, Lt-Col John Roberts; TD (1954), DL (1973); s of David James Haydn Evans (d 1961); *b* 16 Jan 1917; *Educ* Llandovery Coll, Exeter Univ; *m* 1945, Sheila Rita, da of Richard Ball (d 1940); 1 s, 1 da; *Career* served in WW II with HAC and RA (India and Far E), with Welch Regt (TA) 1947-66, Lt-Col 6 (Glam) Bn Welch Regt 1963-66; admitted slr 1952; pres Cardiff and Dist Law Soc 1981-82 (former vice-pres), hon slr Welsh Rugby Union, govr and hon slr Welsh Sports Aid Fndn, chm Tstees Uandovery Coll, memb Ct of Govrs Univ Coll Cardiff; *Recreations* rugby football, music and fishing; *Clubs* Army and Navy, Cardiff and County; *Style*— Lt-Col John Evans, TD, DL; Greenbanks, Highfields, Llandaff, Cardiff, S Glam (☎ 0222 562480)

EVANS, John Russell; s of Henry Claude Evans, of Hamilton, Scotland; *b* 2 August 1945; *Educ* King James I GS Bishop Auckland, City Univ London (BScEng); *m* (m dis); 1 s (Jonathan), 1 da (Nicola); *Career* apprentice Rolls Royce 1960-70, with Ford 1970-72, General Motors 1972-77, gen mangr Butec Electrics (BL) 1977-78, md Park Bros 1978-79, md Bonser Engineering 1980-85, mfrg dir Lansing Henley 1979-81, md 1981-85, mfrg dir Data Magnetics 1985-87, md Renold Conveyor 1988-; CEng, FIProdE; *Recreations* reading, rugby, sailing, squash; *Style*— John Evans Esq; Dunmor House, Tower Rd, Burton on Trent, Staffs DE15 0NH; Renold Conveyor, Horninglow Rd, Burton on Trent, Staffs DE14 2PS (☎ 0283 32881, fax 0283 510136)

EVANS, Hon Mrs (Juliet); *née* Wilson; only da of 2 Baron Moran, KCMG; *b* 29 Sept 1950; *Educ* St Mary's Sch Calne, Newnham Coll Cambridge; *m* 1972, Hon Jeffrey Richard de Corban Evans *qv*; 2 s (Alexander, Julian); *Style*— Hon Mrs Evans; 42 Gloucester Walk, London W8 4HU

EVANS, (William) Kenneth; s of Judge William Hugh Evans, ICS (d 1969), of Bournemouth, and Gladys Gertruse, *née* Williamson (d 1975); *b* 19 July 1925; *Educ* Corpus Christi Coll Oxford (MA); *m* 11 Dec 1954, Lorna Maureen, da of Capt Basil Woodd Cahusac (d POW Far East); 1 s (Christopher b 1955), 1 da (Jennifer-Ann b 1964); *Career* enlisted RE 1943, trg OTS Kirklee India 1944-45, 2 Lt RE Lahore India 1945, Capt 854 Bridge Co Curma 1946, Adj to CRE Maymyo Burma 1946-47, demob 1947; local purchase buyer Uganda, asst Utd Africa co Kampala 1950-52, produce buying asst Dar Es Salaam and Kampala 1952-54, buyer Pirelli Ltd 1954-56, Peak Marwick Mitchell & Co London 1956-60, qualified CA 1960; Commercial Union Gp: joined 1960, taxation mangr 1968, gen mangr 1974, dir 1980 (main bd and 25 subsid cos), ret 1985; chm: Reffet Ltd (insur indust consortium) 1981, Cogent Ltd (technol co) 1982-84; chm taxation ctee Br Insur Assoc 1973-80; former memb taxation ctees of: VBI, Life Offices Assoc, IOD, business and indust ctee OECD; former memb: cncl Inst of Fiscal Studies, UK ctee Int Fiscal Assoc; cncllr: Met Borough of Hampstead 1959-62, London Borough of Camden 1964-71 (chm public bldgs ctee, dep chm building works and servs ctee); ACA 1960, FCA 1966 ; *Books* Tax Consequences of Changes in Foreign Foreign Exchange Rates (1972), The Effects of Losses in One Country on the Income Tax Treatment in Other Countries of an Enterprise or of Associated Companies Engaged in International Activities (UK Reports to Contress of the Int Fiscal Assoc, 1979); *Clubs* Carlton, IOD; *Style*— Kenneth Evans, Esq; Reffet Ltd, St Helens, 1 Undershaft, London EC3P 3DQ (☎ 01 283 7500, ext 2851, fax 01 283 7500, ext 2420, telex 887626)

EVANS, Rt Rev (Edward) Lewis; s of Rev Edward Foley Evans (d 1933), and Mary, *née* Walker; *b* 11 Dec 1904; *Educ* St Anselm's Croydon, Tonbridge Sch, Bishop's Coll Cheshunt, London Univ (external, BD, MTh); *m* 1967, Vera Lydia (d 1981), da of John Percival Groome; *Career* ordained: deacon 1937, priest 1938; curate St Mary's Prittlewell Chelmsford, warden St Peter's Coll Jamaica 1940, rector: Kingston Parish Church Jamaica 1949-52, Woodford-Craigton Jamaica 1952-57, suffragan bishop of Kingston Jamaica, 1957-60, bishop of Barbados 1960-71, ret 1971; *Style*— The Rt Rev Lewis Evans; No 1 Bungalow, Terry's Cross, Brighton Rd, Henfield, West Sussex BN5 95X (☎ 0273 493334)

EVANS, The Hon Liesel Morwenna; o da of Thomas Charles Evans (1985), and Baroness Bladestone, *qv*; *b* 17 Sept 1966; *Educ* Campden Sch for Girls, Bristol Univ; *Recreations* drama, socialising; *Style*— The Hon Liesel Evans; 2 Gower St, London WC1

EVANS, Lionel James Carlyon; OBE (1959); s of Lionel Lewis Carlyon Evans, BA (d 1949), of Bucks, and Margaret Etheldreda Mary Gore Browne (d 1978); *b* 12 July 1916; *Educ* Bradfield, Wye Coll, London Univ, (DipAgric); *m* 1942, Beryl Eulalie, da of Thomas Eyre McKenzie (d 1973), of Barbados; 1 s (Robin b 1944), 2 da (Margaret b 1947, Janet b 1950); *Career* sr lectr Imperial Coll of Tropical Agriculture Trinidad 1939-50, agric advsr Colonial Devpt Corp 1950-61; dir Agric Dept The World Bank Washington DC, USA 1961-73, dir Booker Agriculture Int Ltd 1975-88; chm Booker Farming Ltd 1979-; *Style*— L J C Evans, Esq; Little Acre, Alderpark Meadow, Long Marsdon, Tring, Herts HP23 4RB (☎ 0296 668237) Shaftesbury (0747) 2750)

EVANS, Hon Lucinda Mary Deirdre; did not assume husband's surname on marriage; da of 2 Baron Mountevans (d 1974), and Deirdre, Lady Mountevans; *b* 8 Jan 1951; *Educ* Queen's Gate Sch London; *m* 19 July 1980, John Edward Hooper, journalist, o s of W J Hooper, of Wimbledon; *Career* journalist with Daily Telegraph; *Recreations* reading about antarctic exploration; *Style*— Hon Lucinda Evans; c/o The Daily Telegraph, South Quay Plaza, 181 Marsh Wall, London E14

EVANS, (Ieuan) Lynn; s of Rev Thomas John Evans (d 1973), of Ealing Green, London W5, and Jenny, *née* Lloyd-Williams (d 1958); *b* 15 July 1927; *Educ* Bradford GS, Haverfordwest GS, St Marys Hosp Med Sch (MB BS); *m* 6 June 1956, Menna, da of Rev Evan James (d 1966), of Porthcawl; 1 s (Rowland b 1961), 1 da (Siân b 1963); *Career* Nat Serv jr surgical specialist RAMC Queen Alexandra's Mil Hosp 1951-53; conslt surgn: Lewisham & St John's Hosp 1965-87, Guys Hosp 1982-84; surgical tutor Guys Hosp Med Sch 1970-87; hon conslt surgn: St Lukes Hosp for the Clergy 1983-87, Royal Soc of Musicians of GB; cncl memb: Assoc of Surgns of GB & Ireland, section of surgery Royal Soc of Med, Med Soc of London, Harveian Soc; pres W Kent Medico-Chirurgical Soc, elder Utd Reform Church; memb Worshipful Soc of Apothecaries of London 1975, Freeman City of London 1975; FRCS 1954; *Recreations* skiing, gardening, travel; *Style*— I Lynn Evans, Esq; 34 Birchwood Rd, Petts Wood, Orpington, Kent; Emblem House Consulting Rooms, London Bridge Hospital, London SE1 2NP (☎ 01 403 3817)

EVANS, Lady; Madge - Margaret; da of John B and S J Gribbin, of Heaton Moor, Cheshire; *m* 1930, Sir Trevor Maldwyn Evans, CBE (d 1981), late dir Beaverbrook Newspapers; 1 s (Richard), 1 da (Marilyn); *Style*— Lady Evans; 17 Wolsey Close, Kingston Hill, Surrey (☎ 01 942 6016)

EVANS, Mark Singleton; s of Arthur Singleton Evans, RA (d 1954), of Torquay, and Constance Mary, *née* Jenkins (d 1980); *b* 27 Oct 1933; *Educ* Winchester, New Coll Oxford (BA); *Career* Nat Serv 2 Lt The Royal Dragoons 1952-54; pres Scarborough Cons Assoc 1981, chm Kensington Cons Assoc 1986-89;; *Clubs* Whites, Swinley Forest Golf, Easton Golf; *Style*— Mark Evans, Esq; 6 Argyll Rd, London W8 7DB (☎ 01 937 1182); Manor House, Brompton-by-Sawdon, nr Scarborough, N Yorks (☎ 0723 85233); C L Alexander Laing & Cruickshank, Piercy House, 7 Copthall Ave, London EC2 (☎ 01 588 2800, fax 01 256 9545)

EVANS, Lady (Mary); *née* Darby; *m* 1937, Prof Sir David Gwynne Evans, CBE (d 1984); 1 s, 1 da; *Style*— Lady Evans; 4 Craig Wen, Rhos-on-Sea, Clwyd LL28 4TS

EVANS, Dr Philip Rainsford; CBE (1968); s of Charles Irwin Evans, MA (d 1941), and Katherine Susan, *née* Bracher (d 1936); *b* 14 April 1910; *Educ* Sidcot Sch Winscombe, Leighton Park Sch Reading, Manchester Univ (MSc, MD), Columbia Univ New York; *m* 1935, Dr Barbara Dorothy Fordyce, da of Bernard Hay-Cooper (d 1931), of 2 Murray Rd, Wimbledon; 3 s (Nicholas, Jonathan, Charles), 1 da (Caroline); *Career* served 1939-45 War as Lt-Col RAMC (N Africa and Italy) (despatches), advsr in med CMF 1946; dir paediatric dept Guy's Hosp Med Sch 1946-71, physician Hosp for Sick Children 1946-75, physician-paediatrician to HM The Queen 1971-76; ldr Br Med Team, Saigon 1966-67; *Recreations* light verse; *Clubs* Royal Soc Med; *Style*— Dr Philip Evans, CBE; 24 Abbey Rd, London NW8 9AX (☎ 01 624 1668)

EVANS, Lt-Col Richard; MC (1944), JP (1965 N Herefordshire); o s of Robert Henry Evans, MBE, JP (d 1960), of Eyton Old Hall, Leominster, and Phyllis Eleanor, *née* Eden (d 1982); descended through the Evans family of Henblas, Anglesey, from

Llywarch ap Bran and from Ednyfed Vychan (*see* Burke's Landed Gentry, 1925 edn and 18 edn, vol III, 1972); *b* 15 Jan 1920; *Educ* Stowe, Worcester Coll Oxford; *m* 22 May 1965, Marian Elizabeth Magee, o child of Maj-Gen Brian Cuff, CB, CBE (d 1970), of Fleetham House, Kirkby Fleetham, Northallerton, Yorkshire; 1 s ((Richard) Jonathan b 5 April 1966); *Career* cmmnd KSLI 1940, served WWII in N Africa and Italy, subsequently in Palestine, Syria, Sudan, and in Korea 1952 (wounded); cmd KSLI 1960-63, ret; Bronze Star (USA) 1945; *Recreations* field sports; *Style*— Lt-Col Richard Evans, MC, JP; The Mead House, Eyton, Leominster, Herefordshire HR6 0AQ (☎ 0568 2109)

EVANS, Sir Richard Mark; KCMG (1984), CMG (1978, KCVO 1986); s of Edward Walter Evans, CMG (d 1985), and Anna Margaret, *née* Young (d 1976); *b* 15 April 1928; *Educ* Repton, Magdalen Coll Oxford (BA); *m* 1973, Rosemary Grania Glen Birkett; 2 s; *Career* Diplomatic Service: served London, Peking, Berne, London; head of Near Eastern and subsequently Far Eastern Dept FCO 1970-74, commercial cnsllr Stockholm 1975-77, min (econ) Paris 1977-79, dep under-sec of state FO 1982-84 (previously asst under-sec), ambassador Peking 1984-88; sr res fell Wolfson Coll Oxford; Int Bd of Advice, ANZ Banking Gp; *Style*— Sir Richard Evans, KCMG, KCVO; Sevenhampton House, Sevenhampton, Highworth, Wiltshire SN6 7QA

EVANS, Robert; CBE (1987); s of Gwilym Evans, and Florence May Evans; *b* 28 May 1927; *Educ* Old Swan Coll Liverpool, City Tech Liverpool, Blackburn Tech, Liverpool Univ; *m* 1950, Lilian May, *née* Ward; 1 s, 1 da; *Career* dep chm N Thames Gas 1975-77, chm E Midlands Gas Region 1977-, md Br Gas 1982- (bd memb and chief exec 1983-); pres Inst of Gas Engrs 1981; *Recreations* reading, DIY, golf; *Style*— Robert Evans Esq, CBE; Br Gas Corpn, Rivermill House, 152 Grosvenor Rd, London SW1V 3JL; 165 The Albany, Manor Road, East Cliff, Bournemouth, Dorset (☎ 0202 294108)

EVANS, Robert George; s of George Cecil Evans, of Northampton, and Francis Ennis, *née* Townsend; *b* 15 Nov 1947; *Educ* Northampton GS, Newcastle Univ (LLB, LSE, LLM); *m* 3 March 1973, Judith Evans, da of Thomas Edward Bartlett (d 1976); 2 s (Michael Robert, Peter David); *Career* slr, ptnr Cockburn & Evans Gosforth, sr lectr Law Newcastle-upon-Tyne Poly; memb: Law Soc 1975, Inc Law Soc Newcastle-upon-Tyne; *Recreations* cricket, cycling, fell walking; *Style*— Robert Evans, Esq; 1 The Bridle Path, Howden-le-Wear, Crook, Co Durham (☎ 0388 702 008); 167 High St, Gosforth Newcastle-upon-Tyne NE3 1HE (☎ 091 285 7100); 53 Parkwood Precinct, Speungmoor, Co Durham DL16 6AB (☎ 0388 815 317)

EVANS, Robert John Weston; s of Thomas Frederic Evans, of Cheltenham, and Margery, *née* Weston; *b* 7 Oct 1943; *Educ* Dean Cross Sch Cheltenham, Jesus Coll Cambridge (BA, MA, PhD); *m* 10 May 1969, (Catherine) Kati, da of Ferenc Róbert, (d 1972), of Budapest; 1 s (David b 1973), 1 da (Margaret b 1979); *Career* univ lectr Oxford 1969- (res fell Brasenose Coll 1968-), jt ed English Historical Review 1986-; chm Cumnor & Dist Hist Soc; FBA 1984; *Books* Rudolf II and his World (1984), The Making of the Habsburg Monarchy (1984); *Style*— Robert Evans, Esq; Brasenose College, Oxford OX1 4AJ (☎ 0865 277890)

EVANS, (David) Roderick; s of Thomas James Evans, of 3 Pine Crescent, Morriston, Swansea, and Dorothy, *née* Carpenter; *b* 22 Oct 1946; *Educ* Bishop Gore GS Swansea, UCL (LLB, LLM); *m* 6 Nov 1971, Kathryn Rebecca, da of Leonard Thomas Lewis, of 6 Mount Crescent, Morriston, Swansea; 3 s (Ioan b 1972, Gwion b 1974, Gruffudd b 1978), 1 da (Saran b 1976); *Career* called to the Bar Gray's Inn 1970, rec Crown Ct attached to the Wales and Chester circuit 1987-; *Style*— Roderick Evans, Esq; Angel Chambers, 94 Walter Road, Swansea SA1 5QA (☎ 0792 464623)

EVANS, Roderick Michael; s of Michael White Evans, of Monaco, and Helga Ingeborg, *née* Schneider; *b* 19 April 1962; *Educ* Millfield; *Career* dir of numerous companies incl Astra House Ltd, Furnival Estates Ltd, Garpool Ltd, Mulgate Investmts Ltd, Studfair Ltd, Lichfield Securities Ltd, Speylands Ltd, Evans Universal Ltd, Roando Holdings ltd, and Rowite Properties Ltd; *Recreations* motorcycling, shooting, flying; *Clubs* RAC, Royal Yorkshire YC; *Style*— Roderick Evans, Esq; Evans of Leeds plc, Millshaw, Ring Road Beeston, Leeds 11 (☎ 0532 711 888)

EVANS, Roger Kenneth; s of Gerald Raymond Evans, and Dr Annie Margaret Evans; *b* 18 Mar 1947; *Educ* Bristol GS, Trinity Hall Cambridge (MA); *m* 6 Oct 1973, (Doris) June, da of James Rodgers, of Co Down NI; 2 s (Edward Arthur, Henry William); *Career* chm Cambridge Univ Cons Assoc 1969; pres: Cambridge Georgian Gp 1969, Cambridge Union 1970; called to Bar Middle Temple (ad eundeum Inner Temple) MO circuit; parly candidate (cons): Warley West Oct 1974 and 1979, Ynŷs Môn (Anglesey) 1987; vice chm City of London Cons 1987-; memb exec ctee Friends of Friendless Churches 1983-; Freeman City of London 1976; *Recreations* architectural history; *Clubs* Carlton, Coningsby (chm 1976-77, tres 1983-87); *Style*— Roger Evans, Esq; 2 Harcourt Building, Temple, London, EC4Y 9DB (☎ 01 353 6961, fax 01 353 6968, telex 269871 MONREF G; 74 NFL 3053, Telecom Gold NFL 3053)

EVANS, Roy Lyon; s of David Lewis Evans (d 1937), of Pontarduulais, West Glam (d 1937), and Sarah, *née* Lyon (d 1960); *b* 13 August 1931; *Educ* Gowerton GS; *m* 17 Sept 1960, Brenda Yvonne, da of William George Jones (d 1972), of Gorseinon, West Glam; 1 s (Ian b 1967), 2 da (Julie b 1963, Lisa b 1973); *Career* Nat Serv RAF 1949-51; operator tin plate strip mill 1948-49 and 1951-64; gen sec Iron & Steel Trades Confedn 1985- (organiser 1964-73, asst gen sec 1973-85); chm TUC steel ctee 1985; memb NEC Lab Pty 1981-84, Euro Metalworkers Fedn, TUC Gen Cncl 1985-, ECSC Consultative Ctee 1985- (pres 1986-88), Bd BSC Industries Ltd; pres Industrial Orthopaedic Soc 1986-; *Style*— Roy L Evans, Esq; 26 Crecy Gdns, Redbourn, St Albans, Herts (☎ Redbourn 2174); ISTC, Swinton House, 324 Gray's Inn Rd, London WC1 (☎ 01 837 6691)

EVANS, Russell Wilmot; MC (1945); s of late William Henry Evans and Ethel Williams, *née* Wilmot; *b* 4 Nov 1922; *Educ* King Edward's Sch Birmingham, Birmingham U (LLB); *m* 1956, Pamela Muriel, *née* Hayward; 2 s, 1 da; *Career* chm The Rank Organisation 1981-83 (dep chm 1981, gp md 1975); dir: Rank Xerox Ltd 1973-, Southern Television 1974-, Fuji Xerox Ltd 1976-; chm Butlin's Ltd 1975-82, Rank City Wall Ltd 1975-; *Recreations* tennis, squash, photography; *Clubs* English Speaking Union, Roehampton; *Style*— Russell Evans, Esq, MC; Walnut Tree, Roehampton Gate, London SW15 (☎ 01 876 2433)

EVANS, Hon Sarah Louise Cynlais; da of Baron Evans of Claughton (Life Peer); *b* 1966; *Style*— Hon Sarah Evans

EVANS, Stephen Graham; s of William Campbell Evans, OBE, of Bradley Green, Redditch, Worcs, and Sarah Annie Evans, *née* Duckworth; *b* 20 May 1944; *Educ* Northampton Town and Co GS, W Bromwich GS, Hall Green Tech Coll Birmingham, S Birmingham Tech Coll; *m* 11 May 1968, Gillian Kathleen, da of John Skidmore; *Career* engr and sr engr Cooper MacDonald 1970-78, sr engr and assoc Peel and Fowler 1979-85 (ptnr 1985-); FIStrucE (former chm Midland Co Branch) CEng, memb Assoc of Consulting Engrs 1986 ; *Recreations* sport, music, (memb cte Birmingham Jazz Soc), the arts, travel; *Style*— Stephen Evans, Esq; Peel and Fowler, Griffin House, Ludgate Hill, Birmingham B3 1DW (☎ 021 236 7207, fax 021 236 6918)

EVANS, Stuart John; s of John Redshaw Evans, and Mabel Elizabeth, *née* Brown (d 1974); *b* 31 Dec 1947; *Educ* Royal GS Newcastle-upon-Tyne, Leeds Univ (LLB); *m* 2 Jan 1971, Margaret Elizabeth, da of Edgar John Evans (d 1966); 2 s (John Daniel b 1976, Thomas b 1977), 1 da (Elizabeth b 1983); *Career* articled clerk Stanley Brent & Co 1970-72, asst slr Slaughter & May 1972-79, ptnr Simmons & Simmons 1981- (asst slr 1979-80); reader St Stephens Church Canonbury; Freeman Worshipful Co of Slrs of the City of London; *Books* A Practitioner's Guide to the Stock Exchange Yellow Book (contrib 1989); *Recreations* squash, pictures; *Style*— Stuart Evans, Esq; London; Lodeve; Simmons & Simmons, 14 Dominion St, London EC2M 2RJ (☎ 01 628 2020, fax 01 588 4129, telex 888562 Simmon G)

EVANS, Doctor Trevor John; o s of Evan Alban (John) Evans, of Market Bosworth, Leics, and Margaret Alice, *née* Hilton; *b* 14 Feb 1947; *Educ* King's Sch Rochester, UCL, (BSc, PhD); *m* 1973, Margaret Elizabeth, da of Felix Whitham, of Anlaby, Hull; 3 s (Thomas b 1979, Owen b 1984, Jacob b 1988), 1 da (Jessica b 1981); *Career* chemical engr; gen sec The Inst of Chemical Engrs 1976-, jt hon sec Euro Fedn of Chemical Engrg, bd memb of Cncl of Sci and Technol Insts, memb exec ctee Cwlth Engrs Cncl; CEng, FIChemE, FBIM; *Recreations* renovation of home, travel; *Style*— Dr T J Evans; The Bakery Cottage, 2 Rectory Lane, Market Bosworth, nr Nuneaton, Warwicks CV13 0LS (☎ 0455 290480); Geo E Davis Bldg, 165-171 Rlwy Terrace, Rugby, Warwickshire CV21 3HQ (☎ 0788 78214, telex 311780)

EVANS, Trevor Mills; s of William Arthur Evans (d 1966), of Swansea, and Alma, *née* Mills (d 1945); *b* 28 Sept 1924; *Educ* Swansea GS; *m* 4 Oct 1952, Margaret, da of Evan James Jones (d 1986), of Narberth, Pembrokeshire; 3 s (Eifrion b 1954, Adrian b 1962, Meirion b 1966), 1 da (Susan Alma b 1957); *Career* slr in private prictice, HM coroner for S Powys; ACIS, ATII; *Recreations* dogs, sports interests, photography; *Clubs* Kennel; *Style*— Trevor Evans, Esq; Plasnewydd, Broadway, Builth Wells, Powys LD2 3DB; Sydney G Thomas & Co, West End House, West St, Builth Wells, Powys LD2 3AH

EVANS, Sir (William) Vincent (John); GCMG (1976), KCMG (1970, CMG 1959, MBE 1945, QC 1973); s of Charles Herbert Evans (d 1978), and Elizabeth, *née* Jenkins (d 1965); *b* 20 Oct 1915; *Educ* Merchant Taylors', Wadham Coll Oxford (BA 1937, BCL 1938, MA 1941, hon fell 1981); *m* 4 Jan 1947, Joan Mary, da of Angus Bryant Symons (d 1964), of 112 Powys Lane, Palmer's Green, London N13; 1 s (David b 1950), 2 da (Marion b 1948, Jane b 1952); *Career* serv WWII Lt-Col GB and N Africa; barr Lincoln's Inn 1939 (hon bencher 1983); asst legal advsr FO 1947-54, legal cnsllr UK Perm Mission to UN NY 1954-59, dep legal advsr FO 1960-68, legal advsr FCO 1968-75, chm Bryant Symons & Co 1964-85, chm Euro Ctee on Legal Co-operation, Cncl of Europe 1969-71, UK rep Cncl of Europe Steering Ctee on Human Rights 1976-80 (chm 1979-80), memb Human Rights Ctee (set up under Int Covenant on Civil and Political Rights) 1976-84, judge of Euro Ct of Human Rights 1980-, memb Permanent Ct of Arbitration 1987-; Hon DUniv Essex 1986; *Recreations* gardening; *Clubs* Athenaeum; *Style*— Sir Vincent Evans, GCMG, MBE, QC; 2 Hare Court, Temple, EC4 (☎ 01 583 1770); 4 Bedford Road, Moor Park, Northwood, Middx (☎ 09274 24085)

EVANS, William; s of late Eben Evans, of Tregaron, Cardiganshire; *b* 24 Nov 1895; *Educ* Univ Coll of Wales Aberystwyth, London Hosp Medical Coll; *m* 1936, Christine (d 1964), da of late John Lessels Downie, of Kirkcaldy; *Career* Offr 19 Lancashire Fusiliers 1917-19; consulting cardiologist: London Hosp, Nat Heart Hosp, Inst of Cardiology, Roy Soc of Musicans and RN (1946); author of several text books of diseases of the heart and contributor to various scientific journals; High Sheriff Cardiganshire 1959; hon memb Order of Druids 1960; *Recreations* writing, farming, fishing; *Style*— William Evans Esq; Bryndomen, Tregaron, Dyfed (☎ 097 44 404)

EVANS, William Emrys; CBE (1981); s of Richard Evans (d 1965), Bwlch Y Pentre, Foel, Llangadfan, Welshpool, Powys, and Mary Elizabeth Evans (d 1956); *b* 4 April 1924; *Educ* Llanfair Caereinion County Sch; *m* 26 May 1946, Mair, da of Evan Thomas (d 1953); 1 da (Ceridwen Eleri); *Career* WWII RN 1942-46 (despatches 1944); Midland Bank Ltd 1941-84: asst gen mangr 1967-72, regnl dir South Wales 1972-74, regnl dir Wales 1974-76,sr regn dir Wales 1976-84; dir: Align-Rite Ltd 1984-, Module 2 Ltd 1988-, Nat Welsh Omnibus Serv Ltd 1988-; chm: CBI Wales 1979-81, cncl Univ Coll of Wales Swansea 1982-, Welsh Ctee for Economic and Industl Affairs 1982-, Midland Bank Advsy Cncl for Wales 1984-, Wishing Well Appeal in Wales 1987-, Barnados Centernary in Wales Appeal 1987-88, Menter a Busnes 1988-, Welsh Sports Aid Fndn 1988-; vice-chm Executive Secondment Ltd 1984-; pres: Royal Nat Eisteddfod of Wales 1980-83, Welsh Congregational Church 1988-; vice pres Royal Welsh Agricultural Soc 1972-; dir: Devpt Corpn for Wales 1974-78, Wales Industl Devpt Advsy Bd, Devpt Bd for Rural Wales 1976-89 (chm fin and mktg ctee); tres: Welsh Congregational Church 1975-87, Mansfield Coll Oxford 1977-88; tstee: Catherine and Lady Grace James Fndn 1973-, John and Rhys Thomas James Fndn 1973-, Llandovery Coll 1980-, Mansfield Coll Oxford 1988-; memb: ct and cncl Univ Coll Swansea 1972-, Cncl for the Welsh Language, ct and cncl Univ of Wales 1973-, Prince of Wales Ctee 1975-87; High Sheriff County of South Glamorgan 1985-86; Hon LLD Univ of Wales 1983; FCIB; *Recreations* golf, gardening, music; *Clubs* Cardiff and County; *Style*— W Emrys Evans, Esq, CBE; Maesglas, Penyturnpike, Dinas Powis, South Glamorgan CF6 4HH (☎ 0222 512 985)

EVANS, Hon Mrs; Hon Winifred; *née* Gormley; da of Baron Gormley, OBE; *b* 1940; *m* 1960, Arthur Evans; *Style*— Hon Mrs Evans; c/o The Rt Hon the Lord Gormley, OBE, 1 Springfield Grove, Sunbury-on-Thames, Surrey

EVANS, Rev (Charles) Wyndham; s of William Lloyd Evans, of Brookside Cottage, Corwen, and Ada Henrietta,*née* Wright; *b* 16 Oct 1928; *Educ* Bala Church in Wales Sch, Bala GS, Univ Coll of N Wales (BA), St Catherines Coll Oxford (BA, MA), St Stephens House Oxford; *m* 2 Aug 1961, Sheila Huw, da of Hugh Jones, JP, MBE (d 1975), of Fern Bank, Llanfairfechan, Gwynedd; 1 s (Johnathan b 1966), 1 da (Helen b 1965); *Career* ordained: deacon 1952, priest 1953, curate Denbigh 1952-55, chaplain and housemaster Llandovery Coll 1958-67, Chaplain and sr lectr in educn Trinity Coll Carmarthen 1967-79, vicar Llanrhaeadr YC 1979-, chaplain Ruthin Sch 1979-, rural dean Denbigh 1984-; tstee St Mary's Tst, memb Welsh Nat Religious Educn Centre Bangor; *Books* Bible Families (1965); *Style*— The Rev Wyndham Evans; The Vicarage, Llanrhaeadr, Denbigh, Clwyd LL16 4NN; Parciau, 12 The Close, Llanfairfechan, Gwynedd, (☎ 074 578 250)

EVANS, (John) Wynford; s of Gwilym Everton Evans, of Llanelli (d 1968), and Margaret Mary Elfreda, *née* Jones (d 1982); *b* 3 Nov 1934; *Educ* Llanelli GS, St John's Coll Cambridge (MA); *m* 20 April 1957, Sigrun, da of Gerhard Brethfeld; 3 s (Mark, Chris, Tim); *Career* dep chm London Electricity 1977-84, chm South Wales Electricity 1984-, dir Nat Garden Fest Wales 1987-88, Welsh Nat Opera 1988-; memb Welsh Languages Bd 1988-, Prince of Wales Ctee 1988-; *Recreations* fly fishing, cross-country skiing, golf; *Clubs* Flyfishers, Cardiff & County, London Welsh; *Style*— Wynford Evans, Esq; South Wales Electricity, St Mellons, Cardiff

EVANS LOMBE, Capt Peter Michael; s of Maj John Michael Evans Lombe, MC (d 1938), and Patricia Routledge, *née* Gibson; *b* 5 June 1933; *Educ* Wellington Coll, RMA Sandhurst; *m* 1964, Vera-Alexandra, da of Laurens Rijnhart Boissevain (d 1986), of Monte Carlo; 2 s (James Nicholas b 1967, Charles Patrick Laurens b 1971); *Career* Army 1951-60, cmmnd 3 Carabiniers Prince of Wales Dragon Gds 1953, 15/19 Kings Royal Hussars 1954, resigned 1960; ptnr and memb Stock Exchange, Kitcat and Aitken Stockbrokers 1960-83, dir Hambros Bank 1983; Liveryman Worsipful Co of Skinners; *Recreations* fishing, shooting, sailing, golf; *Clubs* Royal West Norfolk GC; *Style*— Capt Peter Evans Lombe; 10 Child's St, London SW5 9RY (☎ 01 370 5381); Roydon Lodge, Roydon, nr King's Lynn, Norfolk (☎ 0485 600 215); Hambros Bank Ltd, 41 Tower Hill EC3 (☎ 01 480 5000)

EVANS OF CLAUGHTON, Baron (Life Peer UK 1978); (David Thomas) Gruffydd Evans; s of Maj John Cynlais Evans and Nellie Euronwy Evans; *b* 9 Feb 1928; *Educ* Birkenhead Sch, Friars Sch Bangor, Liverpool Univ (LLB); *m* 1956, Moira Elizabeth, da of late James Rankin; 1 s, 3 da; *Career* slr 1952, pres Lib Party 1977-78 (chm 1965-68), Lib spokesman on Local Govt and Housing in House of Lords, chm Gen Election Ctee 1979 and 1983, chm Marcher Sound Ltd (independent local radio for Wrexham/Chester), dir Granada TVl pres Nat Assoc of Wharehouse keepers 1983-88; *Recreations* golf, watching Welsh rugby and Liverpool Football Club; *Clubs* Nat Liberal, Wirral Golf, Oxton CC (pres), Birkenhead Squash Racquets, MCC; *Style*— The Rt Hon Lord Evans of Claughton; House of Lords, London SW1 (☎ 01 219 3121)

EVANS-BEVAN, David Gawain; s and h of Sir Martyn Evans-Bevan, 2 Bt; *b* 16 Sept 1961; *m* 7 Nov 1987, Philippa Alice, yst da of Patrick Sweeney, of East Moors, Helmsley, N Yorks; *Style*— David Evans-Bevan, Esq

EVANS-BEVAN, Sir Martyn Evan; 2 Bt (UK 1958); s of Sir David Martyn Evans-Bevan, 1 Bt (d 1973); *b* 1 April 1932; *Educ* Uppingham; *m* 12 Oct 1957, Jennifer Jane Marion, da of Robert Hugh Stevens, of Lady Arbour, Eardisley, Herefords; 4 s; *Heir* s, David Evans-Bevan, *qv*; *Career* High Sheriff of Breconshire 1967-68, Freeman of City of London, Liveryman Worshipful Co of Farmers; company dir; *Clubs* Carlton; *Style*— Sir Martyn Evans-Bevan, Bt; Felin-Newydd, Llande Falle, Brecon, Powys

EVANS-FREKE, Hon John Anthony; 2 s of 11 Baron Carbery, *qv*; *b* 9 May 1949; *Educ* Downside, RAC Cirencester; *m* 1972, Veronica Jane, yst da of Maj Eric Williams, of House of Lynturk, Alford, Aberdeenshire; 2 s (James Eric b 1976, Charles William Anthony b 1981), 1 da (Flora Mary b 1979); *Career* Cluttons Chartered Surveyors 1975-84 (ptnr 1980-), ptnr Humberts Chartered Surveyors 1984-88, land agent to Northumberland Estates 1988-; FRICS; *Style*— Hon John Evans-Freke; Abbeylands House, Alnwick, Northumberland; Estates Office, Alnwick Castle, Northumberland (☎ 0665 602207)

EVANS-FREKE, Hon Michael Peter; s and h of 11 Baron Carbery; *b* 11 Oct 1942; *Educ* Downside, Christ Church Coll Oxford (MA), Strathclyde Univ (MBA); *m* 9 Sept 1967, Claudia Janet Elizabeth, o da of late Capt Percy Lionel Cecil Gurney, of Little Chart, Penshurst, Kent; 1 s (Dominic Ralfe Cecil b 1969), 3 da (Richenda Clare b 1971, Isabel Lucy b 1973, Anna-Louise b 1979); *Style*— Hon Michael Evans-Freke; Sandpit House, Toot Hill, Romsey, Hants

EVANS-FREKE, Hon Stephan Ralfe; s of 11 Baron Carbery; *b* 2 Mar 1952; *Educ* Downside, Trinity Coll Cambridge (BA); *Career* sr vice-pres Blythe Eastman PaineWebber Inc (USA)l pres PaineWebber Devpt Corpn (USA); dir PaineWebber Inc (USA) (a maj US fin servs firm), Genertech Devpt Corpn, Centocor Devpt Corpn, Amgen Devpt Corp, BBN Advanced Computers Inc; *Clubs* Brooks'; *Style*— Hon Stephan Evans-Freke; norfol, Connecticut 96058, USA; 140 Riverside Drive, New York NY 10024

EVANS-LOMBE, Edward Christopher; QC (1978); only s of Vice Adm Sir Edward Evans-Lombe, KCB, JP, DL (himself gs of Rev Henry Lombe, who took the name Lombe *vice* Evans 1862 under the terms of the will of his great-uncle, Sir John Lombe, 1 Bt. Sir John was bro of Mary, the Rev Henry's mother, who m Thomas Browne Evans). The surname of the Admiral's f, Alexander, became Evans Lombe following the marriage of his f with a cousin, Louisa Evans; *b* 10 April 1937; *Educ* Eton, Trinity Coll Cambridge; *m* 1964, Frances Marilyn, er da of Robert Ewen Mackenzie, of Lincoln; 1 s, 3 da; *Career* served Roy Norfolk Regt 1955-57, 2 Lt; barr Inner Temple 1963, standing counsel to Dept of Trade in Bankruptcy Matters 1971, rec SE Circuit 1982-; chm Agric Land Tribunal SE Area 1983; master of bench Inner Temple 1985; *Style*— Edward Evans-Lombe, Esq, QC; 4 Stone Buildings, Lincolns Inn WC2 A3XT (☎ 01 242 5524); Marlingford Hall, Marlingford, nr Norwich (☎ 0603 880319)

EVE, Robin Anthony; s of late Frederick Latymer Eve; *b* 20 April 1934; *Educ* City of London Freemens Sch; *m* 1953, Anne Augusta, *née* Mead; 2 s, 2 da; *Career* dir Midland Bank Industrial Finances Ltd, common councilman Corpn of London Ward of Cheap 1980; FCIS, FCCA, AJII, MIMC; *Recreations* sailing (yacht Contessa 32 'Picardy II'), music, fishing; *Clubs* City Livery, City Livery Yacht Club; *Style*— Robin Eve, Esq; 36 Poultry, EC2 (☎ 01 638 8861); Aldersmead, Shepherds Hill, Merstham, Surrey (☎ Merstham 2540)

EVE, Hon Simon Rupert; s and h of 2nd Baron Silsoe; *b* 17 April 1966; *Style*— Hon Simon Eve

EVE, William Raymond Cedric; s of John Harvey Sutcliff Eve, JP, DL, of Kingswood, Surrey, and Yvonne Audrey, *née* Alabaster; *b* 26 Oct 1944; *Educ* Tonbridge; *m* 12 Oct 1973, Susan Margaret, da of Dermot Whelan, of Epsom, Surrey; 2 s (Andrew Michael Patrick b 1971, Charles William Harvey b 1978), 1 da (Juliette Amanda b 1979); *Career* md Carter-Parratt (Visisystems) Ltd; dir Carter-Parrett Ltd the Holding Co 1973- (Carter-Parrett are the leading suppliers of micro-computer systems based on IBM to the motor trade in the UK); *Recreations* squash, tennis, golf, cricket, bridge; *Clubs* RAC, South Hatch Racing, Brockham Conservative Assoc (treas); *Style*— William R C Eve, Esq; Mowillands, Reigate Road, Betchworth, Surrey (☎ 0737 784 2176); Carter-Parratt (Visisystems) Ltd, Visidata House, Kimpton Road, Sutton, Surrey (☎ 01 644 4355, telex 915431, car telephone 0836 272462)

EVELEIGH, Hon Mrs (Deborah Gay Le Messurier); da of Baron Wolfenden, CBE (d 1985), and Eileen Le Messurier, *née* Spilsbury; *b* 14 Nov 1943; *m* 1966, Francis Michael James Eveleigh, s of Prof Francis Hedley Arthur Eveleigh; 1 s (Daniel b 1972), 1 da (Christian b 1971); *Style*— Hon Mrs Eveleigh; Quorn Lodge Farmhouse, Leicester Road, Loughborough

EVELEIGH, Rt Hon Sir Edward Walter Eveleigh; PC (1977), ERD; s of Walter William Eveleigh (d 1952), and Daisy Emily Eveleigh; *b* 8 Oct 1917; *Educ* Peter Symonds Sch, BNC Oxford (MA); *m* 1, 1940, Vilma Bodnar; m 2, 1953, Patricia Helen Margaret, da of Marcel Bury; 2 s (and 1 s decd); *Career* cmmnd RA (SR) 1936, served WW II (despatches), Maj; barr Lincoln's Inn 1945, QC 1961, rec Burton-upon-Trent 1961-64, rec Gloucester 1964-68, bencher Lincoln's Inn 1968, judge High Court of Justice (Queen's Bench) 1968-77, presiding judge SE Circuit 1971-76, Lord Justice of Appeal 1977-85; memb Royal Cmmn on Criminal Procedure 1978-80; pres: Br-German Jurists' Assoc 1974-85, Bar Musical Soc 1980-; chm Statute Law Soc 1985-, tres Licolns Sun; kt 1968; *Clubs* Garrick; *Style*— The Rt Hon Lord Justice Eveleigh, ERD; Royal Courts of Justice, Strand, London WC2

EVELEIGH, Hon Mrs (Victoria Morina); *née* Butler; da of Judge The Lord 28 Baron Dunboyne, and Anne Marie, *née* Mallet; *b* 19 Dec 1959; *Educ* Benenden, St Andrew's Univ (BSc), Wye Coll Univ of London (MSc); *m* 27 Sept 1986, Christopher Eveleigh; 1 s (George Jethro b 1987); *Career* self employed in farm tourism, working on family farm; *Recreations* horse riding, painting, campanology; *Style*— The Hon Mrs Eveleigh; West Ilkerton Farm, Lynton, North Devon EX35 6QA (☎ Lynton 52310)

EVELEIGH-ROSS DE MOLEYNS, Hon Mrs John; Olivia Phoebe; da of Capt Percy Neave Leathers, of Robertsbridge, E Sussex; *m* 1, 25 March 1950, Lord John Conyngham (d 31 May 1963), s of 6 Marquess Conyngham; m 2, 4 Aug 1963, as his 4 w, Hon Francis Alexander Innys Eveleigh-Ross-de-Moleyns (d 29 April 1964), s of 6th Baron Ventry; *Style*— Hon Mrs Francis Eveleigh-Ross de Moleyns; 317 The Water Gdns, Hyde Park, London W2

EVELYN, (John) Michael; CB (1976); s of Edward Ernest Evelyn, ISO (d 1950), and Kate Rosa, *née* Underwood (d 1954); *b* 2 June 1916; *Educ* Charterhouse, Christ Church Oxford (MA); *Career* WWII 1939-46 Oxfordshire and Buckinghamshire LI, demob temp Maj; called to the Bar 1939; dir of Public Prosecutions Dept 1946-76, ret asst dir/under sec; author of over 40 crime novels since 1954 under the pseudonym Michael Underwood; *Recreations* reading, listening to music; *Clubs* Garrick, Detection; *Style*— Michael Evelyn, Esq, CB; 100 Ashdown, Eaton Rd, Hove, E Sussex BN3 3AR (☎ 0273 776104)

EVELYN, (John) Patrick Michael Hugh; DL (Surrey 1983); s of Maj Peter Evelyn, Grenadier Gds (presumed d of wounds 1943, ggs through his paternal grandmother of Rev George Chichester, bro of 1 Baron O'Neill and hence of the oldest traceable family in Europe, the O'Neills, of the Irish Royal House of Tara); *b* 16 Oct 1939; *Educ* Eton; *m* 1, 1965 (m dis 1974), Jennifer Browne; 1 s; m 2, 1974, Anne, da of Richard Lindsell, DFC, of Northwood House, Sharpthorne, Sussex; 2 s; *Career* farmer; High Sheriff Surrey 1982-83; cllr Surrey; *Recreations* winter and field sports, Italian 19th century opera; *Clubs* Boodle's; *Style*— Patrick Evelyn, Esq, DL; The Estate Off, Wotton, Dorking, Surrey

EVENNETT, David Anthony; MP (C) Erith and Crayford 1983-; s of Norman Thomas Evennett and Irene Evennett; *b* 3 June 1949; *Educ* Buckhurst Hill County HS for Boys, LSE (MSc); *m* 1975, Marilyn Anne, da of Ronald Stanley Smith; 2 s; *Career* sch teacher 1972-74; Lloyds: broker 1974-81, memb 1976-, dir underwriting agency 1982-; memb Redbriodge Borough Cncl 1974-78; contested (C) Hackney S and Shoreditch 1979; memb select ctee of Educn Sci and the Arts 1986-; *Recreations* family, reading novels and biographies, going to theatre; *Clubs* Carlton, Priory (Belvedere); *Style*— David Evennett Esq, MP; House of Commons, London SW1

EVERALL, Mark Andrew; s of John Dudley Everall, of 122 Harley St, London, and Pamela, *née* Odone; *b* 30 June 1950; *Educ* Ampleforth, Lincoln Coll Oxford (MA); *m* 16 Dec 1978, (Elizabeth) Anne, da of (Thomas) Hugh Richard Perkins; *Career* barr Inner Temple 1975, W Circuit; *Style*— Mark Everall, Esq; 5 Kings Bench Walk, Temple, London EC4 (☎ 01 353 2882)

EVERARD; *see*: Welby-Everard

EVERARD, Francis Vincent; s of Francis Over Everard, of Burrow Down, S Devon (d 1951), and Ada Miriam, *née* Simpson (d 1962); *b* 27 Dec 1907; *Educ* Bradfield, Birmingham Centl Tech Coll, Manchester Univ; *m* 19 Jan 1935, Margaret Isabel (d 1988), da of Stephen Barrett, of Ryburndale, W Yorks (d 1940); 2 s (Christopher Vincent b 1936, Philip Francis b 1939), 1 da (Miriam Rosalind b 1943); *Career* city magistrate, Birmingham 1947-62, memb Birmingham Accident Hosp Bd 1940-48; pres: Engrg Employers' Fedn 1960-61, Birmingham Engrg Employers' Assoc Bd 1939-63; tstee James Watt Meml Fund 1955-67, pres St John's Ambulance Assocn, Birmingham Co 1955-63; Liveryman Worshipful Co of Turners 1966; hon assoc Aston Univ, assoc Manchester Coll of Technol; CEng, FIMechE (cncl 1962-63), FIMARE, MRINA, MBIM; CStJ 1963; *Recreations* walking, swimming; *Style*— F Vincent Everard, Esq; 20 Abbey Walk, Gt Missenden, Bucks (☎ 024 06 2020)

EVERARD, Sir Robin Charles; 4 Bt (UK 1911); s of Lt-Col Sir Nugent Henry Everard, 3 Bt (d 1984), and Frances Audrey, *née* Jesson (d 1975); *b* 5 Oct 1939; *Educ* Harrow, Sandhurst; *m* 28 Sept 1963, Ariel Ingrid, er da of Col Peter Cleasby-Thompson, MBE, MC (d 1981), of Blackhill House, Little Cressingham, Norfolk; 1 s (Henry Peter Charles b 1970), 2 da (Catherine Mary b 1964, Victoria Frances b 1966); *Heir* s, Henry Peter Charles b 6 Aug 1970; *Career* three year cmmn Duke of Wellington's Regt; md P Murray-Jones Ltd 1961-75, mgmnt conslt 1975-; *Style*— Sir Robin Everard, Bt; Church Farm, Shelton, Long Stratton, Norwich NR15 2SB

EVERARD, Simon; TD (1967), DL (Leics 1984); s of Charles Miskin Everard (d 1953), and Monica Mary Barford (d 1970), of Werrington Hall, Peterborough; *b* 30 Oct 1928; *Educ* Uppingham Sch, Clare Coll Cambridge; *m* 1955, Joceline Margaret, da of Francis Jaime Wormold Holt (d 1985), of Seaview, Isle of Wight; 3 s (Nicholas b 1956, Mark b 1958, James b 1962), 1 da (Serena b 1967); *Career* Capt Leics and Derbys Yeo TA; chm Ellis & Everard plc (industrial chemical distributor), vice-chm Leicester Building Soc 1982-; High Sheriff of Leics 1983-84, DL Leics 1984-; *Recreations* shooting, gardening, tennis; *Clubs* Cavalry & Guards; *Style*— Simon Everard, Esq, TD, DL; Sludge Hall, Cold Newton, nr Billesdon, Leics (☎ Billesdon 236); c/o Ellis & Everard plc, 140 New Walk, Leicester LE1 7JL (☎ 0533 542323, telex 341047)

EVERED, David Charles; s of Thomas Charles Evered (d 1959), of Bannatyne, Furzefield Road, Beaconsfield, Bucks, and Enid Christian, *née* Frost; *b* 21 Jan 1940; *Educ* Cranleigh Sch Surrey, Univ of London (BSc, MB, BS, MD); *m* 6 June 1964, Anne Elizabeth Massey, da of John Massey Lings (d 1944), of Bolton, Lancashire; 1 s (Alexander b 1975), 2 da (Elizabeth b 1966, Susanna b 1969); *Career* physician and dir of Ciba Fndn 1978-88, formerly conslt physician Royal Victoria Infirmary Newcastle upon Tyne; memb: Assoc of Med Research Charities Ctee 1980-84 (vice-chm 1987-), St George's Hosp Med Sch Cncl 1983 (fin ctee 1984-), Fndn Louis Jeanet de Médecine (Geneva) 1984- (vice-pres Sch ctee 1984-); memb: Zoological Soc of London (Cncl 1985-), Scientists Inst for Public Information (New York), Media Resource Service Advsy Ctee 1985-; second sec Med Research Cncl 1988-; *Books* Diseases of the Thyroid (1976), Atlas of Clinical Endocrinology (1979), Collaboration in Medical Research in Europe (1981); *Recreations* reading, history, tennis, sailing; *Clubs* Roehampton; *Style*— Dr David Evered, Esq; Medical Research Council, 20 Park Crescent, London W1N 4AL (☎ 01-636 5422)

EVEREST, Dr David Anthony; s of George Charles Everest (d 1957), and Ada Bertha, *née* Wheddon (d 1950); *b* 18 Sept 1926; *Educ* Lower Sch of John Lyon Harrow, UCL (BSc, PhD); *m* 1956, Audrey Pauline, da of Reginald Holford Sheldrick, of Herts; 3 s (Peter b 1958, Michael b 1960, Richard b 1966); *Career* environmental scientist, sr res assoc CEED (UK Centre for Economic and Environmental Devpt), res fell Dept of Environmental Sciences Univ of East Anglia; chief Scientific offr environmental pollution DOE 1979-86, energy conservation and research in materials and metrology DTI 1977-79 (superintendent of divs: inorganic and metallic structure 1970-75, chemical standards 1975-77), The Nat Physical Laboratory, bd memb Hydraulics Res Ltd 1982-86; FInstD; *Publications* The Chemistry of Beryllium, Elsevier (1964); chapter on beryllium in "Comprehensive Inorganic Chemistry" 1972; The Greenhouse Effect: Issues for Policy Makers (1988); numerous papers and patents in inorganic chemistry, materials science, thermal plasmas energy conservation and the environment; *Recreations* walking, reading; *Style*— Dr David Everest; "Talland", Chorleywood Road, Chorleywood, Herts WD3 4ER (☎ 0923 773253)

EVERETT, Maj Anthony Michael; s of Cyril Frederick Cunningham Everett (d 1941), of Hinton House, Hinton St Michael, New Forest, Hampshire, and Marcella,*née* Lawless (d 1957); *b* 25 Nov 1921; *Educ* Stonyhurst Coll, Staff Coll Camberley; *m* 7 May 1955, Sara, da of Vice Adm Sir Hector MacLean, KBE, CB, DSC; 2 s (Simon b 12 May 1956, Rupert b 29 May 1959); *Career* WW11 serv: cmmnd Wiltshire Regt 1939 (became Duke of Edinburgh Royal Regt 1957), active serv with 1 Bn Wiltshire Regt Burma, GSO2 (ops), Tactical HQ 15 Corps Burma 1944-45, Bde Maj 13 Br Inf Bde BLA Germany 1945-46; regtl and staff appts 1946-62 incl: dep COS Combat Intelligence HQ NATO Copenhagen, 2 i/c 1 Bn Duke of Edinburgh Royal Regt (Berks and Wilts), chief instr tactics RMA Sandhurst; ret 1962; Laurie Milbank & Co (stockbrokers): ptnr 1962-81, sr ptnr 1975-81, conslt 1981-83; fin advsr and conslt to various tsts and orgns 1984-; tstee: Duke of Edinburgh Royal Regt (Berks & Wilts), The Wardrobe Bldg Salisbury Cathederal Close, Wilts Regt Museum; fund raising Wilts St John Ambulance; memb Stock Exchange 1964; *Recreations* travel, photography, bloodstock and race horse owner, art and architectural drawings; *Clubs* Turf; *Style*— Maj Anthony Everett; Enford Grange, Enford Nr Pewsey, Wiltshire; 32 Stanhope Gdns, London SW7; Casa Diamoa Tangier, Morocco; Windsor House, 50 Victoria St, London SW1 (☎ 0980 70475, fax 0980 70872, off 01 799 2233, fax 01 799 1321, telex 883356 CALCOM G)

EVERETT, Bernard Jonathan; s of Arnold Edwin Everett, of Adderbury, Oxon, and Helene May, *née* Heine; *b* 17 Sept 1943; *Educ* Kings College Sch Wimbledon, Lincoln Coll Oxford (BA); *m* 1 Oct 1970, (Maria) Olinda, *née* Goncalves de Albuquerque, da of Raul Correia de Albuquerque, of Faro, Portugal; 2 s (Christopher b 1980, Edward b1981), 2 da (Caroline b 1974, Diana b 1976, d 1979); *Career* Dip Serv 1966-; third (later second) sec Lisbon 1967-71, consul Luanda 1975, first sec and head od chancery Lusaka 1978-80, consul (commercial) Rio de Janeiro 1980-83, asst head information dept FCO 1983-84, head Sub Saharan Africa Branch DTI 1984-87, ambassador Guatemala 1987-; *Recreations* reading, the performing arts, walking, numismatics; *Style*— Bernard Everett, Esq; Foreign and Commonwealth Office, London SW1

EVERETT, Edwin Arthur; CBE (1975); s of Ernest George Everett (d 1964); *b* 20 May 1917; *Educ* Hampton Sch; *m* 1, 1944, Joan Margaret (d 1980), da of Capt Arnold George Stanford (d 1916); 2 s; m 2, 1984, Daphne Margaret, da of Robert Heywood; *Career* The Queen's Westminsters (KRRC) 1935-39, Royal West African Frontier Force 1940-43, RAOC 1943-49 (Capt TA), ME 1943, Normandy, Holland and Germany 1944-46 (war crimes trials); slr of Supreme Court 1939-47, registrar County Court 1947-, district registrar of High Court 1979-; memb of County Court Rule Ctee 1968-79, pres Assoc of County Court and District Registrars 1975; *Recreations* photography, gardening and travel; *Clubs* Roy Overseas League; *Style*— Edwin Everett, Esq, CBE; 37 West Ave, Worthing, W Sussex BN11 5LT (☎ 0903 48025)

EVERETT, Martin Thomas; s of Dr Thomas Everett (d 1975), and Ingeborg Maria, *née* Vogt; *b* 24 Sept 1939; *Educ* Clayesmore Preparatory Sch, Bryanston; *m* 14 Sept 1963, Susan Mary, da of John Peter Sworder, MC, TD (d 1987); 2 s (Oliver b 2 July 1965, George b 8 Sept 1967), 1 da (Daisy b 14 May 1975); *Career* Nat Serv 2 Lt 9/12 Royal Lancers 1959-61; Mayor Sworder and Co Ltd Wine Shippers: joined 1962, dir 1967, jt md 1974, md 1980; tstee St Olaves Southwark Church Act of 1918; Freeman City of London, Liverman Worshipful Co of Glass sellers and Glaziers; memb Inst of Masters of Wine 1968; *Recreations* gardening, walking; *Style*— Martin Everett, Esq; Sydenham, London SE26 (☎ 01 778 2569); Mayor Sworder & Co Ltd, 21 Duke St Hill, London SE1 2SW (☎ 01 407 5111, fax 01 378 1804, telex 8954102 MAYOR SWORDER)

EVERETT, Nigel Peter; s of Dennis Reginald Everett, of Bournemouth, Dorset, and Charlotte Evelyn, *née* Saunders; *b* 20 Dec 1953; *m* 3 June 1978, Yvonne Teresa Jane; 1 da (Holly Everett b 4 April 1986) ; *Career* appt gen mangr: Playhouse Theatre Bournemouth 1976, Strand Theatre 1982; Strand Theatre and Theatre Royal Haymarket 1988-; *Style*— Nigel P Everett, Esq; The Theatre Royal, The Haymarket, London, W1

EVERETT, Oliver William; LVO (1980); s of Walter George Charles Everett, MC, DSO (d 1979), of Streete ct, Victoria Drive, Bognor Regis, and Gertrude Florence Rothwell, *née* Hellicar; *b* 28 Feb 1943; *Educ* Felsted Sch Essex, Western Res Acad Ohio USA, Christs Coll Cambridge (MA), Fletcher Sch of Law & Diplomacy Tufts Univ Mass USA (MA), LSE; *m* 28 Aug 1965, Theffania, da of Lt Robert Vesey Stoney (d 1944), of Rosturk Castle, Co Mayo, Ireland; 2 s (Toby b 1979, William b 1982), 2 da (Kathleen b 1966, Grania b 1969); *Career* Dip Serv: first sec Br High Cmmn New Delhi 1969-73, first sec FCO 1973-78, asst private sec to HRH The Prince of Wales 1978-80, head chancery Br Embassy Madrid 1980-81, private sec to HRH The Princess of Wales and comptroller to TRH The Prince and Princess of Wales 1981-83, asst librarian Windsor Castle 1984, librarian and asst Keeper of the Queen's archives Windsor Castle 1985-; *Recreations* skiing, rackets, real tennis; *Clubs* Ski Club of GB; *Style*— Oliver Everett, Esq, LVO; Garden Hse, Windsor Castle, Berks SL4 1NG (☎ 0753 868 286); The East Wing, Kirtlington Pk, Oxon OX5 3JN (☎ 0869 50589); The Royal Library, Windsor Castle, Berks SL4 1NJ (☎ 0753 868 286, fax 0753 854 910)

EVERETT, Peter; s of Henry Everett (d 1984, of Edinburgh, and Kathleen Isabel, *née* Cudderford (d 1961); *b* 24 Sept 1931; *Educ* George Watson's Boys Coll Edinburgh, Edinburgh Univ; *m* 1 Oct 1955, Annette Patricia, da of George Edward Hyde (d 1988), of London: 3 s (David b 1959, Michael b 1962, John b 1964), 1 da (Judith Anne b 1957); *Career* Nat Serv RE 1953-55, 2 Lt 1954; Shell Int Petroleum Co 1955-: trainee engr The Hague 1955-57, petroleum engr Indonesia 1957-61, prodn engr Brunei 1963-64 (petroleum engr 1961-63), chief petroleum engr Trinidad 1968-70 (sr prodn engr 1964-68), exploration and prodn economist projects and agreements dept The Hague 1970, chief petroleum engr Brunei 1970-72 (Sr ops engr 1970), gen ops mangr Nigeria 1977-79 (petroleum engr mangr 1972-76, div mangr western div 1976-77), md Brunei 1979-84; md: Shell UK Ltd 1984-, Shell UK Exploration and Prodn 1984-; memb: Cncl UK Offshore Operators Assoc, Dept of Energy's Offshore Energy Bd; advsy bd memb petroleum engrg depts: Heriot Watt Univ, Imperial Coll London; MBIM 1985; Sen Paduka Mahkota (Brunei) 1984; *Recreations* golf,squash; *Clubs* Watsonian, Wimbledon Park; *Style*— Peter Everett, Esq; 12 Newstead Way, Wimbledon, London SW19 5HS (☎ 01 946 6594); Shell UK Ltd, Shell Mex House, Strand, London WC2R 0DX (☎ 01 257 4414)

EVERETT, Thomas Henry Kemp; s of Thomas Kemp Everett (d 1934), of Bristol, and Katharine Ida Everett, *née* Woodward (d 1972); *b* 28 Jan 1932; *Educ* Queen Elizabeth's Hosp Bristol, Univ of Bristol (LLB Hons) 1957; *m* 1954, June, da of Edward Howard Bryce Partridge (d 1972), of Bristol; 3 s (Rupert Charles Kemp Everett b 1961, Richard Jolyon Kemp Everett b 1965, Robert Edward Kemp Everett b 1968); *Career* special cmmr of Income Tax 1983-; slr 1960, ptnr Meade-King & Co 1963-83, clerk to gen cmmr 1965-83; chm: Service 9 1972-75, Bristol Cncl of Voluntary Service 1975-80, St Christopher's Young Persons' Residential Tst 1976-83; vice-chm Governors of Queen Elizabeth's Hospital 1980-; memb Governing Cncl of St Christophers Sch 1983-, tstee of Freeways Tst (for the mentally handicapped), hon tres and vice-chm of Rowberrow PCC; memb of Axbridge Deanery Synod; *Recreations* music, reading, walking, gardening, badminton; *Style*— Thomas Everett, Esq; Dolebury Cottage, Dolberrow, Churchill, Bristol BS19 5NS; 5th Floor, Turnstile House, 98 High Holborn, London WC1V 6LQ (☎ 01 438 7358)

EVERITT, William Howard; s of Howard George Everitt (d 1978); *b* 27 Feb 1940; *Educ* Brentwood Sch, Leeds Univ (BSc); *m* 1963, Anthea Cecilia, da of late William Nield; 2 children; *Career* dir Associated Engineering Group Ltd 1978-; *Recreations* golf, squash; *Style*— William Everitt, Esq; Horley House, Hornton Lane, Horley, nr Banbury, Oxon (☎ 029 573 603)

EVERS, (Frank) Michael; s of Frank Anthony Evers, of 19 Norton Rd, Stourbridge, W Mids, and Ida Rosemary, *née* Watson; *b* 2 August 1937; *Educ* Rugby, Univ (LLB); *m* 21 Dec 1968 (m dis 1981), Elaine, *née* Priestly; 2 s (Richard 31 Jan 1971, Andrew b 21 May 1972); *Career* slr 1961, dep coroner N Worcs 1966-, clerk to Stourbridge Cmmrs of Income Tax 1966- (Warley Cmmrs 1972-); pres Dudley Law Soc; memb Stourbridge Rotary club 1980-, chm Claverley cc 1984-87, govr Redhill Sch Stourbridge 1988; memb Law Soc 1961-; *Recreations* cricket, squash, walking, gardening; *Style*— Michael Evers, Esq; 19 Norton Rd, Stourbridge, W Mids (☎ 0384 396 417); 1 Worcester St, Stourbridge W Mids (☎ 0384 378 821, fax 0384 378 898)

EVERSHED, Ralph Jocelyn; s of Norman William Evershed (d 1983), and Jocelyn Slade, *née* Lyons; *b* 16 Nov 1944; *Educ* St Albans Boys GS, Univ of Strathclyde (BA); *m* 6 Sept 1968, Carol Ann, da of Jerry Esmond Cullum, RAF (d 1987); 3 s (Timothy b 1973, David b 1974, John b 1982), 2 da (Ruth b 1977, Susannah b 1980); *Career* md Verulam Properties Ltd 1981, chm J E Properties Hldgs Ltd 1987, chm Evershods Gp Ltd 1987 (md 1974-75, dir 1975-81, dir estates Ltd Ltd 1982-87) dir Woodsilk Properties Ltd 1988, memb bd Inter-Varsity Press 1988; youth ldr Independent Chapel St Albans, lay preacher; FInstD; *Style*— Ralph Evershed, Esq; Eversheds Ltd, Alma Rd, St Albans, Herts AL1 3AS (☎ 0727 54652, fax 0727 43908, car 0836 599244)

EVERSON, Sir Frederick Charles; KCMG (1968), CMG (1956); s of Frederick Percival Everson (d 1946); *b* 6 Sept 1910; *Educ* Tottenham Co Sch, London Univ; *m* 1937, Linda Mary (d 1984), da of Samuel Clark; 3 s (eldest of whom d 1984), 1 da; *Career* entered Foreign Serv 1934, ambassador to El Salvador 1956-60, commercial counsellor Stockholm 1960-63, min (econ) Paris 1963-68; *Style*— Sir Frederick Everson, KCMG; 8 Gainsborough Court, College Rd, Dulwich, London SE21 7LT (☎ 01 693 8125)

EVERSON, John Andrew; s of Harold Leslie Everson (d 1976), of Surrey, and Florence Jane, *née* Stone (d 1982); *b* 26 Oct 1933; *Educ* Tiffin Boys Sch Kingston-upon-Thames, Christs Coll Cambridge (MA), Kings Coll London (PGCE); *m* 1961, Gilda, da of Osborne Ramsden (d 1956), of Manchester; 2 s (Simon John b 1965, Benedict David b 1967); *Career* 2 Lt RA 1952-54; schoolmaster: Haberdashers Sch Elstree 1958-65, City of London Sch 1965-68; HM inspr of schools: HMI 1968-78, staff inspr 1978-81, ch inspr for Secondary Educn 1981-; sch cncl - chief offr of examination unit 1971-76; *Clubs* opera, chess, walking; *Style*— John Everson, Esq; Dept of Educn and Sci Elizabeth House, York Rd, London SE1 7PH

EVERY, Sir Henry John Michael; 13 Bt (E 1641); o s of Sir John Simon Every, 12 Bt (d 1988), and his 2 w Janet Marion, *née* Page; *b* 6 April 1947; *Educ* Malvern; *m* 1974, Susan, da of Kenneth Beaton, JP; 2 s; *Heir* s, Edward James Henry Every b 3 July 1975; *Style*— Henry Every, Esq; 5 Thornhill Close, Barton-under-Needwood, Staffs

EVERY, Dowager Lady; Janet Marion; *née* Page; eldest da of John Page, of Blakeney, Norfolk; *m* 1943, as his 2 w, Sir John Simon Every, 12 Bt (d 1988); 1 s (Sir

Henry John Michael, 13 Bt), 2 da (Celia Jane b 1944, Juliet Frances b 1945); Egginton, Derby

EVES, David Charles Thomas; s of Harold Thomas Eves (d 1967), and Violet, *née* Edwards (d 1972); *b* 10 Jan 1942; *Educ* King's Sch Rochester, Univ of Durham (BA); *m* 1 Aug 1964, Valerie Ann, da of George Alexander Carter, of Pinner, Middx; 1 da (Catherine Alice b 1969); *Career* HM chief inspr of factories 1985-88, dir of resources and planning Health and Safety Exec 1988-, under sec Employment Dept Gp; *Recreations* sailing, walking, painting, golf, gardening, reading; *Style—* David Eves, Esq; Helath and Safety Exec, Baynards House, Chepstow Place, London (☎ 01 243 6450)

EVETTS, Hon Mrs (Susan Katharine Lucy); da of 1 and last Baron Ismay (d 1965), and Laura Kathleen, *née* Clegg; *b* 29 May 1922; *m* 1 28 April 1942 (m dis 1946), Maj Neville Ewart Hyde Chance, o s of William Hyde Chance; 1 da; m 2, 16 Dec 1949, Lt-Col Michael John Evetts, MC, RHF, o s of Lt-Gen Sir John Fullerton Evetts, CB, CBE, MC; 2 s; *Style—* Hon Mrs Evetts; Wormington Grange, Broadway, Worcs

EVISON, Lady Beatrix Dora; *née* Alexander; JP; da of 1 and last Earl Alexander of Hillsborough (d 1965), and Esther Ellen, *née* Chapple, CBE (d 1969); *b* 7 May 1909; *Educ* London Univ; *m* 26 Sept 1936, William Bernard Evison, s of Henry Evison, of Scunthorpe, Lincs; 1 s, 1 da; *Style—* Lady Beatrix Evison; Cranleigh, 101 Old Park Ave, Enfield, Middx

EWAN, Gordon Francis David; s of Albert Francis Ewan, of Herts, and Rosemary, *née* Orchard (d 1988); *b* 9 Oct 1938; *Educ* St Audreys Hatfield, The Northern Poly London (Dipl Arch); *m* 28 Nov 1959, Anne Freda, da of Norman McCard (d 1985), of Herts; 2 s (Simon b 1960, Mark b 1964), 1 da (Lesley b 1961); *Career* architect; sr dir (and ptnr) Vincent and Gorbing Architects and Planners 1982-; RIBA; *Recreations* golf, fine wines, Rotary Int; *Style—* Gordon Ewan, Esq; 5 Long Ridge, Aston, Stevenage, Herts SG2 7EW (☎ 0438 88206); Vincent and Gorbing Ltd, Sterling Ct, Norton Rd, Stevenage, Herts SG1 2JY (☎ 0438 316331, fax 0458)

EWANS, Sir Martin Kenneth; KCMG (1987), CMG (1980); s of John Ewans; *b* 14 Nov 1928; *Educ* St Paul's, Corpus Christi Coll Cambridge (MA); *m* 1953, Mary Tooke; 1 s, 1 da; *Career* head E African dept FCO 1973-78, min New Delhi 1978-82; high cmmr: Zimbabwe 1983-85, Nigeria 1986-88; *Recreations* ornithology; *Clubs* Royal Cwlth Society; *Style—* Sir Martin Ewans, KCMG; The Barn, Old Hall Farm, South Walsham, Norfolk NR13 6DS

EWARD, Paul Anthony; s of The Rev Harvey Kennedy Eward (d 1969), and Delphine Eugenie Louise, *née* Pain; *b* 22 Dec 1942; *Educ* Radley; *m* 6 Sept 1966, Dene Kathleen, da of Geoffrey Louis Bartrip, of Ross-on-Wye; 2 da (Sarah b 1969, Lucy b 1971); *Career* slr; ptnr Leslie J Slade & Co, Newent, and Orme, Dykes & Yates Ledbury; chm Newent Business & Professional Assocn 1981-83, sec PCC Ross-on-Wye 1972-88, layco chm Ross and Archenfield Deanery Synod 1988- (hon tres 1980-88); memb: Hereford Diocesan: Synod, bd of fin revence ctee Vacancy in Sec ctee 1985, pastoral ctee 1988-; *Clubs* Gloucester Model Railway, Archenfield Investors, EM Gauge Soc; *Style—* Paul Eward, Esq; Oakleigh, Gloucester Rd, Ross-on-Wye, Herts HR9 5NA (☎ 0989 63845); Leslie J Slade & Co, 5 Broad St, Newent, Glos GL18 1AX (☎ 0531 820281)

EWART, David John; s of John Henry Ewart (d 1976); *b* 30 April 1936; *Educ* Harrow; *m* 1973, Janet Law; 4 children; *Career* former dep chm Guinness Mahon and dir Guinness Peat to Nov 1981; former dir Linfood Hldgs to Sept 1981, chm RHP Gp plc 1979-, exec dir Morgan Grenfell Corporate Finance Dept 1981-85, grp fin dir Morgan Grenfell 1985-; dir: Pirelli, Talbot Designs; Majedie Investmts plc; FCA; *Recreations* hunting, shooting, sailing; *Clubs* Boodle's; *Style—* David Ewart, Esq; The Old Rectory, Stoke Lyne, Oxfordshire OX6 9RU; c/o Morgan Grenfell & Co, 23 Great Winchester St, London EC2 (☎ 01 588 4545)

EWART, Gavin Buchanan; s of George Arthur Ewart (d 1942), of London, and Dorothy Hannah, *née* Turner (d 1979); *b* 4 Feb 1916; *Educ* Wellington, Christ's Coll Cambridge (BA, MA); *m* 24 March 1956, Margaret Adelaide (Margo), da of Selwyn George Bennett, MC (d 1950), of New Malden; 1 s (Julian Robert b 4 July 1958), 1 da (June Susan b 21 Oct 1956); *Career* E Surreys 1940-41, OCTU 1941, RA 1941-46, LAA and AAOR, Capt 1946; salesman Contemporary Lithographs 1938-39, ed Editions Poetry London 1946, Br Cncl 1946-52, SH Benson Ltd 1952-57, various advertising agencies, J Walter Thompson 1966-71, freelance writer 1971-; memb: Poetry Soc, Soc of Authors, Int PEN; *Books include : Poems and Songs (1939), Londoners (1964), Pleasures of the Flesh (1966), The Deceptive Grin of the Gravel Porters (1968), The Gavin Ewart Show (1971), Be My Guest (1975), No Fool Like and Old Fool (1976), Or Where a Young Penguin Lies Screaming (1978), The Collected Ewart 1933-80, The Penguin Book of Light Verse (ed 1980), The New Ewart (1982), Other People's Cherihews (ed 1983), The Ewart Quarto (1984), The Young Pobble's Guide to his Toes (1985), The Complete Little Ones (1986), Late Pickings (1987); in the USA: Selected Poems 1983-88, The Gavin Ewart Show (1986); Recreations* reading, listening to music; *Style—* Gavin Ewart, Esq; 57 Kenilworth Court, Lower Richmond Rd, London SW15 1EN (☎ 01 788 7071)

EWART, Sir (William) Ivan (Cecil); 6 Bt (UK 1887) of Glenmachan, Strandtown, Co Down and of Glenbank, Belfast, Co Antrim; DSC (1945), JP; s of late Maj William Basil Ewart, gs of 1 Bt; suc kinsman, Sir Talbot Ewart, 5 Bt, 1959; *b* 18 July 1919; *Educ* Radley; *m* 21 July 1948, Pauline Chevallier (d 5 Sept 1964), da of late Wing-Cdr Raphael Chevallier Preston, OBE, AFC, JP; 1 s, 2 da; *Heir* s William Michael Ewart; *Career* Lt RNVR WWII (POW Germany); chm William Ewart and Son Ltd 1968-73, Ewart New Northern Ltd 1973-77; East Africa rep Roy Cwlth Soc for the Blind 1977-84; admin Ngora Freda Carr Hosp, Ngora, Uganda (Association of Surgeons of East Africa) 1984; pres NI C of C and Indust 1974-; memb Belfast Harbour Cmmn 1968-77; High Sheriff Co Antrim 1976; *Clubs* Naval, Ulster Reform, Nairobi; *Style—* Sir Ivan Ewart, Bt, DSC, JP; Hill House, Hillsborough, Co Down BT26 6AE (☎0846 683000); PO Box 30171, Nairobi, Kenya (☎ Naindi 02 725726)

EWART, John Walter Douglas; s of Maxwell Douglas Ewart; *b* 27 Jan 1924; *Educ* Beaumont Coll Old Windsor Berks; *m* 1946, Joan Valerie, *née* Hoghton; 1 da (Lavinia Anne (Mrs C Peng) b 1947); *Career* Lt Royal Horse Gds 1942-46; md Paterson Ewart Gp Ltd 1958-70; Carclo Engrg Gp plc (md 1973-, chm 1982-), memb: Northants CC 1970-, Oxford RHA; High Sheriff Northamptonshire 1977-78; *Recreations* hunting, sailing; *Clubs* Cavalry and Guards', Royal London Yacht; *Style—* John Ewart, Esq; Astrop, Banbury, Oxfordshire (☎ 0295 811210)

EWART, William Michael; s and h of Sir Ivan Ewart, 6 Bt; *b* 10 June 1953; *Style—* William Ewart, Esq; Kelsey Hall, Great Steeping, Spilsby, Lincolnshire PE23 5PY

EWART-BIGGS, Hon Henrietta; er da of Baroness Ewart-Biggs (Life Peeress) *qv*; *b* 1961; *Style—* Hon Henrietta Ewart-Biggs; 31 Radnor Walk, London SW3

EWART-BIGGS, Baroness (Life Peer UK 1981); (Felicity) Jane; da of Major Basil Fitzherbert Randall (d 1930), and Rena May; *b* 22 August 1929; *Educ* Downe House Newbury; *m* 1960, Christopher Thomas Ewart, CMG, OBE (assassinated 1976, ambass to Dublin), s of Henry Ewart-Biggs (d 1957); 1 s, 2 da; *Career* sits as Lab Peer in Lords; front bench spokesman on House affairs, active on matters relating to children and young people; pres Peace People's Movement in Br 1977; freelance journalist, broadcaster and lecturer; *Recreations* travel, discussion, foreign affairs; *Style—* The Rt Hon Lady Ewart-Biggs; 31 Radnor Walk, London SW3 4BP

EWART-BIGGS, Hon Kate; yr da of Baroness Ewart-Biggs (Life Peeress) *qv*; *b* 1967; *Style—* Hon Kate Ewart-Biggs

EWART-BIGGS, Hon Robin Thomas Fitzherbert; only son of Baroness Ewart-Biggs (Life Peeress) *qv*; *b* 1963; *Style—* Hon Robin Ewart-Biggs

EWBANK, Hon Mr Justice; Hon Sir Anthony Bruce; s of Rev Harold Ewbank, Rector of Windermere, and Gwendolen, *née* Bruce; *b* 30 July 1925; *Educ* St John's Sch Leatherhead, Trin Coll Cambridge (MA); *m* 1958, Moya, da of Peter McGinn; 4 s, 1 da; *Career* RNVR 1945-47 and 1951-56; barr Gray's Inn 1954, jr counsel to the Treasury in probate matters 1969, QC 1972, rec of Crown Court 1975-80, bencher Gray's Inn 1980, judge of the High Court of Justice Family Divn 1980-; chm Family Law Bar Assoc 1978-80; kt 1980; *Style—* Hon Mr Justice Ewbank; Royal Courts of Justice, Strand, London WC2

EWEN, Peter; s of Alexander Hutcheon Ewen (d 1947), of Liverpool, and Elizabeth Ewen; *b* 4 June 1903; *Educ* Merchant Taylors'; *m* 1932, Janet Howat (d 1982), da of David Howat Allan (d 1943); 2 da; *Career* ptnr Allan Charlesworth & Co 1938-69; chm: Westinghouse Brake and Signal Co Ltd 1962-74, Scruttons; dir Michelin Tyre Co Ltd 1942-84; FCA 1927; *Clubs* Oriental; *Style—* Peter Ewen Esq; Kestor, Howton Rd, Moretonhampstead, Devon TQ13 8PP (☎ 0647 40307)

EWENS, John Qualtrough; CMG (1971), CBE (1959, QC 1983); s of Leonard John Ewens (d 1963), of Adelaide, S Aust, and Amy Effie Qualtrough (d 1959); *b* 18 Nov 1907; *Educ* St Peter's Coll Adelaide, Univ of Adelaide (LLB); *m* 1935, Gwendoline, da of Warren Ashley Wilson (d 1955); 2 s (Warren, Peter); *Career* barr, first parly counsel Aust 1948-72; *Recreations* bowls, reading, music; *Clubs* Univ of Canberra; *Style—* John Ewens, Esq, CMG, CBE, QC; 57 Franklin St, Manuka, ACT 2603, Aust (☎ 010 61 62 959283)

EWIN; *see*: Floyd Ewin

EWING; *see*: Orr-Ewing

EWING, Vice Adm Sir (Robert) Alastair; KBE (1962), CB (1959, DSC 1943); s of Maj Ian Alastair Ewing (d 1971), of Mounthooly, Jedburgh, and Muriel Adèle, *née* Child (d 1930); *b* 10 April 1909; *Educ* Fernden Haslemere, RNC Dartmouth; *m* 1, 18 Aug 1940, Diana Smeed (d 1980), da of Maj Harry Archer, DSO (ka 1917); 1 s (David b 1949); m 2, 1984, Anne, da of Capt C G Chichester, DSO, RN, and wid of Cdr Henry Wilkin; *Career* cmd destroyers 1939-47 (despatches 1940, 1941); Capt 1947; Capt (Plans) on Staff of Adm BJSM and naval memb Standing Gp Int Planning Team Washington 1949; IDC 1952; cmd HMS Vanguard last RN battleship; dir RN Staff Coll; naval sec to First Lord, actg Rear Adm 1956; Flag Offr Flotillas Med 1958; Adm Cmdg Reserves 1960, Vice Adm 1960, inspr recruiting RNVSR; ret 1962; *Clubs* Army and Navy, Naval Member, Royal Yacht Sqdn, Jed Forest; *Style—* Vice-Adm Sir Alastair Ewing, KBE, CB, DSC; 19 Reyntiens View, Odiham, Hampshire (☎ 0256 703 509)

EWING, Harry; MP (Lab) Falkirk East 1983-; s of William Ewing; *b* 20 Jan 1931; *Educ* Beath HS Cowdenbeath; *m* 1954, Margaret Greenhill; 1 s, 1 da; *Career* memb PO Workers' Union; contested (Lab) Fife E 1970; MP (Lab) Stirling Falkirk & Grangemouth 1974-83, sec Scottish Parly Lab Gp 1972-74, parly under-sec Scottish Off 1974-79, sr v-chm Trade Union Gp of Labour MPs 1979-; oppn front bench spokesman: Scottish Affrs 1981-83, Trade and Industry 1983-; specialist on Health Service matters; *Style—* Harry Ewing, Esq, MP; 16 Robertson Ave, Leven, Fife (☎ 0333 26123)

EWING, Winifred Margaret; MEP (SNP) Highlands and Islands 1979-; da of George Woodburn and Christina Bell Anderson; *b* 10 July 1929; *Educ* Queen's Park Sr Secondary Sch, Glasgow Univ (MA, LLB); *m* 1956, Stewart Martin Ewing; 2 s, 1 da; *Career* MP: (Scottish Nat) Hamilton 1967-70, (SNP) Moray and Nairn Feb 1974-79; memb Euro Parl 1975-; vice-pres Euro Democratic Alliance 1984-, pres Scottish Nat Pty 1987-; *Style—* Mrs Winifred Ewing, MEP; 52 Queen's Drive, Glasgow G42 8DD

EXETER, Archdeacon of; *see*: Richards, Ven John

EXETER, 69 Bishop of (cr 1050) 1985-; Rt Rev (Geoffrey) Hewlett Thompson; patron of 121 livings and of two alternately with the Crown, the Precentorship, Chancellorship, Subdeanery, 4 Canonries and 29 Prebends in his Cathedral, and the Archdeaconries of Exeter, Totnes, Barnstaple and Plymouth; this see, created 1050, consists of Devon (except) seven parishes) and one parish in Somerset; s of Lt Col Ralph Reakes Thompson, MC (d 1960), late RAMC and Eanswythe Frances, *née* Donaldson; *b* 14 August 1929; *Educ* Aldenham Sch, Trinity Hall Cambridge (MA); *m* 29 Sept 1954, Elizabeth Joy, da of Col Geoffrey Fausitt Taylor, MBE (d 1982), late IMS; 2 s (Andrew b 1957, Benjamin b 1963), 2 da (Mary Clare b 1955, Louise b 1961); *Career* 2 Lt Royal West Kents 1948-49; curate St Matthew Northampton 1954-59; vicar: St Augustine Wisbech 1959-66, St Saviour Folkestone 1966-74; bishop of Willesden 1974-85; *Clubs* United Oxford and Cambridge; *Style—* The Rt Rev the Bishop of Exeter; The Palace, Exeter EX1 1HY (☎ 0392 72362)

EXETER, 8 Marquess of (UK 1801; a previous Marquessate of Exeter was enjoyed by Henry Courtenay, Earl of Devon and gs of Edward IV, 1525-39); William Michael Anthony Cecil; also Baron Burghley (E 1571) and Earl of Exeter (E 1605; the de Reviers Earls of Devon, who enjoyed that title 1141-1262, were sometimes called Earls of Exeter), Hereditary Grand Almoner, and Lord Paramount of the Soke of Peterborough; s of 7 Marquess of Exeter (d 1988) (14 in descent from the Lord Burghley who was Elizabeth's I chief minister), and his 1 w Edith Lilian (d 1954), o da of Aurel Csanady de Telegd, of Budapest, Hungary; *b* 1 Sept 1935; *Educ* Eton; *m* 1967, Nancy Rose, da of Lloyd Arthur Meeker; 1 s, 1 da (Lady Angela Kathleen, b 1975); *Heir* s, Lord Burghley, *qv*; *Career* businessman and lecturer; *Books* The Rising Tide of Change (1986); *Style—* The Most Hon the Marquess of Exeter; 100 Mile House, PO Box 8, British Columbia VOK 2EO, Canada (☎ 604 395 2323)

EXMOUTH, Maria Luisa, Viscountess; Maria Luisa; also Marquesa de Olias (Sp cr 1652 of Philip IV); da of Luis de Urquijo, Marquøes de Amurrio, of Madrid, by his w Marquesa de Zarreal; *m* 1, Don Gonzalo Alvarez-Builla y Alvera (decd); m 2, 2 Jan 1938, 9 Viscount Exmouth (d 1970); 2 s (including 10 Viscount), 2 da; *Style*— The Rt Hon Maria Luisa, Viscountess Exmouth; c/o Lloyds Bank, High St, Exeter, Devon

EXMOUTH, 10 Viscount (UK 1816); Sir Paul Edward Pellew; 10 Bt (GB 1796); also Baron Exmouth (UK 1814); patron of one living; s of 9 Viscount (d 1970) and Maria Luisa, Marquesa de Olias (Sp cr of 1625), da of late Luis de Urquijo, Marques de Amurrio, of Madrid; *b* 8 Oct 1940; *Educ* Downside; *m* 1, 10 Dec 1964 (m dis 1974), Maria Krystina, o da of late Don Recaredo de Garay y Garay, of Madrid; 1 da (Hon Patricia b 1966); m 2, 1975, Rosemary Frances, da of Francis Harold Scoones, MRCS, LRCP, JP, and formerly w of Earl of Burford (now 14 Duke of St Albans, *qv*); 2 s (Hon Edward, Hon Alexander b (twin) 30 Oct 1978); *Heir* s, Hon Edward Francis Pellew b 30 Oct 1978; *Career* sits as Conservative Peer in House of Lords; memb IOD; *Style*— The Rt Hon Viscount Exmouth; Canonteign, nr Exeter, Devon (☎ 0647 52666)

EXTON, Clive Jack Montague; s of Jack Ernest Brooks (d 1970), of Eastbourne, Sussex, and Marie, *née* Rolfe (d 1984): name changed by deed poll; *b* 11 April 1930; *Educ* Christ's Hosp; *m* 1, 1951 (m dis 1957), Patricia Fletcher, *née* Ferguson (d 1983); 2 da (Frances (Mrs N Morgan), *née* Brooks b 1952, Sarah Brooks b 1954); m 2, 30 Aug 1957, Margaret Josephine (Mara); 1 s (Saul b 1965), 2 da (Antigone b 1961, Plaxy b 1964); *Career* Nat Serv 1948-50; actor 1951-59, writer 1959-; films: Night Must Fall, Isadora (with Melvyn Bragg), 10 Rillington Place, Entertaining Mr Sloane; tv plays: No Fixed Abode 1959, Where I Live 1960, I'll Have You to Remember 1961, Hold My Hand Soldier 1961, The Trial of Doctor Fancy 1963, The Big Eat 1963, Land of My Dreams 1964, The Bone Yard 1965, The Close Prisoner 1965, The Boundary (with Tom Stoppard); tv dramatizations of works by authors incl: Agatha Christie, Jean Cocteau, Daphne Du Maurier, Graham Greene, Somerset Maugham, Ruth Rendell, Georges Simenan, H G Wells; theatre prodn: Have You Any Dirty Washing Mother Dear 1969; *Style*— Clive Exton, Esq; 3 Blenheim Cottages, Church Cres, Hackney, London E9 7DH; c/o A D Peters, 5th Floor, The Chambers, Chelsea Harbour, London SW10 (☎ 01 376 7676)

EXTON, Rodney Noel; JP (Surrey 1968); s of Maj Noel Exton (d 1969), and Winifred *née* Stokes (d 1963); *b* 28 Dec 1927; *Educ* Clifton Coll, Lincoln Coll Oxford (MA Mod Langs), CCC Cambridge (PGCE); *m* 1961, Pamela Beresford, da of Alan Hardie, of Rose Bay, Sydney, New South Wales (d 1947) and widow of Ian Menzies Sinclair, of Glen Innes, NSW; 2 step s (Andrew, Colin), 2 step da (Virginia, Jane); *Career* Royal Hampshire Regt 1946-48; Hampshire Cricketer 1946; master Eton 1951-52, asst master (later housemaster) Mill Hill Sch 1952-63, Int Res Fund Scholarship to USA 1952, in Australia with NSW State Educn Dept 1959-60, headmaster Reed's Sch Cobham 1964-77 md Exton Hotels Co Ltd 1966-80;; ESU/HMC Page Scholar to USA 1971; memb Nat Working Pty on Disadvantaged Children 1972, memb Br Atlantic Educn Ctee 1974, GAP Cncl of Mgmnt 1978-, dir Independent Schools Careers Orgn (ISCO) 1978-88 conslt to the Vocational Guidance Assoc 1988-; French Inspector for Johansens Guide to Hotels 1988-; Pres Flycatchers CC 1989-; *Publications* Industrial Cadets (1972); *Recreations* collecting old lithographs, guitar-playing; *Clubs* East India, MCC, Inst of Directors, Royal Mid-Surrey Golf, Vincent's (Oxford); *Style*— Rodney Exton; 85 Mount Ararat, Richmond, Surrey T@10 6PL (☎ 01 940 0305)

EYERS, Patrick Howard Caines; CMG (1985), LVO (1964); s of Arthur Leopold Caines Eyers (d 1952), of Bristol, and Nora Lilian, *née* Carpenter (d 1938); *b* 4 Sept 1933; *Educ* Clifton Coll, Gonville and Caius Coll Cambridge (BA), Institut Universitaire des Hautes Etudes Internationales Geneva; *m* 1960, Jutta Lindheide (Heidi), da of Werner Rüsch (d 1978), of Vorarlberg, Austria; 2 s (Simon, Sam), 1 da (Sophie); *Career* HM Diplomatic Service, served ME Centre for Arabic Studies 1960, Dubai 1961, Brussels 1964, FO 1966, Aden 1969, Abidjan 1970, Br Mil Govt Berlin 1971, FCO 1974; cnsllr Bonn 1977, head of Republic of Ireland Dept FCO 1981, Royal Coll of Def Studies 1984, HM ambass to Zaire, Congo, Rwanda and Burundi 1985-; *Recreations* music, ski-ing, sailing; *Clubs* Kandahar, Hurlingham; *Style*— Patrick Eyers, Esq, CMG, LVO; Br Embassy, Ave Des Trois Z, BP 8049, Kinshasa, Zaire (☎ 31257); Br Embassy, Ave de L'Equateur, BP 8049, Kinshasa, Zaire (☎ 25767)

EYLES, Andrew Michael; s of Edward Joseph Eyles (d 1969), and Dorothy Beryl, *née* Martin; *b* 16 Sept 1941; *Educ* Rutlish Sch, London Univ (BDS); *m* 19 Dec 1964, Helen Margaret, da of Edward George Wiseman (d 1979); 1 s (Robin b 1969), 1 da (Bridget b 1970); *Career* cmmd Maj RADC 1964-69; gen dental practitioner 1969-; organising sec Ashdon Church Restoration Appeal Fund 1985-; *Recreations* gardening; *Style*— Andrew M Eyles, Esq; The Old Fox, Ashdon, Saffron Walden, Essex (☎ 079984 339); 3 The Square, Sawbridgeworth, Herts (☎ 0279 724121)

EYLES, Peter George; s of George Henry Eyeles MBE, of Surrey, and Louise Cleeves; *b* 22 April 1946; *m* 1975 (m dis) Fallulah Jane, da of Sir Maxwell Joseph (d 1983); 1 s (Kieren b 1978), 1 da (Marelka b 1980); *Career* gp md Norfolk Capital Gp plc; chm: Norfolk Capital Hotels, Norfolk Capital Inns, Norfolk Capital Securities, Celebrated Country Hotels, Norfolk Capital Devpts, St James Club Ltd; *Recreations* work, shooting, skiing; *Clubs* St James; *Style*— Peter Eyles, Esq; 8 Cromwell Place, London SW7 (☎ 01 581 0601)

EYNON, (Richard) Mark; s of Capt Melville Victor Eynon, of The Cedars, Lodge Road, Caerleon, Gwent, and Phyllis Bertha, *née* Aitken-Smith, MBE, JP; *b* 9 Nov 1953; *Educ* Monmouth Sch, Manchester Univ (BSc), Manchester Business Sch (MBA); *m* 18 Oct 1980, Susan Elspeth, da of Dr J T D Allen, of 5 Linden Ave, Liverpool; *Career* vice pres Bank of America 1982-86; dir: London Int Fin Futures Exchange 1984-, Warburg Securities 1986-; *Recreations* rugby, cricket; *Style*— Mark Eynon, Esq; Warburg Securities, 1 Finsbury Avenue, London EC2M 2PA (☎ 0628 26829, 01 382 4477)

EYRE, Hon Mrs; (Edith Joy Marion); *née* Best; o da of 7 Baron Wynford (d 1943), and his 1 wife Evelyn Mary Aylmer, *née* May (d 1929); *b* 14 August 1915; *m* 3 April 1937, Cdr Walpole John Eyre, RN (ret), s of Rev George Frederick Eyre, MA, of West Hill, Lyme Regis, Dorset; 1 s, 1 da, and 1 adopted da; *Style*— Hon Mrs Eyre; Sadborow, Myll, Thorncombe, Chard, Somerset

EYRE, Sir Graham Newman; QC (1970); s of Cdr Newman Eyre, RNVR (d 1970); *b* 9 Jan 1931; *Educ* Marlborough, Trinity Coll Cambridge (MA, LLB); *m* 1954, Jean Dalrymple, da of late A D Walker; 1 s, 3 da; *Career* barr 1954, bencher Middle Temple, Recorder Crown Court 1975-; memb Lincoln's Inn; inspr Airport Inquiries (held at Quendon and Heathrow) 1981-83, Eyre Report on Airports submitted Nov 1984; kt 1989; *Clubs* Athenaeum; *Style*— Graham Eyre, Esq, QC; Walberton House, Walberton, W Sussex (☎ 0243 551205); Chambers; 8 New Square, Lincoln's Inn, London WC2 (☎ 01 242 4987)

EYRE, Maj-Gen James Ainsworth Campden Gabriel; CVO (1978), CBE (1980, OBE 1975); 2 s of Edward Joseph Eyre (d 1962), by his w, Hon Dorothy Elizabeth Anne Pelline, *née* Lyon-Dalberg-Acton, *qv*, 2 da of 2 Baron Acton; *b* 2 Nov 1930; *Educ* Harvard Univ (BA, LLB); *m* 1967, Monica Ruth Esther, da of Michael Joseph Smyth (d 1964), of Harley Street, London; 1 s (James b 1969), 1 da (Annabelle b 1970); *Career* RHG 1955; sec Chiefs of Staff Ctee MOD 1980-82; dir Def Programmes Staff 1982-83; GOC London Dist and Maj-Gen Commanding Household Div 1983-; *Recreations* shooting, racing; *Clubs* Turf; *Style*— Maj-Gen James Eyre, CVO, CBE; c/o HQ London District, Horse Guards, Whitehall, London SW1

EYRE, Maj John Vickers; s of Nevill Cathcart Eyre (d 1971), of Bristol, and Maud Evelyn Wallace, formerly Eyre, *née* Truscott; *b* 30 April 1936; *Educ* Winchester; *m* 19 Oct 1974, Sarah Margaret Aline, da of Maj Geoffrey Beresford (Tim) Heywood, MBE, of North Farm, Edgeworth, Glos; 1 s (Charles b 8 Jan 1980), 1 da (Georgina b 1 Jan 1977); *Career* Nat Serv RA 1955-57, cmmnd RA 1957-59, RHA 1959-62, Capt 14/20 Kings Hussars 1962 served Cyprus Emergency 1963-64, Regtl Adj 1964-66, Gen Staff 4 div 1966-67, Maj 1968, Army Staff Coll 1969, gen staff 1970-71, regtl duty 1971-72, serv N Ireland Emergency 1972, ret 1973; TA, Royal Gloucestershire Hussars 1980-83; asst to chm Savoy Hotel plc 1973-75, administrator Brian Colquhoun and Ptnrs Consulting Engrs 1975-79, proprietor Haresfield Gdn Centre 1981-86, md George Truscott Ltd 1986-(dir 1969-86); JP 1987-, Parish Cncllr 1988-, govr Haresfield Sch 1985-, dist cmmr Berkeley Hunt Pony Club 1986-, memb Haresfield PCC 1984-, memb ctee Berkeley Hunt 1988-; *Recreations* hunting, gardening, skiing; *Style*— Maj John Eyre; Cromwell House, Haresfield, Stonehouse, Glos (☎ 0452 720 410); George Truscott Ltd, College Court, Glos (☎ 0452 24914)

EYRE, Hon Mrs; (Dorothy Elizabeth Anne) Pelline; *née* Lyon-Dalberg-Acton; 2 da of 2 Baron Acton (d 1924); *b* 25 June 1906; *m* 6 June 1928, Edward Joseph Eyre (d 6 Oct 1962), s of Edward Eyre, of New York and London; 5 s (including James Ainsworth Campden Gabriel, *qv*), 2 da; *Style*— Hon Mrs Eyre; 18 Petersham House, Harrington Rd, London SW7

EYRE, Sir Reginald Edwin; s of Edwin Eyre, of Birmingham; *b* 28 May 1924; *Educ* King Edward's Camp Hill Sch Birmingham, Emmanuel Coll Cambridge; *m* 1978, Anne Clements; 1 da; *Career* served WW II, RNVR, Midshipman and Sub-Lt; slr 1950; sr ptnr Eyre & Co; contested (C) Birmingham Northfield 1959; chm: W Midlands Area Cons Political Centre 1960-63, Nat Advsy Ctee 1964-66; MP (C) Birmingham Hall Green 1965-87; oppn whip 1966-70, lord cmmr Treasury 1970, comptroller of HM Household 1970-72; parly under-sec: Environment (Housing and Construction) 1972-74, vice-chm Conservative Party, responsible for Urban Areas 1974-79, PUSS Trade 1979-82, Tport 1982-83; kt 1984; *Publications* Hope for our Towns and Cities (1977); *Clubs* Carlton; *Style*— Sir Reginald Eyre; 1041 Stratford Rd, Birmingham B28 8AS; 45 Aylesford St, London SW1

EYRE, Richard Hastings Charles; s of Richard Galfrious Hastings Giles, of Dorset, and Minna Mary Jessica Royds; maternal gf was antarctic explorer - Scott's 1st Lt; *b* 28 Mar 1943; *Educ* Sherborne Sch, Cambrige (BA);; *m* 1973, Susan Elizabeth Birtwistle; 1 da (Lucy b 1974); *Career* theatre and film dir, assoc dir Lyceum Theatre Edinburgh 1968-71, dir Nottingham Playhouse 1973-78, prodr Play For Today BBC TV 1978- 80, assoc dir Nat Theatre 1980-86 (dir NT 1988-); films: The Ploughman's Lunch (Evening Standard Award for Best Film 1983), Loose Connestions (1983), Laughterhuose (TV Prize Venice Film Festival 1984); TV films: The Imitation Game, Pasmore (1980), Country (1981), The Insurance Man (1986), Past Caring (1986), Tumbledown (winner Italia RAi Prize 1988); SWET Dir of the Year 1982, Standard Best Dir 1982; STV Awards for Best Production: 1969, 1970, 1971;; *Style*— Richard Eyre, Esq; National Theatre, South Bank, London SE1 9PX (☎ 01 928 2033, fax 01 620 1197, telex 297306 NATTRE G)

EYRE, Very Rev Richard Montague Stephens; s of Montague Hemy Eyre (d 1974), (supt Indian Police), and Ethel Mary, *née* Raw (d 1975); memb of Derbys branch of Eyre family; *b* 16 May 1929; *Educ* Charterhouse, Oriel Coll Oxford (MA); *m* 28 Dec 1963, Anne Mary, da of Canon G B Bentley, of 5 The Cloisters, Windsor Castle; 2 da (Chantal b 1966, Henrietta b 1972); *Career* asst curate St Mark Portsea 1956-59, tutor and chaplain Chichester Theol Coll 1959-62, chaplain Eastbourne Coll 1962-65; vicar: of Arundel with Tortington and South Stoke 1965-73, Good Shepherd Brighton 1973-75; archdeacon of Chichester 1975-80, tres Chichester Cathedral 1978-81, dean of Exeter 1981-; *Recreations* golf, travel, wine, music; *Clubs* United Oxford & Cambridge; *Style*— The Very Rev the Dean of Exeter; The Deanery, Exeter EX1 1HT (☎ 0392 72697)

EYSTON, Lady Anne Priscilla; *née* Maitland; 2 da of Viscount Maitland (ka in N Africa 1943), o s of 15 Earl of Lauderdale, (d 1953); granted the rank and precedence of an Earl's da 1953; *b* 4 May 1940; *m* 6 Feb 1968, John Joseph Eyston, *qv*, 1 s, 2 da; *Style*— Lady Anne Eyston; Mapledurham House, Reading, (☎ (0734 723350)

EYSTON, John Joseph; s of Capt Thomas More Eyston (d 1940 of wounds received in action in Belgium; ggs of Charles Eyston, whose w, Agnes, was of the Blount family, of Mapledurham House), and Lady Agnes Savile, *qv*, da of 6 Earl of Mexborough; younger bro of Thomas Eyston, *qv*; *b* 27 April 1934; *Educ* Ampleforth, Trinity Coll Cambridge; *m* 6 Feb 1968, Lady Anne Maitland, *qv*; 1 s, 2 da; *Style*— J J Eyston, Esq; Mapledurham House, Reading (☎ 0734 723350)

EYSTON, Michael Charles; s of Major Charles John Eyston (d 1957), of Channel Islands, and Olive Gertrude O'Rorke (d 1980); *b* 9 Feb 1923; *Educ* Stowe; *m* 1 June 1949, Eileen Maureen Hitchmough, da of Brig Col Francis Gerald Russell Brittorous, CBE, DSO, MC (d 1974), of Hants; 1 s (Charles Martin Russell b 1954), 3 da (Ilynne Sabina Marty b 1950, Anne Thérèse b 1958, Michaela Domine Prisca b 1969); *Career* Capt RB 1941-46, served Europe, M East Italy; elected memb Nat Coursing Club 1966; *Recreations* coursing, shooting, deerstalking; *Clubs* London, Royal Greenjackets; *Style*— Michael C Eyston, Esq; Pound Croft House, East Hanney, Wantage, Oxon OX12 0HP (☎ 023 587 222); Pound Croft Kennels, East Hanney, Wantage, Oxon OX12 0HP (☎ 023 587 222)

EYSTON, Thomas More; Lord of the Manor of Arches, Abbey Manor and Catmore; s of Thomas More Eyston, JP, and Lady Agnes Savile, da of 6 Earl of Mexborough; bro of John Eyston, of Mapledurham, *qv*; *b* 24 Dec 1931; *Educ* Ampleforth, Trinity Coll

Cambridge; *Style*— Thomas Eyston, Esq; Hendred House, East Hendred, Wantage, Oxon (☎ 0235 833203)

EZEKIEL, David Richard Simon; s of Victor David Oscar Ezekiel (d 1976), and Sarah Ethel Ezekiel (d 1963); *b* 27 Sept 1930; *Educ* St John's Sch Leatherhead Surrey; *m* 27 Oct 1960, Carolyn Joan, da of Kenneth Gordon Gale, of South Devon; 2 s (Marcus b 1962, William b 1964); *Career* Nat Serv RAF (FO) 1953-55; qualified CA, Moore Stephens 1948-53, and 1953-57, co sec Controls & Communications Ltd 1961-69, fin dir Celestion Industries plc 1969- (dir associated cos incl: Slix Ltd 1978-, Truvox Engrg Co Ltd 1968-, Wood Bastow Hldgs plc 1978-, Celestion Int Ltd); FCA, FCT; *Recreations* music, bridge, sailing, watching sport - particularly rugby; *Clubs* Lansdowne, Little Ship, Chichester Yacht; *Style*— David R S Ezekiel, Esq; 130 Mount Street, London W1Y 5HA (☎ 01 499 5641)

EZRA, Baron (Life Peer UK 1982), of Horsham in Co of West Sussex; Derek; MBE (1945); s of late David and Lillie Ezra; *b* 23 Feb 1919; *Educ* Monmouth Sch, Magdalene Coll Cambridge; *m* 1950, Julia Elizabeth , da of Thomas Wilkins, of Portsmouth, Hants; *Career* memb UK Delegation to Euro Coal and Steel Community 1952-56; regnl sales mangr Nat Coal Bd 1958-60 (dir-gen Marketing 1960-65, bd memb 1965-67, dep chm 1967-71, chm 1971-82), chm Br Iron & Steel Consumers' Cncl 1983-; dir: Redland plc 1982-, Sankey Building Supplies, Associated Heat Servs Ltd, Br Fuel Co; chm Br Inst of Mngmt 1976-78, conslt on industl matters to Morgan Grenfell 1982-; pres: Coal Indust Soc 1981-, Inst of Trading Standards Admin 1987-; kt 1974; *Style*— The Rt Hon Lord Ezra, MBE; Nat Coal Board, Hobart House, Grosvenor Place, SW1 (☎ 01 235 2020)

F

FABER, Lady (Ann) Caroline; *née* Macmillan; da of 1 Earl of Stockton (d 1986); *b* 1923; *m* 1944, Julian Tufnell Faber; 4 s, 1 da; *Style*— Lady Caroline Faber; Bay House, Sandwich, Kent; 3 Chester Square, London SW1W 9HH

FABER, Hon Mrs (Diana Catriona); *née* Howard; da of 3 Baron Strathcona and Mount Royal (d 1959), and Hon Diana Evelyn, *née* Loder (d 1985), da of 1 Baron Wakehurst; *b* 13 Mar 1935; *m* 7 June 1956, Michael Leslie Ogilvie Faber, er s of George Valdemar Faber (d 1958), of 97 Oakwood Court, W14; 2 s, 2 da (twins); *Style*— The Hon Mrs Faber; The Combe, Glynde, Lewes, Sussex BN8 6RP (☎ 079159 402)

FABER, Sir Richard Stanley; KCVO (1980), CMG (1977); er s of Sir Geoffrey Cust Faber (d 1961), and Enid Eleanor, da of Sir Henry Erle Richards, KCSI, KC; bro of Thomas Erle Faber, *qv*; *b* 6 Dec 1924; *Educ* Westminster, Christ Church Oxford (MA); *Career* served RNVR 1943-46; entered HM Diplomatic Service 1950; serv: Baghdad, Paris, Abidjan, Washington; cnsllr: The Hague 1969-73, Cairo 1973-75; asst under-sec of state FCO 1975-77, ambass Algiers 1977-81, ret; *Books* Beaconsfield and Bolingbroke (1961), The Vision and the Need: Late Victorian Imperialist Aims (1966), Proper Stations: Class in Victorian Fiction (1971), French and English (1975), The Brave Courtier (Sir William Temple) (1983), High Road to England (1985), Young England (1987); *Clubs* Travellers'; *Style*— Sir Richard Faber, KCVO, CMG

FABER, Thomas Erle; yr s of Sir Geoffrey Cust Faber (d 1961); bro of Sir Richard Faber, KCVO, CMG, *qv*; *b* 25 April 1927; *Educ* Oundle, Trinity Coll Cambridge (MA, PhD); *m* 1, 5 Sept 1959, Penelope Morton; 2 s (Matthew b 1963, Tobias b 1965), 2 da (Henrietta b 1961 (d 1983), Polly b 1971); m 2, 1986, Elisabetta van Houts; 1 da (Sophie b 1986); *Career* Fell Corpus Christi Coll Cambridge 1953-, Lecturer in physics Cambridge Univ 1959-; chm Faber & Faber (Publishers) Ltd 1977- (dir 1969-); *Recreations* shooting, fishing, walking; *Style*— Thomas Faber, Esq; The Old Vicarage, Thompson's Lane, Cambridge (☎ 0223 356685)

FABER, Thomas Henry; s of Capt F S Faber (d 1954), of Ampfield House, Romsey Hants, and Amy, *née* Purcell-Gilpin (d 1957); *b* 5 Nov 1922; *Educ* Ampleforth, Christ Church Oxford; *m* 28 July 1951, Jennifer Mary, da of A E L Hill, OBE, DL (d 1986), of Twyford Lodge, Twyford, Winchester, Hants; 1 s (Robin H G Faber b 1955), 2 da (Caroline (Mrs Faber-Zini) b 1952, Juliet (Mrs Moore) b 1959); *Career* WWII Capt Grendier Gds served N Africa, Italy (wounded 1944), Palestine and Egypt; chartered surveyor; ptnr James Harris & Son Winchester (sr ptr 1980); dir: Strong & Co 1967-73, Whitbread Wessex 1973-81; chm Hants branch CLA 1976-79; ARICS 1950, FRICS 1956; *Recreations* hunting, shooting; *Style*— Thomas Faber, Esq; The Drove, West Tytherley, Salisbury, Wilts (☎ 0794 40 378); Mssrs James Harris & Son, Jewry Chambers, Winchester, Hants (☎ 0962 841 842)

FABER, Trevor Martyn; s of Harry Faber (d 1986), of Edgbaston, Birmingham, and Millicent, *née* Waxman (d 1988); *b* 9 Oct 1946; *Educ* Clifton, Merton Coll Oxford (MA); *m* 16 Aug 1985, Katrina Sally, da of George James Clay, of Harborne, Birmingham; *Career* called to the Bar Gray's Inn 1970, practices MO circuit, memb Tanworth in Arden Assoc for the Prosecution of Felons; *Recreations* theatre, literature, sport, music, food and wine; *Clubs* Vincent's, Oxford; *Style*— Trevor Faber, Esq; Woodside House, Salter Street, Earlswood, Warwickshire B94 6BY (☎ 056 46 3499); 3 Fountain Court, Steelhouse Lane, Birmingham B4 6DR (☎ 021 236 5854, fax 021 236 7008)

FABIAN, Andrew Paul; s of Andrew Taggart Fabian, of Kew Gardens, Richmond, Surrey, and Edith Mary, *née* Whorwell (d 1964); nephew of Robert Honey Fabian ('Fabian of the Yard'); *b* 23 May 1930; *Educ* St Paul's, Wadham Coll Oxford (MA); *m* 1, 1957 (m dis), Elizabeth Vivienne Chapman; 1 s (Andrew b 1961), 2 da (Susan b 1958, Jill b 1960); m 2, 29 Oct 1983, Eryll Francesca, da of Ronald Sigmund Dickinson, CMG (d 1985); *Career* Mil serv 1952-54 (Lt RE) Singapore Engr Regt; Dist Offr Tanganyika 1955-64; seconded 1961-64 to FO as vice-cnsl later 2 sec Ruanda-Urundi; HM Diplomatic Serv 1964-, served in Lusaka, Ankara, New Delhi, Islamabad and Karachi before present appt as Br High Cmmr at Nuku'alofa; *Recreations* chess, bird watching; *Clubs* Utd Oxford and Cambridge Univ 71 Pall Mall; *Style*— Andrew Fabian, Esq; c/o FCO King Charles St, SW1; British High Commission Nuku'alofa, PO Box 56, Kingdom of Tonga (☎ 21020, telex 66226 UKREP a/b)

FABLING, The Hon Mrs (Fiona Faith); *née* Campbell-Gray; el da of Maj Hon Lindsay Stuart Campbell-Gray, MC, Master of Gray (d 1945), and Doreen McClymont, *née* Tubbs (d 1948); sis of 22 Lord Gray; raised to rank of Baron's da 1950; *b* 12 Jan 1933; *m* 11 June 1955, Maj (Ronald Hugh) Desmond Fabling (d 1974), served in 14 PWO Scinde Horse (IA) then 1 Royal Dragoons, twin son of Hugh Fabling (d 1972), of Moat House, Grandborough, nr Rugby; 2 da (Victoria b 1958, Fenella b 1963); *Clubs* Sloane; *Style*— The Hon Mrs Fabling; Victoria House, Ampleforth, York YO6 4DA (☎ 043 93 330)

FACER, Roger Lawrence Lowe; s of John Ernest Facer (d 1983), of Epsom, and Phyllis, *née* Lowe (d 1979); *b* 28 June 1933; *Educ* Rugby, St John's Coll Oxford (MA); *m* 2 April 1960, Ruth Margaret, da of Herbert Mostyn Lewis, PhD (d 1985), of Gresford, Clwyd; 3 da (Sian b 1961, Lucinda b 1961, Emma b 1965); *Career* East Surrey Regt 2 Lt 1951-53, WO 1959, asst priv sec to sec of state 1958, cabinet office 1966-68, priv sec to min of state (equipment) MOD 1970, Int Inst for Strategic Studies 1972-73, cnsllr UK Delegation MBFR Vienna 1973-75, priv sec to sec of state for defence 1976-9, cabinet office 1981-83, Rand Corporation Santa Monica USA 1984; asst under sec of state MOD 1984-; *Recreations* alpine gardening, hill walking, opera; *Style*— Roger Facer, Esq; Ministry of Defence, London SW1

FACETTI, Hon Mrs; Hon Mary Frances; *née* Crittall; yst da of 1st and last Baron Braintree (d 1961); *b* 30 Dec 1922; *Educ* Langford Grove, Maldon; *m* 21 July 1950, Germano Luigi Facetti, s of Mario Giovanni Facetti, of Milan, Italy; 1 da (Lucia Olivia Josephine b 1954); *Style*— The Hon Mrs Facetti

FACEY, Mathew George Charles; s of William Facey; *b* 11 Dec 1937; *Educ* Cardiff HS for Boys; *m* 1967, Judith Ann, *née* Davies; 1 s, 1 da; *Career* dir: Everbright Fasteners Ltd, Baestan Ltd, Gordian Everbright Tstees Ltd, Everbright Fasteners Inc USA; pres Schnitzer Alloy Products Co USA; *Recreations* music, literature; *Style*— Mathew Facey, Esq; The Beeches, 19 Park Rd, Hampton Hill, Middx (☎ 01 979 1743); Everbright Fasteners Ltd, Stainless House, 4-6 Edwin Rd, Twickenham TW1 4JN (☎ 01 891 0111, telex 933506); 220 W Jersey Street, Elizabeth, NJ 07208, USA

FAGE, Prof John Donnelly; s of Arthur Fage, CBE, FRS (d 1977), and Winifred Eliza, *née* Donnelly (d 1951); *b* 3 June 1921; *Educ* Tonbridge, Magdalene Coll Cambridge; *m* 1949, Jean, da of late Frederick Banister; 1 s, 1 da; *Career* sr lectr Univ Coll of the Gold Coast 1949-55, prof of History 1955-59, dep principal 1957-59, lectr african history London Univ 1959-63, prof of african history and dir of w african studies Birmingham Univ 1963-84, pro vice-chllr Birmingham Univ 1979-84 (dean Faculty of Arts 1975-78, vice-principal 1981-84); pres African Studies Assoc of the UK 1968-69; jt editor The Journal of African History 1960-73, gen editor The Cambridge History of Africa 1975-86; chm culture advsy ctee of UK Nat Cmmn for UNESCO 1978-85; *Books* An Introduction to the History of W Africa (1955), Atlas of African History (1958), Ghana, a Historical Interpretation (1959), A Short History of Africa (with Roland Oliver 1962), A History of W Africa (1969), Africa Discovers her Past (ed 1970), Papers on African Prehistory (ed with Roland Oliver 1970), A History of Africa (1978), A Guide to Original Sources for pre-colonial Western Africa (1987); *Recreations* doing things to houses and gardens; *Clubs* Athenaeum; *Style*— Prof John Fage; 17 Antringham Gdns, Birmingham, B15 3QL (☎ 021 455 0020)

FAGG, William Buller; CMG (1967); s of William Percy Fagg (d 1934), of Upper Norwood, London, and Lilian Fagg; *b* 28 April 1914; *Educ* Dulwich, Magdalene Coll Cambridge; *Career* anthropologist, tribal art historian and consultant, writer; keeper Dept of Ethnography, Br Museum 1969-74 (asst keeper 1938-55, dep keeper 1955-69), conslt on tribal art to Christie's 1974-; hon sec Royal Anthropological Inst 1939-56, vice-pres 1969-72, hon ed Man 1947-65; *Recreations* photography, music, cycling, travel; *Style*— William Fagg Esq, CMG; 6 Galata Road, Barnes, London SW13 9NQ (☎ 01 748 6620)

FAGGE, John Christopher; s and h of Sir John Fagge, 11 Bt; *b* 30 April 1942; *Style*— John Fagge, Esq

FAGGE, Sir John William Frederick; 11 Bt (E 1660); s of William Archibald Theodore Fagge (d 1924), 4 s of 8 Bt, and Nellie, *née* Wise (d 1924); suc unc, Sir John Harry Lee Fagge, 10 Bt, 1940; *b* 25 Sept 1910; *m* 11 May 1940, Ivy Gertrude, da of William Edward Frier, of Newington, Kent; 1 s, 1 da; *Heir* s, John Christopher Fagge; *Career* farmer; *Style*— Sir John Fagge, Bt; 26 The Mall, Faversham, Kent

FAHERTY, Colman James Bernard; s of Patrick Faherty, of London, and Elizabeth Cristina, *née* Devlin; *b* 1 Sept 1949; *Educ* St Josephs Coll, Galway; *m* 4 Oct 1969, Jacqueline Francis, da of Robert Richard Ford, of Southend-on-Sea, Essex; 2 s (Paul b 16 Jan 1975, Adam b 23 Oct 1977), 1 da (Clare b 2 Aug 1972); *Career* dir Foreign and Colonial: Unit Mgmnt Ltd 1983-, Mgmnt Ltd 1985-, Pensions Mgmnt Ltd 1986-, Nominees Ltd 1986-, Mgmnt (Jersey) Ltd 1988-; chm Circa Leisure plc 1988-, dir SE Essex Technol Centre 1988-; memb Rochford DC 1986-; IOD 1986-; *Recreations* golf, tennis, snooker; *Style*— Colman Faherty, Esq; 26 Gladstone Rd, Hockley, Essex (☎ 0702 202 844); 1 Laurence Pountney Hill, London EC4R 0BA (☎ 01 623 4680, fax 01 623 4680, telex 886197)

FAINT, John Anthony Leonard; s of Thomas Leonard Faint (d 1976), and Josephine Rosey, *née* Dunkerley; *b* 24 Nov 1942; *Educ* Chigwell Sch, Magdalen Coll Oxford (BA), Fletcher Sch Mass USA (MA); *m* 24 June 1978, Elizabeth Theresa, da of Walter Winter (d 1960); *Career* Min of Overseas Dvpt 1965-71 (1974-80 and 1983-86); study leave Cambridge Mass 1968-69, first sec (aid) Blantyre Malawi 1971-73; head SE Asia Devpt Div Bangkok 1980-83, UK alternate exec dir IBRD/IMF Washington 1986-; *Recreations* music, bridge, chess, squash, tennis; *Style*— J Anthony L Faint, Esq; UK Delegation to IMF/IBRD, c/o British Embassy, 3100 Massachusetts Avenue NW, Washington DC 20008, USA (☎ 202 623 4555)

FAIRBAIRN, Sir (James) Brooke; 6 Bt (UK 1869), of Ardwick, Lancs; s of Sir William Albert Fairbairn, 5 Bt (d 1972), and Christine Renée Cotton, *née* Croft; *b* 10 Dec 1930; *Educ* Stowe; *m* 5 Nov 1960, Mary Russell, o da of late William Russell Scott, 2 s (Robert William b 1965, George Edward b 1969), 1 da (Fiona Mary b 1967); *Heir* s, Robert Fairbairn, b 1965; *Career* proprietor of J Brooke Fairbairn & Co Newmarket (furnishing fabric converters); *Clubs* City Livery; *Style*— Sir Brooke Fairbairn, Bt; Barkway House, Bury Rd, Newmarket, Suffolk CB8 7BT (☎ 0638 662733); (business) The Railway Station, Newmarket, Suffolk CB8 9BA (☎ 0638 665766, fax 0638 665124)

FAIRBAIRN, David; JP; s of Ernest Hulford Fairbairn (d 1981; past master Loriners and Gold & Silver Wyre Drawers), and Iva May Shilling (d 1968); *b* 9 August 1924; *Educ* Haileybury, Trinity Hall Cambridge (MA); *m* 1946, Helen Merriel de la Cour, da of Harold Lewis Collingwood (d 1983); 2 s (Michael b 1947, Christopher b 1949), 2 da (Linda b 1952, Joy b 1958); *Career* Lt RNVR 1939-45; called to the Bar Middle Temple 1949; Met Stipendiary Magistrate 1971; dep CJ 1972, dep chm Surrey Quarter Sessions 1969-71; Freeman City of London 1958; *Recreations* golf, tennis, country life;

Style— David Fairbairn, Esq, JP; Wollards Farm, Mayes Green, Nr Dorking, Surrey RH5 5PN

FAIRBAIRN, Hon Sir David Eric; KBE (1977), DFC (1944); s of Clive Prell Fairbairn (d 1961), of NSW Australia, and Marjorie Rose, *née* Jowett (d 1951); *b* 3 Mar 1917; *Educ* Geelong GS, Jesus Coll Cambridge (MA); *m* 1945, Ruth Antill, da of late Dr Robert Affleck Robertson, of NSW; 3 da; *Career* farmer, politician, diplomat, memb House of Reps 1949-75, minister for Air 1962-64, minister for Nat Dvpt 1964-69, minister for Education and Science 1971, minister for Defence 1971-72, Australian ambass to the Netherlands 1977-80; Hon Col 1981-85; *Recreations* golf, gardening; *Clubs* Melbourne, Cwlth (Canberra), Hawks (Cambridge), Leander, Royal Canberra Golf; *Style—* Hon Sir David Fairbairn, KBE, DFC; 18 Yarralumla Bay, 51 Musgrave St, Yarralumla, ACT 2600, Australia (☎ 814659)

FAIRBAIRN, David Ritchie; s of George Forrester Fairbairn (d 1967), and Eileen Bartlett; *b* 4 July 1934; *Educ* Mill Hill, Gonville and Caius Coll Cambridge (BA); *m* 6 Sept 1958, Hon Susan, da of Baron Hill of Luton (Life Peer); 1 s (Charles b 1963), 2 da (Carolyn b 1960, Heather b 1965); *Career* 2 lt RA (Korea) 1952-54; co dir and md James Martin Assoc UK Ltd 1985-; overseas mkt mangr Arthur Guinness Son & Co Ltd 1960; pres: Cambridge Union Soc 1958, Guinness Harp Corp NY 1964, mktg dir Guinness Overseas Ltd 1969; md: ICC Dataset Ltd 1970; mangr Retail and Distribution Sector Int Computers Ltd 1975; dir: The Nat Computing Centre 1980-86, Mkt EMI Medical Ltd 1976, British Standards Inst and chm Automation and Information Technology Cncl 1985; has various other directorships; vice-chm Parliamentary Information Technol ctee 1982; memb: Focus Ctee on Standards 1982, Monopolies and Mergers Cmmn 1985; liveryman The Co of Information Technologists 1987-; FIDpm; FBCS, FID; *Recreations* sailing, skiing, water-skiing; *Clubs* Institute of Directors; *Style—* David Fairbairn, Esq; Oak End, 11 Oak Way, Harpenden, Herts (☎ 05827 5820); James Martin House Littleton Rd, Ashford, Middx (☎ 0784 245058, telex 928230 SMA UKG, fax 0784 243003)

FAIRBAIRN, Hon Mrs Elizabeth Mary; *née* Mackay; da of 13 Lord Reay (d 1963); *b* 21 June 1938; *m* 29 Sept 1962 (m dis 1979), Nicholas Fairbairn, QC, MP; 3 da (and 1 s, 1 da decd); *Style—* The Hon Mrs Fairbairn

FAIRBAIRN, John Sydney; s of Capt Sydney George Fairbairn, MC, and Angela Maude, *née* Fane; *b* 15 Jan 1934; *Educ* Eton, Trinity Coll Cambridge (BA); *m* 18 March 1968, Mrs Camilla Fry, da of Geoffrey Norman Grinling, of Belmont, Hoathly, Sussex; 1 s (John b 1969), 2 da (Rose b 1969, Flora b 1972); *Career* Nat Serv 2 Lt 17/21 Lancers 1952-54; with Monkhouse Stoneham & Co 1957-60, dep chm M&E Group plc 1980- (dir 1974, joined 1961), dep chm LAUTRO Ltd 1986-; memb exec ctee Unit Tst Assoc 1980-, chm Esmee Fairbairn Charitable Tst 1988- (tstee 1965-), hon tres and memb Cncl King's Coll London 1972-84, memb Cncl Univ of Buckingham 1987; hon FKC, FCA; *Clubs* Brooks's, MCC; *Style—* John Fairbairn, Esq; Harvey Hill, Cuckfield, West Sussex

FAIRBAIRN, Robert William; s and h of Sir Brooke Fairbairn, 6 Bt; *b* 10 April 1965; *Educ* King's Sch Ely, Durham Univ (BA); *Career* investmt mangr GT Mgmnt plc 1987-; *Clubs* City Univ; *Style—* Robert Fairbairn, Esq; GT Management plc, 8 Devonshire Sq, London EC2 M4YJ

FAIRBAIRN, Maj Ronald; TD; s of John Douglas Fairbairn (d 1964), and Letitia Ellen Fairbairn (d 1966); *b* 15 April 1916; *Educ* Dulwich; *m* 5 Oct 1940, Doris Edith, da of David Sydney Stevens (d 1948), of 7 Western Terrace, Falmouth; *Career* cmmnd 24 London Regt (later 1/7 Queen's Royal Regt) TA 1935, Capt 1939, served France 1940, joined 8 Army 1942, joined 7 Armd Div (The Desert Rats') and promoted Major 1942, served Alamein (severely wounded) 1942, returned UK and served non-combat units 1943, demob 1946 (disabled with partial paralysis); Bank of England: continued after war 1946-, head of accounting servs 1968, asst sec 1970; staff conslt Ctee of London Clearing Bankers and Br Bankers Assoc 1972-78, ret 1978; hon tres: The Queen's (Southwark) Regtl Assoc, Albury and St Marthas branch Mole Valley Cons Assoc, fabric fund tst St Michael's Church Faley Green; tstee Queen's Royal Surrey Regt Museum (memb working pty for devpt and maintenance), govr Central Fndn Schs 1966-76; Freeman City of London 1962, memb Worshipful Co of Bakers 1962; assoc Chartered Inst of Bankers; *Recreations* sailing until recent years, music, local activities, stock market investment; *Style—* Maj Ronald Fairbairn, TD; Lowingfold, Farley Green, Albury, Surrey GU5 9DN (☎ 048 641 2254)

FAIRBAIRN, Hon Mrs (Susan); *née* Hill; yst da of Baron Hill of Luton, PC (Life Peer); *b* 27 Dec 1936; *m* 6 June 1958, David Ritchie Fairbairn, s of late George Forrester Fairbairn; 1 s, 3 da; *Style—* Hon Mrs Fairbairn; 11 Oak Way, West Common, Harpenden, Herts

FAIRBAIRN OF FORDELL, Sir Nicholas Hardwick; QC (Scotland 1972), MP (C) Perth and Kinross 1983-; holder of territorial Barony of Fordell; s of William Ronald Dodds Fairbairn, MD, DPsych, FRSE (d 1966), and Mary, *née* More-Gordon of Charlton and Kinnaber (d 1951); *b* 24 Dec 1933; *Educ* Loretto, Edinburgh Univ (MA, LLB); *m* 1, 29 Sept 1962 (m dis 1979), Hon Elizabeth Mary Mackay, da of 13 Lord Reay; 1 s (Edward Nicholas d 1965), 4 da (Charlotte Elizabeth b 22 Dec 1963, Micheline b (twin) 22 Dec 1963 d 10 April 1964, Anna Karina b 13 May 1966, Francesca Katharine Nichola b 15 Jan 1969); m 2, 28 May 1983, Suzanne Mary, da of Col George Hilary Wheeler (d 1987); *Career* Capt RA (TA); called to Scots bar 1957; chm Traverse Theatre Edinburgh 1964-72, MP (C) Kinross & Perths W Oct 1974-83; slr-gen Scotland 1979-82; cmmr of northern lighthouses 1979-82; hon pres Soc Preservation Duddingston Village; tstee Nat Museum of Scotland 1987-; FSA (Scot); kt chevalier Order of Polonia Restituta 1988; kt 1988; *Books* A Life is too Short (1987); *Clubs* Beefsteak, Buck's, Puffin's (Edinburgh), New (Edinburgh), Carlton; *Style—* Sir Nicholas Fairbairn of Fordell, QC, MP; Fordell Castle, by Dunfermline, Fife

FAIRBANKS, Douglas Elton Jr; Hon KBE (1949), DSC (1944); o s of Douglas Fairbanks Sr (d 1939), and his 1 wife, Anna Beth, *née* Sully (d 1967); *b* 9 Dec 1909,New York City; *Educ* Bovée Sch, Knickerbocker Greys Mil Sch, Harvard Mil, Poly (New York and Los Angeles); *m* 1, 3 June 1929 (m dis 1933), Joan Crawford, the film actress (d 1977); m 2, 22 April 1939, Mary Lee (d 1988), da of Dr Giles Epling, of Bluefield, W Virginia, and formerly w of George Huntington Hartford; 3 da; *Career* theatre, cinema and television actor; prodr; co dir, writer, sculptor and painter; former vice-pres Franco-Br War Relief and nat vice-pres ctee Defend America by Aiding the Allies 1939-40, former presidential envoy; Capt USNR, ret; chm: Douglas Fairbanks Ltd, Fairtel Inc (US), Boltons Trading Co Inc and dir other cos; KStJ 1950; has received a great number of foreign decorations; *Films include* Stella Dallas, The Green Hat, The Dawn Patrol, Morning Glory, Catherine The Great, Mimi (La Boheme), The Prisoner of Zenda, Gunga Din, The Corsican Brothers, Sinbad the Sailor, The Exile, State Secret (The Great Manhunt), Ghost Story, *Plays include* Young Woodley, The Jest, Romeo and Juliet, My Fair Lady, The Pleasure of His Company, The Secretary Bird, Present Laughter, Out on a Limb, Sleuth; *Style—* Douglas Fairbanks Jr, KBE, DSC; 575 Park Ave, New York, NY 10021, USA (☎ 212 home: 838 4900; office: 980 5283); c/o Countess Benckendorf, 29-A Chalcot Rd, London NW1

FAIRBROTHER, Dr Jeremy Richard Frederick; s of Prof Fred Fairbrother (d 1983), of 8 Athol Rd, Bramhall, Stockport, and Grace, *née* Spann; *b* 4 June 1939; *Educ* Cheadle Hulme Sch, Balliol Coll Oxford (MA, DPhil), Manchester Business Sch (MBA); *m* 12 Nov 1979, Linda Alison, da of Fred Reilly, of 16 Linkside, New Malden; 1 s (Edmund b 1988), 2 da (Laura b 1983, Lucy b 1985); *Career* banker; dir Baring Bros & Co Ltd 1982; sr advsr Saudi-Arabian Monetary Agency 1979-86; *Recreations* skiing, tennis, sailing; *Style—* Dr Jeremy R F Fairbrother; 41 Sheen Rd, Richmond, Surrey TW9 1AJ; Baring Bros & Co Ltd, 8 Bishopsgate, London EC2N 4AE (☎ 01 283 8833)

FAIRCLOTH, John Duncan Ibberson; s of John Ibberson Faircloth, of Flat 2, Oxton House, Kenton, Exeter, Devon, and Yvonne Alastair, *née* Hall; *b* 18 Nov 1942; *Educ* Haileybury and Imp Serv Coll; *m* 23 Oct 1971, Nicola Margaret, da of Prof John Kenneth Sinclair St Joseph, of Histon Manor, Cambridge; 1 da (Clare b 1975); *Career* insur exec Excess Insur Gp; dir: Excess Insur Co 1984, Reinsur Underwriting 1987; *Recreations* golf, swimming, running, gardening, music; *Clubs* RAC, Jesters; *Style—* J D I Faircloth, Esq; 1 Southfield Gardens, Strawberry Hill, Twickenham, Middlesex (☎ 01 892 0529); Excess Insurance Co, 13 Fenchurch Avenue, London EC3 (☎ 01 626 0555)

FAIRCLOUGH, Ian Walter; s of Walter Amedee Fairclough (d 1978), and Ella Mildred, *née* Watson (d 1970); *b* 29 May 1938; *Educ* St Andrew's Sch Eastbourne, Malvern; *m* 2 Sept 1967, Patricia Margaret Anne, da of Brig Thomas Patrick Keene (d 1979); 1 s (William Thomas b 1977), 3 da (Annabel Caroline b 1968, Celia Beatrice b 1970, Katharine Patricia b 1972); *Career* 5 Royal Inniskilling Dragoon Gds, Lt Nat Serv 1957-59; rep Agent for Int Sos Assistance (med repatriation service); dir : Fairclough Dodd & Jones (I & P) Ltd, Clover Greeting Cards Ltd, Pernvale Publications Ltd, Ethos Candles Ltd; memb of Cncl of the Sailing Tning Assoc, govr St Andrew's Sch Eastbourne, Liveryman of Worshipful Co of Girdlers; *Style—* Ian W Fairclough, Esq; Merrow Farm, Dunsfold, Godalming, Surrey GU8 4NX (☎ Dunsfold 215)

FAIRCLOUGH, John Whitaker; *b* 23 August 1930; *Educ* Manchester Univ (BSc); *m* Margaret Ann; 2 s, 1 da; *Career* chm IBM (UK) Laboratories Ltd; dir mfrg and devpt IBM(UK) Ltd; memb Engineering Cncl 1982-; dep pres Br Computer Soc, memb Govt Advisory Cncl Applied Research and Devpt (ACARO), Hon DSc (Southampton) 1983; CEng, FBCS, FIEE; *Style—* John Fairclough, Esq; IBM United Kingdom Ltd, PO Box 41, North Harbour, Portsmouth, Hants

FAIRCLOUGH, Mark; OBE, TD; s of Harry Fairclough (d 1966), of Warrington, and Elsie Marian Rhondda Briggs (d 1977); *b* 20 Dec 1919; *Educ* Oundle; *m* 30 April 1953, Nance Marjorie, da of Herbert Hayes (d 1946); 2 da (Belinda Ann, Philippa); *Career* served S Lancs Regt and RE (Maj): N Africa, Italy, Greece, Middle East; chm: Harry Fairclough Ltd, Fairmitre Ltd; *Recreations* golf, bridge; *Clubs* Warrington; *Style—* Mark Fairclough, Esq, OBE, TD; Southworth Hall, Croft, Warrington, Cheshire (☎ 092 576 3189); Harry Fairclough Ltd, Building & Civil Engineering Contractors, Howley, Warrington (☎ 0925 32214); Fairmitre Ltd, Warrington (☎ 0925 574848)

FAIRCLOUGH, Philip; OBE (1986); s of Albert Edward (d 1947), and Sarah (d 1973); *b* 17 July 1926; *Educ* Oldershaw GS; *m* 15 Sept 1950, Marjorie, da of William Holmes (d 1973); 2 da (Jane b 1951, Ann b 1953); *Career* Castrol Ltd: dir 1970, md 1985; dir Burmah Oil plc 1985; memb Worshipful Coach and Harness Makers Livery 1982; FInst Pet 1975; *Style—* Philip Fairclough, Esq, OBE; Mill Ridge, Field Rise, Swindon, Wilts (☎ 0793 38594)

FAIRFAX, Hon Hugh Nigel Thomas; 2 s of 13 Lord Fairfax of Cameron (d 1964), and Sonia, *née* Gunston; *b* 29 Mar 1958; *m* 25 Feb 1984, Victoria Janet, elder da of Digby Sheffield Neave, of Champflour, Marly-le-Roi, France; 1 s (Alexander b 8 Feb 1986), 1 da (Laura b 1987); *Style—* Hon Hugh Fairfax; 13 Kassala Rd, London SW11

FAIRFAX, Lady; Mary; *née* Wein; OBE; o da of K Wein; *Educ* Presbyterian Ladies Coll Univ of Sydney; *m* 1959, as his 3 w, Sir Warwick Oswald Fairfax (d 1987), o s of Sir James Oswald Fairfax, KBE (d 1928); Hon Consul of Monaco 1979, dir Industrial Equity Ltd 1985; chm Australian Region Metropolitan Opera Auditions NY 1981; Life Governor, founder and dir Opera Foundation, Aust Founder Aust; Opera Auditions in co-op Metropolitan Opera, NY Founder Aust, Opera Scholarships to Bayreuth (Germ), La Scala (Italy), London Opera Centre (UK) founder and pres Friends of the Ballet, memb Cultural Grants Ctee of Ministry for Culture, Sport and Recreation NSW former pres, Smith Family Summer Ctee, formerly an Exec of Ladies Ctee Elizabethan Theatre Trust and Red Cross; founder Julliard Scholarship Lincoln Centre NY 1977; Hon Consul of Monaco 1979, founder of Lady James Fairfax Memorial Prize for photography as art-portraiture for the Art Gallery of NSW; founder of Lady James Fairfax Memorial Prize for Painting (Australian Birds and Flowers for the Royal Agricultural Soc of New South Wales; *Recreations* working, the arts, writing, poetry, sculpture, fashion, entertaining, reading, swimming, walking, travel; *Clubs* Royal Yacht Squadron (Sydney), Assoc Union (Sydney), American National (Sydney), Lansdowne (London); *Style—* Lady Fairfax, OBE; Fairwater, 560 New South Head Road, Double Bay, NSW 2028, Australia

FAIRFAX, Hon Peregrine John Wishart; yr s of 12 Lord Fairfax of Cameron (d 1939); *b* 8 Mar 1925; *Educ* Eton, Trinity Coll Cambridge; *m* 5 Oct 1965, Virginia Alexandra de L'Etang, yr da of Hon Philip Leyland Kindersley; 1 s, 1 da; *Career* late Lt 12 Royal Lancers; *Clubs* White's, Northern Counties (Newcastle); *Style—* The Hon Peregrine Fairfax; Mindrum, Northumberland (☎ 089 085 246)

FAIRFAX, Hon Rupert Alexander James; MVO (1988); s of 13 Lord Fairfax of Cameron (d 1964), and bro of 14 Lord; *b* 21 Jan 1961; *Educ* Eton; *Career* asst private sec to HRH The Prince of Wales 1986-88; Hanson plc 1988-; *Recreations* polo, hunting, skiing; *Clubs* Brooks's; *Style—* The Hon Rupert Fairfax, MVO; 165 Draycott Ave, London SW3 (☎ 01 589 8220)

FAIRFAX, Sir Vincent Charles; CMG (1960); s of John Hubert Fraser Fairfax (d 1950), of Sydney, NSW; *b* 26 Dec 1909; *Educ* Geelong C of E GS, Brasenose Coll Oxford (BA); *m* 1939, Nancy, OBE, da of Charles Brehmer Heald, CBE, MD, FRCP (d 1974); 2 s, 2 da; *Career* dir John Fairfax & Sons Pty Ltd 1946-53, dir John Fairfax Ltd (Publishers Sydney Morning Herald) 1956, chm Aust Section Cwlth Press Union 1950-73, dir Bank of NSW 1953-82, nat pres Scout Assoc 1977-; kt 1971; *see Debrett's Handbook of Australia and New Zealand for further details*; *Style—* Sir Vincent Fairfax, CMG; Elaine, 550 New South Head Rd, Double Bay, NSW 2028, Australia

FAIRFAX OF CAMERON, 14 Lord (S 1627); Nicholas John Albert Fairfax; s of 13 Lord (d 1964; ninth in descent from the bro of the 2 Lord who defeated Prince Rupert at Marston Moor, and unc of the 3 Lord who, as C-in-C of the Parliamentarians, was the victor at Naseby, and who hired the poet, Andrew Marvell, as a tutor for his da Mary who m another poet, the 2 Duke of Buckingham); *b* 4 Jan 1956; *Educ* Eton, Downing Coll Cambridge; *m* 24 April 1982, Annabel, er da of late Nicholas Morriss, of 36 Cambridge Rd, SW11; 2 s (Hon Edward Nicholas Thomas b 20 Sept 1984, Hon John Frederick Anthony b 27 June 1986); *Heir* s, Hon Edward Nicholas Thomas b 20 Sept 1984; *Career* sits as Con in House of Lords; barr Gray's Inn 1977; *Recreations* sailing, skiing; *Clubs* Queen's; *Style—* The Rt Hon the Lord Fairfax of Cameron; 10 Orlando Rd, London SW4 0LF

FAIRFAX OF CAMERON, Sonia Lady; Sonia Helen; JP (Berks 1957); yr da of Capt Cecil Bernard Gunston, MC (d 1934; er bro of Sir Derrick Gunston, 1 Bt), and Lady Doris Gwendoline Hamilton-Temple-Blackwood (da of 2 Marquess of Dufferin and Ava); sis of Mrs G W Luttrell; *m* 17 April 1951, 13 Lord Fairfax of Cameron (d 8 April 1964); 3 s (including 14 Lord), 1 da (Hon Mrs Bell); *Career* temp lady of the bedchamber to HM The Queen 1967-71; *Style—* The Rt Hon Sonia, Lady Fairfax of Cameron, JP; The Garden House, Stanford Dingley, Reading, Berks

FAIRFAX-LUCY, Hon Lady (RAMSAY-) (Alice Caroline Helen); *née* Buchan; o da of 1 Baron Tweedsmuir, GCMG, GCVO, CH (d 1940); *b* 1908; *m* 29 July 1933, Maj Sir Brian Fulke (Ramsay-)Fairfax-Lucy, 5 Bt (d 1974); 1 s (Sir Edmund, 6 Bt), 1 da (Emma b 1946, m 1, 1967, James Scott, 2 da; m 2, 1982, James Louis Lambe, only s of late Adm of the Fleet Sir Charles Lambe); *Career* writes as Alice Buchan and Alice Fairfax-Lucy; *Books* A Scrap Screen (1979), Mistress of Charlecote (1983); *Style—* The Hon Lady Fairfax-Lucy; 15 Sylvester Close, Burford, Oxon; Charlecote Park, Warwick

FAIRFAX-LUCY, Duncan Cameron Ramsay; s of Capt Ewen Aymer Robert Ramsay-Fairfax-Lucy (d 1969), and Margaret Westall, o da of Sir John Westall King, 2 Bt; hp of kinsman, Sir Edmund Ramsay-Fairfax-Lucy, 6 Bt; *b* 18 Sept 1932; *Educ* Eton; *m* 26 Sept 1964, Janet Barclay, o da of late P A B Niven and Mrs K Niven, of Malt Cottage, Charlecote, Warwick; 1 s (Spencer Angus Ramsay b 1966), 1 da (Anna Margaret Barclay); *Career* bursar Queen's Coll Birmingham 1981-; FCA; *Clubs* Army and Navy; *Style—* Duncan Fairfax-Lucy, Esq; The Malt House, Charlecote, Warwick CV35 9EW

FAIRFAX-LUCY, Sir Edmund John William Hugh Ramsay-; 6 Bt (UK 1836); life-tenant under the Nat Tst of Charlecote Park; s of Maj Sir Brian Fulke Ramsay-Fairfax-Lucy, 5 Bt (d 1974), and Hon Alice, *née* Buchan, *qv*, da of 1 Baron Tweedsmuir, GCMG, GCVO, CH, PC; *b* 4 May 1945; *Educ* Eton, Royal Acad of Arts (Dip); *m* 1, 1974 (m dis), Sylvia, da of Graeme Ogden; m 2, 1986, Lady Lucinda, *née* Lambton; *Heir* 1 cous, Duncan Cameron Ramsay-Fairfax-Lucy; *Career* painter; has had several one-man shows, exhibits yearly at the Royal Acad 1967-; *Recreations* landscape gardening, building, waterworks; *Style—* Sir Edmund Ramsay-Fairfax-Lucy, Bt; Charlecote Park, Warwick

FAIRFIELD, Ian McLeod; CBE (1982); s of late Geoffrey Fairfield, and Inez Helen Thorneycroft Fairfield (d 1977); br of Sir Ronald McLeod Fairfield, CBE (d 1978); *b* 5 Dec 1919; *Educ* Monkton House Sch Cardiff, Manchester Coll of Technol, Engrg Trainee Callenders Cables & Construction Co Ltd (now BICC plc); *m* 1941, Joyce Ethel, da of Percy Fletcher (d 1965); 2 s (Clive, Julian); *Career* cmmnd RNVR Electrical Branch 1940-45; area sales mangr St Helens Cable & Rubber Co 1945-51, gp chm Chemring Gp plc 1985- (sales dir 1951, md 1952, dep chm and md 1967, chm and gp chief exec 1980, chm 1984, chm and gp chief exec 1985); *Recreations* motor boat cruising (Tsmy Gwenna III); *Clubs* Athenaeum, Royal Naval Sailing Assoc; *Style—* Ian Fairfield, Esq, MBE; Chemring Gp plc, Alchem Works, Fratton Trading Estate, Portsmouth PO4 8SX (☎ Portsmouth 735457, telex 86242)

FAIRGRIEVE, Sir (Thomas) Russell; CBE (1974), TD (1959), JP (Selkirkshire 1962); s of late Alexander Fairgrieve, OBE, MC, JP, of Galashiels, and Myma Margaret, *née* Crow; *b* 3 May 1924; *Educ* St Mary's Sch Melrose, Sedbergh, Scottish Coll of Textile Galashiels; *m* 7 Dec 1952, Millie, da of Alexander Mitchell; 1 s (Sandy), 3 da (Patricia, Rosemary, Marjorie); *Career* cmmnd 8 Gurkha Rifles IA 1943, Co Cdr 1/8 Gurkha Rifles 1944-46, GSO (2) (Ops) 15 Indian Corps SE Asia 1964; TA, 4 KOSB 1947-63, Maj 2 i/c; pres Scottish Cons Assoc 1965-66, memb exec ctee Euro Movement (Scotland) 1970-74, MP (C) W Aberdeenshire 1974-83, chm Scottish Cons Gp for Europe 1974-78, Scottish Cons whip 1975, chm Scottish Cons Party 1975-80 (vice-chm 1971), Parly under-sec of state Scotland 1979-81; md Laidlaw & Fairgrieve Ltd 1958-68 (dir 1953-58); dir: Dawson Int plc 1961-73, William Baird & Co plc 1975-, Hall Advertising Ltd 1981-; conslt Saatchi & Saatchi Co 1976-; chm: Scottish Woollen Spinners' Assoc, Scottish Cncl of Independent Schs; memb: exec ctee Scottish Cncl, cncl Scottish Woollen Mfrs Assoc; govr: St Mary's Sch Melrose, Scottish Coll of Textiles; kt 1981; *Recreations* golf; *Clubs* Carlton, New (Edinburgh), Royal and Ancient (St Andrews); *Style—* Sir Russell Fairgrieve, CBE, TD; Pankalan, Boleside, Galashiels, Selkirkshire TD1 3NX (☎ 0896 2278)

FAIRHALL, Hon Sir Allen; KBE (1970); s of Charles Edward and Maude Fairhall; *b* 24 Nov 1909; *Educ* East Maitland Boys' HS; *m* 1936, Monica Clelland, da of James Ballantyne; 1 s; *Career* MHR (Lib) for Paterson NSW 1949-69, min for Interior and Works 1956-58, min for Supply 1961-66, min for Defence 1966-69; company dir; FRSA; *Style—* Hon Sir Allen Fairhall, KBE; 7 Parkway Ave, Newcastle, NSW 2300, Australia

FAIRHAVEN, 3 Baron (UK 1961); Ailwyn Henry George Broughton; JP (S Cambs 1975); s of 2 Baron (d 1973), and Hon Diana (d 1937), da of Capt Hon Coulson Fellowes (s of 2 Baron De Ramsey, JP, DL, and Lady Rosamond Spencer-Churchill, da of 7 Duke of Marlborough, KG); *b* 16 Nov 1936; *Educ* Eton, RMA Sandhurst; *m* 23 Sept 1960, Kathleen Patricia, er da of Col James Henry Magill, OBE; 4 s (Hon James, Hon Huttleston Rupert b 1970, Hon Charles Leander b 1973, Hon Henry Robert b 1978); 2 da (Hon Diana Cara, Hon Mrs Thornton *qv*, Hon Melanie Frances b 1966); *Heir* s, Hon James Broughton b 25 May 1963; *Career* RHG 1957-71, Maj; Vice Lord-Lt Cambridgeshire 1977-85 (DL Cambridgeshire and Isle of Ely 1977-); Kt of the White Rose (Finland) 1970, CStJ 1983; *Recreations* shooting, cooking; *Clubs* Jockey (sr steward 1985-89), Turf; *Style—* The Rt Hon the Lord Fairhaven, JP, DL; Anglesey Abbey, Cambridge (☎ 0223 811746)

FAIRHOLM, David Victor; s of Albert Fairholm, of Nottingham, and Doreen Lilian, *née* Dennis; *b* 15 August 1945; *Educ* High Pavement GS Nottingham; *m* 25 Jan 1965, Angela Dolores, da of John Townsend Hanson, of Nottingham; 5 s (Richard b and d 1965, Thomas b 1968, Robert b 1970, Jonathan b 1976, Christopher b 1984); *Career* ptnr: Dexter and Co 1971-86, Saul Fairholm and Co 1987-, tres Rotary Club, sec Round Table 41 Club; FCA; *Recreations* golf, cycling; *Clubs* Woodhall Spa Golf; *Style—* David Fairholm, Esq; Pendling, Tattershall Road, Woodhall Spa, Lincolnshire LN10 6TW (☎ 0526 52103); Saul Fairholm and Co, Chartered Accountants, Lewer House, 12 Tentercroft St, Lincoln LN5 7DB (☎ 0522 537 575, fax 0522 43506)

FAIRHURST, Harry Marshall; s of Philip Garland Fairhurst (d 1987), and Janet Meikle, *née* Marshall; *b* 18 June 1925; *Educ* Clifton, Clare Coll Cambridge (MA), Northern Poly (Dip Arch); *m* 20 June 1959, Elizabeth Mary, da of Bernard Hudson Thorp, of Cheadle, Cheshire; 1 s (Timothy b 1968), 3 da (Katharine b 1960, Rachel b 1962, Philippa b 1964); *Career* architect in private practice; architect and surveyor to Fabric of Manchester Cathedral 1970-, cmmnd architect for English Heritage 1978-; buildings for commerce, industry, education, medicine and scientific res; Hon MA Manchester Univ, Hon FUMIST, FRIBA; *Recreations* forestry, contemporary art, design and crafts; *Clubs* St James's Manchester; *Style—* Harry M Fairhurst, Esq; 22 Macclesfield Rd, Wilmslow, Cheshire SK9 2AF (☎ 0625 523784)

FAIRHURST, Jack Leslie; s of Enoch Fairhurst, RMS, and Adeline, *née* Perry; *b* 1 April 1905; *Educ* Camberwell Sch of Art, RCA; *m* 19 Oct 1935, Barbara Domaire, da of Donald Angus Cooper; 2 s (Robin b 1941, Timothy b 1945), 1 da (Phyllida b 1949); *Career* portrait painter; art master: Leighton Buzzard GS 1928-33, Richmond County GS 1933-38, Sheen County 1938-70; headmaster Richmond Sch of Art 1941-57; works shown RA, RSPP and leading English Galleries; one man exhibitions in Woodbridge, Ipswich, Framlingham and Bury St Edmunds; *Clubs* Ipswich Art; *Style—* Jack L Fairhurst, Esq; Highgate, Dallinghoo, Woodbridge, Suffolk IP13 0LS (☎ 047 337 326)

FAIRLEY, Eric Claude William; s of Robert Alexander (d 1966), of Glasgow, and Euphemia Mitchell, *née* Murrie (d 1979); *b* 10 Sept 1925; *Educ* Alan Glen's Sch Glasgow, Bearsden Acad, West of Scotland Agric Coll, Glasgow Univ (MA, DipEd); *m* 2 July 1956, Stella Thorlow, da of John William Lindley (d 1958), of Hillfoot Drive, Bearsden, Glasgow; 3 da (Lois Elizabeth Mitchell b 1960, Karen Ann Mackenzie b 1963, Jan Thurlow Murrie b 1978); *Career* science teacher, Possil sr Secdy Sch 1956-62; asst organiser West of Scotland Ctee for Technical Educn 1962-63; asst sec Scottish Assoc for Nat Certificates and Diplomas 1963-73; educn offr Scottish Technical Educn Cncl 1973-85; asst dir Scottish Vocational Educn Cncl 1985-87; advsr to Open Coll 1987-; chm and sec The Dullator Assoc; chm Dullator Community Cncl; *Recreations* hill walking, cross country skiing, photography; *Clubs* Dullator Golf; *Style—* Eric Fairley, Esq; 11 Victoria Terrace, Dullator Glasgow G68 0AQ (☎ Cumberwould 724202); The Open College, Corunna House, Cadogan St, Glasgow (☎ 041 248 3492)

FAIRLIE OF MYRES, Capt David Ogilvy; MBE (1984), JP (Fife 1975), DL (Fife 1981); s of James Ogilvy Fairlie of Myres (d 1960), of Myres Castle, Auchtermuchty, Fife, and Constance Gertrude, *née* Lascelles (d 1981); *b* 1 Oct 1923; *Educ* Ampleforth, Oriel Coll Oxford; *m* 19 April 1969, Ann Constance (d 1986) da of Dermot Francis Bolger (d 1974), of Quinta Avista Navios, Funchal, Madeira; *Career* Bde Signal Offr 32 Gds Bde UK 1943, PA to Maj-Gen C M F White France and Belgium 1944, Signal Offr HQ Allied Land Forces SE Asia Ceylon and Singapore 1945, Bde Signal Offr 37 Indian Bde Java and Malaya 1946, Signal Regt Scottish Cmd Edinburgh 1947-48, Signal Regt Northern Cmd Catterick 1949-50, Bde Signal Offr 29 Inf Bde Korea 1951-52, 2 i/c Signal Sqdn SHAPE 1953, Adj 51 Highland Divnl Signals Trg Regt 1958-59; dist cmmr Cupar Scout dist 1960-65, co cmmr Fife Scouts 1966-85, chm E Fife branch Arthritis and Rheumatics Cncl 1986-; memb Royal Co of Archers Queen's Bodyguard for Scotland 1964-; Knight of the Equestrian order of the Holy Sepulchre of Jerusalem (chllr of the order in Scotland) 1988;; *Books* Fairlie of that Ilk (history and genealogy of the family, 1987); *Recreations* gardening, bee keeping, photography, genealogy; *Clubs* Army and Navy, Royal Overseas, Royal and Ancient Golf; *Style—* Capt David Fairlie of Myres, MBE, JP, DL; Myres castle, Auchtermuchty, Fife, KY14 7EW (☎ 0337 28350)

FAIRLIE-CUNINGHAME, Sir William Henry; 16 Bt (NS 1630), of Robertland, Ayrshire; s of Sir William Fairlie-Cuninghame, 15 Bt, MC (d 1981), and Irene Alice (d 1970), da of late Henry Margrave Terry; *b* 1 Oct 1930; *m* 1972, Janet Menzies, da of late Roy Menzies Saddington; 1; *Heir* s, William Robert Henry; *Style—* Sir William Fairlie-Cuninghame, Bt; 29A Orinoco Rd, Pymble, New South Wales 2073, Australia

FAIRLIE-CUNINGHAME, William Robert Henry; s and h of Sir William Henry Fairlie-Cuninghame, 16 Bt; *b* 19 July 1974; *Style—* William Fairlie-Cuninghame, Esq; 29A Orinoco Rd, Pymble, New South Wales 2073, Australia

FAIRMAN, Dr Martin John; s of Henry Douglas Fairman, FRCS, of Bristol, and Stella Margaret, *née* Sheath; *b* 8 May 1945; *Educ* Monkton Combe Sch Bath, London Hosp Med Coll (FRCP); *m* 12 Aug 1967, Marianne Alison Louis, da of Sqdn Ldr Roland Ernest Burton, of Limousin, France; 2 s (James b 1969, Jack b 1978), 2 da (Jocelyn b 1971, Lydia b 1980); *Career* conslt physician, S Lincolnshire Health Authy 1979-, hon snr lectr Medicine Leicester Univ 1979-, fell Gastroenterology Cincinnati 1976-77, MBBS, FRCP; *Recreations* golf, sailing; *Style—* Dr Martin J Fairman; Teviot Lodge, 65 Sleaford Road, Boston, Lincs (☎ 0205 60743); Pilgrim Hosp, Boston, Lincs (☎ 0205 64801)

FAIRRIE, Lt-Col (Adam) Angus; s of Lt-Col Adam Grainger Fairrie, MBE (d 1956), and Elizabeth, *née* Dobie (d 1983); *b* 9 Dec 1934; *Educ* Stowe, RMA Sandhurst; *m* 16 April 1966, Elizabeth Rachel, da of Rev Archibald Selwyn Pryor (ka 1944); 1 s (Adam Hugh b 1967), 1 da (Elizabeth Margaret Emma b 1968); *Career* regular army offr, cmmnd The Queen's Own Cameron Highlanders 1955, to Queen's Own Highlanders 1961, attended Staff Coll Camberley 1966, attended Nat Defence Coll 1973, cmd 1 Bn Queen's Own Highlanders 1974-77, ret 1978, Regimental Sec 1978-, (ret 1978); *Books* Cuidich 'n Righ - A History of the Queens Own Highlanders (1983), "The Northern Meeting 1788-1988" (1988); *Recreations* painting, photography; *Clubs* Naval and Military; *Style—* Lt-Col Angus Fairrie; Craighill, N Kessock, Ross and Cromarty (☎ 046 373 616); RHQ Queens Own Highlanders, Cameron Barracks, Inverness (☎ 0463 224 380)

FAIRTLOUGH, Gerard Howard; s of Maj-Gen Eric Victor Howard Fairtlough, DSO, MC (d 1944), and Agatha Zoë, *née* Barker; *b* 5 Sept 1930; *Educ* Marlborough, King's Coll Cambridge; *m* 1954, Elizabeth Ann, *née* Betambeau; 2 s, 2 da; *Career* Lt RA; md Shell UK Ltd 1974-78; div dir NEB 1978-80; chief exec Celltech Ltd 1980-; *Recreations* walking, theatre, yoga; *Style*— Gerard Fairtlough, Esq; 5 Belmont Grove, London SE13 (☎ 01 852 4904); Celltech Ltd, 216 Bath Rd, Slough SL1 4EN (☎ 0753 35655)

FAIRWEATHER, Brig Claude Cyril; CB (1967), CBE (1965, OBE 1944, TD 1944, JP (N Yorks 1963), DL 1949); s of late Nicholas Fairweather, of Middlesbrough; *b* 17 Mar 1906; *Educ* St Peter's Sch York; *m* 1930, Alice Mary, da of Sir William Henry Crosthwaite, JP (d 1968), of Middlesbrough; 1 s, 1 da; *Career* 2 Lt Royal Corps of Signals 1928, Lt-Col 1941, Col 1943, Brig 1945, CSO Wingate Exp 1943-44, CSO 34 Ind Corps 1944-45, Hon Col 50 Inf Div TA RAOC 1955-67, Hon Col 34 (N) Signal Regt (V) 1967-75; former chm N Riding T&AFA and memb TA Ctees, chm N of England TAVRA 1968-71; chm: St Luke's Hosp Mgmnt Ctee 1959-74, Cleveland Area Health Authy 1973-76; Vice Lord-Lt for Cleveland 1977-82; Cdr N Yorks St John Ambulance Bde 1972-77 (formerly county cmmr N Riding), chm Order of St John Cncl 1977-84; memb Mental Health Review Tribunal 1960-70; KStJ 1978 (OStJ 1967, CStJ 1974); *Recreations* golf, cricket, rugby football; *Clubs* Army and Navy, Cleveland (Middlesbrough), Royal and Ancient (St Andrews); *Style*— Brig Claude Fairweather, CB, CBE, TD, JP, DL; The White Lodge, Hutton Rudby, Yarm, Cleveland TS15 0HY (☎ 0642 700598)

FAIRWEATHER, Hon Mrs (Jean Simpson); *née* Mackie; er da of Baron John-Mackie (Life Peer); *b* 2 July 1937; *m* Alexander Fairweather; *Style*— Hon Mrs Fairweather; 31 Arbirlot Road, Arbroath, Scotland

FAIRWEATHER, Virginia Eileen Cecilie Jessie; *née* Winter; da of Cyril Charles Winter (d 1982), and Jessie Amelia, *née* Thorpe (d 1940); *b* 25 Jan 1923; *Educ* privately and abroad; *m* 1, 8 July 1939, Leslie Jones (d 1972), s of Julian Jones (d 1930), musical dir London Hippodrome and Alhambra; m 2, 24 July 1963, David Carnegy Fairweather (d 1983), s of David Fairweather, MD, JP (d 1936); *Career* former actress (as Virginia Winter); trained Old Vic Sch; 1st London appearance in review Come Out of Your Shell (1940), Rise Above It (1941), It's About Time (1942), Brighton Rock (1943), My Sister Eileen (1944), Better Late (1946), etc; broadcaster and radio and TV actress; films include Brighton Rock; left stage to help launch Chichester Festival Theatre 1962 (press rep during Sir Laurence Olivier's dirship); *Books* Cry God for Larry (biog of Lord Olivier) (1969); *Recreations* Times crossword, embroidery, arguing, Yorkshire terriers; *Style*— Mrs David Fairweather; 8 Russell St, Chichester W Sussex

FAITH, (Irene) Sheila; MEP (C) for Cumbria and Lancashire North 1984-; yr da of late I Book; *b* 3 June 1928; *Educ* Central HS Newcastle, Durham Univ (LDS); *m* 1950, Dennis Faith; *Career* dental surgeon; memb: Northumberland CC 1970-74, Newcastle City Cncl 1975-77; vice-chm Jt Consultative Ctee on Educn for District of Newcastle 1973-74; contested (C) Newcastle Central Oct 1974, MP (C) Belper 1979-83; memb select ctee Health and Soc Servs 1979-83; sec Cons backbench Health and Social Servs Ctee 1982-83; memb: exec ctee of Cons Medical Soc 1979-84, ctee on Unopposed Bills 1980-83, Br-American Parly Gp, Cwlth Parly Assoc, Inter-Parly Union, UN Parly Gp, Euro Movement; memb Euro Parl Tport Ctee and Regional Devpt Ctee 1984-86; vice-chm Swiss Delegation, memb Parly and Scientific Ctee; Parliamentary Maritime Gp 1984; Euro Parl Road Safety Report 1985-86; memb Euro Parl Energy Research & Technology Ctee 1987-, has served as chm of several sch governing bodies and mangr of community homes; JP: Northumberland 1972-74, Newcastle 1974-78, Inner London 1978; *Style*— Mrs Dennis Faith, JP, MEP; Pinewood Cottage, Sedgwick, nr Kendal, Cumbria LA8 0JP; Flat 2, 39 Royal Ave, London SW3 4QE (☎ 01 823 4993); office: No 1, The Square, Milnthorpe, Cumbria LA7 7QJ (☎ 04482 2358);

FAITHFUL, Lt-Col Nicholas Cornish; TD (1953), DL (1976); s of Edward Wilson Faithful (d 1957), of Tenbury Wells, and Laura Cornish (d 1935); *b* 25 May 1911; *Educ* Ludlow GS; *m* 11 March 1939, Barbara Constance, da of Dr Alfred Hollier Clough (d 1951), of Shropshire; 1 s (Simon b 1940), 1 da (Jane b 1942); *Career* joined Shropshire Yeo as trooper 1938 cmmnd RA 1940-46; cmd: Shropshire RHA (TA) 1946-50, 639 Worcestershire and Shropshire Heavy Regt RA (TA) 1950-53, ret to reserve with rank of substantive Lt-Col; active memb: Royal Br Legion (former Co chm), Save the Children; fndr memb and vice pres The Hawk Tst; runs a bird hosp for birds of prey; *Recreations* ornithology, falconry, fishing, fox hunting; *Style*— Lt-Col Nicholas C Faithfull, TD, DL; Penkridge Hall, Leebotwood, Church Stretton, Shropshire SY6 6LZ (☎ 06945 215)

FAITHFULL, Baroness (Life Peeress UK 1975), of Wolvercote, Co of Oxfordshire; Lucy Faithfull; OBE (1972); da of Lt Sydney Leigh Faithfull, RE (ka 1916), and Elizabeth Adie, *née* Algie; *b* 26 Dec 1910; *Educ* Talbot Heath Sch Bournemouth, Birmingham Univ (Social Sciences Dip, Child Care and Family Case Work Certificates); *Career* sits as Cons Peer in House of Lords; social worker; sub warden Birmingham Settlement 1932-35; organiser LCC Care Ctee 1935-40, evacuation welfare offr Miny of Health 1940-45, inspr Home Off (Children's Branch) 1946-58, children's offr Oxford City 1958-70, dir Social Servs Oxford City Cncl 1970-74; govr: Bessells Leigh Sch for Maladjusted Children Oxford, Caldecott Community Sch Merstham-le-Hatch Kent; pres Nat Children's Bureau; chm All Party Parly Gp Children, Westminster; vice-pres: British Assoc for Counselling, Nat Assoc of Voluntary Hostels; Hon MA (Oxon), Hon DLitt (Warwick); *Recreations* travel; *Style*— The Rt Hon Baroness Faithfull, OBE; 303 Woodstock Rd, Oxford OX2 7NY (☎ 0865 55389)

FALCON, Michael Gascoigne; CBE (1979), JP (Norfolk 1967), DL (Norfolk 1981); s of Michael Falcon, JP (d 1976), by his w Kathleen Isabel Frances, *née Gascoigne (d 1985);*; *b* 28 Jan 1928; *Educ* Stowe, Heriot-Watt Coll; *m* 1954, April Daphne Claire, *née* Lambert; 2 s (Michael b 1956, Andrew b 1958), 1 da (Claire b 1960); *Career* former head brewer and jt md E Lacon & Co Gt Yarmouth; exec dir Edgar Watts (Bungay Suffolk) 1968-73; tstee E Anglian Tstee Savings Bank 1963-75; chm Norwich Union Insur Gp 1981- (dir 1963, vice-chm 1979), Lloyds Bank Eastern Counties Regnl Bd 1979- (dir 1972-), Nat Seed Devpt Orgn Ltd 1972-82, Pauls & Whites Ltd 1976-85 (dir 1973-); dir: Securicor East Ltd 1969-72, Lloyds Bank (UK) Mgmnt Ltd 1979-85, Matthew Brown plc 1981-87, Greene King & Sons plc 1988-, Br Rail Anglia Regnl Bd 1988-; chm Norwich Kist Health Authy 1988; High Sheriff of Norfolk 1979-80; high steward Boro' Gt Yarmouth 1984-; Hon LLD Nottingham Univ 1988; CStJ (1986, OStJ 1968); *Recreations* country pursuits; *Clubs* Norfolk County, Royal Norfolk and Suffolk Yacht; *Style*— Michael Falcon, Esq, CBE, JP, DL; Keswick Old Hall, Norwich, Norfolk NR4 6TZ (☎ 0603 54348); Kirkgate, Loweswater, Cockermouth, Cumbria (☎ 090 085 271)

FALCONER, Hon Mr Justice; Hon Sir Douglas William Falconer; MBE (1946); s of William Falconer (d 1956), of South Shields; *b* 20 Sept 1914; *Educ* Westoe S Shields, King's Coll Durham Univ; *m* 1941, Joan Beryl Argent, da of late Archibald Samuel Bishop, of Hagley, Worcs; 1 s, 1 da; *Career* barr 1950, QC 1967, bencher Middle Temple 1972, appointed to exercise appellate jurisdiction of Bd of Trade under Trade Marks Act 1970, memb Standing Advsy Ctee on Patents 1975-79, on Trade Marks 1975-79, chm Patent Bar Assoc 1971-80, memb Senate of Four Inns of Court 1973-74, of Four Inns of Court and Bar 1974-77, a judge of High Court of Justice 1981-; *Recreations* music, theatre; *Style*— Hon Mr Justice Falconer, MBE; Royal Courts of Justice, Strand, London WC2A 2LL

FALCONER, Peter Serrell; s of Thomas Falconer, FRIBA (eighth in descent from Patrick Falconer of Newton, unc of 1 Lord Falconer of Halkerton, S Lordship cr 1646, which was subsequently held by the Earls of Kintore, with the death of the tenth of whom in 1966 the Lordship became dormant; Peter is the presumed heir), and Florence Edith Falconer; *b* 7 Mar 1916; *Educ* Bloxham; *m* 1941, Mary, da of Rev C Hodson; 3 s, 1 da; *Career* architect; FRIBA; *Style*— Peter Falconer, Esq; St Francis, Minchinhampton, Glos (☎ office: Stroud 3404, telex 43418)

FALCONER OF HALKERTON, Lordship (S 1646); *see*: Falconer, Peter Serrell

FALETAU, 'Inoke Fotu; 2 s of 'Akau'ola Siosateki Faletau (d 1954), and Cecelia Lyden (d 1962); *b* 24 June 1937; *Educ* St Peters Sch, Auckland GS NZ, Tonga HS, Univ of Wales, Univ of Manchester; *m* 'Evelini Ma'ata Hurrell; 3 s, 3 da; *Career* diplomat; high cmmr for Tonga to UK 1972-82 (concurrent ambass to: W Germany, France, Luxembourg, Netherlands, Belgium, Denmark, Italy, USSR, USA); dir mgmnt devpt programme Cwlth Secretariat 1983-84, dir Cwlth Fndn 1985-; Kt Grand Cross: Order of Merit (W Germany) 1980, Order of Merit (Luxembourg) 1982; *Clubs* Royal Overseas League, Royal Cwlth Soc; *Style*— Inoke Faletau, Esq; Commonwealth Foundation, Marlborough House, Pall Mall, London SW1Y 5HY (☎ 01 930 3783/4)

FALK, Fergus Antony; TD (1979); s of Leonard Solomon Falk, of 4A Abercorn Place, London NW8 9XR and Lucy Meg, *née* Cohen (d 1970); *b* 30 August 1941; *Educ* Uppingham, London Univ (BSc); *m* 5 May 1973, Vivian Dundas, da of Leonard Cockburn Dundas Irvine (d 1968 Surgn-Capt RNVR) of Hove; 1 s (Sebastian b 1980), 2 da (Harriet 1976, Annabel 1979); *Career* Maj HAC 1961-80; accountant; dept mangr: John Lewis and Co Ltd 1959-63, C Ulysses Williams Ltd 1964-65, Touche Ross and Co 1965- (ptnr 1975); chm: All Saints Little Canfield Restoration Appeal, tres Islington South and Finsbury (C) Assoc 1974-76 and Radwinter Branch 1976-79; memb: Ct of Assistants HAC 1975-, Ct of Common Cncl 1984-, candidate (C) Islington Borough Elections 1974; memb Worshipful Co of Chartered Accountants; ACA 1969, FCA 1973; *Recreations* small children, gardening; *Clubs* HAC, MCC, Farringdon Ward, City Livery, Aldeburgh YC; *Style*— Fergus Falk, Esq, TD; Canfield Moat, Little Canfield, Gt Dunmow, Essex CM6 1TD (☎ 0371 2563); Hill House, 1 Little New Street, London EC4A 3TR (☎ 01 353 8011, fax 01 583 8317)

FALK, Sir Roger Salis; OBE (Mil 1945); s of Lionel David Falk (d 1949), of London; *b* 22 June 1910; *Educ* Haileybury, Geneva Univ; *m* 1938, Margaret Helen (d 1958), da of Albert Stroud (d 1946); 1 s, 2 da; *Career* served WWII Wing Cdr RAFVR 1943; md D J Keymer & Co 1945-49 (dir 1935-49, vice-chm 1950); chm: P E Int Ltd 1973-76, London Bd Provincial Insur Co Ltd; dir gen BETRO 1950-52, dep chm Gaming Bd of GB 1978-81, vice pres Sadlers Wells Fndn 1986- (chm 1976-86); memb: Cncl of Industl Design 1958-67, Monopolies Cmmn 1965-79, cncl RSA 1968-74, cncl Imperial Soc of Kts Bachelor 1979-; life govr Haileybury 1971- (cncl memb 1978-); Hon DLitt City Univ 1984; CBIM; kt 1969; *Books* Business of Management (5 edns, 1961); *Recreations* music, writing, reading; *Clubs* Garrick, MCC; *Style*— Sir Roger Falk, OBE; 603 Beatty House, Dolphin Sq, London SW1 (☎ 01 828 3752)

FALKENDER, Baroness (Life Peeress UK 1974); Marcia Matilda Falkender; *née* Field; CBE (1970); da o: Harry Field; assumed by deed poll 1974 surname Falkender in lieu of Williams; *b* 1932,March; *Educ* QMC London; *m* 1955 (m dis 1960), George Edmund Charles Williams; *Career* private sec Morgan Phillips (gen sec of Labour Pty) 1955-56; private and political sec to Rt Hon Lord Wilson of Rievaulx, formerly Rt Hon Sir Harold Wilson, KG, OBE, MP; political columnist Mail on Sunday 1983-, memb Screen Advisory Cncl and Film Ctee 1976-; dir: Peckham Building Soc 1986-; *Books* Inside No 10 (1972), Perspective on Downing Stree (1983); *Recreations* reading, film; *Clubs* Reform; *Style*— The Rt Hon Lady Falkender, CBE; 3 Wyndham Mews, Upper Montagu St, London W1

FALKINER, Benjamin Simon Patrick; s and h of Sir Edmond Charles Falkiner, of Herts, and Janet Iris, *née* Darby; *b* 16 Jan 1962; *Educ* Queen Elizabeth Boys' Sch Barnet; *Career* retail outlet mangr; *Recreations* rugby, cricket, music (drummer), youth work; *Clubs* Old Elizabethans RFC, Old Elizabethans CC; *Style*— Benjamin Falkiner, Esq; 111 Wood Street, Barnet, Herts (☎ 01 440 2426); 50 Colerige Road, Crouch End (☎ 01 340 1845 9)

FALKINER, Sir Edmond Charles; 9 Bt (I 1778), of Annmount, Cork; s of Sir Terence Falkiner, 8 Bt (d 1987); *b* 24 June 1938; *Educ* Downside; *m* 8 Oct 1960, Janet Iris, da of Arthur Edward Bruce Darby, of The Park, Stoke Lacey, Bromyard, Herefords; 2 s (Benjamin b 1962, Matthew b 1964); *Heir* s, Benjamin Simon Patrick Falkiner, *qv*; *Career* pacifist; probation officer 1968-; *Clubs* Ronnie Scott's; *Style*— Sir Edmond Falkiner, Bt; 111 Wood St, Barnet, Herts EN5 4BX (☎ 01 440 2426)

FALKLAND, Master of; Hon (Lucius) Alexander Plantagenet Cary; s and h of 15 Viscount of Falkland, *qv*; *b* 1 Feb 1963; *Educ* Westminster, Loretto, RMA Sandhurst; *Career* 2 Lt 2 Bn Scots Guards 1985; Rifle Platoon Cdr 1985-88; Milan Platoon Cdr 1988-; *Recreations* drawing, skiing, tennis; *Clubs* Cavalry and Guards'; *Style*— Master of Falkland

FALKLAND, 15 Viscount of (S 1620); Premier Viscount of Scotland; Lucius Edward William Plantagenet Cary; also 15 Lord Cary (S 1620); s of 14 Viscount (d 1984), and his 2 w Constance Mary, *née* Berry; *b* 8 May 1935; *Educ* Wellington Coll; *m* 26 April 1962, Caroline Anne, da of late Lt Cdr George Gerald, RN, of Astron House, Ashton Keynes, Wilts; 1 s, 2 da (Hon Samantha b 1973, Hon Lucinda b 1974) (and 1 da decd); *Heir* s, Master of Falkland, *qv*; *Career* 2 Lt 8 King's Royal Irish Hussars; export marketing conslt C T Bowring Trading (Hldgs) Ltd (former chief exec), memb House of Lords select ctee overseas trade 1954-85; UBERM/SDP Alliance Spokesman Film Industry House of Lords; *Recreations* golf, cinema; *Clubs* Brooks's, Turf, Sunningdale Golf; *Style—* The Rt Hon Viscount of Falkland; 137 Sabine Road, London SW11 5LU

FALKNER, Sir (Donald) Keith; s of John Charles Falkner (d 1937), school master, and Alice Hannah, *née* Wright (d 1928); *b* 1 Mar 1900; *Educ* New Coll Sch, Perse Sch, RCM, private study Berlin, Vienna, Paris; *m* 1930, Christabel Margaret, o da of Thomas Fletcher Fullard (d 1911); 2 da (Julia b 1936, Philippa b 1938); *Career* served WW I Sub Lt RNAS 1917-1919, served WW II Sqdn Ldr RAFVR 1940-45; asst lay vicar St Paul's Cathedral 1922-26; professional singer (lead in three Warner Bros musicals, Mayfair Melody, The Singing Cop, Thistledown 1936-37) 1923-40; music offr Br Cncl Italy 1946-50; prof of music Cornell Univ NY USA 1950-60; dir RCM 1960-74; jt artistic dir King's Lynn Festival 1981-83; editor Voice (with 24 contributors) 1983; Hon DMus (Oxon); ARCM, FRCM; Royal Humane Soc Medal for Life Saving at Sea 1918-19; kt 1967; *Recreations* present: golf, gardening; *Clubs* Athenaeum, MCC, Free Foresters, RAC, Norfolk County; *Style—* Sir Keith Falkner; Low Cottages, Ilketshall St Margaret, Bungay, Suffolk (☎ 0986 2573)

FALKNER, (Frederic Sherard) Neil; s of Francis Sherard Melville Falkner (d 1972), of Louth, Lincs, and Doris Mary, *née* Matthews; *b* 28 August 1927; *Educ* Northampton Sch, Lincoln Coll Oxford (MA), Oberlin Coll Ohio USA (MA); *m* 27 June 1951, Maria Luisa, da of Max Aub (d 1974), of Mexico City; 1 s (Martin b 1959), 2 da (Elaine b 1954, Lynne b 1956) ; *Career* marketing exec Procter & Gamble 1951-56; marketing mangr Mars 1956-61; ch exec Cheesebrough-Ponds 1961-66; ran own manufacturing business 1966-77; chm and ch exec Development Capital Gp 1977-89; dir Lazard Bros 1985-89; chm and ch exec FMS Ptnrs 1989-; Liveryman Worshipful Co of Painter-Stainers 1971; *Recreations* music, medieval history; *Clubs* East India, City Livery; *Style—* Neil Falkner, Esq; 10 Emmanuel Road, Cambridge CB1 1JW (☎ 0223 461750)

FALKUS, Christopher Hugh; s of Hugh Edward Lance Falkus, *qv* of Ravenglass, Cumbria; *b* 13 Jan 1940; *Educ* St Boniface Coll Plymouth, Univ Coll London (BA); *m* 1977, Gila Ann, da of Brig Francis Curtis, of Cambridge; 4 children; *Career* publisher; md Weidenfeld & Nicholson Ltd 1972-79; chm General Book Div of Assoc Book Publishers 1980-; dir Associated Book Publishers 1981-; *Recreations* cricket; *Clubs* MCC; *Style—* Christopher Falkus, Esq; 89 Portland Rd, London W11; Associated Book Publishers plc, 11 New Fetter Lane, London EC4 (☎ 01 583 9855)

FALKUS, Hugh Edward Lance; s of James Everest Falkus (d 1959), and Alice, *née* Musgrove (d 1962); *b* 15 May 1917; *Educ* The East Anglian Sch Culford; *m* ; 1 s (*see* Christopher Falkus); *Career* former RAF fighter pilot writer and film dir; films incl: Shark Island, Drake's England, Signals for Survival, The Gull Watchers, The Beachcombers, The Sign Readers, The Tender Trap, Portrait of a Happy Man, Highland Story, Animal War Animal Peace, Salmo the Leaper; film awards: Italia Prize, American Blue Ribbon, Royal Geographical Soc, Cherry Kearton Medal and Award; currently teaches game fishing and spey casting; *Books* Sea Trout Fishing, Salmon Fishing, Freshwater Fishing, Successful Angling, The Stolen Years, Nature Detective, Master of Cape Horn, Sydney Cove to Duntroon, Signals for Survival; *Recreations* fishing, shooting, sailing; *Style—* Hugh Falkus, Esq; Cragg Cottage, Ravenglass, Cumbria CA18 1RT (☎ 06577 247)

FALL, Brian James Proetel; CMG (1984); s of John William Fall and Edith Juliet, *née* Proetel; *b* 13 Dec 1937; *Educ* St Paul's, Magdalen Coll Oxford, Univ of Michigan Law Sch; *m* 1962, Delmar Alexandra Roos; 3 da; *Career* joined HM Dip Serv 1962, served in FO UN Dept 1963, Moscow 1965, Geneva 1968, Civil Service Coll 1970, FO Eastern Euro and Soviet Dept and Western Orgns Dept 1971, New York 1975, Harvard Univ Center for Int Affrs 1976, cnsllr Moscow 1977-79; head of Energy, Sci and Space Dept FCO 1979-80; head of Eastern Euro and Soviet Dept FCO 1980-81, princ private sec to Sec of State for Foreign and Cwlth Affrs 1981-84; dir private off, sec gen NATO 1984-86, asst under sec (Def) FCO 1986-88; min Washington 1988-1986-; *Style—* Brian Fall, Esq, CMG; c/o Foreign & Commonwealth Office, King Charles Street, London SW1

FALLA, Paul Stephen; s of late Brig Norris Stephen Falla, CMG, DSO, of Wellington, New Zealand, and Audrey Frances, *née* Stock; *b* 25 Oct 1913; *Educ* Wellington and Christ's Coll NZ, Balliol Coll Oxford; *m* 1958, Elizabeth Mary, *née* Shearer; 1 da; *Career* HM Foreign Service 1936-67, cnsllr (Foreign Off, FCO) 1950-67 (dep dir of Research 1958-67); editor Oxford English-Russian Dictionary published 1984; Scott Moncrieff Prize for translation from French 1972 and 1981, Schlegel-Tieck Prize for translation from German 1983; translated about 45 books from various languages on politics, history, art; *Recreations* reading (history, politics, philosophy, belles-lettres), studying languages; *Clubs* Travellers'; *Style—* P S Falla, Esq; 63 Freelands Rd, Bromley, Kent BR1 3HZ (☎ 01 460 4995)

FALLE, Sir Sam(uel); KCMG (1979, CMG 1964), KCVO (1972), DSC (1945); s of Theodore de Carteret Falle (d 1966), of Ickenham, Middx, and Hilda Falle (d 1979); *b* 19 Feb 1919; *Educ* Victoria Coll Jersey; *m* 1945, Merete, da of Paul Rosen, of Fredensborg, Denmark; 1 s, 3 da; *Career* RN 1937-48; FO 1948, Shiraz and Tehran 1949-52, Beirut 1952-55, Baghdad 1957-61, consul-gen Gothenburg 1961-63, head of UN Dept, FO 1963, dep high cmmr Kuala Lumpur, Malaysia 1967, Aden 1967, ambass to Kuwait 1969-70, Br high cmmr in Singapore 1970-74, ambass to Sweden 1974-77, Br high cmmr to Nigeria 1977-78, ret; delegate Cmmn of the Euro Communities, Algeria 1979-82, conslt chm of the Euro Communities, Zambia 1983; *Recreations* swimming, skiing, languages; *Style—* Sir Sam Falle, KCMG, KCVO, DSC; Slattna, 57030 Mariannelund, Sweden

FALLER, John Benson; s of Albert Faller (d 1967); *b* 26 Sept 1921; *Educ* Downside, Jesus Coll Cambridge (MA); *m* 1947, Mary, da of Sir Joseph Sheridan (d 1964), former Ch Justice of Kenya and Pres Court of Appeal for E Africa; 1 s (decd), 2 da (Juliet b 1948 m T L Hunter-Tilney, o s of Dame Guinevere Tilney, DBE, and stepson of Sir John Tilney, Clare b 1952 m M S Copeman, s of late Vice Adm Sir Nicholas Copeman, KBE, CB, DSC); *Career* serv WWII Lt Coldstream Gds, N Africa and Italy (wounded) 1944); formerly chm Henry W Peabody Grain Ltd and its subsidiaries; *Recreations* shooting; *Clubs* Boodle's, MCC; *Style—* John Faller, Esq; Benton House, Worplesdon Hill, nr Woking, Surrey

FALLON, Michael Cathel; MP (C) Darlington 1983-; s of Martin Fallon, OBE, and Hazel Fallon; *b* 14 May 1952; *Educ* St Andrews Univ (MA 1974); *Career* lectr, advsr to Rt Hon Lord Carrington 1974-77, EEC desk offr CRD 1977-79, PPS to Rt Hon Cecil Parkinson, MP, Sec of State for Energy 1987-88, asst govt whip 1988-; *Style—* Michael Fallon, Esq, MP; House of Commons, London SW1

FALLON, Nicholas Raven; s of Col James Fallon, RAMC (d 1944), of Henleaze, Bristol, and Katharine Frances, *née* Powell (d 1964); *b* 19 April 1920; *Educ* Clifton, Clare Coll Cambridge (MA); *m* 25 June 1958, Gladys Georgina, da of William Briggs (d 1943); *Career* conslt Oil and ME Econ Studies, ME Capt Surrey Service 1940-46, Iraq Petroleum Gp 1946-79; *Recreations* gardening, reading; *Style—* Nicholas R Fallon, Esq; 2 Lansdowne, Carleton Drive, London SW15 2BY (☎ 01 789 2488)

FALLON, Padraic Matthew; s of Padraic Fallon (d 1974), and Dorothea *née* Maher (d 1985); *b* 21 Sept 1946; *Educ* St Peter's Coll Wexford, Blackrock Coll Co Dublin, Trinity Coll Dublin (Bachelor of Business Studies); *m* 8 April 1972, Gillian Elizabeth, da of Graham Hellyer, of Drewton Manor South Cave N Humberside; 1 s (Jolyon b 1975), 3 da (Nicola b 1977, Harriet and Annabel (twins b 1980); *Career* md Euromoney 1974-85, md Euromoney Pubns plc 1985-; dir Associated Newspapers Hldgs plc 1985-, Allied Banks plc 1988-; *Recreations* fishing, shooting, tennis; *Style—* Padraic Fallon, Esq; 20 Lower Addison Gardens, London W14 8BQ (☎ 01 602 1253; Euromoney Publications plc, Nestor House Playhouse Yard, London EC4 5EX (telex: 8814985, fax: 329 4349)

FALLOWFIELD, Richard Gordon; s of Capt Walter Herman Gordon Fallowfield, RN (d 1954), and Elizabeth Burnett, *née* Baker (d 1956); *b* 25 Jan 1935; *Educ* Marlborough; *m* 21 Sept 1963, Elfrida Charlotte, da of Sir Timothy Calvert Eden, 8 Bt (d 1963); 2 s (Timothy Gordon b 1965, Nicholas John b 1967), 1 da (Laura Louise b 1974); *Career* Capt Argyll and Sutherland Highlanders 1952-54; dir: Young and Rubicam Inc 1973-80, McCann Erickson Ltd 1980-84; dep chm Grandfield Rork Collins Fin 1985-; memb IPA; *Recreations* squash, tennis, walking, reading biographies; *Clubs* RAC; *Style—* Richard Fallowfield, Esq; 78 West Side, Clapham Common, London SW4 9AY (☎ 01 228 4428); Prestige House, 14-18 Holborn, London EC1 (☎ 01 242 2002)

FALLSIDE, Prof Frank; s of William Thomas Fallside (d 1979), of Edinburgh, and Daisy Helen Kinnear Madden Fallside (d 1981); no other known bearers of the name Fallside; *b* 2 Jan 1932; *Educ* George Heriot's Sch Edinburgh, Edinburgh Univ (BSc), Univ of Wales (PhD), Univ of Cambridge (MA); *m* 8 March 1958, Maureen Helen, da of Matthew Michael Couttie (d 1969), of Tir-Nam-Oig, Portland, Victoria, Aust; 2 s (David b 1958, Hamish b 1967), 1 da (Helen b 1973); *Career* prof of info engrg Cambridge Univ 1983; fell Trinity Hall Cambridge Univ 1962; *Recreations* sailing, maritime history; *Style—* Professor Frank Fallside; 37 Earl St, Cambridge (☎ 0223 353966); Cambridge University Engineering Dept, Trumpington St, Cambridge (☎ 0223 332752)

FALMOUTH, 9 Viscount (GB 1720); George Hugh Boscawen; also 26 Baron Le Despencer (E 1264) and Baron Boscawen-Rose (GB 1720); patron of five livings; 2 s of 8 Viscount (d 1962), and Mary Margaret Desirée, Viscountess Falmouth (d 1985); *b* 31 Oct 1919; *Educ* Eton, Trinity Coll Cambridge; *m* 9 May 1953, (Beryl) Elizabeth Price, er da of Arthur Harold Browne, of Spring Field, W Peckham, Kent; 4 s (Hon Evelyn, Hon Nicholas b 1957, Hon Charles b 1958, Hon Vere b 1964); *Heir* s, Hon Evelyn Boscawen; *Career* served WWII, Italy (despatches, wounded), Capt Coldstream Gds; Lord Lt of Cornwall 1977- (DL 1968); Master Clockmakers Co 1986; *Clubs* Athenaeum, Army and Navy; *Style—* The Rt Hon Viscount Falmouth; Tregothnan, Truro, Cornwall; Buston, Hunton, Kent

FALVEY, Sir John Neil; KBE (1976), QC (1970); s of John and Adela Falvey; *b* 16 Jan 1918; *Educ* Eltham and New Plymouth Convent Schs, Whangarei HS, Otago Univ Auckland; *m* 1943, Margaret Katherine, da of Stanley Weatherby; 3 s, 2 da (and 1 da decd); *Career* barr; MLC Fiji 1953-72, senator and ldr of Govt Business 1972-79; attorney-gen 1970-77; *Style—* Sir John Falvey, KBE, QC; PO Box 1056, Suva, Fiji

FANE, Hon Mrs Mountjoy; Agatha Isabel; da of Lt-Col Arthur Acland-Hood-Reynardson, OBE (2 s of Sir Alexander Fuller-Acland-Hood, 3 Bt); *b* 3 Oct 1903; *m* 29 April 1926, Lt-Col Hon Mountjoy John Charles Wedderburn Fane, TD (d 1963), s of 13 Earl of Westmorland; 1 s, 1 da; *Style—* The Hon Mrs Mountjoy Fane; The Thatched House, Teigh, Oakham, Leics

FANE, (Harry Frank) Brien; CMG (1967), OBE (1957, MBE); s of late Harry Lawson Fane, of Islington, and Edith, *née* Stovold; *b* 21 August 1915; *Educ* William Ellis Sch, Birkbeck Coll London (BSc); *m* 1947, Stella, yr da of late John Hopwood, of Great Harwood, Lancs; 2 da; *Career* HM forces 1940-45, N Africa, Italy, Maj RCS; 1 sec Br Embassy Washington 1950-56, cnsllr 1960-66, regnl controller Midlands MOE and Productivity 1966; ret 1968; *Style—* Brien Fane, Esq, CMG, OBE; 40 Winterbourne Rd, Solihull, W Midlands (☎ 021 705 2195)

FANE, Hon Harry St Clair; 2 s of 15 Earl of Westmorland; *b* 19 Mar 1953; *Educ* Harrow; *m* 6 Jan 1984, Tessa, da of Capt Michael Philip Forsyth-Forrest; 1 da (Sophie Jane b 1987); *Career* page of honour to HM 1966-68; *Style—* Hon Harry Fane

FANE, Hon Julian Charles; s of 14 Earl of Westmorland (d 1948), and Diana (d 1983), da of 4 and last Baron Ribblesdale (d 1925); *b* 25 May 1927; *Educ* Harrow; *m* 1976, Gillian, yr da of John Kidston Swire and sis of John and Adrian Swire of the Far East trading empire; *Style—* Hon Julian Fane; 32 Blenheim Terrace, London NW8

FANE, Julian Francis; JP (Lincs 1978); s of Lt Francis Fane, RN (4 in descent from Hon Henry Fane, MP, 2 s of 8 Earl of Westmorland); *b* 2 Oct 1938; *Educ* Marlborough, Emmanuel Coll Cambridge (MA); *m* 5 June 1965, (Mary) Julia, da of Michael William Allday, of the Shrubbery, Hartlebury, Worcs; 1 s, 1 da; *Career* farmer; High Sheriff Lincs 1981; *Style—* Julian Fane, Esq, JP; Fulbeck Manor, Grantham, Lincs

FANE, Col Julian Patrick; MC (1940, bar 1945); o s of Col Cecil Fane, CMG, DSO (d 1960), by his wife, Gladys Dorothy, *née* MacGeorge (d 1983); *b* 17 Feb 1921; *Educ* Stowe, RMA Sandhurst; *m* 1, 27 April 1949, Lady Ann Mary Lowther (d 23 Aug 1956), da of Anthony Edward, Viscount Lowther, s of 6 Earl of Lonsdale; 1 s, 1 da; m 2, 1959, Diana Ewart, da of Ivan Hill; 1 s, 1 da; *Career* 2 Lt Gloucestershire Regt 1939, serv WWII, 2 Bn GHQ Liaison Regt and Staff (despatches), 12 Royal Lancers 1946, Life Gds 1960, ret 1969; former dir Samuel Montagu & Co; dir Orion Bank Ltd; Croix de Guerre 1943; *Recreations* shooting, riding; *Style—* Col Julian Fane, MC; Winterley House, Inkpen Road, Kintbury, Berks (☎ 04884 357)

FANE, Peter Francis George; s of F J Fane Wheatley (d 1963), of Oxfordshire, and Violet Bower (d 1970); *b* 15 Dec 1917; *Educ* Marlborough, Emmanuel Coll Cambridge (MA); *m* 31 Oct 1939, Diana, da of G H Hodgkinson Bembridge; 1 s (Michael b 1941), 2 da (Victoria b 1947, Sarah b 1962); *Career* Capt RA 1939-49, served Far East (POW); merchant banker Merchant Bank of Centl Africa Ltd 1957-65, dir NM

Rothschild & Sons Ltd 1965-78; *Recreations* golf, shooting, horticulture; *Clubs* Carlton, MCC; *Style*— Peter Fane, Esq; Wildermere, Baughurst, Hants RG26 5JR (☎ 08356 4383)

FANE, Vere John Alexander; s of John Lionel Richards Fane (d 1945; whose gf Robert was 7 s of Hon Henry Fane, 2 s of 8 Earl of Westmorland), and Barbara, da of Falconer Wallace of Candacraig; *b* 21 April 1935; *Educ* Eton, Trinity Coll Cambridge; *m* 30 May 1964, Tessa Helen Murray, o da of John Murray Prain, DSO, OBE, DL, and Helen, *née* Skene; 1 s (Rupert b 1967), 1 da (Miranda b 1968); *Career* former Lt Coldstream Gds; previously chm Wallace Brothers & Co (Hldgs); dep chm D A L Gp plc; *Recreations* shooting, adventure; *Clubs* White's, Pratt's, Leander, Royal and Ancient, Swinley; *Style*— Vere Fane, Esq; 7 Cavendish Sq, London W1

FANE DE SALIS, Gp Capt Arthur Regester; OBE (1944), DL (Worcs 1963); s of Sir Cecil Fane De Salis, KCB (d 1948, gs of Jerome, 4 Count De Salis and his 3 wife Henrietta, da of Rt Rev William Foster); *b* 18 Nov 1911; *Educ* Stowe, Trinity Coll Cambridge; *m* 1937, Nancy Mary, da of Cdr Gerald Hubbard Welch, RN (d 1928); 1 s, 1 da; *Career* joined RAF 1935, served 1939-45 S Rhodesia 1940, W Desert AF 1942, 2 TAF 1944, Gp Capt 1945 (ret 1957), county cmmr Worcs Scouts 1963-75; *Style*— Gp Capt Arthur Fane De Salis, OBE, DL; Woodside, Crossway Green, Stourport-on-Severn, Worcs

FANE GLADWIN, Col Peter Francis; OBE (1954, MBE 1951); s of Ralph Hamilton Fane Gladwin, Scots Gd (ka 1914), and Isabelle Mary, *née* Douglas-Dick later Mrs Fletcher (d 1956); *b* 27 Feb 1915; *Educ* Ampleforth, RMC Sandhurst; *Career* cmmnd Scots Gds 1935, served W Desert 1941 (wounded), cmd 1 Bn Scots Gds 1951, Col 1959, ret 1963; Highland TA Assoc 1963-81; memb Queens Bodyguard for Scotland Royal Co of Archers (non active list); Cadet Cmdt Argyll and Bute 1963-79, chm W Loch Fyne Community Cncl 1970-76, memb Children's Panel Argyll and Bute, pres SSAFA Argyll an Bute, gen cmmr of income tax 1974; fell Royal Cwlth Soc, FSA Scotland, memb Cncl for Scottish Archaeology; memb High Order of St Sebastitanus of Schutzenbund of Germany; *Books* archaeological papers: Excavating on the Line of the Roman Wall in Hadrian's Camp Carlisle (1980), The Solar Alignment at Brainport Bay Minard Argyll (1985); *Clubs* New (Edinburgh); *Style*— Col Peter Fane Gladwin, OBE; Braigh Varr, Minard, Argyll, Scotland PA32 (☎ 0546 86217)

FANE TREFUSIS, Hon Caroline Harriet; da of 22 Baron Clinton; *b* 23 May 1960; *Educ* North Foreland Lodge; *Style*— Hon Caroline Fane Trefusis

FANE TREFUSIS, Hon Charles Patrick Rolle; s and h of 22 Baron Clinton; *b* 21 Mar 1962; *Style*— Hon Charles Fane Trefusis

FANE TREFUSIS, Hon Henrietta Jane; da of 22 Baron Clinton; *b* 31 Jan 1964; *Style*— Hon Henrietta Fane Trefusis

FANNER, His Hon Judge Peter Duncan; s of Robert William Hodges Fanner (d 1945), slr, of Sheffield, and Doris Kitty, *née* Whiffin (d 1981); *b* 29 May 1926; *Educ* Pangbourne Coll; *m* 23 April 1949, Sheila Eveline, da of George England, of Bromley (d 1946); 1 s (Roger b 1953), 1 da (Elizabeth b 1957); *Career* slr 1951, memb of Cncl of Justices Clerks Soc 1966-72, assessor memb of Departmental Ctee on Liquor Licensing 1971-72, co-editor of Stone's Justices Manual 1968-73; dep CJ 1974-80, rec Crown Ct 1980-86, Metropolitan Stipendiary Magistrate 1972-86, since when CJ; served as pilot Fleet Air Arm 1944-47, Lieut (A) RNVR; *Style*— His Hon Judge Peter D Fanner; Bristol Crown Court

FANNING, John K; s of John Fanning, MBE (d 1940); *b* 24 June 1925; *Educ* Victoria Coll, Alexandria, Stainsby Hall, Univ Coll Durham Univ, King's Coll London (MB BS); *m* 8 Nov 1952, Janet Fay, da of Leonard Stuart Brock (d 1935); 1 s (Benedict b 1960), 1 da (Geraldine b 1954); *Career* RAF 1942-47, Flt Offr Aircrew Pilot; GP 1955-; *Recreations* walking, fishing, music, reading; *Style*— John Fanning, Esq; Beeches End, Wendens Ambo, Saffron Walden, Essex CB11 4LQ (☎ 0799 41580)

FANSHAWE, Lady Beatrix Lilian Ethel; *née* Cadogan; er da of 6 Earl Cadogan, CBE (d 1933); *b* 12 May 1912; *m* 1, 22 Jan 1931 (m dis 1941), (Henry Peregrine) Rennie Hoare (d 1981), of Gasper House, Stourton, Warminster, Wilts, er s of Henry Hoare, of Ellisfield, Hants; 1 s, 1 da; 2, 22 Aug 1942, Col Edward Leighton Fanshawe (d 1982), eldest s of Lt-Gen Sir Edward Arthur Fanshawe, KCB (d 1952), of Rathmore, Naas, Co Kildare; 2 da; *Style*— Lady Beatrix Fanshawe; 174 Cranmer Court, Sloane Avenue, London SW3 3HF

FANSHAWE, Hon Mrs (Maura Clare); *née* Evans-Freke; er da of 11 Baron Carbery, *qv*; *b* 13 Sept 1946; *m* 10 Sept 1966, Richard Henry William Fanshawe, o s of Capt Peter Evelyn Fanshawe, CBE, RN; 1 da (Louisa Mary Constance b 1987); *Career* admin asst Royal Coll of Music 1987; Hon RCM 1986; *Style*— The Hon Mrs Fanshawe; 30 Bark Place, London W2 4AT

FANSHAWE, DFC Peter Douglas; s of Brig George Hew Fanshawe, CBE (d 1974), and Mary Holm, *née* Wiggin (d 1969); *b* 28 Feb 1930; *Educ* Ampleforth, RMA Sandhurst; *m* 18 June 1955, Clemency Mary Marcia, da of Lt-Col Rudolph Philip Elwes, OBE, MC (d 1962); 3 s (John b 1956, Damian b 1959, Anthony b 1964), 1 da (Susanna b 1961); *Career* enlisted 1948, cmmnd the Queens Bays, 2 Dragoon Gds 1950, seconded 1 RTR, served Korean War 1952-53, attached USAF 1953; Distinguished Flying Cross and Air Medal (USA); dir UMECO Hldgs Gp 1969-77; fndr dir James Yorke Hldgs 1976-; *Recreations* gardening, photography, conservation; *Style*— Peter Fanshawe, Esq; Welltown Manor, Boscastle, Cornwall PL35 0DY (☎ 08405 242); James Yorke Holdings Ltd, Yorke House, Corpus Street, Cheltenham, Gloucestershire GL52 6XH (☎ 0242 584224, fax 0242 222445, telex 43269 ROMPAC G)

FANSHAWE, Capt Peter Evelyn; CBE (1966, OBE 1946), DSC (1952); s of Capt Guy Dalrymple Fanshawe, RN (d 1962, himself s of Adm of the Fleet Sir Arthur Fanshawe, GCB, GCVO), and Louisa Charlotte, *née* Crichton (d 1948); *b* 13 Sept 1911; *Educ* Twyford Sch Nr Winchester, RNC Dartmouth; *m* 1936, Helen Mary, da of Maj Sigismund William Joseph Trafford (d 1953), of Wroxham Hall, Norwich; 1 s (Richard Henry William b 1939, m, 1966 Hon Maura Claire Evans Freke, *qv*), 1 da (Veronica Evelyn b 1947, m, 1977 Maj Charles Napier St Pierre Bunbury, MBE); *Career* RN Atlantic Fleet 1929, China Station 1930 1937 and 1950, Med Station 1933, Home Fleet 1936 and 1940, POW Germany 1940-45, HMS Vengeance 1946-47, cmd HMS Amethyst 1950-52, cmd Royal Aust Naval Air Station Nowra NSW 1955-57, Naval Staff Admty 1959-61, Naval Asst to Naval Sec MOD 1962-66; Sec Royal Navy Club of 1765 and 1785 (United 1889) 1975-; *Recreations* gardening, yachting; *Clubs* Army and Navy, Royal Yacht Sqdn (Naval memb), RNSA; *Style*— Capt Peter Fanshawe, CBE, DSC, RN; 12 Lincoln Ave, Wimbledon, London SW19 5JT (☎ 01 947 1323); The Royal Navy Club of 1765 and 1785, 37 Queen's Gate Terrace, London SW7 5PW (☎ 01 584 7665)

FANSHAWE OF RICHMOND, Baron (Life Peer UK 1983), of South Cerney, Co Glos; Sir Anthony Henry Fanshawe Royle; KCMG (1974); er s of Sir Lancelot Carrington Royle, KBE (d 1978), and Barbara Rachel, *née*, Haldin (d 1977); *b* 27 Mar 1927; *Educ* Harrow, RMC Sandhurst; *m* 1957, Shirley, da of John Ramsay Worthington (d 1953); 2 da (Hon Susannah Caroline Fanshawe b 1960, Hon Lucinda Katherine Fanshawe b 1962); *Career* served with Life Gds: Germany, Egypt, Palestine and Transjordan 1945-48, 21 SAS Regt (TA) 1948-51; MP (C) Richmond (Surrey) 1959-83, PPS to: under-sec state Colonies 1960, sec state for Air 1960-62, min Aviation 1962-64; memb Assembly Cncl of Europe and WEU 1965-67, oppn whip 1967-70, parly under-sec state FCO 1970-74, vice-chm Cons Parly Orgn and chm Cons Int Off 1979-84; awarded Most Esteemed Family Order of Brunei (1st class); *Clubs* Pratt's, White's, Brooks's; *Style*— The Rt Hon Lord Fanshawe of Richmond, KCMG; The Chapter Manor, South Cerney, Glos; 47 Cadogan Place, London SW1

FANTONI, Barry Ernest; s of late Peter Nello Secondo Fantoni, of 74 Dumbarton Ct London SW2, and Sarah Catherine, *née* Deverell; *b* 28 Feb 1940; *Educ* Archbishop Temple Sch, Camberwell Sch of Arts & Crafts; *m* 1972, Teresa Frances, da of Col Charles James Reidy, OBE, of 52 Carlyle Rd, Egbaston, Birmingham; *Career* writer; artist; musician; broadcaster; memb ed staff Private Eye 1963, cartoonist: The Listener 1968, Times Diary 1983; dir Barry Fantoni Merchandising Co Ltd 1985; *Clubs* Chelsea Arts, Stocks; *Style*— Barry Fantoni, Esq; c/o Fraser & Dunlop, 91 Regent St, London W1R 8RV

FARAM, Hon Mrs (Felicity Lilla); *née* Wallace; o da of Baroness Dudley *qv*, and Guy Raymond Hill Wallace (d 1967); *b* 14 Feb 1944; *m* 29 July 1967, Philip Neil Faram, eldest s of Ewart Faram, of Penkhull, Stoke-on-Trent; 3 s; *Style*— Hon Mrs Faram; Heath Hill, Queenhill, Upton-on-Severn, Worcs

FARGUS, Col Brian Alfred; OBE (1964), DL (Midlothian 1986); s of late Lt-Col Nigel Harry Skinner Fargus, of 26 Kingsburgh Rd, Edinburgh, da of Charlotte Mary, *née* Trimmer (d 1962); gggf was Col James Skinner, CB, who raised Skinner's horse, sr Cavalry Regt of the Indian Army; *b* 3 Jan 1918; *Educ* Rugby, RMC Sandhurst; *m* 21 Sept 1945, Shiona Margaret Lay, da of Alexander Somerled MacKichan, of Hong Kong and Redlynch, Popp's Lane, Cooden, Sussex; 1 s (David b 1947), 1 da (Diana b 1951); *Career* cmmnd Royal Scots (The Royal Regt) 1938, served Hong Kong 1938-41, Adj 8 Bn Royal Scots 1943-45, NW Europe (despatches), Nigeria Regt 1951-54; active ser with 1 Bn Royal Scots, Egypt 1956, cmd Depot Royal Scots 1957-59, GSO 1, Fedn Army, Malaya 1961-64, GSO 1 1st Br Corps 1964-66, Sr Intelligence Offr, Middle East Cmd, Aden 1966-67, Col GS Hq Scotland 1968-70, Mil Attaché Br Embassy Pretoria 1971-73; ret 1973; re-employed as Asst Regt Sec Royal Scots 1973-78, Regiment Sec 1978-83; DL for Midlothian 1986; *Recreations* golf, fishing; *Clubs* Army and Navy, Honourable Company of Edinburgh Golfers; *Style*— Col Brian Fargus, OBE, DL; St Arvans, Nisbet Rd, Gullane, E Lothian (☎ 0620 842440)

FARINGDON, 3 Baron (UK 1916); Sir Charles Michael Henderson; 3 Bt (UK 1902); s of Lt-Col Hon Michael Thomas Henderson, 16/5 Lancers (d 1953), 2 s of 1 Baron; suc unc 1977; *b* 3 July 1937; *Educ* Eton, Trinity Coll Cambridge (BA 1961); *m* 30 June 1959, Sarah Caroline, o da of Maj John Marjoribanks Askew Eskdale and Lady Susan Askew, *qv*; 3 s (Hon James, Hon Thomas b 1966, Hon Angus b 1969), 1 da (Hon Susannah b 1963); *Heir* s, Hon James Henderson; *Career* ptnr Cazenove & Co 1968-, chm Witan Investmt plc 1980-, bd of govrs Royal Marsden Hosp 1980-85, HM tres of Nat Arts Collections Fund 1985-; *Style*— The Rt Hon the Lord Faringdon; Barnsley Park, Cirencester, Glos; Buscot Park, Faringdon, Oxon

FARLEY, Prof Martyn Graham; s of Herbert Booth Farley (d 1985), of Bristol, and Hilda Gertrude, *née* Hendey (d 1963); *b* 27 Oct 1924; *Educ* Bristol Aeroplane Tech Coll, Merchant Venturers Tech Coll; *m* 20 March 1948, Freda, da of Fred Laugharne (d 1958), of Coventry; 2 s (Robin Laugharne b 1949, d 1984, Simon Laugharne b 1952), 1 da (Jane Elizabeth b 1958); *Career* engine div Bristol Aeroplane Co 1939-55: design apprentice, devpt engr, sr gas turbine designer; Bristol Siddeley Engines 1955-65: asst chief devpt engr, asst chief mechanical engr, chief devpt engr, chief engr (design and devpt) SED; Rolls Royce Ltd 1965-75: chief engr, gen works mangr, mfrg and prodn dir, HQ exec to vice-chm; RMCS and Cranfield Inst of Technol: prof mgmnt sci 1975-85, vice-chm sch mgmnt and mathematics 1984-, emeritus prof 1986-; chm: RC Ltd 1985-, Br Mgmnt Data Fndn Ltd 1979-; dir: World Tech Ventures Ltd 1984-87, Harwell Computer Power Ltd 1986-; memb RN Engr Coll advsy cncl; memb ct: Loughborough Univ 1977-, Cranfield Inst 1977-, Brunel Univ 1877-80, Bath Univ 1983-; pres RAES 1983-84, CGIA Assoc 1984=, I PROD E 1984-85; vice-pres IIM 1979-; memb: sr awards ctee CGLI 1979, C & G Cncl (hon memb); hon fell: American IIM, American Soc Mfrg Engrs, Aust IIM, Indian I Prod E; hon CGIA; Freeman City of London, Liveryman Worshipful Co of Coachmakers and Harness Makers; CEng, FRAeS, FIProdE, FIMechE, FIIM, CBIM, MAIAA; *Recreations* gardening, walking, watching rowing and rugby; *Clubs* Athenaeum, Shrivenham, Ariel Rowing; *Style*— Prof Martyn Farley

FARMBROUGH, Stuart Charles Yalden; JP (1969); s of Charles Luton Farmbrough (d 1973), and Ida Mabel, *née* French (d 1976); *b* 24 July 1923; *Educ* Bedford Sch, Coll of Estate Mgmnt; *m* 28 Oct 1957, Jean Patricia, da of Godfrey Osborn Luton (d 1988); 2 s (Simon b 1959, James b 1961); *Career* Lt RE 1942-47, Madras Sappers and Miners IA 1945-47; self employed chartered surveyor Luton 1958-85; High Sheriff Beds 1984-85; pres Luton Dunstable and Dist C of C and Indust 1977, co cmmr St John Ambulance Beds 1987-; FRICS 1952; *Recreations* country life, beagling; *Style*— Stuart Farmbrough, Esq, JP; Lee Cross High St, Pavenham, Bedford MK43 7PD (☎ 02302 2403)

FARMER, Dr (Edwin) Bruce; s of Edwin Bruce Farmer and Doris, *née* Darby; *b* 18 Sept 1936; *Educ* King Edward's Birmingham, Univ of Birmingham (BSc, PhD); *m* 1962, Beryl Ann, da of late William Alfred Griffiths of Birmingham; 1 s (Andrew b 1967), 1 da (Amanda b 1969); *Career* dir gen mangr Brico Metals 1967-69, md: Brico Engrg 1970-76 (tech dir 1969-70) Wellworthy Ltd 1976-81; dir The Morgan Crucible Co plc 1981-83, gp md 1983-; other dir: Morganite Aust Pty Ltd; CBIM, FRSA; *Recreations* squash, cricket, music; *Style*— Dr Bruce Farmer; Weston House, Bracken Close, Wonersh, Surrey GU5 0QS (☎ 0483 898182); The Morgan Crucible Co plc, Chariot House, Victoria St, Windsor, Berks SL4 1EP (☎ 0753 850331, telex 849025, fax 0753 850872)

FARMER, David William Horace; VRD (1969); s of Horace Edwin Farmer, OBE (d

1979), and Marion, *née* Blain; *b* 19 Oct 1935; *Educ* Tonbridge, St John's Coll Cambridge (MA); *Career* Lt RM 1954-56, RM reserve (Capt) 1956-69; admitted slr 1962, private practice Slaughter and May 1962-66; dir: Standard Chartered Merchant Bank Ltd 1979- (dir 1984-); gp sec Lonrho Ltd 1976-79; *Recreations* travel; *Style*— David Farmer, Esq, VRD; 29A Warwick Square, London SW1V 2AD (☎ 01 834 3541); 33-36 Gracechurch Street, London EC3V 0AX (☎ 01 623 8711)

FARMER, Sir (Lovedin) George Thomas; s of Lovedin George Farmer (d 1952), of Droitwich Spa; *b* 13 May 1908; *Educ* Oxford HS; *m* 1, 1938, Editha Mary (d 1980), da of late F W Fisher, of Worcs; m 2, 1980, Muriel Gwendoline Mercer Pinfold; *Career* chm Rover Co Ltd 1963-73, dep chm Br Leyland Ltd 1970-73, chm Zenith Carburetter Co Ltd 1973-77, dir Rea Bros (Isle of Man) Ltd 1976-88; pres: Birmingham C of C 1960-61, Soc of Manufacturers and Traders 1962-64 (dep pres 1964-65, chm exec ctee 1968-72), Loft Theatre; past memb ECGD (Bd of Trade); govr, chm fin ctee and chm exec cncl of Royal Shakespeare Theatre 1955-75; pro-chllr Birmingham Univ 1966-75; Hon LLD (Birmingham) 1975; FCA; JDipMA; kt 1968; *Recreations* theatre, golf, fishing; *Clubs* Royal and Ancient (St Andrews); *Style*— Sir George Farmer; Longridge, The Chase, Ballakillowey, Colby, Isle of Man (☎ 0624 832603)

FARMER, Hugh Robert Macdonald; CB (1967); s of Charles Edward Farmer (d 1935), of Nonsuch Park, Surrey, and Emily, *née* Randolph; *b* 3 Dec 1907; *Educ* Eton, New Coll Oxford; *m* 1, 1934, Penelope Frances (d 1963), da of late Capt Evelyn Leonard Beridge Boothby, RN; 1 s, 3 da; m 2, 1966, Jean Mary (d 1988), da of late Col Lancelot Mare Gregson, OBE, and widow of Peter Bluett Winch; *Career* asst clerk House of Commons 1931, sr clerk 1943; clerk of Private Bills 1958-60, clerk of ctees 1960-65, clerk/administrator 1965-72; *Recreations* golf and gardening; *Clubs* MCC; *Style*— Hugh Farmer, Esq, CB; The Coach House, Hammer Lane, Grayshott, Hindhead, Surrey GU26 6JD (☎ 0428 3129)

FARMER, Michael Keith; s of Frederick Charles Farmer, of London, and Winifred Nora, *née* Hartigan; *b* 5 April 1942; *Educ* Highgate Sch, Spoehrerschule Calw, West Germany; *m* 1970 (m dis 1987); 2 da (Sonja b 1972, Ingrid b 1974); *Career* jt md: Interwood Ltd, H & F Investments Ltd, Stafford Engrg Co Ltd; chm Woodworking Machinery Suppliers Assoc 1988-; MIOD 1964; *Recreations* classical music, opera, walking; *Style*— Michael Farmer, Esq; 26 Orchard Mead, Finchley Rd, London NW11 8DJ (☎ 01 209 1747); Interwood Ltd, Stafford Ave, Hornchurch, Essex RM11 2ER (☎ 04024 52591, fax 04024 57813, telex 896801)

FARMER, Prof Richard Donald Trafford; s of Hereward Anderton Farmer (d 1987), and Kate Elizabeth Farmer (d 1986); *b* 14 Sept 1941; *Educ* Ashville Coll Harrogate, King's Coll London (MB BS), Univ of London (PhD); *m* 20 Nov 1965, Teresa, da of Kenneth Roland Rimer, of Beckenham, Kent; 2 s (Dominic Michael Trafford b 5 Sept 1966, Christopher Kenneth Trafford b 24 June 1968); *Career* lectr Birmingham Univ 1971-74, sr lectr Westminster Med Sch 1974-84, Boerhaave prof Univ of Leiden 1985, sr lectr Charing Cross & Westminster Med Sch 1986, prof community medicine Univ of London 1986-; MRCS 1963, LRCP 1965, MRCGP 1968, MFCM 1979; *Books* The Suicide Syndrome (1979), Lecture notes on Epidemology and Community Medicine (1977, 1983), Epidemiology of Distress (1982); *Style*— Prof Richard Farmer; Sandtiles, 55 Leight Hill Rd, Cobham, Surey (☎ 0932 62561); Westminster Hosp, London SW1 (☎ 01 823 9811)

FARMER, Thomas; s of John Farmer, and Margaret, *née* Mackie; *b* 10 July 1940; *Educ* Holy Cross Acad Edinburgh; *m* 10 Sept 1966, Anne Drury, da of James Scott; 1 s (John Philip b 14 June 1968), 1 da (Sally Anne b 4 July 1967); *Career* sales rep 1961-64, fndr Tyre and Accessory Supplies 1964-68, dir Albany Tyre Serv 1968-70, fndr md Kwik-Fit Holdgs Ltd 1971-84, chm chief exec Kwik-Fit Hldgs plc 1984-; *Recreations* swimming, tennis, skiing; *Style*— Thomas Farmer, Esq; Kwik-Fit Holdings plc, 27 Corstorphine Rd, Edinburgh (☎ 031 337 9200, fax 031 337 0062, telex 727625)

FARNCOMBE, Hon Mrs (Jenefer Anne); *née* Lawson; da of 5 Baron Burnham, *qv*; *b* 17 Dec 1949; *Educ* The Downs Seaford, Heathfield Sch Ascot, Guildhall Sch of Music and Drama (AGSM), Inchbald Sch of Design; *m* 20 April 1985, Andrew Farncombe, s of G F Farncombe, of Ipswich, Suffolk; 1 s (Frederick Alexander Edward b 1987); *Career* formerly specialist drama teacher; now kitchen designer (own co: Jenefer Lawson); *Recreations* sailing, diving; *Clubs* Island Sailing, Br Sub-Aqua; *Style*— The Hon Mrs Farncombe; c/o Lloyds Bank plc, The Broadway, Wycombe End, Beaconsfield, Bucks

FARNDALE, Gen Sir Martin Baker; KCB (1983, CB 1980); s of late Alfred Farndale, of Leyburn, N Yorks, and Margaret Louise, *née* Baker; *b* 6 Jan 1929,Alberta, Canada; *Educ* Yorebridge Sch Yorks, RMA Sandhurst; *m* 1955, Margaret Anne, da of late Percy Robert Buckingham; 1 s; *Career* RA 1948, 1 Regt RHA 1949-54 (Egypt and Germany 1951-54), HQ 7 Armd Div Germany 1955-56, Staff Coll 1959, HQ 17 Gurkha Div Malaya 1960-62, Mil Ops War Off 1962-64, cmd Chestnut Troop 1 Regt RHA South Arabia 1964-66, instr Staff Coll 1966-69, cmd 1 Regt RHA 1969-71, (UK, N Ireland, Germany); sec defence policy staff MOD 1971-73, Cdr 7 Armd Bde Germany 1973-75, dir PR (Army) MOD 1975-78, dir Mil Ops MOD 1978-80, GOC 2 Armd Div BAOR 1980-83, cmd 1 Br Corps 1983-85, C in C BAOR and Cmd Northern Army Gp Germany 1985-87, ret Jan 1988; Col Cmdt RA 1982-, Col Cmdt AAC 1980-88, Hon Col 3 Bn Yorks Volunteers 1983-, Hon Col 1 Regt RHA 1984-, Master Gunner St James' Park 1988-, Col CMOH RHA 1988-; pres 2 Div Dinner Club 1983-; sr def advsr: Short Bros 1988-, Touche Ross 1988-; *Books* History of Royal Artillery France 1914-18 (1987); *Recreations* gardening, military history; *Clubs* E India, Sports, Public Schs, Devonshire; *Style*— Gen Sir Martin Farndale, KCB; c/o Lloyds Bank, 6 Pall Mall, London SW1

FARNELL, Alan Chaffer; s of late William Sugden Farnell of Birkenshaw, Bradford; *b* 9 Mar 1904; *Educ* Giggleswick; *m* 1933, Pamela, da of late Ernest Bridge; 3 s; *Career* Flying Offr RAF, chm Farnell Electronics Ltd group of cos 1966-76, life pres 1976-; *Recreations* foreign travel; *Style*— Alan Farnell Esq; Apartado 101, A Vista de Pájaro, (Urb) La Noria, Mijas (Malaga), Spain (☎ Malaga 48 53 56)

FARNELL, Graeme; s of Wilson Elliot Farnell, of Nottingham, and Mary Montgomerie Wishart, *née* Crichton (d 1987); *b* 11 July 1947; *Educ* Loughborough GS, Univ of Edinburgh (MA), London Film Sch; *m* 19 July 1969, Jennifer Gerda, da of William Holroyd Huddlestone, of Nottingham; 1 s (Paul b 1983); *Career* asst keeper Museum of E Anglian Life Stowmarket 1973-76, curator Inverness Museum and Art Gallery 1976-79; dir Scottish Museums Cncl 1979-86, dir gen Museums Assoc 1986-; FMA, MBIM, FSA (Scotland); *Recreations* Baroque opera; *Style*— Graeme Farnell, Esq; 8 Faraday Dr, Shenley Lodge, Milton Keynes MK5 7DA (☎ 0908 660 629); Museums Association, 34 Bloomsbury Way, London WC1A 25F (☎ 01 404 4767, fax 01 430 0167)

FARNHAM, 12 Baron (I 1756); Sir Barry Owen Somerset Maxwell; 14 Bt (NS 1627); s of Hon Somerset Arthur Maxwell, MP (died of wounds received in action 1942); suc gf 1957; *b* 7 July 1931; *Educ* Eton, Harvard Univ; *m* 19 Jan 1959, Diana Marion, er da of Nigel Eric Murray Gunnis; 2 da (adopted); *Heir* bro, Hon Simon Kenlis Maxwell; *Career* dir Brown Shipley & Co (merchant bankers) 1959-; chm: Brown Shipley Hldgs plc 1976-, Avon Rubber plc 1978-; asst grand master United Grand Lodge of England 1982-; *Clubs* Boodle's, Kildare St and Univ, City of London; *Style*— The Rt Hon the Lord Farnham; 11 Earl's Court Gdns, London SW5 0TD; Farnham, Co Cavan; Founders Court, Lothbury, London EC2R 7HE

FARNHAM, (Edward) George Adrian; DL (1984 Leics); er s of John Adrian George Farnham (d 1930), of 36 Earls Ct Sq, London, and Lilian Edith, *née* Powell; descended from Thomas Farnham, of the Nether Hall, Quorndon, living 16 cent (*see* Burke's Landed Gentry, 1952 edn); *b* 20 July 1927; *Educ* Harrow, RMA Sandhurst; *m* 20 Aug 1948, Barbara Elizabeth, eldest da of Charles Mathers (d 1976), of Holly Lodge, Rothley, Leics; 3 s (John, Charles, Matthew), 1 da (Georgina); *Career* cmmnd Gordon Highlanders 1946, Bde Intelligence Offr 153 Highland Bde BAOR 1947-48; CC Leics 1958-84 (chm 1977-80), High Sheriff of Leics 1986; chm Leics Health Authy 1986-, pres E Midlands Heraldry Soc; *Recreations* art, history, architecture, conservation; *Style*— George Farnham, Esq; Quorn Hse, Quorn, Loughborough (☎ 0509 412502); Leicestershire Health Authority, Princess Rd West, Leicester (☎ 0533 559777)

FARNSWORTH, Jonathan Bower; s of William Farnsworth (d 1964); *b* 9 Dec 1929; *Educ* Oundle; *m* 14 Nov 1953, Ann Isobel, *née* Scott; 3 s (Anthony b 1955, Adam b 1956, Rupert b 1961), 1 da (Joanna b 1959); *Career* chartered surveyor; *Style*— Jonathan Farnsworth, Esq; The Old Rectory, Thorpe Achurch, Oundle, Peterborough PE8 5SL;

FARQUHAR, David Michael; s of Col Noel Percival Farquhar, and Patricia Mary, *née* Giblin; *b* 29 Mar 1941; *Educ* Edinburgh Acad, Scotch Coll, Melbourne Aust; *m* 6 April 1972, Juliette Diana Galer, da of Konrad Maximillian Hellman (d 1979); 1 s (James b 29 April 1980), 1 da (Rebecca b 4 March 1975); *Career* PR mangr F & T Industs Aust 1963-66, dir Lonsdale Hands Info 1967-71, PR and advtg mangr Toyota 1972-77, corporate and PR mangr Nissan 1977-78, md Juliette Hellman Ltd 1979-; memb PR Inst of Aust 1964; *Recreations* sailing, golf, motor cars; *Clubs* West Sussex Golf, Sea View Yacht; *Style*— David Farquhar, Esq; Media house, Petworth, West Sussex, (☎ 0798 43737, car tel 0836 282896, fax 0798 43391)

FARQUHAR, Gordon Ferguson; s of George Frederick Farquhar (d 1967), and Minnie Margaret, *née* Smith (d 1977); *b* 20 April 1933; *Educ* Hutcheson's GS, Univ of Glasgow (BSc), Imperial Coll London (DIC); *m* 24 July 1957, Jill Elizabeth, da of John David Banner, of Uddingston, nr Glasgow; 1 s (Michael Frank Banner b 1964), 2 da (Shirley Elizabeth b 1959, Fiona Ann b 1962); *Career* Nat Serv Sgt RE 1956-58 mainly as lectr/demonstrator RMC Shrivenham; asst in design and devpt dept atomic power div GEC 1958-59, sr agent Monier Construction Co Nigeria 1959-61; W A Fairhurst & Ptnrs consulting civil and structural engrs: sr engr 1962-66, ptnr 1967-86, managing ptnr 1986-; responsible for maj civil and structural projects on motorways and bldgs, Inst Struct E Oscar Faber Medal 1971; former pres Stepps Lawn Tennis Club 1963-66, Capt Kilmacolm GC 1988-; CEng, FICE, FIStructE, FIHT, MConsE; *Recreations* golf; *Clubs* Royal Scottish Auto, Kilmacolm Golf; *Style*— Gordon Farquhar, Esq; 2 Hatfield Ct, Kilmacolm, Renfrewshire PA13 4LY (☎ 050 587 2245); W A Fairhurst Ptnrs, 11 Woodside Terr, Glasgow G3 7XQ (☎ 041 332 8754)

FARQUHAR, Sir Michael FitzRoy Henry; 7 Bt (GB 1796); s of Lt-Col Sir Peter Walter Farquhar, 6 Bt, DSO, OBE (d 1986), and Elizabeth Evelyn, *née* Hurt (d 1983); *b* 29 June 1938; *Educ* Eton, RAC Cirencester; *m* 29 June 1963, Veronica Geraldine, er da of Patrick Rowan Hornidge, of Helford Passage, nr Falmouth, Cornwall; 2 s (Charles Walter FitzRoy b 21 Feb 1964, Edward Peter Henry b 6 Dec 1966); *Heir* s, Charles Walter FitzRoy b 21 Feb 1964; *Recreations* fishing, shooting, gardening; *Clubs* White's; *Style*— Sir Michael Farquhar, Bt; Manor Farm, West Kington, Chippenham, Wilts SN14 7JG (☎ 0249 782671)

FARQUHARSON, Capt Colin Andrew; JP (Aberdeenshire 1969), DL (1966); s of late Norman Donald Farquharson of Whitehouse, Alford, Aberdeenshire; *b* 9 August 1923; *Educ* Rugby; *m* 1948, Jean Sybil Mary (d 1985), da of late Brig-Gen John George Harry Hamilton, DSO, JP, DL, of Skene House, Aberdeenshire; 2 da (1 decd) (*see* Master of Arbuthnott); m 2, 1987, Clodagh, JP, DL, 2 da of late Sir Kenneth Murray JP, DL, of Geanies, Ross-shire and widow of Major Ian Houldsworth DL, of Dallas Morayshire; 3 s, 2 da (*see* Earl of Haddo); *Career* Capt Grenadier Guards 1942-48; chartered surveyor (land agent); memb Royal Cornhill and Assoc Hosps Bd of Mgmnt 1962-74, chm Gordon Dist Local Health Cncl 1975-81, memb Grampian Area Health Bd 1981-; memb Royal Co of Archers (Queen's Body Guard for Scotland); dir MacRobert Farms (Douneside) Ltd 1971-87, Vice Lord Lt for Aberdeenshire 1983-87; Lord Lt of Abserdeenshire 1987: FRICS; *Recreations* shooting, fishing; *Clubs* Royal Northern, Univ (both Aberdeen); MCC; *Style*— Capt Colin Farquharson of Whitehouse, JP; Whitehouse, Alford, Aberdeenshire AB3 8DP (☎ 0336 2503); Estate Off, Mains of Haddo, Haddo House, Aberdeen AB4 0ER (☎ 06515 664)

FARQUHARSON, Hon Mr Justice; Hon Sir Donald Henry; yr s of Charles Anderson Farquharson (d 1929), of Logie Coldstone, Aberdeenshire, and Florence Ellen, *née* Fox; *b* 26 Feb 1928; *Educ* Royal Commercial Travellers Schs, Keble Coll Oxford; *m* 1960, Helen Mary, er da of Cdr H M Simpson, RN (ret), of Abbots Brow, Kirkby Lonsdale, Westmorland; 3 s (and 1 da decd); *Career* barr Inner Temple 1952, dep chm Essex QS 1970-72, QC 1972, rec Crown Cts 1972-81, legal assessor Gen Med Cncl and Gen Dental Cmmn 1978-81, bencher Inner Temple 1979, High Ct judge (Queen's Bench) 1981-; kt 1981; *Recreations* opera going; *Style*— Hon Mr Justice Farquharson; Royal Courts of Justice, Strand, London WC2A 2LL (☎ 01 405 7641)

FARQUHARSON, Sir James Robbie; KBE (1960, CBE 1948, OBE 1944); s of Frank Farquharson, of Cortachy, Augus, and Agnes Jane, *née* Robbie; *b* 1 Nov 1903; *Educ* Royal Tech Coll Glasgow, Glasgow Univ (BSc); *m* 1933, Agnes Binny, da of James Graham, of Kirriemuir, Angus; 2 s; *Career* chief engr Tanganyika Railways 1941-45 (gen mangr 1945-48), chief engr and dep gen mangr E African Railways 1948-52; gen mangr: Sudan Railways 1952-57, E African Railways 1957-61; asst crown agent and engr-in-chief Crown Agents for Overseas Govts and Admins 1961-65; chm Millbank Tech Servs Ordnance Ltd 1973-75, fell Scottish Cncl Devpt and Indust 1986; farmer; *Style*— Sir James Farquharson, KBE; Kinclune, by Kirriemuir, Angus, Scotland (☎

0575 74710)

FARQUHARSON, Robert Alexander (Robin); CMG (1975); s of Capt JP Farquharson, DSO, OBE, RN (d 1960), of Homington Manor, Salisbury, and Phyllis Ruth, *née* Prescott-Decie (d 1969); *b* 26 May 1925; *Educ* Harrow, King's Coll Cambridge (MA); *m* 4 Feb 1955, Jean Elizabeth, da of Sir Ivo Mallet, GBE, KCMG (d 1988) 3 s (John James b 1956, William b 1961, d 1984, Edward b 1962), 1 da (Charlotte b 1959); *Career* Sub Lt RNVR 1943-46; Dip Serv (formerly Foreign Serv): third sec Moscow 1950, seconded sec FO 1952, first sec Bonn 1955, Panama 1958, Paris 1960, FO 1964, cnsllr and dir of trade devpt S Africa 1967, min Madrid 1971, HM Consul-Gen San Francisco 1973, ambassador Yugoslavia 1977; econ advsr Davy McKee Int 1980; chm local Parish Cncl, memb Deanery and Diocesan Synods, Lord of the Manor of Bockleton; *Recreations* country; *Clubs* Naval and Military, Flyfishers, Bohemian (San Francisco); *Style—* R A Farquharson, Esq, CMG; Tollard Royal, Salisbury SP5 5PS (☎ 07256 278)

FARQUHARSON OF FINZEAN, Angus Durie Miller; DL; s of Dr Hugo Durie Newton Miller (d 1984), and Elsie Miller, *née* Duthie; *b* 27 Mar 1935; *Educ* Trinity Coll Glenalmond, Downing Coll Cambridge (MA); *m* 1 July 1961, Alison Mary, da of William Marshall Farquharson-Lang, CBE, LLD; 2 s (Donald b 1963, Andrew b 1969), 1 da (Jean b 1962); *Career* chartered surveyor, Factor Finzean Estate; memb regnl advsy ctee Forestry Cmmn E Scotland 1980-84 and N Conservancy 1985-; memb: Red Deer Cmmn 1986-, Nature Conservancy Cncl Ctee for Scotland 1986-; cncl memb Scottish Landowners Fedn 1980-88; vice lord lieutenant of Aberdeenshire 1987-; pres Deeside Field Club; chm Deeside Woodland Products; memb Presbytery of Kincardine/Deeside; dir Lathallan Sch; FRICS; *Recreations* shooting, fishing, gardening, nature conservation; *Clubs* New (Edinburgh); *Style—* Angus D M Farquharson of Finzean, DL; Finzean House, Finzean, Aberdeenshire AB3 5ED (☎ 033045 229)

FARR, Dennis Larry Ashwell; s of Arthur William Farr (d 1961), and Helen Eva, *née* Ashwell; *b* 3 April 1929; *Educ* Luton GS, London Univ, Courtauld Inst of Art; *m* 1959, Diana (author), da of Capt H J Pullein-Thompson, MC; 1 s, 1 da; *Career* asst keeper Tate Gallery 1954-64, curator Paul Mellon Collection, Washington DC 1965-66, sr lectr and dep keeper Univ Art Collections Glasgow Univ 1967-69, dir Birmingham City Museums Art Gallery 1969-80, tstee Birmingham Museum & Art Gallery Appeal Fund 1980-, memb UK exec bd Int Cncl of Museums 1976-84, dir Courtauld Inst Galleries London Univ 1980-, chm Assoc of Art Historians 1983-86 (memb exec ctee 1981); JP Birmingham 1977-80; Hon DLitt Birmingham; FRSA, FMA; *Publications* William Etty (1958), Tate Gallery Modern British Sch Catalogue, 2 vols (with Mary Chamot and Martin Butlin, 1964), English Art 1870-1940 (1978), Impressionist and Post-Impressionist Paintings from the Courtauld Collections (with William Bradford, 1984), The Northern Landscape (with William Bradford, 1986), Impressionist and Post Impressionist Masters: The Courtauld Collection (with John House and others, 1987), 100 Masterpieces from The Courtauld Collections (ed and contrib, 1987); *Recreations* reading, riding, music, foreign travel; *Clubs* Athenaeum, Inst of Contemporary Arts; *Style—* Dr Dennis Farr; 35 Esmond Rd, Bedford Park, Chiswick, London W4 1JG (☎ 01 995 6400)

FARR, Diana; da of Capt Harold James Pullein-Thompson, MC (d 1957), and Joanna Maxwell, *née* Cannan; *b* 1 Oct 1930; *Educ* Wychwood Sch Oxford; *m* 6 June 1959, Dennis Larry Ashwell Farr, s of Arthur William Farr; 1 s (Benedict Edward b 7 March 1963), 1 da (Joanna Helen b 6 July 1964); *Career* professional author 1946-; dir Grove Riding Schs Peppard and Oxford 1946-52, PA literary agent Rosica Colin 1952-54, memb Public Lending Right Ctee 1960-64, fndr memb Children's Writers Gp 1963-65, hon sec Save the Mere Campaign 1970-73; memb Soc Authors; *Books* as Diana Pullein - Thompson books incl: I Wanted a Pony (1946), The Boy and The Donkey (1958), Cassidy In Danger (1979); as Diana Farr: Gilbert Cannan, A Georgian Prodigy (1978), Five at 10: Prime Minister's Consorts Since 1957 (1985), Choosing (1988), Dear Pup, Letters To A Young Dog (1988); *Recreations* walking, cinema, travel; *Style—* Mrs Dennis Farr; 35 Esmond Rd, Bedford Park, Chiswick, London W4 1JG (☎ 01 995 6400)

FARR, Jennifer Margaret; JP (1979); da of Charles Percival Holliday, of Nottingham, and Vera Margaret Emily, *née* Burchell; *b* 20 July 1933; *Educ* Nottingham Girls HS, Middx Hosp and Royal Victoria Infirmary Newcastle-upon-Tyne; *m* 28 July 1956, Sydney Hordern Farr (d 1981), s of Col Sydney Farr, MC, DL, JP (d 1967), of Nottingham; 2 s (Timothy b 1957, Charles b 1961), 1 da (Rosemary b 1959); *Career* physiotherapist 1954-56; chm Nottingham and Dist NSPCC; *Recreations* golf, tennis, gardening, music; *Clubs* Notts Golf; *Style—* Mrs Jennifer Farr, JP; Lanesmeet, Epperstone, Notts NG14 6AU

FARR, Sir John Arnold; MP (C) Harborough 1959-; 2 and er surv s of Capt John Farr, JP (d 1951) of Worksop Manor, Notts, and Margaret Anne, *née* Heath; *b* 25 Sept 1922; *Educ* Harrow; *m* 26 Aug 1960, Susan Ann, yr da of Sir Leonard John Milburn, 3 Bt (d 1957); 2 s (Jonathan b 1962, George b 1967); *Career* RN 1940-46, demob Lt Cdr RNVR; memb of Lloyd's, landowner, dir Home Brewery Co Ltd 1950-55, pres Worksop Boys' Club 1951-55, contested (C) Ilkeston 1955, sec Cons agric ctee 1970-74 and v-chm 1979-84, memb UK delgn to WEU and Cncl of Europe 1973-78, vice-chm Cons NI ctee 1974-78; chm: Anglo-Irish Parly Gp 1977-80, Br Korea Parly Gp 1980-, Br Zimbabwe Parly Gp 1980-; memb Select Ctee on Standing Orders 1981-, sec All Pty Conservation Ctee, chm All Pty Knitwear Gp; kt 1984; *Clubs* Boodle's, MCC; *Style—* Sir John Farr, MP; 11 Vincent Square, London SW1; Shortwood House, Lamport, Northampton (☎ 060 128 260)

FARR, Suzanne Elizabeth; da of Tom Priday Farr, JP, of Worcestershire, and Anne Farr, *née* Thomas; *b* 14 August 1936; *Educ* The Alice Ottley Sch, Bedford Coll of Physical Educn, Lady Margaret Hall Oxford (MA, MSc); *Career* house mistress Wycombe Abbey 1963-75, Head mistress Downe House 1978-; memb English Lacrosse Team 1963-67; Girls Schs Assoc; *Recreations* gardening, showing & breeding Irish Setters; *Clubs* Lansdowne, Kennel; *Style—* Miss Suzanne E Farr; St Peter's, Cold Ash, Newbury, Berkshire RG16 9JJ; Downe House, Cold Ash, Newbury, Berks (☎ 0635 200 286)

FARRANCE, Roger Arthur; s of Ernest Thomas Farrance (d 1985), and Alexandra Hilda May, *née* Finch; *b* 10 Nov 1933; *Educ* Trinity Sch of John Whitgift, LSE (BSc); *m* 8 Dec 1956, Kathleen Sheila, da of Henry Stephen Owen (d 1974); 1 da (Denise Lesley b 1957); *Career* HM Inspector of Factories Manchester, Doncaster and Walsall 1956-64, asst sec W of England Engng Employers' Assoc Bristol 1964-67, indus relations and personnel mangr Foster Wheeler John Brown Boilers Ltd 1967-68, dep dir Coventry and District Engng Employers Assoc also Coventry Management Tng Centre 1968-75, dep indus relations advsr Elec Cncl 1975-76; indus relations advsr Elec Cncl 1976-79; full time memb Elec Cncl 1979-; memb cncl ACAS 1983- and CBI 1983-; FIPM, OStJ; *Style—* Roger Farrance, Esq; 7 Melville Avenue, Wimbledon, London SW20 0NS (☎ 01 946 9650); The Electricity Council, 30 Millbank, London SW1P 4RD (☎ 01 834 2333, fax: 01 834 6453)

FARRANDS, Dr John Law; CB (1981); s of Harold Rawlings Farrand (d 1976), of Melbourne, and Hilda Elizabeth, *née* Bray (d 1961); *b* 11 Mar 1921; *Educ* Dandenong HS, Univ of Melbourne (BSc), Univ of London (PhD) Imperial Coll London (DIC); *m* 11 Sept 1946, Jessica, da of Harold Nelson Ferguson; 4 s (John Harold, David Robert, Donald James, Peter Graham b 1958, d 1981), 1 da (Rosemary Jennifer); *Career* Lt 1942, Capt 1943 ALF 1942-46; Physicist Dep Laboratories 1946-56; Mil Bd: Scientist advsy 1957-61, asst controller R & D 1961-64; supt res MSL 1964-74, chief aeronautical Res Laboratories 1964-71, chief def scientist 1971-77, sec: Dept Sci and Environment, Dept Sci and Technol 1977-81; chm: Aust Inst of Marine Sci 1982-, OTC Bd R & D 1982-83; chcllr Aust Acad Technol Scis and Engrg 1975-88; Finstp 1948, FTS 1975, FIE (Aust) 1987, FAIP, C Eng, C Phys; *Books* Changing Disease Patterns and Human Behaviour (jtly 1980), 200 Years of Technology in Australia (jtly 1988); *Recreations* fishing, music; *Clubs* Naval and Military, Melbourne, Sciences (Melbourne); *Style—* Dr John Farrands; 20 The Boulevard, Glen Averley Victoria 3150 (☎ 01061 03 232 8195, fax 01061 03 232 3232); 7 Hender St, St Martha Victoria Australia

FARRANT, Malcolm George; s of Andrew Cecil Farrant, (d 1956), of Roskrow, Penryn, Cornwall, and Winifred Mary, *née* Fox, (1974); *b* 1 July 1937; *Educ* Eton; *m* 1, 1963 (m dis 1965, Dorothy, da of Robert Farrow (d 1972) of Melbourne, Australia; m 2, (m dis 1987), Angela Margery Smith-Bosanquet, *née* Moore, da of John Edward Hugh Moore (d 1957); 2 s (Henry Malcolm b 22 Jan 1970, Oliver Jasper b 28 March 1974); *Career* Nat Serv, Duke of Cornwall's LI served Jamaica and Germany 1956-57; Stock Exhange London 1954-55 and 1957-59; property devlpr and estate agent Perth Australia 1963-73, property devlpr Bath England 1973-88, local dir Gold Estates of Australia (1903) Ltd 1970-82 (local chm 1970-73); chm and md Moore Farrant Ltd 1987-; *Recreations* fishing, golf, model making; *Clubs* Landsdowne; *Style—* Malcolm Farrant, Esq; 4 Charlotte St, Bath, Avon BA1 2NE (☎ 0225 332047); Manvers Chambers, Manvers St, Bath, Avon BA1 1PE (☎ 0225 65951, fax 0225 69845, cartel 0860 220026, telex 63614)

FARRAR, Rex Gordon; LVO (1975); s of John Percival Farrar and Ethel Florence, *née* Leader; *b* 22 August 1925; *Educ* Latymer's Sch Edmonton, London Univ (BA); *m* 1, 1955, Mary Katharine Shutts (d 1977); 1 s; m 2, 1978, Masako Ikeda, 1 s, 1 da; *Career* served RN 1944-47; FO 1947-, vice-consul New Orleans 1953, second sec Jakarta 1960 (first sec 1963), first sec: Commercial Caracas 1964, head of chancery and consul San Salvador 1968, Commercial Tokyo 1971, head chancery and consul Rangoon 1978-80; consul-gen at Osaka 1980-85, ret; regnl dir (Tokyo) The De La Rue Co plc 1985-; *Style—* Rex Farrar, Esq, LVO; c/o The De La Rue Co plc, 1-11-45 Akasaka, Kowa No 3 Building, 4th Floor, Chiyoda-ku 107, Tokyo, Japan

FARRAR-HOCKLEY, Gen Sir Anthony Heritage; GBE (1981, MBE 1957), KCB (1977), DSO (1953) and bar (1964), MC (1944); s of Arthur Farrar-Hockley; *b* 8 April 1924; *Educ* Exeter Sch; *m* 1945, Margaret Bernadette Wells (d 1981); 2 s (and 1 s decd); m 2 1983, Linda Wood; *Career* Gloucestershire and Parachute Regt WWII; serv: Mediterranean, Europe, Palestine, Korea 1950-53, later Cyprus, Port Said, Jordan, Aden; chief instr RMA Sandhurst 1959-61, princ staff offr to dir Borneo Ops 1965-66, Cdr 16 Parachute Bde 1966-68, defence fellowship Exeter Coll Oxford (BLitt) 1968-70, Div PR Army 1970, Cdr Land Forces NI 1970-71, GOC 4 Div 1971-73, dir Combat Devpt Army 1974-77, Lt-Gen 1977, GOC SE Dist 1977-79, Gen 1979, C-in-C Allied Forces N Europe 1979-82, ret 1983; ADC Gen to HM The Queen 1981-83; Col Cmdt Para Regt 1977-83, Col The Gloucestershire Regt 1978-84; memb: steering ctee for Defence Begins at Home 1983-, cncl Outward Bound 1983-; *Style—* Gen Sir Anthony Farrar-Hockley, GBE, KCB, DSO, MC; Pye Barn, Moulsford, Oxon

FARRELL, Arthur Denis; CMG (1970), QC (1957); s of Joseph Jessop Farrell, CBE (d 1949), and Emma Louise, *née* Martyn (d 1938); *b* 27 Jan 1906; *Educ* St Paul's, Balliol Coll Oxford (MA); *m* 1953, Margaret Madeline, *née* Cox; 1 s (Nigel); *Career* called to the Bar Middle Temple 1937, crown counsel Singapore 1947-51; legal draftsman Fedn of Malaya 1951-55, slr gen 1955-58, Puisne Judge Kenya 1958-69 (acting chief justice 1968); chm Med Appeal Tribunals 1974-78; Coronation Medal 1953; *Recreations* golf, bridge, music; *Style—* Denis Farrell, Esq, CMG, QC

FARRELL, Charles; MD (1945); s of Gerald William Farrell (d 1919); *b* 10 Feb 1919; *Educ* Ampleforth, Christ Church Oxford (MA); *m* 1949, Lady Katharine, *qv*; 1 s, 3 da; *Career* Maj Scots Gds NW Europe 1944-45 (despatches); For Serv: joined 1947, with Cmmr Gens Off Singapore 1949-51, first sec Br Embassy Brussels 1955-57, resigned 1957; md Br Sidac Ltd 1960-71, chm Sidex Ltd (jt co with ICI Ltd) 1966-71, memb trade and policy ctee CBI 1970-74, chm Montagu Fine Art Ltd 1972-79, dir Christie's Publications Ltd 1972-85, chm CCA Publications plc 1985-; memb: Oxon Health Authy 1981-85, Oxon CC 1981-87; *Recreations* skiing, tennis; *Clubs* White's, Beefsteak; *Style—* Charles Farrell, Esq, MC; Cuttmill House, Watlington, Oxon OX9 5BA (☎ 049 161 2327); CCA Publications plc, 8 Dover St, London W1 (☎ 01 499 6701)

FARRELL, Hon Mrs (Clodagh Mary); *née* Morris; yr da of 2 Baron Morris (d 1975); *b* 8 Nov 1936; *Educ* St Mary's Ascot and New Hall Chelmsford; *m* 2 May 1964, Thomas Hugh Francis Farrell, TD, DL, *qv*; 1 s, 1 da; *Style—* Hon Mrs Farrell; 20 New Walk, Beverley, North Humberside (☎ 0482 869367)

FARRELL, Lady Katharine Mary Veronica; *née* Paget; yst da of 6 Marquess of Anglesey, GCVO (d 1947), and Lady Marjorie Manners (d 1946), eldest da of 8 Duke of Rutland; twin sis of 7 Marquess; *b* 8 Oct 1922; *m* 1, 16 April 1941 (m dis 1948), Lt-Col Jocelyn Eustace Gurney, DSO, MC (d 1973), Welsh Gds, 2 s of Sir Eustace Gurney, of Walsingham Abbey, Norfolk; 1 da; m 2, 21 Jan 1949, Charles Farrell, MC, *qv*; 1 s, 3 da; *Style—* Lady Katharine Farrell; Cuttmill House, Watlington, Oxon OX9 5BA (☎ 049 161 2327)

FARRELL, Thomas Hugh Francis; TD (1969), DL (E Riding Yorks 1971, Humberside 1974); s of Hugh Farrell (d 1959); *b* 3 Feb 1930; *Educ* Ampleforth, Univ Coll Hull, (LLB London); *m* 2 May 1964, Hon Clodagh Mary, *qv*; 1 s, 1 da; *Career* slr 1952; cmmnd The Queen's Bays 1953-55, Lt-Col cmdg Prince of Wales's Own Yorkshire Territorials 1967-69; Sheriff of Hull 1960-61; chm: Hull Cons Fedn 1963-68, Beverley Civic Soc 1970-74; tres Hull Univ 1976-1980, chm cncl Hull Univ 1980-; Hon

LLD (Hull) 1983; *Clubs* Cavalry and Guards'; *Style—* Thomas Farrell, Esq, TD, DL; 20 New Walk, Beverley, North Humberside (☎ Hull 0482 869367); King William House, Market Place, Hull (☎ 0482 23239)

FARREN, Graham Richard; s of Dennis Henry Saunders Farren (d 1985), and Doris Margaret, *née* Francis; *b* 19 Jan 1947; *Educ* Hemel Hampstead GS, Churchill Coll Cambridge (MA); *m* 12 April 1975, Bridget Mary, da of late William Hardisty; 1 s (Richard), 1 da (Frances); *Career* Bacon Woodrow & De Souza 1973-77, ptnr Bacon & Woodrow 1977- (joined 1969); Freeman: City of London, Worshipful Co of Actuaries; FIA 1972, ASA 1974, APMI 1980; *Recreations* gardening, travelling, photography; *Style—* Graham Farren, Esq; Beltrees, Park Rd, Stoke Poges, Bucks SL2 4PA (☎ 0753 224 84); Bacon & Woodrow, Ivy Hse, 107 St Peters St, St Albans, Herts AL1 3EW (☎ 0727 555 66, fax 0727 410 77)

FARRER, Hon Anne Lucy; 3 da (only da by 2 w) of 2 Baron Farrer (d 1940) (title ext 1964); *b* 12 July 1908; *Educ* Downe House; *Style—* Hon Anne Farrer; Newby Cote, Clapham, via Lancaster, Lancs (☎ 046 85 204)

FARRER, His Hon Judge Brian Ainsworth; QC (1978); s of Albert Ainsworth Farrer (d 1966), and Gertrude, *née* Hall (d 1985); *b* 7 April 1930; *Educ* King's Coll Taunton, UCL (LLB); *m* 1960, Gwendoline Valerie, JP, da of William Waddoup (d 1986), of Lichfield; 2 s, 1 da; *Career* barr Gray's Inn 1957, MO Circuit 1958-85, rec Crown Ct 1974-85, circuit judge 1985-; *Recreations* golf, bridge, chess; *Clubs* Aberdovey Golf; *Style—* His Hon Judge Brian Farrer, QC; Shutt Cross House, Aldridge, W Mids (☎ 065 472 0922 53602); Ardudwy Cottage, Ty Ardudwy, Aberdovey, Gwynedd (☎ 065 472 397)

FARRER, Sir (Charles) Matthew; KCVO (1983, CVO 1973); s of Sir (Walter) Leslie Farrer, KCVO (d 1984), and Hon Lady (Marjorie Laura) Farrer (d 1981), da of 1 Viscount Hanworth, KBE, PC; *b* 3 Dec 1929; *Educ* Bryanston, Balliol Coll Oxford; *m* 1962, Johanna Creszentia Maria Dorothea, da of Prof Hans-Herman Bennhold, of Tübingen, Germany; 1 s, 1 da; *Career* slr 1956; ptnr Messrs Farrer & Co 1959-; private slr to HM The Queen 1965-; *Style—* Sir Matthew Farrer, KCVO; 6 Priory Ave, Bedford Park, London W4; Messrs Farrer & Co, 66 Lincoln's Inn Fields, London WC2A 3LH (☎ 01 242 2022)

FARRER, (John) Philip (William); s of William Oliver Farrer, of Popmoor, Fernhurst, Haslemere, Surrey, and Margery Hope Farrer (d 1976); *b* 12 Mar 1958; *Educ* Eton, Sandhurst; *m* 19 July 1986, Maria Jane Margaret da of Cuthbert Peter Ronald Bowlby, of Liphook, Hants; 2 da (Beatrice Hope b 27 July 1987, Katherine Isabella Caroline b 17 March 1989); *Career* Lt 2 Bn Coldstream Gds 1978-82; Grievson Grant & Co 1982-84, UBS Phillips & Drew 1985, SBC Stockbroking 1986-; memb Stock Exchange; *Recreations* skiing, golf, tennis; *Style—* Philip Farrer, Esq; 25 Killiester Ave, London SW2 (☎ 671 5792); SBC Stockbroking, Swiss Bank House, 1 High Timber St, EC4V 3SB (☎ 01 329 0329, fax 01 329 8700, telex 88 74 34)

FARRER, Trevor Maurice; s of William Maurice Farrer, and Dorothy Joyce Farrer; *b* 21 Dec 1931; *Educ* The Knoll Sch Woburn Sands, Dauntsey's Sch Devizes; *m* 2 April 1960 (m dis 1986), Eileen Mary; 2 s (Stewart William b March 1961, Noel Ecroyd b 25 Dec 1963), 1 da (Xanthe Rachel (twin) b 25 Dec 1963); *Career* Nat Serv Kings Own RR 1950-52; farmer 1952-82; cncl memb NFU 1965-74 (co chm 1970-73); memb: Agric Land Tbnl 1974-, Cons Nat Union Exec 1988-; memb: S Westmorland RDC 1963-66, Lancs River Authy and NW Water Authy 1966-84, Cumbria CC 1977-89; cncl memb Westmorland Cons 1963-, memb NW area Cons exec 1981-; Freeman City of London 1986; *Recreations* music, travel, politics; *Clubs* Farmers; *Style—* Trevor Farrer, Esq; Whitbarrow Stables, Grange over Sands, Cumbria LA11 6SL (☎ 0448 52235)

FARRER, William Oliver; s of John Oliver Farrer, MC (d 1942); *b* 23 June 1926; *Educ* Eton, Balliol Coll Oxford; *m* 1, 1955, Margery Hope (d 1976), da of William Yates (d 1931); 2 s, 1 da; m 2, 1979, Hazel Mary, da of Robert Clark Taylor (d 1963); *Career* Lt Coldstream Guards; slr; ptnr Farrer & Co 1955, sr ptnr 1976; *Recreations* golf, music; *Clubs* Brooks's, MCC, Royal and Ancient; *Style—* William Farrer, Esq; Popmoor, Fernhurst, Haslemere, Surrey (☎ 0428 2564)

FARRER-BROWN, Leslie; CBE (Civil 1960); s of late Sydney Brown, and Annie, *née* Brearley (d 1944); *b* 2 April 1904; *Educ* Southgate Secondary Sch, LSE (BSc); *m* 8 Dec 1928, Doris Evelyn (d 1986), da of Herbert Jamieson (d 1910); 2 s (Malcolm Jamieson b 15 July 1930, Geoffrey b 26 May 1934); *Career* asst registrar LSE 1927-28, admin staff Univ of London 1928-36, called to the Bar Gray's Inn 1932, sec Central Midwives Bd 1936-45, seconded to Miny of Health 1941-44, sec Interdepartmental ctee on Med Schs 1942-44, sec first dir Nuffield Fndn 1944-64 (tstee Nuffield Provincial Hosp Tst 1955-67), pres Sussex and Surrey Rent Assessment Panel 1965-76, dir Alliance Building Soc 1969-85, chm Alliance Building Soc 1975-81; JP: Middx 1947-65, Sussex 1966-81; chm Highgate Juvenile Ct 1952-61, Highgate Magistrates Ct 1961-65; chm: Malta Med Servs Ctee 1956, Rhodesia Med Sch Ctee 1956-57, Nat Cncl Soc Serv 1960-73, Inst of Child Health Univ of London 1966-76, UK govr Cwlth Fndn 1966-, cncl and pro-chllr Univ of Sussex 1976-80; chm: Overseas Visual Aid Ctee 1958-70, Centre for Educnl TV Overseas 1962-70, ctee on Res and Devpt in Modern Languages 1964-70, vol ctee on overseas Aid and Devpt 1965-76, Centre for Info on Language Teaching 1966-72; *Recreations* travel, painting; *Clubs* Athenaeum; *Style—* Leslie Farrer-Brown, Esq, CBE; 3 Kennet Ct, Woosehill, Wokingham, Berkshire RG11 9BD

FARRIMOND, Herbert Leonard; CBE (1977); s of late George and Jane Farrimond, of Newcastle-upon-Tyne; *b* 4 Oct 1924; *Educ* St Cuthbert's GS Newcastle, Durham Univ; *m* 1951, Patricia Sara, da of Col James Craig McGrath, MC; 1 s; *Career* Lt HM RM; former personnel dir ICI (IMI) and Dunlop Ltd, full-time memb BR Bd 1971-77, chm Br Tport Hotels Ltd 1976-78, memb of ACAS 1974-78, dir Portsmouth & Sunderland Newspapers Ltd 1978-80, chm H L Farrimond & Associates (Advisers to Industrial/Commercial Organisations) 1978-, pt-time memb Br Waterways Bd 1980-; *Style—* Herbert Farrimond, Esq, CBE; Crinan, 26 Box lane, Boxmoor, Hemel Hempstead, Herts (☎ 0442 52348); 9 Ardgare, Shandon, Helensburgh, Dunbartonshire (☎ 0436 820803)

FARRINGTON, Col Sir Henry Francis Colden; 7 Bt (UK 1818); s of Sir Henry Anthony Farrington, 6 Bt (d 1944); *b* 25 April 1914; *Educ* Haileybury; *m* 22 March 1947, Anne, eldest da of late Maj William Albert Gillam, DSO, Border Regt; 1 s, 1 da (Susan Maria b 1949); *Heir* s, Henry William Farrington (*qv*); *Career* 2 Lt RA 1936, Maj 1942, ret 1960, Hon Col 1966; *Recreations* shooting; *Style—* Col Sir Henry Farrington, Bt; Higher Ford, Wiveliscombe, Taunton, Somerset TA4 2RL (☎ 0984 23219)

FARRINGTON, Henry William; s and h of Col Sir Henry Farrington, 7 Bt, *qv*; *b* 27 Mar 1951; *Educ* Haileybury, RAC Cirencester; *m* 1979, Diana Donne, da of Albert Geoffrey Broughton, of North Petherton, Somerset, 2 s (Henry John Albert b 1985, Charles George Donne b 1988); *Career* ARICS; farmer; landowner; *Style—* Henry Farrington, Esq; Castle, Wiveliscombe, Taunton, Somerset TA4 2TJ (☎ 0984 23606)

FARROR, Shelagh Ann (Mrs Nicholas Jones); da of Robert Maitland Farror, of Maidenhead, Berks, and Rosemary Beatrice, *née* Croft (d 1975); *b* 25 Mar 1947; *Educ* St Michael's Sch Limpsfield, St Annes Coll Oxford (BA, MA); *m* 25 Sept 1976, Nicholas Graham Jones, s of Albert Jones; 1 s (Benjamin Nicholas Farror b 5 Aug 1986); *Career* called to the Bar 1970, family law practice; memb Family Law Bar Assoc; *Recreations* sailing, walking, reading, golf; *Clubs* Bar Yacht, Frensham Pond Sailing; *Style—* Miss Shelagh Farror; 3 Hare Ct, Temple, London EC4 (☎ 01 353 7561)

FARROW, Nigel Alexander Emery; s of Arthur Hemsworth Farrow, of Bentley, Hants, and Estelle Frances *née* Emery; *b* 24 Mar 1939; *Educ* Cheltenham Coll, Queens' Coll Cambridge (MA); *m* 2 Dec 1961, Susan, da of Thomas Bertram Daltry (d 1974); 3 da (Miranda b 1965, Sarah b 1967, Imogen b 1970); *Career* publisher; editor Business Mgmnt 1964-67; chm: Xerox Publishing Gp Ltd 1972-82, Ginn & Co Ltd 1972-78, University Microfilms Ltd 1972-82; dir and chm Gower Publishing Gp Ltd, Ashgate Publishing Ltd, Information Publications Int Ltd, Information Billicatruss PTE Ltd, Singapore; pres Cheltonian Soc 1988-; memb Cheltenham Coll Council; tstee New Ashgate Gallery; *Publications* Gower Handbook of Management (ed); The English Libarary (ed); numerous articles: business & management; *Recreations* reading books, looking at pictures; *Style—* Nigel Farrow, Esq; Dipenhall Gate, Dippenhall, Farnham, Surrey; 19 Whitehall, 9-11 Bloomsbury Sq, London; Gower House, Croft Road, Aldershot, Hants

FARROW, Victoria Elizabeth (Mrs Nicholas Elton); *née* Farrow; da of Douglas Henry Farrow, and Belle, *née* Goldberg; *b* 13 June 1960; *Educ* Francis Holland Sch, Chelsea Sch of Art (BA); *m* 7 Dec 1985, Nicholas George Stephen Elton, s of Paul Elton; *Career* mktg mangr J Trevor & Sons 1985-, mktg conslt Allsop & Co 1987-, currently md Victoria Farrow Publicity; *Recreations* freelance journalism, design; *Style—* Miss Victoria Farrow; 45 Burnaby Street, London SW10 OPW; 58 Grosvenor Street, London WIX ODD (☎ 01 629 8151, fax 01 499 5555, car tel 0860 251 468)

FARSTAD, Jan-Arne; s of Petter N Farstad (d 1982), of Aalesund, Norway, and Klara, *née* Bjoerhovde; *b* 9 Sept 1950; *Educ* Jacksonville State Univ USA (BS), Univ of California Berkeley USA (MBA); *m* 9 Sept 1977, Marie-France, da of Edouard Durand (d 1966), of Rio de Janeiro, Brazil; 1 da (Anne-Christine b 29 June 1980); *Career* vice-pres Wells Fargo Bank 1975-83, sr vice-pres Bank of Montreal 1983-87, md Royal Tst Bank 1988-; *Recreations* golf, skiing, classical music; *Clubs* RAC; *Style—* Jan-Arne Farstad, Esq; Royal Trust Bank, Royal Trust Ho, 48-50 Cannon St, London EC4N 6LD (☎ 01 236 6044, fax 01 248 0828, telex 8952879)

FARTHING, (Richard) Bruce (Crosby); s of Col Herbert Hadfield Farthing (d 1978), and Marjorie Cora, *née* Fisher (d 1981); *b* 9 Feb 1926; *Educ* Alleyns Sch, St Catharine's Coll Cambridge (BA, MA); *m* 1, 14 Feb 1959 (m dis 1986), (Anne) Brenda, da of Capt Thomas Williams (d 1961); 1 s (Richard Crosby b 24 July 1962), 1 da (Anne Crosby b 30 Nov 1959); m 2, 6 Nov 1986, Moira Jess Roupell, da of Lt-Col Curties RA (d 1970); *Career* joined RA 1944, RA OCTU 1945-46, cmmnd 1946, served various field regts and 7 RHA in Europe, Egypt and Palestine 1946-47, demobbed as Lt 1948; barr Inner Temple 1954; govt legal serv 1954-59, Chamber of Shipping of the UK: legal advsr 1959, asst gen mangr 1966, sec Ctee of Euro Nat Shipowners 1967-74, sec Ctee of Euro Shipowners Assoc 1967-74, sec gen Cncl of Euro and Japanese Nat Shipowners Assoc (CENSA) 1974- 76, dir gen Cncl of Br Shipping 1976-80, (dep dir gen 1980-83); Rapporteur Sea Tport Cmmn Int C of C 1976 to ICC on maritime affairs 1983-, conslt dir Int Assoc of Dry Cargo & Shipowners 1983-; memb ct of common cncl Corpn of London (Ward of Aldgate) 1982-, pres Aldgate Ward Club 1985 (vice-pres 1984); govr: City of London Sch 1983- (vice-chm Bd of Govrs 1988), SOAS 1985; chm reception ctee for state banquet to King of Norway 1988, tstee Nautical Museums Tst 1983-; Freeman City of London 1978, Liveryman Worshipful Co of Shipwrights 1982 (Freeman 1978); FBIM 1983; Cdr Royal Norwegian Order of Merit 1988; *Books* Aspinalls Maritime Law Cases (ed vol 20, 1961), International Shipping: an introduction to the Policies, Politics and Institutions of the Maritime World (1987); *Recreations* sailing, golf, music; *Clubs* Royal Ocean Racing, MCC, Incogniti Cricket, Rye Golf; *Style—* Bruce Farthing, Esq; Snaylham House, Broad St, Icklesham, East Sussex TN36 4AJ (☎ 0424 812983); 44 St Georges Dr, London SW1V 4BT (☎ 01 834 1211); Fifth Floor, 39 Dover St, London W1X 3RB (☎ 01 629 7079, fax 01 493 7865, telex 291705 HNLON G)

FARTHING, Thomas William; OBE (1983); s of late Thomas Farthing; *b* 19 Dec 1927; *Educ* Middlesbrough HS, Jesus Coll Cambridge (MA, PhD); *m* (m dis); 1 s, 1 da; *Career* metallurgist; IMI Res 1951-58, Beryllium project mangr IMI 1958-62, res mangr Traditional Metals IMI 1962-64, Euro res dir Int Copper Res Assoc 1964-66; md: Wolverhampton Metal Ltd 1966-74, IMI Titanium 1974-, additional responsibility for corporate res and devpt 1983-; cncl memb: The Inst of Metals, SBAC; chm SBAC Materials Gp Ctee, tres and cncl memb BNF Metals Technol Centre Wantage; memb DTI Aviation Ctee, DTI Metals and Minerals Ctee; FEng; *Recreations* walking, reading, music, gardening; *Style—* Thomas Farthing, Esq, OBE; c/o IMI Titanium Ltd, PO Box 704, Birmingham B6 7UR (☎ 021 356 1155, telex 336771)

FATCHETT, Derek John; MP (Lab) Leeds Central 1983-; s of Herbert and Irene Fatchett; *b* 8 August 1945; *Educ* Lincoln Sch, Birmingham Univ, LSE; *m* 1969, Anita Bridgens, *née* Oakes; 2 s; *Career* univ lecturer, cllr Wakefield Met Boro; *Style—* Derek Fatchett, Esq, MP; House of Commons, London SW1

FATHERS, Antony; *b* 27 June 1931; *Educ* Charterhouse, Oxford Univ (MA); *m* 21 July 1962, Elizabeth Margaret, da of Frederick Brewer (d 1963), late Mayor of Oxford; 1 s (Richard b 1967, d 1979), 1 da (Victoria b 1970); *Career* md Czech & Speake 1984-; FID; *Recreations* squash, opera, gardening; *Clubs* IOD; *Style—* Antony Fathers, Esq; 613 Upper Richmond Rad, West Richmond, Surrey; Czech & Speake, 39 Jermyn St, London (☎ 01 980 4567)

FATTORINI, Joseph; MBE (1945), TD; s of Edward Joseph Fattorini (d 1950), of Bradford, and Lilian Mary, *née* Harrop (d 1956); *b* 8 Nov 1912; *Educ* Stonyhurst; *m* 5 June 1941, Mary, da of Maj Edward Joseph Collingwood; 2 s (Peter b 2 May 1942, Edward b 25 Sept 1943), 1 da (Jane (Mrs de Halpert) b 14 Nov 1948); *Career* 2 Lt

West Yorks Regt TA 1938, WWII 1939-45 Maj 2 i/c 601 Regt RA (West Yorks) TA; Empire Stores (Bradford) Ltd: md 1945-65, chm 1965-72, vice chm 1972-75; chm Yorks and Lancs Investmt Tst Ltd until 1975, vice chm and dir Arbathnot Securities (CL) Ltd and Assoc investmt tsts 1975-85, chm Singer & Friedlander (CI) Ltd; non exec dir: Colonnade Reinsurance Ltd, Guernsey Catholic Nat Mutual Ltd (Guernsey); chm: St Bedes GS Bradford until 1973, Cardinal Hinsley and St Margaret Clitheroe GS until 1975, Leeds Area Health Authy Teaching 1973-75; memb: Leeds Regnl Hosp Bd (chm fin and geriatrics) 1952-67, Bradford B Mgmnt Ctee 1948-51, Guernsey Soc for Cancer Relief, Ct Leeds Univ; govr Leeds Utd Teaching Hosp 1966-74, pres Stonyhurst Old Boys Assoc 1974; JP (City of Bradford 1955-75); FBIM, FRSA; Knight of St Gregroy 1963, Knight of the Holy Sepulchre 1963; *Recreations* golf, skiing; *Clubs* Utd Guernsey, Royal Channel Islands YC; *Style—* Joseph Fattorini, Esq, MBE, TD; Saumarez Lodge, The Queens Rd, St Peter Port, Guernsey (☎ 0481 229 11)

FAUCONBERG AND CONYERS, Baronies of (E 1283 and 1509); *see*: Miller, Lady Diana and Lycett, Lady Wendy

FAULDER, Carolyn Mary; *née* Calburn; da of Charles Clement Calburn (d 1977) (*see* Burke's Landed Gentry 18th Edn, vol.3), and Maria Clemencia, *née* Echeverria (d 1969); *b* 13 Feb 1934; *Educ* Convent of the Holy Child Jesus St Leonards on Sea, Bedford Coll, London Univ (BA); *m* 2 June 1956, (m dis 1989), John Sewell Faulder, s of Ronald Sewell Faulder (d 1983); 1 s (Dominic b 1958), 2 da (Sarah b 1957, Clemencia b 1961); *Career* journalist, author and lectr; specialist in: career devpt and work opportunities particularly for women and in socio-medical issues; *Books include* Treat Yourself to Sex, Breast Cancer: A Guide To Its Detection and Early Treatment, Whose Body is It? The Troubling Issue of Informed Consent; *Recreations* gardening, travelling, the company of friends; *Style—* Ms Carolyn Faulder; 25 Belsize Park Gdns, London NW3 4JH (☎ 722 5557)

FAULDS, Andrew Matthew William; MP (Lab) Warley E 1974-; s of Rev Matthew Faulds and Doris Faulds; *b* 1 Mar 1923; *Educ* George Watson's Coll Edinburgh, King Edward VI GS Louth, Daniel Stewart's Sch Edinburgh, Stirling HS, Glasgow Univ; *m* 1945, Bunty Whitfield; 1 da; *Career* actor; formerly with Shakespeare Meml Co Stratford, also TV, radio and films; MP (Lab) Smethwick 1966-74; PPS to min of state for aviation Miny of Technol 1967-68, PMG 1968-69; oppn front bench spokesman arts 1970-73 and 1979-82 (sacked for opposing official Labour policy on Falklands crisis); memb: exec ctee GB China Centre, chm Parly Assoc Euro-Arab Cooperation (UK branch) 1974-, All-Party Heritage Gp, Br Delegation to Cncl of Europe and WEU 1975-80 and 1987-, exec ctee IPU (Br Section) 1983-; *Style—* Andrew Faulds Esq, MP; 14 Albemarle St, London W1 (☎ 01 499 7589)

FAULDS, Ian Craig; s of Basil Craig Faulds, of Bromsgrove, and Paula, *née* Klausner; *b* 4 July 1948; *Educ* Rossall, Univ of Durham (BA, Cert Ed); *m* 20 July 1974, Clare, da of Albert Wiliam Harper (d 1979); 2 s (Matthew b 1977,William b 1984); *Career* asst master King William's Coll IOM 1971-74, dir Shearwater Press Ltd 1975-80, ed The Manxman 1976-78, md Trafalgar Press Ltd 1982-; ed: The Peel City Guardian 1986-, The Ramsey Chronicle 1987-, Manx Life 1988-; chm Peel Chamber of Trade 1986-88; *Recreations* antiques, gardening, walking; *Style—* Ian Faulds Esq; The Lynague, German, Isle of Man, (☎ 0624 842045) 14 Douglas St, Peel, Isle of Man, (☎ 0624 843882)

FAULKNER, Hon Mrs (Deborah Jane); da of 2 Baron MacAndrew; *b* 1956; *Educ* Tudor Hall, Wykham Park Banbury, Winkfield; *m* 1979, Maj Mark William Bingham Faulkner, 5 Royal Inniskillen Dragoon Gds; 2 s (b 1983 and 1987); *Recreations* riding, skiing, tennis, bridge; *Style—* Hon Mrs Faulkner; c/o Dilston House, Aldborough St John, Richmond, Yorks

FAULKNER, Hon (Lucy) Claire; da of Baron Faulkner of Downpatrick (Life Peer, d 1977); *b* 1954; *Educ* Hillcourt Dublin, Moreton Hall Shropshire, Univ of Edinburgh; *Career* Brit Tourist Authy 1979-84; started own business Project Planning (conference and exhibition organiser) 1984; *Recreations* eventing, hunting; *Style—* Hon Claire Faulkner; The Gate Lodge, Spa Road, Ballynahinch, Co Down, Northern Ireland

FAULKNER, Hon David; s of Baron Faulkner of Downpatrick (Life Peer, d 1977); *b* 1951; *Educ* Glenalmond Coll Perthshire, Aberdeen Univ (MA); *m* 28 Aug 1982, (Belinda) Gail, eldest da of James Elliott Wilson, OBE, DL, of White Lodge, Boardmills, Co Down; 2 s, 1 da; *Career* haulage contractor; *Recreations* hunting, sailing; *Style—* The Hon David Faulkner; Highlands, Seaforde, Downpatrick, Co Down, Northern Ireland

FAULKNER, David Edwart Riley; CB (1985); s of Harold Ewart Faulkner (d 1968), of Manchester and London, and Mabel, *née* Riley (d 1960); *b* 23 Oct 1934; *Educ* Manchester GS, Merchant Taylor's, St John's Coll Oxford (MA); *m* 16 Sept 1961, Sheila Jean, da of James Stevenson (d 1985), of Buckinghamshire; 1 s (Martin b 1962), 1 da (Rosemary b 1965); *Career* Nat Serv RA and Intelligence Corps, 2 Lt 1957-59; Home Office: asst princ 1959, princ 1963, asst sec 1969, private sec to the Home Sec 1969, Prison Dept 1970, Police Dept 1975, asst under sec of state 1976 (seconded to the Cabinet Office 1978-79), dir of operational policy Prison Dept 1980, dep under-sec of state Criminal and Res and Statistical Depts 1982; memb: United Nations Ctee on Crime Prevention and Control, advsy bd of Helsinki Inst for Crime Prevention and Control; *Style—* David Faulkner, Esq, CB; Home Office, 50 Queen Anne's Gate, London SW1 (☎ 01 273 2143)

FAULKNER, Sir Eric Odin; MBE (1945), TD; s of Sir Alfred Edward Faulkner, CB, CBE (d 1963), and Edith Florence, *née* Nicoll; *b* 21 April 1914; *Educ* Bradfield, Corpus Christi Coll Cambridge (hon fell); *m* 1939, Joan Mary, da of Lt-Col F A M Webster; 1 s, 1 da; *Career* WWII Lt-Col RA; banker; chm Glyn Mills & Co 1963-68, dir: Hudson's Bay Co 1950-70, Vickers plc 1957-79; advsy dir Unilever plc 1979-84, dir and dep chm Finance for Indust 1977-80; chm: Union Discount Co 1959-70 (dir 1949-70), Lloyds Bank Ltd 1968-77, Industrial Soc 1973-76; pres Br Bankers Assoc 1979-83; warden Bradfield Coll 1965-83; kt 1974; *Recreations* fishing (formerly cricket and associaton football (CUAFC XI 1935)); *Style—* Sir Eric Faulkner, MBE, TD; Farriers Field, Sevenoaks Rd, Ightham, Kent TN15 9AA

FAULKNER, Hugh Branston; OBE (1980); s of Frank Faulkner (d 1964), and Ethel, *née* Branston (d 1968); *b* 8 June 1916; *Educ* Lutterworth GS; *m* 1954, Anne Carlton, *née* Milner; 1 s (Anthony), 1 da (Jane); *Career* admin asst City of Leicester Educn Ctee 1936-46, organising sec Fellowship of Reconciliation 1946-54, christian peace delegate USSR 1952, lectr int affrs USA 1953, hon dir Voluntary and Christian Serv 1954-79 (tstee); dir Help the Aged (fndg memb) 1961-83, delegate and speaker UN World Assembly on Ageing Vienna 1982, dir: Asthma Research Cncl 1983-88; charity conslt 1988-; tstee: Phyllis Tst, World in Need Tst; Lester Tst; Quest for a Test for Cancer Tst; memb exec ctee Cncl for Music in Hosps 1983-; *Recreations* music, gardening; *Clubs* Nat Liberal; *Style—* Hugh Faulkner, Esq, OBE; Longfield, 4 One Tree Lane, Beaconsfield, Bucks HP9 2BU (☎ 0494 674 769)

FAULKNER, Cdr Hugh Douglas Younger; s of Rear Adm Hugh Webb Faulkner, CB, CBE, DSO, DL (d 1969), and Olave Mary, *née* Younger, DStJ; *b* 17 May 1931; *Educ* West Downs Winchester, RNC Dartmouth; *m* 28 July 1956, Fiona Naomi, da of Brigadier Dominick Andrew Sidney Browne, CBE (d 1981), of Breaghwy, Castlebar, Co Mayo; 2 s (Christopher Gerald b 15 Aug 1958, Anthony Dominick Hugh b 5 April 1961); *Career* HMS Liverpool 1949-50, HMS Sheffield 1952-54, HMS Hornet (CO MTB Dark Antagonist) 1954-56, HMS Mercury (signal offr qualifying course) 1957-58, staff of C in C Home Fleet (FCA) 1959-60, HMS Mercury 1961-62, staff of SNO W Indies 1962-64, staff course RNC Greenwich 1964, HMS Mercury 1965-66, MOD 1967-70, Cdr HMS Mercury 1970-72, 2 i/c HMS Collingwood 1973-75, staff of C in C Naval Home Cmd 1975-78, ret 1978; sec Royal Warrant Holders Assoc 1979-; hon field trial sec Labrador Retriever Club 1989; *Recreations* shooting, fishing, golf, working and training gundogs; *Clubs* Army and Navy; *Style—* Cdr Hugh Faulkner; Grenville Hall, Droxford, Hants (☎ 0489 877 576); 7 Buckingham Gate, London SW1 (☎ 01 828 2268)

FAULKNER, John Richard Hayward; s of Capt Richard Hayward Ollerton Faulkner (d 1943), and Lilian Elizabeth, *née* Carrigan; *b* 29 May 1941; *Educ* Archbp Holgate's Sch, Keble Coll Oxford (BA); *m* 1970, Janet Gill, da of Alfred George Herbert Cummings; 2 da (Abigail b 1976, Emma b 1984), 2 step da (Zoe b 1963, Amanda b 1966); *Career* worked with sev cos inc: Prospect Theatre Co (fndr memb), Cambridge Theatre Co, Sixty-Nine Theatre Co 1964-72; drama dir Scottish Arts Cncl 1972-76, Arts Cncl of GB 1976-83, assoc producer and later head of artistic planning Nat Theatre 1983-88; theatre and mgmnt conslt 1988-, UK rep American-Anglo-Soviet Theatre Initiative 1988-; non-exec dir Galactic Smallholdings Ltd, govr Arts Educnl Schs, chm Assoc of Br Theatre Technicians; *Recreations* intricacies and wildernesses; *Style—* John Faulkner, Esq; 33 Hadley Gdns, London W4 4NU (☎ 01 995 3041)

FAULKNER, John Selway; s of Joseph Robert Faulkner, of Witts Cottage, Arlington Green, Bibury, Cirencester, Glos, and Rosalind Violet, *née* Selway; *b* 30 May 1933; *Educ* Univ Coll Sch, Coll of Estate Mgmnt London Univ; *m* 22 June 1963, Patricia Ann, da of Alfred Richard Harrold; 1 s (Julian Miles b 2 Dec 1971); *Career* cmmnd RA 1956, 3 Div HQ Staff 1956-57; chartered surveyor; with Folkard & Hayward 1959-66, equity ptnr Keith Cardale Groves 1972- (joined 1967-); vice-pres Execs Assoc of GB 1986- (chm 1985-86); Freeman City of London 1984, Worshipful Co of Farriers 1985; FRICS 1974; *Recreations* national hunt racing, rugby union, cricket, music; *Style—* John Faulkner, Esq; 65 Sheringham Queensmead, St John's Wood Park, London NW8 6RB (☎ 01 586 1205); 22 Grosvenor Square, Mayfair, London W1X 9LF (☎ 01 629 6604, fax 01 495 0150, car tel 0836 661 0568, telex 27839)

FAULKNER, Hon (James) Michael (Sewell); s of Baron Faulkner of Downpatrick (Life Peer, d 1977); *b* 1956; *Educ* Glenalmond Univ of Aberdeen (LLB); *Career* business; *Style—* Hon Michael Faulkner; 1 Grassmarket, Edinburgh

FAULKNER, Richard Oliver; s of Harold Ewart Faulkner (d 1968), and Mabel, *née* Riley; *b* 22 Mar 1946; *Educ* Merchant Taylors', Worcester Coll Oxford (MA); *m* 5 July 1968, Susan, da of Donald James Heyes (d 1978); 2 da (Julia b 1969, Tamsin b 1970); *Career* communications advsr: Railway Trade Unions 1976-77, Br Railway Bd 1977-, Br Gas plc 1980-, TSB Gp plc 1987-, Interparly Union 1987-, Civil Aviation Authy 1988-; vice chm Tport 2000 Ltd, md Westminster Communications Ltd 1988-; parly candidate (Lab): Devizes 1970 and Feb 1974, Monmouth Oct 1974, Huddersfield W 1979; memb Merton Borough Cncl 1971-78, communications advsr to opposition leader gen election 1987, co-fndr pty jl The House Magazine; dep chm The Football Tst 1986- (fndr tstee 1979-83, sec 1983-86), chm Camden Assoc 1986-, memb Sports Cncl 1986-88, chm Womens FA 1988-; MIPR 1977; *Recreations* collecting Lloyd George memorabilia, tinplate trains, watching association football, travelling by railway; *Clubs* Reform; *Style—* Richard Faulkner, Esq; Crusader House, 14 Pall Mall, London SW1Y 5LU (☎ 01 321 0699, fax 01 925 2206, telex 917700)

FAULKNER OF DOWNPATRICK, Baroness; Lucy Barbara Ethel; CBE; da of William John Harkness Forsythe (d 1960), of Bangor, and Jane Ethel, *née*, Sewell; *b* 1 July 1925; *Educ* Trinity Coll Dublin; *m* 1951, Baron Faulkner of Downpatrick (Life Peer d 1977); 2 s, 1 da; *Career* nat govr BBC NI 1978-85; chm Broadcasting Cncl NI 1981-85; co dir; former journalist with Belfast Telegraph; genealogist; tstee Ulster Historical Fndn 1980-, govr Belfast Linen Hall Library, 1983-; memb NI Tourist Bd 1985-; chm NI Advsy Bd of Salvation Army; *Recreations* hunting, dressage, gardening, book collecting; *Clubs* Royal Overseas League; *Style—* The Rt Hon Lady Faulkner of Downpatrick, CBE; Toberdoney, Seaforde, Downpatrick, Co Down, NI

FAULKS, Edward Peter Lawless; s of Judge Peter Faulks, MC, of Downs Cottage, Boxford, Berks, and Pamela, *née* Lawless; *b* 19 August 1950; *Educ* Wellington, Jesus Coll Oxford (MA); *Career* called to the Bar Middle Temple 1973, practises SE circuit; *Recreations* cricket; *Clubs* Garrick; *Style—* Edward Faulks, Esq; 26 Colville Rd, London W11 (☎ 01 221 4168); 6 King's Bench Walk, Temple, London EC4 (☎ 01 353 9901)

FAULKS, Esmond James; s of Sir Neville Major Ginnel Faulks, MBE, TD (d 1985), and Bridget Marigold, *née* Bodley (d 1962); *b* 11 June 1946; *Educ* Uppingham, Sidney Sussex Coll Cambridge (MA); *m* 12 Sept 1972, Pamela Margaret, da of William Arthur Ives, of Almora, Rockcliffe, Kircudbright; 1 s (Sam b 17 Oct 1973), 1 da (Nicola b 6 March 1976); *Career* barr; rec Crown Ct 1987; *Recreations* country pursuits; *Style—* Esmond Faulks, Esq; Chesterwood, Haydon Bridge, Northumberland (☎ 0434 84 329); 51 Westgate Road, Newcastle-upon-Tyne (☎ 091 2320541)

FAULKS, His Hon Judge; Peter Ronald; MC (1943); s of late Maj James Faulks, of Reigate Heath, Surrey, and A M, *née* Ginner; *b* 24 Dec 1917; *Educ* Tonbridge, Sidney Sussex Coll Cambridge; *m* 1949, Pamela Brenda, da of late Philip Henry (Peter) Lawless; 2 s; *Career* slr 1949-80, rec Crown Ct 1972-80, dep chm Agricultural Land Tribunal (SE England) 1972-80, a circuit judge 1980-; *Recreations* country life; *Clubs* MCC, Farmers'; *Style—* His Hon Judge Faulks, MC; Downs Cottage, Boxford, Newbury, Berks (☎ 048 838 382)

FAULL, David Wenlock; s of Eldred Faull (d 1964), of Newquay, Cornwall, and Mary Jessie, *née* Wenlock (d 1982) ; *b* 25 Feb 1929; *Educ* Taunton Sch; *Career* admitted slr 1954; registrar and legal sec Diocese of: Chelmsford 1963, Southwark 1963, St Albans 1963-78, London; legal sec to Bishop of Rochester 1963, chapter clerk St Paul's

Cathedral; sr ptnr Winckworth & Pemberton; chm Ecclesiastical Law Assoc, tres Ecclesiastical Law Soc; considerable involvement in charitable housing; FRSA; *Recreations* walking, theatre; *Clubs* Athenaeum; *Style—* David Faull, Esq; c/o Winckwork & Pemberton, 35 Great Peter Street, Westminster, London SW1P 2LR (☎ 01 222 7381, fax 01 222 1614, car tel 0860 823 212, telex 895 5719)

FAURE, Eric Simon Noel; s of Henry Martin Frederick Faure (d 1937), and Anna Elizabeth Van Der Graf; *b* 25 Dec 1913; *Educ* Rugby, Ecole d'Commerce Neuchâtel Switzerland, Univ Coll Oxford; *m* 25 June 1941, Irene, da of Edward Battes (d 1933); 2 s (Andrew b 1948, John (twin) b 1948), 1 da (Caroline b 1949); *Career* Sqdn Ldr RAF, posted to Air Miny 1942, seconded as air advsr Bletchley Park 1942-46; dir HMF Fayre & Co 1937-, chm Faure Fairclough Ltd 1977; jt pres United Oilseeds Marketing until 1987; memb of Baltic Exchange (as princ 1937-) pres Baltic Golfing Soc 1972-87; semi ret but still active in arbitration and ctees concerning vegetable seeds and oils; Liveryman Worshipful Co of Skinners 1943-; *Recreations* golf, bridge; *Clubs* Rye & Thorpeness Golf; *Style—* Eric S N Faure, Esq; 15 Pishiobury Drive, Sawbridgeworth, Herts; Federation of Oils Seeds & Fats Associations (☎ 01 283 5511)

FAURE WALKER, Mrs Roderick; Diana Constance; o da of Maj Kenneth Arthur Seth-Smith, and his 1 wife Doris Roberta, *née* McKergow; *b* 3 June 1921; *m* 1, 2 Sept 1948 (m dis 1956), Charles Stewart M'Donnell Vane-Tempest (gggs of 3 Marquess of Londonderry); 1 s, 1 da; m 2, 23 Jan 1961, as his 2 w, 2 Viscount Buckmaster (d 1974); m 3, 31 Aug 1982, as his 2 wife, Roderick Edward Faure Walker, *qv*; *Career* served in War Organisation of the British Red Cross Soc 1934-45 (despatches 1945); *Style—* Mrs Roderick Faure Walker; Ringwold House, Middle Wallop, Hants; 74 Cheyne Court, Roy Hospital Rd, SW3 (☎ 01 352 2593)

FAURE WALKER, Henry (Harry) John; s of Lt-Col Henry William Faure Walker, and Elizabeth Alice Catherine, *née* Fordham; *b* 25 July 1940; *Educ* Eton, Trinity Coll Cambridge (BA); *m* 5 Nov 1966, Elizabeth, da of Maj William Boyd Kennedy Shaw, OBE, of Elford, Staffordshire; 2 s (William b 1970, Henry b 1972), 1 da (Alice b 1968); *Career* regnl dir: Barclays Bank plc, Cambridge regn; dir H W Faure Walker Farms Ltd 1969-; *Recreations* field sports, garden; *Style—* Harry Faure Walker, Esq; c/o Barclays Bank plc, Cambridge Regional Office, Cambridge

FAURE WALKER, Hon Mrs (Angela) Mary; *née* Chaloner; da of 2 Baron Gisborough, TD, JP; *b* 5 April 1925; *m* 27 Nov 1946 (m dis 1973), as his 1 wife, Roderick Edward Faure Walker *qv*; 2 s (Rupert, *qv*, James b 1948, m Vivian Knight), 1 da (Camilla b 1953 d 1981); *Style—* Hon Mrs Faure Walker; Geranium Cottage, Ditchling, Sussex

FAURE WALKER, Roderick Edward; yr s of Henry Faure Walker (d 1940) of Highley Manor, Balcombe, Sussex (and bro of Lt-Col Henry Faure Walker of Sandon Bury, Herts), and his 2 wife, Edith Ina, *née* Bartholomew (d 1940); *b* 26 Jan 1914; *Educ* Eton, Corpus Christi Coll Oxford; *m* 1, 27 Nov 1946 (m dis 1973), Hon (Angela) Mary Chaloner, *qv*, da 2 Baron Gisborough (d 1951); 2 s, 1 da (d 1981); m 2, 31 Aug 1982, Viscountess Buckmaster (Diana Constance, *qv*); *Career* slr 1947, ptnr Allen & Overy (Slrs) 1950-56; dir Hall Bros Steamship Co Ltd 1955-80; memb Lloyd's; former CC E Sussex, memb cncl Royal Coll of Music 1979-84; churchwarden St George's Hanover Sq 1949-; *Clubs* Boodle's; *Style—* Roderick Faure Walker, Esq; Ringwold House, Middle Wallop, Stockbridge, Hants (☎ 0264 781230)

FAURE WALKER, Rupert Roderick; er s of Maj Roderick Faure Walker and Hon Mrs Angela Faure Walker, *qv*; *b* 9 Sept 1947; *Educ* Eton, Bristol Univ (BSc); *m* 1975, Sally Anne Vivienne, MB, BChir da of Lt-Cdr Francis John Sidebotham, RN; 1 s (Nicholas b 1978), 2 da (Julia b 1980, Joanna b 1984); *Career* dir Samuel Montagu 1982-; FCA; *Style—* Rupert Faure Walker, Esq; Abbotswood, Wickham Bishops, Essex; c/o Samuel Montagu & Co Ltd, 10 Lower Thames St EC3 (☎ 01 260 9000)

FAUSSET, Robin John; *b* 6 Jan 1925; *Educ* Haileybury, Magdalene Coll Cambridge (MA); *m* 10 July 1965, Sarah Elizabeth, da of Hamilton Walters (d 1983); 2 s (Rupert b 1966, Adam b 1968); *Career* cmmnd 2 Cavalry IA 1946, transferred 17/21 Lancers 1947; served Syria, Lebanon, Egypt, India, Palestine; copywriter Masius & Ferguson 1951, sales promotion mangr Readers Digest (Canada) 1954, account dir Ogilvy & Mather 1955-68, md Mathers & Streets 1969, chm and chief exec: Mathers & Bensons 1971-78, Foster Turner & Benson 1977-78; farmer 1979-; cncl memb: Devonshire Assoc 1983-84, Devon Gardens Tst 1987-; *Books* The Creation of the Gardens at Castle Hill; *Recreations* writing, sheep, garden design, architecture; *Style—* Robin Fausset, Esq; Pyne Farm, Black Dog, Crediton, Devon (☎ 0884 860695)

FAVELL, Anthony Rowland; MP (Cons Stockport 1983-); s of Arnold Rowland Favell and Hildegard Wilhelmene Marie Weevpas; *b* 29 May 1939; *Educ* St Bees Cumbria, Sheffield Univ; *m* 1966, Susan Rosemary Taylor; 1 s, 1 da; *Career* slr, contested (C) Bolsover 1979; parly private sec to Rt Hon John Mayor MP (chief sec to the Treasy) 1987-; *Style—* Anthony Favell, Esq, MP; House of Commons, London SW1

FAWCETT, Sir James Edmund Sandford; DSC (1942), QC (1984); s of Rev Joseph Fawcett (d 1942), and Edith Annie, *née* Scattergood (d 1942); *b* 16 April 1913; *Educ* Rugby, New Coll Oxford; *m* 7 Aug 1937, (Frances) Beatrice, 2 da of late Dr Elias Avery Lowe; 1 s (Edmund b 1946), 4 da (Sarah b 1939, Charlotte b 1942, Philippa b 1950, Sophia b 1957); *Career* WWII served RN; barr 1937-39 and 1950-55, asst legal advsr to FO 1945-50, gen counsel IMF 1955-60, dir of studies Royal Inst of Int Affairs 1969-73, pres Euro Cmmn of Human Rights 1972-78 (memb 1962-84), prof of int law King's Coll London 1976-80 (emeritus prof 1980), memb Inst of Int Law 1973-, chm Br Inst 1977-81; kt 1984; *Style—* Sir James Fawcett, DSC; 20 Murray St, 80 Banbury Rd, Oxford

FAWCETT, Robert; MBE (1945), TD (1946); s of late Percival Charles Fawcett; *b* 16 June 1917; *Educ* Rugby, Trinity Coll Oxford; *m* 1939, Esmé Boileau, da of Lt-Col Nevill George Boileau Henderson, DSO; 1 s, 1 da (and 1 child decd); *Career* Lt Col RA; serv: UK, NW Europe; ptnr Messrs Jackson Taylor Abernethy & Co 1948-1976; company directorships included: Andrew Weir & Co Ltd, Utd Baltic Corpn Ltd, Spink & Son Ltd 1977-84; ret 1984; gen cmmr of Income Taxes 1984-; chm: investmt ctee Merchant Navy Offrs Pension Fund, Ensign Tst plc, Merchant Navy Investmt Mgmnt Ltd; dep chm: CDFC Tst plc, Kent and E Sussex Regnl Ctee of Nat Tst; FCA; *Recreations* reading, travelling; *Clubs* MCC; *Style—* Robert Fawcett, Esq, MBE, TD; Vine House, Appledore, Ashford, Kent TN26 2BU (☎ 023 383 260)

FAWCUS, Maj-Gen Graham Ben; s of Col Geoffrey Arthur Ross Fawcus, OBE (d 1972), of 39 St Catherine's Rd, Hayling Island, Hants, and Helen Sybil Graham, *née* Stronach; *b* 17 Dec 1937; *Educ* Wycliffe Coll Stonehouse Glos, RMA Sandhurst, King's Coll Cambridge (BA, MA); *m* 23 July 1966, Diana Valerie, da of Dr Patrick John Spencer-Philips, of Levells Hall, Bildeston, Suffolk; 2 s (Jeremy b 1967, Caspian b 1969), 1 da (Abigail b 1972); *Career* cmmnd RE 1958, 2 Lt (later Lt) troop cmd 33 Ind FD Sqdn RE Cyprus 1959-60, Lt (later Capt) troop cmd 25 Corps Engr Regt BAOR 1963-65, GSO3 (Ops) HQ 19 Inf Bde Borneo and UK (Colchester) 1965-68, Adj 35 Corps Engr Regt 1968, Capt (later Maj) RMCS Shrivenham and Staff Coll Camberley 1969-70, Maj GS02 (W) MG0 Sec 3 MOD 1971-72, OC 39 FD Sqdn RE BAOR 1973-75, DAAG AG7 MOD 1975-76, Lt-Col GSO1 (DS) Staff Coll Camberley 1977-78, CO 25 Engr Regt BAOR 1978-81, Col Cabinet Off 1981, Brig Cmdt RSME 1982-83, ACOS HQ 1 (Br) Corps BAOR 1984-85, Maj-Gen Chief Jt Servs Liaison Orgn, Maj-Gen COS Live Oak SHAPE 1986-89; *Recreations* skiing, tennis, wind surfing, furniture restoring, bird watching, Scottish Dancing; *Style—* Maj-Gen Graham Fawcus; c/o Lloyds Bank Ltd, Cox's & King's Branch, 6 Pall Mall, London SW1Y 5NH; Chief of Staff, Live Oak Shape BFPO 26 (☎ 01032 6544 2600)

FAWCUS, Sir (Robert) Peter; KBE (1964), CMG (1960); s of Arthur Francis Fawcus, OBE (d 1950), of Claygate, Surrey; *b* 30 Sept 1915; *Educ* Charterhouse, Clare Coll Cambridge; *m* 1943, Isabel Constance, da of late Simon Ethelston; 1 s, 1 da; *Career* serv WWII RNVR; barr 1941; Overseas Civil Serv: admin Basutoland 1946-54, govt sec Bechuanaland Protectorate 1954-59, resident cmmr 1959-63, Queen's cmmr 1963-65, ret; *Recreations* gardening; *Clubs* Royal Cwlth Soc; *Style—* Sir Peter Fawcus, KBE, CMG; Dochart House, Killin, Perthshire (☎ 056 72 225)

FAWCUS, Judge Simon James David; s of Gp Capt Ernest Augustus Fawcus (d 1966), and Joan Shaw (Jill), *née* Stokes; *b* 12 July 1938; *Educ* Aldenham, Trinity Hall Cambridge (BA, MA); *m* 12 March 1966, Joan Mary, da of William John Oliphant, of Morgans Farm, Drayton Beauchamp, nr Aylesbury, Bucks; 1 s (Adrian John Oliphant b 10 April 1974), 4 da (Juliet Jane b 11 March 1970, Meriel Ann b 13 Dec 1972, Madeline Clare b 22 Sept 1975, Annabel Barbara (twin) b 22 Sept 1975); *Career* called to the Bar Gray's Inn 1961, N circuit 1962-85, rec Crown Ct 1981-85, circuit judge 1985-; memb Ctee of Cncl of Circuit Judges 1985-; *Recreations* tennis, rackets, golf, music, bridge; *Clubs* MCC, Manchester Tennis and Racquet; *Style—* His Hon Judge Simon Fawcus; Rosehill, Brook Lane, Alderley Edge, Cheshire; Courts of Justice, Crown Sq, Manchester

FAWKE, Pamela; OBE (1981); da of Laurence Drader (d 1963), of Lyndon, Leics, and Mabel Blanche, *née* Kidner (d 1987); *b* 14 May 1919; *Educ* Hamilton House Tunbridge Wells; *m* 3 May 1947, Leslie Arthur Fawke (d 1982), s of Arthur Fawke (d 1945); 2 s (William Laurence b 1948, Richard Arthur Leslie b 1950); *Career* 2 Offr WRNS 1941-47; dir Rudgwick Brickworks 1978-82, chm 1982- ; *Style—* Mrs Pamela Fawke, OBE; The Cottage, The Common, Cranleigh, Surrey GU6 8SJ; Rudgwick Brickworks, Lynwick Street, Rudgwick, W Sussex (fax 0483 72 3357)

FAWKES, Brig Lindsay Valentine Francis; DSO (1943), OBE (1958), MC (1942); s of Valentine Hawkesworth Francis Fawkes (d 1954), and Blanche Isobel Mary, *née* Neill (d 1931); *b* 6 May 1913; *Educ* Cheltenham, RMA Woolwich; *m* 30 May 1945, Marjorie Josephine, da of Lt Col William Edward Kemble (d 1954); 1 s (Francis Antony b 1953), 1 da (Gillian Mary b 1950); *Career* cmd RA 1933; served India 1934-39; active service in Western Desert, Sicily, Italy, Korea 1950-51, Malaysia and Suez 1956; Lt-Col 1955, cmdg 33 Parachute Field Regt RA; Col 1958, Brig 1961; ret 1968; *Recreations* fishing, shooting, gardening; *Clubs* Naval and Military; *Style—* Brig Lindsay V F Fawkes, DSO, OBE, MC; Lanvean Churt (☎ 025 125 2815)

FAWKES, Sir Randol Francis; s of Edward Ronald Fawkes and Mildred, *née* McKinney; *b* 20 Mar 1924; *Educ* in the Bahamas; *m* 1951, Jacqueline *née* Bethel; 3 s, 1 da; *Career* attorney-at-law Bahamas 1948-; MHA for Progressive Lib Party 1956, fndr and pres Bahamas Fedn of Labour, fndr People's Penny Savings Bank 1951; kt 1977; *Style—* Sir Randol Fawkes; PO Box N 7625, John F Kennedy Drive, Nassau, NP, Bahamas

FAWSSETT, Robert Seymour; s of Capt Arthur Charles Fawssett, DSO, RN (d 1961), of Lindfield, Sussex, and Sybil Frieda, *née* Salaman (d 1977); *b* 4 May 1931; *Educ* Bradfield, Pembroke Coll Cambridge (BA); *m* 17 May 1958, Philippa Karen, d of George Philip Fox, MBE (d 1970), of Glasshouses, nr Harrogate, Yorks; 1 s (Edward b 1962), 2 da (Nicola b 1961, Katherine b 1965); *Career* Nat Serv 2 Lt RA 1950-51, TA 1951-58, ret Actg Capt RA; admitted slr 1957, sr ptnr Biddle & Co 1976- (ptnr 1958-); memb Lowtonian Soc 1977; *Recreations* gardening, tennis, opera; *Clubs* Naval, City Univ; *Style—* Robert Fawssett, Esq; Biddle & Co, 1 Grisham St, London EC2V 7BU (☎ 01 606 9301, fax 01 606 3305, telex 888197)

FAY, His Hon Judge Edgar Stewart; QC (1956); s of Sir Sam Fay (d 1953), of Romsey, Hants, and Beatrice Charlotte Scamell (d 1957); *b* 8 Oct 1908; *Educ* Courtenay Lodge Sch, McGill Univ (BA), Pembroke Coll Cambridge (MA); *m* 1, Kathleen Margaret, eld da of Charles Hewitt Buell, of Montreal, Quebec, and Brockville, Ontario; 3 s (Charles, Peter, William); m 2, Jenny Julie Marie Henriette, yr da of Dr William Roosegaarde Bisschop (d 1945), of Lincoln's Inn London; 1 s (Francis); *Career* barr Inner Temple 1932, master of the bench Inner Temple 1962, practised at common law and parly bars 1932-71, rec: Andover 1956-61, Bournemouth 1961-64, Plymouth 1964-71; dep chm Hants Quarter Sessions 1960-71; official ref of the Supreme Ct and Circuit Judge 1971-80; memb: Bar Cncl 1955-59 and 1966-70, Senate of Four Inns of Court 1970-72, Compton Ctee on NI 1971; chm Inquiry into Munich Air Disaster 1960 and 1969, Inquiry into Crown Agents 1975-77; FCIArb 1981; *Books* Life of Mr Justice Swift (1939), Official Referee's Business (1983, 2 edn 1988); *Style—* His Hon Judge Fay, QC; Knox End, Ashdon, Saffron walden, Essex (☎ 079 984 275); 13 Egbert St, London NW1 (☎ 01 586 0725); 3 Temple Gardens, Temple, London EC4 (☎ 01 353 0832)

FAYRER, Sir John Lang Macpherson; 4 Bt (UK 1896); s of Lt-Cdr Sir Joseph Herbert Spens, 3 Bt, DSC, RNVR (d 1976), and Helen Diana Scott, *née* Lang (d 1961); *b* 18 Oct 1944; *Educ* Edinburgh Acad, Strathclyde Univ; *Heir* none; *Career* memb HCIMA; chief catering officer 1973-77; hotel night mangr 1977-80; clerical offr Edinburgh Univ 1980-; *Recreations* reading, walking, riding; *Clubs* Univ of Edinburgh Staff; *Style—* Sir John Fayrer, Bt; Overhailes, Haddington, E Lothian (☎ (062 086) 0444); 9 Westfield St, Edinburgh 11; Tourism and Recreation Research Unit, Univ of Edinburgh (☎ 031 667 1011)

FAZAKERLEY, (Andrew) Neil; s of George Fazakerley of Denmead, Portsmouth, and Muriel Boyd, Fazakerley (d 1968); *b* 22 Mar 1950; *Educ* Abergele GS, Manchester Poly (BA); *m* 25 Sept 1976, Vibeke Lunn, da of Lt-Col Jens Christian Axel Eric Lunn (d 1959), of Copenhagen; 3 s (Sam b 1979, Jack b 1980, Pip b 1987);

Career creative dir and bd dir: Davidson Pearce Ltd 1982-87, Boase Massimi Pollitt Ltd 1987-88; memb D & AD; *Style*— Neil Fazakerley, Esq; Hope Cottage, 42 Nelson Rd, Harrow on the Hill, Middx HA1 3ET (☎ 01 864 0309); BMP Davidson Pearce Ltd, 12 Bishops Bridge Rd, London WC2 6AA (☎ 01 258 3979)

FEAR, (Kenneth) Winston; s of Herbert Fear (d 1935), of Taunton, and Lillie Ida, *née* Gillard (d 1953); *b* 28 Feb 1917; *Educ* Taunton Sch, RMCS; *m* 15 May 1943, Eileen Mary, da of Dr Harry Reginald Allingham (d 1946), of Totnes; 2 s (Patrick b 1949, Michael b 1951); *Career* served as Maj RAOC 1940-59, Inspecting Ordnance Offr 1942, Italian Campaign 1943-47, Gen Stockwell's HQ Suez Operation 1956-57, dir UK Tning Royal Inst of Public Admin 1961-77; Gen Cmmr Income Tax St Marylebone 1976-87, D L Freeman & Co Slrs 1977-80; sec: Nat Food and Drink Fedn 1980-81, Inst of Maintenance and Building Mgmnt 1980-87; fell Inst of Mgmnt Services 1970, hon fell Inst of Maintenance and Building Mgmnt 1987; *Recreations* photography, gardening, carpentry, philately; *Clubs* RAC; *Style*— Winston Fear, Esq; Cutlers Close, Pilton, Shepton Mallet, Somerset BA4 4NY (☎ Pilton 683)

FEARN, Alan d'Arcy; s of Charles Henry Fearn, MM (d 1982), and Gladys Lily, *née* d'Arcy Jones; *b* 24 July 1924; *Educ* Bury GS, Terra Nova Sch Southport, Shrewsbury, Guy's Hosp Dental Sch; *m* 1, 1947, (m dis 1947), Kathleen, da of Frank Humphries (d 1955); 2 da (Gail b 1947, Cheryl b 1950); m 2, 19 Aug 1966, Doreen, da of Walter Milne, of Rochdale; *Career* RAF Air Gunner Sgt 1942-46; Dental surgeon LOS RCS (Eng); elected memb Gen Dental Cncl 1962- (longest serving elected memb); pres Br Dental Assoc 1986-87; Parly (C) candidate; Ashton under Lyne 1970, Accrington Feb 1974, Middleton & Prestwich Oct 1974, Ashton under Lyne 1979, Rochdale 1983; dep ldr Tameside MBC 1978-89, Generalist Tameside and Glossop Area Health Authy 1976-85; sr steward Nat Greyhound Racing Club 1988- (steward 1974-); *Recreations* greyhound racing, gardening, theatre; *Clubs* Naval and Military London, The Royal Soc of Medicine London; *Style*— Alan Fearn, Esq; Tall Trees, Bent Meadows, Rochdale OL12 6LF (☎ 0706 45276)

FEARN, (Charles) Barry d'Arcy; s of Charles Henry Fearn (d 1982), and Gladys Lily, *née* d'Arcy Jones (d 1983); *b* 4 Mar 1934; *Educ* Shrewsbury, Gonville and Caius Coll Cambridge (MA, MB, BChir), St Mary's Hosp Univ of London; *m* 21 April 1962, Gay Barbara Ann, da of Capt Edward Smythe (d 1940); 1 s (Giles b 1964), 3 da (Alexandra b 1967, Victoria b 1971, Jocasta b 1973); *Career* Nat Serv Capt RAMC, MO Royal Irish Fusiliers 1960, Capt RAMC (V) TAVR Regtl Surgn Kent and Co of London Yeo 1966, Maj RAMC (V) TA Regtl MO 71 YEO Signal Regt 1981; sr lectr and hon conslt Orthopaedic Surgn Khartoum Univ Sudan 1969-70, sr registrar Nuffield Orthopaedic Centre Oxford 1970-72; conslt orthopaedic surgn 1972-: Royal Sussex County Hosp Brighton, Cuckfield Hosp W Sussex; memb Hove Civic Soc, Haywards Heath Amenity Soc; Freeman City of London, Liveryman Worshipful Soc of Apothecaries of London; memb RSH, FRCS (Eng and Edin) 1967; memb Société Internationale de Chirurgie Ortopaedique et Traumatologie 1982; *Recreations* rowing coaching, opera, the theatre, territorial army, racing; *Clubs* Leander; *Style*— Barry Fearn, Esq; Colwell House, Haywards Heath, West Sussex

FEARN, Brian Leslie; s of Leslie Fearn, of Stonycroft, Stevenage, and Eileen Lily, *née* Keeley (d 1966); *b* 5 April 1954; *Educ* Hitchin Boys Grammar; *m* March 1980, Shree Devi, da of Pradip Patul Rayarappan, of Kuala Lumpur; *Career* information technology strategist; corporate structure conslt; ACMA, ACCA, JdipMA; *Recreations* DIY, swimming, piano, golf; *Style*— Brian L Fearn, Esq; Furnace House Farm, Four Elms, Edenbridge, Kent; Midland Bank plc, Poultry, London EC2P 2BX

FEARN, Ronnie; OBE (1985), MP (Lab) Southport 1987; s of James Fearn (d 1972), of 201 Meolscop Rd, Southport, and Martha Ellen, *née* Hodge; *b* 6 Feb 1931; *Educ* King George V GS Southport; *m* 11 June 1955, Joyce Edna, da of John Dugan (d 1945) of 51 Salisbury St Southport; 1 s (Martin John b 1962), 1 da (Susan Lynn b 1959); *Career* Nat Serv 2 tours RN as first class electrician; sr asst bank mangr with Royal Bank of Scotland plc 1947-87; pres Southport and Waterloo Athletic Club; FIB; *Recreations* badminton, athletics, drama, politics; *Clubs* Nat Lib; *Style*— Ronnie Fearn, Esq, MP; Norcliffe, 56 Norwood Ave, Southport (☎ 0704 28577); House of Commons, London SW1A 0AA

FEARON, Daniel; s of Henry Bridges Fearon, of Maidenhead, Berks, and Alethea, *née* McKenna; *b* 14 Oct 1944; *Educ* Canford; *m* 20 Feb 1971, Karen Dawn, da of Clifford M Wark, of Toronto, Canada; 1 s (James Adrian b 1978), 1 da (Letitia Jane b 1981); *Career* Sotheby & Co 1963-69, Parke Bernet NY 1969-70, Spink & Son 1970-86, md Glendining & Co 1988- (joined 1986); memb Worshipful Co of Drapers 1970; FRNS 1968, memb Br Numismatic Soc 1960 (cncl memb 1986), FRSA; *Books* Catalogue of British Commemorative Medals (1984), Victorian Souvenir Medals (1986); *Clubs* Savage; *Style*— Daniel Fearon, Esq; Glendining & Co, 7 Bleinheim St, New Bond St, London W1Y 9LD (☎ 01 493 2445, fax 01 491 9181, telex 298855 BLEN G)

FEATHER, Baroness; Alice Helena; da of John Fernyhough; *m* 1930, Baron Feather (Life Peer, d 1976); 1 s (Hon Harry *qv*), 1 da (Hon Mrs Stanley Palmer); *Career* JP, ret 1978; *Style*— The Rt Hon Lady Feather; Mill House, Sudborough, Kettering, Northants NN14 3BT (☎ 08012 3763)

FEATHER, Hon Harry Alexander; s of Baron Feather (Life Peer, d 1976), and Alice Helena, *née* Fernyhough, *qv*; *b* 3 August 1938; *m* 1972, Patricia Lesley, JP, da of Gilbert Victor Green; 2 da (Victoria, Jessica); *Career* master mariner; nat staff offr The Iron and Steel Trades Confedn; *Style*— The Hon Harry Feather; The Mill, Sudborough, Kettering, Northants NN14 3BT; The Iron and Steel Trades Confedn, Swinton House, 324 Gray's Inn Rd, London WC1X 8DD

FEATHER, William Anderson; George Medal (1941); s of George Feather (d 1958), of Earby, Yorks, and Annie Garbutt, *née* Anderson (d 1976); *b* 29 July 1909; *Educ* Ermysted's GS Skipton, Univ of Leeds (BSc Civil Engrg); *m* 29 June 1945, Marian Melita (SO, WAAF) (d 1985), da of Bertram Coughlin (d 1936), of Whitchurch, Cardiff; 1 da (Penelope Melita b 1946); *Career* emergency commission Royal Engineers 1940; No 4 Bomb disposal Co RE 1940-42; Staff Capt SME and GHQ Home forces 1942-45; contractor's engr/agent 1934-40; assit ed "Water and Water engineering" 1945-46; Lemon and Blizard 1946-80 (eng asst 1946, chartered eng 1949 ptnr and snr ptnr 1952, conslt 1977); life memb RE Assoc 1950 (Badge of Merit 1987); pres Inst of Public Health Eng 1974-75; memb Yorks County RFU and Woodford RUFC; CEng; FICE; Hon FIWEM; *Style*— William Feather, Esq; 45 Monkhams Drive, Woodford Green, Essex IG8 0LE (☎ 01 504 6832)

FEAVER, Rt Rev Douglas Russell Feaver; s of late Ernest Henry Feaver, of Bristol; *b* 22 May 1914; *Educ* Bristol GS, Keble Coll Oxford (scholar, MA); *m* 1939, Katharine, da of Rev Wilfrid Thomas Stubbs (d 1968); 1 s, 2 da; *Career* canon and sub-dean of St Albans 1946-58, vicar and rural dean of Nottingham 1958-72; 35 bishop of Peterborough 1972-84, ret; *Style*— The Rt Rev Douglas Feaver; 10 Spens Avenue, Cambridge CB3 9LS

FEBEN, Eric Graham; s of late Stanley Oswald Feben; *b* 4 July 1916; *Educ* Cncl Educn (Matriculation); *m* 1939, Ernestine Paula, da of late Ernest Alfred White; 2 da (1 decd); *Career* road transport operator (ret); high sheriff Co of Isle of Wight 1979-80, mayor South Wight Borough Cncl 1974-75, chm IOW Rural Dist Cncl 1968-71, sec and mangr Shanklin & Sandown Golf Club; *Recreations* golf; *Style*— Eric Feben, Esq; Pound Cottage, Calbourne, Newport, IOW (☎ Calbourne 276)

FEDER, Ami; s of Joseph Feder (d 1985), and Nicha, *née* Dornstein; *b* 17 Feb 1937; *Educ* Hebrew Univ of Jerusalem Tel-Aviv (LLB); *m* 26 March 1970, Frances Annabel, da of late Michael August; 1 s (Ilan b 1974), 1 da (Shelley b 1972); *Career* Israeli Army 1956-58; called to the Bar Inner Temple 1965, SE Circuit, advocate practising at the Israeli Bar; memb Hon Soc Inner Temple; *Recreations* sport, music, theatre; *Style*— Ami Feder, Esq; 118 King Henry's Rd, London NW3 3SN (☎ 01 586 4339); Chambers: Lamb Building, Temple, London EC4Y 7AS (☎ 01 353 0774, fax 01 353 0535); Off: 10 Malchei, Israel Square, Tel-Aviv 64951 (☎ 03 265 272, fax 03 250 764)

FEELY, Terence John; s of Edward John Feely (d 1961), of Liverpool, and Mary Maude, *née* Glancy; *b* 20 July 1935; *Educ* St Francis Xavier Jesuit Coll Woolton Lancs, Univ of Liverpool (BA); *m* 15 Aug 1959, Elizabeth, da of Alphonsus William Adams (d 1963), of Southampton; *Career* has written theatre plays, films, television and books; plays: Shout For Life (1963), Don't Let Summer Come (1965), Adam's Apple (1967), Who Killed Santa Claus ? (1972), Murder in Mind (1982), The Team (1985); creator of tv series: Callan (with James Mitchell), Arthur of The Britons (Writers' Guild Award), Affairs of The Heart (New York Literary Circle Award), Number Ten, The Gentle Touch, Cats' Eyes, Eureka (1989); memb Cncl of PDSA; memb Cncl of The Writers' Guild; *Books* Rich Little Poor Girl (1981), Limelight (1984), Number 10 (1982); *Recreations* travel, shooting, boxing (spectator), Shakespearian research; *Clubs* Garrick, Carlton; c/o Douglas Rae Management, 28 Charing Cross Road, London WC2H ODB

FEENY, Anne Dudley; da of Robert Dudley Best (d 1984), and Beryl Gladys, *née* Smith (d 1939); *b* 14 July 1920; *Educ* Bedales, Univ of Neuchatel, Birmingham Coll of Art; *m* 7 Feb 1948, Peter Joseph, s of Gerard Feeny (d 1972); 1 s (William b 17 Feb 1951), 3 da (Mary Anne (Mrs Tooke) b 15 Nov 1945, Katy (Mrs Burness) b 26 Dec 1953, Frances Xavier Feeny-Sohiez b 30 Nov 1959); *Career* WAAF ection Offr Photographic Interpretation 1941-46; dir Best & Lloyd Ltd; memb Arthritic and Rheumatism Cncl for res; *Clubs* RAF; *Style*— Mrs Anne Feeny; 2 Greening Dr, Edgbaston, Birmingham B15 2XA, Ran de Mar, Puerto, Andraitx, Mallorca (☎ 021 454 4002, Mallorca 671 285)

FEENY, Peter Joseph; DL (W Midlands 1975); s of Gerard Feeny (d 1966); *b* 19 Mar 1916; *Educ* Stonyhurst; *m* 1948, Anne Dudley, *née* Best; 4 children; *Career* Maj WW II; memb Stock Exchange 1952, hon consul for Thailand 1960, pres Birmingham Consular Assoc 1969-70, consultant Smith Keen Cutler (stockbrokers, London and Birmingham); *Recreations* travel, squash rackets, lawn tennis; *Clubs* All England Lawn Tennis; *Style*— Peter Feeny Esq, DL; 2 Greening Drive, Edgbaston, Birmingham B15 2XA (☎ 021 454 4002); Smith Keen Cutler, Exchange Buildings, Stephenson Place, Birmingham B2 4NN (☎ 021 643 9977)

FEHR, Basil Henry Frank; CBE (1979); s of Frank Emil Fehr, CBE (d 1948), and Jane Poulter, LRAM (d 1961); *b* 11 July 1912; *Educ* Rugby, Ecole de Commerce Neuchatel Switzerland; *m* 1, 1936 (m dis 1951), Jane Marner, *née* Tallent; 2 s (Richard, James), 1 da (Ann); m 2, 1951 (m dis 1974), Greta Constance, *née* Bremner; 1 da (Olinda); m 3, 1974, Anne Norma, *née* Cadman; 1 da (Amanda); *Career* served WWII HAC, later instr Gunnery Sch of Anti-Aircraft RA, ret Maj; joined family firm Frank Fehr & Co 1934, ptnr 1936, governing dir (later chm) Frank Fehr & Co Ltd London 1948, pres (later chm) Fehr Bros (Mfrs) I nc NY 1949; chm: Cocoa Assoc of London 1952, London Commodity Exchange 1954, London Oil and Tallow Trades Assoc 1955, Copra Assoc London 1957, Inc Oilseed Assoc 1958, United Assocs Ltd 1959, Colyer Fehr Pty Ltd Sydney 1984; elected to Baltic Exchange 1936, dir Baltic Merchantile and Shipping Ex change 1963-69 and 1970- (vice-chm 1973-75, chm 1975-77); landowner; jurat of liberty of Romney Marsh 1979; *Recreations* sports, farming; *Clubs* City Livery (Aldate Ward), MCC, RAC, West Kent CC, Littlestone GC, Little Ship; *Style*— Basil Fehr, Esq, CBE; Slodden Farm, Dymchurch, Romney Marsh, Kent (☎ 0303 872 241); Frank Fehr & Co Ltd, Prince Rupert House, 64 Queen St, London EC4 (☎ 01 248 5066)

FEILDEN, Sir Bernard Melchior; CBE (1976, OBE 1969); s of Maj Robert Humphrey Feilden, MC, RHA (d 1925), of BC, Canada, and Olive, *née* Binyon (d 1971); *b* 11 Sept 1919; *Educ* Bedford Sch, UC, Architectural Assoc (AADip); *m* 1949, Ruth Mildred, da of Robert John Bainbridge, of Apple Tree Farm, Gt Plumstead, Norfolk; 2 s (Henry, Francis), 2 da (Harriet, Mary); *Career* architect to Norwich Cathedral 1962-77; surveyor to York Minster 1965-77, St Paul's Cathedral 1969-77; conslt architect to Univ of E Anglia 1968-77; dir: ICCROM 1977-81, Emeritus 1983; kt 1985; *Books* The Wonder of York Minster (1976), Introduction to Conservation (1979), Conservation of Historic Buildings (1982), Between Two Earthquakes; *Recreations* sketching, photography, chess, sailing; *Clubs* Norfolk, Norwich; *Style*— Sir Bernard Feilden, CBE; Stiffkey Old Hall, Wells next the Sea, Norfolk NR23 1QJ (☎ 0328 75585, telex 97250 STIRNG)

FEILDEN, Henry Rudyard; s and h of Sir Henry Feilden, 6th Bt, and Lady (Ethel May) Feilden, *née* Atkinson; *b* 26 Sept 1951; *Educ* Kent Coll Canterbury, v of Bristol, (BVSC); *m* 1982, Anne, da of William Frank Bonner Shepperd (d 1985); 1 s (William Henry b 5 April 1983); *Career* veterinary surgn in small animal and equine practice 1975-84; Tuckett Gray and Partners Aylesbury Bucks 1976-78, Fraser and Smith Binfield Berks 1978-83, LA Gould Rossendale Lancs 1983-84, currently veterinary advsr Duphar Veterinary Ltd Southampton 1984-; MRCVS; *Recreations* gardening, DIY, fine wine, antiques, good company; *Clubs* Old Canterburians; *Style*— Henry Feilden, Esq; 30 Manor Close, Wickham, Fareham, Hants PO17 5BZ (☎ 0329 832805; Duphar Veterinary Ltd, Solvay House, Flanders Rd, Hedge End, Southampton SO3 4QH (☎ 04892 81711)

FEILDEN, Sir Henry Wemyss; 6 Bt (UK 1846), of Feniscowles, Lancashire; s of Col Wemyss Feilden, CMG (3 s of Sir William Feilden, 3 Bt, JP); suc 1 cous, Sir William Feilden, 5 Bt, MC, 1976; *b* 1 Dec 1916; *Educ* Canford Sch, King's Coll London; *m* 25

Aug 1943, Ethel May, da of late John Atkinson, of Annfield Plain, Co Durham; 1 s, 2 da (Mrs Graham Donald b 1944, Mrs William Stokoe b 1947); *Heir* s, Henry Rudyard Feilden, *qv*; *Career* served in RE WW II; civil servant (ret); *Recreations* gardening, watching cricket; *Clubs* MCC; *Style*— Sir Henry Feilden, Bt; Little Dene, Heathfield Rd, Burwash, Etchingham, E Sussex TN19 7HN (☎ 0435 882205)

FEILDEN, Lady; Mary Joyce; only da of Sir John Frecheville Ramsden, 6th Bt, DL, and sis of Maj Sir William Pennington-Ramsden, 7th Bt; *b* 12 Nov 1907; *m* 1929, Maj-Gen Sir Randle Guy Feilden, KCVO, CB, CBE, DL, sometime sr steward of the Jockey Club, High Sheriff Oxon, and VQMG (d 1981); 2 s (Randle Joseph b 1931, *see also* Lady Caroline Gosling; Andrew James b 1941) and 1 s decd; *Style*— Lady Feilden; 3 Kingston House South, SW7 (☎ 01 589 7135); Cot Farm, Minster Lovell, Oxfon OX8 5RS

FEILDEN, Dr (Geoffrey Bertram) Robert; CBE (1966); s of Maj Robert Humphrey Feilden, MC, RHA (d 1925), of Canada, and Olive, *née* Binyon (d 1971); *b* 20 Feb 1917; *Educ* Bedford Sch, King's Coll Cambridge (BA, MA); *m* 1, 1945, Elizabeth Ann, da of Rev J P Gorton (d 1952); 1 s (Richard b 1950), 2 da (Jane b 1948, Fiona b 1953); m 2, 1972, Elizabeth Diana, da of P C Lloyd (d 1961); *Career* chartered mechanical engr, Lever Bros and Unilever Ltd 1939-40, Power Jets Ltd 1940-46, Ruston & Hornsby Ltd - chief engr and engrg dir 1946-59, md Hawker Siddeley Brush Turbines and dir Hawker Siddeley Industries Ltd 1959-61, gp technical dir Davy Ashmore Ltd and dir of principal operating companies 1961-68, dep dir gen British Standards Institution 1968-70, dir gen British Standards Institution 1970-81, non exec dir Avery's Ltd 1974-79, sr ptnr Feilden Associates Ltd 1981-, non exec dir Plint & Ptnrs Ltd 1982-; Hon DTech Loughborough Univ 1970, Hon DSc Queen's Univ Belfast 1971; jt winner MacRobert Award for Engineering Innovation 1983; FRS 1959, FEng 1976, Sr FRCA 1986; *Recreations* sailing, skiing, photography; *Clubs* Athenaeum; *Style*— Dr Robert Feilden, CBE; Verlands, Painswick, Gloucestershire GL6 6XP (☎ 0452 812112; Feilden Associates Ltd, Verlands, Painswick, Glos GL6 6XP (☎ 0452 812112, telex 437244 CMINTL, fax 0 452 812912)

FEILDING, Viscount; Alexander Stephen Rudolph Feilding; s and h of 11 Earl of Denbigh and Desmond; *b* 4 Nov 1970; *Style*— Viscount Feilding

FEILDING, Hon Mrs David; Elizabeth; 2 da of William Fletcher (d 1920), of Arcledon, Cumberland; *m* 19 Oct 1938, Hon David Charles Feilding (d 1966), bro of 10 Earl of Denbigh; 3 s (William b 1939, Michael b 1946, Charles b 1949); *Style*— Hon Mrs David Feilding; Newnham Paddox, Rugby, Warwicks

FEILDING, Hon Henry Anthony; MC; yrt s of Lt-Col Rudolph Edmund Aloysius, Viscount Feilding, CMG, DSO (d 1937; eld s of 9 Earl of Denbigh, who *d* 1939); *b* 27 Feb 1924; *Educ* Ampleforth, King's Coll Cambridge (MA) (FRICS); *m* 2 Aug 1950, Dunia Maureen, yr da of late Gordon Spencer, MD, of Putley, nr Ledbury, Herefordshire; 1 s (Jasper b 1953), 1 da (Penelope b 1954); *Career* late Capt Coldstream Gds, High Sheriff of Warwicks 1978, land agent; *Style*— Hon Henry Feilding, MC; The Manor House, Pailton, nr Rugby

FEILDING, Hon Hugh Richard; 4 s of Lt-Col Rudolph Edmund Aloysius, Viscount Feilding, CMG, DSO (d 1937, eld s of 9 Earl of Denbigh, who d 1939); *b* 15 July 1920; *Educ* Ampleforth; *m* 28 March 1944, Sheila Katharine, o da of Brig Charles Arthur Bolton, CBE; 1 s (John b 1945); *Career* Sqdn Ldr RAFVR (despatches); FCA; co dir in Mauritius & UK, dir Country Landowners Assoc; FCA; *Recreations* fishing, shooting; *Clubs* RAF; *Style*— Hon Hugh Feilding; Home Farm, Bainton, Driffield, E Yorks YO25 9NJ

FEILDING, Hon Mrs Basil; Rosemary; da of late Cdr (Frederick) Neville Eardley-Wilmot, RN (d 1956), and Dorothy, *née* Little (d 1959); sis of Sir John Eardley-Wilmot, 5 Bt; *b* 17 July 1920; *m* 14 Sept 1939, Capt Hon Basil Egerton Feilding (d 1970), bro of 10 Earl of Denbigh; 3 s (Peter b 1941, Giles b 1950, Crispin b 1960), 2 da (Jennifer Crawley b 1947, Imelda b 1958); *Style*— Hon Mrs Basil Feilding; The Park Cottage, Monks Kirby, Rugby, Warwicks

FEINBERG, Peter Eric; s of Leon Feinberg (d 1976), of Bradford, and May, *née* Frais (d 1969); *b* 26 Oct 1949; *Educ* Bradford GS, UCL (LLB); *m* 13 Aug 1988, Tina, da of James Flannery, of Leeds; *Career* barr Inner Temple 1972, SE circuit; *Recreations* music, opera, squash; *Style*— Peter Feinberg, Esq; 1 Crown Office Row, Temple, London EC4 (☎ 01 583 3724, fax 01 353 3923)

FELD, Alfred; s of Rueben Feldman (d 1941), and Betsy Feldman (d 1968); *m* 27 April 1941, Lily, da of Albert Green (d 1958); 1 s (Robert Philip b 3 Jan 1953), 1 da (Roberta Arleen (Mrs Stenson) b 15 May 1946); *Career* WWII served N Staffs Regt 1941-45; band leader Mecca Dancing 1936-41; hotelier 1945-, pres Resort Hotels plc 1988-; memb: Brighton BC 1964-88 (Mayor 1978-79), (and asst pres) Brighton & Hove Hotels Assoc 1966-; Freeman City of London 1962, Liveryman Worshipful Co of Loriners 1971; FHCIMA; Chevalier du Tasteuin (France), Officier Jurade du St Emilion (France); *Recreations* music; *Clubs* Carlton, City Livery; *Style*— Alfred Feld, Esq; Norfolk Resort Hotel, Kings Rd, Brighton BN1 2PP (☎ 0273 738 201, fax 0273 821 752, telex 877247)

FELD, Robert Philip; s of Alfred Feld, and Lily, *née* Green; *b* 3 Jan 1953; *Educ* Brighton & Hove Sussex GS, Imperial Coll of Sci and Technol; *m* 6 March 1987, Tara Louise, da of Edward Scannell; 1 s (Daniel Mark Joseph b 1988); *Career* md Resort Hotels plc; hon sec Brighton Regency Round Table, non-exec dir Guide Dogs for the Blind Assoc Recreational Servs Ltd; Freeman City of London, Liveryman Worshipful Co of Loriners; MHCIMA, FInstD, MCFA; *Recreations* private pilot, yachting; *Clubs* Carlton, City Livery, Sussex Motor YC; *Style*— Robert Feld, Esq; Resort Hotels plc, Resort House, Clifton Mews, Clifton Hill, Brighton BN1 3HR (☎ 0273 207671, fax 0273 729552, telex 877247 RESORT G)

FELDMAN, Sir Basil Samuel; s of Philip and Tilly Feldman; *b* 23 Sept 1926; *Educ* Grocers' Sch; *m* 1952, Gita, da of Albert Julius (d 1964); 2 s, 1 da; *Career* contested (C) GLC Richmond 1973; Cons Pty: pres Nat Union Cons and Unionist Assocs (Gtr London) 1981-85 (dep chm 1975-78, chm 1978-81), memb Nat Union Exec Ctee 1975-, jt Nat chm Cons Pty's Impact 80s Campaign 1982-86; patron Hampstead Cons Assoc 1981 (memb 1965-); Lloyd's underwriter 1979-; dir Young Entrepreneurs Fund 1985-; pres Richmond 1976-84 and Hornsey Cons Assoc 1978-82; vice-pres Gtr London Young Cons 1975-77, chm: Martlet servs Gp Ltd 1973-81, Solport Ltd 1980-85, Clothing EDC (NEDO) 1978-85, Better Made in Britain Campaign 1983-, Watchpost Ltd 1983-; vice pres Nat Union 1986-(chm 1985-86, vice chm 1982-85), chaired Cons Cont Blackpool; memb: Free Enterprise Loan Soc 1977-84, Policy Gp for London 1975-81 and 1984-, Nat Campaign Ctee 1976 & 1978, advsy ctee on Policy 1981-86, Ctee for London 1984-87, GLC Housing Mgmnt Ctee 1973-77, GLC Arts Ctee 1976-81, (membre Consultatif) Institut Int de Promotion et de Prestige Geneva 1978-, PO Users Nat Cncl 1978-81, Tariffs Sub-Ctee 1980-81, Job Opportunities Task Force (NEDO) 1985-, Eng Tourist Bd 1986-; kt 1982; *Books* Constituency Campaigning- A Guide for Conservative Party workers, some thoughts on Jobs Creation (for NEDO) 1984; several other pty booklets and pamphlets; *Recreations* travel, golf, tennis, theatre, opera, writing; *Clubs* Carlton; *Style*— Sir Basil Feldman; c/o Nat Union of Conservative & Unionist Associations, 32 Smith Sq, London SW1 (☎ 01 222 9000)

FELDMAN, Dr Geoffrey Vivian; s of Leonard Feldman (d 1963), and Fanny, *née* Messer (d 1962); *b* 3 April 1920; *Educ* Manchester GS, Manchester Univ (MB, ChB), DCH (London); *m* 18 Sept 1963, (Doris) Anne, da of William Hall Walton (d 1975); *Career* Capt RAMC 1945-47; house physician Manchester Royal Infirmary 1945, house physician and registrar Royal Manchester Childrens Hosp 1947-49, lectr dept of child health Univ of Manchester 1953-84 (res asst and asst lectr 1949-53); hon conlst paediatrician St Mary's Hosp Manchester and Royal Manchester Childrens Hosp 1961-63, conslt paediatrician S Manchester Health Authy 1963-84; memb Manchester Univ RFC; FRCP, memb Br Paediatric Assoc, Neonatal Soc, Manchester Med Soc, BMA; *Recreations* fishing, gardening, painting; *Style*— Dr Geoffrey V Feldman

FELL, Sir Anthony; s of Cdr David Mark Fell, RN; *b* 18 May 1914; *Educ* Bedford Sch and in NZ; *m* 1938, June Warwick; 1 s, 1 da; *Career* contested (C): Brigg 1948, Hammersmith S 1949 and 1950; MP (C): Yarmouth 1951-66 (resigned pty whip 1956 in protest at withdrawal from Suez), Yarmouth 1970-83; kt 1981; *Style*— Sir Anthony Fell; 11 Denny St, London SE11 4UX (☎ 01 735 9021)

FELL, David; s of Ernest Fell (d 1964), of Belfast, NI, and Jessie, *née* McCreedy (d 1981); *b* 20 Jan 1943; *Educ* Royal Belfast Academical Inst, Queen's Univ Belfast (BSc); *m* 22 July 1967, Sandra Jesse, da of Hubert Moore (d 1982), of Co Fermanagh, NI; 1 s (Nicholas b 1976), 1 da (Victoria b 1972); *Career* sales mangr Rank Hovis McDougall 1965-66, teacher Belfast Model Sch 1966-67, res assoc Queen's Univ Belfast 1967-69; NI civil serv 1969-: asst princ Miny of Agric 1969-72, princ Miny of Commerce 1972-77, under sec Dept of Commerce 1981-82 (asst sec 1977-81), dep chief exec Industl Devpt Bd for NI 1982-84, permanent sec Dept of Econ Devpt 1984-; CBIM 1985; *Recreations* golf, rugby, coaching, listening to and playing music; *Clubs* Belfast Old Instonians; *Style*— David Fell, Esq; Dept of Econ Devpt, Netherleigh, Massey Ave, Belfast BT4 2JP (☎ 0232 63244)

FELL, John Arnold; s of Charles Arthur Fell, of James House, 2 Sandy Lodge Way, Northwood, Middx, and Susannah, *née* Arnold (d 1978); *b* 31 August 1928; *Educ* Merchant Taylor's, Pembroke Coll Oxford (MA); *m* 10 Aug 1963, Janet Eva, da of Irvine Charles Parr, of Greenhollow, Lower Broadoak Rd, West Hill, Ottery St Mary, Devon; 2 da (Ruth Anne b 19 June 1966, Rachel Elizabeth b 18 May 1968); *Career* slr 1955; article clerk Kimbers 1952-56; asst slr: Conquest Clare & Binns 1956-58, asst slr Hatchett Jones & Co 1958-63; Wilde Sapte 1963- (ptnr 1964-); dir: Portman Family Settled Estates Ltd, Portman Burtley Estate Co, Moor Park (1958) Ltd, Seymour Street Nominees Ltd; chm Tstees of Truro Fund; tstee: Royal Acad of Arts, Housing Assoc Charitable Tst, Lord Mayor's 800th Anniversary Awards Tst; govr City of London Sch, donation govr of Christ's Hosp, former chm Broad St Ward Club, chm Queenhithe Ward Club (commcn councilman Corpn of London 1982-); Freeman City of London 1980, Liveryman Worshipful Co of Gardeners 1982; *Recreations* walking, gardeing, youth work with Crusaders; *Clubs* Old Merchant Taylor's Soc Guildhall, City Livery; *Style*— John Fell, Esq; Dellfield, 43 Sandy Lodge Lane, Moor Park, Northwood, Middx HA6 2HX (☎ 092 74 26508); Queensbridge House, 60 Upper Thames St, London EC4V 3BD (☎ 01 236 3050, fax 01 236 9624, telex 887793)

FELLOWES, Hon Andrew Edward; s of 3 Baron De Ramsey, KBE, TD; *b* 24 Mar 1950; *m* 1974, Anne Mary, da of Roy Tweedy, of Mungle, North Star, NSW, Australia; 1 s, 2 da; *Career* agriculture; *Recreations* motor racing; *Clubs* Pratt's; *Style*— Hon Andrew Fellowes; Bodsey House, Ramsey, Huntingdon, Cambridgeshire

FELLOWES, Hon (John) David Coulson; s of late Capt Hon Coulson Churchill Fellowes (eld s of 2 Baron De Ramsey) and half-bro of 3 Baron; *b* 1 May 1915; *Educ* Eton, Univ Coll Oxford (BA); *m* 1, 31 May 1946 (m dis 1962), Louise (d 1975), yr da of Lt Sir James Henry Domville, 5 Bt, RN, and formerly w of Leslie Alexander Mackay; 1 s (Peter b 1948), 1 da (Jacqueline b 1955); m 2, 4 April 1963, Joan Lynette (d 1965), o da of Edgar G Rees, of Llanelly, and formerly w of Richard Dewar Neame; m 3, 1977, Mervyn, da of late Reinold de Toll, and former w of Peter Sherwood; *Career* WWII Lt Rifle Brigade (wounded, POW Colditz, despatches); *Style*— Hon David Fellowes; Flat 3, 117 Elgin Cres, W11

FELLOWES, David Lyon; s of Brig Reginald William Lyon Fellowes (d 1982), of Cladich, and Dulcie Margaret Blessing Hurt, *née* Peel (d 1957); *b* 16 May 1931; *Educ* Winchester; *m* 13 Oct 1955, Elizabeth Mary, da of Maj-Gen Errol Arthur Edwin Tremlett, CB, TD (d 1982), of Devon; 1 s (Mark b 1967), 1 da (Emma b 1965); *Career* farming; *Style*— David Fellowes, Esq; Inistrynich, Dalmally, Argyll PA33 1BQ (☎ 08382256); Cladich Farms, Dalmally, Argyll PA33 1BQ (☎ 08282256)

FELLOWES, Lady (Cynthia) Jane; da (by 1 m) of 8 Earl Spencer, LVO, JP, DL, *qv*; sis of HRH The Princess of Wales (*see* Royal Family); *b* 11 Feb 1957; *Educ* West Heath; *m* 20 April 1978, Robert Fellowes, CB, LVO, *qv*; 1 s, 2 da; *Style*— Lady Jane Fellowes; 5a The Old Barracks, Kensington Palace, W8

FELLOWES, Hon John Ailwyn; s and h of 3 Baron De Ramsey, KBE; *b* 27 Feb 1942; *Educ* Winchester; *m* 1, 1973 (m dis 1983), Phyllida Mary, da of Philip Athelstan Forsyth; 1 s (Freddie John b 1978); m 2, 1984, Alison Mary, da of Archibald Birkmyre, *qv*; 1 s (Charles Henry b 1986), 1 da (Daisy b 1988); *Career* farmer; chm Cambridge Water Co; *Recreations* fishing; *Clubs* Boodle's; *Style*— Hon John Fellowes; Abbey House, 6 Church Green, Ramsey, Huntingdon, Cambs P17 1DW

FELLOWES, Julian Alexander; s of Peregrine Edward Launcelot Fellowes, of Chipping Campden, and Olwen Mary, *née* Stuart-Jones (d 1980); forebears include Sir John Fellowes, sub-govr of South Sea Bubble, and naval hero Sir Thomas Fellowes; *b* 17 August 1949; *Educ* Ampleforth, Magdalene Coll Cambridge (BA, MA); *Career* actor, prodr; West End appearances incl: Joking Apart (Globe), Present Laughter (Vaudeville), Futurists (Nat Theatre); Film and TV appearances incl: Baby (Walt Disney), Swallows and Amazons (BBC), Knights of God (TVS), Sophia and Constance (BBC); as dir of Lionhead co-prodns incl: Married Man (with LWT), Little Sir Nicholas (with BBC); *Recreations* history, building; *Style*— Julian Fellowes, Esq; 15 Moore St, London SW3

FELLOWES, Lady Maureen Thérèse Josephine; *née* Noel; o da of 4 Earl of Gainsborough (d 1927), and Alice Mary, *née* Eyre; *b* 7 Mar 1917; *m* 1, 18 Feb 1944, 15 Baron Dormer (d 1975); 2 da (Hon Mrs Glennie, Hon Mrs Bird); m 2, 22 July 1982, Peregrine Edward Launcelot Fellowes (who m 1935, as his first w, Olwen Stuart-Jones (d 1980), by whom he has 4 s); *Style*— Lady Maureen Fellowes; The Court, Chipping Campden, Gloucestershire (☎ 0386 840201)

FELLOWES, Peregrine Edward Launcelot; s of Henry Shirley Morant Fellowes (d 1915), of Hurstborn Priors, Hants, and Georgiana Maria Hulton, *née* Wrightson, (d 1956); *b* 8 July 1912; *Educ* Ampleforth, UCL (BSc); *m* 1, 27 July 1935, Olwen Mary, (d 1980), da of James Stuart-Jones, CBE (d 1948), of Welwyn, Herts; 4 s (Nicholas b 1937, David b 1944, Roderick b 1946, Julian b 1949); m 2, 22 July 1982, Lady Maureen Thérèse Josephine, *née* Noel, da of, 4 Earl of Gainsborough (d 1927), of Exton Park, Oakham; *Career* civil engnr 1933-40; mil serv 1940-44, Capt Sudan, Ethiopia, E Africa; HM For Serv 1946-53; Shell Int 1953-69 (co-ordinator of Trade Relations 1967-69); conslt to Ford Fndn 1969-73; dir Lionhead Prodns 1980-; memb Br Cncl of Churches 1969-87; Kt of Hon and Devotion, SMO Malta; *Recreations* religion and politics; *Clubs* Athenaeum; *Style*— Peregrine Fellowes, Esq; The Court, Chipping Campden, Gloucestershire GL55 6JQ (☎ 0386 840 201)

FELLOWES, Robert; CB (1987) LVO (1982); s of Sir William Albemarle Fellowes, KCVO (d 1986), agent to HM at Sandringham 1936-64, and Jane Charlotte (d 1986), da of Brig-Gen Algernon Francis Holford Ferguson, bro Thomas Fellowes *qv*; *b* 11 Dec 1941; *Educ* Eton; *m* 20 April 1978, Lady (Cynthia) Jane Spencer, da of 8 Earl Spencer; 1 s (Alexander Robert b 1983), 2 da (Laura Jane b 1980, Eleanor Ruth b 1985); *Career* Lt Scots Guards 1960-63; dir Allen Harvey & Ross (discount brokers and bankers) 1968-77, asst private sec to HM The Queen 1977-86 (since when dep private sec); *Recreations* cricket, shooting, golf; *Clubs* White's, Pratt's, MCC; *Style*— Robert Fellowes, Esq, CB, LVO; 5a The Old Barracks, Kensington Palace, London W8 4PU

FELLOWES, Robert; s of Lt-Col Percy Ailwyn Fellowes, MBE (d 1964), of Kings Sombourne, Hants, and Joyce Madelaine, *née* Fordham (d 1976); *b* 30 June 1931; *Educ* Charterhouse, RAC Cirencester; *m* 26 Aug 1961, Sarah Ann, da of John White (d 1961), of Fyfield, Glos; 2 s (Nicholas John Ailwyn b 23 Feb 1964, James Robert William b 3 July 1966); *Career* RHA 1949-51; agent to the Jockey Club 1964-; tstee: Stable Lads Welfare Tst, New Astley Club, Nat Horse Racing Museum; pres Links Golf Club Newmarket; co cncllr 1981-85; FRICS; *Recreations* golf, tennis, shooting, fishing, racing; *Style*— Robert Fellowes, Esq; Portland Lodge, Newmarket, Suffolk CB8 0NQ (☎ 0638 662252); Jockey Club Office, Newmarket (☎ 0638 665122, fax 0638 662490, car ☎ 0860 528865)

FELLOWES, Thomas William; s of Sir William Albermarle Fellowes, KCVO, DL, FRICS (d 1986), and Jane Charlotte Fellowes (d 1986), br Robert Fellowes, CB, LVO *qv*; *b* 3 Nov 1945; *Educ* Eton; *m* 1, 1968, Caroline Moira (m dis 1972), da of Capt D J R Ker; m 2, 1975, Rosamund Isobelle, da of Bernard Van Cutsem (d 1975), and Lady Margaret Fortesque; 2 da (Catherine b 1977, Mary b 1978); *Career* dir Gerrard and Nat Disc Co Ltd 1973; md Gerrard & Nat Hldgs plc and subsidiary cos; govr Queen Elizabeth Fndn for the Disabled; *Recreations* shooting, fishing; *Clubs* White's, Pratt's; *Style*— Thomas Fellowes; Barking Old Rectory, Ipswich, Suffolk IP6 8HH (☎ 0449 720734); c/o Gerrard & National Hldgs, 33 Lombard Street, London EC3V 9BQ

FELLOWS, Derek Edward; s of Edward Frederick Fellows (d 1986), of Sussex, and Gladys Marguerite, *née* Parker; *b* 23 Oct 1927; *Educ* Mercers Sch; *m* 1948, Mary, da of William George Watkins (d 1977), of Surrey; 2 da (Angela b 1954, Nicola b 1959); *Career* memb Occupational Pensions Bd 1974-78; ch actuary Prudential Assur Co Ltd 1981-88; vice-pres Inst of Actuaries 1980-82, dir Secutiries and Investmts Bd; fell of Pensions Mgmnt Inst: FIA; *Recreations* music, gardening, bridge; *Clubs* Actuary's, Gallio; *Style*— Derek Fellows, Esq; 20 Fairbourne, Cobham, Surrey KT11 2BT (☎ 0932 65488)

FELLS, Prof Ian; s of Dr Henry Alexander Fells, MBE (d 1975), of Sheffield, and Clarice, *née* Rowell; *b* 5 Sept 1932; *Educ* King Edward VII Sch Sheffield, Trinity Coll Cambridge (MA, PhD); *m* 17 Aug 1957, Hazel Denton, da of Donald Murgatroyd Scott, of Sheffield; 4 s (Nicholas Scott b 1959, Jonathan Wynne b 1961, Alastair Rowell b 1963, Crispin Denton b 1966); *Career* cmmnd RCS 1951, Chief Wireless Offr Br Troops in Austria 1952; lectr and dir of studies dept of fuel technol and chemical engrg 1958-62, reader in fuel sci Univ of Durham 1962-75; Univ of Newcastle upon Tyne: public orator 1971-74, prof of energy conversion 1975-; exec David Davies Inst of Int Affairs 1975-; pres Inst of Energy 1978-79; memb: Sci Consultative Gp BBC 1976-81, Electricity Supply Res Cncl 1979-, Cncl for Nat Academic Awards 1988-; Hadfield Meml Medal & Prize 1974, Beilby Meml Medal & Prize 1976, Sir Charles Parsons Meml Medal & Prize 1988; involved with various tv series including Young Scientist of the Year, The Great Egg Race, Earth Year 2050, Take Nobody's Word for It; tstee Northern Sinfonia Orchestra; FEng 1979, FInstE, FRSC, FIChemE; *Books* Energy for the Future (1973, 2 edn 1986); *Recreations* sailing, guitar, energy conversation; *Clubs* Naval and Military; *Style*— Prof Ian Fells; 29 Rectory Terrace, Newcastle upon Tyne NE3 1YB (☎ 091 285 5343); Dept of Chemical & Process Engineering, University of Newcastle upon Tyne NE1 7RU (☎ 091 232 8511)

FELTON, Ralph; s of Robert Forrester Felton (d 1947), of The Rest, Colnbrook, Buckinghamshire, and Maude Isobel, *née* Gray (d 1956); *b* 28 April 1911; *Educ* Kings Coll Sch Wimbledon; *m* 1, 1 May 1939 (m dis), Elizabeth; m 2, 27 June 1969, Mabel Clara, da of Lodge Frederick Charles, of Brighton; *Career* wireless instr 1 Bn Bovington Rtc; conslt dir (former dir) Felton & Sons Ltd; former chm: Vintry & Dowgate Word Club, City of London Retail Traders Assoc; Freeman City of London, Liveryman Worshipful Co Fruiterers 1957; *Recreations* golf; *Clubs* City Livery, Little Ship Sailing; *Style*— Ralph Felton Esq; 63A Thorneyhedge Rd, Chiswick, London W4 5SB (☎ 01 995 5935)

FELTON, Timothy John Fowler; s of Maj William Fowler Felton, RAMC, and Felicity Anne Hamilton, *née* Hervey; *b* 8 Mar 1954; *Educ* Brighton Coll, Leeds Univ (LLB), Seale Hayne Coll (Dip Farm Mgmnt); *m* 18 Sept 1982, Sarah Elizabeth, da of Peter Norman Whitley, of Leighland House, Leighland, Somerset; 2 da (Emily b 21 July 1985, Chloë b 17 June 1987); *Career* barr Middle Temple Trinity 1977; share farmer Gogwell Share farm 1984-; memb Stoke Hill Beagles, Liveryman Worshipful Co of Carpenters 1975; *Recreations* running, hill walking; *Clubs* Tiverton Harriers Athletic

FELTWELL, Ray Parker; s of Henry Augustus Feltwell (d 1966), of Forest Row, Sussex, and Flora, *née* MacDonald Stewart (d 1977); *b* 13 July 1915; *Educ* Plumpton Agric Coll, Harper Adam's Agric Coll Newport Salop, (Nat Dip of Poultry Husbandry); *m* 27 Jan 1940, Edna Mary, da of Robert William Edmonds (d 1955), of Croydon; 2 s (Robert Leslie BSc b 1944, Dr John Edmonds b 1948); *Career* WWII 1939-43, Capt RASC served Guards Armd Div (invalided 1943); poultry advsy offr Miny of Agric 1938-56; poultry devpt mangr Vitamins Ltd (later Beechams) and dir assoc cos (inc: Norfolk Newlay Ltd, Mainline Eggs Ltd, Nicholas Italiano SPA) 1956-70; int agric conslt 1970-; memb: Br Govt Delegation to World Poultry Congress (Australia 1962, Kiev USSR 1966), chm Poultry Indust Conf Ltd 1965-70; former chm Br Eggs Assoc, past vice chm Br Chicken Assoc; winner Poultry Assoc of GB award 1969; Freeman City of London 1954, Liveryman Worshipful Co of Poulters 1955; *Books* Small Scale Poultry Keeping (1980, 1987), Practical Poultry Feeding (Co-Author, 1978), Turkey Farming (1953, 1963), Turkeys (1959), Intensive Methods of Poultry Farming (1953, 1958); *Recreations* riding; *Clubs* Farmers, Whitehall Court; *Style*— Ray Feltwell, Esq

FENBY, Dr Eric William; OBE (1962); s of Herbert Henry Fenby (d 1954), of Scarborough, and Ada, *née* Brown (d 1974); *b* 22 April 1906; *Educ* Municipal Sch Scarborough, Articled Pupil to A C Keeton (B Mus, FRCO); *m* 22 July 1944, Rowena Clara Teresa da of Rev Percy Marshall (d 1950) of Scarborough; 1 s (Roger Delius), 1 da (Ruth b 1949); *Career* amannuensis to Frederick Delius 1928-34: A Song of Summer for orchestra, Songs of Farewell; composer film score Jamacia Inn 1939, prof of composition RAM 1964-77, numerous lectrs on Delius and his music 1935-82; memb: Composers' Guild of Great Br, Soc of Authors; hon memb Royal Philharmonic Soc; Hon D Music Jacksonville Univ Florida 1978; Hon D Litt: Bradford Univ 1978, Warwick Univ 1978; *Books* Delius As I Knew Him (1936), Delius (1971); Menuhin's House of Music (1969); *Recreations* chess, walking; *Style*— Dr Eric Fenby, OBE ; 1 Raincliffe Court, Stepney Rd, Scarborough, North Yorks 12 5BT (☎ 0723 372 988)

FENBY, Jonathan Theodore Starmer; s of Charles Fenby (d 1974), and June, *née* Head; *b* 11 Nov 1942; *Educ* King Edward's Sch Birmingham, Westminster, New Coll Oxford (BA); *m* 1 July 1967, Renée; 1 s (Alexander b 1972), 1 da (Sara b 1970); *Career* 1963-77: corr bureau chief Reuters ed Reuters World Serv; corr The Economist France and West Germany 1982-86, home ed and asst ed The Independent 1986-88, dep ed the Guardian 1988-; *Books* The Fall of the House of Beaverbrook (1979), Piracy and the Public (1983), The International News Services (1986); *Style*— Jonathan Fenby, Esq; c/o The Guardian, 119 Farringdon Rd, London EC1 (☎ 01 278 2332)

FENDALL, Prof (Neville) Rex Edwards; s of Francis Alan Fendall (d 1967), and Ruby, *née* Matthews (d 1975); *b* 9 July 1917; *Educ* Wallingbrook HS Devon, UCL and UCH (BSc, MB BS, MD, MRCS, LACP), London Sch of Tropical Med and Hygiene (DPH), FFCM 1972; *m* 11 July 1942, Margaret Doreen, da of William Beynon (d 1917), of Pontadawe, S Wales; *Career* Overseas Med Serv 1944-64: Nigeria, Malaya, Singapore, Br Mil Admin Malaya 1945-46, Kenya 1948-64 dir of med srvs; Rockefeller Fndn NYC 1964-67, regnl dir the Population Cncl NYC 1967-71, Middlemass Hunt prof of tropical community health Liverpool Sch of Tropical Med 1971-81, emeritus prof Univ of Liverpool 1982-, visiting prof of public health Boston Univ 1982-, adjunct prof of community health sciences Univ of Calgary Canada 1983-, visiting lectr Harvard Univ 1965; memb panel of experts WHO 1957-, conslt SE Asia WHO 1960, memb UK UNSCAT Delgn 1963, lead speaker Cwlth Mins' of Health Conf Colombo 1974, memb econ devpt advsy panel WHO Ochocerciasis 1976-77, UK project mangr CENTO (Low Cost Rural Health Care) 1977-79, memb UK Delgn WHO/UNICEF Primary Health Care ALMA ATA 1978; memb exec bd Cwlth Human Ecology Cncl; conslt and advsr to numerous int orgns and developing countries since 1981; BMA 1942, FFCM 1972; Gold Medal Nigrendra Med Tst Nepal 1983; memb: Soc Community Med, Soc Social Med, American Public Health Assoc;; *Books* Auxiliaries in Health Care (1972); (jointly with J H Paxman, F M Sharprock) Use of Paramedicals for Primary Health Care in the Commonwealth (1979), contrib of various articles to specialists pubns;; *Recreations* travel, gardening;; *Clubs* Royal Cwlth Soc, Athenaeum; *Style*— Prof Rex Fendall; Berwyn, North Close, Bromborough, Wirral L62 2BU (☎ 051 334 2193)

FENHALLS, Richard Dorian; s of Roydon Myers and Maureen Fenhalls; *b* 14 July 1943; *Educ* Hilton Coll Univ of Natal (BA), Christ's Coll Cambridge (MA LLM); *m* 1967, Angela Sarah, *née* Allen; 1 s, 1 da; *Career* Goodricke & Son, Attorney SA 1969-70, Citibank 1970-72, sr vice-pres: Marine Midland Bank 1972-77, American Express Bank 1977-81, dep chm and chief exec Guinness Mahon & Co Ltd 1981-85; chm Henry Ansbacher & Co Ltd; grp chief exec Henry Ansbacher Hldgs plc 1985-; *Recreations* sailing, skiing; *Clubs* Royal Ocean Racing, Royal Southern Yacht (Hamble), Ski Club of Great Britain, Campden Hill Lawn Tennis; *Style*— R D Fenhalls, Esq; 15 St James's Gardens, London W11 4RE; Henry Ansbacher & Co Ltd, 1 Mitre Sq, London EC3A 5AN (☎ 01 283 2500, telex: 884580 & 886738)

FENN, HE Nicholas M; CMG (1980); s of Rev Prof J Eric Fenn, of Worcs, and Kathleen M, *née* Harrison; *b* 19 Feb 1936; *Educ* Downs Sch, Kingswood Sch, Peterhouse Cambridge (MA); *m* 1959, Susan Clare, da of Rev Dr G L Russel, of Dorset; 2 s (Robert b 1962, Charles b 1963), 1 da (Julia b 1974); *Career* Flying Offr RAF 1954-56; Burmese studies SOAS 1959-60 , vice-consul Mandalay Burma 1960-61; third sec Br Embassy Rangoon Burma 1961-63, asst private sec to four successive secs of state for Foreign and Cwlth Affrs 1963-67, first sec and head of chancery Br Interests Section Swiss Embassy Algiers Algeria 1967-69, first sec for public affrs UK Mission to the UN 1969-72, dep head successively of sci and technol dept and energy dept FCO 1972-75; counsellor head of chancery and consul-gen Br Embassy Peking 1975-77; RCDS 1978, head of News Dept FCO, spokesman of the FCO and press sec successively to Lord Carrington and Francis Pym 1979-82; pres Sec to Lord Soames, last Governor of S Rhodesia now Zimbabwe 1979-80); HM Ambassador: Rangoon Burma 1982-86, Dublin Republic of Ireland 1986-;; *Recreations* sailing; *Clubs* Utd Oxford and Cambridge Univ, Hibernian Utd Servs Dublin; *Style*— HE Sir Nicholas Fenn, CMG British Embassy, 33 Merrion Rd, Dublin 4, Republic of Ireland (☎ 0001 695211)

FENN-SMITH, Clive Antony Kemp; s of Gurth Kemp Fenn-Smith MRCVS, of 2 Otter Road, Poole, Dorset, and Mary Esmée, da of Malcolm Watson (d 1977); *b* 13 Mar 1933; *Educ* Charterhouse, Cambridge Univ (MA); *m* 29 April 1961, Jane Hester, da of Rt Rev Edward Barry Henderson (d 1986), formerly Bishop of Bath and Wells; 2 s (Oliver b 1965, Edward b 1974), 1 da (Emma b 1962); *Career* late 4/7 Royal Dragoon Gds, Lieut 1952; slr: Messrs Letcher & Son Ringwood 1958-64, M & G Gp Ltd 1968-80 (md 1977); dir: Barclays Bank Tst Co Ltd 1984-, Barclays de Zoete Wedd Asset Mgmnt Ltd 1986-, Barclays Fin Services Ltd 1986-, Barclays Life Assur Co Ltd

1980-, Barclays Unicorn (Tstees) Ltd 1980-, Barclays Unicorn Ltd 1980-, Barclayshare Ltd 1986-, and Ebbgate Hldgs Ltd 1987, and other cos Investmt Mgmnt Regulatory Orgn 1986-;; *Recreations* sailing, gardening; *Clubs* Calvalry and Gds'; *Style—* Clive A K Fenn-Smith, Esq; 23 West End Terrace, Winchester, Hampshire SO22 5EN; 94 St Paul's Churchyard, London EC4M 8EH (☎ 01 248 9155, fax ext 3031)

FENNELL, (John) Desmond Augustine; OBE (1982), QC (1974); s of Dr Augustine Joseph Fennell (d 1980), of Lincoln, and Maureen Eleanor, *née* Kidney; *b* 17 Sept 1933; *Educ* Ampleforth, Corpus Christi Coll Cambridge (MA); *m* Feb 1966, Susan Primrose, da of John Marshall Trusted (d 1979); 1 s (Simon b 1969), 2 da (Alexandra b 1967, Charlotte b 1972); *Career* Lt Grenadier Gds 1956-58; barr Inner Temple 1959; dep chm Beds Quarter Sessions 1971-72; Crown Court Recorder 1972-; pres Buckingham Div Cons Assoc (chm 1976-79), vice-chm Wessex Area Cons 1978-80, chm WARA (formed to oppose siting of third London Airport in Bucks) 1968-70 and 1979-; Master of the Bench Inner Temple 1983-; ldr M & O Circuit 1983-88; memb Senate 1983; gen Cncl of the Bar: memb 1984, vice chm 1988, chm 1989; Judge of the Ct of Appeal of Jersey and Ct of Appeal of Guernsey 1984-; inspector King's Cross Underground Fire Investigation 1987-88 (produced report into King's Cross Underground Fire 1988); *Clubs* Boodle's Pilgrims; *Style—* Desmond Fennell, Esq, OBE, QC; Lawn House, Winslow, Buckingham MK18 3AJ (☎ 029 671 2464); 2 Crown Off Row, Temple, London EC4Y 7HJ (☎ 01 353 1365, fax 01 353 4591)

FENNELL, Hon Mrs; (Sarah Elizabeth Jane); *née* Hawke; da of 10 Baron Hawke; *b* 10 Nov 1935; *Educ* Tudor Hall; *m* 5 Oct 1957, John Norris Fennell, er s of late Col Harold Percival Fennell, of Hove, East Sussex; 1 s (Adrian Martin Alexander b 1963), 1 da (Olivia Louise b 1961); *Career* care of elderly people; County DGAA Ctee; *Recreations* art and craft pursuits, flower arrangement/decoration; *Clubs* Sloane; *Style—* The Hon Mrs Fennell; Hawke Mount, Polruan-by-Fowey, Cornwall PL23 1PG (☎ 072 687 717)

FENNEMORE, Roger Arnold; s of Joseph Percy Fennemore (d 1983), of Paulerspury, Northants, and Dorothy, *née* Francis (d 1985); *b* 14 April 1943; *Educ* Bedford Sch, Coll of Law (slr); *m* 21 Sept 1968, Susan Mary, da of Dr Alastiar Marshall , of Aspley Heath, Beds; 3 da (Katie b 1971, Juliet b 1972, Lucinda b 1977); *Career* lst sr ptnr Fennemores Milton Keynes 1984; chief exec Butlers Wharf Ltd 1984-; Capt Woburn Golf & Country Club 1985; pres Milton Keynes Rotary Club 1981; Liveryman Co of Coopes; *Recreations* golf, politics, gardening; *Clubs* Woburn Golf, Oriental, Bedford Rugby Football; *Style—* Roger A Fennemore, Esq; Yew Tree Farm, Sherington, Bucks; Butlers Wharf Ltd, Shad Thames, London SE1 2NP

FENNER, Dame Peggy Edith; OBE (1987), MP (Cons Medway 1983-); *b* 12 Nov 1922; *Educ* LCC Sch Brockley, Ide Hill Sevenoaks; *m* 1940, Bernard S Fenner, s of F W Fenner, of Sevenoaks, Kent; 1 da; *Career* chm Sevenoaks UDC 1962 & 1963 (memb 1957-71), vice-pres UDCs Assoc 1971, Parly candidate (C) Newcastle-under-Lyme 1966, MP (Cons) Rochester and Chatham 1970-74 and 1979-83; Parly sec MAAF 1972-74 and 1981-86, govt co-chm Womens Nat Cmmn 1983-; memb: Br delgn to Euro Parl 1974, Cncl of Europe 1987, Western Euro Union (Def) 1987;; *Style—* Dame Peggy Fenner, MP; 12 Star Hill, Rochester, Kent (☎ 0634 42124)

FENNESSY, Sir Edward; CBE (1957, OBE Mil 1944); s of Edward Patrick Fennessy (d 1955), of London, and Eleanor, *née* Arkwright (d 1942); *b* 17 Jan 1912; *Educ* West Ham GS, QMC London (BSc); *m* 1 1937, Marion (d 1983), da of late Albert Edwin Banks, of Sheffield; 1 s, 1 da; m 2, 1984, Leonora Patricia, widow of Trevor Birkett; *Career* 1939-45 War 60 Gp RAF; md: Decca Radar 1950-65, Plessey Electronics 1965-69, PO Telecommunications 1969-77; dep chm: PO 1975-77, Muirhead to 1982, LKB Instruments Ltd 1978-87; chm: Biochrom 1978-87, Br Medical Data Systems Ltd 1981-; D Univ Surrey; FIEE, FRIN; kt 1975; *Recreations* gardening, sailing; *Clubs* RAF, Island Sailing; *Style—* Sir Edward Fennessy, CBE; Northbrook, Littleford Lane, Shamley Green, Guildford, Surrey (☎ 0483 892444)

FENNEY, Roger Johnson; CBE (1973, MBE 1945); s of James Henry Fenney (d 1952), of St Helens, and Annie Sarah Fenney; *b* 11 Sept 1916; *Educ* Cowley GS, Manchester Univ; *m* 1942, Dorothy Porteus; 2 da; *Career* Maj Field Artillery, N Africa, Italian Campaigns (despatches); sec Statutory Bd 1947-80, first Nuffield fellow for Health Affrs USA 1968, field dir Int Jt Study Gp (Accra, Yaounde, Nairobi, Dakar, San José, Bogota) 1972-76, chm Tstees of Charing Cross Hosp 1980-; *Style—* Roger Fenney, Esq, CBE; 11 Gilray House, Gloucester Terrace, London W2 (☎ 01 262 8313); Chiltern Cottage, Lower Assendon, Henley-on-Thames, Oxon

FENTON, Dr Alexander; CBE (1986); s of Alexander Fenton (d 1960), and Annie Stirling, *née* Stronach; *b* 26 June 1929; *Educ* Turriff Acad, Aberdeen Univ (MA), Cambridge Univ (BA), Edinburgh Univ (DLitt); *m* 1956, Evelyn Elizabeth, *née* Hunter; 2 da; *Career* sr asst ed Scottish Nat Dictionary 1955-59, asst keeper Nat Museum of Antiquities of Scotland 1959-75 (dep keeper 1975-78, dir 1978-85), res dir Nat Museums of Scotland 1985-; Hon DLitt Edinburgh 1981; author; Books incl: The Various Names of Shetland, Scottish Country Life, The Island Blackhouse, The Northern Isles: Orkney and Shetland, The Rural Architecture of Scotland, The Shape of the Past (2 vol), Wirds an' Wark 'e Seasons Roon', Country Life in Scotland; *Recreations* languages; *Clubs* New (Edinburgh); *Style—* Dr Alexander Fenton, CBE; 132 Blackford Ave, Edinburgh EH9 3HH (☎ 667 5456)

FENTON, Charles Miller; OBE (1982); s of Sir William Charles Fenton, MC, JP (d 1976), of Fieldhead, Cleckheaton, W Yorks, and Margaret, *née* Hirst; *b* 24 Feb 1931; *Educ* Uppingham, Leeds Univ (Dip Textile Industs); *m* 1963, Shirley Jane, da of George Arthur Windsor (d 1982), of Priestley Green, Halifax, W Yorks; 1 s, 1 da; *Career* chm: Fenton Hldgs Ltd, BBA Gp plc; High Sheriff W Yorks 1981, non-exec chm Br Mohair Hldgs plc, non exec dir Barr & Wallace Arnold Tst plc; FTI, CBIM; *Recreations* gardening, fishing; *Clubs* Carlton; *Style—* Charles Fenton, Esq, OBE; Priestley Green, Norwood Green, Halifax, W Yorks (☎ 0422 202373); PO Box 20, Cleckheaton, W Yorks BD19 6HP

FENTON, Rev Christopher Miles Tempest; s of Dr Victor Norman Fenton (d 1983), of Farnham Surrey, and Doril, *née* Trewartha-James (d 1966), of Itchenor West Sussex; descended from Sir Geoffrey Fenton, Princ Sec of State in Ireland for Elizabeth I; *b* 24 Jan 1928; *Educ* Bradfield, Queens' Coll Cambridge (BA, LLB, MA); *m* 1964, Elizabeth Christine, da of Robert Sutherland Macadie (d 1957), of Kington, Herefs; 2 s (Jonathan b 1968, Daniel b 1971); *Career* RAEC, Sergeant BAOR 1946-48; asst curate Welling Parish Church 1954-57, chaplain The Malsis Sch West Yorkshire 1957-63, asst curate Bp Hannington Church, Hove 1963-65, vicar Christ Church Ramsgate 1965-71, priest-in-charge St Albans Mottingham 1971-73; Westminster Pastoral Fndn London: staff psychotherapist 1971-72, supervisor and head of Dept of Gp Studies 1972-83; in private practice as an analytical psychotherapist; conslt: Assoc for Pastoral Care and Counselling, Cambridgeshire Consultancy in Counselling; memb Gp Analytic Soc; founding memb Inst of Pastoral Educn and Counselling; fndr and head of house The Coll of St-Anne's-on-the-Hill Ledbury Herefs 1984-; editor Foundation 1983-; *Recreations* design and typography, literature, walking, food and wine; *Clubs* East India and Sports; *Style—* The Reverend Christopher Fenton; Under Down, Ledbury, Herefs HR8 2JE (☎ (0531) 2669)

FENTON, Derek Risian; MVO (1977), MBE (1973); s of Arthur Fenton (d 1954), and Gladys, *née* Donaldson (d 1968); *b* 20 July 1921; *Educ* Clark's Coll; *m* 1943, Iris May, da of Sidney Francis Rendle Diamond (d 1958); 1 s, 1 da; *Career* md Heston Codan Rubber Ltd 1978-86, memb St John Ambulance 1935-, now Cdr London (Prince of Wales's) dist 1983-; Chapter Gen Order of St John 1982-, Liveryman Worshipful Soc of Apothecaries 1984-, Freeman City of London 1977; KStJ 1975; *Recreations* St John Ambulance, grandchildren; *Clubs* Directors, St John House; *Style—* Derek Fenton, Esq, MVO, MBE; 11 Links Rd, West Acton, London W3 0ER (☎ 01 993 4353); office: Edwina Mountbatten House, 63 York St, London W1H 1PS (☎ 258 3456)

FENTON, Ernest John; s of Forbes Duncan Campbell Fenton (d 1970), of Angus, Scotland, and Janet Burnfield, *née* Easson (d 1978); *b* 14 Oct 1938; *Educ* Harris Acad Scotland; *m* 2 March 1965, Ann Ishbel, da of Robert Ramsay; 1 s (Forbes b 1965), 2 da (Joanna b 1969, Elizabeth b 1976); *Career* CA, ptnr W Greenwell & Co Stockbrokers 1968-81, dir Greenwell Montagu & Co 1986-87; chief exec: Greenwell Stockbrokers 1988-, Smith Keen Cutler Ltd 1988-; ASIA; *Recreations* shooting, curling; *Style—* Ernest Fenton, Esq; Dundale Farm, Tunbridge Wells, Kent (☎ 089 282 2175); 406 Seddon Ho, The Barbican, London; 114 Old Broad St, London EC2P 2HY (☎ 01 588 8817)

FENTON, Hon Mrs (Geraldine Jane); *née* Milner; er da of 2 Baron Milner of Leeds; *b* 24 Nov 1954; *m* 1978, Mark Anthony Fenton; 1 s (Harry b 1982); *Style—* Hon Mrs Fenton; 5 Crofton Terrace, Shadwell, Leeds LS17 8LD

FENTON, Air Cdre Harold Arthur; CBE (1945), DSO (1942), DFC (1942); s of Ernest George Fenton, FRCSI, DPH (d 1938), of Castletown House, Easky, Co Sligo, and Julia, *née* Ormsby (d 1962); *b* 9 Feb 1909,Gallegos, Patagonia, Argentina; *Educ* Sandford Park Sch, Trinity Coll Dublin (BA) 1927; *m* 1935, Helier Georgina (d 1950), da of St George de Carteret, of Bullswater Lodge, Pirbright, Surrey; *Career* RAF, Sqdn Cdr Battle of Britain, Wing and Gp Cdr Werten Devet, OC 212 Gp al Alamein, Chief of Staff 83 Gp France and Germany 1944-45; md: Deccan Airways Ltd, Peter Jones Ltd 1952-58; ops mangr BOAC 1948-52; *Clubs* RAF; *Style—* Air Cdre Harold Fenton, CBE, DSO, DFC; Le Vallon, St Brelade, Jersey C1 (☎ 41172)

FENTON, John Hirst; s of Col Sir William C Fenton, MC (d 1976), of Fieldhead, Cleckheaton, W Yorks, and Lady Margaret, *née* Hirst (d 1972); *b* 6 July 1928; *Educ* Uppingham, RMA Sandhurst; *m* 1, 23 June 1956 (m dis 1981), Juanita, da of Hadleigh Seaborne (d 1962), of Knowle, West Midlands; 2 s (William b 29 Sept 1957, Marcus b 25 March 1966), 1 da (Suzanne (twin) b 29 Sept 1957); m 2, 29 May 1981, Shirley, da of Aston Hayes Mayhall (d 1975), of Alvanley, Cheshire; *Career* RAC 1946-47, Sandhurst 1947-48, RTR 1948-53 served Germany and Korea; ret Capt 1953; BBA Gp plc 1953-70, dir and flying instr Yorks Flying Servs 1970-; represented GB in two Aviation World Champs; chm Spen Valley Civic Soc; Freeman City of London, Upper Freeman Guild of Air Pilots and Air Navigators; *Recreations* fishing, vintage motor cycles; *Style—* John Fenton, Esq; Fieldhead, Cleckheaton, W Yorks BD19 3UE; Yorkshire Flying Services Ltd, Leeds/Bradford Airport, Leeds LS19 7TU (☎ 0532 503 840)

FENTON, Maria Elizabeth Josephine; *née* Neuman; da of Karol Kurt Neuman, of Surrey, and Betty Joan, *née* Hine; *b* 9 May 1956; *Educ* St Mary's Providence Convent, Kingston Poly Coll of Law, Breabouef Manor Guildford (BA); *m* 14 Nov 1981, William James Timothy, s of Wing Cdr William James Ferguson Fenton (ret), of Surrey; *Career* admitted slr of the Supreme Ct 1980, ptnr Aldrich Crowther & Wood; memb: Law Soc, Sussex Law Soc; *Clubs* Network; *Style—* Mrs Maria Fenton; The Warenne, Hurstpierpoint, Sussex BN6 9BD; Aldrich Crowther & Wood, The Old Ho, 199 Preston Rd, Brighton, East Sussex BN1 6AW; 1 Market Square, Norsham, West Sussex

FENTON, Thomas James; Capt James Edmund Fenton, OBE (d 1959), and Margaret Dorothea, *née* Cripps (d 1979); *b* 28 July 1948; *Educ* Elstree Sch, Berks; Bradfield Coll, Berks; *m* 1 April 1978, Deborah Clare, da of Arthur John Medcalf, of Harwell, Oxon; 2 da (Olivia b 1979, Georgina b 1981); *Career* memb Glos Cath Choir; found memb Friends of Highnam Church; Lord of Manor of Highnam (suc Highnam Ct 1966) Linton and Over, Patron of Living of Highnam; tstee Ely stained Glass Museum; *Recreations* music, architecture; *Style—* Thomas Fenton, Esq; The Old Rectory, Highnam, Glos GL2 8DG (☎ Glos 412341)

FENTON, Tom; s of Thomas Fenton and Anne Mary, *née* Palethorpe; *b* 29 August 1933; *Educ* Barnsley GS, Nat Coal Bd (colliery mangr's cert); *m* 1963, Dorothy Anne, *née* Race; 1 s (Charles b 1964), 1 da (Joanne b 1966); *Career* md Huwood (mining equipment mfrs subsidiary of Babcock Int) Aug 1981-; former md Becorit (GB); dir Br Coal Int; pres (int) Assoc of Br Mining Equipment Companies 1983-; cncl memb Instn of Mining Engrs (chm conference ctee 1983); fellow Inst Mining Electrical and Mining Mechanical Engrs 1983-; memb NEDO Mining Machinery Sector Working Pty; CEng; *Recreations* golf, fishing, shooting; *Clubs* IOD; *Style—* Tom Fenton Esq; Glebe House, Kirkwhelpington, Northumberland NE19 2RS (☎ 0830 40305); Huwood Ltd, Team Valley, Gateshead, Tyne and Wear NE11 0LP (☎ 0632 878888, telex HUWOOD G 53368)

FENTON-JONES, Michael Langford; s of Charles Langford Fenton-Jones (d 1946), of Kent, and Rita Beryl Violet, *née* Webster; *b* 1 June 1930; *Educ* Cranbrook Sch Kent; *m* 1956, Gillian Mary, da of Elford Charles Pimble (d 1985), of Surrey; 3 s (Richard b 1959, Jonathan b 1960, David b 1963); *Career* chm: Commercial Union Properties Ltd 1982-, Central Station Properties Ltd 1983-; jt chm Midland Hotel & Conference Centre 1984-, property advsr DOE 1979-81, memb Fin Inst Gp, property advsr Br Airways plc 1983-, Provincial Insur plc 1982-; chm of Int Christian C of C (UK) 1986-; tstee: Christians in Educn, The Carpenters Tst, The Durleston Tst; *Recreations* golf, swimming, reading; *Clubs* National (at Carlton); *Style—* Michael Fenton-Jones, Esq; Eastlea, Felix Lane, Shepperton, Middx; TW17 8NN (☎ 0932 227228); British Airways, Trident House, Heathrow Airport, London, Hounslow TW6 2JA (☎ 01 562 0185)

FENWICK, Maj Charles Xtafer Sebastian; LVO (1977); s of David Fenwick (d 1982); *b* 7 April 1946; *Educ* Ampleforth; *Career* Maj, Regt Offr Grenadier Guards 1965-78, tutor to Sheik Maktoum Bin Rashid Al Maktoum of Dubai 1968-69, equerry to HRH The Duke of Edinburgh 1975-77; dir: By Pass Nurseries Ltd 1978-, By Pass Nurseries (Seeds) Ltd 1978-; chm Int Garden Centre Assoc (Br Gp) Ltd 1984-; md The Chelsea Gardener 1984-; *Clubs* Turf; *Style—* Maj Charles Fenwick, LVO; Barhams Manor, Higham, nr Stoke by Nayland, Suffolk (☎ 0206 37231); 125 Sydney Street, Chelsea, London SW3; Bypass Nurseries Ltd, Ipswich Rd, Colchester, Essex

FENWICK, John James; DL (Tyne and Wear 1986); s of James Frederick Trevor Fenwick (d 1979), and Elizabeth Vere, *née* Meldrum; *b* 9 August 1932; *Educ* Rugby, Pembroke Coll Cambridge (MA); *m* 27 April 1957, (Muriel) Gillian, da of George Robert Hodnett (d 1978); 3 s (Andrew b 8 Oct 1959, Adam b 20 Oct 1960, Hugo b 29 Dec 1964); *Career* md Fenwick Ltd 1972-82, dep chm 1972-79, chm 1979-; regnl dir Lloyds Bank plc 1982-86; dir Northern Rock Bldg Soc 1984-; tstee Civic Tst (North East) 1979-; govr Royal GS Newcastle-upon-Tyne 1975-, chm 1987-; memb Worshipful Co of Mercers 1981; *Recreations* travel, theatre, shooting; *Clubs* Garrick, MCC; *Style—* J J Fenwick, Esq, DL; 27 St Dionis Rd, London SW6 4UQ; 35 Osborne Road, Necastle-upon-Tyne NE2 2AH

FENWICK, Maj Justin Francis Quintus; s of David Fenwick (d 1982), of Barhams Manor, Higham, nr Colchester, Suffolk, and Maita Gwladys Joan, *née* Powys-Keck; *b* 11 Sept 1949; *Educ* Ampleforth, Clare Coll Cambridge (MA); *m* 21 June 1975, Marcia Mary, da of Archibald Dunn (d 1977), of Overbury Hall, Layham, Hadleigh, Suffolk; 3 da (Corisande Mary b 1983, Rosamond Xanthe b 1985, Madeleine Isobel b 1988); *Career* Grenadier Gds 1968-81: Maj and Adj 2 Bn 1977-79, Extra Equerry to HRH Duke of Edinburgh 1979-81; barr Temple 1981, dir By Pass Nurseries Ltd 1982-; chm Soc of Chelsea Res Assoc 1988-; *Recreations* shooting, reading, wine; *Clubs* Garrick, Travellers, Cavalry and Guards'; *Style—* Maj Justin Fenwick; 27 Oakley St, London SW3 (☎ 01 376 5072); Lamb Building, The Temple, London, EC4 (☎ 01 353 6701, fax 01 353 4686)

FENWICK, Mark Anthony; s of John Fenwick, 7 Chesterfield House, South Audley St, London, and Sheila E M, *née* Edwards; *b* 11 May 1948; *Educ* Millfield, Univ of Business Studies Switz; *m* 9 Nov 1972, Margaret Kathleen, da of Col Frederick Boger Hue-Williams (d 1987), of Newbury, Berks; 1 s (Leon b 26 Sept 1980), 1 da (Mia b 14 April 1978); *Career* dir EG Mgmnt Ltd 1971-77, md EG Records Ltd 1977-88, chm EG Gp Ltd 1980-, dir Fenwick Ltd 1981-, dep chm Yeoman Security Gp plc 1986-, chm Old Chelsea Gp plc 1986-, dir Ridmans (Hldgs) Ltd 1986-, chm Fenwick of Bond St 1988-, ptnr Athol & Co Ltd 1989-; tstee LSO Tst 1988-, memb appeals ctee Royal Acad of Music Fndn 1989-; *Recreations* shooting, reading; *Style—* Mark Fenwick, Esq; Old Chelsea Group plc, 63A Kings Rd, London SW3 4NT, (☎ 01 730 2162, fax 01 730 1330)

FENWICK, Thomas Richard Featherstone; s of Edwin Arthur Featherstone Fenwick (d 1978), of Foresters Lodge, Wolsingham, Co Durham and Marjorie Newton *née* Weeks; *b* 11 Dec 1926; *Educ* Charterhouse, Jesus Coll Cambridge; *m* 27 April 1957, Sarah Mary da of Thomas Alexander Page (d 1970); 3s, 1 da; *Career* RA 1945; landowner, farmer, forester; JP Co Durham 1966-79, High Sheriff Co Palatine of Durham 1975-76; *Recreations* shooting; *Clubs* Farmers; *Style—* Thomas Fenwick, Esq; Bishop Oak, Wolsingham, Bishop Auckland, Co Durham DL13 3LT (☎ 0388 527 435)

FENWICKE-CLENNELL, (Geoffrey Thomas) Warren; s of Lt Col Geoffrey Edward Fenwicke-Clennell (d 1963), of Claydon, Oxon, and Barbara Enid, *née* Jolliffe (d 1977); *b* 15 Jan 1928; *Educ* Winchester, RMA Sandhurst; *m* 1, June 1957, Caroline Ann, da of Maj Sir Charles Douglas Blackett, 9 Bt (d 1968), of Northumberland; 2 s (Nicholas b 1959, Luke Thomas b 1961), 1 da (Katherine Mary b 1963); *Career* Capt 11 Hussars PAD resigned 1958; sales mangr Taplows 1962-64, prod mangr IDV/WA Gilbey 1964-69, dir Watney-Mann 1971-72, dir of Free Trade Watney-Mann & Truman Brewers 1972-76 (comm dir 1981-83), md Truman Ltd 1976-81; comptroller The Earl of Harewood from May 1984, dir Harewood Property Co, Harewood House Tst Ltd, Diacteon Property Ltd; *Recreations* country sports, gundogs, poultry; *Clubs* Cavalry and Gds'; *Style—* Warren Fenwicke-Clennell, Esq; Kirk Hammerton House, York (☎ 0423 331016); 8 Donne Place, London SW3 (☎ 01 584 2350); Estate Office, Harewood, Leeds (☎ 0532 886331)

FERENS, Lt-Col Michael Radcliffe; MBE (1943), TD (1945), JP (Durham 1961), DL (1982); s of Henry Radcliffe Ferens, of Bishop Auckland; *b* 25 Sept 1912; *Educ* Aysgarth, Sedbergh; *m* 1939, Mary, yr da of Rev Charles Henry Surtees, Rector of Brancepeth, Durham 1919-45 (d 1955); 2 s, 2 da; *Career* served Durham LI (TA) 1936-45, Lt-Col in France, N Africa, Sicily, Italy, NW Europe; dir: Ferens Bros 1938-66, Nitrovit Ltd 1961-66; High Sheriff Durham 1976-77; MFH 1968-71; *Recreations* gardening, hunting; *Style—* Lt-Col Michael Ferens, MBE, TD, JP, DL; The Old Vicarage, Bolam, Darlington, Co Durham DL2 2UP (☎ 0388 832499)

FERENS, (Charles) Richard; s of John Leslie Ferens (d 1987), of Harrogate, and Joan, *née* Mannington; *b* 23 Dec 1936; *Educ* Trinity Hall (MA); *m* 17 Sept 1960, Penelope Jane, da of Lt-Col Stuart Dewes Hayward (d 1983), of Suffolk; 3 da (Emma b 1962, Caroline b 1963, Sophie b 1965); *Career* Lt E Yorks Regt 1955-57; Hon Sec Land Agency and Agric Div RICS 1977-80 (chm E Anglian Branch): Hon Dir Royal Show 1982-87, vice-pres Royal Agric Soc of England, chm Lincs branch Br Food and Farming; Arbitrator to Ld Chllr; *Recreations* shooting, fishing, gardening; *Clubs* Farmers, Anglo Belgian; *Style—* Richard Ferens, Esq; Casthorpe Lodge, Barrowby, Grantham, Lincs (☎ 0476 63559)

FERENS, Sir Thomas Robinson; CBE (1952); s of John Johnson Till Ferens, of Hull (d 1957), and Marion, *née* Runton; *b* 4 Jan 1903; *Educ* Rydal, Leeds Univ (BSc); *m* 1 Sept 1934, Jessie (d 4 May 1982), da of late P G Sanderson, of Hull and Scarborough; 2 da; *Career* engr, md Shipham & Co Ltd, George Clark & Son (Hull) Ltd, dir Newman Hender Ltd, ret 1970; kt 1957; *Recreations* fly fishing; *Style—* Sir Thomas Ferens, CBE; Sunderlandwick House, Driffield, Humberside (☎ 0377 42323)

FERGUS, John Graham; s of Leslie Fraser Fergus (d 1987), of Glasgow, and Barbara Ireland, *née* Pringle; *b* 2 July 1933; *Educ* Glasgow HS, Glasgow Acad, Kings Park Sch (Glasgow); *m* 1958, Helen Davidson, da of Andrew Davidson McLay (d 1982); 2 s (Alasdair b 1965, Colin b 1967), 1 da (Linda b 1972); *Career* Nat Serv PO RAF, serv UK; CA; md Scottish Lowland Hldgs Ltd and Subsidiaries 1974-82; dir Arbuckle Smith & Co Ltd 1972-74, md Castlegreen Warehousing Co Ltd 1966-72; chm Beithcraft Furniture Ltd 1984-85, Antartex Ltd 1984-87, Scottish Tanning Industries Ltd 1982-, dir: Barr and Wray Ltd 1982-, AA Bros Ltd 1987-, Thomas Auld & Son Ltd 1988-; cncl memb Br Leather Confed Ltd 1986-; *Recreations* garden, golf, church affairs, city of Glasgow; *Clubs* RSAC; *Style—* John Fergus, Esq; Carleith, Kilmacolm, Renfrewshire PA13 4AS (☎ 050 587 2520); Scottish Tanning Industries Ltd, Bridge of Weir, Renfrewshire (☎ 050 561 2953, telex 778057, fax 050 561 4964)

FERGUSON; *see*: Johnson-Ferguson

FERGUSON, Andrew John Duncan; s of James Duncan Ferguson (d 1980), of Heath Drive, Sutton, Surrey, and Kathleen Ann Ferguson (d 1985); *b* 9 June 1940; *Educ* Epsom Coll, St John's Coll Cambridge (MA); *m* 1967, Elizabeth Mary, da of Cdr Leslie Edward Wright, of 4 Glebe Way, Wisborough Green, W Sussex; 1 s (Ian b 1968), 3 da (Joanna b 1970, Kate b 1979, Gillian b 1983); *Career* chm and chief exec Rayne Med Indust Ltd; FCA; *Recreations* sailing, squash, horse riding; *Clubs* RAC, Caledonian; *Style—* Andrew Ferguson, Esq; Mundys Hill, Shere Road, Ewhurst, Surrey (☎ 0483 277237);

FERGUSON, David Allen; s of Sir David Gordon Brukewich Ferguson (d 1969), and Lady (Rosemary Lelia) Ferguson, *née* Brass; *b* 29 Oct 1928; *Educ* Marlborough, Worcester Coll Oxford (MA); *m* 1960, Margaret Beatrice, da of Harold Wilmot CBE (d 1966); 1 s (Antony b 1961); *Career* CA; fin dir: Lloyds Bank Int 1970-79, London & Scottish Marine Oil Plc 1980-; *Recreations* mountain walking, music, golf, gardening, keep fit; *Clubs* Canning; *Style—* David Ferguson, Esq; LASMO, 140 London Wall (☎ 01 600 8021)

FERGUSON, George Robin Paget; s of Robert Spencer Ferguson, MVO, of Manningford Bruce House, Pewsey, Wilts, and Eve Mary, *née* Paget; *b* 22 Mar 1947; *Educ* Wellington, Bristol Univ (BA, BArch); *m* 24 May 1969, (Aymée) Lavinia, da of Sir John Clerk, 10 Bt, of Penicuik House, Midlothian; 1 s (John b 1974), 2 da (Alice b 1971, Corinna b 1979); *Career* architect; fndr practice 1973, ptnr Ferguson Mann 1979-87 (md 1988-), fndr and chm Acanthus Assoc Architectural Practices Ltd 1986; ptnr Concept Planning Gp 1988; Univ of Bristol ct, tstee Bristol Exploratory, chm Bristol Adventure Play Assoc, memb Cncl for Preservation of Ancient Bristol, ctee memb Bristol Civic Soc, pres Bristol West Democrats; Bristol City cncllr (Lib) 1973-79, party candidate (alliance) Bristol West 1983-87; RIBA 1972; *Books* Races Against Time (1983); *Recreations* writing, broadcasting, skiing, painting; *Style—* George Ferguson, Esq; Ferguson Mann Architects/Acanthus Bristol, Royal Colonnade, 18 Great George St, Bristol BS1 5RH (☎ 0272 273140, fax 0272 225027)

FERGUSON, James Gordon Dickson; s of Col James Dickson Ferguson, OBE, ERD, DL (d 1979), of Aghaderg Glebe, Loughbrickland, Banbridge, Co Down, and Jean, *née* Gordon; *b* 12 Nov 1947; *Educ* Winchester, Trinity Coll Dublin (BA); *m* 20 June 1970, Nicola Hilland, da of Walter G H Stewart, of Lausanne, Switzerland; 2 s (Jim, William), 1 da (Jessica); *Career* dir Stewart Ivory & Co Ltd (formerly Stewart Fund Mangrs Ltd) 1974- (joined 1970), dep chm Assoc of Investmt Tst Cos 1984-86, dir Value & Income Tst plc; *Recreations* country pursuits; *Clubs* New; *Style—* James Ferguson, Esq; 25 Heriot Row, Edinburgh, EH3 6EN, Aghaderg Glebe, Loughbrickland, Banbridge, Co Down; Stewart Ivory & Co Ltd, 45 Charlotte Square, Edinburgh EH2 4HW (☎ 031 226 3271, fax 031 226 5120, telex 72500)

FERGUSON, Jeremy John; s of Archibald John Lindo Ferguson (d1976) of Great Missenden, Bucks, and Ann Meryl, *née* Thomas; *b* 12 Nov 1935; *Educ* Stowe; *m* 19 July 1958, Joesphine Mary, da of Authur William John Hitchcock (1969), of - Coombe Vale, Sandymere Road, Northam, Bideford, Devon; 1 s (Paul b 1962), 1 da (Elizabeth b 1966); *Career* ptnr: Seldon Ward & Nuttal 1960-74, Jeremy Ferguson & Co 1974-, Chanters Barnstaple 1986-; dep coroner for N. Devon 1964-74, memb N. Devon Manufacturers Assoc, hon slr (memb and past pres) Bideford C of C, fndr and sec Bideford Devpt Project, pres Law Soc Motor club, memb Legal aid Area Ctee; *Recreations* motor racing, video photography; *Style—* Jeremy Ferguson, Esq; Langleys, 25 Bay View Rd, Northam, Bideford, Devon EX39 1BH (☎ 02372 74855); 17 The Quay, Bideford, North Devon EX39 2EN (☎ 02372 78751, fax 02372 70893); Bridge Chambers, Barnstaple, North Devon EX31 1HF (☎ 0271 42268)

FERGUSON, Col Kenneth Dubois; DSO (1944), TD, DL (Dorset 1977); s of H W G Ferguson MC (d 1963), of Gosforth, Newcastle-upon-Tyne, and A E Raine (d 1962); *b* 22 Dec 1917; *Educ* Uppingham, Clare Coll Cambridge (BA); *m* 20 Sept 1983, Pauline, da of Samuel Garthwaite Edgar, CBE (d 1947), of Minister of Works, Jodhpur, India; (by previous m) 2 s (Christopher b 1944, Michael b 1947), 1 da (Sarah b 1949); *Career* served Army, N Africa 1940-43, NW Europe 1944-45, directing staff, Staff Coll Camberley 1945-46, CRE 50th (N) TA 1955-59; commadant Army Cadet Force Dorset 1959-65; steel manfacturer 1946-58; Proprietor Knoll House Hotel, Studland Bay, Dorset 1959-; memb Dorset CC 1970-85; high sheriff of Dorset 1986-87; *Recreations* golf; *Clubs* Army and Navy; *Style—* Kenneth Ferguson, DSO, TD, DL; Studland Bay House, Studland, Dorset (☎ 092 944 253)

FERGUSON, Nicholas Eustace Haddon; s of Capt Derek Ferguson, of Craigard, Tighnabruaich, Argyll, and Betsy, *née* Eustace; *b* 14 Oct 1948; *Educ* Winchester Coll, Edinburgh Univ (BSc Ordinary, First-Class Econs), Harvard Business Sch (MBA); *m* 18 Dec 1976, Margaret Jane Dura, da of Robert Collin, Wheatsheaf House, Hook Norton, Oxon; 2 s (Alexander b 1978, Thomas b 1985), 1 da (Cornelia b 1979); *Career* banker; UK dirships: chm Schroder Ventures, J Henry Schroder Wagg and Co Ltd, Schroder Venures Ltd, Int Students Club (C of E) Ltd; overseas dir: Singapore Int Merchant Bankers Ltd, Schroder Real Estate Investment Inc, Schroder Venure Mangrs (Guernsey) Ltd, Schroder Securities (Japan) Ltd, Schroder PTV Ptnrs KK; *Recreations* sailing, skiing; *Clubs* Brooks; *Style—* Nicholas Ferguson, Esq; 18 Queensdale Road, London W11 4QB (☎ 01 229 0503); 120 Cheapside, London EC2V 6DS (☎ 01 382 6896, telex 885029, fax 01 382 6878)

FERGUSON, Richard; QC (NI 1973, UK 1986); s of Wesley Ferguson (d 1973), of Enniskillen, and Edith, *née* Hewitt; *b* 22 August 1935; *Educ* Methodist Coll, Queen's Univ Belfast (LLB), Trinity Coll Dublin (BA); *m* 8 Sept 1961, Janet, da of Irvine H M Gowan, CB (d 1978), of Mount Norris, Co Armagh; 4 s (Richard b 1964, William b 1966, James b 1968, Patrick b 1988), 1 da (Kathrine b 1962); *Career* Lt Royal Irish Fus TA 1958-61; barr Gray's Inn 1956, sr counsel Rep of Ireland 1983; chm Mental Health Review Tribunal (NI), govr Methodist Coll, chm Mountain Trg Bd, memb Irish Sports Cncl, MP S Antrim 1986-88; FRGS; *Recreations* swimming, hill walking; *Clubs* Kildare St (Dublin); *Style—* Richard Ferguson, Esq, QC; Sandhill House, Derrygonnelly, Fermanagh, NI; 84 Buckingham Rd, London N1; 1 Crown Office Row, Temple, London EC4 (☎ 01 583 3724, fax 01 353 3923)

FERGUSON, Maj Robert Spencer; MVO (1954); s of Maj Spencer Ferguson OBE (d 1958), of Brockenhurst, and Agnes (d 1957), *née* Irwin; *b* 15 May 1918; *Educ*

Wellington, RMC Sandhurst; *m* 19 June 1945, Eve, da of Maj Kenneth Paget (d 1966), of Itchen Abbas; 2 s (George b 1947, Richard b 1949); *Career* 2 Lt Royal Northumberland Fusiliers 1938, served Western Desert 1939-42 POW Italy/Germany 1942-45, Maj 1951, Comd Depot Royal Northumberland Fusiliers 1950-53, mil sec to Govr & C in C Gibraltar 1953-56, RMA Sandhurst 1956-59, HQ AFNE Oslo 1959-61, Sch of Inf Netheravon 1961-68, Master Staff Coll Drag Hunt 1957-59, ret 1969; *Recreations* gardening, shooting, fishing, woodwork; *Clubs* Army and Navy; *Style*— Maj Robert Ferguson, MVO; Manningford Bruce House, Pewsey, Wiltshire (☎ Stonehenge 630265)

FERGUSON DAVIE, Sir Antony Francis; 6 Bt (E 1641, revived UK 1847 in favour of Gen Henry Ferguson, who m Frances sis of Sir John Davie, 9 Bt, and who assumed by Royal Licence the additional surname and arms of Davie); s of Rev Sir (Arthur) Patrick Ferguson Davie, 5 Bt, TD (d 1988); *b* 23 Mar 1952; *Educ* Stanbridge Earls Sch, Birkbeck Coll London; *Style*— Sir Antony Ferguson Davie, Bt

FERGUSON DAVIE, Lady; Iris Dawn; *née* Cable-Buller; o da of Capt Michael Francis Buller, of Devon, and Hon Dawn Weston, da of 1 and last Baron Cable; *b* 7 Mar 1929; *m* 8 Dec 1949, Rev Sir (Arthur) Patrick Ferguson Davie, 5 Bt (d 1988); 1 s (Sir Antony, 6 Bt, *qv*); *Style*— Lady Ferguson Davie; Skalatos House, Girne, Mersin 10, Turkey

FERGUSSON, Adam Dugdale; yr s of Sir James Fergusson, 8 Bt, of Kilkerran (d 1973) and bro of Sir Charles, 9 Bt *qv*; *b* 10 July 1932; *Educ* Eton, Trinity Coll Cambridge (BA); *m* 11 Dec 1965, (Elizabeth Catherine) Penelope, eldest da of Thomas Peter Hughes, of Furneaux Pelham Hall, Buntingford, Herts; 2 s (James b 1966, Marcus 1972), 2 da (Petra b 1968, Lucy b 1970); *Career* politician, author and journalist; Glasgow Herald 1956-60 (ldr writer, diplomatic correspondent), Statist 1961-67 (foreign ed 1964-67); Times, feature writer 1967-77; MEP (Con) W Strathclyde 1979-84; political affrs spokesman for Euro Democratic Gp 1979-82, vice-pres Political Affrs Ctee Euro Parl 1982-84; special adviser European Affairs FCO 1985-; *Publications* Roman Go Home (1969), The Lost Embassy (1970), When Money Dies (1975), The Sack of Bath (1973); *Clubs* Brooks's; *Style*— Adam Fergusson Esq; 15 Warwick Gardens, London W14 (☎ 01 603 7900)

FERGUSSON, Sir Ewen Alastair John; KCMG (1987); s of Sir Ewen MacGregor Field Fergusson (d 1974), and Winifred Evelyn Fergusson; *b* 28 Oct 1932; *Educ* Rugby, Oriel Coll Oxford (MA); *m* 19 Dec 1959, Sara Carolyn, da of late Brig-Gen Lord Esmé Gordon-Lennox KCVO, CMG, DSO; 1 s (Ewen b 30 Nov 1965), 2 da (Anna b 15 June 1961, Iona b 7 May 1967); *Career* 2 Lt 60 Rifles KRRC 1954-56; Dip Serv 1956, asst private sec MOD 1957-59, Br Embassy Addis Ababa 1960, FO 1963, Br Trade Devpt Off NYC 1967, cnsllr and head of Chancery Off UK Perm Rep to Euro Communities 1972-75, private sec for and with cwlth sec 1975-78, asst under sec State FCO 1978-82, ambass SA 1982-84, dep under sec state FCO 1984-87, ambass France 1987-; govr Rugby 1985-, hon fell Oriel Coll Oxford 1987; *Clubs* RAC, Jockey, Cercle de l'Union Interalliée (Paris); *Style*— Sir Ewen Fergusson, KCMG; c/o Foreign and Commonwealth Office, London SW1A 2AH

FERGUSSON, Hon George Duncan Raukawa; s of Baron Ballantrae (Life Peer), KT, GCMG, GCVO, DSO, OBE (d 1980), 3 s of Sir Charles Fergusson, 7 Bt, of Kilkerran), by his w Laura Margaret Grenfell (d 1979) (*see* Peerage Baron Grenfell 1976); *b* 30 Sept 1955; *Educ* Hereworth Sch NZ, Eton, Magdalen Coll Oxford (BA); *m* 10 Jan 1981, Margaret Sheila, da of Michael John Wookey, of Camberley, Surrey; 1 s (Alexander b 1984), 2 da (Laura, b 1982, Alice v 1986); *Career* civil servant 1978-; 1 sec Br Embassy Dublin 1988-; *Style*— G D Fergusson, Esq; c/o Outward Bag Room, Foreign and Commonwealth Office (Dublin), King Charles Street, London SW1

FERGUSSON, (Frederick) James; s of Frederick Peter Fergusson, of Yalding, Kent, and Oenone Barbara, *née* Wicks; *b* 28 Mar 1943; *Educ* Haileybury, ISC, Univ Coll Oxford (BA); *m* 11 Nov 1966, Diane Frances (Sophie), da of Leslie Eric Duncan Darley (d 1986), of Rochester, Kent, 2 s (William b 1975, Edward b 1984), 2 da (Polly b 1973, Isobel b 1982); *Career* joined James Capel and Co: joined 1969, ptnr 1976, dir 1984, dep chm 1987; *Recreations* skiing, tennis, music, reading; *Style*— James Fergusson, Esq; James Capel and Co, 6 Bevis Marks, London EC3A 7JQ (☎ 01 621 0011, fax 01 621, telex 888866 JC LDN G)

FERGUSSON, William Gordon; s of Capt John Gordon Fergusson, of Sandy Brow, Tarporley, Cheshire, and Marielou, *née* Gaggero (d 1988); *Educ* Ampleforth; *Career* 9/12 Royal Lancers (Prince of Wales) 1978-81, ret as Lt; assoc dir Walter Judd Ltd (practitioners in fin advertising and pr) 1987 (joined 1982); MIPA 1987; *Recreations* skiing, golf, shooting, watersports; *Style*— William Fergusson, Esq; Walter Judd Ltd, 1A Bow Lane, London EC4 (☎ 01 236 4541, fax 248 8139)

FERGUSSON-CUNINGHAME OF CAPRINGTON, Capt Robert Wallace; DL (Ayrshire 1960); 17 of Caprington; Lord of the Barony of Caprington; er s of Lt-Col William Wallace Smith Cuninghame, DSC (d 1959), of Caprington, and Ella Cutlar Fergusson (d 1928), 20 of Craigdarroch, Dumfries; *b* 4 August 1919; *Educ* Eton, RMC; *m* 1958, Rosemary Elisabeth Euing, er da of Brig Alastair W E Crawford, of Auchentroig, Buchlyvie, Stirling; 1 s; *Career* 2 Lt Scots Gds 1939, served WWII; Capt RARO 1949; memb Queen's Body Gd for Scotland (Royal Co of Archers) 1948-; *Clubs* Turf, Pratt's, New (Edinburgh); *Style*— Capt Robert Fergusson-Cuninghame, DL; Caprington Castle, Kilmarnock, Ayrshire (☎ 0563 26157)

FERMOR-HESKETH, Hon Flora Mary; da of 3 Baron Hesketh; *b* 31 July 1981; *Style*— Hon Flora Fermor-Hesketh

FERMOR-HESKETH, Hon John; s of 2 Baron Hesketh (d 1955); *b* 15 Mar 1953; *Educ* Ampleforth; *m* 2 Dec 1980, Anna, o da of Hamish Wallace, of Old Corromony, Glen Urquhart, Inverness; *Style*— Hon John Fermor-Hesketh

FERMOR-HESKETH, Hon Robert; s of 2 Baron Hesketh (d 1955); *b* 1 Nov 1951; *Educ* Ampleforth; *m* 10 Oct 1979, Jeanne, da of Patrick McDowell, of Co Clare; 1 s (Blaise b 1987); *Style*— Hon Robert Fermor-Hesketh

FERMOY, Lady; Lavinia Frances Elizabeth; *née* Pitman; o da of late Capt John Pitman (d 1943), of Foxley House, Malmesbury, Wilts, and Elizabeth Cattanach, *née* Donaldson; *b* 18 April 1941; *m* 22 June 1964, 5 Baron Fermoy (d 1984), 2 s (6 Baron, *qv*, Hon Edmund Hugh Burke b 1972), 1 da (Hon Frances Caroline Burke b 1965); *Style*— The Rt Hon Lady Fermoy; Axford House, nr Marlborough, Wiltshire

FERMOY, 6 Baron (I 1856); (Patrick) Maurice Burke Roche; s of 5 Baron Fermoy (d 1984), and Lady (Lavinia) Fermoy, *qv*, *née* Pitman; br of Hon Hugh Roche, *qv*, and Hon Frances Roche, *qv*; *b* 11 Oct 1967; *Educ* Eton, RMA Sandhurst; *Heir* br, Hon (Edmund) Hugh Burke Roche b 5 Feb 1972; *Career* page of honour to HM Queen Elizabeth The Queen Mother 1982-85; The Blues and Royals 1987-; *Clubs* Cavalry and Guards'; *Style*— The Rt the Hon Lord Fermoy; Axford House, Marlborough, Wilts

FERMOY, Ruth, Lady; Ruth Sylvia; *née* Gill; DCVO (1979, CVO 1966), OBE (1952), JP (Norfolk 1944); grandmother of HRH The Princess of Wales; *see* Spencer, 8 Earl; da of Col William Smith Gill, CB, VD (d 1957), of Dalhebity, Bieldside, Aberdeenshire, and Ruth, *née* Littlejohn (d 1964); *b* 2 Oct 1908; *m* 17 Sept 1931, 4 Baron Fermoy (d 8 July 1955); 1 s (5 Baron, decd), 2 da (Hon Mrs Anthony Berry *see* Peerage Viscount Kemsley, Hon Mrs Shand Kydd *qv*); *Career* an extra woman of the bedchamber to HM Queen Elizabeth The Queen Mother 1956-60, since when a woman of the bedchamber; Freedom of King's Lynn 1963; Hon MusD, E Anglia 1975; Hon FRCM 1984; *Style*— The Rt Hon Ruth, Lady Fermoy, DCVO, OBE, JP

FERNAU, (Francis) Guy; s of Maj Francis John Fernau (d 1968), Joyce Fernau *née* Barnes (d 1973), (f clerk of the Privy Cncl 1952); *b* 25 May 1929; *Educ* Canford, Corpus Christi Coll Cambridge (BA); *m* 5 Nov 1972, Janet Elspeth; 1 s (John b 1974), 1 da (Sarah b 1976); *Career* chm and md Fernau Avionics Ltd 1970-87; *Recreations* sailing; *Style*— Francis Fernau, Esq; The White Lodge, Hawkshead Rd, Potters Bar, Herts EN6 1LU; Fernau Avionics Ltd, Holywell Hill, St Albans, Herts AL1 1HS (☎ 0727 31215, telex 894570, fax 0727 54307)

FERNYHOUGH, Rt Hon Ernest; PC (1970); s of Harry Fernyhough (d 1927), of Wood Lane, Stoke-on-Trent, and Fanny, *née* Franklin (d 1957); *b* 24 Dec 1908; *Educ* Wood Lane Cncl Sch; *m* 1934, Ethel, da of Arthur Edwards (d 1970), of King Street, Talke Pits, Staffs; 2 s (John, Harry (decd)), 1 da (Margaret); *Career* miner 1923-25; Trade Union Official (USDAW) 1926-36; MP (L) Jarrow 1947-79, under sec of State Dept Employment 1967-69; PPS to PM 1964-66, jt Parly under-sec Employment and Productivity 1967-69; memb: Privy Cncl 1970 Cncl of Europe 1970-73; freeman of Jarrow; *Style*— The Rt Hon Ernest Fernyhough; 35 Edwards Rd, Lache Park, Chester (☎ 0632 671 522)

FEROZE; *see*: Moolan-Feroze

FERRALL, Sir Raymond Alfred; CBE (1969); s of Alfred Charles Ferrall (d 1955), and Edith Maud Ferrall (d 1963); *b* 27 May 1906; *Educ* Launceston Church GS; *m* 1931, Lorna Lyttleton, da of late Percy A Findlay; 2 s, 2 da; *Career* master warden Port of Launceston Authy 1961-80, assoc cmmr Hydro-Electric Cmmn Tas 1970-80, pres Launceston Bank for Savings 1976-82, chm Tas Coll Advanced Educn 1976-80, dir various public and private cos; Silver Jubilee Medal 1977; kt 1982; *see Debrett's Handbook of Australia and New Zealand for further details*; *Style*— Sir Raymond Ferrall, CBE; Quamby, Hagley, Tasmania 7292 (☎ 93 1606)

FERRANTI; *see*: de Ferranti

FERRERS, 13 Earl (GB 1711); Sir Robert Washington Shirley; 19 Bt (E 1611), PC (1982), DL (Norfolk 1983); also Viscount Tamworth (GB 1711); s of 12 Earl Ferrers (d 1954, 17 in descent from Sir Hugh Shirley, Grand Falconer to Henry IV and victim of mistaken identity at the Battle of Shrewsbury through being accoutred as the king; 16 in descent from Sir Ralph Shirley, one of the principal commanders at Agincourt; 9 in descent from Dorothy, da of Elizabeth I's, favourite Essex, through whom Lord Ferrers descends from Edward III, hence the quartering of the arms of Fr and Eng on the Shirley escutcheon; 5 in descent from Hon Walter Shirley, yr bro of 4 Earl, the last Lord to be tried for homicide by his Peers; *b* 8 June 1929; *Educ* Winchester, Magdalene Coll Cambridge (MA); *m* 21 July 1951, Annabel Mary, da of Brig William Greenwood Carr, CVO, DSO, JP, DL (d 1982), of Ditchingham Hall, Norfolk; 2 s (Viscount Tamworth b 1952, Hon Andrew b 1965), 3 da (Lady Angela Ellis b 1954, Lady Sallyanne b 1957, Lady Selina b 1958); *Career* sits as (C) Peer in the House of Lords; served Coldstream Gds, Lt, Malaya; chm S Norfolk Cons Assoc 1953-65 (pres 1971-); lord-in-waiting and govt whip Lords 1962-64 and 1971-74, oppn whip Lords 1964-67, jt-dep ldr oppn Lords 1976-79, parly sec Ag Fish and Food 1974, min state Ag Fish and Food 1979-83, dep ldr Lords 1979-83 and 1988-, min state Home Office 1988-; memb: Cncl Food from Britain 1985-88, Armitage Ctee on Political Activities of Civil Servants 1976, central bd TSB 1977-79; tstee: E Anglian TSB 1957-75 (v-chm 1971-75), TSB of E England 1975-79 (chm 1977-79), Central TSB Ltd 1978-79, TSB Trustcard 1978-79; dir: Economic Forestry Gp plc 1985-88, Norwich Union Insurance Gp 1975-79 and 1983-88, Chatham Historic Dockyard Tst 1984-88, Goving By of Rothamstead Agric Station 1984-88; pres (eastern counties region) MENCAP 1979-88; chm British Agric Export Cncl 1984-88; high steward Norwich Cathedral 1979-; chm R Commn on Historical Monuments (England) 1984-88; Fell Winchester Coll 1988; *Recreations* shooting, music, travel; *Clubs* Beefsteak; *Style*— The Rt Hon Earl Ferrers, PC, DL; Ditchingham Hall, Bungay, Suffolk (☎ 050 844 250)

FERRERS-WALKER, Thomas Weaving; s of Thomas Ferrers (d 1970), and Undine Ferrers, *née* Weaving (d 1962); *b* 24 Sept 1925; *Educ* Bradfield Coll; *m* 1, 1948, Pamela Mary Beer (decd); 2 s (Richard b 1949, John b 1952); m 2, 1956, Shirley, wid of Edward Kenneth Dunlop, and da of Herbert Cordingley (d 1950); 1 s (Edward b 1961), 1 da (Undine b 1965); *Career* WWII served RNVR combined ops Europe and Pacific 1942-46; TNVSR 1947-65, Lieut RNR 1965-71; chm and chief exec Thomas Walker plc 1971-; tstee: Shakespeare Birthplace Tst (exec ctee 1986-) 1985-, RN Museum 1987-; pres Stratford-on-Avon Nat Tst Assn 1985-, vice-pres Solihull Nat Tst Centre 1980-, patron of the living of Baddesley Clinton, achieved transfer at Baddesley Clinton to Nat Tst 1980; memb Regnl Ctee Historic Houses Assoc Heart of England Region 1975-; Cncl of the Order of St John for the County of W Midlands 1970-; OStJ (1985); *Recreations* gardening, photography for recording purposes, historical and naval research and preservation, conservation of historic and natural landscape and buildings; *Style*— Thomas Ferrers-Walker, Esq; Westfield, 30 Fiery Hill Rd, Barnt Green, Worcestershire B45 8LG (☎ 021 445 1785); 39 St Paul's Square, Birmingham B3 1QY (☎ 021 236 5565, telex 338836, fax 021 236 6275)

FERRIER, Maj (Richard) Anthony Plowden Gournay; s of Capt Richard Gournay Ferrier (d 1985) of Hemsby Hall, Hemsby, Norfolk and Doris Esperanza Rosemary Chichele *née* Plowden (d 1967); *b* 13 Jan 1920; *Educ* Old Buckenham Hall, Radley, RMC, Sandhurst, Staff Coll, Camberley; *m* 15 Oct 1946, (m dis 1975), Eelin Ailsa da of William Campbell, Boroughbridge, Yorks (d 1944); 2 s (Richard b 1948, Michael b 1949); m2, 8 July 1977, Peta Ann da of Gp Capt David Christie, CBE, AFC, of Sheringham, Norfolk; *Career* cmmnd Royal Norfolk Regt - 1939, served India, Far East 1939-45, POW 1942-45, Adj, Royal Norfolk Regt, 1946-47, General Staff HQ 7 Armd Div 1947-49, Chief Instr Rhine Army Trag Centre, 1949-50, Parachute Regt, Middle East, 1952-53, DAAG HQ 16 Airborne Div 1953-55, Royal Norfolk Reg,

Cyprus, 1955-57, GHQ UK Lane Forces GSO 11 (Plans) 1957-59, ret 1960; regnl sec and chief exec Country Landowners Assoc East Anglia 1964-85; Area Pres and cncl memb St John Ambulance Brig - Norfolk 1960-70, cdr Bn Norfolk Army Cadet Force, 1963-66, County trg offr Norfolk Army Cadet Force, 1966-69, Pres Central Norfolk Far East POW Assoc 1967-; CS & J (1970); *Recreations* shooting, golf, sailing, ornithology; *Clubs* Naval and Military, Norfolk County; *Style—* Maj Anthony Ferrier

FERRIER, Prof Robert Patton; s of William McFarlane Ferrier (d 1963) and Gwendoline Melita, *née* Edward (d 1976); *b* 4 Jan 1934; *Educ* Glebelands Sch, Morgan Academy, Univ of St Andrews (BSc, PhD), Univ of Cambridge (MA); *m* 2 Sept 1961, Valerie Jane, da of Samuel George Duncan (d 1986); 2 s (Hamish b 1965, Alan b 1969), 1 da (Elizabeth b 1967); *Career* Sci Offr UKAERE Harwell 1959-61, res assoc MIT USA 1961-62, Sr Asst in res 1962-66, Cavendish Lab Univ of Camb (asst dir of res 1966-73), guest scientist IBM Res Div San Jose Calif USA 1972-73, prof of nat philosophy Univ of Glasgow 1973-; memb: of local Episcopal Church, various ctees of Sci and Engrg, Res Cncl 1970-85 (former chm); FInstP 1964, FRSE 1977; *Recreations* tennis, gardening, reading crime novels; *Style—* Prof Robert Ferrier; Glencoe, Thorn Road, Bearsden G61 4BS, Scotland; Department of Physics and Astronomy, The University, Glasgow G12 8QQ (☎ 041 330 5388, 041 339 8855, 4707, fax 041 334 9029, telex 777070 UNIGLA)

FERRIER, Baron (Life Peer UK 1958); Victor Ferrier Noel-Paton; ED (1945), DL (Lanarks 1960); s of Frederick Waller Ferrier Noel-Paton (d 1914), of Edinburgh, dir-gen Commerical Intelligence to Govt of India, and Ethel Margaret, *née* Alt (d 1963); *b* 29 Jan 1900; *Educ* Edinburgh Acad; *m* 9 March 1932, Joane Mary (d 1984), er da of Sir Gilbert Wiles, KCIE, CSI (d 1961); 1 s (Hon Ranald b 1938), 3 da (Hon Lady Fergusson, Hon Mrs Laird, Hon Mrs Hacking); *Career* Maj (ret) Bombay Light Horse Aux Force India and IA Reserve of Offrs 19 KGVO Lancers, Hon ADC to Govr of Bombay; East India merchant and industrialist; formerly MLC Bombay, former dir Imperial Bank of India (among other directorships), pres Bombay Chamber of Commerce; past chm: Fedn of Electricity Undertakings of India, Indian Road and Tport Dvpt Assoc Bombay, Edinburgh Pharmaceutical Industries; memb Queen's Body Gd for Scotland (Royal Co of Archers); dep speaker & chm of Ctees House of Lords 1970-73; *Recreations* field sports; *Clubs* New (Edinburgh), Cavalry and Guards', Beefsteak; *Style—* The Rt Hon Lord Ferrier, ED, DL; Kilkerran, Maybole, Ayrshire KA19 7SJ (☎ 065 54 515)

FERRIS, Neil Jeremy; s of Oscar Ferris, and Benita, *née* Lewis; *b* 5 April 1955; *Educ* Brighton Hove and Sussex GS; *m* 25 Jan 1980, Jill Denise, da of William Charles Anderson, of London; 1 s (Daniel Mark); *Career* jr PR dept EMI Records 1974; PR dept: NEMS Records 1976, CBS Records 1977; formed The Ferret Plugging Co 1980 representing: UB40, Erasure, Depeche Mode, Spandau Ballet, XTC, Bros, S-Express, Howard Jones among others; produced tv special about Erasure for BBC 2 1988 and TV documentary on Depeche Mode BBC TV 1989; speaker on various subjects relating to the music indust and the media; *Recreations* photography, power-boats, antiques (early oak furniture); *Style—* Neil Ferris, Esq; 50 Lisson St, London NW1 5DF (☎ 01 402 2401, fax 01 723 0069, car tel 0836 211 045)

FERRY, Alexander; MBE (1978); s of Alexander Ferry (d 1932), and Susan Cavan Ferry (d 1987); *b* 14 Feb 1931; *Educ* Saint Patrick's Sr Secdy Sch, Dunbartonshire Scotland; *m* 15 Feb 1958, Mary, da of late Patrick M'Alaney; 3 s (Alexander b 1958 d 1977, Andrew b 1966, Carlann b 1960), 1 da (Mary b 1962); *Career* Nat Serv RAF 1952-54; engr 1951-64, trade union offr AEU 1964-78, gen sec Confedn of Shipbldg and Engng Unions 1978-; adtive in Br (Lab) Pty, memb Monopolies and Mergers Cmmn 1986-; bd memb: Harland Wolff Belfast 1984-, SE Electricity 1986-; *Recreations* golf, reading, crosswords; *Style—* Alexander Ferry, Esq, MBE; 190 Brampton Rd, Bexley Heath, Kent DA7 4YS (☎ 01 303 5338); 140/142 Walworth Rd, London SE17 (☎ 01 703 2215, fax 01 252 7397)

FERRY, Brig (John) Peter; s of Col John Geoffrey Ferry, of Wymering Lodge, Farnborough, Hants (d 1961), and Barbara, *née* Hussey (d 1964); *b* 23 June 1928; *Educ* Sherborne, RMA Sandhurst; *m* 1, 23 Feb 1952 (m dis 1969), Jane, da of James Stephen Neave, of Greenhayes, Connaught Rd, Fleet, Hants (d 1971); 2 s (Timothy b 1953, Andrew b 1960), 2 da (Georgina b 1955, Stephanie b 1956); m 2, 5 Nov 1969, Ann Margaret, da of George Sydney Thompson, of Nelson House, The Beacon, Exmouth, Devon (d 1987); 1 da (Katherine b 27 Jan 1971); *Career* cmmnd RA 1948; served: UK, BAOR (cmd 20 Heavy Regt, Falling-Bostel 1969-71), Hong Kong, Malaya, Borneo (cmd 70 Light Battery 1964-65, despatches), Sch of Tank Technology 1956, RMC of Sci 1958-60, Staff RMCS 1965-67 (Lt-Col) and 1972-75 (Col), R&D Attaché USA 1975-78, dir Heavy Weapons Projects MoD (PE) 1978-80; Brig; vol ret 1980; Marconi Space and Def Systems 1981, (asst dir responsible for NATO business Marconi Cmd and Control Systems); *Recreations* restoration, riding veteran and vintage motorcycles; *Clubs* Army and Navy, Vintage Motorcycles; *Style—* Brig John Ferry, Esq; Lane End Cottage, Porton, Salisbury, Wilts SP4 0LN (☎ 0980 610378); Marconi Command and Control Systems Ltd, Chobhaw Rd, Frimley, Camberley, Surrey (☎ 0276 63311 ext 3140, telex 858289, fax 0276 29784)

FERSHT, Prof Alan Roy; s of Philip Joseph Fersht (d 1970), and Betty, *née* Mattleson; *b* 21 April 1943; *Educ* Sir George Monoux GS, Gonville and Caius Coll Cambridge (MA, PhD); *m* 14 Oct 1966, Marilyn, da of Montague Persell (d 1975); 1 s (Philip b 1972), 1 da (Naomi b 1970); *Career* memb scientific staff MRC laboratory of molecular biology Cambridge 1969-77, Wolfson res prof Royal Soc and prof of chemistry Imperial Coll 1978-88, Herchel Smith prof of organic chemistry Univ of Cambridge 198-; memb EMBO 1980, FRS 1983, FRSC 1986, hon memb American Acad of Arts and Sciences 1988; *Books* Enzyme Structure and Mechanism (1978, 1985); *Recreations* chess, horology; *Style—* Prof Alan Fersht; 82 Mill End Rd, Cambridge CB1 4JP (☎ 0223 212 377); Univ Chemical Laboratory, Lensfield Rd, Cambridge CB2 1EW (☎ 0223 336 341, fax 0223 336 362)

FETHERSTON, Alexander Haigh; CBE (1977); s of Christopher Albert (d 1968), of 26 Bristow Park Belfast, and Grace Haigh, *née* Potter (d 1979); *b* 16 Mar 1917; *Educ* Royal Belfast Academical Inst, Queen's Univ of Belfast (LLB); *m* 1941, Helen Sinclair, da of Sydney Herbert Jackson (d 1948), of Derryvolgie Ave, Belfast; 1 s (John), 1 da (Mary); *Career* slr; ptnr J C Taylor & Co Belfast 1944-54, dep chm and chief exec V F Corpn (UK) Ltd 1955-79; dep chm Spence Bryson Ltd 1979-82; memb: NI Housing Tst, NI Econ Cncl, NI Industs Devpt Advsy Ctee, NI Electricity Serv 1979-85; *Recreations* golf; *Style—* Alexander Fetherston Esq, CBE; 12 Tarawood, Farmhill Rd, Holywood, Co Down BT18 0HS (☎ 02317 2958)

FETHERSTON-DILKE, Michael Charles; s of Capt Charles Beaumont Fetherston-Dilke, of Maxstoke Castle, Coleshill, Warwicks and Pauline *née* Stanley-Williams; *b* 30 Dec 1948; *Educ* Rugby, Univ of Bristol (BSc); *m* 25 June 1983, Rosemary Ann, da of Michael Telfair Keith (d 1966), of Hoe Hall, Dereham, Norfolk; 2 s (George b 1985, Edward b 1986); *Career* Peat Marwick Mitchell London, Nat Enterprise Bd 1978-79, BET plc (Indust Hldg Co) 1980-, various subsidiary co directorships; exec dir: Utd Tport Int plc; FCA; *Recreations* archery, photography, country pursuits; *Clubs* Boodle's, MCC; *Style—* Michael Fetherston-Dilke, Esq; 29 Princedale Rd, London W11 4NW (☎ 01 221 5447); Utd Tport Int plc, Stratton House, Piccadilly, London W1X 6DD (☎ 01 491 2633)

FETHERSTON-DILKE, Lt Cdr (John) Timothy; CBE (1986); s of Dr Beaumont Albany Fetherston-Dilke, MBE, MRCS (d 1968), of Warks, and Phoebe Stella Bedford (d 1968); family resident at Maxstoke Castle since 1598; *b* 4 Feb 1926; *Educ* RNC Dartmouth; *m* 1, 1956 (m dis), Idonea, da of Sir Hugh Chance, CBE, DL (d 1981), of Worcs; 1 s (Timothy b 1958), 1 da (Miranda b 1956); m 2, 1966, Olivia, da of Dr E C Turton, FRCS (d 1983), of Hants; 1 s (Edmund b 1969), 1 da (Natalia b 1967); *Career* RN 1939-59: sea service during WWII and Korean War; ret 1959 Lt Cdr; patent agent 1959-65; HM Coastguard Serv 1966-86 (Chief Coastguard 1978-86); Int Marine Conslt 1986-; *Recreations* gardening, carpentry, archery, music; *Style—* Lt Cdr Timothy Fetherston-Dilke, CBE; 85 Christchurch Road, Winchester, Hants SO23 9QY (☎0962 68661)

FETHERSTONE-DILKE, Capt Charles Beaumont; JP (Warwicks 1969-), DL (Warwicks 1974-); s of Dr Beaumont (Albany) Fetherston-Dilke, MBE (d 1968), of Maxstoke Castle, Warwickshire, and (Phoebe) Stella, *née* Bedford (d 1968); *b* 04 April 1921; *Educ* RN Coll Dartmouth; *m* 12 May 1943, Pauline, da of Maj Horatio Stanley-Williams, DSO (d 1936), of Ebbw Lodge, Irthlingborough; 1 s (Michael b 1948), 1 da (Anne b 1945); *Career* RN 1935-68; WWII served: Home Fleet, Med, Battle of the Atlantic; torpedo and anti-submarine specialist, served Korean War 1952-54, 8 Destroyer Sqdn, Cdr 1955 Danish Naval Staff 1955-57, ops offr S Atlantic and S America Station 1960-61, Capt 1961, naval def to UK nat mil rep SHAPE 1962-64; cmd: HMS Maidstone, HMS Adamant, HMS Forth; cmd HMS St Vincent 1964-66, dep policy staff MOD 1966-68, ret 1968; pres cncl Kingsley Sch Leamington Spa, govr Lady Katherine Leveson Hosp, govr (chm) Coleshill GS Endowment Fndn, pres T S Stirling Sea Cadet Unit Birmingham; chm Warwicks CLA 1984-87; chm Warwicks CC 1978-80 (memb 1970-81); High Sheriff Warwicks 1974; SBStJ; *Recreations* country pursuits; *Clubs* Army and Navy; *Style—* Capt Charles Fetherson-Dilke, RN; Keeper's Cottage, Coleshill Rd, Maxstoke, Coleshill, Birmingham B46 2QA (☎ 0675 65100)

FEVERSHAM, Countess of; Lady Anne Dorothy; *née* Wood; OBE (1979, MBE 1950); da of 1 Earl of Halifax; *b* 31 July 1910; *m* 9 May 1936, 3 and last Earl of Feversham (d 1963) the Barony devolving to his kinsman *qv*; 1 da (Lady Clarissa Collin); *Career* MFH Sinnington; county organiser, WRVS N Yorks; JP Ryedale N Yorks; *Books* Strange Stories of the Chase; *Style—* The Rt Hon Countess of Feversham, OBE; Bransdale Lodge, Fadmoor Kirbymoorside, N Yorks (☎ 0751 31500)

FEVERSHAM, 6 Baron (UK 1826; the full designation is 'Feversham of Duncombe Park'); Charles Antony Peter Duncombe; s of Col Antony John Duncombe-Anderson, TD (d 1949; gggs of 1 Baron Feversham), and Gloranna Georgina Valerie, *née* McNalty (d 1989); suc to Barony of kinsman, 3 Earl of Feversham and Viscount of Helmsley, which became extinct 1963; *b* 3 Jan 1945; *Educ* Eton; *m* 1, 12 Sept 1966, Shannon (d 1976), da of late Sir Thomas Foy, CSI, CIE; 2 s (Hon Jasper b 1968, Hon Jake b 1972), 1 da (Hon Melissa b 1973); m 2, 6 Oct 1979, Pauline, da of John Aldridge, of Newark, Notts; 1 s (Hon Patrick b 1981); *Heir* s; *Career* journalist and author; chm: Yorks Arts Assoc 1969-80, Standing Ctee of Regional Arts Assocs 1969-76, Tstees Yorks Sculpture Park 1982-; co-pres Arvon Foundation 1976-86; pres: Yorks Parish Cncls Assoc 1977-, Yorks Arts Assoc 1986-, Nat Assoc Local Cncls 1986-; *Books* A Wolf in Tooth (1967), Great Yachts (1970); *Style—* The Rt Hon Lord Feversham; Duncombe Park, Helmsley, York (☎ 0439 70217)

FFOLKES, Sir Robert Francis Alexander; 7 Bt (GB 1774); s of Sir (Edward John) Patrick Boschetti Ffolkes, 6 Bt (d 1960); *b* 2 Dec 1943; *Educ* Stowe, Christ Church Oxford; *Career* involved with Save The Children Fund 1974-; *Clubs* Turf; *Style—* Sir Robert Ffolkes, Bt; Coastguard House, Morston, Holt, Norfolk

FFOOKS, Roger Cambridge; s of Edward Cambridge Ffooks (d 1965), and Eileen Catharine, *née* Gordon (d 1988); *b* 3 Oct 1924; *Educ* Edinburgh Acad, Durham Univ (BSc); *m* 1, 28 July 1951 (m dis 1988), Gillian Melville, da of Lt-Col B R Turner, DSO, of Tittlesfold Farm Cottage, Billingshurst, Sussex; 2 s (Anthony b 11 Dec 1952, Adrian b 27 May 1955), 1 da (Stephanie (Mrs Trafford) b 24 Dec 1963); m 2, 9 Sept 1988, Barbara Joyce; *Career* Shell Int Marine 1946-76 (tech dir Conch Methane Servs 1973-76), ind conslt naval architect 1976-; memb Br Tech Ctee, American Bureau of Shipping 1970-, rep Br Maritime League (W Dorset), chm local resident's assoc; FRINA; *Books* Natural Gas by Sea; The Development of a New Technology (1979), Gas Carriers (ed 1984); *Recreations* books, boating, music; *Style—* Roger Ffooks, Esq; Priors Dean, Long Lane, Bothenhampton, Bridport, Dorset DT6 4BX (☎ 0308 23122)

FFORDE, Lady Jean (Sybil Violet); *née* Graham; DL (Ayr and Arran); yr da of 6 Duke of Montrose, KT, CB, CVO, VD, LLD (d 1954); *b* 7 Nov 1920; *m* 8 Oct 1947 (m dis 1957), Col John Patrick Ilbert Fforde, yr s of Maj Charles Annesley Lilbraham Ford; 1 s (Charles b 1948); *Style—* Lady Jean Fforde, DL; Strabane, Brodick, Isle of Arran KA27 8DD (☎ 0770 2276)

FFOWCS WILLIAMS, Prof John Eirwyn; s of Rev Abel Ffowcs Williams (d 1989), and Elizabeth, *née* Davies; *b* 25 May 1935; *Educ* Friends' Sch Gt Ayton, Derby Tech Coll, Southampton Univ (BSc, PhD), Cambridge Univ (MA, ScD); *m* 10 Oct 1959, Anne Beatrice, da of Percy Cecil Mason (d 1984); 2 s (Aled Ceiriog b 1969, Gareth Idris b 1980), 1 da (Awena Lynn b 1966); *Career* Rolls-Royce prof of applied mathematics Imperial Coll London 1969- 72; Rank prof of engrg Cambridge Univ 1972-; dir Vicker Ship and Engrg Ltd plc 1988-; FEng; *Recreations* friends and cigars; *Clubs* Athenaeum, Danish; *Style—* Prof John Ffowcs Williams; Emmanuel College, Cambridge (☎ 0223 332629)

FFRENCH, Hon Clare Katherine Grace Mary; yr da of 7 Baron ffrench (d 1986); *b* 18 July 1958; *Style—* Hon Clare Ffrench; Castle Ffrench, Ballinasloe, Co Galway, Ireland

FFRENCH, 8 Baron (I 1758); Sir Robuck John Peter Charles Mario; also Bt (I

1779); s of 7 Baron Ffrench (d 1986), and Katherine Sonia, da of late Maj Digby Coddington Cayley; *b* 14 Mar 1956; *m* 20 June 1987, Dörthe Marie-Louise Schauer-Lixfeld, da of Capt Wilhelm Schauer, of Zürich, Switzerland, and Mrs Marie-Louise Schauer-Lixfeld, of Attymon House, Co Galway; *Style*— The Rt Hon Lord Ffrench; Castle Ffrench, Ballinasloe, Co Galway, Ireland

FFRENCH, Hon Rose Sophia Iris Mary; er da of 7 Baron Ffrench (d 1986); *b* 27 Jan 1957; *Style*— Hon Rose Ffrench; Castle Ffrench, Ballinasloe, Co Galway, Ireland

FFRENCH BLAKE, Lady Caroline Anne de Vere; *née* Beauclerk; da (by 2 m) of 13 Duke of St Albans, OBE (d 1988); *b* 19 July 1951; *Educ* Fritham House, Queen's Gate Sch; *m* 1970 (m dis 1986), Neil St John Ffrench Blake, *qv*; 2 da (Clare Eleanor de Vere b 1972, Kate Juliana de Vere b 1977); *Style*— Lady Caroline Ffrench Blake; Barn House, Midgham, Reading, Berks RG7 5UG

FFRENCH BLAKE, Neil St John; s of Lt-Col Robert Lifford Valentine ffrench Blake, DSO, of Midgham Park Farm, Woolhampton, Berks, and Grania Bryde, *née* Curran; *b* 4 Nov 1940; *Educ* Eton; *m* 1970, (m dis 1986) Lady Caroline de Vere Beauclerk *qv*, da of 13 Duke of St Albans by his 2 w; 2 da; *Career* BBC producer 1963-69, md Network Broadcasting Ltd 1969-73, Programme Controller Thames Valley B'dcasting Ltd 1975-80; md CTV Productions Ltd 1980-82; snr advsr to ASEAN 1983-; communications conslt and author; *Recreations* skiing, golf; *Clubs* Brooks's; *Style*— Neil Ffrench Blake, Esq; 560/286 Dindaeng Road, Klaosiam Condominium 286, Samsannai Payatai, Bangkok 10400, Thailand (☎ Bangkok 2452544/2452610)

FFRENCH BLAKE, Col Robert John William; s of Lt Col Desmond O'Brien Evelyn Ffrench Blake (d 1943), of Hants, and Elizabeth Iris Hogg, *née* Cardale; *b* 21 June 1940; *Educ* Eton, RMA Sandhurst; *m* 21 Sept 1976, Ilynne Sabina Mary, da of michael Charles Eyston, of Oxon; 3 da (Nicola b 1977, Alice b 1980, Emily b 1983); *Career* GSO2 Tactics Br Army Tning Unit 1973-75, Sqdn Cmdr 13/18 Royal Hussars (QMO) 1975-77, DAMS MOD 1977-78, GSO1 directing staff Camberley 1979-80, cmding offr 13/18 Royal Hussars (QMO) 1981-83, cmdr Combined Arms Tactics Div 1983-85 asst mil attache Washington DC 1985-; *Recreations* farming, shooting, riding, travel; *Clubs* Cavalry and Gds'; *Style*— Col Robert J W Ffrench Blake; c/o Hoares Bank, 37 Fleet Street, London EC4P 4DQ; c/o British Army Staff, British Embassy BF P02 (☎ 202 898 4303)

FFYTCHE, Timothy John; s of Louis E S ffytche (d 1987), of Wilbraham Place, London, and Margaret Law; *b* 11 Sept 1936; *Educ* Lancing, King's Coll London, St Georges Hosp (MB BS, DO, FRCS); *m* 13 May 1961, Bärbl, da of Günther Fischer, of W Germany; 2 s (Dominic b 1962, Mattias b 1965); *Career* Consultant Ophthalmic Surgeon: St Thomas's Hosp London, Moorfields Hos, King Edward VII Hosp London; Surgeon Oculist Royal Household; author of articles and papers on retinal disease and ocular leprosy; *Recreations* fishing, occasional cricket; *Style*— Timothy Ffytche, Esq; 1 Wellington Square, London SW3 4NJ; 149 Harley Street, London W1N 2DE

FICKLING, Benjamin William; CBE (1973); s of late Robert Marshall Fickling, LDS, and Florence, *née* Newson; *b* 14 July 1909; *Educ* Framlingham Coll, St George's Hosp, Royal Dental Hosp; *m* 1942, Shirley Dona, er da of late Albert Latimer Walker; 2 s, 1 da; *Career* dental surgn: St George's Hosp 1936-74, Royal Dental Hosp of London 1935-74; oral surgn to dept of dental and oral surgery Mount Vernon Hospital (formerly Hill End Hospital) 1941-74; dean Faculty of Dental Surgery; Royal Coll of Surgeons of England 1968-71, dir Medical Sickness Annuity & Life Assur Soc 1967-, dir Perm Insur Soc and Medical Sickness Fin Corpn; FRCS, FDS, MGDS RCS; *Books* Injuries of the Jaws and Face (jtly 1940); *Recreations* travel, gardening; *Clubs* Ski Club of GB; *Style*— Benjamin Fickling, Esq, CBE; 29 Maxwell Road, Northwood, Middx (☎ Northwood 22035)

FIDGEN, Roger Stewart; s of Eric Frank Fidgen, and Vera, (*née* Clark; *b* 14 May 1946; *Educ* Sherborne; *m* 1, 10 Nov 1971 (m dis 1988) Sarah Dorothy, da of William Nevill Dashwood Lang (d 1988); 2 s (Patrick b 1973, Robert b 1976), 1 da (Joanna b 1979); m 2, 20 May 1988 (m dis 1988), Jennifer Godesen, da of Stanley Angold; *Career* Sub Lt RNR 1969-72; chartered quantity surveyor; articled to George Walford, worked with family firm before joining Gardiner and Theobald Cptnr 1975-), non-exec dir Winglaw Gp 1988-; Liveryman: Worshipful Co of Barbers 1973, Worshipful Co of Chartered Surveyors 1980; FRICS; *Recreations* fishing, shooting, sailing, skiing; *Clubs* Royal Thames YC, Flyfishers; *Style*— Roger Fidgen, Esq; Wield House Farm, Wield, Alresford, Hants (☎ 0420 64292); 49 Bedford Sq, London WC1B 3EB (☎ 01 637 2468)

FIDLER, Brian Harvey; s of Philip Fidler, of Manchester, and Esther, *née* Levy; *b* 19 Oct 1938; *Educ* Manchester GS, Manchester Univ (LLB); *m* 12 Aug 1962, Wendy, da of Abraham Gouldman; 1 s (Benjamin Philip b 1970), 2 da (Sarah Jane b 1964, Ruth Yvette b 1966); *Career* chief accountant Pressed Steel Fisher Coventry 1967-70 (fin accountant Cowley 1962-67), gp mgmnt accountant Amey Roadstone plc 1970-73, chief fin exec Northern Foods plc 1974-85, gp fin dir Christian Salvesen plc 1985-; *Style*— Brian Fidler, Esq; 'Broompark', 1001 Liberton Drive, Edinburgh EH16 6TH (☎ 031 666 1346); 24 Langford Green, Camberwell, London SE5; Christian Salvesen Plc, 50 East Fettes Ave, Edinburgh EH4 1EQ (☎ 031 552 7101, fax 031 552 5809, telex 72222)

FIDLER, Ian Douglas Field; s of Reginald Douglas Field Fidler (d 1944), and Lillian Dorothy, *née* Gregor-Pearse (d 1988); *b* 17 April 1927; *Educ* St Georges Putney Hill, Surbiton GS; *m* 25 Oct 1958, Elizabeth Jean, da of Maj James Morton, RA (d 1977); 4 da (Caroline Elizabeth b 8 May 1962, Alexandra Louise b 31 Oct 1964, Charlotte Anne b 22 Dec 1965, Henrietta Mary Sirkka b 18 Oct 1973); *Career* RM 1943-47, 42 Commando, 3 Commando Bde, Substantive Lt; trainee Albert E Reed Co Ltd 1947; asst mangr: London Paper Mills Ltd 1947-54, Empire Papers Mills Ltd 1954-56; sales dir Reed Paper and Bd Sales Ltd 1958-68 (formerly tech mangr 1956-58), dep md Lamco Paper Sales 1976-86 (formerly sales dir 1968-75), chm Hunt and Broadhurst Ltd 1983-86, md Lamco Servs Ltd 1987-; memb Stationers Social Soc, past pres Paper Agents Assoc, tstee Lamco Pension Fund Mgmnt; Freeman City of London 1982, Liveryman Worshipful Co of Stationers and Newspaper Makers; Knight First Class of the Order of the Lion of Finland 1986; *Recreations* golf, gardening, walking dogs; *Clubs* Burhill CC, Norwegian, RAC; *Style*— Ian Fidler, Esq; Brackens, Heathdown Rd, Pyrford, Surrey GU22 (☎ 093 23 496 03); Norfolk Hse, 31 St James's Sq, London SW1Y 4JJ (☎ 01 895 0077, fax 01 895 0039, car tel 0836 223 688, telex 8950107)

FIDLER, Dr John Havelock; s of William Thomas Fidler (d 1965), of Reading, and Adrienne Selkirk, *née* Potts (d 1963); *b* 12 Mar 1910; *Educ* Clifton, Sidney Sussex Coll Cambridge (MA), Univ of Reading (PhD); *m* 9 Sept 1939, Anne, da of William Simpson (d 1955); *Career* Philip Buckle res fell, Manchester Univ 1935-36, advsy entomologist Miny of Agric Fisheries and Food 1936-70; since retirement res into the relationship between dowsing and science, contributor to various scientific journals; *Books* Preservation of Natural History Specimens (1955, 1968), Ley Line:- a dowsers investigation (1983), Earth Energy (1988); *Recreations* hill walking; *Clubs* pres Reading Univ Boat 1933-34; *Style*— Dr John Fidler, Esq; Rhu-na-Bidh, Shieldaig Strathcarron, Ross-shire, Scotland IV54 8XN (☎ 05205 230)

FIDLER, Michael M; JP (Lancs 1958); s of late Louis Fidler and Golda, *née* Sherr; *b* 10 Feb 1916; *Educ* Salford GS, Salford Royal Tech Coll; *m* 1939, Maidie, da of Jack Davis; 1 s, 1 da; *Career* business conslt in clothing industry; md: H & L Fidler Ltd 1941-70, Michael Lewis Ltd 1942-70, Wibye Ltd 1968-; former mayor and alderman Borough of Prestwich; MP (C) Bury and Radcliffe 1970-74; pres bd of deputies of Br Jews 1967-73; pres Gen Zionist Orgn of GB 1973-; fndr and nat dir Cons Friends of Israel 1974-; chm Int Orgn Cmmn World Jewish Congress 1975-; Fndr and Int Dir Friendship with Israel Gp (All-Pty) Euro Parl 1979-; vice pres Zionist Fedn of GB and Ireland 1981-; life pres Holy Law South Broughton Hebrew Congregation 1984-; life vice-pres Manchester Jewish Social Servs 1967-; *Style*— Michael Fidler, Esq, JP; 51 Tavistock Ct, Tavistock Sq, London WC1H 9HG (☎ 01 387 4925); 1 Woodcliffe Lodge, Sedgley Park Rd, Prestwich, Manchester M25 8JX (☎ 061 773 1471); office: 45B Westbourne Terrace, London W2 3UR (☎ 01 262 2493)

FIDLER, Peter John Michael; s of Dr Harry Fidler, of Bramhall, nr Stockport, Cheshire, and Lilian, *née* Kahn; *b* 16 Mar 1942; *Educ* Bradford GS, St John's Coll Oxford (MA); *m* 19 July 1984, Barbara Julia Gottlieb, da of Harold Pinto, of Wembley, Middx; 1 s (David Robert b 1985), 1 step s (Richard Charles b 1979), 2 step da (Clare Rachel b 1973, Katherine Anna b 1977); *Career* slr 1967; articled Peacock Fisher & Finch (now Field Fisher & Martineau) 1964-67, Coward Chance 1967-72, DJ Freeman & Co 1972-84, Stephenson Harwood 1984-; rep GB at Croquet 1974; memb City of London Solicitors Co; memb: Law Soc, City of London Law Soc; *Books* Sheldon's Practise, Law of Banking (now Sheldon and Fidlers) (asst ed 1972, ed 1982); *Recreations* music, theatre; *Style*— Peter Fidler, Esq; 237 West Heath Rd, London NW3 7UB (☎ 01 455 2247); Stephenson Harwood, One St Paul's Churchyard, London EC4M 8SH (☎ 01 329 4422, fax 01 606 0822, telex 886789 SHSPC G)

FIELD, Alan Frank; s of Frank William Field, of Holme Pierrepoint, Notts, and May Field; *b* 26 Sept 1937; *Educ* Trent Bridge; *m* 1970, Olga Ann, da of Charles Keightley (d 1972), of Leics; *Career* Creative Dir & Chm Garratt Baulcombe Ltd 1972-; dir Foote Cone & Belding Ltd 1984-; *Recreations* music, fly fishing, illustration, cooking; *Style*— Alan Field, Esq; Bridgford House, Trent Bridge (☎ Nottingham 822022)

FIELD, Brig Anne; CB (1980); da of Capt Harold Derwent and Annie Helena, *née* Hodgson; *b* 4 April 1926; *Educ* Keswick Sch, St George's Harpenden, LSE; *Career* joined ATS 1947, cmmnd 1948; WRAC 1949-: Lt-Col 1968, Col 1971, Brig 1977-82, Dep Controller Cmdt 1984-; Hon ADC to HM The Queen 1977-82; regional dir Lloyds Bank plc London (West) Regnl Bd 1982-; freeman City of London 1981; *Style*— Brig Anne Field, CB; c/o Lloyds Bank plc, 6 Pall Mall, London SW1Y 5NH

FIELD, Arnold; OBE (1965); s of Wilfred Field (d 1933); *b* 19 May 1917; *Educ* Sutton Coldfield Royal Sch, Erdington C of E, Birmingham Tech Coll; *m* 1943, Kathleen Dulcie, da of Albert Bennett (d 1930); 1 s, 1 da; *Career* serv WWII, RAF, Sqdn Ldr, Coastal Cmd and Air Miny Special Duty List 1940-46; air traffic control offr 1946-61, divnl air traffic control offr 1961-65, supt London Air Traffic Control Centre 1965-71, dir Civil Air Traffic Ops 1971-74, dir gen Nat Air Traffic Serv 1974-77; aviation conslt technical journalist, 1977-; memb aviation/space writers assocn; *Books* The Control of Air Traffic (1980), Int Air Traffic Control mgmnt of the worlds airspace (1985); Int Directory of Mil Simulation and Training Aids (1988); *Recreations* vintage motor cars, flying; *Clubs* Bentley Drivers; *Style*— Arnold Field, Esq, OBE; Footprints, Stoke Wood, Stoke Poges, Bucks SL2 4AU (☎ 02814 2710)

FIELD, Barry John Anthony; TD (1984); MP (Cons Isle of Wight 1987-); s of Edward Ernest Field, of Crawley, Sussex, and Marguerite Eugenie, *née* Bateman (d 1979); *b* 4 July 1946; *Educ* Collingwood Boys Sch, Mitcham GS, Bembridge Sch, Victoria Street Coll; *m* 11 Oct 1969, Jaqueline Anne, da of Cdr Alfred Edward Joseph Miller, RN, of Emsworth, Hants; 1 s (Jason b 1977), 1 da (Penny b 1978); *Career* dir: Gt Southern Cemetery and Crematoria Co Ltd 1969-86, J D Field and Sons 1981-; cncllr Horsham Dist Cncl 1983-86, vice chm Housing Ctee 1984-85, memb IOW CC 1986-; *Recreations* sailing, skiing, theatre; *Clubs* Island Sailing; *Style*— Barry Field, Esq, TD, MP; Medina Lodge, 25 Birmingham Rd, Cowes, Isle of Wight PO31 7BH; House of Commons (☎ 01 219 3453, office 0983 522645)

FIELD, Derek Harold; s of Harold Field (d 1945), of Lion House, Chichester, Sussex, and Edith Muriel, *née* Harrison (d 1980); *b* 26 Mar 1923; *Educ* Marlborough, St John's Coll Cambridge (MA); *m* 3 July 1948, (Catherine) Rosemary, da of Leonard Howson Jones (d 1968), of Beechcliffe, Trentham, Staffs; 4 s (Christopher b 1951, Godfrey b 1953, Stephen b 1956, Mark b 1960); *Career* WWII Capt REME, served Palestine 1943-47; Dorman Long & Co: engr and designer 1947-48, engr i/c Vila Franca Brdige over River Tagus 1949-51; gen mangr Shelton Iron, Steel & Coal Co (subsidiary of John Summers & Sons Ltd) 1968-78 (structural engr 1953-62, works mangr 1963, dir 1964); dir N Staffs C of C & Indust 1980-84, dir Tableware Distributors Assoc 1984; dep chm W Midlands Regn TSB Eng & Wales 1985-; MICE (1956), CEng; *Recreations* tennis, fell walking, country pursuits, philately, reading; *Clubs* Army and Navy; *Style*— Derek Field, Esq; The Dairy House, Trentham Park, Stoke-on-Trent, Staffs ST4 8AE (☎ 0782 657 908); Commerce House, Festival Park, Stoke-on-Trent, Staffs ST1 5BE (☎ 0782 202 222, fax 0782 202 448, telex 36250 CHAMCOM G)

FIELD, Frank; MP (Lab) Birkenhead 1979-; s of late Walter Field, and Annie Field; *b* 16 July 1942; *Educ* St Clement Danes GS, Hull Univ; *Career* former teacher, memb TGWU, cncllr Hounslow 1964-68, contested (Lab) S Bucks 1966; dir: Child Poverty Action Gp 1969-79, Low Pay Unit 1974-80; oppn spokesman on educn 1979-81, Parly conslt to Civil and Public Servs Assoc, front bench oppn spokesman Health and Social Security 1983-; *Books* author: Unequal Britain (1974), Inequality In Britain: Freedom, Welfare and The State (1981), Poverty and Politics (1982), The Minimum Wage: Its Potential And Dangers (1984), Freedom And Wealth In A Socialist Future (1987), The Politics of Paradise (1987); co author To Him Who Hath: A Study of Poverty And Taxation (1976); ed: 20th Century State Education (jtly 1971), Black Britons (jtly 1971), Low Pay (1973), Are Low Wages Inevitable (1976), Education And The Urban Crisis (1976), The Conscript Army: A Study of Britain's Unemployed (1976), The

Wealth Report (1 edn 1979, 2 edn 1983), Policies Against Low Pay: An International Perspective (1984); *Style—* Frank Field, Esq, MP; House of Commons, London SW1

FIELD, Guy; s of Norman Field (d 1985), and Marie-Therese Leonie Henriette, *née* Bouchet; *b* 28 Dec 1926; *Educ* Lycee Condorcet Paris France, Wallasey GS Wirral Cheshire; *m* 23 May 1953, Dorothy Evelyn, da of John Reginald Blakely (d 1959); 1 s (Alastair b 1961), 1 da (Sonya b 1958); *Career* RM 1945-47; exec dir Samuel Montagu & Co Ltd 1954-77, dir Derby & Co Ltd 1977-82, sr vice-pres Morgan Guaranty Tst Co of NY London 1982-88, vice-chm London Bullion Market Assoc 1987-88; chm Buckland branch Cons Assoc, vice-chm govrs Croham Hurst Sch S Croydon Surrey; Freeman City of London 1983, Liveryman Worshipful Co of Fan Makers; *Recreations* gardening, walking, music, opera, photography, philately; *Style—* Guy Field, Esq; Little Perrow, Old Rd, Buckland, Betchworth, Surrey RH3 7DY (☎ 073784 3227)

FIELD, John Arthur; s of Lt-Col Arthur William Henry Field, MBE (d 1980), of Bromley, Kent, and Rebecca Annie Rose, *née* Bolt (d 1986); *b* 28 Feb 1932; *Educ* Bromley GS, Keble Coll Oxford (BA), London Univ (BSc, PGCE, Ac Dip Ed); *m* 11 May 1955, Heather Mavis, da of Eric Douglas Liddiard (d 1986), of Enfield, Middx; 3 s (Andrew b 1962, Richard b 1963, Martin b 1968), 1 da (Alison b 1965); *Career* asst master: City of Norwich Sch 1956-59, Dauntsey's Sch 1953; head of Sci dept Dover GS 1964-68; headmaster: Springhead Sch Northfleet 1969-81, Wombwell Hall Sch Northfleet 1977-81, Northfleet GS 1981-88 co inspector of secdy educn Kent 1988-; lay reader at Fawkham and Hartley, dir of reader trg Rochester Diocese, dep county cmmr Scout movement Kent, fndr chm Gravesham Town Twinning Assoc 1981-85; memb: SHA, Assoc for Sci Educn, Botanical Soc of Br Isles, Br Biological Soc, Freshwater Biological Assoc; FIBiol 1979; *Recreations* foreign travel, railways, choral music; *Style—* John Field, Esq; Kent County Council, Springfield, Maidstone, Kent ME14 2LJ

FIELD, (Edward) John; s of Lt-Col Arthur Field, MC, OBE, TD, of 4 Fox Hill, Northam, nr Bideford, N Devon, and Dorothy Agnes, *née* Strouts (d 1943); *b* 11 June 1936; *Educ* Highgate Sch, Corpus Christi Coll Oxford (MA), Univ of Virginia USA; *m* 16 July 1960, Irene Sophie du Pont, da of Colgate Whitchead Darden (d 1981), of Norfolk, Virginia, USA; 1 s (Edward b 12 July 1968), 1 da (Dorothy b 24 March 1964); *Career* Nat Serv RA 1954-55, 2 Lt Intelligence Corps 1955-56; Courtaulds 1960-63; FO: second sec (later first sec) Br Embassy Tokyo 1963-68, American Dept 1968-70, cultural attaché Br Embassy Moscow 1970-72, first sec Br Embassy Tokyo 1973-76, asst head S Asia Dept 1976-77, head exports to Japan unit DTI 1977-79, cnsllr UK Mission to Un (econ and social cncl rep), min Br Embassy Tokyo 1988-; *Recreations* tennis, riding, music; *Style—* John Field, Esq; Br Embassy, Tokyo, Japan (☎ 03 265 5511)

FIELD, Malcolm David; s of Maj Stanley Herbert Raynor Field (d 1970), of Link Cottage, Selsey, Sussex, and Constance Frances, *née* Watson; *b* 25 August 1937; *Educ* Highgate Sch, London Business Sch; *m* 1, 1963 (m dis 1970), Jane, da of James Barrie, of 11 South Grove House, Highgate Villiage; m 2, 1974 (m dis 1982), Anne Carolyn, *née* Churchill; 1 da (Joanna Clare b 1974); *Career* 2 Lt WG 1956-58; dir: WH Smith & Son Ltd 1970, WH Smith Canada Ltd 1973; WH Smith & Son Holdings Ltd: dir 1974, Wholesale md 1978, retail md 1978, gp md 1982; chm WH Smith Gp (USA) Inc 1988; NAAFI (non-exec): dir 1973, dep Chm 1985, Chm 1986; CBIM 1988; *Recreations* tennis, cricket, golf, collecting water colours, civil aviation,; *Clubs* Garrick, MCC, Vanderbilt; *Style—* Malcolm Field, Esq; 47 Cadogan Gdns, London SW3 (☎ 01 581 2576); Strand House, 7 Holbein Place, London SW1 (☎ 01 730 1200, fax 730 1200, ext 5563, telex 887777 WHS G)

FIELD, Marshall Hayward; CBE (1985); s of Maj Harold Hayward Field (d 1973), and Hilda Maud, *née* Siggers (d 1983); *b* 19 April 1930; *Educ* Dulwich; *m* 9 July 1960, Barbara Evelyn, da of Douglas Richard Harris (d 1950); 2 da (Alexandra b 1962, Katherine b 1964); *Career* Nat Serv Intelligence Corps 1955-57, serv Cyprus; Phoenix Assur: joined 1958, actuary 1964, gen mangr and actuary 1972-85, dir 1980-85; chm Life Offs Assoc 1983-85, memb Fowler Enquiry into Provision for Retirement 1984, conslt Securities and Investmts Bd 1985-86, conslt ptnr to Bacon Woodrow 1986-, non exec dir TSB Tst Co 1985-, chm Dulwich Estates 1988- (bd memb 1973); govr: Dulwich Coll 1987-, James Allen's Girls Sch 1981-, memb Dulwich Picture Gallery Ctee 1985-; Freeman City of London 1980, Liveryman Worshipful Co of Actuaries 1984; FIA 1957 (cncl memb 1966, hon sec 1975-77, vice pres 1979-82, pres 1986-88); *Recreations* theatre, art generally; *Style—* Marshall Field, Esq, CBE; 35 Woodhall Drive, London SE21 7HJ (☎ 01 693 1704); Bacon & Woddrow, Empire House, St Martin's-le-Grand, London (☎ 01 600 2747)

FIELD, Philip Sidney; TD; s of Sidney Field (d 1943) 17 Motspur Park, New Malden, and Edith Mary, *née* Duggin (d 1958); *b* 19 Jan 1917; *Educ* Dulwich, Oxford Univ (BA); *Career* enlisted TA 1938, Actg Maj TARO, ret 1967; clerk Cargo Superintendents (London) Ltd 1936-39, cost accountant second asst sec Aplin & Barrett Gp 1946-52; in practice as accountant 1952-; managing tstee many local charities 1954-; controller of Civil Def Corps Evesham Dist 1959 (until disbanding), served on mgmnt ctee Evesham Co of Sea Cadets 1962-66, memb Royal Utd Servs Inst 1965-78; church tres 1960- (warden 1960-72), area supt St John Ambulance Bde 1958-74; vice pres: Broadway CC, Broadway FC; OStJ 1924; *Recreations* music; *Clubs* St John House; *Style—* P S Field, Esq, TD; Little Hill, Evesham Rd, Broadway, Worcs WR12 7DG (☎ 0386 852 405)

FIELD, Richard David; OBE (1987); s of Col G W H Field, of Lancaster, and Pesita Mary; *b* 9 April 1945; *Educ* Malvern; *m* 15 July 1967, Shirley Philippa (Pippa), da of F P Mountford (d 1968), of Sheffield; 2 da (Catherine b 1969, Elizabeth b 1971); *Career* CA 1968; chief accountant Briden Wire 1973-75 (fin dir 1975-78); Manchester Business Sch 1978; Bamford Business Services, conslt 1978- (dir 1980-); chm: Dysan Refractories Ltd 1980-87, Friends of Sheffield Children's Hosp, of gov Queen Margarets Sch Eserick York, (dep) Young Enterprise Sheffield, J & J Dyson plc, Bamford Business Services Ltd; dep chm: J & J Dyson plc, T K R Ltd; memb: Nat cncl (Sheffield pres) Chamber of Commerce, cncl (exec memb, finance ctee chm) Industrial Soc, Industry Matters (Sheffield ctee chm), RSA Industry Refractories Assoc of GB, careers advsy bd Sheffield Univ, Cncl St Williams Fndn York; pres Sheffield Centre for Science & Technol; FCA, CBIM, FITD, FRSA; *Recreations* martial arts (black belt in ju-jitsu), walking, reading, collecting glass; *Style—* Richard D Field, Esq; 134 Townhead Road, Dore, Sheffield S17 3AQ; J & J Dyson plc, 381 Fulwood Rd, Sheffield S10 3GB (☎ 0742 303921, fax 308583)

FIELD, Robin Shaun; s of Harold Ivor Field (d 1988), of Highworth, Wilts, and Margaret Gleaves, *née* Doyle; *b* 10 May 1938; *Educ* Cheltenham, Corpus Christi Coll Cambridge (MA); *m* 23 July 1960, da of Joseph Addison Brace (d 1963); 2 s (Mark b 28 Dec 1961, Michael b 9 Dec 1964), 1 da (Alison b 3 Nov 1973); *Career* Shell Int Petroleum Co 1960-66, mgmnt servs mgr John Waddington Ltd 1967-70, commercial dir (later dir and gen mgr) Plastona (John Waddington) Ltd 1970-76, ptnr Touche ross Mgmnt Conslts 1980- (joined 1976); CEng, MIProdE, FCIMA, FSS; *Recreations* squash, sailing, skiing, opera, gardening; *Clubs* Wing and Pen; *Style—* Robin Field, Esq; Touche Ross Mgmnt Consultants, Hill House, Little New St, London EC4A 3TR (☎ 01 936 3000)

FIELD, Roy William; s of William Laurie Field, and Cicely May, *née* Holland; *b* 19 August 1934; *Educ* Eton Coll Choir Sch, Buckingham Coll Harrow; *m* 13 Sept 1958, Patricia Ann, da of William Muston; 2 s (Timothy William b 1961, Peter Michael b 1962), 1 da (Alison Louise b 1965); *Career* RAOC 1952-54, NCO Austria; Br Film Indust 1952-, Rank Organisation 1956-71; md: Field Films Ltd 1971-, Optical Film Effects Ltd 1981-; Hollywood Oscar for achievement in Visual Effects Superman the Movie, Br Acad Award Sir Michael Balcon Award for outstandintg achievement in Br Cinema Superman, nomination for BAFTA Award Visual Effects Dark Crystal, nomination for BAFTA Award Visual Effects Labyrinth; Br soc of Cameramen, FRKSTS, memb: Guild of Br Camera Technicians, Br Acad of Film and TV Arts; *Style—* Roy Field, Esq; Redroof Cottage, Tempiewood Lane, Farnham Common, Bucks S22 3HA (☎ 02814 4156); Optical Film Effects Ltd, Pinewood Studios, Iver Heath Bucks SLO0 ONH (☎ 0753 655486, fax 0753 656844, telex 847505 PINEW G)

FIELD-FISHER, Thomas Gilbert; TD 1949, QC (1969); s of Caryl Hillyard Field-Fisher (d 1953), of Torquay, Devon, and Dora Kate, *née* Purvis (d 1946); *b* 16 May 1915; *Educ* Kings Sch Bruton, Peterhouse Cambridge (BA, MA); *m* 8 Sept 1945, Ebba da of Max Larsen, of Linwood Utah USA; *Career* QVR KRRC WW II 1939-47, BEF 1940 (POW, despatches), Maj i/c war crimes dept DJAG CMF (Italy) 1945-47; called to Bar Middle Temple 1942 (bencher 1976), joined Western circuit 1947; rec Crown Ct 1972-86; memb Bar Cncl 1962-66; chm Maria Colwell Inquiry 1973-74; dep chm: SW Agric Claims Tbnl 1962-82, Cornwall QS 1967-72; vice-chm London Cncl of Social Serv 1966-79, vice-pres London Vol Serv Cncl 1979-, memb Home Off ctee on Animal Experiments 1980-87, (memb Animal Procedures Ctee 1987-) chm Dogs Home Battersea 1982-, chm and fdr Assoc of Br Dogs Homes 1985-, pres Cornwall Magistrates Assoc 1985-; *Books* Animals and the Law (1964), Rent Regulation and Control (1967), contribs to Halsbury's Laws of England (3 and 4 edns) and other legal pubns; *Recreations* dogs, collecting watercolours, gardening, lawn tennis; *Clubs* Hurlingham, Int Lawn Tennis of (GB); *Style—* Thomas Field-Fisher, Esq, TD, QC; 38 Hurlingham Court, London SW6 3UW (☎ 01 736 4627); 2 Kings Bench Walk, Temple, London EC4Y 7DE (☎ 01 353 1746)

FIELDEN, (John) Anthony Haigh; s of Lt-Col John Haigh Fielden, TD, of 1 Willow Crescent, Broughton Gifford, Melksham, Wilts, and Jean, *née* Turnbull; *b* 18 Mar 1937; *Educ* Rossall, Keble Coll Oxford (MA); *m* 29 Sept 1962, Deryl Anne, da of Arthur Leonard Collinson, of 16 Hampton Grove, Bury, Lancs; 1 s (Nicholas b 30 May 1964), 1 da (Tiffany b 23 Nov 1965); *Career* slr; ptnr: Emerson & Fielden 1962-68, Whitworths 1968-70; sr ptnr: Leak Almond & Parkinson 1985-87 (ptnr 1970-85), Cobbett Leak Almond 1987-; clerk to tstees Manchester Guardian Soc Charitable Tst, memb bd of mgmnt Wood St Mission; memb Law Soc; *Recreations* cricket, squash rackets, real tennis; *Clubs* MCC, Manchester Tennis and Racquet; *Style—* Anthony Fielden, Esq; Rosehill, Rostherne, Knutsford, Cheshire WA16 6RT (☎ 0565 830 430); The Old Manor Hse, Westington, Chipping Campden, Glos; Cobbett Leak Almond, Ship Canal Hse, King St, Manchester M2 4WB (☎ 061 833 3333, fax 061 833 3030)

FIELDEN, Dr Christa Maria; *née* Peix; da of Ludwig Robert Peix (d 1974), and Margaret Freer-Hewish, *née* von Neumann; *b* 28 June 1943; *Educ* Hamps Co HS for Girls, Univ of London (BSc, MSc, PhD); *m* 29 Jan 1964 (m dis 1983), Christopher James Fielden; 2 s (James b 15 July 1966, William b 4 Oct 1968); *Career* with Civil Serv 1970-74, head of computer dept CNAA 1974-75, barr Lincolns Inn 1982, practises SE circuit; FSS 1982; *Recreations* skiing, psychology; *Style—* Dr Christa Fielden; 9 Woburn Ct, Bernard St, London WC2 (☎ 01 837 8752); 12 Old Sq, Lincolns Inn, London WC2 (☎ 01 242 4289, fax 01 831 6736)

FIELDEN, Christopher Thomas; s of Wilfred Fielden of Nottingham (d 1968), and Nellie *née* Shaw; *b* 22 Nov 1942; *Educ* Nottingham HS, Downing Coll Cambridge (MA, LLB); *m* 30 Mar 1964, Pauline Mary, da of Joseph Frederick Hoult of Nottingham (d 1982); 2 s (Henry b 1964, Timothy b 1968); *Career* slr 1967; dir: Gallaher Ltd 1987- (gp legal advsr 1972), Gallaher Tobacco Ltd 1986, Forbuoys plc 1984; memb ctee Tilford Bach Soc; Law Soc 1967; *Recreations* golf; *Style—* Christopher Fielden, Esq; Evergreens, Elstead Rd, Tilford, Farnham, Surrey GU10 2AJ (☎ 02518 2407); Gallaher Ltd, Members Hill, Brooklands Rd, Weybridge, Surrey KT13 0QU (☎ 0932 859777, fax 0932 857829)

FIELDEN, Mark; s of Cyril Lupton Fielden (d 1985), and Annie Mary Gladys *née* Air (d 1979); *b* 17 Oct 1934; *Educ* Mill Hill, Worcester Coll Oxford (MA); *m* 20 June 1959, Margaret Helen; 4 s (Roger b 1962, Gavin b 1965, Nicholas and Philip b 1970); *Career* Nat Serv RA; CA 1961, ptnr Bland Fielden & Co Colchester 1961-65; chief acct Sundour Fabrics 1966-69; md Firth Carpets Ltd 1983-, (fin dir 1969-83), dir Readcut Int plc 1984-; *Recreations* reading and walking; *Style—* Mark Fielden, Esq; The Moorings, 47 Station Road, Baildon, Shipley, W Yorks BD17 6HS (☎ Bradford 586477); Firth Carpets Ltd., Clifton Mills, Brighouse, W Yorks (☎ Brighouse 713371)

FIELDHOUSE, Adm of the Fleet Sir John David Elliott; GCB (1982, KCB 1980), GBE (1982); s of Sir Harold Fieldhouse, KBE, CB; *b* 12 Feb 1928; *Educ* RNC Dartmouth; *m* 1953, Margaret Ellen Cull; 1 s, 2 da; *Career* RN 1941, cmd HMS Acheron, Tiptoe, Walrus, Dreadnought, Hermes, Diomede; dir Naval Warfare MOD 1973-74, Flag Offr Second Flotilla 1974-76, Flag Offr Submarines 1976-78, Controller of Navy 1979-81, Admiral 1981; C-in-C Fleet, Allied C-in-C Channel and C-in-C Eastern Atlantic Area 1981-82, was in overall command during Falklands Islands operation Spring 1982; First Sea Lord and Chief of Naval Staff; First and Principal Naval ADC to HM The Queen 1982-85; Adm of the Fleet 1985, Chief of the Defence Staff 1985-; *Recreations* sailing; *Clubs* Royal Yacht Sqdn; *Style—* Adm of the Fleet Sir John Fieldhouse, GCB, GBE; Ministry of Defence, Main Building, Whitehall, London SW1A 2HB (☎ 01 218 6190)

FIELDING, Claude Eric; s of Frederick Fischl (d 1943), and Elisabeth, *née* Medola (d 1937); *b* 29 June 1926; *Educ* King's Sch Canterbury; *m* 8 Feb 1953, Olga Rachel, da of Dr Jacob Micahel Raphael (d 1972); 2 da (Rachel b 1956, Jenny b 1959); *Career* slr, clerk Stephens and Scown Slrs St Austell 1941-43, managing clerk in articles Crawley & de Reya London 1943-50, admitted slr 1950; ptnr Crawley & de Reya (film, entertainment and media law) 1950-78, head entertainments and communications law dept Bartletts de Reya 1978-88, (Michon de Reya 1988-); hon clerk Oxshott Heath Conservators 1971-; Liveryman Worshipful Co of Slrs 1960; memb: Law Soc 1950, Int Bar Assoc 1976; Commendatore Republic of Italy; *Recreations* sailing, skiing; *Clubs* Bosham Sailing, Warsash Sailing, Downhill Only, Royal Over-seas League; *Style*— Claude Fielding, Esq; Windfalls, 29 Prince's Drive, Oxshott, Surrey KT22 0UL (☎ 037284 292); 125 High Holborn, London WC1V 6QP (☎ 01 405 3711, fax 01 404 5982, telex 21455 MISLEX)

FIELDING, Hon Mrs (Daphne Winifred Louise); da of 4 Baron Vivian, DSO (d 1940); *b* 11 July 1904; *m* 1, 27 Oct 1926 (m dis 1953), 6 Marquess of Bath, *qv*; 2 s (Viscount Weymouth, Lord Christopher Thynne, *qqv*) and 1 s decd, 1 da (Duchess of Beaufort, *qv*); m 2, 11 July 1953 (m dis 1978), Major Alexander Wallace Fielding, DSO, s of Alexander Lumsden Wallace (d 1966), of Kirkcaldy; *Career* writer; *Books* Mercury Presides (autobiography), The Nearest Way Home (autobiography), The Duchess of Jermyn Street (biography of Rosa Lewis), Emerald and Nancy (biography of Emerald and Nancy Cunard), The Rainbow Picnic (biography of Nancy Tree), The Face on the Sphinx (biography of Gladys Deacon, Duchess of Marlborough), The Adonis Garden (fiction); *Style*— Hon Mrs Fielding; Old Laundry, Badminton, Avon GL9 1DD

FIELDING, John Lewis; JP (1987); s of Capt Kenneth Hubert Fielding (d 1957), of The End House, Church Ave East, Christ Church Rd, Norwich, and Olive, *née* Colman (d 1965); *b* 20 Sept 1922; *Educ* Felsted; *m* 19 Sept 1959, Ann Mary, da of Canon Stanley Clarke (d 1965), of Norwich; 2 da (Charlotte b 3 July 1960, Rachel b 6 Dec 1962); *Career* WWII SAS 1939-45; qualified as chartered surveyor auctioneer and estate agent 1952, sr ptnr Fielding & Son Norwich (now Hambros plc), dir Ipswich Building Soc; memb: mgmnt ctee Norwich Housing Soc, local valualtion panel; dep chm local bench 1975-87, chm licensing ctee 1974-87; cricketer for Norfolk (Minor Counties) 1952-57; FRICS 1952; *Recreations* sport, gardening; *Clubs* Strangers (Norwich), Special Forces ; *Style*— John Fielding, Esq, JP; The End House, Church Avenue, East Christ Church Rd, Norwich (☎ 0603 53 781); 6 Princes St, Norwich (☎ 0603 633 200, fax 0603 622 282)

FIELDING, Sir Leslie; KCMG (1988); o s of Percy Archer Fielding (d 1963), and Margaret, *née* Calder Horry; *b* 29 July 1932; *Educ* Queen Elizabeth's Sch Barnet, Emmanuel Coll Cambridge (MA), SOAS London, St Antony's Coll Oxford (MA); *m* 1978, Dr Sally Patricia Joyce, da of late Robert Stanley Thomas Stibbs Harvey; 1 s, 1 da; *Career* diplomat; Foreign Serv 1956, Tehran 1957-60, FO 1960-64, Phnom Penh (chargé d'affaires) 1964-66, Paris 1966-70, FCO 1970-73; transferred to European Cmmn in Brussels 1973-, head of delgn cmmn of Euro Communities in Japan 1978-82, dir gen for external rels Euro Cmmn in Brussels 1982-1987, vice-chllr Univ of Sussex 1987-; memb high and Euro Univ Inst Florence 1988; Kt Cdr Order of the White Rose of Finland 1987; *Recreations* living in the country; *Clubs* Travellers'; *Style*— Sir Leslie Fielding, KCMG; Vice-Chancellor, University of Sussex, Falmer, Brighton, Sussex BN1 9RH

FIELDING, Michael; s of Maurice Frisch (d 1982), and Ides, *née* Kessler; *b* 27 Mar 1946; *Educ* Hackney Downs GS, Univ of Sheffield (LLB) ; *m* 1, Sept 1968, Sandra Estelle, da of Sidney Shulman, of 35 Danescroft, Brent St, London NW4; 2 s (Jeremy Richard b 1972, Nicholas James b 1975); *Career* slr, ptnr Brecher & Co, dep chm, Land Investors plc 1986, vice-chm Palmerston Hldgs plc 1987, memb Law Soc; *Recreations* tennis, travel, reading, work; *Clubs* Harry's Bar, Annabels; *Style*— Michael Fielding, Esq; 6 Hanover Terrace, Regents Park, London NW1 (☎ 01 262 2017; 78 Brook St, London W1 (☎ 01 493 5141, telex 263486, fax 493 6255)

FIELDING, Richard Walter; s of Walter Harrison, MBE (d 1988), of Burnleigh, Ashley Common Road, New Milton, Hants, and Marjorie Octavia Adair, *née* Roberts; *b* 9 July 1933; *Educ* Clifton ; *m* 1, 27 Apr 1961, Felicity Ann (d 1981), da of the late Dr V D Jones; 1 s (Timothy b 1965), 3 da (Vanessa b 1962, Anabel, Lucinda (twins) b 1968); m 2, 1983, Jacqueline Winifred Digby, *née* Hussey; *Career* Nat Serv Lt Royal Engrs 1951-58; broker to dir Bland Welch & Co Ltd 1954-68; dir and md C E Heath & Co Ltd 1968-75; fndr chm and chief exec offr Fielding and Ptnrs 1975-86; chief exec offr C E Heath plc 1986; chm and chief exec C E Heath plc 1987-; *Style*— Richard Fielding, Esq; C E Heath plc, Cuthbert Heath House, 150 Minories, London EC3N 1NR (☎ 01 488 2488)

FIELDS, Terry (Terence); MP (Lab) Liverpool Broadgreen 1983-; s of late Frank Fields; *b* 8 Mar 1937; *m* 1962, Maureen Mongan; 2 s, 2 da; *Career* fireman, former memb NW Regional Exec Ctee Lab Pty; *Style*— Terry Fields Esq, MP; House of Commons, London SW1A 0AA (☎ 01 219 6342; home: 051 521 6413)

FIENNES *see also*: Twisleton-Wykeham-Fiennes

FIENNES, Hon Martin Guy; s (twin) of 21 Baron Saye and Sele; *b* 27 Feb 1961; *Educ* Eton, Brasenose Coll Oxford; *Style*— Hon Martin Fiennes; Broughton Castle, Banbury, Oxon (☎ 0295 62624); 44 Cathcart Rd, London SW10 (☎ 01 352 8606)

FIENNES, Hon Richard Ingel; s and h of 21 Baron Saye and Sele; *b* 19 August 1959; *Style*— Hon Richard Fiennes; Broughton Castle, Banbury, Oxon

FIENNES, Hon Susannah Hersey; da (twin) of 21 Baron Saye and Sele; *b* 27 Feb 1961; *Style*— Hon Susannah Fiennes; Broughton Castle, Banbury, Oxon (☎ 0295 62624)

FIENNES, Hon William John; s of 21 Baron Saye and Sele; *b* 7 August 1970; *Style*— Hon William Fiennes; Broughton Castle, Banbury, Oxon

FIENNES-CLINTON, Hon Edward Gordon; o s and h of 18 Earl of Lincoln, *qv*; *b* 7 Feb 1943; *m* 1970, Julia, da of William Howson, of Westminster Street, Victoria Park, Perth, W Australia; 2 s (Robert Edward b 1972, William Roy b 1980), 1 da (Marion Dawn b 1973); *Style*— The Hon Edward Fiennes-Clinton; 8 Jasminium Road, Torcoola, Pinjarra, W Australia 6208

FIFE, Eugene Vawter (Gene); s of Clark E Fife, and Margaret Ellen, *née* Morton; *b* 23 Sept 1940; *Educ* Virginia Poly Inst (BS), Univ of Southern California (MBA); *m* 1, 4 June 1966, Susan Schucker (d 1981); 1 s (David b 1971), 1 da (Amy b 1974); m2, 16 June 1984, Anne, da of Waldo Leisy; 1 s (Alexander b 1985), 1 da (Elizabeth b 1988); *Career* Lt US Air Force 1962-65; assoc Blyth & Co Inc 1968-70, Goldman Sachs & Co NY, Los Angeles, San Francisco 1970-76, chm and md Goldman Sachs Int Ltd 1986-; *Clubs* Union Club (NY); *Style*— Gene Fife, Esq; Goldman Sachs Ltd, 8-10 New Fetter Lane, London EC4A 1DB (☎ 01 489 2000, fax 01 489 5431, telex 887902)

FIFE, 3 Duke of (UK 1900); James George Alexander Bannerman Carnegie; also Earl of Macduff (UK 1900), Lord Carnegie, Master of Southesk, Master of Carnegie, Master of Kinnaird and Leuchars; el s of 11 Earl of Southesk and HH Princess Maud Alexandra Victoria Georgina Bertha (*née* Lady Maud Duff; granted title of Princess, style of Highness, and special precedence immediately after all members of Royal Family bearing style of Royal Highness 1905), 2 da of 1 Duke of Fife and HRH The Princess Royal, eldest da of HM King Edward VII; *b* 23 Sept 1929; *Educ* Gordonstoun, RAC Cirencester; *m* 11 Sept 1956 (m dis 1966), Hon Caroline Cecily Dewar, da of 3 Baron Forteviot (she m 2 Gen Sir Richard Worsley, *qv*); 1 s (Earl of Macduff b 1961), 1 da (Lady Alexandra b 1959); *Heir* s; *Career* served in Malaya 1948-50 Scots Guards; landowner, farmer; Freeman City of London 1954, Liveryman Worshipful Co of Clothworkers 1954; pres ABA 1959-73, vice-patron 1973; vice-patron of Braemar Royal Highland Soc; vice-pres British Olympic Assoc; *Clubs* Turf; *Style*— His Grace the Duke of Fife; Elsick House, Stonehaven, Kincardineshire AB3 2NT, Scotland

FIGG, Sir Leonard Clifford William; KCMG (1981), CMG (1974); s of late Sir Clifford Figg (d 1947), of Gt Missenden, Bucks, and Eileen Maud (d 1968), *née* Crabb; *b* 17 August 1923; *Educ* Charterhouse, Trinity Coll Oxford; *m* 1955, Jane, eldest da of late Judge Harold Brown; 3 s; *Career* Diplomatic Serv 1947: consul-gen and min Milan 1973-77, asst under-sec of state 1977-80, ambass to Repub of Ireland 1980-83; v-chm Br Red Cross Soc 1983-; pres Aylesbury Div Cons Assoc 1985-, Bucks Assoc of Youth Clubs 1987-; *Clubs* Brooks's; *Style*— Sir Leonard Figg, KCMG; Court Field House, Little Hampden, Great Missenden, Bucks

FIGGESS, Sir John George; KBE (1969, OBE 1949), CMG (1960); eldest s of Percival Watts Figgess, and Leonora, *née* McCanlis; *b* 15 Nov 1909; *Educ* Whitgift Sch; *m* 1948, Alette, da of Dr P J A Idenburg, of The Hague; 2 da; *Career* cmmnd Intelligence Corps 1939, Japanese linguist, liaison offr with C-in-C Eastern Fleet WWII (India, Burma), Maj 1942, Temp Lt-Col 1943, Temp Col 1956; mil attaché Tokyo 1956-61, cnsllr (info) Br Embassy Tokyo 1961-68, cmmr-gen for Britain at EXPO 70 Osaka 1968-70, dir Christie, Manson and Woods Ltd 1973-82; *Style*— Sir John Figgess, KBE, CMG; The Manor House, Burghfield, Berks

FIGGINS, Hon Mrs (Sarah Rachel Jane); *née* Kay-Shuttleworth; da of 4 Baron Shuttleworth (d 1975); *b* 18 July 1950; *Educ* Southover Manor, City and Guilds Art Sch; *m* 1, 1970 (m dis 1984), Richard Francis Foster, 2 s of William Robert Brudenell Foster, *qv*; 1 s, 2 da; m 2, 20 Dec 1988, Peter R Figgins, o s of Robert Figgins; Flat 15, 16 Pembridge Square, London W2 4EH

FIGGIS, Dermot Samuel Johnstone; s of Terence Samuel Ernest Figgis, of Heath Drive, Potters Bar, Herts, and Irene Elizabeth, *née* Arnold; *b* 31 Dec 1933; *Educ* Uppingham; *m* 24 Sept 1960, Penelope Jane, da of Leslie Harris East OBE, of Chaffcombe House, Chard, Som; 2 s (Andrew b 1962, Matthew b 1970), 1 da (Charlotte b 1965); *Career* chm and md S Figgis & Co Ltd; *Recreations* gardening, tennis, country pursuits, sailing; *Clubs* MCC; *Style*— Dermot S J Figgis, Esq; The Limes, Essendon, Hatfield, Herts (☎ 07072 61400); 53-54 Aldgate High Street, London EC3 (☎ 01 488 4511)

FIGGURES, Sir Frank Edward; KCB (1970, CB 1966), CMG (1959); s of Frank Figgures (d 1950), and Alice Figgures; *b* 5 Mar 1910; *Educ* Rutlish Sch, New Coll Oxford; *m* 1, 1941, Aline (d 1975), da of Prof Hugo Frey; 1 s, 1 da; m 2, 1975, Ismea, da of George Napier Magill, and widow of Jack Barker; *Career* served WW II RA; dir Julius Baer Int 1975-, chm: Central Wagon Co 1976- and BBC Gen Advsy Cncl 1978-82, also Pay Bd 1973-74; dir-gen Nat Ec Dvpt Off 1971-73; with Tresy 1946-71 (2 perm sec 1968-71, 3 sec 1965-68, under-sec 1955-60); sec-gen EFTA 1960-65, Dir Tde & Finance Orgn Euro Ec Cooperation 1948-51; *Style*— Sir Frank Figgures, KCB, CMG; 7A Spring Lane, Glaston, Uppingham, Rutland LE15 9BX (☎ Uppingham 822777)

FIGURES, Sir Colin Frederick; KCMG (1983, CMG 1978), OBE (1969); s of Frederick and Muriel Figures; *b* 1 July 1925; *Educ* King Edward's Sch Birmingham, Pembroke Coll Cambridge (MA); *m* 1956, Pamela Ann Timmis; 1 s, 2 da; *Career* FO 1951; first sec Vienna 1966, FCO 1969-; *Style*— Sir Colin Figures, KCMG, OBE; c/o Foreign and Cwlth Off, King Charles St, London SW1

FILBY, The Venerable William Charles Leonard; s of William Richard Filby (d 1946), of Middx, and Dorothy, *née* Evans (d 1980); *b* 21 Jan 1933; *Educ* Ashford Co Sch Middx, London Univ (BA); *m* 1958, Marion Erica, da of Prof T W Hutchinson, of Birmingham; 4 s (Jonathan b 1959, Andrew b 1961, Christopher b 1963, William b 1968), 1 da (Rebecca b 1966); *Career* archdeacon of Horsham 1983-, vicar of Holy Trinity Richmond 1965-71, of Bp Hannington Hove 1971-79, rector of Broadwater 1979-83, rural dean of Worthin 1980-83; chm: Redcliffe Missionary Tning Coll 1970, Diocesan Stewardship Ctee 1983-, Sussex Churches Bdcasting Ctee 1984-; govr: St Mary's Hall Brighton 1984-, W Sussex Inst of High Educn 1985-; memb Keswick Convention Cncl 1973-; bishop's advsr for Hosp Chaplains 1986-; *Recreations* sport, music; *Style*— The Venerable the Archdeacon of Horsham; The Archdeaconry, Itchingfield, Horsham, N Sussex RH13 7NX

FILER, Denis Edwin; TD 1962 and 1974; s of Edwin Francis Filer (d 1951), of Manchester and Sarah Ann, *née* Stannard (d 1984); *b* 19 May 1932; *Educ* Manchester Central GS, Manchester Univ (BSc), Open Univ (BA); *m* 17 Aug 1957, Pamela, da of Sam Armitage of Manchester; 1 s (Nigel John Denis b 1967), 2 da (Fiona Anne b 1962, Katharine Helen b 1964); *Career* Nat Serv 2 Lt REME served BAOR 1953-55; TA serv culminating: Lt-Col ADEME 1970-75, Col 1975-78, hon col REME(v) West 1978-87; ICI: project mangr (Holland, Grangemouth and Hillhouse) 1953-73, asst works mangr (Wilton Works) 1973-76, engrg mangr (Welwyn) 1976-78, engrg and production dir (Welwyn) 1978-81, dir of engrg 1981-88; dir gen The Engrg Cncl 1988-; (memb cncl), FEng, FIMechE, FIChemE; *Recreations* squash; *Clubs* Wilton Castle; *Style*— Denis Filer, Esq, TD; Brambles, Watton Green, Watton-at-Stone, Hertford SG14 3RB (☎ 0920 830207); The Engineering Council, 10 Maltravers St, London WC2R 3ER (☎ 01 240 7891)

FILER, Michael Harold; s of Louis Horace Filer, of Bournemouth, Dorset, and Raie, *née* Behrman (d 1978); *b* 11 August 1939; *Educ* Clifton, Inst of Taxation (ATII); *m* 5 Dec 1965, Anne Brenda, da of Peter Packer; 1 s (Samuel b 1978), 3 da (Lucy b 1967, Katy b 1970, Sadie b 1981); *Career* CA 1963; Inst of Taxation ATII admitted 1965; currently sr ptnr Filer, Knapper & Co; cncllr Bournemouth CC 1969-79 and 1983-87; Mayor of Bournemouth 1984-85; numerous charitable ctees; FCA; *Recreations* cricket (played in 1957 Clifton Coll Cricket Team at Lords, player mangr UK Cricket Team in

Maccabiah Games Israel 1974), tennis; *Style*— Michael H Filer, Esq; 8 Boscombe Cliff Rd, Bournemouth, Dorset BH5 1JL (☎ 0202 36 302); Filer Knapper & Co, Chartered Accountants, 10 Bridge St, Christchurch, Dorset BH23 1EF (☎ 0202 483 341, fax 0202 483 550)

FILLING, Roy Paul; OBE (1988); s of William Arthur Filling (d 1960), of Egham, Surrey, and Alice May, *née* Field (d 1925); *b* 18 May 1924; *Educ* Ashford Secdy Sch Ashford Middx; *m* 19 July 1945, Audrey Margaret, da of Fred Wilfred Highland (d 1972), of Staines, Middx; 1 da (Ann Linda); *Career* air crew navigator RAFVR 1943-47; trainee accountant Mackay Indust Equipment Feltham Middx 1948-54, fin dir Isacc Walton & Co Ltd London 1954-66, chm and md Wellsway Garage Ltd Bath 1966-77, counselling advsr Dept of Employment Business Devpt Serv & Small Firms Serv 1977-, chm Corintech Ltd Salisbury & Fordingbridge 1986-87; *Recreations* travel, swimming, model aircraft; *Clubs* Mansion House (Poole), Luncheon; *Style*— Roy Filling, Esq, OBE; 37 Beauchamps Gdns, Castledean, Bournemouth, Dorset BH7 7JE (☎ 0202 433 166)

FINBOW, Roger John; s of Frederick Walter Finbow, of Sudbourne, Woodbridge, Suffolk, and Olivia Francis *née* Smith; *b* 13 May 1952; *Educ* Woodbridge Sch Suffolk, Mansfield Coll Oxford (MA); *m* 23 May 1984, Janina Fiona (Nina), da of John Doull of Shorne, Kent; 2 da (Romy b 1985, Georgina b 1987); *Career* Ashurst Morris Crisp London: articled clerk 1975-77, asst 1977-83, (Paris 1978-79), assoc 1983-75, ptnr 1985-; former pres Old Woodbridgian Soc; cncl memb Mansfield Coll, (memb appeal ctee), pres Mansfield Assoc, chm Business Sub Gp; memb: Law Soc, Slrs Euro Gp; *Recreations* cars, collecting model cars, badminton, football spectating; *Clubs* Ipswich Town Football; *Style*— Roger Finbow, Esq; 32 Allerton Rd, London N16 (☎ 01 802 3805); Broadgate House, 7 Eldon St, London EC2M 7HD (☎ 01 247 7666, fax 01 377 5659, telex 887067)

FINCASTLE, Viscount; Malcolm Kenneth Murray; er s and h of 11 Earl of Dunmore and Margaret Joy, *née* Cousins (d 1976); *b* 17 Sept 1946; *Educ* Queechy HS, Launceston Schools' Bd 'A' certificate; *m* 1970, Joy Anne, da of A Partridge (d 1987), of Launceston, Tasmania, 1 s (Leigh b 1977), 1 da (Elisa b 1980) (both adopted); *Career* electrical tech offr, Civil Aviation Authy, licenced aircraft maintenance engnr; *Recreations* flying, astronomy, builder of an amateur built aircraft Thorp T18; *Clubs* Soaring of Tasmania; *Style*— Viscount Fincastle; PO Box 100E, E Devonport, Tas 7310, Australia; Devonport Airport, Tas

FINCH, Nigel Lucius Graeme; s of Harold George Graeme, and Elizabeth, *née* Turner; *b* 1 August 1949; *Educ* Ravensbourne Boys Sch, Sussex Univ (BA, Dip Ed); *Career* Arena, BBC TV 1985-; dir: Chelsea Hotel, Raspberry Ripple, Your Honor I Object; Freedom New Orleans USA 1988; *Recreations* listing, I list therefore I am; *Style*— Nigel Finch, Esq; The Bishopric, 80 Culverden Road, London SW12 (☎ 01 673 0896)

FINCH, Peter John; s of Richard Stuart Finch (d 1981), of Essex, and Charlotte Betsy, *née* Finch; *b* 17 April 1948; *Educ* Plaistow GS, City of London Poly; *m* 1, 1967, Angela Ruth, da of George Herbert Harold Watkins (d 1982); m 2, 1986, Carol Joyce, da of Douglas Arthur Wilson (d 1985), of Kent; *Career* dir: M & G Life Assurance Co Ltd 1979-, M & G Pensions and Annuity Co Ltd 1979-; pres Insurance Inst of Chelmsford 1980-81; *Recreations* sailing, squash; *Clubs* Royal Corinthian Yacht; *Style*— Peter Finch, Esq; 17 Barnmead Way, Burnham on Crouch, Essex CM0 8QD (☎ 0621 784309); M & G Life, M & G House, Victoria Road, Chelmsford CM1 1FB (☎ 0245 266266, fax 0245 267789)

FINCH HATTON, Hon Robin Heneage; 2 s of 15 (and 10) Earl of Winchilsea and Nottingham; *b* 1 Nov 1939; *Educ* Gordonstoun; *m* 7 Sept 1962, Molly Iona, da of the late Col Palgrave Dawson Turner Powell, MBE, TD; 2 s (Christopher b 1966, Rupert b 1968), 1 da (Louisa b 1971, Nicola b 1964 d 1967); *Style*— Hon Robin Finch Hatton; Town House Farmhouse, Clemsfold, Horsham, Sussex

FINCH-KNIGHTLEY, Hon Anthony Heneage; JP (Huntingdon); s of 10 Earl of Aylesford (d 1958); *b* 27 April 1920; *Educ* Oundle; *m* 12 June 1948, Susan Mary, o da of Maj-Gen Geoffrey Woodroffe Palmer, CB, CBE; 2 da (Minette b 1950, Joanna b 1954); *Career* Lt and temp Capt Black Watch, served ME 1940-44 (despatches); formerly with ICI; dep chm Huntingdon Bench; pres Huntingdon Cons; *Recreations* shooting, fishing, archery; *Clubs* The Bean; *Style*— Hon Anthony Finch-Knightley, JP; Broomleigh House, Brampton, Huntingdon, Cambs (☎ Huntingdon 53163)

FINDLAY, Brig (William Francis) Allan; OBE (1973); s of James Arthur Findlay (d 1966), of London SW19, and Gladys Anna, *née* Ker (d 1971); *b* 30 Nov 1929; *Educ* Wellington, RMA Sandhurst; *m* 21 April 1956, Bridget Gay, da of Air Vice Marshal Augustus Henry Orlebar, CBE, AFC (d 1943), of Sandy, Beds; 2 s (Giles b 1959, Oliver b 1962); *Career* CO Queens Own Yeomanry 1971-73, Brig 1977, Col 5 Royal Inniskilling Dragoon Gds 1981-86, ADC to HM The Queen 1982; marketing exec MEL Defence Electronics 1982-; master Catterick Beagles 1955-56; *Recreations* gardening, field sports; *Clubs* Cavalry and Guards'; *Style*— Brig Allan Findlay, OBE; Upmeadow Lodge, Graffham, Petworth, West Sussex (☎ 079 86 236); MEL, Manor Royal, Crawley, West Sussex (☎ 0293 28787)

FINDLAY, Donald Russell; QC (1988); s of James Findlay (d 1980), of Edinburgh, and Mabel, *née* Muirhead (d 1985); *b* 17 Mar 1951; *Educ* Harris Acad Dundee, Univ of Dundee (LLB); *m* 28 Aug 1982, Jennifer Edith, *née* Borrowman; *Career* lectr in law Heriot Watt Univ Edinburgh 1975-76, advocate 1975-; vice chm Leith Cons and Unionist Assoc, memb Lothian Health Bd 1987, memb Faculty of Advocates 1975; *Recreations* Glasgow Rangers Football, egyptology, wine, american football, sumo; *Clubs* Caledonian, Edinburgh, Royal Burgess Golfing Soc, Glasgow Rangers Premier; *Style*— Donald R Findlay, Esq, QC; 26 Barnton Park Crescent, Edinburgh EH4 6EP (☎ 031 336 3734); Advocates Library, Parliament House, Edinburgh EH1 1RF (☎ 031 226 2881, fax 031 225 3642, car tel 0860 410 749, tlx 727856 FACADV 9)

FINDLAY, Ian Herbert Fyfe; s of late Prof Alexander Findlay, CBE (d 1966), of Aberdeen, and Alice Mary, *née* de Rougemont; *b* 5 Feb 1918; *Educ* Fettes; *m* 1950, Alison Mary, da of late Bernard George Ashby; 2 s, 1 da; *Career* chm Price Forbes (Hldgs) Ltd 1967-72; chm Sedgwick Forbes (Hldgs) Ltd 1974-77, (dep chm 1972-74); chm Lloyd's Insur Brokers Assoc 1969-70, chm Lloyd's 1978-79 (dep chm 1977), chm Br Insurance Brokers Assoc 1980-82; memb cncl Guide Dogs for the Blind Assoc 1980-87, (chm 1981-87); tstee St George's Eng Sch Rome 1980-, govr Brighton Coll 1981-88; *Recreations* golf, postal history; *Clubs* City of London, Royal and Ancient Golf, Addington Golf; *Style*— Ian Findlay, Esq; 24 Forest Ridge, Keston Park, Kent BR2 6EQ (☎ 0689 52993)

FINDLAY, Martin Charles; s of Cdr Noel Charles Mansfeldt Findlay, RN (d 1976), of Court Lodge, Hastingleigh, Kent, and Lady Mary Cecilia, *née* Legge, da of 7 Earl Dartmouth, GCVO, JP, DL; *b* 27 June 1935; *Educ* Marlborough, St John's Coll Cambridge (MA); *m* 26 May 1966, Davina Margaret da of Sir Thomas Dundas Bart, MBE, (d 1970), of The Old Rectory, Slaugham, Sussex; 2 s (Mark b 1967, Adam b 1969); *Career* Nat serv 2 Lt Royal Dragoons 1953-55; Whitbread & Co: personnel dir 1976-86, vice chm 1982-; dir Business in the Community, memb cncl London Educn Business Partnership; Freeman: City of London 1986, Worshipful Co of Brewers; M Inst D, FRSA 1988; *Recreations* country pursuits which lead to peace; *Style*— Martin Findlay, Esq; Ledburn Manor, Leighton Buzzards, Bedfordshire (☎ 0525 373110); Whitbread & Co, Chiswell St, London EC1 (☎ 01 606 4455)

FINDLAY, Lady Mary Cecilia; *née* Legge; eldest da of 7 Earl of Dartmouth, GCVO (d 1958); *b* 27 Oct 1906; *m* 17 Oct 1929, Cdr Noel Charles Mansfeldt Findlay, RN (d 1976), s of Sir Mansfeldt de Cardonnel Findlay, GBE, KCMG, CB; 2 s (Jonathan b 1933, Martin b 1935), 1 da (Mrs J Debenham b 1930); *Style*— Lady Mary Findlay; 2 South Close, The Precincts, Canterbury, Kent CT1 2EJ

FINDLAY, Paul Hudson Douglas; s of Prof John Niemeyer Findlay (d 1987), and Aileen May, *née* Davidson; *b* 26 Sept 1943; *Educ* Univ Coll Sch London, Balliol Coll Oxford (BA), London Opera Centre; *m* 9 Sept 1966, Francoise Christiane, da of Albert Victor Willmott (d 1987); 1 s (Anthony b 4 May 1968), 1 da (Lucy b 4 June 1972); *Career* prodn and tech mangr New Opera Co 1967, dir London Sinfonietta 1967-, stage mangr Glyndebourne Touring Opera and English Opera Gp 1968, chm Opera 80 1987, opera dir Royal Opera House Covent Gdn 1987- (asst dir 1976-87, PA to gen dir 1972-76, asst press offr 1968-72); Cavaliere Ufficiale Del 'Ordine Al Merito Della Repubblica Italiana; *Recreations* tennis, gardening, walking; *Style*— Paul Findlay, Esq; Royal Opera House, Covent Gdn, London WC2 (☎ 01 240 1200, telex 27988 COVGAR G)

FINDLAY SHIRRAS, Richard George; s of Prof George Findlay Shirras (d 1953), of Greystones, Ballater, Aberdeenshire, and late Amy Zara, *née* McWatters; *b* 4 Oct 1913; *Educ* Clifton, RMC Sandhurst; *m* 16 Sept 1946 (m dis), Yolaine Elizabeth Claridge, da of late R O C Johnsen; 3 s (Douglas Richard b 10 Dec 1947, Alasdair Robert b 6 Feb 1949, Nigel John b 14 June 1951); *Career* cmnd Gordon Highlanders 1934 serv: Gibralter 1935-37, Singapore 1937-40, Capt Western Desert 1941; POW 1941-45 (Italy and Germany); 1 Bn Gordon Highlanders BAOR 1947, posted Highland Bde HQ Fort George 1947-48, 1 Bn Argyll and Sutherland Highlanders Colchester, sr offrs Sch Earls Earlstoke Park, 2 i/c 4/7 Gordon Highlanders Aberdeen, 1 Bn, Gordon Highlanders Malaya; Trg offr St Andrew CCF 1955-56; ret (UK) 1956; John Harvey & Sons Ltd 1956: trg Bristol, No 2 Glasgow HQ, Scotland 10 Years, No 1 to John Harvey Pall Mall, ret 1979; memb Worshipful Co of Distillers 1963; *Recreations* golf, curling; *Clubs* Whites, Boodles; *Style*— Maj Richard Findlay Shirras; 50 Dean Path, Edinburgh EH4 3AU (☎ 031 332 8834)

FINESTEIN, His Hon Judge; Israel Finestein; QC (1970); yst s of Jeremiah Finestein (d 1957), of Hull, Yorks; *b* 29 April 1921; *Educ* Kingston HS Hull, Trinity College Cambridge (MA); *m* 1946, Marion Phyllis, er da of Simon Oster, of Hendon, Middx; *Career* formerly major scholar and prizeman of Trinity Coll Cambridge; memb Cncl of Utd Synagogue, pres Cncl of Jewish Historical Soc of England; barr Lincoln's Inn 1953, a circuit judge 1972-; author; *Books* Short History of the Jews of England, Sir George Jessel; *Style*— His Hon Judge Finestein, QC; 18 Buttermere Court, Boundary Rd, London NW8

FINGALL, Countess of; Clair Hilda Plunkett; *née* Salmon; MBE; da of late Henry Robert Salmon, of Ballarat, Victoria, Australia; *b* 2 Feb 1903; *m* 1, Frank Richardson (decd), of Geelong, Vic, Australia; m 2, 4 May 1966, as his 2 w, 12 Earl of Fingall (d 5 March 1984, when title became extinct); *Clubs* RACV (Melbourne); *Style*— The Rt Hon the Countess of Fingall; 13 Lock Wood St, Point Lonsdale, Victoria, Australia

FINGERHUT, John Hyman; s of Abraham Fingerhut (d 1931), of Manchester, and Emily, *née* Roe (d 1913); *b* 2 Nov 1910; *Educ* Manchester GS, Manchester Univ; *m* 1950, Beatrice, da of late Michael and Kitty Leigh; 2 s, 2 da; *Career* md Merck Sharp & Dohme Ltd 1963-67, chm Merck Sharp & Dohme Ltd 1967-72, regnl dir Merck Sharp & Dohme Int (conslt 1975-77), chm Thomas Morson & Son Ltd 1967-72, conslt to pharmaceutical indust; *Recreations* music, reading, gardening, washing-up; *Style*— John H Fingerhut, Esq; 76 Green Lane, Edgware, Middx HA8 7QA (☎ 01 958 6163)

FINGLAND, Sir Stanley James Gunn; KCMG (1979, CMG 1966); s of Samuel Gunn Fingland (d 1969), of Edinburgh, and Agnes Christina, *née* Watson; *b* 19 Dec 1919; *Educ* Royal HS Edinburgh; *m* 1946, Nell, da of late Charles Lister; 1 s, 1 da; *Career* Maj Royal Signals (despatches Italy) 1939-47; Dip Serv; dep high cmmr Port of Spain 1962, Salisbury Rhodesia 1964, high cmmr Freetown 1966-69, asst under-sec of state FO 1969-71, ambassador Havana 1972-75, high cmmr Nairobi 1975-79 (concurrently Br rep to the UN Environmental Programme and to UN Habitat HQ in Nairobi); *Recreations* fishing; *Style*— Sir Stanley Fingland, KCMG; 34 Ashdown, Eaton Rd, Hove, Sussex (☎ 0273 723324)

FINGLETON, David Melvin; s of Lawrence Arthur Fingleton and Norma Phillips, *née* Spiro; *b* 2 Sept 1941; *Educ* Stowe Sch, UC Oxford (MA); *m* 1975, Clare, yr da of Ian Colvin (d 1975); *Career* barr 1965-80; Met Stipendiary magistrate 1980; music critic Daily Express, stage design corr Arts Review; *Books* Kiri (biography of Dame Kiri Te Kanawa, 1982); *Recreations* music, travel; *Clubs* Garrick, MCC; *Style*— David Fingleton, Esq; Wells Street Magistrates Court, Wells Street, London W1A 3AE (☎ 01 825 2343)

FINGRET, Peter; s of Iser Fingret (d 1975), and Irene, *née* Jacobs (d 1979)d; *b* 13 Sept 1934; *Educ* Leeds Modern Sch, Leeds Univ (LLB); *m* m 1 (m diss) 11 Dec 1960, June Gertrude; 1 s (Andrew b 1963), 1 da (Kathryn b 1966); m 2 14 March 1980, Ann Lilian Mary; *Career* slr 1960-82; stipendiary magistrate: County of Humberside 1982-85, metropolitan 1985-; Crown Ct Recorder 1987-; RSM; *Recreations* golf, music, open univ; *Clubs* Reform; *Style*— Peter Fingret, Esq; Dairy Cottage, Richmond, TW10 7DB; 6 Herring House, Holy Island, Northumbria (☎ 01 703 0909)

FINIGAN, John Patrick; s of John Joseph Finigan, of Sale, Ches, and Mary Matilda Finigan (d 1983); *b* 12 Nov 1949; *Educ* Ushaw Coll Durham, St Bedes Coll Manchester, Council of Legal Educn London, Univ of Manchester, Harvard Law Sch; *m* 6 Dec 1976, Elizabeth Liew, da of Joseph Liew, of Banda Seri Begawan Brunei; 1 s (Damien b 1980), 1 da (Emily E Jane b 1982); *Career* slr, Standard Chartered Bank 1967-78, Nat Bank of Abu Dhabi 1978-82; asst gen mangr The Nat Bank of Kuwait SAK 1982-; AIB 1970, ACIS 1973, FCIB 1980; memb Hon Soc of Lincolns Inn;

Recreations tennis, squash, music, literature; *Clubs* Oriental, Overseas Bankers; *Style—* John Finigan, Esq; The Old Orchard, Odiham, Hants; Delorain, Newton Ferrers, Devon The National Bank of Kuwait SAK, 13 George St, London W1H 5PB (☎ 01 224 2277, fax 01 224 2101, telex 892348)

FINKELSTEIN, Prof Ludwik; s of Adolf Finkelstein (d 1950), of London and Amelia, *née* Diamanstein (d 1980); *b* 6 Dec 1929; *Educ* London Univ (BSc, MSc), City Univ (DSc); *m* 1957, Mirjam Emma, da of Dr Alfred Wiener (d 1964), of London; 2 s (Anthony b 1959, Daniel b 1962), 1 da (Tamara b 1967); *Career* scientist intsrument branch mining res establishment NCB 1952-59; Northampton Coll City Univ 1959-: prof of instrument and control engrg, dean sch of electrical engrg and applied physics, head dept pf physics, head dept of Systems Sci, dir of measurment and instrumentation centre dean sch of engrg; Queen's Silver Jubilee Medal 1977; Liveryman Worshipful Co Sci Instrument Makers; FEng 1986, FIEE, FInstP, FInstMC, CPhys; *Recreations* books, conversation, Jewish studies; *Style—* Prof Ludwik Finkelstein; 9 Cheyne Walk, Hendon, London NW4 3QH (☎ 01 202 6966); City Univ, Northampton Sq, London EC1V 0HB (☎ 01 253 4399 ext 4400, fax 01 250 0837)

FINLAISON, Brig Alexander Montagu; CBE (1957), DSO (1944); s of late Maj-Gen John Bruce Finlaison, CMG, late RM (d 1950), of Dedham, Essex, and Isabel, da of Lt-Gen Sir John Hudson, KCB; *b* 14 Mar 1904; *Educ* RNCs Osborne and Dartmouth, RMC Sandhurst; *m* 1935, Monica Mary Louisa, da of T W Donald, of Grendon, Stirling; 1 da and 1 da dec'd; *Career* Cameronians (Scottish Rifles) 1924, served Sudan Def Force 1932-38, BGS Scottish Cmd 1954-57, ADC to HM The Queen 1955-57, ret 1957; Cmdt Queen Victoria Sch Dunblane 1957-64; *Clubs* Naval and Military; *Style—* Brig Alexander Finlaison, CBE, DSO; Gledenholm, Ae, Dumfries (☎ Parkgate 242)

FINLAY, Sir David Ronald James Bell; 2 Bt (UK 1964), of Epping, Co Essex; s of Sir Graeme Finlay, 1 Bt, ERD (d 1987); *b* 16 Nov 1963; *Educ* Marlborough, Grenoble Univ, Bristol Univ; *Career* trainee CA, Peat Marwick Mclintock; *Recreations* shooting, ski-ing, photography; *Style—* Sir David Finlay, Bt; The Garden Flat, 106 Chesterton Rd, London W10 6EP

FINLAY, Air Cdre Denis; CBE (1950); s of James Finlay (d 1921), and Kezia Jane, *née* Osborne (d 1958); *b* 4 Jan 1912; *Educ* King Edward VI GS Southampton, RAF Coll Cranwell; *m* 1938, Pamela Mary (d 1969), da of late Sydney Barrett; 1 s (Jeremy b 1940); *Career* Air Cdre RAF, Europe NW Africa Italy, dir of Personal Serv Air Miny, Cmdt Aircrew Selection Centre; *Style—* Air Cdre Denis Finlay, CBE; Casa Pamela, Benisa, Alicante, Spain; Lloyd's Bank (Cox's and Kings) 6 Pall Mall, London

FINLAY, (Robert) Derek; s of William Templeton Finlay (d 1972), and Phyllis, *née* Jefferies (d 1948); *b* 16 May 1932; *Educ* Kingston GS, Emmanuel Coll Cambridge (BA, MA); *m* 1956, Una Ann, da of late David Smith Grant; 2 s (Rory, James), 1 da (Fiona); *Career* Lt Gordon Highlanders Malaya 1950-52, Capt Gordon Highlanders TA 1952-61; Mobil Oil Co UK 1955-61; assoc McKinsey & Co Inc 1961-67 (princ 1967-71, dir 1971-79); md H J Heinz Co Ltd 1979-81, sr vice-pres World HQ H J Heinz Co Pittsburgh PA, USA 1981-; *Recreations* tennis, rowing, music, theatre; *Clubs* Highland Brigade, Leander, Allegheny Country, Duquesne, Annabels; *Style—* Derek Finlay, Esq; Backbone Rd, Sewickley Heights, Pennsylvania 15143, USA (☎ 412 741 4763); World Headquarters, H J Heinz Co, PO Box 57, Pittsburgh, Pa 15230, USA (☎ 412 456 5707)

FINLAY, Frank; CBE (1984); s of Josiah Finlay (d 1951), of Farnworth, Lancs, and Margaret Griffin (d 1974); *b* 6 Aug 1926; *Educ* St Gregory's Farnworth Lancs, Bolton Tech Coll, RADA (Dip); *m* 27 Sept 1954, Doreen Joan, da of Joseph Shepherd; 2 s (Stephen b 1955. Daniel b 1965), 1 da (Cathy b 1957); *Career* actor; theatre: repertory 1950-52 and 1954-57; Belgrade (Covenrty) 1958, Epitath for George Dillan (NY) 1958, Royal Court 1958; 1959-62: Sugar in the Morning. Sergeant Musgrave's Dance, Chicken Soup with Barley, Roots, I'm Talking About Jerusalem, The Happy Haven, Platonov, Chips with Everything (Royal Court then transferred to Vaudeville 1962, Clarence Derwent Best Actor Award); St Joan (Chichester Festival 1963), Hobson's Choice and Othello (Chichester Festival 1964), The Crucible 1965, Much Ado About Nothing 1965, Mother Courage 1965, Juno and the Paycock 1966, Dikey in the Storm 1966, After Haggerty (Aldwych, Criterion), Son of Man (Leicester Theatre and Round House, first actor to play Jesus Christ on the English stage) 1970, Kings and Clowns (musical, Phoenix) 1978, Filumena (Lyric 1978, US tour 1979-80), The Girl in Melanie Klein 1980, The Cherry Orchard (tour and Haymarket 1983), Mutiny (musical, Piccadilly) 1985-86, Beyond Reasonable Doubt (Queen's 1987, Australian tour 1988-89); Nat Theatre Co: Saturday, Sunday, Monday 1973, The Party 1973, Plunder, Watch it Come Down, Weapons of Happiness 1976, Amadeus 1982; films incl: The Longest Day, Private Potter, The Informers, A Life for Ruth, Lonliness of the Long Distance Runner, Hot Enough for June, The Comedy Man, The Sandwich Man, A Study in Terror, Othello (nominated for American Acad Award, best actor award San Sebastian 1966), The Jokers, I'll Never Forget What's 'is Name, The Shoes of the Fisherman, Deadly Bees, Robbery, Inspector Clouseau, Twisted Nerve, Cromwell, The Molly Maguires, Assault, Victory for Danny Jones, Gumshoe, Shaft in Africa, Van Der Valk and the Girl, Van Der Valk and the Rich, Van Der Valk and the Dead, The Three Musketeers, The Ring of Darkness, The Wild Geese, The Theif of Baghdad, Sherlock Holmes - Murder by Decree, Enigma, Return of the Soldier, The Ploughman's Lunch 1982, La Chiave (The Key, Italy) 1983, Sakharov 1983, Christmas Carol, Arch of Triumph 1919 1984, Life Force 1985, Return of the Musketeers 1988; TV appearances incl: Julius Caesar, Les Miséables, This Happy Breed, the Lie (SFTA Award), Casanova (series), The Death of Adolph Hitler, Don Quixote (SFTA Award), Voltaire, Merchant of Venice, Bouquet of Barbed Wire (series, Best Actor Award), 84 Charing Cross Road, Saturday, Sunday, Monday, Count Dracula, The Last Campaign, Napoleon in Betzi, Dear Brutus, Tales of the Unexpected, Tales from 1001 Nights, Aspects of Love - Mona, In the Secret State, Verdict on Erebus (NZ); Freeman City of Baltimore USA 1979; *Recreations* reading, theatre, films, the countryside; *Clubs* Garrick; *Style—* Frank Finlay, Esq, CBE; c/o Al Parker Ltd, 55 Park Lane, London W1

FINLAY, (William) Ian (Robertson); CBE (1965); s of William Robertson Finlay (d 1961), and Annie M, *née* Somerville; *b* 2 Dec 1906,Auckland, NZ,; *Educ* Edinburgh Acad, Edinburgh Univ; *m* 1933, Mary Scott, da of Prof William Henderson Pringle, (d 1967); 2 s, 1 da; *Career* art historian and author; keeper of dept of art and archaeology Royal Scottish Museum 1956-61 (dir 1961-71); hon prof of antiquities to Royal Scottish Acad 1966- (HRSA); Freeman City of London, Liveryman Worshipful Co of Goldsmiths; *Books* Art in Scotland (1948), Scotland (1945), A History of Scottish Gold and Silver Work (1956), Celtic Art (1973), Priceless Heritage: the Future of Museums (1977), Columba (1979); *Style—* Ian Finlay Esq, CBE; Currie Riggs, Balerno, Midlothian (☎ 031 449 4249); High Corrie Isle of Arran (☎ 077 081 689)

FINLAY, Lady; June Evangeline; *née* Drake; da of Col Francis Collingwood Drake, OBE, MC, DL (d 1976), 10 Royal Hussars; *m* 22 May 1953, Sir Graeme Finlay, 1 Bt, ERD (d 1987); 1 s (Sir David Finlay, 2 Bt); 2 da; *Style—* Lady Finlay; La Campagne, Rozel, St Martin, Jersey, CI (☎ 0534 51194)

FINLAY, Ronald Adrian (Ron); s of Harry Finlay, of London NW3, and Tess, *née* Matz; *b* 4 Dec 1956; *Educ* Univ Coll Sch London, St John's Coll Cambridge (BA, MA); *Career* Br Market Res Bureau 1979-81, Merrill Lynch 1982-83, Valin Pollen Ltd 1983-86 (dir 1986-); sec SDP Hendon S 1984-85; assoc memb Market Res Soc 1980; *Recreations* squash, bridge, hill-walking; *Style—* Ron Finlay, Esq; 24B Belsize Grove, London NW3 4TR (☎ 01 586 8716); Valin Pollen Ltd, 18 Grosvenor Gardens, London SW1W ODH (☎ 01 730 3456, fax 01 730 7445, telex 296846 BIZCOM G)

FINLAY-MAXWELL, David Campbell; s of Luke Greenwood Maxwell (d 1937), and Lillias Maule Finlay (d 1955); *b* 2 Mar 1923; *Educ* St Paul's, Heriot-Watt Edinburgh (CEng, MIEE), Leeds Univ (PhD); *m* 1954, Constance Shirley, da of James Douglas Hood, CBE (d 1981); 1 s (Douglas), 1 da (Carol); *Career* Maj Royal Signals SOE Operations 1939-45, serv: Europe, India and Malaysia; dir and chm John Gladstone & Co Ltd and John Gladstone & Co (Engrg) Ltd 1948-; chm: Manpower Working Party NEDO 1970-73, Wool Industs Research Assoc 1974-77, Textile Research Cncl 1977-82, Wool Textile EDC 1977-79; cncllr and dir Br Textile Cncl 1977-84; UK rep Consultative Ctee for R & D Brussels 1979-84; memb: Cncl Textile Inst 1972-74 (granted fellowship), Textile Industry Advsy Ctee, Leeds Univ Cncl 1974- (hon lectr), Soc of Dyers & Colourists 1950- (granted fellowship), Scientific Devpt Sub Ctee, CBI Science & Research Ctee 1980-87; dir The Wool Foundation (IWS) 1985-; pres Comitextil Science and Research Ctee Brussels 1979-85; EEC reviewer Esprit prog 1986-; dir and vice-chm Sound Recording Bd of Dirs RNIB; hon organizer UK Technical Volunteer Helpers for Blind; MIEE, FTI, FSDC; *Recreations* radio propagation, satellite tracking; *Clubs* RSAC, Special Forces; *Style—* Dr David Finlay-Maxwell; Folly Hall Ho, Cross Lane, Kirkburton, Huddersfield HD8 0ST; John Gladstone & Co Ltd, Wellington Mills, Huddersfield HD3 3HJ (☎ 0484 653 437, fax 0484 647 321, telex 51442)

FINLAYSON, George Ferguson; CMG (1979), CVO (1983); s of late G B Finlayson; *b* 28 Nov 1924; *Educ* N Berwick HS; *m* 1, 1951, Rosslyn Evelyn (d 1972), da of late E N James; 1 da (Carolyn b 1952); m 2, 1982, Anthea Judith Perry; *Career* FO 1949; consul-gen: Toronto 1978-81, Los Angeles 1981-84; ret; *Style—* George Finlayson, Esq, CMG, CVO; 141B Ashley Gardens, London SW1; Romola, Westgate, North Berwick, East Lothian

FINLEY, Michael John; s of Walter Finley (d 1940), and Grace Marie Butler, *née* Sykes,; *b* 22 Sept 1932; *Educ* King Edward VII Sch Sheffield; *m* 19 March 1955, Sheila Elizabeth, da of late Harold Cole of Osbournby Lincs; 4 s (Nicholas b 1955, Andrew b 1959, Jonathan b 1967, Robert b 1968); *Career* ed Sheffield Telegraph 1964-69, gen mangr and dir Kent Messenger Gp 1979-82 (editorial dir 1969-79), exec dir Periodical Publishers Assoc 1982-88, dir Fedn Int de la Presse Periodique 1989-; memb advsy cncl BBC 1975-80, govr Int Press Fndn 1988-; chm Kent IOD 1980-82, govr Cranbrook Sch 1977-; *Books* Advertising And The Community (contrib 1969); *Recreations* tennis, golf, snooker, watching rugby, walking; *Style—* Michael Finley, Esq; Sorrento, Staplehurst, Kent; Fipp, Suite 19, Grosvenor Gdns House, 35-37 Grosvenor Gdns, London SW1W OBS (☎ 01 828 1366)

FINLEY, Sir Peter Hamilton; OBE (1974), DFC (1944); s of Dr Cecil Aubert Finley (1957), and Evelyn, *née* Daniels (d 1944); *b* 6 Dec 1919; *Educ* The King's Sch Paramatta; *m* 1947, Berenice Mitchell, da of William Victor Armstrong (d 1964); 1 s, 1 da; *Career* CA 1949-72, co dir; chm: Boral Ltd 1976, Email Ltd 1974, Custom Credit Corpn Ltd 1973-, Avery Aust Ltd 1972-, dep chm Cadbury Schweppes Aust Ltd 1971; dir: Nat Aust Bank Ltd 1970-, Nat (vice-chm 1986), Burns Philip & Co Ltd 1980, Sir Robert Menzies Meml Tst 1979-; kt 1981; *see Debrett's Handbook of Australia and New Zealand for further details*; *Style—* Sir Peter Finley, OBE, DFC; 50 Treatts Rd, Lindfield, NSW 2070, Australia

FINLINSON, Alastair John; s of Malcolm Everard Finlinson (d 1960), of Brayfield House, Olney, Bucks, and Violet Marion, *née* Leventhorpe (d 1983); *b* 25 Feb 1929; *Educ* Radley, RMA Sandhurst; *m* 19 Jan 1980, Anne Elizabeth, da of Norman Stanley Holland (d 1945), of Saxbys Cowden, Kent; *Career* dist agent Lord Falmouths Tregothnan Estates 1955-58, asst land cmmr MAFF Som 1958-59, asst area agent Cornwall and SW Devon Nat Tst 1966-71, regnl dir Severn Regn Nat Tst 1971-87; ministerial appointee Exmoor Nat Park Ctee 1989; FRICS; *Recreations* gardening, walking, music, conservation; *Style—* Alastair Finlinson, Esq

FINN, Hugh Roderick; CBE (1974), DL (Kent 1979); s of George William Finn; *b* 12 April 1911; *Educ* Haileybury; *m* 1954, Muriel Enid (Mel), da of Walter Dale; 2 s; *Career* farmer and company dir; chm: Stonegatefarmers Ltd, Kent Salads Ltd, SSP Ltd; chm Kent Agric Exec Ctee 1954-68, BBC Agric Advsy Ctee, Gen Advsy Ctee BBC 1966-75, Miny of Agric Regnl Advsy Ctee 1974-80, ARC Hops Tech Ctee 1976-86; memb Lord Chllrs Advsy Ctee (Kent) 1976-86; memb Cncl Protection Rural England 1954-85 (chm Kent Branch 1981-); govr Wye Coll London and chm Estates Panel 1954-85; FRZS, FRAgS; *Clubs* Athenaeum; *Style—* Hugh Finn, Esq, CBE, DL; Nackington Farmhouse, Canterbury, Kent CT4 7AD (☎ home: 0227 463 169, office: 0227 763 100)

FINN, John Wilson; s of Edwin Finn (d 1968), and Frances Evelyn Finn, *née* Moody (d 1975); *b* 4 Feb 1916; *Educ* Westminster; *m* 24 Aug 1940, Mildred Mary, da of George Edward Bermingham (d 1966); 1 s (Martin Anthony b 1942), 1 da (Susan Mary b 1944); *Career* joined TA 1939 and served WWII Maj RA 1939-45; qualified CA 1938; co sec De la Rue Co Ltd 1974-78 (joined 1958); FCA; *Recreations* construction of miniature antique furniture, beagling, opera; *Style—* John Finn, Esq; Pond Oast, Frittenden, Kent TN17 2BE (☎ 058 080 431); Lloyds Bank, High St, Cranbrook, Kent

FINNEY, His Hon Judge Jarlath John; s of Victor Harold Finney (d 1970), of Dorking, Surrey, and Aileen Rose, *née* Gallagher, of Dorking, Surrey; Lib MP for Hexham 1923-24, subsequently sec gen Lloyd George's cncl of action for peace and reconstruction; *b* 1 July 1930; *Educ* Wimbledon Coll; *m* 27 April 1957, Daisy Emöke, da of Dr Matyas Veszy, formerly of Budapest (d 1959); 2 s (Mark b 1960, Gavin b 1963), 2 da (Patricia b 1958, Victoria b 1965); *Career* Nat Serv 1953-55, 2 Lt 8 RTR

1953-55 (Lt 1955); called to the Bar Gray's Inn 1953, Rec of the Cn Ct 1980-86, Circuit judge 1986; *Books* Gaming, Lotteries, Fundraising and The Law (1982), Sales Promotion Law (1986, with others); *Recreations* books, wild flowers, walking in the country; *Clubs* Wig and Pen; *Style*— His Hon Judge Finney; c/o Ground Floor, 1 Essex Court, Temple, London EC4Y 9AR

FINNEY, Malcolm James; s of Alfred James Finney (d 1983) and Audrey, *née* Saynor; *b* 19 Mar 1948; *Educ* Univ Hull, Sheffield, and Bradford (M Sc, B Sc); *m* m and sep; 2 s (Matthew b 1977, Nicholas b 1980); *Career* Spear and Jackson Int 1970-72, Duncan C Fraser and Co 1972-73, J Henry Schroder Wagg and Co Ltd 1973-76, J F Chown and Co Ltd 1976-79, Grant Thornton 1979-; memb MBIM 1975, AFIMA 1972; *Books* Captive Insurance Cos: Tax Strategy 1979, Business Tax Handbook 1978 , Companies Operating Overseas and Tax Strategy 1983; *Recreations* photography, cars, cycling, reading; *Style*— Malcolm Finney, Esq; Grant Thornton House, Merton Street, Euston Square, London (☎ 01 383 5100)

FINNIGAN, John Howard; s of Alan Finnigan, and Kathleen, *née* Shackleton; *b* 5 Mar 1947; *Educ* Woodhouse Grove Sch Bradford, Gonville and Caius Coll Cambridge (MA); *m* 19 Oct 1974, Hilary Jill, da of Conrad Edward Pronger, DFC; 2 s (Barnabas Vincent b 1981, Timothy Caleb b 1983); *Career* ptnr Hepworth & Chadwick Slrs 1974-; memb Leeds City Cncl 1973-76, Law Soc 1971; *Style*— John Finnigan, Esq; 1 Dawson Lane, Tong Village, Bradford BD4 0ST; Hepworth & Chadwick Cloth Hall Court, Infirmary Street, Leeds LS1 2JB (☎ 0532 430391, fax 0532 456188, telex 557917)

FINNIS, John Mitchell; s of Maurice Meredith Steriker Finnis, of Adelaide, and Margaret McKellar, *née* Stewart; *b* 28 July 1940; *Educ* St Mark's Coll, St Peter's Coll Adelaide (LLB), Univ Coll Oxford (DPhil); *m* 20 June 1964, Marie Carmel, *née* McNally; 3 s (John-Paul b 1967, Jerome b 1977, Edmund b 1984), 3 da (Rachel b 1965, Catherine b 1971, Maria b 1974); *Career* assoc in law Univ of California Berkeley 1965-66, fell and praelector in jurisprudence University Coll Oxford 1966-, Rhodes reader in laws of Br Cwlth and US Oxford Univ 1972-, prof and head of law dept Univ of Malawi 1976-78; barr Grays Inn 1970, special advsr to Foreign Affrs Ctee of House of Commons on the role of UK Parl in Canadian Constitution 1980-82; memb Int Theological Cmmn Vatican 1986-; *Books* Natural Law and Natural Rights (1980), Fundamentals of Ethics (1983), Nuclear Deterrence, Morality and Realism; *Style*— Dr John Finnis; 12 Staverton Road, Oxford OX2 6XJ (☎ 0865 58660, fax 0865 310874); University College, Oxford OX1 4BH (☎ 0865 276602); 12 Gray's Inn Sq, London WC1R 5JP (☎ 01 405 8654)

FINNISTON, Sir Harold Montague (Monty); s of late Robert and Esther Finniston; *b* 15 August 1912; *Educ* Allan Glen's Sch Glasgow, Glasgow Univ, Strathclyde Univ, Royal Coll of Sci and Technol; *m* 1936, Miriam Singer; 1 s, 1 da; *Career* RN Scientific Serv 1940-46, seconded to Miny of Supply Chalk River Canada 1946-47; lectr Royal Coll of Sci and Technol 1933-35, metallurgist Stewarts & Lloyd's Steel Co 1935-37, chief res offr Scottish Coke Res Ctee 1937-40; chief metallurgist Harwell 1948-58; chm: Int R & D Co (formerly Nuclear Res Centre) 1968-77 (md 1959-66), Sears Hldgs Ltd 1973-76 (chief exec 1971-73), Sears Engrg Ltd 1976-79, Anderson Strathclyde 1980-83, Butterfield-Harvey plc 1981-84, Inst Technol Securities Ltd 1984, Marcus Hartley Engrg Centre Ltd 1985-, Mulholland Ltd 1987-, Nene Instruments Ltd 1987-, The Urban Tst 1987-, Abacus Simulations Ltd 1988-; dep chm: Br Steel Corpn 1967-76, Drake & Scull Hldgs 1980-83, H M Finniston Ltd 1980-, Taddale Investmts plc (formerly Branon plc) 1980-, Future Technol Systems plc 1981-85, Metal Sciences Hldgs plc 1983-85, Clyde Cable Vision Ltd 1983-87, KCA Drilling Gp plc 1983-; dir: Bodycote Int plc 1980-84, Finance for Housing Ltd 1981, Caledonian Heritable Estates Ltd 1982-, Cluff Resources plc 1976-, Br Nutrution Fndn 1982-, Combined Capital Ltd 1983-, GKN 1976-83, Sherwood Int Ltd 1984-, Info Technol Trg Accreditations Ltd 1985; pres: Metals Soc 1974-75, Inst of Metallurgists 1975-76, ASLIB 1976-78, Assoc of Br Cs of C 1980-83, Indust Mktg Res Assoc 1983-, Industl Building Bureau 1983-, Occupational Pensions Advsy Serv 1983-, British Export Assoc 1984-, Assoc of Projects Mangrs 1984-, Engrg Industs Assoc 1984-, Surrey Retirement Assoc 1985-, Soc of Environmental Engrs 1986-; chm: Govt Ctee of Inquiry into Engrg Profession 1977-79, Young Enterprise Scotland 1987-; dir: Scottish Business Sch 1978-87, Building Econ Ctee (NEDO) 1980-87, Prison Reform Tst 1981-88, Scottish Enterprise Fndn 1982; chllr Stirling Univ 1978-88, pro-chllr Surrey Univ 1977-85; govr: Carmel Coll 1973-, KQC London 1985-; chm award ctee Engrg Cncl 1984-; vice pres: Inst Mktg 1980-, Royal Soc 1971-72; City and Guilds of London Inst Insignia Award In Technol (Hon CGIA) 1987; FRS, FIM, ARCT, FRSA, FRSE, FEng; *Recreations* reading, writing, spectator sports; *Clubs* Athenaeum; *Style*— Sir Monty Finniston; 6 Manchester Sq, London W1A 1AU (☎ 01 486 3658)

FINSBERG, Sir Geoffrey; MBE (1959), JP (Inner London 1962), MP (C) Hampstead and Highgate 1983-; o s of Montefiore Finsberg, MC (d 1972), and May, *née* Grossman (d 1979); *b* 13 June 1926; *Educ* City of London Sch; *m* 1969, Pamela Benbow (d 1989), da of Roland Benbow Hill (d 1973); 1 step s; *Career* memb Hampstead Boro Cncl 1949-65, Camden Boro Cncl 1964-74, industl relations advsr Gt Universal Stores 1968-79 and 1983, dir London and SE TSB 1963-75, dep chm S E regnl b TSB 1986-; memb: cncl CBI 1968-79, POUNC 1970-77; former nat chm Young Cons, chm Greater London Cons local govt ctees, MP (C) Hampstead 1970-1983, vice chm Cons Party Orgn 1975-79 and 1984-87, opposition spokesman Greater London 1974-79; parly under sec: Environment 1979-81, DHSS 1981-83; memb Parly Assembly of the Cncl of Europe 1983- (delgn ldr 1987-); Freeman City of London; kt 1984; *Recreations* bridge; *Clubs* Royal Overseas League; *Style*— Sir Geoffrey Finsberg, MBE, JP, MP; 80 Westbere Rd, London NW2 3RU (☎ 01 435 5320); Rosewell, White Rd, Methwold, Norfolk

FINTRIE, Lord; James Alexander Norman Graham; el s of Marquess of Graham; *b* 16 August 1973; *Educ* Eton; *Style*— Lord Fintrie; Auchmar, Drymen, Glasgow

FIREMAN, Bruce Anthony; s of Michael Fireman; *b* 14 Feb 1944; *Educ* Kilburn G S, Jesus Coll Cambridge; *m* 1968, Barbara, *née* Mollett; *Career* slr 1970, merchant banker, chm Fireman Rose Ltd 1986-, dir Newspaper Publishing plc (The Independent) 1986-, dir D G Durham Gp plc 1988-; *Style*— Bruce Fireman, Esq; c/o Fireman Rose Ltd, Black Lion House, 45 Whitechapel Rd, London E1 1DU (☎ 01 377 6189); 19 Southwood Hall, London N6 (☎ 01 444 7125)

FIRMIN, David; s of Eric Henry, of 2 Bay Walk, Aldwick Bay, W Sussex, and Margaret Freda, *née* Hales; *b* 20 Sept 1937; *Educ* The Leys Sch Cambridge, Brixton Sch of Bldg; *m* 20 Sept 1979, Zara Synolda, da of Maj John Atholl Duncan MC (d 1983) and Hon (Doreen) Synolda, *née* Butler el da 27 (17) Baron Donboyne, of Sloane St, SW1; 2 s (Philip Duncan b 1981, Robert Charles b 1985), 1 da (Zoe Charlotte b 1980); *Career* sr ptnr Sidney Kaye Firmin Partnership 1968-; ARIBA 1965, FRIBA 1970; *Recreations* golf; *Clubs* Carlton, New Zealand GC Surrey; *Style*— David Firmin, Esq; 11 Westmoreland Place, London SW1V 4AA (☎ 01 834 2520); SKF Architects, Thavies Inn House, 5 Holborn Circus, London EC1 (☎ 01 583 8811)

FIRMSTON-WILLIAMS, Peter; CBE (1987, OBE 1979); s of Geoffrey Firmston-Williams (d 1964), and Muriel Firmston-Williams; *b* 30 August 1918; *Educ* Harrow; *m* 1945, Margaret, da of Wilfred Butters Beaulah (d 1967); 1 s, 1 da; *Career* Capt (mil) N Africa, Low Countries and Germany, md: Cooper and Co's Stores Ltd 1958-62, Key Markets Ltd 1962-71; Asda Stores Ltd 1971-81; dir: Assoc Daries Ltd 1973-81, BAT Stores 1981-82; dep chm Woolworth Hldgs 1982-; chm: Covent Garden Market Authy 1982-, Retail Consortium 1984-, Flowers and Plants Assoc 1985-; *Recreations* golf, water skiing, wind surfing; *Style*— Peter Firmston-Williams, Esq, CBE; Oak House, 12 Pembroke Road, Moor Park, Northwood, Middx

FIRNBERG, David; s of Leopold Bernard Firnberg (d 1984), and Karin Lubof Ernestine, *née* Kellgren; *b* 1 May 1930; *Educ* Merchant Taylors'; *m* 1957, Sylvia Elizabeth, da of William C du Cros; 1 s (Jonathan b 1969), 3 da (Nichola b 1960, Sarah b 1961, Virginia b 1965); *Career* dir Nat Computing Centre 1975-80, chm Eosys Ltd 1989- (md 1980-88); chm The Networking Centre Ltd 1985-; pres: Assoc of Project Managers 1979-84, Br Computer Soc 1983-84; FID, FBCS, FIIS; *Books* Cassel's Spelling Dictionary; Computers, Management and Information; *Recreations* writing; *Clubs* Wig and Pen; *Style*— David Firnberg, Esq; The Great House, Buckland Common, nr Tring, Herts HP23 6NX; Albas, 11360 Durban-Corbieres, France

FIRTH, (David) Colin; s of Jack Firth, of Wakefield, Yorks, and Muriel, *née* Wood; *b* 29 Jan 1930; *Educ* Rothwell GS, Sheffield Univ (BSc, Dip Ed); *m* 29 April 1954, Edith Mary, da of Harold Scanlon; 3 s (John b 1967, Ian b 1958, Timothy b 1964), 1 da (Susan b 1960); *Career* 2 Lt RCS 1952-54; teacher Stand GS Lancs 1954-58, head of E Barnet GS 1958-62, dep head Bristol GS 1962-73; head: The Gilberd Sch Essex 1973-77, Cheadle Hulme Sch 1978-; *Books* A Practical Organic Chemistry (1966), Elementary Chemical Thermodynamics (1969), Introductry Physical Science (1971); *Recreations* gardening, fell walking, reading modern novels, talking about cricket; *Style*— Colin Frith, Esq; Cheadle Hulme School, Claremont Rd, Cheadle Hulme, Cheshire SK8 6EF (☎ 061 485 8697)

FIRTH, Geoffrey Shipston; s of Harold Firth (d 1959), of Halifax, and Gladys, *née* Shipston (d 1961); *b* 27 Jan 1934; *Educ* Silcoates Sch Wakefield; *m* 16 April 1960, Patricia Anne, da of Thomas Henry Mines (d 1984), of Hove; 2 da (Pamela Anne b 1961, Angela Mary b 1963); *Career* RAPC 1952-54; md James Royston Co Ltd 1959-80 (co sec 1956-59), dir Hawkins & Tipson Ltd 1969-82, md Smith Wires Ltd 1982-; chm: Wire and Wire Rope Indust Trg Assoc, Young Enterprise Area Bd (Calderdale); memb Rotary Club Halifax Calder; under warden Worshpful Co of Tinplate Worker (alias Wire Workers) 1988/89 (memb 1965); memb IOD 1960; *Recreations* golf, walking, photography; *Clubs* City Livery; *Style*— Geoffrey S Firth, Esq; Fourways, Hammerstone Leach Lane, Elland, West Yorkshire HX5 0QW (☎ 0422 72077); Smith Wires Ltd, Charlestown Rd, Halifax, West Yorks HX3 6AB (☎ 0422 341211, telex 51188 SMITH G)

FIRTH, Rt Rev Peter James; *see*: Malmesbury, Bishop of

FIRTH, Prof Sir Raymond William; s of Wesley Hugh Bourne Firth (d 1977), and Marie Elizabeth Jane, *née* Cartmill (d 1962); *b* 25 Mar 1901; *Educ* Auckland GS NA, Auckland Univ Coll (MA), LSE (PhD); *m* 1936, Rosemary, da of Sir Gilbert Upcott, KCB (d 1967); 1 s; *Career* lectr and acting prof of anthropology Sydney Univ 1930-32, lectr in anthropology LSE 1933-35 (reader 1936-44), prof of anthropology Univ of London 1944-68 (now emeritus), visiting prof various USA Univs, life pres Assoc Social Anthropologists; Hon degrees: Oslo, Michigan, Exeter, E Anglia, Br Columbia, Chicago, Australian NU Auckland, Cracow, London; research in Tikopia Solomon Islands and Kelantan Malaysia; author of numerous pubns on anthropological subjects; hon fell LSE 1970; FBA; kt 1973; *Recreations* Romanesque painting and sculpture, early music; *Clubs* Athenaeum; *Style*— Prof Sir Raymond Firth; 33 Southwood Ave, London N6 (☎ 01 348 0768)

FISCH, Isadore Ian; s of Solomon Fisch (d 1985), of Leeds, and Rebecca, *née* Swift; *b* 28 Dec 1924; *Educ* Nether Edge GS Sheffield, Sheffield Univ (LLB); *m* 2 March 1952, Phyllis Miriam, da of Leon Elgrod (d 1983); 1 s (Nigel Ian b 1959), 3 da (Suzanne Joy b 1953, Juliet Diane b 1955, Alison Jane b 1963); *Career* slr, chm: Arncliffe Hldgs plc, Wakefield Social Services Appeal Tribunal, Bd of Inquiry Dept of Tport; Pres NSPCC Leeds Childrens Centre Appeal; former pres: Leeds Lodge B'nai B'rith, Street Lane Gardens Synagogue; memb ctee Home Farm Trust; former chm: Children's Aid Soc (Leeds), Leeds Friends of Bar-Ilan Univ; fndr The Isadore Fisch Charitable Fndn; Lord of the Manor of Sutton Holland; memb Law Soc and Leeds Law Soc; *Recreations* swimming, skiing, tennis, reading ; *Clubs* RAC; Fairfield, 620 Harrogate Road, Leeds LS17 8EN (☎ 0532 683775); 114 Monarch Court, Lyttelton Road, London NW2; office, Follifoot Hall, Follifoot Ridge, Pannaz Road, Harrogate, N Yorkshire HG3 1RU (☎ 0423 879988, fax 0423 873495); car telephone, 0860 620989

FISCHEL, John Roy; s of late Roy Fischel, MC; *b* 2 Sept 1924; *Educ* Cheltenham and RN; *m* 1952, Anita, da of late Capt Maximilian Despard, DSC, RN; 2 s, 3 da; *Career* commodity merchant, chm: L M Fischel & Co Ltd 1966- (dir 1960-), non-exec dir 1984-; Baltic Mercantile & Shipping Exchange 1975-80; underwriting memb Lloyd's; *Recreations* shooting, sailing (yacht 'Matawa'); *Clubs* Castaways, RCC, RNSA, MCC, KCCC; *Style*— John Fischel, Esq; The Mount, Shoreham, nr Sevenoaks, Kent (☎ 095 92 2071)

FISCHER, Christopher Robert; s of Frank Ignacu Fischer (d 1979), of Alicante, Spain, and Krystna, *née* Sawostianik; *b* 12 August 1953; *Educ* Salesian Coll, Lanchester Poly (BA, HND); *Career* md Jenex SA (Belgium) 1976-85, dir Michael Ross Knitwear Ltd 1978-82; chm/md: Christopher Fischer Ltd 1982-, Christopher Fischer (Knitwear) Ltd 1981-, H K Knitwear (Hawich) Ltd 1985-; *Style*— Christopher Fischer, Esq; Redcliffe Gardens, London SW10; East 86th Street, New York City, NY 10028; Christopher Fischer Ltd, Units 103-105, Brune Street Workshops, 16 Brune Street, Spitalfields, London E1 7NJ (☎ 01 247 3777, fax 01 247 1830, telex 8813271)

FISH, Prof Francis (Frank); OBE (1989); s of William Fish (d 1980), of Houghton-le-Spring, Tyne & Wear, and Phyllis Fish, *née* Griffiths (d 1983); *b* 20 April 1924; *Educ* Houghton-Le-Spring GS, Sunderland Tech Coll (BPharm, ext London Univ), Univ of Glasgow (PhD); *m* 10 Aug 1949, Hilda Mary, da of James Percy Brown (d 1980), of Houghton-le-Spring; 2 s (David James Francis, Andrew William); *Career* Univ of

Strathclyde (formerly The Royal Coll of Sci and Tech Glasgow): asst lectr and lectr 1946-62, sr lectr 1962-69, reader in Pharmacognosy and Forensic Sci 1969-76, prof and head Forensic Sci Unit 1976-78, dean Sch of Pharmaceutical Sci 1977-78 (vice-dean 1974-77); Univ of London: dean sch of pharmacy 1978-88, prof pharmacy 1988, emeritus prof 1989-; memb: The Br Pharmacopoeia Commn, Ctee on Review of Medicines, UGC Medical Sub Ctee; chm: UGC Panel on Studies Allied to Medicine, Post Qualification Educ Bd for Health Serv Pharmacists in Scotland; former memb: Ctee on Safety of Meds, Nuffield Fndn Ctee of Inquiry into Pharmacy; former vice chm DHSS Standing Pharmaceutical Advsy Ctee, former vice-pres Cncl of Forensic Sci Soc; FRPharmS 1946; *Books* res papers in pharmaceutical and forensic journals; *Recreations* gardening, golf, wine-making; *Clubs* Grieff Golf; *Style—* Prof Frank Fish, OBE; Trollheim, Connaught Terrace, Crieff, Perthshire

FISH, George Marshall; s of George Frederick Fish (d 1940), of Hamilton House, and Dorothy, *née* Creswell (d 1984); *b* 26 June 1928; *Educ* Sedbergh Sch Yorks; *m* 9 Feb 1952, Josephine Lilian, da of Joseph Sydney Plant Lowater; 3 s (George, Thomas, Charles); *Career* Capt RA 1946-48, Capt S Notts Hussars, 350 Heavy Dept RA (TA) 1948-52; chartered builder, currently chm Notts Magistrates Cts Ctee (chm bldgs and boundaries sub-ctee); tstee Nottingham Assoc of Builders, tres Nottingham Bldg Employers Confedn; FCIOB, FFB; *Recreations* walking, golf, gardening; *Style—* George Fish, Esq; The Manor House, Old Main Rd, Bulcote, Notts NG14 5GU (☎ 0602 313159); Great Freeman St, Nottingham

FISH, William Francis (Frank); s of William Francis Fish, of Lancs, and Marie, *née* Williams (d 1942); *b* 26 Feb 1940; *Educ* St Josephs Coll Darjeeling, St Anne's Prep Manchester, Xaverian Coll, Manchester Univ (LLB); *m* 6 Jan 1967, Mary Rosetta Hughes, da of Dr Peter Esmond Gosgrove, of NI; 1 s (Kevin b 1969), 3 da (Paula b 1968, Anne-Marie b 1971, Helen b 1980); *Career* slr; lectr (pt/t) in law, Univ of Manchester; memb area ctee of No.10 Legal Aid Area; an ed of "Butterworths Family Law Service"; sometime dep dist registrar of the High Ct and Dep County Ct Registrar 1974-76; sometime asst dep coroner of the High Peak Derbys 1978; awarded at Univ: Dauntesy Jnr Legal Scholarship 1960, Dauntsey Snr Legal Scholarship (1962); awarded Stephen Hellis Gold Medal and other Local Law Soc Awards; *Recreations* walking, swimming, angling, gardening; *Style—* Frank Fish, Esq; Mount Delphi, 11 Melia Close, Rawtenstall, Rossendale, Lancashire (☎ 0706 220 487); 61 Mosley Street, Manchester M2 3HZ (☎ 051 236 0321)

FISHBOURNE, Joseph Russell; CBE (1957), DL (Essex 1962); s of Lt-Col C E Fishbourne (late 5 Fusiliers, ka 1916), of Ashfield Hall, Queens County, Eire; *b* 18 Nov 1909; *Educ* Harrow, RMC Sandhurst, Army Staff Coll; *m* 1937, Jean Caroline, da of Col L G Harrison, of Morant Bay, Jamaica (d 1950); 1 s, 1 da; *Career* Brig commissioned 5 Fusiliers 1929, transferred to 3 Carabiniers 1937, CO 1950-53, Col of Regt 1957-66, regional sec Country Landowners Assoc 1963-78; *Recreations* shooting, fishing and countryside; *Clubs* Cavalry, Essex; *Style—* Brig Joseph Fishbourne, CBE, DL; Lime House, Earls Colne, nr Colchester, Essex (☎ Earls Colne 2493)

FISHBURN, J Dudley; s of late Eskdale Fishburn and Mrs Peter Murray-Lee; *b* 8 June 1946; *Educ* Eton, Harvard; *m* 1981, Victoria, da of Sir Jack Boles and step da of Lady Anne Boles (da of 12 Earl Waldegrave); 2 da (Alice b 1982, Honor b 1984); *Career* exec ed The Economist; (C) candidate IOW 1979; pres Harvard Club of London; tstee Open Univ Foundation; tres Br American Arts Assoc; dir Aidcom Int plc; *Clubs* Harvard (NY), Brooks's; *Style—* Dudley Fishburn Esq; 16 West Halkin St, London SW1 (☎ 01 235 1184); The Old Rectory, Englefield, Berkshire (☎ 0734 302497)

FISHER, (Jervis) Andrew; s of John George Fisher, of Birmingham, and Joyce, *née* Horton; *b* 23 Oct 1955; *Educ* Malvern, London Univ (LLB); *m* 3 April 1982, Catherine Maura, da of Peter Phillimore Swatman, of Gwynedd; 1 s (Alexander b 1984), 1 da (Lara b 1986); *Career* barr; called to the Bar Gray's Inn 1980, MO Circuit; *Style—* Andrew Fisher, Esq; The Ark, Noah's Green, Feckenham, Worcs; Coleridge Chambers, 177 Corporation St, Birmingham B4 6RG (☎ 021 233 3303, fax 01 236 6966)

FISHER, Hon Mrs; (Audrey Joan); *née* Vernon; 3 da of 5 Baron Lyveden (d 1973); *b* 1922; *m* 1, 14 Nov 1940 (m dis), Russell Parker; 3 s, 1 da; m 2, 17 Nov 1983, Maurice Fisher; *Style—* The Hon Mrs Parker

FISHER, Hon Benjamin Vavasseur; s (by 1 m) of 3 Baron Fisher; *b* 21 Sept 1958; *m* 31 Aug 1985, Pamela M, only da of A Cooper, of Tolcarne, Rough Close, Staffs; 1 s (Peter Vavasseur b 13 Oct 1986), 1 da (Rose Kathleen b 31 Oct 1988); *Style—* Hon Benjamin Fisher

FISHER, Charles Murray; s of Hon Alderman K J Fisher of Cheltenham; *b* 24 Dec 1949; *Educ* Cheltenham, Oxford Univ; *m* Denise; 2 da (Louise, Jasmine); *Career* chief exec Sharpe and Fisher plc, chm Bayshill Estates Ltd; *Recreations* travel, sport; *Clubs* MCC, Annabel's; *Style—* Charles Fisher, Esq; Rossetti Gd Mansions, Flood St, SW3 (☎ 01 352 7548); Hampnett Lodge, Hampnett, Glos (☎ Cotswold 60596)

FISHER, Dudley Henry; s of Arthur Fisher (d 1926), and Mary Eliza, *née* Greenacre (d 1965); *b* 22 August 1922; *Educ* City of Norwich Sch; *m* 1, 1946, Barbara Lilian Sexton (d 1984); 1 s (Christopher), 2 da (Pamela, Angela); m 2, 1985, Jean Mary Livingstone, da of Dr R B Miller (d 1954), of Stafford House, Cowbridge, S Glam; *Career* Flt Lt RAF 1941-46; chm Wales Region Br Gas Corpn 1974-87 (dir of finance 1968-70, dep chm 1970-74); memb: Audit Commn for Local Authorities in Eng & Wales 1983-88, cncl Univ of Wales Coll of Cardiff 1988-; chm: CBI Cncl for Wales 1987- (memb 1984-), admin ctee WEC 1986; hon tres Br Nat Ctee World Energy Conference 1987- (memb 1974), nat tstee Help the Aged Charity; High Sheriff of South Glamorgan 1988-89; *Recreations* golf, music, reading; *Clubs* Cardiff & Co; *Style—* Dudley Fisher, Esq; Norwood Edge, 8 Cyncoed Ave, Cardiff CF2 6SU (☎ 0222 757958)

FISHER, Francis St George; s of George Forster Fisher (d 1947), of Higham, Bassenthwaite Lake, Cockermouth, Cumberland, and Florence Maude,*née* Deuchar (d 1962); *b* 30 Mar 1911; *Educ* Harrow, Trinity Hall Cambridge (MA); *m* 1, Sept 1934, Patricia (d 1955), da of Maj Edward Lycett Lyon (ka 1915); 1 s (Keith Plunket b 1935), 2 da (Lucy Carolyn b 1938, Lee b 1941); m 2, Sept 1964, Elizabeth Campbell Scott (d 1982), *née* Dibben, wid of Wilson Young; *Career* Corpl RE TA 1937, Maj Grenadier Gds 1940-45; underwriting memb Lloyds 1945-64, dir Thomas Armstrong (Holdings) Ltd(formerly Thomas Armstrong Ltd) 1950-; landowner Higham Estate 1947-; RBKC: cncllr and ald 1949-74, mayor 1956-58 and 1966-67; chm Setmurthy Parish Cncl 1975-82, memb Embleton Dist Cncl 1982; *Recreations* country sports; *Style—* Francis Fisher, Esq; Cragg, Bassenthwaite Lake, Cockermouth, Cumbria (☎ 059 681 277)

FISHER, Hon Geoffrey Robert Chevallier; 5 s of Baron Fisher of Lambeth, GCVO, PC (Life Peer, d 1972), formerly 99 Archbishop of Canterbury, and Rosamond Chevallier, *née* Forman (d 1986); *b* 4 April 1926; *Educ* Repton, Emmanuel Coll Cambridge (BA, MB, BChir); *m* 20 May 1961, Jill Audrey, eldest da of James Henry Cooper, of New Malden, Surrey; 2 s, 1 da; *Career* D (Obst) RCOG 1952, Surg Lt RN (Emergency Res); *Style—* The Hon Geoffrey Fisher; 3 Wendover Drive, New Malden, Surrey

FISHER, Geoffrey Wilson O'Neill; OBE (Mil 1943), DFC (1941 and Bar 1943); s of Rev Walter Francis O'Neill Fisher (d 1955), and Elizabeth Gladys Fisher, *née* Wilson (d 1959); *b* 10 July 1921; *Educ* HMS Worcester, RAF Staff Coll, Joint Servs Staff Coll; *m* 1, 1945, Kathleen Helliwell, *née* Forester Parker (d 1960); m 2, 12 July 1961, Olive Mary, da of Arthur Dunwell (d 1960), of Otley, Yorks; 3 s (Simon b 1962, Michael b 1964, Paul b 1966; *Career* Wing Cdr RAF 1939-61 active serv in 149 and 101 Sqdns Bomber Cmd as Pilot and Flt Cdr; cmd: 207 Sqdn B29 (Washington) 1952-53, 139 Jamaica Sqdn (Canberra) 1958-59, ret 1961, co dir 1970-73; farmer; *Recreations* history, biography, sailing; *Clubs* Cruising Assoc; *Style—* Geoffrey Fisher, OBE, DFC; Cotswold, Jack Straw's Lane, Headington, Oxford OX3 0DW (☎ 0865 62033)

FISHER, Sir George Read; CMG (1961); s of George Alexander and Ellen Harriett Fisher; *b* 23 Mar 1903; *Educ* Prince Alfred Coll, Adelaide Univ (BE); *m* 1, 1927, Eileen Elaine (d 1966), da of A J; 1 s, 3 da; m 2, 1973, Marie C Gilbey; *Career* mining engineer, chm Mount Isa Mines Ltd Qld 1953-70, former pres MIM Hldgs Ltd, former chllr James Cook Univ Qld; kt 1967; *Recreations* shooting, bowls; *Clubs* Queensland, Brisbane; *Style—* Sir George Fisher, CMG; c/o MIM Holdings, GPO Box 2236, Brisbane, Qld 4001, Australia

FISHER, Gerald (Gerry); s of Oliver Charles Fisher (d 1980), and Margaret, *née* Eyles (d 1978); *b* 23 June 1926; *Educ* Bishopshalt Sch Hillingdon Middx, Watford Tech Sch; *m* 20 Jan 1951, Jean Aline, da of late John Hawkins; 1 s (Cary Adam); *Career* RN 1943-46; draughtsman De havilland Aircraft Co 1943, clapper leader loader Alliance Films 1946, asst cameraman Br Lion 1949, camera operator on 18 films mostly with Jack Hildyard 1957-67, first film as cinematographer Accident 1967, cinematographer on 50 films including 8 with Joseph Losey, notably The Go-Between and Don Giovanni; memb: Br Soc Cinematographers 1967, BAFTA 1975; *Style—* Gerry Fisher, Esq; Pebble Cottage, River Bank, Hurstfield Rd, W Molesey, Surrey KT8 9QX (☎ 01 979 5498)

FISHER, Hon Mrs (Gwen Elfrida Penelope); *née* Abbott; da of 4 Baron Tenterden (d 1939, when the Barony became extinct), and Elfrida Charlotte, *née* Turner (d 1970); *b* 22 July 1908; *m* 1941, William Fisher, s of Alexander Fischer, of Budapest, Hungary; 2 s; *Style—* Hon Mrs Fisher

FISHER, Hon Sir Henry Arthur Pears; el s of Most Rev and Rt Hon Baron Fisher of Lambeth, GCVO, PC (d 1972), formerly 99 Archbishop of Canterbury and Lady (Rosamond) Fisher (d 1986), da of Rev Arthur Forman; br Hon Geoffrey Fisher *qv*, and Hon Humphrey Fisher *qv*; *b* 20 Jan 1918; *Educ* Marlborough, Christ Church Oxford; *m* 18 Dec 1948, Felicity, da of late Eric Sutton, of Cheyne Place, Chelsea; 1 s (Thomas Henry Sutton b 1958), 3 da (Emma b 1949, Lucy b 1951, Francesca b 1955); *Career* served WWII Leics Regt & at Staff Coll Quetta, also as Staff Offr (GSO 14th Army 1945, rank of Hon Lt-Col 1946); chm Appeal Ctee of Panel on Take-overs & Mergers 1981-; pres Wolfson Coll Oxford 1975-, fell (emeritus 1976-) All Souls Oxford 1946-73 (sub-warden 1965-67), memb cncl Marlborough Coll 1965-82, chm Governing Body Imperial Coll, tstee Pilgrim Tst (chm 1979-83 and 1989-); barr 1947, QC 1960, rec Canterbury 1962-68, High Ct Judge (Queen's Bench) 1968-70, chm Gen Cncl Bar 1966-68 (v-chm 1965-66, memb 1959-63 & 1964-68); v-pres Senate of Inns of Court 1966-68 & of Bar Assoc for Commerce Finance & Industry 1973-; chm various ctees of inquiry (most recently (1979-80) into self-regulation at Lloyd's); chm Jt Lib/Soc Democrat Cmmn on Constitutional Reform; former memb Cncl on Tbnls and Law Reform Ctee; memb BBC Programmes Complaints Cmmn 1972- -79; kt 1968; *Style--* Hon Sir Henry Fisher; c/o Wolfson College, Oxford (☎ 0865 56711)

FISHER, Hon Humphrey Richmond; 4 s of Baron Fisher of Lambeth GCVO, PC (*d* 1972, Life Peer); br Hon Sir Henry and Hon Geoffrey Fisher *qv*; *b* 21 August 1923; *Educ* Repton; *m* 22 July 1959, Diana Beresford (writer for the Australian magazine *Woman's Day*), o da of C Beresford Davis; *Career* Lt RA, film technician and producer 1946-54, exec producer BBC TV 1954-64, rep Australia and NZ 1964-67 and head of science and features BBC TV 1967-69, dir of TV features Australian Broadcasting Cmmn 1969-; *Style—* Hon Humphrey Fisher; 32 South St, Edgecliff, NSW 2027, Australia

FISHER, Lady Jane Angela; da of George Cecil Paulet (d 1961), and sis of 18 Marquess of Winchester, *qv*; *b* 15 Nov 1939; *m* 1972, Christopher John Fisher; *Career* raised to rank of Marquess's da 1970; *Style—* Lady Jane Fisher

FISHER, Col Jocelyn; CBE (1967); yr da of late William Thomas Fisher; *b* 10 April 1913; *Educ* Barrow-in-Furness GS, City of Leeds Training Coll; *Career* Col WRAC; *Clubs* Naval and Mil; *Style—* Col Jocelyn Fisher CBE; 21 Victoria Rd, Topsham, Exeter (☎ Topsham 3061)

FISHER, John Adrian; s of Henry William Fisher (d 1986), and Bessie, *née* Clymer; *b* 8 July 1943; *Educ* Ross-on-Wye GS (Herefs), Aston Univ (BSc); *m* 28 Jan 1966, Julie Anne, da of Cyril Joseph Smith (d 1971); 2 da (Karen b 1966, Claire b 1972); *Career* md: Chance Pilkington Group plc 1987, Change Pilkington Ltd 1984-87 (marketing dir 1980-), Chance Pilkington 1987- (chm and dir various subsidiaries 1980-87); former pres Colnyn Bay Lions; *Recreations* wine, food; *Style—* John Fisher, Esq; Carreg-y-Bryn, Llanfair Road, Abergele, Clwyd (☎ 0745 824565); Change Pilkington Ltd, Glascoed Road, St Aspah Clwyd (☎ 0745 583301, fax 0745 584913)

FISHER, John Mortimer; CMG (1962); s of Capt Mortimer Fisher (ka 1914), and Margaret Sarah, *née* Bailey (d 1982); *b* 20 May 1915; *Educ* Wellington, Trinity Coll Cambridge (BA); *m* 1949, Helen Bridget Emily, da of Capt Maurice Copland Du Quesne Caillard (d 1957); 2 s (Mark Ashley b 1949, Timothy James b 1952); *Career* former memb HM Dipl Serv (ret 1970); *Recreations* working with my hands indoors and out; *Style—* John Fisher, Esq, CMG; The North Garden, Treyford, Nr Midhurst, W Sussex GU29 0LD (☎ 073085 448)

FISHER, 3 Baron (UK 1909); John Vavasseur Fisher; DSC (1944), JP (Norfolk 1970); s of 2 Baron (d 1955, himself s of Adm of the Fleet 1 Baron (Sir John) Fisher, GCB, OM, GCVO); *b* 24 July 1921; *Educ* Stowe, Trinity Coll Cambridge; *m* 1, 25 July

1949 (m dis 1969), Elizabeth Ann Penelope, yr da of late Maj Herbert P Holt, MC; 2 s (Hon Patrick *qv*, Hon Benjamin b 1958), 2 da (Hon Frances b 1951, Hon Bridget b 1956); m 2, 1970, Hon Rosamund Anne, da of 12 Baron Clifford of Chudleigh and formerly w of Geoffrey Forrester Fairbairn (*see* Fisher, Baroness); *Heir* s; *Career* sometime Lt RNVR WWII; dir Kilverstone Latin American Zoo 1973, memb Eastern Gas Bd 1961-70, memb E Anglian Economic Planning Cncl 1972; DL Norfolk 1968-82; *Style*— The Rt Hon the Lord Fisher, DSC, JP; Kilverstone Hall, Thetford, Norfolk (☎ 0842 2222)

FISHER, Jonathan Simon; s of Aubrey Fisher; *b* 24 Feb 1958; *Educ* St Dunstan's Coll, N London Poly (BA), St Catharine's Coll Cambridge (LLB); *m* 21 Dec 1980, Paula Yvonne, da of Rev Louis Goldberg (d 1988); 1 s (Benjamin b 1984), 1 da (Hannah b 1986); *Career* barr: Gray's Inn 1980, Inner Temple 1985; pt/t visiting lectr City Univ, UK case corr and regular contrib Jl of Int Banking Law; memb: Justice, Selden Soc, The Maccabaens; *Style*— Jonathan Fisher, Esq; 5 King's Bench Walk, Temple, London EC4 (☎ 01 353 4713, fax 01 353 5459)

FISHER, Lady Karen Jean; *née* Carnegie; da of 13 Earl of Northesk; *b* 22 Dec 1951; *Educ* Queen's Coll London; *m* 1977, Hon Patrick Vavasseur Fisher, *qv*; 2 s (John b 1979, Benjamin b 1986), 3 da (Juliet b 1978, Penelope b 1982, Suzannah b 1984); *Career* dir Macrae Farms Ltd 1981-; *Style*— Lady Karen Fisher; Highwayman's Vineyard, Heath Barn Farm, Risby, Bury St Edmunds, Suffolk

FISHER, Kenneth John; s of Stanley Joseph Fisher (d 1983), of High Beckside, Dalton-in- Furness, Cumbria, and Gertrude Isabel, *née* Ridding (d 1980); *b* 26 June 1927; *Educ* Uppingham, St John's Coll Cambridge (MA, LLM); *m* 8 May 1954, Mary Florence, da of William Isaac Towers, JP (d 1971), of The Croft, Abbey Road, Barrow-in-Furness, Cumbria; 1 s ((Stephen) John b 6 Oct 1957), 1 da (Anne Rosemary (Mrs Biggar) b 24 April 1956); *Career* Sub Lt RNVR 1945-48; slr 1953; sr ptnr W C Kendall & Fisher of Barrow-in-Furness, Dalton-in-Furness, Ulverston, Grange-over-Sands and Millom; chm: Agric Land Tbnl (Northern Area), Supplementary Benefit Appeal Tbnl; memb Cumbria Family Practitioners Ctee; chm Med Servs Ctee and Opthalmic Services Ctee for Cumbria, memb area ctee The Law Soc; former pres: N Lonsdale Law Assoc, N Lonsdale Lowick and Cartmel Agric Soc, Barrow-in-Furness Branch Royal Soc of St George; chm Govrs of Chetwynde Sch, life memb Furness RFC and Lancs RFC, chm Dalton and Dist Recreational Charity Tst; *Recreations* rugby, cricket, skiing, gardening; *Clubs* Hawks, Cambridge LX, Uppingham Rovers; *Style*— Kenneth J Fisher, Esq; Glenside House, Springfield Road, Ulverston, Cumbria LA12 OEJ (☎ 0229 53437); 68 Market Street, Dalton-in-Furness, Cumbria LA15 8AD (☎ 0229 62126, fax 0229 62083)

FISHER, Margery Lilian Edith; da of Sir Henry Samuel Edwin Turner (d 1978), and Edith Emily Rose (d 1948); *b* 21 Mar 1913; *Educ* Amberley Ho Sch New Zealand, Somerville Coll Oxford (MA, BLitt); *m* 1936, James Maxwell McConnell Fisher (d 1970) s of Kenneth Fisher (d 1945), 3 s (Edmund, Crispin, Adam), 3 da (Selina, Anstice, Clemency); *Career* freelance writer; *Books* Intent upon Reading (1961), Matters of Fact, Who's Who in Children's Books (1975), The Bright Face of Danger (1986), sole writer ed and publisher Growing Point, bi-monthly journal of reviews of books for children and young people; *Recreations* music, gardening; *Style*— Mrs Margery Fisher; Ashton Manor, Northampton NN7 2JL (☎ Roade 862277)

FISHER, Mark; MP (Lab) Stoke-on-Trent Central 1983-; s of Sir Nigel Thomas Loveridge Fisher, MC, *qv*, by his 1 w, Lady Gloria Vaughan, da of 7 Earl of Lisburne; *b* 29 Oct 1944; *Educ* Eton, Trinity Coll Cambridge; *m* 1971, Ghilly (Mrs Ingrid Hunt), da of late James Hoyle Geach; 2 s, 2 da; *Career* former princ Tattenhall Educn Centre; former documentary writer and film producer; contested (Lab) Leek 1979; memb Staffs CC 1981-85, Treasy and Civil Service Select Ctee 1983-86; opposition whip 1985-86, shadow min for Arts and Media 1987-; *Style*— Mark Fisher, Esq, MP; House of Commons, London SW1A 0AA

FISHER, Max Henry (Fredy); s of Dr Friedrich Fischer (d 1971), of Locarno, and Sophia Baks (d 1965); *b* 30 May 1922; *Educ* Fichte Gymnasium Berlin, Rendcomb Coll, Lincoln Coll Oxford (MA); *m* 1952, Rosemary Margaret, da of Dr Leslie Algernon Ivan Maxwell (d 1964), of Melbourne; 2 s (Stephen, Andrew), 1 da (Caroline); *Career* ed Financial times 1973-80; dir: S G Warburg & Co Ltd 1981-, Commercial Union Assur Co plc 1981-; govr LSE 1980-; *Recreations* music; *Clubs* Reform; *Style*— Fredy Fisher; 16 Somerset Sq, Addison Rd, W14 8EE; 1 Finsbury Ave, EC2M 2PR

FISHER, Michael Laurens Jeremy; s of Edwin Fisher, of Barleys, Offham, Lewes (d 1947), and Theodora Cecilia (d 1976); *b* 13 Feb 1929; *Educ* Eton, Christ Church Oxford (MA); *m* 1958, Susan, da of Capt Richard Lovatt, OBE, RN (d 1941); 2 s (Nicholas, James); *Career* ptnr: Colegrave & Co 1961-75, Grenfell & Colegrave 1975-86 (conslt 1986-87); memb: Stock Exchange 1960- (cncl memb 1976-86), C Cncls Membership and Quotations Ctees 1987-89; *Style*— Michael Fisher, Esq; 21 Flood St, London SW3

FISHER, Sir Nigel Thomas Loveridge; MC (1945); s of Cdr Sir Thomas Fisher, KBE, RN, by his w Aimée Constance (who m 1926, subsequent to Sir Thomas's death (1925), and as his 1 w, Sir Geoffrey Shakespeare, 1 Bt, PC); through his mother Sir Nigel is half-bro of Sir William Shakespeare, 2 Bt, *qv*; Sir Nigel is also 3 cous twice removed of late Lord Fisher of Lambeth; *b* 14 July 1913; *Educ* Eton, Trinity Coll Cambridge (MA); *m* 1, 1935 (m dis 1952), Lady Gloria Vaughan, da of 7 Earl of Lisburne; 1 s (Mark Nigel Thomas Vaughan, MP, *qv*), 1 da (Amanda Gloria Morvyth Vaughan b 1939); m 2, 1956, as her 2 husb, Patricia, only da of Lt-Col Sir Walter Smiles, CIE, DSO, DL, MP; *Career* volunteered Welsh Gds 1939, Capt 1940, Maj 1944, served Hook of Holland and Boulogne 1940 (despatches), NW Europe 1944-45, wounded; Parly Cand (C) Chislehurst 1945; MP (Cons): Hitchin 1950-55, Surbiton 1955-74, Kingston-upon-Thames, Surbiton 1974-83; PPS to min Food 1951-54, to home sec 1954-57, Parly under-sec Colonies 1962-63, Cwlth Rels and Colonies 1963-64, oppn spokesman Cwlth Affrs 1964-66; vice-pres Bldgs Socs Assoc, dep chm Cwlth Parly Assoc 1979-83; kt 1974; *Books* Ian Macleod (1973), The Tory Leaders (1977), Harold Macmillan (1982); *Clubs* MCC, Boodle's; *Style*— Sir Nigel Fisher, MC; 45 Exeter Ho, Putney Heath, London SW15 (☎ 788 6103)

FISHER, Hon Patrick Vavasseur; s (by 1 m) and h of 3 Baron Fisher; *b* 14 June 1953; *m* 1977, Lady Karen Jean Carnegie, *qv*, da of 13 Earl of Northesk; 2 s (John, Benjamin), 3 da (Juliet, Penelope, Suzannah); *Style*— Hon Patrick Fisher; Highwayman's Vineyard, Heath Barn Farm, Risby, Bury St Edmunds, Suffolk

FISHER, Hon Richard Temple (Tim); 6 and yst s of Most Rev and Rt Hon Baron Fisher of Lambeth, GCVO, PC (Life Peer) (d 1972), and Rosamond Chevallier, *née* Forman (d 1986); *b* 26 Jan 1930; *Educ* St Edward's Sch Oxford, King's Coll Cambridge (MA); *m* 17 May 1969, Clare Margaret, da of J Lewen Le Fanu; 1 s (Paul b 1970), 1 da (Rosamond b 1973); *Career* Hon Maj TA Gen List late 16/5 Queen's Royal Lancers; asst master and housemaster Repton 1953-69, headmaster Bilton Grange Prep Sch 1969-; dir Bilton Grange Shop Ltd; dir (govr) Leicester HS for Girls; dir (memb of cncl) Inc Assoc of Prep Schs (vice chm 1986, chm 1987); *Recreations* skiing, sailing, music, drama, travel; *Style*— The Hon Richard Fisher; Bilton Grange, Dunchurch, Rugby (☎ 0788 810958; business 0788 810217)

FISHER, (Francis George) Robson; s of John Henry Fisher (d 1941), and Hannah Clayton Fisher (d 1969); *b* 9 April 1921; *Educ* Liverpool Coll, Oxford Univ; *m* 1965, Sheila Vernon, o da of late David Dunsire; 1 s; *Career* schoolmaster; housemaster and head of english Kingswood Sch Bath 1950-59, headmaster Bryanston Sch Blandford 1959-74, chief master of King Edward's Sch Birmingham and headmaster of King Edward VI Schs in Birmingham 1974-82; dep sec Headmasters' Conference 1982-86; *Recreations* music, sailing, reading, gardening; *Style*— Robson Fisher, Esq; Craig Cottage, Lower St, Dittisham, S Devon TQ6 0HY

FISHER, Capt Roger Roland Sutton; CBE (1973), DSC (1944); s of Surgn-Capt Arthur Roland Fisher, RN (d 1973); *b* 3 August 1919; *Educ* Clifton; *m* 1949, June Audrey, da of Neville John Acland Foster OBE, MC (d 1978); 1 s, 1 da; *Career* served RN, cadetship 1937, cmdg HM Naval Base Bahrain 1957-59, dep sec to Chiefs of Staff 1964-66, Ch Naval Judge Advocate 1967-70, cmdg HMS Pembroke 1971-73, ret 1973; barr Gray's Inn 1950, dep circuit judge SE Circuit 1973-83, legal chm Indstl Tbnls 1976-85; marine artist, FRSA 1978, memb Wapping Gp of Artists 1982-, RSMA 1983; *Recreations* painting, sailing; *Clubs* Army and Navy; *Style*— Capt Roger Fisher, CBE, DSC, RN; High Ridge, Snape, Saxmundham, Suffolk IP17 1SU (☎ 072 888 333)

FISHER, Dr Ronald Albert; JP; s of Albert Edward (d 1963), and Hannah Jackson, *née* Byrom (d 1986); *b* 3 June 1917; *Educ* Heversham Sch, Cumbria, Downing Coll Cambridge (MA), Middx Hosp London; *m* 23 Feb 1952, Gwyneth Ena, da of Harold Arthur Mackinnon (d 1983); 2 da (Deborah Anne b 22 March 1956, Teresa b 2 Dec 1963); *Career* Surgn Lt RNVR 1943-46, convoy duties 1943-45 (Western Approaches, Russia, Gibraltar), landing in Java and MO Port Souabaya 1945-46; Bournemouth and E Dorset Gp of Hosps: conslt anaesthetist and admin 1953-73, memb hosp mgmnt ctee 1960-71, chm med exec ctee 1965-71 (memb med advsy ctee to Wessex Regnl Health Bd), dir postgrad educn 1963-67; founded and became conslt physician to the Macmillan Unit at Christchurch Hosp Dorset (pioneering hospice care in the NHS) 1974-82, started first home - care serv (Mcmillan Serv) in the NHS 1975, started first day-care unit in the NHS 1977; chm select ctee of experts on 'problems relating to death' Cncl of Europe Strasbourg 1977-80, opened new hospice Riverside Side Hosp Columbus Ohio and gave first Libby Bradford Meml lecture 1989, hon conslt in continuing cancer care to Cancer Relief (tstee); chm bd of dirs Palace Ct Theatre Bournemouth; formerly: chm Bournemouth Little Theatre Club, dir LM Theatres Ltd; President's Medal Cancer Relief; MRCS, LRCP, FFARCS; memb: BMA, Nat Soc for Cancer Relief; *Recreations* philosophy, theatre, literature, family; *Style*— Dr Ronald Fisher, JP; "Waders", 6 Lagoon Rd, Lilliput, Poole, Dorset BH14 8JT (☎ 0202 708867)

FISHER, Baroness; Hon Rosamund Anne; *née* Clifford; da of 12 Baron Clifford of Chudleigh (d 1964); *b* 22 May 1924; *Educ* St Mary's Convent Ascot; *m* 1, 21 July 1945 (m dis 1965), Geoffrey Forrester Fairbairn (decd); 2 s (James b 1950, Charles b 1956), 1 da (Katrina b 1947); m 2, 1970, 3 Baron Fisher, DSC, *qv*; *Career* zoo dir and author; *Style*— The Rt Hon Lady Fisher; Kilverstone Hall, Thetford, Norfolk; Marklye, Rushlake Green, Heathfield, Sussex

FISHER OF CAMDEN, Baroness; Millie; da of Isaac Gluckstein; *m* 1930, Baron Fisher of Camden (Life Peer, d 1979); 1 da; *Style*— The Rt Hon Lady Fisher of Camden; 48 Viceroy Ct, Prince Albert Rd, NW8

FISHER OF REDNAL, Baroness (Life Peeress UK 1974); Doris Mary Gertrude Fisher; JP (Birmingham 1961); da of late Frederick James Satchwell, BEM; *b* 13 Sept 1919; *Educ* Tinker's Farm Girls' Sch, Fircroft Coll, Bournville Day Continuation Coll; *m* 1939, Joseph Fisher (d 1978); 2 da; *Career* sits as Lab peer in House of Lords; joined Lab Pty 1945, memb Birmingham City Cncl 1952-74, MP (Lab) Birmingham (Ladywood) 1970-74, MEP 1975-79, hon alderman Birmingham 1974, memb Warrington New Town Dvpt Corpn 1974-, memb Gen Medical Cncl 1974-79, vice-pres Assoc of Municipal Authorities, Assoc of District Cncls, Guardian Birmingham Assay Off 1982-; pres Birmingham Royal Institution for the Blind 1983-; *Style*— The Rt Hon Lady Fisher of Rednal JP; 60 Jacoby Place, Priory Road, Birmingham B5 7UW

FISHER-HOCH, Hon Mrs (Nesta Donne); *née* Philipps; TD (1947), DL (Carmarthenshire); da of late 1 Baron Kylsant; *b* 20 Nov 1903; *m* 1, 17 Sept 1921, 10 Earl of Coventry (ka 1940); 1 s, 2 da; m 2, 17 Jan 1953, Maj Terrance Vincent Fisher-Hoch, RA (d 1978), s of John Henry Fisher-Hoch, of Basle, Switzerland; *Career* chief cdr ATS 1939-45; *Style*— Hon Mrs Fisher-Hoch, TD, DL; Plâs Llanstephan, Carmarthen, Dyfed, Wales SA33 5JP

FISHLOCK, Dr David Jocelyn; OBE (1983); s of William Charles Fishlock (d 1958), of Bath, and late Dorothy Mary Fishlock; *b* 9 August 1932; *Educ* City of Bath Boys' Sch (now Beechen Cliff Sch), Bristol Coll of Tech (now Bath Univ); *m* 21 Dec 1959, Mary Millicent, *née* Cosgrove; 1 s (William David b 12 June 1960); *Career* assoc ed McGraw-Hill Publishing Co 1959-62, technol ed New Scientist 1962-67, sci ed Fin Times 1967-, DLitt Royal Univ of Salford 1982; FIBiol 1988, Companion Inst of Energy 1988; ; *Books* author and ed of twelve books incl The Business of Science (1975), Biotechnology - Strategies for Life (with Elizabeth Antebi, 1987); *Clubs* Athenaeum; *Style*— Dr David Fishlock, OBE; Traveller's Joy, Copse Lane, Jordans, Bucks, HP9 2TA (☎ 02707 3242); Financial Times, Number One Southwark Bridge, London SE1 9HL (☎ 01-873 3000)

FISHWICK, Avril; DL (Gtr Manchester 1982); da of Frank Platt Hindley (d 1966), and Charlotte Winifred, *née* Young (d 1940); *b* 30 Mar 1924; *Educ* Woodfield Pte Sch, Wigan HS for Girls, Liverpool Univ (LLB, LLM); *m* 4 Feb 1950, Thomas William Fishwick, s of William Fishwick of Rainford; 2 da (Lizbeth Joanna b 1951, Hilary Alean b 1953); *Career* FO Bletchley Park 1942-45, slr 1949, ptnr Frank Platt & Fishwick 1958-; pres: Wigan branch RSPCA 1974-, Wigan Little Theatre 1985-; hon memb Soroptimist Int 1973-,Countryside Cmmn rep Groundwork Tst 1986-, dir N Advsy Bd Nat West Bank 1984-; memb: Wigan and Leigh Hosp Mgmnt Ctee 1960-73 (exec cncl 1966-73), appeals ctee Prince of Wales Youth Business Tst, ct Manchester Univ

1984-; chm Wigan area Health Authy 1973-82; DL Gtr Manchester 1982-, High Sheriff Gtr Manchester 1983-84, Vice Lord Lt Gtr Manchester 1988-; memb Law Soc; *Recreations* countryside, natural history; *Style*— Mrs Avril Fishwick, DL; Haighlands, Haigh Country Park, Haigh, Wigan (☎ 0942 831 291); Victoria Buildings, King Street, Wigan (☎ 0942 43281, fax 0942 495 522)

FISHWICK, Lady Mary Louise; *née* Northcote; da of 4 Earl of Iddesleigh; *b* 14 April 1959; *Educ* St Mary's Convent Shaftesbury Dorset; *m* 12 Sept 1981, Maj Simon Nicholas Fishwick, 13/18 Royal Hussars (Queen Mary's Own), yr s of Clifford Fishwick, of Salisbury House, Monmouth Street, Topsham, Devon; 2 s (James Nicholas b 1983, Hugh Simon b 1984 d 1987), 1 da (Lucy Mary b 1988); *Style*— Lady Mary Fishwick; Lower Woodrow, Brampford Speke, nr Exeter, Devon EX5 5DY

FISKE, Hon Giles Geoffrey; s (by 1 m) of late Baron Fiske (Life Peer, d 1975); *b* 1935; *Style*— Hon Giles Fiske

FISKE, Baroness; Josephine; da of Alan Griffiths Coppin, JP, of Hong Kong; *m* 1955, as his 2 w, Baron Fiske (Life Peer, d 1975); *Style*— The Rt Hon Lady Fiske

FISON, Sir (Richard) Guy; 4 Bt (UK 1905), DSC (1944); s of Capt Sir (William) Guy Fison, 3 Bt, MC (d 1964); *b* 9 Jan 1917; *Educ* Eton, New Coll Oxford; *m* 28 Feb 1952, Elyn (d 1987), da of Mogens Hartmann, of Bordeaux, and formerly wife of Count Renaud Doria; 1 s, 1 da; *Heir* s, Charles William Fison; *Career* Lt RNVR; serv: Atlantic, N Sea, Channel; chm Fine Vintage Wines plc, non-exec dir Whitehead Mann 1982-84, former chm Saccone and Speed Int (dir 1952-83); pres Wine and Spirit Assoc of GB 1976-77, Upper Warden Worshipful Co of Vintners 1982-83, Master 1983-84; chm Wine Devpt Bd 1982-83, dir Wine Standards Bd 1984-87; *Clubs* MCC; *Style*— Sir Guy Fison, Bt, DSC; Medwins, Odiham, Hants RG25 1NE (☎ 025 671 2125)

FISTOULARI, Anatole; s of Gregor Fistoulari (d 1942 in Paris; conductor, pianist, composer), and Sophie Fistoulari (d 1965); *b* 20 August 1907; *m* 1, 1943 (m dis 1956), Anna, da of Gustav Mahler, the composer (d 1911); 1 da (Marina b 1943); m 2, 1957, Mary Elizabeth, da of James Lockhart (d 1943), of Edinburgh; *Career* principal conductor London Philharmonic Orchestra 1943-44; hon dir Madrid Sinfonica; princ conductor and musical dir London International Orchestra 1946; *Recreations* reading; *Style*— Anatole Fistowlari, Esq; 65 Redington Road, Hampstead, London NW3

FITCH, Adrian Hill; s of Brian Hill Fitch, of 'Grayleigh', St Huberts Lane, Gerrards Cross, Bucks, and Susan Margeret, *née* Edwards; *b* 2 Mar 1959; *Educ* Merchant Taylors'; *Career* money broker Eurobrokers Sterling Ltd; dir London & Westminster Property Co Ltd 1980-; registered representative on Stock Exchange 1986; *Recreations* squash, shooting, wind surfing, classic car collecting; *Clubs* Cannons Sports, MG Owners; *Style*— Adrian H Fitch, Esq; 1 Elystan Walk, Cloudesley Rd, Islington, London N1 (☎ 01 833 1806); Eurobrokers Sterling Ltd, Adelaide House, London Bridge, London EC4 (☎ 01 626 8471)

FITCH, Brian Hill; s of Stanley Hill Fitch (d 1961), of Hampstead, and Marjorie Winifred, *née* Browne; *b* 19 May 1930; *Educ* Haileybury; *m* 1955, Susan Margaret, da of Cyril Rex Edwards, LDS (d 1935), of Scarborough; 1 s, 1 da; *Career* Lloyd's Insurance broker 1950-65, md The London & Westminster Property Co Ltd 1965- (dir 1956-), chm Caledonian Municipal Investmts Ltd 1970-80, chm and md The London & Westminster (Sterling Brokers) Ltd 1972-80, licensed dealer in securities 1974-, md London Financial Agency Ltd 1980-, underwriting memb Lloyd's 1982-; *Recreations* curio and antique collector, vintage motor cars, shooting, swimming; *Clubs* IOD (fell and life memb), Rolls Royce Enthusiasts, Mongewell Shoot; *Style*— Brian Fitch Esq; Grayleigh, St Hubert's Lane, Gerrards Cross, Bucks (☎ 0753 884702, fax 888302); Cheviot Court, Broadstairs, Kent (☎ 0843 63293)

FITCH, Colin Digby Thomas; s of Thomas Charles Fitch, of Itayling Island, Hampshire, and Grace Leila Fitch; *b* 2 Jan 1934; *Educ* St Paul's, St Catharine's Coll Cambridge (MA, LLM); *m* 15 Dec 1956, Wendy Ann, da of Edward Davis (d 1961); 4 s (Alanc b 1959, Quentin b 1960, Joshua b 1971, Felix b 1972), 1 da (Cressida b 1964); *Career* Nat Serv 1951-53, cmmnd into The Queens Own Royal W Kent Regt TA 1953-58; called to the Bar Inner Temple 1970, ptnr Rowe and Pitman 1968-76, md Wardley Middle E Ltd 1976-80, ptnr Grieveson Grant and Co 1980-86, dir Kleinwort Benson Securities Ltd 1986-; memb Stock Exchange 1968, FCIS 1970, FRSA 1987; *Clubs* Brooks's; *Style*— Colin Fitch, Esq; The Coach House, Royston, Hertforshire (☎ 0763 242 072); Bouyon, Mayrinhac, Lentours, Gramat Lot, France; 20 Fenchurch St, London EC3 (☎ 01 623 8000, fax 01 29 2657, telex 8873480)

FITCH, (John) Derek; s of John Dowson Fitch (d 1979) and Nora (d 1984); *b* 22 Sept 1937; *Educ* Rutherford GS Newcastle on Tyne, Univ of Durham (BA); *m* 22 June 1963, Maureen Rose; 1 s (John Stephen b 1968); *Career* dir: Hill Samuel Registrars 1979, Devpt Planning Ltd 1982, Hill Samuel & Co 1985, Hill Samuel Life Assur Co 1987, Hill Samuel Investmt Servs Gp 1987; md; Universal Credit Ltd 1979, Hill Samuel Personal Fin 1987; *Recreations* golf, swimming (ex British record holder); *Style*— Derek Fitch, Esq; Douglas Cottage, Coombe End, Kingston, Surrey KT2 7DQ (☎ 01 942 8009; 6 Greencoat Place, London SW1P 1PL (☎ 01 828 5241)

FITCH, Douglas Bernard Stocker; s of William Kenneth Fitch (d 1970), and Hilda Alice, *née* Barrington (d 1953); *b* 16 April 1927; *Educ* St Albans Sch, Abbey Gateway St Albans, RAC Cirencester; *m* 1952, Joyce Vera, da of Arthur Robert Griffiths-Cirencester (d 1941), of Glos; 3 s (Christopher b 1958, Simon b 1961, Adrian b 1964); *Career* RE, (Germany, Belgium, Netherlands) 1944-48; chartered surveyor, under sec, dir land and water serv MAFF 1980-87 (ret); memb gen cncl RICS 1980-86; pres land agency and agric divnl cncl RICS 1985-86; chm RICS standing conference marine resources; govr the Royal Agric Coll 1986-; FRICS, MRAC, FAAV; *Clubs* Farmers, Civil Service; *Style*— Douglas Fitch, Esq; 71 Oasthouse Crescent, Hale, Farnham, Surrey GU9 0NP (☎ 0252 716742)

FITCH, Adm Sir Richard George Alison; KCB (1985); s of Instr Capt Edward William Fitch, RN (d 1953), and Agnes Jamieson, *née* Alison (d 1979); *b* 2 June 1929; *Educ* RNC Dartmouth (13 year-old entry); *m* 1969, Kathleen Marie-Louise, da of Robert Igert (d 1984), of Biarritz, France; 1 s (Richard b 1972); *Career* cmd HMS Hermes 1976-78, Dir Naval Warfard (MOD) 1978-80, Naval Sec 1980-83, Flag Offr 3 Flotilla and Cdr Anti-Submarine Gp Two 1983-85; Chief of Naval Personnel, Second Sea Lord and Adm, pres RNC Greenwich 1986-88; ret 1988; Liveryman Worshipful Co of Coachmakers and Coach Harness Makers; CBIM; *Recreations* gardening, following sport, the family; *Style*— Adm Sir Richard Fitch, KCB; West Hay, 32 Sea Lane, Middleton-on-Sea, West Sussex (☎ 0243 69 2361)

FITCH, Rodney Arthur; s of Arthur Francis Fitch (d 1982), of Wilts, and Ivy Fitch; *b* 19 August 1938; *Educ* Willesdon Poly, Sch of Architecture, Central Sch of Arts & Crafts, Hornsey Sch of Art; *m* 28 Aug 1965, Janet Elizabeth, da of Sir Walter Stansfield, CBE, QPM (d 1984); 1 s (Edward b 18 Aug 1978), 4 da (Polly Jane b 27 May 1967, Emily Kate b 18 June 1968, Louisa Claire b 7 Nov 1971, Tessa Grace b 29 Oct 1974); *Career* Nat Serv RAPC 1958-60; trainee designer Hickman Ltd 1956-58, Charles Kenrick Assoc 1960-62, Conran Design Gp Ltd 1962-69, CDG (design conslts) Ltd 1969-71, fndr Fitch-RS plc (formerly Fitch & Co) 1971-; memb Design Cncl 1988-, dep chm ct of govrs London Inst 1989-, CSD (formerly SIAD) pres 1988-90 (vice pres 1982-86, hon tres 1984-87), former pres Designers & Arts Directors Assoc 1983; FRSA 1976; *Recreations* cricket, tennis, opera, theatre, family; *Style*— Rodney Fitch, Esq; 4-6 Soho Square, London W1 (☎ 01 580 3060, fax 01 734 0448)

FITT, Baron (Life Peer UK 1983), of Bell's Hill, Co Down; Gerard Fitt; s of George Patrick Fitt, and Mary Ann Fitt; *b* 9 April 1926; *Educ* Christian Brothers Sch Belfast; *m* 1947, Susan Gertrude, *née* Doherty; 5 da (and 1 da decd); *Career* merchant seaman 1941-53; cncllr Belfast Corpn (alderman) 1958-61; MP (Lab Eire) Parl of N Ireland for Dock Div of Belfast 1962-72; MP (Repub Lab) Belfast W 1966; dep chief exec NI Exec 1974; fndr and ldr Social Democratic and Labour Party NI, MP (SDLP) 1970-79, MP (Socialist) Belfast West 1979-83; *Style*— The Rt Hon Lord Fitt; House of Lords, London SW1A 0PW

FITTER, Richard Sidney Richmond; s of Sidney H Fitter (d 1962), of Banstead, Surrey, and Dorothy Isacke, *née* Pound (d 1926); *b* 1 Mar 1913; *Educ* Eastbourne Coll, LSE (BSc); *m* 19 April 1938, Alice Mary Stewart (Maisie), da of Dr R Stewart Park (d 1945), of Huddersfield, Yorks; 2 s (Julian Richmond b 1944, Alastair Hugh), 1 da (Jenny Elizabeth (Mrs Graham) b 1942); *Career* RAF Ops Res Section Coastal Cmd 1942-45; res staff: PEP (Political & Econ Planning) 1936-40, Mass Observation 1940-42; sec Wild Life Conservation Special Ctee Miny of Town & Country Planning 1945-46, asst ed The Countryman 1946-59, open air corr The Observer 1958-66, dir intelligence unit Cncl for Nature 1959-63; Fauna Preservation Soc: hon sec 1964-81, vice chm 1981-84, chm 1984-87, vice pres 1987-; Berks Bucks & Oxon Naturalists Tst 1959-: hon sec, vice chm chm, pres; memb survival serv cmmn Int Union for Conservation of Nature 1963- (chm steering ctee 1975-88), tstee and cncl memb World Wildlife Fund UK 1977-85; cncl memb: RSPB, Royal Soc for Nature Conservation; sci FZS; *Books* London's Natural History (1945), Wildlife for Man (1986), and 28 other books of wildlife, mainly field guides on birds and wild flowers, most recent being the Field Guide to the Countryside in Winter (1988, with Alastair Fitter 1988); *Recreations* bird watching, botanising, reading; *Clubs* Athenaeum; *Style*— Richard Fitter, Esq; Drifts, Chinnor Hill, Oxford OX9 4BS (☎ 0844 51223)

FITTON, Lady Eileen Cecil Theo; *née* Paulet; yr da of Capt Charles Standish Paulet, MVO (d 1953), and Lillian Jane Charlotte, *née* Fosbery; sis of 17 Marquess of Winchester (d 1968); raised to rank of Marquess's da 1970; *b* 1916; *m* 1, H Martin (d 1947); 2 children; m 2, 1949, Joseph Fitton; 6 children; *Style*— Lady Eileen Fitton; 1610E 11th Ave, Vancouver 12, BC, Canada

FITZ-CLARENCE, Lady Georgina; da of 7 Earl of Munster by his 2 w; *b* 1966; *Style*— Lady Georgina Fitz-Clarence

FITZALAN HOWARD, Lord Mark; s of Lord Howard of Glossop (d 1972), and Baroness Beaumont (*née* Tempest) (d 1971); *b* 28 Mar 1934; *Educ* Ampleforth Coll; *m* 17 Nov 1961, Jacynth Rosemary, da of Sir Martin Lindsay (d 1981); 1 s (Timothy b 1987), 2 da (Amelia b 1963, Eliza b 1964, m 1987 Timothy Bell); *Career* late Coldstream Gds; chm Assoc of Investmt Tst Cos 1981-83; dir Robert Fleming Hldgs Ltd 1971-, non-exec dir BET plc 1983-, dir Nat Mutual Life Assur Soc; *Style*— Lord Mark Fitzalan Howard; 13 Campden Hill Square, London W8 7LB (☎ 01 727 0996); 25 Copthall Ave, London EC2 (☎ 01 638 5858)

FITZALAN HOWARD, Lord Martin; JP (N Riding of Yorks 1966), DL (N Yorks 1982); 3 s of 3 Baron Howard of Glossop, MBE (d 1972), and Baroness Beaumont, OBE; bro of 17 Duke of Norfolk, KG, GCVO, CB, CBE, MC; *b* 22 Oct 1922; *Educ* Ampleforth, Trinity Coll Cambridge; *m* 5 Oct 1948, Bridget Anne, da of late Lt-Col Arnold Ramsay Keppel (fourth in descent from Hon Frederick Keppel, sometime Bp of Exeter and 4 s of 2 Earl of Albemarle, KG, KB); 1 s, 4 da; *Career* served WW II (wounded), Palestine 1945-46, Capt Grenadier Gds; High Sheriff N Yorks 1979-80; *Style*— Lord Martin Fitzalan Howard, JP, DL; 3/E Whittingstall Rd, SW6 (☎ 01 736 0520); Brockfield Hall, Warthill, York (☎ 0904 489298)

FITZALAN HOWARD, Maj-Gen Lord Michael; GCVO (1981, KCVO 1971, MVO 4 Class 1952), CB (1968), CBE (1962, MBE 1949), MC (1944), DL (Wilts 1974); 2 s of 3 Baron Howard of Glossop, MBE, and Baroness Beaumont, OBE (Barony called out of abeyance in her favour 1896); bro of 17 Duke of Norfolk, KG, GCVO, CB, CBE, MC; granted rank of Duke's s 1975; *b* 22 Oct 1916; *Educ* Ampleforth, Trinity Coll Cambridge (MA); *m* 1, 4 March 1946, Jean Marion (d 1947), da of Sir Hew Hamilton-Dalrymple, 9 Bt; 1 da ; m 2, 20 April 1950, Jane Margaret, yr da of Capt William Particle Meade Newman; 4 s, 1 da; *Career* served WW II, Scots Gds, Europe and Palestine, subsequently Malaya, GOC London Dist and Maj-Gen cmdg Household Div 1968-71, Marshal Dip Corps 1972-82; Col Life Gds 1979-, Gold Stick to HM The Queen 1979-; pres cncl TAVR Assocs 1981- (chm 1973-81); Freeman City of London 1985; Kt SMO Malta; *Clubs* Pratt's, Buck's; *Style*— Maj-Gen Lord Michael Fitzalan Howard, GCVO, CB, CBE, MC, DL; Fovant House, Fovant, Salisbury, Wilts (☎ 072 270 617)

FITZALAN-HOWARD, Lord Gerald Bernard; s of 17 Duke of Norfolk, KG, CB, CBE, MC; *b* 13 June 1962; *Style*— Lord Gerald Fitzalan Howard; Bacres House, Hambleden, nr Henley-on-Thames, Oxon

FITZGEORGE-BALFOUR, Sir (Robert George) Victor; KCB (1968, CB 1965), CBE 1945, DSO 1950, MC 1939, DL (W Sussex 1977); o s of Robert Shekleton Balfour (d 1942), of Stirling, and (Mabel) Iris *née* FitzGeorge (d 1976), who m subsequently (as his 2 w) Prince Vladimir Emmanuelovitch Galitzine (*see* Prince George Galitzine); Iris was da of Col George William Adolphus FitzGeorge (d 1907), Royal Welch Fusiliers, who was in his turn s of HRH Prince George, 2 Duke of Cambridge (whose f was 7 s of King George III); *b* 15 Sept 1913; *Educ* Eton, King's Cambridge; *m* 4 Dec 1943, Mary Diana, er da of Adm Arthur Henry Christian, CB, MVO, descended from an ancient family of Manx landowners; 1 s (Robin b 1951), 1 da (Diana b 1946); *Career* served Coldstream Gds 1934-73 in M East, NW Europe (WW II), later Dir Mil Ops MOD, Sr Army Instructor IDC, Vice CGS 1968-70, UK Mil Rep NATO 1971-73; Col Cmdt HAC 1976-84; former chm Nat Fund for Res into Crippling Diseases 1975-89; *Clubs* Army and Navy; *Style*— Gen Sir Victor FitzGeorge-Balfour, KCB, CBE, DSO, MC, DL; The Old Rectory, W Chiltington, W Sussex (☎ 2255)

FITZGERALD, Adrian James Andrew Denis; s and h of Sir George FitzGerald, 5 Bt, MC, 23 Knight of Kerry, *qv*; *b* 24 June 1940; *Educ* Harrow; *Career* hotelier; cncllr Royal Borough of Kensington and Chelsea 1974- (Mayor 1984-85); *Clubs* Pratt's; *Style*— Adrian FitzGerald, Esq; 16 Clareville St, London SW7; Lackaneask, Valentia Island, Co Kerry

FITZGERALD, Brian John; s of John Fitzgerald, of Glasgow, and Margaret, *née* McCaffrey; *b* 17 Sept 1946; *Educ* Salesian Coll Farnborough Hants, Univ of Glasgow (BSc); *m* 1969, Maren Lina, da of Capt George Hunter (d 1972), of Glasgow; 2 s (Michael b 1973, Philip b 1977); *Career* civil engr; nrothern area dir bldg div John Laing Costruction Ltd, dir Norcity plc; CEng, FICE; *Recreations* squash; *Clubs* Royal Scottish Automobile; *Style*— Brian Fitzgerald, Esq; John Laine Construction Ltd, Page St, London NW7 2ER (☎ 01 959 3636, telex 8958741)

FITZGERALD, Christopher Francis; s of Lt Cdr Michael Francis FitzGerald RN, of Hove, E Sussex, and Anne Lise, *née* Winther; *b* 17 Nov 1945; *Educ* Downside, Lincoln Coll, Oxford (MA); *m* 1, 1968 (m dis 1984); 1 s (Matthew b 1973), 2 da (Francesca b 1975, Julia b 1978O); m 2, 31 Oct 1986, Jill, da of Dr Douglas Gordon Freshwater, of Upton-on-Severn, Worcs; 2 step da (Joanna b 1978, Victoria b 1979); *Career* slr; ptnr Slaughter and May 1976 (exec ptnr fin 1986-); *Recreations* travelling, music, reading; *Style*— Christopher FitzGerald, Esq; 21 Palace Gardens Terr, London W8 4SA; 35 Basinghall St, London EC2V 5DB

FITZGERALD, Rev Daniel Patrick; s of late Sir John Fitzgerald, 2 Bt and hp of bro, Rev (Sir) Edward Fitzgerald (3 Bt); *b* 28 June 1916; *Style*— Rev Daniel Fitzgerald

FITZGERALD, Desmond John Villiers; *see*: Glin, Knight of

FITZGERALD, Capt (Peter) Desmond; s of Lt-Col (Peter) Francis FitzGerald, DSO (d 1968), and Adrienne Marie Jacoba (d 1973), da of Baron Gustave de Geer, of Zeist, Holland; ggs of Sir Peter George Fitzgerald, 1 Bt, Knight of Kerry; *b* 22 May 1910; *Educ* Lancing, RMC Sandhurst; *m* 27 June 1945, Elizabeth Janet Cameron, da of late Donald Norman; 1 s (Anthony b 1953), 4 da (Caroline b 1946, Olivia b 1948, Louise b 1951, Georgina b 1960, d 1962); *Career* company dir, memb of Lloyds; SMOM 1983; *Recreations* travel, hunting, skiing, yachting, preservation of rural England; *Clubs* Army and Navy; *Style*— Capt Peter FitzGerald; Querns House, Cirencester, Glos (☎ 0285 653418); 65 Eaton Terrace, London SW1 (☎ 01 730 4848)

FITZGERALD, Rev (Sir) Edward Thomas; (3 Bt, UK 1903); s of Sir John Joseph Fitzgerald, 2 Bt (d 1957); suc his father but does not use title; *b* 7 Mar 1912; *Heir* bro, Rev Daniel Patrick Fitzgerald; *Career* Roman Catholic priest; *Style*— The Rev Edward Fitzgerald; Mayfield, Cork

FITZGERALD, Frederick Patrick; s of Thomas FitzGerald (d 1959), of Waterford, Ireland, and Margaret, *née* Power (d 1969); *b* 1 Feb 1905; *Educ* Clongowes Sch Co Kildare Ireland, Trinity Coll Dublin (MA, MB, BCh, BAO); *m* 21 Sept 1942, Zina Eveline, da of George Moncrieff (d 1959), of Drumlithie, Scot; 1 s (Richard Kieran b 1945), 1 da (Susanna Patricia (Mrs Clough) b 1950); *Career* conslt surgn: Royal Northern Hosp London 1945-72, St Anthony's Hosp London 1945-72, St Anthony's Hosp Cheam 1945-72, Royal Free Hosp London 1962-72; fell Internat Coll of Surgns (former pres Br Section 1969-84); FRCS (Ireland); hon fell Czechoslovakian Coll of Surgns 1978, Silver Medal of Paris for Servs to Internat Surgery; *Recreations* riding, fishing, horticulture; *Style*— Frederick Fitzgerald, Esq; 129 Harley St, London W1N 1DJ (☎ 01 935 1777); Wadhurst Castle, Wadhurst, Sussex

FITZGERALD, Garret; s of Desmond FitzGerald (Min External Affrs Irish Free State 1922-27, Min Def 1927-32) and Mabel, *née* McConnell; *b* 9 Feb 1926; *Educ* St Brigid's Sch Bray, Colaiste na Rinne Waterford, Belvedere Coll Dublin, Univ Coll Dublin & King's Inns Dublin; *m* 1947, Joan, da of late Charles O'Farrell; 2 s, 1 da; *Career* barr 1946, res and schedules mangr Aer Lingus 1947-58; Rockefeller res asst Trinity Coll Dublin 1958-59, lectr in Political Econ Univ Coll Dublin 1959-73; memb: Nat Univ of Senate, Seanad Eireann 1965-69, TD, Dail Eireann for Dublin SE 1969; ldr and pres Fine Gael 1977-87; min Foreign Affrs 1973-77, Taoiseach (meaning chieftain; title used by Irish PMs) of Eire 1981-82, 1982-87; pres: cncl of Mins of EEC Jan-June 1975, Euro Cncl July-Dec 1984, Irish Cncl of Euro Mvmnt 1977-81, 1982; formerly vice-pres Euro People's Pty, Euro Parly, Irish corr: BBC, Financial Times, Economist and other overseas papers; formerly econ corr Irish Times, md Economist Intelligence Unit of I; hon LLD: NY, St Louis, St Mary's Univ Halifax Canada, Univ of Keele, Boston Coll Mass, Oxford Univ; *Publications* State-Sponsored Bodies (1959), Planning in Ireland (1968), Towards a New Ireland (1972), Unequal Partners (UNCTAD 1979), Estimates for Baronies of Minimum Level of Irish Speaking amongst Successive Decennial Cohorts 1771-1781 to 1861-1871 (1984); *Style*— Garret FitzGerald Esq; Leinster House, Kildare St, Dublin 2, Ireland

FITZGERALD, Sir George Peter Maurice; 5 Bt; *see*: Kerry, Knight of; *Style*— Sir George Fitzgerald

FITZGERALD, James Gerard; s of John Fitzgerald (d 1974), and Josephine, *née* Murphy (d 1952); *b* 22 May 1935; *m* 22 March 1978, Jane Latta, da of A C Leggat, of Lindsaylands, Biggar, Lanarks; 1 s (by previous m Timothy John b 1962), 2 da (Lisa Siobhan, by previous m, b 1964, Kirsty Isobel b 1985); *Career* racehorse trainer; major races won include: Tote Cheltenham Cup, Power Gold Cup, Vincent O'Brien Irish Gold Cup, Arkle Challenge trophy Cheltenham, Hennessy Cognac Gold Cup, Tote Cesarewitch, NBA Northumberland Plate, Sun Alliance Chase Cheltenham, Timeform Chase Haydock (twice), Philip Corner, Saddle of Gold Final Newbury, WM Hill Scottish Nat Ayr (twice), SGB Chase Ascot, Hermitage Chase Newbury, Coral Golden Hurdle Final Cheltenham; best horses trained include: Androma, Brave Fellow, Bucko, Canny Danny,Danish Flight, Fairy King, Fair Kitty, Forgive N' Forget, Galway Blaze, Kayudee, Tickite Boo, Treasure Hunter; *Recreations* shooting; *Style*— James Fitzgerald, Esq; Norton Grange, Norton, Malton, N Yorkshire YO17 (☎ 0653 692718, fax 0653 600214)

FITZGERALD, Lord John; 2 s of 8 Duke of Leinster by his 2 w Anne, yr da of late Lt-Col Philip Eustace Smith, MC; *b* 3 Mar 1952; *Educ* Millfield, RMA Sandhurst; *m* 11 Dec 1982, Barbara, eldest da of late Andreas Zindel by his w Daniele, of Lausanne, Switzerland; 1 s (Edward b 27 Oct 1988), 1 da (Hermione b 11 Oct 1985); *Career* Capt 5 Royal Inniskilling Dragoon Gds; racehorse trainer (Graham Place, Newmarket); *Recreations* shooting, fishing; *Clubs* Turf, Naval and Military; *Style*— Lord John FitzGerald; Graham Lodge, Newmarket, Suffolk CB8 OWE (☎ 0638 669879)

FITZGERALD, Michael Frederick Clive; QC (1980); s of Sir William James FitzGerald MC, QC, and late Erica Critchley, *née* Clarke; *b* 9 June 1936; *Educ* Downside, Christ's Coll Cambridge (MA); *m* 15 Feb 1966, Virginia Grace, da of Col William Sturmy Cave DSO, TD (d 1953); 1 s (Hamilton b 14 March 1971), 3 da (Emma Grace b 2 Feb 1967, Charlot Grace b 7 June 1968, Harriet Grace 4 Aug 1969); *Career* 2 Lt Queens Royal Lancers 1954-56, barr Middle Temple 1961, Master of the Bench 1987; *Recreations* fishing, shooting; *Clubs* Athenaeum, Special Forces; *Style*— Michael FitzGerald, Esq; East Lymden, Ticehurst, Sussex TN5 7JB; 2 Mitre Court Buildings, Temple, London EC4 (☎ 01 583 1380, fax 01 353 7772)

FITZGERALD, Michael John; s of Albert William Fitzgerald (d 1980), of Dynerth, Heather Lane, West Chiltington, and Florence Margaret, *née* Stannard (d 1981); *b* 14 May 1935; *Educ* Caterham Sch; *m* 9 June 1962, Judith-Ann, da of Dr A C Boyle of The Barn, Iping; 2 s (Alistair b 1964, Malcolm b 1966), 1 da (Aimee-Louise b 1970); *Career* CA, vice pres Occidental Int Oil Inc 1987, vice-pres and gen mangr Occidental Int (Libya) Inc 1985; dir: Occidental Petroleum (Caledonia) Ltd, Langham Publishing Ltd, Arundale Sch Tst; *Recreations* golf, gardening opera; *Clubs* West Sussex G; *Style*— Michael J Fitzgerald, Esq; Fir Tops, Grove Lane, West Chiltington, Sussex (☎ (07983) 2258); 16 Palace St, London SW1 (☎ 01 828 5600)

FITZGERALD, Niall William Arthur; s of William FitzGerald (d 1972), and Doreen, *née* Chambers; *b* 13 Sept 1945; *Educ* St Munchins Coll Limerick, Univ Coll Dublin (M Com); *m* 2 March 1970, Monica Mary, da of John Cusack (d 1985); 2 s (Colin b 30 Jan 1976, Aaron b 24 March 1982), 1 da (Tara b 5 Dec 1973); *Career* N American commerical memb Unilever plc 1978-80 (overseas commercial offr 1976-78), md Unilver SA 1982-85 (fin dir 1980-82), dir Unilever NV & Unilever plc 1987- (gp tres 1985-86); memb: ctee on indust and fin NEDC, Accounting Standards Review Ctee; FCT 1986; *Recreations* opera, running, golf, and an active family; *Clubs* RAC; *Style*— Niall W A FitzGerald, Esq; Unilever, Blackfriars, London EC4P 4BQ (☎ 01 822 6328)

FITZGERALD, Penelope Mary; da of Edmund Valpy Knox (poet and editor of Punch, d 1971) and Christina Frances Knox (d 1935); *b* 17 Dec 1916; *Educ* Wycombe Abbey Sch, Somerville Coll Oxford (BA); *m* 15 Aug 1942, Desmond John Lyon Fitzgerald, MC, s of Thomas Fitzgerald (d 1960); 1 s (Edmund Valpy b 1947), 2 da (Christina Rose b 1950, Maria b 1953); *Career* writer; FRLS 1988; *Books* biography: Edward Burne-Jones (1975), The Knox Brothers (1977), Charlotte Mew and Her Friends (1984, Br Academy Mary Rose Crawshay award); fiction: The Bookshop (1978, Offshore (1979, Booker McConnell award for fiction), At Freddies (1982), Innocence (1986), The Beginning of Spring (1988); *Recreations* gardening, counting blessings; *Clubs* PEN, William Morris Soc; *Style*— Mrs Penelope Fitzgerald; c/o Collins Publishers, 8 Grafton St, London W1X 3LA

FITZGERALD, Peter Gilbert; s of P H Fitzgerald, and H E Fitzgerald, *née* Clark; *b* 13 Feb 1946; *Educ* Harvey GS Folkestone; *m* 5 Dec 1970, Elizabeth T, da of F L Harris (d 1970), of Cornwall; 1 s (Timothy b 1973); *Career* chartered accountant; dir: Valor Vanguard Ltd 1965-66, Fitzgerald Lightring Ltd 1973-80; md: Fitzgerald Lightring Ltd 1980-, Bodmin & Wenford Railway plc 1985-; FCA; *Recreations* cycling, model railways; *Style*— Peter G Fitzgerald, Esq; 1 Tower Park, Lanivet, Bodmin, Cornwall PL30 5BL; Fitzgerald Lightring Ltd, Normandy Way, Bodmin, Cornwall (☎ 0208 5611, telex 45389, fax 0208 4893)

FITZGERALD, Lady Rosemary Ann; *née* FitzGerald; da of 8 Duke of Leinster by his 1 w Joane, da of late Maj Arthur MacMurrough Kavanagh, MC; *b* 4 August 1939; *Educ* Lady Margaret Hall Oxford; *m* 9 Feb 1963 (m dis 1967), Mark Killigrew Wait, o s of Peter Lothian Killigrew Wait, of 10 Pembroke Square, W8; reverted to maiden name; *Career* botanist; *Style*— Lady Rosemary FitzGerald; West House, East Quantoxhead, Nr Bridgwater, Somerset TA5 1EL

FITZGERALD, Sir William James; MC (1918), QC (1936); s of Joseph FitzGerald, MB (d 1926); *b* 19 May 1894; *Educ* Blackrock Coll Dublin, Trinity Coll Dublin (Hon LLD 1940); *m* 1, 1933 (m dis 1946), Erica, da of F J Clarke, JP, of Chikupi Ranch, Northern Rhodesia; 1 s; m 2, 1956, Cynthia Mary Mangnall, da of late William Foster, OBE, of Jerusalem; 1 step s; *Career* barr 1922, crown counsel Nigeria 1924, attorney-gen N Rhodesia 1932-36 (Palestine 1937-44), chief justice Palestine 1944-48, pres Lands Tribunal England 1950-65; Croix de Guerre (France); kt 1944; *Clubs* Athenaeum; *Style*— Sir William FitzGerald, MC, QC; 51 Vicarage Court, Vicarage Gate, London W8 4HE

FITZGERALD, Dr William Knight; CBE (1981), JP (1958), DL (1974); eldest s of John Alexander Fitzgerald (d 1963), of Brunton, Fife, and Janet 1938, Elizabeth (d 1980), da of Alexander Grant Knight (d 1979); *b* 19 Mar 1909; *Educ* Robertson Acad SA; *m* 1 1938, Elizabeth (d 1980), da of Alexander Grant; 3 s (Alexander, John, William); m 2, 1984, Margaret Eleanor, da of George Baird Bell (d 1965); *Career* co dir (ret); local govt Dundee City tres 1967-70, lord provost Dundee Cncl 1970-73, dep convener Tayside Rgnl Cncl 1974-77 (convener 1977-86); chm Tay Road Bridge Bd, pres Dundee Bn Boys' Bde; ex pres COSLA; *Recreations* gardening, walking; *Clubs* Univ of Dundee; *Style*— Dr W K Fitzgerald, CBE, JP, DL; 1 Roxburgh Terrace, Dundee (☎ 68475); Tayside Rgnl Cncl, Tayside Ho, Dundee (☎ 23281)

FITZGIBBON, Louis Theobald Dillon; Comte Dillon in France; s of Lt Cdr Robert Francis Dillon FitzGibbon, RN (d 1954), and Kathleen Clare, *neée* Atcheson (d 1950); *b* 6 Jan 1925; *Educ* St Augustine's Abbey Sch Ramsgate, RNC Dartmouth, London Univ (Sch of Eastern European and Slavonic Studies) for Naval Polish Interpreters' Course; *m* 1, 1950 (m dis 1962), Josephine Miriam Maud Webb; m 2, 15 Aug 1962, Madeleine Sally Hayward-Surry (d 1980); 1 s (James b 7 Nov 1963), 2 da (Simone b 16 Nov 1962, Michèle b 24 April 1965); m 3, 12 Sept 1980, Joan Elizabeth Jevons; *Career* Midshipman RN 1942, Sub Lt 1944, Lt 1946, Lt Cdr (ret) 1954; dir De Leon Properties Ltd 1954-72; hon sec jt ctee for Preservation of Historic Portsmouth 1959-61; slrs articled clerk 1960-63; Anglo-Polish Conf Warsaw 1963; PA to Rt Hon Duncan Sandys, MP (later Lord Duncan-Sandys) 1967-68; gen sec Br Cncl for Aid to Refugees 1968-72; UN Mission to S Sudan 1972-73; dir of a med charity 1974-76; exec offr Nat Assoc for Freedom 1977-78; gen sec of a trade assoc 1978-80; memb missions to: Somalia 1978 and 1980-81; Sudan and Egypt 1982; Sudan, German Parl, Somalia and Euro Parl 1984; UN 1984, 1986, 1987, 1988, 1989; memb: RIIA 1982; Anglo-Somali Soc; Ethiopian Soc; UN Assoc; won first Airey Neave Meml Scholarship 1981; hon sec Katyn Memorial Fund 1971-77; area pres St John Ambulance Bde (Hants East) 1974-76; Kt of Honour and Devotion SMHOM; Polish Gold Cross of Merit 1969; Order of Polonia Restituta (Polish govt in exile), Offr 1971, Cdr 1972, Kt Cdr 1976; Katyn Meml Medal Bronze (USA) 1977; Laureate van de Arbeid (Netherlands) 1982; hon sec Br Horn of Africa Cncl 1984-; *Books* Katyn - A Crime without Parallel (1971), The Katyn Cover-up (1972), Unpitied and Unknown (1975), Katyn - Triumph of Evil (Ireland 1975), The Katyn Memorial (1976), Katyn Massacre (paper 1977, 2nd edn

1979) Katyn (USA 1979), Katyn Horror (in German 1979), The Betrayal of the Somalis (1982), Straits and Strategic Waterways in the Red Sea (1984), Ethiopia Hijacks the Hijack (1985), The Evaded Duty (1985), When the Killing has to Stop (1988); also reports and contributions to int and national journals; *Recreations* travel, politics, writing, reading, history, languages, refugee problems, Horn of Africa affairs, Islamic matters, Anglo-Irish understanding; *Clubs* Beefsteak; *Style—* Louis FitzGibbon, Esq; 8 Portland Place, Brighton BN2 1DG (☎ 0273 685661)

FITZHARRIS, Viscount; James Carleton Harris; s and h of 6 Earl of Malmesbury; *b* 19 June 1946; *Educ* Eton, Queen's Coll St Andrews Univ (MA); *m* 14 June 1969, Sally Ann, da of Sir Richard Newton Rycroft, 7 Bt; 3 s (Hon James, Hon Edward b 1972, Hon Guy b 1975) 2 da (Hon Frances b 1979, Hon Daisy b 1981); *Heir* s, Hon James Hugh Carleton Harris b 29 April 1970; *Style—* Viscount FitzHarris; Heather Row Farm House, Heather Row, Nately Scures, Basingstoke, Hants RG27 9JP (☎ 025 672 3138)

FITZHERBERT, Giles Eden; CMG (1985); er s of Capt Henry Charles Hugh FitzHerbert, and Sheelah, *née* Murphy; *b* 8 Mar 1935; *Educ* Ampleforth, Christ Church Oxford; *m* 1962, Margaret (d 1986), da of Evelyn Waugh, the novelist; 2 s, 3 da; *Career* 2 Lt 8 King's Royal Irish Hussars; formerly with Vickers da Costa & Co; fought Fermanagh and S Tyrone in Lib interest 1964; Diplomatic Serv: first sec Rome 1968-71, cnsllr Kuwait 1975-77 and Nicosia 1977-78, head European Community Dept (External) FCO 1978-81, sabbatical year 1982, inspr 1983, min Rome 1983-87, ambass Caracas 1988-; *Clubs* Beefsteak, Kildare St Univ (Dublin); *Style—* Giles FitzHerbert, Esq, CMG; Cove House, Cove, Tiverton, Devon

FITZHERBERT, Nicholas John; s of Cuthbert Fitzherbert (d 1986), and Barbara, *née* Scrope (d 1975); *b* 3 Nov 1933; *Educ* Ampleforth; *m* 26 March 1968, Countess Teréz Szapáry, da of Count Gyula Szapáry (d 1985); 1 s (Henry Laszlo b 1972), 1 da (Elizabeth Magdolna b 1970); *Career* Coldstream Gds BAOR 1952-54; Kleinwort Benson Ltd 1960-77, currently business devpt dir Ketson plc; *Books* Robert Fleming Holdings 1845-1982; *Clubs* The Cavalry and Guards; *Style—* Nicholas Fitzherbert, Esq; Dane Bridge House, Much Hadham, Herts SG10 6JB

FITZHERBERT, Hon Philip Basil; 3 s of 14 Baron Stafford (d 1986); *b* 7 Oct 1962; *Educ* Ampleforth Coll; sporting agents; *Recreations* shooting, cricket, golf, snooker, darts, reading, photography, beer tasting; *Clubs* I Zingari, MCC, Free Foresters, Staffordshire Gentlemen, Old Amplefordians; *Style—* Hon Philip Fitzherbert; c/o Rt Hon Lord Stafford, Swynnerton Park, Stone, Staffordshire

FITZHERBERT, Richard Ranulph; only s of Rev David FitzHerbert, MC, by his w Charmian Hyacinthe, yr da of late Samuel Ranulph Allsopp, CBE, DL (gs of 1 Baron Hindlip), by Samuel's w Hon Norah Littleton (2 da of 4 Baron Hatherton); hp of unc, Sir John FitzHerbert, 8 Bt; *b* 2 Nov 1963; *Educ* Eton; *Clubs* Bachelor's, Flappers; *Style—* Richard FitzHerbert Esq; Alsa Lodge, Stansted, Essex

FITZHERBERT, Hon Thomas Alastair; 2 s of 14 Baron Stafford (d 1986); *b* 9 August 1955; *Educ* Ampleforth; *m* 8 May 1982, Deborah S, yr da of late P A Beak, of The Coach House, Englefield Green; 2 da (Tamara Frances b 1986, Purdita Aileen b 1987); *Career* marketing; *Style—* Hon Thomas Fitzherbert; 72 Foxbourne Rd, London SW17

FITZHERBERT-BROCKHOLES, Francis Joseph; eldest s of Michael John Fitzherbert-Brockholes, *qv*; *b* 18 Sept 1951; *Educ* Oratory Sch, Corpus Christi Coll Oxford (BA, MA); *m* 7 May 1983, Jennifer, da of Geoffrey George Watts, of Grassdale, Wandering, W Aust; 2 s (Thomas Antony b 8 Nov 1985, George Frederick b 1 March 1988), 1 da (Susannah Louise b 23 Feb 1984); *Career* barr 1975; admitted New York bar 1978; memb of chambers, Manchester 1976-77; assoc Cadwalader, Wickersham & Taft 1977-78; ptnr White & Case 1985 (assoc 1978-85); *Style—* Francis Fitzherbert-Brockholes, Esq; 11 Hesper Mews, London SW5 0HH; Bailiff's Cottage, Claughton-on- Brock, nr Garstang, Lancs PR3 0PN; White & Case, 66 Gresham Street, London EC2V 7LB (☎ 01 726 6361, fax 01 726 8558, telex 884757)

FITZHERBERT-BROCKHOLES, Michael John; OBE (1989), JP (Lancashire 1960), DL (1975); s of John William Fitzherbert-Brockholes, CBE, MC, JP, DL (d 1963, sometime Privy Chamberlain of Sword and Cape to Pope Pius XI), and Hon Eileen French, da of 4 Baron de Freyne; the Brockholes have been seated at Claughton since the 14 cent and the estate passed through female descent to the Hesketh in 1751 and from them to the Fitzherberts in 1783, when William Fitzherbert assumed the additional surname and arms of Brockholes (*see* Burke's Landed Gentry, 18 edn, vol II, 1969); *b* 12 June 1920; *Educ* Oratory Sch, New Coll Oxford; *m* 28 Sept 1950, Mary Edith, da of Capt Charles Joseph Henry O'Hara Moore, CVO, MC, late Irish Guards (d 1965), of Mooresfort, Co Tipperary, by his w Lady Dorothie Feilding, da of 9 Earl of Denbigh, GCVO; 4 s (Francis Joseph, *qv*, Antony John b 23 Nov 1952, Simon Peter b 15 March 1955, William Andrew Charles b 1 Dec 1958); *Career* Maj Scots Gds (Italy and N W Europe) 1940-46; memb Lancashire CC 1967-89 (chm education ctee 1977-81); Vice Lord-Lieut Lancs 1977-; Kt of St Gregory 1978, OStJ; *Recreations* gardening; *Style—* Michael Fitzherbert-Brockholes, Esq, OBE, JP, DL; Claughton Hall, Garstang, nr Preston, Lancashire (☎ Brock 40286)

FITZMAURICE, Lt-Col Sir Desmond FitzJohn; CIE (1941); s of John Day Stokes Fitzmaurice, ICS (d 1897), and Emily Grace Ellen, *née* Cooke (d 1954); *b* 17 August 1893; *Educ* Bradfield Coll, RMA, Cambridge; *m* 1926, Nancy (d 1975), da of Rev John Sherlock Leake (d 1934), of Grayswood, Surrey; 1 s, 3 da; *Career* RE (France, Belgium, Italy), WW I, Lt-Col; former instr RMA Woolwich and Sch of Mil Engrg Chatham; chief engr Callenders Cable and Construction Co 1928-29, dep master of the Mint Bombay and Calcutta 1929-33, Master Security Printing India and controller of stamps India and Burma 1934-46; kt 1946; *Recreations* genealogy, wine-making, travel, languages; *Style—* Lt-Col Sir Desmond Fitzmaurice, CIE; Lincombe Lodge, Fox Lane, Boars Hill, Oxford OX1 5DN

FITZPATRICK, Christopher Hugh Eugene; s of Hugh Joseph Fitzpatrick (d 1979) of Cleator Moor, Cumbria, and Monica Alice, *née* Piper; *b* 5 Oct 1940; *Educ* Priory Sch Bishops Waltham; *m* 3 April 1971, Margaret Anne, da of John Thomas Bell (d 1974), of Florence Rd, Sanderstead, Surrey; 3 da (Clare Marie b 1972, Charlotte Ellen b 1974, Victoria Jane b 1979); *Career* md Transtar Ltd 1976-81, dep md Victor Products plc 1981-84 (md 1984-88), dir Scholer Gp plc, chm amd md Wylex Ltd; current dierctorships: PDL-Wylex SDN BDH Malaysia, WSK (Electricals) Ltd, Pentland Electronics Ltd, Aptec Ltd; *Recreations* motoring, caravanning, golf; *Clubs* Ponteland Lions, Catenians, Caravan; *Style—* Christopher Fitzpatrick, Esq; 35 Bow green Rd, Bowdon, Cheshire WA14 3LF (☎ 061 928 6247); Sharston Rd, Wythenshawe, Manchester M22 4RA

FITZPATRICK, David Beatty; CB (1969), OBE (1951), AFC (1949 and Bar 1958); s of Cdr Daniel Thomas Fitzpatrick, RN (d 1968) and Beatrice Anne, *née* Ward (d 1986); *b* 31 Jan 1920; *Educ* Kenilworth Prep Sch Exeter Midhurst Sussex; *m* 23 May 1941, Kathleen Mary (d 1988), da of Alfred John Miles (d 1928); 1 da (Anne b 1943); *Career* RAF cadet 1937, cmmnd 1938; served WWII Med, North Atlantic and Far East theatres 1939-45; cmd 209 Sqdn 1944, cmd first jet flying schs wings 1949-51, RAF Flying Coll, Manby 1954-57, GW specialist Aeronautics Engrg Coll Henlow 1957-58, cmd RAF Christmas Island (Br nuclear trials) 1959-60, NATO Def Coll Paris 1961, JSSC 1961, sr staff appts MOD (Air) 1961-64, Cmdg Offr RAF Akrotiri and RAF Nicosia Cyprus 1964-66 (Air Cdr 1966, dir (Q) RAF 1966-69, dir Guided Weapons (Trials and Ranges) MOD (PE) 1969-75; ret RAF 1975, sr master Fernden (Ind) Sch West Sussex 1975-85; pres RAF Swimming Assoc 1966-75; *Recreations* swimming, writing; *Style—* David Fitzpatrick, Esq, CB, OBE, AFC; 'Whistledown', 38 Courts Mount Road, Haslemere, Surrey GU27 2PP (☎ 0428 4589)

FITZPATRICK, (Gen) Sir (Geoffrey Richard) Desmond; GCB (1971, KCB 1965, CB 1961), DSO (1945), MBE (1942), MC (1940); o s of Brig-Gen Sir (Ernest) Richard Fitzpatrick, CBE, DSO (d 1949), and Georgina Ethel, *née* Robison; *b* 14 Dec 1912; *Educ* Eton, RMC Sandhurst; *m* 22 April 1944, Mary Sara, o da of Sir Charles Campbell, 12 Bt, of Auchinbreck (d 1948); 1 s (Brian), 1 da (Sara); *Career* Royal Dragoons 1932, served Palestine 1938-48 (MC), Middle E, Italy, N-W Europe 1939-40 (despatches, DSO, MBE), Brevet Lt-Col 1951, Col 1953, ADC to HM the Queen 1959, Asst Chief of Def Staff (Maj-Gen) 1959-61, Dir of Mil Ops, WO 1962-63, COS BAOR 1964-65, GOCIC NI Cmd 1965, Lt-Gen 1965, Vice CGS 1966-68, C in C BAOR and Cdr NAG 1968-70, Gen 1968, Dep Supreme Cdr Allied Forces Europe 1970-74; Lt-Govr and Cin C Jersey 1974-79; Dep Col Blues and Royals 1969-74, Col 1979-, Gold Stick to the Queen 1979-; Col Cmdt RAC 1971-74; *Recreations* sailing, shooting; *Clubs* RYS, Cavalry and Guards; *Style—* Sir Desmond Fitzpatrick, GCB, DSO, MBE, MC; Belmont, Otley, Ispwich, Suffolk IP6 9PF (☎ 047 339 206)

FITZPATRICK, James Bernard; CBE (1983), DL (1985), JP (1977); s of Bernard Arthur Fitzpatrick (d 1963) and Jessie Emma *née* Blunt; *b* 21 April 1930; *Educ* Bootle GS, London Univ (LLB Law Society Solicitor); *m* 2 Sept 1965, Rosemary, da of Capt Edward Burling Clark, RD RNR of Glust Hendre N Wales; 1 s (Simon b 1967), 1 da (Susan b 1970); *Career* md: Mersey Docks & Harbour Company 1977-84 (chm 1984-87); chm Liverpool Health Authority 1986-, dir: Plan Invest plc 1984-; *Recreations* fell walking, gardening; *Clubs* Oriental, Pilgrims, Racquet (Liverpool); *Style—* James Fitzpatrick Esq, CBE DL JP; 30 Abbey Rd, West Kirby, Wirral L48 7EP (☎ 051 625 9612); Liverpool Health Authority, 1 Myrtle St, Liverpool L7 7DE (☎ 051 709 9290)

FITZPATRICK, Air Marshal Sir John Bernard; KBE (1984), CB (1982); s of Joseph Fitzpatrick (d 1947), and Bridget Fitzpatrick; *b* 15 Dec 1929; *Educ* St Patrick's Sch Dungannon, NI; RAF Coll Cranwell; *m* 1954, Gwendoline Mary, da of Edwin Abbott (d 1971); 2 s, 1 da; *Career* RAF officer: SASO HQ Strike Cmd 1980-83, Air Marshal 1983, AOC No 18 Gp 1983-; *Recreations* reading, DIY; *Clubs* RAF; *Style—* Air Marshal Sir John Fitzpatrick, KBE; c/o Lloyd's Bank Ltd, 1-2 Market Place, Reading, Berks RG1 2EQ

FITZPATRICK, Michael Francis; s of Francis Michael Fitzpatrick, of Northampton, and Elizabeth Mary, *née* Wafer; *b* 7 July 1952; *Educ* St Marys RC, Secondary Sch, Coll of Law Guildford, Surrey; *m* 5 July 1981, Pauline Teresa, da of Paul Panayis Panle, of Northampton; 2 da (Victoria b 1982, Laura b 1984); *Career* slr, chm fell Inst Legal Execs, Northamptonshire Young Slrs Gp 1987-88, ex officio memb Cncl of Northamptonshire Law Soc 1987-88, ptnr Fitzpatrick Dyte & Co; *Recreations* motor, motor cycle sport, family and roundtable activities; *Clubs* Northampton; *Style—* Michael F Fitzpatrick, Esq; (☎ (0604) 844707, (0604) 231467, fax (0604) 231459); 3 The Parade, Market Square, Northampton (fax (0604) 231459)

FITZPATRICK, (Francis) Michael John; s of Francis Latimer FitzPatrick (d 1982), of E Bergholt, Suffolk, and Kathleen Margaret FitzPatrick, *née* Gray; *b* 14 July 1938; *Educ* Brentwood Sch; *m* 4 April 1964, Patricia Hilbery, da of Sir George Frederick Chaplin, CBE, DL, JP (d 1975), of Great Warley, Essex; 1 s (Richard b 1965), 1 da (Kathryn b 1967); *Career* chartered surveyor, ptnr Messrs Hilbery Chaplin (chartered surveyors); Freeman of City of London, Liveryman Worshipful Co of Chartered Surveyors; FRICS; *Recreations* music, travel, gardening; *Clubs* Royal Overseas League; *Style—* Michael FitzPatrick, Esq; Wood House, Stratford St Mary, Suffolk CO7 6LU (☎ 0206 322266); 19 Eastern Rd, Romford, Essex (☎ 0708 45004)

FITZPATRICK, Nicholas David; s of Prof Reginald Jack Fitzpatrick, of Norwoods, Rectory Lane, Heswall, Wirral, Merseyside, and Ruth, *née* Holmes; *b* 23 Jan 1947; *Educ* Bristol GS, Nottingham Univ (BA); *m* 23 Aug 1969, (Patricia) Jill, da of Peter Conway Brotherton; 1 s (Daniel b 12 Jan 1976), 1 da (Paula b 14 Dec 1973); *Career* trainee analyst Friends Provident 1969-72, equity mangr Abbey Life 1972-76, equity mangr then investmt mangr BR Pension Fund 1976-86, ptnr and investmt specialist Bacon & Woodrow 1986-; memb of Soc Investmt Analysts 1972, FIA 1974; *Recreations* rugby, woodwork, reading; *Style—* Nicholas Fitzpatrick, Esq; 9 Grovelands Rd, Purley, Surrey (☎ 01 668 2412); Bacon & Woodrow, Empire Ho, St Martins-le-Grand, London EC1A 4ED (☎ 01 600 2747, fax 01 726 6519)

FITZPATRICK;, Roger; s of Charles Fitzpatrick, and Mary; *b* 8 May 1944; *Educ* Leeds Central HS; *m* 23 June 1976, Patricia Norma, da of Leonard Boniface; 1 s (Nicholas Mark), 1 da (Leanne); *Career* chm & md: Instagraphic Products Ltd, Instagraphic Ltd, Ashfield Gp Ltd, Greenhill Devpts Ltd, Ward Software Ltd; *Recreations* business; *Clubs* IOD; *Style—* Roger Fitzpatrick, Esq; work: (☎ 0532 589893, fax 0532 580720, telex 557266)

FITZROY, Charles; o s of 4 Baron (cr of GB 1780) Southampton (d 1958; descended from the 1 Baron, who was yr bro of 3 Duke of Grafton), and Lady Hilda Mary Dundas (d 1957), da of 1 Marquess of Zetland; disclaimed his peerage for life 1964; *b* 3 Jan 1904; *Educ* Harrow; *m* 1, 22 June 1927, Margaret (d 3 Feb 1931), da of Rev Prebendary Herbert Mackworth Drake, Vicar of Berry Pomeroy, Devon; 1 s; m 2, 12 Jan 1940 (m dis 1944), Mrs Phyllis Joan Leslie, da of Francis Archibald Lloyd; m 3, 3 Feb 1951, Rachel Christine, da of Charles Zaman, of Lille, France; *Heir* (to disclaimed Barony) s, Hon Charles FitzRoy; *Career* late Lt Royal Horse Guards; *Style—* Charles FitzRoy Esq; Preluna Hotel, Sliema, Malta

FITZROY, Hon Charles James; s (by 1 m) and h of Charles FitzRoy, 5 Baron Southampton who disclaimed his peerage for life; *b* 12 August 1928; *Educ* Stowe; *m* 29 May 1951, Pamela Anne, da of Edward Percy Henniker, of Clematis, Yelverton, S

Devon; 1 s (Edward Charles (m Rachel Caroline Vincent *née* Millett) b 1955), 1 da (Geraldine Anne (Mrs Richard Fuller) b 1951); *Style*— Hon Charles FitzRoy

FITZROY, Lord Charles Patrick Hugh; yr s of 11 Duke of Grafton, KG; *b* 7 Jan 1957; *Educ* Eton, Magdalene Coll Cambridge (BA); *m* 16 July 1988, Diana, da of Hubert Miller-Stirling, of Cape Town, SA; *Style*— Lord Charles FitzRoy; Euston Hall, Thetford, Norfolk

FITZROY, Lord Edward Anthony Charles; DL (Norfolk 1986); s of 10 Duke of Grafton (d 1970), and his 2 wife Lucy Eleanor, *née* Barnes (d 1943); *b* 26 August 1928; *Educ* Eton, RMA Sandhurst; *m* 26 April 1956, Veronica Mary, da of Maj Robert Francis Ruttledge, MC, of Doon, Newcastle Greystones, Co Wicklow; 1 s (Michael b 1958), 2 da (Joanna b 1957, Shauna b 1963); *Career* joined Coldstream Gds 1948, Capt 1954, ret 1955; chm Ross Poultry Ltd 1969-75, chm and md Imperial Foods Int Technical Services 1975-82; dir: Imperial Foods Ltd 1969-82, Ross Breeders Ltd, Ross Poultry (New Zealand) Ltd 1982-, Ross Breeders Peninsular (Spain) 1984-, National Poultry Breeders (S Africa) Ltd 1987-; chm: Caledonian Cartridge Co 1987-, Norfolk Playing Fields Assoc 1980-; High Sheriff of Norfolk 1987; cncl memb Norfolk Naturalists Trust; memb Lloyd's; *Recreations* shooting, stalking, gardening, travel; *Clubs* Pratt's, Norfolk; *Style*— Lord Edward FitzRoy, DL; Norton House, Norwich, Norfolk NR14 6RY (☎ 050 846 303); 40 Eland Rd, Battersea, London SW11 (☎ 01 585 2526); office 61-65 Rose Lane, Norwich (☎ 0603 612415, telex 97237)

FITZROY, Lady (Olivia) Rose Mildred; yst da of 11 Duke of Grafton, KG; *b* 1 August 1963; *Style*— Lady Rose FitzRoy; Euston Hall, Thetford, Norfolk

FITZROY NEWDEGATE, Hon James; s and h of 3 Viscount Daventry, JP, DL; *b* 27 July 1960; *Style*— The Hon James Fitzroy Newdegate

FITZSIMMONS, Rt Hon William Kennedy; PC (NI) 1965, JP (Belfast 1951); *b* 31 Jan 1909; *Educ* Skegoniell National School, Belfast Junior Technical School; *m* 1935, May Elizabeth Lynd; 2 da; *Career* memb Royal Soc of Health; chm Belfast City and Dist Water Cmmrs 1954-55 (member 1948-57); pres Duncairn (Belfast) Unionist Assoc; Northern Ireland Parl: MP Duncairn 1956-72; parly sec: Min of Commerce 1961-65, Min of Home Affrs 1963-64; at Devpt Min 1964-65; min of Educn 1965-66 and 1968-69; min of: Devpt 1966-68, Health and Social Servs 1969-72; *Style*— The Rt Hon William Fitzsimmons, JP; 16 Cleaver Court, Cleaver Ave, Malone Road, Belfast BT9 5JA

FITZWALTER, 21 Baron (E 1295); (Fitzwalter) Brook Plumptre; JP (Kent 1949); s of George Beresford Plumptre (d 1934), yr bro of 20 Baron (d 1932, but the present Lord FitzWalter was not summoned to Parl till 1953); Lord FitzWalter is eleventh in descent from Frances, w of Sir Thomas Mildmay and half sis of 3 Earl of Sussex (whose 2 w Frances, da of Sir William Sydney, of Penshurst, left £5,000 to establish a Cambridge Coll to be called 'Sydney-Sussex'); Frances was twelfth in descent from Robert FitzWalter, the leading enforcer among the Barons of Magna Carta; by his w (and cousin) Mary Augusta, *née* Plumptre (d 1953); *b* 15 Jan 1914; *Educ* Diocesan Coll Cape Town, Jesus Coll Cambridge; *m* 29 Sept 1951, Margaret Melesina, 3 da of Herbert William Deedes, JP (d 1966), and sis of William Deedes, sometime ed of the Daily Telegraph; 5 s (Julian, Henry, George, William, Francis); *Heir* s, Hon Julian Plumptre; *Career* served WW II Capt; landowner & farmer (2,500 acres); *Recreations* shooting, gardening; *Style*— The Rt Hon the Lord FitzWalter; Goodnestone Park, Canterbury, Kent (☎ (0304) 840218)

FITZWILLIAM, Countess; Joyce Elizabeth; da of Lt-Col Philip Langdale, OBE, TD, JP, DL (ggs of 17 Baron Stourton); *b* 25 April 1898; *m* 1, 9 May 1922 (m dis 1955), 2 and last Viscount FitzAlan of Derwent, OBE (d 1962); 2 da (Hon Mrs Edward Ward, Hon Lady Hastings, *qqv*); m 2, 3 April 1956, 10 and last Earl Fitzwilliam (d 1979); *Style*— The Rt Hon Countess Fitzwilliam; Milton, Peterborough PE6 7AA

FITZWILLIAMS, Maj Reginald Clixby Lloyd; JP (1958), DL (1970); yr s of Maj Cuthbert Collingwood Lloyd Fitzwilliams, MC (d 1960), and Hilda Wynnefred, *née* Burkinshaw (d 1962); first cous of Maj Robert Campbell Lloyd Fitzwilliams, *qv*; *b* 2 Dec 1916; *Educ* Eton, Magdalene Coll Cambridge; *m* 13 Feb 1943, Pauline Agatha, da of Jordayne Cave; 2 da; *Career* chartered accountant, chm Humberside CC 1980-81; *Style*— Maj Reginald Fitzwilliams, JP, DL; Hazeldene, The Avenue, Healing, Grimsby

FITZWILLIAMS, Maj Robert Campbell Lloyd; TD; er s of late Duncan Campbell Lloyd Fitzwilliams, CMG, Lt-Col RAMC (TF) (d 1954), of The Temple, nr Bray, Berks, and his 1 wife Mary Elizabeth, *née* Filley (d 1919); first cous of Maj Reginald Clixby Lloyd Fitzwilliams, *qv*; *b* 9 Feb 1909,, London; *Educ* Oundle, CCC Cambridge; *m* 1, 10 Aug 1948, Natalie Jura Stratford (d 1965), o da of Col George Stratford Mardall, OBE, JP, of Cape, S Africa; 1 s (Richard, ed Int Who's Who, m 1981, Gillian Savill); m 2, 1973, Mary (d 1976), widow of Bernard Sunley and John R V Sunley-Cooper, and da of William Goddard, of Waxlow Manor, Southall, Berks; m 3, 1978, Joan Lucy (former cllr Royal Boro of Kensington and Chelsea, dep mayor 1976), da of Francis R M Davis, of Manor Farm, Upton St Leonards, Glos; *Career* served WW II RA, Norway, Western Desert (despatches Tobruk 1942), Germany; late dir Bernard and Mary Sunley Ltd; Freeman City of London; memb of the Soc of Genealogists; *Recreations* shooting, fishing, golf; *Clubs* Naval & Military, Royal St George's Golf (Sandwich); *Style*— Maj Robert Fitzwilliams, TD; 84 North End Road, London NW11 7SY (☎ 01 455 7393)

FLANAGAN, Prof Terence Patrick (Terry); OBE (1987); s of Thomas Flanagan (d 1933), of Dudley, Worcs, and Harriet Selina, *née* Beard (d 1978); *b* 25 Sept 1924; *Educ* St Josephs Sch Dudley, Queen Mary Coll London Univ (BSc, MSc); *m* 1, 9 July 1949 (m dis 1980), Marian Margaret, da of Horace Riddleston (d 1954), of Chesterfield, Derbys; 3 da (Helen (Mrs Russell) b 6 Feb 1955, Jane b 19 Jan 1957, Margaret b 19 Sept 1959); m 2, 31 Jan 1981, Sheila Mary, da of John Wallace McDonald, of Bromley, Kent; *Career* Fl-Sgt RAF Aircrew 1943-47; electronics designer Marconi Instruments 1950-57; SIRA Ltd: head of nucleonics dept 1957-63, head of indust measurement div 1963-74, exec dir 1974-79, md 1979-87; chm: Ometron Ltd 1981-87, pres Inst of Measurement & Control 1983, Honeywell Int Medallist 1987; conslt: UKAEA 1964-88, indust conslt 1987-; memb Metrology & Standards Requirements Bd DTI 1980-87, visiting prof City Univ, 2nd chm Sch of Engrg Advsy Ctee 1980-; ed Measurement & Control series 1987-; non-exec dir: Ometron Ltd 1987-, SIRA Safety Servs Ltd 1987-; govr Ravensbourne Coll of Design & Communication 1984-; Freeman City of London 1982, Liveryman Worshipful Co of Scientific Instrument Makers 1982; FIEE, FInstP, FInstMC; *Recreations* cricket, music, DIY, Local Affairs; *Clubs* 54; *Style*— Prof Terry Flanagan, OBE; 11 Eastgate Rd, Tenterden, Kent (☎ 05806 4070); 19 Foxleas Ct, Spencer Rd, Bromley, Kent

FLANDERS, Dennis; s of Bernard Charles Flanders (d 1964), of Woodford, London E18, and Jessie Marguerite, *née* Sandell (d 1964); *b* 2 July 1915; *Educ* Merchant Taylors', various art schs; *m* 1952, Dalma Joan Darnley, da of Jack Darnley Taylor (d 1949); 1 s (Julian b 1956), 1 da (Alison b 1953); *Career* Staff Sergeant RE 1942-46; artist (drawings of Britain, particularly elaborate architectural compositions - townscapes and landscapes in black and white and water-colour); has had series of drawings in Yorkshire Post, Birmingham Post, Sunday Times, Illustrated London News; has occupied the last 50 yrs in proclaiming the superior beauties of the landscapes and townscapes of England, Wales, Scotland and Ireland in more than 3000 drawings and water-colours, 224 of which (half in colour and half in black and white) are reproduced in book (*see below*); RBA 1970, ARWS 1970, RWS 1976; *Books* Dennis Flanders' Britannia (1984); *Recreations* travel; *Clubs* Art Workers' Guild (master 1975); *Style*— Dennis Flanders Esq; 51 Gt Ormond St, London WC1N 3HZ (☎ 01 405 9317); Baker's Cross House, Cranbrook, Kent TN17 3AQ (☎ 0580 712018)

FLANNERY, Martin Henry; MP (Lab) Sheffield Hillsborough Feb 1974-; s of Martin Flannery of Sheffield; *b* 2 Mar 1918,Sheffield,; *Educ* De La Salle GS, Sheffield Teacher Training Coll; *m* 1949, Blanche Mary; 1 s, 2 da; *Career* Middle Sch head teacher 1969-74 (dep head 1965-69), exec memb NUT 1969-1974, sponsored by ASTMS, former sec PLP Chile gp, chm Tribune Gp 1980-82, chm PLP N Ireland Ctee, memb Select Ctee on Educn Science and Arts 1981-; *Recreations* music, literature, rambling; *Style*— Martin Flannery, Esq, MP; 53 Linaker Road, Sheffield (☎ 0742 334911)

FLATHERS, Keith Arthur; s of Willie Flathers (d 1978), of Batley, York, and Ethel Barbara, *née* Sykes; *b* 15 Jan 1935; *Educ* Dewsbury Wheelwright, Univ of Leeds (LLB); *m* 8 April 1961, Shirley Ann, da of Jack Campin Wheeler, BEM; 2 s (John, Christopher), 1 da (Elizabeth); *Career* Nat Serv 1960-62, RASC attached to legal aid section BAOR; slr Sharrott Barnes & Co Lichfield (now sr ptnr) served local and area legal aid ctee 1971; memb: Guild of Stewards Lichfield Cathedral, Law Soc 1959; *Recreations* music, cricket, gardening; *Style*— Keith Flathers, Esq; Pool Furlong, 33 The Friary, Lichfield, Staffs WS13 6QH (☎ 0543 251 846); 30-32 St John Street, Lichfield, Staffs WS13 6PE (☎ 0543 414 426, fax 0543 250 623)

FLAVELL, Geoffrey; s of William Alfred Flavell, JP, of Dunedin, New Zealand (d 1953); *b* 23 Feb 1913; *Educ* Waitaki and Otago HS, Univ of Otago, St Bartholomew's Hosp London; *m* 1943, Joan Margaret, o da of late Sydney Ewart Adams, of Hawkwell, Essex; *Career* served RAF 1942-46, advsr in surgery, Mediterranean and M East Cmd, Wing Cdr, ret 1958; former conslt cardio-thoracic surgn to Hosps: NE Thames Regnl Health Authy, Royal Masonic Hosp, LCC and British Legion Hosp; hon conslt cardio-thoracic surgn to: The London Hosp (and former head of dept of Cardio-Vascular and Thoracic Surgery), Chelmsford Gp Hosps, Harlow and Epping Gp, Whipps Cross Hosp 1978-; travelling British Cncl lectr Middle East and Far East 1961; chm advsy ctee on cardiothoracic surgery to RHA 1970-78; FRCS, FRCP; *Books* Introduction to Chest Surgery (1957), The Oesophagus (1963), Chest Diseases (1963), Scientific Foundations of Surgery (1974); *Recreations* architecture, art, history, wine & food; *Clubs* RAF; *Style*— Geoffrey Flavell, Esq; 9 Camden Cres, Bath BA1 5HY (☎ 0225 444903)

FLAVELLE, Sir (Joseph) David Ellsworth; 3 Bt (UK 1917); s of Sir (Joseph) Ellsworth Flavelle, 2 Bt (d 1977), and Muriel, *née* McEachren (d 1982); *b* 9 Nov 1921; *m* 1 Sept 1942, Muriel Barbara, da of David Reginald Morton; 3 da; *Heir* none; *Career* Lt-Cdr RCNVR, ret; *Clubs* Albany, Canadian, Empire (all Toronto); *Style*— Sir David Flavelle, Bt; 1420 Watersedge Rd, Clarkson, Ontario L5J 1A4, Canada

FLAWN THOMAS, Lady Rose Alice Elizabeth Gascoyne; *née* Cecil; da of 6 Marquess of Salisbury, *qv*; *b* 11 Sept 1956; *Educ* privately; *m* 9 Feb 1985, Mark Flawn Thomas, yst s of Peter Flawn Thomas, of Shortbrige Hill, Sussex; *Career* artist; *Recreations* travelling, squash, opera, films; *Style*— Lady Rose Flawn Thomas

FLAXMAN, Charles; s of William Henry Flaxman, and Amy, *née* Williams; *b* 12 April 1926; *Educ* Owen's Sch London; *m* 7 April 1947, (Muriel) Jane, *née* Colbear; 2 s (Roger b 1951, Jeremy b 1954), 1 da (Sara b 1953); *Career* Nat Serv 1944-48, cmmnd Royal Fusiliers 1945 (Capt 1947); worked for various Lloyd's Brokers 1942-61, underwriter Frank Barber & Ors Lloyds 1982-86 (dep underwriter 1962-81), ptnr Morgan Fentiman & Barber Lloyds 1982-, conslt Bowring Professional Indemnity Fund Ltd 1987-; memb Saffron Walden Town Cncl 1979-87; memb Worshipful Co of Insurers 1984; ACII 1952; *Recreations* music, walking, reading, work; *Style*— Charles Flaxman, Esq; Birbecks, Redgate Lane, Sewards End, Saffron Walden, Essex (☎ 0799 27364)

FLAXMAN, Edward (Ted) Wasley; s of Edward George Flaxman of Forest Lodge, The Common, Southwold, Suffolk, and Ellen Ashton *née* Youngman; *b* 7 April 1928; *Educ* Culford Sch, Imperial Coll, (BSc 1952, DIC 1957); *m* 2 Apr 1955, Joan Edwina, da of the late Edwin John Knight, 2 s (Peter Edward b 1959, John Wasley, b 1962) 1 da (Penelope Ann, b 1957); *Career* Nat Serv 2 Lt RE 1947-49; FICE memb Int Soc for Trenchless Engrg, fell Fellowship of Engrg, pntr Binnie and Partners 1973 (assoc 1968- 72, res engr 1958-60, joined 1952; *Recreations* bird watching, genealogy; *Style*— Ted Flaxman Esq; The Coach House, Capenor, Coopers Hill Road, Nutfield, Surrey RH1 4HS (☎ 0737 823454); Binnie and Partners, Grosvenor House, 69 London Road, Redhill, Surrey RH1 1LQ (☎ 0737 774155, fax 0737 772767, telex 24552)

FLECKER, James William; s of Henry Lael Oswald, CBE (d 1958), and Mary Patricia, *née* Hessey; *b* 15 August 1939; *Educ* Marlborough, Brasenose Coll Oxford (BA); *m* 22 July 1967, Mary Rose, da of Noel Jeremy Firth, of Sandal Yorks; 3 da (Rachel b 1969, Lara b 1970, Brontë b 1974); *Career* asst master: Sydney GS NSW 1962-63, Latymer Upper Sch Hammersmith 1964-67; housemaster Marlborough 1975-80 (asst master 1967-80), headmaster Ardingly 1980-; *Recreations* hockey, flute playing, writing children's operas; *Style*— James Flecker, Esq; Headmaster's House, Ardingly Coll, Haywards Heath, W Sussex RH17 6SQ (☎ 0444 892330)

FLEET, Kenneth George; s of Frederick Major Fleet, and Elizabeth Doris, *née* Brassey; *b* 12 Sept 1929; *Educ* Calday Grange GS Cheshire LSE (BSc Econ); *m* 1953, Alice Brenda, da of Capt H R Wilkinson, RD, RNR; 3 s (Ian b 1957, Malcolm b 1959, Graham b 1964), 1 da (Elizabeth b 1962); *Career* journalist of commerce Liverpool 1950-52; Sunday Times 1955-56; dep city ed Birmingham Post 1956-58; dep fin ed Guardian 1958-63, dep city ed Daily Telegraph 1963; city ed: Sunday Telegraph 1963-66, Daily Telegraph 1966-77; ed - business news Sunday Times 1977-78; city ed Sunday Express 1978-82, city editor-in-chief Express Newspapers plc 1982-83, exec ed (fin and indust) The Times 1983-87; dir Young Vic 1976-83, chm Chichester Festival Theatre 1985- (dir 1984); Wincott Award (1974); *Recreations* theatre, books, sport; *Clubs* MCC, Lord's Taverners, Piltdown GC; *Style*— Kenneth Fleet, Esq; Chetwynd House, 24 St Swithin's Lane, London EC4N 8AE

FLEET, Dr Stephen George; s of George Fleet (d 1976), of Lewes, Sussex, and Elsie Fleet; *b* 20 Sept 1936; *Educ* Brentwood Sch, Lewes County GS, St John's Coll Cambridge (BA MA PhD); *Career* registrary Univ of Cambridge 1983-, univ lectr in mineralogy at Cambridge 1967-83, bursar Downing Coll 1974-83 (pres 1983-85, vice master 1985-88); chm: Bd of Examinations 1974-83, Bursars' Ctee 1980-83; tstee of Fndn of Edward Storey 1977-; memb: Cncl of Senate Univ of Cambridge 1979-83, Ctee of Mgmnt of Charities Property Unit Tst 1983-88, Fin Ctee of Int Union of Crystallography 1987-; tstee Mineralogical Soc of GB 1977-87; fell: Fitzwilliam House Cambridge 1963-66, Downing Coll 1973-; fndn fell Fitzwilliam Coll 1966-73; FInstP; *Recreations* books, music, history of Sussex; *Clubs* Athenaeum; *Style*— Dr Stephen G Fleet; Downing College, Cambridge CB2 1DQ (☎ 0223 334843); University Registry, Old Schools, Cambridge (☎ 0223 332294)

FLEMING, Lady (Francesca Georgina) Caroline; *née* Acheson; er da of 6 Earl of Gosford (d 1966), and his 1 wife Francesca Augusta Maria, *née* Cagiati; *b* 23 April 1940; *m* 15 Sept 1967, David Wallace Fleming, s of Wallace Fleming, of Santa Barbara, Cal, USA; 1 s (Alexander b 1968); *Style*— Lady Caroline Fleming; 1045 5th Ave, New York 10028, NY, USA

FLEMING, Christopher Michael; 2 s of Capt Michael Valentine Fleming (d 1940), and Letitia Blanche (later Mrs James Currie Thomson), da of Hon Malcolm Algernon Borthwick (granted rank of a Baron's son 1913), s of Sir Thomas Borthwick, 1 Bt; *b* 8 May 1937; *Educ* Eton; *m* 1975, Judith Marion, da of Col Godfrey Jeans, of Salisbury, Wilts ; 2 da; *Career* dir Thomas Borthwick & Sons Ltd; *Recreations* shooting, fishing, racing; *Clubs* Turf; *Style*— Christopher Fleming Esq; Briff Farm, Bucklebury Common, nr Reading, Berks RG7 6SS (☎ 0635 63814); Thomas Borthwick & Sons plc, Priory House, St Johns Lane, London EC1M 4BX (☎ 01 253 8661)

FLEMING, Ven David; s of John Frederick Fleming, BEM (d 1976), of Norfolk, and Emma Fleming; *b* 8 June 1937; *Educ* King Edward VII GS Kings Lynn, Kelham Theol Coll; *m* 1966, Elizabeth Anne Marguerite, da of Bernard Bayleys Hughes (d 1947), of Birmingham; 3 s (Christopher b 1967, Nicholas b 1968, Matthew b 1972), 1 da (Fiona b 1970); *Career* curate St Margaret Walton on the Hill 1963-67, chaplain HM Gaynes Hall, vicar Great Staughton 1968-76, rural dean St Neots 1972-76, vicar Whittlesey 1976-85, rural dean March 1977-82, hon canon Ely Cathedral 1982-, archdeacon of Wisbech 1984-, vicar of Wisbech St Mary 1985-88; *Recreations* television, tennis, extolling Hunstanton; *Clubs* Whittlesey rotary; *Style*— The Ven the Archdeacon of Wisbech; 20 Barton Rd, Ely, Vambs CB7 4DE (☎ 0353 663632)

FLEMING, Hon Mrs (Dorothy Charmian); *née* Hermon-Hodge; 3 da of 2 Baron Wyfold, DSO, MVO (d 1942), by Dorothy, *née* Fleming, aunt of Peter and Ian, the writers; *b* 4 Jan 1913; *m* 12 May 1938, her 1 cous, Maj Richard Evelyn Fleming, MC, 3 son of late Maj Valentine Fleming, DSO, MP, and yr bro of Peter and Ian; 5 s (two of whom m sisters, daughters of Sir Hereward Wake, 14 Bt), 3 da; *Style*— Hon Mrs Fleming; Leygore Manor, Northleach, Glos (☎ 60234)

FLEMING, Dr Ian; s of John Fleming (d 1939), of Glasgow, and Catherine, *née* McLean (d 1970); *b* 19 Nov 1906; *Educ* Hyndland Sch Glasgow, Glasgow Sch of Art, Jordanhill Trg Coll Glasgow; *m* 27 April 1943, Catherine Margaret, da of Walter John Weetch (d 1948); 1 s (Alisdair Ian b 4 Dec 1949), 2 da (Elspeth Jane b 15 Oct 1944, Fiona Margaret b 10 Oct 1947); *Career* WWII serv, Police War Res Glasgow Police F Div 1940-43, cmmn into Army, 2 Lt Pioneer Corps 1943-46, serv Normandy, Holland and Germany, 30 Corps Capt 1945; sr lectr Glasgow Sch of Art 1946-48 (asst lectr 1931-41), warden Patrick Allen and Fraser Art Coll Hospitalfield Arbroath 1948-54, head Grays Sch of Art RGIT Aberdeen 1954-72; chm: Peacock Printmakers Workshop Aberdeen 1972-85, Cyrenians Workshop 1985-; artworks in many public galleries in Britain, France, Norway and private collections in America, Canada, Germany, South Africa; Hon LLD Univ of Aberdeen 1984; memb RSW 1947, ARSA 1956; memb: RSA, Royal W of Eng Acad 1975, Royal Glasgow Inst of Fine Arts 1984; *Recreations* art only (being as good an artist as I can be); *Style*— Dr Ian Fleming; 15 Fonthill Rd, Aberdeen AB1 2UN (☎ 0224 580680)

FLEMING, Rear Adm Sir John; KBE (1960), DSC (1944); s of James Fleming, of Jarrow, Co Durham; *b* 2 May 1904; *Educ* County Sch Jarrow, St John's Coll Cambridge; *m* 1930, Jean Law, da of James Stuart Gillitt, of S Shields, Co Durham; *Career* RN 1925, Instr Cdr 1939, served at Admty (Naval Weather Service) 1939-42, Fleet Instr and Fleet meteorlogical offr on Staff of C-in-C Home Fleet 1942-44, Fleet meteorlogical offr to Allied Naval Cdr Expeditionary Force 1944-45, asst dir Naval Weather Serv 1945-47, dep dir 1947-49, Instr Capt 1950, Fleet instr and meteorlogical offr on Staff of C-in-C Home Fleet 1950-51, cmd instr offr on staff of C-in-C The Nore 1951-52, on staff of Dir Naval Educn Serv 1952-56, Instr Rear Adm 1956, dir Naval Educn Serv 1956-60, ret; *Style*— Rear Adm Sir John Fleming, KBE, DSC; Mullion Cottage, Tanners Lane, Haslemere, Surrey (☎ 0428 2412)

FLEMING, John Grierson; s of Richard Grierson Fleming of Riseholme, Lincoln (d 1966), and Mildred Mary, *née* Birkett (d 1984); *b* 2 Feb 1926; *Educ* Lincoln Sch Lincoln, Trinity Coll Cambridge (BA later MA, LLB later LLM); *m* 29 Aug 1953, Margaret, da of John Edward Rayner, of Lincoln (d 1960); 1 s (Alistair b 1958), 2 da (Amanda b 1955, Nicola b 1961); *Career* RA short course Edinburgh Univ 1944-45, primary trg corps trg OCTU 1945-46, cmmnd RA 1946, ADC to GOC 5AA Gp 1946-48, (Capt 1947); articled clerk Johnson Jecks and Landons 1950-52, admitted solr 1953 (first in order of merit Law Soc final exam); awarded Scott scholarship, Clements Inn, Maurice Nordon, City of London Solrs Co Grotius, and John Mackerell prizes, asst slr Reynolds Perry Jones and Crawford 1953-54, ptnr Evill and Coleman 1955-58 (asst solr 1954-55); admin ptnr Stephenson Harwood 1983- (joined 1958 head of law dept 1973-83, ptnr 1959-); club Capt Beaconsfield CC 1979- (hon sec 1962-79); freeman: Gardeners Co (clerk 1969-83) Solicitors Co; craftsman Gardeners of Glasgow; *Recreations* cricket, golf, gardening, travel, maps, watercolours; *Clubs* Western (Glasgow), Gresham, RSO, MCC; *Style*— John G Fleming, Esq; Quantocks, 73 Burkes Road, Beaconsfield, Bucks, HP9 1PP (☎ (0494) 674 264); Stephenson Harwood, One St Paul's Churchyard, London, EC4M 8SH (☎ 01 329 4422), fax 01 606 0822, telex 886 789

FLEMING, John Marley; s of David A Fleming, of Methuen, Massachusetts USA, and Mary L, *née* Marley; *b* 4 April 1930; *Educ* Harvard (BA), Harvard Sch of Business Admin (MBA); *m* 1961, Jeanne Claire, da of Edward Retelle, of Lawrence, Massachusetts; 1 s, 2 da; *Career* served Lt USN; chm and chief exec Vauxhall Motors 1982-; *Recreations* skiing, sailing, golf; *Clubs* Harpenden Golf, Harvard (London); *Style*— John Fleming Esq; Barnards, Oakhurst Ave, Harpenden, Herts AL5 2ND; c/o Vauxhall Motors plc, Kimpton Rd, Luton, Beds (☎ (0582) 21122)

FLEMING, Rt Rev (William) Launcelot Scott; KCVO (1976); yst s of Robert Alexander Fleming, MD, LLD, FRCPE, of Innerhadden, Kinloch Rannoch, Perthshire, and Edinburgh; *b* 7 August 1906; *Educ* Rugby, Trinity Hall, Cambridge (MA), (Westcott House Cambridge, (DD), Commonwealth Fund Fellowship Yale Univ (MS); *m* 1965, Jane, widow of Anthony Agutter; *Career* ordained 1933, chaplain and geologist British Graham Land Expedition to Antarctic 1934-37 (Polar Medal), fell and chaplain Trinity Hall Cambridge 1933-49, dean 1937-49, chaplain RNVR 1940-44 (hon chaplain RNR 1950), dir Service Ordination Candidates 1944-46, dir Scott Polar Research Inst Cambridge 1947-49, Bishop of Portsmouth 1949-59, Bishop of Norwich 1959-71, dean of Windsor 1971-76, domestic chaplain to HM The Queen 1971-76; register Order of the Garter 1971-76; chm govrs: Portsmouth GS 1950-59, Canford Sch 1954-60; chm: Church of England Youth Cncl 1950-61, Archbp's Cmmn of Church's Needs and Resources 1963-73; hon vice-pres Royal Geographical Soc 1961; vice-chm Parly Gp on World Govt 1969-71; memb Royal Cmmn on Environmental Pollution 1969-71; pres Young Explorers Trust 1976-79; memb governing body United World Coll of the Atlantic; hon fell Trinity Hall, Cambridge 1956, Hon DCL (E Anglia) 1976; visitor (formerly govr) Bryanston Sch 1984; FRSE; *Style*— The Rt Rev Launcelot Fleming, KCVO; Tithe Barn, Poyntington, nr Sherborne, Dorset DT9 4LF (☎ 096 322 479)

FLEMING, Robert Atholl; s of Atholl Fleming, MBE (d 1972), and Phyllis Wallace, *née* Best (d 1983); *b* 19 July 1933; *Educ* Cranbrook Sch, Sydney; *m* 15 Sept 1982, Marion Heather, da of Maurice Leigh (d 1969); *Career* TV Documentary prodr, dir and writer; md ARGO Prodns Ltd ; *Clubs* Garrick, MCC, Royal Sydney GC; *Style*— Robert Fleming, Esq; 5 South Villas, Camden Square, London NU11 9BJ (☎ 01 267 3316)

FLEMING, (Dr) Thomas (Tom) Kelman; OBE (1980); s of Rev Peter Fleming (d 1939); *b* 29 June 1927; *Educ* Daniel Stewart's Coll Edinburgh; *Career* actor, writer, producer, broadcaster, co-founder Edinburgh Gateway Co 1953-65, RSC 1962-64, founder and dir Royal Lyceum Theatre Co 1965-66, govr Scottish Theatre Tst 1980-82, dir Scottish Theatre Company 1982-, BBC Radio commentator Coronation 1953, BBC TV commentator on over 250 national and state occasions incl: Silver Wedding 1972, Princess Anne's Wedding 1973, Prince of Wales's Wedding 1979, State visits to USA and Japan, Silver Jubilee 1977, The Queen Mother's 80 Birthday Celebrations 1980, The Queen's 60 Birthday 1986, Queen's Birthday Parade annually since 1970, Cenotaph Service of Remembrance 1961, and annually since 1965, Installations of Archibishop of Canterbury (1975, 1980), two Papal Inaugurations (1978), funerals of Duke of Gloucester, Duke of Windsor, Montgomery of Alamein, Mountbatten of Burma, King Frederick of Denmark, Marshal Tito, Princess Grace, Cardinal Heenan, Pope John Paul I; DUniv (Heriot-Watt 1984); FRSAMD (1986); *Books* So That Was Spring (poems), Miracle at Midnight (play), Voices Out of the Air; *Recreations* hill-walking, music; *Clubs* Royal Cwlth Soc, Scottish Arts (Hon), Royal Scottish Pipers' Soc (Hon); *Style*— Tom Fleming Esq, OBE; 56 Murrayfield Gdns, Edinburgh; Tomfarclas, Ballindalloch, Banffshire

FLEMINGTON, Roger; s of Walter Harold Flemington (d 1977), of Market Drayton, Shrops, and Mary Elizabeth Julia, *née* Stone (d 1985); *b* 7 May 1932; *Educ* Nantwich and Acton GS; *m* 3 Sept 1955, Doreen Helen, da of Claude George Smyter (d 1968), of London; *Career* Nat Serv RAF 1950-52; Nat West Bank Gp 1948-: md The Diners Club Ltd 1975-77, sr int exec 1978-79, chief int exec Asia, Australasia and Africa 1979-81, asst gen mangr int banking div 1981-84, dir Westments Ltd 1984-, gen mangr premises div 1984-86, gen mangr domestic banking div 1986-88, chief exec UK fin Serv 1989-; dir: Coutts & Co 1986-, dir Nat West Bank plc 1988-, Lombard North Central plc 1989-; memb: cncl Chartered Inst of Bankers 1986- (gen purposes ctee 1987-), London & Scottish Bankers Ctee on Private Fin for Housing 1988-; Freeman City of London 1979, Liveryman Worshipful Co of Woolmen; FCIB 1986; *Recreations* music, flyfishing, country pursuits, antiques, travel, reading; *Clubs* MCC; *Style*— Roger Flemington, Esq; Larkrise, Rectory Lane, Buckland, Betchworth, Surrey (☎ 073 784 4522); National Westminster Bank plc, 41 Lothbury, London EC2P 2BP (☎ 01 726 1616)

FLEMMING, John Stanton; s of Sir Gilbert Nicolson Flemming, KCB (d 1981), and Virginia, *née* Coit; *b* 6 Feb 1941; *Educ* Rugby, Trinity Coll Oxford, Nuffield Oxford (BA); *m* 1963, Jean Elizabeth, da of George Briggs (d 1982); 3 s (Edward b 1968, Thomas b 1970, William b 1973), 1 da (Rebecca b 1966); *Career* economist; offical fell and bursar Nuffield Coll Oxford 1965-80, ed Economic Journal 1976-80; chief advsr Bank of England 1980-83, economic adviser to the Gow Bank of England 1983-88, memb exec dir Bank of England 1988 cncl and exec ctee Royal Economic Soc 1980-; memb Advsy Bd on Res Cncls 1986-; *Clubs* Reform; *Style*— John Flemming, Esq; Bank of England, Threadneedle Street, London (☎ 01 601 4444)

FLEMMING, Lady; Virginia; da of Stanton Coit, of London; *m* 1935, Sir Gilbert Flemming, KCB (d 1981), sometime memb Restrictive Practices Court and s of Percy Flemming, FRCS, of London; 2 s, 2 da; *Style*— Lady Flemming; G3 Burton Lodge, Portinscale Rd, SW15 (☎ 01 874 9375)

FLEMONS, Kenneth John; s of Sidney Flemons (d 1968), of Eastbourne, and Amy Elizabeth, *née* Davies (d 1972); *b* 27 Jan 1924; *Educ* All Saints Sch, Bloxham & Cathedral Sch Shanghai, Northampton Engrg Coll London (now City Univ); *m* 19 March 1955, Margaret Joan Ogilvy, da of Sydney Duncan Main (d 1961), of Purley; 1 s (Gordon b 4 July 1959), 1 da (Rosemary (Mrs C Bayford) b 18 March 1957); *Career* interned by Japanese in Lunghwa Camp Shanghai (as civilian) 1941-45; chartered civil engr; Taylor Woodrow Construction 1949-53, Air Miny Works Directorate 1953-55, Sir Frederick Snow & Ptnrs 1955-88 (assoc 1964-88, conslt 1988-); hon fell Inst of Water and Environmental Mgmnt (memb cncl 1987-88); CEng, FICE, Hon FIPHE (memb cncl 1979-87, pres 1986-87); *Recreations* walking, gardening; *Clubs* Royal Overseas League; *Style*— Kenneth Flemons, Esq; Belgrove, 45 Rose Bushes, Epsom Downs, Surrey KT17 3NT (☎ 0737 354 821)

FLETCHER; *see*: Aubrey-Fletcher

FLETCHER, Adrian James; s of Col Michael J R Fletcher MBE, of Folkestone, Kent, and Marguerite, *née* Sproule; *b* 16 Dec 1943; *Educ* Sir Roger Manwood's Sch Sandwich Kent, Imperial Coll London Univ (BSc, MSc, DIC); *m* 20 April 1974, Carolyn Lennox, da of Arthur E Davis (d 1975), of Sydney, Australia; 2 s (James E Fletcher b 1975, Nicholas A L Fletcher b 1980), 1 da (Emily C Fletcher b 1978);

Career lectr in business policy Graduate Business Sch Univ NSW Aust 1972-75, mangr corporate planning Glass Containers Ltd Sydney 1975-79, princ Adrian Fletcher & Assocs Sydney 1979-80, chm Petroleum Securities Group 1981-, fir Morganite Aust Pty Ltd 1981-, exec ctee memb and gen mangr gp planning Westpac Banking Corpn Sydney 1983-87 (chief mangr 1980-83), gen mangr global investmt banking Westpac Banking Corpn London 1987-;ARCS, FAIM; *Recreations* music, reading; *Clubs* Australian (Sydney), Union (Sydney), Royal Sydney Yacht Squadron; *Style*— Adrian Fletcher, Esq; Westpac Banking Corporation, Walbrook House, 23 Walbrook, London EC4N 8LD (☎ 01 867 7500, fax 01 626 2171, telex 888641)

FLETCHER, Alan; s of Bernard Fletcher (d 1936), and Dorothy Murphy; *b* 27 Sept 1931; *Educ* Christ's Hosp, Royal Coll of Arts (ARCA), Sch of Design and Architecture Yale Univ (MFA); *m* 5 July 1956, Paola, da of Raffaele Baigi (d 1935); 1 da (Raffaella b 1961); *Career* graphic designer; NY clients: Container Corp, Fortune Magazine, IBM -1959; co founder Fletcher/Forhes/Gill, (clients: Pirelli, Cunard, Olivetti, Reuters) 1959-; founder memb Pentagram (clients: Lloyds, Daimler-Benz, IBM Europe, Mandarin Oriental Gp) 1972-; consultant OUN Int Tokyo; gold awards: Designers & Art Director's Assoc, NY 'One Show'; outstanding achievement medal SIAD 1982; Royal Designer for Industry; FSIAD; former pres Designers & Art Directors Assoc, internat pres Alliance Graphique Internationale 1982-85; *Publications* co-author: Identity Kits - a pictorial survey of visual signs, Graphic-Design - a visual comparison, A sign systems manual, Living by design, Ideas on design; *Style*— Alan Fletcher, Esq; Pentagram, 11 Needham Rd, London W11 2RP (☎ 01 229 3477, telex 8952000 Penta G, fax 727 9932)

FLETCHER, Hon Sir Alan Roy; s of Alexander Roy Fletcher (d 1957), of Pittsworth, Qld, and Rosina Wilhelmina, *née* McIntyre; *b* 26 Jan 1907; *Educ* Pittsworth State Sch Qld, Scots Coll Warwick Qld; *m* 1934, Enid Phair, da of James Thompson (d 1945), of Ashburton, New Zealand; 1 s (and 1 decd), 2 da; *Career* MLA Qld (Country Party) for Cunningham 1953-74, speaker 1957-60, min for Lands 1960-68, min for Education and Cultural Activities 1968-75; kt 1972; *Recreations* shooting, billiards, croquet; *Style*— The Hon Sir Alan Fletcher; Te Mata, Mount Tyson, Qld 4356, Australia (☎ Irongate 938184)

FLETCHER, Sir Alexander MacPherson (Alex); s of Alexander Fletcher (d 1960), of Greenock, and Margaret Muirhead; *b* 26 August 1929; *Educ* Greenock HS, Inst of CAs; *m* 1950, Christine Anne Buchanan; 2 s, 1 da; *Career* CA; mktg mangr IBM 1956-64, dir Gaskell & Chambers 1964-70, in private practice 1971-; memb East Kilbride Devpt Corpn 1971-73; Parly candiate (Cons) Renfrewshire West 1970, MP (Cons): Edinburgh North 1973-1983, MP (Cons) Edinburgh Central 1983-87, memb Euro Parliament Strasbourg 1976-77, oppn front bench spokesman Scottish Affrs 1977-79, under-sec state Scottish Off 1979-83, min for Corporate and Consumer Affrs DTI 1983-85, kt 1987; *Recreations* golf, music; *Style*— Sir Alex Fletcher; 8A Symons Street, Sloane Square, London SW3 2TJ, (☎ 01823 5567 fax 01 730 0612)

FLETCHER, Allan William Macpherson; s of Rev John Fletcher, of Edinburgh, and Elizabeth, *née* Stoddaart (d 1966); *b* 27 July 1950; *Educ* Trinity Coll Glenalmond, Univ of Aberdeen (BSc); *m* 30 Oct 1976, Marjorie, da of George Daniel (d 1984), of Aberdeen; 1 s (James b 1979), 1 da (Elizabeth-Anne b 1978), 3 steps (Antony Sherlock b 1965, Michael Sherlock b 1966, Nicholas Sherlock b 1973); *Career* mangr McLaren Marine Queensland Aust 1973-75, proprietor Balavil Estate 1975-, dir Badenoch Land Mgmnt Ltd 1975-, mangr Bell-Ingram Sporting Dept 1987-; dir and govr Butterstone Sch Hldgs Ltd 1988-; memb: Northern Meeting Soc, Scottish Landowners Fedn, Game Conservancy, Kingussie Sheep Dog Trial Assoc; memb Lloyds 1983; *Recreations* shooting, stalking, fishing, skiing, sailing, travel, wine; *Clubs* The Highland; *Style*— Allan Fletcher of Balavil;; Balavil, Kingussie, Inverness-shire (☎ 05402 413); 10 Glencairn Crescent, Edinburgh; 13 Sandend, Portsoy, Banffshire; Durn, Isla Rd, Perth PH2 7HF (☎ 0738 21121, fax 0738 30904, telex 76538)

FLETCHER, Andrew Fitzroy Stephen; s of (Maj) Fitzroy Fletcher, of Lodge House, Ansford, Castle Cory, Somerset, and Brygid, *née* Mahon; *b* 20 Dec 1957; *Educ* Eton, Magdalene Coll Cambridge (MA); *m* 1 Sept 1984, Felicia, da of Maj John Philip Pagan Taylor (d 1986), of Egland House, nr Honiton, Devon; 2 s (Thomas b 1987, James b 1989); *Career* barr Inner Temple 1980; Freeman, City of London 1986; *Recreations* travel, fishing, reading; *Clubs* Boodle's; *Style*— Andrew Fletcher, Esq; 4 Pump Ct, Temple London EC4 (☎ 01 353 2656)

FLETCHER, Archibald Peter; s of Walter Archibald Fletcher (d 1970), and Dorothy Mabel Fletcher; *b* 24 Dec 1930; *Educ* Kingswood Sch Bath, London Hosp Medical College, St Mary's Hosp Medical Sch; *m* 1972, Patricia Elizabeth Samson, *née* Marr; 3 s, 2 da; *Career* sr lectr chemical pathology St Mary's Hosp London 1967-70, head of biochemistry American Nat Red Cross 1970-73, princ med offr, medical assessor to Ctee on Safety of Medicines 1977-, chief scientific offr, sr med offr DHSS 1978, res physicican Upjohn Int 1978-80, sr med offr DHSS; ptnr Documenta Biomedica, md CTC International, medical dir IMS International; *Recreations* gardening, cooking; *Clubs* Wig and Pen, Royal Society of Medicine; *Style*— Archibald Fletcher Esq; Hall Corner Cottage, Little Maplestead, Halstead, Essex (☎ Halstead 475465)

FLETCHER, Audrey Littledale; da of Lt-Col Geoffrey Littledale Fletcher, JP (d 1945), and Lilian Steuart, *née* Gladstone (d 1960); *b* 14 Jan 1910; *Career* hon life memb BRCS 1943-, chm local branch Cons Assoc 1937-39, asst co cmmr GG Assoc, asst co VAD controller 1940-45, co dir BRCS 1945-50, staff offr special ctees BRCS Nat HQ London 1950-72, petrol offr War Orgn Red Cross and St John 1940-56, VAD cdr N Cmd Catterick Mil Hosp, JP Co Denbigh 1945-80; SSStJ 1962; *Clubs* Ladies Carlton, VAD Ladies; *Style*— Miss Audrey Fletcher

FLETCHER, Prof Charles Montague; CBE (1952); s of Sir Walter Morley Fletcher, KBE, CB, MD, FRCP (d 1933), and Mary Francis Cropper (d 1971); *b* 5 June 1911; *Educ* Eton Coll, Trinity Coll Cambridge, St Bartholomews Hosp Medical Sch MD (Cantab); *m* 24 Oct 1941, Louisa Mary Sylvia; 1 s (Mark b 1941), 2 da (Susanna b 1945, Caroline b 1949); *Career* physician Michael Foster res student Trinity Coll 1934-36; Nuffield Res Student Oxford 1940-42; asst phys EMS 1943-44; dir MRC Pneumoconiosis Res Unit 1945-52; physician Hammersmith Hosp 1952-76; prof clinical epidemiology 1973-76; (reader 1960-73, sr lectr 1952-60) sec MRC Ctee on Bronchitis Res 1954-76; (cncl memb 1959-62, vice pres 1975), Royal Coll of Phys; sec Ctee on Smoking and Health 1961-71; Goulstonian lectr 1947; Bisset-Hawkins Gold Medal 1969; WHO: conslt Pulmonary Heart Disease 1960, Chronic Bronchitis 1962, Smoking and Health 1970; vice-chm Health Education Cncl 1967; pres Action on Smoking and Health (ASH) 1979- (chm 1971-76); appeared on many TV medical programmes incl: Matters of Medicine 1952, Hurt Mind 1955, Your Life in Their Hands 1958-65, Television Doctor 1969-70; Editorial Board Jnl Med Educ 1975-; vice-pres Coll of Health 1983-; memb: Central Health Services Cncl and Standing Med Adv Ctee 1966-76, British Diabetic Assocn (chm education section 1973-78), governing body Inst of Med Ethic 1973-77, Asthmas Res Ctee 1968; (SOC memb exec and med adv ctee 1979); Rock Carling fell Nuffield Provincial Hosps Fund 1973; *Books* Communication on Medicine (1973), Natural History of Chronic Bronchitis and Emphysema (1976), Talking and Listening to Patients (1989); many papers on: First Use Penicillin (1941), Dust Diseases on Lungs (1946-55), Bronchitis and Emphysema (1953-76); *Recreations* gardening, music, beekeeping; *Clubs* Brooks's; *Style*— Professor Charles M Fletcher, CBE, MD, FRCP, FFCM; 24 West Square, London SE11 4SN (☎ 01 735 8753); 2 Coastguard Cottages, Newtown, Newport, Isle of Wight PO30 4PA (☎ 0983 76321)

FLETCHER, Rev Hon David Clare Molyneux; s of Baron Fletcher, PC (Life Peer); *b* 15 May 1932; *Educ* Repton, Worcester Coll Oxford (MA); *m* 1970, Susan Charlotte, da of late Alan Stockdale Langford, of Jersey; 2 children; *Career* ordained 1958, curate of St Mary's Islington 1958, Scripture Union staff worker 1962, rector of St Ebbe's Oxford 1986; *Style*— Rev Hon David Fletcher; St Ebbe's Rectory, 2 Roger Bacon Lane, Oxford OX1 1QE

FLETCHER, Baron (Life Peer UK 1970); Eric George Molyneux Fletcher; PC (1967); s of late Clarence George Eugene Fletcher, town clerk of Islington; *b* 26 Mar 1903; *Educ* Radley, London Univ; *m* 1929, Bessie Winifred, da of late James Butt, of Enfield; 2 s, 1 da; *Career* sits as Labour Peer in House of Lords; slr 1924, former sr ptnr Denton Hall & Burgin, now conslt; former dir Assoc of Br Picture Corpn Ltd and other cos; memb LCC 1934-39 (chm fin ctee); MP (Lab) Islington 1945-70, min Without Portfolio 1964-66, dep speaker and chm Ways and Means House of Commons 1966-68; pres Br Archaeological Assoc 1960-63, tstee British Museum 1968-77; kt 1964; *Style*— The Rt Hon Lord Fletcher, PC; 90 Chancery Lane, London WC2 FSA; (☎ 01 242 1212); 51 Charlbury Road, North Oxford, OX2 6UX (☎ Oxford 52292)

FLETCHER, Geoffrey; MBE (1944), TD (1947), JP (Kent 1965), DL (1979); s of Brig Harold Fletcher, OBE, TD, JP (d 1964); *b* 27 April 1920; *Educ* Repton; *m* 1947, Cynthia Diana Howard, da of David Howard Lloyd (d 1966), of Newmarket; 2 s, 2 da; *Career* Major BEF 1940 and 1944; engineer; chm Drake & Fletcher Ltd; FIAgrE; *Recreations* golf, bridge, gardening; *Clubs* Farmers', Royal St Georges Golf; *Style*— Geoffrey Fletcher, Esq, MBE, TD, JP, DL; Thornham Friars, Pilgrims Way, Thurnham, Kent; Drake & Fletcher, Parkwood, Sutton Rd, Maidstone, Kent (☎ (0622) 55531)

FLETCHER, Geoffrey Bernard Abbott; s of James Alexander Fletcher (d 1945), of Burgess Hill, Sussex, and Ursula Constance (d 1962), da of William Richard Rickett, of Hampstead; *b* 28 Nov 1903; *Educ* Rugby, King's Coll Cambridge (MA); *Career* asst lectr in Classics Leeds Univ 1927-28, lectr in Greek Liverpool Univ 1928-36, prof of classics Durham Univ King's Coll Newcastle-upon-Tyne 1937-46, prof of Latin 1946-63, prof of Latin Newcastle-upon-Tyne Univ 1963-69, now emeritus prof; *Publications* an appendix on Housman's poetry in: Housman 1897-1936 by Grant Richards (1941), Annotations on Tacitus (1964); *Recreations* music, reading, art galleries, travel; *Clubs* Athenaeum; *Style*— Professor G B A Fletcher; Thirlmere Lodge, Elmfield Rd, Gosforth, Newcastle-upon-Tyne NE3 4BB (☎ Tyneside 091 2852873)

FLETCHER, Giles; s of Thomas Simons Fletcher (d 1985), of Nunton Cottage, Nunton, Salisbury, and Janet, *née* Bigg (d 1987); *b* 12 August 1936; *Educ* Marlborough; *m* 18 Jan 1964, Jennifer Marion Edith, da of Sir Eric Cecil Heygate Salmon, MC, DL (d 1946), of The Vale House, Old Church St, London SW3; 2 s (James b 1965, Timothy b 1974), 1 da (Alice b 1967); *Career* Fletcher and Partners: ptnr 1964-77, senior ptnr 1977-; govr Godolphin Sch, tres Southern Cathedrals Festival, tstee Charitable Tsts; churchwarden; FCA 1961; *Recreations* hill walking, English and French Cathedrals and Churches; *Style*— Giles Fletcher, Esq; Apple Tree House, Middle Woodford, Salisbury SP4 6NG (☎ 0722 733 29); c/o Fletcher and Partners, Crown Chambers, Bridge Street, Salisbury SP1 2LZ (☎ 0722 278 01, fax 0277 238 39)

FLETCHER, Ian Macmillan; WS; s of John Malcolm Fletcher, JP, of Gourock, Scotland, and Jane Ann Cochran Fletcher (d 1980); *b* 16 Feb 1948; *Educ* Greenock Acad, Univ of Glasgow (LLB); *m* 15 Jan 1977, Jennifer Margaret, da of Capt John Brown William Daly, MN (d 1972), of Glasgow; 1 s (Richard John Malcolm b 13 Jan 1980), 2 da (Elizabeth Jane b 4 Aug 1978, Eleanor Kathleen b 21 Aug 1985); *Career* asst slr Richards Butler 1977-79; ptnr: MacRoberts 1980-87, Richards Butler 1987-; co sec Chilton Bros Ltd; LTCL, LRAM, ARCO; memb: Law Soc, Law Soc of Scotland, Soc WS, Int Bar Assoc (memb ctee of section on business law), Soc of Scottish Lawyers London (vice pres); MInstD; *Books* The Law and Practice of Receivership in Scotland (jtly 1987); *Recreations* music, golf, swimming; *Clubs* Western (Glasgow); *Style*— Ian Fletcher, Esq; Beaufort House, 15 St Botolph St, London EC3A 7EE (☎ 01 247 6555, fax 01 247 5091, telex 949494 RBLAW)

FLETCHER, Major John Antony (Tony); MBE (1952); s of Alexander Ernest Fletcher (d 1946) of Heath Cross Cottage Whitestone Nr Exeter and Abbey *née* Wheeler (d 1969); *b* 4 May 1918; *Educ* Cheltenham Coll Junior, Abingdon Sch, Royal Military Academy Woolwich; *m* 1, 27 Jan 1951, Elizabeth, da of Reginald George Cross (d 1953) of Kenya; 1 s (Geoffrey b 1954), 3 da (Sara b 1952, Alice b 1957, Jane b 1960); 2 m, Susan Mary, da of Henry Eggerton Brown of 384 Coniscliffe Road Darlington Co Durham; *Career* Cmmd 2 Lt RA 1938, served Malta, Middle East, Far East (2 despatches, Malaya 1946, Korea 1952), staff and regimental duty, army and RAF staff colls PSC and PAC; sec and chief exec Inst of Road Transport engrgs 1963; chm Assoc of Care Takers and Care Seekers; *Recreations* travel, caravanning; *Clubs* Ex Playing Member MCC, ex Sheringham and other golf clubs, ex member United Hunts Club; *Style*— Tony Fletcher Esq, MBE; Milford Cottage, 10 Cudnall Street, Charlton Kings, Cheltenham, Glos GL53 8HT (☎ 0242 522367)

FLETCHER, John Duncan; s of Joseph Fletcher, of Farnham, nr Knaresborough, N Yorks; *b* 20 Oct 1942; *Educ* Leeds GS, St Catherine's Coll Oxford, Harvard Business Sch (MBA); *m* 1967, Gloria; 1 s; *Career* former chief exec Oriel Foods; dir Assoc Dairies Gp plc, md Asda Foods 1981-; *Recreations* golf, walking; *Clubs* RAC, Pannal Golf; *Style*— John Fletcher Esq; c/o Asda, Asda House, Britannia Rd, Morley, Leeds LS27 0BT (☎ 0532 539141); The Priory, Follifoot, Harrogate, N Yorks HG3 1DT (☎ Harrogate (0423) 871537)

FLETCHER, Dr (Timothy) John; s of George Spencer Fletcher (d 1981, of Silsden, W Yorks, and Pattie Margaret Beaver; *b* 12 Sept 1946; *Educ* The Leys Sch

Cambridge, Glasgow Univ (BVMS), Magdalene Coll Cambridge (Phd); *m* 8 July 1972, Nichola Rosemary, da of Hubert Henry Ormerod Chalk (d 1981); 2 da (Stella b 1978, Martha b 1980); *Career* chm Br Deer Farmers' Assoc 1982-84, dir Br Deer Producers Soc Ltd 1983-, pres Veterinary Deer Soc, dir Scottish Deer Centre 1987-, fndr first Br Deer Farm 1973; *Recreations* food, wine, travel, collecting deer literature and ephemera, gardening; *Style—* Dr John Fletcher, Esq; Reediehill Farm, Auchtermuchty, Fife KY14 7HS (☎ 0337 28369, telex 72165G, fax 0337-28369)

FLETCHER, Rev the Hon Jonathan James Molyneux; s of Baron Fletcher, PC (Life Peer); *b* 22 Sept 1942; *Educ* Dragon Sch, Repton, Hertford Coll Oxford; *Career* ordained: deacon 1968, priest 1969; curate: Christ Church Cockfosters 1968-72, Holy Sepulchre Church Cambridge 1972-76, St Helen's Bishopsgate 1976-81; incumbent Emmanuel Wimbledon 1982-; *Style—* Rev the Hon Jonathan Fletcher; Emmanuel Parsonage, 8 Sheep Walk Mews, Ridgway, Wimbledon, London SW19 4QL (01 946 4728)

FLETCHER, Kenneth William Ian; s of William Walter Fletcher (d 1983), and Minnie Ena, *née* Day (d 1983); *b* 17 Sept 1927; *Educ* Coopers' Company's Sch; *m* 23 July 1949, Alice Harriett, da of James George Fewtrell (d 1978); 1 s (Martin Andrew b 1954), 1 da (Susan Carol b 1950); *Career* Nat Serv signalman RCS 1947-49; Pearl Assur Co Ltd 1949-81, chm and pres The Monarch Insur Co of Ohio 1981-85, asst gen mangr 1986-87 and gen mangr Pearl Assur plc 1987-; pres First New York Syndicate Corpn 1986-; FCII 1959; *Style—* Kenneth Fletcher, Esq; Brimley Lodge, Megg Lane, Chipperfield, Kings Langley, Herts WD4 9JN (☎ 09277 60883), Pearl Assurance plc, 252 High Holborn, London WC1V 7EB (☎ 01 405 8441, fax 01 831 6251, telex 296350 PEARL G)

FLETCHER, Sir Leslie; DSC (1945); s of Ernest Fletcher (d 1960), and Lily Fletcher; *b* 14 Oct 1922; *Educ* Nether Edge Sec Sch Sheffield; *m* 1947, Audrey Faviell, da of William Faviell Jackson (d 1972); 1 s, 1 da; *Career* served WW II, Lt (A) RNVR, Europe and Far East; Fleet Air Arm 1942-46; Rolls Royce Ltd 1938-39, Nat Provincial Bank 1939-42, 1946-47 articled clerk 1947; dir: J Henry Schroder Wagg & Co Ltd 1955-57, Glynwed Int plc 1966-86 (chm 1971-86), RMC Gp plc 1983-, The Rank Organisation plc 1984-, West Midlands Ind Dev Assoc Ltd 1984, Standard Chartered Overseas Holdings Ltd 1978-; dep chm: Standard Chartered plc 1972-, Bank Africa plc 1971-; chm Standard Chartered Merchant Bank: Ltd 1983-, Holding Ltd 1983-; Scimitar Asset Management Ltd 1985-; FCA; kt 1982; *Recreations* golf, gardening, photography; *Clubs* MCC, RAC, Brooks's, R and A; *Style—* Sir Leslie Fletcher, DSC; Hafod, The Green, Sherfield on Loddon, Basingstoke, Hants

FLETCHER, Hon Mrs (Louisa Mary Sylvia); *née* Seely; yst da of 1 Baron Mottistone, CB, CMG, DSO, TD (d 1947), and his 1 wife Emily Florence, *née* Crichton (d 1913); *b* 9 August 1913; *m* 24 Oct 1941, Prof Charles Montague Fletcher, CBE, MD, FRCP, s of Sir Walter Morley Fletcher, KBE, CB, MD, ScD, FRS (d 1933); 1 s, 2 da; *Style—* Hon Mrs Fletcher; 24 West Sq, London SE11 4SN (☎ 01 735 8753)

FLETCHER, Mandie Elizabeth; da of Sqdn Ldr C W Fletcher (ret), of Homefield, Lodsworth, Midhurst, Sussex, and Shirley, *née* Hull; *b* 27 Dec 1954; *Educ* Guildford HS Surrey; *Career* prodr/dir: The Fainthearted Feminist 1985 (ACE award winner best comedy dir), Brushstrokes 1987-88, Blackadder II 1988 (ACE award winner- best comedy series), Blackadder III 1988 (BAFTA award winner - best comedy series), No Frills 1988; *Recreations* cycling; *Style—* Miss Mandie Fletcher; 34 Inglethorpe St, London SW6 6NT (☎ 01 385 5465)

FLETCHER, Cmdt Marjorie Helen Kelsey; CBE (1988);; da of Norman Farler Fletcher, and Marie Amelie, *née* Adams; *b* 21 Sept 1932; *Educ* Avondale HS, Sutton Coldfield HS for Girls; *Career* slr's clerk 1948-53; WRNS: telegraphist 1953, Third Offr 1956, Second Offr 1960, First Offr 1979, Chief Offr 1976, ndc 1979, Directing Staff RN Staff Coll 1980-81, psc 1981, Supt 1981, Int Mil Staff NATO HQ 1981-84, Asst Dir Naval Staff Duties 1984-85, Cmdt 1986, dir WRNS 1986-88; ADC to HM the Queen 1986-88; CBIM 1987; *Recreations* reading, collecting pictures, needlework, fishing, natural and English history; *Style—* Cmdt Marjorie Fletcher, CBE

FLETCHER, Nathan; CBE (1984); s of Nathan Fletcher (d 1937), of York, and Mary Hannah Maria, *née* Gledhill (d 1980); *b* 8 August 1920; *Educ* Welbeck Boys Sch Castleford, Whitwood Technical Coll Yorks; *m* 1946, Iris Hilda, da of Richard Jackson (d 1961), of Cheshire; 1 da (Lesley b 1950); *Career* chm Kadek Press Ltd 1968-; memb Taylor Woodrow exec Bd 1972-; dir Taylor Woodrow plc 1974-; vice pres of Small Business Bureau 1982-; pres Ealing North C Assoc 1985; vice pres (life) Tug of War Assoc 1987 (pres 1985-86); *Recreations* reading, music; *Style—* Nathan Fletcher, CBE; Whitwood, 7 Oak Tree Drive, Englefield Green, Surrey (☎ Egham 37489); Taylor Woodrow plc, 345 Ruislip Road, Southall, Middlesex (☎ 01 578 2366, telex 24428, fax 01 575 4701)

FLETCHER, Brig (Bolton) Neil Littledale; CBE (1976); s of Maj Bolton Littledale Fletcher (d 1943), and Vera Marguerite, *née* Edmondson (d 1977), later Mrs David Ritchie, OBE, MC (d 1974); *b* 19 August 1923; *Educ* Stowe; *m* 30 July 1947, Mary Elizabeth, former w of Maj Dennis William Seddon-Brown (ka 1944), and da of Col John Hugh Lovett, DSO, DL (d 1974); 1 da (Elizabeth Caroline Anne b 1950), 1 step s (Jonathan Lovett Seddon-Brown); *Career* cmmnd KSLI 1943, cmd Depot KSLI 1959-60, DSD Staff Coll Camberley 1960-63, cmd 1 KSLI in UK Singapore and Malaysia 1965-67, Army's author 1968-69, Col GS Hong Kong 1970-71, cmd 2 Inf Bde 1973-75, dep constable Dover Castle 1973-75; ret 1978; ADC to HM the Queen 1976-78; *Recreations* shooting, golf; *Clubs* Army and Navy; *Style—* Brig Neil Fletcher CBE;; Old Vicarage, Shipton Bellinger, Tidworth, Hants

FLETCHER, Sir Norman Seymour; s of Thomas Fletcher, of Nottingham, and Ivy Clarice, *née* Jeffrey; *b* 20 Sept 1905; *m* 1937, Constance Catherine, *née* Coombes; 1 s; *Career* Capt Adj Pacific Is 16 Bn AIF, (despatches) AASA; agriculturalist and pastoralist, Hereford stud breeder (pioneered the introduction to WA of the Hereford cattle breed), past pres Royal Agr Soc of WA; outstanding service to Agr in WA; kt 1977; *Recreations* bowls; *Clubs* Weld, Western Australia (both Perth); *Style—* Sir Norman Fletcher; Unit 1, Haddon Place, 39 The Esplanade, South Perth, 6151 W Australia

FLETCHER, Paul Thomas; CBE (1959); s of Stephen Baldwin Fletcher (d 1971) of Maidstone, and Jessie Carrie, *née* Rumsby (d 1963); *b* 30 Sept 1912; *Educ* Nicholson Institute Isle of Lewis, Maidstone GS, Medway Technical Coll (BSc Eng); *m* 12 April 1941, Mary Elizabeth, da of Percy Howard King (d 1936), of Maidstone; 3 s (John b 1947, David b 1949, Peter b 1952); *Career* chartered engrg; Miny of Works 1939-54 (chief engr 1951-54), engrg dir UKAEA Industrial Group 1954-61, dir United Power Co 1961-65, md GEC Process Engrg Ltd 1965-70, md Atomic Power Construction Ltd 1970-75 (dep chm 1976-80), conslt 1980-; pres InstMechE 1975-76, chm Br Standards Inst 1979-81 (dep pres 1981-); FEng; FICE; FIMechE; FIEE; *Recreations* motoring, photography; *Style—* Paul T Fletcher, Esq, CBE

FLETCHER, Air Chief Marshal Sir Peter Carteret; KCB (1968), OBE (1944), DFC (1942), AFC (1952); s of Frederick Wheeler Trevor Fletcher (d 1964), of Norton, S Rhodesia, and Dora, *née* Clulee; *b* 7 Oct 1916; *Educ* St George's Coll S Rhodesia, Rhodes Univ; *m* 1940, (Marjorie) Isobel, da of Gilbert Percival Kotzé (d 1953), s/r, of Grahamstown. S Africa; 2 da (Anne, Elizabeth); *Career* transferred from S Rhodesian Air Force to RAF 1941, CO 135 Fighter Sqdn and 258 Fighter Sqdn 1940-42, CO 25 Elementary Flying Training Sch 1942-43, DSD of RAF Staff Coll 1943-44, of Jt Services Staff Coll 1945-46, and IDC 1956-57, CO RAF Abingdon 1958-60, DOR (B) Air Miny 1961-63, Air Cdre 1961, Air Vice-Marshal 1964, Asst Chief of Air Staff (Policy and Planning) 1964-66, AOC 38 Gp, Transport Cmd 1966-67, Air Marshal 1967, vice-Chief of Air Staff 1967-70, Controller of Aircraft, Miny of Aviation Supply 1970, Air Systems Controller Def Procurement Exec 1971-73; dir: Hawker Siddeley Aviation Ltd 1974-77, Corporate Strategy and Planning, Br Aerospace 1977-82, Airbus Industry Supervisory Bd 1979-82, ret Br Aerospace 1982; aerospace conslt 1983-; *Recreations* books, travel; *Clubs* RAF; *Style—* Air Chief Marshal Sir Peter Fletcher; Woodlands, Sandy Lane, Tilford, Surrey GU10 2ET (☎ Frensham 2897)

FLETCHER, Philip John; s of Alan Philip Fletcher, QC, of Royston Herts and Annette Grace, *née* Wright; *b* 2 May 1946; *Educ* Marlborough, Trinity Coll Oxford (MA); *m* 12 Feb 1977, Margaret Anne, da of J E Boys, of Witley, Surrey; 2 da (Helen b 1978, Sarah b 1982); *Career* teacher VSO 1967-68; DOE 1968- (formerly Miny Public Building and Works); asst princ 1968, W Midlands Regnl Off 1973-76, private sec to perm sec 1978, asst sec Private Sector Housebuilding 1980, local govt expenditure 1982-85, under sec fin 1986-; lay reader St Michael's Stockwell; *Style—* Philip Fletcher, Esq; Department of the Environment, 2 Marshall St, London SW1P 3EB (☎ 01 276 3560)

FLETCHER, Piers Michael William; s of Col Michael James Rex Fletcher, MBE, of Folkestone, Kent, and Mary Anita, *née* Williams; *b* 10 August 1956; *Educ* Wellington Coll, Christ Church Oxford (MA); *m* 8 Aug 1986, Paula Harvey Anne, da of Brig John Levey, of Burghfield Common, Hampshire; *Career* 2 Lt 6 QEO Gurkha Rifles 1975; dir: GNI Ltd 1984, Baltic Futuras Exchange 1988-; *Recreations* polo, cooking, photography; *Style—* Piers Fletcher, Esq; 46 Lessar Avenue, London SW4 (☎ 01 673 8508); GNI Ltd, Colechurch House, 1 London Bridge Walk, London SE1 2SX (☎ 01 378 7171, car tel 0860 834174)

FLETCHER, (Leopold) Raymond; s of Leopold Raymond Fletcher, of Ruddington, Notts; *b* 3 Dec 1921; *Educ* overseas, Humboldt Univ Berlin; *m* 1, 1947, Johanna Klara Elisabeth (d 1973), da of Karl Ising, of Berlin; m 2, 1977, Dr Catherine Elliott (fndr memb SDP), widow of Jasper Fenn; *Career* served WW II Indian Army Ordnance Corps and Intelligence BAOR; journalist (columnist with The Times); MP (Lab) Ilkeston 1964-83; former leader UK Delegn to WEU and Cncl of Europe (where ldr Socialist Gp) and vice pres Consultative Assembly; fndr Airship Assoc 1970; *Style—* Raymond Fletcher, Esq; 23 Ilkeston Rd, Heanor, Derbyshire DE7 7DT (☎ (077 37) 12682)

FLETCHER, Dr Robin Anthony; OBE (1984), DSC (1944); s of Maj P C Fletcher, MC, TD (d 1961), of Hinton Priory, Hinton Charterhouse, Bath, and Edith Maud, *née* Okell, JP (d 1978); *b* 30 May 1922; *Educ* Marlborough, Trinity Coll Oxford (MA, DPhil); *m* 9 Dec 1950, Jenny May; 2 s (Clive b 1951, Denys b 1954); *Career* WWII: Ordinary Seaman RN HMS Gambia 1941-42, Sub Lt (later Lt) RNVR 1943-46 (Levant Schooner Flotilla Med, minesweeping trawlers UK); Univ of Oxford: lectr Modern Greek 1949-79, domestic bursar Trinity Coll 1950-74, sr proctor 1966-67, memb Hebdomedal Cncl 1967-74; sec Rhodes House and warden Rhodes Tst 1980-89, tstee Oxford Preservation Tst; former memb bd of govrs: Kelly Coll Cheltenham Coll, Marlborough Coll, Radley Coll, Sherborne Sch; bronze medallist GB hockey team Olympic Games 1952, hockey player for England 1949-55, pres Hockey Assoc 1972-83; *Books* Kostes Palamas (1984); *Recreations* golf, listening to music; *Clubs* Naval, Vincent's; *Style—* Dr Robin Fletcher, OBE, DSC; Rhodes House, Oxford OX1 3RG (☎ 0865 271902)

FLETCHER, Wilfred Leslie; CBE (1977); s of Frederick Smith Fletcher, OBE (d 1970), of Marton, Cleveland, and Isabella, *née* Litler (d 1967); *b* 25 July 1913; *Educ* Rossall Sch Durham Univ; *m* 20 May 1939, (Margaret) Joan Hird, da of John Coates Hird (d 1947), of Yarm; 1 s (John b 1940), 1 da (Penelope b 1942, d 1975); *Career* dir; Teeside Bridge Engrg Co Ltd 1945-70 (md 1950-70), Br Structural Steel Co 1956-67, Dorman Long (Steel) Ltd 1959-67 Dorman Long (Africa) Ltd 1959-67, Dorman Long (Steel)lLtd 1959-67, Dorman Long (Nigeria) 1962-67, Redpath Dorman Long Ltd 1967-73, BSC Works Gp 1969-71, BSC Costructional E Div 1971-73; md Dorman Long (Bridge Engrg) Ltd 1962-67; pres: Cleveland Sci Inst 1969-70, Br Constructional Steelwork Assoc 1972-75; govr Teesside Poly 1963-72, chm NSG Engrg Employers Fedn 1964-67, Rear Cdre Salcombe YC 1978-81, dep chm Salcombe and Kingsbridge Estuary Assoc 1987-89; MICE 1939, FIStructE 1959, CEng 1970; *Recreations* yachting, beekeeping, philately; *Clubs* Salcombe YC; *Style—* Wilfred Fletcher, Esq, CBE; Whitehorses, Salcombe, Devon (☎ 054 884 2652); Waterfoot Lodge, Pooley Bridge, Cumbria

FLETCHER, Winston; s of Albert Fletcher (d 1963), of London, and Bessie, *née* Miller (d 1955); *b* 15 July 1937; *Educ* Westminster City Sch, St John's Coll Cambridge (MA); *m* 14 June 1963, Jean, da of Alfred Brownston (d 1968), of Bristol; 1 s (Mathew b 5 Nov 1970), 1 da (Amelia b 1 Jan 1966); *Career* dir Sharps Advertising 1964-69 (joined as trainee 1959), md MCR Advertising 1970, chm Fletcher Shelton Delaney 1981-83 (md 1974-81, fndr 1974), chm and chief exec Ted Bates UK 1983-85; chm Delaney Fletcher Delaney 1985-; advertising conslt SDP, reg author for nat business and advertising trade press; memb cncl Advertising Standard Authy; FIPA (pres 1989-); *Books* The Admakers (1972), Teach Yourself Advertising (1978), Meetings, Meetings (1983), Commercial Breaks (1984), Supereffiency (1986), The Manipulator (1988); *Recreations* reading, writing, arithmetic; *Clubs* Reform, Royal Institution, Annabels, Thirty, Mosimanns; *Style—* Winston Fletcher, Esq; Souldern Mill, Bicester, Oxon (☎ 08696 497); 12 Bourdon St, Berkeley Sq, London W1 (☎ 01 629 4844); 5-11 Shorts Gardens, London WC2 (☎ 01 240 7871, car tel 0860 345 869)

FLETCHER ROGERS, David Geoffrey; s of Murray Rowland Fletcher Rogers, of

Flat 10, Mount View Rd, London N4, and Dorothy Lilian, *née* Bardsley (d 1950); *b* 20 May 1927; *Educ* St Edward's Sch Oxford; *m* 28 Sept 1972, Helen Susan, da of Peter Alexander Stewart, of 5 Windsor Lodge, Windsor Rd, Ansdell, Lytham St Annes; 2 s (Anthony, Jonathan) 1 da (Karen Elizabeth); *Career* cmmnd RNVR; barr Grays Inn; mangr legal dept Monotype Corpn 1957-65; legal advsr: NRDC 1965-69, Dunlop Co Ltd (Dunlop Ltd) 1969-85; advsr to and dir of Various cos 1985-; chm local Cons Assoc; first chm Anti Counterfeiting Gp; memb: Inst of Patent Agents, Licensing Exec Soc; *Books* Butterworths Encyclopaedia of Forms and Precedents vols 16 and 16a (princ contrib chapter on patents and designs); *Recreations* sailing (cruising), enjoying pleasant company; *Clubs* Army and Navy, Conway Cruising Assoc; *Style*— David Fletcher Rogers, Esq; Conway House, Furlong Lane, Totternhoe, Dunstable, Beds LU6 1QR (☎ 0582 472300); AWD Ltd, Boscombe Rd, Dunstable, Bedfordshire (☎ 0582 472244)

FLETCHER-COOKE, Sir Charles; QC (1958); yr s of Capt Charles Arthur Fletcher-Cooke (d 1924), and Gwendolen May Fletcher-Cooke; bro of Sir John Fletcher-Cooke, CMG, *qv*; *b* 1914; *Educ* Malvern and Peterhouse Cambridge; *m* 1959 (m dis 1967), Diana Many Margaret Westcott, yr da of Capt Edward Westcott King, RA, and formerly wife of 3 Baron Avebury; *Career* barr 1938, contested East Dorset Div (Lab) 1945, later resigned from Labour Party, MP (C) Darwen 1951-83, jt parly under-sec of state Home Office 1961-63, MEP 1977-79; Dato of the Kingdom of Brunei 1978; kt 1981; *Clubs* Garrick, Pratts; *Style*— Sir Charles Fletcher-Cooke, QC; 2 Paper Buildings, Temple, London EC4 (☎ 01 353 1853)

FLETCHER-COOKE, Sir John; CMG (1952); er s of Capt Charles Arthur Fletcher-Cooke (d 1924), and Gwendolen May, *née* Bradford; *b* 8 August 1911; *Educ* Malvern, Université de Paris, St Edmund Hall Oxford; *m* m 1, 8 Aug 1935 (m dis 1949), (Margaret) Louise, da of James Paterson Brander, of Edinburgh; 1 s (Charles Louis Brander b 1947); m 2, 10 Sept 1949 (m dis 1971), Alice Elizabeth, da of Dr Russell Forest Egner, of Washington, DC, USA; 1 s (Richard Mark Forest b 1951), 1 da Anne Gillian b 1953); m 3, 1977, Marie-Louise, da of Roger Jonchim Ducasson, French Colonial Service (d 1947), and wid of Louis, Viconte Fournier de la Barrer; *Career* Colonial Office 1936-42 and 1946, POW Japan 1942-45, und-sec to Govt of Palestine 1946-48, colonial sec and occasional actg govr Cyprus 1951-55, occasional actg govr Tanganyika 1959-61, stood for (C) Luton 1963, MP (C) Southampton Test 1964-66, author; kt 1962; *Recreations* writing, building dry Cotswold stone walls; *Clubs* Travellers', Royal Commonwealth Soc; *Style*— Sir John Fletcher-Cooke, CMG; c/o Lloyds Bank Ltd, Finsbury Circus Branch, 3 Broad St Pla, EC2

FLETCHER-MOULTON, Hon Sylvia May Fletcher; CBE (1961), JP (1949); da of Baron Moulton, GBE, KCB, PC (Life Peer) (d 1921), and his 2 wife Mary, *née* Davis (d 1909); *b* 15 June 1902; *Educ* schools in USA and GB, Girton Coll Cambridge (BA); *Career* barr Middle Temple 1929; regnl admin for Women's Vol Services for Civil Defence Midland Region during WW II; chm Westfield Coll Cncl; *Recreations* travelling; *Clubs* University Women's; *Style*— Hon Sylvia Fletcher-Moulton, CBE, JP; Court House, Barcombe, nr Lewes, Sussex BN8 5TS (☎ (0273) 400 235)

FLETCHER-VANE; *see*: Vane

FLETT, David John; s of Alec Flett, DFC, QPM, of Acle, Norfolk, and Catherine May, *née* Read; *b* 13 Dec 1946; *Educ* Colfes GS; *m* 11 May 1974, Susan Hilda Georgina, da of Sidney Rimmington (d 1972); 1 s (Jonathon Alexander b 2 May 1980), 1 da (Claire Susannah b 24 April 1977); *Career* RBT Bradford Ltd 1963-64, active underwriter Syndicate 250 Lloyds 1983- (jr underwriting asst 1964-83); dir: RBT Bradford Holdings Ltd 1983, Wren Underwriting Agencies Ltd 1987; ACII 1971; *Recreations* fishing, metal detecting; *Style*— David Flett, Esq; Wren Underwriting Agencies Ltd, Minster House, Arthur St, London EC4R 9AB (☎ 01 623 3050)

FLETT, Lady; Mary; er da of Sir Alec Martin, KBE (d 1971), and Ada Mary, *née* Fell; *m* 1936, Sir Martin Teall Flett, KCB (d 1982), sometime dir Siebe Gorman Hldgs; 2 s, 1 da; *Style*— Lady Flett; 45 Campden Hill Rd, W8 (☎ 01 937 9498)

FLEURY, Noel Wilfred; s of Gerald Wilfred Fleury (d 1949), and Claire Maud Fleury; *b* 1 Dec 1908; *Educ* Central Sch of Arts and Crafts (NDD); *m* 4 Feb 1961, Helen Amy, da of James McLean; 1 s (Simon Marc b 31 Jan 1964), 1 da (Samantha b 28 May 1965); *Career* chief designer Bakelite Xylonite Ltd 1966-70; Bissell Appliances Ltd: design dir 1970-84, md 1984-88, sr vice pres 1988-; memb: Design Ctee Plastics Inst, Selection Ctee Design Cncl, Duke of Edinburgh Design Prize and outside assesor Design Cncl, Bursary Ctee RSA; Plastics Design Prize 1969; Freeman Worshipful Co of Horners; FCSD; *Recreations* golf; *Clubs* Old Ford Manor GC; *Style*— Noel Fleury, Esq; Bissell Appliances Ltd, 2 Jubilee Ave, Highams Park Ind Est, Highams Park, London E4 9HN (☎ 01 531 7241)

FLEW, Prof Antony Garrard Newton; o s of Rev Dr R Newton Flew (d 1962); *b* 11 Feb 1923; *Educ* Kingswood Sch Bath, St John's Oxford; *m* 1952, Annis Ruth Harty, da of Col Frank Siegfred Vernon Donnison; 2 da; *Career* prof of philosophy: Keele Univ 1954-71, Calgary Univ 1972-73, Reading Univ 1973-82, York Univ Toronto 1983-85; fndr memb Cncl of Freedom Assoc; dir: Academic Cncl Adam Smith Instit Educn Gp of the Centre for Policy Studies; *Books Incl:* Hume's Philosophy of Belief (1961), God and Philosophy (1967), Crime or Disease (1973), Sociology, Equality and Education (1976), The Presumption of Atheism (1976), A Rational Animal (1978), The Politics of Procrustes (1981), Darwinian Evolution (1984), Thinking about Social Thinking (1985); *Recreations* walking, house maintenance; *Style*— Prof Antony Flew; 26 Alexandra Rd, Reading, Berks RG1 5PD (☎ 0734 61848); Social Philosophy and Policy Center, Bowling Green State University, Bowling Green, Ohio 43403, USA

FLICK, (Michael) Tony; s of Maj Samuel Godfrey Flick, of The Laurels Saxmundham Suffolk, and Madge, *née* Brownlow; establishment by great great grandfather of auctioneering business in 1833 (now known as Flick & Son), presentation of clock in Saxmundham Church Tower in his memory in about 1880 by his family; *b* 15 May 1935; *Educ* Eversley Sch Southwold, Dover Coll, RAC Cirencester (Dip); *Career* 2 Lt Suffolk Regt, seconded Somaliland Scouts Br Somaliland (acting Capt for 7 mths); chartered surveyor Flick and Son, dir and chm, Stanford Broom and Stanford, Halesworth Market Ltd, dir: Suffolk Agricultural Assoc, E Anglian Water Co, Guildgold Ltd; farmer; FRICS, FAAV, MRAC; *Recreations* shooting, gardening; *Style*— Tony Flick, Esq; Westering Middleton, Saxmundham, Suffolk IP17 3NY (☎ Westleton 382); Ashford House, Saxmundham, Suffolk (☎ 0728 3232)

FLIGHT, Howard Emerson; s of Bernard Thomas Flight, of Devon, and Doris Mildred Emerson, *née* Parker; *b* 16 June 1948; *Educ* Brentwood Essex, Magdalene Coll Cambridge (MA), Univ of Michigan Business Sch (MBA); *m* 1973, Christabel Diana Beatrice, da of Christopher Paget Norbury (d 1975), of Worcestershire; 1 s (Thomas b 1978), 2 da (Catherine b 1975, Josephine b 1986, Mary Anne b 1988); *Career* jt md Guinness Flight Global Asset Mgmnt (formerly Invest div of Guinness Mahon; dir: Guinness Mahon & Co Ltd, Guinness Flight Int Fund Ltd, Guinness Flight Global Strategy Fund Ltd, Guinness Mahon Asset Mgmnt Ltd; memb Lloyds; C party candidate Cons Bermondsey, Southwark both elections 1974, c Parly candidate Cons approved list; *Books* All You Need to Know About Exchange Rates (jtly 1988); *Recreations* skiing, classical music, fruit farming; *Clubs* Carlton, Winchester House; *Style*— Howard Flight, Esq; 6 Ruvigny Gardens, Putney, London SW15 (☎ 01 789 0923); The Norrest, Leigh Sinton, Worcestershire; Guinness Flight Global Asset Management Ltd, 32 St Mary at Hill, London EC3 (☎ 01 626 9333)

FLINDALL, Jacqueline; JP (Oxford and Salisbury Bench 1982); da of Henry Flindall (d 1940) brought up by unc Alfred Thomas Evans, OBE late Chief Constable of Pembrokeshire, and Lilian, *née* Evans (d 1940); *b* 12 Oct 1932; *Educ* St David's Sch Ashford, Middlesex; *Career* srn Univ Coll Hosp, scm: St Lukes Guildford, Watford Maternity Hosp, asst matron Wesham Park Hosp 1957-63, dep supt of Nursing Prince of Wales Hosp 1964-66, chief nursing offr: Northwick Park Hosp 1969- 73, Oxfordshire Health Authy 1973-83; (regnl nursing offr Wessex Health Authy 1985-; assoc conslt PA Mgmnt Conslts; pres UCH Nurses League, govr St Davids Sch; hon FRCN Royal Coll of Nursing 1983; *Recreations* painting; *Style*— Miss Jacqueline Flindall; Greenways Cottage, Cowesfield Green, White Parish, Salisbury, Wilts SP5 2QS (☎ 0794 884836)

FLINN, Donal Patrick; s of Hugo Victor Flinn (d 1943), sometime Parly Sec Dept of Finance, of Coleen, Co Cork; *b* 8 Nov 1923; *Educ* Christian Brothers Coll Cork, Univ Coll Cork (BComm); *m* 1954, Heather Mary, da of Fred W Cole (d 1979); 2 s (Hugo, Richard b 1958), 1 da (Jennifer b 1961); *Career* chm: Barclays Bank plc (Irish Branch), Barclays Bank Ireland Ltd, De La Rue Smurfit Ltd; dir: Aer Lingus, Fitzwilton Ltd, Abbey Life Assurance Co (Ireland) Ltd; cncl and exec memb Irish Mgmnt Inst; bd memb and vice pres US C of C in Ireland; FICA (pres 1976-77); *Recreations* golf, tennis, fishing; *Clubs* Portmarnock Golf, Fitzwilliam Lawn Tennis, Royal St George YC; *Style*— Donal Flinn, Esq; 44 Orwell Park, Rathgar, Dublin 6, Eire; Hurrican Lodge, Glenbeigh, Co Kerry (☎ Glenbeigh 55)

FLINT, Christopher Gardiner; s of George Elmslie Flint (d 1973), and Mary Turner (d 1966); *b* 2 Jan 1922; *Educ* Edinburgh Acad, Edinburgh Univ (BSc); *m* 8 April 1942, Kathlyn Ellen, da of Frederick George Vallance, Mus Doc (d 1960), USA; 1 s (Christopher b 1947), 1 da (Kathlyn Robin b 1943); *Career* Military Serv Maj REME (despatches) Burma and Indo China 1940-46; chm James Fleming & Co Ltd 1983-89; dir: Fleming Howden Ltd 1967-85, George Dunbar (1928) Ltd 1967-85; pres Edinburgh Chamber of Commerce and Manufactures 1987-88; dir: Chamber Devpts Ltd 1985-, William Hunters Fund 1985-, John Wilson Bequest 1987-, Edinburgh's Capital Ltd 1985-; vice-pres (Fin) Edinburgh C of C and Mfrs 1984-; gen cmmr of Income Tax 1983-; memb of Court The Co of Merchants of The City of Edinburgh 1971-74; vice-convenor Daniel Stewart's and Melville Coll 1972-74;; *Recreations* golf, fishing, gardening; *Clubs* New (Edinburgh) Royal Burgess Golfing Society; *Style*— Christopher G Flint, Esq; EAS Sarachan, Strathlachlan, Argyll (☎ (036) 986 636); 14 Almond Court East, 5 Braehead Park, Barnton, Edinburgh (☎ 031 339 4169)

FLINT, Prof David; TD (1950); s of David Flint, JP (d 1940), and Agnes Strang Lambie; *b* 24 Feb 1919; *Educ* HS Glasgow, Univ of Glasgow (MA, BL); *m* 1953, Dorothy Mary Maclachlan, *née* Jardine; 2 s, 1 da; *Career* served WW II (despatches 1945), Maj; ptnr Mann Judd Gordon & Co 1950-71; Univ of Glasgow: prof of accountancy 1964-85, dean of faculty of law 1971-73, vice-princ 1981-85; pres: Inst of CAs of Scotland 1975-76, Euro Accounting Assoc 1983-84; FCA; FRSA; *Books* A True and Fair View in Company Accounts (1982), Philosophy and Principles of Auditing: An Introduction (1988); *Recreations* golf; *Style*— Prof David Flint; 16 Grampian Avenue, Auchterarder, Perthshire PH3 1NY (☎ 0764 63978)

FLINT, Gillian (Julie) Margaret; da of Percy Sydney George Flint, of Sevenoaks, and Joyce Marjorie Peggy, *née* Papworth; *b* 1 Jan 1948; *Educ* Talbot Heath Sch Bournemouth, Girton Coll Cambridge (BA); *Career* Rome corr Assoc Press 1974-76; United Press Int: Madrid corr 1976-81, Middle East corr 1982-84; radio corr Beirut ABC News 1983-, corr Beirut Guardian 1985-, corr Beirut Observer 1986-; runner up foreign radio reporter of the year Overseas Press Club of America 1984, foreign reporter of the year What the Papers Say 1988; *Recreations* swimming, reading, tennis; *Style*— Ms Julie Flint; c/o Courtlands, Kippington Rd, Sevenoaks, Kent (☎ 0732 455638); c/o Guardian, 119 Farringdon Rd, London EC1R 3ER (☎ 01 278 2332, fax 01 837 2114, 01 833 8342, telex 8811746)

FLINT, Colonel John Montagu; MBE (1954); s of Maj Eric Charles Montagu Flint, DSO (d 1962), of Torrington, Devon, and Frances Sarah Nancy Hulbert (d 1938); *b* 31 Jan 1917; *Educ* Eton, RMA Woolwich, Trinity Coll Cambridge (MA); *m* 5 Jan 1951, Anne Margaret, JP, DL, da of Lt Col Ulick Otway Vortigern Lloyd Verney, OBE (d 1979), of Cheriton, Hants; 2 s (Charles b 1952, Michael b 1956), 2 da (Sarah b 1955, Elizabeth b 1958); *Career* jnd RE 1937; served France 1939-40, N Africa and Sicily 1943, Italy 1943-44 (despatches) Middle East 1945; Col Cmdg 29 Engr Gp (TA) 1960-63; bursar Woodard Sch (Midland Div) 1966-82; hon fell Woodward Sch 1984; *Recreations* gardening, carpentry, travel; *Clubs* MCC; *Style*— Col John M Flint, MBE; The Dower House, Great Ness, Shrewsbury SY4 2LE (☎ 074381 288)

FLINT, Hon Mrs; Hon Pamela Margaret; *née* Lee; only child of Baron Lee of Newton, PC (Life Peer) (d 1984); *b* 19 Sept 1945; *Educ* Newton-le-Willows GS; *m* 1965, Rodney Owen Flint, s of Edwin Arnold Flint: 3 s (Mark b 1965, Jason b 1966, Daniel b 1970); *Style*— Hon Mrs Flint; The Willows, Church Drive, Newton-le-Willows, Merseyside WA12 9SR (☎ 09252 6970); Keyspools Ltd, Mono Lodge, Bridge Street, Golborne, Warrington WA3 3QA (☎ 0942 712566, telex 67228)

FLOCKHART, (David) Ross; s of Very Rev D J Flockhart (d 1965), and Jean Isobel, *née* Ingram (d 1955); *b* 20 Mar 1927; *Educ* Knox GS Sydney NSW (BA), Edinburgh (BD); *m* 1 March 1951, Pamela Ellison, da of Ellison Macartney, BA, LLB (d 1956); 3 s (David b 1952, Andrew b 1955, Patrick b 1961), 2 da (Carola b 1965, Fiona decd); *Career* minister Church of Scotland; chaplain to overseas students Edinburgh 1955-58, minister Northfield Aberdeen 1958-63, warden Carberry Tower 1963-66, lectr and sr lectr Moray House Coll of Educ 1966-72; dir Scottish Cncl for Voluntary Orgns 1972-; *Recreations* beekeeping, sailing; *Clubs* New (Edinburgh); *Style*— Ross Flockhart, Esq; Longwood, Humbie, East Lothian EH36 5PN (☎ 087 533 208); Scottish Cncl for Voluntary Organisations, 19 Claremont Crescent, Edinburgh EH7 4QD

FLOOD, David Andrew; s of Frederick Joseph Alfred Flood, of Selsey, W Sussex, and June Kathleen, *née* Alexander; *b* 10 Nov 1955; *Educ* Royal GS Guildford, St Johns Coll Oxford (MA), Clare Coll Cambridge (PGCE); *m* 26 June 1976, Alayne Priscilla, da of Maurice Ewart Nicholas, of Farnborough, Hants; 2 s (Christopher Nicholas b 1982, Joshua Samuel b 1986), 1 da (Oliva Kathryn b 1979); *Career* asst organist Canterbury Cathedral 1978-86, music master King's Sch Canterbury 1978-86; organist and master of choristers: Lincoln Cathedral 1986-88, Canterbury Cathedral 1988-; organist for enthronement of Archbishop Runcie 1979, organist for visit of Pope John Paul II 1982; asst dir Canterbury Choral Soc 1978-85, fndr and dir Canterbury Cantata Choir 1985-86, musical dir Lincoln Choral Soc 1986-88, Canterbury Music Club 1984-86 and 1988-, hon sr memb Darwin Coll Univ of Kent; FRCO 1976 (ch 1975); *Recreations* travel, motoring, DIY; *Style*— David Flood, Esq; 6 The Precincts, Canterbury, Kent CT1 2EE (☎ 0227 765 219, office 0227 762 862, fax 0227 762 897)

FLOOD, Prof John Edward; OBE (1986); s of Sydney Edward Flood (d 1983), of London, and Elsie Gladys Flood (d 1967); *b* 2 June 1925; *Educ* City of London Sch, QMC London (BSc, PhD, DSc); *m* 23 April 1949, Phyllis Mary, da of John Charles Groocock (d 1978), of Worthing; 2 s (Nicholas John b 20 Oct 1951, Stephen Charles b 25 May 1954); *Career* experimental offr admiralty signals estab 1944-46, devpt engr Standard Telephones and Cables Ltd 1946-47, exec engr PO Res Station 1947-52, chief engr advanced devpt laboratories telecommunications div Assoc Electrical Industries Ltd 1952-65; Aston Univ: prof electrical engrg 1965-, head dept 1967-81 and 1983-, dean of faculty engrg 1971-74, sr pro vice chancellor 1981-83; chm: IEE professional gp on Telecommunications Systems & Networks 1974-77, univs cttee on Integrated Sandwich Courses 1981-82, Br Standards ctee on Telecommunications 1981-; memb monopolies and mergers cmmn 1985-; memb cncl Selly Oak colls 1966-85, chm S Midland centre IEE 1967-68 vice pres Birmingham Electrical club 1988-89; Freeman City of London 1957, Liveryman Worshipful Co Engrs 1984; FIEE 1959, FInstP 1987; *Books* Telecommunication Networks (1975); *Recreations* swimming, writing, winemaking; *Clubs* Royal Overseas; *Style*— Prof John Flood; 60 Widney Manor Rd, Solihull, West Midlands B91 3JQ (☎ 021 705 3604); Aston University, Aston Triangle, Birmingham, B4 7ET (☎ 021 359 3611, fax 021 359 7358, telex 336 997)

FLOOD, Brig (George) Robert; MC (1945); s of Rev J C Flood (d 1963); *b* 26 Nov 1919; *Educ* Lancing Coll, Reading Univ; *m* 1945, Jeanette Mary Lapage, da of late Col John Sydney Lapage Norris; 1 s, 1 da; *Career* Royal Berks Regt 1939, Parachute Regt 1958; Cdr 44 Para Bde (V) 1965-68, Asst Cdr Sandhurst 1968-71, ADC 1972-74; *Recreations* gardening; *Clubs* MCC, Free Foresters, Army & Navy; *Style*— Brig Robert Flood, MC; Cheverell Mill, Little Cheverell, Devizes, Wilts (☎ 0380 812 481)

FLOREY, Hon Charles du Vé; s of late Baron Florey, OM, FRS, MD (Life Peer) (d 1968), and his 1 wife Mary Ethel, *née* Reed (d 1966); *b* 11 Sept 1934; *Educ* Rugby, Cambridge Univ (MD), Yale Univ (MPH); *m* 14 April 1966, Susan Jill, da of Cecil Hopkins, of Tuttle Hill, Nuneaton, Warwicks; 1 s, 1 da; *Career* prof Dept of Community Medicine at Ninewells Hosp and Medical Sch; FFCM; FRCPE; *Style*— The Hon Charles Florey; Ninewells Hospital and Medical Sch, Dundee DD1 9SY (☎ 0382 60111)

FLOREY, Baroness; Hon Margaret Augusta; *née* Fremantle; 2 da of 3 Baron Cottesloe, CB, VD, TD (d 1956) and Florence, *née* Tapling (d 1956); sis of 4 Baron Cottesloe; *b* 2 Dec 1904; *Educ* Oxford Univ (MA, DM 1950); *m* 1, 9 April 1930 (m dis 1946), Denys Arthur Jennings, BM, BCh, o s of A E Jennings, of Budleigh Salterton, Devon; m 2, 6 June 1967, as his 2 w, Baron Florey, OM, FRS (d 21 Feb 1968); scientist who pioneered the use of penicillin); *Career* lecturer Oxford Univ (Pathology) 1945-72, research fellow of LMH Oxford 1952-72; *Books* Antibiotics (contrib, 1949); contrib to scientific journals 1939-67; *Style*— The Rt Hon Lady Florey; 4 Elsfield Rd, Old Marston, Oxford

FLOWER, Dr Anthony John Frank (Tony); s of Frank Robert Edward Flower (d 1977), of Clyst Hydon, Devon, and Dorothy Elizabeth, *née* Williams; *b* 2 Feb 1951; *Educ* Chipping Sodbury GS, Univ Exeter (BA, MA, MS), Univ of Leicester (PhD); *Career* graphic designer 1973-76, first gen sec Tawney Soc 1982-88, co-ordinator Argo Venture 1984-; fndr memb SDP 1981, memb cncl for Soc Democracy; dir: Res Inst for Econ and Socl Affrs 1982-, Argo Tst 1986-, Healthline Health Info Serv 1986-88, Health Info Tst 1987-88 (tstee 1988-), centre for Educ Choice 1988-; tstee: Health Info Tst 1982, GAIA: ed Tawney Journal 1982-88, assoc Open Coll of the Arts 1988-, co-fndr and managing ed Samizdat magazine 1988-; *Recreations* making & restoring musical instruments; *Style*— Dr Tony Flower; 18 Victoria Park Sq, London, E2 9PF, (☎ 01 980 6263)

FLOWER, Hon Anthony John Warburton; yr s of 10 Viscount Ashbrook, KCVO, MBE, *qv*; *b* 6 June 1938; *Educ* Eton; *m* 1970, Bridget Karen, yr da of J Duncan; 1 da (Alexandra Jane b 1972); *Style*— Hon Anthony Flower; Prouts Farm, Hawkley, Liss, Hampshire

FLOWER, Dennis Lowndes; CBE (1987), DL (Warwicks 1982); only s of Spenser Aldborough Flower (whose maternal gf was John Morley Dennis, himself 4 s of Rev Meade Swift, who took the surname Dennis after inheriting the estates of his mother Frances's bro, 1 and last Baron Tracton who d 1782. Frances's husb Thomas Swift was s of Meade Swift of Lynn, JP, who was in his turn 1 cous of Jonathan Swift, the writer); *b* 30 May 1915; *Educ* Stowe, Clare Cambridge; *Career* with Flower & Sons (brewers, Stratford-on-Avon, later Whitbread Flowers) 1939-77; chm exec cncl Shakespeare Birthplace Tst 1966-, vice chm exec cncl Royal Shakespeare Theatre; High Sheriff Warwicks 1981; *Recreations* fishing; *Clubs* Boodle's; *Style*— Dennis FLower, Esq, CBE, DL; Ilmington Manor, Shipston-on-Stour, Warwicks CV36 4LA (☎ 060 882 230)

FLOWER, Dr Desmond John Newman; MC (1944); s of Sir Walter Newman Flower (d 1964), and his 1 wife Evelyne, *née* Readwin; *b* 25 August 1907; *Educ* Lancing, King's Coll Cambridge (MA); *m* 1, 1931 (m dis 1952), Margaret Cameron Coss; 1 s; m 2, 1952 (m dis 1972), Anne Elizabeth Smith; 1 s, 2 da; m 3, 1987, Sophie Rombeyko; *Career* Maj NW Europe (despatches 1945); publisher Cassell & Co: dir 1931, chm 1958, ret 1972; pres des Comités de L'Alliance Française en Grande Bretagne 1963-72; dir Michael Joseph Ltd 1963-71; chm Folio Society 1948-72; Offr de la Légion d'Honneur D Litt(hc) Univ Caen;; *Books* Complete Poetical Works of Ernest Dowson (ed, 1934), The Pursuit of Poetry (1939), Voltaire's England (1950), History of 5 Battalion Argyll and Sutherland Highlanders (1950), The War 1939-45 (ed, 1960), Letters of Ernest Dowson (ed, 1967), New Letters of Ernest Dowson (ed, 1984); *Clubs* Royal and Ancient St Andrews; *Style*— Dr Desmond Flower, MC; 26 Grovedale Rd, London N19 3EQ (☎ 01 281 0080)

FLOWER, Lady Gloria Regina Malet; *née* Vaughan; eldest da of 7 Earl of Lisburne (d 1965), and Maria Isabel Regina Aspasia, *née* de Bittencourt (d 1944); *b* 1916; *m* 1, 7 June 1935 (m dis 1952), Sir Nigel Thomas Loveridge Fisher, MC, s of late Cdr Sir Thomas Fisher, KBE, RN; 1 s, 1 da; m 2, 10 June 1952, Ronald Philip Flower, OBE, o s of late Philip Arthur Flower; 1 s; *Style*— Lady Gloria Flower; Manor Farm Cottage, Weston Patrick, nr Basingstoke, Hants

FLOWER, Keith David; s of Frank Leslie Flower (d 1976), of 20 St Ursula Grove, Pinner, Middx, and Catherine Elizabeth, *née* Millo (d 1981); *b* 20 Jan 1945; *Educ* Merchant Taylors; *m* 11 May 1973, Jennifer, da of Edward Arthur Howick; 1 da (Melanie b 1976); *Career* admitted slr 1969, HJ Heinz Ltd 1970-73, John Laing Properties Ltd 1973-76; sr ptnr Keith Flower & Co 1976-; memb Rotary Club of Pinner; memb Law Soc; *Clubs* Sloane, Durrants; *Style*— Keith Flower, Esq; Lane End, Sandy Lodge Rd, Moor Park, Rickmansworth, Herts WD3 1LJ; 25/27 Pinner Green, Pinner, Middx HA5 2AF (☎ 01 868 1277, fax 01 868 1356, car tel 0836 281 058, telex 8951947 FLOWER G)

FLOWER, Hon Michael Llowarch Warburton; DL (Cheshire 1982), JP (Cheshire 1983); s and h of 10 Viscount Ashbrook, KCVO, MBE; *b* 9 Dec 1935; *Educ* Eton, Worcester Coll Oxford (MA); *m* 8 May 1971, Zoë Mary, da of Francis Henry Arnold Engleheart, of The Priory, Stoke-by-Nayland, Suffolk (d 1963); 2 s (Rowland b 1975, Harry b 1977), 1 da (Eleanor b 1973); *Career* 2 Lt Gren Gds 1955; landowner; slr 1963, ptnr Farrer & Co 1966-76; ptnr March Pearson & Skelton Manchester 1986-; chm Taxation sub-ctee CLA 1984-86; *Recreations* gardening, shooting; *Clubs* Brooks's, St James's Manchester; *Style*— The Hon Michael Flower, JP, DL; The Old Parsonage, Arley Green, Northwich, Cheshire CW9 6LZ (☎ 056 585 277); 41 Spring Gardens, Manchester M2 2BB (☎ 061 832 7290)

FLOWERS, Baron (Life Peer UK 1979); Brian Hilton Flowers; o s of late Rev Harold Joseph Flowers, of Swansea; *b* 13 Sept 1924; *Educ* Bishop Gore GS Swansea, Gonville and Caius Cambridge, Birmingham Univ; 1951, Mary Frances, er da of Sir Leonard Frederick Behrens, CBE (d 1978); 2 step s; *Career* physicist; head of theoretical physics Div at AERE Harwell 1952-58, prof of theoretical physics Manchester Univ 1958-61, Langworthy prof of physics Manchester Univ 1961-72, rector Imperial Coll of Science and Technol 1973-85; chm: SRC 1967-73, Royal Cmmn on Environmental Pollution 1973-76, Standing Cmmn on Energy and Environment 1978-81; joined SDP 1981, managing tstee Nuffield Fndn 1982- (chm 1987-); chm Ctee of Vice-Chllrs and Princs 1983-85; vice-chllr Univ of London 1985-; Rutherford Medal and Prize IPPS 1968, Glazebrook Medal IPPS 1987, Chalmers Medal Sweden 1980; FInstP 1961, Hon FCGI 1975, Hon MRIA 1976, Hon FIEE 1975; MA (Oxon) 1956; Hon DSc (Sussex) 1968, (Wales) 1972, (Manchester) 1973, (Leicester) 1973, (Liverpool) 1974, (Bristol) 1982, Oxford (1985); Hon DEng (Nova Scotia) 1983; sr fellow RCA 1983; Offr de la Légion d'Honneur 1981; Hon ScD (Dublin); Hon LLD (Dundee) Hon LLD (Glasgow) 1987; FRS; kt 1969; *Style*— The Rt Hon Lord Flowers; University of London, Senate House, Malet Street, London WC1E 7HU (☎ 01 636 8000)

FLOWERS, Lady Mary Joy; *née* Abney-Hastings; da of Countess of Loudoun, *qv* and (3 husb), Peter Abney-Hastings; *b* 18 Mar 1957; *Educ* Leicester Univ (BA, MA); *m* 11 Sept 1982, David John Flowers; 1 da (Clare Hannah Flowers b 1987); *Style*— Lady Mary Flowers

FLOYD, David Henry Cecil; s and h of Sir Giles Floyd, 7 Bt; *b* 2 April 1956; *Educ* Eton; *m* 20 June 1981, Caroline Ann, da of John Henry Beckly, of Manor Farm, Bowerchalke, Wilts; 2 da (Suzanna b 1983, Claire b 1986); *Career* Lt 15/19 The King's Royal Hussars; ACA 1982; merchant banker; *Clubs* Cavalry & Guards; *Style*— David Floyd, Esq; Tinwell Manor, Stamford, Lincs

FLOYD, Sir Giles Henry Charles; 7 Bt (UK 1816); s of Lt-Col Sir John Duckett Floyd, 6 Bt, TD (d 1975); *b* 27 Feb 1932; *Educ* Eton; *m* 1, 23 Nov 1954 (m dis 1978), Lady Gillian Moyra Katherine Cecil, da of 6 Marquess of Exeter, KCMG; 2 s; m 2, 1985, Mrs Judy Sophia Lane, er da of William Leonard Tregoning, CBE, of Landue Launceston, Cornwall; *Heir* s David Henry Cecil Floyd; *Career* farmer dir Burghley Estate Farms 1958-, High Sheriff of Rutland 1968; *Recreations* fishing; *Clubs* Turf, Farmers'; *Style*— Sir Giles Floyd, Bt; Tinwell Manor, Stamford, Lincs (☎ 0780 62676)

FLOYD, John Anthony; s of Lt-Col Arthur Bowen Floyd, DSO, OBE (d 1965, himself grandson of Major-General Sir Henry Floyd, 2 Bt), and Iris Clare, *née* Belding; *b* 12 May 1923; *Educ* Eton; *m* 5 Oct 1948, Margaret Louise, o da of late Major Hugo Rosselli, of Worlington Old Hall, Suffolk; 2 da (Elizabeth b 1951, Caroline b 1953); *Career* served WW II in KRRC; chm: Christie Manson & Woods Ltd 1974-, Christies International Ltd 1976-; *Clubs* Boodle's, White's, MCC; *Style*— John Floyd, Esq; Ecchinswell House, Newbury, Berkshire (☎ 0635 298237)

FLOYD, Peter Joseph; s of Arthur Floyd, CBE (d 1978), and Nora Floyd, *née* Poulton (d 1978); *b* 2 Dec 1928; *Educ* Charterhouse (scholarship), Balliol Coll Oxford (BA, MA); *m* 29 July 1972, Madeline Edna Clare, da of Charles Samuel Lincoln Whiteley, of Wantage, Oxon; *Career* admitted slr 1954; dep clerk Devon CC 1971-73, county sec Oxon CC 1973, county slr Oxon CC 1980; clerk Oxon Magistrates Cts Ctee 1974-, Probation Ctee 1974-; sec Oxon Ld-Lt's Advsy Ctee 1976; chm Soc of County Secs 1985-86; *Recreations* inactivity, reading; *Clubs* Sloane; *Style*— Peter J Floyd, Esq; The Stables, East Hanney, Wantage, Oxon OX12 0JJ (☎ 023587 240); County Hall, Oxford (☎ 0865 815367, fax 0865 726155)

FLOYD, Richard Eaglesfield; s of Harold Bailey Floyd, FCA, of Purley, Surrey, and (Edith) Margaret, *née* Griffith (d 1954); *b* 9 June 1938; *Educ* Dean Close Sch Cheltenham; *m* 16 June 1973 (m dis 1984), Caroline, da of Maurice Clement Jones (d 1957); 1 da (Emilia Margaret b 1974); *Career* articled clerk Fincham Vallance & Co 1956-61, sr clerk 1961-62, 1964-65 insolvency admin Cork Gully 1965-70; ptnr Floyd Nash & Co (later styled Floyd Harris) 1971-82, when firm merged with Moores & Rowland 1982-; held appointments as admin receiver, administrator, liquidator and tstee; memb Assoc Européenne des Practiciens des Procédures, Collectives; FCA 1962, FIPA 1976; Freeman of the City of London 1985; *Books* Administration, Voluntary Liquidation and Receivership (2 edn 1987), Personal Insolvency - A Practical Guide (1987), Company Administration Orders and Voluntary Arrangements (1988);; *Publications* author of many articles on insolvency matter in specialised journals; member of editorial advisory board of Insolvency Law & Practise; *Recreations* writing, lecturing, mountain walking; *Style*— Richard Floyd, Esq; 9 Beaufort Road, Kingston-upon-Thames, Surrey KT1 2TH (☎ 01 546 5833); Moores & Rowland, Clifford's Inn, Fetter Lane, London EC4A 1AS (☎ 01 831 2988/01 831 2345, telex 886504, fax 01 831 6123)

FLOYD EWIN, Sir David Ernest Thomas; LVO (1954), OBE (1965); 7 s of Frederick P Ewin (d 1929), and Ellen, *née* Floyd, of Blackheath; *b* 17 Feb 1911; *Educ* Eltham, MA (Lambeth); *m* 1948, Marion Irene, da of William Robert Lewis, of Paignton, S Devon; 1 da; *Career* notary public; lay admin St Paul's Cathedral 1939-43, registrar and receiver 1944-78, conslt to the Dean and Chapter 1978-; chm: Tubular Exhibition Group plc 1978-, memb of court Common Cncl for Ward of Castle Baynard (dep 1972-), vice-pres Castle Baynard Ward Club (chm 1962 and 1988); chm Corpn of London Gresham Ctee 1975-76; memb Lord Mayor and Sheriffs Ctee 1976, 1978 chm 1988; court of assts Hon Irish Soc 1976-79; surrogate for Province of Canterbury; tstee: City Parochial Fndn 1967- (chm pensions ctee 1978-), St Paul's Cathedral Tst 1978-, Temple Bar Tst 1979-, City of London Endowment Tst for St Paul's Cathedral (dep chm 1982-), Allchurches Tst; hon dir British Humane Soc; govr: Sons of the Clergy Corpn (memb of court), St Gabriel's Coll Camberwell 1946-72: past master Scriveners Co, Liveryman Wax Chandlers Co, Freeman City of London, sr past master Guild of Freemen of City of London; gold staff offr at Coronation of HM 1953; KStJ 1970 (OStJ 1965); kt 1974; *Books* A Pictoral History of St Paul's Cathedral (1970), The Splendour of St Paul's (1973); *Recreations* tennis, fishing, gardening; *Clubs* City Livery, Guildhall; *Style—* Sir David Floyd Ewin, LVO, OBE; Silver Springs, Stoke Gabriel, South Devon (☎ 080 428 264); Chapter House, St Paul's Churchyard, London EC4M 8AD (☎ 01 248 2705); St Augustine's House, 4 New Change, London EC4M 9AB (☎ 01 248 0683)

FLOYDE, Marilyn Ysanne; da of Kenneth Arthur Floyde (d 1970); *b* 7 Oct 1950; *Educ* Royal Tunbridge Wells GS, Dartington Hall Devon; *m* m 1985, Richard Sutcliffe; 1 s (William b 1980), 1 da (Olivia b 1985); *Career* teacher; lectr Dovecot Arts Centre 1976-78; theatre and dance offr South West Arts 1978-81; memb IBA Gen Advsy Cncl; acting chm Dance Tales; dir Exeter & Devon Arts Centre 1983-; *Recreations* walking, choreography, piano; *Style—* Ms Marilyn Floyde; Exeter & Devon Arts Centre, Bradninch Place, Gandy Street, Exeter, Devon (☎ 0392 219741)

FLOYER, Prof Michael Antony; s of Cdr William Antony Floyer, RN, Legion of Honour (d 1943), of Inglewood, Camberley, Surrey, and Alice Rosalie, *née* Whitehead (d 1979); *b* 28 April 1920; *Educ* Sherborne, Trinity Hall Cambridge (MB, ChB, MD); *m* 8 June 1946, Lily Louise Frances, da of H P Burns (d 1940); 2 s (David b 1947, Christopher b 1951), 1 da (Jennifer b 1948); *Career* Sqdn-Ldr RAF 1946-48, med specialist RAF Hosps at Karachi and Cawnpore; London Hosp Med Coll 1948-86: lectr 1948, sr lectr 1951, asst dir of med unit 1953, reader 1967, prof of medicine 1974, dean 1982, fell 1988-; The London Hospital-; Hon conslt physician 1958-86, conslt in charge emergency and accident dept 1976-86, consulting physician 1986-, locum consultant 1987; seconded as prof of medicine to Nariobi Unvi 1973-75; sec Med Res Soc 1962-67 (memb 1949-), memb Tower Hamlets Dist Health Authy 1982-86; pres and tres The London Hosp Clubs Union: pres RFC, climbing and backpacking club, History Soc; MD 1952, FRCP 1963; *Recreations* wild things and wild places, music, rugby football; *Style—* Prof Michael Floyer; Duke's Cottage, Willingale, Ongar, Essex CM5 OSW (☎ 0277 86270); Medical Unit, The London Hosp Med Coll, London E1 2AD (☎ 01 377 7602)

FLOYER-ACLAND, Brig Stafford Nugent; CBE (1967), DL (Dorset 1975); o s of Lt-Gen Arthur Nugent Floyer-Acland, CB, DSO, MC, DL (d 1980), and Evelyn Stafford, *née* Still (d 1973); *b* 23 Dec 1916; *Educ* Marlborough Coll, RMC Sandhurst; *m* 14 April 1950, Patricia Egidia Hastings, da of Lt-Col Richard St Barbe Emmott (d 1949), of Stafford House, Dorchester; 2 s (Richard b 1952, Andrew b 1955), 1 da (Victoria b 1962); *Career* DCLI 1937-59; CO 1 Bn KOYLI 1959-61; instr Australian Army Staff Coll 1962; cdr 130 (West Country) Bde 1963-65; dep cdr Land Forces Borneo, Brig i/c admin and cdr Force Troops Sabah 1965-66; Brig AQ Northern Cmd 1966-67; High Sheriff of Dorset 1974-75; *Recreations* shooting, fishing, gardening; *Style—* Brig Stafford Floyer-Acland, CBE, DL; The Dairy House, West Stafford, Dorchester, Dorset DT2 8AL (☎ 0305 64005)

FLYNN, Prof Frederick Valentine; eldest s of Frederick Walter Flynn (d 1957), and Jane Laing, *née* Valentine; *b* 6 Oct 1924; *Educ* UCL, UCH Med Sch London (MB, BSc, MD); *m* 1955, Catherine Ann, o da of Dr Robert Walter Warrick (d 1950); 1 s (David b 1956), 1 da (Frances b 1959); *Career* prof of chemical pathology Univ Coll Sch of Med 1970-, conslt chemical pathologist to UCH London 1960-, civil conslt in chemical pathology to RN 1978- FRCP, FRCPath; *Recreations* photography, gardening; *Style—* Prof Frederick Flynn; 20 Oakleigh Ave, Whetstone, London N20 9JH (☎ 01 445 0882); Dept of Chemical Pathology, University College and Middx School of Medicine, Windeyer Building, Cleveland St, London W1P 6DB (☎ 01 636 8333)

FLYNN, Paul Phillip; MP (Lab) Newport W 1987-; s of James Flynn (d 1939), and Kathleen Rosien *née* Williams (d 1988); *b* 9 Feb 1935; *Educ* St Illtyd's Coll Cardiff, Univ Coll Cardiff; *m* 1, 6 Feb 1962, Ann Patricia; 1 s (James Patrick b 1965), 1 da (Rachel Sarah b 1963 d 1979); m 2, 31 Jan 1985, Lynne Samantha; *Career* chemist in the steel industry 1955-81, since worked in local radio and as research asst to Euro MP Llewellyn Smith; Labour Party: front bench spokesman Welsh Affrs May 1988-, front bench spokesman Social Security Nov 1988-; *Clubs* Ringland Labour, Pill Labour; *Style—* Paul Flynn, Esq, MP; House of Commons, London SW1A 0AA (☎ 01 219 3468)

FLYTE, Ellis Ashley; da of Thomas Hynd Flyte, and Anne Margaret Paterson Little Duncan; *Educ* The Mary Erskine Sch for Young Ladies Edinburgh, London Coll of Fashion (Dip in Art and Fashion Design); *Career* fashion and costume designer, bunny girl Dorchester Hotel; costumes: RSC, Royal Opera House, Thames TV; designed costumes for films incl: Dark Crystal, Out of Africa, Labyrinth, Camden Town Boy; set up Ellis Flyte Fashion Design Showroom London 1984; ACTT, NATTKE; *Recreations* travel, photography, film, dance, jacuzzis, music, art, dressing up; *Clubs* Le Petit Opportune Paris, Chelsea Arts, Blast R101, Bill Stickers, The Ritz Casino Gamblin C; *Style—* Ms Ellis Flyte; 18 Parliament Hill, Hampstead, London, NW3 (☎ 01 267 9653); 12 Greenland St, Camden, London, NW1 0ND (☎ 01 267 9653)

FOALE, Air Commodore Colin Henry; s of William Henry Foale (d 1979), of Galmpton, Devon, and Frances Margaret, *née* Muse (d 1969); *b* 10 June 1930; *Educ* Wolverhampton GS, RAF Coll Cranwell, RAF Staff Coll Bracknell, Jt Servs Staff Coll Latimer, Royal Coll of Def Studies Belgrave Sq; *m* 19 Sept 1954, Mary Katherine, da of Prof Samuel Bannister Harding (d 1925), of Minneapolis, USA; 2 s (Michael b 6 Jan 1957, Christopher b 13 March 1958, d 1979) 1 da (Susan b 2 May 1962); *Career* pilot 13 photo recce sqdn (Meteor) Kabrit Egypt 1952-53, Flt Cdr 32 fighter sqdn (Vampire), Deversoir Egypt 1953-54, RAF flying coll Manby (fighter instr Hunters) 1954-57, instr in selection techniques offr Selection Centre RAF Hornchurch 1958-60, Sqdn Cdr 73 light Bomber Sqdn Akrotiri Cyprus 1960-63, organiser Biggin Hill Battle of Br display 1963, chm cockpit ctee TSR2 MOD (PE) 1965, Wing Cdr air plans HQ RAF Germany 1965-68, Co 39 photo recce sqdn (Canberras) Luqa Malta 1969-71, Gp Capt SO flying MOD (PE) 1971-74, station cdr RAF Luqa Malta 1974-76, dir RAF PR 1977-79, ret at own request 1979; aviation advsr Yorks TV Drama 1979-80, trg advsr to chm Cons Pty Central off 1980-81, pilot to ctee for aerial photography Cambridge Univ 1981-; memb: Nat Tst, Woodland Tst, RSPB, RYA, St Catherines Coll Cambridge 1981; hon memb Univ Air Sqdn Cambridge 1981, dining memb Selwyn Coll Cambridge 1981, fndr memb RAF Historical Soc 1986; Cormoraunt 1969, RCDS 1977, RSVI 1980, FBIM 1980, FIWM 1981; *Recreations* flying, sailing (yacht Wrabness Aeolus), travel. theatre, music, writing; *Clubs* RAF; *Style—* Air Cdre Colin Foale; 37 Pretoria Rd, Cambridge CB4 1HD, (☎ 0223 352684); Aerial Photography, The Mond Building, Free School Lane, University of Cambridge CB2 3RF, (☎ 0223 334577, fax 0223 334748, telex 81240 CAMSPL G)

FOALE, Lady Emma Cecile; *née* Gordon; er da of 6 Marquess of Aberdeen and Temair, *qv*; *b* 26 May 1953; *m* 6 Sept 1980, Dr Rodney Foale, eldest s of Maurice Spencer Foale, of Melbourne, Australia; 2 s (Archie Alexander b 17 Sept 1984, Jamie b 1 April 1986); *Style—* Lady Emma Foale

FOALE, Graham Douglas Kenneth; JP (1981); s of Hubert Douglas Foale (d 1985), of Essex, and Lilian Kate, *née* Tolchari (d 1985); *b* 27 May 1938; *Educ* Clifton Coll Bristol; *m* 30 May 1964, Jean Barbara, da of Frederick Kershaw Sunderland (d 1949), of Sunderland; 2 s (Robin b 1967, Matthew b 1969); *Career* ptnr Bishop Fleming CAs Plymouth 1969-; memb S W Regnl Ind Devpt Bd 1977-83, Plymouth Round Table 1974-75; chm: Cornwall & Plymouth Branch of CAs 1979-80; memb: Small Practitioners Ctee, Inst of CAs 1982-86; FCA; *Recreations* walking, toy collecting; *Style—* Graham D K Foale, JP; 8, Blue Haze Close, Plymbridge Road, Glenholt, Plymouth, PL6 7HR; 2 Marlborough Rd, North Hill, Plymouth PL4 8LP (☎ 0752 262611)

FOCKE, Lady Tana Marie; *née* Alexander; da of 6 Earl of Caledon (d 1980), by 1 w, Ghislaine, o da of Cornelius Willem Dresselhuys, of Long Island, NY; *b* 2 Mar 1945; *m* 1973, Paul Everard Justus Focke, QC, s of Frederick Justus Focke; 2 da; *Style—* Lady Tana Focke; 7 Cheyne Walk, London SW3

FODEN, Edwin Peter; s of Edwin Richard Foden (d 1950), and Mary, *née* Cooke; *b* 24 Feb 1930; *Educ* Rossall, N Staffs Tech Coll; *m* 1957, Judith, da of James Harding Baxter, of Nantwich, Cheshire; 3 s; *Career* Lt REME (UK and Germany), fndr ERF Ltd, chm and chief exec ERF (Hldgs) plc, chm ERF Ltd, ERF S Africa (Pty) Ltd, ERF Plastics; vice-pres: SMMT 1971-83, Inst of Motor Industry 1981-; pres Congleton Cons Assoc;; *Recreations* golf, shooting, motor racing; *Clubs* REME Officers', Annabels; *Style—* Edwin Foden Esq; Oak Farm, The Heath, Sandbach, Cheshire (☎ 09367 2732); ERF Ltd, Sun Works, Sandbach, Cheshire (telex 36152)

FOGARTY, Christopher Winthrop; CB (1973); s of Philip Christopher Fogarty (d 1942), and Hilda Spencer Fogarty; *b* 18 Sept 1921; *Educ* Ampleforth, Christ Church Oxford (MA); *m* 1961, Elizabeth Margaret (d 1972), da of late Dr E L Ince; *Career* Lt RA; HM Treasury 1946-76: treasy rep in S Asia and Far East 1967-72, dep sec 1972-76; overseas devpt admin FCO 1976-81; *Recreations* Travellers'; *Style—* Christopher Fogarty, Esq, CB; 7 Hurlingham Ct, Ranelagh Gdns, London SW6 3SH (☎ 01 731 3948)

FOGG, Cyril Percival; CB (1973); s of Henry Fogg (d 1961), and Mabel May, *née* Orton (d 1981); *b* 28 Nov 1914; *Educ* Herbert Strutt Sch Belper, Gonville and Caius Coll Cambridge; *m* 1, 1939, Margaret Amie Millican, *née* Belper (d 1982); 2 da; m 2, 1983, Mrs June Adele McCoy (widow), of Bosham, Sussex; *Career* def scientist MOD, dir gen of Electronics Res & Devpt 1964-67, dep controller of Electronics 1967-73, dir Admty Surface Weapons Estab 1973-75, ret 1975; *Recreations* bird watching, continental caravan touring; *Style—* Cyril Fogg, Esq, CB; 10 Miles Cottages, Taylors Lane, Old Bosham, Chichester, W Sussex PO18 8QG (☎ 0243 573082)

FOGG, Prof Gordon Elliott (Tony); CBE (1983); s of Rev Leslie Charles Fogg (d 1951), of Ranmoor, Sheffield, and Doris Mary, *née* Elliott (d 1976); *b* 26 April 1919; *Educ* Dulwich Coll, Queen Mary Coll London (BSc), St John's Coll Cambridge (Phd, ScD); *m* 7 July 1945, Elizabeth Beryl, da of Rev Thomas Llechid Jones (d 1946), of Old Colwyn, Clwyd; 1 s (Timothy b 1951), 1 da (Helen b 1947); *Career* seaweed survey of Br Isles Miny of Supply 1942, plant physiologist Pest Control Ltd Cambridge 1943-45, asst lectr, lectr and reader dept botany UCL 1945-60, prof botany Westfield Coll Univ of London 1960-71, prof marine biology Univ Coll of N Wales 1971-85, prof emeritus marine biology Univ of Wales 1985-; govr Marine Biol Assoc 1973-, pres section K Br Assoc 1973 (biological gen sec 1967-72), chm cncl Freshwater Biological Assoc 1974-85, pres Inst Biology 1976-77, tstee Br Museum (Natural History) 1976-85, memb Royal Cmmn Environmental Pollution 1979-85, tstee Royal Botanic Gdns Kew 1983-; hon LLD Univ of Dundee 1974; FIBiol 1960, FRS 1965; *Books* The Metabolism of Algae (1953), The Growth of Plants (1963), Photosynthesis (1968), The Bluegreen Algae (with WDP Stewart, P Fay and AE Walsby, 1973), Algal Cultures and Phytoplankton Ecology (with B Thake, 1987); *Recreations* walking, antarctic history, listening to music; *Clubs* Athenaeum; *Style—* Prof Tony Fogg, CBE; Bodolben, Llandegfan, Anglesey, Gwynedd LL59 5TA (☎ 0248 712 916); Sch of Ocean Scis, Marine Sci Laboratories, Menai Bridge, Anglesey, Gwynedd ll59 5EY (☎ 0248 351 151)

FOGGIN, Erica; da of Wilhelm Myers Foggin, CBE (d 1986), of London, and Lotte Lina, *née* Breitmeyer; *b* 24 Sept 1957; *Educ* Francis Holland Sch, Westminster, Somerville Coll Oxford (MA); *m* 28 June 1986, Hugo Timothy Neville Barwick, s of Neville Barwick, of Bath; *Career* barr Middle Temple 1980; *Recreations* skiing, riding, swimming, cooking; *Style—* Miss Erica Foggin; 11 Kings Bench Walk, Temple, EC4 (☎ 01 353 2484, fax 353 1261)

FOLDES, Hon Mrs; Hon Elizabeth; da of Baron Roll of Ipsden, KCMG, CB (Life Peer); *b* 1946; *m* Peter Foldes; 1 s (Phineas), 1 da (Abigail); *Style—* Hon Mrs Foldes

FOLEY, 8 Baron (GB 1776); Adrian Gerald Foley; s of 7 Baron Foley (d 1927), and Minoru, *née* Greenstone (d 1968); *b* 9 August 1923; *m* 1, 23 Dec 1958 (m dis 1971), Patricia, da of Joseph Zoellner III, of Pasadena, California, and formerly w of Minor de Uribe Meek; 1 s, 1 da (Hon Alexandra Mary); m 2, 1972, Ghislaine, da of

Cornelius Willem Dresselhuys, of Long Island, USA and formerly w of (1) Maj Denis James Alexander, later 6 Earl of Caledon, and (2) 4 Baron Ashcombe, *qv*; *Heir* s, Hon Thomas Henry Foley; *Career* composer and pianist; *Clubs* White's; *Style*— The Rt Hon Lord Foley; c/o Marbella Club, Marbella, Malaga, Spain

FOLEY, Johanna Mary (Jo) (Mrs Desmond Quigley); da of John Andrew Foley, of Leamington Spa, Warwichshire, and Elizabeth Monica, *née* Savage; *b* 8 Dec 1945; *Educ* St Joseph's Convent Kenilworth, Univ of Manchester (BA); *m* 6 Jan 1973, Desmond Francis Conor, s of Thomas Francis Quigley (d 1969); *Career* womans ed Walsall Observer 1968, reporter Birmingham Post 1970, Eng teacher Monwick Secdy Mod Sch Colchester and More House Sch London 1972-73, launched and ed Successful Slimming Magazine 1976, sr asst ed Woman's Own 1978 (dep beauty ed 1973), woman's ed The Sun 1980; ed Woman 1982, exec ed (features) The Times 1984-85, managing ed Daily Mirror 1985-86; ed: Observer Magazine 1986-88, Options Magazine 1988; Ed of Year Br Soc Magazine Eds 1983; memb gen advsy ctee BBC 1984-88; *Style*— Miss Johanna Foley; Options Magazine, Kings Reach Tower, Stamford St, London SE1 9LS (☎ 01 261 5000)

FOLEY, Sir (Thomas John) Noel; CBE (1967); s of late Benjamin Foley, of Brisbane; *b* 1914; *Educ* Brisbane GS, Qld Univ (BA, BCom); *Career* dir: CSR Ltd, Aust United Corpn Ltd; chm: Allied Mfrg and Trading Industs Ltd, Courage Breweries Ltd, Westpac Banking Corpn (formerly Bank of NSW/CBA, pres Bank of NSW 1978-); founding pres World Wildlife Fund Aust 1978-80; kt 1978; *Style*— Sir Noel Foley, CBE; c/o Bank of New South Wales, 60 Martin Place, Sydney, NSW 2000, Australia

FOLEY, Hon Thomas Henry; s (by 1 m) and h of 8 Baron Foley; *b* 1 April 1961; *Style*— Hon Thomas Foley

FOLJAMBE, (George) Michael Thornhagh; s of Capt Robert Francis Thornhagh Foljambe, MC, RA (d 1987), and Zaida Nell, *née* Priestman (d 1985); *b* 28 May 1934; *Educ* Eton, Magdalene Coll Cambridge (BA); *Career* Nat Serv 2 Lt 15/19 Hussars; pres Notts Branch of Country Landowners Assoc 1986-; FLAS 1966-70, FRICS 1970; Bledisloe Gold Medal (RASE) 1983; *Recreations* riding, shooting, fishing; *Style*— Michael Foljambe, Esq; Mill Farm, Osberton, Worksop, Notts (☎ 0909 472206); Estate Office, Osberton (☎ 0909 472206)

FOLJAMBE, Hon Ralph Edward Anthony Savile; s of 5 Earl of Liverpool; *b* 24 Sept 1974; *Style*— Hon Ralph Foljambe; The Grange Farm, Exton, Oakham, Rutland LE15 8BN

FOLKESTONE, Viscount; William Pleydell-Bouverie; s (by 1 m) and h of 8 Earl of Radnor; *b* 5 Jan 1955; *Educ* Harrow, RAC Cirencester; *Style*— Viscount Folkestone; Round House, Charlton All Saints, Wilts (☎ 0722 330295)

FOLKMAN, Peter John; s of Eric Folkman; *b* 30 August 1945; *Educ* Oxford University (BA); *m* 25 July 1969, Judith Lella, da of Sir Hugh Weeks; 3 s (Michael Philip b 1972, David Thomas b 1975, James Peter b 1980); *Career* Burroughs Machines Ltd 1967-70, Rank Xerox Ltd 1971-73, 3i plc 1973-88 (dir 1986-88); md North of England Ventures Ltd 1989-; dir Salford Univ Hldgs plc; Skiing: Br Trg Team 1962-64, Oxford Univ Team 1968-69; *Recreations* skiing, squash; *Clubs* St James (Manchester), The Club of GB; *Style*— Peter Folkman, Esq; 6 Oakfield Rd, Manchester M20 0XA (☎ 061 434 5489); North of England Ventures Ltd, Cheshire House, Booth Street, Manchester M2 4AN (☎ 061 236 6600, fax 061 236 6650)

FOLL, John; s of Wallace Arthur Foll (d 1945), of Bucks, and Ethel Emmeline Oakley (d 1960); *b* 29 April 1923; *Educ* Berkhamsted Sch; *m* 7 July 1952 (m dis 1979), Chica, da of John Douglas Lea (d 1963), of Warwickshire; 4 s (Stephen b 1955, Charles b 1960, Guy b 1963, Ian b 1965), 1 da (Caroline b 1956 (d 1958)); *Career* Flt-Lt Navigator 3 Gp Bomber Cmd RAF 1942-46; ptnr Brown & Merry 1965-86, FRICS; *Recreations* yachting; *Clubs* Aldeburgh Yacht; *Style*— John Foll, Esq; Park House, The Avenue, Aspley Guise, Milton Keynes MK17 8HH; Brown & Merry, 8 High Street, Woburn Sands, Milton Keynes MK17 8RG

FOLLETT, Lady Helen Alison; da of Alexander Wilson, of Herne Bay, and Ellen Coote, *née* Cranfield; *b* 8 Jan 1907; *Educ* Castelnau Coll; *m* 1932, Sir David Follett (d 1982, sometime dir Science Museum); 3 s decd; *Recreations* conservation and animal welfare; *Style*— Lady Follett; 3 Elm Bank Gdns, Barnes, London SW13 (☎ 01 876 8302)

FOLLETT, Martin John; s of Claude Michael Trevor Follett, of Cornwall, and Maria Lyn, *née* Warne; *b* 14 Nov 1949; *Educ* Marlborough Coll, Sidney Sussex Coll, Cambridge (MA); *m* 12 Aug 1977, Orla Josephine; 2 s (Michael b 1978, James b 1985), 1 da (Sarah b 1980); *Career* slr; ptnr with Coodes; registrar of the diocese of Truro; dir Mount Edgcumbe Hospice Ltd; *Recreations* sailing; *Style*— Martin J Follett, Esq; Ingestre, Agar Road, Truro TR1 1JU (☎ 0872 73542); Coodes, 2 Princes Street, Truro TR1 2EZ

FOLLOWS, Lady; Claire Camille; da of late Julien Lemarchand; *m* 1922, Sir (Charles) Geoffrey Shield Follows, CMG (d 1983), rep Northern Rhodesia on Federal Interim Public Service Cmmn 1953-59; *Style*— Lady Follows; c/o Mrs C H Dawson, Craggen House, Oakhill Rd, Sevenoaks, Kent TN13 1NT

FOLLOWS, Lady; Mary Elizabeth; *née* Milner; *m* 1938, Sir Denis Follows, CBE (d 1983), chm Br Olympic Assoc; 2 da; *Style*— Lady Follows; 116b Barrowgate Rd, Chiswick, London W4 (☎ 01 994 5782)

FONE, Michael; s of Lawrence Fone, of Chippenfield, Herts, and late Mabel Edith Fone ; *b* 21 Feb 1933; *Educ* Hemel Hempstead GS, QMC London; *Career* md Rea Bros Ltd 1972-88 (dir 1969-72), dir Jupiter Tarbutt Ltd 1988-; dir St Peter's Res Tst 1975-; *Recreations* gardening, the arts ; *Clubs* Garrick; *Style*— Michael Fone, Esq; 29 Huguenot House, 19 Oxendon St, London SW1Y 4EH (☎ 01 839 3978); Marshfield Chippenham, Wilts SN14 8NU; Jupiter Tarbutt Ltd Knightsbridge House, 197 Knightsbridge, London SW7 1RB (☎ 01 581 8015)

FONSECA, Julian Francis Amador; s of Amador John Gabriel Fonseca (d 1984), and Mary Kathleen, *née* Jones; *b* 20 April 1951; *Educ* Prior Park Coll Bath, Reading Univ, Coll of Law; *m* 27 Aug 1977, Clarissa Julia, da of Harry Kerr Aitken; 1 s (Louis Charles Amador b 1984), 3 da (Emma Ruth Mary b 1980, Amy Frances Ann b 1982, Isabel b 1985); *Career* slr, ptnr Fonseca & Co at Ebbw Vale Abergavenny and Newport, Rutland Properties of Brecon; pt/t chm Social Security Appeal Tbnl; *Recreations* tennis, walking; *Style*— Julian F A Fonseca, Esq; White House Farm, Llanvetherine, Abergavenny, Gwent (☎ 0873 863 02); County Buildings, Market Street, Ebbw Vale, Gwent

FONTEYN, Dame Margot; DBE (1956, CBE 1951); Dame Margot Fonteyn de Arias; *b* 18 May 1919; *m* 1955, Roberto Arias, *qv*; *Career* prima ballerina; pres Royal Academy of Dancing 1954-, chllr Durham Univ 1982-; hon Doctor of Music Durham 1982; *Style*— Dame Margot Fonteyn, DBE; c/o Royal Opera House, Covent Garden, WC2

FOOKES, Dame Janet Evelyn; DBE (1989), MP (Cons) Plymouth Drake 1974-; da of Lewis Aylmer Fookes (d 1978), and Evelyn Margery, *née* Holmes; *b* 21 Feb 1936; *Educ* Hastings and St Leonards Ladies' Coll, Hastings HS for Girls, Royal Holloway Coll London (BA); *Career* teacher 1958-70; memb Hastings County Boro Cncl 1960-61 and 1963-70 (chm educn ctee 1967-70); MP (C) Merton and Morden 1970-74; sometime chm Educn Arts and Home Off sub-ctee of former Expenditure Ctee, former sec Parly Animal Welfare Gp; memb: Speaker's Panel of Chairmen, select ctee on Home Affrs 1984-, Cwlth War Graves Cmmn 1987-; vice-chm all-pty Mental Health Gp; fell Indust & Parl Tst, chm RSPCA 1979-81; memb cncl: RSPCA, Stonham Housing Assoc, SSAFA; *Recreations* keep-fit exercises, theatre, gardening; *Clubs* Royal Overseas League; *Style*— Dame Janet Fookes, DBE; House of Commons, London SW1A 0AA

FOOKS, John Anthony; JP; s of William John Fooks; *b* 24 August 1933; *Educ* Shrewsbury, Trinity Coll Cambridge; *m* 1959, (Maureen) Heather, da of Percival Charles Jones, sometime High Sheriff of Gwent; 3 s, 1 da; *Career* gen cmmr Inland Revenue; chm Cardiff & Provincial Properties plc 1980; dirs include: Fooks Property Co Ltd, Garnar Booth plc, Pittard Garnar plc; chm: East Surrey Water Co, The Bradford Property Tst plc, The Sutton District Water Co; memb Lloyds 1975; Freeman City of London 1976, Liveryman Worshipful Co Broderers; FCA; *Recreations* golf, shooting, music, bridge; *Clubs* Cardiff and County, Rye GC, Golf Match, Oxford and Cambridge University, MCC, Lloyds YC; *Style*— John Fooks, Esq, JP; 52 Trinity Church Sq, London SE1; Dale Hill Farm House, Ticehurst, E Sussex TN5 7DQ

FOORD, Derek Fergus Richard; *b* 19 August 1931; *m* 1985, Kate; 1 s (John b 1965), 1 da (Rachel b 1963) from previous m; 2 step da (Vanessa b 1968, Sandra b 1971); *Career* fin dir TSL Gp plc (UK); 1981-; dir: Thermal American Fused Quartz Inc (USA), TSL Quadrant Ltd (UK), TSL Semicon Ltd (UK), vice-pres Japan High Purity Silica Ltd (Akita Japan); FCA; *Recreations* fell walking; *Style*— Derek Foord, Esq; 3 Riverside, Darras Hall, Northumberland NE20 9PU (☎ 0661 72447); TSL Group plc, PO Box 6, Wallsend, Tyne & Wear NE28 6DG (☎ 091 2625311)

FOOT, Hon Benjamin Arthur; yst s of Baron Caradon, GCMG, KCVO, OBE, PC (Life Peer), *qv*; *b* 19 August 1949; *Educ* Leighton Park Sch, Univ Coll Swansea; *m* 18 April 1981, Sally Jane, o da of Maj M F S Rudkin, MC (d 1953); 1 s (Alexander Mark Isaac b 1986), 1 da (Joanna b 1983); *Career* Save the Children Fund: dep dir Karamoja-Uganda 1980-82; field dir: Pakistan 1982-84, Nepal 1985, Somalia 1986-88; regnl advsr E Africa 1988-; *Style*— Hon Benjamin Foot; c/o Save The Children Fund, Overseas Dept, 17 Grove Lane, London SE5 8RD

FOOT, Sir Geoffrey James; s of James Portrey Foot (d 1973), and Susan Jane, *née* Shields (d 1964); *b* 20 July 1915; *Educ* Launceston HS; *m* 1940, Mollie Winifred, da of Ernest E Snooks (d 1937); 2 s (Gregory b 1942, Warwick b 1946), 1 da (Jocelyn b 1948); *Career* memb legislative cncl of Tasmania 1961-72, ldr for govt 1969-72, memb of cncl of Univ of Tasmania 1971-85; chm Hydro-Electric Cmmn of Tasmania; Hon LLD Univ of Tasmania 1988; kt 1984 (for community serv in Australia); *Clubs* Tasmanian and Launceston; *Style*— Sir Geoffrey Foot; 85 Arthur Street, Launceston, Tasmania 7250 Australia (☎ 003 340573)

FOOT, Baron (Life Peer UK 1967); John Mackintosh Foot; 3 s of Rt Hon Isaac Foot, PC (d 1960), and his 1 w Eva, *née* Mackintosh (d 1946); bro of Lord Caradon and Michael Foot, former ldr of Lab Pty; *b* 17 Feb 1909; *Educ* Bembridge Sch, Balliol Coll Oxford; *m* 25 June 1936, Anne Bailey, da of Dr Clifford Bailey Farr, of Bryn Mawr, Pa, USA; 1 s, 1 da; *Career* WWII Maj RASC; admitted slr 1934, sr ptnr Foot & Bowden of Plymouth), chm UK Immigrants Advsy Serv 1970-78; Lib candidate: Basingstoke 1934 and 1935, Bodmin 1945 and 1950; pres Dartmoor Preservation Assoc 1976-; chm Cncl of Justice 1983-; *Recreations* Royal Western Yacht; *Style*— The Rt Hon Lord Foot; Yew Tree, Crapstone, Yelverton, Devon (☎ Yelverton 853417)

FOOT, Hon John Winslow; s of Baron Foot (Life Peer); *b* 23 Oct 1939; *Educ* Sidcot Sch, Philadelphia Coll of Art USA; *Style*— Hon John Foot; Yew Tree, Crapstone, Yelverton, Devon

FOOT, Michael David Kenneth Willoughby; s of Kenneth Willoughby Foot (d 1980), and Ruth Joan, *née* Cornah; *b* 16 Dec 1946; *Educ* Latymer Upper Sch, Pembroke Coll Cambridge (BA, MA), Yale Univ USA (MA); *m* 16 Dec 1972, Michele Annette Cynthia, da of Michael Stanley Macdonald, of Kingsgate, Kent; 1 s (Anthony b 5 June 1978), 2 da (Helen b 28 Oct 1980, Joanna b 22 July 1985); *Career* Bank of England 1969-: mangr gilt-edged div 1983, mangr money market div 1983, head foreign exchange div 1988-; UK alternate dir to IMF 1985-87; AIB 1973; *Recreations* church singing, chess, youth work, soccer referee; *Style*— Michael Foot, Esq; Bank of England, Threadneedle St, London EC2R 8AU (☎ 01 601 4123 fax 01 601 4822, tlx 885001

FOOT, Rt Hon Michael Mackintosh; PC (1974), MP (Lab) Blaenau Gwent 1983-; 4 s of Rt Hon Isaac Foot, PC (d 1960), MP (Lib) for Bodmin 1922-24 and 1929-35, pres Lib Party Orgn 1947, and 1 wife Eva, *née* Mackintosh (d 1946); bro of Lords Caradon and Foot; *b* 23 July 1913; *Educ* Forres Sch, Leighton Park, Wadham Coll Oxford; *m* 21 Oct 1949, Jill, *née* Craigie, former w of Jeffrey Dell; *Career* pres Oxford Union 1933; contested (Lab) Monmouthshire 1935; MP (Lab): Devonport (now Rt Hon David Owen's constituency) 1945-55, (contested Devonport 1959), Ebbw Vale 1960-1983; ed Tribune 1948-52 and 1955-60 (md 1945-74), actg ed Evening Standard 1942, later book critic, wrote column for Daily Herald 1944-64; oppn spokesman on Power and Steel Industries 1970-71, shadow ldr of House 1971-72, spokesman EEC Affairs 1972-74, sec of state Employment 1974-76, lord pres of Cncl and leader House of Commons 1976-79, succeeded Rt Hon James Callaghan as ldr of Oppn 1980-Oct 1983; Freedom of City of Plymouth 1982, Freedom of Borough of Blaenau Gwent 1983; hon fellow Wadham Coll; *Books* Guilty Men (with Frank Owen and Peter Howard, 1940), Armistice 1918-39 (1940), Trial of Mussolini (1943), Brendan and Beverley (1944), Still at Large (1950), Full Speed Ahead (1950), Guilty Men (with Mervyn Jones, 1957), The Pen and the Sword (1957), Parliament in Danger (1959), Aneurin Bevan Vol I 1897-1945 (1962), Vol II 1945-60 (1973), Debts of Honour (1980), Another Heart and Other Pulses (1984); *Style*— The Rt Hon Michael Foot, MP; House of Commons, London SW1A 0AA

FOOT, Michael Richard Daniell; TD (1945); s of Brig Richard Cunningham Foot (d 1969), and Nina Foot, *née* Raymond (d 1970); *b* 14 Dec 1919; *Educ* Winchester, New

Coll Oxford (MA, BLitt); *m* 1, 1945, Philippa Ruth Bosanquet; m 2, 1960, Elizabeth Mary Irvine King; 1 s, 1 da; m 3, 1972, Miriam Michaela, yst da of Prof Carl Paul Maria Romme (d 1980); *Career* WW II Major RA, parachutist served NW Europe (POW); historian; prof of modern hist Manchester 1967-73; Croix de Guerre; *Books* Gladstone and Liberalism (with J L Hammond, 1952), British Foreign Policy since 1898 (1956), Men in Uniform (1961), SOE in France (1966), Resistance (1976), Six Faces of Courage (1978) MI 9 (with J M Langley, 1979), SOE: an outline history (1984) ed: The Gladstone Diaries Vols I & II (1968), War and Society (1973), The Gladstone Diaries Vols III and IV (with H C G Matthew, 1974); ; *Clubs* Savile, Special Forces; *Style—* Michael R D Foot, Esq; 45 Countess Road, London NW5 2XH

FOOT, Hon Oliver Isaac; 2 s of Baron Caradon, GCMG, KCVO, OBE, PC (Life Peer), *qv*; *b* 19 Sept 1946; *Educ* Leighton Park Sch, RAC Cirencester, Goddard Coll Vermont USA; *m* 1967 (m dis 1975), Nancy Foot; 1 s (Jesse Isaac b 1973), 1 da (Mary Rachel b 1971); *Style—* Hon Oliver Foot; 16 Cedar Avenue, Locust Valley, NY 11560, USA

FOOT, Hon Paul Mackintosh; eldest s of Baron Caradon (Life Peer); *b* 8 Nov 1937; *Educ* Univ Coll Oxford; *m* 23 June 1962 (m dis 1970), Monica, da of Dr Robert P Beckinsale; 2 s (John b 1964, Matthew b 1966); m 2, 27 July 1971, Roseanne, da of Robert Harvey; 1 s (Tom b 1979); *Career* journalist; *Books* Immigration and Race in British Politics (1965), The Politics of Harold Wilson (1968), The Rise of Enoch Powell (1969), Who Killed Hareatty (1971), Why You Should Be a Socialist (1977), Red Shelley (1981), The Helen Smith Story (1983), Murder at the Farm: Who Killed Carl Bridgewater (1986); *Style—* Hon Paul Foot; Daily Mirror, Holborn Circus, London EC1

FOOTE, Maj-Gen (Henry) Robert Bowreman; VC (1944), CB (1952), DSO (1942); s of Lt-Col Henry Bruce Foote, RA (d 1932), and Elizabeth Jennie, *née* Jessett; *b* 5 Dec 1904; *Educ* St Cyprians Eastbourne, Bedford, Sandhurst; *m* 1, 1944, Anita Flint (d 1970), da of Carey Howard, of California, USA; m 2, 1981, Mrs Audrey Mary Ashwell, *née* Thompson; *Career* cmmnd RTC 1925, Capt RTR 1936, served Western Desert, instr Staff Coll 1941, attached Br Army Staff Mission Washington USA 1941, Palestine 1942 (despatches), cmd 7 RTR 1942, Italy (despatches), Brig RAC MELF 1945-47, Lt-Col 1946, cmd 2 RTR 1947-48, Col 1948, cmd Automotive Wing Fighting Vehicles Proving Estab, Miny of Supply 1948-49, temp Brig 1949, cmd 7 Armd Bde 1949-50, Cdr 11 Armd Div 1950-53, dir-gen Fighting Vehicles Min of Supply 1953-55, Maj-Gen 1951, dir RAC War Off 1955-58, ret 1958; Col Cmdt RTR 1957-64; vice-chm Victoria Cross and George Cross Assoc; *Recreations* golf; *Clubs* Army and Navy; *Style—* Maj-Gen Henry Foote, VC, CB, DSO; Furzefield, W Chiltington, Pulborough, Sussex (☎ 079 83 2130)

FOOTMAN, Charles Worthington Fowden; CMG (1952); s of William Llewellyn Footman (d 1923), and Mary Elizabeth, *née* Fowden (d 1961); *b* 3 Sept 1905; *Educ* Rossall Sch, Oxford Univ (BA); *m* 1947, Joyce Marcelle, da of Sir Charles Ewan Law (d 1974), of Worthing; 1 s (Robert), 2 da (Elizabeth, Catherine); *Career* HM Overseas Civil Serv, admin offr Zanzibar 1930, asst sec E African Govrs Conference 1942, seconded to Colonial Off 1943, fin sec Nyasaland 1947, chief sec 1951, acted govr on four occasions, ret 1960; chm Public Serv Cmmn Tanganyika 1960-61, Cwlth Rels Off 1962, min of Overseas Devpt 1964-70; *Recreations* golf, tennis; *Style—* Charles Footman, Esq, CMG; c/o Nat West Bank, 27 South St, Worthing

FOOTS, Sir James William; *b* 12 July 1916; *Educ* Melbourne Univ (BME); *m* 1939, Thora Hope Thomas; 1 s, 2 da; *Career* mining engr; pres: Aust Inst Mining and Metallurgy 1974, Aust Mining Indust Cncl 1974 and 1975; chm MIM Holdings 1970-83, dep chm 1983-87, dir Bank of NSW (now Westpac Banking Corpn) 1971-89 (chm 1987-89); chllr Univ of Queensland 1985-; kt 1975; *Recreations* golf; *Clubs* Brisbane, Queensland; *Style—* Sir James Foots; PO Box 662, Brisbane, Qld 4069, Australia (☎ 07 374 1043)

FOPP, Dr Michael Anton; s of Sqdn-Ldr Desmond Fopp, AFC, AE, of Tarporly, Cheshire, and Edna Meryl, *née* Dodd; *b* 28 Oct 1947; *Educ* Reading Blue Coat Sch, Met Police Coll, Met Police Trg Estab, City Univ (MA, PhD); *m* 5 Oct 1968, Rosemary Ann, da of V G Hodgetts, of Ashford, Kent; 1 s (Christopher Michael b 5 April 1973); *Career* Met Police Cadet Corps 1964-66, constable 1966-69, Met Police Mounted Branch 1969-79, ret due to injury on duty; Keeper Battle of Britain Museum 1982-85 (dep keeper 1979-81), co sec Hendon Museums Trading Co Ltd 1981-85, visiting lectr City Univ 1984-; dir: London Tport Museum 1985-87, RAF Museum 1988-; chm London Tport Flying Club, vice pres Friends of RAF Museum, vice pres London Underground Railway Soc; Freeman: City of London 1980, Guild of Air Pilots and Navigators 1987; MBIM 1980; *Books* Washington File (1983), The Battle of Britain Museum (1981), The Bomber Command Museum (1982), The Royal Air Force Museum (1984), RAF Museum Children's Activity Book (ed 1985); *Recreations* flying light aircraft, Chinese cookery, walking, writing; *Clubs* Royal Air Force; *Style—* Dr Michael A Fopp; Royal Air Force Museum, Hendon, London NW9 5LL (☎ 01 205 2266, fax 01 200 1751)

FORBES; *see*: Stuart-Forbes

FORBES, Alastair (Cameron); 3 s of James Grant Forbes (d 1955), of Boston, USA, and St Briac, France; *b* 2 May 1918; *Educ* Winchester, King's Coll Cambridge; *m* 1 (m dis 1960), Charlotte, da of Fleming Bergsøoe, of Copenhagen; 1 s; m 2, 7 Dec 1966 (m dis 1970), Hon Georgina Anne Ward, o da of 1 Viscount Ward of Witley; *Career* Finland Volunteer 1940, Lt RM 1940-41; diplomatic and war correspondent 1941-45: Observer, Sunday Times, France Libre, Daily Mail; contested (Lib) Hendon in Gen Election 1945; columist Sunday Dispatch 1945-57; conslt Brainstorm Centre 1969-79; journalist and literary critic: Times Literary Supplement, Spectator, Listener, Literary Review; *Recreations* reading, conversation, walking, cross-country skiing; *Clubs* White's, Beefsteak; *Style—* Alastair Forbes, Esq; 1837 Château D'Oex, Switzerland (☎ 29 4 76 50); Les Essarts, St Briac, I & V France (☎ 99 88 32 66)

FORBES, Hon Sir Alastair Granville; s of Granville Forbes (d 1943), and Constance Margaret, *née* Davis; *b* 3 Jan 1908; *Educ* Blundell's, Clare Coll Cambridge; *m* 11 Jan 1936, Constance Irene Mary, da of late Capt Charles Everard Hughes White, DSO, DSC, RN; 2 da (Anne Margaret b 1936, Elizabeth Mary b 1938); *Career* barr; HM Colonial Serv 1936, HM Overseas Judiciary 1956, puisne judge Kenya 1956, justice of appeal, ct of Appeal for Eastern Africa 1957 (vice-pres of the Ct 1958); federal justice Federal Supreme Ct of Rhodesia and Nyasaland 1963; pres Cts of Appeal for: Seychelles, St Helena, Falkland Is and Br Antarctic Territories 1965-88, Gibralter 1970-83, Br Indian Ocean Territory 1986-88; pres Pensions Appeal Tbnl for England and Wales 1973-80; kt 1960; *Recreations* gardening, fishing; *Clubs* Royal Cwlth Soc; *Style—* Hon Sir Alastair Forbes; Badgers Holt, Church Lane, Sturminster Newton, Dorset DT10 1DH

FORBES, Anthony David Arnold William; s of Lt-Col David Walter Arthur William Forbes, MC, Coldstream Guards (ka 1943), and Diana Mary, *née* Henderson (who m 2, 6 Marquess of Exeter; he d 1981, she d 1982); *b* 15 Jan 1938; *Educ* Eton; *m* 1, 14 June 1962 (m dis 1973), Virginia June, yr da of Sir Leonard Ropner, 1 Bt, MC, TD (d 1977); 1 s (Jonathan David b 1964), 1 da (Susanna Jane b 1966); m 2, 1973, Belinda Mary, da of Sir Hardman Earle, 5 Bt (d 1979); *Career* Lt Coldstream Gds 1956-59; memb Stock Exchange 1965, jt sr ptnr Cazenove & Co (stockbrokers); chm: Hosp and Homes of St Giles, Wellesley House Educn Tst; govr: Cobham Hall, Royal Choral Soc; *Recreations* music, shooting, gardening; *Style—* Anthony Forbes, Esq; 16 Halsey St, London SW3 (☎ 01 584 4749); Cazenove & Co, 12 Tokenhouse Yard, London EC2R 7AN (☎ 01 588 2828; telex 886758)

FORBES, Maj Anthony David Knox; s of Lt-Col William John Herbert Forbes of Rothiemay, DSO, *qv*, and Diana Burrel de Ker, *née* Knox; *b* 20 May 1944; *Educ* Eton, RMA Sandhurst; *m* 1985, Reidun, *née* Setane, of Norway; *Career* Maj Scots Gds, memb Royal Co of Archers Queen's Body Guard for Scotland; *Recreations* skiing, mountaineering, shooting, sailing (yacht Viking Spirit); *Clubs* RHYC; *Style—* Maj Anthony Forbes, yr of Rothiemay; c/o RHQ Scots Guards, Wellington Barracks, Birdcage Walk, London SW1E 6HQ

FORBES, Sir Archibald Finlayson; GBE (1957); s of Charles Forbes, of Johnstone, Renfrewshire; *b* 6 Mar 1903; *Educ* Paisley, Glasgow Univ; *m* 1, 1937 (m dis 1943), Elliot, da of Maj Ronald Elliot Krickenbeck; m 2, 9 Nov 1943, Angela Gertrude (d 1969), o da of Horace Ely, of 55 Arlington House, London SW1; 1 s, 2 da; *Career* chartered accountant; dep sec Miny of Aircraft Prodn 1940-43, controller of Repair, Equipment and Overseas Supplies 1943-45, memb Aircraft Supply Cncl 1943-45; pres: FBI 1951-53, Midland Bank Ltd 1975- (chm 1964-75), Spillers 1969-80 (exec dir 1935, chm 1965-68); former chm first Iron and Steel Bd; chm: Cent Mining and Investmt Corpn 1959-64, Midland and Int Banks 1964-76; former chm Br Millers' Mutual Pool Ltd and Debenture Corpn Ltd; former dir: Dunlop Hldgs Ltd, Shell Tport and Trading Co Ltd, English Electric Co Ltd; pres Br Bankers Assoc 1970-72, chm Ctee of London Clearing Bankers 1970-72; Hon Dip MA; kt 1943; *Style—* Sir Archibald Forbes, GBE; 40 Orchard Court, Portman Sq, London W1 (☎ 01 935 9304); Mattingley Green Cottage, Mattingley, Hants (☎ Heckfield 247)

FORBES, Archibald Peter Sturrock; CBE (1960); s of Alexander Manzies Forbes (d 1970), and Elizabeth Lilian, *née* Campbell (d 1960); *b* 5 May 1913; *Educ* George Heriot's Edinburgh, Univ of Edinburgh (BSc), Univ of Cambridge (Dip Ag); *m* 10 June 1939, Mary, da of Capt Robert William Manning (d 1936); 1 s (Maj Alexander Robert Menzies b 23 April 1940), 1 da (Heather Mary Menzies (Mrs Loxton) b 20 March 1942); *Career* Colonial Serv: agric offr 1937, chief agric offr Nyasaland 1953 (sr agric offr 1946), perm sec Miny of Agric and Cooperative Devpt Tanganyika 1960 (dep dir of agric 1954, dir of agric 1958); consultancy work 1963-78 in Africa and Asia: World Bank, Food and Agric Orgn, UN, Nordic Bd (Finland, Norway, Sweden, Denmark), engrg and tech firms in natural resources field; Oxfam 1963-85: tstee, memb admin ctee, chm ctee dealing with East; memb and chm PPC Bledington 1976-,; *Recreations* rugby, cricket, tennis, gardening; *Style—* Archibald Forbes, Esq, CBE; The Chesnuts, The Gn, Bledington, Oxford OX7 6XQ (☎ 060 871 308)

FORBES, Bryan; *b* 22 July 1926; *Educ* Westham Secdy Sch, RADA; *m* 1958, Nanette Newman *qv* ; 2 da (one of whom, Sarah, m Sir John Leon, 4 Bt, *qv*); *Career* actor 1948-60; formed Beaver Films with Sir Richard Attenborough 1959; writer dir and prodr of numerous films incl: The League of Gentlemen, Only Two Can Play, Whistle down the Wind 1961, The L-Shaped Room 1962, Seance on a Wet Afternoon 1963, King Rat 1964, The Wrong Box 1965, The Madwoman of Chaillot 1968, The Raging Moon 1970, The Tales of Beatrix Potter 1971, The Stepford Wives 1974, The Slipper and the Rose 1975, International Velvet 1978, The Sunday Lovers 1980, Better Late than Never 1981, The Naked Face 1983; dir and prodr for tv incl: Edith Evans I Caught Acting Like the Measles Yorkshire TV 1973, Elton John Goodbye Norma Jean and other Things ATV 1973, Jessie BBC 1980; theatre dir incl: Macbeth Old Vic 1980, Killing Jessica Savoy 1986; acted in: December Flower Granada 1984, First Among Equals Granada 1986; winner of: Br Academy Award 1960, Writers Guild Award (twice), numerous int awards; md and head of prodn ABPC Studios 1969-71, md and chief exec EMI-MGM Elstree Studios 1970-71, dir Capital Radio Ltd 1973-; memb: BBC Gen Advsy Cncl 1966-69, BBC Schs Cncl 1971-73; pres: Beatrix Potter Soc 1982-, Nat Youth Theatre 1984-; tstee Writers Guild of GB; *Publications* : Truth Lies Sleeping (1950), The Distant Laughter (1972), Notes for a Life (1974), The Slipper and the Rose (1976), Ned's Girl (biog of Dame Edith Evans, 1977), International Velvet (1978), Familiar Strangers (1979), That Despicable Race (1980), The Rewrite Man (1983), The Endless Game (1986); *Recreations* running a bookshop, reading, photography, landscape gardening; *Style—* Bryan Forbes, Esq; Bryan Forbes Ltd, Seven Pines, Wentworth, Surrey

FORBES, Derek Francis Kemball; s of Fl Lt Francis William Forbes (d 1972), of E Finchley, and Vera Maud Roaslind Forbes; *b* 2 Feb 1943; *Educ* City of London Sch, Law Soc Sch of Law; *m* 1 Aug 1972, Carol Ann, da of Colin Robert Knight (d 1986), of Highgate, London; *Career* sr assoc Abbey Life 1971-79 (advertising mangr 1968-71) sr branch mangr Crown Life 1979-84, asst head of sales Sun Alliance 1984-88, agency mangr Sun Life 1988; Life Insur Assoc: chm nat ctee of mangrs forum 1984-87, hon sec 1985, tres 1986, elected to nat exec 1984-87; Freeman City of London 1964, Liveryman Worshipful Co of Gold and Silver Wyre Drawers; memb Million Dollar Round Table 1976; fell Life Insur Assoc 1971; *Books* The Save and Prosper Book of Money (jtly 1968); *Style—* Derek Forbes, Esq; 22 Cherry Tree Rd, E Finchley, London N2 9QL (☎ 01 883 2985); Orford, Suffolk; Sun Life Unit Services, 10-12 Ely Place, London EC1 (☎ 01 242 2905)

FORBES, Donald James; s of Andrew Forbes (d 1960), of Hythe, Southampton, and Amy Forbes (d 1969); *b* 6 Feb 1921; *Educ* Oundle, Clare Coll Cambridge (MA), Santander Univ; *m* 21 Dec 1945, Patricia Muriel, da of Percival Douglas Yeo (d 1966); 2 s (Ian b 1947, Anthony b 1949), 1 da (Elizabeth b 1961); *Career* Sandhurst 1941, cmmnd Scots Gds 1941, Signals Offr 1942, 1 Bn Scots Gds: Platoon Cdr, 2 i/c C Co, Co Cdr HQ Co served in N Africa and Italy 1943-46; asst master Dulwich Coll 1946-55; headmaster: Dauntsey's Sch West Lavington Wilts 1956-69, Merchiston Castle Sch Edinburgh 1969-81; capt Cambridge Univ Rugby Fives 1941; chief invigilator ICA

Scotland, sec Cystic Fibrosis Res Tst SE Scotland, librarian and memb Edinburgh Chamber Orchestra, sec Wengen Reunion Curling Club; *Recreations* golf, curling; *Clubs* Hon Co Edinburgh Golfers Muirfield, Wengen & Forest Hills; *Style*— Donald Forbes, Esq;; 33 Coates Gardens, Edinburgh EH12 5LG (☎ 031 346 0844), Breachacha (New) Castle, Isle of Coll, Argyleshire

FORBES, Lady Georgina Anne; yr da of 9 Earl of Granard; *b* 19 Sept 1952; *Style*— Lady Georgina Forbes; Le Vivarais, Bettens, Vaud, Switzerland

FORBES, Very Rev Graham John Thomson; s of John Thomson Forbes (d 1986), of Edinburgh, and Doris, *née* Smith; *b* 10 June 1951; *Educ* George Heriots Sch Edinburgh, Univ of Aberdeen (MA), Univ of Edinburgh (BD), Edinburgh Theol Coll; *m* 25 Aug 1973, Jane, da of John Tennant Miller, of Edinburgh; 3 s (Duncan, Andrew, Hamish); *Career* curate Old St Paul's Edinburgh 1976-82, provost St Ninians Cathedral Perth 1982-; non-exec dir Radio Tay, chm Radio Tay Charity Auction, fndr Canongate Youth Project Edinburgh; pres Lothian Assoc of Youth Clubs 1986-; memb: Scottish Community Educn Cncl 1981-87, Childrens Panel Advsy Ctee Tayside; *Recreations* discovering dry rot, fly fishing, running, visiting Russia; *Style*— The Very Rev the Provost of St Ninians Cathedral Perth; St Ninian's House, Hay St, Perth PH1 5HS (☎ 0738 26 874); St Ninian's Cathedral, N Methven St, Perth (☎ 0738 27 982)

FORBES, Maj Sir Hamish Stewart; 7 Bt (UK 1823) of Newe, MBE (1945), MC; s of late Lt-Col James Stewart Forbes (d 1957, gs of 3 Bt) and Féridah Frances, da of Hugh Lewis Taylor; suc cousin, Col Sir John Stewart Forbes, 6 Bt, DSO, JP, DL (d 1984); *b* 15 Feb 1916; *Educ* Eton, Lawrenceville USA, SOAS London; *m* 1, 2 June 1945 (m dis 1981), Jacynthe Elizabeth Mary, o da of late Eric Gordon Underwood; 1 s, 3 da; m 2, 1981, Mary Christine, MBE, da of late Ernest William Rigby; *Heir* s, James Thomas Stewart Forbes, b 28 May 1957, *qv*; *Career* Maj WG, served WW II (POW) France, Germany, Turkey, ret; KJStJ 1983; Patron Lonach Highland and Friendly Society; hon dir Br Humane Assoc, hon dir Inc Soc The Church Lads' and Girls' Bde; *Recreations* shooting, sculpture; *Clubs* Turf, Chelsea Arts, Pilgrim, Royal Asian Soc; *Style*— Maj Sir Hamish Forbes, Bt, MBE, MC; 36 Wharton St, London WC1X 9PG (☎ 01 833 1235)

FORBES, James; s of Maj Donald Forbes (d 1963), of Edinburgh, and Rona Ritchie, *née* Yeats (d 1963); *b* 2 Jan 1923; *Educ* Christ's Hospital, Offrs Training Sch Bangalore S India; *m* 14 Aug 1948, Alison Mary Fletcher, da of Maj George K Moffat (d 1979), of Dunblane, Perthshire; 2 s (Lindsay b 11 Oct 1953, Moray b 29 June 1962); *Career* WWII cmmnd 15 Punjab Regt 1942, transferred to IAOC qualifying as Inspecting Ordnance Offr, CO (Capt) Mobile Ammunition Inspection Unit 1943-44, Maj DADOS Amm GHQ (1) 1945-46, released with rank of Hon Maj 1947; Peat Marwick Mitchell 1952-58; Schweppes plc 1958-69: ops res mangr 1960-63, gp chief accountant and dir subsid cos 1963-69; gp fin dir Cadbury Schweppes 1970-78 (fin advsr on formation 1969- 70), vice-chm Tate & Lyle 1980-84 (sr exec dir 1978-80, chm pension fund 1978-85); non exec dir: Br Tport Hotels 1978-83, Br Investmts 1980-84, Steetley plc 1984-, Compass Hotels Ltd 1984-, Lautro Ltd 1986-; tres and chm cncl of almoners Christs Hospital 1987- (chm resources ctee 1985-87) Forestry cmmr 1982-88; memb Worshipful Co Accountants in England and Wales; FCA 1966 (memb cncl 1971-88, tres 1984-86); memb Highland Soc of London; *Recreations* golf; *Clubs* Caledonian; *Style*— James Forbes, Esq; Lower Ridge, Courts Mount Rd, Haslemere, Surrey GU27 2PP (☎ 0428 52 461); Great Eastern Hotel, Liverpool Street, London EC2M 7QN (☎ 01 626 6647)

FORBES, James Duncan Mallen; VRD; s of James Alexander Forbes (d 1986), and Marjorie Beckley, *née* Mallen (d 1978); *b* 19 Dec 1926; *Educ* City of London Sch; *m* 1960, June, da of Harry De Behr Acheson-Gray (d 1952); 1 s (Patrick), 1 da (Susan); *Career* Lt Cdr RNR 1944-47; dir: Booker Line Ltd 1960-84 (md 1969-83, chm 1983-84), Clarkson Booker 1965-66, Booker Bros (Liverpool) Ltd 1966-84 (chm 1982-84); chm W India Assoc of Liverpool 1967-71, dir Liverpool Maritime Terminals Ltd 1972-84, memb Merchant Navy Trg Bd 1974-76, chm Such & Schosley Ltd 1974-84; memb Port of Preston Advisory Board 1977-79, dir London Steamship Owners Mutual Insur Assoc 1978-84; memb North West Economic Planning Cncl 1978-79; chm: Merseyside C of C 1980-82, Liverpool Steamship Owners Assoc 1977-78; dir Coe Metcalf Shipping Ltd 1983-84,; vice-chm Merseyside Residuary Body 1985-, dir N American Fishing Insur Mutual Assoc Ltd 1988; *Style*— James Forbes Esq, VRD; 30 Boundary Rd, West Kirby, Wirral, Merseyside L48 1LF (☎ 051 625 5598)

FORBES, James Thomas Stewart; s and h of Sir Hamish Stewart Forbes, 7 Bt, MBE, MC; *b* 28 May 1957; *Educ* Eton, Bristol Univ (BA); *m* 1986, Kerry Lynne, o da of Rev Lee Toms, of Sacramento, California, USA; *Career* proprietor: Spats Catering Co (film location and party catering), Scotch Malt Club of America (whiskey retailers in USA); *Clubs* Pratt's; *Style*— James Forbes, Esq; The Cottage, Hambleden, nr Henley-on-Thames Oxon RG9 6RT (☎ 0491 575 914); 47 Kendal St, London W2 (☎ 0836 201 216)

FORBES, Hon Mrs John; Joan; 3 da of A Edward Smith, of Sherlockstown House, Sallins, Co Kildare; *m* 23 Jan 1947, Hon John Forbes (d 1982), yr s of 8 Earl of Granard (d 1948), and bro of 9 Earl, *qv*; 1 s (Peter A E H Forbes, *qv*), 3 da; *Style*— Hon Mrs John Forbes; Le Royale, 13 Boulevard de Suisse, Monte Carlo, Monaco

FORBES, Vice Adm Sir John Morrison; KCB (1978); s of Lt-Col Robert Hogg Forbes, OBE (d 1976), and Gladys M, *née* Pollock; *b* 16 August 1925; *Educ* RNC Dartmouth; *m* 1950, Joyce Newenham, da of late Addison Perrit Hadden, of Ireland; 2 s, 2 da; *Career* 2 i/c and Operational Cdr Royal Malaysian Navy 1966-68, directorate of Naval Plans 1969-71, Capt HMS Triumph 1971-72, Capt RN Coll Dartmouth 1972-74, Naval sec 1974-76, Vice Adm 1977, Flag Offr Plymouth 1977-79, Cdr Central Sub Area Eastern Atlantic and Cdr Plymouth Sub Area Channel 1977-79; chm Civil Serv Cmmrs Interview Panel 1980-; charity govr; Naval ADC to HM The Queen 1974; awarded Kesatria Manku Negara 1968; *Recreations* country pursuits; *Clubs* Army & Navy, RNSA; *Style*— Vice Adm Sir John Forbes, KCB; c/o Nat Westminster Bank, Waterlooville, Portsmouth, Hants

FORBES, Hon Jonathan Andrew; 2 s of 23 Lord Forbes, KBE; *b* 20 August 1947; *Educ* Eton; *m* 10 Jan 1981, Hon Nichola Frances, da of 10 Baron Hawke, *qv*; 1 s (James Frederick Nicholas b 1987), 2 da (Camilla Rose b 1983, Annabella Jane b 1985); *Career* Capt Gren Gds; md Profile Security Services Ltd; *Style*— Hon Jonathan Forbes; Tullynessle House, Alford, Aberdeenshire AB3 8QR (☎ 0336 2509)

FORBES, Master of; Hon Malcolm Nigel Forbes; s and h of 23 Lord Forbes, KBE, *qv*; *b* 6 May 1946; *Educ* Eton, Univ of Aberdeen; *m* 1, 30 Jan 1969 (m dis 1982), Carole Jennifer Andrée, da of Norman Stanley Whitehead (d 1981), of Aberdeen; 1 s (Neil Malcolm Ross b 10 March 1970), 1 da (Joanne Carole b 23 April 1972); m 2, 15 Feb 1988, Mrs Jennifer Mary Gribbon, da of Ian Peter Whittington, of Tunbridge Wells, Kent; *Heir* s, Neil Malcolm Ross Forbes b 1970; *Career* dir Instock Disposables Ltd; farmer and landowner; sec Donside Ball; *Recreations* skiing, cricket, croquet; *Clubs* Hurlingham, Royal Northern and University (Aberdeen), MCC; *Style*— The Master of Forbes; Castle Forbes, Alford, Aberdeenshire AB3 8BL (☎ 09755 62574); Forbes Estate Office, Alford, Aberdeenshire AB3 8DR (☎ 0336 2524)

FORBES, 23 Lord (Premier S Lordship before July 1445); Nigel Ivan Forbes; KBE (1960), JP (Aberdeenshire 1955), DL (1958); s of 22 Lord Forbes (d 1953), and Lady Mabel Anson (d 1972), da of 3 Earl of Lichfield; *b* 19 Feb 1918; *Educ* Harrow, RMC Sandhurst; *m* 23 May 1942, Hon Rosemary Katharine Hamilton-Russell, da of 9 Viscount Boyne; 2 s, 1 da; *Heir* s, Master of Forbes; *Career* served WW II, France and Belgium (wounded), N Africa, Sicily, NW Europe, Adj Grenadier Gds, Staff Coll 1945-46, mil asst high cmmr Palestine 1947-48, Maj Gren Gds; pres Royal Highland and Agric Soc for Scotland 1958-59; min of state Scottish Off 1958-59; chm Don Dist River Bd 1961-73; bd memb: Scottish Nature Conservancy 1961-67, Aberdeen Milk Mktg Bd 1962-72; memb Sports Cncl for Scot 1966-71; dep chm Tennant Caledonian Breweries Ltd 1964-74, chm Rolawn Ltd; dir: Blenheim Travel Ltd 1981-88, Grampian TV 1960-88; pres Scottish Scouts Assoc 1970-88; chm Nat Playing Fields Assoc (Scottish Branch) 1965-80; farmer and landowner; *Recreations* wildlife, conservation, travel; *Clubs* Army & Navy; *Style*— The Rt Hon the Lord Forbes, KBE, JP, DL; Balforbes, Alford, Aberdeenshire AB3 8DR (☎ 09755 62516, office 09755 62574)

FORBES, Peter Arthur Edward Hastings; er s of Hon Mrs John Forbes, *qv*, and late Hon John Forbes; hp of unc, 9 Earl of Granard, *qv*; *b* 15 Mar 1957; *m* ; 1 s (b 1982); *Style*— Peter Forbes Esq; Le Royale, 13 Boulevard de Suisse, Monte Carlo, Monaco

FORBES, Lt-Col William John Herbert of Rothiemay; DSO (1945); Representor of the House of Forbes of Rothiemay, formerly of Dunira, by Comrie, Perthshire; descendant of John Forbes, of Newe (6 in descent from Sir William Forbes, 1 of Kynaldy and Pitsligo 1419-46 and bro of Sir Alexander, who was cr 1 Lord Forbes, a Barony which is now extinct); s of Cdr William Stronach Forbes, OBE, RN (d 1949), and Helen, da of George Herbert Strutt, of Kingairloch, Argyll; *b* 25 Sept 1912; *Educ* Downe House; *m* 1941, Diana Burrell de Ker, only child of late William Barr Knox, of Ryefield House, Dalry, Ayrshire; 2 s (and 1 s decd), 1 da; *Heir* s, Anthony Forbes, yr of Rothiemay; *Career* Argyll and Sutherland Highlanders, served NW Frontier, India 1934-39 (medal and clasp), served WW II NW Europe (despatches), instr Staff Colls Haifa and Camberley, GSO Mil Intelligence War Off, invalided out of Services 1949; farming in Norfolk and Perthshire until 1978 (breeder of Supreme Ayrshire Champion Royal Shows 1955/56); *Recreations* stalking, shooting, fishing, gardening; *Clubs* New, Army and Navy, Royal Highland Yacht, Puffins (Edinburgh); *Style*— Lt-Col William Forbes of Rothiemay, DSO; Son Rocaflor, Puerto de Andraitx, Palma, Majorca, Spain

FORBES ADAM, Sir Christopher Eric; 3 Bt (UK 1917), of Hankelow Court, Co Chester; s of Eric Forbes Adam, CMG (2 s of Sir Frank Forbes Adam, 1 Bt, CB, CIE, JP, DL), by his w Agatha, widow of Sidney Spooner and eldest da of Reginald Walter Macan, sometime Master Univ Coll, Oxford; suc unc, Gen Sir Ronald Forbes Adam, 2 Bt, GCB, DSO, OBE, 1982; *b* 12 Feb 1920; *Educ* Abinger Hill Sch Surrey, privately; *m* 17 Sept 1957, Patricia Anne Wreford, yr da of John Neville Wreford Brown, of Maltings, Abberton, Colchester, Essex; 1 adopted da (Sarah, Anne b 1960); *Heir* 1 cous, Rev Timothy Forbes Adam; *Career* sometime journalist with *Yorkshire Post*; *Style*— Sir Christopher Forbes Adam, Bt; 46 Rawlings St, London SW3

FORBES ADAM, Nigel Colin; JP (1960); s of Colin Forbes Adam, CSI, DL (d 1982, 3 s of Sir Frank Forbes Adam, 1 Bt) and Hon Mrs (Irene Constance) Forbes Adam, *née* Lawley (d 1976), da of 3 Baron Wenlock, PC, GCSI, GCIE, KCB; bro of Rev Timothy, *qv*; *b* 7 Dec 1930; *Educ* Eton, King's Coll Cambridge (BA); *m* 1954 (m dis 1987), Teresa Hermione Idena, o da of Cdr David Lambert Robertson, RN (d 1979); 4 s; m 2, 1987, Malise, formerly w of David Ropner, *qv*, and da of late Col Armitage, MC, TD, of Newburgh House, Coxwold, Yorks; *Heir* S Charles David Forbes Adam; *Career* landowner and farmer; High Sheriff N Yorks 1976; chm Yorks Region Nat Tst 1985-; *Recreations* tennis, shooting, gardening; *Clubs* Brooks's; *Style*— Nigel Forbes Adam, Esq, BA, JP; Skipwith Hall, Selby, Yorks (☎ 0757 85434)

FORBES ADAM, Rev (Stephen) Timothy Beilby; er s of Colin Gurdon Forbes Adam, CSI, JP, DL (d 1982, 3 s of Sir Frank Forbes Adam, 1 Bt, CB, CIE, JP, DL), by his w Hon Mrs (Irene Constance) Forbes Adam (d 1976), bro of Nigel Forbes Adam, *qv*; hp to 1 cous, Sir Christopher Forbes Adam, 3 Bt; *b* 19 Nov 1923; *Educ* Eton, Balliol Coll Oxford, RADA, Chichester Theol Coll; *m* 28 Sept 1954, Penelope, da of George Campbell Munday, MC, of Leverington Hall, Wisbech, Cambs; 4 da; *Career* served Rifle Bde 1942-47 in France and Far East; ordained 1962, rector of Barton-in-Fabis with Thrumpton, Southwell, Notts 1964-70, priest-in-charge: Southstoke 1974-84, Bath & Wells 1984-; *Style*— Rev Timothy Forbes Adam; 1 Bakers Lane, Tadmaston, Banbury, Oxon OX15 5SS (☎ 0295 8305)

FORBES ADAM, Hon Mrs Vivien Elisabeth; *née* Mosley; da of Sir Oswald Mosley, 6 Bt (d 1986), of Temple de la Gloire, 91400 Orsay, France, and Lady Cynthia (d 1933), da of 1 Marquess Curzon of Kedleston; *Educ* Francis Holland Sch, Owlstone Croft Cambridge; 15 Jan 1949, Desmond Francis Forbes Adam (d 1958), s of Colin Forbes Adam, CSI (d 1982), of Skipwith Hall, Selby, Yorks; 1 s (Rupert b 1957), 2 da (Cynthia (Mrs Chaddock) b 1950, ARabella b 1952); *Style*— The Hon Mrs Vivient Forbes Adam; 11 Mulberry Walk, London SW3 6DZ (☎ 01 352 2107)

FORBES OF CRAIGIEVAR, Hon Sir Ewan; 11 Bt (NS 1630), of Craigievar, Aberdeenshire, JP (Aberdeenshire 1969); s of late 18 Lord Sempill; suc to Btcy only of bro, 19 Lord Sempill, AFC, 1965; *b* 6 Sept 1912; *Educ* Munich, Aberdeen Univ (MB, ChB); *m* 10 Oct 1953, Isobel, da of late Alec Mitchell, of Glenrinnes, Banffshire; *Heir* kinsman, John Alexander Cumnock Forbes-Sempill; *Career* Senior Casualty Officer Aberdeen Royal Infirmary; *Books* The Aul' Days (1984); *Recreations* shooting, fishing, Highland dancing; *Style*— Hon Sir Ewan Forbes of Craigievar, Bt, JP; Brux, Alford, Aberdeenshire (☎ Kildrummy 223)

FORBES TURNER, Rev, CF Timothy John; s of Maj Henry John Richard Turner, of Whitstable, Kent, and Hazel Forbes, *née* Burnett; *b* 10 Jan 1946; *Educ* Canterbury Tech HS for Boys, Pontifical Beda Coll Rome; *Career* clerk in Holy Orders at present serving Chaplain to H M Forces (Army); *Recreations* work with the RLSS, country pursuits; *Style*— Rev Timothy Forbes Turner, CF; St Patrick's House, St Patrick's Ave, Tidworth, Hants SP9 7BP (☎ 0980 42284; RC Chaplain, Headquarters, 8th

Infantry Brigade, BFPO 807 (☎ 0504 40288)

FORBES-BELL, Barry Russell; s of Frederick George Bell (d 1963), and Hilda Marion, *née* Stanfield (d 1971); *b* 9 April 1941; *Educ* Leeds Univ (LLB); *m* 1, Sept 1966 (m dis 1971), Margaret Rutherford; 1 s (Russell James Bell, now Goater b 1969); m 2, 4 April 1971, Penelope Beryl, da of John Forbes, of Saltburn, Cleveland; 2 s (Christian b 1974, Philip b 1979), 3 da (Charlotte b 1971, Eleanor b 1976, Olivia b 1983); *Career* slr; hon sec Harrogate Law Soc; former professional footballer with Charlton Athletic and Millwall FC 1957-60; MBIM; *Recreations* sport, theatre, amateur dramatics, travel, music; *Style*— Barry R Forbes-Bell, Esq; Tiree, New Lane, Nun Monkton, York YO5 8EP; Osborne House, 20 Victoria Ave, Harrogate HG1 5QY (☎ 0423 523 011, 0423 711 327); High St, Pakeley Bridge, W Yorks

FORBES-LEITH, George Ian David; s and h of Sir Andrew George Forbes-Leith of Fyvie, 3 Bt; *b* 26 May 1967; *Style*— George Forbes-Leith, Esq; Estate Office, Fyvie, Turriff, Aberdeenshire (☎ 06516 246)

FORBES-LEITH OF FYVIE, Sir Andrew George; 3 Bt (UK 1923); s of Sir (Robert) Ian (Algernon) Forbes-Leith of Fyvie, 2 Bt, KT, MBE (d 1973), and Ruth Avis, *née* Barnett (d 1973); *b* 20 Oct 1929; *Educ* Eton; *m* 1962, Jane Kate (d 1969), da of late David McCall-McCowan, of Dalwhat, Moniaive, Dumfries; 2 s, 2 da; *Heir* s, George Ian David Forbes-Leith b 26 May 1967; *Style*— Sir Andrew Forbes-Leith of Fyvie, Bt; Dunachton, Kingussie, Inverness-shire (☎ 054 04 226)

FORBES-MICHIE, Captain Stanley Allan; s of Allan Black Wyness Michie (d 1958), and Isobel Joan Forbes Michie (d 1944); *b* 23 Feb 1934; *Educ* Bankhead Acad Aberdeen; *m* 1959, Marjorie, da of Joseph Elliott Robson (d 1986); 1 da (Susan Elizabeth b 1968); *Career* former Capt RA, served Egypt, Malta, Cyprus, BAOR; John Goschen Meml Prize 1951; hon sec SSAFA South Tynside 1961-80, chief probation offr Sunderland Tyne and Wear 1973-81; fndr memb SDLP; Cdr with Star Order Polonia Restituta 1984; received grant of arms from Lord Lyon 1981; *Books* Poems of a Probation Officer (1978); *Recreations* heraldry, poetry, tapestry, genealogy; *Style*— Captain Stanley Forbes-Michie; Marstan, St John's Terrace, East Boldon, Tyne and Wear NE36 0LL (☎ 091 5362142)

FORBES-ROBERTSON, Cdr Kenneth Hugh; s of Col James Forbes-Robertson, VC, DSO, MC, DL (d 1955), and Hilda Forster, ARRC (d 1986); *b* 12 Sept 1933; *Educ* Rugby, Britannia RNC; *m* 25 July 1959, Elspeth Janet, da of Marvin Arundel Puttock (d 1970), of Lancing, Sussex; 3 da (Fiona b 1960, Kirsten b 1962, Grania Helen b 1966); *Career* RN, cmmnd HMS Yarnton 1965, HMS Russell 1967, HMS Londonderry 1973, HMS Kent 1981-83, served in submarines and various other ships on the Home, E Indies and Far East Stations, ret Cdr 1983; farmer in Hants; *Recreations* fishing, shooting; *Clubs* Farmers, IOD; *Style*— Cdr Kenneth Forbes-Robertson; West Barn, Soberton, Hampshire (☎ 0489 877563)

FORBES-SEMPILL, Hon Janet Cecilia; da of late Lord Sempill (19 in line), by 2 w, Cecilia, *née* Dunbar-Kilburn; half-sis of Lady Sempill, *qv*; *b* 4 May 1942; *Educ* Colchester Coll of Art; *Career* artist; *Style*— Hon Janet Forbes-Sempill

FORBES-SEMPILL, John Alexander Cumnock; JP; s (by 3 m) of late Rear Adm Hon Arthur Lionel Ochoncar Forbes-Sempill, s of 17 Lord Sempill; hp of kinsman, Hon Sir Ewan Forbes of Craigievar, 11 Bt, JP; *b* 29 August 1927; *Educ* Stowe; *m* 1, 26 June 1956 (m dis 1963), Penelope Margaret Ann, da of Arthur Gordon Grey-Pennington; m 2, 1966, Jane Carolyn, da of C Gordon Evans, of Chelsfield, Kent; *Career* Capt Seaforth Highlanders; memb: Scottish Cncl, Br Show Jumping Assoc; *Clubs* Naval and Military, RSAC; *Style*— John Forbes-Sempill, Esq, JP; Auchendoon House, Newton Stewart, Wigtownshire DG8 6AN (☎ 0671 2533)

FORD; *see*: St Clair-Ford

FORD, Rev Adam; s of Rev John Ford, and Jean Beattie, *née* Winstanley; *b* 15 Sept 1940; *Educ* Minehead GS, King's Coll London (BD, AKC), Lancaster Univ (MA); *m* 2 Aug 1969, Veronica Rosemary Lucia, da of David Cecil Wynter Verey, Capt Royal Fusiliers (d 1984), of Barnsley House, Cirencester, Glos; 2 s (Nathaniel b 1972, Joshua b 1977), 2 da (Imogen b 1970, Natasha b 1973); *Career* asst Ecumenical Inst of World Cncl of Churches Geneva 1964, curate Cirencester Parish Church Glos 1965-69, vicar Hebden Bridge W Yorks 1969-76, chaplain St Paul's Girls' Sch London 1976-, head Lower Sch 1986-; priest in ordinary to HM the Queen Chapel Royal 1984-; regular contributor to Prayer for the Day BBC Radio 4 1978-, author of several articles in the Times and science jls on the relationship between science and religion; FRAS 1960; *publications* Star Gazers Guide to the Night Sky (audio guide to astronomy 1982), Spaceship Earth (1981), Weather Watch (1982), Universe: God Man and Science (1986), Whose World? (6 video programmes for TV, 1988); *Recreations* astronomy, dry stone walling, field walking; *Style*— The Rev Adam Ford; 55 Bolingbroke Rd, Hammersmith, London W14 0AH (☎ 01 602 5902); Saintbridge Cottage, Barnsley, Cirencester, Glos (☎ 0285 74 246); St Paul's Girls School, Brook Green, London W6 (☎ 01 603 2288)

FORD, Andrew Russell; s and h of Sir Henry Ford, Bt, TD, JP; *b* 29 June 1943; *Educ* Winchester, New Coll Oxford; *m* 8 Aug 1968, Penelope Anne, o da of Harold Edmund Relph, of West Kirby, Wirral; 2 s, 1 da; *Style*— Andrew Ford, Esq; 20 Coniston Road, Chippenham, Wilts

FORD, Sir (Richard) Brinsley; CBE (1978); eldest s of Capt Richard Ford (d 1940), by his w Rosamund Isabel (d 1911), da of Sir John Ramsden, 5 Bt (and gggda of Richard Brinsley Sheridan, the orator and dramatist); ggs of Richard Ford, author of Handbook to Spain; *b* 10 June 1908; *Educ* Eton, Trinity Coll Oxford; *m* 1937, Joan Mary, da of Capt Geoffrey Vyvyan, Royal Welch Fus (ka 1914); 2 s (Francis, Augustine), 1 da (Marianne); *Career* joined TA 1939, served for one year as Troop Sgt Maj RA; cmmnd 1941, and transferred to Intelligence Corps, Maj 1945; memb: Nat Art-Collections Fund 1927- Memb exec ctee 1960-88, vice-chm 1974-75, chm 1975-78); tstee Watts Gallery Compton 1955- (chm 1974-84), jt hon advsr on paintings to the Nat Tst 1980, tstee Nat Gallery 1954-61, chm Nat Tst Fndn for Art Ctee 1986-; hon fell RA 1981, sec of Soc of Dilettanti 1972-88; pres Walpole Soc 1986-; FSA 1973; owner Ford Collection of Richard Wilsons; Order of Isabel la Catolica of Spain (First Class A 1986), Belgian Order of Leopold II (1945), US Bronze Star (1946), Médaille d'Argent de la Reconaissance, Française (1947); kt 1984;; *Publications* The Drawings of Richard Wilson (1951), contributor Burlington Magazine and Apollo; *Clubs* Brooks's; *Style*— Sir Brinsley Ford, CBE; 14 Wyndham Place, Bryanston Square, London W1H 1AQ (☎ 01 723 0826)

FORD, Hon Mrs; (Caroline Jane); *née* Nelson; er da of 2 Baron Nelson of Stafford; *b* 11 Jan 1942; *m* 2 April 1964, Michael John Henry Ford, *qv*; 2 s (James, Andrew), 1 da (Annabel); *Style*— Hon Mrs Ford; Lower Moorhayne Farm, Yarcombe, nr Honiton, Devon EX14 9BE (☎ Upottery 284)

FORD, Colin John; s of John William Ford, and Helene Martha, *née* Jones; *b* 13 May 1934; *Educ* Enfield GS, Univ Coll Oxford (MA); *m* 1, 12 Aug 1961, Margaret Elizabeth, da of Ernest Cordwell, 1 s (Richard John b 1970), 1 da (Clare Michaela Elizabeth b 1972); m 2, 7 Sept 1984, Susan Joan Frances Grayson; 1 s (Thomas Grayson b 1985); *Career* mangr and prodr Kidderminster Playhouse 1958-60, gen mangr Western Theatre Ballet 1960-62, visiting lectr English and drama California State Univ at Long Beach & UCLA 1962-64, dep curator Nat Film Archive 1965-72, organiser Thirtieth Anniversary Congress of Int Fedn of Film Archives London 1968, dir Cinema City exhibition 1970, programme dir London Shakespeare Film Festival 1972, keeper of film and photography Nat Portrait Gallery 1972-81, keeper Nat Museum of Photography Film and TV 1982-; film: Masks and Faces 1966 (BBC tv version Omnibus 1968); *Books* An Early Victorian Album (with Roy Strong, second edn 1977), The Cameron Collection (1975), Happy and Glorious: six reigns of Royal Photography (ed 1977), Rediscovering Mrs Cameron (1979), People in Camera (1979), A Hundred Years Ago (with Brian Harrison, 1983), Portraits (Gallery World of Photography, 1983), Oxford Companion to Film (princ contrib), Andre Kertesz: The Manchester Collection (contrib 1984), The Story of Popular Photography (ed 1989); *Recreations* travel, music, small boats; *Style*— Colin Ford, Esq; Nat Museum of Photography, Film and Television, Prince's View, Bradford, West Yorks BD5 0TR (☎ 0274 727 488, fax 0274 723 155)

FORD, Hon Mrs (Diana Elizabeth); *née* Maxwell; da of Cdr (John) David Maxwell, RN, *qv*, and 27 Baroness de Ros (d 1983); sister of 28 Baron de Ros, *qv*; *b* 6 Jun 1957; *Educ* Godstowe Sch High Wycombe, Hillcourt Sch Dunlaoghaire; *m* 1, 1976 (m dis 1978), Jonathon Watkins; m 2, 1978 (m dis 1981), Don Richard Bell; m 3, 1987, Eric Ford; 1 da (Neesha b 10 May 1988); *Style*— The Hon Mrs Ford

FORD, Sir Edward William Spencer; KCB (1967, CB 1952), KCVO (1957, MVO 1949), ERD (1987), DL; s of Very Rev Lionel George Bridges Justice Ford, Dean of York (d 1932), and Mary Catherine, *née* Talbot; bro of Neville M Ford, *qv*; *b* 24 July 1910; *Educ* Eton, New Coll Oxford; *m* 1 Dec 1949, Hon Virginia, *qv*, da of 1 and last Baron Brand; 2 s; *Career* WWII Lt-Col Grenadier Gds; barr 1937, in practice 1937-39; asst private sec to HM King George VI 1946-52 and to HM The Queen 1952-67 (extra equerry 1955-); sec Pilgrim Tst 1967-75, sec and registrar Order of Merit 1975-; dir: Eydon Hall Estates Ltd 1963-83, London Life Assoc Ltd 1970-83; High Sheriff Northants 1970; OStJ 1976; hon fell New Coll Oxford 1982; memb Ct of Assts Worshipful Co of Goldsmiths 1970- (Prime Warden 1979); *Clubs* White's, MCC, Beefsteak; *Style*— Sir Edward Ford, KCB, KCVO, ERD, DL; Canal House, 23 Blomfield Road, London W9 1AD (☎ 01 286 0028)

FORD, Major Frederick John Vivian; s of Col Frederick William Ford (d 1974), of Farnham, Surrey, and Brenda Mary, *née* Vivian (d 1978); *b* 13 Oct 1917; *Educ* Imperial Service Coll, RMC Sandhurst; *m* 11 Sept 1945, Patricia Joan, da of Lt Gen Sir Wentworth Harman, of Marnhull, Dorset; 1 s (Jeremy David); *Career* Maj Welch Regt cmmnd 1938, served Palestine, W Desert, Crete (POW), Greek War Cross; winner Public Sch quarter mile 1936; played rugby for: Harlequins, Army, Surrey, capped for Wales 1938-39; *Recreations* sailing, fishing; *Clubs* Army and Navy, MCC; ; *Style*— Major Frederick J V Ford; c/o Lloyds Bank, Ilminster Br, Ilminster, Somerset TA19 0UL

FORD, Air Marshal Sir Geoffrey Harold; KBE (1979), CB (1974); s of Harold Alfred Ford (d 1961), of Lewes; *b* 6 August 1923; *Educ* Lewes GS, Bristol Univ; *m* 1951, Valerie, da of late Douglas Hart Finn, of Salisbury; 2 s; *Career* served RAF WW II, cmmnd Tech Branch 1942, Air Offr Engrg Strike Cmd 1973-76, dir-gen Engrg and Supply 1976-78, chief engr 1978-81; dir Metals Soc 1981-84, sec Inst of Metals 1985-88; FEng; *Clubs* RAF; *Style*— Air Marshal Sir Geoffrey Ford, KBE, CB; c/o Barclays Bank plc, The Old Bank, Lewes, E Sussex

FORD, Harold Frank; yr s of Sir Patrick Johnston Ford, 1 Bt (d 1945), and Jessie Hamilton, *née* Field (d 1962); *b* 17 May 1915; *Educ* Winchester, Univ Coll Oxford, Edinburgh Univ; *m* 29 July 1948, Lucy Mary, da of late Sheriff John Rudolph Wardlaw Burnet, KC; 1 s, 3 da; *Career* Capt WW II Lothians and Border Yeo (POW), Maj Home Guard; advocate 1945, legal adviser to UNRRA and IRO (Germany) 1947; Sheriff Substitute Forfar 1951-71, Sheriff Perth 1971-80; *Recreations* gardening, golf, shooting; *Clubs* New (Edinburgh), Hon Co Edinburgh Golfers, Royal Perth Golfing Soc; *Style*— Harold Ford, Esq; Millhill, Meikleour, Perthshire PH2 6EF (☎ 073 871 311)

FORD, Sir Henry Russell; 2 Bt (UK 1929), TD (1954), JP (E Lothian 1951); er s of Sir Patrick Johnston Ford, 1 Bt (d 1945), and Jessie Hamilton, *née* Field (d 1962); *b* 30 April 1911; *Educ* Winchester, New Coll Oxford; *m* 8 Aug 1936, Mary Elizabeth, da of late Godfrey FitzHerbert Wright, JP, of Whiddon, Bovey Tracey; 1 s, 3 da; *Heir* s, Andrew Russell Ford; *Career* 2 Lt RA 1939, Lt-Col 1945 (despatches), served Africa, Italy; *Recreations* golf, gardening, viewing scenery; *Clubs* Hon Co of Edinburgh Golfers; *Style*— Sir Henry Ford, Bt, TD, JP; 1 Broadgait Green, Gullane, E Lothian (☎ 0620 842214)

FORD, Prof Sir Hugh; s of Arthur Ford (d 1969), of Welwyn Garden City, Herts, and Constance Ford; *b* 16 July 1913; *Educ* Northampton Sch, Imperial Coll London (DSc, PhD); *m* 1942, Wynyard Scholfield; 2 da; *Career* res engr ICI 1939-42, chief engr Br Iron & Steel Fedn 1942-48; Imperial Coll London: prof of applied mechanics (formerly reader) 1948-65, prof of mechanical engrg and head of dept 1965-78, pro rector 1978-80, prof of mechanical engrg 1969-82, currently emeritus prof; memb Agric Research Cncl 1976-81, pres Inst of Mechanical Engrs 1976-77, chm Sir Hugh Ford & Assocs Ltd 1982- (formerly of Ford & Dain Ptnrs Ltd); dir: Air Liquide UK, RD Projects Ltd 1982-; vice-pres Fellowship of Engrg 1981-84, pres Welding Inst 1983-85, fellow Imperial Coll 1983; pres Inst of Metals 1985-87; Hon Doctorate Univ of Sheffield 1984; James Watt Int Gold Medal 1985; FRS 1967, FEng, Hon MASME, FCGI, FICE, Hon FIMechE, Hon FIChemE, FIM; Hon Dsc: Salford Univ, Queen's Univ Belfast, Aston Univ, Bath Univ, Sheffield Univ; *Recreations* gardening, music, model engineering; *Clubs* Athenaeum; *Style*— Prof Sir Hugh Ford; 18 Shrewsbury House, Cheyne Walk, London SW3; Shamley Cottage, Shamley Green, Surrey

FORD, James Allan; CB (1978), MC (1946); 2 s of Douglas Ford (d 1948), and Margaret Duncan, *née* Allan; *b* 10 June 1920; *Educ* Royal HS Edinburgh, Edinburgh Univ; *m* 1948, Isobel, *née* Dunnett; 1 s, 1 da; *Career* WWII Capt 2 Bn The Royal Scots Hong Kong; civil servant: registrar gen for Scotland 1966-69, princ estab offr SO

1969-79, ret 1979; tstee Nat Library of Scotland 1981-; novelist; *Books* The Brave White Flag (1961), Season of Escape (1963, Frederick Niven Award 1965), A Statue for a Public Place (1965), A Judge of Men (1968, Scottish Arts Cncl Award 1968), The Mouth of Truth (1971); *Recreations* trout fishing; *Clubs* Scottish Arts, Royal Scots; *Style*— James Ford, Esq, CB, MC; 29 Lady Rd, Edinburgh, EH16 5PA (☎ 031 667 4489)

FORD, James Glyn; s of Ernest Benjamin Ford, of Glos, and Matilda Alberta James (d 1986); *b* 28 Jan 1950; *Educ* Marling Stroud, Reading Univ (BSc), UCL, (MSc); *m* 1973, Hazel Nancy, da of Hedley John (d 1969), of Guernsey; 1 da (Elise Jane b 1981); *Career* undergraduate apprentice BAC 1967-68, course tutor in oceanography Open Univ 1976-78, teaching asst UMIST 1977-78; res fell: Sussex Univ 1978-79, Manchester Univ 1976-79; lectr Manchester Univ 1979-80, sr res fell Programme of Policy Res in Engrg Sci and Technol 1980-84, visiting prof Univ of Tokyo 1983, hon visiting res fell 1984-; MEP (Lab, Gtr Manchester East) 1984-; contested (Lab) Hazel Grove gen election 1987; chm Ctee of Inquiry into Growth of Racism and Fascism in Europe for Euro Parl 1984-86; vice chm Security and Disarmament Sub Ctee of Euro Parl 1987-; *Publications* The Future of Ocean Technology (1987), various articles in journals of Science and Technology; *Style*— Glyn Ford, Esq, MEP; 149 Old Road, Ashton-under-Lyne, Lancs OL6 9DA (☎ 061 330 9299); 3 Market Place, Ashton-under-Lyne, Lancs OL6 7JD (☎ 061 344 3000)

FORD, Sir John Archibald; KCMG (1977, CMG 1967), MC (1945); s of Ronald Mylne Ford (d 1963), of Newcastle-under-Lyme, Staffs, and Margaret Jesse Coghill; *b* 19 Feb 1922; *Educ* Sedbergh, Oriel Coll Oxford; *m* 1956, Emaline, da of late Mahlon Burnette, of Leesville, Virginia, USA; 2 da; *Career* served WW II as Maj RA Field Regt; HM Dip Serv: consul-gen NY, dir-gen Br Trade Devpt in USA 1971-75, Br ambassador Jakarta 1975-78, high cmmr Ottawa 1978-81, ret 1981; lay administrator Guildford Cathedral to co-ordinate admin of all cathedral's secular activities 1982-84; chm Voluntary and Christian Service 1985-88; *Publications* Honest to Christ (1988); *Recreations* walking, writing, sailing; *Clubs* Farmers, Yvonne Arnaud Theatre, RHS; *Style*— Sir John Ford, KCMG, MC; Loquats, Guildown, Guildford, Surrey

FORD, Lt Cdr John Worthington; s of William Ernest Ford (d 1961), of Bradford on Tone, Somerset, and Agnes Mary, *née* Worthington (d 1979); *b* 8 Sept 1932; *Educ* Royal Naval Coll Dartmouth; *m* 7 June 1968, Anne, da of Maj Harold Vandeleur Phelps, of Priors Marston, Warwickshire; 1 s (Nicholas Worthington b 1973); *Career* RN 1950-65: serv HM submarines UK and abroad 1954-62, Flag Lt to Flag Offr Scotland and N Ireland 1963-65, ret Lt Cdr; clerk of the course: Wolverhampton Racecourse 1970-74, Stratford Racecourse 1974, Uttoxeter Racecourse 1974-88; cdr and co cmmr St John Ambulance Northamptonshire 1974-79; OStJ 1978; *Recreations* hunting; *Style*— Lt Cdr J W Ford; The Gables, Everdon, Daventry, Northamptonshire NN11 6BL (☎ 032 736 221)

FORD, Leslie John; s of Sidney George Frederick Ford (d 1971), and Doris Irene, *née* Davies; *b* 16 Mar 1936; *Educ* Sir Walter St John Sch, London Univ (BSc); *m* 24 Sept 1960, Janet Loraine, da of Max Gilbert Frost (d 1972); 1 s (Samuel b 1964), 1 da (Madeleine b 1966); *Career* prof chemical engrg ICI plc 1959-86, conslt chemical engr 1986-; co-ordinator for the Sci and Engrg Res Cncl's Programme in Particulate Technol 1984; pres Int Fine Particle Res Inst Inc 1985-; vice-chm of the Bd of Dirs of IFPRI 1979-85; vice-chm Hitchin UDC 1974-75; CEng, FIChemE, ACMA; *Recreations* squash, badminton, politics; *Clubs* Naval; *Style*— Leslie Ford, Esq; 2 High View, Helsby, Cheshire WA6 9LP (☎ 09282 3886); G1, Waterloo Centre, Waterloo Rd, Widnes, Cheshire WA8 0PR (☎ 051 420 1850, telex 265871 MONREF G Attn: CQQ1012)

FORD, Michael John Henry; s of Lt-Col Mortimer Noel Ford, TD, DL, and Miriam Margaret Ford; *b* 23 May 1936; *Educ* Harrow; *m* 2 April 1964, Hon Caroline Jane, *qv*, da of 2 Baron Nelson of Stafford; 2 s (James, Andrew), 1 da (Annabel); *Career* 2 Lt KAR also Devonshire Regt; dir estate agents firm, memb cncl of Sail Trg Assoc, vice pres West of England Deaf Sch; regnl sec Game Conservancy Devon; Freeman Worshipful Co of Gunmakers; Kenya Medal 1956; *Recreations* sailing, shooting, fishing; *Clubs* Royal Ocean Racing; *Style*— Michael Ford, Esq; Lower Moorhayne Farm, Yarcombe, nr Honiton, Devon EX14 (BE (☎ 040 486 284)

FORD, Neville Montague; 2 s of Very Rev Lionel George Bridges Justice Ford, Dean of York (d 1932), and Mary Catherine, da of D Edward Talbot and Hon Lavinia, *née* Lyttelton; bro of Sir Edward W S Ford, KCB, KCVO, *qv*; *b* 18 Nov 1906; *Educ* Summer Fields, Harrow, Oriel Coll Oxford (BA); *m* 1, 1941 (m dis 1956), Patricia (MP North Down 1953-55), da of Lt-Col Sir Walter Smiles, CIE, DSO, DL, MP (drowned 1953); 2 da (er da m Michael Grylls, MP, *qv*; yr da m Brig A D Myrtle, CBE); m 2, 1975, Beatrice Mary Colyear (d 1988), widow of Roy Hudson, of Singleton, Sussex; 1 step s, 1 step da; *Career* winner Public Schs Rackets Championship 1925; Derbyshire Co cricketer 1926-32; served WW II Norway 1940, ADC to Gen Sir Adrian Carton de Wiart, VC, and with RHG (N W Europe) 1944-45; memb Grand Cncl of Royal Acad of Dancing, dir Theatre Royal Windsor, dir Wiggins Teape & Co (Sales) Ltd 1935-70; *Recreations* swimming, golf, travel, lawn tennis; *Clubs* Army & Navy, MCC, Huntercombe Golf; *Style*— Neville Ford Esq; 14 Cranmer Court, Sloane Ave, London SW3 (☎ 01 589 0458)

FORD, (John) Peter; CBE (1969); s of late Ernest Ford, of Westminster, and Muriel Ford; *b* 20 Feb 1912; *Educ* Wrekin Coll, Gonville and Caius Coll Cambridge; *m* 1939, Phoebe Seys, da of Herbert McGregor Wood, of Hampstead; 1 s, 2 da; *Career* md: Brush Export/Assoc Brit Oil Engines Export Ltd 1949-58, Coventry Climax Int Ltd 1958-63; dir Plessey Overseas Ltd 1963-70, chm Inst of Export 1954-56 and 1965-67, vice-pres London C of C 1972-, chm Br Shippers Cncl 1972-75, chm and md Int Jt Ventures Ltd 1974-; Master Worshipful Co of Ironmongers 1981; *Recreations* athletics (Cambridge Univ and Int teams); *Clubs* United Oxford & Cambridge, City Livery, MCC, Hawks (Cambridge), Royal Wimbledon Golf; *Style*— Peter Ford, Esq; 40 Fairacres, Roehampton Lane, London SW15 (☎ 01 876 2146, office: 01 222 9871)

FORD, Richard James Cameron; s of Bernard Thomas Ford (d 1967), of Little Estcotts, Burbage, Wilts, and Eveline Saumaez Ford (d 1952); *b* 1 Feb 1938; *Educ* Marlborough; *m* 27 Sept 1975, Mary Elizabeth, da of James Arthur Keevil; 3 s (James Richard Keevil b 26 July 1976, Charles John Cameron b 26 July 1978, William Bernard Saumarez b 29 May 1980); *Career* admitted slr 1961, ptnr Ford and Ford 1965, sr ptnr Ford Gunnigham and Co 1970-, dir Ramsbury Bldg Soc 1984-86, dir West of England Bldg Soc 1986-89, dir Regency and West of England Bldg Soc 1989-; tstee Glos and Wilts Law Soc 1983-(pres 1982-83); Salisbury Diocesan Synod 1985-, chm Pewsey Synod 1987-; memb: Wyverm Hosp Mgmnt Ctee 1967-70, Swindon Home Mgmnt Ctee 1970-74, Wiltshire Area Health Authy 1974-82, vice chm Swindon Health Authy 1982-87; memb Law Soc; *Recreations* riding, sailing; *Clubs* Royal Solent Yacht; *Style*— Richard Ford, Esq; Little Estcotts, Burbage, Wilts SN8 3AG; Kingsbury House, Marlborough, Wilts (☎ 0672 52265)

FORD, Gen Sir Robert Cyril; GCB (1981, KCB 1977, CB 1973), CBE (1971, MBE 1958); s of John Stranger Ford (d 1970), and Gladys Ford (d 1986), of Yealmpton, Devon; *b* 29 Dec 1923; *Educ* Musgrave's Coll; *m* 1949, Jean Claudia, da of Gp Capt Claude Luther Pendlebury, MC, TD (d 1961), of Yelverton; 1 s; *Career* served WW II 4/7 Royal Dragoon Gds NW Europe (despatches), Egypt and Palestine 1947-48 (despatches); instr Mons OCS 1949-50, trg offr Scottish Horse (TA) 1952-54, Staff Coll Camberley 1955, GSO2 Mil Ops War Off 1956-57, GSO1 to Adm of Fleet Earl Mountbatten 1964-65, Cdr 4/7 Royal Dragoons 1966-67, Cdr 7 Armd Bde 1968-69, princ staff offr to CDS 1970-71, Maj-Gen 1971, Cdr Land Forces NI 1971-73, Cmdt RMA Sandhurst 1973-76, Lt-Gen 1976, mil sec MOD 1976-78, General 1978, Adj-Gen 1978-81 and ADC Gen to HM The Queen 1980-81, ret 1981; Col Cmdt RAC 1980-82 and SAS 1980-85, Col 4/7 Royal Dragoon Gds 1984-88; govr: Royal Hosp Chelsea 1981-87, Corps of Commissionaires 1981-; chm: Army Benevolent Fund 1981- (pres 1986-), Royal Cambridge Home for Soldiers' Widows 1981-87; nat pres Forces Help and Lord Roberts Workshops 1981-; cmmr Cwlth War Graves Cmmn 1981-88 (vice chm 1989-); CBIM; *Recreations* tennis, cricket, war studies; *Clubs* Cavalry & Guards, MCC; *Style*— General Sir Robert Ford, GCB, CBE; c/o National Westminster Bank, 45 Park Street, Camberley, Surrey GU15 3PA

FORD, Robert Webster; CBE (1982); s of Robert Ford, and Beatrice,*née* Webster; *b* 27 Mar 1923; *Educ* Alleyne's Sch; *m* 2 June 1956, Monica Florence, da of Ernest George Tebbett; 2 s (Martin b 1957, Giles b 1964); *Career* WWII RAF 1939-45; radio offr 1945-50: Br Mission, Lhasa Tibet, Political Agency Sikkin and Bhutan, Tibetan Govt Serv; political prisoner communist China 1950-55, freelance writer and broadcaster Tibetan and Chinese affrs 1955-56; HM Dip Serv 1956-83: Saigon 1957-58, Djakarta 1959, Washington 1960-62, FO 1962-67, Tangier 1967-70, Luanda 1970-74, Bordeaux 1974-78, Gothenburg 1978-80, Geneva 1980-83; memb cncl Tibet Soc; FRGS 1956, FRComS 1956; *Books* Captured in Tibet (1956); *Recreations* skiing, gardening, travelling; *Style*— Robert Ford, Esq, CBE; Cedar Garth, Latimer Rd, Monken Hadley, Barnet, Herts EN5 5NU

FORD, Lady; Sheila; *née* Simon; *m* 1965, as his 2 w, Sir Sidney William George Ford, MBE (d 1983, pres Nat Union of Mineworkers 1960-71); *Style*— Lady Ford; 18 Woodland Way, Winchmore Hill, London N21 (☎ 01 882 4220)

FORD, Dr Sydney John; s of Sidney James Ford (d 1983), of West Huntspill, Burnham on Sea, Somerset; *b* 23 August 1936; *Educ* Bishop Gore Sch Swansea, Wales Univ (BSc, PhD, Dip Math Statistics); *m* 1960, Beryl, da of Albert G Owen; 2 s; *Career* chm: Aluminium Corpn, British Alcan Sheet Ltd (dep md to 1985); md. The British Aluminium Co 1982-, (dep md to 1982), dir William Hldgs 1985-; *Recreations* rugby referee and coach; *Style*— Dr S John Ford; Christian Salvesen plc, 50 East Fettes Ave, Edinburgh EH4 1EQ

FORD, Timothy Graham; s of John Hamilton Ford (d 1974), of Charleston, Cornwall, and Dorothy Joyce Ford; *b* 27 Jan 1945; *Educ* Bancrofts Sch Woodford Green Essex, Coll of Law Lancaster Gate; *m* 4 March 1972, Marian Evelyn, da of Charles Bernard Frederick Hayward, MBE, of 2 Orchard Close, Mersham, nr Ashford, Kent; 2 s (Paul b 1973, Simon b 1977); *Career* Inns of Ct and City Yeo 1965-67, cmmd RCS TA 1967, 36 Eastern Signal Regt V; admitted slr 1969, ptnr Park Nelson slrs 1971, gen sec Nat Pawnbrokers Assoc 1988-, contrib to professional press, particularly in architectural press on business and planning law matters; parly candidate (Alliance) Greenwich constituency Gen Election 1983; memb London Legal Aid Ctee; Freeman: City of London 1978, City of London Slrs Co; Liveryman Worshipful Co of Painter Stainers; memb: Law Soc 1969, IOD 1987; *Books* practice manual on procedures under the Consumer Credit Act 1974 for lending insts; *Recreations* golf, fly fishing, cricket, music, reading Charles Dickens; *Clubs* Royal Black GC, East India, MCC; *Style*— Timothy Ford, Esq; The Pavilion, Manorbrook, Blackheath, London SE3 9AW (☎ 01 318 9817); 1 Bell Yard, London WC2A 2JP (☎ 01 404 4191, fax 01 405 4266, car tel 0836 237 577)

FORD, Hon Lady; Hon Virginia; *née* Brand; er da of 1 and last Baron Brand, CMG (d 1963), by his wife, Phyllis (d 1937), sis of the celebrated Lady Astor, both das of Chiswell Dabney Langhorne, of Greenwood, Va, USA; *b* 31 August 1918; *m* 1, 9 Dec 1939, John Metcalfe Polk (d 12 Jan 1948), s of Frank Polk, of USA; 2 s; m 2, 1 Dec 1949, Sir Edward William Spencer Ford, KCB, KCVO, ERD, *qv*; 2 s; *Style*— Hon Lady Ford; Canal House, 23 Blomfield Rd, London W9 1AD (☎ 01 286 0028)

FORDE, Lady Anthea Geraldine; *née* Lowry-Corry; er da of 7 Earl Belmore, JP, DL (d 1960); *b* 16 Feb 1942; *m* 24 April 1965, Patrick Mathew Desmond Forde, s of late Lt-Col Desmond Charles Forde, DL, of Seaforde, Co Down; 3 s, 1 da; *Style*— Lady Anthea Forde; Seaforde, Co Down, N Ireland (☎ 225)

FORDE, Dr Harold McDonald; s of Harold McDonald Forde (d 1978), of Bridgetown, Barbados, and Gertrude, *née* Williams (d 1920); *b* 10 Jan 1916; *Educ* Harrison Coll Barbados, Univ Coll Hosp London (MD); *m* 1949, Alice Elaine, da of William Leslie, of Belize City; 1 s (William), 2 da (Stella, Ann); *Career* medical offr Govt of Belize 1947-52, conslt physician Miny of Health 1957-84, sr lectr in medicine Univ of WI 1967-78; high cmmr for Barbados to UK 1984- (concurrent ambass to: Norway, Sweden, Denmark, Finland, Iceland, Holy See); FRCP (Ed), Hon FRCP, DPH, OTH & H (London); *Recreations* cricket, soccer, bridge; *Clubs* Surrey CC, Lancashire CC, Athenaeum (hon memb); *Style*— Dr Harold Forde; Iverta, Burtenshaw Road, Boyle Farm, Thames Ditton, Surrey (☎ 01 398 1873); Barbados High Commission, 6 Upper Belgrave Street, London SW1X 8AZ (☎ 01 235 8686)

FORDE, Ivo Mathew Leopold Dieskau; OBE (1944), TD (1946); s of Henry Bligh Forde (d 1910), and Hedwig Alice von Dieskau (d 1970); mother Lady-in-Waiting to Princess Charlotte, eldest da of the Empress Frederick (The Princess Royal of England) 1896-1900; *b* 24 Sept 1906; *Educ* Christ's Hosp, St Catharine's Coll Cambrige (MA); *m* 1940, Margaret Pamela, da of Cdr Clive Robinson, DSC, RN (d 1982); 1 da (Penelope Jane b 1945); *Career* mil serv 1939-45, Lt-Col RA Home and Eur; merchant banking; dir: Kleinwort Sons and Co 1948-61, Kleinwort Benson Lonsdale plc 1960- 87, Kleinwort Benson Ltd 1961-71, English and New York Investmt Tst 1963-87 (chm 1968-80); govr St Thomas's Hosp 1963-74, chm John Bright and Co Ltd 1965-79, chm Schlumberger & Co (UK) Ltd 1976-86, dep chm

Christ's Hosp 1974-80; *Recreations* big game photography, shooting, fishing; *Clubs* Brooks's, MCC; *Style*— Ivo Forde, Esq; Norther Farm, Cranleigh, Surrey GU6 8LT (☎ 0483 273881); Kleinwort Benson Lonsdale Ltd, 20 Fenchurch Street, London EC3 (☎ 623 8000)

FORDER, Hon Mrs Elizabeth Sarah; *née* David; da of Baroness David (Life Peer); *b* 1947; *Educ* Badminton Sch, Centl Sch of Speech and Drama; *m* 1966 (m dis 1977), Martin Anthony Potter; 2 da; m 2, John Forder; 1 da; *Career* photojournalist; *Books* Open Fell Hidden Dale (1985), Faces of Lakeland (1987); *Style*— The Hon Mrs Eliza Forder; Sedgwick Cottage, Dent, Cumbria

FORDER, Kenneth John; s of James A Forder (d 1973), and Elizabeth, *née* Hammond (d 1952); *b* 11 June 1925; *Educ* West Cliff Sch, Hertford Coll Oxford (MA); *m* 1948, Dorothy Margot, da of Nelson Burles; 2 da (Jane, Lamorna); *Career* RAF Flt-Lt Aircrew 1943-47; barr Gray's Inn; registrar of the Architects Registration Cncl of the UK 1977-; colonial magistrate 1951-63; *Recreations* tennis; *Clubs* Hurlingham; *Style*— Kenneth Forder Esq; Steeple Close, Church Gate, London SW6 (☎ 01 736 3958); 73 Hallam St, London W1 (☎ 01 580 5861)

FORDHAM, Cecil Frank Alan (Dick); s of Joseph Anthony Quinton Fordham (d 1955), of London, and Sarah Louisa, *née* Waite (d 1979); *b* 3 Sept 1921; *Educ* Christ Coll Finchley, Centl Navigation Sch RAF; *m* 18 Dec 1948, Eileen Joyce, da of Thomas Charles Higby (d 1966), of Nottingham; 1 s (Nigel b 1951), 1 da (Susan b 1952); *Career* RAF 1942-46, Fl Lt Europe; co sec: Foodtech Ltd 1958-68, Multivac Packaging Systems Ltd; *Recreations* bellringing; *Style*— Dick Fordham, Esq; 11 Vicarage Close, Northan, Potters Bar, Herts EN6 4NY (☎ 0707 59929)

FORDHAM, John Anthony; s of Lt Cdr J H Fordham, CBE (d 1967), and Ebba Fordham; *b* 11 June 1948; *Educ* Gresham's Sch Holt Norfolk; *m* 25 June 1974, Lynda Patricia, da of Bernard Green, of Weston-Super-Mare; 2 s (Michael b 28 Dec 1979, Timothy b 3 Aug 1983); *Career* with Bowater Corpn Ltd 1973-81, head of mergers and acquisitions Hill Samuel and Co Ltd 1986- (joined 1981, dir 1985); *Recreations* squash, running, golf, gardening; *Clubs* Royal Wimbledon GC, Rye GC, The Jesters, The Escorts; *Style*— John Fordham, Esq; Sandgate, 81 Thurleigh Road, London SW12 8TY (☎ 01 675 7950); Hill Samuel and Co Ltd, 100 Wood Street, London EC2P 2AJ (☎ 01 628 8011, fax 01 588 5292, car 0860 330772)

FORDHAM, Hon Mrs (June Jane Coupar); *née* Barrie; er da of 1 and last Baron Abertay, KBE (d 1940), and Ethel, *née* Broom (d 1983); *b* 27 Feb 1928; *m* 1, 19 April 1952 (m dis 1977), Brig Alan Norman Breitmeyer, Gren Guards, o s of late Louis Cecil Breitmeyer, of Shape Hill, Rickingshell, Suffolk; 1 s, 1 da; m 2, 1977, Christopher Jeremy King Fordham; *Style*— Hon Mrs Fordham; Odsey Park, Ashwell, Herts (☎ 046 274 2237)

FORDY, (George) Malcolm; s of George Laurence Fordy (d 1970), and Louise, *née* Birdsall; *b* 27 August 1934; *Educ* Durham Sch; *m* 7 June 1957, Pauline, da of William Stanley Thompson, of Thirsk Rd, Northallerton, North Yorks; 1 s (Nicholas b 1960), 2 da (Susan b 1958, Sarah b 1965); *Career* chm and chief exec FT Construction Gp and Fordy Hldgs, chm BEC Pension Tstee Ltd; pres Nat Fedn Bldg Trades Employers 1982-83, bd memb Construction Indust Trg Bd, chm Vocational Trg Cmmn of the Fedn de L'Industrie Europeene de la Construction, dir Guild of Business Travel Agents Ltd; chm N Tees Hosp Womens Cancer Appeal; FCIOB 1978, FBIM 1978; *Recreations* the countryside, travel; *Clubs* Cleveland (Middlesbrough); *Style*— Malcolm Fordy, Esq; High Farm House, Ingleby Greenhow, Great Ayton, North Yorks TS9 6RG; Construction House, Northallerton, North Yorks DL7 8ED (☎ 0609 780 700, fax 0609 777 236, telex 58376 FORDYS G)

FORDYCE, Lt-Col (Alexander) Alastair; MBE (1944), JP (1959), DL (Lancs 1975); s of Alexander Fordyce (d 1926); *b* 30 Sept 1916; *Educ* Perth Acad; *m* 1942, Christian Margaret, *née* Smith; 2 s; *Career* Lt-Col WW II; jt md: Perrite Ltd 1957-80, Manchester Rubber Co Ltd 1966-80; dir: Harvey & Sons Ltd 1959-69, Perrite (Ireland) Ltd 1977-80; ret.; High Sheriff Lancs 1982-83; *Recreations* travel; *Clubs* Army & Navy; *Style*— Lt-Col Alexander Fordyce, MBE, JP, DL; Whitelands, 824 Livesey Branch Rd, Feniscowles, Blackburn, Lancs BB2 5EG (☎ 0254 21352)

FORDYCE, (John) Alistair; s of Thomas Fordyce (d 1935), and Marion Fordyce, *née* Broadley (d 1970); *b* 14 May 1921; *Educ* Merchant Taylors'; *m* 7 Oct 1950, Hazel Ethel Robertson Stone; 2 s (Stuart Alistair b 1951, Andrew Murray b 1955), 1 da (Elspeth Lindsay Mary b 1960); *Career* CA; ptnr Fordyce Curry & Co; dir various private cos; sec Butchers & Drovers Charitable Inst; Liveryman Worshipful Co of Butchers; *Recreations* choral music, gardening, golf; *Clubs* MCC; *Style*— J Alistair Fordyce, Esq; 61 West Smithfield, London EC1 (☎ 01 606 5711)

FORECAST, Trevor Cecil; s of Cecil Arthur Forecast (d 1989), of St Albans, Herts, and Daisy Edith, *née* Lovell; *Educ* St Albans Sch; *m* 29 June 1963, Christine Kay, da of Keith Lionel Stephens (d 1978); 2 da (Katie Jane b 1967, Emma Kay b 1969); *Career* RAF 1956-58; mktg mangr Polymer Corpn (UK) Ltd 1968-72; md and proprietor: Crown Hotel Downham Mkt Ltd 1972-82, Congham Hall Country House Hotel Kings Lynn Norfolk 1982-, dir Pride of Britain Ltd 1988-; pres Kings Lynn Hotels & Catering Assoc; ctee memb: BHRCA Eastern Regn, West Norfolk Tourism Forum; former pres Downham Mkt Chamber of Trade, fndr pres Downham Market RC, pres Grimston CC; MIPE 1955, CEng 1956, MInstM 1968; *Recreations* shooting; *Clubs* Old Albanian, IOD; *Style*— Trevor Forecast, Esq; Congham Hall, Country House Hotel & Restaurant, Grimston, Kings Lynn, Norfolk PE32 1AH (☎ 0485 600 250, telex 81508 CHOTEL)

FOREMAN, Keith; OBE (1986); s of John Foreman (d 1977), of Kettering, Northants, and Phyllis, *née* Barker (d 1982); *b* 19 May 1935; *Educ* Kettering GS, Univ of Durham (BA, MEd), Univ of Cambridge (PGCE); *m* 5 Jan 1957, Ruth Mary, da of Haydn Lawrence Sail (d 1972), of Kettering; 1 s (Paul b 1967), 2 da (Helen b 1964, Anne b 1966); *Career* warden Comberton Village Coll Cambridge 1969-86, princ Burleigh Community Coll Loughborough 1986-, memb sch mgmt Task Force DES 1988-; memb Trinity Methodist Church Loughborough; FRSA 1983; *Recreations* sailing, walking; *Style*— Keith Foreman, Esq, OBE; 5 De Verdun Ave, Belton, Loughborough, Leics LE12 9TY (☎ 0530 222 832); Burleigh Community Coll, Loughborough, Leics (☎ 0509 268 996)

FOREMAN, Sir Philip Frank; CBE (1972), DL (Belfast 1975); s of late Frank and Mary Foreman; *b* 16 Mar 1923; *Educ* Soham GS, Loughborough Coll; *m* 1971, Margaret, da of John Petrie Cooke, of Belfast; 1 s; *Career* with RN Scientific Serv 1943-58; chm chief exec and md Short Brothers Ltd (aerospace mfrs) 1983-88 (joined 1959, md 1967); dir: Renaissance Hldgs, Simon Engrg plc; Progressive Building Soc, Ricardo Gp plc; chm BSI 1988-, conslt Foreman Assoc; hon FRAeS, hon DSc, hon DTech; FEng, FIMechE, FIProdE, CBIM; kt 1981; *Style*— Sir Philip Foreman, CBE, DL; Ashtree House, 26 Ballymenoch Rd, Holywood, Co Down BT18 0HH (☎ 02317 5767)

FORESTER, 8 Baron (UK 1821); (George Cecil) Brooke Weld-Forester; s of 7 Baron Forester (d 1977), and Marie Louise Priscilla (d 1988), da of Col Sir Herbert Perrott, 6 and last Bt, CH, CB; *b* 20 Feb 1938; *Educ* Eton, RAC Cirencester; *m* 14 Jan 1967, Hon (Elizabeth) Catherine Lyttelton, 2 da of 10 Viscount Cobham, KG, GCMG, GCVO, TD, PC; 1 s (Hon George b 1975), 3 da (Hon Selina b 1968, Hon Alice b 1969, Hon Alexandra b 1973); *Heir* s, Hon (Charles Richard) George Forester b 8 July 1975; *Career* Patron of 3 livings; this nobleman has in his possession a licence of the time of Henry VIII, giving to John Forester of Watling St, Co Salop, the privilege of wearing his hat in the Royal presence; *Style*— The Rt Hon Lord Forester; Willey Park, Broseley, Shropshire (☎ Telford 882146); 21 Whiteheads Grove, London SW3 3HB

FORESTER, Baroness; Hon (Elizabeth) Catherine; *née* Lyttelton; 2 da of 10 Viscount Cobham, KG, GCMG, GCVO, TD, PC (d 1977); *b* 7 Feb 1946; *m* 14 Jan 1967, 8 Baron Forester *qv*; *Style*— The Rt Hon Lady Forester; Willey Park, Broseley, Shropshire TF12 5JJ (☎ 0952 882146) 21 Whiteheads Grove, London SW3 3HB (☎ Telford 589 8543)

FORESTIER-WALKER, Alan David; s of Urbain Evelyn Forestier-Walker, 2 s of Ivor Augustus Forestier-Walker (5 s of 2 Bt); hp of cous, Sir Michael Forestier-Walker, 6 Bt; *b* 29 August 1944; *Educ* Prior Park Coll Bath; *m* 7 Nov 1969, Adela Judith, da of Simon Phillip Davies, of Hampstead; 1 s 2 da; *Career* Capt 7 Duke of Edinburgh's Own Gurkha Rifles; *Style*— Capt Alan Forestier-Walker

FORESTIER-WALKER, Maj (George) Clive; s of Edmund Annesley Forestier-Walker, of Broombank, Aldeburgh, Suffolk (gggs of Sir George Walker, 1 Bt, GCB), by his w Bridget, da of Cdr Sir Geoffrey Hughes-Onslow, KBE, DSC, JP, DL, RN (kin to the Earls of Onslow), and Hon Eileen, da of 4 Baron Crofton; *b* 17 April 1946; *Educ* Wellington; *m* 8 April 1970, (Ruth) Christian, yst da of John Gurney, *qv*, of Walsingham Abbey, Norfolk; 4 da (Camilla b 1973, Susanna b 1976, Liza b 1980, Mary b 1983); *Career* Major Coldm Gds; stockbroker; *Recreations* shooting, skiing, sailing (yacht: Casalamy); *Clubs* Cavalry & Guards, Royal Yacht Squadron; *Style*— Maj Clive Forestier-Walker; Plum Tree Cottage, North Heath, Chieveley, Newbury, Berks RG16 8UD (☎ 0635 248673)

FORESTIER-WALKER, Sir Michael Leolin; 6 Bt (UK 1835); s of Lt-Col Alan Ivor Forestier-Walker, MBE, 7 Gurkha Rifles (ka Malaya 1954, s of Ivor Forestier-Walker, 5 s of 2 Bt) and Margaret Joan, da of Maj Henry Bennet Marcoolyn, MBE; suc kinsman, Sir Clive Radzivill Forestier-Walker, 5 Bt, 1983; *b* 24 April 1949; *Educ* Wellington, Royal Holloway Coll London (BA); *m* 16 July 1988, Elizabeth, da of Joseph Hedley, of Bellingham, Northumberland; *Heir* cous, Alan David Forestier-Walker, b 29 Aug 1944; *Career* teacher Feltonfleet Sch Cobham; *Recreations* sailing, electronics, computing; *Style*— Sir Michael Forestier-Walker, Bt; 91 Tartar Road, Cobham, Surrey KT11 2AS (☎ work: 0932 64870)

FORMAN, Sir (John) Denis; OBE (1956); s of Rev Adam Forman, CBE (d 1977), of Dumcrieff, Moffatt, Scotland, and Flora, *née* Smith; *b* 13 Oct 1917; *Educ* Loretto Musselburgh, Pembroke Coll Camb; *m* 1948, Helen Blondel de Moulpied (d 1987); 2 s; *Career* Lt-Col (OSDEF Battle Sch, North Africa, Italy); dir Granada TV 1955-87 (chm 1974-87), dir Granada Gp 1964 (dep chm 1984), chm Novello and Co 1971-88; chief prodn offr Central Off of Information Films 1947, dir Br Film Inst 1948-55, chm bd of govrs Br Film Inst 1971-73; Royal Opera House: dir 1980, dep chm 1984, chm Opera Bd 1988; cncl memb Royal Northern Coll of Music 1977; Hon Doctorate: Stirling Univ 1982, Univ of Essex 1986; Hon LLD Manchester 1983; kt 1976; *Recreations* music; *Clubs* Garrick, Saville; *Style*— Sir Denis Forman, OBE; The Mill House, Howe St, Chelmsford, Essex CM3 1BG; Granada Group Ltd, 36 Golden Sq, London W1P 4AH (☎ 01 734 8080)

FORMAN, (Francis) Nigel; MP (Cons) Carshalton and Wallington 1983-; s of late Brig J F R Forman; *b* 25 Mar 1943; *Educ* Shrewsbury, New Coll Oxford, Coll of Europe Bruges, Harvard Univ, Sussex Univ; *Career* former asst dir CRD, contested (C) Coventry NE Feb 1974, MP (C) Sutton Carshalton 1976-83, memb Select Ctee on Sci and Technol 1976-79; sec Cons ctees: Educn 1976-79, Energy 1977-79; PPS to Douglas Hurd as Min of State FCO 1979-1983; vice-chm Conservative Finance Ctee 1983-87, PPS to the Chllr of the Exchequer, Nigel Lawson 1987-; *Style*— Nigel Forman, Esq, MP; House of Commons, London SW1

FORMAN, Phyllis Maude; *née* Warner; da of William Thomas Warner (d 1963), of Coleshill, Warwickshire, and Maude Alicia Rowley (d 1933); paternal family tree available back to 1640; *Educ* Nuneaton HS, Lady Margaret Hall Oxford (MA); *m* 1951, Winston Oswald Forman (d 1968), s of George Forman (d 1963), of Boston, Lincs; *Career* Legal and Parly sec to Royal Assoc for Disability and Rehabilitation 1969-80; trg offr Nat Old People's Welfare Cncl 1955-69; formerly educn offr Sch Broadcasting Cncl; currently chm Merton Assoc for the Disabled; *Recreations* travel, gardening, voluntary work; *Style*— Phyllis M Forman; 84 Arthur Road, Wimbledon, London SW19 7DT (☎ 01 947 1680); National Westminster Bank, 149 Arthur Road, London SW19

FORMAN HARDY, Col Thomas Eben; CBE (1966), MC (1943), TD (1945), DL (Notts 1963); s of William Eben Hardy, of Bramcote Hills, Notts; *b* 30 August 1919; *Educ* Harrow, Trinity Coll Cambridge; *m* 1946, Marjorie Senior, da of Edward Senior Edgar, of Nottingham; 1 s, 1 da (and 1 decd); *Career* cmmnd S Notts Hussars Yeo 1939, served WW II with RA, cmd S Notts Hussars Yeo as Lt-Col 1958, Dep Bde Cdr 148 Bde 1962-64 as Col, Hon Col SNH Yeo 1976-83; jt acting master S Notts Hunt 1957-65, High Sheriff Notts 1960, ADC (TA) to HM The Queen 1966-71; chm: T Bailey Forman Ltd (proprietors of Nottingham Evening Post), Forman Hardy Farms; chm E Midlands TAVR 1980-85;; *Recreations* shooting, sailing; *Clubs* Cavalry & Guards, Royal Cornwall YC; *Style*— Col Thomas Forman Hardy, CBE, MC, TD, DL; Car Colston Hall, Bingham, Notts (☎ 0949 20254)

FORMARTINE, Viscount; George Ian Alastair; s and h of Lord Haddo, *qv*, (himself s and h of 6 Marquess of Aberdeen and Temair, *qv*), and Joanna Clodagh, da of late Maj Ian George Henry Houldsworth; *b* 4 May 1983; *Style*— Viscount Formartine

FORMBY, Roger Myles; s of Myles Landseer Formby, CBE, of Storrington, W Sussex, and Dorothy Hussey, *née* Essex; *b* 15 Mar 1938; *Educ* Winchester, Oxford Univ (BA); *m* 15 Sept 1962, (Alice) Jane, da of Herbert Victor Woof (d 1950), of Bedford; 2 da (Kate b 1965, Emily b 1967); *Career* Nat Serv 2 Lt Oxford and Bucks

LI 1957; slr 1965, managing ptnr MacGarlanes 1987- (ptnr 1967-, head of property 1970-86); *Recreations* golf, skiing, travel; *Clubs* City of London; *Style*— Roger M Formby, Esq; 10 Norwich St, London EC4A 1BD (☎ 01 831 9222, fax 01 831 9607, telex 296381)

FORRES, 4 Baron (UK 1922); Sir Alastair Stephen Grant Williamson; 4 Bt (UK 1909); s of 3 Baron Forres (d 1978), by his 1 w, Gillian Ann Maclean, *née* Grant; *b* 16 May 1946; *Educ* Eton; *m* 2 May 1969, Margaret Ann, da of late George John Mallam, of Mullumbimby, NSW; 2 s (Hon George, Hon Guthrie b 1975); *Heir* s, Hon George Archibald Mallam Williamson b 16 Aug 1972; *Career* chm Agriscot Pty Ltd; dir Jaga Trading Pty Ltd; Australian rep Tattersalls; *Clubs* Australian Jockey, Tattersalls (Sydney), Sydney Turf; *Style*— The Rt Hon the Lord Forres; c/o Clark Oliver, Solicitors, Brothobank House, Arbroath, Angus DD11 1NJ

FORRES, Cecily, Baroness; Cecily Josephine; da of Maj Sir Alexander Gordon-Cumming, 5 Bt, MC, by Elizabeth, *née* Richardson, who later m 5 Earl Cawdor; *b* 11 Dec 1925; *m* 1, 25 June 1957, as his 2 w, 2 Earl of Woolton (d 7 Jan 1969); m 2, 22 Sept 1969 (m dis 1974), 3 Baron Forres (d 1978); *Style*— Cecily, Lady Forres; Glenogil, by Forfar, Angus; 31 Tite St, SW3 (☎ 01 352 1333)

FORREST, Prof (William) George Grieve; s of William Downie Forrest, of 19b East Heath Rd, London NW3, and Ina Mitchell Grieve, *née* Welsh; *b* 24 Sept 1925; *Educ* LCC Merton Pk, UCS Hampstead, New Coll Oxford (BA); *m* 14 July 1956, Margaret Elizabeth Mary, da of Frederick Hall (d 1955); 2 da (Catherine b 1957, Alison b 1959); *Career* served RAF 1943-47, Actg Corp; fell Wadham Coll 1951-76; visiting prof: Toronto 1961, Yale 1968; Wykeham prof of ancient hist Oxford Univ 1976-, visiting fell Br Sch of Athens 1986; Univ memb Oxford City 1962-65; *Books* Emergence of Greek Democracy (1966), History of Sparta (1968); *Recreations* socialism; *Style*— Prof George Forrest; 9 Fyfield Rd, Oxford (☎ 0865 56187); New Coll, Oxford OX1 3BN (☎ 0865 248451)

FORREST, Sir James Alexander; s of John Forrest (d 1945), and Mary Gray Forrest (d 1950); *b* 10 Mar 1905; *Educ* Caulfield GS, Melbourne Univ; *m* 1939, Mary Christina, da of William Duke Armit (d 1945); 3 s; *Career* chm: Chase NBA Group Ltd 1969-80; Alcoa of Australia Ltd 1970-78; dir: Nat Bank of Australia Ltd 1950-78, Australian Consolidated Industries Ltd 1950-77; FAA; kt 1967; *see Debrett's Handbook of Australia and New Zealand for further details*; *Recreations* golf, fishing; *Clubs* Melbourne, Australian (Melbourne); *Style*— Sir James Forrest; 11 Russell St, Toorak, Vic 3142, Australia (☎ 20 5227)

FORREST, John Orchover; *b* 4 May 1918; *Educ* Centl Fndn Sch, Univ of London, Guy's Hosp Dental Sch; *m* 1944, Irene, *née* Leanse; 2 s; *Career* sr hosp dental offr Guy's Hosp 1961-68, hon Guy's Dental Hosp 1969-71, Gibbs Prize Scholar 1968; pres: Br Periodontal Soc 1964, Br Endodontic Soc 1966, Br Dental Assoc Metropolitan branch 1977, Euro Dental Soc 1983-85; UK Regent Int Coll Dentists 1980-86; vice pres Int Coll Dentists 1987, (pres Euro section 1989-); *Books* The Good Teeth Guide (2 edn 1985), Preventive Dentistry (1981), A Guide to Successful Dental Practice (1984), The Good Teeth Guide (2 edn 1985), A Handbook for Dental Hygienists (2 edn 1985); *Recreations* photography, writing, collecting snuff bottles and rejection slips; *Clubs* RAF; *Style*— John Forrest, Esq; 74 Lawn Rd, Hampstead, London NW3 2XB (☎ 01 722 8589); c/o Coutts & Co, 16 Cavendish Square, London W1

FORREST, Dr John Richard; s of Prof John Samuel Forrest, and Ivy May Ellen, *née* Olding; *b* 21 April 1943; *Educ* King's Coll Sch Wimbledon, Sidney Sussex Coll Cambridge (BA, MA), Keble Coll Oxford (DPhil); *m* 8 Sept 1973, Jane Patricia Robey, da of John Robey Leech, of Little Hockham Hall, Great Hockham, Norfolk; 2 s (Nicholas John b 1975, Alexander Iain b 1980), 1 da (Katherine Elizabeth b 1977); *Career* UCL: lectr 1970-79, reader 1979-82, prof 1982-84; tech dir Marconi Def Systems Ltd, dir of engr IBA 1986-; FIEE 1980, FEng 1985, FRSA 1987; *Recreations* theatre, music, reading, walking; *Style*— Dr John Forrest; Hilfield Farm House, Hilfield Lane, Aldenham, Watford, Herts WD2 8DD (☎ 01 950 1820); Independent Broadcasting Authority, Crawley Court, Winchester, Hants SO21 2QA (☎ 0962 822 455, fax 0962 822 434, cartel 0836 692 278, telex 477211)

FORREST, Michael William; s of William Edward Forrest (d 1969), of St Clement, Jersey, CI, and Kathleen Honor, *née* Foxall (d 1985); *Educ* Victoria Coll Jersey CI; *m* 25 July 1973, Linda Mary, da of William Giles, of Manchester; 2 s (Richard b 1975, Thomas b 1979), 1 da (Laura b 1981); *Career* sr ptnr Robson Rhodes Jersey CI, chm The Langtry House Gp of Cos; memb: Jersey Race and Hunt Club, Jersey Motor Cycle and Light Car Club, Riding Club, IOD; FCA, FCCA, ACIArb; *Recreations* hunting, riding, skiing; *Clubs* Old Victorians Assoc, IOD; *Style*— Michael Forrest, Esq; La Sergente, St Mary, Jersey, CI (☎ 0534 838 24); Les Chevrons, Les Diablerets, Vaud, Switzerland; Langtry House, La Motte St, St Helier, Jersey, CI (☎ 0534 739 21, fax 0534 246 68, car tel 0860 740 240, telex 4192069 FIDES G)

FORREST, Nigel; s of Wing Cdr Gerald Vere Forrest, of Sydney New South Wales, Aust, and Elizabeth, *née* Burnett; *b* 12 Sept 1946; *Educ* Harrow, Oriel Coll Oxford (MA), Insead European Business Sch (MBA); *m* 22 Nov 1980, Julia Mary, da of Philip Nash (d 1970), of Dorking, Surrey; 1 s (Dominic b 18 Aug 1982), 1 da (Harriet b 9 Feb 1984); *Career* commercial technol sales mangr 1972 (graduate trainee 1969) Rolls Royce Ltd, mangr 1978 (exec 1973) Lazard Bros & Co Ltd, assoc md 1986 (mangr 1981, exec dir 1983) Nomura Int Ltd; chm fundraising ctee Highbury Roundhouse 1978-81; *Books* The Channel Tunnel - Before The Decision (1973); *Style*— Nigel Forrest, Esq; Nomura Int Ltd, 24 Monument St, London EC3R 8AJ (☎ 01 283 8811, fax 01 929 4489, car tel 0860 615 712, 0836 526 920)

FORREST, Prof Emeritus Sir (Andrew) Patrick McEwen; s of Rev Andrew James Forrest (d 1960), and Isabella Pearson; *b* 25 Mar 1923; *Educ* Dundee HS, St Andrews Univ (BSc, MB ChB, ChM, MD); *m* 1, 1955, Margaret Beryl (d 1961), da of Capt Frederick Hall, MBE; 1 s, 1 da; m 2, 1964, Margaret Anne, da of Harold Edward Steward (d 1976); 1 da; *Career* Surgn Lt RNVR 1946-48; civilian conslt to RN in Surgery Researching 1977-88; Prof of surgery Welsh Nat Sch of Med 1962-71, regius prof of clinical surgery Edinburgh 1971-88; numerous memb: Med Res Cncl 1976-80, Advsy Bd for Res Cncls 1982-85; chief scientist to Scottish Home and Health Dept 1981-87; pres Assoc of Surgns GB and Ireland 1988-9; FRCS, FRSE; hon DSc: Wales, Chinese Univ. of HK; hon LLD (Dundee); hon FACS, FRACS, FRCR, FRCCPS, Lister Medal RCSEng 1987; author of papers on breast cancer and gastro-intestinal disease; *Recreations* sailing; *Style*— Sir Patrick Forrest; 19 St Thomas Road, Edinburgh EH9 2CR

FORREST, Rear Adm Sir Ronald Stephen; KCVO (1975), JP (Honiton 1978), DL (Devon 1985); s of Dr Stephen Forrest (d 1957), of Edinburgh, and Maud M McKinstry; *b* 11 Jan 1923; *Educ* Belhaven Hill, RNC Dartmouth; *m* 1, 1947, Patricia (d 1966), da of Dr E N Russell, of Alexandria, Egypt; 2 s, 1 da; m 2, 1967, June, widow of Lt G Perks, RN, and da of L W Weaver (d 1945), of Budleigh Salterton; 1 step s, 1 step da; *Career* RN: serv at sea 1940-72, dir Seamen Offrs Appts 1968, CO HMS London 1970, def serv sec 1972-75, Rear Adm 1972; co cmmr St John Ambulance Bde Devon 1976-81, county cdr St Ambulance Devon 1981-87; KStJ; *Clubs* Naval, Army & Navy; *Style*— Rear Adm Sir Ronald Forrest, KCVO, JP, DL; Higher Seavington, Stockland, Honiton, Devon EX14 9DE

FORREST, Surgn Rear Adm (D) William Ivan Norman; CB (1970); s of Eng Lt James Forrest (d 1916), and Alice Amelia, *née* Honeyben; *b* 8 June 1914; *Educ* Christ's Hosp, Guy's Hosp (LDS, RCS Eng); *m* 1943, Mary Margaret McMordie, da of John Millen Black; 3 s (John, Robin, Peter); *Career* Christ's Hosp 1923-31, Guy's Hosp 1931-37; RN 1937-71, Surgn Rear Adm 1968, dir Naval Dental Servs 1968-71; conslt in dental surgery, HM The Queens hon dental surgn 1966-71, HMS Birmingham (China) 1938-40, RN Hosp Bermuda 1947-49, RN Hosp Malta 1961-63; SE Hants Health Authy 1972-84; *Recreations* gardening, golf; *Clubs* RN; *Style*— Surgn Rear Adm (D) William Forrest, CB; 16 Queen's Rd, Waterlooville, Hants PO7 7SB

FORRESTER, John Stuart; MP (Lab) Stoke-on-Trent North 1966-; s of Harry Forrester (d 1961), of Stoke-on-Trent, and Nellie Forrester; *b* 17 June 1924; *Educ* Eastwood Cncl Sch, City Sch of Commerce, Stoke-on-Trent, Alsager Teachers' Trg Coll; *m* 1945, Gertrude H, da of Harold Weaver (d 1969), of Stoke-on-Trent; *Career* teacher, PPS to min state DHSS Feb-June 1970, NUT, memb Stoke-on-Trent: exec ctee City Lab Pty 1958-, city and dist cncls 1970-, memb Speaker's Panel of Chairmen; *Style*— John Forrester Esq, MP; House of Commons, London SW1

FORRESTER, Maj-Gen Michael; CB (1969), CBE (1963, OBE 1960), DSO (1943) and bar (1944), MC (1939) and bar (1941); 2 s of James Forrester (d 1962), of Chilworth, Hants, and Elsie, *née* Mathwin (d 1961); *b* 31 August 1917; *Educ* Haileybury; *m* 1947 (m dis 1960), Pauline Margaret Clara, da of late James Fisher, of Crossmichael, Kirkcudbright; 2 s; *Career* 2 Lt SRO Queen's Royal Regt 1936, 2 Lt QRR 1938, served WW II (Middle E, Greece, Crete, N Africa, Italy and NW Europe), Cdr 16 Parachute Brigade Gp 1961-63, GOC 4 Div (Maj-Gen) 1965-67, dir of Infantry MOD 1968-70; Col Cmdt Queen's Div 1968-70, ret 1970; Lay co-chm Alton Deanery Synod 1984-; *Recreations* countryside, gardening; *Style*— Maj-Gen Michael Forrester, CB, CBE, DSO, MC; Hammonds, West Worldham, Alton, Hants GU34 3BH (☎ 0420 84470)

FORRESTER, Prof Peter Garnett; CBE (1981); s of Arthur Forrester (d 1949), of Cheshire, and Emma, *née* Garnett (d 1962); *b* 7 June 1917; *Educ* Manchester GS, Manchester Univ (BSc, MSc), Hon DSc (Cranfield); *m* 1942, Marjorie Hewitt, da of Robert Berks (d 1940), of Staffs; 2 da (Patricia b 1945, Claire b 1954); *Career* metallurgist; Royal Aircraft Estab Farnborough, Tin Research Inst; chief metallurgist Glacier Metal Co 1948-63, conslt John Tyzack & Ptnrs 1963-66, prof of Industrial Mgmnt Cranfield Inst of Technol 1966-82, dir Cranfield Sch of Mgmnt 1967-82, pro-vice chllr Cranfield Inst of Technol, dir Jackson Taylor Int Gp Ltd 1984-88, dir Faculties Ptnrship Ltd; hon DSc Cranfield Inst of Technol 1983, Burnham Medal 1979; FIM, CBIM, FRSA; *Recreations* research, writing, gardening, walking, sailing; *Style*— Prof Peter Forrester, CBE; Strawberry Hole Cottage, Ewhurst Lane, Northiam, nr Rye, E Sussex TN31 6HJ (☎ 079 74 2255)

FORRESTER-PATON, His Hon Douglas Shaw; QC (1965); s of Alexander Forrester-Paton, JP (d 1954), and Hon Mary Emma Louise Shaw (d 1974), da of 1 Baron Craigmyle (d 1937); *b* 22 June 1921; *Educ* Gresham's, Queen's Coll Oxford (BA); *m* 1948, Agnete, da of late Hr Ingenior Holger Tuxen, of Denmark; 1 s (Thomas), 2 da (Kirsten, Elspeth); *Career* Sqdn Ldr RAFVR; barr 1947, rec of Middlesbrough 1963-68, rec of Teesside 1968-70, co ct judge 1970-71, circuit judge 1972-86; *Recreations* gardening, walking; *Style*— His Hon Douglas Forrester-Paton, QC; 24 Kirkby Lane, Gt Broughton, Middlesbrough (☎ Stokesley 0642 712301)

FORSBERG, Cdr (Charles) Gerald; OBE (1955); s of Charles G Forsberg (d 1913), of Vancouver, and Nellie, *née* Wallman; *b* 18 June 1912; *Educ* Poly sch, trg ship Mercury, Sir John Cass Coll; *m* 1952, Joyce Whewell, da of Dr Frederick Whewell Hogarth, (d 1976); 1 s, 1 da; *Career* recovered deeply sunk Comet airliner 1955; Br long-distance swimming champion 1957-59, (England to France record 1957-59, first to swim Loch Lomond and Lough Neagh 1959); Cdr RN, cmd HM Ships Vega (despatches), Mameluke, Chaplet, Z39, Thames, Isis; war serv in Norway, Malta convoys, Greece, Crete, Indian Ocean, Tobruk, N Sea convoys; master mariner 1938; dep dir Marine Services (Naval) 1958-72 (asst dir 1972-75); author and journalist; *Books* Modern Long Distance Swimming, Salvage from The Sea, Pocket Book for Seamen, Thirty Years of Distance Swimming; *Recreations* marathon swimming; *Clubs* Otter Swimming; *Style*— Cdr Gerald Forsberg, OBE, RN; c/o Barclays Bank, 19 Euston Rd, Morecambe, Lancs LA4 5DE

FORSTER, Alan Roger; s of Harold Edgar Forster (d 1979), and Annie Dorothy, *née* Wenham; *b* 27 Oct 1933; *Educ* Eastbourne GS; *m* 1, 1956, Diana, da of Herbert Raymond Love; 1 s (Paul b 1957), 1 da (Emma b 1966); m 2, 1979, Valerie, da of James Fisk; *Career* chm Booker Overseas Trading Ltd, Bookers Sugar Co Ltd, Such & Schooley Ltd; memb exec ctee of West India Ctee; *Recreations* horse racing (owner), watching cricket; *Clubs* MCC; *Style*— Alan R Forster, Esq; Little Ridge, Chislehurst Rd, Chislehurst, Kent (☎ 01 467 1094, 01 467 3684); 177/179 Southwark Bridge Road, London SE1 0EE (telex 8952713, fax 01-403 3631)

FORSTER, Sir Archibald William; s of William Henry Forster (d 1955), and Matilda (d 1969); *b* 11 Feb 1928; *Educ* Tottenham GS, Univ of Birmingham (BSc, Cadman Medallist); *m* 1954, Betty Margaret, da of Edgar Norman Channing (d 1984); 3 da (Nicola b 1959, Jacqueline b 1961, Amanda b 1967); *Career* RAF (FO) 1949-51; chm Esso Pension Tst 1980-, chief exec Esso Petroleum Co Ltd 1980-, exec bd memb Lloyds Register of Shipping 1981-; chm & chief exec: Esso UK plc 1983-, Esso Exploration and Prodn UK Ltd 1983-; non-exec bd memb: Midland Bank 1986-, Rover Gp plc 1986-88; FEng; kt 1987; *Recreations* sailing; *Clubs* Royal Southampton Yacht; *Style*— Sir Archibald Forster; Esso House, Victoria St, London SW1E 5JW (☎ 01 245 3294, telex 24942, fax 01 245 2556)

FORSTER, Rev Bennet Fermor; s of Lt-Gen Alfred Leonard Forster, CB, DSO (d 1963), and Gladys Maud Godfrey-Faussett; *b* 27 May 1921; *Educ* Lancing, Brasenose Coll Oxford (MA); *m* 31 March 1951, Anthea Monica, da of Raymond Walter Beall (d 1949); 1 s (Keith b 1953), 1 da (Clare b 1954); *Career* Maj Royal Marine 1940-46,

ME, Far E, Normandy; vicar St Cuthbert Copnor Portsmouth 1957-65, chaplain Bedford Sch 1965-72, sr teacher Newnham Sch Bedford 1972-78, vicar Hawkley and Froxfield Hants 1978-; *Recreations* walking, tennis; *Clubs* RM Assoc; *Style*— The Rev Bennet Forster; Flat 2, Holywell House, Holywell Rd, Malvern Wells, Worcs WR14 4LF (☎ 06845 72170)

FORSTER, Donald; CBE; s of Bernard Forster (d 1983), and Rose, *née* Deutsch (d 1975); *b* 18 Dec 1920; *Educ* Manchester GS; *m* 1942, Muriel Steinman; 1 s (Steven), 2 da (Susan, Vanessa); *Career* served 1940-45 RAF Pilot (Flt Lt); md B Forster & Co Ltd Textile Mfrs 1946-81, (chm 1981-85); bd memb Skelmersdale Devpt Corpn; chm: Warrington Runcorn Devpt Corpn 1981-85, Merseyside Devpt Corpn 1984-87; *Recreations* golf, music, art; *Clubs* Dunham Forest, Whitefield; *Style*— Donald Forster, Esq, CBE; 6 The Dell, South Downs Rd, Hale, Altrincham, Cheshire WA14 3HU (☎ 061 926 9145)

FORSTER, His Honour Judge Donald Murray; s of John Cameron Forster (d 1970), and Maisie Constance, *née* Nicoll; Tom Forster led the English Jacobites to defeat at Preston in 1715; Nicolls were a Skye clan - Nicolson; *b* 18 June 1929; *Educ* Wrekin Coll Shropshire, St Edmund Hall Oxford; *Career* circuit judge 1984, assigned to N circuit; *Recreations* sport; *Clubs* Liverpool Ramblers Football, Liverpool Racquet, Mersey Bowmen Tennis; *Style*— His Hon Judge Donald Forster; Flat 8, Sutcliffe House, Edmond Castle, Wetheral, Carlisle CA4 8QE

FORSTER, (Charles) Ian Kennerley; CBE (1964); s of Douglas Wakefield Forster (d 1963), of Bishop Middleham, and Nora Scott, *née* Leggatt (d 1964); *b* 18 July 1911; *Educ* Rossall Sch; *m* 1, 1942 (m dis 1974), Thelma Primrose, da of late Augustus Selwyn Horton; 1 s, 1 da; m 2, 1975, (Violet) Loraine, *née* Sperling, wid of Sqdn-Ldr Brian Huxtable; *Career* Capt RA WW II (AA Cmd and BAOR); Sun Life Assurance Soc 1928-46, Govt Statistical Service Admty 1946-54, Miny of Power 1954 (chief statistician 1955-65, dir Statistics 1965-69), Miny of Technol 1969, under-sec Economics and Statistics DTI 1970-72, energy conslt Nat Coal Bd 1972-81; FIA; *Recreations* stamp collecting, bridge; *Style*— Ian Forster, Esq, CBE; 140 Watchfield Court, Sutton Court Rd, Chiswick, London W4 (☎ 01 994 3128)

FORSTER, John Henry Knight; s of Henry Knight Forster, of Salcombe, Devon, and Margaret Rutherford, *née* Metcalf; *b* 14 Feb 1941; *Educ* Dean Close Sch Cheltenham; *m* 1, 1965 (m dis 1985), Hilary; 1 s (Gregory), 2 da (Heidi, Hayley); m 2, 1986, Carol Ann, *née* Lamond; *Career* sec The Kaye Orgn Ltd; dir and sec: Color Steels Ltd, Elvetham Hall Ltd, Hadley Garages Ltd, Industl Modernisation Ltd, Kingfield Wholesale Office Supplies Ltd, Lansing Henley Ltd, Pegasus Retirement Homes Ltd, Pool & Sons (Hartley Wintney) Ltd, FCA, FCT; *Recreations* riding to hounds; *Style*— John Forster, Esq; Hunters Moon, Little Fallow, Danes Mead, Old Basing, Hampshire RG24 0UN (☎ 0256 64638); Hart Ho, Hartley Wintney, Hampshire RG27 8PE (☎ 025126 377, telex 858393 KAYORG)

FORSTER, Margaret; da of Arthur Gordon Forster, and Lilian, *née* Hind; *b* 25 May 1938; *Educ* Somerville Coll Oxford; *m* 1960, (Edward) Hunter Davies, *qv*; 1 s, 2 da; *Career* author; *Books Incl:* Georgy Girl (1965); *Style*— Margaret Forster; 11 Boscastle Rd, London NW5

FORSTER, Neil Milward; s of Norman Milward Forster and Olive Christina, *née* Cockrell; bro of Sir Oliver Forster *qv*; *b* 29 May 1927; *Educ* Hurstpierpoint, Pembroke Coll Cambridge (BA); *m* 1954, Barbara Elizabeth Smith; 1s, 2 da; *Career* dir Brit and Cwlth Shipping Co plc 1982-; *Style*— Neil Forster, Esq; c/o British & Commonwealth Shipping Co plc, Queens House, 64/65 St James's Street, London SW1 (☎ 01 493 2682); 18 Carlton Rd, Ealing, London W5

FORSTER, Norvela F; MEP (EDG) Birmingham S 1979-84; *b* 1931; *Educ* South Wilts GS Salisbury, London Univ (BSc); *m* 1981, Michael Jones, s of Norman Jones; *Career* fndr chm and md IAL Conslts Ltd (formerly Industl Aids Ltd, consultancy co; former memb: Hampstead Borough Cncl, cncl Bow Gp; memb: cncl Mgmnt Consults Assoc, W European Ctee of London C of C; *Clubs* Royal Ocean Racing, Royal Mid-Surrey Golf; *Style*— Miss Norvela Forster; c/o IAL Comsultants Ltd, 14 Buckingham Palace Rd, London SW1W 0QP (☎ 01 828 5036); 6 Regency House, Regency St, London SW1 (☎ 01 821 5749)

FORSTER, Sir Oliver Grantham; KCMG (1983, CMG 1976), LVO (1961); 2 s of Norman Milward Forster and Olive Christina, *née* Cockrell; bro of Neil Milward Forster, *qv*; *b* 2 Sept 1925; *Educ* Hurstpierpoint, King's Coll Cambridge; *m* 1953; 2 da; *Career* Cwlth Relations Office 1951, first sec 1959, min Br High Cmmn New Delhi 1975, asst under-sec of state and dep chief clerk FCO 1975-79, ambass Pakistan 1979-84; *Style*— Sir Oliver Forster, KCMG, LVO; The White House, 71 Raglan Road, Reigate, Surrey

FORSTER, Robert Anthony; s of Capt Henry Knight Forster MBE, of Fernbank, Coronation Rd, Salcombe, South Devon, and Margaret Rutherford, *née* Metcalf; *b* 26 July 1945; *Educ* Llandaff Cathedral Sch Llandaff, Dean Close Sch Cheltenham; *m* 12 Sept 1970, Christine Elizabeth, da of Frederick William Milward, of 3 St Michael's Rd, Llandaff, Cardiff; 1 da (Annabel b 16 May 1973); *Career* accountant 1952-74: EM Manufacturing Co Ltd, Western Mail & Echo Ltd, Standard Telephone & Cables Ltd, Aeroquip UK Ltd; fin dir Biomet Ltd 1974-, vice-pres Cardiff C of C; ctee memb: IOD Wales Div (past sec), Chartered Inst of Mgmnt Accountants S Wales Branch (past sec, chm, pres); memb Peterston-Super-Ely Parish Church Cncl; FCMA 1973, FIOD 1977; *Recreations* travel, gardening, fine arts; *Clubs* Fredericks; *Style*— Robert Forster, Esq; 7 Duffryn Crescent, Peterston-Super-Ely, South Glamorgan CF5 6NF (☎ 0446 760162); BIOMET Ltd, Waterton Indust Estate, Bridgend, South Glamorgan CF31 3YN (☎ 0656 55221, fax 0656 645454, telex 497920)

FORSTER, Hon Mr Justice; Sir William Edward Stanley Forster; AE (1953); s of F B Forster; *b* 15 June 1921; *Educ* St Peter's Coll Adelaide, Adelaide Univ (LLB); *m* 1950, Johanna B, da of Brig A M Forbes; 1 s, 2 da; *Career* master Supreme Ct SA and district registrar High Ct of Australia 1966-71, judge Fed Ct of Aust 1977; chief Justice Supreme Ct of the Northern Territory 1979-; kt 1982; *Style*— Hon Mr Justice Forster, AE; Judges' Chambers, Supreme Court, Darwin, NT 5790, Australia (☎ 89 5511)

FORSYTH, Alastair Elliott; s of Maj Henry Russell Forsyth (d 1941), and Marie Elaine, *née* Greensmith (d 1958); *b* 23 Oct 1932; *Educ* Christ's Hosp, Keble Coll Oxford Univ (MA); *m* 21 July 1973, Margaret Christine, da of Maj Royston Ivor Vallance, of Lark Rise, Weasenham St Peter, nr King's Lynn Norfolk; 4 s (Angus b 1963, Jamie b 1966, Alexander b 1975, John b 1978); 1 da (Arethusa b 1980); *Career* banker; dir J Henry Schroder Wagg & Co Ltd 1982-; *Recreations* Colombian and Venezuelan history; *Clubs* Annabels; *Style*— Alastair Forsyth, Esq; The Old Rectory, Foulsham, Norfolk NR20 5SF; J Henry Schroder Wagg & Co Ltd, 120 Cheapside, London EC2V 6DS (☎ 01 382 6000)

FORSYTH, Cyril Theodore; CBE (1969); s of Edwin Forsyth (d 1979), of Nottingham; *b* 9 Sept 1899; *Educ* People's Coll Nottingham, Nottingham Univ; *m* 1921, Mary Agnes, da of John Kerr, of Nottingham; 2 da; *Career* accountant; chief exec offr Nottingham Co-op Soc Ltd 1943-65; *Recreations* golf, cricket; *Clubs* Victory Services; *Style*— Cyril Forsyth Esq, CBE; Redlands, 45 Loughborough Rd, Ruddington, Nottingham (☎ 211454)

FORSYTH, Gordon Scott; s of George Stirling Forsyth (d 1982), of Rutherglen, Scotland, and Betty Agnes Forsyth, *née* Scott; *b* 20 April 1926; *Educ* Glasgow HS; Glasgow Univ (MA); *m* 6 March 1954, Nancy Scott, da of John Molesworth Reid (d 1971), of Hale, Cheshire; 1 s (Andrew b 1969), 1 da (Fiona b 1966); *Career* Military Serv 1945-48, Lt The Highland LI; CA; chief accountant The Br Petroleum Co plc 1974-81; dir: BP Petroleum Devpt Ltd 1976-86, BP Oil Devpt Ltd 1976-86 fin dir BP Exploration Co Ltd 1981-86; hon tres The Inst of Petroleum 1985-; ; *Recreations* golf, walking; *Clubs* Langley Park GC; *Style*— Gordon Forsyth, Esq; 89 Barnfield Wood Rd, Beckenham, Kent; The Inst of Petroleum, 61 New Cavendish St, London W1M 8AR (☎ 01 636 1004, telex 264380)

FORSYTH, James Law; s of Richard Forsyth (d 1970), of Glasgow, and Jessie, *née* Law (d 1967); *b* 5 Mar 1913; *Educ* HS of Glasgow, The Glasgow Art Sch (Dip); *m* 1, 1938 (m dis 1945), Helen Stewart; 2 s (Antony b 1940, Richard b 1948); m 2, 5 Aug 1955, Dorothy Louise Tibble; *Career* WWII 1940-46: trained Scots Gds Chelsea, cmmnd 2 Monmouthshire Regt South Wales Borderers, Capt Signals Inf (serv Normandy, NW Euro Theatre), Adj Italy (decorated for gallantry 1946); artist: exhibitions 1934-35, designer GPO film unit 1936-40, illustrator Basic English Project 1936-40, Sussex annual exhibitions 1981-88; playwright: active serv and writing 1940-46 (poetry incl Poetry in Wartime 1942, The War Poets 1945), in residence Old Vic 1946-48; stage plays incl: The Medicine Man 1950, Heloise 1951, The Other Heart 1952, The Pier 1958, Trog 1959, Emmanuel 1960, Dear Wormwood 1965, If My Wings Heal 1966, Lobster Back 1975; TV plays incl: The English Boy 1969, Four Triumphant 1969, The Last Journey 1972, The Old Man's Mountain 1972; radio plays incl: The Bronze Horse 1948, Christophe 1958, Every Pebble on the Beach 1962, When the Snow Lay Round About 1978, Fifteen Strings of Cash 1979, The Threshing Floor 1982; visiting prof of drama: Howard 1962, Tufts Univ 1963, Florida State Univ 1964; memb: exec ctee League of Dramatists 1950-75, Theatres Advsy Cncl 1962-67; dir: Tufts in London, overseas drama programme Tufts Univ Mass 1967-71; artistic dir Forsyth's Barn Theatre Sussex 1971-83; awarded Civil List Pension for servs to Literature 1984; memb Soc of Authors (1946-); Bronze Cross Netherlands 1946; *Recreations* walking, gardening, music, reading; *Style*— James Forsyth, Esq; Grainloft, Ansty, West Sussex RH17 5AG (☎ 0444 413 345)

FORSYTH, John Howard; s of George Howard Forsyth, MBE, DSC, (d 1980), of Cartmel, Cumbria, and Marjorie Christine, *née* Cook; *b* 23 August 1945; *Educ* Oundle, St Johns Coll Cambridge; *m* 19 Sept 1968, Barbara, da of Major Gwd Cook of Ockbrook, Derbyshire; 2 s (Mark b 1977, James b 1980), 1 da (Alicia b 1975); *Career* merchant banker; chief economist Morgan Grenfell & Co Ltd 1973; dir: Morgan Grenfell & Co Ltd 1979; memb of cncl Royal Inst of Int Affair 1983-; *Recreations* books, country pursuits; *Clubs* City of London; *Style*— John Forsyth, Esq; 38 Well Walk, London NW3 (☎ 01 794 3523); 20 Finsbury Circus, Londn EC2 (☎ 01 588 4545)

FORSYTH, Michael Bruce; MP (C) Stirling 1983-; s of John Tawse Forsyth and Mary Watson; *b* 16 Oct 1954; *Educ* Arbroath HS, St Andrews Univ (MA); *m* 1977, Susan Jane, da of John Brian Clough; 1 s, 1 da; *Career* nat chm Fedn of Cons students 1976; Westminster City cllr 1978-83, PPS to Foreign Sec 1986-1987, Parly under-sec of state at the Scottish Office June 1987-; *Recreations* mountaineering, photography, astronomy; *Clubs* Reform; *Style*— Michael Forsyth, Esq, MP; House of Commons, London SW1

FORSYTH OF THAT ILK, Alistair Charles William; Chief of the Name and Clan of Forsyth; s of Capt Charles Forsyth of Strathendry, FCA (d 1981), and Ella Millicent Hopkins (d 1983); *b* 7 Dec 1929; *Educ* St Paul's Sch; *m* 1958, Ann OStJ, da of Col Percy Arthur Hughes, IA (d 1950); 4 s; *Career* cmmnd The Queen's Boys (2 dragoon Gds) 1948-50; commodity broker 1950-68; chm: Caledonian Produce (Hldgs) Ltd and Subsidiaries 1968-87; cncllr Angus DC, convenor Industl Devpt Ctee, memb Highland TAVRA, JP Angus; *Recreations* hill walking, Scottish antiquities; *Clubs* Cavalry & Guards, New (Edinburgh); *Style*— Alistair Forsyth of that Ilk; Ethie Castle, by Arbroath, Angus

FORSYTH-JOHNSON, Bruce Joseph; s of John Frederick Forsyth-Johnson, (d 1961), and Florence Ada Forsyth-Johnson (d 1957); *b* 22 Feb 1928; *Educ* Latimer Sch Edmonton; *m* 1, 1951, Olivia, da of Calvert, of NI; 3 da (Debbie b 1955, Julie b 1958, Laura b 1964); m 2, 24 Dec 1973, Anthea, da of Bernard Redfern, of Torquay; 2 da (Charlotte b 1976, Louisa b 1977); m 3, 15 Jan 1983, Wilnelia, da of Enrique Merced, of Puerto Rico; 1 s (Jonathan Joseph b 1986); *Career* theatre: Little Me original British prod 1964, Travelling Music Show 1978, One Man show, Winter Garden NY 1979, Huntington Hartford Los Angeles 1979, London Palladium; numerous extensive tours: UK, NZ, Aust; film: Star 1968, Can Heironymous Merkin Ever Forgive Mercy Humppe and Find True Happiness 1969, Bedknobs and Broomsticks 1971, The Seven Deadly Sins 1971, Pavlova 1984; TV: Sunday Night at the London Palladium 1958-63, Piccadilly Spectaculars, Bruce Forsyth Show ATV, The Generation Game BBC 1971-77 (seven series), Bruces Big Night LWT 1978, Play Your Cards Right 1980-87 (ten series), Slingers Day Thames 1985-86, Hollywood or Bust 1984, You Bet! LWT 1987-89; numerous specials incl: Bring on the Girls Thames 1976, Bruce and More Girls Thames 1977, Bruce Meets the Girls; The Forsyth Follies; Sammy and Bruce (with Sammy Davis Jr): The Entertainers (with Rita Moreno), The Muppet Show, The Mating Season, The Canterville Ghost; awards: Daily Mirror National TV Award 1961, Variety Club Showbusiness Personality of the Year 1975, The Sun TV Personality of the Year (twice) 1976 and 1977, TV Times Favourite TV Personality (male; three times 1975, 1976, 1977) TV Times Favourite Game Show Host 1984; *Recreations* golf, tennis; *Clubs* Tramp, Crockfords; *Style*— Bruce Forsyth-Johnson, Esq; Bruce Forsyth Enterprises Ltd, Straidarran, Wentworth Dr, Virginia Water, Surrey GU25 4NY (☎ 09904 4056)

FORSYTHE, Clifford James; MP (OUP) South Antrim 1983-; *b* 1929; *Career* former professional footballer Linfield and Derry City, plumbing and heating contractor, Mayor of Newtonabbey 1982-83, memb NI Assembly 1982-86, vice-chm Health & Social Servs Ctee, memb Environment Ctee, party spokesman Tport, Communications and Local Govt; fell Indust and Parly Tst, pres NI section of Inst of Plumbing, chm Chest, Heart and Stroke Assoc Glengormley branch; *Style—* Clifford Forsythe Esq, MP; House of Commons, London SW1 (☎ 01 219 4144); constituency office: 19 Fountain St, Antrim BT41 4BG (☎ 08494 60776)

FORSYTHE, Dr (John) Malcolm; s of Dr John Walter Joseph Forsythe (d 1988), and Dr Charlotte Constance Forsythe, *née* Beatty (d 1981); *b* 11 July 1936; *Educ* Repton Sch Derby, Guy's Hosp Med Sch London Univ (BSc, MB BS, MRCS, DObstRCOG), Univ of N Carolina, London Sch Hygiene and Tropical Med, Univ of London (MSc); *m* 1, 1961 (m dis 1983), Delia Kathleen da of the late Dr J K Moore; 1 s (Marcus b 1965), 3 da (Suzanne b 1962, Nicola b 1962, Sarah b 1969); m2, 1984, Patricia Mary Murden, *née* Barnes; *Career* house surgn Guys Hosp 1961-62, house offr Farnborough 1962, house physician Lewisham 1962-63, GP Beckenham 1963-65, MO Birmingham Regnl Hsp Bd 1965-68, princ asst sr admin med offr SE Met RHB 1973-74 (dep 1972-73), area MO Kent area Health Authy 1974-78; regnl MO SE Thames RHA 1978- (dir of planning 1983, dir of pub health 1988-); FRCP, FFCM; *Clubs* RSM, RSA; *Style—* Dr Malcolm Forsythe; Harewood, 27 Withyham Rd, Cooden, Bexhill-on-Sea, E Sussex TN39 3BA; Thrift House, Collington Ave, Bexhill-on-Sea, E Sussex TN39 3NQ (☎ 04243 730 073)

FORTE, Baron (Life Peer UK 1982); Sir Charles Forte; s of Rocco (Giovanni) Forte, of Casalattico, Italy; *b* 26 Nov 1908; *Educ* Alloa Acad, Dumfries Coll, Mamiani Rome; *m* 1943, Irene Mary, da of Giovanni and Olga Chierico, of Venice; 1 s, 5 da (Hon Olga (Hon Mrs Polizzi di Sorrentino), Hon Marie Louise (Hon Mrs Burness), Hon Irene (Hon Mrs Danilovich), Hon Giancarla (Hon Mrs Alen-Buckley), Hon Portia b 7 Feb 1964); *Career* chm Trusthouse Forte Ltd (started as milk bar in Regent St 1935); hon consul-gen for San Marino; FRSA, FBIM; kt 1970; *Books* Forte (autobiography); *Recreations* music, fencing, golf, fishing, shooting; *Clubs* Carlton, Caledonian, Royal Thames Yacht; *Style—* The Rt Hon Lord Forte; 166 High Holborn, London WC1V 6TT

FORTE, Maj John Knox; MBE (1971); s of Philip Leslie Forte (d 1943), and Winifred Mary Forte (d 1980); *b* 2 Nov 1915; *Educ* Bradfield Coll, RMC Sandhurst, Staff Coll Camberley; *m* 28 June 1947, Nadine, da of Demetrius Curcumelli-Rodostamo (d 1951), of Afra, Corfu; 4 da (Melita b 1952, Danae b 1953, Thalia b 1957, Daphne b 1960); *Career* Maj The Royal Norfolk Regt 1935-58; vice-consul Corfu 1958-71, hon life govr The Intercontinental Church Soc; *Books* Corfu Venus of the Isles, Wheeler on Corfu, Rock of Ages, The Commodore and the Colonels, Plays The Thing - A Medley of Corfu and Cricket; *Recreations* erstwhile jack of all games and master of some, activities now confined to bridge, golf; *Clubs* The East India, MCC, Queens; *Style—* Maj John Forte, MBE; Paleocastritsa, Corfu (☎ 01030 66341205)

FORTE, Hon Rocco John Vincent; o s of Baron Forte of Ripley (Life Peer), *qv*; *b* 18 Jan 1945; *Educ* Downside, Pembroke Coll Oxford (MA); *m* 15 Feb 1986, Aliai, da of Prof Giovanni Ricci, of Rome; 2 da (Lydia Irene b 1987, Irene Alisea b 1988); *Career* chief exec Trusthouse Forte plc; memb: Br Tourist Authy, Grand Cncl Hotel & Catering Benevolent Assoc; vice-pres Cwlth Games Cncl; memb Worshipful Co of Bakers; FMICA, ACA; Cavaliere Ufficiale of Order of Merit of the Italian Republic 1988; *Recreations* golf, fishing, shooting, running; *Clubs* Garrick, Turf; *Style—* The Hon Rocco Forte; 166 High Holborn, London WC1V 6TT (☎ 01 836 7744, fax 01 240 9993, telex 264678 THF PLC)

FORTE DELLE MANDRIOLE, Marchese (Marquis of Mandriole, creation of the Republic of San Marino 1963, AD, and in year 1663 of the Republic) Olimpio; Grand Cordon of the Order of Polonia Restituta, Grand Cross Ordre of Merit Legion de Honor de la Republica de Cuba, Grand Croix de l'Ordre de l'Encouragement Public Francais, Medaille d'Honneur d'Or de Societe d'Encouragement au Progress, Kt Cdr Ordre du Merite Francais D'Outre Mer, Kt Cdr Royal Order of St Sava, Kt Sov Mil Order of Malta, Kt Cdr Italian Republic, Kt Grand Offr Holy Sepulchure of Jerusalem, Kt Order St Gregory the Great, Grand Offr Royal Crown of Yugoslavia; s of Francesco Forte (d 1940), and Maria Ciaraldi, original founder of family: Angelo Forte di Lecce who was granted the title of Baron by Charles VIII, King of France, on 1 April 1485, in Naples. Giovanni Forte was among the first fifty people to be made a Kt of Justice of the Order of Constantine St George 19 March 1834; *b* 8 Mar 1918,Casalattico Frosinone, Italy,; *Educ* in Casalattico; *m* 1948, Iolanda Dese (b in Scotland), da of Silviano Forte (d 1956); 1 s (Francesco Pietro, m 1984, Rosalin Good; 1 s, Gino Olimpio b 1985), 1 da (Sandra Francesca Maria); *Heir* s, *see above*; *Career* 1940-46 Italian Army, memb Allied Resistance Force Underground Movement First Lt Italian Army 1945, Lt-Col Allied Resistance Forces IMOS 1947; DSC, IMOS (first class), Monte Cassino Cross, War Cross of the Royal Yugoslav Army 1941-45 and Sword of Honour, Military Cross Virtuti Military (silver), Commemorative War Medal Dwight D Eisenhower 1939-45, Commemorative War Medal Gen George Patton 1944-45, Certificate of Gratitude from Field Marshal Alexander 1939-45, Grand Cross of the Fed of Partisan 1939-45, Euro Cross, DDL, Nat Univ of Canada 1947; present day, financier, Institute des Relations Diplomatique: Ordre du Merite Diplomatique; Medaille D'Or of Association Nationale Franco-Britannique, Etoile du Mérite Franco-Allié (of Union et Mérite Franco Alliés) 1939-45; landowner and dir of various cos; *Recreations* golf; *Style—* Marchese Forte delle Mandriole; Montforte, Cassalattico, Frosinone, Italy; San Marino House, Bexhill-on-Sea, E Sussex (☎ 0424 216 737)

FORTESCUE, Lady Laura Margaret; da (by 2 m) of 7 Earl Fortescue; *b* 1 May 1962; *Style—* Lady Laura Fortescue

FORTESCUE, Lady Margaret; eldest da of 5 Earl Fortescue, KG, PC, CB, OBE, MC (d 1958), and Hon Margaret Helen Beaumont, CBE (d 1958), eldest da of 1 Viscount Allendale; *b* 13 Dec 1923; *m* 30 July 1948 (m dis 1968), Bernard van Cutsem (d 1975), s of late Henry Harcourt van Cutsem; 2 da (*see* Earl of Arran); *Career* resumed surname Fortescue 1966; *Style—* Lady Margaret Fortescue; Castle Hill, Barnstaple, N Devon (☎ 05986 227)

FORTESCUE, Hon Martin Denzil; yr s of 6 Earl Fortescue, MC, TD (d 1977), and his 1 wife Marjorie Ellinor, OBE, *née* Trotter (d 1964); *b* 5 Jan 1924; *Educ* Eton; *m* 23 April 1954, Prudence Louisa, yr da of Sir Charles Samuel Rowley, 6 Bt, TD; 2 s, 2 da; *Career* Lt RN (Emergency List); *Style—* Hon Martin Fortescue; Wincombe Park, Shaftesbury, Dorset

FORTESCUE, 7 Earl (GB 1789); Richard Archibald Fortescue; JP (Oxon 1964); also Baron Fortescue (GB 1746), Viscount Ebrington (GB 1789); s of 6 Earl, MC, TD (d 1977), by his 1 w Marjorie, OBE; *b* 14 April 1922; *Educ* Eton, Christ Church Oxford; *m* 1, 24 Oct 1949, Penelope Jane (d 28 May 1959), yr da of late Robert Evelyn Henderson, by his w Beatrice, da of Sir William Clerke, 11 Bt; 1 s, 1 da; m 2, 3 March 1961, Margaret Anne, da of Charles Michael Stratton; 2 da; m 3, 5 Jan 1989, Carolyn Mary, eld da of Clement Hill, by his w Violet da of Charles Phillimore; *Heir* s, Viscount Ebrington; *Career* sits as Cons in House of Lords; late Capt Coldstream Gds; *Clubs* White's; *Style—* The Rt Hon Earl Fortescue, JP; House of Lords SW1

FORTESCUE, Lady Sarah Jane; da (by 2 m) of 7 Earl Fortescue; *b* 16 August 1963; *Style—* Lady Sarah Fortescue

FORTESCUE, Hon Seymour Henry; s of 6 Earl Fortescue, MC, TD (d 1977), and his 2 w Hon Sybil Mary (d 1985), da of 3 Viscount Hardinge (d 1985); *b* 28 May 1942; *Educ* Eton, Trinity Coll Cambridge, London Graduate Sch of Business Studies; *m* 25 July 1966, Julia, o da of Sir John Arthur Pilcher, GCMG; 1 s (James Adrian b 1978), 1 da (Marissa Clare b 1973); *Career* chief exec Barclaycard July 1982-85, gen mangr Barclays Bank plc 1985-87; dir: Barclays Bank UK Ltd, Mercantile Credit Company Ltd, UK Retail Services, Barclays Bank plc 1987-; *Style—* Hon Seymour Fortescue; 7 The Terrace, Barnes, London SW13 0NP (☎ 01 876 8457)

FORTEVIOT, 3 Baron (UK 1917); Sir Henry Evelyn Alexander Dewar; 3 Bt (UK 1907), MBE (Mil 1943), DL (Perth 1961); s (by 2 m) of 1 Baron (d 1929), suc half-bro 1947; *b* 23 Feb 1906; *Educ* Eton, St John's Oxford; *m* 25 April 1933, Cynthia Monica (d 1986), da of late Piers Cecil Le Gendre Starkie and his w Cicely , 2 da of Sir James de Hoghton, 11 Bt; 2 s, 2 da; *Heir* s, Hon John James Evelyn Dewar; *Career* chm John Dewar & Sons Ltd 1954-76, late dir Buchanan-Dewar Ltd and Distillers Co; *Clubs* Brook's; *Style—* The Rt Hon Lord Forteviot, MBE, DL; Dupplin Castle, Perth, Perthshire PH2 0PY

FORTH, Eric; MP (C) Mid-Worcestershire 1983-, MEP (EDG) Birmingham North 1979-84; s of William and Aileen Forth; *b* 9 Sept 1944; *Educ* Jordanhill Coll Sch Glasgow, Glasgow Univ; *m* 1967, Linda St Clair, 2 da; *Career* memb Brentwood UDC 1968-72, contested (C) Barking Feb and Oct 1974, chm Euro Democratic Gp backbench ctee, House vice-chm Euro Affairs backbench ctee House of Commons 1986-88 (vice-chm 1983-86), PPS to min of State Dep of Educn and Sci 1986-87, Parly under sec of state for indust and consumer affrs OTI 1988-; *Clubs* Carlton; *Style—* Eric Forth, Esq, MP; House of Commons, London SW1

FORTUNE, Lt-Col (John) Bruce; MC (1943); s of Maj Gen Sir Victor Morven Fortune, KBE, CB, DSO (d 1949), of Bengairn, Castle Douglas, Scotland, and Eleanor Steel (d 1971); *b* 19 July 1921; *Educ* Winchester; *m* 23 Oct 1945, Susan Mary, da of Charles James Mackie (d 1934), of Aberdeen; 2 s (David Victor b 1946, John Philip b 1955), 1 da (Angela Morven b 1949); *Career* Lt-Col Black Watch cmmnd 1941, wounded N Africa 1943, ADC to HE the Viceroy and Govr Gen of India 1943-45, DAMS HQ Allied Forces Netherlands E Indies 1945-46; Staff Coll 1953, Staff and RD 1954-60, instr RMA Sandhurst 1960-62, cmd 6/7 Bn The Black Watch 1962-65; AA and QMG 51 Highland Div 1965-68, GSOI Supreme HQ Allied Powers Europe 1968-71; ret; landowner, farmer, forester; memb: Scottish Landowners Fedn, Timber Growers UK Ltd, Game Conservancy; *Recreations* all countryside pursuits, music; *Clubs* MCC; *Style—* Lt-Col Bruce Fortune, MC; Bengairn, Auchencairn, Castle Douglas, Kirkcudbrightshire DG7 1QN (☎ 055 664 209)

FORTUNE, Ernest Forrester; MBE; s of Ernest George Fortune (d 1962), of Buchlyvie Lodge, Buchlyvie, Stirlingshire, and Sophia Farley Kennedy (d 1934); *b* 26 May 1911; *Educ* Glasgow Acad, Uppingham; *m* 1948, Dorothy Frances, da of Sir Thomas Dunlop, 3Bt, (d 1963), of Helensburgh, Dumbartonshire; 1 s (George Dunlop b 1953), 1 da (Susan Elizabeth b 1949); *Career* Maj RA, N Africa 1942, Italy 1943, Normandy and NW Europe 1944-46; paper maker 1928, dir Textile Merchanting Co 1950-; formerly: pres Fife Kinross and Clackmannon Charitable Soc 1948, chm Edinburgh branch Action Research for the Crippled Child 1968-75; Deacon Incorpn of Bakers Glasgow 1960, memb Incorpn of Hammerman Glasgow, memb Merchants House Glasgow; CStJ 1978 (priory of Scotland 1973-77) ; *Recreations* golf, walking, enjoying two dogs, painting, gardening; *Clubs* Elie Golf House; *Style—* Ernest Fortune, Esq, MBE, TD; 'Allanton', 31 South St, Elie, Fife KY9 1DN (☎ 0333 330 352)

FORWELL, Dr George Dick; s of Harold Cecil Forwell (d 1955), and Isabella L Christie; *b* 6 July 1928; *Educ* George Watson's Coll, Edinburgh Univ (MB, ChB, PhD); *m* 1957, Catherine Forsyth Campbell, *née* Cousland; 2 da; *Career* lectr Dept of Public Health & Social Medicine, asst dean Faculty of Medicine Edinburgh Univ 1959-63, sr admin med offr Eastern Regnl Hospital Bd 1963-67, princ med offr Scottish Home & Health Dept 1967-73, chief admin med offr Greater Glasgow Health Bd 1973-; QHP 1980-83; Gen Medical Cncl 1984-; *Recreations* running; *Clubs* RAF (London); *Style—* Dr George Forwell; 60 Whittingehame Dr, Glasgow (☎ 334 7122)

FORWOOD, Sir Dudley Richard; 3 Bt (UK 1895), of The Priory, Gateacre, Childwall, Co Palatine of Lancaster; s of Lt-Col Sir Dudley Baines Forwood, 2 Bt, CMG (d 1961), and Norah Isabel, *née* Lockett (d 1961); gs of Rt Hon Sir Arthur Bower Forwood, 1 Bt, Lord Mayor of Liverpool, Privy Cncllr, MP; *b* 6 June 1912; *Educ* Stowe; *m* 27 May 1952, Mary Gwendolene, da of Basil Foster (she m 1, Inigo Brassey, Viscount Ratendone (later 2 Marquess of Willingdon), m 2, Frederick Robert Cullingford, m 3, Brig Donald Croft-Wilcock); 1 adopted s (Rodney Simon Dudley); *Heir* cous, Peter Noel Forwood; *Career* Scots Guards (Capt); hon attaché British Legation Vienna 1934-37, equerry to HRH the Duke of Windsor 1937-39, underwriting memb of Lloyd's; master New Forest Buckhounds 1957-65, vice-pres Royal Agric Soc of England (hon dir 1972-77); chm: New Forest Agric Soc 1964-82 (pres 1983-), New Forest Consultative Panel 1970-82, Crufts Dog Show 1970-87; official verderer New Forest 1974-82; vice pres The Kennel Club, chm British Deer Soc 1984-87; *Recreations* hunting, wildlife conservation; *Style—* Sir Dudley Forwood, Bt; Uppacott, Bagnum, nr Ringwood, Hants (☎ 0425 471480); 43 Addison Rd, London W14 (☎ 01 603 3620)

FORWOOD, Nicholas James; QC (1987); s of Lt-Col Harry Forwood, RA of Cobham, Surrey, and Wendy, *née* French-Smith; *b* 22 June 1948; *Educ* Stowe, St Johns Coll Cambridge (BA, MA); *m* 4 Dec 1971, Sally Diane, da of His Hon Judge Basil Gerrard, of Knutsford, Cheshire; 3 da (Victoria b 1974, Genevra b 1976, Suzanna b 1979); *Career* called to the Bar 1970, called to the Irish Bar 1982; *Recreations* golf, skiing, sailing, shooting; *Clubs* United Oxford and Cambridge, Ski

Club of GB; *Style*— Nicholas Forwood, Esq, QC; 11 Avenue Juliette, 1180, Brussels, Belgium (☎ 02 3752542); 4 Pump Ct, Temple, London EC4 (☎ 01 353 2656)

FORWOOD, Peter Noel; s (by 2 m) of Arthur Noel Forwood (d 1959), 3 s of 1 Bt; hp of cousin, Sir Dudley Richard Forwood, 3 Bt; *b* 15 Oct 1925; *Educ* Radley; *m* 1950, Roy, da of James Murphy, MBE, FRCS, LRCP, of Horsham, Sussex; 6 da; *Career* Welsh Gds WW II; *Style*— Peter Forwood, Esq; Newhouse Farm, Shillinglee, Chiddingfold, Surrey

FORWOOD, William Grantham Lewis; s of Philip Lockton Forwood (d 1976), of Bucks, and Barbara Muriel Lewis, *née* Richards (d 1982); *b* 3 August 1927; *Educ* Kings Coll Choir Sch Cambridge, Eton coll, Clare Coll Cambridge (MA, LLM); *m* 22 Dec 1951, Joyce Barbara Addenbrooke, da of Lt Col Gordon Spencer Marston, DSO, MC, of Bucks; 4 s (Kemeys b 1954, Edward b 1959, Richard b 1961, Henry b 1963), 2 da (Philippa b 1957, Felicia b 1966); *Career* slr 1954, legal & fin conslt; cmmnd Royal Welsh Fusiliers 1947; dir: Mercantile Credit Co of Ireland Ltd 1971-; Sedgwick Dineen Gp Ltd 1976-, Thorn Home Entertainment Ltd 1982-, Applied Chemical Ireland Ltd 1983-; *Recreations* shooting, rough gardening, book collecting; *Clubs* Kildare Street Univ (Dublin); *Style*— William G L Forwood, Esq; Woodstock, Newtownmountkennedy, Co Wicklow (☎ 0001 874151); 30 Uper Pembroke Street, Dublin 2 (☎ 0001 765888, telex 93238, fax 613409)

FOSKETT, Douglas John; OBE (1978); s of John Henry Foskett (d 1959), and Amy Florence Foskett; *b* 27 June 1918; *Educ* Bancroft's 1929-36, Queen Mary Coll London Univ 1939, Birkbeck Coll London Univ 1955; *m* 1948, Joy Ada, *née* McCann; 1 s, 2 da; *Career* librarian: Metal Box Co Ltd 1948-57, London Univ Inst of Educn 1957-78; dir of Central Library Services and Goldsmiths' librarian London Univ 1978-83; Freeman City of London 1980; *Recreations* travel, reading, writing, cricket; *Clubs* MCC, Sussex CC; *Style*— Douglas Foskett, Esq, OBE; 1 Daleside, Gerrards Cross, Bucks (☎ 0753 882835)

FOSS, Prof Brian Malzard; s of Rev Francis S Foss (d 1978), and Ann Eliza, *née* Malzard (d 1950); *b* 25 Oct 1921; *Educ* Emmanuel Coll Cambridge (MA), Oxford Univ (Dip Psychology, MA); *Career* experimental offr Army Op Res Gp, Mil Op Res Unit 1942-46; jr lectr Oxford Univ 1948-51, lectr Birkbeck Coll 1951-64; London Univ: prof educnl psychology 1964-65, prof psychology 1968-87; pres: Br Psychology Soc 1974, Section J Br Assoc for the Advancement of Sci 1974; *Books* New Horizons in Psychology (1966), Determinants of Infant Behaviour (1961-69);; *Style*— Prof Brian Foss

FOSS, Hon Janet Mary Penrose; *née* Lewis; yr da of 1 & last Baron Brecon (d 1976); *b* 2 Oct 1944; *Educ* Cheltenham Ladies Coll; *m* 1969, Christopher John Foss, er s of K J Foss, of Greenwood, Torquay; 2 da; *Style*— Hon Mrs Foss; 3 Sterling St, Montpelier Sq, London SW7

FOSS, Kate; *née* Arden; da of George Arden (d 1958), and May Elizabeth (d 1959); *b* 17 May 1925; *Educ* Northampton HS, Whitelands Coll; *m* 1951, Robert, s of Laurence Foss (d 1957); 1 s (Jonathan b 1959); *Career* chm Insur Ombudsman Bureau 1985-, memb Bd and Cncl Direct Mail Servs Standards Bd 1983-, Cncl Licensed Conveyancers 1985-88, Standing Ctee Licenced Conveyancing 1985-88, memb data protection tribunal 1986-, Nat Consumer Cncl 1981-84, chm of bd WI Books Ltd 1982-; *Recreations* golf; *Style*— Mrs Kate Foss; Merston, 61 Back Lane, Knapton, York (☎ 0904 782549); Insurance Ombudsman Bureau, 31 Southampton Row, London

FOSTER, Andrew Gerard; s of Sydney Edward Lancelot Foster, MC (d 1963), of The Shieling, Oak Hill, Wethersfield, Braintree, Essex, and Elsa Glyn, *née* Barnett (d 1979); *b* 9 August 1936; *Educ* Braintree Co HS, Univ of Nottingham (LLB); *m* 1, 21 March 1962, da of John Adams (d 1943), of Stour House, Sudbury, Suffolk; 1 s (Roland b 1965), 2 da (Ann b 1963, Jane b 1967); m 2, 7 Aug 1980, (Shirley) Jennifer, da of Joseph Harold Davies, of Tudor Cot, Styal, Cheshire; *Career* slr 1961, sr ptnr Steed & Steed 1985, Notary Public 1979; memb Law Soc; *Recreations* rugby union football, rowing, fell walking; *Style*— Andrew Foster, Esq; 6 Gainsborough St, Sudbury, Suffolk CO10 6ET (☎ 0787 73387, fax 0787 880287)

FOSTER, Brendan; MBE (1976); s of Francis and Margaret Foster; *b* 12 Jan 1948; *Educ* St Joseph's GS Co Durham, Sussex Univ (BSc), Carnegie Coll Leeds (DipEd); *m* 1972, Susan Margaret, da of Kenneth Frank Alston, of, Clacton, Essex; 1 s (Paul b 1977), 1 da (Catherine b 1979); *Career* sch teacher St Joseph's GS Hebburn 1970-74, recreation mangr Gateshead Metropolitan Borough Cncl 1974-81, chm Nike (UK) Ltd 1981-87 (md Nike Europe); Cwlth Games medals include: Bronze 1500 m 1970, Silver 5000 m 1974, Silver 5000 m 1978, Gold 10000 m 1978; Euro Games medals include: Bronze 1500 m 1971, Gold 5000 m 1974; Olympic Games Bronze medal 10000 m 1976; World record holder: 2 miles 1973, 3000 m 1974; UK record holder: 10000 m 1978 (still current UK record), 1500 m, 3000 m, 2 miles, 5000 m; *Style*— Brendan Foster, Esq, MBE; Whitegates, 31 Meadowfield Road, Stocksfield, Northumberland

FOSTER, Brian Joseph; s of Joseph Robert Foster, of Letchworth Garden City, Herts, and Mabel, *née* Picton (d 1957); *b* 28 Sept 1925; *Educ* Letchworth GS, London Hosp Med Coll London Univ (MB, BS, DPM); *m* 25 Aug 1950, Elizabeth Joan, da of Arthur Charlton (d 1954), of Newcastle Upon Tyne; 1 s (Timothy Huw b 12 May 1950), 2 da (Christine Gwynneth (Mrs Schmidhaüsler) b 17 July 1851, Vanessa Jane (Mrs Paminger) b 3 Aug 1954); *Career* Nat Serv Capt RAMC 1950-52 area psychiatrist Northern Cmd; GP 1952-, special interest in community psychiatry; local med conslt: BP Oil and Shell Oil 1960, Texaco Oil Co 1982; hosp practitioner in psychogeriatric med Moorgreen Hosp London 1964-, hon teacher primary med care Southampton Univ; fndr memb and current med conslt Bitterne & Woolston Rotary Club Housing Soc for the Elderly; sec Southampton Flower Fund Homes, pres Bitterne and Woolstan Rotary Club 1970-71; MRCS 1949, LRCP 1949, MRCGP, memb BMA; *Recreations* gardening, walking, foreign travel (Europe and Middle East; *Clubs* Royal Southern YC; *Style*— Dr Brian Foster; Landor House, 59 St Cross Rd, Winchester SO23 9RE; Blackthorn Surgery, Netley Abbey, Southampton (☎ 0703 4539720)

FOSTER, Charles Arthur; ERD (1969); s of Arthur William Foster (d 1974), and Alice Katherine Mabel, *née* Browne; *b* 25 June 1926; *Educ* Blundell's, St Thomas's Hosp Med Sch (MB, BS); *m* 1, 18 Dec 1948 (m dis 1963), Elizabeth Darby, da of late Alec Draper; 2 s (Richard Charles Darby b 6 Jan 1951, Simon John Darby b 22 April 1957); m 2, 9 March 1963, Virginia Caroline Juniper Delap; 1 da (Tiffany Victoria b 18 Nov 1966); *Career* conslt anaesthetist: St Thomas's Hosp London 1958-86, Royal Masonic Hosp 1970-86; tres Sternfield PCC, church warden St Mary Magdalene Sternfield; Freeman City of London, Liveryman Worshipful Co of Barbers 1980; FCA, MRCS, LRCP; *Books* An Introduction to Anaesthetics (1966), Anaesthesia for Operating Theatre Technicians (jtly 1968); *Recreations* bird watching, gardening; *Style*— Dr Charles Foster, ERD; Glebe Farm, Sternfield, nr Saxmundham, Suffolk IP17 1ND (☎ 0728 2579)

FOSTER, Sir Christopher David; s of Capt George Cecil Foster (d 1978), and Phyllis Joan, *née* Mappin (d 1964); *b* 30 Oct 1930; *Educ* Merchant Taylor's, King's Coll Cambridge (MA); *m* 26 July 1958, Kay Sheridan, da of Hubert Percy Bullock, (d 1987), of Horsehay, Shropshire; 2 s (Oliver Drummond b 1960, Sebastian Luke b 1968), 3 da (Henrietta Sheridan Jane b 1959, Cressida Imogen Dakeyne b 1963, Melissa Catherine Mappin b 1964); *Career* RAOC 1949, cmmd 1 Bn The Seaforth Highlanders Malaya 1949-50, 1 Bn The London Scottish TA 1950-53, General Service Medal Malaya 1950; res fellowship 1954-64: Univ of Pennsylvania, King's Coll Cambridge, Univ of Manchester, Jesus Coll Oxford; official fell and tutor in econs Jesus Coll Oxford 1964-66, dir-gen of econ planning Miny of T'port 1966-69, visiting prof of econs and urban studies 1969-70, visiting fell dept of city planning Univ of California Berkeley 1970; LSE: head of centre for urban econs 1970-75, prof of econs and urban studies 1975-78, visiting prof of econs 1978-79; dir Centre for Environmental Studies 1976-78; Coopers and Lybrand: head of econs and pub policy div 1978-84, head of business devpt 1984-85, memb mgmnt ctee and MCS mgmnt ctee (econs practic ldr 1988); commercial advsr to the bd Br Telecom 1986-88; memb Speed Ctee on Road Pricing 1962-63, pt/t econ advrs to DOE 1974-77, chm ctee of inquiry into Civil Serv Pay 1981-82, memb Audit Cmmn 1983, econ assessor Sizewell B Inquiry 1982-86, ERSC 1985-, memb London Docklands Devpt Cmmn 1987; *Books* The Transport Problem 91963), Politics, Finance and the Role of Economics (with R Jackson and M Perlman, 1972), Local Government Finance (1980); *Recreations* opera, theatre; *Clubs* Reform, RAC; *Style*— Sir Christopher Foster; 6 Holland Park Avenue, London W11 (☎ 01 727 4757); Coopers and Lybrand, Plumtree Court, London EC4A 4HT (☎ 01 822 4652, car 0860 533735, telex 887470)

FOSTER, Christopher Kenneth; s of Kenneth John Foster, of Sunningdale, and Christina Dorothy, *née* Clark; *b* 05 Nov 1948; *Educ* Harrow HS; *Career* dir Chase Corpn plc 1985-88, chm and dir Springwood Books Ltd 1975-; Lord of the Manor Little Hale; *Recreations* golf, music, art; *Clubs* Wentworth GC; *Style*— Christopher Foster, Esq; Springwood Hse, The Avenue, Ascot, Berks SL5 7LY (☎ 0990 287 53); 1 Berkeley St, London W1 (☎ 01 499 9020, telex 8813271)

FOSTER, Christopher Norman; s of Maj Gen Norman Leslie Foster, CB, DSO, *qv*; *b* 30 Dec 1949; *Educ* Westminster; *m* 1981, Anthea Jane, da of Geoffrey Tait Sammons; 2 s (Nicholas b 1983, Piers b 1986); *Career* Cooper Bros & Co 1965-73, Weatherbys 1973- (dir 1976); sec to the Jockey Club 1983-; memb cncl Westminster Sch Soc 1972-; ACA, FCA; *Recreations* racing, shooting, fishing, gardening; *Clubs* MCC; *Style*— Christopher Foster Esq; 29 Homefield Rd, Chiswick, London W4 2LW (☎ 01 995 9309); 42 Portman Sq, London W1 (☎ 01 486 4921)

FOSTER, David Carrick; s of Ernest John Thomas Carrick Foster (d 1949), and Evelyn Claire Hilda Hunter, *née* Lynes (d 1985); *b* 9 Oct 1936; *Educ* Repton, Leeds Univ (LLB); *m* 27 July 1963, Joan Margaret, da of Lt Col Ronald Reginald Waugh, OBE, ED (d 1977); 1 s (Daniel b 1973), 2 da (Sarah b 1965, Clair b 1967); *Career* slr 1960, sr ptnr Watson Burton Newcastle 1981 (ptnr 1966-); memb Law Soc; *Recreations* playing the piano and harpsichord; *Style*— David Foster, Esq; 12 Castleton Close, Jesmond, Newcastle upon Tyne, NE2 2HF (☎ 091 281 0859), Watson Burton, 20 Collingwood St, Newcastle upon Tyne NE1 1LB (☎ 091 232 3801, fax 091 232 0532 telex 53529 WATSON G)

FOSTER, David Kenneth Dudley; s of Kenneth Dudley Foster, MBE (d 1972), and Amy Margaret, *née* Walduck (d 1970); *b* 20 April 1931; *Educ* Charterhouse, Pembroke Coll Cambridge; *m* 1 Aug 1962, Hon Susan Elizabeth, *qv*, 2 da of 2 Viscount Bridgeman, KBE, CB, DSO, MC; 3 s (Robert b 1966, Edward b 1967, Simon b 1969); *Career* Accountancy Mgmnt Services Ltd; *Recreations* skiing, chess; *Style*— David Foster, Esq; Beech House, Shifnal, Shropshire (☎ 0952 460261)

FOSTER, Derek; MP (Lab) Bishop Auckland 1979-; s of Joseph Foster (d 1959), and Ethel, *née* Ragg (d 1982); *b* 25 June 1937; *Educ* Bede GS Sunderland, St Catherine's Coll Oxford; *m* 1972, (Florence) Anne, da of Thomas Bulmer, of Sunderland; *Career* youth and community worker 1970-73, further educn organiser 1973-74, asst dir of educn Sunderland Cncl 1974-79, chm N of England Devpt Cncl 1974-76, memb Tyne & Wear CC and Sunderland Borough Cncl; additional oppn spokesman Social Security 1982, oppn whip 1982, PPS to Neil Kinnock 1983-, opposition chief whip 1985-; vice-chm Youthaid 1979-; *Recreations* brass bands, male voice choirs; *Style*— Derek Foster, Esq, MP; 3 Linburn, Rickleton, Washington, Tyne and Wear (☎ 091 4171580)

FOSTER, (John) Francis Harold; DSO (1945), OBE (1944), TD (and 3 bars), DL (Sussex 1968); s of Capt William Thomas Benjamin Foster (d 1945), and Lilian Frances, *née* Lea (d 1975); *b* 6 Feb 1904; *Educ* Uckfield GS; *m* 1, 1930, Dorothy Christian (d 1962), *née* Brooke; m 2, 1963, Gwendolene Rebecca, *née* Funnell; 2 step da; *Career* cmmnd RE TA 1924, Maj 1936, WWII BEF 1940 (despatches), CRE 4 Corps Troops, CRE 1 Div 1942-45 (despatches), Substantive Col 1950; Hon Col RE 44 Div 1950-67, Cmdt Sussex ACF 1960-69; chartered architect, private practise at Seaford 1933-73; memb RIBA; *Clubs* Sussex; *Style*— Col Francis Foster, DSO, OBE, TD, DL; Wildbees, 11 Kings Ride, Seaford, E Sussex BN25 2LN (☎ 0323 895526)

FOSTER, Giles Henry; s of Stanley William Foster (d 1986), and Gladys Maude, *née* Moon; *b* 30 June 1948; *Educ* Monkton Combe Sch, Univ of York (BA), RCA (MA); *m* 28 Sept 1974, Nicole Anne, da of Alan Coates, of London; 2 s (George b 1982, William b 1987); *Career* film and TV dir; TV films incl: Northanger Abbey, Hotel du Lac (BAFTA Award), Silas Marner, Dutch Girls, The Aerodrome, Last Summers Child, The Obelisk, and five scripts by Alan Bennett; cinema films: Devices and Desires (Grierson Award), Consuming Passions, Tree of Hands; *Clubs* Grouchos; *Style*— Giles Foster, Esq; c/o Anthony Jones, Peters Fraser and Dunlop, 5 Floor, The Chambers, Chelsea Harbour, Lots Rd, London SW10OXF (☎ 01 376 7676)

FOSTER, Hon Mrs (Gillian Rosemary); o da of 22 Lord Forbes, KBE, *qv*; *b* 3 April 1949; *Educ* St Mary's Sch Wantage; *m* 26 March 1969, Alexander Neil Foster, o s of Lt-Col (Brevet Col) Neil Phipps Foster, DL, of Whittlebury Cottage, Towcester, Northants; 1 s (Michael Alexander b 1 March 1973), 1 da (Lucia Katharine b 12 Feb 1970); *Style*— The Hon Mrs Foster; Church Farmhouse, Blakesley, Towcester, Northants (☎ 0327 860364); Bury Walk, London SW3 (☎ 01 589 7678)

FOSTER, Jerome; s of Cecil William Foster, of East Sheen, London, and Rosaleen, *née* Game (d 1988); *b* 3 August 1936; *Educ* Wellington Coll, Univ of Grenoble; *m* 27

May 1961, Joanna, da of Michael Mead, OBE; 1 s (Hugo b 1969), 1 da (Kate b 1972); *Career* Nat Serv 2 Lt Oxfordshire & Bucks L1 (now 1 Green Jackets) 1954-56; advertisement mangr Benn Bothers Ltd 1957-61, mangr TLS Times Newspapers Ltd 1961-67, dir Euro offs Benn Gp 1967-72, dir continuing educn INSEAD 1972-79, assoc dean: exec educn Carnegie-Mellon Univ Pittsburgh 1979-82, Templeton Coll Oxford 1982-84, exec educn INSEAD 1984-87; chief exec Ambrosetti Europe (mgmnt consits) 1987-; FRSA; *Recreations* family, Europe, singing, sailing; *Style—* Jerome Foster, Esq; 43 Bainton Rd, Oxford OX2 7AG (☎ 0865 514 400); Ambrosetti Europe, 8 Clifford St, London W1X 1RB (☎ 01 434 9091, fax 01 439 1598)

FOSTER, Joanna; *née* Mead; da of Edward Michael Mead, and Lesley Mead, of Winterbourne Bristol; *b* 5 May 1939; *Educ* Benenden Sch Kent, Grenoble Univ France (Dip); *m* 1961, Jerome Foster; 1 s (Hugo b 1969), 1 da (Kate b 1972); *Career* Press attachée INSEAD Fontainebleau France 1975-79, dir of educn corporate servs Western Psychiatric Inst and Clinic Univ of Pittsburgh USA 1980-82; head Youth Trg Industl Soc London 1983-85, head Pepperell Unit at the Industl Soc 1985-88, chair Equal Opportunities Cmmn 1988-; *Recreations* family, food, friends; *Style—* Mrs Joanna Foster; 43 Bainton Rd, Oxford OX2 7AG (☎ Oxford 0865 514400) Equal Opportunities Cmmn, Overseas House, Quay St, Manchester M3 3HN (☎ 061 833 9244)

FOSTER, John; CBE (1985); s of David Little Foster (d 1985), of Lochside House, Castle Douglas, Kircudbrightshire, and Isabella, *née* Livingston, JP (d 1979); *b* 13 August 1920; *Educ* Whithill Sch Glasgow, Royal Tech Coll Glasgow; *m* 10 June 1950, Daphne, da of Charles Frederick Househam (d 1965); 1 s (Alasdair Graham b 4 June 1954), 1 da (Caroline Mary b 10 May 1957); *Career* WWII staff Air Miny 1940-45; surveyor in private practice 1937-40, asst planning offr Kirkcudbright CC 1945-47, planning offr Holland CC 1948-52, dir Peak Nat Park Bd 1954-68 (dep planning offr 1952-54), dir Countryside Cmmn for Scotland 1968-85; pt/t conslt in countryside and recreation 1985-; hon vice pres Countryside Holidays Assoc, vice pres Ramblers Assoc (Scotland), cncl memb RICS; memb: Cmmn on Nat Parks, Int Union for the Conservation of Nature; hon fell Royal Scottish Geographical Soc, ARICS 1943, FRTPI 1946, RIBA 1950, FRICS 1954, ARIAS 1968; *Recreations* hillwalking, swimming, philately, reading, travel; *Clubs* Cwlth; *Style—* John Foster, Esq, CBE; Birchover, Ferntower Rd, Crieff, Perthshire PH7 3DH (☎ 0764 2336)

FOSTER, Sir John Gregory; 3 Bt (UK 1930); o s of Sir Thomas Saxby Gregory Foster, 2 Bt (d 1957), and Beryl, *née* Ireland; *b* 26 Feb 1927; *Educ* Michaelhouse Coll Natal, Witwatersrand Univ (MB, BCh); *m* 24 Nov 1956, Jean Millicent, eldest da of late Elwin Watts, of Germiston, S Africa; 1 s, 3 da; *Heir* s, Saxby Gregory Foster; *Career* MRCP Edinburgh 1955, med registrar 1955-56, med offr 1957, physician 1961; FRCP Edinburgh 1984; *Style—* Sir John Foster, Bt; 7 Caledon Street, PO Box 1325, George 6530, Cape Province, S Africa (☎ George 3251)

FOSTER, John Leonard William; s of Herbert Frederick Brudnell Foster, JP, TD, of Park Hse, Drumdak, Kincardineshire, and Christine Leonard Lucas, *née* Tooth; *b* 20 July 1948; *Educ* Stambridge Earls, Aberdeen Univ (HSDA); *m* 1 March 1973, Clarinda Anna, da of Maj Bruce William Cottell (d 1985); 2 s (William Francis Edward b 8 July 1976, Edward John Frederick b 25 June 1983), 1 da (Alice Clarinda Edith b 18 Oct 1978); *Career* farming and forestry; dir John Foster & Son plc 1982-87; chm: Kameruka Estates Ltd 1976-, Drumoak Investmts Ltd 1978-, Faskally Investmts Ltd 1978-, Drumoig Ltd 1987-; organiser of the Ecurie Ecosse Historic Motor Show, organiser St Andrews Horse Trails; *Recreations* motor racing, fishing, shooting, skiing, sailing; *Clubs* Royal Northern (Aberdeen); *Style—* John Foster, Esq; Craigie, Leuchars, St Andrews, Fife; Estates Office, Craigie Farm, Leuchars, St Andrews

FOSTER, Jonathan Rowe; s of Donald Foster (d 1980), and Hilda Eaton, *née* Rowe; *b* 20 July 1947; *Educ* Oundle J Keble Coll Oxford; *m* 18 Mar 1978, Sarah; 3 s (Thomas b 1980, Henry b 1982, Edward b 1986); *Career* barr, recorder Crown Ct 1988-; *Recreations* children, golf, bridge; *Clubs* St James Manchester, Hale Golf, Bowdon Lawn Tennis; *Style—* Jonathan Foster, Esq; 18 St John Street, Manchester (☎ 061 834 0843)

FOSTER, Maj-Gen Norman Leslie; CB (1961), DSO (1945); s of Col Arthur Leslie Foster (d 1956), of Wimbledon; *b* 26 August 1909; *Educ* Westminster, RMA Woolwich; *m* 1937, Joan Constance, da of late Canon Thomas W E Drury, of Dublin; 2 s (*see* Christopher Norman Foster); *Career* WW II, CRA 11 Armoured Div 1955-56, dep mil sec (War Off) 1958-59, Maj-Gen 1959, GOC Royal Nigerian Army 1959-62, pres Regular Cmmns Bd 1962-65, ret 1965, dir Security (Army) MOD 1965-73, security advsr Civil Serv Dept 1974-79, Col Cmdt Royal Regt of Artillery 1966-74; chm Truman & Knightley Educnl Tst 1977-80 (pres 1982-87); *Style—* Maj-Gen Norman Foster, CB, DSO; Besborough, Heath End, Farnham, Surrey (☎ 0252 23540)

FOSTER, Norman Robert; s of Robert Foster (d 1976), and Lily, *née* Smith (d 1971); *b* 1 June 1935; *Educ* Manchester Univ (Dip Arch), Yale Univ; *m* 18 Aug 1964, Wendy Ann, da of late Reginald George Lewis Cheesman; 4 s (Ti b 1965, Steve b 1966, Cal b 1967, Jay b 1986); *Career* Nat Serv RAF 1953-55; fndr Foster Assocs 1967; winner of int competitions 1979-88 for projects incl: Hong Kong and Shanghai Bank, BBC Radio Centre, Nat German Athletics Centre Frankfurt, Telecommunications Tower Barcelona, Bilbao Metro System; conslt architect Univ of East Anglia 1978-87; teacher 1967-77: London Poly, Bath Acad of Arts, Univ of Pennsylvania, Architectural Assoc; numerous awards incl: Royal Gold Medal for Architecture 1983, Civic Tst Award 1984, RIBA Awards 1969, 72, 77, 78, 81, RS Reynolds Award 1976, 1979 & 1986, Fin Times Industl Architecture Award 1967, 1970, 1971, 1974, 1981, Premio Compasso d'Oro Award 1987, Ambrose Congreve Award 1980, Kunstpreis Berlin Award 1989, Structural Steel Award 1972, 1980, 1984, 1986, International Prize for Architecture 1976, 1980, Br Tourist Bd Award 1979; tv documentaries incl BBC Omnibus 1981 and Anglia Enterprise 1983, featured in int publications and jls; exhibitions of work held in: London, New York, Paris, Tokyo, Berlin, Madrid, Barcelona, Milan; work in permanent collection of Museum of Modern Art New York; vice pres AA 1974 (memb cncl 1973), memb RIBA visiting bd of educn 1971 (external examiner 1971-73); Hon LittD East Anglia 1980, Hon DSc Bath 1986; memb RIBA 1965, FCSD 1985, ARA 1983, RDI 1988, hon memb Bund Deutscher Architekten 1983, hon fell American Inst of Architects 1980; *Recreations* flying aircraft, helicopters and sailplanes, skiing, running; *Style—* Norman Foster, Esq; Foster Associates 172 Great Portland St, London W1N 5TB (☎ 01 637 5431, fax 01 637 2640, telex 261571)

FOSTER, (John) Peter; s of Francis Edward Foster (d 1953), of Newe Strathdon, and Evelyn Marjorie Forbes (d 1953); *b* 2 May 1919; *Educ* Eton, Trinity Hall Cambridge (MA); *m* 1944, Margaret Elizabeth, da of George John Skipper (d 1948); 1 s (Edward Philip John b 1949), 1 da (Elizabeth Anne b 1946); *Career* cmmnd RE 1941, served Norfolk Div, joined Gds Armd Div 1943, served France and Germany, Capt (SORE2) 30 Corps 1945, discharged 1946; joined Marshall Sisson architect 1948, later ptnr, sole ptnr 1971; architect ARIBA 1949, surveyor of the Royal Acad of Arts 1965-80; ptnr with John Peters of Vine Press Hemingford Grey 1957-63; memb Art Workers Guild 1971 (master 1980, tstee 1985); surveyor of the Fabric of Westminster Abbey 1973-; pres Surveyor's Club 1980, memb of Historic Bldgs Cncl for England 1977-84; fell of Soc of Antiquaries 1973; memb: of tech panel of the Soc for Protection of Ancient Bldgs 1976, of advsy bd for Redundant Churches 1979; govr of Suttons Hosp Charterhouse 1982, exec ctee of Georgian Gp 1983; chm of Cathedral Architects Assoc 1987, memb of the Fabric Ctee Canterbury Cathedral 1987; OStJ; *Recreations* painting, shooting, books; *Clubs* Athenaeum; *Style—* Peter Foster, Esq; Harcourt, Hemingford Grey, Huntingdon, Cambs PE18 9BJ (☎ 0480 61101)

FOSTER, Peter Martin; CMG (1975); s of Capt Frederick Arthur Peace Foster, RN (d 1948), and Marjorie Kathleen, *née* Sandford; *b* 25 May 1924; *Educ* Sherborne, CCC Cambridge; *m* 1947, Angela Hope, *née* Cross; 1 s, 1 da; *Career* Maj Royal Horse Gds WW II; HM Diplomatic Serv 1948, HM Embassy Vienna 1948-52, FO 1952-54, Warsaw 1954-56, FO 1956-59, S Africa 1959-61, FO 1961-64, Bonn 1964-66, Kampala (dep high cmmr) 1966-68, Imperial Def Coll 1969, Tel Aviv (cnsllr) 1970-72, FCO (head of Central and S Africa Dept) 1972-74, Strasbourg (ambass and UK perm rep to Cncl of Europe) 1974-78, ambass German Democratic Repub 1978-81, ret 1981; dir Cncl for Arms Control 1984-86; chm Int Soc Serv (GB) 1985-; *Clubs* Athenaeum; *Style—* Peter Foster Esq, CMG; Rew Cottage, Abinger Common, Dorking, Surrey (☎ 730114); c/o Midland Bank Ltd, 455 Strand, WC2R 0RH

FOSTER, Peter Walter; CBE (1983, OBE 1959), MC (1943), TD (1947), DL (Gtr London 1967); s of Harold Foster, of London; *b* 8 Dec 1919; *Educ* Oundle, Imperial Coll; *m* 1949, Anne, da of Arthur Thomas Sturgess, of London; 2 s, 2 da; *Career* served TA 1939-61 (Col), chartered electrical engr; chm William White and Co (Switchgear) Ltd; *Style—* Peter Foster, Esq, CBE, MC, TD, DL; 27 Peckerman's Wood, London SE26 6RY

FOSTER, Richard Anthony; s of Eric Kenneth Foster (d 1945), of Bournemouth, and Sylvia Renee, *née* France, now Mrs Westerman; *b* 3 Oct 1941; *Educ* Kingswood Sch, LSE (BSc), Manchester Univ (MA); *m* 31 Aug 1964, Mary Browning, da of Arthur Leslie James, OBE, of Saltburn, Cleveland; 2 s (James b 28 May 1970, William b 27 May 1973), 1 da (Polly b 12 Aug 1979); *Career* student asst Leicester Museum 1964-66, museum asst Bowes Museum 1967-68, keeper i/c Durham LI Museum and Arts Centre 1968-70; dir: Oxford City and Co Museum 1970-78, Oxon Co Museums 1974-, Merseyside Co Museums 1978-86, Nat Museums and Galleries on Merseyside 1986-, Merseyside Tourism Bd; memb: bd NW Museums and Art Galleries Serv, bd Inst of Western Popular Music Univ of Liverpool; tstee Boat Museum Ellesmere Port; advsr fabric ctee Liverpool Cathedral; FSA 1976, FMA 1980; *Recreations* sailing, watching football; *Style—* Richard Foster, Esq; National Museums and Galleries on Merseyside, Liverpool Museum, William Brown St, Liverpool, L3 8EN (☎ 051 207 0001, fax 051 207 3759)

FOSTER, Sir Robert Sidney; GCMG (1970, KCMG 1964, CMG 1961), KCVO (1970); s of late Sidney Charles Foster, and late Jessie Edith, *née* Fry; *b* 11 August 1913; *Educ* Eastbourne Coll, Peterhouse Cambridge; *m* 1947, Margaret, da of Joseph Charles Walker; *Career* serv 2 Bn N Rhodesian Regt (Agrica and Madasgar) 1940-43; entered Colonial Serv N Rhodesia 1936, sr dist offr 1953, prov cmmr 1957, sec min of Native Affairs 1960, chief sec Nyasaland 1961-63, dep govr 1963-64, high cmmr for Western Pacific 1964-68, govr and C-in-C Fiji 1968-70, govr-gen Fiji 1970-73; Offr Légion d'Honneur, tstee The Beit Tst; KStJ 1968; *Clubs* Leander, Henley on Thames, Royal Overseas League; *Style—* Sir Robert Foster, GCMG, KCVO; Kenwood, 16 Ardnave Cres, Southampton (☎ 0703 769412)

FOSTER, Rosalind Mary (Mrs R M Englehart); da of Ludovic Anthony Foster, of Greatham Manor, Pulborough, W Sussex, and Pamela Margaret, *née* Wilberforce; *b* 7 August 1947; *Educ* Cranborne Chase Sch Tisbury Wiltshire, Lady Margaret Hall Oxford (BA); *m* 2 Jan 1971, Robert Michael Englehart, s of Gustav Axel Englehart (d 1969), of London; 1 s (Oliver b 1982), 2 da (Alice b 1976, Lucinda b 1978); *Career* barr Middle Temple 1969, recorder Crown Ct 1987-; *Recreations* music, theatre, travel; *Style—* Miss Rosalind Foster; 2 Temple Gardens, The Temple, London EC47 9AY (☎ 01 583 6041)

FOSTER, Roy William John; s of Francis Edwin Foster, of Hawkchurch, Axminster, Devon, and Marjorie Florence Mary, *née* Chapman (d 1944); *b* 25 May 1930; *Educ* Rutlish Sch Merton; *m* 6 Sept 1957, Christine Margaret, da of Albert Victor Toler (d 1972); 2 s (Nicholas Charles Roy b 23 April 1960, d 1969, Richard James b 25 March 1964); *Career* Nat Serv RAF 1953-54, cmmnd PO 1953; qualified CA 1955, ptnr Deloitte Haskins and Sells 1960-; cncl memb CBI, Freeman City of London, Liveryman Worshipful Co of Painter Stainers, Liveryman Worshipful Co of CAs; FCA 1965, ATII 1964; *Recreations* rugby, cricket watching, music, theatre, food and wines; *Clubs* RAC, HAC, MCC, City Livery; *Style—* Roy Foster, Esq; Deloitte Haskins and Sells, 128 Queen Victoria St, London EC4P 4JX (☎ 01 248 3913, fax 01 248 3623)

FOSTER, Saxby Gregory; s and h of Sir John Gregory Foster, 3 Bt; *b* 3 Sept 1957; *Style—* Saxby Gregory Esq

FOSTER, Hon Mrs (Susan Elizabeth); *née* Bridgeman; 2 da of 2 Viscount Bridgeman, KBE, CB, DSO, MC; *b* 19 Oct 1935; *m* 1 Aug 1962, David K D Foster, *qv*; 3 s; *Career* former lady-in-waiting to Lady May Abel Smith, when Lady May's husband was govr of Queensland 1958-60; *Style—* Hon Mrs Foster; Beech House, Shifnal, Shropshire (☎ 0952 460261)

FOSTER, William Robert Brudenell; s of Col Herbert Anderton Foster (d 1930), of Faskally, Pitlochry and Frances Edith Agnes, *née* Brudenell-Bruce (d 1976); *b* 14 April 1911; *Educ* Wellington, CCC Oxford (MA); *m* 1942, Jean Leslie, (d 1986) da of Leslie Urquhart, of Brasted Place, Kent; 3 s (Neil b 1943, Richard b 1945, Charles b 1955), 1 da (Melanie (Mrs Boyle) b 1948); *Career* Capt 6 Black Watch RHR, (TA) invalided 1940, Col 30 Middx HG; barr Inner Temple 1936, dir and chm John Foster & Son Ltd 1939-76, dir and vice-chm Enfield Rolling Mills Ltd 1941-1976, dir MIM Hldgs, Mount Isa Mines Ltd 1955-78; dir and chm St Piran Mining Ltd 1943-76, dir and vice-chm London Brick 1970-82; hon vice-pres Br Field Sports Soc; High Sheriff Norfolk 1969-70, high steward's ctee Norwich Cathedral 1970-80; Liveryman Worshipful Co of Cloth

Workers (Master 1976-77); FRSA; landowner (3800 acres); *Recreations* field sports, architecture, art, travel; *Clubs* Carlton, Pratt's, Norfolk; *Style*— William Foster, Esq; Lexham Hall, King's Lynn, Norfolk PE32 2QJ (☎ 0328 701239)

FOSTER-SUTTON, Sir Stafford William Powell; KBE (1957, OBE 1945), CMG 1948, QC (1938 Jamaica, 1948 Fedn of Malaya); s of G W Foster-Sutton; *b* 24 Dec 1898; *Educ* St Mary Magdalen Sch; *m* 1919, Linda Dorothy, da of John Humber Allwood, OBE, of Enfield, St Anne, Jamaica; 1 da (and 1 s decd); *Career* served WW I and in Army to 1926, also in RFC and RAF; barr Gray's Inn 1926, solicitor-gen Jamaica 1936, attorney-gen Cyprus 1940, Col Cmdg Cyprus Volunteer Force and inspr Cyprus Forces WW II; attorney-gen Kenya 1944-48, actg govr Kenya 1947, attorney-gen Malaya 1948-50, actg high cmmr Aug-Dec 1950, chief justice Fedn Malaya 1950-51, pres W African Court Appeal 1951-55, chief Justice Fedn Nigeria 1955-58 (actg govr-gen 1957); pres Pensions Appeal Tbnl for England and Wales 1958-72; chm: Zanzibar Cmmn of Inquiry 1961, Kenya Regional and Electoral Cmmns 1962-, Malta Referendum Observers 1964-; Master Tallow Chandlers' Co 1981, (dep master 1982-83); kt 1951; *Style*— Sir Stafford Foster-Sutton, KBE, CMG, QC; 7 London Rd, Saffron Walden, Essex

FOTHERGILL, (Arthur) Brian; s of John Smirthwaite Fothergill (d 1938), of Kendal, Cumbria, and Kathleen Anderson Entwisle (d 1957); *b* 3 April 1921; *Educ* Wycliffe Coll, King's Coll London (AKC 1942); *Career* mil serv with Intelligence Corps in India and Singapore 1944-47; vice-pres and chm cncl RSL 1986- (cncl memb 1977-); FSA 1970-; Silver Pen Prize 1970, Heinemann Award for Literature 1969 and 1980; *Books* The Cardinal King (1958), Nicholas Wiseman (1963), Mrs Jordan (1965), Sir William Hamilton (1969), The Mitred Earl (1974), Beckford of Fonthill (1979), The Strawberry Hill Set (1983); *Recreations* reading, opera; *Clubs* Royal Overseas League, PEN; *Style*— Brian Fothergill, Esq; 7 Union Square, London N1 7DH (☎ 01 359 2355)

FOTHERGILL, Michael John; s of Frederick Samuel Abraham Fothergill, of Pembridge, Herefords, and Ethel Irene, *née* Frappell; *b* 23 Mar 1945; *Educ* Latymer Upper Sch, Jesus Coll Cambridge (MA); *m* 28 Aug 1970, Christina Ann, da of Maj Charles Frederick Bushell, OBE, of Milton Keynes; 2 s (Alexander b 1974, Julian b 1979); *Career* founded M J Fothergill Assocs 1973 (now Fothergill and Co Ltd), Consulting Civil and Structural Engineers; int rowing umpire; CEng, FICE, MIStructE, MConsE; *Recreations* family, rowing, skiing; *Clubs* London Leander; *Style*— Michael Fothergill, Esq; 14 Bolton Rd, Chiswick, London, W4 3TB; Fothergill and Company, 62 Hill St, Richmond, Surrey TW9 1TW (☎ 01 948 4165, fax 01 948 5705)

FOTHERINGHAM, John; OBE; s of David Fotheringham, and Elizabeth Fotheringham, *née* Sorley; *b* 5 June 1923; *Educ* Dunfermline HS; *m* 1946, Isobel Mary, da of William Ballantyne, of Falkirk; 1 s (David Ian b 1948), 2 da (Lynda Mary b 1950, Elizabeth Jean b 1952); *Career* WWII Lt RNVR 1941-47; Nat Bank of Scotland Ltd 1940-41 and 1947-49, dist mangr J Bibby & Sons Ltd 1949-53, Barclay Ross & Hutchison 1953-55, md Northern Agric & Lime Co Ltd 1955-64, Sales Dir Br Oil & Cake Mills Unilever Ltd; md United Agric Merchants 1964-72, md North Eastern Farmers Ltd 1972-85, dir Nat Pig Devpt Co (Scotland) 1972-85, chm Grampian Tractors Ltd 1976-85, dep chm Ellis & McHardy Ltd 1984-86; dir: Esk Foods 1985-, Stewart Milne Gp Ltd 1985-, chm Agribusiness (Scotland) Ltd 1987-; memb cncl Scottish Agric Organisation Soc 1973-86, chm GOGECA Animal Feeds Ctee Brussels 1974-86, EEC Animal Feeds Ctee Brussels 1974-86, pres UK Agricultural Suply Trade Assoc 1977-78, memb Aberdeen Harbour Bd 1978-87, pres UKASTA (Scotland) 1979-80, pres Scottish Animal Feed Compounders Assoc Ltd 1979-80, chm Scottish Seed Potato Devpt Cncl 1981-87, Grampian Industrialist of the year 1983, Coop Devpt Agency 1984-87, chm Desside Salmon Fish Bd 1984-87, memb Aberdeen Chamber of Commerce 1985-87, vice-chm Fedn Agric Coops 1985-86, Grampian Regnl Transport 1987-; Aberdeen Univ: memb ct 1984-, Res and Ind Serv Ltd 1984-; convenor Rotary Youth Leadership Awards 1984-, Indust fell Edinburgh Univ 1985, North of Scotland Innovation Serv Ltd 1985-87, memb Industl Tribunals Panel 1986 Paul Harris Fellowship (Rotary Int) 1988; FRAGS; *Recreations* golf; *Clubs* Royal Northern and University; *Style*— John Fotheringham, Esq; St Helens, Earlsferry, Fife

FOTHRINGHAM, Mr Walter Steuart; s of Maj Thomas Steuart Fothringham, MC, TD, JP, DL (d 1979), of Fothringham, Forfar, Angus, and Carola Mary, *née* Noel; *b* 26 Mar 1939; *Educ* Fort Augustus Abbey Sch, RAC Cirencester; *m* 8 Jan 1972, Patricia Anne, da of Sir David Charles Watherston KBE, KStJ, CMG (d 1977); 1 s (David Frederick b 1979), 1 da (Teresa Catherine Frances b 1975); *Career* Lt Scots Gds 1958-63; dir Malcolm Innes Gallery, kt of Obedience, Sov Mil Order of Malta 1978, offr of Merit with Swords; *Recreations* golf, bird watching; *Clubs* R and A, New; *Style*— Walter Fothringham, Esq; Kennacoil House, Dunkeld, Perthshire (☎ 03503 237)

FOUCAR, Antony Emile; s of Emile Charles Victor Foucar (d 1963), of Devon, and Mabel Emma, *née* Harris (d 1956); *b* 3 August 1926; *m* 1959, Anne, da of Arthur Otway Gosden (d 1950), of Sussex; 2 s (Adam b 1960, James b 1961), 1 da (Charlotte b 1964); *Career* barr Middle Temple 1950; dir F & C Alliance Investmt plc 1973; chm: River & Mercantile Tst plc 1985, F & C Pacific Investmt Tst plc 1985, Arthur J Gallagher Investmt Inc 1986; *Clubs* Oriental; Royal Wimbledon Golf; *Style*— Antony Foucar, Esq; Greystock, 5 Peek Crescent, London SW19 5ER (☎ 9468973); Cutlers Gdns, 6 Devonshire Square, London EC2M 4YE (☎ 6235511, fax 6266894, telex 887355)

FOULDS, Gordon Lang; s of William Foulds (d 1987), of Paisley, and Elizabeth Young, *née* Lang (d 1988); *b* 7 May 1937; *Educ* Paisley GS; *m* 29 Aug 1959, Margaret Mortimer, da of William Crawford (d 1947); 1 s (Paul b 1961), 1 da (Natalie b 1970); *Career* W Lang Jr & Co Ltd (later W Lang Paisley Ltd): dir 1965-67, md 1967-85; dir: Brownlee plc 1985-87, Sinclair Lang Ltd 1987-; dir St Mirren Football Club 1977-81, memb Rotary Club Paisley (pres 1986-87); FInstD; *Recreations* golf, bowls; *Clubs* Whitecraigs GC, Whitecraigs Bowling; *Style*— Gordon Foulds, Esq; 7 Broomcroft Rd, Little Broom, Newton Mearns, Glasgow G77 5ER (☎ 041 639 1539); Earls Rd, Grangemouth, Stirlingshire FK3 8UU (☎ 0324 482 778, fax 0324 665397, telex 778464); 102 New Sneddon St, Paisley, Renfrewshire PA3 2BH (☎ 041 889 8826, fax 041 889 5541, telex 778950, car tel 0860 413113)

FOULIS; *see*: Liston-Foulis

FOULIS, Sir Iain Primrose Liston; 13 Bt (NS 1634), Bt of Colinton (1634), and Bt of Ravelston (1661, But for the Attainder); s of Lt-Col James Alastair Liston Foulis (d 1942, s of Lt-Col Archibald Primrose Liston Foulis (ka 1917), 4 s of 9 Bt), by his w Kathleen, da of Lt-Col John Moran and Countess Olga de la Hogue, yr da of Marquis De La Houge (Isle of Mauritius); suc kinsman Sir Archibald Charles Liston-Foulis, 12 Bt (d 1962); Sir James Foulis, 2 Bt, was actively engaged in the wars of Scotland after the death of Charles I and was knighted during his f's lifetime; distant cous of Sir Archibald Primrose, Bt of Ravelston who took arms and name of Primrose; fought with Hussars at Culloden, beheaded at Carlisle 1746. Title of Ravelston and Estates forfeited; *b* 9 Aug 1937; *Educ* Stonyhurst, Cannington Farm Inst Bridgewater Somerset; *Career* nat serv Argyl and Sutherland Highlanders 1957-59, Cyprus 1958; language tutor Madrid 1959-61 and 1966-; trainee-exec Bank of London and S America 1962, Bank of London and Montreal Ltd Bahamas, Guatemala and Nicaragua 1963-65, Sales Toronto Canada 1966; landowner 1962-; *Recreations* mountain walking, country pursuits (Hunting Wild Boar), swimming, camping, travelling, car racing and rallies, looking across the plains of Castille to the mountains; *Clubs* RACE, Friends of Castles, Friends of St James' Way (all in Spain); *Style*— Sir Iain Foulis, Bt; Residencial Cuzco, Calle Soledad 11, Portal 5-2-C, San Augustin de Guadalix, 28750 Madrid, Spain (☎ 91 8418978)

FOULKES, George; JP (Edinburgh 1975), MP (Lab Carrick, Cumnock and Doon Valley 1983-); s of late George Foulkes, and Jessie M A W Foulkes; *b* 21 Jan 1942; *Educ* Keith GS, Haberdashers' Aske's, Edinburgh Univ; *m* 1970, Elizabeth Anna, da of William Hope; 2 s, 1 da; *Career* pres Edinburgh Univ Students Representative Cncl 1963-64, Scottish Union of Students 1965-67, rector's assessor at Edinburgh Univ, dir Enterprise Youth 1968-73, dir Age Concern Scotland 1973-79, cncllr and bailie Edinburgh City Cncl 1970-75, cncllr Lothian Regnl Cncl 1975-79; chm: Lothian Region Educn Ctee 1974-79, Educn Ctee Convention of Scottish Local Authys 1976-79, Scottish Adult Literacy Agency 1977-79; MP (Lab) S Ayrshire 1979-1983, memb Commons Select Ctee on Foreign Affrs, jt chm Commons All-Party Pensioners' Ctee; front bench oppn spokesman: Euro and Community Affairs Nov 1983-85, Foreign Affrs 1985-; *Recreations* boating, supporting Heart of Midlothian FC; *Clubs* Edinburgh University Staff; *Style*— George Foulkes, Esq, JP, MP; 8 Southpark Rd, Ayr, Scotland (☎ 0292 265776); House of Commons, London SW1A 0AA

FOULKES, Sir Nigel (Gordon); s of Louis Augustine Foulkes and Winifred Foulkes; *b* 29 August 1919; *Educ* Gresham's Sch Holt, Balliol Coll Oxford (MA); *m* 1 s, 1 da; m 2, 1948, Elisabeth, da of Ewart B Walker, of Toronto; *Career* WWII Sqdn Ldr RAF; formerly with: H P Bulmer, P E Management Gp, Int Nickel, Rank Xerox (dep md 1964-67, md 1967-70); dir: Charterhouse Gp 1972-83, Bekaert Gp 1973-85, Stone-Platt Industs 1975-80; chm: Br Airports Authy 1972-77, CAA 1977-82, Equity Capital for Indust 1983-86 (vice-chm 1982-83), ECI Mgmnt Jersey 1986-, ECI Int Mgmnt Ltd 1987-, Equity Capital Trustee Ltd 1983-; CBIM, kt 1980; *Clubs* RAF; *Style*— Sir Nigel Foulkes; ECI Ventures, Brettenham Ho, Lancaster Place, London WC2E 7EN (☎ 01 606 1000)

FOUNTAIN, Eric Dudley; OBE (1986); s of William Arthur Fountain (d 1957), of Markyate, Herts, and Lily Eva, *née* Severn; *b* 15 Mar 1929; *m* 18 May 1957, Yvonne Ruby, da of Edward Blacknell (d 1967); 2 s (Roderic Mark, Gregory Richard), 1 da (Lynn Janette); *Career* chm: Inst of Motor Indust, Becenta (Beds and Chiltern Enterprise Agency), Indust Matters for E Anglia; vice pres Luton Town FC (chm working pty); Royal Warrant holder for Vauxhall Motors, pres Luton Beds and Dist C of C; FIMI, FInstD; *Recreations* golf, football, tennis; *Style*— Eric Fountain, Esq, OBE; 13 Hammondswick, Harpenden, Herts AL5 2NR (☎ 0582 72137); Vauxhall Motors Ltd, Kimpton Road, Luton, Beds (☎ 0582 426060)

FOUNTAIN, Hon Mrs (Wendy Shona Coulter); *née* Macpherson; da of 2 Baron Macpherson of Drumochter by his 1 w Ruth; *b* 30 Sept 1950; *m* 1972, Brian Anthony Fountain; 1 s (Stewart James Coulter); *Style*— The Hon Mrs Fountain; 40 Station Av, Wickford, Essex

FOURMAN, Prof Michael Paul; s of Prof Lucien Paul Rollings Fourman (d 1968), of Leeds, and Dr Julia Mary, *née* Hunton (d 1981); *b* 12 Sept 1950; *Educ* Allerton Grange Sch Leeds, Bristol Univ (BSc), Oxford Univ (MSc, D Phil); *m* 12 Nov 1982, Jennifer Robin, da of Hector Grainger Head (d 1970), of Sydney Aust; 1 s (Maximillian b 1987), 1 da (Paula b 1984); *Career* jr res fell Wolfson Coll Oxford 1974-78, JF Ritt asst prof mathematics Columbia Univ NY 1976-82, dept of electrical and electronic engg Brunel Univ: res fell 1983-86, Hirst reader in integrated circuit design 1986, prof of formal systems 1986-88, prof computer systems Edinburgh Univ 1988-; *Recreations* cooking, sailing; *Style*— Prof Michael Fourman; Department of Computer Science, University of Edinburgh, James Clerk Maxwell Building, The King's Buildings, Edinburgh EH9 3JZ (☎ 031 667 1081 ext 2733, fax 031 662 4712)

FOWDEN, Sir Leslie; s of Herbert Fowden and Amy D Fowden; *b* 13 Oct 1925; *Educ* UCL (PhD); *m* 1949, Margaret Oakes; 1 s, 1 da; *Career* UCL: lectr plant chemistry 1950-55, reader 1956-64, prof 1964-73, dean faculty of sci 1970-73; dir: Rothamsted Experimental Station 1973-, AFRC Inst of Arable Crops Res 1986-88; chm agric vet advsy ctee Br Cncl 1987; memb: Cncl Royal Soc 1970-72, scientific advsy panel Royal Botanic Gardens Kew 1977-, (bd of trustees 1983-); FRS; kt 1982; *Style*— Sir Leslie Fowden; 31 Southdown Rd, Harpenden, Herts

FOWKE, Sir David Frederick Gustavus; 5 Bt (UK 1814), of Lowesby, Leicestershire; s of late Lt-Col Gerrard Fowke, 2 s of 3 Bt; suc unc, Sir Frederick Fowke, 4 Bt (d 1987); *b* 28 August 1950; *Style*— Sir David Fowke, BT

FOWLER, Prof Alastair David Shaw; s of David Fowler (d 1939), and Maggie, *née* Shaw (d 1978); *b* 17 August 1930; *Educ* Queens Park Sch Glasgow, Glasgow Univ, Edinburgh Univ (MA), Pembroke Coll Oxford (MA), Queen's Coll Oxford (DPhil, DLitt); *m* 23 Dec 1950, Jenny Catherine, da of Ian James Simpson (d 1981), of Giffnock House, Helensburgh; 1 s (David b 1960), 1 da (Alison b 1954); *Career* jr res fell Queen's Coll Oxford 1955-59, visiting instr Indiana Univ 1957-58, lectr Univ Coll Swansea 1959-61, fell and tutor Eng Lit BNC Oxford 1962-71; visiting prof: Columbia Univ 1964, Virginia Univ 1969, 1979 and 1985-; regius prof rhetoric and Eng lit Edinburgh Univ 1972-84, visiting fell cncl humanities Princeton Univ 1974, fell humanities Res Centre Canberra 1980, visiting fell All Souls Coll Oxford 1984, univ fell Edinburgh Univ 1984-87, memb Inst Advanced Study Princeton 1966 and 1980; external assessor Open Univ 1972-77: advsy ed: New Literary Hist, Eng Literary Renaissance, Spenser Encyclopaedia, Word and Image, Swansea Review, The Seventeenth Century; memb: Harrap Academic Advsy Ctee, Scottish Arts Cncl 1972-74, nat printed books panel; FBA 1974, AUT 1971-84; memb: Carlyle Soc (hon vice pres 1972), Eng Union Edinburgh (pres 1972), Renaissance Soc, Renaissance Eng Text Soc, Soc Emblem Studies, Spenser Soc, Bibliographical Soc Virginia; *Books* Spenser and the Numbers of Time (1964), The Poems of John Milton (with John Carey

1968), Triumphal forms (1970), Conceitful Thought (1975), Catacomb Suburb (1976), From the Domain of Arnheim (1982), Kinds of Literature (1982), A History of English Literature (1987); *Recreations* swimming; *Clubs* United Oxford and Cambridge; *Style*— Prof Alastair Fowler; Dept of English Literature, Univ of Edinburgh, George Sq, Edinburgh EH8 9JX (☎ 031 667 1011 ext 6259, 031 667 7681) Dept of English, Univ of Virginia, Wilson Hall, Charlottesville, VA 22903, USA (☎ 804 924 7105, 804 979 9119)

FOWLER, Gerald Teasdale; s of James A Fowler, (d 1964), of Long Buckby, Northants, and Alfreda, *née* Teasdale; *b* 1 Jan 1935; *Educ* Northampton GS, Lincoln Coll, Univ of Oxford, Univ of Frankfurt-am- Main (BA, MA) 1960; *m* 1982, Lorna Fowler, da of William LLoyd (d 1983), of Ribbleton Preston; 1 s (Julian Giles); *Career* pt/t lectr Pembroke Coll Oxford 1958-59, lectr Hertford and Lincoln Coll Oxford 1959-65, Huddersfield Polytechnic, 1970-72, prof of educnl studies Open University 1972-74, prof assoc dept of govr Brunel Univ 1977-80, dep dir Preston Poly 1980-81, rector N London Poly 1982-; pres: Comparative Educn in Euro Soc 1980, Assoc of Business Exec 1979-81; memb: Oxford City cncl 1960-64, The Wrekin 1966-70 and 1974-79; it parly sec Min of Tech 1967-69, min of State DES Oct 1969-June 1970, March-Oct 1974 and Jan-Sept 1976; FBIM 1984, FRSA 1985, FABAC 1986, HonFABE 1981; *Books* edited: Education In Britain & Ireland 1973, Decision-Making In British Education Systems 1974, Development in Current & Lifelong Education 1987; author num educnl articles and Open Univ Units; *Clubs* Reform Club; *Style*— Prof Gerald Fowler; North East London Polytechnic, Romford Road, London E15 4LZ (☎ 01 590 7722, fax 01 519 3740)

FOWLER, Ian; s of Maj Norman William Frederick Fowler, OBE, QPM, of Herne Bay, Kent, and late Alice May, *née* Wakelin ; *b* 20 Sept 1932; *Educ* The King's Sch Canterbury, St Edmund Hall Oxford (MA); *m* 3 April 1961, Gillian Cecily, da of late Desmond Allchin; 2 s (Aidan Lewis b 12 May 1966, Edmund Ian Carloss b 18 March 1970), 1 da (Sarah May (Mrs Kaliszewska) b 1964); *Career* Nat Serv 2 Lt (Lt TA) 2 Bn The Green Howards 1951-53; barr Gray's Inn 1957; joined Inner London Magistrates' Cts Serv 1959, principal ch clerk and clerk to the ctee of magistrates 1979-; cllr Herne Bay UDC 1961-74; cllr Canterbury City Cncl 1974-83, Mayor 1976-77; memb Ct of Univ of Kent 1976-; *Recreations* reading; *Style*— Ian Fowler, Esq; 6 Dence Park, Herne Bay, Kent (☎ 0227 375530); ILMCS, 3rd Floor, North West Wing, Bush House, Aldwych WC2 (☎ 01 836 9331, fax 01 3796694)

FOWLER, Lady Jennifer Evelyn; *née* Chichester; da of 7 Marquess of Donegall; *b* 3 April 1949; *m* 1971, John Robert Henry Fowler; 2 s; *Style*— Lady Jennifer Fowler; Clegarrow, Enfield, Co Meath

FOWLER, John; s of Jack Fowler, Porlock, Somerset, and Ida Annie, *née* Odgen; *b* 3 Oct 1947; *Educ* Bury GS, Southampton Univ (BA); *m* 17 Feb 1979, Lesley Margaret, da of Melvyn Samuel Jeffries (d 1984), of Fulham; *Career* dir research and planning: United Biscuits Ltd 1967-74, Cadbury Schweppes 1974-78, McCann Erickson Advtg 1978-85, Burson-Marstella 1985-; memb Market Research Soc; *Recreations* reading, eating, drinking, driving, France; *Clubs* Chelsea Arts; *Style*— John Fowler, Esq; 77 Santos Rd, London SW18 (☎ 01 870 9245); Burson Marsteller, 24-28 Bloomsbury Way, London WC1A 2PX (☎ 01 831 6262, fax 01 430 1033, telex 267531)

FOWLER, Keith Harrison; s of late Lancelot Harrison Fowler; *b* 20 May 1934; *Educ* Aldenham; *m* 1961, Vicki Belinda, *née* Pertwee; 3 c; *Career* Lt Army Suez Canal; exec chm Edman Communications Gp plc 1977-88, chief exec Cresta Corporate Servs Ltd 1988-, dir Cresta Hldgs Ltd 1988-; memb Cncl Nat Advtg Benevolent Soc 1978-, govr Winchester House Sch 1968-, dir Pertwee Hldgs 1982-; ACIS; *Recreations* sailing, riding, crested china, pictures; *Clubs* Arts, Solus; *Style*— Keith Fowler, Esq; Little Hundridge Farm, Little Hundridge Lane, Great Missenden, Bucks (☎ 024 06 2034); Edman Group plc, Edman House, 17-19 Maddox St, London W1R 0EY (☎ 01 499 0477)

FOWLER, Lionel Albert; s of Alan Jack Fowler (d 1976), of 17 The Terrace, Finchfield, Wolverhampton, and Violet Florence Fowler; *b* 23 May 1952; *m* 10 May 1975, (Margaret) Mary, da of George Griffin (d 1985); 1 s (James Alexanda Lionel b 23 May 1983), 1 da (Suzanne Louise b 28 May 1981); *Career* buyer Alcan Metal Centres 1968-74, salesman RTZ Metal Stockholders 1974-86 (full bd memb 1983), sales and mktg dir Skipper Gp 1987-; memb IOD 1988; *Recreations* golf; *Clubs* Brocton Hall GC; *Style*— Lionel Fowler, Esq; Skipper Gp, Furness Hse, Trafford Rd, Salford, Manchester (☎ 061 848 7801, car tel 0860 832 832, home 078 571 4023)

FOWLER, Lady; Margaret; da of Dr John MacFarquhar MacLeod (d 1957); *m* 1939, Sir Robert William Doughty Fowler, KCMG (sometime High Cmmr Tanzania and Ambass Khartoum; d 1985), s of William Fowler (d 1944); 1 s, 1 da; *Style*— Lady Fowler; 17 Adam Court, Henley-on-Thames, Oxon RG9 2BJ (☎ 0491 572 404)

FOWLER, Rt Hon (Peter) Norman; PC (1979), MP (C) Sutton Coldfield Feb 1974-; s of N F Fowler (d 1964), of Chelmsford, and Katherine Fowler; *b* 2 Feb 1938; *Educ* King Edward VI Sch Chelmsford, Trinity Hall Cambridge; *m* 1979, Fiona Poole, da of John Donald; 2 da (Kate Genevieve b Nov 1981, Isobel Geraldine b July 1984); *Career* with The Times 1961-70 (special correspondent 1962-66, home affrs 1966-70), memb editorial bd Crossbow 1962-69; MP (C) Nottingham S 1970-74; chief oppn spokesman: Tport 1976-79, Social Servs 1975-76, oppn spokesman Home Affrs 1974-75, PPS NI Office 1972-74, min Tport 1979-81, sec of state Tport Jan-Sept 1981, sec of state Social Servs 1981-87, sec of state Employment 1987-; *Style*— The Rt Hon Norman Fowler, MP; House of Commons, London SW1A 0AA

FOWLER, Prof Peter Howard; s of Prof Sir Ralph Howard Fowler, OBE (d 1944), and Eileen, *née* Rutherford (d 1930); *b* 27 Feb 1923; *Educ* Winchester, Univ of Bristol (BSc, DSc); *m* 23 July 1949, Rosemary Hempson, da of Rear-Adm (E) George Herbert Hempson Brown RN, CBE (d 1977); 3 da (Mary b 1950, Anne b 1952, Susan b 1962); *Career* PO RAF 1942-46; Royal Soc Res Prof Univ of Bristol 1964-88: asst lectr 1948-50, lectr 1950-59, res fell in physics 1959-63, reader 1963-64; Royal Soc Rutherford Meml Lectr 1971, Royal Soc Hughes Medal 1974; memb of various sci and engrg res cncl bds in astronomy and space area 1971-88, Meteorological ctee 1983-; FRS 1964, FRAS 1962, FR Met Soc 1983; *Books* The Study of Elementary Particles by the Photographic Method (with CF Powell and DH Perkins, 1959), Solid State Nuclear Track Detectors 1981, with VM Clapham, Forty Years of Particle Physics (with B Foster, 1988); *Recreations* gardening, meteorology ; *Clubs* Roy Soc Dining; *Style*— Professor Peter Fowler; HH Wills Physics Laboratory, Royal Fort, Tyndall Avenue, Bristol BS8 1TL (☎ 0272 303 030 ext 3605, fax 0272 732 657, telex 0272 445938)

FOWLER, Ronald Frederick; CBE (1950); s of Charles Frederick Fowler (d 1942), and Amy Beatrice, *née* Hollyoak (d 1976); *b* 21 April 1910; *Educ* Bancroft's Sch, LSE (BCom), Sir Ernest Carsel Travelling Scholar, Univs of Lille and Brussels; *m* 17 April 1937, Brenda Kathleen, da of Henry William Smith (d 1970); *Career* asst and lectr in commerce LSE 1932-40' cabinet office and central statistical office 1940-50, dir of statistics and under sec Miny of Labour 1950-68, dir statistical res DOE 1968-72, statistic cnslt Prices Div Ottawa Statistics Canada 1971-74, statistic cnslt Prices Cmmn 1973-77; memb Retail Prices Index Advsy Ctee 1956-86; Royal Statistical Soc (hon tres 1950-60); *Books* The Depreciation of Capital (1934), The Duration of Unemployment (1968), Some Problems of Index Number Construction (1970), Further Problems of Index Number Construction (1973); contrib num articles in Br and Us Learned jnls; *Clubs* Reform; *Style*— R F Fowler, Esq, CBE; 10 Silverdale Rd, Petts Wood, Orpington, Kent

FOWLES, John; OBE (1986), JP (1972); s of Harold Fowles (d 1983), and Helen (d 1983); *b* 28 June 1932; *Educ* Reading Collegiate Sch, Harvard Business Course; *m* 22 April 1961, Diana Mary, da of Victor Urrey Oldland; 2 s (Charles b 1962, James b 1964), 1 da (Jayne b 1963); *Career* RAF Tech Trg Cmd, Fighter Cmd 90 Gp 1949-53; joined Gowring Gp 1953 presently chm and md; CBI: memb Southern Regn Cncl 1979-(chm 1983-85, vice chm 1981-83), memb Nat Cncl, chm's ctee and pres ctee 1981-86; dir Newbury Racecourse plc 1983; chm Berkshire Industry Year 1986; Freeman City of London; HM gen cmmr for Inland Revenue 1981-; *Recreations* fishing, shooting, golf; *Clubs* MCC, Guild of Freemen, City Livery; *Style*— John Fowles, Esq, OBE; Burghclere Manor, Near Newbury, Berkshire; Gowrings Ltd, 18-21 Church Gate, Thatcham, Berkshire (☎ 0635 64464)

FOWLIE, Dr Hector Chalmers; s of Hector McIntosh Fowlie (d 1954), and Agnes Blue, *née* Turner (d 1966); *b* 21 June 1929; *Educ* Harris Academy Dundee, Univ of St Andrews (MB ChB); *m* Christina Napier Morrison, da of Peter Walker (d 1967); 2 s (Stephen b 1956, Peter b 1962), 1 da (Kay b 1958); *Career* psychiatrist; formerly dep physician supt Gartnavel Royal Hosp Glasgow and physician supt Royal Dundee Liff & Strathmartine Hosps Dundee, conslt psychiatrist Tayside Health Bd Dundee, vice-chm Mental Welfare Cmmn for Scotland; *Style*— Dr Hector Fowlie; 21 Clepington Road, Dundee (☎ 0382 41926)

FOX; *see*: Scott Fox

FOX, Allan Spencer; s of Joseph Bower Fox (d 1964), of Bradford, and Florence Mary, *née* Farrow (d 1986); *b* 3 Feb 1932; *Educ* Bradford GS, Univ of Sheffield (BA, DipEd); *m* 15 Aug 1959, Margaret Seddon, da of Reginald Charles Eveleigh (d 1933), of Reading; 2 da (Susan b 1962, Carolyn b 1967); *Career* Flying Offr RAF (Educn Branch) 1955-58; asst Master: Excelsior Sch Kingston Jamaica 1958-62, Bedford Lower Sch Bedford Sch 1962-67; headmaster jr Sch: Daniel Stewarts' Coll Edinburgh 1967-74, Daniel Stewarts' and Melville Coll Edinburgh 1974-77; Master Highgate Jr Sch 1977-; Capt Sheffield Univ CC 1953 and 1955, memb mgmnt ctee Highgate Literary and Scientific Inst 1984-86, tstee The Whipple Tst 1984-; FRGS 1960; *Recreations* hill walking, gardening, painting; *Style*— Allan Fox, Esq; Cholmeley House, 3 Bishopswood Rd, Highgate, London N6 (☎ 01 340 9193)

FOX, Christopher Jonathan; s of Richard Glanfield Fox, of Penlea, Freshwater Lane, St Mawes, Truro, Cornwall, and Ella Tweed, *née* Bingley; *b* 2 June 1948; *Educ* LSE (BSc); *m* 26 June 1982, Susan Agnes Bridget, da of John Charles McNicol (d 1971), of Maidenhead, Berks; *Career* CA, former jt tres and chm Fin and Admin Bd Lib Pty, ldr SLD Gp Guildford Borough Cncl, contested (Lib) Guildford Feb and Oct 1974; Liveryman Workshipful Co of Weavers; *Recreations* reading, history, politics, genealogy; *Clubs* Guildford Cncl Sports and Social; *Style*— Christopher Fox, Esq; 173 Worplesdon Rd, Guildford, Surrey GU2 6XD (☎ 0483 31739)

FOX, David John; s of Frederick Oswald Fox (d 1966), and Beatrice, *née* Roberts-Clarke (d 1988); *b* 13 Mar 1935; *m* Norma Kathleen, da of (Ernest) Norman Parkes (d 1973); 1 s (Travis John b 15 March 1975); *Career* Grenadier Gds 1953-56; legal exec; memb: Dorset CC 1975- (chm Public Protection Ctee 1980-), Christchurch Borough Cncl 1973- (Mayor 1987-88); chm fire and emergency planning ctee Assoc CCs; area sec Cons Club Advsy Ctee, chm Christchurch Age Concern; *Recreations* Genealogy; *Style*— David Fox, Esq; 1 Canberra Rd, Christchurch, Dorset BH23 2HL (☎ 0202 482 787); 194 Seabourne Rd, West Southbourne, Bournemouth (☎ 0202 423 232, fax 0202 423 232)

FOX, Edward Charles Morice; eldest s of late Maj Robin Box, RA, of Sussex, and Angela Muriel Darita, *née* Worthington; *b* 13 April 1937; *Educ* Harrow; *m* 1958, Tracy Reed (m dis), da of Anthony Pelissier, of Sussex; 1 da (Lucy Arabella b 1950); *Career* late Coldstream Gds, 2 Lt Royal N Lancs Regt; stage, screen and tv actor 1958-; *Recreations* music, gardening; *Clubs* Garrick, Savile; *Style*— Edward Fox, Esq

FOX, Freddie Frank; OBE (1977); s of Ing Arnost Fuchs (d in holocaust 1944/45), of Prague, and Alice Fuchs (d in holocaust 1944/45); *b* 6 July 1919; *Educ* Tech Coll Prague; *m* 11 May 1944, Gertrude, da of Leopold Preiss (d in holocaust 1943/4), of Zilina, Czech; 1 s (John b 1946), 1 da (Vivienne (Mrs Erdos) b 1949); *Career* md: Record Food Prods Ltd 1947-64, Record Bakery Equipment Co Ltd 1947-; md and chm Pasta Foods Co Ltd (RHM) 1964-81; currently chm: Adv Hldgs Co Ltd, Javin Property Co (London) Ltd; memb sci and technol bd MAFF, chm Bakery Equipment Mfrs Soc 1960-63, cncl & exec memb Food Mfrg Fedn 1958-80, chm external relations ctee FMF 1970-74, pres UNAFPA (Union of Pasta Mfrs in EEC) 1977-78, tres Hammerson Memorial Home for the Elderly Hampstead 1980-88, memb Inst of Br Engrs 1958; Freeman: City of London 1968, Worshipful Co of Bakers 1968; *Recreations* golf, skiing, theatre; *Style*— Freddie Fox, Esq, OBE; Unit 10, Verulam Industrial Estate, London Rd, St Albans, Herts AL1 1JF (☎ 0727 43136, fax 0727 43123, telex 265192 RECORD G)

FOX, Lady Hazel Mary; da of John Matthew Blackwood Stuart, CIE (d 1941), and Joan Daria, *née* Elliot Taylor; *b* 22 Oct 1928; *Educ* Roedean, Somerville Coll Oxford (MA); *m* 5 June 1954, Rt Hon Sir Michael John Fox, s of Michael Fox (d 1926); 3 s (Matthew b 1957, Patrick b 1958, Charles b 1968), 1 da (Jane b 1962); *Career* called to the Bar 1950, practising 1950-54, lectr in jurisprudence Somerville Coll 1951-58, fell 1976-81, lectr Cncl of Legal Educn 1962-76; chm: London Rent Assessment Panel 1977-, London Leasehold Valuation Tbnl 1981-; dir Br Ins of Int and Comparative Law 1982-, memb Home Off Departmental Ctee on Jury Serv 1953-65, chm Tower Hamlets Juvenile Ct 1968-76; JP London 1956-77; *Books* International Arbitration (with J L Simpson, 1959), International Economic Law and Developing States (ed 1988); *Style*— Lady Fox; British Institute of International and Comparative Law, Charles

Clore House, 17 Russell Sq, London WC1B 5DR (☎ 01 636 5802)

FOX, James Ewart; s of Ewart Lyndall Fox (d 1963), Gwendoline Rose Hann (d 1988); *b* 30 Sept 1941; *Educ* Wellington, Royal West of England Acad, Bristol Univ (BArch, DiplArch); *m* 18 Dec 1976, Bridget Ann, da of Maj Basil Frank Jones, of Chilton Cantelo, Somerset; 1 s (Sebastian James b 1985), 2 da (Charlotte Ann b 1978, Melanie Sarah b 1981); *Career* princ architect 1964-; underwriting memb Lloyds of London 1978-; ARIBA 1964-; *Recreations* salmon fishing, pheasant/partridge shooting, tennis, skiing, flying, golf; *Clubs* Conservative, Lloyds of London, Flying; *Style*— James E Fox, Esq; Nether Compton, Sherborne, Dorset; 55 The Park, Yeovil, Somerset BA20 1DF (☎ 0935 20831)

FOX, James George; s of George Romney Fox (d 1968), of Trewardreva Constantine, Falmouth, Cornwall, and Barbara Muriel, *née* Twite; *b* 14 May 1943; *Educ* Eton, Univ of Newcastle-on-Tyne (BA), Univ of Pennsylvania (MBA); *m* 4 May 1974, Rebecca Jane, da of Charles Wright of Canyon, Texas; 2 s (Francis b 1977, Romney b 1981), 2 da (Rachel b 1975, Sarah b 1979); *Career* dir: Hill Samuel Investment Mgmnt 1968-78, Warburg Investment Mgmnt 1982-85; md Morgan Grenfell Tst Mangrs 1985-, chm Falmouth Hotel plc 1981-; *Recreations* sailing; *Clubs* Athenaeum, Penn; *Style*— James Fox, Esq; Trewardreva, Constantine, Falmouth, Cornwall; 57 St Andrewes House, Barbican, London EC2 (☎ 0326 40207, 01 638 9103); 46 New Broad St, London EC2 (☎ 01 256 7500)

FOX, Capt John Rupert Anselm; s of Sqdn Ldr John Arnold Fox, MBE, RAF (d 1984), of Worcestershire, and Eleanor Margaret, *née* Green (d 1986), (gs of William Owen design and architect for Port Sunlight for 1 Lord Leverhulme); *b* 10 Dec 1935; *Educ* Stonyhurst Coll; *m* 10 Oct 1965, Isabel June Mary Jermy Fox, da of H E Le Bailli Quintin Jermy Gwyn, former Grand Chancellor Sov and Mil Order of Malta; 5 s (Oliver b 1967, d 1986, Benjamin b 1969, Justin b 1970, Quintin b 1972, Anthony b 1980), 1 da (Eleanor b 1966); *Career* 2 Lt RASC BAOR 1955-56, Capt Cheshire Yeo 1958-65; slr; Notary Public 1965 under sheriff City of Worcester 1964-76, ptnr Whatley Weston & Fox (Worcester, Malvern, Hereford) 1963-76, ptnr John Fox Slrs 1978-; chm: Carewell Housing Assoc Ltd, Carewell Second Housing Assoc Ltd, Warminster (young persons) Housing Assoc Ltd; tstee order of Malta Homes; Kt of Magisterial Grace, Sov of Mil Order of Malta 1975-, Offr of Merit, Pro Merite Melitensi; *Recreations* interior decoration, gardening, picture collector, water colourist; *Clubs* Travellers; *Style*— Capt John Fox; Condicup Farm, Willersey Rd, Badsey, Worcestershire (☎ 0386 830327); Keil Close, 32 High St, Broadway, Worcs (☎ 0386 858436/858794, fax 0386 853254)

FOX, The (O'Sionnaigh); John William Fox; s of James George Fox (d 1957), of Gypsum, Tempsey, NSW, and Ethel, *née* Laidlaw; suc his kinsman, Nial Arthur Hubert Fox, The Fox, as Chief of his Name 1959; *b* 22 August 1916; *m* 1939, Margaret Frances Wilson; 4 s, 1 da; *Heir* s, Douglas John Fox b 23 Aug 1942; *Style*— The Fox; Koorlong, Vic 3501, Australia

FOX, Dr Levi; OBE (1964), DL (1967 Warwickshire); s of John William Fox (d 1952), of Coleorton, Leics; *b* 28 August 1914; *Educ* Ashby De La Zouch Boys' GS, Oxford Univ, Manchester Univ; *m* 1938, Jane Richards, of Coleorton, Leics; 1 s, 2 da; *Career* dir and sec: Incorporated Tst, Shakespeare Birthplace Trust 1945-; author of books on Shakespeare, Stratford-upon-Avon, and Warwickshire; dep chm Int Shakespeare Assoc; Hon DLitt Birmingham Univ, FSA, FRHistS, FRSL; *Recreations* gardening, local history; *Style*— Dr Levi Fox OBE, DL, MA; Silver Birches, 27 Welcombe Rd, Stratford-upon-Avon, Warwickshire (☎ 0789 292648); The Shakespeare Centre, Stratford-upon-Avon, Warwickshire (☎ 0789 204016)

FOX, Sir (John) Marcus; MBE (1963), MP (C) Shipley 1970-; s of late Alfred Hirst Fox; *b* 11 June 1927; *Educ* Wheelwright GS, Dewsbury; *m* 1954, Ann, da of F W J Tindall; 1 s, 1 da; *Career* served Duke of Wellington's Regt and The Green Howards 1945-48; memb Dewsbury Boro Cncl 1957-65, contested (C): Dewsbury 1959, Huddersfield W 1966; memb race relations and immigration select ctee 1970-72, asst govt whip 1972-73, Lord Cmmr of the Treasury 1973-74, oppn front bench spokesman: environment 1974, housing 1974-75, transport 1975-76; vice-chm Cons Pty (responsible for candidates) 1976-79, under-sec state DOE 1979-81, memb Select Ctee on Members' Salaries 1981-82, vice-chm 1922 Ctee 1983-; chm Ctee of Selection 1984-; nat chm Assoc of Cons Club 1988-; kt 1986; *Style*— Sir Marcus Fox MBE, MP; House of Commons, London SW1A 0AA

FOX, Lord Justice; Rt Hon Sir Michael John; PC (1981), QC (1968); s of Michael Fox; *b* 8 Oct 1921; *Educ* Drayton Manor Sch Hanwell, Magdalen Coll Oxford; *m* 1954, Hazel Mary (formerly fellow Somerville Oxford, dir Br Inst Int & Comparative Law 1982-), da of John Matthew Blackwood Stuart, CIE; 3 s, 1 da; *Career* serv Admty 1942-45; barr Lincoln's Inn 1949, judge High Ct (Chancery) 1975-81, Lord Justice of Appeal 1981-; kt 1975;; *Style*— The Rt Hon Lord Justice Fox; Royal Courts of Justice, Strand, WC2 (☎ 01 405 7641)

FOX, Michael Pease; s of Julian Pease Fox (d 1979), of Pennant, Wellington, Som, and Marjorie Ellis, *née* Gibbins (d 1981); *b* 21 August 1921; *Educ* Leighton Park Sch, Reading, Corpus Christi Coll, Cambridge (MA); *m* 24 July 1948, Yvonne Hotham, da of Joel Hothan Cadbury (d 1946), of King's Norton, Birmingham; 2 s (Julian b 1949, Roger b 1953), 2 da (Jeanie b 1951, Diana b 1955); *Career* Friends Ambulance Unit China Convoy 1942-46; main bd dir Friends Provident Life Off 1967-; chm and md 1968-: Fox Bros & Co Ltd (joined 1948, dir 1952, vice-chm 1964), William Bliss & Son; memb Wool Textile EDC 1965-69, chm W of Eng Wool Textile Assoc 1968- (chm jt industl cncl 1968-); chm public health cncl RDC 1966-69, pres Rotary Club Wellington 1967; assoc memb ATI 1966; *Recreations* sailing, gardening, mountain walking; *Style*— Michael Fox, Esq; Legglands, Wellington, Somerset TA21 9NU (☎ 082 347 2119); Fox Bros & Co Ltd, Tonedale, Wellington, Somerset (☎ 082 347 2271, fax 082 347 6963, telex 46158)

FOX, Sir (Henry) Murray; GBE (1974); s of Sidney Joseph Fox (d 1962), of London, and Molly Button; *b* 7 June 1912; *Educ* Malvern, Emmanuel Coll Cambridge; *m* 1941, Helen Isabella Margaret (d 1986), da of late J B Crichton; 1 s, 2 da; *Career* Alderman Ward of Bread St 1966-82, Sheriff City of London 1971-72, Lord Mayor of London 1974-75, one of HM Lts City of London 1976-82; pres City & Metropolitan Building Soc, chm Trehaven Tst Ltd; dir: Municipal Mutual Ins Ltd, Toye Kenning & Spencer Ltd 1976-; Order of Rising Sun and Sacred Treasure (Japan) 1971, Order of Stor (Afghanistan) 1971, Order of Orange (Netherlands) 1972; *Style*— Sir Murray Fox, GBE; 80 Defoe House, Barbican, London EC2; 20-24 Kirby St, Hatton Garden, London EC1N 8TU (☎ 01 242 5205)

FOX, Philip Hamilton; DL (1977); s of Maj Cuthbert Lloyd Fox MC (d 1972), of Glendurgan, Mawnan Smith, Falmouth, and Moyra Florence, *née* Sulivan (d 1988); family business G C Fox & Co established 1762 in Falmouth previously in Fowey about 1646, still an operating partnership; *b* 11 Mar 1922; *Educ* Harrow, Magdalene Cambridge; *m* 1948, Rona, da of late Kenneth D Briggs; 3 s (Robert, Charles, William); *Career* Lt Northern Europe 1944-45, High Sheriff of Cornwall 1973-74; chm Fed Cncl of UK and Irish Co Membs of Inst of Chartered Shipbrokers 1985-87; travel agent; dir: Shipping Servs (Falmouth) Ltd, Falmouth Syndicate Ltd; FICS, FID, MInstTT; Orders of Orange Nassau (Neth), Vasa (SW), Polar Star (SW), Olaf (Nor) and Order of Merit (Nor), and Danneborg (Danish); *Recreations* sailing (aux sloop 'Quaker Girl'), gardening; *Clubs* Royal Cruising, Royal Ocean Racing, Royal Cornwall Yacht; *Style*— Philip Hamilton Fox Esq, DL; Stable Court, Mawnan Smith, Falmouth, Cornwall TR11 5JZ (☎ 0326 311300, telex 45-237, fax 0326 317913)

FOX, Raymond Charles Hayne; s of Henry James fox (d 1949), of Muswell Hill, and Dora Lilian, *née* Welch (d 1929); *b* 10 July 1914; *Educ* City of London Sch, King's Coll London Univ (LLB); *m* 1, 26 July 1947, Dorothea Cunliffe (d 1974), da of Ernest Hamilton Sharp, OBE, KC (d 1922), of Surrey and Hong Kong; m 2, 11 Oct 1975, Geraldine Mary Brett, da of Capt Thomas Gerald Cahill, MC (d 1969), of Kingsgate, Kent; *Career* WWII Royal Mil Coll 1939-40, Royal Wech Fusiliers 1940-46 serv Normandy and Hamburg (Capt 1944); Town Clerk's Dept City of London 1934-39 and 1946-76 (asst Town Clerk 1973-76), involved in Barbican devpt 1960-76); dir Tally-Ho Estates Ltd 1948-; memb Wimbledon Guild of Social Welfare; Freeman City of London 1935, Liveryman Worshipful Co of Cutlers 1936; Offr Orden de Mayo al Merito Argentine Republic 1961, Knight Official, Order of African Redemption Republic of Liberia 1962, Chevalier of L'Ordre de la Valeur Camerounaise 1963, Offr of the Nat Order of Niger 1969; *Recreations* reading, gardening, music, walking, shooting; *Style*— Raymond Fox, Esq; 1 Wilberforce Way, Wimbledon, London SW19 4TH (☎ 01 946 3362)

FOX, Robert Trench; s of Waldo Trench Fox (d 1953), of Penjerrick, Falmouth, Cornwall; *b* 1 Jan 1937; *Educ* Winchester, Univ Coll Oxford (BA); *m* 1962, Lindsay Garrett, da of Sir Donald Forsyth Anderson (d 1973); 2 s, 2 da; *Career* dir: Kleinwort Benson Ltd 1972-, Westpac Banking Corpn London 1974-; *Recreations* shooting, walking, sailing; *Clubs* Brooks's; *Style*— Robert Fox, Esq; Kleinwort Benson Ltd, 20 Fenchurch St, London EC3P 3DB (01 623 8000); Cheriton House, Cheriton, Alresford, Hants (☎ 096 279 230)

FOX, Stephen Howard; s of Louis Fox, and Augusta; *b* 8 Oct 1948; *Educ* Manchester GS, Coll of Law; *Career* admitted slr 1973, sr ptnr Betesh Fox & Co Slrs, dir Fox Bros (warehousemen) Ltd, md Van Daele Chocolatier Ltd; *Recreations* squash, writing; *Style*— Stephen Fox, Esq; 17 Ralli Ct, West Riverside, Manchester M3 5FT (☎ 061 832 6131, fax 061 832 8172)

FOX, Sir Theodore (Fortescue); 3 s of Robert Fortescue Fox, MD (d 1940); *b* 26 Nov 1899; *Educ* Leighton Park, Pembroke Coll Cambridge; *m* 1930, Margaret Evelyn (d 1970), eldest da of late W S McDougall, of Wallington, Surrey; 4 s (2 decd); *Career* Major RAMC, dir Family Planning Association 1964-67, ed The Lancet 1944-64 (joined staff 1925); kt 1962; *Recreations* gardening, family history; *Clubs* Athenaeum; *Style*— Sir Theodore Fox; Green House, Rotherfield, E Sussex (☎ 089 285 2870)

Fox, Hon Mrs; (Virginia Sarah); yr da of Baron Carr of Hadley (Life Peer); *b* 1957; *m* 1984, Michael Frederick Fox; *Style*— Hon Mrs Fox

FOX, William; JP (Cumbria); s of Philip Henry Fox, JP (d 1937), of High House, St Bees, and Hilda Mary, *née* Brinton (d 1969); *b* 13 Jan 1922; *Educ* St Bees Sch, Univ of Oxford (MA); *m* 28 Jan 1948, (Lillian) Esme, da of Maj LB Hogarth, OBE (d 1966), of Whitehaven; 1 s (Anthony b 29 Nov 1948), 2 da (Prudence b 31 July 1951, Joanna b 2 April 1960); *Career* Capt 18 Royal Garhwal Rifles IA 1942-46, Malayan CS 1946-58; bursar St Bees Sch 1958-83; chm or memb numerous local orgns incl dep chm Cumbria Probation Ctee; *Recreations* golf, skiing, windsurfing, fell walking; *Style*— William Fox, Esq, JP; High House, St Bees, Cumbria CA27 0BZ (☎ 0946 822 228)

FOX, Winifred Marjorie (Mrs Eustace Gray Debros); *née* Fox; da of Frederick Charles Fox (d 1968), and Charlotte Marion Ogborn; *b* 31 Mar 1915; *Educ* Streatham County Sch, St Hugh's Oxford; *m* 1953, Eustace Gray Debros, formerly Eustacius Debroswki (d 1954); 1 da, *Career* entered Home Civil Service, asst princ Unemployment Assistance Board 1937, War Cabinet Office 1942, princ 1943, min of Town & Country Planning 1944, asst sec 1948, min of Housing & Local Govt 1952, under-sec Local Government 1963, resident chm Civil Service Selection Bd 1971-72, under-sec DOE (Planning) 1972-77; *Recreations* reading, listening to music; *Style*— Miss Winifred Fox; (☎ Brackley 702100)

FOX, Yvonne Hotham; da of Joel Hotham Cadbury (d 1946), and Margery; *b* 27 July 1921; *Educ* Sidcot Sch Avon, and The Mount Sch York; *m* 24 July 1948, Michael Pease Fox, s of Julian Pease Fox, of Pennant, Wellington, Somerset (d 1979); 2 s (Julian b 1949, Roger b 1953), 2 da (Jeanie b 1951, Diana b 1955); *Career* memb: Chartered Soc of Physiotherapists, Assoc of Chartered Physiotherapists in Obstetrics and Gynaecology ret; SSStJ (1976), County Pres for Somerset 1988; *Recreations* caligraphy, gardening, dress making, mountain walking; *Style*— Mrs Yvonne Fox; Legglands, Wellington, Somerset TA21 9NU (☎ 082 347 2119)

FOX BASSETT, Nigel; s of Thomas Fox Bassett (d 1960), of London, and Catherine Adriana, *née* Wiffen (d 1960); *b* 1 Nov 1929; *Educ* Taunton Sch, Trinity Coll Cambridge (MA); *m* 9 Sept 1961, Patricia Anne, da of Stanley William Lambourne (d 1986), of E Horsley, Surrey; 1 s (Jonathan b 30 July 1966), 1 da (Emma (Mrs Lines) b 19 Jan 1964); *Career* Nat Serv 2Lt RA 1949-50 (serv Canal Zone Egypt with Mauritian Gds), Capt 264 (7 London) Field Regt RA TA 1950-60; admitted slr 1956, ptnr Clifford Chance (formerly Coward Chance) 1960- (articled 1953); chm exec ctee Br Inst of Int and Comparative Law 1986- (cncl memb 1977); cncl memb Int Assoc for the Protection of Industl Property (Br Gp) Inc 1984-, memb cncl Int Law Assoc (Br branch) 1974-86, chm intellectual property sub-ctee City of London Slrs Co 1982-87 (cncl memb 1969-87), ctee memb business section of IBA (anti-tst, patents and trademarks, securities ctees) 1969-, memb: Law Soc Euro Gp 1969-, American Bar Assoc (Futures Regulation Ctee) 1979-, Assoc Europeenne d'Etudes Juridiques et Fiscales (UK memb) 1969-; cncl memb Taunton Sch, hon legal advsr to Partially Sighted Soc; memb Glyndebourne Festival Opera Soc and Kent Opera, memb The Pilgrims of GB 1988-, vice pres Dulwich Hockey Club, chm Old Tautonians Sports Club; Freeman Worshipful Co of Slrs 1960; memb Law Soc; *Books* English Sections of: Branchs and Subsidiaries in the European Common Market (1976), Business Law in Europe (1982); *Recreations* shooting, beagling, cricket, art, opera; *Clubs* Garrick, City of London, MCC, Seaview YC; *Style—* Nigel Fox Bassett, Esq; Clifford Chance, Royex House, Aldermanbury Square, London EC2V 7LD (☎ 01 600 0808, fax 01 726 8561, telex 8959991)

FOX-ANDREWS, James Roland Blake; QC (1968); step s of Norman Roy Fox-Andrews, QC (d 1971), and s of Mary Gammell, *née* Stuart (d 1973); *b* 24 Mar 1922; *Educ* Stowe, Pembroke Coll Cambridge; *m* 1950, Angela Bridget da of Brig Charles Swift OBE, MC; 2 s (Mark b 1952, Piers b 1954); *Career* called to the Bar 1949, recorder of Winchester 1971-72 (hon recorder 1972-, recorder 1972-85); bencher Grays Inn 1974; circuit judge assigned to official referee work 1985; ldr W Circuit 1982-84; dep chm Devon GS 1969-71; *Style—* James Fox-Andrews, Esq, QC; 20 Cheyne Gdns, London SW3

FOX-ANDREWS, (Jonathan) Mark Piers; s of Judge James Fox-Andrews, QC, and Bridget, *née* Swift, JP; *b* 7 May 1952; *Educ* Eton, Trinity Hall Cambridge (BA, MA); *m* 22 Sept 1984, Rosemary Anne, da of Dennis Jenks; 1 s (Macimillian George b 28 Mar 1987); *Career* Drexel Burnham Lambert: trader 1977-80, mangr Singapore Off 1980-83, mangr Sydney Off 1984, md (Ltd) London Off 1984-; *Style—* J M P Fox-Andrews, Esq,; Drexel Burnham Lambert Ltd, 1 Alie St, London E1 8DB (☎ 01 325 9797)

FOX-ROBINSON, Robert Andrew; Lancing, Trinity Coll Dublin (MA); s of Wilfred Henry Fox-Robinson, of London, and Jane Mary, *née* Home; *b* 11 Dec 1940; *m* 7 Oct 1972, Anne Thornton, da of Humphrey Challis (d 1958), of Essex; 3 s (Richard Charles b 14 Oct 1973, John Edward b 2 Feb 1976, William Robert b 23 March 1979); *Career* TAVR IV HAC London Gunner B Battery 1966-69; slr of supreme ct 1970-88, dir of various co's; tstee Boothby Hall Tst Lincolnshire 1968-84; former memb Ely Diocesan Synod, former memb Linton Deanery Synod; memb Law Soc, Westminster C of C; *Recreations* squash, sailing and chess; *Clubs* Oriental; *Style—* Robert Fox-Robinson, Esq; 307 Grays Inn Rd, London WC1X 8DY (☎ 01 833 4099/8222, fax 01 833 8319)

FOX-STRANGWAYS, Hon Raymond George; 2 s of 8 Earl of Ilchester (d 1970), and hp of bro, 9 Earl; *b* 11 Nov 1921; *Educ* Exeter Sch, Seale Hayne Agric Coll; *m* 15 Nov 1941, Margaret Vera, da of late James Force, of North Surrey, BC, Canada; 2 s; *Career* served RAF WW II; Civil Service 1949-76, ret; *Recreations* walking, riding, ornithology; *Style—* Hon Raymond Fox-Strangways; Cherry Orchard Yews, Trull, Taunton, Somerset TA3 7LF (☎ 0823 282879)

FOXALL, Colin; s of Alfred George Foxall, of Chatham, Kent, and Ethel Margaret, *née* Hall; *b* 6 Feb 1947; *Educ* Gillingham GS; *m* 2 Feb 1980, Diana Gail, da of John Edward Bewick; 2 s (Ian b 1981, Neil b 1984); *Career* DOT 1974-75, under sec ECGD 1986 (joined 1966, asst sec 1982), gp dir ECGD Insur Servs; *Recreations* clay pigeon shooting; *Style—* Colin Foxall, Esq; ECGD, Crown Building, Cathays Park, Cardiff (☎ 0222 82 4664, fax 0222 82 4003, telex 0222 497305/497522)

FOXELL, Alan William Humphrey; s of The Rev Maurice Frederick Foxell, KCVO, (d 1981), and Mariana Helene Emily, *née* Fountain (d 1975); *b* 25 June 1916; *Educ* Lancing, Univ of London (BA, MB, BS, FRCPath); *m* 28 Sept 1948, Maureen Daphne, da of Sir Frederick Rebbeck (d 1965), of N Ireland; 4 s (Richard b 1950, Martin b 1953 (decd), Anthony b 1958, Peter b 1961); *Career* former conslt haematologist The London Hosp; liveryman Worshipful Soc of Apothecaries of London, freeman City of London; *Recreations* golf, watercolour painting, bookbinding; *Style—* Alan W H Foxell, Esq

FOXELL, Clive Arthur Peirson; CBE; s of Arthur Turner Foxell (d 1955), and Lillian, *née* Ellerman (d 1979); *b* 27 Feb 1930; *Educ* Harrow HS, London Univ (BSc); *m* 1956, Shirley Ann Patey, da of Idwal Morris; 1 da (Elizabeth); *Career* mangr GEC Semiconductor Labs 1968, md GEC Semiconductors Ltd 1971; dep dir of res PO 1975, dept dir PO Procurement Exec 1978-79, dir of purchasing PO 1980, dir of procurement Br Telecom 1981, dir Br Telecommunications Systems Ltd 1982-, chief exec procurement Br Telecom 1983-85, chm Fulcrum Communications Ltd 1985-86; memb: Cncl IEE 1975-78 and 1982-85 and 1987- (vice-chm Electronics Div 1980-81, dep chm 1982-83, chm 1983-84), SRC Engrg Bd 1977-80, SERC cncl 1986-, DTI CS Ctee 1985-88, ACARD Working Pty on Inf Tech 1981, Bulgin Premium IERE 1964, Bd Br Telecom 1986-; Liveryman Worshipful Co of Engrs; FEng, FIEE, FInst P, FIP & S; *Books* Low Noise Microwave Amplifiers (1968), numerous articles and papers on electronics; *Recreations* photography, railways; *Style—* Clive Foxell Esq; 4 Meades Lane, Chesham, Bucks (☎ 0494 785737); Br Telecom, Btcentre, 81 Newgate St, London EC1A 7AJ

FOXLEY-NORRIS, Air Chief Marshal Sir Christopher Neil; GCB (1973, KCB 1968, CB 1966), DSO (1945), OBE (1956); s of Major John Perceval Foxley-Norris, Cheshire Regt (d 1922), and Dorothy Brabant Smith; *b* 16 Mar 1917; *Educ* Winchester, Trinity Coll Oxford (hon fellow 1974), Middle Temple; *m* 1948, Joan Lovell, da of Major Percy H Hughes (d 1953), of Crondall, Hants; *Career* Air Chief Marshal 1970, chief of personnel and logistics MOD 1971-74, ret; chm: Battle of Britain Fighter Assoc 1978-, Leonard Cheshire Fndn 1974-82 (chm emeritus 1982-), General Portfolio Life Insur Co, Gardening for the Disabled Tst 1980-; chm Ex-RAF and Dependants Severely Disabled Holiday Trust 1984-; vice-pres Royal United Services Inst; CBIM; *Recreations* golf, cricket, writing, bridge; *Clubs* RAF, Huntercombe Golf, Lucifers; *Style—* Air Chief Marshal Sir Christopher Foxley-Norris, GCB, DSO, OBE; Tumble Wood, Northend Common, Henley-on-Thames, Oxon (☎ Turville Heath 457)

FOXON, (Harold) Peter; OBE (1976); s of William Henry Foxon (d 1967), and Kathleen Avis, *née* Perry; *b* 7 April 1919; *Educ* Bancrofts; *m* 1948, Elizabeth Mary, da of Capt Harold Butterfield (d 1974); 1 s, 3 da; *Career* Capt RCS E Africa and ME, dep chief exec and md Inchcape & Co Ltd 1979-84; *Recreations* golf; *Clubs* Oriental, City; *Style—* Peter Foxon, Esq, OBE; 48 Abingdon Court, W8 (☎ 01 937 8113); Tanglin, Second Avenue, Frinton on Sea, Essex

FOXWELL, Lady Edith Sybil; *née* Lambart; only child of Capt Hon Lionel John Olive Lambart, DSO, RN (ka 1940, 2 s of late 9 Earl of Cavan; bro of 10 and 11 Earl), and Adelaide Douglas, *née* Randolph; raised to the rank of an Earl's da 1947; *b* 11 June 1918; *m* 28 Feb 1940 (m dis 1975), Maj Ivan Cottam Foxwell, *qv*, 2 da (Zia b 1940, Atalanta Edith b 1956); *Career* public relations consultant; *Recreations* travelling, swimming, charitable activities; *Clubs* Windsor Polo, Cirencester Polo; *Style—* Lady Edith Foxwell; Home Farm, Sherston, Wilts (☎ Malmesbury 840200)

FOXWELL, Ivan Cottam; er s of Lt-Col Herbert Somerton Foxwell (died on active service 1943); *b* 22 Feb 1914; *Educ* Stubbington House, Wellington, RMC Sandhurst; *m* 28 Feb 1940 (m dis 1975), Lady Edith, *qv*; 2 da (Zia b 1940, m 1968 David Kruger, 1 s; and Atalanta b 1956, m Prince Stefano Massimo, *qv*); *Career* substantive Maj Royal Norfolk Regt, served BEF France 1940, France and Germany 1944-45, film prodr and screenwriter 1947-; prodns incl: No Room at the Inn, Guilt is my Shadow, Stephan Zweig's Twenty Four Hours of a Woman's Life, The Intruder, The Colditz Story, Manuela, A Touch of Larceny, Tiara Tahiti, The Quiller Memorandum, Evelyn Waugh's Decline and Fall; *Recreations* reading, writing, swimming; *Clubs* Buck's, Pratt's; *Style—* Ivan Foxwell, Esq; c/o Baker Tilley, Clement House, 99 Aldwych, London WC2 4JY

FOXWELL, Rupert Edward Theodore; s of Peter Cottam Foxwell, of Farnham, Surrey, and Marika, *née* Soutzos, of London; *b* 24 Nov 1954; *Educ* Radley, Magdalene Coll Cambridge (MA); *m* 5 May 1979, Penelope, da of Brig Sir Nicholas Somerville, of Greywell, Hants; 3 s (Jonathan, Mark, Edward); *Career* slr Allen and Overy 1979, dir Barclays de Zoete Wedd Ltd 1983-86, md euro investmt banking div Prudential-Bache London 1986-88, curr exec dir UBS-Phillips and Drew; memb Law Soc 1979; tstee First Challenge Tst; *Recreations* shooting, driving; *Style—* Rupert Foxwell, Esq; UBS-Phillips & Drew, Broadgate, London EC3 (☎ 01 628 4444, car tel 0860 372 651)

FOXWOOD, Capt Philip Anthony; o s of Maj Prince Ibrahim Fazil, RA (d 1978; naturalized a British subject 1920; of Franco-Turkish descent; gggs of Muhammad Ali Pasha, Vali of Egypt), by his w Kate (d 1973), o da of Calvin Amory Stevens and his w Jessie Isabelle *née* Prendagast, of NY; assumed the additional christian name of Anthony in lieu of forename Ali; assumed the neological surname of Foxwood 1969; *b* 5 Sept 1935; *Educ* Harrow, RMA Sandhurst; *m* 12 July 1971, (Rose) Mary, o da of Clifford Mansel Reece, QC (d 1973), of Oakford Bridge, nr Tiverton, Devon; 1 s (Hugo Charles Amory b 1973); *Career* 2 Lt Coldstream Gds 1955, Capt No 1 (Gds) Ind Co The Parachute Regt 1961, Adjt 2 Bn Coldstream Gds 1964, severely wounded Aden, invalided 1966; individual memb Royal Assoc for Disability and Rehabilitation 1977- and Oxon War Pensions Ctee 1986-; Hon Tres W Oxon Cons Assoc 1985-; *Recreations* gardening, genealogy; *Clubs* Boodle's, Elmfield Cons Club (Witney), Pratt's; *Style—* Captain Philip Foxwood; Ann's Cottage, Ramsden, Oxford OX7 3AZ (☎ 099386 592)

FOYLE, Christina Agnes Lilian; da of William Alfred Foyle (d 1963), and Christina Tulloch (d 1976); *b* 30 Jan 1911; *Educ* Aux Villas Unspunnen, Interlaken Switzerland; *m* 1938, Ronald Frederick Batty; *Career* began Foyle's Literary Luncheons, where distinguished writers and artists meet the reading public, 1930; memb ctee Univ of Essex, cncl memb Royal Soc of Arts 1963-69 (chm E Anglican Region 1978); landowner (1000 acres);; *Recreations* book collecting, reading; *Style—* Miss Christina Foyle; Beeleigh Abbey, Maldon, Essex; Foyles, Charing Cross Rd, London WC2

FOYLE, (William Richard) Christopher; s of (William) Richard Foyle (d 1957), and Alice, da of Eugen Kun, of Vienna; the Foyles are an ancient W Country family (*see* Burke's Landed Gentry, 18 Edn, vol 3); *b* 20 Jan 1943; *Educ* Radley; *m* 27 July 1983, Catherine Mary, da of Rev David William Forrester Jelleyman, of Melbourn, Cambs; 3 da (Charlotte b 1984, Annabel b 1985, Christine b 1987); *Career* trained in publishing and bookselling in London, Tuebingen, Berlin, Helsinki and Paris; mangr W & G Foyle Ltd 1965-72, ptnr Emson & Dudley and dir Emson & Dudley Securities Ltd 1972-78; proprietor Christopher Foyle Aviation (Leasing) Co Ltd; md: Air Foyle Ltd 1978-, Air Foyle Executive Ltd; memb: air tport devpt ctee Gen Aviation Mfrs and Traders Assoc 1986-, small business ctee Aviation Trg Assoc 1987-; *Recreations* travel, skiing, flying, reading non-fiction, wine and food; *Clubs* White's; *Style—* Christopher Foyle, Esq; c/o Lloyds Bank plc, 16 St James's St, London SW1A 1EY; Air Foyle Ltd, Halcyon House, Luton Airport, Luton, Beds LU2 9LU (☎ 0582 419792, telex 825538 AFOYLE G, fax 0582 400958)

FOYLE, Grace Joan; da of Frederick Joseph Hayball (d 1948), of Devon, and Alice Harriet, *née* Bondfield; *b* 9 April 1918; *Educ* The Kings Sch Ottery St Mary, Inchbold Sch of Design (Dip Fine Arts); *m* 25 July 1942, Gilbert Eric Foyle (d 1975), s of Gilbert Samuel Foyle (d 1971); 1 s (Roger John b 1944), 1 da (Angela Fenella b 1956); *Career* pres Foyles Educnl Ltd 1988- (dir 1973-88), cncllr Worthing Borough Cncl 1966-72, chm Friends of Worthing Museum 1972-74; *Recreations* tennis, local ctee work and fund raising; *Clubs* West Worthing Tennis, Parrot; *Style—* Mrs Grace J Foyle; Dukes Cottage, The Street, Patching, W Sussex; Foyles Educnl Ltd, Feldon House, Victoria Way, Burgess Hill, Sussex (☎ 04446 2797)

FOYLE, John Ernest; s of Gilbert Foyle (d 1971), of Eastbourne (founder of W & G Foyle Ltd, booksellers, 1903), and Ethel, *née* Cook (d 1981); *b* 9 Oct 1920; *Educ* Christ's Coll, Finchley; *m* 29 March 1952, Margaret Patricia, da of William White, of Haywards Heath; 2 s (Lance b 14 Aug 1954, Robert 2 May 1958), 1 da (Deborah b 16 May 1961); *Career* served RE 1940-46 as Lt in Africa and Italy; dir: Foyles Educnl Ltd 1947-, Unifoyle Ltd 1977-, Croom Helm Publishers 1972-78; govr Gilbert Foyle Educnl Tst; *Recreations* fishing, bowls, travel; *Clubs* IOD, Royal Cwlth; *Style—* John Foyle, Esq; Feldon House, Victoria Way, Burgesshill, W Sussex (☎ 04446 2797)

FOYLE, John Lewis; s of Roland Bernard Foyle, of Portsmouth, Hants, and Rose Vera, *née* Taylor; *b* 7 June 1948; *Educ* Portsmouth Northern GS, St John's Coll Cambridge (MA); *m* 19 Feb 1972, Patricia Mary, da of John Victor Ketteringham (d 1986), of Ruthin, Clwyd; 3 s (James b 1972, Thomas d 1978, William b 1980); *Career* sec: Inflation Accounting Steering Gp 1976-78, jnt Exchanges Ctee 1982-; md ops and market sec London Int Fin Futures Exchange, dir Assoc Futures Brokers and Dealers 1985-; FCA 1973; *Recreations* sport, music; *Style—* John Foyle, Esq; Brookmead, Moat Farm Chase, Chipping Hill, Witham, Essex CM8 2DE; Liffe, Royal Exchange, London EC3V 3PJ (☎ 01 623 0444, fax 01 588 3624)

FOZARD, Dr John William; OBE (1981); s of John Fozard (d 1958), and Eleanor, *née* Paulkit (d 1948); *b* 16 Jan 1928; *Educ* London Univ (BSc), Coll of Aeronautics (Dip), Cranfield Inst of Technol; *m* 1, 1951 (m dis 1985), Mary, da of late RSM Charles Burley Ward, VC; 2 s; *m* 2, 1985, Gloria Ditmars Stanchfield, wid of Alan Roberts, of Alexandria, Virginia, USA; *Career* chief designer Harrier 1963-78, exec dir Hawker Siddeley Avn 1971-78, mktg dir Kingston-Brough Div, Br Aerospace 1978-84 vice-pres Royal Aeronautical Soc 1980-84 (pres 1986-87); dir of Special Projects Mil Aircraft Divn, Br Aerospace 1984-89 (ret 1989); Br Silver Medal for Aeronautics; Hon DSc Strathclyde 1983; fell of UK Fellowship of Engrg 1984, fell of Royal Soc of London 1987; RAes 1977, CEng, FRAeS, FIMechE, FAIAA, FRSA; James Clayton Prize, Inst of Mech Engrs 1983, The Mullard Award (with RS Hooper) Royal Soc 1983; Lindbergh Prof of Aerospace History, Smithsonian Inst Nat Air & Space Museum,

Washington DC, USA for 1988; visiting prof in aircraft design Univ of Michigan at Ann Arbor 1989-; visiting prof in Aeronautics Kingston Poly 1983-87; *Books* many papers in specialist aeronautical jnls and tech press 1958-; *Recreations* music, engrg history; *Style*— Dr John Fozard, OBE; 1. 306 N Columbus St, Alexandria, VA 22314, USA (☎ 703 549 5142); Smithsonian Institution, National Air and Space Museum, Washington DC, 20560, USA (☎ 202 357 2515)

FRAENKEL, Peter Maurice; s of Ernest Fraenkel and Luise, *née* Tessmann; *b* 5 July 1915; *Educ* Battersea Poly, Imperial Coll London (BSc); *m* 1946, Hilda Muriel, da of William Norman; 2 da; *Career* sr ptnr Peter Fraenkel and Ptnrs (consulting engrs), chm Peter Fraenkel Int Ltd; Queen's Award for Export 1982); FEng, FICE, FIStructE; *Clubs* Athaneum; *Style*— P M Fraenkel Esq; Peter Fraenkel and Partners, Tuition House, 27-37 St George's Rd, Wimbledon, London SW19 3EU (☎ 01 879 0335)

FRAKER, Ford McKinstry; s of Harrison Shedd Fraker, and Marjorie Tomlinson Fraker (d 1987); *b* 15 July 1948; *Educ* Phillips Acad Andover Mass USA, Harvard (BA); *m* 24 Dec 1984, Linda Margaret, da of T Hanson; 1 s (Jonathan b 2 May 1987), 1 da (Antonia b 21 Jan 1986); *Career* vice pres and regnl mangr Chemical Bank (NY) Bahrain Arabian Gulf 1977-79; Saudi Int Bank London: mangr Middle East 1979-82, asst gen mangr, hd Gen Banking 1982-85, hd credit 1985-; dir Saudi Int Bank Nassau 1987-; *Recreations* tennis, art, travel; *Clubs* Nantucket Yacht, RAC, Overseas Bankers; *Style*— Ford M Fraker, Esq; 51 Clarendon Rd, London W11; (☎ 01 727 2567); 12 Mt. Vernon St, Nantucket, Mass 02554

FRAKES, Ronald Alfred; s of Alfred Henry Frakes (d 1946), of London, and Edith Amelia, *née* Marsden (d 1981); *b* 2 June 1928; *m* 27 May 1950, (Joan) Heather, da of John Austen Chamberlain (d 1977), of London; 2 da (Janet b 1958, Alison b 1960); *Career* Wireless operator serv Malaya (SEAC) RAF 1946-48; freelance heraldic artist 1972-; numerous commissions include: painting Arms of Queen Elizabeth I and Queen Elizabeth II plus Heraldic symbols of England, Scotland, Ireland and Wales in the border of a Royal Charter presented to the Painter-Stainers in 1981; memb: Richard III Soc, Heraldry Soc; Freeman: City of London 1972, Worshipful Co of Painter-Stainers 1972 (Liveryman 1981); FRSA 1981; *Recreations* study of medieval history; *Clubs* Queenhithe Ward; *Style*— Ronald Frakes, Esq; 77 Highfield Rd, Woodford Green, Essex IG8 8JB (☎ 01 504 6717)

FRAME, Sir Alistair Gilchrist; s of Alexander Frame and Mary, *née* Fraser; *b* 3 April 1929; *Educ* Glasgow Univ, Cambridge Univ; *m* 1953, Sheila, *née* Mathieson; 1 da; *Career* dir Britoil 1982, chm RTZ Corpn 1985-(dir 1973-85), dir Plessey Co Ltd 1978, currently dir Glaxo Holding plc Eurotunnel; former : memb Engrg Cncl, memb NEB, dir Reactor and Res Gps UKAEA; FEng, BSc; kt 1981; *Style*— Sir Alistair Frame; 6 St James's Square, London SW1Y 4LD

FRAME, Frank Riddell; *b* 15 Feb 1930; *Educ* Hamilton Acad, Glasgow Univ (MA, LLB); *m* 1958, Maureen; 1 s, 1 da; *Career* slr; dep chm The Hongkong and Shanghai Banking Corpn; dir: The British Bank of the Middle East, Marine Midland Banks Inc, Swire Pacific Ltd; chm South China Morning Post Ltd 1981-87; *Clubs* The Hong Kong; *Style*— Frank Frame, Esq; 19 Middle Gap Rd, Hong Kong (☎ 5 8496143); The Hongkong and Shanghai Banking Corp, 1 Queen's Rd Central, Hong Kong (☎ 5 8221133)

FRAME, Roger Campbell Crosbie; s of Andrew Crosbie Frame, of Giffnock, Glasgow, and Jessie Caldwell, *née* Campbell; *b* 7 June 1949; *Educ* Glasgow Acad; *m* 10 Sept 1973, Angela Maria, da of Louis Evaristi, of Giffnock, Glasgow; 2 s (Nicholas Roger b 1976, Mark Christopher b 1980), 1 da (Lauren Charlotte b 1988); *Career* CA; sr ptnr Frame & Co; dir: Camos Ltd, Frame & Co mgmnt servs Ltd; tres Glasgow Gp of Artists 1983-; sec: Glasgow Eastern Merchants and Tradesman Soc, Royal Scottish Soc of Painters in Watercolour (RSW) 1986-, chm James Custator Wards Fund (Glasgow Univ) 1984-, offr Incorpn of Weavers of Glasgow; Freeman City of Glasgow, Freeman City of London; *Recreations* clay pigeon shooting, art; *Clubs* Glasgow Art; *Style*— Roger C C Frame, Esq; Dunglass, 56 Manse Rd, Bearsden, Glasgow G61 3PN; Frame & Co Chartered Accountants, 29 Waterloo St, Glasgow G2 6BZ (☎ 041 226 3838)

FRANCE, Sir Arnold William; GCB (1972, KCB 1965, CB 1957); s of William Ernest France (d 1939), of Knutsford, Cheshire, and Southport, Lancs; *b* 20 April 1911; *Educ* Bishop's Stortford Coll; *m* 1940, Frances Margaret Linton, da of Dr Charles John Linton Palmer (d 1926), of Gosport; 4 da (*see* J N B Penny); *Career* served WWII, Capt, Middle East; civil servant; HM Treasy 1945-63, Miny of Health 1963-68 (perm sec 1964-68), chm Bd Inland Revenue 1968-73, ret; *Recreations* reading; *Clubs* Reform; *Style*— Sir Arnold France, GCB; Thornton Cottage, Lingfield, Surrey (☎ 0364 832278)

FRANCIS, The Ven Edward Reginald; s of Alfred John Francis (d 1978), of 43 Moning Rd, Dover, Kent, and Elsie Hilda, *née* Hiscock; *b* 31 Jan 1929; *Educ* Monmouth, Dover GS, Rochester Theol Coll; *m* 21 Oct 1950, Joyce Noreen, da of George James Atkins (d 1935); 3 s (Paul, Nigel, Jonathan); *Career* ordained 1961, chaplain Training Ship Arethusa and asst curate All Saints Frindsbury Rochester 1961-64, vicar St Williams Chatham 1964-73, vicar and rural dean Rochester 1973-79, archdeacon of Bromley 1979-; memb Gen Synod 1981-, jt chm Canterbury and Rochester Diocesan Cncl for Social Responsibility 1983-88; ACII 1958; *Recreations* ornithology, walking, rugby football, poetry; *Style*— The Ven the Archdeacon of Bromley

FRANCIS, Gp Capt Geoffrey; DSO (1941), DFC (1940); s of F S Francis (d 1950), and Lillian, *née* Drake; *b* 13 Jan 1907; *Educ* Wellington, RAF Cadet Coll Cranwell; *m* 1, 6 June 1936 (m dis 1947), Patience Elinor, da of Lt-Col Sir Thomas Salt, DSO (d 1946); 1 da (Jessica b 1 Jan 1942); m 2, 4 March 1949, Joan Millicent Kirkland Vavasour, da of Arthur John Robb (d 1956); 1 s (Andrew b 29 Nov 1951), 3 da (Rosemary b 14 July 1950, Jilly b 12 March 1955, Miranda b 4 June 1957); *Career* 202 Flying Boat Sqdn Malta 1928, i/c Station Flt Malta 1930, pa to C in C Coast Cmd Lee on Solent 1932, 201 Flying Boat Sqdn Calshot 1933-34, HQ Coastal Cmd Lee-on-Solent 1935-36, HQ Far East Cmd Singapore 1936, 230 Flying Boat Sqdn Singapore 1938, Ceylon 1939, i/c Alexandria 1940-41 (despatches 1940), 201 Gp temp i/c Alexandria 1941, No 4 (C) Operational Trg Unit, i/c Invergordon 1941-42, (despatches 1942), HQ Coastal Cmd Air Staff 1943, attached C in C US Pacific Fleet 1943; HQ SE Asia Cmd: Planning Staff Delhi 1944, Air Cmd, Air Staff Delhi 1944; RAF Station Kogalla i/c Ceylon 1944-45, RAF Station Seletar, i/c Singpore 1945, Air Miny 1946, HQ 38 Gp Sr Offr Admin 1947, RAF Station i/c Netheravon 1948, RAF Station i/c Bassingbourn 1949, resigned cmmn 1951; farmer Sussex 1951-56; owned and operated Sandwich Boatyard Kent 1956-70, athletics; runner up for Victor Ludorum Cranwell, broke Cranwell record for 120 yard Hurdles 1926; sailed from Hong Kong to Singapore 1938, fndr memb RAF YC; Freeman City of London 1928, memb Worshipful Co of Cordwainers 1927; Greek Flying Cross 1946; *Recreations* yachting; *Clubs* Royal Cruising Club, RAF YC, Royal Lymington YC; *Style*— Gp-Capt Geoffrey Francis, DSO, DFC; 28 Stanley Rd, Lymington, Hants SO41 9SG (☎ 0590 74616)

FRANCIS, George Carwardine; s of Guy Lancelot Brereton Francis (d 1962); *b* 15 April 1929; *Educ* Malvern; *m* 1960, Barbara Peggy, da of John Francis Brooke (d 1977), of W Chiltington; 2 da; *Career* slr; md The Chepstow Racecourse plc 1963-, vice chm Racecourse Assoc Ltd 1986-; *Recreations* cricket, racquets, real tennis, squash, shooting; *Clubs* MCC, Free Foresters, I Zingari; *Style*— George Francis, Esq; East Cliff, Chepstow, Gwent NP6 7PT (☎ 02912 622072)

FRANCIS, Capt John Lionel; DL (Dyfed 1971); s of Maj John Francis, DSO, TD, DL (d 1960); *b* 4 July 1921; *Educ* Cheltenham, RAC Cirencester; *m* 1947, Susan Mary Macleod (d 1986), da of Arthur Macleod Clarke (d 1932), and gda of Ven A F Clarke, Archdeacon of Lancaster; 2 da (Sophie Patricia Marguerite (Mrs Boggis-Rolfe), Judith Joanna Mary (Mrs Bromley-Davenport); *Career* served WWII as Capt 17/21 Lancers in N Africa, Sicily and Italy (wounded twice), Capt Reserve; High Sheriff of Carmarthenshire 1969; pres Carmarthen Con Assoc (chm 1973-77), chm Mid-West Wales Con Cncl, vice-pres Carmarthen & Cardigan Country Landowners Assoc (chm 1957-60), dir Carmarthen Journal Co; OStJ 1977; FRICS; *Clubs* Cavalry & Guards; *Style*— Capt John Francis, DL; Llwynhelig, Llandeilo, Dyfed SA19 6AZ (☎ 0558 822 302)

FRANCIS, Dr John Michael; s of William Winston Francis (d 1939) of Haverfordwest, Pembrokeshire, and Beryl Margaret, *née* Savage; *b* 1 May 1939; *Educ* Gowerton Co GS, Royal Coll of Science, Imperial Coll London (BSc, ARCS, PhD, DIC); *m* 14 Sept 1963, Eileen, da of Hugh Foster Sykes (d 1977), of Hutton Mount, Shenfield, Essex; 2 da (Sarah Katherine b 1966, Rachel Victoria b 1968); *Career* res offr R & D Dept Berkeley Nuclear Labws CEGB 1963-70, first dir Soc religion Church of Scotland 1970-74, sr res fell energy studies Heriot-Watt Univ 1974-76, asst sec SO 1981- (princ 1976-80); conslt sci technol and social ethics World Cncl of Churches Geneva 1971-73; chm: sub ctee on religion and technol Church of Scotland 1980-, Edinburgh Forum 1986-; dir: Nature Conservancy Cncl Scotland 1984; memb: Oil Devpt cncl for Scotland 1973-76, Scottish advsy ctee Nature Conservancy Cncl 1974-76, Independent Cmmn on Tport 1974-, cncl Nat Tst for Scotland 1984-, St Giles Cathedral Edinburgh; assoc memb Scottish Inst of Human Relations; *Books* Scotland in Turmoil (1973), Changing Directions (jtly 1974), The Future as an Academic Discipline (1975), Facing up to Nuclear Power (1976), The Future of Scotland (1977), contrib to scientific and professional jls and periodicals; *Recreations* ecumenical travels, hill walking, theatre; *Style*— Dr John Francis; 49 Gilmour Rd, Newington, Edinburgh EH16 5NU (☎ 031 667 3996); Scottish Headquarters, Nature Conservancy Council, 12 Hope Terrace, Edinburgh EH9 2AS (☎ 031 447 4784)

FRANCIS, His Excellency Sir Laurie Justice; *b* 30 August 1918; *Educ* Otago Boys HS, Victoria Univ of Wellington, Univ of Otago (LLB); *m* 1952, Heather Margaret McFarland; 3 da; *Career* barr and slr, sr partner in Dunedin firm of Gilbert, Francis, Jackson and Co 1964-76; New Zealand high cmmr to Aust 1976-; kt 1982; *Recreations* jazz and classical music; *Style*— His Excellency Sir Laurie Francis, NZ High Commissioner to Aust; 21 Mugga Way, Red Hill, ACT 2603, Australia

FRANCIS, His Hon Judge (William) Norman; s of Llewellyn Francis (d 1953), of Llanishen, Cardiff, and Margaret Ceridwen, *née* Davis (d 1963); *b* 19 Mar 1921; *Educ* Bradfield Coll, Lincoln Coll Oxford (BCL, MA); *m* 1951, Anthea Constance, da of James Leslie Kerry (d 1951), of Llanishen, Cardiff; 1 s, 1 da; *Career* serv WWII Lt RA Europe; barr Gray's Inn 1946; dep chm Brecklock Qtr Sessions 1962-71, county ct judge 1969 (converted to circuit judge 1972); cncllr diocese of Llandaff 1979; *Recreations* hockey, walking; *Style*— His Hon Judge Norman Francis; 2 The Woodlands, Lisvane, Cardiff (☎ 0222 753070)

FRANCIS, Richard Trevor Langford; s of Eric Roland Francis and Esther Joy, *née* Todd; *b* 10 Mar 1934; *Educ* Uppingham, Univ Coll Oxford (MA); *m* 1, 1958 (m dis), Beate Ohlhagen; 2 s; m 2, 1974, Elizabeth Penelope Anne Fairfax Crone; 2 s; *Career* joined BBC 1958; former asst ed Panorama and 24 Hours; headed Euro Broadcasting Union coverage of US presidential elections 1968 and 1972, also Apollo missions 1969-72; asst head Current Affrs TV 1971-73; controller BBC N Ireland 1973-77, dir News and Current Affrs BBC 1977-82, md BBC Radio 1982-86; dep chm Visnews 1979-82; vice-chm Br Exec IPI 1982-86; dir-gen Br Cncl 1987-; *Recreations* offshore sailing, photography, the children; *Clubs* Reform; *Style*— Richard Francis, Esq; The British Council, 10 Spring Gardens, London SW1A 2BN (☎ 01 930 8466)

FRANCIS, Rita Winifred; da of James Stone (d 1962), of Manchester, and Winifred, *née* Myatt; *b* 10 Dec 1947; *Educ* Alderman Newtons GS for Girls; *m* 7 Jan 1967 (m dis 1983), Graham Francis; 1 s (Scott James b 4 June 1968), 1 da (Keely b 26 March 1970); *Career* dir: Ensign Computers Ltd 1985, Ensign Systems Ltd 1986, Ensign Computer Hldgs Ltd 1986-, T F Services Ltd 1986; T F Gp of Cos 1988-; *Style*— Mrs Rita Francis; The Lodge, Stanhope Gdns, Wigston, Leics; Ensign House, Vaughan Way, Leicester LE1 4SG (☎ 0533 532 555, fax 0533 536 834, car tel 0860 387 510)

FRANCKE, John Valdemar Gordon; s of Frederick Francke (d 1955), of 263 Sheen Lane, London SW14, and Helen, *née* Craven (d 1970); gs of Max Francke (b 1867) holder of the Order of the Red Eagle (Prussia); *b* 1933,; *Educ* Harrow, St Catharines Coll Cambridge Univ; *m* 1, 23 March 1957, Joan Deirdre, da of Sydney Bolster (d 1979); 1 da (Caroline b 1958); m 2, 29 June 1968, Elizabeth Ann, da of John Geoffrey Lax Lovell (d 1965), of Haywards Heath; 1 s (Giles b 1973), 2 da (Alison b 1969, Angela b 1975); *Career* Offr Cadet 15/19 Hussars 1953; Selection Tst Ltd 1955-57, Hawker (Aircraft) Ltd 1957-59, Vickers Armstrong Aircraft Ltd 1959-60, Handley Page Ltd 1960-70, Sci Museum 1970, BUA, Br Caledonian V 1971-87, fndr own company J F Aircraft 1987-; *Style*— John Francke, Esq; Glengarriff, Stone Quarry Rd, Chelwood Gate, Haywards Heath, Sussex RH17 7LS

FRANCKLIN, Cdr (Mavourn Baldwin) Philip; DSC (1940); s of Capt Philip Francklin, MVO, RN (ka 1914), by his w Irene, da of Vice Adm Sir Baldwin Wake Walker, 2 Bt, CVO, CMG; The Captain's mother was Hon Alice Jervis, da of 3 Viscount St Vincent; *b* 15 Jan 1913; *Educ* RNC Dartmouth; *m* 1949, Xenia Alexandra Riddel, da of Alexander Davidson, of Tinna Park, Co Wicklow; 2 s (Liell b 1952, William b 1958) and 1 s decd; 1 da (Rose b 1960); *Career* Cdr RN Norway, N and S

Atlantic 1940-43 (despatches twice), Naval-Air Asst to 5 Sea Lord 1947-49, Korea 1950-51, asst Naval attaché Paris 1952-53, Lord-Lieut Notts 1972-83 (DL 1963-68, Vice-Lieut 1968-72); Croix de Guerre (France) 1940; KStJ 1972; *Recreations* shooting, golf; *Clubs* Boodle's; *Style—* Cdr Philip Francklin, DSC; Gonalston Hall, Notts NG14 7JA (☎ 0602 663635)

FRANCOME, John; MBE (1986); s of Norman John Francome and Lillian Maud Francome; *b* 13 Dec 1952; *Educ* Park Sr High Sch Swindon; *m* 1976, Miriam, da of Andrew Stringer, London; *Career* champion jockey seven times, 1138 wins (Nat Hunt Record); racehorse trainer; *Books* Born Lucky (autobiography (1985), Eavesdropper (1986), Riding High (1987); *Recreations* tennis, music; *Style—* John Francome Esq, MBE; Windy Hollow Stud, Sheepdrove, Lambourn, Berks

FRANK, Sir (Robert) Andrew; 4 Bt (UK 1920), of Withyham, Sussex; s (by 2 m) of Sir Robert John Frank, 3 Bt (d 1987), and his 2 w Margaret Joyce, *née* Truesdale; *b* 16 May 1964; *Educ* Eton; *Heir* none; *Career* actor, prodr; *Recreations* theatre, travel; *Style—* Sir Andrew Frank, Bt; 50 Under-the-Wood, Bisham, Marlow, Bucks (☎ 06284 75298)

FRANK, Sir (Frederick) Charles; OBE (1946); s of Frederick Frank (d 1971), and Medora Frank; *b* 6 Mar 1911; *Educ* Thetford GS, Ipswich Sch, Lincoln Coll Oxford; *m* 1940, Maia Maita, yst da of Prof Boris Michaelovich Asché (d1943); 1 c (d at birth); *Career* scientist; Air Scientific Intelligence 1940-46, Bristol Univ dept of physics 1946-76, prof 1954, head of dept 1969-76; vice-pres Royal Soc 1967-69, Royal Medallist 1979; FRS; kt 1977; *Recreations* gardening; *Clubs* Athenaeum; *Style—* Sir Charles Frank, OBE; Orchard Cottage, Grove Rd, Coombe Dingle, Bristol BS9 2RL (☎ 0272 681708)

FRANK, David Thomas; s of Thomas Frank (d 1984), of Robertsford, Shrewsbury, and Margaret McCrea, *née* Cowan; *b* 29 April 1954; *Educ* Shrewsbury, Bristol Univ (LLB); *m* 10 July 1982, Diane Lillian, da of Stephen Nash Abbott, of Farnham Common, Bucks; 1 s (Charles b 1988), 1 da (Lucinda b 1986); *Career* admitted slr 1979, ptnr Slaughter and May 1986- (asst slr 1979-86); *Recreations* lawn tennis, golf; *Style—* David Frank, Esq; Slaughter and May, 35 Basinghall St, London EC2V 5DB (☎ 01 600 1200, fax 01 726 0038, telex 883486)

FRANK, Sir Douglas George Horace; QC (1964); s of late George Maurice Frank, of Osterley, and Agnes Winifred Frank; *b* 16 April 1916; *Educ* City of London Sch and privately; *m* 1, 1939, Margaret Clara, da of Alfred William Shaw, OBE; 1 s, 2 da; m 2, 1963, Sheila Frances, da of late Cdre Lawrence King Beauchamp, RN, and widow of Jack Eric Jones; 2 da; m 3, 1979, Audrey, yr da of Charles Leslie Thomas, of Neath, Glam; *Career* served Lt RA 1939-43; barr Gray's Inn 1946, bencher 1970; memb ctee for Public Participation in Planning 1968; pres Lands Tribnl 1973- 89; dep judge of the High Court 1975-; hon pres Anglo American Real Property Inst 1980-; one time dep boundary cmmr for England and Wales; kt 1976; *Style—* Sir Douglas Frank, QC; 1 Verulam Buildings, London WC1 (☎ 01 242 5949); Lands Tribunal, 49 Chancery Lane, London WC2 (☎ 01 831 6611)

FRANKEL, Sir Otto (Herzberg); s of late D. Ludwig Herzberg Frankel, of Vienna, and Teresa Herzberg Frankel; *b* 4 Nov 1900, Vienna; *Educ* Ag Univ of Berlin (DAgSc), Univ of New Zealand (DSc); *m* 1939, Margaret, da of F W Anderson, of Christchurch, NZ; *Career* geneticist; dir Crop Research Div Dept of Scientific and Indust Res NZ 1949-51, chief of Div of Plant Industry CSIRO Aust 1951-62 (memb of exec CSIRO 1962-6, hon res fell 1966); FAA, FRS; kt 1966; *Recreations* skiing, angling, gardening; *Style—* Sir Otto Frankel; 4 Cobby St, Campbell, ACT 2601, Australia (☎ (47 9460)

FRANKEL, William; CBE (1971); s of Isaac Frankel (d 1963), of London, and Anna, *née* Lecker (d 1946); *b* 3 Feb 1917; *Educ* Poly Secdy Sch Regent St London, Univ of London (LLB); *m* 1, 1939 (m dis 1972), Gertrude Freda, da of Louis Reed, of London; 1 s (John), 1 da (Anne); m 2, 1973, Mrs Claire Neuman, da of Herold J Schwab, of Birmingham, Alabama USA; *Career* barr Middle Temple; ed (now dir) Jewish Chronicle 1958-77; chm: Social Security Appeal Tbnl 1977-, Mental Health Review Tbnl 1978-; special advsr to The Times 1977-81, London corr Statesman (Calcutta and Delhi), ed Survey of Jewish Affairs (annual); *Books* Israel Observed: an anatomy of the state (1981); *Clubs* Athenaeum, MCC; *Style—* William Frankel, Esq, CBE; 30 Montagu Sq, London W1H 1RJ

FRANKISH, (John) Keith; s of Fred Skelton Frankish (d 1985), and Mary Frankish, *née* Ellerby (d 1983); *b* 1 August 1927; *Educ* Humberside Fndn Sch Cleethorpes; *m* 2 April 1955, Mary Hilda, da of Charles William Brunton (d 1970); 2 s (Simon Charles b 1961, John Anthony b 1964), 1 da (Susan Mary b 1957); *Career* slr; employed by Vauxhall Motors for nearly 30 years; sec and legal advsr 1971-81 (and pres 1974-79, tres 1979-81); sec and gen counsel all Gen Motors Corpns UK operations 1981-87; dir to A C Spark Plug Overseas, Delco Products Overseas and many other G M Assoc Cos 1982-87; chm Legal Ctee SMMT 1985-87, pres Luton Bedford and Dist Chamber of Commerce & Ind 1980-81; ret 1987; *Recreations* birdwatching, travel; *Style—* Keith Frankish, Esq; Garden Cottage, Cobbett Lane, Flitton, Bedford MK45 5DX (☎ 0525 60562)

FRANKLAND, Hon Mrs Barbara Mary; *née* Frankland; da of Baroness Zouche (17 holder of the title) and Sir Frederick Frankland, 10 Bt; aunt of 18 Baron Zouche; *b* 1906; *m* 1, 6 July 1926 (m dis 1937), Brig (now Sir) Otho Prior-Palmer, DSO (d 1986); 1 s (decd), 1 da (Diana de Marco b 1929); m 2, 5 July 1937 (m dis 1943), 5 Earl of Normanton (d 1967); m 3, 4 Feb 1944 (m dis 1962), Peter Lucas; resumed name of Frankland by deed poll 1958; *Style—* Hon Mrs Frankland; Ridge House, Stockland, Honiton, Devon (☎ Wilmington 325)

FRANKLAND, Dr Alfred William (Bill); s of Rev H Frankland (d 1960), of Scotby, Carlisle, and Rose, *née* West (d 1947); *b* 19 Mar 1912; *Educ* St Bees Sch, Oxford Univ (MA, DM, BCh); *m* 27 May 1941, Pauline Margaret Wrench, da of Rowland Bower Jackson (d 1972); 1 s (Andrew William b 1956) 3 da (Penelope Jane b 1946, Jenifer Rosemary b 1949, Hilary Fern b 1951); *Career* WWII serv: Lt (later Capt) RAMC 1939-46 (Far East); conslt physician (allergy) St Mary's Hosp hon sec Asthma Res Cncl 1959; Church sidesman; Liveryman Worshipful Co of Drapers 1959; memb RSM; *Books* Allergies Questions and Answers (with Doris Raff 1980), numerous articles on aerobiology and related allergic diseases; *Recreations* medicine, gardening, foreign travel; *Style—* Dr Bill Frankland; 46 Devonshire Close, London W1N 1LN (☎ 6371994); 139 Harley St, London W1N 1DJ (☎ 935 5421)

FRANKLAND, Dr (Anthony) Noble; CB (1983), CBE (1971), DFC (1944); s of Dr Edward Percy Frankland (d 1958), of Ravenstonedale, Westmorland, and Maud, *née* Metcalfe-Gibson (d 1979); *b* 4 July 1922; *Educ* Sedbergh, Trinity Coll Oxford (Open Scholar, MA, DPhil); *m* 1944, Diana Madeline Fovargue (d 1981), da of late G V Tavernor, of Madras and Southern Mahratta Rly, India; 1 s (Roger), 1 da (Linda); m 2, 1982, Sarah Katharine, da of His Hon Sir David Davies QC (d 1964); *Career* served RAF 1941-45 (Bomber Cmd 1943-45); demob Flt Lt; Narrator Air Historical Branch Air Miny 1948-51, official mil historian Cabinet Off 1951-60, dep dir of Studies Roy Inst of Int Affrs 1956-60; dir: Imp War Museum 1960-82, Imp War Museum at Duxford Airfield nr Cambridge 1976-82, Imp War Museum Ship HMS Belfast 1978-82; Rockerfeller fell Inst for Advanced Studies Princeton USA 1953, Lees Knowles lectr Trinity Coll Cambridge 1963; historical advsr Thames Television series 'The World at War' (1971-74); vice-chm: Br Nat Ctee for the Study of the Second WW 1976-82, HMS Belfast Tst 1972-78; *Books* Documents on International Affairs for 1955 (1958), For 1956 (1959), For 1957 (1960), Crown of Tragedy, Nicholas II (1960), The Strategic Air Offensive Against Germany 1939-45 (4 Volumes, jointly with the late Sir Charles Webster, 1961), The Bombing Offensive against Germany, Outlines and Perspectives (1965), Bomber Offensive, The Devastation of Europe (1970), Prince Henry Duke of Gloucester (1980); numerous articles, reviews and broadcasts; *Style—* Dr Noble Frankland; Thames Ho, Eynsham, Oxford OX8 1DA

FRANKLAND, Timothy Cecil; s of Hon Roger Nathaniel Frankland, *qv*; *b* 4 Oct 1931; *Educ* Charterhouse; *m* 4 Sept 1957 (m dis 1968), Lynette, da of Lt-Cdr Ian Hope Dundas, RNVR; 3 s; *Career* Lt 15/19 Hussars 1950-52; Binder Hamlyn & Co CAS 1952-67; dir: Hill Samuel & Co 1967-, Newman Tonks Gp; chm: James Neill Hldgs, Jarvis Porter Gp plc; FCA 1957; *Clubs* MCC, Berks GC ; *Style—* Timothy Frankland Esq; Hill Samuel & Co, 100 Wood St, London EC2 (☎ 01 628 8011)

FRANKLAND MOORE, Dr (Violet) Elizabeth; OBE (1963, MBE 1950); da of Henry Guy Bangerter (d 1915), and Eda Sarah Bangerter (d 1964); *b* 10 Dec 1901; *Educ* Private London and Switzerland; *m* 1, 17 Nov 1927 (m dis), Harold Bellet Miller, m 2, 1949, Maj Charles Frankland Moore, OBE; *Career* WWII Civil Def 1939-45, ret WVS 1962; res asst to Mr Lloyd George for Cncl of Action 1937-38, political sec to Eleanor Rathbone MP 1938-42, hon chief exec and organiser Spanish Relief Ctee 1939, organising sec Br United Aid to China 1942, hon sec Int Family Planning Assoc 1934, tstee Basque Children and After Care Tst 1942; currently: chm and tstee Sino-Br Fellowship Tst, hon dir Nat Appeal BLESMA, co fndr and dir Nat Star Centre Disabled Youth, memb cncl Distressed Gentlefolk Aid Assoc, memb cncl Prospect Hall Selly Oak Birmingham, vice-pres Youth Clubs UK United; Freeman City of London, 1984, (only woman) Liveryman Worshipful Co Bakers 1984; hon LLD Univ of Hong Kong 1974; Brilliant Star of China 1946; *Recreations* music, golf, bridge; *Clubs* Special Forces, Royal Mid-Surrey GC; *Style—* Dr Elizabeth Frankland Moore, OBE, MBE; Bede House, Manor Fields, Putney Heath, London SW15 3LT (☎ 01 788 6252)

FRANKLIN, Sir Eric Alexander; CBE (1952); s of William John Franklin (d 1942), and Sarah, *née* Hutton (d 1958); *b* 3 July 1910; *Educ* English Sch Maymyo Burma, Emmanuel Coll Cambridge; *m* 1936, Joyce Stella, da of late George Oakes Lucas, of Cambridge; *Career* Indian Civil Service 1935, dist and sessions judge Arakan 1941-42, dep sec to Govt Burma 1942-45, registrar High Court Rangoon 1946-48; dep sec to Govt Pakistan 1949-52, estab offr 1953-56, estab sec 1956-57; chm Sudan Govt Terms of Service Cmmn 1958-59, UN admin advsr to Jordanian Govt 1960-63, sr admin advsr to Nepalese Govt 1964-67; chm Cambridgeshire Soc for the Blind 1969-74 (vice-pres 1974-); Star of Jordan 1963; kt 1954; *Recreations* walking in alpine valleys, gardening; *Style—* Sir Eric Franklin, CBE; 16 Cavendish Ave, Cambridge CB1 4US (☎ 0223 248661)

FRANKLIN, George Henry; s of George Edward Franklin, RN (d 1975), and Annie Franklin; *b* 15 June 1923; *Educ* Hastings GS, Hastings Sch of Art, Architectural Assoc Sch of Architecture (AADip), Sch of Planning and Res for Regnl Devpt London (SPDip); *m* 1950, Sylvia Daisy, *née* Allen; 3 s, 1 da; *Career* WW II Capt RE; served Europe (Parachute Sqdn RE), SE Asia, Bengal Sappers and Miners Royal Indian Engrs; architect-planner Finchley Borough Cncl 1952-54, architect Christian Med Coll Punjab India 1954-57; physical planning advsr: Republic of Indonesia 1958-62, Govt of Malaysia 1963-64; Overseas Devpt Admin FCO 1966-83, conslt Third World planning and devpt; hon prof Dept of Town Planning UWIST 1982-, sr advsr Devpt Planning Unit UCL, memb Int Advsy Bd Centre for Devpt and Environmental Planning Oxford Poly, hon sec Cwlth Assoc of Planners 1984-88 (memb exec ctee 1970-80, pres 1980-84), memb exec ctee Cwlth Human Ecology Cncl 1970-; memb ed bd: Third World Planning Review 1979-, Cities 1983-; memb overseas/world service ctee United Bible Socs 1968-77; RIBA, assoc Indian Inst of Architects, FRTPI, Assoc Inst of Town Planners India, FRSA; *Recreations* bible society, third world, environmental interests and activities, promotion of physical planning, fly fishing; *Clubs* Royal Commonwealth Soc, Victory Services; *Style—* George Franklin, Esq; The Manse, Sutton Veny, Warminster, Wiltshire BA12 7AW (☎ 0985 40072)

FRANKLIN, The Hon Mrs Joan Edith; *née* Eden; JP (Essex 1966); er da of 7 Baron Auckland, MBE (d 1955), and Dorothy Ida, *née* Harvey (d 1964); *b* 31 Jan 1920; *Educ* North Foreland Lodge, Chelsea Art Sch; *m* 1, 6 Sept 1941, Rev Alfred Lisinea Pond (d 21 July 1947), s of late Chaloner Pond; 2 da (Rosemary b 1942, Sally b 1945); m 2, 31 Aug 1948, Rev Arthur Harrington Franklin, MBE, TD, er s of late Maj Percival Charles Franklin; 2 da (Elizabeth b 1949, Caroline b 1952); *Career* ATS 1939-41; chm: Chelmsford Bench 1987, govr Chelmsford Co HS for Girls; *Recreations* gardening; *Style—* The Hon Mrs Franklin, JP; Hea Corner, Mill Rd, Felsted, Dunmow, Essex CM6 3HQ (☎ 0371 820519)

FRANKLIN, John Andrew; s of Bernard Franklin (d 1979); *b* 21 Nov 1943; *Educ* Rugby, Pembroke Cambridge (MA Law and Economics); *m* 1976, Elizabeth Anthea, da of Samuel John Noel Bartley, of Constantine Bay, Cornwall; 2 s; *Career* slr Slaughter and May 1968-72, dir Morgan Grenfell & Co Ltd 1979- (joined 1972), chm First Mortgage Securities Ltd 1987-, govr Utd World Coll of the Atlantic; *Recreations* skiing, sailing, wine, golf, shooting; *Clubs* Boodle's, Royal Harwich Yacht, Hurlingham, HAC, The Leash, New York; *Style—* John Franklin Esq; Morgan Grenfell & Co Ltd, 23 Great Winchester St, London EC2P 2AX (☎ 01 588 4545)

FRANKLIN, Sir Michael David Milroy; KCB (1983), CB (1979), CMG (1972); s of Milroy Llewellyn Capon Franklin, of Trowbridge; *b* 24 August 1927; *Educ* Taunton Sch, Peterhouse Cambridge; *m* 1951, Dorothy Joan, da of James Stuart Fraser, of Wallasey, Cheshire; 2 s, 1 da; *Career* joined Miny Ag Fish and Food 1950, UK delgn to OEEC (now OECD) 1959-61, private sec to min 1961-64, under-sec Ag Fish and Food 1968-73; dep dir-gen to Directorate-Gen of Agric EEC 1973-77, dep sec Head

European Secretariat Cabinet Office 1977-82; perm under-sec Dept of Trade 1982-83, perm sec Miny Agric Fish and Food 1983-87; Dir Barclays plc 1988-; memb cncl Henley Management Coll, memb Internat Policy Cncl on Agric and Trade, memb cncl RIIA; *Clubs* Utd Oxford and Cambridge; *Style*— Sir Michael Franklin, KCB, CMG; 15 Galley Lane, Barnet, Herts EN5 4AR

FRANKLIN, Col Peter Howard Arthur Louis; DL (Essex 1977); s of Howard William Franklin (d 1961); *b* 11 Feb 1915; *Educ* Felsted, Sandhurst; *m* 1967, Vera Mary, *née* Stubbs; 1 s (step); *Career* cmmnd Essex Regt 1935, served Palestine 1936-39, Sudan 1940, Syria, Iraq and Tobruk 1941, Burma 1942-45 (despatches); Cmdt Essex ACF 1963-67; Hon Col: Essex ACF 1969-81, Royal Anglian (Essex) 1975-80; pres Essex Regimental Assoc 1962-83; chm Essex ctee East Anglian TAVR 1969-80; dir J G Franklin & Sons 1960-70; dep dir Essex Red Cross 1971-80; *Recreations* sailing, golf; *Style*— Col Peter Franklin, DL; 79 Lexden Rd, Colchester, Essex CO3 3QF (☎ 0206 576728)

FRANKLIN, Prof Raoul Norman; s of Norman George Franklin, JP (d 1977), of Auckland, NZ, and Thelma Brinley, *née* Davis; *b* 3 June 1935; *Educ* Howick DHS NZ, Auckland GS NZ, Auckland Univ (BE, BSc, ME, MSc), Oxford Univ (DPhil, MA, DSc); *m* 29 July 1961, Faith, da of Lt-Col Harold Thomson Carew Ivens (d 1951), of Beaconsfield; 2 s (Robert b 1965, Nicholas b 1967); *Career* Capt NZ Def Scientific Corps 1957-63; sr res fell RMCS Shrivenham 1961-63; Univ of Oxford: fell and tutor Keble Coll 1963-78, univ lectr 1966-78, vice chm gen bd 1971-74, memb hebdomadal cncl 1971-74 and 1976-78; vice chllr and princ City Univ 1978-; chm City Technol Ltd 1978- (3 Queens Awards), dep ed Jl of Physics D 1986-; memb: equipment sub ctee UGC 1974-78, Int Conf on Phenomena in Ionized Gases 1971-77 (chm 1976-77), plasma physics cmmn IUPAP 1976-86, science bd SERC 1982-85; tstee Ruskin Sch of Art 1974-78, memb Business in the Community 1982-, govr Ashridge Mgmnt Coll 1986-; Freeman City of London 1981, Liveryman Worshipful Co of Curriers 1984; hon fell Keble Coll Oxford 1981; FInstP, FIMA, FIEE, CBIM, FRSA; *Books* Plasma Phenomena in Ionized Gas (1976), Physical Kinetics (ed 1981), Interaction of Intense Electromagnetic Fields with Plasma (1981); *Recreations* walking, gardening, tennis; *Clubs* Athenaeum; *Style*— Prof Raoul Franklin; 20 Myddelton Square, London EC1R 1YE; The City University, Northampton Square, London EC1V 0HB (☎ 01 253 4399 ext 3000, fax 01 250 0837)

FRANKLIN, Richard Harrington; CBE (1973); s of late Percival Charles Franklin, of Twickenham, and late Winifred Eliza Mary; *b* 3 April 1906; *Educ* Merchant Taylors', Univ of London (MBBS); *m* 5 Oct 1933, Helen Margaret (d 1987), da of Sir Henry Dixon Kimber (d 1950), of Maidenhead; 2 s (Richard b 15 Jan 1936, Peter b 28 Feb 1948, d 1984); *Career* WWII surgn EMS 1940-45; hon visiting surgn Royal Postgrad Med Sch, emeritus conslt surgn Kingston and Longrove Gp Hosps 1946-71, hon conslt surgn Royal Star and Garter Home 1957-85 (govr 1969-85), conslt surgn emeritus to RN; RCS: Hunterian prof 1947, Bradshaw lectr 1973, Hunterian orator 1977, memb Ct of Examiners 1956-66; examiner in surgery Univ of Cambridge 1958-69, vis prof Univ of California 1972; memb cncl Imperial Cancer Research Fund 1967-82 (vice chm 1975-79, life govr 1975); Freeman: City of London 1950, Worshipful Co of Apothecaries; FRCS (vice-pres 1974-76), FRSM (pres surgns 1969-70), fell Assoc of Surgns of GB and Ireland, memb Med Soc of London, Br Assoc of Paediatric Surgeons, hon memb Hellenic Surgns Soc; *Books* Surgery of the Oesophagus (1952); *Recreations* sailing, gardening; *Clubs* Aldeburgh YC, Ranelagh Sailing; *Style*— Richard Franklin, Esq, CBE; The Stern Walk, Crespigny Rd, Aldeburgh, Suffolk IP15 5EZ (☎ 072 885 2600)

FRANKLIN, Stephen Roy; s of Prof George Henry Franklin, of Wilts, and Sylvia Daisy, *née* Allen; *b* 10 Dec 1954; *Educ* St Lawrence Coll Ramsgate; *m* 7 Dec 1985, Amanda Patricia, da of Keith Clegg, of St Albans, Herts; 2 da (Hannah b 1986, Sophie b 1987); *Career* ca; snr ptnr Franklin Chartered Accountants; FCA; *Recreations* hockey, squash, fishing; *Clubs* RAC; *Style*— Stephen R Franklin, Esq; Locksley Hall, North Somercotes, Nr Louth, Lincs (☎ 050785 305); 242 Battersea Bridge Rd, London SW11 3AA (☎ 01 223 9536, fax 01 924 3217, car tel 0836 231 976)

FRANKLIN, Stephen Roy; s of Prof George Henry Franklin, of Wiltshire, and Sylvia Daisy, *née* Allen; *b* 10 Dec 1954; *Educ* St Lawrence Coll; *m* 7 Dec 1985, Amanda Patricia, da of Keith Clere, of St Albans; 2 da (Hannah b 1986, Sophie b 1987); *Career* CA; ptnr George Hay & Co 1979, sr ptnr Franklin Chartered Accountants 1982-; FCA; *Recreations* hockey, squash, fishing; *Clubs* RAC; *Style*— Stephen Franklin, Esq; Locksley Hall, North Somercotes, Nr Louth, Lincolnshire (☎ 050785 305); 242 Battersea Bridge Rd, London SW11 3AA (☎ 01 223 9536, fax 01 924 3217, car tel 0836 231976)

FRANKLIN, Rt Rev William Alfred; OBE (1965); s of George Amos Franklin (d 1956) and Mary Ann Catherine, *née* Scott (d 1980); *b* 16 July 1916; *Educ* Church Sch in London, Kelham Theol Coll Nottingham; *m* 1945, Winifred Agnes, *née* Jarvis; 1 s, 1 da; *Career* ordained: deacon 1940, priest 1941; curate St John Bethnal Green 1940-43, St John Palmer's Green London 1943-45; asst chaplain St Saviour's Anglican Church Buenos Aires 1945-48, rector Holy Trinity Lomas De Zamora Buenos Aires 1948-58, rector, canon and sub dean St Andrew's Santiago Chile 1958-65, rector St Alban's Anglican Church Bogota and archdeacon of Colombia (Episcopal church of USA) 1965-71, consecrated lord bishop of Columbia 1972, resigned 1978; full-time asst bishop Diocese Peterborough (England) and hon canon Peterborough Cathedral 1978-86; hon canon emeritus of Peterborough Cathedral 1987, hon asst bishop of Canterbury 1985-; *Recreations* fishing, writing, study of Church growth; *Clubs* Royal Cwlth Soc; *Style*— The Rt Rev William Franklin, OBE; Flat 26c, The Beach, Walmer, nr Deal, Kent CT14 7HJ

FRANKLIN, William John; s of William Thomas Franklin (d 1958), and Edith Hannah Franklin (d 1954); *b* 8 Mar 1927; *Educ* Monkton House Sch Cardiff; *m* 1951, Sally, da of David Roderick Davies (d 1967); 1 da (Ann Elizabeth b 1952); *Career* chief exec Powell Duffryn plc 1976-85; dep chm Chartered Tst plc 1986-; chm: Powell Duffryn Wagon Ltd 1986-, Howells Motors Ltd 1986-; dep tres Univ of Swansea 1988-; FCA; *Recreations* Royal Porthcawl Golf; *Style*— John Franklin, Esq; 80 South Road, Porthcawl, Mid Glam CF36 3DA (☎ 0656 715194)

FRANKLYN, William Leo; s of Leo Franklyn (d 1975), of London, and Mary Victoria, *née* Rigby; *b* 22 Sept 1925; *Educ* Wesley Coll Melbourne, Haileybury Coll Melbourne, Leas House Sch London; *m* 1969, Susanna Jane, da of Edmund Jupp (d 1943), of Hong Kong; 3 da (Sabina, Francesca, Melissa); *Career* actor; films incl: The Snorkel, The Flesh is Weak, Danger Within, Fury at Smuggler's Bay, Pit of Darkness, The Legend of Young Dick Turpin, The Intelligence Men, Cul-de-Sac, The Satanic Rites of Dracula; BBC TV serials: The Makepeace Story, No Wreath for the General, No Cloak, No Dagger; ITV TV series: Top Secret, What's On Next, Paradise Island, Masterspy, The Steam Video Company; London theatre includes: The Tunnel of Love, Girl in my Soup, Deathtrap, Dead Ringer, A Touch of Danger; TV film series incl: The Scarlet Pimpernel, Charlie Chan, The Avengers, The Saracens, Troubleshooters, Public Eye; theatre dir incl: There's a Girl in my Soup, Tunnel of Love, Subway in the Sky, Later Leonardo, That's No Lady (re-titled The Bedwinner), Castle in the Air, Rope, Same Time Next Year; *Recreations* cricket, squash, tennis, Italy; *Clubs* MCC, Hurlingham; *Style*— William Franklyn, Esq; c/o John Redway & Associates, 16 Berners Street, London W1

FRANKS, Anthony Kenric Stapleton; s of Maurice Kenric Franks (d 1955); *b* 13 June 1928; *Educ* Nautical Coll Pangbourne; *m* 1960, Sarah Georgina Cochrane, *née* Watson; 3 s; *Career* md Phicom plc (previously Plantation Hldgs Ltd) 1971-84 (chm and chief exec 1984-86), chm Beck Electronics Ltd 1986-; chm Royal Hosp and Home Putney 1988; *Recreations* shooting, sailing; *Clubs* Boodle's, Royal Yacht Sqdn, City of London; *Style*— Anthony Franks, Esq; Becketts Grove, Matfield, Tonbridge, Kent TN12 7LH (☎ 089 272 2175)

FRANKS, Cecil Simon; MP (C) Barrow Furness 1983-; *b* 1 July 1935; *Educ* Manchester GS, Manchester Univ; *Career* s/r, ldr of (C) Gp Manchester City Cncl; *Style*— Cecil Franks, Esq, MP; House of Commons, London SW1

FRANKS, His Hon Judge; Desmond Gerald Fergus Franks; s of late Frederick Franks, MC; *b* 24 Jan 1928; *Educ* Cathedral Choir Sch Canterbury, Manchester GS, Univ Coll London; *m* 1952, Margaret Leigh, da of late Clarence Daniel; 1 da; *Career* barr 1952 Middle Temple, N Circuit, asst rec Salford 1966, dep rec Salford 1971, rec of Crown Ct 1972, circuit judge 1972-, pres SW Penine Magistates Assoc Liaison Judge to Oldham Magistrates; *Recreations* music, photography; *Style*— His Hon Judge Franks; 4 Beathwaite Drive, Bramhall, Cheshire

FRANKS, Sir Dick (Arthur Temple); KCMG (1979, CMG 1967); s of late Arthur Franks, of Hove, Sussex; *b* 13 July 1920; *Educ* Rugby, Queen's Coll Oxford; *m* 1945, Rachel Marianne, da of Rev A E S Ward, DD, of Thame, Oxon; 1 s, 2 da; *Career* served WWII (despatches); entered Foreign Ser 1949, Br Mid East Off 1952, Tehran 1953, Bonn 1962, FCO 1966-81, ret; *Clubs* Travellers', Army and Navy, Aldeburgh Golf, Sunningdale Golf; *Style*— Sir Dick Franks, KCMG; Roefield, Alde Lane, Aldeburgh, Suffolk

FRANKS, John Alexander; s of Morris Franks, JP, and Jennie, *née* Alexander; *b* 10 Dec 1928; *Educ* Shaftesbury GS, Univ Coll London (LLB), Inst of Advanced Legal Studies (LLM); *m* 1, 1952, Golda Yacha (d 1976), da of Michael Lawrence (d 1950); 2 s (Michael b 1954, Gerald b 1958), 1 da (Jane b 1961); m 2, 1983, Sheila, da of William J J Clark (d 1969), 1 da (Sara b 1954); *Career* slr (1952); chm: Sunlight Service Gp (merged Godfrey Davis Gp plc 1987) 1974-, Disciplinary Ctee of Architects Registration Cncl, Appeal Ctee of Nat House Builders' Registration Cncl; memb cncl Law Soc 1974-; FCI Arb; *Books* Company Director and the Law (5th edn 1986); *Recreations* collecting Vanity Fair Caricatures and English Cottage Glass; *Clubs* City Livery, United Wards, Royal Automobile; *Style*— John Franks, Esq; Chethams, 84 Baker Street, London W1M 1DL (☎ 01 935 7360, telex: 24932 JETAMS, fax: 01 935 4068)

FRANKS, Air Vice-Marshal John Gerald; CB (1954), CBE (1949); el s of James Gordon Franks (d 1941, er s of late Sir John Hamilton Franks, of Dublin), and Margaret (d 1938), yr da of Lord Justice Gerald FitzGibbon, of 10 Merrion Square, Dublin; *b* 23 May 1905; *Educ* Cheltenham, RAF Cadet Coll Cranwell; *m* 1936, Jessica Rae, da of Donald William West, (d 1955), of Nairobi; 2 da (Rachel Anne, Rosemary Juliet); *Career* RAF, cmmnd Gen Duties Branch 1924, Pilot No 56 Fighter Sqdn 1925-26, Fleet Air Arm (HMS Courageous) 1927-28, flying duties on NW Frontier of India 1930-35, Trans Jordan and Egypt 1935-36, specialised in air armament dvpt, aeroplane experimental establishment Boscombe Down 1944; RAF Staff Coll 1939, Dir of Armament Res and Dvpt 1944, Imperial Def Coll 1951, Cmdt RAF Tech Coll 1952AOC No 24 Gp RAF 1952-55, Pres Ordnance Bd 1959-60; ret; Cdr US Legion of Merit 1948; *Recreations* motoring in rural Ireland, walking in West of Ireland; *Style*— Air Vice-Marshal John Franks, CB, CBE; The Sextant, Schull, Co Cork, Republic of Ireland (☎ 028 28317)

FRANKS, Michael John Alan; s of Jacob Franks MD (d 1976); *b* 6 May 1928; *Educ* Epsom Coll, Merton Coll Oxford (MA); *m* 1, 3 Nov 1962 (m dis 1978), Anne, yr da of Sir David George Home, 13 Bt; 2 da (Lucinda b 1964, Miranda b 1966); m 2, 1980, Nicola Stewart, da of Col George Harcourt Stewart Balmain (d 1962); *Career* barr Gray's Inn 1953, Chancery Bar 1953-59; with Royal Dutch Shell 1959-69; dir Beaverbrook Newspapers 1969-73; chm: Clyde Paper Co 1971-76, Schwarzkopf 1981-86, Woodbury Chillcott, Innsite Hotel Servs; A Grantham Hldgs, Silicon Bridge, dep-chm Goodhead Gp plc 1985-; non-exec dir: Int Laboratires, Unipower Vehicles, Select Appointments plc; *Recreations* sailing, skiing, travel; *Clubs* Royal Thames Yacht; *Style*— Michael Franks, Esq; Field House, Mapledurwell, Basingstoke, Hants (☎ 0256 464861)

FRANKS, Baron (Life Peer UK 1962); Oliver Shewell Franks; OM (1977), GCMG (1952), KCB (1946), CBE (1942), PC (1949), KCVO (1986), DL (Oxon 1978); s of Rev Robert Sleightholme Franks (d 1964), of Leppington, Winscombe, Somerset, and Katharine, *née* Shewell; *b* 16 Feb 1905; *Educ* Bristol GS, Queen's Coll Oxford; *m* 3 July 1931, Barbara Mary, da of Herbert George Tanner, JP, LLD, of Llanfuist, Clifton Down, Bristol; 2 da (Hon Mrs John Dinwiddy b 1939, Hon Mrs Stanley Wright b 1945); *Career* prof of moral philosophy Glasgow Univ 1937-45; Miny of Supply 1939-46 (perm sec 1945-46); provost Queen's Coll Oxford 1946-48; chm Marshall Plan Negotiations (Paris) 1947; ambass to USA 1948-52; dir Lloyds Bank 1953-75 (chm 1954-62); provost Worcester Coll Oxford 1962-76; chllr E Anglia Univ 1965-84; chm: Wellcome Trust 1965-82, ctee on Official Secrets Act (Section 2) 1971-72, ctee on Ministerial Memoirs 1976, Political Honours Scrutiny Ctee 1976-86, ctee of PCs on the Falklands Invasion 1982-83; lord warden of the Stannaries and dep chm of the cncl of the Duchy of Cornwall 1983-85 (memb cncl Duchy of Cornwall 1966-85); FBA; *Style*— The Rt Hon Lord Franks, OM, GCMG, KCB, CBE, PC, DL; Blackhall Farm, Garford Rd, Oxford OX2 6VY (☎ 0865 511286)

FRAPPELL, Charles Edward; s of Charles Joseph Frappell (d 1972), and Kate Lilian, *née* Smith (d 1969); *b* 26 April 1919; *Educ* Plaistow Municipal Secdy Sch, Univ of London; *m* 25 March 1945, Violet Eileen, da of Richard Edward Batcheler (d 1950), of

Rainham, Essex; 3 da (Carole Eileen b 15 Oct 1946, Susan Ellen b 26 Sept 1948, Hazel Elizabeth b 24 Aug 1957); *Career* 54 (EA) Divnl Signals TA 1939, 4 Divnl Signals 1939, Intelligence Corps Ciphers ATT 4 Div 1941, No 3 Intelligence Sch WO 1942, posted HQ E Africa Cmd-ATT HQ Eastern Fleet Mombasa (Ciphers) 1942, posted Fortress HQ Diego Suarez Madagascar (Ciphers), posted HQ 11 (E African) Div (Ciphers Section) Kenya, serv Ceylon, Burma and India 1943-44, returned UK 1945, demobbed 1946; trainee Grieveson Grant & Co Stockbrokers London 1935 (mangr 1946-58); W Greenwell & Co joined 1959, ptnr 1961, ptnr i/c gilt edged securities 1965, ret 1985, memb London and SE Bd Bradford & Bingley Bldg Soc 1985; common councilman ward of Bread Street City of London (memb Ct 1973), chm Spitalfields Mkt Ctee 1977-80, fndr memb City of London Branch IOD; Freeman City of London 1973, Liveryman Worshipful Co of Gold and Silver Wyre Drawers 1973; memb Stock Exchange 1961, FIOD 1968, FBIM 1978; *Recreations* golf, puzzles, conversation, travelling; *Clubs* RAC, City Livery, Guildhall; *Style—* Charles Frappell, Esq; White Oaks, Forest Road, Burley, Ringwood, Hants BH24 4DE

FRASER, Hon (Alexander) Andrew Macdonell; o s of Baron Fraser of Tullybelton, PC (Life Peer) (d 1989); *b* 1946; *m* 28 April 1982, Sarah J, da of Henry Jones, of Kitsbury Orchard, Oddinton, Moreton-in-Marsh, Glos; 1 s (b 1984); *Style—* Hon Andrew Fraser; c/o 35 Cleaver Square, London SE11

FRASER, Hon Andrew Roy Matthew; s of 17 Lord Lovat, DSO, MC, TD; *b* 24 Feb 1952; *Educ* Ampleforth, Magdalen Coll Oxford; *m* 10 Sept 1979, Lady Charlotte Anne Greville, o da of 8 Earl of Warwick; 2 da (Daisy b 1985, Laura b 1987); *Career* dir China Trading Int, Cordle & Co; memb Queens Bodyguard for Scotland The Royal Co of Archers; Col in Chief 78 Fraser Highlanders; SMOM; *Clubs* Turf, Puffin's, Pratt's; *Style—* Hon Andrew Fraser; 1 Petyt Place, London SW3 5DJ; China Trading Int Ltd, 97 Drayton Gardens, London SW10 9QN (☎ 01 835 1229)

FRASER, Sir Angus McKay; KCB (1985), CB (1981, TD 1965); s of late Thomas Douglas Fraser; *b* 10 Mar 1928; *Educ* Falkirk HS, Glasgow Univ, Bordeaux Univ; *m* 1955 (m dis 1968), Margaret Neilson; 1 s, 1 da; *Career* RA 1950-52; 44 Para Bde (TA) 1953-66; Customs and Excise 1952-61, 1965-73, 1976-80 (dep chm 1978, chm bd 1983-87), Treasy 1961-64, CSD 1973-76, dep sec CSD 1980-83, first civil serv cmmr 1981-83; *Clubs* Reform, City Livery, Royal Over-Seas League, Caledonian, Norfolk (Norwich); *Style—* Sir Angus Fraser, KCB, TD; 84 Ennerdale Rd, Kew, Richmond, Surrey TW9 2DL (☎ 01 940 9913)

FRASER, Hon Ann Lewis; o da of 1 Baron Fraser of Allander (d 1966), and Baroness Fraser of Allander, *née* Hutcheon Lewis; bro disclaimed his peerage for Life 1966, Sir Hugh Fraser 2 Bt (d 1987 when extinct); *b* 5 April 1932; *Educ* Westbourne Sch Glasgow; *Style—* Hon Ann Fraser

FRASER, Air Cdre Anthony Walkinshaw; s of Robert Walkinshaw Fraser (d 1956), and Evelyn Elisabeth, *née* Watts (d 1955); *b* 15 Mar 1934; *Educ* Stowe; *m* 1955, Angela Mary Graham, da of George Richard Shaw (d 1983), of Darlington, Co Durham; 1 s (Robert), 3 da (Amanda, Antonia, Alexandra); *Career* RAF Pilot, Instr and Staff Offr, Air Cdre 1979, Cmdt Central Flying Sch, ret; ADC to HM The Queen 1977-79; dir Soc of Motor Mfrs & Traders Ltd 1980-88, pres Organisation Internationale des Constructeurs d'Automobiles 1983-87; Goddard Kay Rogers (Northern) Ltd 1988-;; *Recreations* golf, shooting, fishing, languages; *Clubs* Boodles, RAF, Sunningdale; *Style—* Air Cdre Anthony Fraser; 32 Cliveden Place, London SW1; Goddard Kay Rogers Ltd, Park House, Park Sq, Leeds LS1 2PS (☎ 0532 449922)

FRASER, Lady Antonia; *née* Pakenham; da of 7 Earl of Longford, PC, and Lady Longford, the biographer of Queen Victoria and the Duke of Wellington; *b* 27 August 1932; *Educ* Dragon Sch, St Mary's Convent Ascot, Lady Margaret Hall Oxford; *m* 1, 25 Sept 1956 (m dis 1977), Rt Hon Sir Hugh Fraser, MBE, PC, MP (d 1984), s of 16 Lord Lovat; 3 s (Benjamin b 1961, Damian b 1964, Orlando b 1967), 3 da (Rebecca (Mrs Edward Fitzgerald) b 1957, Flora (Mrs Robert Powell-Jones) b 1958, Natasha b 1964); m 2, 1980, Harold Pinter, CBE, *qv*; *Career* writer: Mary Queen of Scots (James Taite Black Memorial Prize 1969), Cromwell our chief of Men (1973), James I & VI of England and Scotland (1974), ed Kings and Queens of England (1975), King Charles II (1979), The Weaker Vessel (Wolfson History Award 1984), Boadicea's Chariot: The Warrior Queens (1988), Quiet as a Nun (1977), Cool Repentance (1980), The Wild Island (1978), Oxford Blood (1985), Your Loyal Hostage (1987), A Splash of Red 1981 (basis TV series Jemima Shore 1983), Jemima Shore's First Case (1986); chm Soc of Authors 1974-75; chm Crimewriters' Assoc 1985-86; pres English PEN 1988-; *Recreations* gardening, swimming; *Style—* Lady Antonia Fraser; Curtis Brown, 167 Regent Street W1

FRASER, Sir Basil Malcolm; 2 Bt (UK 1921); s of Sir (John) Malcolm Fraser, 1 Bt, GBE (d 1949), and Irene, *née* Brightman; *b* 2 Jan 1920; *Educ* Eton, Queens' Coll Cambridge; *Heir* none; *Career* Capt RE WWII, Madras Sappers and Miners (despatches); *Style—* Sir Basil Fraser, Bt; 175 Beach St, Deal, Kent

FRASER, Hon Belinda Ann; 2 da (by 1 m) of Sir Hugh Fraser, 2 Bt (2 Baron Fraser of Allander, who disclaimed his peerage for life 1966 d 1987 when title extinct); *b* 19 Jan 1964; *Style—* Hon Belinda Fraser

FRASER, Sir Bruce Donald; KCB (1961, CB 1956); s of Maj-Gen Sir Theodore Fraser, KCB, CSI, CMG (d 1953), and Constance Ruth, *née* Stevenson (d 1918); *b* 18 Nov 1910; *Educ* Bedford Sch, Trinity Coll Cambridge (MA); *m* 12 May 1939, Audrey (d 1982), da of Lt Col Evan Leigh Croslegh (d 1942); 1 s (decd), 1 da (decd); *Career* entered Civil Service Scottish Office 1933, transferred Treasury 1936; permanent sec Miny of Health 1960-64, jt perm under-sec of state DES 1964-65, perm sec Miny of Land and Natural Resources 1965-66, comptroller and auditor general Exchequer and Audit Dept 1966-71; *Books* The Complete Plain Words by Sir Ernest Gowers (revised edition, 1973); *Clubs* Athenaeum; *Style—* Sir Bruce Fraser, KCB; Jonathan, St Dogmael's, Cardigan, Dyfed (☎ Cardigan 0239 612387)

FRASER, Sir (James) Campbell; s of Alexander Ross Fraser and Annie McGregor Fraser; *b* 2 May 1923; *Educ* Glasgow Univ, McMaster Univ (Hamilton Canada), Dundee Sch of Economics; *m* 1950, Maria Harvey, *née* McLaren; 2 da; *Career* pres CBI 1982-84 (former chm CBI Industrial Policy Ctee); chm Dunlop Hldgs 1978-83; chm Scottish TV 1975-; dir (non-exec): vice-pres BP, BAT Industries, Bridgewater Paper Co, Tandem Computers, Britoil Alexander Proudfeet; vice-pres Scottish Opera; tstee The Economist 1978-; memb NEDC 1982-84; pres Soc of Business Economists 1972-84; FRSE, CBIM, FPRI, Hon LLD (Strathclyde), DUniv (Stirling); visiting prof Sterling Univ; kt 1978; *Style—* Sir Campbell Fraser; 114 St Martins Lane, London WC2N 4AZ

FRASER, Hon Caroline Emily; 3 da (by 1 m) of Sir Hugh Fraser, 2 Bt (2 Baron Fraser of Allander, who disclaimed his peerage for life 1966); *b* 29 Sept 1966; *Style—* Hon Caroline Fraser

FRASER, Sir Charles Annand; KCVO (1989, CVO 1985, LVO 1968), DL (1985), WS (1956) ; s of Very Rev Dr John Annand Fraser, MBE, TD (d 1985), and Leila, *née* Campbell, of 4-3 Gillsland Rd Edinburgh; *b* 16 Oct 1928; *Educ* Hamilton Acad Lanarkshire, Edinburgh Univ (MA, LLB); *m* 1957, Ann, da of William Francis Scott-Kerr (d 1974), of Sunlaws Roxburghshire; 4 s (Simon, Ian, James, Robert); *Career* WS; purse bearer to Lord High Cmmr to Gen Assembly of Church of Scotland 1969-87; vice-chm Utd Biscuits Hldgs Ltd 1977-; dir: Etrick Nominees Ltd 1968-, Br Assets Tst 1972-, W & J Burness Tstees Ltd 1971-, Signetics (UK) Ltd 1969-, Solsgirth Invstmt Tst Co Ltd 1981-, Scottish Widows' Fund and Life Assur Soc 1976-, Scottish Widow's Unit Funds Ltd 1981-, Scottish TV plc 1979-, Scottish Business in the Community 1982-, The Patrons of the Nat Galleries of Scotland 1984-, The John Muir Tst Ltd 1984-, Selective Assets Tst plc (until 1987 Japan Assets Tst plc) 1981-, Grosvenor Dvpts Ltd 1981, Anglo Scottish Investmt Tst plc 1984, Walter Alexander plc 1981, Adam & Co plc 1983; tstee Scottish Civic Tst 1978-; memb cncl Law Soc of Scotland 1966-72 memb ct Heriot-Watt Univ 1972-78; *Clubs* New (Edinburgh), Caledonian (London); *Style—* Sir Charles Fraser, KCVO, WS, DL; Shepherd House, Inveresk, Midlothian (☎ 031 665 2570); Wester Dalvoult, Boat of Garten, Inverness-shire (☎ 047 983 343); W & J Burness, 16 Hope St, Charlotte Sq, Edinburgh EH2 4DD (☎ 031 226 2561, telex 72405)

FRASER, Lady Charlotte Anne; *née* Greville; da of 8 Earl of Warwick and Sarah (now Mrs H Thomson Jones), da of Alfred Chester Beatty, the financier; *b* 6 June 1958; *Educ* Heathfield; *m* 10 Sept 1979, Hon Andrew Roy Matthew Fraser, *qv*, 4 s of 17 Lord Lovat; 2 da; *Style—* Lady Charlotte Fraser; 1 Petyt Place, London SW3 5DJ

FRASER, Gen Sir David William; GCB (1980, KCB 1973), OBE (1962), DL (Hants 1982); er s of Brig Hon William Fraser, DSO, MC (d 1964, yst s of 18 Lord Saltoun), and Pamela Cynthia, *née* Maude (d 1975); *b* 30 Dec 1920; *Educ* Eton, Christ Church Oxford; *m* 1, 26 Sept 1947 (m dis 1952), Anne, yr da of Brig Edward William Sturgis Balfour, CVO, DSO, OBE, MC; 1 da (Antonia Isabella b 1949); m 2, 11 Oct 1957, Julia Frances, yr da of Maj Cyril James Oldridge de la Hey; 2 s (Alexander James b 1960, Simon b 1963), 2 da (Arabella b 1958, Lucy b 1965); *Career* cmmnd Grenadier Gds 1941, served UK and NW Europe 1939-45, Malaya 1948, Egypt 1952-54, Cyprus 1958, British Cameroons 1961, Borneo 1965, NATO Brussels 1975-77, GOC 4 Div 1969-71, ACDS 1971-73, Vice CGS 1973-75, British Mil Rep to NATO 1975-77, Cmdt RCDS 1977-80, ADC Gen to HM The Queen 1977-80, Col The Royal Hampshire Regt 1981-87; pres Soc for Army Historical Research 1980-; chm Treloar Tst and Governing Body Lord Mayor Treloar Coll 1982-; *Books* Alanbrooke (1982), And We Shall Shock Them (1983), The Christian Watt Papers (1983), August 1988 (1983), A Kiss for the Enemy (1985), The Killing Times (1986), The Dragon's Teeth (1987), The Seizure (1988), A Candle for Judas (1989); *Recreations* shooting; *Clubs* Turf, Pratt's; *Style—* Gen Sir David Fraser, GCB, OBE, DL; Vallenders, Isington, Alton, Hants (☎ 0420 23166)

FRASER, Sir Douglas Were; ISO (1962); s of Robert John Fraser and Edith Harriet, *née* Shepherd (both decd); *b* 24 Oct 1899; *Educ* State HS Gympie; *m* 1927, Violet (d 1968), da of late Alfred Pryke; 3 s; *Career* cmmr Pub Service Brisbane 1956-66 (ret), formerly chm Qld Conservatorium of Music Cncl, memb Senate Qld Univ, pres State Cncl Qld Ambulance Tport Bde; kt 1966; *Recreations* gardening, fishing, music, reading; *Style—* Sir Douglas Fraser, ISO; 76 Prince Edward Parade, Redcliffe, Qld 4020, Australia (☎ 203 4393)

FRASER, Hon Mrs; Hon Elizabeth Penelope; *née* Methuen; o da of 5 Baron Methuen (d 1975); *b* 4 July 1928; *Educ* Downe House, Newbury; *m* 8 Dec 1956, Malcolm Henry Alastair Fraser, er s of (Hugh) Alastair Hamilton Fraser, JP, of Mill Place, Stanton Drew, Somerset; 2 da (Elizabeth b 1957, Anne b 1961); *Career* former county pres Somerset YFC; SW Area Pres YFC 1987-, nat dep pres NFYFC 1988-; area pres St Johns Ambulance; memb of SWEB consumer consultative cncl ctee for Bath and Bristol; *Recreations* travel, the arts; *Clubs* ESU Dartmouth Ho, The GB-China Centre; *Style—* Hon Mrs Fraser; Grey Gables, Pilton, Shepton Mallet, Somerset BA4 4DB (☎ 074 989 370)

FRASER, Dr Ewan John Stanley; s of Maj IM Fraser MC (d 1988), of Chipstead, Surrey, and Mary Stanley (d 1964); *b* 15 May 1947; *Educ* Eton, Christ Church Oxford (MA, DPhil); *Career* investmt analyst James Capel and Co (Stockbrokers) 1975 - (sr exec 1985)); memb (Co) Oxford City Cncl 1969-70 and 1971-72; memb Int Stock Exchange 19843; *Recreations* fly fishing, reading, ballet; *Clubs* Carlton; *Style—* Dr Ewan Fraser; 80 Hadley Highstone, Barnet, Herts EN5 4PY (☎ 01 440 5386); PO Box 551, 6 Bevis Marks, London EC3A 7JQ (☎ 01 621 0011, fax 01 621 0496, telex 888866)

FRASER, George MacDonald; s of William Fraser, of Carlisle, and Anne Struth, *née* Donaldson; *b* 2 April 1925; *Educ* Carlisle GS, Glasgow Academy; *m* 1949, Kathleen Margarette, da of George Hetherington, of Carlisle; 2 s (Simon, Nicholas), 1 da (Caroline); *Career* served Br Army 1943-47, infantryman Border Regt Burma, Lt Gordon Highlanders; journalist 1947-69, dep ed Glasgow Herald; author; *Books* the Flashman novels and various other books; *film screenplays include* The Three Musketeers (1973), The Four Musketeers (1974), Octopussy (1983), Casanova (1987), The Return of the Musketeers (1989); *Recreations* writing, history, talking to wife, Scrabble; *Style—* George Fraser, Esq; Baldrine, Isle of Man

FRASER, Iain Michael; er s (and h) of Prof Sir James Fraser, 2 Bt, and Lady Fraser, *née* Maureen Reay; *b* 27 June 1951; *Educ* Trinity Coll Glenalmond, Edinburgh Univ (BSc); *m* 30 Jan 1982, Sherylle Ann, da of Keith Gillespie, of Wellington, NZ; 1 s (Benjamin b 1986), 1 da (Joanna b 1983); *Career* shipping co mangr; mktmktg mangr American President Lines Hong Kong; *Style—* Iain Fraser, Esq; 16B Barnton Court, Canton Rd, Hong Kong

FRASER, Brig Sir Ian; DSO (1944), OBE (1941), DL (Belfast 1955); s of Robert Moore Fraser, MD, of Knock, Belfast, and Margaret Boal, *née* Ferguson; *b* 9 Feb 1901; *Educ* Royal Belfast Academical Inst, Queen's Univ Belfast; *m* 2 Sept 1931, Eleanor Margaret, da of Marcus Adolphus Mitchell, of Quarry House, Belfast; 1 s, 1 da; *Career* served WWII RAMC (W Africa, N Africa, France, India), Brig 1945; Hon Col: No 4 Field Amb 1948-71, 204 General Hosp TA 1961-71; sr surgeon: Royal Victoria Hosp Belfast 1955-66, Royal Belfast Hosp for Children 1955-66, now consltg surg; surg in ordinary to the Govr of N Ireland, hon consulting Surg to the Army in N

Ireland; chm Police Authy Royal Ulster Constabulary 1970-76; GCStJ 1974, Ordre de la Couronne (Belgium) 1963, Ordre des Palmes Académiques (France) 1964, Order of Orange Nassau 1969, Chevalier de la Légion d'Honneur (France) 1981, Kt Cdr Commandery of Ards (Ulster); Hon DSc Oxon, Hon DSc New Univ of Ulster; FRSE, FRCS, FRCSI, FACS; kt 1963; *Style*— Brig Sir Ian Fraser, DSO, OBE, DL; 19 Upper Malone Rd, Belfast, N Ireland (☎ 0232 668235); 35 Wellington Park, Belfast, N Ireland (☎ 0232 665543)

FRASER, Lt Cdr Ian Edward; VC (1945), DSC (1943, RD and Bar 1948), JP (Wirral 1957); s of Sydney Fraser (d 1976), of Bourne End, Bucks; *b* 18 Dec 1920; *Educ* Royal GS High Wycombe, HMS Conway 1936-38; *m* 1943, Melba Estelle, da of late Stanley Hughes; 2 s, 4 da; *Career* Lt Cdr RNR Atlantic, Pacific, N Africa, N Sea; dir Star Offshore Services Ltd 1975-82, chm Nordive (W Africa Ltd), md North Sea Diving Services Ltd 1965-77, md Universal Divers Ltd 1946-87; *Books* Frogman VC (1952); *Recreations* golf, model ships; *Clubs* Hoylake Sailing, New Brighton Rugby, Leasowe Golf (1 capt 1975); *Style*— Lt Cdr Ian Fraser, VC, DSC, RD, JP; Sigyn, 1 Lyndhurst Rd, Wallasey, Merseyside L45 6AX

FRASER, Sir Ian James; CBE (1972), MC (1945); s of Hon Alastair Thomas Joseph Fraser, DSO, Lovat Scouts (d 1949, s of 13 Lord Lovat) and Lady Sibyl, *née* Grimston (d 1968), da of 3 Earl of Verulam; *b* 7 August 1923; *Educ* Ampleforth, Magdalen Coll Oxford; *m* 25 Oct 1958, (Evelyn Elizabeth) Anne (d 1984), yr da of Maj Alastair Edward George Grant, DSO, 9 Lancers, of Nutcombe Manor, Clayhanger, Tiverton; 2 s, 2 da; *Career* Lt Scots Gds WWII (despatches); FRSA, CBIM; former Reuter correspondent; dir S G Warburg & Co 1959-69, dir gen city Panel on Take-overs and Mergers; dir: Davy International, BOC International 1972-73, S Pearson & Son, Pearson Longman, EMI; chm Rolls Royce Motors 1971-80, Datastream 1976-77; chm Lazard Bros 1980-85, Accepting House Ctee 1981-85, dep chm Vickers 1980-, dep chm TSB Gp plc 1985-; Kt of Honour and Devation, Sov Mil Order of Malta 1971; kt 1986; *Style*— Sir Ian Fraser, CBE, MC; South Haddon, Skilgate, Taunton, Somerset TA4 2DR; Skilgate, Taunton, Somerset (☎ 0398 247); Lazard Brothers, 21 Moorfields, London EC2P 2HT (☎ 01 588 2721)

FRASER, Very Rev Ian Watson; CMG (1973); s of Malcolm Fraser, CVO, OBE (d 1949), of 29 Rawhiti Terrace, Wellington, NZ, and Caroline, *née* Watson (d 1959); *b* 23 Oct 1907; *Educ* Scots Coll Wellington, NZ, Victoria Univ of Wellington, NZ (BA, MA), Theological Hall, Knox Coll Dunedin (BD Melbourne), Edinburgh Univ, Univ Bonn Germany, Union Theol Seminary NY (STM, ThD); *m* 1932, Alexa Church, da of George Leighton Stewart, of Wellington, NZ; 1 s (Malcolm), 2 da (Sheila, Mairi); *Career* military serv as chaplain NZ; minister: St Andrew's Church Levin 1933-39; chaplain St Andrew's Coll Christchurch 1942-48, minister: St John's Church Papatoetoe 1948-61, St Stephen's Church Lower Hutt 1961-73; moderator of Gen Assembly of Presbyterian Church of NZ 1968-69; convenor Ctee on Position of Women in the Church 1948-55 (secured opening of eldership to women and later the ministry); memb jt cmmn on Church Union 1962-73; Refugee Award of the NZ Nat Cncl of Churches 1970; ret; *Books* Understandest Thou? (1946), Understanding the Old Testament (1958), Journey into the Shadows (1958), The Story of Nansen Home (1984); *Recreations* walking, woodworking; *Style*— Very Rev Ian Fraser, CMG; 19a Bloomfield Terrace, Lower Hutt, NZ (☎ Wellington 697269)

FRASER, James (Edward); s of Dr James Fowler Fraser, TD (d 1979), of Aberdeen, and Dr Kathleen Nevill Blomfield (d 1974); *b* 16 Dec 1931; *Educ* Aberdeen GS, Univ of Aberdeen (MA), Christ's Coll Cambridge (BA); *m* 10 Oct 1959, Patricia Louise, da of John Henry Stewart (d 1970), of Perth; 2 s (Paul Anthony b 1960, Mark Edward b 1962); *Career* Capt RA HQ Tel-el-Kebir garrison 1954-55; civil servant; private sec permanent under-sec Scottish Off 1960-62, parly under-sec Scottish Off 1962-64; Cabinet Off 1964-66; HM Treasy 1966-68; under-sec Scottish Off Local Govt Fin Gp 1976-81, Scottish Home & Health Dept 1981-; pres Scottish Hillonic Soc of Edinburgh and Eastern Scotland 1987-; FSA(Scot);; *Recreations* reading, music, walking, greece ancient and modern; *Clubs* Scottish Arts (Edinburgh); *Style*— J Edward Fraser, Esq; c/o St Andrews House, Edinburgh, EH1 3DE (☎ 031 244 2131)

FRASER, Col James Andrew; MC (1943 and Bar 1944); s of Cdr John Fraser, OBE, RN (d 1969) of Leckmelm, Rosshire, and Catherine, *née* Whittier (d 1979); *b* 14 Jan 1921; *Educ* RMA Woolwich; *m* 4 Oct 1947, Jean Pamela, da of Lt-Col Walter Murray, OBE, MC (d 1945) of Chilton Polden, Somerset, 2 s (Simon b 1950, Donald b 1951), 1 da (Jean b 1954); *Career* cmmnd 1939, 80 Scottish Horse RA 1940-45, instr Sch of Artillery 1946-49, Lovat Scouts RA 1949-50 (Adj), 1 Regt RHA 1951-54, instr RMA Sandhurst 1954-55, instr Guided Weapons 1956-58, 4 Regt RHA 1959-61, (Battery cmd and 2i/c), 27 Guided Weapons Regt 1962-64, (cmmd offr), sr instr Guided Weapons Sch of Artillery 1964, Chief instr Locating Wing Sch of Artillery, 1966-68, ret 1969; farmer Guisachan Farm Invernesshire 1969-86; *Recreations* fishing, stalking, photography; *Clubs* Army & Navy; *Style*— Col James Fraser, MC; Tomuaine, Tomich, Beauly, Invernesshire, (☎ 045 65 220)

FRASER, Prof Sir James David; 2 Bt (UK 1943), of Tain, Co Ross; o s of Sir John Fraser, 1 Bt, KCVO, MC (d 1947), and Agnes Govane, *née* Herald (d 1983); *b* 19 July 1924; *Educ* Edinburgh Acad, Magdalen Coll Oxford, Edinburgh Univ (MB, ChB, ChM); *m* 16 Sept 1950, Edith Maureen, da of late Rev John Reay, MC; 2 s; *Heir* s, Iain Fraser; *Career* late Maj RAMC, served Far East 1949-51; sr lectr in Clinical Surgery Edinburgh Univ and hon conslt surgn Edinburgh Royal Infirmary 1963-70, prof of Surgery Southampton Univ 1970-80, hon conslt surgn Southampton Univ Hosp Gp 1970-80, Postgrad dean Edinburgh Univ Med Sch 1981-; pres RCS Edinburgh 1982-85; *Recreations* golf, gardening; *Style*— Prof Sir James Fraser, Bt; 2 Lennox St, Edinburgh (☎ 031 332 3205)

FRASER, Hon Mrs; Hon Jane Bronwen; *née* Short; only da of Baron Glenamara, CH, PC (Life Baron); *b* 1945; *m* 1970, James Weir Fraser; *Style*— Hon Mrs Fraser; 303 Montagu Village, Nassau, Bahamas

FRASER, John Denis; MP (Lab) Norwood 1966; s of Archibald and Frances Fraser; *b* 30 June 1934; *Educ* Sloane GS (Chelsea), Loughborough Co-Op Coll, Law Soc Law Sch; *m* 1960, Ann Hathaway; 2 s, 1 da; *Career* memb Lambeth Cncl 1962-68, MP (Lab): Lambeth Norwood 1966-; former slr with: Royal Army Educatnl Corps, Aust & NZ Bank; pps to Barbara Castle as Employment and Productivity sec 1968-70, oppn front bench spokesman Home Affrs 1972-74, Parly under-sec Employment 1974-76, min state Prices and Consumer Protection 1976-79, front bench oppn spokesman: Trade Prices and Consumer Protection 1981-83, Housing and Construction 1983-87, Shadow Law Officer 1987-; *Recreations* music, walking; *Style*— John Fraser, Esq, MP; House of Commons SW1 A0AA

FRASER, John Stewart; s of Donald Stewart Fraser, of Seacliff Park, Adelaide, Aust; *b* 18 July 1931; *m* 1955, Diane Louise, da of late William Frederick Witt; 3 children; *Career* mktg mangr Ilford (Australia) Pty Ltd 1968-73, head of mktg Ilford 1973-78, md and chief exec Ilford Ltd 1978-84, gp md Ciba-Geigy (plastics and additives) 1982-84, gp md and chief exec Ciba-Geigy plc (gp md 1984-87); chm: The Clayton Aniline Co Manchester, Ciba-Geigy Chemicals Ltd, Gretag-CX Ltd 1987; *Recreations* tennis; *Style*— John Fraser, Esq; Ciba-Geigy plc, 30 Buckingham Gate, London SW1E 6LH (☎ 01 828 5676); Carters Farm, High Wych, Sawbridgeworth, Bishop's Stortford, Herts CM21 0LB (☎ 0279 725619)

FRASER, June (Mrs Allen Cull); da of Donald Stuart Denholm Fraser (d 1986), of Dorset and Myrtle Josephine *née* Ward; *b* 30 August 1930; *Educ* Talbot Health Sch Bournemouth, Bekenham Coll of Art, RCA; *m* 7 Oct 1963, Allen Hans, s of Earnest Albert Cull, of Burridge, Southampton, Hants; 1 s (Zoë Gail b 27 July 1970); *Career* dir Design Res Unit 1968 (ptnr 1963), head of graphic design John Lewis Partnership 1980-84, head of the industl design div The Design Cncl 1984-88; own design practice 1988; former pres Chartered Soc of Designers 1983-85, memb of the ct RCA, 1986; govr: London Inst, Kent Inst, and Bournemouth & Poole Coll of Art; ARCA 1957, PPCSD 1960, MInst P 1968; *Recreations* travel, horticulture, design, tennis, piano, films, theatre; *Style*— Miss June Fraser; 5 Combermartin Rd, London SW18 5PP (☎ 01 788 2353, fax 01 877 1173)

FRASER, Kenneth John Alexander; s of Jack Sears Fraser and Marjorie Winifred, *née* Savery; *b* 22 Sept 1929; *Educ* Thames Valley GS, LSE (BSc); *m* 1953, Kathleen Grace, da of Herbert Bramwell Booth; 2 s (Neil, Alexander), 1 da (Julie); *Career* joined: Erwin Wasey & Co Ltd 1953, Lintas Ltd 1958; md Res Bureau Ltd 1962; head of mktg analysis and evalutation gp Unilever 1965, head of mktg div Unilever 1976; memb: Consumer Protection Advsy Ctee, Dept of Prices and Consumer Protection 1975; chm: CBI Mktg and Consumer Affairs Ctee 1977, Int Chamber of Commerce Mktg Cmmn 1978-; secondment to NEDO as industl dir 1979-81; head of mktg div and int affairs Unilever plc; *Clubs* Royal Cwlth, Wig and Pen; *Style*— Kenneth Fraser, Esq; 14 Coombe Lane, West Kingston, Surrey KT2 7BX; Unilever House, Blackfriars (☎ 01 822 5971)

FRASER, Hon Kim Maurice; 2 s of 17th Lord Lovat, DSO, MC, TD; *b* 4 Jan 1946; *Educ* Ampleforth; *m* 1975, Joanna Katherine, da of Maj Geoffrey Edward Ford North, MC; 3 s (Tom (Thomas) Oswald Mungo b 1976, Joe b 197-, Max b 1981); *Career* Lt Scots Gds; *Style*— Hon Kim Fraser; c/o Beaufort Castle, Beauly, Inverness-shire

FRASER, Rt Hon (John) Malcolm; PC (1976), AC (1988), CH (1977); s of John Neville Fraser (d 1962), of Victoria, and Una Arnold, *née* Woolf; gf Sir Fraser elected to first Federal Senate 1901, and delegate to convention with framed Federal Constitution; *b* 21 May 1930; *Educ* Tudor House, Melbourne C of E GS, Magdalen Coll Oxford; *m* 1956, Tamara Margaret Sandford, da of Sandford R Beggs (d 1984); 2 s (Mark, Hugh), 2 da (Angela, Phoebe b 1966); *Career* memb Federal Parl (Lib) Australia from 1955-83, min for: Army 1966-68, Educn and Science 1968-69, Def 1969-71, Educn 1971-72; ldr of the Oppn 1975, ldr Lib Pty March 1975 - March 1983 (resigned); PM of Australia 1975- March 1983; chaired UN Hearings in NY on Role of Multi Nationals in S Africa and Namibia 1985; co-chm Cwlth Ctee of Eminent Persons to Encourage Dialogue and Reform in S Africa 1985-86; *Recreations* fishing, shooting, photography; *Clubs* Melbourne, Cwlth (Canberra), Brook; *Style*— The Rt Hon Malcolm Fraser, AC, CH; 44th Floor, Anz Tower, 55 Collins St, Melbourne, Vic 3000, Australia (☎ 03 6541822, telex 34884); Nareen, Vic 3315, Australia (☎ 055 798575)

FRASER, Hon Mrs George; Margaret Elizabeth; 2 da of Reginald Barnes, of St Ermin's, Westminster; *m* 1934, as his 2 w, Rear Adm Hon George Fraser, DSO, RN (d 1970), 2 s of 18 Lord Saltoun; 2 s; *Style*— Hon Mrs Fraser

FRASER, Nicholas Andrew; s of W Lionel Fraser, CMG (d 1965), of London and Cynthia Elizabeth *née* Walter, OBE; *b* 2 Mar 1935; *Educ* Eton, King's Coll Cambridge (MA); *m* 1, 19 June 1964 (m dis 1979), Jill, da of Roy Butterfield (d 1985), of Yorkshire; 1 s (Tom b 1968), 2 da (Kate b 1960, Emily b 1966); m 2, 23 April 1981, Charlotte Ann, da of John Warren-Davis, of Dyfed, Wales; *Career* Helbert Wagg & Co Ltd 1957-62, Bank of London & America 1965-67; James Capel & Co 1967-; head of institutional equity sales 1977, head of investmt mgmnt 1983-, dir 1986; Liveryman Worshipful Co of Fishmongers; *Style*— Nicholas Fraser, Esq; James Capel House, 6 Bevis Marks, London, EC3A 7JQ (☎ 01 621 0011, fax 01 621 0496, telex 888866)

FRASER, Air Marshal Rev Sir (Henry) Paterson; KBE (1961, CBE 1945), CB (1953), AFC (1937); s of late Harry Paterson Fraser, MBE (d 1956), of Johannesburg, and Edith May, *née* Coxhead; *b* 15 July 1907; *Educ* St Andrews Coll Grahamstown S Africa, Pembroke Coll Cambridge (MA); *m* 1933, Avis Gertrude, da of Hugh Charles Haswell, of Johannesburg (d 1962); 2 s; *Career* joined RAF 1929, directorate War Organization 1938-40, CO Experimental Flying Section (Royal Aircraft Estab) 1940-42, Gp Capt 1941, memb RAF element Combined Chiefs of Staff Washington 1942, dep AOA 2 TAF 1944, Air Cdre cmdg Aircraft and Armament Experimental Estab 1945, SASO Fighter Cmd 1952-54, Air Vice-Marshal 1953, COS AAFCE (actg Air Marshal) 1954-56, AOC 12 Gp Fighter Command 1956-58, Air Marshal 1959, dir RAF Exercise Planning 1959, UK rep on Perm Military Deputies Gp Central Treaty Orgn Ankara 1960-62, Inspr-Gen RAF 1962-64, ret; CEng, FRAeS; concrete conslt (former technologist with Readymix (IOM) Ltd); ordained Dec 1977; *Style*— Air Marshal Rev Sir Paterson Fraser, KBE, CB, AFC; 803 King's Court, Ramsey, Isle of Man (☎ 0624 813069)

FRASER, Hon Patricia Lydia; eldest da (by 1 m) of Sir Hugh Fraser, 2 Bt (2 Baron Fraser of Allander, who disclaimed his peerage for life 1966, d 1987 when title became extinct); *b* 20 Jan 1963; *Style*— Hon Patricia Fraser

FRASER, (Rowland) Roley Lovat; s of William Lovat Fraser, CBE (d 1968), of Parkfield House by Perth, and Belle, *née* Ballantyne (d 1952); *b* 11 Mar 1931; *Educ* Merchiston Castle Sch; *m* 22 May 1954, Lilian Mary, da of Sir Frederick Archibald Bell (d 1972), of Chapelbank, Auchterarter; 2 s (Simon b 1957, Mark b 1958), 2 da (Sarah Jane b 1960, Nina b 1962); *Career* Lt Royal Scots Fus 1950, Capt Scottish Horse 1955; dir: United Auctions (Scotland) Ltd 1962 (chm 1982-), UA Eastern Ltd, UA Western Ltd; chm: Fraser Tennant Ltd 1970-, Perth City Auctions Ltd, W Bosonworth & Sons Ltd, Robertson & Hunter (Engnr) Ltd, UA Properties Ltd, UA Forestry Ltd, Holiday Cottages (Scotland) Ltd, chm Perth Beef Breeds Assoc 1984-, vice-chm Scotch Quality Beef and Lamb Assoc 1984; Fell Inst of Auctioneers in

Scotland 1966- (pres 1981-82); *Recreations* vintage cars; *Clubs* Bentley Drivers; *Style*— R L Fraser, Esq; Parkfield House, By Perth, Scotland (☎ 0738 51745); 17 Caledonian Rd, Perth, Scotland (☎ 0738 38462)

FRASER, Ronald Petrie; CB (1972); yr s of late Thomas Petrie Fraser, of Elgin; *b* 2 June 1917; *Educ* Daniel Stewart's Coll Edinburgh, Edinburgh Univ, Queen's Coll Oxford; *m* 1962, Ruth Wright, da of late James Baillie Anderson, of Edinburgh; 1 da; *Career* entered HM Civil Serv 1940, undersec Scottish Educn Dept 1963-67, undersec Miny of Agric Fisheries and Food 1968-70 (dep sec 1971), sec Scottish Home and Health Dept 1972-77, chief counting offr for Referendum under Scotland Act 1978; *Recreations* music, walking; *Clubs* New (Edinburgh); *Style*— Ronald Fraser, Esq, CB; 40A Lygon Rd, Edinburgh EH16 5QA (☎ 031 667 8298)

FRASER, William Hamilton; s of William Hamilton Fraser (d 1978), of Scotland, and Agnes Pender, *née* Pate; *b* 20 Feb 1938; *Educ* Hamilton Acad Scotland, Strathclyde Univ Glasgow (BSc metallurgy); *m* 1968, Evelyn Christine, da of Richard Henry Chapman (d 1954), of London; 2 s (Mark William b 1969, John Richard b 1972), 1 da (Lauren Eve b 1972); *Career* md Foster Wheeler Offshore Ltd 1973-78, dir and vice pres McDermott Marine Engrg 1978-85, chm and chief exec Humpreys & Glasgow Ltd 1985-; CEng; *Recreations* tennis, skiing, swimming, shooting, local politics; *Clubs* Caledonian, Les Ambassadeurs, Oil Industries; *Style*— William Hamilton Fraser, Esq; Humphreys & Glasgow Ltd, Chestergate House, 253 Vauxhall Bridge Road, London SW1V 1HD (01-828 1234)

FRASER, Sir William Kerr; GCB (1984, KCB 1979, CB 1978); s of late Alexander Macmillan Fraser and Rachel, *née* Kerr; *b* 18 Mar 1929; *Educ* Eastwood Sch, Glasgow Univ (MA, LLB); *m* 1956, Marion Anne, *née* Forbes; 3 s, 1 da; *Career* joined Scottish Home Dept 1955, perm under-sec of state Scottish Office 1978-88 (dep sec 1975-78); princ and vice-chllr Univ of Glasgow 1988-; *Clubs* New (Edinburgh); *Style*— Sir William Fraser, GCB; Principals Lodging, The University Glasgow G12 8QG (☎ 031 339 8855)

FRASER OF ALLANDER, Baroness; Kate Hutcheon; *née* Lewis; da of Sir Andrew Jopp Williams Lewis, LLD (d 1952), and Anne, *née* Walker (d 1940); *b* 2 April 1910; *Educ* St Margarets Aberdeen, LA Casita Lausanne; *m* 2 April 1931, 1 Baron Fraser of Allander (d 6 Nov 1966); 1 s (Sir Hugh Fraser, 2 Bt - he disclaimed his Peerage and d 1987), 1 da (Hon Ann Fraser); *Career* tstee Hugh Fraser Fndn; Hon LLD Aberdeen Univ 1984; *Style*— The Rt Hon Lady Fraser of Allander; Allander Lodge, 39 Craigmillar Avenue, Milngavie, Glasgow G62 8AX

FRASER OF CARMYLLIE, Baron (Life Peer UK 1989), of Carmyllie in the District of Angus; Peter Lovat Fraser; PC (1989), QC (Scot) (1982); s of Rev George Robson Fraser and Helen Jean, *née* Meiklejohn; *b* 29 May 1945; *Educ* Loretto, Gonville and Caius Coll Cambridge, Edinburgh Univ; *m* 1969, Fiona Macdonald Mair; 1 s, 2 da; *Career* advocate (Scotland) 1969-; lectr constitutional law Heriot-Watt Univ 1972-74; standing jr counsel (Scotland) to FCO 1979; contested (C) Aberdeen North Oct 1974, MP (C) Angus South 1979-83, Angus East 1983-89; PPS to George Younger (sec state Scotland) 1981-82, slr-gen for Scotland 1982-89, Lord Advocate 1989-; Hon Bencher of Lincoln's Inn 1989; *Style*— The Rt Hon Lord Fraser of Carmyllie, PC, QC; Slade House, Carmyllie by Arbroath, Angus (☎ 024 16 215)

FRASER OF KILMORACK, Baron (Life Peer UK 1974); Sir (Richard) Michael; CBE (1955), MBE (Mil 1945); yr s of Dr Thomas Fraser, CBE, DSO, TD, DL (d 1951), and Maria-Theresia, *née* Kayser (d 1965); *b* 28 Oct 1915; *Educ* Fettes, King's Coll Cambridge (BA, MA); *m* 1944, Elizabeth Chloë, da of Brig Cyril Alexander Fraser Drummond, OBE (d 1979); 1 s (Angus b 1945) (and 1 s Hugo b 1949, d 1970); *Career* served WWII RA, Lt-Col, GSO1 1945; entered Cons Res Dept 1946 (head of Home Affrs Section 1950-51, dir 1951-64, chm 1970-74), sec to Cons Pty Advsy Ctee on Policy 1951-64 (dep chm 1970-75), sec to Cons Leader's Consultative Ctee 1964-70 and 1974-75, dep chm Cons Pty Orgn 1964-75; dir: Glaxo Hldgs plc 1975-85, Glaxo Gp Ltd 1975-85, Whiteaway Laidlaw Bank Ltd 1981-, Glaxo Enterprises Inc (USA) 1983-85; Glaxo Tstees Ltd 1975-86; kt 1962; *Clubs* Brooks's, Carlton, St Stephens Constitutional (hon), Coningsby (hon); *Style*— The Rt Hon Lord Fraser of Kilmorack, CBE; 18 Drayton Ct, Drayton Gdns, London SW10 9RH (☎ 01 370 1543)

FRASER OF TULLYBELTON, Baroness; (Mary Ursula) Cynthia Gwendolen; o da of Lt-Col Ian H Macdonell, DSO, late HLI, of Connel, Argyllshire; *m* 1943, Baron Fraser of Tullybelton, PC (Life Peer; d 1989); 1 s (Hon (Alexander) Andrew Macdonell Fraser, *qv*); *Style*— The Rt Hon Lady Fraser of Tullybelton; Tullybelton House, Bankfoot, Perthshire (☎ 073 887 312)

FRASER-TYTLER, Christian Helen; *née* Shairp; CBE (1940), TD; da of John Campbell Shairp (d 1913), of Houston, W Lothian, and H Caroline, *née* Erskine (d 1979); *b* 23 August 1897; *m* 1919, Col Neil Fraser-Tytler, DSO and bar, TD, DL (awarded Croix de Guerre avec palme, d 1937), of Aldourie and Balnain, Inverness, s of Col E G Fraser-Tytler; 2 da (Ann b 1920 m Sir David Erskine, 5 Bt; Mary Hermione b 1922 m Sir Patrick Morgan); *Career* FO 1917-19, WO 1939-43; ATS 1938-45; senior controller AA Command 1945 (TD), former JP Inverness; landowner (Old Clune House, Albourie, Inverness, and farm); *Recreations* fishing, reading; *Style*— Mrs Neil Fraser-Tytler, CBE, TD; 116 Market St, St Andrews, Fife (☎ 0334 76826)

FRATINI, Gina Georgina Carolin Eve; da of The hon Somerset Butler, CIE (d 1960), and Barbara, *née* Jackom-Hood (d 1978); *b* 22 Sept 1931; *Educ* in Canada, Burma, India and UK, RCA (Dip Fashion); *m* 1, 1954 (m dis), David Goldberg, s of David Goldberg; m 2 1960 (m dis 1964), Renato Fratini, s of Fernucio Fratini, of Rome,; m 3 1966 (m dis 1985), Jimmy Logan; *Career* fashion and theatre designer, involved in various art colls, communities and lectures; *Recreations* gardening, horse racing; *Style*— Mrs Gina Fratini; Wandle Rd, London SW17; Church Cottage Wilts, Marvic House, Bishops Rd, London SW6 (☎ 01 381 8759)

FRAYLING, Prof Christopher John; s of Maj Arthur Frederick Frayling and Barbara Kathleen, *née* Imhof; *b* 25 Dec 1946; *Educ* Repton, Churchill Coll Cambridge (MA, PhD); *m* 1981, Helen Ann Snowdon; *Career* lectr in history Exeter Univ 1971-72; film archivist Imperial War Museum 1972-73; lectr in history of ideas Bath Univ 1973-79; prof of cultural history (and head of dept) RCA 1979-; tstee Victoria & Albert Museum 1983-; govr Br Film Inst 1982-86; chm Educn Ctee BFI 1983-86; memb: Crafts Cncl 1982-85, del visual arts panel (chm) Arts Cncl of GB 1983-87, photography panel 1983-85, chm Arts Projects Cttee 1985-; chm: Crafts Study Centre Bath, 1981-, Free Form Arts Trust 1984-; memb Nat Advsy Body linking party on higher educn in the Arts 1985-; *Publications include* Napoleon Wrote Fiction (1972), The Vampyre (1977), Spaghetti Westerns (1981), The Royal Coll of Art: one hundred and fifty years of art and design (1987) and numerous articles in learned and less learned journals; *Recreations* finding time; *Style*— Prof Christopher Frayling; 12 Macaulay Buildings, Widcombe Hill, Bath, Avon; Department of Cultural History, Royal College of Art, Kensington Gore, London SW7 (☎ 01 584 5020)

FRAYN, Michael; s of late Thomas Allen Frayn, and late Violet Alice, *née* Lawson; *b* 8 Sept 1933; *Educ* Kingston GS, Emmanuel Coll Cambridge; *m* 1960 (m dis 1989), Gillian, *née* Palmer; 3 da; *Career* author and playwright; columnist The Guardian 1959-62 (reporter 1957-59), columnist The Observer 1962-68; stage plays: The Two of Us 1970, The Sandboy 1971, Alphabetical Order 1975, Donkeys' Years 1976, Clouds 1976, Balmoral 1978 (new version Liberty Hall 1980), Make and Break 1980, Noises Off 1982, Benefactors 1984; tv plays incl: Jamie, On a Flying Visit 1968, Birthday 1969; tv documentaries incl: Second City Reports 1964, Beyond a Joke 1972, Making Faces (series) 1975, One Pair of Eyes 1968, Laurence Sterne Lived Here 1973, Imagine a City Called Berlin 1975, Vienna: The Mask of Gold 1977, Three Streets in the Country 1979, The Long Straight (Great Railway Journeys of the World) 1980, Jerusalem 1984; translations of plays incl: The Cherry Orchard, Three Sisters, The Seagull, Uncle Vanya, Wild Honey, The Fruits of Enlightment (Tolstoy), Exchange (Trifonov), Number One (Anouilh); The Sneeze (adaption of Chekhov Short Stories) Aldwych Theatre 1988-89, Clockwise (script for film) 1985; recipient of numerous drama awards; hon fell Emmanuel Coll Cambridge 1985; *Books novels* incl: The Tin Men 1965, The Russian Interpreter 1966, Towards the End of the Morning 1967, A Very Private Life 1968, Sweet Dreams 1973; *non-fiction* incl: Constructions (philosophy) 1974, several volumes of collected writings and translations; *Style*— Michael Frayn, Esq; c/o Elaine Green Ltd, 31 Newington Gn, London N16

FRAZER, Ian William; s of William George Frazer (d 1982), of Hutton, Essex, and Grace Marjorie, *née* Willis (d 1979); *b* 26 Jan 1933; *Educ* Framlington Coll Suffolk; *m* 3 March 1964, Priscilla, da of Capt John Daniell (ka 1943), of Kimpton, Herts; 3 da (Annabel b 30 May 1965, Katharine b 14 Nov 1966, Henrietta b 5 March 1970); *Career* Nat Serv cmmnd The Queen's Bays (2 Dragoon Gds) 1955-57; Army Emergency Reserve 1957-64, ret Lt 1 Queen's Dragoon Gds; qualified CA 1955, sr ptnr (formerly ptnr) Littlejohn Frazer (formerly Frazer Whiting & Co) 1971-; govr: Morpeth Sch Tower Hamlets 1984-, St Mary's Sch Wantage 1967-; cncl memb Chelsea Soc 1972-; FCA 1955; *Recreations* music, reading, shooting, skiing; *Clubs* Cavalry and Guards, City of London; *Style*— Ian Frazer, Esq; 6 Edith Terrace, Chelsea, London SW10 0TQ (☎ 01 352 3310); Irish Hill Cottage, Hamstead Marshall, Newbury, Berks RG15 0JB; Littlejohn Frazer, 2 Canary Wharf, London E14 9SY (☎ 01 987 5030)

FRAZER, Lady Juliet Clare; *née* Chichester; yr da of 7 Marquess of Donegall; *b* 2 Nov 1954; *m* April 1983, Andrew David Frazer, yr s of I W Frazer, of Hillmount, Cullybackey, Co Antrim; 1 s (William John Andrew b 1985), 1 da (Mary Emma b (twin) 1985); *Style*— Lady Juliet Frazer; Hillmount, Cukkybackey, Co Antrim, Northern Ireland

FRAZER, Oliver Haldane; s of Wilson Ray Frazer, OBE (d 1963), and Grace Haldane, *née* Robbs (d 1966); *b* 13 July 1913; *Educ* Dulwich, Coopers Hill Trg Coll; *m* 18 Feb 1950, Dorothy Adeline, da of Kingsley Newman, MM (d 1965); *Career* WWII Staff Sgt Glider Pilot Regt, served D-Day and Arnhem; teacher of biology and gen sci (ret); lectr, broadcaster and author, conservation conslt and advsr; voluntary bat warden for Nature Conservancy Cncl; pres IOW Natural History and Archaeological Soc 1960-63 (vice-pres 1963-); author and presenter of 'What's in a Habitat?' (a series of 12 educational radio broadcasts with supporting slides and info pack for schs, for BBC Radio Solent 1974); co-author with J F D Frazer (cousin) 'Amphibians' in the Wykeham Science Series (No 25) 1973; contrib to the AA Leisure Guide to the IOW; *Recreations* natural history, photography; *Style*— Oliver Frazer, Esq; Mottistone Mill, Brighstone, Newport, IOW PO30 4AW (☎ 0983 740318)

FREAN, Denis Edward; CBE (1973, OBE 1964); s of Charles Frean (d 1921), of Bournemouth; *b* 23 Sept 1913; *Educ* Stowe; *m* 1943, Margareta, da of the late Leonard Bucknall Eyre, MBE, of Sweden; 3 s; *Career* slr until 1939, Helsingfors Univ 1940-41, Br Cncl Serv: Finland 1945-47, Turin 1947-51, London 1951-52, Melbourne 1952, Br Guiana 1952-54, Warsaw 1954-56, Dublin 1956-59, Baghdad 1959-64, Lisbon 1964-66, London 1966-68; British Cncl rep and cultural attaché Br Embassy, Pretoria 1968-75; Freedom Medal second class Finland 1940; *Recreations* enamelling, photography; *Style*— Denis Frean, Esq, CBE; 1 St Martins Row, Upton Grey, Basingstoke, Hants (☎ 0256 862416)

FREDERICK, Sir Charles Boscawen; 10 Bt (GB 1723), of Burwood House, Surrey, JP (Bucks); s of Lt-Col Sir Edward Boscawen Frederick, 9 Bt, CVO (d 1956), and Edith Katherine (Kathleen) Cortlandt, *née* Mulloy (d 1970); *b* 11 April 1919; *Educ* Eton; *m* 8 Oct 1949, Rosemary, er da late Lt-Col Robert John Halkett Baddeley MC; 2 s, 2 da; *Heir* s Christopher St John Frederick; *Career* Maj (ret) Grenadier Gds; memb: London Stock Exchange 1954-62, gen cmmr Income Tax 1966-, Stock Exchange Cncl 1973-75; chm Provincial Unit of Stock Exchange 1973-75; *Recreations* woodwork, fishing; *Style*— Sir Charles Frederick, Bt, JP; Virginia Cottage, Stoke Trister, Wincanton, Somerset BA9 9PQ

FREDERICK, Christopher St John; s and h of Sir Charles Frederick, 10 Bt; *b* 28 June 1950; *Style*— Christopher Frederick, Esq

FREDJOHN, Dennis; s of late Maurice Fredjohn; *b* 22 Feb 1925; *Educ* Westminster City Sch, St John's Coll Cambridge; *m* 1947, Pamela Jill, *née* Samms; 1 s, 2 da; *Career* Fl Offr RAF, served WWII, Lt RN; exec dir Rio Tinto Zinc 1970-73; dir Arbuthnot Latham Holdings 1973-76; md Alusuisse (UK) Ltd 1976-80, Capital Ventures Ltd 1981-; memb of cncl Lloyd's of London 1982-84; *Recreations* squash, farming, bridge; *Style*— Dennis Fredjohn, Esq; Fairfields, Redmarley, Glos GL12 3JU (☎ 053 181 477)

FREEBORN, David Michael; s of Herbert Aubury Freeborn (d 1976), of Whetstone, London, and May Beatrice, *née* Inwards; *b* 15 May 1950; *Educ* Christ Church Secondary Sch London, Tottenham Tech Coll, St Albans Coll of Further Education; *m* 25 Feb 1983, Janis, da of Roy James Lambert, of Maidstone; 1 da (Claire b 27 June 1983); *Career* md J A Elliott (Holdings) Ltd 1988 (dir 1982), chm J A Elliott Ltd 1988 (dir 1979, md 1983), chm J A Elliott (Layford) Ltd 1988 (dir 1978, md 1980), chm J A Elliott (Developments) Ltd 1988 (dir 1980), chm J A Elliott (New Homes) Ltd 1988 (dir 1985), chm J A Elliott (Projects) Ltd 1988 (dir 1988), chm J A Elliott (Plant) Ltd 1988 (dir 1988), dir Seedbed Centres Ltd 1985, non-exec dir Land & Urban plc 1986, dir Fedn Industl Assocs 1987, chm Moorcroft Construction (Ellesmere Port) ltd 1988 (dir 1988); MCIOB 1972, FRICS 1983, IOD; *Recreations* golf; *Clubs* RAC, Pall Mall;

Style— David Freeborn, Esq; c/o J A Elliott Ltd, 133 Stansted Rd, Bishops Stortford, Herts CM23 5NT (☎ 0279 755 962, fax 0279 55504, telex 818853 JAE G)

FREEDMAN, Cyril Winston; s of Sydney Freedman (d 1951), and Irene Rosalind, *née* Anekstein; *b* 31 August 1945; *Educ* Brighton Coll, Brighton Coll of Art and Design (Dip Graphic Art and Design); *m* 25 Mar 1970, Christine Mary, da of Cecil Shipman of Swanwick, Derbys; 1 s (Mark b 1973) 1 d (Anna b 1977); *Career* chm: CWF Advertising Ltd 1971-74, Halls Homes and Gardens 1978-80 (md 1977-78 dir 1974-81); dir Pentos plc and subsidiaries 1979-81, chm Serco Ryan Ltd 1982-87, chief exec WBH Group Ltd (subsidiary of Lopex plc) 1985-88, dir Armour Automotive Products Gp 1985-; chm Deeko plc 1988-, Hennell Hldgs Ltd 1988-; dir Alan Patricof Assocs Ltd 1988-; MInstM; *Recreations* painting, collecting fine art; *Style*— Cyril Freedman, Esq; Alan Patricof Associates Ltd, 24 Upper Brook St, London W1 (☎ 01 493 3633)

FREEDMAN, Ivor Stuart Douglas Andrew; s of Mordka (Mick) Freedman (d 1980), of 21 Glebe Crescent, Hendon, London, and Rita, *née* Isaacs; *b* 18 July 1947; *Educ* Hendon County GS; *m* 15 Oct 1972, Linda, da of Samuel Tischler, 41 Greenacres, Finchley, London; 1 s (Michael James b 15 Sept 1980), 1 da (Emma Jane b 26 March 1975); *Career* chm: WIMTA Credit Bureau 1976-83, Western Int Wholesale Fruit 1977- 82, jt mgmnt ctee Hounslow Borough 1978-81, H Freedman Ltd 1980-83, Fruita-Plan (UK) Ltd 1980-, Gammalodge Ltd 1983-87, London Market Corpn 1987-, ISI Int Holdings, 1987-, Moordale Enterprises Ltd 1987-, memb: Cons Pty, Variety club of GB 1970-82, Fruit Importers Assoc 1975-82;; *Recreations* tennis, football, cricket, snooker, stamp collecting, general music; *Style*— Ivor Freedman, Esq; LMC House, 74-76 Cheshire Street, London E2 6EH (☎ 01 739 9900, fax 01 739 9400, car telephone 0836 284213, car answerphone 0836 862420, telex 297073 COPRA G)

FREEDMAN, Prof Lawrence David; s of late Lt Cdr Julius Freedman, RN, and Myra, *née* Robinson; *b* 7 Dec 1948; *Educ* Whitley Bay GS, Manchester Univ (BA), York Univ (BPhil), Oxford Univ (DPhil); *m* 1974, Judith Anne, da of Harry Hill; 1 s (Samuel b 1981), 1 da (Ruth b 1984); *Career* head policy studies, Royal Inst for International Affairs at Chatham House to April 1982; prof of war studies King's Coll London 1982-; *Books* The Evolution of Nuclear Strategy (1981); US Intelligence and the Soviet Strategic Threat (1977), Britain and Nuclear Weapons (1980), The Atlas of Global Strategy (1985), The Prize of Peace (1986), Britain and the Falklands War (1988); *Style*— Prof Lawrence Freedman; Department of War Studies, King's College, London University, Strand, London WC2R 2LS (☎ 01 836 5454)

FREELAND, James Gourlay; s of James Gourlay, of Surrey, and Jessie McRobie, *née* Brown; *b* 3 August 1936; *Educ* Haileybury & ISC, Trinity Hall Cambridge (MA); *m* 27 May 1961, Diana, da of Bryce Graham Dewsbury (d 1971); 1 s (Jeremy b 1963), 2 da (Joanna b 1965, Stephanie b 1971); *Career* Nat Serv: RM Malta 1955-57; shipbroker; dir: H Clarkson & Co Ltd London 1970-, Clarkson Res Studies Ltd London 1986-, Distribution Consulting Servs Inc Dallas USA 1986-; underwriting memb Lloyd's 1985-; Liveryman Worshipful Co of Shipwrights 1963- (Asst to Ct 1984-); *Recreations* golf, shooting; *Clubs* MCC, Jesters; *Style*— James G Freeland, Esq; 122 Rivermead Court, Ranelagh Gardens, London SW6 3SD (☎ 01 7361511; Grenna House, Chilson, Oxford OX7 3HU (☎ 060 876 349); H Clarkson & Co Ltd, 12 Camomile Street, London EC3A 7BP (☎ 01 283 9020)

FREELAND, Sir John Redvers; KCMG (1984, CMG 1973), QC 1987; o s of Clarence Redvers Freeland and Freda, *née* Walker; *b* 16 July 1927; *Educ* Stowe, Corpus Christi Coll Cambridge; *m* 1952, Sarah Mary, er da of late Sidney Pascoe Hayward, QC; 1 s (Nicholas b 1956), 1 da (Petra b 1959); *Career* RN 1945 and 1948-51, barr Lincoln's Inn 1952, bencher 1985, asst legal advsr FO 1954-63 and 1965-67; legal advsr HM Embassy Bonn 1963-65, legal cnsllr FCO 1967-70 and 1973-76, cnsllr (legal advsr) UK Mission to UN NY 1970-73, second legal advsr FCO 1976-84, legal advsr 1984-87; judge Arbitral Tbnl and Mixed Cmmn for the Agreement on German External Debts 1988-; memb US-Chile Int Cmmn of Investigation 1989-; *Clubs* Travellers'; *Style*— Sir John Freeland, KCMG, QC

FREELING, Nicolas; s of Heathfield Walter Partridge (d 1939), of Norfolk, and Anne Freeling Davidson (d 1974); a collateral of freeling, Bt (extinct 1940); *b* 3 Mar 1927; *m* 1954, Cornelia, da of Laurens Termes (d 1970); 4 s (Conrad, Hugo, Wolf, Yvan), 1 da (Andrea); *Career* author of some thirty novels; *Style*— Nicolas Freeling, Esq; Grandfontaine, 67130 Schirmeck, France

FREEMAN, Brig Alfred Francis; MC (1940); s of Henry Alfred Freeman (d 1975), and Murielle Theodora, *née* Cameron-Stuart (d 1975); *b* 24 Mar 1916; *Educ* Imperial Serv Coll Windsor, RMA Woolwich; *m* 6 April 1944, Dorothy Peart, da of Capt Ivo Peart Robinson (d 1950); 2 s (Francis b 1948, Nigel b 1953), 2 da (Susan b 1950, Judith b 1957); *Career* cmmnd Royal Signals 1936, Sch of Signals Catterick 1936-37, 3 Divnl Signals Bulford 1937-39, signal offr 7 Gds Bde 1939, SO3 to Chief Signal Offr 3 Corps France 1939-40, SO2 to Chief Signal Offr 6 Corps NI 1940-41, Staff Coll Camberley 1941-42, SO2 WO Signals 1 1942-44, 2 i/c (later cmd) 8 Corps Signals 1944, cmd 1 Corprs Signals 1944-45, SO1 to Signal Offr in Chief SE Asia Cmd Ceylon 1945, SO1 to Chief Signal Offr Malaya 1946-47, instr RMA Sandhurst 1947-49, long telecommunications course Catterick 1949-50, SO2 Signals Div Allied Land Forces Central Europe 1951-53, 2 i/c Cwlth Signal Regt Korea 1953-54, instr and SO1 planning wing Sch of Signals Catterick 1954-59, cdr 54 Divnl Signal Regt TA 1959-60, cdr Royal Signals Singapore 1960-62, Col GS Signals MOD 1963-65, chief signal offr Northern Cmd 1965-68, ret 1968; membership recruitment offr Oxon and N Cotswold Royal Agric Soc of England 1969-80; chm Brailes branch Royal Br Legion, former chm and pres Annual Brailes Show, life govr Three Counties Agric Soc; *Recreations* gardening; *Clubs* Army and Navy; *Style*— Brig Alfred Freeman, MC

FREEMAN, David Alexander; s of John Freeman (d 1963), of Hampstead, and Betty, *née* Morris (d 1970); *b* 13 May 1928; *Educ* Univ Coll Sch London, Sorbonne, Univ of St Andrew's (MA); *m* 4 Sept 1956, Margaret (Meg) Joan (Meg), da of Lt-Col Sir Geoffrey Stewart Tomkinson, OBE, MC (d 1963), of Whitville, Kidderminster, Worcs; 1 s (Charles Geoffrey John b 1963), 2 da (Victoria Frances Margaret b 1960, Alexandra Jane b 1969); *Career* air raid messenger School Boy Civil Def Hampstead 1942-44; md: Spa Brushes Ltd Chesham 1954-62, Freeman Dawson & Co Ltd 1965-83, Guarantee Protection Tst 1983-; Parly candidate (Lib) East Fife 1950; memb cncl Br Wood Preserving Assoc; *Books* Choosing The Right School (1983); *Recreations* chatting, trombone, biking; *Clubs* Lansdowne, Nat Lib, Leander; *Style*— David Freeman, Esq; Stoneleigh, Naphill, Nr High Wycombe, HP14 4QX (☎ 024 024 2905); The Guarantee Protection Trust, P O Box 77, High Wycombe HP11 1BW (☎ 0494 447 049, fax 0494 465 194)

FREEMAN, David John; s of Meyer Henry Freeman (d 1984), of London, and Rebecca, *née* Lubinsky (d 1980); *b* 25 Feb 1928; *Educ* Christ's Coll Finchley; *m* 19 March 1950, Iris Margaret, da of Cyril Henry Alberge (d 1980), of London; 2 s (Michael Ian b 1951, Peter Geoffrey b 1955), 1 da (Jill Barbara b 1953); *Career* Army Lt 1946-48; slr 1952; fndr and sr ptnr DJ Freeman & Co 1952-; Dept of Trade Inspector into affairs of AEG Telefunken (UK) Ltd and Credit Collections Ltd 1977; govr Royal Shakespeare Theatre 1979-; memb Law Soc; *Recreations* reading, theatre, gardening; *Clubs* Reform, Huntercombe Golf; *Style*— David J Freeman, Esq; 6 Hyde Park Gardens, W2 (☎ 01 262 0895); Old Greenfield House, Christmas Common, Watlington, Oxon (☎ 049 161 2272); 43 Fetter Lane, London EC4A 1NA (☎ 01 583 4055, fax 01 353 7377, telex 894579)

FREEMAN, Frederick Clement; s of (Clement) Sidney Freeman (d 1985), and Margaret, *née* Yorke (d 1947); *b* 14 Mar 1921; *Educ* Repton; *m* 20 July 1946, Yvonne, da of John Pye Bibby; 2 s (Andrew b 1950, Richard b 1953), 1 da (Hazel b 1947); *Career* Maj King's (Liverpool) Regt and Para Regt, served Burma (Chindits); chm and md Freemans (Liverpool) Ltd and subsiduary cos 1948-; chm and hon dir: United Way (reg charity) 1972-, United Tsts 1987- (reg charity 1988; bd memb Interphil (internat philanthropy) 1975-85; author of The SUVOC Application (1983) (Soc of United Vol Organisations within Community); FBIM, JP (ret); *Recreations* charitable work, gardening, golf; *Clubs* Army and Navy, London, Anthenaeum Liverpool; *Style*— Frederick Freeman, Esq; Broughshane, Croft Drive West, Caldy, Wirral, Merseyside L48 2JQ (☎ 051 625 8306); PO Box 14, 8 Nelson Rd, Edge Hill, Liverpool L69 7AA (☎ 051 709 8252)

FREEMAN, Prof Hugh Lionel; s of the late Bernard Freeman, and Dora Doris, *née* Kahn; *b* 4 August 1929; *Educ* Altrincham GS, St John's Coll Oxford (DM, MSc, MA); *m* 1957, Sally Joan, BSc, MEd, PhD, FBPS, da of Philip Casket; 3 s, 1 da; *Career* Capt RAMC 1956-58; house surg Manchester Roy Inf 1955, registrar Bethlem Roy and Maudsley Hosps 1958-60, sr registrar Littlemore Hosp Oxford 1960-61; conslt psychiatrist Salford Royal Hosp 1961-70, hon conslt Salford Health Authy Univ of Manchester Sch of Medicine 1988-; WHO conslt: Grenada 1970, Chile 1978, Philippines 1979, Bangladesh 1981, Greece 1985; Rapporteur: WHO conf on Mental Health Services Trieste 1984, WHO Ruanda 1985, Cncl of Europe conf on Health in Cities 1985; ed Br Jl of Psych 1983- (asst ed 1978-83), has lectured to and addressed univs, confs and hosps worldwide; vice chm MIND 1983-87; vis fell Greer Coll Oxford; memb: Morcian Regnl Ctee Nat Tst, Mental Health Cmmn 1983, Mental Health Review Tbnls, City of Manchester Historic Bldgs Panel, hon memb: Chilean Soc of Psych Neurol and Neurosurgery, Egyptian Psychiatric Assoc, Polish Psychiatric Assoc; Hon Prof Univ of Manchester, vice chm Manchester Heritage Tst, Freeman City of London, Liveryman Soc of Apothecaries; FRC Psych, FRSH; publications: Trends in Mental Health Services (1963), New Aspects of the Mental Health Service (ed jtly 1968), Mental Health Services in Europe (1985), Mental Health 7 the Environment (ed 1985), Dangerousness (ed jtly 1982); *Recreations* architecture, travel, music; *Clubs* United Oxford & Cambridge, Whitefriars; *Style*— Hugh Freeman, Esq; Wykeham, Alan Drive, Hale, Cheshire WA15 0LR (☎ 061 980 4597)

FREEMAN, Ifan Charles Harold; CMG (1964), TD (1960); s of C E D W Freeman (d 1970), of Woodhall Spa, Lincs; *b* 11 Sept 1910; *Educ* Friars Sch Bangor, Univ of Wales; *m* 1937, Enid Marguerite, da of late Edward W Hallum, of Cheltenham; 2 da; *Career* served with RA 1939-45; Colonial Serv: Kenya 1946-58, Nyasaland 1958-71, dir of Education 1958-61, perm sec 1961-65, registrar Univ of Malawi 1965-71; *Recreations* gardening,; *Style*— Ifan Freeman, Esq, CMG, TD; Swyn Y Wylan, Marianglas, Anglesey, Gwynedd LL73 8PG (☎ 0248 853 746)

FREEMAN, (Edgar) James (Albert); MC (1945); s of Horace Freeman (d 1954), of London, and Beatrice Mary, *née* Craddock (d 1946); *b* 31 Dec 1917; *Educ* Westminster, Trinity Coll Cambridge (MA); *m* 15 May 1948, Shirley Lake (d 1988), da of William Henry Whatmough (d 1963), of Streatham; 1 s (Peter b 1 March 1951), 2 da (Catherine b 22 Sept 1955, Ruth b 12 Feb 1958); *Career* Suffolk Regt 1939, 2 Lt The Durham Light Infantry 1940-44 (Maj 1944) served UK, India, Burma; barr Lincoln's Inn 1947, Chancery Bar 1947-72, VP Value Added Tax Tribunals 1972-, chm of Industl Tbnls 1975-84 (regnl chm 1984-); *Recreations* sailing, cycling; *Clubs* Royal Cruising, Bar Yacht; *Style*— James Freeman, Esq, MC; Regional Office of the Industrial Tribunals, Southgate St, Bury St Edmunds, Suffolk IP33 2AQ

FREEMAN, His Eminence James Darcy; KBE; *see*: Cardinal Archbp (RC) of Sydney

FREEMAN, Sir James Robin; 3 Bt (UK 1945), of Murtle, Co Aberdeen; s of Sir Keith Freeman, 2 Bt (d 1981), and Patricia, Lady Freeman, *qv*; *b* 21 July 1955; *Heir* none; *Style*— Sir James Freeman, Bt; c/o Midland Bank, 151 Hoe St, Walthamstow, E17

FREEMAN, Rt Hon John; PC (1966), MBE (1943); eldest s of Horace Freeman, barrister-at-law (d 1954); *b* 19 Feb 1915; *Educ* Westminster, Brasenose Coll Oxford; *m* 1, 1938 (m dis 1948), Elizabeth Allen Johnston; m 2, 1948, Margaret Ista Mabel Kerr (d 1957); 1 adopted da; m 3, 1962 (m dis 1976), Catherine, da of Harold Dove and formerly wife of Charles Wheeler; 2 s, 1 da; m 4, 1976, Judith Mitchell; 2 da; *Career* serv WWII; MP (Lab) Watford Div of Herts 1945-50, Borough of Watford 1950-55; ed (asst ed 1951-58, dep ed 1958-60) New Statesman 1961-65; Br high cmmr in India 1965-68, ambass in Washington 1969-71; vice-pres Roy Televison Soc 1975-84; chm LWT 1971-84, LWT (Hldgs) 1976-84; winner of Royal TV Soc Gold Medal 1981 for distinguished service to ind broadcasting; chm Ind TV News 1976-81, Hutchinson Ltd 1978-83, Page & Moy (Hldgs) 1979-84; visiting Prof of Int Relations at the Univ of Calif; Hon Fell Brasenose Coll Oxford, Hon LLD Univ of S Carolina; *Style*— The Rt Hon John Freeman, MBE; c/o Barclay's Bank, 58 Southampton Row, London WC1B 4AT

FREEMAN, John Frederick; s of Albert George Freeman (d 1985), of Salisbury, and Catherine Sarah, *née* Crowe (d 1977); *b* 11 Dec 1937; *Educ* Bishop Wordsworth Sch Salisbury, Durham Univ (BA); *m* 12 Aug 1960, Betty, *née* Wolstencroft (d 1960); 1 s (Ivan Xenon (b England) b 25 May 1965); *Career* teacher with Stockport LEA 1965-; chief moderator for Eng NW Reg Exam bd 1982-87 (moderator 1978-82); info tech dept and educnl admin software devpt N Area Coll 1987-; *Books* Creative Writing (1965); play Xenona (1968); *Recreations* travel; *Style*— John Freeman, Esq; 42 Ravenork Rd, Davenport, Stockport SK2 7BQ (☎ 061 483 4903); North Area Sixth Form College, Buckingham Rd, Heaton Moor, Stockport SK4 4RA (☎ 061 442 7494)

FREEMAN, Matthew Philip George; s of Philip Edmund Freeman, of Great

Yarmouth, Norfolk, and Thelma Doreen, *née* Pike (d 1962); *b* 13 Mar 1953; *Educ* Great Yarmouth GS, RCM (GRSM, ARCM), Univ of London; *Career* musical dir: theatre recording tv; memb BAHAI Assoc for the Arts; Freeman City of London, memb Worshipful Co of Musicians 1977; *Style—* Matthew Freeman, Esq; Leighton House, Glade Rd, Marlow, Bucks

FREEMAN, Michael Alexander Reykers; s of Donald George Freeman (d 1937), of Gatton Manon, Ockley, Surrey, and Florence Julia, *née* Elms (d 1962); *b* 17 Nov 1931; *Educ* Stowe, Corpus Christi Coll Cambridge (BA, MB, BCh), London Hosp Med Coll; *m* 1, 1951 (m dis), Elizabeth Jean; 1 s (Jonathan b 29 May 1954), 1 da (Julianne b 5 June 1952); m 2, 1959 (m dis), Janet Edith; 1 s (dominic b 3 April 1965), 1 da (Emma b 18 May 1962); m3, 26 Sept 1968, Patricia, da of Leslie Gill (d 1976), of Bristol; 1 s (James b 14 April 1971, d 18 May May 1971), 1 da (Clare b 31 Dec 1972); *Career* clinical trg in med surgery and orthopaedic surgery London Hosp, Westminster Hosp, Middx Hosp, awarded Copeman Medal, Robert Jones Gold Medal, co-fndr and dir biomechanics unit dept of med engrg Imperial Coll London 1966-79, sr lectr orthopaedic surgery London Hosp Med Coll 1968-, conslt orthopaedic surgn London Hosp 1968-, co-dir bone & it res unit London Hosp Med Coll 1975; pre Br Hip Soc, past pres Int Hip Soc; past memb: bd of govrs London Hosp, Clinical Res Bd, MRC; memb advsy ctee health unit Inst of Econ Affrs; Yeoman Worshipful Co of Apothecaries; AAOS, BOA, RSM, BES, ORS, IHS, SICOT, FRCS; *Books* ed: Adult Articular Cartilage (1973), The Scientific Basis of Joint Replacemnet (with S A V Swanson 1977), Arthritis of the Knee (1980), Osteoarthritis in the Young Adult Hip (with D Reynolds 1984); *Clubs* Athenaeum; *Style—* Michael Freeman, Esq; 79 Albert St, London NW1 (☎ 01 387 0817); 149 Harley St, London W1 (☎ 01 935 4444 ext 4004, fax 01 935 4771)

FREEMAN, Nicholas Hall; OBE (1985); s of William Freeman, of Devon, and (Ada) Grace Ellen, *née* Hall (d 1987); *b* 25 July 1939; *Educ* Stoneygate Sch, King's Sch Canterbury; *Career* slr 1962-68, barr Middle Temple 1968-, rec Crown Court 1985-; cncllr RBK&C 1968-, chm Town Planning Ctee 1975-77, ldr Cncl 1977-, chllr Dioc Leic, Parly Candidate (C) 1974, vice-chm General Purposes Ctee London Borough Assoc 1978; Freeman City of London; *Recreations* reading, particularly biography, holidays in France, theatre; *Clubs* Carlton, Leicestershire (Leicester); *Style—* Nicholas Freeman, Esq, OBE; 51 Harrington Gardens, London SW7 (☎ 01 370 3197); 4 Brick Ct, Temple EC4 (☎ 01 583 8455)

FREEMAN, Patricia, Lady; Patricia Denison; yr da of late Charles W Thomas, of Sandown, IOW; *m* 21 Dec 1946, Sir (John) Keith Noël Freeman, 2 Bt (d 5 June 1981); 1 s (Sir James, 3 Bt), 1 da (and 1 s decd); *Style—* Patricia, Lady Freeman; c/o Child & Co (Royal Bank of Scotland), 32 St Giles, Oxford OX1 3ND

FREEMAN, Sir Ralph; CVO (1964), CBE (1952, MBE (mil) 1945); s of Sir Ralph Freeman (d 1950), and Mary, *née* Lines (d 1958); *b* 3 Feb 1911; *Educ* Uppingham, Worcester Coll Oxford (BA, MA); *m* 19 May 1939, Joan Elizabeth, da of Col John George Rose, DSO, VD (d 1973), of Wynberg, Cape Town, South Africa; 2 s (Anthony b 29 March 1946, Hugh b 16 Feb 1949), 1 da (Elizabeth b 10 May 1942); *Career* temp Maj RE 1939-45 WWII, Col Engr and Tport Staff Corps RE (TA), Col Cmdg 1969-74, ret 1976; chartered engr; construction engr: Dorman Long & Co (S Africa, Rhodesia and Denmark) 1932-36, 1937-39, Braithwaite & Co 1936-37; on staff of Freeman Fox and Ptnrs 1939-44, Admiralty and other war work, served RE (see above) 1943-45 at Experimental Bridging Estab, later seconded as bridging advsr to CE 21 Army Gp HQ NW Europe campaign; conslt Freeman Fox & Ptnrs 1979- (ptnr 1947-79, sr ptnr 1963-79); pres Inst Civil Engrs 1966-67, chm Assoc Consltg Engrs 1974-75, pres Welding Inst 1974-76; consltg engr Sandringham Est 1949-76, memb Royal Fine Art Cmmn 1968-85; hon fell Worcester Coll Oxford 1980, Hon D Univ Surrey, Hon MConsE, Hon MIRoyE, Hon FIMechE, hon fell Zimbabwe Inst of Engrs, memb Emeritus Smeatonian Soc, FEng, FICE, FWeldI, FRSA, FCIT, FASCE; kt (4th class) Order of Orange Nassau 1945; kt bach 1970; *Recreations* carpentry, metal work, writing letters; *Clubs* Army and Navy, Leander; *Style—* Sir Ralph Freeman, CVO, CBE; Ballards Shaw, Ballards Lane, Limpsfield, Oxted, Surrey RH8 0SN (☎ 0883 723284)

FREEMAN, Prof Raymond; s of Albert Freeman (d 1940), and Hilda Frances, *née* Bush (d 1983); *b* 6 Jan 1932; *Educ* Nottingham HS, Lincoln Coll Oxford (MA, DPhil, DSc); *m* 19 April 1958, Anne-Marie Catherine, da of Philippe Périnet-Marquet (d 1969); 2 s (Jean-Marc b 1964, Lawrence b 1969), 3 da (Dominique b 1959, Anne b 1960, Louise b 1962); *Career* engr Centre D'Etudes Nucléaires de Saclay France 1957-59, sr sci offr Nat Physical Laboratory Teddington Middx 1959-63, mangr Nuclear Magnetic Resonance Res Varian Assoc Palo Alto California 1963-73; Oxford Univ: lect in physical chemistry 1973-87, fell Magdalen Coll 1973-87, aldrichian praelector in chemistry 1982-87; Cambridge Univ: John Humphrey Plummer Prof of Magnetic Resonance 1987-, Jesus Coll 1987-; FRS 1979; *Books* A Handbook of Nuclear Magnetic Resonance (1987); *Style—* Prof Raymond Freeman; 29 Bentley Rd, Cambridge CB2 2AW (☎ 0223 323 958); Dept of Physical Chemistry, Univ of Cambridge, Lensfied Rd, Cambridge CB2 1EP (☎ 0223 336 450)

FREEMAN, Roger John; s of Lt Cdr Harold Cecil Freeman, MBE, VRD (d 1984), of Much Hadham, Herts, and Jacqueline Mary Freeman; *b* 21 June 1944; *Educ* Wellington, Exeter Univ (BA), Wharton Sch Univ of Pennsylvania (MBA); *m* 12 May 1971, Kitty, da of Juan Carlos Yegros (d 1966), of Asuncion, Paraguay; 2 s (Jonathan b 1981, Christopher b 1989); *Career* Bank of London and S America 1968-72, Harris Tst 1974-79, Libra Bank 1979- (gen mangr 1985-); *Recreations* sport; *Clubs* MCC; *Style—* Roger Freeman, Esq; 11 Grove Terrace, London NW5 (☎ 01 485 2685); Libra Bank plc, 140 London Wall, London EC2 (☎ 01 600 1700, Fax 01 726 2392, Telex 885 869)

FREEMAN, Roger Norman; MP (C) Kettering 1983-; s of Norman and Marjorie Freeman; *b* 27 May 1942; *Educ* Whitgift Sch, Balliol Coll Oxford (MA); *m* 1969, Jennifer Margaret Watson; 1 s, 1 da; *Career* pres Oxford Univ Cons Assoc 1964, md Bow Pubns 1968 (former cncl memb and tres Bow Gp), contested (C) Don Valley 1979; FCA 1978; merchant bank dir; md Lehman Brothers 1972- (joined Lehman Bros (US merchant bank) 1969; first Englishman invited to join US ptnrship); non-exec dir: Martini & Rossi Ltd, McCormick Int Investmts Ltd; fndr memb Hundred Gp of UK CA Fin Dirs; Parly under-sec of State: Armed Forces MOD 1986-88, Dept of Health 1988-; *Publications include* Pensions Policy, Professional Practice, A Fair Deal for Water; *Recreations* sailing, shooting; *Clubs* City of London, Carlton, Kennel; *Style—* Roger Freeman, Esq, MP; House of Commons, London SW1A 0AA (☎ 01 219 6436)

FREEMAN, Roland John Michael; JP (1972); s of Cornelius Alexander Freeman (d 1972), of London, and Marjorie Dolores Kathleen, Freeman (d 1974); *b* 7 May 1927; *Educ* Chippenham GS, St Joseph's Coll Beulah Hill, LSE; *m* 18 Dec 1976, Marian, da of Mr John Kilroy, of Rugby; *Career* sch master 1947-53, Cons Res Dept 1958-59, dir London Municipal Soc 1959-61, campaign mangr Aims of Indust 1961-65; md: PR (Indust) Ltd 1965-69, Welbeck City Ltd 1969-76, Roland Freeman Ltd 1976-89; dir LWT Ltd 1981-89; Wandsworth Borough Cncl: memb 1949-65, ldr and fin chm; GLC: memb and fin chm 1967-70, memb 1975-81; pty candidate: (C) Nuneaton 1974, (SDP/Alliance) Tonbridge and Malling 1983, (SDP) London Central Euo Constituency 1989; memb Alliance Central Ctee 1987 Gen Election; govr LSE 1961-85; Liveryman Worshipful Co of Tallow Chandlers 1970; FCIS 1962, MIPR 1986; *Books* Becoming a Councillor (second edn 1975); *Recreations* music (piano, organ), mountain walking, gardening; *Clubs* Reform; *Style—* Roland Freeman, Esq; Gayfere House, 22/23 Gayfere St, Westminster, London SW1P 3HP (☎ 01 222 8161/222 1337, fax 01 799 1457)

FREEMAN, Lady Winefride Alice; *née* Fitzalan-Howard; yst da of 15 Duke of Norfolk, KG, PC, CVO (d 1917), and his 2 wife Gwendolen Mary, Lady Herries of Terregles (d 1945); *b* 31 Oct 1914; *m* 7 May 1943, Lt-Col John Edward Broke Freeman (d 1986), s of late Sir Philip Horace Freeman, KCVO, KBE; 1 s, 2 da; *Career* JP Suffolk, pres Suffolk Red Cross 1972-84, ret; *Style—* Lady Winefride Freeman; St Catherine's Cottage, Hook Lane, Aldingbourne, West Sussex

FREEMAN-ATTWOOD, Maj (Harold) Warren; s of Maj-Gen Harold Augustus Freeman-Attwood, DSO, OBE, MC (d 1963), and Jessie (d 1958), da of Hon William Carson Job, of Newfoundland, and Liverpool; the family claims descent from the ancient Worcestershire house of Attwood of Park Attwood, Wolverly and Perdiswell (*see* Burke's Landed Gentry, 18 Edn, vol 3); *b* 20 Sept 1923; *Educ* Marlborough, RMC Sandhurst; *m* 1, 9 July 1947 (m dis 1960), Elizabeth, da of Lt-Col Roger Mostyn-Owen, DSO, JP (d 1947); 1 s (Julian b 1953), 1 da (Rosamond b 1951); m 2, 15 Oct 1960, Mrs Marigold Diana Sneyd Wedderburn, da of Edward Mark Philips, OBE (d 1937); 1 s (Jonathan b 1961); *Career* cmmnd Grenadier Gds 1942, serv WWII: N Africa, Italy and Austria (despatches); psc 1952; DAA and QMG 32 Guards Bde 1953-54, Regtl Adj Grenadier Gds 1957-59, 2 i/c 3 Bn Grenadier Gds 1959-60; ret 1960; memb: London Stock Exchange 1962-85, Baltic Exchange 1969-85; *Recreations* music, fine woodwork; *Style—* Maj Warren Freeman-Attwood; West Flexford, Wanborough, Guildford, Surrey (☎ 0483 810 884)

FREEMAN-GRENVILLE, Dr Greville Stewart Parker; s of Ernest Charles Freeman (d 1946), of Shipton-under-Wychwood Oxen, and Agnes Mary Gibson, *née* Parker (d 1966); surname changed from Freeman to Freeman-Grenville by Decree of the Lord Lyon King of Arms 1950; *b* 29 June 1918; *Educ* Eastbourne Coll, Worcester Coll Oxford, (BA, BLitt, MA, DPhil); *m* 29 Aug 1950, The Rt Hon Beatrice Mary Grenville, Lady Kinloss, da of Rev The Hon Luis Francis Chandos Temple Morgan-Grenville, Master of Kinloss (d 1944); 1 s (Bevil David Stewart Chandos b 1953), 2 da (Teresa Mary Nugent b 1957, Hester Josephine Ann b 1960); L.....; *Career* WWII Capt Royal Berks Regt, Personnel Selection Staff 1939-46; HM Overseas Civil Service Tanganyika 1951-60; educnl advsr Aden Protectorate 1961-64; sr res fell: Univ of Ghana 1964-66, Univ of York 1966-69, hon fell Univ of York 1969-, Prof History State Univ of NY 1969-74; author and writer; memb Br Acad Ctee on Fontes Historiae Africanae 1972-, memb Cncl of the Hakluyt Soc 1986-; fell Royal Numismatic Soc 1956, fell Soc of Antiquaries of London 1961, fell Royal Asiatic Soc 1966; contributor Encyclopaedia Britannica, Encyclopaedia of Islam, various journals; *Books* The Medieval History of the Coast of Tanganyika (1982), The East African Coast: Select Documents (1962), The Moshim and Christian Calendars (1963), Chronology of African History (1973), Chronology of World History (1976), Modern Atlas of African History (1976), The Queen's Lineage: from AD 495 to HM The Queen Elizabeth II (1977), Atlas of British History (1977), The Mombassa Rising of 1631 (1980), The Beauty of Jerusalem (second edn 1988), The Beauty of Rome (1988) The Swahili Coast 2nd to 19th Centuries (1988), Papal Cross Pro Ecclesia et Poutifice 1984; *Recreations* travel, gardening; *Clubs* Royal Cwlth Soc; *Style—* Dr Greville Freeman-Grenville; North View House, Sheriff Hutton, York YO6 1PT (☎ 034 77 477)

FREEMAN-GRENVILLE, Hon Teresa Mary Nugent; er da of Lady Kinloss and Greville Stewart Parker Freeman-Grenville; *b* 20 July 1957; *Style—* Hon Teresa Freeman-Grenville; North View House, Sheriff Hutton, York

FREEMAN-THOMAS, Hon Mrs (Moyra); *née* Marjoribanks; da of 3 and last Baron Tweedmouth (d 1935); *b* 1902; *m* 1, 12 June 1923, Lt-Col Reginald Francis Heyworth, of 1 Royal Dragoons (ka 1941); 1 s, 1 da; m 2, 5 Nov 1943, Maj Reginald Brodrick Freeman-Thomas, KOYLI; *Style—* Hon Mrs Freeman-Thomas; Kingswall House, nr Malmesbury, Wilts (☎ 066 62 2338)

FREER, (Charles) Edward Jesse; DL; s of late Canon S Thorold Winckley, FSA, and Elizabeth, *née* Freer; assumed surname of Freer by Deed Poll 1922; *b* 4 Mar 1901; *Educ* Radley; *m* 1, 1927, Violet Muriel (d 1944), da of Harry Percy Gee (d 1962), of Leicester; 2 s, 2 da; m 2, 1945, Cynthia Lilian, da of Leonard R Braithwaite, of Leeds; 2 da; *Career* WWII Lt-Col 1943-44, served in France and Iceland; slr, chm Leics QS 1949-72, chm Mental Health Tbnl Sheffield Regional Bd 1960-72, a chm of indust tbnls 1966-72; *Recreations* reading, walking, travel; *Clubs* East India, Sports and Public Schools; *Style—* Edward Freer, Esq, DL; Shoal House, 48 Pearce Ave, Parkstone, Poole, Dorset BH14 8EH (☎ 0202 748393)

FREER, Air Chief Marshal Sir Robert William George; GBE (1981, CBE 1966), KCB (1977); s of William Freer (d 1979), of Stretton, Cirencester, Glos, and Margaret Jane, *née* Clements (d 1957); *b* 1 Sept 1923; *Educ* Gosport GS; *m* 1950, Margaret Tinkler, 2 da of late John William Elkington, of Ruskington Manor, nr Sleaford, Lincs; 1 s (Adrian), 1 da (Anna); *Career* Queen's Commendation 1955; cmd 92 Fighter Sqdn 1955-57, station cdr RAF Seletar 1963-66, Air ADC to HM The Queen 1969-71, dep cmdt RAF Staff Coll 1969-71, SASO HQ Near East Air Force 1971-72, AOC 11 Gp 1972-75, dir-gen Orgn MOD Air 1975, AOC 18 Gp 1975-78, dep C-in-C RAF Strike Cmd 1979-80, Air Chief Marshal, cmdt RCDS 1980-82, ret; CBIM; dir: Rediffusion 1982-88, Rediffusion Simulation Ltd 1985-88; chm: BM Pension Trustees Ltd 1985-88; Br Manufacture and Res Co Ltd 1984-88; dir Pilatus Britten-Norman 1988-; CBIM; *Recreations* tennis, golf; *Clubs* RAF, Hankley Common GC, All England Lawn Tennis; *Style—* Air Chief Marshal Sir Robert Freer, GBE, KCB; c/o Lloyds Bank, 75 Castle St, Farnham, Surrey; Pilatus Britten-Norman Ltd, Bembridge, IOW (☎ 0983 872511)

FREESON, Rt Hon Reginald Yarnitz; PC (1976); *b* 24 Feb 1926; *Educ* Jewish Orphanage W Norwood; *m* (m dis); 1 s, 1 da; *Career* served in Army 1944-47;

journalist 1948-64; leader Willesden Cncl 1958-65 (chm Brent Cncl 1964-65); MP (Lab) Willesden E and Brent E 1964-87, PPS to Min Transport 1964-67; Parly sec: Miny Power 1967-69, Miny Housing and Local Govt 1969-7; oppn front bench spokesman Housing, Construction and Urban Affairs 1970-74, min of Housing and Construction (responsible for inner cities, planning, land and local govt) 1974-79, oppn front bench spokesman Social Security 1979-81, memb: Select Ctee on the Environment 1982-87 (chm 1982-83), Cncl of Europe Parly Assembly 1984-87, Western Euro Assembly 1984-87; dir JBG Housing Soc 1982-83; fndr Reg Freeson & Associates (Urban Renewal Conslts) 1987-; chm Neighbourhood Regeneration Team 1988-; memb: Housing Centre Tst 1987-, Jewish Welfare Bd 1971-74 (memb exec 1973-74), NCCL, IVS, UNA Int Serv; fndr memb: War on Want, CND; *Recreations* gardening, reading, theatre, music, country walking; *Style*— The Rt Hon Reginald Freeson; 159 Chevening Rd, London NW6

FREESTON, Hon Mrs (Anne Boswall); *née* Jackson; er da of Baron Jackson of Burnley (Life Peer) (d 1970), and Mary Elizabeth, *née* Boswall; *b* 9 Oct 1939; *Educ* Sutton HS, Froebel Educational Inst Roehampton (Teachers Dip); *m* 18 March 1967, David Garner Freeston, s of Charles Garner Freeston (d 1969) of Stonewall, Philpots Lane, Hildenborough, Kent; 2 children; *Career* teacher 1961-65, secretary 1980-; *Recreations* painting, cooking, conservation, German; *Style*— Hon Mrs Freeston; Hazel Cottage, North Heath, Chieveley, Newbury, Berks (☎ 0635 248 654)

FREETH, Denzil Kingson; s of late Walter Kingson Freeth, and Alice Vera Freeth; *b* 10 July 1924; *Educ* Sherborne, Trinity Hall Cambridge; *Career* Flying Offr RAF; pres Union Soc Cambridge 1949, chm Cambridge Union Cons Assoc 1949, MP (Cons) Basingstoke 1955-64, Parly sec to Min for Sci 1961-63; memb London Stock Exchange 1964-; churchwarden All Saints Margaret St London W1 1977-; *Recreations* good food, wine, conversation; *Clubs* Carlton, Pitt (Cambridge); *Style*— Denzil Freeth, Esq; 3 Brasenose House, 35 Kensington High St, London W8 (☎ 01 937 8685)

FREETH, (Frederic) Fred; s of Frederic George Freeth (d 1926), and Emily Jane Freeth (d 1946); *b* 14 Jan 1907; *Educ* Jenners Sch Cricklade Wilts, Cirencester GS Glos; *m* 1935, Ruby Ethel, da of George King; 1 s (Richard George b 1937); *Career* farmer Calcutt Farm Cricklade (ret); Hayward for Gt and Little Chelworth for Common Land out of the Borough of Cricklade 1928-; feoffee and memb Waylands Estates 1962-88; memb: Wilts CC 1974-82, Thames Water Authy and Bristol Avon local Land Drainage Ctee 1977-83, Cricklade Utd Charities; High Bailiff for the Manorial Court for the Hundred and Borough of Cricklade 1981-; hon vice-pres Thames Amenity Forum 1982; memb Stroud Water and Thames Severn Canal Tst 1980; freeman of Cricklade 1987; *Style*— Fred Freeth, Esq; Kingshill House, Cricklade, Swindon (☎ 750224)

FREETH, Hon Sir Gordon; KBE (1978); s of Rt Rev Robert Evelyn Freeth (d 1979), and Gladys Mary, *née* Snashall (d 1984); *b* 6 August 1914; *Educ* Sydney C of E GS, Guildford GS, Univ of W Australia; *m* 1939, Joan Celia Carew, da of Vincent Brice Carew Baker (d 1943); 1 s, 2 da; *Career* served RAAF (pilot) 1942-45; Australian high commissioner to UK 1977-80; barr WA 1938, in practice 1939-49, memb Ho of Reps 1949-69; min: Interior & Works 1958-63, Shipping & Tport 1963-68; asst attorney-gen 1962-64; min for Air & min assisting Treasurer 1968, min for External Affrs 1969; ambass to Japan 1970-73; law practice Perth 1973-77; chm Australian Consolidated Minerals 1981-; *Clubs* Weld, Royal Perth, Lake Karrinyup Country; *Style*— Hon Sir Gordon Freeth, KBE; Tingrith, 25 Owston St, Mosman Park, W Australia 6012 (☎ 384 6524)

FREETHY, Norman Derek; s of Arthur Thomas Freethy (d 1961), and Helen Maud, *née* Cook (d 1977); *b* 23 Feb 1923; *Educ* Pinner County Sch; *m* 1, 1958; 2 s (Simon Julian b 1964, Conrad Stephen Mark b 1971); 1 da (Nicola b 1962); m 2, 1985, Alison Lesley Vaughan, da of William Arthur Sparke (d 1978); 1 da (Sophie Dawn Vaughan b 1987); *Career* fell of the Institute of Actuaries, qualified 1957; sr ptnr Hymans Robertson & Co Cnsltg Actuaries; frequent writer and speaker on Pensions and Investmt Matters; dir City of London Computer Services Ltd, Coulter Pension Tstees, Liveryman Worshipful Co of Actuaries; *Recreations* music, gardening, golf; *Clubs* RAC, Addington Golf, Royal Mid-Surrey Golf; *Style*— Norman Freethy; Overcombe, 87 Harvestbank Road, West Wickham, Kent; Hymans Robertson & Co, Consulting Actuaries, 190 Fleet Street EC4A 2AH (☎ 01 831 9561, telex 881 3786, fax 01 831 6800)

FREMANTLE, Hon Cecilia Jane; da of 4 Baron Cottesloe; *b* 28 August 1962; *Style*— Hon Cecilia Fremantle

FREMANTLE, Hon Christopher Evelyn; 4 s of 3 Baron Cottesloe (d 1956); *b* 17 Dec 1906; *Educ* Eton, Balliol Coll Oxford; *m* 12 Nov 1930, Anne Marie Huth, da of late Rt Hon Frederick Huth Jackson; 3 s; *Style*— Hon Christopher Fremantle; 252 East 78th St, New York, NY 10021, USA

FREMANTLE, Hon Edward Walgrave; s (by 2 m) of 4 Baron Cottesloe; *b* 18 June 1961; *Style*— Hon Edward Fremantle

FREMANTLE, Hon Flora Catherine; da of 4 Baron Cottesloe; *b* 12 Sept 1967; *Style*— Hon Flora Fremantle

FREMANTLE, Cdr the Hon John Tapling; JP (Bucks 1984); s and h of Lt-Col 4 Baron Cottesloe, GBE, DL, *qv*; *b* 22 Jan 1927; *Educ* Eton; *m* 26 April 1958, (Elizabeth Ann), er da of Lt-Col Henry Shelley Barker, DSO (d 1970), of Rugby; 1 s (Tom), 2 da (Betsy, Fanny); *Career* joined RN 1945, Lt 1949, Lt Cdr 1957, Cdr 1962, ret 1966; chm: Bucks County Show 1977-82, Oxon-Bucks Div Royal Forestry Soc 1981-83; pres: Bucks branch CLA (chm 1976-79); vice-pres: Hosp Savings Assoc, BASC (previously WAGBI); cncl memb Royal Agric Soc of England 1974-; Radcliffe tstee; govr Stowe Sch; High Sheriff of Bucks 1969- 70, Lord Lt 1984-; KStJ (1984); *Recreations* shooting, stalking, crosswords; *Clubs* Travellers', RN and Royal Albert (Portsmouth); *Style*— Cdr the Hon John Fremantle, RN (ret); The Old House, Swanbourne, Milton Keynes, Bucks MK17 0SH (☎ 029 672 263); The Estate Office, Home Farm, Swanbourne, Milton Keynes, Bucks MK17 0SW (☎ 029 672 256)

FREMANTLE, Hon Katharine Dorothy Honor; yr da of 3 Baron Cottesloe (d 1956); *b* 23 May 1919; *Educ* Girton Coll Cambridge; *Career* PhD London 1956; *Style*— Hon Katharine Fremantle; Dennenlaan 48, Hollandsche Rading, Netherlands

FRENCH, Dr Cecil Charles John; s of late Ernest French, of Shoreham-by-Sea, and late Edith Hannah, *née* Norris; *b* 16 April 1926; *Educ* Newport Sch Essex, King's Coll London (MSc), Columbia Univ NY, London Univ (DSc); *m* 1, 14 July 1956, (Olive) Joyce (d 1969), da of late Arthur James Edwards, of Lancing, Sussex; 2 da (Alison b 1957, Hilary b 1961); m 2, 23 Oct 1971, Shirley Frances, da of late Montague Charles Outten, of Colchester, Essex; 1 s (Matthew b 1975), 1 da (Elizabeth b 1973); *Career* vice-chm Ricardo Gp plc; pres: IMechE 1988, Int Cncl on Combustion Engines 1983; visiting prof in mechanical engrg King's Coll 1983; FEng; *Books* numerous papers on internal combustion engineering; *Recreations* folk dancing, photography; *Clubs* Shoreham and Southwick Rotary; *Style*— Cecil French Esq; 303 Upper Shoreham Rd, Shoreham-by-Sea, W Sussex BN43 5QA (☎ 0273 452050); Ricardo Gp plc, Bridge Works, Shoreham-by-Sea, W Sussex BN43 5FG (☎ 0273 455611, telex 87383)

FRENCH, Hon (Fulke) Charles Arthur John; s (by 1 m) of 7 Baron De Freyne; *b* 21 April 1957; *Educ* Downside, RAC Cirenester; Dip Polytechnic of the South Bank London; *m* 12 April 1986, Julia Mary, o da of Dr James H Wellard, PhD, FLA, FRGS, of Hampstead, London; 1 s (Alexander James Charles b 22 Sept 1988); *Career* planning and dvlpt conslt; *Recreations* sailing, tennis, photography, literature, travel; *Style*— The Hon Charles French; 72c Sinclair Road, London W14 0NJ

FRENCH, (Edward Frank) Christopher; s of Frank Charles French, of W Malling, Kent, and Mary, *née* Parish; *b* 28 July 1950; *Educ* Roan GS for Boys; *m* 29 March 1969, Rita Margaret, da of Brian Stewart; 1 s (James b 1983), 1 da (Sally b 1977); *Career* Nationwide Bldg Soc: trainee mangr 1971, branch mangr 1978, sec 1985; asst gen mangr Nationwide Anglia Bldg Soc 1988 (sec 1987); chm: Nationwide Bldg Soc Staff Assoc 1983-85, Fedn of Bldg Soc Staff Assocs 1984-85; FCBSI 1978, DMS 1985; *Recreations* music, horticulture; *Style*— Christopher French, Esq; Nationwide Anglia Building Society, Chesterfield House, Bloomsbury Way, London WC1V 6PW (☎ 01 242 8822, fax 01 242 8822 ext 4391, telex 264549 NBS GRP G)

FRENCH, Hon Mr Justice; Hon Sir Christopher James Saunders; s of Rev Reginald French, MC (d 1961), hon chaplain to HM The Queen and to the late King George VI, and Gertrude Emily Mary, *née* Haworth; *b* 14 Oct 1925; *Educ* Denstone Coll, Brasenose Coll Oxford; *m* 1957, Philippa, da of Philip Godfrey Price, of Abergavenny, Mon; 1 s, 1 da; *Career* barr Inner Temple 1950, dep chm Bucks QS 1966-71, QC 1966, rec Coventry 1971, rec and hon recorder Coventry 1972-79, High Ct judge (family) 1979-82, Queen's Bench Div 1982-, presiding judge SE circuit 1982-86; memb Lord Chllr's Advsy Ctee on Trg Magistrates 1974-80; kt 1979; *Books* Agency Halsbury's Laws of England (4th edn); *Recreations* walking, music, painting; *Clubs* Garrick; *Style*— The Hon Mr Justice French; Royal Courts of Justice, Strand, London WC2

FRENCH, David; s of Capt Godfrey Alexander French, CBE, RN, (d 1988), of Stoke Abbott, Dorset, and Margaret Annis, *née* Best; *b* 20 June 1947; *Educ* Sherbourne, St John's Coll, Durham Univ (BA); *m* 3 Aug 1974, Sarah Anne, da of Rt Revd Henry David Halsey, Bishop of Carlisle; 3 s (Thomas b 1978, Alexander b 1980, William b 1983); *Career* with Nat Cncl of Social Services 1971-74, head social services dept RNID 1974-78, dir of serv C of E Childrens Soc 1978-87; dir RELATE, Nat Marraige Guidance Cncl 1987-; memb of MIPM; *Recreations* children; *Style*— David French, Esq; 21 Prospect Rd, St Albans, Herts AL1 2AT; Relate: National Marraige Guidance, Herbert Gray College, Little Church Street, Rugby CV21 3AP (☎ 0788 73241)

FRENCH, Douglas Charles; MP (C) Gloucester 1987-; s of Frederick Emil French, of Surrey, and Charlotte Vera, *née* Russell; *b* 20 Mar 1944; *Educ* Glyn GS Epsom, St Catharine's Coll Cambridge (MA), Inns of Court Sch of Law; *m* 1978, Sue, da of late Philip Arthur Phillips; 2 s (Paul b 1982, David b 1985), 1 da (Louise b 1983); *Career* barr Inner Temple 1975; md Westminster & City Programmes 1979-87; special advsr to Chllr of Exchequer 1982-83 (asst to Rt Hon Sir Geoffrey Howe QC, MP 1976-79); P W Merkle Ltd (exec 1966-71, dir 1972-87); Parly candidate Sheffield Attercliffe 1979, chm Bow Gp 1978-79; *Recreations* skiing, gardening, squash; *Clubs* Metropolitan Sports, RAC Country, Coningsby; *Style*— Douglas French, MP; The Fields, Tuffley Ave, Gloucester; House of Commons, SW1A 0AA (☎ 01 219 6210)

FRENCH, Jeremy Godfrey; s of Capt Godfrey Alexander French, CBE (d 1988), *qv*, and Mary Neville, *née* Gilhespy (d 1965); *b* 26 May 1930; *Educ* Sherborne, RMA Sandhurst; *m* 1, 11 Aug 1954, Ann Mary, *née* Rowland; 1 da (Caroline Mary Hudson b 1957); m 2, 1963, June Mary Prescott, da of Aidan Arnold Wallis, of Ashdown House, Forest Row, Sussex; 1 step s (Lt Cdr J A Prescott), 1 step da (Mrs N A Mièville); *Career* The Duke of Cornwall's Light Infantry, Capt 1950-62; joined Shell Mex and BP Ltd 1962, regnl mangr Shell UK Oil 1978-80, mangr public affairs Shell UK Oil 1980-82; *Recreations* gardening, music, woodwork; *Clubs* Army and Navy; *Style*— Jeremy French, Esq; Jasmine Lodge, School Lane, Stoke Poges, Bucks (☎ 02816 2484)

FRENCH, Hon Mrs Hubert; Mary Frances; da of Charles Hasslacher, of 3 Kensington Park Gdns, W11; *m* 19 Jan 1937, Hon Hubert John French (d 7 Dec 1961), 8 s of 4 Baron de Freyne (d 1918); 2 s, 2 da; *Style*— Hon Mrs Hubert French; Stychfield, Stychens Lane, Bletchingley, Redhill, Surrey

FRENCH, Neville Arthur Irwin; CMG (1976), LVO (1968); s of Maj Ernest French (d 1960), of Punjab and Kenya, and Alice Winifred Irwin, *née* Powell (d 1946); *b* 28 April 1920; *Educ* LSE, Univ of London (BSc); *m* 1945, Joyce Ethel, yr da of Henry Robert Greene (d 1926), of Kilkea, Co Kildare, Argentina and Uruguay; 1 s (Christopher), 2 da (Deborah, Barbara); *Career* Fleet Auxiliary 1940-45, chief radio offr all theatres of war; Colonial Admin Serv (later HMOCS) 1948-62, Tanganyika dist cmmr 1949-61, princ asst sec (external affrs) 1961-62; Dip Serv 1963-80: princ Central African Off 1963-64, first sec Br High Cmmn Salisbury 1964-66, head of chancery Br Embassy Rio de Janeiro 1966-69, asst head Western Orgns Dept FCO 1970-72, cnsllr and charge d'affaires Havana 1972-75, govr and C-in-C Falkland Islands and high cmmr Br Antarctic Territory 1975-77, dep high cmmr Southern India 1977-80; *Recreations* books and scepticism, fly fishing; *Clubs* Royal Cwlth Soc, Madras (India); *Style*— Neville French, Esq, CMG, LVO

FRENCH, Peter Reginald; **RD (1965)**; s of Rev Reginald French, MC, QHC (d 1961), and Gertrude Emily Mary, *née* Haworth (d 1968); *b* 22 July 1921; *Educ* Rugby, St Thomas's Hosp London Univ; *m* 29 March 1958, (Norna Elizabeth) Ann, da of Capt David Norman Drybrough (d 1925); 2 s (James b 1965, Michael b 1966); *Career* Surgn Lt RNVR 1945-47, Naval Hosp Hong Kong 1945-46, Naval Res HMS President London, Surgn Lt-Cdr RNR, ret 1966; orthopaedic surgn: St George's Hosp London 1961-86, Royal Masonic Hosp London 1963-88; private orthopaedic practice London 1961-; Freeman City of London, Liveryman Worshipful Soc of Apothecaries; FRCS 1952, FRSM, fell Br Orthopaedic Assoc; *Books* contributions to numerous surgical books and jls; *Recreations* golf, swimming, fishing, gardening; *Clubs* Garrick, Hurlingham, Naval, Berkshire GC, Royal Wimbledon, Royal Cinque Ports; *Style*— Peter French, Esq, RD; 1 Hurlingham Gdns, London SW6 3PL (☎ 01 736 3547); 30A Wimpole St, London W1M 7AE (☎ 01 580 2115)

FRENCH, Ralph John; OBE; s of Alfred William French (d 1965), and Flora Regan (d

1972); *b* 22 June 1935; *Educ* Haberdashers' Aske's, Waldschulheim Breuer Aachen, Coll of Law London, Inns of Ct Sch of Law, Manchester Business Sch & Ashridge Coll Bucks; *m* 1, 1964 (m dis 1982), m 2, 1982, Rosemary Joan (Rosie), da of John Frederick Wearing, MA, FCO (d 1974); 1 s (Rupert John Wolfe b 6 Nov 1967), 2 da (Charlotte Elizabeth b 25 Jan 1966, Juliette Louise b 22 July 1970), and 2 step da; *Career* Royal Welch Fusiliers 2 Lt 1954-56, HMOCS 1957-62; ICI: asst sec plastics div 1965-71, div sec and business res mangr plastics div 1971-75, head East Euro Dept Corp HQ 1975-85, dir East Euro Relations and ICI (Export) 1985-; fndr memb Welwyn Gdn City YMCA 1965 and chm 1967-75, Bar Assoc for Fin, Comm & Indust 1965-, memb E Euro Cncl BOTB 1980-, memb cncl BSCC 1975- and chm 1980-; leader first and second British Trade Missions to Mongolia 1987 and 1988; Freedman City of London 1972, Freedman and Liveryman of Worshipful Co of Masons 1972; 1300th Anniversary of Fndn of Bulgarian State Medal for servs to Bulgaria 1981, NY 1988 for services to export; *Recreations* climbing, sailing, water sports, wine; *Clubs* Athenaeum; *Style*— Ralph French, Esq, OBE; 7 Dartmouth Place, London W4 2RH (☎ 01 995 7959)

FRENCH, Lady Rosemary; *née* Mackay; da of 2 Earl of Inchape (d 1939); *b* 5 Nov 1936; *m* 19 Jan 1957, Francis Martin French, s of late Francis Holroyd French; 1 s, 3 da; *Style*— Lady Rosemary French; Little Offley, Hitchin, Herts

FRENCH, Lady Sarah Mary Essex; 2 da of 3 Earl of Ypres by his 1 w Maureen; *b* 22 May 1953; *Style*— Lady Sarah French

FRENCH, Hon Vanessa Rose Bradbury; da (by 1 m) of 7 Baron De Freyne; *b* 19 Sept 1958; *Style*— Hon Vanessa French

FRERE, Richard Burchmore; s of Harold Arthur Frere (d 1945), of Maryfield, Inverness, and formerly of Roydon Hall, Diss, Norfolk, and Finningham, Suffolk (both of which he sold 1934), and Mary Elvira Carter, *née* Harrison; the Frere family can be traced back to John Frere, of Sweffling, Suffolk, living in the reign of Henry III; Finningham was in their possession from the 17 cent and Roydon Hall was purchased by Shepherd Frere in 1766 (*see* Burke's Landed Gentry, 18 edn, vol II, 1969); *b* 8 June 1922; *Educ* Inverness Acad, privately; *m* 8 Sept 1943, Joan, da of Arthur Pareezer, formerly of Hove, Sussex; 1 s (Richard Tudor b 28 Nov 1947), 2 da (Heather Stephanie b 20 Feb 1945, Jane Gwendoline b 2 Dec 1959); *Career* served WWII with RAF Motor Transport 1941-45, rising to rank of full corporal; memb Soc of Authors, Woodland Tst, and John Muir Tst; *Books* Thoughts of a Mountaineer (1952), Maxwell's Ghost (1976), Beyond the Highland Line (1984), Loch Ness (1988); contributor to Scots Magazine, Scotsman, Scottish Field, etc, and to Dictionary of National Biography; *Recreations* hill walking, rock climbing, gardening, DIY; *Style*— Richard Frere, Esq; Drumbuie House, Drumnadrochit, Inverness-shire (☎ 04562 210)

FRESNES; *see*: de Fresnes

FRETER, Michael Charles Franklin; s of Leslie Charles Freter, 1 The Browns, Sidmouth, Devon, and Myra, *née* Wilkinson; *b* 29 Oct 1947; *Educ* Whitgift Sch, St Edmund Hall Oxford (BA); *m* 2 June 1979, Jan, da of Brian Wilson, of Ealing, London; *Career* sr brand mangr Elida Gibbs Ltd 1970-76, account dir BBDO Advertising Ltd 1976-78; executive dir McCann-Erickson Advertising Ltd 1988- (joined 1978, dir 1980-); *Style*— Michael Freter, Esq; 17 Beaufort Close, Lynden Gate, Putney Heath, SW15; McCann-Erickson Ltd, 36 Howland Street, London W1

FRETWELL, Sir (Maj) John (Emsley); GCMG (1987, KCMG 1982, CMG 1975); s of Francis Thomas Fretwell, of Chesterfield; *b* 15 June 1930; *Educ* Chesterfield GS, Lausanne Univ, King's Coll Cambridge; *m* 1959, Mary Ellen Eugenie, da of Frederick Charles Dubois; 1 s, 1 da; *Career* Army 1948-50; joined FO 1953, served Hong Kong and Peking, first sec Moscow 1959-62, FO 1962-67, first sec (commercial) Washington 1967-70, cnsllr (commercial) Warsaw 1971-73, head EID 1973-76, asst under-sec FCO 1976-79, min Washington 1980-81, ambassador France 1982-87, political dir FCO 1987-; *Style*— Sir John Fretwell, CGMS ; c/o Foreign and Commonwealth Office, King Charles St, London SW1

FREUD, Sir Clement Raphael; s of late Ernst Freud and Lucie Freud; bro of Lucian Freud, *qv* (gs of Prof Sigmund Freud); *b* 24 April 1924; *Educ* Dartington Hall, St Paul's; *m* 1950, Jill, 2 da of H W Flewett; 3 s, 2 da; *Career* Royal Ulster Rifles 1942-47, liaison off Int Mil Tribunal Nuremburg 1946-47; writer, broadcaster, rector Dundee Univ 1974-80, MP (Lib) Isle of Ely (by-election) July 1973-1983, sponsor Official Info Bill 1978-79; MP (Lib) NE Cambridgeshire 1983-87; master Open Univ 1989; kt 1987; *Books* Grimble (1968), Grimble at Christmas (1973), Freud on Food (1978), Below the Belt (1983), Book of Hangovers (1981); Below the Belt (1983), No-one else has Complained (1988); *Clubs* MCC, Br Rail Staff Assoc, March, Groucho's; *Style*— Sir Clement Freud; 22 Wimpole Street, London W1 (☎ 01 580 2222)

FREUD, Lucian; CH (1983); s of late Ernst and Lucie Freud; bro of Clement Freud, *qv*; *b* 8 Dec 1922; *Educ* Central Sch of Art, E Anglia Sch of Painting and Drawing; *m* 1, 1948 (m dis 1952), Kathleen Garman, da of Jacob Epstein; 2 da; m 2, 1953 (m dis 1957), Lady Caroline Maureen Blackwood, da of 4 Marquess of Dufferin and Ava (*see* Lowell, Lady Caroline); *Career* painter; former teacher Slade Sch of Art; *Style*— Lucian Freud, Esq, CH; c/o Anthony d'Offay, 9 Dering St, London W1

FREWEN, William Kingswell; s of William Frewen, of Tipperary, and Edith, *née* Burke; *b* 25 August 1913; *Educ* Beaumont Coll Windsor, London Univ, St Bart's Hosp (MB BS); *m* 29 Jan 1957, Eileen Mary, da of Dr Louis Courtney, of Nenagh, Co Tipperary; 1 s (William b 1959); *Career* surgeon 1950-80 Royal Berkshire Hospital Reading; served WWII Capt RAMC, Egypt, Sudan, Eritrea, Western Desert (MO 4 Bn Cameron Highlanders, despatches), POW 1942-45; research work on the bladder and urethral function, 20 publications in English and American journals of urology 1970-83; *Recreations* literature, golf, bridge; *Clubs* Huntercombe Golf (Nuffield); *Style*— William Frewen, Esq; Orchards, Kingswood Common, Henley-on-Thames, Oxon (☎ 04917 322)

FREWER, Richard John Barrett; s of Dr Edward George Frewer (d 1972), and Bridget Audrey Christina Penefather, *née* Ford, of Girton, Cambs; *b* 24 Jan 1942; *Educ* Shrewsbury, Gonville and Caius Coll Cambridge (MA), AA (Dipl Arch); *m* 19 July 1969, Carolyn Mary, da of Thomas Arthur Butler (d 1969); 1 da (Emelye b 1971); *Career* architect, Arup Assoc 1966-, (ptnr 1977); major works incl: Sir Thomas White Bldg St John's Coll Oxford (with Sir Philip Dowson), Theatre Royal Glasgow, Liverpool Garden Festival Hall, Baburgh DC Offs Suffolk, Stockley Park Arena Heathrow; lectr & teacher at schs of architecture, pt/t professional tenor soloist, Bach Specialist Lieder and Oratorio repertoire; memb: cncl House of St Barnabas-in-Soho, bursary jury RSA; RIBA, FRSA; *Recreations* painting, music; *Style*— Richard Frewer, Esq; Avebury Cottage, High St, Fulbourn, Cambs; Flat 5 Lansdowne Crt, 42 Lansdowne Cresc, London W11; Arup Associates, 2-4 Dean St, London W11 (☎ 01 734 8494, fax 01 439 1457)

FREWIN, Dr Tom; s of Noel Frewin, and Sylvia Maude, *née* Lindsey, of Kent; *b* 9 Dec 1946; *Educ* Borden GS, Univ of Bristol (MB, ChB); *m* 12 Dec 1970, Susan Elizabeth, da of Anthony George Williams, of Gwent; 2 s (Charles b 1971, Hugo b 1980), 2 da (Joanna b 1973, Alice b 1976); *Career* medical practitioner; *Style*— Dr Tom Frewin; 13 Mortimer Rd, Clifton, Bristol BS8 4EY (☎ 0272 736407); 52 Clifton Down Rd, Clifton, Bristol BS8 4AM (☎ 0272 732178)

FREYBERG, Hon Annabel Pauline; eldest da of 2 Baron Freyberg, OBE, MC; *b* 16 August 1961; *Style*— Hon Annabel Freyberg

FREYBERG, 2 Baron (UK 1951); Col Paul Richard; OBE (Mil 1965), MC (1945); s of 1 Baron Freyberg, VC, GCMG, KCB, KBE, DSO and 3 bars (d 1963) and Barbara, GBE (d 1973), da of Sir Herbert Jekyll, KCMG, niece of Getrude Jekyll and widow of Hon Francis Walter Stafford MacLaren, MP, s of 1 Baron Aberconway, KC; *b* 27 May 1923; *Educ* Eton; *m* 23 July 1960, Ivry Perronelle Katharine, o da of late Cyril Harrower Guild, of Aspall Hall, nr Debenham, Suffolk; 1 s, 3 da; *Heir* s, Hon Valerian Bernard Freyberg b 15 Dec 1970; *Career* Col late Gren Gds; with New Zealand Expeditionary Force 1940-42, with Gren Gds 1942-45, AAG HQ London Dist 1962-65, cmd HAC Inf Bn 1965-68, on Defence Policy Staff MOD 1968-71, dir Volunteers Territorials and Cadets 1971-75, Col Gen Staff 1975-78; *Style*— Col the Rt Hon Lord Freyberg, OBE; Munstead House, Godalming, Surrey (☎ 048 68 6004)

FREYBERG, Hon Venetia Rose; 2 da of 2 Baron Freyberg, OBE, MC; *b* 28 May 1963; *Style*— Hon Venetia Freyberg

FREYD, Michael; s of Cecil Freyd (d 1971), and Joan, *née* Woodhead (d 1960); *b* 5 June 1948; *Educ* Burnage GS Manchester, Univ of Hull (BSc); *m* 21 March 1971, Marilyn (Lyn) Sharon, da of Ivor Paul Levinson (d 1960); 1 s (Mark b 29 Aug 1979), 2 da (Danielle b 14 June 1972, Elana b 7 May 1976); *Career* UBS Phillips & Drew (formerly Phillips & Drew) 1969-: ptnr 1980, dir; appointed Option Ctee 1986; memb United Synagogue Investment ctee; memb soc Investmt Analysts; *Recreations* golf, skiing, bridge, chess; *Style*— Michael Freyd, Esq; UBS Phillips & Drew, 120 Moorgate, London EC2M 6XP (☎ 01 628 4444)

FRICKER, Alan Derek; s of late Norman Fricker, OBE; *b* 20 June 1924; *Educ* Charterhouse, Trinity Coll Oxford; *m* 1950, Margaret Mary, *née* Snelgrove; 2 s, 4 da; *Career* barr 1949 ret; dir Cawoods Solid Fuels Ltd; *Recreations* sailing, fishing, walking; *Clubs* Naval, New (Cheltenham); *Style*— A D Fricker, Esq; The Cottage, Mill St, Prestbury, Cheltenham, Glos (☎ 0242 244 555)

FRICKER, Colin Frank; s of Frank Charles Fricker, of Eastbourne, and Hilda Emily, *née* Ingle (d 1955); *b* 9 April 1936; *Educ* Dulwich, London Univ (LLB); *m* 20 June 1964, Elizabeth Ann Brooke, da of John Douglas Skinner, of Eastleigh, Hants; 2 s (Henry b 1975 (d 1975), Robert), 1 da (Annabel); *Career* Nat Serv RAF 1954-56; asst dir C E Heath Home Ltd 1968-70, dir Assoc of Br Launderers & Cleaners 1979-84, ldr Employers' Side of Laundry Wages Cncl 1979-84, dir-gen Br Direct Mktg Assoc 1985-; and memb CBI 1979-84; Freeman City of London, memb Worshipful Co of Launderers 1979; FCII 1960; *Recreations* cricket, rugby, genealogy; *Clubs* MCC; *Style*— Colin Fricker, Esq; 34 Hill Rise, Rickmansworth, Herts WD3 2NZ (☎ 0923 776813); BDMA, Grosvenor Grdns, London SW1W OBS (☎ 01 630 7322, fax 01 828 7125, telex 8951182)

FRICKER, (Anthony) Nigel; QC (1977); s of late Dr William Shapland Fricker and Margaret, *née* Skinner; *b* 7 July 1937; *Educ* King's Sch Chester, Liverpool Univ (LLB); *m* 1960, Marilynn Ann, da of August L Martin, of Pennsylvania, USA; 1 s (Joseph b 1969), 2 da (Deborah b 1962, Katherine b 1964); *Career* barr; prosecuting counsel to DHSS Wales and Chester circuit (North) 1975-77, rec Crown Court 1975-84, asst cmmr Boundary Commn Wales 1981-84; a circuit judge in Yorks 1984-; *Articles Paper in Civil Justice Quarterly and 2nd Family Law periodical; Clubs* Yorkshire (York); *Style*— His Honour Judge Fricker, QC; 6 Park Sq, Leeds LS1 2LW (☎ 0532 459763)

FRIEBE, John Percy; s of Charles Friebe (d 1962); *b* 9 May 1931; *Educ* Glasgow HS, Glasgow Univ; *m* 1966, Laura Mary, da of Archibald Fleming (d 1961); *Career* dir: Smith and MacLaurin Ltd 1957-64, Millard Bro Ltd 1964-70; gp md Stoddard Hldgs plc 1970-83; md Carpets Int (UK) 1984-86 (mktg dir 1983-84), dir Carpets Int plc 1984-86 ;dir John Crowther Gp plc 1986, vice chm Intersport GB Ltd 1986-, dir John Letters (1918) Ltd 1986-; chm Fleming Friebe Assoc; memb Inst of CAs of Scotland, FICMA; *Recreations* golf, gardening; *Style*— John Friebe Esq; Hunters Heights, Uphampton, Ombersley, Worcs (☎ 0905 620 854

FRIEDMAN, Bernard Marcus; s of Mayer Freidman, (d 1945), of Chichele Mansions, London, and Rosie, *née* Lipman (d 1946); *b* 18 Sept 1913; *Educ* Private; *m* 31 March 1946, Hilda Phyllis, da of Ernest Solk, (d 1944), of Teignmouth Rd, London NW2; 2 da (Susan Elaine (Mrs Stoney) b 1947, Anne Michelle (Mrs Curran) b 1951); *Career* WWII 1940-46, RAOC Donnington Base Depot 1940, Egypt and Palestine 1940-43, ME Army Personnel Unit 1943-45, Germany control cmmn 1945-46, rank of War Substansive Sgt; works mangr Rotorohms 1929-35; mangr and tech exec Marks and Spencer plc, except war years (post war took control of all store devpts and design of all bldg and equipment incl devpt and employment world wide of eight foot hot cathode flourescent lighting tube peculiar to Marks and Spencer and still in use); ret 1977; chm Embassy Ct Lessees Assoc 1985-; Freeman City of London, Freeman Worshipful Co of Plumbers 1955; *Style*— Bernard Freidman, Esq; 84 Embassy Court, Kings Road, Brighton, BN1 2PY, E Sussex (☎ 0273 726 182)

FRIEND, Bernard Ernest; CBE (1986); s of Richard Friend (d 1972), and Ada Florence Friend (d 1952); *b* 18 May 1924; *Educ* Dover GS; *m* 1951, Pamela Florence, da of Frederick Henry Amor Alcester; 1 s (Nigel Andrew b 1963), 2 da (Gillian Diana b 1952, Penelope Elaine b 1955); *Career* Flying Offr RAF 1943-47; CA; dir British Aerospace plc 1977-; non-exec dir: Iron Trades Gp 1981, SD-Scicon, Ballast Nedam BV; chm Grahams Rintoul Investmt Tst; *Recreations* cricket; *Clubs* RAF, RAC, MCC; *Style*— Bernard Friend, Esq, CBE; British Aerospace plc, 11 Strand, London WC2N 5JT

FRIEND, Peter Henry; s of Henry Eugene Friend, and Anne, *née* Richards; *b* 1 Oct 1950; *Educ* Colfe's GS; *m* 8 Nov 1980, Christine Megan, da of William Herbert Hames, of London; 2 da (Aimi Christina b 29 June 1981, Lucy Amanda b 16 Oct 1982); *Career* CA; audit mangr Hill Vellacott 1969-74, controller of ops and fin Salomon Bros Int Ltd 1974-78, mangr ops Salomon Bros New York 1979, vice pres ops planning and control Merrill Lynch Int Co 1979-83, exec dir ops Goldman Sachs Int Ltd 1983-; dir: Goldman Sachs Govt Securities (UK) Ltd, Goldman Sachs Equity Securities (UK) Ltd, FCA; *Style*— Peter H Friend, Esq

FRIEND, Dame Phyllis Muriel; DBE (1980, CBE 1972); da of Richard Edward Friend; *b* 28 Sept 1922; *Educ* Herts & Essex HS Bishop's Stortford, London Hosp (SRN), Royal Coll Nursing (RNT); *Career* dep matron St George's Hosp 1956-59; chief nursing offr: London Hosp 1969-72 (matron 1961-68, dep matron 1959-61), DHSS 1972-82; *Style*— Dame Phyllis Friend, DBE; Barnmead, Start Hill, Bishop's Stortford, Herts (☎ 0279 54873)

FRIER, (Gavin Austin) Garry; s of Gavin Walter Rae Frier (d 1985), and Isabel Fraser, *née* Austin (d 1981); *b* 18 May 1953; *Educ* Hutchesons' Boys GS Glasgow, Univ of Strathclyde (BA); *m* 1978, Jane Carolyn, da of John Keith Burton, of Glasgow; 1 s (Stuart Austin Frier b 1981); *Career* CA; dir County Bank Ltd (renamed County Natwest Ltd) 1985-87; currently fin dir Floyd Energy plc; memb Scottish Inst of CA's 1978; *Recreations* tennis, photography; *Clubs* Western, Galsgow; *Style*— Garry Frier, Esq; Old Carpenters, Dares Lane, Ewshot nr Farnham, Surrey GU10 5BS (☎ 0252 850401); Floyd Energy plc, Brettenham House, Lancaster PLace, Londo WC2E 7EN (☎ 01 379 5190)

FRIGGENS, William Godfrey; *b* 18 August 1926; *Educ* Univ Coll Univ of London (BSc); *m* 1, 1946, Betty Eileen Swinnerton (decd); 2 s; m 2, 1981, Janet Patricia Gunn; 1 da; *Career* dir: Manufacturers Equipment Co Ltd 1960-68, J H Fenner & Co Ltd 1962-68, Mastabar Mining Equipment Co 1962-68, Pioneer Laura NV (Holland) 1964-68, Rapistan Lande NV (Holland) 1964-71; Fenner GMBH (1964-68), J H Fenner & Co Hldgs Ltd 1965-68, Pioneer Oilsealing & Moulding Co Ltd 1962-71, F Pratt Engrn Corpn plc 1969-84, Pratt Burnerd Int Ltd 1969-84, Crawford Collets Ltd 1969-84, Pratt Woodworth Ltd 1970-84, Precor Investmts Ltd 1970-84, Precor VB 1979-84, Jiltward Ltd 1981-84, Trojan Structures Ltd 1983-84, Prenco Prods Ltd 1984, Prenco Dairy Prods Ltd 1984, Engrg Ind Trg Bd 1985-88; CEng, FIMechE, MIEE; *Recreations* swimming, tennis, reading, music; *Style*— William Friggens, Esq; Trevelyan, 17 Greenhill Road, Farnham, Surrey GU9 8JP

FRINK, Dame Elisabeth Jean; DBE (1981, CBE 1969); *b* 14 Nov 1930; *Educ* Convent of the Holy Family Exmouth, Guildford Sch of Art, Chelsea Sch of Art; *m* 1, 1955 (m dis 1963), Michel Jammet; 1 s; m 2, 1968 (m dis 1974), Edward Pool, MC; m 3, 1974, Alexander Csáky; *Career* RA 1977 (ARA 1971); sculptor tstee Br Museum 1975-, memb Royal Fine Art Cmmn 1976-81; Hon DUniv Open Univ 1983, Hon DLitt Warwick Univ 1983, Hon DUniv of Cambridge 1988, Hon DUniv of Exeter 1988; *Style*— Dame Elisabeth Frink, DBE; Woolland, Blandford, Dorset

FRISBY, Terence Peter Michael; s of William Alfred Frisby (d 1968), of Kent, and Kathleen Campbell, *née* Casely; *b* 28 Nov 1932; *Educ* Dartford GS, Central Sch of Speech Training and Dramatic Art; *m* 1963, Christine, da of Luigi Vecchione (d 1967); 1 s (Dominic b 1969); *Career* playwright, actor, dir, prodr (over 200 acting and directing roles in theatre, TV, film, West End and rep for over 32 years); most notable prodn: Woza Albert at Criterion Theatre, Picadilly 1983-84; WGGB, Equity; published plays: The Subtopians (1964), There's a Girl in MY Soup 1967 (film 1971 starring Peter Sellers and Goldie Hawn - winner Writers' Guild of GB Award for Best Br Comedy 1971), The Bandwagon 1970, It's All Right If I Do It 1977, Seaside Postcard 1978; radio plays: Just Remember Two Things, It's Not Fair And Don't Be Late (Giles Couper Award) (published 1989); many TV plays and two TV series: Lucky Feller (LWT 1976), That's Love (TVS 1988-89); *Recreations* golf; *Clubs* Richmond Golf; *Style*— Terence Frisby, Esq; 72 Bishops Mansions, Bishops Park Rd, London SW6 (☎ 01 736 2450)

FRISCHMANN, Wilem William; s of Lajos Frischmann (d 1944), of Hungary, and Nelly Frischmann (d 1945); *b* 27 Jan 1931; *Educ* Hammersmith Coll of Art and Building, Imperial Coll of Sci and Technol (DIC), City Univ of London (PhD); *m* 1 Sept 1957, Sylvia, da of Maurice Elvey (d 1980), of Glasgow; 1 s (Richard Sawdor), 1 da (Justine Elnor); *Career* CJ fell Ptnrs 1956-68 (ptr 1961-68), sr ptnr Fell Frischmann & Ptnr 1968-, chm Fell Frischmann Gp 1984-; F Eng, FCGI, FI Struct E, MConsE, MASCE, MSocCE (Fr); *Recreations* tennis, swimming, skiing; *Clubs* Arts; *Style*— Dr Wilem Frischmann; Haversham Grange, Haversham Close, Twickenham TW1 2JP 5 Manchester Square, London W1A 1AU (☎ 01 486 3661, fax 01 487 4153, telex 21536 Consec G)

FRITH, Donald Alfred; OBE (1980); yr s of late Charles Henry Frith and Mabel, *née* Whiting; *b* 13 May 1918; *Educ* Whitgift, Christ's Coll Cambridge; *m* 1941, Mary Webster, yr da of late Raymond Tyler; 4 s, 1 da; *Career* teacher and Deme warden Univ Coll Sch 1946-52, headmaster Richmond Sch Yorks 1953-59, headmaster Archbishop Holgate's Sch York 1959-78, sec Headmasters' Conf and Secondary Heads Assoc 1979-836; chm N Yorks Forum for Voluntary Orgns 1983-89; *Recreations* music, reading, walking, gardening; *Clubs* Athenaeum, Yorkshire (York); *Style*— Donald Frith, Esq, OBE; Kilburn, York (☎ 034 76 517)

FRITH, John William Gabriel; s of Canon Herbert Charles Frith (d 1953), of Chichester, and Nora Frith, *née* Gabain (d 1974); *b* 25 Mar 1925; *Educ* Marlborough, Magdalene Coll Cambridge; *m* 21 June 1952, Cherry Jill, da of Frank Anthony Dorset Challoner, of Blackheath (d 1954); 2 s (Simon b 1955, Michael b 1957), 1 da (Gilliam b 1953); *Career* Lt RNVR 1943-47; CA; fin dir C J Clark Ltd 163-85, memb Cncl Inst Chartered Accountants 1966-74; tstee Wells Cathedral Preservation Tst, tres Friends Wells Cathedral; chm Somerset Health Authy 1977-82, chm St Margarets Hospice Somerset; chm Malvern Girls Coll; *Recreations* walking, gardening; *Style*— John W G Frith, Esq; 35 New Street, Wells BA5 2LE (☎ 0749 73221); 5 Market Place, Wells BA5 2RF (☎ 0749 74241)

FRITH, Stanley William; s of Reuben Stanley Frith, and Isabella Evelyn, *née* Bilke; *b* 15 July 1943; *Educ* Southern Methodist Univ (MBA); *m* 17 June 1972, Gillian Anne, da of Lt-Col W W Bailey; 2 s (Jason Anthony b 22 March 1976, Rory Nicholas b 8 Jan 1981); *Career* accountant 1964-66, chief accountant GS Int SA Tripoli Libya 1966-70, fin controller GSI (Singapore) Pre 1970-73, gp fin controller Texas Instruments Dallas USA 1973-78, personnel dir Texas Instruments (UK) Ltd 1978-81, euro personnel dir Texas Instruments HQ Nice France 1981-85, gp personnel dir House of Fraser plc 1985-; patron Christian Childrens Fund; memb Chartered Inst of Secs and Admins; *Books* The Expatriate Dilemma (1978), A Step in the Right Direction (1981); *Style*— Stanley Frith, Esq; House of Fraser plc, 1 Howick Place, London SW1P 1BH (☎ 01 834 1515, fax 01 318 2820, telex 896429)

FRIZZELL, Colin Frazer; s of Thomas Norman Frizzell (d 1976), of Grosvenor House Hotel, London, and Susanna Alice Clogh *née* Boyd (d 1979); *b* 8 April 1939; *Educ* Oundle; *m* 9 June 1962, Anna Georgina, da of Thomas Stewart-Johnstone (d 1986); 2 da (Nicola b 1963, Sarah b 1965); *Career* Lt Royal Fusiliers 1958-59; chm The Frizzell Gp Ltd (with the Gp 1957-), Insurance Brokers and Fin Services and at Lloyds; *Recreations* fly fishing, golf, music; *Clubs* Royal and Ancient Golf (St Andrews); *Style*— Colin Frizzell, Esq; Chuffs House, Holyport, Maidenhead, Berkshire SL6 2NA (☎ 0628 20827); Frizzell House, 14/22 Elder St, London E1 6DF (☎ 01 247 6595, telex 8811077, fax 01 377 9114, car ☎ 0860 337330)

FRODSHAM, Anthony Freer; CBE (1978); s of George William Frodsham (d 1929), and (Constance) Violet Neild (d 1949); descendant of Charles Frodsham (1810-71), the London clockmaker; *b* 8 Sept 1919; *Educ* Ecole Lacordaire Paris, Faraday House Engrg Coll London (DFH); *m* 1953, Patricia Myfanwy, da of Cdr A H Wynne-Edwards, DSC, RN (d 1971); 2 s (Simon, David); *Career* Lt (E) RN 1940-46, served in China, E Indies and Med (despatches); mgmnt conslt and co dir, chief exec P E Consulting Gp 1963-72; dir: Tace plc 1973-75, UDT Industs Ltd 1973-75, F Pratt Engrg Corpn 1982-85, Greyfriars Ltd 1984-87; dir gen Engrg Employers' Fedn 1975-82, ind chm Int Compressed Air and Allied Machinery Ctee 1977-, vice-chm Br Export Fin Advsy Cncl 1982-87; chm: Mgmnt Conslts Assoc 1968-70, Machine Tools EDC 1973-79; Advsy ctee Euro Business Ist 1982-; pres: Inst of Mgmnt Conslts 1966-68, Inst of Linguists 1986-89; memb: Engrg Indust Trg Bd 1975-79, Employers Policy Ctee 1975-79, Employment Policy Ctee 1975-82, Grand Cncl 1975-82, CBI President's Ctee 1979-82; gen cmmr of taxes 1975-, underwriting memb Lloyds 1977-, chm cncl Euro Business Sch 1983-, memb cncl Royal Naval Engrg Coll 1988-, DTI Enterprise cnsllr 1988-; conducted study for MOD on the provision of Engr Offrs for the Armed Forces 1983; *Clubs* Carlton, RAC; *Style*— Anthony Frodsham, Esq, CBE; 36 Fairacres, Roehampton Lane, London SW15 5LX (☎ 01 878 9551)

FROGGATT, Sir Leslie Trevor; s of late Leslie Froggatt and Mary Helena, *née* Brassey; *b* 8 April 1920; *Educ* Birkenhead Park Cheshire; *m* 1945, Jessie Elizabeth, da of P M Grant; 3 s; *Career* chm and chief exec offr Shell Gp of Cos Australia 1969-80, chm Ashton Mining Ltd 1981-, dir Aust Indust Devpt Corpn, cmmr Aust Nat Airlines Cmmn (TAA), v-chm Dunlop Olympic Ltd; dir Aust Inst of Petroleum Ltd 1983-; kt 1981; *Recreations* golf, music, racing; *Clubs* Melbourne, Australian, Commonwealth Golf; *Style*— Sir Leslie Froggatt; 20 Albany Rd, Toorak, Vic 3142, Australia (☎ 03 20 1357)

FROGGATT, Sir Peter; s of Albert Victor Froggatt (d 1964), of Belfast, and Edith, *née* Curran (d 1949); *b* 12 June 1928; *Educ* Royal Belfast Acad Inst, Trinity Coll Dublin (MB, MA, MD, LLD), Queen's Univ Belfast (DPH, PhD); *m* 1958, Norma Alexandra Irene, da of Robert Alexander Cochrane (d 1976), of Belfast; 4 s (Mark b 1961, Richard b 1964, Ian b 1968, Keith b 1970); *Career* medical conslt 1963-86; QUB: prof of Epidemiology 1968-76; Dean sch of Med 1971-76; vice-chllr and pres 1976-86; dir (non-exec) Allied Irish Banks plc; Inst of Clinical Pharmacology plc; FRCP (1979), FFCM, FRCP (Ire), FFCM (Ire), FFOM (Ire), DSc (hc NUI), FRCS (Ire) (hc), MRIA, CBIM; kt 1985; *Recreations* golf, music, travel; *Clubs* Royal Cwlth Soc; *Style*— Sir Peter Froggatt; c/o Allied Irish Banks plc, 2 Royal Ave, Belfast 1 (☎ 0232 246 559)

FROHLICH, Herbert; s of late Julius Jakob Fröhlich, of Munich; *b* 9 Dec 1905; *Educ* Munich Univ; *m* 1950, Audrey Fanchon, *née* Aungst; *Career* physicist; prof and head dept of theoretical physics Univ of Liverpool 1948-73; FRS; *Clubs* Royal Soc; *Style*— Herbert Frohlich, Esq; The Univ, Oxford St, Liverpool (☎ 051 709 6022)

FROOD, Alan Campbell; CBE; s of James Campbell Frood, MC (d 1964), and Margaret Helena Frood (d 1969); *b* 15 May 1926; *Educ* Cranleigh Sch, Peterhouse Cambridge (BA); *m* 1960, Patricia Ann, da of Frederick Wynn Cotterel; 2 s, 2 da; *Career* RN 1944-47, Sub-Lt RNVR; Bank of England 1949, Colonial Admin Servs 1952, Bankers' Tst Co 1962, dir Bankers' Trust Int; Crown Agents: gen mangr banking dept 1975, md 1978-88, crown agent 1980, ret 1988; *Recreations* gardening; *Clubs* Royal Cwlth Soc; *Style*— Alan Frood, Esq; West Orchard, Holmbush Lane, Henfield, W Sussex BN5 9TJ;

FROSSARD, Sir Charles Keith; s of Rev Edward Louis Frossard, CBE (d 1968), formerly Dean of Guernsey, and Margery Smith, *née* Latta (d 1958); *b* 18 Feb 1922; *Educ* Elizabeth Coll Guernsey, Univ of Caen (Bachelier en Droit); *m* 10 April 1950, Elizabeth Marguerite, da of John Edmund Leopold Martel, OBE (d 1973), of Grange Court, Guernsey; 2 da (Marguerite, Jeanne); *Career* WWII: enlisted Gordon Highlanders 1940, cmmnd IA 1941, Capt 17 Dogra Regt, seconded Tochi Scouts and Chitral Scouts, NW Frontier India 1942-46; barr Gray's Inn 1949, advocate of the Royal Court of Guernsey 1949; People's Dep States of Guernsey 1958, conseiller States of Guernsey 1967, solicitor-general 1969, attorney-gen 1973, dep bailiff 1977, bailiff of Guernsey 1982; ACIArb; KGStJ 1987; Médaille de Vermeil Ville de Paris 1984; kt 1983; *Recreations* golf; *Clubs* Naval and Military; *Style*— Sir Charles Frossard; Les Lierres, Rohais, St Peter Port, Guernsey, Channel Islands (☎ 0481 22076); The Bailiff's Chambers, Royal Court House, Guernsey, Channel Islands (☎ 0481 26161)

FROST, Alan John; s of Edward George Frost (d 1981), and Ellen Lucy *née* Jamieson (d 1979); *b* 6 Oct 1944; *Educ* Stratford Co GS, Manchester univ (BSc); *m* 15/Dec 1933, Valerie Jean, da of Francis David Bennett; 2 s (Christopher, Patrick); *Career* asst gen mangr (investmts): London & Manchester Assur Gp plc 1980- 84, Sun Life Assur Soc plc 1984-86; investmt dir Abbey Life Gp 1986- 89; md Life Assur Co Ltd 1989-; Freeman City of London 1986, Liveryman Worshipful Co of Actuaries 1986, FIA 1970; *Books* A General Introduction to Institutional Investment (with D P Hager 1986); *Recreations* reading, gardening, genealogy; *Clubs* East India; *Style*— Alan Frost, Esq; Rondels, 20 Little Forest Rd, Bournemouth, Dorset BN4 9NW; Abbey Life House, PO Box 33, 80 Holdenhurst Rd,Bournemouth, Dorset BN8 8AL (☎ 0202 292373, fax 0202 296816, telex 41310)

FROST, Albert Edward; CBE (1983); s of Charles Albert Frost (d 1953), and Minnie Frost; *b* 7 Mar 1914; *Educ* Oulton Sch Liverpool, London Univ; *m* 1942, Eugénie Maud Barlow; *Career* barr Middle Temple; HM inspr of taxes 1937-49, dep head taxation ICI Ltd 1949-57, dep treasurer 1957-60, treasurer 1960-68, finance dir 1968-76; dir: Marks & Spencer 1976-, S G Warburg 1976-83, BL Ltd 1977-80, Br Airways 1976-80, Br Steel Corpn 1980-83, Remploy Ltd (chm 1983-), Guinness Mahon & Co Ltd (chm 1984-), Guinness Mahon Hldgs Ltd 1984-, The Guinness Peat Gp plc 1984-; memb: Panel on Take-overs and Mergers, cncl United Med Schs of Guy's and St Thomas's Hosps (and chm fin ctee), cncl and fin ctee Morley Coll London to 1983; dir

Youth Music Ltd, chm Robert Mayer Trust for Youth and Music 1981-, dir City Arts Trust Ltd 1982-, chm London Soc of Chamber Music 1983-; memb: Royal Academy of Arts Appeal Ctee, cncl British United Industrialists, advsy cncl Assoc for Business Sponsorship of the Arts, orgn ctee Carl Flesch Int Violin Competition London, exec ctee for dvpt appeal Royal Opera House, Arts Cncl of GB 1982-83; *Recreations* violinist, swimming, athletics, walking, arts generally; *Clubs* RAC; *Style—* Albert Frost, Esq, CBE; Guinness Mahon & Co Ltd, 32 St Mary Axe Hill, London EC3 (☎ 01 623 9333)

FROST, David Paradine; OBE (1970); s of late Rev W J Paradine Frost, of Tenterden, Kent; *b* 7 April 1939; *m* 1, 1981 (m dis 1982), Lynne Frederick, widow of Peter Sellers; m 2, 1983, Lady Carina Mary Anne Gabrielle, da of 17 Duke of Norfolk, KG, GCVO, CB, CBE, MC, *qv*; 3 s (Miles b 1984, Wilfred b 1985, George Paradine b 1987); *Career* television presenter, prod, author; programmes incl That Was the Week that Was, The Frost Report, The Frost Programme, The David Frost Show and interviews including The Sir Harold Wilson Interviews, The Nixon Interviews; jt fndr and dir TV-AM; *Style—* David Frost, Esq, OBE

FROST, Maj-Gen John Dutton; CB (1964), DSO and bar (1943, 1945), MC (1942), DL (W Sussex 1982); s of Brig-Gen Frank Dutton Frost, CBE, MC (d 1968), and Elsie Dora, *née* Bright (d 1952); *b* 31 Dec 1912; *Educ* Wellington, RMC Sandhurst; *m* 1947, Jean MacGregor, da of Philip Lyle (d 1955), of Waterside, nr Liphook, Hants; 1 s, 1 da; *Career* cmmnd Cameronians 1932, served WWII in Iraq Levies, Cameronians and Parachute Regt, Bt Lt-Col 1953, Col 1956, Brig 1960, cmdg 44 Independent Parachute Bde Gp (TA) 1958-61, Cdr 52 Lowland Div Dist 1961-64, Cdr Malta Land Force 1965-67 (when ret), GOC Troops Malta & Libya 1964-66; now farming; Cross of Grand Offrs SMO Malta 1966; *Recreations* golf, shooting; *Clubs* Army & Navy; *Style—* Maj-Gen John Frost, CB, DSO, MC, DL; Northend Farm, Milland, Liphook, Hants (☎ Milland 206)

FROST, Air Commodore John William; CBE (1966), DFC (1945, DL (Berkshire 1986)); s of John Frost (d 1974), of Stoke-on-Trent, Staffs; *b* 30 July 1921; *Educ* Longton HS Stoke-on-Trent; *m* 1950, Shelagh, da of George Frederick Baldock (d 1982); 1 s, 2 da; *Career* joined RAF 1941, pilot training/flying instr US Army Air Corps 1941-43, 2 TAF BAFO Germany 1944-49, Fighter Cmd 1949-53 and 1957-60, RAF Staff Coll Bracknell 1954, Far East Air Force 1955-57, jt serv Staff Coll 1960, RAF Staff Coll 1961-64, Station Cdr RAF El Adem Libya 1964-66, dep dir RAF Projects MOD 1967-68, Air Cdre 1968, dir Personnel Services RAF MOD 1968-70, Dep Cmdt Jt Warfare Estab 1970-72, COS UK Mil Rep HQ NATO 1972-76, ret RAF 1976; head Protocol MOD 1977-83; vice chm Air TAVR Eastern Wessex 1979-87; Chevalier Order Leopold II, Croix de Guerre Belge (1947); *Recreations* reading, rough shooting, photography, country interests; *Clubs* RAF; *Style—* Air Commodore John Frost, CBE, DFC, DL; 20 Wise's Firs, Sulhamstead, Reading, Berks RG7 4EH (☎ 073 529 2372)

FROST, (Cecil) John William; s of Benjamin John (d 1963), and Gladys *née* Raynes (d 1979); *b* 27 May 1942; *Educ* Royal Liberty GS; *m* 1 Sept 1962, Janice Rhoda, da of Herbert Cook (d 1971); 2 s (Stephen John, Jeremy William); *Career* md Cater Allen Ltd 1977-, dir Cater Allen Hldgs plc 1983-; hon sec Lombard Assoc London; FCIB 1965; *Recreations* sailing, opera, jazz; *Style—* John Frost, Esq; Redwalls, Frairs Close, Shenfield, Essex, (☎ 0277 224753), Cater Allen Ltd, 1 Kinng William St, London ECHN 7AU, (☎ 623 2070)

FROST, Hon Mrs; Hon Marygold; *née* Mills; da of 3 Baron Hillingdon (d 1952); *b* 19 Oct 1924; *m* 1948, Kenneth Frost; 2 s, 4 da; *Style—* Hon Mrs Frost

FROST, Patrick Edward; s of Richard Edward Frost (d 1980), of Kingsley Green, Surrey, and Audrey Kate, *née* Jenkins (d 1986); *b* 22 Nov 1948; *Educ* Midhurst GS, Guildford Coll (HND); *m* 19 Feb 1977, Susan Anne, da of Col Leonard Bindon Arrowsmith Thacker; *Career* area surveyor Marshall-Andrew Construction 1974-81, chief surveyor C J Sims Ltd 1981-84, chm and md Patrick Frost Assocs Ltd 1985-; Freeman: City of London 1982, Worshipful Co of Carmen 1983; memb Royal Soc of St George (City of London branch); *Recreations* sailing, shooting, golf, antiques restoration; *Clubs* City Livery; *Style—* Patrick Frost, Esq; Furnace Ct, Haslemere, Surrey GU27 2EJ (☎ 0428 52255)

FROST, Dame Phyllis Irene; DBE (1974, CBE 1963); da of Harry Caleb Turner, of Croydon, Vic (d 1977), and Irene Anna Clarke, *née* Rickard (d 1973); *b* 14 Sept 1917; *Educ* Presbyterian Ladies' Coll, Melbourne Univ; *m* 1941, Glenn Neville Frost, LDS, BDSc, JP, s of Ernest Arthur Frost (d 1949), of Canterbury, Victoria; 3 da (Elizabeth, Pauline, Christine); *Career* chm: Victorian Relief ctee 1975- (memb 1964-), Fairlea Women's Prison Cncl 1953-; chm: Brain Behaviour Research Inst Latrobe Univ, Keep Australia Beautiful Cncl, Australian Contact Emergency Service; memb: Environment Protection Authority Waste Recycling Advsy ctee 1981-, State Disaster Welfare ctee 1983-; v-chm: Clean World Int 1980-, Victorian Assoc for Care and Resettlement of Offenders 1977-, memb many other Federal and State cncls, delegate to many int conferences; *Clubs* RAC (Victoria); *Style—* Dame Phyllis Frost, DBE, CBE, JP; 4 Jackson Street, Croydon, Vic 3136, Australia; Keep Australia Beautiful Council, 220 Bay St, Port Melbourne, Vic, Australia (☎ 03 6462141)

FROST, Hon Raymond; s of Baroness Gaitskell by her 1 husb, David Frost; *b* 6 May 1924; *Educ* Oundle, Worcester Coll Oxford; *m* 6 Sept 1958, June Virginia Johnston Gonzalez, da of Eduardo Rodriguez del Rey, of Cienfuegos, Cuba; 1 s, 1 da; *Career* dir Econ Dvpt Inst at World Bank, Washington, DC; *Style—* Hon Raymond Frost; 2917 Q Street NW, Washington, DC 20007, USA

FROST, Ronald Edwin; s of Charles Henry Frost, and Doris, *née* Foggin; *b* 19 Mar 1936; *m* 19 Sept 1959, Beryl, da of Leonard Ward, of Windsor (d 1964); 1 s (Stephen Charles b 1962), 2 da (Jane Samantha b 1965, Louise Karen b 1966); *Career* chief exec: Hays plc 1986-, Hays Farms Hursley Ltd 1986; dir: HWC Superannuation Tst Ltd 1983-, Chainpoint Ltd 1986-, Hays Chemical Distribution Ltd 1983, Hays Commercial Servs Ltd 1983, Hays Distribution Servs Ltd 1983, Hays Marine Servs Ltd 1986, Hays Personnel Servs Ltd 1986; *Recreations* game shooting, sailing; *Clubs* RAC, St James's, IOD; *Style—* Ronald Frost, Esq; Shamley Wood, Shamley Green, Nr Guildford, Surrey GU5 0SP (☎ 0483 893338); Hays plc, Hays House, Millmead, Guildford, Surrey GU2 5HJ (☎ 0483 302203, telex 85904, fax 300388, car 0836 222159)

FROST, Hon Sir (Thomas) Sydney; s of late Thomas Frost; *b* 13 Feb 1916; *Educ* Melbourne Univ (LLM); *m* 1943, Dorothy Gertrude, *née* Kelly; 2 s, 1 da; *Career* barr 1945, QC 1961, judge of the County Ct of Victoria 1964, judge of Supreme Ct of Papua New Guinea 1964-75 (chief justice 1975-78); chm: Aust Govt Inquiry into Whales and Whaling 1978, Royal Cmmn Inquiry into Housing Cmmn Land Purchases and Valuation Matters 1979-81; bd of accident inquiry into aircraft crash at Sydney Airport Feb 1980; pres Med Serv Review Tribunal 1979-85; kt 1975; *Recreations* golf; *Clubs* Australian (Melbourne), Royal Melbourne Golf; *Style—* The Hon Sir Sydney Frost; Park Tower, 201 Spring St, Melbourne, Vic 3000, Australia (☎ 662 3239)

FROSTICK, Raymond Charles; DL (Norfolk 1979); s of Harry Frostick, of Hoveton, Norfolk (d 1965), and Ethel Marion, *née* Preston (d 1983); *b* 18 May 1931; *Educ* Norwich Sch, Corpus Christi Coll Cambridge (MA, LLM); *m* 27 July 1957, (Rosemary) Claire, da of Sir George Harold Banwell, of Lincoln (d 1982); 2 s (Richard b 1960, Andrew b 1963), 2 da (Marion b 1958, Elizabeth b 1961); *Career* Nat Serv RAF 1949-51; slr 1957, chm ptnrship bd Daynes Hill & Perks 1988-(ptnr 1962-), ptnr Daynes Hill Paterson Wieringa Amsterdam, dir RG Carter (Hldgs) Ltd 1975-, vice-chm Radio Broadland (Hldgs) plc 1987-(dir 1984-); chm: Norfolk Area Health Authy 1978-82, Norwich Health Authy 1982-85; pres Norwich and Norfolk C of C and Industry 1985-88; Univ of E Anglia: memb of cncl 1972-, tres and vice-chm cncl 1985-, chm Centre of E Anglian Studies 1986-; cllr Norwich City Cncl 1966-79, Lord Mayor of Norwich 1976-77, cllr Norfolk CC 1973-85(chm 1983-84), chm nat exec Nat Marriage Guidance 1986-; memb Law Soc 1957, FRSA 1985; *Books* The Dutch Connection: Some Norfolk Maps and Their Makers (1988); *Recreations* cartography, travel; *Clubs* Royal Cwlth Soc; *Style—* Raymond Frostick, Esq, DL; 425 Unthank Rd, Norwich, Norfolk NR4 7QB (☎ 0603 52937); Daynes Hill & Perks, Holland Ct, The Close, Norwich, Norfolk NR1 4DX (☎ 0603 611 212, fax 0603 610 535, telex 97197)

FROWEN, Prof Stephen Francis; s of Adolf Frowein (d 1964), and Anna *née* Bauer (d 1968); *b* 22 May 1923; *Educ* Univ of: Cologne, Wuerzburg, Bonn, London (BSc, MSc); *m* 21 March 1949, Irina, da of Dr Sam Minskers; 1 s (Michael b 17 Jan 1950), 1 da (Tatiana b 20 Sept 1955); *Career* ed The Bankers Magazine (now Banking World) 1954-60, econ advsr Indust and Commercial Fin Corpn 1960-61, res offr Nat Inst of Econ and Social Res 1961-62, sr lectr Thames Poly 1962-67, sr lectr Univ of Surrey 1967-87, prof of econ Univ of Frankfurt 1987, Bundesbank prof of monetary econs Free Univ of Berlin 1987-88; numerous journal articles and editing of conf transactions in the field of monetary econs; hon fell UCL 1989-; *Recreations* numismatics, painting, music, tennis; *Clubs* Reform; *Style—* Prof Stephen Francis Frowe; 40 Gurney Drive, London N2 0DE (☎ 01 458 0159)

FROY, Robert Anthony Douglas; s of Hienz Louis Froy (d 1981), and Giezela Anna, *née* Salomon; *b* 23 August 1936; *Educ* Clarks Coll; *m* 8 July 1960, (Diana) Wendy, da of Maj Clifford Anderson Likeman (d 1980); 2 s (Stephen b 4 April 1963, Nicholas b 21 Feb 1965); *Career* statistician David A Bevan Simpson & Co 1957-60, equity salesman J & A Scrimgeour 1960-69, md Montagu Loebl Stanley 1969-87, dep md Lloyds Bank Stockbrokers 1987-; dir: Lloyds Merchant Bank Ltd, Betram Investmt Tst plc; non-exec: The Otford Gp, Hanover Property Unit Tst; dep chm Chambers & Remington Ltd Stockbrokers, chm Sennocke Services Ltd, memb Int stock Exchange; Mayor Sevenoaks 1975 (former cncllr), former chm Citizen's Advice Bureau, chm govrs Sevenoaks Sch; AMSIA Freeman City of London, Liveryman Worshipful Co of Pattenmakers; *Recreations* sport, walking, gardening; *Clubs* City of London; *Style—* Robert Froy, Esq; Little Chart, Oakhill Rd, Sevenoaks, Kent TN13 1NS (☎ 0732 453 475); Lloyds Bank Stockbrokers Ltd, 40-66 Queen Victoria St, London EC4P 4EL (☎ 01 248 2244, fax 01 236 1632, telex 888301)

FRY, Lady Cosima Maria Gabriella; *née* Vane-Tempest-Stewart; yr da (by his 1 w) of 9 Marquess of Londonderry; *b* 25 Dec 1961; *Educ* St Paul's Girls' Sch; *m* 1 Oct 1982, Cosmo Joseph Fry, s of Jeremy Fry, of 7 Royal Crescent, Bath, by his former w, now Mrs Camilla Fairbairn, of Harvest Hill Farm, Cuckfield, Sussex; *Style—* Lady Cosima Fry

FRY, Donald William; CBE (1970); s of William Joseph Fry (d 1946) of Weymouth and Mary Jane *née* Symonds (d 1963); *b* 30 Nov 1910; *Educ* Weymouth GS, King's Coll London (MSc); *m* 7 July 1934, Jessie Florence, da of Robert Joseph Wright (d 1937) of Weymouth; 3 s (David b 1937, John b 1939, Peter b 1945); *Career* Chief Physicist and Electrical Eng Radio Communications and Radar 1932-45, PSO Atomic Energy Research Establishment Harwell 1946; head General Physics Div 1950-54, chief physicist AERE 1954-57; dep dir: AERE 1958; dir: Winfrith Atomic Energy Establishment 1959-73; *Recreations* travelling, bridge; *Clubs* Came Down Golf; *Style—* D W Fry Esq, CBE; 25 Bowleaze Coveway, Overcombe, Weymouth DT3 6PL (☎ 0352 833276)

FRY, Dr John; CBE (1988); s of Dr Ansel Fry (d 1972), and Basia Fry (d 1979); *b* 16 April 1922; *Educ* Whitgift Middle Sch, London Univ, Guy's Hosp Med Sch (MD); *m* 2 April 1944, Joan Lilian, da of James Sabel (d 1941); 1 s (James b 26 Feb 1946), 1 da (Dimity Jane (Mrs Dawson) b 28 May 1947); *Career* GP 1947-, memb cncl RCGP 1957-88, governing tstee Nuffield Provincial Hosp Tst 1957-88, memb Gen Med Cncl 1970-88, Jephcott prof Oxford Univ 1981-82; conslt ed Update 1968-88, civilian conslt in Gen Practice to the Br Army 1967-87; Queen Elizabeth the Queen Mother fell and lectr 1988; FRCS, FRCGP, FRSM;; *Books* Medicine in Three Societies (1969), Common Diseases (4 edn 1985), Disease Data Book (1986); *Recreations* reading, writing, running; *Style—* Dr John Fry, CBE; 138 Croydon Rd, Beckenham, Kent BR3 4DG (☎ 01 650 0568)

FRY, John Marshall; s of Montague Philip Fry, and Margery Maud, *née* Marshall; *b* 3 Mar 1936; *Educ* Tonbridge, Trinity Hall Cambridge (MA); *m* 12 Aug 1967, Diana Margaret, da of John Wybert Nowell Clark; 2 da (Amanda b 1969, Susannah b 1971); *Career* Royal Dragoons 1954-56; mgmnt trainee Marshall Ltd Cambridge 1959-61; Abbey Nat Bldg Soc: mangr personnel and trg 1965-72, divnl mangr 1972-79, gen mangr 1979, dir 1984, dir and gen mangr gp servs 1988; pres Chartered Bldg Socs Inst 1986-87 (cncl memb 1979), chm govrs St Mary's Sch Gerrards Cross, govr Queenswood Sch Herts; FCIS 1972; *Recreations* gardening, equestrian activities; *Clubs* Cavalry and Guards'; *Style—* John Fry, Esq; Clonmel, Flaunden, nr Hemel Hempstead, Herts HP3 0PP (☎ 0442 832 204); Abbey Ho, Baker St, London NW1 6XL (☎ 01 486 5555, fax 01 486 555, ext 4230, telex 266103 ABBNAT G)

FRY, Jonathan Michael; s of Stephen Fry (d 1979), of London, and Gladys Yvonne, *née* Blunt; *b* 9 August 1937; *Educ* Repton, Trin Coll Oxford (MA); *m* 21 Feb 1970, Caroline Mary, da of Col Vincent Ashforth Blundell Dunkerly, DSO, JP (d 1968); 4 da (Lucy b 1971, Camilla b 1973, Victoria b 1977, Sophie b 1979); *Career* account exec Pritchard Wood & Ptnrs 1961-65, account supervisor Norman Craig & Kummel 1965-66, engagement mangr McKinsey & Co 1966-72, dir and chief exec foods div Unigate Ltd 1972-77, chief exec speciality chemicals div The Burmah Oil plc, chief exec and dir

Castrol 1978-; chm: Beechingstoke PC 1978-; chm Woodborough Conservative Assoc 1976-83, St Francis Sch Pewsey 1984-; *Recreations* cricket, skiing, archaeology; *Clubs* MCC, Vincent's (Oxford); *Style*— Jonathan Fry, Esq; Beechingstoke Manor, Pewsey, Wilts; Burmah Oil plc, Burmah House, Piper's Way, Swindon, Wilts (☎ 0793 512 712, fax 0793 513 419, car tel 0836 230 387)

FRY, Dr Lionel; s of Dr Ancel Fry (d 1972), and Barbara, *née* Mintzman (d 1979); *b* 19 Mar 1933; *Educ* King's Coll, London Univ (BSc, MD, BS); *m* 27 Nov 1955, Minné, da of Dr Jack Sidney Zidel; 1 s (Michael b 1959), 2 da (Tessa Joanne b 1961, Kathrine b 1963); *Career* conslt dermatologist St Mary's Hosp London; author: Dermatology, An Illustrated Guide; Immunological Aspects of Skin Disease; *Recreations* tennis, walking, music, theatre; *Style*— Dr Lionel Fry; 16 Caroline Place, London W2 4AN (☎ 01 229 7790); St Mary's Hosp, London W2 1NY; 96 Harley St, London W1 (☎ 01 935 2421)

FRY, Maurice Alec; s of Edward Stanley Fry; *b* 11 Dec 1915; *Educ* Bancroft Sch; *m* 1; 3 children; m 2, 1977, Cozette, da of Edward Cordwell-Green; *Career* served WWII, Maj, 2 i/c 1 Bn Indian Parachute Regt; chm Electronics Rental Gp; *Recreations* golf; *Clubs* Army & Navy, Inst of Directors, St George's Hill Golf; *Style*— Maurice Fry, Esq; 4 Belgrave Sq, London SW1 (☎ 01 235 3544); c/o Electronic Rental Group Ltd, Electronic House, Churchfield Rd, Weybridge, Surrey

FRY, Nicholas Rodney Lowther; s of Rodney William Lowther Fry, of Derby, and Mary Winifred Rosalind, *née* Ellis; *b* 28 April 1947; *Educ* Malvern, Christ's Coll Cambridge (MA); *m* 1972, Christine Sarah, da of Edmund De Chazal Rogers (d 1967), of London; 1 s (Jonathan b 1976), 2 da (Emma b 1974, Lucy b 1981); *Career* merchant banker; dir S G Warburg & Co Ltd 1983-; FICA; *Recreations* music, gardening, recreational sport; *Style*— Nicholas Fry, Esq; 38 Lyford Rd, London SW18 3LS (☎ 01 874 7608); S G Warburg & Co Ltd, 2 Finsbury Ave, London EC2M 2PA (☎ 01 860 1090, telex 920301, fax 01 860 0901)

FRY, Peter Derek; MP (C) Wellingborough 1969-; s of Harry Walter Fry, of High Wycombe, Bucks, and late Edith Fry; *b* 26 May 1931; *Educ* Royal GS High Wycombe, Worcester Coll Oxford (MA); *m* 1, 1958 (m dis 1982), Edna, da of John Roberts, of Liverpool; 1 s, 1 da; m 2, 1982, Helen Claire Mitchell, da of late James Gregson; *Career* memb Bucks CC 1961-67, insurance broker 1963-, London area political educn offr CCO 1961-63, contested (C): Nottingham N 1964, Willesden E 1966; memb transport select ctee 1979-, vice-pres British Yugoslav Soc, ptnr Political Research and Communications Int (chm 1982-); chm Political Research & Communications Int Ltd 1982-; dir CBA Public Affairs Ltd 1984-; *Clubs* RAC; *Style*— Peter Fry, Esq, MP; Glebe Farm House, Church Lane, Cranford, Kettering, Northants; House of Commons, London SW1

FRY, Stephen John; s of Alan John Fry, ARCS (Lt REME), of Booton, Norfolk, and Marianne Eve, *née* Newman; *b* 24 August 1957; *Educ* Uppingham, Queens' Coll Cambridge (MA); *Career* actor and writer; appeared with Cambridge Footlights in revue The Cellar Tapes at Edinburgh Festival 1981 (Perrier Award); plays: Latin (Scotsman Fringe First Award 1980 and Lyric Hammersmith 1983), Forty Years On (Chichester Festival and Queen's Theatre London) 1984 The Common Pursuit (Phoenix Theatre London) 1988; TV series: Alfresco 1982-84, The Young Ones 1983, Happy Families 1984, Saturday Night Live 1986-87, A Bit of Fry and Laurie 1987 and 1989, Blackadder's Christmas Carol 1988; radio: Whose Line Is It Anyway? 1987, Saturday Night Fry 1987, Loose Ends 1986-87; weekly column in the Listener, re-wrote script for musical Me and My Girl 1984 (London, Broadway, Sydney); patron: Studio 3 (arts for young people) Freeze (nuclear disarmament charity); memb: Amnesty Int, Comic relief; *Recreations* chess, computing, dining out, light alcoholic refreshments; *Clubs* Oxford and Cambridge's Chelsea Arts, Groncho, Freds, Zanzibar; *Style*— Stephen Fry, Esq; c/o Noel Gay Artists, 24 Denmark St, London WC2 (☎ 01 836 3941)

FRY, (Hon) Sir William Gordon; JP; s of Alfred Gordon Fry (d 1942), and Edith Elizabeth Fry (d 1950); *b* 12 June 1909; *Educ* Victorian Teachers' Coll, Melbourne Univ; *m* 1936, Lilian Gwendoline, da of Alexander William Macrae (ka 1915); 4 s; *Career* MLC Vic (Lib) for Higinbotham 1967-79 (ret), pres Legislative Cncl of Vic 1976-79 (ret); kt 1981; *see Debrett's Handbook of Australia and New Zealand for further details*; *Recreations* golf, bowls, billiards; *Clubs* West Brighton, VRC, Kooyong Tennis, Legacy (Melbourne); *Style*— The Hon Sir William Fry, JP; 16 Mariemont Ave, Beaumaris, Vic 3193, Australia

FRYBERG, Sir Abraham; MBE (1942); s of Henry Fryberg (d 1938), of Bendigo, and Rose Fryberg (d 1942); *b* 26 May 1901; *Educ* Wesley Coll Melbourne, Queen's Coll Melbourne Univ, (MB BS(MECD), DPH DM), Hon (MD) Qld Hon Fell RCMA, Fell Qld Reerch; *m* 1939, Vivian Greensill, da of late Henry Greensill Barnard; 1 s (George); *Career* dir-gen Health and Med Services Qld 1947-67, memb of Senate Qld Univ 1946-68, chm Med Bd of Qld 1947-67, ret; SBStJ 1958; kt 1968; *Recreations* racing; *Clubs* United Services; *Style*— Sir Abraham Fryberg, MBE; 19 Dublin St, Clayfield, Qld 4011, Australia (☎ 262 2549)

FRYE, Eric; s of William Barnard Frye (d 1949); *b* 15 Mar 1923; *Educ* Tom Hood Coll, SE Essex Tech Coll; *m* 1947, Doreen Joan, da of Edward Thomas Day (d 1958); 2 c; *Career* warrant offr, air observer Europe, POW Japan 1941-45; FCA 1952; sr exec Ford Motor Co 1964; dir: Staveley Industries 1964-67, The Plessey Co plc 1969-78 (dep chief exec 1976-78), H Brammer plc 1978-87, Deborah Services plc 1979-86; chm and chief exec Arcotronics Holding BV 1982-86; CBIM; *Recreations* golf, travel, bridge, carpentry; *Style*— Eric Frye, Esq; Little Orchard, 209 Cooden Sea Rd, Cooden, Bexhill-on-Sea, E Sussex TN39 4TR (☎ 04243 3995); Casa Doric, Quinta do Paraiso, Praia do Carvoeiro, Algarve, Portugal

FRYER, Maj-Gen (Wilfred) George; CB (1956), CBE (1951, OBE 1941); s of James Fryer (d 1948), and Marion, *née* Cook (d 1950); gn of William Raikes Hodson (1821-58), mutiny hero, founder Hodson's Horse, killed at relief Lucknow; *b* 1 May 1900; *Educ* Christ Coll Brecon, RMA Woolwich; *m* 1951, Jean Eleanore Graham, da of Graham Binny, RSW, of Edinburgh; 3 s (Graham decd, Angus, Robert); *Career* cmmd RE 1919; WWII 1940-45: SO1 to chief engr 8 Army 1941, DOWE & M GHQ Middle East 1942, dep chief engr 8 Corps France and Germany 1945, chief engr Br Army Staff Washington DC 1945, Brig chief engr Southern Cmd UK 1951-53, chief engr MELF 1954-57; chm Warminster Press 1960-87; *Recreations* skiing (Lauberhorn Cup 1928), sailing (Nat champion Wayfarer Dinghy class 1960), flying (held A air pilot's licence); *Clubs* Hurlingham, Royal Ocean Racing (Transatlantic Race 1931), Army and Navy, Royal Lymington Yacht; *Style*— Maj Gen George Fryer, CB, CBE; 47 Belmore Lane, Lymington, Hants SO41 9NR (☎ 0590 72608)

FRYER, John Albert; CBE (1970); s of George Albert Fryer, RN; *b* 17 Jan 1925; *Educ* Portsmouth Northern Secdy Sch, Southern Coll Art Winchester, Camborne Sch of Mines, Univ Coll London, Southampton Univ; *m* m 1, 1960, Brenda Sheila (d 1984), da of Reginald Charles Frederick Baugh, of Cardiff; 1 s; m 2, 1986, Audrey Jean, da of Eric Gilbert Wells, of Hove; *Career* Lt RE, FARELF; Colonial Survey Serv N Borneo 1948, dir lands and surveys Sabah Malaysia 1966-70; transportation res offr GLC 1970-86; ARICS 1960; *Recreations* genealogy; *Clubs* MENSA; *Style*— John Fryer, Esq, CBE; New Orchard, 6 Meadowlands, Havant, Hants

FRYER-SPEDDING, John Henry Fryer; OBE, DL; s of Lt-Col James Eustace Spedding, OBE (d 1969), of Windebrowe, Keswick, Cumbria, and Mary Catherine, *née* Fryer; *b* 23 Jan 1937; *Educ* Harrow, Trinity Coll Cambridge (MA); *m* 15 Aug 1968, Clare Caroline, da of Ven Walter Frederick Ewbank, of High Rigg, Castle Sowerby, Cumbria; 2 s (James b 1970, Jack b 1972); *Career* Royal Green Jackets 1958-68 serv: Germany, Cyprus, Borneo, ret Maj 1968; DLI (TA) 1969-78 CO 7 Bn LI (TA) 1976-78, ret Lt Col 1978; barr Grays Inn 1970, practising Newcastle-upon-Tyne; tstee: Wordsworth Tst, Calvert Tst for Disabled People; vice-pres Tennyson Soc; *Recreations* forestry, beekeeping; *Style*— John Fryer-Spedding, Esq, OBE, DL; Mirehouse, Keswick, Cumbria CA12 4QE (☎ 07687 72287); Trinity Chambers, 12 Trinity Chare, Quayside, Newcastle NE1 3DF (☎ 091 2321927, fax 091 232 7975)

FRYERS, (Charles) Geoffrey; s of Charles Ronald Fryers, of Bradley W Yorks, and Margaret, *née* Mattock; *b* 4 June 1950; *Educ* Ermysteds GS Skipton; *m* 25 Sept 1971, Elizabeth Ame, da of Fred Hird Hodgson, of Bradley, W Yorks; 1 s (Paul b 1975), 1 da (Rachel b 1973); *Career* dir and co sec: Merrit & Fryers Ltd 1975-, Nicholas Smiths Garages Ltd 1981-, E Midgley & Co (Builders Merchants) Ltd 1976-; capt Bradford League Side, Keighley CC 1972, capt Lancashire League Side, Colne CC 1984 and 1985; apptd Nat Cricket Assoc Coach 1987; *Recreations* cricket player, snooker player, football spectator and lover of all sports; *Clubs* Colne Cricket; *Style*— Geoffrey Fryers, Esq; Harden Clough Farm, Skipton Old Road, Colne, Lancashire BB8 7ER (☎ Earby 843777); Merritt & Fryers Ltd, Firth Street Works, Skipton N Yorks BD23 2PX

FUCHS, Sir Vivian (Ernest); s of Ernest Fuchs (d 1957), of Heatherdene, Tilford, Surrey, and Annie Violet, *née* Watson; *b* 11 Feb 1908; *Educ* Brighton Coll, St John's Coll Cambridge (MA, PhD); *m* 1933, Joyce, 2 da of John Alexander Connell (d 1914), of Langley, Putney; 1 s (Peter), 1 da (Rosalind decd), 1 da (Hilary); *Career* Maj, West Africa, NW Europe; geologist, expeditions include: Greenland 1929, East Africa 1930-31, 1934, 1937-38, field cdr Falkland Islands Dependencies Survey 1947-50, dir FIDS Scientific Bureau 1950-55, dir Br Antarctic Survey 1958-73, leader Commonwealth Trans-Antarctic Expedition 1955-58; pres: Br Assoc for the Advancement of Science 1972, Royal Geographical Soc 1981-83; author; FRS; kt 1958; *Books* Of Ice and Men (1982), Crossing of Antarctica (1958), Antarctic Adventure (1959), Forces of Nature (Ed) (1977); *Recreations* sailing, gardening; *Clubs* Athenaeum; *Style*— Sir Vivian Fuchs; 78 Barton Rd, Cambridge (☎ 0223 359238)

FUGARD, Maj-Gen Michael Teape; s of Rev Theodore Charles William Cooper Teape Fugard (d 1985), of Malton, Yorks, and Lilian Rhodes, *née* Freeman Baker (d 1954); *b* 27 Mar 1933; *Educ* Sherborne; *m* 22 Dec 1961, Theresia, da of Anton Hollensteiner (d 1952), of Leiben, Lower Austria; 2 s (Robert b 1963, William b 1970), 2 da (Alison b 1962, Berenice b 1966); *Career* slr 1957; cmmnd Army Legal Servs (now Army Legal Corps) 1958: Maj CO Army Legal Aid FARELF 1960-74, Lt-Col asst dir BAOR 1971, Col Legal Staff HQUKLF 1979-82, Brig cdr Army Legal Gp UK 1983-86, dir of Army Legal Servs 1986, Maj-Gen; memb Law Soc's Salaried Slr's Ctee 1973-78, asst rec 1986-, chm UK Gp Int Soc for Military Law of War 1988; hon legal advsr Kingston-on-Thames CAB 1965-66, govr Royal Sch Bath 1984-, memb spire appeal ctee Salisbury Cathedral 1985-86, chm govrs Leadenhall Sch Salisbury 1988-; *Recreations* walking preferably with a dog, reading, coarse gardening; *Clubs* Lansdowne; *Style*— Maj-Gen Michael Fugard; Dir of Army Legal Servs, Empress State Bldg, Lillie Rd, London SW6 1TR (☎ 01 385 1244 ext 2297)

FULCHER, Derick Harold; DSC (1944); s of Percy Frederick Fulcher (d 1951), of London and Gertrude Lilian, *née* Robinson (d 1971); *b* 4 Nov 1917; *Educ* St Olave's GS; *m* 2 Dec 1943, (Florence Ellen) May, da of John Barr Anderson (d 1956), of Glasgow; 1 s (Derick John b 19 Aug 1945), 1 da (Moira Joy b 12 Dec 1949); *Career* RN 1940-46, Lt RNVR; asst accountant WO 1936, princ Miny of Nat Insur 1950-56 (asst princ 1947-50), princ HM Treasy 1957-59, asst sec Miny of Social Security 1959, asst undersec of state Dept of Health and Social Security 1969-70, Admin Staff Coll Henley 1952, interviewer Civil Serv Cmmn 1971-79, chm Supplementary Benefit Appeals Tribunals 1971-75, head of UK res project in W Euro into social security provision for disablement 1971-72, res conslt Off of Manpower Econs 1972-73; chm: NATO Mgmnt Survey Ctee 1970-71, Cncl of Euro Mgmnt Survey Ctee 1971-72; conslt on mgmnt servs to Govt of Indonesia 1973, conslt on social security to: Govt of Trinidad and Tobago 1967-69, ILO 1973-80, EEC Statistical Off 1974, Govt of Thailand 1978-79 and 1981; fell Inst for Euro Health Servs res Leuven Univ Belgium 1974; *Books* Medical Care Systems (1974), Social Security for the Unemployed (1976); *Recreations* photography, travel; *Clubs* Civil Service; *Style*— Derick Fulcher, Esq, DSC; 100 Downs Rd, Coulsdon, Surrey CR3 1AF (☎ 0737 554231)

FULFORD, Francis Christopher; s of Lt-Col Francis Edgar Anthony Fulford (d 1969), and Joan Shirley, *née* Blackman, who m 2, 1979, Sir John Carew Pole, 12 Bt (*qv*); Fulfords have been seated at Fulford, Devon, since *temp* Richard I; *b* 31 August 1952; *Educ* Milton Abbey; *Career* memb Lloyd's; dir Hargreaves Reiss and Quinn Ltd (Lloyds Brokers); landowner (3000 acres); Liveryman Worshipful Co of Fishmongers; *Recreations* shooting, territorial army, books, trees; *Clubs* Turf; *Style*— Francis Fulford, Esq; Great Fulford, Dunsford, nr Exeter, Devon (☎ Cheriton Bishop 205); 212-210 Borough High St, London SE1 (☎ 01 403 306)

FULHAM, Bishop of 1985-; Rt Rev (Charles) John Klyberg; s of Charles Augustine Klyberg (Capt MN, 1975), and Ivy Lilian, *née* Waddington, LRAM (d 1978); *b* 29 July 1931; *Educ* Eastbourne Coll, Lincoln Theol Coll; *Career* 2 Lt 1 Bn The Buffs 1952-53; asst estates mangr Cluttons 1953-57, curate St John's E Dulwich 1960-63, rector Fort Jameson Zambia 1963-67, vicar Christ Church and St Stephen Battersea 1967-77, dean Lusaka Cathedral Zambia and rector of parish 1977-85 (vicar gen 1978-85), chm Church Property Devpt Gp 1978-85, dean emeritus 1985, UK Commissary for Anglican Church in Zanbia 1985-; ARICS; *Recreations* reading, music, travel; *Clubs* Athenaeum; *Style*— The Rt Rev the Bishop of Fulham; 4 Cambridge Place, London W8 5PB

FULLARD, Hon Mrs - Hon Glenys; *née* Macdonald; da of 1 Baron Macdonald of Gwaenysgor, KCMG, PC (d 1966), and Mary, *née* Lewis (d 1967); *b* 1923; *m* 1949, Robert Fullard, BSc, yst s of Herbert Fullard (d 1958), of Werneth, Lancs; 2 da; *Career* JP Lancs; *Style—* Hon Mrs Fullard; 2 Thornley Lane, Grotton, Oldham

FULLENWIDER, Fran; da of Dale Fullenwider (d 1975), and Kelsey La Verrier-Stuart Fullenwider (d 1963); *b* 16 Nov 1945; *Educ* Univ of Maryland (BA), New York Univ (Graduate Study in Film, TV and Radio), RADA (Stage Mgmnt Diploma); *Career* actress, starring in romantic film comedies in Italy 1976-, dir Pilgrim Productions 1987-; *Recreations* writing, interior decoration, food; *Clubs* Groucho; *Style—* Miss Fran Fullenwider

FULLER, Anthony Gerard Fleetwood; 2 s of Maj Sir Gerard Fuller, 2 Bt, JP (d 1981), and his 1 w, Lady Fiona Pratt (later Countess of Normanton, d 1985), yr da of 4 Marquess Camden; *b* 4 June 1940; *Educ* Eton; *m* 19 Nov 1964, Julia Mary, er da of Lt-Col Eric Astley Cooper-Key, MBE, MC; 1 s (William Gerard Fleetwood b 13 July 1968), 1 da (Camilla Fleetwood b 16 Feb 1966); *Career* Lt Life Gds 1959-62; Lloyd's underwriter; dir Fuller Smith & Turner plc (brewers) 1967-, md 1978-, and md and chm 1982-; Freeman, Liveryman and Past Master Worshipful Co of Brewers, chm Brewers Soc 1986-89; *Recreations* shooting, gardening; *Style—* Anthony Fuller Esq; Griffin Brewery, Chiswick, London W4 2QB (☎ 01 994 2162); Little Chalfield Manor, Melksham, Wilts SN12 8NN (☎ 022 16 5934)

FULLER, Charles Christopher Fleetwood; s of Lt-Col CMF Fuller, TD (d 1976), of Jaggards, Corsham, Wilts, and Beatrice Susan *née* Mambro (d 1977); *b* 24 June 1945; *Educ* Winchester; *m* 9 March 1984, Bryony Jane *née* Kup; 1 s (George b 3 April 1985), 1 da (Claire b 16 July 1987); *Career* 5 Royal Inniskilling Dragoon Gds 1964-67; Royal Wiltshire Yeo 1970-74; *Clubs* Pratts; *Style—* Charles Fuller, Esq, JP; Jaggards, Corsham, Wilts

FULLER, David William; s of Edward William Jack Fuller (d 1969), of Suffolk, and Alice Marjorie, *née* Budd (d 1956); *b* 27 May 1935; *Educ* Forest Sch; *m* 25 Jan 1969, Sheila Mary, da of Erst Ellis (d 1952); 1 s (Julian b 1971), 1 da (Katharine b 1972); *Career* Nat Serv with RN; marine broker Lloyds 1956-58, Arthur Ackermann & Son Ltd 1958- (dir 1965, jt md 1985); Masks Worshipful Co Tylers & Bricklayers 1988-189; *Clubs* Arts; *Style—* David W Fuller, Esq; Barnards Bridge, Duton Hill, nr Dunmow, Essex (☎ 037 184 255); 33 New Bond St, London W1 (☎ 01 493 3288)

FULLER, Hon Sir John Bryan Munro; s of Bryan Cecil Fuller, QC (d 1956), and Isobel Mary, *née* Deane; *b* 22 Sept 1917; *Educ* Knox GS Sydney; *m* 1940, Eileen, da of Oswald Sidmouth Webb, of Bathurst, NSW; 1 s, 1 da; *Career* MLC NSW 1961-78, min for Planning and Environment 1973-76, min for decentralisation and devpt 1965-73, vice-pres Exec Cncl 1968-76, ldr of govt in Legislative Cncl 1968-76, ldr oppn in Legislative Cncl 1976-78; pres: Barnardo's Aust 1985-, Aust Inst of Export 1986-, Athritis Fndn of Aust 1980; kt 1974; *see Debrett's Handbook of Australia and New Zealand for further details*; *Recreations* tennis, bowls; *Clubs* Australian (pres 1984-87); *Style—* Sir John Fuller; 54/8 Fullerton St, Woollahra, NSW 2025, Australia (☎ 02 328 7674)

FULLER, Sir John William Fleetwood; 3 Bt (UK 1910), of Neston Park, Corsham, Wiltshire; s of Maj Sir (John) Gerard Henry Fleetwood Fuller, 2 Bt (d 1981), by his 1 w, Lady Fiona Pratt yr da of 4 Marquess Camden; *b* 18 Dec 1936; *Educ* Bradfield; *m* 9 Jan 1968, Lorna Marian, o da of F Richard Kemp-Potter, of Findon, Sussex; 3 s (James, Andrew William Fleetwood b 1972, Edward Richard Fleetwood b 1977); *Heir* s, James Henry Fleetwood Fuller b 1 Nov 1970; *Career* Maj (ret) Life Gds; *Style—* Sir John Fuller, Bt; Neston Park, Corsham, Wilts SN13 9TG (☎ 0225 810211)

FULLER, Martin Elliot; *b* 09 Feb 1943; *Educ* Mid-Warwickshire Coll of Art, Hornsey Coll of Art; *Career* awarded Guggenheim-McKingley Scolarship (American Art Workshop, Italy) 1964, worked in Italy and America, now London; one-man exhibitions incl: Arnolfini Gallery (Bristol) 1968, Midland Art Centre (Birmingham) 1968, Centaur Gallery (Bath) 1969, Bristol Art Gallery 1970, Arnolfini Gallery (Bristol) 1971, Bear Lane Gallery (Oxford) 1971, Camden Art Centre (London) 1971, Bear Lane Gallery (Oxford) 1973, Festival Gallery (Bath) 1973, Grabowski Gallery (London) 1973, Thumb Gallery (London) 1976 and 1979, Oxford Gallery 1983, RZA Galerie (Dusseldorf) 1983, Austin Desmond Fine Art 1985, On The Wall Gallery (Belfast) 1987, Hendriks Gallery (Dublin) 1987; *Clubs* Chelsea Arts; *Style—* Martin Fuller, Esq; 29 Blenheim Gardens, London SW2 (☎ 01 678 6008)

FULLER, Mary, Lady; (Katherine) Mary; da of Douglas Leigh Spence, (d 1965), of Melksham, Wilts; *b* 26 Dec 1918; *m* 1, E H Leventon (decd); 1 s decd, 1 da; m 2, 21 Oct 1966, as his 3 w, Maj Sir Gerard Fuller, 2 Bt, JP, Maj Life Gds (d 1981); *Style—* Mary, Lady Fuller; Bay Tree Cottage, Chapel Lane, Neston, Corsham, Wilts SN13 9TD (☎ 0225 810497)

FULLER, Paul Malcolm; s of John Taylor Fuller of Billericay, Essex; *b* 4 Nov 1946; *Educ* Southend HS for Boys; *m* 1969, Jenifer Mary Elizabeth, da of Percy Beere (d 1955); 1 s, 2 da; *Career* accountant; memb IOD, fin dir: Lacrinoid Products Ltd 1973-78, TKM Foods Ltd 1978-83, Touche Ross 1983-, (consulting ptnr Touche Ross 1987); *Recreations* walking, the arts; *Style—* Paul Fuller, Esq; Pen-Y-Bryn House, 1 Buckingham Rd, Hockley, Essex SS5 4UE

FULLER, Roy Broadbent; CBE (1970); s of Leopold Charles Fuller (d 1920), of Oldham, and Nellie, *née* Broadbent (d 1949); *b* 11 Feb 1912; *Educ* private; *m* 1936, Kate (Kathleen), da of Henry North Smith; 1 s (John Leopold b 1937); *Career* Ordinary Seaman RN 1941-42, leading radar mechanic 1942-43, Petty Offr radar mechanic 1943-44, Lt RNVR 1944-46; asst slr private practice 1934-38; Woolwich Equitable Building Soc: asst slr 1938-56, slr 1958-69, dir 1969-87; prof of poetry Oxford Univ 1968-73, govr BBC 1972-79; *Books* many books of verse, novels autobiography and criticism; *Clubs* Athenaeum; *Style—* Roy Fuller, Esq, CBE; 37 Langton Way, London SE3 7TJ (☎ 01 858 2334)

FULLER-ACLAND-HOOD, Dr Hon Mrs John; Phyllis Lily Frances; o da of Dr Denys Bouhier Imbert Hallett (d 1969); *b* 14 Oct 1915; *Educ* Cheltenham Ladies' Coll, UCL, Univ Coll Hosp London; *m* 1 June 1939, Hon (Arthur) John Palmer Fuller-Acland-Hood (d 2 Nov 1964), yr s of 1 Baron St Audries (d 1917), and Hon Mildred Rose Eveleigh de Moleyns (d 1949), da of 4 Baron Ventry; 3 da; *Career* Flt Lt RAF Med Service 1942-43; registered med practitioner house surg Univ Coll Hosp 1940-41, Govt Health Service Singapore 1952-53, psychiatrist Mendip Hosp Wells 1964-79; *Recreations* gardening, bridge; *Clubs* New Cavendish; *Style—* Dr Hon Mrs John Acland-Hood; Wootton House, nr Glastonbury, Somerset BA6 8TX (☎ 0458 42348)

FULLER-ACLAND-HOOD, Sir (Alexander) William; 8 Bt (UK 1806), of Hartington, Co Derby, and 6 Bt (UK 1809), of St Audries, Co Somerset; in remainder to Irish Barony of Bridport; naturalised an American citizen 1926; s of late William Fuller-Acland-Hood (d.1933), 5 s of 3 Bt (cr 1809); suc cous, 2 Baron St Audries (also 7 and 5 Bt) 1971, and Elizabeth, *née* Kirkpatrick (d 1966); gggf commanded Mars in famous battle between Mars and Hercules and died at moment of victory 21 April 1796; *b* 5 Mar 1901; *Educ* Wellington, RMA Woolwich (Lieut RE), Univ of California (BSMA); *m* 1925, Mary Violet, da of late Augustus Edward Jessup, of Philadelphia, USA (d 1925); 1 da (Elisabeth), (1 s John d 1947); *Heir* none; *Career* formerly Lt RE; prof Los Angeles City Coll, ret;; *Books* (co-author with Mary V Hood) Nature and the Camper, Wildflowers of Yosemite and their Story; *Recreations* photography; *Style—* Sir William Acland-Hood, Bt; SR2 Box 577, 29 Palms, Calif 92277, USA (☎ 714 3679345)

FULLERTON, Edward; s of Thomas Henry (d 1924), and Mary Dickson (d 1987); *b* 27 April 1921; *Educ* St Mary's Catholic Sch Grimsby; *m* 10 July 1943, Irene Ivy, da of Harry Whiteley (d 1954), of Hull, N Humberside; 1 da (Margaret Ivy b 1949); *Career* design engnr, fndr md and chm Turbo Tools (Hull) Ltd 1957-; fndr chm Trinity Graphics Ltd 1970-; memb Inst of Patentees and Inventors; fell IOD; *Recreations* pencil drawings, water colour painting, computer programming; *Style—* Edward Fullerton, Esq; 177 Westella Road, Westella, Hull, N Humberside HU10 7RP (☎ 0482 659212); Turbo Tools (Hull) Ltd, 1 Gillett Street, Hull, N Humberside (☎ 0482 25651, telex 597626); car telephone 0860 363731

FULLERTON, Fiona Elizabeth; da of Brig B V H Fullerton, CBE, ADC, RAPC, and Pamela Fullerton, *née* Crook; *b* 10 Oct 1956; *Educ* Elmhurst Ballet Sch; *m* (m dis 1982) Simon MacCorkindale *qv*; *Career* actress: films include: Run Wild, Run Free (1968), Nicholas and Alexandra (1970, as Anastasia), Alice's Adventures in Wonderland (1972, title role), The Human Factor (1979), The Ibiza Connection (1984), A View to a Kill (1984); stage includes: Cinderella (1976-77, title role), I am A Camera (1979, as Sally Bowles), The Beggar's Opera (1980, as Polly Peachum), Gypsy (1981, as Gypsy Rose Lee), The Boyfriend (1982), Camelot (1982-83, as Queen Guinevere), The Royal Baccarat Scandal 1988-89; tv includes: Angels (1975-76 Angels, Gaugin, The Savage (1979), Lev Tolstoy: A Question of Faith (1979); Shaka Zulu 1985, Hold the Dream 1986, The Charmer 1986, Hazard of Hearts 1987, The Life of Hemingway 1987, A Taste for Death 1988; dir Savoy Theatre Ltd; *Style—* Miss Fiona Fullerton; c/o Jean Diamond, London Mgmnt, 235 Regent St, London W1

FULLERTON, John Charles Mark; s of Capt John Robert Rankin Fullerton (d 1966), by his 2 wife Evelyn Mary (d 1960), 2 da of Sir Alfred Molyneux Palmer, 3 Bt; *b* 21 Dec 1924; *Educ* Eton; *m* 1, 1955, Pamela Blanche Gwynedd (d 1982), da of Robert Crespigny Gwynedd Vivian (d 1984), of Jersey; 2 s (John, David), 1 da (Carolin); m 2, 1984, Philippa Nancy Le Marchant, *née* Denby; *Career* Staff Capt 60 Rifles KRRC; MIPA; advertising exec; md Ogilvy & Mather Ltd Hong Kong 1978-79 (dir 1967), chm Assoc of Accredited Advertising Agents (Hong Kong) 1979; *Novels include* If Chance is a Stranger, Beloved Enemy, The Man Who Spoke Dog; *Recreations* writing novels, sailing (aux sloop 'Myschief'); *Clubs* Royal Lymington Yacht; *Style—* John Fullerton, Esq; The Old Estate House, Heytesbury, Wiltshire BA12 0HQ (☎ 0985 40727); 25 St George's Court, 87 St George's Drive, London SW1V 4DB (☎ 01 828 5275)

FULLERTON, William Hugh; s of Maj Arthur Hugh Theodore Francis Fullerton, RAMC (d 1950), and Mary, *née* Parker; *b* 11 Feb 1939; *Educ* Cheltenham, Queens' Coll Cambridge (MA); *m* 1968, Arlene, da of late Dr J Jacobowitz; 1 da (Elizabeth b 1970); *Career* Shell Int Petroleum Co Uganda 1963-65; joined FO 1965, MECAS Lebanon 1965-66; info offr Jedda 1966-67, UK Mission to UN (NYC) 1967, FCO 1968-70; head of Chancery: Kingston Jamaica 1970-73, Ankara 1973-77; FCO 1977-80, cnsllr (econ and commercial) 1980-83, consul gen Islamabad 1981-83; HM ambassador Mogadishu 1983-87, on loan to MOD London 1987-88; 1988: govr of the Falkland Islands, cmmr South Georgia and South Sandwich Islands, high cmmr Br Antartic Territory; *Recreations* travelling in remote areas, sailing, reading, walking; *Clubs* Travellers'; *Style—* William Fullerton, Esq; c/o FCO, King Charles St, London SW1

FULLWOOD, Keith Saxon; s of Percy Fullwood; *b* 9 May 1928; *Educ* HS Sheffield; *m* 1962, Rosemary Anne, *née* Law; 2 s; *Career* chartered sec, accountant John Brown Gp 1954-60, gp chief accountant Bestwood Gp 1960-62, gp sec Sprite Gp 1962-67; dir Autopack Ltd, Scientific & Educnl Aids Ltd 1967-82, chm Wayfeed 1983-1987 (mgmnt conslt 1983-), exec dir Falcon Packaging Ltd 1987-; Freeman City of London; Liveryman: Worshipful Co of Scriveners, Workshipful Co of Chartered Secs; FCIS, FBIM; *Style—* Keith Fullwood, Esq; Shazam, Upper St, Defford, Worcs (☎ 0386 750241, office 0386 45925)

FULLWOOD, Neville; CBE (1974); s of John William Fullwood (d 1968), of Shrewsbury; *b* 5 Sept 1914; *Educ* Priory Sch Shrewsbury, Trinity Coll Oxford; *m* 1946, Daphne Fay, *née* Bush; 1 da; *Career* HM inspr of schs (Scotland) 1951, HM chief inspr 1966, HM dep sr chief inspr 1973-74, ret 1974; *Recreations* reading, music; *Style—* Neville Fullwood, Esq, CBE; Roskeen, 17 Glenbrook, Balerno, Edinburgh (☎ 449 3925)

FULTHORPE, Jonathan Mark; s of Henry Joseph Fulthorpe, and Betty May, *née* Forshew; *b* 21 Mar 1949; *Educ* Sir Joseph Williamson's Mathmatical Sch Rochester, UCL (LLB), Univ of London (LLM); *m* 1, 1973 (m dis 1978), Clare Elizabeth *née* Stephenson; m 2, 1979, Carol Margaret, da of late Stanley Gordon Greensfield, of Brantford, Ontario, Canada; 1 s (James Mark Charles b 1981), 3 step da (Sarah Lynne b 1970, Jennifer Anne b 1972, Alison Claire b 1975); *Career* called to the Bar Inner Temple 1970, practising Western circuit 1973-; FRGS 1972-; *Recreations* watching cricket and soccer, the study of geography; *Clubs* Hampshire (Winchester), Hampshire CCC, Bentham; *Style—* Jonathan Fulthorpe, Esq; 16 Abbotts Way, Southampton, Hants SO2 1QT (☎ 0703 584879/584743); 17 Carlton Crescent, Southampton SO1 2ES (☎ 0703 636036, fax 0703 223877); 3 Paper Buildings, Temple, London EC4 (☎ 01 583 8055, fax 01 353 6271)

FULTON, Hon Alan Scott; 2 s of Baron Fulton (Life Peer) (d 1986); *b* 27 June 1946; *Educ* Eton, Balliol Coll Oxford; *m* 2 July 1983, (Herminie) Jane, da of Geoffrey J Bulman, of Pool House, Harpenden, Herts; 1 s (Christopher John b 1986); *Style—* Hon Alan Fulton

FULTON, Hon Duncan John Rowntree; yst s of Baron Fulton (Life Peer) (d 1968); *b* 12 Mar 1949; *Educ* Eton, Balliol Coll Oxford; *Style—* The Hon Duncan Fulton

FULTON, Sidney James; CMG (1952); s of Lt-Col Henry Fulton, DSO, (d 1944), of Lisburn, Sevenoaks, Kent; *b* 28 Feb 1912; *Educ* St Paul's, Christ Church Oxford; *m* 1946, Cynthia Mary, eldest da of Capt (John) Leslie Morton Shaw (d 1925), Duke of Wellington's Regt, by his wife Hon Isabel Alexander, sister of 13 Baron Cobham; 1 s,

2 da; *Career* Control Cmmn for Germany 1946, Office of the Cmmr Gen for the UK in SF Asia 1952-57, FO 1958-66; *Recreations* gardening; *Clubs* Travellers'; *Style—* Sidney Fulton, Esq, CMG; The Old Farmhouse, Tainfield, Kingston St Mary, Somerset

FUMMI, Lady (Cynthia) Anne; *née* Lindsay; da of late 27 Earl of Crawford and 10 of Balcarres, KT, PC and Constance, da of Sir Henry Carstairs Pelly, MP, 3 Bt; *b* 21 June 1904; *m* 1, 12 Nov 1931, Per Erik Folke Arnander (d 26 Feb 1933), first sec Swedish Legation Rome; 1 s; m 2, 2 April 1934, Giovanni Fummi d 1970), s of Pietro Fummi; 1 da; *Style—* Lady Anne Fummi; 10 Lochmore House, Cundy St Flats, Ebury St, London SW1W 9JX

FUNG, Hon Sir Kenneth Ping-fan; CBE (1965, OBE 1958), JP (Hong Kong 1952); yr s of Fung Ping-shan, JP; *b* 28 May 1911; *Educ* Govt Vernacular Sch, Sch of Chinese Studies Hong Kong Univ; *m* 1933, Ivy, Shiu-Han, OBE, JP, da of late Kan Tong-Po, JP; 4 s, 1 da; *Career* unofficial memb Urban Cncl 1951-60, unofficial MLC 1959-65, MEC 1962-72; chm Fung Ping Fan & Co; dir (ch mangr ret) The Bank of East Asia Ltd Hong Kong; life memb Court of Univ of Hong Kong; cmdr St John Ambulance Bde (first Chinese to serve) 1953-58, KStJ 1958; Order of the Sacred Treasure (Japan) 1969; kt 1971; *Style—* Hon Sir Kenneth Fung, CBE, JP; home: 14 South Bay Rd, Hong Kong (☎ 92514); office: Fung Ping Fan & Co Ltd, 2705-2715 Connaught Centre, Hong Kong (☎ 220311)

FUNG-ON, Eton Gregory; s of Leslie Rupert Fung-On, of Kent, and Avis Christabel *née* Woon-Shing; *b* 14 Oct 1947; *Educ* Beckenham and Penge GS; *m* 3 July 1971, Patricia Helen, da of Frederick Ernest Dodd, of Sussex; 2 s (Richard b 1973, Neil b 1974); *Career* CA, mgmnt conslt; various sr fin and mgmnt positions public, commercial, indust orgns 1966-86; fin & investmt advsr Ficci Investmts Ltd 1986-; FCA; *Recreations* church activities, gardening & sports; *Style—* Eton G Fung-On, Esq; 412 Upper Shoreham Road, Shoreham-by-sea, W Sussex BN4 5NE (☎ 0273 462656); Ficci Investments Ltd, 13th Floor, Bowatar House, 1 Edinburgh Gate, London SW1X 7LT (☎ 01 589 9600)

FUNNELL, Barry Oliver Bevan; OBE (1969), JP; s of Hubert John Funnell (d 1957), of Sussex, and Kathleen Doris, *née* Bevan (d 1942); *b* 29 Sept 1924; *Educ* Preston Coll Brighton, Montpellier Coll; *m* 1942, Pamela Margery Maud, da of Frederick Joseph Harding (d 1971); L.....; *Career* chm & md: Bevan Funnell Ltd (John Lawrence & Co (Dover) Ltd, A K Verity Ltd, Shard Stebbing Ltd, H & A G Alexander Ltd, Reprodux Inc North Carolina USA, Bevan SA; ex chm BFM Exports Ltd; Major of Hove 1960-61, E Sussex magistrate 1974; *Recreations* yachting; *Clubs* IOD; *Style—* Barry Funnell, Esq, OBE, JP; Innisfree, Cuckmere Rd, Seaford, Sussex; Le Beaupre, Sark, Channel Islands; Reprodux House, Norton Road, Newhaven, Sussex (☎ 0273 513762)

FUNSHINE, Geoffrey Nicholas Christopher Peter; s of Leonard Funshine (d 1976); *b* 16 Nov 1936; *Educ* Shrewsbury; *m* 1962, Barbara Joan, *née* Foxcroft; 1 s, 2 da; *Career* chm The Grand Theatre Tst Ltd 1981-, md BPB Corpn 1976, dir The 525 Co and subsidiaries 1959; *Recreations* pleasure, ice skating, squash, travel; *Clubs* Cambridge Union, Primrose, Fylde Cons, Travellers and Explorers; *Style—* Geoffrey Funshine, Esq; Grosvenor House, Grosvenor rd, Poulton-le-Fylde

FURBER, (Robert) John; s of Frank Robert Furber, of 8 Pond Road, Blackheath, London SE3, and Anne Wilson, *née* McArthur; *b* 13 Oct 1949; *Educ* Westminster Sch, Gonville and Caius Coll Cambridge (MA); *m* 16 April 1977, (Amanda) Cherry, da of Frederick Colbran Burgoyne Varney, OBE, of 21 Lock Chase, Blackheath, London SE3; 1 s (Thomas b 1980), 1 da (Sophia b 1983); *Career* called to the Bar Inner Temple 1973; *Books* jt ed: Halsbury's Laws of England (Landlord and Tenant) 1981, Hill and Redman's Law of Landlord and Tenant (1988); *Recreations* wine, literature, music, cricket; *Clubs* Buck's; *Style—* John Furber, Esq; 52 Southbrook Rd, Lee, London SE12 (☎ 01 852 5770); 2 Paper Buildings, Temple, London EC4 (☎ 01 353 5835)

FURLONG, Monica; da of Alfred Gordon Furlong (d 1972), of Harrow, and Bessie Winifred Esther, *née* Simpson (d 1985); *b* 17 Jan 1930; *Educ* Harrow Co Girls Sch, Univ Coll London; *m* 12 Aug 1953 (m dis 1977), William John Knights; 1 s (Alexander William b 1961), 1 da (Charlotte Ann b 1957); *Career* Daily Mail 1961068, prodr BBC 1974-78; moderator Mvmnt for the Ordination of Women 1982-85, co fndr St Hilda Community 1987; DD gen Theol Seminary NY 1986; *Books* With Love To The Church (1964), Travelling In (1974), The Cat's Eye (1976), Merton (1980), Cousins (1983), Genuine fake (1986), Thérèse of Lisieux (1987), Wise Child (1987); *Clubs* Soc of Authors; *Style—* Mrs Monica Furlong; c/o Anthony Sheil Associates, 43 Doughty St, London WC1

FURMSTON, (Bentley) Edwin; s of Rev Edward Bentley Furmston (d 1959), and Mary, *née* Bennett (d 1983); *b* 7 Oct 1931; *Educ* Nelson Sch Wigton, Manchester Univ (BSc); *m* 1957, Margaret, da of Thomas Jackson (d 1970); 2 s (Michael, Robin), 1 da (Susan); *Career* surveyor; Directorate of Overseas Surveys Colonial Off: surveyor 1953, princ surveyor 1967, asst dir 1971; dep dir Ordnance Survey 1974; dir and survey advsr: Min, for Overseas Devpt, Directorate of Overseas Surveys 1980, DOS merged with Ordnance Survey 1984, dir overseas surveys Ordnance Survey 1984-; *Recreations* gardening, mountain walking; *Style—* Edwin Furmston, Esq; Ordnance Survey, Romsey Road, Southampton (☎ 0703 792000, telex 477843)

FURNER, Air Vice-Marshal Derek Jack; CBE (1973, OBE 1963), DFC (1943), AFC (1954); s of Vivian Jack Furner (d 1933); *b* 14 Nov 1921; *Educ* Westcliff HS Essex; *m* 1948, Patricia, da of Richard Charles Donnelly, of Norwich; 3 s; *Career* joined RAF 1941, Bomber Cmd 1943-44, served Far East 1944-47; dep dir Manning MOD (Air) 1966-67, OC RAF Scampton 1968, AOC Central Reconnaissance Estab 1969-70, sec NATO Mil Ctee Brussels 1970-73, asst air sec MOD 1973-76; dir-gen mangr Harlequin Wallcoverings Ltd 1976-81; *Clubs* RAF; *Style—* Air Vice-Marshal Jack Furner, CBE, DFC, AFC; 1D South Cliff Tower, Bolsover rd, Eastbourne, E Sussex BN20 7JN (☎ 0323 33 447)

FURNESS, Alan Edwin; s of Edwin Furness (d 1985), and Marion *née* Senton (d 1988); *b* 6 June 1937; *Educ* Eltham Coll, Jesus Coll Cambridge (BA, MA); *m* 27 Nov 1971, (Aline) Elizabeth Janine, da of Cdr R Barrett RN (d 1972); 2 s (Roderick b 1972, Christian b 1975); *Career* CRO 1961, private sec to Parly Under Sec of State, CRO (Duke of Devonshire) 1961-62, third later second sec Br High Cmmn New Delhi 1962-66, with DSAO 1966-69; first sec: UK Delegation to Euro Communities Brussels 1967-72, Br Embassy Dakar 1972-75; FCO 1975-78; cnsllr Br Embassy: Jakarta 1978-81, Warsaw 1982-85, head of S Pacific Dept FCO 1985-88; *Clubs* United Oxford and Cambridge; *Style—* Alan Furness, Esq; Foreign and Commonwealth Office, King Charles Street, London, SW1A 2AH (☎ 01 270 3000)

FURNESS, Michael Fitzroy Roberts; s and h of Sir Stephen Furness, 3 Bt, and Mary, (*née Cann*; *b* 12 Oct 1962; *Educ* Sedbergh, Askham Bryan Coll of Agric and Hort, Higher Nat Diploma in Agric (HND); *Career* farmer, pig husbandry; *Recreations* rugby, shooting, travelling, contemplation, music; *Style—* Michael Furness, Esq; Stanhow Farm, Great Langton, Northallerton, North Yorks (☎ Northallerton 748614)

FURNESS, Michael John; s of Stanley Charles Furness, of Eastbourne, E Sussex and Gladys Violet Furness; *b* 20 Mar 1941; *Educ* Rutlish Sch, Royal Dental Hosp and St George's Hosp Univ of London (MB BS, BDS); *m* 23 Sept 1972, Mary Elizabeth, da of Rev William Clifford Smallman (d 1980), of Sheffield; 3 da (Cordelia b 1973, Nadine b 1976, Eleanor b 1977); *Career* house surgn oral surgery St Georges Hosp London 1964, house physician Whittington Hosp London 1970; house surgn: ENT surgery Charing Cross Hosp 1971, and subsequently clinical asst head and neck surgery Royal Marsden Hosp London 1972-75; private dental practitioner 1972-; pre Coll Union at London Univ; Freeman City of London 1983, Liveryman Worshipful Co of Apothecaries 1978; FRSA 1979, FRHS 1980; *Recreations* fishing, shooting, antiques, swimming; *Clubs* Athenaeum, MCC; *Style—* Dr Michael Furness; 31 Wilton Place, London SW1 (☎ 01 235 3824); Clifton House, Clifton Hill, Winchester, Hants; Tyddyn Bach, Cwm Cynfal, Ffestiniog, Gwynedd

FURNESS, Lt-Col Simon John; DL (Berwickshire 1984-); s of Sir Christopher Furness, 2 Bt (d 1974), of Netherbyres, Eyemouth, Berwickshire, and Flower, *née* Roberts; *b* 18 Aug 1936; *Educ* Charterhouse, RMA Sandhurst, Royal Naval Staff Coll; *Career* cmmnd Durham LI 1956, cmd 5 Bn 1976-78, ret Lt-Col 1978; Dep Col (Durham) The Light Inf 1989-; memb exec Nat Tst for Scotland (chm gardens ctee), chm Eyemouth Museum Tst; *Recreations* gardening, field sports; *Clubs* Army and Navy, Durham Co; *Style—* Lt-Col Simon Furness, DL; Netherbyres, Eyemouth, Berwickshire TD14 5SE (☎ 08 907 50 337)

FURNESS, Sir Stephen Roberts; 3 Bt (UK 1913), of Tunstall Grange, W Hartlepool; s of Sir Christopher Furness, 2 Bt (d 1974, 2 cous of 2 Viscount Furness), and Violet Flower Chipchase, *née* Roberts; *b* 10 Oct 1933; *Educ* Charterhouse; *m* 6 April 1961, Mary, er da of Jack Fitzroy Cann, of Newland, Cullompton, Devon; 1 s, 1 da; *Heir* s, Michael Fitzroy Roberts Furness; *Career* late Lt RN, ret 1962; farmer and sporting artist (as Robin Furness); jt MFH Bedale Foxhounds 1979-87; *Recreations* hunting, racing, looking at paintings; *Style—* Sir Stephen Furness, Bt; Stanhow Farm, Great Langton, Northallerton, Yorks DL7 0TJ (☎ 0609 748614)

FURNISS, Air Vice-Marshal Peter; DFC (1944), TD (1964); s of John Furniss (d 1930), and Mary Furniss; *b* 16 July 1919; *Educ* Sedbergh Sch; *m* 1954, Denise Andrée Gisèle, da of Charles Cotet, of S France; 1 s, 2 da; *Career* cmmnd Liverpool Scottish TA, Queens Own Cameron Highlanders 1939, seconded to RAF 1942, served in Med theatre of ops, cmd 73 fighter sqdn, demobilised 1946, slr 1948, cmmnd in Legal Branch RAF 1950, dir of Legal Servs HQ Air Forces M East, Aden 1961-63, HQ Far East Air Force Singapore 1969-71, HQ RAF Germany 1973-74, dep dir of Legal Servs RAF 1975-78, (dir 1978-82); *Recreations* country pursuits; *Clubs* RAF; *Style—* Air Vice-Marshal Peter Furniss, DFC, TD; 18 Sevington Park, Loose, Maidstone, Kent (☎ 0622 744620)

FURNIVAL, John Stephen; s of Thomas Bourne Furnival (d 1967), and Phyllis Elizabeth *née* Corke (d 1983); *b* 13 August 1939; *Educ* Kimbolton Sch, Mander Coll Bedford, Coll of Estate Mgmnt; *m* 1, June 1961 (m dis 1981), Susan Marilyn, *née* Everett; 1 s (John Everett b 8 Oct 1971), 2 da (Clare Susan b 11 Jan 1962, Victoria Merrie Louise b 31 March 1964); m 2, 17 July 1981, Patricia Mary, da of William Geoffrey Herbert (d 1988) 1 s (Roger Smith b 9 Oct 1983);; *Career* patrol offr Br S Africa Police 1958-60; agric farm mangr and dir 1960-64, ptnr gen practice Estate Agency 1964-69, property and projects mangr UK Hertz Int 1969-71, estates mangr Granada TV Rental 1971-80, gp property dir George Oliver (Footwear) plc 1988- (estates mangr 1980-81, property dir 1981-88), divnl md Castle Acres Devpts Ltd 1988-; dir incl: George Oliver Distributors Ltd, Hiltons Footwear Ltd, Timpson Shoes Ltd, William Timpson Ltd, Timpson Shoe Sales Ltd, Brick Studio and Manufacturing Ltd, Timpson Shops Ltd; fndr memb and former pres Property Mangrs Assoc 1975, memb real estates ctee Br Retailers Assoc 1985, dir Cr Cncl of Shopping Centres 1987-, dir and cncl memb The Land Inst 1987, memb Charter Soc Coll of Estate Mgmnt 1988; chm of govrs Walnuts Special Sch for Handicapped Children Milton Keynes 1978-80; memb: IOD, RSPB, Nat Autistic Soc; FFAS FLandInst, FFB 1971, ACIArb 1982, FBIM 1984, FRSA 1987; *Recreations* country pursuits, walking, rugby, reading; *Clubs* Farmers; *Style—* John S Furnival, Esq; 4 Warrington Drive, The Spinney, Groby, Leicester LE6 0YS (☎ 0533 879986); George Oliver (Footwear) plc, Grove Way, Castle Acres, Narborough, Leicester, LE9 5BZ (☎ 0533 630444, fax 0533 630014, car tel 0836 527588, telex 341270)

FURNIVAL JONES, Sir (Edward) Martin; CBE (1957); s of Edward Furnival Jones (d 1946); *b* 7 May 1912; *Educ* Highgate Sch, Gonville and Caius Coll Cambridge (MA); *m* 1955, Elizabeth Margaret, da of Bartholomew Snowball, AMIEE; 1 da; *Career* served WWII GSO SHAEF and War Office (despatches); slr 1937; attached to MOD; chm of bd Frensham Heights 1973-76 (pres 1977); kt 1967; *Style—* Sir Martin Furnival Jones, CBE; Lindum, First Drift, Wothorpe, Stamford, Lincolnshire PE9 3JL (☎ 0780 63085)

FURNIVALL, Barony of (E 1295); *see*: Hon Rosamond Dent, Hon Mrs Bence

FURSDON, (Edward) David; o s of Maj-Gen (Francis William) Edward Fursdon, CB, MBE, *qv*, and Joan Rosemary, *née* Worssam; s uncle as owner of Fursdon family estate in Devon 1981; Lord of the Manors of Cadbury and South Zeal, Devon; *b* 20 Dec 1952; *Educ* Sherborne, St John's Coll Oxford (BA, MA); *m* 7 Oct 1978, Catriona Margaret, da of Geoffrey Crichton McCreath, of Berwick-upon-Tweed; 3 s (Oliver b 1980, Thomas b 1982, Charles b 1986); *Career* short service limited cmmn as 2 Lt 6 QEO Gurkha Rifles 1972; assoc ptnr Stags auctioneers 1988-; Gov Blundell's Sch 1984-; ARICS 1988, FAAV 1988; *Recreations* sport; *Clubs* MCC; Fursdon, Cadbury, Exeter, Devon; business, c/o Stags, 19 Bampton Street, Tiverton, Devon (☎ 0884 256331)

FURSDON, Maj-Gen (Francis William) Edward; CB (1980), MBE (1958), KStJ (1980); s of George Ellsworth Sydenham Fursdon (d 1936), and Aline Lucinda, *née* Gastrell (d 1982); family resident at Fursdon in Devon since 1251; *b* 10 May 1925; *Educ* Westminster, Aberdeen (MLitt), Leiden (DLitt); *m* 1950,Joan Rosemary, da of Charles Archie Worssam, OBE (d 1971); 1 s ((Edward) David, *qv*), 1 da (Sabina b

1956); *Career* RE 1942; Cmd 25 Engr Regt BAOR 1967-69; AA&QMG HQ Land Forces Gulf 1970-71, Dep Cmd and COS Land Forces Gulf 1971, Col Qtg HQ BAOR 1972-73, dir Defence Policy MOD (Europe and NATO) 1974-77, dir MOD Mil Asst Off 1977-80, advsr to Rhodesian Govr and sr Br offr Zimbabwe 1980; ret as Maj-Gen 1980; Def and Mil corr Daily Telegraph 1980-86; dir of Ceremonies Order of St John 1980-, independent defence conslt, author and freelance corr 1986-; Freeman City of London; *Books* Grains of Sand (1971), There are no Frontiers (1973), The European Defence Community - a History (1980), Falklands Aftermath (1988); *Recreations* travel, writing, gardening; *Clubs* Special Forces, St John House; *Style*— Maj-Gen Edward Fursdon, CB, MBE; c/o The National Westminster Bank, 1 St James's Square, London SW1Y 4JX

FYFE, (James) Gordon; TD (1956), WS, DL (Peeblesshire 1966),; s of Alexander Fyfe (d 1978), of Kendalmere, Peebles; *b* 5 May 1918; *Educ* George Watson's Coll, Edinburgh Univ; *m* 1, 1942, Phyllis Una (d 1956), da of Maj J W Goodford, of Chilton Cantelo, Som; 1 s; m 2, 1958, Katherine Jean Wolfe, da of Capt George Wolfe Murray, of Meldonfoot, Peebles; *Career* Maj WWII; *Recreations* fishing, curling; *Clubs* Caledonian (Edinburgh); *Style*— Gordon Fyfe, Esq, TD, WS, DL; Meldonfoot, Peebles, Pebblesshire, Scotland (☎ Kirkton Manor 252)

FYSHE, (Robert) Alexander Dennis; s of Alexander Gordon Fyshe, of Hurstans, Sollershope, Hereford, and Gwendoline Joan, *née* Dennis; *b* 15 Nov 1938; *Educ* Sherborne; *m* 29 April 1965, (Angel) Margaret, da of Lt-Col Geoffrey Babington (d 1956), of Easter Ross, Comrie, Nr Crieff, Perthshire; 1 s (Henry b 21 Dec 1975); *Career* Nat Serv 2 Lt KSLI 1957-59; md Artscope Int Insur Servs Ltd 1979; dir: Seascope Insur Hldgs Ltd 1984, APS Int Ltd 1988, APS Insur Brokers Inc 1988; memb of Lloyds 1964; *Recreations* shooting, classic italian cars; *Clubs* Boodle's; *Style*— Alexander Fyshe, Esq; St Peter's Square, London

FYSON, Lt Cdr RN retd Richard Hugh; s of Philip Furley Fyson (d 1947), s of P K Fyson, Missionary Bp of Japan 1974-83, and Diana Ruth, *née* Wilson (d 1969); *b* 30 Oct 1917; *Educ* King's Sch, Worcs; *m* 9 April 1943, Isabella Marguerite, da of Reuben Woodland Payne (d 1974); 3 s (Jonathan b 1944, Christopher b 1945, Oliver b 1953), 2 da (Susan b 1948, Miranda b 1958); *Career* RN 1935-49: midshipman 1936, Sub Lt 1938, Lt 1939, Lt Cdr 1947, specialised in navigation 1942; served in combined operations Reconnaissance Pty COPP, CO COPP 2 1944-45; cabinet maker and antique furniture restorer 1949, memb Witney Rural DC 1960-74, memb Oxford and District Water Bd 1967-74; *Clubs* flat green bowls; *Style*— Lt Cdr Richard Fyson, Esq; Manor Farm, Kencot, Lechlade GL7 3QT

G

GABRIEL, Christopher Waithman; s of Christopher Parton Gabriel, OBE (d 1974), of Suffolk, and Rosemary, *née* Waithman; *b* 28 Feb 1941; *Educ* Charterhouse; *m* 20 May 1981, Diana Lesley Sharman, da of Everard Lesley Campion Gwilt (d 1976), of Surrey; 1 da (Lucinda Rose b 1984); *Career* md Christopher Gabriel Ltd 1979-; memb: Exec Ctee Nat Panel Products Assoc, exec ctee Agents Section of Timber Trade Fedn; Liveryman Worshipful Co of Goldsmiths'; *Recreations* sailing, shooting, tennis; *Clubs* Royal Ocean Racing; *Style—* Christopher W Gabriel, Esq; Binley Cottage, Binley, nr Andover, Hants SP11 6HA (☎ 026473 261); Christopher Gabriel Ltd, 21 Swan St, Longsclere, Newbury, Berks RG15 8PP (☎ 0635 297705, telex 846252 ANGEL G, car tel 0836 272852)

GABRIEL, David Charles; s of Richard Trevor Gabriel, of Lansdowne House, St Julian St, Tenby, Dyfed, and Beatrice Anne Victoria, *née* Foulger; *b* 29 July 1950; *Educ* Selwyn House PS, Hereford Cathedral Sch, Univ of Bristol (BVSc); *Career* veterinary surgn; mixed practise: J M Brook Leamington Spa 1973-74, Fairfield Vet Gp Hinckley 1974-77; exotic practise JV Aspinall Howletts and Port Lympne Wild Life Parks 1977; mixed practise: Fairfield Vet Gp 1977-84, Les Eturs Vet Clinic Guernsey 1984-86; mixed practise (with emphasis on equine work) Fairfield Vet Gp Hinckley 1986-; Atherstone Hunt Supporter; MRCVS (1973); *Recreations* skiing, boardsailing, squash, equestrian activities, surfing, books; *Clubs* Ski Club of GB; *Style—* David Gabriel, Esq; 8 Barwell Rd, Kirkby Mallory, Leics LE9 7QA (☎ 0455 45793); Fairfield Veterinary Gp, 51 Leicester Rd, Hinckley, Leics LE10 1LW (☎ 0455 637 642/0455 611 715, car tel 0836 253 049)

GABRIELCZYK, Ryszard January; s of Józef Gabrielczyk (d 1981), of Poland, and Helena, *née* Sykut (d 1931); *b* 19 Sept 1927; *Educ* State Sch Poland, Brixton Coll (HND); *m* 28 Aug 1949, Barbara Zofia, da of Lt Jozef Sadowski, Polish Army (d 1981), of London; 3 s (Jorge Jozef b 7 March 1952, Marek Ryszard b 25 July 1955, Jacek Robert b 15 Dec 1959); *Career* Polish Army under Br Cmmd 1942-47 Palestine, Br Army 1947-49; structural engr Felix Samuely Construction Engrs 1954-56; managing ptnr Taylor Whalley & Spyra 1968-88 (ptnr 1961-67, sr structual engr 1957-60): various projects incl Leeds Univ, Richmond Terrace Devpt Whitehall; memb ctee Polish Benevolent Fund UK, pres Polish Educn Soc UK; CEng, FIStructE, FINuce, MConsE, MFrSCE; Polish Order of Merit 1967, Order of Polonia Restituta 1974, Order of St Sylvester (Knight) Vatican 1978, KSS; *Recreations* gardening, bee keeping; *Clubs* RAC; *Style—* Ryszard Gabrielczyk, Esq; 33 Alexandra Grove, Finchley, London N12 8HE (☎ 01 445 4352); 3 Dufferin Ave, Barbican, London EC1Y 8PQ (☎ 01 253 2626, fax 01 253 2767)

GADD, (John) Staffan; s of late John Gadd and Ulla Olivecrona; *b* 30 Sept 1934,Stockholm,; *Educ* Stockholm Sch of Economics (MBA); *m* 1958, Margaretha, da of Gösta Löfborg; 1 s, 1 da; *Career* sec Confedn of Swedish Industs 1958-61; Skandinaviska Banken 1961-69 (London rep 1964-67); Scandinavian Bank Ltd in London 1969-80 (dep md 1969-71, chief exec and md 1971-80); chief exec Samuel Montagu & Co 1980-84 (chm and chief exec 1982-84); chm Montagu & Co AB Stockholm 1982-85; dir Guyerzeller Zurmont Bank AG Switzerland 1983-84; chm: Sage Securities Ltd 1985-, J S Gadd & Co Ltd; *Recreations* skiing, shooting; *Style—* Staffan Gadd, Esq; Locks Manor, Hurstpierpoint, Sussex; Office: J S Gadd & Co Ltd, 45 Bloomsbury Square, London WC1A 2RA (☎ 01 242 5544)

GADSBY, G (ordon) Neville; CB (1972); s of William George Gadsby (d 1978), and Margaret Sarah Gadsby; *b* 29 Jan 1914; *Educ* King Edward VI Sch Stratford-upon-Avon, Birmingham Univ (BSc, DipEd); *m* 1938, Jeanne, *née* Harris; 2 s, 1 da; *Career* dir Army Operational Res Estab 1961-64, dir Biological and Chemical Def MOD 1965-67, dep ch scientist (Army) MOD 1967-68, dir Chemical Def Estab 1968-72, min (def res and dvpt) Br Embassy Washington 1972-75; gp ldr The MITRE Corpn USA 1976-80, conslt NUS Corpn USA 1980-; FRSC; *Recreations* oil painting; *Style—* G Neville Gadsby, Esq, CB; Ruan House, Cliff Rd, Sidmouth, Devon EX10 8JN (☎ 03955 77842)

GADSDEN, Sir Peter Drury Haggerston; GBE (1979), AC (1988), JP (City of London 1971, Greater London Inner London Area 1969-71); er s of Rev Basil Claude Gadsden, ACT, ThL (d 1958), of Whitney-on-Wye, Hereford, and Mabel Florence, *née* Drury (d 1964); *b* 28 June 1929; *Educ* Wrekin Coll, Jesus Coll Cambridge (MA); *m* 16 April 1955, Belinda Ann de Marie, eld da of Capt Sir (Hugh) Carnaby de Marie Haggerston, 11 Bt (d 1971); 4 da (Juliet Mary (Mrs Cartwright) b 4 March 1956, Caroline Mabel (Mrs Simpson) b 4 Aug 1957, Clare Louise (Mrs McWhirter) b 29 June 1960, Elizabeth Ann b 28 Feb 1962); *Career* served as 2 Lt King's Shropshire LI 1948-49; alderman City of London 1971-, lord mayor 1979-80; dir: City of London (Arizona) Corpn 1970-, Ellingham Estate Ltd 1974-, Clothworkers' Fndn 1978-, Williams Jacks 1984-; mktg economist to UNIDO; chm Private Patients Plan plc 1984-; Lloyd's underwriter, mineral marketing consultant, memb London Metal Exchange; pres: Nat Assoc of Charcoal Mfrs 1970-, Embankment Rifle Club, City of London Branch of Leukaemia Research Fndn, Metropolitan Soc for Blind; tstee Chichester Festival Theatre, memb Mgmnt Cncl Shakespeare Theatre Tst, chm The Britain-Australia Bicentennial Ctee 1984-, pt/t memb Crown Agents for Overseas Govts and Admin, also Crown Agents' Hldg & Realisation Bd 1981-; Fndr Master Worshipful Co of Engineers; vice-pres Robert Jones and Agnes Hunt Orthopaedic Hosp, pres Ironbridge Gorge Museum Devpt Trust; Liveryman Worshipful Co of Clothworkers' (Sr Warden 1982-83, Master 1989-90); Hon Liveryman: Worshipful Co of Plaisterers', Worshipful Co of Marketers'; Hon Freeman Worshipful Co of Actuaries'; memb Guild of Freemen (Master 1984); Master Guild of World Traders in London 1987; DSc City Univ 1980; FInstM 1976, CEng 1979, FEng 1980, FIMM 1979; KStJ (1980, OStJ 1977); Officier de l'Etoile Equatoriale de la Republique Gabonaise 1970; *Recreations* farming, forestry, shooting, fishing, sailing, walking, photography, skiing; *Clubs* City Livery, City of London, Guildhall, Royal London YC, Pilgrims; *Style—* Sir Peter Gadsden, GBE, JP; 606 Gilbert House, Barbican, London EC2Y 8BD (☎ 01 638 9968)

GADSDEN, Peter John; s of Lt-Col George Edward Graham Gadsden, DSO, OBE, TD (d 1981), and Doris Lillian, *née* Benson; *b* 28 May 1929; *Educ* Eton, Worcester Coll Oxford (MA); *m* 19 Dec 1953, Yvonne, da of Issa Khalil Shousha (d 1964); 3 s (Paul Martin b 1954, Mark b 1956, James Michael b 1964 (d 1983)), 2 da (Mary Anne b 1958, Jane Chrstine b 1963); *Career* slr; clerk Stroud RDC 1965-73, superintendent registrar 1965-; vice-chm Stroud Bldg Soc, chm Co of the Proprietors of the Stroudwater Navigation, ctee memb Glos and Wilts Incorporated Law Soc, dep asst Coroner 1965-68; *Recreations* travel, sailing, reading; *Clubs* Leander; *Style—* Peter Gadsden, Esq; Bournestream, Wotton-under-Edge, Glos GL12 7PA (☎ 0453 842202); 4/7 Rowcroft, Stroud, Glos GL5 3BJ (☎ 04536 3381, fax 04536 71997)

GAFFNEY, Maj Edward Fane Travers; s of Capt Edward Desmond Gaffney (d 1940), and Irene Mary, *née* Travers; *b* 7 Jan 1937; *Educ* Cheltenham, RMC Sandhurst; *m* 10 June 1961, Fiona Esmé Gildroy, da of George Richard Shaw (d 1983); 3 s (Edward William b 1962, Richard Desmond Travers b 1963, Adrian Toby George Hannaford b 1972), 1 da (Miranda Mary b 1967); *Career* Bn Welsh Gds 1957-68, Maj BAOR 1961-66, Aden 1966-67; slr 1976; dep under sheriff of Durham & Cleveland 1982; *Recreations* tennis, squash, shooting, fishing; *Style—* Maj Edward F T Gaffney; Crossbank Hill, Hurworth-on-Tees, Darlington DL2 2JB (☎ 0325 720537); 64 Stanhope Rd, Darlington DL3 7SE (☎ 0325 466 545)

GAFFNEY, Thomas Francis; s of Thomas F Gaffney (d 1954), and Margaret *née* Carroll; *b* 2 April 1932; *Educ* St John's Univ NY (BA), St John's Law Sch, American Inst of For Trade Phoenix Arizona; *m* 30 Oct 1954, Carmen, da of Benito Vega Luna, of Bucaramanga, Colombia; 2 s (Thomas b 30 Dec 1957, Peter b 21 Sept 1968), 1 da (Elisa b 14 Jan 1960); *Career* Chase Manhattan Bank NY 1954-87, seconded to several Industl Latin-American Banks (inc period as chief exec Banco Continental, Lima) 1962-72, chief exec Libra Bank plc London 1972-84, pres: Chase Investmt Bank, London 1984-87, chief exec and md West LB UK Ltd 1988-; author numerous article on econ and fin matters in professional magazines; registered rep Securities Assoc; *Recreations* art appreciation, music, theatre; *Clubs* Mark's, Ends of the Earth, Oriental; *Style—* Thomas Gaffney, Esq; Marvells, Five Ashes, Mayfield, East Sussex TN20 6NL (☎ 0435 873030); Westlb UK Ltd, 51 Moorgate, London EC2R 6AE (☎ 01 638 6141, fax 628 1843, telex, 887984/5)

GAGE, Sir Berkeley Everard Foley; KCMG (1955, CMG 1949); s of Brig-Gen Moreton Foley Gage, DSO (d 1953), and his 1 wife Anne Massie, *née* Strong (d 1915); *b* 27 Feb 1904; *Educ* Eton, Trinity Coll Cambridge; *m* 1, 15 Jan 1931 (m dis 1954), Hedwig Maria Gertrud Eva (who m 2, 1954, as his 3 wife, HH Prince Rostislav Alexandrovich of Russia, who d 1978), da of Carl von Chapuis, of Liegnitz, Silesia; 2 s; m 2, 4 Oct 1954, Mrs Lillian Riggs Miller, da of Vladimir Vukmirovich, sometime Yugoslav Consul-Gen in Chicago; *Career* joined Diplomatic Serv 1928, Consul-Gen Chicago 1950-54, ambass to Thailand 1954-57, ambass to Peru 1958-63; memb: Cncl for Volunteers Overseas 1964-66, Br Nat Export Cncl 1964-66; chm Anglo-Peruvian Soc 1969-71, Grand Cross Order of the Sun (Peru) 1964, Ctee of the Exports to Latin America; *Clubs* Beefsteak, Buck's, Tavern (Chicago); *Style—* Sir Berkeley Gage, KCMG; 24 Ovington Gdns, London SW3 1LE (☎ 01 589 0361)

GAGE, Viscountess; Diana; 4 da of Col Rt Hon Lord Richard Cavendish, CB, CMG (bro of 9 Duke of Devonshire, KG, GCMG, GCVO, PC, JP, DL), and Lady Moyra Beauclerk, da of 10 Duke of St Albans; *b* 15 Sept 1909; *m* 1, 21 March 1935 (m dis 1937), as his 1 w, Robert (Bob) Boothby, MP (later Baron Boothby, KBE, who d 1986); m 2, 7 July 1942, Lt-Col Hon Ian Douglas Campbell-Gray (d 1946), 3 s of Henry Craig-Campbell and Lady Gray (holder of the Scottish Lordship in her own right and gm of 22 Lord Gray); m 3, 1971, as his 2 w, 6 Viscount Gage, KCVO (d 1982); *Style—* The Rt Hon Viscountess Gage; The Cottage, Charwelton, Daventry, Northants

GAGE, Lady Diana Adrienne; *née* Beatty; el da of 2 Earl Beatty, DSC (d 1972); *b* 13 Sept 1952; *Educ* St Paul's Girls' Sch, London; *m* 1974, Hon (Henry) Nicolas Gage, yr s of 6 Viscount Gage, KCVO (d 1982); 2 s; *Style—* Lady Diana Gage; The Cottage, Charwelton, Daventry, Northants (☎ Byfield (0327) 205

GAGE, 7 Viscount; Sir George John St Clere Gage; 14 Bt (E 1622); also Baron Gage of Castlebar (I 1720) and Baron Gage of High Meadow (GB 1790, title in House of Lords); er s of 6 Viscount Gage, KCVO (d 1982) and Viscountess Gage, *qv*; *b* 8 July 1932; *Educ* Eton; *m* 1971 (m dis 1975), Valerie Ann, da of Joseph E Dutch, of Horam, Sussex; *Heir* bro, Hon (Henry) Nicholas Gage; *Style—* The Rt Hon the Viscount Gage; White Friars, Alciston, E Sussex; Firle Place, Lewes, Sussex

GAGE, Hon (Henry) Nicolas; yr s of 6 Viscount Gage, KCVO; hp to bro, 7 Viscount; *b* 9 April 1934; *Educ* Eton, Ch Ch Oxford; *m* 1974, Lady Diana Adrienne Beatty, da of 2 Earl Beatty; 2 s (Henry William b 1975, David Benedict b 1977); *Career* 2 Lt Coldstream Gds 1953; *Style—* Hon Nicholas Gage; The Cottage, Charwelton, Rugby, Warwickshire (☎ Byfield (0327) 205)

GAGE, Quentin Henry Moreton; s of Brig-Gen Moreton Foley Gage, DSO, DL (d 1953), and Frances, *née* Lippitt (d 1955); *b* 22 August 1955; *Educ* Eton, Christ Church Oxford; *m* 16 April 1949, Hazel, da of Col George Archibald Swinton Home, DSO, OBE (d 1961); 1 s (Jonathan Moreton b 26 1954), 1 da (Deborah Pamela b 31 March 1950); *Career* Grenadier Gds 1940-40; Adj-Maj, Capt served in Tunisa, Italy, Palestine (wounded Anzio 1944), insur broker East, Central and S Africa, USA, UK; *Style—* Quentin Gage, Esq; Pelham Cottage, Church Lane, Hellingly, Sussex BN27 4 HA (☎ 0323 843902)

GAGE, William Marcus; QC (1982); s of His Honour Conolly Hugh Gage (d 1984), ret circuit judge, and Elinor Nancy, *née* Martyn; *b* 22 April 1938; *Educ* Repton, Sidney Sussex Coll Cambridge (MA); *m* 16 June 1962, Penelope Mary, da of Lt-Col James Jocelyn Douglas Groves, MC (d 1985); 3 s (Marcus b 1964, Timothy b 1966, Hugh b 1970); *Career* Nat Serv 1956-58, 2 Lt Irish Gds; barr 1963; chllr diocese of Coventry 1980-; Rec 1985-; memb Criminal Injuries Compensation Bd 1987-; *Recreations* shooting, fishing, travel; *Clubs* Beefsteak; *Style—* William Gage, Esq, QC; Evershaw House, Biddlesden, Brackley, Northants; 2 Harcourt Bldgs, Temple, London SC4Y 9DB (☎ 01 583 9020)

GAGGERO, John George; OBE (1981), JP (1972); s of Sir George Gaggero, OBE, JP (d 1978), of Gibraltar, and Mabel, *née* Andrews-Speed (d 1986); *b* 3 Mar 1934; *Educ* Downside; *m* 1961, Valerie, da of John Malin, OBE, JP, of Gibraltar; 2 s, 2 da; *Career* Lt 12 Royal Lancers Malaya; dep chm Bland Gp (includes Gibraltar Airways, Rock Hotel, and Cadogan Travel) 1970-86, chm M H Bland & Co Ltd 1986-; MRINA; *Recreations* boating; *Clubs* Royal Gibraltar YC; *Style—* John Gaggero, Esq, OBE, JP; 15 Bayside Rd, Gibraltar (☎ 77274); office: Cloister Building, Gibraltar (☎ 72735)

GAHAN, Lt-Col Gerald Patrick; s of Revell Patrick Gahan, of Abbotsbury, Dorset, and Mary Bannerman McKenzie, *née* McLean (d 1954); *b* 30 April 1933; *Educ* George Watson's Coll Edinburgh, RMA Sandhurst; *m* 11 May 1957, Jean Mary, da of Brig Andrew McGregor Stewart (d 1967); 1 s (Paul b 1962), 2 da (Susan b 1958, Caroline b 1960); *Career* Army Offr RA 1954-84; Lt-Col; served in Cyprus (GSM), N Ireland (GSM), Aden, Trucial Oman, BOAR, UK; civil servant 1984-89; *Recreations* music, drama, field sports; *Clubs* Lansdowne; *Style—* Lt-Col Gerald Gahan; c/o Royal Bank of Scotland, 14 Minster St, Salisbury, Wilts SP1 1TP

GAILEY, John Lowry Dunseath Pat; OBE (1983); s of John Taylor Gailey (d 1953), of Holywood, Co Down NI, and Mary Lilian, *née* Dunseath (d 1988): original family name Buchanan changed to Gaylea and subsequently Gailey when family arrived in NI around 1740 from Scotland; *b* 13 Sept 1926; *Educ* Portora Royal Sch Enniskillen NI, Edinburgh Univ; *m* 1, 1952, Lilian (d 1987), da of Howard Donaldson (d 1957), of Belfast, NI; 2 s (Andrew, John); m 2, 1988, Winifred, da of Francis Bisset (d 1970); *Career* served RNVR 1944-47, Sub-Lt Minesweepers, 4 MS Flotilla Home Waters and Norway; md Giddings & Lewis-Fraser Ltd 1977; pres Machine Tool Trades Assoc 1981-83, vice-pres CECIMO 1983; *Recreations* golf, gardening, classical music; *Clubs* Naval & Military; *Style—* Mr Pat Gailey, Esq, OBE; 30 Albany Rd, Westferry, Dundee, Angus, Scotland (☎ 0382 75947); Giddings & Lewis-Fraser Ltd, Wellgate Works, Arbroath, Angus (☎ 0241 73811)

GAINFORD, 3 Baron (UK 1917); Joseph Edward Pease; s of 2 Baron Gainford, TD (d 1971), by Veronica, Baroness Gainford, *qv*; *b* 25 Dec 1921; *Educ* Eton, Gordonstoun; *m* 21 March 1953, Margaret Theophila Radcliffe, da of Henry Edmund Guide Tyndale (d 1948), of Winchester Coll, and Ruth Isabel Walcott, da of Alexander Radcliffe, of Bag Park, S Devon; 2 da; *Heir* bro, Hon George Pease; *Career* serv WWII as Sgt RAF; with Hunting Aerosurveys Ltd 1947, Directorate of Colonial Surveys 1951; Soil Mechanics Ltd 1953; employed by LCC 1958, GLC 1965; UK delegate to UN 1973; memb Coll Guardians Nat Shrine of Our Lady of Walsingham 1979-; memb Plaisterers' Co 1976; FRGS, MSST; *Clubs* MCC, Pathfinder; *Style—* The Rt Hon the Lord Gainford; 1 Dedmere Court, Marlow, Bucks SL7 1PL (☎ 062 84 4679)

GAINFORD, The Dowager Lady; Veronica Margaret; o da of Sir George John William Noble, 2 Bt (d 1937), and Mary Ethel, *née* Walker-Waters; *b* 3 Mar 1900; *m* 3 Feb 1921, 2 Baron Gainford (d 1971); 3 s; *Style—* The Rt Hon Dowager Lady Gainford; Taigh na Seanamhair, Tayvallich, Argyll

GAINSBOROUGH, 5 Earl of (UK 1841); Sir Anthony Gerard Edward Noel; 7 Bt (GB 1781), JP (Leics 1974, formerly Rutland 1957); also Baron Barham (UK 1805), Viscount Campden and Baron Noel (both UK 1841); patron of two livings (but being a Roman Catholic cannot present); s of 4 Earl of Gainsborough, OBE, TD, JP (d 1927), sometime Private Chamberlain to Popes Benedict XV and Pius XI; *b* 24 Oct 1923; *Educ* Worth Sussex, Georgetown Maryland USA; *m* 23 July 1947, Mary, er da of Hon John Joseph Stourton, TD, of Miniature Hall, Wadhurst, 2 s of (24) Baron Mowbray, (25 Baron) Segrave, and (21 Baron) Stourton; 4 s, 3 da (and 1 da decd); *Heir* s, Viscount Campden; *Career* vice pres Caravan Club; chm Rutland CC 1970-73, pres Assoc of Dist Cncls 1974-80; Bailiff Grand Cross SMO Malta (pres Br Assoc 1968-74); Hon FICE, chm Multitrust plc; KStJ; *Clubs* Boodle's, Brooks's, Bembridge Sailing, Royal Yacht Squadron; *Style—* The Rt Hon the Earl of Gainsborough, JP; Exton Park, Oakham, Leics (☎ 0572 812209)

GAINSBOROUGH, Dr George Fotheringham; CBE (1973); s of Rev William Anthony Gainsborough (d 1972), and Alice Edith *née* Fennell (d 1941); *b* 28 May 1915; *Educ* Christ's Hosp, King's Coll London (BSc, PhD); *m* 28 April 1937, Gwendoline Berry (d 1976), da of John Berry (d 1944); 2 s (Michael b 1938, John b 1942); *Career* barr Gray's Inn; scientific staff Nat Physical Laboratory 1938-46, radio physicist Br Cwlth Scientific Off Washington DC 1944-45, admin civil serv Minys Supply and Aviation 1946-62, Imp Def Coll 1960, sec Inst of Electrical Engrs 1962-80, dir external relations Int Electrotechnical Cmmn 1980-83; papers in proceedings of Inst of Electrical Engrs; *Clubs* Athenaeum; *Style—* Dr George Gainsborough, CBE; 19 Glenmore House, Richmond Hill, Richmond, Surrey (☎ 01 940 8515); Moncorbon, 41360 Savigny-sur-Braye, France (☎ 54 23 99 25)

GAINSFORD, Ian Derek; s of Rabbi Dr Morris Ginsberg (d 1969), and Anne Freda, *née* Aucken (d 1950); *b* 24 June 1930; *Educ* Thames Valley GS, King's Coll London (BDS, RCS (MS, LDS, FDS, MGDS), Toronto Univ (DDS); *m* 13 June 1957, Carmel, da of Dr Lionel Bertram Liebster; 1 s (Jeremy Charles b 1961), 2 da (Ann Marietta b 1959, Deborah Jane b 1965); *Career* jr staff King's Coll Hosp 1955-57, lectr (later sr lectr) London Hosp Med Coll 1957-70; King's Coll Hosp Med Sch 1970-: sr lectr (later consultant) conservative dentistry dept, dep dean of dental studies 1973-77, dean of dental studies 1977-87, dean of med and dentistry 1988-; London Univ ctees: Senate, Academic cncl, standing ctee in med, FKC 1984; Hon memb American Dental Assoc; FICD, FACD; *Books* Silver Amalgam in Clinical Practise; *Recreations* canal cruising, theatre ; *Clubs* Carlton, Athenaeum; *Style—* Ian Gainsford, Esq; 31 York Terrace East, London NW1 4PT (☎ 01 935 8659); 16 Sloane Square, London SW1; Kings Coll School of Medicine & Dentristy, Denmark Hill, London SE5 (☎ 01 730 1616, 01 326 3000)

GAIR, Alan Graham; s of Sydney Gair (d 1968), and Margaret Evelyn, *née* Graham (d 1975); *b* 12 Nov 1930; *Educ* Ashville Coll Harrogate Yorks, Manchester Univ (MBA), Leeds Univ; *m* 1, 28 March 1957, Marion Edith, *née* Farson (m dis 1984) 1 s (Crispin Robert William b 1966), 2 da (Camilla Jane b 1962, Miranda Kate b 1963); m 2 Francine Gaye, *née* Hutchins of USA, 2 s (Justin b 1985 (decd), Alexander Thomas William b 1988); *Career* Nat Serv RAF; The Distillers Co; Lewis's, Selfridges; dir: Royds McCann (Manchester) Ltd, advertising agency 1973- (exec dir 1987-; md: McCann Business Devpt, McCann Recruitment and Corporate Recruitment; FBIM, MInstM, FIIM; memb Results (non-pty political lobby group for third world); *Recreations* fencing (foil), AFA coach; *Style—* Alan G Gair, Esq; Endon Hall West, Oak Lane, Kerridge, Cheshire SK10 5AL (☎ 0625 74 147); Royds McCann Manchester, Bonis Hall, Prestbury, Cheshire (☎ 0625 828 274)

GAIRY, Rt Hon Sir Eric Matthew; PC (1977); s of Douglas Gairy, of St Andrew's, Grenada; *b* 18 Feb 1922; *Educ* St Andrew's RC Sch; *m* 1949, Cynthia Clyne; 2 da; *Career* pm and min of external affairs Grenada 1974-79, Premier (before independence) 1967-74; kt 1977; *Style—* The Rt Hon Sir Eric Gairy, PC

GAISFORD, Ven John Scott; s of Joseph Gaisford, and Margaret Thompson, *née* Scott; *b* 7 Oct 1934; *Educ* Burnage GS, Durham Univ (BA, MA, Dip Theol); *m* 6 Oct 1962, Gillian, da of Francis Murdo Maclean; 1 s (Giles Gregory John b 6 July 1972), 1 da (Sophia Elizabeth Eve b 9 July 1970); *Career* Sr Aircraftsman RAF 1953-55; asst curate: St Hilda Audenshaw 1960- 62, Bramhall 1962-65; vicar St Andrew Crewe 1965-86, rural dean Nantwich 1974-85, archdeacon of Macclesfield 1986-; memb: Gen Synod 1975-, C of E Pensions Bd 1982-; church cmmr 1986-; *Recreations* fell walking, caravanning; *Clubs* Victory Services; *Style—* The Ven the Archdeacon of Macclesfield; 2 Lovat Drive, Knutsford, Cheshire WA16 8NS (☎ 0565 4456)

GAISFORD, Philip David; s of late (George) David Gaisford, and Vera Elizabeth, *née* Webb; *b* 15 Sept 1942; *Educ* Chigwell Sch, Southampton Univ (LLB); *m* 27 Aug 1984, Petra, da of Walter Hammer, of Inzlingen, W Germany; 2 da (Julia b 1 Nov 1988, Victoria (twin)); *Career* barr Gray's Inn 1969, practices SE Circuit; *Style—* Philip Gaisford, Esq; 15 Warwick Sq, London SW1; 3 Serjeants Inn, London EC4Y 1BQ (☎ 01 353 5537, fax 01 353 0425)

GAISMAN, Jonathan Nicholas Crispin; o s of Peter Gaisman, of Kirdford, West Sussex; *b* 10 August 1956; *Educ* Eton, Worcester Coll Oxford (BA, BCL, MA); *m* 24 Apr 1982, Tessa Nignon, eld da of Sir John Jardine Paterson, of Norton Bavant, Wilts; 2 da (Clementine b 1986, Imogen b 1987); *Career* called to the Bar Inner Temple 1979; memb Old Etonian Assoc Ctee 1982; Freeman Worshipful Co of Grocers; *Recreations* the arts, travel, country pursuits; *Clubs* I Zingari, Brooks's; *Style—* Jonathan Gaisman, Esq; 32 Grafton Square, London SW4 (☎ 01 622 6485); 7 King's Bench Walk, Temple, London EC4 (☎ 01 583 0404)

GAITSKELL, Baroness (Life Peeress UK 1963); Anna Dora; *née* Creditor; da of Leon Creditor, immigrant from Lithuania 1903 and fndr *Jewish Voice*; *m* 1, 15 March 1921 (m dis 1937), David Frost, s of Louis Frost; 1 s; m 2, 1937, Rt Hon Hugh Todd Naylor Gaitskell, CBE, MP (d 1963), s of Arthur Gaitskell, ICS (d 1915); 2 da; *Career* sits as Labour peeress in House of Lords; tstee Anglo-German Fndn 1974-, memb House of Lords All Pty Ctee on Human Rights 1977-; *Style—* The Rt Hon The Baroness Gaitskell; c/o The House of Lords, London SW1

GALBRAITH, Hon David Muir Galloway; 5 but 3 surviving s of 1 Baron Strathclyde, PC, JP (d 1985); *b* 8 Mar 1928; *Educ* Wellington, RAC Cirencester; *m* 5 Aug 1967, Marion Bingham, o da of Maj Bruce Bingham Kennedy, TD, of Doonholm, Ayr; 1 s, 3 da; *Career* chartered land agent, chartered surveyor; *Recreations* country pursuits; *Style—* Hon David Galbraith; Burnbrae Lodge, Mauchline, Ayrshire (☎ 50210)

GALBRAITH, Hon Heather Margaret Anne Galloway; yr da of 1 Baron Strathclyde (d 1985); *b* 27 Feb 1930; *Style—* Hon Heather Galbraith; Barskimming, Mauchline, Ayrshire

GALBRAITH, Hon Ida Jean Galloway; er da of 1 Baron Strathclyde (d 1985); *b* 21 Jan 1922; *Educ* Queen Ethelburga's Sch; *Career* served WW II as 3 Offr WRNS; *Recreations* riding, gardening, wildlife, country pursuits; *Style—* Hon Ida Galbraith; Barskimming, Mauchline, Ayrshire

GALBRAITH, Hon James Muir Galloway; CBE (1984); 3 but eldest surviving s of 1 Baron Strathclyde, PC, JP (d 1985); *b* 27 Sept 1920; *Educ* RNC Dartmouth, Ch Ch Oxford, RAC Cirencester; *m* 27 Sept 1945, Anne, er da of late Maj Kenneth Paget, of Old Rectory House Itchen Abbas, Hants; 3 s, 1 da; *Career* served with RN WW II (wounded); chm Forestry Indust Ctee GB, dir Buccleuch Estates Ltd; JP Inverness-shire 1953-54; FRICS; *Clubs* Army & Navy, New (Edinburgh); *Style—* Hon James Galbraith, CBE; Rawflat, Ancrum, Roxburghshire (☎ 083 53 302)

GALBRAITH, Hon Norman Dunlop Galloway; 4 but 2 surviving s of 1 Baron Strathclyde, PC, JP (d 1985); *b* 24 Jan 1925; *Educ* Wellington; *m* 9 Sept 1950, Susan Patricia, er da of Cdr Jan Herbert Farquharson Kent, RN, of La Coupe, St Martin, Jersey; 1 s, 2 da; *Career* served WW II, Sub-Lt RNVR, HMS Malaya 1943, HMS Undine 1943-46, Normandy landing 1944, Br Pacific Fleet 1944-46; dir Ben Line Steamers Ltd 1968-86; farmer; *Recreations* farming, country pursuits; *Clubs* New (Edinburgh); *Style—* The Hon Norman Galbraith; Over Newton, by Haddington, East Lothian (☎ 062 081 470)

GALBRAITH, William Campbell; QC (1977); s of William Campbell Galbraith and Margaret, *née* Watson; *b* 25 Feb 1935; *Educ* Merchiston, Pembroke Coll Cambridge, Edinburgh Univ; *m* 1959, Mary Janet Waller; 3 s; *Career* barrister; *Style—* William Galbraith, Esq, QC

GALE, Capt Douglas William; s of William Charles Gale (d 1980), and Helen Sophia Watt (d 1985); *b* 16 Sept 1935; *Educ* Wandsworth GS, Harrow Sch of Art, Sch of Military Survey RE, London Coll of Printing; *m* 7 May 1962 (m dis 1982), Donna Marion, da of John Herbert de Kewer Williams (d 1974), of Oxford; 2 step s (Nicholas Gregory Harding b 1951, Mark Cedric Harding b 1955); *Career* RE: land surveyor, joined Corps 1956, cmmnd and served 42 Survey Engr Regt Cyprus, 22 Litho Sqdn Sch of Mil, 13 Field Survey Sqdn Aden, Print Troop Cdr Sch of Mil Survey UK, Tech Adj 42 Survey Engr Regt; ret RARO 1972; estab De Kewer Gale Bldg Co 1975 (specialising in renovation of timber frame bldgs) won Suffolk Assoc of Architects Craftmanship award Best New House 1984; *Recreations* shooting, sailing, skiing; *Clubs* Inst of Royal Engrs, Inst of Printing, Br Cartographic Soc, Suffolk Preservation Soc; *Style—* Capt Douglas W Gale; The Maltings, Bacton, Stowmarket, Suffolk IP14 4LF

(☎ 0449 781 227, 0449 781 324)

GALE, Hon George Alexander; CC (1977), QC (KC 1944); s of Robert Henry Gale (d 1950), and Elma Gertrude Gale; *b* 24 June 1906; *Educ* Prince of Wales HS, Vancouver BC, Toronto Univ (BA), Osgoode Hall Law Sch Toronto; *m* 1934, Hilda Georgina, da of William Arthur Daly (d 1943); 3 s; *Career* barrister; Supreme Ct of Ontario 1946, Ct of Appeal for Ontario 1963, chief justice of the High Ct of Justice 1964, chief justice of Ontario 1967-76; vice-chm Ontario Law Reform Cmmn 1977-81; hon pres: Lawyers Club 1970, Ontario Curling Assoc 1978; *Recreations* golf; *Clubs* York, University, Chippewa; *Style—* The Hon George Gale, CC, QC; 2 Brookfield Rd, Willowdale, Ontario, Canada (☎ 416 488 0252)

GALE, George Edwin; CBE (1973); s of James Edmund Gale (d 1951); *b* 11 Dec 1910; *Educ* Royal GS High Wycombe, Selhurst GS Croydon, London Univ (PhD); *m* 1935, Carole Fisher, da of late Isaac Joseph Frank Waldron; 1 s, 2 da; *Career* sci (chemist) with Admty (later RN Scientific Serv) 1939-64, Lt RNVR scientific intelligence 1944-45, seconded to Indian Navy as scientific advsr 1951-54, dir Scientific & Technical Servs Branch DHSS; FRSC; *Recreations* writing, philately; *Clubs* Royal Naval and Royal Albert Yacht (Portsmouth); *Style—* Edwin Gale, Esq, CBE; 23 St Helen's Court, St Helen's Parade, Southsea, Hants (☎ 0705 818095)

GALE, George Stafford; s of George Pyatt Gale (d 1966), of Hutton, Somerset, and Anne Watson *née* Wood; *b* 22 Oct 1927; *Educ* Royal GS Peterhouse Cambridge (BA, MA), Gottingen Univ Germany; *m* 1, 24 Nov 1951 (m dis 1983), Patricia Marina, da of Louis Holley (d 1951), of Leatherhead, Surrey; 4 s (Ben b 1952, Mark b 1954 James b 1956, Rupert b 1967); m 2, 6 Aug 1983, Mary Kierman, da of Louis Dillon-Malone (d 1957), of Dublin and Cannock, Staffs; *Career* leader writer (reporter, dep lab corr, lab corr) Manchester Guardian 1950-55, special writer and for corr Daily Express 1955-67, columnist Daily Mirror 1967-69, freelance broadcaster and journalist 1969-81, ed The Spectator 1970-73, phone-in host LBC 1973-78, commentator Thames TV 1975-76, columnist Daily Express 1976-86, assoc ed Daily Express 1981-86, chief leader writer 1981-82, freelance journalist and broadcaster 1986-; columnist: Daily Mirror 1986-87, Daily Mail 1987-; fndr memb and first chm Wivenhoe Arts Club and Wivenhoe Soc; *Books* No Flies in China (1955), 1 Highland Jaunt (with Paul Johnson, 1973); *Clubs* Garrick; *Style—* George Gale, Esq; Titlington Hall, Alnwick, Northumberland NE66 2EB (☎ 0665 78 435)

GALE, John Robert; s of George Joseph Albert Gale, and Irene Christine, *née* Lock (d 1978); *b* 11 June 1955; *Educ* Rutlish Sch; *Career* (as practitioner) dir Light Impressions Europe Ltd ACA; *Recreations* Boys' Bde Offr, organist, swimming; *Clubs* Wig and Pen; *Style—* John Gale, Esq; 415 Hillcross Ave, Morden, Surrey (☎ 01 542 7869)

GALE, (Thomas Henry) John; OBE (1986); s of Frank Haith Gale (1970), and Martha Edith Gale; *b* 2 August 1929; *Educ* Christ's Hosp, Webber Douglas Sch of Drama; *m* 24 Nov 1950, Liselotte Ann, da of Ian Dennis Wratten, CBE (d 1988); 2 s (Timothy Simon b 1956, Matthew Ian b 1959); *Career* 2 Lt RASC 1948; former actor; dir: Gale Enterprises Ltd 1960-, John Gale Prodns Ltd 1960-, West End Mngrs Ltd 1972-, Lisden Prodns Ltd 1975-, Chichester Festival Theatre 1985-89, (exec prodr 1983-84); prodr and co prodr more than eighty plays around the world incl: Candida 1960, On The Brighter Side 1961, Boeing-Boeing, Devil May Care 1963, Windfall 1963, Where Angels Fear to Tread 1963, The Wings of the Dove 1963, Amber for Anna 1964, Present Laughter 1964, and 1981, Malgret and the Lady 1965, The Platinum Cat 1965, The Sacred Flame 1966, An Evening With GBS 1966, A Woman of No Importance 1967, The Secretary Bird 1968, Dear Charles 1968, Highly Confidential 1969, The Young Churchill 1969, The Lionel Touch 1969, Abelard and Heloise 1970, No Sex Please - We're British 1971 (the longest running comedy in Br theatre history), Lloyd George Knew My Father 1972, The Mating Game 1972, Parents Day 1972, At the End of the Day 1973, Birds of Paradise 1974, A Touch of Spring 1975, Separate Tables 1977, The Kingfisher 1977, Sextet 1977, Cause Celebre 1977, Shut Your Eyes and Think of England 1977, Can You Hear Me At The Back? 1979, Middle Age Spread 1979, Private Lives 1980, A Personal Affair 1982; pres Soc West End Theatre Mngrs 1972-75, govr and almoner Christ's Hosp 1976-, chm Theatres Nat Ctee 1979-85, memb Amicable Soc Blues 1981-; Liveryman Worshipful Co Gold and Silver Wyredrawers 1974-; *Recreations* travel, rugby; *Clubs* Garrick and Greenroom, London Welsh RF; *Style—* John Gale, Esq, OBE; Chichester Festival Theatre, Oaklands park, Chichester, W Sussex PO19 4AP (☎ 0243 784 437, fax 0243 787 288)

GALE, Michael; QC (1979); s of Joseph and Blossom Gale; *b* 12 August 1932; *Educ* Cheltenham GS, Grocers Sch, King's Coll Cambridge; *m* 1963, Joanna Stephanie Bloom; 1 s, 2 d; *Career* Royal Fus 1956-58, barr of Middle Temple 1968, rec of Crown Court 1977-, bencher; memb Gen Cncl of the Bar; *Recreations* arts, country pursuits; *Clubs* United Oxford & Cambridge, MCC; *Style—* Michael Gale, Esq, QC; 6 Pump Court, Temple EC4 (☎ 01 353 7242)

GALE, Michael Sadler; MC (1945); s of Rev John Sadler Gale (d 1939), of Canterbury, Kent, and Ethel Maude Victoria, *née* Woollatt (d 1940); *b* 5 Feb 1919; *Educ* Tonbridge, Oriel Coll Oxford (MA); *m* 1950, Philippa Jean, da of Sidney Terence Evelyn Pook Ennion (d 1966), of Apple Tree Cottage, Calbourne, IOW; 3 s (Jonathan, Matthew (decd), Patrick), 1 da (Catharine); *Career* cmmnd The Queens Own Royal West Kent Regt 1940, served in N Africa (wounded 1942) and NW Europe, Maj; joined prison serv of Eng & Wales 1946; govr: HM Prison Portland 1952-57, HM Prison Camp Hill IOW 1957-62, HM Prison Wandsworth 1962-66; asst dir and inspr of prisons Prison Dpt Home Off 1966-69; controller: Planning and Dvpt 1969-75, Operational Admin 1975-79; memb Prisons Bd 1969-79; asst under sec of state Home Off 1972-79; *Recreations* walking, reading, gardening; *Style—* Michael Gale, Esq, MC; 21 Christchurch Rd, Winchester, Hants (☎ Winchester 53836)

GALE, Roger James; (C) North Thanet 1983-; s of Richard Byrne Gale and Phyllis Mary, *née* Rowell (d 1948); *b* 20 August 1943; *Educ* Hardye's Sch Dorchester, Guildhall Sch of Music and Drama ; *m* 1, 1964 (m dis 1967), Wendy Dawn Bowman; m 2, 1971 (m dis), Susan Sampson; 1 da (Misty); m 3, 1980, Suzy Gabrielle, da of Thomas Leopold Marks (d 1972); 2 s (Jasper, Thomas); *Career* formerly: reporter BBC Radio, prodr BBC Radio 4 Today Show, dir BBC Children's TV prodr/dir Thames Children's TV, editor teenage unit Thames; contested (C) Birmingham Northfield (by-election) 1982; *Recreations* swimming, sailing; *Clubs* Parkstone YC, Garrick; *Style—* Roger Gale, Esq, MP; House of Commons, London SW1A 0AA (☎ 01 219 4021)

GALE, Valence Errol; s of Hon Valence Chenery Gale (d 1963, memb Legislative Cncl Barbados), of Barbados, and Elsie Frances, *née* Grell; *b* 9 Sept 1918; *Educ* Harrison Coll Barbados, Reading Univ (BSc); *m* 26 March 1947, Ruth Beynon, da of David John Lloyd (d 1952); 2 s (Timothy David Valence b 1949, Matthew Valence b 1959), 1 da (Stephanie Frances b 1955); *Career* asst dir agric (prev agric offr) Colonial Serv Nigeria 1944-59; farmer (and res offr Oxford Univ Sch of Agric) 1960-66; memb UN FAO 1966-78; working in: Cuba, Chile, Indonesia, Malawi and Columbia; cnslt Indust Cncl for Devpt, NY 1979- (memb advsy missions to Ivory Coast, Somalia, Sudan, Senegal, Mali, Ethiopia and W Samoa); *Recreations* previously cricket and polo now gardening, rare breeds survival tst; *Clubs* Royal Cwlth Soc; *Style—* Valence Gale, Esq; Popes Close, Greenfield, Watlington, Oxfordshire OX9 5NG (☎ 049 161 2439)

GALITZINE, Prince (Russian kniaz, cr 1408 confirmed 1798) George; name also spelt Golitsyn and Gallitzinn; 2 s of Prince Vladimir Emanuelovitch Galitzine (d 1954), by his 1 w Countess Catherine von Carlow (d 1940; product of the morganatic m between Natalia, *née* Wonlarsky, cr Countess von Carlow, and HH Duke Georg of Mecklenburg-Strelitz; the latter's maternal gf was yst s of Tsar Paul I of Russia, while through his mother's mother Georg was fifth in descent from HRH Princess Augusta, sis of George III; hence Prince George Galitzine is sixth cous once removed of HM The Queen); *b* 3 May 1916; *Educ* Lancing, St Paul's, BNC Oxford (MA); *m* 1, 11 Sept 1943 (m dis 1954), Baroness Anne-Marie von Slatin, da of Maj-Gen (Baron) Sir Rudolf von Slatin Pasha, GCVO, KCMG, CB (d 1928); 2 s (Alexander b 1945, George b 1946), 1 da (Caroline b 1944); m 2, 5 May 1963, Jean, da of Frederick Dawnay; 1 da (Katya b 1964); *Career* formerly Maj Welsh Gds Gen Staff Europe; company dir; Royal Humane Soc med 1936; *Recreations* travel, photography, skiing; *Style—* Prince George Galitzine; Mulberry Cottage, Brown Candover, Alresford, Hants; 113 Eaton Sq, SW1 (☎ 01 235 3113)

GALL, Henderson Alexander (Sandy); CBE (1988); s of Henderson Gall (d 1963), of Banchory, Scotland, and Jean, *née* Begg (d 1970); *b* 1 Oct 1927; *Educ* Glanalmond Perthshire, Univ of Aberdeen (MA); *m* 11 Aug 1958, Eleanor Mary Patricia Anne, da of Michael Joseph Smyth (d 1964), of London; 1 s (Alexander Patrick Henderson b 17 June 1960), 3 da (Fiona Deirdre b 7 May 1959, Carlotta Marie-Jean b 2 Nov 1961, Michaela Monica b 27 March 1965); *Career* Corpl RAF 1945-48; for corr Reuters 1953-63: Berlin, Bonn, Nairobi, Suez, Geneva, Budapest, Johannesburg; ITN 1963-: roving reporter, newscaster; maker of seven TV documentaries; rector Univ of Aberdeen 1978-81, Sitara-i-Pakistan RSAA 1985, Laurence of Arabia Medal 1987, Hon LLD Univ of Aberdeen 1981; *Books* Gold Scoop (1977), Chasing the Dragon (1981), Don't Worry About the Money Now (1983), Behind Russian Lines (in Afghan Journal 1983), Afghanistan: Agony of a Nation (1986); *Recreations* golf, Cresta Run; *Clubs* Turf, Special Forces, Rye GC, Royal St Georges GC; *Style—* Sandy Gall, Esq, CBE; Doubleton Oast Hse, Penshurst, Kent TN11 8JA; ITN, 48 Wells St, London W1 (☎ 01 637 2424, fax 0892 870 871)

GALLACHER, John; s of John Gallacher (d 1983), of Garrowhill, Glasgow, Scotland, and Catherine, *née* Crilly; *b* 16 July 1931; *Educ* Our Lady's HS Motherwell; *m* 8 Feb 1956, Eileen Agnes, da of John McGuire (d 1965); 1 s (John Kevin b 1964); *Career* RAF Nat Serv 1950-52, superintendent Kenya Police 1953-65, advsr to Ministry of Interior Libyan Govt 1965-67; counsellor HM Dip Serv 1967-85; gp security advsr Gallacher Ltd 1985; *Recreations* golf, travel, reading; *Clubs* Royal Overseas League; *Style—* John Gallacher, Esq; 1 Clive Rd, Strawberry Vale, Twickenham, Middx TW1 4SQ; Gallacher Limited, Weybridge, Surrey

GALLAGHER, (Francis George) Kenna; CMG (1963); s of George Gallagher (d 1981), and Joanna, *née* Sullivan; *b* 25 May 1917; *Educ* London Univ (LLB); *Career* HM Dip Serv 1945-77; served in Marseilles, Paris, Damascus, Berne and FO; asst under sec of state FCO 1968-71, ambass and permanent UK rep to OECD 1971-77; conslt on Int Trade Policy to CBI 1978-80; *Recreations* music; *Style—* Kenna Gallagher, Esq, CMG; The Old Courthouse, Kirkwhelpington, Northumberland NE19 2RS (☎ 0830 40373)

GALLAGHER, Hon Mrs; Hon Kristin; er da of Baron Wynne-Jones (Life Peer) (d 1982); *b* 1931; *Educ* Cheltenham Ladies' Coll, Somerville Coll Oxford (MA, BSc); *m* 1956, Dr Charles Joseph Gallagher (d 1964); children; *Style—* Hon Mrs Gallagher

GALLAGHER, Dame Monica Josephine; *née* McInerney; DBE (1976); da of late James Francis McInerney, and late Mary Josephine McInerney (arrived 1909 from USA); *b* 5 April 1923; *m* 1946, Dr John Paul Gallagher, KCSG, KM, s of John Paul Gallagher; 2 s, 2 da; *Career* nat pres Catholic Women's League 1972-74 (gen and state pres 1972-80), vice pres ctee Order of the British Empire 1979-, memb Queen Elizabeth Silver Jubilee Ctee 1981-88; Pro Ecclesia et Pontifice (Papal Decoration) 1981; chm YWCA Appeal Ctee Sydney; memb: Dr Horace Newland Travelling Scholarship Selection Ctee, Aust Church Women (NSW div), Catholic Coll of Educ, Sydney (nursing external advisory ctee); Vice chm Friends of St Mary's, St Mary's Cathedral Sydney, Advsy Bd, Festival of Light; Tour Guide St Mary's Cathedral 1970-,(pres Flower festival ctee 1987-) bd memb Gertrude Abbott Nursing Home 1986-; past pres: Catholic Women's Club Sydney, Catholic Central Ctee Care of the Aged Sydney, Exec bd Mater Misericoriae Hosp N Sydney, Catholic Inst of Nursing Studies Sydney, YWCA Appeal Planning Ctee Sydney; former memb: UN Nations, (NSW div), UN Status of Women Ctee NSW, Austcare; *Recreations* ballet, symphony concerts, reading; *Style—* Dame Monica Gallagher, DBE; 1 Robert St, Willoughby, NSW 2068, Australia (☎ 958 8874 or 958 7639)

GALLAGHER, Patrick Joseph; DFC (1943); s of Patrick Gallagher and Mary Berndine, *née* Donnellan; *b* 15 April 1921; *Educ* Prior Park Bath; *m* 1950, Veronica Frances Bateman (d 1981); 1 s; *Career* md Patrick Gallagher Associates 1979-; *Style—* Patrick Gallagher, Esq, DFC; 12 Parsons Green, London SW6

GALLAGHER, Patrick Joseph David; s of Matthew Gallagher, of Cashel, Co Sligo; *b* 28 Feb 1909; *Educ* Trinity Coll Dublin, Temple Univ Philadelphia USA; *m* 1944, Mary, da of Joseph Gleason, of Philadelphia; 3 s, 2 da; *Career* chm Abbey Ltd Dublin 1977-; dir Abbey Homesteads Ltd London and Cyprus; *Recreations* golf, football; *Clubs* Kildare Street Univ; *Style—* Patrick Gallagher, Esq; Liskilleen, Shankill, Dublin, Eire (☎ 01 852426)

GALLEWAY, William Henry; s of Major Harold Galleway, JP (d 1963), and Marjorie, *née* Frankland; *b* 30 July 1931; *Educ* Whitby GS, Leeds Univ (B Com); *Career* articled to M Wasley Chapman 1949; ptnr: Carlill Burkinshaw Ferguson 1963-, Hodgson impey 1970 (previously Hodgson Harris); pres Humberside and Dist Soc CA's 1982 and 83; memb cncl ICEAW 1982; Worshipful Co of CAs 1988; ACA 1955, FCA 1966; *Recreations* antique collecting, philately; *Clubs* Landsdowne; *Style—* William Galleway,

Esq; 26 Argyle Road, Whitby, N Yorks, (☎ 0947 602280); Queen Victoria House, Guildhall Road, Hull, HU1 1HH (☎ 0482 224111, fax 0482 27479, telex 597641F)

GALLEY, Dr Robert Albert Ernest; s of John Atkinson Galley (d 1971), of Hayling Island, and Jane Alice, *née* James (d 1970); *b* 23 Oct 1909; *Educ* Colfe's GS, Sir John Cass Coll and Imperial Coll London (BSc, DIC, PhD); *m* 1, 29 July 1933, (Elsie) Marjorie (d 1985), da of late John Stannix Walton, of London; 1 s (John b 1936), 2 da (Gillian b 1939, Susan b 1944); m 2, 27 April 1988, Ann Louise, da of Wing Cdr John Henry Dale (d 1946); *Career* research chemist Wool Industs Res Assoc 1932-34, dept WD Chemist 1934-37, lectr in chemistry dept Sir John Cass Coll 1937-39, princ exp offr flax estab Miny of Supply 1945-46 (sr exp offr 1939-45), sr princ sci offr Agric Res Cncl 1946-50 (sec interdepartmental insecticides ctees), various short term consultancies WHO and FAO 1948-72, Off of the Lord Pres of the Cncl (advsy cncl's sci policy, natural resources ctee) 1950-52; dir: Tropical Prods Inst Colonial Off 1953-60, Woodstock Agric Res Centre Shell Research Ltd 1960-69; memb 1970-82: Bredgar Parish Cncl, Bredgar Village Hall Ctee, Bredgar Village Fete Ctee; ARSC 1930, FRSC; *Recreations* bowls, gardening, foreign travel; *Style*— Dr Robert Galley; 10 Riverside Ct, River Reach, Teddington, Middx TW11 9QN (☎ 01 943 1884); ATICO 7 Bloque 7, Javea Park, Javea (Alicante) Spain

GALLEY, Roy; s of Kenneth Haslam Galley, and Letitia Mary, *née* Chapman; *b* 8 Dec 1947; *Educ* King Edward VII GS Sheffield, Worcester Coll Oxford; *m* 1976, Helen Margaret Butcher; 1 s, 1 da; *Career* PO mangr; contested (C) Dewsbury 1979, memb Calderdale Met Boro Cncl 1980-83, MP (C) Halifax 1983-87; Social Services Select ctee 1983-87, sec Cons Backbench Health Ctee 1983-87; *Style*— Roy Galley, Esq

GALLIANO, John Charles; s of John Joseph Galliano, of London, and Anita, *née* Guillen; *b* 28 Nov 1960; *Educ* Wilsons GS, St Martins Sch of Art; *Career* fashion designer 1984-; elected Br Designer of the Year 1988; *Style*— John Galliano, Esq

GALLICHAN, Richard Raymond Grandin; DSC (1944); s of Cdr Sydney Gallichan RNR (d 1975); *b* 16 July 1918; *Educ* Portsmouth GS; *m* 1948, Barbara Jean, *née* Robshaw; 2 children; *Career* served WWII, Lt RNVR; slr; sr ptnr Cameron Kemm 1964-80, joint sr ptnr Cameron Markby 1980-81; dir Hill Samuel & Co (Jersey) Ltd 1981-88; cmmr of appeal for Income Tax States of Jersey; underwriting memb Lloyd's 1977; *Recreations* golf, swimming, snooker, bridge; *Style*— Richard Gallichan, Esq, DSC; La Vallée, rue des Landes, Archirondel, Jersey, CI (☎ 0534 55087)

GALLIE, Thomas Holmes (Tom); TD; s of Henry Holmes Gallie (d 1947), of Glasgow, Rangoon and Tunbridge Wells, and Marion Evelyn, *née* Morphew (d 1970); *b* 1 Sept 1917; *Educ* Edinburgh Acad, Fettes; *m* 21 Aug 1943, Doreen Yvonne Lily (Dee), da of George Charles Sydney Pike (d 1967), of London; 2 da (Rosemary b 1944, Josephine b 1949); *Career* WWII Bde Maj 69 HAA Regt RA TA UK and India; metals div ICI 1936-75: overseas dir 1961, later md copper div and gen mangr mktg and overseas; dir Irish Metal Industs 1963-75; cncl memb Br Non-Ferrous Metals Fedn and Br del to Int Wrought Copper Cncl (pres 1973-75); chm Birmingham Marriage Guidance Cncl 1969-77; memb: Stratford-on-Avon DC 1976- (chm 1982-83), S Warwicks Community Health Cncl 1976-79; tstee Brandwood Tst; gen cmmr for income tax 1974-, JP Birmingham 1971-87; *Recreations* gardening, bridge, family; *Clubs* Special Forces; *Style*— Tom Gallie, Esq, TD; Greenacres, Gilberts Green, Tanworth in Arden, Warwickshire B94 5EA (☎ 054 44 2550)

GALLIERS-PRATT, Rupert Anthony; s of Anthony Malcolm Galliers-Pratt, CBE, and Angela, 2 da of Sir Charles Cayzer, 3 Bt; *b* 9 April 1951; *Educ* Eton; *m* 1973, Alexandra Mary, da of Major Hugh Rose; 2 s (George b 1979, Frederick b 1980), 2 da (Isabella b 1985, Alexandra b 1988); *Career* chm Harvey & Thompson plc 1983- (dir 1982-); *Clubs* White's, Turf; *Style*— Rupert Galliers-Pratt, Esq; Mawley Hall, Cleobury Mortimer, Worcs (☎ 0299 270711)

GALLIFORD, Peter; OBE (1981); s of T J Galliford; *b* 21 Oct 1928; *Educ* King Edward VI Sch Nuneaton; *m* 1963, Rona, *née* Pearson; 3 s; *Career* fndr dir Galliford & Sons Ltd, md Galliford Gp of Cos 1952-73, chm Galliford plc (Wolvey Leics) 1973-; chm: Fedn of Civil Engrg Contractors 1978 (currently vice-pres and chm fin ctee), Construction Indust Res and Info Assoc; tres and UK rep Fedn of Int Euro Construction, dir Birmingham Heartlands Ltd (urban renewal agency); memb: Warwicks CC 1964-70, Seven Trent Water Authy 1973-76, civil engrg ctee NEDO 1978-84; vice-pres Warwicks Rural Community Cncl; *Recreations* rugby football, motor sport (competed at int level); *Style*— Peter Galliford, Esq, OBE; Hunters Gap, Ashlawn Rd, Rugby CV22 5QE (☎ 0788 543835)

GALLINER, Peter; s of Dr Moritz Galliner and Hedwig Isaac; *b* 19 Sept 1920; *Educ* Berlin and London; *m* 1948, Edith Marguerite Goldschmidt; 1 da; *Career* Reuters 1942-45, for mangr Fin Times 1945-61, chm and md Ullstein Publishing Gp (Berlin) 1961-64, vice chm and md British Printing Corp Publishing Gp 1967-70, int publishing conslt 1965-67 and 1970-75; chm Peter Galliner Assocs 1970-; dir International Press Inst 1975-; Federal Cross of Merit (first class, FDR), Ecomienda Orden de Isabel la Catolica (Spain); *Recreations* music, reading; *Style*— Peter Galliner, Esq; 27 Walsingham, St John's Wood Park, London NW8 6RH (☎ 01 722 5502); Untere Zäune 15, Zürich 8001, Switzerland (☎ 01 251 8664)

GALLON, Col Anthony William; s of John Walter (d 1971), and Alice Maud Ellen (d 1957); *b* 10 July 1929; *Educ* King Edward VI Totnes, RMA Sandhurst, JSSC; *m* 17 Dec 1953, Muriel, da of Victor Oliver Baldwin (d 1985); 3 s (Robin b 1955, Peter b 1958, Martin b 1961); *Career* served Regular Army 1947-78; asst mil attaché Khartoum 1962-65, Regt Cdr 1966, Col Logistics HQBOAR; business mangr The American Sch London 1978-81, bursar Sherborne Sch 1981-; *Recreations* fishing, shooting, gardening; *Clubs* MCC; *Style*— Col Anthony W Gallon; The Old Coach House, Holnest Park, Holnest, Sherborne, Dorset (☎ Holnest 428); The Bursary, Abbey Road, Sherborne, Dorset

GALLOWAY, David Richard; s of John Campbell Galloway (d 1963), of Kent, and Kathleen Adelaide Galloway, *née* Herbert; *b* 5 Nov 1931; *Educ* Blackrock Coll Dublin, Lincoln Coll Oxford (MA); *m* 18 May 1963, Ann Penelope Clare, da of William John Clare Gaskell (d 1965), of Kent; 1 s (James b 1969), 2 da (Lucinda b 1964, Natasha b 1967); *Career* writer & financial conslt; dep city ed Sunday Telegraph 1964-67; research ptnr Spencer Thornton (stockbroker) 1967-77; money columnist ('David Hume') Harpers & Queen 1970-; conslt GT Mgmnt (fund mangrs) 1977-; chm Imagine (computer graphics) 1985-; *Books* The Public Prodigals (1976), Outbid (as 'David Hume', 1984); *Recreations* theatre, opera, concert going, gardening, swimming, skiing, croquet; *Clubs* Garrick; *Style*— David R Galloway, Esq; 78 Neal Street, London WC2 (☎ 836-6115)

GALLOWAY, George; MP (Lab) Glasgow Hillhead 1987-; s of George Galloway, of Dundee, and Sheila Reilly; *b* 16 August 1954; *Educ* Harris Acad; *m* 1979, Elaine, da of James Fyffe, of Dundee; 1 da (Lucy b 1982); *Career* labourer jute & flax industry 1973, prodn worker Michelin Tyres 1973, organiser Dundee Lab Pty 1977, dir War on Want 1983; *Recreations* sport, films, music; *Style*— George Galloway, MP; House of Commons, London SW1

GALLOWAY, Bishop of; Rt Rev Maurice Taylor; s of Maurice Taylor (d 1967), of Hamilton, and Lucy, *née* McLaughlin (d 1975); *b* 5 May 1926; *Educ* Our Lady's HS Motherwell, Pontifical Scots Coll Rome, Pontifical Gregorian Univ Rome; *Career* RAMC 1944-47 served in UK, India, Egypt; rector Royal Scots Coll Valladolid 1965-74, parish priest Our Lady of Lourdes East Kilbride 1974-81; bishop of Galloway 1981-; vice-pres Catholic Inst for Int Relations (London); *Books* The Scots College in Spain (1971); *Style*— The Rt Rev The Bishop of Galloway, DD; Candida Casa, 8 Corsehill Rd, Ayr, KA7 2ST (☎ 0292 266750)

GALLOWAY, 13 Earl of (S 1623); Sir Randolph Keith Reginald Stewart; 12 Bt (of Corsewell S 1627 and 10 Bt of Burray S 1687); also Lord Garlies (S 1607) and Baron Stewart of Garlies (GB 1796); s of 12 Earl of Galloway, JP (d 1978); *b* 14 Oct 1928; *Educ* Harrow; *m* 1975, Mrs May Lily Budge, yst da of late Andrew Miller, of Duns, Berwickshire; *Heir* kinsman, Andrew Stewart; *Style*— The Rt Hon the Earl of Galloway; Lothlorien Community, Corsock, Castle Douglas, Kirkcudbrightshire, Dumfries and Galloway DG7 3DR

GALLWEY; *see*: Frankland-Payne-Gallwey

GALPERN, Baron (Life Peer UK 1979); Myer Galpern; JP (City of Glasgow), DL (Co of City of Glasgow 1962); s of Maurice Galpern (d 1939); *b* 1903; *Educ* Hutcheson's Boys' GS, Glasgow Univ; *m* 1940, Alice Campbell, JP, da of late Thomas Stewart; 1 s, 1 da; *Career* ld-lt Co of City of Glasgow 1958-59, ld provost Glasgow 1958-60; MP (L) Glasgow Shettleston 1959-79, first dep chm Ways & Means 1974-79; kt 1960; *Style*— Rt Hon Lord Galpern, JP, DL; 42 Kelvin Court, Glasgow

GALPIN, Rodney Desmond; s of Sir Albert James Galpin, KCVO, CBE (d 1984), and Vera Alice, *née* Tiller (d 1980); *b* 5 Feb 1932; *Educ* Haileybury, Imperial Serv Coll; *m* 1956, Sylvia, da of Godfrey Craven (d 1981); 1 s (Paul), 1 da (Fenella); *Career* exec dir Bank of Eng 1984-; chm Standard Chartered plc 1988-; OStJ; *Style*— Rodney Galpin, Esq; Standard Chartered plc, 38 Bishopsgate, London EC2N 4DE (☎ 01 280 7001)

GALSWORTHY, Anthony Charles; CMG (1985); s of Sir Arthur Norman Galsworthy, KCMG (d 1986), and Margaret Agnes, *née* Hiscocks (d 1973); *b* 20 Dec 1944; *Educ* St Pauls, Corpus Christi Coll Cambridge (BA, MA); *m* 30 May 1970, Jan, da of Dr A W Dawson-Grove; 1 s (Andrew b 1974), 1 da (Carolyn b 1975); *Career* Dip Serv; Far East dept FCO 1966-67, language student Hong Kong 1967-69, third sec (later second sec) Peking 1970-72, Rhodesia dept FCO 1972-74, private sec Min of State 1974-77, first sec Rome 1977-81, first sec (later cnsllr and head of chancery) Peking 1982-84, head Hong Kong dept FCO 1984-86, princ private sec to Sec of State Foreign and Cwlth Affrs 1986-88; visiting res fell Roy Inst Int Affrs 1988-; Order of the Lion of Finland 1975, Order of Adolph of Nassau Luxembourg 1976; *Recreations* ornithology, wildlife; *Clubs* Oxford and Cambridge; *Style*— Anthony Galsworthy, Esq, CMG, FCO; FCO, King Charles St, London SW1A 2AH

GALSWORTHY, Sir John Edgar; KCVO (1975), CMG (1968); s of Capt Arthur Galsworthy (d 1957), and Violet Gertrude, *née* Harrison (d 1964); bro of Sir Arthur Norman Galsworthy (d 1986); *b* 19 June 1919; *Educ* Emanuel Sch, Corpus Christi Coll Cambridge; *m* 1942, Jennifer Ruth, da of George Horace Johnstone, OBE; 1 s, 3 da; *Career* serv 1939-41 in HM Forces; entered FO 1941, first sec Athens 1951, first sec Bangkok 1958-61, cnsllr Brussels (UK delegation to EEC) 1962-64, cnsllr (economic) Bonn 1964-67, Paris 1967-69, min (European economic affairs) Paris 1970-71; ambass Mexico 1972-77, ret; UK Observer to El Salvador elections March 1982; *Style*— Sir John Galsworthy, KCVO, CMG; Lanzeague, St Just in Roseland, Truro, Cornwall TR2 5JD

GALT, Hon Mrs; Catriona Mary; *née* Morrison; da (by 1 m) of 2 Viscount Dunrossil; *b* 10 July 1952; *Educ* Cheltenham Ladies' Coll; *m* 1973, John James Galt; 2 s, 1 da; *Style*— Hon Mrs Galt; 64 Templeton St, Sandy Hill, Ottawa, Ontario K1N 6X3, Canada

GALTON, Prof Maurice James; s of James Galton (d 1948), and Olive, *née* Prendergast (d 1987); *b* 31 May 1937; *Educ* Salesian Coll Oxford, Univ of Durham (BSc), Univ of Newcastle (MSc), Univ of Leeds (MEd); *m* 19 March 1960, Pamela Jean, da of Rev Canon Albert John Bennitt (d 1985); 3 s (Simon b 1960, Giles b 1963, Matthew b 1964), 3 da (Philippa b 1968, Bridget b 1969, Su b 1977); *Career* asst master St Pauls Sch 1960-65, instr Univ of Leeds 1965-70, prof Univ of Leicester 1982- (lectr 1970-82); Parly (and Lib) Bosworth 1974-75; conslt Cncl of Europe Primary Project 1982-88, memb Primary Ctee Nat Curriculum Cncl (NCC) 1988-; memb Leicester Theatre Tst 1975-81; FRSA 1986; *Books* Inside The Primary Classroom (1980), Moving From The Primary Classroom (1984), Primary Teaching (1988), Handbook of European Primary Education (1989); *Recreations* golf, cricket, walking, theatre; *Style*— Prof Maurice Galton; Brookside House, Main St, Tilton on the Hill, Leics LE7 9RF (☎ 053 754 268); Sch of Educn, 21 Univ Rd, Leics LE1 7RF (☎ 0533 523 680)

GALTON, Raymond Percy; s of Herbert and Christina Galton; *b* 17 July 1930; *Educ* Garth Sch Morden; *m* 1956, Tonia Phillips; 1 s, 2 da; *Career* scriptwriter and author; television scripts (with Alan Simpson): Hancock's Half Hour (1956-61), Citizen James (1961), BBC Comedy Playhouse, Steptoe and Son (1962-74), Milligan's Wake, Frankie Howerd, Casanova (1973), Dawson's Weekly (1975), The Galton and Simpson Playhouse (1976-77); (with John Antrobus): Room at the Bottom; films (with Alan Simpson): The Rebel (1960), The Bargee (1963), The Wrong Arm of the Law (1964), The Spy with the Cold Nose (1966), Loot (1970), Steptoe and Son (1971), Steptoe and Son Ride Again (1973); theatre (with Alan Simpson): Way Out In Piccadilly (1966-67), The Wind in the Sassafras Trees (1968); (with John Antrobus) When Did You Last See Your Trousers (1987-88); radio (with Alan Simpson): Hancock's Half Hour (1954-59), The Frankie Howerd Show, Back with Braden, Steptoe and Son (1966-73); awards: John Logie Baird for outstanding contribution to TV, Writers Guild Award (twice), The Guild of TV Producers and Directors 1959 Merit Awards Scriptwriters of the Year; *Works include* Hancock's Half Hour (1963), Steptoe & Son (1974); *Style*— Raymond Galton, Esq; The Ivy House, Hampton Court, Middx (☎ 01 977 1236)

GALVIN, Patrick Derek Thomas; s of Maj Thomas Derek Galvin (d 1952), and

Teresa Christina, *née* Innes; *b* 26 Mar 1939; *Educ* Downside, Christ's Coll Cambridge; *m* 23 Jan 1982, (Hilda) Juliana Mary, da of Conrad Marshall Swan, CVO, York Herald of Arms, *qv*; 4 s (Thomas b 23 Jan 1984, Edward b 9 June 1985, Nicholas b 3 Dec 1986, Alexander b 8 Sept 1988), 1 da (Elizabeth b 12 Nov 1982); *Career* investmt analyst Equity and Law Life 1960-62, property ed Investors Chronicle 1963-68, assoc Rowe Rudd and Co 1971 (joined 1968), memb London Stock Exchange 1971, ptnr De Zoete Wedd Int Equities 1986-; AMSIA 1970 (memb of cncl 1979-84, tres 1982-83); *Recreations* gardening, wine, opera, skiing, sailing, travel; *Clubs* Royal Harwich Yacht; *Style—* Patrick Galvin, Esq; Longwood Ho, Nayland, nr Colchester, Essex (☎ 0206 262 482); Barclays De Zoete Wedd, Ebbgate Ho, 2 Swan Lane, London EC4R 3TS (☎ 01 623 2323, fax 01 975 1193, telex 8953239)

GALWAY, 12 Viscount (I 1727); George Rupert Monckton-Arundell; CD; also Baron Killard (I 1727); s of Philip Marmaduke Monckton (d 1965), and Lavender, *née* O'Hara; suc 1 cous once removed, 11 Viscount, 1980; *b* 13 Oct 1922; *Educ* Victoria Coll; *m* 1944, Fiona Margaret, da of Capt W de P Taylor (d 1979), of Sooke, Br Columbia; 1 s, 3 da; *Heir* s, Hon (John) Philip Monckton; *Career* Lt-Cdr RCN, WWII; stockbroker, ret; *Recreations* painting, 'birding', golfing, travelling; *Style—* The Rt Hon the Viscount Galway, CD; 583 Berkshire Drive, London, Ontario N6J 3S3, Canada

GALWAY, James; OBE (1977); s of James Galway; *b* 8 Dec 1939; *Educ* RCM, Guildhall Sch of Music, Conservatoire National Supérieur de Musique (Paris); *m* 1; 1 s; m 2; 1 s, 2 da (twin); m 3, 1984, Jeanne Cinnante; *Career* flute-player; princ flute: London Symphony Orch 1966, Royal Philharmonic Orch 1967-69, Berlin Philharmonic Orch 1969-75; solo career 1975-; Hon MA Open Univ 1979; Hon DMus: Queen's Univ Belfast 1979, New England Conservatory of Music 1980; *Publications* Flute (Yehudi Menuhin Music Guide Series, 1982), James Galway - An Autobiography (1978); *Recreations* music, swimming, walking, theatre, films, TV, chess, backgammon, talking to people; *Style—* James Galway, Esq, OBE; c/o London Artists, 73 Baker St, London W1M 1AH (☎ 01 935 6244, telex 299115)

GAMBLE, Sir David Hugh Norman; 6 Bt (UK 1897), of Windlehurst, St Helens, Co Palatine of Lancs; s of Sir David Gamble, 5 Bt (d 1984), and Dawn Adrienne, da of late David Hugh Gittins, (Pilot Offr RAF); *b* 1 July 1966; *Style—* Sir David Gamble, Bt; c/o Keinton House, Keinton Mandeville, Somerton, Somerset

GAMBLE, David Martin; s of Rev Alfred Edward Gamble, of Scotland, and Yvonne, *née* Cornforth (d 1973); *b* 10 Mar 1953; *Educ* Soham Village Coll, Ealing Sch of Photography; *m* 21 Feb 1981, Pantip, da of Montri Vipatasilan, of Thailand; *Career* photographer Observer Magazine 1984-; other magazines incl: Independent, Femail, Telegraph, She, NY Life, NY Fortune, NY Face, Time, Paris Match, World of Interiors, Town and Country; photographic subjects incl: Margaret Thatcher at No 10, Dali Lama, Capt Mark Phillips, Nigel Lawson, Lord Caernarvon, Richard Branson, Alastair Cooke, Edward Heath; exhibitions incl: Arles 1987 (jtly), Assoc of Fashion, Advtg and Eds Photographers gallery 1987, Kodak Euro exhibition 1988; winner Kodak Grande Prix Euro Award France 1987; memb of Assoc Fashion Advtg Editorial Photographers; *Recreations* watching cricket, photography; *Style—* David Gamble, Esq

GAMBLE, Evelyn, Lady; (Olga) Evelyn; yr da of Robin Arthur Norman Gamble (gs of Sir Josias Christopher Gamble, 2 Bt, JP), by his 1 w, Cissie Emily, *née* Goodall (d 1944); *b* 23 Jan 1944; *m* 9 Dec 1965, as his 2 w, her father's 1 cous, Sir David Arthur Josias Gamble, 4 Bt, JP (d 1982); AIQPS; *Style—* Evelyn, Lady Gamble; Wood End, Tregony, Truro, Cornwall (☎ 087 253 277)

GAMBLE, (Horace) Roy; s of Mary Alice Elizabeth, *née* Pike; *b* 4 Oct 1922; *Educ* Gateway Sch Leicester; *m* 1946, Muriel, da of William Elliott of Leicester; 1 s (Richard), 1 da (Susan); *Career* gen mangr Midland Bank plc until 1982, chm Joseph Rochford & Sons Ltd, dir Royal Tst Bank; *Clubs* MCC, RAC; *Style—* Roy Gamble, Esq; River Lodge, 1 Ravensbury Dr, Dartmouth, Devon

GAMBLING, Prof William Alexander; s of late George Alexander Gambling, of Port Talbot, and late Muriel Clara, *née* Bray; *b* 11 Oct 1926; *Educ* Port Talbot Co GS, Univ of Bristol (BSc), Univ of Liverpool (PhD), Univ of Bristol (DSc); *m* 25 Jul 1952, Margaret da of the late Wilfred Alan Pooley 1 s (Paul b 1956), 2 da (Alison b 1960, Vivien b 1962); *Career* lectr Univ of Liverpool 1950-55, NRC fell Univ of Br Columbia 1955-57; Univ of Southampton: lectr and reader 1957-64, head dept of electronics 1974-79, dean of engrg 1972-75, prof of electronics 1964-; visiting prof: Univ of Colorado 1966-67, Bhabha Atomic Res Centre India 1970, Osaka Univ Japan 1977, Univ of Cape Town SA 1979; memb: Nat Electronics Cncl 1977-78 and 1984-, Engrg Cncl 1983-88, Engrg Indust Trg Bd 1985-88; chm Cmmn D Int Union of Radio Sci 1984-87; dir: York Ltd, York Technol Ltd 1980-; Selby fell Aust Acad of Sci 1982, foreign memb Polish Acad of Sci 1985; Hon DSc Eurotech Res Univ Calif; hon prof Huazhong Univ and Beijing Univ, hon dir Beijing Optical Fibre Res Lab; Freeman City of London, Liveryman Worshipful Co of Engrs; Hon FIEE 1983, FEng 1979, FRS 1983, FRSA 1979; *Books* author several books and over 200 res papers on optical fibres, quantum electronics, microwave engrg and plasma physics; *Recreations* music, travel, walking; *Style—* Prof Alex Gambling; Dept of Electronics and Computer Science, University of Southampton, Southampton, SO9 5NH (☎ 0703 559122 ext 3373, fax 0703 559308)

GAMBON, Michael John; s of Edward Gambon, and Mary Gambon; *b* 19 Oct 1940; *Educ* St Aloysius Sch for Boys London; *m* 1962, Anne Miller; *Career* actor; formerly engr apprentice; first stage appearance Edwards/Mac Liammair Dublin 1962, Nat Theatre, Old Vic 1963-67, RSC Aldwych 1970-72; London Theatre Critics Award Best Actor For Galileo Nat Theatre 1980, RSC 1982-83, numerous TV and film appearances; *Recreations* flying, gun collecting, clock making; *Style—* Michael Gambon; c/o Larry Dazell Associates, 126 Kennington Park Road SE11 4DJ

GAMESTER, Lady Jane Margaret; *née* Annesley; eld da of 10 Earl of Annesley; *b* 15 June 1948; *Educ* Marist Convent Sunninghill, Croydon Coll of Art; *m* 1966, Vernon Hugh Gamester, o s of Edward Arthur Gamester, of The Retreat, 23 Wendover Rd, Staines, Middx; 1 s (Carl b 1970), 2 da (Colette b 1967, Juliet b 1969); *Style—* Lady Jane Gamester; The Retreat, 23 Wendover Road, Staines, Middlesex

GAMINARA, Albert William; CMG (1963); s of Albert Sidney Gaminara (d 1929), of London, and Katherine Helen, *née* Copeman; *b* 1 Dec 1913; *Educ* City of London Sch, St John's Coll Cambridge (MA), Oriel Coll Oxford; *m* 1947, Monica, da of Eric Watson, of Harlow, Essex; 1 s, 3 da; *Career* Colonial Admin Serv 1936-66; admin sec N Rhodesia Govt 1961-64, sec to the Cabinet Zambia Govt 1964-65, ret; *Recreations* beagling; *Clubs* Hawks (Cambridge); *Style—* Albert Gaminara, Esq, CMG; Stratton House, Over Stratton, South Petherton, Somerset (☎ 0460 40295)

GAMMELL, David Scott; s of William Sidney Gammell, of Surrey, and Mary Muriel, *née* Haywood; *b* 12 Mar 1945; *Educ* Bradfield, Reading Univ (Coll of Estate Mgmnt); *m* 1, 20 June 1970, Mia Elizabeth, da of James Child, of Hants; 3 s (Archie b 1972, Alistair b 1973, Evan b 1974), 1 da (Caroline b 1976); m 2, 6 Aug 1982, Sally Ann, da of David Townsend, of Stockton on Tees; 1 s (Harry b 1984), 1 da (Isla b 1983); *Career* chartered surveyor and co dir; md Killearn Estates Ltd 1986-; FRICS; *Recreations* shooting, cricket; *Clubs* Naval and Military, MCC; *Style—* David S Gammell, Esq; 37 Queen Anne Street, London W1M 9FB (☎ 01 631 1778)

GAMMELL, James Gilbert Sydney; MBE (1944); eld s of Lt-Gen Sir James Andrew Harcourt Gammell, KCB, DSO, MC (d 1975), of Alrick, Glenisla, Angus, and Gertrude, *née* Don (d 1960); *b* 4 Mar 1920; *Educ* Winchester; *m* 1944, Susan Patricia, yr da of late Edward Bowring Toms, of Melbury Ct, London W8, and Harbour Light, Sandbanks, Dorset; 5 s 1 da; *Career* CA 1949; chm: Cairn Energy plc, Personal Assets Tst plc; dir: Standard Life Assur Co 1954-, Bank of Scotland 1969-; *Style—* James Gammell, Esq, MBE; Foxhall, Kirkliston, W Lothian, (☎ 031 333 3275); Cairn Energy plc, 64 Queen St, Edinburgh EH2 3AT (☎ 031 225 2092, telex 727905 G CAIPEM)

GAMMIE, Gordon Edward; CB (1981); eld s of late Dr Alexander Edward Gammie, and Ethel Mary, *née* Miller; *b* 9 Feb 1922; *Educ* St Paul's, Queen's Coll Oxford (MA); *m* 1949, Joyce, da of late Arthur Arnold Rust; 2 s (David, Peter); *Career* WWII Capt 1 Bn Argyll and Sutherlands Highlanders served Western Desert and Itlay; under sec Cabinet Off 1975-77; dep Treasy slr 1977-79, legal advsr and slr to MAFF 1979-83, counsel to the Speaker (Euro legislation) 1983; *Recreations* tennis, music; *Clubs* Athenaeum; *Style—* Gordon Gammie, Esq, CB; 52 Sutton Lane, Banstead, Surrey SM7 3RB (☎ 073 73 55287); Ho of Commons, London SW1A 0AA (☎ 01 219 5561)

GAMMIE, William Forbes Petrie; DL (W Sussex 1988); s of Robert Petrie Gammie, OBE, of Bishop's Stortford, and Margaret Marr, *née* Forbes (d 1971); *b* 1 Dec 1926; *Educ* Bishop's Stortford Coll, Oxford Univ (BM, BCh, MA), London Hosp Med Coll; *m* 13 May 1955, (Elsa) Verena, da of Max Muller (d 1969), of Zurich; 1 s (Walter b 1956), 2 da (Susan b 1957, d 1960, Catherine b 1961); *Career* Nat Serv Flt Lt med branch RAF 1952-54; conslt surgn: Royal W Su Hosp Chichester 1964-, King Edward VII Hosp Midhurst 1969-; memb: W Sussex Area Health Authy 1977-83, Chichester Dist Health Authy 1982-87, Med Appeals Tbnl 1988-; Freeman City of London, Liveryman Worshipful Soc Apothecaries 1962; FRCS 1956; *Recreations* walking, gardening; *Style—* William Gammie, Esq, DL; Field Place, Church lane, Clymping, Littlehampton, West Sussex BN17 5RR; West Street, Chichester, West Sussex PO19 1QP (☎ 0243 789 630)

GAMON, Hugh Wynell; CBE (1979), MC (1944); s of His Hon Judge Hugh Reece Percival Gamon (d 1953), of The Lodge, Acomb, York, and Eleanor Margaret Gamon, *née* Lloyd, of Hartford House, Hartley Wintney, Hants; *b* 31 Mar 1921; *Educ* St Edwards Sch Oxford, Exeter Coll Oxford (MA); *m* 17 Dec 1949, June Elizabeth, da of William Temple (d 1986), of Underriver, Sevenoaks, Kent; 1 s (Charles b 1956), 3 da (Mary-Anne b 1952, Sarah b 1954, Jane b 1959); *Career* WWII 1940-46, Maj 1 Div Signals; served: N Africa, Italy, Palestine; slr and parly agent; sr ptnr Sherwood & Co 1972; HM Govt Agent 1970; *Recreations* gardening, motoring; *Clubs* St Stephens and Constitutional, Westminster; *Style—* Hugh W Gamon, CBE, MC; Black Charles, Underriver, Sevenoaks, Kent TN15 0RY (☎ 0732 833036); Messrs Sherwood & Co, Queen Annes Chambers, 3 Dean Farrar St, Westminster SW1H 9LG (☎ 01 222 0441)

GANDELL, Sir Alan Thomas; CBE (1959); s of William Gandell (d 1914), of Greymouth, NZ, and Emma Gandell (d 1952); *b* 8 Oct 1904; *Educ* Greymouth Dist HS; *m* 1933, Edna Marion, da of Rev Thomas Jackson Wallis (d 1943), of Turakina, NZ; 1 s; *Career* chancellor OStJ NZ 1972-78, memb NZ Nat Ports Authy 1969-81; GCStj (1983), FCIT; kt 1978; *Style—* Sir Alan Gandell, CBE; Wesley Haven, Nae Nae, Lower Hutt, Wellington, New Zealand

GANE, Barrie Charles; CMG (1988), OBE (1978); s of Charles Ernest Gane, and Margaret, *née* Price; *b* 19 Sept 1935; *Educ* King Edward's Sch Birmingham, Corpus Christi Coll Cambridge (MA); *m* 1, (m dis 1974); 2 da (Christine Anne b 1963, Nicola Vanessa b 1966); m 2, 5 July 1974, Jennifer Anne, da of Lt Cdr George Pitt; *Career* Nat Serv RN 1955-57, Sub Lt RNVR; FO 1960, third sec Vientiane 1961-63, seconded staff HM Govr Sarawak 1963, second sec Kuching 1963-66, FO 1966, first sec Kampala 1967-70, FCO 1976, on loan to HQ Br Forces Hong Kong 1977-82, FCO 1982-; *Recreations* reading, walking; *Style—* Barrie Gane, Esq, CMG, OBE; c/o Foreign & Cwlth Office, King Charles St, London SW1

GANE, Denis; s of Granville Gane (d 1970), of Pontypool, and Elizabeth, *née* Buckley; *b* 6 July 1939; *Educ* Jones W Monmouth GS, Univ of Wales (MSc); *m* 5 June 1965, Joyce, da of Percival Rosser, of Pontypool; *Career* Nat Serv RCS 1960-62; news ed Western Mail Cardiff 1974-88, news and features ed Wales on Sunday Cardiff 1989-; *Style—* Denis Gane, Esq; 26 Llandegveth Close, Croesyceiliog, Cwmbran, Gwent NP44 2PE (☎ 06333 4339); Thomson House, Cardiff CF1 1WR (☎ 0222 342530)

GANE, Michael; s of Rudolf E Gane and Helen Gane; *b* 29 July 1927; *Educ* Colyton GS, Edinburgh Univ, London Univ, Oxford Univ; *m* 1954, Madge Stewart Taylor; 1 da; *Career* dir England Nature Conservancy Cncl 1974-81; international conslt on economic forestry and environmental matters 1982-; *Style—* Michael Gane, Esq; 1 Ridgeway Close, Sidbury, Sidmouth, Devon EX10 0SW (☎ 039 57 510)

GANELLIN, Prof (Charon) Robin; s of Leon Ganellin (d 1969), and Beila, *née* Cluer (d 1972); *b* 25 Jan 1934; *Educ* Harrow County GS, Queen Mary Coll of London (BSc, PhD), Univ of London (DSc); *m* 27 Dec 1956, Tamara, da of Jacob Greene (d 1988); 1 s (Mark b 1963) 1 da (Nicole b 1960); *Career* res chemist Smith Kline & French Labs Ltd 1958-59, res assoc MIT 1960, vice pres Smith Kline & French Res Ltd 1984-86 (vice pres res 1980-84, dir 1978-86, head of chemistry 1962-78, medicinal chemist 1961-62); Smith Kline & French prof of medicinal chemistry UCL 1986-, dir Upjohn Euro Discovery Centre UCL 1987-; hon prof Univ of Kent 1979-, Prix Charles Mentzer 1978; Royal Soc of Chemistry: medicinal chemistry medal 1977, Tilden Medal 1982, Messel Medal 1988; chm Soc for Drug Res 1985-87; memb Soc Chem Indust, FRSC 1968, FRS 1986; *Books* Phamacology of Histamine Receptors (1982), Frontiers in Histamine Research (1985); *Recreations* music, sailing, walking; *Style—* Prof Robin Ganellin ; Department of Chemistry, University College London, 20 Gordon St, London WC1H OAJ (☎ 01 387 7050)

GANILAU, Ratu Sir Penaia Kanatabatu; GCMG (1983, CMG 1968), KCVO (1982, CVO 1970), KBE (1974, OBE 1960), DSO (1956), ED (1974); s of late Ratu Epeli Gavidi Ganilau; *b* 28 July 1918; *Educ* Queen Victoria Memorial Sch Fiji, Wadham Coll

Oxford; *m* 1, 1949, Adi Laisa Delaisomosomo (decd), da of Livai Yavaca; 5 s, 2 da; m 2, 1975, Adi Davila Vunivalu (decd); *Career* Fiji Mil Forces 1940-46; entered Colonial Admin Serv 1947, dist offr 1948-53; memb of cmmn on Fijian Post Primary Educn 1953; Fiji Mil Forces 1953-56, Lt-Col 1956; Fijian economic devpt offr and Roko Tui Cakaudrove 1956, tour mangr and Govt rep Fiji Rugby Football tour of NZ 1957, dep sec for Fijian Affrs 1961, ldr of Govt Business and min Home Affrs, lands and mineral resources 1970, min Communications, Works and Tourism 1972, memb Cncl of Mins, official MLC; chm: Fijian Affrs Bd, Fijian Devpt Fund Bd, Native Land Trust Bd, Great Cncl of Chiefs; dep PM and min Fijian Affrs and Rural Devpt 1973-83, govr-gen Fiji and C-in-C of Mil Forces 1983-88; Pres and C-in-C of Mil Forces 1988-; Hon Col 2 Bn (TA) Fiji Inf Regt 1973; *Recreations* rugby; *Clubs* Defence, Suva, Fiji; *Style*— Ratu Sir Penaia Ganilau, GCMG, KCVO, KBE, DSO, ED; Government House, Suva, Fiji (☎ Suva 314244)

GANS-LARTEY, Joseph Kojo; s of Charles Botway Lartey (d 1977), of Ghana, and Felicia Adoley, *née* Gans-Boye; *b* 28 August 1951; *Educ* Presbyterian Secdy Sch X'Borg Accra Ghana, Croydon Coll Surrey (HNC), Ealing Coll of Higher Educn (LLB), LSE (LLM); *m* 28 Oct 1978, Rosmarie, da of Harold Ramrattan (d 1987), of Trinidad and Tobago; 1 da (Josephine Annmarie Laatele b 11 Sept 1985); *Career* sr enrolled psychiatric nurse 1978-82 (trainee 1974-76, enrolled 1976-78), sr legal asst RAC 1985-86, Crown Prosecutor 1986-; voluntary legal advsr Croydon Community Rels Cncl; memb: Hon Soc of Lincoln's Inn 1983, Bar of Trinidad and Tobago 1984; *Recreations* tennis, squash, table tennis; *Clubs* Crystal Palace Sports; *Style*— Joseph Gans-Lartey, Esq; 10 Willow Wood Crescent, Selhurst, London WE25 5PZ (☎ 01 684 8058); Crown Prosecution Service, Ground Floor, 10 Furnival St, London EC4A 1PE (☎ 01 831 3038 ext 2276, fax 01 430 0154, Britdoc-DX 499 Chancery Lane)

GANZONI, Hon (Mary) Jill; DL (Suffolk 1988); only da of 1 Baron Belstead (d 1958); *b* 27 Mar 1931; *Educ* Crofton Grange Sch, Eastbourne Sch of Domestic Economy; *Career* memb Gen Synod of Church of England 1970-, church cmmr 1978-; *Recreations* bridge; *Style*— Hon Jill Ganzoni; Rivendell, Spring Meadow, Playford, nr Ipswich (☎ 0473 624662)

GAON, Dr Solomon; s of Isaac Gaon, and Rachael Gaon; *b* 15 Dec 1912; *Educ* Jesuit Secdy Sch Travnik Yugoslavia, Jewish Teachers' Seminary Sarajevo, Jews Coll London Univ; *m* 1944, Regina Hassan; 1 s, 1 da; *Career* Haham (Chief Rabbi) Assoc of Sephardi Congregations 1977-80; Haham of Communities affiliated to World Sephardi Fedn in the Diaspora 1978-; *Style*— Dr Solomon Gaon; 25 Ashworth Rd, London W9 (☎ 01 289 1575)

GARBER, Hon Mrs (Fiona); *née* Spring Rice; 3 and yst da of 6 Baron Monteagle of Brandon; *b* 10 April 1957; *m* 26 March 1982, Andrew Louis Garber, yst s of S Garber, of St John's Wood; 2 da (Rose Anne b 13 July 1985, Eliza Kate b 8 Aug 1987); *Style*— Hon Mrs Garber; 6 Amies St, London SW11

GARCIA, Russell Simon; s of Julie Ann, *née* Carter; *b* 20 June 1970; *Educ* City of Portsmouth Boys Sch, Portmouth Coll of Art; *Career* hockey player; yst GB capped player 17, under 21 Silver Medalist Euro Cup 1988, Gold Medallist 5 Nation Tournament Malaysia 1988, yst Gold Medallist Seoul Olympics 1988; memb: Hockey Assoc 1988, GB Men's Hockey Bd 1988; *Recreations* hockey; *Clubs* Havant Hockey, Fareham Indoor Hockey; *Style*— Russell Garcia, Esq; 9 Sandhurst Ct, Victoria Grove, Southsea, Hants (☎ 0705 815 577)

GARDAM, Susan Rosemary; *née* Martin; da of Louis Thomas Martin, of Milford-on-Sea, Hants, and Margaret Hilda, *née* Hinder; *b* 18 July 1953; *Educ* St Albans HS for Girls, LSE, Guildford Coll of Law (LLB); *m* 15 June 1985, Robert Alan (Head of Outside Bdcast TVS), s of Gerald Frederick Gardam (d 1985), of Potters Bar, Herts; 2 s (Paul Robert b 1981, Ian Thomas b 1982), 1 da (Victoria Margaret b 1986); *Career* slr; private practice; *Recreations* sailing, riding, antiques, travel, swimming; *Clubs* Royal Lymington Yacht, Careys Manor Carat; *Style*— Mrs Susan R Gardam; Gateways, Partridge Road, Brockenhurst, Hants (☎ 0590 23810); Martins, The New House, 32 Brookley Road, Brockenhurst (☎ 0590 23252)

GARDAM, Timothy David; s of David Hill Gardam, QC, of Sandwich, and Jane, *née* Pearson; *b* 14 Jan 1956; *Educ* Westminster, Gonuile and Caius Coll Cambridge (BA); *m* Kim Scott, da of Capt Gordon Walwyn, RN, CVO, of Warblington; *Career* BBC: trainee 1977, prodr Newsnight 1979-82, exec prodr Timewatch 1982-85 and Bookmark 1984-85, output ed Newsnight 1985-86, dep ed Gen Election 1987, ed Panorama 1987-; *Recreations* gardening, ruins; *Style*— Timothy Gardam, Esq; 28 School Rd, Kidlingto, Oxford; BBC TV, Wood Lane, London W12 (☎ 01 576 1957)

GARDINER, Hon Carol Susan; o da of Baron Gardiner, CH, PC, QC, (Life Peer); *b* 5 Dec 1929; *Style*— Hon Carol Gardiner

GARDINER, David Alfred William; s of Neil William Gardiner (d 1973), of Burghfield Common, Berks; *b* 11 April 1935; *Educ* Winchester, Imperial Coll London, Harvard Business Sch; *m* 1963, Carolyn Georgina, da of Thomas Humphrey Naylor (d 1966), of Ashton, Chester; 2 s (James b 1965, Andrew b 1971), 1 da (Georgina b 1968); *Career* Lt Grenadier Gds 1953-55; dir Huntley & Palmers Ltd and assoc companies 1961-83; farmer and landowner; High Sheriff of Berkshire 1988-89; chm Berks CLA 1989; *Recreations* field sports; *Style*— David Gardiner, Esq; The Old Rectory, Lilley, Newbury, Berks RG16 0HH (☎ 048 82 227)

GARDINER, (John) Duncan (Broderick); s of Frederick Keith Gardiner, JP, and Ruth, *née* Dixon (d 1985); *b* 12 Jan 1937; *Educ* St Edward's Sch Oxford; *m* 1965, Geraldine Mallen; 1 s, 1 da; *Career* author and broadcaster; ed Western Mail 1974-81; *Style*— Duncan Gardiner, Esq; 145 Pencisely Rd, Llandaff, Cardiff (☎ 0222 33022)

GARDINER, George Arthur; MP (C) Reigate 1974-; s of Stanley Gardiner (d 1958), of Maldon, Essex, and Emma Gardiner; *b* 3 Mar 1935; *Educ* Harvey GS Folkestone, Balliol Coll Oxford; *m* 1, 1961 (m dis 1980), Juliet Wells; 2 s, 1 da; m 2, 1980, Helen, *née* Hackett; *Career* dep political corr The Sunday Times 1966-70, chief political corr Thomson Regnl Newspapers 1964-74; contested (C) Coventry S 1970; ed Cons News 1972-79, memb exec 1922 ctee and vice chm Cons For Affrs ctee, memb Home Affrs and Race Rels Select Ctee and Immigration Sub-Ctee 1979-82, chm Cons Euro Affairs Ctee 1980-87 (former sec 1976-79, vice chm 1979-80); *Books* The Changing Life of London (1972); Margaret Thatcher, from Childhood to Leadership (1975); *Recreations* gardening; *Style*— George Gardiner, Esq, MP; House of Commons, London SW1A 0AA

GARDINER, Baron (Life Peer UK 1963); Gerald Austin Gardiner; CH (1975), PC (1964); s of Sir Robert Septimus Gardiner (d 1939), and Baroness Alice Marie (d 1953), da of Baron Hermann Ludwig Wilhelm Karl Georg von Ziegesar; *b* 30 May 1900; *Educ* Harrow, Magdalen Coll Oxford; *m* 1, 3 Dec 1925, Lesly Doris (d 1966), da of Alderman Edwin Trounson, JP, of Penzance; 1 da; m 2, 1970, Muriel, da of Charles Baker, and formerly w of Sydney Box; *Career* served WW I, 2 Lt Coldstream Gds; barr 1925, KC 1948, chm Gen Cncl Bar 1958 and 1959; LCC Alderman 1961-63; lord high chllr 1964-70; elected to Int Cmmn of Jurists 1971; chllr The Open Univ 1973-78; pres Help the Aged; *Style*— The Rt Hon Lord Gardiner, CH, PC; Mote End, Nan Clark's Lane, Mill Hill, London NW7

GARDINER, Guy Clavell Inge; CBE (1960); s of Charles Herbert Inge Gardiner (d 1922), and Rufa Flora Clavell, *née* Hore (d 1975); *b* 18 July 1916; *Educ* Westminster; *m* 9 Sept 1939, Louise Mabelle (Jane), da of Walter Clerk Randolph Rose (d 1938); 3 s (Micheal b 12 March 1942, Colin b 25 Sept 1943, David b 13 March 1945); *Career* De Havilland Aircraft Co Ltd: aeronautical tech sch 1936-38, designer undercarriage and hydraulics (Mosquito) 1938-45; De Havilland Propellor Co Ltd: chief designer 1945-47, chief engr 1947-52, tech dir and chief engr 1952-59, chief exec (Blue Streak) 1959-61; tech dir (guided weapons) Hawker Siddeley Aviation 1961-63; Hawker Siddeley Dynamics: dir and gen mangr 1963-67, md 1967-71, conslt 1971; Freeman Worshipful Co of Coach and Coach Harness Makers 1971 FRAeS 1956, FIMechE 1955; *Recreations* shooting, golf, sailing; *Clubs* Naval & Military; *Style*— Guy Gardiner, Esq, CBE; Heron Cottage, Heronsgate, Rickmansworth, Herts (☎ 092 782 584)

GARDINER, Dame Helen Louisa; DBE (1961, CBE 1952) MVO (1937); yst da of late Henry Gardiner, of Bristol; *b* 24 April 1901; *Educ* Clifton HS; *Career* formerly in Private Secretary's Office, Buckingham Palace (chief clerk 1946-61); *Recreations* reading, gardening; *Style*— Dame Helen Gardiner, DBE; Lostwithiel, Cornwall

GARDINER, Ian David; s of Maj David Gardiner, MC (d 1939), and Dorothea, *née* Caswell (d 1985); *b* 14 April 1928; *Educ* Harlow Coll, Univ of London (BSc); *m* 12 Aug 1950, Dorothy Anderson, da of Frank Arnold Onians (d 1985); 2 s (David b 1954, Andrew b 1969), 2 da (Elizabeth b 1951, Anne b 1958); *Career* TA RE 1972, Col 1984; The Eng Electric Co 1948-70: mangr Bombay 1957, mangr Calcutta 1959, mangr Victoria Aust 1960-65, commercial mangr diesel div 1965-70; BR Engrg Ltd 1970-81: commercial dir 1970-73, engrg dir 1973-76, md 1976-81; dir of engrg BR 1981-85; chm convocation City Univ 1978-81, memb of cncl City Univ 1982-, memb of cncl and chm prodn ctee CBI 1980-84, memb of bd BSI 1982-84, vice pres IMechE 1984-; Freeman City of London 1982, Liveryman Worshipful Co of Engrs 1984; FIMechE 1970, FIEE 1971, FRSA 1975, FEng 1982; *Recreations* gardening, swimming, fishing, choral singing; *Style*— Ian Gardiner, Esq; Cottesloe, 8 Barrs Ave, New Milton, Hants BN25 5HJ (☎ 0425 638039)

GARDINER, Patrick Lancaster; s of Alfred Clive Gardiner (d 1960), and Lilian, *née* Lancaster (d 1973); *b* 17 Mar 1922; *Educ* Westminster, Christ Church Oxford (MA); *m* 7 July 1955, (Kathleen) Susan, da of Herbert Booth (d 1984); 2 da (Josephine b 1956, Vanessa b 1960); *Career* Army 1942-45: Lt 1943, Capt 1945, serv N Africa and Italy; lectr in philosophy Wadhar Coll Oxford 1949-52, fell in philosophy St Anthony's Coll Oxford 1952-58, fell and tutor philosophy Magdalen Coll Oxford 1958-89, visiting prof Columbia Univ NY 1955, author; FBA 1985; *Books* The Nature of Historical Explanation (1952), Schopenhauer (1963), Kierkegaard (1988), ed: Theories of History (1959), Nineteenth-Century Philosophy (1969), The Philosophy of History (1974); *Style*— Patrick Gardiner, Esq; The Dower house, Wytham, Oxford (☎ 0865 242205); Magdalen Coll, Oxford (☎ 0865 276000)

GARDINER, Peter Ambrose; s of Harold Gardiner (d 1963), of Beaconsfield, and Constance Mabel, *née* Hare (d 1946); *b* 13 Oct 1913; *Educ* Westminster Sch, London Univ (MD); *m* 19 April 1941, Bridget Mary Cameron, da of Sir Francis Carnegie (d 1946), of Blackheath; 2 s (Michael b 1942 d 1943, Richard b 1945), 2 da (Annabel b 1944, Catherine b 1951); *Career* conslt opthalmic surgn (emeritus) Guys Hosp, past pres Swedenborg Soc; *Style*— Peter Gardiner, Esq

GARDINER, Brig Richard; CB (1954), CBE (1946, OBE 1944); s of Maj Alec Gardiner, RE (ka 1914); *b* 28 Oct 1900; *Educ* Uppingham, RMA Woolwich; *m* 1, 1924, Catherine Dod (d 1982), da of Capt Victor Oliver, RN; 2 s; m 2, 1982, Barbara Mary Whatmore; *Career* Army serv 1920-53, India, M East BAOR; dir Transportation and dir Engr Stores War Office 1948-53, md Peruvian Corpn Peru 1954-63; memb Surrey CC 1970-77; FCIT; *Recreations* music, gardening; *Style*— Brig Richard Gardiner, CB, CBE; Botolph House, Botesdale, Diss, Norfolk IP22 1BX (☎ 0379 898413)

GARDINER, Hon Mrs (Susanna Catherine Crawshay); da of Baron Greenwood of Rossendale, PC (d 1982; Life Peer); *b* 1943; *m* 1970, Christopher Gardiner; 1 s (Thomas b 1982), 1 da (Anna b 1980); *Style*— Hon Mrs Gardiner; 1 Oak Tree House, Redington Gdns, London NW3; Greenwoods, East Mersea, Essex

GARDINER, Victor Alec; OBE (1977); *b* 9 August 1929; *Educ* Whitgift and City and Guilds Schs; *m* ; 1s, 2 da; *Career* dir and gen mangr London Weekend TV 1971-; dir London Weekend TV (Hldgs) Ltd and London Weekend Services Ltd 1976-; chm Dynamic Technol Ltd and Standard Music Ltd 1972-; *Style*— Victor Gardiner, Esq, OBE; The Gables, Sulhamstead, Reading, Berks

GARDINER, William Griffiths; s of James Gardiner (d 1962), of Glasgow, and Muriel, *née* Griffiths; *b* 8 Mar 1938; *Educ* Glasgow HS; *m* 7 July 1967, Una, da of David Anderson (d 1945); 2 s (David b 1969, Ian b 1971); *Career* CA 1960, co sec Stenhouse Hldgs plc 1970-84, head fin investmt small business div Scottish Devpt Agency 1984-87, fin dir Glasgow Investmt Mangrs Ltd 1987-; *Recreations* golf, curling, music; *Clubs* Glasgow HS, Glasgow GC; *Style*— William Gardiner, Esq; 5 Ardoch Rd, Bearsdew, Glasgow (☎ 041 942 7338); Glasgow Investment Managers Ltd, 29 St Vincent Place, Glasgow G1 2DR (☎ 041 226 4585, fax 041 226 3632, telex 779503)

GARDNER; *see*: Bruce-Gardner

GARDNER, Cecil John; *b* 11 June 1912; *m* 1936, Marjorie Isobel; 2 da (Pamela, Diana); *Career* Gardners Transformers Ltd (Queen's Award for Export 1980); founded business as Gardners Radio 1928, incorp 1934, name changed to Gardners Transformers 1962, now chm; *Recreations* sailing; *Clubs* Royal Solent YC, Royal Lymington YC, Christchurch SC (CSC); *Style*— Cecil Gardner, Esq; Willow Close, Bridge Street, Christchurch, Dorset BH23 1DY (☎ 0202 482827); Gardners Transformers Ltd, Christchurch, Dorset BH23 3PN (☎ 0202 482284, telex 41276 GRSXCH G)

GARDNER, David Maitland; MBE, TD; s of John James Maitland Gardner (d 1945), of Culdees Castle, Muthill, Perthshire, and Margaret, *née* Thomson (d 1953); *b* 3 April 1914; *Educ* Charterhouse, Clare Coll Cambridge (MA); *m* 5 Oct 1946, Barbara Helen, da of David John Wauchope Dundas (d 1938), of Woodhouselee, Milton Bridge, Midlothian; 1 s (Colin b 1960), 2 da (Jane b 1947, Margaret b 1949); *Career* cmmnd 2

Lt RA (TA) 1937, Staff Capt 1939, served GSO2 N Africa and Italy (despatches 1943), DAQMG Br Army Staff France 1944, transferred TARO (hon rank of Maj) 1945; A Gardner & Son Ltd (family furniture mfrs and retailers estab Glasgow 1832): dir 1938-46, md 1946-83, chm 1983-85); commercial farming interests in Perthshire 1953-; rep Scottish House Furnishers' Fedn on trade Wages Cncl 1950-54 (pres 1951-54), hon pres Scottish Furniture Trades Benevolent Assoc 1957- (pres 1954-55), chm Kinross & W Perthshire Cons Assoc 1960-65 (vice chm 1951-60), pres Perth & Kinross Cons Assoc 1983-89; pres Strathearn Agric Soc 1961-64, elder Church of Scotland 1951-, Deacon of the Incorpn of Hammermen of Glasgow 1964-65; *Recreations* golf, curling, shooting; *Clubs* Western (Glasgow), Royal & Ancient Golf of St Andrews; *Style—* D Maitland Gardner, MBE, TD; Culdees Castle, Muthill, Crieff, Perthshire PH5 2BA (☎ 0764 81 280)

GARDNER, Cdr Derek George Montague; VRD, RNVR (ret); s of Alfred Charles Gardner (d 1952), and Florence Mary, *née* Johnson (d 1955); *b* 13 Feb 1914; *Educ* Oundle; *m* 14 July 1951, Mary, da of Joseph Harry Dalton; 1 s (Charles Henry Penn b 11 May 1954), 1 da (Angela Mary b 2 June 1952); *Career* Midshipman RNVR (Clyde Div) 1934, mobilised HMS Proserpine 1939, HM (trawler) Ocean Fisher 1939-41, HMS Osprey 1941, HMS Broke (despatches) 1942, HMS Highlander 1942-43, Lt Cdr Staff of C in C Western Approaches HMS Eaglet 1943-45, Cdr Asst CSO to Flag Offr Ceylon HMS Lanka 1945-46, Cdr RNVR 1946, ret 1947; chartered civil engr Miny of Works Kenya HMOCS 1947-63, regnl engr Kenya 1953-63, ret HMOCS 1963; elected memb RSMA 1966; works in: Nat Maritime Museums Greenwich and Bermuda, RNC Dartmouth; one man shows Polak Gallery London: 1972, 1975, 1979, 1982, 1987; hon vice pres for life RSMA; lay vice patron of the Missions to Seamen 1983; RSMA, CEng, FICE; *Clubs* Naval; *Style—* Cdr Derek Gardner, VRD; High Thatch, Corfe Mullen, Wimborne, Dorset BH21 3HJ (☎ 0202 693211)

GARDNER, Douglas Frank; s of Lt Ernest Frank Gardner, of 32 Bramshill Gardens, London NW5, and Mary, *née* Chattington; *b* 20 Dec 1943; *Educ* Woolverstone Hall, Coll of Estate Mgmnt, Univ of London (BSc); *m* 5 Sept 1978, Adèle, da of Major Charles Macmillan Alexander, of Broome Cottage, The Drive, Angmering-on-Sea, Sussex; 1 s (Mark b 1972), 2 da (Teresa b 1971, Amy b 1979); *Career* md Brixton Estate plc 1983-, chief exec properties div, Tarmac plc 1976-83; chm: Estates Improvement Ltd, Brixton Investments Ltd; dir Brixton France SA; *Recreations* tennis; *Style—* Douglas Gardner, Esq; 2 Woodstock Rd, Bedford Park, Chiswick, London W4 (☎ 01 994 0152); Brixton Estate plc, 22/24 Ely Place, London EC1 (☎ 01 242 6898, fax 01 405 1630, telex 22838)

GARDNER, Sir Edward Lucas; QC (1960); s of late Edward Walker Gardner, of Fulwood, Preston, Lancs; *b* 10 May 1912; *Educ* Hutton GS; *m* 1, 1950 (m dis 1962), Noreen Margaret, da of late John Collins, of Moseley, Birmingham; 1 s, 1 da; m 2, 1963, Joan Elizabeth, da of late B B Belcher, of Bedford; 1 s, 1 da; *Career* served WWII, Cdr RNVR; former journalist; barr Gray's Inn 1947, dep chm QS: E Kent 1961-71, Kent 1962-71, Essex 1968-71; recorder Crown Court 1972-85; chm Soc Cons Lawyers 1975-85, vice-pres 1985-, chm exec ctee 1969-75); contested (C) Erith & Crayford 1955; MP (C): Billericay 1959-66, South Fylde 1970-1987; PPS to attorney-gen 1962-63; Bencher Gray's Inn 1968; cmmr Commonwealth War Graves Cmmn 1971-77; govr Thomas Coram Fndn for Children 1962-; steward British Boxing Bd Control 1975-84; kt 1982; *Clubs* Pratt's, Garrick; *Style—* Sir Edward Gardner, QC; 1 Raymond Bldgs, Gray's Inn, London WC1 (☎ 01 242 4719); Outlane Head, Chipping, Lancs PR3 2NQ (☎ 09956 430)

GARDNER, Dame Frances Violet; DBE (1975); da of Sir Ernest Gardner (d 1925, yeoman farmer and sometime MP), and Amy Inglis, *née* Laurie; *b* 28 Feb 1913; *Educ* Headington Sch Oxford, Westfield Coll London (BSc), Royal Free Hosp Sch of Med (MB, BS, MD); *m* 1958, George Qvist (d 1981); *Career* med registrar Royal Free Hosp 1943, clinical asst Nuffield Dept of Med Oxford 1945, fell in med Harvard Univ USA 1946, conslt physician Royal Free Hosp 1946-78, chief asst Nat Hosp for Diseases of the Heart 1947, late physician Royal Nat Throat Nose and Ear Hosp London, former dean Royal Free Hosp Sch of Med, visitor med faculty Khartoum 1981, Cwlth travelling fell 1962, rep Gen Med Schs on senate Univ of London 1967, memb Gen Med Cncl 1971, pres Royal Free Hosp Sch of Med 1979, former chm London/Riyadh Univs Medical Faculty, tstee Hilda Martindale Educational Tst; MRCP 1943, FRCP 1952, FRCS 1953; *Style—* Dame Frances Gardner, DBE; Fitzroy Lodge, Fitzroy Park, Highgate, London N6 6JA (☎ 01 340 5873)

GARDNER, (Ralph Roland) Gay; s of Ralph Rodman Gardner, The Old Hall, Malpas, Cheshire, SY14 8NG, and Mima Elaine, *née* Forrester (d 1976); *b* 9 August 1934; *Educ* Eton; *m* 15 Oct 1966, Susan Blakeley, da of Cdr Vincent Russell, RN (d 1983); 1 s (Charles b 1968), 2 da (Louise b 1966, Chloë b 1973); *Career* cmmnd Scots Gds Nat Serv; md Smith St Aubuyn and Co Ltd, UK tres and dir Kleinwort Benson Ltd, exec dir Mees and Hope Securities Hldgs, dir Univ Life Assur Soc; *Style—* Gay Gardner, Esq; Leamington Hastings Manor, Rugby, CV23 8DY; Mees and Hope Securities 95 Gresham St, London, EC2V 7NA (☎ 01 600 9331, fax 01 606 1404, telex 946003

GARDNER, Hon Joanna; yst da of Baroness Gardner of Parkes, *qv*; *b* 14 Nov 1964; *Educ* Univ of Essex (BA), Coll of Law Chancery Lane London; *Career* articled clerk McKenna & Co; *Style—* Hon Joanna Gardner; 15 Lancelot Place, London SW7 1DR

GARDNER, (Arthur) John; s of Harold John Gardner (d 1967), of Shipham, Somerset, and Lily Mary, *née* White (d 1985); *b* 19 Oct 1930; *Educ* Huish GS Taunton, London Univ (LLB); *m* 16 May 1953, Patricia Beatrice Mary, da of James Hooper (d 1954), of Ilminster, Somerset; 3 da (Rosemary b 1958, Caroline b 1963, Joanne b 1965); *Career* slr; pres Somerset Law Soc, memb Cheddar PC 1970- (chm 1973 and 1985); former chm Somerset CCC; *Recreations* philately, cricket; *Style—* John Gardner, Esq; Staddles, Station Road, Cheddar, Somerset (☎ 0834 742261); Gardner Jackson, Roley House, Church St, Cheddar, Somerset (☎ 0934 743321)

GARDNER, John Linton; CBE (1976); s of Capt Alfred Linton Gardner, RAMC (ka 1918), of Ilfracombe, and Muriel, *née* Pullein-Thompson; *b* 2 Mar 1917; *Educ* Wellington Coll, Exeter Coll Oxford; *m* 1955, Jane Margaret Mary, da of Nigel James Abercrombie, of Ringmer, Lewes, E Sussex; 1 s, 2 da; *Career* composer; chief music master Repton 1939-40, on music staff Royal Opera House 1946-52, prof of harmony and composition RAM 1956-86; dir of music: Morley Coll 1965-69, St Paul's Girls' Sch 1962-75; dep chm Performing Rights Soc 1983; *Compositions include* the opera The Moon and Sixpence; two symphonies; three string quartets; concertos for piano, trumpet and organ; many large scale choral works; *Recreations* tesseraphily; *Style—* John Gardner, Esq, CBE; 20 Firswood Ave, Ewell, Epsom, Surrey KT19 0PR

GARDNER, Capt Nicolas Charles Eric; s of Maj Laurie Gardner (d 1969), and Erica Sylva Margareta Herta, *née* Steinmann (d 1976); *b* 23 July 1946; *Educ* Eton, Keble Coll Oxford (MA); *m* 3 Oct 1974, Roseanne Serena, da of Charles Douglas Neville Walker, MM, of 58 Rue Singer, 75016 Paris; *Career* cmmnd Irish Gds 1966, Capt 1971, ADC to C-in-C UKLF 1972-74, ret 1974; ptnr: Town & Country Estate Agents 1975-83, Somerley Crayfish 1984-; Queen's Messenger 1987-; Liveryman Worshipful Co of Drapers 1983; *Recreations* shooting, gardening; *Style—* Capt Nicholas Gardner; Breamore Cottage, Breamore, Fordingbridge, Hampshire SP6 2DB (☎ 0725 22 265); Foreign & Commonwealth Office, King Charles St, London SW1

GARDNER, Peter Louis; s of Jack Louis Gardner (d 1976), and Joan Miriam, *née* Stokvis; *b* 22 June 1949; *Educ* NW Kent Coll of Technol (Dip GaI); *m* 30 Sept 1972, Maureen Elizabeth, da of William George Collis (d 1977); 2 s (Adam b 5 Aug 1977, Neil b 24 May 1979), 1 da (Charlotte b 21 Feb 1984); *Career* aachitechural conslt Newman Tonks plc 1972-75, sales mangr G & S Allgood Ltd (architectural ironmongers) 1975-78; DA Thomas Ltd 1978-88: sales mangr, sales dir; sales dir Hewi UK Ltd, gp sales dir D A Thomas Gp plc; chm Inst of Architectural Ironmongers 1984-85, pres Guild of Architectural Ironmongers 1987-88; parent govr: Pickhurst Infants Sch, Pickhurst Jr Sch; memb ctee Langley Park GC; memb: Inst IAI, IAM; *Recreations* golf, driving; *Clubs* Langley Park GC; *Style—* Peter Gardner, Esq; Beaver Construction Supplies Ltd, Unit B2 Ullswater Crescent, Coulsdon, Surrey (☎ 01 668 0731, fax 01 668 5319)

GARDNER, Hon Rachel; *née* Gardner; 2 da of Baroness Gardner of Parkes, *qv*; *b* 8 April 1961; *m* 24 Sept 1988, Dr Alvan J Pope, s of Kenneth Pope, of the Old Rectory, Chastleton, Glos; *Style—* Hon Rachel Gardner; 10 Loudoun Rd, London NW8

GARDNER, Hon Sarah; el da of Baroness Gardner of Parkes, *qv*; *b* 3 Mar 1960; *Style—* Hon Sarah Gardner; 3 Northwick Close, London NW8

GARDNER, Trevelyan Codrington; CBE (1960); s of Lt-Cdr Thomas Gardner, DSC, RN (d 1928); *b* 3 August 1917; *Educ* Taunton's Sch, Queen's Coll Oxford (MA); *m* 1944, Briege Theresa, da of Patrick Feehan, of Castle Carra, Dundalk; 2 s, 3 da; *Career* Maj Royal Hampshire Regt 1939-45, Italy; Colonial Serv 1946-64, sec for finance N Rhodesia 1958-60, Miny of Fin N Rhodesia 1960-64; tres Cambridge Univ until 1983, emeritus 1983-; administrator: American Friends of Cambridge Univ, 1983-87, Friends of the Oxford and Cambridge Boat Race 1988-; chm Cambridge Education Consultants 1982-; fell Wolfson Coll Cambridge; Hon Fell: Robinson Coll Cambridge, Darwin Coll Cambridge; *Recreations* golf, gardening; *Clubs* Army and Navy, Gog Magog GC; *Style—* Trevelyan Gardner, Esq, CBE; Hill Court, Station Rd, Whittlesford, Cambridge (☎ 0223 832483); Friends of the Oxford and Cambridge Boat Race, Pitt Bldg, Trumpington St, Cambridge CB2 1RP (☎ 0223 311201)

GARDNER OF PARKES, Baroness (Life Peer UK 1981); (Rachel) Trixie Anne; JP (N Westminster Inner London 1971); da of Hon (John Joseph) Gregory McGirr (d 1949; MLA, NSW State Govt), and Rachel, *née* Miller; *b* 17 July 1927; *Educ* Monte Sant Angelo Coll N Sydney, Sydney Univ (BDS); *m* 1956, Kevin Anthony Gardner (Lord Mayor of Westminster 1987-88), s of George Gardner, of Sydney, Australia; 3 da (Sarah, Rachel, Joanna, *qqv*); *Career* dental surgeon; memb: Westminster City Cncl 1968-78, GLC Havering 1970-73, Enfield-Southgate 1977-; contested (C): Blackburn 1970, N Cornwall 1974 Gen Elections; govr National Heart Hosp 1974-, memb Industrial Tribunal Panel for London 1974-, British chm European Union of Women 1978-82, National Women's vice-chm Cons Party 1978-82, UK rep on UN Status of Women Cmmn 1982-, memb London Electricity Board 1984-; dir Gateway Building Society 1987-; *Recreations* gardening, cooking, travel, historic buildings, family life; *Style—* The Rt Hon Lady Gardner of Parkes; House of Lords, London SW1 OPW

GARDNER-THORPE, Dr Christopher; s of Col Sir Ronald Gardner-Thorpe, GBE, TD, JP, qv, and Lady Hazel, *née* Dees; *b* 22 August 1941; *Educ* St Philips Sch London, Beaumont Coll Old Windsor Berks, St Thomas' Hosp Med Sch London (MB, BS), Univ of London (MD); *m* 1 April 1967 (m dis 1988), Sheelah, da of Dr Edward Irvine, of Exeter; 2 s (Damian, James), 3 da (Catherine, Anne, Helen); *Career* registrar in neurology: Wessex Neurological Centre Southampton Gen Hosp 1967-69, Gen Infirmary Leeds 1969-71, Special Centre for Epilepsy Bootham Park Hosp York 1969-71; sr registrar in neurology Newcastle Gen Hosp and Royal Victoria Infirmary Newcastle upon Tyne 1971-74, conslt neurologist SW Regnl Health Authy (duties Exeter and N Devon) 1974-, hon tutor in neurology Post Grad Med Sch Univ of Exeter 1983-; memb: Int League Against Epilepsy 1969-; fndr memb and hon tres SW Eng Neurosciences Assoc 1981, fndr memb S Eng Neurosciences Assoc; memb: Harveian Soc 1966-, SW Physicians Club 1974-, Devon and Exeter Med Soc 1974- (hon asst sec 1978-81, hon sec 1981-85), advsy ctee Northcott Devon Med Fndn; fndr hon med advsr Devon Sports Assoc for the Disabled 1976-, memb Northumbrian Pipers Soc 1976-; Order of St John 1980, HM Lt City of London 1981; Freeman City of London 1978, Liveryman Worshipful Co of Barbers 1980; FRSM 1968, FRCP 1985; *Books* James Parkinson 1755-1824 (1987), ed various books and papers on epilepsy and other neurological topics; *Recreations* music, travel, reading, photography, sailing, gardening; *Clubs* Starcross Yacht; *Style—* Dr Christopher Gardner-Thorpe; The Coach House, 1A College Rd, Exeter EX1 1TE (☎ 0392 433 941)

GARDNER-THORPE, Col Sir Ronald Laurence; GBE (1980), TD (1950) and 3 bars, JP (Inner London 1965, City of London 1969); s of Joseph Alfred Gardner, of Ulverston, Lancs, and Hannah Coulthurst, *née* Thorpe; *b* 13 May 1917; *Educ* St John's De La Salle Coll Southsea Hants, Univ of Padua; *m* 1938, Hazel Mary St George, Dame of Magistral Grace SMO Malta, da of Adrian Bernard Dees, of Norfolk; 1 s (Christopher); *Career* served Heavy Regt TA Hants (2 Lt 1939, Capt 1939, Maj 1940, Lt-Col 1944, Col 1960) Europe, Mediterranean, USA, cmd 5 Bn The Buffs 1956-60; fin memb Kent TA 1954-65; govr: St John's Coll Hants 1963 (dep chm of govrs 1976), St Joseph's Sch London 1966-76; memb Governing body Assoc Pub Schs 1963; alderman of the Ward of Bishopgate 1972; tstee: Utd Westminster Fndn 1975, The Buffs Royal East Kent Regt Museum 1976, Rowland Hill Benevolent Fund 1978, Morden Coll 1980, Mental Health Fndn 1981, Royal Fndn of Grey Coat Hosp 1982, Duke of Edinburgh's Award; vice pres BRCS 1978; pres: SSAFA Central London 1982, Friends of the Hosp of St John and St Elizabeth 1982, 25th Anniversary Appeal of the Duke of Edinburgh's Award; Sheriff City of London 1978, Admiral Port of London 1980, chllr City Univ 1980, Lord Mayor of London 1980-81, HM Lieut for the City of London 1980; chm Distressed Gentlefolk's Aid Assoc; memb cncl of the Magistrates Assoc, hon memb World Trade Centre; hon citizen Kansas City,

Baltimore, Norfolk Virginia, Cusco (Peru), State of Arizona; court memb: Worshipful Co of Painter-Stainers, Worshipful Co of Builders Merchants; Lloyds underwriter 1979; Hon DCL City Univ 1980, Hon DH Lewis Univ Chicago 1981; KStJ 1980 (OStJ 1979), kt SMOM 1982, KASG, kt Cdr Royal Order of the Daneborg (Denmark) 1960, kt Cdr Order of the Infante Henrique (Portugal) 1978, kt Cdr Order of Gorka Dakshina Bahu (Nepal) 1980, kt cdr Order of King Abdul Aziz (Saudi Arabia) 1981; *Clubs* Bishopsgate Ward, City Livery, Utd Wards, Royal Soc of St George, The Belfry, Variety (vice-pres), Anglo-Danish Soc (cncl); *Style*— Col Sir Ronald Gardner-Thorpe, GBE, TD, JP; 8 Cadogan Square, London SW1X 0JU (☎ 01 235 0413)

GAREL-JONES, (William Armand Thomas) Tristan; MP (C) Watford 1979-; s of Bernard Garel-Jones, of Madrid, and Meriel, *née* Williams; *b* 28 Feb 1941; *Educ* King's Sch Canterbury; *m* 1966, Catalina, da of Mariano Garrigues, of Madrid; 4 s, 1 da; *Career* pps to Barney Hayhoe 1981-82, asst whip 1982-83, lord cmmr to the Treasury 1983-86; vice-chamberlain of H M Household 1986-; *Recreations* collecting books; *Clubs* Beefsteak, Carlton, Club de Campo Madrid; *Style*— Tristan Garel-Jones, Esq, MP; House of Commons, London SW1A 0AA

GARFIELD, Leon; s of David Kalman Garfield (d 1951), of London, and Rose, *née* Blaustein (d 1964); *b* 14 July 1921; *Educ* Brighton GS; *m* 23 Oct 1948, Vivien, da of John Foster Alcock, OBE (d 1980); 1 da (Jane Angela b 1964); *Career* RAMC 1941-45; hosp biochemist until 1966; author; winner of: Guardian Award 1967, Carnegie Medal 1970, Whitbread Literary Award 1980; FRSL 1985; *Books* Jack Holborn (1964), Devil in The Fog (1966), Smith (1967), Black Jack (1968), The Boy and The Monkey (1968), Mr Corbett's Ghost (1969), The Drummer Boy (1970), The Strange Affair of Adelaide Harris (1971), The Ghost Downstairs (1972), Child O' War (1972), The Sound of Coaches (1974), The Prisoners of September (1975), The Pleasure Garden (1976), The House of Hanover (1976), The Confidence Man (1978), Bostock and Harris (1969), The Apprentices (1976-79), John Diamond (1980), The Mystery of Edwin Drood (by Dickens completed by Garfield in 1980), The House of Cards (1982), Guilt and Gingerbread (1984), Shakespeare Stories (1985), The December Rose (1986), The Empty Sleeve (1988), Blewcoat Boy (1988); with Edward Blishen: The God Beneath The Sea (1970), and The Golden Shaw (1973); Picture Books: Fair's Fair (1981), King Numrod's Tower (1982), The Writing on The Wall (1983), The King in The Garden (1984), The Wedding Ghost (1985); *Recreations* collecting Staffordshire China; *Clubs* Pen; *Style*— Leon Garfield, Esq; 59 Wood Lane, Highgate, London N6 5UD (☎ 01 340 5785); c/o John Johnson (Authors' Agent) Ltd, Clerkenwell House, 45/47 Clerkenwell Green, London EC1R 0HT (☎ 01 251 0125)

GARFIELD, Lewis Aubrey; s of John Garfield (d 1975), and Celia Garfield; *b* 11 June 1934; *Educ* Secondary Modern; *m* 28 April 1972, Agnes Maria, da of Prof John Morrison, of Great Shelford, Cambs; 1 s (Neill David b 1977), 1 da (Emma Rose b 1980); *Career* chm: Garfield Lewis Ltd and subsidiaries, Aluminium Stockholders Assoc; *Recreations* hunting, racing, tennis; *Clubs* Reform, Lansdowne; *Style*— Lewis A Garfield, Esq; The Hall, Thorpe Mandeville, Northamptonshire; PO Box 21, Banbury, Oxon (☎ 0295 710001, telex 837501, fax 0295 712201)

GARFIT, Thomas Noel Cheney; s of Edward Christopher Cheney Garfit (d 1982), of Louth, Lincolnshire, and Dorothy Marguerite, *née* Morris (d 1978); *b* 27 Feb 1925; *Educ* Bryanston, Trinity Coll Cambridge (BA); *m* 3 May 1958, Elizabeth Mary, da of Lt-Col John Wilton Watts (d 1984), of Warminster, Wilts; 2 da (Frances Jane b 1962, Emma Anne b 1965); *Career* RA 1944-47 (cmmnd 1945); HMOCS N Rhodesia 1950-66, dist offr and private sec to the govr 1956-57; Oil & Chemical Plant Constructors' Assoc 1966- (dir 1975-); *Clubs* Royal Cwlth Soc; *Style*— Thomas N C Garfit, Esq; Meadows Court, Fir Tree Close, Esher, Surrey KT10 9DS (☎ 0372 66061); 87 Regent St, London W1R 7HF (☎ 01 734 5246)

GARFITT, His Hon Judge Alan; s of Rush Garfitt and Florence Garfitt; *b* 20 Dec 1920; *Educ* King Edward VII GS King's Lynn, Metropolitan Coll, Inns of Court Sch of Law (LLB); *m* 1, 1941, Muriel Ada Jaggers; 1 s, 1 da; m 2, 1973, Ivie Maud Hudson; m 3, 1978, Rosemary Lazell; 1 s, 1 da; *Career* barrister Lincoln's Inn 1948, circuit judge 1977-, judge Cambridge County Court and Wisbech Crown Court 1978-; memb Assoc of British Riding Schs 1960- (pres 1977-); *Style*— His Hon Judge Garfitt; Leap House, Barcham Rd, Soham, Ely, Cambs

GARFORTH-BLES, Michael William; s of Capt George Garforth-Bles, of Knutsford and London (d 1954; Hon Consul for The Netherlands, Capt MI5 in WWI, gs of David Bles, famous Dutch painter, and Helen Kathleen (d 1969), da of Sir William Garforth; *b* 28 July 1913; *Educ* Rugby; *m* 29 Nov 1947, Pamela Joan, da of Maj Nigel Fairholt Paton, of Covehithe, Suffolk (d 1945); 2 s (Robert, b 1949, Hugh b 1951), 1 da (Jill b 1952); *Career* Maj Royal Signals WWII; FCA; *Recreations* hunting, gardening; *Clubs* English Speaking Union, Herts 100; *Style*— Michael Garforth-Bles, Esq; Darfield, Berkhamsted, Herts (☎ 86 5211)

GARLAND, Nicholas Withycombe; s of Thomas Ownswoth Garland, and Margaret, *née* Withycombe; *b* 1 Sept 1935; *Educ* Rongotai Coll NZ, Slade Sch Fine Art; *m* 1, 1964 (m dis 1968), Harriet Crittall; m 2, 19 Dec 1969, Caroline Beatrice, da of Sir Peter Medawar; 3 s (Timothy William b 1957, Alexander Medawar b 1970, Theodore Nicholas b 1972), 1 da (Emily b 1964); *Career* political cartoonist: Daily Telegraph 1966-1986, The Independent 1986-; *Style*— Nicholas Garland, Esq; 27 Heath Hurst Rd, London NW3 2RU (☎ 01 435 3808); The Independent, 40 City Rd, London EC1 (☎ 01 253 1222)

GARLAND, Patrick; s of Capt Ewart Garland, DFC, RFC (d 1985), of Brockenhurst Hants, and Rosalind (d 1984), da of Herbert Granville Fell; *b* 10 April 1935; *Educ* St Mary's Coll Southampton, St Edmund Hall Oxford (MA); *m* 1980, Alexandra Bastedo; *Career* artistic dir Festival Theatre Chichester 1981-85; prodr: Fanfare for Europe at Covent Garden 1975, Fanfare for Elizabeth (for HM the Queen's 60 birthday) 1986, Celebration of a Broadcaster Westminster Abbey 1987; interviews on television: Laurence Olivier 1987, Rex Harrison 1987; dir: Brief Lives, Forty Years On, Billy, Snow Goose (film), The Doll's House (film); *Books* Wings of the Morning (1988); *Recreations* idling in Corsica; *Clubs* Garrick; *Style*— Patrick Garland, Esq

GARLAND, Hon Mr Justice; Sir Patrick Neville; s of Frank Neville Garland (d 1984), and Marjorie, *née* Lewis (d 1972); *b* 22 July 1929; *Educ* Uppingham, Sidney Sussex Coll Cambridge (MA, LLM); *m* 1955, Jane Elizabeth, da of Harold John Bird (d 1970), of Troston, Suffolk; 2 s, 1 da; *Career* barr Middle Temple 1953, asst rec Norwich 1971, Crown Court Ct rec 1972, QC 1972, bencher Middle Temple 1979, dep High Ct judge 1981, High Ct judge Queen's Bench 1985; chm Official Referees' Bar Assoc of Probation Ctees 1986-, memb Parole Bd 1988-; kt 1985; *Recreations* gardening, shooting, industl archaeology; *Clubs* Cumberland Lawn Tennis, Norfolk; *Style*— Hon Mr Justice Garland; 9 Ranulf Rd, London NW2; 23 Grove Rd, Norwich; c/o Royal Courts of Justice, Strand, London WC2

GARLAND, Dr Peter Bryan; s of Frederick George Garland (d 1978), and Molly Kate, *née* Jones; *b* 31 Jan 1934; *Educ* Hardye's Sch Dorchester, Downing Coll Cambridge, Kings Coll Hosp London (MA, MB BChir, PhD); *m* 7 Feb 1959, Ann, da of Arthur Apseley Bathurst (d 1951); 1 s (James b 1964), 2 da (Joanna b 1961, Clare b 1962); *Career* lectr in biochemistry Bristol Univ 1964-68 (reader 1969-70), prof of biochemistry Dundee Univ 1970-84, princ scientist and head of biosciences Unilever Research Colworth House Laboratory 1984-87; memb MRC 1980-84 (chm cell biology disorders bd 1980-82), memb scientific policy ctee Cancer Res Campaign 1985-, chm Cancer Res Campaign Technol Ltd 1988-; visiting prof Johnson Res Fndn Philadelphia 1967-69, visiting fell Aust Nat Univ Canberra 1983; Colworth Medal of the Biochemical Society 1970; memb EMBO 1981, FRSE 1977; author of numerous original articles on biochemistry and biophysics; *Recreations* sport (Athletics Blue Cambridge 1954-55), skiing, windsurfing, sailing; *Style*— Dr Peter B Garland; Hope Cottage, Sunnyway, Bosham, W Wussex (☎ 0243 572524); Amersham Int plc, Pollards Wood, Nightingales Lane, Chalfont St Giles, Bucks HP8 4SP (☎ 02404 4400)

GARLAND, Hon Sir (Ransley) Victor; KBE (1981); s of Idris Victor Garland; *b* 5 May 1934; *Educ* Hale Sch W Australia Univ (BA); *m* 1960, Lynette May Jamieson; 2 s, 1 da; *Career* memb House Reps (Lib) for Curtin W Aust 1969-81, Aust min Supply 1971-72, opposition chief whip 1974-75, chm Expenditure Ctee 1975-77; min: Special Trade Rep 1977-79, Business and Consumer Affairs 1979-81; Aust high cmmr London 1981-83, dir Prudential Corpn plc 1984-; dep chm South Bank Bd; FCA; *Clubs* White's, Weld (Australia); *Style*— Hon Sir Victor Garland, KBE; Wilton Place, Knightsbridge, London SW1

GARLAND, William John Harley; s of Patrick John Garland, of Pitmarston Ct, Moseley, Birmingham, and Ruth, *née* Massey; *b* 14 Jan 1942; *Educ* Bloxham Sch, Univ of Aston (BSc); *m* 1 Oct 1966, Carol Ann, da of Eric Arley Whitehouse (d 1982), of Birmingham Rd, Dudley, W Midlands; 2 s (Simon b 1968, Edward b 1972), 1 da (Catherine b 1978); *Career* chm and co-fndr Anglo-Holt Gp Inc 1969; former pres BEC Birmingham, cncl memb Birmingham Chamber of Indust and Commerce; MICE 1971; *Recreations* the English countryside, model steam railways, antiques; *Style*— William Garland, Esq; Parkdale, 594 Warwick Rd, Solihull B91 1AD (☎ 021 705 4062); Anglo-Holt Gp Ltd, 290 High St, W Bromwich, W Midlands B70 8EN (☎ 021 525 6717, fax 021 553 4701)

GARLICK, Sir John; KCB (1976), CB (1973); s of late Charles Garlick; *b* 17 May 1921; *Educ* Westcliff HS Essex, London Univ (BSc); *m* 1945, Frances Esther, da of late Edward Stanley Munday; 3 da; *Career* entered Miny of Tport 1948, private sec to Ernest Marples 1959-60, second perm sec Cabinet Off 1974-77, perm sec Dept Environment 1978-81; dir Abbey National Bldg Soc 1981-; memb London Docklands Devpt Corpn 1981-; *Style*— Sir John Garlick, KCB, CB; 16 Astons Rd, Moor Park, Northwood, Middx (☎ 092 74 24628)

GARLICK, Dr Kenneth John; s of David Ernest Garlick (d 1947), of Glastonbury, and Annie, *née* Hallifax (d 1962); *b* 1 Oct 1916; *Educ* Elmhurst GS, Balliol Coll Oxford (MA), Courtauld Inst of Art, Univ of London; *Career* WWII RAF Signals served in UK, N Africa, Italy demobbed 1946 Flt-Lt; lectr art history and librarian Bath Acad of Art 1946-48, fine art dept Br Cncl London 1948, asst keeper City Art Gallery Birmingham 1948-50, sr lectr Barber Inst of Fine Arts Univ of Birmingham 1950-68 (PhD 1960), keeper of Western Art Ashmolean Museum Oxford Univ 1968-84; govr Royal Shakespeare Theatre Stratford Upon Avon, ctee memb Oxford Preservation Tst, memb Cncl of Friends & Ashmolean, emeritus fell Balliol Coll 1984- (fell 1968-84); FMA, FSA, FRSA; *Books* Sir Thomas Lawrence (1954), Lawrence Catalogue Raisonné (1964), ed The Farington Dairy Vol I IV (with Angus MacIntyre, 1977-78); *Recreations* travel in France, Italy, music; *Clubs* Reform; *Style*— Dr Kenneth Garlick; 39 Hawkswell House, Hawkswell Gdns, Oxford OX2 7EX (☎ 0865 53 731)

GARMOYLE, Viscount; Simon Dallas Cairns; s and h of 5 Earl Cairns; *b* 27 May 1939; *Educ* Eton, Trinity Coll Cambridge; *m* 4 Feb 1964, Amanda Mary, o da of late Maj Edgar Fitzgerald Heathcoat-Amory, RA; 3 s (Hon Hugh Sebastian, Hon David Patrick b 1967, Hon Alistair Benedict b 1969); *Heir* s, Hon Hugh Sebastian Cairns b 26 March 1965; *Career* jt chm S G Warburg & Co Ltd, jt vice chm Mercury Securities 1987, dir S G Warburg Gp plc; formerly with J A Scrimgeour; chm Voluntary Servs Overseas 1981; *Clubs* Turf; *Style*— Viscount Garmoyle; Bole Hyde Manor, Allington, Chippenham, Wilts (☎ 0249 652105)

GARNELL, Lady Caroline Louise; *née* Bridgeman; yr da of 6 Earl of Bradford (d 1981); *b* 18 April 1952; *Educ* Benenden; *m* 1974, Brian Martin Garnell; 1 s (Thomas), 1 da (Tara); *Style*— Lady Caroline Garnell; 2 Cranley Place, London SW7

GARNER, Alan; s of Colin Garner (d 1983), of Cheshire, and Marjorie, *née* Greenwood Stuart; *b* 17 Oct 1934; *Educ* Manchester GS, Magdalen Coll Oxford; *m* 1, 1956, Ann, da of Harry Cook (d 1976), of Oxford; 1 s (Adam), 2 da (Ellen, Katharine); m 2, 1972, Griselda, da of Paul Greaves (d 1986), of Cheshire; 1 s (Joseph b 1973), 1 da (Elizabeth b 1975); *Career* Mil Serv Lt RA; author; *plays*: Holly from the Bongs (1965), Lamadload (1978), Lurga Lom (1980), To Kill a King (1980), Sally Water (1982), The Keeper (1983); *dance drama*: The Green Mist (1970); *libretti*: The Bellybag (1971), Potter Thompson (1972); *films*: The Owl Service (1969), Red Shift (1978), Places and Things (1978), Images (1981, First Prize Chicago Int Film Festival); *Books* The Weirdstone of Brisingamen (1960), The Moon of Gomrath (1963), Elidor (1965), Holly from the Bongs (1966), The Old Man of Mow (1967), The Owl Service (1967, Library Assoc Carnegie Medal 1967; Guardian Award 1968) The Hamish Hamilton Book of Goblins (1969), Red Shift (1973), The Breadhorse (1975), The Guizer (1975), The Stone Book (1976), Tom Fobble's Day (1977), Granny Reardun (1977), The Aimer Gate (1978), Fairy Tales of Gold (1979), The Lad of the Gad (1980), A Book of British Fairy Tales (1984), A Bag of Moonshine (1986); *Recreations* work; *Clubs* The Portico Library; *Style*— Alan Garner, Esq; Blackden, Holmes Chapel, Cheshire CW4 8BY

GARNER, Anthony James; s of Lt Cdr Frederick Ernest Garner, DSC, RN (d 1976), of Carysfort, Malford Grove, Snaresbrook, Essex, and Sunshine, The Parade, Birchington-on-Sea, Kent, and Gertrude Eleanor, *née* Penwarden (d 1988); *b* 2 May 1925; *Educ* Uppingham, Hertford Coll Oxford (MA); *m* 16 April 1955, Catherine, da of William Talbot (d 1926), of 14 King St, Ramsgate; 2 s (Anthony Frederick John b 1956, William Talbot b 1970), 3 da (Elizabeth Catherine b 1957, Julia Nonie (Mrs

Bouverat) b 1962, Mary Ann Frances b 1966); *Career* WWII volunteered RNVR 1943; Ordinary Seaman: HMS Ganges 1943, HMS Dauntless 1944, HMS King Alfred 1944; Midshipman 1944, Temp Actg Sub Lt 1944, HMS Woolston 1945; articled clerk Reid Sharman & Co 1947-51, admitted slr 1951, Freshfields 1951-53, Wray Smith Paterson & Co 1954, legal asst to Official Slr the Church Cmmrs 1954, conveyancing slr ICI plc 1957-81, dir Levancroft Ltd 1978-, underwriting memb Lloyds 1964-; hon slr 625 Sqdn RAF Assoc; memb numerous orgns and socs incl: Uppingham Assoc and School Soc, Chelsea Cons Assoc, Huguenot Soc, CLA, Friends of Bodleian; Freeman City of London, Memb Worshipful Co of Loriners; memb Law Soc 1951; *Recreations* bibliophile, gardening, swimming, music; *Clubs* Boodle's Hurlingham, St Stephen's Constitutional, Royal Temple YC, City Livery, Canning (Oxford); *Style*— Anthony Garner, Esq; 7 Iverna Ct, Kensington, London W8 6TY (☎ 01 937 1313), The Manor House, Great Mongeham, Deal, Kent CT14 9LR

GARNER, Sir Anthony Stuart; s of Edward Henry Garner, MC (d 1953), and Dorothy May Garner; *b* 28 Jan 1927; *Educ* Liverpool Coll; *m* 1967, Shirley Doris, da of William Henry Taylor (d 1963), of East Grinstead; 2 s; *Career* Grenadier Gds 1945-48; Cons agent Halifax 1951-56, nat organising sec of Young Cons Movement 1956-61, Cons Central Off agent: London area 1961-64, Western area 1964-66, NW area 1966-77; dir of orgn Cons Central Off 1976-88, parly consit 1988-; kt 1984; *Recreations* boating, theatre; *Clubs* Carlton, St Stephen's; *Style*— Sir Anthony Garner; 1 Blomfield Rd, London W9 (☎ 01 286 5972)

GARNER, Hon Christopher John Saville; s of Baron Garner, GCMG (d 1983; Life Peer); *b* 28 Feb 1939; *Educ* Highgate, Jesus Coll Cambridge; *m* 6 April 1962, Janet Mary, o da of Maj Harold Vaughan Rees, of Winnersham, Wokingham, Berks; 1 s; *Career* British Council officer 1963-71, asst rep Freetown Sierra Leone 1964-67, Staff Recruitment Dept British Council London 1967-70, asst rep Athens Greece 1970-71; lectr College of Technology Bournemouth 1971; *Style*— Hon Christopher Garner

GARNER, Frank Harold; s of (Bertie) Harold Garner (d 1974), of Culverton Farm, Princes Risborough, Bucks, and (Gertrude) May, *née* Chapman (d 1918); *b* 4 Dec 1904; *Educ* Swindon Secondary Sch, Cambridge Univ (MA), Oxford Univ (MA), Minnesota USA (MSc); *m* 5 Aug 1929, Hilda May (d 1988), da of Arthur Sheppard (d 1961), of Swindon; 1 da (Frances May b 1939); *Career* Univ lectr in agric 1927-39; War Agric Ctee: Cambridge 1939-40, Suffolk 1940-44; gen Mangr F Hiam Ltd Cambridge 1944-58, princ Royal Agric Coll Cirencester 1958-71, ed Modern Br Farming Systems 1972; rowing: Fitzwilliam first Eight 1922-24, New Coll Oxford first Eight 1925; Worshipful Master Masonic Lodges: Cambridge, Cirencester, Gloucester; past chm: NFU Co Cambridgeshire and Bucks, Lacey Green Cons, Farmers Club London, Oxford Farming Con, Br Grassland Soc, Animal Prodn Soc; memb PCC Lacey Green Princes Risborough; Master Worshipful Co of Farmers London 1971-72; FRAgS England; *Books* Feeding Farm Animals (1940), Farmers Animals (1942), Cattle of Britain (1943), British Dairy Farming (1946); *Recreations* rowing, shooting; *Clubs* Farmers; *Style*— Frank Garner, Esq; Brooklyn, 29 Park St, Princes Risborough, Bucks (☎ 084 44 5402); Culverton Farm, Princes Risborough, Bucks

GARNER, Frederic Francis; CMG (1959); o s of Frank Hastings Garner (d 1920), of Santa Cruz, Tenerife; *b* 9 July 1910; *Educ* Rugby, Worcester Coll Oxford; *m* 1946, Muriel, da of Alfred John Merrick, of New Malden, Surrey; *Career* entered Br Consular Serv China 1932, served various consular posts China and elsewhere; ambass Phnom Penh 1958-61, ambass Costa Rica 1961-68, ret 1968; *Style*— Frederic Garner, Esq, CMG; The Grand Hotel, Esplanade, St Helier, Jersey, CI

GARNER, Frederick Leonard; s of Leonard Frank Garner (d 1968), and Florence Emily Garner; *b* 7 April 1920; *Educ* Sutton Co Sch; *m* 1953, Giovanna Maria, da of Pietro Anzani (d 1975), of Milan, Italy; *Career* pres Pearl Assurance Co 1983-87 (dir 1971-75, dep chm 1975-77, chm 1977-83), pres Pearl Group plc 1986-; *Clubs* RAC; *Style*— Frederick Garner, Esq; 98 Tudor Ave, Worcester Park, Surrey KT4 8TU (☎ 01 337 3313)

GARNER, Lady; Hilda Annie; da of late John E Green, of Redhill; *b* 9 August 1898; *m* 1921, Sir Harry Mason Garner, KBE, CB, (d 1977); 1 s, 1 da; *Style*— Lady Garner; Montford, 8 Grange Rd, Camberley, Surrey GU15 2DH (☎ 0276 22763)

GARNER, Hon Joseph Jonathan; s of Baron Garner, GCMG (d 1983, Life Peer); *b* 29 Dec 1940; *Educ* Highgate, Jesus Coll Cambridge; *m* 3 May 1969, Brigitte, da of Louis Pittet, of Sens, France; 1 s; *Style*— The Hon Joseph Garner; 44 Holmewood Rd, SW2

GARNER, His Hon Judge Michael Scott; s of William Garner (d 1968), and Doris Mary, *née* Scott (d 1958); *b* 10 April 1939; *Educ* Huddersfield Coll, Manchester Univ (LLB); *m* 1, 30 July 1964, Sheila Margaret (d 1981), da of Edward Frederick Garland (d 1973); 1 s (John William Scott b 1968), 1 da (Caroline Louise b 1966); m 2, 12 Aug 1982, Margaret Anne, da of Philip Senior (d 1985); *Career* admitted slr 1965, asst rec 1978, rec 1985-88, circuit judge 1988-; pres Huddersfield Incorporated Law Soc 1985-86; *Recreations* walking, motoring; *Style*— His Hon Judge Michael Garner; 22 Longley Rd, Almondbury, Huddersfield HD5 8JL

GARNER, Peter Frederick; s of Lt Cdr Frederick Ernest Garner, DSC, RN, and Gertrude Eleanor, *née* Penwarden; *b* 24 Feb 1936; *Educ* Uppingham; *m* 14 Oct 1961, (Elizabeth) Wendy, da of Benjamin John Jones, of Lampeter, Dyfed; 2 s (Robert Charles b 1964, Julian Peter b 1966); *Career* bisomess devpt cnslt Minet Hldgs plc 1975-89; memb: Minet Fellowship, Minet Employees Charitable Tst; memb: Nat Cncl Christian Standards in Soc, Nat Congress for Christians in the World of Work, Just Working Fellowship in the City (Indust Year 1986 project); speaks on christian standards in business mgmnt; Anglian churchman (lay preacher and Evangelist); Freeman City of London, Liveryman Worshipful Co Loriners; MBIM; *Recreations* golf, sailing, conversation, gardening; *Style*— Peter Garner, Esq; Flat B, 50 Old Rd, Frinton-on-Sea, Essex CO13 9BZ (☎ 02556 73117); Minet House, 100 Leman St, London E1 8 HG (☎ 01 481 0707, fax 01 488 9786, telex 8813901)

GARNER, Stephen; s of Arthur Garner (d 1964), of Pedley Hill, Adlington, nr Macclesfield, Ches, and Madeline, *née* Turner; *b* 4 April 1901; *Educ* Ryleys Sch Cheshire, Univ of Liverpool (BARCH, MCD); *Career* Nat Serv RN 1949-50, Serv HMS Illustrious; architect, formed Garner Preston & Strebel 1960; awards: Dumbarton central area redevpt (first prize), town square and riverfront Dumbarton (civic tst), St Peter's Church Dumbarton (RIBA); ctee memb Housing Partnership Ltd, memb Richmond Soc; *Recreations* travel, water colour painting, poetry & music; *Style*— Stephen Garner, Esq; 1A Limpsfield Ave, Wimbledon, London SW19 6DL (☎ 01 788 6477); Garner, Preston & Strebel, 14 The Green, Richmond, Surrey 1PX (☎ 01 940 8244, fax 01 948 0367)

GARNETT, Hon Mrs (Anne Jeanetta Essex); *née* Cholmondeley; yr da of 4 Baron Delamere (d 1979); *b* 2 Sept 1927; *m* 30 Nov 1951, Conrad Peter Almeric Garnett, s of Dr Donald Goddard Garnett, of Maresfield, E Sussex; 1 s (and 1 s decd 1981); *Style*— Hon Mrs Garnett; Half Acre, Maresfield, Sussex TN22 2HJ

GARNETT, Hon Mrs; Hon Dariel; *née* Rawlinson; 2 da of Baron Rawlinson of Ewell, QC, by his 1 w; *b* 1943; *m* 1965, Harry Garnett; 2 da; *Style*— Hon Mrs Garnett; 32 Northumberland Place, London W2

GARNETT, Gerald Archer; s of Leslie Pearson Garnett (d 1985), of Westcliff-on-sea, Essex, and Betty Gladys, *née* Archer; *b* 1 Mar 1937; *Educ* Framlingham Coll Suffolk, Insead Fountainbleau; *m* 24 Feb 1973, Sheila Mary, da of Col David Bruce Ronald, CBE, of West Byfleet, Surrey; 1 s (Rupert b 13 Feb 1978), 1 da (Clare b 20 May 1980); *Career* RAF 1955-57; sec Ranks Hovis McDougall plc 1979 - (asst sec 1971-79); Freeman City of London, Liveryman Worshipful Co of Armourers and Brasiers; FCIS; *Recreations* gardening, squash; *Clubs* Naval and Military; *Style*— Gerald Garnett, Esq; Southbury Farmhouse, Ruscombe, Berks (☎ 0739 340 132); Ranks Hovis McDougall plc, RHM Centre, Windsor, Berks (☎ 0753 857123, fax 0753 846537, telex 847314)

GARNETT, (William) John Poulton Maxwell; CBE (1970); s of Dr (James Clerk) Maxwell Garnett, CBE (d 1958), and Margaret Lucy Poulton; *b* 6 August 1921; *Educ* Rugby, Kent Sch (USA), Trinity Coll Cambridge; *m* 1, 1943 (m dis), Barbara, da of Dr Rex Rutherford-Smith; 2 s, 2 da (*see* Bottomley, Virginia, MP); m 2, 3 April 1985, Julia Cleverdon, *qv*; 1 da (Victoria b 1987); *Career* with ICI 1947-62, former dep chm UNA; dir: Spencer Stuart and Assocs Mgmnt Consits (chm 1979-81), Industl Soc; chm West Lambeth Health Authy; *Style*— John Garnett, Esq; 3 Carlton House Terrace, London SW1

GARNETT, Hon Mrs (Sylvia Jane); da of Baron Swann (Life Peer); *b* 1 April 1947; *Educ* St Andrews Univ (BSc); *m* 1970, Christopher William Maxwell Garnett; 1 s, 2 da; *Style*— Hon Mrs Garnett; 40 Caledonia Place, Clifton, Bristol 8

GARNETT-ORME, Ion; CBE (1983); er s of George Hunter Garnett-Orme (d 1957), and Alice Richmond (d 1933), da of Sir William Richmond Brown, 2nd Bt; *b* 23 Jan 1910; *Educ* Eton, Magdalene Coll Cambridge; *m* 23 Feb 1946, Katharine Clifton, 2 da of Brig-Gen Howard Clifton Brown (d 1946); *Career* served WWII Welsh Gds; dir: Brown Shipley Hldgs Ltd 1946-81 (chm 1963-75), United States Debenture Corpn Ltd 1951-81 (chm 1958-78), London-Scottish American Tst 1951- (chm 1957), Avon Rubber 1956-66, Ellerman Lines Ltd 1971-75; vice pres: St Dunstans 1983- (memb cncl 1958-83, chm 1975-83); *Clubs* Carlton; *Style*— Ion Garnett-Orme, Esq, CBE; Cheriton Cottage, Cheriton, nr Alresford, Hants

GARNHAM, Dr John Claude; s of Percy Cyril Claude Garnham, CMG, of Southernwood, Farnham Common, Bucks, and Esther Long, *née* Price; *b* 7 May 1932; *Educ* Merchant Taylor's, Univ of Paris (Dip de CF), Univ of London (MB BS), Med Coll of St Barts Hosp London (MRCS, LRCP); *m* 11 Dec 1954, Frances Joan, da of Frank Kirkup (d 1951); 3 s (Timothy Claude b 1956, Frank Jasper b 1959, Simon Philip b 1960), 1 da (Francesca b 1971); *Career* med practice 1957-65, clinical res 1965-, vice-pres med affrs Abbott Laboratories USA 1970-71, private med practice 1980-; chm Chiltern Int Ltd Barbican Med plc, med dir Haventern Laboratories Ltd, dir Cardiac Res Wexham Park Hosp Slough; Freeman City of London, ct memb Worhsipful Co of Farriers; fell Royal Soc of Tropical Med and Ayciene, FRSM, fell Med Soc of London, fell Amercian Soc of Clinical Pharmacology & Therapeutics; memb: BMA, Br Soc of Pharmacology; *Recreations* fishing, clay pigeon shooting, bridge, golf, tennis, riding; *Clubs* Guards Polo, City Livery; *Style*— Dr John Garnham; Kynance, Manor Rd, Penn, Bucks HP10 8JB (☎ 0494 812 177); Barbican Medical plc, 3 White Lyon Ct, Barbican, London EC1 (☎ 01 588 3146)

GARNHAM, Roy Richard; s of Alfred Joseph Garnham, of Gilbey Hse, Hackney, London, and Elizabeth Louise, *née* Stannard (d 1986); *b* 7 July 1938; *Educ* Parmiters GS London; *m* 10 Feb 1962, Sylvia, da of Joseph Derwent, of Oliver Rd, Shenfield, Essex; 3 s (Ian Roy Cuckow b 8 Aug 1966, Matthew Richard b 5 Nov 1968, Peter Joseph b 9 June 1971); *Career* princ for exchange dealer Bank of London & S America London 1955-73, exec dir London & Continental Bankers London 1973-77; gen mangr: Euro Arab Bank Bahrain 1977-80, DG Bank London 1980-; non-exec dir Product Fin Ltd 1985-; memb: Overseas Bankers Club, Forex Club of London, Lombard Assoc, For Banks Assoc; *Recreations* gardening, golf; *Clubs* Warley Park GC; *Style*— Roy Garnham, Esq; Wellmead, Fryerning La, Ingatestone, Essex (☎ 0277 353 705); DG Bank, 10 Aldersgate, London, EC1A 4XX (☎ 01 726 6791, telex 886647)

GARNIER, Edward Henry; s of Col William d'Arcy Garnier, RA, and Hon Mrs Garnier, (*née* Hon Lavender Hyacinth de Grey), *qv*; *b* 26 Oct 1952; *Educ* Wellington, Jesus Coll Oxford (BA, MA); *m* 17 April 1982, Anna Caroline, da of Michael James Mellows (d 1974), of Belton House, Rutland; 1 s (George b 1986), 1 da (Eleanor b 1983); *Career* barr Middle Temple 1976; vice-pres Hemsworth (C) Assoc; contested: Hemsworth W Yorks in 1987 gen election, Tooting in 1986 ILEA election, Wandsworth Borough Cncl by-election 1984; govr Graveney Sch Tooting; *Books* contrib to Halsbury's Laws of England (4 edn); *Recreations* cricket, shooting, opera; *Clubs* United and Cecil; *Style*— Edward Garnier, Esq; 70 Streathbourne Rd, London SW17 (☎ 01 767 4961); Chambers, 1 Brick Ct, Temple, London EC4Y 9BY (☎ 01 353 8845, fax 01 583 9144)

GARNIER, Maj Edward Hethersett Charles; MC (1942); s of Edward Thomas Garnier (d 1924), and Dorothy Maude, *née* Hemsworth (d 1962); *b* 7 Mar 1920; *Educ* Eton, RMC, Sandhurst; *m* 4 July 1946, Alice Mary, da of Charles Henry Hale Monro (d 1966); 2 s (Edward b 1948, Simon b 1950); *Career* cmmnd The Rifle Bde 1939, A/Maj 1942, Sub/Maj 1952, 1 Bn The Rifle Bde served UK, M East, Italy 1939-44; (despatches 1941 and 1943); instr 165 OTU 1944, Staff Coll (psc)1944-45, BM 184 Inf Bde 1945, DAQMG Br troops Siam 1945-47, DAA and QMG 56 Arm'd Div 1949-51, DAA and QMG 29 Bde Korea 1953-54, MA to C-in-C FARELF 1956-57, DAA and QMG 20 Armd Bde 1959-61; fruit farmer 1968-; chm and vice chm Shropham Parish Cncl 1970-, churchwarden Shropham Church 1968-, patron 5 livings, patronage bd for 8 livings, chm Hockham and Wretham Br Legion 1976-, memb Breckland DC 1970-78, area pres St John Amb Bde 1980-84 (area cmmnr 1972-80), gen cmmnr Income Tax 1976-; OStJ; *Recreations* shooting, gardening; *Clubs* Army and Navy, I Zingazi, Free Foresters; *Style*— Maj Edward Garnier, MC; Shrophan House, Attleborough, Norfolk (☎ 095 382 241)

GARNIER, Rear Adm John; CBE (1982), LVO (1965); s of Rev Thomas Vernon

Garnier (d 1939), and Helen David, *née* Stenhouse, of Stour View, The Bridge, Sturminster, Newton, Dorset; *b* 10 Mar 1934; *Educ* Berkhamsted Sch, Britannia Royal Naval Coll; *m* 30 Dec 1966, Joanna Jane (Dodie), da of Alan Cadbury, of Haffield, Ledbury, Herefords; 2 s (Thomas b 1968, William b 1970), 1 da (Louisa b 1972); *Career* joined RN 1950, served in HM Yacht Britannia 1956-67, HMS Tyne 1956, qualified navigation specialist 1959; naval equerry to HM The Queen 1962-65, Cdr HMS Dundas 1968-69, directorate of Naval Ops and Trade 1969-71, Cdr HMS Minerva 1972-73, Def Policy Staff 1973-75, exec offr HMS Intrepid 1976, asst dir Naval Manpower Planning 1976-78, RCDS 1979, Cdr HMS London 1980-81; dir Naval Ops and Trade 1982-84, Cdr Amphibious Warfare 1985, flag offr Royal yachts 1985-; fell The Institute of Linguists (FIL) 1965; younger bro of Trinity House 1974; Freeman City of London 1982; govr of Sherborne Sch for Girls 1985-; *Recreations* sailing, gardening, opera, computers; *Style—* Rear Adm John Garnier, CBE, LVO; Flag Officer Royal Yachts, HM Yacht Britannia, BFPO Ships

GARNIER, Hon Mrs; Hon Lavender Hyacinth; *née* de Grey; el da of Lt-Col 8 Baron Walsingham, DSO, OBE, JP, DL (d 1965), and Hyacinth Lambart, *née* Bouwens 9d 1968); *b* 14 Oct 1923; *m* 9 April 1946, Col William d'Arcy Garnier, RA, yst s of Brig Alan Parry Garnier, CB, MBE, MC (whose paternal gf was Very Rev Thomas Garnier, fell of All Souls and successively dean of Lincoln and of Ripon, while the Brig's paternal grandmother was Lady Caroline Keppel, yst da of 4th Earl of Albemarle; the Dean was eighth in descent from Guillemin Garnier, of Joussecourt in the Champagne area of France and Seigneur du Tron, who flourished in sixteenth century); 3 s, 1 da; *Career* served WWII First Aid Nursing Yeo N Africa, Italy, India, Ceylon; *Style—* Hon Mrs Garnier; College Farm, Thompson, Thetford, Norfolk (☎ 095 383 318)

GARNIER, Peter; s of Geoffrey Sneyd Garnier (d 1970), and Jessie Caroline Dunbar Garnier (d 1966); *b* 3 Sept 1918; *Educ* Cheltenham Coll Junior, Charterhouse, Kings Coll London Univ; *m* 1, 21 Nov 1944 (m dis 1951), June Patricia, da of Sqdn Ldr L J St George Bayly (ka WWI); 1 da (Rowan Patricia b 1946); m 2, 16 June 1951, Patricia Elizabeth, da of A P Dowden (d 1986), of Bucks; 1 s (Mark Robery Timothy b 1963); *Career* served RN WWII, Lt MTBs E and S Coast England, wounded 1942; joined Autocar Magazine 1950 (art ed, sports ed, dep ed and ed until 1975), managing ed and special publications sec IPC Transport Press (ret 1981); sec and hon tres Grand Prix Driver Assoc 1960-67, chm Guild of Motoring Writes 1970 and 1971; Liveryman Worshipful Co of Coachmakers and Coach Harness Makers (chm ctee 1975-76); memb RNLI (chm Penlee Station branch); co-driver with Stirling Moss 1957 Tour de France, competed as memb Br Moto Corpn Factory Team 1958-60 (Austin Healy cars); *Books* 16 on The Grid, The Art of Gordon Crosby, Goodwood; *Recreations* sailing, model engineering, photography; *Clubs* British Racing Drivers' (assoc memb), Royal Naval Sailing Assoc; *Style—* Peter Garnier, Esq; Orchard Cottage, Newlyn, Penzance, Cornwall TR18 5EB (☎ 0736 68737)

GARNIER, Thomas Stenhouse (Tom); s of Rev Thomas Vernon Garnier, OBE (d 1939), and Helen, *née* Stenhouse (later Mrs Davis); *b* 26 Oct 1932; *Educ* Berkhamsted Sch, Trinity Coll Oxford (MA); *m* 11 Feb 1961, Heather Colquhoun, da of James Grant (d 1981); 2 s (Edward b 20 May 1966, James b 27 March 1981), 2 da (Rachel b 20 May 1968, Elisabeth b 7 Dec 1977); *Career* Kalamazoo plc: asst overseas sales mangr 1956-63, asst to md 1963-66, personnel divnl mangr 1966-68, dir i/c personnel and printing 1968-72, dir i/c sales and personnel 1972-74, dep md 1974-77, gp md 1977-85, gp chm 1985-; chm: Kalamazoo Fin Ltd 1978-, MBM Systems & Equipment Ltd Hong Kong 1982-, K3 Software Servs Ltd 1984-, Alfred Gilbert & Sons Ltd 1984-86; Birmingham Chamber of Indust & Commerce: memb educn and trg ctee 1973-, ctee chm 1979-85, memb working pty on industl democracy 1977, memb cncl 1980-, memb gen purposes ctee 1981-, vice pres 1987-, chm overseas trade policy ctee 1987-; Br Inst of Mgmnt: memb working pty on indust educn and mgmnt 1976-77, memb mgmnt devpt servs and educn ctee 1978-, memb cncl 1979-85, memb new business panel 1982-83, memb West Midlands regnl bd; memb West Midlands regnl bd Confedn of Br Indust 1982-; tstee Middlemore Homes 1968-, memb West Midlands Econ Planning Cncl 1978-79, tstee RALI Fndn 1985-; CBIM 1982; *Recreations* languages, bridge, reading, riding, swimming; *Style—* Tom Garnier, Esq; Manor Farm House, Alderton, nr Tewkesbury, Gloucs GL20 8NL (☎ 0242 62 419); Kalamazoo plc, Northfield, Birmingham B32 2RW (☎ 021 411 2345, fax 021 476 4293, telex 336700)

GARNOCK, Viscount; James Randolph Lindesay-Bethune; s and h of 15 Earl of Lindsay by his 1 w, Mary, *née* Douglas-Scott-Montagu (*see* Hon Mrs Horn); *b* 19 Nov 1955; *Educ* Eton, Univ of Edinburgh (MA), Univ of California Davis (BA); *m* 2 March 1982, Diana Mary, er da of Nigel Chamberlayne-Macdonald, OBE, LVO, of Cranbury Park, Winchester; 2 da (Frances Mary b 1986, Alexandra Penelope b 1988); *Career* landscape architect; tstee of gardens for the disabled; cncl memb of London Gardens Soc; *Clubs* Turf; *Style—* Viscount Garnock

GARNSWORTHY, Baroness Sue; da of Harold Taylor; *m* 1, Michael Farley; m 2, 1973, as his 2 w, Baron Garnsworthy, OBE (d 1974); 1 s (Hon Charles Edyvean b 1974); *Style—* The Rt Hon Lady Garnsworthy; Little Dormers, Smithy Lane, Lower Kingswood, Tadworth, Surrey

GARRAN, Sir (Isham) Peter; KCMG (1961, CMG 1954); s of Sir Robert Randolph Garran, GCMG, QC (d 1956), and Hilda, *née* Robson (d 1936); *b* 15 Jan 1910; *Educ* Melbourne GS, Trinity Coll Melbourne (BA); *m* 1935, Mary Elisabeth, da of Sir Richard Rawdon Stawell, KBE (d 1935); 2 s, 1 da; *Career* Nat Serv 1934-70; Chief Political Div Control Cmmn Germany 1947-50, inspr Foreign Serv Estabs 1952-54, min (commercial) Br Embassy Washington 1954-60, ambass to Mexico 1960-64, ambass to the Netherlands 1964-70 (ret); dir: Lend Lease Corpn 1970-78, UK Branch AMP Soc 1970-82; chm: Quality Assur Cncl Br Standards Inst 1971-82, Securicor Nederland BV 1976-82; *Recreations* gardening; *Clubs* Boodles; *Style—* Sir Peter Garran, KCMG; The Coach House, Collingbeams, Donhead St Mary, Shaftesbury, Dorset SP7 9DX (☎ 074 788 8108)

GARRATT, Stephen Kearsley; s of Maj George Herbert Garratt (d 1961), of Heron Bridge, Chester, and Aline Mary, *née* Norman (d 1960); *b* 17 May 1916; *Educ* Shrewsbury; *m* 17 Nov 1951, Felicity Ann De Laune, da of Capt Antony Percival Williams; 1 s (Jonathan), 2 da (Charlotte, Victoria); *Career* WWII serv: Middx Regt 1939, cmmnd 2 Lt Royal Berks Reg 1940, volunteered for RWAFF 1940, serv Sierra Leone Regt and Staff Capt Gen Woolher's HQ 1940-43, GSO3 to 21 Army Gp 1 Corps HQ (D Day planning staff) 1943-44, GSO3 Liason Offr 1 Corps 1944 (D Day until after Battle of Arnhem), Staff Coll Camberley 1944, magistrate in mil cts legal section of mil govt Berlin Dec 1944-45, demobbed with rank of Maj 1945; admitted slr 1939, official Slrs Off Royal Cts of Justice 1946, Shell Int (China, Sri Lanka, Nigeria, London) 1947-61, private advsr to Railways Bd 1961-66, pr sec to Law Soc 1966-69; currently ind art dealer specialising in pictures; memb London Diocesan Cncl; memb Law Soc 1939-89; *Recreations* polo, skiing; *Clubs* Garrick, Rhinefield Polo; *Style—* Stephen Garratt, Esq; 60 Addison Rd, London W14 (☎ 01 603 0681); Old Stagbury, Furzley, Bramshaw, Hants (☎ 0794 22298)

GARRATT, Timothy George; s of George Herbert Garratt (d 1976), of Chichester, Sussex, and Hylda Joyce, *née* Spalton (d 1958); *b* 7 Sept 1942; *Educ* Stowe; *m* 24 April 1965, Vanessa Ann, da of Charles Albert Wright (d 1980), of Chichester, Sussex; 2 s (Alastair b 1969, James b 1973); *Career* chartered surveyor RICS 1966; memb: gen cncl RICS 1969-73, Devon and Cornwall branch agric div ctee; vice chm Devon and Cronwall branch RICS, ctee memb Western Counties Agric Valuers Assoc, ptnr Rendells Auctioneers Valuers & Estate Agents S Devon 1976-; pres: Chagford and Dist Lions Club 1984-85, Lions Club Int Zone (chm 1985-86); FAAV 1968, FRICS 1975; *Recreations* farming, sporting shooting, gardening; *Clubs* Lions Int, RICS 1913; *Style—* Timothy Garratt, Esq; Baileys Hey, Chagford, Devon TQ13 8AW (☎ 06473 3396); Rock House, Chagford, Devon TQ13 8AX

GARRET, Richard Anthony (Tony); CBE (1986); s of Charles Victor Garrett (d 1945), and Blanche, *née* Michell (d 1968); *b* 4 July 1918; *Educ* Kings Sch Worcester; *m* 5 Jan 1946, Marie Louise, da of Rear Adm Robin Campsie Dalglish (d 1937); 1 s (Rupert Charles Anthony b 8 July 1961), 2 da (Anne b 8 Jan 1947, Amanda b 2 Feb 1955); *Career* Royal Gloucs Hussars TA 1938, RMC Sandhurst 1940, WW II 22 Dragoons 1941-46; chm and md Imperial tobacco ltd 1971-79 (joined 1936), dep chm HTV Gp plc 1976-83, dir Standard Commercial Corpn USA 1981-; chm NABC 1980-87, tstee Glynebourne Arts Tst 1976-88; Worshipful Co of Tobacco Pipe Makers; CBIM, FID; *Recreations* golf, gardening, music; *Clubs* Naval & Military, MCC; *Style—* Tony Garrett, Esq; Marlwood Grange, Thornbury, Bristol BS12 2JB (☎ 0454 412630)

GARRETT, Anthony David (Tony); s of Sir William Garrett (d 1977), of Eastbourne, Sussex, and Lady Marion, *née* Houghton (d 1967); *b* 26 August 1928; *Educ* Ellesmere Coll, Clare Coll Cambridge (MA); *m* 17 May 1952, Monica, da of Richard V Harris (d 1976), of Sidmouth, Devon; 3 s (Nicholas b 1954, David b 1959, Mark b 1962), 1 da (Jennifer b 1956); *Career* Nat Serv 4 Queens Own Hussars 1946-8; md Proctor & Gamble UK & Italy 1969-73, vice pres int The Procter & Gamble Co 1973-82; bd memb The Post Office 1983-87, dep master and chief exec The Royal Mint 1988-; *Recreations* golf, bridge, chess, sailing, mountain walking, gardening; *Clubs* Utd Oxford & Cambridge; *Style—* Tony Garrett, Esq; Cammock House, Goldsmith Ave, Crowborough, E Sussex TN6 1RH

GARRETT, Colin Noël; s of Ernest Leslie Garrett, of Southwold, Suffolk, and Eileen Gladys, *née* May; *b* 3 June 1942; *Educ* Leighton Park Sch Reading, Kings Coll Cambridge (BA, MA), Univ De Nancy France; *m* 16 Sept 1967, Sarah Hamilton, da of Maj Geoffry Clemow Smith, MBE, of Cambridge; 2 da (Marion b 17 Dec 1971, Jill b 21 Feb 1974); *Career* articled clerk and asst slr Waterhouse & Co 1965-67, asst slr Few & Kester Cambridge 1968-69, co sec and slr AMOCO (UK) Ltd 1969-71, legal advsr Shell Int Petroleum Co London 1971-77, attorney Scallop Corpn NY 1977-79, legal advsr Shell London 1979-81, gp slr 3i Gp plc London 1981-; memb Law Soc 1967, ABA 1977, NY Bar 1978; FBIM 1986; *Recreations* music, violin-making; *Clubs* Law Soc; *Style—* Colin Garrett, Esq; 17 North Rd, Berkhamsted, Herts HP4 3DX (☎ 0442 866 694); 91 Waterloo Rd, London SE1 8XP (☎ 01 928 7822, fax 01 928 0058, telex 917844)

GARRETT, (William) Edward; MP (Lab) Wallsend 1964-; s of John Garrett, of Prudhoe-on-Tyne, Northumberland, and Frances, *née* Barwise; *b* 21 Mar 1920; *Educ* LSE; *m* 1, 1946, Beatrice (d 1976), da of John Kelly, of Prudhoe; 1 s; m 2, 1980, Noel Stephanie Ann Johnson; *Career* engr; memb AEU 1935, formerly with ICI; parly candidate (Lab) Hexham 1955, Doncaster 1959; memb: Northumberland CC 1956, Expenditure Ctee House Commons 1971-79, parly advsr Machine Tool Trade Assoc 1973-; memb Cncl of Europe 1979-; *Style—* Edward Garrett, Esq, MP; House of Commons, London SW1

GARRETT, Godfrey John; OBE (1982); s of Thomas Garrett (d 1978), and May Louisa, *née* Botten; *b* 24 July 1937; *Educ* Dulwich, Sidney Sussex Coll Camb (MA); *m* 23 March 1963, Elisabeth Margaret, *née* Hall; 4 s (Mark b 1964, Edward b 1967, William b 1968, Richard b 1970), 1 da (Anna b 1974); *Career* FO: joined 1961, third sec Kinshasa (ex Leopoldville) 1963-65, second sec Prague 1965-68, first sec Buenos Aires 1971-73, first sec (later cnsllr) Stockholm 1981-83, cnsllr Bonn 1983-88; *Recreations* skiing, mountain walking, gardening, languages, photography; *Style—* Godfrey J Garrett, Esq, OBE; White Cottage, Henley, Haslemere, Surrey (☎ 0428 52172)

GARRETT, Maj Gen Henry Edmund Melvill Lennox; CBE (1975); s of John Edmund Garrett (d 1978), and Mary, *née* Jamieson; *b* 31 Jan 1924; *Educ* Wellington, Clare Coll Cambridge (MA); *m* 1973, Rachel Ann; 1 step s (Richard Beadon b 1962), 1 step-da (Sarah Beadon b 1962); *Career* cmmnd 1944, Staff Coll 1956, US Armed Forces Staff Coll 1960, OC 7 Field Sqdn 1960, CO 35 Engr Regt 1965, Col GS, MOD 1968, Cdr 12 Engr Bde 1969, Royal Coll of Def Studies 1972, COS NI 1972, Maj Gen i/c admin ULLF 1975, Vice Adj Gen 1976, dir Army Security 1978-; *Recreations* walking, riding; *Clubs* Army and Navy; *Style—* Maj Gen Henry Garrett; c/o National Westminster Bank, 1 Market St, Bradford, W Yorks; MOD London

GARRETT, John Laurence; s of Laurence Garrett and Rosina Garrett; *b* 8 Sept 1931; *Educ* Sir George Monoux GS (London), Univ of Oxford, UCLA Business Sch; *m* 1959, Wendy Ady; 2 da; *Career* former: lab offr in chemical indust, head of market res in car indust, pub serv mgmnt conslt; dir Int Management Consultancy Practice; MP (Lab) Norwich South 1987- (formerly 1974-83, contested 1983); pps to: Civil Service min 1974, Social Security min 1977-79; oppn spokesman: Treasy 1979-80, Indust 1980-83; Energy 1987, Indust 1988-; *Style—* John Garrett, Esq

GARRETT, Prof John Raymond; s of Charles Raymond Garrett, MM (d 1976), of Winchester, and Irene Lily, *née* Rogers (d 1978); *b* 28 Mar 1928; *Educ* Peter Symonds Sch, King's Coll Hosp Dental Sch (LDS, RCS), King's Coll (BSc), King's Coll Hosp Med Sch (MB BS, PhD); *m* 28 April 1958, Daphne Anne, da of Edwin Owen Parr (d 1953); 1 s (Malcolm b 1964), 1 da (Claire b 1963); *Career* RADC Lt 1950-51, Capt 1951-52, Nat Serv active parachutist in Airbourne Servs in 23 Para Field Ambulance; res fell Nuffield 1961-64, sr lectr pathology King's Coll Hosp Med Sch 1964-, prof and head of dept of oral pathology King's Coll Hosp Dental Sch 1971 (reader 1968);

Freeman City of London 1971, memb Worshipful Soc of Apothecaries; MD London Univ 1985; MRCPath 1965, FRCPath 1977; *Books* Histochemistry of Secretory Processes (1976); *Recreations* med history; *Style*— Prof John Garrett; 15 Deepdene Rd, London SE5 8EG (☎ 01 274 6488); The Rayne Inst, King's Coll Med Dental Sch, 123 Coadharbour Lane, London SE5 9NU (☎ 01 326 3019)

GARRETT, Nicholas Young; s of Geoffrey Elmer Garrett (d 1988), of 13 New Cavendish St, W1, and Josephine Honor Franklin, *née* Bishop (d 1988); *b* 5 June 1936; *Educ* Sherborne, Worcester Coll Oxford (MA); *Career* Nat Serv 1954-56, 2 Lt, RA; slr 1962, sr ptnr Ingledew Brown Bennison and Garrett 1974-; *Recreations* reading, opera, television; *Clubs* Garrick; *Style*— Nicholas Garrett, Esq; 26 Creechurch Lane, London EC3 (☎ 01 623 8899, fax 01 626 3073, telex 885420)

GARRETT, Hon Sir Raymond William; AFC (1943), AEA (1945), JP; s of James John Percival Garrett (d 1914), of Kew, Victoria, Australia; *b* 19 Oct 1900; *Educ* Royal Melbourne Tech Coll, Melbourne Univ; *m* 1934, Vera Halliday, da of Charles Edward Lugton (d 1927, of East Kew, Victoria; 1 s, 2 da; *Career* dir Cine Serv Pty Ltd 1940-73, pres Legislative Cncl Victoria 1968-76, chm Parly Library Ctee and vice-chm House Ctee 1968-76, chm of dirs Ilford (Aust) Pty Ltd 1969-75; life govr Lady Nell Seeing Eye Dog Sch; Freeman City of Doncaster and Templestowe 1988; kt 1973; *see Debrett's Handbook of Australia and New Zealand for further details*; *Recreations* photography, motoring; *Clubs* Air Force, Royal Auto of Victoria; *Style*— Hon Sir Raymond Garrett AFC, AEA, JP; 22/330 Springvale Rd, Donvale, Vic 3111, Australia

GARRETT, Terence; CBE (1967); s of Percy Herbert Garrett (d 1972), and Gladys Annie, *née* Budd (d 1972); *b* 27 Sept 1929; *Educ* Alleyn's Sch, Gonville and Caius Coll Cambridge (MA); *m* 1960, Grace Elizabeth Bridgeman, yr da of Rev Basil Kelly Braund (d 1981); 2 s (Andrew b 1960, Charles b 1963) 3 da (Bridget b 1966, Katharine b (twin) 1969, Ruth b 1969); *Career* instr Lt RN 1952-55; lectr Ewell County Tech Coll 1955-56, sr lectr RMC of Science Shrivenham 1957-62, programmes analysis unit Miny of Technol 1967-70, cnsllr (scientific) Br Embassy Moscow 1970-74 (1962-66), int technol unit Dept of Trade 1974-76, sec to bd govr and gen conf IAEA Vienna 1976-78, cnsllr (science & tech) Br Embassy Bonn 1978-82; res and technol policy div Dept of Trade and Industry 1982-87, cnsllr (science & tech) Br Embassy Moscow 1987-; *Recreations* squash, travel; *Style*— Terence Garrett, Esq, CBE; c/o FCO (Moscow), King Charles St, London SW1A 2AH

GARRETT, Thomas John; s of Thomas John Garrett, of Belfast (d 1977), and Violet, *née* Dudgeon (d 1982); *b* 13 Sept 1927; *Educ* Royal Belfast Academical Inst, Queen's Univ Belfast (BA), Heidelberg Univ; *m* 9 August 1958, Sheenah Agnew, da of Grey Marshall (d 1960), of Drymen, Dumbartonshire, Scotland; 1 da (Catrione b 1960); *Career* asst master: Royal Belfast Academical Inst 1951-54, Nottingham HS for Boys 1954-56; house master Campbell Coll Belfast 1956-73, headmaster Portora Royal Sch Enniskillen, princ Royal Belfast Academical Inst 1978-; cncl memb BBC NI; memb Queen's Univ Belfast Schs Cncl; *Books* Modern German Humour (1969), Two Hundred Years at the Top (1977); *Recreations* hill-walking, angling, broadcasting; *Clubs* East India, Devonshire, Sports and Public Schools; *Style*— Thomas Garrett, Esq; RBAi College Sq East, Belfast BT1 (☎ 0232 240461)

GARRETT, Hon Mrs (Valda Jean); *née* Vernon; 2 da of 5 Baron Lyveden (d 1973), and his 1 wife Ruby, *née* Shandley (d 1932); *b* 11 July 1918; *m* 10 July 1937, Basil George Garrett; 1 s, 3 da; *Style*— Hon Mrs Garrett; 18 Tarikaka St, Ngaio, New Zealand

GARRICK, Ronald; s of Thomas Garrick and Anne, *née* MacKay; *b* 21 August 1940; *Educ* Roy Coll of Science and Technology Glasgow, Glasgow Univ; *m* 1965, Janet Elizabeth Taylor Lind; 2 s, 1 da; *Career* md Weir Pumps Ltd; md Weir Gp 1982-; *Style*— Ronald Garrick, Esq; c/o Weir Pumps Ltd, 149 Newlands Rd, Glasgow 44 (☎ 041 637 7141)

GARRIOCH, Sir (William) Henry; s of Alfred Garrioch and Jeanne Marie Madeleine Colin; *b* 4 May 1916; *Educ* Royal Coll Mauritius; *m* 1964, Jeanne Louise Marie-Thérèse Desvaux de Marigny; *Career* barrister 1952; chief justice Mauritius 1977-78; kt 1978; *Style*— Sir Henry Garrioch; Lees St, Curepipe, Mauritius (☎ 862708)

GARROD, Lt-Gen Sir (John) Martin Carruthers; KCB (1988), OBE (1980); s of late Rev William Francis Garrod, and late Isobel Agnes, *née* Carruthers; *b* 29 May 1935; *Educ* Sherborne; *m* 1963, Gillian Mary, da of Lt-Col Robert Granville Parks-Smith, RM (ka 1942); 2 da (Catherine, Fenella); *Career* Lt-Gen RM, cdr 3 Commando Bde RM 1983-84 (despatches NI 1974); ADC to HM The Queen 1983-84, chief of staff to Cmdt Gen RM 1984-87, Cmdt Gen RM 1987-; *Recreations* portrait photography; *Clubs* East India; *Style*— Lt-Gen Sir Martin Garrod, KCB, OBE; c/o Lloyds Bank, Petersfield, Hants

GARROD, Norman John; s of Frank Albert Garrod (d 1965); *b* 10 July 1924; *Educ* Alleyns Sch Dulwich; *m* 1945, Beryl Portia Betty, *née* Bastow; 2 children; *Career* served WW II, Fl-Lt RAF, UK, Middle East, Far East; master printer; chm Garrod Ltd 1952-; chm Printers Charitable Corpn 1981; vice pres Variety Club of Great Britain (chief barker 1984); *Recreations* dogs, fishing; *Clubs* Garrick, RAC, No 10; *Style*— Norman Garrod, Esq; Great Common, Big Common Lane, Bletchingley, Surrey (☎ 0883 843375); Garrod Offset Ltd, Kelvin Way, Crowley, Sussex RH10 2LX (☎ 0293 21133)

GARSIDE, Roger Ramsay; s of Capt Frederick Rodney Garside, CBE, RN, and Margaret Ada Beatrice, *née* Ramsay; *b* 29 Mar 1938; *Educ* Eton, Clare Coll Cambridge (MA), Sloane Sch of Mgmnt (MIT, MSc); *m* 11 Oct 1969, Evelyne Madeleine Pierrette, da of André René Émile Guérin (d 1982); 3 da (Juliette b 1972, Alice b 1974, Rebecca b 1978); *Career* Nat Serv cmmnd offr 1/6 Queen Elizabeth's Own Gurkha Rifles; Dip Serv 1962-71: London, Rangoon, Hong Kong, Peking; World Bank Washington 1972-74; Dip Serv 1975-87: London, Peking, Paris; dir public affairs Int Stock Exchange London 1987-; *Books* Coming Alive: China After Mao (1981); *Recreations* tennis, riding; *Clubs* Reform; *Style*— Roger Garside, Esq; 36 Groveway, London SW9 0AR; Int Stock Exchange, Old Broad St, London EC2N 1HP (☎ 01 588 2355, fax 01 256 8972)

GARSON, Cdre Robin William; CBE (1975); s of Peter James Garson (d 1922), and Ada Frances, *née* Newton (d 1965); *b* 13 Nov 1921; *Educ* Sch of Oriental and African Studies (Japanese interpreter); *m* 1946, Joy Ligertwood Taylor, *née* Hickman; 1 s (Simon), 1 da (Nicola); *Career* entered RN 1937, served WWII 1939-45; HM Ships: Resolution, Nigeria, Cyclops; HM Submarines: Seawolf, H33; Spark in command HM submarines 1945-54: Universal, Uther, Seraph, Saga, Sanguine, Springer, Thule, Astute; Chief Staff Offr Intelligence Far East 1966-68, Sr Polaris UK Rep Washington 1969-71; Capt 1 Submarine Sqdn 1971-73; Cdre HMS Drake 1973-75; ADC to HM The Queen 1974, advsr to AMA on Arts and Recreation 1976; memb Library Advsy Cncl (Eng) 1977-81; dir leisure services London Borough of Hillingdon 1975-85, advsr Sports Cncl 1979-85; *Recreations* golf, ski-ing, tennis; *Clubs* Moor Park, Army & Navy, Hunstanton GC; *Style*— Cdre Robin Garson, CBE; "Gateways", Hamilton Bay West, Old Hunstanton, Norfolk, PE36 6JB

GARSTON, Eric Michael; s of Dr Maurice Kopelowitz (d 1971), of Newcastle-upon-Tyne, and Mabel, *née* Garston (d 1949); *b* 23 May 1931; *Educ* Malvern, Durham Univ (LLB); *m* 20 Nov 1960 (m dis 1976), Jill Rosemary, da of Jack Kleeman (d 1983), of Regents Park, London NW1; 1 s (Jeremy b 1963), 1 da (Annabel b 1966); *Career* slr; sr ptnr Reynolds Porter Chamberlain 1988-; exec ctee Anglo Austrian Soc, ctee memb legal gp Friends of Hebrew Univ, chm bd of tstees The World Resource Fndn, non exec dir numerous private co (incl Tetra Pak Fin and Trading SA of Switzerland); Liveryman Worshipful Co of Glaziers (1986); memb Law Soc 1954, Int Bar Assoc 1966; *Recreations* swimming, walking, theatre; *Clubs* MCC, RAC; *Style*— Michael Garston, Esq; 97 Abbotsbury Rd, Holland Park, London W14 (☎ 01 603 2903); Chichester House, 278-282 High Holburn, London WC1V 7HA (☎ 01 242 2877, fax 01 242 1431)

GARTHWAITE, (William) Mark Charles; s and h of Sir William Garthwaite, 2 Bt, DSC, and Patricia Beatrice Eden Allen, *née* Neate; *b* 4 Nov 1946; *Educ* Gordonstoun, Univ of Pennsylvania (BSc); *m* 1979, Victoria Lisette, da of Gen Sir Harry Tuzo, GCB, OBE, MC, and former wife of Robert Hohler; 1 s (William b 1982), 2 da (Rosie b 1980, Jemima b 1984); *Career* md Seascope Insurance Serv (Marine insurance broker) 1979; *Recreations* yachting, trekking, skiing; *Clubs* Turf; *Style*— Mark Garthwaite, Esq; The Old Vicarage, 12 Foxmore Street, London SW11 4PL (☎ 01 488 3288)

GARTHWAITE, Hon Mrs; Waveney Mancroft; *née* Samuel; er da of 1 Baron Mancroft (d 1942); *b* 25 Feb 1916; *m* 1 Dec 1950, Anthony William Garthwaite (d 1972), 2 s of Sir William Garthwaite, 1 Bt (d 1956); 1 s (Nicholas Anthony William Mancroft b 1952); m 2, 1982, Caroline, da of Thomas Willbourne, of Peterborough; *Style*— Hon Mrs Garthwaite; 98 Bickenhall Mansions, W1

GARTHWAITE, Sir William Francis Cuthbert; 2 Bt (UK 1919), DSC (1941) and bar (1942); s of Sir William Garthwaite, 1 Bt (d 1956), and his 1 w, Francesca Margherita, *née* Parfett; *b* 3 Jan 1906; *Educ* Bradfield Coll, Hertford Coll Oxford; *m* 1, 23 July 1931 (m dis 1937), Hon Dorothy, o da of 1 Baron Duveen; m 2, 27 June 1945 (m dis 1952), Patricia Beatrice Eden, er da of late Cdr Charles Eden Neate, RN; 1 s; m 3, 4 April 1957, Patricia Merriel, o da of Sir Philip d'Ambrumenil; 3 s (inc twins), 1 da (decd); *Heir* s, William Mark Charles Garthwaite; *Career* Lt-Cdr (A) RNR, RN Pilot and with RAF WW II (despatches thrice); underwriter and broker at Lloyds 1927-; contested three Parliamentary elections as Cons candidate 1931 Hemsworth, 1935 Isle of Ely, 1945 Wolverhampton; *Recreations* flying, golf, skiing; *Clubs* Portland, Naval, Royal Thames YC, Jockey (Paris), Royal Navy Sailing Assoc; *Style*— Sir William Garthwaite, Bt, DSC; Matfield House, Matfield, Kent TN12 7JT (☎ 089 272 2454)

GARTON, Dr (George) Alan; s of William Edgar Garton, DCM, (d 1966), and Frances Mary Elizabeth, *née* Atkinson (d 1967); *b* 4 June 1922; *Educ* Scarborough HS, Univ of Liverpool (BSc, PhD, DSc); *m* 21 Aug 1951, Gladys Frances, da of Francis James Davison (d 1978), of Glasgow; 2 da (Dr Alison Francis b 7 Sept 1952, Dr Fiona Mary b May 1955); *Career* war serv in Miny of Supply; Johnston res and teaching fell Univ of Aberdeen 1949-50, dep dir Rowett Res Inst 1968-83 (Head Lipid Biochemistry dept 1963-83, biochemist 1950-63); hon res assoc Rowett Res Inst 1984-, hon res fell Univ of Aberdeen 1987-; vis prof biochemistry Univ of North Carolina 1967, chm Br nat ctee for Nutritional and Food Science 1985-87, memb cncl Br Nutritional Fndn 1982-, pres Int Conferences on Biochemistry of Lipids 1982-; SBStJ 1986; FRSE 1966, frs 1978; *Books* contributor to several multi-author books on ruminant physiology and lipid biochemistry; *Recreations* gardening, golf, philately, foreign travel; *Clubs* Farmers', Deeside GC; *Style*— Dr Alan Garton; Ellerburn, 1 St Devenick Crescent, Cults, Aberdeen AB1 9LL (☎ 0224 867 012)

GARTON, Hon Mrs (Annabel Jocelyne); da of 2 & last Viscount Hudson (d 1963); *b* 11 August 1952; *m* 9 Feb 1970, (Anthony) Juan Garton, eldest s of Anthony Charles Garton (d 1982); 1 s, 3 da; *Style*— Hon Mrs Garton; 8 Moncorvo Close, London SW7

GARTON, Charles Herbert Stanley; MBE (1949); s of Arthur Stanley Garton (d 1948), of Danesfield, Medmenham, Marlow, Bucks, and Mona, *née* Macaulay (d 1986); *b* 5 Feb 1920; *Educ* Eton, Magdalen Coll Oxford; *m* 14 April 1948, Sheelagh Mary Georgiana, da of Thomas Harrison Greene, OBE (d 1963); 3 da (Georgiana b 12 Aug 1949, Jane, Anne (twins) b 19 July 1951); *Career* FO 1940-54, farmer 1954-; *Recreations* shooting, fishing, stalking; *Clubs* Leander; *Style*— Charles Garton, Esq, MBE; Wadeford Hse, Wadeford, Chard, Somerset (☎ 046 06 3222)

GARTON, Hon Mrs (Ines Monica); *née* Wilson; twin da of 4 Baron Nunburnholme; *b* 13 Feb 1963; *m* 1 Oct 1988, Anthony Richard Leslie Garton, yst s of Anthony Charles Garton (d 1982); 23 Sutherland Street, London SW1

GARTON, John Leslie; CBE (1974, MBE 1946); er s of Charles Leslie Garton (d 1940), and Madeline Laurence; *b* 1 April 1916; *Educ* Eton, Magdalen Coll Oxford (MA); *m* 1939, Elizabeth Frances, da of Sir Walter Erskine Crum, OBE (d 1923); 1 s (and 2 s decd); *Career* Maj TA 1938-51; chm: Coca-Cola Bottling Co Oxford Ltd 1951-65, Coca-Cola Western Bottlers Ltd 1966-71; Thames Conservator 1970-74; High Sheriff Bucks 1977; pres CUBS 1939, chm Henley Royal Regatta 1966-77 (pres 1978-), pres Amateur Rowing Assoc 1969-77 (hon life vice pres 1978-), pres Leander Club 1980-83 (capt 1946, chm 1958-59); chm World Rowing Championships 1975, fin and gen purposes ctee Br Olympic Assoc 1969-77; *Recreations* shooting, fishing, supporting the sport of rowing; *Clubs* Leander; *Style*— John Garton, Esq, CBE; Mill Green House, Church St, Wargrave, Berks RG10 8EP (☎ 073 522 2944)

GARTON, Lady Lucy Catherine Mary; *née* Primrose; er da of 7 Earl of Rosebery, DL; *b* 24 Dec 1955; *Educ* Benenden; *m* 1976, (Anthony Gavin) Charles Garton, s of Anthony Charles Garton (d 1982), of Hyde Pk Gdns; 1 s (James Anthony Leo b 1986), 1 da (Camilla Mary Eva b 1982), and 1 child decd; *Style*— Lady Lucy Garton; 9 North Terrace, Alexander Sq, London SW3 2BA (01 589 8338)

GARTON JONES, Lt Col John; MBE (1953); s of William John Garton Jones (d 1947), of Lucknow, United Provinces, India, and Mavis Noreen *née* Mauger (d 1986); *b* 19 Sept 1930; *Educ* Bedford Sch; *m* 29 Dec 1960, Mary (d 1983), da of Lt Col Edward Roger Nanney-Wynn DL (d 1982), of Llanfendigaid, Tywyn, Gwynedd; 2 s (William b 1961, Charles b 1970), 1 da (Edwina b 1964); *Career* Nat Serv joined Army

1949, Eaton Hall OCS 1950, cmmn serv with Jamaica Bn 1950-51, regular cmmn Depot Royal Norfolk Regt 1951-54, 1 Bn Royal Norfolk Regt 1954-60 serv in Cyprus BAOR Berlin, HQ Mid East Cmd Aden 1960-62, 4 Bn Royal Norfolk Regt 1963-65, on loan to Malaysian Government in Barawak 1965-66, 4 Royal Anglian Regt serv Malta and Eng 1967-69, MOD 1969-71, Depot The Queens Div 1971-73, HQ NI 1973-75, HQ Wales 1975-80, HQ Western Dist 1980-82, ret 1982; burser Outward Bound Tst Sch Aberdovey 1982-84, freelance journalist (nat and provincial pubns); memb: ctee of Shrewsbury Theatre Guild, Attingham Writers, Shrewsbury Sch Community Choir, Shrewsbury Arts and Drama Assoc; *Recreations* journalism, photography, singing, golf, tennis, skiing; *Clubs* Army and Navy; *Style—* Lt-Col John Garton Jones, MBE

GARTSIDE, Edmund Travis; TD (1968); s of Col J B Gartside, DSO, MC, TD, DL, JP (d 1964), of Crimble Cottage, Bamford, Rochdale, and Cora Maude, *née* Baker; *b* 11 Nov 1933; *Educ* Winchester, Trinity Coll Cambridge (MA); *m* 1, 29 Aug 1959 (m dis 1982), Margaret Clare, *née* Nicholls; 1 s (Michael Travis b 1969), 1 da (Vanessa Perry Anne (Mrs Anderson) b 1962); m 2, 5 May 1983, Valerie Cox, da of Cyril Vowels, of Prospect Cottage, Marine Parade, Instow, N Devon; *Career* Nat Serv 2 Lt RE and Lancs Fusiliers 1952-54; TA: Lancs Fusiliers (Maj) 1954-67, E Lancs Regt 1967-68; chm and md Shiloh plc (formerly Shiloh Spinners Ltd) 1966- (mgmnt trainee 1957, dir 1960, gen mangr Roy Mill 1961-65, dep chm 1963-66, md 1965); chm Amberguard Ltd 1977-; dir Oldham & Dist Textile Employers' Assoc 1965- (pres 1971-75), memb central ctee Br Textile Employers' Assoc 1969- (pres 1976-78), pres Eurocoton 1985-87, memb ct Manchester Univ 1979-, govr Manchester GS 1984-; CBIM, FIOD; *Clubs* Army & Navy; *Style—* Edmund Gartside, Esq; Shiloh plc, Holdenfold, Royton, Oldham, Lancs OL2 5ET (☎ 061 624 8161, fax 061 627 3840, telex 667558)

GARVAGH, 5 Baron (UK 1818); (Alexander Leopold Ivor) George Canning; s of 4 Baron Garvagh (d 1956) by his 2 w, Gladys Dora May (d 1982), da of William Bayley Parker, of Edgbaston, and widow of Lt-Col D M Dimmer, VC; *b* 6 Oct 1920; *Educ* Eton, Christ Church Oxford; *m* 1, 12 July 1947 (m dis 1973), Edith Christine, da of Jack H Cooper, of Worplesdon, Surrey; 1 s, 2 da; m 2, 1974, Cynthia Valerie Mary, da of Eric Ernest Falk Pretty, CMG, of Kingswood, Surrey; *Heir* s, Hon Spencer George Stratford de Redcliffe Canning; *Career* served Indian Army WW II in Burma (despatches); chm: Garvagh & Ptnrs; accredited rep trade and industry Cayman Islands 1981-, memb court Painter and Stainers Livery; MBIM, FInstD, MIEx; *Clubs* Royal Overseas League; *Style—* The Rt Hon the Lord Garvagh; Casa Canning, Costera del Mar, Moraira, Alicante, Spain

GARVEY, Sir Ronald Herbert; KCMG (1950, CMG 1947), KCVO (1953), MBE (1940); s of Rev Herbert Richard Garvey (d 1955), and Alice M Lofthouse; *b* 4 July 1903; *Educ* Trent Coll, Emmanuel Coll Cambridge; *m* 30 Oct 1934, Patricia Dorothy Edge, da of Dr Victor William Tighe McGusty, CMG, OBE; 1 s (Richard b 1935), 3 da (Grania b 1939, Lavinia b 1946, Julia b 1947); *Career* entered Colonial Serv 1926, W Pacific High Cmmn, actg govr Windward Is BWI 1946-48, govr and c-in-c Br Honduras 1948-52, govr and c-in-c Fiji, and govr Pitcairn Is, consul-gen Western Pacific, sr cmmr for UK in S Pacific Cmmn 1952-58, Lt-Govr Isle of Man 1959-66; dir Garveys (London) SA 1966-82; memb East Anglian Tourist Bd; KStJ 1954; *Books* Gentleman Pauper; Happy Days in the Isle of Man; *Recreations* golf, gardening, eating, drinking Garvey sherry, writing; *Clubs* Royal Cwlth Soc; *Style—* Sir Ronald Garvey, KCMG, KCVO, MBE; The Priory, Wrentham, Beccles, Suffolk (☎ 0502 75274); Gilmooka House, 57-61 Mortimer St, London W1N 7TD

GARVIN, Michael John Moore; s of Stephen Garvin, MBE, of Sussex, and Gilda Constance, *née* Moore (d 1955); *b* 12 Sept 1943; *Educ* Rugby; *m* 22 Sept 1976, Bridget, da of Thomas A Tolhurst (d 1969); 2 s (Patrick b 1978, Fergus b 1983), 1 da (Melissa b 1981); *Career* CA 1966; dir: Barclay Securities 1972-73, Hampton Areas 1973-79, Trident Television 1979-83, Condé Nast 1983-; *Clubs* Travellers', Oriental, Hurlingham; *Style—* Michael Garvin, Esq; 46 Guildford Road, London SW8 2BV; Witney Street, Burford, Oxon; The Conde Nast Publications Ltd, Vogue House, Hanover Square, London W1R 0AD

GASCOIGNE, Hon Mrs; Hon (Elizabeth) Ann; *née* Harcourt; eldest da of 2 and last Viscount Harcourt, KCMG, OBE (d 1979), by his 1 w Hon (Maud) Elizabeth Grosvenor (da of 4 Baron Ebury); *b* 17 Feb 1932; *m* 19 Jan 1954, Crispin Gascoigne, o s of Maj-Gen Sir Julian Alvery Gascoigne, KCMG, KCVO, CB, DSO, *qv*; 1 s, 2 da; *Style—* Hon Mrs Gascoigne; The Manor House, Stanton Harcourt, Oxon

GASCOIGNE, (Arthur) Bamber; s of Derick (Ernest Frederick) Orby Gascoigne, TD (of the old Yorks family dating back to the 14 century, and gggs of Gen Isaac Gascoigne, whose er bro's da Frances was the Gascoigne heiress who m 2 Marquess of Salisbury, whence also the Salisbury family name of Gascoyne-Cecil) and Hon Mary (Midi) Louisa Hermione O'Neill, sis of 3 Baron O'Neill (through which connection Mr Gascoigne belongs to one of the oldest traceable lineages in Europe, the O'Neills of the Irish Royal House of Tara, records of which date from AD 360); nephew of Sir Julian Alvery Gascoigne, *qv*; *b* 24 Jan 1935; *Educ* Eton, Magdalene Coll Cambridge; *m* 1965, Christina Mary, da of late Alfred Henry Ditchburn, CBE; *Career* publisher: proprietor of St Helena Press; author and TV presenter, notably of University Challenge and The Christians; FRSL; *Style—* Bamber Gascoigne, Esq; St Helena Terrace, Richmond, Surrey

GASCOIGNE, Crispin; s of Maj-Gen Sir Julian Gascoigne, KCMG, KCVO, CB, DSO, qv, of Sanders, Stokefleming, Dartmouth, Devon, and Joyce Alfreda, *née* Newman (d 1981); *b* 10 Oct 1929; *Educ* Eton, RMA Sandhurst; *m* 19 Jan 1954, Hon (Elizabeth) Ann, da of 2 Viscount Harcourt, KCMG, OBE (d 1979), of The Manor House, Stanton, Harcourt, Oxon; 1 s (William Harcourt Crisp b 1955), 2 da (Elizabeth Laura b 1958, Mary Ann b 1960); *Career* Grenadier Gds 1949-54; Morgan Grenfell & Co Ltd 1956-66, ptnr Panmure Gordon 1966-80; memb Stock Exchange Cncl 1973-80; chm Oundle Schs ctee 1987-; Memb Ct Worshipful Co of Grocers (Master 1974); *Recreations* gardening, fishing, shooting; *Style—* Crispin Gascoigne, Esq; The Manor House, Stanton Harcourt, Oxford

GASCOIGNE, Maj-Gen Sir Julian Alvery; KCMG (1962), KCVO (1953), CB (1949), DSO (1943), JP (Devon 1966), DL (Devon 1966); s of Brig-Gen Sir Ernest (Frederick) Orby Gascoigne, KCVO, CMG, DSO, JP, DL (d 1944), of Ashtead, Surrey, and Laura Cicely, *née* Clive (d 1954); *b* 25 Oct 1903; *Educ* Eton, RMA Sandhurst; *m* 26 Nov 1928, Joyce Alfreda (d 22 Aug 1981), da of Robert Lydston Newman, JP, of Dartmouth, and sis of Sir Ralph Newman, 5 Bt; 1 s (Crispin m 1954 Hon Anne Harcourt, *qv*; 1 s, 2 da), 1 da (Merida, m 1956 Andrew Drysdale, s of Sir Mathew Drysdale; 3 da); *Career* cmmnd 1923, psc 1939, served WWII cmdg 1 Bn Grenadier Gds, 201 Gds Bde N Africa and Italy, idc 1946, Dep Cdr Br Army Staff Washington 1947-49, GOC London Dist and Maj-Gen cmdg Household Div 1950-53; Col Cmdt HAC 1954-59; memb Stock Exchange & ptnr Grieveson Grant 1954-59; cmmr Royal Hosp Chelsea 1958-59; govr and C-in-C Bermuda 1959-64; chm Devon & Cornwall Ctee Nat Tst 1965-75; patron Union Jack Club 1980 (cncl memb 1937, vice pres 1955-64, pres 1964-76); KStJ 1959; *Style—* Maj-Gen Sir Julian Gascoigne, KCMG, KCVO, CB, DSO, JP, DL; Sanders, Stoke Fleming, Dartmouth, S Devon

GASCOYNE, David Emery; s of Leslie Noel Gascoyne (d 1968), of IOW, and Winifred Isobel Emery Gascoyne (d 1970); *b* 10 Oct 1916; *Educ* Salisbury Cathedral Choir Sch, Regent St Poly Secdy Sch; *m* 17 May 1975, Mrs (Lorna) Judith Lewis, da of Capt Guy Tyler, MC (d 1966), of Upper Redpits, Marlow, Bucks; 4 stepchildren; *Career* writer and poet; FRSL 1951; *Books* A Short Survey of Surrealism (1936), Holderlin's Madness (1938), Poems 1937-42 (1943, illustrated by Graham Sutherland), A Vagrant and Other Poems (1950), Night Thoughts (1956), Collected Poems (1965), Paris Journal 1937-39 (1978), Journal 1936-37 (1980), Journal de Paris and D'Ailleurs (1984), Collected Poems (1988); *Style—* David Gascoyne, Esq

GASCOYNE-CECIL; *see*: Cecil

GASELEE, Nick - Nicholas Auriol Digby Charles (Nick); s of Lt-Col Auriol Stephen Gaselee, OBE (d 1987), of Tonbridge; *b* 30 Jan 1939; *Educ* Charterhouse; *m* 1966, Judith Mary, da of Dr Gilmer; 1 s (James b 1968), 1 da (Sarah, *qv*); *Career* Life Gds 1958-63; racing trainer to HRH The Prince of Wales; *Recreations* coursing; *Clubs* Turf; *Style—* Nick Gaselee, Esq; Saxon Cottage, Upper Lambourn, Berks (☎ 0488 71503)

GASELEE, Sarah Jane; da of Nick Gaselee, *qv*; *b* 2 June 1970; *Educ* Southover Manor Lewes, Hatherop Castle Cirencester, Clenord, France, Beechlawn Oxford; *Career* bridesmaid to Lady Diana Spencer at her marriage to HRH The Prince of Wales 1981, shop assistant in Harvey Nicholls; *Style—* Miss Sarah Jane Gaselee; Saxon Cottage, Upper Lambourn, Berks (☎ 0488 71503)

GASH, Michael Alfred; s of Benjamin Thomas Gash (d 1969), of Solihull, and Brenda Aileen, *née* Crockett; *b* 24 Oct 1943; *Educ* Sharmans Cross HS for Boys; *m* 24 Oct 1967, Sandra Ruth, da of Albert Ernest Wright (d 1977), of Kidderminster; 1 da (Kate b 1 April 1972); *Career* CA 1967; articled Cox & Furse Birmingham 1962-67, sr, supervisor and mangr Coopers & Lybrand London 1967-72, ptnr Kidsons Birmingham 1974- (mangr 1972-74); memb Rotary Club of Edgbaston Convention; FCA 1967, ATII 1970; *Recreations* golf, reading, theatre, cooking; *Clubs* The Edgbaston Priory, Harborne GC; *Style—* Michael Gash, Esq; Charnwood, 54 Richmond Hill Road, Edgbaston, Birmingham B15 3RZ (☎ 021 455 8440); Kidsons Chartered Accountants Ltd, Bank House, 8 Cherry St, Birmingham B2 5AD (☎ 021 631 2631, fax 021 631 2632, telex 338973)

GASK, Mrs Daphne Irvine Prideaux; O B E (1976); da of Capt Roger Prideaux Selby (d 1975), and Elizabeth May, *née* Stirling (d 1958); *Educ* St Trinnean's Edinburgh, Chateau Brillamont Lausanne Switzerland, O U (BA); *m* 31 July 1945, Dr John Gask, s of George Ernest Gask, CMG, DSO (d 1951); 1 s (Anthony Gask b 1947), 1 da (Zebee Gask b 1959); *Career* WWII third offr WRNs 1940-45; magistrate: shrops 1952-80, Inner London 1982-86, asst sec Int Assoc of Juvenile and Family Ct Magistrates 1974-86; memb: Royal Cmmn on Criminal Procedure 1978-81, NACRO cncl 1982-, Defence for Children Int UK exec ctee 1986-, shrop cc 1964-76, chm St Peter's Housing Plymouth, Cab Cornwall, Melo Mattos Medal Brazil 1986; *Recreations* photography, travel; *Clubs* Univ Women's; *Style—* Mrs Daphne Gask, O B E; 5 The Old School House, Garrett St, Cowsand, Cornwall PL10 1PD (☎ 0752 822 136)

GASKELL, (Richard) Carl; s of (Henry) Brian Gaskell (d 1982), and Doris (Winnifred), *née* Taylor; *b* 23 Mar 1948; *Educ* Gatewqay Sch Leicester, Univ of Newcastle upon Tyne (LLB); *m* 29 Dec 1973, Margaret Annette, da of Stanley Walter Humber; 1 s (Philip b 1975), 3 da (Victoria b 1976, Elizabeth b 1979, Gillian b 1983); *Career* called to Bar Lincoln's Inn 1971, MO circuit; chm Desford branch Bosworth Cons Assoc; *Style—* Carl Gaskell, Esq; Nova Rustica, Church Lane, Desford, Leicestershire LE9 9GD (☎ 14557 2717);'2 New St, Leicester LE1 5NA (☎ 0533 625 906, fax 0533 512 023)

GASKELL, Dr Colin Simister; CBE (1987); s of James Gaskell (d 1987), of Dukinield, Ches, and Carrie, *née* Simister (d 1968); *b* 19 May 1937; *Educ* Manchester GS, Manchester Univ (BSc), St Edmund Hall Oxford (DPhil); *m* Aug 1961, Jill, da of A Travers Haward (d 1980), of Torquay Devon; 1 s (John b 1970), 1 da (Sarah b 1974); *Career* tech dir Herbert Controls 1971-74, md Marconi Instruments Ltd 1979- (dir 1977-79), dir St Albans Enterprise Agency; CEng, FIEE (memb fin ctee and inspection bd), FIEEIE (vice pres), FBIM, FRSA; *Recreations* reading, theatre, horse riding; *Style—* Dr Colin Gaskell, CBE; Marconi Instruments Ltd, St Albans, Herts AL4 OJN (☎ 05827 59292, car tel 0560 316 312)

GASKELL, Richard Kennedy Harvey; s of Dr Kenneth Harvey Gaskell, of 18 Downleaze, Bristol, and Jean Winsome, *née* Beaven; *b* 17 Sept 1936; *Educ* Marlborough; *m* Oct 1965, Judith (Judy), da of Roy Douglas Poland (d 1963), of Gerrards Cross; 1 s (Simon b 1966), 1 da (Susanna b 1968); *Career* slr 1960; articled to Burges Salmon Bristol 1955-60, asst slr Tuckett Williams and Kew (later Tucketts) 1960-63, ptnr Tucketts 1963-85, ptnr Lawrence Tucketts Bristol 1985-; legal advsr The Laura Ashley Fndn 1988-; memb: Crown Ct Rules Ctee 1977-83, Lord Justice Watkins Working Pty on the Criminal Trials 1981-88, Lord Chllr's Efficiency Cmmn 1986-88, Marre Ctee on Future of Legal Profession 1986-88; Law Soc; nat chm Young Slrs Gp of Law Soc 1964-65, Cncl 1969-; chm: Contentious Business Ctee 1979-82, Advocacy Trg Team 1974-87; dir: Law Soc Tstees 1974- (chm 1982-, dep vice pres 1986-87), Law Servs Ltd 1987- (vice pres 1987-88, pres 1988-) Bristol Law Soc 1965- (memb, pres 1978-79); memb Som Law Soc, pres Assoc of S Western Law Socs 1980-81; Wild Fowl Tst: memb of cncl 1980-, memb exec ctee 1982-, chm 1983-87; memb mgmnt ctee Bristol 5 Boys Club 1960-66, hon cases sec Bristol branch NSPCC 1966-76, memb of Ct of Bristol Univ 1973-, cncl memb Bristol Zoo 1988-; *Recreations* people, furniture, things mechanical, farming, conservation; *Clubs* Farmers; *Style—* Richard Gaskell, Esq; Grove Farm, Yatton Keynell, Chippenham, Wiltshire SN14 7BS (☎ 0249 782289); Shannon Court, Corn Street, Bristol BS99 7JZ (☎ 0272 294861)

GASKELL, William Peter; CBE (1964), MBE (1953); s of late William Gaskell, late headmaster Lawrence Royal Mil Sch Sanawar, India; *b* 9 June 1914; *Educ* Dragon Sch Oxford, Blundell's, Sch of Metaliferous Mining Camborne; *Career* Capt Royal W Africa Frontier Force; mining engr Colonial Serv 1937-64 (chief inspr of mines Nigeria 1952-

64); lectr Sch of Mgmnt and Business Studies Brooklands Coll Weybridge 1965-74; *Recreations* badminton, music, motoring, travel; *Clubs* Royal Commonwealth Soc; *Style*— William Gaskell, Esq, CBE; 3 Cove Row, Weymouth, Dorset (☎ 0305 774067)

GASKIN, Catherine Majella Sinclair; da of James Gaskin (d 1980), and Mary Harrington (d 1952); *b* 2 April 1929; *Educ* Holy Cross Coll Australia; *m* 1955, Sol Cornberg, s of Joseph Cornberg (d 1928); *Career* author; *Books* This Other Eden (1946), With Every Year (1947), Dust in Sunlight (1950), All Else is Folly (1951), Daughter of the House (1952), Sara Dane (1955), Blake's Reach (1958), Corporation Wife (1960), I Know My Love (1962), The Tilsit Inheritance (1963), The File On Devlin (1965), Edge of Glass (1967), Fiona (1970), A Falcon For A Queen (1972), The Property of A Gentleman (1974), The Lynmara Legacy (1975), The Summer of The Spanish Woman (1977), Family Affairs (1980), Promises (1982), The Ambassador's Women (1985); *Recreations* music, reading; *Style*— Miss Catherine Gaskin; White Rigg, East Ballaterson, Maughold, Isle of Man (☎ 0624 812145)

GASKIN, James Joseph; s of James Joseph Gaskin (d 1979), of Berks, and Caroline, *née* Myers (d 1988); *b* 23 April 1945; *Educ* Wembley Co GS; *m* 26 Oct 1968, Linda, da of Thomas William Arundel, of Middlesex; 1 s (Matthew b 1972), 1 da (Sarah b 1974); *Career* dir 1976-84 of Hull Blyth & Co Ltd, Oakwool Gp Ltd, Seatronics (UK) Ltd, Wm Jacks (UK) Ltd, Suttons Gp Ltd; fin dir Ocean Cory Energy 1980-82 & Ocean Cory Investmt 1979-80, md Repcon (UK and Ireland) Ltd 1982-84,dir of External Services Fimbra, memb of Securities Indust Exec Liaison Ctee; *Recreations* riding, classical music; *Style*— James Gaskin, Esq; 21 Sandiland Crescent, Hayes, Bromley, Kent BR2 7DP (☎ 01 462 4156); Fimbra, Hertsmere House, Marsh Wall, London E14 9RW (☎ 01 538 8860)

GASKIN, Prof John Charles Addison; s of Harry James Gaskin, of Mixbury, Oxfordshire, and Evelyn Mary Addison Gaskin, *née* Taylor; *b* 4 April 1936; *Educ* City of Oxford Sch, Oxford Univ (MA, BLitt); *m* 20 May 1972, Diana Katherin, da of Morice Dobbin (d 1969); 1 s (Rupert John Addison b 1974), 1 da (Suzette Jane Addison b 1975); *Career* Royal Bank of Scotland 1959-61, prof of philosophy Trinity Coll Dublin 1983- (prev jr dean and lectr); FTCD; *Books* inc: Hume's Philosophy of Religion (1978, 1988), The Quest for Eternity (1984); *Recreations* riding, writing ghost stories, shooting, gardening, walking; *Clubs* Kildare St, University; *Style*— Prof John C A Gaskin; Trinity College Dublin, Dublin 2, Irish Republic (☎ 772941); Crook Crossing, Netherwitton, Northumberland

GASKIN, Malcolm Graeme Charles; s of Charles Augustus Gaskin (d 1981), of Blyth, Northumberland, and Jean, *née* Denton; *b* 27 Feb 1951; *Educ* Blyth GS, Manchester Poly, Sch of Art and Design; *m* Deborah Ann, da of Michael Loftus, of Osterley, Middx; 2 s (Jack Alexander b 1983, Lewis Ross (twin) b 1983), 1 da (Francesca Vita b 1985); *Career* art dir Leo Burnett 1973-77, creative dir TBWA 1977-81, creative dir Woollams Moira Gaskin O'Malley 1987-, inventor of Eau in Perrier; advertising awards for Lego, Land Rover, CIGA, Nursing Recruitment, Aids; memb: Design and Art Direction, Creative Circle, Aids Drugs and Alcohol Assoc; ctee memb Fulham Palace Allotments Assoc; memb Design and Art Dirs Assoc 1975; *Books* Design and Art Direction (1975); *Recreations* gardening, angling, hiking, art; *Clubs* Zanaibar; *Style*— Malcolm Gaskin, Esq; 33 Clonmel Road, Fulham, London SW6; Woollams Moira Gaskins O'Malley, Portland House, 12-13 Greek St, London W1 (☎ 01 494 0770, fax 01 734 6684)

GASKIN, Prof Maxwell; DFC (1944, Bar 1945); s of Albert Gaskin (d 1960), and Beatrice Ada, *née* Boughey (d 1967); *b* 18 Nov 1921; *Educ* Quarry Bank Sch, Univ of Liverpool (BA, MA); *m* 24 July 1952, Brenda Patricia Rachel, da of Rev William Dale Stewart (d 1954), of Crieff Perthshire; 1 s (Richard b 1960), 3 da (Rosemary b 1953, Hilary b 1957, Fiona b 1962); *Career* WWII Flt Engr RAF Bomber Cmd 1941-46, 161 Sqdn, 7 (PFF) Sqdn; sr lectr (formerly lectr) economics Univ of Glasgow 1951-65; Univ of Aberdeen: Jaffrey prof political economy 1965-85, prof emeritus political economy 1985-; chm bd of mgmnt Foresterhill & Assoc Hosps 1972-74, memb Scottish Agric Wages Bd 1972-, chm Retail Bespoke Tailoring Wages Cncl 1978-, memb Civil Engrg EDC 1978-84, chm section F Br Assoc 1978-79; memb Royal Economic Soc 1951, Scottish Economic Soc 1951 (pres 1981-84); *Books* Scottish Banking (1965), North East Scotland: A Survey of its Development Potential (jtly 1969), The Economic Impact of North Sea Oil on Scotland (jlty 1978), The Political Economy of Tolerable Survival (jlty 1981); *Recreations* music, gardening; *Style*— Prof Maxwell Gaskin, DFC; Westfield, Ancrum, Roxburghshire TD8 6XA (☎ 08353 237)

GASS, Lady; Elizabeth Periam; *née* Acland-Hood; da of Hon (Arthur) John Palmer Fuller-Acland-Hood (d 1964; s of 1 Baron St Audries, Barony extinct 1971); *b* 2 Mar 1940; *Educ* Cheltenham Ladies' Coll, Girton Coll Cambridge (MA); *m* 1975, Sir Michael David Irving Gass, KCMG (d 1983, sometime HM Overseas Civil Serv in W Africa, colonial sec Hong Kong, high cmmr for W Pacific, British high cmmr for New Hebrides); *Career* memb Somerset County Cncl 1985-; *Style*— Lady Gass; Fairfield, Stogursey, Bridgwater, Somerset (☎ 0278 732251)

GASSON, Andrew Peter; s of Sidney Samuel Gasson and Elsie; *b* 18 July 1943; *Educ* Dulwich Coll PS, Henry Thornton GS, City Univ; *Career* in pte practice (specalising in contact lenses) 1972-; pres Contact Lens Soc 1974-75, examiner: Spectacle Makers Co, Br Coll of Optometrists 1975-84, memb: cncl Br Contact Lens Assoc 1986, contact lens ctee of BSI 1980-82; lectr numerous sci meetings; sec Wilkie Collins Soc 1981-; Freeman City of London, Liveryman Worshipful Co of Spectacle Makers; FBOA, FSMC, FBCO, DCLP,GFell Amer Acad of Optometry; *Recreations* antiquarian books, travel, photography, cricket, motoring; *Clubs* MCC; *Style*— Andrew Gasson, Esq

GATEHOUSE, Graham Gould; s of George Gatehouse (d 1953), of West Coker, Somerset, and Gwendoline Maud, *née* Gould; *b* 17 July 1935; *Educ* Crewkerne Sch Somerset, Exeter Univ, LSE, Birmingham Univ; *m* 31 Jan 1960, Gillian Margaret, da of Dr Norman Wade Newell (d 1964); 2 s (Mark b 1960, John b 1963), 1 da (Jane b 1962); *Career* served RA 1954-56, subaltern; soc worker Somerset CC 1957-67, dep co welfare offr Worcestershire CC 1967-70, asst dir soc servs Norfolk CC 1970-73, dep dir soc servs W Sussex CC 1973-81, dir soc servs Surrey CC 1981-; advsr to educn and soc sers ctees ACC, Dept of Sociology Advsry Bd Surrey Univ, chm assoc dirs soc sers parly ctee; ADSS 1981, BASW 1969, FRSA 1987; *Recreations* music, rugby, theatre, cricket; *Clubs* RAC; *Style*— Graham Gatehouse, Esq; Surrey County Council, Social Services Dept, 7 Penrhyn Rd, Kingston Upon Thames KT1 2DS (☎ 01 541 9600, fax 01 541 9654)

GATEHOUSE, The Hon Mr Justice; Sir Robert Alexander Gatehouse; s of Maj-Gen Alexander Hugh Gatehouse, DSO, MC (d 1964), and Helen Grace, *née* Williams (d 1969); *b* 30 Jan 1924; *Educ* Wellington Coll, Trinity Hall Cambridge (BA); *m* 1, Oct 1950, Henrietta, da of Air Vice-Marshal Sir Oliver Swann (d 1948); m 2, 18 Aug 1966, Pamela Riley, da of late Frederick Fawcett; *Career* WW II 1939-45, cmmnd Royal Dragoons, 1944 N West Europe; called to the Bar Lincoln's Inn 1950; QC 1969; High Court Judge (Queen's Bench Div) 1985; gov Wellington Coll 1970; kt 1985; *Recreations* golf; *Style*— The Hon Mr Justice Gatehouse; Royal Courts of Justice, Strand, London WC2A 2LL

GATES, Malcolm Gilbert; s of Douglas Gilbert Gates (d 1953); *b* 6 Mar 1940; *Educ* Wallington Sch Surrey, Southampton Univ; *m* 1963, Valerie Diane, da of Harold William Hudson; 3 children; *Career* vice pres (international) Royal Trust Toronto; md: Royal Trust Bank (Jersey) Ltd, Royal Trust Co Canada (CI) Ltd; dir: Royal Trust International Fund Mgmnt, International Investment Trust; MInstD; *Recreations* golf, sailing; *Clubs* City of London, Victoria, Royal Commonwealth; *Style*— Malcolm Gates, Esq; Royal Trust, PO Box 7500, Station A, Toronto, Ontario, Canada

GATHERCOLE, Richard Benjamin David; s of Evan Frederick James Gathercole, and Kathleen Mary, *née* Burrows; *b* 28 Sept 1956; *Educ* Salesian Coll, Leicester Univ (BSc), University Coll (MSc); *Career* dir and head govt sales Hoare Govett Ltd 1981-88, dir UK Govt sales Credit Suisse First Boston 1988-; *Recreations* rugby, racing, ballet; *Style*— Richard Gathercole, Esq; 13 Landgrove Road, Wimbledon Sw19 7LL; Lindham Ho, Wells-next-the-Sea, Norfolk NR23 1E7 (☎ 01 947 2260); 2A Great Titchfield Street, London W1 (☎ 01 322 4000)

GATHORNE-HARDY, Hon Hugh; s of 4 Earl of Cranbrook (d 1978), and his 2 w, Fidelity (*see* Dowager Countess of Cranbrook); *b* 30 Dec 1941; *Educ* Eton, CCC Cambridge; *m* 1971, Caroline Elisabeth, da of William Nigel Ritchie (gs of 1 Baron Ritchie of Dundee) and Baroness Sibylla, da of late Baron von Hirschberg, of Murnau, Bavaria; 2 s, 2 da; *Career* timber merchant; *Style*— Hon Hugh Gathorne-Hardy; The Hall Farm, Great Glemham, Saxmundham, Suffolk (☎ 072 878 420)

GATHORNE-HARDY, Hon Mrs Antony; Mary Catherine; da of Bernard Joseph Smartt (d 1963); *b* 26 Mar 1917; *Educ* Varndean Sch for Girls, Brighton Teachers Trg Coll; *m* 1974, as his 2 w, Surgn Cdr Hon Antony Gathorne Gathorne-Hardy, RN, OstJ, MB, ChB (d 1976), s of 3 Earl of Cranbrook (d 1911), and Lady Dorothy Montagu Boyle, da of 7 Earl of Glasgow; *Recreations* painting, golf; *Clubs* Richmond Art Society; *Style*— Hon Mrs Antony Gathorne-Hardy; 21 Cranebrook, Manor Rd, Twickenham, Middx TW2 5DJ (☎ 01 894 1174)

GATTY, Trevor Thomas; OBE (1974); s of Thomas Alfred Gatty (d 1959), of Looe, Cornwall, and Lilian, *née* Wood (d 1980); *b* 8 June 1930; *Educ* King Edwards Sch Birmingham; *m* 21 April 1956 (m dis 1983), Jemima Silver, da of Thomas Bowman; 2 s (Timothy James b 1957, Nicholas Trevor b 1959), 1 da (Jane Margaret (Mrs Clay), b 1960); *Career* Nat Serv 1948-50, 2 Lt Royal Warwickshire Regt, TA 1950-54, Lt Royal Fusiliers; HM Dip Serv 1950-85; vice-consul Leopoldville, first sec Bangkok; commercial consult: San Francisco, Zurich; cnsllr 1977, head Migration and Visa Dept FCO, dip serv inspr FCO, consul gen Atlanta 1981-85; conslt: Ernst & Whinney (Atlanta) 1985-, MGT Int 1988-; *Recreations* reading, English Springer Spaniels, physical fitness, railway history; *Style*— Trevor Gatty, Esq, OBE; 4026 Land O'Lakes Drive, Atlanta, Georgia, USA, 30342 (☎ 0101 404 264 9033); MGT International, PO Box 550328, Atlanta, Georgia, USA 30355 (☎ 0101 404 264 9033, fax 0101 404 256 2602)

GATWARD, (Anthony) James; s of George James Gatward (d 1964), and Lillian Georgina, *née* Strutton; *b* 4 Mar 1938; *Educ* George Gascoigne Sch Walthamstow, SW Essex Tech Coll and Sch of Art; *m* 1969, Isobel Anne Stuart, da of Ian Stuart Black, of Devon; 3 children; *Career* gp chief exec TVS Entertainment plc (instigated and led preparation of application for south and south east England TV franchise 1979-80), dir: TVS Television Ltd Solent Cablevision Ltd 1983-, C4 TV Co 1984-, Midem Organisation SA ITV News Ltd 1986-, TVS Ltd; TVS Northern American Hldgs Inc 1986; chm Telso Communications Ltd 1987; former dir and producer of films and TV dramas in GB and abroad (Br series incl Minder, West End Tales); *Recreations* farming, sailing, music; *Clubs* Reform, Royal Thames; *Style*— James Gatward, Esq; TVS Entertainment plc, Television Centre, Southampton SO9 5HZ (☎ 0703 634211)

GAUDRY, Roger; *b* 15 Dec 1913; *Educ* Laval Univ (BA, BSc, DSc), Oxford Univ (Rhodes Scholar); *m* 1941, Madeleine Vallée; 2 s, 3 da; *Career* rector Univ of Montreal 1965-75; chm UN Univ 1974-76; pres International Assoc of Universities 1975-80; chm Science Cncl of Canada 1972-75; CC (1968); FRSC; *Style*— Roger Gaudry, Esq; 445 Beverley Ave, Mount Royal, Montréal, Québec, Canada (☎ home 514 342 4759; office 514 343 7761)

GAULD, Alastair William Mitchell; s of William Mitchell Gauld (d 1950), of Rocquaine, Woking, Surrey, and Freda Caroline, *née* Condrop (d 1961); *b* 26 Sept 1914; *Educ* Roy GS Guildford, Oriel Coll Oxford (MA, Dip Econ); *m* 29 Nov 1947, Cynthia Rowena, da of Thomas Steel Downie, OBE (d 1931), of Chenar, Woking; 1 s (Andrew b 1955), 1 da (Fiona b 1949); *Career* WWII served Argyll and Sutherland Highlanders 1941-46 (demobbed as Major); Scottish Amicable Life Assur Soc 1937-40, Gresham Life Assur Soc 1946-70; chm: Old Woking branch, Woking Cons Assoc 1951-54, Wood St branch Guildford Cons Assoc 1970-75; pres Puttenham Garden Club 1987-, chief steward Wimbledon LT Championships 1973-; Freeman City of London 1957, Liveryman Worshipful Co of Farriers 1963; *Recreations* gardening, golf, reading; *Style*— A W M Gauld, Esq; Pilgrims Way Cottage, The Heath, Puttenham, Guildford, Surrey GU3 1AL (☎ 0483 810288)

GAULT, David Hamilton; s of Leslie Hamilton Gault, and Iris Hilda Gordon Young; *b* 9 April 1928; *Educ* Fettes; *m* 1950, Felicity Jane Gribble; 3 s, 2 da; *Career* exec chm Gallic Management 1974-; *Recreations* gardening, walking; *Clubs* Boodle's, City of London; *Style*— David Gault, Esq; Telegraph House, N Marden, Chichester, W Sussex (☎ 073 085 206, office 01 628 4851)

GAULTER, Derek Vivian; CBE (1978); s of Jack Rudolf Gaulter, MC (d 1967), slr and Cmmr for Oaths, of Newport House, Clarence Ave Cleveleys, Nr Blackpool, and Muriel, *née* Westworth (d 1982); *b* 10 Dec 1924; *Educ* Denstone Coll, Peterhouse Cambridge ; *m* 1 Jan 1949, Edith Irene, da of Frederick Norman Shackleton (d 1964), of 10 St Edmumds Ave, Hunstanton, Norfolk; 1 s (Andrew b 1951), 3 da (Briony b 1953, Catherine b 1959, Deborah b 1964); *Career* Sub Lt RNVR 1943-46 (serv MTBs in N Sea and minesweepers in Far East); barr Grays Inn 1949, practising Common Law bar (Manchester) 1955-56, Fedn of Civil Engrg Contractors: legal sec, gen sec, dep dir-gen, dir-gen (1967); chm Construction Indust Trg Bd 1985-; memb cncl and pres's ctee CBI; former memb Civil Engrg Econ Devpt Ctee companion of The Inst of Civil Engrs 1983; *Recreations* golf, gardening, travel, photography; *Clubs* IOD; *Style*— Derek Gaulter, Esq, CBE; Construction Industry Training Board, 24-30 West Smithfield, London EC1A 9JA (☎ 01 489 1662, fax 01 236 2875, car tel 0836 510 948)

GAUNT, David; s of Edgar Gaunt, of Hawksworth Hall, Guiseley, Yorks; *b* 29 June 1920; *Educ* Winchester, Magdalene Coll Cambridge; *m* 1965, Elizabeth, da of William Robertson, of Helensburgh; *Career* served WW II, Capt, N Africa, Italy, Balkans; chm Reuben Gaunt & Sons, pres Bradford Chamber of Commerce 1961; High Sheriff W Yorks 1977-78; *Recreations* fishing, shooting, gardening; *Clubs* Special Forces, Shrievalty Assoc; *Style*— David Gaunt, Esq; The Nunnery, Arthington, Otley, W Yorks (☎ 0532 886236)

GAUNTLETT, John Wilson; s of Reginald Wilson Gauntlett (d 1916), and Kate Susanna Gauntlett, *née* Gibbs (d 1974); *b* 11 Jan 1914; *Educ* Christ's Hosp; *m* 29 July 1948, Alice Betty Magee, da of Rev Deane (d 1941); 1 step s (Sean b 1943), 1 step da (Mary b 1941); *Career* WWII RA, Maj 1939-46; slr 1936, ptnr Linklater & Paines 1951, ret 1978; dep chm: RMC Gp plc, Malcolm Sargent Cancer Fund for Children 1987; *Recreations* carpentry, reading; *Style*— John W Gauntlett, Esq; High Hammerden, Stonegate, Wadhurst, E Sussex TN5 7ES (☎ 0580 200183); RMC Group plc, 32 Chesham Place, London SW1X 8HB (☎ 01 235 0711)

GAUNTLETT, Malcolm Victor; s of Michael Errington Gauntlett (d 1971), and Adele Sylvia Dolores Gauntlett, *née* Montgomerie; *b* 20 May 1942; *Educ* St Marylebone GS; *m* 22 Oct 1966, Jean, da of James Brazier, of Shropshire; 3 s (Michael b 1971, Mark b 1981, Richard b 1982), 1 da (Sarah b 1969); *Career* exec chm Aston Martin Lagonda Ltd 1981-, chm Aston Martin Lagonda Gp Ltd 1984-; former chm Pace Petroleum Ltd (fndr dir 1972, company sold to Kuwait Investmt Office 1983); *Recreations* motor racing, aviation; *Clubs* Carlton, Cavalry and Guards', MCC; *Style*— Victor Gauntlett, Esq; 37 Chesham Place, SW1; Aston Martin Lagonda Ltd, Tickford St, Newport Dagnell, Bucks (☎ 0908 610620), telex 892341, fax 0908 613708)

GAUSSEN, Hon Mrs (Diana Bridget); da of Hon Robert Godfrey de Bohun Devereux (d 1934; only s of 17 Viscount Hereford); raised to the rank of a Viscount's da 1953; *b* 25 Mar 1931; *m* 16 Oct 1967, Col Samuel Charles Casamajor Gaussen, Welsh Gds, o surv s of late James Archibald Casamajor Gaussen, of Pegglesworth, Glos; 1 s, 1 da; *Style*— Hon Mrs Gaussen; 60 Alder Lodge, Stevenage Rd, London SW7; Nutbeam, Duntisbourne Leer, Cirencester, Glos GL7 7AS

GAUTREY, Peter; CMG (1972), CVO (1961); s of Robert Harry Gautrey (d 1961), of Surrey, and Hilda Morris (d 1972); *b* 17 Sept 1918; *Educ* Abbotsholme Sch Derbyshire; *m* 1947, Marguerite Etta, da of Horace Ewart Uncles (d 1963); 1 s (Christopher b 1948), 1 da (Sarah Jennifer b 1951); *Career* WWII Capt Army 1939-46; Home Off 1936; CRO 1948; first sec: Br Embassy Dublin 1950-53, New Delhi 1955-57; counsellor New Delhi 1960-63; dep high cmmr Bombay 1963-65; Corps of Dip Serv Insp 1965-68; high cmmr: Swaziland 1968-72, Brunei 1972-75, Guyana 1975-78; concurrently ambassador Suriname; DK (Brunei) 1972; *Recreations* walking, music; *Style*— Peter Gautrey, CMG, CVO; 24 Fort Rd, Guildford, Surrey GU1 3TE (☎ 0483 68407)

GAUVAIN, Col Anthony de Putron; s of Roland de Putron Gauvain, (ka Singapore 1943), and Marcelle Iris Clisson (now Mrs Hugo), *née* Mitchell; *b* 11 Jan 1941; *Educ* Wellington Coll, RMA Sandhurst; *m* 9 Dec 1967, Avril, da of Brig Pat Hancock, (d 1987) of Aynho: 2 da (Claire b 1973, Bonamy b 1975); *Career* cmmnd Cheshire Regt 1961, Trucial Oman Scouts 1966, Staff Coll 1972, Cmd 1 Bn Cheshire Regt 1981, (despatches 1983), MA to CDS Oman 1984; DACOS G2 Int HQ BAOR 1987-;; *Recreations* tennis, water and snow skiing, sailing, amateur dramatics; *Clubs* Army and Navy; *Style*— Colonel A de P Gauvain; DACOS, E2, Int HQ, BAOR

GAVIN, Maj-Gen James Merricks Lewis; CB (1967), CBE (1963, OBE 1953); s of Joseph Merricks Gavin (d 1945), of Antofagasta, Chile, and Frances Edith, *née* Lewis (d 1955); *b* 28 July 1911; *Educ* Uppingham Sch, Univ of Cambridge (MSc); *m* 1942, Barbara Anne Elizabeth, da of Gp Capt Charles Geoffrey Murray, CBE (d 1962), of Hayling Island, Hants; 1 s (Angus), 2 da (Lindy, Janine); *Career* cmmnd 2 Lt RE 1931, served WWII Far East, ME, Italy, France, also post-war in USA, Germany and France, Maj-Gen at SHAPE 1964-67; memb Everest Expedition 1936; *Recreations* yachting (Corruna), skiing, climbing; *Clubs* Royal Yacht Sqdn, Royal Cruising, Alpine; *Style*— Maj-Gen James Gavin, CB, CBE; Slathurst Farm, Milland, Liphook, Hants

GAY, Barrie; s of Walter Lionel Gay (d 1970), and Florence Emily, *née* Upson (d 1983); *b* 9 Sept 1938; *Educ* Peter Symonds Sch Winchester; *m* 15 Oct 1966, Sylvia Ann, da of Charles Allen Parsons (d 1978); 1 s (James b 1969), 1 da (Catherine b 1971); *Career* CA; sr ptnr Weeks Green Southampton 1979-; FCA; *Style*— Barrie Gay, Esq; 9 The Abbey, Romsey, Hampshire SO51 8EN (☎ 0794 523413); 21 Cumberland Place, Southampton SO9 5SS (☎ 0703 632023)

GAY, Bramwell Clifford (Bram); s of Clifford Gay, of Wolverhampton, and Effield, *née* Brown; *b* 19 Sept 1930; *Educ* Porth County Sch, Birmingham Sch of Music (LRAM 1949); *m* 10 Jan 1954, Margaret Ivy, da of Augustus Bywater; 3 s (Peter John Noel, David, Jonathan Michael); *Career* served Scots Guards 1949-53; principal trumpet: City of Birmingham Symphony Orch 1954-59, Halle Orch 1959-69, Royal Opera House Covent Garden 1969-74; orch dir Royal Opera House 1974-; fndr: CBSO Brass Ensemble, Halle Brass Ensemble, Granada Brass Band Festival 1971-87; ed Brass Music (Novello & Co) 1967-; *Recreations* music, boating; *Style*— Bram Gay, Esq; Royal Opera House, Covent Garden, London WC2 (☎ 01 240 1200)

GAY, Lt Col Geoffrey Charles Lytton; s of Charles Millne Gay (d 1952), and Ida Lytton Gay (d 1978), e da of Sir Henry Lytton (famous savoyard); *b* 14 Mar 1914; *Educ* St Pauls; *m* 6 Sept 1947, Dorothy Ann, da of Maj Eric Rickman; 2 s (Charles, Vivien), 1 da (Louise (Mrs Fox)); *Career* WWII 1939-45, Durham LI Bef 1940, psc, Lt-Col Chief of Staff Dist India; Knight Frank and Rutley: joined 1929, ptnr 1952, sr ptnr 1969 (ret 1975), conslt 1975-80; chm and vice pres Westminster Chamber of Commerce; K St J; memb Worshipful Co of Brokerers; FRICS, FSVA, FRSA, FRSS, LRPS; Chevalier De L'Ordre De L'Economie Nationale 1960, Vermeille Medal of Paris; *Recreations* photography, fishing, music, theatre; *Clubs* Carlton, Flyfishers, MCC; *Style*— Lt-Col Geoffrey Gay; Brookmans Old Farm, Iwerne Minster, Blandford Forum, Dorset DT1 8NG

GAY, Rear Adm George Wilsmore; CB (1969), MBE (1946, DSC 1943, JP (1970 Plymouth)); s of George Murch Gay, Engr Cdr RN (d 1933), and Olive Trounsell, *née* Allen (d 1971); *b* 2 Oct 1913; *Educ* Eastmans Sch Southsea, The Nautical Coll Pangbourne, RN Engrg Coll Keyham; *m* 15 Feb 1941, Nancy Agnes, da of Robert John Hinton Clark, MBE (d 1976), of 29 Whiteford Rd, Mannamead, Plymouth, Devon; 2 s (John b 1943, Paul b 1945), 1 da (Jane b 1948); *Career* RN 1930-69; WWII submarines; Cdr 1947, Capt 1958; CO HMS Sultan 1960-3; Chief Staff Offr material to Flag Offr Submarines 1963-66; Rear-Adm 1967; dir gen Naval Trg 1967-69; ret 1969; FIMechEng; *Recreations* fishing, gardening; *Clubs* Army and Navy; *Style*— Rear Adm George Gay, CB, MBE, DSC, JP; 29 Whiteford Rd, Mannamead, Plymouth, Devon PL3 5LU (☎ 0752 664486)

GAYMER, Vivien Murray; *née* Gall; da of Dr Louis Adrian Murray Gall (d 1973), of Spalding, Lincs and Patricia Violet, *née* Boothby, ARRC, JP; *Educ* Felixstowe Coll, English Speaking Union Scholar at Northfield Sch Mass USA, Univ of Sheffield (LLB); *m* 12 Aug 1978, Keith Edward (Sam) Gaymer, s of Ernest Edward Gaymer; 1 step da (Victoria b 1961); *Career* called to the Bar, Middle Temple, 1971; lectr London Coll of Printing 1970-74, asst sec Inst of Practioners in Advertising 1974-75, counsel Mobil Oil in London and NY 1975-84, head of Legal Affrs Enterprise Oil plc 1984-; tstee Petroleum and Mineral Law Educn Tst, fndr memb and sec UK Oil Lawyers Gp 1985-87, dir St Christophers Fellowship 1983-85; *Recreations* cooking and eating; *Style*— Mrs Vivien Gaymer; 5 Strand, London WC2N 5HU (☎ 01 930 1212, fax 01 930 0321, telex 8950611 EPRISE G)

GAYTON, Alan William; JP (Leicester 1963); s of Frank Gayton (d 1961), of Leicester, and Susannah Edith Anne Drackley (d 1975); *b* 21 June 1923; *Educ* Wyggeston GS Leicester, LSE, Sandhurst; *m* 1, Dec 1948 (m dis), Jean Urquhart; 1 s (John Charles b 1956), 1 da (Susan Mary b 1953); m 2, Feb 1974, Jean Frances, da of Frank Kelly (d 1976), of Leicester; *Career* WWII served N Africa and Italy Capt 17/21 Lancers; dir Gayton Advtg Ltd Leicester, chm Leicester City Bench 1987; FIPA; *Recreations* golf, theatre; *Style*— Alan W Gayton, Esq, JP; Old Boot Cottage, Main St, Houghton-on-the-Hill, Leics (☎ 0533 414 131)

GAZE, Dr (Raymond) Michael; s of William Mercer (d 1959), of Blue Mills, Wickham Bishops, Essex, and Kathleen Grace, *née* Bowhill (d 1974); *b* 22 June 1927; *Educ* Sch of Med of the Royal Colls Edinburgh, Oxford Univ (BA, DPhil); *m* 20 March 1957, Robinetta Mary, da of Prof Roger Noel Armfelt (d 1955), of Woodlea, Shadwell Lane Leeds; 1 s (Julian Mercer b 1959), 2 da (Harriet Carlin b 1958, Hannah Mary (twin) b 1959); *Career* Med Offr RAMC 1953-55; house Physician Chelmsford and Essex Hosp 1949, lectr in physiology Edinburgh Univ 1955-62, Alan Johnston Lawrence and Moseley research Fellow of the Royal Soc 1962-66, reader in physiology Edinburgh Univ 1966-70, head div of Developmental Biology Nat Inst Med Res London 1970-83, head MRC Neural Devpt and Regeneration Gp Dept of Zoology Edinburgh Univ 1984-; FRSE 1964, FRS 1972; *Books* The Formation of Nerve Connections (1970), and numerous scientific papers; *Recreations* hill walking, drawing, music; *Style*— Dr Michael Gaze; Dept of Zoology, Univ of Edinburgh, West Mains Rd, Edinburgh EH9 3J

GAZZARD, Roy James Albert; s of James Henry Gazzard, MBE (d 1976), of New Milton, Hants, and Ada Gwendoline, *née* Willis (d 1973); *b* 19 July 1923; *Educ* Stationers' Company's Sch Hornsey Middx, Architectural Assoc Sch of Architecture (Dip), Sch of Planning & Res for Regnl Devpt (Dip); *m* 6 Jan 1947, (Muriel) Joy, da of Frederick William Morgan (d 1952), of Higher Odcombe, Somerset; 2 s (Paul b and d 1948, Mark b 1953), 2 da (Sarah (twin) b 1953, Naomi b 1958); *Career* cmmnd Middx Regt 1942, Glider Pilot Regt 1943, Support Capt HQ 6 Airlanding Bde 6 Airborne Div 1944, demobbed Maj 1947; govt town planner Uganda 1949-54 (devpt plans for Jinja 1954), staff architect Barclays Bank 1953-60, chief architect planner Peterlee New Town Devpt Corpn 1960-62, dir of devpt Northumberland CC 1962-70, dir of postgrad studies urban geography and planning Univ of Durham 1970-76, under sec DOE 1976-79, dir centre for Middle Eastern and Islamic studies Univ of Durham 1984; memb Sec of State's Working Party preparing UK evidence for UN conf on the environment 1972, chief professional advsr Sec of States Environmental Bd 1976-79; chm Northern region RIBA 1970, vice chm BBC NE advsy cncl 1970-73, govr Sunderland Poly 1972-76, cncl memb Northern Arts 1970-76, chm BBC Radio Newcastle advsy cncl 1980-83, tstee City of Durham Tst 1970-89; Liveryman Worshipful Co of Stationers 1970 (Renter Warden 1985-86); Hon Fell Centre for Middle Eastern and Islamic Studies Univ of Durham 1988; FRTPI 1957, FRIBA 1967; *Books* Durham: Portrait of a Cathedral City (1983); *Recreations* independent travel in remote locations, esp Arabia, dry stone walling, castles and castle towns; *Clubs* City Livery, Victory; *Style*— Roy Gazzard, Esq; 13 Dunelm Ct, South St, Durham City DH1 4QP (☎ 091 386 4067)

GEARING, Eric Gerard; s of Bertrand John Gearing (d 1969), of Wallasey, and Winifred Anastasia Gearing, *née* Smith (d 1964); *b* 21 Sept 1922; *Educ* Private, Liverpool Collegiate Sch, Liverpool Univ (LLB); *m* 7 Nov 1959, Pauline Mary, da of Charles Ebo (d 1964), of Crosby; 1 da (Maria Winefride b 1971); *Career* Army 1941-45, Lt (actg capt) wounded N Africa; slr Gearing and Wilde; pt/t chm Social Security Appeal Trib, former Borough Cllr and Parly Candidate (Cons); pres: Wallasey Operatic Soc (ex chm), Wallasey YMCA; vice-pres The Rotary Club of Wallasey ex pres Wallasey Cons Assoc (vice-chm, tres), pres Wallasey Civic Soc (ex chm), chm Wallasey Soc for Mentally Handicapped, life govr Cancer Research Fund, County Borough Cllr; *Recreations* amateur drama & operatics, politics, painting, photography, theatre, spectator, sports, music; *Clubs* Rotary, Catenians, YMCA; *Style*— Eric G Gearing, Esq; Tarsus, 6 Gorsehill Road, Wallasey, Wirral (☎ 051 639 5802); 110 Wallasey Road, Wallasey, Wirral (☎ 051 638 2113, telex 628761 BUTEL G, fax 051 658 8688)

GEARING, Graham David; s of Jack Gearing (d 1974), and Clara Elizabeth, *née* Patterson; *b* 17 Oct 1932; *Educ* East Ham GS; *m* 25 April 1981, Kathleen Elizabeth, da of Patrick Cardinall Mason Sedgwick, CMG (d 1985); 1 s (Patrick b 1985), 1 da (Nicola b 1982) ; *Career* md G D Gearing Electronics Ltd 1975-; *Recreations* power boating, mountaineering; *Style*— Graham Gearing, Esq; Tarskavaig, Sleat, Isle of Skye, Scotland IV46 8SA (☎ 047 15 263)

GEARING, Ian Martin; s of Jack Gearing (d 1974), and Clara Elizabeth,*née* Patterson (now Mrs Walker); *b* 23 Sept 1950; *Educ* East Ham GS, Thames Poly (BA); *m* 24 Aug 1974, Liselotte, da of Herr Konrad Roder, of Bayreuth, West Germany; 1 s (David Alexander b 14 Oct 1980), 1 da (Andrea Elizabeth b 31 July 1982); *Career* advertising exec J Walter Thomson Ad Agency Frankfurt W Germany 1973-74, mktg mangr Bunzl Paper Subsiduary London 1974-76 (gen mangr Antwerp 1976-79), mktg mgmnt Utd Rum Merchants Int Ltd London 1980-87, pres and md Tia Maria Int London; vice pres Camberley Rugby FC; MInstM; *Recreations* sport and music; *Style*— Ian Gearing, Esq; Tia Maria Int Ltd, Heritage House, 21 Inner Park Rd,

London SW19 6ED (☎ 01 788 4400, fax 01 788 4323, telex 919396 HIWALKG)

GEARY, Michael John; s of John Geary (d 1980), of Hemel Hempstead, Herts, and Joyce Nellie, *née* Lee; *b* 18 June 1950; *Educ* Apsley GS Hemel Hempstead, Worcester Coll Oxford (BA, MA); *m* 4 Jan 1975, Susan Mary, da of Henry Spilman Wood, of Turweston, Northants; 2 s (John b and d 1979, Malcolm b 1980), 1 da (Hazel b 1982); *Career* exec engr PO Telecommunications (now Br Telecom) 1971-74, controller Industl and Commercial Fin Corpn Ltd (now 3I) 1974-79, investmt exec Charterhouse Devpt Ltd 1979-82, md Munford White plc 1982-85; dir: Tunstall Devpt Ltd 1985-86, Prudential Venture Mangrs Ltd 1986-; *Recreations* sailing, skiing; *Clubs* Royal Southern YC, Ski (GB); *Style*— Michael Geary, Esq; Audrey House, Ely Place, London EC1N 2NH (☎ 01 831 7747)

GEBBETT, Stephen Henry; s of Albert Gebbett, of Hundon, Suffolk, and Elsie Mary, *née* Kettle; *b* 24 Jan 1949; *Educ* Raynes Park CGS, Univ of Wales (BSc); *m* 22 Dec 1973, Linda Margaret; 1 s (Timothy Giles b 5 Oct 1976), 1 da (Kimberley Sarah b 13 May 1981); *Career* graduate trainee and assoc dir F J Lyons PR Consultancy 1970-76; Charles Barker Lyons 1976-: assoc dir 1976-79, dir 1979-86, md 1986-88, chief exec 1988-; MIPR 1976; *Recreations* squash, gardening, humour; *Style*— Stephen Gebbett, Esq; Charles Barker Lyons, 30 Farringdon St, London EC4A 4EA (☎ 01 634 1014)

GEDDES, Hon David Campbell; TD; s of 1 Baron Geddes, GCMG, KCB, PC (d 1954); *b* 11 Mar 1917; *Educ* Stowe, Gonville and Caius Coll Cambridge; *m* 31 Dec 1948, Gerda, da of State Cllr Gerdt Meyer Bruun, of Bergen, Norway (d 1945); 2 da (Jane, Harriet); *Career* joined RA 1938, served 1939-45 on staff, Maj 1943; dir Jardine Matheson Hongkong 1953-58 & assoc cos; civil servant Foreign & Cwlth Off, Overseas Devpt Admin (princ 1969-77); FRGS; *Clubs* Brooks's; *Style*— Hon David Geddes, TD; Clayfield, Etchingham, East Sussex TN19 7QJ

GEDDES, Enid, Baroness; Enid Mary; *née* Butler; o da of late Clarance Howell Butler, of Shanghai and Tenterden, Kent; *m* 26 Jan 1931, 2 Baron Geddes (d 1975); 2 s (3 Baron and 1 s decd), 1 da (Hon Mrs van Koetsveld); *Style*— The Rt Hon Enid, Lady Geddes; 12 Courtenay Place, Lymington, Hants (☎ 0590 73333)

GEDDES, 3 Baron (UK 1942), of Rolvenden; Euan Michael Ross Geddes; s of 2 Baron, KBE (d 1975), and Enid, Lady Geddes, *née* Butler; *b* 3 Sept 1937; *Educ* Rugby, Gonville and Caius Cambridge (MA), Harvard Business Sch; *m* 7 May 1966, Gillian, yr da of the late William Arthur Butler, of Henley-on-Thames; 1 s (James b 1969), 1 da (Clair b 1967); *Heir* s, Hon James George Neil Geddes; *Career* Lt Cdr RNR (ret); chm: Geddes & Co Ltd 1985-, Jenny Maclean & Co 1975-, Dawson Strange Photography Ltd 1988-, Parasol Portrait Photography Ltd 1988-; dep chm: Faber Prest Holdings plc 1987-; dir: Barchester Shipping Ltd 1984-, John Broadwood & Sons Ltd 1986-, Alfred Bishop & Son Ltd 1987-, City Harbour Hotel Ltd 1987-, Eurospa (Chelsea) Ltd 1987-, Harbour Inns Ltd 1988-, Stewart Consultants & Offshore Technol Servs Ltd 1986-; *Recreations* golf, skiing, bridge, gardening; *Clubs* Brooks's, Aldeburgh GC, Hong Kong, Royal Hong Kong GC; *Style*— The Rt Hon the Lord Geddes; The Manor House, Long Sutton, Basingstoke, Hants RG25 1ST (☎ 0256 862105, fax 0256 862029)

GEDDES, Ford Irvine; MBE (Mil 1943); s of Irvine Campbell Geddes (d 1962), bro of 1 Baron Geddes), and Dorothy Jefford, *née* Fowler; *b* 17 Jan 1913; *Educ* Loretto, Gonville & Caius Cambridge; *m* 8 Dec 1945, Barbara Gertrude Vere, o da of Charles Fitzmaurice Parry Okeden, JP; 1 s (David (m Sahra Mellor)), 4 da (Jennian (Mrs Nicholas Montagu), Merryn (Mrs Michael Lloyd), Fiona (Mrs Colin Goodwille), Ailie (Mrs Adrian Collins)); *Career* dir Anderson Green & Co Ltd 1947-68, The Equitable Life Assurance Soc 1955-76 (pres 1963-71), The Peninsular & Oriental Steam Navigation Co 1960-72 (chm 1971-72); memb London Advsy Bd Bank of New South Wales 1950-81; *Clubs* City of London, Union (Sydney); *Style*— Ford Geddes, Esq, MBE; 18 Gordon Place, London W8 4JD

GEDDES, Keith Irvine; DFC; s of Irvine Campbell Geddes (d 1962), and Dorothy Jefford, *née* Fowler (d 1976); *b* 25 Oct 1918; *Educ* Loretto Sch, Gonville & Caius Coll Cambridge (BA); *m* 1, 1946 (m dis 1967), Marion Olive, da of late Sir John Stirling; 2 s (Rorie b 1948, Angus b 1954), 2 da (Rona b 1947, Shian b 1951); m 2, 1968, Anne Mary, da of Richard Pullen; 1 s (Marcus b 1975), 2 da (Katherin b 1970, Serena b 1973); *Career* cmmnd RAFVR 1939, 604 Fighter Sqdn 1940-41, staff HQ Fighter Cmd 1943-45 (demobilised 1945 rank of Sqdn Ldr); dir Anderson Green & Co Ltd 1950-62; fndr memb and dir Economic Forestry Gp 1959-87, memb Lloyds 1961; rugby football blue 1938; Capt 1944-47: Scotland RF XV, RAF RFC, London Scottish RFC; *Recreations* shooting; *Clubs* City of London; *Style*— Keith I Geddes, DFC; Westbrook House, Upwey, Weymouth, Dorset (☎ 0305 812929, 036982 284)

GEDDES, Philip Clinton; s of David Geddes, and Audrey Clinton, *née* Phillips; *b* 26 August 1947; *Educ* Sherborne, Queens' Coll Cambridge; *m* 27 Oct 1984, Selina Valerie, da of Capt Derek Head, RNR; 1 s (David b 1985); *Career* gen trainee BBC 1970, prodr BBC features 1973-80, exec prodr TVS and head of sci and indust programmes 1981-88, currently writer and conslt to business; churchwarden St James Wield; *Books* In The Mouth Of The Dragon (1981), Inside The Bank of England (1988); *Recreations* cricket; *Clubs* Ooty; *Style*— Philip Geddes, Esq; Manor Farm, Upper Wield, Alresford, Hants (☎ 0420 62361)

GEDDES, Sir (Anthony) Reay Mackay; KBE (1968), OBE (1943); s of Rt Hon Sir Eric Campbell Geddes, GCB, GBE (bro of 1 Baron Geddes, d 1937), and Ada Gwendolen, *née* Stokes (d 1945); *b* 7 May 1912; *Educ* Rugby, Magdalene Coll Cambridge; *m* 14 April 1938, Imogen, da of Capt Hay Matthey; 2 s (Duncan, Piers), 3 da (Alison, Lindsay, Candida); *Career* chm Dunlop Hldgs 1968-78, dep chm Midland Bank 1978-83 (dir 1967-83); dir: Shell Tport & Trading 1968-82, Rank Orgn 1975-84; pres the Abbeyfield Soc; chm Charities Aid Fndn; ; *Style*— Sir Reay Geddes, KBE, OBE; 49 Eaton Place, London, SW1X 8DE (☎ 01 235 5179)

GEDDES TAYLOR, Hon Mrs (Pamela Margaret); has used name of Geddes Taylor since 1960; o da of Baron Geddes of Epsom, CBE (Life Peer, d 1983), and Julia, *née* Burke; *b* 27 Sept 1925; *m* 11 Oct 1957 (m dis 1966), Louis Patrick Taylor, s of Louiss Herbert Taylor, of Cambridge; *Career* Coll lect; ret; *Recreations* bridge, wine making; *Style*— Hon Mrs Geddes Taylor; North Cottage, Pump Lane, Framfield, Sussex TN22 5RQ (☎ 082 584 512)

GEDDIS, (Andrew) David Roberston; s of Andrew Geddis (d 1975), and Jean Baikie, *née* Gunn (d 1976); *b* 13 Oct 1915; *Educ* Merchiston Castle Sch Edinburgh; *m* 3 Dec 1955, Enid Joan Millicent (d 1979), da of George Edward Lambert Houghton (d 1961); 1 da (Jean b 1959); *Career* Maj 2 King Edwards VII own Gurkha Rifles, Western Desert, Italy, Greece (despatches); vice chm Bombay Exchange Banks Assoc 1940-66, fell of the Indian Inst of Bankers and memb cncl 1960-66; memb: mgmnt ctee Labour Secretariat of Banks in Indian (chm 1965-66), gen ctee Bombay C of C 1963-66, mgmnt ctee UK Citizen's Assoc Bombay Branch 1961-66 (chm 1965-66); vice pres and memb cncl Centl Admin of The UK Citizen's Assoc in India 1965-66, asst gen mangr Nat Grindlays Bank London 1967-69 (gen mangr 1970-72), ret 1973; *Recreations* golf, travel; *Clubs* Overseas Bankers (London); *Style*— David Geddis, Esq; c/o Grindlays Bank plc, 13 St James Square, London SW1Y 4LF

GEE, Anthony Francis (Tony); s of Frank Gee, of Hazel Grove, Cheshire (d 1959), and Hilda May, *née* McHaffie (d 1942); *b* 16 Feb 1934; *Educ* Malvern, Selwyn Coll Cambridge (MA); *m* 1, 26 Dec 1958 (m dis 1979), Patricia Ann (Pat), da of Sqn Ldr Harry Millington, of Lower Withington, Ches; 1 s (Timothy b 1962), 1 da (Sally b 1961); m 2, 30 March 1984, Patricia Louise Rudham (Patti), da of George Simmons, of Sutton, Surrey; *Career* conslt Tony Gee & Ptnrs 1988- (fndr 1974, dir Far East 1982-), conslt Tony Gee & Quandel Atlanta USA 1986- (fndr 1982); FICE 1959, MIMechE 1975, FIStructE 1962, FIMechE 1975; *Books* Civil Engineering Reference Book (jtly 1961); *Recreations* golf, bridge; *Clubs* Walton Heath GC, Cherokee T & C C (Atlanta USA); *Style*— Tony Gee, Esq; Atlanta, Arbour Close, The Mount, Fetcham, Leatherhead, Surrey KT22 9DZ (☎ 0372 376 787); 290 Halah Circle, Sandy Springs, Atlanta, Georgia 30328, USA; Tony Gee and Ptnrs, TGP House, 45-47 High St, Cobham, Surrey KT11 3DP (☎ 0932 68277, fax 0932 66003, telex 928496 TGANDP)

GEE, Christopher John; s of Victor George Gee, of Bucks, and Rene, *née* Yule; *b* 7 Nov 1940; *Educ* Wycombe RGS; *m* 1 Jan 1966, Nanette, da of Philip Pedley Walley (d 1967); 2 s (Thomas John Philip b 1970, Toby Quintin Alleyne (adopted 1976)), 2 da (Anne Louise b 1967, Alison Christine b 1968); *Career* CA public practice 1968-, now ptnr MacIntyre Hudson; FCA; *Recreations* farming; *Clubs* Reform; *Style*— Christopher Gee, Esq; MacIntyre Hudson, Chartered Acctnts, 28 Ely Place, London EC1N 6RL

GEE, David William; s of William George Gee (d 1975), and Gladys Elizabeth Gee; *b* 4 Dec 1930; *Educ* Univ of Birmingham (BSc Hons Phys); *m* 31 August 1957, Margaret, da of James Harvey Rowson (d 1949), of Lancashire; 2 s (Steven William b 1962, Martin Philip James b 1965), 1 da (Janet Elizabeth Sara b 1960); *Career* Royal Navy Instr Lt 1942-55; chartered patent agent, european patent attorney; dir Trade Marks, Patents, Designs Fedn 1977-86; jt fndr Anti-Counterfeiting Gp 1974; vice-pres: North Warwickshire Small Business Bureau, North Warwickshire Constituency Cons Assoc; chm: North Warwickshire Ctee British Horse Soc; fndr and prop: David W Gee Patent and Trade Mark Agents, Gee Computer Services; *Recreations* riding, golf; *Style*— David W Gee, Esq; The Farmhouse, Marston, W Midlands B76 0DW (☎ 0675 70202); Farmhouse Court, Marston, W Midlands (☎ 0675 70621)

GEE, Prof Geoffrey; CBE (1958); s of Thomas Gee (d 1962), of Overdale Rd, New Mills, Derbyshire, and Mary Ann Gee; *b* 6 June 1910; *Educ* New Mills Sch, Manchester Univ, Cambridge Univ; *m* 1934, Marion, da of late Fred Bowden, of New Mills; 1 s, 2 da; *Career* dir of research Br Rubber Producers Research Assoc 1947-53, prof of chemistry Manchester Univ 1953-77 (with periods of appointment as pro-vice-chllr), now emeritus prof; Hon DSc (Manchester 1983); FRS; *Recreations* gardening; *Clubs* Royal Society; *Style*— Prof Geoffrey Gee, CBE; 8 Holmfield Drive, Cheadle Hume, Cheshire (☎ 061 485 3713)

GEE, Ronald Davenport; s of Fred Davenport Gee (d 1975); *b* 16 May 1925; *Educ* Manchester GS, Balliol Coll Oxford; *m* 1950, Marianne, da of Prof Paul Kalbeck, of Vienna (d 1949); 2 da; *Career* Lt RNVR (Fleet Air Arm) 1942-45, served Pacific, Torpedo Dive Bomber Sqdns; company director; chm London Gold Futures Market 1983- (vice chm 1982); dir Metal Market & Exchange Co; *Recreations* opera, golf; *Clubs* Sunningdale, Vincents; *Style*— Ronald Gee, Esq; BICC Cables Ltd, PO Box 5, 21 Bloomsbury St, London WC1B 3QN (☎ 01 637 1300, telex 62881 BICC G)

GEE, Steven Mark; s of Dr Sidney Gee, of 42 Chester close North, Regent's Park London NW1 and Dr Hilda *née* Elman; *b* 24 August 1953; *Educ* Tonbridge Sch, Brasenose Coll Oxford (MA); *Career* barr Middle Temple in commercial practice, standing jr counsel in export credit guarantee matters DTI; MCC Sporting memb London Maritime Arbitrators Assoc; *Books* The Law and Practice of Mareva Injunctions (1987); *Recreations* marathon running; *Clubs* Serpentine Running; *Style*— Steven Gee, Esq; 38 Eaton Terrace, London, SW1 (☎ 823 4660), 4 Essex Court, Temple, London, EC4 (☎ 583 9191, fax 353 3421)

GEERING, Kenneth Redman; s of Walter Redman Geering (d 1937), of Wootton Manor, Charing, Kent, and Edith Amelia, *née* Giles (d 1960); *b* 26 Jan 1910; *Educ* Bedford Sch; *m* 6 June 1934, Mary Pauline, da of William Davis (d 1937), Ashford, Kent; 1 s (Christopher b 1937, 1976); *Career* Aux Fire Serv Ashford Cmdt 1942, Nat Fire Serv Column Offr E Kent 1943; chm Ashford Chamber of Trade 1952-53; chm Off Machinery Ltd 1964-70, chm Business Machines (SE) Ltd 1974-79, Geerings of Ashford Ltd 1938-; co-fndr Ashford Childrens Day 1949; pres: Ashford Cattle Show 1974, Typewriter Trades Fedn of GB and Ireland 1955-56, Ashford Cricket Club 1973-78; chm Assoc of Imperial Typewriter Agents 1963-64; pres: Town Div St John Ambulance Bde 1947-59, Ashford GC 1973-, Wengen Curling Club 1986-87, Ashford Rotary Club 1946; Paul Harris fell 1985, cncllr Ashford Urban Dist Cncl 1939-49 (chm 1947); *Recreations* curling, golf, cricket; *Clubs* MCC Paternosters; *Style*— Kenneth Geering, Esq; Wootton Manor, Charing, Kent TN27 0DU (☎ 0233 71 2310); Cobbs Wood House, Chart Rd, Ashford, Kent TN23 1EP (☎ 0233 33366, telex 965009, fax 39404)

GEERING, Michael William; s of John George William Geering, of London, and Winifred, *née* Green; *b* 5 August 1944; *Educ* Stationers' Company's Sch, Univ of Southampton (BSc); *m* 19 Sept 1970, Jean Mavis, da of Samuel Frederick George Fletcher, of Cardiff; 1 s (Jonathan b 3 July 1974), 1 da (Nicola b 4 Aug 1972); *Career* CA 1965; articled clerk Binder Hamlyn 1965-68, trainee analyst Laing & Cruickshank Stockbrokers 1968-69, audit sr Ernst & Whinney 1969-72; James Capel & Co 1973-: investmt analyst, head UK Equity res 1985-, memb bd 1987-, dir for UK equity div 1987-; FCA; *Recreations* golf, swimming, tennis, horse racing; *Clubs* Gnomes; *Style*— Michael Geering, Esq; Lion Hill, West Rd, St George's Hill, Weybridge, Surrey KT13 OLZ (☎ 0932 843302); James Capel & Co, James Capel House, PO Box 551, 6 Bevis Marks, London EC3A 7JQ (☎ 01 621 0011, fax 01 621 0496, car tel 0836 254 848, telex 888866)

GEFFERS, Maj Iain George Huntly; s of Col Frederick William Geffers (d 1980), of Berks, and Mildred Maud Sumner (d 1979); *b* 27 Jan 1932; *Educ* Haileybury, RMA Sandhurst; *m* 8 Nov 1958, Johanna Jane Frances, da of Francis Raymond George Nason Sherrard (d 1974); 2 da (Georgina b 1960, Fiona b 1961); *Career* cmmnd 2 Lt

12 Lancers 1952 (served Malaya, Korea, Cyprus), ret Maj 1968; conservation of paintings 1968-; memb: Assoc of Br Picture Restorers, Int Inst for Conservation; *Recreations* hunting; *Clubs* Cavalry; *Style*— Maj Iain Geffers; The Manor House, Piddletrenthide, Dorchester, Dorset DT2 7QX (☎ 03004 203)

GELBER, David; s of Edward Gelber, of Toronto (d 1970), and Anna *née* David (d 1974); *b* 10 Nov 1947; *Educ* Whittinghame Coll Brighton, Hebrew Univ Jerusalem (BSc), Univ of London (MSc); *m* 1, 1969 (m dis 1979), Laura Beare; 1 s (Jeremy Edward b 1973), 1 da (Amy b 1975); m 2 1962, Vivienne da of Harry Cohen of Weybridge; *Career* Morgan Guaranty Tst 1975-76, vice pres Citibank/Citicorp 1976-85; md (head global SWAPS and foreign exchange options) Chemical Bank 1985-; *Recreations* tennis, squash; *Clubs* RAC Cumberland Lt; *Style*— David Gelber, Esq; 6 Clorane Gardens, London, NW3 7PR (☎ 01 794 1352); Chemical Bank, 180 Strand, London, WC2R 1ET (☎ 01 380 8366), fax 01 380 5948, car tel (0836) 202 187

GELBER, Lady Henrietta Mary; *née* Spencer-Churchill; da of 11 Duke of Marlborough, by his 1 w, Susan Mary, *née* Hornby (now Mrs Jo Gough, *qv*); *b* 7 Oct 1958; *Educ* St Mary's Wantage, Inchbald Sch of Design; *m* 14 March 1980 (m dis 1989), Nathan Gelber, s of Aba Gelber; 2 s (David b 1981, Maximilian b 1985); *Career* interior decorator; dir: Woodstock Designs, Spencer-Churchill Designs Ltd; *Style*— Lady Henrietta Gelber; 35 Redcliffe Road, London SW10 9NJ (☎ 01 352 6804); Woodstock Designs, 7 High St, Woodstock, Oxon OX7 9XX; 55 Hollywood Road, London SW10 9HX

GELDARD, Robin John; s of Cyril John Geldard (d 1984), of Thornton Dene, South Glam, and Gertrude Nellie Lawrence (d 1971); *b* 9 August 1935; *Educ* Aldenham Sch, Coll of Law; *m* 4 Sept 1965, Susan Elizabeth, da of Sir Martin Llewellyn Edwards (d 1987), of Pentwyn Farm, Lisvane, nr Cardiff; 2 s (Bruce b 1967, Michael b 1972), 1 da (Anna b 1972); *Career* recruit RM 1958, Mons Offr Cadet Sch, cmmnd RM 1959, 2 Lt Commando Trg Unit, RM rugby team 1958-60; slr and ptnr Edwards Geldard 1962, asst registrar 1980-85; dir: Thames Valley Lift Co Ltd 1987-, The Bigtlis Co Ltd 1980-, Highfield Holiday Park Ltd 1979-, Hendre Gritstone Ltd 1980-87, Hadley Wholesale Suppliers Ltd 1980-; pres Cardiff Incorporated C of C and Indust 1987-89; vice pres Cardiff Incorporated Law Soc 1987-88 (pres 1988-), vice pres Federated Welsh C of C 1987-88, memb cncl Nat Cncl of the Assoc Br C of C memb Lloyds 1987; *Recreations* sailing, flyfishing, music, photography; *Clubs* Naval, Cardiff and Co, Royal Porthcawl GC; *Style*— Robin Geldard, Esq; Llanquian Farm, Aberthin nr Cowbridge, South Glam CF7 7HB (☎ 044 63 2484); 16 St Andrews Crescent, Cardiff CF1 3RD (☎ 0222 238239)

GELDER, Prof Michael Graham; s of Philip Graham Gelder (d 1972), and Alice Margaret, *née* Graham (d 1985); *b* 2 July 1929; *Educ* Bradford GS, Queens Coll Oxford, Univ Coll Hosp Med Sch; *m* 21 Aug 1954, Margaret Constance, da of Lt-Col John William Smith Anderson (d 1984); 1 s (Colin b 31 May 1960), 2 da (Fiona b 31 May 1960), 2 da (Fiona b 12 Jan 1963, Nicola b 9 May 1964); *Career* Capt RAMC 1955-57; sr house physician Univ Coll Hosp 1957 (house physician 1955), registrar Bethlem Royal and Maudsley Hosps 1958-61, MRC fell in clinical res 1962-63; Inst of Psychiatry: lectr 1964-65, sr lectr 1965-67, vice dean 1967-68; prof of psychiatry Univ of Oxford 1969-, fell Merton Coll Oxford 1969-, hon conslt Oxfordshire Health Authy 1969-; chm Neurosciences Bd MRC 1978-79 (memb 1976-78), vice pres RC Psych 1982-84; FRCP 1970, FRCPsych 1973; *Books* Psychological Aspects of Medical Practice (ed 1973), Agrophobia: Nature and Treatment (jtly 1981), Oxford Textbook of Psychiatry (jtly 1983); *Recreations* real tennis, reading, photography; *Clubs* Athenaeum; *Style*— Prof Michael Gelder; Univ Dept of Psychiatry, Warneford Hosp, Oxford; Merton Coll, Oxford

GELL, Peter Donald Marriott; s of Harold Marriot Gell, MC, of Chipping Campden, Glos; *b* 17 Mar 1929; *Educ* Sherborne, Worcester Coll Oxford (MA); *m* 1960, Jean, da of Lt-Col David Livingstone Graham, of Crowborough; 1 s, 3 da; *Career* dir Bunzl plc, chm Industrial Division Bd; FCA, FCIS; *Recreations* music, field sports; *Style*— Peter Gell, Esq; Shearings, Witheridge Lane, Penn, Bucks (☎ (049 481) 3243)

GELLHORN, Hon Mrs (Olive Shirley); 3 da of 1 Baron Layton, CH, CBE (d 1966), and Eleanor Dorothea, *née* Osmaston (d 1959); *b* 18 Dec 1918; *m* 18 May 1943, Peter Gellhorn, prof GSM 1981-, s of late Dr Alfred Gellhorn; 2 s, 2 da; *Style*— Hon Mrs Gellhorn; 33 Leinster Ave, London SW14 7JW

GELLHORN, Peter; s of Dr Alfred Gellhorn (d 1972), and Else Agathe, *née* Fischer (d 1950); *b* 24 Oct 1912; *Educ* Schiller Real Gymnasium Charlottenburg, Univ of Berlin, Berlin Acad of Music, (passed with distinction final exams as pianist 1932 and conduct 1934; *m* 18 May 1943, Olive Shirley, 3 da of 1 Baron Layton of Danehill, CH, (d 1966); 2 s (Martin b 1945, Philip b 1951), 2 da (Mary b 1959, Barbara b 1960); *Career* musical dir Toynbee Hall London 1935-39, asst conductor Sadler's Wells Opera 1941-43, indust war serv 1943-45, conductor Royal Carl Rosa Opera 1945-46, conductor and head music staff Royal Opera House Covent Gdn 1946-53, conductor and chorus master Glyndebourne Festival Opera 1945-61, dir BBC chorus (incl conducting Promenade Concerts) 1961-72, rejoined Glyndebourne 1974-75, co fndr and musical dir Opera Barga Italy 1967-69; conductor: The Elizabethan Singers 1976-80, Morley Coll Opera Gp 1973-79, Barnes Choir 1973-; on opera sch staff RCM 1980-88, prof Guildhall Sch of Music and Drama 1981-, lectr and adjudicator GB and overseas; compositions incl: music for the silhouette and puppet films of Lotte Reiniger, "Aucassin and Nicolette" (Festival of London 1972); Royal Philharmonic Soc, ISM; *Recreations* swimming, walking, going to plays; *Style*— Peter Gellhorn, Esq; 33 Leinster Ave, East Sheen, London SW14 7JW (☎ 01 876 3949)

GELLINER, Ernest André; s of Rudolf Cellner (d 1987), and Anna, *née* Fantl (d 1954) ; *b* 9 Dec 1925; *Educ* Balliol Coll Oxford (MA), London (PhD); *m* 23 Sept 1954, Susan, da of Curteis Norwood Ryan, CB, CMG, MC, DSO (d 1969); 2 s (David b 18 Nov 1957, Benjamin b 3 July 1963), 2 da (Sarah b 8 March 1959, Deborah 10 Feb 1961); *Career* WWII Private Czechoslovak Armed Bde BLA 1944-45; LSE 1949-84 (prof 1962-), William Wyse prof of soc anthropology Cambridge 1984- professional fell King's Coll Cambridge 1984-; Hon DSc Bristol 1986; FBA 1974; hon foreign memb American Academy of Arts and Scis 1988; *Books* Words and Things (1959), Thought and Change (1964), Saint of the Atlas (1969), Contemporary Thought and Politics (1974), The Devil in Modern Philosophy (1974), Legitimation of Belief (1975), Spectacles and Predicaments (1979), Muslim Society (1981), Nations Nationalism (1983), The Psychoanalytic Movement (1985), Culture, Identity and Politics (1987), State and Society in Soviet Thought (1988), Plough, Sword and Book (1988); *Clubs* Reform; *Style*— Prof Ernest Gelliner; 9 Claredon St, Cambridge CB1 1JU (☎ 0223 66 155); Department of Social Anthropology Univ of Cambridge, Free School Lane, Cambridge CB2 3RF (☎ 0223 334 599)

GELLING, Robert Raisbeck (Robin); s of Douglas Raisbeck Gelling, of Millersdale, Derbyshire, and Marjorie Nicklin, *née* Roberts (d 1977), formerly Gelling and Mann; *b* 29 Nov 1930; *Educ* Bishop Veseys GS Sutton Coldfield; *m* 29 July 1961, Shelagh Mary, da of Arthur Kenneth Hannah (d 1979), of Sutton Coldfield; 3 da (Susan b 1962, Sarah b 1964, Louise b 1966); *Career* Nat Serv 1954-56, Intelligence Corps Cyprus; CA; ptnr Wenham Major; *Recreations* golf, gardening, travel; *Clubs* Little Aston, Blackwell, Sutton Coldfield; *Style*— Robert Gelling, Esq; 4 Oaklands Road, Four Oaks, Sutton Coldfield, W Midlands B74 2TB (☎ 021 308 1298); 89 Cornwall Street, Birmingham B3 3BY (☎ 021 236 1866, fax 021 200 1389)

GEMMELL, Gavin John Norman; s of Maj Gilbert Anderson Sloan Gemmell, of Gullane, E Lothian, and Dorothy Maud, *née* Mackay; *b* 7 Sept 1941; *Educ* George Watson's Coll; *m* 18 March 1967, Kathleen Fiona (Kate), da of Alexander Drysdale, of Edinburgh; 1 s (John Gilbert b 9 Sept 1971), 2 da (Alison Fiona b 22 Aug 1969, Lynsey Jane b 4 April 1975); *Career* CA 1964; apprentice John M Geoghegan 1959; Baillie Gifford & Co: investmt trainee 1964, ptnr 1967, ptnr i/c pension fund clients 1973; dir: Accountants Publishing Co 1983, Scottish Widows Fund & Life Assur Soc 1984, Baillie Gifford Shin Nippon plc 1985; vestry memb St Peters Episcopal Church 1966-84, pres Watsonian Squash Rackets Club 1986-, Capt Watsonian GC 1988; chm AITC Tax Ctee 1980-88; *Recreations* golf, squash, travel; *Style*— Gavin Gemmell, Esq; 14 Midmar Gdns, Edinburgh EH10 6DZ (☎ 031 447 8135); Springwell, Gullane, E Lothian; Baillie Gifford & Co, 3 Glenfinlas St, Edinburgh EH3 6YY (☎ 031 225 2581, fax 031 225 2358, telex 72310 BGCO G)

GEMMELL, James Henry Fife; s of James Walter Shanks Gemmell (d 1962), and Vera McKenzie, *née* Scott; *b* 17 May 1943; *Educ* Dunfermline HS, Edinburgh Univ; *m* 27 Dec 1972, (Catherine) Morna Davidson, da of John Wilson Gammie, of Elgin, Morayshire; 2 da (Caroline b 1974, Catriona b 1976); *Career* CA 1965; ptnr: Fryer Whitehill and Co 1975-82, Clark Whitehill (on merger of Fryer Whitehill and Co and Clark Pixley) 1982-; memb: disciplinary ctee Insur Brokers Registration Cncl 1985, cncl ICAS 1988; *Books* RICS Accounts Rules (1978), Insurance Brokers Accounts and Business Requirement Rules (1979), How to Value Stock (1983); *Recreations* gardening; *Style*— James Gemmell, Esq; Clark Whitehill, 25 New St Sq, London EC4A 3LN (☎ 01 353 1577, fax 01 583 1720, telex 887422)

GENT, (John) David Wright; s of Pilot Offr Reginald Philip Gent, RAFVR (d 1942), and Stella Eve Wright (d 1988); *b* 25 April 1935; *Educ* Lancing Coll; *m* 19 Aug 1970, Anne Elaine, da of John Leslie Hansen (d 1988), of Ilkley, Yorks; *Career* admitted slr 1959, dep dir SMMT 1971-80 (sec 1965-70, asst sec 1964, legal advsr 1961-63), gen mangr Lucas Service UK Ltd 1980-82, gp PR mangr Lucas Indus plc 1982-83, dir Br Road Fedn 1983-85; dir gen Motor Agents Assoc 1985- ; chm: MAA Pensions Ltd, GPA Hldgs Ltd 1985-, memb Road Tport Indust Trg Bd 1985-; Freeman City of London 1985, Liveryman Worshipful Co of Coach Makers and Coach Harness Makers 1985; FIHT (1984), FIMI (1985); *Recreations* farming, gardening; *Clubs* RAC; *Style*— David W Gent, Esq; 44 Ursula St, London SW11 3DW (☎ 01 228 8126); 219 High St, Henley in Arden, Warwickshire B95 5BG (☎ 05642 3922); Motor Agents Assoc Ltd, 201 Great Portland St, London W1N 6AB (☎ 01 580 9122, fax 01 580 6376)

GENT, Marcus James; OBE (1974); s of of Sir (Gerard) Edward James Gent, KCMG, DSO, OBE, MC (d 1948), and Gwendolen Mary, *née* Wyeth; *b* 5 Feb 1925; *Educ* Malvern, Trinity Coll Oxford; *m* 1952, Marian Elizabeth, da of Lancelot Newling Rawes (d 1976); 4 da; *Career* barr 1950; dir: The Guthrie Corpn plc (rubber and palm oil gp) 1970- (chm 1979-81); Phoenix Assurance Co 1979-85; *Style*— Marcus Gent, Esq, OBE; c/o Thge Guthrie Corporation plc, 6 Devonshire Square, London EC2

GENTLEMAN, David William; s of Tom Gentleman (d 1966), and Winifred Murgatroyd (d 1966); *b* 11 Mar 1930; *Educ* Hertford GS, Royal Coll of Art; *m* 1, 1953 (m dis 1966), Rosalind Dease; 1 da (Fenella); m 2, 1968, Susan, da of George Ewart Evans (d 1988), of Brooke, Norfolk; 1 s (Tom), 2 da (Sarah, Amelia); *Career* painter and designer, work includes: watercolours of landscape, bldgs and people; lithography, wood engraving, book illustration; Eleanor Cross platform mural designs for Charing Cross Underground 1979; posters and postage stamps; *Books* David Gentleman's Britain (1982), David Gentleman's London (1985), A Special Relationship (1987), David Gentleman's Coastline (1988); *Style*— David Gentleman, Esq; 25 Gloucester Cres, London NW1 7DL (☎ 01 485 8824)

GENTRY, Maj-Gen Sir William George; KBE (1957, CBE 1947, OBE 1941), CB (1954), DSO (1942 and bar 1945); s of Maj Frederick Charles Gentry, MBE, and Eliza Amy Gentry; *b* 20 Feb 1899; *Educ* Wellington Coll NZ, Roy Mil Coll of Aust; *m* 1926, Alexandra Nina, da of Charles Robert Caverhill (d 1951); 1 s (Steven), 1 da (Sally); *Career* regular soldier GSO1 2 NZ Div 1941-42, Cdr 6 NZ Inf Bde 1942-43, ANU 9 NZ Inf Bde 1945, Adj Gen NZ Army 1949-52, CGS NZ Army 1952-55, served Greece, Crete, Western Desert, Libya, Italy; *Recreations* walking; *Clubs* Wellington (NZ), United Services (NZ); *Style*— Maj-Gen Sir William Gentry, KBE, CB, DSO; 52 Kings Crescent, Lower Hutt, NZ (☎ 660208)

GEORGE, Rear Adm Anthony Sanderson; CB (1983); s of Sandys Parker George, and Winifred Marie George; *b* 8 Nov 1928; *Educ* RNC Dartmouth, RN Engrg Coll Manadon; *m* 1953, Mary Veronica Frances Bell; 2 da; *Career* Captain 1972 (served aboard HMS Nelson), Rear Adm 1981; dir Dockyard Production & Support 1981-82, chief exec Royal Dockyards 1983-; *Style*— Rear Adm Anthony George, CB; c/o Dockyard Dept, Ministry of Defence, Whitehall, SW1

GEORGE, Sir Arthur Thomas; AO; s of Thomas George; *b* 17 Jan 1915; *Educ* Sydney Boys' HS, Slrs' Admission Bd Course; *m* 1939, Renee, da of Anthony Freeleagus; 1 da; *Career* slr and co dir; chm and md George Investmt Pty Gp Ltd 1943-; dir: Thomas Nationwide Tport Ltd 1973-, Ansett Tport Industs Ltd, Aust Solenoid Hldgs Ltd, G & P Hotels Ltd, Quadrax Investments Ltd, Wyndhanm Wines Ltd; chm Assoc classical Archaelogy Sydney Univ 1966- (endowned chair of classic archelogy, hon fell 1985); pres Aust Soccer Fedn 1969-88, hon pres Ctee Oceania Football Confedn, exec memb FIFA; chm and govr the Arthur T George Fndn Ltd 1972-, fell Confedn Aust Sport 1985; Queen's Silver Jubilee Medal, Elizabethan Medal, Gold Cross Order of Phoenix (Greece), Grand Cdr and keeper Cross of Mt Athos Greek Orthodox Church; Offr of the Order of Australia 1987; kt 1972; *Recreations* swimming, theatre; *Clubs* American Nat, Royal Motor YC; *Style*— Sir Arthur George, AO; 1 Little Queen's Lane, Vaucluse, NSW 2030, Australia (☎ 371 4030)

GEORGE, Bruce Thomas; MP (Lab) Walsall South 1974-; s of Edgar Lewis George of Mountain Ash, Glam; *b* 1 June 1942; *Educ* Mountain Ash GS; Univ Coll of Wales Swansea and Univ of Warwick; *Career* asst lectr politics Glamorgan Coll of Technol 1964-66, lectr in politics Manchester Poly 1968-70, contested (Lab) Southport 1970, sr lectr politics Birmingham Poly and part-time tutor Open Univ 1971-74, memb Select Ctee on Defence 1979-; *Recreations* football; *Style*— Bruce George, Esq, MP; 42 Wood End Road, Walsall, W Midlands (☎ 0922 27898)

GEORGE, (William Norman) Bruce; s of Norman Macdonald George (d 1922), and Isobella Elizabeth Dunn (d 1964); *b* 3 Dec 1915; *Educ* Liverpool Univ Sch of Architecture, Sch of Planning and Research for Regnl Devpt (BArch); *Career* WWII Lt RA 1940-46 (POW Malaya); architect; formerly sr ptnr George/Trew/Dunn/Beckles Willson/Bowes, ret 1984; served: practice ctee and panel of arbitrators RIBA, CNAA ; princ buildings: The Guards Chapel 1963, Wellington Barracks London 1984, Huddersfield Royal Infirmary 1966, Aberdeen Royal Infirmary 1967 and 1976; other works at: Kings Coll Hosp London, Kings Coll Hosp Med Sch, Halifax Gen Hosp, New Cross Hosp, Wolverhampton; ARIBA, AMTPI; *Books* The Architect in Practice; *Recreations* sculpture, portrait painting, music, cricket; *Style*— Bruce George, Esq; 1 Copley Dene, Wilderness Rd, Chislehurst, Kent (☎ 01 467 5809)

GEORGE, Edward Alan John; s of Alan George, and Olive Elizabeth George; *b* 11 Sept 1938; *Educ* Dulwich, Emmanuel Coll Cambridge (BA, MA); *m* 1962, Clarice Vanessa, *née* Williams; 1 s, 2 da; *Career* Bank of England 1962-: seconded to Bank for Int Settlements and later to Int Monetary Fund 1972-74, dep chief cashier 1977-80, asst dir gilt-edged div 1980-82, exec dir 1982-; *Style*— E A J George, Esq; c/o Bank of England, Threadneedle St, London EC2R 8AH (☎ 01 601 4444)

GEORGE, Hywel; CMG (1967), OBE (1963); s of Rev William Morris George (d 1970), of Llys Hywel, Llanfairfechan, and Catherine Margaret, *née* Lloyd (d 1984); *b* 10 May 1924; *Educ* Llanelli GS, UC of Wales Aberystwyth (BA), Pembroke Coll Cambridge (MA); *m* 1955, Edith, da of Karl Pirchl (d 1959), of Offensee, Austria; 3 da (Carol, Tamara, Frances); *Career* mil serv RAF Flying Offr 1942-46; colonial admin serv N Borneo 1949-63, resident Tawau Malaysia 1963-66, admin St Vincent 1967-69, govr St Vincent 1969-70, admin Br Virgin Islands 1971; fell and bursar Churchill coll Cambridge 1972-; CStJ 1968, PDK (Malaysia) 1964, JMN (Malaysia) 1966; *Recreations* walking, watching rugby; *Style*— Hywel George, Esq, CMG, OBE; Churchill Coll, Cambridge (☎ 0223 336112)

GEORGE, John Charles Grossmith; er s of Col Edward Harry George, OBE, WS (d 1957), and Rosa Mary, Papal medal Benemerenti (d 1988), da of George Grossmith, OStJ, Chev de la Légion d'Honneur, Gold Cross of the Order of the Redeemer, Cross Pro Ecclesia et Pontefice; *b* 15 Dec 1930; *Educ* Ampleforth; *m* 1972, Margaret Mary Maria Mercedes (late sec to Garter King of Arms), Dame of Honour and Devotion SMO Malta, Offr of Order Pro Merito Melitense, da of Maj Edric Humphrey Weld, TD, JP (d 1969), and Maria Mercedes, da of Henry Scrope, of Danby; *Career* Lt Hertfordshire Yeo (RA, TA); College of Arms 1963-72, Earl Marshal's liaison offr with Churchill family for State Funeral of Sir Winston Churchill 1965, Green Staff Offr Investiture of HRH Prince of Wales 1969, Kintyre Pursuivant of Arms 1986-; Garioch Pursuivant of Arms 1976-86; cncl memb: The Heraldry Soc 1976-84; The Heraldry Soc of Scotland 1986-; co-designer Royal Wedding Stamp (Crown Agents Issue 1981); vice-pres BBC Mastermind Club 1979-81; FSA (Scot) 1975, FHS 1980; Kt of Obedience SMO Malta 1975, Kt of Grace and Devotion 1971, dir of ceremonies British Assoc SMOM 1976-80, Cdr of Order Pro Merito Melitense 1983, Offr 1980; *Books* The Puffin Book of Flags; *Recreations* nineteenth century English operetta, musical comedy, hagiography, watching sport principally racing, rugby and golf; *Clubs* New (Edinburgh); *Style*— J C G George, Esq, Kintyre Pursuivant of Arms; 115 Henderson Row, Edinburgh EH3 5BB (☎ 031 557 1605); Court of the Lord Lyon, HM New Register House, Edinburgh EH1 3YT (☎ 031 556 7255)

GEORGE, Prof Kenneth Desmond; s of Horace Avory George (d 1962), of Craig-Cefn-Parc, Nr Swansea, and Dorothy Margaret, *née* Hughes; *b* 11 Jan 1937; *Educ* Ystalyfera GS, Univ Coll of Wales, Aberystwyth; *m* 18 July 1959, Elizabeth Vida, *née* Harries; 2 s (Alun Michael b 30 Nov 1962, David Keith b 16 Feb 1964), 1 da (Alison Elizabeth b 5 March 1969); *Career* lectr in econs: Univ WA 1960-63, Univ Coll N Wales 1963-64, Cambridge Univ 1966-73; Cambridge Univ: res fell Dept Applied Econs 1964-66, fell Sidney Sussex Coll 1965-73; prof econs and head dept; Univ Coll Cardiff 1973-88, Univ Coll Swansea 1988-; pt/t memb MMC 1978-86; memb cncl of the Royal Econ Soc 1987-; *Books* The Allocation of Resources (with J Shorey, 1978), Industrial Organization (with C Joll, 1981), The Welsh Economy (ed with Dr L Mainwaring, 1988); *Recreations* walking, photography, music; *Style*— Prof Kenneth George; Dept Econs, Univ Coll Swansea, Singleton Park, Swansea, (☎ 0792 295168, fax 0792 295618, telex 48358)

GEORGE, Llewellyn Norman Havard; s of late Cdr Benjamin William George, DSO, RNR, and the late Annie Jane George; *b* 13 Nov 1925; *Educ* Cardiff HS, Fishguard GS; *m* 30 Aug 1950, Mary Patricia Morgan, da of the late David Morgan Davies Fishguard; 1 da (Sarah b 1957); *Career* slr; HM Coroner 1965-80; rec Wales and Chester circuit 1980-; pres: West Wales Law Soc 1973-74, Pembs Law Soc 1982-3; chm (no5) S Wales Law Soc Legal Aid Ctee 1979, dep chm Agric Land Tbnl (Wales) 1985-; *Recreations* golf, reading, chess; *Clubs* Newesault Pembs GC, Pembs Country; *Style*— Llewellyn George, Esq; Four Winds, Tower Hill, Fishguard, Pembs (☎ 0348 873894); Gaeskwide House Chambers, West Road, Fishguard (☎ 0348 873691)

GEORGE, Nicholas; s of Wallace Yowdall Evelyn George and Joy Isabel Gilbert, *née* Hickey; *b* 1 Feb 1954; *Educ* Radley Coll; *Career* articled clerk Edward Moore & Sons 1973-77, Joseph Sebag & Co 1977-79, Rowe & Pitman; dir: WI Carr Sons & Co 1981-86, BZW Securities 1986-; FCA 1978, ASIA 1980; *Recreations* shooting, fishing, travelling; *Style*— Nicholas George, Esq; 47 Ursula St, London SW11 (☎ 01 228 1513); BZW, Ebbgate Ho, Swan Lane, London EC4 (☎ 01 623 2323)

GEORGE, Peter Michael Christol; s of Col E H George, OBE, WS (d 1957), and Rosa Mary, *née* Grossmith (d 1988); *b* 12 Jan 1935; *Educ* Ampleforth; *m* 14 Aug 1971, Denise Dowding, da of Maj Charles Davenport, RM (d 1951); 6 s (Jamie b 1972, Charles b 1974, Columba b 1975, Kentigern (twin), Gervase b 1980, Tom b 1984), 1 da (Talitha b 1978); *Career* Nat Serv cmmnd 2Lt RA; admitted slr 1962, ptnr Charles Russell & Co 1964-, currently ptnr Charles Russell Williams & James; memb Law Soc; *Recreations* reading, chess, bridge, music; *Style*— Peter George, Esq; Hydeacre Worthy Rd, Winchester; Hale Court, New Square, Lincoln's Inn, London WC2 (☎ 01 242 1031, fax 01 430 0388, telex 23521 LAWER G)

GEORGE, Philip William; s of Capt Rex George (d 1986), of Melbourne, Aust, and Marie Cecil, *née* Soutar; *b* 15 August 1951; *Educ* Chigwell Sch Essex, Magdalene Coll Cambridge (MA); *m* 10 Jul 1982, Lorraine, da of Dennis James Whiting (d 1985); 2 s (Thomas b 1984, Samuel b 1987); *Career* admitted slr 1975, Beachcrofts of Chancery Lane 1973-75, asst slr Smith Morton & Long (Colchester, Halstead, Clacton-on-Sea) 1975-76 (ptnr 1976-); Cricket: Essex second eleven 1970-72, Essex League 1975-87, memb South Woodford CC 1965-79, memb Colchester and East Essex CC 1980-88; memb Colchester Round Table (chm 1987-88); memb Law Soc 1976; *Recreations* cricket, squash; *Clubs* MCC, Colchester Garrison Offrs; *Style*— Philip George, Esq; Smith, Morton & Long, Essex House, 22 Crouch St, Colchester, Essex 303 3ES

GEORGE, Rowland David; DSO (1944), OBE (1943); s of John Ellis George (d 1935), of Combe Park, Bath, and Mary Louisa, *née* Fear; *b* 15 Jan 1905; *Educ* Wycliffe Coll, Lincoln Coll Oxford (MA); *m* 22 April 1933, Hon Sylvia Beatrice, *née* Norton, da of 1 Baron Rathcreedan (d 1930); 3 s (Kester William Norton b 21 July 1934, Ryan Cecil Norton b 11 Oct 1936, Sebastian Piers Norton b 23 Feb 1947 d 16 July 1951), 1 da (Eiluned Mary Norton (Mrs Patrick Alan Crozier-Cole) b 11 Feb 1940); *Career* RAFVR 1939-45, in equipment branch, Wing-Cdr 1943, RAuxAF 1948-51, CO 3619 (Co of Suffolk) Fighter Control Unit, Fighter Cmd, RAuxAF Res 1951-; chm Bath Cncl of Social Service 1960-75; *Recreations* rowing; *Style*— Rowland George, Esq; Pythouse, Tisbury, Wilts SP3 6PB (☎ 0747 870841)

GEORGE, Susan Melody; da of Norman Alfred George, of Wraysbury, Berks, and Eileen, *née* Percival; *b* 26 July 1950; *Educ* Corona Acad; *m* 1984, Simon MacCorkindale, *qv*; *Career* actress; films include: Billion Dollar Brain 1965, The Sorcerers 1966, The Strange Affair 1967, Eye Witness 1969, Fright 1970, Straw Dogs 1971, Dirty Mary, Crazy Larry 1972, Dr Jekyll and Mr Hyde 1972, Mandingo 1973, Tiger Shark 1975, Tomorrow Never Comes 1977, Venom 1980, A Texas Legend 1980, Enter The Ninja 1981, The House Where Evil Dwells 1982, The Jigsaw Man 1984, Czech Mate 1985; The White Stallion Ltd; dir AMY Int Prodns; exec prodr: Stealing Heaven 1988-89, White Roses 1988-89; Valentino award for best actress, Virgin Islands Film Festival award for best actress; *Books* Songs to Bedroom Walls (1987); *Clubs* St James; *Style*— Ms Susan George; c/o Jean Diamond, London Mgmnt, 235 Regent St, London W1A 2JT (☎ 01 493 1610)

GEORGE, Dr William Richard Philip; s of William George (d 1967), and Anita Williams (d 1943); *b* 20 Oct 1912; *Educ* Friars Sch Bangor Gwynedd, Wrekin Coll, Wellington; *m* 19 Dec 1953, Margarete, da of Leonhard Bogner (d 1956), of Nurnberg; 1 s (Philip b 1956), 3 da (Anita b 1959, Elizabeth b 1961, Gwen b 1966); *Career* slr 1934, pt/t clerk to Justices Barmouth 1948-75, dep circuit judge 1975-80; co cncllr rep Criccieth Ward Gwynedd CC 1967- (cncl chm 1982-83, currently chm gen purposes ctee); memb: ACC, Welsh Counties ctee; chm Criccieth Meml Hall Ctee, sec Criccieth Welsh Baptist Church 1958-; winner Poetry Crown-Royal Nat Eisteddfod of Wales 1974; Hon DLitt Univ of Wales 1988; memb Law Soc 1934; *Books* 5 vols Welsh verse (1947, 1969, 1974, 1979), The Making of Lloyd George (1976), Lloyd George: Backbencher (1983), Gyfaill Hoff (the letters of Welsh Patagonian authoress Eluned Morgan, ed 1982); *Recreations* golf and (formerly) boating; *Clubs* Criccieth; *Style*— Dr William George; Garthcelyn, Criccieth, Gwynedd (☎ 76652 2625); 103 High St, Porthmadog, Gwynedd (☎ 76651 2011, 76651 2474, fax 076651 4363)

GERAGHTY, Lady Lilian Irene; *née* Travis; da of Frederick Glover Travis, of New Malden, Surrey; *m* 1946, Sir William Geraghty, KCB (d 1977); *Style*— Lady Geraghty; 11 Kelvin Grove, Chessington, Surrey (☎ Lower Hook 3721)

GERARD, Anthony Robert Hugo; s of Maj Rupert Gerard, MBE (d 1978, great nephew of 2 Baron); hp to 2 cous once removed, 4 Baron Gerard; *b* 3 Dec 1949; *Style*— Anthony Gerard, Esq

GERARD, Hon Heloise Katherine Marie; 3 da of of 3 Baron Gerard (d 1953); *b* 21 June 1911; *Career* a nun; *Style*— Hon Heloise Gerard; Blakesware, Ware, Herts (☎ 3665)

GERARD, 4 Baron (UK 1876); Sir Robert William Alwyn Frederick Gerard; 16 Bt (E 1611); s of 3 Baron, MC (d 1953), by his cous Mary, da of Sir Martin Gosselin, GCVO, KCMG, CB, and Hon Katharine Gerard (2 da of 1 Baron); *b* 23 May 1918; *Educ* Ampleforth; *Heir* 2 cous once removed, Anthony Gerard; *Recreations* nature study, poetry writing; *Style*— The Rt Hon the Lord Gerard; Portwood House Blakesware, Ware, Herts (☎ 3665)

GERARD LEIGH, Col William Henry; CVO (1983), CBE (1981); s of Lt Col J C Gerard Leigh (d 1965), of Thorpe Satchville Hall, Melton Mowbray, Leics, and Helen, *née* Goudy (d 1964); *b* 5 August 1915; *Educ* Eton, Cambridge Univ; *m* 29 Oct 1946, (Nancy) Jean, da of Wing Cdr Sir Norman Leslie Bt CMG, CBE (d 1937); 2 s (John b 24 Jan 1949, David b 28 Aug 1958), 2 da (Carolyn (Mrs Benson) b 12 Nov 1947, Camilla (Mrs Seymour) b 4 July 1952); *Career* LG: joined 1937, Lt Col Cmdg 1953-56, Col Cmdg Household Cavalry and Silver Stick in Waiting to HM The Queen 1956-59, Gentleman Usher to HM The Queen 1967-85; chm Nat Cncl YMCA,S 1974-81;; *Clubs* Whites; *Style*— Col W H Gerard Leigh, CVO, CBE; Hayes, East Woodhay, Newbury, Berks (☎ 048 84228); 15 Eaton Mansions, London SW1 (☎ 01 730 5900)

GERHARD, Dr (Derek James) Jeremy; CB (1986); s of Frederick James Gerhard (d 1983), of Banstead, Surrey, and Lily Muriel, *née* Hubbard (d 1984); *b* 16 Dec 1927; *Educ* Highgate, Fitzwilliam Coll Cambridge (MA, hon fell), Reading Univ (PhD); *m* 5 April 1952, Dr Sheila Decima, da of Dr Gerald Kempster Cooper, (d 1979); 3 s (Timothy b 1955, Mark b 1961, Christopher b 1965), 2 da (Jane b 1957, Julia b 1963); *Career* civil servant 1951-88; Air Miny, Dept of Scientific and Industl Res, BOT, DTI; dep master and comptroller (chief exec) Royal Mint 1978-88, business conslt 1988-; *Recreations* woodwork, gardening; *Style*— Dr Jeremy Gerhard, CB; Little Dowding, Walton Heath, Surrey KT20 7TJ (☎ 0737 813045)

GERKEN, Vice Adm Sir Robert William Frank; KCB (1986), CBE (1975); s of Francis Sydney Gerken, and Gladys Gerken; *b* 11 June 1932; *Educ* Chigwell Sch, RNCs Dartmouth and Greenwich; *m* 1, 1966, Christine Stephenson (d 1981); 2 da; m 2, 1983, Mrs Ann Fermor, widow of Graham Fermor, née Blythe; *Career* Capt of the Fleet (C-in-C Fleet's Staff at Northwood Middx) 1978-81, Rear Adm and Flag Offr 2 Flotilla 1981-83, dir-gen Naval Manpower and Trg 1983-84, Vice Adm 1984-87, Flag Offr Plymouth and Port Adm Devonport, placed on Retired List April 1987; govr Chigwell Sch; pres Port of Plymouth Lifeboat (RNLI), chm of tstees China Fleet Club (UK) 1987, dir Pilgrim Promotions Ltd, show dir Daily Express West of Eng Int Boat Show 1989; *Recreations* tennis, moor walking; *Clubs* Army & Navy, Royal Western YC of England; *Style*— Vice Adm Sir Robert Gerken, KCB, CBE; Faunstone Cottage, Shaugh Prior, Plymouth, Devon PL7 5EW (☎ 075 539 445)

GERLACHE; *see*: de Gerlache de Gomery

GERMAN, Lady; Dorothy; *née* Sparks; da of Richard Sparks; *m* 1931, Sir Ronald Ernest German, KCB, CMG (d 11 May 1983, dir-gen Post Office 1960-66); *Style*— Lady German; Flat 1, 8A Grassington Rd, Eastbourne, E Sussex BN20 7BU

GEROSA, Peter Norman; s of Enrico Cecil Gerosa (d 1944), and Olive Doris Minnie, *née* Harry (d 1931); *b* 1 Nov 1928; *Educ* Whitgift Sch, Birkbeck Coll London Univ (BA); *m* 1955, Dorothy Eleanor, da of Newton Cunningham Griffin; 2 da (Susan, Catherine); *Career* Civil Serv 1945-82, served in: FO, Home Office, Customs & Excise, Dept of Tport; under sec DOE 1972-82; sec Tree Cncl 1983-, vice pres ROSPA 1984-, chm Nat Automobile Safety Belt Assoc 1986-; *Recreations* languages, numismatics, singing, enjoying architecture and the countryside; *Style*— Peter Gerosa, Esq; 17 Friths Drive, Reigate Surrey RH2 0DS (☎ 0737 243771); The Tree Cncl, 35 Belgrave Sq, London SW1X 8QN (☎ 01 235 8854)

GERRARD, His Hon Basil Harding; s of Lawrence Allen Gerrard (d 1955), of Lancs, and Mary, *née* Harding (d 1972); *b* 10 July 1919; *Educ* Bryanston Sch, Cambridge Univ (BA); *m* 1948, Sheila Mary Patricia, da of C J Coggins (d 1972) and widow of Walter Dring, DSO, DFC (ka 1945), 1 s (Christopher b 1982), 2 da (Sally Diane b 1949, Rosemary Anne b 1950), 1 step da (Susan Dring); *Career* RN (MTBs) 1942-44; asst naval attaché Washington DC 1945; barr 1947; recorder Barrow in Furness 1969-70; circuit judge 1970 (ret 1982); memb Parole Bd England, Wales 1974-76; chm Selcare Tst 1971-78 (vice pres 1978-); *Recreations* golf, gardening, croquet; *Clubs* Knutsford Golf, Bowdon Croquet (Cheshire); *Style*— His Hon Basil Gerrard; North Wood, Toft Road, Knutsford

GERRARD, Peter Noël; s of Sir Denis Gerrard (d 1965), of Fulbourn, Cambs, and Lady (Hilda Goodwin) Cantley, *née* Jones; *b* 19 May 1930; *Educ* Rugby, Christ Church Oxford (MA); *m* 15 June 1957, Prudence, da of Herbert Lipson-Ward (d 1937), of Shanghai; 1 s (Hugo b 1963), 2 da (Phyllida b 1958, Deborah b 1960); *Career* Nat Serv 2 Lt XII Royal Lancers Malaya; slr 1959, sr ptnr Lovell White & King 1980-88 (ptnr 1960-80), sr ptnr Lovell White Durrant 1988-; memb: City Capital Mkts Ctee 1974-, cncl of St George's Hosp Med Sch 1982-, ctee of mgmnt Inst of Advanced Legal Studies, cncl of the Law Soc 1972-82; *Recreations* walking, music; *Clubs* Athenaeum; *Style*— Peter Gerrard, Esq; Pightle Cottage, Ashdon, Saffron Walden, Essex CB10 2HG (☎ 079 984 374); 40 Canonbury Park North, London N1 2JT (☎ 01 354 0481); 21 Holborn Viaduct, London EC1A 2DY (☎ 01 236 0066, fax 01 248 4212, telex 887122 LWD G)

GERRARD, Ronald Tilbrook; s of Henry Thomas Gerrard and Edith Elizabeth, *née* Tilbrook; *b* 23 April 1918; *Educ* Imperial Coll of Sci and Technol, London Univ; *m* 1950, Cecilia Margaret Bremner; 3 s, 1 da; *Career* sr ptnr Binnie and Ptnrs consulting engrs 1974-; *Style*— Ronald Gerrard, Esq; 6 Ashdown Rd, Epsom, Surrey (☎ 24834)

GERRARD-WRIGHT, Maj-Gen Richard Eustace John; CB (1985), CBE (1977, OBE 1971, MBE 1965); s of Rev R L Gerrard-Wright; *b* 9 May 1930; *Educ* Christ's Hosp, RMA Sandhurst; *m* 1960, Susan Kathleen Young; 2 s, 2 da; *Career* Dep Col Royal Anglian Regt 1975-80, Col Cmdt The Queen's Div 1981-84, GOC Eastern Dist 1980-82, dir TA & Cadets MOD 1982-85; *Style*— Maj-Gen R E J Gerrard-Wright, CB, CBE; Welney House, Welney, Wisbech, Cambs

GERSON, Michael Joseph; s of Maj John Leslie Gerson, TD (d 1980), and Jeanne Ida, *née* Marx (d 1981); *b* 2 Nov 1937; *Educ* Greshams Sch Holt; *m* 28 Oct 1962, Shirley Esther, da of Alfred Simons; 3 s (Anthony, Peter, Simon); *Career* RNVR 1952-58; chm Michael Gerson Ltd 1980- (md 1961-80), chm Inst of Furniture Warehousing and Removal Indust, pres Fedn Internationaux Brussels 1982-83, govr Barnet Coll; Freeman City of London 1984, Liveryman Worshipful Co of Carmen 1984; MCIT, FInstFF, FWRI; *Recreations* sailing; *Clubs* City Livery; *Style*— Michael Gerson, Esq; Downland Close, Whetstone, London N20 9LB (☎ 01 446 1300, fax 01 446 5088, telex 23965)

GERVAISE-BRAZIER, Colin Peter; s of Reginald Ernest (d 1957), and Joan Otto Bridie, *née* Babbe; *b* 5 April 1943; *Educ* Elizabeth Coll Guernsey; *m* 1971, Lynne Elizabeth, da of James Wilson, of Ikeringill; 1 s (James b 1976), 1 da (Alexandra b 1980); *Career* represented Guernsey at football, cricket, swimming, water polo, athletics, basketball; powerboat Br class I Champion (offshire) 1984; non-exec dir Airwaves Media Ltd; dir: Theodore Allen & Co Ltd, City Vision plc 1986-, Baldwin plc chief exec 1987-; *Clubs* Lord Taverners, Guernsey Yacht, Royal Yachting Assoc UKOBA; *Style*— Colin Peter Gervaise-Brazier, Esq; La Trappe, Berget, Ruette De La Generotte, Câtel, Guernsey, Channel Islands; PO Box 240, St Peter Pont, Guernsey (☎ 0481 20622, telex 4191623, fax 0481 712482)

GERVASE-WILLIAMS, Kenneth; s of George Herbert Williams (d 1978), and Edith Esther, *née* Shipway (d 1980); *b* 25 Feb 1929; *Educ* Brockenhurst Co GS Hampshire; *m* 1, 13 July 1960 (m dis 1982), Shirley Elizabeth, da of HW Barritt, OBE (d 1967); 2 s (Christopher b 26 Feb 1961, Anthony b 26 Feb 1963); m 2, 8 March 1982, Gillian, da of Dr James Burns, CBE GM; *Career* RAF 1947-49; quantity surveyor 1949-63, md Gervase Instruments Ltd 1964-88 (devpt of Ginflo Primary Flow Sensor), pres Gervase Metering Inc USA 1987; chm Gervase Instruments Ltd 1988-; Freeman City of London, Worshipful Co of Blacksmiths; FIOD 1987, MISA 1988; *Recreations* golf, tennis; *Clubs* City Livery, West Hill GC Surrey ; *Style*— Kenneth Gervase-Williams, Esq; Craneswood, Cranleigh, Surrey (☎ 0483 273 452); Gervase Instruments Limited, Britannia Works, Cranleigh, Surrey GU6 8ND (☎ 0483 275 566, fax 0483 2 71 923, car tel 0836 766 137, telex 859 473)

GESTETNER, David; s of Sigmund Gestetner (d 1956), of 12 Charles St, W1, and Henny Gestetner; er bro of Jonathan Gestetner, *qv*; *b* 1 June 1937; *Educ* Midhurst GS, Bryanston, Univ Coll Oxford (MA); *m* 16 Oct 1961, Alice Floretta, er da of Oliver Robert Marne Sebag-Montifiore, TD, of Brook Hall, Finchingfield, Essex; *Career* pres and md Gestetner Hldgs; *Recreations* sailing, tennis; *Style*— David Gestetner, Esq; Gestetner Holdings plc, PO Box 466, London N17 9LT (☎ 01 808 1050)

GESTETNER, Jonathan; s of Sigmund Gestetner (d 1956), of 12 Charles St, W1, and Henny Gestetner; yr bro of David Gestetner, *qv*; *b* 11 Mar 1940; *Educ* Bryanston, MIT (BSc); *m* 1968, Jacqueline Margaret Strasmore; *Career* jt chm Gestetner Hldgs plc 1972-; *Style*— Jonathan Gestetner, Esq; Gestetner Holdings plc, PO Box 466, 41 Fawley Rd, Tottenham, London N17 9LT (☎ 01 808 1050)

GETHIN, Fara, Lady; Fara; *née* Bartlett; yst da of late Joseph Henry Bartlett, of Garrick's Villa, Hampton, Middx; *m* 8 May 1946, Lt-Col Sir Richard Patrick St Lawrence Gethin, 9 Bt (d 1988); 1 s, 4 da; *Career* former 2 Offr WRNS; *Style*— Lady Gethin; Easter Cottage, Bredon, Tewkesbury, Glos

GETHIN, Maj Sir Richard Joseph St Lawrence; 10 Bt (I 1665), of Gethinsgrott, Cork; *b* 29 Sept 1949; *Educ* Oratory, RMA Sandhurst, RMC Shrivenham BSc), Cranfield Inst of Technol (MSc); *m* 1974, Jacqueline Torfrida, da of Cdr David Cox; 3 da; *Heir* uncle, Lt-Col William Allan Tristram Gethin, MC, RA b 13 Oct 1913; *Career* serv HM Forces, Maj, N Ireland, Germany and UK; MCIT; *Recreations* tennis, carpentry; *Style*— Maj Sir Richard Gethin, Bt; Greystones, 16 Coxwell Rd, Faringdon, Oxon (☎ 0367 21003)

GETHIN-JONES, Richard Llewellyn; s of Rev James Gethin-Jones, MC (d 1971), and Gwendoline Margaret, *née* Lewis (d 1942); *b* 6 Jan 1935; *Educ* Haileybury; *m* 8 Oct 1964, Rosemary Jennifer, da of William Arthur Hicklin (d 1969); 2 da (Amanda b 1966, Kate b 1968); *Career* Nat Serv Welsh Gds 1955-58; ptnr Ernst Whinney 1975-83; dir: Kingsley Underwriting Agencies Ltd 1983-, Kingsley Gethin-Jones and Assocs 1983-; FCA 1971; *Recreations* sailing, skiing, tennis, theatre; *Clubs* City of London; *Style*— Richard Gethin-Jones, Esq; 48 Queen's Gate Gdns, London SW7 5ND (☎ 01 584 6949); Fleur de Lys House, London EC3A 7BD (☎ 01 626 8331, fax 01 626 3943, telex 8814671 KINSLE G)

GETHING, Brian Constantine Peter; s of Lt-Col Burton William Eills Gething, of 5 Royal Northumberland Fus (d 1936), and Lady Donatia Faith Mary, *née* Wentworth-Fitzwilliam, 3 da of 7 Earl Fitzwilliam, KCVO, CBE, DSO; *b* 11 June 1926; *Educ* RNC Dartmouth; *m* 6 Jan 1954, (Ann) Sigrid, da of Sir John Musker, of Shadwell Park, Thetford, Norfolk; 1 s (William b 1959), 1 da (Caroline b 1957); *Career* served RN 1943-52, Lt 1948, ADC to HE Govr of Trinidad and Tobago 1950-52; dir: Hurst Park Club Syndicate Ltd 1957-63, Br Bloodstock Agency plc 1964-; underwriting memb of Lloyds; *Recreations* shooting; *Clubs* White's, Pratt's, MCC; *Style*— Brian Gething, Esq; British Bloodstock Agency plc, Queensberry House, High Street, Newmarket, Suffolk CB8 9BD (☎ 0638 665021)

GETHING, Air Cdre Richard Templeton; CB (1960), OBE (1945), AFC (1939); s of George A Gething, of Wilmslow, Cheshire; *b* 1911,Aug; *Educ* Malvern, Sydney Sussex Cambridge; *m* 1940, Margaret Helen, da of Sir Herbert William Gepp (d 1954), of Melbourne, Vic, Australia; 1 s, 1 da; *Style*— Air Cdre Richard Gething, CB, OBE, AFC; Garden Hill, Kangaroo Ground, Vic 3097, Australia

GHAFFARI, Dr Kamran; s of Mir Jalil Ghaffari, of Milan, Italy, and Aschraf Ghaffari; *b* 17 July 1948; *Educ* King's Sch Ely, Univ of Milan (MD, MRCPsych); *m* 8 Nov 1986, Farnaz, da of Mir Jafar Ghaffari-Tabrizi; *Career* sr registry lectr in psychiatry St Thomas' Hosp 1984-86, locum conslt psychiatrist West Middx Univ Hosp 1986-87, md and conslt psychiatrist Psychiatric and Psychological Conslt Servs Ltd 1987-; MRCPsych; assoc memb: Br Psychoanalytic Soc, Assoc Psychoanalytic Psychotherapy; *Recreations* theatre, bridge, chess, computer sciences; *Style*— Dr Kamran Ghaffari; 14 Devonshire Place, London W1N 1PB (☎ 01 935 0640)

GIBB, Andrew (McArthur); s of William Gibb (d 1983), and Ruth Margaret, *née* Railton; *b* 8 Sept 1927; *Educ* Sedbergh, Cambridge (MA); *m* 6 Sept 1956, Olga Mary, da of Leonard Marlborough Morris (d 1977); 3 da (Rosalind Emily (Mrs Morrill) b 1958, Fiona Margaret b 1959, Vanessa Grace b 1964); *Career* serv FAA and RN; barr Middle Temple 1957; dep circuit judge 1972-76; rec of the Crown Ct 1976-79; chm ctee of enquiry into fire at Wensley Lodge Old Peoples Home 1978, and other non-public enquiries; *Recreations* music, reading, watching golf, cricket; *Clubs* MCC, LCCC; *Style*— Andrew Gibb, Esq; 263 Colne Road, Sough, Earby, via Colne, Lancs BB8 6SY; Steele & Son, Solicitors, Castlegate, Clitheroe, Lancs, BB7 1AZ (☎ 0200 27431)

GIBB, Sir Francis Ross; CBE (1982); s of Robert Gibb (d 1932) and Violet Mary Gibb; *b* 29 June 1927; *Educ* Loughborough Coll (BSc); *m* 1950, Wendy Marjorie, da of Bernard Fowler (d 1957), 1 s, 2 da; *Career* dir Taylor Woodrow Int 1969-85; chm: Taywood Santa Fe 1975-85, Taylor Woodrow Construction 1978-85 (jt md 1979-84); chm and chief exec Taylor Woodrow plc 1985-(jt md 1979-85, jt dep chm 1983-85); pres Fedn of Civil Engrg Contractors 1984-87, (vice chm 1978-79, chm 1979-80, vice pres 1980-84); dir: Holiday Pay Scheme 1980-83, Tstees Benefits Scheme 1980-83, Bldg and Civil Engrg Tstees 1980-83; chm: Agreement Bd 1980-82, Nat Nuclear Corpn 1981-88; dir Br Nuclear Assocs 1980-88; memb: CBI Cncl, governing body London Business Sch, vice pres Inst Civil Engrs 1988-; FICE; kt 1987; *Recreations* ornithology, gardening, walking, music; *Clubs* Arts; *Style*— Sir Francis Gibb, CBE; Taylor Woodrow plc, 10 Park St, London, W1 (☎ 01 575 4373, telex 24428)

GIBB, Walter Frame; DSO (1945), DFC (1943); s of Robert Gibb, and Mary Florence, *née* Davies; *b* 26 Mar 1919; *Educ* St Peter's Weston-super-Mare, Clifton Coll Bristol; *m* 26 Feb 1944, (Pauline) Sylvia, da of Edward Baines Reed (d 1972); 3 da (Philippa Jane b 1947, Alison Mary b 1950, Anne Charlotte b 1956); *Career* RAFVR 1940, Night Fighter Mosquitos 264, 6O5, 515, 239 Sqdns, Wing Cdr 1944, CO 239 Sqdn, Wing Cdr Flying TFU 1945, RAF Defford, demobed 1946; Bristol Aeroplane Co: apprentice engine div 1937-40, war service until 1946, test pilot, chief test pilot 1956; achieved World Altitude Record in Olympus Canberra WD 952 1953 and 1955 (65, 890 fleet), flew Brabazon and Britannia Aircraft; sales and service mangr Br Aircraft Corpn (now Br Aerospace plc) 1961, chm and md Br Aerospace Aust Ltd 1978, ret 1984; JP Bristol 1974; *Recreations* sailing, swimming; *Clubs* RAF, Royal Sydney Yacht Sqdn, Thornbury Sailing; *Style*— Walter Gibb, Esq, DSO, DFC; Merlin Haven Lodge, 21 Merlin Haven, Wotton-under-Edge, Glos GL12 7BA (☎ 0453 844 889)

GIBB, William (Bill) Elphinstone; s of George Gibb and Jessie, *née* Reid, of Brae Neuk, New Pitsligo, Aberdeenshire; *b* 23 Jan 1943; *Educ* Fraserburgh Acad Scotland, St Martin's Sch of Art (Dip AD), Royal Coll of Art (Des RCA); *Career* couturier; Vogue Designer of the Year 1970, fell Soc of Industl Artists and Designers 1975, chm Glenclair Ltd; works are included in following museum collections: Bath, V & A, Leeds, Royal Ontario (Canada), National Museum of Antiques Edinburgh; *Recreations* travel, history of costume research, illustration; *Clubs* The Gardens, Ritz Casino, The Saddle Room, Legends, Hippodrome, Chelsea Arts; *Style*— Bill Gibb, Esq; 38 Drayton Ct, Drayton Gdns, London SW10; 12 Queensdale Rd, Holland Park, London W11 (☎ 01 727 4994)

GIBBERD, Frederick (Brian); s of Dr George Frederick Gibberd, CBE (d 1976), and Margaret Erica Gibberd, *née* Taffs (d 1976); *b* 7 July 1931; *Educ* Aldenham Sch, Cambridge Univ (BA, MB BChir), Westminster Med Sch, Cambridge (MD); *m* 3 Sept 1960, Margaret Clare, da of David James Sidey (d 1939); 4 da (Ruth b 1962, Judith b 1965, Lucy b 1966, Penelope b 1968); *Career* conslt physician Westminster Hosp London 1965-; cncl memb RSM 1972 and 1975-79; chm standing ctee of membr RCP

1970-72; (examiner 1973-); chm medical ctee: Westminster Hosp 1983-85, Riverside Dist Health Authy 1985-87 (conslt memb 1987); hon librarian RSM 1975-79; (pres clinical section 1972-74); Liveryman Worshipful Soc of Apothecaries 1968-; FRCP 1972; *Style*— Dr Brian Gibberd, Esq; 7A Alleyn Park, London SE21 8AU (☎ 01 670 2197); Westminster Hospital, London SW1 (☎ 01 828 9811)

GIBBERD, Lady; Patricia; *née* Spielman; *b* 17 Oct 1926; *m* 1, Fox-Edwards; m 2, 1972, as his 2 w, Sir Frederick Gibberd, CBE, RA, FRIBA, FRTPI, FILA (d 1984, architect of Liverpool Met Cathedral, Inter-Continental Hotel London, London Airport Terminal Buildings and Chapel); *Career* memb: Crafts Cncl, Eastern Arts Assoc, Harlow Art Tst, Yorkshire Sculpture Park, Kettles Yard; *Style*— Lady Gibberd; Marsh Lane, Harlow, Essex CM17 0NA

GIBBINGS, Hon Lady (Louise Barbara); *née* Lambert; da of 2 Viscount Lambert, TD; *b* 29 Mar 1944; *m* 1975, as his 2 wife, Sir Peter Walter Gibbings, *qv*; 1 s ; *Style*— Hon Mrs Gibbings; 10 The Vale, Chelsea, SW3

GIBBINGS, Sir Peter Walter; s of Walter White Gibbings (d 1963), and Margaret Russell, *née* Torrance (d 1963); *b* 25 Mar 1929; *Educ* Rugby, Wadham Coll Oxford (MA); *m* 1953, Elspeth, da of Cedric Macintosh; 2 da (Sarah b 1957, Jane b 1959); m 2, 1975, Louise Barbara, da of 2 Viscount Lambert, of Switzerland; 1 s (Dominic b 1976); *Career* 2 Lt, 9 Queens Royal Lancers, Capt Northants Yeomanry (TA); barr Middle Temple 1953; dir The Observer Ltd 1964-67, The Guardian and Manchester Evening News plc 1967-88 (chm 1973-88), The Press Assoc 1983-88 (chm 1986-87); Reuters Hldgs plc 1984-88, Anglia TV Gp plc 1981- (chm 1988-); The Economist Ltd 1987-; kt 1989; *Recreations* tennis, skiing, gardening; *Style*— Peter Gibbings, Esq; c/o Anglia TV Gp plc, 48 Leicester Sq, London WC2 (☎ 01 321 0101)

GIBBON, Gen Sir John Houghton; GCB (1977, KCB 1972, CB 1970), OBE (1945, MBE 1944); er s of Brig John Houghton Gibbon, DSO (d 1960), of The Manor House, Little Stretton, Salop, and Jessie Willoughby, *née* Campbell; *b* 21 Sept 1917; *Educ* Eton, Trinity Coll Cambridge; *m* 1951, Brigid Rosamund, da of Dr David Armitage Bannerman, OBE, of London; 1 s; *Career* cmmnd RA 1939, served France, Western Desert, Sicily and Europe WWII, 6 Airborne Div Palestine 1945-47, instr and chief instr RMA Sandhurst 1947-51, AQMG War Office 1955-58, Co Field Regt 1959-60, Bde Cdr Cyprus 19 62, dir Def Plans MOD 1962-65, Maj-Gen 1966, Sec Chiefs of Staff Ctee and dir Def Ops Staff MOD 1966-68, DSD (Army) 1969-71, Lt-Gen 1971, Vice-Chief of Def Staff 1971-74, Gen 1974, Master Gen of the Ordnance 1974-77, ADC Gen to HM the Queen 1976-77; Col Cmdt RA 1972-82; *Recreations* fishing, shooting, rowing; *Clubs* Naval and Military, Leander; *Style*— Gen Sir John Gibbon, GCB, OBE; Beech House, Northbrook Close, Winchester, Hants SO23 8JR (☎ 0962 66 155)

GIBBON, His Hon Judge Michael; QC (1974); s of Frank Oswald Gibbon (d 1959) of Ty-Draw Road, Caridd and Jenny Muriel *née* Leake (d 1958); *b* 15 Sept 1930; *Educ* Brightlands, Charterhouse, Pembroke Coll Oxford (MA); *m* 15 Feb 1956, Malveen Elliot, da of Capt John Elliot Seager, MC, DL, JP, OStJ (d 1955); 2 s (Nigel Elliot b 1958, David Frank b 1960), 1 da (Juliet Rebecca b 1963); *Career* Royal Artillery 1949-50; TA lt 1950-58; called to bar 1954; chm: Electoral Advisory Ctee to Home Sec 1972; Crown Court Recorder 1972-74; dep chm Local Gvt Boundary Comm for Wales 1974-78 chm: 1978-9; QC 1974; circuit judge 1979; memb Parole Bd for England & Wales 1986-88; hon recorder of the City of Cardiff 1986-; *Recreations* music, golf; *Clubs* Cardiff and County, Royal Porthcawl Golf; *Style*— His Honour Judge Gibbon; Newport (Gwent) Crown Court, Civic Centre, Newport, Gwent (☎ Newport Gwent 66211)

GIBBONS, Christopher Adney Walter; s of Adney Walter Gibbons (d 1941), of London, and Lady Taylor, *née* Constance Ada Shotter; *b* 14 May 1930; *Educ* Charterhouse, Trinity Coll Cambridge; *m* 1, Jan 1953 (m dis 1964), Gillian Elizabeth Sugden Temperley; 1 da (Virginia b 10 March 1954); m 2, Sept 1964, Charlotte Sophia, da of Sir George Bull Bt (d 1986); 2 da (Jemima b 31 Aug 1965, Loveday b 8 Nov 1967); *Career* 2 Lt Grenadier Gds 1949-50; barr Middle Temple 1954, practised at Bar 1954-60, slr 1961, asst slr Linklater and Paines 1961-66, ptnr Stephenson Harwood 1966-; non-exec dir: The Throgmorton Tst plc, The New Throgmorton Tst plc, The Throgmorton Dual Tst plc and Framlington Investmt Tst Servs Ltd 1983-, Framlington Gp plc 1986-, TT Fin plc 1986-, The Fifth Throgmorton Co plc 1988-; City of London Slrs Co: dep chm Professional Business Ctee 1982-84 (memb 1976-84), chm Banking Law Sub-Ctee 1980-84, memb Co Law Sub Ctee 1968-86; memb: Law Soc Standing Ctee on Co Law 1978-, Law Soc Ethics and Guidance Ctees Incopn Rules Sub-Ctee 1987; cncllr Hammersmith Met Borough 1968-71 (vice-chm fin ctee); memb mgmnt ctee: Hammersmith Cncl of Community Rels 1968-74, Fulham Legal Advice Centre 1968-74, Shepherds Bush Housing Assoc 1968-80; Freeman City of London 1978, Liveryman City of London Slrs Co; memb Law Soc; *Recreations* racing, walking; *Style*— Christopher Gibbons, Esq; 1 St Paul's Churchyard, London EC4M 8SH (☎ 01 329 4422, fax 01 606 0822, telex 886789 SHSPC G)

GIBBONS, Hon Sir (John) David; KBE (1985), JP (Bermuda 1974); s of Edmund Graham Gibbons, CBE (d 1972), and Winifred Gladys, MBE, *née* Robinson (d 1972), of Palm Grove, Devonshire, Bermuda; *b* 15 June 1927; *Educ* Saltus GS Bermuda, Hotchkiss Sch Connecticute USA, Harvard Univ (BA); *m* 1958, Lully, da of Johannes Jorgen Lorentzen, of Oslo; 3 s (William, John, James), 1 da by former marriage (Edith); *Career* MP (Utd Bermuda Pty) 1972-75, min health and social services 1974-75, min fin 1975-84 (post held concurrently with premiership), premier of Bermuda 1977-82; chm Bermuda Monetary Authy 1984-86; chm Bank of N T Butterfield & Son Ltd 1986-; *Recreations* tennis, golf, skiing, swimming; *Clubs* Lyford Cay (Bahamas), Royal Bermuda YC, Royal Hamilton Dinghy, Mid Ocean, Riddells Bay, Harvard (New York); *Style*— Hon Sir David Gibbons, KBE, JP; Leeward, Point Shares, Pembroke, Bermuda (☎ 809 29 5 2396); Apt 7A 3 East 71 Street, NY 10021, USA; 29 Montpelier Walk, London SW7 1JF; Bank of N T Butterfield & Son Ltd, Hamilton, Bermuda (☎ 809 295 8154) 5276)

GIBBONS, David Paul; *née* Baynes; s of Geoffrey Albert Gibbons of Milton Keynes, and Lorna June, *née* Howard; *b* 20 Nov 1957; *Educ* Weymouth GS, Bristol Univ (BSc) ; *Career* CA; Arthur Andersen & Co (articles) 1979-82, investmt analyst electronics James Capel & Co 1982-; ACA 1981; *Recreations* windsurfing, skiing; *Style*— David Gibbons, Esq; 48 Clapham Manor St, London SW4 6DZ (☎ 01 627 4652) James Capel & Co, 6 Bevis Marks, London EC3A 7JQ (☎ 01 621 0011)

GIBBONS, Dr John Ernest; s of John Howard Gibbons (d 1979), and Lilian Alice, *née* Shale (d 1982); *b* 20 April 1940; *Educ* Oldbury GS, Birmingham Sch of Architecture (Dip Arch, Dip TP), Edinburgh Univ (PhD); *m* 3 Nov 1962, Patricia, da of Eric John Mitchell, of Albany, WA; 2 s (Mark b 16 March 1963, Carey b 20 May 1964), 1 da (Ruth b 29 July 1967); *Career* lectr: Aston Univ 1964-66, ARU Edinburgh Univ 1969-72 (res fell 1966-69); Scot Devpt Dept: princ architect 1972-74 and 1976-78, superintending architect 1978-82; res scientist CSIRO Melbourne Aust 1975; SO: dep dir Bldg Directorate 1982-84, dir of bldg 1984-, chief architect 1984-; memb cncl: Edinburgh Architectural Assoc 1977-80, Royal Incorpn of Architects in Scot 1977-80, Architects Registration Cncl of UK 1984-; memb Design Cncl 1984-88; RIBA 1964, ARIAS 1967, FSA (Scot) 1984, FRSA 1987; *Style*— Dr John Gibbons; Crichton Ho, Pathhead, Midlothian EH37 5UX (☎ 0875 320 085); Scottish Office, New St Andrews House, Edinburgh EH1 3SZ (☎ 031 244 4149)

GIBBONS, Ven Kenneth Harry; s of Harry Gibbons (d 1968), and Phyllis, *née* Priday (d 1963); *b* 24 Dec 1931; *Educ* Blackpool GS, Chesterfield GS, Manchester Univ (BSc), Cuddesdon Coll Oxford; *m* 2 June 1962, Margaret Ann, da of Bertie Tomlinson (d 1962), of Billinghay, Lincoln; 2 s (David Austen b 1963, Andrew Kenneth b 1964); *Career* RAF 1952-54; ordained 1956, asst curate of Fleetwood 1956-60, sec Student Christian Movement in Schs 1960-62, sr curate St Martin-in-the-Fields Westminster 1962-65; vicar: St Edward New Addington 1965-70, Portsea 1970-81, Weeton 1981-85, St Michaels-on-Wyre 1985-; rural dean Portsmouth 1973-79 (hon canon 1974), acting chaplain to the Forces at Weeton Barracks 1981-85, diocesan dir of Ordination Candidates 1982-; archdeacon of Lancaster 1981-; *Recreations* gardening, cinema; *Clubs* Reform; *Style*— The Ven the Archdeacon of Lancaster; The Vicarage, Hall Lane, St Michael's-on-Wyre, nr Preston, Lancs PR3 0TQ (☎ 099 58 242)

GIBBONS, Robert Frank; s of Robert Rex Maynard Gibbons (d 1986), of Lawers Ho, Comrie, Perthshire, and Maria Carmella, *née* Difelice (d 1976); *b* 19 Mar 1937; *Educ* Downside, Coll of Law; *m* 14 May 1964, Rita Ann; 3 s (Nigel b 1965, Charles b 1966, Edward b 1972), 1 da (Amelia b 1969); *Career* slr 1962, sr ptnr Fox & Gibbons; memb Law Soc; *Recreations* shooting, fishing, carriage driving; *Style*— Robert Gibbons, Esq; 67 Eccleston Sq, London SW1 (☎ 01 439 8271); Lawers, Comrie, Perthshire PH6 2LT; 2 Old Burlington St, London W1X 2QA (☎ 01 439 8271, fax 01 734 8843, telex 267108 GIBLAW G)

GIBBONS, Stella Dorothea; da of C P J T Gibbons, and Maud Standish Williams; *b* 5 Jan 1902; *Educ* N London Collegiate Sch, UCL; *m* 1933, Allan Bourne Webb (d 1959, former singer and actor); 1 da (Laura Caroline); *Career* poet and novelist; FRSL; *Books Incl:* Cold Comfort Farm (1932), Bassett (1934), Christmas at Cold Comfort Farm (short stories, 1940), The Rich House (1941), The Bachelor (1944), The Matchmaker (1949), Conference at Cold Comfort Farm (1949), Swiss Summer (1951), Beside the Pearly Water (short stories, 1954) The Shadow of a Sorcerer (1955), Here Be Dragons (1956), White Sand and Grey Sand (1958), A Pink Front Door (1959), The Weather at Tregulla (1962), The Wolves were in the Sledge (1964), The Charmers (1965), Starlight (1967), The Snow Woman (1969), The Woods in Winter (1970); *Recreations* music, reading; *Style*— Miss Stella Gibbons; 19 Oakeshott Ave, Highgate, London N6

GIBBONS, Sir William Edward Doran; 9 Bt (GB 1752), of Stanwell Place, Middlesex; s of Sir John Edward Gibbons, 8 Bt (d 1982), and Mersa Wentworth, *née* Foster; *b* 13 Jan 1948; *Educ* Pangbourne, RNC Dartmouth, Bristol Univ; *m* 1972, Patricia Geraldine Archer (LLB, barr), da of Roland Archer Howse; 1 s, 1 da; *Heir* s, Charles William Edwin Gibbons b 28 Jan 1983; *Career* mangr Harwich Sealink UK Ltd 1985-87, gen mangr Isle of Wight Services Sealink UK Ltd 1987-; chm Manningtree Parish Cncl 1985-87; *Style*— Sir William Gibbons, Bt; 5 Yarborough Road, Southsea, Hants

GIBBS, Maj Andrew Antony; MBE (1945), TD (1945); s of Ven Hon Kenneth Francis Gibbs, DD (d 1935) 5 s of 1 Baron Aldenham), Archdeacon of St Albans, and Mabel Alice, *née* Barnett (d 1953); *b* 31 Mar 1914; *Educ* Winchester, Ch Ch Oxford (MA); *m* 9 May 1947, Elizabeth Joan, widow of Capt Peter George William Savile Foljambe (ka 1944), and da of Maj Eric Charles Montagu Flint, DSO (d 1962); 2 s; *Career* served WWII, Maj Herts Regt; dir: Barclays Bank 1962-84, Barclays UK Mgmnt Ltd 1971-79, Barclays Insur Servs Co Ltd 1970-75, York Waterworks Co 1969-89; memb York Diocesan Bd of Fin 1964-85, chm Dean & Chapter of York Fin Ctee 1969-; hon life memb BRCS; fell of the Midland Div of Woodard Corpn 1959-84 (hon fell 1985), chm of Sch Cncl Worksop Coll 1962-84, govr St Edward's Sch Oxford 1948-88; *Recreations* shooting; *Clubs* Travellers', Pratt's, MCC; *Style*— Maj Andrew Gibbs, MBE, TD; Kilvington Hall, Thirsk, N Yorkshire YO7 2NS (☎ Thirsk 0845 537213)

GIBBS, Hon Antonia Mary; o da of 5 Baron Aldenham and 3 Baron Hunsdon of Hunsdon (d 1986); *b* 10 July 1958; *Style*— Hon Antonia Gibbs

GIBBS, Bryan Somerset Andrew; s of Somerset Bryan Gibbs (Capt Welsh Gds), of Witcham House, Witcham, Cambs, and Elspeth Oriana Elisabeth, *née* Russi; *b* 30 Nov 1950; *Educ* Ampleforth; *m* 12 Oct 1974, Suzette Elizabeth, da of Maj Ronald John Stephens, of Southrepps, Norfolk; 3 da (Lucy b 1981, Gemma b 1983, Alice b 1987); *Career* audit mangr (formerly articled clerk) Coopers & Lybrand 1969-78, gp chief accountant (latterly gp fin controller) Phicom plc (formerly Plantation Hldgs Ltd) 1978-86; Corporate Communications plc (formerly City Commercial Communications plc): fin dir 1986-89, gp fin dir 1989-; FCA; *Recreations* golf, tennis, table tennis, chess, old house restoration; *Clubs* Royal Worlington & Newmarket Golf; *Style*— Bryan Gibbs, Esq; Keepers Cottage, Knights Hill, Westmill, Buntingford, Herts SG9 9LX (☎ 0920 821856); Corporate Communuications plc, Bell Court House, 11 Blomfield Street, London EC2M 7AY (☎ 01 588 6050, fax 01 920 9405, car tel 0836 233717, telex 883502 CCC G)

GIBBS, Christopher Henry; 5 and yst s of Hon Sir Geoffrey Cokayne Gibbs, KCMG (d 1975; 2 s of 1 Baron Hunsdon of Hunsdon, 4 s of 1 Baron Aldenham, JP), and Helen Margaret, CBE, JP, *née* Leslie (d 1979); *b* 29 July 1938; *Educ* Eton, Stanbridge, Université de Poitiers; *Career* art dealer; dir: Christopher Gibbs Ltd, and Faversham Oyster Fishery Co; tstee: Edward James Fndn, J Paul Getty Jr Charitable Tst, J Paul Getty Jr Endowment Inst (Nat Gallery), Serpentine Gallery; memb Oxford Diocesan Ctee for the Care of Churches; *Recreations* antiquarian pursuits, gardening; *Clubs* Beefsteak; *Style*— Christopher Gibbs, Esq; Manor House, Clifton Hampden, Abingdon, Oxon; L6 Albany, Piccadilly; Christopher Gibbs Ltd, 118 New Bond St, London W1Y 9AB (☎ 01 629 2008/9)

GIBBS, David Charles Leslie; eldest s of Hon Sir Geoffrey Cokayne Gibbs, KCMG (d 1975; 2 s of 1 Baron Hunsdon of Hunsdon, JP, himself 4 s of 1 Baron Aldenham,

JP), and Helen Margaret, CBE, JP, *née* Leslie; *b* 15 August 1927; *Educ* Eton, Ch Ch Oxford; *m* 20 March 1965, (Charmian) Fleur, da of Dalzell Pulteney Mein, of Toolang, Coleraine, Victoria, Australia; 2 s, 2 da; *Career* Antony Gibbs Gp in Eng and Aust 1949-80, (dir Antony Gibbs & Sons, chm Gibbs Bright & Co); chm: Baillieu Bowring 1977-81, Baillieu Bowring Marsh & McLennan 1981-85, Marsh & McLennan 1985-87, BGJ Hldgs 1982-; dir: Australia & NZ Banking Gp 1979-, Folkestone Ltd 1976- (chm 1983-), John Swire & Sons Pty Ltd 1983-, Parbury Henty Hldgs 1984-, Marsh and McLennan 1987-, Victoria State Opera 1985-; cncl memb: Museum of Victoria 1979-85, World Wildlife Fund Aust 1983- (vice pres), Victoria State Opera Fndn 1982- (pres), Victoria Cncl, Aust Bicentennial Authy 1984-; *Recreations* fishing, opera, ornithology, farming, old master drawings; *Clubs* Pratt's, Flyfishers, Melbourne, Australian (Melbourne), Australia (Sydney) Queensland; *Style*— David Gibbs, Esq; 21 William St, S Yarra, Melbourne, Vic 3141, Australia

GIBBS, David Evelyn; s of Brig Lancelot Merivale Gibbs, CVO, DSO, MC (d 1966), and Hon Marjory Florence, *née* Maxwell (d 1939), da of 11 Baron Farnham, DSO; *b* 22 Mar 1931; *Educ* Eton; *m* 6 June 1959, Phyllida Lovaine (county rep for Hants on Nat Gardens Scheme; fund raiser for Macmillan Nurses Hospices), da of Col Piers Standish Plowden, OBE, of East Wing, Somborne Park, Kings Somborne, Hants; 2 s (Giles b 6 Nov 1962, Crispin b 14 Dec 1966), 1 da (Quenelda); *Career* cmmnd Lt Coldstream Gds 1949-51, served in UK and Tripoli; Gold Staff Offr Westminster Abbey at Coronation of HM The Queen 1953; memb London Stock Exchange; ptnr Norris Oakley Richardson & Glover/ Capel Cure Myers until incorpn 1975; *Recreations* shooting, tennis, underwater diving, gardening; *Clubs* Pratt's; *Style*— David Gibbs, Esq; The Clock House, Sparsholt, Winchester, Hants SO21 2LX (☎ 0962 72 461)

GIBBS, David Phillip; s of William Charles Gibbs (d 1961); *b* 6 May 1941; *Educ* Cranleigh Sch; *m* 1, 1964 (m dis 1981), Gillian; 2 s, 1 da; m 2, 1982, Vanessa Susan Jane; *Career* dir Hambros Bank Ltd 1973-; *Recreations* golf, tennis, jogging; *Style*— David Gibbs, Esq; 42 Hove St, Hove, Sussex; Hambros Bank, 41 Bishopsgate, London EC2 (☎ 01 588 2851)

GIBBS, Hon Mrs (Elizabeth Beatrice); *née* Baring; yr da of 1 Baron Howick of Glendale, KG, GCMG, KCVO (d 1973); *b* 10 Jan 1940; *m* 15 Jan 1962, Capt Nicholas Albany Gibbs, 9 Royal Lancers (d 14 April 1984), yr s of Capt Lionel Cyril Gibbs (d 1940); 1 s (Andrew b 1966), 2 da (Mary b 1964, Eliza b 1968); *Style*— Hon Mrs Gibbs; c/o Rt Hon Lord Howick of Glandale Howick, Alnwick, Northumberland; Drayton House, East Meon, Hants

GIBBS, Hon Sir Eustace Hubert Beilby; KCVO (1986), CMG (1982); 4 s of 1 Baron Wraxall, TD, PC, JP, DL (d 1931), yr s by his 2 w (Hon Ursula Mary Lawley, OBE, er da of 6 and last Baron Wenlock); hp to bro, 2 Baron; *b* 3 July 1929; *Educ* Eton, Ch Ch Oxford; *m* 23 Oct 1957, Veronica, o da of Sydney Keith Scott, of Reydon Grove Farm, Southwold; 3 s (Hubert b 1958, Andrew b 1965, Jonathan b 1969), 2 da (Miranda b 1961, Alexandra b 1971); *Career* entered Foreign Serv 1954 retd 1986; HM The Queen's Vice-Marshal of the Dip Corps 1982-86; RCDS 1974-75, served Bangkok, Rio de Janeiro, Berlin, Caracas, Vienna & Paris, RET 1986; HM The Queen's Vice-Marshal of the Dip Corps 1982-; *Recreations* music, golf; *Clubs* Brooks's, Pratt's, Beefsteak; *Style*— Hon Sir Eustace Gibbs, KCVO, CMG; Coddenham House, Coddenham, Ipswich, Suffolk (☎ Coddenham (044 979) 332)

GIBBS, Hon George Henry Paul; 2 s of 5 Baron Aldenham, and 3 Baron Hunsdon of Hunsdon (d 1986); *b* 17 June 1950; *Educ* Rannoch; *m* 1973, Janet Elizabeth, da of Harold Leonard Scott; 2 s (Piers Antony Scott b 1973, Corin William Tyser b 1976); *Style*— Hon George Gibbs; Chetwode Priory, Buckingham

GIBBS, Air Marshal Sir Gerald Ernest; KBE (1954, CBE 1945), CIE (1946), MC (1918, and two bars 1918); s of Ernest William Cecil Gibbs (d 1933), and Fanny Wilmina Gibbs (d 1944); *b* 3 Sept 1896; *m* 1938, Margaret Jean, da of Henry Hulatt Bradshaw (d 1962); 1 s (John), 1 da (Pamela); *Career* served WWI 7 Wilts Regt and RFC, transferred RAF 1918, cmd 47 Sqdn Sudan and RAF Kenya 1935-36, SASO 11 Fighter Gp 1940-41 (Battle of Britain), dir Overseas Ops 1942-43, SASO 3 TAF Air Cmd SE Asia 1944, chief air staff offr HQ Supreme Allied Cmd SE Asia 1945-46, SASO Transport Cmd 1946-48, head Serv Advsrs to UK Delgn at UNO NY and chm UK Membs of Mil Staff Ctee UN 1948-51, CAS and C-in-C IAF 1951-54; Air Cdre 1940, Air Vice-Marshal 1944, Air Marshal 1951, ret 1954; Legion of Honour, Croix de Guerre 1918; *Books* Survivor's Story (1956); *Recreations* golf, sailing, skiing; *Clubs* RAF, Royal Wimbledon GC, Trevose GC, Seaford GC (E Blatchington); *Style*— Air Marshal Sir Gerald Gibbs, KBE, CIE, MC; Lone Oak, 170 Coombe Lane West, Kingston upon Thames, Surrey KT2 7DE

GIBBS, Rt Hon Sir Harry Talbot; GCMG (1981), AC (1987), KBE (1970), PC (1972); s of Harry Victor Gibbs (d 1969), of Ipswich, Qld, and Flora Macdonald Gibbs (d 1972); *b* 7 Feb 1917; *Educ* Ipswich GS, Qld Univ; *m* 1944, Muriel Ruth, da of Hugh Hector Harold Dunn (d 1970), of Maryborough, Queensland; 1 s, 3 da; *Career* QC 1957; barr Queensland 1939, justice High Court Australia 1970, chief justice Australia 1981-87; *see Debrett's Handbook of Australia and New Zealand for further details*; *Recreations* tennis, theatre; *Clubs* Australian (Sydney); *Style*— The Rt Hon Sir Harry Gibbs, GCMG, AC, KBE, PC; 27 Stanhope Rd, Killara 2071, Australia (☎ 498 6924)

GIBBS, Lady Hilaria Agnes; *née* Edgcumbe; eld da of 6 Earl of Mount Edgcumbe, TD, DL (d 1965), and Lilian Agnes, *née* Arkwright (d 1964); *b* 16 Jan 1908; *m* 17 Oct 1933, Lt-Col Denis Lucius Alban Gibbs, DSO (d 27 April 1984), 3 s of Rev Canon Reginald Gibbs (d 1940) and gs of Rev John Gibbs, yr bro of 1 Baron Aldenham; 4 da (Jillianne, Margaret, Rosamund, Penelope); *Career* former pres: Tavistock Branch Red Cross, Plymouth League of Pity; *Style*— Lady Hilaria Gibbs; Aldenham, Deer Park Lane, Tavistock, Devon (☎ 0822 2731)

GIBBS, Rt Hon Sir Humphrey Vicary; GCVO (1969, KCVO 1965), KCMG (1960), OBE (1959), PC (1969); 3 s of 1 Baron Hunsdon of Hunsdon (d 1935), and Anna Maria, *née* Durant (d 1938); *b* 22 Nov 1902; *Educ* Eton, Trinity Coll Cambridge; *m* 17 Jan 1934, Molly Peel, DBE, CStJ, 2 da of John Peel Nelson, of Bulawayo; 5 s; *Career* govr of Rhodesia 1959-69; KStJ 1959; Hon LLD Birmingham 1969, Hon DCL East Anglia 1969; *Clubs* Bulawayo (Bulawayo, Zimbabwe), Harare (Zimbabwe); *Style*— Rt Hon Sir Humphrey Gibbs, GCVO, KCMG, OBE; 22 Dornie Rd, Borrowdale, Harare, Zimbabwe

GIBBS, Jeremy Herbert; s of Rt Hon Sir Humphrey Gibbs, GCVO, KCMG, OBE (3 s of 1 Baron Hunsdon of Hunsdon), and Dame Molly Gibbs, DBE; *b* 26 May 1935; *Educ* Bishops Sch Cape Town, Christ Church Oxford (MA); *m* 8 April 1958, Alison Douglas, da of Col Douglas McCrone Martin, of Dunchattan, Troon, Ayrshire; 4 da; *Career* insur broker; govr: St Mary's Sch Wantage, London House for Overseas Students; *Recreations* fishing; *Clubs* Bulawayo (Zimbabwe); *Style*— Jeremy Gibbs, Esq; Upper Kennards, Leigh, Kent TN11 8RE (☎ 0732 832160; office: 0732 362444)

GIBBS, Rt Rev John; s of late Arthur Edgar Gibbs, of Bournemouth; *b* 15 Mar 1917; *Educ* London Univ, Bristol Univ, Western Coll Bristol, Lincoln Theological Coll; *m* 1943, G Marion, da of late W J Bishop, of Poole, Dorset; 1 s, 1 da; *Career* ordained 1955, examining chaplain to bishop of Norwich 1968-73, bishop suffragan of Bradwell 1973-76, 6 bishop of Coventry 1976-85; *Style*— The Rt Rev John Gibbs; Farthingloe, Southfield, Minchinhampton, Stroud, Glos GL6 9DY (☎ 0453 886211)

GIBBS, Julian Herbert; 3 s of Hon Sir Geoffrey Cokayne Gibbs, KCMG (2 s of 1 Baron Hunsdon of Hunsdon, JP, himself 4 s of 1 Baron Aldenham, JP), and Helen Margaret, CBE, *née* Leslie (d 1977); *b* 26 Nov 1932; *Educ* Eton; *Career* 2 Lt KRRC 1951-53, Lt Queen's Westminsters (TA) 1953-56; with Antony Gibbs & Sons Ltd (merchant bankers) 1953-74; chm Antony Gibbs Personal Fin Planning Ltd; chm Julian Gibbs Associates Ltd 1975-82; chm First Mkt Intelligence Ltd 1983-; dir Mencap Unit Tst; former vice-chm London Fedn of Boys' Clubs; former chm P M Club; former memb ctee: Distressed Gentlefolks' Assoc, Queen's Inst of Dist Nursing; Freeman City of London, Liveryman Worshipful Co of Grocers 1961; FCII (vice-pres); *Books* Living with Inflation; a Simple Guide to Lump Sum Investment; *Recreations* travel, theatre, opera, France; *Clubs* Carlton, Beefsteak, Pratt's, MCC; *Style*— Julian Gibbs, Esq; 35A Colville Terrace, London W11 (☎ 01 221 8034); 824 Johnson Lane, Key West, Florida, USA; First Market Intelligence Ltd, 56A Rochester Row, London SW1P 1JU (☎ 01 834 9192, fax 01 630 0194)

GIBBS, Hon Mrs ((Sarah) Marcia); *née* Kimball; er da of Baron Kimball (Life Peer); *b* 8 Feb 1958; *m* 1982, David Alexander Somerset Gibbs, 2 son of Patrick Somerset Gibbs, of Hazeley House, Mortimer, Reading; 1 s (James Patrick b 1983), 1 da (Emily Rose b 1985); *Style*— Hon Mrs Gibbs; Kentmere House, Castor, Peterborough PE5 7BY

GIBBS, Maj Martin Antony; JP (Wilts 1966), DL (1977); s of Col William Otter Gibbs, JP, DL (d 1960), of Barrow Court, Barrow Gurney, Somerset, and Janet Blanche Gibbs (d 1974), his cous and sis of 1 Baron Wraxall; *b* 12 Mar 1916; *Educ* Eton, Sandhurst; *m* 17 Jan 1947, Elsie Margaret Mary, er da of Sir Hew Hamilton-Dalrymple, 9 Bt, of North Berwick; 1 s (Antony), 5 da (Blanche, Bridget, Cecily, Katharine, Julian); *Career* Maj Coldstream Gds, regular soldier joined 1 Bn Coldstream Gds 1936, 3 Bn 1939; serv: Palestine, Egypt, Western Desert (Long Range Desert Gp), 2 Bn 1947,Malaya 1948-50; ret 1952; now open house and garden to the public; landowner (500 acres); *Recreations* horticulture, dendrology, travel; *Clubs* Pratt's; *Style*— Maj Martin Gibbs, JP, DL; Sheldon Manor, Chippenham, Wilts (☎ 0249 653120)

GIBBS, Col Martin St John Valentine (Tim); CB (1958), DSO (1942), TD, JP (Glos 1965); s of Maj Guy Melvil Gibbs, TD, of Cirencester (yr bro of William Otter Gibbs, *see* Gibbs, Martin Antony), and Margaret, da of Henry St John (gs of Hon Ferdinand St John, 2 s of 3 Viscount Bolingbroke and (4) St John by his 2 w Isabella Baroness Hompesch) by his w Maud (da of Hon Pascoe Glyn, sometime MP E Dorset and 5 s of 1 Baron Wolverton); *b* 14 Feb 1917; *Educ* Eton; *m* 1947, Mary Margaret, er da of Lt-Col Philip Mitford (seventh in descent from Humphrey Mitford, whose yr bro John was ancestor of the Barons Redesdale) by his w Alice, yst da of Sir John Fowler, 2 Bt, and widow of Capt Michael Wills, MC; 2 da, 3 step s; *Career* 2 Lt Royal Wilts Yeo 1937, Maj 1942, Lt-Col 1951, Bt-Col 1955, Col 1958, Ld-Lt for Glos 1978-; Hon Col Royal Wilts Yeomanry Sqdn TAVR 1972, Col Cmdt Yeomanry RAC 1975-82; High Sheriff Glos 1958; *Recreations* country pursuits; *Clubs* Cavalry and Guards, MCC; *Style*— Col Martin Gibbs, CB, DSO, TD, JP; Ewen Manor, Ewen, Cirencester, Glos (☎ 028 577 206)

GIBBS, Michael John; s of Harold Percy Gibbs (d 1980), of Solihull, and Alice, *née* Groom (d 1974); *b* 8 April 1931; *Educ* Solihull Sch, Univ of Bristol (BA); *m* 22 June 1957, Pamela Jessie, da of Jesse Pane, of Bristol; 1 s (Alexander b 22 April 1964); *Career* sec Leicester Perm Bldg Soc 1968-71; Gateway Bldg Soc: asst gen mangr 1971-75, dep chief exec 1975-81, md 1981-88; exec vice chm Woolwich Equitable Bldg Soc 1988-; chm Met Assoc of Bldg Socs 1984-85, cncl memb Bldg Socs Assoc 1982-88; CBIM; *Recreations* golf, cricket; *Clubs* MCC, British Sportsmens; *Style*— Michael Gibbs, Esq; Woolwich Equitable Building Society, Gateway House, Worthing, Sussex (☎ 0903 68 555)

GIBBS, Dame Molly (Peel); DBE (1969); (Lady Gibbs); da of John Peel Nelson; *b* 13 July 1912; *Educ* Girls' HS Barnato Park Johannesburg; *m* 1934, Rt Hon Sir Humphrey Gibbs, *qv*; 5 s; *Style*— Dame Molly Gibbs, DBE; 22 Dornie Rd, Borrowdale, Harare, Zimbabwe

GIBBS, HE Mr Oswald Moxley; GMG (1976); s of Michael Gibbs, Planter (d 1958), of Moliniere, St George's, Grenada, W Indies, and Mary Emelda Gibbs, *née* Cobb (d 1963); *b* 15 Oct 1927; *Educ* Happy Hill RC, St George's Sr Boys RC, Grenada Boys Secdy Sch, City of London Coll (BSc); *m* 8 Oct 1955, Dearest Agatha, da of Sendall Mitchell (d 1969), of Grand Anse, Grenada, W Indies; 2 s (Marius b 1949 (adopted), Dr Kenyatta b 1957), 2 da (Beatrice b 1960, Patricia b 1963); *Career* economist and diplomat; trade sec and cmmr Eastern Caribbean Mission London 1965-75, high cmmr for Grenada, London 1974-78, conslt Centre for Industl Devpt Brussels 1979-81, high cmmr for Grenada (London 1984-, ambass to EEC 1985-, ambass to Belgium 1987-, Queen's Silver Jubilee Medal 1977; *Recreations* gardening, photography, DIY; *Style*— HE Mr Oswald M Gibbs, CMG; Woodside Green, London SE25; Grenada High Commission, 1 Collingham Gardens, London SW5 (☎ 01 373 7800/7808, telex 889183 GRENCOM-G)

GIBBS, Rachel Elizabeth; da of Lt-Col Geoffrey Bernard Youard, MBE (d 1987), of Gwernowddy Old Farmhouse, Llandrinio, Llanymynech, Powys, and Hon Rosaline Joan, *née* Atkin (d 1973); *b* 26 Feb 1930; *Educ* Benenden Sch Kent, St Paul's Girls Sch London; *m* 11 April 1953, Denis Dunbar Gibbs, s of Very Rev Michael McCausland Gibbs, Dean of Chester (d 1962); 1 s (Nicholas b 1954), 1 da (Sarah b 1956); *Career* Lib Pty Orgn 1949-65 sec: Arthur Holt MP (Bolton West), Alasdair Mackenzie MP (Ross and Cromarty), Sir Russell Johnston MP (Inverness-shire); Lib Pty res dept (4 yrs); memb: ctee of Inquiry UK prison serv 1979, bd visitors HM Prison Swinfon Hall 1970-76 (chm 1975-76), bd of visitors HM Prison Pentonville 1977-83 (chm 1981-83), Parole Bd 1987; fndr memb: Lichfield Marriage Guidance Cncl, Lichfield CAB, Lichfield Adventure Playground Assoc 1965-76, ctee Friends of Christchurch Spitalfields 1979-82, ctee Prisons and Penal Concerns Gp (Diocese of

London and Southwark 1984-, chm Albion Sq Res Assoc 1988-; JP: Lichfield 1971-76, Inner London 1977-; *Books* Pedigree of the Family of Gibbs of Pytte in the Parish of Clyst St George (ed fourth edn 1981); *Recreations* gardening, china mending, family history, lurchers, carpentery; *Style—* Mrs Rachel Gibbs, JP; 21 Albion Square, London E8 4ES (☎ 01 249 8211)

GIBBS, Richard John Hedley; QC (1984); s of Brian Conaway Gibbs (d 1946), Asst Dist Cmmr Colonial Admin Serv, and Mabel Joan, *née* Gatford; *b* 2 Sept 1941; *Educ* Oundle, Trin Hall Cambridge (MA); *m* 26 June 1965, Janet, da of Francis Herbert Whittall, of Reigate, Surrey; 1 s (Christopher b 1979), 3 da (Sarah b 1966, Susannah b 1966, Julia b 1971); *Career* barr Inner Temple 1965; rec of the Crown Ct 1981; chm Birmingham Friendship Housing Assoc 1987;; *Style—* Richard Gibbs, Esq, QC; 4 King's Bench Walk, Temple, London EC4Y 7DL (☎ 01 353 3581); 1 Fountain Court, Steelhouse Lane, Birmingham B4 6DR (☎ 021 236 5721)

GIBBS, Roger Geoffrey; 4 s of Hon Sir Geoffrey Gibbs, KCMG (2 s of 1 Baron Hunsdon of Hunsdon, JP, who himself was 4 s of 1 Baron Aldenham) and Hon Lady Gibbs, CBE, JP, *qv*; *b* 13 Oct 1934; *Educ* Eton, Millfield; *Career* chm Gerrard and Nat holdings plc 1975-, memb cncl Royal Nat Pension Fund for Nurses 1975-; dir Arsenal FC 1980, Wellcome trustee 1983-, govr London Clinic 1983-, special tstee Guy's Hosp 1985-, memb cncl Imperial Cancer Res Fund; *Recreations* sport; *Clubs* Pratt's, Swinley; *Style—* Roger Gibbs, Esq; 23 Tregunter Rd, London SW10 9LS (☎ 01 370 3465)

GIBBS, Field Marshal Sir Roland Christopher; GCB (1976, KCB 1972), CBE (1968), DSO (1945), MC (1943), DL (Wilts 1980); yr s of Maj Guy Melvil Gibbs, TD (d 1959), of Parkleaze, Ewen, Cirencester, and Margaret, *née* St John (d 1964); bro of Col Martin Gibbs, CB, DSO, TD, *qv*, Ld-Lt Glos; *b* 22 June 1921; *Educ* Eton, Sandhurst; *m* 1955, Davina, da of Lt-Col Eion Merry, MC (d 1966), of Lucknam Park, Chippenham, and Jean (da of Hon Arthur Crichton, 3 s of 4 Earl of Erne, KP, PC, sometime MP Enniskillen), 2 s, 1 da; *Career* served WW II: N Africa, Italy and NW Europe, 2 Lt 60 Rifles 1940; Lt-Col 1960, Brig 1963, cmd 16 Para Bde 1963-66, COS Middle East Cmd 1966, IDC 1968, Cdr Br Forces Gulf 1969, Maj-Gen 1969, Lt-Gen 1971, GOC1 (Br) Corps 1971-74, GOC-in-C UKLF 1974, Gen 1974, ch of gen staff 1976-79, ADC Gen to HM The Queen 1976-79, Field Marshal; Col Cmdt: 2 Bn Royal Green Jackets 1971-78, Parachute Regt 1973-77; Vice Ld-Lt Wilts 1982-; constable HM Tower of London 1985-; *Recreations* out of door recreations, painting; *Clubs* Turf; *Style—* Field Marshal Sir Roland Gibbs, GCB ,CBE, DSO, MC, DL; Patney Rectory, Devizes, Wilts (☎ 038 084 733)

GIBBS, Lady Sarah; *née* Bingham; yr da of 6 Earl of Lucan, MC (d 1964); *b* 5 Sept 1936; *Educ* Badminton Sch Bristol; *m* 17 June 1958, Rev William Gilbert Gibbs, yr s of late Col Ralph Crawley Boevey Gibbs, of Little Gaddesden, Herts; 1 s, 3 da; *Career* magistrate for Daventry 1987; *Style—* Lady Sarah Gibbs; The Vicarage, Guilsborough, Northampton

GIBBS, Somerset Bryan; s of Maj Bryan Northam Gibbs, MBE; *b* 16 Jan 1926; *Educ* Eton; *m* 1950, Elspeth, da of Maj F Russi, MC; 3 s, 1 da; *Career* memb Stock Exchange 1952-77, chm Capel-Cure Myers 1975-77; chm Directorship Appointments Ltd 1977-; dir: Rotaflex plc, Moray Firth Maltings Ltd, Equity Consort Investmt Tst plc, New Ct Tst plc; *Recreations* golf, sailing, photography; *Clubs* Boodle's, Royal Worlington & Newmarket GC, Royal London YC; *Style—* Somerset B Gibbs, Esq; 62 Oakwood Court, London W14 (☎ 01 602 2633); Withcam House, Headley's Lane, Witcham, Ely, Cambs CB6 2LH (☎ 0353 778212); Directorship Appointments Ltd, 66 Great Cumberland Place, London W1H 8BP (☎ 01 402 3233)

GIBBS, Stephen; CBE (1981); s of Arthur Edwin and Anne Gibbs; *b* 12 Feb 1920; *Educ* Oldbury GS, Birmingham Univ; *m* 1941, Louise Pattison; 1 s, 1 da; *Career* chm Turner & Newall plc (plastics and chemicals); fellow Plastics and Rubber Inst; *Style—* Stephen Gibbs, Esq, CBE; Turner & Newall plc, 20 St Mary's Parsonage, Manchester M3 3NL (☎ 061 833 9272, telex 669281)

GIBBS, Stephen Cokayne; 2 s of Hon Sir Geoffrey Gibbs, KCMG (d 1975, 2 s of 1 Baron Hunsdon of Hunsdon, JP, himself 4 s of 1 Baron Aldenham, JP), and Hon Lady Gibbs, CBE, JP, *qv*; *b* 18 July 1929; *Educ* Eton; *m* 1972, Lavinia Winifred, 2 da of Sir Edmund Bacon, 13 Bt, KG, KBE, TD (d 1982); 2 s, 1 da; *Career* 2 Lt KRRC, Maj QVR (TA) 1960-63 and Royal Greenjackets; dir: Charles Barker plc 1962-87, Vaux Group plc 1971-; *Recreations* shooting, gardening; *Clubs* White's, Pratt's; *Style—* Stephen Gibbs, Esq; Dougarie, Isle of Arran KA27 8EB (☎ 077 084 229)

GIBBS, Lady; Sylvia Madeleine; *née* Knight; da of late Henry Knight, of Buenos Aires, Argentina; *m* 1944, Sir Frank Stannard Gibbs, KBE, CMG (d 1983, ambass to The Philippines 1954-55); 1 s, 1 da; *Style—* Lady Gibbs; El Rincón, High St, Old Woking, Surrey (☎ Woking 70147)

GIBBS, Lady Virginia; *née* Rous; da of 5 Earl of Stradbroke (d 1983), and Hon Mrs Keith Rous, *qv*; *b* 13 June 1954; *m* 1974, Antony William Hew Gibbs, s of Maj Martin Antony Gibbs, Coldstream Gds and Elsie, da of Sir Hew Clifford Hamilton-Dalrymple, 9 Bt; 2 s (Abram b 1976) (William b 1986), 3 da (Mary b 1975, Emily-Anna b 1978, Elizabeth b 1979); *Style—* Lady Virginia Gibbs; The Home Farm, Barrow Gurney, nr Bristol

GIBBS-SMITH, Lavinia Marie; *née* Snelling; da of George Edward Snelling (d 1961), and Maisie Binder (d 1961); descendant of Thomas Snelling whose collection of coins and medals founded the numismatic collection in Br Museum; *b* 20 Dec 1946; *Educ* Hollington Park Sch, St Leonards, Guildhall Sch of Music, Univ of Cologne (Musikhochschule); *m* 24 Jan 1974, Charles Harvard Gibbs-Smith, s of Dr E G Gibbs; *Career* prof de Luth Centre d'Etude de Musique Baroque Beziers France 1983-; flute accompanist to soloists; festival organiser 'Le Petit Festival des Baux en Provence'; dir Les Bons Vins Occitans; hon memb Int Lyceum; *Recreations* gardening, walking, skiing, reading; *Clubs* IOD; *Style—* Lavinia Gibbs-Smith; c/o Messeurs Coutts & Co, 1 Cadegau Place, SW1

GIBRALTAR IN EUROPE, Bishop of, 1980-; Rt Rev John Richard Satterthwaite; diocese of Gibraltar in Europe created 1980; s of William and Clara Elisabeth Satterthwaite; *b* 17 Nov 1925; *Educ* Leeds Univ (BA), Community of the Resurrection Mirfield; *Career* history master St Luke's Sch Haifa 1946-48; curate: St Barnabas Carlisle 1950-53, St Aidan Carlisle 1953-54, St Michael Paternoster Royal London 1955-59 (curate-in-charge 1959-65); gen sec C of E Council on Foreign Relations 1959-70 (asst gen sec 1955-9); gen sec Archbishop's Cmmn on Roman Catholic Relations 1965-70; vicar St Dunstan in the West 1959-70; bishop suffragan of Fulham 1970, bishop of Gibraltar 1970 (known as bishop of Fulham and Gibraltar until creation of new diocese 1980); Canon of Canterbury 1963-70; Canon of the Old Catholic Cathedral, Utrecht 1968-; (ChStJ 1972); *Clubs* Athenaeum; *Style—* The Rt Rev the Lord Bishop of Gibraltar in Europe; 5A Gregory Place, London W8 4NG (☎ 01 937 2796)

GIBSON, Sir Alexander Drummond; CBE (1967); s of James McClure Gibson (d 1946), and Wilhelmina, *née* Williams; *b* 11 Feb 1926; *Educ* Dalziel HS Motherwell, Glasgow Univ, RCM, Mozarteum (Salzburg), Accademia Chigiano (Siena); *m* 1959, Ann Veronica, *née* Waggett; 3 s (James b 1959, Philip b 1962, John b 1965), 1 da (Claire b 1968); *Career* orchestral conductor: princ conductor and musical dir Scottish Nat Orchestra 1959-84 (guest conductor), fndr and artistic dir Scottish Opera 1962-85, (music dir 1985-87), princ guest conductor Houston Symphony Orch 1981-83; Arnold Bax Medal for Conducting 1959, Distinguished Musician of the Year Award ISM 1976, Sibelius Medal 1978, British Music Year Book Musician of the Year 1980; OStJ 1975, hon pres of the Scottish National Orchestra 1985-; founder and conductor Laureate Scottish Opera 1987-; FRSE, FRSA; kt 1977; *Recreations* music, reading; *Clubs* Garrick, Oriental; *Style—* Sir Alexander Gibson, CBE; 15 Cleveden Gdns, Glasgow G12 (☎ 041 339 6668)

GIBSON, Anthony Gair; TD (1971); s of Wilfrid Humble Gibson, of Linnel Hill, Hexham, Northumberland, and Joan Margaret, *née* Gair; *b* 10 Nov 1937; *Educ* Ampleforth, Lincoln Coll Oxford (BA); *m* 23 July 1966, (Jennifer) Bryony, da of Maj Timothy Basil Ellis, of Trinity Hall, Bungay; 4 s (Benjamin Timothy b 7 Jan 1968, Toby James b 12 Sept 1969, Richard Gair (twin) b 12 Sept 1969, Anthony Daniel b 30 April 1975); *Career* Kings Dragoon Gds 1956-58 (despatches), N'merland Hussars & Queens Own Yeo 1958-77; slr 1965; memb Slrs Disciplinary Tbnl 1980-, pres (elect) Newcastle-upon-Tyne Incorporated Law Soc 1989-90, dir Hexham Steeplechase Co Ltd, govr Mowden Hall Sch, sec Haydon point-to-point 1962-88; memb Law Soc; *Recreations* shooting, fishing, forestry; *Clubs* Cavalry & Guards, Northern Counties; *Style—* Anthony G Gibson, Esq, TD; Newbiggin, Hexham (☎ 0434 602 649); Barclays Bank Chambers, Denton Burn, Newcastle-upon-Tyne (☎ 091 274 1241, fax 091 274 2164)

GIBSON, Cdr Bryan Donald; s of Donald Gibson (d 1983), of Barnston, Wirral, Cheshire, and Inez Margaret, *née* Lawrence (d 1983); *b* 21 Jan 1937; *Educ* Birkenhead Park HS, Victoria Univ of Manchester (BSc, MSc); *m* 1 Jan 1966, (Frances) Mary, da of Reginald Herbert Greenhalgh (d 1982), of Swinton, Lancashire; 1 s (James b 1968), 1 da (Helen b 1970); *Career* cmmnd RN 1962, lectr RN Engrg Coll 1963-66; served: HMS Bulwark 1967, HMS Sultan (Nuclear Propulsion Sch) 1968-70; sr lectr dept of nuclear sci and technol RNC Greenwich 1970-72, head of materials technol RN Engrg Coll Manadon Plymouth 1973-78, ret 1978; academic sec Chartered Assoc of Certified Accountants 1978-82, sec Inst of Metallurgists 1982-84, dep sec Inst of Metals 1985-; former ctee memb: CNAA, RSA, Engrg Cncl, CSTI; vice pres Inst Nuclear Engrs 1976-78; Freeman City of London 1984, Liveryman Worshipful Co of Engrs 1984 (Clerk 1986-); hon memb CGLI; FIM 1975, CEng 1977; *Recreations* gardening, DIY; *Clubs* Anglo Belgian, City Livery; *Style—* Cdr Bryan Gibson, RN; Kiln Bank, Bodle St Green, nr Hailsham, E Sussex BN27 4UA (☎ 0323 833 554); 1 Carlton House Terrace, London SW1Y 5DB (☎ 01 839 4071, 01 839 3097, fax 01 839 2289, telex 8814813)

GIBSON, Rev Christopher Herbert; CP; s and h of Sir Christopher Gibson, 3 Bt, *qv*; *b* 17 July 1948; *Career* ordained priest 1975; *Style—* Rev Christopher Gibson, CP; Holy Cross, Buenos Aires, Argentina

GIBSON, Sir Christopher Herbert; 3 Bt (UK 1931); s of Sir Christopher Herbert Gibson, 2 Bt (d 1962); *b* 2 Feb 1921; *Educ* St George's Coll Argentina; *m* 16 Aug 1941, Lilian Lake, da of late Dr George Byron Young, of Colchester, Essex; 1 s, 3 da; *Heir* s, Rev Christopher Gibson, CP; *Career* mangr Leach's Argentine Estates 1946-51, of Encyclopaedia Britannica 1952-55, design draughtsman Babcox & Wilcox USA 1956-57, tea plantation mangr then ranch mangr Liebig's Extract of Meat Co 1958-64, bldg inspector Indust Kaiser Argentina 1964-68, mangr and part owner Lakanto Poultry Farms 1969-76; *Style—* Sir Christopher Gibson, Bt; Suite 107, 6660 Buswell St, Richmond, British Columbia V6Y 2G8, Canada

GIBSON, Hon Clive Patrick; s of Baron Gibson (Life Peer), and Elizabeth, da of Hon Clive Pearson (2 s of 1 Viscount Cowdray, GCVO, PC, DL) and Hon Alicia Knatchbull-Hugessen, da of 1 Baron Brabourne; *b* 24 Jan 1948; *Educ* Eton, Oxford; *m* 1974, Anne, da of late Comte Jacques de Chauvigny de Blot; 1 s (Patrick b 1975), 1 da (Beatrice b 1978); *Career* Cmmn of the Euro Communities 1973-74, Pearson Gp 1974-83; dir: Château Latour (chm), Pearson Longman 1979-82, Financial Times 1978-83, The Economist 1978-83, Penguin Books 1978-82, Longman Gp 1978-82, J Rothschild Hldgs 1985-; *Recreations* music, shooting, skiing; *Clubs* Brooks's; *Style—* Hon Clive Gibson; 15 St James's Place, London SW1A 1NW

GIBSON, Craigie Alexander; s of Cdr James Brown Gibson, RNR (d 1984), of Stenhousemuir, Stirlingshire, and Cora Jessie, *née* Craigie; *b* 19 Sept 1927; *Educ* Falkirk HS, Edinburgh Univ (BSc); *m* 26 Nov 1955, Margaret Louise, da of Albert Frederick De Villiers Richter (d 1967), of Shanghani, Rhodesia; 2 da (Kate b 1962, Sandra b 1965); *Career* Navigators Yeoman RN 1945-48; exploration geologist Anglo American Corpn 1952-57; Rio Tinto Rhodesia Ltd: exploration geologist 1957-60, mine mangr 1960-67, exec dir 1967-76, md 1976-78; md: Rossing Uranium Ltd 1978-82, RTZ Metals Ltd 1982-83, mining dir Rio Tinto Zinc Corpn 1983-87, chief exec Rossing Uranium Ltd 1988; pres Chamber of Mines: Rhodesia 1976-78, SW Africa/Namibia 1981-82; chm Rossing Fndn 1979-82; FGS 1952, FIMM 1983; *Recreations* geology, snooker; *Clubs* RAC, Harare, Windhoek; *Style—* Craigie Gibson, Esq; 15 Westminster Palace Gardens, Artillery Row, Westminster, London SW1P 1RL (☎ 01 222 2596); 6 St James Sq, London SW1Y 4LD

GIBSON, Rev Sir David Ackroyd; 4 Bt (UK 1926); s of Sir Ackroyd Herbert Gibson, Bt (d 1975); *b* 18 July 1922; *Educ* Cathedral GS Wells, Warfleet Trg Coll Dartmouth, Greenwich Coll, Oscott Coll; *Career* Lt RNVR 1939-46: N Sea and N Atlantic 1940-41, Med 1941-43, Indian and Pacific Ocens 1944-45; Roman Catholic priest: Plymouth 1956-60, Weymouth 1960-66; fndr Societas Navigatorum Catholica (Catholic Mariner's YC) 1958; Capt, RA chaplain: Germany 1967-69, NI 1969-70; RC priest: Helston 1971-75, Liskeard 1975-85; *Recreations* sail cruising, history of marine shipwrighting, English and Roman law, producing the perfect English marmalade; *Clubs* Societas Navigatorum Catholica; *Style—* The Rev Sir David Gibson, Bt; c/o Barclay's Bank plc, 19 Princess St, Plymouth, PL1 2HA

GIBSON, David Horsburgh; s of George Paterson Gibson (d 1977), of Pencaitland,

East Lothian, and Marguerite Gladys Mary, *née* Primrose, MBE (d 1955); *b* 25 June 1937; *Educ* Gordonstoun; *m* 30 June 1962, (Elizabeth) Christine, da of Foster Neville Woodward, CBE (d 1985); 2 s (Jonathan b 1963, Duncan b 1966), 1 da (Juliette b 1969); *Career* Nat Serv RN 1956-58: Home and Med fleets Suez campaign 1956; CA; Mollins Machine Co Ltd 1966-71, commercial dir Penelectro Int Ltd 1971-81, dir King Taudevin & Gregson Ltd 1978-81, jt md Hargreaves Reiss & Quinn Ltd 1981-83, dir fin and admin Henderson Admin Gp plc 1983-; memb Royal Br Legion; Freeman City of London, memb Worshipful Co Distillers; MICAS 1963, FBIM 1980; *Recreations* golf, skiing, music, gardening; *Clubs* City of London, Sloane; *Style—* David Gibson, Esq; Paprills Farmhouse, East Hanningfield, Essex CM3 5BW (☎ 0245 400 294); Henderson Administration Gp plc, 3 Finsbury Ave, London EC2M 2PA (☎ 01 638 5757, fax 01 377 5742, telex 884616)

GIBSON, Hon (William) David; OBE (1944), TD; s of Hon Edward Gibson (d 1928), and gs of 1 Baron Ashbourne; bro of 3 Baron Ashbourne, CB, DSO, JP; raised to rank of Baron's s 1943; *b* 22 Mar 1914; *Educ* Sherborne, Trinity Coll Cambridge (MA); *m* 6 Jan 1947, Sabina, da of late Dr Ernst Landsberg, of Cape Town; 3 da (Celia b 1948, Monica b 1951, Philippa b 1953); *Career* served army WW II (France, N Africa, Italy), Col; second master Clifton Coll 1966-74 (housemaster 1948-65), memb of Council of World Disarmament Campaign 1985-88; *Recreations* sailing, skiing, bridge; *Style—* Hon David Gibson, OBE, TD; Buckley Cottage, Batson, Salcombe, Devon (☎ 054 884 3143)

GIBSON, Maj (William) David; s of George Cock Gibson, OBE, of Landwade Hall, Exning, Newmarket, Suffolk, and Angela Madelaine, *née* Llewellin-Evans; *b* 26 Feb 1925; *Educ* Harrow, Trinity Coll Cambridge; *m* 1, 16 Jan 1959, Charlotte Henrietta (d 1973), da of Norman Selwyn Pryor, JP, DL (d 1982), of Manuden House, Bishops Stortford, Herts; 3 s (Martin, George, Edward), 1 da (Anna); m 2, 1975, Jane Marion, da of Brig Ladas L Hassell, DSO, MC (d 1963); *Career* serv Welsh Guards 1944-57 (Palestine 1947, Egypt 1953-56), Maj; dir W J Tatem Ltd 1957, chm 1970-; dir Atlantic Shipping & Trading Co Ltd 1957, chm 1970-77; dir West of England Ship Owners Mutual Protection & Indemnity Assoc: London 1959-86, Luxembourg 1970-83; dir Int Shipowners Investmt Co 1970-83, chm 1977-83; Nat Hunt Ctee steward 1963-66, sr steward 1966; dep sr steward Jockey Club 1969-71; memb Tattersalls Ctee 1963-69 and chm 1967-69; memb Farriers Registration Cncl, master Worshipful Co of Farriers 1979; *Recreations* racing, sailing (Klaxton), shooting; *Clubs* Jockey, Royal Yacht Squadron, Royal Thames Yacht, Cavalry and Guards; *Style—* Maj David Gibson; Bishopswood Grange, nr Ross on Wye, Herefordshire HR9 5QX (☎ 0594 60444)

GIBSON, Sir Donald Evelyn Edward; CBE (1951); s of Prof Arnold Hartley Gibson (d 1959), of Beech House, Alderley Edge, Manchester, and Amy, *née* Quarmby; *b* 11 Oct 1908; *Educ* Manchester GS, Manchester Univ (MA); *m* 1, 19 Oct 1935, Winifred Mary (d 1977), da of Dr Sinclair McGowan, of Oldham, Lancs; 3 s, 1 da; m 2, 1978, Mrs Grace Haines; 2 step s; *Career* RA (TA) Western Cmd 1938-40; Building Res Station 1935-37, dep county architect Isle of Ely 1937-39, city architect and planning offr Coventry 1939-55, county architect Nottingham 1955-58, dir-gen of works WO 1958-62, dir-gen of res and devpt Miny of Public Building and Works 1962-67, Hoffman Wood prof of architecture Leeds Univ 1967-68; controller-gen Miny of Public Building and Works 1967-69, currently conslt; pres RIBA 1964-65; Hon DCL Durham; FRIBA, FRTPI; kt 1962; *Style—* Sir Donald Gibson, CBE; Bryn Castell, Llanddona, Beaumaris, Gwynedd LL58 8TR (☎ 0248 810399)

GIBSON, Lt-Col Edgar Matheson; MBE (1986), TD (1975), DL (1976); s of James Edgar Gibson (d 1976); *b* 1 Nov 1934; *Educ* Kirkwall GS, Gray's Coll of Art; *m* 1960, Jean, *née* McCarrick; 2 s, 2 da; *Career* Lt-Col, Nat Serv 1958-60, TA & TAVR Lovat Scouts 1961-, Cadet Cmdt Orkney 1979-86, JSLO Orkney 1980-85; schoolmaster, Hon Col Orkney Lovat Scouts A C F 1986, head of art Kirkwall GS; chm: St Magnus Cathedral Fair 1982-, Northern Area Highland TA&VR Assoc 1987; *Recreations* painting, sculpture, whisky tasting; *Clubs* Highland Bde; *Style—* Lt-Col Edgar M Gibson, MBE, TD, DL; Transcona, New Scapa Rd, Kirkwall, Orkney (☎ 0856 2849)

GIBSON, Hon Mrs; Hon Frances Phoebe; *née* Phillimore; granted 1949, title, rank and precedence of a Baron's da, which would have been her's had her f survived to succeed to title of Baron Phillimore; da of Capt Hon Anthony Francis Phillimore (ka 1940, s and h of 2 Baron Phillimore), of Coppid Hall, Henley-on-Thames, Oxon, and Anne Julia, *née* Pereira; *b* 24 June 1938; *Educ* St Mary's Convent Ascot; *m* 1, 11 Feb 1961, Colin John Francis Lindsay-MacDougall of Lunga, o s of Maj John Stewart Lindsay-MacDougall of Lunga, DSO, MC, Argyll and Sutherland Highlanders; 3 s, 2 da; m 2, 8 Nov 1980, Joseph Peter Gibson, s of Charles Gibson, of Kelty Hill, Kelty, Fife; *Style—* The Hon Mrs Gibson; Quinta das Madres, Ulgueira, Colras, 2710 Sintra, Portugal (☎ Lisbon 929-0956)

GIBSON, Hon Hugh Marcus Thornely; eldest s of Baron Gibson, *qv*; *b* 23 June 1946; *Educ* Eton, Magdalen Coll Oxford (BA); *m* 31 March 1967, Hon Frances Towneley, da of Hon Anthony Strachey (d 1955); 1s, 2 da; *Career* md Royal Crown Derby and Minton, dir Royal Doulton Ltd; *Recreations* National Trust, book collecting, wine, fishing; *Style—* Hon Hugh Gibson; The Fold, Parwich, Ashbourne, Derbys

GIBSON, Ian Robert; s of John Wilfred Gibson (d 1971), of Bridlington, and Eileen Margaret, *née* Pudsey (d 1965); *b* 19 August 1948; *Educ* St Peter's York, The Queens Coll Oxford (BA); *m* 9 Sept 1972, Valerie Ann, da of Capt Frederick Alfred Armitage, MBE, GM, SGM (d 1968); 1 s (Edward b 1984), 2 da (Alison b 1975, Anna b 1978); *Career* admitted slr 1972, ptnr Frere Cholmeley 1978-; memb Law Soc; *Recreations* music, walking; *Style—* Ian Gibson, Esq; Parkgate, Aldwickbury, Harpenden, Herts AL5 1AB; 28 Lincoln's Inn Fields, London WC2A 3HH (☎ 01 405 7878, fax 01 405 9056, telex 27623)

GIBSON, Dr Joseph; CBE (1980); s of George Gibson (ka 1918), and Mary Ann Scott, *née* Mordy (d 1980); *b* 10 May 1916; *Educ* Washington GS; King's Coll Now Univ of Newcastle upon Tyne (MSc, PhD), Durham Univ; *m* 22 Dec 1944, Lily McFarlane, da of late David McCutcheon Brown; 1 s (David McFarlane b 1950), 1 da (Carole Ann b 1954); *Career* res Northern Coke Res Lab 1938-46; head Chemistry Dept Sunderland Tech Coll and lectr Durham Univ 1947-55, chief sci Northumberland and Yorkshire Divisions NCB 1956-64, dir Coal Res Establishment 1968-75, dir Coal Utilisation Res 1975-77, memb Nat Coal Bd Responsible for Sci 1977-81, coal sci advsr 1981-83, dir several NCB Cos 1977-81; pres Institute of Fuel 1975-76; BCURA: chm 1972-77, pres 1977-81; meml lectures: Cadman 1980 and 1982, Prof Moore 1981; coal sci lectr and medal 1977, carbonization sci medal 1979; Hon Fellowship Inst Chem Engrs 1977; Engrg (FEng) 1979; Hon DCL Univ of Newcastle 1981; *Publications* many articles on coal utilisation and conversion; Carbonisation of Coal (1971, co-author), Coal and Modern Coal Processing (1979), Coal Utilisation: Technology, Economics and Policy (1981); *Recreations* bridge, gardening; *Style—* Dr Joseph Gibson, CBE; 31 Charlton Close, Charlton Kings, Cheltenham, Glos GL53 8DH (☎ 0242 517832)

GIBSON, Joseph David; CBE (1979); s of late Charles Ivan Gibson and Mamao Lavenia Gibson; *b* 26 Jan 1928; *m* Emily Susan Bentley; 3 s, 2 da; *Career* high cmmr for Fiji London 1976-81 (NZ 1981-83), ambass for Fiji Japan 1984-; *Style—* Joseph Gibson, Esq, CBE; 2-1 Todoroki, 8-Chome, Setagaya-Ku, Tokyo

GIBSON, Lt-Col Kenneth Charles Robert; TD (1968); s of Charles Robert Gibson (d 1974), and Jane Boyd Young, *née* Aitken (d 1978); *b* 16 Sept 1935; *Educ* Monkton Combe Sch Bath, Clare Coll Cambridge (MA, LLM); *m* 10 June 1964, Jill Seaton, da of Douglas Campbell Connor (d 1964); 3 s (Douglas b 1966, James b 1970, Mark b 1971), 1 da (Elizabeth b 1967); *Career* Nat Serv 5 Bn Kings African Rifles Kenya 1954-56, Somerset LI (TA) 1956-71, CO 6 Bn LI (vol) 1971-74, hon Col Avon ACF 1987-; admitted slr 1962, ptnr Wansbroughs 1965-85 (sr ptnr 1985-), pres Bristol Law soc 1985-86; DL County of Avon 1986; reader Diocese of Bristol; *Style—* Lt-Col Kenneth Gibson, TD, DL; Rosewell, Bitton, Bristol BS15 6LJ (☎ 0272 322 122); Wansbroughs, 8 Broad Quay, Bristol BS99 7UD (☎ 0272 268 981, fax 0272 291 582)

GIBSON, Col Leonard Young; CBE (1961, MBE 1940), TD (1947, Clasp and 3 Bars 1961), DL (Northumberland 1971); s of William McLure Gibson (d 1959), of The Grove, Gosforth, Northumberland, and Wilhelmina Mitchell, *née* Young (d 1930); *b* 4 Dec 1911; *Educ* Royal GS Newcastle upon Tyne, Paris, Germany; *m* 1949, Pauline Mary, da of Newsam Cawcutt Anthony, of Newcastle-upon-Tyne; 1 s, 1 da; *Career* CSM RGS Newcastle-upon-Tyne OTC 1928-29, TA 1931-61, 2 Lt, Lt Capt The Elswick Battery, 72 (N) Fd Regt RA TA, Staff Coll Camberley 1939, Bde Maj RA 50 (N) Div Rearguard Dunkirk 1940 MBE (despatches) BMRA 43 (W), Div GSO2 SE Army 1941-1942, GSO2 Directing Staff, Staff Coll Camberley 1942-43, GSO1 ops Eastern Cmd 1943-44; 2-in-C 107 med Regt S Notts Hussars RHA TA: France, Belgium, Holland, Germany 1944-45 (despatches, French Croix de Guerre Gold Star); GSO1 Mil Govt Westphalia Germany 1945, Bty Cmd The Elswick Bty 272 (N) Fd Regt TA 1947-51, 2-in-c, CO 272 (N) Fd Regt RA TA 1956-58, Dep Cdr RA 50 (N) Div TA 1959-61, Col TA; memb Northumberland TA and AF Assoc 1958-68, pres Master's Harriers and Beagles Assoc 1968, master Newcastle and District Beagles 1946-83, elected pres 1983; *Recreations* beagling, breeding hounds and horses; *Clubs* Army & Navy, Northern Counties; *Style—* Col Leonard Gibson, CBE, TD, DL; Simonburn Cottage, Humshaugh, Hexham, Northumberland (☎ 043 481 402)

GIBSON, Capt Michael Bradford; s of Lt-Col B T Gibson; *b* 20 Mar 1929; *Educ* Taunton Sch, Sandhurst, Sidney Sussex Coll Cambridge; *m* 1953, Mary Helen Elizabeth Legg; 2 s; *Career* md Racquet Sports Int 1976-; *Style—* Capt Michael Gibson; Olde Deene, Warnham, Horsham, Sussex (☎ 65589)

GIBSON, Baron (Life Peer UK 1975), of Penn's Rocks, Co of East Sussex; (Richard) Patrick Tallentyre Gibson; o s of Thornely Carbutt Gibson (d 1969), of 2 Kensington Gate, W8, and late Elizabeth Anne Augusta, *née* Coit; *b* 5 Feb 1916; *Educ* Eton, Magdalen Coll Oxford (hon fell 1977); *m* 14 July 1945, Elizabeth Dione, 3 da of Hon Clive Pearson (d 1965; 2 s of 1 Viscount Cowdray), and Hon Alicia Knatchbull-Hugessen da of 1 Baron Brabourne; 4 s; *Career* serv WWII, Middx Yeo, Maj (POW 1941-43); sits as Ind Peer in House of Lords; chm S Pearson & Son 1978-83 (former chm Financial Times, dir Economist Newspaper, Pearson Longman); chm: Arts Cncl of GB 1972-77, Nat Tst 1977-86; tstee Glyndebourne Festival Opera 1965-72 and 1977-87; memb bd Royal Opera House 1977-87; tres Sussex Univ 1983-87; Hon DLitt Reading 1980; *Clubs* Brooks's, Garrick; *Style—* The Rt Hon Lord Gibson; 4 Swan Walk, SW3 (☎ 01 351 0344); Penn's Rocks, Groombridge, Sussex (☎ 0892 864 244)

GIBSON, Rear Adm Peter Cecil; CB (1968); 2 s of Alexander Horace Cecil Gibson (d 1968), and Phyllis Zéline, *née* Baume (d 1948); *b* 31 May 1913; *Educ* Ealing Priory; *m* 1938, Phyllis Anna Mary, da of Norman Haliburton Hume (d 1936); 2 s, 1 da; *Career* entered RN 1931; service mainly marine and aeronautical engrg, maintenance test flying, staff and Admty aviation appts; dir engr offr's appts 1961-63, dep controller aircraft (RN) Ministries Aviation and Technol 1966-69, ret RN 1969; business mgmnt conslt 1973-; *Recreations* bridge, fly-fishing; *Clubs* Army & Navy; *Style—* Rear-Adm Peter Gibson, CB

GIBSON, Gp Capt Peter Hurst; MBE (1959); s of Stanley Silvers Gibson (d 1955), of Leeds, and Florence Muriel, *née* Blackie (d 1971); *b* 10 Dec 1930; *Educ* Leeds Modern Sch, Leeds Univ (BA, MA); *m* 19 June 1965, June Carlisle, da of Capt Arthur Brierley (d 1944), of Tideswell; 1 da (Caroline Spirett b 1966); *Career* RAF 1955; served in Germany, Singapore, Huntington, Wilts and MOD, ret Gp-Capt 1977; Bilston Coll 1977-80, princ Aylesbury Coll 1980-; chm Local Review Ctee Aylesbury; FBIM 1980, FRSA 1982, hon memb City & Guilds Inst; *Recreations* theatre, music, cooking, gardening; *Style—* Gp Capt Peter Gibson, MBE; Fairlands Terrick, Aylesbury, Bucks HO22 5XL (☎ 0296 61 2591); Aylesbury Coll, Oxford Rd, Aylesbury, Bucks HO21 8PD (☎ 0296 43 4111, fax 0296 392 133)

GIBSON, Hon Mr Justice Peter; Hon Sir Peter Leslie Gibson; s of Harold Leslie Gibson and Martha Lucy, *née* Diercking; *b* 10 June 1934; *Educ* Malvern, Worcester Coll Oxford; *m* 1968, Katharine Mary Beatrice Hadow; 2 s, 1 da; *Career* barr Inner Temple 1960, Treasy counsel (Chancery) 1972-81, bencher Lincoln's Inn, High Ct judge (Chancery) 1981-, judge of Employment Appeal Tribunal 1984-6; kt 1981; *Style—* Hon Mr Justice Peter Gibson; Royal Courts of Justice, Strand, London WC2A 2LL (☎ 01 405 7641)

GIBSON, Hon Piers Nathaniel; 4 and yst s of Baron Gibson (Life Peer), *qv*; *b* 15 Mar 1956; *Educ* Eton, Magdalen Coll Oxford (BA); *m* 19 Oct 1981, Melanie Jane Stella, er da of Jack Walters, OBE, of La Torre, Gavirate, Varese; 1 s, 1 da; *Career* furniture maker; *Recreations* music, running, skiing; *Clubs* Annabel's, Oxford and Cambridge; *Style—* The Hon Piers Gibson; 41 Ovington St, London SW3 (☎ 01 589 2830)

GIBSON, Prof Robert Donald Davidson; s of Nicol Aitken Gibson (d 1976), of 4 Westmorland Rd, London E17, and Ann, *née* Campbell (d 1977); *b* 21 August 1927; *Educ* Leyton Co HS, Kings Coll London (BA), Magdalene Coll Cambridge (PhD), Ecole Normale Supérieure Paris; *m* 21 Dec 1953, Sheila Elaine, da of Bertie Goldsworthy (d 1983), of 83 Sandford St, Exeter; 3 s (Ian b 1956, Graham b 1958, Robin b 1962); *Career* served RAF 1948-50, Flying Offr (education branch); asst lectr

St Andrews Univ 1954-55; lectr: Queens Coll Dundee 1955-58, Aberdeen Univ 1958-61; prof of french: Queens Univ Belfast, Kent Univ 1965-; master Rutherford Coll Kent Univ 1985-; govr: Eversley Coll 1967-74, Sittingbourne Coll 1968-76, Ninnington Coll 1966-85; memb Soc for French Studies; *Books* The Quest of Alain Fournier (1961), Modern French Poets on Poetry (1961), Le Grand Meaulnes by Alain Fournier (1 edn 1968), The Land Without a Name (1975), Annals of Ashdon (1988), Studies in French Fiction (ed 1968); *Recreations* writing, reading, walking; *Style*— Prof Robert Gibson; 7 Sunnymead, Tyler Hill, Canterbury, Kent (☎ 0227 472373); Rutherford Coll, The Univ of Kent, Canterbury, Kent (☎ 0227 764000)

GIBSON, Sir Ronald George; CBE (1970, OBE 1961), DL (Hants 1983-); s of George Edward Gibson and Gladys Muriel, *née* Prince; *b* 28 Nov 1909; *Educ* Mill Hill, St John's Coll Cambridge, St Bartholomew's Hosp London, (MA); *m* 1934, Dorothy Elisabeth Alberta, da of Thomas Alfred Rainey, of Southampton; 2 da; *Career* served WWII (E Africa, Somalia) RAMC, Lt Col; former MO Winchester Coll and St Swithun's Sch; former chm Med Insurance Agency, chm cncl BMA 1966-71 (memb 1950-72), memb GMC 1974-79, former chm Standing Med Advsy Ctee DHSS; former memb: Personal Soc Servs Cncl DHSS, Home Office Advsy Cncl on Misuse of Drugs; vice-chm Centl Health Servs Cncl; govr Eastleigh Coll Further Educn 1977-86; Master Apothecaries Co 1981-82 (liveryman 1964, memb Ct of Assts 1971); memb Ct Southampton Univ 1979-86; Hon DM Southampton, Hon LLD Wales, pres Brendoncare Fndn 1984-; high steward Winchester Cathedral 1985; Gold Medal for distinguished merit BMA; FRCS, FRCGP, FRSA; kt 1975; *Publications* Care of The Elderly in General Practice (Gold Medal) 1956, Young People Growing Up (1978), Becoming a Doctor (1980), The Family Doctor, His Life and History (1981) etc; *Recreations* cricket, music, medicine, gardening; *Clubs* Athenaeum, MCC; *Style*— Sir Ronald Gibson, CBE, DL; 21 St Thomas's St, Winchester, Hants (☎ 0962 54582)

GIBSON, Ven Terence Allen; s of Fred William Allen Gibson, of Boston, Lincs, and Joan Hazel, *née* Bishop; *b* 23 Oct 1937; *Educ* Boston GS, Jesus Coll Cambridge (MA), Cuddesdon Coll Oxford; *Career* curate St Chad Kirkby Liverpool 1963-66, warden Centre 63 C of E Youth Centre and vicar for Youth Work 1966-75, rector of Kirkby Liverpool 1975-84, rural dean Walton Liverpool 1979-84; archdeacon of: Suffolk 1984-87, Ipswich 1987-; *Style*— The Ven The Archdeacon of Ipswich; 99 Valley Rd, Ipswich, Suffolk 1PI 4NF (☎ 0473 50333)

GIBSON, Hon William Knatchbull; s of Baron Gibson, *qv*, and Elizabeth Dione, da of Hon Clive Pearson; *b* 26 August 1951; *Educ* Eton, Oxford Univ; *Career* newspaper mangr with Westminster Press (industl rels specialist 1976-82), Sloan fell London Grad Sch of Business Studies 1983, dir of Admin Financial Times 1984-, publisher of Financial Times magazines 1986-; *Recreations* opera, shooting, skiing; *Clubs* Garrick; *Style*— The Hon William Gibson; 11 Paultons Sq, London SW3 5AP; Financial Times Magazines, Greystoke Place, London EC4

GIBSON FLEMING, Selina Littlehales; da of Lt-Col Sir Randolf Littlehales Baker, 4 and last Bt, DSO, DL (d 1959), of Ranston; *b* 26 Oct 1925; *m* 23 July 1955, Maj William Harry Gibson Fleming, RA (d 1981), o s of late Harry Gibson Fleming, of Englemere Wood, Ascot, Berks; 1 s (James b 1958), 1 da (Anthea b 1956); *Career* landowner; *Style*— Mrs Selina Gibson Fleming; Ranston, Blandford, Dorset (☎ 0258 860271)

GIBSON-CRAIG-CARMICHAEL, Sir David Peter William; 15 Bt of Keirhill (NS 1702) and 8 Bt of Riccarton (UK 1831); s of Sir (Archibald Henry) William Gibson-Craig-Carmichael, 14 and 7 Bt (d 1969), and Rosemary Anita, *née* Crew (d 1979); *b* 21 July 1946; *Educ* Queen's Univ Kingston Canada (BSc); *m* 1973, Patricia, da of Marcos Skarnic, of Santiago, Chile; 1 s, 1 da; *Heir* s, Peter William Gibson-Craig-Carmichael b 29 Dec 1975; *Style*— Sir David Gibson-Craig-Carmichael, Bt

GIBSON-CRAIG-CARMICHAEL, Emily, Lady - Emily Ellen; o da of Henry Rummell, of Falkland Islands; *m* 2 Sept 1914, Sir Eardley Gibson-Craig-Carmichael, 13 and 6 Bt (d 24 Feb 1939); 1 s (14 and 7 Bt, decd), 2 da; *Style*— Emily, Lady Gibson-Craig-Carmichael

GIBSON-WATT, Baron (Life Peer UK 1979); (James) David Gibson-Watt; MC (1943 and 2 bars), PC (1974, JP, DL) (formerly Radnorshire 1968, now Powys); s of Maj James Miller Gibson-Watt, JP, DL (d 1929; himself ggs of James Watt the engineer and the father of the steam engine) and Marjorie Adela, *née* Ricardo, MBE (herself gggda of David Ricardo, the political economist); *b* 11 Sept 1918; *Educ* Eton, Trinity Coll Cambridge; *m* 10 Jan 1942, Diana, 2 da of Sir Charles Hambro, KBE, MC (d 1963); 2 s (and 1 s decd), 2 da; *Career* served WW II Welsh Gds (North African and Italian campaigns); contested Brecon and Radnor 1950 and 1951, MP (C) Hereford 1956-74, lord cmmr of the Treasury 1959-61, minister of state Welsh Office 1970-74; memb Historic Buildings Cncl Wales 1975-79, a forestry commissioner 1976-; chm: Cncl of Royal Welsh Agricultural Soc 1978-, Council on Tribunals 1980-86; FRAgs; *Clubs* Boodle's, Pratt's; *Style*— The Rt Hon Lord Gibson-Watt, MC, PC, JP, DL; Doldowlod, Llandrindod Wells, Powys LD1 6HF (☎ 059 789 208)

GIBSON-WATT, Hon Robin; 3 s of Baron Gibson-Watt, MC, PC, JP, DL; *b* 25 Mar 1949; *Educ* Eton; *m* 1971, Marcia Susan, da of Sir Roger Hugh Cary, 2 Bt; 3 s, 1 da; *Career* High Sheriff Powys 1981; *Style*— The Hon Robin Gibson-Watt; Gelli Garn, Llanyre, Llandrindod Wells, Powys

GIBSON-WATT, Hon Sian Diana; yr da of Baron Gibson-Watt, MC, PC, JP, DL; *b* 1 April 1962; *Style*— Hon Sian Gibson-Watt

GIDDINGS, Air Marshal Sir (Kenneth Charles) Michael; KCB (1975), OBE (1953, DFC 1945, AFC and bar 1950, 1955); s of Charles Giddings and Grace, *née* Gregory; *b* 27 August 1920; *Educ* Ealing County Sch, UCL; *m* 1946, Elizabeth, da of Joseph McConnell; 2 s, 2 da; *Career* Test Pilot; Dep Chief Def Staff Op Requirements 1973-76; ind panel inspector DOE 1978-, dir National Counties Building Soc 1982-85; *Recreations* golf, gardening, music; *Clubs* RAF; *Style*— Air Marshal Sir Michael Giddings, KCB, OBE, DFC, AFC; 159 Long Lane, Tilehurst, Reading, Berks (☎ 0734 23012)

GIDDINS, Alan Clifford Bence; s of Dr Alan Grey Giddins, of Blacknest Hall, Grant Ave, Worthing, Sussex, and Dr Esther Anne, *née* Bence; *b* 25 August 1965; *Educ* Eton, Belmont Hill Sch, USA and Durham Univ (BA); *Career* accountant; public schs singles and doubles rackets finalist, and Br Univs doubles finalist; rep English and Welsh Univs athletics union, lawn tennis; *Recreations* lawn tennis, rackets, real tennis, golf; *Clubs* Lansdowne; *Style*— Alan Giddins, Esq; Blacknest Hall, Grand Ave, Worthing, Sussex BN11 5AG (☎ 202965); NoA2 Quay West, Westferry Rd, Isle of Dogs, London; Peat Marwick McLintock, 1 Puddle Doc, London EC2 (☎ 01 236 8000)

GIDLOW-JACKSON, Charles Michael; s of Lt Col Roger Myles Gidlow-Jackson, DSO (d 1945), of Glos, and Norah Gildow-Jackson, *née* Ramsay (d 1982); *b* 12 Sept 1944; *Educ* Eton Coll, Ch Ch Oxford; *m* 30 March 1968, Nuala Wynne, da of Patrick Griffin, of Oxfordshire; 1 s (Mark b 1972), 1 da (Ratia b 1970); *Career* dir of sales York Ltd 1986-; *Recreations* travel, shooting; *Clubs* Naval and Military; *Style*— Charles M Gidlow-Jackson, Esq; 84 Exeter St, Salisbury, Wilts SP1 2SE (☎ 0722 339 213)

GIDMAN, Richard Hippsley; s of Towers Halcott Gidman (d 1963), and Phyllis Mary, *née* Hippsley, MBE (d 1979); *b* 15 June 1928; *Educ* Nottingham HS, RAF Coll Cranwell; *m* 15 March 1952, Mary Elizabeth Whiteway, da of Lt-Col Cyril Harry Sands (d 1941); 2 s (Simon b 1953, Alastair b 1954); *Career* RAF pilot (gen duties), Sqdn-Ldr Bomber Cmmnd and MEAF 1946-60; mgmnt conslt 1970-87, vice-pres Towers Perrin Forster & Crosby 1970-83; *Recreations* gardening, cooking; *Clubs* RAF; *Style*— Richard H Gidman, Esq; Frieth Court, Little Frieth, nr Henley on Thames, Oxon RG9 5NU (☎ 0494 881080)

GIDNEY, Norman; CBE; s of George Gidney (d 1953), of Birmingham, and Abia (d 1969); *b* 26 Dec 1931; *Educ* Billesley Secdy Modern Birmingham; *m* 1957, Carol Ann, da of Alfred Mole (d 1957), of Birmingham; 3 s (Simon Mark b 1961, Daniel George b 1969, Jonathan Alfred (twin) b 1969), 1 da (Rachel Elizabeth b 1963); *Career* staff rgt RMO Italy, Austria; chm Warwick Industries Ltd, Industrial Hldg Co; *Recreations* tennis, squash, horse-riding, reading, philosophy & theology; *Style*— Norman Gidney, CBE; Haven Pastures, Henley-in-Arden, Solihull B95 5QS (☎ 05642 2734 & 3289); Gidney Securities Ltd, 66 High Street, Henley-in-Arden B95 5BX (telex 339358, fax 05642 2743)

GIDWANEY, Dhanras Chatamal Telkchand Hassasingh; s of Dewan Chatamal Telkchand Hassasingh Gidwaney (d 1974), of Giddubhamdar, and Mohini, *née* Jhagiani; *b* 3 Dec 1949; *Educ* Delhi Univ (BSc); *m* 1 (m dis 1979), Nagina; m 2, 26 June 1987, Tina, da of Dig Manley, of Chandigarh, India; *Career* CA; dir EW Ract plc 1981-83, chm and md Accountancy Tutors Ltd 1983; ACA 1981; *Recreations* cricket, tennis, polo; *Style*— Dhandras Gidwaney, Esq; Accountancy Tutors Ltd, 7-13 Melior St, London SE1 (☎ 01 403 3767, fax 01 403 7191)

GIEDROYĆ, Michal Graham Dowmont (Miko); s of Michal Jan Henryk Giedroyć, of Oxford, and Rosemary Virginia Anne, *née* Cumpston; *b* 5 May 1959; *Educ* Ampleforth Coll York, New Coll Oxford (BA); *m* 1 Nov 1986, Dorothee Ulrike Alexandra, da of Dr Ernst Friedrich Jung, of Botschafter; *Career* investmt div J Henry Schroder Vagg and Co Ltd 1980-83, vice pres Schroder Captital Mgmnt Inc 1984-85, dir of div Warbury Securities 1985-; *Recreations* jass piano; *Style*— Miko Giedroyć, Esq; Warburg Securities, 1 Finsbury Ave, London EC2M 2PA (☎ 01 382 4677, fax 01 382 4800)

GIELGUD, Sir (Arthur) John; CH (1977); s of Frank Gielgud, stockbroker (d 1949), and Kate Terry Lewis (d 1958, niece of Dame Ellen Terry 1847-1928); *b* 14 April 1904; *Educ* Westminster, Lady Benson Sch of Drama, RADA; *Career* actor, stage director and producer; stage debut Old Vic 1921 as the herald in Henry V, suc Noel Coward as Nicky Lancaster in The Vortex 1925 and as Lewis Dodd in The Constant Nymph 1927, Richard II in Richard of Bordeaux 1932, alternated Mercutio and Romeo with Laurence Olivier in Romeo and Juliet 1935 (also dir); appeared in Hamlet 1930, 1934, 1936, 1939, 1944, 1945, 1946 (over 500 appearances in this role); John Worthing in The Importance of Being Earnest 1930, 1939, 1942; Prosquero in The Tempest 1930, 1940, 1957, 1974; King Lear 1931, 1950, 1955; dir: The Heiress 1949, The Lady's Not For Burning 1949, The Cherry Orchard 1954, The Chalk Garden 1956, Hamlet (starring Richard Burton) USA 1964, Private Lives 1972; played Oedipus in Seneca's Oedipus 1968, headmaster in 40 Years On 1968, Home 1970, No Man's Land 1975, Julius Caesar 1977, Volpone 1977, Half-Life 1977, The Best of Friends 1988; films include: Richard III 1955, Chimes at Midnight 1966, Oh, What a Lovely War! 1968, Murder on the Orient Express 1974, The Elephant Man 1979, Arthur 1982 (Oscar for Best Supporting Actor), Wagner 1983, Plenty 1985; Hon LLD St Andrew's, Hon DLitt Oxon, Hon DLitt London, companion Légion d'Honneur 1960; kt 1953; *Books* Early Stages (1938), Stage Directions (1963), Distinguished Company (1972), An Actor and His Time (autobiog 1979); *Recreations* music, painting; *Clubs* Garrick, Arts, Players (New York); *Style*— Sir John Gielgud, CH; South Pavilion, Wotton Underwood, Aylesbury, Bucks

GIELGUD, Maina Julia Gordon; da of Lewis Evelyn Gielgud (d 1953), and Elisabeth Sutton (author and actress under name of Zita Gordon); niece of Sir John Gielgud; *b* 14 Jan 1945; *Educ* BEPC France; *Career* ballerina with Cuevas Co and Roland Petit Co to 1963; Grand Ballet Classique de France 1963-67; principal ballerina: Béjart Co 1967-71, Berlin 1971, London Festival Ballet 1972-76, Sadler's Wells Ballet 1976-78; freelance ballerina and guest artist 1978-82, rehearsal dir London City Ballet 1982, artistic dir Australian Ballet 1983-; creations and choreographies: Steps Notes and Squeaks (London) 1978, Petit Pas et Crac (Paris) 1979, Ghosties and Ghoulies (London City Ballet) 1982, The Sleeping Beauty (Australian Ballet) 1984, Giselle (Australian Ballet) 1986; *Style*— Miss Maina Gielgud; 11 Mount Alexander Rd, Flemington, 3031 Australia (☎ 03 376 1400); Stirling Court, 3 Marshall St, London W1 (☎ 01 734 6612)

GIFFARD, Adam Edward; o s and h of 3 Earl of Halsbury (but does not use courtesy title Viscount Tiverton); *b* 3 June 1934; *Educ* Stowe, Jesus Cambridge; *m* 1, 1 Aug 1963, Ellen, da of late Brynjolf Hovde, and formerly w of Matthew Huxley; m 2, 1976, Joanna Elizabeth, da of Frederick Harry Cole; 2 da (Sarah b 1976, Emma b 1978); *Career* late 2 Lt Seaforth Highlanders; *Style*— Adam Giffard, Esq; PO Box 13, North Branch, New York 12766, USA

GIFFARD, Peter Richard de Longueville; DL (1984); s of Thomas Giffard, MBE, JP, DL (d 1971), and Angela, da of Sir William Trollope, 10 Bt; is sr male rep of the Giffards of Chillington, one of the few English families to be able to trace their ancestry from pre-Conquest times, who flourished in Normandy in the tenth century, came over with William the Conqueror, are mentioned in Domesday and have held Chillington since 1178; bro of Baroness Airey of Abingdon; *see also* Bellew, Hon Patrick; *b* 20 May 1921; *Educ* Eton, Ch Ch Oxford; *m* 1949, Mary Roana, da of Ronald Gandar Dower (d 1963), of Old Park, Warninglid, Sussex; 1 s, 1 da; *Career* barr 1947; dir S Staffs Waterworks Co 1974; pres CLA 1983-85; chm Mercia Region Nat Trust; pres: Staffordshire Soc 1979, European Landowners Orgn 1985-87; FRSA 1987; *Recreations* shooting, tree planting; *Clubs* Army & Navy, Boodle's, MCC; *Style*— Peter Giffard, Esq, DL; Chillington Hall, Codsall Wood, Wolverhampton (☎ 0902 850236)

GIFFARD, Sir (Charles) Sydney Rycroft; KCMG (1984), CMG (1976); s of Walter Ernest Giffard, JP (d 1970), of Gypsy Furlong, Lockeridge, Wilts, and Minna Kathleen Douglas, *née* Cotton (d 1966); *b* 30 Oct 1926; *m* 1, 1951 (m dis 1976), Wendy Patricia, da of late (Charles) John Vidal, of Newbury, Berks; 1 s (Charles b 1959), 1 da (Theresa b 1960); m 2, 1976, Hazel Beatrice Coleby Roberts, OBE; *Career* joined Foreign Service 1951, ambassador Tokyo 1984-; *Style—* Sir Sydney Giffard, KCMG, CMG; c/o Foreign and Commonwealth Office, King Charles St, London SW1; British Embassy, Chiyoda-ku, Tokyo 102, Japan

GIFFIN, Michael; s of John Metcalfe Giffin (d 1984); *b* 2 May 1935; *Educ* Sevenoaks Sch; *m* 1963, Jane Agnes, da of Col Howard Watson Wright (d 1974); 2 s, 1 da; *Career* md St Olaf Bonding Co Ltd 1974-81; chm: Hays Business Services Ltd 1981-, Britdoc Ltd 1981-; md Hays Commercial Services Ltd 1985-; FCA; *Recreations* sailing; *Clubs* RAC, Medway Yacht; *Style—* Michael Giffin, Esq; Tussocks, 19 Burntwood Rd, Sevenoaks, Kent TN13 1PS (☎ 0732 451536)

GIFFORD, 6 Baron (UK 1824); Anthony Maurice Gifford; QC (1982); s of 5 Baron Gifford (d 1961); *b* 1 May 1940; *Educ* Winchester, King's Coll Cambridge; *m* 22 March 1965, Katherine Ann, da of Max Mundy, MRCS, of 52 Hornton St, Kensington; 1 s, 1 da (Hon Polly Anna b 1969); *Heir* s, Hon Thomas Adam Gifford b 1 Dec 1967; *Career* sits as Lab Peer in Lords; barr 1962; chm Ctee for Freedom Mozambique, Angola & Guiné 1968-75, N Kensington Law Centre 1974-77, Legal Action Gp 1978-81, Mozambique Angola Ctee 1984, vice-chm Briton Defence Aid Fund 1985, chm Broadwater Farm Inquiry 1986; *Books* Where the Justice (1986); *Style—* The Rt Hon the Lord Gifford, QC; 35 Wellington St, WC2 (☎ 01 836 5917)

GIFFORD, Baroness; (Ellice) Margaret; 2 da of late Arthur Wigram Allen, of Merioola, Woollahra, NSW; *b* 9 Sept 1896; *Educ* Private Education; *m* 5 March 1939, 5 Baron Gifford (d 16 April 1961); 1 s (6 Baron); *Publications* I Can Hear the Horses (1983); *Clubs* Queens (Sydney), Naval & Military (London); *Style—* The Rt Hon the Dowager Lady Gifford; Hollington House, Woolton Hill, Newbury, Berks

GIGGALL, Rt Rev (George) Kenneth; OBE (1960); s of Arthur William Giggall (d 1959), and Matilda Hannah, *née* Granlese (d 1964); *b* 15 April 1914; *Educ* Manchester Central HS, Univ of Manchester (BA), St Chad's Coll Univ of Durham (Dip Theol); *Career* ordained: deacon 1939, priest 1940; curate: St Alban's Cheetwood 1939-41, St Elisabeth's Reddish 1941-45; chaplain RNVR and RN: HMS Braganza 1945, 34 Amphibious Support Regt RM 1945-46, Sch of Combined Ops Fremington 1946-47, HMS Norfold 1947-49, Ocean 1949- 50, Flotilla Cmd Med and HMS Phoenicia 1950-52, HMS Campania for Op Hurricane 1952, BRNC Dartmouth 1952-53, HMS Centaur 1953-56, Ceylon 1956-58, Frisgard 1958-60, Royal Arthur and lectr RAF Chaplains' Sch 1960-63, HMS Eagle 1963-65, Dratee 1965-69; QHC 1967-, dean of Gibraltar and officiating chaplain HMS Rooke 1969- 73, Flag Offr Gibraltar 1969-73, Bishop St Helena 1973-79, consecrated St Saviours Church E London, Cape Province, RSA, chaplain San Remo with Bordighera 1979-81, Auxilliary Bishop Diocese of Gibraltar (subsequently Europe) 1978-81, Asst Bishop Diocese of Blackburn 1982-; *Recreations* music; *Clubs* Commonwealth Soc, Sidn Coll Exiles (Ascension Island); *Style—* The Rt Rev Kenneth Giggall, OBE; Fosbrooke House, Clifton Drive, Lytham St Annes FY8 5RQ (☎ 0253 735 683)

GIGNOUX, Peter Alan; s of Frederick Evelyn Gignoux, Jr (d 1968); *b* 17 June 1945; *Educ* St Albans Sch, The Gunnery Sch, Boston Univ, Columbia Univ; *m* 26 Jan 1984, Katherine Elizabethe Phillips; *Career* London mangr Int Energy Desk; sr vice pres Shearson/Lehman Brothers Inc; *Recreations* shooting, travelling, yacht cruising; *Clubs* Buck's, Mark's, Hurlingham, St Anthony (New York); *Style—* Peter Gignoux, Esq; 22 Woodfall St, Chelsea, London SW3 (☎ 01 730 4132); Shearson/Lehman Brothers Inc, 1 Broadgate, London EC2

GILBART-DENHAM, Lt Col Seymour Vivian; s of Major Vivian Vandeleur (d 1940), of Norway, and Diana Mary Gilbart-Denham, *née* Beaumont (d 1983); *b* 10 Oct 1939; *Educ* Ludgrove, Tabley House; *m* 1 April 1976, Patricia Caroline, da of Lt Col Granville Brooking, of E Sussex; 2 da (Sophie b 1977, Georgina b 1980); *Career* cmmnd Life Gds 1960, (adjutant 1965-67), cmd Household Cavalry Regt 1986-87, Crown Equerry 1987; *Recreations* riding, shooting, fishing, skiing; *Clubs* Cavalry and Guards; *Style—* Lt Col Seymour V Gilbart-Denham; The Royal Mews, Buckingham Palace, London SW1W 0QH (☎ 01 930 4832); Chicksgrove Manor, Chicksgrove, Tisbury, Wilts SP3 6NA (☎ 072 276 414)

GILBART-SMITH, (Oliver) Denham; s of Oliver Brian Gilbart-Smith (d 1988), and Doris Florence, *née* Martin-Harvey; *b* 24 May 1947; *Educ* St Columbas Coll nr Dublin Eire; *m* 1 Nov 1975, Lesley Anne, da of Michael Gordon Evans, of Devon; 3 s (Matthew b 1981, Luke b 1983, Adam b 1987), 1 da (Ruth b 1980); *Career* ptnr Geo H Fryer & Co Lloyd's Brokers 1968-71, Bryant and Shaw Lloyds Brokers 1971-74, self employed insur broker assoc with F Bolton & Co and Frizzell Gp 1974-86, md F Bolton & Co Marine Ltd 1987, dir Haggai Inst for Advanced Leadership Trg Ltd 1988; pastor River Church Marlow & Maidenhead; Freeman: City of London, Worshipful Co of Poulters; memb of Lloyds 1968-; *Recreations* swimming, travel; *Style—* Denham Gilbart-Smith, Esq; The Stables, Job's Lane, Cookham Dean, Berks; 103 Mallon Dene, Rustington, Sussex; RCF House, Victoria Rd, Marlow, Bucks (☎ 0628 890 292, fax 0628 890 667)

GILBERT, Brian Geoffrey; s of Donald William Gilbert (d 1968); *b* 18 July 1927; *Educ* Bishopshalt Sch Hillingdon, Middx; *m* 1978, Maxine, da of George Hadley (d 1971); 2 da; *Career* md and gp chief exec Low & Bonar plc 1973-84; chm: BMG Ltd, Elgin City Sawmills Ltd, Faulds Advertising Ltd; dep chm A T Mays Gp plc, chm Richards plc; dir: Graphic Information Services Ltd, Polbeth Packaging Ltd, Polbeth Packaging (Corby) Ltd, McClintock Assocs Ltd (Australia), Klearfold Inc (USA), chm New Park Sch; CBIM; *Recreations* golf, fishing; *Clubs* Royal & Ancient, Caledonian; *Style—* Brian Gilbert, Esq; Beechfield, 29 Balgrove Rd, Gauldry, Newport-on-Tay, Fife DD6 8SH (☎ 082 624 228)

GILBERT, Dennis; s of Gordon S Gilbert (d 1973), and Beatrice Maskell-Hall (d 1968); *b* 7 Jan 1922; *Educ* Lewisham Sch, South-West Essex Tech Coll, St Martins Sch of Art (NDD); *m* 14 July 1949 (m dis 1976), Joan, da of Harold Musker, OBE, MC (d 1974); 3 s (Hugh b 1952, Michael b 1957, Joseph b 1963), 1 da (Mary b 1965); *Career* WWII Warrant Offr and Navigator 1942-46; lectr (visiting): Hammersmith Coll of Art 1950-65, Wimbledon Coll of Art 1954-60, Kingston Coll of Art 1958-65; lectr Hammersmith Coll of Art 1965-75, sr lectr Chelsea Sch of Art 1975-84; exhibitions incl: RA, Paris Salon, Royal Festival Hall, Royal Soc of Portrait Painters (annually 1959-81), Contemporary Portrait Soc, Royal Soc of Br Artists, Royal Inst Portrait Painters, New English Art Club (annually 1959-), Nat Soc of Painters (annually 1957-), Chelsea Art Soc, Ben Uri Gallery, Browse and Darby Gallery, Chenil Gallery, Redfern Gallery, Wildenstein Gallery, Woodstock Gallery, Century Gallery, Compton Gallery, Phoenix Gallery, Southwell Brown Gallery; memb: New English Art Club , Int Assoc of Artists, Comtemporary Portrait Soc (chm 1984-86), Nat Soc of Painters, Chelsea Art Soc, Nine Elms Gp of Artists; *Clubs* Arts, Chelsea Arts; *Style—* Dennis Gilbert, Esq; Top Studio, 11 Edith Grove, London SW10 OJZ (☎01 352 9476)

GILBERT, Lt-Col Ernle Reginald Forester; s of Capt Humphrey Gilbert, of Bishopstone House, Bishopstone, Hereford; *b* 1 June 1921; *Educ* Marlborough, Staff Coll Camberley; *m* 1946, Helene Maria Margarete, da of Prof Dr Hans Reiter, of Graz, Austria; 1 da (Sybella); *Career* Reg Army Offr 1940-61, served N Africa, Italy, Greece, Palestine, Malaya; merchant banker; consultant: Save and Prosper 1966-70, Keyser Ullmann 1971-75; High Sheriff Herefordshire 1973-74, chm Herefordshire and Radnorshire Nature Trust; *Recreations* cricket, natural history, shooting, fishing; *Clubs* Army & Navy; *Style—* Lt-Col Ernle Gilbert; Bishopstone House, Bishopstone, Hereford HR4 7JG (☎ 098 122 277)

GILBERT, Maj-Gen Glyn Charles Anglim; CB (1974), MC (1944); s of C G G Gilbert, OBE, MC, and Marjory Helen Gilbert, MBE of Bermuda; *b* 1920; *Educ* Eastbourne Coll, RMC Sandhurst; *m* 1943, Heather Mary, widow of Pilot Offr A E Jackson, DFM, and da of late F Green; 3 s, 1 da; *Career* served: NW Europe 1944-45, Palestine 1945-47, Cyprus 1951, Egypt 1951, Malaya 1955-56, Cyprus 1958-59, IDC 1966, Maj-Gen 1970, cmd 1944 Para Bde 1963-65, cmd Sch of Infantry 1967-70, GDC 3 Div 1970-72; cmd Jt Warfare Establishment 1972-74, ret 1974; dir Riverside Holidays 1974-80, md Fitness for Indust Ltd 1980-85 (vice- chm 1985), dir Windward Rum Co Ltd 1987; *Recreations* following the sun; *Clubs* Army & Navy, Royal Bermuda Yacht; *Style—* Maj-Gen Glyn Gilbert, CB, MC; c/o Lloyds Bank, Warminster, Wilts

GILBERT, Ian Grant; s of Capt Alexander Grant Gilbert, DCM (d 1943), and Marion Patrick, *née* Cruickshank (d 1963); *b* 18 June 1925; *Educ* Fordyce Acad Banffshire Scot, Royal HS of Edinburgh, Univ of Edinburgh (MA); *m* 1 July 1960, Heather Margaret, da of Rev Francis Cantlie Donald (d 1974), of Lumphanan, Scotland; *Career* WWII 1943-47, RA; seconded to Indian Artillery (Capt): 10 Indian Field Regt 1944-45, Sch of Artillery Deolali India 1946-47; entered Home CS as asst princ Miny of Nat Insur 1950, private sec to perm sec (Sir Geoffrey S King, KCB) 1953, private sec to parly sec (Rt Hon Ernest Marples, MP) 1955, princ Miny of Pensions and Nat Insur 1956, princ HM Treasury 1962-66, asst sec Miny of Soc Sec (later DHSS) 1966-, under sec Internat Rels Divn DHSS 1979-85, memb UK delegation to World Health Assembly Geneva 1979-84, clerk and advsr Select Ctee on Euro Legislation House of Commons 1987-; Session Clerk Crown Ct Church of Scot Covent Gdn 1975-80, Church of Scot memb Churches Main Ctee 1986-; *Recreations* keeping half-an-acre, choral singing, local history; *Clubs* Royal Cwlth Soc London; *Style—* Ian Gilbert, Esq; Wellpark, Moorside, Sturminster Newton, Dorset DT10 1HJ (☎ 0258 820306); House of Commons (Overseas Office), London SW1A 0AA (☎ 01 219 3307)

GILBERT, (Cecil) James; s of T C Gilbert (d 1958), of Edinburgh, and Mabel (d 1945); *b* 15 May 1923; *Educ* Edinburgh Acad, Edinburgh Univ, RADA (Dip); *m* 10 July 1951, Fiona, da of George Clyne (d 1957), of Moss House, Wick, Caithness, 1 s (Colin b 1952), 2 da (Susan (Mrs Gilmore) b b 1953, Julia b 1962); *Career* WII RAF Flt LT 1942-46 (bomber pilot); composer,lyricist: Grab me a Gondola (Lyric Theatre,1957), Golden Touch (Piccadilly Theatre 1960), Good Time Johnny (Birmingham Rep 1973); prodr/dir BBC TV 1956-73 (3 BAFTA Awards, Golden Rose, Montreaux)) head: Comedy BBC TV 1973-77, Light Entertainment BBC TV 1977-82, Comedy Progs Thames TV 1982-88; *Recreations* walking, music, reading, theatre; *Clubs* RAF; *Style—* James Gilbert, Esq; 29 Sydney Rd, Richmond, Surrey (☎ 01 940 1240); Tarden Cottage, Chalford, Glos; Thames TV, Broom Rd, Teddington, Middx (☎ 01 977 3252)

GILBERT, John Arthur; *b* 11 August 1932; *Educ* Kings Norton GS for Boys, Birmingham Coll of Technol (later Univ of Aston) (HNC, BSc); *m* 1, 19 Nov 1955, late Marion Audrey; 2 s (Simon Gerard b 11 April 1958, Andrew Boyd b 1 Jan 1960), 1 da (Rosamund Grace (Mrs Jackson), b 25 Feb 1964); m 2, 22 April 1983, Nicola Ann; *Career* trainee engr S Willis 1949, ptnr James-Carrington & Ptnrs 1967- (assoc 1964-67), work includes: maj town redevelopment schemes, large retail stores, hosps, refurbishment of listed bildgs, developing on deep landfill sites; awarded Inst Civil Engrs George Stephenson Medal for paper on maj Belfast project 1988; FICE 1961, FIStructE 1963, ACIArb 1979; *Style—* John A Gilbert, Esq; White Lodge, Bevere, Worcs WR3 7RQ (☎ 0905 51285); James-Carrington & Ptnrs, Kennedy Tower, St Chads Queensway, Birmingham B4 6JH (☎ 021 236 9988)

GILBERT, Rt Hon Dr John William; PC (1978), MP (Lab) Dudley East 1974- (Dudley 1970-); *b* 5 April 1927; *Educ* Merchant Taylors', St John's Coll Oxford, New York Univ (PhD); *m* 1; 2 da; m 2, 1963, Jean Olive Ross Skinner; *Career* MP Dudley 1970-74, financial sec Treasury 1974-75, min for Transport DOE 1975-76, min state MOD 1976-79; *Style—* The Rt Hon Dr John Gilbert, MP; House of Commons, London SW1

GILBERT, Jonathan Sinclair; s of Brian Hamlyn Gilbert (d 1978), and Joan, *née* Sinclair; *b* 29 Sept 1937; *Educ* Bilton Grange PS, Rugby; *m* 10 Aug 1962, Lene, da of Palle Palsby (d 1988); 3 s (Andrew b 12 Nov 1964, Nicholas (twin) b 12 Nov 1964, Peter b 22 July 1967); *Career* Nat Serv, Lt Kings Hussars 1955-57; bd dir Bland Payne Ltd 1968, chm Bland Payne 1977, dir Bland Payne Hldgs Ltd 1978, chm Sedgwick Offshore Resources Ltd 1980, dir Sedgwick Gp plc 1981-; memb Lloyds; *Recreations* golf; *Clubs* Burhill Folf, Royal St George's Golf, Lloyd's Golf, MCC; *Style—* J.S Gilbert, Esq; Nash House, 6 The Quillot, Burwood Park, Walton-on-Thames, Surrey KT12 5BY (☎ 0932 227 214); Sedwick House, The Sedgwick Centre, London E1 8DX (☎ 01 377 3153, fax 01 377 3199, telex 882 131)

GILBERT, Martin James; s of James Robert Gilbert, of Papua and New Guinea, and Winifred, *née* Walker; *b* 13 July 1935; *Educ* Robert Gordons Coll, Univ of Aberdeen (MA, LLB); *m* 4 June 1981, Dr Fiona Jane Gilbert, da of Dr John K Davidson; 1 s (Jamie); *Career* CA with: Deliotte Haskins and Sells 1978-81, Brander and Cruickshank 1982-83, Aberdeen Fund Mangrs 1983-; memb Inst of CA of Scotland; *Recreations* golf, hockey, skiing; *Clubs* Royal Aberdeen GC, Royal Selangor GC, Gordonians HC; *Style—* Martin Gilbert, Esq; Balgranach, Milltimber, Aberdeen (☎ 0224 733231); Aberdeen Fund Mangers Ltd, 10 Queens Tce, Aberdeen AB9 1QJ (☎ 0224 631999)

GILBERT, Michael Francis; CBE (1980), TD (1950); s of Bernard Samuel Gilbert (d 1927), and Berwyn Minna, *née* Cuthbert (d 1966); *b* 17 July 1912; *Educ* Blundell's Sch, Univ of London (LLB); *m* 26 July 1947, Roberta Mary, da of the late Col R M W

Marsden; 2 s (Richard b 1956, Gerard b 1960), 5 da (Harriett b 1948, Victoria b 1950, Olivia b 1952, Kate b 1954, Laura b 1958); *Career* WWII HAC (Major) served N Africa, Italy (despatches 1943) 1939-45; slr Trower, Still & Keeling 1947 (ptnr 1952-83), legal advsr to Ruler of Bahrain 1960; memb: Royal Literary Fund Ctee 1964, cncl Soc of Authors 1975; *Books* 24 novels of detection and suspense, over 200 short stories, 4 stage plays and critical articles, editor of 2 anthologies; *Recreations* walking; *Clubs* Garrick; *Style*— Michael Gilbert, Esq; The Old Rectory, Luddesdown, Gravesend, Kent DA13 0XE (☎ 0474 814272)

GILBERT, Stuart William; CB (1983); s of Rodney Stuart Gilbert (d 1978), and Ella Edith, *née* Esgate; *b* 2 August 1926; *Educ* Maidstone GS, Emmanuel Coll Cambridge (MA); *m* 1955, Marjorie Laws, da of Stanley Aloysius Vallance (d 1975); 1 s, 1 da; *Career* served WW II Sgt RAF, India, Burma; civil servant; dep sec and dir Dept for National Savings 1981-86; *Recreations* sailing, music, electronics, woodwork; *Clubs* Oxford and Cambridge, Bewl Valley Sailing; *Style*— Stuart Gilbert, Esq, CB; 3 Westmoat Close, Beckenham, Kent BR3 2BX (☎ 01 650 7213)

GILBERT, Brig Sir William Herbert Ellery; KBE (1976), OBE (1945, DSO 1944); s of Ellery George Gilbert, and Nellie, *née* Hall; *b* 20 July 1916; *Educ* Wanganui Collegiate Sch NZ, RMC Duntroon Australia; *m* 1944, Patricia Caroline Anson, da of O R Farrer; 2 s, 1 da; *Career* director NZ Security Intelligence Service 1956-76; ret; *Style*— Brig Sir William Gilbert, KBE, OBE, DSO; 38 Chatsworth Rd, Silverstream, New Zealand (☎ 04 286570)

GILBERTSON, Arthur Geoffrey; JP (Glam 1959); s of Charles Geoffrey Gilbertson (d 1963), of Gellygron, Pontardawe; *b* 18 May 1913; *Educ* Shrewsbury; *m* 1937, Hilarie Annette, da of Hubert S Williams-Thomas, of Stourbridge; 3 da (Phebe, Ruth, Diana); *Career* md Brown Lenox & Co of Pontypridd 1949-71; memb Western Railway Bd 1963-77, dir Royal Briersley Crystal 1965-82; High Sheriff Glamorgan 1970-71, pres S Glamorgan British Red Cross Soc 1974-81, chm Vale of Glamorgan Magistrates 1981; former hon sec Llandaff Diocesan Conference; former memb: cncl St David's Univ Coll Lampeter, governing and rep body and Electoral Coll of The Church in Wales; CStJ; *Recreations* cricket, fishing, shooting, gardening; *Clubs* MCC; *Style*— Arthur Gilbertson, Esq, JP, CStJ; Castle Cottage, Llanblethian, Cowbridge, S Glamorgan (☎ 044 63 2809)

GILBERTSON, David Stuart; s of Donald Stuart Gilbertson, and Jocelyn Mary, *née* Sim; *b* 21 Sept 1956; *Educ* Birkenhead Sch Merseyside, Trinity Hall Cambridge Univ (MA); *Career* corr Reuters 1980-81, ed Metal Bulletin 1981-87, ed Lloyds List 1987-; NUJ; *Style*— David Gilbertson, Esq

GILBERTSON, (Cecil) Edward (Mark); s of Francis Mark Gilbertson, of Ham, Hungerford, Wilts, and Elizabeth Margaret, *née* Dawson, of USA; *b* 2 June 1949; *Educ* Maidwell Hall PS, Eton; *m* 3 Sept 1986, Nicola Leslie Bellairs, yr da of Maj J A B Lloyd Philipps (d 1974), of Dale Castle, Dale, Dyfed; 1 da (Georgina Charlotte Bellairs b 29 Oct 1987); *Career* stockbroker 1976, memb Lloyds 1989; *Recreations* cricket, shooting, squash, tennis; *Clubs* MCC, County (Cardiff); *Style*— Edward Gilbertson, Esq; Cathedine Hill, Bwlch, Nr Brecon, Powys; Llangwarren Estate, Letterston, Dyfed SA62 5UL

GILBERTSON, Sir Geoffrey; CBE (1972); s of Albert James and M O Gilbertson; *b* 29 May 1918; *Educ* Durham Sch, Jesus Coll Cambridge; *m* 1940, Dorothy Ness, da of Percy Barkes, MBE; 4 children; *Career* served WW II, 4/7 Royal Dragoon Guards; chm: NEDC Shipbuilding 1974-77, Nat Advsy Ctee Employment of Disabled People 1975-81; former memb Pay Bd, with ICI 1946-74 (gp gen manager 1967-74); Croix de Guerre; FIPM, FRSA; kt 1981; *Style*— Sir Geoffrey Gilbertson, CBE; Greta Bridge, Barnard Castle, Co Durham (☎ 0833 27276)

GILBEY, Hon Anthony William; s and h of 10 Baron Vaux of Harrowden by his 1 cous Maureen Gilbey; *b* 25 May 1940; *Educ* Ampleforth; *m* 4 July 1964, Beverley, o da of Charles Alexander Walton, of Cooden, Sussex; 2 s (Richard b 1965, Philip b 1967), 1 da (Victoria b 1969); *Career* farmer; *Recreations* fishing, shooting; *Style*— Hon Anthony Gilbey; Rusko, Gatehouse of Fleet, Kirkcudbrightshire

GILBEY, Sir (Walter) Derek; 3 Bt (UK 1893); s of Walter Ewart Gilbey (d 1941), and Alice Dora, *née* Sim (d 1961); suc gf, Sir (Henry) Walter Gilbey, 2 Bt, 1945; *b* 11 Mar 1913; *Educ* Eton; *m* 1948, Elizabeth Mary, da of Col Keith Gordon Campbell, DSO, of Standen House, Newport, Isle of Wight; 1 s, 1 da (Camilla Elizabeth b 1953); *Heir* s, (Walter) Gavin Gilbey; *Career* Lt Black Watch 1940-45; export dir W & A Gilbey Ltd to 1970; *Clubs* Portland; *Style*— Sir Derek Gilbey, Bt; Grovelands, Wineham, nr Henfield, West Sussex (☎ 044 482 311)

GILBEY, (Walter) Gavin; s and h of Sir Derek Gilbey, 3 Bt; *b* 14 April 1949; *Educ* Eton; *m* 1980, Mary, da of late William E E Pacetti, of Florida, USA; *Style*— Gavin Gilbey, Esq; 9615 SW 118th St, S Miami, Fla, USA

GILBEY, Mark Newman; s of Henry Newman Gilbey (d 1956; s of Newman Gilbey, JP, who was both n of Sir Walter Gilbey, 1 Bt, and great unc of 9 and 10 Barons Vaux of Harrowden), and his 1 wife Myn Beatrice, *née* Brunwin (d 1936); *b* 21 Nov 1923; *Educ* Beaumont, Trinity Coll Cambridge; *Career* served Italy 1944-45 as Capt Gren Gds; fndr and former chm Duncan Gilbey & Matheson Gp of Cos; hon cnsl as Ecuador to Morocco 1967-; *Recreations* travel, reading, antique and picture collecting; *Clubs* Boodle's, Buck's; *Style*— Mark Gilbey, Esq; Ile de Gorée, Dakar, Senegal (216966); Dar el Bab, Casbah, Tangier, Morocco (☎ 32942); c/o United African Distilleries Ltd, 4 Great Portland St, London W1N 5AA (☎ 01 580 0342); 1510 Diamond Mountain Rd, Calistoga, California 954575 (☎ 707 942 9448)

GILBEY, Hon Mary Agnes Margaret; da of Baroness Vaux of Harrowden (d 1958); *b* 13 April 1928; *Style*— Hon Mary Gilbey; Glenmore House, Orlingbury Road, Gt Harrowden, Wellingborough, Northants

GILBEY, Hon Michael Christopher; 3 s of 10 Baron Vaux of Harrowden, and Maureen, nee Gilbey (a 1 cous, da of Hugh Gilbey, yr bro of William Gilbey who m Baroness Vaux of Harrowden, m of 9 and 10 Barons); *b* 29 Dec 1949; *Educ* Ampleforth, St Andrews Univ (MA); *m* 1971, Linda, da of Arthur Sebastian Gilbey (d 1964, ggs of Sir Walter Gilbey, 1 Bt) and his 3 cous once removed; 3 s (Henry b 1973, Julian b 1975, William b 1979); *Career* chartered surveyor 1974-; dir: The Eton Wine Bar 1975-, M & W Gilbey Ltd (Wine Merchants) 1981-; *Recreations* tennis, golf, sailing; *Style*— Hon Michael Gilbey; Red Hatch, Harpsden Woods, Henley-on-Thames, Oxon RG9 4AF (☎ 0491 573202); (☎ office 0491 579104, telex 846565 GILBEY)

GILBEY, Lady Penelope Anne; *née* Rous; yr da of 4 Earl of Stradbroke (d 1983); *b* 31 July 1932; *m* 1, 19 June 1950 (m dis 1960), Cdr Ian Dudley Stewart Forbes, DSC, RN, s of late Lt-Col James Stewart Forbes (gs of late Sir Charles Forbes, 3 Bt) by his 2 w, Feridah; 1 s (Charles b 1956, farms at Henham), 2 da (Catriona, m 1981 Michael Bradley; 1 s, 1 da; Caroline, photographer, m 1977 (m dis 1982) Katsuhisa Sakai, of Tokyo, Japan, 1 s); m 2, 15 May 1961 (m dis 1969), John Cator, s of late Col Henry Cator, MC, JP, DL, of Woodbastwick Hall, Norfolk; m 3, 27 Sept 1984, as his 3 w, Anthony James Gilbey, s of Quintin Holland Gilbey, gn of Sir Walter Gilbey, 1 Bt; *Career* dir: David Carritt Ltd (picture gallery) 1972-82, Artemis Fine Arts UK Ltd (art dealers) 1972-82, Gilbey Collections Ltd 1983-; *Style*— Lady Penelope Gilbey; 26 Cambridge St, London SW1V 4QH

GILBEY, Walter Anthony; MHK Glenfaba IOM 1982-; s of Sir Henry Walter Gilbey, 2 Bt, JP (d 1945), of Portman Sq, London W1, and his 2 w Marion, *née* Robert; half-bro of Sir Derek Gilbey, 3 Bt; *b* 26 Feb 1935, (as Anthony Walter, present order of names by Deed Poll 195; *Educ* Eton; *m* 2 April 1964, Jenifer Mary, eldest da of Capt James Timothy Noël Price, of Brookfield, Ramsey, IOM, and his w, Hon Anne Younger, yr da of 2 Viscount Younger of Leckie; 1 s (Walter Anthony b 20 Jan 1966), 2 da (Caroline Anne b 2 Oct 1967, Sarah Elizabeth b 3 Nov 1969); *Career* merchant banker with Kleinwort Benson Ltd London 1954-62; fin dir Gilbeys Ltd (int distillers and vintners) 1962-72; chm: Mannin Tst Bank Ltd IOM 1972-82, Mannin Int Ltd IOM 1982-88; dir and chm Mannin Int Securities Ltd IOM 1972-; dir IOM Steam Packet Co Ltd 1976-; chm Mannin Industries Ltd IOM 1972-; dir Gilbey Farms Ltd IOM 1974-; ptnr Gilbey Grianagh Horses IOM 1978-; chm: Manx Telecom Ltd 1986-, Civil Service Cmmn and Whitley Cncl IOM 1985-; memb Dept of Local Govt & The Environment IOM 1987-; chm Planning Ctee Dept of Local Govt IOM 1987-; Sr Master IOM Bloodhounds; sec Manx Horse Cncl; chm gp of almshouses; memb: European Atlantic Gp, European League for Economic Co-operation, Coaching Club, Br Driving Soc, Br Horse Soc, Shire Horse Soc, Masters of Drag Hounds Assoc; Cons Parly Candidate for Ealing Southall 1971-74; memb Berkshire CC 1966-74; memb Vintners' Co; *Recreations* horses, riding, driving; *Style*— Walter Gilbey, Esq, MHK; Ballacallin Mooar, Crosby, Marown, IOM (☎ 0624 851450)

GILBEY, Hon William John; s of 10 Baron Vaux of Harrowden; *b* 24 Feb 1944; *Educ* Ampleforth; *m* 1971, Caroline Susan, da of Alan Ball, of Ramsbury, Wilts; 2 s (Thomas, James), 1 da (Charlotte); *Career* dir M & W Gilbey Ltd; *Recreations* golf, tennis, fishing, sailing, photography; *Style*— The Hon William Gilbey; The Grange, Waltham St Lawrence, Twyford, Berks RG10 0JJ

GILCHRIST, Sir Andrew Graham; KCMG (1964, CMG 1956); eldest s of James Graham Gilchrist (d 1945), of Kerse, Lesmahagow, Lanarkshire; *b* 19 April 1910; *Educ* Edinburgh Acad, Exeter Coll Oxford; *m* 1946, Freda Grace (d 1987), da of Alfred George Slack (d 1947), of London; 2 s, 1 da; *Career* served Force 136 (India, Burma and Siam, despatches) 1944-46, Maj; Consular Service Siam 1933, first sec Bangkok 1946, consul-gen Stuttgart 1951-54, cnsllr Office of UK Cmmr-Gen in S E Asia 1954-56, ambass: Iceland 1956-60, Indonesia 1963-66, Republic of Ireland 1966-70; chm Highlands and Islands Devpt Bd 1970-76; *Books* Bangkok Top Secret (1970), Cod Wars and How to Lose Them (1979), The Russian Professor (1984), The Watercress File (1985), The Ultimate Hostage (1986), South of Three Pagodas (1987); *Recreations* outdoor, opera; *Clubs* Special Forces, New (Edinburgh); *Style*— Sir Andrew Gilchrist, KCMG; Arthur's Crag, Hazelbank, by Lanark ML11 9XL (☎ Crossford (055 586) 263)

GILCHRIST, Archibald; s of James Gilchrist (d 1972); *b* 17 Dec 1929; *Educ* Loretto Sch, Pembroke Coll Cambridge (MA); *m* 1958, Elizabeth Jean, da of Robert Cumming Greenlees (d 1983); 2 s, 1 da; *Career* Capt Glasgow Yeomanry (TA); engr and shipbuilder, md Vosper Private Ltd Singapore 1980-, dir (non exec) Vosper plc; *Recreations* golf, reading, music; *Clubs* Hon Co of Edinburgh Golfers, Western (Glasgow); *Style*— Archibald Gilchrist, Esq; 19 Victoria Park Rd, Singapore (☎ Singapore 4662354); Vosper Private Ltd, PO Box 95 Maxwell Rd, Singapore 9001

GILCHRIST, Graeme Elder; s of Sir Finlay Gilchrist, OBE (d 1987), of South Cottage, Hapstead Farm, Ardingly, Sussex, and Dorothy Joan, *née* Narizzano (d 1986); *b* 4 Dec 1934; *Educ* Sherborne, Queens' Coll Cambridge (MA); *m* 2 April 1981, Susan Elizabeth, da of Douglas William Fenwick, of Bluebell Cottage, The Croft, Lodsworth, W Sussex; 1 s (Thomas William Elder b 1982); *Career* Lt RA 1953-55, Col HAC 1971-73, hon Col RA 1973-75; mangr Baring Bros 1963-71, md and dep chm Union Discount Co of London 1971-; *Recreations* tennis, golf, music; *Clubs* Brooks's, Hurlingham; *Style*— Graeme Gilchrist, Esq; 50 Holmbush Road, Putney, London SW15 3LE (☎ 01 788 1667); 39 Cornhill, London EC3V 3NV (☎ 01 623 1020)

GILCHRIST, Raymond King; DL (Northumberland); s of Robert Gilchrist (d 1981), of 6 Howick Terrace, Tweedmouth, Berwick-upon-Tweed, and Mary, *née* Ray (d 1975); *b* 7 May 1922; *Educ* Berwick-upon-Tweed Co Schs; *m* 18 Sept 1950, Olive May, da of Charles Edward Dixon (d 1974); 1 s (David Robert b 1962), 1 da (Susan King b 1957); *Career* PT Instr RAF 1942, Sgt 1943, WO 1945; gen mangr Tweedside Co-op Soc 1968, div mangr N Northumberland NE Co-op Soc 1971 (sales mangr 1976-); memb Berwick Borough Cncl 1964- (mayor 1983-84), vice chm Northumberland CC 1984- (chm 1987-88) memb Northumberland: Health Authy, Family Practioners Tstees, Salmon Queen Ctee; pres Old Peoples Organisations, chm of First Schs; *Style*— Raymond Gilchrist, Esq; 17 Highcliffe, Spittal, Berwick-upon-Tweed, Northumberland (☎ 0280 206787)

GILCHRIST, Roderick Munn Renshaw; s of Ronald Renshaw Gilchrist (d 30 June 1971), and Vera Gilchrist, *née* Ashworth; *b* 6 Dec 1934; *Educ* MillHill Sch; *m* 19 March 1959, Patricia Frances, da of late Robert Charles Durrant; 2 s (Adam Munn Renshaw b 1959, Luke Ronald Renshaw b 1965); *Career* slr of Supreme Ct of England and Wales, a cmmr for Oaths, former princ of Bennett and Gilchrist Guildford, ptnr Renshaw Gilchrist Slrs Fleetwood and Garstang; FSA (Scot); *Recreations* hunting (beagle hounds), heraldry, celtic mythology; *Clubs* Old Millhillians; *Style*— Roderic Gilchrist, Esq; Sion Hill, Garstang PR3 1ZB (☎ (09952) 2389); 9 St Peters Place, Fleetwood FY7 6ED (☎ (03915) 3569)

GILES, Christopher Henry; s of Gp Capt Henry Giles (d 1986), and Yvonne Molly, *née* Wiseman; *b* 7 Oct 1943; *Educ* Harrow Tech Coll; *m* 12 Oct 1962, Ann Margaret, *née* Huinsby; 1 s (Henry b 1963), 1 da (Emma b 1966); *Career* licenced conveyance financier and property developer in private practise; memb Brighton Borough Cncl 1983; Liveryman of the City of London, memb Worshipful Co of Loiners; FIMBRA 1988; *Clubs* Reform, Hove; *Style*— Christopher Giles, Esq; 8 Wykeham Terrace, Brighton BN1 3FF (☎ 0273 29372); Giles House, Old Steyne, Brighton, BN1 1NH (☎ 0273 23618, fax 730587)

GILES, Frank Thomas Robertson; s of Col Frank Lucas Netlam Giles, DSO, OBE, of Barn Close, Finchampstead, Berks; *b* 31 July 1919; *Educ* Wellington, Barenose Coll Oxford; *m* 29 June 1946, Lady Katharine Pamela, *qv*; 1 s (Sebastian b 1952), 2 da (Sarah b 1950, Belinda b 1958); *Career* serv WWII as ADC to govr Bermuda, then WO Directorate of Mil Ops; with FO 1945-46 (priv sec to Ernest Bevin); Sunday Times: dep ed 1967-81, foreign ed 1966-77, ed 1981-83 (formerly with The Times 1946-60: asst correspondent Paris 1947, chief correspondent Rome 1950-53, Paris 1953-60); dir Times Newspapers 1981-85; memb exec ctee GB-USSR Assoc; govr: Wellington Coll, Sevenoaks Sch; chm Painshill Park Ist; memb Governing Body of Br Inst in Florence; author; *Books* A Prince of Journalists: the life and times of de Blowitz (1962), Sundry Times, (autobiography), 1986; *Style—* Frank Giles, Esq; Bunns Cottage, Lye Green, Crowborough, E Sussex N6 1UY (☎ 089 26 3701); 42 Blomfield Rd, W9 1AH (☎ 01 286 5706)

GILES, Lady Katharine Pamela; *née* Sackville; only da of 9 Earl De La Warr, GBE, PC (d 1976), and his 1 wife Diana, *née* Leigh (d 1966); *b* 4 Mar 1926; *m* 29 June 1946, Frank Thomas Robertson Giles, *qv*; 1 s, 2 da; *Career* JP (1966) Inner London; chm North Westminster P S D; *Style—* Lady Katharine Giles; 42 Blomfield Rd, London W9 (☎ 01 286 5706)

GILES, (Derryck) Peter Fitzgibbon; s of Arthur Frederick Giles CBE (d 1960), of 21 Princes Ct, Brompton Rd, Knightsbridge, London SW1, and Gladys Adelaide Giles, *née* Hird; *b* 17 Nov 1928; *Educ* Sherborne, Bristol Univ (LLB); *Career* barr Gray's Inn 1954, Stewarts and Lloyds Ltd 1955-62; Charity Cmmn 1962-69, 1974-84 (asst cmmnr 1967), legal Advsr Glaxo Hldgs 1970- 72, Soc of Authors 1973, Sec of Crosby Hall 1973; *Recreations* heraldry, genealogy, music, reading, pipe smoking; *Clubs* Savile, East India; *Style—* Peter Giles, Esq; 22 Petworth Rd, Haslemere, Surrey GU27 2HR (☎ 0428 4425)

GILES, Robert William; s of William George Giles (d 1968); *b* 30 Dec 1937; *Educ* Archbishop Tenisons GS, London Univ (BSc); *m* 1961, Doreen June; 3 children; *Career* md Bovis Civil Engrg Ltd 1981-; CEng, FICE, FCIOB; *Recreations* golf, running; *Style—* Robert Giles, Esq; The Rockery, 25 High St, West Lavington, Wilts SN10 4HQ (☎ 038 081 3256); Bovis Civil Engineering Ltd, Bridge House, Station Rd, Westbury, Wilts (☎ 0373 864444)

GILKES, Dr Jeremy John Heming; s of Lt Col Geoffrey Heming Gilkes, and Mary Stella, *née* Richardson; *b* 2 Dec 1939; *Educ* Charterhouse, St Bartholomew's Hosp Med Coll (MB BS), London Univ; *m* 8 July 1978, Robyn Vanessa, da of Maj Nigel Bardsley (d 1962); 2 s (Alexander, Charles), 3 step da (Emma, Sara, Katrina); *Career* conslt dermatologist: Univ Coll Hosp, Middx Hosp, Whittington Hosp, Eastman Dental Hosp, London Foot Hosp; memb RSM, MD, FRCP; *Clubs* The Hurlingham; *Style—* Dr Jeremy J H Gilkes; 115A Harley Street, London W1N 1DG

GILKISON, Sir Alan Fleming; CBE (1972); s of John Gilkison, of Invercargill, NZ, and Margaret, *née* Thomson; *b* 4 Nov 1909; *Educ* Southland Boys' HS, Timaru Boys' HS; *m* 1950, Noeline, da of A A Cramond; 2 s; *Career* kt 1980 for services to export, aviation and the community; *Style—* Sir Alan Gilkison, CBE

GILKISON, (Charles) Anthony; s of Capt Dugald Stewart Gilkison (ka 1914), and Janet Kate, *née* Harcourt-Vernon (d 1968); *b* 3 June 1913; *Educ* Dragon, Stowe, Prof Erlers Art Sch Munich; *m* 1, 1937; 2 da; m 2, 1972, Brita Margareta, da of Julius Andersson; *Career* serv WWII 1939-45; various jr jobs in film indust 1932-39; prodr int current affairs film series Spotlight (20th Century Fox) 1946; md Payant Pictures Ltd; chm: Anthony Gilkinson Assoc Ltd, Viscom Ltd, Viscom Prodn Ltd, A G Associates pty S Africa, Viscomarket Ltd; int conslt to govts and multi-nat cos on audiovisual communications; Cross of Freedom Finland 1940; *Recreations* gardening; *Style—* Anthony Gilkison, Esq; Huish Old Rectory, Merton, Okehampton, Devon EX20 3EH

GILKS, (Geoffrey) Paul; s of Geoffrey Lewis Gilks, of 110 Widney La, Solihull, W Mids, and Evelyn Marie, *née* Parkinson; *b* 12 May 1954; *Educ* Tudor Grange GS, Univ Coll London (LLB); *m* 1 June 1985, Josephine Verrier, da of Capt Basil Edward Holman Elwin (d 1976), of Kingsdown, Kent; *Career* DGIX EEC Cmmn Brussels 1977, asst slr Allen & Overy 1979-85 (articled clerk 1977-79, seconded as legal advsr to Int Airports Projects MOD and Aviation Saudi Arabia 1982-83), ptnr Berwin Leighton 1987-(asst slr 1985-87); memb Nat Ctee of the Trainee Slrs' Gp 1978-79, memb: Law Soc, Slrs Euro Gp; *Recreations* yachting, squash, raquets; *Style—* Paul Gilks, Esq; Adelaide House, London Bridge, London EC4R 9HA (☎ 01 623 3144, fax 01 623 4416)

GILL, Anthony Keith; s of Frederick William Gill (d 1955), of Colchester, Essex, and Ellen, *née* Davey; *b* 1 April 1930; *Educ* Colchester HS, Imperial Coll London (BSc); *m* 4 July 1953, Phyllis, da of Maurice Cook (d 1954), of Colchester; 1 s (Simon b 2 Oct 1964), 2 da (Joanna b 21 Feb 1958, Sally b 5 May 1960); *Career* REME (Nat Serv Offr) 1954-56; Lucas Bryce Ltd 1956-72 (md 1965-72), dir Lucas CAV Ltd 1967- (gen mngr 1974), divnl md and dir Lucas Industs plc 1978; gp md Lucas Indust plc 1980 (Group md 1984, Dep chm 1986); chm and chief exec Lucas Industs plc; 1987 chm: Lucas Aerospace Ltd, Lucas Automotive Ltd, Lucas Industl Systems Ltd, Lucas Industs Inc USA, Lucas France SA; pres IProdE 1986-87; memb ACOST; memb TRB; vice-pres EEF; Fell City of Birmingham Poly 1989; FIMechE, FIProdE, FCGI 1979, FEng 1983; *Recreations* sailing; *Style—* Anthony Gill, Esq; Mockley Close, Gentleman's Lane, Ullenhall, nr Henley-in-Arden, Warwicksshire (☎ 0564 442337); Lucas Industries plc, 44-46 Park Street, London W1Y 4DJ (☎ 01 493 6793, fax 01 491 0096)

GILL, Hon Mrs (Celia Mary); *née* Gore-Booth; da of Baron Gore-Booth, GCMG, KCVO (d 1984, Life Peer), and his w, Patricia Mary, da of late Montague Ellerton, of Yokohama, Japan; *b* 6 Jan 1946; *Educ* Downe House Sch, London Acad for Music and Dramatic Art, York Repertory Theatre 1967, Jacques Lecoq Sch Paris 1968-69; *m* 21 May 1983, Douglas George Gill; *Style—* Hon Mrs Gill; 29 The Vale, London SW3

GILL, Hon Mrs; (Charlotte Mary Magdalen); *née* Hunt; da of Baron Hunt of Tanworth, GCB, and his 1 wife Hon Magdalen Mary Robinson (d 1971), da of 1 Baron Robinson; *b* 1947; *m* 1976, Dr Herbert Gill; 1 da (Julia Magdalen b 1980); *Style—* Hon Mrs Gill; 22230 Drums Court, Woodland Hills, California 91364, USA

GILL, Christopher J F; RD (1971), MP (C) Ludlow 1987-; s of F A Gill, and D H Gill, *née* Southan; *b* 28 Oct 1936; *Educ* Shrewsbury Sch; *m* 2 July 1960, Patricia, da of late E V Greenway; 1 s (Charles b 1961), 2 da (Helen b 1963, Sarah b 1967); *Career* Lt-Cdr RNR (ret 1979); butcher and farmer; dir F A Gill Ltd 1968; *Recreations* walking, sailing, skiing; *Style—* Christopher Gill, Esq, RD, MP; c/o House of Commons, Westminster, London SW1A 0AA

GILL, Donald Phillott Chapple; yr s of Robert Carey Chapple Gill (d 1960), of Brynderwen, Bwlch-y-Cibau, Montgomeryshire, and Mildred, *née* Pretty; *b* 16 May 1918; *Educ* Shrewsbury; *m* 1, 3 April 1944, Anne Irvine (d 1961), widow of Maj Hon John Yarburgh Cunliffe-Lister (d on active serv 1943, eld s of 1 Earl of Swinton); yr da of Rev Canon Robert Sumner Medlicott, Rector of Burghclere, Newbury; 1 s (Sandy Timothy Chapple b 1955); m 2, 1965, Angela Faith, *née* Barker; *Career* Lt 17/21 Lancers 1941 Tunisia; *Recreations* shooting, fishing; *Style—* Donald Gill, Esq; Greenage, Llanfyllin, Powys (☎ 069 184 305)

GILL, Col (Geoffrey) Douglas; MBE (1950); s of Geoffrey Murton Gill (d 1949), and Hilda Violet Clavering, *née* Forhergill (d 1966); *b* 8 Oct 1916; *Educ* Lancing Coll; *m* 27 May 1958, Mabel Dorothy, da of Capt the Hon Sir Archibald Douglas Cochrane, GMCG, KCSI, DSO, RN (formerly Govr of Burma); 1 s (Peter b 1966); *Career* naval and mil attaché Br Embassy: Warsaw 1961-63, NATO intelligence ctee Washington DC 1964-66; def attaché Embassy Rome 1967-71, asst dir of operations Int Ctee of the Red Cross Geneva 1972-80; *Recreations* skiing; *Clubs* Army and Navy; *Style—* Col Douglas Gill; Tierce, 14 Verbier, Switzerland; Camino Son Toells 5, San Agustin, Palma de Mallorca, Spain

GILL, Frank Maxey; 5 s of Frederick Gordon Gill, DSO, and Mary Gill; *b* 25 Sept 1919; *Educ* Marlborough, De Havilland Aeronautical Tech Sch; *m* 1, 1942, late Sheila Rosemary Gordon; 3 da; m 2, 1952 Erica Margaret Fulcher; 1 s; *Career* dir Gill and Duffus Gp Ltd 1957-80; *Style—* Frank Gill, Esq; Tile House, Reigate Heath, Reigate, Surrey

GILL, Air Vice-Marshal Harry; CB (1979), OBE (1968); s of John William Gill, of Newark, Notts, and Lucy Gill; *b* 1922,Oct; *Educ* Barnby Rd Sch, Newark Tech Coll; *m* 1951, Diana, Patricia, da of Colin Wood, of Glossop; 1 da; *Career* Dir-Gen Supply RAF 1976-79; *Recreations* fishing, shooting, cycling; *Clubs* RAF; *Style—* Air Vice-Marshal Harry Gill, CB, OBE; Gretton Brook, S Collingham, Notts

GILL, Maj-Gen Ian Gordon; CB (1972), OBE (1959, MBE 1949), MC (1940) and bar (1945); s of Brig Gordon Harry Gill, CMG, DSO (d 1962), and Doris Gill; *b* 9 Nov 1919; *Educ* Repton; *m* 1963, Elizabeth Vivian, MD, MRCP, o da of A F Rohr, of London; *Career* cmmnd 4/7 Royal Dragoon Gds 1938, served BEF France 1939-40, NW Europe 1944-45 (despatches), Palestine 1946-48, Tripolitania 1950-51, cmdg 4/7 Royal Dragoon Gds 1957-59, Coll Cdr RMA Sandhurst 1961-62, Cdr 7 Armoured Bde 1964-66, dep mil sec (1) MOD 1966-68, head Br Def Liaison Staff Canberra 1968-70, Asst Chief Gen Staff Operational Requirements MOD 1970-72, ret 1972; Col 4/7 Royal Dragoon Gds 1973-78; Hon Liveryman Worshipful Co Coachmakers and Coach Harness Makers; *Recreations* equitation, skiing, squash, rackets, cricket; *Clubs* Cavalry & Guards, MCC; *Style—* Maj-Gen Ian Gill, CB, OBE, MC; Cheriton House, Thorney, Peterborough, PE6 0QD (☎ 0733 270246)

GILL, Jack; CB (1984); s of Jack and Elizabeth Gill; *b* 20 Feb 1930; *Educ* Bolton Sch; *m* 1954, Alma Dorothy; 3 da (Alison b 1957, Helena b 1959, Alexandra b 1961); *Career* govt serv; under-sec and princ fin offr Export Credits Guarantee Dept 1975-79; sec Monopolies and Mergers Cmmn 1979-81; dep sec and dir Industl Devpt Unit Dept of Indust 1981-83; chief exec Export Credits Guarantee Dept 1983-87; memb: BOTB 1981-87, British Aerospace plc 1987-; dir Govt Relations BICC plc, advsr Northern Eng Ind plc 1987-; *Recreations* music, chess problems; *Clubs* Overseas Bankers; *Style—* Jack Gill, Esq, CB; 9 Ridley Road, Warlingham, Surrey CR3 9LR (☎ 08832 2688)

GILL, John Nicol; s of William Gill, MBE (d 1959), of Llandaff, Cardiff, and Jane Nicol, *née* Adamson; *b* 10 April 1930; *Educ* Boston GS, Chesterfield GS, St Edmund Hall Oxford (MA); *m* 20 Aug 1958, Ann Therese Frances, da of Charles Clifford Turner (d 1970), of Chesterfield; 1 s (Richard b 1963), 2 da (Susan (Micklethwaite) b 1960, Stephanie b 1965); *Career* Nat Serv 1948-49, with Royal Corps of Signals; asst Slr Stanton and Walker (Slrs) Chesterfield in 1956 following articles with same firm, ptnr 1959, sr ptnr 1978; chm Chesterfield Round Table 1967-68; pres Chesterfield and N E Derbyshire Law Soc 1980-81; part-time chm Social Security Appeal Tbnls 1988-; memb: Law Soc 1956, cmmt for Oaths 1962; *Recreations* golf, hill-walking; *Clubs* Chesterfield Golf; *Style—* John Gill, Esq; The White House, 38 Summerfield Road, Chesterfield, Derbyshire, S40 2LJ (☎ 0246 232681): Stanton and Walker, Solicitors, 12 Soresby Street, Chesterfield S40 1JL (☎ 0246 236926, fax 0246 221321)

GILL, (James) Kenneth; s of late Alfred Charles Gill and Isabel Gill; *b* 27 Sept 1920; *Educ* Highgate; *m* 1948, Anne Bridgewater; 1 s; *Career* pres Saatchi & Saatchi Co plc 1985- (chm 1976-85); FIPA; *Style—* Kenneth Gill, Esq; c/o Saatchi & Saatchi Co plc, 80 Charlotte St, W1 (☎ 01 636 5060)

GILL, Air Vice-Marshal Leonard William George; DSO (1944); s of Leonard William Gill (d 1963), Marguerite, *nér Dutton (d 1955)*; *b* 31 Mar 1918; *Educ* UC Sch London; *m* 1, 1943 (m dis), Joan Favill; 2 s (David b 1946, James b 1958), 2 da (Rosemary b 1945, Frances b 1947); m 2, 1982, Constance Mary Cull, da of late James Henry Button; *Career* RAF, Far East 1937-42, then UK, cmd 68 Sqdn 1945 (despatches 1941), cmd 85 and 87 Sqdn, directing Staff RAF Staff Coll, Stn Cdr Linton on Ouse 1957-60; dir Overseas Ops 1960-62; Nat Def Coll of Canada 1962-63; Dir of Organization (Estabs) 1963-66; SASO RAF Germany 1966-68; dir Gen Manning RAF MoD 1968-73 ret; planning advsr P+O Steam Navigation Co 1973-79; vice pres RAF Assoc 1973-79, Merton Assocs (Conslts) Ltd, chm 1985-; FIPM, FBIM; *Recreations* shooting, cricket, boats, amateur woodwork; *Clubs* RAF; *Style—* Air Vice-Marshal Leonard Gill, DSO; 3 Wickham Court, 7 Ashburn Gardens, Kensington, London SW7 4DG (☎ 01 370 2716); Merton Associates (Conslts) Ltd, Merton House, 70 Grafton Way, London W1P 4LE (☎ 01 388 2051)

GILL, Malcolm Alexander; TD (1972); s of Alexander Gill (d 1972), ARIBA, FRIAS, of Cults, Aberdeenshire, and Galdys Muriel, *née* Bullock; *b* 22 Mar 1940; *Educ* St Edward's Sch Oxford, Univ of Aberdeen (MA); *m* 13 July 1968, Jane Quincey, da of Col William Quincey Roberts, CVO, CBE, DSO, TD (d 1981), of Newton St Loe, Bath, Avon; 2 da (Suzanna b 3 April 1970, Philippa b 18 Feb 1971); *Career* md Thomson Pubns SA (PTY) Ltd 1974-88, md Standbrook Pubns Ltd 1978-83; md Int Thomson Publishing Ltd 1984-; pres Int Fedn of the Periodical Press 1987-89; Liveryman Worshipful Co of Stationers and Newspaper Makers 1981; *Recreations* skiing, travel; *Clubs* Travellers, Naval and Military, City Livery; *Style—* Malcolm Gill, Esq, TD; Pleasant Cottage, Woodend Green, Henham, nr Bishops Stortford, Herts CM22 6AZ (☎ 0279 850 792); First Floor, The Quadrangle, 180 Wardour St, London W1A 4YG (☎ 01 437 9787)

GILL, Peter; OBE (1980); s of George John Gill (d 1986), and Margaret Mary, *née* Browne (d 1966), union representative Spillers Flower Mill General Strike 1926; *b* 7

Sept 1939; *Educ* St Illtyd's Coll Cardiff; *Career* dir, dramatic author and former actor; actor 1957-65; directed his first prodn A Collier's Friday Night at the Royal Ct 1965; plays directed since then include: The Ruffian on the Stair 1966, A Provincial Life 1966, Crimes of Passion 1967, Much Ado About Nothing 1969, The Fool 1975, Small Change 1976; dir Riverside Studios 1976- where his prodns include: The Cherry Orchard (own version), The Changeling 1978, Julius Caesar 1980; apptd assoc dir Nat Theatre 1980 where his prodns include: Month in the Country 1981, Don Juan 1981, Major Barbara 1982, Tales from Hollywood 1983, Venice Preserv'd 1984, Fool for Love 1984; wrote and produced: The Sleepers Den 1966 and 69, Over Garden's Out 1969, Kick For Touch 1983, Mean Tears, Murderers, In the Blue 1985; dir Nat Theatre Studio 1984-where his prodns include: As I Lay Dying 1985, The Garden of England 1984; his prodn of The Daughter-in-Law won first prize at the Belgrade Int Theatre Festival 1968; assoc artistic dir Royal Ct Theatre 1970-72, A Provincial Life (1966 Royal Ct); *Style*— Peter Gill, Esq, OBE; National Theatre, South Bank, London SE1 (☎ 01 928 2033, telex 297306 NATTRE G)

GILL, Robin Denys; s of Thomas Henry Gill (d 1931), of Hastings, NZ, and Marjorie Mary, *née* Butler; *b* 7 Oct 1927; *Educ* Dulwich, Brasenose Coll Oxford (MA); *m* 5 Oct 1951, Mary Hope (d 1986), da of John Henry Alexander (d 1953), of Harrogate, Yorks; 3 s (Stephen b 23 July 1953, Richard b 9 Sept 1955, Jonathan b 25 March 1957); *Career* sales mangr: Van der Berghs (Unilever Ltd) 1949-54, UK Newsprint Br Int Paper Ltd 1954-59; founded Border TV Ltd (md 1960-64), md and Assoc TV Ltd 1964-69; chm: ITN Ltd 1968-69, Tst Ltd 1970-, Avsvar Insur Co Ltd 1975-; dir: Reed Roger Gp Ltd 1970-75, Hewlett Packard 1975-, Baring Hambreckt Alpine Ltd 1986-, SO Scicon plc 1988-; bd memb in local church, chm Standard Ind Tst 1970-81, former Bd memb Claremount Far Ct Sch; memb: Nat Advsy Bd for Higher Educn, Manpower Education GP, Vix Ctee of RCA, Oxofrd Univ Appts Ctee, Oxford Univ Devpt Ctee, NW Regnl Cncl for Higher Educn; bd memb IESTE (UK); *Recreations* golf, opera, travel, art collecting; *Clubs* Vincents (Oxford); *Style*— Robin Gill, Esq; 1970 Trust Ltd, 52 Queen St, London, W1M 9LA (☎ 04865 5290)

GILL, Hon Mrs (Rosemary Eva Gorell); *née* Barnes; o da of 3 Baron Gorell, CBE, MC (d 1963); *b* 9 July 1925; *Educ* Priors Field, Masters Sch Dobbs Ferry New York, NFF Roehampton, Bedford Coll London; *m* 16 July 1961, Peter Douglas Gill, s of Charles Douglas Gill, CBE; 1 s, 2 da; *Career* teacher; chm: Yorks Regnl European Movement 1970-74, Fawcett Soc 1976-80; memb: Ripon Diocesan Synod 1979-, General Synod of C of E 1981-; serving sister OStJ; *Recreations* reading, gardening, observing; *Style*— Hon Mrs Gill; c/o The Midland Bank plc, 34 Westgate, Ripon, N Yorks HG4 2BL

GILL, His Hon Judge Stanley Sanderson; s of Sanderson Henry Briggs Gill, OBE (d 1966), of Snow Hill Grange, Wakefield and Dorothy Margaret, *née* Bennett (d 1977); *b* 3 Dec 1923; *Educ* Queen Elizabeth's Sch Wakefield, Magdalene Coll Cambridge (MA); *m* 1954, Margaret Mary Patricia, da of James Grady (d 1976), of Coventry; 1 s, 2 da; *Career* Flt Lt Bomber Cmmd Europe 1941-46; barr 1950-71; memb York Rent Assessment Ctee 1966-71; dep chm West Riding Quarter Sessions 1968-72; county court judge 1971, circuit judge 1972-, memb County Court Rule Ctee 1980-84; *Recreations* reading, (mainly history), cooking, walking; *Style*— His Hon Judge Gill; Arden Lodge, Thirkleby, Thirsk, N Yorks YO7 2AS

GILLAM, Gp Capt Denys Edgar; DSO and 2 bars (1940), DFC and bar (1940), AFC (1938), DL (W Riding Yorks 1959); s of Maj Thomas Henry Gillam (d 1946), and Doris, *née* Homfray (d 1988); *b* 18 Nov 1915; *Educ* Wrekin Coll, RAF Staff Coll; *m* 1, 1946, (Nancye) Joan (d 1986), da of late Godfrey Short, of S Africa; 1 s (Christopher James b 17 April 1952), 2 da (Marilyn b 3 May 1947, Penelope b 31 May 1948); m 2, 1987, Mrs Irene Scott; *Career* RAF 1935, Gp Capt 1944, ret 1946; md Br Furtex Ltd, chm Homfray & Co Ltd 1971, ret 1981; *Recreations* sailing, shooting, fishing; *Clubs* Royal Ocean Racing; *Style*— Gp Capt Denys Gillam, DSO, DFC, AFC, DL; The Glebe, Brawby, Malton, N Yorks (☎ 0751 31530)

GILLAM, Patrick John; s of Cyril Bryant Gillam (d 1978), and Mary Josephine Gillam; *b* 15 April 1933; *Educ* LSE (BA); *m* 1963, Diana Echlin; 1 s (Luke b 1973), 1 da (Jane b 1970); *Career* FO 1956-57; BP Co 1957-, vice-pres BP N America Inc 1971-74, gen mangr Supply Dept 1974-78, dir BP Int Ltd (formerly BP Trading Ltd) 1978-; chm: BP Shipping Ltd 1981-, BP Minerals Int Ltd 1982-, BP Coal Ltd 1986; md BP Co plc 1981-; *Recreations* gardening; *Style*— Patrick Gillam, Esq; c/o BP International Ltd, Britannic House, Moor Lane, EC2Y 9BU (☎ 01 920 6615, telex London 888811)

GILLARD, Isabelle; da of Prof Robert Gillard, of Univ of Wales, Cardiff, and Diana, *née* Laslett; *b* 17 Dec 1959; *Educ* Howell's Sch LLandaff, Univ of Birmingham (LLB), London Hosp; *Career* called to the Bar Middle Temple 1980, practising SE circuit; *Recreations* movies; *Style*— Miss Isabelle Gillard; 1 Crown Off Row, Temple, London EC4 (☎ 01 583 3724)

GILLES, Prof Dennis Cyril; s of Cyril George Gilles (d 1970), of Sidcup, Kent, and Gladys Alice Annesley, *née* Bachelor (d 1971); *b* 7 April 1925; *Educ* Chislehurst and Sidcup GS, Imperial Coll London Univ (BSc PhD); *m* 10 Dec 1055, Valerie Mary, da of Gerald Gardiner (d 1988), of Abbey Wood, Kent; 2 s (Christopher b 1957, Andrew b 1962), 2 da (Susan b 1960, Julia b 1969); *Career* asst lectr:mathematics dept Imperial Coll 1945-47, oceanography dept Univ of Liverpool 1947-49; mathematician Sci Computing Serv Ltd 1949-55, res fell computing machine laboratory Univ of Manchester 1955-57, prof computing sci Univ of Glagow 1966- (dir computing laboratory 1957-65); FRSE, FIMA, FBCA, FRSA; *Style*— Prof Dennis Gilles; 21 Bruce Rd, Glasgow G41 5EE (☎ 041 429 7733); University of Glasgow G12 8QQ (☎ 041 330 5391)

GILLESPIE, Prof Iain Erskine; s of John Gillespie (d 1974), of Glasgow, and Flora, *née* MacQuarie (d 1978); *b* 4 Sept 1931; *Educ* Hillhead HS, Univ of Glasgow (MB, ChB, MD), Univ of Manchester (MSc); *m* 5 Sept 1957, (Mary) Muriel, *née* McIntyre; 1 s (Gordon McIntosh b 1963), 1 da (Rhona Kirstine b 1960); *Career* Nat Serv Cmmnd Lt RAMC 1954, Regtl Med Offr, Capt till 1956; prof of surgery Manchester Univ 1970 (dean faculty of med 1983-86), hon conslt Manchester Royal Infirmary 1970; memb med sub-ctee UGC 1975-86, off bearer Br Soc of Gastroenterology, surgical Res Soc of GB and Ireland, Assoc of Surgeons of GB and Ireland, Assoc of Profs of Surgery, memb sub-ctee Hong Kong Univs and Poly's Grants Ctee 1985-, ed bds of several surgical and gastroenterological jls; memb NW RHA 1982-86, govr Stockport GS (formerly fndn chm parents assoc), pres Manchester branch Royal Scottish Dance Soc; FRCSE 1959, FRCS 1963, FRCSG 1970; *Books* Gastroenterology - An Integrated Course (ed with T J Thomson 3 edn 1983), Current Opinion in Gastroenterology - Stomach Duodenum (with TV Taylor, 1986, 1987, 1988); *Recreations* golf, gardening, music; *Clubs* New GC (St Andrews); *Style*— Prof Iain Gillespie; 27 Athol Rd, Bramhall, Cheshire SK7 1BR (☎ 061 439 2811); Univ Dept of Surgery, Manchester Royal Infirmary, Oxford Rd, Manchester M13 9WL (☎ 061 276 4033)

GILLESPIE, Capt (Thomas) Patrick; CBE (1966, MBE 1943), RN; s of David Bryce Gillespie (ka 1916), and Louise Gwendoline, *née* Mutlow-Williams (d 1962); *b* 5 Nov 1914; *Educ* Bedford Sch; *m* 17 Feb 1940, (Helen) Diana, da of the late Thomas Bayntun Ching, of Auckland, NZ; 2 s (Patrick Michael b 1944, Anthony Bayntun b 1949); *Career* RN 1931-67, (despatches 1941); regl dir SE Region Mission to Seaman 1967-70, sec Nuffield Tst for the Forces of the Crown 1970-88; ADC to HM The Queen 1964; Freeman City of London 1970, Liveryman Worshipful Co of Shipwrights 1970; *Style*— Capt Patrick Gillespie, CBE, RN

GILLETT, (John) Anthony Cecil Walkey; s of Eric Walkey Gillett, FRSL, Hon RCM (d 1978), and Joan, *née* Edwards (d 1956); *b* 17 Mar 1927; *Educ* Malvern, Brasenose Coll Oxford (MA); *m* 18 Oct 1952, Jacqueline Eve, da of Philippe Leslie Caro Carrier, CBE, MB, MRCP (d 1975), of Ashdown House, St Anne's House, St Anne's Hill, Lewes, Sussex; 2 s (Charles b 1954, Jon b 1958), 1 da (Amanda b 1961); *Career* served as Lt RM 1945-47 barr Inner Temple 1955; colonial serv district offr Somaliland Protectorate 1950-58, magistrate Aden (sometime acting chief Justice, Puisne Judge and chief Magistrate) 1958-63, crown cnsl, asst attorney gen of Aden and dep advocate gen Fedn of S Arabia 1963-68, temp legal asst Cncl on Tribunals (UK) 1968-70, legislative draftsman States of Guernsey 1970-83, Stipendiary Magistrate of Guernsey; auth of State of Aden Law Reports (1959-60); played polo for Somaliland Protectorate and Aden; hon sec Oxford Univ Tennis Club (Royal Tennis); *Recreations* lawn tennis, reading; *Clubs* Royal Channel Islands YC, MCC, Vincents (Oxford); *Style*— Anthony Gillett, Esq; Bellieuse Farm, St Martin's, Guernsey, CI (☎ 0481 36986; The Magistrate's Chambers, Royal Court Hse, Guernsey, CI (☎ 0481 25277)

GILLETT, Charlie; s of Anthony Walter Gillett, and Mary Diana, *née* Maltby; *b* 20 Feb 1942; *Educ* Grangefield GS Stockton-on-Tees, Cambridge Univ (BA), Columbia Univ NY (MA); *m* 19 Dec 1964, Elizabeth (Buffy), da of Kenneth Chessum; 1 s (Ivan b 28 July 1970), 2 da (Suzy b 18 May 1966, Jody b 5 Sept 1968); *Career* lectr Kingsway Coll 1966-71, researcher BBC TV 1971, presenter BBC Radio London 1972-78; co-dir Oval Records & Music 1972-, presenter Capital Radio 1980-, presenter The Late Shift Channel 4 TV 1988; *Books* The Sound of the City (1970, 1983), Making Tracks (1974, 1985); *Recreations* athletics, soccer, African holidays, cinema; *Style*— Charlie Gillett, Esq; 11 Liston Rd, London SW4 (☎ 01 622 0111); Oval Records & Music, 326 Brixton Rd, London SW9 7AA (☎ 01 326 4907)

GILLETT, Christopher John; yr s of Sir Robin Gillett, 2 Bt, GBE, RD, *qv*; *b* 16 May 1958; *Educ* Durlston Court Sch, Pangbourne Coll, King's Coll Cambridge (choral scholar, MA), RCM, Nat Opera Studio; *m* 7 Jan 1984, Julia A, yr da of late W H Holmes, of Tunbridge Wells; 1 da (Tessa Holmes b 1987); *Career* opera singer: New Sadlers Wells, Glyndebourne, Kent Opera, Covent Garden; Liveryman Worshipful Co of Musicians 1981; *Style*— Christopher Gillett, Esq; 41 Stanhope Gardens, Highgate, London N6

GILLETT, Nicholas Danvers Penrose; er s and h of Sir Robin Gillett, 2 Bt, GBE, RD; *b* 24 Sept 1955; *Educ* Durlston Court Sch, Pangbourne Coll, Imperial Coll London (BSc); *m* 3 Jan 1987 Haylie Brooks, eld da of Dennis Brooks of Swansea, Glamorgan; *Career* trials engr Br Aerospace 1977-84; Product Assur mangr Br Aeorspace 1984-; Liveryman Worshipful Co of Coachmakers 1982; ARCS, FBIS; *Recreations* photography, sub-aqua, computing, reading, skiing, DIY; *Style*— Nicholas Gillett, Esq; Yew Tree Cottage, The Batch, Butcombe, Bristol BS18 6UX

GILLETT, Maj-Gen Sir Peter Bernard; KCVO (1979, CVO 1973), CB (1966), OBE (1955); s of Bernard George Gillett, OBE, of Cross Bush, Milford on Sea, Hants; *b* 8 Dec 1913; *Educ* Marlborough, RMA Woolwich; *m* 1952, Pamela Graham, da of Col Spencer Graham Walker, of Winsley, Wilts, and widow of Col R J Lloyd Price; 3 step s; *Career* cmmnd RA 1934, appointed to RHA 1945; serv WWII: India, Burma, WO, BAOR; Mil Asst GOC E Africa 1953-55, CO 5 RHA 1955-58, Col Gen Staff SHAPE 1958-59, Cdr RA 3 Div 1959-61, IDC 1962, Maj-Gen 1962, COS HQ Eastern Cmd 1962-65, GOC 48 Div (TA) W Midland Dist 1965-68, ret; Col Cmdt RA 1968-78, sec Central Chancery of the Orders of Knighthood 1968-79, govr Military Knights of Windsor 1980-; *Recreations* shooting, sailing, gardening, travel; *Clubs* Army and Navy, Royal Ocean Racing, MCC; *Style*— Maj-Gen Sir Peter Gillett, KCVO, CB, OBE; Mary Tudor Tower, Windsor Castle, Windsor, Berks SL4 1NJ (☎ 075 53 868286, ext 416)

GILLETT, Sir Robin Danvers Penrose; 2 Bt (UK 1959), of Bassishaw Ward, City of London, GBE (1976), RD (1965); s of Sir Sydney Harold Gillett, 1 Bt, MC, FCA (d 1976; lord mayor London 1958-59), and Audrey Isabel Penrose (d 1962), da of late Capt Edgar Penrose Mark-Wardlaw; *b* 9 Nov 1925, (lord mayor's day); *Educ* Hill Crest Sch, Pangbourne NC; *m* 22 Sept 1950, Elizabeth Marion Grace, er da of late John Findlay, JP, of Busby House, Lanarks; 2 s (Nicholas, Christopher, *qqv*); *Heir* s, Nicholas D P Gillett; *Career* Canadian Pacific Steamships Ltd 1945-60 (cadet 1943-45), master mariner 1951, staff cdr 1957; dir: Wigham Poland Home Ltd, Wigham Poland Mgmnt Services Ltd 1965-86, St Katherine Haven Ltd; conslt Sedgwich Insurance Brokers 1987-; underwriting memb Lloyd's; common councilman for Ward of Bassishaw 1965-69 (alderman 1969-), sheriff City of London 1973-74 (HM Lieutenant 1975, lord mayor 1976-77); RLSS: UK pres 1979-82, dep Cwlth pres 1982-; vice-chm PLA 1979-84, er brother Trinity House 1978- (yr brother 1973-78), fellow and fndr memb Nautical Inst, tstee Nat Maritime Museum, pres Inst of Admin Mgmnt 1980-84; vice-pres: City of London Red Cross, City of London Outward Bound Assoc; memb Hon Co of Master Mariners 1962- (warden 1971-85, master 1979-80); Hon DSc City of London Univ 1976 (chllr 1976-77); Offr Order of Leopard (Zaire) 1974, Cdr Order of Dannebrog 1974, Order of Johan Sedia Mahkota (Malaysia) 1974, Grand Cross Municipal OM (Lima) 1977, Gold Medal Admin Mgmnt Soc (USA) 1983; FInstD; KStJ 1976; Gentleman Usher of the Purple Rod 1985; *Recreations* photography, sailing (yacht 'Lady Libby'); *Clubs* City Livery, Guildhall, City Livery Yacht (Admiral), Royal Yacht Sqdn, Royal London Yacht (Cdre 1984-85), St Katherine Yacht (Cdre); *Style*— Robin Gillett, Bt, GBE, RD, RNR; Elm Cottage, Biddestone, Wilts; 4 Fairholt St, London SW7 1EQ (☎ 01 589 9860)

GILLHAM, Dr Anthony John; s of Leslie James Gillham; *b* 17 May 1939; *Educ* Whitgift Sch, Imperial Coll London, St Catharine's Coll Cambridge (PhD); *m* 1969, Shiela Marion, *née* Adnitt; 2 s (Charles, Richard); *Career* cmmnd Cheshire Yeomanry 1968; chemical engr, md Chemoxy Int plc 1984-; CEng; *Recreations* fishing; *Clubs*

IOD; *Style—* Dr Anthony Gillham; The Grange, Chop Gate, Middlesbrough, Cleveland (☎ 043 96 351); Chemoxy Int Ltd, All Saints Refinery, Cargo Fleet Rd, Middlesborough, Cleveland TS3 6AF (☎ 0642 248557/9, telex 587185 Cemint Mbro)

GILLHAM, Paul Maurice; s of Gerald Albert Gillham, and Doris, *née* Kinsey; *b* 26 Nov 1931; *Educ* RCM, GSM (LGSM), Christ's Coll Cambridge (BA, MA); *m* 3 Sept 1960, Jane Marion, da of Sir George Pickering (d 1982); 2 s (Adam b 27 Dec 1965, Dan b 13 Apr 1968), 1 da (Carola b 7 July 1963); *Career* chm: Keith Prowse Gp 1970-80, St Giles Properties Ltd 1980-, Patent Devpts Int Ltd 1980-, Acton Barn Ltd 1983-, CP Roberts and Co Ltd 1985-; chm LPO cncl 1983-87; *Recreations* playing cello and piano, walking; *Style—* Paul Gillham, Esq; Edmonds Farmhouse, Gomshall, Guildford, Surrey GU5 9LQ (☎ 048641 2299); CP Roberts & Co Ltd, Roberts House, Station Close, Potters Bar, Herts EN6 3JW (☎ 0707 51277, fax 0707 44942)

GILLIAM, Lady Zara Lison Josephine; *née* Jellicoe; da of 2 Earl Jellicoe, DSO, MC, PC; *b* 24 Sept 1948; *m* 9 May 1983, Bruce Gilliam, s of Alvin Bruce Gilliam, of Houston, Texas, and of Mrs Robert Wright, of Carmel, Calif; *Style—* Lady Zara Gilliam; 214 Villa Garden Drive, Mill Valley, California 94941, USA

GILLIAT, John Martyn; s of George Nicholas Earle Gilliat (d 1968), and Marjorie Florence, *née* Stott (d 1968); *b* 4 Dec 1923; *Educ* William Hulme's GS Manchester, Brasenose Coll Oxford, Manchester Univ (BA); *m* 25 July 1953, Mary Patricia, da of John Wadsley Rollitt (d 1954); 1 s (Simon Timothy Francis b 1958), 1 da (Joanna Mary Frances b 1961); *Career* served RCS (Capt) India 1944-47; CA, ptnr Dearden Gilliat & Co (and successor firms) 1958-84; sole practitioner John M Gilliat 1984-; memb: Ct of Univ of Manchester 1987, VAT Tbnl Panel Manchester 1987; bursar Wilmslow Prep Sch 1984-, pres Manchester Soc CA's 1972-73; FCA, FICA (memb cncl 1975-); *Clubs* Royal Overseas League; *Style—* John Gilliat, Esq; Sycamore Cottage, Bonis Hall Lane, Butley, Macclesfield, Cheshire SK10 4LP; Bracondale House, 141 Buxton Rd, Heaviley, Stockport SK2 6EQ

GILLIAT, Lt-Col Sir Martin John; GCVO (1981, KCVO 1962, CVO 1954), MBE (1946); s of Lt-Col John Babington Gilliat, DSO (d 1949), and Muriel Helen Lycette Gilliat; *b* 8 Feb 1913; *Educ* Eton, RMC; *Career* 2 Lt KRRC 1933, serv BEF WWII (despatches, POW), Temp Lt-Col 1953, Dep Mil Sec to Viceroy and Govr-Gen of India 1947-48, comptroller to UK Cmmr-Gen SE Asia 1948-51, mil sec to Govr-Gen of Australia 1953-55, private sec and equerry to HM Queen Elizabeth the Queen Mother 1956-, memb Nat Hunt Ctee 1964, vice-lt for Herts 1971- (DL 1963); hon bencher Middle Temple 1977, Hon LLD London 1977; KStJ 1983; *Style—* Lt-Col Sir Martin Gilliat, GCVO, MBE; Appletrees, Welwyn, Herts (☎ 043 871 4675); 31A St James's Palace, London SW1 (☎ 01 930 1440)

GILLIBRAND, Alec Lindow; OBE (1975); s of Harold Lindow Gillibrand (d 1953), of Accrington, Lancs, and May, *née* Ramsbottom (d 1983); *b* 30 Mar 1932; *Educ* Queen Mary's Royal GS Clitheroe; *m* 29 June 1957, Jennifer Bridget, da of Maj Jasper Cyril Holmes, MC (d 1976), of Tavistock, Devon; 1 s (Guy Nigel b 1962), 1 da (Susan Jane (Mrs Massie) b 1960); *Career* Nat Serv 1960-62; banker, served over 32 yrs overseas with British Bank of the Middle East and Hongkong and Shanghai Banking Corpn in Bahrain, Doha, Aden, Jordan, Kuwait, Abu Dhabi, Beirut, Iran, Saudi Arabia, Hong Kong and India; ret as chief exec offr India; dir British and South Asian Trade Assoc; memb exec ctee British Cwlth Ex-Services League; ACIB 1975; *Recreations* walking, sport, reading, Arab affairs; *Clubs* Oriental, Bombay Gymkhana, Bombay Willingdon; *Style—* Alec Gillibrand, Esq, OBE; 181A Ashley Gardens, Emery Hill St, London SW1P 1PD (☎ 01 834 5626); British and South Asian Trade Association (BASATA), Centre Point, 103 New Oxford St, London WC1A 1DU (☎ 01 379 7400, fax 01 240 1578, telex 21332)

GILLIE, Dr Oliver John; s of John Calder gillie, of Tynemouth, Northumberland, and Ann, *née* Philipson; *b* 31 Oct 1937; *Educ* Bootham Sch York, Edinburgh Univ (BSc, PhD), Stanford Univ; *m* 3 Dec 1969 (m dis 1987), Louise, da of Col Phillip Panton; 2 da (Lucinda Kathrine b 1970, Juliet Ann b 1972); *Career* lectr in genetics Edinburgh Univ 1961-65, Nat Inst for Med Res Mill Hill 1965-68, IPC Magazines 1968-70, Haymarket Publishing 1970-72, med corr The Sunday Times, med ed The Independent 1986-; *Books* The Sunday Times Book of Body Medicine (jtly 1978), The Sunday Times guide to the World's Best Food (jtly 1981), The Sunday Times Self-Help Directory (jtly 1982), The ABC Diet and Bodyplan (jtly 1984); *Recreations* sailing, wind-surfing; *Clubs* RSM; *Style—* Dr Oliver Gillie; The Independent, 40 City Rod, London EC1Y 2DB (☎ 01 253 1222)

GILLIES, (Maurice) Gordon; TD (1946), bar (1952); s of James Brown Gillies (ka 1916, Advocate in Aberdeen), and Rhoda Ledingham (d 1952); *b* 17 Oct 1916; *Educ* Aberdeen GS, Merchiston Castle, Edinburgh Univ (MA, LLB); *m* 1954, Anne Bethea, da of Bryce McCall-Smith, OBE (d 1977), of Pencaitland, E Lothian; *Career* served RA 1939-46, Maj, France 1940, Europe 1944-46; advocate 1946, advocate dep 1953-58; sheriff of Lanarkshire at Lanark 1958-82; sheriff princ of South Strathclyde, Dumfries and Galloway 1982-; *Recreations* golf, gardening; *Clubs* New (Edinburgh) Hon Co of Edinburgh Golfers; *Style—* Sheriff Principal Gordon Gillies, QC, TD; Redwalls, Biggar, Lanarkshire ML12 6HA (☎ Biggar 20281)

GILLIES, John Sydney Henry; s of Sydney Alfred Gillies, (d 1969), of London, and Lena Florence, *née* Dersley-Macer (d 1978); *b* 13 Oct 1921; *Educ* St Ignatius London; *m* 22 July 1950, Margaret Catherine, da of Hon Michael Whelton-(d 1957) of Cork, Ireland; 2 s (John b 1951, Peter b 1955), 1 da (Anne b 1960); *Career* WWII RAF-1946; MAFF 1947-54, official receivers BOT (later DTI) 1954-71, insolvency practitioner 1971-88; pres Insolvency Practitioners' Assoc 1987 (cncl memb 1978); pres Anti Modern Packaging Soc; Freeman City of London 1978, Worshipful Co of Chartered Secs and Administrators; FSCA, ACIS, FIPA; *Books* Insolvency Law and Practice (1988); *Recreations* sailing; *Clubs* City Livery; *Style—* John Gillies, Esq; 47 Hatton Garden, London EC1M 8EX (☎ 01 404 3059, fax 01 405 6244); Whitegates, Lodwick, Shoeburyness, Essex

GILLIGAN, Timothy (Tim) Joseph; DL; s of Timothy Gilligan (d 1928) of Rosscommon Eire and Mary *née* Greevy (d 1924); *b* 18 April 1918; *Educ* Handsworth Tech Coll Birmingham; *m* 2 Nov 1944, Hazel (Bunty), da of William Ariel Farmer, (k/a 1918); 2 s (Simon b Oct 1945, Peter b 17 Jan 1952), 2 da (Anita b 29 Jan 1949 (d 1952), Rosemary b 7 Apr 1957); *Career* WWII, Maj RASC serv BEF France, ME and N Africa, Germany (despatches 1944 and 1945) 1939-46; exec offr (1 sec grade) FO (German section) 1946-53; sales and mgmnt Dictaphone Co Ltd and WH Smith & Sons 1953-63; chm Pitney Bowes plc 1983- (joined 1963, chief exec 1967); chm: The Tree Cncl 1983-85, fndr Conservation Fndn 1982-86, Herts Groundwork Tst 1984-; memb Hertsmere BC 1983, CBIM 1983, FRSA 1927; *Recreations* the countryside and environment; *Style—* TJ Gilligan, Esq, DL; The White Cottage, Mimms Lane, Shenley Radlett, Herts WD7 9AP (☎ 0923 857 402); Pitney Bone plc, The Plinnacles, Harlow, Essex CM19 5BD (☎ 0279 26731, fax 0279 34861, telex 81244)

GILLILAND, Elsie; da of James Lauder McCuly (d 1985), of Belfast, and Mary Agnes, *née* Calvert; *b* 6 Dec 1937; *Educ* Richmond Lodge, Queen's Univ Belfast (LLB); *m* 22 July 1961, James Andrew David Gilliland (d 1984), of Exmouth, Devon; 2 s (Jeremy b 1964, Jonathan b 1967); *Career* slr in private practice, memb Manchester Family Practitioner Ctee; *Recreations* skiing, opera, painting; *Style—* Mrs Elsie Gilliland; The Shieling, Highfield, Prestbury, Cheshire (☎ 0625 828029); 13 Somerford Way, Nelson's Reach, London SE16 (☎ 01 232 0144); Towns Needham & Co, John Dalton House, 121 Deansgate, Manchester M3 2AR

GILLING, Lancelot Cyril Gilbert; OBE (1985); s of Gilbert Joseph Gilling (d 1949), of Somerset, and Esther Marianne Clapp (d 1969); *b* 7 Mar 1920; *Educ* Shebbear Coll Beaworthy Devon, Reading Univ (BSc); *m* 1951, Brenda, da of Jack Copp (d 1974); 2 da (Jennifer b 1952, Hilary b 1955); *Career* Capt Royal Northumberland Fus 2nd Batt UK N Africa, Palestine, Greece 1940-46, warden and lectr Dorset Coll of Agric 1949-51; head dept of agric Writtle Coll Chelmsford Essex; princ Askham Bryan Coll of Agric and Horticulture York 1957-84; pres: Agric Educn Assoc (hon memb 1987) 1981-82, Assoc of Agric Educn Staffs 1979-80, Yorks Agric Soc 1981-82; vice pres Yorks Philosophical Soc; chm exec ctee Yorks Agric Soc; memb Min of Agric Northern Regnl Panel of Advrs; lectr Int Centre for Agric Educn Berne, Switzerland 1968-76; conslt UNESCO and Br Cncl 1975, 1976 and 1982, memb Royal Cmmn on Environmental Pollution 1985-; FIBiol, FRAgS, CBiol; *Recreations* tennis, badminton, music (choral); *Style—* Lancelot Gilling, OBE; The Spinney, Brandsby, York YO6 4RG

GILLINGHAM, Prof (Francis) John; CBE (1981), MBE (1945); s of Herbert John Gillingham Elwell Lea (d 1958), and Lily Gillingham (d 1962); *b* 15 Mar 1916; *Educ* Hardye's Sch Dorset, Univ of London (MB BS); *m* 30 Aug 1945, Irene Judy, da of F W Jude (d 1947), of Norfolk; 4 s (Jeremy, Timothy, Simon, Adam); *Career* surgn Mil Hosp (for head injuries) Oxford 1941-42, Maj RAMC (No 4 Mobile Neurosurgical Unit) 1942-45; conslt surgical neurologist Royal Infirmary & Western Gen Hosp Edinburgh 1950-80, prof (now emeritus) surgical neurology Univ of Edinburgh 1963-80, hon conslt St Bartholomew's Hosp London 1980-, conslt neurosurgn Army in Scotland 1963-81, prof (now emeritus) Univ of King Saud 1983-85 (advsr MOD Saudi Arabia 1981-85), pres RCS Edinburgh 1974-82; coll lectr Irish Coll of Surgns 1974, Haveian Oration Edinburgh 1980, 17th Elsbery lecture NY 1967, Syme Derby lecture (and medal) Hong Kong 1982; hon MD (Thessaloniki), hon FRACS, hon FCM (S Africa), hon FRCP (Glasgow), hon FRCSI, hon memb Royal Acad of Med (Valencia); *Publications* papers on neurosurgical subjects in learned magazines, ed 4 books; *Recreations* gardening, sailing, photography, travel; *Clubs* New (Edinburgh), Bruntsfield Link's Golfing Soc Edinburgh, Club Nautico Alicante Spain; *Style—* Prof John Gillingham, CBE, MBE; Easter Park House, Barnton Avenue, Edinburgh EH4 6JR (☎ 031 336 3528); Las Colinas, Jesus Pobre, Denia, Alicant, Spain (☎ 010 34 65 75 70 62)

GILLINGS, Ronald James; s of Joames Oliver Gillings (d 1952), of Surrey, and Ivy Edith Gillings (d 1962); *b* 11 July 1931; *Educ* Dorking GS, Kingston on Thames Sch of Architecture; *m* Mary, da of Arthur Williams Enfield (d 1964); 2 da (Katharine b 1958, Sarah b 1964); *Career* architect, ptnr Gerald Murphy Burles Newton 1962-; chm Highbury Div Cmmrs of Inland Revenue 1982- (memb Finsbury Advsy Ctee 1986-); chm: tourism ctee London Borough of Islington 1986-, consultative gp of Gtr London C of C 1982-83, Islington Chamber of Commerce 1980-82, Indust Year London N Centl 1986 (Indust Matters 1987); memb: bd Islington Enterprise Centre, co-op London Borough of Islington Employment & Econ Devpt Ctee 1970-; pres Islington Rotary Club 1976-77; ARIBA; *Recreations* boating, photography, building; *Style—* Ronald Gillings, Esq; The Japanese Garden, Codicote, Hitchin, Herts (☎ Stevenage 820430); Stanhope House, 4 Highgate High Street, London N6 (☎ 01 341 1307, fax 01 341 0851)

GILLIONS, Paul; s of William Stanley Gillions (d 1972), and Marie Lilian, *née* Crawley; *b* 15 May 1950; *Educ* St Albans GS for Boys; *m* 5 June 1976, Grace Kathleen, da of David Adam Smith; 2 da (Jennie b 1980, Laura b 1983); *Career* int PR conslt main bd dir Burson-Marsteller Ltd 1987-; dir of Public Affairs; *Recreations* reading; *Style—* Paul Gillions, Esq; 3 Hitehurst Ave, Hitchin, Herts (☎ 0462 55513); 24-28 Bloomsbury Way, London WC1 (☎ 01 831 6262)

GILLMAN, Gerry; s of Elias Gillman (d 1988), Rotterdean, Sussex, and Gladys Maud, *née* Willomatt; *b* 14 April 1927; *Educ* Archbishop Tenison's GS; *m* 21 July 1951, Catherine Mary, da of Thomas Harvey (d 1966), of Berkenhead; *Career* Soc Civil Servants: asst sec 1953, gen sec 1973-85; memb Police Complaints Authy 1986-; *Clubs* MCC; *Style—* Gerry Gillman, Esq; 10 Gt George St, London SW1 (☎ 01 273 6469)

GILLMORE, David Howe; CMG (1982); s of Air Vice-Marshal Alan David Gillmore, CB, CBE, of Burnham-on-Sea, and Kathleen Victoria, *née* Morris; *b* 16 August 1934; *Educ* Trent Coll, King's Coll Cambridge (MA); *m* 1964, Lucile, da of Jean Morin (d 1972), of Paris; 2 s (Julian b 1967, Paul b 1970); *Career* RAF 1953-55; Reuters 1958-60, Polypapier SA 1960-65; schoolmaster ILEA 1965-69; FCO 1970-72; first sec Br Embassy Moscow 1972-75; cllr Br Delgn to MBFR Talks Vienna 1975-78; head of Def Dept FCO 1979-81; asst under-sec of state FCD 1981-83; Br high cmmnr to Malaysia 1983-86; dep under-sec of state FCO 1986-; *Recreations* books, music, exercise; *Style—* David Gillmore, Esq; Foreign & Commonwealth Office, King Charles St, London SW1

GILLOTT, Nicholas Richard; TD (1948); s of Bernard Henry Gillott (d 1954), and Dorothy, *née* Mann (d 1965); *b* 2 August 1917; *Educ* Oundle; *m* 1966, Isobel Barrett, da of John Varley (d 1952), of Elmbank, Leamington Spa; *Career* serv Royal Signals: UK, Middle East, Br Columbia, Germany; Capt; md Joseph Gillott & Sons Ltd 1948-72; chm Best & Lloyd Ltd 1972-74; md Br Castors Ltd 1974-79, chm 1979-80; hon tres Birmingham C of Indust and C 1979-82; *Recreations* gardening, property maintenance, wine making; *Style—* Nicholas Gillott, Esq; Orchard House, Mickleton Rd, Ilmington, Shipston-on-Stour, Warwicks CV36 4JQ (☎ 060 882 494)

GILLOTT, Roland Charles Graeme; s of John Arthur Gillott (d 1982), of Northwood, Middx, and Ursula Mary, *née* Bailey (d 1983); *b* 22 August 1947; *Educ* Haileybury; *m* 25 Oct 1975, (Bridget) Rae, da of Lesley Bentley Jones (d 1959), of Northwood; 1 s (Adrian b 20 Oct 1979), 2 da (Shanta b 21 April 1978, Lissa b 1 Jan 1981); *Career* admitted slr 1972, ptnr Radcliffes & Co 1979; chm Amersham and Chesham Bois Churches Ctee 1988-89 (memb), memb St Michaels & All Angels Amersham PCC; Liveryman Worshipful Co of Merchant Taylors 1979; memb Law Soc; *Recreations* walking, photography, watching cricket, birdwatching; *Clubs* MCC, RAC, City Livery; *Style—* Roland Gillott, Esq; 10 Little Coll St, Westminster, London SW1P 3SJ

GILLUM, John Reginald; s of Sidney Julius Gillum (d 1953); *b* 25 Jan 1928; *Educ* Winchester, King's Coll Cambridge; *m* 1953, Mary Rosalind, da of Alan Frederick Graham Ayling, of The Garden Cottage, Holwell Manor, Hatfield, Herts; 3 children; *Career* Lt The Buffs; joined Robert Benson, Lonsdale & Co Ltd (subsequently Kleinwort Benson) 1956, hd of corporate fin Samuel Montagu & Co Ltd 1971, dir (corporate fin) N M Rothschild & Sons Ltd 1981-; BR (Eastern) Bd, Criterion Hldgs Ltd, Gillow plc; Leonard Grouse Associates Ltd; dep chm: Ratners Gp plc, Sketchley plc; chm: Blagden Industs plc, Atlantic Computers plc; *Recreations* golf; *Clubs* Brooks's; *Style—* John Gillum, Esq; Holwell Manor, Hatfield, Herts (☎ Hatfield 61232); N M Rothschild & Sons Ltd, New Court, St Swithin's Lane, London EC4 (☎ 01 280 5000)

GILMORE, Brian Terence; s of John Henry Gilmore, of 48 Rockdale Gdns, Sevenoaks, Kent, and Edith Alice, *née* Johnson; *b* 25 May 1937; *Educ* Wolverhampton GS, Christ Church Oxford (MA); *m* 17 Feb 1962, Rosalind, da of Sir Robert Fraser (d 1986); *Career* civil servant, under sec HM Treasury; *Recreations* walking, music, Greece; *Clubs* Athenaeum; *Style—* Brian T Gilmore, Esq; c/o HM Treasury, Parliament St, London SW1

GILMORE, David; s of David Gilmore, and Dora, *née* Baker; *b* 7 Dec 1945; *Educ* Alleyn's; *m* 3 Sept 1978, Fiona, da of J P R Mollison; 2 s (Charles b 1982, George b 1985); *Career* artistic dir: Watermill Theatre, Nuffield Theatre Southampton; West End prodns incl: Nuts Whitehall Theatre, Daisy Pulls it Off Globe Theatre, Lend Me a Tenor Globe Theatre, The Irresistible Rise of Arturo Ui Queens Theatre, Beyond Reasonable Doubt Queens Theatre, The Hired Man Astoria Theatre; other prodns incl: Cavalcade Chichester Festival Theatre, Song and Dance Sydney (also Melbourne and Adelaide), Glen Garry Glenross Brussels; memb: DGGB, TMA; *Recreations* golf, gardening; *Style—* David Gilmore, Esq; 4 Wilton Cres, Wimbledon, London SW19

GILMORE, Fiona Catherine; da of Robin (Dick) Triefus (d 1983) and Jean Margaret, *née* Herring; *b* 7 Nov 1956; *Educ* Queenswood Sch Hatfield Herts, Cambridge (MA); *m* 5 May 1979, Richard John Maurice, s of Richard Thomas Gilmore, of Maldon, Essex; 1 s (Daniel b 1986); y; *Career* Ted Bates Advertising Agency London 1977-78, Benton & Bates Advertising Agency London 1978-84, md Michael Peters & Ptnrs 1987- (account mangr 1977, account dir 1979, devpt dir 1984, mktg dir 1985); memb NEDO Maker User Working Pty 1988, govr Centre for Info on Language Teaching and Res 1987, memb Milk Mktg Bd 1988; speaker CBI conference 1986, memb CBI vision 2010 Gp 1986-87, chm Design Effectiveness Awards Scheme 1988-89; memb: IOD, Mktg Soc; *Recreations* family, skiing, tennis, walking, singing; *Style—* Mrs Fiona Gilmore ; Michael Peters & Ptnrs, 3 Olaf St, London W11 4BE (☎ 01 229 3424, fax 01 221 7720, car telephone 0836 685997, telex 21726 DESIGN G)

GILMORE, John Franklin; s of John Franklin Gilmore (d 1987), and Evelyn Maude Exum (d 1974); *b* 30 June 1927; *Educ* Univ of Florida (B Mech Eng); *m* 1950, Norma Rhea, da of Carl Leo Jones (d 1985), of Kentucky; 1 s (Mark b 1967), 2 da (Rebecca, Brenda); *Career* quartermaster USN 1944-46, USS Hornet CV-12, South Pacific, pres Unit Citation 1945; Blaw-Knox Co Oklahoma 1950-55; Stearns Catalytic Corp 1955-86, engr, project man, Philadelphia 1955-73, vice-pres Catalytic Int London 1973-76 (pres 1976-81), vice-pres Marketing Philadelphia 1981-86; pres Life Science Inc Philadelphia Pennsylvania USA 1986-; registered professional engr State of Oklahoma and the Cwlth of Pennsylvania, memb: Pennsylvania soc of professional engrs, Nat Soc of Professional Engrs, American Soc of Mech Engrs, founding memb American Assoc of Cost Engrs, memb American Inst of chemical engrs; 'Man of Merit to the Polish Petrochemia' Commemorative Medal Krakow Poland 1980; Winner of Queen's Award for Export Achievement 1979; *Recreations* shooting, swimming, sailing, riding; *Clubs* Clinkers (Philadelphia), Sugar Mill Country (Florida); *Style—* John Gilmore, Esq; 398 Lakeside Road, Ardmore, Pennsylvania, USA (☎ 215/896 6151 and 215/896 0173, office: 1818 Market Street, Philadelphia, Pennsylvania, USA (☎ 215/299 8700, telex 845192 CABLE: DAYZIM

GILMORE, Maj Michael Maurice Allan; s of Lt-Col Edward Maurice Blunt Gilmore, DSO (d 1965), and Dorothy Hill, *née* Drury; third successive generation cmmnd into 51 Foot/Gloucestershire Regt; *b* 18 Dec 1931; *Educ* Dauntsey's Sch W Lavington, RMA Sandhurst; *m* 28 Sept 1963, Marion Patricia Studdy, da of Cecil John Edmonds, CMG, CBE (d 1979); 1 s (Edward b 1974), 2 da (Alexandra b 1967, Elizabeth b 1976); *Career* Army Offr (Glosters) 1952-69, ret as Maj, serv Kenya 1955-56, Aden 1956, Bahrain 1956-57, Cyprus 1957, Turkey 1958-59, Cyprus 1962-65, S Arabia 1966-67; exec offr Tata Ltd London 1969-71; Maj Dubai Def Force UAE 1972-76; branch mangr MAR Albahar Oman 1976-77; branch mangr Binladen Telecommunications Co EP Saudi-Arabia 1978-80; YBA Kanoo Branch mangr, reg mangr 1980-86; *Recreations* all equitation, skiing, beagling, shooting, singing, reading, amateur dramatics, gliding; *Clubs* Royal Aero, British Horse Soc, IOD (Associate), Inst of Linguists, Brit Inst of Mgmnt; *Style—* Maj Michael Gilmore; The Old Forge, Pyrton, Watlington, Oxon OX9 5AP (☎ Watlington 049 161 2459)

GILMORE, Owen Jeremy Adrian; s of Dr Owen Dermot Gilmore, of Inigo House, Highworth, Wilts, and Carmel, *née* Cantwell; *b* 27 Dec 1941; *Educ* Beaumont Coll, St Bartholomew's Hosp Med Sch (MB BS); *m* 19 Nov 1986, Hilary Ann Frances; 2 s (Hugh Inigo b 1969, Quentin Roderick b 1977), 4 da (Anna Benedicta Claire b 1967, Deborah Emma Frances b 1968, Katherine Laura Matilda b 1971, Natasha Olivia Polly b 1973); *Career* consult surg St Bartholomew's Hosp London 1976, consult in charge Breast Unit St Bartholomew's Hosp, consult surgn Homerton Hosp London 1976; prizes: Begley prize RCS 1966, Moynihan Prize and Medal Assoc surgeons GrBr 1975, Hamilton Bailey Prize Int Coll Surgeons 1975, Hunterian Prof Royal Coll of Surgeons England 1976; MRCS (England), LRCP (London) 1966, FRCS (England) 1971, FRCS (Edinburgh) 1971, MS (London 1976); *Books* Diagnosis and Treatment of Breast Disease, Diagnosis and Treatment of Surgical Gastro-intestinal Disease; *Recreations* skiing, squash, swimming, rugby football, wine and dining; *Style—* Owen Gilmore, Esq; 30 Harley St, London W1N 1AB (☎ 01 637 8820, 01 323 4799, 01 631 4448)

GILMOUR, Dr Alan Breck; CBE (1984); s of Andrew Gilmour, CMG (d 1988), of Edinburgh, and Nelle, *née* Twigg (d 1984); *b* 30 August 1928; *Educ* Clayesmore Sch, King's Coll Hosp London Univ (MB BS); *m* 8 June 1957, Elizabeth, da of late Henry Heath; 2 da; *Career* Nat Serv 1947-49; 2 Lt RSF, Bde Liaison Offr Trieste 1948-49; GP 1957-67, BMA Secretariat 1967-79, dir NSPCC 1979-89; former memb: Standing Med Advsy Ctee, cncl BMA, educnl ctee RCGP; former tres ASME; Liveryman Worshipful Co of Apothecaries 1973; FRCGP 1974, LMSSA 1956; *Books* Innocent Victims - The Question of Child Abuse (1988); *Recreations* walking, gardening, music; *Clubs* RSM, Royal Overseas League, City Livery; *Style—* Dr Alan Gilmour, CBE; 106 Crock Lane, Bothenhampton, Bridport, Dorset; NSPCC, 67 Saffron Hill, London EC1; 222 Bunyan Ct, The Barbican, London EC2 (☎ 01 242 1626)

GILMOUR, Alexander Clement (Sandy); s of Sir John Gilmour, 2 Bt (d 1977), and Lady Mary Gilmour, *qv*, da of 3 Duke of Abercorn; half bro of Rt Hon Sir Ian Gilmour, 3 Bt, MP, *qv*; *b* 23 August 1931; *Educ* Eton; *m* 1, 2 Dec 1954 (m dis 1983), Barbara Marie-Louise Constance, da of Hon Denis Gomer Berry, TD, *qv*; 2 s, 1 da; *m* 2, 1983, Susan Janet, eld da of late Capt Voltelin James Howard Van der Byl, BSC, RN (ret), and formerly wife of (1) Alwyn Richard Dudley Smith and (2) 2 Baron Chetwode; *Career* stockbroker; dir (head corp fin dept) Carr Sebag and Co 1972-82, conslt with Grieveson Grant 1982-83; Gilmour & Associates Ltd 1983-84; Equity Fin Tst Ltd 1984-; *Recreations* fishing, gardening, tennis skiing; *Clubs* White's, HEEG; *Style—* Sandy Gilmour, Esq; Knighton Farm House, Ramsbury, Wilts (☎ 0672 204 71)

GILMOUR, Col Allan Macdonald; OBE (1961), MC (and bar 1942, 1943); o s of Capt Allan Gilmour, of Rosehall, Sutherland (ka Salonica 1916), and Mary H M Macdonald; *b* 23 Nov 1916; *Educ* Winchester; *m* 1941, Jean, da of Capt E G Wood (d 1980), of Gollanfield, Inverness-shire; 3 s, 1 da; *Career* served WW II Seaforth Highlanders M East, Sicily, Italy, NW Europe (despatches 1944); Col Queen's Own Highlanders, served 1944-66: Germany, M East, UK, and as Instr Staff Coll Pakistan, CGS Ghana, ret 1966; chm Sutherland DC, memb Highland Regnl Cncl and chm Highland Health Bd; HM Lord Lieut Sutherland 1972- (DL 1971); DSC (USA) 1945; *Recreations* fishing; *Style—* Col Allan Gilmour, OBE, MC; Invernauld, Rosehall, Sutherland (☎ 054 984204)

GILMOUR, Lady Caroline Margaret; *née* Montagu Douglas Scott; yr da of 8 Duke of Buccleuch, KT, GCVO, TD, PC (d 1973); *b* 17 Nov 1927; *m* 10 July 1951, Rt Hon Sir Ian Hedworth John Little Gilmour, 3 Bt, MP; 4 s, 1 da; a bridesmaid to HRH The Princess Elizabeth 20 Nov 1947; *Style—* Lady Caroline Gilmour; The Ferry House, Old Isleworth, Middlesex

GILMOUR, David Robert; s and h of Rt Hon Sir Ian Gilmour, 3 Bt, MP, *qv*; *b* 14 Nov 1952; *Educ* Eton, Balliol Coll Oxford; *m* 1975, Sarah Anne, da of Michael Bradstock, of Falconer's House, Crichel, Dorset; 1 s (Alexander b 1980), 3 da (Rachel b 1977, Katharine b 1984, Laura b 1985); *Career* writer; *Books* Dispossessed: The Ordeal of The Palestinians 1917-80 (1980), Lebanon: The Fractured Country (1983), The Transformation of Spain: From Franco to the Constitutional Monarchy (1985); *Style—* David Gilmour, Esq; Ruchlaw House, Stenton, East Lothian

GILMOUR, Ewen Hamilton; s of Lt Cdr Patrick Dalrymple Gilmour (d 1978), and Lorna Mary, *née* Dore; *b* 16 August 1953; *Educ* Rugby, Downing Coll Cambridge; *m* 3 June 1978, Nicola, da of Maarten Van Mesdag, 3 s (James b 27 Feb 1980, Rowallan b 3 April 1982, Fergus b 4 May 1985); *Career* Peat Marwick McLintock 1974-80, Charterhouse Bank Ltd 1980- (dir 1987); FCA 1977; *Recreations* cricket, golf, gardening; *Clubs* MCC; *Style—* Ewen Gilmor, Esq; 20 Arthur Rd, London SW19 7DZ (☎ 01 947 6805); 1 Paternoster Row, St Pauls, London EC4 (☎ 01 248 4000, fax 01 248 1998, telex 884276)

GILMOUR, Rt Hon Sir Ian Hedworth John Little; 3 Bt (UK 1926), PC (1973), MP (C) Chesham and Amersham 1974-; s of Sir John Little Gilmour, 2 Bt (d 1977), by his 1 w; *see* Hon Mrs Gilmour, OBE, TD; half bro of Sandy Gilmour *qv*; *b* 8 July 1926; *Educ* Eton, Balliol Coll Oxford; *m* 10 July 1951, Lady Caroline Margaret Montagu Douglas Scott, da of 8 Duke of Buccleuch and Queensberry; 4 s, 1 da; *Heir* s, David Robert Gilmour; *Career* late Gren Gds; barr 1952; ed The Spectator 1954-59; MP Norfolk Central 1962-74, parly under-sec MOD 1970-71, min of state: Defence Procurement MOD 1971-72, Defence 1972-74; sec state Defence 1974, chm Cons Research Dept 1974-75, Lord Privy Seal and dep Foreign Sec 1979-81; *Books* The Body Politic (1969), Inside Right: A Study of Conservatism (1977), Britain Can Work (1983); *Style—* The Rt Hon Sir Ian Gilmour, Bt, MP; The Ferry House, Old Isleworth, Middx (☎ 01 560 6769)

GILMOUR, John; s and h of Col Sir John Gilmour, 3 Bt, DSO, TD, JP; *b* 15 July 1944; *Educ* Eton, Aberdeen Coll of Agric; *m* 6 May 1967, Valerie Jardine, yr da of late George Walker Russell and Mrs William Wilson, of Hilton House, Cupar; 2 s, 2 da; *Career* Capt Fife and Forfar Yeo/Scottish Horse (TA); farmer; memb Royal Co of Archers (Queen's Body Guard for Scotland); MFH 1972-; company dir; *Recreations* riding, fishing, reading; *Clubs* New (Edinburgh); *Style—* John Gilmour, Esq; Balcormo Mains, Leven, Fife (☎ 033336 229)

GILMOUR, Col Sir John Edward; 3 Bt (UK 1897), of Lundin and Montrave, Parishes of Largo and Scoonie, Co Fife, DSO (1945), TD, JP (Fife 1957); s of Col Rt Hon Sir John Gilmour, 2 Bt, GCVO, DSO, sometime MP E Renfrewshire and Glasgow Pollok (d 1940), by his 1 w, Mary (d 1919), da of Edward Lambert, of Telham Court, Sussex; *b* 24 Oct 1912; *Educ* Eton, Trinity Hall Cambridge, Dundee Sch of Economics; *m* 24 May 1941, Ursula Mabyn, da of Frank Oliver Wills, of Cote Lodge, Westbury-on-Trym; 2 s (John, *qv*; Andrew, b 1947 (d 1972) m Mary, adopted da of Sir Henry Campbell de la Poer Beresford-Peirse, 5 Bt (d 1972); *Heir* s, John Gilmour; *Career* Bt-Col 1950; MP (C) E Fife 1961-79, chm Cons and Unionist Party Scotland 1965-67; HM lord-lieut Fife 1980-87 (vice ld-lt 1979-80, DL 1953); lord high cmmr to Gen Assembly of Church of Scotland 1982 and 1983; Capt Royal Co of Archers (Queen's Body Guard for Scotland); *Recreations* hunting, gardening, shooting; *Clubs* Royal and Ancient St Andrews, Cavalry and Guards'; *Style—* Col Sir John Gilmour, Bt, DSO, TD, JP; Montrave, Leven, Fife KY8 5NZ (☎ 0333 26159)

GILMOUR, Hon Mrs; Hon (Katherine Pulcheria) Katia; *née* Grenfell; er da (by 2 w) of 2 and last Baron St Just (d 1984); *b* 23 May 1957; *m* 1981 (m dis 1985), Oliver John Gilmour, 2 s of Rt Hon Sir Ian Hedworth John Little Gilmour, 3 Bt, MP, *qv*; 1 da; *Style—* Hon Mrs Gilmour; c/o The Rt Hon Lady St Just, 30 Cambridge Street, London SW1

GILMOUR, Hon Mrs Victoria Laura; OBE (1927), TD; da of Henry Arthur Cadogan, Viscount Chelsea (d 1908, s of 5 Earl Cadogan) and Hon Mildred, *née* Sturt, da of 1 Baron Alington; *b* 22 Oct 1901; *m* 22 July 1922 (m dis 1929), John Little Gilmour (afterwards 2 Bt, d 1977); 1 s (Rt Hon Sir Ian Gilmour, Bt, MP, *qv*) 1 da; *Career*

Controller ATS; acted as lady-in-waiting to HM Queen Elizabeth the Queen Mother when Duchess of York on tour of Australia and New Zealand 1927; *Style—* The Hon Mrs Gilmour, OBE, TD; Dacres, Bentworth, Alton, Hants (☎ 0420 62040)

GILPIN, Adrian (formerly Adrian Charles Scrymsour Slattery); s of Peter Anthony Slattery, and Joanella Elizabeth Agnes, *née* Scrymsour-Nichol; *b* 9 August 1956; *Educ* Holmewood House Sussex, Ampleforth, Skinners Sch Tunbridge Wells, Guildhall Sch of Music and Drama; *m* 26 Feb 1983, Francesca, *née* Marks; *Career* actor 1974-, work incl: rep, West End, tours, film, tv (incl Don't Wait up, Hot Metal); fndr Adrian Gilpin Assocs theatre consultancy (UK, USA, Australia, M East), gen mangr Theatre of Comedy Co Ltd 1982-84, md Artatack (stage) Ltd theatre prodrs 1986-; work incl: Now We are Sixty Cambridge Arts Theatre 1986, If Winter Comes Melbourne Australia 1986; md Unicorn Heritage plc 1986-89 (fndr Royal Britain Exhibition, London), md Adrian Gilpin TV Ltd 1989-; memb: Assoc of Ind Prodrs 1986, Ind Programme Prodrs Assoc; MInstD 1987, memb Tourism Soc 1988; *Style—* Adrian Gilpin, Esq; Kilchurn House, South St, Rotherfield, East Sussex TN6 3LU; Castlelough, Portroe, Nenagh, Co Tipperary, Eire

GILROY, Dr Beryl Agatha; *née* Alnwick; da of Frederick Alnwick (d 1928), and M Alnwick, *née* Hooper; *b* 30 August 1924; *Educ* London Univ (BA), Sussex Univ (MA), Century Univ LA California (PhD); *m* 4 July 1954, P E Gilroy (d 1975); 1 s (Paul b 1956), 1 da (Darla-Jane b 1959); *Career* educn conslt, counselling psychologist, Univ lectr, author; memb Race Relations Bd 1964-69, 1976-; *Books* In for a Penny (1978), Frangipani House (1985); *Recreations* walking, reading, needlework; *Clubs* Network; *Style—* Dr Beryl Gilroy; 86 Messina Ave, NW6 4LG (☎ 01 624 1494); Institute of Education, 20 Bedford Way, W1

GILROY, Darla-Jane; da of Patrick Eric Gilroy (d 1976), and Beryl Agatha, *née* Answick; *b* 9 Jan 1959; *Educ* Camden Girls Sch, Brighton Coll of Art, St Martin's Sch of Art (BA); *Career* costume design David Bowie Ashes to Ashes video 1980, first major show Olympia 1981, London designers collections 1981; major press features: Vogue, Options, Company, Cosmopolitan 1982; opened retail outlet 1983, freelance collection Topshop 1984, second retail outfit Kings Rd 1984; exhibited: Milan, New York, London 1986-; commenced manufacture Hong Kong 1987, lectr St Martins Sch of Art 1987-, 30 min video of career and achievements Design Cncl 1987; *Recreations* horse riding, breeding dogs, film, travel; *Clubs* Chelsea Arts, Groucho's, Fred's; *Style—* Miss Darla-Jane Gilroy; Studio 23, Ransome's Dock, 35-37 Parkgate Road, London SW11 (☎ 223 9145/352 2095, fax 350 2389)

GILROY, Sandy; s of Alexander Gilroy (d 1952), and Thelma Mercy McClymont, *née* Tubbs (d 1980); *b* 22 June 1935; *Educ* Winchester; *m* 1959, Marion (d 1985), da of Maj David Brodie (d 1966), of Nairn; *Career* 2 Lt The Black Watch (RHR); merchandise controller Br Home Stores; chm Alexander Gilroy Gp Ltd, fndr Savoir Vivre (Information Exchange); *Recreations* writing, miniatures, country pursuits; *Style—* Sandy Gilroy, Esq; Glen Shinnel, Tynron by Thornhill, Dumfriesshire DG3 4LE (☎ 084 82551, 08482 611)

GIMENA, Lady Anne-Marie Ines; *née* Ward; da (twin, by 1 m) of 4 Earl of Dudley; *b* 26 May 1955; *m* 1978, Laureano Perez-Andujar Gimena, of Madrid; *Style—* Lady Anne-Marie Gimena

GIMSON, Maj Richard Allynne Stanford; MC (1944), TD (1956), JP (1961); s of Harold Gimson (d 1939), of Daneway, Leiston, Suffolk, and Janet Marjorie, *née* Stanford (d 1946); *b* 12 Dec 1922; *Educ* Uppingham, Clare Coll Camb; *m* 12 July 1947, Elspeth Primrose, yst da of Col Sholto Stuart Ogilvie, CBE, DSO, of Ness House, Sizewell, Suffolk (d 1964); 1 s (Alexander Edward Stanford b 1951), 2 da (Wendy Louise b 1948, Caroline Ann b (twin) 1948); *Career* serv WWII cmmnd RE 1941-47 in Egypt, Greece, Italy, Yugoslavia and NW Europe, TA Royal Lincs Regt 1947-59 as Maj; co dir: Ruston and Hornsly Ltd 1960-66, English Electric Diesels 1966-70, Davey Paxman Ltd 1966-70, Babcock and Wilcox (Operations) Ltd 1970-78, Gimson and Co Ltd 1979-87, Coastal Trg Services 1984-; JP Lincoln 1961-70, Essex 1970-78; chm Middle East Assocn 1978; memb: Br Overseas Trade Bd, European Trade Ctee 1970-77, Scottish Cncl for Devpt Mission (China 1974 and USSR 1976); *Recreations* swimming, stalking, sailing, music; *Clubs* Naval and Military, Aldeburgh Yacht; *Style—* Maj Richard Gimson, MC, TD, JP; Ness House, Sizewell, Suffolk IP16 4UB (☎ 0728 830007)

GIMSON, (George) Stanley; QC (1961); s of George William Gimson (d 1949), of Glasgow, and Mary, *née* Hogg (d 1950); *b* 6 Sept 1915; *Educ* HS of Glasgow, Glasgow Univ (BL); *Career* RA TA 1938, cmmnd 1941, Lt 2 HAA Regt Indian Artillery Singapore 1941-, POW Changi (Singapore) and River Kwai (Thailand); called to the Scottish Bar 1949; standing cousel 1956-61: Dept of Agric for Scotland, Forestry Cmmn; Sheriff Princ: of Aberdeen Kincadine and Bauff 1972-74, of Grampion Highland and IS 1975-82; chm: Pensions Appeals Tribunals Scotland 1971-, Med Appeals Tribunals Scotland 1985-; dir Scottish Nat Orchestra Soc Ltd 1962-80, chm RSPCC (Edinburgh) 1972-76; chm bd of mgmnt Edinburgh Central Hosps (memb 1960-70), vice chm Edinburgh Victoria Hosps 1970-74, tstee Nat Library of Scotland 1963-76; hon LLD Aberdeen Univ 1981; memb Faculty of Advocates 1949; *Recreations* travel, forestry, sketching, history; *Clubs* Royal Northern & Univ (Aberdeen), Edinburgh Univ Staff; *Style—* Stanley Gimson, Esq, QC; 11 Royal Circus, Edinburgh EH3 6TL

GINGELL, Air Chief Marshal Sir John; GBE (1984, CBE 1973, MBE 1962), KCB (1978); eldest s of Ernest John Gingell; *b* 3 Feb 1925; *Educ* St Boniface's Coll Plymouth; *m* 1949, Prudence Mary, da of Brig Roy Frank Johnson; 2 s, 1 da; *Career* RAF 1943, Sub-Lieut RNVR Fleet Air Arm 1945-46, RAF 1951, Air Plans Staff HQ NEAF 1960-63, OC No 27 Sqdn (Vulcans) 1963-65, Defence Ops Staff MOD 1966-68, Mil Asst to Chm Mil Ctee NATO Brussels 1968-70, AOA RAF Germany 1971-72, AOC No 23 Gp RAF 1973-75, asst chief of Defence Staff (Policy) MOD 1975-78, air memb for Personnel 1978-80, AOC-in-C RAF Support Cmd 1980-81, Dep C-in-C Allied Forces Central Europe 1981-85; Gentleman Usher of the Black Rod and Serjeant at Arms, House of Lords, sec Lord Great Chamberlain 1985-; Cmmnr Cwlth War Graves; *Clubs* RAF; *Style—* Air Chief Marshal Sir John Gingell, GBE, KCB; House of Lords, London SW1A 0PW

GINSBURY, Norman; s of Samuel Jacob Ginsbury (d 1904), and Rachel Cecily Schulberg (d 1929); *b* 8 Nov 1903; *Educ* Grocers' Co Sch, London Univ (BSc); *m* 1945, Dorothy Agnes, da of William Jennings, of 54 Greenbank Ave, Plymouth, Devon; *Career* produced plays include: Viceroy Sarah 1934 and 1935, Ibsen's Ghosts 1937 and 1958, Ibsen's An Enemy of The People 1939, Walk in The Sun 1939, Take Back Your Freedom 1940, (Take Back Your Freedom was derived from a play by Winifred Holtby called "Hope of Thousands"), The Forefathers 1940, Ibsen's Peer Gynt 1944, The First Gentleman 1945 and 1946, The Gambler 1946, Ibsen's A Doll's House 1946, The Happy Man 1949, The School for Rivals 1949, Portrait By Lawrence 1950, The Forefathers 1951, Ibsen's Rosmersholm 1960, Ibsen's The Pillars of Society 1961, Ibsen's John Gabriel Borkman 1960, Strindberg's The Dance of Death 1966, The Wisest Fool 1974, The Forefathers 1970; *Books* Viceroy Sarah (1935), Take Back Your Freedom (1939), The First Gentleman (1940 and 1946), Peer Gynt (1946); *Clubs* Dramatists'; *Style—* Norman Ginsbury, Esq; 10 Bramber House, Michael Grove, Eastbourne, East Sussex BN21 1LA (☎ 0323 29603)

GINTELL, Burton; *b* 11 May 1935; *Educ* City Univ of New York; *Career* md J G Turney & Son Ltd, winner of a Queen's Award for Export 1980, William Whiteley & Co, Glenforres Glenlivet Distillery Co Ltd 1978-; *Style—* Burton Gintell, Esq; Atlas House, 57a Catherine Place, SW1, (☎ 01 834 3771)

GIORDANO, Richard Vincent; s of Vincent and Cynthia Giordano; *b* 1934,March; *Educ* Harvard (BA, LLB, PhD); *m* 1956, Barbara Claire Beckett; 1 s, 2 da; *Career* head Airco Corpn to 1978;chief exec offr The BOC Gp 1979- (chm 1985-); part-time memb CEGB 1982-; pt-t bd memb Georgia Pacific Corp, Atlanta GA 1984-; bd memb Grand Metropolitan plc 1985-; *Recreations* ocean sailing, tennis; *Clubs* The Links, New York Yacht, Edgartown Yacht (Mass), Duquesne (Pittsburgh PA); *Style—* Richard Giordano, Esq; The BOC Group plc, Chertsey Rd, Windlesham, Surrey GU20 6HJ

GIOVENE, Laurence; s of Andrea Giovene, Duca Di Girasole, of Palazzo Ciervo St Agata Del Goti, BV, Italy, and Adeline Constance, *née* Schuberth; *b* 21 Nov 1936; *Educ* Solihull Sch, St Catharines Coll Cambridge (MA); *Career* barr, standing counsel to Italian Govt 1965-85, dep Circuit judge 1978, recorder 1986; contested (Cons) East-Ham North 1965, Fulham Borough cncllr 1962-64; pres CU 1960; MCIA; *Recreations* sailing, oil painting; *Clubs* Garrick, Bar Yacht; *Style—* Laurence Giovene, Esq; 2 Pump Court, Temple EC4 (☎ 01 583 2122)

GIRDWOOD, Prof Ronald Haxton; CBE (1984); s of Thomas Girdwood (d 1933), of Polwarth Grove, Edinburgh, and Mary Elizabeth, *née* Haxton (d 1952); *b* 19 Mar 1917; *Educ* Daniel Stewart's Coll Edinburgh, Univ of Edinburgh (MB, ChB, MD, PhD), Hon FACP, FRCPath, FRSEd (1978); *m* 1945, Mary Elizabeth, da of Reginald Ralph Williams (d 1965), of Woodcroft, Calstock, Cornwall; 1 s (Richard), 1 da (Diana); *Career* RAMC Offr 1942-46, A/Lt-Col, served in India and Burma; lectr in medicine Univ of Edinburgh 1946-51, sr lectr then reader Edinburgh Univ 1951-62, prof of therapeutics and clinical pharmacology Edinburgh Univ 1962-82, dean Faculty of Medicine Edinburgh Univ 1975-79; conslt physician Royal Infirmary of Edinburgh 1948-82; pres Royal Coll of Physicians of Edinburgh 1982-85 (vice-pres 1980-82); chm Nat Blood Transfusion Assoc 1980-, chm Medico Pharmaceutical Forum 1985-87; Freedom of township of Sirajgunj Bangladesh 1984; FRCPEd, FRCPLond, FRCPI, Hon FRACPP,; *Books* Blood Disorders due to Drugs and other Agents (ed 1973), Clinical Pharmacology (1976, 1979, 1984), Malabsorption (co-ed, 1969), Textbook of Medical Treatment (1971, 1974, 1978, 1987); about 300 papers in medical journals, particularly relating to haematology, clinical pharmacology and medical history; *Recreations* photography, painting in oils; *Clubs* East India, Edinburgh Univ Staff; *Style—* Prof Ronald Girdwood, CBE; 2 Hermitage Drive, Edinburgh EH10 6DD (☎ 031 447 5137)

GIRI, Surg Capt George Anand Rurik; OBE (1970); s of D V Giri (d 1958), conslt ophthalmic surg, and Princess Marina Kossatkine-Rostoffsky (d 1979), da of Prince Feodor Kossatkine-Rostoffsky, Col Simeonovsky Guards, poet and playwright; *b* 28 April 1923; *Educ* Charterhouse, Jesus Coll Cambridge, St Bartholomew's Hosp (MA (Hons), LMSSA (Lond), DPH, MFCM, AFOM); *m* 26 Jan 1957, Karin Francesca Dora Margaretha, da of Count Eric Audley Lewenhaupt (d 1968), and Dora Florence (d 1953) (artist Dora Crockett), da of Sir James Crockett; 2 s (Michael George Rurik b 1958, Christopher Audley b 1959), 1 da (Alexandra Georgina Francesca b 1961); *Career* Surg Capt RN 1950-78; Asst Dir-Gen RN Med Service 1965-69; SE Asia Treaty Organisation 1970-72; dir Studies Ins Naval Medicine 1973-75; Ch Staff Offr Med Miny Defence 1975-78; asst sec BMA 1978-82; RN ski team Germany 1954, Capt RN hockey Far East 1963; *Recreations* music, arts, gardens; *Clubs* Naval and Military, Veteran Squash GB; *Style—* Capt George Giri, OBE; Es Figuerelet, Mancor del Valle, Mallorca, Spain (☎ 50 36 77)

GIRLING, Hon Mrs (Eleanor Brigit); *née* Addison; er da of 3 Viscount Addison; *b* 1938; *m* 1972, Michael Girling; *Style—* The Hon Mrs Girling; 9 Levana Close, SW19

GIRLING, Maj Gen Peter Howard; CB (1972), OBE (1961); *b* 18 May 1915; *m* 1942, Stella Muriel, da of Sydney Harcourt Hope (d 1931); 2 da (Carolyn, Susan); *Career* dir Electrical and Mechanical Engrg (Army) 1969-72, Maj Gen; dir of operations Open Univ 1972-80; liveryman Turners Co 1973, ret 1980; *Recreations* sailing, travelling; *Clubs* Army and Navy; *Style—* General Peter Girling, CB, OBE; The Folly, Wicken, Milton Keynes MK19 6BH

GIROLAMI, Paul; s of Peter Girolami (d 1956); *b* 25 Jan 1926; *Educ* LSE; *m* 1952, Christabel Mary Gwynne, *née* Lewis; 3 children; *Career* jt pres Shin Nihon Jitsugyo Co Ltd, pres: Glaxo Finanziaria SpA Italy, Glaxo Insurances (Bermuda) Ltd, Glaxo Finance Bermuda Ltd; chm Glaxo Holdings plc, dir Nippon-Glaxo Ltd Japan, Glaxo-Sankyo Ltd, Japan, Vestric Ltd, National Westminster Bank plc (inner London Bd); FCA; *Style—* Paul Girolami, Esq; Burghley Rd, London SW19 5BH (☎ 01 946 0608); Glaxo Holding plc, Clarges House, 6-12 Clarges St, London W1Y 8DH (☎ 01 493 4060; telex 25456)

GIROUARD, Mark; s of Richard Désiré Girouard (s of Col Sir Percy Girouard, KCMG, DSO, sometime govr N Nigeria and British E Africa Protectorates, and Mary, da of Hon Sir Richard Solomon, GCMG, KCB, KCVO), and Lady Blanche, *née* de la Poer Beresford, da of 6 Marquess of Waterford, KP; *b* 7 Oct 1931; *Educ* Ampleforth, Ch Ch Oxford, Courtauld Inst of Art, Bartlett Sch, UCL; *m* 1970, Dorothy N Dorf; 1 da; *Career* writer and architectural historian; Slade prof of fine art Oxford 1975-76; memb Royal Fine Art Cmmn, Royal Cmmn Hist Monuments, Hist Bldgs Advisory Ctee, Cncl Victorian Soc; Hon FRIBA; *Style—* Mark Girouard, Esq; 35 Colville Rd, London W11

GISBOROUGH, 3 Baron (UK 1917); Thomas Richard John Long Chaloner; JP; s of 2 Baron Gisborough, TD, JP (d 1951); *b* 1 July 1927; *Educ* Eton, RAC Cirencester; *m* 26 April 1960, Shane, er da of Sidney Arthur Newton, of Hyde Park Gate, SW7 (2 s of Sir Louis Newton, 1 Bt); 1 s, 2 da (decd); *Heir* s, Hon Thomas Peregrine Long Chaloner; *Career* served 16th/5th Lancers, Northumberland Hussars TA; sits as Cons peer in House of Lords; former Lt-Col Green Howards (TA); farmer and landowner; cllr of North Riding and then Cleveland 1964-77; ld-lt Cleveland 1981-; hon Col Cleveland Cadet Force Devpt Cmmn 1985-, pres Nat Ski Fedn; KStJ; *Recreations* gliding, bridge, piano, tennis, field sports, skiing; *Clubs* Northern Counties (Newcastle); *Style—* The Rt Hon the Lord Gisborough, JP; 37 Bury Walk, London SW3 (☎ 01 581 0260); Gisborough House, Guisborough, Cleveland (☎ 0287 32002)

GITTINGS, Robert William Victor; CBE (1970); s of Surg-Capt Frederick Claude Bromley Gittings, RN (ret) (d 1963), of Bosham, Sussex, and Dora Mary Brayshaw (d 1963): maternal ggf created Baron of the Austrian Empire; *b* 1 Feb 1911; *Educ* St Edward's Oxford, Jesus Coll Cambridge (BA, MA, LittD); *m* 1, 1934 (m dis 1947), Katherine Edith Cambell; 2 s; m 2, 1949, Joan Grenville, da of Edwin Grenville Manton, of Broxbourne, Herts; 1 da; *Career* res student and fell Jesus Coll 1933-38; prodr BBC 1947-63, hon fell Jesus Coll 1979-; *Books* John Keats (1968), Young Thomas Hardy (1975), The Older Hardy (1978), Collected Poems (1976); *Style—* Robert Gittings, Esq; The Stables, East Dean, West Sussex (☎ 024 363 328)

GLADMAN, Ronald John; s of Ronald Arthur Gladman (d 1940), of Deptford, and Johanna Patricia Fifield, *née* O'Connor; *b* 19 Feb 1941; *Educ* St Edmund's Coll Ware, Pembroke Coll Cambridge (MA, LLB); *m* 29 July 1972, Wendy Anne Urling, da of John Harold Stenning, of Ringles Cross, Uckfield; 2 s (Anthony b 1974, Richard b 1977); *Career* slr 1967, worked on Cmmn of Euro Communities 1971-74, asst sec and gp legal advsr Reuters Hldgs Plc 1976-; memb Law Soc; *Recreations* reading, music, walking, skiing; *Style—* Ronald Gladman, Esq; Reuters, 85 Fleet Street, London EC4P 4AJ (☎ 01 250 1122, fax 01 583 1538, telex 23222)

GLADSTONE, Charles Angus; s and h of Sir William Gladstone, 7 Bt, DL; *b* 11 April 1964; *Educ* Eton, Worcester Coll Oxford; *m* 16 April 1988, Caroline, o da of Sir Derek Thomas, KCMG, of the British Embassy, Rome; *Career* music publishing; *Recreations* theatre, film, music, television, shooting, fishing; *Style—* Charles Gladstone, Esq; 57 Gratton Road, London, W14 (☎ 01 603 6805)

GLADSTONE, David Arthur Steuart; CMG (1988); s of Thomas Steuart Gladstone (d 1971), and Muriel Irene Heron, *née* Day; *b* 1 April 1935; *Educ* Ch Ch Coll (BA); *m* 29 July 1961, (Mary Elizabeth) April, da of Wing Cdr Patrick O'Brien Burnner (d 1966), of Wotton Ho, nr Aylesbury, Bucks; 1 s (Patrick b 1969), 1 da (Perdita b 1965); *Career* Nat Serv 2 Lt 4 RHA 1954-56; articled to Annan Dexter & Co 1959-60; FO 1960-: Arabic Language Student of Mecas Lebanon 1960-62, 3 sec political agency Bahrain 1962-63, FO 1963-65 and 1969-72, 2 later 1 sec HM Embassy Bonn 1965-69, 1 sec and hd of chancery Cairo 1972-75, political advsr BMG Berlin 1976-79, hd of Western Euro Dept FCO 1979-82, HM Consul-Gen Marseillers 1983-87, High Cmmr Sri Lanka 1987-; fndr memb and chm the Barnsbury Assoc 1964-65, chm Homes for Barnsbury 1970-72, fndr memb Sinharaja Soc; *Recreations* domestic architecture, real tennis, German lit; *Style—* David Gladstone, Esq, CMG; 2 Mountfort Terr, London N1 1JJ (☎ 01 607 8200); c/o FCO, King Charles St, London SW1A 2AH

GLADSTONE, Hon Mrs Josephine; da of Baron Elwyn-Jones, CH, PC (Life Peer); *m* 1972, as his 2 w, James Francis Gladstone, s of 6 Bt (gs of Rt Hon William Gladstone, PM); 1 s; *Style—* The Hon Mrs Gladstone

GLADSTONE, Sir (Erskine) William; 7 Bt (UK 1846), of Fasque and Balfour, Kincardineshire; JP (Clwyd 1982); s of (Sir) Charles Andrew Gladstone (6 Bt) (d 1968), and Isla Margaret, *née* Crum (d 1987); ggs of Rt Hon William Gladstone, PM; *b* 29 Oct 1925; *Educ* Eton, Ch Ch Oxford; *m* 10 Sept 1962, Rosamund Anne, yr da of Maj Robert Alexander Hambro (d 1943), of Milton Abbey, Dorset; 2 s, 1 da; *Heir* s, Charles Angus Gladstone; *Career* asst master Eton 1951-61, headmaster Lancing 1961-69, chief scout of the UK and Overseas Branches 1972-82 (ret 1982), chm World Scout Ctee 1979-81; chm Representative Body of the Church in Wales 1977-, chm cncl Glenalmond Coll 1982-; DL Flintshire 1969, Clwyd 1974; HM lord-lieut of Clwyd 1985-; *Style—* Sir William Gladstone, Bt, JP, DL; Hawarden Castle, Clwyd CH5 3PB (☎ 0244 520210); Fasque, Laurencekirk, Kincardineshire

GLADSTONE OF CAPENOCH, Robert Hamilton; er s of John Gladstone of Capenoch, TD (d 1977), and his 2 w, Diana Rosamond Maud Fleming, *née* Hamilton; gggs of Thomas Steuart Gladstone, JP, who acquired Capenoch 1850; *b* 17 July 1953; *Educ* Eton, Magdalene Coll Camb (MA); *m* 16 Jan 1982, Margaret Jane, da of Brig Berenger Colborne Bradford, DSO, MBE, MC, of Kincardine, Kincardine O'Neil, Aberdeenshire; 2 s (John b 3 March 1983, Harry b (twin) 3 March 1983), 1 da (Catharine b 13 April 1986); *Career* chartered surveyor; with John Sale & Ptnrs 1974-78, Smiths-Gore 1978-; memb Scottish Landowners' Fedn Cncl 1984-87; memb Timber-Growers UK South-West Scotland Ctee 1987-; vice-pres Penpont Community Cncl 1986-; ARICS 1977; *Recreations* home-brewing, shooting, fishing, trees; *Clubs* Whistle, '71; Capenoch, Penpont, Dumfrieshire (☎ 0848 30261); office, Smiths-Gore, 28 Castle Street, Dumfries (☎ 0387 63066)

GLADWELL, Dennis Arthur; s of Arthur Frederick Gladwell (d 1987), and Alice May Gladwell, *née* Liquorish (d 1973); *b* 20 June 1923; *Educ* Westcliff HS; *m* 1, 1945, Joyce Barbara; 3 s 2 da; m 2, 1855, Yvonne Carey, da of Albert Huband Hall (d 1966); *Career* WWII Lieut RNVR served Home Fleet and Russian Convoy duties; banker; chief acct Midland Bank plc 1967-72, gen mangr (gp fin) Midland Bank plc 1972-83, chm BACS Ltd 1970-81; dir: East India, Devonshire, Sports and Public Schs Clubs 1968-83; chm Wimborne, Ferndown and Blandford Citizens Advice Bureau 1987-; *Recreations* golf, gardening; *Clubs* Poole Harbour Yacht; *Style—* Dennis Gladwell, Esq; Serampore, 8 Martello Rd South, Canford Cliffs, Poole, Dorset BH13 7HH (☎ 0202 709237)

GLADWYN, 1 Baron (UK 1960); (Hubert Miles) Gladwyn Jebb; GCMG (1954, KCMG 1949, CMG 1942), GCVO (1957), CB (1947); s of Sydney Gladwyn Jebb, JP (d 1950), of Firbeck Hall, Rotherham, and his 1 wife Rose Eleanor, da of Maj-Gen Hugh Chichester, of Pilton House, Barnstaple, Devon; *b* 25 April 1900; *Educ* Eton, Magdalen Coll Oxford (First in History 1922, Beit Prize Essay); *m* 22 Jan 1929, Cynthia, da of Sir Saxton William Armstrong Noble, 3 Bt; 1 s, 2 da (Vanessa, m 1963 Baron Thomas, of Swynnerton (*qv*), Stella, m 1959 Baron Joel de Rosnay, Director of Reseasrch, Institut Pasteur); *Heir* s, Hon Miles Jebb; *Career* sits as Lib Peer in House of Lords; dep ldr Libs and spokesman on Foreign Affrs and Defence 1965-; served Foreign Service 1924-60: Dep Under Sec of State Foreign Office 1948; first (acting) sec gen of United Nation 1947; perm rep UN 1950-54, ambass France 1954-60; created hereditary Peer before his retirement from Foreign Service; stood as Lib MEP candidate Suffolk 1979; chm Campaign for European Political Community; vice-chm European Movement; pres: Afghanistan Support Ctee, UK Cncl for Overseas Students Affrs; patron Cncl for Educn in the Cwlth; former pres Atlantic Treaty Assoc; author of various works and articles on de Gaulle and French foreign policy and nuclear matters; Grand Cross Legion of Honour; hon fell Magdalen Coll Oxford; Hon DCL: Oxon, Essex, Syracuse; *Books* The European Idea (1965), Halfway to 1984 (1967), Memoirs of Lord Gladwyn (1970); *Clubs* Garrick; *Style—* The Rt Hon Lord Gladwyn, GCMG, GCVO, CB; 62 Whitehall Court, London SW1 (☎ 01 930 3160); Bramfield Hall, Halesworth, Suffolk (☎ 098 684 241)

GLAISTER, Catherine Victoria Jane; *née* Blount; da of Christopher Charles Blount, of Manor Farm, Barkway, Hertfordshire, and Hon Mrs Susan Victoria, *née* Cobbold; *b* 15 Dec 1962; *Educ* Downe House Berks, St Mary's Convent Cambs; *m* 12 Nov 1988, Richard Martin Glaister, s of Thomas Stephen Glaister, of Croft Head, Kendal, Cumbria; *Career* mktg dept London Int Fin Futures Exchange 1982-84, ptnr (mktg and PR Christopher Morgan 1985) Christopher Morgan & Ptnrs 1988, dir Trimedia Communications Ltd 1988; *Recreations* eating, walking, talking; *Clubs* Scribes; *Style—* Mrs Richard Glaister; Trimedia Communications Ltd, 15 John Adam St, London WC2N 6LV (☎ 01 930 7642, fax 01 839 3579)

GLANDINE, Viscount; Richard James; s and h of 6 Earl of Norbury; *b* 5 Mar 1967; *Style—* Viscount Glandine

GLANUSK, 4 Baron (UK 1899); Sir David Russell Bailey; 5 Bt (UK 1852); s of Hon Herbert Crawshay Bailey (d 1936; 4 s of 1 Baron) and Kathleen Mary (d 1948), da of Sir Shirley Harris Salt, 3 Bt; suc 1 cous, 3 Baron, 1948; *b* 19 Nov 1917; *Educ* Eton; *m* 25 Jan 1941, Lorna Dorothy, da of late Capt Ernest Courtenay Harold Andrews, MBE, RA; 1 s, 1 da; *Heir* s, Hon Christopher Russell Bailey; *Career* Lt-Cdr RN 1935-51; MEL Ltd 1954-64, Elliott Automation Ltd 1964-66, md Wandel & Goltermann (UK) Ltd 1966-81; chm W & G Ltd 1981-; liveryman Clockmakers & Scientific Instrument Makers; *Style—* The Rt Hon Lord Glanusk; 16 Clarendon Gardens, London W9 1AY

GLANVILL-SMITH, John Seeley; s of Arthur Glanvill-Smith, MC (d 1965), of Madeira House, Littlestone, nr New Romney, Kent, and Margaret, *née* Harris (d 1930); *b* 26 June 1924; *Educ* Bishop's Stortford Coll; *m* 1, Alison Mary (d 1972), da of Charles Aldworth Gifford Campion (d 1963); 4 da (Virginia Mary b 1948, Mary b 1950, Angela Rosemary b 1955, Fiona Frances b 1958); m 2, 3 June 1978, Barbara Joan, *née* Young; *Career* WW11 1939-45, cmmnd Lt Royal Norfolk Regt 1943; chm Glanvill Enthoven & Co Ltd 1976-80 (dep chm 1973-76, dir 1954), chm Jardine Glanvill 1980-82, dep chm Jardine Matheson (insur brokers) 1980-82; dir: Clarkson Pudde (insur brokers) 1982-87, Haris & Dixon Ltd 1987-; memb Lloyds 1956-; pres Buckingham branch Br Limbless Ex-servicemen's Assoc; Freeman City of London, memb Worshipful Co of Gardeners; *Recreations* golf, gardening, cricket; *Clubs* MCC, Surrey CCC, Landsdowne, Norwegian; *Style—* John Glanvill-Smith, Esq; The Old Grange, Great Kimble, Nr Aylesbury, Buckinghamshire HP17 OXS (☎ 084 447 289); Harris & Dixon Ltd, 21 New St, London EC2 (☎ 01 623 6622)

GLANVILLE, Brian Lester; s of James Arthur Glanville (d 1960), and Florence, *née* Manches (d 1984); *b* 24 Sept 1931; *Educ* Charterhouse; *m* 1959, Elizabeth Pamela de Boer, da of Fritz Manasse (d 1961); 2 s (Mark, Toby), 2 da (Elizabeth, Josephine); *Career* novelist, journalist, playwright, football corr and sports columnist The Sunday Times 1958-, lit advsr Bodley Head 1958-62; *Books* novels include: Along The Arno, The Bankrupts, Diamond, The Olympian, A Roman Marriage, A Second Home, The Financiers, A Cry of Crickets, Kissing America; The Catacomb short story collections: A Bad Streak, The Director's Wife, The Thing He Loves, The King of Hackney Marshes, Love is Not Love; stage musical: Underneath The Arches (1982-83 co author); *Recreations* playing football; *Clubs* Chelsea Casuals; *Style—* Brian Glanville, Esq; 160 Holland Park Ave, London W11 4UH (☎ 01 603 6908)

GLANVILLE, John Foster; DSC (1942), VRD (1951); s of Leonard Foster Glanville (d 1975), of Cosham, Portsmouth, and Harriet Ann, *née* Drew; *b* 1 Jan 1918; *Educ* Bradfield Coll; *m* 26 April 1952, Judith Anne (Judy), da of Martyn Dorey (d 1958), of St Sampsons, Guernsey; 1 s (Charles b 1956), 2 da (Pippa b 1954, Louise b 1959); *Career* RNVR 1938-54; served: E Indies Fleet 1939, Med Fleet HMS Eagle and HMS Formidable 1940, Mobile Naval Base Def Orgn Crete 1941, Inshore Sqdn Western Desert 1942, HMS Tracker Western Approaches N Atlantic 1943-44, HMS Arbiter Br Pacific Fleet 1945-46; slr 1947, sr ptnr Glanvilles Wells & Way 1972-82; coroner Portsmouth 1979 and SE Hants 1988-; pres Hants Incorporated Law Soc 1971, memb Southern Legal Aid Area Ctee 1972-80; dir: Portsmouth Water Co 1964, Slrs Benevolent Assoc 1966- (chm 1982); memb Portsmouth Diocesan Bd of Fin 1964-83; cdre: Royal Albert YC 1962-65, Emsworth SC 1971-72; cmmr Sea Scouts Portsmouth 1953-63 (and sec Solent Scout Ctee); memb Law Soc; *Recreations* sailing, music, country walking; *Clubs* Royal Ocean Racing, Royal Naval (Portsmouth); *Style—* John Glanville, Esq, DSC, VRD; Fowley Cottage, Emsworth, Hants PO10 7HH, (☎ 0243 372249); 16 Land Port Terrace, Portsmouth PO1 2QT, (☎ 0705 827231)

GLANVILLE, Lt-Col Robert Cardew; OBE (Mil 1954), MC (1941), DL (Derbys 1967); s of Gerald Glanville, of St Germans Cornwall; *b* 28 Feb 1912; *Educ* Blundell's, Sandhurst; *m* 1947, Alice, da of John Allen, of Ilford; *Career* Reg Army Offr 1932-58; served WW II: E Africa and Ethiopia, Ceylon and Burma, NW Europe; Cdr Support Bn Supreme HQ Allied Powers Europe 1956-58, ret; TA sec Derbys 1958-68; *Recreations* gardening; *Clubs* Army and Navy, County (Derby); *Style—* Lt-Col Robert Glanville, OBE, MC, DL; Catchfrench, Bridge Hill, Belper, Derbys (☎ 077 382 3255)

GLASGOW, David George; s of Tom Glasgow, 55 Embercourt Road, Thames Ditton, Surrey, and Betty Madelaine, *née* Wells; *b* 18 Oct 1942; *Educ* Kings Coll Sch Wimbledon, RNC Dartmouth; *m* 5 Oct 1985, Bridget Gay Elizabeth, da of Joseph Stanley (John) Watson, MBE, QC of The Old Dairy, Micleham, Surrey; *Career* Lieut RN; serv naval interpreter (Italian) 1967, HMS Arethusa 1965- 67, HMS Albion 1967-70, HMS Cleopatra 1970-72 ret 1973; clerk Burge & Co Stockbrokers 1973-74, tech dir Schlesinger Tst Mangrs Ltd 1976-79 (joined 1974), Abbey Link Gp 1979-87: investmt mktg dir and md Abbey Unit Tsts Mangrs Ltd; Kleinwort Benson Investmt Mgmnt 1987-: dir and md Kleinwort Barrington Ltd, chm Unit Tst Customer Servs Ctee 1986, chm Unit Tst Assoc Info Ctee 1986; hon sec Castaway Club; memb Int Stock Exchange 1987; *Recreations* sailing, music, theatre, skiing; *Clubs* Royal Ocean Racing, Royal London YC; *Style—* David Glasgow, Esq; Inwardleigh Cottage, Rockbourne, Hants (☎ 072 53 500); 117 The Colonnades, Porchester Square, London W2; 31 Gordon Road, Cowes Isle of Wight; Kleinwort Benson Investment Management Ltd, 10 Fenchurch Street, London EC3M 3LB (☎ 01 623 8000, fax 01 929 2655)

GLASGOW, 10 Earl of (S 1703); Patrick Robin Archibald Boyle; also Lord Boyle

(S 1699), Lord Boyle of Kelburn (S 1703), Baron Fairlie (UK 1897); s of Rear Adm 9 Earl of Glasgow, CB, DSC (d 1984), and his 1 wife Dorothea, only da of Sir Archibald Lyle, 2 Bt, now Dorothea, Viscountess Kelburn; *b* 30 July 1939; *Educ* Eton, Sorbonne; *m* 1975, Isabel Mary, da of George Douglas James; 1 s (Viscount of Kelburn), 1 da (Lady Alice Dorothy b 1981); *Heir* s, Viscount of Kelburn, *qv*; *Career* Sub-Lt RNR; television documentary producer, dir and admin of Kelburn Country Centre; *Recreations* skiing, theatre, cinema; *Style*— The Rt Hon the Earl of Glasgow; Kelburn Estate, Fairlie, Ayr (☎ 047 556 685); 93 Hereford Rd, London W2 (☎ 01 727 9725)

GLASGOW, Archbishop of (RC) 1974-, and Metropolitan; Most Rev Thomas Joseph Winning; s of Thomas Winning (d 1959), and Agnes, *née* Canning (d 1951); *b* 3 June 1925; *Educ* Our Lady's HS Motherwell, Blairs Coll Aberdeen, St Peter's Coll Bearsden, Pontifical Scots Coll and Pontifical Gregorian Univ Rome (STL, DCL); *Career* ordained priest 1948; spiritual dir Pontifical Scots Coll Rome 1961-66, pres Scottish Catholic Tribunal 1970-71, aux bp Glasgow 1971-74; Hon DD Glasgow Univ 1983; pres Bishops' Conf of Scotland 1985; *Recreations* golf; *Style*— His Grace the Archbishop of Glasgow; The Oaks, 40 Newlands Rd, Glasgow G43 2JD; vicariate: 18 Park Circus, Glasgow G3 6BE (☎ 041 332 9473/4)

GLASGOW AND GALLOWAY, Bishop of; Rt Rev Derek Alec Rawcliffe; OBE (1971); s of James Alec Rawcliffe (d 1947), and Gwendoline Alberta Rawcliffe, *née* Dee; *b* 8 July 1921; *Educ* Sir Thomas Rich's Sch Gloucester, Univ of Leeds (BA, Eng Hons), Coll of the Resurrection Mirfield; *m* 10 Sept 1977, Susan Kathryn (d 22 July 1987), da of William Arthur Rawson Speight, certified accountant, of Kitkatts, Wetherby Rd, Bardsey, Leeds LS17 9BB; *Career* ordained priest 1945, asst priest St George's Claines, Worcester 1944-47, All Hallow's Sch Pawa, Solomon Is 1947-56 (headmaster 1953-56), St Mary's Sch Maravovo Sol Is 1953-58, archdeacon of Southern Melanesia 1958-74, asst bishop Melanesia 1974-75, bishop of New Hebrides 1975-80, bishop of Glasgow and Galloway 1981; *Recreations* music, numismatics; *Style*— The Rt Rev the Bishop of Glasgow and Galloway, OBE; Bishop's House, 48 Drymen Road, Bearsden, Glasgow G61 2RH (☎ 041 943 0612); Diocese of Glasgow & Galloway, 5 St Vincent Place, Glasgow G1 2DH (☎ 041 221 5720)

GLASS, Alick; s of Harry Glass, of Edinburgh, and Bessie, *née* Shemenski; *b* 10 August 1936; *Educ* Royal HS Edinburgh; *m* 5 Sept 1961, Ruth Marion, da of William Wolenberg; 1 s (Richard Andrew b 8 May 1966), 1 da (Suzanne Lesley b 10 Aug 1962); *Career* md Young Glover & Co Ltd 1958-62, chm and chief exec Glass Glover Gp plc 1962-, md Glass Assoc Ltd 1988; dir: Nat Fed of Fruit and Potato Trades Ltd, Fresh Fruit and Vegetable Info Bureau; memb The Fruiterers Co 1979; FIFP 1980; *Recreations* oratory, travel; *Style*— Alick Glass, Esq; Glass Assoc Ltd, 12 York Gate, London NW1 4QS (☎ 01 348 7913, fax 01 341 3783)

GLASS, Martin; JP (1986); s of Harry Glass (d 1959, of Swansea, and Bella, *née* Cohen (d 1975); *b* 27 Sept 1935; *Educ* Swansea GS, UWIST (Dip Arch), RIBA; *m* 12 May 1963, Norman Marcia, da of Hyman Corrick (d 1983), of Swansea; 2 da (Deborah b 1965, Judith b 1967); *Career* CA; princ of Martin Glass Chartered Architects 1960-; *Clubs* Rotary (Swansea); *Style*— Martin Glass, Esq, JP; 6 Richmond Villas, Ffynone, Swansea, W Glamorgan SA1 6DQ (☎ 0792 472331); 101 Walter Rd, Swansea, W Glamorgan SA1 5QF (☎ 0792 464123)

GLASS, William Ian; s of William Glass of Weybridge (fndr Glass's Guide to Used Car Values, d 1949), and Evelyn Ellen Glass (d 1963); *b* 13 Mar 1916; *Educ* George Watson's Coll Edinburgh, Univ of Grenoble France; *m* 1, Ruthene Eveline Marcia, *née* Driver-Williams; 1 s (David Ian b 1942), 1 da (Patricia Lynn Ruthene b 1947); m 2, Irene Joyce (Jill), da of Edward Claud Maby, of Nether Cerne, Dorset (d 1967); *Career* WWII 1939-46; Maj GSO2 RA(AA), 8 Army GSO2 Allied Armies in Italy; CA 1938; sec William Glass Ltd and Used Motor Shows, dir Brit Air Conditioners Ltd 1938-39, ptnr Tansley Witt & Co 1946-47, ptnr and dir Stevenson Jordan & Harrison 1947-67, dir William Glass Ltd (publishers Glass's Guides) 1950-63 (chm 1963-65); MBIM, MIMC, FInstD; *Recreations* sailing, skiing, rough shooting; *Clubs* Royal Lymington YC; *Style*— W Ian Glass, Esq; Blazemore Farm, Royden Lane, Boldre, Lymington, Hampshire (☎ 0590 23047)

GLASSE, Lady Margaret Nicola; *née* Sinclair; 2 da of 19 Earl of Caithness, CVO, CBE, DSO, JP, DL (d 1965), and Grizel Margaret, *née* Cunningham (d 1943); *b* 11 Sept 1937; *Educ* Seymour Lodge Sch Crieff; *m* 1, 29 Aug 1959, Capt (David) Colin Kirkwood Brown, late Gordon Highlanders, yr s of Gp Capt Hugh Mitchell Kirkwood Brown, of Croft Butts, Kingsbarns, Fife; 2 da (Nicola b 1960, Olivia b 1962); m 2, 9 July 1983, John James Maxwell Glasse, s of John Glasse, of Easton House, Corsham, Wilts; *Career* JP 1970-71; *Style*— Lady Margaret Glasse; The Old Rectory, Milton Bryan, Beds (☎ 0525 210 043)

GLASSON, Christopher Paul; s of Donald Trelawney Glasson; *b* 4 Jan 1941; *Educ* Latymer Upper Sch, Emmanuel Coll Cambridge; *m* 1964, Julie, *née* Gill; 2 children; *Career* chief exec Business Equipment Div Vickers plc 1981-87; dir: Roneo SA (France), Roneo Vickers Ltd (India) 1981-87; chm: Comforto Inc (USA) 1985-87, Comforto Systems (Switzerland) 1985-87, Pres Allsteel Inc 1987-, Koni Inc 1987-; *Recreations* golf, squash, music, philately; *Clubs* Naval and Military, Cambridge Union, MCC; *Style*— Christopher Glasson, Esq; 6N422 Woodhill Lane, St Charles, Illinois 60174, USA. Office ☎ 312 844 7201; 47 Rue des Dunes, 85680 La Gueriniere, France (☎ 51 39 85 76)

GLASSPOLE, Sir Florizel Augustus; ON (1973), GCMG (1981), GCVO (1983), CD (1970); s of late Rev Theophilus A Glasspole, and Florence, *née* Baxter; *b* 25 Sept 1909; *Educ* Wolmer's Boys' Sch, Ruskin Coll Oxford; *m* 1934, Ina Josephine Kinlocke; 1 da; *Career* accountant 1932-44, dir City Printery Ltd 1944-50, gen sec Jamaica TUC 1939-52, memb House of Representatives Jamaica 1944-73, min of Educn 1957-62 and 1972-73, ldr of House 1955-62 and 1972-73, min of Labour 1955-57, govr-gen of Jamaica 1983-; *Recreations* sports, gardening; *Style*— H E Sir Florizel Glasspole, ON, GCMG, GCVO, CD; King's House, Kingston 10, Jamaica

GLAUERT, Dr Audrey Marion; JP (Cambridge 1975); da of Hermann Glauert (d 1934), of Farnborough, Hants, and Muriel, *née* Barker (d 1949); *b* 21 Dec 1925; *Educ* Perse Sch for Girls Cambridge, Bedford Coll London (BSc, MSc), Clare Hall Univ of Cambridge (MA, DSc); *Career* asst lectr physics Royal Holloway Coll London 1947-50, Sir Halley Stewart fell and memb sci staff Strangeways Res Lab Cambridge 1950-, fell Clare Hall Univ of Cambridge 1966-; chm: Br Jt Ctee for Electron Microscopy 1968-72, Fifth Euro Congress of Electron Microscopy 1972; pres Royal Microscopical Soc 1970-72; hon: Societe Francaise de Microscopie Electronique, FRMS; *Books* Fixation, Dehydration and Embedding of Biological Specimens (1974); *Recreations* sailing, gardening; *Style*— Dr Audrey Glauert, JP; 29 Cow Lane, Fulbourn, Cambridge CB1 5HB (☎ 0223 880 463); 19 High Street, Blakeney, Holt, Norfolk NR25 7NA; Strangeways Research Laboratory, Worts Causeway, Cambridge CB1 4RN (☎ 0223 243 231)

GLAZE, Michael John Carlisle (James); s of Derek Glaze (d 1970), and Shirley Winifred Gardner, formerly Glaze, *née* Ramsay; *b* 15 Jan 1935; *Educ* Repton, St Catharine's Coll Cambridge (MA), Worcester Coll Oxford; *m* 1965, Mrs Rosemary Duff, da of Thomas McIntosh (d 1971), of Monifieth; 2 step da (Fiona, Deirdre); *Career* HM Overseas Civil Serv Lesotho 1959-70, dep permanent sec Miny of Fin; consul-gen: Abu Dhabi 1975-78, Rabat 1978-80, Bordeaux 1980-84; ambassador Republic of Cameroon 1984-; *Style*— James Glaze, Esq; c/o British Embassy, Yaoundé, c/o Foreign and Cwlth Office

GLAZEBROOK, Col David; OBE (1973); s of Col Arthur Rimington Glazebrook, MC, TD, and Joan Annie Glazebrook; *b* 28 Jan 1933; *Educ* Queen Elizabeth's GS Wakefield, RMA Sandhurst; *m* 30 Aug 1975, Clara Jane (Wink), da of Maj Harry Collett Bolt, MBE; 2 da (Samantha b 1977, Emma b 1978); *Career* cmmnd RTR 1953, seconded Malaysian Armed Forces 1957-60, seconded Trucial Oman Scouts 1965-67, seconded Sultan of Oman's Armed Forces 1970-73, CO 9 Bn UDR 1975-77, instr Nat Def Coll 1977-79, def attache Khartoum Sudan 1979-81, def attache Jakarta Indonesia 1983-85, def advsr Kuala Lumpur Malaysia 1985-87, ret 1988; Omani Distinguished Serv Medal 1973; *Recreations* golf, shooting, gardening; *Style*— Col David Glazebrook, OBE; Streete Farmhouse, Hope Mansell, Ross-on-Wye, Herefordshire HR9 5TJ)

GLAZEBROOK, (Reginald) Mark; s of Reginald Field Glazebrook (d 1986), and Daisy Isabel, *née* Broad; *b* 25 June 1936; *Educ* Eton, Pembroke Coll Cambridge (MA), Slade Sch of Fine Art; *m* 1 1965 (m dis 1969), Elizabeth Lea, *née* Claridge; 1 da (Lucy b 22 April 1966); m 2, 27 Sept 1974, Wanda Barbara, da of Ignacy Piotr Osinski, of Warsaw, Poland; 1 da (Bianca b 25 March 1975); *Career* Nat Serv 2 Lt Welsh Gds 1953-55; art critic London Magazine 1967-68, dir Whitechapel Art Gallery 1969-71, head of modern british pictures Colnaghi & Co Ltd 1972-75, gallery dir San Jose Univ USA 1976-78; dir: Editions Alecto 1979-81, Albemarle Gallery 1986-; princ exhibition catalogues written and edited: Artists and Architecture of Bedford Park 1875-1900, David Hockney Paintings Prints Drawings 1960-70 (1970), Edward Wadsworth Paintings Drawings and Prints (1974), John Armstrong (1957), John Tunnard (1977), The Seven and Five Soc (1979), Unit One Spirit of the 30's (1984), Mark Twain USA 1977, FRSA 1971; *Recreations* travelling, theatre, tennis, swimming; *Clubs* Beefsteak, Lansdowne; *Style*— Mark Glazebrook, Esq; Albemarle Gallery, 18 Albemarle Street, London W1X 3HA (☎ 01 355 1880)

GLAZEBROOK, William Field; s of Reginald Field Glazebrook (d 1986), of Brynbella, St Asaph, Clwyd, and Daisy Isabel, *née* Broad; *b* 18 June 1929; *Educ* Eton, Pembroke Coll Cambridge (MA); *m* 19 Sept 1959, Sara Elizabeth, da of Lt Cdr Arthur Frederick Whalley Boumphrey, DSC, DL (d 1988), of Maesmor Hall, Corwen, Clwyd; 3 s (Charles b 19 March 1961, Jonathan b 2 April 1964, Neil b 30 Oct 1966, d 2 Jan 1989); *Career* 2 Lt South Wales Borderers 1948-49; Capt Cheshire Yeo TA 1952-59; admitted slr 1956, ptnr Lace Mawer Liverpool and Manchester; chm Liverpool Merchants Guild; legal advsr Br Assoc for Shooting and Conservation; memb Law Soc 1956-; *Recreations* tennis, golf, fishing, shooting, gardening; *Clubs* Liverpool Racquet; *Style*— William Glazebrook, Esq; Pontruffydd Hall, Bodfari, Denbigh, Clwyd LL16 4BP (☎ 074 575 322); Castle Chambers, 43 Castle St, Liverpool L2 9SU (☎ 051 236 1634, fax 051 236 2585, telex 627229)

GLAZIER, Barry Edward; s of Edward Thomas Glazier (d 1976), of San Antonio, Ibiza, Spain, and Gladys Mabel, *née* Faulkner; *b* 1 July 1941; *Educ* Hurstpierpoint, St Peter's Coll Oxford (MA); *m* 1, 5 Aug 1970 (m dis), Lesley, da of John Richard Kirby (d 1986); 2 da (Anna b 1973, Rachael b 1976); m 2, 5 April 1984, Mrs Patricia McGregor, da of Cecil Mears (d 1977), of Wareham, Dorset; 1 da (Becky b 1985), 1 adopted step-da (Emma Sarah b 1981); *Career* slr 1966; sr ptnr Mooring Aldridge 1984-88, ptnr Lester Mooring Aldridge and Russell 1988-; hon slr Dorset Chamber of Commerce and Industy; memb Dorset War Pensions Ctee; memb Law Soc 1966; *Recreations* concerts, theatre, bird watching, gardening; *Clubs* Lanz (Bournemouth), The Wimborne; *Style*— Barry Glazier, Esq; Quarter Jack House, The Cornmarket, Wimborne, Dorset BH21 1JL (☎ 0202 885128); Lester Mooring Aldridge & Russell, Vandale House, Post Office Road, Bournemouth, Dorset BH1 1BT (☎ 0202 21426, fax 0202 290725, telex 417196)

GLEAVE, John Reginald Wallace; s of Rev Canon John Wallace Gleave (d 1979), of Cambridge, and Dorothy Littlefair, *née* Green (d 1978); *b* 6 April 1925; *Educ* Uppingham, Magdalen Coll Oxford (MA, BM, BCh); *m* 6 Sept 1952, (Margaret) Anne, da of Michael Robert Newbolt (d 1956), of Chester; 3 s (Mark b 1957, Humphry b 1959, Arthur b 1964), 3 da (Frances b 1954, Charity b 1961, Emily b 1965); *Career* Nat Serv Maj RAMC OIC Army Neurosurgical Unit 1952-54; neurosurgeon; dir E Anglian Neurosurgical and Head Injury Serv Addenbrookes Hosp Cambs, lectr in neurosurgery Univ of Cambridge; fell and praelector St Edmund's Coll Cambridge and lectr Magdalene Coll; OUBC 1946-48 (won boat race 1946), Leander 1948-49 (won grand 1949); FRCS 1957, FRSM 1975, SBNS 1962; *Recreations* coach to LMBC, gardening, travel; *Clubs* Vincent's, Leander, Utd Oxford and Cambridge; *Style*— John R W Gleave, Esq; Riversdale, Gt Shelford, Cambridge CB2 5LW (☎ 0223 843309); Neurosurgical Unit, Addenbrookes Hospital, Cambridge (☎ 0223 216762)

GLEDHILL, Anthony John; GC (1967); s of Harold Victor Gledhill, of 60 Meon Rd, Milton, Portsmouth, Hants, and Marjorie Edith, *née* Prout; *b* 10 Mar 1938; *Educ* Doncaster Tech HS; *m* 3 Sept 1958, Marie Lilian, da of William Hughes, of 43 Eastry Ave, Hayes, Bromley, Kent; 1 s (Stewart b 1 Sept 1961), 1 da (Rachel b 13 Sept 1963); *Career* accounts clerk offr's mess RAF Bruggen Germany 1953-56; Met Police: cadet 1956-57, police constable 1957-75, detective sgt 1976-87; PO Investigation Dept 1987, md FCA Ltd 1988-; memb Royal Br Legion Kent; *Recreations* football, carpentry; *Style*— Anthony Gledhill, Esq, GC; 98 Pickhurst Lane, Hayes, Bromley, Kent, BR2 7JD (☎ 01 462 4033); 6/7 Queen Street, London EC4N 1SP (☎ 01 236 8702)

GLEDHILL, Keith Ainsworth; DL (Lancashire 1986-); s of Norman Gledhill (d 1970), of Blackpool, and Louise, *née* Ainsworth (d 1988); *b* 28 August 1932; *Educ* Arnold Sch Blackpool; *m* 21 July 1956, Margaret Irene, da of Joseph Bramwell Burton (d 1970); 1 s (Ian C b 1958); *Career* jr offr MN 1950-54; Nat Serv RAF 1954-56; Norman Gledhill & Co Ltd 1956-65, Delta Metal Co Ltd 1965 (sr exec contract 1972); fndr: Gledhill

Water Storage Ltd 1972, Nu-Rad Ltd 1974, Thermal Sense (energy conservation systems) Ltd 1979; chm: bd govrs Arnold Sch Ltd, Lancs Youth Clubs Assoc, Talking Newspaper for the Blind Fylde Soc for the Blind, past offr Rotary Int, rotarian tstee Foxton Dispensary, govr Skelton Bounty Tst; MInstP 1970, FInstD 1968; *Recreations* golf; *Clubs* Royal Lytham and St Annes GC, Fylde RFC; *Style*— Keith Gledhill, Esq, DL; Broken Hill, 35 South Park Drive, Blackpool, Lancashire FY3 9PZ (☎ 0253 64 462); Gledhill Water Storage Ltd, Sycamore Estate, Squires Gate, Blackpool, Lancashire FY4 3RL (☎ 0253 401 494, fax 0253 49 657, telex 677631)

GLEDHILL, Michael William; s of George Eric Louis Gledhill (d 1986), of Shelf, nr Halifax, W Yorks, and Sarah Jane, *née* Green (d 1979); *b* 28 Oct 1937; *Educ* Rishworth Sch Halifax; *m* 18 Oct 1962, Margaret, da of Cyril Ira Fletcher (d 1965), of Hanson Lane, Halifax, W Yorks; 3 s (Marc b Nov 1963, Andrew b May 1966, Jonathan b June 1969); *Career* slr; ptnr Finn Gledhill & Co 1962-; Notary Public Halifax 1980; clerk: Waterhouse Charity Halifax 1965-, Tstees Abbotts Ladies Home Halifax 1967-, Wheelwright Charity (Rishworth Sch) 1985-; dir: G W Estates Ltd 1968, Michaels Estates Ltd 1970, Hanson Coach Servs Ltd 1980, Bellsounds Ltd 1983, Red Seal Ltd 1985, Gold Seal (Conveyancing) Ltd 1985, Halifax Incorporated Law Soc Ltd 1986, Hillodge Ltd 1987; *Recreations* golf, gardening, rugby; *Style*— Michael W Gledhill, Esq; Whiteshaw, Denholme, Bradford, BD13 4DE (☎ 0274 832665); Finn, Gledhill & Co, 2 Harrison Rd, Halifax, HX1 2AG (☎ 0422 53771, fax 0422 42604)

GLEESON, Dermot James; s of Patrick Joseph Gleeson, of 160 Sandy Lane, Cheam, Surrey, and Margaret Mary, *née* Higgins; *b* 5 Sept 1949; *Educ* Downside, Fitzwilliam Coll Cambridge (MA); *m* 6 Sept 1980, Rosalind Mary Catherine, da of Lt-Col Charles Edward Moorhead (d 1955), of Chipping, Campden, Glos; 1 s (Patrick b 1984), 1 da (Catherine b 1981); *Career* Cons Res Dept 1974-77 (asst dir 1979), Euro Cmmn (cabinet of C Tugendhat) 1977-79, EEC rep of Midland Bank (Brussels), dep chm MJ Gleeson Gp PLC 1982-88 (md, chief exec 1988); *Clubs* Utd Oxford and Cambridge, RAC; *Style*— Dermot Gleeson, Esq; Hook Farm, White Hart Lane, Wood Street, Surrey GU3 3EA (☎ 0483 236210); M J Gleeson Gp plc, Haredon House, London Road, North Cheam, Sutton, Surrey SM3 9BS (☎ 01 644 4321, fax 01 644 6366, car 0836 777972, telex 927762)

GLEESON, Judith Amanda Jane; *née* Coomber; da of Derek Young Coomber, of 10 Wraylands Drive, Reigate, Surrey and Jennifer Isabel, *née* Strudwick, JP; *b* 24 August 1955; *Educ* Reigate Co Sch for Girls, Lady Margaret Hall Oxford (MA), Université Libre de Bruxelles (Dip in Civil and Community Law); *m* 5 Jan 1980, Donald Frank Gleeson, s of George Aubrey Gleeson (d 1957); *Career* slr; pres West Surrey Law Soc 1987-88, chm Surrey Assoc of Women Slrs, vice-pres Oxford Univ Law Soc 1974-75; *Recreations* reading, study of language; *Clubs* Oxford Union; *Style*— Mrs Judith Gleeson; Hedleys, 6 Bishopsmead Parade, East Horsley, Surrey (☎ 04865 4567, fax 04865 4817, telex 265871 MONREF G, ref SJJ099)

GLEN, Sir Alexander Richard; KBE (1967, CBE 1964), DSC (1942, bar 1945); s of Richard Bartlett Glen, of Glasgow; *b* 18 April 1912; *Educ* Fettes Coll, Balliol Coll Oxford; *m* 1947, Baroness Zora Cartuyvels de Collaert, da of Ago Bukovac, of Dubrovnik; 1 s; *Career* served RNVR 1939-59; chm H Clarkson & Co 1958-73, dir BICC 1964-70, chm Br Tourist Authy 1969-77, dep chm Br Tport Hotels 1978-83; memb: Horserace Totalisator Bd 1976-84, Historic Bldgs Cncl 1976-80; chm V & A Museum Advsy Cncl 1978-83; former: explorer (Arctic), banker in New York, bd memb BEA and Nat Ports Cncl 1964-70; Gold Medallist Royal Geographical Soc 1940, Medallist Royal Soc of Edinburgh and Swedish Geographical and Anthropological Soc 1938; *Books* Under the Pole Star (1937), Footholds against a Whirlwind (1978); *Recreations* travel; *Clubs* City of London, Explorers (NYC); *Style*— Sir Alexander Glen, KBE, DSC; The Dower House, Stanton, Glos (☎ 038 673 301)

GLEN, (James) Hamish Robert; s of William Glen (d 1969), of Perthshire, and Irene Marjorie Stewart, *née* Sutherland; *b* 27 May 1930; *Educ* Merchiston Castle Sch Edinburgh; *m* 1956, Alison Helen Margaret, da of Robin Archibald Brown (d 1948); 3 s (William b 1957, Graeme b 1959, Iain b 1961); *Career* 2 Lt RA 1955-56 serv Hong Kong; CA Investmt Mgmnt, md The Scottish Investmt Tst plc 1981, dir The Scottish Life Assurance Co 1971 (chm 1987); *Recreations* golf, fishing; *Clubs* New (Edinburgh), Hon Co of Edinburgh Golfers; *Style*— Hamish Glen, Esq; 6 Albyn Place, Edinburgh (☎ 031 225 7781)

GLENAMARA, Baron (Life Peer UK 1977); Edward Watson Short; CH (1976), PC (1964); s of Charles and Mary Short, of Warcop, Westmorland; *b* 17 Dec 1912; *Educ* Bede Coll Durham Univ; *m* 1941, Jennie, da of Thomas Sewell, of Newcastle-upon-Tyne; 1 s, 1 da; *Career* WWII Capt DLI; sits as Labour peer in House of Lords; MP (L) Newcastle upon Tyne Central 1951-76, Oppn Whip (N) 1955-62, dep chief oppn whip 1962-64, govt ch whip (and Parly sec Treasy) 1964-66, Postmaster Gen 1966-68, sec state Educn and Sci 1968-70, ld pres Cncl and ldr Commons 1974-76, dep ldr Lab Pty 1972-76, chllr Newcastle upon Tyne Poly, pres Finchale Abbey Trg Coll for Disabled, chm Cable Wireless Ltd 1976-80; *Publications* Education in a Changing World, Birth to Five, I Knew my Place, Story of The Durham Light Infantry, The Infantry Instructor; *Style*— The Rt Hon Lord Glenamara, CH, PC; Glenridding, Cumbria (☎ 085 32273); 21 Priory Gardens, Corbridge, Northumberland (☎ 043 471 2880)

GLENAPP, Viscount; (Kenneth) Peter Lyle Mackay; s and h of 3 Earl of Inchcape; *b* 23 Jan 1943; *Educ* Eton; *m* 7 June 1966, Georgina, da of Sydney Charles Nisbet; 1 s, 2 da (Hon Elspeth b 1972, Hon Ailsa b 1977); *Heir* Hon Fergus James Kenneth Mackay b 9 July 1979; *Career* 2 Lt 9/12 Royal Lancers served: Aden, Arabian Gulf, BAOR; dir: Duncan MacNeill & Co Ltd, Inchcape (UK) Ltd, Inchcape Family Investments Ltd; AIB; *Recreations* shooting, fishing, golf, farming; *Clubs* White's, Oriental, City of London; *Style*— Viscount Glenapp; Manor Farm, Clyffe Pypard, nr Swindon, Wilts; 63E Pont St, London SW1; office: Sir John Lyon House, 5 High Timber St, Upper Thames St, London EC4

GLENARTHUR, Dowager Baroness; Margaret Risk; o da of late Capt Henry James Howie, of Stairaird, Mauchline; *m* 1 Sept 1939, as his 2 w, 3 Baron Glenarthur (d 1976); 2 s (4 Baron, Hon Matthew Arthur), 1 da (Hon Mrs Vernon); *Style*— The Rt Hon the Dowager Lady Glenarthur; Stairaird, Mauchline, Ayrshire (☎ 0290 50211)

GLENARTHUR, 4 Baron (UK 1918); Sir Simon Mark Arthur; 4 Bt (UK 1903); s of 3 Baron Glenarthur, OBE, DL (d 1976), by his 2 w (*see* Glenarthur, Dowager Baroness); *b* 7 Oct 1944; *Educ* Eton; *m* 12 Nov 1969, Susan, yr da of Cdr Hubert Wyndham Barry, RN, and Violet, da of Col Sir Edward Ruggles-Brise, 1 Bt; 1 s, 1 da (Hon Emily Victoria b 1975); *Heir* s, Hon Edward Alexander Arthur b 9 April 1973; *Career* sits as Cons peer in House of Lords; served Royal Hussars: cmmnd 1963, Capt 1970, Maj 1973, ret; served Royal Hussars TA 1975-80; MCIT; Capt Br Airways Helicopters Ltd 1976-82, dir Aberdeen & Texas Corporate Fin Ltd 1977-82; Govt whip (lord in waiting) 1982-83, parly under-sec state DHSS 1983-85, Parly under-sec Home Off 1985-86; min of State: for Scotland 1986-87, FCO 1987-; memb Queen's Body Guard for Scotland (Royal Co of Archers); *Recreations* field sports, flying, gardening, choral singing; *Clubs* Cavalry and Guards'; *Style*— The Rt Hon Lord Glenarthur; c/o House of Lords, London SW1A 0PW (☎ 01 270 2093)

GLENAVY, Baroness; Vivienne; o da of late Charles Knight, MC, of Ipswich, Suffolk; *m* 1, Eric Drake (decd); m 2, Hartley Sharpe (decd); m 3, Charles Orme; m 4, 24 Nov 1966, as his 3 w, 3 Baron Glenavy (Patrick Campbell, the author, who d 1980); *Style*— The Rt Hon Lady Glenavy; La Tranche, Le Rouret 06, France

GLENCONNER, Baroness; Lady Anne (Veronica); *née* Coke; eldest da of 5 Earl of Leicester, MVO (d 1976); *b* 16 July 1932; *m* 12 April 1956, 3 Baron Glenconner; 3 s, 2 da; *Career* an extra lady-in-waiting to HRH The Princess Margaret, Countess of Snowdon 1971-; *Books* The Picnic Papers (with Susanna Johnstone, 1983); *Style*— The Rt Hon Lady Glenconner; 50 Victoria Road, London W8; The Glen, Innerleithen, Peebleshire

GLENCONNER, 3 Baron (UK 1911); Sir Colin Christopher Paget Tennant; 4 Bt (UK 1885); s of 2 Baron Glenconner (d 1983), and his 1 w, Pamela, Baroness Glenconner, *qv*; *b* 1 Dec 1926; *Educ* Eton, New Coll Oxford; *m* 12 April 1956, Lady Anne Veronica Coke (*see* Glenconner, Baroness); 3 s, twin da (Hon May and Hon Amy b 1970); *Heir* s, Hon Charles Tennant; *Career* Lt Irish Gds; governing dir Tennants Estate Ltd 1967-, chm Mustique Co; *Style*— The Rt Hon Lord Glenconner; The Glen, Innerleithen, Peeblesshire; 50 Victoria Rd, London W8

GLENCONNER, Baroness Elizabeth; er da of late Lt-Col Evelyn George Harcourt Powell, Grenadier Gds, of 31 Hillgate Place, London W8; *m* 25 March 1935, as his 2 w, 2 Baron Glenconner (d 1983); 1 s, 2 da; *Style*— The Rt Hon Elizabeth, Lady Glenconner; Rovinia, Liapades, Corfu, Greece

GLENCONNER, Pamela, Baroness; Pamela Winifred; da of Sir Richard Arthur Surtees Paget, 2 Bt (d 1955), and his 1 wife, Lady Muriel Evelyn Vernon Finch-Hatton, CBE (d 1938), o da of 12 Earl of Winchilsea and Nottingham; *m* 25 Sept 1925 (m dis 1935), 2 Baron Glenconner (d 1983); 2 s; *Style*— Pamela, Lady Glenconner; Hill Lodge, Hillsleigh Rd, London W8

GLENCROSS, David; s of John William Glencross, of Salford, Lancs (d 1962), and Elsie May, *née* Ward; *b* 3 Mar 1936; *Educ* Salford GS, Trinity Coll Cambridge (BA); *m* 1965, Elizabeth Louise, da of Jack Turner Richardson (d 1977), of Birmingham; 1 da (Juliet b 1966); *Career* BBC gen trainee various posts in radio and TV prodn 1958-70, sr programme offr 1970-76, head programme offr 1976-77, dir TV IBA 1983- (dep dir 1977-83); fell Royal TV Soc, FRSA; *Recreations* music, reading, walking, idling; *Style*— David Glencross, Esq; IBA, 70 Brompton Rd, London SW7 1EY

GLENDEVON, 1 Baron (UK 1964); of Midhope, Co Linlithgow; John Adrian Hope; ERD (1988); yr (twin) s of 2 Marquess of Linlithgow, KG, KT, PC, GCSI, GCIE, OBE, TD (d 1952); *b* 7 April 1912; *Educ* Eton, Christ Church Oxford (MA); *m* 21 July 1948, Elizabeth Mary, o da of (William) Somerset Maugham, CH, FRSL, and former w of Vincent Paravicini; 2 s; *Heir* s, Hon Julian John Somerset Hope, *qv*; *Career* Maj Scots Gds Res; WWII 1939-45; serv; Narvik, Salerno, Anzio (despatches twice); MP (C): Midlothian N and Peebles 1945-50, Edinburgh Pentlands 1950-64; min Works 1959-62 (jt Parly under-sec Scotland 1957-59, Parly under-sec of state Cwlth Rels 1956-57 and Foreign Affrs 1954-66); chm: Royal Cwlth Soc 1963-66, Historic Bldgs Cncl England 1973-75, Geigy (UK) Ltd 1967-71; dir and dep chm Ciba-Geigy (UK) Ltd 1971-78; dir: Colonial Mutual Life Assur Soc Ltd 1952-54 and 1962-82, British Electric Traction Omnibus Serv 1947-52 and 1962-82; FRSA 1962; *Books* The Viceroy at Bay (1971); *Clubs* White's; *Style*— The Rt Hon Lord Glendevon, PC; Mount Lodge, Mount Row, St Peter Port, Guernsey, CI (☎ 0481 21516)

GLENDINNING, James Garland; OBE (1973); s of George Moffat Glendinning (d 1965), of Edinburgh, and Isabella, *née* Green (d 1951); *b* 27 April 1919; *Educ* Boroughmuir Edinburgh, Military Coll of Sci; *m* 1, 28 Aug 1943, Margaret Euphemia (decd), da of James Donald (d 1916); 1 da (Jennifer Ann b 1948 d 1986); m 2, 23 Oct 1980, Anne Ruth, da of Adalbert Horn (d 1984), of Reutlingen; *Career* WWII 1939-46 London Scottish (Gordon Highlanders) and REME (cmmnd Capt); HM inspr of taxes 1946-50; Shell Petroleum Co Ltd in London 1950-58; dir: Shell Egypt, Anglo Egyptian Oilfields in Egypt 1959-61; gen mangr PT Shell (Indonesia) in Borneo and East Java 1961-64, Shell Int London 1964-67, vice-pres (Japan) Shell Sekiyu KK, Shell Kosan KK 1967-72, md Japan Shell Technol KK, dir Showa Sekiyu KK 1967-72, chm Br C of C in Japan; bd memb London Tport Exec 1972-80; chm North American Property Unit Tst 1975-80, dir The Fine Art Soc plc 1972-; md Gestam Int Realty Ltd 1980-84; chm Masterpack Ltd 1980-, dir LE Vincent & Ptnrs Ltd 1984-; *Clubs* Caledonian, Oriental; *Style*— James Glendinning, Esq, OBE; 20 Albion Street, London W2 2AS; 162/168 Regent Street, London W1R 5TB

GLENDINNING, Prof Robert; s of James Watson Glendinning (d 1953), and Isabella Butters, *née* Smeaton (d 1954); *b* 11 August 1912; *Educ* Glasgow HS, Glasgow Univ (MA); *m* 25 Sept 1941, Helena Lilian, da of John Greig Fenton (d 1953); 2 da (Aileen b 1944, Lorna b 1947); *Career* CA; various financial and accounting appts, Br Tport Cmmn 1948-62, BR Bd 1962-72, conslt (mainly tport and engrg accounting and fin) 1972-, pt/t lectr in fin and mgmnt accounting Stirling Univ visiting prof of accounting Queen's Univ of Belfast, prof of financial mgmnt Int Mgmnt Centre Buckingham; contrib: The Accountant, Accountancy Age, Management Accounting; FCMA, FCIT, FIOD, JDipMA; *Recreations* lawn tennis; *Clubs* IOD; *Style*— Prof Robert Glendinning; 10 Copperfields, Beaconsfield, Bucks HP9 2NS (☎ 09496 4341)

GLENDINNING, Hon Victoria (Hon Mrs de Vere White); *née* Seebohm; da of Baron Seebohm, TD (Life Peer), and Evangeline, da of His Hon Sir Gerald Hurst, QC; *b* 23 April 1937; *Educ* St Mary's Wantage, Millfield, Somerville Coll Oxford (BA, MA, Dip Social Admin); *m* 1, 6 Sept 1958 (m dis 1981), Prof (Oliver) Nigel Valentine Glendinning; 4 s; m 2, 1982, Terence de Vere White, *qv*; *Career* author and journalist; FRSL; *Books* A Suppressed Cry, Elizabeth Bowen: Portrait of a Writer, Edith Sitwell: A Unicorn among Lions, Vita, Rebecca West, Hertfordshire, The Grown Ups; *Recreations* gardening; *Style*— The Hon Victoria Glendinning; c/o David Higham Associates, 5-8 Lower John St, Lower W1R 4HA

GLENDYNE, 3 Baron (UK 1922); Sir Robert Nivison; 3 Bt (UK 1914); s of 2 Baron Glendyne (d 1967); *b* 27 Oct 1926; *Educ* Harrow; *m* 25 April 1953, Elizabeth, yr da of Sir (Stephen) Cecil Armitage, CBE, JP, DL, of Hawksworth Manor, Notts; 1 s, 2 da; *Heir* s, Hon John Nivison; *Career* WWII Lt Grenadier Gds; sr ptnr R Nivison & Co (stockbrokers) 1967-86; *Clubs* City of London; *Style*— The Rt Hon the Lord Glendyne; Hurdcott, Barford St Martin, Salisbury, Wilts (☎ Wilton 2221)

GLENKINGLAS, Baroness; Anne; da of Sir Neville Pearson, 2 Bt, by his 1 w, Hon Mary Angela Mond (da of 1 Baron Melchett); *b* 5 Feb 1923; *m* 11 Sept 1940, Baron Glenkinglas, PC (Life Peer, d 1984); 4 da; *Style*— The Rt Hon Lady Glenkinglas; 7 Egerton Gardens, London SW3 2BP

GLENN, Sir (Joseph Robert) Archibald; OBE (1965); s of Joseph Robert Glenn (d 1946), of Sale, Victoria, Australia, and Evelyn, *née* Lockett (d 1939); *b* 24 May 1911; *Educ* Scotch Coll Melbourne, Melbourne Univ, Harvard Univ, La Trobe Univ Victoria (Hon Doctor of Univ); *m* 1939, Elizabeth Mary Margaret, da of James Schofield Balderstone (d 1954); 1 s, 3 da; *Career* professional engr and co dir; chm and md ICI Aust 1963-73, dir Bank of NSW (now Westpac Banking Corpn) 1967-84, dir ICI Ltd London 1970-75, chm IMI Aust 1970-78, govr Atlantic Inst of Int Affrs 1973-78, chllr La Trobe Univ 1964-72; kt 1966; *see Debrett's Handbook of Australia and New Zealand for further details*; *Style*— Sir Archibald Glenn, OBE; 1A Woorigoleen Rd, Toorak, Vic 3142, Australia (☎ 241 6367)

GLENNIE, Hon Mrs (Jane Maureen Thérèse); *née* Dormer; er da of 15 Baron Dormer (d 1975), and Lady Maureen Fellowes, *née* Noel; *b* 20 Nov 1945; *m* 1, 21 July 1966 (m dis 1978), (Henry Alistair) Samuel Sandbach; 1 s (James), 1 da (Emma); m 2, 1980, Sqdn Ldr Geoffrey E Meek, RAF (d 1984); m 3, 16 Jan 1988, Lt Cdr R N F Glennie; *Career* landowner; *Recreations* travel; *Clubs* Itchenor SC; *Style*— The Hon Mrs Glennie; 44 Homefield Rd, Chiswick, London W4 (☎ 01 994 4795); Church Farm Cottage, East Wintering, West Sussex (☎ 0243 673226)

GLENNY, (Alexander) Keith; s of Lt-Col Clifford Roy Glenny, TD, of 28 Crosby Rd, Westcliff-On-Sea, Essex, and Eileen Winifred, *née* Smith (d 1974); *b* 19 July 1946; *Educ* Charterhouse, Gonville and Caius Coll Cambridge (MA, LLM); *m* 19 April 1975, Rachel Elizabeth, da of Rev A C Fryer, of Byfield House, Byfield, Northants; 2 s (Christopher b 5 Jan 1977, Matthew b 31 Oct 1986), 1 da (Anna b 24 May 1979); *Career* slr British Oxygen Co Ltd 1970-72; Hatten Asplin Channer and Glenny Barking Essex: slr 1972-74, ptnr 1974-88, sr ptnr 1988-; clerk Barking and Ilford Utd Charities and Barking Gen Charities, govr Barking Abbey Sch; Freeman Worshipful Co of Poulters 1978; memb Law Soc; *Clubs* Wig and Pen, City Livery; *Style*— Keith Glenny, Esq; Netherfield, Powdermill Lane, Leigh, Tonbridge, Kent TN11 8PY (☎ 0732 833 320); 4 Town Quay Wharf, Abbey Rd, Barking IG11 7BZ (☎ 01 591 4131, fax 01 591 1912)

GLENNY, (Reginald Thomas) Rex; CBE (1964); s of Walter Glenny (d 1955), of Beckenham, Kent, and Mary Elizabeth, *née* Dawes (d 1962); *b* 10 July 1914; *Educ* Alleyn's Sch Dulwich; *m* 1, 1939, Edith Hawthorne (d 1957), da of late Harry Stevenson; 1 da (Margaret, d 1950) m 2, 1960, Florence Eliza (Betty), da of Joseph Wilson (d 1956), of St Marylebone, London W1; *Career* WWII Capt TA served France 1940, cmmnd IA 1942, discharged Capt 1946; stockbroker 1948-, ptnr Charles Stanley & Co 1975-, chm bd of fin London Diocese C of E 1977-, Gtr London Area Cons Assoc 1969-72, F-GP Age Concern, Westminster, vice-pres Alexandra Rose Day; *Recreations* church and charitable work; *Clubs* MCC; *Style*— Reginald Glenny Esq, CBE; 22 Clarewood Court, Seymour Place, London W1 (☎ 01 262 8217); Charles Stanley and Co, Gardenhouse, 18 Finsbury Circus, London EC2M 7BL (☎ 01 638 5717)

GLENTON, Anthony Arthur Edward; MBE (1983), TD (1974); s of Lt Col Eric Cecil Glenton (d 1978), of Gosforth, Newcastle, and Joan Lydia, *née* Taylor; *b* 21 Mar 1943; *Educ* Merchiston Castle Sch Edinburgh; *m* 8 April 1972, Caroline Ann, da of Maurice George Meade-King, of Clifton, Bristol; 1 s (Peter b 1977), 1 da (Sophie b 1974); *Career* joined TA 1961, Lt-Col 1984, cmd 101 (Northumbrian) Field Regt RA (V) 1984-86, Col 1986, dep cdr 15 Inf Bde; ADC to HM the Queen 1987; sr ptnr Ryecroft Glenton & Co; dir: Port of Tyne Authy 1987, Newcastle Bldg Soc 1987; Liveryman Worshipful Co of Chartered Accountants England & Wales, Freeman City of London; FCA 1971; *Recreations* shooting, skiing, sailing; *Clubs* Army & Navy; *Style*— Anthony Glenton, MBE, TD; Whinbank, Rothbury, Northumberland (☎ 0669 20361); 27 Portland Terrace, Jesmond, Newcastle upon Tyne NE2 1QP (☎ 091 2811292)

GLENTORAN, 2 Baron (UK 1939); Sir Daniel Stewart Thomas Bingham Dixon; 4 Bt (UK 1903), KBE (1973), PC (NI 1953); s of 1 Baron, OBE, PC, JP, DL (d 1950), and Hon Emily, *née* Bingham (da of 5 Baron Clanmorris); *b* 19 Jan 1912; *Educ* Eton, Sandhurst; *m* 20 July 1933, Lady Diana Mary, *née* Wellesley, er da of 3 Earl Cowley; 2 s (Hon Thomas b 1935, Hon Peter b 1948, 1 da (Hon Mrs Rudolph Agnew b 1937); *Career* served WWII and as regular Gren Gds, Lt-Col ret; Hon Col 6 Bn RUR (TA); MP (U) NI Parl Belfast Bloomfield 1950-61, min Commerce 1953-61, min NI Senate 1961-72 (speaker 1964-72); HM Lieut Belfast 1950-76, Lord-Lieut 1976-85; *Style*— The Rt Hon Lord Glentoran; Drumadarragh House, Doagh, Co Antrim, N Ireland (☎ Doagh 222)

GLENTWORTH, Viscount; Edmund Christopher Pery; s and h of 6 Earl of Limerick, KBE; *b* 10 Feb 1963; *Educ* Eton, New Coll Oxford, Pushkin Inst Moscow, City Univ; *Career* called to the Bar Middle Temple 1987; HM Dip Serv: FCO 1987-88, Ecole Nationale d'Adminstration 1988-89; *Recreations* skiing, travel, music; *Style*— Viscount Glentworth; 30 Victoria Road, London W8 (☎ 01 937 1954)

GLENWRIGHT, Harry Donald; s of late Harry Glenwright, and Minnie Glenwright; *b* 25 June 1934; *Educ* Stockton-on-Tees Sec Sch, Durham Univ (BDS), Newcastle Univ (MDS); *m* 29 Dec 1966, Gillian Minton, da of late Arthur Holland Thacker; 1 s (Robert b 1970), 1 da (Kate b 1973); *Career* house surgn Newcastle Dental Hosp 1957-58, Surg Lt (D) RN 1958-61, registrar Eastman Dental Hosp 1961-63, lectr in dental surgery Birmingham Univ 1963-66, lectr in periodontics Queens Univ of Belfast 1966-69, Br Cncl scholar Oslo Univ 1968, Cncl of Europe scholar Aarhus and Oslo Univs 1971, Br Cncl scholar Colombo Univ 1985, sr lectr in periodontology Birmingham Univ 1969-; external examiner: Dublin Univ 1978, London Univ 1979-81, Manchester Univ 1979-86, Belfast Univ 1980-83, Leeds Univ 1985-87, RCS 1988-; pres Br Soc of Periodontology 1980-81, and section of odontology Birmingham Med Inst 1981-82, cncl memb conslt in Restorative Dentistry Gp 1987-, memb: specialist advsy ctee in Restorative Dentistry 1987-, centl ctee for Hosp Dental Servs 1988, Dental Health and Sci Ctee 1988; FDSRCS; *Recreations* gardening, reading; *Style*— Harry Glenwright, Esq; White House, Rushbrook Lane, Tanworth-in-Arden, Warwickshire B94 5HP (☎ 056 44 2578); The Dental School, St Chads Queensway, Birmingham B4 6NN (☎ 021 236 8611)

GLICHER, Julian Harvey; s of Samuel Glicher (d 1982), and Dorothy Glicher (d 1983); *b* 15 June 1948; *Educ* Haberdashers' Aske's Sch Elstree, Ashridge Sch of Mgmnt; *m* 18 Aug 1976, Adrienne, da of Phillip Rose, of Elstree; 2 s (Toby Oliver b 1978, Nicholas David b 1980); *Career* CA; sr exec Price Waterhouse Paris 1968-72, mangr Hambros Bank 1972-77, asst dir Lloyds Merchant Bank 1977-85, ptnr and nat dir corporate fin Clark Whitehill 1987- (dir 1985); FCA 1978; *Recreations* badminton, cycling, sailing, family; *Style*— Julian H Glicher, Esq; 25 New St Sq, London EC4A 3LN (☎ 01 353 1577, fax 01 353 2803, telex 887422)

GLIDEWELL, Rt Hon Lord Justice; Rt Hon Sir Iain Derek Laing; PC (1985); s of Charles Norman Glidewell, and Nora Glidewell; *b* 8 June 1924; *Educ* Bromsgrove Sch, Worcester Coll Oxford; *m* 1950, Hilary, da of late Clinton D Winant; 1 s, 2 da; *Career* barr 1949, QC 1969, chm Panels for Examination Structure Plans: Worcs 1974, W Midlands 1975; rec Crown Ct 1976-80, conducted Heathrow Fourth Terminal Enquiry 1978, appeal judge IOM 1979-80, High Ct judge (Queen's Bench) 1980-85, memb Supreme Ct Rule Ctee 1980-83, presiding judge NE circuit 1982-85; kt 1980; *Style*— Rt Hon Sir Iain Glidewell; Royal Courts of Justice, Strand, London WC2

GLIN, 29 Knight of (The Black Knight, Irish hereditary knighthood dating c 1300-30, though first authenticated use dates from 1424); Desmond John Villiers FitzGerald; s of 28 Knight of Glin (Desmond Windham Otho FitzGerald, d 1949, descended from John Fitz-Thomas FitzGerald (d 1261), father of three bros, The White Knight, The Knight of Glin and The Knight of Kerry (*qv*); *b* 13 July 1937; *Educ* Stowe, Univ of British Columbia, Harvard; *m* 1, 6 Oct 1966 (m dis 1970), Lulu (Louise) Vava Lucia Henriette, da of Alain, Marquis de la Falaise de la Coudraye, of Paris; m 2, 12 Aug 1970, Olda Anne, o da of Thomas Willes, of Brompton Sq, London SW; 3 da; *Career* asst and dep keeper furniture and woodwork dept Victoria and Albert Museum 1965-75, Irish agent Christie's 1975-; vice-pres Irish Georgian Soc, dir Irish Georgian Fndn, dir and past chm Historic Irish Tourist Houses Assoc, tstee Castletown Fndn; author of books and articles on Irish art and architecture; FSA; *Books* Ireland Observed (with Maurice Craig, 1975), Lost Demesnes (with Edward Malins, 1976), The Painters of Ireland (with Anne Crookshank, 1978), Vanishing Country Houses of Northern Ireland (jtly 1988); *Recreations* art, history; *Clubs* White's, Beefsteak, Kildare and Univ (Dublin); *Style*— The Knight of Glin; 52 Waterloo Rd, Dublin 4 (☎ 0001 680585); Glin Castle, Co Limerick, Eire (☎ 068 34173 and 34112)

GLOAK, Graeme Frank; CB (1980); s of Frank Gloak, MBE (d 1979), of Kent, and Lilian Phoebe; *b* 9 Nov 1921; *Educ* Brentwood; *m* 1944, Mary Beatrice, da of Stanley James Thorne (d 1953), of Essex; 2 s (Nigel (decd), Malcolm b 1951), 1 da (Karen b 1960); *Career* RN 1941-45, Lt RNVR served Atlantic, North Sea, France; slr 1947; slr for Customs and Excise 1978-82; vice-chm Agric Wages ctee for Essex and Herts 1987-, chm Agric Dwellings Housing advsy ctee for Essex and Herts 1984-, memb Barking and Havering Family Practitioners ctee 1986-; *Publications* Customs and Excise Halsbury's Laws of England; *Recreations* badminton, walking, watching cricket; *Clubs* MCC, Essex CCC (Chelmsford); *Style*— Graeme Gloak, CB; Northwold, 123 Priests Lane, Shenfield, Essex (☎ 0277 212748)

GLOCK, Sir William Frederick; CBE (1963); s of William George Glock; *b* 3 May 1908; *Educ* Christ's Hosp, Caius Coll Camb; *m* 1, 1944, Clemency, da of Swinburne Hale; m 2, 1952, Anne Genevieve, da of Charles Geoffroy-Dechaume; *Career* dir Summer Sch of Music: Bryanston 1948-52, Dartington Hall 1953-79; former music critic The Observer and New Statesman, controller of music BBC 1959-72, former memb bd dir Royal Opera House and Arts Cncl, dir Bath Festival 1975-84, chm London Orch Concerts Bd 1975-; kt 1970; *Style*— Sir William Glock, CBE; Vine House, Brightwell cum Sotwell, Wallingford, Oxon (☎ 0491 37144)

GLOSSOP, Peter; s of Cyril Glossop, and Violet Elizabeth Glossop; *b* 6 July 1928; *Educ* High Storrs GS Sheffield; *m* 1, 1955 (m dis 1977), Joyce Elizabeth Blackham; m 2, 1977, Michèle Yvonne Amos; 2 da; *Career* singer (baritone) guest artist: Royal Opera House (Covent Garden), La Scala (Milan), Met Opera (NY); *Style*— Peter Glossop, Esq; c/o Green Room, 8 Adam St, London WC2

GLOUCESTER, Archdeacon of; *see*: Wagstaff, Ven Christopher John Harold

GLOUCESTER, 37 Bishop of (cr 1541) 1975-; Rt Rev John Yates; patron of 80 livings and Archdeaconries of Gloucester and Cheltenham; See (formerly part of Diocese of Worcester) founded by Henry VIII (along with Bristol, with which Gloucester was combined 1836-97); s of Frank Yates and Edith Ethel Yates, of Burslem; *b* 17 April 1925; *Educ* Battersea GS, Blackpool GS, Jesus Coll Cambridge, Lincoln Theological Coll; *m* 1954, Jean Kathleen Dover; 1 s, 2 da; *Career* served RAFVR 1943-47; took seat in House of Lords Nov 1981; curate Christ Church Southgate 1951-54, tutor and chaplain Lincoln Theological Coll 1954-59, vicar Bottesford-with-Ashby 1959-65, princ Lichfield Theological Coll 1966-72, suffragan bishop Whitby 1972-75; *Clubs* RAF; *Style*— The Rt Rev the Lord Bishop of Gloucester; Bishopscourt, Pitt St, Gloucester GL1 2BQ (☎ (0452) 24598)

GLOVER, Anthony Richard Haysom; 2 s of Arthur Herbert Glover (d 1941), and Margorie Florence Glover; *b* 29 May 1934; *Educ* Emmanuel Coll Cambridge; *m* 1960, Ann Penelope, da of John Scupham, OBE, of Harpenden, Herts; 2 s, 1 da; *Career* dep controller HMSO 1976-; *Style*— Anthony Glover, Esq; 7 Hillside Rd, Thorpe St Andrew, Norwich (☎ 33508)

GLOVER, Lady; (Margaret) Eleanor; *m* 1, Erwin Hurlimann (decd), of Schloss Freudenberg; m 2, 1976, as his 2 w, Col Sir Douglas Glover, TD, sometime MP (C) for Ormskirk (d 15 Jan 1982); *Style*— Lady Glover; Schloss Freudenberg, 6343 Rotkreuz, Kanton Zug, Switzerland (☎ 042 641126); 94 Avenue d'Iéna, 75116 Paris, France (☎ 720 0481)

GLOVER, Eric; s of William Arthur Glover (d 1965), of Liverpool, and Margaret, *née* Walker; *b* 28 June 1935; *Educ* Liverpool Inst HS, Oriel Coll Oxford (MA); *m* 1960, Adele Diane, da of Col Cecil Geoffrey Hilliard, of Bournemouth; 3 s (Ian, Paul, Jason); *Career* sec-gen Chartered Inst of Bankers 1982-89 (dir of studies 1968-82); *Recreations* golf, squash, tennis; *Clubs* Overseas Bankers; *Style*— Eric Glover, Esq; 12 Manor Park, Tunbridge Wells (☎ 0892 31221); The Chartered Inst of Bankers, 10 Lombard St, London EC3V 9AS

GLOVER, Gen Sir James Malcolm; KCB (1981), MBE (1964); s of Maj-Gen Malcolm Glover, CB, OBE (d 1970), and Jean Ogilvie, *née* Will; *b* 25 Mar 1929; *Educ* Wellington, RMA Sandhurst; *m* 1959, Janet Diones, da of Maj Hugo De Pree; 1 s, 1

da; *Career* cmmnd RA 1949, RHA 1950-54, instr RMA Sandhurst 1955-56, transferred to Rifle Bde 1956, Bde Maj 48 Gurkha Bde 1960-62, directing staff Staff Coll 1966-68, CO 3 Bn Royal Green Jackets 1970-71, Col Gen Staff MOD 1972-73, cdr 19 Airportable Bde 1974-75, Brig Gen Staff (Intelligence) MOD 1977-78, Cdr Land Forces NI 1979-80, Lt-Gen 1981, dep chief Def Staff (Intelligence) 1981-83, vice-chief Gen Staff MOD and memb Army Bd of Def Cncl 1983-85, C-in-C UKLF 1985-87, Col Cmdt Royal Green Jackets 1983-88, ret 1987; chm Delta Data Systems Ltd; dir: Br Petroleum plc, Airship Industs; *Recreations* shooting, hillwalking, gardening; *Clubs* Boodle's; *Style—* Gen Sir James Glover, KCB, MBE; c/o Lloyd's Bank Ltd, 6 Pall Mall, London SW1

GLOVER, Dr Jane Aliston; da of Robert Finlay Glover, TD, of Malvern, Worcs, and Jean, *née* Muir; *b* 13 May 1949; *Educ* Monmouth Sch for Girls, St Hugh's Coll Oxford, (BA, MA, DPhil); *Career* freelance conductor; musical dir: Glyndebourne Touring Opera 1982-85, London Choral Soc 1983-; artistic dir London Mozart Players 1984-; appeared with many orchestras and opera cos incl: BBC Proms 1985-, Royal Opera House Covent Garden 1988; sr res fell St Hughs Coll Oxford 1982-; memb Worshipful Co of Haberdashers; Hon: DMus Exeter Univ 1986, Hon DUniv Open Univ 1988, Hon DLitt Loughborough 1988; RMA 1974, RSA 1988; *Books* Cavalli (1978); *Recreations* Times Crossword, theatre; *Style—* Dr Jane Glover; c/o Lies Askonas Ltd, 186 Drury Lane, London WC2B 5RY (☎ 01 405 1708)

GLOVER, Gp Capt John Neville; CMG (1963), QC (Western Pacific Territories, 1961); s of John Robert Glover (d 1965), and Sybil, *née* Cureton (d 1983), of Hayes Barton, Exbourne, Devon; *b* 12 July 1913; *Educ* Tonbridge; *m* 1, 1940, Margaret Avice, da of Stanley George Burdick, MBE; 1 s; m 2, 1956, June Patricia Bruce, da of late Wing Cdr Arthur Bruce Gaskell, DSC; *Career* served RAF 1934-46; SASO 44 Gp 1943; RAF Res of Offrs 1946-59; barr 1949; legal advsr Western Pacific High Cmmn and attorney-gen Br Solomon Islands 1957-63, law revision cmmr and legal draftsman for various overseas territories 1967-; *Recreations* fly fishing; *Clubs* RAF; *Style—* Group Capt John Glover, CMG, QC; Clam End, Trebullett, Launceston, Cornwall PL15 9QQ (☎ 0566 82347)

GLOVER, Malcolm; *b* 3 Nov 1943; *Educ* Doncaster GS, Univ of Bristol (LLB); *m* 30 March 1973, Diane Marilyn; 1 s (Matthew b 1977), 2 da (Katie b 1975, Caroline b 1983); *Career* Wilde Sapte 1970-: slr 1970-71, ptnr 1971-88, dep sr ptnr 1988-; memb Worshipful Co Slrs; memb Law Soc; *Recreations* tennis, theatre; *Style—* Malcolm Glover, Esq; 31 Ossulton Way, Hampstead Gdn Suburb, London N2 0JY; Wilde Sapte, Queensbridge House, 60 Upper Thames St, London EC4V 3BD (☎ 01 236 3050, fax 01 236 9624, telex 887793 WILDES G)

GLOVER, Maj Gen Peter James; CB (1966), OBE (1948); s of George Herbert Glover, CBE (d 1955), of Sheephatch House, Tilford Surrey, and Constance Eliza, *née* Sloane (d 1965); *b* 16 Jan 1913; *Educ* Uppingham, Emmanuel Coll Camb (MA); *m* 1946, Wendy, da of Henry George Fuller Archer, OBE (d 1944), of Trevone, Weybridge, Surrey; 1 s (Jeremy), 2 da (Philippa, Elizabeth); *Career* 2 Lt RA 1934, served WWII BEF France and Far East, Lt-Col 1956, Brig 1961, Cmdt Sch of Artillery Larkhill 1960-62, Dir RA 1966-69, ret Col Cmdt RA 1970-78; *Recreations* sailing (Trisul); *Clubs* Royal Western YC; *Style—* Maj-Gen Peter Glover, CB, OBE; Lukesland, Diptford, Nr Totnes, Devon (☎ 054882 229)

GLOVER, Dr Richard Berry; s of Henry Graham Glover (d 1931), of Hove, Sussex, and Marjorie Florence, *née* Covell (d 1978); *b* 9 Dec 1928; *Educ* Charterhouse, Middx Hosp London Univ (MB BS); *m* 24 April 1957, (Joan Elizabeth) Ann, da of C Stuart Chiesman (d 1969), of Bickley, Kent; 1 s (Mark Berry b 24 April 1959), 1 da (Sarah Jane (Mrs Tice) b 23 May 1962); *Career* Flt Lt surgical div med branch RAF; RAF Hosps: Nocton Hall, Uxbridge, Halton 1954-58; house surgn and ENT house surgn Middx Hosp 1952-53, sr ptnr med practice Oxshott (joined 1958); MO: Sandown Park Racecourse 1973, Epsom Racecourse 1978, Kempton Park Racecourse 1986, Reed's Sch Cobham 1985; memb Worshipful Co of Innholders 1961; MRCS, LRCP 1952; memb: BMA, Med Equestrian Assoc; *Recreations* sailing; *Clubs* RAC, Royal Corinthian YC, Royal Lymington YC; *Style—* Dr Richard Glover; Spinnycroft, Leatherhead Rd, Oxshott, Surrey KT22 0ET; 5 Totland Ct, Victoria Rd, Milford-On-Sea, Hants SO41 0NR (☎ 0372 843 088); Oxshott Med Centre, Holtwood Rd, Oxshott, Surrey KT22 0QL (☎ 0372 842 503)

GLOVER, Robert Finlay; TD (1954); s of Dr Terrot Reaveley Glover (d 1943), and Alice Emily Cornelia, *née* Few (d 1956); *b* 28 June 1917; *Educ* The Leys Sch, Corpus Christi Coll Oxford (BA, MA); *m* 28 June 1941, Jean, da of Norman Gordon Muir (d 1962), of Lincoln; 1 s (Richard b 1952), 2 da (Catherine b 1947, Jane b 1949); *Career* Maj RA (TA) 1939-46, Staff Coll Camberley 1944; asst master Ampleforth Coll 1946-50, head of classics The Kings Sch Canterbury 1950-53; headmaster: Adams' GS Newport Shropshire 1953-59, Monmouth Sch 1959-76; dep sec HMC 1977-82; Fell Woodard Corpn 1982-87; Liveryman Worshipful Co of Haberdashers 1976; *Books* Notes on Latin (1954), Latin for Historians (1954); *Recreations* normal; *Clubs* East India, Devonshire, Sports and Public Schs; *Style—* Robert Glover, Esq, TD; Brockhill Lodge, West Malvern Rd, The Wyche, Malvern, Worcs WR14 4EJ (☎ 0684 564 247)

GLOVER, Timothy Mark; s of John Stafford (d 1958), and Francess Mary, *née* Hodson; *b* 22 Feb 1951; *Educ* Sir Anthony Browne's Sch, Brentwood; *m* 26 June 1976, Sally Alexandra, da of Col Peter Anthony Stevens, of Chatley Lodge, Norton St Philip, Bath, Somerset; 2 da (Rebecca Kate b 15 Aug 1982, Jessica Fleur b 11 Sept 1984); *Career* dir sales and mktg Border TV plc 1984-; *Recreations* sailing, shooting, fishing, squash, music; *Clubs* IOD; *Style—* Timothy M Glover, Esq

GLYN, Dr Alan; ERD, MP (C) Windsor and Maidenhead 1974-; s of John Paul Glyn (d 1938), and Margaret, *née* Johnston; *b* 26 Sept 1918; *Educ* Westminster, Gonville and Caius Coll Cambridge, Bart's and St George's Hosps; *m* 4 Jan 1962, Lady Rosula Caroline, *née* Windsor-Clive, *qv*, 3 da of 2 Earl of Plymouth, PC, and Lady Irene, *née* Charteris, da of 11 and 7 Earl of Wemyss and March; 2 da; *Career* WWII served Far East 1942-46, psc 1945; re-employed as Capt (Hon Maj) Royal Horse Gds 1967; attached French Foreign Legion 1960 (by special permission of French Govt) doctor 1948, barrister 1955; co-opted memb LCC Educn Ctee 1956-58; MP (C): Wandsworth Clapham 1959-64, Windsor 1970-74; memb: No 1 LCC Divnl Health Ctee 1959-61, Chelsea Borough Cncl 1959-62, Inner London Med Ctee 1967-, GLC Valuation Panel 1967-; former govr of Henry Thornton and Aristotle Schs ; one of the Earl Marshal's Green Staff Offrs at Investiture of HRH The Prince of Wales at Caernarvon 1969; govr body of Br Postgrad Med Fedn London Univ 1968-81, memb bd of govrs Nat Heart and Chest Hosps 1982-; Freeman City of London 1961, memb Soc of Apothecaries 1961; (with freedom fighters in Hungarian Revolution 1956) awarded Pro-Hungarian Medal of Sov Mil Order of Malta; war corr in Vietnam; *Publications* Witness to Vietnam the Containment of Communism in SE Asia, Let's Think Again; *Clubs* Pratt's, Carlton, Special Services; *Style—* Dr Alan Glyn, ERD, MP; 17 Cadogan Place, London SW1 (☎ 01 235 2957); House of Commons, London SW1

GLYN, Hon Andrew John; yr s of 6 Baron Wolverton, CBE (d 1988); bro and h of 7 Baron; *b* 30 June 1943; *Educ* Eton, New Coll Oxford (MA); *m* 1, 1965 (m dis 1986), Celia Laws; 1 s (Miles John b 1966), 1 da (Lucy Abigail b 1968); m 2, 1986, Wendy Carlin; *Career* fell Corpus Christi Coll Oxford; 64 Hurst Street, Oxford

GLYN, Sir Anthony Geoffrey Leo Simon; 2 Bt (UK 1927); s of Sir Edward Rae Davson, 1 Bt, KCMG (d 1937), and Margot Elinor, OBE (d 1966), da of Clayton Louis Glyn, and Elinor Sutherland (the novelist Elinor Glyn); assumed by deed poll 1957 the surname of Glyn in lieu of his patronymic and the additional forename of Anthony; *b* 13 Mar 1922; *Educ* Eton; *m* 2 Oct 1946, Susan Eleanor, da of Lt-Col Sir Rhys Rhys Williams, 1 Bt, DSO, QC; 1 da (and 1 da decd); *Heir* bro, Christopher Michael Edward Davson; *Career* Capt Welsh Gds 1941-46; author; Vermeil Medal City of Paris 1985; *Principal works* The Ram in the Thicket, Elinor Glyn (a biography), I Can Take It All, The Seine, The Dragon Variation, The Blood of a Britishman, The Companion Guide to Paris (1985); *Recreations* skiing, music, chess; *Clubs* Pratt's; *Style—* Sir Anthony Glyn, Bt; Marina Baie des Anges, Ducal Apt U-03, 06270 Villeneuve Loubet, Alpes Maritimes, France

GLYN, Barbara Louvain; da of William Charles Ritchie Jardine, of Oxford; *m* 1, Gp Capt Francis Henwood, DFC; m 2, 1970, as his 2 w, Sir Richard Hamilton Glyn, 9 Bt, OBE, TD, DL (d 1980); *Clubs* Kennel; *Style—* Barbara, Lady Glyn; 53 Belgravia Court, Ebury St, London SW1W 0NY (☎ 01 730 1963)

GLYN, Hilary Beaujolais; s of Maurice Glyn, of Albury Hall, Ware, and Hon Maud, *née* Grosvenor, da of 2 Baron Ebury, DL, by his w, Hon Emilie White yr da of 1 Baron Annaly; *b* 12 Jan 1916; *Educ* Eton, New Coll Oxford; *m* 1938, Caroline, da of William Perkins Bull, QC (d 1948), of Toronto, Canada; 1 s (James b 1939), 2 da (Ann b 1941, Sarah b 1948); *Career* md Gallaher Ltd 1975-76; ret; *Recreations* gardening, shooting; *Style—* Hilary Glyn, Esq; Castle Hill Cottage, Boothby, Graffoe, Lincoln LN5 0LF (☎ 0522 810885)

GLYN, Dr John Howard; s of Sidney Glyn, and Clair Beatrice, *née* Vos; *b* 18 May 1921; *Educ* Harrow, Jesus Coll Cambridge (BA, MA), Middx Hosp Med Sch, NY Univ Med Sch; *m* 2 April 1947, Daphne Barbara, da of Hugh Robert Bayley, of Chingford; 1 s (Ian Robert Howard b 14 Feb 1951), 1 da (Gillian Clair Philippa (Mrs Readman) b 2 Sept 1954); *Career* Flt Lt RAFVR nemopsychiatric unit Princess Mary RAF Hosp Halton 1947-49; conslt physician: Prince of Wales Hosp Tottenham 1957, St Charles Hosp London W2 1969, Osborne House, St Dunstan; Liveryman Worshipful Co of Apothecaries; FRCP; *Books* Cortisone Therapy (1959); *Recreations* tennis, skiing, golf, photography; *Clubs* Hurlingham, Royal Society, Medicine, Sonning GC; *Style—* Dr John Glyn; 35 Sussex Sq, London W2 2PS (☎ 01 262 9187); Pool Ct, Thames St, Sonning-on-Thames (☎ 0734 693116)

GLYN, Sir Richard Lindsay; 6 Bt (1800) of Gaunt's House, Dorset, and 10 Bt (1759); s of Sir Richard Hamilton Glyn, OBE, TD, 5 and 9 Bt (d 1980), and Lyndsay Mary Baker; *b* 3 August 1943; *Educ* Eton; *m* 1970 (m dis 1979), Carolyn Ann, da of Roy Frank Williams, of Pasadena, Calif, USA (1979); 1 s, 1 da; *Heir* s Richard Rufus Francis Glyn b 8 Jan 1971; *Career* 2 Lt Royal Hamps Regt 1962-65; Studio Orange Ltd (Photography and Design) 1966-71, Gaunts Estate 1972, farmer 1976-; underwriting memb Lloyd's 1976-; *Style—* Sir Richard Glyn, Bt; Ashton Farmhouse, Stanbridge, Wimborne, Dorset (☎ Witchampton 840585)

GLYN, Lady Rosula Caroline; *née* Windsor-Clive; yst da of 2 Earl of Plymouth, PC (d 1943); *b* 30 April 1935; *m* 4 Jan 1962, Dr Alan Glyn, ERD, MP, *qv*; 2 da (Mary b 1963, Anne b 1964); *Career* OStJ; *Style—* Lady Rosula Glyn; 17 Cadogan Place, SW1

GLYNN, Prof Ian Michael; s of Hyman Glynn (d 1984), and Charlotte, *née* Fluxbaum; *b* 3 June 1928; *Educ* City of London Sch, Trinity Coll Cambridge (MA, PhD, MD), Univ Coll Hosp; *m* 9 Dec 1958, Jenifer Muriel, da of Ellis Arthur Franklin, OBE (d 1964); 1 s (Simon b 1964), 2 da (Sarah b 1959, Judith b 1961); *Career* Nat Serv Flt Lt RAF Med Branch 1956-57; house physician Centl Middx Hosp 1952-53; Univ of Cambridge: fell Trinity Coll 1955-, demonstrator in physiology 1958-63, lectr 1963-70, reader 1970-75, prof of membrane physiology 1975-86, vice master Trinity Coll 1980-86, prof of physiology 1986-; visiting prof Yale Univ Sch of Med 1969-; memb: MRC 1976-80, cncl of Royal Soc 1979-81, Agric and Food Res Cncl 1981-86; Hon MD Aarhus (Denmark) 1988; FRS 1970, FRCP 1987, Hon Foreign memb American Acad of Arts & Sciences 1984; *Books* The Sodium Pump (ed with C Ellory 1985), The Company of Biologists; *Style—* Prof Ian Glynn; Daylesford, Conduit Head Rd, Cambridge CB3 0EY (☎ 0223 353 079); Physiological Laboratory, Downing St, Cambridge CB2 3EG (☎ 0223 333 869, fax 0223 333 840, telex CAMSPL G)

GLYNN, Stanley Frederick Henry; *b* 5 August 1918; *Educ* Mercers'; *m* 1943, Mary Keith, *née* Dewdney; 2 da; *Career* served with army in N Africa, Egypt, Italy, Greece; Maj; auctioneer, estate agent, Knight Frank and Rutley 1935-79; govr BUPA 1970, chm BUPA Med Fndn 1979; v-chm Regency Building Soc 1970-; chm: Chislehurst & Mottingham Housing Assoc, Sidcup Housing Assoc; memb Lloyd's, Freeman City of London, Liveryman Worshipful Co Tallow Chandlers and Glass-sellers; *Recreations* tennis, walking, gardening, watching cricket; *Clubs* Carlton, MCC, Farmers', Inst of Dirs; *Style—* Stanley Glynn, Esq; Rosemount, Cricket Ground Rd, Chistlehurst, Kent (☎ 01 467 5197); 21 Cliffe House, Radnor Cliff, Folkestone, Kent (☎ 0303 48008)

GLYNNE-WALTON, Hon Mrs (Caroline Jane Grenville); *née* Morgan-Grenville; raised to the rank of a Baron's da 1947; yst da of Rev Hon Luis Chandos Francis Temple Morgan-Grenville, Master of Kinloss (d 1944), els 11 Baroness Kinloss; sis of Lady Kinloss, *qv*; *b* 21 Mar 1931; *Educ* Privately, Ravens Croft School Eastbourne; *m* 18 Sept 1958, Gordon Glynne-Walton, FRGS, FRMetSoc, FRAS, FGS, late Duke of Wellington's Regt, s of late Thomas Henry Walton, of Batley, Yorks; 1 da (Charlotte b 1961); *Recreations* gardening, reading, walking, music; *Style—* Hon Mrs Glynne-Walton; White Lea Grange, Batley, W Yorks

GOAD, Sir (Edward) Colin Viner; KCMG (1974); s of late Maurice George Viner Goad, of Cirencester, Glos, and Caroline, *née* Masters; *b* 21 Dec 1914; *Educ* Cirencester GS, Gonville and Caius Coll Camb (BA); *m* 1939, Joan Olive Bradley (d 1980); 1 s; *Career* under-sec Min of Tport 1963, sec-gen Intergovernmental Maritime Consultative Orgn 1968-74 (dep sec-gen 1963-68), ret 1974; memb Advsy Bd Int Bank Washington DC 1975-, conslt Liberian Shipowners' Cncl 1976-; *Recreations* gardening,

18th Century furniture; *Style*— Sir Colin Goad, KCMG; The Paddock, Ampney Crucis, Cirencester, Glos (☎ Poulton 028 585 353)

GOADBY, Dr Hector Kenneth; s of Sir Kenneth Weldon Goadby, KBE (d 1959), of 83 Harley St, London W1, and Eva, *née* Olding (d 1962); *b* 16 May 1902; *Educ* Winchester Coll, Cambridge (MD); *m* 22 May 1937, Margaret Evelyn, da of Richard Boggon (d 1956), of Seaton, Hillside Ave, Worthing, Sussex; 1 s (Jack Weldon b 14 March 1978), 2 da (Juliet Mary b 8 Oct 1940, Hilary Jane b 3 Feb 1953); *Career* RAMC 1942-45; physician: St Thomas's Hosp London 1937-46, St Peters Hosp Chertsey 1940-46; Beckley Hort Soc: sec 1971, chm 1977, pres 1988; memb TOCH 1971-; Freeman Worshipful Co of Grocers; FRCP 1937-; *Recreations* golf, sailing; *Clubs* Royal Cruising, Rye GC; *Style*— Dr Hector Goadby; Dolphin Cottage, Rye, East Sussex TN31 7PT (☎ 079 78355)

GOBBO, Hon Sir James Augustine; s of Antonio Gobbo and Regina, *née* Tosetto; *b* 22 Mar 1923; *Educ* Xavier Coll, Melbourne Univ (BA), Rhodes Scholar 1952, Magdalen Coll Oxford (MA); *m* 1957, Shirley, da of S Lewis; 2 s, 3 da; *Career* barr 1956; ind lectr in Evidence Melbourne Univ 1964-68, QC 1971, Judge of Supreme Ct of vic 1978-; chm: Aust Refugee Cncl 1977, Victoria's 150 Advsy Panel 1984-85, Aust Bicentennary Multicultural Task Force 1982, Mercy Private Hosp 1977-87, supervisory ctee Childrens Protection Soc 1982-, Italian Historical Soc 1980-, Task Force for the Italian Aged 1983-, Caritas Christi Hospice 1986-, Order of Malta Hospice Home Care Serv 1986-, Reference Gp into Public Library Funding 1987, Aust Cncl of Multicultural Affrs 1987-, Aust Bicentennial Multicultural Fndn 1988-; pres Sovereign Mil Order of Malta (Aust) 1987- (vice pres 1984-87), CO AS IT Italian Assistance Assoc 1979-84 and 1986-, Scout Assoc (Victorian branch) 1987-; memb: Aust Population and Immigration Cncl 1975-83, Victoria Law Fndn 1972-84, Newman Coll Cncl 1970-85, RC Archdiocese Fin Advsy Cncl 1970, Mercy Maternity Hosp Bd 1972-, Sisters of Mercy Health Care Cncl 1977-, Cncl of the Order of Aust 1982-, Italo-Aust Educn Fndn 1974-, exec Cncl of Judges 1986-, Victorian Health Promotion Fndn 1988-, Palladio Fndn 1989-; pt/t cmmr Law Reform Cmmn of Victoria 1985-88; tstee Opera Fnd (Victoria) 1983-; hon fell Aust Inst of Valuers 1985; Commendatore all'Ordine di Merito of the Republic of Italy 1973; kt of Magistral Grace Sov Mil Order of Malta; kt 1982; *Books* ed Aust edn Cross on Evidence, numerous papers; *Style*— Hon Sir James Gobbo; 6 Florence Ave, Kew, Vic 3101, Australia (☎ 03 817 1669, business ☎ 03 603 6149)

GOBERT, Gerald; s of Dr Richard Gobert (d 1954), of Meadway Court, Hampstead, and Greta, *née* Kaufman (d 1954); *b* 20 June 1925; *Educ* King Edward VI Sch, Regent St Poly; *m* 27 Aug 1960, Rosemary, da of Dr Bertram Shires (d 1943), of Welbeck St, London W1; 4 da (Julia 10 March 1961, Loretta b 16 Oct 1962, Rachel b 24 Aug 1965, Gina b 18 June 1968); *Career* fndr Gallwey Chem Co 1951, Protim and Gallwey 1954 (plc 1967, merger with FOSECO MINSEP 1969) chm Chemplant Stainless; inventor Protimer 1954, two Royal Warrants for Protim and Gallwey (wood preservative and timber treatment); memb ctee for local Sch's (Godstowe, St Helen's, Northwood); memb: NSPCC, political ctees, active in numerous local fundraising events; Freeman City of London, liveryman Worshipful Co of Clockmakers 1973; CEng, MIMechE, MIWSc, MInst BEng, FFBldg, FInstD; *Recreations* travel, the garden, my family; *Style*— Gerald Gobert, Esq; Woodchester, Knotty Green, Beaconsfield HP9 2TN; Chemplant, Rickmansworth, Herts (☎ 089582 2466/8, fax 089582 2469, telex 933969 CHEMPT G)

GOBLE, James Blackley Hague; s of Leslie Herbert Goble, CMG (d 1969), of The Pound House, Brabourne Lees, Ashford, Kent, and Lilian Miriam, *née* Cunningham; *b* 21 July 1927; *Educ* Marlborough, Corpus Christi Coll Cambridge; *m* 1, 24 Nov 1951, Barbara Mary (d 1986), da of Sir Thomas Claude Harris Lea Bt (d 1985), of Worcs; 2 s (Timothy b 1957, Jonathan b 1961); m 2, 4 June 1988, Yvonne Patricia Jane Coke-Wallis, da of Lt-Col John Stone (d 1988); *Career* Coldstream Gds 1945, Gdsman O/ Cadet Worcs Regt 1946-48, Capt; admin offr HM Overseas Civil Serv Gold Coast Ghana: class 4 1950, class 3 1956, class 2 1959; J Walter Thompson London: assoc dir 1967, sr assoc dir 1970, dir 1971-86, sr vice-pres int 1983-86; dir: Pillar Pubns 1987-, Winston Churchill Travelling Fellowships Fndn Inc USA 1988-; memb Br Standards Inst Advsy Panel on Publicity 1971-84, advsy cnsllr English Speaking Union 1976-83;MIPA 1971-86; *Recreations* ornithology, shooting, building; *Style*— James Goble, Esq; Court Farm, Upton Snodsbury, Worcs WR7 4NN (☎ 0905 60 314)

GODBER, (Robert) Christopher; s of Geoffrey Chapman Godber, CBE, DL, *qv*; *b* 3 Nov 1938; *Educ* Bedford, Merton Coll Oxford; *m* 1962, Frances Merryn Candy, da of Capt Ernest Howard Stanley Bretherton (d 1960); 3 s, 1 da; *Career* Lt Nat Serv 1956-58, served Kenya, Mau Mau Emergency; dir main bd Travis Perkins plc, dir Travis Perkins Trading Co Ltd, dir Travis & Arnold plc (responsible for group policy on timber and forest products) 1973-88 (branch mangr Travis & Arnold Rugby 1969-73, branch mangr Travis & Arnold Camb 1967-69), dir King's Lynn Wood Preservation 1973-, Sussex Timber Preservation 1975-, chm East Anglian Timber Trade Assoc 1988-; *Recreations* sailing (yacht 'Minnow'), shooting; *Clubs* Banbury Sailing, Leander, Royal Agric Soc of England; *Style*— Christoper Godber, Esq; Staverton Acres, Staverton, Daventry, Northamptonshire NN11 6JY (☎ 0327 71223); Travis & Perkins plc, Lodge Way House, Harlestone Rd, Northampton NN5 7UG (☎ 0604 52424, telex 311386)

GODBER, Geoffrey Chapman; CBE (1961), DL (W Sussex 1975); s of Isaac Godber (d 1957), of Willington Manor, Beds, and Bessie Maud, *née* Chapman; bro of Sir George Edward Godber, *qv*, and late Baron Godber, of Willington; *b* 22 Sept 1912; *Educ* Bedford Sch, London Univ (LLB); *m* 1937, Norah Enid, da of Reginald John George Fletcher Finney (d 1942), of Derbys; 3 s (Christopher b 1938, *qv*, Jonathan b 1942, Peter b 1945); *Career* slr 1936; clerk of CC and Lieutenancy Shropshire 1944-66 and West Sussex 1966-75; memb sundry govt ctees 1953-75 incl Central Advsy Water Ctee 1961-70, SE Econ Planning Cncl 1969-75; chm Weald and Downland Museum 1975-82 (pres 1988-), memb Br Waterways Bd 1975-81; dep chm: Chichester Harbour Conservancy 1975-78, Shoreham Port Authy 1976-82; *Recreations* sailing; *Clubs* Naval & Military, Sussex; *Style*— Geoffrey Godber, Esq, CBE, DL; Pricklows, Singleton, Chichester, W Sussex (☎ 024 363 238)

GODBER, Sir George Edward; GCB (1971, KCB 1962, CB 1958); s of Isaac Godber (d 1957), of Willington Manor, Beds and Bessie Maud, *née* Chapman; bro of Geoffrey Chapman Godber, *qv*, and late Baron Godber of Willington; *b* 4 August 1908; *Educ* Bedford Sch, New Coll Oxford (BA, DM), London Hosp; *m* 1935, Norma Hathorne, da of W H T N Rainey; 2 s, 1 da (and 2 s, 2 da decd); *Career* dep chief med offr Miny of Health 1950-60, QHP 1953-56, chief med offr DHSS, DES and Home Office 1960-73; chm Health Educn Cncl 1976-78; DPH, FRCP, FFCM; *Style*— Sir George Godber, GCB; 21 Almoners' Avenue, Cambridge CB1 4NZ (☎ Cambridge 0223 247 491)

GODBER, Hon Richard Thomas; s of Baron Godber, of Willington, PC, DL (Life Peer, d 1980), and Baroness Godber, of Willington, *qv* (*née* Miriam Sanders); *b* 4 June 1938; *Educ* Bedford Sch; *m* 1962, Candida Mary, da of late Albert Edward Parrish; 1 s 2 da; *Career* Lt Royal Lines 1956-58 (served Malaya); farmer, horticulturist; vice-pres Bucks Assoc Boys Clubs (chm 1977-86); chm: CLA Game Fair, Stowe 1981, Bucks CLA 1987-; Cncl memb RASE 1970-; Hon Dir Royal Show 1987-; *Recreations* shooting, gardening; *Clubs* Farmers', Anglo-Belgian, Bedford; *Style*— Hon Richard Godber; Hall Farm, Little Linford, nr Milton Keynes, Bucks

GODBER, Hon (Andrew) Robin; yr s of Baron Godber, of Willington, PC, DL, of Willington Manor, Bedford (Life Peer, d 1980), and Baroness Godber, of Willington, *qv*; *b* 7 Sept 1943; *Educ* Bedford Sch; *m* 1969 Genevieve, da of late Kenneth Parrish, of Higham Gobion, Herts; 2 s; *Career* author, boat builder; *Recreations* sailing; *Clubs* Sandwich Bay Sailing; *Style*— Hon Robin Godber; Tan House, Tanhouse Lane, Peasmarsh, Rye, Sussex TN31 6UY

GODBER, Baroness; Violet Ethel Beatrice; JP; da of George Albert Lovesy, of Cheltenham, Glos; *m* 29 Aug 1914, 1 and last Baron Godber (d 1976); 2 da (Hon Mrs Andrew Agnew b 1917, Hon Mrs A Debenhom b 1923); *Style*— The Rt Hon Lady Godber, JP; Cranesden, Mayfield, Sussex (☎ 3271)

GODBER OF WILLINGTON, Baroness; Miriam; da of Haydon Sanders, of Lowestoft; *m* 1936, Baron Godber of Willington, PC (Life Peer, d 1980); 2 s (Hon Richard *qv*, Hon Robin *qv*); *Style*— The Rt Hon Lady Godber of Willington; Willington Manor, nr Bedford

GODDARD, Anthony John; s of Henry Gordon Goddard, DSO, DFC, AFC, and Nicolette Julienne Louise Arluison; *b* 27 May 1941; *Educ* The Oratory Sch Oxford, Leicester Univ (Dip Arch), Univ of Illinois (MArch); *m* 16 March 1968 (m dis 1987), Gretchen Drew, da of Stanley Damon (d 1975), of USA; 1 s (Sam b 1979); *Career* architect; asst prof of architecture Univ of Illinois 1967-68; ptnr Goddard Manton Partnership London 1969-, specialising in the redevpt of London's Dockland, FRIBA, FIAVE (1972); *Recreations* travel, motor racing; *Style*— Anthony J G Goddard, Esq; The Manor House, Newton Harcourt, Leicestershire (☎ Gret Glen 2986); 60 Weston Street, London SE1 (☎ 01-403 4741, fax 01-403 2705)

GODDARD, David Rodney; MBE (1985); s of Air Marshall Sir Victor Goddard, KCB, CBE (d 1987), of Brasted, Kent, and Mildred Catherine Jane, *née* Inglis (d 1979); *b* 16 Mar 1927; *Educ* Bryanston, Wanganui Collegiate Sch NZ, Peterhouse Coll Cambridge (MA); *m* 14 April 1951, Susan, da of Maj Gilbert Ashton, MC (d 1981), of Abberley, Worcester; 3 s (Stephen b 1952, Anthony b 1 54, Thomas b 1958), 1 da (Tessa b 1963); *Career* Lt 44 Commando RM 1945-47; Lt Somerset LI 1952 served: Germany 1952, Malaya 1952-55, regtl depot Taunton 1955-58; KAR 1959-62, army DS with RM offrs Wing 1963-66, staff duties Bahrain 1966-68, ILI N Ireland 1968, ret with rank of Maj at own request 1968; fndr Int Sailing Craft Assoc Ltd 1965, chief ldr Br Schs Exploring Soc Expdn to Arctic Norway 1965, dir Exeter Maritime Museum 1969-; *Recreations* shooting, fishing, sailing, photography; *Style*— David Goddard, Esq, MBE; The Mill, Lympstone Exmouth, Devon EX8 5HH (☎ 0392 265575); ISCA Ltd, The Haven, Exeter, Devon EX2 8DT (☎ 0392 58075)

GODDARD, Maj Douglas George; *b* 4 Nov 1920; *Educ* Roan Sch Blackheath, Brighton Tech Coll; *m* Eve; 1 s (Nigel Johnson), 1 da (Christina Lynne); *Career* reg cmmn RA; serv: Normandy landing, NW Europe Campaign (Germany, Egypt and Jordan), instr Royal Sch of Artillery, resigned 1959 (awarded BAOR C-in-C's certificate 1946);1959-64: div sec Sulzer Bros Ltd, asst sec and chief accountant Mallery Batteries Ltd; Chartered Inst of Bldg 1964-85: sec and dir central servs, dep chief exec, controller nat project Bldg Tommorrow's Heritage 1984; Wokingham DC: cncllr rep Wargrave and Remenham 1978-, chm recreation and amenities ctee 1980-83, vice-chm fin and gen purposes ctee 1985, vice-chm 1986-88, chm 1988-89; memb: tsteeship ctee Nat Info Age Project, governing body and local ctee Bulmershe Coll Higher Educn, St Mary's PCC and stewardship ctee (sidesman), ctee Wargrave Cons Branch, ctee Wargrave Housing Assoc, mgmnt ctee Wargrave News (chm), ctee Wargrave Resident's Assoc (former tres), Woodclyffe Alnishouse Tstee Ctee, mgmnt ctee Lower Early Youth and Community Centre, policy and resources ctee Southern Cncl for Sport and Recreation, Bracknell and Wokingham Jt Golf Courses Ctee (chm 1983-); rotarian Rotary Club Ascot 1973-79; memb: Chatham Dining Club, Friends of Henley Festival, Friends Wokingham Choral Soc, Phyllis Ct Club Henley-on-Thames, Royal Br Legion Wargrave, Royal Soc St George, Wargrave and Shiplake Regatta, Wargrave Local Hist Soc; patron Henley Running Club; hon sec Berks Industry Year 1986 Campaign 1985, co chm Industry Matters Campaign 1987; Queen's Sister Jubilee Medal 1977; Liveryman (Freeman) City of London; FCIS; *Clubs* MCC, Reading CC, Reading Hockey, Sonning GC; *Style*— Maj Douglas Goddard

GODDARD, Harold Keith; QC (1979); s of Harold Goddard (d 1979), of Stockport, Cheshire, and Edith Goddard; *b* 9 July 1936; *Educ* Manchester GS, CCC Cambridge; *m* 1, 1963 (m dis), Susan Elizabeth, yr da of late Ronald Stansfield, of Wilmslow, Cheshire; 2 s; m 2, 1983, Maria Alicja, da of Czeslaw Lazuchiewicz (d 1981), of Lodz, Poland; *Career* barr 1959; recorder Crown Ct 1978-; *Style*— Harold Goddard, Esq, QC; 1 Dean's Court, Crown Square, Manchester (☎ 061 834 4097)

GODDARD, Maj-Gen John Desmond; MC (1944); s of Maj J Goddard, HAC (d 1968), of Bombay and Gerrards Cross, Bucks; *b* 13 Jan 1919; *Educ* Sherborne, RMA Woolwich; *m* 1948, Sheila Noel Vera, da of C W H P Waud (d 1976), of Bombay and St John, Jersey; 3 s, 1 da; *Career* cmmnd RA 1939, served WW II France, N Africa, Italy (despatches), CRA 3 Div 1965-56, BGS Mil Ops MOD 1966-69, dir Mil Assistance Office MOD 1969-72, ret 1972; *Recreations* yachting (yacht 'Amoret'); *Clubs* Army & Navy, Royal Lymington Yacht; *Style*— Maj-Gen John Goddard, MC; Cranford, Pinewood Hill, Fleet, Hants

GODDEN, Rumer; da of late Arthur Leigh Godden, of Lydd House, Aldington, Kent, and Katherine Norah Hingley; *b* 10 Dec 1907; *Educ* Moira House Eastbourne Sussex; *m* 1, 1934, Laurence Sinclair Foster; 2 da (Jennifer, Janaki); m 2, 1949, James Haynes-Dixon, OBE (d 1973); *Career* author; chief books incl: Chinese Puzzle (1935), The Lady and The Unicorn (1937), Black Narcissus (1939), Breakfast with the Nikolides (1941), Fugue in Time (1944), The River (1946), A Candle for St Jude (1948), Kingfishers Catch Fire (1952), An Episode of Sparrows (1955), The Greengage Summer (1959), China Court (1961), The Battle of the Villa Fiorita (1963),

In This House of Brede (1969), Prayers from the Ark (trans, 1962), Two Under the Indian Sun (autobiography, 1965), Swans and Turtles (1968), The Raphael Bible (1970), Shiva's Pigeons (with Jon Godden, 1979), Gulbadan (1980), The Dark Horse (1981), Thursday's Children (1984), Time To Dance: No Time to Weep (1987, autobiography Vol I), A House with Four Rooms (autogiog Vol II 1989); *Style—* Miss Rumer Godden; Ardnacloich, Moniaive, Dumfriesshire DG3 4H2

GODDIN, Richard William; s of William Frederick Goddin (d 1967), and Audrey Joan, *née* Stearn; *b* 17 May 1943; *Educ* Perse Sch, London Poly (DMS); *m* 15 June 1985, Margaret Ann, da of Reginald Barlow (d 1957); 1 s (James b 1987); *Career* sr mangr Nat West Bank plc 1977-83, tres Lombard North Central plc 1983-86, dep tres Nat West plc 1986-87, exec dir County Nat West Ltd 1987-; ACIB 1967; *Recreations* sailing, croquet, country life; *Style—* Richard Goddin, Esq; Belmington Close, Meldreth, Cambs SG8 6NT (☎ 0763 600 61); Co Natwest Ltd, Drapers Gdns, Throgmorton Ave, London EC2P 2ES (☎ 01 826 8354, fax 01 628 2436, telex 882121)

GODFREY, Dr Gerald; s of Mr Phillip Godfrey, of Stanmore, Middx, and Sophie, *née* Godfrey; *b* 22 August 1926; *Educ* Dunstable GS, Glasgow Univ; *m* 9 April 1951, Florence, da of Leon Jaffé (d 1958), of Glasgow; 1 da (Leone b 1958); *Career* Southern Gen Hosp Glasgow 1951-52 (gen med, casualty surgery, psychiatry), civilian med offr RAF 1953-60, police med offr 1953-62, clinical asst med offr of Barking Hosp 1954-61, asst MOH Lewisham, Wandsworth and Croydon 1963-67; med referee insur cos: Prudential, Colonial, Mutual, Crusader, Forester, Pearl, Royal London, NEM Assur; GP: Dagenham and Streatham 1953-, Harley St 1966; LRCP 1951, MRCS 1951, MRGP 1960, BMA; *Recreations* sail board, tennis, squash, sailing, shooting; *Clubs* Kensington Rifle and Pistol, Tir Club d'Antibes; *Style—* Dr Gerald Godfrey; 86 Eaton Square, London SW1W 9AG (☎ 01 235 7676); 68 Harley St, London W1N 1AE (☎ 01 935 3980)

GODFREY, Howard Anthony; s of Emanuel Godfrey, of London, and Amy, *née* Grossman; *b* 17 August 1946; *Educ* William Ellis Sch, LSE (LLB); *m* 3 Sept 1972, Barbara, da of John Ellinger, of London; 2 s (Timothy b 1975, James b 1980); *Career* barr Middle Temple 1970, practicing SE circuit 1972-, asst rec Crown Ct 1987-; *Recreations* wine and food, walking; *Style—* Howard Godfrey, Esq; The Red House, Swallowfield Rd, Arborfield Cross, Berks RG2 9JZ (☎ 0734 760 657); 3 Hare Ct, Temple, London EC4Y 7BJ (☎ 01 353 7561, fax 01 353 7741)

GODFREY, Laurence Howard; s of William Herbert Godfrey (d 1978), of 9 Cyncoed Place, Cyncoed, Cardiff, and Elizabeth, *née* Peel (d 1960); *b* 6 Dec 1935; *Educ* LLandaff Cathedral Sch, Cranleigh Sch; *m* 12 Oct 1963, Audrey Elizabeth , da of Donald Ernest Blake (d 1962), of The Chase, LLyswen Rd, Cyncoed, Cardiff; 1 s (Ian Blake b 1971), 1 da (Amanda Jane b 1973, d 1980); *Career* sr ptnr Fooks & Co 1982- (ptnr 1965-82); represented S Wales and Glamorgan at hockey, golf and cricket, sec tres chm and vice pres Glamorgan Co Golf Union tstee Cardiff GC(former capt); FCA 1963; *Recreations* cricket, hockey, golf; *Style—* Laurence Godfrey, Esq; Coedllys, Sherborne Ave, Cyncoed, Cardiff (☎ 0222 751 732), 14 High St, Bargoed, M Glam (☎ 0443 834 047)

GODFREY, Hon Mrs; Hon (Sonja) Lois; *née* Mitchison; er da of Baron Mitchison, CBE, QC (Life Peer) (d 1970), and Naomi Mary Margaret (the authoress Naomi Mitchison), *née* Haldane; *Educ* Lady Margaret Hall, Oxford (BA); *m* 21 March 1959 (m dis), John Godfrey, s of Arthur Corfield Godfrey; 2 da; *Style—* Hon Mrs Godfrey

GODFREY, Dr Malcolm Paul Weston; s of Harry Godfrey (d 1945), of London, and Rose Kaye; *b* 11 August 1926; *Educ* Hertford GS, Univ of London (MBBS); *m* 1955, Barbara, da of Louis Goldstein (d 1963), of London, and Brighton; 1 s (Richard), 2 da (Jennifer, Claire); *Career* dean Royal Postgraduate Med Sch Univ of London 1974-83, second sec Med Res Cncl 1983-86; RSM; *Recreations* reading, theatre, walking; *Style—* Dr Malcolm Godfrey; 17 Clifton Hill, St John's Wood, London NW8 0QE (☎ 01 624 6335);

GODFREY, Robert John; s of Capt Thomas Mason Godfrey (d 1968), of E Molesey, Surrey, and Winifred Alice, *née* Beresford (d 1980); *b* 10 Oct 1931; *Educ* Tiffin Sch; *m* 31 Aug 1957, Jean Barbara, da of Dr Robert Alexander Frazer, DSC (d 1959), of Ockham, Surrey; 3 s (Christopher b 1960, Peter b 1962, Stephen b 1964); *Career* publisher and ed Hayling Islander Newspaper 1973-; sub-ed: Daily Telegraph 1960-70 (later foreign chief sub), News Chronicle 1960, Morning Advertiser 1954-60; *Recreations* photography; *Style—* Robert J Godfrey, Esq; Simon's Place, Alderney, Channel Islands (☎ 0481 82 2085, fax 0481 82 2110); Regal House, Hayling Island, Hampshire PO11 9BS (☎ 0705 463473, fax 0705 461685)

GODLEY, Hon Christopher John; s and h of 3 Baron Kilbracken, DSC; *b* 1 Jan 1945; *Educ* Rugby, Reading Univ (BSc); *m* 10 May 1969, Gillian Christine, yr da of Lt-Cdr Stuart Wilson Birse, OBE, DSC, RN (d 1981), of Alverstoke, Hants; 1 s (James b 1972), 1 da (Louisa b 1974); *Career* agriculturalist with ICI: Agric Div 1968-78, Head Office London 1978-82, Plant Protection Div Fernhurst Haslemere 1982-; *Style—* Hon Christopher Godley; Four Firs, Marley Lane, Haslemere, Surrey (☎ Haslemere 2814; office: 4061)

GODLEY, Georgina Jane (Mrs Conran); da of Michael Godley, and Heather, *née* Couper; *b* 11 April 1955; *Educ* Putney HS, Thames Valley GS, Wimbledon Art Sch, Brighton Poly (BA), Chelsea Sch of Art (MA); *m* 16 April 1988, Sebastian Conran s of Sir Terence Conran; *Career* picture restorer 1978-79, menswear designer Browns London and Paris 1979, ptnr designer Crolla London 1980-85, fndr and designer own label Georgina Godley (retail outlets from London to USA and Japan, and illustrations and articles in all major fashion pubns); *Style—* Ms Georgina Godley; 19 All Saints Road, London W11 1HE (☎ 01 221 1906)

GODLEY, Lt Cdr Peter Brian; s of Brig Brian Richard Godley, CBE (d 1954), and Margaret Valiant, *née* Livingstone-Learmonth (d 1979); *b* 4 Oct 1933; *Educ* Cheltenham, RNC Dartmouth; *m* 7 Jan 1960, Jean, da of Col James Forbes Robertson, VC, DSO, MC; 1 s (John b 9 July 1962), 2 da (Sarah b 21 Dec 1960, Joanna b 25 Feb 1968); *Career* submarines 1955-62, minesweepers 1963-65, RN Staff Coll 1966, first Lt HMS Minerva 1967-68, asst to Chief of Allied Staff Med 1969-70, RAF Coll Cromwell 1971-73; Charterhouse Gp plc 1974-83 (md Charterhouse Pensions Ltd 1978-83), dir Europa Investmt Servs Ltd 1987-, Royal Br Legion 1988; memb PCC Westoctt; Liveryman Worshipful Co Coachmakers and Coach Harness Makers 1976; *Recreations* off shore sailing, walking; *Clubs* Army & Navy; *Style—* Lt Cdr Peter Godley, RN; Down House, Westcott, Dorking, Surrey RH4 3JX (☎ 0306 881 555); Royal Br Legion, 48 Pall Mall, London SW1Y 5JY (☎ 01 930 8131)

GODLEY, Prof Hon Wynne Alexander Hugh; yr s of 2 Baron Kilbracken, CB, KC (d 1950), and his 1 wife Elizabeth Helen Monteith, *née* Hamilton; *b* 2 Sept 1926; *Educ* Rugby, New Coll Oxford (BA); *m* 3 Feb 1955, Kathleen Eleanora, da of Sir Jacob Epstein, KBE, and formerly wife of the painter Lucian Freud; 1 da (Eve b 1967); *Career* former professional oboist; served Treasy 1957-70; dir: Investing in Success Equities Ltd 1970-85, Royal Opera House (Covent Gdn) 1976-; Cambridge Univ: dir of dept applied econs 1970-85, fell Kings' Coll 1970-, actg dir of dept 1985-87, prof applied econs 1980-; *Style—* Prof Hon Wynne Godley; 16 Eltisley Ave, Cambridge

GODMAN, Arthur; s of Arthur Andrew Godman (d 1958), of London, and Mary Adelbine Newman (d 1946); *b* 10 Oct 1916; *Educ* Univ Coll London (BSc) Inst of Educn (Dip Ed); *m* 24 June 1950, Jean Barr, da of James Morton, OBE (d 1973), of Scotland; 2 s (Ian b 1951, Brian b 1953), 1 da (Diana b 1953); *Career* WWII Capt RA 1939: served France, India, Malaya, (POW Far E 1946); colonial civil serv educn dept Malaya, Hong Kong priv sec Min of Ed UCN Malaysia 1946-63; author 1963-; educn conslt Longman Gp 1966-77; hon fell Eliot Coll Univ of Kent 1978-, res fell dept of SE Asian studies Univ of Kent; CChem, MRSC,FFRAS; *Books* Dictionary of Scientific Usage (with E M F Payne, 1979), Illustrated Science Dictionary (1981), Illustrated Dictionary of Chemistry (1981); Cambridge Illustrated Thesaurus of Computer Science (1984), Health Science for the Tropics (1962), Chemistry: A New Certificate Approach (with S T Bajah 1969), Human and Social Biology (1973), Energy Supply (1989); *Recreations* bridge, reading, oriental languages; *Clubs* Royal Overseas League; *Style—* Arthur Godman, Esq; Sondes House, Patrix Bourne, Canterbury, Kent CT4 5DD (☎ 0227 830 322); Room L47, Gliot College, Univ of Kent, Canterbury, Kent

GODMAN, Desmond Frederick Shirley; JP (Glos 1962), DL 1987; s of Lt-Col Edward Shirley Godman, OBE, of Chetcombe House, Mere, Wilts; *b* 31 Jan 1927; *Educ* Winchester, Cambridge Univ; *m* 1954, Angela Janice, da of Rev John Corlett Rowson, of Ivy Cottage, Kirk Michael, IOM; 2 s, 2 da; *Career* High Sheriff of Glos 1976; *Clubs* Farmers; *Style—* Desmond Godman, Esq, JP, DL; Compton Abdale Manor, Cheltenham, Glos GL7 4DR

GODMAN, Dr Norman Anthony; MP (Lab) Greenock and Port Glasgow 1983-; *b* 19 April 1937; *Educ* Westbourne St Boys' HS Hull, Hull Univ (BA), Heriot-Watt Univ (PhD); *m* Patricia; *Career* former shipwright, teacher; joined Lab Pty 1962, contested (Lab) Aberdeen S 1979, TGWU sponsored; *Style—* Dr Norman Godman, MP; House of Commons, London SW1

GODSAL, Lady Elizabeth Cameron; *née* Stopford; 2 da of 8 Earl of Courtown, OBE, TD (d 1975), by his 1 w; *b* 10 April 1939; *m* 24 April 1962, Alan Anthony Colleton Godsal, o s of late Hugh Godsal, of Haines Hill, Twyford; 1 s (Hugh b 1965), 2 da (Lucy b 1964, Laura b 1968); *Career* CStJ; *Style—* Lady Elizabeth Godsal; Haines Hill, Twyford, Berks (☎ 0734 345 678); 7 Herbert Crescent, London SW1 (☎ 01 581 0937)

GODSAL, Philip Caulfeild; s of Maj Philip Hugh Godsal (d 1982), of Iscoyd Park, Whitchurch, Shropshire, and Pamela Ann Delisle, *née* Caulfeild; *b* 10 Oct 1945; *Educ* Eton; *m* 1, 29 Nov 1969 (m dis 1985), Lucinda Mary, da of Lt Cdr Percival Royston Dancy; 3 s (Philip Langley b 28 June 1971, Benjamin Rupert Wilmot b 17 June 1976, Thomas Henry b 3 Aug 1977), 1 da (Laura Sophie b 24 May 1973); m 2, 2 July 1986, Selina Baber, da of Thomas William Brooke-Smith, of Canford Cliffs; *Career* farmer, land agent and chartered surveyor; formerly ptnr Savills Norwich, ptnr John German Shrewsbury 1984-; chm Historic Houses Assoc for Wales, vice chm N Wales sub-region Timber Growers UK, ctee memb Shropshire branch CLA, sec Shropshire Rural Housing Assoc, govr Higher Wych C of E primary sch, pres Iscoyd and Fenns Bank CC; FRICS; *Recreations* shooting, forestry, reading; *Clubs* Farmers, Salop; *Style—* Philip Godsal, Esq; Iscoyd Park, Whitchurch, Shropshire SY13 3AT; John German, Chartered Surveyors, 43 High St, Shrewsbury SY1 1ST (☎ 0743 231661)

GODSAL, Capt Walter Edward Browning; s of Lt Col Philip Godsal, MC (d 1963), of Salop, and Violet Mary, *née* Browning (d 1978); *b* 3 Dec 1924; *Educ* Eton; *m* 7 Nov 1970, Pamela Anne De Lisle, da of Lt-Col Wilmot Smyth Caulfeild (d 1980), of Norwich; 6 step children; *Career* RN 1943-79, Capt Underwriter Weapons Accpetance Portland 1972-74, Asst Naval Attaché Washington, Capt HMS Saker 1974-76, Dep UK Nat Mil Rep at SHAPE 1976-79; porcelain restorer; *Recreations* shooting, walking; *Clubs* Army & Navy; *Style—* Capt Walter Godsal; Edbrooch House, Winsford, nr Minehead, Somerset TA24 7AE (☎ 064385-239)

GODWIN, Dame (Beatrice) Anne; DBE (1962, OBE 1952); da of William Goodwin (d 1932); *b* 6 July 1897; *Career* gen sec Clerical and Admin Workers' Union 1956-62, chm TUC 1961-62, govr BBC 1962-68, memb Industrial Ct 1963-69; *Recreations* talking, gardening, reading; *Style—* Dame Anne Godwin, DBE; 25 Fullbrooks Ave, Worcester Park, Surrey KT4 7PE

GODWIN, Charles Richard; s of Maj John Percival Godwin (d 1961), and Nancy, *née* Lee; *b* 23 August 1933; *Educ* Ardingly Coll Sussex; *m* 19 Nov 1976, Gwendoline Janet, da of Geoffrey Thomas Le Butt, of Leicester; *Career* Lt Essex Regt and Somaliland Scouts 1953-54; CA; sr ptnr Price Waterhouse Manchester Office 1975-; *Recreations* golf, skiing, wine, antiques; *Style—* Charles Godwin, Esq; York House, York Street, Manchester (☎ 061 228 6541, telex 669591, fax 061 228 1420)

GODWIN, Jeremy Purdon; s of Dr Eric George Godwin, of Tillington, Petworth, W Sussex, and Hannah (Nancy), *née* Rook; *b* 16 April 1943; *Educ* Epsom Coll, Lincoln Coll Oxford (MA), UCL (Dip of Archive Admin); *Career* archivist; asst archivist Northumberland 1969-71, Cumbria 1971-; reader The Diocese of Carlisle 1978-; sec (and ex chm) The Penrith Cncl of Churches; part of a medieval res gp; corr to: The Orcadian, Shetland Times, The Scotsman, Cumberland and Westmorland Herald; Scottish Record Soc, Diocesan Synod of Carlisle, (Bishops Cncl), English Place Name Soc; FSA (Scot) 1988; *Books* ed Jo Bens Description of Orkney 1529; *Recreations* research (local history), walking, music; *Style—* Jeremy Godwin, Esq; 15 Drovers Lane, Penrith, Cumbria CA11 9EP (☎ 64038); Cumbria Record Office, The Castle, Carlisle CA3 8UR (☎ 23456 ext 2416)

GODWIN, Peter Raymond; *b* 16 May 1942; *Educ* Harrow Co Boys' GS; *m* 3 June 1967, Wendy Dorothy; 1 s (Philip b 1972), 1 da (Helen b 1969); *Career* banker; dir Lazard Bros & Co Ltd 1979-85; Korea Merchant Banking Corpn Seoul 1976-86; The Int Investmt Corp for Yugoslavia SA Luxembourg 1981-85; dir: Standard Chartered Merchant Bank Ltd Standard Chartered Export Fin Ltd, Fin Merchant Bank Ltd Lagos; pres Anglo-Taiwan Trade Ctee; organist, St Andrews Church, Roxbourne, Harrow; ACIB; *Clubs* Overseas Bankers'; *Style—* Peter R Godwin, Esq; 16 Newquay Crescent, Harrow, Middx HA2 9LJ (☎ 01 422 1801); 33-36 Gracechurch St, London

EC3V 0AX (☎ 01 623 8711, fax 01 626 1610)

GOEHR, Prof Alexander; s of Walter and Laelia Goehr; *b* 10 August 1932; *Educ* Berkhamsted, Royal Manchester Coll of Music, Paris Conservatoire; *m* 1, 1954 (m dis 1971), Audrey Baker; 3 da; m 2, 1972, Anthea Staunton; 1 s; m 3, 1982, Amirakatz; *Career* composer; prof of music and fell Trinity Hall Cambridge 1976-; *Style*— Prof Alexander Goehr; Trinity Hall, Cambridge

GOFF, Hon Mrs (Angela Estelle); *née* Kitson; 7 and yst da of 2 Baron Airedale (d 1944), and Florence, *née* Baroness von Schunk (d 1942); *b* 1905; *m* 12 Nov 1927, George Herbert Goff (d 1957), s of late George Charles Golf, of Birchington, Kent; 1 s (George b 1928), 1 da (Mrs Brian Richardson b 1932); *Style*— Hon Mrs Goff; 20 Field Way, Broad Oak, Brede, E Sussex

GOFF, Lady; Marjorie Morwenna; *née* Curnow; da of Rev A Garfield Curnow (d 1965), of Wallington, Surrey; *b* 7 May 1917; *Educ* James Allens Girls' Sch Dulwich, Lewisham Prendergast Sch; *m* 1944, Rt Hon Lord Justice (Sir Reginald William) Goff (d 1980); 2 da; *Style*— Lady Goff; Tamarisk, 24 Waverleigh Road, Cranleigh, Surrey GU6 8BZ (☎ Cranleigh 271440)

GOFF, Martyn; OBE (1977); s of Jacob Goff (d 1971), and Janey Goff (d 1978); *b* 7 June 1923; *Educ* Clifton; *Career* dir Nat Book League 1970-, author, fiction reviewer The Daily Telegraph 1975-; chm: School Bookshop Assoc, Soc of Bookmen; chief exec Book Tst for 1986 (formerly Nat Book League); FRSA, fell Int Inst of Arts and Letters; *Novels* The Plaster Fabric, A Season with Mammon, A Sort of Peace, The Youngest Director, The Flint Inheritance, Indecent Assault, The Liberation of Rupert Bannister; *Music* A Short Guide to Long Play, A Further Guide to Long Play, LP Collecting, Record Choice; *Miscellaneous* Victorian Surrey, The Royal Pavilion, Why Conform?; *Recreations* picture collecting, travelling; *Clubs* Athenaeum, Savile; *Style*— Martyn Goff, Esq, OBE; 95 Sisters Ave, London SW11 5SW (☎ 01 228 8164)

GOFF OF CHIEVELEY, Baron (Life Peer UK 1986), of Chieveley, Co Berkshire; Sir Robert Lionel Archibald Goff; PC (1982); s of Lt-Col Lionel Trevor Goff (d 1953), of Queen's House, Monk Sherborne, Basingstoke, Hants, and his wife, *née* Denroche-Smith; *b* 12 Nov 1926; *Educ* Eton, New Coll Oxford; *m* 1953, Sarah, er da of Capt G R Cousins, DSC, RN, of Child Okeford, Dorset; 1 s (and 1 s decd), 2 da; *Career* served Scots Guards 1945-48; fell and tutor Lincoln Coll Oxford 1951-55; barr Inner Temple 1951, QC 1967, recorder 1974-75, High Ct judge (Queen's Bench) 1975-82, chm Cncl Legal Educn 1976-, judge i/c Commercial List and chm Commercial Court Ctee 1979-81, lord justice of Appeal 1982-; lord of appeal in ordinary 1986-; hon prof legal ethics Birmingham Univ 1980-81, Maccabaean lectr 1983; chm: Ct of Univ of London 1986-, Br Inst of Int and Comparative Law 1986-; pres: the Bentham Club 1986, Holdsworth Club 1986-87; FBA 1987, hon fell: New Coll Oxford 1986, Lincoln Coll Oxford 1983; hon DCL Oxon 1972, Hon DLitt City Univ; kt 1975; *Books* The Law of Restitution (with Prof Gareth Jones, 1966); *Style*— The Rt Hon Lord Goff of Chieveley; House of Lords, London SW1

GOLD, Sir Arthur Abraham; CBE (1974); s of late Mark Gold and Leah Gold; *b* 10 Jan 1917; *m* 1942, Marion, da of late N Godfrey; 1 s (Jonathan); *Career* international athlete (high jumper); leader athletics team Mexico Olympics 1968, Munich 1972, Montreal 1976; hon sec Br Amateur Athletic Bd 1965-77, life vice pres 1977; pres: Counties Athletic Union, Euro Athletic Assoc; chm Cwlth Games Cncl for England 1979-; vice-chm Br Olympic Assoc, memb Sports Cncl 1980-; kt 1984; *Clubs* London Athletic, City Livery, MCC; *Style*— Sir Arthur Gold, CBE; 49 Friern Mount Drive, Whetstone, London N20 9DJ (☎ 01 445 2848)

GOLD, Jack; *b* 28 June 1930; *Educ* London Univ; *m* 1957, Denyse, *née* Macpherson; 2 s, 1 da; *Career* film director; ed Film Dept BBC 1955-60, dir TV and film documentaries and fiction 1960; BAFTA Award: Death in the Morning 1964, World of Copperd 1968, Stockers Copper 1972; Peabody Award 1974, Italia Prize 1976, Int Emmy and Critics Award 1976, Int Emmy 1981, jt winner Martin Luther King memorial prize 1980; Monte Carlo: Catholic Award 1981, Critics Award 1981, Grand Prix 1971; *stage play* The Devils Disciple; *Style*— Jack Gold, Esq; 18 Avenue Rd, N6

GOLD, Hon Mrs (Jocelyne Mary); *née* Boot; da of 2 and last Baron Trent (d 1956); *b* 6 Feb 1917; *m* 19 Nov 1947, Major Harcourt Michael Scudamore Gold, MC (d 1982), s of Sir Harcourt Gilbey Gold, OBE (d 1952); 1 s (John b 1958), 1 da (Mrs James Nicholson b 1950, *see Baronetage* Nicholson (r 1912); *Style*— Hon Mrs Gold; Wheathill, Sparsholt, Winchester, Hants

GOLD, Sir Joseph; *b* 12 July 1912; *Educ* London Univ, Harvard Univ; *m* 1939, Ruth Schechter; 1 s, 2 da; *Career* joined IMF 1946, gen counsel and dir Legal Dept 1960-79, sr conslt 1979-; author of numerous pubns on monetary matters; kt 1980; *Style*— Sir Joseph Gold; 7020 Braeburn Pl, Bethseda, Maryland 20817, USA

GOLD, Nicholas Roger; s of Rev Guy Alastair Whitmore Gold, TD, of Gt Bealings nr Woodbridge, Suffolk, and Elizabeth Weldon, *née* Maythem, JP; *b* 11 Dec 1951; *Educ* Felsted, Univ of Kent (BA); *m* 23 April 1983, (Siena) Laura (Joy), da of Adam Sebastian Arnold-Brown, of Salcombe, Devon; 1 s (James Mortimer Fearon b 8 Oct 1987), 1 da (Siena Jane b 9 Jan 1985); *Career* CA Touche Ross & Co 1973-76, slr Freshfields 1977-86, Baring Bros & Co Ltd 1986- (dir corp fin dept 1987-); ACA 1977, FCA 1982; *Recreations* sailing, the arts, stalking, travel; *Style*— Nicholas Gold, Esq; 14 Northumberland Place, London W2 (☎ 01 229 4773); North Sands Cottage, Salcombe, Devon; Baring Brothers & Co Ltd, 8 Bishopsgate, London EC2 (☎ 01 283 8833, fax 01 283 2224, telex 883622)

GOLDBERG, Prof Sir Abraham; s of Julius Goldberg (d 1953), and Rachel, *née* Varinofsky; *b* 7 Dec 1923; *Educ* George Heriot's Sch Edinburgh, Univ of Edinburgh (MB ChB, MD), Univ of Glasgow (DSc); *m* 1957, Clarice, da of Jacob Cussin, of 130 Menock Rd, Glasgow; 3 children; *Career* Maj RAMC M East; Univ of Glasgow Regius prof of: Materia Medica 1970-78, Practice of Medicine 1978-; chm Ctee on Safety of Medicines 1980-86; FRCP (London, Edinburgh, Glasgow), FRSE; Kt 1983; *Books* co-author: Diseases of Porphyrin Metabolism (1962), Clinics in Haematology - The Porphyrias (1980); *Recreations* swimming, writing; *Clubs* Royal Society of Medicine (London); *Style*— Prof Sir Abraham Goldberg; 16 Birnam Crescent, Bearsden, Glasgow G61 2AU (☎ office 041 339 2800)

GOLDBERG, David Gerard; s of Arthur Goldberg (d 1982), of Plymouth, and Sylvia, *née* Stone; *b* 12 August 1947; *Educ* Plymouth Coll, LSE (LLB, LLM); *m* 22 Dec 1981, Alison Ninette, da of Jack V Lunzer, of London; 1 s (Arthur b 1986), 1 da (Selina b 1984); *Career* barr Lincoln's Inn 1971, in practice at Revenue Bar, case note ed British Tax Review 1975-87, author of numerous articles on taxation and company law; *Books* An Introduction to Company Law (jty 1987), The Law of Partnership Taxation (jty 1987); *Recreations* reading, letter writing, thinking; *Style*— David Goldberg, Esq, QC; Grays Inn Chambers, Grays Inn, London WC1R 5JA (☎ 01 242 2642, fax 01 831 9017)

GOLDBERG, Ivan Jeffrey; s of Myer Goldberg (d 1945), and Florence, *née* Jacobson (d 1952); *b* 26 Dec 1930; *Educ* Queen Elizabeth's GS Blackburn; *m* 14 July 1957, Audrey Githa, *née* Prepsler (d 1980); 1 s (Adam b 1964), 1 da (Sarah b 1966); *Career* mgmnt conslt; chm Michael Adam Assoc Ltd, Teleconsultants (UK) Ltd, visiting lecturer, Manchester Business Sch, Univ Manchester; CEng, FIMechE, MIMC; *Recreations* horse riding; *Clubs* Royal Overseas; *Style*— Ivan Goldberg, Esq; 50 Wilmslow Road, Cheadle, Cheshire SK8 1NF

GOLDBERG, Jonathan Jacob; s of Rabbi Dr Percy Selvin Goldberg, and Frimette, *née* Yudt; *b* 13 Nov 1947; *Educ* Manchester GS, Trinity Hall Cambridge (MA, LLB); *m* 8 Nov 1980, Alexis Jane, da of George Martin, CBE; 1 s (Saul Percy Lawrence b 22 Sept 1985), 1 da (Natasha Jane Frimette b 22 Dec 1982); *Career* called to the Bar Middle Temple 1971, practising SE circuit, fndr with Robert Watson of chambers at 3 Temple Gdns 1985, asst recorder 1987; memb NY State Bar; *Recreations* reading, music; *Style*— Jonathan Goldberg, Esq; Springfield Lodge, 348 Upper Richmond Road, Putney, London SW15 (☎ 788 3376); 3 Temple Gardens, Temple, London EC4Y 9AU (☎ 583 1155, fax 353 5446)

GOLDEN, Lewis Lawrence; OBE (1978), JP (1968); s of Samuel Arthur Golden (d 1951), and Julia, *née* Lee (d 1976); *b* 6 Dec 1922; *Educ* East Sheen Co Sch, Manchester Univ; *m* 15 Jan 1953, Jacqueline Esther, da of Maurice Frances (d 1966); 2 s (David b 1954, Jonathan b 1961), 2 da (Deborah b 1957, Sara b 1959); *Career* WWII RCS 1941-46: cmmnd 2 Lt (later Lt) 1942, 8 Armd Div England 1942, 1 Airborne Div 1942-45 (served: England, N Africa, Sicily, Italy, Holland, Norway), Capt 1944, Adj Arnhem 1944, 2 (Indian) Airborne Div India 1945-46, released Maj 1946); CA and asst sec Emu Wool Industs Ltd 1949-50, Lewis Golden & Co CAs 1950-, fin dir Home Insulation Ltd 1965-88; beef and corn farmer 1971; currently tres: London Library, Friends of the Nat Libraries, Friends of the British Library, Friends of the Lambeth Palace Library, Wiener Library Endowment Appeal; pres Westminster Synagogue; tstee: Chalk Pits Museum Devpt Tst Amberley, Dove Cottage Grosmere until 1986; memb advsy cncl Chichester Cathedral Tst, memb Wisborough Green Parish Cncl until 1987; Freeman City of London 1980, memb Worshipful Co of CAs 1980, ACA 1947, FCA 1951; *Books* Echoes From Arnhem (1984); *Recreations* walking, reading; *Style*— Lewis Golden, Esq, OBE, JP; Pallingham Manor Farm, Wisborough Green, Billingshurst, W Sussex RH14 0EZ; Lewis Golden & Co, 40 Queen Anne St, London W1M 0EL

GOLDENBERG, Philip; s of Nathan Goldenberg, OBE, and Edith, *née* Dee; *b* 26 April 1946; *Educ* St Pauls, Pembroke Coll Oxford; *m* 1, 16 Aug 1969 (m dis 1975), Dinah Mary Pye; m 2, 12 Oct 1985, Lynda Anne, *née* Benjamin; 1 s (Jonathan b 1986), 1 da (Philippa b 1988); *Career* admitted slr 1972; asst slr with Linklaters & Paines 1972-82, ptnr S J Berwin & Co 1983 (asst slr 1982-83); sec Oxford Univ Lib Club 1966, pres Watford Lib Assoc 1980-81, vice chm Home Counties Regnl Lib Pty 1976-78 and 1980-81; memb: Lib Pty Cncl 1975-88, Nat Exec Ctee 1977-87, Candidates Ctee 1976-85, Assembly Ctee 1985-87; parly candidate: (Lib) Eton and Slough 1974 (twice) and 1979, (Lib/SDP Alliance) Woking 1983 and 1987; elected Woking Borough Cncl 1984- (chm highways ctee); former memb exec ctee Wider Share Ownership Cncl, cncl memb Electoral Reform Soc 1978-82, memb London regnl cncl CBI, jt author Constitution of the Social and Lib Democrats, jt ed New Outlook 1974-77; govr Slough Coll of Higher Educn 1980-86; memb Law Soc; *Books* Fair Welfare (1968), Sharing Profits (with David Steel, 1986), The Businessman's Guide to Directors' Responsibilities (1988); *Recreations* family, friends; *Clubs* National Liberal; *Style*— Philip Goldenberg, Esq; Toad Hall, White Rose Lane, Woking, Surrey GU22 7LB (☎ 04862 65377); 236 Grays Inn Rd, London WC1X 8HB (☎ 01 278 0444, fax 01 833 2860, telex 8814928 WINLAW G)

GOLDIE, William Law; s of Hugh Goldie (d 1964), of Norwood, Academy Street, Coatbridge, and Agnes Pettigrew Law (d 1984); *b* 16 April 1922; *Educ* Coatbridge HS, Glasgow Univ (BSc); *m* 2 Jun 1955, Sheila Veronica Mary, da of Jack Robertson Lamberton (d 1973), of Arden, Charlotte Street, Helensburgh; 3 s (William b 1958, Andrew b 1962, Angus b 1968); *Career* RAF volunteer res flt-Lt pilot coastal command, W Africa; engr; pres: Metalworking Plantmakers Fedn 1979-80; chm: Lamberton (Hldgs) Ltd and Lamberton & Co Ltd, Lamberton Robotics Ltd, Scomagg Hydraulics Ltd, Scoforr Engr Ltd; CEng, MIMechE; *Recreations* maintenance, restoration; *Clubs* Caledonian, RAF; *Style*— William Goldie, Esq; Woodburn House, Milton of Campsie, Glasgow G65 8AN (☎ 0236 823249); Sunnyside Works, Coatbridge ML5 2DL (☎ 0236 20101, fax: 0236 29136)

GOLDINER, Hon Mrs (Sigrid); yr da of Baron Wynne-Jones (Life Peer d 1982); *b* 1935; *m* 1962, Dr Marvin Goldiner, of Oakland, Cal, USA; *Style*— Hon Mrs Goldiner

GOLDING, Dr Anthony Mark Barrington; s of Dr Mark Golding (d 1954), of 29 Dawson Place, London W2, and Marian Rosalie, *née* Benjamin (d 1965); *b* 21 August 1928; *Educ* Marlborough, Cambridge Univ (MA, MB, BChir), Middx Hosp Med Sch; *m* 29 Aug 1962, (Olwen) Valery, da of Reginald Francis Orlando Bridgeman, CMG, MVO (d 1968), of 105 Waxwell Lane, Pinner, Middx; 1 s (Richard b 1965), 3 da (Rosemary b 1963, Catherine b 1967, Charlotte b 1970); *Career* RAMC 1954-56 (Lt and Capt), jr specialist in ophthalmology Cambridge Mil Hosp; med offr DHSS 1968-72, princ asst sr med offr SE Metropolitan RHB 1972-74, dist community physician Kings Health Dist (Teaching) 1974-82; Camberwell Health Authy: dist med offr 1982-86, sr conslt in community med 1986-88, hon conslt 1988-; hon sr lectr: King's Coll Hosp Med Sch 1977-, King's Coll Sch of Med & Dentistry; ed Health and Hygiene 1988-; cncl memb: RID H and H 1987-; Section of Epidemiology and Community Med, Royal Soc of Med 1987-, tstee Ctee Against Drug Abuse; DO 1956, MFCM 1973, FFCM 1979, FRIPH & H 1983; contributor to various pubns incl Public Health, The Lancet and British Medical Journal; *Recreations* walking the dogs; *Style*— Dr Anthony Golding; 12 Clifton Hill, London NW8 0QG (☎ 01 624 0504); Keepers, Byworth, nr Petworth, W Sussex

GOLDING, John; s of Peter John Golding, of Birmingham; *b* 9 Mar 1931; *Educ* Chester GS, London Univ, Keele Univ; *m* 1, 1958, Thelma, da of S G Gwillym, of Birmingham; 1 s; m 2, 1980, Llinos Lewis, *née* Edwards,; *Career* political and parly offr Post Office Engrg Union 1969-86; MP (Lab) Newcastle-under-Lyme 1969-86; PPS to Min State Technol 1970, oppn whip 1970-74, ld cmmr Treasy 1974, parly under-sec Employment 1976-79; memb Labour NEC 1978-83 and chm Home Policy Ctee 1982-

83; chm Select Ctee Employment 1979-82; made 11 hr 15 min speech in Commons against privatisation of Br Telecom 1983; gen sec Nat Communications Union 1986-; memb gen Cncl TUC; govr Ruskin Coll; *Recreations* flyfishing, horseracing; *Style—* John Golding, Esq; c/o National Communications Union, Greystoke House, Brunswick Rd, Ealing, London W5

GOLDING, Llinos; MP (Lab) Newcastle under Lyme 1986-; da of Ness Edwards (d 1968, MP for Caerphilly 1939-68), and Elina Victoria (d 1988); *b* 21 Mar 1933; *Educ* Caephilly Girls GS, Cardiff Royal Infirmary Sch of Radiography; *m* 1, June 1957 (m dis 1971), John Roland Lewis; 1 s (Steven), 2 da (Caroline (Mrs Hopwood), Janet); m 2, 8 Aug 1980, John Golding *qv*; *Career* Memb Soc of Radiographers; *Style—* Mrs Llinos Golding; House of Commons, London

GOLDING, Brig Dame (Cecilie) Monica; DBE (1958), RRC (1950, ARRC 1940); o da of Ben Johnson and Clara, *née* Beames; *b* 6 August 1902; *Educ* Croydon Secdy Sch; *m* 1961, as his 2 wife, Brig the Rev Harry Golding, CBE (d 1969); *Career* Royal Surrey County Hosp Guildford 1922-25, Louise Margaret Hosp Aldershot and Queen Victoria's Inst of Dist Nursing; joined Army Nursing Servs 1925: India 1929-34, France 1939-40, M East 1940-43 and 1948-48; Southern Cmd 1943-44 and 1950-52, WO 1945-46, Eastern Cmd 1955-56, matron-in-chief and dir of Army Nursing Serv 1956-60, ret 1960; Col Cmdt Queen Alexandra's Royal Army Nursing Corps 1961-66; OStJ; *Recreations* motoring, nature study; *Clubs* UNS; *Style—* Brig Dame Monica Golding, DBE, RRC; 9 Sandford Court, 32 Belle Vue Rd, Southbourne, Bournemouth, Dorset BH6 3DR (☎ 431608)

GOLDING, Dr Richard James Arthur; s of Arthur Bertram Golding, and Bridget Elizabeth, *née* Mahoney; *b* 13 April 1952; *Educ* Queen Elizabeth's Sch for Boys Barnet, Wadham Coll Oxford (BA, MA, DPhil); *Career* stockbroker 1976-, with Simon and Coates 1976-81, ptnr Grieveson Grant and Co 1984-86 (joined 1981), Kleinwort Benson Ltd 1986-, dir Kleinwort Benson Gilts, head of bond mkt res Kleinwort Benson, chm taxation ctee Gilt-Edged Mkt Makers Assoc 1986-; *Clubs* Utd Oxford and Cambridge Univ; *Style—* Dr Richard Golding; 20 Fenchurch St, London EC3P 3DB (☎ 01 623 8000, fax 01 623 4069)

GOLDING, Terence Edward; s of Sydney Richard and Elsie Golding; *b* 7 April 1932; *Educ* Harrow County GS; *m* 1955, Sheila Jean, *née* Francis; 1 s, 1 da; *Career* chief exec Nat Exhibition Centre 1978, chm Exhibition Liaison Ctee 1979 and 1980; dir: Br Exhibitions Promotions Cncl 1981-83, Birmingham Convention and Visitor Bureau, 1981-, Heart of England Tourist Bd 1984-, Birmingham Heartbeat 1986 Ltd, 1986-87, Sport Aid Promotions Ltd 1986-87; chief exec designate Int Convention Centre Birmingham 1987-; *Style—* Terence Golding, Esq; Pinn Cottage, Pinner Hill, Pinner, Middx (☎ 01 866 2610; office 021 780 4141)

GOLDING, Terry; s of Gordon Eric Golding, of Berks, and Olive Lillian, *née* Gilbert (d 1972); *b* 23 May 1948; *Educ* Hownslow Coll, Park High, Bristol Coll of Commerce; *m* 8 March 1980, Penelope, da of Arthur Wilson (d 1975), of Gwent; 1 s (Nicholas b 1980), 1 da (Sarah-Jane b 1982), 2 step s (Jonathan b 1969, Simon b 1972); *Career* admitted slr 1975, Cartel Investmts 1978-; *Recreations* salmon and trout fishing; *Clubs* RAC; *Style—* Terry Golding, Esq; Ouseley House, Ipsden, Oxon OX9 6AR (☎ 0491 680083); 10 Market Place, Henley on Thames, Oxon RG9 2AA (☎ 0491 573931, fax 0491 572482, car phone 0836 250966)

GOLDING, William Gerald; CBE (1966); s of Alec A Golding, and Mildred A Golding; *b* 7 April 1932,Cornwall,; *Educ* Marlborough GS, Brasenose Coll Oxford; *m* 1939, Ann, da of late E W Brookfield, of the Homestead, Bedford Place, Maidstone, Kent; 1 s, 1 da; *Career* served RN WW II; former actor, writer and prodr with various small theatre cos, teacher Bishop Wordsworth's Sch Salisbury until 1961, author; winner of: Booker Prize 1980 (for Rites of Passage), Nobel Prize for Literature 1983; CLit 1984; FRSL 1955; *Books* Lord of the Flies (1954, filmed 1963), The Inheritors (1955), Free Fall (1959), The Spire (1964), The Pyramid (1967), Darkness Visible (1979), Rites of Passage (1980), A Moving Target (essays, 1982), The Paper Men (1984); *Recreations* Greek literature, riding, pianoforte; *Style—* William Golding, Esq, CBE; c/o Faber & Faber, 3 Queen St, London WC1

GOLDKORN, Geoffrey; s of David Goldkorn, and Judith, *née* Yudt; *b* 14 Jan 1945; *Educ* City of London, Jesus Coll Cambridge (MA); *m* 16 June 1978, Lindy, da of Leon Berman, of Flat 16a, 15 Grosvenor Sq, London W1; 1 s (Benjamin b 1980), 1 da (Gabriella b 1983); *Career* slr, sr ptnr Goldkorn Davies & Co; ctee memb The Br Technion Soc, tstee The Kennedy Leigh Charitable Tst; assoc memb Chartered Inst of Arbitrators; *Recreations* cycling, tennis, opera, philosophy; *Clubs* Coolhurst Lawn Tennis, Squash Rackets; *Style—* Geoffrey Goldkorn, Esq; 4 Sheldon Ave, London N6 4JT (☎ 01 348 1028); 6 Coptic St, London WC1A 1NH (☎ 01 631 1811, fax 01 631 0431)

GOLDMAN, Sir Samuel; KCB (1969, CB 1964); yst s of Philip Goldman (d 1958), and Sarah Goldman; *b* 10 Mar 1912; *Educ* Raine's Sch, LSE; *m* 1, 1933, Pearl Marre (d 1941); 1 s (Antony b 1940); M 2, 1943, Patricia Rosemary, *née* Hodges; *Career* Bank of Eng 1940-47, Civil Serv 1947; Treasy: chief statistician 1948, asst sec 1952, under-sec 1960-62, third sec 1962-68, second perm sec 1968-72; exec dir Orion Bank 1972-74, (md 1974-76); chm: Henry Ansbacher Ltd and Henry Ansbacher Hldgs 1976-82, Covent Gdn Marketing Authy 1976-81; hon fell LSE; *Style—* Sir Samuel Goldman, KCB; White Gate, Church Lane, Haslemere, Surrey (☎ 0428 4889)

GOLDREIN, Iain Saville; s of Capt Neville Clive Goldrein, of Torreno, St Andrew's Rd, Crosby, Liverpool, and Sonia Hannah Jane, *née* Sumner; *b* 10 August 1952; *Educ* Merchant Taylors', Pembroke Coll Cambridge; *m* 18 May 1980, Margaret Ruth, da of Josef De Haas, of Grove Park, Wanstead, London; 1 s (Alastair Philip b 1 Oct 1982), 1 da (Alexandra Ann b 22 Feb 1985); *Career* called to the Bar Inner Temple 1975, practising Northern circuit; memb: Br Insur Law Assoc, Br Acad of Experts, Int Litigation Forum; *Books* Personal Injury Litigation, Practice and Precedents (with Margaret R De Haas, 1985), Ship Sale and Purchase, Law and Technique (1985), Commercial Litigation, Pre-Emptive Remedies (with K H P Wilkinson, 1987), Butterworths' Personal Injury Litigation Service (with Margaret R De Haas); *Recreations* law, new ideas, the family, riding; *Clubs* Athenaeum (Liverpool); *Style—* Iain Goldrein, Esq; 4 Linden Ave, Crosby, Liverpool L23 8UL (☎ 051 924 2610); 48 Castle St, Liverpool, L2 7LQ (☎ 051 227 5009, fax 051 227 5488, car tel 0836 583 257)

GOLDREIN, Neville Clive; s of Saville Goldrein (d 1946), of Hull, and Nina, *née* Aronoff (d 1977); *Educ* Hymers Coll Hull, Pembroke Coll Cambridge (MA); *m* 30 Oct 1949, Sonia Hannah Jane, da of Myer Sumner (d 1966), of Newcastle Upon Tyne; 1 s (Iain b 1952), 1 da (Nadine b 1954); *Career* served East Yorks Regt as Actg Capt East Africa; slr Supreme Ct; memb: Crosby Borough Cncl 1957-71 (Mayor 1966-67, Dep Mayor 1967-68), Lancs CC 1965-74, NW Planning Cncl 1966-72; cncl of Liverpool Univ 1973-81, Merseyside CC 1973-86 (dep ldr Cons Gp 1975-77); ldr: Merseyside CC 1980-81 (vice chm 1977-80), Cons Gp 1981-86; dir Merseyside Econ Devpt Co Ltd 1980-87, chm Cons Constit Assoc 1986-89; memb cncl Merseyside C of C; govr Merchant Taylors' 1965-74, vice pres Crosby Mencap, chm St John Ambulance (South Sefton) 1965-87; *Recreations* videography, swimming, music, grandchildren; *Clubs* Athenaeum Liverpool; *Style—* Neville C Goldrein, Esq; Torreno, St Andrew's Road, Blundellsands, Merseyside L23 7UR (☎ 051 924 2065); Peel House, 5 Harrington St, Liverpool L2 9XP (☎ 051 255 0611, fax 051 236 3319)

GOLDRING, Timothy John; s of Stephen Spencer Goldring (d 1979), and late Joan Francis Goldring; *b* 22 Jan 1930; *Educ* Christ's Hosp Horsham; *m* 6 Aug 1960, Penelope Mary (Penny), da of Bruin Milner-White (d 1976); 3 s (Colin b 18 May 1961, Simon b 8 Nov 1962, Dougal b 10 May 1966), 1 da (Helen b 18 April 1970); *Career* Sgt RAF 1948-49; prep sch master 1947-55, sales and sales mgmnt Kenwood Mfrg Ltd 1955-63, sales mgmnt Simplex Electric Co (Tube Investmts) 1963-66, mktg dir Bath Cabinet Makers & Arkana Ltd 1967-73, Times Furnishing (part of GU5) 1973-dir owner Goldring & Assocs (sales and mktg conslts) 1977-84, mktg dir Ercol Furniture Ltd 1984-; memb Round Table 1963-70, Liveryman Worshipful Co of Furnituremakers 1974; MBIM 1970-85, MIMC 1986, MInstM 1959; *Recreations* travel, gardening; *Clubs* Harlequin FC, Ashridge GC; *Style—* Timothy Goldring, Esq; Ercol Furniture Ltd, London Rd, High Wycombe, Bucks HP13 7AE (☎ 0494 21261, fax 0494 462 467, telex 83616)

GOLDS, Anthony Arthur; CMG (1971), LVO (1961); s of Arthur Oswald Golds (d 1934), of Macclesfield, and Florence, *née* Massey (d 1943); *b* 31 Oct 1919; *Educ* The King's Sch Macclesfield, New Coll Oxford (MA); *m* 9 Oct 1944, Suzanne MacDonald, da of Dr John Miller Young, MC (d 1947), of Glasgow; 1 s (Richard b 1947), 1 da (Laura (Mrs Russell) b 1952); *Career* WWII RAC 1939-46; Cwlth Off 1948, first sec Calcutta and Delhi 1951-59, Karachi 1959-61, cnsllr FCO 1962-65, ambass Cameroon Gabo and Equatorial Guinea 1970-72, high cmmr Bangladesh 1972-74; sr civilian instr RCDS 1975-76, Br dir Int C of C 1977-83; *Recreations* golf, literature; *Clubs* Dulwich and Sydenham Hill GC; *Style—* Anthony Golds, Esq, CMG, LVO; 4 Oakfield Gardens, London SE19 1HF (☎ 01 670 7621)

GOLDSACK, Alan Raymond; s of Raymond Frederick Goldsack, MBE (d 1985), of Hastings, and Mildred Agnes, *née* Jones; *b* 13 June 1947; *Educ* Hastings GS, Leicester Univ (LLB); *m* 21 Aug 1971, Christine Marion, da of Frank Leslie Clarke, MBE; 3 s (Ian b 1974, Richard b 1977, Stephen b 1980), 1 da (Tessa b 1975); *Career* barr Grays Inn 1970, rec 1988; *Recreations* gardening, walking; *Style—* Alan Goldsack, Esq; The Old Rectory, Braithwell, Rotherham (☎ 0709 812 167); 12 Paradise Sq, Sheffield (☎ 0742 738 951)

GOLDSMID, John Michael Francis; s of Cyril Julian Goldsmid (d 1971), and Anna Emily, *née* McGillycuddy (d 1969); *b* 28 June 1922; *Educ* Eton, Univ of Oxford (BA); *m* 24 July 1954, Virginia Marguerite, da of Thomas Agnew Ansdell (d 1966); 1 s (Nicholas b 1958, m 1981, Sara Gillian, da of Gen Sir Roland Guy, GCB, CBE, DSO, *qv*), 1 da (Miranda b 1955); *Career* WW II Capt 9 Queens Royal Lancers served N Africa and Italy; farmer; *Style—* J M F Goldsmid, Esq; Copyhold Farm, Goring Heath, Oxon RG8 7RT (☎ 07357 2291)

GOLDSMITH, Lady Annabel; *née* Vane-Tempest-Stewart; da of 8 Marquess of Londonderry (d 1955), and Romaine, *née* Combe (d 1951); *b* 11 June 1934; *Educ* Southover Manor Lewes; *m* 1, 10 March 1954 (m dis 1975), Marcus Oswald Hornby Lecky Birley, s of Sir Oswald Hornby Lecky Birley, MC (d 1952); 2 s (Rupert b 1955, Robin b 1958), 1 da (Mrs Julian Colchester b 1961); m 2, 1978, Sir James Michael Goldsmith, *qv*; 2 s (Zacharias b 1975, Benjamin b 1980), 1 da (Jemima Marcelle b 1974); *Style—* Lady Annabel Goldsmith; Ormeley Lodge, Ham Common, Surrey (☎ 01 940 5677/8)

GOLDSMITH, Carl Stanley; s of Stanley Thomas Goldsmith (d 1956), and Ida, *née* Rawlinson (d 1965); *b* 14 Oct 1936; *Educ* King James GS, UCL (LLB); *m* 1958, Margaret Violetta, da of Stanley Olley (d 1966); 3 da (Delia, Sallie, Belinda); *Career* slr; ptnr in Hill Dickinson & Co; dir incl: Dvpt Capital Gp Ltd, Motofax Ltd, Anglo American Agric plc, Barbury Properties Ltd, Eletson Maritime Ltd, Trenchdean Ltd, W S Moody Hldgs plc; FInst D; *Clubs* MCC, XL; *Style—* Carl Goldsmith, Esq; 59 Grange Gdns, Pinner, Middx (☎ 01 866 2909); Irongate House, Dukes Place, London EC3

GOLDSMITH, Edward René David; s of Frank Benedict Hayum Goldsmith, OBE, TD (d 1967; MP (C) Stowmarket 1910-18), by his w Marcelle, *née* Mouiller (d 1985); er bro of Sir James Goldsmith, *qv*; *b* 8 Nov 1928; *Educ* Millfield, Magdalen Coll Oxford (MA); *m* 1, 1953, Gillian Marion Pretty; 1 s (Alexander), 2 da (Dido, Clio); m 2, 1981, Katherine Victoria, da of John Anthony James, CMG, of 136 Vipond Rd, Whanga Paraoa, Auckland, NZ; 1 s (Benedict); *Career* ed The Ecologist 1970-; author, ed; *Books* Can Britain Survive? (Tom Stacy 1971), A Blueprint for survival (co-ed 1972), The Stable Society (1977), The Social and Environmental Effects of Large Dams Vol I (with Nicholas Haldyard 1984); *Clubs* Travellers, Paris; *Style—* Edward Goldsmith, Esq; Whitehay, Withiel, Bodmin, Cornwall (☎ 0208 831237); 254 Fanbours St Honoré, Paris; The Ecologist, Whitehay, Withiel, Bodmin, Cornwall

GOLDSMITH, Sir James Michael; s of Frank Benedict Hayum Goldsmith, OBE, TD (d 1967) and Marcelle, *née* Mouiller; yr bro of Edward Goldsmith, *qv*; *b* 26 Feb 1933; *Educ* Eton; *m* 1, 7 Jan 1954, Maria Isabel (d 15 May 1954), da of Don Antenor Patiño y Rodriguez (d 1982), sometime Bolivian ambass in London, and Maria Cristina, 3 Duchess of Durcal (*see* Vol I Burkes Royal Families of the World); 1 da (Isabelle); m 2, Ginette Lery; 1 s, 1 da; m 3, 1978, as her 2 husband, Lady Annabel Vane Tempest Stewart (*see* Goldsmith, Lady Annabel); 2 s, 1 da and 2 step s, 1 step da; *Career* fndr: Generale Occidentale SA (France), Cavenham Ltd (UK); fndr and chm Gen Oriental (Hong Kong); *Books* Counterculture (1985, vol II 1988), Pour la Revolution permanente dans la diversite (1986); *Clubs* Brooks's, Buck's, Traveller's (Paris); *Style—* Sir James Goldsmith; Swan House, Madeira Walk, Windsor, Berks SL4 1EV (☎ 0753 830707)

GOLDSMITH, John Stuart; CB (1984); o s of R W Goldsmith and S E Goldsmith; *b* 2 Nov 1924; *Educ* Whitgift Middle Sch, St Catharine's Coll Cambridge; *m* 1948, Brenda Goldsmith; 2 s, 1 da; *Career* Royal Signals 1943-47; WO 1948, joined MOD 1964, dir gen Def Accounts MOD 1980-84; *Style—* John Goldsmith, Esq, CB; Cobthorne House,

Church Lane, Rode, Somerset (☎ 0373 830681)

GOLDSMITH, Peter Henry; QC (1987); s of Sydney Elland Goldsmith, and Myra, *née* Nurick; *b* 5 Jan 1950; *Educ* Quarry Bank HS Liverpool, Gonville and Caius Coll Cambridge (MA), UCL (LLM); *m* Joy; 3 s (James b 1978, Jonathan b 1983, Benjamin b 1985), 1 da (Charlotte b 1981); *Career* called to the Bar Gray's Inn 1972, SE circuit, jr counsel to the Crown Common Law 1985-87; *Style*— Peter Goldsmith, Esq, QC; Fountain Court, Temple, London EC4Y 9DH (☎ 01 583 3335)

GOLDSMITH, Stuart Andrew; s of Kenneth Ernest Goldsmith (d 1968), of Bournemouth, and Frances Ruby, *née* Wratten; *b* 1 April 1945; *Educ* Ashford GS, Univ of Bristol (BA); *m* 22 June 1968, Cherry Ann, da of Thomas John Kempton (d 1980), of Chichester; 2 s (Andrew b 1972, James b 1976), 2 da (Katherine b 1971, Amanda b 1975); *Career* deputy chm and chief exec Fredericks Place Hldgs plc 1985-; non-exec and dir: CCL Fin Gp plc 1985, Stanley Gibbons Hldgs plc 1986, Hallwood Gp Inc 1987; dir: Britannia Arrow Hldgs plc, subsidiaries and managed investmt companies 1978-84 (investment dir 1978-81, md, fund mgmnt div 1981-84); *Recreations* wine, opera, philately, trees; *Style*— Stuwart A Goldsmith, Esq; Ketton House, Kedington, Suffolk; 1 Fredericks Place, Old Jewry, London EC2R 8HR (☎ 01 600 3677, fax 01 726 8619, telex 8953861)

GOLDSMITH, Walter Kenneth; s of Lionel Goldsmith (d 1981), and Phoebe Goldsmith; *b* 19 Jan 1938; *Educ* Merchant Taylors'; *m* 1961, Rosemary Adele, da of Joseph Salter (d 1970); 2 s, 2 da; *Career* mangr Mann Judd & Co 1964; joined Black & Decker Ltd 1966: dir of investmt, finance and admin Europe 1967, gen mangr 1970, md 1974, chief exec and Euro dir 1975, Black & Decker USA 1976-79); corporate vice pres and pres Pacific Int Operation; dir gen IOD 1979-84; chm: Korn Ferry Int Ltd 1984-86 (chief exec 1984-85), Leisure Devpt Ltd 1984-85; dir: Bank Leumi (UK) Ltd 1984-, Bestobell plc 1980-85, The Lesser Gp 1983-85, BUPA Med Centre 1980-84, Pubns Ltd 1983-84, Trusthouse Forte Inc 1985-87, The Winning Streak Ltd 1985, Reginald Watts Associates Ltd 1987-, Spong plc 1987, Isus Ltd (dep chm 1987-); gp planning and marketing dir Trusthouse Forte plc 1985-87; memb: cncl Br Exec Service Overseas 1979-84, Eng Tourist Bd 1982-84, Br Tourist Authy 1984-86, BOTB for Israel 1984- (chm 1987-), Policy Planning Gp Inst of Jewish Affairs 1983-; tstee Israel Diaspora Tst 1982-, chm of tstees Stress Fndn 1984-; pres Inst of Word Processing 1983-; Free Enterprise Award Aims for Industry 1984, cncl memb Co-op Ireland 1985, tres Leo Baeck Coll 1987-, chm Food Frm Britain 1987-; Liveryman Worshipful Co of CAs in England and Wales 1985; FCA; *Publications* The Winning Streak (with D Clutterbuck 1984), The Winning Streak Workout Book (1985); The New Elite (with Berry Ritchie 1987); *Recreations* music, boating, painting, property; *Clubs* Carlton, Durbar (vice pres 1984-); *Style*— Walter Goldsmith, Esq; IOD, 116 Pall Mall, London SW1Y 5ED (☎; c/o Trusthouse Forte plc, 86 Park Lane, London W1A 4AA (☎ 01 493 4090) 01 839 1233, telex 21614)

GOLDSTEIN, Dr Michael; s of Jacob Goldstein (d 1945), of London, and Sarah, *née* Goldberg (now Mrs Hyman); *b* 1 May 1939; *Educ* Hackney Downs GS London, Northern Poly (BSc, PhD, DSc); *m* 5 May 1962, Janet Sandra, da of Henry Arthur Skevington (d 1979), of London; 1 s (Richard b 1968); *Career* lectr (later sr lectr and princ lectr) Poly of North London (formerly Northern Poly) 1963-73; Sheffield Poly: head of dept of chemistry 1974-83, dean of the faculty of science 1979-83; dir Coventry Poly 1987- (dep dir 1983-87); author of several review chapters in books 1966-77; chm Chemistry Bd CNAA 1978-84, involved with local regnl and nat sections of Royal Soc of Chemistry and with W Midlands Regnl Advsy Cncl for further educn; CChem, MRSC 1967, FRSC 1973; *Recreations* jogging, DIY, Coventry City FC; *Style*— Dr Michael Goldstein; Coventry Poly, Priory St, Coventry CV1 5FB (☎ 0203 838212, fax 0203 258597, telex 931210228 CP G)

GOLDSTEIN-JACKSON, Kevin Grierson; s of Harold Grierson Jackson, and Winifred Miriam Emily, *née* Fellows; *b* 2 Nov 1946; *Educ* Univ of Reading (BA), Univ of Southampton (MPhil); *m* 6 Sept 1975, Jenny Mei Leng, da of Ufong Ng, of Malaysia; 2 da (Sing Yu b 1981, Kimberley b 1984); *Career* staff rels dept London Tport 1966, Scottish Widows Pension and Life Assur Soc 1967, programme organizer Southern TV 1970-73, asst prodr HK - TVB Hong Kong 1973, freelance writer and TV prodr 1973-75, fndr and dir Thames Valley Radio 1974-77, head film Dhofar Region TV Serv Sultanate of Oman 1975-76, asst to head of drama Anglia TV 1977-81; TV SW: fndr, controller and dir of programmes 1981-85, jt md 1981-82, chief exec 1982-85; dir Ind TV Pubns 1981-85, contrib Financial Times 1986-, dir private cos; govr Lilliput First Sch Poole; FRSA 1978, FBIM 1982, FInstD 1982, FFA 1988; *Books* incl: The Right Joke for the Right Occassion (1973), Encyclopaedia of Ridiculous Facts (1975), Experiments with Everyday Objects (1976), Dictionary of Essential Quotations (1983); *Recreations* writing, tv, films, travel, music, walking; *Style*— Kevin Goldstein-Jackson, Esq; c/o Barclays Bank, 49 St Leonard's Rd, Windsor, Berks SL4 3BP

GOLDSTONE, David Israel; CBE (1971), JP (Manchester 1958-), DL (1978); s of Philip Goldstone, and Bessie Goldstone; *b* 1908,Aug; *m* 1931, Belle, da of L A Franks; *Career* fndr and chm Sterling McGregor Ltd Gp of Cos, fndr memb NW Telecommunications Bd 1974-84, chm Prince's Tst in Gtr Manchester Co 1979-84; exec memb: Queen's Jubilee Ctee for Gtr Manchester Co 1978-84, Br Ctee of Int Chambers of Commerce (ICC) 1975-84; dir Manchester Chamber of Commerce & Ind 1958- (vice-pres 1968-70, pres 1970-72, emeritus dir Ind 1978-); vice-pres: Gtr Manchester Youth Assoc, Gtr Manchester Assoc of Physically Handicapped and Able Bodied Clubs 1972-; fndr memb and vice-pres NW Museum of Science and Ind 1973-, fndr memb Clothing Neddy Ctee, exec memb St John's Cncl 1980-, govr Manchester Victoria Hosp, memb Miny of Pensions Nat Insur Tbnls, Wage Cncls and Br Standard Ctee; Hon MA Manchester 1979; *Style*— David Goldstone, Esq, CBE, JP, DL; Dellstar, Elm Rd, Didsbury, Manchester M20 0XD (☎ 061 445 1868)

GOLDSTONE, David Joseph; s of Solomon Goldstone, and Rebecca, *née* Degotts; *b* 21 Feb 1929; *Educ* Dynevor Swansea, LSE (LLB); *m* 21 March 1957, Cynthia, da of Walter George Easton; 1 s (Jonathan Lee b 3 Nov 1957), 2 da (Debra Ann b 24 Aug 1959, Karen Ella b 22 Oct 1964); *Career* legal practice 1955-66, chief exec Regalian Properties plc 1970-; memb incl: Football Assoc of Wales 1970-72, Welsh Nat Opera 1984-; memb ct of govrs: LSE 1985-, Atlantic Coll 1987-; *Recreations* family, reading, farming, sport; *Clubs* RAC, Lansdowne; *Style*— David Goldstone, Esq; P O Box 4NR, 44 Grosvenor Hill, London W1A 4NR (☎ 01 493 9613, fax 01 491 0692)

GOLLANCZ, Livia Ruth; da of Sir Victor Gollancz (d 1967), and Ruth, *née* Lowy (d 1973); *b* 25 May 1920; *Educ* St Paul's Girls' Sch, RCM; *Career* hornplayer 1940-53; governing dir and joint md Victor Gollancz Ltd 1967-87, (chm 1983-); ARCM; *Recreations* singing, gardening, mountain walking; *Style*— Miss Livia Gollancz; Victor Gollancz Ltd, 14 Henrietta St, London WC2 (☎ 01 836 2006)

GOLLINGS, Raymond Dennis; s of George Robert Gollings (d 1985), and Renee Mary, *née* Greves; *b* 5 June 1943; *Educ* Bexleyheath Sch for Boys; *m* 4 Oct 1975, Anne Elizabeth, da of Raymond Lavallan Nugent, JP, of Knockbarragh Park, Rostrevor, Co Down, NI; *Career* dir Hill Samuel Securities Ltd 1983-85, Hill Samuel Bank Ltd 1985-, Hill Samuel Int Banking Corp NY 1986-; *Recreations* golf, photography, music; *Clubs* North Down GC; *Style*— Raymond Gollings, Esq; 36 Pickhurst Park, Bromley, Kent (☎ 01 460 8753); Hill Samuel Bank Ltd, 100 Wood St, London (☎ 01 606 1422, fax 01 606 8175, telex 888471)

GOLT, Sidney; CB (1964); s of Wolf Golt (d 1939), of W Hartlepool, and Fanny, *née* Mossman (d 1923); *b* 31 Mar 1910; *Educ* Portsmouth GS, Christ Church Oxford (MA); *m* 1947, Jean Amy McMillan, da of Ralph Oliver (d 1978), of Lyme Regis; 2 da (Deborah, Isobel); *Career* econ conslt; sec Central Price Regulation Ctee 1945-46, ldr UK Delgn to UN Conf on Trade and Devpt New Delhi 1968, dep sec DTI 1968-70, chm Linked Life Assur Gp 1971-81, advsr on trade policy Int C of C 1978-, dir Malmgren Golt Kingston & Co Ltd 1978-; *Recreations* travel, bridge; *Clubs* Reform; *Style*— Sidney Golt, Esq, CB; 37 Rowan Rd, London W6; The Gore Cottage, Burnham, Bucks

GOMBRICH, Prof Sir Ernst Hans Josef; OM (1988), CBE (1966); s of Dr Karl B Gombrich (d 1950) and Prof Leonie, *née* Hock; *b* 30 Mar 1909; *Educ* Theresianum Akademie, Univ of Vienna (PhD); *m* 1936, Ilse, da of Gustav Heller, of Neuötting, Bohemia; 1 s (Richard Francis b 1937); *Career* Slade prof of fine art: Oxford Univ 1950-53, Cambridge Univ 1961-63; dir of Warburg Inst and prof of history of the classical tradition London Univ 1959-76 (emeritus prof 1976-); *Books* Ehrenkreuz Für Wissenschaft und Kunst (1975), Pour le Mérite (1977), Ehrenzeichen Für Wissenschaft Und Kunst (1984); FBA, FSA; kt 1972; *Style*— Prof Sir Ernst Gombrich, OM, CBE; 19 Briardale Gdns, London NW3 7PN (☎ 01 435 6639)

GOMER, Sara Louise; da of Derek Colin Gomer, of Torquay, Devon, and Elaine Barbara, *née* Slack; *b* 13 May 1964; *Educ* Torquay GS for Girls, Eastbourne Further Educn Coll; *Career* memb: Wightman Cup Team 1985-, Fedn Cup Team 1987-, Euro Cup Team 1986-; competed in Seoul Olympics 1988, winner Plate Event Wimbledon 1987 (runner up 1988), winner Northern Californian Open 1988; *Recreations* cycling, music, squash, photography, cinema; *Clubs* Riverside Sports; *Style*— Miss Sara Gomer; Brecklands, 21 Childs Hall Rd, Bookham, Surrey KT23 3QF (☎ 0372 54415)

GOMERSALL, Richard; s of Willie Gomersall, of Rotherham, and Mary, *née* Hardman; *b* 18 Oct 1945; *Educ* Mexborough GS; *m* 13 June 1970, Christine Mary Magdalene, da of Marrian Zgoda; 1 s (Nicholas b 1975), 1 da (Vanessa b 1972); *Career* CA; ptnr Montgomery & Co Rotherham; chm: Abel Data Ltd 1986-, Poll Tax Consultancy Ltd 1988; *Recreations* lay reader C of E, property developing; *Clubs* Rotherham; *Style*— Richard Gomersall, Esq; Dale View House, 14 Wignall Avenue, Wickersley, Rotherham (☎ 0709 546441); Montgomery & Co, Chartered Accountants, 55 Moorgate Street, Rotherham (☎ 0709 376313, fax 0709 703026)

GOMEZ, Jill; *b* Trinidad, British and Spanish parents; *Educ* RAM, Guildhall Sch of Music; *Career* Br opera and concert singer; operatic debut with Glyndebourne Festival Opera 1969 and has since sung leading roles incl: Melisande, Calisto and Ann Truelove in the Rake's Progress; has appeared with The Royal Opera, English Opera and Scottish Opera in roles incl: Pamina, Ilia, Fiordiligi, the Countess in Figaro, Elizabeth in Elegy for Young Lovers, Tytania, Lauretta in Gianni Schicchi, and the Governess in The Turn of the Screw; created the role of Flora in Tippett's The Knot Garden (Covent Garden), the Countess in Thea Musgrave's Voice of Ariadne (Aldeburgh) 1974, sang title role in Massenet's Thais (Wexford) 1974, Jenifer in The Midsummer Marriage (WNO) 1976, created title role in William Alwyn's Miss Julie for radio 1977, Tatiana in Eugene Onegin (Kent Opera) 1977, Donna Elvira in Don Giovanni (Ludwigsburg Festival) 1978, title role in BBC world prepiere of Prokoviev's Maddalena 1979, Fiordiligi Cosi fan Tutte (Bordeaux) 1979, sang in premiere of the 8th Book of Madrigals (Zurich Monteverdi Festival) 1979, Violetta in Kent Opera's production of La Traviata (Edinburgh Festival) 1979, Cinna in Lucio Silla (Zurich) 1981, The Governess in The Turn of the Screw (Geneva) 1981, Cleopatra in Giulio Cesare (Frankfurt) 1981, Teresa in Benvenuto Cellini, (Berlioz Festival, Lyon) 1982, Leila in Les Pecheurs de Perles (Scottish Opera) 1982-83; Governess in The Turn of the Screw (English Nat Opera) 1984, Helena in Glyndebourne's production of Britten's A Midsummer Night's Dream; Donna Anna in Don Giovanni (Frankfurt Opera) 1985, Amyntas in IL RE Pastore (Kentopera) 1987, Donna Anna in Don Giovanni (Kent Opera) 1988; Regular engagements incl recitals in: France, Austria, Belgium, Netherlands, Germany, Scandinavia, Switzerland, Italy, Spain and the USA ; Festival appearances incl: Aix-en-Provence, Spoleto, Bergen, Versailles, Flanders, Netherlands, Prague, Edinburgh and BBC Promenade concerts; numerous recordings incl: Vespro della Beata Vergine 1610 (Monteverdi), Acis and Galatea (Handel), The Knot Garden (Tippett), three recital discs of French, Spanish and Mozart songs, Quatre Chansons Francaises (Britten), Trois Poemes de Mallarme (Ravel), Chants d'Auvergne (Canteloube), Les Illuminations (Britten), Bachianas Brasileiras No 5 (Villa Lobos); *Books* Knoxville Summer of 1915 (Samuel Barber Cabaret Classics with John Constable); *Style*— Miss Jill Gomez; 16 Milton Park, London N6 5QA

GOMM, Douglas Rubert; s of Horace Gomm (d 1962), of Canterbury, and Gladys Carden Elizabeth, *née* Weeks; *b* 12 Jan 1937; *Educ* Simon Langton GS For Boys; *m* 22 Dec 1973, Sheila, da of Victor George Arthur Coombes; 2 s (Dominic b 1975, Russell b 1980); *Career* Nat Serv 1955-57, RAPC attached to 1 Bn KOSB; sr accountant E Clarke Williams; cncllr Canterbury City Cncl 1983-, Sheriff of Canterbury 1987-88, govr Briary Co Primary Sch Herne Bay; hon life memb and vice pres Canterbury and Dist Table Tennis Assoc (past chm); FFA 1975; *Style*— Douglas Gomm, Esq; Hawthorns, 89A Greenhill Rd, Herne Bay, Kent CT6 7QW (☎ 0227 372 091); E Clarke Williams, 41/43 William St, Herne Bay, Kent (☎ 0227 373 271)

GONZALEZ-MORENO, Anna; da of Mahmood Taghavy-Shirzi, of Tehran, Iran, and Charmaine Hassen; *b* 12 Dec 1956; *Educ* Lucée Francais Turkey, Sorbonne Paris, Licence es Sciences Sociales, UCL (MA Anthropology); *m* 12 July 1986, Simon Gonazlez-Moreno, s of Jaime Gonzalez-Moreno, of Lausanne, Switzerland; *Career* Lloyds Insurance Broker specialising in political risks insurance; *Recreations* skiing, scuba diving; *Style*— Mrs Anna Gonzalez-Moreno; Lloyd Thompson Ltd, 14 Lovat Lane, London EC3

GOOCH, Brig Arthur Brian Sherlock Heywood; ADC 1989; s of Col Brian

Sherlock Gooch, DSO, TD, JP (d 1968), of Tannington Hall, Woodbridge, Suffolk, and Monica Mary, *née* Heywood (d 1975); *b* 1 June 1937; *Educ* Eton; *m* 27 July 1963, Sarah, da of Lt Col John Francis George Perceval (d 1980), of Templehouse, Co Sligo; 2 da (Rowena b 1965, Katherine b 1967); *Career* cmmnd Life Gds 1956, Oman and Aden 1958-59, Adj 1960-63, instr RMA Sandhurst 1964-65, Malaysia and Hong Kong 1966-68 GS03 (Ops) HQ 4 Gds Armd Bde 1969-70, NI 1972, asst mil attaché Tehran 1973-75, CO Life Gds 1978-81, dir staff Army Staff Coll 1981-82, cmdt jr div Staff Coll 1982-86, cdr Royal Armd Corps Centre 1987-89; *Recreations* field sports, gardening, food and wine; *Style*— Brig Arthur Gooch

GOOCH, Charles Albert; s of Ernest Edward Gooch; *b* 15 Sept 1938; *Educ* Coleman St Ward Sch London; *m* 1974, June Margaret, *née* Reardon; 2 da (Charlotte b 1976, Jessica b 1978); *Career* former chm Shaw & Marvin plc, chm and md Buckland Securities Ltd Gp of cos; *Recreations* squash, football; *Style*— Charles Gooch, Esq; Buckland Securities Ltd, 28 Redchurch St, London E2 7DP (☎ 01 739 3604)

GOOCH, Sir (Richard) John Sherlock; 12 Bt (GB 1746), JP (Suffolk 1970); s of Sir Robert Eric Sherlock Gooch, 11 Bt, KCVO, DSO, JP, DL (d 1978), and Katharine Clervaux (d 1974), da of Maj-Gen Sir Edward Walter Clervaux Chaytor, KCMG, KCVO, CB; *b* 22 Mar 1930; *Educ* Eton; *Heir* bro, Maj Timothy Gooch, MBE; *Career* Capt Life Gds; *Style*— Sir John Gooch, Bt, JP; Benacre Hall, Beccles, Suffolk (☎ 0502 740333)

GOOCH, Michael Edwin; s of Edwin George Gooch MP (d 1964), of Wymondham, Norfolk, and Ethel Banham (d 1953); *b* 6 Feb 1923; *Educ* Norwich Sch, CCC Cambridge (MA, AA Dip); *m* 24 May 1942, Sheila Mary, da of Frederick Ward (d 1981), of Winchester; 1 s (Simon b 1955), 1 da (Joanna b 1957); *Career* WW II 1942-46 Capt; architect, winner of numerous awards incl: Europa Nostra Awards, Civic Tst Awards, 'Times' Conservation Award; RIBA; *Style*— Michael Gooch, Esq; 11 Willow Lane, Norwich, Norfolk NR2 1EU (☎ 0603 627506)

GOOCH, Richard Christopher Wyard; s of Rev Henry Wyard Gooch (d 1962), and Gwendolen, *née* Brutton (d 1988); *b* 9 Nov 1927; *Educ* Marlborough, Sidney Sussex Coll Cambridge (MA); *m* 23 Aug 1958, Joan Hemsley, da of John Hemsley Longrigg; 1 s (Nicholas b 12 July 1966), 3 da (Phillipa (Mrs Lark) b 21 May 1959, Belinda (Mrs Humphry) 1 May 1961, Amanda b 20 Aug 1963); *Career* RASC 1946-48, Lt; admitted slr 1954, ptnr Maslen & Maslen Bournemouth 1956-71, sr ptnr Thos Coombs and Son Dorchester 1967-; registrar Archdeaconry of Sherborne 1970-; chm: Social Security Appeal Tbnl 1984-, Medical Appeal Tbnl 1987- (dep registrar 1986-); legal advsr Dorset Relate (formerly Marriage Guidance Cncl) 1970-, parish cncllr 1970-86; memb: Archbishops Advsy Panel on Divorce Law Reform 1968-69, Hodson Cmmn on Synodical Govt 1967-68, Diocesan Synod 1958-87, Salisbury Diocesan Bishop's Cncl 1973-88; clerk to Hardye's Sch Dorchester 1970-76; pres Dorset Law Soc 1986, memb Law Soc 1954; *Recreations* riding, gardening, reading; *Style*— Richard Gooch, Esq; The Garden Hse, Frome Whitfield, Dorchester, Dorset (☎ 0929 471 480); Thos Coombs & Son, Savernake Hse, 42 High West St, Dorchester, Dorset, DT1 1UU (☎ 0305 62901)

GOOCH, Sir Robert Douglas; 4 Bt (UK 1866); s of Sir Daniel Fulthorpe Gooch, 3 Bt (d 1926); *b* 19 Sept 1905; *Educ* Brighton Coll; *m* 1, 5 Jan 1928 (m dis 1930), Moyra Katharine, o da of Charles Howard Saunders, MB; m 2, 18 Aug 1930, Mary Eileen (d 1979), da of late Colin George Barrett, and wid of Maj H L Gifford; 1 da; *Heir* kinsman, Trevor Sherlock Gooch, VRD, *qv*; *Style*— Sir Robert Gooch, Bt

GOOCH, Maj Timothy Robert Sherlock; MBE (1970); s of Sir Robert Eric Sherlock Gooch, KCVO, DSO, JP, DL, 11 Bt (d 1978), of Benacre Hall, Suffolk, and Katharine Clervaux (d 1974), da of Maj-Gen Sir Edward Walter Clervaux Chaytor, KCMG, KCVO, CB; hp of bro, Sir (Richard) John (Sherlock) Gooch, 12 Bt; *b* 7 Dec 1934; *Educ* Eton, RMA Sandhurst; *m* 17 Dec 1963, Susan Barbara Christie, da of Maj-Gen Kenneth Christie Cooper, CB, DSO, OBE (d 1981), of West End House, Donhead St Andrew, Wilts; 2 da (Lucinda b 1970, Victoria b 1974); *Career* Maj Life Gds; company dir; Memb HM Body Gd of Hon Corps of Gentlement at Arms 1986-; *Clubs* White's, Cavalry & Guards; *Style*— Maj Timothy Gooch, MBE; The Cedars, Covehithe, Wrentham, Beccles, Suffolk (☎ 050 275 266)

GOOCH, Trevor Sherlock; VRD; s of Charles Trevor Gooch (d 1963), and Hester Stratford, *née* Sherlock (d 1957); hp to Btcy of kinsman, Sir Robert Gooch, 4 Bt, *qv*; *b* 15 June 1915; *Educ* Charterhouse; *m* 1, 1956, Denys Anne (d 1976), o da of Harold Victor Venables, of Edificio la Vileta Camino Vechinal la Vileta 215, Palma, Mallorce, 1 s (Miles b 1963), 4 da (Beverly b 1957, Vanda b 1958, Yvonne b 1961, Rowan b 1971); m 2, 1978, Jean, da of John Joseph Wright; 1 child; *Career* Fl-Lt RAFVR; *Style*— Trevor Gooch, Esq, VRD; Jardin de la Roque, Mont de la Roque, St Aubin, Jersey, CI

GOOD, Anthony Bruton Meyrick; *b* 18 April 1933; *Educ* Felsted; *m* ; 2 da; *Career* mgmnt trainee Distillers Gp 1950-52; editorial asst Temple Press Ltd 1952-55, PR offr Silver City Airways (gp PR/marketing Br Aviation Servs Ltd) 1955-60, fndr and chm Good Relations Gp plc 1960-, chm Cox & Kings Ltd 1975- (joined bd 1971); dir: Britcar (Hldgs), Subaru (UK), John E Wiltshier Group Ltd, Blue Sea Ltd, Frog Hollow Ltd, Norfolk Capital Gp plc 1983-; Nolton plc 1984-; FIPR; *Recreations* travel, reading, theatre; *Clubs* RAC; *Style*— Anthony Good, Esq; 2 Campden House Close, London W8 (☎ 01 937 9737); Good Relations Group plc, 59 Russell Sq, London WC1B 4HJ (☎ 01 631 3434, telex 265903)

GOOD, Anthony Richard; s of Richard George Good; *b* 20 April 1930; *Educ* Reading Univ; *m* 1956, Sallie Lorraine, da of Archibald Wilson; 2 s, 2 da; *Career* former dir Grand Metropolitan Ltd (chief exec milk and foods div), chm Express Dairy Co Ltd; farmer; *Recreations* shooting, fishing; *Style*— Anthony Good, Esq; Warborough Farm, Letcombe Regis, Nr Wantage, Oxfordshire (☎ Wantage 3244)

GOOD, Charles Anthony; s of William Marsh Good (d 1953), of Dublin, and Doris Audrey, *née* Scott; *b* 8 May 1946; *Educ* Charterhouse, Univ of Kent (BSc); *m* 12 Jan 1966, Averil Ray, da of Lt Cdr Frank William Haxworth, RNVR, of Chobham, Surrey; 3 da (Charlotte b 1967, Natasha b 1968, Elinor b 1978); *Career* Robson Rhodes 1968-71, S G Warburg and Co Ltd 1972-75, chm CA Good and Co 1976-, md J S Gadd and Co Ltd 1987-, dep md J S Gadd Hldgs plc 1987-, dir Embassy Property Gp plc 1986-; govr Flexlands Sch 1974- (dep chm 1983-); FCA 1972; *Recreations* tennis, squash, sailing, skiing; *Style*— Charles Good, Esq; Burchetts, Chobham, Surrey; Carlyle Court, Chelsea Harbour, London (☎ 01 376 8164); J S Gadd and Co Ltd, 45 Bloomsbury Sq, London WC1A 2RA (☎ 01 242 5544, fax 01 405 0077, car 0836 614 247, 0860 399544, telex 23260 ARLADY G)

GOOD, Brig Ian Henry; DSO (1943); s of Rev Henry Brodie Good (d 1941), of Balrothery, Co Dublin, and Greystones, Co Wicklow, and Evelyn Francis, *née* Carroll (d 1951); *b* 11 Nov 1905; *Educ* St Columba's Coll Rathfarnham Co Dublin, RMC Sandhurst; *m* 1, 3 Sept 1930 (m dis 1962), Monica Norah, da of Hamilton Coffey (d 1938), of Clobeman, Co Wexford; 2 s (Brian Rupert b 5 Feb 1935, Ian David b 1 Oct 1938); m 2, 3 Feb 1963, Anne Vivienne Vanrenen; *Career* cmmnd RUR 1925, served 1 Bn RUR Germany 1925-27, RWAFF Nigeria 1928-30, 1 Bn RUR 1930-39: Egypt, Palestine, Hong Kong, Shanghai, India; Adj 2 Bn RUR: Palestine 1939, BEF France 1939-40; Staff Capt France 1940, Bde Maj UK 1940-41, GSO2 HQ 1 Corps 1941, CO 1 Bn London Irish Rifles (RUR) 1942-44 (despatches twice): UK, Iraq, Sicily Landings, Italian Campaign (incl Anzio 1944), chief instr M East Staff Coll 1944-45, chief of staff NI Cmd 1945-46, Cmdt Middle East Sch of Inf 1946, cmd 29 Br Bde Gp 1947-48 (last Br bde to evacuate India 1948), Col co-ordination Adj Gen's Off 1948-51, COS Br Army Staff Washington DC 1951-54, dep dir inf WO 1954-56, vice pres Regular Cmmn's Bd 1956-57, Col RUR 1956-62, ret 1957; ADC to HM The Queen 1956-57; staff offr to inspr-gen RUC (orgn, training and ops of the Ulster Special Constabulary) 1957-62, sec Veteran Car Club of GB 1962-66, chm Royal Br Legion Hindon branch 1966-72 (pres 1979-86), memb Hindon PCC; pres London Irish Rifles Regtl Assoc 1976-87; *Recreations* formerly hockey and tennis; *Style*— Brig Ian Good, DSO; Coppers, Fieldway, Hindon, Salisbury, Wilts (☎ 0747 202)

GOOD, Robert Philip; s of Robert Stanley Good (d 1981), and Amy Edith, *née* Grainge; *b* 23 Sept 1928; *Educ* Trinity GS, LSE (BSc); *m* 25 April 1959, (Penelope) Ann, da of Philip Kidson, of Aincroft, Devon Rd, Merstham, Sy; 2 s (Robert b 1963, Richard 1965), 1 da (Fiona b 1961); *Career* served RAF 1946-49 Union Int Co Ltd 1952-57, Thorn EMI plc 1957 - (investmt mangr Thorn EMI Pension Fund); memb mgmnt ctee: Mim North American Exempt Tst 1973, Mim Australian & Asian Exempt Tst 1974, Mim Far Eastern Exempt Tst 1980; dir: County Nat West's American Sunbelt Exempt Tst 1981, County Nat West's Int Venture Capital Exempt Tst 1984; memb: FCIS 1955, AC11 1961, AMSIA 1970, APMI 1976; *Recreations* tennis, painting watercolours, watching old movies; *Style*— Robert Good, Esq, The White House, Henham, Nr Bishop's Stortford, Herts CM 22 6AR (☎ 0279 850 470); Thorn EMI Pension Trust Ltd., Atlas House, Lincoln Road, Enfield, Middlesex EN1 1SE (☎ 01 366 1166, fax 01 366 1166 ext 2863, telex 915 891); The White House, Henham, nr Bishop's Stortford, Herts CM22 6AR (☎ 0279 850 470); Thorn EMI Pension Trust Ltd, Atlas House, Lincoln Rd, Enfield, Middlesex EN1 1SE (☎ 01 366 1166, fax 01 366 1166 ext 2863, telex 915 891)

GOODACRE, (John) Michael Kendall; s of Kenneth Goodacre, TD, DL, of London, and Dorothy, *née* Kendall; *b* 19 August 1941; *Educ* Shrewsbury, Keble Coll Oxford (MA); *m* 29 July 1967, Yvonne Scott, da of John Milsom (d 1985); 2 s (William Henry Kendall b 5 Mar 1971, Edward James Scott b 2 Feb 1972); *Career* slr 1969, asst slr with messrs Coffin Mew & Clover 1969-71 (ptnr 1971); memb: bd of visitors HM Prison Kingston (chm 1987 and 1988), Promotion of Int Gastronomy Soc Portsmouth (chm 1988-89); memb: Law Soc, Hants Inc Law Soc; *Recreations* eating, drinking, reading, skiing, raising beef cattle; *Clubs* Royal Naval, Royal Albert YC (Portsmouth); *Style*— Michael Goodacre, Esq; Crofton Old Farm, Titchfield, Hants PO14 3ER (☎ 0329 43298); 17 Hampshire Terr, Portsmouth, Hants PO1 2PU (☎ 0705 812 511, fax 0705 291 847)

GOODALE, Hon Mrs (Pamela Muriel Dorine); *née* Hirst; MBE (1983); da of Harold Hugh Hirst (d 1919; s of 1 Baron Hirst, barony extinct 1943), and Carol Iris Hirst, MBE, *née* Lindon; raised to the rank of a Baron's da 1943; *b* 16 April 1918; *Educ* Luckley Wokingham; *m* 1, 29 Nov 1940 (m dis 1947), Capt Arthur George Bevington Colyer, RA, o s of Dr Arthur Colyer, of Old Way House, Charing, Kent; m 2, 9 Dec 1949, Roy Edward Goodale (d 1 Aug 1969), s of late William Thomas Goodale, of Laleham-on-Thames; 1 s (Hugh b 1953); *Career* served WWII as Staff Capt ATS; chm: Lingfield Parish Cncl 1957-69 (memb 1955-69), Godstone RDC 1969-72 (memb 1955-76); memb Tandridge Cncl 1974-75, hon Alderman Tandridge DC; dir and company sec H R Goodale Ltd; *Recreations* voluntary work (political and public); *Style*— Hon Mrs Goodale, MBE; Peartrees, Dormansland, nr Lingfield, Surrey RH7 6QY (☎ 0342 832368; office: 0732 863993)

GOODALL, His Hon Anthony Charles; MG (1942), DL (Devon) 1987; s of Charles Henry Goodall (d 1968), of Wilts, and Mary Helen, *née* Walker (d 1956); *b* 23 July 1916; *Educ* Eton, Kings Coll Cambridge (MA); *m* 1947, Anne Valerie, da of John Reginald Chichester (d 1968), of Devon; 1 s (Charles b 1948), 2 da (Clarissa b 1950, Diana b 1959); *Career* served WWII 1939-45, 1 Royal Dragoons in M East, Italy, France, Beglium, Holland; (POW twice 1944), Capt; barr 1939, practised at the bar 1946-67, county ct judge and circuit judge 1968-86; pres Plymouth Magistrates Assoc 1976-84, memb County Ct Rule Ctee 1978-83, jt vice-pres cncl of HM Circuit Judges 1985 (joint pres 1986), ret 1986; DL Devon 1987-; *Style*— His Hon Anthony Goodall; Mardeon, Moretonhampstead, Devon (☎ 40239)

GOODALL, Caroline Mary Helen; da of Capt Peter Goodall, CBE, TD, of Wetherby, W Yorks, and Sonja Jeanne, *née* Burt; sis of Charles Peter Goodall, *qv*; *b* 22 May 1955; *Educ* Queen Ethelburgh's Sch, Newham Coll (MA); *m* 1 Oct 1983, (Vesey) John, s of Maj Vesey Michael Hill (d 1972); *Career* asst slr Slaughter & May 1980-84 (articled clerk 1978-80), ptnr Herbert Smith 1987- (asst slr 1984-87); memb Worhsipful Co Slrs; memb: Law Soc, London Young Slrs GP; *Recreations* tennis, theatre, windsurfing, fell walking; *Clubs* Roehampton; *Style*— Miss Caroline Goodall; Watling House, 35 Cannon St, London EC4M 5SD (☎ 01 489 8000, 01 236 5733, telex 886 633)

GOODALL, Charles Peter; s of Capt Peter Goodall, CBE, TD, of Springfield House, Sickinghall Rd, Wetherby, West Yorks, and Sonja Jeanne, *née* Burt; bro of Caroline Mary Helen Goodall, *qv*; *b* 14 July 1950; *Educ* Sherborne, St Catherine's Coll Cambridge (MA, LLM); *Career* asst slr Slaughter and May 1976-82 (articled clerk 1974-76), ptnr Simmons and Simons 1984- (asst slr 1982-84); memb Law Soc; *Recreations* squash, golf, sailing; *Clubs* Utd Oxford and Cambridge Univ, Hawks, Cambridge, Royal Wimbledon GC; *Style*— Charles Goodall, Esq; Simmons and Simmons, 14 Dominion St, London EC2M 2RJ (☎ 01 628 2020, fax 01 588 4129, telex 888562 SIMMON G)

GOODALL, Sir (Arthur) David (Saunders); KCMG (1987, CMG 1979); o s of Arthur William Goodall (d 1968), of Whaley Bridge, Derbys, and Maisie Josephine, *née* Byers; *b* 9 Oct 1931; *Educ* Ampleforth, Trinity Coll Oxford (MA); *m* 1962, Morwenna, yst da of Percival George Beck Peecock (d 1972), of Goring, Sussex; 2 s, 1 da;

Career 2 Lt 1 Bn KOYLI 1955-56: Kenya, Aden, Cyprus; HM Dip Serv: head of W Euro dept FCO 1975-79, min Bonn 1979-82, seconded to Cabinet Off dep sec 1982-84, deputy under sec of State FCO 1984-87, Br High Cmmr to India 1987-; *Recreations* water colour painting, social history; *Clubs* United Oxford and Cambridge Univs; *Style*— Sir David Goodall, KCMG; c/o Foreign and Commonwealth Office (New Delhi), London SW1A 2AH

GOODALL, Francis Richard Cruice; s of William Cruice Goodall (d 1958), of Liverpool, and Joan Mary, *née* Berrill (d 1955); *b* 4 Oct 1929; *Educ* Ampleforth, Queens' Coll Cambridge (MA), Architectural Assoc (Dip Arch); *m* 21 Jan 1978, Vivienne, da of Thomas Vyvyan More (d 1956), of E London and S Africa; *Career* Nat Serv 1948-49, cmmnd RE, serv N Africa, Malta; ptnr Frederick MacManus & Ptnrs 1963-, (assoc 1958-63); memb cncl: Soc of Construction Law 1988, Architects' Registration Cncl UK 1984-; Freeman City of London 1982, Liveryman Worshipful Co of Arbitrators 1982 (memb Ct of Assts 1987-); FRIBA, FCIArb; *Clubs* Garrick, Travellers; *Style*— Francis Goodall, Esq; 37 Molyneux St, Marylebone, London W1H 5HW (☎ 01 723 4701); 41 Upper Montagu St, Marylebone, London W1H 1FQ (☎ 01 262 6651, fax 01 402 0433)

GOODALL, Geoffrey Trevor; s of Thomas Henry Goodall (d 1947), of London, and Jane, *née* Bird (d 1980); *b* 15 Oct 1929; *Educ* Haberdashers' Askes's, Corpus Christi Coll Oxford (MA); *m* 6 Sept 1952, Marion Rosemary, da of Arthur William Smith, MBE (d 1980), of London; 3 s (Ashley b 1956, Howard b 1958, Adrian b 1961), 1 da (Sally b 1967); *Career* craftsman REME 1948-50; languages teacher Haberdashers' Aske's 1954-58, head of modern languages Uppingham 1960-64, (teacher 1958-60); headmaster: Lord William's Sch Thame 1964-79, Exeter Sch Devon 1979-; nat pres SHA 1982, chm SW Div HMC 1985, del for Oxford local Examination Bd 1974-; ed Maigret series for Macmillans 1965-; *Books* Themes Anglais pour toute la grammaire (1963); *Recreations* music, theatre, sport; *Style*— Geoffrey Goodall, Esq; High Meadow, Barrack Rd, Exeter, Devon, EX2 5AB (☎ 0392 73679) Exeter School, Exeter, Devon EX2 4NS

GOODALL, Peter; CBE (1983), TD (1950); s of Maj Tom Goodall, DSO, MC (d 1977), and Alice, *née* Black; *b* 14 July 1920; *Educ* Ashville Coll Harrogate; *m* 1948, Sonja Jeanne, da of Victor Charles Burt (d 1960); 1 s (Charles b 1950), 1 da (Mrs John Hill b 1955); *Career* Capt, Duke of Wellington's and Parachute Regts 1939-46; slr 1948; practised with family firm Goodall & Son, Whitfield Son & Hallam 1948-67; dir: Hepworth Iron Co 1967-70, Hepworth Ceramic Hldgs plc (producers of refractories, clayware, plastics, foundry resins and equipment, engineering products) 1970-71 (md 1971-77, exec chm 1977-86); memb cncl: CBI 1981-, Br Utd Industrialists 1984-; *Recreations* shooting, fishing; *Style*— Peter Goodall, Esq, CBE, TD; Springfield House, Sicklinghall Road, Linton, Wetherby, W Yorks (☎ 0937 61297)

GOODALL, Sir Reginald; CBE (1975); *b* 13 July 1901; *m* 1932, Eleanor Gipps; *Career* conductor Royal Opera House 1947; Hon DMus Oxford; kt 1985; *Style*— Sir Reginald Goodall, CBE; Barham Court, Barham, Canterbury, Kent

GOODALL, Rodney David; s of Cecil Ernest Goodall (d 1972), of Reading, and Ellen May, *née* Farr (d 1982); *b* 30 June 1934; *Educ* Reading Sch, Oxford Sch of Architecture (DipArch); *m* 15 Aug 1964, Lesley Ann, da of Walter Leslie Chapman, of Thurloxton, Somerset; 1 s (Timothy b 1965), 1 da (Rachel b 1967); *Career* chartered architect; princ Rodney D Goodall, Frome 1968-; Civic Tst Awards: EAHY Award 1975, Commendation 1980 (for historic building repairs/conversion); restoration of St James' Church Trowbridge 1987; Somerset co cncllr 1975-80, town cncllr Frome 1971-87, Mayor of Frome 1977-79; C of E lay reader 1984-; RIBA, DCHM, FRSA; *Recreations* walking, music making, theatre, history; *Style*— Rodney D Goodall, Esq; The Gables, 28 Somerset Road, Frome, Somerset BA11 1HD (☎ 0373 65756); 8 Bath Street, Frome, Somerset BA11 1DH (☎ 0373 62284)

GOODBAND, Philip Haydon; s of Philip Aubrey Goodband, of 61 The Ave, Camberley, Surrey, and Edith Emma Haydon, *née* Cooper; *b* 26 May 1944; *Educ* Strodes Sch Dijon France, Academie Du Champagne (MW); *m* 18 Dec 1971, Lynne Wendy, da of Brig Lindsey Jerment Aspland, OBE, of Vine Cottage, Ridgeway Rd, Dorking, Surrey; 2 s (Charles Lindsey Haydon b 19 June 1976, d 24 Nov 1976, Henry Lindsey Charles b 24 Oct 1978), 1 da (Emily Victoria b 19 Sept 1973) ; *Career* dir: Gilbey SA France 1972-73, Wine Devpt Bd 1980-, purchasing and quality Stowells of Chelsea 1981-86 (buyer 1973-80); chm Inst Masters of Wine 1984-85, tstee Wine and Spirit Trade Benevolent Soc 1986-, wine buying and quality logistics Grants of St Jame's 1986-88, md Grants of St James's Wholesale (Whitbread) 1988-; lectr and broadcaster in London, Paris, Milan, San Francisco, chm Redbourn Tennis Club 1975-82, judge Newdigate; Freeman: City of London 1972, Worshipful Co Haberdashers 1972 (Clothed 1975); FBBI 1968; Compagnon du Beaujolais 1978, membre de L'Ordre St Etienne France 1981, Cavaleiro da Confraria do Vinho do Porto Portugal 1987; *Recreations* competition carriage driving, riding, tennis; *Clubs* Naval and Military, Brockham Harness, British Driving Soc; *Style*— Philip Goodband, Esq; Long Meadow, Parkgate Rd, Newdigate, Dorking, Surrey, RH5 5DX (☎ 030677 342); Grants of St Jame's Wholesale, Guildford Cellars, Moorfield Rd, Guildford, Surrey GU1 1RU (☎ 0483 64861, fax 0483 506691, telex 859328)

GOODBODY, Michael Ivan Andrew; s of Llewellyn Marcus Goodbody (see Burkes Irish Family Records), of Ardclough Lodge, Straffan, Co Kildare, Ireland, and Eileen Elizabeth, *née* Bourke; *b* 23 Jan 1942; *Educ* Kingstown Sch Dublin; *m* 9 March 1968, Susannah Elizabeth, da of Donald Guy Pearce (Capt Ayrshire Yeomanry RA, ka 1944); 1 s (Guy b 1972), 2 da (Sarah b 1970, Perry b 1976); *Career* Lt TA, 289 Parachute Battery RHA; stockbroker Smith Rice & Hill 1962-74, private client stockbroker Capel-Cure Myers 1974-; memb Int Stock Exchange; *Books* The Goodbody Family of Ireland (1979); *Recreations* family history; *Style*— Michael Goodbody, Esq; The Old Rectory, Wickham St Paul's, Halstead, Essex CO9 2PJ; Capel-Cure Myers Capital Management Ltd, 65 Holborn Viaduct, London EC1A 2EU

GOODCHILD, Peter Robert Edward; s of Douglas Richard Geoffrey Goodchild, MBE, of Angmering Village W Sussex, and Lottie May, *née* Ager; *b* 18 August 1939; *Educ* Aldenham, St John's Coll Oxford (MA); *m* 1968, Penelope-Jane, da of Dr William Pointon-Dick (d 1956); 2 da (Abigail b 1971, Hannah b 1974); *Career* prodr Horizon BBC TV 1965-69 (1967, 1968, 1969 winner Soc of Film and TV Arts, Mullard Award for Science Broadcasting), ed Horizon BBC TV 1969-76 (1972 and 1974 winner BAFTA Award for Best Factual Series, 1973 and 1975- winner Italia Prize for Factual Programmes), exec prodr drama prodns 1977-80 (including Marie Curie 1977 and Oppenheimer 1980 which both won BAFTA Awards for Best Series), prodr Bread or Blood 1980, head of Science and Features BBC TV 1980-84, head of plays BBC TV 1984-; CChem, FRSC; *Books* Shatterer of Worlds (the life of J Robert Oppenheimer, 1980); *Recreations* tennis, music; *Clubs* Phyllis Ct; *Style*— Peter Goodchild, Esq; Brockdale Ho, Cricketer's Lane, Warfield, Berks (☎ Winkfield Row 882492); BBC Television Centre, Wood Lane, London W12 (☎ 01 743 8000)

GOODDEN, Benjamin Bernard Woulfe; o s of Cecil Phelips Goodden, JP (d 1969), of The Old House, North Cheriton, Templecombe, Som, and Hylda Maud (d 1970), da of Stephen Roland Woulfe, of Tiermaclane, Co Clare; *b* 16 July 1925; *Educ* Harrow, Trinity Coll Oxford (MA 1950); *m* 1, 1952 (m dis 1966), Elizabeth Sarah, da of GI Woodham-Smith, by his w Cecil Blanche FitzGerald (the authoress); 1 s, 2 da; m 2, 1973, Rose Emma Margaret, 2 da of Lt-Cdr Hon Douglas David Edward Vivian, DSC, RN (d 1973, 2 s of 4 Baron Vivian), and formerly wife of James Collet Norman; 1 s; *Career* barr 1951; ptnr James Capel & Co 1957-71, dir M & G Securities Ltd 1974-; hon tres Bach Choir 1972-; underwriting memb Lloyd's 1972-; *Recreations* cricket, choral music; *Clubs* MCC; *Style*— Benjamin Goodden, Esq; Ferryside, Riverside, Twickenham, Middlesex TW1 3DN (☎ 01 892 1448)

GOODDEN, Rev John Maurice Phelips; er s of John Henry Goodden (d 1974), of Compton House, Sherborne, Dorset, and his 1 w, Valerie Mary, *née* Llewellyn-Evans (d 1959); descended from Robert Goodden (d 1764), of Bower Hinton and Martock, who purchased Compton House and the lordship of the manor of Over Compton and Nether Compton from George Abington in 1736 (*see* Burke's Landed Gentry, 18 edn, vol I, 1965); *b* 17 May 1934; *Educ* Salisbury Cathedral Sch, Sherborne, Trinity Coll Oxford, Sarum and Wells Theological Coll; *m* 1, 12 Oct 1957 (m dis 1974), Ann Rosemary, o child of Alec Vincent Tucker, of Stirling, Nether Compton, Dorset; 3 da (Sarah Helen b 12 Dec 1958, Victoria Ann b 13 Sept 1962, Maria Jeane b 24 May 1968); m 2, 12 Nov 1983, Mrs Madeleine Hilary Wilson; 1 step s, 1 step da; *Career* ordained deacon 1972, priest 1975, Curate of Holy Trinity Weymouth 1972-74, Curate of Harlow New Town with Little Parndon 1974- 78; Industl Chaplain and Chaplain Princess Alexandra Hosp, Harlow 1978-82; Incumbent of St John, Moulsham 1986-; St John's Vicarage, Vicarage Rd, Chelmsford, Essex CM2 9PH (☎ 0245 352344)

GOODDEN, Robert Crane; yr s of John Henry Goodden (d 1974), of Compton House, and his 1 w, Valerie Mary, *née* Llewellyn-Evans (d 1959); bro of Rev John Maurice Phelips Goodden, *qv*; *b* 2 April 1940; *Educ* Salisbury Cathedral Choir Sch, Dauntsey's Sch; *m* 1 June 1968, Rosemary Joan Frances, da of Lt-Col Arthur Edward Bagwell Purefoy (d 1986); 2 s (John b 6 April 1973, Michael b 23 June 1976), 1 da (Sally b 11 May 1971); *Career* trainee: L Hugh Newman, The Butterfly Farm Ltd Bexley Kent 1957, Harrods Knightsbridge 1959; fndr and md Worldwide Butterflies Ltd 1960; co-fndr, tstee and vice-chm Br Butterfly Conservation Soc, owner Lullingstone Silk Farm, advsr to govt of Papua-New Guinea on butterfly farming; memb mgmnt ctee Almshouses of St John Sherborne; memb Sherborne Chamber Choir; FRHS; *Books* nine books on lepidoptera and entomology, incl: Butterflies (1971), The Wonderful World of Butterflies (1973), Field Guide to the Butterflies of Britain (1978), Beningfield's Butterflies (1978); *Recreations* gardening, music, photography, walking, natural history, botany, travel, computer programming, arts and crafts; *Style*— Robert Godden, Esq; Compton House, nr Sherborne, Dorset DT9 4QN (☎ 0935 74608)

GOODE, Joseph Pugh; s of Robert James Goode (d 1954), of USA, and Grace Edward Pugh (d 1972); *b* 28 June 1919; *Educ* Univ of Alabama USA; *m* 1952, Marie Louise Sheila, da of Capt James Allan Dysson Perrins, MC (d 1972), of Co Tipperary; 1 s (Allan b 1959); *Career* served WWII USAF, fighter pilot Europe (Maj); flying instr USA 1942-47; formerly cattle rancher for 27 yrs in Rhodesia, hon game conservation offr; USAF DFC 1944; *Recreations* shooting, fishing, travel; *Clubs* Bulawayo (Zimbabwe); *Style*— Joseph P Goode, Esq; The Tee Farm, Martley, Worcestershire WR6 6QT (☎ 08865 240)

GOODE, Michael Andrew; s of Edwin Eardley Bentley Goode (d 1943), and Winifred Beatrice Whittaker, *née* Glenn; *b* 30 Nov 1924; *Educ* Pocklington Sch, Sheffield Univ (LLB 1949); *m* 30 Aug 1951, Auriel Jean, da of Charles Louis Emy (d 1961); 3 da (Nicola b 1954, Helen b 1956, Catherine b 1958); *Career* slr 1950-; pres: Sheffield Junior C of C 1959-60, Sheffield Chamber of Trade 1968-69, Sheffield and Dist Law Soc 1986-87; chm Social Security Appeal Tbnl 1987-; Hon MPhil 1986; *Recreations* fly fishing; *Clubs* Sheffield; *Style*— Michael Goode, Esq; Bridge End Cottage, Brough, Bradwell, Sheffield (☎ 0433 20015); Taylor & Emmet 2 Norfolk Row, Sheffield (☎ 0433 766 111)

GOODE, Raymond Arthur; s of late Arthur Thomas Goode, of London, and Elsie Florence, *née* Hayes; *b* 24 April 1934; *Educ* Colindale Secdy Sch; *m* 1, 23 Aug 1956 (m dis 1976), Iris Margaret, da of Thomas Horn (d 1980); 2 da (Janette Ann b 15 July 1965, Karen Elizabeth b 4 Nov 1966); m2, 28 Aug 1976, Yvonne, da of Philip Conway Cattral; 2 da (Catherine b 27 Dec 1979, Helen b 23 April 1985); *Career* lighting cameraman; Rank Orgn Ltd Pinewood Studios 1956-61, Granada TV Ltd 1961-69, Brideshead Revisited (BAFTA nominee) 1981, Jewel in The Crown (BAFTA nominee) 1984; memb BSC; *Recreations* golf; *Clubs* New North Manchester GC; *Style*— Raymond Goode, Esq; 4 Johnson Grove, Archer Park, Middleton, Manchester M24 4AE (☎ 061 654 8262)

GOODE, Prof Royston Miles (Roy); OBE (1972); s of Samuel Goode (d 1968), of Portsmouth, Hants, and Blooma, *née* Davies (d 1984); *b* 6 April 1933; *Educ* Highgate, London Univ (LLB, LLD); *m* 18 Oct 1964, Catherine Anne, da of Jean Marcel Rueff; 1 da (Naomi b 1965); *Career* Nat Serv RASC 1955-57; admitted slr 1955, ptnr Victor Mishcon & Co 1966-71 (conslt 1971-88); Queen Mary Coll: prof law 1971-75, Crowther prof credit and commercial law 1973-, dean faculty laws and head dept 1976-80; fndr and dir Centre Commercial Law Studies 1979-, transferred to Bar, Inner Temple 1988; UK rep and memb cncl govrs UNIDROIT Rome 1989-; Freeman City of London; FBA 1988; *Books* Hire-Purchase Law & Practice (2 ed 1970), Proprietary Rights & Insolvency in Sales Transactions (1985), Commercial Law (3 ed 1986), Legal Problems of Credit & Security (2 ed 1988); *Recreations* chess, walking, browsing in bookshops; *Clubs* Wig & Pen; *Style*— Prof Roy Goode; 20 Hocroft Rd, London NW2 2BL (☎ 01 435 7778); Centre for Commercial Law Studies, Queen Mary College, 339 Mile End Rd, London E1 4NS (☎ 01 980 4811, fax 01 980 1079, telex 893750)

GOODENOUGH, Frederick Roger; 3 (but 2 surviving) s of Sir William Macnamara Goodenough, 1 Bt (d 1951), and Dorothea Louisa (d 1987), da of Ven the Hon Kenneth Gibbs, DD, 5 s of 1 Baron Aldenham; *b* 21 Dec 1927; *Educ* Eton, Magdalene Coll Cambridge (MA); *m* 15 May 1954, Marguerite June, o da of David Forbes Mackintosh, sometime headmaster of Loretto; 1 s (David b 1955), 2 da (Annabel b

1957, Victoria b 1961); *Career* RN 1946-48; joined Barclays Bank Ltd 1950; local dir: Birmingham 1958-60, Reading 1960-69, Oxford 1969-87; dir: Barclays Bank UK Ltd 1971-87, Barclays Int Ltd 1977-87, Barclays plc 1985-, Barclays Bank plc 1979-; advsy dir Barclays Bank Thames Valley Region 1988-; memb London Ctee Barclays Bank DCO 1966-71, Barclays Bank Int Ltd 1971-80; sr ptnr Broadwell Manor Farm 1968-; curator Oxford Univ Chest 1974-; tstee: Nuffield Med Tst 1968- (chm 1987), Nuffield Dominions Tst 1968- (chm 1987-), Nuffield Orthopaedic Tst 1978- (chm 1981-), Oxford & Dist Hosps Improvement & Devpt Fund 1968- (chm 1982-88), Oxford Prservation Tst 1980-; govr: Shiplake Coll 1963-74 (chm 1966-70), Wellington 1968-74; fell Linnean Soc (memb cncl 1968-75, tres 1970-75); FRSA; govr London House for Overseas Graduates 1985-, tstee Radcliffe Med Foundation 1987-; High Sheriff of Oxfordshire 1987-88; *Recreations* shooting, fishing, photography, ornithology; *Clubs* Brooks's; *Style*— Frederick Goodenough, Esq; Broadwell Manor, Lechlade, Glos GL7 3QS (☎ 036 786 326)

GOODENOUGH, Gary; s of Le Roy Goodenough (d 1960), of Rochester, Minnesota, USA, and Mary Wright, *née* Remington; *b* 1 Nov 1947; *Educ* Phillips Exeter Acad, Dartmouth Coll, Wharton Sch of Univ of Pennsylvenia (MBA); *m* 12 July 1969, Nancy Lee, da of Ellis Jensen; 1 s (Jason Edward b 1979); *Career* Saloman Brothers Inc: joined 1975, vice pres 1978, dir 1986, md 1987-; *Recreations* swimming; *Style*— Gary Goodenough, Esq; Salomon Bros Int Ltd, 111 Buckingham Palace Rd, London SW1W 0SB (☎ 01 721 3110)

GOODENOUGH, Sir Richard Edmund; 2 Bt (UK 1943); s of Sir William Macnamara Goodenough, 1 Bt (d 1951); *b* 9 June 1925; *Educ* Eton, Christ Church Oxford; *m* 22 Dec 1951, Jane Isobel, da of Harry Stuart Parnell McLernon (d 1950), of Gisborne, NZ; 1 s (William b 1954), 2 da (Rosemary b 1952, Joanna b 1958); *Career* Coldstream Gds WWII; *Style*— Sir Richard Goodenough, Bt

GOODENOUGH, William McLernon; s & h of Sir Richard Goodenough, 2 Bt; *b* 5 August 1954; *Educ* Stanbridge Earls; *m* 12 June 1982, Louise Elizabeth, da of Capt Michael Ortmans, RN, LVO of 48 Bishops Rd, Fulham; 1 da (Sophie Julia b 1986); *Career* design conslt, md; *Recreations* shooting, fishing, tennis; *Style*— William Goodenough, Esq

GOODEVE, (John) Anthony; s of Cdr Sir Charles Frederick Goodeve, OBE (d 1980), of London NW11, and Janet Irene, *née* Wallace; *b* 4 August 1944; *Educ* Canford; *m* 2 Oct 1965, Susan Mary, da of Sydney John Tupper (d 1988), of Petts Wood, Kent; 1 da (Claire Michelle b 29 May 1982); *Career* RNR 1963-66; Shell Mktg Ltd 1964-68 (latterly sr indust asst Shell UK Oil), md Dupré Vermiculite Ltd 1978-79, gp mktg exec Wood Hall Bldg Gp Ltd 1979-80, chief exec and md Grosvenor Property & Fin Ltd 1980-, proprietor Mr Quickpix Photolabs 1985-; Freeman City of London 1969, Liveryman Worshipful Co of Salters 1969; FInstD, LRPS; *Recreations* work, swimming; *Clubs* IOD; *Style*— Anthony Goodeve, Esq

GOODEVE, Lady - Janet Irene; *née* Wallace; PhD; da of Rev J M Wallace, of Winnipeg, Canada; *m* 1932, Sir Charles Frederick Goodeve, OBE (d 17 April 1980); 2 s; *Style*— Lady Goodeve; 38 Middleway, London NW11 (☎ 01 455 7308)

GOODEVE-DOCKER, Michael Lee; s of Capt George Arthur Murray Docker (ka 1914), and Anna Louisa Maude Josephine (d 1964); *b* 9 Nov 1911; *Educ* Gresham's, Oriel Coll Oxford (MA); *m* 14 Aug 1937, Phyllis Mary, da of William Henry Chedzen Stiling (d 1962), of Burnham-on-Sea Somerset; *Career* Maj RE Home Serv 1941-46; headmaster 1946-75; capt Oxford Univ hockey 1932-33, played hockey for Somerset, Oxon, Lancs, Kent, golf for Somerset; *Recreations* bridge, gardening; *Style*— Michael L Goodeve-Docker, Esq; Bygrove, Rectory Rd, Burnham-on-Sea, Somerset TA8 2BZ (☎ 027 783044)

GOODFELLOW, Mark Aubrey; s of Alfred Edward Goodfellow, Tonbridge, Kent, and Lucy Emily Goodfellow; *b* 7 April 1931; *Educ* Preston Manor Co Sch Wembley, LSE; *m* 10 Oct 1964, Madelyn Susan, 1 s (Adam b 1969), 1 da (Venetia b 1967); *Career* Nat Serv RAF 1949-51; Dip Serv 1951-; Br Mil Govt 1954-56, second sec Br Embassy Khartoum 1956-59, FO 1959-63, Br Embassy Yaounde Cameron 1963-66, Br trade cmmnr Hong Kong 1966-71, FCO 1971-74, Br Embassy Ankara 1974-78, HM consul Atlanta USA 1978-82, Br Embassy Washington DC (cnsllr Hong Kong commercial affairs also accreditted to Ottawa) 1982-84, cnsllr commercial Br high cmmn Lagas 1984-87, HM ambassador Libreville Gabon 1987-; *Clubs* Traveller's, Hong Kong, Ikoyi, Lagos; *Style*— Mark Goodfellow, Esq; British Residence, BP 476 Libreville, Republic of Gabon (☎ 010 421 740707, telex 5538 GO)

GOODGER, Donald; s of Charles Thomas Goodger (d 1986), and Miriam, *née* Rowe (d 1979); *b* 1 Oct 1930; *Educ* Wyggeston GS Leicester, Leicester Coll of Tech (BSc); *m* 29 Aug 1959, (Anne) Priscilla, da of Percy Dalton (d 1968); 1 s (Anthony b 1963), 1 da (Katherine b 1960); *Career* eng Scott Wilson Kirkpatrick 1957-64; Pick Everard Keay and Gimson: engr 1964-67, assoc 1982-; FICE 1975, FIStructE 1972, MConsE 1985; *Recreations* beagling; *Clubs* Leicestershire; *Style*— Donald Goodger, Esq; 37 Grenfell Rd, Leicester LE2 2PA (☎ 0533 705750); Pick Everard Keay and Gimson, 7 Friar Lane, Leicester LE1 5JD (☎ 0533 573311)

GOODHART, Hon Lady (Celia McClare); *née* Herbert; er da of 2 Baron Hemingford; *b* 25 July 1939; *Educ* St Hilda's Coll Oxford U (MA); *m* 21 May 1966, Sir William Howard Goodhart, 2 s of Prof Arthur Lehman Goodhart, KBE (hon), QC, of Whitebarn, Boars Hill, Oxford; 1 s (Benjamin b 1972), 2 da (Annabel b 1967, Lavra b 1970); *Career* selected 1982 as prospective parly candidate (SDP) Kettering; *Style*— Hon Mrs Goodhart; 43 Campden Hill Sq, London W8 (☎ 01 221 4830)

GOODHART, Margaret, Lady - Margaret Mary Eileen; da of late Morgan Morgan, of Cray, Powys; *m* 19 Feb 1944, Sir John Gordon Goodhart, 3 Bt (d 1979); 1 s (Sir Robert *qv*), 1 da (Mrs John Soul b 1945); *Style*— Margaret, Lady Goodhart; Holtye, 17 Mavelstone Close, Bromley

GOODHART, Lt-Col Mark Henry; s of Harry Goodhart (d 1976), of W Thorpe, Lymington, Hants, and Mary Suzette, *née* Haworth (d 1986); *b* 2 May 1931; *Educ* Stowe; *m* 8 Feb 1964, Angela, da of Cdr Eric May, OBE, RN; 1 s (Jonathan b 24 July 1965), 1 da (Caroline b 29 April 1967); *Career* 14/20 Kings Hussars 1949-86; graduate Armed Forces Staff Coll (USA) 1973-74, GOS1 Fort Knox USA 1974-76; Cdr RAC Tactical Sch 1976-79, GSO1 Liasison 1 Dutch Corps 1979-81, Cdr Salisbury Plain Trg Area 1982-86; chm Rainbow Conslts, yacht master examiner DTI RYA; Freeman City of London 1952, Liveryman Worshipful Co of Grocers 1959; *Recreations* sailing, country sports; *Clubs* Cavalry & Guards, Royal Yacht Sqdn; *Style*— Lt-Col Mark Goodhart; The Barn House, Hurstbourne Priors, Whitchurch, Hants (☎ 0256 893133)

GOODHART, Rear Adm (Hilary Charles) Nicholas; CB (1973); s of Gavin Caird Goodhart (d 1974), of Newbury, Berks, and Evelyn Winifred Alphega, *née* Mahon; ggf Jakob Emanuel Guthardt came to Eng in 1755 in Ct of George II; *b* 28 Sept 1919; *Educ* RNC Dartmouth, RN Engrg Coll Keyham; *m* 1975, Molly, da of Robert Copsey (d 1956), of Langstone, Farlington, Hants; 1 step s (Ian), 2 step da (Alyson, Fiona); *Career* Engrg Offr RN, served in Med 1941-43, Pilot 1944, Fighter Pilot Indian Ocean 1945, Test Pilot 1946, Naval Test Flying 1947-51, Br Naval Staff Washington 1952-55, Navy Staff Serv and MOD, Rear Adm 1970, ret 1973; dir: Brassey's Def Publishers Ltd, Res Engrgs Ltd, Southdown Aero Servs Ltd, Octavian Unit Tst Mangrs Ltd, Lancashire & Yorks Assur Soc, Grocers Tst Co Ltd; competition glider pilot 1956-72, competed as memb Br team in 7 World Gliding Championships (world champion 1956, runner up 1958), competed in 9 Br Nat Championships (three times Nat Champion, three times runner-up), competed in 2 US Nat Championships (winner 1955), holds Br Gliding Record of flight of 579 km to a declared goal, first UK pilot to get Int Diamond Gliding Badge, Royal Aero Club Silver Medal 1956, Fedn Aeronautique Int Tissandier Diploma 1972; invented mirror deck-landing system for aircraft carriers; designed and built 42 m span man-powered aircraft, led team bldg the Sigma advanced glider; FRAeS; Legion of Merit (US) 1958; *Recreations* bee keeping, genealogy, computing; *Clubs* Army & Navy; *Style*— Rear Adm Nicholas Goodhart, CB; Church House, Uffculme, Cullompton, Devon EX15 3AX

GOODHART, Sir Philip Carter; MP (C) Beckenham 1983-; eld s of Prof Arthur Lehman Goodhart, KBE (hon), QC, FBA, and Cecily, *née* Carter; *b* 3 Nov 1925; *Educ* Hotchkiss Sch USA, Trinity Coll Cambridge; *m* 1950, Valerie Forbes, da of Clinton Winant, of NY; 3 s, 4 da; *Career* served KRRC and Para Regt 1943-47; ed staff: Daily Telegraph 1950-55, Sunday Times 1955-57; contested (C) Consett Co Durham 1950; MP (C) Bromley Beckenham 1957-1983, memb Cncl Consumers' Assoc 1959-68 and 1970-79, vice-pres Consumers' Assoc 1983; jt sec 1922 Ctee 1960-79; memb: Cons Advsy Ctee on Policy 1973-79, exec ctee Br Cncl 1974-79; chm Parly NI Ctee 1976-79, memb Advsy Cncl on Public Records 1979; parly under-sec state: NI Office 1979-81, MOD 1981; chm Sulgrave Manor Bd 1982-; kt 1981; *Books* Fifty Ships That Saved The World (1965), The 1922: The History of the 1922 Ctee (1973), Full-Hearted Consent (1975); *Pamphlets incl* Stand On Your Own Four Feet - a Study of Work Sharing and Job Splitting (1982); *Clubs* Beefsteak, Carlton, Garrick; *Style*— Sir Philip Goodhart, MP; Whitebarn, Boars Hill, Oxford (☎ 0865 735294); 27 Phillimore Gardens, London W8 (☎ 01 937 0822)

GOODHART, Sir Robert Anthony Gordon; 4 Bt (UK 1911); s of Sir John Goodhart, 3 Bt, FRCGP (d 1979), and Margaret Lady Goodhart *qv*; *b* 15 Dec 1948; *Educ* Rugby, London Univ, Guy's Hosp Med Sch (MB BS); *m* 1972, Kathleen Ellen, da of Rev Alexander Duncan MacRae, MA (d 1979), of 45 Laggan Rd, Inverness; 2 s, 2 da; *Heir* s, Martin Andrew Goodhart b 9 Sept 1974; *Career* medical practitioner 1976-; MRCGP; *Recreations* cricket, sailing, music; *Style*— Sir Robert Goodhart, Bt; The Old Rectory, Netherbury, Bridport, Dorset DT6 5NB (☎ 030 888 248)

GOODHART, Sir William Howard; QC; 2 s of Prof Arthur Lehman Goodhart, KBE (hon), QC (d 1978), and Cecily, *née* Carter; *b* 18 Jan 1933; *Educ* Eton, Trinity Coll Cambridge, Harvard Law Sch; *m* 21 May 1966, Hon Celia Herbert, da of 2 Baron Hemingford, qv; 1 s, 2 da; *Career* barr 1957; QC 1979; kt 1989; *Style*— Sir William Goodhart, QC; 43 Campden Hill Sq, London W8 (☎ 01 214 830); Youlbury House, Boars Hill, Oxford (☎ 735477)

GOODHEW, Sir Victor Henry; s of late Rudolph Goodhew, of Mannings Heath Sussex, and late Rose, *née* Pullen; *b* 30 Nov 1919; *Educ* King's Coll Sch; *m* 1, 1940 (m dis 1951), Sylvia Johnson; 1 s, 1 da; m 2, 1951 (m dis 1972), Suzanne Gordon-Burge; m 3, 1972 (m dis 1981), Eva Rittinghausen; *Career* serv WWII RAF, Sqdn Ldr; memb: Westminster City Cncl 1953-59, LCC 1958-61; contested (C) Paddington N 1955; MP (C) St Albans 1959-83; PPS to: Civil Lord Admty 1962-63, jt parly sec Transport 1963-64; asst Govt whip 1970, ld cmmr Treasy 1970-73; vice-chm Cons Def Ctee 1965-70 and 1974-83; memb: Speaker's Panel of Chairmen 1975-83, Select Ctee House of Commons Servs 1978-83, House of Commons Cmmn 1979-83; jt sec 1922 Ctee 1979-83; kt 1982; *Clubs* Buck's; *Style*— Sir Victor Goodhew; The Coach House, St Leonard's Dale, Winkfield Road, Windsor, Berkshire SL4 4AQ (☎ 0753 859073, 01 235 4911)

GOODIER, Roger Banks; s of Benjamin Bancroft Goodier (d 1967), and Adi Irene Goodier (d 1986); *b* 7 Sept 1944; *Educ* Moseley Hall GS, Univ of Sheffield (LLB); *m* 20 July 1974, Denise, da of Eric Forshaw; 2 s (Benjamin b 1975, Oliver b 1978); *Career* admitted slr 1970, sr ptnr Rowley Ashworth slrs; *Recreations* soccer, rugby union, cricket; *Clubs* Wig & Pen; *Style*— Roger Goodier, Esq; 69 Popes Ave, Twickenham, Middx (☎ 01 894 1355); Rowley Ashworth, 247 The Broadway, Wimbledon, London SW19 1SE (☎ 01 543 2277, telex 8951693, fax 01 543 0143)

GOODIN, Frederick Glanville; s of Benjamin Henry Chorley Goodin (d 1937), of Ensworth, Hants, and Elizabeth, *née* Gower (d 1955); *b* 24 April 1903; *Educ* Cambridge and Co HS, Bartlett Sch of Architecture, London Univ; *m* 27 July 1929, Ursula Afra Willmer, da of Alfred Willmer Pocock, LRIBA (d 1968); 1 da (Elizabeth b 1931); *Career* RE, Garrison Engr, E Anglia 1941-43; chartered architect: worked with Sir John Simpson on Br Empire Exhibition 1924, and Sir Edwin Lutyens on Imp Delhi 1925-29; ch designer architectural dept of Sunlife Assurance Co Montreal 1929-31, in private practice in UK 1931-; princ lectr Dept of Building and Civil Engrg Central Coll of Technol Birmingham 1932-41, 1944; princ of Building Sch Newcastle-upon-Tyne 1944-46; head dept of architecture, Building and Surveying Coll of Estate Mgmnt London 1952-63; examiner on various bds of estate mgmnt etc; chm Special Sub-Ctee RICS 1952-55; FRIBA, FRSH; *Recreations* hill walking, golf, reading, chess, photography; *Clubs* Army and Navy, Pall Mall, London; *Style*— Frederick G Goodin, Esq; Awelon, Llanelltyd, Dolgellau, Gwynedd LL40 2TA (☎ 0341 422414)

GOODING, Air Vice-Marshal Keith Horace; CB (1966), OBE (1951); s of Horace Milford Gooding (d 1953), of Romsey, Hants; *b* 2 Sept 1913; *Educ* King Edward VI Sch Southampton; *m* 1, 1943, Peggy Eileen (d 1962), da of Albert William Gatfield, of Guildford, Surrey; 1 s; m 2, 1968, Jean, da of Maurice Stanley Underwood, of Andover, Hants; 2 s, 1 da; *Career* cmmnd RAF 1938, Air Vice-Marshal 1965, Air Offr Administration HQ Maintenance Cmmd 1965-68, Dir-Gen Supply (RAF) MOD 1968-71, ret 1971; chm: Crohn's in Childhood Research Appeal; *Recreations* tennis, bridge; *Clubs* RAF; *Style*— Air Vice-Marshal Keith Gooding, CB, OBE; c/o Lloyds Bank Ltd, Guildford Surrey

GOODISON, Sir Alan Clowes; KCMG (1985, CMG 1975), CVO (1980); o s of Harold Clowes Goodison, and Winifred, *née* Ludlam; *b* 20 Nov 1926; *Educ* Colfe's GS

Lewisham, Trinity Coll Cambridge; *m* 1956, Anne Rosemary, o da of Edward Fitton, of Leeds; 1 s, 2 da; *Career* entered FO 1949; serv: Cairo, Tripoli, Khartoum, Lisbon, Amman, Bonn, Kuwait; head Southern European Dept FCO 1973-76, min Rome Embassy 1976-80, asst under-sec state FCO 1981-83, ambass to Irish Republic 1983-86; dir The Wates Fndn 1988-; Grande Ufficiale dell'Ordine Al Merito (Italy); *Clubs* Travellers'; *Style*— Sir Alan Goodison, KCMG, CVO; 12 Gardnor Mansions, Church Row, London NW3 6UR; The Wates Foundation, 1260 London Rd, Norbury, London SW16 4EG

GOODISON, Sir Nicholas Proctor; yr s of Edmund Harold Goodison, of Longacre, Radlett, Herts, and Eileen Mary Carrington Proctor; *b* 16 May 1934; *Educ* Marlborough, King's Coll Cambridge (PhD); *m* 18 June 1960, Judith Nicola, only da of Capt Robert Eustace Abel Smith (ka 1940), Gren Gds *see* Burke's Landed Gentry 1967; 1 s, 2 da; *Career* chm The Stock Exchange 1976- (memb Cncl 1968-); chm Quilter Goodison Co Ltd 1975- (formerly: H E Goodison & Co, Quilter Goodison & Co; ptnr 1962-); pres Int Fndn at Stock Exchange 1985-86; vice-chm ENO; dir: City Arts Tst, Burlington Magazine; hon keeper Furniture Fitzwilliam Museum Cambridge; chm: Exec Cmmn Nat Art Collection Fund, Courtauld Inst of Art; pres Antiquarian Horological Soc, hon tres Furniture History Soc; author; CBIM, FRSA, FSA; kt 1982; *Books* English Barometers 1680-1860 (1968, 2nd edition 1977), Ormolu: the Work of Matthew Boulton (1979); many papers on history of furniture, metalwork, barometers and associated subjects; *Style*— Sir Nicholas Goodison; The Stock Exchange, London EC2 (☎ 01 588 2355)

GOODLAD, Alastair Robertson; MP (C) Eddisbury 1983-; yst s of late Dr John Fordyce Robertson Goodlad, MB, of Lincoln, and Isobel, *née* Sinclair; *b* 4 July 1943; *Educ* Marlborough, King's Coll Cambridge (MA, LLB); *m* 1968, Cecilia Barbara, 2 da of Col Richard Hurst (s of Sir Cecil Hurst, GCMG, KCB) by his w Lady Barbara, *née* Lindsay (6 da of 27 Earl of Crawford (and Earl Balcarres), KT, PC); 2 s; *Career* contested (C) Crewe 1970, MP (C) Northwich Feb 1974-83; asst Govt whip 1981-82, lord cmmr Treasy 1982-84, jt vice-chm Cons Pty Trade Ctee 1979- (jt hon sec 1978-), hon sec All Party Heritage Gp 1979-; memb: Select Ctee Agriculture 1979-, House of Commons Bridge Team in matches against Lords 1982-85, parly under sec of state at Dept of Energy 1984; *Clubs* Brooks's; *Style*— Alastair Goodlad, Esq, MP; c/o House of Commons, London SW1

GOODMAN, Baron (Life Peer UK 1965); Arnold Abraham Goodman; CH (1972); s of Joseph and Bertha Goodman; *b* 21 August 1913; *Educ* UCL, Downing Coll Cambridge; *Career* slr 1936, sr ptnr Messrs Goodman Derrick & Co; serv WWII RA TA as Maj; chm: Jewish Chronicle Tst 1970-, Theatres' Tst 1976-, ABSA 1976-, Motability (charity helping the disabled) 1977-, Cnc for Charitable Support 1986-; pres: Theatres Advsy Cncl 1972-, Inst Jewish Affrs; 2 ENO 86- Theat Investmt 1 fund 85-; dep chm Br Cncl 1974-; Master UC Oxford 1976-86; *Style*— The Rt Hon Lord Goodman, CH; 9-11 Fulwood Place, Gray's Inn, London WC1V 6HQ (☎ 01 404 0606)

GOODMAN, Cyril Joshua; s of Paul Goodman (d 1949), and Romana, *née* Manczyk (d 1955); *b* 10 May 1915; *Educ* St Paul's Sch; *m* 16 Dec 1948, Ruth, da of Percy Perez Ernest Sabel (d 1946), of London and Burnham-on-Crouch; 5 s (Paul b 1952, Martin b 1953, Andrew b 1955, Roger b 1960, Thomas b 1961), 1 da (Sarah b 1950); *Career* WWII 1939-45: Field Security Police 1940, instr Intelligence Trg Centre Matlock 1941, cmmnd Intelligence Corps 1941; serv: Cairo, Haifa, Beirut 1942, Asst Adjt Palestine Trg Depot Sarafand 1943, Bde Intelligence Offr Jewish Inf Bde Gp 1944-45, GSO3 1945 (despatches); admitted slr 1937, sr ptnr Lindo & Co 1949-70, ptnr Nicholson Graham & Jones 1971-81; hon slr Royal Corinthian YC 1959-81, memb Bd of Deputies Br Jews 1948-50, chm Exec Cncl Assoc for Jewish Youth 1948-50, chm Camperdown House Tst 1978-, memb Crouch Harbour Authy 1975 (first chm 1975-82); Freeman City of London 1947, Liveryman City of London Slrs Co; memb Law Soc 1937; *Recreations* sailing, gardening, reading, travelling; *Clubs* Royal Corinthian YC, Little Ship; *Style*— Cyril Goodman, Esq; Tideways, Creeksea, Burnham-on-Crouch, Essex CM0 8PL (☎ 0621 782 679)

GOODMAN, Maj-Gen (John) David Whitlock; CB (1987); s of Brig Eric Whitlock Goodman, DSO, MC (d 1981), and Norah Dorothy, *née* Stacpoole (d 1986); *b* 20 May 1932; *Educ* Wellington, RMA Sandhurst; *m* 21 Dec 1957, (Valerie) Ann, da of D H H McDonald (d 1974), of Tates, Burley, Ringwood, Hants; 1 s (Jeremy b 1961), 2 da (Amanda b 1959, Pippa b 1971); *Career* Army Offr; Dir Army Air Corps 1983-87; cmmnd into RA 1952, serv: Eng, NI, Germany, Aden, Hong Kong, Sudan; Instr at Sandhurst and Staff Coll, cmnd 26 Field Regt RA and Royal Sch of Artillery; pres Army Flying and Gliding Assocs, chm Army Athletics; ret from Army 1987; dir Aspen Spafax TV; Hon Col 26 Field Regt RA and 3 Regt Army Air Corps; memb Guild of Air Pilots and Air Navigators 1986; *Recreations* gardening, tennis, country pursuits; *Style*— Maj-Gen David Goodman, CB; c/o Lloyds Bank Ltd, 6 Pall Mall, London SW1Y 5NH

GOODMAN, Frederick; s of Hyman Goodman (d 1924); *b* 4 Nov 1910; *Educ* London Univ, Chelsea Poly and business schs; *m* 1974, Iris Gene; *Career* conslt accountant and dir of Brilaw Properties Ltd, Keystone Credits Ltd, RS Hldgs Ltd, Headtown Ltd, Powerlistic Ltd, Upton Heath Properties Ltd, St James Court Estate (1977) Ltd; underwriting memb of Lloyd's; *Recreations* charity work; *Style*— Frederick Goodman, Esq; 11 Warwick Place, London W9 (☎ 01 286 0970); 29/30 Fitzroy Sq, London W1 (☎ 01 388 2444)

GOODMAN, Hon Mrs (Janet Teresa); *née* Addington; 3 da of 7 Viscount Sidmouth; *b* 4 Oct 1949; *m* 1972, Anthony Goodman; 3 da; *Style*— Hon Mrs Goodman; 68 Wierda Rd, Wierda Valley, Sandton 2196, S Africa

GOODMAN, Prof John Francis Bradshaw; s of Edwin Goodman (d 1979), and Amy Bradshaw, *née* Warrener; *b* 2 August 1940; *Educ* Chesterfield Sch, LSE (BSc), Univ of Manchester (MSc), Univ of Nottingham (PhD); *m* 12 Aug 1967, Elizabeth Mary, da of Frederick William Towns, of Romiley, Ches; 1 s (Richard b 1972), 1 da (Clare b 1970); *Career* personnel offr Ford Motor Co 1962-64, lectr in industl econs Univ of Nottingham 1964-69, industl rels advsr NBPI 1969-70, sr lectr in industl rels Univ of Manchester 1970-74, Frank Thomas prof of industl rels UMIST 1975-(head of sch 1977-79 and 1986-88, vice princ 1979-81); visiting prof of industl rels: Univ of WA 1981 and 1984, Mc Master Univ 1985; govr Withington Girls Sch; memb: ctee of mgmnt Wood St Mission Manchester, cncl Manchester Business Sch; pres: Manchester Industl Rels Soc, Br Univs Industl Rels Assoc 1983-86; memb: cncl ACAS, panel of arbitrators ACAS; CIPM 1986; *Books* Shop Stewards (1973), Rule-making and Industrial Peace (1977), Ideology and Shop-floor Industrial Relations (1980), Employee Participation (1981), Employment Relations in Industrial Society (1984), Unfair Dismissal Law and Employment Practice (1985); *Recreations* squash, fell walking; *Style*— Prof John Goodman; Manchester School of Management, Umist, PO Box 88, Manchester M60 1QD (☎ 061 236 3311, fax 061 228 7040, telex 666094)

GOODMAN, Nathanial; s of Samuel Morris Goodman (d 1948), of London, and Sarah, *née* Feldman (d 1959); *b* 28 Mar 1915; *Educ* Battersea GS; *m* 7 Jan 1947, Edith, da of Samuel Glekin (d 1963), of Glasgow; 1 s (Louis Melville b 1951); *Career* VR Sargent RAF India 1943-45, England 1939-43; City Site Estates plc; chm and dir: City Site Construction Ltd, City Site South Ltd, City Site North Ltd, Baltic Chamber Ltd, Daniel Ross Ltd, James Allan & Son North Ltd, Cameron Hoxaxi Ltd, Hascasci Ltd, Mademoiselle Anne Ltd, City Site Properties Ltd, Queensbridge Estates Ltd; *Clubs* RNVR Scotland; *Style*— Nathanial Goodman, Esq; 50 Wellington St, Glasgow (☎ 041 248 2534/01 133 135); Stockwell St, Glasgow (☎ 041 525 2986)

GOODMAN, Perry; s of Cyril Goodman (d 1982), and Anne, *née* Rosen (d 1985); *b* 26 Nov 1932; *Educ* Haberdashers' Aske's Hampstead Sch, Univ Coll, London Univ (BSc); *m* 1958, Marcia Ann, da of Samuel Morris (d 1982); 1 s (Nicholas b 1959), 1 da (Rachel b 1964); *Career* 2 Lt Royal Corps of Signals 1956; jt head Chemistry Res Lab, Morgan Crucible Co 1960, sr scientific offr Dept of Scientific and Industl Res (DSIR) 1964; princ scientific offr Miny of Technol 1965; cnsllr (Scientific) Br Embassy Paris 1970; hd Policy and Perspectives Unit Dept of Indust 1980; hd Electrical Engr Branch DTI 1987; MICeram; FRSA; *Recreations* walking, talking, birdwatching; *Style*— Perry Goodman, Esq; 118 Westbourne Terrace Mews, London W2 6QG (☎ 01 262 0925); Ashdown House, 123 Victoria St, London SW1 (☎ 01 212 5806)

GOODMAN, Richard Thomas; s of Thomas Henry Goodman (d 1957), of Hanbury Rd, Tottenham, and Alma Florence, *née* Harben (d 1969); *b* 10 Jan 1920; *Educ* Tottenham GS, City of London Coll; *m* 1, 1940 (m dis 1960), Joan Doris Hutcherson; 1 s (Stephen b 1946), 1 da (Diane b 1948); m 2, Shelagh Marie, da of Arthur Brown (d 1969), of Arnwood Cottage, Ringwood, Hants; 2 s (James b 1963, Geoffrey b 1966); *Career* WWII 1940-45, served Cambridge Regt seconded Intelligence Corps (POW Singapore 1942-45); dir Erwin Wasey 1949-60, md Green Shield Trading Stamps Ltd 1960-78, dir Argos Distributors 1975-78 (mktg conslt 1978-); Freeman City of London 1974, Liveryman Worshipful Co of Carmen 1974; MCAM, FInstM, FBIM; *Recreations* fly fishing, golf, reading; *Style*— Richard Goodman, Esq; 3 Latchmoor Way, Gerrards Cross, Bucks SL9 8LW (☎ 0753 885 165)

GOODRICH, Hon Mrs Audrey; er da of 1 Baron Elton (d 1973), and Dedi, *née* Hartmann (d 1977); *b* 22 June 1922; *m* 1 May 1948, Rev Brian William Frere Goodrich (d 1977), former Asst Cmmr Singapore Police, eld s of late Albert Frere Goodrich, of The Thicket, Linksway, Northwood, Middx; 5 s (John b 1952, Peter b 1954, Simon b 1957, Justin b 1962, Alexander b 1968), 1 da (Sarah b 1949); *Career* took holy order 1962, vicar of Cheveley Berks, rector of Frant Sussex; *Style*— Hon Mrs Goodrich; Hill House, Enford, Pewsey, Wilts

GOODRICH, David; s of William Boyle Goodrich (d 1984), of Sunderland, and Florence Bosenquett, *née* Douglas (d 1984); *b* 15 April 1941; *m* 5 June 1965, Margaret, da of Andrew Robertson Riley, of Sunderland; 1 s (John b 1981), 3 da (Helen b 1968, Kathryn b 1970, Alison b 1972); *Career* md Br Martime Technol ltd, constructor RCNC MOD (Navy) 1970-80, md Br Ship Res Assoc 1980-88, chief exec Br Maritime Technol Ltd 1988-; CEng, memb RCNC, FRINA; *Recreations* squash, walking; *Clubs* East India; *Style*— David Goodrich, Esq; Whitecroft, Hatton Hill, Windlesham, Surrey GU20 6AB; British Maritime Technology, Orlando House, 1 Waldegrave Rd, Teddington, Middlesex TW11 8LZ (☎ 01 943 5544, fax 01 943 5347, telex 263118)

GOODRICH, Rt Rev Philip Harold Ernest; *see*: Worcester, Bishop of

GOODSON, Sir Mark Weston Lassam; 3 Bt (UK 1922); o s of Maj Alan Richard Lassam Goodson (d 1941) 2 s 1 Bt, and Clarisse Mary Weston, *née* Adamson; suc Sir Alfred Lassam Goodson, 2 Bt 1986; *b* 12 Dec 1925; *Educ* Radley, Jesus Coll Cambridge; *m* 4 May 1949, Barbara Mary Constantine, da of Surgn Capt Reginald Joseph McAuliffe Andrews, RN, of Crandel, Ferndown, Dorset; 1 s, 3 da (Phyllida b 1950, Hilary b 1953, Christian b 1958); *Heir* s, Alan Reginald Goodson b 15 May 1960; *Style*— Sir Mark Goodson, Bt; Kilham, Mindrum, Northumberland TD12 4QS (☎ 089 085 217)

GOODSON-WICKES, Dr Charles; s of the late Ian Goodson Wickes (d 1972), of Stock Harvard, Essex, and Monica Frances Goodson-Wickes; *b* 9 Nov 1945; *Educ* Charterhouse, St Bart's Hosp, Inner Temple; *m* 17 April 1974, Judith Amanda, da of the late Cdr John Hopkinson, RN (d 1978), Sutton Grange, Nr Stamford, Lincs; 2 s (Edward b 1976, Henry b 1978); *Career* house surgn Addenbrooke's Hosp Cambridge 1972, surgn capt The Life Gds (serv BAOR, N I, Cyprus) 1973-77, Silver Stick mo, Household Cavalry 1977, Capt RARO, specialist physician St Bart's Hosp 1977-80, conslt physician BUPA 1977-86, occupational physician, barr; med advsr: Barclays Bank, RTZ, Standard Chartered Br Alcan, McKinsey, Hogg Robinson, Meat and Livestock cmms; memb: Med Advsy Ctee, Indust Soc, Fitness Advsy Panel, IOD; govr Highbury Grove Sch 1977-85; *Books* The New Corruption (1984); *Recreations* hunting, shooting, real tennis, gardening, travel, history; *Clubs* Boodle's, Pratt's, MCC, Melton Hunt, Guards and Saddle, Pogasus formerly Pitt (Cambridge); *Style*— Dr Charles Goodson-Wickes; Watergate House, Bulford, Wilts (☎ 0980 32344); 37 St James's Pl, London SW1 (☎ 01 629 0981); 8 Devonshire Pl, London W1 (☎ 01 935 5011)

GOODWILL, Geoffrey Mortimer; s of Reginald Mortimer Goodwill, FRICS (d 1978), and Jane Margaret King; *b* 13 Jan 1944; *Educ* Nunthorpe GS for Boys York; *m* 23 June 1973, Anne, da of James Henry Jewitt (d 1981), of York; 2 s (Russell b 1975, Robert b 1983), 1 da (Catherine b 1977); *Career* chartered surveyor; co dir appointed main bd Mountleigh Gp plc 1985; school govr; FRICS; *Recreations* squash; *Style*— Geoffrey Goodwill, Esq; 17 Adel Towers Ct, Leeds LS16 8ER (☎ 0532 677594); Leigh House, Leeds LS28 7XG (☎ 0532 555555, fax 0532 555556)

GOODWIN, Hon Mrs; Hon Gillian Theodora Marianne; *née* Chorley; only da of 1 Baron Chorley QC (d 1978), and Katharine Campbell, *née* Hopkinson; *b* 5 April 1929; *Educ* Liverpool Coll for Girls, St Anne's Coll Oxford; *m* 19 Jan 1965, (Francis) Godfrey Goodwin, yr s of Robert Goodwin (d 1923), of Lisbon; 1 s (Robert b 1969); *Style*— Hon Mrs Goodwin; 29 Chalcot Sq, London NW1

GOODWIN, Sir Matthew Dean; CBE (1980); s of Matthew Dean Goodwin (d 1965), of Bothwell, and Mary Gertrude, *née* Barrie (d 1965); *b* 12 Dec 1929; *Educ* Glasgow Acad; *m* 15 Sept 1955, Margaret Eileen, da of Harold Campbell Colvin (d 1959), of Bearsden; 2 da (Frances Margaret, Carol Elizabeth); *Career* Flying Offr RAF (Nat

Serv); CA 1952; ptnr Davidson Down McGown 1959-68; chm Hewden Stuart Plant plc 1978- (fin dir 1968-78); dir: Irvine Devpt Corpn 1980-, Rocep Hldgs Ltd, Murray Technol plc, F S Assur Co Ltd, Murray Ventures plc; tres Scottish Cons Pty 1984-; kt 1989; *Recreations* bridge, shooting, fishing, farming, politics; *Clubs* Western (Glasgow); *Style*— Sir Matthew Goodwin, CBE; 87 Kelvin Ct, Anniesland, Glasgow (☎ 041 339 7541); Hewden Stuart Plant plc, 135 Buchanan St, Glasgow

GOODWIN, (Trevor) Noel; s of Arthur Daniel Goodwin (d 1937), and Blanche, *née* Stephens (d 1956); more than three generations of master mariners and seafarers; *b* 25 Dec 1927; *Educ* educated in France, Univ of London (BA); *m* 1, 1954 (m dis 1960), Gladys Marshall Clapham; m 2 1963, Mrs Elizabeth Anne Myers, *née* Mason; 1 step s (Richard); *Career* areelance critic, writer, ed and broadcaster specializing in music and dance; asst music critic: News Chronicle 1952-54, Manchester Guardian 1954-55; music and dance critic Daily Express 1956-78; London dance critic Int Herald Tribune Paris 1978-83; exec ed Music and Musicians 1963-71, ed Royal Opera and Royal Ballet Yearbook 1978, 1979 and 1980; frequent broadcaster musical topics BBC Home and World Servs and Br Forces Broadcasting Serv (MOD) 1950-, interviewer and commentator on music and arts matters, programme annotator for Royal Opera, Royal Ballet and other cos and major orchestras; overseas news ed Opera; regular reviewer for: The Times, Opera News, Ballet News, Dance and Dancers; cncl memb Arts Cncl of GB 1979-81, chm Dance Advsy Panel (memb 1973-81), dep chm Music Advsy Panel (memb 1974-81); memb: Dance Advsy Panel Calouste Gulbenkian Fndn UK branch 1972-76, Fndn's Nat Enquiry into Dance Educn and Trg in Br 1980), Br Cncl's Drama and Dance Advsy Ctee 1973-, HRH The Duke of Kent's UK Ctee for Euro Music Year 1985 (chm of its sub-ctee for Writers and Critics 1982-84); tstee-dir Int Dance Course for Prof Choreographers and Composers 1975-; pres The Critics' Circle 1977 (memb 1958-, jt tstee and memb cncl 1977-); *Books* London Symphony: Portrait of an Orch (1954), A Ballet for Scotland (1979), A Knight at the Opera (with Sir Geraint Evans, 1984), author of history of Theatre Music in Encyclopedia Britannica (15 edn, 1976) and of Dance (Europe) entries in Britannica Books of the Year (1980-), area ed and contributor The New Grove Dictionary of Music and Musicians (1981), contributor to Encyclopaedia of Opera (1976), The Dictionary of Composers (1977), Cambridge Encyclopaedia of Russia (1982), The Encyclopedia of Dance (NY, in preparation), Handbuch des Musiktheaters (Munich, in preparation, vol 1 (1987)); *Recreations* travel; *Style*— Noel Goodwin, Esq; 76 Skeena Hill, London SW18 5PN (☎ 01 788 8794)

GOODWIN, (Francis) Norman; s of Norman Parkes Goodwin (d 1968), and Phylis Mary, *née* Hume (d 1975); *b* 30 Dec 1923; *Educ* HM Sch Ship Conway, Wye Coll London (BSc); *m* 14 June 1956, Ann Gillian (Gill), da of Roy Edward Furniss (d 1929); 1 s (Timothy b 1958), 2 da (Josephine b 1959, Hilary b 1961), 1 adopted s (Richard b 1963); *Career* Midshipman RNR 1940, serv HMS Canton S Atlantic Patrol, HMS Abdiel Eastern Mediterranean (Crete, Tobruk), HMS Abdiel mining of Andaman Islands, HMS Sheffield Western Mediterranean and N Africa Landings, HMS King George V Sicily, HMS Sheffield Arctic Convoys incl: Battle of the North Cape Convoy JWSIB, HMS Tintagel Castle N Atlantic, HMS Allington Castle Fishery Protection, demob Lt RNR 1946; staff Agric Dept of N Nigeria 1953-63, Hunting Tech Servs 1963-76, Booker Agric Int 1976-79, independent agric conslt 1979-(working mainly with the Asian Devpt Bank and the Int Fund for Agric Devpt (IFAD); major projects/ devpts incl: Lower Indus, Chasma Barrage, Right Bank Canal and Pat Feeder Canal rehabilitation (Pakistan), South Chad of Kano River Phase II (Nigeria), Nat Cropping Plan (Brazil), advsy work in connection with Federal Funded Irrigation devpts; memb Tropical Agric Assoc 1986; *Recreations* motor caravanning, photography, pottering around son-in-law's farm; *Style*— Norman Goodwin, Esq; The Mount, Aston Munslow, Craven Arms, Shropshire SY7 9ER (☎ 058476 328, fax 0743 253 678, telex 8954667 VBSTLX Ref SHC)

GOODWIN, Peter Austin; CBE (1986); s of Stanley Goodwin, London 1967, and Louise, *née* Skinner; *b* 12 Feb 1929; *Educ* Harrow Co Sch; *m* 1950, Audrey Vera, of John Webb (d 1969), of Surrey; 1 da (Julia b 1960); *Career* RAF 1947-49; exec offr Public Works Loan Cmmn 1950 (asst sec 1976, sec 1979); princ Civil Aviation Authy 1973-76; chm Pensions Commutation Bd 1980-84; comptroller gen Nat Debt Off 1979; dir Nat Investmt and Loans Off 1979; memb ctee of experts advising on investmt of superannuation fnd moneys of European Patent Off Munich; *Recreations* theatre, opera, ballet, country dancing, model railways; *Style*— Peter Goodwin, CBE; 87 Woodmansterne Rd, Carshalton Beeches, Surrey SM5 4JW; National Investmt & Loans Office, Royex House, Aldermanbury Square, London EC2V 7LR (☎ 01 606 7321)

GOODWIN, (Neville) Rex; s of Hubert Victor Goodwin (d 1978), of London Rd, Yaxley, Peterborough, Cambs, and Lilian Gertrude Goodwin; *b* 7 Feb 1932; *Educ* Deacons Sch Peterborough Cambs, Sch of Architecture, Leicester Coll of Art (Dip Arch); *m* 5 Sept 1957, Mary Alice, da of Cecil Capp, 22 Earlswood Dr, Edwalton, Notts; 1 s (Mark Goodwin b 22 Oct 1964), 1 da (Kate Goodwin b 21 March 1961); *Career* Nat Serv RAF 1952-54; architect Notts CC 1957-61, dep chief architect Brockhouse Steel Structures 1961-65, ptnr Goodwin Warner & Assocs 1965-, visiting lectr in bldg design Dept of Civil Engng Loughborough Univ of Tecnol 1970-; vice-pres Loughborough Colls Rugby Union Club; RIBA 1959; *Recreations* aviation, watching cricket and rugby; *Style*— Rex Goodwin, Esq; 9A, Hallfields, Edwalton, Nottingham (☎ 0602 234 283); 39 Granby St, Loughborough, Leics LE11 3DU (☎ 0509 239 131), fax 0509 610 128)

GOODWIN, Ronald; s of William Henry Goodwin (d 1951), and Kathleen Florence, *née* Vizor (d 1977); *b* 6 May 1927; *Educ* Keighley Tech Coll; *m* 11 Aug 1957, (Brenda) Molly, da of Francis (d 1987); 3 s (David, Glynn, Alan); *Career* 2 Bn The Glos Regt 1945-48; CA; ptnr Benten & Co 1954-, dir Blyth & Pawsey Ltd 1955-86, chm Saffron Walden & Essex Bldg Soc; chm Royal Soc of St George Saffron Walden branch, pres Saffron Walden Rotary Club 1968-69, vice-chm Uttlesford CAB, tstee and tres Mid Essex Doctors Emergency Care Scheme; FCCA 1952; *Recreations* gardening and travel; *Style*— Ronald Goodwin, Esq; Orchard Bungalow, Debden Rd, Saffron Walden, Essex CB11 4AB (☎ 0799 23 098); Benten & Co Abbey House, 51 High St, Saffron Walden, Essex (☎ 0799 23 053)

GOODWIN, Ronald Alfred (Ron); s of James Goodwin (d 1952), of Ruislip, Middx, and Bessie Violet, *née* Godsland (d 1966); *b* 17 Feb 1925; *Educ* Willesden Co Sch, Pinner Co Sch; *m* 1, 3 July 1947 (m dis 1986), Ellen Gertrud, da of William Drew, of Ruislip, Middx; 1 s (Christopher Russell b 16 Sept 1951); m 2, 22 Sept 1986, Heather Elizabeth Mary, da of Harold Wesley Dunsden, of Blewbury, Berks; *Career* composer and conductor; 61 film scores incl: Battle of Britain, 633 Squadron, Frenzy, Where Eagles Dare, Those Magnificent Men in their Flying Machines; other compositions incl: The New Zealand Suite, The Drake 400 Suite, The Armada 400 Suite, The Brimpton Suite, Suite No 1 for Brass Quintette; guest conductor with many orchestras incl: Royal Philharmonic Orchestra, The Bournemouth Symphony Orchestra, The Scottish Nat Orchestra, The New Zealand Symphony Orchestra; vice pres: Br Acad of Songwriters Composers and Authors, The Stars Orgn for Spastics; cncl memb The Composers Guild of GB, bd memb Young Persons Concert Fndn; pres Worthing Youth Orchestra, vice pres The Friends of the Hants Co Youth Orchestra; Liveryman Worshipful Co of Musicians 1971; *Recreations* walking, swimming, amateur computer programming; *Style*— Ron Goodwin, Esq; Blacknest Cottage, Brimpton Common, Reading RG7 4RP

GOODWIN, Shirley Ann; da of Harold Harper Goodwin, of Burwash Surrey, and Jean Patricia, *née* Richmond; *b* 5 Oct 1947; *Educ* Royal Tunbridge Wells County GS for Girls, Univ of Surrey (Dip in Health Visiting), NE London Poly (BSc); *Career* health visitor Ealing West London 1971-83, gen sec Health Visitors' Assoc 1984- (in designate post 1983-84); part-time youth worker Ealing 1974-78, hon sec Health Visitors' Assoc 1980-83; memb: Health Educn Cncl 1981-83, Eng Nat Bd for Nursing Midwifery and Health Visiting 1983-, fndr memb Babymilk Action Coalition 1980 (lect health visitors' role in promoting breastfeeding, advsr Nat Childbirth Tst), teacher relaxation classes 1974-; contributor to the nursing press 1979-, regular columnist and editorial advsr Nursing Mirror 1980-83; *Publications* articles published in Nursing Times, Self and Society, the British Medical Journal, New Generation (journal of the NCT), Health Visitor; *Style*— Miss Shirley Goodwin; 14 Fairlea Place, London W5 1SP (☎ 01 998 0125); 36 Eccleston Sq, London SW1V 1PF (☎ 01 834 9523)

GOODWIN, Timothy John Medlicott; s of Lt-Col Edward Guy Medlicott Goodwin, MC, RA, of Claverdon, Warwick; *b* 27 Mar 1935; *Educ* Stonyhurst, Lanchester Coll; *m* 1961, Elizabeth Joan, da of Roland Wills, of Leamington Spa; 1 s, 1 da; *Career* Lt Royal Artillery, BAOR, thereafter QOWWY (TA); mgmnt conslt 1961-67, with GEC (US) 1968-77, md The Charles Rickards Gp Ltd 1979-82, dir Giltspur Precision Industries Ltd 1977-, md Caranex UK 1982-; *Recreations* ornithology, forestry; *Style*— Timothy Goodwin, Esq

GOODWORTH, Simon Nicholas; s of Michael Thomas Goodworth, 10 Manor Green, Stratford-Upon-Avon, Warwickshire CV37 7ES, and Lorna Ruth, *née* Skerrett; *b* 9 August 1955; *Educ* Solihull Sch Solihull W Midlands, Univ of Manchester (LLB); *Career* ptnr Theodore Goddard 1986 (admitted slr 1980); memb Law Soc; *Recreations* tennis, squash, music, theatre; *Style*— Simon Goodworth, Esq; 22 Oakhill Rd, London SW15 (☎ 01 874 5431); Theodore Goddard, 16 St Martins-le-Grand, London EC1A 4EJ (☎ 01 606 8855, fax 01 606 4390)

GOODYEAR, Andrew William Raeside; s of Capt Maxwell William Goodyear (d 1957), and Gwendolen Moyra Raeside (d 1975); *b* 26 April 1939; *Educ* Merchiston; *m* 17 April 1971, Elizabeth Mary, da of George Hay Marshall Surgeon, of The Thicket, Beech Avenue, Worcester; *Career* teacher and co dir; md: PB Books Ltd 1969-77, Oho Enterprises 1986-; *Recreations* golf, amateur dramatics, writing; *Style*— Andrew Goodyear, Esq; The Sundial Cottage, Essen Lane, Kilsby, Rugby, Warks (☎ 0788 822454); Bilton Grange, Dunchurch, Rugby, Warks (☎ 0788 810217, car tel 0860 511742)

GOOLD, Sir George Leonard; 7 Bt (UK 1801), of Old Court, Co Cork; s of Sir George Ignatius Goold, 6 Bt (d 1967, and Rhoda, *née* Benn; *b* 26 August 1923; *Educ* St Mark's Sch, St John's Coll Port Piere S Australia; *m* 8 Dec 1945, Joy Cecelia, da of William Percival Cutler, of Melbourne; 1 s (George*qv*), 4 da (Dianne b 1946, Georgina b 1948, Michelle b 1956, Louise b 1962); *Career* mechanical engr, ret 1981; *Recreations* fishing, bowls, shooting; *Clubs* Probus; *Style*— Sir George Goold, Bt; 60 Canterbury Rd, Victor Harbour, S Australia 5211 (☎ 085 52 2872)

GOOLD, George William; s and h of Sir George Goold, 7 Bt; *b* 25 Mar 1950; *m* 1973, Julie Anne, da of Leonard Crack, of Whyalla; 2 s (George b 1975, Jon b 1977); *Style*— George Goold, Esq; 2 Ambleside Ave, Mount Keira, NSW 2500, Australia

GOOLD, Baron (Life Peer UK 1987), of Waterfoot, in the District of Eastwood; Sir James Duncan Goold; DL (Renfrewshire 1985); s of John Goold, CA (d 1934), and Janet Agnes, *née* Kirkland; *b* 28 May 1934; *Educ* Glasgow Acad, Inst of Chartered Accountants Scotland; *m* 1959, Sheena, da of Alexander David Paton, OBE, CA, (d 1986), of Troon, Ayrshire; 2 s (Hon Michael b 1966, Hon James b 1968), 1 da (Hon Anna b 1962); *Career* CA 1958; pres: Scottish Building Contractors Assoc 1971, Scottish Building Employers Fedn 1977; chm CBI Scotland 1981-83, dir Mactaggart & Mickel Ltd; hon tres Scottish Cons Pty 1980-83 (chm 1983-); dir American Tst plc, Morgan Grenfell (Scotland) Ltd, Edinburgh Oil & Gas plc 1986-, Gibson & Goold Ltd; DL Renfrewshire; kt 1983; *Recreations* gardening, hill walking, golf, tennis; *Clubs* Carlton, RSAC, Western (Glasgow), Royal Troon GC; *Style*— The Rt Hon Lord Goold, DL; Sandyknowe, Waterfoot, Clarkston, Glasgow G76 8RN (☎ 041 644 2764); Linden Lea, Lamlash, Isle of Arran (☎ 077 06 340); Mactaggart & Mickel Ltd, 107 West Regent St, Glasgow G2 (☎ 041 332 0001)

GOOLD, Peter Anthony; s of Ernest George Goold, of Spencer Brook, Chelford Rd, Prestbury, Cheshire, and Vera Rose, *née* Wilks; *b* 5 Oct 1943; *Educ* Shrewsbury, London Univ (LLB); *m* 1, 6 May 1967 (m dis 1982), Angela Moira, da of Cedric Iliffe, of Woodbury, Salerton, Devon; 1 s (Simon b 16 Nov 1970), 1 da (Georgina b 16 Jan 1973); m 2, 11 Feb 1982 (Valerie Elizabeth) Lorraine, da of Arnold Richard Holden, of Prestwich, Manchester; *Career* CA; Spicer & Oppenheim 1962-68, jt md Whitecroft plc 1969-; dir Salford Univ Hldgs plc; FCA 1967; *Recreations* mountain walking; *Style*— Peter Goold, Esq; Kingswood, Macclesfield Rd, Alderley Edge, Cheshire SK9 7BH (☎ 0625 582 725); Whitecroft plc, Water Lane, Wilmslow, Cheshire SK9 5BX (☎ 0625 524 677, fax 0625 535 821, telex 666150)

GOOLD-ADAMS, Richard John Moreton; CBE (1974); s of Sir Hamilton Goold-Adams, GCMG (d 1920, sometime govr of Queensland), formerly of Jamesbrook, Midleton, Co Cork, and Elsie, *née* Riordon, of Ontario and Montreal; *b* 24 Jan 1916; *Educ* Winchester, New Coll Oxford; *m* 1939, Diana Mary Ponsonby Deenagh (a horticultural author), da of Richard Francis Ponsonby Blennerhassett, only s of Rowland Ponsonby Blennerhassett, MP Kerry 1872-1885; *Career* Maj Italy 1945; ed staff The Economist 1947-55, dir within Guthrie Gp of Cos 1954-69; chm: Int Inst for Strategic Studies 1963-73, SS Great Britain Project 1968-82; economist, co dir, journalist, broadcaster, lectr, and author; *Books Incl:* The Time of Power: a Reappraisal of John Foster Dulles; The Return of the Great Britain; *Recreations* photography; *Clubs* Travellers'; *Style*— Richard Goold-Adams, Esq, CBE; c/o National Westminster Bank, 116 Fenchurch Street, London EC3M 5AN

GOOLDEN, Douglas Cyril Aubrey; s of Cdr Cyril Goolden, RN (d 1942), and Eustine, *née* Turner (d 1958); *b* 16 Dec 1914; *Educ* Gresham's, Oriel Coll Oxford; *m* 7 July 1945, Hon Rosemary, *qv* da of maj Hon Christopher William Lowther (d 1935); 2 s (Michael b 1947, Alastair b 1954), 1 da (Jill b 1949); *Career* WW II RNVR 1939-45 (Lt), Naval ADC to Govr of Bermuda 1942-44; *Recreations* tennis, croquet, bridge; *Clubs* MCC; *Style*— Douglas Goolden, Esq; Forge Cottage, Withyham, Hantfield, East Sussex (☎ 089277 351)

GOOLDEN, Hon Mrs (Rosemary); *née* Lowther; er da of Maj Hon Christopher William Lowther (d 1935, er s of 1 Viscount Ullswater); raised to the rank of a Viscount's da, 1950; *b* 25 Feb 1922; *m* 7 July 1945, Lt Douglas Cyril Aubrey Goolden, RNVR, s of late Cdr Cyril Goolden, DSO, RN; 2 s, 1 da; *Career* served in World War II as 2nd Offr WRNS; *Recreations* painting, horses; *Style*— The Hon Mrs Goolden; Forge Cottage, Withyham, Hartfield, E. Sussex

GOONETILLEKE, Lady; Phyllis Mary; *née* Millar; *m* 1968, as his 2 w, Sir Oliver Ernest Goonetilleke, GCMG, KCVO, KBE (d 1978); *Style*— Lady Goonetilleke; 14 Albion Gate, Hyde Park Place, London W2

GORARD, Anthony John; s of William James and Rose Mary Gorard, of Cleveland Rd, Ealing; *b* 15 July 1927; *Educ* Ealing County Sch for Boys; *m* 1954, Barbara Kathleen, da of Hubert Clifford Hampton, OBE (d 1971), of Acton; 1 s, 3 da; *Career* hotel proprietor, exec dir Anglia TV 1959-67, chief exec HTV and dir Independent TV Publications and ITN 1968-78, chief exec Cardiff Broadcasting Co 1979-81; FCA; *Recreations* tennis, rambling, pottery, art galleries, theatre; *Style*— A J Gorard, Esq; The Old Market House, Cerne Abbas, Dorset DT2 7JE (☎ 030 03 680)

GORDON; *see*: Smith-Gordon

GORDON; *see*: Duff-Gordon

GORDON, Sir Alexander John (Alex); CBE (1974), OBE (1967); s of John Tullis Gordon (d 1959), of Swansea, and Euphemia Baxter Borrowman, *née* Simpson (d 1942); *b* 25 Feb 1917; *Educ* Swansea GS, Welsh Sch of Architecture; *Career* Maj RE 1940-46; architect in partnership with T Alwyn Lloyd 1948-60, sr ptnr Alex Gordon & Partners 1960-82, conslt The Alex Gordon Partnership 1982-88; memb: Welsh Arts Cncl 1959-73, Design Cncl 1973-77, Bd of British Cncl 1980-87; Royal Fine Art Cmmr 1973-; pres RIBA 1971-73; Hon LLD Univ of Wales 1972; FCSD 1975, ARICS 1987, Hon Fell ISE 1980, Hon Fell CIBSE 1975, Hon Memb BDA 1980, Soc of Mexican Architects 1972, and corresponding memb Danish Architects 1976, Hon FRAIC 1974, Hon FAIA 1974; kt 1988; *Recreations* reflecting on past skiing, visual arts; *Clubs* Arts, Cardiff and County; *Style*— Sir Alex Gordon, CBE, OBE; River Cottage, Llanblethian, nr Cowbridge, S Glam CF7 7JL (☎ 04463 3672); Flat 3, 32 Grosvenor St, London W1X 9FF (☎ 01 629 7910)

GORDON, Andrew David; er adopted son of 4 Marquess of Aberdeen and Temair (d 1974); bro James Gordon *qv*; *b* 6 Mar 1950; *Educ* Harrow; *Style*— Andrew Gordon, Esq

GORDON, Aubrey Abraham; s of Isaac Gordon (d 1962), of Sunderland, and Fanny, *née* Benjamin (d 1975); *b* 26 July 1925; *Educ* Bede Collegiate Boys Sch Sunderland, Durham Univ (LLB); *m* 28 June 1949, Reeva Rebecca, da of Myer Cohen (d 1941), of Sunderland; 1 s (David Myer b 1956), 2 da (Anne b 1950, Susan b 1950); *Career* admitted slr 1947; rec of the Crown Ct 1978-; pres: Houghton le Spring Chamber of Trade 1955, Helton le Hole Rotary Club 1967, Sunderland Law Soc 1976; chm Houghton Round Table 1959, Sunderland Victims Support Scheme 1978-80, Sunderland Guild of Help 1984-; vice-pres NE Joel Intract Memorial Home for Aged Jews; *Recreations* communal activities, photography, walking; *Style*— Aubrey A Gordon, Esq; 1 Acer Court, Sunderland, Tyne & Wear SR2 7EJ (☎ 091 565 8993)

GORDON, Boyd; s of David Gordon (d 1986), of Musselburgh, and Isabella, *née* Leishman; *b* 18 Sept 1926; *Educ* Musselburgh GS; *m* 26 Sept 1951, Elizabeth Mabel, da of Thomas Smith (d 1963); 2 da (Ruth b 1953, Pamela b 1955); *Career* served Royal Scots (WO 2) 1944-48; Dept of Ag & Fish Scotland: asst sec EEC and gen econ matters 1978-82, Fisheries sec 1982-86; dir fish Galore plc 1987-; conslt Scottish Fishermens Orgn 1987-; *Recreations* golf, gardening, local church matters; *Style*— Boyd Gordon, Esq; 87 Duddingston Rd, Edinburgh (☎ 031 669 4380); Scottish Fishermen's Organisation, Braehead, Queensferry Rd, Edinburgh

GORDON, Catherine (Kate); JP (Inner Manchester 1969); da of William Alexander Keir (d 1963), of Ayr, Scotland, and Marion Watson, *née* Prentice (d 1987); *b* 28 April 1923; *Educ* Ayr Acad, Open Univ (BA); *m* 20 Aug 1955, (Donald) Hugh McKay Gordon, s of James Bremner Gordon, of Huntly, Aberdeenshire; 1 s (Alistair Keir b 10 Sept 1956), 1 da (Marion Louise (Mrs Livingstone Jones) b 31 July 1959); *Career* Civil Serv and PA to chm of nationalised indust 1945-56; local and met dist cncllr 1969-, chm Trafford Ethical Ctee 1984-; memb· Trafford Health Authy 1976-, Trafford Cts Ctee 1972-88, Gtr Manchester Probation Ctee 1974-; chm Inner Manchester Magistrates 1985-; YWCA: nat pres and chm bd of govrs 1980-84, govr 1970-, del World Cncl YWCA Forces rep (BAOR and Cyprus) 1984-; memb cncl Nat Magistrates Assoc 1985-; FRSA 1980; *Recreations* music, family, friends, fun; *Clubs* YWCA; *Style*— Mrs Hugh Gordon, JP; 3 West Lynn, Devisdale Rd, Bowdon, Cheshire WA14 2AT (☎ 061 928 6038, fax 061 941 5394, telex 66-88-00)

GORDON, Sir Charles Addison Somerville Snowden; KCB (1981), (CB 1970); s of Charles Gordon Snowden Gordon, TD (d 1961); *b* 25 July 1918; *Educ* Winchester, Balliol Coll Oxford; *m* 1943, Janet Margaret, da of late Douglas Porteous Beattie, of Dewsbury, Yorks; 1 s, 1 da; *Career* served 1939-45 in Fleet Air Arm (Lt (A) RNVR); asst clerk House of Commons 1946, sr clerk 1947, fourth clerk at the Table 1962, princ clerk of the Table Office 1967, second clerk asst 1974, clerk asst 1976, clerk of the House of Commons 1979-83; *Books* ed 20th edition Erskine May's Parliamentary Practice (1983); *Style*— Sir Charles Gordon, KCB, CB; 279 Lonsdale Rd, Barnes, London SW13 9QB (☎ 01 748 6735)

GORDON, Colin Malcolm; s of Colin Pithie Gordon, of Cobham, Surrey, and Elsie Isabella, *née* Brown; *b* 19 May 1946; *Educ* Badingham Coll, Merrist Wood Agric Coll; *m* 1, 4 May 1968 (m dis 1987), Jill Margaret, da of John Walter Lawrence, of Fetcham, Leatherhead, Surrey; 2 s (Stuart Colin b 29 Oct 1970, Alisdair Robert b 29 Dec 1973); m 2, 30 April 1988, Sandra Dawn Gordon, da of Raymond Gordon Smith (d 1975); *Career* farmer 1963-73, agric fin specialist NW Securities Ltd 1973-76, area then regnl mangr Highland Leasing Ltd 1976-82, chief exec Humberclyde Fin Gp Ltd 1986- (sales and mktg dir 1982-86); IOD 1986; *Recreations* walking, rugby, golf, gardening; *Style*— Colin Gordon, Esq; Byand H Welham Road, Norton, Malton, N Yorkshire YO17 9DP (☎ 0653 692266); United House, Piccadilly, York YO1 1PQ (☎ 0904 645 411, car 0860 548 455)

GORDON, David Michael; s of Nathian Gordon, of London, and Diana, *née* MacKoffsky; *b* 12 Dec 1940; *Educ* Davenant Foundation GS; *m* 9 June 1968, Patricia Anne, da of Alfred Melamed (d 1982); 1 s (Andrew b 27 Oct 1971), 1 da (Nicola b 2 July 1974); *Career* actuary Pearl Assurance Plc 1984-(asst actuary 1975-83, dep actuary 1983-84); dir: Pearl Assurance Plc 1987, Pearl Assurance (Unit Funds) Ltd 1987, Pearl Assurance (Unit Linked Pensions) Ltd 1987, Pearl Tst Mangrs Ltd 1987, Pearl Gp Plc 1988, Insur Overweight Disease Tst; memb: Ctees of the Assoc of Br Insurers, the Lautro Selling Practices Ctee; FIA 1968, FSS 1970; *Recreations* reading, gardening, swimming; *Clubs* 59, Denarius; *Style*— David Gordon, Esq; Pearl Assurance Plc, 252 High Holborn, London, WC1V 7EB (☎ 405 8441, fax 01 831 6251, telex 296350 PEARL G)

GORDON, Maj-Gen Desmond Spencer; CB (1961), CBE (1952, DSO 1943, JP (Hants 1968), DL (Hants 1980)); s of Harold Easty Gordon (ka 1917), and Gwendoline, *née* Blackett; *b* 25 Dec 1911; *Educ* Haileybury Coll, RMC Sandhurst; *m* 1940, Sybil Mary, da of Allan Crewe Thompson; 1 s, 1 da; *Career* Green Howards 1932, Brig comd 151 Durham Bde 1944, 146 Bde 1945, 131 Lorried Inf Bde Berlin 1945 and 16 Indep Para Bde Gp 1952-55; DA & QMG HQ 1 (BR) Corps 1959, GOC 4 Div 1959-61, chief army instr Imperial Def Coll 1962-64, ACDS MOD 1964-66, Col The Green Howards 1965-74, ret 1968; cmmr in chief St John Ambulance 1973-78; Order of Orange Nassau with Swords 1945; KStJ 1973; *Clubs* Army and Navy; *Style*— Maj-Gen Desmond Gordon, CB, CBE, DSO, JP, DL; Southfields, Greywell, Basingstoke, Hants (☎ 025 671 2088)

GORDON, Donald; s of Nathan Gordon (d 1978), and Sylvia (Sheila), *née* Shevitz (d 1984); *b* 24 June 1930; *Educ* King Edward VII Sch, Johannesburg Univ of Witwatersrand; *m* 21 Jan 1958, Peggy, da of Max Cowan (d 1950); 2 s (Richard Michael b 1958, Graeme John b 1963), 1 da (Mrs Appelbaum b 1960); *Career* CA, registered public accountant and auditor; chm: Charter Life Ins Co Ltd (dir 1985), Continental & Industl Tst plc (UK dir 1986), Guardian Nat Ins Co Ltd (dir 1980), GuardBank Mgmnt Corp Ltd (dir 1969), First Union General Investmt Tst Ltd (dir 1977), Liberty Asset Mgmnt Ltd (dir 1969), Liberty Hldgs Ltd (dir 1968), Liberty Investors Ltd (dir 1971), Liberty Life Assoc of Africa Ltd (dir 1957), Rapp & Maister Hldgs Ltd (dir 1968), and TransAtlantic Hldgs plc (UK dir 1981); dir: Capital & Counties plc 1982-, Guardian Royal Exchange plc 1984-, Guardian Royal Exchange Assur plc 1971-, Placor Hldgs Ltd 1982-, Plate Glass & Shatterprufe Industries Ltd 1982-, Premier Gp Hldgs Ltd 1983-, S African Breweries Ltd 1982-, Standard Bank Investmt Corp 1979-, UBS Hldgs Ltd 1986-, UBS Insur Co Ltd 1986-, and Utd Bldg Soc Ltd 1972-; *Recreations* tennis; *Clubs* Houghton Golf, Johannesburg Country, Plettenberg Bay Country, Rand; *Style*— Donald Gordon, Esq; Liberty Life Assoc of Africa Ltd, 4th Floor, Liberty Life Centre, 1 Ameshoff Street, Braamfontein 2017, PO Box 10499, Johannesburg 2000, S Africa; TransAtlantic Holdings plc, St Andrew's House, 40 Broadway, London SW1H 0BR, (☎ SA 011 712 2100, London 01 222-5496, fax: SA 011 403 3171, London 01 222 5840)

GORDON, Lord Douglas Claude Alexander; DSO (1945); yst s of Lt-Col (Granville Cecil) Douglas Gordon, CVO, DSO (d 1930, s of Lord Granville Armyne Gordon, 6 s of 10 Marquess of Huntly), and Violet Ida, *née* Streatfeild (d 1968); bro of 12 Marquess of Huntly; granted the rank of a Marquess's s 1937; *b* 30 July 1916; *Educ* Eton, RMC Sandhurst; *m* 1, 21 Dec 1940 (m dis 1961), Suzanne (d 1983), da of late Lt-Col Arthur Houssemayne du Boulay, DSO; 2 s (Andrew b 1942, Douglas b 1947), 1 da (Lady Robert Nairne *see* Peerage M Lansdowne b 1950); m 2, 1963, Bridget, da of late Gerald Bryan Ingram, and formerly wife of Maj Alexander Hutchison; 1 da; *Career* page of honour to HM 1930-33, Lt-Col Black Watch, memb Queen's Body Gd for Scotland (Royal Co of Archers) Palestine 1937-1940, Italy 1943-45 (DSO), Greece 1945-46, Staff Coll Haifa 1947, Egypt 1948-49, instr RMA Sandhurst 1949-52, ret 1953; *Recreations* antiques, fishing, horticulture; *Style*— Lord Douglas Gordon, DSO; The Old Rectory, Stockbridge, Hants (☎ 0264 810662)

GORDON, Frederick William; s of George Gordon (d 1980), and Susan, *née* McNelis (d 1973); *b* 13 June 1949; *Educ* Bletchley GS; *m* 14 Feb 1976, Barbara Ann, da of Sidney Clarke (d 1964); 1 s (Neil b 1980), 1 da (Anna b 1977); *Career* gen sales mangr Pergeot Talbot Motor Co 1985-; *Recreations* cricket; *Clubs* Bletchley Town; *Style*— Frederick W Gordon, Esq; Fariholme, Bon, Brickhill, Bucks (☎ 0908 642530); Luton Rd, Dunstable, Bedfordshire (☎ 0582 64171)

GORDON, George; s of Dr Adam Smith Gordon, RAMC (d 1951), of Ferniebank, Markinch, Fife, and Agnes Forbes, *née* Smith; *b* 4 Sept 1936; *Educ* Bell Baxter Sch Cupar Fife, Edinburgh Univ (MB ChB); *m* 11 June 1966, Rosemary Gould, da of Rev Alexander Hutchison; 1 s (David b 4 Jan 1971), 1 da (Fiona b 27 March 1967); *Career* house surgn: Western Gen Hosp Edinburgh 1959-60, Royal Infirmary Edinburgh 1960; house physician Royal Hosp Sick Children Edinburgh 1961, sr house offr Simpson Meml Maternity Pavilion 1962, registrar Eastern Gen Hosp Edinburgh 1962-66, sr registrar Western Gen Hosp Edinburgh 1966-69, conslt obstetrician and gynaecologist Dumfries 1969-, admin conslt Alexandra Hospice Unit Dumfries ; pres: Dumfries div BMA (formerley sec), Edinburgh Obstetrical Soc; chm confidential enquiry into Maternal Deaths Scotland, sec Scottish exec ctee RCOG; pres Dumfries Music Club 1987-; fell BMA 1988; FRCS (Edin) 1967, FRCOG 1977; *Recreations* Scots literature, gardening, golf, music; *Clubs* New (Edinburgh); *Style*— George Gordon, Esq; Dumfries & Galloway Royal Infirmary, Dumfries (☎ 0387 53151)

GORDON, Sheriff Gerald Henry; er s of Simon Gordon (d 1982), of Glasgow, and Rebecca, *née* Bulbin (d 1956); *b* 17 June 1929; *Educ* Queen's Park Sr Secdy Sch Glasgow, Glasgow Univ (MA, LLB, PhD), Edinburgh Univ (LLD); *m* 1957, Marjorié, yr da of Isaac Joseph, of Glasgow; 1 s (David), 2 da (Susan, Sarah); *Career* prof of scots law Edinburgh Univ 1972-76; sheriff of: South Strathclyde, Dumfries and Galloway at Hamilton 1976-77, Glasgow and Strathkelvin 1978-; *Books* Criminal Law (1 ed 1968, 2 ed 1978), Criminal Procedure (ed 4th and 5th edn); *Recreations* Jewish studies, swimming; *Style*— Sheriff Gerald H Gordon; 52 Eastwoodmains Rd, Giffnock, Glasgow G46 6QD (☎ 041 638 8614); Glasgow Sheriff Ct (☎ 041 429 8888)

GORDON, Ian; s of James Donald Gordon, of Montrose, Angus, and Winifred, *née* Thomson (d 1985); *b* 15 August 1957; *Educ* Biggar HS, Edinburgh Univ (LLB); *m* 22 July 1988, (Mary) Angela Joan, da of Donald Macdonald, of Isle of Lewis; *Career* McGrigor Donald (formerly Moncrieff Warren Paterson & Co Slrs Glasgow):

apprentice 1979-81, slr 1981, ptnr 1983-; memb: Law Soc of Scotland 1981, Assoc of Pension Lawyers 1986; NP (1981); *Recreations* getting out and about especially on wheels; *Style*— Ian Gordon, Esq; Hughenden, Glasgow; Pacific Ho, 70 Wellington St, Glasgow G2 6SB (☎ 041 248 6677, fax 041 221 1390, telex 778744 MGDGLWG)

GORDON, James Drummond; yr adopted son of 4 Marquess of Aberdeen (d 1974); bro Andrew Gordon, *qv*; *b* 11 April 1953; *Educ* Harrow; *Style*— James Gordon, Esq

GORDON, James Stuart; CBE (1984); s of James Edward Gordon (d 1975), of Glasgow, and Elsie Riach (d 1984); *b* 17 May 1936; *Educ* St Aloysius' Coll, Glasgow Univ (MA); *m* 1971, Margaret Anne, da of Andrew Kirkwood Stevenson (d 1968), of Glasgow; 2 s (Michael Stevenson b 1974, Christopher James b 1976), 1 da (Sarah Jane b 1972); *Career* political ed STV 1965-73, md Radio Clyde 1973-, chm Scottish Exhibition Centre 1983-; memb: Scottish Devpt Agency 1981-; Ct Univ of Glasgow 1984, Ctee of Inquiry into Teachers' Pay and Conditions 1986; *Recreations* walking, genealogy, golf; *Clubs* New (Edinburgh), Prestwick Golf, Buchanan Castle Golf; *Style*— James S Gordon, Esq, CBE; Deil's Craig, Strathblane, Glasgow G63 9ET (☎ 0360 70604); Radio Clyde plc, Clydebank Business Park, Clydebank G81 2RX (☎ 041 941 1111, telex 779537, fax 041 952 0080)

GORDON, Rt Hon John Bowie (Peter); PC (1978); s of Dr William Patteson Pollock Gordon, CBE, MB, FRCSE, and Dr Doris Clifton Gordon, OBE, MD, FRCSE, FRCOG, *née* Jolly; *b* 24 July 1921; *Educ* St Andrew's Coll Ch Ch NZ, Lincoln Coll Canterbury, Nuffield Scholar 1954; *m* 1943, Dorothy Elizabeth, da of Robert Morton; 2 s, 1 da; *Career* MP (Clutha) 1960-78; min of Tport, Railways, Aviation, Marine and Fisheries 1966-72, and Labour and State Services 1975-78; ret 1978; co dir banking, insurance, transport; *Books* Some Aspects British Farming (1955); *Recreations* golf, cooking, gardening; *Clubs* Otago Officers, Tapanui Services; *Style*— The Rt Hon John Gordon; Tapanui, Otago, New Zealand

GORDON, John Edwin; s of Dennis Lionel Shute (d 1940); *b* 14 Dec 1939; *Educ* Tonbridge, Queens' Coll Cambridge; *m* 1968, Monica Anne, *née* Law; 1 s, 2 da; *Career* dir: Robert Fleming & Co 1974-77, Laing & Cruickshank (stockbrokers) 1978-82, Jackson Exploration Inc 1982-85, British Waterways Bd; head of Corporate Finance Capel-Cure Myers, tres of Br Postgraduate Med Fedn; FCA; *Recreations* fishing; *Clubs* Boodle's, Leander; *Style*— John Gordon, Esq; 50 Castelnau, Barnes, London SW13 (☎ 01 748 1715); 65 Holborn Viaduct, London EC1A 2EU (☎ 01 236 5080, telex 886653)

GORDON, Sir Keith Lyndell; CMG (1971); 3 s of George S E and Nancy Gordon; *b* 8 April 1906; *Educ* St Mary's Coll St Lucia; *m* 1947, Ethel King; 1 da; *Career* justice of Appeal WI Associated States Supreme Court 1967-72, chief justice W Cameroon 1963-67, Puisne judge: Br Guiana 1959-62 and Windward and Leeward Islands 1954-59, former magistrate Trinidad and Tobago; chm Public Service Bd of Appeal 1978-; kt 1979; *Style*— Sir Keith Gordon, CMG; Vigie, Castries, St Lucia, W Indies

GORDON, Lady Marion; *née* Wright; 3 da of James B Wright, of Springfield, Neutral Bay, N Sydney, NSW; *m* 26 Sept 1928, Sir John Charles Gordon, 9 Bt (d 1982); 1 s, 1 da; *Style*— Marion, Lady Gordon; 61 Farrer Brown Ct, Nuffield Village, Castle Hill, NSW, Australia

GORDON, Murray Graham; s of Solomon Gordon; *b* 13 May 1922; *Educ* Collegiate Sch Liverpool, Univ of Liverpool Sch of Art; *m* 1950, Vera, *née* Denby; 2 s; *Career* Lt-Col (acting) India and Burma; chm and md Combined English Stores Gp Ltd 1970-87; *Recreations* golf, tennis, squash; *Clubs* Carlton, RAC; *Style*— Murray Gordon, Esq; Chelsea House, 3 The Vale, London SW3 (☎ 01 352 9311); Pythingdean Farmhouse, Coombelands Lane, Pythingdean, nr Pulborough, West Sussex (☎ 079 82 3654)

GORDON, Richard John Francis; s of John Bernard Basil Gordon, of 10 Ingelow House, Kensington Church Walk, London, and Winifred Josephine *née* Keenan; *b* 26 Nov 1948; *Educ* St Benedicts Sch, Christ Church Oxford (MA), UCL (LLM); *m* 13 Sept 1975, Jane Belinda, da of Anthony George Lucey, of Rosedale House, Welburn, Yorks; 2 s (Edmund John Anthony b 17 June 1982, Adam Richard Cosby b 25 Oct 1985); *Career* called to the Bar Middle Temple 1972; ed Crown Off Digest 1988-, broadcasts and articles on admin law in legal periodicals and other pubns; Freeman City of London; FRGS, ACIArb; *Books* The Law Relating to Mobile Homes and Caravans (second edn 1985), Judicial Review Law and Procedure (1985); *Recreations* modern fiction, theatre, cricket; *Style*— Richard Gordon, Esq; 24 Clonmel Rd, London SW6 5BJ (☎ 01 731 2126); 2 Harcourt Buildings, Temple, London EC4 (☎ 01 353 6961, fax 01 353 6968)

GORDON, Cdr Richard Redmond; OBE (1968), VRD (1959); s of Eric Redmond Sutton Gordon (d 1946), and Nancy Margaret, *née* Roff; *b* 1 Mar 1925; *Educ* Radley; *m* 4 Dec 1948, Ruth, da of Joseph Geoffrey Brooks (d 1953); 2 da (Elizabeth b 1953, Helen b 1955); *Career* War Serv 1943-46, London Div RNR 1946-68 (Cdr 1966-68); chm Jantar Nigeria Ltd 1965-71, dir and sec Cavendish Land Ltd 1968-73; pres Euro Fedn of Sea Anglers 1988-(chm 1976-88); Freeman City of London 1963, Liveryman Worshipful Co of Shipwrights 1965; FCIS 1955; *Recreations* sea angling, golf; *Clubs* Victory Servs; *Style*— Cdr Richard Gordon, OBE, VRD; 29 Alleyne Way, Elmer Sands, Bognor Regis, W Sussex PO22 6JZ (☎ 024 369 4057)

GORDON, Sir Robert James; 10 Bt (NS 1706), of Afton and Earlston, Kirkcudbrightshire (but has not yet proved his succession), probably next in remainder to the Viscountcy of Kenmure and Lordship of Lochinvar (dormant since 1872); s of Sir John Charles Gordon, 9 Bt (d 1982), and Marion, Lady Gordon, *qv*; *b* 17 August 1932; *m* 1976, Helen Julia Weston, da of Margery Perry, of Cammeray, Sydney, NSW; *Style*— Sir Robert Gordon, Bt; Earlstoun, Guyra, NSW 2365, Australia

GORDON, Robert Wilson; MC (1944); s of late Malcolm Gordon and Blanche Fayerweather Gordon; *b* 3 Mar 1915; *Educ* Harrow; *m* 1, 1946, Joan Alison (d 1965), da of Brig Arthur George Kenchington, CBE, MC (d 1966); 1 da; m 2, 1967, Diana Evelyn Venice (d 1980), eldest da of Edward Thomas Tyrwhitt-Drake, JP (d 1933), of Shardeloes, Bucks, former w of Robert Edward Ansell, and previously widow of Lt Arthur Michael William Blake, RN; *Career* dep chm Stock Exchange 1965-68, ptnr Pidgeon de Smitt (stockbrokers); *Style*— Robert Gordon Esq, MC; 41 Cadogan Sq, SW1 (☎ 01 235 4496)

GORDON, Lord Roderic Armyne; MBE (1943), TD; 3 s of Lt-Col (Granville Cecil) Douglas Gordon, CVO, DSO (d 1930, s of late Lord Granville Armyne Gordon, 6 s of 10 Marquess of Huntly), and Violet Ida, *née* Streatfeild (d 1968); bro of 12 Marquess; *b* 20 Jan 1914; *Educ* Stowe; *m* 1, 7 Jan 1937 (m dis 1949), Anne, yr da of late Lt-Col Hon Sir Osbert Eustace Vesey, KCVO, CMG, CBE; 2 s; m 2, 26 Aug 1949, Joana Alexandra, 2 da of Ion Bujoiu, of Bucharest, Romania, and formerly wife of (1) Prince Serban Ghica and (2) Baron de Stuers; *Career* N Africa 1943; Major 72nd (Hampshire) Anti-Aircraft Brig RA (TA); *Style*— Lord Roderic Gordon, MBE, TD; 101 The Davenport, 1011 12th Ave SW, Calgary, Alberta, Canada

GORDON, Rt Rev (Archibald) Ronald McDonald; s of Sir Archibald McDonald Gordon, CMG (d 1974), and Dorothy Katharine (d 1959), da of Charles Silvester Horne, MP, by his w Hon Katharine Maria, elder da of 1 Baron Cozens-Hardy; *b* 19 Mar 1927; *Educ* Rugby Sch, Balliol Oxford, Cuddesdon Theol Coll; *Career* deacon 1952, priest 1953, curate of Stepney 1952-55, chaplain Cuddesdon Coll 1955-59, vicar of St Peter Birmingham 1959-67, residentiary canon Birmingham Cathedral 1967-71, vicar of Univ Church of St Mary the Virgin with St Cross and St Peter in the East Oxford 1971-75, bishop of Portsmouth 1975-84, took seat in House of Lords 1981 (relinquished 1984), sr memb archbishop of Canterbury's Staff 1984-; also bishop to HM Forces 1985-; memb Church Assembly and Gen Synod, and proctor in convocation 1965-71, chm ACCM 1976-83, select preacher Oxford Univ 1985; *Style*— The Rt Rev Ronald Gordon; Lambeth Palace, London SE1 7JU

GORDON, Sir Sidney Samuel; CBE (1968, OBE 1965), JP (Hong Kong 1961); s of late P S and Angusina Gordon; *b* 20 August 1917; *Educ* Hyndland Sch Glasgow, Glasgow Univ; *m* 1950, Olive W F, da of late T A Eldon; 2 da; *Career* chartered accountant; sr ptnr Lowe, Bingham & Matthews (chartered accountants) Hong Kong 1956-70; MLC Hong Kong 1962-66, MEC 1965-80; chm Sir Elly Kadoorie Continuation Ltd 1970-; dep chm China Light & Power Co; chm Univ and Poly Grants Ctee 1974-76; steward Royal Hong Kong Jockey Club; Hon LLD Chinese Univ of Hong Kong 1970; kt 1972; *Recreations* golf, racing; *Clubs* Oriental, Hong Kong, Royal Hong Kong Jockey, Royal Hong Kong Golf; *Style*— Sir Sidney Gordon, CBE, JP; 7 Headland Rd, Repulse Bay, Hong Kong (☎ 5-8122577)

GORDON, Lady Sophia Catherine; da of 6 Marquess of Aberdeen and Temair, *qv*; *b* 20 July 1960; *Style*— Lady Sophia Gordon; c/o Quick's Green, Ashampstead, Berks RG8 8SN

GORDON, Lt-Col William Howat Leslie; CBE (1957), MBE (1941, MC 1943 and bar 1944); s of Frank Leslie Gordon, Indian Civil Service, FSCE (d 1974, designer of Sukkur barrage on the Indus), and Madelaine Ker (d 1982); *b* 8 April 1914; *Educ* Rugby, RMA Woolwich; *m* Nov 1944, Margot Evelyn (Wimbledon and Wightman Cup lawn tennis player), da of late Charles Lumb, of Ballard Coombe, Kingston Hill; 1 s (Raymond Francis b 1948), 3 da (Eleonora Lesley b 1947, Fiona Claire b 1952, Margo b 1955); *Career* Cmmnd Royal Signals 1934; Palestine, Africa, Italy, NW Europe; 1 Armoured, 1 Airborne Divs (despatches); Instr, Staff Coll Camberley 1947-49; chief exec The Uganda Co Ltd 1949-60, John Holt & Co (Liverpool) Ltd and Lonrho Exports Ltd 1960-71, MLC Uganda 1952-57; chm: Rickmansworth Water Co, St John Cncl, Bucks 1974-82; KStJ 1982; *Recreations* shooting, fishing, golf; formerly squash rackets army player, lawn tennis, cricket; *Clubs* White's, Rye Golf, MCC, Institute of Directors; *Style*— Lt-Col W H L Gordon, CBE, MBE, MC; Acre End, Maplefield Lane, Chalfont St Giles, Bucks HP8 4SN (☎ 02404 2047, office 02404 3645); Rickmansworth Water Co, Batchworth, Herts (☎ 0923 776633)

GORDON, William John (Bill); s of Sidney Frank Gordon (d 1982), and Grace, *née* Louie; *b* 24 April 1939; *Educ* King Edward VI Sch Birmingham; *m* 17 Oct 1963, Patricia, da of Thomas Rollason; 2 s (Bruce b 1967, Lewis b 1971); *Career* with Barclays Bank 1955-80; dir UK corporate servs Barclaycard 1987- (asst gen mangr 1980-82, regnl gen mangr Central Region 1983-87); memb London Regnl Cncl CBE 1988-; ACIB 1959, FCIB 1981 ; *Recreations* bridge, golf, chess, classical music; *Style*— Bill Gordon, Esq; 4 Beech Way, Blackmore End, Wheathampsted, Herts AL4 8LY (☎ 0438 832054); Barclays Bank Plc 54 Lombard Street, London EC3P 3AH (☎ 01 626 1567, fax 01 929 0394)

GORDON CUMMING, Sir William; 6 Bt (UK 1804); s of Maj Sir Alexander Penrose Gordon Cumming, MC, 5 Bt (d 1939); *b* 19 June 1928; *Educ* Eton; *m* 1, 1953 (m dis 1972), Elisabeth, da of Maj-Gen Sir William Robert Norris Hinde, KBE, CB, DSO; 1 s, 3 da; m 2, 1972 (m dis 1976), Lady Pauline Anne, sis of 13 Earl of Seafield, and former w of James Henry Harcourt Illingworth; *Heir* s, Alexander Gordon Cumming; *Career* late Lt Royal Scots Greys; *Style*— Sir William Gordon Cumming, Bt; Altyre, Forres, Morayshire

GORDON DILL, Maj Richard Patrick Murray; s of Major John Martin Gordon Dill (d 1949), of Stream Hill, Doneraile, Co Cork, and of Ethné Charlton Murray (d 1979); *b* 24 Nov 1923; *Educ* Eton, Trinity Coll Cambridge (not completed due to war serv); *m* 1, 27 June 1959, Mary Chichester (m dis 1967), da of James Paul Mills (d 1987), of Middleburg, VA, USA; m 2, 1968, Kari Penelope, da of Grahan Hugh Sheppard MC, TD (d 1973); 1 s (Marcus Patrick Gordon b 5 March 1974); *Career* landowner/farmer; served with the 8 King's Royal Irish Hussars N Africa, Middle East, NW Europe (despatches), personal liason offr to Gen Sir Myles Depmsey (cmdr 2 Army), and on staff, mil asst to Hd of Standing Gp NATO Washington DC 1957-59, Maj ret (on amalgamation of Regt 1959); subsequent to retirement from Army farmed, trained and bred racehorses, amateur jockey 1945-64 (Grand Mil Gold Cup 1957), local Jockey Club steward, Master of Foxhounds & Field Master (Warwickshire) 1965-75; Master of the Worshipful Co of Carpenters 1985-86; FRSA 1986; *Recreations* field sports, racing, travel, the arts; *Clubs* Cavalry & Guards; *Style*— Major Richard Gordon Dill; Idlicote House, Idlicote, nr Shipston-on-Stour, Warwics (☎ 0608 61473); Treshnish, Salen, Argylli (☎ 096 785 642); Estate Office Idlicote House, Idlicote, Nr Shipston-on-Stour, Warwics (☎ 0608 61381)

GORDON JONES, Air Marshal Sir Edward; KCB (1967) CB (1960, CBE 1956, OBE 1945, DSO 1941, DFC 1941); s of Lt-Col Albert Jones, DSO, MC, MD, DPH, of Dulverton House, Widnes; *b* 31 August 1914; *Educ* Wade Deacon Sch, Liverpool Univ; *m* 1938, Margery Thurston Hatfield, BSc; 2 s; *Career* served WW II (despatches), Air Vice-Marshal 1961, AOC RAF Germany 1961-63, AOC Malta and dep C-in-C (Air) Allied Forces Mediterranean 1965-66, Air Marshal 1966, AOC-in-C NEAF and admin Sovereign Base Areas 1966-69, Cdr British Forces Near East 1967-69, ret; Greek DFC 1941, Cdr Order of Orange Nassau 1945; *Recreations* music, opera, photography, sport; *Clubs* RAF; *Style*— Air Marshal Sir Edward Gordon Jones, KCB, CB, CBE, OBE, DSO, DFC; 20 Marlborough Court, Grange Road, Cambridge CB3 9BQ (☎ 0223 63029)

GORDON LENNOX, Maj-Gen Bernard Charles; CB (1986), MBE (1968); s of Lt-Gen Sir George Gordon Lennox, *qv*, and Nancy Brenda, da of Maj Sir Lionel Edward Hamilton Marmaduke Darell, 6 Bt, DSO; *b* 19 Sept 1932; *Educ* Eton, Sandhurst; *m*

1958, Sally-Rose, da of John Weston Warner (d 1981); 3 s (Edward b 1961, Angus b 1964, Charles b 1970); *Career* page of honour to HM The King 1946-49; cmmnd 1 Bn Grenadier Gds, 1974-75, GSO 1 RAF Staff Coll 1976-77, Brig 1977, Cdr Task Force H, Dep Cdr and COS SE Dist UKLF 1981-83, Maj-Gen 1982, Br Cmdt and Goc British Sector Berlin 1983-85, sr army memb Royal Coll of Defence Studies 1986-87; *Recreations* fishing, shooting, cricket, squash, music; *Clubs* Army and Navy, MCC; *Style—* Maj Gen B C Gordon Lennox; c/o Lloyds Bank, Cox's & King's Branch, 6 Pall Mall, London

GORDON LENNOX, Lt-Gen Sir George Charles; KBE (1964), CB (1959, CVO 1952, DSO 1943); er s of Lord Bernard Gordon Lennox (ka 1914); *b* 29 May 1908; *Educ* Eton, Sandhurst; *m* 1931, Nancy, da of Maj Sir Lionel Darell, 6 Bt, DSO, and Eleanor, da of Capt Justinian John Edwards-Heathcote, of Apedale, Staffs; 2 s (Maj-Gen Bernard, Colonel David); *Career* served Gren Gds 1928-52 (staff and regt WW II), GOC 3 Inf Div 1958-59, Cmdt Sandhurst 1960-63, Dir Gen Mil Trg 1963-64, GOC-in-C Scottish Cmd and govr Edinburgh Castle 1964-66, King of Arms Order British Empire 1968-83, ret; *Clubs* Cavalry and Guards'; *Style—* Lt-Gen Sir George Gordon Lennox, KBE, CB, CVO, DSO; Gordon Castle, Fochabers, Morayshire (☎ 0343 820275)

GORDON LENNOX, Capt Michael Charles; s of Rear Adm Sir Alexander Henry Charles Gordon Lennox KCVO, CB, DSO (d July 1987, gs of 7 Duke of Richmond and Gordon), and Barbara, *née* Steele (d Oct 1987); *b* 30 Sept 1938; *Educ* Eton, RNC Dartmouth; *m* 1974, Jennifer Susan, da of Capt Hon Vicary Gibbs (ka 1944); 1 s (Hamish b 1980), 2 da (Lucinda b 1975, Charlotte b 1978); *Career* chief Staff to Flag Offr Scotland and N Ireland 1985-8; *Recreations* gardening, shooting, fishing, golf, cricket; *Clubs* Naval and Military, Pratt's; *Style—* Capt Michael Gordon Lennox, RN; Fishers Hill, Iping, Midhurst, W Sussex GU29 0PF (☎ 073 081 3474)

GORDON-CLARK, Guy Lawrence; OBE (1983), JP (1970); s of Henry Michael Gordon-Clark (d 1976), of Wyatt House, Dorking, Surrey, and Gwendolyn Emily, *née* Marriner (d 1986); *b* 13 Mar 1928; *Educ* Winchester; *m* 3 Oct 1953, Pauline Guise; 2 da (Catherine b 1955, Lucinda b 1959); *Career* wine and spirit shipper; dir Matthew Clark & Sons Ltd (family firm) 1952-; chm: J E Matther & Son Ltd, British Wine Producers 1971-, Wine & Spirit Assoc 1969-71, 1981-83, West Sussex Probation Ctee 1979-85; *Recreations* gardening; *Clubs* City of London; *Style—* Guy Gordon-Clark, Esq, OBE, JP; Itchingfield House, Horsham, West Sussex (☎ 0403 790393); 183-185 Central Street, London EC1V 8DR (☎ 01 253 7646)

GORDON-CUMMING, Alastair Alexander Penrose; s and h of Sir William Gordon-Cumming, 6 Bt; *b* 15 April 1954; *Style—* Alastair Gordon-Cumming, Esq

GORDON-CUMMING, Gp Capt Alexander (Sandy) Roualeyn; CMG (1977), CVO (1969); s of Lt Cdr Roualeyn Geoffrey Gordon-Cumming, RN (d 1928), and Mary Violet Katharine, *née* Marter (d 1984); *b* 10 Sept 1924; *Educ* Eton; *m* 1, 1965, Beryl Joyce MacNaughton (d 1973), da of late Naughton Dunn, of Edgbaston; 1 da (Ann Penrose b 1968); m 2, 1974, (Elizabeth) Patricia (d 1983), da of Travers Robert Blackley (d 1982), of Co Cork; 1 da (Mary Elizabeth b 1975); *Career* RAF 1943-69 (ret), Gp Capt and Dep Capt of The Queen's Flight; Bd of Trade 1969-73; seconded HM Diplomatic Service 1974-78 (cnsllr Aviation and Shipping HBM Embassy Washington); Dept of Trade and Industry 1978-84; dir Invest in Britain Bureau; chm W Sussex Branch of English Speaking Union; *Recreations* gardening; *Clubs* RAF; *Style—* Gp Capt Alexander Gordon-Cumming, CMG, CVO; Woodstock, West Way, Chichester, Sussex PO19 3PW (☎ 0243 776413)

GORDON-DUFF, Maj John Beauchamp; MBE (1942); s of Archibald Hay Gordon-Duff (d 1938), and Lady Frances (d 1950), da of 3 Earl Fortescue; *b* 15 Feb 1899; *Educ* Winchester, RMC Sandhurst; *m* 1937, Ellen Susan, da of Hon Charles Platt Williams (d 1944), of NY, USA; 1 s (decd), 1 da; *Career* Maj Rifle Bde WW I (wounded); served WW II Malta, Palestine, ADC to Viceroy of India (Lord Irwin), mil sec to Field Marshal Viscount Gort, VC; DL Aberdeenshire 1942-64; *Style—* Maj John Gordon-Duff, MBE; Lindridge Priory, Tenbury Wells, Worcs WR15 8JQ (☎ 058 470 274)

GORDON-DUFF, Hon Mrs; Hon Sheila Beatrice; *née* Davison; yr da of 1 Baron Broughshane, KBE (d 1953), by his 1 w; *b* 14 June 1907; *m* 1936, Gp Capt George Edward Gordon-Duff, CBE (d 1966); 1 s; *Style—* The Hon Mrs Gordon-Duff; 10 Jameson St, London W8

GORDON-DUFF, Col Thomas Robert; MC (1945), JP (Banffshire 1959); s of Capt Lachlan Gordon-Duff, DL (ka 1914, s of Thomas Duff-Gordon-Duff, CBE, JP, by his w Pauline, sis of 1 Baron Glenconner, Lady Ribblesdale and Margot Asquith and half-sis of Ladies Wakehurst, Elliot of Harwood and Crathorne (ie the children of Sir Charles Tennant, 1 Bt)); *b* 5 Oct 1911; *Educ* Eton, Sandhurst; *m* 1946, Jean, da of Leslie Moir, of Bicester; 1 s; *Career* Brevet Col TA Gordon Highlanders, CO 5/6 Bn 1947-51; POW Calais 1940; DL Banffshire 1948, vice-ld lt 1961, ld-lt 1964; ccllr 1949-75, convenor Banff CC 1962-71; landed proprietor; *Recreations* fishing, shooting; *Clubs* Army and Navy; *Style—* Col Thomas Gordon-Duff, MC, JP; Drummuir, Keith, Banffshire (☎ 054 281 224)

GORDON-FINLAYSON, Air Vice-Marshal James Richmond; DSO (1941), DFC (1940); s of Gen Sir Robert Gordon-Finlayson, KCB, CMG, DSO, DL (d 1956), Leslie Mary, OBE, *née* Richmond; *b* 19 August 1914; *Educ* Winchester, Pembroke Coll Cambridge (MA); *m* 1, 1939, Suzanne Sim; 1 s (Christopher), 1 da (Penelope Ann); m 2, 1953, Margaret Ann (d 1964), da of Col C C Richardson, DSO MC; m 3, 11 Feb 1981, Iracema Philippina; *Career* RAF 1936, ADC to govt of Kenya 1938-39, Libya 1940-42, Greece 1940-41 (despatches) Syria 1941, Sqdn Ldr 1940; RAF Staff Coll 1942, staff Air Min 1942-45, RAF Liaison Offr USAAF Guam 1945, Air Staff Air Cmd SEA 1945-46, SASO AHQ Burma 1946, OC 48 Sqdn 1946-47, directing staff JSSC, Gp Capt 1951, Air Staff Air Min 1951-54, OC RAF Deversoir 1954, OC RAF Kharmaksar 1954-56, staff HQ Bomber Cmd 1956, asst cmdt RAF Staff Coll Bracknell, Air Cdre 1958, Air Vice-Marshal 1961, dir gen of Personal Services Air Min 1960-63, ret; barr Inner Temple 1935, Greek DFC 1941; *Books* Epitaph for a Squadron (1965), Their Finest Hour (1976); *Recreations* travel, sailing, literary interests; *Clubs* Naval and Military; *Style—* Air Vice-Marshal James Gordon-Finlayson, DSO, DFC; Villa Aqui, Avenida del Cobre 9-11, PO Box 187, Algeciras (Prov de Cadiz) Spain (☎ 603399)

GORDON-FINLAYSON, Maj-Gen Robert; OBE (1957, MBE 1945), JP (1972), DL (Notts 1974); s of Gen Sir Robert Gordon-Finlayson, KCB, CMG, DSO, DL (d 1956); *b* 28 Oct 1916; *Educ* Winchester, RMA Woolwich; *m* 1945, Alexandra, da of John Bartholomew, of Rowde Court, Devizes, Wilts (d 1953); 2 s; *Career* served RA and RHA 1936-59 (Regt and Staff, WW II, served Europe, Mid E, Far E, Suez Ops 1956), GOC 49 Inf Div TA 1966-67, Maj-Gen 1966, GOC E Midland Dist 1967-70, ret; Hon Col Worcs & Sherwood Foresters Regt TAVR 1971-78, chm Notts Co Army Benevolent Fund 1970-85, pres Notts Co Royal British Legion 1971-79, vice-pres Notts Co SSAFA 1970-; vice-pres Notts Co Scouts 1971-80, High Sheriff 1974; *Recreations* shooting, fishing, gardening, skiing, walking; *Style—* Maj-Gen Robert Gordon-Finlayson, OBE, JP, DL; South Collingham Manor, Newark, Notts (☎ 892204)

GORDON-HALL, Maj-Gen Frederick William; CB (1958), CBE (1945); s of Col Frederick William George, CB (d 1942), and Clare Frances, *née* Taylor (d 1963); *b* 28 Dec 1902; *Educ* Winchester Coll; *m* 1930, Phyllis Dorothy, da of Augustus Miller (d 1947), of Sharia Sheik Yussef, Gezira, Cairo, Egypt; 1 s (Anthony), 1 da (Jill); *Career* Regular Army Tank Corps, WO 1935-39, Min of Supply 1939-43, Italy 1943-45, Mill Coll of Science 1946-49, Tech Services Washington 1949-52, dir of inspection 1952-55, dir gen F V 1955-58; *Style—* Maj-Gen Frederick Gordon-Hall, CB, CBE; Whitegates, Salisbury Rd, Horsham, W Sussex RH13 7AL (☎ 53304)

GORDON-HARRIS, William; s of William Gordon-Harris (d 1952), of Bexhill-on-Sea, and Florence May, *née* Doughty (d 1973); *b* 2 May 1918; *Educ* Bexhill GS, Coll of Estate Mgmnt; *m* 2 Nov 1946, Margot Wynn, da of John William Edwards (d 1971), of Oswestry; 1 s (John William b 15 March 1948), 2 da (Angela Margot (Mrs Chivers) b 26 April 1954, Jennifer Jane b 3 Oct 1955); *Career* RNVR: Ordinary Seaman 1938, Contraband control 1939, serv HMS Hood (Homefleet N Atlantic convoys, Med malta convoys) 1940-41, cmmnd 1941, HMS Anson (Homefleet Russian Convoys) 1941-44, HMS Glenoy (Combined Ops Burma and Malaya) 1944-45, demobbed as Lt 1945; articled to Cdr John Bray 1936-39, Valuation off Inland Revenue 1945-48, princ in private practice as surveyor and estate agent 1948-, chm Hastings and Dist Estate Agents Assoc 1960 (sec 1958-60), chm gen practice div of Sussex branch RICS 1972, memb Lloyds 1978-; surveyor to Rent Assessment Ctee and Rent Tbnl for SE Eng; memb benevolent fund RICS, chm Old Bexhillian Assoc; Freeman City of London 1980, Liveryman Worshipful Co of Chartered Surveyors; FRICS 1948, FSVA 1958; *Recreations* sailing (holding an ocean yacht masters cert), vintage cars; *Clubs* Sussex RNVR, RNR Offr's Assoc, Bexhill SC, Royal Naval Sailing Assoc, HMS Hood Assoc, Capital Ships Assoc; *Style—* William Gordon-Harris, Esq; Bexhill-on-Sea, E Sussex

GORDON-JONES, Lady Frances Christina; *née* Knox; yr da of 7 Earl of Ranfurly, *qv*; *b* 13 Feb 1961; *m* 1981, Henry Gordon-Jones; *Style—* Robert Davies, Esq; Plant Cottage, Friston, Saxmundham, Suffolk

GORDON-JONES, Michael Philip; s of Cyril Gordon-Jones (d 1964), and Brenda Mary Blaker (d 1962); *b* 29 August 1926; *Educ* Haileybury; *m* 1, 1 May 1954, Jennifer (d 1979), da of Alan Bostock Baker (d 1965); 1 s (Henry b 1956), 3 da (Alison b 1955, Victoria b 1960, Diana b 1963); m 2, 16 Aug 1980, Teresa, da of Philip John Fortin (d 1985); *Career* slr; dir Edward Baker Holdings Ltd (chm 1983-86); *Style—* Michael P Gordon-Jones, Esq; Esplanade House, 32 Kings Quay Street, Harwich, Essex CO12 3ES (☎ 0255 506917); 61/65 Station Road, Clacton on Sea, Essex (☎ 0255 421248, fax 0255 476485)

GORDON-LENNOX, Lady Ellinor Caroline; da of Earl of March and Kinrara; *b* 28 July 1952; *Educ* Elmhurst Ballet Sch, De Vos Studio of Ballet; *Career* ballet teacher, also of dance therapy and modern dance, dancer with John Curry in Coventry Cathedral, solo dance in Chichester Cathedral 'Sweet Messenger', painter of nature in watercolour; *Recreations* walking, poetry writing, singing; *Style—* Lady Ellinor Gordon-Lennox; Goodwood House, Chichester, W Sussex PO18 OP7 (☎ Chichester 0243 774760, office: Haslemere 2647)

GORDON-LENNOX, Lady Louisa Elizabeth; da of Earl of March and Kinrara; *b* 14 Mar 1967; *Educ* Bishop Cuffa C of E Sch, Lancing Coll, Balliol Coll Oxford; *Style—* Lady Louisa Gordon-Lennox; Goodwood House, Nr Chichester, W Sussex PO18 OPY (☎ Chichester 0243 774760)

GORDON-LENNOX, Lord Nicholas Charles; KCMG (1986, CMG 1978), LVO (1957); yr son of 9 Duke of Richmond and (4 of) Gordon; *b* 31 Jan 1931; *Educ* Eton, Worcester Coll Oxford; *m* 1958, Mary, o da of late Brig Hudleston Noel Hedworth Williamson, DSO, MC; 1 s, 3 da; *Career* late 2 Lt KRRC; entered HM Foreign Service 1954; ambass to Spain 1984-; Grand Cross Order of Isabel La Catolica (Spain); *Style—* Lord Nicholas Gordon-Lennox, KCMG, LVO; c/o Foreign and Commonwealth Office, King Charles St, London SW1

GORDON-SMITH, David Gerard; CMG (1971); s of late Frederic Gordon-Smith, and Elsie Florence, *née* Foster; *b* 6 Oct 1925; *Educ* Rugby, Trin Coll Oxford (BA), Sch of Jurisprudence Oxford; *m* 26 July 1952, Angela Eugenie Kirkpatrick, da of late Conrad Kirkpatrick Pile, of Bridgetown, Barbados; 1 s (James Gerard b 1961, deceased), 1 da (Caroline Jane b 1958); *Career* RNVR 1944-46 Sub-Lt; barr Inner Temple 1949; legal dept, Colonial Office and CRO 1950-66; legal cnsllr Cwlth Off 1966-68, FCO 1968-72, dep legal advsr FCO 1973-76, dir gen in legal serv cncl of European Communities 1976-87, ret; *Recreations* bird watching, tennis, music, gardening; *Clubs* RAC; *Style—* David Gordon-Smith, Esq; Kings-Cote, Westcott, Dorking, Surrey RH4 3NX (☎ Dorking 885702)

GORDON-SMITH, Lt Cdr Peter Russell; s of Lt Cdr Russell Claude Gordon-Smith, DSC, RN (ka 1940), and Anne Cunitia Keen, *née* Morris (d 1986); *b* 12 June 1938; *Educ* Winchester Coll, RNC Dartmouth; *m* 8 June 1963, Marion Elizabeth, da of Cdr Sydney Arthur Morehouse Else, OBE (d 1979); 2 s (Russell b 1964, David b 1968), 1 da (Louise b 1965); *Career* served RN 1956-78, ret as Lt-Cdr; farmer 1975-; *Recreations* shooting, skiing, stamps, model railways; *Clubs* Naval and Military, W Sussex County; *Style—* Lt Cdr Peter Gordon-Smith; Lower Farm, Up Marden, Chichester, Sussex PO18 9LA (☎ 024359 274)

GORDON-WALKER, Hon Alan Rudolf; er (twin) s of Baron Gordon-Walker, CH, PC (Life Peer, d 1980); *b* 1946; *Educ* Wellington Coll, Ch Ch Oxford (MA); *m* 1976, Louise Frances Amy, da of Gen Sir Charles Henry Pepys Harington, GCB, CBE, DSO, MC; 1 s (Thomas b 1978), 1 da (Emily b 1981); *Career* md Pan Books Ltd; *Style—* The Hon Alan Gordon-Walker; c/o The Hon Mrs Gowar, The Homestead, Cuddington, Bucks

GORDON-WALKER, Dr the Hon Ann Marguerite; da of Baron Gordon-Walker, CH, PC,; *b* 1944; *Educ* N London Collegiate Sch, Queen's Coll Dundee, St Andrews Univ, Oxford Univ; *m* 1968 (m dis 1983), Laurence Andrew Ball; 2 da (Jennifer b 1974, Katherine b 1976); *Style—* Dr the Hon Ann Gordon-Walker; 1230 University Bay Drive, Madison, Wisconsin 53705, USA

GORDON-WALKER, Baroness; Audrey Muriel; da of Norman Rudolf, of Jamaica; *m* 1935, Baron Gordon-Walker, CH, PC (Life Peer, d 1980); 2 s, 3 da; *Style*— The Rt Hon the Lady Gordon-Walker; 105 Frobisher House, Dolphin Sq, London SW1V 3LL (☎ 01 821 8270)

GORDON-WALKER, Hon Robin Chrestien; yr (twin) s of Baron Gordon-Walker, CH, PC (Life Peer, d 1980); *b* 15 May 1946; *Educ* Wellington Coll, E Anglia Univ (BA); *m* 1, 1974 (m dis 1985), June Patricia, da of Patrick Barr, of Eversholt, Beds; 1 s, 1 da; m 2, 1987, Magally, da of Gilberto Flores, of Valencia, Venezuela; 1 s; *Career* sr information offr Department of Employment; *Recreations* cricket, politics, racing, rugby union; *Clubs* MCC, Surrey CCC; *Style*— The Hon Robin Gordon-Walker; 16 Hexham Road, London SE27 (☎ 01 670 5925)

GORDON-WATSON, Brig Michael; OBE (1949), MC (1938, 2 bars 1940 and 1944), JP (Dorset 1964); s of Sir Charles Gordon-Watson, KBE, CMG, FRCS; *b* 23 Feb 1913; *Educ* Downside, Ch Ch Oxford; *m* 1942, Thalia, da of Charles Gordon; 3 s, 2 da; *Career* cmmnd Irish Gds 1934, served Palestine; WWII: Norway, N Africa, Italy, NW Europe; Lt-Col 1945; mil attaché Washington 1950-52, Lt-Col cmdg Irish Gds 1953-55, Brig 1959, BGS BAOR 1959, dep cdr Aldershot Dist 1961, vice-pres Regnl Cmmns Bd 1962, ret 1963; farmer and bloodstock breeder; memb: Cncl SMO Malta, St John's and St Elizabeth's Hosp Management Bd, Tattersall's Ctee; *Recreations* shooting, stalking, fishing, racing; *Clubs* White's; *Style*— Brig Michael Gordon-Watson, OBE, MC, JP; East Blagdon Farm, Cranborne, Dorset (☎ 072 54 304)

GORE; *see*: Ormsby-Gore

GORE, Lady Barbara Susan; *née* Montgomerie; er da of 16 Earl of Eglinton and Winton (d 1945); *b* 23 August 1909; *m* 1930, Capt Christopher Gerald Gore, Coldstream Gds (d 1954); 1 s, 1 da; *Style*— Lady Barbara Gore; 31 Sloane Court West, London SW3 (☎ 01 730 2998)

GORE, Charles John; s of John Francis Gore, CVO, TD (d 1983, gggs of 2 Earl of Arran, KP), of Ringwood, Hants, and Lady Janet Helena, *née* Campbell (d 1982), er da of 4 Earl of Cawdor; *b* 11 June 1932; *Educ* Eton; *m* 10 June 1961, Jean, da of Maj C I Fraser, CBE (d 1963), of Kirkhill, Invernessshire; 2 s (Simon b 1965, John b 1971), 1 da (Helena b 1962); *Career* promotion and print design conslt humorous book illustrator, writer of guide books and ephemera; *Recreations* traditional Scottish fiddle music, boats, history; *Style*— Charles J Gore, Esq; PO Box Taynuilt, Argyll PA35 1HU (☎ 08662 678)

GORE, Lady Mary Sophia; *née* Palmer; da of 3 Earl of Selborne (d 1971), and his 1 w, Hon Grace, da of 1 Viscount Ridley and Hon Mary Marjoribanks, da of 1 Baron Tweedmouth; *b* 6 Sept 1920; *m* 1, 11 Nov 1944, Maj Hon (Thomas) Anthony Edward Towneley Strachey (d 1955) (only s of 3 Baron O'Hagan), who assumed by deed poll surname of mother (Hon Frances, da of 1 Baron Strachie) and additional christian name of Towneley; 2 s (*see* 4 Baron O'Hagan and Hon Richard Strachey), 2 da (*see* Hon Mrs (F T) Gibson and Hon Jane Strachey; m 2, 1981, (Francis) St John Gore, *qv*; *Style*— Lady Mary Gore; 25 Elvaston Place, London SW7 (☎ 01 584 6994)

GORE, Michael Balfour Gruberg; s of Dr Victor Gore (d 1985), of London and Victoria, *née* Slavouski; *b* 25 Oct 1937; *Educ* Felsted, Peterhouse Cambridge (BA); *m* 11 April 1972, Mozella, da of Geoffrey Ransom; 2 s (Benjamin b 1974, Daniel b 1977), 1 da (Camilla b (twin) 1977); *Career* Kemp, Chatteris & Co 1959-64; S G Warburg & Co Ltd 1964- (dir 1969-); chm: S G Warburg & Co (Jersey) Ltd 1979-87; dir: Mercury Securities plc 1984-, Mercury Int Gp plc 1985-; gp finance dir Mercury Int Gp plc (now S G Warburg Gp plc) 1986-; chm: Rowe & Pitman Moneybroking Ltd 1986-; joint chm S G Warburg Gp Mgmnt Ltd 1986-; FCA, FRSA; *Style*— Michael Gore, Esq; S G Warburg Group plc, 1 Finsbury Avenue, London EC2M 2PA (☎ 01 382 4314)

GORE, Nigel Hugh St George; yr s of St George Richard Gore (d 1952), who was gn of 9 Bt; hp of n, Sir Richard Gore, 13 Bt; *b* 23 Dec 1922; *m* 3 Sept 1952, Beth Allison, *née* Hooper; 1 da (Seonaid Beth b 1955); *Style*— Nigel Gore, Esq; Hillhaven, Preston Road, M/S 852, Hodgsonvale, Qld 4350, Australia

GORE, Paul Annesley; CMG (1964), CVO (1961); s of Charles Henry Gore, OBE (d 1941), s of Sir Francis Gore KCB, whose f (yr bro of 4 Earl of Arran) m Lady Augusta Ponsonby, 2 da of 4 Earl of Bessborough; hp of 9 Earl of Arran, *qv*; *b* 28 Feb 1921; *Educ* Winchester, Ch Ch Oxford (MA); *m* 1946, Gillian Mary, da of Tom Allen-Stevens (d 1941); 2 s (and 1 s decd); *Career* Capt 16/5 Lancers (N Africa, Italy) 1941-46, Colonial Admin Serv 1948-65, dep govr Gambia 1962-65; JP: Oxford 1972-74, Suffolk 1976-84; *Recreations* sailing (yacht, 'Mandora of Deben'); *Clubs* Cruising Assoc; *Style*— Paul Gore, Esq, CMG, CVO; 1 Burkitt Rd, Woodbridge, Suffolk

GORE, Sir Richard Ralph St George; 13 Bt (I 1622); s of Sir St George Ralph Gore, 12 Bt (d 1973; gn of 9 Bt); *b* 19 Nov 1954; *Educ* The King's Sch Parramatta, New England Univ, Queensland Coll of Art (Dip Art); *Heir* unc, Nigel Gore; *Career* artist; *Recreations* tennis, golf, handcrafts; *Clubs* Assoc of Illustrators, Soc of Scribes and Illuminators, Buddhist Soc (London); *Style*— Sir Richard Gore, Bt; c/o 14 Brodie St, Toowoomba, Qld 4350, Australia; Wycanna, Talwood, Qld, 4322 Australia

GORE, Lady Shirley; da of of C Tabor, of Wauchope NSW; *m* 1950, Sir St George Ralph Gore, 12 Bt (d 1973); ls, 3 da; *Style*— Lady Gore; Wycanna, Talwood, Queensland 4322, Australia

GORE, (Francis) St John Corbet; CBE; s of Francis William Baldock Gore (gs of Rev William Gore, who was uncle of Sir St George Ralph Gore, 9 Bt, and gn of Lt-Gen Sir Ralph Gore, 6 Bt, who was cr Earl of Ross (1772), Viscount Bellisle (1768) and Baron Gore of Manor Gore (1764), all in the peerage of Ireland. His Lordship was C-in-C Ireland 1788 and d 1802, when his peerage honours became extinct); *b* 8 April 1921; *Educ* Wellington, Courtauld Inst of Art; *m* 1, 1951 (m dis 1976), Priscilla Margaret, da of Cecil Harmsworth King; 1 s (William b 1951), 1 da (Catharine (Mrs Richard Gayner)); m 2, 1981, Lady Mary Strachey, *see* Gore, Lady M S; *Career* late Capt Royal Northumberland Fusiliers, served WWII; Nat Tst: advsr on pictures 1956-86, historic bldgs sec 1973-81; exec ctee Nat Art Collections Fund 1963-; tstee: Wallace Collection 1975, Nat Gallery 1986; FSA; *Recreations* viewing pictures and architecture; *Clubs* Boodle's, Beefsteak; *Style*— St John Gore, Esq, CBE; 25 Elvaston Place, London SW7 (☎ 01 584 6994); Grove Farm, Stoke-by-Nayland, Suffolk

GORE, Maj Toby Clements; s of Brig Adrian Clements Gore, DSO, of Horton Priory, Sellindge, Kent, and Enid Amy, *née* Cairnes; *b* 8 Dec 1927; *Educ* Eton, Sandhurst; *m* 28 July 1959, (Isolde) Marian, da of Edward Hyde Macintoch (d 1970), of Rebeg, Kirkhill, Invernesshire; 4 da (Fiona b 1960, Juliet b 1962, Tessa b 1968, Stephanie b 1969); *Career* cmmnd Rifle Brigade 1948-70; memb Stock Exchange 1973; ptnr: Roger Mortimer 1973-75, Sheppards & Chase; memb: Ctee of West Berkshire, Macmillan Cancer Care Appeal; Played cricket for Army 1948-52; *Recreations* golf, fishing, shooting; *Clubs* Naval and Military; *Style*— Maj Toby Gore; Monks Alley, Binfield, Bracknell, Berks (☎ 0344 428200); 49 Smith St, London SW3

GORE BROWNE, Anthony Giles Spencer; s of (John) Giles Charles Gore Browne (d 1980), of Manton, nr Oxham, Leics, and Pamela Helen, *née* Newton; *b* 20 April 1944; *Educ* Rannoch Sch Perthshire; *m* 14 March 1970, Penelope Anne Courtenay, da of Prebendary Clarke Edward Leighton Thomson, (vicar of Chelsea Old Church), of Chelsea London; 1 s (Edward b 1973), 1 da (Alexandra b 1975); *Career* stockbroker 1964-, with Sheppards & Co 1964-65, Sheppards and Chase 1965-73, ptnr R C Greig & Co Glasgow (London Off) 1973-82, dir of dealing Greig Middleton & Co Ltd 1986- (ptnr 1982-86), dir Riverside Racquets plc 1988-, memb Int Stock Exchange; Liveryman Worshipful Co of Fishmongers 1965, Freeman City of London 1965; *Clubs* City of London, Riverside Racquets; *Style*— Anthony Gore Browne, Esq; 20 Melville Rd, Barnes, London SW13 9RJ (☎ 01 741 0701); Greig Middleton & Co Ltd, 66 Wilson St, London EC2A 2BL (☎ 01 2470007, fax 01 377 0353, telex 887296)

GORE BROWNE, James Anthony; s of Sir Thomas Gore Browne, (d 1988), and Lady Gore Browne, *née* Loyd; *b* 26 Mar 1947; *Educ* Eton, Univ of Dundee (MA), Aston Univ (Dip Business Admin); *m* 16 April 1983, Jane Anne, da of Col Seton Grahame Dickson, of Field House, Symington, Ayrshire; 2 s (Freddie b 21 Jan 1987, Harold b 20 April 1988), 1 da (Marina b 19 Dec 1984); *Career* Casanove & Co 1969-75, asst to chm EMI Ltd 1976-79, Thames TV 1979-80, Lead Industs Gp 1980-81, admitted slr 1986; SDP candidate: Doncaster Central 1987, Bristol Bath Euro Elections 1989; Liveryman Worshipful Co of Fishmongers; memb Law Soc; *Recreations* golf, studying portraiture; *Clubs* Whites; *Style*— James Gore Browne, Esq; 38 Winsham Grove, London SW11 6NE (☎ 01 228 6816)

GORE LANGTON, (Walter) Grenville Algernon (Temple); s of Cdr Hon Evelyn Arthur Temple-Gore-Langton, DSO, RN (d 1972) (yst s of 4 Earl Temple of Stowe); hp of kinsman, 7 Earl Temple of Stowe; *b* 2 Oct 1924; *m* 1, 1954, Zillah Ray (d 1966), da of James Boxall, of Tillington, Petworth, Sussex; 2 s, 1 da; m 2, 1968, (Margaret) Elizabeth Graham, da of late Col Henry William Scarth of Breckness, of Skaill House, Orkney; *Style*— Grenville Gore Langton, Esq; The Cottage, Easton, Winchester (☎ 096 278 300)

GORE-ANDREWS, Russell William; *Career* chm: More O'Ferrall Sales (UK) Ltd, More O'Ferrall Devpt (UK) Ltd; chm: More O'Ferrall plc, More O'Ferrall International Advertising Ltd, More O'Ferrall Publicité Int SA, SAGA SA, Adshel Ltd, More O'Ferrall SE Asia Ltd; dir Outdoor Advertising Assoc of GB Ltd; memb IOD; *Style*— Russell Gore-Andrews, Esq; More O'Ferrall plc, 19 Curzon St, London W1Y 8BJ (☎ 01 499 8146, telex 23602)

GORE-BOOTH, Sir Angus Josslyn; 8 Bt (I 1760), of Artarman, Sligo; s of Sir Josslyn Augustus Richard Gore-Booth, 6 Bt, JP, DL (d 1944); suc bro Sir Michael Savile Gore-Booth, 7 Bt (d 1987); *b* 25 June 1920; *Educ* Radley, Worcester Coll Oxford (BA); *m* 1948 (m dis 1954), Hon Rosemary Myra Vane, da of 10 Baron Barnard, CMG, MC (d 1964); 1 s (Josslyn b 1950), 1 da (Eirenice b 1949); *Heir* s, Josslyn Henry Robert, *qv*; *Career* Capt Irish Gds 1939-45; *Style*— Sir Angus Gore-Booth, Bt; 25 Gorst Road, London, SW11

GORE-BOOTH, Hon Christopher Hugh; yr (twin) s of Baron Gore-Booth, GCMG, KCVO (Life Peer, d 1984), and his w, Patricia Mary, da of Montague Ellerton, of Yokohama, Japan; *b* 15 May 1943; *Educ* Eton, Durham Univ; *m* 1979, Mrs Jolanta Nicholls, da of late Dr L S Bernacinski; 1 s (Oliver Lucian Ralph b 1980); *Style*— The Hon Christopher Gore-Booth; 42 Ringford Rd, SW18

GORE-BOOTH, Hon David Alwyn; er (twin) s of Baron Gore-Booth, GCMG, KCVO (Life Peer, d 1984), and Patricia Mary, o da of late Montague Ellerton, of Yokohama, Japan; *b* 15 May 1943; *Educ* Eton, Christ Church Oxford (MA); *m* 1, 1964 (m dis 1970), Jillian Sarah, da of James Wyatt Valpy, of Somerset West, S Africa; 1 s (Paul Wyatt Julian b 1968); m 2, 1977, Mary, da of Sir David Muirhead, KCMG, CVO; 1 step-s (Riccardo Gambetta b 1970); *Career* HM Dip Serv 1964-: third sec Baghdad 1966, third later second sec Lusaka 1967, FCO 1969, second sec Tripoli 1969, FCO 1971, first sec UK permanent representation to European Communities Brussels 1974, asst head of financial relations dept FCO 1978, cnsllr (Commercial) Jeddah 1980-83, cnsllr and head of chancery UK mission to UN NY 1983-86, head of policy planning staff FCO 1987-; *Recreations* tennis, squash, the Island of Hydra; *Clubs* MCC; *Style*— The Hon David Gore-Booth; 28 Chesilton Rd, SW6 5AB (☎ 01 736 8757)

GORE-BOOTH, Josslyn Henry Robert; s and h of Sir Angus Gore-Booth, 8 Bt, and Hon Mrs Rosemary Myra Gore-Booth, *née* Vane, da of 10 Baron Barnard; *b* 5 Oct 1950; *Educ* Eton, Balliol Coll Oxford (BA), INSEAD (MBA); *m* 1970, Jane Mary, da of Hon Sir (James) Roualeyn (Hovell-Thurlow-) Cumming-Bruce, *qv*; 2 da (Mary b 1985, Caroline b 1987); *Career* mgmnt conslt; *Recreations* shooting, fishing, cooking; *Clubs* Brooks's, Kildare Street and Univ (Dublin); *Style*— Josslyn Gore-Booth, Esq; 25 Gorst Road, London SW11 (☎ 01 223 2581); Hartforth, Richmond, Yorks (☎ 0748 2410)

GORE-BOOTH, Hon Mrs (Rosemary Myra) Vane; *née* Vane; da of 10 Baron Barnard, CMG, OBE, MC (d 1964); *b* 1921; *m* 1948 (m dis 1954), Angus Josslyn Gore-Booth; 1 s, 1 da; *Style*— The Hon Mrs Gore-Booth; The White House, Gainford, Darlington, Co Durham (☎ 730386)

GORE-BROWNE, Sir Thomas Anthony; s of Sir Eric Gore Browne, DSO (d 1965); *b* 20 June 1918; *Educ* Eton, Trinity Coll Cambridge; *m* 1946, Lavinia Georgina, da of Gen Sir Charles Loyd, GCVO, KCB, DSO, MC (d 1973); 3 s, 1 da; *Career* served Grenadier Gds 1938-48: WWII in France, N Africa, Italy, Maj; ptnr Mullens & Co (stockbrokers) 1949, sr Govt broker 1973-81; tres Imp Cancer Res Fund 1980-, dir SW Region Nat West Bank 1981-; kt 1980; *Clubs* Brooks's, White's, MCC; *Style*— Sir Thomas Gore-Browne; 62 Melton Court, London SW7 3JH (☎ 01 589 0530)

GORE-RANDALL, Philip Allan; s of Alec Albert Gore-Randall, of Uxbridge, and Joyce Margaret, *née* Gore; *b* 16 Dec 1952; *Educ* Merchant Taylors Sch, Univ Coll Oxford (MA); *m* 15 Dec 1984, Alison Elizabeth da of Harold Arthur Armstron While, MBE, TD (d 1983); 2 s (William b 1986, Edward b 1987); *Career* ptnr Arthur Andersen & Co 1986- (joined 1975); FCA 1978, MInstPet; *Recreations* classical music, good food, travel; *Clubs* Vincents; *Style*— Philip Gore-Randall, Esq; 21 Rylett Road, London W12 9SS (☎ 01 743 7054); The Old Forge, Windrush, nr Burford, Oxon (☎ 04514 225); Arthur Andersen & Co, 1 Surrey Street, London WC2R 2PS (☎ 01 836 1200, fax 01 831 1133, car tel 0860 380406, telex 8812711)

GORELL, 4 Baron (UK 1909); Timothy John Radcliffe Barnes; s of 3 Baron

Gorell, CBE, MC, (d 1963, sometime ed Cornhill Magazine and under sec state Air), and (Maud) Elizabeth Furse (d 1954), eld da of Alexander Radcliffe, of Bag Park, S Devon; first cous of Sir William van Straubenzee, MBE, MP; *b* 2 August 1927; *Educ* Eton, New Coll Oxford; *m* 1954, Joan, da of John Collins, MC; 2 adopted da; *Heir* bro, Hon Ronald Barnes; *Career* late Lt Rifle Bde; barr 1951; sr exec Royal Dutch Shell Gp 1959-84; *Recreations* golf, tennis, gardening, skiing; *Clubs* Roehampton Golf; *Style*— The Rt Hon the Lord Gorell; 4 Roehampton Gate, London SW15 (☎ 01 876 5522)

GORHAM, Richard Arthur; s of Arthur Percy Gorham (d 1979), of Bristol, and Pamela Joan, *née* Burkitt; *b* 18 Feb 1942; *Educ* Clifton Coll Bristol, Bristol Univ (BDS); *m* 9 Jan 1969, Alison Jill, da of Kenneth Percy Wortley, N Poole, Dorset; 1 s (Andrew b 1971), 1 da (Catherine b 1974); *Career* house offr Bristol Dental Hosp 1966, gen dental practitioner Poole 1967, clinical asst orthodontic dept Boscombe Hosp 1982-86, regnl advsr in gen dental practice Wessex; chm: Bournemouth Section Br Dental Assoc 1977-78, Dorset Local Dental Ctee 1977-80, pres Wessex Branch Br Dental Assoc 1981-82, memb Nat Panel of Examiners for Dental Surgery Assts, lectr Bournemouth & Poole Coll of FE; *Books* Dentistry in East Dorset (1986); *Recreations* gardening, philately, DIY, local heritage; *Style*— Richard Gorham, Esq; 14 Charborough Rd, Broadstone, Dorset BH18 8NE (☎ 0202 697 176); 68 Wimborne Rd, Poole, Dorset BH15 2BZ (☎ 0202 673 037)

GORICK, Robert Lionel; s of John Gorick, of Llandudno, N Wales; *b* 24 Feb 1927; *Educ* Blackburn Tech Coll; *m* 1968, Jean Audrey, da of Frank Harwood (d 1976), of Wilpshire, nr Blackburn; 3 children; *Career* chm and md Liquid Plastics Ltd 1963- (mfr of plastics-based waterproof coatings and fire retardant finishes; Queen's Award for Export 1982), Flexcrete Ltd, Industrial Copolymers Ltd; *Recreations* reading, horticulture, modern music, wining and dining; *Clubs* Preston Rotary, Preston GC; *Style*— Robert Gorick, Esq; Liquid Plastics Ltd, PO Box 7, London Rd, Preston, Lancs PR1 4AJ (☎ 0772 59781); The Stone House, Whittingham Lane, Broughton, nr Preston, Lancs (☎ 0772 864872)

GORING, Hon Lady; Caroline; *née* Thellusson; da of 8 Baron Rendlesham (by 1 w); *b* 2 April 1941; *m* 1960, Sir William Burton Nigel Goring, 13 Bt, *qv*; *Style*— The Hon Lady Goring; 16 Linver Rd, London SW6 (☎ 01 736 6032)

GORING, Edward Yelverton Combe; s of Maj Frederick Yelverton Goring (d 1938), and bro and hp of Sir William Goring, 13 Bt; *b* 20 June 1936; *Educ* Wellington, RNC Dartmouth, RNC Greenwich; *m* 1969, Daphne Christine Seller; 2 da; *Career* Lt Cdr RN (ret); dep sec and slr Stratford-upon-Avon Dist Cncl; *Style*— Edward Goring, Esq; Walcote, Dark Lane, Tiddington, Stratford-upon-Avon, Warwicks

GORING, Lady Hersey Margaret; *née* Boyle; 2 da of 8 Earl of Glasgow, DSO, DL (d 1963); *b* 11 July 1914; *m* 1, 1940, Cdr Hon John Waldegrave DSC, RN (ka 1944), s of 5 and last Baron Radstock; 2 da; m 2, 1947, John Goring, CBE, TD, DL, s of Charles Goring, JP, DL (ggs of Sir Charles Goring, 5 Bt); 2 s (John James, Richard Harry), 2 da (Corinna Jane, Anne Elizabeth); *Style*— Lady Hersey Goring; Shirley House, Wiston, Steyning, Sussex BN4 3DD

GORING, Marius; s of Dr Charles Goring; *b* 23 May 1912; *Educ* Perse Sch Cambridge, Frankfurt Univ, Vienna Univ, Munich Univ, Paris Univ; *m* 1, 1931 (m dis), Mary Steel; 1 da; m 2, 1941, Lucie Mannheim (d 1976); m 3, 1977, Prudence FitzGerald; *Career* actor, vice-pres Equity 1975-; *Style*— Marius Goring, Esq; Middle Court, The Green, Hampton Court, Surrey (☎ 01 977 4030)

GORING, Sir William Burton Nigel; 13 Bt (E 1678, with precedency of 1627), of Highden, Sussex; s of Maj Frederick Yelverton Goring (d 1938), 6 s of 11 Bt; suc unc, Sir Forster Gurney Goring, 12 Bt, 1956; the Goring family is of great antiquity in Sussex and were MPs from fifteenth to the nineteenth century; *b* 21 June 1933; *Educ* Wellington; *m* 1960, Hon Caroline Thellusson, da of 8 Baron Rendlesham (*see* Goring, Hon Lady); *Heir* bro, Edward Goring; *Career* Lt 1 Royal Sussex Regt; memb London Stock Exchange 1963, ptnr Quilter Goodison & Co 1976; *Recreations* squash; *Clubs* Hurlingham; *Style*— Sir William Goring, Bt; 16 Linver Rd, London SW6 (01 600 4177)

GORMAN, John Reginald; CVO (1961), CBE (1974), MC (1944), DL; s of Maj J K Gorman, MC (d 1980); *b* 1 Feb 1923; *Educ* Rockport, Haileybury and ISC, Portora Harvard Business Sch; *m* 1948, Norah Heather, *née* Caruth; 2 s, 2 da; *Career* Capt Irish Guards WWII; personnel dir BOAC 1963-70, vice chm and chief exec Northern Ireland Housing Exec 1979-85; dir: NI IOD, NI Airports, Nationwide Anglia Building Soc, Cooperation North; High Sheriff Co Down 1987; FCIT, MIH; *Recreations* gardening, fishing, beekeeping; *Clubs* Cavalry and Guards', Ulster Reform; *Style*— John Gorman, Esq, CVO, CBE, MC, DL; The Forge, Jericho Road, Killyleagh, Co Down, Ireland

GORMANSTON, 17 Viscount (I 1478, Premier Viscount of Ireland); Jenico Nicholas Dudley Preston; also Baron Gormanston (I 1365-70 and UK 1868, which latter sits as); s of 16 Viscount (ka 1940), and Pamela, *née* Hanly (whose mother was Lady Marjorie, *née* Feilding, da of 9 Earl of Denbigh); *b* 19 Nov 1939; *Educ* Downside; *m* 1974, Eva Landzianowska (d 1984); 2 s (Hon Jenico, Hon William b 3 May 1976); *Heir* s, Hon Jenico Francis Tara Preston b 30 April 1974; *Style*— The Rt Hon the Viscount Gormanston; 8 Dalmeny House, Thurloe Place, London SW7 2RY

GORMLEY, Antony Mark David; s of Arthur John Constantine Gormley (d 1977), of Hampstead, London, and Elspeth, *née* Braüninger; *b* 30 August 1950; *Educ* Ampleforth, Trinity Coll Cambridge (BA, MA), Goldsmiths Coll London Univ (BA), Slade Sch of Fine Art UCL (Dip FA); *m* 14 June 1980, Emilyn Victoria (Vicken), da of Maj (Ian) David Parsons, of Baas Manor, Broxbourne, Herts; 2 s (Ivo b 16 March 1982, Guy b 17 June 1985), 1 da (Paloma b 20 July 1987); *Career* artist; one man exhibitions incl: Whitechapel Art Gallery 1981, Coracle Press 1983, Riverside Studios London, Chapter Cardiff 1984, Salvatore Ala Gallery NY 1985 (twice), 1986, 1987, Stadtishes Gallerie Regensburg, Franfurt Kuntsverein 1985, Serpentine Gallery 1987, Burnett Miller LA 1988 Louisiana Museum Denmark 1989; gp exhibits: Objects and Sculpture ICA 1981, Venice Biennale 1982 and 1986, Beinnale De Sao Pavlo 1983, An International Survey Museum of Modern Art NY 1984, The British Show Aust 1985, Between Object and Image Madrid 1986, Documenta 8 Kassel 1987, ROSC Dublin 88; catalogues: Salvatore Ala NY 1984, Regensburg W Germany 1985, Salvatore Ala NY 1985, Contemporary Sculpture Centre Tokyo 1988, Louisiana 1989; collections incl: Arts Cncl of GB, Tate Gallery, CAS, Br Cncl, Southampton Art Gallery, Neue Museum Kassel, Stadt Kassel, Walker Arts Centre Minneapolis, Leeds City Art Gallery; *Recreations* sailing, skiing, walking; *Style*— Antony Gormley, Esq; 49 Talfourd Rd, London SE15 5NN (☎ 01 701 7718); 153 Bellenden Rd, London SE15 5NN (☎ 01 639 1303)

GORMLEY, Baron (Life Peer UK 1982), of Ashton-in-Makerfield in Gtr Manchester; Joseph Gormley; OBE (1969); s of John Gormley, of Ireland; *b* 5 July 1917; *Educ* St Oswald's RC Sch Ashton-in-Makerfield; *m* 1937, Sarah Ellen, da of Levi Mather, of Ashton-in-Makerfield; 1 s, 1 da; *Career* miner 1931-, memb NEC 1957, gen sec NW Area NUM 1961, memb Labour Pty NEC 1963- (former chm Int and Orgn Ctee), pres NUM 1971-82, memb TUC Gen Cncl 1973-80; govr BBC June-July 1982; hon fell Univ of Manchester Inst of Sci and Technol; dir: Utd Racecourses, Br Investt Tst 1978-; Cdr's Cross Order of Merit (W Germany) 1981; *Books* Battered Cherub (autobiography 1982); *Style*— The Rt Hon the Lord Gormley, OBE

GORMLY, Allan Graham; s of William Gormly, and Christina Swinton Flockhart, *née* Arnot; *b* 18 Dec 1937; *Educ* Paisley GS, Glasgow Univ; *m* 30 June 1962, Vera Margaret, da of late Alexander Grant; 1 s (Alisdair William b 10 Sept 1965), 1 da (Lynn Margaret b 15 Nov 1963); *Career* chm John Brown Engrg Ltd 1983-, gp md John Brown plc 1983-; dir: Trafalgar House plc 1986-, Trafalgar House Construction Hldgs Ltd 1986-, Dartford River Crossing Co Ltd 1987-; chm Overseas Projects Bd 1988, memb: BOTB 1988, Export Guarantees Advsy Cncl 1987; MICAS 1961; *Recreations* music, golf; *Style*— Allan Gormly, Esq; 20 Eastbourne Terr, London W2 6LE (☎ 01 724 0801, fax 01 262 0387, telex 8950033 JBPLC G)

GORNA, Anne Christina; da of John Gorna, of Oak Bank, Hill Top, Hale, Altrincham, Ches, and Muriel Theresa Gorna; *b* 19 Feb 1937; *Educ* Loreto Convent Llanddudno, Univ of Manchester (LLB), Univ of Neuchatel (Diploma Swiss and Int Law), Univ of The Sorbonne Paris (Dip in French Civilisation); *m* 6 July 1963, Ian Davies, s of Reginald Beresford Davies, of 55 Brook Lane, Timperly, Altrincham, Ches; 1 s (Caspar Dominick John b 11 May 1966), 1 da (Samantha Jane b 14 Jan 1964); *Career* barr, writer, broadcaster, columnist, legal agony aunt; barr Middle Temple 1960, sr lectr Lanchester Poly 1973-79; in practice specialising criminal, family, med negligence, media law and int law 1980-; numerous tv and radio appearances inc: ITV Summer Sunday Question Time 1988, BBC4 Any Questions? 1988, Kilroy BBC1 1989; contrib legal advice column Prestel 1988; *Books* Company Law (1961), Leading Cases on Company Law (1961), Questions and Answers on Company Law (1961); *Recreations* swimming, dance, theatre, ballet, music, visiting, galleries, cherishing friendships, writing, painting; *Clubs* Network (exec memb), Nat Liberal, Via; Friend of: Tate Gallery, Royal Ct Theatre, Lyric Theatre Hammersmith, Royal Academy; *Style*— Miss Christina Gorna; Ida Kempsford Gardens, London SW5; 1, The Old Warehouse, Denver Rd, Topsham, Devon; (☎ 01 370 0434); 4, Pader Buildings, Temple, London EC4Y 7EX (☎ 01 353 3366)

GORODICHE, Nicolas; s of Dr Jean Gorodiche, OBE, of Arles, France; *b* 21 July 1938; *Educ* Ecole Nationale Supérieure de l'Aéronautique, Ecole Personnel Naviguant d'Essais et de Réception, Harvard Business Sch; *m* 1968, Isabelle, da of Gen Henri Ziegler, MVO, OBE; 3 da; *Career* test pilot and Lt French Air Force; commercial pilot with Air Alpes, gen mangr UK and Ireland Air France 1981- (joined 1970), chm Air France Holidays; *Recreations* mountaineering, skiing, tennis, golf, music; *Clubs* Hurlingham, Royal Mid-Surrey Golf; *Style*— Nicolas Gorodiche, Esq; Air France, 69 Boston Manor Rd, Brentford, Middx TW8 9JQ (☎ 01 568 4411)

GORONWY-ROBERTS, Hon Ann Elizabeth; da of Baron Goronwy-Roberts, PC (Life Peer, d 1981); *b* 1947; *Educ* Pwlheli GS, Univ of Wales Cardiff, Sch of Educn; *Career* adult and secdy teaching; *Recreations* classical music and jazz, Times crossword, chess; *Style*— The Hon Ann Goronwy-Roberts; Plas Newydd, Pwllheli, Gwynedd, North Wales

GORONWY-ROBERTS, Baroness; Marian; da of David Evans, of Aberdare; *m* 1942, Baron Goronwy-Roberts, PC (Life Peer d 1981), Min State FCO and Dep Ldr House of Lords 1975-79; 1 s, 1 da; *Style*— Rt Hon Lady Goronwy-Roberts; Plâs Newydd, Pwllheli, Gwynedd

GORONWY-ROBERTS, Hon Owen Dafydd; s of Baron Goronwy-Roberts, PC (Life Peer) (d 1981); *b* 1946; *m* 1, 1979, Milana Majka Bartonova, da of Dr M M Jelinek, of London; m 2, 1987, Sharon Jennifer, da of Terence Taylor, of Duncan, BC, Canada; *Style*— The Hon Owen Goronwy-Roberts; c/o The Rt Hon Lady Goronwy-Roberts, Plas Newydd, Pwllheli, Gwynedd, N Wales

GORRINGE, Christopher John; s of Maurice Sydney William Gorringe (d 1981), of Newick, Nr Lewes, Sussex, and Hilda Joyce, *née* Walker; *b* 13 Dec 1945; *Educ* Bradfield Coll Reading Berks, RAC Cirencester Glos; *m* 17 April 1976, Jennifer Mary, da of Roger Arthur Chamberlain (d 1979), of Ramsbury Wilts; 2 da (Kim b 13 April 1978, Anna b 24 Feb 1981); *Career* asst land agent Iveagh Tstees Ltd (Guinness Family) 1968-73, chief exec The All Eng Lawn Tennis and Croquet Club Wimbledon 1983-(asst sec 1973-79, sec 1979-83); ARICS 1971; *Recreations* lawn tennis; *Clubs* The All England LTC, The Queen's, Jesters, Int (GB), St George's Hill LTC; *Style*— Christopher Gorringe, Esq; The All England Lawn Tennis Club, Church Road, Wimbledon, London, SW19 5AE (☎ 01 946 2244, fax 01 947 8752, telex 265180 AELTC)

GORROD, Prof John William; s of Ernest Lionel Gorrod (d 1981), of 29 Manton Ave, Hanwell, London W7, and Caroline Rebecca, *née* Richardson; *b* 11 Oct 1931; *Educ* London Univ (DSc, PhD), Chelsea Coll (Dip), Brunel CAT (HNC); *m* 3 April 1954, Doreen Mary, da of George Douglas Collins, of 114 Huntingfield Rd, Putney, London; 2 s (Simon b 1962, Nicholas b 1966) 1 da (Julia b 1959); *Career* res fell dept of biochem Univ of Bari Italy 1964, res fell of Royal Cmmn for the Exhibition of 1851 1965-67, lectr in biopharmacy Chelsea Coll Univ of London 1968-80, (reader 1980-84) prof biopharmacy and head of Chelsea dept of pharmacy Kings Coll London 1984-, head of div of health sciences Faculty of Life Science Kings Coll London 1988-; FRSC 1980, FRC Path 1984, MRPham S (hon) 1982; *Books* Drug Metabolism in Man (1978), Drug Toxicity (1979), Testing for Toxicity (1981), Biological Oxidation of Nitrogen in Organic Molecules (1985), Biological Oxidation of Nitrogen (1978), Metabolism of Xenobiotics (1988), Development of Drugs and Modern Medicines (1986); *Recreations* Badminton, Running; *Clubs* Athenaeum, Hillingdon Athletic; *Style*— Prof John Gorrod; Kingsmead, 13 Park Lane, Hayes, Middx (☎ 01 561 3851); The Rest Orchard, Polstead Heath, Nr Colchester; King's College London, Chelsea Department of Pharmacy, Manresa Road, London, SW3 6LX (☎ 01 351 2488)

GORSKY, David; s of Dr J A Gorsky (d 1962), of London, and Sylvia, *née* Coles (d 1935); *b* 24 Oct 1930; *Educ* Kings Sch Bruton Somerset, Trinity Coll Oxford (MA), Univ of London (Dip Archaeology); *m* 7 April 1955, Margaret, JP, da of Dr Sproull (d 1978), of Port Isaac, Cornwall; 1 s (Martin b 1957), 2 da (Diana (Mrs Hensher) b 1959, Helen b 1961); *Career* Nat Serv 1949-50, NCO Intelligence Corps; barr Inner

Temple 1955; md Peter Jones Sloane Sq 1967-70; John Lewis Partnership: dir servs 1971-86, ptnrs cnsllr 1986-89 (dir main bd); tres Village Carnival Day Ctee Hartley Wintney, ed Hartley Row Jl (half yearly), memb Christian Aid Ctee and PCC, chm planning ctee and fin and gen purposes ctee Hart DC 1976-82; memb Bar Assoc for Commerce Fin and Indust; *Books* The Old Village of Hartley Wintney (1970, 4 ed 1978), Great Grandfather's Village (1975); *Recreations* local history, archaeology, fell and footpath walking; *Clubs* Oriental; *Style—* David Gorsky, Esq; Hartley Grange, Hartley Wintney, Hants RG27 8HH (☎ 025 126 2457), John Lewis plc, 11-12 Old Cavendish St, London W1A 1EX (☎ 01 637 3434)

GORST, John Marcus; s of Maj James Marcus Gorst of South Stack, Fornham All Saints, Bury St Edmunds, Suffolk, and Frances Gladys *née* Espley; *b* 13 Jan 1944; *Educ* Culford Sch, Selwyn Coll Cambridge (MA); *m* June 1974 (m dis 1977) Marian, da of James Anthony Judge of 2 Rockall Drive, Glasgow; *Career* md Drayson Property Hldgs Ltd 1971-, chm Folkard and Hayward Servs Ltd 1984-; Freeman Worshipful Co of Bakers; *Recreations* golf, shooting; *Clubs* Oxford and Cambridge Univ; *Style—* John Gorst, Esq; Mill Farm, Higham, Bury St Edmunds, Suffolk; 35 Tedworth Square, London SW3 (☎ 01 351 2036); 20 Crawford St, London WIH 2AR (☎ 01 935 7799, fax 01 486 6877, car tel 0836 249 857)

GORST, John Michael; MP (C) Hendon North 1983-; s of Derek Charles Gorst; *b* 28 June 1928; *Educ* Ardingly, Corpus Christi Coll Cambridge; *m* 1954, Noël Harington, da of Austin Walker, of E Kilbride; 5 s; *Career* fndr of Assocs 1974: Telephone Users, Local Radio, Middle Class; advertising and PR mangr Pye Ltd 1953-63, PR conslt John Gorst and Assocs Ltd 1964-, contested (C): Chester-le-Street 1964, Bodmin 1966; MP (C): Hendon North 1970-74, Barnet 1974-1983; memb select ctee on Employment 1979-; *Clubs* Garrick; *Style—* John Gorst, Esq, MP; House of Commons, London SW1

GORT, 8 Viscount (I 1816); Colin Leopold Prendergast Vereker; JP (Castletown IOM 1962-1986); also Baron Kiltarton (I 1810); s of Cdr Leopold Vereker, RNR (gs of 4 Viscount); suc first cous once removed, 7 Viscount, 1975; *b* 21 June 1916; *Educ* Sevenoaks; *m* 1946, Bettine, da of Godfrey Green, of Douglas, IOM, and formerly w of Arthur Jarand; 2 s, 1 da; *Heir* s, Hon Foley Vereker; *Career* Lt Cdr RNVR, served WW II (despatches), Mediterranean, Africa, Indian Ocean, Home Fleet, Atlantic, Russian Convoy; dir Royal Bank of Scotland (IOM), Royal Skandia Life Assur, Britannia Gilt Fund (IOM); memb House of Keys IOM 1966-71; *Recreations* golf, gardening, antique restoration; *Style—* The Rt Hon the Viscount Gort, JP; Westwood, The Crofts, Castletown, IOM (☎ 822545)

GORTON, Rt Hon Sir John Grey; GCMG (1977), CH (1971), PC (1968); s of J R Gorton; *b* 9 Sept 1911; *Educ* Geelong GS, Brasenose Coll Oxford (MA); *m* 1935, Bettina, *née* Brown; 2 s, 1 da; *Career* MHR (Lib) for Higgins Vic Aust 1968-75, Prime Minister Aust 1968-71, min for def and dep ldr Lib Party 1971, memb Parly Lib Pty Exec and Lib Pty spokesman on environment, conservation and urban and regnl devpt 1973-75, ret; *see Debrett's Handbook of Australia and New Zealand for further details*; *Style—* The Rt Hon Sir John Gorton, GCMG, CH; Suite 3, 9th Floor, 197 London Circuit, Canberra City, ACT 2601, Australia

GORTON, Philip Murray; s of Rev John Percival Page Gorton (d 1951), and Muriel Gladys, *née* Murray; *b* 24 Nov 1928; *Educ* Bedford Sch, Coll of Estate Mgmnt London; *m* 3 July 1954, Rosalind Angela Mary, da of Lt-Col Sir James Edmond Henderson Neville, 2 Bt, MC (d 1983); 3 s (Simon b 24 Feb 1957, Mark b 25 Dec 1960, Colin b 24 Aug 1962), 1 da (Clare (Mrs Hill) b 7 Aug 1958); *Career* Civil Serv; Miny of Agric: asst land cmmr Norwich 1966, sr asst land cmmr London 1970, div surveyor Northampton 1975, supt surveyor London 1981, regnl mangr (land use and countryside) Cambridge 1984, ret 1988; RICS: rural div cncl memb 1988-, memb (RD) Educn and Membership Ctee 1981-88, assessor Test of Professional Competance 1984-89, assessor RAC Cirencester 1988-; Liveryman Worshipful Co of Fishmongers; FRICS; *Recreations* conservation, shooting; *Clubs* Civil Service; *Style—* Philip Gorton, Esq; The Emplins, Gamlingay, Cambridgeshire SG19 3ER (☎ 0767 50581)

GORVIN, Roger John; s of Dennis Richard Gorvin (d 1986), and Edith Mary, *née* Lockyer; *b* 16 June 1938; *Educ* Chippenham GS, Cheltenham GS, Witney GS; *m* 3 April 1961, Josephine Edwina Stamford, da of late Frederick George Hamilton Cooper; 3 da (Fiona b 1966, Alison b 1969, Kirsty b 1973); *Career* dir: Co-operative Bank plc, Leslie Bilsby Devpts Ltd, EftPos UK Ltd, Scottish Co-operative Society Nominees Ltd, Unity Tst Bank plc (alternate), Fastline Credit Fin Ltd, Holyoake Insur Brokers Ltd, Co-operative Bank Insur Servs Ltd, Cleveland Finance Ltd, First Co-operative Finance Ltd; *Recreations* cricket, gardening, photography, hi-fi; *Style—* Roger Gorvin, Esq; Rhodewood House, 140 Prestbury Road, Macclesfield, Cheshire SK10 3BN (☎ 0625 32244); Co-operative Bank plc, P O Box 200, Delt Hse, Southway, Skelmersdale, Lancs WN8 6NY (☎ 0695 24151, fax 0695 3366J, telex 629300)

GOSCHEN, Viscountess - Alvin Moyana Lesley; yr da of late Harry England, of Durban, Natal, S Africa; *m* 18 Aug 1955, as his 2 w, 3 Viscount Goschen, KBE (d 1977); 1 s (4 Viscount *qv*), 1 da; *Style—* The Rt Hon the Viscountess Goschen; Hilton House, Crowthorne, Berks

GOSCHEN, Hon Caroline Elizabeth; da of 3 Visc Goschen, KBE (d 1977); *b* 24 July 1963; *Style—* The Hon Caroline Goschen

GOSCHEN, Edward Alexander; s and h of Sir Edward Christian Goschen, 3 Bt, DSO, and Cynthia, da of late Rt Hon Sir Alexander Cadogan, OM, GCMG, KCB; *b* 13 Mar 1949; *Educ* Eton; *m* 1976, Louise Annette, da of Lt-Col Ronald Chance, MC, and Lady Ava, *née* Baird (da of 1 Viscount Stonehaven and Lady (Ethel) Sidney, *née* Keith-Falconer, who was Countess of Kintore in her own right); 1 da (Charlotte, b 1982); *Style—* Edward Goschen, Esq; Pixton Stables, Dulverton, Taunton, Somerset

GOSCHEN, Sir Edward Christian; 3 Bt (UK 1916), DSO (1944); s of Sir Edward Goschen, 2 Bt (d 1933; s of Sir (William) Edward Goschen, 1 Bt, GCB, GCMG, GCVO, HM ambass in Berlin in 1914), and Countess Mary Danneskiold-Samsöe (d 1964), 7 da of 5 Count (Christian) Danneskiold-Samsöe; *b* 2 Sept 1913; *Educ* Eton, Trinity Coll Oxford; *m* 1946, Cynthia, da of Rt Hon Sir Alexander Cadogan, OM, GCMG, KCB, PC, sometime perm under sec at the FO (7 s of 5 Earl Cadogan), by his w Lady Theodosia Acheson, da of 4 Earl of Gosford; 1 s, 1 da; *Heir* s, Edward Alexander Goschen; *Career* memb Stock Exchange Cncl (dep chm 1968-71); Cwlth War Graves cmmr 1977-87; *Style—* Sir Edward Goschen, Bt, DSO; Lower Farm House, Hampstead Norreys, Newbury, Berks (☎ 0635 201270)

GOSCHEN, 4 Viscount (UK 1900); Giles John Harry Goschen; s of 3 Viscount Goschen, KBE (d 1977), and his 2 w Alvin, *née* England; *b* 16 Nov 1965; *Heir* none; *Style—* The Rt Hon The Viscount Goschen; Hilton House, Crowthorne, Berks

GOSFORD, 7 Earl of (I 1806); Sir Charles David Alexander John Sparrow Acheson; 13 Bt (NS 1628); also Baron Gosford (I 1776), Viscount Gosford (I 1785), Baron Worlingham (UK 1835, sits as), and Baron Acheson of Clancairny (UK 1847); s of 6 Earl of Gosford, OBE (d 1966), by his 1 w, Francesca, er da of Francesco Cagiati, of Rome; *b* 13 July 1942; *Educ* Harrow, Byam Shaw Sch of Drawing and Painting, Royal Academy Schs; *m* 1983, Lynnette Redmond; *Heir* unc, Hon Patrick Acheson; *Career* artist; oneman shows: Barry Stern Exhibition Gallery, Sydney 1983 and 1986, Von Bertouch Galleries, Newcastle, NSW 1983 and 1986; *Style—* The Rt Hon The Earl of Gosford; c/o House of Lords, Westminster, London SW1

GOSFORD, Cynthia, Countess of; Cynthia Margaret; da of late Capt Henry Cave West, RHA; *m* 1, Maj James Pringle Delius, 13/18 Royal Hussars (d 1944); m 2, 1960, as his 2 w, 6 Earl of Gosford, OBE (d 1966); *Style—* The Rt Hon Cynthia Countess of Gosford; Heath Cottage, Camberley, Surrey

GOSKIRK, (William) Ian MacDonald; CBE (1986); s of William Arthur Goskirk (d 1984), of Scotby, Carlisle, and Flora Rennie, *née* MacDonald; *b* 2 Mar 1932; *Educ* Carlisle GS, Queen's Coll Oxford (MA); *m* 7 June 1969, Hope-Ann, da of John Knaizuk, of New York, USA; 1 da (Nadia Anna b 1970); *Career* Lt REME 1950-52; Shell Int Petroleum 1956-74; md Anschutz Petroleum Ltd 1974-76; Br Nat Oil Corpn 1976-85; md BNOC (Trading) Ltd 1980- 82, chief exec 1982-85; dir Coopers & Lybrand Assocs 1986-; CBIM 1984, FInstPet 1975; *Recreations* gardening; *Clubs* Naval and Military; *Style—* Ian Goskirk, Esq, CBE; c/o Coopers & Lybrand Associates Ltd, Plumtree Court, London EC4A 4HT (☎ 01 583 5000, telex 887470)

GOSLING, Lady Caroline Victoria; *née* Wood; er da of 2 Earl of Halifax, JP, DL; *b* 10 Sept 1937; *m* 1, 1958 (m dis 1970), Randle Joseph, eldest s of late Maj-Gen Sir Randle Feilden, KCVO, CB, CBE, DL, and Lady Feilden, *qv*; 1 s (Randle Charles Roderick b 1961), 2 da (Virginia Mary b 1959, Fiona Caroline b 1965); m 2, 1970, John V Gosling; *Style—* Lady Caroline Gosling; The Claw, Brushford, Dulverton, Somerset (☎ 0398 23493)

GOSLING, Sir (Frederick) Donald; *b* 2 Mar 1929; *m* 1959, Elizabeth Shauna, *née* Ingram; 3 s; *Career* joined RN 1944, served Med HMS Leander; jt chm Nat Car Parks Ltd 1950-, chm Palmer & Harvey Ltd 1967-, dir Lovell Hldgs Ltd 1975-; memb cncl of mgmnt White Ensign Assoc 1970- (chm 1978-83, vice-pres 1983-); chm Selective Employment Scheme 1976-; tstee: Fleet Air Arm Museum Yeovilton 1974-, RYA Seamanship Fndn; patron Submarine Meml Appeal 1978-; chm Berkeley Square Ball Charitable Tst; kt 1976; *Style—* Sir Donald Gosling; National Car Parks Ltd, PO Box 4NH, 21 Bryanston St, Marble Arch, London W1A 4NH (☎ 01 499 7050)

GOSLING, Peter Alfred; s of late William Thomas Gosling; *b* 29 April 1924; *Educ* Clacton on Sea Co HS; *m* 1947, Doris Eva Emily, *née* Smith; 1 s (David), 1 da (Susan); *Career* WWII RE Burma; FCIS; *Recreations* hunting, gardening; *Style—* Peter Gosling, Esq; Pinfarthings, Great Somerford, Chippenham, Wilts (☎ Seagry 720374)

GOSLING, Col Richard Bennett; OBE (1957), TD (1948), DL (Essex 1954); s of Thomas Spencer Gosling, JP (d 1946), of Dynes Hall, Halstead, Essex, and Miriam Gwendolyn Wickham, *née* Wyles (d 1952), ancestors founded Goslings Bank, 19 Fleet St, London 1650, amalgamated with Barclays Bank 1896; *b* 4 Oct 1914; *Educ* Eton, Magdalene Coll Cambridge (MA), Birmingham Univ (Dip Industl Admin); *m* 1, 21 April 1950, Marie Terese (d 1976), o da of Philip Ronayne (d 1944), of Castle Redmond, Midleton, Co Cork; 1 s (Timothy Philip b 11 May, d 18 Nov 1953), 1 adopted s (Aidan Bennett b 27 Feb 1960), 1 adopted da (Francine Mary b 26 Jan 1959); m 2, 22 July 1978, Sybilla Jacoba Margaretha, da of Wilhelmus Matthias Jan Van Oyen (d 1935), of Venlo, Netherlands, and wid of Bernard Burgers, of Kasteel Weurt, Nijmegen, Netherlands; *Career* Essex Yeomany 1939-53, CO 1950-53, Dep CRA E Anglia Div (full cmd) 1953-56; professional engr, dir gen Br Agric Export Cncl 1971-73; dir: PE Consulting Gp 1957-69, PE Int Ltd 1969-76, Royal Doulton Gp 1964-72; chm: Constructors 1965-68, Hearne & Co 1966-80, Revertex Chems Ltd 1974-84, Press Mouldings Ltd 1980-; pres Univ of Essex Assoc; int steward Royal Show 1974-; High Sheriff of Essex 1982-83; French Croix de Guerre with Gold Star 1945; CEng, MBIM 1950, FIME 1969, FID 1967, FIMC 1985; *Recreations* shooting, farming, country pursuits; *Clubs* Naval and Military, MCC, Beefsteak; *Style—* Col Richard Gosling, OBE, TD, DL; Canterburys Lodge, Margaretting, Essex CM4 OEE (☎ 0277 353073)

GOSLING, William; s of Harold William Gosling (d 1980), of Cograve, Notts, and Aida Maisie, *née* Webb; *b* 25 Sept 1932; *Educ* Mundella Sch Nottingham, Imperial Coll London (BSc, ARCS), Univ of Bath (DSc) ; *m* 5 July 1953, Patricia Mary, da of Charles Harold Best, of Rode, Somerset; 2 s (Richard b 1956 d 1958, Ceri b 1959), 1 da (Melanie b 1954); *Career* prof of electrical engrg Univ of Wales 1966, vice-princ Univ Coll Swansea 1972, prof of electronic engrg Univ of Bath 1974; tech dir Plessey Co plc 1981- (formerly Plessey Electronic Sys Ltd) 1981-; hon prof of communication engrg Southampton Univ 1981; pres: Euro Convention of Soc of Electronic Engrs 1977-78, Inst of Electronic and Radio engrs 1979-80; Freeman City of London 1980; Liveryman Worshipful Co of: Scientific Instrument Makers 1980, Engrs 1985; Hon Fell (UMIST) 1987; FIEE 1968, FInstD 1982; *Books* Design of Engineering Systems (1962), Field Effect Electronics (1971), Radio Receivers (1986),; *Recreations* music, poetry; *Clubs* Athenaeum; *Style—* Prof William Gosling; White Hart Cottage, Rode, Bath (☎ 0373 830901); The Plessey Company plc, Roke Manor, Romsey, Hants (☎ 0794 515222 ext 2353, fax 0794 515222 ext 2545, car tel 0860 319846, telex 47311)

GOSLING, William Douglas; MBE (1949), TD, DL (Essex 1952); s of William Sullivan Gosling (d 1952), and Lady Victoria Kerr, 5 da of 9 Marquess of Lothian; *b* 11 Sept 1904; *Educ* Eton, Cambridge; *m* 1935, Rosemary (d 1986), da of Hon Victor Alexander Frederick Russell, CBE (3 s of 1 Baron Ampthill); *Career* Lt-Col cmdg Essex Yeo 1951, Maj RA (TA) Middle East WW II; farmer; local dir Barclays Bank; High Sheriff Essex 1958, patron of living of Farnham Essex; *Style—* William Gosling, Esq, MBE, TD, DL; Thrimley House, Farnham, Bishop's Stortford CM23 1HX

GOSS, Major (William) Raymond; s of Vernon William Goss (d 1968), of Whalley, Lancs, and Mary Elizabeth, *née* Kingston (d 1983); *b* 29 Dec 1925; *Educ* Kings Sch Worcester, RMCS; *m* (m dis); 5 s (Robert b 1954, Richard b 1956, Patrick b 1957, Geoffrey b 1959, Quentin b 1961), 1 da (Laurel b 1965); *Career* cmmnd RA 1946, served India 1946-47, active service 45 Field Regt Korea 1952-53, instr Armours Sch RAC Centre 1966-69, MOD as ret offr 1983-; dir Steam Marine Ltd; CEng, MRAeS; *Recreations* sailing, swimming, woodcarving, sculpture; *Style—* Maj Raymond Goss; 22 Derwent Ave, Mill Hill, London NW7 3DZ (☎ 01 959 1999)

GOSS, Prof Richard Oliver; s of Sqdn-Ldr Leonard Arthur Goss (d 1956), and Hilda Nellie, *née* Casson (d 1986); *b* 4 Oct 1929; *Educ* Christs Coll Finchley, HMS

Worcester, Kings Coll Cambridge (BA, MA, PhD); *m* 21 June 1958 (m dis 1983), Lesley Elizabeth, da of William Thomas Thurbon; 2 s (David Anthony b 1963, Stephen Peter b 1966), 1 da (Catherine Alice b 1960); *Career* MN: Cadet to Chief Offr 1947-56, Master Mariner 1956; statistics clerk and subsequently PA to gen mangr NZ Shipping Co Ltd (London) 1958-63; Civil Serv 1963-80: econ conslt on shipping, ship bldg and parts, sr econ advsr on aviation shipping and marine, under sec for advice on shipping, civil aviation, prices and consumer protection, wholesale prices etc; econ advsr Ctee of Inquiry into Shipping (Rochdale Ctee) 1967-70, prof maritime econs Univ of Wales Cardiff 1980-; fndr memb Nautical Inst (cncl memb 1972-76), ed (later ed-in-chief) Maritime Policy and Mgmnt; memb Hon Co of Master Mariners; Assoc Inst NA 1969, FNI 1977; *Books* Studies in Maritime Economics (1968), Advances in Maritime Economics (1977); *Recreations* cruising; *Clubs* Wyre Mill (Pershore, Worcs); *Style*— Prof Richard Goss; 8 Dunraven House, Westgate St, Cardiff CF1 1DL (☎ 0222 344 338); University of Wales College of Cardiff, Dept of Maritime Studies, Aberconway Building, Colum Drive, Cardiff (☎ 0222 874000, fax 0222 874478, telex 498635)

GOSSELIN, Peter John Nicholas; s of René Jean Gosselin (d 1977), and Edith May, *née* Bouchere; *b* 7 June 1944; *Educ* De Lasalle Coll, Somerset Coll of Agric (NCA); *m* 1 Oct 1977, Joan Elizabeth, da of Gordon Arthur Gaudin; *Career* formerly agric foreman and haulage contractor; fishing tackle dealer; memb: Jersey Records Ctee, Jersey Sea Fisheries Advsy Panel; chm Jersey Fedn of Sea Anglers; *Recreations* fishing, reading; *Clubs* Jersey Light Tackle Group, States Airport Social; *Style*— Peter J N Gosselin, Esq; Nouages, Neuvaine, Golf Lane, Grouville, Jersey (☎ 0534 74875)

GOSWELL, Brian Laurence; s of Albert George Goswell (d 1971), and Florence Emily, *née* Barnett (d 1980); *b* 26 Nov 1935; *Educ* St David's Sch High Wycombe, Durham Univ; *m* 1961, Deirdre Gillian, da of Harold Stones, of Cadby Hall, Cadby, Leics; 2 s (Paul b 1964, Angus b 1967); *Career* dep sr ptnr Healey & Baker, fell and past pres Incorporated Soc of Valuers and Auctioneers, assoc Chartered Inst of Arbitrators, chm Healey & Baker Inc New York, dir Roux Restaurants Ltd, hon tres Carlton Club Political ctee, chm Friends of Royal Soc for Nature Conservation Inc, New York, vice chm Br Wildlife Appeal, dir London Handel Orchestra; *Recreations* shooting, horse racing, cricket; *Clubs* Turf, Carlton, City of London, City Livery, United and Cecil, MCC; *Style*— Brian Goswell, Esq; 118 Old Broad St, London EC2N 1AR (☎ 01 628 4361); Pipers, Camley Park, Pinkneys Green, Berks SL6 6QF (☎ 0628 30768); 555 Madison Ave, New York, NY 10022, USA (☎ 212 935 7251)

GOTELL, Walter; s of Jakob Gotell (d 1964), of Berlin, and London, and Margaret, *née* Cohn (d 1980); *b* 15 Mar 1924; *Educ* Seaford Coll Sussex, Leighton Park Sch Reading, Northern Poly; *m* 1, 6 Sept 1958, Yvonne (d 1974), da of Col RJT Hills (d 1968), latterly of Buenos Aires; 1 da (Carol Verity b 23 March 1960); m 2, 1975, Celeste Fitzgerald Mitchell, of New York; *Career* actor and engr; student Old Vic 1945, appeared in numerous plays incl: Adventure Story (at St James), Othello (for Ken Tynan); films incl: African Queen, Bismarch, Ice Cold in Alex, The Guns of Navarone, Road to Hong Kong, 55 Days at Peking, Black Sunday, The Boys from Brazil; played Gen Gogol in Seven James Bond films, and Chief Constable Cullen for six years in Softly, Softly; mechanical engr in 1950's, fndr own co 1970's, ret; govr Box Hill Sch Dorking Surrey; Hon Memb of the Guildhall Sch of Music and Drama (HMGSM) 1975, FIMH 1975; *Style*— Walter Gotell, Esq

GOTHARD, Dr Richard Sherwin; s of late Henry Alexander Sherwin Gothard, and Amy Rubina, *née* Baxter; *b* 22 May 1923; *Educ* Cranbrook; *m* 1955, late Margaret Eileen Milligan; 1 step s, 2 step da; *Career* joined RAF 1939, served 29 Sqdn, 174 Sqdn, 2 Tactical Airforce, 133 RAF/US Sqdn UK, RAFVR until 1963; ptnr Alexander Gothard and Ptnrs 1947, fndr md Adelphi Mfrg Co; chm: RS Gothard and Co Ltd (fndr 1962), Gothard House Pubns Ltd, RS Gothard Export Co Ltd, RS Gothard (S America) Resources Ltd, Int Subscriptions Ltd, GHG Info and Library Servs Co Ltd, Info Resources Ltd; sr ptnr Hythe Books and Gothard Investmt Co, dir Noyes Data Corpn USA, chm and chief exec Gothard House Gp of Cos Ltd; pres: Fruit Culture Cncl 1982, RNLI Henley-on-Thames; Freeman City of London, Freeman and Liveryman Worshipful Co of Fruiterers (Master 1982); former fell IOD, former MInstM; memb: Assoc of Info Offrs in the Pharmaceutical Indust, Soc of Pharmaceutical Medicine, East Malling Res Assoc; *Books* Information Resources Guides Britain, Glossary of Terms, Professionally and Commonly Used in Health, History of Worshipful Co of Fruiterers 1912-1975; *Recreations* sailing, engraving, gardening, writing; *Clubs* Royal Cinque Ports YC, MCC, RAF, City Livery, United Wards, Royal Soc of St George; *Style*— Dr Richard S Gothard; Sherwins, Park Place Farm, Remenham, Henley-on-Thames, Oxon; Gothard House, Henley-on-Thames, Oxon RG9 1AJ (☎ 0491 573602)

GOTTO, Arthur Charles Corry; s of Charles Corry Gotto (d 1958), and Ethel Millar, *née* Pinion (d 1950); *b* 5 June 1911; *Educ* Campbell Coll Belfast, Dauntseys; *m* 15 Sept 1939, Margaret Charly, da of Cdr Charles Frederick Ballard (ka 1915); 1 s (Charles b 1943), 1 da (Margaret Mavis b 1940); *Career* WWII Maj Devonshire Regt served France, Germany (despatches) 1939-45; dir family linen firm N Ireland 1945-60; pres Confedn of Ulster Socs (pres cncl memb); exec memb Embroiderers' Guild; played lawn tennis for GB against Norway, Spain, Malta and in 1987 (in 77 year) against Hungary; Freeman City of London, Past Master Worshipful Co of Broderers 1977-78; *Recreations* lawn tennis, travel, shooting; *Clubs* Royal Automobile, International Lawn Tennis (GB), Veterans Lawn Tennis; *Style*— Arthur Gotto, Esq; Lansallos, Miles Lane, Cobham, Surrey KT11 2EA (☎ 0932 63853)

GOTZ, Lady (Mary Spencer); da of Hector Ranson, of NZ; *m* 1962, as his 2 w, Sir Frank Götz, KCVO (d 1970); *Style*— Lady Gotz; 327 Fenton St, Rotorua, New Zealand

GOUBET, Jean-Claude Jules André; s of Jules Sylvain Goubet (d 1965), and Olga Zelie, *née* Leroy; *b* 31 Dec 1943; *Educ* Lycee Carnot Paris, Institut National de Sciences Appliquees Lyons France; *m* 29 June 1964, Francoise Anette Monique; 2 s (Lionel Jean-Claude b 1963, Stephane Jules Aisène b 1969); *Career* Credit Lyonnais: joined 1966, trainee account mangr 1966-70, project and planning/mgmnt info 1970-74, branch mangr in Lorient Brittany 1974-77, head of corporate relations New York 1977-79, mangr Californian Branches 1979, head of US credit dept New York 1980-81, md Luxembourg 1981-84, dep gen mangr UK branches 1984-87, md UK branches 1987-; vice pres French C of C in GB 1987, Conseiller du Commerce Exterior de la France 1983; *Recreations* skiing, sailing; *Clubs* Foxhills, Overseas Bankers; *Style*— Jean-Claude Goubet, Esq; 169 Oakwood Ct, London, W14 (☎ 01 602 3153); 6 Avenue Emile Zola, Paris; Credit Lyonnais, 84-94 Queen Victoria Street, London, EC4P 4LX (☎ 01 634 8000, fax 01 489 1909)

GOUDE, Lt-Col (Clarence Henry) Peter; MBE (1943); s of James Henry Goude (d 1957), of Shirley Ave, Leicester, and Ruth, *née* Botwright (d 1969); *b* 8 Mar 1909; *Educ* Mill Hill Leicester, Univ Coll Leicester; *m* 27 Sept 1952, Jean, da of John Edward Rawding (d 1970), of E Retford, Notts; 1 s (Nicholas b 1953), 2 da (Amanda b 1958, Jennifer b 1958); *Career* slr; private practise London, Norwich, Leics 1930-39; enlisted RA 1939, cmmnd 1940, Capt 1942, Major 1943, Actg Lt-Col 1945; Western Desert 1941-43, Greece/Crete 1941, Sicily 1943, Italy 1943-45; cmdt 12 German/Italian POW camp (UK) 1945; Lt-Col Co of Lincoln Regt RA 1950, dep coroner N Notts 1946-52; clerk to cmmrs of taxes (Maelor) 1953-84, conslt to Lucas, Butter (slrs); *Recreations* reading, music, freemasonry; *Style*— Lt-Col Peter Goude, MBE; Littlegrove, Church Meadows, Whitchurch, Shropshire (☎ 0948 2944)

GOUDIE, Prof Andrew Shaw; s of William Cooper Goudie, and Mary Isobel, *née* Pulman; *b* 21 August 1945; *Educ* Dean Close Sch Cheltenham, Trinity Hall Cambridge (BA, MA, PhD); *m* 21 March 1987, Heather Ann, da of John Viles, of Chelmsford; 1 da (Amy Louise b 7 June 1988); *Career* Univ of Oxford: lectr in geography and fell Hertford Coll 1976-84, prof of geography and head of dept 1984-; vice pres RGS, chm Br Geomorphological Res Gp, hon vice pres Geographical Assoc; FRGS (1970), MIBG (1970); *Books* The Human Impact, The Nature of the Environment, Environmental Change, Geomorphological Techniques, Duricrusts, The Warm Desert Environment, Land Shapes, Discovering Landscape in England and Wales, The prehistory and palaeogeography of the Great Indian Desert, Chemical Sediments in Geomorphology; *Recreations* old books, old records, gardening; *Clubs* Geographical; *Style*— Prof Andrew Goudie; School of Geography, Mansfield Rd, Oxford OX1 3TB (☎ 0865 271 921, telex 83147 VIA OR G)

GOUDIE, (Thomas) James Cooper; QC (1984); s of late William Cooper Goudie, and Mary Isobel, *née* Pulman; *b* 2 June 1942; *Educ* Dean Close Sch Cheltenham, LSE (LLB); *m* 30 Aug 1969, Mary Teresa, da of Martin Brick; 2 s (Martin b 5 July 1973, Alexander b 14 July 1977); *Career* slr 1966-70, barr Inner Temple 1970, SE circuit 1970-, rec 1985-; fndr memb and ctee memb Admin Law Bar Assoc; memb Brent Cncl 1967-78 (latterly ldr); parly candidate (Lab) Brent North 1974; *Style*— James Goudie, Esq, QC; 11 Kings Bench Walk, Temple EC4Y 7EQ (☎ 01 583 0610, telex 884620 BARLEX, fax 01 583 9123)

GOUDIE, (James) Sandford; s of James Sand Goudie (d 1981), of South Shields, and Sarah Elizabeth Hartley, *née* Harcus (d 1986); *b* 5 May 1935; *Educ* Harleys of South Shields; *m* 7 Feb 1961, June, da of Harry Hilton (d 1969), of South Shields; 1 s (J Sandford b 25 Nov 1965), 1 da (Janice S b 28 Feb 1962); *Career* Nat Serv 15/19 QOH; jt md: Be Modern Ltd 1964, Mellinate Prods Ltd 1973-78, Academy Crafts Ltd 1980, exec dir Aquarius Bathrooms Ltd 1983-88; jt md: Lister Moudlings Ltd 1983, Marcraft Ltd 1988; chm S Shields: Mentally Handicapped Parents Assoc 1975-77, Amateur Operatic Soc 1980-88; JP 1967-81; *Recreations* amateur and professional theatre; *Style*— Sandford Goudie, Esq; Villa in Menorca; Pine Lodge in Cumbria; Be Modern Ltd, Western Approach, S Shields, Tyne & Wear NE38 5DP (☎ 091 455 3571, fax 091 456 556, telex 537307 MERGER G)

GOUDIE, Hon William Henry; MC (1944); s of Henry Goudie; *b* 21 August 1916; *Educ* Bristol GS; *m* 1948, Mourilyan Munro; 2 s; exec dir and dep chm Tasmania Law Reform Cmmn 1974-; *Style*— Hon William Goudie; 24 Nimala St, Rosny, Hobart, Tasmania 7018, Australia

GOUGH, (Anita Norma) Annie; da of Horace Kilian (d 1987), of Baddow Park, Gt Baddow, Essex, and Ruby Kilian; *b* 28 May 1930; *Educ* Benenden Sch Kent; *m* 22 July 1950 (m dis 1970), Hugh Patrick Gough, s of Hubert Vincent Gough (d 1986), of 33 Shooters Hill, Pangbourne, Berks; 2 da (Deirdre Caroline b 26 Sept 1952, Henrietta Joanna Louise b 22 July 1954); *Career* memb Ballet Rambert Co 1948-50, fndr Fachion Design Co 1968-85; numerous private cmmns incl: HRH Princess Michael of Kent, Deborah Kerr, Hannah Gordon, Lisa Goddard; chm Gp of Packaging Cos 1981-; *Recreations* vintage cars, interior design, country persuits; *Style*— Mrs Annie Gough; The Stables, Little Horwood Manor, Little Horwood, Bucks NK17 0PH (☎ 029671 3703); H Kilian Ltd, Baddow Park, Gt Baddow, Essex CM2 7SY (☎ 0245 72361, telex 885225)

GOUGH, (Charles) Brandon; s of Charles Richard Gough (d 1957), and Mary Evaline, *née* Goff; *b* 8 Oct 1937; *Educ* Douai Sch, Jesus Coll Cambridge (MA); *m* 24 June 1961, Sarah, da of Maurice Evans Smith (d 1987); 1 s (Richard b 1962) 2 da (Lucy b 1964, Katherine b 1967); *Career* Nat Serv Army 1956-58; joined Coopers and Lybrand (formerly Cooper Bros and Co) 1964 (ptnr 1968-83, sr ptnr 1983-), memb exec ctee Coopers and Lybrand Int 1982- (chm 1983), chm Coopers and Lybrand Europe 1989-; chm CCAB Auditing Practices Ctee 1981-84 (memb 1976-84), memb Accounting Standards Review (Dearing) Ctee 1987-88; memb: Cambridge Univ Careers Serv Syndicate 1983-86, cncl for Indust and Higher Educn 1985-, cncl City Univ Business Sch 1986-, City advsy panel City Univ Business Sch 1980- (chm 1987-), Cncl of Lloyd's 1983-86 (Lloyd's Silver Medal 1986), governing cncl Business in the Community 1984-88, cncl Business in the Community 1988-, mgmnt cncl GB-Sasakawa Fndn 1985-; govt dir Br Aerospace plc 1987-88; Freeman: City of London 1983, Worshipful Co of CAs (1983); FCA 1974 (cncl 1981-84); *Recreations* music, gardening; *Style*— Brandon Gough, Esq; Long Barn, Weald, Sevenoaks, Kent TN14 6NH (☎ 0732 463714); Coopers and Lybrand, Plumtree Court, London EC4A 4HT (☎ 01 583 5000, fax 01 822 4652, telex 887470 answerback: 887470 COLYLN G)

GOUGH, Cecil Ernest Freeman; CMG (1956); s of Ernest John Gough, of Hockley, Essex; *b* 29 Oct 1911; *Educ* Southend HS, LSE; *m* 1938, Gwendolen Lily Miriam, da of Martin Longman, of Hockley; 1 s, 1 da; *Career* formerly civil servant: Inland Revenue, MOD, FO, Admty; md Airwork Overseas Ltd 1968-71; asst dir-gen Br Property Fedn 1978-80 (actg dir-gen 1980-81); Medal of Freedom USA 1946; *Recreations* cookery, gardening, reading; *Clubs* Naval and Military, Civil Service; *Style*— Cecil Gough, Esq, CMG; 23 Howbridge Rd, Witham, Essex (☎ 0376 518969)

GOUGH, Brig Clifford Thomas William; OBE (1952, MBE 1946); s of Sgt Maj Thomas William Gough (ka The Somme 1916), and Kate (d 1989), *née* Dare; *b* 10 Sept 1911; *Educ* Mil Coll of Sci Tech Sch Woolwich; *m* 1, 27 Dec 1933, Lilian Mary (d 1981), da of John Brace (d 1931); 1 s (Terence William Brace b 6 April 1936); m 2, 15 Aug 1983, Olive Mary, da of Norman Griffith Thomas; *Career* apprentice artificer RA 1926-31, transferred to engrg branch RAOC 1937; WWII served Middle East 1939-43 (despatches 1941), cmmnd RAOC in the field (Alamein) 1942, transferred to REME on its formation 1942, Capt 1943, served Normandy and NW Europe 1943-45, Maj 1945,

Lt Col cmdg REME 7 Armd Div BAOR 1949-52, Sr Offrs' Sch 1953, seconded dir of tech servs Arab Legion 1955-56, Col 1956, Admin Coll Henley 1957, cmd Trg Bde REME 1959-61, ret 1961; with Friary-Meux Ltd (brewers) 1961-65; Bass Charrington Ltd (formerly Charrington Utd Breweries): joined 1965, dir of distribution and tport 1970, ret 1974, special projects conslt 1974-78 (set up Bass Museum of Brewing 1977); co vice pres Royal Br Legion Pembrokeshire 1983-; hon organiser Royal Br Legion Poppy Appeal: Berkswich branch Stafford 1974-78, Pembroke and Pembroke Dock branch 1980-; pres: Pembrokeshire branch Normandy Veterans Assoc, Pembroke Dock Volunteer Artillery; sec Pembrokeshire branch REME Assoc; CEng, FIMechE 1960, FBIM 1961, FRSA; *Recreations* sailing, walking; *Style—* Brig Clifford Gough, OBE, MBE; Adlestrop, St Florence, Tenby, Dyfed SA70 8LJ (☎ 0834 871 200)

GOUGH, Rt Rev Hugh Rowlands; CMG (1965), OBE (Mil 1945), TD (1945); s of Rev Charles Massey Gough (d 1943), and Lizzie Middleton (d 1946); *b* 19 Sept 1905; *Educ* Weymouth Coll, Trinity Coll Cambridge, London Coll of Divinity; *m* 1929, Hon Madeline Elizabeth, *qv*, da of 12 Baron Kinnaird; 1 da, *see* 4 Baron Swansea; *Career* chaplain London Rifle Bde (Western Desert, wounded) 1939-43, sr chaplain 1 Armoured Div 1943, dep asst chaplain gen 10 Corps (Italy) 1943-45 (despatches); vicar and rural dean Islington 1946-48, prebendary of St Paul's Cathedral 1948, archdeacon of West Ham 1948-58, bishop of Barking 1948-59, archbishop of Sydney and primate of Australia 1959-66; DL County of Essex 1952-59; Sub-Prelate OStJ 1959; *Clubs* National; *Style—* The Rt Rev Hugh Gough, CMG, OBE, TD, DD; Forge House, Over Wallop, Stockbridge, Hants (☎ 0264 781315)

GOUGH, John Osborne; MBE (1984); s of Reginald Osborne Gough (d 1972); *b* 26 Mar 1932; *Educ* Tonbridge, Bristol Univ (BA); *m* 1, 1958 (m dis 1983), Patricia Annette, da of Kenneth Blandford Lalonde; 2 children; m 2, 1983, Susan Mary, da of Michael Hornby and Nicolette, gda of 1 Earl of Dudley (Susan m 1, 1951 (m dis), Marquess of Blandford, now 11 Duke of Marlborough; 1 s (Marquess of Blandford, *qv*), 1 da (Lady Henrietta Gelber, *qv*); m 2, 1962, Alan Heber-Percy); *Career* chm: Kleeneze Hldgs 1987-, CBI (SW region) 1982-84; cncl memb RSA 1988-; *Recreations* fishing; *Style—* John Gough, Esq; Kleeneze Holdings plc, Hanham, Bristol; Church House, Little Coxwell, Faringdon, Oxon

GOUGH, Hon Mrs; Madeline Elizabeth; da of 12 Baron Kinnaird, KT, KBE, JP, DL (d 1972), and Frances, JP, da of Thomas Clifton, of Lytham Hall, Lancs; *b* 30 Jan 1908; *m* 1929, Rt Rev Hugh Gough, CMG, OBE, TD, DD, *qv*; 1 da, *see* 4 Baron Swansea; *Style—* The Hon Mrs Gough; Forge House, Over Wallop, Stockbridge, Hants (☎ Andover 0264 781315)

GOUGH, 5 Viscount (UK 1849); Sir Shane Hugh Maryon Gough; 5 Bt (UK 1842); also Baron Gough of Chinkangfoo and of Maharajpore and the Sutlej (UK 1846); s of 4 Viscount Gough, MC, JP, DL (d 1951, ggs of Field Marshal 1 Viscount, KP, GCB, GCSI, PC, whose full title was Viscount Gough of Goojerat in the Punjab and of the City of Limerick. His brilliant exploits in the two Sikh Wars resulted in the annexation of the Punjab to British India), by his w Margaretta Elizabeth, da of Sir Spencer Maryon-Wilson, 11 Bt; *b* 26 August 1941; *Educ* Winchester; *Career* late Lt Irish Gds; stockbroker with Laurence Keen & Co; memb Royal Co of Archers (Queen's Body Guard for Scotland); *Clubs* White's, Pratt's; *Style—* The Rt Hon the Viscount Gough; Keppoch Estate Office, Strathpeffer, Rosshire IV14 9AD (☎ (0997) 21224); 17 Stanhope Gdns, London SW7 5RQ; Laurence Keen & Co, 7 Moorgate, London EC2R 6AH (☎ 01 600 9100)

GOUGH, Thomas Hugh John; s of Cecil Ernest Freeman Gough, CMG, of Witham, Essex, and Gwendolen Lily Miriam, *née* Longman; *b* 7 June 1947; *Educ* King's Sch Rochester, N Western Poly (Dip Bus); *m* 2 Aug 1969, Beryl Ann Gough; 1 s (Michael b 26 Aug 1973), 1 da (Catie b 2 March 1976); *Career* musical dir Tower Theatre 1967-69, Kent Youth Orchestra (double bass) 1968, Hammersmith Philharmonic Orchestra (double bass) 1969-71, Newgate Singers (bass) 1970-72, dir Longmans Ltd Florists 1974-, chm Interflora Dist One 1982-84, Keyboard player with Vertically Horizontal 1986-, govr Parkhill Infant and Jr Sch's; sec St Laurence PCC 1986-, ctee memb London in Bloom 1988 (Judge, 1982); Freeman City of London 1974, Liveryman Worshipful Co of Gardeners 1976; *Books* How to Care for Palms and Ferns (1983), How to Care for Flowering Houseplants (1983), How to Care for More Flowering Houseplants (1983); *Recreations* music, cooking, gardening, active Christian; *Clubs* L'Ordre Mondial Des Gourmets Degustateurs; *Style—* Thomas Gough, Esq; 46 Holborn Viaduct, London EC1A 2PB (☎ 01 583 1440, fax 01 583 7881, telex 883497 FLOWER G)

GOULD, Bryan Charles; MP (Lab) Dagenham 1983-; s of Charles Terence Gould, of Hamilton, NZ; *b* 11 Feb 1939; *Educ* Auckland Univ, Balliol Coll Oxford; *m* 1967, Gillian Anne Harrigan; 1 s, 1 da; *Career* FO 1964-66, 2 sec Br Embassy Brussels 1966-68, fell Worcester Coll Oxford 1968-74, MP (Lab) Southampton Test Oct 1974-79 (contested same Feb 1974), PPS to Sec State: Trade 1975-76, Environment 1976-77; former memb Select Ctee on Euro Legislation, television journalist, oppn front bench spokesman Trade and Industry Nov 1983-; memb Shadow Cabinet 1986, campaign co-ordinater 1987, shadow sec of state Trade and Industry 1987; *Recreations* food, wine, gardening; *Style—* Bryan Gould, Esq, MP; House of Commons, London SW1

GOULD, Cecil Hilton Monk; s of Lt Cdr Rupert Thomas Gould (d 1948), of Ashtead, and Muriel Hilda, *née* Estall (d 1979); *b* 24 May 1918; *Educ* Westminster; *Career* WWII RAF VR : Pilot Offr 1940, Flying Offr 1941, Flt Lt 1942, Sqdn Ldr 1945; Nat Gallery: asst keeper 1946, dep keeper 1961, keeper and dep dir 1973-78; FRSA; *Books* Introduction to Italian Renaissance Painting (1957), Trophy of Conquest (1965), Leonardo da Vinci (1975), Correggio (1976), Bernini in France (1981); *Recreations* music, travel; *Clubs* Reform; *Style—* Cecil Gould, Esq; Jubilee House, Thorncombe, Chard, Somerset (☎ 046 030 530)

GOULD, Edward John Humphrey; s of Roland Akehurst Gould, of London, and Winifred Ruth Lee, *née* Dixon; *b* 31 Oct 1943; *Educ* St Edwards Oxford, St Edmund Hall Oxford Univ (BA, MA, DipEd); *m* 4 April 1970, Jennifer Jane, da of Ian Hunter Lamb of Edinburgh; 2 da (Karen Penelope b 1971, Nicola Mary b 1973); *Career* Harrow Sch: joined 1967, asst master head of geography dept 1974-79, housemaster 1979-83; headmaster Felsted Sch 1983-, memb: Ind Schs Curriculum Ctee 1985-, Common Entrance Ctee 1988-, Ct of Essex Univ 1985-, Br Atlantic Educn Ctee 1987-; govr : Heathfield Sch, Ascot & Orwell Park Sch Ipswich; Oxford rugby blue 1963-66 and swimming half blue 1965; rep GB rowing 1967; FRGS; *Recreations* music; *Clubs* East India, Devonshire Sports and Public Schools, Vincents (Oxford); *Style—* Edward Gould, Esq; Headmasters House, Felsted Sch, Dunmow, Essex (☎ 0371 820258)

GOULD, Maj-Gen John Charles; CB (1975); s of Alfred George Webb Gould (ka 1917), and Hilda, *née* Bewsey (d 1971); *b* 27 April 1915; *Educ* Brighton Hove and Sussex GS; *m* 1941, Mollie, da of Alan James Bannister (d 1963); 1 s (Robert), 1 da (Elizabeth); *Career* paymaster-in-chief and inspr of Army Pay Services 1972-75, ret 1975; *Recreations* golf; *Clubs* Lansdowne, Piltdown Golf; *Style—* Maj-Gen John Gould, CB; Squirrels Wood, Ringles Cross, nr Uckfield, E Sussex TN22 1HB (☎ 0825 4592)

GOULD, Jonathan; s of Cedric Gould (d 1956), of London, and Joan Wilson, *née* Spiers (d 1983); *b* 1 April 1952; *Educ* Hurstpierpoint Coll, Bristol Univ (LLB); *Career* Allen & Overy 1974-: articled 1974-76, asst slr 1976-81, ptnr 1982-, res ptnr Hong Kong 1988-; Freeman Worshipful Co of Slrs; memb: Law Soc, Law Soc of Hong Kong; *Style—* Jonathan Gould, Esq; 44 Halsey St, London SW3 2PT; 23A Century Tower, 1 Tregunter Path, Hong Kong (☎ 58400208); Allen & Overy, 9 Cheapside, London EC2V 6AD (☎ 01 248 9898, fax 01 236 2192, telex 8812801); Allen & Overy, 9th Floor, Three Exchange Sq, Hong Kong (☎ 58401282, fax 58400515, telex 68757)

GOULD, Kenneth; CBE (1973), TD; s of Capt William Charles Gould (d 1929), and Ethel Edna, *née* Board; *b* 5 Feb 1919; *Educ* Manchester GS, Victoria Univ Manchester (LLB); *m* 1946, Kathleen Ann, da of Dr Thomas O'Connell (d 1975); 1 s, 1 da; *Career* Lt-Col RA (TA), served Pacific, Burma; slr 1947; advocate and slr Singapore and Malaya 1948; chm and md Borneo Berhad/Inchcape Berhad 1966-73, chm Singapore Int CofC 1971-73; govr London Sch Oriental & African Studies; dir: Inchcape & Co 1971-81, Norwich Union Insur Gp, Goal Petroleum plc; *Recreations* shooting, golf, cricket; *Clubs* Oriental (chm), City of London, MCC, Singapore Cricket, Royal Island Country (Singapore), Tanglin (Singapore); *Style—* Kenneth Gould, Esq, CBE, TD; Tithe Barn, Courts Mount Rd, Haslemere, Surrey GU27 2PP (☎ (0428) 2879)

GOULD, Michael John Rodney; s of Capt Edward Russell Gould (d 1980), and Nancy Olivia Marion, *née* Johnson (d 1983); *b* 4 Feb 1930; *Educ* Summerfields Oxford, Wellington; *m* 1, 1951 (m dis 1968), Delia, da of Maj WE Johns (d 1960); 1 s (Nicholas b 18 April 1958); m 2, 25 Jan 1969, Valerie Mary, da of Maurice St John-Perry (d 1987); 2 s (Philip b 16 Dec 1970, Christopher b 16 Jan 1973); ; *Career* dir: BICC (Export) Ltd 1957-62, Nat Standard Co Ltd 1962-75, Michael Gould & Co Ltd 1980-, Bislex Engrg Ltd -; chm Kentredder Ltd 1975- 79, Eurowine Ltd (Jersey) 1986-, Bejex Electrical (Jersey) 1986-, Echo Industl & Consulting Servs Ltd (Jersey) 1987-, Med Equipment Ltd (Jersey) 1986-, Sense Engrg Ltd (Jersey) 1686-, Eurocables & Engrg (overseas) Co Ltd (Jersey) 1988-, Callon Electric Ltd (Jersey) 1986-, Techno Steel Wire & Engrg Ltd (Jersey) 1989-, Transelectric (Europe) Ltd (Jersey); *Recreations* Bibliophilism; *Style—* Michael Gould, Esq; The Oaks, St John, Jersey (☎ 0534 61142); PO Box 364 Jersey (☎ 0534 62320, fax 0534 64129, telex 4192113)

GOULD, Michael Philip; s of John Gould, of Clayhall, Ilford, Essex, and Amelia, *née* Cohen (d 1983); *b* 29 Jan 1947; *Educ* SW Essex Tech Coll; *m* 29 Aug 1971, Linda, da of Philip Keen, of Loughton, Essex; 2 da (Rosemary Julia b 1974, Jennifer Karen b 1977); *Career* sr ptnr Haslers, CA; memb Inst of Taxation; dir: Kaymere Ltd 1978, Brontree Ltd 1982, Scopeprop Ltd 1982, Tametree Properties Ltd 1982, Veryshield Ltd 1978; FCA; *Recreations* amateur pianist, music generally, theatre, good food, skiing, travel; *Clubs* Local Sports and Recreation Centre; *Style—* Michael P Gould, Esq; Laurels, Park Hill, Upper Park, Loughton, Essex IG10 4ES (☎ 508 1586); Johnston House, 8 Johnston Rd, Woodford Green, IG8 0XA (☎ 504 3344, car ☎ 0860 321837)

GOULD, Peter; s of Rupert Gould, and Vera Alberta Louise Gould; *b* 28 Mar 1945; *Educ* Priory Sch, Manchester Univ (LLB); *m* 2 Sept 1978, Diana Elizabeth, da of Allan Humphreys Hart; 2 da (Stephanie b 1981, Rosalind b 1983); *Career* slr; sr ptnr Gould Fowler & Co; clerk to govrs Priory Sch 1973-80; *Recreations* squash, reading, charitable activities; *Clubs* Rotary; *Style—* Peter Gould, Esq; Upton, Lyth Hill, Shrewsbury SY3 0BS (☎ 0743 874792); The Mill House, 139 Abbey Foregate, Shrewsbury SY2 6AP (☎ 0743 235161)

GOULD, Sidney; s of Jack Gould, of Birnbeck Court, Temple Fortune, and Rachel Gould, *née* Mintz (d 1950); *b* 1 Feb 1932; *Educ* Hinkley GS, Cambridge Univ (MA); *m* 13 June 1956, Jean, da of Simon Diamond, of Northways, Swiss Cottage; 3 s (Lawrence Jonathon b 1959, Simon Hilary b 1961, Matthew Stephen b 1971); *Career* dep chm and fin dir Tibbett & Britte Gp plc 1984-; dir Tibbett & Britte: Int Ltd, (NI) Ltd; dir: RDC Properties Ltd, Retail Consolidation Serv Ltd, Dartford Securities Ltd; fin dir SPD Gp 1969-84; *Recreations* golf, bridge; *Style—* Sidney Gould, Esq; 39 Pebworth Rd, Harrow, Middx HA1 3UD (☎ 01 422 6898); Tibbett & Britte Group plc, 691-697 High Rd, Tottham N17 9AZ (☎ 01 808 3040, telex 923700, fax 01 801 5682)

GOULD, Lady Sylvia Davina; *née* Brudenell-Bruce; da of 8 Marquess of Ailesbury; *b* 19 June 1954; *Educ* Lawnside, Redlynch Park; *m* 10 Oct 1987 Peter Malcolm Gould; *Style—* Lady Sylvia Gould; Springtide, La Pulente, St Brelade, Jersey, C I

GOULDING, Hon Mrs (Caroline Laurence Patricia); *née* Cavendish; da of 7 Baron Waterpark; *b* 3 Mar 1952; *Educ* French Lycée London, St Anns Oxford; *m* 1979, (Richard Michael) George Goulding; 1 s (Rory b 1983), 1 da (Laura b 1986); *Career* slr; *Recreations* antiques, travel, reading, skiing; *Style—* The Hon Mrs Goulding

GOULDING, Sir (Ernest) Irvine; s of Dr Ernest Goulding (d 1938); *b* 1 May 1910; *Educ* Merchant Taylors', St Catharine's Coll Cambridge (MA, Hon Fell 1971-); *m* 1935, Gladys Ethel (d 1981), da of Engr Rear-Adm Marrack Sennett (d 1935); 1 s (Marrack Irvine, *qv*), 1 da; *Career* served as Instr Offr (Lt-Cmdr) RN 1931-36, 1939-45; barr Inner Temple 1936, QC 1961; bencher Lincoln's Inn 1966-, tres 1983; judge of High Court (Chancery Div) 1971-85; *Clubs* Travellers'; *Style—* Sir Irvine Goulding; Penshurst, Wych Hill Way, Woking GU22 0AE (☎ 048 62 61012)

GOULDING, Sir (William) Lingard Walter; 4 Bt (UK 1904), of Millicent, Clane, co Kildare, and Roebuck Hill, Dundrum, co Dublin; er s of Sir Basil Goulding, 3 Bt (d 1982), and Hon Lady Goulding, *qv*. Sir Lingard is tenth in descent from William Goulding, who arrived in Ireland as a member of Oliver Cromwell's army; *b* 11 July 1940; *Educ* Winchester, Trinity Coll Dublin; *Heir* yr bro, Timothy Adam Goulding (b 1945, educated Winchester, m 1971 Patricia Mohan, of Dublin); *Career* formerly with Conzinc Rio Tinto of Aust; former mangr Rionore; racing driver; headmaster Headfort Sch 1977- (asst master 1974-76); *Style—* Sir Lingard Goulding, Bt; Dargle Cottage, Enniskerry, Co Wicklow, Eire

GOULDING, Marrack Irvine; CMG (1983); s of Sir (Ernest) Irvine Goulding, *qv*, and

Gladys Ethel, *née* Sennett (d 1981); *b* 2 Sept 1936; *Educ* St Paul's, Magdalen Coll Oxford (BA); *m* 1961, Susan Rhoda, da of Air Marshal Sir John D'Albiac, KCVO, KBE, CB, DSO (d 1963); 2 s, 1 da; *Career* HM Dip Serv 1959-85; serv Lebanon, Kuwait, London, Libya, Egypt, London (priv sec to Min State FCO, seconded Cabinet Off CPRS), Portugal, UN (New York); ambass to Angola and (concurrently but non-resident) to Sao Tome and Principe 1983-85, UN Secretariat 1986-, under sec gen for special political affrs UN, New York 1986-; *Recreations* travel, bird-watching; *Clubs* Royal Over-Seas League; *Style—* Marrack Goulding, Esq, CMG; 82 Claverton St, London SW1V 3AX (☎ 01 834 3046); 40 East 61st St, NY, NY 10021, USA (☎ 212 935 6157)

GOULDING, Timothy Adam; s of Sir (William) Basil Goulding, 3 Bt (d 1982), and Hon Lady Goulding, *qv*; hp of bro, Sir (William) Lingard Goulding, 4 Bt; *b* 1945; *m* 1971, Patricia Mohan, of Dublin; *Style—* Timothy Goulding, Esq; Dargle Cottage, Enniskerry, Co Wicklow

GOULDING, Hon Lady (Valerie Hamilton); *née* Monckton; da of 1 Viscount Monckton of Brenchley, GCVO, KCMG, MC, PC, QC (d 1965); *b* 1918; *Educ* National Univ of Ireland; *m* 28 Aug 1939, Wing Cdr Sir (William) Basil Goulding, 3 Bt (d 1982); 3 s (Sir Lingard G, 4 Bt, *qv*; Timothy b 1945; Hamilton Paddy b 1947); *Career* ATAS 1941-45, late Subaltern WRAC (Reserve); stood as Fianna Fail candidate for Dun Laoghaire for Dail Gen Election 1982 (former senator of Republic of Ireland); chm Central Remedial Clinic Ireland; fndr memb: Nat Rehabilitation Bd, Union of Voluntary Orgns for the Handicapped; memb: bd of govrs St Patrick's Hosp, mgmnt ctee Mater Hosp, advsy ctee American/Ireland Fund; dir Ansbacher Merchant Bank Ireland; Hon LLD NIU; Dame of Honour and Devotion SMO Malta; *Style—* The Hon Lady Goulding; Dargle Lodge, Enniskerry, Co Wicklow; Central Remedial Clinic, Penny Ansley Memorial Building, Vernon Avenue, Clontarf, Dublin 3 (☎ 332206)

GOUMAL, Jose Luis; s of Gregorio Goumal, of London and Barcelona, and Ana, *née* Jimenez; *b* 5 Jan 1946; *Educ* St Michaels and Acland (UK), Don Manuel (Spain); *m* 1, 17 Sept 1966, Madeleine, da of Edward Raymond Yescombe, MBE, of Bedfordshire; 1 da (Amanda b 1967); m 2, 1 March 1978, Sandie Bennett, da of Joseph Edward Bennett (d 1981), of Buckinghamshire; 2 s (Jamie b 1978, Dominic b 1980); *Career* CA; princ Anderson Goumal & Co, ptnr Anderson Shaw & Co; dir: Sanchez Fin Servs Ltd, Atext Ltd, Counthurst Ltd, LBJ Conslts Ltd, Film Fin and Devpt Ltd, Voices Dance Co; FCA, FCCA, FBIM; *Recreations* music, the arts, golf, country walks, work; *Style—* Jose L Goumal, Esq; Clive Court, Maida Vale, London W9; 169-173 Regent Street, London W1 (☎ 01 439 1371, telex 265951 (GOUMAL G), fax 01 439 4108)

GOURIET, Maj John Prendergast; s of Sqdn Ldr Alfred (Wings) William Edward Gouriet, RFC, RAF (d 1973), of Luxborough, Som, and Mary Douglas, *née* Prendergast (d 1977); *b* 1 June 1935; *Educ* Charterhouse, RMA Sandhurst, RMC Shrivenham and Staff Coll Camberley; *m* 4 April 1963, Sarah Julia Wheate, da of Maj Frank Henry Wheate Barnett (ka Dunkirk); 3 s (James Edward Frank b 1966, Michael David b 1967, Rupert John b 1969); *Career* 15/19 Hus, S/Ldr and Ops Offr NATO 1956-70, CO 2 i/c Somaliland Scouts 1959-60, Adj Trucial Oman Scouts 1961-63, Staff GSO 3 Intelligence, dir of Ops Borneo 1965-66, DAA & QMG MOD (Ops and Plans) 1971-72; dir Nat Assoc for Freedom 1975-78, co dir Conslt Wild Life Conservation Project (USA); dir: Park Air Travel Ltd, Gtr Joynson Ltd; chm Freedom in Action, PR dir CHREST (charitable res and film making on christian origins), memb Govt Int Policy Forum (US think tank); hon memb: Inst of Econ Affrs, Nat Right to Work Ctee (US), Colditz Soc; lectr; Polish Gold Cross; *Books* incl Checkmate Mr President; *Recreations* all forms of sport, hunting, polo, racing, fishing, mountaineering, big game hunting, stalking; *Style—* Maj John Gouriet; Upper Enham House, nr Andover, Hants (☎ 0264 51495);

GOURLAY, Gen Sir (Basil) Ian (Spencer); KCB (1973), OBE (1956, MBE 1948), MC (1944); s of Brig K I Gourlay, DSO, OBE, MC (d 1970); *b* 13 Nov 1920; *Educ* Eastbourne Coll; *m* 1948, Natasha, da of late Col Dimitri Zinovieff, and Princess Elisaveta Galitzine; 1 s, 1 da; *Career* cmmnd RM 1940, Capt 1949, Maj 1956, Lt-Col 1963, CO 42 Commando 1963, Col 1965, actg Brig 1966, cdr 3 Commando Bde RM 1966, Maj-Gen 1968, cdr Trg Gp RM 1968-71, Lt-Gen 1971, Gen 1973, Cmdt-Gen RM 1971-75, ret; dir-gen Utd World Colleges 1975-; *Clubs* MCC, Army & Navy; *Style—* Gen Sir Ian Gourlay, KCB, OBE, MC; c/o Lloyds Bank Ltd, 15 Blackheath Village, London SE3

GOURLAY, Hon Mrs (Patricia Drake); *née* Normand; da of Baron Normand (Life Peer) (d 1962); *b* 1917; *m* 1948, Douglas William Gourlay; *Style—* The Hon Mrs Gourlay; c/o Craigmuie, Moniaive, Thornhill, Dumfriesshire

GOURLAY, Dr Robert John; OBE (1983); s of Robert James Gourlay (d 1965), of Kilmacolm, Renfrewshire, Scotland, and Annie, *née* Patterson (d 1958); *b* 28 August 1912; *Educ* Morrison's Acad Crieff Perthsire, Glasgow Univ (MB ChB, MD) Leeds Univ (DPH), Oxford Univ (BSc); *m* 1, 1940 (m dis), Elizabeth Thackeray; 1 s (Robin b 1941), 1 da (Elizabeth b 1943); m 2, 1962, Joan Glenys (d 1985); m 3, 3 Aug 1986, Jacqueline Dorothy Juanita, da of Maj John Edward Power, (d 1938), of Camden to Bletchingly; *Career* supt Wharfedale Isolation Hosp 1939-46, dep MOH Oxford City 1948-51, asst SMO NW Metro Regnl Hosp Bd London 1951-57, sr lectr and head dept social and preventative med Univ of W Indies 1957-66, chief MO (formerly SMO) Bermuda 1966-82; memb (Bermuda): 1966-72 Kiwanis Club, Age Concern, Probus; memb: CGA, Oxford Soc, Local Cons Assoc; Freeman City of Glasgow (qua weaver) 1945; FFCM 1985, FRSH 1960; *Recreations* golf, woodwork, music; *Clubs* Bermuda Mid-Ocean GC 1970-85, The Naval; *Style—* Dr John Gourlay, OBE; Lyneham, High Ham, Langport, Somerset TA10 9DF (☎ 0458 250 091)

GOVAN, Sir Lawrence Herbert; s of Herbert Cyril Charles Govan (d 1957), and Janet Armour Govan, *née* Edmiston (d 1948); *b* 13 Oct 1919; *Educ* Christchurch Boys HS; *m* 1946, Clara, da of John Wilcox Hiscock, of Brigus Newfoundland (d 1964); 1 s (Herbert), 3 da (Edith, Elizabeth, Pamela); *Career* Mil Serv 1941-45, 2 Lt, served in Egypt and Italy; dep chm Lichfield NZ Ltd 1950-; dir: Utd Bldg Soc 1964-, Allied Mortgage Ctee Co Ltd 1986-, Superannuation Investmts Ltd 1974-, Reserved Bank of NZ 1973-85, Broadbank Corpn Ltd 1969-86, Mair Astley Ltd 1978-84; pres Canterbury Med Res Fndn 1985-; kt 1984; *Recreations* golf; *Style—* Sir Lawrence Govan; 11 Hamilton Avenue, Christchurch 4, New Zealand (☎ 519557); 179 Tuam Street, Christchurch, New Zealand; Box 1471 Christchurch

GOVETT, (Clement) John; s of Clement Charles Govett (d 1963), and Daphne Mary, *née* Norman (d 1964); *b* 26 Dec 1943; *Educ* St Paul's, Pembroke Coll Oxford (MA); *m* 14 June 1975, Rosalind Mary, da of Geoffrey Fawn (d 1988); 3 da (Helen b 1977, Sarah b 1978, Joanna b 1981); *Career* Price Waterhouse 1966-69, dir J Henry Schroder Wagg & Co Ltd 1980- (joined 1964); dir: Fundinvest plc 1981-, City & Commercial Investt Tst plc 1981-, Schroder Ventures Ltd 1985-, SIM Unit Tst Mgmnt Ltd 1987-; chm: Schroder Properties Ltd 1987-; dep chief exec: Schroder Investmt Mgmnt Ltd 1987-; *Recreations* bridge, tennis, gardening; *Style—* John Govett, Esq; 29 Marchmont Road, Richmond, Surrey TW10 6HQ (☎ 01 940 2876); 36 Old Jewry, London EC2 R8BS (☎ 01 382 6000)

GOVETT, Peter John; s of late Francis Govett; *b* 3 Sept 1935; *Educ* Harrow; *m* 1, 1964, Janet Adorian; 1 s, 1 da; m 2, 1978, Carolyn Odhams; *Career* commodity broker; dir Shearson Lehman Brothers Ltd; *Recreations* theatre; *Style—* Peter Govett, Esq; 114 Pavilion Rd, London SW1 (☎ 01 235 7381); The Old Chapel, Ashampstead Green, Newbury, Berks (☎ 063522 512)

GOVETT, William John Romaine; s of John Ramaine Govett, and Anglea Mostyn, *née* Pritchard; *b* 11 August 1937; *Educ* Sandroyd, Gordonstoun; *m* 1, (m dis 1970), Mary Hays; 2 s (Charles b 20 March 1965, Alexander b 3 May 1967), 1 da (Laura b 12 Dec 1968); m 2, 1970, Penelope Ann Irwin; 1 s (Romaine b 4 Jan 1973); *Career* Nat Serv cmmnd Royal Scots Greys; chm John Govett and Co Ltd 1974-87 (dep chm 1986-); numerous dirs incl: Legal & Gen Gp plc 1972-, Basinghall Securities Ltd 1975-, Gen Overseas Investmts Ltd 1975-, Govett Equity TST LTD 1975-, Govett Strategic Investmts Tst plc 1975-, Scottish Eastern Investmt Tst plc 1977-, Corney & Barrow Ltd 1979-, Govett Atlantic Investmt Tst plc 1979-, Energy & Resources Int Ltd 1981-, Union Jack Oil Co Ltd 1981-, LEP Gp plc 1983-, Investors in Indust Gp plc 1984-, CIN Mgmnt Ltd 1985-, Berkeley Atlantic Income Ltd 1986-, Berkeley Govett & Co Ltd 1986-, Govett American Endeavour Fund Ltd 1988-, Ranger Oil (UK) Ltd 1988-; *Recreations* modern art, fishing; *Style—* William Govett, Esq; 62 Glebe Place, London SW3 5JB; Fosbury Manor, Marlborough, Wilts SN8 3NJ; John Govett & Co Ltd, Shackleton House, 4 Battle Bridge Lane, London SE1 2HR (☎ 01 378 7979, fax 01 638 6468, telex 884266)

GOW, Ian; TD (1970), MP (C) Eastbourne Feb 1974-; s of Dr Alexander Edward Gow (d 1952), of London; *b* 10 Feb 1937; *Educ* Winchester; *m* 1966, Jane Elizabeth Mary, yr da of Maj Charles Packe (ka 1944), and Hon Margaret, *née* Lane Fox, yst da of 1 Baron Bingley, PC; 2 s; *Career* serv 15/19 King's Royal Hussars, Brevet Major; slr 1962; PPS to PM (Rt Hon Margaret Thatcher) 1979-83, min housing and construction 1983-85, min of State Treasy 1985; *Recreations* cricket, tennis, gardening; *Clubs* MCC, Cavalry and Guards', Carlton, Pratt's, Beefsteak; *Style—* Ian Gow, Esq, TD, MP; 25 Chester Way, Kennington, London SE11 (☎ 01 582 6626); The Dog House, Hankham, Pevensey, E Sussex (☎ 0323 763316)

GOW, John Stobie; s of David Gow (d 1988), of Sauchie, Alloa, Scotland, and Ann Frazer, *née* Scott (d 1984); *b* 12 April 1933; *Educ* Alloa Acad, St Andrews Univ (BSc, PhD); *m* 29 Dec 1955, Elizabeth, da of James Henderson (d 1963), of Alloa; 3 s (Iain b 1958, Alan b 1961, Andrew b 1964); *Career* prodn mangr Chem Co of Malyasia 1966-68; ICI: res mangr agric div 1968-72, gen mangr catalysts agric div 1972-74, res dir organics div 1974-79, dep chm organics div 1979-84, md speciality chemicals 1984-86; non exec dir W & J Foster Ltd 1984; sec gen Royal Soc of Chem 1986-, cncl memb Fedn Euro Chem Socs, assessor SERC; elder Utd Reformed Church; FRSE 1978, FRSC 1986, FRSA; *Style—* John Gow, Esq; 19 Longcroft Ave, Harpenden, Herts AL5 2RD (☎ 05827 64889); Royal Society of Chemistry, Burlington House, Piccadilly, London (☎ 01 437 8656, fax 01 437 8883, telex 268001)

GOW, Gen Sir (James) Michael; GCB (1982, KCB 1979); s of J C Gow (d 1927); *b* 3 June 1924; *Educ* Winchester; *m* 1946, Jane Emily, da of Capt Mason H Scott, RN (ret); 1 s, 4 da; *Career* served WWII 2 Lt Scots Gds, Lt-Col cmdg 2 Bn Scots Gds 1964-67, Brig cmdg 4 Gds Bde 1967-70, Brig-Gen Staff (Intelligence & Security) HQ BAOR 1971-73, Col Cmdt Intelligence Corps 1972-86, GOC 4 Div 1973-75, dir Army Training MOD 1975-78, GOC Scotland and Govr Edinburgh Castle 1979-80, C-in-C BAOR and cdr NATO N Army Gp 1980-83; ADC Gen to HM The Queen 1981-84; Cmdt RCDS 1984-86; Brig Queen's Body Guard for Scotland (Royal Co of Archers); cmmr British Scouts Western Europe 1980-83, vice-pres Royal Patriotic Fund Corpn 1984-; pres: Royal British Legion Scot, Earl Haig Fund Scot 1986-; *Recreations* sailing, travel, music, reading; *Clubs* Pratt's, New (Edinburgh); *Style—* Gen Sir Michael Gow, GCB

GOW, Sheriff of South Strathclyde at Ayr Neil; QC (Scot 1970); s of Donald Gow, of Glasgow; *b* 24 April 1932; *Educ* Merchiston Castle Sch, Univ of Edinburgh, Univ of Glasgow (MA, LLB); *m* 1959, Joanna, da of Cdr S D Sutherland, of Edinburgh; 1 s; *Career* Capt Intelligence Corps (BAOR); Carnegie scholar in History of Scots Law 1956, advocate 1957-76, Standing Cncl to Miny of Soc Security (Scot) 1964-70, Contested (C) Kircaldy Burghs Gen Elections 1964 and 1966, Edinburgh East 1970, memb regnl cncl Scottish Con Assoc, Sheriff of Lanarkshire 1971; pres Auchinteck Boswell Soc; FSA (Scot); *Books* A History of Scottish Statutes (1959), An Outline of Estate Duty in Scotland (jt ed 1970), and numerous articles and broadcasts on legal topics and Scottish affairs; *Recreations* golf, books, antiquities; *Clubs* Prestwick GC, Western (Glasgow); *Style—* Sheriff Gow, QC; Old Auchenfail Hall, By Mauchline, Ayrshire (☎ 0290 50822)

GOWAN, Lt-Col Christopher D'Olier; s of Sir Hyde Gowan, KCSI, CIE (d 1938), and Edna, *née* Brown (d 1968); *b* 4 August 1910; *Educ* Rugby, Hertford Coll Oxford; *m* 4 Aug 1933, Margaret Anne, da of George Smith McNair (d 1943), of NZ; 3 da (Elizabeth Ann b 1934, Juliet Mary b 1935, Cecilia Margaret b 1941); *Career* schmaster, Eton Coll, housemaster 1947-64, hd of Modern Language Dep 1959-69; hon Lt-Col; *Recreations* gardening, fell walking; *Style—* Lt-Col Christopher Gowan; Wood Cottage, Newby Bridge, Ulverston, Cumbria LA1 8NP (☎ Newby Bridge 31275)

GOWANS, Hon Sir (Urban) Gregory; s of late James, and Hannah Theresa Gowans; *b* 9 Sept 1904; *Educ* Christian Brothers Coll, Univ of WA, Univ of Melbourne (BA, LLB); *m* 1937, Mona Ann Freeman; 1 s, 4 da; *Career* barr Vic 1928, QC 1949, judge of Supreme Court of Vic 1961-76; kt 1974; *Recreations* bush walking; *Style—* The Hon Sir Gregory Gowans; 68 Studley Park Rd, Kew, Melbourne, Vic 3101, Australia (☎ (861) 8714)

GOWANS, Sir James Learmonth; CBE (1971); s of John Gowans and Selma Josefina Ljung; *b* 7 May 1924; *Educ* Trinity Sch Croydon, King's Coll Hosp Med Sch, Lincoln Coll Oxford, Pasteur Inst Paris, Exeter Coll Oxford; *m* 1956, Moyra Leatham; 1 s, 2 da; *Career* dep chm MRC 1978-87 (memb 1965-69, assessor 1973-75, sec 1977-87, hon dir MRC Cellular Immunology Unit 1963-77); memb advsy bd for Res Cncls 1977-, FRCP, FRS (Prof 1962-77, vice pres and memb Cncl 1973-75), Hon MD Edinburgh and Southampton, Hon ScD Yale, Hon DSc Chicago, Birmingham and Rochester New York, Royal Soc Royal Medal, Foreign Associate US Nat Acad of Sciences, fell St Catherine's Coll Oxford; hon fell Exeter Coll Oxford 1983; hon fell Lincoln Coll, Oxford 1984; kt 1981; *Style—* Sir James Gowans, CBE; 75 Cumnor Hill, Oxford OX2 9HX

GOWARD, Russell John; s of Alan John Goward, of Canberra, and Betty Helen, *née* Fiedler; *b* 15 Jan 1954; *Educ* Aust Nat Univ; *m* 18 Dec 1976, Catherine Ann, da of Bailey Thomas Walsh, of New South Wales; 1 s (Richard John b 1986), 2 da (Elizabeth Jane b 1980, Alison Louise b 1981); *Career* chief exec Industl Equity Gp Ltd 1983-86; chm and md: Westmex Gp Ltd 1986-, Charterhall plc 1986-; chm Tandem Shoes Ltd 1988-; *Recreations* deer farming, motor cars, tennis; *Style—* Russell Goward, Esq; Charterhall plc, Mezzanine Floor, 105 Victoria Street, London SW1E (☎ 01 834 8644, fax 01 630 1813, telex 27600)

GOWENLOCK, Prof Brian Glover; CBE (1986); s of Harry Hadfield Gowenlock (d 1976), of Oldham, and Hilda, *née* Glover (d 1977); *b* 9 Feb 1926; *Educ* Hulme GS Oldham, Univ of Manchester (BSc, MSc, PhD), Univ of Birmingham (DSc); *m* 24 July 1953, Margaret Lottie, da of Luther John Davies (d 1981), of Swansea; 1 s (Stephen b 1958), 2 da (Cathren b 1959, Judith b 1964); *Career* lectr in chem Univ Coll of Swansea Univ of Wales 1951-55 (asst lectr 1948-51), sr lectr in chem Univ of Birmingham 1964-66 (lectr 1955-64); Heriot-Watt Univ Edinburgh: prof of chem 1966-, dean faculty of sci 1987-(and 1969-72); Erskine visiting fell Univ of Canterbury NZ 1976; memb Univ grants ctee 1976-85 (vice chm 1983-85); local preacher Methodist Church 1948-; FRSC 1966, FRSE 1969; *Books* Experimental Methods in Gas Reactions (with Sir Harry Melville, 1964), First Year at The University (with James C Blackie, 1964); *Recreations* genealogy, foreign travel; *Style—* Prof Brian Gowenlock, CBE; 49 Lygon Rd, Edinburgh EH16 5QA (☎ 031 667 8506); Dept of Chemistry, Heriot-Watt Univ, Edinburgh EH14 4AS (☎ 031 449 5111)

GOWER, David Ivon; s of Richard Hallam Gower (d 1973), and Sylvia Mary, *née* Ford (d 1986); *b* 1 April 1957; *Educ* King's Sch Canterbury, Univ Coll London; *Career* cricketer, Leicestershire and England, Capt England 1984-86 and 1988- ;7000 test runs including 14 test centuries; dir: David Gower Promotions Ltd; dir: Gelling Travel (IOM) Ltd, Ten Tenths Travel Int Ltd; *Recreations* tennis, golf, skiing, Cresta run; *Clubs* St Moritz Tobagganing, East India; *Style—* David Gower, Esq; Leicestershire CCC, Grace Road, Leicester LE2 8AD (☎ 0533 832128)

GOWER, His Hon Judge John Hugh; QC (1967); s of Henry John Gower, JP (d 1951), of Penbury, Kent, and Edith, *née* Brooks (d 1926); *b* 6 Nov 1925; *Educ* The Skinners' Co Sch Tunbridge Wells, Inns of Court Sch of Law; *m* 20 Feb 1960, Shirley Maureen, da of William Henry Darbourne (d 1977), of Carshalton Beeches, Surrey; 1 s (Peter b 1960), 1 da (Anne b 1962); *Career* RA Serv Corps 1945-48, Staff Sgt; barr Inner Temple 1948, circuit judge 1971-, resident judge and liaison judge East Sussex Crown Courts 1986-; pres: Kent Assoc of Parish Cncllrs 1962-71, Tunbridge Wells and DC of Voluntary Serv 1974-; vice-pres Kent Cncl of Voluntary Serv 1971-86, chm Southdown and Eridge Hunt 1985-; *Recreations* fishing, fox-hunting, gardening; *Style—* His Hon Judge Gower, QC; The Coppice, Lye Green, Crowborough, E Sussex TN6 1UY (☎ 08926 4395); The Crown Court, Lewes, Sussex

GOWER-SMITH, Nicholas Mark; s of Charles Samuel Smith (d 1983), of Tunbridge Wells, and Margaret Brenda, *née* Isaac; *b* 20 Mar 1955; *Educ* The Skinners' Sch Tunbridge Wells; *m* 25 July 1987, Christine Lorraine, da of Leslie Frank George Allan, (d 1981); *Career* CA; sr ptnr Norman Cox & Ashby 1984-, proprietor Gower-Smith & Co 1984-; ACA 1981; *Recreations* music, photography, philately; *Clubs* Royal Cwlth Soc; *Style—* Mark Gower-Smith, Esq; Grosvenor Lodge, 72 Grosvenor Rd, Tunbridge Wells, Kent TN1 2AZ (☎ 0892 22551)

GOWING, Prof Sir Lawrence Burnett; CBE (1952); s of Horace Burnett Gowing; *b* 21 April 1918; *Educ* Leighton Pk; *m* 1, 1952 (m dis 1967), Julia Frances, widow of Hon Stephen Tomlin (d 1937, yr s of Baron Tomlin, Life Peer) and da of Oliver Strachey, CBE (d 1960, 3 s of Lt-Gen Sir Richard Strachey), by his 1 w Ruby, da of Julius Mayer; m 2, Jennifer Akam, da of Sydney Herbert Wallis; 3 da; *Career* painter and author; former pupil of William Coldstream; works exhibited nat and int, incl Tate Gallery, Ashmolean Museum (Oxford); prof fine art Durham Univ and princ King Edward VII Sch of Art Newcastle-upon-Tyne 1948-58, princ Chelsea Sch Art 1958-65, keeper Br Collection and dep dir Tate Gallery 1965-67, prof fine art Leeds Univ 1967-75, Slade Prof Fine Art UCL 1975-; adjunct prof history of art Univ of Pennsylvania 1977-, memb Arts Cncl and dep chm Art Panel 1977-81 (previously 1970-72); tstee: Nat Portrait Gallery 1960-, Br Museum 1976-81; Hon DLitt Heriot-Watt 1980, Hon LLD Leicester 1983; kt 1982; *Publications include* Renoir (1947), Vermeer (1952 and 1961), Goya (1965), Turner: Imagination and Reality (1966), Matisse (1979); *Style—* Prof Sir Lawrence Gowing, CBE; 49 Walham Grove, London SW6 (☎ 01 385 5941)

GOWLLAND, Robin Anthony Blantyre; s of Reginald Blantyre-Gowlland (d 1974), of London and Hawkley, Hants, and Pauline, *née* Broomfield (d 1981); *b* 6 Sept 1932; *Educ* RNC Dartmouth and Greenwich, IMEDE Lausanne (Dip), Harvard Business Sch (MBA); *Career* RN 1946-62, served UK, Med, Far East and Suez Campaign 1956 (ret as Lt); mgmnt conslt and dir Egon Zehnder Int 1969- (md UK 1969-81, chm 1981-); chm: Southampton Cable 1986-, Wandsworth Cable 1986-, ERI 1973-, ABGH 1979-, G & B Media 1988-, Fairway Pubns 1989-; sr res fell Cramfield Inst of Technol 1964-66; sr conslt engrg ptnr Harbridge House Inc 1966-69, vice-chm London Fedn of Boys Clubs 1976- (cncl memb Nat Assoc), dep chm Christian Assoc of Business Execs (chm 1976-80), chm Downside Settlement 1983-, (hon sec 1966-73, vice chm 1973-83); KSG 1983, KHS 1985; Hon Lt Cl Alabama State Militia (USA), Hon Citizen City of Mobile (USA); *Recreations* cricket, squash, real tennis, sailing, travel, theatre, art; *Clubs* Brooks's, Royal Yacht Sqdn, MCC, Naval and Military, Royal Thames, Anglo-Belgian, Army and Navy, Jesters, Harvard (NY); *Style—* Robin A B Gowlland, Esq; Tann House, Crondall, Hants GU10 5QU (☎ 0252 850700); 4 Sloane Gate Mansions, London SW1X 9AG (☎ 01 730 2121); Egon Zehnder International, Devonshire House, Mayfair Place, London W1X 5FH (☎ 01 493 3882)

GOWRIE, 2 Earl of (UK 1945); Alexander Patrick Greysteil Hore Ruthven; PC (1984); also Baron Ruthven of Gowrie (UK 1919), Baron Gowrie (UK 1935), and Viscount Ruthven of Canberra (UK 1945); in remainder to Lordship of Ruthven of Freeland (officialy recognised in the name of Ruthven by Warrant of Lord Lyon 1957); s of Maj Hon Patrick Hore Ruthven (s of 1 Earl of Gowrie, VC, GCMG, CB, DSO, PC, who was govr-gen and C-in-C of Australia 1936-44 and 2 s of 9 Lord Ruthven of Freeland); suc gf 1955; *b* 26 Nov 1939; *Educ* Eton, Balliol Coll Oxford, Harvard; *m* 1, 1962 (m dis 1974), Xandra, yr da of Col Robert Bingley, CVO, DSO, OBE; 1 s; m 2, 1974, Countess Adelheid, yst da of Count Fritz-Dietlof von der Schulenburg; *Heir* s, Viscount Ruthven of Canberra; *Career* former lectr and tutor: State Univ of New York, UCL, Harvard; Cons whip 1971-72, lord in waiting 1972-74, oppn spokesman Economic Affrs 1974-79; min of state; Dept of Employment 1979-81, Min of State NI Off 1981-83, Privy Cncl Office (and min for The Arts) 1983-84; chllr of the Duchy of Lancaster (and min for The Arts) 1984-85; chm: Sotheby's Int 1985-86, Sotheby's UK 1987-; *Books* A Postcard from Don Giovanni 1971; jtly: The Genius of British Painting (1975), Derek Hill, An Appreciation (1985), The Conservative Opportunity (1976); *Style—* The Rt Hon the Earl of Gowrie, PC; House of Lords SW1

GOYDER, Daniel George; s of George Armin Goyder, CBE, of Long Melford, Suffolk, and Rosemary Bernard Goyder; *b* 26 August 1938; *Educ* Rugby, Cambridge Univ (MA, LLB), Harvard Law Sch (LLM); *m* 28 July 1962, Jean Mary, da of Kenneth Godfrey Arthur Dohoo (d 1944) of Malaysia; 2 s (Andrew b 1968, Richard b 1970), 2 da (Joanna b 1963, Elizabeth b 1965); *Career* admitted slr 1962, cnslt Birketts Ipswich 1983- (ptnr 1968-83), pt/t lectr law dept Essex Univ 1981-; memb Monopolies and Mergers Cmmn 1980-, chm St Edmundury and Ipswich Diocesan Bd of Fin 1977-85; memb Law Soc; *Books* The Antitrust Laws of the USA (with Sir Alan Neale third edn 1980), EEC Competition Law (1988); *Recreations* sport, choral singing; *Clubs* Ipswich and Suffolk (Ipswich); *Style—* Daniel Goyder, Esq; Manor Hse, Old London Rd, Capel St Mary, Ipswich, Suffolk (☎ 0473 310 583); Birketts Solictors, 20-28 Museum St, Ispwich (☎ 0473 232 300, fax 0473 230 524, telex 98597)

GOYMER, Andrew Alfred; s of Richard Kirby Goymer (d 1986), of Keston, Kent, and Betty Eileen, *née* Thompson; *b* 28 July 1947; *Educ* Dulwich Coll, Pembroke Coll Oxford (BA, MA); *m* 30 Sept 1972, Diana Mary, da of Robert Harry Shipway, MBE, of Heathfield, E Sussex; 1 s (Patrick b 1977), 1 da (Eleanor b 1980); *Career* barr Gray's Inn 1970, SE circuit 1972-, asst rec 1987-, admitted to bar NSW Aust 1988; Gerald Moody entrance scholar 1968, Holker sr exhibitioner 1970, Arden Atkin and Mould prizeman 1971; *Style—* Andrew Goymer, Esq; 6 Pump Court, Temple, London EC4Y 7AR (☎ 01 353 7242, fax 01 583 1667)

GRAAFF, David de Villiers; s and h of Sir de Villiers Graaff, 2 Bt, MBE; *b* 3 May 1940; *Educ* Diocesan Coll S Africa, Stellenbosch Univ, Grenoble Univ, Magdalen Coll Oxford; *m* 1969, Sally, da of Robin Williams; 3 s, 1 da; *Career* farmer Hex River; dir: Graaff's trust, Milnerton Estates, Deciduous Fruit Bd, MP Wynberg; *Recreations* tennis; *Clubs* West Province Sports, West Province Cricket, City and Civil Service; *Style—* David Graaff, Esq; PO Box 1, Hex River, Cape, South Africa 6855 (☎ 02322 8708)

GRAAFF, Sir de Villiers; 2 Bt (UK 1911), of Cape Town, Cape of Good Hope Province of Union of South Africa; MBE (1947); s of Sir David Pieter de Villiers Graaff, 1 Bt, sometime high cmmr for Union of S Africa in London, Cabinet minister and mayor of Cape Town (d 1931); *b* 8 Dec 1913; *Educ* Diocesan Coll Cape Town, Cape Town Univ (BA), Magdalen Coll Oxford, Leyden Univ Holland (BCL); *m* 1939, Ena, da of Frederick Voigt; 2 s, 1 da; *Heir* s, David de Villiers Graaff; *Career* war service in SA Forces 1941 (POW); advocate S Africa Supreme Ct 1938-, leader of the Oppn in SA 1957-77 (MP 1948-77); farmer of pedigree Friesian cattle; dir: Graaff's Trust, Southern Life, Milnerton Estates; Decoration for Meritorious Serv 1978; *Recreations* fishing, riding, cricket; *Clubs* Civil Service, Kelvin Grove, Western Province Cricket; *Style—* Sir de Villiers Graaff, Bt, MBE; De Grendel, Private Bag, GPO, Cape Town 8000, S Africa (☎ home 582068, office 466613)

GRABHAM, Anthony Herbert; *b* 19 July 1930; *Educ* St Cuthberts GS Newcastle-upon-Tyne, Durham Univ (MB, BS); *m* 1960, Eileen Pamela; *Career* conslt Surgn Kettering Gen Hosp 1965-; chm: jt consult ctee 1984-, BMA Cncl 1979-84; *Clubs* Army and Navy; *Style—* Anthony Grabham, Esq; Rothesay House, Headlands, Kettering, Northants NN15 6DG; BMA House, Tavistock Sq, London WC1 (☎ 01 387 4499)

GRABINER, Anthony Stephen; QC (1981); s of Ralph Grabiner (d 1985), and Freda, *née* Cohen; *b* 21 Mar 1945; *Educ* Central Fndn Boys' GS London, LSE, London Univ (LLB LLM); *m* 18 Dec 1983, Jane Aviva, da of Dr Benjamin Portnoy, of Hale, Cheshire; 1 s (Joshua b 1986); *Career* called to the Bar 1968 Lincoln's Inn; standing counsel to the DTI Export Credits Guarantee Dept (1976-81); jr counsel to the Crown (1978-81); *Books* Sutton & Shannon on Contracts (seventh edn 1970), Banking Documents: Encyclopedia of Forms and Precedents (1986); *Recreations* theatre, swimming; *Clubs* Garrick, MCC; *Style—* Anthony Grabiner, QC; 1 Essex Court, Temple, London EC4Y 9AR (☎ 01 583 2000)

GRABOWSKI, Stanislaw; s of Col Zygmunt Grabowski (Polish Army), MC, TD (d 1968), of Barons Court, London, and Anna, *née* Edemska (d 1959); *b* 6 Sept 1919; *Educ* Mil Academy (Poland), Cambridge Univ, Polytechnic Sch of Architecture (MA Cantab, Dip Arch); *m* 19 Sept 1948, Maria, da of Col Benedykt Chlusewicz (d 1951), Col Polish Army; 1 s (Marek Bohdan b 1948); *Career* Capt Polish Army CO Squadron of Tanks 1 Polish Armd Div 1944-45, France, Belgium, Holland and Germany; Platoon Cdr in France 1940; architect in private practice, conslt since 1986; FRIBA; Knight Order of Leopold 1946, Croix de Guerre 1946, War Cross 1944, Cross of Merit 1946 (TD); *Clubs* White Eagle; *Style—* Stanislaw Grabowski, Esq; 99 The Ridgeway, Gunnersbury Park, London W3 8LP (☎ 01 992 8196); 12 Sutton Row, London W1V 6AB (fax: 01 734 1793)

GRACEY, Howard; s of Charles Douglas Gracey (d 1968), and Margaret Gertrude Gracey; *b* 21 Feb 1935; *Educ* Birkenhead sch; *m* 8 June 1960, Pamela Jean, da of William Thomas Bradshow (d 1988); 1 s (Mark), 2 da (Kathryn, Rachel); *Career* Nat Serv 2 Lt RA 1959-61; Royal Insur Co 1953-69, consulting actuary and ptnr R Watson & Sons 1970-; pres Pensions Mgmnt Inst 1983-85; memb: General Synod C of E 1970-, C of E Pensions Bd 1970- (chm 1980-); Church Cmmr 1978-, tres and vice chm South American Missionary Soc 1975-; FIA 1959, FIAA 1982, FPMI 1977, ASA 1978; *Recreations* fell walking, photography; *Clubs* Army and Navy; *Style—* Howard Gracey, Esq; Timbers, Broadwater Rise, Guildford, Surrey GU1 2LA (☎ 0483 659 63); R Watson & Sons, Watson Ho, London Rd, Reigate, Surrey RH2 9PA (☎ 073 72 41144)

GRACEY, John Halliday; CB (1984); s of Halliday Gracey and Florence Jane, *née* Cudlipp; *b* 20 May 1925; *Educ* City of London Sch, Brasenose Coll Oxford (MA); *m* 1950, Margaret Procter; 3 s; *Career* served Army 1943-47; joined Inland Revenue 1950, HM Treasy 1970-73; dir: Gen (Mgmnt) 1981-85, Bd of Inland Revenue 1973-85; hon tres Nat Assoc for Care and Resettlement of Offenders 1987; *Recreations* walking, beekeeping; *Clubs* Reform; *Style—* John Gracey, Esq, CB; 3 Woodberry Down, Epping, Essex (☎ (0378) 72167)

GRACEY, Lionel Rodney Hubert; s of Dr Ivan Hubert Gracey, of 8 Clarendon Place, Leamington Spa, and Kathleen Gracey, *née* McCarthy (d 1984); *b* 31 July 1928; *Educ* Beaumont Coll, Jesus Coll Cambridge, St Bartholomew's Hosp (MA, MB, MChir (Cantab), FRCS (England)), FRCS (Edin); *m* 13 Feb 1971, Angela Mary Fleming, da of Edmund Henry Fleming (d 1972); 3 s (John b 1971, Charles b 1973, Thomas b 1982); 3 da (Emma b 1974, Laura b 1975, Sarah b 1977); *Career* conslt surgn: Royal Free Hosp, King Edward VII Hosp for Offrs, Hosp of St John and St Elizabeth; hon consulting surgn, Italian Hosp; *Recreations* golf, tennis, skiing; *Clubs* Royal and Ancient, Sunningdale, Hawks, Ski (GB); *Style—* Lionel Gracey, Esq; 149 Harley St, London W1N 2DH (☎ 01 935 4444)

GRACEY, Peter Bosworth Kirkwood; s of Lt-Col H M K Gracey (d 1972), of Tonbridge, Kent, and E M Gracey (d 1946); *b* 12 Dec 1921; *Educ* Wellington Coll, Brasenose Coll Oxford (MA); *m* 1, June 1953 (m dis 1982), Ruth Mary, da of Charles Young (d 1960), of Berrow Manor, Burnham-on-Sea, Somerset; 1 s (Guy b 1958), 2 da (Sylvia b 1960, Pippa b 1962); m 2, May 1982, Jane (d 1987), da of Vernan Owen (d 1980), of Mockbeggar, Playden, Rye, E Sussex; m 3, 4 Feb 1989, Andra Julia Mary, da of Capt A C A C Duckworth, DSO, DSC, RN (d 1987), of Myskyns, Ticehurst, E Sussex; *Career* WWII cmmnd RE 1941, 2 Lt 280 Parachute Sqdn RE, 81 Inf Div HQ, West African Engrs RWAFF, Capt RE OC Gold Coast Field Co 1946; Tate & Lyle Ltd 1948-62 (London mangr tport 1955), gen mangr and dir Sturgeons Tport 1963, gen mangr Marley Tile Tport 1968, distribution dir Lyons Bakery Ltd 1973, dir Bosworth & Co Ltd (music publishers) 1973, Hill Samuel Investmt Servs Ltd; memb ctee Nat Freight Tport Assoc 1976; pres Oxford and Cambridge Golfing Soc 1987- (hon sec 1959-64, capt 1970-71); Freeman City of London 1970, memb Worshipful Co of Wax Chandlers 1970; *Recreations* golf, sport; *Clubs* Naval and Military, Royal and Ancient GC; *Style—* Peter Gracey, Esq; The Oast House, Houghton Green Lane, Playden, Rye, E Sussex TN31 7PJ (☎ 079 78 269)

GRADE, Baron (Life Peer UK 1976); Lew Grade; s of Isaac and Olga Winogradsky; bro of Lord Delfont; *b* 25 Dec 1906; *Educ* Rochelle St Sch London; *m* 1942, Kathleen, da of John Moody; 1 s (adopted); *Career* jt md Lew and Leslie Grade to 1955; pres ATV 1977-82, chm and chief exec: ACC 1973-82, Embassy Communications Int 1982-; chm and md ITC Entertainment 1958-82; chm: Bentray Investmts 1979-82, Stoll Moss Theatres 1969-82, ACC Enterprises Inc 1973-82, chm and chief exec The Grade Co 1985-; Kt Cdr of St Silvester; OStJ; kt 1969; *Style—* The Rt Hon the Lord Grade; Embassy House, 3 Audley Sq, London W1Y 5DR

GRADE, Michael Ian; s of late Leslie Grade and n of Lords Grade and Delfont; *b* 8 Mar 1943; *Educ* St Dunstan's Coll; *m* 1967 (m dis 1981), Penelope Jane, *née* Levinson; 1 s, 1 da; m 2, 1982, Sarah Jane, *née* Lawson, *qv*, yst da of Lt-Col 5 Baron Burnham, JP, *qv*, of Hall Barn, Beaconsfield, Bucks; *Career* trainee journalist Daily Mirror 1960 (sports columnist 1964-66), theatrical agent Grade Orgn 1966, jt md London Mgmnt and Representation 1969-73, dep controller of progs LWT 1973 (dir of Progs and bd memb 1977-81), pres Embassy TV Los Angeles 1982-83, chm and chief operating offr The Grade Co Ind TV and Motion Picture Prodn Co 1983-84, controller BBC 1 1984-86, dir of progs BBC TV 1986 -87, chief exec Channel 4 1987-; memb cncl LAMDA 1981-; *Recreations* entertainment; *Style—* Michael Grade, Esq; Channel Four Television, 60 Charlotte St, London W1P 2AX (☎ 01 631 4444)

GRADE, Paul Nicholas; only child (adopted) of Baron Grade; *b* 1952; *m* Lisa, *née* Pearce; 1 s (Daniel b 1978), 1 da (Georgina b 1980); *Career* dir The Ivy Restaurant; book and record publisher; *Style—* Paul Grade, Esq; c/o ATV House, Great Cumberland Place, W1

GRADE, Hon Mrs (Sarah Jane); *née* Lawson; da of Lt-Col 5 Baron Burnham, JP, DL, *qv* ; *b* 7 Oct 1955; *Educ* Heathfield; *m* 1982, as his 2 w, Michael Ian Grade, *qv*; *Career* slr Macfarlanes 1976-80, agent Curtis Brown 1980-82, vice-pres Devpt TV D L Taffner Ltd 1982-84, pres Taft Entertainment/Lawson Group 1985-; *Recreations* theatre; *Style—* The Hon Mrs Grade; 1300 Sierra Alta Way, Los Angeles, California 90069, USA (☎ 213 859 4822); Wycombe End House, Beaconsfield, Bucks HP9 1NB; 1st Floor, 35 Piccadilly, London W1 (☎ 01 439 8985, telex 23116); 10th 10960 Wilshire Blvd, Los Angeles, California 90024 (☎ 213 208 2000, telex 677462 TECO LSA)

GRADIDGE, (John) Roderick Warlow; s of Brig John Henry Gradidge, OBE, QVO, Corps of Guides (Cavalry), and Lorraine Beatrice Warlow, *née* Warlow-Harry; *b* 3 Jan 1929; *Educ* Stowe, Arch Assoc Sch of Arch; *Career* Master Art Workers Guild 1987 (hon-sec 1978-84), vice-chm The Thirties Soc, tstee Lutyens Tst Ctee Vict Soc; as architect specialises in repair, alteration and additions to major country houses particularly work of Edwin Lutyens and contemporaries, recently completed interior Nat Portrait Gallery, Bodelwyddan Castle, Clwyd and extension to St Edmund's Coll Cambridge; property corres The Field 1984-87, contrib Country Life; *Books* Dream Houses — The Edwardian Ideal (1980), Edwin Lutyens — Architect Laureate (1981); *Recreations* enjoyment of early twentieth century architecture and appreciation of its potential; *Clubs* Art Workers Guild; *Style—* Roderick Gradidge, Esq; 21 Elliott Rd, London W4 1PF (☎ 01 995 6490, fax 01 995 6490)

GRADON, Air Cdre Oswald; CBE (1970, OBE 1951); s of James W Gradon, (d 1939) of Hetton-le-Hole, Co Durham, and Alice, *née* Robinson (d 1916); *b* 8 Nov 1915; *Educ* Houghton Sch, RAF Staff Coll, Joint Servs Staff Coll; *m* 1955, Judith, da of Wilfrid Foster; 2 s; *Career* dir: external liaison RCAF 1944-46, RAF personnel policy 1958-61, Station Cmd RAF Kenley 1962-64, Cmd Accountant Maintenance and Tech Trg Cmd 1964-66; Dir of RAF Manning 1967-71; bursar Oundle Sch 1971-78; FCA, FIPM; *Recreations* tennis and real tennis; *Clubs* RAF; *Style—* Air Cdre Oswald Gradon, CBE; 34 Thornton Court, Thornton Rd, Girton, Cambridge CB3 0N5 (☎ 0223 277201)

GRAESSER, Col Sir Alastair Stewart Durward; DSO (1945), OBE (1963), MC (1944), TD (1950); s of Norman Hugo Graesser, JP (d 1970), and Annette (d 1970), da of James Durward; *b* 17 Nov 1915; *Educ* Oundle, Gonville and Caius Coll Cambridge; *m* 1939, Diana Aline Elms Neale; 1 s (Simon), 3 da (Dawn, Camilla, Emma); *Career* served WWII (France and Germany): cmmnd 4 Bn (TA) Royal Welsh Fus 1939, cmd 158 Bde Anti Tank Co (later became 53 Welsh Div Reconnaissance Regt) 1940-46, Cheshire Yeo 1949-64, Hon Col 3 RWF 1972-80; md R Graesser Ltd 1947-1972, dir Lancashire Tar Distillers Ltd 1949-1972, chm Welsh Industl Estates Corpn 1971-75, former pres Industl Assoc Wales and Monmouth; former chm: Wales Regnl Cncl CBI, Central Trg Cncl for Wales; former memb: Merseyside N Wales Electricity Bd, Devpt Corpn Wales and Monmouth, Wales and the Marches Postal Bd, Welsh Cncl; former managing tstee Municipal Mutual Insurance Ltd, former dir Chester Grosvenor Hotel Co Ltd, tstee Wales and Border Counties TSB; hon vice-pres Nat Union Cons and Unionist Assoc (chm 1974-75, pres 1984-85); High Sheriff Flintshire 1963, Vice Lord-Lt Clwyd 1980-83; JP 1956-78; CStJ 1980; kt 1973; *Recreations* boxing (half Blue), rugby football, rowing, shooting, gardening; *Clubs* Hawks (Cambridge), Leander, Naval and Military; *Style—* Col Sir Alastair Graesser, DSO, OBE, MC, TD; Sweet Briar, Berghill Lane, Babbinswood, Oswestry, Salop SY11 4PF (☎ 0691 662395)

GRAESSER, (Norman) Rhidian; s of Norman Hugo Graesser (d 1970), and Annette Stewart, *née* Durward (d 1970); *b* 21 Oct 1924; *Educ* Oundle, RNC Dartmouth; *m* 2 July 1952, Stella Ainley, da of Philip Nicholson Hoyle (d 1982); 2 s (Jonathan b 1953, Max b 1957), 1 da (Fern b 1970); *Career* RN 1942-48, invalided out with rank Lt; served Mediterranean, N Atlantic, E and W Indies; dir James Lithgow Ltd 1953-86; *Recreations* countryside, golf, bridge; *Clubs* Lansdowne; *Style—* Rhidian Graesser, Esq; Fron Fanadl, Llandyrnog, Denbigh, Clwyd LL16 4HR (☎ 08244 349)

GRAFFTEY-SMITH, John Jeremy (Jinx); s of Sir Laurence Barton Grafftey-Smith, KCMG, KBE (d 1989), and Mrs Vivien Isobel Tennant-Eyles, *née* Alderson; *b* 13 Oct 1934; *Educ* Winchester, Magdalen Coll Oxford (MA); *m* 23 Jan 1964, Lucy, da of Major John Fletcher, MBE, of Sussex; 2 s (Alexander b 1967, Toby b 1970), 1 da (Camilla b 1968); *Career* banker; 2 Lt Oxfordshire & Bucks LI 1953-55; European rep Nat Commercial Bank of Saudi-Arabia 1982-; with Samuel Montagu 1958-66, Wallace Bros 1966-76, res dir Allied Med Gp Saudi-Arabia 1977-81, dir Saudi NCB Securities Ltd (IMRO memb), Brendoncare; memb Saudi Br Soc Ctee; *Recreations* golf, shooting, tennis, jogging, music, wine, bridge; *Clubs* Cavalry and Guards', City of London, Hong Kong, Green Jackets, Ashridge Golf; *Style—* Jinx Grafftey-Smith, Esq; Burcott Hill House, Wing Leighton Buzzard, Bedfordshire LU7 0JU; National Commercial Bank, Bevis Marks House, Bevis Marks, London EC3A 7SB

GRAFFTEY-SMITH, Roger Tilney; s of Sir Laurence Barton Grafftey-Smith, KCMG, KBE (d 1989), and Mrs Vivien Isobel Tennant-Eyles, *née* Alderson; *b* 14 April 1931; *Educ* Winchester, Trinity Oxford (PPE Hons); *m* 28 March 1962, Jane Oriana Mary, da of Sir John Pollen-Bart; 2 s (Simon b 1968, Max b 1974), 1 da (Selina b 1971); *Career* 2 Lt Queens Bays 1949-51; md Galban Lobo (England) Ltd 1962-72, vice-chm North Wilts Dist Cncl 1980-82; chm Dermalock Med Corp 1985, mangr ptnr Grafftey-Smith & Associates Financial Conslts 1982; *Recreations* shooting, fishing; *Style—* Roger T Grafftey-Smith, Esq; Monks Farm House, Sherborne, Cheltenham, Glos; Grafftey Smith Assocs, 25 Wormwood Street, London EC2 (☎ 01 638 6626, fax 01 638 6628)

GRAFTON, Duchess of; (Ann) Fortune FitzRoy; GCVO (1980, DCVO 1970, CVO 1965), JP; o da of late Capt (Evan Cadogan) Eric Smith, MC, LLD; *m* 12 Oct 1946, 11 Duke of Grafton, *qv*; 2 s, 3 da; *Career* SRCN Great Ormond St 1945, pres W Suffolk Mission to the Deaf, vice-pres Suffolk Br Royal British Legion Women's Section; govr: Felixstowe Coll, Riddlesworth Hall; JP: County of London 1949, County of Suffolk 1972; memb bd of govrs The Hosp for Sick Children Great Ormond St 1952-66; lady of the bedchamber to HM The Queen 1953-66, mistress of the robes to HM The Queen 1967-; pres W Suffolk Decorative and Fine Art Soc; *Style—* Her Grace the Duchess of Grafton, GCVO, JP; Euston Hall, Thetford, Norfolk IP24 2QP (☎ 0842 3282)

GRAFTON, 11 Duke of (E 1675); Hugh Denis Charles Fitzroy; KG (1976), DL (Suffolk 1973); also Earl of Euston, Viscount Ipswich and Baron Sudbury (E 1672); patron of four livings; Hereditary Ranger of Whittlebury Forest; s of 10 Duke of Grafton (d 1970), and Lady Doreen Buxton, 2 da of 1 Earl Buxton; *b* 3 April 1919; *Educ* Eton, Magdalene Coll Cambridge; *m* 12 Oct 1946, Fortune (*see* Grafton, Duchess of, GCVO); 2 s, 3 da; *Heir* s, Earl of Euston; *Career* Grenadier Gds ADC to Viceroy of India 1943-46; memb: Historic Bldgs Advsy Ctee to English Heritage, Nat Tst Properties Ctee; chm: Soc for the Protection of Ancient Buildings, Architectural Heritage Tst; chm jt ctee Soc for Protection of Ancient Buildings, Georgian Gp, Victorian Soc and Civic Tst; nat pres Cncl of Br Soc of Master Glass Painters; chm Cathedrals Advsy Cmmn for England, chm of tstees Historic Churches Preservation Tst, memb Royal Fine Art Cmmn, chm trustees Sir John Soane's Museum, vice-chm tstees Nat Portrait Gallery, patron Hereford Herd Book Soc; Hon Air Cdre No 2633 RAuxAF Regt Sqdn 1982-; *Clubs* Boodle's; *Style—* His Grace the Duke of Grafton, KG, DL; Euston Hall, Thetford, Norfolk IP24 2QP (☎ 0842 3282)

GRAFTON, Col Martin John; CBE (1976, OBE 1964, MBE 1944), TD (1958); s of Vincent Charles Grafton (d 1949), of Worcester and Tewkesbury, and Maud Isabel, *née* Brazier (d 1968); *b* 28 June 1919; *Educ* Bromsgrove Sch; *m* 7 Aug 1948, Jean Margaret (Jennifer), da of James Drummond-Smith, OBE (d 1945), of Daventry; 2 da (Fiona, Caroline); *Career* WWII RE 1940-46; cmmnd 1941, Capt 1943, served Normandy and NW Europe 1944-46; RE (TA) 1947-66: served 101 (London) FD Engr Regt, Maj 1954, Lt-Col 1960, cmd 101 FD Engr Regt 1960-64, Col 1964, Dep Chief Engr E Anglian dist 1964-66; John Lewis Partnership: joined 1948, gen mangr Peter Jones 1951-53, dir bldg 1954-60, md 1960-63; dir gen Nat Fedn Bldg Trades Employers (now Bldg Employers Confedn) 1964-79, dir Alfred Booth & Co Ltd 1979-80; memb: EDC for Bldg 1964-75, cncl CBI 1964-79, Nat Consultative Cncl for Bldg and Civil Engrg 1964-79; DL Gtr London 1967-83; Freeman City of London 1978, memb Co of Builders 1977-80; FFB 1968-80, hon FCIOB 1978; *Recreations* travel, reading, music; *Style—* Col Martin Grafton, CBE, TD; Urchfont Hse, Urchfont, nr Devizes, Wilts SN10 4RP (☎ 038 084 404)

GRAFTON, Peter Witheridge; CBE (1972); s of James Hawkins Grafton and Ethel Marion, *née* Brannan; *b* 19 May 1916; *Educ* Westminster City Sch, Sutton Valence Sch, Coll of Estate Mgmnt; *m* 1, 1939, Joan (d 1969), da of late Eng Rear Adm Hubert Bleackley, CBE, MVO; 3 da and 1 s (1 s and 1 da decd); m 2, 1971, Margaret Ruth, da of John Frederick Wark; 2 s; *Career* served WWII Queen's Westminster Rifles, Dorsetshire Regt and RE, UK and Far E (Capt); chartered quantity surveyor, sr ptnr G D Walford & Partners to 1982; pres Royal Inst Chartered Surveyors 1978-79 (vice-pres 1974-78, first chm policy review ctee), memb and past chm Quantity Surveyors Cncl (first chm Building Cost Info Service), memb cncl Construction Industs Res and Info Assoc 1963-69, memb Res Advsy Cncl to Min of Housing and Construction 1967-71, memb Nat Cncl for Building and Civil Engrg Industs 1968-76, chm Nat Jt Consultative Ctee for Building Indust 1970-77, memb Br Bd of Agrément 1973-; tstee United Westminster Schs, chm govrs Sutton Valence

Sch, past chm Old Suttonians Assoc; contested (Lib) Bromley 1959; master Worshipful Co of Chartered Surveyors 1983-84; FRICS, FCIArB; *Publications* numerous articles on technical and other professional subjects; *Recreations* golf (fndr and chm Public Schs Old Boys Golf Assoc, co-donor Grafton Morrish Trophy, past capt Chartered Surveyors Golfing Soc), writing; *Clubs* Reform (W Sussex), Tandridge; *Style—* Peter Grafton, Esq, CBE; Corner Cottage, 10 Stanhopes, Limpsfield, Surrey RH8 0TY (☎ Oxted 6685)

GRAHAM, (John) Alistair; s of Robert Graham (d 1968), and Dorothy, *née* Horner; *b* 6 August 1942; *Educ* Royal GS Newcastle upon Tyne; *m* 1967, Dorothy Jean, da of James Clark Wallace, of Morpeth, Northumberland; 1 s (Richard b 1974), 1 da (Polly b 1972); *Career* gen sec The Civil and Public Servs Assoc 1982-86, Industl Soc 1986; *Recreations* music, theatre; *Clubs* RAC; *Style—* Alistair Graham, Esq; The Industrial Soc, Peter Runge House, 3 Carlton House Terrace, London SW1Y 5DG (☎ 01 839 4300)

GRAHAM, Major Andrew John Noble; s and h of Sir John Alexander Noble Graham, 4 Bt, GCMG, *qv*; *b* 21 Oct 1956; *Educ* Eton, Trinity Coll Cambridge; *m* 7 July 1984, Susan Mary Bridget, da of Rear Adm John Patrick Bruce O'Riordan, of Long House, Chitterne, Wilts; 2 da (Katharine b 1986, Louisa b 1988); *Career* Major Argyll and Sutherland Highlanders; *Recreations* outdoor sports, piping; *Clubs* MCC, RGS; *Style—* Major Andrew Graham; c/o 8 St Maur Rd, London SW6 (☎ 01 731 4884)

GRAHAM, Andrew Winston Mawdsley; s of Winston Graham, OBE, of Abbotswood, Buxted, Sussex, and Jemm Mary, *née* Williamson; *b* 20 June 1942; *Educ* St Edmund Hall Oxford (MA); *m* 1970, Peggotty, da of E L Fawssett; *Career* econ asst: Nat Econ Devpt Off 1964, Dept of Econ Affairs 1964-66, asst to the econ advsr to the cabinet 1966-68, econ advsr to the PM 1968-69, fell and tutor in econs Balliol Coll Oxford 1969-(lectr 1970-), policy advsr to the PM 1974-76, estates bursar Balliol Coll Oxford 1978 (investmts bursar 1979-83, vice master 1988); memb: The Wilson Ctee on the Functioning of Fin Insts 1977-80, econs ctee SSRC 1978-80; non exec dir of the Br Tport Docks Bd 1979-82, memb ILO/JASPA employment advsy mission to Ethiopia 1982, head of Queen Elizabeth House, Food Studies gp advising the govt of the Rep of Zambia 1984; *Recreations* windsurfing; *Style—* Andrew Graham, Esq; Balliol Coll, Oxford OX1 3BJ

GRAHAM, Antony Richard Malise; s of Col Patrick Ludovic Graham, MC, (d 1958), and Barbara Mary Jury (d 1964); *b* 15 Oct 1928; *Educ* Nautical Coll Pangbourne; *m* 1958, Gillian Margaret, da of L Bradford Cook (d 1941); 2 s (Ludovic b 1961, Thomas b 1962); 1 da (Lucy b 1965); *Career* Merchant Navy 1945-55 (Master Mariners Certificate 1955); contested Leeds East (Cons) 1966; mgmnt conslt; Stewarts and Lloyds Ltd 1955-60, PE Cnsltg Gp 1960-72, under sec & regnl industl dir DTI 1972-76; dir: Barrow Hepburn Gp plc, Maroquinere Le Tanneur du Bugey SA 1976-81; chm Paton & Sons (Tillicoultry) Ltd 1981-82; dir Clive & Stokes Int 1983-; *Style—* Antony Graham, Esq; 1 The Gardens, Nun Appleton Hall, York YO5 7BG (☎ 0904 84533); 17 Waldemar Ave, London SW6 5LB (☎ 01 731 3896)

GRAHAM, Arthur William; JP (1979); s of William Douglas Graham (d 1970), and Eleanor Mary Scott, *née* Searle; *b* 18 Nov 1949; *Educ* Monkton Coll, Coll Estate Mgmnt London; *m* 20 June 1981, Elizabeth Hannah, da of Joshua Griffiths, of Gwent; 1 s (William James b 1982), 2 da (Sarah Jane Mary b 1984, Hannah Victoria b 1987); *Career* FRICS 1980; cncllr Gwent 1985, elected to Newport BC 1988; *Recreations* breeder of pedigree suffolk sheep; *Clubs* IOD; *Style—* William Graham, Esq, JP; The Volland, Lower Machen, Newport, Gwent NP1 8UY (☎ 440419, 54825); 114 Commercial St, Newport, Gwent NP9 1LW

GRAHAM, Beatrice, Lady; Beatrice Mary; *née* Spencer-Smith; OBE (1982); o da of Lt-Col Michael Seymour Spencer-Smith, DSO, MC (d 1928, yr bro of Sir Drummond Hamilton-Spencer-Smith, 5 Bt), and (Evelyn) Penelope (d 1974, having m 2, 1934, Elliot Francis Montagu Butler), yr da of Rev Arthur Delmé Radcliffe and Beatrice, da of Hon Frederick Dudley Ryder, 3 s of 1 Earl of Harrowby.; *b* 27 Mar 1909; *m* 16 Sept 1939, Sir Richard Bellingham Graham, 10 Bt, OBE, JP, DL, chm Yorkshire TV (d 1982); 3 s; *Career* museum service; *Style—* Beatrice, Lady Graham; Norton Conyers, Melmerby, Ripon, N Yorks (☎ 076 584 333)

GRAHAM, Lord Calum Ian; s of 7 Duke of Montrose; *b* 22 July 1958; *Educ* St Andrew's Coll, Grahamstown; *Style—* Lord Calum Graham

GRAHAM, Maj Sir Charles Spencer Richard; 6 Bt (GB 1783), of Netherby, Cumberland; s of Lt-Col Sir (Frederick) Fergus Graham, 5 Bt, KBE, TD (d 1978), and Mary Spencer Revell, CBE (d 1985), da of Maj-Gen Raymond Northland Revell Reade, CB, CMG; *b* 16 July 1919; *Educ* Eton; *m* 1944, Susan, da of Maj Robert Lambton Surtees, OBE; 2 s, 1 da; *Heir* s, James Fergus Surtees Graham; *Career* Maj Scots Gds, served 1940-50, NW Europe (despatches), Malaya; High Sheriff of Cumberland 1955-56, Ld-Lt Cumbria 1983- (DL Cumberland 1970); pres Country Landowners Assoc 1971-73, memb Nat Water Cncl 1973-83; master Worshipful Co of Farmers 1982-83; KStJ; *Clubs* Brooks's, Pratt's; *Style—* Maj Sir Charles Graham, Bt; Crofthead, Longtown, Cumbria CA6 5PA (☎ 0228 791231)

GRAHAM, Brig Cyril Carew; CBE (1958), DSO (1950); s of Capt E C Graham (d 1935); *b* 26 Oct 1907; *Educ* Haslebury and Imperial Serv Coll, RMC Sandhurst; *m* 1959, Kathleen Margaret Colley, *née* Robertson (d 29 July 1987); *Career* Bde Maj 43 Gurkha Lorried Inf Bde 1944, cmd 2 Bn (DEO) 7 Gurkha Rifles 1945, 1 Bn 10 Princess Mary's Own Gurkha Rifles 1948-50, Col HQ Bde of Gurkhas Malaya 1952-54, cmd: 99 Gurkha Inf Bde 1952-53, North Malaya Dist 1953-55, HQ Br Gurkhas in India 1954-58; *Recreations* golf; *Clubs* Army and Navy; *Style—* Brig Cyril Graham, CBE, DSO; Broadmead, Ludham, Norfolk NR29 5PH (☎ 069 262 590)

GRAHAM, Hon Mrs (Daphne); *née* Bootle-Wilbraham; da of 6 Baron Skelmersdale (d 1973), and Ann, da of Percy Quilter (d 1974), (s of 1 Bt); *b* 14 Oct 1946; *m* 1980, Jocelyn Peter Gore Graham, s of Brig Peter Alastair John Gore Graham, of Chalkpit Cottage, Blewbury, Oxon; 1 da (Tamsin b 1985); *Style—* The Hon Mrs Graham; 11 Rosenhall Rd, London SW11 4QN

GRAHAM, David James Ogle; s of Dr Frank Ogle Graham, of Stokesly, Cleveland, and Annie Campbell, *née* McLeod; *b* 7 May 1932; *Educ* Taunton Sch Taunton Somerset; *m* 6 Sept 1960, Marion Emma, da of David William Ralph Knighton (d 1983); 1 s (Robert b 7 April 1985), 1 da (Sarah Jane b 8 May 1983); *Career* slr; former: ptnr Bentleys Stokes & Lowless, chm Admty Slrs Gp, memb Admty Ct Ctee; govr St Albans HS for Girls; memb Law Soc; *Recreations* golf, fly fishing; *Style—* David Graham, Esq; Fairway, 38 The Ave, Potters Bar (☎ 0707 55909)

GRAHAM, (Stewart) David; QC (1977); s of Lewis Graham (d 1985), of Harrogate, and Gertrude, *née* Markman; *b* 27 Feb 1934; *Educ* Leeds GS, St Edmund Hall Oxford (MA, BCL); *m* 20 Dec 1959, Corinne, da of Emile Carmona (d 1984), of London; 2 da (Jeanne (Mrs Zane), Angela); *Career* called to the Bar Middle Temple 1957, Harmsworth Law Scholar 1958, ret from Bar 1985, dir Coopers and Lybrand and Cork Gully 1985-; chm: law parly and gen purpose ctee of Bd of Deputies of Br Jews 1983-88, Editorial Bd of Insolvency Intelligence 1988-; memb: Cncl of Justice 1976-, Insolvency Rules Advsy Ctee 1984-86; editor of various works on Insolvency Law; *Recreations* biography, travel, music, history of insolvency law; *Style—* David Graham, Esq, QC; 133 London Rd, Stanmore, Middx HA7 4PG (☎ 01 954 3783); Shelley House, 3 Noble St, London EC2V 7DQ (☎ 01 606 7700, fax 01 606 9887, telex 884730 CORK GXG)

GRAHAM, Lord Donald Alasdair; s of 7 Duke of Montrose; *b* 28 Oct 1956; *Educ* St Andrew's Coll Grahamstown, Univ of St Andrew's Scotland (BSc), INSEAD (MBA); *m* Dec 1981, Bride Donalda Elspeth, da of Maj Allan John Cameron, of Allangrange, Munlochy, Ross-shire; 1 s (Alasdair b 1986, d 1988), 1 da (Caitriana b 1984); *Career* memb Br Computer Soc; *Recreations* windsurfing, tennis, piping; *Clubs* New; *Style—* Lord Donald Graham; Nether Tillyrie, Milnathort, Kinross-shire, Scotland; Adam & Company plc, 22 Charlotte Square, Edinburgh EH2 4DF

GRAHAM, Donald Henry; s of Alan Wilson Graham (d 1985), of Woodvale, Storrs Park, Windermere, and Mary Margaret, *née* Addison; *b* 13 July 1945; *Educ* Heversham GS; *m* 12 May 1973, (Norah) Christine, da of John O'Connor (d 1979), of Wigan; 1 s (Michael b 11 Oct 1976), 1 da (Anna b 6 May 1983); *Career* CA; ptnr Jackson and Graham 1968-; sidesman St Mary's Church Windermere, govr St Mary's Sch Windermere 1982-88; hon auditor for various local charities: Save the Children, St Mary's Church, St Martin's Church, Windermere Jr Sch; FICA 1973 (assoc memb 1968); *Style—* Donald Graham, Esq; Maudlands, Maude Street, Kendal, Cumbria (☎ 0539 20526)

GRAHAM, Dr Douglas; s of David Sims Graham, (d 1974), of Cheshire, and Freda Wilson, *née* Pearce; *b* 18 Jan 1946; *Educ* Rutherford Coll of Technol (BSc), Newcastle Univ (PhD); *m* 16 April 1966, Rosemary Anne Graham; 1 s (Anthony Edmund b 5 Aug 1967), 1 da (Rosalynde Michelle b 11 Nov 1969); *Career* res engr CA Parsons 1966-71, fin controller ICFC 1972-76; chief exec Indespension Ltd 1977-; chm Bolton Business Ventures, MIMech E (1972); *Style—* Dr Douglas Graham; Moorlands, Chapeltown Rd, Bromley Cross, Bolton (☎ 0204 53 850); Indespension Ltd, Belmont Rd, Bolton, Lancs (☎ 0204 58 434, fax 0204 595 197, car tel 0860 619 635, telex 635264)

GRAHAM, Rev Douglas Leslie; s of Very Rev George Frederick Graham, Dean of Kildare (d 1962), and Mirabel (d 1971), da of W P Odlum; *b* 4 Oct 1909; *Educ* Portora Royal Sch, Trinity Coll Dublin; *m* 1935, Gladys Winifred Ann, *née* Brittain; 3 s; *Career* chaplain RNVR (home and N Atlantic); asst master Eton 1934-41; ordained 1937, head Portora Royal Sch 1945-53, head Dean Close Sch 1954-68, asst master Williston Massachusetts 1968-72; *Recreations* the three R's, birds; *Style—* The Rev Douglas Graham; Forest Cottage, West Woods, Lockeridge, Marlborough, Wiltshire SN8 4EG (☎ 067 286 432)

GRAHAM, (Malcolm Gray) Douglas; s of Malcolm Graham, of Farmcote Hall, Claverley, nr Wolverhampton, and Annie Jeanette Sankey, *née* Robinson (d 1976); *b* 18 Feb 1930; *Educ* Shrewsbury; *m* 18 April 1980, Sara Ann, da of William Patrick Whitelaw Anderson (d 1976), of Feckenham, Worcs; 2 step s (Colin William Edward Elwell b 12 Jan 1971, James Peter Elwell b 24 April 1973); *Career* chm: The Midland News Assoc Ltd 1984-, Express & Star Ltd, Shropshire Newspapers Ltd 1980-; pres: Young Newspapermen's Assoc 1969, West Midlands Newspaper Soc 1973-74; chm Evening Newspaper Advertising Bureau 1978-79; *Recreations* shooting; *Style—* Douglas Graham, Esq; Roughton Manor, Worfield, nr Bridgnorth, Shropshire (☎ 074 64 209); Express and Star, Queen St, Wolverhampton, W Midlands (☎ 0902 313131)

GRAHAM, Duncan Gilmour; CBE (1987); s of Robert Gilmour Graham, of Glasgow, and Lilias Turnbull, *née* Watson; *b* 20 August 1936; *Educ* Hutchesons' Sch Glasgow, Univ of Glasgow (MA), Jordanhill Coll of Educn (Cert Ed); *m* 26 Dec 1962, Margaret Gray, da of James Brown Cairns (Maj R E d 1984), of Eaglesham; 2 s (Roderick b 1966, Duncan b 1969), 1 da (Kirsty b 1967); *Career* teacher of history Whitehill and Hutchesons' Sch's Glasgow 1959-65, lectr Craigie Coll of Educn Ayr 1965-68, asst later sr dep dir of educn Renfrewshire 1968-74, sr dep dir of educn Strathclyde Regnl Cncl 1974-79, co educn offr Suffolk CC 1979-87, chief exec Humberside CC 1987-88, chm and chief exec Nat Curriculum Cncl 1988-; advsr to Convention of Scottish Local Authorities and Scottish Teachers' Salaries Ctee 1974-79, advsr Assoc of CC 1983-88, memb Burnham Ctee 1983-87, chm Assoc of Educn Offrs 1984, sec Soc of Co Educn Offrs 1985-87; Arts Cncl nominee on Lincoln and Humberside Arts, chm LRAC Radio Humberside and BBC; FBIM 1972, FRSA 1981; *Books* Those Having Torches (1985), In the Light of Torches (1986), Mathematics For Ages 5-16 (1988); *Recreations* golf, sailing, the Arts; *Clubs* Western Gailes, Royal Overseas League; *Style—* Duncan Graham, Esq, CBE; Westwood Garth, N Dalton YO25 9XA (☎ 037 781 277); National Curriculum Council, 15-17 New St, York YO1 2RA (☎ 0904 622533, fax 0904 622921)

GRAHAM, Euan Douglas; CB (1985); yr s of Brig Lord (Douglas) Malise Graham, CB, DSO, MC (d 1979; 2 s of 5 Duke of Montrose), and Hon Rachael Mary Holland (d 1977), da of 2 Viscount Knutsford; *b* 29 July 1924; *Educ* Eton, Ch Ch Oxford (MA); *m* 1, 3 June 1954 (m dis 1970), Pauline Laetitia, eldest da of Hon David Francis Tennant, and former w of Capt Julian Lane-Fox Pitt Rivers; m 2, 1972, Caroline Esther, da of Sheriff Kenneth Middleton, of Ledwell, Oxon; 2 da (Sarah b 1973, Alexandra b 1976); *Style—* Euan Graham, Esq, CB

GRAHAM, Geraldine, Lady; Geraldine; *née* Velour; da of Austin Velour, of Brooklyn, NY; *m* 1949, as his 2 w, Sir Ralph Wolfe Graham, 13 Bt (d 1988); 2 s (Sir Ralph Stuart, 14 Bt, *qv*, Robert Bruce b 1953); *Style—* Geraldine, Lady Graham; 134 Leisureville Boulevard, Boynton Beach, Florida 33435, USA

GRAHAM, Gordon; CBE (1980); s of late Stanley Bouch Graham and Isabel Hetherington; *b* 4 June 1920; *Educ* Creighton Sch, Nottingham Sch of Architecture (Dip Arch 1949); *m* 1946, Enid Pennington; 3 da; *Career* sr ptnr Gordon Graham and Ptnrs, pres RIBA 1977-79; *Style—* Gordon Graham, Esq, CBE; Lockington Hall, Lockington, Derby DE7 2RH

GRAHAM, (William) Gordon; MC (1944); s of Thomas Graham (d 1944), and Marion Walker Hutcheson (d 1979); *b* 17 July 1920; *Educ* Hutchesons' GS Glasgow, Glasgow Univ (MA); *m* 1948, Friedel, da of Emil Gramm (d 1966); 2 da (Fiona, Sylvia); *Career* Queen's Own Cameron Highlanders 1941-46, Capt 1944, Maj 1945, GSO II India

Office 1946 serving in India and Burma; newspaper corr and publishers' rep in India 1946-55; vice-pres McGraw-Hill Book Co NY 1961-74 (int sales mangr 1956-63, md 1963-74) gp, chm 1974- and chief exec 1974-88 Butterworth Publishers; chm: Int Electronic Publishing Res Centre Ltd 1981-84, Publishers Databases Ltd 1982-84, R R Bowker NY 1985-; dir: W & R Chambers Edinburgh 1974-83, Int Publishing Corpn 1975-82, Reed Publishing Gp 1982-; pres Publishers' Assoc of GB 1985-87 (cncl memb 1972-88), memb bd Br Library 1980-86; FRSA; *Recreations* reading, writing, ski-ing, gardening; *Style*— Gordon Graham, Esq, MC; 5 Beechwood Drive, Marlow, Bucks SL7 2DH (☎ Marlow 3371); Butterworth & Co (Publishers) Ltd, 88 Kingsway, London WC2B 6AB (☎ 01 405 6900)

GRAHAM, Henry Trevenen Davidson (Harry); s of William Graham, CMG, OBE, MM, Croix de Guerre, Order of the Nile (d 1956), of Cairo, and Edith Frederica, *née* Davidson (d 1972); *b* 17 Feb 1932; *Educ* Eton, Christ Church Coll (MA); *m* 26 July 1958, Mary Hermione, qv, da of Sir Arthur Hobhouse, KBE (d 1965), of Hadspen House, Castle Cary, Som; 1 s (Francis Henry b 1960), 1 da (Harriet Konradin b 1964); *Career* Nat Serv 2 Lt Intelligence Corps 1950-52; furniture designer and architect; ptnr Graham Stollar Assocs Ltd (formerly Hugh Robert and Graham Architects) 1973-; memb: Bath Preservation Tst, Bath Soc, Walpole Soc, Royal Inst Cornwall Georgian GP, Soc Protection Ancient Buildings (Victorian Soc), RIBA, Architectural Assoc; *Recreations* painting in water colour, music, travelling, reading; *Style*— Harry Graham, Esq; 29 Royal Crescent, Bath BA1 2LT (☎ 0225 331656); The Old Malthouse, Clarence St, Bath BA1 5NS (☎ 0225 25254)

GRAHAM, Col Ian Derek; TD, DL (Humberside 1974-); s of Maj Ernest Frederic Graham, MBE, MC (d 1985), of Rowan, The Park, Swanland, N Humberside, and Muriel, *née* Fell (d 1970); *b* 27 Feb 1928; *Educ* Sedbergh, Univ of Hull, London (LLB); *m* 1, 24 July 1955 (m dis 1984), Margaret Edwards; 3 da (Fiona Clare b 1956, Janet Elaine b 1958, Sally Anne b 1962); m 2, 1985, Betty, da of Thomas Vessey Whittaker (d 1954); *Career* conscripted 1946, cmmnd RA 1947, demob 1948; TA 1949-; Lt-Col 440 LAD Regt RA 1967, Col Cmdt Humberside ACF 1971-79, memb nat cncl ACF Assoc (presently chm shooting ctee vice chm Yorks and Humberside TAVRA 1987-; qualified slr 1954; local chm Nat Insur and Social Security Appeal Tbnl 1970-; memb Law Soc; *Recreations* game shooting; *Style*— Col Ian Graham, TD, DL; Kelsey Cottage, Hariff Lane, Burstwick, North Humberside (☎ 0964 622429; Graham & Rosen, 8 Parliament St, Hull (☎ 0482 23123)

GRAHAM, Hon Ian Stuart; s of Baron Graham of Edmonton (Life Peer); *b* 2 Mar 1959; *Style*— The Hon Ian Graham

GRAHAM, Marquess of; James; s and h of 7 Duke of Montrose; *b* 6 April 1935; *Educ* Loretto; *m* 1970, Catherine Elizabeth MacDonnell, da of Capt Norman Alexander Thompson Young (d 1942), Queen's Own Cameron Highlanders of Canada; 2 s (Lord Fintrie, Lord Ronald John Christopher b 1975), 1 da (Lady Hermione Elizabeth b 1971); *Heir* s, Lord Fintrie; *Career* Brig Royal Co of Archers (Queen's Body Guard for Scotland) 1986-; memb cncl Scottish Nat Farmers' Union 1981-86 and 1987-88; OStJ 1978; *Clubs* Hon Memb RNVR (Scotland), Royal Scottish Pipers Soc, Royal Highland and Agricultural Soc of Scotland; *Style*— Marquess of Graham; Auchmar, Drymen, Glasgow (☎ 0360 60307)

GRAHAM, Sir James Bellingham; 11 Bt (E 1662), of Norton Conyers, Yorkshire; er s of Sir Richard Graham, 10 Bt, OBE, JP, DL (d 1982); *b* 8 Oct 1940; *Educ* Eton, Christ Church Oxford; *m* 1986, Halina, yr da of late Major Wiktor Grubert; *Heir* yr bro, William Reginald Graham, *qv*; *Career* Res Asst Cecil Higgins Museum and Art Gallery Bedford; *Books* Guide to Norton Conyers (1976), Cecil Higgins, Collector Extraordinary (jtly with wife 1983), A Guide to the Cecil Higgins Museum and Art Gallery (1987); *Recreations* history, sightseeing; *Style*— Sir James Graham, Bt; 1 Oberon Court, Shakespear Rd, Bedford MK40 2EB

GRAHAM, James Fergus Surtees; s and h of Maj Sir Charles Graham, 6 Bt; *b* 29 July 1946; *Educ* Milton Abbey; *m* 1975, Serena Jane, da of Ronald Frank Kershaw; 1 s (Robert b 1985), 2 da (Catherine b 1978, Iona b 1980); *Style*— James Graham, Esq; Scaurbank, Longtown, Cumbria (☎ 0228 791262); 35 Drayton Ct, Drayton Gdns, London SW10 (☎ 01 370 7245)

GRAHAM, James Lionel Malin; s of Christopher Colin Graham (d 1980), of Offchurch, Leamington Spa, and Evelyn Gladys, *née* Pridmore (d 1987); *b* 2 Sept 1927; *Educ* All Saints Sch Bloxham, Lincoln Coll Oxford; *m* 28 Oct 1961, Valerie Maddalena, da of Dr William Henry Cotton Croft, of Kineton, Warwick; 2 s (Christopher b 1962, Stephen b 1963), 1 da (Sarah b 1969); *Career* Army 1945-48, cmmnd RASC, demobbed Lt; Thomson McLintock & Co 1948-52, qualified as CA 1953, md J & J Cash Ltd 1953-74, dir Coventry Provident Bldg Soc 1970-81, fin dir John Trelawny Ltd 1975-77, md Br Transfer Printing co Ltd 1978-88, ret 1988; pt/t dir Display Prodrs and Screenprinters Assoc London 1989-; tstee Coventry Tstee Savings Bank 1966; magistrate Coventry Bench 1969-75, gen cmmr of income tax 1979; High Sheriff Warwicks 1985-86; memb Coventry C of C 1970-82, regnl bd memb Tstee Savings Bank of England and Wales Birmingham 1984-; former pres: Coventry Textile Soc, Warwicks Soc of CAS; tstee Bonds Hosp Estates Charity 1958, Samuel Smith's Charity 1965, Newfield Charitable Tst 1966, Sir Thomas White's Charity 1971, Coventry Church Charities 1978; Liveryman Worshipful Company of Weavers 1966 (Upper Bailiff 1986-87); Fellowship: Drapers Coventry 1959 (past master), Broadweavers and Clothiers 1957 (past master); FCA 1953; *Recreations* skiing, gardening, philately, golf, collecting and hoarding generally; *Style*— James Graham, Esq; Gable House, Offchurch, Leamington Spa, Warwicks CV33 9AP; La Coquille, Braye Rd, Alderney, CI

GRAHAM, Sir John Alexander Noble; 4 Bt (UK 1906), of Larbert House, Larbert and Househill, Dunipace, Co Stirling; GCMG (1985, KCMG 1979, CMG 1972); s of Sir Reginald Graham, 3 Bt, VC, OBE (d 1980), and Rachel, *née* Sprot (d 1984); *b* 15 July 1926; *Educ* Eton, Trinity Coll Cambridge; *m* 1956, Marygold Elinor Gabrielle, da of Lt-Col Clive Austin, JP, DL (d 1974), and Lady Lilian Lumley, sis of 11 Earl of Scarbrough, KG, GCSI, GCVO, TD, PC; 2 s, 1 da; *Heir* s, Capt Andrew Graham; *Career* joined FO 1950, served Amman, Kuwait, Bahrain, Belgrade, Benghazi and as cnsllr and head of Chancery Washington; ambass Iraq 1974-77, FCO dep under-sec 1977-79 and 1980-82, ambass Iran 1979-80, ambass and UK perm rep NATO in Brussels 1982-; *Recreations* outdoor activities; *Clubs* Army and Navy; *Style*— Sir John Graham, Bt, GCMG; Ditchley Park, Enstone, Oxford OX7 4ER

GRAHAM, Maj-Gen John David Carew; CB (1978), CBE (1973, OBE 1967); s of Col John Alexander Graham (d 1957), of The White House, Nettlestone, IoW, and Constance Mary, *née* Carew-Hunt (d 1987); *b* 18 Jan 1923; *Educ* Fernden Sch Haslemere, Cheltenham; *m* 17 Nov 1956, Rosemary Elaine, da of James Basil Adamson (d 1946), of Georgetown, British Guiana; 1 s (John Christopher Malcolm b 1959), 1 da (Jacqueline Patricia Anne b 1957); *Career* cmmnd Argyll and Sutherland Highlanders 1942 (despatches), served 5 Bn The Parachute Regt 1946-49, Br Embassy Prague 1949-50, HQ Scottish Cmd 1956-58, mil asst to CINCENT Fontainebleau 1960-62, cmd 1 Bn The Parachute Regt 1964-66, instr Staff Coll Camberley 1967, Regt Col The Parachute Regtl 1968-69, cdr Sultan's Armed Forces Oman 1970-72, Indian Nat Def Coll 1973, asst chief of Staff HQ AFCENT 1974-76; GOC Wales 1976-78, Hon Col Kent ACF 1981-88 (chm Kent ACF Ctee 1979-86), Hon Col 203 Welsh Gen Hosp, RAMC, TA 1983-89 OStJ (chm St John Cncl for Kent 1978-86); CStJ, Order of Oman; *Recreations* gardening, walking, travel; *Clubs* The Hurlingham, London SW6; *Style*— Major-General John Graham, CB, CBE; c/o National Westminster Bank, Riverhead, Sevenoaks, Kent TN13 2DA

GRAHAM, Sir John Moodie; 2 Bt (UK 1964), of Dromore, Co Down; s of Sir Clarence Johnston Graham, 1 Bt (d 1966); *b* 3 April 1938; *Educ* Trinity Coll Glenalmond, Queen's Univ Belfast; *m* 1970 (m dis 1982), Valerie Rosemary, da of late Frank Gill, of Belfast; 3 da; *Career* pres N Ireland Leukaemia Res Fund, dir John Graham (Dromore) Ltd, Electrical Supplies Ltd, Concrete (NI) Ltd, Ulster Quarries Ltd, G H Fieldhouse Plant (NI) Ltd; ret 1983; *Style*— Sir John Graham, Bt; Superservicio Jesus, Jesus, Ibiza, Spain (☎ 34 71 30 46 16)

GRAHAM, Lady Lilias Catriona Maighearad; yst da of 7 Duke of Montrose, *qv*; *b* 16 Feb 1960; *Educ* St Andrew's Univ (Robert T Jones Meml Scholarship); *Career* Executive Search Conslt; *Style*— Lady Lilias Graham; Montrose Estates, Drymen, by Glasgow

GRAHAM, Malcolm Gray Douglas; s of Malcolm Graham, of Shropshire, and Annie Jeanette Graham (d 1976); *b* 18 Feb 1930; *Educ* Shrewsbury Sch; *m* 1980, Sara Ann, da of William Patrick Whitelaw Anderson (d 1976); 2 step-s (Colin Elwell b 1961, James Elwell b 1963); *Career* RM 1948-50; chm: Midland News Assoc Ltd, Express & Star Ltd, Shropshire Newspapers Ltd; Precision Colour Printing Ltd; dir: Claverley Co, Stars News Shops Ltd; pres: Young Newspapermen's Assoc 1969, West Midlands Newspaper Soc 1973-74, Newspaper Advertising Bureau 1978-79; *Recreations* shooting; *Style*— Douglas Graham, Esq; Roughton Manor, Worfield, Bridgnorth, Shropshire (☎ 074 64 209); Wolverhampton (☎ 0902 313131, telex 335490, fax 0902 21467)

GRAHAM, Marigold Evelyn; JP (Clwyd 1983); da of Sir J Crosland Graham (d 1946), and Violet Kathleen, *née* Brinkley (d 1985); *b* 17 Feb 1931; *Educ* St Leonard's Sch, St Andrew's; *Career* farmer; High Sheriff Clwyd 1981; N Wales regnl rep Riding for Disabled Assoc 1970-77; vice pres BRCS Denbighshire; chm: Clwyd Special Riding Tst 1987-, Clwyd Fine Arts Tst; *Recreations* hunting, travel, sport, fine arts; *Style*— Miss Marigold Graham, JP; Plas-yn-Rhos, Ruthin, Clwyd (☎ 08242 2048)

GRAHAM, Hon Martin Nicholas; s of Baron Graham of Edmonton (Life Peer); *b* 17 Jan 1957; *Style*— The Hon Martin Graham

GRAHAM, (Alexander) Michael; JP; s of Dr Walter Graham (d 1985), of 66 Acacia Rd, London NW8, and Suzanne, *née* Simon (d 1976); *b* 27 Sept 1938; *Educ* St Paul's; *m* 6 June 1964, Carolyn, da of Lt-Col Alan Wolryche Stansfeld, MBE, of Dellview Cottage, St Ippollytts, Hitchin, Herts; 3 da (Lucy b 1967, Catriona b 1969, Georgina b 1970); *Career* nat serv Lt The Gordon Highlanders 1957-59, 4/7 Bn The Gordon Highlanders, 3 Bn and HQ 152 Highland Bde (TA) 1959-67; underwriting memb Lloyd's; joined Frizzell Gp Ltd (insurance brokers) 1957, md 1973-; Common Councilman City of London 1978-79, Alderman for Ward of Queenhithe 1979-, Sheriff of City of London 1986-87; govr: St Paul's Sch, St Paul's Girls' Sch, The Hall Sch, Christ's Hosp, King Edward's Whitley; memb: cncl Gresham Coll, tstees Morden Coll; pres Queenhithe Ward Club; Churchwarden All Saints, St Paul's Walden 1981-84; Freeman of City of London, Liveryman Worshipful Co of Mercers 1971 (Master 1983-84); FCII 1964, FBIIBA 1970, FRSA 1980, MBIM 1971; CStJ 1987; Ordre de Wissam Alouite (Morocco) 1987; Sheriff City of London 1986-87; *Recreations* golf, swimming, shooting, tennis, wine, silver, bridge; *Clubs* Carlton, City Livery, Highland Brigade, Royal Worlington Golf; *Style*— Michael Graham, Esq, JP; Walden Abbotts, Whitwell, Hitchin, Herts (☎ 0438 87223); The Frizzell Gp Ltd, Frizzell House, 14-22 Elder St, London E1 6DF (☎ 01 247 6595, fax 01 377 9114, car tel 0860 339 399)

GRAHAM, Norman Sidney; s of Sidney Graham (d 1975), of Cheshire, and Esther, *née* Shipley (d 1983); *b* 19 Sept 1928; *Educ* Birkenhead Sch, St Catharine's Coll Cambridge (MSc); *m* 1954, Gwendolen Mary, da of William Hughes (d 1965), of Cheshire; 1 s (Philip b 1958); *Career* chm Intermediaries Ctee Assoc of Br Insurers; ex pres Manchester Actuarial Soc; Actuary to three Charitable Disaster Funds; govr cncl Coll of Insurance; gen mangr chief Actuary, General Accident Life Assurance Ltd York 1980 (dir 1983); FIA, FCII; *Recreations* golf, bridge, music, hill-walking; *Clubs* Yorkshire, Gallio Dining; *Style*— Norman Graham, Esq; 41 Hillcrest Ave, Nether Poppleton, York YO2 6LD (☎ 0904 795 111); General Accident Life Assurance Ltd, Rougier St, York YO1 1HR (☎ 0904 28 982)

GRAHAM, Sir Norman William; CB (1961); s of late William McLeod Graham; *b* 11 Oct 1913; *Educ* Glasgow HS, Glasgow Univ; *m* 1949, Catherine Mary, *née* Strathie; 2 s, 1 da; *Career* PPS to Min of Aircraft Production 1944-45, asst sec Dept of Health for Scotland 1945, under-sec Scottish Home and Health Dept 1956-63, sec Scottish Edun Dept 1964-73; kt 1971; *Clubs* New (Edinburgh); *Style*— Sir Norman Graham, CB; Chesterhall Steading, Longniddry, East Lothian (☎ 0875 52130)

GRAHAM, Hon Mrs (Pamela Winifred); *née* Whitelaw; yst da of 1 Viscount Whitelaw, *qv*; *b* 1951; *m* 1974, Malise Charles Richard Graham; 4 da (Arabella Mary Susan b 1975, Georgina Carol Cecilia b 1977, Laura Meliora Winifred b 1981, Victoria Malise Samantha b 1985); *Style*— The Hon Mrs Graham; The Cottage, Sproxton, Melton Mowbray, Leicestershire (☎ 0476 860266)

GRAHAM, Sir (John) Patrick; s of Alexander Graham (d 1942), of Shrewsbury; *b* 26 Nov 1906; *Educ* Shrewsbury, Gonville and Caius Coll Cambridge; *m* 1931, Annie Elizabeth Newport, da of Newport Granger Willson, of Fordham, Ely; 4 s; *Career* served WWII Gp Capt RAFVR, chief planning branch PR Div SHAEF; barr Middle Temple 1930, QC 1953, bencher 1961, Tres 1979, dep-chm Salop Quarter Sessions 1961-69, judge of the High Court of Justice (Chancery Div) 1969-81; memb Standing Ctee on Structural Safety 1975-; kt 1969; *Books* Awards to Inventors; *Recreations* golf, fishing; *Style*— Sir Patrick Graham; Tall Elms, Radlett, Herts WD7 8JB (☎ 09276 6307)

GRAHAM, Peter; CB (1982); s of Alderman Douglas Graham, CBE (d 1981), of Huddersfield, Yorkshire, and Ena May, *née* Jackson (d 1982); f was Mayor of Huddersfield 1966-67, and Freeman of Borough 1973; *b* 7 Jan 1934; *Educ* St Bees Sch Cumberland (Scholar), St John's Coll Cambridge (MA, LLM, Scholar); *m* 1, Judith Mary Dunbar; 2 s (Ian b 1960, Alistair b 1962); m 2, Anne Silvia, o da of Benjamin Arthur Garcia; *Career* barr 1958, parly counsel 1972-86, second parly counsel 1987-; *Recreations* village organist, gardening, bridge; *Clubs* The Sette of Odd Volumes; *Style*— Peter Graham, Esq, CB; Parliamentary Counsel Office, 36 Whitehall, SW1

GRAHAM, Sir Peter Alfred; OBE (1969); s of Alfred Graham and Margaret, *née* Winder; *b* 25 May 1922; *Educ* St Joseph's Coll Beulah Hill; *m* 1953, Luned Mary, *née* Kenealy-Jones; 2 s, 2 da; *Career* chm: Standard Chartered Merchant Bank 1977-83, Standard Chartered Bank Ltd 1987-, Crown Agents 1983-; FIB, CBIM; kt 1987; *Style*— Sir Peter Graham, OBE; 3 Somers Crescent, London W2 2PN

GRAHAM, Maj-Gen Peter Walter; CBE (1981, OBE 1978, MBE 1972); s of D Walter Graham (d 1985), of London, and Suzanne, *née* Simon (d 1976); *b* 14 Mar 1937; *Educ* Hall Sch Hampstead, St Pauls Sch London, RMA Sandhurst; *m* 23 March 1963, Alison Mary, da of David Begg Morren, TD, of Huntly Aberdeenshire; 3 s (James b 1964, Roderick b 1967, Douglas b 1970); *Career* cmmnd The Gordon Highlanders 1959; regtl appts 1957-62: Dover, BAOR, Scotland, Kenya; Staff Capt HQ Highland Bde Perth 1962; Adj 1 Gordons 1963: Kenya, Scotland, Borneo (despatches); Staff Capt HQ 1 Bde Corps BAOR 1966-68, Staff Coll Aust 1968, Co Cdr 1 Gordons BAOR 1969, BH 39 Inf Bde Ulster 1970-72; 2 i/c 1 Gordons 1972-74: Scotland, Ulster, Singapore; MA to Adj Gen MOD 1974-76; OC 1 Gordons 1976-78: Scotland, Ulster, Chester; COS HQ 3 Armd Div BAOR 1978-82, Cdr UDR (despatches) 1982-84, Nat Def Coll Canada 1984, Dep Mil Sec B MOD 1985-87, GOC Eastern Dist 1987-, Col The Queen's Bodyguards for Scotland Royal Co of Archers 1985; memb RUSI; *Books* Gordon Highlanders Pipe Music Collection (with Pipe Major B McRae vol 1 1983, vol 2 1985); *Recreations* shooting, fishing, hill walking, gardening under wifes supervision, pipe music; *Clubs* Caledonian; *Style*— Maj-Gen Peter Graham, CBE; c/o National Westminster Bank, Cropthorne Court, Maida Vale, London W9 1TA

GRAHAM, Sir Ralph Stuart; 14 Bt (E 1629); er s of Sir Ralph Wolfe Graham, 13 Bt (d 1988), and his 2 w, Geraldine, *née* Velour; *b* 5 Nov 1950; *Educ* Hofstra Univ; *m* 1, 1972, Roxanne (d 1978), da of Mrs Lovette Gurzan, of Elmont, Long Island, New York; m 2, 1979, Deena Louise, da of William Robert Vandergrift, of 2903 Nemesis, Waukegan, Illinois; 1 child; *Career* self-employed (maintenance company); singer/songwriter (recorded three gospel albums, including Star of the Show, One by One); *Recreations* bible fellowships, performing music; *Style*— Sir Ralph Graham, Bt; 904 Earps Court, Nashville, Tennessee 37221, USA

GRAHAM, Robert Martin; s of Francis P Graham (d 1979), of Dublin, and Margaret M, *née* Broderick; *b* 20 Sept 1930; *Educ* CBS Synge St Dublin; *m* 8 Sept 1959, Eileen, da of Francis Hoey (d 1981); 2 s (Peter b 2 July 1960, James b 11 July 1962), 2 da (Susan b 14 May 1965, Catherine b 28 Jan 1972); *Career* chief exec BUPA 1984- (dep chief exec 1982-84); pres Int Fedn of Voluntary Health Serv Funds 1988-, memb bd of govrs Int Assoc of Mutualities (AIM); *Clubs* RAC, St Stephens Green, London Irish RFC; *Style*— Robert Graham, Esq; Provident Hse, Essex St, London WC2R 3AX (☎ 01 353 5212)

GRAHAM, Stuart Twentyman; CBE (1981), DFC (1943); s of Twentyman Graham (d 1923); *b* 26 August 1921; *Educ* Kilburn GS; *m* 1948, Betty June, *née* Cox; 1 s (Neil); *Career* Sqdn Ldr RAF 1940-46; joined Midland Bank Ltd 1938, jt gen mangr 1966-70, asst chief gen mangr 1970-74, chief gen mangr 1974-81 and dir 1974-85, gp chief exec 1981-82, ret; chm: Northern Bank Ltd (head office, Belfast) 1982-85, Int Commodities Clearing House Ltd 1982-86; dir: Allied-Lyons plc 1981-, Sheffield Forgemasters Holdings plc 1983-85, Aitken Hume Int plc 1985-, Efamol Holdings plc 1985-; *Recreations* music, reading, photography; *Clubs* St James's, RAF; *Style*— Stuart Graham, Esq, CBE, DFC

GRAHAM, Rear Adm Wilfred Jackson; CB (1979); s of William Bryce Graham (d 1955), of Kilmacolm, Scotland, and Jean Hill, *née* Jackson; *b* 17 June 1925; *Educ* Rossall; *m* 15 Dec 1951, Gillian Mary, da of Capt A W J Finlayson, RN (d 1960), of Burley, Hants; 3 s (Angus, Simon, Robin), 1 da (Victoria); *Career* joined RN as cadet 1943; War Serv HM Ships: Sheffield, Howe, Teazer; specialised in Gunnery 1951, cdr 1960, staff of CBNS Washington 1961-63, cmd HMS Tartar 1964-65, cdr RNC Dartmouth 1965-67, Capt 1967, cmd HMS Scarborough and Dartmouth Trg Squad 1971-72, cmd HMS Ark Royal 1975-76, Rear Adm 1976, Flag Offr Portsmouth 1976-79, ret from RN 1979; dir and sec Royal Nat Lifeboat Inst 1979 (ret 1987); *Recreations* walking, sailing; *Clubs* Royal Yacht Squadron, Army and Navy; *Style*— Rear Admiral Wilfred Graham, CB; Bank of Scotland, 110 Queen St, Glasgow G1 3BY

GRAHAM, William Reginald; 2 s of Sir Richard Bellingham Graham, 10 Bt, OBE (d 1982); bro and h of Sir James Graham, 11 Bt, *qv*; *b* 7 July 1942; *Educ* privately; *Style*— William Graham, Esq; Norton Conyers, nr Ripon, N Yorks

GRAHAM, Winston Mawdsley; OBE (1983); s of Albert Henry Graham, and Anne, *née* Mawdsley; *b* 30 June 1912; *m* 1939, Jean Mary, da of Cdr Samuel Arthur Williamson, RN; 1 s (Andrew), 1 da (Rosamund); *Career* publishing novelist since age of 23, books translated into 17 languages, six novels made into feature films incl: Marnie (directed by Alfred Hitchcock); TV films made of: The Sleeping Partner 1967, The Forgotten Story (six instalments) 1983, The Poldark novels (twenty-nine instalments) 1975-77; Other works incl: Angell, Pearl and Little God, The Walking Stick, The Grove of Eagles, The Spanish Armadas, Poldark's Cornwall, The Green Flash, The Tumbled House; FRSL; *Clubs* Savile, Beefsteak; *Style*— Winston Graham, Esq, OBE; Abbotswood Hse, Buxted, Sussex TN22 4PB

GRAHAM BRYCE, Dame Isabel; *née* Lorrain-Smith; DBE (1968); da of late Prof J Lorrain-Smith, FRS; *b* 30 April 1902; *Educ* St Leonards Sch, St Andrew's Edinburgh Univ (MA); *m* 1934, Alexander Graham Bryce (d 1968); 2 s; *Career* investigator Industl Fatigue Res Bd 1926-27, HM inspector of factories 1928-34, organizer WVS Manchester 1938-39; dir Orgn Ontario div Canadian WVS 1941-42, tech advsr American WVS 1942-43, res fell Fatigue Lab Harvard Univ 1943-44, chm Manchester br Nat Cncl of Woman 1947-50, vice-chm Education Ctee 1950-51, vice-pres Princess Christian Coll Manchester, JP and memb Juvenile Ct Panel Manchester City 1949-55, vice-chm Assoc of HMC's 1953-55; memb: Gen Nursing Cncl 1956-61, Nurses and Midwives Whitley Cncl 1954-60; Public Health Insp Education Bd 1958-64, ITA 1960-65, ATV Network Ltd 1968-72, chm: Oxford Regional Hosp Bd 1963-72, Nat Staff Ctee and Nat Nursing Staff Ctee of NHS 1967-75; memb bd: Br Tport Hotels 1962-78, Oxford Polytechnic 1969-70; pres Goring & Dist Day Centre for the Elderly, life memb Br Fedn Univ Women; Hon memb Oxford Br Zouta Int; memb: Edinburgh Univ Club of Oxford, Oxford Branch Nat Cncl of Women; pres League of Friends Radcliffe Infirmary Oxford; *Clubs* New Cavendish (London); *Style*— Dame Isabel Graham Bryce, DBE; 23 Russell Court, Woodstock Rd, Oxford OX2 6JH (☎ 0865 513168)

GRAHAM OF EDMONTON, Baron (Life Peer UK 1983); (Thomas) Edward Graham; s of Thomas Edward Graham, of Newcastle-upon-Tyne; *b* 26 Mar 1925; *Educ* WEA Co-Op Coll, Open Univ (BA); *m* 1950, Margaret Golding, da of Frederick and Alice Golding, of Dagenham; 2 s; *Career* memb and leader Enfield Cncl 1961-68, national sec Co-Op Party 1967-74, MP (Lab and Co-Op) Enfield Edmonton Feb 1974-83, PPS to Min of State Prices and Consumer Protection 1974-76, lord cmmr Treasury 1976-79; oppn front bench spokesman on: Environment 1981-, Sport, Defence, N Ireland; oppn whips off, sec All Pty Gp on Retail Trade; *Style*— The Rt Hon the Lord Graham of Edmonton; 17a Queen Anne's Grove, Bush Hill Park, Enfield, Middx EN1 1BP (☎ 01 363 3013); House of Lords, London SW1

GRAHAM-CAMPBELL, Hon Mrs (Sarah); *née* Peyton; da of Baron Peyton of Yeovil (Life Peer); *b* 4 Sept 1948; *m* 1971, Dugald Graham-Campbell; *Style*— The Hon Mrs Graham-Campbell; 14 Ewald Rd, London SW6

GRAHAM-CLARKE, Philip Audley; s of Gerald Graham-Clarke (d 1961); *b* 6 Oct 1924; *Educ* Eton, Edinburgh Univ; *m* 1960 (m dis 1974), Nora Margaret, *née* Keep; 1 da (Emma Marjorie b 1962); *Career* Maj RA (India, BAOR, W Africa, USA); chartered accountant 1966; DL Monmouthshire 1963-73, county cmmr for Scouts Monmouthshire 1962-69; *Style*— Philip Graham-Clarke, Esq; Hortons, The Street, Broughton Gifford, Melksham, Wiltshire (☎ 0225 782586); Norman & Pike, 11 Edward St, Westbury, Wilts (☎ 0373 822290)

GRAHAM-DIXON, Anthony Philip; QC (1973); Leslie Charles Graham-Dixon QC (d 1986), and Dorothy, *née* Rivett (d 1979); *b* 5 Nov 1929; *Educ* Westminster, Christ Church Oxford (MA); *m* 15 Dec 1956, Margaret Suzanne, s of Edgar Hurmon Villar (d 1953); 1 s (Andrew b 1960), 1 da (Elizabeth b 1965); *Career* Mid Special Branch RN 1953-55, Lt Special Branch RNVR 1956; called to the Bar Inner Temple 1956, bencher 1982; memb advsy bd Competiton Law in Western Europe and the USA 1976-87; chm London Concertino Ltd 1982-, memb cncl Charing Cross Hosp Med Sch 1976-83, dep chm Public Health Laboratory Serv 1988 (bd memb 1987); tstee Soc for Promotion of New Music 1988, govr Bedales Sch 1988; Liveryman Worshipful Co of Goldsmiths; *Recreations* music, gardening, tennis, walking, trees; *Style*— Anthony Graham-Dixon, Esq, QC; 31 Hereford Sq, London SW7 4NB (☎ 01 370 1902), Maslelts Manor, Nutley, East Sussex (☎ 082 571)

GRAHAM-HARRISON, Robert Montagu; s of Francis Laurence Theodore Graham-Harrison, CB, of London, and Carol Mary St John, *née* Stewart; *b* 16 Feb 1943; *Educ* Eton, Magdalen Coll Oxford (BA); *m* 30 April 1977, Kathleen Patricia, *née* Maher; 2 da (Emma b 24 July 1978, Laura b 15 Aug 1980); *Career* VSO India 1965, ODA (formerly Miny of Overseas Dept) 1967, World Bank Washington 1971-73, private sec Min of Overseas Devpt 1978, asst sec ODA 1979; head: Br Devpt Div Eastern Africa 1982, Eastern Asia Dept ODA 1986-; *Style*— Robert Graham-Harrison, Esq; Overseas Devpt Admin, Eland House, Stag Place, London SW1 (☎ 01 273 3000)

GRAHAM-JONES, Oliver; s of late Andrew Vaughan Jones, and Ethel Mabel, *née* Smith; *b* 17 Feb 1919; *Educ* King Edward's GS, RVC London Univ; *m* 23 March 1958, Gillian Margaret, da of Basil Dent (d 1948); 2 s (Piers Dominic b 1965, Peregrine Jasper b 1967); *Career* WWII cmmnd RAVC served Italy 1943-44; vet surgn in private practice 1941-50, sr vet offr Zoological Soc of London 1960-66 (vet offr 1951-60), sr lectr RVC 1966-79 (asst lectr 1950-51); conslt vet offr: Nat Hosp for Nervous Diseases 1967-, London Hosp Med Sch 1967-, Sultan of Oman 1972-79; past pres: Br Small Animal Vet Assoc, Central Vet Soc; vet steward Nat Greyhound Racing Club; expert witness in many cases involving wild animals, licensed zoo inspector under Govt; awarded: The Livesey Medal RCVS, The Victory Medal, Sir Arthur Keith Medal; RCS; FRCVS; *Books* author of numerous contributions to learned journals and magazines; *Recreations* horse driving, polo, Legion of Frontiersman Mounted Sqdn; *Clubs* RSM; *Style*— Oliver Graham-Jones, Esq; 45 Clayton Rd, Selsey, Chichester PO20 9DF (☎ 0243 602838/0243 605956)

GRAHAM-MOON, Sir Peter Wilfred Giles; 5 Bt (UK 1855), of Portman Square, Middx; s of Sir Wilfred Graham Moon, 4 Bt (d 1954), by his 2 w, Doris, *née* Jobson (d 1953); *b* 24 Oct 1942; *Educ* Lancing; *m* 1967, Mrs Sarah Chater, da of Lt-Col Michael Smith, MC, of The Grange, Headley, Hants (gs of Sir Thomas Smith, 1 Bt, KCVO, Hon Serjeant-Surgeon to King Edward VII); 2 s; *Heir* s, Rupert Graham-Moon; *Career* chm and md Joblux Ltd; *Recreations* golf, shooting, horse racing; *Clubs* Royal Cork Yacht; *Style*— Sir Peter Graham-Moon, Bt; Old Whistley Farm, Potterne, Wiltshire SN10 5TD (☎ 0380 4388)

GRAHAM-MOON, Rupert Francis Wilfred; s and h of Sir Peter Graham-Moon, 5 Bt; *b* 29 April 1968; *Educ* Marlborough; *Style*— Rupert Graham-Moon, Esq

GRAHAM-SMITH, Prof Sir Francis; s of Claud Henry Smith, of April Cottage, Fairlight, Sussex (d 1963), and Cicely Winifred Kingston (d 1946); *b* 25 April 1923; *Educ* Epsom Coll, Rossall Sch, Downing Coll Cambridge (MA, PhD); *m* Dorothy Elizabeth, da of Reginald Palmer, of Ecclestone House, Mildenhall, Suffolk (d 1949); 3 s, 1 da; *Career* dir Royal Greenwich Observatory 1976-81, pres Royal Astronomical Soc 1975-77, prof of radio astronomy Manchester Univ 1964-74 and 1981-, dir Nuffield Radio Astronomy Laboratories 1981-88, Astronomer Royal 1983-; physical sec Royal Soc 1988-, pro vice chllr Manchester Univ 1988-; FRS; kt 1986; *Recreations* sailing, badminton, gardening; *Style*— Prof Sir Francis Graham-Smith; Old School House, Henbury, Macclesfield, Cheshire (☎ 0625 612657); Nuffield Radio Astronomy Laboratories, Jodrell Bank, Macclesfield, Cheshire (☎ 0477 71321)

GRAHAM-VIVIAN, Henry Richard; TD (1955), JP (Cornwall 1970), DL (1982); s of (Richard) Preston Graham-Vivian, MVO, MC, sometime Norroy and Ulster King of Arms (d 1979, himself 2 s of Sir Richard Graham, 4 Bt, JP, DL, and Lady Mabel Duncombe, who in her turn was da of 1 Earl of Feversham), by his w Audrey, da of Henry Wyndham Vivian (which surname Preston assumed by Royal Licence 1929), himself n of 1 Baron Swansea and gn of 1 Baron Vivian; *b* 13 April 1923; *Educ* Eton, Ch Ch Oxford; *m* 1955, Rosemary, da of Lt-Col Giffard Loftus Tyringham (d 1976); 1 s, 1 da; *Career* Capt Coldstream Guards Normandy, territorial serv with Duke of Cornwall Light Infantry 1946-60, High Sheriff Cornwall 1965; *Recreations* shooting, fishing; *Clubs* Army and Navy; *Style*— Henry Graham-Vivian, Esq, TD, JP, DL; Bosahan, Manaccan, nr Helston, Cornwall TR12 6JL (☎ 032 623 330)

GRAHAM-WOOD, David; TD (1952); s of Sir Edward Graham Wood, JP (d 1930), and Dorothy, MBE, *née* Harwood (d 1956); *b* 14 Mar 1919; *Educ* Oundle, Univ of London; *m* 15 April 1950, Joan Helen, da of Lt-Col John Stratton Storrar, MC (d 1946); 2 s (Malcolm b 1957, Maxwell b 1959), 2 da (Fiona b 1951, Gillian b 1954); *Career* TA 42 (E Lancs) Div, WWII serv UK, BEF (despatches), N Africa, Italy; chm and fndr Graham Wood Steel Gp plc 1952-78, dir and later chm Lilleshall Co plc 1979-87; serv on Surrey CC and later Finance Office for the Euro Constituency of Surrey; Freeman City of London, Liveryman Worshipful Co of Glaziers and Painters of Glass (Master 1977/78); OStJ 1986; *Recreations* sailing, stained glass; *Clubs* Royal Thames Yacht, City Livery, MCC; *Style—* David Graham-Wood, Esq, TD; Little Chartham, Shalford, Guildford, Surrey GU4 8AF (☎ 0483 62429)

GRAINGER, (Leonard) Cherry; s of George Grainger (d 1936), and Lucy, *née* Cherry (d 1974); *b* 12 Mar 1919; *Educ* Westminster Catering Coll (Dip), Ecole Des Hoteliers Zurich; *m* 17 June 1944, (Yvonne) Claudia Marshall, da of Victor Stanley Chambers, OBE (d 1954); 1 s (Lt Cdr Robert Marshall b 1955), 2 da (Lynne b 1945, Jacki b 1947); *Career* RN: Fleet Air Arm 1940-42, Paymaster 1942-46; fndr and chm Graison (Caterers) Ltd 1946-; Chevalier Du Tastevin 1964; chm: London ctee Catering Trades Benevolent Assoc, tstees Reunion Des Gastronomes (former pres); memb: ctee Br Hotels & Restaurants Assoc, mgmnt ctee City & Guilds; govr Westminster Coll 1981-; Freeman City of London 1964, Liveryman Worshipful Co of Distillers 1964-, Master Worshipful Co of Cooks 1988-89; FCA, FHCIMA, FRSH; *Recreations* swimming, travel; *Clubs* City Livery, RAC; *Style—* Cherry Grainger, Esq; 102 Hayes Way, Beckenham, Kent BR3 2RS (☎ 01 650 4727, 01 650 4727); Casa 22, Puebla Blanca, Torreblanca, Malaga, Spain

GRANARD, 9 Earl of (I 1684); Sir Arthur Patrick Hastings Forbes; 10 Bt (S 1628), AFC (1941); also Viscount Granard, Baron Clanehugh (both I 1675) and Baron Granard (UK 1806, title in House of Lords); s of 8 Earl of Granard (d 1948, eighth in descent from 1 Earl, who was himself ggs of Hon Patrick Forbes, 3 s of 2 Lord Forbes); *b* 10 April 1915; *Educ* Eton, Trinity Coll Cambridge; *m* 1949, Marie, da of Jean Maurel, of Millau, Aveyron, and formerly w of Prince Humbert de Faucigny Lucinge (cr of Charles X of France 1828); 2 da (HH Princesse Charles (Lady Moira) de Ligne de La Tremoille, of the family of mediatised Princes of the Holy Roman Empire; Lady Georgina Forbes); *Heir* nephew, Peter A H Forbes, *qv*; *Career* Air Cdre RAFVR, served WW II (despatches, Cdr Legion of Honour, offr of American Legion of Merit, 4 Class Order of George I of Greece with crossed swords, French Croix de Guerre, Polish Cross of Valour); *Clubs* White's; *Style—* The Rt Hon the Earl of Granard, AFC; Castle Forbes, Newtown Forbes, Co Longford, Eire; 11 Rue Louis de Savoie, Morges, Switzerland

GRANBY, Marquis of; David Charles Robert Manners; s & h of 10 Duke of Rutland, CBE, JP, DL, by his 2 w, Frances; *b* 8 May 1959; *Educ* Wellesley House Broadstairs Kent, Stanbridge Earls; *Career* dir Belvoir Arms and Armour; Freeman City of London, Liveryman Worshipful Co of Gunsmiths; *Recreations* shooting, fishing, gliding; *Clubs* Turf, Annabel's; *Style—* Marquis of Granby

GRANBY, Nicholas Charles; s of Paul Granby (d 1982), of London, and Lydia Barbara, *née* Goulding; *b* 19 Nov 1945; *Educ* Westminster Sch, London Sch of Film Technique (Dip); *m* Pauline Sylvia, da of Arthur Hapgood Rice (d 1975); 1 da (Sarah b 1967); *Career* film & TV dir, writer and prodr; *films incl* Closed Circuit (1987, prize winner Barcelona Film Festival); *documentaries incl* : The Queen in Arabia 1979, To Win at All Costs - The Story of the America's Cup 1983-84 (prize-winner Houston Int Film Festival and UK Video Awards), The Queen in Jordan 1984; *stage musical* Mesmer (1988); dir: Nicholas Granby Prodns Ltd, Orbit TV and Film Ltd, Para-Shoot Enterprises Ltd; *Clubs* BAFTA; *Style—* Nicholas C Granby, Esq; c/o Valerie Hoskins, Eagle House, 109 Jermyn Street, London SW1Y 6HB (☎ 01 839 2121)

GRANDY, Marshal of the RAF Sir John; GCB (1967, KCB 1964, CB 1956), GCVO (1988), KBE (1961), DSO (1945); s of Francis Grandy (d 1932), and Nellie, *née* Lines (d 1948); *b* 8 Feb 1913; *Educ* Univ Coll Sch; *m* 1937, Cecile, CStJ, yr da of Sir Robert Rankin, first and last Bt (d 1960); 2 s; *Career* RAF 1931, Adj and Flying Instr London Univ Air Sqdn 1937-39, cmd 249 Sqdn Battle of Britain, Wing Cdr Flying RAF Coltishall 1941, cmd RAF Duxford 1942, cmd HQ 210 Gp No 73 Operational Training Unit and Fighter Conversion Unit Abu Sueir 1943, cmd 341 Wing SE Asia 1944-45, Air Cdre 1956, AVM 1958, Cdr 2 TAF and C-in-C RAF Germany 1961-63, Air Marshal 1962, AOC-in-C Bomber Cmd 1963-65, C-in-C Br Forces Far East and UK Mil Advsr SEATO 1965-67, Air Chief Marshal 1965, Chief of Air Staff 1967-71, Marshal of RAF 1971, govr and C-in-C Gibraltar 1973-78, constable and govr Windsor Castle 1978-88; chm tstee Imperial War Museum, dep chm cncl RAF Benevolent Fund, vice-pres Burma Star Assoc, tstee Shuttleworth Remembrance Trust and chm Aerodrome Ctee, past sr pres Offrs Assoc, vice-pres Offrs Pension Soc, pres Disablement in City; tstee: St Clement Danes RAF Church, Prince Philip Trust Fund Royal Borough of Windsor and Maidenhead; vice-pres: Nat Assoc of Boys Clubs, RNLI; dir Brixton Estate 1971-73 and 1978-83; memb ctee Royal Humane Soc, patron Polish Air Force Assoc in GB; pres Air League 1984-87; Freeman City of London, Hon Liveryman Haberdashers Co; KStJ; *Clubs* White's, Pratt's, Royal Yacht Sqdn, RAF; *Style—* Marshal of the RAF Sir John Grandy, GCB, KBE, DSO; c/o White's, St James's Street, London SW1

GRANGE, Hugh; s of James Grange (d 1968), of Inver Green House, Inver, Larne, Co Antrim, and Ruth, *née* Gourley; *b* 26 Nov 1943; *Educ* Trinity Coll Dublin (MA, LLB); *m* 18 Sept 1971, Janet, da of Maj K C B Golding, TD, JP (d 1977), of Court Farm, Hedgerley, Bucks; *Career* barr NI 1970, practised NI 1970-73, barr Gray's Inn 1974, worked for HM Procurator Gen and Treasy Slr 1974-87, seconded Attorney Gen Chambers Law Offrs Dept 1987- (responsible for NI matters), protocol offr Law Offrs Dept 1988; memb: RSL, compilation team Burkes Irish Family Records (1975); *Recreations* history, literature, genealogy, walking, travel; *Style—* Hugh Grange, Esq; The Dean Cottages, Village Lane, Hedgerley, Bucks SL2 3UY (☎ 028 14 5949); The Attorney General's Chambers, Law Officers Dept, Royal Cts of Justice, Strand, London WC2

GRANGE, Kenneth Henry; CBE (1984); s of Harry Alfred Grange, and Hilda Gladys, *née* Long; *b* 17 July 1929; *Educ* Willesden Coll of Art; *m* 13 Oct 1984, Apryl, da of Deric Swift; *Career* tech illustrator RE 1947-48; architectural asst Bronek Katz & Vaughan 1949-50; designer: Gordon Bowyer 1950-52, Jack Howe & Ptnrs 1952-58; fndr Kenneth Grange Design London 1958, fndr ptnr Pentagram Design 1972-; winner of 10 Design Cncl awards and Duke of Edinburgh Prize for Elegant Design 1963; work represented in collections of: V & A, Design Museum London, State Museum Munich; one man shows: Kenneth Grange at the Boilerhouse V & A 1983, The Product Designs of Kenneth Grange of Pentagram XSITE Tokyo Japan 1989; master faculty of Royal Design for indust 1985-87 (memb 1969), Design Cncl: Cncl memb, industl design advsr 1971, memb advsy bd on product design; chm Br Design Export Gp, conslt design dir Wilkinson Sword Ltd, cncl memb and ct memb RSA; Hon Dr RCA 1985, Hon DUniv Herriot-Watt Univ 1986; FCSD 1965 (pres 1987-99); RDI 1969; *Books* Living by Design (jtly 1977); *Recreations* tennis, skiing; *Clubs* RAC; *Style—* Kenneth Grange, Esq, CBE; Acrise Cottage, Christchurch Hill, London NW3; 11 Needham Rd, London W11 2RP (☎ 01 229 3477, fax 01 727 9932)

GRANGER, Dr John Douglas; s of Dr Edmund Douglas Granger (d 1961), of Dorset, and Kathryn Edith Emily Granger (d 1982); *b* 16 August 1926; *Educ* Stowe, Magdalen Coll Oxford, St Thomas's Hosp (BM, BCL, MRCCP, QRCOG); *m* 25 March 1961, Mary Sylvia, da of George William Back, of Kent; 2 s (William b 1965, Oliver b 1966), 2 da (Cressida b 1963, Annabel b 1969); *Career* gen med practitioner; MO, Fl Lt, RAF Malaya 1952-54; house surgn St Thomas's Hosp 1951; *Recreations* golf; *Clubs* Parkstone GC; *Style—* Dr John D Granger; St Just, Sandbourne Rd, Bournemouth (☎ 0202 752550); Westbourne Medical Centre, Milburn Rd, Bournemouth (☎ 0202 752550)

GRANGER, Penelope Ruth; da of Eric Frank Hardy, of Stowmarket, Suffolk, and Ruth Susannah, *née* Turner; *b* 14 July 1947; *Educ* Norwich HS for Girls, Univ of Sheffield (BA), Homerton Coll Cambridge; *m* 11 July 1970, Richard John; 1 s (Timothy b 1976), 1 da (Caroline b 1973); *Career* memb Gen Synod of the C of E 1980, church cmmr 1983, GS Standing Ctee 1985, chm Ely Diocesan Synod House of Laity 1988; broadcaster, musician; *Recreations* walking; *Clubs* Royal Cwlth Soc; *Style—* Mrs Penny Granger; 88 Queen Edith's Way, Cambridge, CB1 4PW (☎ 0223 246392)

GRANT; *see*: Macpherson-Grant

GRANT, Alexander Marshall; CBE (1965); s of Alexander Gibb Grant, and Ealther May, *née* Marshall; *b* 22 Feb 1925; *Educ* Wellington Coll New Zealand; *Career* princ dancer Royal Ballet 1946-76, dir Ballet for All 1971-76, artistic dir Nat Ballet of Canada 1976-83, princ dancer London Festival Ballet 1985-; judge at int ballet competitions: Moscow, Mississippi, Helsinki; created many ballet roles particularly for Sir Frederick Ashton, guest artist with Royal Ballet and Joffrey Ballet; *Recreations* gardening, cooking; *Style—* Alexander Grant, Esq, CBE; London Festival Ballet, Festival Ballet Hse, 39 Jay Mews, London SW7 2ES (☎ 01 581 1245)

GRANT, (Duncan) Alistair Antoine; s of Duncan George Grant (d 1968), of London, and Germaine Victoria, *née* Ramet Cousin (d 1970); *b* 3 June 1925; *Educ* Froebel E Sheen, Whitehall Glasgow, Birmingham Sch of Art, RCA; *m* Phyllis (d 1988), da of late William Fricker, of Guildford; 1 da (Emma b 12 Sept 1954); *Career* Aircrew RAF 1943-47; artist, painter and printmaker; art teacher 1951-53: St Martin's Sch of Art, Hammersmith Sch of Art, Sidcup Sch of Art, Colchester Sch of Art; RCA: tutor printmaking dept 1955- 1970, head printing dept 1970-84, chair printmaking 1984-; numerous exhibitions 1951- including: Redfern Gallery London 1952-54, Nat Arts Cncl of Southern Rhodesia 1957, Tel Aviv Museum Israel 1959, Zwemmer Gallery London 1961 and 1962, AAA Gallery NY 1967, Portland Museum Oregon 1971, Carcow Print Biennale (prize) 1972, Calgary Graphics Canada 1973, Limited Editions London 1979, Mullhouse Print Biennale 1982 and 1986, Le Cadre Gallery Hong Kong 1985; works in the collection of: V & A Museum, The Arts Cncl, The Tate Gallery, Dallas Museum USA, Museum of Modern Art NY USA, Vancouver Art Gallery Canada, Tel Aviv Museum Israel, Cairo Art Gallery Egypt, Nat Gallery of S Aust, Mobil Oil, BP Int, Unilever; memb RBA; *Clubs* Chelsea Arts; *Style—* Alistair Grant, Esq; Royal College of Art, London SW7 (☎ 01 584 5020)

GRANT, Allan Wallace; OBE (1974), MC (1941), TD (1947); s of Henry Grant (d 1929), and Rose Margaret, *née* Sheppard (d 1947); *b* 2 Feb 1911; *Educ* Dulwich, London Univ (LLB); *m* 31 Aug 1939, Kathleen Rachel, *née* Bamford; 1 da (Hilary b 1944); *Career* Sharpshooters: Trooper 23 London Armd Car Co 1929 (2 Lt 1938), Capt 3 Co London Yeo 1940, (Maj 1941, 2 i/c 1942); md Ecclesiastical Insur Off Ltd 1952-75 (chm 1975-81, pres 1981-87); pres Sharpshooters Regimental Assoc 1969-, chm Clergy Orphan Corpn 1967-80 (vice pres 1980-), govr St Mary's Sch Wantage 1967-81; memb: Worshipful Co of Coopers (Master 1984-85), Worshipful Co of Insurers (asst from fndn); Hon Dr Canon Law Lexington USA 1970; FCII 1970-71 (pres); *Recreations* golf; *Clubs* City Livery's, Richmond GC (Capt 1974); *Style—* Allan Wallace, Esq, OBE, MC, TD; 24 Alexandra Lodge, Monument Hill, Weybridge, Surrey KT13 8RY (☎ 0932 858 179)

GRANT, Andrew Francis Joseph; CB (1971); er s of Francis Herbert Grant (d 1976), and Clare Grant; *b* 25 Feb 1911; *Educ* St Joseph's Coll, King's Coll London Univ (BSc, CEng); *m* 1934, Mary Harrison; 2 s (Peter, Jeremy), 2 da (Clare, Susan); *Career* civil engr, entered civil engr-in-chief's dept Admiralty 1937, fleet civil engr Med 1960-63, dir for Wales Min of Public Building & Works 1966-6, dir Far East Region 1966-68, dir Home Regional Service Dept of Environment 1968-71, Civil Serv Appeal Bd 1972-81, FICE; *Recreations* painting, golf, travel; *Clubs* Civil Service; *Style—* Andrew Grant, Esq, CB

GRANT, Anne Caroline; da of Maj Gen Ferris Nelson Grant, of Ropley, Hants, and Patricia Anne Grant (d 1988); *b* 18 Feb 1951; *Educ* Hall Sch Wincanton, Exeter Tech Coll, Royal Naval Sch of Physiotherapy; *Career* NHS Univ Coll Hosp 1974-75, Hosp de Zone Payerne Switzerland 1975-76, Hosp Orthopaedic Lausanne Switzerland 1976-78, La Cassage Home Ecole FMC Lausanne 1978-80, Catholic Relief Servs Thailand 1980-82, personnal physiotherapist to HRH Sheik Rashid Dubai 1983, private practice London 1984-; memb Chartered Soc Physiotheraphy, MCSP, SRP; *Recreations* tennis, skiing, travel, photography; *Style—* Miss Anne Grant; 10 Gowrie Rd, London SW11 (☎ 01 228 4748); Cannons, Cousin Lane, London EC4R 3TE (☎ 01 283 0108)

GRANT, Anthony Ernest; s of Ernest Grant (d 1986), of Sheffield, and Doris, *née* Hughes; *b* 23 April 1940; *Educ* King Edward VII GS Sheffield, Keble Coll Oxford (MA); *m* 14 April 1962, Darel Avis, da of Frederick John Atkinson (d 1980), of Sheffield; 3 da (Henrietta b 1965, Sarah b 1966, Philippa b 1969); *Career* Coopers & Lybrand CA 1961-: Sheffield 1961-68 (qualified 1964, mangr 1966, later ptnr), E Malaysia and Brunei 1968-72, London 1972-73, Madrid 1973-75, Leeds 1976- (off ptnr 1984-); dep chm Leeds Poly, tres Leeds C of C, memb ctee Friends of Br Limbless Ex-Servicemen's Assoc Leeds; FCA 1965; *Recreations* riding, bridge; *Clubs* Leeds; *Style—* Anthony Grant, Esq; Albion Ct, 5 Albion Pl, Leeds (☎ 0532 431343, fax 0532 424009, telex 556230)

GRANT, Sir (John) Anthony; MP (C) S W Cambridge 1983-; s of Arthur Ernest Grant; *b* 1925,May; *Educ* St Paul's, BNC Oxford; *m* 1953, Sonia Isobel, da of late George Henry Landen; 1 s, 1 da; *Career* solicitor 1952; serv WWII Capt 3 Dragoon Gds; MP (C) Harrow Cen 1964-1983, oppn whip 1966-70, parly sec BOT 1970, parly under-sec (Trade 1970-72, Industl Devpt 1972-74) DTI; chm Cons back bench Trade Ctee 1979-, memb Foreign Affrs Select Ctee 1980-; chm Econ Ctee Cncl of Europe 1980-; Liveryman Worshipful Co of Slrs; kt 1982; *Style—* Sir Anthony Grant, MP; House of Commons, London SW1

GRANT, Bernard Alexander Montgomery (Bernie); MP (L) Tottenham 1987-; s of Eric and Lily Grant; *b* 17 Feb 1944; *Educ* Stanislaus Coll Guyana, Tottenham Technical Coll; *m* separated; 3 s; *Career* analyst Demerara Bauxite Co Guyana 1961-63, clerk British Rail 1963-65, telephonist Int Telephones 1969-78, area offr NUPE 1978-83, devpt worker Black Trade Unionists Solidarity Movement 1983-84, sr housing offr London Borough Newham 1985-87; fndr memb and chair Parly Black Caucus 1987; ldr Harringay Cncl London; *Style—* Bernard Grant, Esq, MP; House of Commons, London SW1A 0AA

GRANT, His Hon (Hubert) Brian; *b* 5 August 1917; *Educ* Trinity Coll Cambridge (MA); *m* 1946, Jeanette Mary; 1 s (Paul), 3 da (Susan, Elizabeth, Jane); *Career* served WWII, No 10 Commando 1942-44; barr Gray's Inn 1945, circuit judge Sussex and Kent (formerly judge County Courts) 1965-82, memb Lord Chllr's Law Reform Ctee 1970-74; vice-chm Nat Marriage Guidance Cncl 1970-72; fndr pres Parenthood 1979; hon librarian Br Deaf Assoc 1985-87; *Publications* Marriage, Separation and Divorce (1946), Family Law (1970), Conciliation and Divorce (1981), The Quiet Ear (1987); *Clubs* Penrith Golf; *Style—* His Hon Brian Grant; Eden Hill, Armathwaite, Carlisle CA4 9PQ

GRANT, Dr Douglas; s of Robert Grant (d 1957) and Ierne Grant (d 1963); *b* 6 Jan 1918; *Educ* George Watson's Coll, St Andrews Univ; *m* 1948, Enid Whitsey, da of Raymond Whitsey Williams (d 1985); 3 s (William Neil b 1953, Richard Martin b 1955, Peter Michael b 1958); *Career* WWII Lt Col RA (served W Africa and staff) 1939-46; Scottish Widows Fund 1936-39; dir: Oliver and Boyd Ltd 1947-67, Edinburgh C of C 1952-56, New Education Ltd 1962-66, Bracken House Publications Ltd 1963-67, Sprint Productions Ltd 1963-80, E & S Livingston Ltd 1963-67, Darien Press Ltd 1963-68, R & R Clark Ltd 1963-80, Port Seton Offset Printers Ltd 1965-75, T & A Constable ltd 1965-75, Br Jl of Educnl Psychology 1970-, Pindar (Scotland) Ltd 1986-, Macdonald Lindsay (Printers) Ltd 1988; chm: Scottish Journal of Theology Ltd 1948-, Robt Cunningham & Sons Ltd 1952-76, Ch of Scotland Publications Ctee 1958-76, Hunter and Foulis Ltd 1963-75, Port Seton Offset Printers Ltd 1965-75, Multi Media (AU) Services Ltd 1967-75; Scottish Academic Press Ltd 1969-, Scottish Int Review Ltd 1970-75, The Handsel Press Ltd 1975-, Scottish Academic Press (Jls) Ltd 1976, Clark Constable Printers Ltd 1978-89; pres: Edinburgh Bookseller Soc 1977-80, Edinburgh Amateur Angling Club 1978-80; tstee: The Lodge Tst (Natural History) 1949-85, Darling (Ogilvy) Investment Tst 1955-78, Kilwarlin Tst 1964-, Esdaile Tst 1975; ctee memb: The Scottish Cncl of Law Reporting 1950-, Police Dependents Tst (Lothian and Borders Police) 1956-, NEDO 1968-75, New Coll Univ of Edinburgh (Fin) 1970, Edinburgh Univ Ct 1972-84, The Scottish Arts Cncl 1975-79; Hon D Litt St Andrew's Univ; FRSE (1949); *Clubs* New (Edinburgh), Hon Co of Edinburgh Golfers; *Style—* Dr Douglas Grant; 2 Pentland Road, Edinburgh EH13 0JA (☎ 031 441 3352)

GRANT, Brig Eneas Henry George; CBE (1951), DSO (1944, and bar 1945), MC (1936), JP (1957); s of Col Hugh Gough Grant, CB (d 1922), and Isabel, *née* Mackintosh (d 1960); *b* 14 August 1901; *Educ* Wellington, RMC Sandhurst; *m* 20 Oct 1926, Lilian Marion (d 1978), da of S O'Neill, of Cumberstown, Co Westmeath; 2 s (Patrick Angus b 8 Aug 1927, ka Korea 1951, Donald John Arthur); *Career* 2 Lt Seaforth Highlanders 1920, Capt and Adj Lovat Scouts 1928-33, Palestine 1933-34 and 1936, Maj 1937, France 1940, Temp Lt-Col 1942 (Lt-Col 1947), France and Germany 1944, Temp Col 1944 (Col 1948), Bde Cdr 1944-49, Temp Brig 1944 (Brig 1952), Cdr Gold Coast Dist and Col Cmdt Gold Coast Regt RWAFF 1949-52, Dep Cdr Northumbrian Dist 1952-55, ret 1955; chm Inverness-shire TA & AFA 1961-65; farmer 1956-71; DL Inverness-shire 1958-76; *Recreations* country pursuits; *Clubs* Highland (Inverness); *Style—* Brig Eneas Grant, CBE, DSO, MC, JP; Inverbrough Lodge, Tomatin, Inverness-shire, Scotland (☎ 08082 216)

GRANT, Maj Gen Ferris Nelson; CB (1967); s of Lt-Gen Harold George Grant (d 1948), and Norah Lindsey Bucknal Grant, *née* Barker (d 1968); *b* 25 Dec 1916; *Educ* Cheltenham; *m* 1, 1940, Patricia Anne (d 1988), da of Maj-Gen Thomas Henry Jameson, CBE, DSO (d 1985); 1 s (Alastair), 1 da (Anne); m 2, 1988, Mrs M L Bagwell; *Career* RM 1935, HMS Suffolk 1940, GSO 1 HQS ACSEA 1943, Bde Major Commando Bde, Cmdg 41 Indep Commando, Amphibious Trg Unit RM, Depot RM, ITC, RM, GOC Commando Forces, ret 1968; dep dir Printing & Publishing Training Bd, chm Sch for Visually Handicapped Children, memb panel of Ind Inspectors, lay reader; offr Legion of Merit USA 1955; *Recreations* gardening, painting, ex chm RN&RM Boxing, Rear Cdre RNSA, pres RN Canoe Club; *Clubs* RNSA, Army & Navy; *Style—* Maj Gen Ferris Grant, CB, BA

GRANT, Francis Tollemache; s of late Capt Sir Francis Grant, 12 Bt; hp of bro, Sir Archibald Grant, 13 Bt; *b* 18 Dec 1955; *Recreations* salmon, fishing; *Style—* Francis Grant, Esq; The Malt House, Kingston House Estate, Kingston Bagpuize, Abingdon, Oxon OX13 5AX

GRANT, Geoffrey Clive; *b* 7 August 1932; *Educ* Liverpool Coll, Liverpool Univ (LLB); *m* Feb 1956, Valerie; 3 da (Deborah b 1958, Andrea b 1961, Emma b 1966); *Career* slr (honours 1955); sr ptnr Grant Saw & Sons slrs Greenwich 1957-; chm Greenwich Building Society 1987-, (vice-chm 1985-87, dir 1982); Liveryman: Loriners Co 1968, City of London Slrs Co 1969; pres South London Law Soc 1972-73; FBIM 1985; ACIArb 1986; *Recreations* playing clarinet and saxophone; *Style—* Geoffrey Grant, Esq; 21 Hitherwood Drive, Dulwich, London SE19; 181/83 Trafalgar Rd, Greenwich, London SE10 (☎ 01 858 6971, fax 01 858 5796)

GRANT, Dr James Shaw; CBE (1968, OBE 1956); s of William Grant (d 1932), of Stornoway, Isle of Lewis, and Johanna, *née* Morison (d 1952); *b* 22 May 1910; *Educ* Nicolson Inst Stornoway, Glasgow Univ (MA); *m* 25 July 1951, Catherine Mary (1988), da of Norman Stewart (d 1945), of Back Isle of Lewis; *Career* journalist and author; editor Stornoway gazette 1932-63, chm Crofters Common 1963-78, dir Grampian TV 1969-80; plays incl: Tarravore (1944), The Magic Rowan (1947), Legend is Born (1948), Comrade the King (1951); books incl: Highland Villages (1977), Their Children will See (1979), The Hub of My Universe (1982), Surprise Island (1983), The Gaelic Vikings (1984), Stornoway and the Lewis (1985), Discovering Lewis and Harris (1987); memb Highlands and Islands Advsy Panel 1954-65, Highlands and Islands Devpt Bd 1970-82, Scottish Advsy Ctee Br Cncl 1972-; hon LLD (Aberdeen) 1979; FRSE (1982), FRAGS (1973); *Recreations* walking, photography; *Clubs* Royal Overseas League, Highland; *Style—* Dr James Shaw Grant, CBE; Ardgrianach, Inshes, Inverness (☎ 0463 231 476)

GRANT, John Donald; s of Ian Campbell Grant (d 1960), and Eleanor Sage, *née* Maley (d 1984); *b* 31 Oct 1926; *Educ* Univ of Cambridge (MA); *m* 14 July 1951, Helen Bain Fairgrieve, da of James Wilson (d 1984); 2 s (Alasdair b 1953, Robin b 1956); *Career* Lt REME 1947-49, Lt London Rifle Bde 1949-56; N Thames Gas Bd 1949-60, ICI plc 1960-83, chief exec FIMBRA (formerly NASDIM) 1983-88, ptnr Grant and Fairgrave 1988-; *Clubs* United Oxford and Cambridge; *Style—* John Grant, Esq

GRANT, John Douglas; *b* 16 Oct 1932; *Educ* Stationers' Company's Sch Hornsey; *m* 1955, Patricia Julia Ann; 2 s, 1 da; *Career* reporter Daily Express 1955-70 (chief industl corr 1967-70); Parly candidate (L) Beckenham 1966, MP (L) Islington East 1970-74 (Islington Central 1974-83, (L) to Nov 1981, SDP to 1983); chm Lab and Industl Correspondents' Gp 1967, oppn front bench spokesman Broadcasting and Press Policy 1974, parly sec CSD 1974; parly under-sec state: Overseas Devpt Miny 1974-76, DOE 1976-79; oppn (L) front bench spokesman employment 1979-81, SDP employment and industry spokesman 1982-83, parly advsr to First Div Assoc (a sr civil servants' trade union) 1982-83; head of communication Electrical Electronic Telecommunication Union 1984-; *Style—* John Grant, Esq; 1 Betts Close, Beckenham, Kent (☎ 01 650 8643)

GRANT, Keith Wallace; s of Randolph Grant (d 1977), and Sylvia, *née* Hawks (d 1983); *b* 30 June 1934; *Educ* Trinity Coll Glenalmond, Clare Coll Cambridge (MA); *m* 1968, Deanne, da of Dr Arnold Bergsma (d 1972), of S Africa; 1 s (Sam b 1975), 1 da (Katherine b 1977); *Career* account exec W S Crawford Ltd 1958-62; gen mangr Royal Opera Co Covent Garden and English Opera Gp 1962-73; sec RSA 1973-77, dir Design Cncl 1977-82, dean faculty of design Kingston Poly 1988-; *Recreations* music, reading, gardening; *Clubs* Garrick, Arts; *Style—* Keith Grant, Esq; c/o Garrick Club, Garrick St, London WC2

GRANT, Sir (Kenneth) Lindsay; OBE (1956), ED (1944); s of Thomas Geddes Grant (d 1934); *b* 10 Feb 1899; *Educ* Queen's Royal Coll Trinidad, Maritime Business Coll Halifax Canada; *m* 1923, Edith Grace, da of Charles Bennett Norman (d 1911, Supt of Police Trinidad); *Career* served WWI British West Indies Regt, RFC and RAF (Victory Medals WWI), served Trinidad Volunteers WWII, 2 in Cmd; chm T Geddes Grant Ltd 1946-64 (joined 1919), pres 1964-69 and 1980-; hon life pres, fndr and former pres Trinidad Leprosy Relief Assoc; on West Indies Cricket Bd for 11 years to 1970; memb Trinidad and Tobago Elections and Boundaries Cmmn 1963; Chaconia Medal of Trinidad 1969; co dir and memb many govt ctee; kt 1963; *Recreations* formerly soccer, cricket, golf; *Clubs* cricket: MCC, Middlesex, Trinidad Union, Country, Queen's Park; *Style—* Sir Lindsay Grant, OBE, ED; 50 Ellerslie Park, Maraval, Trinidad (☎ 25202); Geddes Grant Ltd, Box 171, Port of Spain, Trinidad (☎ 54805)

GRANT, Very Rev Malcolm Etheridge; s of Donald Etheridge Grant, and Nellie Florence May, *née* Tuffey; *b* 6 August 1944; *Educ* Dunfermline HS, Univ of Edinburgh (BSc, BD); *m* 1984, Katrina Russell, da of David Burn Skinner Dunnett; 1 da (Alison b 1987); *Career* asst curate St Mary's Cathedral Glasgow 1969-72, team vicar of Earlesfield Grantham 1972-78, priest-in-charge St Ninian's Invergordon 1978-81, examining chaplain to Bishop of Moray Ross & Caithness 1979-81, provost and rector St Mary's (Scottish Episcopal) Cathedral Glasgow 1981-; memb Highland Cncl Educ Ctee 1979-81; *Style—* The Very Rev Malcolm Grant; 45 Rowallan Gardens, Glasgow G11 7LH (☎ 041 339 4956); St Mary's Cathedral, 300 Great Western Road, Glasgow G4 9JB (☎ 041 339 6691)

GRANT, Lady; Margaret Katharine; da of J W Milne; *m* 1936, Rt Hon Lord (William) Grant, TD (d 1972; sometime Lord Justice-Clerk of Scotland); *Style—* Lady Grant; 30 Moray Place, Edinburgh (☎ 031 225 4406)

GRANT, Newton Keene; s of Cyril Ernest Newton Oscar Grant (d 1947), of London, and Ethel, *née* Keent (d 1958); *b* 25 June 1931; *Educ* Egopus GS Alton Hants; *m* 30 Aug 1950, Mary Elizabeth, da of Joseph Henry Jule Romaguy (d 1971), of Sohsons, France; 3 da (Nicole Mary (Mrs Carbin) b 1962, Carolyn Gillian b 1966, Marie-Anne Hélène b 1969); *Career* Nat Serv RAPC; sr ptnr: Privie Brenster CAs (ptnr 1960), Privie Longman Ceritified Accountants; pres Chartered Assoc of Certified Accountants 1983-84; JP formerly Surrey now City of London 1974, chm Hearing Aid Cncl; memb Worshipful Co of Horners 1971 (Ct of Assts and Hon Tres); FCCA 1955, FCA 1960, FCIArb 1970; *Recreations* music, cookery, antique silver; *Clubs* Savage, City Livery; *Style—* Newton Grant, Esq; Treworas House, Ruanhighlames, Truro, Cornwall TR2 5LN; 96 Thomas More House, Barbican EC2Y 8BU (☎ 0872 501759); Carolyn House, 29-31 Greville St, EC2Y 8BU (☎ 01 831 8821, fax 01 404 3069, telex 296326)

GRANT, (Ian) Nicholas; s of Hugo Moore Grant (d 1987), of Herts and Cara Phyllis, *née* McMullen-Pearson; *b* 24 Mar 1948; *Educ* Durham Sch, Univ of London (LLB), Univ of Warwick (MA); *m* 5 Nov 1977, Rosalind Louise, da of Winston Maynard Pipe; 1 s (Robert b 1979), 1 da (Rosemary b 1981); *Career* public affairs advsr to Robert Maxwell 1985-; dir of info Lab Pty 1983-1985, head of res and P/R Confedn of Health Serv Employees 1972-82; memb: Lambeth Borough Cncl (Lab) 1978-84, West Lambeth Dist Health Authy 1982-84, parly candidate (L) contested Reigate 1979; *Books* Economics of Prosperity (1980), Political Communication for Br General Election (1983); *Recreations* walking, music, photography, sailing, children, reading; *Clubs* Reform; *Style—* Nicholas Grant, Esq; 23 Orlando Rd, Clapham, London SW4 0LD (☎ 01 720 1091); Mirror Group Newspapers (☎ 01 822 2586, telex 896713 PUBMGN G, fax 01 353 2424)

GRANT, (Alastair) Norman; s of Alexander Grant (d 1985), of Carrbridge, Scotland, and May Grant, *née* Robertson; *b* 18 Nov 1943; *Educ* Royal Acad Inverness, Grays Sch of Art Aberdeen, (Dips in silversmithing and graphic design); *m* 3 July 1965, Jess Sloss Innes, da of Dr William Paterson (d 1968), of Glenrothes, Fife; 1 s (Rob b 1973), 1 da (Romany b 1966); *Career* fndr and md Dust Jewellery Ltd 1966-88, co fndr and md Grant Walker Ltd (the first jewellery design conslt working internationally for UN, EEC plus UK and other govts and private co's, art coll business studies advsr); chm Sir John Cass Advsy Ctee (jewellery faculty); Freeman: City of Lonson 1981, Worshipful Co of Goldsmiths 1981,; *Recreations* travel, Scottish cottage; *Style—* Norman Grant, Esq; 55 Ridge Rd, London N8 9LJ (☎ 01 341 6104); Grant Walker Ltd, 4-5 Broadbent Close, Highgate Village, London N6 5JP (☎ 01 341 9119, fax 01

348 0078)

GRANT, Capt Pauline Ann; da of Sqdn Ldr John James Woods, RAF, DFC, of Kipscombe, 15A Church Street, Steeple Ashton, Trowbridge, Wilts, and Nancy Farran, *née* Caldecott; *b* 17 Jan 1956; *Educ* Stover Sch, Newton Abbot Devon, Trowbridge High Sch Wilts, Loughborough Univ of Technol (BA); *Career* WRAC, UK and N Ireland (despatches), Capt 1978-84; project ldr Racal Vodafone 1984-86, sr conslt and information systems mangr Learmonth and Burchett Mgmnt Services plc 1987- (sr conslt 1986-87); *Recreations* being at home; *Clubs* Network, British Computer Soc; *Style*— Capt Pauline Grant; 17 Crawford Road, Camberwell, London SE5 9NF (☎ 01 326 0469); LBMS plc, Evelyn House, 62 Oxford Street, London W1N 9LF (☎ 01 636 4213 ext 233)

GRANT, Robin William; s of Rt Hon Lord (William) Grant (d 1972), Lord Justice-Clerk of Scotland, and Lady Margaret, *née* Milne, *qv*; *b* 14 May 1938; *Educ* Rugby, Oxford Univ (MA); *m* 4 May 1968, Hilary Beryl, da of Air Cdre Peter H Hamley (d 1978); 1 s (Jonathan b 1972), 1 da (Veronica b 1970); *Career* Royal Scots 1956-58, 2 Lt 1957; Baring Bros & Co 1966-71, dir Williams Glyn and Co 1971-75, Charterhouse Bank Ltd 1977- (dir 1983-); MICAS; *Recreations* golf, music, skiing; *Clubs* Denham GC; *Style*— Robin Grant, Esq; 14 Cumberland Rd, Barnes, London SW13 9LY (☎ 01 748 7760); Charterhouse Bank Ltd, 1 Paternoster Row, St Paul's, London EC4M 7DH (☎ 01 248 4000, fax 01 248 1998)

GRANT, Russell John d'Ammerall; s of Frank William Grant and Joan Alice Peverall; *b* 5 Feb 1952; *Educ* Abbotsfield; *Career* TV presenter; presenter Star Choice (ITV), The Zodiac Game (ITV); radio presenter Believe It or Not (BBC Radio 4), original presenter BBC Breakfast Time; pres Emeritus Br Astrological Psychic Soc, hon life memb Astrologer's Guild of GB; *Books* Your Sun Signs, Your Love Signs; *Recreations* collector of Br maps and gazetteers, county of Middlesex memorabilia; *Style*— Russell Grant, Esq; BBC TV (☎ 01 743 8000); TV Times Magazine (☎ 01 323 3222)

GRANT OF DALVEY, Sir Patrick Alexander Benedict; 14 Bt (NS 1688); Chieftain of Clan Donnachy (Donnachaidh); s of Sir Duncan Alexander Grant, 13 Bt (d 1961), of Polmaily, Glen Urquhart, Invernesshire and Joan Penelope, *née* Cope; *b* 5 Feb 1953; *Educ* Fort Augustus Abbey Sch, Glasgow Univ (LLB); *m* 1981, Dr Carolyn Elizabeth, MB, ChB, DRCOG, MRCGP, da of John Highet, of Albert Drive, Glasgow; 2 s (Duncan b 1982, Neil b 1983); *Heir* s, Duncan Archibald Ludovic; *Career* inshore fisherman; chm and md: Grants of Dalvey Ltd, Duncan MacRae Ltd, Grainger and Campbell Ltd; *Recreations* professional competing piper; *Clubs* Royal Scottish Automobile; *Style*— Sir Patrick Grant of Dalvey, Bt; 2 The Crescent, Busby, Glasgow G76 8HT (☎ 041 644 4121); c/o Grants of Dalvey Ltd, 42 Westgarth Place, College Milton N, East Kilbride, Glasgow G74 5NT (☎ 035 52 46516/7, telex 777625 GRANT G, fax 03552 32963)

GRANT OF GARTENBEG, Rear-Adm John; CB (1960), DSO (1942); s of Maj-Gen Sir Philip Grant, KCB, CMG (d 1943), and Lady Annette Mary Grant, *née* Coventry (d 1963); *b* 13 Oct 1908; *Educ* Eastbourne, RNC Dartmouth, RNC Greenwich, JSSC, RCDS; *m* 1935, Ruth Hayward, da of Richard Slade (d 1915); 2 s (Duncan, Andrew), 2 da (Tessa, Grizel); *Career* RN; CO HM Ships: Beverley, Philante (Atlantic, Med, Russia) 1940-43, HMS Opportune, Fame, Crispin, Cleopatra, Vernon 1943-56; Flag Offr cmdg reserve fleet Vanguard 1959-61; ret RN 1961; Rank Orgn 1961-65, dir Conf of Electronics Industry 1965-71; CBIREE, FRSA to 1970; *Clubs* Hurlingham; *Style*— Rear-Adm John Grant, CB, DSO; 9 Rivermead Ct, Ranelagh Gardens, London SW6 3RT

GRANT OF GLENMORISTON, (14 Laird of) Ian Faulconer Heathcoat; DL; s of John Augustus Grant, DL (d 1978), and Gwendolen Evelyn Mary Knight; *b* 3 June 1939; *Educ* Sedbergh Sch Yorks, Liverpool Coll of Commerce; *m* 1964, Sarah Bonita, da of Kenneth Lincoln Hall, CBE (d 1981); 1 s (John b 1976), 3 da (Amabel b 1966, Miranda b 1968, Iona b 1970); *Career* md Glenmoriston Estates Ltd; chm: Pacific Assets Tst plc, MacDougalls Advertising plc; dir: The Royal Bank of Scotland plc, First Charlotte Assets Tst plc, Worldwide Value Fund Inc; *Recreations* gardening; *Clubs* New (Edinburgh); *Style*— Ian Grant of Glenmoriston, Esq, DL; Bhlaraidh House, Glenmoriston; 64 Great King St, Edinburgh; Glenmoriston Estates Ltd, Glenmoriston, nr Inverness IV3 6YA (☎ 0320 51202)

GRANT OF GRANT, Hon Amanda Caroline; da of 5 Baron Strathspey and 32 Chief of the Clan Grant, by his 2 w, Olive; *b* 16 Feb 1955; *Educ* St Margaret's Sch Bushey, Central Sch of Art & Design; *Career* graphic designer; *Style*— The Hon Amanda Grant of Grant; Flat D, 25 Nevern Sq, London SW5

GRANT OF GRANT, Hon (Geraldine) Janet; da of 5 Baron Strathspey; *b* 10 June 1940; *m* 1963 (m dis 1972), Neil Hamish Cantlie, s of Adm Sir Colin Cantlie, KBE, CB, DSC (decd); resumed maiden name of Grant of Grant; *Style*— The Hon Janet Grant of Grant; c/o Royal Bank of Scotland, 14 George St, Edinburgh EH2 2YF

GRANT OF GRANT, Hon Michael Patrick Francis; s of 5 Baron Strathspey; *b* 22 April 1953; *Educ* Harrow, Oriel Coll Oxford (MA); *Career* real estate conslt and fast food restaurateur, franchise conslt, dir Blythe Management Ltd 1984-; ARICS; *Recreations* sailing (yacht 'Blue Daiquiri'); *Style*— The Hon Michael Grant of Grant; 3 Ifield Road, London SW10 9AZ (☎ 01 351 1868)

GRANT OF MONYMUSK, Sir Archibald; 13 Bt (NS 1705), of Cullen, Co Buchan; s of Capt Sir Francis Cullen Grant, 12 Bt (d 1966, himself tenth in descent from Archibald Grant, whose f d 1553 and whose er bro John was ancestor of the Barons Strathspey), by his w Jean, only da of Capt Humphrey Tollemache, RN (s of Hon Douglas Tollemache, 8 s of 1 Baron Tollemache); *b* 2 Sept 1954; *Educ* Trinity Coll Glenalmond, RAC Cirencester (Dip Farm Mgmnt); *m* 31 Dec 1982, Barbara Elizabeth, eldest da of A G D Forbes, of Druminnor Castle, Rhynie, Aberdeenshire, and Mrs Alison Forbes; 2 da (Christian Mariot b 31 March 1986, Catriona Elizabeth b 14 April 1988); *Heir* bro, Francis Tollemache Grant; *Career* farmer; *Recreations* hill-walking, shooting, water-divining; *Clubs* Royal Northern; *Style*— Sir Archibald Grant of Monymusk, Bt; House of Monymusk, Monymusk, Aberdeenshire (☎ 046 77220, office 046 77250)

GRANT OF ROTHIEMURCHUS, John Peter; s of Lt-Col John Grant of Rothiemurchus, MBE (d 1987), and Lady Katherine Grant of Rothiemurchus, *qv*; *b* 22 Oct 1946; *Educ* Gordonstoun; *m* 1973, Philippa, da of John Chance, of Widmer Lodge, nr Princes Risborough; 1 s, 1 da; *Style*— John Grant of Rothiemurchus

GRANT OF ROTHIEMURCHUS, Lady Katherine; *née* Greaves; 2 da of Countess of Dysart (d 1975, the 10 holder of the title) and Maj Owain Greaves, DL, RHG (d 1941); hp to sis, Countess of Dysart (11 holder of the title); *b* 1 June 1918; *m* 1941, Lt-Col John Peter Grant of Rothiemurchus, MBE (d 1987), *qv*, Lovat Scouts, s of Col John P Grant of Rothiemurchus, CB, MC, TD, JP, DL (decd) (see above); 1 s (John Peter, Philippa Chance), 1 da (Jane m A R F Buxton); *Style*— Lady Katherine Grant of Rothiemurchus; Rothiemurchus, Aviemore, Inverness-shire

GRANT-DALTON, Maj Nathaniel Duncan Spry; s of Lt-Col Duncan Grant-Dalton, CMG, DSO (d 1969), of Place House, St Anthony-in-Roseland, Portslatho, Truro, Cornwall, and Gwavas May, *née* Spry (d 1955); *b* 24 July 1922; *Educ* Clifton Coll; *m* 19 Sept 1950, Valentia, da of Hon Francis Alexander Innys Eveleigh-de-Moleyns (d 1964), of Balnagown Castle, Kildary, Ross-Shire, Scotland; 1 s (Kevin Duncan Spry b 23 Dec 1952), 2 da (Miranda b 14 Jan 1955, Nicola b 15 Feb 1957); *Career* joined army 1941, cmmnd RA 1942, War Serv Western Desert and Italy, Flying Instr AOP 1946-53, Long Gunnery Staff Course Larkhill 1954, Gunnery SO Hohne Germany 1955-57, RHA 1957-59, ret 1959; working memb Lloyds 1959-72; High Sheriff of Cornwall 1986-87, local cncllr; *Recreations* shooting, sailing; *Style*— Maj Nathaniel Spry Grant-Dalton ; Place House, St Anthony-in-Roseland, Portscatho, Truro, Cornwall (☎ 087 258 447)

GRANT-FERRIS, The Rev and Hon Dom Piers Henry Michael; s of Baron Harvington, PC, AE (Life Peer), *qv* ; *b* 9 April 1933; *Educ* Ampleforth, Strawberry Hill Teaching Coll; *Career* Lt Irish Gds, served Germany 1953 and Egypt 1954; monk of St Benedict 1959, priest 1964-, teacher Ampleforth Prep Sch 1965-75, asst priest Workington 1977-; chaplain of Magistral Obedience SMO Malta 1980, OSB (1959); *Recreations* mountaineering, swimming, skiing, riding, photography; *Clubs* British Ski, Kandahar Ski, Alpine Ski, Achille Ratti Climbing; *Style*— The Rev and Hon Dom Piers Grant-Ferris, OSB; The Priory, Workington, Cumbria CA14 3EP (☎ 0900 2114)

GRANT-SUTTIE, James Edward; s and h of Sir (George) Philip Grant-Suttie, 8 Bt; *b* 29 May 1965; *Style*— James Grant-Suttie, Esq

GRANT-SUTTIE, Sir (George) Philip; 8 Bt (NS 1702); s of Maj George Grant-Suttie (decd), gs of 2 Bt; suc kinsman, Sir George Grant-Suttie, 7 Bt, 1947; *b* 20 Dec 1938; *Educ* Sussex Composite HS New Brunswick, McGill Univ; *m* 1962 (m dis 1969), Elspeth Mary, da of Maj-Gen Robert Elliott Urquhart, CB, DSO; 1 s; *Heir* s, James Grant-Suttie; *Career* farmer, writer, pilot; *Recreations* fishing, forestry, flying (owner: Entstrom Helicopter and Cessna 206); *Style*— Sir Philip Grant-Suttie, Bt; Sheriff Hall, North Berwick, E Lothian EH39 5BP (☎ 0620 2569; office 3750); 25 Moray Place, Edinburgh (☎ 031 225 4361)

GRANTCHESTER, 2 Baron (UK 1953); Kenneth Bent Suenson-Taylor; CBE (1985), QC (1971); s of 1 Baron Grantchester, OBE (d 1976), and Mamie (d 1976), da of Albert Suenson, of Copenhagen; *b* 18 August 1921; *Educ* Westminster, Christ's Coll Cambridge; *m* 12 April 1947, Betty, da of Sir John Moores, CBE, *qv*; 3 s, 3 da; *Heir* s, Hon Christopher Suenson-Taylor; *Career* former Capt RA; barr Middle Temple 1946, ad eundem Lincoln's Inn; pres VAT Tribunals 1972-87, chm 1988-; a Recorder of the Crown Courts 1975-; chm Licensed Dealers' Tribunal 1976-88; pres Aircraft and Shipping Industs Arbitration Tribunal 1980-83; chm: Dairy @roduce Quota Tribunal 1984-, Financial Services Tribunal 1987-; dep chm in House of Lords 1988-; *Clubs* Buck's; *Style*— The Rt Hon the Lord Grantchester, CBE, QC; The Gate House, Coombe Wood Rd, Kingston Hill, Surrey KT2 7JY (☎ 01 546 9088)

GRANTHAM, Adm Sir Guy; GCB (1956, KCB 1952, CB 1942), CBE (1946), DSO (1941); s of Charles Fred Grantham, JP (d 1922); *b* 9 Jan 1900; *Educ* Rugby; *m* 1934, Beryl Marjory Mackintosh-Walker, CStJ; 2 da; *Career* joined RN 1918, Capt 1937, served WWII (despatches 2), Rear-Adm 1947, Flag Offr Submarines 1948-50, Flag Offr (Air) 2 in Cmd Mediterranean Fleet 1950-51, Vice-Chief of Naval Staff 1951-54, Vice-Adm 1950, Adm 1953, C-in-C Mediterranean Station and Allied Forces Mediterranean 1954-57, C-in-C Portsmouth and Allied C-in-C Channel and S North Sea NATO 1957-59, govr and C-in-C Malta 1959-62, first and princ naval ADC to HM The Queen 1958-59, ret; vice-chm Commonwealth War Graves Cmmn 1963-70; govr Corps of Commissionaires 1964-; *Style*— Adm Sir Guy Grantham, GCB, CBE, DSO; Tandem House, Nayland, Colchester, Essex EO6 4JF

GRANTHAM, (Robert) James; s of Walter Leslie Grantham, and Marcia Anne Howard, *née* Macdonald; *b* 20 Sept 1947; *Educ* Stowe, Wolverhampton Poly (BA); *m* 6 April 1985, Cecilia Anna Eloise, da of Kapten Karol Wickström; 1 da (Isabella b 1986), 1 step s (Marcus b 1971), 2 step da (Matilda b 1970, Emily b 1979); *Career* Spillers 1969-71, investmt analyst Sternberg Thomas Clarke & Co 1972-77, mangr fixed interest and money market servs dept Phillips & Drew 1977-86; dir: Co NatWest (formerly Co Gp) 1986-, i/c convertibles and warrants Co NatWest Woodmac (formerly Co Securities and Co NatWest Securities) 1986-; memb Int Stock Exchange 1986; *Style*— James Grantham, Esq; County NatWest WoodMac, Drapers Gardens, 12 Throgmorton Ave, London EC2P 2ES (☎ 01 588 1818 and 031 243 4205, fax 01 588 4450, telex 72555)

GRANTLEY, Baroness; Lady Deirdre Freda Mary; *née* Hare; da of 5 Earl of Listowel, GCMG, PC; *b* 1935; *Educ* Lady Margaret Hall Oxford; *m* 1955, 7 Baron Grantley, *qv*; *Style*— The Rt Hon the Lady Grantley; Markenfield Hall, Ripon; 53 Lower Belgrave St, SW1

GRANTLEY, 7 Baron (GB 1782); John Richard Brinsley Norton; MC (1944); s of 6 Baron Grantley (d 1954, ggs of George Norton by his w Caroline, herself gda of the playwright Sheridan), and Jean, da of Brig-Gen Sir David Kinloch, 11 Bt, CB, MVO; *b* 30 July 1923; *Educ* Eton, New Coll Oxford; *m* 18 Jan 1955, Lady Deirdre Elisabeth Freda Hare, o da of 5 Earl of Listowel; 2 s; *Heir* s, Hon Richard Norton, *qv*; *Career* served WW II Capt Grenadier Gds; memb Lloyd's; *Clubs* White's, Pratt's; *Style*— The Rt Hon Lord Grantley, MC; Markenfield Hall, Ripon, N Yorks; 53 Lower Belgrave St, London SW1 (☎ 01 730 1746)

GRANVILLE, 5 Earl (UK 1833); Granville James Leveson-Gower; MC (1945); also Viscount Granville, of Stone Park (UK 1815), and Baron Leveson, of Stone (UK 1833, eldest s and h usually styled simply Lord Leveson); s of 4 Earl Granville (d 1953, gs of 1 Earl, who was himself yr bro of 1 Duke of Sutherland) and Lady Rose Bowes-Lyon, da of 14 Earl of Strathmore and sis of HM Queen Elizabeth The Queen Mother; through his mother Lord Granville is therefore first cous of HM The Queen; *b* 6 Dec 1918; *Educ* Eton; *m* 1958, Doon, da of Fl-Lt Hon Brinsley Sheridan Plunket (2 s of 5 Baron Plunket, gs of 1 Marquess of Dufferin and Ava, and gggs of the playwright Sheridan); 2 s, 1 da; *Heir* s, Lord Leveson; *Career* Maj Coldstream Gds, Supply Reserve; pres Navy League 1953-66; served WW II N Africa & Italy; DL Inverness 1974, vice-lord-lieut Western Isles (Islands Area) 1976-83, lord-lieut 1983-; *Style*— The Rt Hon the Earl Granville, MC; Callernish, Sollas, N Uist, Outer

Hebrides, Inverness-shire; 49 Lyall Mews, London SW1 (☎ 01 235 1026)

GRANVILLE, Sir Keith; CBE (1958); *b* 1 Nov 1910; *Educ* Tonbridge Sch; *m* 1, 1933, Patricia Capstick; 1 s, 1 da; m 2, Truda Belliss; 1 s, 4 da; *Career* joined Imperial Airways 1929; chm and chief exec BOAC 1971-72 (commercial dir 1954-58, dep md 1958-60, dep chm 1964, md 1969), dep chm British Airways Bd 1972-74; pres: Institute of Transport 1963-64, IATA 1972-73; chm British Residents' Assoc of Switzerland 1979-81; FCIT, Hon FRAeS 1977; kt 1973; *Style—* Sir Keith Granville, CBE; Speedbird, 1837 Château d'Oex, Switzerland (☎ (029) 4376 03)

GRANVILLE, Hon Linda Elizabeth Mary; only child of Baron Granville of Eye (Life Peer) *qv*; *b* 10 Feb 1949; *Educ* London Univ (BA); *Recreations* eventing and dressage, opera; *Clubs* Lansdowne; *Style—* Hon Linda Granville; c/o Rt Hon Lord Granville of Eye, 112 Charlton Lane, Cheltenham

GRANVILLE, Richard de la Bere; JP; s of Richard St Leger Granville (d 1972), of Frays Weston, Herts, and Barbara Lempriere, *née* Wells (d 1983); descended from Sir Bevil Granville (1595-1648), one of the boldest and most successful of the Cavalier leaders, who represented Cornwall in the Parliaments of James I and Charles I. He was ggs of Sir Roger Granville who drowned when the frigate Mary Rose sank off Portsmouth; *b* 20 June 1938; *Educ* Eton; *m* 1966, Christina Veronica, da of Philip Debell Tuckett (d 1967); 1 da (b 1968); *Career* Coldstream Gds 1957-59, Lt; assoc memb Hoare Govett Ltd (stockbrokers) 1986 (joined Hoare & Co 1959); memb: Stock Exchange 1964, cncl of Stock Exchange 1981-84; dir J S Gadd & Hldgs Ltd and various other cos; *Recreations* country pursuits; *Clubs* Boodle's, Pratt's; *Style—* Richard Granville, Esq, JP; 116 Woodsford Sq, London W14 8DT; J S Gadd & Co Ltd, 45 Bloomsbury Square, London WC1A 2RA (☎ 01 242 5544 telex 23260 ARCADY G)

GRANVILLE OF EYE, Baron (Life Peer UK 1967); Edgar Louis Granville; s of Reginald Granville; *b* 12 Feb 1899; *Educ* High Wycombe, Melbourne; *m* 1943, Elizabeth, da of Rev William Cecil Hunter; 1 da (Linda); *Career* sits in Lords as an Independent Peer; served WW I and II; former md E L Granville & Co; MP (Lib) Suffolk Eye 1929-51; pps to: Sir Herbert Samuel 1931, Sir John Simon (National Govt) 1931-36; *Recreations* skiing, writing autobiographies, poetry and novels, watching 3 day events; *Style—* The Rt Hon the Lord Granville of Eye; Charlton Lane, Cheltenham, Glos

GRANVILLE WEST, Hon Gerald Hugh; s of Baron Granville-West (Life Peer, d 1984); *b* 1942; *m* 1969, Barbara, da of Arthur Strath, of Ellwood Deane, Kilndown, Cranbrook, Kent; children; *Style—* The Hon Gerald Granville West

GRATTAN, Dr Donald Henry; CBE (1989); s of Arthur Henry Grattan (d 1980), and Edith Caroline, *née* Saltmarsh (d 1980); family of Henry Grattan Irish PM; *b* 7 August 1926; *Educ* Harrow, Kings Coll Univ of London (BSc), Open Univ (DUniv); *m* 1950, Valmai, da of Richard Edward Morgan (d 1978); 1 s (David), 1 da (Jennifer); *Career* jr res offr TRE Gt Malvern 1945-46, sch master Chiswick GS 1946-50, sr master Downer GS 1950-56, television prodr BBC 1956-61, ed further educn BBC 1961-63, head continuing educn BBC TV 1963-71, controller educnl broadcasting BBC TV 1971-84; memb: Cncl Open Univ 1972-84, cncl Educnl Technol 1972-84, advsy cncl for Adult and Continuing Educn 1979-83; chm: UDACE (Unit for Devpt of Adult Continuing Educn) 1984-, CET (Cncl for Educnl Technology) 1985-; memb: Mathematical Assoc, Royal TV Soc, Assoc for Sci Educn, Open University Visiting Ctee 1987-, Open Coll Cncl 1987-; FRSA 1988; *Publications* Science and the Builder, Mathematics Miscellany; *Recreations* dinghy sailing, foreign travel; *Style—* Dr Donald Grattan, CBE; Delabole, Gossmore Close, Marlow, Bucks SL7 1QG (☎ 062 8473571)

GRATTON, Col John Steuart Sancroft; OBE (1960); s of Maj John Steuart Gratton, of Glebe House, Woodbridge, Suffolk, and Etheldreda Mary Sancroft, *née* Randall (d 1972); *b* 6 August 1915; *Educ* Winchester, and RMA Sandhurst; *m* 26 July 1943, Anne Lavington, da of Alfred Manderville Turner (d 1964), fo Woodedge, Maresfield, Sussex; 2 s (James b 1944, Robert b 1948); *Career* cmmnd The Hampshire Regt 1935, served Palestine 1936-38, BEF 1939, Dunkirk 1940, 8th Army Egypt, Palestine, Syria and Italy 1943, wounded Cassino 1944, British Army Staff, Washington DC 1945-46, served Palestine 1946-48, Malaya 1953-55 and Cyprus and Suez 1956-57 in cmd 1 Parachute Regt; Garrison Cmdr British Honduras 1960-64; ret 1970; sec Army Sport Control Bd 1970-80, Cmdt Army Cadet Force, Hants and IOW 1977-80; DL Hants 1977; *Recreations* British modern Pentathlon, soccer, rugger, cricket, hockey, tennis, squash, sailing; *Clubs* MCC, Royal Yacht Squadron, Little Ship, SRA Ctee, Football Assoc Ctee, RYA, Royal Commonwealth Soc; *Style—* Col John Gratton, OBE, DL; White Rock, Lamlash, Isle of Arran KA27 8NL

GRATWICK, John; OBE (1978); s of Percival John Gratwick (d 1957), of Brands Hatch Place, Fawkham, Kent, and Kathleen Mary, *née* Lunnon (d 1970); *b* 23 April 1918; *Educ* Cranbrook, Imperial Coll London (BSc); *m* 14 Feb 1944, Ellen Violet, da of W H Wright (d 1942), of Coventry, Warwicks; 2 s (John Michael b 1948, Christopher Andrew b 1950), 2 da (Susan Anne b 1953, Jennifer Jane b 1955); *Career* asst prodn mangr Armstrong Siddeley Motors Ltd, 1941-45; Urwick Orr & Ptnrs Ltd 1945-: dir 1959-, md 1968-, vice-chm 1971-72; vice-chm: Lake & Elliot Ltd 1971-85, George Bassett Hldgs plc 1977-80; dir: R Kelvin Watson Ltd 1976-86, The Export Fin Co Ltd 1984-; chm: Guild Sound & Vision Ltd 1976-85, Empire Stores (Bradford) plc 1973-, Lovat Enterprise Fund Ltd 1980-88, Ladyline Ltd 1984-88; chm Clothing Indust Econ Devpt Ctee 1985- (memb 1967-); memb: Monopolies and Mergers Cmmn 1969-76, Bd of CAA 1972-75; memb Senate Univ of London 1967- (memb Ct 1987-); FCGI, CEng, MIMechE, CBIM, FIMC, FRSA; *Recreations* golf, sailing, photography, philately; *Clubs* RAC, City Livery, Wentworth; *Style—* John Gratwick, Esq, OBE; Empire Stores (Bradford) plc, 18 Canal Rd, Bradford, West Yorks (☎ 0274 729544, fax: 725683, telex: 51675)

GRAUBARD, Lady Mary Jane; *née* Cavendish-Bentinck; da of 9 Duke of Portland, CMG; *b* 1929; *m* 1, 1963 (m dis 1978), Alexander Georgiades; 2 s; m 2 1978, Prof Stephen Graubard; *Style—* Lady Mary Graubard; 83 White's End, Concord, Mass 02138, USA

GRAVE, (George) Frank; s of George Grave (d 1965), and Mary, *née* Litt-Wilson (d 1983); *b* 14 Dec 1928; *Educ* Palmers Sch, The London Hosp Med Coll (MB, BS); *m* 2 Oct 1954, Rosemary Marjorie, da of Walter L Gurd, of 10 Smiths Field, Cirencester; 3 da (Jane b 1956, Joanna b 1958, Catherine b 1966); *Career* sr surgn, head of dept surgery Bulawayo and MPILO Central Hosps Bulawayo Rhodesia 1966-79, conslt surgn The Alexandra Hosp Redditch Worcs 1979-; FRCS (Edin); *Recreations* sailing, golf, gardening; *Clubs* Newquay Yacht; *Style—* George Grave, Esq; Lychgate Cottage, Salwarpe, nr Droitwich (☎ 0905 773696); The Alexandra Hospital, Redditch (☎ 0527 503030)

GRAVELL, David William; s of Canon William James Gravell (d 1968); *b* 9 June 1925; *Educ* Marlborough, Trinity Coll Cambridge; *m* 1955, Cecil Katharine, *née* Eastwood; 3 s, 1 da; *Career* shipbroker; chm: British Philippine Soc Exec Ctee 1966-67, Killick Martin & Co (dir 1954) 1975-89, St Olave's Hart St Patronage Trust 1980-, London C of C S E Asia Ctee 1982-85; pres Malaysia, Singapore and Brunei Assoc 1987-89; memb British Waterways Bd 1980-83; *Recreations* watching cricket, listening to music, seeing the world; *Clubs* MCC, Inst of Dirs; *Style—* David Gravell, Esq; Great Barnetts, Leigh, Kent

GRAVES, Francis Charles; OBE (1983), DL (West Midlands 1982); s of Capt Jack Graves (d 1942), of Whitby, Yorkshire, and Lily, *née* Porter (d 1980); *b* 9 June 1929; *Educ* Whitby GS, Birmingham Coll of Technol (now Aston Univ), Coll of Estate Mgmnt London; *m* 24 Nov 1951, Phyllis May, da of Abraham Arthur Woolhouse (d 1940), of Birmingham; 1 s (Richard John Charles b 22 March 1956), 1 da (Helen Margaret b 28 June 1953); *Career* Capt RE 1953-56; chartered quantity surveyor; articled pupil Maxwell Harrison & Ptnrs 1948-52, asst surveyor Wilfred Hiles & Son 1952-53, chm and ptnr Francis C Graves & Ptnrs 1956-; West Midlands RICS 1960-: chm junior organisation branch ctee 1960-61, chm quanitiy surveyors branch ctee 1969-71, chm branch ctee 1973-74, nat pres quantity surveyors div 1980-81; project controller construction NEC Birmingham 1972-76 (project controller extensions 1978-), memb W Midlands Economic Planning Cncl, 1975-79, chm Bldg Ind Gp W Midlands 1976-80, chm NEDO report Construction for Industl Recovery 1977-78, memb Midlands Electricity Bd 1980-, memb Redditch Devpt Corpn 1981-85, memb PSA Advsy Bd 1981-85; memb cncl: Royal Soc of Health 1969-75, Birmingham Engrg and Bldg Centre 1969-83, Univ of Birmingham 1989-; dir Birmingham Hippodrome Theatre Tst 1979-, pres Birmingham Chamber of Ind and Commerce 1985-86 (memb 1977-, vice-pres 1983-85), memb Home Office Prison Bldg Bd 1987-; High Sheriff Co of West Midlands 1988-89; Freeman City of London, Worshipful Co of Paviors 1977; FRICS 1961, FRSH 1965, FCIOB 1980; *Recreations* sport generally, cricket (memb ctee Warwicks CCC), golf, football, gardening, travelling; *Style—* Francis Graves, Esq, OBE, DL; Aldersyde, Broad Lane, Tanworth in Arden, Solihull, W Midlands B94 5DY (☎ 05644 2324); 9 Frederick Rd, Edgbaston, Birmingham B15 1TW (☎ 021 455 9521, fax 021 454 9643, telex 338024)

GRAVES, John Derek; s of Capt Eric Christie Graves (d 1981), of Harrogate, Yorks, and Joyce, *née* Reffitt (d 1981); *b* 30 April 1938; *Educ* Rossall; *m* 1, 28 April 1962 (d 1978), Lorna Sugden, da of Robin Sugden Moore (d 1976); 2 s (Nicholas Jonathan b 1965, Stephen Robert b 1968), 1 da (Caroline Frances b 1966); m 2, 30 Dec 1978, Pauline, da of Cyril Henry Stoyle (d 1943), of Totnes, Devon; 1 step s (Hedley Triggs b 1970); *Career* chartered surveyor: Hollis & Webb Leeds 1955-63, Frank Richardson & Co Leeds 1963-68; chief valuation surveyor Leeds Perm Bldg Soc 1985- (chartered surveyor 1968-83, sr valuation surveyor 1983-85); memb assessment ctee PRC Homes Ltd; FRICS 1961; *Recreations* golf, gardening, reading; *Clubs* Pannal GC; *Style—* John Graves, Esq; 31 Harlow Manor Park, Harrogate, N Yorks (☎ 0423 68278); Leeds Permanent Building Soc, Permanent House, 72 The Headrow, Leeds LS1 1NS (☎ 0532 438181 ext 2930)

GRAVES, 8 Baron (I 1794); Peter George Wellesley Graves; s of 7 Baron (d 1963); *b* 21 Oct 1911; *Educ* Harrow; *m* 1960, Winifred (the actress Vanessa Lee), da of Alfred Moule and widow of Warde Morgan; *Heir* 2 cous once removed, Maj Evelyn Graves; *Career* actor; *Recreations* lawn tennis (played Wimbledon championships played 1932-3); *Clubs* All England Lawn Tennis; *Style—* The Rt Hon Lord Graves; 505 Nelson House, Dolphin Sq, London SW1

GRAVES-JOHNSTON, Hon Mrs; Carolyn Meliora; da of Rt Hon Viscount Whitelaw (Viscount 1983); *b* 1946; *m* 1, 1973 (m dis 1979), Robert Donald Macleod Thomas; 2 da (Miranda b 1974, Rhoda b 1977); m 2, 1983, Michael Francis Graves-Johnston; 2 da (Cleopatra Frances Graves-Johnston b 1985, Helen Mercedes Graves-Johnston b 1987); *Style—* The Hon Mrs Graves-Johnston; 54 Stockwell Park Rd, London SW9

GRAVESON, Ronald Harry; s of Harry Graveson (d 1951), of Sheffield, and Louisa Gertrude, *née* Rodgers (d 1965); *b* 2 Oct 1911; *Educ* King Edward VII Sch Sheffield, Sheffield Univ (LLM, LLD), Harvard Univ (SJD), London Univ (PHD, LLD); *m* 1937, Muriel, da of John Saunders (d 1975), of Sheffield; 1 s (John), 2 da (Diana, Christine); m 2, 1988, Joan, da of William Franklin (d 1959), of Sheffield; *Career* Lt-Col Control Cmmn for Germany 1945-46; slr 1934, Bar Gray's Inn 1945, bencher 1965, tres 1983; univ teacher, reader in English Law UC London 1946-47, prof of law King's Coll London 1947-74, head of Law Dept 1951-78 (fell 1962), dean of Faculty of Laws London Univ 1951-54 and 1972-74, visiting prof Harvard Law Sch 1958-59; memb: Polish Acad of Sciences 1977, Grand-Ducal Inst of Luxembourg 1985; emeritus prof of Private Int Law London Univ 1978-; memb: Mgmnt Ctee Courtauld Inst of Art, The Br Inst in Paris, Inst of Advanced Legal Studies London Univ pres Int Assoc of Legal Science 1960-62, Harvard Law Sch Assoc of UK 1954-56 and 1977-80, Soc of Public Teachers of Law 1972-73; chm Cncl of Anglo-Belgian Soc 1985-; Liveryman Clockmakers' and Carmens' Cos; Hon LLD: Ghent (1964), Uppsala (1977), Leuven (1978); Doctor Juris Freiberg (1969); Star 1939-45, France and Germany Star, Cdr Order of Crown of Oak (Luxembourg, 1964), Cdr Order of Orange-Nassau (1970), Grand Cross of Order of Merit (Germany 1976), Chevalier of Order of Legion of Hon 1978 (Offr 1970), Cdr of Order of the Crown (Belgium) 1977; *Books* jt ed Int and Comparative Law Quarterly (1955-61), conslt ed The Law Reports and the Weekly Law Reports (1970-75), gen ed Problems of Private Int Law; *Recreations* family, international friendship, works of art; *Clubs* Athenaeum, Royal Cwlth Soc, Anglo-Belgian; *Style—* Prof Ronald Graveson; 2 Gray's Inn Sq, Gray's Inn, London WC1R 5AA (☎ 01 242 8492); 12 Castle Mount Cres, Baslow Rd, Bakewell DE4 1AT

GRAVESTOCK, Peter Stanley; s of Herbert Stanley Gravestock, of W Bromwich, W Mids, and Phyllis Gwendoline, *née* Bye; *b* 6 June 1946; *Educ* West Bromwich GS; *m* 9 Dec 1973, Cynthia Anne, da of Maj Philip John Radford, of Walsall, W Midlands; 1 da (Elisabeth b 1977); *Career* sr lectr W Bromwich Coll of Commerce and Tech 1971-74 (lectr 1967-), fndr ptnr Gravestock and Owen 1974-; pres elect Inst of CA's Wolverhampton branch, memb Staffs Salop and Wolverhampton Dist Soc of Inst of CA's, ctee memb Inst of Taxation Birmingham Branch, lectr in taxation; Inst of Taxation (cncl memb), ICEAW, ICAI, FCA 1967; *Books* Tolleys Taxwise Taxation Workbooks (jtly, published annually); *Recreations* travelling, walking, reading; *Clubs* Nat Trust; *Style—* Peter Gravestock, Esq; 2 Grasmere Ave, Little Aston, nr Lichfield, Staffs (☎ 021 353 5482); Gravestock and Owen, 1 Walsall St, Willenhall, W Midlands

(☎ 0902 601 166, fax 0902 606 925, car tel 0836 237 286)

GRAY; *see*: Campbell-Gray

GRAY, Andrew Aitken; MC (1945); s of John Gray (d 1956), and Margaret Eckford, *née* Crozier (d 1960); *b* 11 Jan 1912; *Educ* Wyggeston Sch Leicester, Christ Church Oxford (MA, BSc); *m* 1, 5 Nov 1939, Eileen Mary (d 1980), da of George Augustus Haines (d 1959), of Leicester; 3 s (John Aitken b 1942, Andrew George Aitken b 1944, Duncan Aitken b 1950); m 2, Jess, *née* Carr; *Career* WWII RE 1939-45 (despatches), Maj 1942; Uniterer 1935-52, Wellcome Fndn Ltd 1952-77 (chm 1970); chm Hertfordshire AHA 1973-77; Commendatore Order of Merit Italy 1976, Ord Merito Agricola Spain 1969; *Recreations* theatre, fishing, gardening; *Clubs* East India; *Style—* Andrew Gray, Esq, MC; Rainhill Spring, Bovingdon, Herts HP3 0DP (☎ 0442 833 277)

GRAY, Master of; Hon Andrew Godfrey Diarmid Stuart Campbell-Gray; Master of Gray; s and h of 22 Lord Gray; *b* 3 Sept 1964; *Educ* Craigflower Prep Sch, Trinity Coll Glenalmond, Edward Greene's Tutorial Estab Oxford; *Style—* The Master of Gray; Airds Bay House, Taynuilt, Argyll PA35 1JR (☎ 086 62 232)

GRAY, 22 Lord (S 1445); Angus Diarmid Ian Campbell-Gray; s of Maj the Hon Lindsay Stuart Campbell-Gray, Master of Gray, MC (d 1945), and Doreen, *née* Tubbs (d 1948); s grandmother, Lady Gray, 21 holder of the title 1946 ; *b* 3 July 1931; *Educ* Eton; *m* 1959, Patricia Margaret (d 1987), da of Capt Philip Alexander (d 1953, gs of 3 Earl of Caledon), of Lismore, Co Waterford, Ireland; 1 s, 3 da; *Heir* s, The Master of Gray; *Clubs* Carlton, MCC; *Style—* The Rt Hon the Lord Gray; Airds Bay House, Taynuilt, Argyll OA35 1TR

GRAY, Charles Antony St John; QC (1984); s of Charles Gray (d 1982), and Catherine Gray, *née* Hughes (d 1986); *b* 6 July 1942; *Educ* Winchester Trinity Coll Oxford (MA); *m* 7 Sept 1967, Rosalind Macleod, da of Capt R F Whinney, DSO, RN, of Lymington, Hants; 1 s (Alexander Charles Macleod b 1974), 1 da (Anya Catherine Macleod b 2 Nov 1972); *Career* barr Gray's Inn 1966, Midlands and Oxford Circuit; *Recreations* tennis, ski-ing, walking; *Clubs* Brooks's; *Style—* Charles Gray, Esq, QC; 79 Ravenscourt Rd, London W6 0UJ (☎ 01 748 1493); Matravers House, Uploders, Dorset (☎ 0308 85222); 10 South Sq, Gray's Inn London WC1R 5EV (☎ 01 242 2902, fax 01 831 2686)

GRAY, Charles Donald Marshall; s of Capt Donald Gray, RE (d 1975), of Bournemouth, and Maude Elizabeth Gray; *b* 29 August 1928; *Career* actor; stage debut Regents Park Open Air Theatre, has acted with the RSC and at the Old Vic; roles include Achilles in Troilus and Crossida, Bolingbroke in Richard II; West End plays incl: Expresso Bongo, Everything in the Garden, Poor Bitos, The Philanthropist; Broadway: Right Honourable Gentlemen, Kean, Poor Bitos; numerous Films incl: You Only Live Twice, The Man Outside, The Night of the Generals, Secret War of Harry Frigg, The Devil Rides Out, The Executioner, Cromwell, Diamonds are Forever, The Beast Must Die, The Rocky Horror Picture Show, The Seven Per Cent Solution, Seven Nights in Japan, The Silver Bears, The Legacy, The Mirror Crack'd, Shock Treatment, The Jigsaw Man; TV: Hay Fever, The Moon and Sixpence, Ross, Richard II, Julius Caesar, An Englishman Abroad, Comedy of Errors, Sherlock Holmes, Bergerac, Small World, Blind Justice; *Style—* Charles Gray, Esq; c/o London Mgmnt, 235/241 Regent St, London W1A 2JT (☎ 01 493 1610)

GRAY, Lt-Col Charles Reginald; MBE (1945), TD (1950); s of Charles Wilson Gray (d 1969); *b* 3 July 1920; *m* 1941, Anne, da of Ewart Bradshaw, of Greyfriars Hall, nr Preston (d 1959); 2 s; *Career* Lt-Col WWII; former md then chm The Dutton-Forshaw Gp Ltd 1969-81; formerly chm: Sterling Wygate Ltd, Wygate Hldgs, Sterling Foods Ltd, William Clarke (Bradford) Ltd, Cabana Soft Drinks Ltd, Tammy Pet Foods Ltd, Cabana (Hldgs) Ltd, former dep chm Jack Barclay Ltd; currently chm: Williams & Gray Ltd, Greyfriars Estates Ltd, Icee (UK) Ltd, Co-ordinate Technol Ltd, PERAM Ltd; dep chm Jack Barday Ltd; *Recreations* shooting; *Clubs* Cavalry and Guards'; *Style—* Lt-Col Charles Gray, MBE, TD; Wennington Old Farm, Wennington, nr Lancaster (☎ 0468 21330)

GRAY, David Francis; s of John Morris Gray (d 1975), and Alice Kathleen, *née* Winsor (d 1982); *b* 18 May 1936; *Educ* Rugby, Trinity Coll Oxford (MA); *m* 11 Sept 1970, Rosemary Alison Elizabeth, da of Horace William Parker (d 1987); 2 s (James b 1975, Oliver b 1981), 1 da (Fiona b 1977); *Career* articled clerk Coward Chance 1957-60, admitted slr 1960; slr: Coward Chance 1960-62, Bischoff & Co 1962-63, Lovell White & King 1963-65 (ptnr 1966-88); ptnr Lovell White Durrant 1988-; asst to the Ct of the City of London Slrs Co 1974- (Almoner 1988-), Master of City of London Slrs Co 1984-85, vice-pres, jt sec and chm ctee of City of London Law Soc 1985-88, memb of Int Bar Assoc 1972- (asst tres 1988-), memb of the Law Soc 1960- (hon auditor 1988-), tstee Trinity Coll Oxford Soc (hon sec 1979-88); Liveryman Worshipful Co of: Solicitors, Glaziers Co; *Recreations* skiing, golf, tennis, swimming; *Clubs* Ski of Gr Britain, Upihook GC; *Style—* David Gray, Esq; 73 Cheapside, London EC2V 6ER (☎ 01 236 0066, fax 01 236 0084)

GRAY, Hon (James Northey) David; er s of Baron Gray of Contin and Judith Waite, *née* Brydon

GRAY, Dr Denis Everett; CBE (1983, MBE 1972), JP (Solihull 1982-); s of late Charles Norman Gray, and Kathleen Alexandra Gray, *née* Roberts; *b* 25 June 1926; *Educ* Bablake Sch Coventry, Univ of Birmingham (BA), Univ of London, Univ of Manchester (PhD); *m* 1949, Barbara Joyce, da of Edgar Ewart Kesterton (d 1970); *Career* sr lectr Univ of Birmingham 1957-84; chm of bench 1971-75; chm: Jt Negotiating Ctees for Justices' Clerks and Magistrates Cts Staff 1978-86, Central Cncl of Magistrates' Cts Ctees 1980-86; memb Magistrates' Cts' Rule Ctee 1982-86; *Books* Spencer Perceval the Evangelical Prime Minister (1963); *Recreations* travel, church architecture, reading; *Style—* Dr Denis Gray, CBE, JP; 11 Brueton Ave, Solihull, West Midlands (☎ 021 705 2935)

GRAY, Prof Denis John Pereira; OBE (1981); s of Dr Sydney Joseph Pereira Gray (d 1975), of Exeter, and Alice Evelyn, *née* Cole; *b* 2 Oct 1935; *Educ* Exeter Sch, St John's Coll Cambridge (MA), St Bart's Hosp Med Sch (MB BChir); *m* 28 April 1962, Jill Margaret, da of Frank Carruthers Hoyte (d 1976), of Exeter; 1 s (Peter b 1963), 3 da (Penelope b 1963, Elizabeth b 1968, Jennifer b 1970); *Career* gen med practice 1962-, sr lectr in surgery Univ of Exeter 1973-86 (prof of gen practice 1986-), advsr in GP Univ of Bristol 1975-, ed Med Annual 1983-87, conslt advsr in GP to chief med off DHSS 1984-87, dir PGMS Exeter 1987-; chm of cncl RCGP 1987- (hon ed RCGP journal 1972-80 and pubns 1976-); Hunterian Soc Gold Medal 1966 and 1969, Sir Charles Hastings Prize 1967 and 1970, James Mackenzie Lecture 1977, George Abercrombie Award 1978, RCGP Fndn Cncl Award 1980, Sir Harry Platt prize 1981; MRCGP 1967, FRCGP 1973; *Books* Training for General Practice (1981), Running a Practice (jtly, 1978); *Recreations* reading; *Style—* Prof Denis Gray, OBE; Alford House, 9 Marlborough Rd, Exeter EX2 4TG (☎ 0392 218080); 34 Denmark Rd, Exeter EX1 1SF (☎ 0392 51661, fax 0392 413449)

GRAY, The Rev Canon Dr Donald Clifford; TD (1970); s of Henry Hackett Gray (d 1959), of Manchester, and Constance Muriel Gray, *née* Bullock; *b* 21 July 1930; *Educ* Newton Heath Tech HS Manchester, King's Coll London (AKC), Liverpool Univ (MPhil), Manchester Univ (PhD); *m* 1955, Joyce, da of Walter Mills Jackson (d 1979), of Oldham; 1 s (Timothy), 2 da (Clare, Alison); *Career* curate Leigh Parish Church 1956-60, vicar St Peter Westleigh 1960-67, vicar of All Saints' Elton 1967-74, rector of Liverpool 1974-87, chaplain TA & TAVR 1958-77, honorary chaplain to HM The Queen 1974-77, chaplain to HM The Queen 1982-, proctor in convocation 1964-74 and 1980-87, rural dean of Liverpool 1975-81, canon diocesan of Liverpool 1982-87, canon of Westminster, rector of St Margaret's Westminster, chaplain to the Speaker of the House of Commons 1987-; memb Liturgical Cmmn 1968-86, chm Soc for Liturgical Study 1978-84, memb Jt Liturgical Gp 1969- (sec 1980-); pres Societas Liturgica 1987-; FRHistS; OStJ 1982; *Books* Earth and Altar (1986), contributions to Worship and the Child (1975), Getting the Liturgy Right (1982), Liturgy Reshaped (1982), Nurturing Children in Communion (1985), ed Holy Week Services (1983), ed The Word in Season (1988); *Recreations* watching cricket, reading modern poetry; *Clubs* Athenaeum (Liverpool), Liverpool Artists'; *Style—* The Rev Canon Dr Donald Gray, TD; 1 Little Cloister, Westminster Abbey, London SW1P 3PL (☎ 01 222 4027)

GRAY, Dulcie Winifred Catherine (Mrs Michael Denison); CBE (1983), Silver Jubilee Medal (1977); da of Arnold Savage Bailey, CBE (d 1935), of Kuala Lumpur, and Kate Edith, *née* Clulow-Gray (d 1942); *b* 20 Nov 1920; *Educ* St Anthony's Wallingford Berks, Luckley Wokingham Berks, Leeson Ho Langton Matravers Dorset, St Mary's Kuala Lumpur; *m* 29 April 1939, (John) Michael (Terence Wellesley) Denison CBE, *qv*, s of Gilbert Dixon Denison (d 1959); *Career* actress 1939-, served with ENSA 1944, first part Sorel in Hay Fever at His Majesty's Aberdeen; more than 40 plays in W End incl: Brighton Rock, Candida, Where Angels Fear to Tread, Bedroom Farce, School for Scandal; tv plays incl: The Governess, The Letter, Beautiful for Ever, Three Up Two Down; currently playing Kate Harvey in BBC tv's Howards' Way; memb exec cncl and finance ctee Actor's Charitable Tst, numerous appearances for charities; FLS, FRSA; *Books* 23 published books incl: Baby Face, Murder in Mind, The Murder of Love, Butterflies on My Mind (winner Times Educnl Supplement Sr Info Award 1978); *Recreations* swimming, butterflies; *Clubs* The Lansdowne ; *Style—* Miss Dulcie Gray, CBE; Shardeloes, Amersham, Bucks; c/o International Creative Managment, 388/396 Oxford St, London W1N 9HE (☎ 01 629 8080)

GRAY, His Eminence Cardinal Gordon Joseph; s of Francis and Angela Gray; *b* 10 August 1910; *Educ* Holy Cross Acad Edinburgh, St Joseph's Coll Mark Cross, St John's Seminary Wonersh, St Andrews Univ (MA); *Career* asst priest St Andrews 1935-41, parish priest Hawick 1941-47, rector Blairs Coll Aberdeen 1947-51, Cardinal 1969; Archbishop of St Andrews and Edinburgh 1951-85; Hon FEIS 1970; Hon DUniv Heriot-Watt 1981, Hon DD St Andrews Univ 1967; *Recreations* joinery, gardening, local historical research; *Style—* His Eminence Cardinal Gordon Joseph Gray; The Hermitage, St Margarets Convent, Whitehouse Loan, Edinburgh EH9 1BB (☎ 031 447 6210)

GRAY, Harold James; CMG (1956); s of John William Gray (d 1930), and Amelia Francis Miller (d 1961); *b* 17 Oct 1907; *Educ* Dover County Sch, London Univ (BSc, MSc, LLB), Harvard Univ USA (MPA); *m* 1928, Katherine, da of Sydney George Starling (d 1956); 1 da (Ann); *Career* civil servant 1927-61, examiner Patent Off 1935-39, asst sec Miny of Supply 1939, under sec BOT 1954, UK sr trade cmmr, economic advsr to: UK High Cmmr Australia 1954-58, S Africa 1958-60; dir: Nat Union of Mfrs 1961-65, Confedn of Br Industs 1965-72, Numas Mgmnt Serv Ltd 1961-70 (chm 1970-74); G Phys, MInstP, FRSA; *Books* Electricity in Service of Man (1949), Economic Survey of Australia (1955), Dictionary of Physics (1956), New Dictionary of Physics (1975); *Recreations* horse riding, swimming, golf; *Style—* Harold Gray, Esq, CMG; Copper Beeches, Tudor Avenue, Maidstone, Kent ME14 5HJ (☎ 0672 685978)

GRAY, Hon J N David; s of Baron Gray of Contin (Life Peer) and Judith Waite, *née* Brydon; *b* 30 April 1955; *Educ* Fettes Coll, Bristol Univ; *m* Lynda Jane, *née* Harlow; 2 da (twins b 1984); *Career* head of english Leeds GS; *Style—* The Hon David Gray; 11 Vancouver Rd, Forest Hill, London

GRAY, Dr James Nicol; s of Capt George Nicol Gray (d 1961), and Elsie May, *née* Scott (d 1966); *b* 29 Mar 1922; *Educ* George Watsons Coll Edinburgh, Univ of Edinburgh, Royal Sch of Med; *m* 28 Nov 1953, Pamela Ann, da of James MacDonald Walker, DFC (d 1942); 1 s (Ian b 1958), 2 da (Lesley b 1954, Moira b 1962); *Career* Canadian mangr Benger Laboraties Ltd 1957-61, res grantee Arthritis and Rheumatism Cncl 1964-66, GP 1965-78, police surgn 1967-87; med advsr 1978-85: Lothian Regnl Cncl, Lothian and Border Police, Lothian and Border Fire Brigade; LRCPE, LRCSE, LRFPS, DMJ, AFOM, FRSM; memb: BMA, BSMDH, Faculty Occupational Medicine RCP; Assoc Police Surgns, AFOM 1981; *Recreations* golf, photography; *Clubs* Luffness New; *Style—* Dr Nicol Gray

GRAY, Sir John Archibald Browne; s of Sir Archibald Montague Henry Gray, KCVO, CBE (d 1967); *b* 30 Mar 1918; *Educ* Cheltenham, Clare Coll Cambridge (MA, MB, ScD); *m* 1946, Vera Kathleen, da of Charles Anthony Mares of Highgate; 1 s, 1 da; *Career* Surgn-Lt RN Pacific Fleet; physiologist; prof of physiology Univ Coll London 1959-66; sec Med Res Cncl 1968-77; memb external scientific staff MRC Marine Biological Assoc Laboratories Plymouth 1977-83; hon fellow Clare Coll 1976; Hon DSc (Exeter) 1985; FIBiol, FRCP, FRS; kt 1973; *Recreations* sailing (35 ft sloop "White Seal II"); *Clubs* Royal Guisings, Royal Plymouth Corinthian Yacht, Royal Western Yacht; *Style—* Sir John Gray; Seaways, North Rock, Kingsand, Torpoint, Cornwall (☎ 0752 822745)

GRAY, John Magnus; CBE (1971, MBE 1945), ERD (1946); s of Lewis Campbell Gray, and Ingeborg Sanderson Gray, *née* Ross; *b* 15 Oct 1915; *Educ* Winchester; *m* 1947, Patricia Mary, *née* Eggar; 1 da; *Career* md William Ewart & Son Ltd (linen mfrs) Belfast 1958-72; chm: Irish Linen Guild 1958-64, Central Cncl of Irish Linen Indust 1968-74, NI Electricity Serv 1974-80, Belfast Branch RNLI 1970-76; memb: FBI Cncl 1956-74, Export Cncl for Europe 1964-70, Design Cncl 1974-80, CBI Cncl 1979-80; *Recreations* golf, gardening; *Clubs* Army and Navy, Royal Co Down GC (Capt 1963);

Style— John Gray, Esq, CBE, ERD; Blairlodge, Dundrum, Newcastle, Co Down, N Ireland (☎ 039 675 271)

GRAY, Vice-Adm Sir John Michael Dudgeon; KBE (1967), OBE (1950, CB 1964); s of Col Arthur Claypon Horner Gray, OBE (d 1963), of Nayland, Suffolk, and Dorothy M, *née* Denham; *b* 13 June 1913; *Educ* RNC Dartmouth; *m* 1939, Margaret Helen, da of Arthur Purvis, of Cairo; 1 s, 1 da; *Career* joined RN 1926, served WWII: in HMS Hermes and Spartan, with US in Anzio, with 8 Army in Italy, with French Army in France (despatches); Cdr 1947, Capt 1952, cmd HMS Lynx 1955, cmd HMS Victorious 1960, Rear Adm 1962, dir-gen Trg MOD (RN) 1962-65, Vice Adm 1965, C-in-C S Atlantic and S America 1965-57, ret; sec The Oriental Ceramic Soc; *Clubs* Naval and Military; *Style*— Vice Adm Sir John Gray, KBE, CB; 55 Elm Park Gdns, London SW10 (☎ 01 352 1757; office: 01 636 7985)

GRAY, Maj-Gen (Reginald) John; CB (1973); s of Dr Cyril Gray (d 1951), and Frances Anne, *née* Higgins (d 1953), of Higginsbrook, Trim, Co Meath; *b* 26 Nov 1916; *Educ* Ascham House, Gosforth, Rossall Sch, Durham Univ; *m* 1943, Esme, da of Maj G R G Ship (decd); 1 s, 1 da; *Career* served 1939-45 in India, Burma, later in NW Europe, Egypt, Malta, BAOR, Gold Staff Offr 1953, dep dir-gen AMS 1967-69, QHS 1970-73, med dir UKLF 1972-73; chief med offr British Red Cross Soc 1974-83, dir Int Generics Ltd 1974-83, Col Cmdt RAMC 1977-81, chm RAMC Assoc 1980-, chm BMA Armed Forces Ctee 1981-85; FRSM, fndr fell Faculty of Community Med RCP: memb BMA and Casualty Surgns Assoc; memb (hon caus) St AAA and Inst of Civil Defence, CStJ 1971 (OStJ 1957); *Recreations* growing some things, repairing others, fermenting grape juice; *Style*— Maj-Gen John Gray, CB; 11 Hampton Close, Wimbledon, London SW20 0RY (☎ 01 946 7429)

GRAY, John Walton David; CMG; s of Myrddin Gray (d 1943), of Llanelly, Carmarthenshire, and Elsie Irene, *née* Jones (d 1983); *b* 1 Oct 1936; *Educ* Queen Elizabeth GS Devon, Blundells Sch Tiverton Devon, Christs Coll Cambridge (BA, MA), ME Centre Oxford, American Univ Cairo; *m* 22 Sept 1957, Anthoula, da of Nicholas Yerasimou, of Nicosia, Cyprus; 1 s (Nicholas Myrddin Christopher b 1971), 2 da (Helen Irene b 1961, Clare Marian b 1963); *Career* 2 Lt RASC 1954-56; Foreign Serv: joined 1962, serv MECAS 1962-63, political offr Bahrain 1964-67, FO 1967-70, Geneva 1970, UK delegation to Conf on Security and Co-operation in Europe 1973-74, head of chancery Sofia 1974-77, cnsllr Jedda 1978-81, head of dept FCO 1982-85, ambass Beirut 1985-88, UK delegation to OECD Paris, ambass 1988-; *Recreations* watching sport, being Welsh, leisurely walking, travel; *Clubs* Athenaeum, Royal Cwlth, Royal Overseas League; *Style*— John Gray, Esq, CMG; Foreign and Commonwealth Office, King Charles St, London SW1A 2AH

GRAY, (Stephen) Marius; s of Basil Gray, CB, CBE, of Long Wittenham, Oxford, and Nicolete Mary, *née* Binyon; *b* 3 August 1934; *Educ* Westminster, New Coll Oxford (MA); *m* 2 Sept 1961, Clare Anthony, da of Sir Anthony Horace Milward, CBE (d 1981); 1 s (Theodore b 1964), 3 da (Emma b 1962, Bridget b 1967, Jacquetta b 1971); *Career* Nat Serv 2 Lt RCS 1953-55; CA 1962; sr ptnr Dixon Wilson 1981 (ptnr 1967); non-exec dir: Davies Turner Ltd 1970-, Abingworth plc 1973-, Spice plc 1977-, Folkestone Ltd 1977-, Br Bio-Technology Ltd 1982-, Assoc Newspapers Hldgs plc 1983-, Daily Mail and Gen Tst plc 1985-; chm: Special Tstees The London Hosp 1974-, mgmnt ctee of the King's Fund 1985-; govr The London Hosp Med Coll 1984-; FCA; *Clubs* Savile; *Style*— Marius Gray, Esq; 47 Maze Hill, London SE10 8XO; Dixon Wilson, Rotherwick House, PO Box 900, 3 Thomas More St, London E1 9YX (☎ 01 628 432, fax 01 702 9769, telex 883967)

GRAY, Dr Michael Ian Hart (Mike); s of Harry Lesley Gray, of London, and Edith Louise, *née* Hart; *b* 12 July 1940; *Educ* Dartford GS, Univ of St Andrews (MB ChB, Dip Aviation Med 1976); *m* 22 July 1964, Patricia Margaret (Trish), da of Capt William Thompson Stewart, of Dundee, Scotland; 1 s (Jeremy Rupert Andrew Hart b 1968); *Career* cmmnd RAMC 1963, Regtl MO 4/7 Royal Dragoon Gds 1966-68, pathologist Queen Alexandra Mil Hosp London 1972-74 (trainee since 1969), trainee in aviation med Army Air Corps Centre 1974-76, awarded Helicopter Wings 1975, specialist in aviation med Army Air Corps Centre 1976-77, advsr in aviation med (Lt-Col) to dir Army Air Corps 1977-79, conslt in aviation med (Flt Surgn) King Abdul Aziz Mil Hosp Tabuk Saudi Arabia 1979-83; chief med offr Gulf Air Bahrain 1986-88 (sr med offr 1983-86); Br Acad of Forensic Sci's 1971, Soc of Occupational Med 1978, MFOM 1981, MRAeS; *Recreations* reading, gardening, flying, sailing, shooting; *Clubs* Cavalry and Guards; *Style*— Dr Michael Gray; Nut Tree Cottage, Lower Chicksgrove, Tisbury, Salisbury, Wiltshire SP3 6NB (☎ 072 270 382)

GRAY, Lt Gen Sir Michael Stuart; KCB (1986), OBE (1971); s of Lt Cdr Frank Gray, RNVR (ka 1940); *b* 3 May 1932; *Educ* Christ's Hosp Horsham, RMA Sandhurst; *m* 1958, Juliette Antonia; 3 children; *Career* reg offr Br Army, memb Royal Coll Def Studies 1976, Cdr 16 Parachute Bde 1977, cdr 6 Field Force and COMUKMF 1977-79, cdr Br Army Staff and mil attaché 1979-81 (with additional responsibilities of head Br Def Staff and Def Attaché) Washington 1981, GOC S W Dist 1981-83, COS HQ BAOR 1984-85, GOC SE Dist 1985-88, ret 1988; Actg Col Cmdt The Parachute Regt; conslt Brittany Ferries 1988-, def industs advsr Wardle Storeys plc 1989-; area organiser (NE England) King Georges Fund for Sailors 1988-; chm: Airborne Assault Normandy Tst, Forces Retirement Assoc; tstee: Air Forces Security Fund, Airborne Forces Charities Assoc; tstee: Air Forces Security Fund, Airborne Forces Charities Devpt Tst; FBIM; *Recreations* military history, gardening and house maintenance, drawing, painting, photography; *Style*— Lt-Gen Sir Michael Gray, KCB, OBE; c/o National Westminster Bank plc, 60 Market Place, Beverley, North Humberside

GRAY, Milner Connorton; CBE (1963); s of Archibald Campbell Gray (d 1952), of Eynsford, Kent, and Katherine May, *née* Hart; *b* 8 Oct 1899; *Educ* Private, Colfe Sch Lewisham, Goldsmiths' Coll London; *m* 12 July 1934, Gnade Grace, da of William Osbourne-Pratt, of Northamton; *Career* 19 London Regt 1917, transferred RE Experimental Section Sch of Camouflage 1917-19, gunner HAC (TA) 1923-31, admitted Veteren Co 1931; fndr and sr ptnr Basset Gray (multi-discipline design practice) 1922-35, sr ptnr Industl Design Ptnrship (reorganisation of former practice) 1935-40, princ Sir John Cass Sch of Art 1937-40, head and princ design advsr exhibitions branch Miny of Info 1940-44, fndr ptnr Design Res Unit 1945-80, conslt 1980-; work incl: rendering of Royal Coat of Arms Crown and Royal Cipher for Coronation Souvenirs 1952-53, design conslt Royal Mint for coin inscriptions 1961-, design of armorial bearings and common seal Post Office 1970, design of official emblem for Queen's Silver Jubilee for use on street decorations and souvenirs; fndr memb FCSD 1930 (pres 1943-49 and 1966-67); memb cncl: Design and Industs Assoc 1935-38, RSA 1959-65; memb: Miny Educn Advsy Ctee for Art Examinations 1947-52, Royal Mint Advsy Ctee 1952-86, fndr ctee Int Cncl Soc Industl Design 1956, Miny Educn Advsy Cncl on Art Educn 1973-76, Alliance Graphique Internationale 1950 (Br pres 1963-71); Design Centre Award 1957, Queen's Silver Jubilee Medal 1977; Freeman City of London 1981; Hon Univ of Manchester 1965, hon fell Soc Typographic Designers 1979, hon Dr RCA 1979; RDI 1938, FInst Pack 1947, AGI 1950; *Books* numerous publications, lectures and broadcasts on design; *Clubs* Arts; *Style*— Milner Gray, Esq, CBE; Felix Hall, Kelvedon, Essex CO5 9DG; 8 Holly Mount, Hampstead London NW3 6SG (☎ 01 435 4238)

GRAY, Nicholas Anthony; s of Sir William Gray, 2 Bt (decd); hp of n, Sir William Hume Gray, 3 Bt; *b* 1934; *m* 1956, Amanda, da of H W Edwards, of Newbury; 1 da; *Style*— Nicholas Gray, Esq; 43 Markham Sq, London SW3; Skutterskelfe House, Hutton Rudby, Yarm, Yorks

GRAY, Nicolete Mary; *née* Binyon; da of Laurence Binyon, CH (d 1943), and Cicely, *née* Powell (d 1962); *b* 20 July 1911; *Educ* St Paul's Girls Sch, Oxford (MA), Br Sch at Rome; *m* 20 July 1933, Basil, s of Charles Gray (d 1915), of London SW7; 2 s (Marius b 1934, Edmund b 1939), 3 da (Camilla b 1936 d 1971, Cecilia b 1940, Sophia b 1943); *Career* asst princ Miny of Food 1940-43, pt/t teacher Convent of Sacred Heart Hammersmith 1948-51, lectr Lettering Central Sch of Art & Design London 1964-81; organised exhibitions of lettering 1963 for Arts Cncl of GB and Assoc Typographique Internationale 1981; Introduction to Helen Sutherland Collection 1970; *Books* XIX Century Types and Title Pages (1938 and 1976), The Paleography of Latin Inscriptions in Italy 700-1000 AD (1948), Rossetti, Dante and Ourselves (1947), Jacob's Ladder (a bible picture book for children from Anglo-Saxon Mss) (1949), Lettering on Building (1960), Lettering as Drawing (1971), The Painted Inscriptions of David Jones (1981), A History of Lettering (1986), Assoc Typographique Internationale; *Clubs* Double Crown; *Style*— Mrs Nicolete M Gray; Dawbers House, Long Wittenham, Abingdon, Oxon OX14 4QQ (☎ 086 730 7995)

GRAY, Peter Francis; s of Rev George Francis Selby Gray; *b* 7 Jan 1937; *Educ* Marlborough, Trinity Coll Cambridge; *m* 1978, Fiona Elspeth Maude Lillias, da of late Arnold Charles Verity Bristol; 2 s; *Career* serv Lt Royal Fusiliers attached to 4 Kings African Rifles, Uganda 1956-58; Coopers & Lybrand 1967-69, Samuel Montagu & Co 1970-77, head of investmt div Crown Agents for Oversea Govts and Admins 1977-83, md and chief exec Touche Remnant & Co and Touche Remnant Hldgs 1983-87, dir TR Industl & Gen Tst plc 1984-88; dep chm The Assoc of Investmt Tst Cos 1985-87; chm Exmoor Dual Investmt Tst 1988,- dir NZ Investmt Tst 1988-; FCA; *Clubs* Buck's; *Style*— Peter Gray, Esq; 1 Bradbourne St, London SW6 (☎ 01 731 4950)

GRAY, Hon Peter L; s of Baron Gray of Contin and Judith Waite, *née* Brydon; *b* 7 Nov 1959; *Style*— The Hon Peter Gray; Achneim House, Flichity, Inverness-shire IV1 2XE

GRAY, Dr (John) Richard; s of Capt A W Gray, RN, of Bournemouth, and Christobel Margaret, *née* Raikes; *b* 7 July 1929; *Educ* Charterhouse, Downing Coll Cambridge (MA), SOAS London (PhD); *m* 30 March 1957, Gabriella, da of Dr Camillo Cattaneo (d 1956); 1 s (Camillo b 1959), 1 da (Fiammetta b 1965); *Career* lectr Univ of Kartoum 1959-61; SOAS: res fell 1961-63, reader 1963-72, prof of African history 1972-; chm: African Centre Covent Garden 1967-72, Br Zimbabwe Soc 1981-84; Equitem Ordinis Sancti Silvestri Papae 1966; *Books* The Two Nations (1960), A History of the Southern Sudan (1961), Cambridge History of Africa (ed vol 4, 1975); *Style*— Dr Richard Gray; 39 Rotherwick Rd, London NW11 7DD; School of Oriental and African Studies, Univ of London, Thornhaugh St, London WC1H 0XG (☎ 01 637 2388, fax 01 436 3844, telex 291829 SOASP)

GRAY, Robert Walker (Robin); CB (1977); s of Robert Walker Gray (d 1985), of Dundee and Dorothy, *née* Lane (d 1974); *b* 29 July 1924; *Educ* John Lyons Sch Harrow, LSE (BSc); *m* 1955, Shirley Matilda, da of Frederick Henry Taylor (d 1958), of Chingford; 2 s (Julian, Alistair), 1 da (Charlotte); *Career* civil servant; BoT 1952-66, commercial cllr Ottawa 1966-70; under-sec: Dept of Trade and Indust 1971-74, Dept of Prices and Consumer Protection 1974-75; dep sec: Dept of Indust 1975, DTI 1975-84, ret 1984; *Recreations* gardening, fishing; *Style*— Robin Gray, Esq, CB

GRAY, Roger Ibbotson; QC (1967); s of Arthur Gray (d 1959), and Mary, *née* Ibbotson (d 1982); *b* 16 June 1921; *Educ* Wycliffe Coll, Queen's Coll Oxford (BA); *m* 1, 1952, Anne Valerie, da of Capt G G P Hewett, CBE, RN (d 1966), of Folkestone; 1 s (Randal b 1952); m 2, 1987, Lynne Jacqueline, da of Eric Towell, FRIA, of Spain; *Career* cmmnd RA 1942 with Ayrshire Yeo 1942-45, Normandy and NW Europe, GSO 3 8 Corps 1945, GSO 3 (Mil Ops) GHQ India 1946; barr Grays Inn 1947; contested (C) Dagenham 1955; Rec of Crown Ct 1972-; *Recreations* cricket, reading; *Clubs* Carlton, Pratt's, MCC; *Style*— Roger Gray, Esq, QC; 6/74 Kensington Park Road, London W11; Queen Elizabeth Building, Temple, London EC4 (☎ 583 7837)

GRAY, Ronald George; s of Henry Gray (d 1958), and Elizabeth Campbell, *née* Cowan (d 1942); *b* 12 July 1929; *Educ* Royal HS Edinburgh, Edinburgh Univ (MA); *m* 26 June 1954, Diana Ravenscroft, da of Francis Henry Houlston (d 1983); 3 da (Karen b 14 Oct 1955, Francesca b 14 Sept 1958, Fiona b 10 March 1960); *Career* trainee Unilever 1953; dir: Elida Gibbs Ltd 1967-72, Unilever Co-ordination 1973-80; chm: Elida Gibbs (Germany) 1981-84, Lever Bros Ltd 1984-; memb: CTFA (Cosmetic Toiletry and Fragrance Assoc) 1970-72, SDIA (Soap and Detergent Industry Assoc) 1985-, pres ISBA 1988-, memb IBA advertising advsy ctee; govr Dulwich Coll and Alleyns Sch; *Style*— Ronald Gray, Esq; Lever Brothers Ltd, Lever Ho, 3 St James's Rd, Kingston-on-Thames, Surrey KT1 2BA (☎ 01 541 8200)

GRAY, Rosemarie Hume; *née* Elliott-Smith; da of Air Cdre C H Elliott-Smith, AFC, of Eggleston Hall, Barnard Castle, Co Durham, and Margot Agnes, *née* Piffard (d 1977); *Educ* privately; *m* 22 April 1954, William Talbot Gray (d 1971), s of Sir William Cresswell Gray, 2 Bt (d 1978); 1 s (Sir William Hume Gray, 3 Bt, *qv*), 2 da (Victoria (Mrs Straker) b 15 July 1958, Emma Mary b 7 Oct 1962); *Career* dir: Eggleston Estate Co, Talbot Gray Ltd; govr Polam Hall Sch; High Sheriff of Co Palatine of Durham 1986; *Recreations* gardening, travel; *Style*— Mrs William Talbot Gray; Eggleston Hall, Barnard Castle, Co Durham (☎ 0833 50403); 483 Fulham Palace Road, London SW6

GRAY, Hon Sally B; da of Baron Gray of Contin and Judith Waite, *née* Brydon; *b* 1957; *Style*— The Hon Sally Gray; c/o Judy Daish Associates, 83 Eastbourne Terrace W2 6LQ

GRAY, Simon James Holliday; s of Dr James Davidson Gray, and Barbara Cecelia Mary, *née* Holliday; *b* 21 Oct 1936; *Educ* Westminster, Dalhousie Univ, Trinity Coll Cambridge (MA); *m* 1965, Beryl Mary, *née* Kevern; 1 s (Ben), 1 da (Lucy); *Career*

res student and Harper-Wood travelling student 1960, sr instr in English Univ of Br Columbia 1963-64, lectr QMC London 1965-85; author and playwright; Plays: Wise Child (1968), Sleeping Dog (1968), Dutch Uncle (1969), The Idiot (1971), Spoiled (1971), Butley (1971), Otherwise Engaged (1975, voted Best Play 1976-77 by NY Drama Critics Circle), Plaintiffs and Defendants (1975), Two Sundays (1975), Dog Days (1976), Molly (1977), The Rear Column (1978), Close of Play (1979), Stage Struck (1979), Quartermaine's Terms (1981), The Common Pursuit (1984), Melon (1987); *Books* Colmain (1963), Simple People (1965), Little Portia (1967 as Hamish Reade), A Comeback for Stark (1968), An Unnatural Pursuit and Other Pieces (1985), How's That For Telling 'em Fat Lady? (1988); *Recreations* watching cricket and soccer; *Clubs* Dramatist; *Style*— Simon Gray, Esq; c/o Judy Daish Assoc, 83 East Bourne News, London W2 6LQ

GRAY, Simon Talbot; s of Dr John Talbot Carmichael Gray (d 1961), of Ealing, and Doris Irene Gray, *née* Baker; *b* 1 June 1938; *Educ* Westminster; *m* 1963, Susan, da of Felix William Grain, of Ealing; 2 s (Nicholas b 1965, Julian b 1968); *Career* CA: sr tax ptnr Smith & Williamson; dir: S & W Securities, S & W Tst Corpn, S & W Nominees, S & W Insur Conslts, Yattendon Investmt Tst Ltd, Syndicate Admin Ltd, Hartridge Investmt Ltd, Havenpace Ltd, Mallmead Ltd, Chichester Est Co, Yattendon Hldgs plc; special tstee of St Bartholomew's and St Marks Hospitals 1982-; memb City & Hackney Health Authy 1983-; memb Ct of Worshipful Co of Glass Sellers (Master 1978); *Recreations* yachting (yacht Fast Anchor); *Clubs* City of London, City Livery, Royal Lymington Yacht, Royal Thames Yacht; *Style*— Simon Gray, Esq; Brackens, Captains Row, Lymington, Hants SO41 9RP (☎ 0590 77101); 44 Minster Court, Hillcrest Road, Ealing W5 1HH (☎ 01 997 6447); 1 Ridinghouse St, London W1 (☎ 01 637 5377, telex 25187, fax 01 631 0741)

GRAY, Sir William (Stevenson); JP (Glasgow 1965), DL (City of Glasgow 1976); s of William Gray; *b* 3 May 1928; *Educ* Glasgow Univ (BL); *m* 1958, Mary Rodger; 1 s, 1 da; *Career* slr and notary public; City of Glasgow: hon tres 1971-72, magistrate 1961-64, memb corpn 1958-75, chm property mgmnt ctee 1964-67; former chm Irvine New Town Devpt Corpn; chm: World of Property Housing Tst Scottish Housing Assoc 1974-, Third Eye Centre 1975-85, Scottish Devpt Agency 1975-79, The Oil Club 1975-, Glasgow Ind Hosp 1982-, The Barrel Selection 1986-; Gap Housing Assoc 1988-, Norcity plc 1988-, Clan Homes plc 1988-; vice-pres Glasgow Citizens' Theatre 1975-; memb: Scottish Opera Bd 1971-72, Nat Tst Scotland 1971-72, Ct of Glasgow Univ 1972-75, Clyde Port Authy 1972-75, advsy cncl Energy conservation 1974-85, Scottish Youth Theatre 1976-86, Scottish Pakistani Soc 1983-; vice-pres Charles Rennie Mackintosh Soc 1974-, Scottish Assoc for Care and Resettlement of Offenders 1975-82; Lord Provost City of Glasgow, Lord-Lt Co of the City of Glasgow 1972-75 (DL 1971-72); kt 1974; *Style*— Sir William Gray, JP, DL; 13 Royal Terrace, Glasgow G3 7NY (☎ 041 332 8877, fax 041 332 2809)

GRAY, Sir William Hume; 3 Bt (UK 1917), of Tunstall Manor, Hart, Co Durham; s of William Talbot Gray (decd), s of 2 Bt; suc gf, Sir William Gray, 2 Bt, 1978; Sir William Cresswell Gray, 1 Bt, was chm William Gray & Co Ltd, a memb of Lloyds Register Ctee and fndr of the S Durham Steel and Iron Co Ltd in 1889; *b* 26 July 1955; *Educ* Eton, Polytechnic of Central London (Dip Arch); *m* 1984, Catherine, yst da of late John Naylor, of The Mill House, Bramley, Hants; 1 s, 1 da (b 1987); *Heir* s William John Cresswell Gray b 1986; *Career* architect; *Style*— Sir William Gray, Bt; Eggleston Hall, Eggleston, Barnard Castle, Co Durham

GRAY OF CONTIN, Baron (Life Peer UK 1983); Hamish - James Hector Northey Gray; PC (1982); s of James Northey Gray, JP (d 1979), of Inverness; *b* 28 June 1927; *Educ* Inverness Royal Acad; *m* 1953, Judith Waite, BSc, da of Noel M Brydon, MBE, BSc, of Ayr; 2 s, 1 da; *Career* served Queen's Own Cameron Highlanders (Lt) 1945-48; memb Inverness Cncl 1965-70; former dir: Drumry Testing Co Hillington, James Gray (Inverness) Ltd, and others; MP (C) for Ross and Cromarty 1970-83; asst govt whip 1971-73, lord cmmr Treasury 1973-74, oppn whip 1974-75, oppn spokesman on energy 1975-79; min of state: Energy 1979-83, Scottish Off 1983-86, public affrs business and parly conslt 1986-; *Recreations* golf, cricket, walking; *Clubs* Highland (Inverness); *Style*— The Rt Hon Lord Gray of Contin, PC; Achneim House, Flichity, Invernessshire IV1 2XE (☎ (08083 211) House of Lords, London SW1

GRAY-CHEAPE, Hamish Leslie; s of Lt-Col Leslie George Gray-Cheape, of Carse Gray, Forfar, Angus, Scotland, and Dorothy Evelyn *née* Thomas (d 1986); Lt-Col L G Gray-Cheape, DL (1969) Angus, JP (1954) Worcs, High Sheriff of Worcs 1953; *b* 18 Mar 1942; *Educ* Eton; *m* 6 Oct 1965, Fiona Mariella, da of Brig Sir Harry Ripley Mackeson (d 1964, 1 Bt late Royal Scots Greys); 2 s (James b 1968, George b 1971); *Career* Capt Grenadier Gds 1961-71; High Sheriff of Warwickshire 1984; farmer 1987-; JP Warwickshire 1985; *Style*— Hamish Gray-Cheape, Esq; Great Alne (☎ (078-981) 420); Hill House, Walcote, Alcester, Warwickshire B49 6LZ

GRAYBURN, Jeremy Ward; s of Sqdn Ldr Robert William Grayburn (d 1982), of Silverdale, Lancs and Moira Wendy, *née* Rice; *b* 24 August 1952; *Educ* Lancaster Royal GS; *m* 7 Feb 1976, Pamela Anne, da of Fl-Lt Graham Ross; 2 da (Nicola, Caroline); *Career* joined Allied Dunbar Assur plc 1971: divnl dir 1984-85, exec dir 1985-; *Style*— Jeremy Grayburn, Esq; York Cottage, Long Lane, Shaw, Newbury, Berks RE16 9LJ (☎ 0635 34437); Allied Dunbar Assurance Plc, Allied Dunbar Centre, Swindon Wiltshire (☎ 0793 514514, fax 0793 512301)

GRAYDON, Air Vice-Marshal Michael James; CBE (1984); s of James Julian Graydon (d 1985), and Rita Mary, *née* Alkan; *b* 24 Oct 1938; *Educ* Wycliffe Coll; *m* 25 May 1963 (Margaret) Elizabeth, da of Arthur Ronald Clark (d 1972); *Career* RAF Coll Cranwell 1957-59, QFI No 1 Fts 1960-62, No 56 Sqdn Wattisham 1963-64, 226 OCU 1965-67, Fl-Cdr No 56 Akrotiri 1967-69, RAF Staff Coll Bracknell 1970, PSO to D/CINCENT HQAFCENT 1971-73, ops staff MOD 1973-75, NDC Latimer 1975-76, OC No 11 Sqdn Binbrook 1977-79, MA to CDS MOD 1979-81, OC RAF Leuchars 1981-83, OC RAF Stanley FI 1983, RCDS London 1984, SASO HQ 11 Gp Bentley Priory 1985-86, ACOS policy SHAPE Belgium 1986-88, Air Marshal and AOC-in-C RAF Support Cmd 1989-; govr Wycliffe Coll; *Recreations* golf, photography; *Style*— Air Vice-Marshal Michael Graydon, CBE; ACOS Policy, SHAPE, Mons, Belgium BF P026 (☎ Mons 065 44 4115)

GRAYSON, Edward; *b* 1 Mar 1925; *Educ* Taunton's Sch Southampton, Exeter Coll Oxford; *m* 27 May 1959, (Myra) Wendy Shockett; 1 s (Harry b 26 March 1966); L.....; *Career* RAF 1943-45; barr Middle Temple 1948: uninterrupted practice: Lincoln's Inn 1949-53, Temple and SE circuit 1953-; author and communicator; contrib: legal, sporting and nat jls, newspapers, BBC, ITV, various radio stations; contrib and conslt to Centl Cncl of Physical Recreation and Sports Cncl, hon legal advsr Freedom in Sport Int; memb Br Assoc of Sports Med; *Books* Corinthians and Cricketers (1955, re-issued as Corinthian-Casuals and Cricketers 1983), The Royal Baccarat Scandal (jtly, second edn 1988), The Way Forward: The Gleneagles Agreement (1982), Sponsorship of Sport, Arts and Leisure (jtly, 1984), Sport and The Law (second edn 1988); *Recreations* working and creative thinking; *Clubs* MCC, Harlequins, Corinthian-Casuals, Sussex, Surrey CC, Littlehampton Town FC; *Style*— Edward Grayson, Esq; 1 Brick Court, Temple, London EC4Y 9BY (☎ 01 583 6287); Temple Gate, Shaftesbury Rd, Rustington, West Sussex (☎ 0903 783823); 4 Paper Buildings, Temple, London EC4Y 7EX (☎ 01 583 7765, fax 01 353 4674: Groups 2 & 3)

GRAYSON, Sir Rupert Stanley Harrington; 4 Bt (UK 1922); s of late Sir Henry Grayson, 1 Bt, KBE (d 1951); suc n Sir Ronald Henry Rudyard Grayson, 3 Bt (d 1987); unc of Lord Rawlinson, of Ewell, QC and the Earl of Munster; *b* 22 July 1897; *Educ* Harrow; *m* 1, 1919, Ruby Victoria, da of Walter Henry Banks; m 2, 1950, Vari Colette, da of Maj Henry O' Shea, Royal Dublin Fus, of Cork; *Heir* n, Jeremy Brian Vincent Grayson b 1933; *Career* Ensign in Irish Gds (twice wounded) 1914-18, King's For Serv Messenger 1939-45; novelist, constant traveller; Kt of Order of Holy Sepulchre; *Books autobiographies* Voyage Not Completed, Stand Fast The Holy Ghost, *fiction* 26 Gun Cotton, Secret Service Adventures; *Style*— Sir Rupert Grayson, Bt; c/o Midland Bank, Hythe, Kent

GRAZEBROOK, Donald McDonald Denis Durley; s of Kenrick Denis Durley Grazebrook (d 1957), and Evelyn, *née* Griffiths; *b* 17 Jan 1927; *Educ* privately, UCL (LLB); *m* 17 April 1953, Mabel, da of Charles Gawler (d 1970), of Stalbridge, Dorset and Anglesey; *Career* barr Lincoln's Inn 1952, entered Govt Legal Serv 1952; serv: Miny of Nat Insur 1952-61, Miny of Lab (later Dept of Employment) 1961-70; legal advsr UKAEA 1982-88 (ind 1979), conslt UKAEA 1988-; memb Conseil d'Administration Assoc Int du Droit Nucléaire 1983 (2 vice pres 1987); *Recreations* fox and stag hunting; *Clubs* East India; *Style*— Donald Grazebrook, Esq; Pine Ridge, Peaslake, Surrey; Atomic Energy Authy, 11 Charles II St, London SW1

GRAZEBROOK, Michael Ward; MC (1944); s of George Ward Grazebrook (d 1948), of Sharpthorne, of Sussex, and Eleanor Blanche, *née* Charrington (d 1972); *b* 27 June 1917; *Educ* Eton, Trinity coll Cambridge (BA); *m* 11 April 1951, Diana Patience, da of Col Huntly Gordon Spencer, DL (d 1953), of Somerset; 2 s (Julian b 1953, Anthony b 1958 (d 1977)), 1 da (Lavinia b 1952); *Career* Maj Grenadier Gds UK and Italy; dir Private Cos 1947-82; *Recreations* gardens, travel; *Clubs* Army & Navy; *Style*— Michael Grazebrook, Esq, MC

GREATBATCH, Sir Bruce; KCVO (1972, CVO 1956), CMG (1961), MBE (1954); s of W T Greatbatch; *b* 10 June 1917; *Educ* Malvern, Barenose Coll Oxford; *Career* serv WWII with RWAFF Nigeria and Burma (despatches), Maj 1944; entered Colonial Serv (N Nigeria) 1939, sec to govr and exec cncl N Nigeria 1957, sec to Premier and head of N Nigerian Civil Serv 1959, cnsllr tech asst Br High Cmmn in Nairobi 1963, dep high cmmr Nairobi 1965, govr and C-in-C Seychelles 1969-73, head of Br Devpt Div in Caribbean 1974-78, freelance conslt 1978-; KStJ 1969; kt 1969; *Clubs* East India, Sports & Public Schools; *Style*— Sir Bruce Greatbatch, KCVO, CMG, MBE; Greenleaves, Painswick, near Stroud, Glos

GREATOREX, Raymond Edward; s of Percy Edward Greatorex (d 1985), and Lilian Alice *née* George (d 1986); *b* 28 August 1940; *Educ* Westcliff HS, Lewes County GS; *m* 1, 3 Sept 1966 (m dis 1982), Brenda Margery, da of Edward James Rands; m 2, 27 May 1982, Barbara Ann, da of Mark Booth; 1 step da (Joanna Dawn Carty b 15 Sept 1974); *Career* CA 1965; ptnr: Sydenham & Co 1970, Hodgson Harris (after merger) 1980, Hodgson Impey (after merger) 1985; memb ctees S Eastern Soc of CA; FCA; *Recreations* travelling, horse racing, gardening; *Style*— Ray Greatorex, Esq; Beeches Brook, Wisborough Green, W Sussex RH14 OHP (☎ 0403 700 796); Peel House, Barttelot Rd, Horsham, Sussex RH1Q 1DQ (☎ 0403 51666, fax 0403 51466, telex 878353)

GREATREX, Geoffrey Harold; s of Harold Victor Greatrex, of Essex, and Henrietta; *b* 3 Mar 1933; *Educ* Gosfield Sch, Durham Univ Newcastle upon Tyne (MB BS), Toronto Univ, Harvard Univ; *m* 1968 (m dis 1976), Tatiana, da of Mikhail Swetchin (d 1967), of Toronto; 1 da (Alexandra b 1973); *Career* Capt RAMC attached parachute regt Cyprus 1958-61; conslt surgn Central Notts Health Authy 1977-, dir Nottingham private med conslts 1983-; memb ct of examiners RCS (Eng) 1986-; *Recreations* arts, fell walking, tree felling; *Clubs* Flyfishers, Royal Society of Medicine; *Style*— Geoffrey Greatrex, Esq; Greenfields, Quaker Lane, Farnsfield, Notts NG22 8EE; Kings Mill Hospital, Sutton-in-Ashfield, Notts

GREAVES, (Ronald) John; s of Ronald Greaves, and Rose Mary, *née* Nugent; *b* 7 August 1948; *Educ* Douay Martyrs Ickenham Middx, Poly of Central London (LLB); *m* 1, 3 July 1970 (m dis 1980), Angela, da of Stanley Menze; m 2, 15 Jan 1983, Margaret Dorothy, da of Denis John O'Sullivan, of Thornhill, Lincoln Drive, Winterton, S Humberside; 1 s (Patrick John b 30 Sept 1987), 1 da (Caroline Frances 28 July 1984); *Career* barr Middle Temple 1973, SE Circuit; Parly candidate (Lab) St Albans 1979; memb justice ctee Compensation for Wrongful Imprisonment 1982; memb Soc of Labour Lawyers; *Style*— John Greaves, Esq; 51 Kingsend, Ruislip, Middx HA4 7DD (☎ 0895 632676); 4 Paper Buildings, Temple, London EC4Y 7EX (☎ 01 583 7765, fax 01 353 4674)

GREELEY, Paul William; s of Thomas Greeley, of London, and Mary Greeley, of London; *b* 5 Oct 1939; *Educ* St Josephs Acad Blackheath; *m* 10 April 1976, Moya Patricia, da of A Basil Pippet; 2 s (Justin b 1978, Andrew b 1984), 2 da (Susanna b 1980, Sophia b 1982); *Career* public practice CA; FCA, ATII; *Recreations* cricket, chess, literature; *Clubs* Challoner; *Style*— Paul Greeley, Esq; Four Stacks, 6 Peaks Hill, Purley, Surrey CR3 (☎ 01 668 5789); 1433B London Rd, Norbury, London SW16 4AW (☎ 01 679 5722, fax 01 773 2267)

GREEN, Alan; CBE (1974); s of Edward Green (d 1929) and Emily *née* Harthill (d 1942); *b* 29 Sept 1911; *Educ* Brighton Coll; *m* 8 Jan 1935, Hilda Mary, da of John Wolstenholme (d 1966) of Sussex Down, Storrington, Sussex; 3 da (Hilary b 1937, Gillian Rosemary b 1939, Judith Penelope b 1946); *Career* Gnr RA 1940, Maj 1946; MP (C) Preston South 1955-64 and 1970-74, Parly Estimates Ctee 1956-61, Parly sec Min of Labour 1961-62; Min of State BOT 1962-3, fin sec Treasy 1963-64; Parly Ctee on Legislation 1971-74, Nationalised Indust Ctee 1970-74, Ctee on Europe 1972-73, Speakers Conference 1973-74; dir: Scapa Gp 1946-76, Walmsley Gp (chm) 1951-78, Wolstenholme Rink 1951-87 (chm 1980-84); *Recreations* cricket, gardening, history, poetry; *Clubs* Carlton, RAC; *Style*— Alan Green, Esq, CBE; The Stables, Sabden, Blackburn, Lancs (car ☎ Padihar 71528)

GREEN, Alison; da of Sam Green, CBE, of Holly Lodge, 39 Westmoreland Rd, Bromley, Kent, and Lilly Green; *b* 18 Mar 1951; *Educ* Bromley HS, Univ Coll London (LLB, LLM), Univ of Louvain; *Career* barr Middle Temple 1974-, lectr in law Univ of Surrey 1976-78; tutor in law: QMC London 1978-79, Univ Coll London 1979-81, practices on Western Circuit; memb: Br Insur Law Assoc, IBA; *Books* Insurance Contract Law (ed advsr 1988), Law Journal (ed); *Recreations* music, tennis, ballet; *Clubs* The Hurlingham; *Style*— Miss Alison Green; 5 King's Bench Walk, The Temple, London EC4Y 7DN (☎ 01 353 2882)

GREEN, Allan David; QC; s of Lionel Green, of 20 Upper Grosvenor St, London W1X 9PB, and Irene Evelyn (later Axelrad, *née* Abrahams) (d 1975); *b* 1 Mar 1935; *Educ* Charterhouse, St Catharine's Coll Cambridge (MA); *m* 21 Feb 1967, Eva Brita Margareta, da of Prof Artur Attman, of Kjellbergsgatan 4, 41132 Gothenburg, Sweden; 1 s (Robin b 1969), 1 da (Susanna b 1970); *Career* serv RN 1953-55; dir Public Prosecutions and head Crown Prosecution Serv 1987; barr Inner Temple 1959 (bencher 1985); jr prosecuting cncl to Crown, Central Criminal Ct 1977-79 (sr 1979-85); first sr prosecuting cncl Crown, Central Criminal Ct 1985-87; rec Crown Ct 1979-87; QC 1987; non-exec dir Windsmoor plc 1986-87; *Recreations* music, studying calligraphy; *Style*— Allan D Green, QC; 4-12 Queen Anne's Gate, London SW1H 9AZ

GREEN, Andrew Fleming; s of Gp Capt Joseph Henry Green, CBE (d 1970), and Beatrice Mary, *née* Bowditch; *b* 6 August 1941; *Educ* Haileybury, Magdalene Coll Cambridge (BA, MA); *m* 21 Sept 1968, Catherine Jane, da of Lt Cdr Peter Norton Churchill, RN (1940); 1 s (Stephen b 1973), 1 da (Diana b 1970); *Career* short serv cmmn Royal Greenjackets 1962-65; Dip Serv: MECAS Lebanon 1966-68, 2 sec Aden 1968-70, asst political agent Abu Dhabi 1970-73, 1 sec FCO 1973-77, 1 sec UK Del OECD Paris 1977-80, 1 SCC FCO 1980-82, political cnsllr Washington 1982-85, consul gen and head of chancery Riyadh 1985-88, cnsllr FCO 1988; *Recreations* tennis, sailing, bridge; *Style*— Andrew Green, Esq; c/o Foreign and Commonwealth Office, King Charles St, London SW1A 2AH

GREEN, Anthony Eric Sandall; s of Frederick Sandall Green (d 1961), of 17 Lissenden Mansions, London, and Marie-Madeleine (Mrs Joscelyne), *née* Dupont (d 1969); *b* 30 Sept 1939; *Educ* Highgate Sch, Slade Sch of Fine Art UCL (Dip Fine Art); *m* 29 July 1961, Mary Louise, da of Gordon Roberts Cozens-Walker (d 1981); 2 da (Katharine Charlotte b 1965, Lucy Rebecca b 1970); *Career* artist; Harkness Fellowship USA 1967-69, over 40 one man shows worldwide; UK public collections: Tate, V & A, Arts cncl of GB, Br Cncl, and others; foreign public collections at: The Met Museum of Art NYC, various museums in Japan and Brazil, and others; RA 1977; *Books* A Green Part of the World (with Martin Bailey, 1984); *Recreations* family, travel; *Clubs* Arts; *Style*— Anthony Green, Esq; 17 Lissenden Mansions, London NW5 1PP (☎ 01 485 1226)

GREEN, Charles Frederick; s of George Frederick Green (d 1987), and Ellen Maud Mary, *née* Brett (d 1987); *b* 20 Oct 1930; *Educ* Harrow Co Sch; *m* 1956, Elizabeth Pauline Anne, da of Egbert Joseph William Jackson, CB, MC (d 1975); 2 s (Nicholas b 1957, Martin b 1959); 1 da (Mary b 1963); *Career* joined Nat Provincial Bank 1946 (sec 1967-70), head of planning Nat West Bank 1970, md Centre File 1974, dir and gen mangr fin control div Nat West Bank 1982, dep gp chief exec Nat West Bank 1984; chm: industl econ affrs ctee C of E 1986, multinational affrs panel CBI/ICC 1982-87, overseas ctee CBI 1987; vice chm: Business in the Community, bd of social responsibility C of E 1983; memb General Synod 1980, tstee Church Urban fund 1987, tres Policy Studies Inst 1984; *Recreations* opera, concert music, drama; *Clubs* National, Langbourn Ward; *Style*— Charles Green, Esq; National Westminster Bank plc, 41 Lothbury, London EC2P 2BP (☎ 01 726 1222)

GREEN, Christopher Edward Wastie; s of James Wastie Green and Margarita, *née* Mensing; *b* 7 Sept 1943; *Educ* St Paul's Sch London, Oriel Coll Oxford (MA); *m* 1966, Mitzie, da of Dr Joachim Petzold, of Lugano Switzerland; 1 s (James b 1971), 1 da (Carol b 1969); *Career* BR mgmnt trainee 1965, area mangr Hull 1973, passenger operations mangr BRB 1978, rgnl operations mangr Scotland 1980, dep gen mangr Scot Rail 1983, gen mangr Scot Rail 1984, dir London & South East 1986; *Recreations* architecture, music, hill walking; *Style*— Chris Green, Esq; British Rail, Waterloo Stn HQ, London SE1 (☎ 01 928 5151)

GREEN, Hon Mrs; Claerwen; *née* Gibson-Watt; er da of Baron Gibson-Watt, MC, PC; *b* 20 Oct 1952; *Educ* Queensgate London, Châtelard Switzerland; *m* 1, 1970 (m dis 1979) Enrique Rene Ulvert, s of Marcel Ulvert-Portocarrero, sometime Nicaraguan Ambass in London; 2 s (b 1971, Marcel David Joaquin Nicholas Charles b 1972); m 2, 4 Sept 1980, John (James) Randal Green, s of John Richard Daniel Green and Hon Jane Smith, da of 2 Baron Bicester; 3 s (Toby James Ralf b 1982, Richard John Daniel b 1984, David Peter Julian (twin)); *Style*— The Hon Mrs Green; Foxboro Hall, Melton, nr Woodbridge, Suffolk IP12 1ND

GREEN, David John Mark; s of John Geoffrey Green, of Woodford Green, Essex, and Margaret Green; *b* 8 Mar 1954; *Educ* Christs Hosp Horsham, St Catherine's Coll Cambridge (MA); *m* 7 June 1980, Katherine, da of James Sharkey, of Woodford Green; 1 s (Dominic James Millican), 1 da (Clemency Alice); *Career* Def Intelligence Staff MOD 1975-78; called to the Barr Inner Temple 1979-; *Style*— David Green, Esq; 5 King's Bench Walk, Temple, London EC4 (☎ 01 353 4713, fax 01 353 5459)

GREEN, Ernest; s of Luke Green (d 1944), and Daisy Sarah Lydia, *née* Smeeton; *b* 22 Dec 1929; *Educ* Westminster Tech Coll; *m* 1 Sept 1951, May, da of John Menzies Kennedy (d 1959), of Scotland; 3 s (Graham Ernest b 1955, Russell Ian b 1959, Elliot Luke b 1973), 1 da (Susan Debra (Mrs Wright) b 1957); *Career* Nat Serv Sgt RE 1949, MONS OTC, cmmnd 1952; served: 3 TRRE, 9 TRRE, 114 Army Engr Regt, 101 Field Engr Regt, ret RE TA 1957; after gaining extensive experience in civil and structural consulting offices, commenced own pratice Ernest Green Hldgs (first consulting engr on London Stock Exchange) 1985; memb Assoc of Community Engrs; Freeman City of London 1960, Liveryman Worshipful Co of Basketmakers 1960, Freeman Guild of Air Pilots and Navigators 1972; FIStructE 1955, FICE 1957; *Recreations* motor yachting, flying; *Clubs* City Livery, Belfry; *Style*— Ernest Green, Esq; The White Hse, L'Eree, St Peters in the Wood, Guernsey, CI (☎ 0481 643 85, fax 0481 650 85)

GREEN, Dr Frank Alan; s of Frank Green (d 1943), and Winifred Hilda, *née* Payne; *b* 29 Oct 1931; *Educ* Mercers Sch, Univ of London (BSc, PhD, CEng, ACT); *m* 30 March 1957, Pauline Eleanor, da of George Edward Tayler (d 1980); 1 s (Paul b 19 July 1963), 2 da (Gail b 17 April 1958, Sally b 18 Sept 1960); *Career* md AE Gp subsidiary 1962-66, tech advsr Consormex SA Mexico City 1966-68, mfrg dir Stewart Warner Corpn 1968-72, dir market dvpt Calor Gp 1972-74, md Br Twin Disc Ltd (dir Twin Disc Int SA) 1974-80, industl advsr (under-sec) DTI 1981-84; currently: princ Charing Green Assoc, sr conslt Gen Technol Systems Ltd, dir Gen Technol Systems (Scandinavia) A/s; advsr to Mexican govt on mfrg 1966-68, dep chm Newcastle Technol Centre 1983, memb professional bd Inst of Metals 1986- (chm gen educn ctee 1986-88, chm initial formation ctee 1988-); memb Kent CBI ctee and CBI SE Regnl Ctee 1974-80; currently involved in Understanding Industry Initiative; Freeman City of London 1953; FIM, FBIM; *Recreations* wine, photography, hill walking, military and local history; *Clubs* Old Mercers; *Style*— Dr Frank Green; Courtwood House, Burleigh Rd, Charing, Kent TN27 OJB (☎ 023 371 3152); General Technology Systems Ltd, Brunel Science Park, Kingston Lane, Uxbridge UB8 3PQ (☎ 0895 56767, fax 0895 32078, telex 295 607 GENTEC G)

GREEN, Geoffrey David; s of Ronald Green (d 1977), of Enfield, and Ivy May, *née* Steggles (d 1988); *b* 17 Mar 1946; *Educ* George Spicer Central Sch Enfield; *m* 3 April 1969, Rosmarie, da of Dominik Raber, of Affoltern Am Albis, Switzerland; 2 da (Natasha b 1970, Vanessa b 1972); *Career* dir: Bisgood 1985, Co Securities 1986, Co Nat West 1986, Co Nat West Wood MacKenzie 1988; memb Stock Exchange 1970; *Recreations* cycling, gardening, travel, reading; *Style*— Geoffrey Green, Esq; Hadleigh, 35 Carnaby Rd, Broxbourne, Hertfordshire, Drapers Gardens, 12 Throgmorton Ave, London EC2P 2ES

GREEN, Maj George Hugh; MBE (1958), MC (1946), DL (Caithness 1965), TD (1947); s of George Green (d 1952), and Charlotte, *née* Steven (d 1952); *b* 21 Oct 1911; *Educ* Wick HS, Edinburgh Univ (MA); *m* 1936, Isobel Elizabeth (d 1987), da of Peter Myron (d 1953); 2 s (George, Patrick); *Career* serv WWII: N Africa, Sicily, NW Europe, TA 1935-63 incl active serv; headmaster until 1977; vice-Lt Caithness 1973-86; *Recreations* gardening, beekeeping; *Clubs* Highland Bde; *Style*— Maj George Green, MBE, MC, TD, DL; Tjaldur, Gerston, Halkirk, Caithness (Tel: 084 783 639)

GREEN, Hon Sir Guy Stephen Montague Green; KBE (1982); s of Clement Francis Montague Green, of Hobart, Tasmania, and Beryl Margaret Jenour, *née* Williams (d 1981); *b* 26 July 1937; *Educ* Launceston Church GS, Univ of Tasmania (LLB); *m* 1963, Rosslyn Mary, da of Clarence Garrow Marshall (d 1967); 2 s (David b 1970, Christopher b 1973), 2 da (Jill b 1966, Ruth b 1968); *Career* chief justice and Lt govr of Tasmania, admitted ot the Bar, Supreme Ct of Tasmania 1960, ptnr Ritchie & Parker Alfred Green & Co 1963-71, pres Tasmanian Bar Assoc 1968-70, magistrate 1971-73, chief justice of Tasmania 1973-, chllr of the Univ of Tasmania 1985-; KGStJ *see Debrett's Handbook of Australia and New Zealand for further details*; *Clubs* Tasmanian, Athenaeum; *Style*— The Hon Sir Guy Green, KBE; 1 Paviour St, Newtown, Tas 7008, Australia; Chief Justice's Chambers, Supreme Ct of Tasmania, Salamanca Place, Hobart, Tasmania, Australia 7000 (☎ 002 303442)

GREEN, Hon Mrs (Jane Beatrix Randal); *née* Smith; yr and o surviving da of 2 Baron Bicester (d 1968); *b* 12 Feb 1928; *m* 21 April 1949, John Richard Daniel Green, *qv*; 1 s, 2 da; *Style*— The Hon Mrs Green; Appleshaw Manor, Nr Andover, Hampshire SP11 9BH (☎ 026477 2255)

GREEN, John Dennis Fowler; s of Capt Henry Green (d 1947), of The Manor, Chedworth, Cheltenham, and Amy Gertrude, *née* Rock (d 1950); *b* 9 May 1909; *Educ* Cheltenham, Peterhouse Cambridge (MA); *m* 6 May 1946, (Diana) Judith, da of Col HC Elwes, MVO, DSO; *Career* called to the bar Inner Temple; controller Talks Div BBC 1956-61, chm Agric Advsy Cncl 1964-70, memb nat exec CPRE 1967-80 (pres Glos branch), pres Nat Pigbreeders Assoc 1954-55, tstee and dep pres RASE 1984; special agric mission to Aust and NZ (MAFF) 1945-47; chm Cirencester and Tewkesbury Cons Assoc 1964-78; *Books* Mr Baldwin: A Study in Post War Conservatism (1933); *Recreations* forestry, field sport; *Clubs* Bucks, Oriental, Naval & Military, Farmers; *Style*— John Green, Esq; The Manor, Chedworth, Cheltenham (☎ 028 57 233)

GREEN, John Michael; CB (1976); s of George Morgan Green (d 1949), and Faith Mary, *née* Sage; *b* 5 Dec 1924; *Educ* Merchant Taylors', Jesus Coll Oxford (MA); *m* 1951, Sylvia, da of Rowland Yorke Crabb (d 1972); 1 s (David), 1 da (Barbara); *Career* Royal Armoured Corps, Capt 1943-46; entered Civil Serv (Inland Revenue) 1948, HM Treasy 1956-57, memb Bd of Inland Revenue 1971 (dep chm of Bd 1973-85); *Recreations* gardening; *Clubs* Reform; *Style*— John Green, Esq, CB; 5 Bylands, Woking GU22 7LA

GREEN, John Richard Daniel; yr s of John Everard Green (d 1966); *b* 8 Oct 1926; *Educ* Harrow, Christ Church Oxford; *m* 4 April 1949, Hon Jane Beatrix Randal Smith, *qv*; 1 s, 2 da; *Career* Sub-Lt RNVR, Home Fleet; chm Blackwall Green Gp Ltd and subsids 1970-, insur broker at Lloyd's; chm Cowes Combined Clubs 1982-; *Recreations* yacht racing, fishing, shooting; *Clubs* Royal Yacht Squadron, Pratt's, City of London, Seawanhaka Corinthian; *Style*— John Green, Esq; Appleshaw Manor, Appleshaw, Andover, Hants SP11 9BH (☎ Weyhill 026 477), Blackwall Green Group Ltd, 4 Botolph Alley, London EC3R 8DR (☎ office 01 626 5161)

GREEN, Sir Kenneth; s of James William Green, and Elsie May Green; *b* 7 Mar 1934; *Educ* Helsky GS, Univ of Wales Bangor (BA), Univ of London (MA); *m* 1961, Glenda, *née* Williams; 1 da (Lindsey); *Career* Nat Serv 2 Lt S Wales Borderers 1955-57; trainess mangr Dunlop Rubber Co Birmingham 1957-58, asst teacher Speke Secdy Modern Sch Liverpool 1958-60, lectr I Widnes Tech Coll 1961-62, lectr II Stockport Coll of Educn (Tech) 1964-68, head of educn City of Birmingham Col of Educn 1968-72, visiting lectr Univ of Warwick 1972-73, dean of Warwick 1972-73, dean of Faculty of Community Studies and Educn Manchester 1973-81, dir Manchester Poly 1981-; memb Manchester Literary and Philosophical Soc; hon memb RNCM 1987; kt 1988; *Recreations* rugby football; *Style*— Sir Kenneth Green; 40 Royden Ave, Runcorn, Cheshire WA7 4SP (☎ 09285 75201); Manchester Polytechnic, All Saints, Manchester M15 6BH (☎ 061 228 6171, fax 061 236 7383)

GREEN, Kenneth Charles; s of Louis Charles Green (d 1948), of Wimbledon, and Rose Elizabeth, *née* Hyatt (d 1965); *b* 18 Feb 1940; *Educ* Hinchley Wood Commercial Sch Esher Surrey; *m* 18 Sept 1971, Margaret Jean Green; *Career* devpt mangr Zurich Insur Gp 1969-72, md Midland Bank Insur Servs Ltd 1972-88, gen mangr Clydesdale Bank plc 1988-; former chm City Forum; Freeman City of London, memb Worshipful Co of Insurers; FCII 1969; *Recreations* cricket, golf, walking, travel; *Clubs* MCC, Reform, Surbiton GC (Tstee); *Style*— Kenneth Green, Esq; Clydesdale Bank plc, 30 St Vincent Place, Glasgow G1 2HL (☎ 041 248 7070)

GREEN, Kenneth David; s of William Haskell Green, of California, USA, and Zelma Grace, *née* Galyean; *b* 11 April 1944; *Educ* El Camino HS, UCLA (BA, MBA); *m* 12 April 1969, Anne Elizabeth, da of late William Fred Fremdling; 1 s (Michael b 1972), 1 da (Melissa b 1975); *Career* sr vice-pres Bank of America 1968-86, md Bank of America Int Ltd 1980-86; dir: Barclays de Zoete Wedd Hldgs Ltd 1986-, Barclays de Zoete Wedd Ltd 1986-; md Barclays de Zoete Wedd Capital Mkts Ltd 1986-, dir Barclays de Zoete Wedd Govt Securities Inc 1987-; *Recreations* tennis, travel, family; *Clubs* St Georges Hill Lawn Tennis, Annabel's; *Style—* Kenneth Green, Esq; The Lake House, 29 Broadwater Close, Walton-on-Thames, Surrey (☎ 0932 247398); 2 Swan Lane, London EC4R 3TS (☎ 01 623 2323, fax 01 895 1525)

GREEN, Prof Leslie Leonard; CBE (1989); s of Leoard Green (d 1978), and Victoria, *née* Lemere (d 1975); *Educ* Alderman Newtons SCh Leicester, Kings Coll Cambridge (MA, PhD); *m* 26 April 1952, Helen Theresa, da of late Francis Morgan; 1 s (Paul Nicholas b 25 April 1959), 1 da (Elizabeth Sarah b 1956); *Career* Univ of Liverpool: lectr 1948, reader 1962, prof (now emeritus) 1964, dean faculty of sci 1976-79, pro vice chllr 1977-80; dir SERC Daresbury Laboratory 1980-88; FInstP, CPhys; *Style—* Prof Leslie Green, CBE; Seafield Cottage, De Grouchy St, West Kirby, Merseyside L48 5DX (☎ 051 625 5167)

GREEN, Lewis Homer; s of Ernest Sydney Green (d 1980); *b* 14 Nov 1935; *Educ* Sherrardswood Sch, London Coll of Printing; *m* 1961, Mary Valentine; 3 children; *Career* printer; md Unwin Brothers Ltd 1963-79; dir Staples Printers Ltd 1975-81, dir and chief exec Martins Publishing Gp 1979-81, dir Taylowe Ltd 1981-; Freeman and memb Worshipful Co of Stationers; *Books* Confessions of a Woodpecker (ed); *Recreations* the wood engravings of George Mackley and Gertrude Hermes, sport, homemaking, private press work; *Style—* Lewis Green, Esq; The Knoll, Shiplake, Henley-on-Thames, Oxon RG9 3JT; Taylowe Ltd, Furze Platt, Malvern Rd, Maidenhead, Berks (☎ 0628 23311)

GREEN, Mrs David; Lucinda Jane; MBE (1977); da of Maj-Gen George Erroll Prior-Palmer, CB, DSO (d 1977), by his 2 w, Lady Doreen, *qv*; *b* 7 Nov 1953; *Educ* St Mary's Wantage Idbury Manor Oxon; *m* 1981, David Michael Green, yr s of Barry Green, of Brisbane, Australia; 1 s (Frederick b 1985), 1 da (b 1989); *Career* formerly known as Lucinda Prior-Palmer; winner Badminton Horse Trials Championships 1973, 1976, 1977, 1979, 1983, 1984; Individual Euro Championships 1975, 1977; memb Olympic Team Montreal 1976, winning Euro Championship Team Burghley 1977, World Championship Team Kentucky 1978; memb World Championship-winning Br 3-Day Event Team Luhmühlen (W Germany) 1982, also winner of individual championship; Silver Medallist Euro Championship Frauenfeld 1983, memb Silver Medal winning Olympic Team 1984, winning Euro Championship Team Burghley 1985; TV co-presenter of Channel 4, 6 part documentary Horses 1987; *Books* Up, Up and Away (1978), Four Square (1980), Regal Realm (1983); Cross Country Riding (1986); *Clubs* Mount Kenya Safari; *Style—* Mrs David Green, MBE; Appleshaw House, Andover, Hants (☎ 026 477 3322)

GREEN, Dr Malcolm; s of James Bisdee Malcolm Green, of 90 Lexden Rd, Colchester, Essex, and Frances Marjorie Lois, *née* Ruffell; *b* 25 Jan 1942; *Educ* Charterhouse, Trinity Coll Oxford (BA, BSc, BM, BCh, MA, DM), St Thomas's Hosp Med Sch; *m* 21 April 1971, Julieta Caroline, da of William Preston (d 1984); 2 s (Andrew b 28 Feb 1974, Marcus b 1979), 2 da (Nicola b 8 March 1972, Camilla b 1980); *Career* lectr in med St Thomas' Hosp 1970-74 (house physician 1968-69), Radcliffe travelling fell Oxford Univ to Harvard Univ Med Sch 1971-73, conslt physician and conslt i/c chest dept St Bartholomews Hosp 1975-87, conslt physician chest med and sr lectr Brompton Hosp 1975-(sr house physician 1969-70), dean Nat Heart & Lung Inst London Univ 1988-; hon tres United Hosps SC 1977-87, chm cncl and exec Br Lung Fndn 1985-; author of chapters, reviews and articles on gen med, respiratory medicine and physiology; Freeman City of London 1968, Liveryman Worshipful Co of Apothecaries 1965; MRCP 1970, FRCP 1980; *Recreations* sailing, skiing; *Clubs* WMYC, Imperial Poona YC; *Style—* Dr Malcolm Green; 38 Lansdowne Gdns, London SW8 2EF (☎ 01 622 8286); The Nat Heart & Lung Inst, Dovehouse St, London SW3 6LY (☎ 01 351 8175)

GREEN, Dr Malcolm Robert; s of Frank Green (d 1980), and Margery Isabel; *b* 4 Jan 1943; *Educ* Wyggeston GS Leicester, Magdelene Coll Oxford (MA, D Phil); *m* 18 Dec 1971, Mary Margaret, da of Leonard Charles Pratley (d 1987); 1 s (Alasdair b 1981), 2 da (Eleanor b 1975, Sally b 1978); *Career* lectr in roman history Univ of Glasgow 1967-; memb Corpn: of Glasgow 1973-75, Strathclyde Reg Cncl 1975-; chm: Scottish Teachers and Lectrs Negotiating Ctee 1977, Nat Ctee for In-Serv Trg of Teachers 1977-86 and Scot ctee for Staff Devpt in Educn, educn ctee Convention of Scottish Local Authys 1978 Scottish cmmnr Manpower Servs Cmmn 1983-85, fin chm Scottish Examination Bd, 1984-, chm Scottish Vtee for Staff Devpt in Educ 1987-; active in community based Housing Assoc Mvmnt 1975-; F Scotvec; *Style—* Dr Malcolm Greem; 46 Victoria Cres Rd, Glasgow G12 9DE (☎ 041 339 2007); Strathclyde House, India St, Glasgow G2 4PF (☎ 041 227 3453)

GREEN, Martin; s of Samuel Green (d 1967); *b* 7 Oct 1933; *Educ* Whittinghame Coll Brighton, Manchester Univ; *m* 1960, (m dis 1980), Gillian Susan; 3 s, 1 da; *Career* md: Adsega Ltd 1960-65, Wrensons Stores Ltd, David Greig Ltd, Lampa Ltd 1971-74; dir: Scottish Heritable Tst Ltd 1976-82, Associated Tooling Industs Ltd 1978-, The Jessel Tst Ltd 1981-; *Style—* Martin Green, Esq; 101 Dovehouse St, London SW3 (☎ 01 352 2783)

GREEN, Dame Mary Georgina; DBE (1968); da of Edwin Green, of Wellingborough; *b* 27 July 1913; *Educ* Wellingborough HS, Westfield Coll London; *Career* govr BBC 1968-73, chm Gen Optical Cncl 1979-85, former headmistress Kidbrooke Sch London; *Recreations* gardening; *Style—* Dame Mary Green, DBE; 45 Winn Rd, London SE12 9EX

GREEN, Michael Philip; s of Cyril Green, and Irene, *née* Goodman; *b* 2 Dec 1947; *Educ* Haberdashers' Askes'; *m* 12 Oct 1972, Janet Francis, da of Lord Wolfson of Marylebone; 2 da (Rebecca b 1974, Catherine b 1976); *Career* chm and chief exec Carlton Communication plc; chm: Open Coll, Tangent Charitable Tst; non-exec dir Hambros Advanced Technol Tst plc; *Recreations* bridge, television; *Clubs* Portland, Carleton; *Style—* Michael P Green, Esq; 15 St George St, Hanover Sq, London W1R 9DE, (☎ 01 499 8050)

GREEN, Sir Owen Whitley; *b* 14 May 1925; *m* Doreen Margaret Spark; 1 s, 2 da; *Career* chm BTR 1984- (formerly md); former Businessman of the Year; FCA; kt 1984; *Style—* Sir Owen Green; Edgehill, Succombs Hill, Warlingham, Surrey; BTR Ltd, Silvertown House, Vincent Sq, London SW1P 2PL (☎ 01 834 3848)

GREEN, Brig Percy William Powlett; CBE (1960, OBE 1956), DSO (1946); s of Brig Gen Wilfrith Gerald Key Green, CB, CMG, DSO (d 1937), and Minnie Lilian, *née* Powlett (d 1962); *b* 10 Sept 1912; *Educ* Wellington, RMC; *m* 27 Nov 1943, Phyllis Margery Fitzgerald, da of late Lt-Col Arthur Henry May, OBE; 1 s (Guy b 24 July 1947), 1 da (Susan b 20 Nov 1944); *Career* cmmnd Northamptonshire Regt, serv ops NW Frontier India 1936-37, BEF France 1939-40; Cdr: 2 Bn W Yorks Regt Burma and Jav 1945-46 (despatches), 1 Bn Malay Regt, 4 Bn KAR (ops in Kenya) 1954-56, (despatches); Col Gen Staff WO 1956-57, Brig COS E Africa Commando 1957-60, dep dir Mil Intelligence WO 1961-63, COS NI Cmd 1963-65, ADC to HM The Queen and Dep Cdr Aldershot Dist 1965-67, Dep Col Royal Anglian Regt 1966-76, ret 1967; *Recreations* field sports; *Clubs* Army and Navy; *Style—* Brig Percy Green, CBE, DSO; Grudds, South Warnborough, Basingstoke, Hants RG25 1RW (☎ 0256 862 472)

GREEN, Peter Frederick; s of Frederick Arthur Green (d 1964); *b* 5 Sept 1922; *Educ* Berkhamsted; *m* 1949, Ruth Joy Griggs; 1 s, 1 da; *Career* dir LCP Hldgs Ltd 1975-85; chm Evans Halshaw Hldgs Ltd 1975-87; non-exec dir Evans Halshaw Hldgs plc; *Recreations* golf, rugby; *Style—* Peter Green, Esq; Windrush, Wawensmere Rd, Wootton Wawen, Warwickshire (☎ (056 42) 2395)

GREEN, Sir Peter James Frederick; er s of John Everard Green, of Eggington House, Leighton Buzzard (himself s of Sir Frederick Green and gs of Sir Frederick Green, KBE, JP, the latter being fifth in descent from one John Green, a landed proprietor of Chelsea, from whom the government bought part of the site of The Royal Hospital in 1682); *b* 28 July 1924; *Educ* Harrow, Christ Church Oxford; *m* 1, 1950, Aileen Pamela (d 1985), only da of Sir Gerald Ryan, 2 Bt; m 2, 1986, Mrs E Whitehead, of Canada; *Career* chm: Janson Green Ltd 1966-87, Janson Green Hldgs Ltd 1986-, Lloyd's 1980-83 (underwriter 1947, memb Ctee 1974-77, dep chm 1979-80); dir Hogg Robinson to 1983; kt 1982; *Recreations* farming, shooting, fishing; *Clubs* Royal Yacht Sqdn, City of London, Pratt's, Royal Ocean Racing, Cruising Club of America; *Style—* Sir Peter Green; Stutton Mill House, Ipswich, Suffolk (☎ Holbrook (0473) 328242); 85 Burton Court, Franklin's Row, London SW3 (☎ 01 730 5948); Janson Green Ltd, 10/11 Crescent, London EC3N 2LX (☎ 01 480 6440, telex 893432)

GREEN, Peter Smart; MBE (1972), MC (1944), DL (Gwent 1978); s of (Abel Arthur) Aylmer Green (d 1949), and (Sarah) Maria, *née* Edwards (d 1955); *b* 8 Dec 1918; *Educ* Colston's Sch Bristol; *m* 26 April 1952, Phyllis Joyce, da of Albert Edmund Edwards (d 1985), of Weston-Super-Mare; 2 s (Martyn b 1953, Richard b 1956), 1 da (Helen b 1962); *Career* WWII RA: 2 Lt 1940, Lt 1941, Capt 1942-46; md Davies Bros (Debee) Ltd Builders Merchants 1947-82 (dir 1944-47), chm and md Davies Bros (Newport) Hldgs Ltd 1961-, chm Monmouthshire Bld Soc 1967- (dir 1962-67), dir Aberthaw Cement Co pl c1972-82; magistrate Gwent 1960; memb: Tax Cmmn Gwent, fin and gen purposes ctee Gwent branch BRCS; chm SSAFA Gwent 1978-; Freeman City of London 1977, Liveryman Worshipful Co Builders Merchants 1977; FIBM; *Recreations* golf, bridge; *Clubs* Newport GC; *Style—* Peter Green, Esq, MBE, MC, JP, DL; 38 Chepstow Rd, Newport, Gwent NP9 1PT (☎ 0633 63963)

GREEN, DR Philip Charles; s of Thomas James Green (d 1979), and Alice, *née* Theakston (d 1953); *b* 13 Nov 1929; *Educ* Bridlington Sch, Cambridge Univ (MA, MB BChir), St Georges Med Sch London; *m* 3 Sept 1955, Judy Frances, da of Francis Harris Lardman, of Stratton Dell, Stratton Rd, Beaconsfield, Bucks; 3 s (Jeremy b 1957, Barnaby b 1958, Leander b 1964), 2 da (Stella b 1962, Candida b 1967); *Career* house offr: St Peters Chertsey 1956, St Georges 1956; res clinical pathologist St Georges 1957-58, princ GP Beaconsfield 1960-, trainer in gen practice 1974-88, visiting MO Katherine Knapp Home for the Blind, Bucks Co MO Red Cross 1974-82 (local MO 1962-74); govr Oakdene Sch for Girls 1982- (chm of bd 1986-88); Freeman City of London 1975, Liveryman Worshipful Co of Barbers; LMSSA 1955, MRCGP 1979; *Recreations* shooting, sailing, bridge; *Style—* Dr Philip Green; 54 Butlers Court Rd, Beaconsfield, Bucks HP9 1SG (☎ 0494 674 326); Simpson Centre, Beaconsfield, Bucks (☎ 0494 671 571)

GREEN, Richard Chevallier; s of Lionel Green, MBE, JP, DL (d 1969), of The Whittern, Lyonshall, Kington, Herefords, and Phyllis Chalmers, *née* Jameson, (d 1977); *b* 22 May 1924; *Educ* Wellington, RAC Cirencester; *m* 1959, Julia, da of Roger de Wesselow (d 1960); 1 s (Jonathan b 1966), 3 da (Nicola, Joanna, Sara); *Career* Lt RNVR 1942-46 Escort Vessels N Atlantic and MTBs English Channel; farmer; (700 acres), dir The Whittern Farms Ltd; High Sheriff Herefords & Worcs 1981-82;; *Recreations* fishing, travel, boating (yacht 'Rondone'); *Clubs* Royal Yacht Sqdn, Farmers'; *Style—* Richard Green, Esq; The Whittern, Lyonshall, Kington, Herefs (☎ 05448 241/205); 65 Burton Court, London SW3 (☎ 01 730 0420) Cancello Rosso, Giuncarico (GR) Italy (☎ 010 39 566 88228)

GREEN, Richard David; s of Bernard Green, and Flora Amelia, *née* Wartski; *b* 25 May 1944; *Educ* Highgate Sch, Queens' Coll Oxon (BA); *Career* pa to chm and md John Wyeth & Co Ltd 1966-67; Keyser Ullman Investmt Mgmnt Ltd 1967-72; gp economist fund mangr Keyser Ullman Investmt Mgmnt Ltd 1970-72, (investmt analyst 1967-68); economist, res and unit tst mgmnt Hill Samuel Investmt Mgmnt Ltd 1973, dir 1979; Inst Funds Mangr 1974-76 (sr Investmt mangr 1976-77); dir: Hill Samuel Asset Mgmnt Ltd 1981, Pensions Investmt 1981; chief investmt offr Daiwa Int Capital Mgmnt Ltd 1988; memb: Soc of Business Economists, London Oil Analysts Gp; *Recreations* skiing, travel, water sports, theatre; *Clubs* Champneys; *Style—* Richard Green, Esq; The Cottage, Whitestone Lane, London NW3 1EA (☎ 435 3497); 45 Beech Street, London EC2P 2LX

GREEN, Richard Desmond; s of Walter Herbert Green, FCA of Winchester and Nina Margaret *née* Hellyar; *b* 3 June 1947; *Educ* Allhallows, Rousdon, Devon; *m* 16 Aug 1986, Margaret Ann, da of Frederick Richard Lisle (d 1985); *Career* CA 1970; dir: Int Thomson Publishing Servs Ltd 1988-, Routledge, Chapman & Hall Ltd 1988-; *Recreations* golf, amateur operatic/dramatic; *Style—* Richard Green, Esq; ABP ITPS Ltd, North Way, Andover, Hants SP10 5BE (☎ 0264 332424)

GREEN, Richard Paul; s of Hugh Claude Green, of Effingham, Surrey, and Betty Rosina, *née* Blake (d 1983); *b* 17 April 1950; *Educ* King's Coll Sch Wimbledon, City of Westminster Coll London; *m* 29 Sept 1973, (Sheila) Marilyn, da of Lionel Francis Guillem, of Fetcham Surrey; 3 da (Nicola b 1976, Elizabeth b 1976, Susannah b 1981); *Career* CA; ptnr Arthur Young 1979-87, dir Svenska Int plc 1987-; chm Guildford Round Table 1988-89, vice-pres French C of C in GB 1984-; Freeman City of London 1981, memb Worshipful Co of Glovers 1981; FCA 1971; *Recreations* gardening, family, motor sport; *Clubs* RAC; *Style—* Richard Green, Esq; Tanglewood, Aldersey Rd,

Guildford, Surrey GU1 2ES (☎ 0483 32 216); Svenska House, 3-5 Newgate St, London EC1A 7DA (☎ 01 329 4467)

GREEN, (Henry) Rupert; CBE (1960); s of Henry Green, JP (d 1947), of Langdale, 2 Clifton Rd, Davenport Park, Stockport, Cheshire, and Margaret Helène, *née* Turner; *b* 29 Dec 1900; *Educ* Charterhouse, Hertford Coll Oxford (MA); *m* 3 April 1937, (Marie Elizabeth) Patricia, da of Dr John Thomas Bailey (d 1953), of Collingwood, Davenport Park, Stockport, Cheshire; 3 s (Christopher, Jonathan, Roger), 1 da (Rosemary); *Career* WWII: cmmnd RAF 1940, Flt-Lt served ops So Siege of Malta 1941-43; barr Lincolns Inn 1926, in practice N circuit 1926-36, legal cmmr Lunacy and Mental Deficiency Bd of Control 1936-53 (sr cmmr 1953-59, served in same capacity Miny of Health 1959-77); pres govrs St Mary's Indep Sch for Girls Gerrards Cross 1976- (govr 1963-, chm 1970-76); memb: Bar Assoc, Hertford Coll Soc; *Books* Persons of Unsound Minds (in Halsbury's Laws of England, 1960); *Recreations* carpentry, literature; *Style—* Rupert Green, Esq, CBE; The Square House, Latchmoor Grove, Gerrards Cross, Buckinghamshire SL9 8LN (☎ 0753 882316)

GREEN, Sam; CBE (1960); s of Fred Green (d 1951), and Alice Ann, *née* Wrigley (d 1950); *b* 6 Feb 1907; *Educ* Oldham Tech Coll (HNC), Manchester Coll of Technol; *m* 18 July 1942, Dr Lilly, da of Lugwig Pollak (d 1942); 1 da (Alison Anne b 18 March 1951); *Career* apprentice Platt Bros electrical and mechanical engrs, Br Northrop Automatic Loom Co 1934-39 (invented Box Motion Automatic Loom), chief engr Betts & Co London 1939-42, works mangr Morphy-Richards 1942-44, gen works mangr Horoplast Ltd 1944-47, indust advsr Industl & Commerical Fin Corpn 1948-52, md Remploy Ltd 1952-65, chm and md Ralli Bros Industs Ltd 1965-70, chm (govt appt) Dula UK Ltd 1969-, chm and chief exec Spears Bros Ltd 1970-; non exec dir: Grampion Lighting Co Ltd 1966-69, J E Lesser Co Ltd 1969-74, New Day Hldgs Ltd 1966-69; lectr Workingmens Coll Crowndale Rd Kings Cross 1949-51, chm and vice pres Inst of Patentees & Inventors 1952-, vice pres Int Fedn of Inventors Assocs 1968-, memb Industl Advsrs to the Blind 1965-72; Royal Br Legion 1965-: memb benevolent ctee, dir and vice chm poppy factory dir of industs Maidstone Kent; CEng, FIEE, FIProdE, Fell IOD; 1984 Gold Medal for services to Invention by WIPO UN; *Recreations* reading, gardening, walking, cycling; *Clubs* Reform, Pickwick Bicycle; *Style—* Sam Green, Esq, CBE; Holly Lodge, 39 Westmoreland Rd, Bromley, Kent BR2 0TF (☎ 01 460 3306); Spear Bros Ltd, 1 Southlands Rd, Bromley, Kent BR2 2QR (☎ 01 460 0039)

GREEN, Lt-Col Simon Lycett; TD, JP (Wakefield), DL (W Riding Yorks); s of Sir Edward Green, 3 Bt (d 1941); hp of bro, Sir (Edward) Stephen Green, 4 Bt, CBE; *b* 11 July 1912; *Educ* Eton, Magdalene Coll Cambridge (BA); *m* 1, 3 Jan 1935 (m dis 1971), Gladys, eldest da of late Arthur Ranicar, JP; 1 da; m 2, 1971, Mary, da of late George Ramsden, of Wakefield; *Career* Lt-Col cmdg Yorks Dragoons Yeo 1947-51; chm Green's Economiser Gp Ltd 1956-83, ret; *Recreations* shooting and racing (owner racehorses: Green Gorse, King's Vale); *Clubs* White's; *Style—* Lt-Col Simon Green, TD, JP, DL; Cliff Bank, N Rigton, Leeds (☎ 0423 74582)

GREEN, Sir (Edward) Stephen Lycett; 4 Bt (UK 1886), CBE (1964), JP (Norfolk 1946, supp list 1980), DL (1961); s of Sir Edward Arthur Lycett Green, 3 Bt (d 1941), and Elizabeth Williams (d 1964); *b* 18 April 1910; *Educ* Eton, Magdalene Coll Cambridge; *m* 1935, Constance Mary, da of Ven Harry Sydney Radcliffe (decd), archdeacon of Lynn; 1 da; *Heir* bro, Simon Lycett Green; *Career* called to the Bar 1933; farmer and landowner; cncllr 1946-49, dep chm Norfolk Quarter Sessions 1948-71, chm E Anglian Regnl Hosp Bd 1959-74, High Sheriff Norfolk 1973-74; *Style—* Sir Stephen Green, Bt, CBE, JP, DL; Ken Hill, Snettisham, King's Lynn, Norfolk (☎ 0485 70001)

GREEN, Stephen Peter; s of James Dean Green, and Ruth, *née* Marley; *b* 2 Jan 1937; *Educ* Kingswood Sch Bath, Univ of Manchester (LLB); *m* (m dis 1979); 3 da (Clarissa Jane b 10 July 1965, Philippa Lucy b 17 Jan 1967, Victoria Alice b 16 Sept 1971) m 2, 2 Aug 1979, Margaret Enid Owen, da of Cdr John Irwin, RD, RNR, of 26 Queensbury Way, Swanland, North Ferriby, North Humberside;; *Career* admitted slr 1963, sr ptnr March Pearson and Skelton Manchester; pres Manchester Consular Assoc 1988, Netherland Consul for Manchester, E Lancs, E Cheshire, NW rep, Netherlands/Br C of C; ctee memb Manchester and Dist Housing Assoc; memb Law Soc, Licensing Exec Soc; *Recreations* opera, music, gardening; *Clubs* St James' (Manchester), British Overseas League; *Style—* Stephen Green, Esq; Cottage of Content, Off London Road, Buxton, Derbyshire SK17 9NL; March Pearson and Skelton, 41 Spring Gdns, Manchester M2 2BB (☎ 061 832 7290, fax 061 832 2655)

GREEN, Rev Vivian Hubert Howard; the man on whom John Le Carré partly modelled the character of George Smiley in Tinker, Tailor, Soldier, Spy, The Honourable Schoolboy and Smiley's People; s of Hubert James Green (d 1963); *b* 18 Nov 1915; *Educ* Bradfield Coll Berks, Trinity Hall Cambridge (MA, DD); *Career* deacon 1939, priest 1940; former chaplain and asst master Sherborne Sch; rector Lincoln Coll Oxford 1983-87 (chaplain 1951-69, fellow and history tutor 1951-83, sr tutor 1953-62 and 1974-77, sub-rector 1970-83, hon fellow 1987-); FRHistS; *Publications* Bishop Reginald Pecock (1945), The Hanoverians (1948), From St Augustine to William Temple (1948), Renaissance and Reformation (1952), The Later Plantagenets (1955), Oxford Common Room (1957), The Young Mr Wesley (1961), The Swiss Alps (1961), Martin Luther and the Reformation (1964), John Wesley (1964), Religion at Oxford and Cambridge (1964), The Universities (1969), Medieval Civilization in Western Europe (1971), A History of Oxford University (1974), The Commonwealth of Lincoln College 1427-1977 (1979), Love in a Cool Climate, Letters of Mark Pattison and Meta Bradley 1879-1884 (1985); Memoirs of an Oxford Don, Mark Pattison, edited with an introduction (1988); A Question of Guilt: the murder of Nancy Eaton (with William Scoular 1989); contributor to Dictionary of English Church History, The Oxford Dictionary of the Christian Church, The Oxford History of the University, Encyclopaedia of Oxford, ed C Hibbert, The Quest for Le Carré, ed Alan Bold (1988); *Style—* The Rev Vivian Green; Lincoln College, Oxford OX1 3DR (☎ 0865 279830); Calendars, Sheep St, Burford, Oxon (☎ 099 382 3214)

GREEN-ARMYTAGE, John McDonald; *m* 1977, Susan Rosemary, da of Lt-Col Hugh Shelley Le Messurier and Rosemary Alice Champney, *née* (maternal gda of 21 Baron Forbes and paternal ggda of Sir James Walker, 1 Bt, of Sand Hutton); 1 s (Matthew b 1978), 3 da (Anna b 1981, Camilla b 1983, Elizabeth b 1985); *Career* md Guthrie Corpn 1982-; *Style—* John Green-Armytage, Esq; c/o The Guthrie Corporation plc, 6 Devonshire Square, London EC2M 4LA

GREEN-PRICE, Lady; Jean Chalmers Scott; da of David Low Stark, of Arbroath, and widow of Thomas Scott; *m* 17 Oct 1956, as his 2 w, Capt Sir John Green-Price, 4 Bt (d 1964); *Style—* Lady Green-Price; Gwernaffel, Knighton, Powys

GREEN-PRICE, Powell Norman Dansey; 2 s of John Powell Green-Price (d 1927, 5 s of Sir Richard Green-Price, 2 Bt) and Julia Helen Ouchterlony Norman, da of Harold Manners-Norman; adopted by his uncle Sir Robert Green-Price, 3 Bt, 1944; hp to his nephew Sir Robert Green-Price, 5 Bt; *b* 22 July 1926,in India; *Educ* Shrewsbury; *m* 1 s (Simon b 1964), 1 da (Stella b 1965); *Career* Lt Welsh Guards; High Sheriff of Powys; chm of Magistrates; MFH; *Style—* Powell Green-Price, Esq; Hivron, Bleddfa, Knighton, Powys LD7 1NY

GREEN-PRICE, Sir Robert John; 5 Bt (UK 1874), of Norton Manor, Radnorshire; s of Capt Sir John Green-Price, 4 Bt (d 1964); *b* 22 Oct 1940; *Educ* Shrewsbury; *Heir* uncle, Powell Norman Dansey Green-Price JP, *qv*; *Career* Capt (ret) RCT; ADC to Govr of Bermuda 1969-72; *Style—* Sir Robert Green-Price, Bt; Gwernaffel, Knighton, Powys (☎ Knighton 528580)

GREENACRE, Andrew John; s of John Edwin Greenacre (decd); *b* 5 May 1931; *Educ* East Ham GS, Trinity Coll Oxford; *Career* 2 Lt Royal Artillery Germany; fin dir: Glaxo Laboratories Ltd 1975-78, Glaxo Operations UK Ltd 1978-82, Glaxo Pharmaceuticals Ltd 1982-85; *Clubs* Oxford and Cambridge Univ; *Style—* Andrew Greenacre, Esq; 10 Hayes court, Sunnyside, Wimbledon, London SW19 (☎ 01 946 9413)

GREENACRE, Major David Laurence; s of Brig Walter Douglas Campbell Greenacre, CB, DSO, MVO (d 1978), and Gwendolene Edith (d 1978); *b* 19 June 1929; *Educ* Eton; m 1, 26 May 1960 (m dis 1970), Lady Elizabeth Marjory Lindesay-Bethune, da of The Earl of Lindsay (d 1986); 2 s (Philip b 1961, Andrew b 1969), 1 da (Louise b 1967); m 2, 1 June 1971, Pauline Daphne, da of Alexander Wilberforce Bird; *Career* Welsh Gds 1953-69, Maj; banker: Page & Gwyther 1969-72, Charterhouse Japhet 1973-84; *Clubs* Pratt's, Ski of GB, Colchester Garrison Officers; *Style—* Maj David L Greenacre; Alresford Lodge, Alresford, Colchester, Essex CO7 8BE (☎ 020622 2926)

GREENACRE, Lady Elizabeth Marjory Beatrice; *née* Lindesay-Bethune; er da of 14 Earl of Lindsay, DL (d 1985); *b* 31 May 1932; *m* 26 May 1960 (m dis 1970), Maj David Laurence Greenacre, late Welsh Gds, eld s of Brig Walter Douglas Campbell Greenacre, CB, DSO, MVO; 2 s, 1 da; *Style—* Lady Elizabeth Greenacre; Selby House, Ham Common, Richmond, Surrey (01 940 8012)

GREENALL, Hon Edward Gilbert; o s and h of 2 Baron Daresbury and his 2 w, Josephine (d 1958), da of Brig-Gen Sir Frederick Laycock, KCMG, DSO, and Katherine 3 da of Hon Hugh Hare, 4 s of 2 Earl of Listowel, KP; *b* 27 Nov 1928; *Educ* Eton; *m* 1, 7 Feb 1952, Margaret Ada, yst da of Charles John Crawford (d 1940), and Ella, sis of Sir Denis Anson, 4 Bt; 3 s, 1 da; m 2, 1986, Mary Patricia, da of Lewis Parkinson (d 1977); *Career* chm: Randall & Vautier Ltd, Grunhalle Lager Int; *Recreations* boating; *Style—* The Hon Edward Greenall; Crossbow House, Trinity, Jersey, CI (☎ 0534 63316)

GREENALL, John Desmond Thomas; s of Thomas Henry Greenall (d 1941), and Joan Clare Walker, *née* Ridgway; *b* 11 April 1939; *Educ* Winchester; *m* 30 Jan 1965, Margaret Anne, da of Sir Iain Maxwell Stewart; 1 s (Damian b 1968), 2 da (Melissa b 1967, Cleonie b 1974); *Career* stockbroker; dir: The Securities Assoc Ltd, Greig Middleton and Co Ltd, Chart Serv plc, Local Stores Ltd, Small Shops Assoc, REES Geophysical Ltd; chm Gavel Securities; *Recreations* shooting, GC, cricket; *Clubs* Prestwick Golf, The Hon Co of Edinburgh Golfers, Royal and Ancient Golf, MCC; *Style—* John Greenall, Esq; Greig, Middleton & Co Ltd, 139 St Vincent St, Glasgow G2 5JP (☎ 041 221 8103)

GREENALL, Peter Gilbort; s of Hon Edward Gilbert Greenall, of Crossbow House, Trinity, Jersey, CI, and Margaret Ada, *née* Crawford; *b* 18 July 1953; *Educ* Eton, Cambridge (BA), London Business Sch (Sloan Fellowship); *m* 11 Sept 1982, Clare Alison, da of Christopher N. Weatherby, MC, of Whaddon House, Whaddon, Bucks; 3 s (Thomas b 1984, Oliver b 1986, Toby b 1988); *Career* md Greenalls Brewery, chm Aintree Racecourse Co Ltd; champion amateur under national hunt rules 1985-86 and 1986-87; *Recreations* hunting, skiing, tennis, golf; *Clubs* Jockey, White's, Turf, MCC; *Style—* Peter Greenall, Esq; Hall Lane Farm, Daresbury, Warrington, Cheshire (☎ 0925 74212); Greenalls Retail Mgmnt, PO Box 2, Wilderspool Brewers, Warrington, Cheshire WA4 6RH (☎ 0925 51234, car tel 0860 336810 and 0836 701526)

GREENAWAY, Sir Derek Burdick; 2 Bt (UK 1933), of Coombe, Co Surrey; CBE (1974), TD, JP (Kent 1962), DL (1973); s of Sir Percy Walter Greenaway, 1 Bt (d 1956); *b* 27 May 1910; *Educ* Marlborough; *m* 28 April 1937, Sheila Beatrice, o da of Richard Cyril Lockett (d 1950); 1 s, 1 da; *Heir* s, John Michael Burdick Greenaway, Lois Weedon House, Weedon Lois, Towcester, Nothants NN12 8PJ; *Career* Hon Col 44 (HC) Signal Regt (unique Ports) (TA) 1966-67, Hon Col 36 (Eastern) Signal Regt (V) 1967-74; High Sheriff Kent 1971-72, life pres Daniel Greenaway & Son Ltd printers; jt master Old Surrey and Burstow Fox Hounds 1958-66, pres Sevenoaks Div Cons Assoc 1963-66 (formerly chm), chm SE Area Nat Union of Cons Assocs 1975-79 (hon tres 1969-75); memb Masters Stationers' & Newspaper Makers' Co 1974-75 (silver medal 1984); *Recreations* hunting, shooting, fishing; *Clubs* Carlton, City of London, MCC; *Style—* Sir Derek Greenaway, Bt, CBE, TD, JP, DL; Dunmore, Four Elms, Edenbridge, Kent TN8 6NE (☎ 073 270 275)

GREENAWAY, John Michael Burdick; s and h of Sir Derek Greenaway, 2 Bt, CBE, TD, JP, DL, of Dunmore, Four Elms, Edenbridge, Kent; *b* 9 August 1944; *Educ* Harrow; *m* 1982, Susan, da of Henry Birch, of Lion House, Tattenhall, Cheshire; 1 s (Thomas), 1 da (Camilla); *Career* Lt Life Gds (ret); dir Daniel Greenaway & Sons Ltd 1970-79; farmer 1980-; *Recreations* skiing, tennis, riding; *Style—* John Greenaway, Esq; Blackford, Cornwood, nr Ivybridge, Devon (☎ Cornwood 297)

GREENAWAY, Michael Philip; s of Alan Pearce Greenaway, of E Sussex, and Patricia Frances Greenaway, *née* Wells (d 1982); gs of Sir Percy Greenaway Lord Mayor of London 1932-33 and Sir Frederick Wells Lord Mayor of London 1947-48; *b* 14 Dec 1949; *Educ* Harrow; *m* 28 Jan 1978, Alison Robyn, da of Geoffrey Douglas Cohen, of W Sussex; 1 s (Daniel Pearce b 1981), 2 da (Hannah Kate b 1980, Rebecca Lucy b 1984); *Career* fin dir: Cormen Ltd 1984-, Tooling Design and Manufacture (Brighton) Ltd 1987-; dir: Charles Clarke Printers Ltd 1984-, Sensystems Ltd 1984-; Dip Mgmnt Studies 1983; FCA; *Recreations* tennis, skiing, family; *Clubs* Royal Automobile, City Livery, Liveryman of Stationers & Newspapers Makers Co; *Style—* Michael P Greenaway, Esq; Criplands, Gravelye Lane, Lindfield, W Sussex RH16 2SL (☎ 044 473196); Cormon House, South Street, Lancing, W Sussex BN15 8AJ (☎

0903 766861, telex 877885, fax 0903 763192)

GREENBAUM, Prof Sidney; s of Lewis Greenbaum (d 1949), and Nellie Greenbaum (d 1963); *b* 31 Dec 1929; *Educ* Hackney Downs (Grocers) GS, Univ of London (BA, MA, PhD); *Career* visiting asst prof Univ of Oregon 1968-69, assoc prof Univ of Wisconsin-Milwaukee 1969-72, visiting prof Hebrew Univ of Jerusalem 1972-73, prof Univ of Wisconsin-Milwaukee 1972-83, Quain prof of english language and literature UCL 1983- (dir of survey of english usage); memb of senate Univ of London 1985-, dean of faculty of arts Univ of London 1986-88 and UCL 1988-; *Books* Studies in English Adverbial Usage (1969), Elicitation Experiments in English (jtly 1970), A Grammar of Contemporary Usage (jtly 1972), A University Grammar of English (jtly 1973), Studies in English Linguistics (co-ed 1980), A Comprehensive Grammar of the English Language (jtly 1985), Verb-Intensifier Collocations in English (1970), Acceptability in Language (ed 1977), The English Language Today (ed 1985), Studying Writing (co-ed 1986), Gowers Complete Plain Words (co-revisor 1987), A College Grammar of English (1988), Good English and the Grammarian (1988), Guide to English Usage (co-author 1988); *Recreations* reading novels; *Clubs* Reform; *Style*— Prof Sidney Greenbaum; Dept of English, Univ Coll London, Gower St, London WC1E 6BT (☎ 01 387 7050)

GREENBOROUGH, Sir John Hedley; KBE (1979, CBE 1975); s of William Greenborough (d 1953), and Elizabeth Marie, *née* Wilson; *b* 7 July 1922; *Educ* Wandsworth Sch London; *m* 1951, Gerta Ebel; 1 step s; *Career* served WWII pilot RAF later Fleet Air Arm; exec vice-pres Shell Argentina 1965-66, area co-ordinator (Far East) Shell International Petroleum Co 1967-68, md (mktg) Shell-Mex & BP Ltd 1969-71, chief exec and md Shell-Mex & BP Ltd 1971-75, md Shell UK 1976-78, dep chm Shell UK 1976-80; chm Newarthill 1980-; dir: Bowater Corpn 1979-, Lloyds Bank 1980- (dep chm 1985), Hogg Robinson Gp 1980-, Laporte Industs (Hldgs) 1983-86; pres: CBI 1978-80, Nat Cncl for Voluntary Orgns 1980-86, Strategic Planning Soc 1986; govr Ashridge Mgmnt Coll 1972- (chm 1977-); chm: governing cncl Utd Med and Dental Schs of Guy's and St Thomas's Hosps 1982-, Nursing and Professions Allied to Medicine Pay Review Body 1983-86, Civic Tst 1983-86; Liveryman Co of Distillers 1975-, Freeman City London; Hon LLD Birmingham 1983; *Style*— Sir John Greenborough, KBE; 30 Burghley House, Oakfield, Somerset Rd, Wimbledon Common, London SW19 5JB; Newarthill plc, 40 Bernard St, London WC1N 1LG (☎ 01 837 3377, telex 22308)

GREENBURY, Richard; s of Richard Oswald Greenbury (d 1974), and Dorothy, *née* Lewis (d 1980); *b* 31 July 1936; *Educ* Ealing County GS; *m* 1, 1959 (m dis), Sian, da of Dr T Eames Hughes, CBE; 2 s (Jonathan Harri b 1963, Adam Richard b 1966), 2 da (Alyson Jane b 1960, Rosalind b 1970); m 2, Gabrielle Mary, *née* McManus; *Career* Marks & Spencer plc: alternate dir 1970, full dir 1972, jt md 1978, chief operating offr 1986, chief exec offr 1988; non-exec dir: British Gas plc 1976-87, Metal Box 1985; memb Br American C of C; *Recreations* tennis; *Clubs* All England Lawn Tennis, Int Lawn Tennis of GB; *Style*— Richard Greenbury, Esq; c/o 27 Baker St, London W1A 1DN; Marks & Spencer plc, Michael House, 47-57 Baker St, London W1A 1DN (☎ 01 935 4422)

GREENCROSS, Sir Alan David; DL (1986); s of Morris Philip Greencross, OBE (d 1970), and Mirian (d 1969); *b* 15 April 1937; *Educ* Trinity Coll Cambridge (MA); *m* 26 April 1954, Sally; 1 s (Peter b 1962), 3 da (Gail b 1960, Joanna b 1961, Claire b 1964); *Career* leader Camden Cncl 1974-79; memb GLC 1977-86; policy leader Planning & Communications Ctee 1979-81, dep leader of oppn GLC 1982-83 (leader 1983-86), dir Port of London Authy 1979-84; govr Univ Coll Sch; kt 1986; *Clubs* Hurlingham; *Style*— Sir Alan Greengross, DL; 9 Dawson Place, London W2

GREENE, Hon Amanda Louise Massy; *née* Edwardes; o da of 8 Baron Kensington; *b* 22 May 1962; *Educ* St Annes Sch for Girls SA; *m* 1984, Anthony Michael Greene; 1 s (James Stuart b 1985), 2 da (Stephanie Louise Massy b 1987, Rachel Delia b 1988); *Style*— Hon Amanda Greene; Mansfield Farm, PO Box 130, Nottingham Road, Natal, S Africa

GREENE, Edward Reginald; CMG (1952); s of Edward Greene (d 1938); *b* 26 Nov 1904; *Educ* Bedales Sch, St John's Coll Cambridge; *m* 1962, Irmingard, da of Herr Spitza (d 1944); *Career* joined E Johnston & Co Ltd (coffee merchants) 1927, Miny of Food 1943-52 (dir of coffee, dir of raw cocoa); chm: Brazilian C of C 1948-60, Coffee Fedn 1952-53, responsible for the formation of the London Coffee Terminal Market 1952; memb Cmmn of Inquiry into Coffee Industry of Uganda Protectorate 1957; hon vice-pres Brazilian C of C 1960-; FRSA; *Clubs* Garrick, City of London; *Style*— Edward R Greene, Esq; Orbell House, Castle Hedingham, Essex (☎ Hedingham 60298)

GREENE, Graham; OM (1986), CH (1966); 3 s of Charles Henry Greene (himself yr bro of Sir Graham Greene, KCB, JP (decd), and 1 cous of Sir Edward Greene, 1 Bt); er bro of Sir Hugh Carleton Greene, KCMG, OBE, *qv*; bro of Elisabeth Dennys (*see* Dennys, Rodney); *b* 2 Oct 1904; *Educ* Berkhamsted, Balliol Coll Oxford (hon fellow 1963); *m* 1927, Vivien Muriel, da of Sidney Roderick Browning, of Clifton; 1 s (Francis b 1936), 1 da (Caroline b 1933); *Career* author, dramatist, story writer, essayist; The Times 1926-30, literary ed The Spectator 1940-41, FO 1941-44, former dir Bodley Head and Eyre & Spottiswoode; Hon LittD Cantab 1962; Hon DLitt: Edinburgh 1967, Oxon 1979; Hon Doctorate Moscow Univ 1988; *Publications* Babbling April (1925), The Man Within (1929), The Name of Action (1930), Stamboul Train (1932), It's a Battlefield (1934), The Old School (ed 1934), The Bear Fell Tree (1935), England Made Me (1935), The Basement Room (short stories 1935), Journey without Maps (1936), A Gun for Sale (1936), Brighton Rock (1938), The Lawless Roads (1939), The Confidential Agent (1939), The Power and the Glory (1940, Hawthornden Prize 1940), British Dramatists (1942), The Ministry of Fear (1943), The Heart of the Matter (1948), The Third Man (1950), The End of the Affair (1951), The Lost Childhood and other essays (1951), Essais Catholiques (1953), Twenty One Stories (1954), Loser Takes All (1955), The Quiet American (1955), Our Man in Havana (1958), A Burnt-Out Case (1961), In Search of a Character, Two African Journals (1961), A Sense of Reality (1963), The Comedians (1966), May we borrow your husband? and other comedies of the Sexual Life (short stories, 1967), Collected Essays (1969), Travels with my Aunt (1969), A Sort of Life (autobiography, 1971), The Pleasure-Dome; the collected film criticism 1935-40 (ed John Russell Taylor, 1972), Collected Stories (1972), The Honorary Consul (1973), Lord Rochester's Monkey (1974), An Impossible Woman: the Memories of Dottoressa Moor of Capri (ed, 1975), The Human Factor (1978), Dr Fischer of Geneva (1980), Ways of Escape (autobiog 1980), J'Accuse: the dark side of Nice (1982), Monsignor Quixote (1982), Getting to Know the General (1984), The Tenth Man (1985); *Plays* The Living Room (1953), The Potting Shed (1957), The Complaisant Lover (1959), Carving A Statue (1964), The Return of A J Raffles (1975), Yes and No (1980), For Whom the Bell Chimes (1980), The Great Jowett (1981), The Captain And The Enemy (1988); *Children's Books* The Little Train (1947), The Little Fire Engine (1950), The Little Horse Bus (1952), The Little Steamroller (1953); *Screenplays* Brighton Rock (1948), The Fallen Idol (1948), The Third Man (1948), Our Man in Havana (1960), The Comedians (1967); *Style*— Graham Greene, Esq, OM, CH; c/o Reinhardt Books, 27 Wrights Lane, London W8 5TZ

GREENE, Graham Carleton; er s of late Sir Hugh Carleton Greene; *b* 10 June 1936; *Educ* Eton, Univ Coll Oxford (MA); *m* 1, 1957 (m dis), Hon Judith Margaret, da of Baron Gordon-Walker, CH, PC (Life Peer) (decd); m 2 , 1976, Sally Georgina Horton, da of Sidney Wilfred Eaton; 1 s; *Career* merchant banking Dublin, New York and London 1957-78; publishing: Secker & Warburg Ltd 1958-62, Jonathan Cape 1962- (dir 1962-, and md 1966-88); dir: Chatto Virago, Bodley Head and Jonathan Cape 1969 (chm 1970-88), Jackdaw Publications (chm 1964-88), Cape Goliard Press 1967-88, Guinness Mahon Hldgs 1968-69, Australasian Publishing Co Pty 1969 (chm 1978-88), Sprint Productions 1971-80, Book Reps (NZ) 1971-88, CVBC Servs Ltd (chm 1972-88), Guinness Peat Gp 1973-87, Grantham Book Storage (chm 1974-88), Triad Paperbacks 1975-88, Chatto Virago, Bodley Head and Jonathan Cape Australia (chm 1977-88), Greene King & Sons 1979, Statesman & Nation Publishing Co 1980-85 (chm 1981-85), Statesman Publishing Co 1980-85 (chm 1981-85), New Society (chm 1984-86); pres Publishers Assoc 1977-79 (memb cncl 1969-88); memb: Book Devpt Cncl 1970-79 (dep chm 1972-73), int ctee Int Publishers Assoc 1977-88 (exec ctee 1981-88), Groupe des Editeurs de Livres de la CEE (EEC) 1977-86 (pres 1984-86), Arts Cncl Working Party Sub-Ctee on Public Lending Right 1970, Paymaster Gen's Working Party on Public Lending Right 1970-72, bd British Cncl 1977-88; chm Nat Book League 1974-76 (dep chm 1971-74), gen ctee Royal Literary Fund 1975; tstee Br Museum 1978-, ldr First Delgn Br Publishers to China 1978; Chevalier L'Ordre des Arts et des Lettres, 1985 (France); *Style*— Graham C Greene, Esq; 11 Lord North St,London SW1P 3LA (☎ 01 799 6808)

GREENE, Jenny; da of James Wilson Greene, (d 1945), of Cork, and Mary Emily, *née* Dickson (d 1971); *b* 9 Feb 1937; *Educ* Rochelle Sch Cork, Trinity Coll Dublin (BA), Univ of Montpellier France (Dip d' Etudes Francais); *m* 1 April 1971 (m dis 1987), John Gilbert, s of Capt James Gilbert (d 1987), of Johannesburg; *Career* researcher 1963-64, account exec Central News 1964-65, Pembertons Advertisers 1965-66, publicity exec Revlon 1966-71, beauty ed Woman' Own 1971-75, features writer and drama critic Manchester Evening News 1975-77, asst ed Woman's Own 1977-78, ed Homes and Gardens 1978-86, fndr ed A la Carte 1984-85, ed Country Life 1986-; contrib to numerous papers and magazines incl: The Times, The Independent, Daily Mail, BBC Today, Observer; memb Good Food Writers; *Recreations* gardening, cookery; *Style*— Miss J Greene; Michaelmas House, Churchyard, Kimbolton, Cambs PE18 OHH; Country Life, IPC Magazines, Kings Reach Tower, Stamford St, London SE1 (☎ 01 261 7070)

GREENE, Hon Judith; *see*: Dawson-Gowar

GREENE OF HARROW WEALD, Baron (Life Peer UK 1974); Sidney Francis Greene; CBE (1966); s of Frank Greene; *b* 12 Feb 1910; *m* 1936, Masel Carter; 3 da; *Career* gen sec NUR 1957-74, chm TUC 1969-70; dir: Bank of England 1970-78, Trades Union Unit Tst 1970-, RTZ 1975-80; independent nat dir Times Newspaper Hldgs 1980-82; JP London 1941-65; FCIT; kt 1970; *Style*— Rt Hon Lord Greene of Harrow Weald, CB; 26 Kynaston Wood, Boxtree Rd, Harrow Weald, Middx

GREENER, Anthony Armitage; s of William Martin Greener, and Diana Marianne, *née* Muir; *b* 26 May 1940; *m* Audrey, da of Patrick Ogilvie (d 1944); 1 s (Charles b 5 May 1981), 1 da (Clare b 20 Oct 1977); *Career* dir and gp mangr Dunhill Hldgs plc 1974-87; dir: Guinness plc 1986-, Reeves Communications (USA) 1986-; md Utd Distillers 1987-; *Recreations* ocean racing; *Clubs* Royal Ocean Racing; *Style*— Anthony Greener, Esq; Holly House, Church St, Chiswick, London W4; Utd Distillers plc, Landmark House, Hammersmith Bridge Rd, Hammersmith, London W6 9DP (☎ 01 846 8040 office)

GREENER, Maj (William) John Martin; s of William James Greener, JP (d 1977), of Huntspill Court, Bridgwater, Som, and Joyce Durbin, *née* Glass Hooper; *b* 19 Sept 1929; *Educ* Abberley Hall Worcs, Harrow; *m* 14 Jan 1964, (Gillian Diana) Juniper, da of Lt-Col (Arthur) Patrick Sykes, MBE, of Lydham Manor, Bishops Castle, Shropshire; 1 s (James b 1967), 1 da (Juliet b 1970); *Career* cmmnd 2 Lt Coldstream Gds 1948, Capt 1952, Adj Mons OCS 1956-58, Maj 1959, MA to MOD (Army) and to Dep Sec of State 1964-67, ret 1968; Wright Deen & Co Ltd 1968-74 (dir 1972-74); Richards Longstaff Ltd: dir 1974-86, md 1977-86, chm 1986-88 (resigned 1988); dir: Lautro Ltd 1986-, Winterbourne Hosp plc 1982-; St John's Ambulance Bde: area cmmr Som 1968-71, cmmr Co of Bristol 1971-73, cmmr Co of Avon 1973-77, cdr Co of Avon 1977-87; chm: Dorset Health Tst, St Christopher's Sch Burnham-on-Sea; KStJ 1984; memb: BIBA 1974, IBRC 1976; Chevalier Legion d'Honneur; *Recreations* gardening, country pursuits; *Clubs* Cavalry and Guards; *Style*— Maj John Greener

GREENFIELD, Hon Julius MacDonald (Julian); CMG (1954), QC (1949); s of Rev C E Greenfield (d 1940), and Jeannie, *née* Henderson (d 1948); f served as chaplain Royal Scots Greys S African War 1899-1902; *b* 13 July 1907; *Educ* Milton HS Bulawayo, Univ of Capetown (BA, LLB), Oxford Univ (BA, BCL); *m* 1935, Florence Margaret, da of John Cardno Ogston Couper (d 1913), of Craigiebuckler Aberdeen; 2 s (Ewen, Thomas), 1 da (Caroline decd); *Career* barr Grays Inn 1933, advocate S Rhodesia, princ legal advsr to Lord Malvern and later to Sir Royal Welensky at numerous conferences with UK Govt 1951-63; memb of: Parliament SR 1948-53, Fedn Rhodesia and Nyasaland 1954-63; min of: Justice SR 1950-54, Law Fedn of Rhodesia and Nyasaland 1954-63; puisne judge High Ct Rhodesia 1948-74; ret; *Books* Testimony of a Rhodesian Federal 1978; *Clubs* Bulawayo, Harare, Cape Town (City and Civil Serv); *Style*— Hon J M Greenfield, CMG, QC; 27 East Common, Redbourn Herts AL3 7NQ (☎ 058 285 2311)

GREENGROSS, Prof Sir Alan; DL (1986); s of Morris Philip Greengross, OBE (d 1970) and Miriam Greengross (d 1969); *b* 15 April 1929; *Educ* Univ Coll Sch, Trinity Coll Cambridge (MA); *m* 26 May 1959, Sally; 1 s (Peter b 1962), 3 da (Gail b 1960, Joanna b 1961, Claire b 1964); *Career* chm Memfagimal Gp; dir: Indusmond Ltd, Blazy and Clement Ltd, BC Blazy and Clement Ltd; former dir Port of London Authy; memb Holborn Borough Cncl 1957-64; memb London Borough of Camden Cncl 1965-: chm planning and communications 1967-71, dep ldr 1971-74, ldr 1974-79; memb GLC 1977-86: chm Covent Gdn ctee, chm N London Area planning ctee, ldr planning and communications policy ctee, dep ldr of oppn 1982-83, ldr of oppn 1983-86; govr Univ Coll Sch, memb London Regnl Passenger Ctee, fndr memb Inst for Met Studies; kt 1986; *Clubs* Hurlingham; *Style—* Prof Sir Alan Greengross, DL; 9 Dawson Place, London W2; Batworthy on the Moor, Devon;

GREENGROSS, Lady Sally; *b* 29 June 1935; *Educ* Brighton & Hove HS, LSE (BA); *m* 26 May 1959, Prof Sir Alan Greengross; 1 s (Mark Peter b 6 Nov 1962), 3 da (Stephanie Gail b 24 April 1960, Joanna Louise b 31 Oct 1961, Claire Juliet b 10 Feb 1964); *Career* former linguist, exec in indust, lectr and researcher; dir Age Concern Eng 1987- (asst dir 1977-82, dep dir 1982-87), jt coordinator Eurolinkage 1981-,presently vice-pres Int Fedn on Ageing, sec gen 1982-87, coordinator Prog for Elderly People Within Second EEC Prog to Combat Poverty 1985-, memb Standing Advsy Ctee on Transport for Disabled and Elderly People 1986-, jt bd chm Age Concern Inst of Gerontology King's Coll London (KQC) 1987-; ind memb: UN Network on Ageing 1983-, WHO Network on Ageing 1983-; former memb: Inner London Juvenile Ct Panel, mgmnt bd Hanover Housing Gp; FRSH; *Books* Ageing, an Adventure in Living (ed, 1985), The Law and Vulnerable Elderly People (ed, 1986), and others; *Recreations* countryside, music; *Clubs* Reform, Hurlingham; *Style—* Lady Greengross; Age Concern England, 60 Pitcairn Rd, Mitcham, Surrey CR4 3LL (☎ 01 640 5431, fax 01 648 7221)

GREENHALF, (William) Douglas George; s of late John William Greenhalf, and Mabel Gertrude Greenhalf (d 1985); *b* 8 May 1918; *m* 1966, Phyllis Doreen; 1 s (Stephen b 1952); *Career* dir Shipton Communications Ltd; *Recreations* golf, work, swimming; *Style—* Douglas Greenhalf, Esq; En-Joie, Henton, Oxford (☎ Kingston Blount 0844 52922; office 0442 47171)

GREENHALGH, Prof Roger Malcolm; s of Maj John Greenhalgh (d 1977), of IOM, and Phyllis, *née* Poynton; *b* 6 Feb 1941; *Educ* Ilkeston Sch, Clare Coll Cambridge (MA, MD, MChir), St Thomas' Hosp (FRCS); *m* 30 July 1964, Karin Maria, da of Dr Karl Gross; 1 s (Stephen John b 4 Sept 1967), 1 da (Christina Elizabeth b 26 June 1970); *Career* house surgn St Thomas' Hosp London 1967, lectr in surgery St Bartholomew's Hosp London 1972, sr lectr in surgery Charing Cross Hosp London 1976 (hon conslt surgn 1976-), head of dept of surgery Charing Cross Hosp Med Sch 1981 (prof of surgery London Univ 1982), prof of surgery Univ of London at Charing Cross and Westminster Hosp Med Schs 1984, cncl memb Assoc of Surgns of GB and Ireland 1987, Hunterian prof RCS of Eng 1980, vice pres section of surgery RSM 1986; chm ed bd Euro Jl of Vascular Surgery 1987, offr and cncl memb Euro Soc for Vascular Surgery 1987, sec gen and chm exec ctee Assoc of Int Vascular Surgn; FRCS 1970; *Books* Progress in Stroke Research (1978), Smoking and Arterial Disease (1979), Hormones and Vascular Disease (1980), Femoro Distal Bypass (1981), Extra Anatomical Bypass and Secondary Arterial Reconstruction (1982), Progress in Stroke Research 2 (1983), Vascular Surgical Tecniques (1984), Diagnostic Techniques and Investigative Procedures (1985), Vascular Surgery: Issues in Current Practice (1986), Indications in Vascular Surgery (1987), Limb Salvage and Amputation in Vascular Surgery (1988); *Recreations* tennis; *Clubs* Roehampton; *Style—* Prof Roger Greenhalgh; 271 Sheen Lane, London SW14 8RN (☎ 01 878 1110); Department of Surgery, Charing Cross Hospital, London W6 8RF (☎ 01 748 2040)

GREENHILL, Dr Basil Jack; CB (1981), CMG (1967); s of Basil Greenhill (d 1979), of Nailsea Somerset, and Edith Greenhill, *née* Holmes (d 1964); *b* 26 Feb 1920; *Educ* Bristol GS, Univ of Bristol (BA, PhD); *m* 1, 1950, Gillian (d 1959); 1 s (Richard); m 2, 1961, (Elizabeth) Ann, da of Walter Ernest Giffard, JP (d 1970), of Lockeridge, Wiltshire; 1 s (James); *Career* Lt RN (Air Branch) 1941-45; HM Dip Serv cnsllr 1946-67; dir Nat Maritime Museum 1967-83; chm: SS Great Britain project 1982-, Dulwich Picture Gallery 1980-88, Exeter Univ Maritime History Project 1985-, govt advsy ctee on Historic Wreck Sites 1986-; The Royal Armouries 1983-88, The Royal Air Force Museum 1987-; princ advsr BBC TV series: The Commanding Sea 1980-81, Trade Winds 1985-86; BBC Radio series The British Seafarer 1980-81; frequent radio and television appearances; fell Univ of Exeter; Order of White Rose Finland 1980; *Books* Boats and Boatmen of Pakistan (1971), Westcountrymen In Prince Edward's Isle (3 edn 1989, filmed and televised, American Assoc award), Archaeology of the Boat (1976), The Merchant Schooners (4 edn 1988), The Life and Death of the Sailing Ship (1980), Seafaring Under Sail (1982), The Grain Race (1986), The British Assault on Finland 1954-55 (with Ann Gifford, 1988), The Evolution of the Wooden Ship (1988); *Recreations* gardening, walking, sailing (Nugget), travel; *Clubs* Arts, Royal Western YC, Nautical (Mariehamn, Finland); *Style—* Dr Basil Greenhill, CB, CMG; West Boetheric Farm, St Dominic, Saltash, Cornwall PL12 6SZ

GREENHILL, Hon Malcolm; yr s of 1 Baron Greenhill, OBE, LLD (d 1967); heir to er bro, 2 Baron; *b* 5 May 1924; *Educ* Kelvinside Acad Glasgow, Glasgow Univ (BSc); *Career* a chartered patent agent; memb of UK Scientific Mission to Washington USA 1950-51, with UKAEA 1954-73, MOD 1973-89; *Recreations* gardening; *Clubs* Civil Serv; *Style—* The Hon Malcolm Greenhill; 28 Gorselands, Newbury, Berks (☎ 45651)

GREENHILL, 2 Baron (UK 1950); Stanley Ernest Greenhill; s of 1 Baron Greenhill, OBE (d 1967); *b* 17 July 1917; *Educ* Kelvinside Acad Glasgow, Glasgow Univ, Toronto Univ, California Univ (MD, DPH); *m* 1946, Margaret Jean, da of Thomas Newlands, of Ontario; 2 da; *Heir* bro, Hon Malcolm Greenhill; *Career* served WWII RAF; former WHO conslt; prof of community medicine Alberta Univ 1959-80, emeritus 1984-; FRSM, FRCP; *Recreations* photography; *Style—* The Rt Hon the Lord Greenhill; 10223, 137th St, Edmonton, Alberta, Canada T5N 2G8 (☎ 403 452 4650)

GREENHILL OF HARROW, Baron (Life Peer UK 1974); Denis Arthur Greenhill; GCMG (1972, KCMG 1967, CMG 1960), OBE (mil 1941); s of James Greenhill, of Loughton, Essex; *b* 7 Nov 1913; *Educ* Bishop's Stortford Coll, Christ Church Oxford (MA); *m* 1941, Angela Doris, da of William McCulloch, of Helensburgh; 2 s; *Career* Col RE, served WWII, Mid E, N Africa, Italy, Asia; FO 1946-73, PUS FCO and head Dip Serv 1969-73; dir BAT Industs 1974-82, govr BBC 1973-78; dir: BP 1973-78, Br Leyland 1974-77, Leyland Int 1977-82, Clerical Med & Gen Life Assurance 1973-, Hawker Siddeley Gp 1974-84, S G Warburg & Co Ltd 1974-, The Wellcome Fndn Ltd 1974-85; dep chm BUPA 1978-84; chm governing body SOAS 1978-85, King's Coll Hosp Med Sch Cncl 1977-83; pres: Royal Soc for Asian Affrs 1976-84, Anglo-Finnish Soc 1981-84; tstee Rayne Fndn 1974-; govr Wellington Coll 1974-83; *Clubs* Travellers'; *Style—* The Rt Hon the Lord Greenhill of Harrow, GCMG, OBE; 25 Hamilton House, Vicarage Gate, London W8 (☎ 01 937 8362)

GREENING, (Pamela) Margaret (Evelyn); da of Philip Vincent Pelly, of Wilts, and Pamela Mary de Veoux (d 1971); *b* 22 July 1933; *Educ* The Study Wimbledon; *m* 6 Jan 1957, Maurice John; 3 s (Harold John b 1958, James Timothy b 1960, Dominic Maurice Vincent b 1964), 1 da (Mary Jacqueline b 1962); *Career* md family firm M J Greening; memb several diocesan ctees, Gloucs Diocese; chm Smooth Coat Chihuahua club, sec West Country Chihuahua club, ctee memb West of England Ladies Kennel Soc; tres Rural Theology Assoc; church warden St Mary's Acton Turville; moderator for Gloucester Movement of Ordination of Women; dioceasan sec SPCK, govr Trinity School Acton Turville, memb Parish Cncl; *Recreations* running, photography, gardening, breeding dogs, church work; *Clubs* Overseas League, IOD; *Style—* Mrs Margaret Greening; Ladyfield, Acton Turville, Badminton (☎ 0454 21 314/628)

GREENING, Rear Adm Sir Paul Woollven; KCVO; s of Capt Charles Greening, DSO, DSC, RN; *b* 1928; *Educ* Mowden Sch Brighton, Nautical Coll Pangbourne; *m* 1951, Monica; 1 s, 1 da; *Career* RN 1946; Capt Britannia Royal Naval Coll 1976-78, naval sec 1978-80, ADC to HM The Queen 1978, Flag Offr Royal Yachts 1981-85, Extra Equerry to HM 1983-; Master of HM Household 1986-; *Style—* Rear Adm Sir Paul Greening, KCVO; Kingsmead Cottage, Kingsmead, Wickham, Hants

GREENLAND, Michael Patrick; s of Patrick John Greenland, and Margaret Elsie, *née* Howlett; *b* 29 Nov 1941; *Educ* Gilbard Sch Colchester (ONC); *m* 28 May 1966, Susan, da of Henry Lavender Frost, OBE, of Tolleshunt Major, Essex; 2 s (Andrew b 1967, Howard b 1969), 1 da (Katherine b 1972); *Career* chm and md MPG Hydraulics Ltd 1971-; *Recreations* drinking fine wines, fishing, reading, charitable activities; *Style—* Michael P Greenland, Esq; MPG Hydraulics Ltd, Lynn Street, Swaffham, Norfolk PE37 7AT (☎ 0760 721707, fax 0760 23708)

GREENLY, Simon Stafford; s of Raymond Henry Greenly, of Corsham, and Brenda Margaret Agnes, *née* Stafford (d 1986); *b* 2 Mar 1945; *Educ* Uppingham, London Univ (BSc); *Career* Beecham Gp 1967-71 (progressed from mgmnt trainee to int mktg exec); dir: Stafford Robert and Ptnrs Mgmnt Conslts 1972-82, Greenly's Mgmnt Conslts 1983-; chm: Les Routiers 1983-, ATA Selection plc 1986-88, Greenley's Serv Gp 1988-; assoc St George's House Windsor; *Recreations* fly fishing, racing, gardening; *Clubs* Carlton, RAC; *Style—* Simon Greenly, Esq; Wayside Cottage, Mincing Lane, Cobham, Surrey GU24 8AW; 211 Piccadilly, London W1V 9LD (☎ mobile 0836 292020)

GREENOCK, Lord; Charles Alan Andrew Cathcart; s and h of 6 Earl Cathcart, CB, DSO, MC, *qv*; *b* 30 Nov 1952; *Educ* Eton; *m* 1981, Vivien Clare, o da of Francis Desmond McInnes Skinner, of North Farm, Snetterton, Norfolk; 1 s (Hon Alan George b 16 March 1986), 1 da (Hon Laura Rosemary b 11 June 1984); *Heir* s, Hon Alan George Cathcart; *Career* late Scots Gds, cmmnd Scots Gds 1972-75; ACA Ernst and Whinney 1976-83, Hogg Robinson plc 1983; *Clubs* Cavalry and Guards', City; *Style—* Lord Greenock; 18 Smith Terrace, London SW3; Gateley Hall, Dereham, Norfolk

GREENOGH, Hon Mrs; Mary Heritage; *née* Banbury; only da of Capt the Hon Charles William Banbury, Coldstream Gds (ka 1914); raised to rank of a Baron's da, 1938; *b* 28 Mar 1914; *m* 1, 1941, Siegfried Guido Buchmayr (d 1963); 3 s; m 2, 1964, Richard D Greenogh; *Style—* Hon Mrs Greenogh; 120 East 79th St, New York, NY 10026, USA

GREENOUGH, Michael Howarth; s of Arthur Greenough (d 1987) of Morecambe, Lancs, and Mary, *née* Morphet (d 1986); *b* 28 Dec 1936; *Educ* Morecambe GS, Fitzwilliam Coll Cambridge (MA); *m* 20 Dec 1958, Julie Margaret, da of Harry Gabbitas (d 1987), of 1 St Margaret's Court, Ilkley, West Yorkshire; 3 da (Amanda b 1960, Lucinda b 1965, Zoë b 1970); *Career* Nat Serv with RE, Farnborough, Chatham, Aldershot 1958-60; 2 Lt RE; assoc dir Burton Gp plc; md Montague Burton Property Inv Ltd; dir: Burton Property Tst Ltd, Freebody Properties Ltd, FPI Devpt Co Ltd, MBPI Securities LTd, Pengap Estates Ltd; FRICS; *Recreations* tennis, golf, skiing, riding, sailing; *Clubs* Royal Yachting Assoc, Great Middenden Lawn Tennis, Ilkley GC; *Style—* Michael Greenough, Esq; 35/36 Grosvenor Street, London W1X 9FG (☎ 01 491 7823, fax 01 493 4075, telex 295253)

GREENTREE, Hedley Anthony; s of Bertram Albert Greentree (d 1963), of The Crossways, Portchester, and Dolly, *née* Snell (d 1956); *b* 17 April 1939; *Educ* St Johns Coll Southsea, Portsmouth Poly (Dip Arch); *m* 1 (m dis), Sandra Caroline, da of late Frank Paige; 1 s (Richard Anthony b 19 March 1971; m 2, 10 Jan 1976, Jennifer Mary, da of Douglas Stuart Edwin Gudgin, of Magnolia Cottage, Friarydene, Prinstead, nr Emsworth, W Sussex; 3 s (Benjamin Hedley b 4 Feb 1977, Thomas Anthony b 7 Aug 1979, Joseph Michael b 27 Oct 1981); *Career* Nat Serv Lance Corpl X-Technician Army Signals Regt 1959-61; fndr Hedley Greentree Ptnrship Hampshire 1968, chm HGP Greentree Allchurch Evans Ltd (incorporating HGP Conslts, Greentree Assoc Ltd and Marintech) 1987-; fndr and exec ctee memb Hampshire Devpt Assoc; former vice pres Portsmouth Junior (of C, former pres Hampshire branch RIBA, former dir Portsmouth Area Enterprise Bd, chm bd of govrs Portsmouth Coll of Art Design and further Educn, memb Portsmouth Cathedral Businessman's Assoc; memb RIBA; *Recreations* windsurfing, tennis, swimming; *Style—* Hedley Greentree, Esq; Dormers, Crofton Ave, Lee-on-Solent, Hampshire(☎ 0329 661347); HGP Greentree Allchurch Evans Ltd, Furzehall Farm, Wickham Rd, Fareham, Hampshire PO16 7JG (☎ 0329 283225, fax 0329 237004, car 0836 598136)

GREENWAY, 4 Baron (UK 1927); Sir Ambrose Charles Drexel Greenway; 4 Bt (UK 1919); s of 3 Baron (d 1975); *b* 21 May 1941; *Educ* Winchester; *m* 1985, Mrs Rosalynne Peta Schenk, da of Lt Col Peter Geoffrey Fradgley, of Upcott Manor, Rackenford, N Devon; *Heir* bro, Hon Mervyn Greenway; *Career* marine photographer and writer, Yr Bro of Trinity House 1987; *Recreations* sailing, swimming; *Clubs* House of Lords Yacht; *Style—* The Rt Hon Lord Greenway; c/o House of Lords, SW1

GREENWAY, Cordelia Baroness; Cordelia Mary; da of Maj Humphrey Campbell Stephen, JP, of Dormansland, Surrey; *m* 1939, 3 Baron Greenway (d 1975); 3 s (incl 4 Baron); *Career* Freeman City of London 1978, memb Worshipful Co at Glovers 1979; *Style—* Cordelia Baroness Greenway; 703 Collingwood House, Dolphin Sq, London SW1

GREENWAY, Harry; MP (C) Ealing North 1979-; s of late John Kenneth Greenway, and Violet Adelaide, *née* Bell; *b* 4 Oct 1934; *Educ* Warwick Sch, Coll of St Mark and St John London, Caen Univ; *m* 1969, Carol Elizabeth Helena, da of Maj John Robert Thomas Hooper, Metropolitan Stipendiary Magistrate (d 1975); 1 s, 2 da; *Career* former schoolmaster, chm British Atlantic Educn Ctee 1970-84; dep headmaster: Sir William Collins Sch 1971-72, Sedgehill Sch 1972-79; chm All Party Adult Educn Ctee

1979-, memb Parly Select Ctee on Educn, Science and Arts 1979-, vice-chm Greater London Members 1981-, vice-chm and hon sec Cons Parly Educn Ctee 1981-, vice chm Cons Pty Sports Ctee 1987; memb cncl Br Horse Soc 1973- (Award of Merit 1980), memb Cncl Open Univ 1982-, tstee Clare Coll Oxford 1982-, pres Nat Equine Welfare Cncl 1989-; *Recreations* riding, hockey (fndr Lords & Commons Hockey Club, capt 1982), tennis, music, cricket, skiing; *Clubs* Ski Club of GB, St Stephen's Constitutional; *Style*— Harry Greenway, Esq, MP; House of Commons, London SW1 (☎ 01 219 4598)

GREENWAY, John Robert; MP (C) Ryedale 1987; s of Thomas William, of 34 Melchett Cres, Rudheath, Northwich, Cheshire, and Kathleen Gregory; *b* 15 Feb 1946; *Educ* Sir John Deane's GS Northwich; *m* 24 Aug 1974, Sylvia Ann, da of James Francis Gant, of 4 Mulgrave Rd, Whitby, N Yorks; 2 s (Stephen, Anthony), 1 da (Louise); *Career* Midland Bank 1964-65, Met Police 1965-69, insur rep 1969-72, insur broker 1972; memb N Yorks Co Cncl 1985-87; pres York City FC; memb House of Commons Select Ctee on Home Affrs; sec Cons Backbench Health Ctee, Cons Yorks Members Gp; *Recreations* opera, football, wine, travel; *Clubs* Yorkshire; *Style*— John R Greenway, MP; 11 Oak Tree Close, Strensall, York YO3 5TE (☎ 0904 490535); Flaxton House, Pigeon Cote Business Park, Malton Rd, York (☎ 0904 644944); House of Commons, London SW1A 0AA (☎ 01 219 3000)

GREENWAY, Hon Mervyn Stephen Kelvynge; s of 3 Baron Greenway; bro and hp of 4 Baron Greenway; *b* 19 August 1942; *Educ* Winchester; unmarried; 1 da (Philippa Mary b 1980); *Career* stockbroker with Capel Cure Myers, dir Australia & New Zealand Merchant Bank; Freeman City of London, liveryman Vintners Co; FCA; *Recreations* racing, bridge, golf, cricket, tennis; *Clubs* Turf, MCC; *Style*— The Hon Mervyn Greenway; 504 Frobisher House, Dolphin Sq, London SW1 (☎ 01-821 1893)

GREENWAY, Hon Nigel Paul; yst s of 3 Baron Greenway (d 1975); *b* 12 Jan 1944; *Educ* Winchester; *m* 1979, Gabrielle, eldest da of late Walter Jean Duchardt, of Obenheim, Alsace; 1 s (Nicholas Walter Paul b 6 Dec 1988); *Style*— The Hon Nigel Greenway; 7ter rue du Colonel Oudot, 75012 Paris, France

GREENWELL, Basil Evelyn; s of Maj A E Greenwell (d 1944), and Beatrice Lilian Greenwell (d 1966); *b* 23 July 1915; *Educ* Cheltenham Coll, London Univ; *m* July 1955, Sarah Carson, da of The Hon Walter Carson; 2 s (Simon Lloyd b 1956, Giles Henry b 1957), 2 da (Joanna Beatrice Taswell b 1962, Virginia Annette b 1965); *Career* WW II RNVR 1939-45, Flag Lt Lord Louis Mountbatten; chartered surveyor 1946-; *Recreations* cricket, golf, field sports; *Clubs* Boodle's; *Style*— Basil E Greenwell, Esq; Tanners, River, Petworth, W Sussex GU28 9AY (☎ (0798) 5242); Strutt & Parker, 13 Hill Street, Berkeley Square, London W1X 8DL (☎ 01 629 7282)

GREENWELL, Sir Edward Bernard; 4 Bt (UK 1906), of Marden Park, Godstone, Co Surrey and Greenwell, Wolsingham, Co Durham; s of Sir Peter Greenwell, 3 Bt, TD (d 1978), and Henrietta, *qv* (she m 2 Hugh K Haig); *b* 10 June 1948; *Educ* Eton, Nottingham Univ (BSc), Cranfield Inst of Technology (MBA); *m* 1974, Sarah, da of Lt-Col Philip Gore-Anley (d 1968), of Sculthorpe House, Fakenham; 1 s, 3 da; *Heir* s, Alexander; *Career* farmer; sometime chm Suffolk Coastal District Cncl; *Clubs* Turf; *Style*— Sir Edward Greenwell, Bt; Gedgrave Hall, Woodbridge, Suffolk (☎ 0394 450440)

GREENWELL, Maj James Peter; JP (1986); 2 s of Sir Peter Greenwell, 3 Bt, TD, DL (d 1978); *b* 27 May 1950; *Educ* Eton; *m* 1979, Serena, da of Hon Colin Dalrymple, DL (4 da of 12 Earl of Stair, KT, DSO, JP, DL), by his 2 w Fiona (da of Adm Sir Ralph Edwards, KCB, KBE); 1 s; *Career* Blues and Royals 1981; farmer 1981-; *Style*— Maj James Greenwell, JP

GREENWELL, (Arthur) Jeffrey; s of George Greenwell (d 1982), of Durham, and Kate Mary, *née* Fleming; *b* 1 August 1931; *Educ* Durham Sch, Univ Coll Oxford (MA); *m* 15 Aug 1958, Margaret Rosemary, da of Sidney David Barnard (d 1949); 1 s (David 1964), 2 da (Jane b 1960, Kate b 1962); *Career* Nat Serv RHA 1950-51; articled to Town Clerk Newcastle upon Tyne 1955-58, admitted slr 1958, law tutor Gibson and Weldon 1958-59, asst slr Birmingham Corpn 1959-61, dep clerk of the Cncl Hants CC 1967-74 (asst clerk 1964-67, asst slr 1961-64) dep clerk of the peace 1967-74, dep clerk Hants River Authy 1967-74, chief exec Northants CC 1974-, clerk of lieutenancy Northants 1977-; pres Northants Assoc of Local Cncls, memb Peterborough Diocesan Synod, govr Nene Coll, tstee Central Festival Opera; hon sec: Assoc of Co Chief Execs 1980-84, Soc of local Authy Chief Execs 1984-88; chm Home Office GP on Juvenile Crime 1987, memb bd 'Crime Concern'; FCIS 1982 (pres 1989); *Recreations* bridge, travel, local history; *Clubs* Royal Overseas League, Northampton and County; *Style*— Jeffrey Greenwell, Esq; County Hall, Northampton NN1 1DN (☎ 0604 236050, fax 0604 236223)

GREENWOOD, Maj (Arthur) Alexander; s of Dr Augustus Charles Greenwood (d 1938), of Horncastle, Lincs; kinsman of: 2 Viscount Greenwood, cous of Gen Sir Roland Guy and Maj-Gen Richard Gerrard-Wright, *qqv*; *b* 8 Mar 1920; *Educ* Oakham Sch, Sidney Sussex Coll Cambridge (PhD); *m* 1, 1946 (m dis 1970), Betty Doreen, da of Brig Sidney Albert Westrop, CBE, DSO, MC (d 1979), of Brattleby, Lincs; 1 s (Nicholas), 1 da (Jane); m 2, 1976, Shirley Knowles, da of Wing Cdr Alec Knowles-Fitton, MBE, CC, of Appletreewick, N Yorks; *Career* regular army, The Royal Lincolnshire Regt 1939-59, serv WWII Norway 1940, Iceland 1940-41, India and Burma 1942-45 (despatches), ADC to FM Sir Claude Auchinleck, GCB 1943-44, GSO 2 (Int) GHQ Middle East Land Forces 1953-54, chief instr Sch of Mil Intelligence 1954-56; memb London Stock Exchange 1963-76; co dir 1977-; dir Lincolnshire Chickens Ltd 1965-87; Liveryman Worshipful Co of: Pattenmakers 1965, Chartered Secretaries 1978; memb Hon Co of Freemen of the City of London of North America 1983; FCIS, FSCA, FRSA, FRGS, FREconS, FInstD; *Books* The Greenwood Tree in Three Continents (1988); *Recreations* cricket, golf, shooting, genealogy; *Clubs* Carlton, Pilgrims, MCC; *Style*— Maj A A Greenwood; RR 1, Box 40, Madrona Drive, Nanoose Bay, BC V0R 2R0, Canada (☎ (604) 468 9770)

GREENWOOD, Allen Harold Claude; CBE (1974), JP (Surrey 1962, Hampshire 1987); s of Lt-Col Thomas Claude Greenwood (d 1958); *b* 4 June 1917; *Educ* Cheltenham, Coll of Aeronautical Engineering London; *Career* Lt-Cdr (A) RNVR, 'pilot' Fleet Air Arm 1942-52; chm: Sepecat SA 1964-73, Panavia GmBh 1969-72, Rookcliff Props 1973-, Europlane Ltd 1974-83, Br Aircraft Corpn 1975-77, Remploy Ltd 1976-79, Br Aerospace Inc (USA) 1977-81; dep chm Br Aerospace 1977-83; pres: Euro Assoc Aero Cos 1974-76, Br Soc Aero Cos 1970-72; vice-pres Engrg Employers' Fedn Feb 1982-83; gen cmmr of Income Tax 1970-74; pres Cheltenham Cncl Coll, chm cncl St John's Sch Leatherhead 1980-84; memb: cncl Cranfield Inst of Technol 1970-79, cncl CBI 1970-77, ctee Governing Body of Public Schs 1981-84; Freeman City of London, Liveryman Coachmakers' Co, memb Guild of Air Pilots; *Recreations* sailing, motoring, travel; *Clubs* White's, RAC, Royal Lymington YC; *Style*— Allen Greenwood, Esq, CBE, JP; 2 Rookcliff, Milford-on-Sea, Lymington, Hampshire SO41 0SD (☎ 0590 42893)

GREENWOOD, (Geoffrey) Brian; JP (1969)-; s of Walter Greenwood (d 1971), of Rawdon, Leeds, and Anne, *née* Nellist (d 1973); *b* 20 August 1927; *Educ* Woodhouse Grove Sch; *m* 31 Aug 1949, Enid Dorothy, da of James Bennet (d 1955), of Stockton Heath, Cheshire; 1 s (David Brian b 1 June 1956), 1 da (Patricia Mary b 16 March 1951); *Career* chm: Greenwoods Menswear Gp 1971-82 (dir 1949-82), Burley House Gp 1982-; chm Woodhouse Grove Sch 1969-, govr St Martin's Coll Lancaster 1986-; *Recreations* shooting, fly-fishing, tennis; *Style*— Brian Greenwood, Esq, JP; Whittington hall, Whittington, Carnforth, Lancashire LA6 2NR (☎ 05242 71249); Burley House, Burley-In-Wharfedale, Ilkley, West Yorks LS29 7DZ (☎ 0943 864333, fax 0943 864362)

GREENWOOD, Christopher John; s of Capt Murray Guy Greenwood, of Singapore, and Diana Maureen, *née* Barron; *b* 12 May 1955; *Educ* Wellingborough Sch, Magdalene Coll Cambridge (MA, LLB); *m* 5 Aug 1978, Susan Anthea, da of Geoffrey James Longbotham; 2 da (Catherine b 1982, Sarah b 1985); *Career* called to the Bar Middle Temple 1978, Cambridge Univ: fell Magdalene Coll 1978-, dir Studies in Law 1982-, dean 1982-87, lectr Faculty of Law 1984- (asst lectr 1981-84); visiting prof West Virginia Univ 1986, asst ed Int Law Reports; *Recreations* politics, reading novels, walking ; *Clubs* Oxford & Cambridge; *Style*— Christopher Greenwood, Esq; 2 Victoria Park, Cambridge CB4 3EL (☎ 0223 31 2105); Magdalene Coll, Cambridge CB3 0AG (☎ 0223 33 2100, fax 0223 63637)

GREENWOOD, 2 Viscount (UK 1937); Sir David Henry Hamar Greenwood; 2 Bt (UK 1915); also Baron Greenwood (UK 1929); s of 1 Viscount Greenwood, PC, KC (d 1948), and Dame Margery Spencer, DBE, da of Rev Walter Spencer (decd), of Fownhope Ct, Herefordshire; *b* 30 Oct 1914; *Educ* privately and Bowers Gifford; *Heir* bro, Hon Michael Greenwood; *Career* farmer; *Recreations* reading, walking, shooting; *Style*— The Rt Hon the Viscount Greenwood; 63 Portsea Hall, Portsea Place, London W2 2BY

GREENWOOD, Derek; s of Cyril Greenwood, of Tunbridge Wells, Kent, and Dorothy Alice Sarah, *née* Macdonald; *b* 5 Nov 1941; *Educ* Dulwich, London Univ (BSc); *m* 17 April 1965, Kathleen Margaret, da of Harry Alderdon; 1 s (Timothy William b 30 Aug 1969), 1 da (Fiona Clare b 20 June 1971); *Career* ptnr Seymour Pierce Stockbrokers 1967-, jt md Seymour Pierce Butterfield 1987-; Freeman City of London; memb Stock Exchange 1967; *Recreations* walking, tennis, classic cars; *Style*— Derek Greenwood, Esq; 10 Old Jewry, London EC2R 8EA (☎ 01 628 4981, fax 01 606 2405)

GREENWOOD, Prof Duncan Joseph; s of Herbert James Greenwood (d 1978), and Alison Fairgrieve Greenwood (d 1968); *b* 16 Oct 1932; *Educ* Hutton GS, Liverpool Univ (BSc), Aberdeen Univ (Phd, DSc); *Career* res fell Aberdeen Univ 1957-59; Nat Vegetable Res Station: scientific offr Chemistry section 1959-62, sr scientific offr 1962-66, head of soil science 1966-87; head of soil science and plant nutrition AFRC Inst of Horticultural Res 1987-; pres Int Ctee of Plant Nutrition 1978-83; Blackman lectr Univ of Oxford 1982, Distinguished Scholars Queens Univ of Belfast 1982, Hannaford lectr Univ of Adelaide 1985; visiting prof in plant sciences Leeds Univ, hon prof agric chemistry Birmingham Univ 1986; Res Medal Royal Agric Soc of England 1979, Sir Gilbert Morgan Medal Soc of Chemical Indust 1962; published over 100 scientific papers; fell of Royal Chemical Soc 1977, fell of Inst of Horticulture; FRS 1985; *Style*— Prof Duncan J Greenwood, FRS; 23 Shelley Rd, Stratford-on-Avon CV35 7JR (☎ 0789 204 735); Institute of Horticultural Research, Wellesbourne, Warwick CV35 9EF (☎ 0789 840 382)

GREENWOOD, John Kenneth; s of Kenneth Greenwood, and Iris, *née* Humphries; *b* 24 Dec 1948; *Educ* Wellington, Manchester; *m* 21 June 1986, Jennifer Joy, da of R Hagan; 1 s (Maximilian Peter b 1983), 1 da (Tzigane Timanfaya Grace b 1985); *Career* dir Intercon Advertising 1971-78, shareholder Gen Advertising Co London Ltd 1978-87, propietor Greenwood Hinds Advertising Ltd 1987-; MInstM, MInst Dir, MBIM, MCAM; *Recreations* writing, golf; *Clubs* Foxhills, St Georges; *Style*— John Greenwood, Esq; Pendrick, Castle Rd, Weybridge, Surrey KT13 9QN (☎ 0932 858 652) Greenwood Hinds Advertising Ltd, 17 Church St, Epsom, Surrey KT17 4PF (☎ 0372 742 066, fax 03727 220 73)

GREENWOOD, Hon Michael George Hamar; yr son of 1 Viscount Greenwood (d 1948); hp of bro, 2 Viscount; *b* 5 May 1923; *Educ* Eton, Christ Church Oxford, Webber-Douglas Sch of Singing and Dramatic Art; *Career* former Royal Signals; actor; West End theatre appearance in Joan of Arc at the Stake (with Ingrid Bergman); *Feature films* The Big Money, House in the Woods, The Bank Raiders, Poor Cow, The Insomniac; *TV appearances* Emergency Ward 10, Falstaff, Great Expectations, Charlie Drake Show, Dixon of Dock Green, Rob Roy, Lloyd George Documentary, Nixon at Nine, Adam Adamant Lives, Broaden Your Mind, Honey Lane, Gnomes of Dulwich, Eric Sykes Show, Nancy Astor; *Recreations* walking, dancing, reading, writing and rhythm; *Style*— The Hon Michael Greenwood; 63 Portsea Hall, Portsea Place, London W2 2BY (☎ 01 402 2975)

GREENWOOD, Prof Norman Neill; s of Prof John Neill Greenwood (d 1981), of Melbourne, Aust, and Gladys, *née* Uhland (d 1976); *b* 19 Jan 1925; *Educ* Univ HS Melbourne, Univ of Melbourne (BSc, MSc, DSc), Cambridge Univ (PhD, ScD); *m* 21 Dec 1951, Kirsten Marie, da of Johannes Rydland (d 1978), of Bergen, Norway; 3 da (Karen b 1952, Anne b 1954, Linda b 1958); *Career* res tutor and lectr Trinity Coll Univ of Melbourne 1946-49, sr lectr (former lectr) inorganic chem Univ of Nottingham 1953-61; prof and head of dept: inorganic chem Univ of Newcastle 1961-71, inorganic and structural chemistry Univ of Leeds 1971-; dean faculty of sci Univ of Leeds 1986-88, numerous visiting professorships Australia, Canada, USA, Denmark; chm Int Cmmn on Atomic Weights; pres: Inorganic Chem Div Int Union of Pure and Applied Chem 1977-81, Dalton div Royal Soc of Chem 1979-81; chm UK ctee of Heads of Univ Chemistry Depts 1985-87; Freeman of Nancy (France) 1977; hon doctorate l'Univ de Nancy I 1977; FRS 1987, FRSC 1960, CChem, M Amer Chem Soc 1958; *Books* author numerous books and res papers incl: Ionic Crystals, Lattice Defects and Nonstoichiometry (1968), Mössbauer Spectroscopy (with T C Gibb 1971), Contemporary British Chemists (with W A Campbell 1971), Boron (1973), Chemistry of the Elements (with A Earnshaw 1984); *Recreations* skiing, music; *Style*— Prof Norman Greenwood; School of Chemistry, Univ of Leeds, Leeds LS2 9JT (☎ 0532

336401, fax 0532 336017, telex 556473 UNILDS G)

GREENWOOD, (John) Richard; s of John Eric Greenwood (d 1975), of The Priory of Lady St Mary, Wareham, Dorset; *b* 18 Mar 1926; *Educ* Eton; *m* 1953, Penelope Anne, da of Lt-Col Sir Walter Raymond Burrell, 8 Bt, CBE, TD, DL (d 1985), of Knepp Castle, Horsham; 2 s (John Simon, James Anthony), 2 da (Anne Lucinda, Fiona Mary); *Career* former Capt Grenadier Gds; JP 1966-74, co cncllr East Sussex 1966-74 West Sussex 1974-85, High Sheriff Sussex 1971; *Recreations* shooting, more shooting, golf, fishing; *Clubs* White's; *Style*— Richard Greenwood, Esq; Stone Hall, Balcombe, West Sussex (☎ 0444 811 371); Lairg Lodge Sutherland (☎ 0549 2004)

GREENWOOD, Walter Holland; s of Herbert Greenwood (d 1979), and Leila Maud, *née* Holland (d 1968); *b* 2 Sept 1925; *Educ* Belle Vue HS Bradford, Jesus Coll Cambridge (MA); *m* 14 Sept 1949, Helen Mary, da of Sydney Charles Douglas (d 1966); 2 s (Adrian b 1951, Dominic b 1956), 1 da (Lucy b 1953); *Career* RNVR 1943-46; called to the bar Gray's Inn 1950, barr N Eastern circuit 1950-59; 1962-83: asst Master of the Crown Off, Queens Coroner and Attorney, asst registrar of criminal and courts-martial appeals; magistrate Hong Kong 1984-87; legal advsr to the Worshipful Co of Haberdashers, Freeman City of London 1978; memb Royal Tunbridge Wells Scout Assoc; *Recreations* history, literature, badminton, sailing, skiing; *Clubs* Naval, Royal Hong Kong YC, Kipling Soc; *Style*— Walter Greenwood, Esq; Haberdashers' Hall, Staining Lane, London EC2V 7DD

GREENWOOD OF ROSSENDALE, Baroness; Gillian; da of Leslie Crawshay Williams (himself s of Arthur John Williams, DL, MP, of Glamorgan) and Joyce, a portrait miniatiaturist and only child of Hon John Collier (2 s of 1 Baron Monkswell) by his 1 w Marian (herself da of Thomas Huxley, the scientist); *b* 11 April 1910; *m* 1940, Baron Greenwood of Rossendale, PC (d 1982), Min of Housing and Local Govt in Sir Harold Wilson's second govt; 2 da (Hon Mrs Gardiner, Hon Mrs Murray); *Style*— The Rt Hon the Lady Greenwood Rossendale

GREEVES, Maj-Gen Sir Stuart; KBE (1955, CBE 1945, OBE 1940), CB (1948), DSO (1944 and Bar 1945), MC (1917 and Bar 1918); s of late J S Greeves, of Northampton; *b* 2 April 1897; *Educ* Northampton Sch; *Career* served WWI and WWII, Lt-Col 1943, Acting Brig 1943, Burma (despatches), Col 1946, Maj-Gen 1947, ret 1957; *Clubs* Naval and Military; *Style*— Maj-Gen Sir Stuart Greeves, KBE, CB, DSO, MC; c/o Lloyds Bank Ltd, 6 Pall Mall, London SW1; Flat 601, Grosvenor Sq, College Rd, Rondebosch, Cape Town, S Africa (☎ Cape Town 6891208)

GREEY, Edward Ronald; s of Derek Edward Horace Greey (d 1979), and Irene Osborne, *née* Taylor; *b* 26 April 1939; *Educ* Malvern; *m* 1 Oct 1966, Gillian Frances Rippon, da of John Sargeant Hughes, of Woodlea, 371 Thorpe Rd, Longthorpe, Peterborough; 3 da (Sally b 1969, Wendy b 1972, Philippa b 1986); *Career* cmmnd 16/5 Queens Own Royal Lancers TA Queens Own Staffs Yeo; stockbroker and co dir; memb Birmingham Stock Exchange 1965 (chm 1975-76), dir Stock Beech & Co; dir: Birmingham Stock Exchange Bldgs Co Ltd, Robinson Bros Ryders Green Ltd; dep chm Stock Exchange Midland and Western Unit, 1977-78 (chm 1979-80); memb governing cncl Stock Exchange 1985-88, dep chm regnl ctee Int Stock Exchange; gen cmmr of Income Tax; govr Malvern Coll; *Recreations* golf, fishing, shooting; *Clubs* Blackwell GC, Edgbaston GC, Royal West Norfolk GC; *Style*— Edward Greey, Esq; Peewit Cottage, Bittell Farm Rd, Barnt Green, Worcestershire B45 8BS (☎ 021 445 1672); Stock Beech & Co Ltd, 75 Edmund St, Birmingham B3 3HL (☎ 021 233 3211)

GREGG, Hubert Robert Harry; s of Robert Joseph (d 1955), of London, and Alice Maud, *née* Bessant (d 1956); *b* 19 July 1914; *Educ* St Dunstan's Coll, Webber-Douglas Acad; *m* 1980, Carmel Josephine, da of Laurence Maguire, of Dublin; 1 s (Robert b 1983), 1 da (Katherine b 1981); *Career* served WWII Private Lincs Regt 1939, cmd 60 Rifles 1940, transferred to Intelligence, political warfare exec 1942 (duties included broadcasting in German); actor, composer, lyric writer, author, playwright and dir; first London appearance Julien in Martine 1933, Shakespearean roles Open Air Theatre Regent's Park, Old Vic 1934/35, 1 NY appearance as Kit Neilan in French Without Tears 1937 (London 1938-39); London appearances incl: Pip in The Convict 1935, Frederick Hackett in Great Possessions 1937, Tom D'Arcy in Off the Record 1947, Peter Scott-Fowler in After The Dance 1939, 'Polly' in Men In Shadow 1942, Michael Carraway in Acacia Avenue 1944, Earl of Harpenden 1945-46, Gabriel Hathaway in Western Wind 1949 (first musical), John Blessington-Briggs in Chrysanthemum 1958, Lionel Toop in Pools Paradise 1961; Chichester Festival Theatre: Alexander MacColgie Gibbs in The Cocktail Party, Antonio in The Tempest, Announcer in The Skin of Our Teeth 1968, Sir Lucius O'Trigger in The Rivals, Brittannus in Caesar and Cleopatra, Marcellin in Dear Antoine (also London) 1971; dir (London): The Hollow (Agatha Christie's first stage success) 1951, The Mousetrap 1953-60, Speaking of Murder 1958, The Unexpected Guest 1958, From The French 1959, Go Back for Murder 1960, Rule of Three 1962, 1 solo performance Leicester 1970, subsequently performances in Britain and America (subjects include Shakespeare, Shaw, Jerome K Jerome, the London Theatre and the 20s, 30s, and 40s); films incl: In Which We Serve, Flying Fortress, Acacia Avenue, The Root of all Evil, Vote for Huggett, Once Upon a Dream, Robin Hood (Walt Disney), The Maggie, Svengali, Doctor at Sea (also wrote music and lyrics), Simon and Laura, Speaking of Murder, Final Appointment, Room in the House, Stars in Your Eyes (also co-dir and wrote music and lyrics); announcer BBC Empire Service 1934-35, weekly radio programmes with accent on nostalgia 1965-, chm BBC TV Brains Tst 1955, 40 week radio series on London theatres 1974-75, biography series I Call it Genius, I Call It Style 1980, ITV solo series 1982, 50 Years of Broadcasting (BBC celebration programme) 1984; directed, lectured and adjudicated at: Webber-Douglas Sch, Central Sch of Speech Training, RADA; patron Cinema Theatre Assoc 1973-; pres: Northern Boys' Club 1975-, Concert Artists Assoc 1979-80; memb Br Academy of Composers, Authors and Song Writers 1982; Freeman City of London, Gold Badge of Merit; plays and screenplays: We Have Company (1953), Cheque Mate (dir and appeared in), Villa Sleep Four (1965), From the French (written under pseudonym of Jean-Paul Marotte), Who's Been Sleeping...?, The Rumpus (1967), Dear Somebody (1984), After the Ball (screenplay adapted from own television biography of Vesta Tilley), Stars in your Eyes (screenplay), Geliebtes Traumbild (1984); author of songs: over 200 incl: I'm Going to get Lit up, Maybe it's Because I'm a Londoner; *Books* April Gentleman (1951), A Day's Loving (1974), Agatha Christie and all that Mousetrap (1980), Thanks for the Memory (1983); L.....; *Clubs* Garrick; *Style*— Hubert Gregg, Esq; 260 King's Drive, Eastbourne, E Sussex BN21 2XD; c/o Broadcasting Ho, London W1A 1AA

GREGORY, Capt Alexander Michael; OBE (1987); s of Vice Adm Sir George David Archibald Oregory, KBE, CB, DSO (d 1975), of Greymount, Alyth, Perthshire, and Florence Eve Patricia, *née* Hill;; *b* 15 Dec 1945; *Educ* Marlborough, Dartmouth; *m* 13 June 1970, Jean Charlotte, da of Cdr Gerald Robin Muir OBE, of Silverton Farm Braco, By Dunblane, Perthshire; 4 da (Charlotte b 1971, Katherine b 1973, Helen b 1979, Sarah b 1982); *Career* 1964-65 BRNC Dartmouth, HMS Albion HMS Aisne 1965-66, HMS Narwhale 1966-67, HMS Otter 1967-68, HMS Warspite 1968-70, HMS Courageous 1970-73, HMS Odin (Based in Australia) 1973-75, HMS Finwhale (In Command) 1976-78, HMS Repulse 1978-80, Staff of US Third Fleet Hawaii 1980-82, HMS Renown (In Command) 1982-85, Cdr Tenth Submarine sqdn and HMS resolution (In Command) 1985-86, jt service Def Coll 1987, Directorate of Naval Warfare 1987-88; HMS Cumberland (In Command) 1988- Memb of Roy Com of Archers (Queens Bodyguard for Scotland); *Recreations* shooting, fishing, skiing, stalking, gardening

GREGORY, Conal Robert; MP (Cons York 1983-); s of Patrick George Murray Gregory and Marjorie Rose, *née* Pointon; *b* 11 Mar 1947; *Educ* King's Coll Sch Wimbledon, Univ of Sheffield (BA); *m* 1971, Helen Jennifer, da of Frederick Craggs; 1 s (Rupert), 1 da (Fiona); *Career* wine buyer Colman's of Norwich 1973-77, broadcaster and corr 1977-, ed Int Wine and Food Soc Jl 1980-83, dir Standard Fireworks 1987; sec All Pty Parly Tourism Ctee; vice chm: Cons Parly Tourism Ctee 1985-, Cons Parly Food and Drinks Industs Ctee 1985-, Cons Parly Tport Ctee 1987-(sec 1983-87); Fell Indust and Parly tst; Norfolk CC; memb 1977-81, vice chm Schs Ctee 1977-78; vice pres: Norwich Jr Chamber 1975-76, York Civic Tst, UN Assoc (York branch); fndr and chm the Bow Gp of E Anglia 1975-82; vice chm: Nat Bow Gp 1976-77, Eastern area Cons Political Centre 1980-83; govr Univ of Sheffield 1978-, chm Norwich N Cons Assoc 1980-82; memb: E Anglia Tourist Bd 1979-81, ct of govrs Univs of Hull and York, York Archaeological Tst; pres York Young Cons 1982-; Master Worshipful Co of Vintners 1979; *Books* Caterer's Guide to Drinks, A Policy for Tourism? (co-author), Beers of Britain (co-author), Food for a Healthy Britain (co-author); *Clubs* Acomb Conservative, York Conservative Central; *Style*— Conal Gregory, Esq, MP; House of Commons, London SW1A 0AA (☎ 01 219 4603)

GREGORY, Derek Edward; s of Edward Gregory Ilkeston (d 1970), and Hilda, *née* Stokeley; *Educ* Ilkeston GS; *m* 16 June 1962, m 1, Marjorie (d 1984), da of LLoyd Priest Newcastle (d 1976); 1 s (Philip Edward b 1965), 1 da (Tina Louise b 1968); m 2, 13 Dec 1986, Kate; *Career* fndr and sr ptnr Gregory Priestley & Stewart CAs Ilkeston, Long Eaton Sutton in Ashfield 1970-; tres Stanton by Dale CC 1958-; FCA 1961; *Recreations* horse racing, cricket, gardening; *Style*— Derek Gregory, Esq; Rosemary Cottage, Bowling Close, Stanton By Dale, Ilkeston, Derby (☎ 0602 322 047); 16 Queen St, Ilkeston, Derbys (☎ 0602 326 726)

GREGORY, John Frederick; s of Arthur Frederick Gregory (d 1955), of London, and Marjorie Phyllis, *née* Williams; *b* 7 April 1935; *Educ* Ashburton HS; *m* 9 June 1956, Ethel Currie, da of Robert Burns, of Preston Lancs; 1 s (David Russell b 14 Nov 1965), 2 da (Linda Ann b 21 May 1957, Alison Joy b 8 Dec 1960); *Career* RAF 1953-55; Capel-Cure Myers (now ANZ McCaughan) 1950-: ptnr 1979-85, dir 1985-89; dir Beeson Gregory plc 1989-, non exec dir Cussins Property Gp plc 1983-; memb Stock Exchange 1972; *Recreations* music, painting, fell walking; *Clubs* Mossimans; *Style*— John Gregory, Esq; 185 Ballards Way, Croydon, Surrey (☎ 01 657 6706); Sefton, Saltcote Lane, Rye, East Sussex; Beeson Gregory plc, The Registry, Royal Mint Court, London EC3

GREGORY, John James Conrad; s of Hubert Conrad Gregory (d 1955), of Newark House, 2 Gloucester Rd, Staple Hill, Bristol, and Mary McLachlan, *née* Drysdale (d 1976); *b* 3 April 1932; *Educ* Chipping Sodbury GS, Merchant Ventures Tech Coll Bristol (ONC), Gosta Green Coll of Technol (HNC); *m* 9 April 1955, Marion Elizabeth, da of Gilbert H Mart, of 49 Raynes Rd, Ashton Gate, Bristol; 1 s (Nigel James b 1959), 1 da (Sarah Louise b 1961); *Career* apprentice and draughtsman Gardiner Sons & Co 1948-55, sr draughtsman Boulton & Paul 1955-58, section ldr Metal Constructions Ltd 1958-61, sr design engr Norris Conslts 1961-64, chief draughtsman Johnson Structures 1964-65, princ Gregory & Assocs 1965-; cmmns include: catering estabs, food and chemical plants, multi-storey office blocks, schools and sports facilities; Chamber of Indust & Commerce Swindon: pres 1986-87, bd rep Swindon Devpt Agency: CEng, FIStructE (former memb cncl London, twice branch chm Bedford), MComsE, FFB 1970, MInstD (Chm S East Midlands branch); *Recreations* propogation of plants, cooking & presentation of food; *Style*— John Gregory, Esq; Redcliffe House, 14 Thrapston Rd, Spaldwick, Huntingdon, Cambridgeshire PE18 0TA (☎ 0480 890 632); Gregory & Associates, Harpur House, 62 Harpur St, Bedford MK40 2RA (☎ 0234 60377/8, fax 0234 211 121); Gregory & Associates, Shaftesbury Centre, Percy St, Swindon, Wiltshire SN2 2AZ (☎ 0293 512 923, fax 0793 616837)

GREGORY, Capt (Alexander) Michael; OBE (1987); s of Vice Adm Sir George David Archibald Gregory, KBE, CB, DSO (d 1975), of Greymount, Alyth, Perthshire, and Florence Eve Patricia, *née* Hill; *b* 15 Dec 1945; *Educ* Marlborough, Dartmouth; *m* 13 June 1970, Jean Charlotte, da of Lt Cdr Gerald Robin Muir, OBE, of Silverton Farm House Braco, By Dunblane, Perthshire; 4 da (Charlotte b 1971, Katherine b 1973, Helen b 1979, Sarah b 1982); *Career* 1964-65 BRNC Dartmouth, HMS Albion and HMS Aisne 1965-66, HMS Narwhale 1966-67, HMS Otter 1967-68, HMS Warspite 1968-70, HMS Courageous 1970-73, HMS Odin (Based in Australia) 1973-75, HMS Finwhale (in Command) 1976-78, HMS Repulse 1978-80, Staff of US Third Fleet Hawaii 1980-82, HMS Renown (in command) 1982-85, cdr Tenth Submarine Sqdn and HMS Resolution (in command) 1985-86, Jt Serv Def Coll 1987, MOD Directorate of Naval Warfare 1987-88, HMS Cumberland (in command) 1988-; memb Royal Co of Archers (Queen's Bodyguard for Scotland); *Recreations* shooting, fishing, skiing, stalking, gardening; *Style*— Capt Michael Gregory, RN, OBE

GREGORY, Michael Anthony; s of Lt Col Wallace James Ignatius Gregory (d 1972), and Dorothy Isabel, *née* Malyon; *b* 8 June 1925; *Educ* Douai Sch, UCL (LLB); *m* 11 Aug 1951, Patricia Ann, da of Frank Thomas Hodges (d 1978); 3 s (Martin, Damien, Tristan), 5 da (Anne, Philippa, Lucy, Bernadette, Jane); *Career* WWII joined RAF 1943, cmmnd 1945, Navigator 1945, demobed as Flying Offr 1947; called to the Bar Middle Temple 1952, in practice 1952-60, legal dept Country Landowners' Assoc 1960-(chief legal advsr 1977-); chm: mgnt ctee Catholic Social Serv for Prisoners 1960-71 and 1974-85 (memb 1952-), Fleet Branch Int Help for Children 1967-77; hon legal advsr Nat Anglers Cncl 1968-, fndr memb Agricultural Law Assoc 1975-, tstee Country Landowners Assoc Charitable Tst 1980-; memb: BSI Ctee on Installation of Pipelines 1965-83, cncl Salmon and Trout Assoc 1980-, cncl Anglers' Cooperative Assoc 1980-, ctee Fedn for Promotion of Horticulture for Disabled People 1981-(tstee

1987), Thames Water Authy Regnl Fisheries Advsy Ctee 1974-, Inland Waterways Amenity Advsy Cncl 1982-; pres Douai Soc 1984-86; Proecclesia Et Pontifice (Papal, 1988); *Books* Organisational Possibilities in Farming (1968), Joint Enterprises in Farming (with C Townsend, second edn 1973), Angling and the Law (second edn 1974), All for Fishing (with R Seymour, 1970), Essential Law for Landowners and Farmers (with Margaret Parrish, second edn 1987); *Recreations* ball games, angling, playing saxophones, kidding kids; *Style*— Michael Gregory, Esq; 63 Gally Hill Rd, Church Crookham, Aldershot, Hants GU13 0RU (☎ 0252 616 473); Country Landowners Assoc, 16 Belgrave Sq, London SW1X 8PQ (☎01 235 0511, fax 01 235 4696)

GREGORY, Peter William; s of William Henry Gregory Esq, of Thamesway, 9 Berkeley Gardens, Walton on Thames, Surrey, and Florence Mabel Gregory, *née* Peters; *b* 3 Oct 1934; *Educ* Surbiton GS, City & Guilds, Imperial Coll, London, BSC (Eng) AC41 1958; *m* 16 Jan 1960, Angela Margaret; 1 s (Timothy b 10 March 1963), 2 da (Sarah b 14 March 1965, Susan b 22 April 1966); *Career* short service cmmn RAF 1958-61, Flt Lieut 5003 Sqn Alb in UK, civil engineer (Mice); deputy chm and jnt mangr dir Laing Mgmnt Contracting Ltd 1986; md LMC 1985; md LMC (Scotland) Ltd; dir John Lain Constr Ltd 1984; dir Laingloy Ltd; *Recreations* game shooting, salmon fishing, gardening, golf; *Style*— Peter W Gregory, Esq; Target House, Hexham, Northumberland NE46 4LD (☎ (0434) 604689); Laing Management Contracting Ltd, 37-39 Grey Street, Newcastle upon Tyne NE1 6EE (☎ (091) 261 7574, fax (091) 261 7288, car ☎ (0836) 204750)

GREGORY, Lt-Col Richard Boutcher; s of Capt Ernest Foster Gregory, CBE, RN (d 1940), and Evelyn Isabelle, *née* Browning; *b* 6 May 1916; *Educ* Cranleigh Sch, RMA Woolwich, RMCS Shrivenham; *m* 30 Aug 1955, Alison, da of Vice-Adm Wion de Malpas Egerton, DSO, RN (ka 1943); 1 s (Andrew b 1957), 1 da (Jane b 1960); *Career* cmmnd RA 1936, served India until 1940, active serv W Desert and Eritrea 1940-42, "D" Day 1944 (wounded); princ regnl inspr (armaments) Scottish and Northern Region 1958-60; joined staff of Sedbergh Sch 1960-72, educn books div Encyclopaedia Britannica 1975-82; *Style*— Lt Col Richard Gregory; Rosslyn, Charmouth Rd, Lyme Regis, Dorset DT7 3DW (☎ 02974 3260)

GREGORY, Richard John; s of John Gregory, and Joan, *née* Slingsby; *b* 18 August 1954; *Educ* Danum GS, Doncaster; *m* 14 Aug 1976, Elaine Margaret, da of (Herbert Charles) Ronald Matthews (d 1971); 2 da (Anna Marie b 11 Feb 1979, Antonia Faye b 11 Dec 1987); *Career* industl corr Morning Telegraph 1977-79, news ed Granada TV 1979-81; Yorkshire TV: news ed 1981-82, prodr 1982-84, ed Calendar 1984-; *Recreations* squash, swimming, riding, hill-walking; *Style*— Richard Gregory, Esq; Brooklands, Castleton Rd, Hope, Derbyshire; Yorkshire Television, Kirkstall Rd, Leeds LS3 1JS (☎ 0532 438283)

GREGORY, Sydney Absell; s of Sydney Buxton Gregory (d 1963), and Elizabeth Florence, *née* Lofting (d 1966); *b* 5 April 1914; *Educ* Bancroft's, Queen Mary Coll (BSc Chem); *m* 21 Oct 1939, Mary, da of Rupert Harry Truelove (d 1967), of Ripon, Yorks; 2 s (Ross b 1943, Bruce b 1945), 3 da (Clare b 1948, Kate b 1953, Flora b 1956); *Career* reader Univ of Aston, ret 1979, visiting res fell RCA 1983-85; over 30 Br patents, advsr Sci Museum London; ed: The Design Method (1966), Creativity and Innovation in Engineering (1972), Design Studies (journal 1979-83); *Recreations* gardening, small animals; *Style*— Sydney Gregory, Esq; 22 Crescent Rd, Stafford ST17 9AL (☎ 0785 51776)

GREGSON, Baron (Life Peer UK 1975); John Gregson; DL (Gtr Manchester 1979); s of John Gregson; *b* 29 Jan 1924; *Career* joined Stockport Base Subsidiary 1939, Fairey R and D team, appointed to bd 1966; pt/t memb Br Steel plc 1976-; exec dir Fairey plc since 1978, Manchester Industrial Centre Ltd 1982-; non exec dir: Lazard Defence Fund Mgmnt Ltd 1982-, Otto-Simon Carves Ltd, Electra Corporate Ventures Ltd; memb House of Lords Select Ctee on Sci and Technol 1980, pres Parly and Scientific Ctee 1986-, chm Finance and Indust Gp of Lab Party 1978-, vice-pres Assoc of Metropolitan Authorities 1984, pres Defence Manufacturers Assoc 1984- (chm 1980-84); memb court Univ Manchester Inst of Sci and Technol 1976; pres Stockport Youth Orch, vice-pres Fedn of Br Police Motor Clubs; Hon Fell Manchester Poly 1983, Hon FIProdE 1982, Hon D Open Univ, Hon DSc Aston Univ; AMCT, CBIM; *Recreations* mountaineering, skiing; *Style*— The Rt Hon the Lord Gregson, DL; Fairey plc, Cranford Lane, Heston, Middx

GREGSON, Sir Peter Lewis; KCB 1988, CB 1983; s of Walter Henry Gregson (d 1961), and Lillian Margaret, *née* Lees; *b* 28 June 1936; *Educ* Nottingham HS, Balliol Coll Oxford (MA); *Career* National Service 1959-61 (2 Lt RAEC, attached Sherwood Foresters); BOT 1961-66, private sec to PM 1968-72, sec Industrial Devpt Advsy Bd 1972-74, sec NEB 1975-77, under-sec Dept of Trade 1977-80, dep sec Dept of Trade 1980-81; dep sec Cabinet Office 1981-85; perm under-sec of state Dept of Energy 1985-; *Recreations* gardening, listening to music; *Style*— Sir Peter Gregson, KCB; Department of Energy, Thames House South, Millbank, London SW1P 4QJ (☎ 01 211 4391)

GREGSON, William Derek Hadfield; CBE (1970), DL (1984); s of W Gregson (d 1929); *b* 27 Jan 1920; *Educ* King William's Coll IOM, Alpine Coll Villars Switzerland, Faraday House Engrg Coll (DFH); *m* 1944, Rosalind Helen, da of R M E Reeves; 3 s, 1 da; *Career* served RAF, Sqdn Ldr NW Europe 1941-45; chm: BIM Advsy Bd Scotland 1970-75, Scottish GPs Research Support Unit 1971-79, Management Assoc of SE Scotland 1980-81; former memb: Electronic Engrg Assoc (pres 1963-64), Electronics EDC 1965-75, Scottish Economic Planning Cncl 1965-71, Soc of Br Aerospace Cos (chm Equipment Gp Ctee 1967), Bd of Livingston New Town 1968-76, Scottish Cncl CBI to 1979, Machine Tool Expert Ctee 1969-70, BIM Cncl 1975-80, jt BIM/NEDO Professional Mgmnt Advsy Ctee on Industl Strategy; pres British Electrical & Allied Manufacturers' Assoc; dep chm: British Airports Authority 1975-85, Scottish Cncl Devpt & Indust, Scottish Nat Orchestra; dir: Ferranti Holdings Ltd 1983-85 (asst gen mangr Ferranti (Scotland) Ltd 1959-83), Anderson Strathclyde plc, Brammer plc, British Telecom (Scotland) 1977-85, East of Scotland Industl Investments; cmmr Northern Lighthouse Bd; memb: Design Cncl, Mgmnt Assoc of SE Scotland; conslt ICI; CEng, FIEE, CBIM, FIIM; *Recreations* reading, cabinet-making, automation in the home; *Clubs* RAF, New (Edinburgh); *Style*— William Gregson, Esq, CBE; 15 Barnton Ave, Edinburgh EH4 6AJ (☎ 031 336 3896)

GREHAN, Maj Denis Stephen; s of Maj Stephen Arthur Grehan, OBE, MC (d 1972), of Clonmeen, Banteer, co Cork, and Cecily Mary, *née* Gaisford St Lawrence (d 1973), of Howth Castle, co Dublin; *b* 24 July 1927; *Educ* Ampleforth, RMA Sandhurst; *m* 9 Aug 1969, Jane, da of Maj Norman McCaskle, of Harefield House, Theale, Berks (d 1968); *Career* Regular Offr Irish Gds 1948-67; with Stewart Wrightson Insur Brokers 1971-; dir: Stewart Wrightson PFP Ltd, Valuers Auctioneers and Estate Agents Gp Insur Servs Ltd; *Recreations* sports, hunting, shooting, fishing, polo; *Clubs* Blue Seal; *Style*— Maj Denis Grehan; Olivers Cottage, Bramley Green, Basingstoke, Hants (☎ 0256 881340); Willis Wrightson House, Wood St, Kingston upon Thames, Surrey KT1 1QG (☎ 01 860 6000)

GREIG, (Henry Louis) Carron; CVO (1972), CBE (1986); s of Gp Capt Sir Louis Greig, KBE, CVO, DL, of Thatched House Lodge, Richmond Park; *b* 21 Feb 1925; *Educ* Eton; *m* 1955, Monica, da of Hon John Stourton, TD, *qv*; 2 s and twin s and da; *Career* Capt Scots Gds N W Europe 1945; gentleman usher to HM The Queen 1962-; chm H Clarkson & Co 1973-85 (md 1962-85, dir 1954-85); chm Horace Clarkson plc 1976-; dir: James Purdey & Sons 1972-, Williams & Glyn's 1983-85; Royal Bank of Scotland 1985-, chm Baltic Exchange 1983-85 (dir 1978-85); vice-chm Not Forgotten Assoc 1979-; *Clubs* White's; *Style*— Carron Greig, Esq, CVO, CBE; Binsness, Forres, Moray; Brook House, Fleet, Hants

GREIG, Prof James; s of James A Greig (d 1936), and Helen Bruce Meldrum (d 1907); *b* 24 April 1903; *Educ* George Watsons Coll, Heriot Watt Univ Edinburgh, Univ Coll London (MSc, PhD); *m* 29 July 1931, Ethel May, *née* Archibald; 1 da (Isabel); *Career* Engr with Gen Electrical Co (Wembley) 1928-33, UCL 1933-36, lectr Univ of Birmingham 1936-39, Northampton Poly head of EE Dept 1939-45, Univ Prof Kings Coll Univ of London 1945-70; *Books* biogs of: Leonard Horner, Silvanus Thompson, John Hopkinson; *Clubs* Athenaeum London; *Style*— Prof James Greig; Inch of Kinnordy, by Kirriemuir, Angus, Tayside; 22 Castle Street, Crail, Fife (☎ Kirriemuir 72350)

GREIG, Lt-Cdr Philip Guy Morland; s of Capt Philip Humphreys Greig, MC (d 1965), and Minnie Sylvia Greig, *née* Baker (d 1966); *b* 19 Jan 1927; *Educ* The Old Malt House, RN Coll Dartmouth; *m* 18 Nov 1953, Susan, da of Harold Owen Stutchbury (d 1966), of W Byfleet; 2 da (Victoria & Charlotte b 1954), 2 s (William b 1956, Stephen b 1959); *Career* Lt Cdr RN, served WW II D Day 1944, Far East; signal offr HMS Belfast 1959-61, fleet electronic warfare ofr Far East Fleet 1961-62, naval liaison offr GCHQ 1967-73; fruit farmer 1977-; fndr and chm Upper Thames Protection Soc 1986; obtained certificate Royal Forestry Soc in arboriculture; *Recreations* watching cricket on TV, growing trees; *Style*— Lt-Cdr Philip Greig; (☎ 028 581 274)

GREIG OF ECCLES, James Dennis; CMG (1967); s of Dennis George Greig, of Eccles (d 1971), and Florence Aileen, *née* Marjoribanks (d 1959); *b* 14 July 1926; *Educ* Winchester, Clare Coll Cambridge, LSE; *m* 1, 1952 (m dis 1960), Pamela Stock; 1 s, 1 da; m 2, 1960 (m dis 1967), Mrs Elizabeth Ettenger Brown, da of Horace Melville Starke, of Charlotte, N Carolina, USA; 1 s; m 3, 1968, Paula, da of Percival Cook, of Gillingham Kent; 1 s (adopted); *Career* Lt The Black Watch RHR and Nigeria Regt 1944-47 served Burma; Colonial Serv: Nigeria 1949-59, fin sec Mauritius 1960-67, head of Africa and Middle East Bureau Int Planned Parenthood Fedn 1968-76, dir Population Bureau Miny of Overseas Devpt 1976-80; trader in commodity and fin futures; *Recreations* national hunt racing, shooting, gardening, bowls; *Clubs* Hurlingham, Annabel's; *Style*— James Greig of Eccles, CMG; The Braw Bothy, Eccles, Kelso, Roxburghshire (☎ 089 084544); 6 Beverley Close, Barnes, London SW13 0EH (☎ 01 876 5354)

GRENFELL, Hon Aline Mary; da of 2 Baron Grenfell (d 1976), by his 2 w; *b* 17 Feb 1950; *Style*— The Hon Aline Grenfell; c/o The Rt Hon Irene, Lady Grenfell, 13 Liphook Crescent, Honor Oak, Forest Hill, London SE23

GRENFELL, Francis Pascoe John; s of Maj Hon Arthur Grenfell (2 s of 1 Baron Grenfell) and Eleanor Dorothy Alice, da of Hon (Mr Justice) Sir Francis James, of Saltash; hp to first cous, 3 Baron Grenfell; *b* 28 Feb 1938; *Educ* Eton, Ch Ch Oxford; *m* 1977, Elizabeth, da of Hugh Kenyon and Mary (da of Sir Peile Thompson, 4 Bt); *Career* Teacher Kitwood Boys' Sch, Boston, Lincs; Justice of the Peace 1977; memb Bd of Visitors HM Prison Northsea Camp 1969-; *Recreations* fishing, restoration of buildings and drains, gardening; *Style*— Francis Grenfell, Esq, JP; Lenton House, Lenton, Grantham, Lincs NG33 4HB

GRENFELL, Irene, Baroness; Irene Lilian; da of Harry Cartwright, of Buenos Aires; *m* 1946, as his 2 w, 2 Baron Grenfell (d 1976); 1 da (Hon Aline Grenfell, *qv*); *Style*— The Rt Hon Irene, Lady Grenfell; 13 Liphook Crescent, Honor Oak, Forest Hill, SE23 (☎ 01 699 8528)

GRENFELL, Hon Isabella Sarah Frances; da of 3 Baron Grenfell and his first wife, Loretta Reali; *b* 1 May 1966; *Educ* Frances Holland Sch; *Recreations* acting, dancing, sports; *Style*— Hon Isabella Grenfell; 55 East 72nd St, New York City, NY 10021, USA

GRENFELL, 3 Baron (UK 1902); Julian Pascoe Francis St Leger Grenfell; s of 2 Baron Grenfell, CBE, TD (d 1976), and his 1 w, Elizabeth (gda of 1 Baron Shaughnessy); *b* 23 May 1935; *Educ* Eton, King's Coll Cambridge; *m* 1, 1961, Loretta, da of Alfredo Reali, of Florence; 1 da; m 2, 1970, Gabrielle, da of Dr Ernst Raab; 2 da (Hon Katharina Elizabeth Anne b 1973, Hon Vanessa Julia Claire b 1976); m 3, 27 June 1987, Mrs Elizabeth Porter, da of Buford Scott, of Richmond, Virginia; *Heir* first cous, Francis Grenfell; *Career* 2 Lt KRRC (60 Rifles), Capt Queen's Westminsters (TA) KRRC; chief of info and pub affrs World Bank Europe 1970, dep dir European office World Bank 1973, special rep for World Bank to UNO 1974-81, special advsr World Bank 1983-87, snr advsr 1987-; *Books* Margot (a novel) (1984); *Recreations* writing; *Clubs* Royal Green Jackets; *Style*— The Rt Hon the Lord Grenfell; The World Bank, 1818 H Street N W, Washington DC, 20433, USA (☎ (202 477) 8843)

GRENFELL, Hon Natasha Jeannine Mary; da of 2 Baron St Just (d 1984), and his 2 w, Maria Britneva, the actress, da of Alexander Vladimirovitch Britnev (decd), of St Petersburg, Russia; *b* 1959; *Style*— The Hon Natasha Grenfell

GRENFELL, Simon Pascoe; s of Osborne Pascoe Grenfell, of Saltburn, N Yorkshire (d 1971), and Margaret Grenfell, *née* Morris; *b* 10 July 1942; *Educ* Fettes Coll Edinburgh, Emmanuel Coll Cambridge (MA); *m* 13 April 1974, Ruth de Jersey, da of John Peter de Jersey Harvard, of Carlton-in-Cleveland, N Yorkshire (d 1981); 1 s (Robin b 1981), 3 da (Rachel b 1975, Amelia b 1976, Philippa b 1978); *Career* barrister; recorder of the Crown Court 1985; *Recreations* music, sailing, coarse gardening; *Clubs* Special Forces; Ripon; *Style*— Simon P Grenfell, Esq; St John's House, Sharow Lane, Sharow, Ripon, N Yorks NG4 5BN (☎ (0765) 5771); Park

Court Chambers, 40 Park Cross Street, Leeds LS1 2QH (☎ (0532) 4332677, telex 666135, fax (0532) 421285)

GRENFELL, (Sybil) Vera; CBE (1961), LVO; da of Col Arthur Grenfell, DSO, TD (d 1958, n of 1 Baron Grenfell), by his 1 w, Lady Victoria Grey, da of 4 Earl Grey; *b* 21 July 1902; *Career* lady-in-waiting to HRH Princess Alice of Athlone (decd) 1942-45; former chm Highway Clubs Incorporated, chm Florence Nightingale Aid in Sickness Tst (1975-80, pres 1981-); *Style*— Miss Vera Grenfell, CBE, LVO; Paddock Cottage, Newlands Dve, Maidenhead, Bucks (☎ 26521)

GRENFELL-BAINES, Prof Sir George; OBE (1960), DL (Lancs 1982); s of Ernest Charles Baines and Sarah Elizabeth, *née* Grenfell; *b* 30 April 1908; *Educ* Roebuck St Council Sch, Harris Coll Preston, Manchester Univ (DIpTp); *m* 1 (m dis 1952), Dorothy Hudson; 2 da; m 2, 1954, Milena Fleischman; 1 s, 1 da; *Career* architect planning consultant; fndr Grenfell Baines Gp 1940, fndr ptnr and chm Building Design Partnership 1959-74, prof and head of Dept of Architecture, Univ of Sheffield 1972-75, Emeritus 1976, fndr and dir The Design Teaching Practice Sheffield 1974-, former vice-pres RIBA, hon fellow Manchester Polytechnic, hon vice-pres North Lancs Soc of Architects, Hon DLitt Sheffield 1981, hon fellow American Inst of Architects 1982; RIBA, FRIBA, FRTPI; kt 1978; *Style*— Prof Sir George Grenfell-Baines, OBE, DL; 60 West Cliff, Preston, Lancs (☎ Preston 55824); office: 56 West Cliff, Preston, Lancs PR1 8HU (☎ 52131)

GRENIER, John Allan; s of Rev George Arthur Grenier; *b* 2 April 1933; *Educ* St John's Sch Leatherhead Surrey; *m* 1980, Valerie, da of James William Cocksey; 2 children; *Career* chm The HLT Group Ltd (ind law & business coll); Queen's Award for Export 1982); elected chm of British Mgmt Training Export Cncl 1985; FCA; *Recreations* off-shore cruising, water skiing; *Clubs* RAC, Inst of Directors; *Style*— John Grenier, Esq; The HLT Group Ltd, 200 Greyhound Road, London W14 9RY (☎ 01 385 3377, telex 266386 fax 3813377); Plovers, Horsmonden, Kent

GRENIER, Rear Adm Peter Francis (Frank); s of Dr Frank William Henry Grenier, MRCS, LRCP (d 1964), and Mabel Corenier, *née* Burgess (d 1985); *b* 27 August 1934; *Educ* Montpelier Prep Paignton, Blundell's Sch; *m* 15 Aug 1957, Jane Susan, da of Bert Bradshaw (d 1973), of Kent; 3 s (Timothy Francis b 1959 (d 1960), Stephen Marcel b 1961, Matthew Peter b 1965); *Career* BRNC Dartmouth special entry scheme 1952, submarine serv HMS Dolphin 1956, first cmd submarine HMS Ambush Far East 1964, 2 i/c HMS Resolution (Polaris) 1968, Cmmnd HMS Valiant (Nuclear Attack) 1972-74, Capt 1976, cmd destroyer HMS Liverpool 1981, Capt Fleet 1983-85, Rear Adm 1985, COS to C in C Naval Home Cmd, Flag Offr submarines and Comsubeastlant; Liveryman Worshipful Co of painters and Stainers, chm RNFG 1982-85; govr Blundells Sch 1985; *Recreations* painting, sketching, glass engraving, golf; *Clubs* Army and Navy, West Wilts Golf; *Style*— Rear Adm Frank Grenier; Dolphin House, Home Farm Road, Richmansworth, Herts (☎ 0923 772862, Northwood 26161, ext 6260); Flag Officer Submarine, Northwood, Middlesex HA6 3HP

GRENSIDE, Sir John Peter; CBE (1974); s of Harold Cutcliffe Grenside (d 1953), and Muriel Grenside (d 1970); *b* 23 Jan 1921; *Educ* Rugby; *m* 1946, Yvonne Thérèse, da of Ernest Albert Grau (d 1959); 1 s, 1 da; *Career* Capt RA, served UK, Europe, India; CA; pres Inst of Chartered Accountants in England and Wales 1975-76, ptnr Peat Marwick Mitchell & Co 1960-86, (sr ptnr 1977-86), chm Peat Marwick Int 1980-83; non-exec dir: Allred-Lyons 1986, Nomura Internat Bank 1987; Master Chartered Accountants' Livery Co 1987-88; ACA, FCA; kt 1983; *Recreations* tennis, bridge; *Clubs* All England Lawn Tennis, MCC, Queens, Hurlingham, Pilgrims; *Style*— Sir John Grenside, CBE; 51 Cadogan Lane, London SW1X 9DT (☎ 01 235 3372)

GRESHAM, Prof (Geoffrey) Austin; TD; s of Thomas Michael Gresham (d 1939), of Wrexham, N Wales, and Harriet Ann, *née* Richards (d 1945); *b* 1 Nov 1924; *Educ* Grove Pk GS, Gonville and Caius Coll Cambridge (MA, DSc, MB BChir, MD), King's Coll Hosp London; *m* 1 July 1950, Gweneth Margery, da of Louis Charles Leigh (d 1983), of Cambridge; 3 s (Christopher b 1951, Andrew b 1955, Robert b 1957); *Career* Lt and Capt RAMC 1950-52, Maj and Lt-Col RAMC (V) 1954-66; house physician King's Coll Hosp London 1949-50 (house surgn 1949); Univ of Cambridge: demonstrator in pathology 1953-58, fell and coll lectr (and sometime pres) Jesus Coll, sec faculty bd of medicine 1956-61, lectr in pathology 1958-62; (sometime dep assessor to regius prof of physic and supervisor of res student dept of pathology); univ morbid anatomist and histologist Addenbrooke's Hosp Cambridge 1962- (jr asst pathologist 1953, conslt pathologist 1960), Home Off pathologist to Mid-Anglia 1966- (prof of morbid anatomy and histology 1973); ed of Atherosclerosis, sci fell Zoological Soc London; FRCPath; *Books* A Colour Atlas of General Pathology (1971), A Colour Atlas of Forensic Pathology (1979), Post Mortem Procedures (1979), A Colour Atlas of Wounds and Wounding (1987); *Recreations* gardening, organ playing, wine, silver; *Style*— Prof Austin Gresham, TD; 18 Rutherford Rd, Cambridge (☎ 0223 841326); Addenbrooke's Hosp, Hills Rd, Cambridge (☎ 0223 217168, fax 0223 242775)

GRESLEY, Lady; Ada Mary; da of George Miller (decd); *m* 1924, Sir William Francis Gresley, 13 Bt (d 1976, when the title became extinct); *Style*— Lady Gresley; 59A Grand Ave, Southbourne, Bournemouth, Dorset

GRESWELL, Air Cdre Jeaffreson Herbert; CB (1967), CBE (1962, OBE 1945), DSO (1944), DFC (1942); s of William Territt Greswell (d 1971); *b* 28 July 1916; *Educ* Repton; *m* 1939, Gwyneth Alice, da of Lt-Cdr Robert Cholerton Hayes, RN (d 1925); 1 s, 2 da (and 1 da decd); *Career* cmmnd RAF 1935, WWII served Coastal Cmd, 217 Sqdn 1937-40 (despatches), OC 179 Sqdn Gibraltar 1943-44, HQ 18 Gp 1944-45, air liaison offr British Pacific Fleet 1946-47, HQ Far East Air Force Admin Plans 1947-49, dep dir JASS Londonderry 1949-52, OC RAF Kinloss 1957-59, HQ Coastal CD Air Plans 1959-61, dep standing gp rep NATO HQ Paris 1961-64, Cmdt Royal Observer Corps 1964-68; *Recreations* croquet; *Style*— Air Cdre Jeaffreson Greswell, CB, CBE, DSO, DFC; Red Cedars, Oddley Lane, Saunderton, Bucks (☎ 084 444684)

GRETTON, Baroness; Jennifer; o da of Edmund Moore, of York; *m* 1970, 3 Baron Gretton (d 1989); 1 s (4 Baron), 1 da (Hon Sarah Margaret b 1971); *Style*— The Rt Hon Lady Gretton; Holygate Farm, Stapleford, Melton Mowbray, Leicestershire LE14 2XQ (☎ 057 284 540)

GRETTON, 4 Baron (UK 1944) John Lysander Gretton; o s of 3 Baron Gretton (d 1989); *b* 17 April 1975; *Style*— The Rt Hon Lord Gretton; Holygate Farm, Stapleford, Melton Mowbray, Leicestershire LE14 2XQ

GRETTON, Margaret, Baroness; (Anna Helena) Margaret; JP (Staffs 1943); er da of Capt Henrik Loeffler (decd), of Grosvenor Sq, W1; *m* 1930, 2 Baron Gretton, OBE (d 1982); 2 s (decd), 2 da ; *Style*— The Rt Hon Margaret, Lady Gretton, JP; The Old Rectory, Ufford, Stamford (☎ 0780 740198)

GREVILLE, 4 Baron (UK 1869); Ronald Charles Fulke Greville; s of 3 Baron, OBE, JP, DL (d 1952, ADC to govr of Bombay (Baron Northcote) 1900-03 and Mil Sec to same as Govr-Gen of Australia 1904-08) and Olive Grace (d 1959), da of J W Grace; *b* 11 April 1912; *Educ* Eton, Magdalen Oxford; *Heir* none; *Recreations* golf, tennis, gardening, reading, swimming; *Clubs* Hurlingham; *Style*— The Rt Hon the Lord Greville; Lionsmead House, Shalbourne, nr Marlborough, Wilts (☎ 0672 870440); 75 Swan Court, Chelsea Manor St, SW3 (☎ 01 352 3444)

GREW, James; JP (1974), DL (Co Armagh 1981); s of James Grew; *b* 25 Oct 1929; *Educ* Downside; *m* 1955, Pauline Peta, da of Prof John Cunningham; 2 s (Jonathan James b 1958, Christopher Nicholas b 1969), 2 da (Michaela Maria b 1962, Philippa Peta b 1967); *Career* memb: NI Economic Cncl 1970-74, NI Community Relations Cmmn 1971-74, Craigavon Devpt Cmmn 1971-73, Crawford Ctee on Broadcasting Coverage 1973-74; dir Mgmnt Devpt Servs Ltd 1975-; memb: BBC Advsy Ctee NI 1976-80, BBC Gen Advsy Cncl London 1976-80; chm Post Office Users Cncl NI 1976-81; memb: Post Office Users Nat Cncl London 1976-81, Standing Advsy Cmmn on Human Rights 1980-82; md Abbicoil Spring Ltd; memb IBA Advisory Ctee N Ireland First and 1983-85; chm Probation Bd for NI 1982-88, dir (Govt appointment) NI Tport Holding Co Ltd 1983-86, dir NI Railways 1986, dep chm TSB Fndn Bd N Ireland 1986; First chm Independent Cmmn for Police Complaints NI 1988; *Recreations* sailing; *Clubs* Challoner Pont Street; *Style*— James Grew, Esq, JP, DL; Peacefield, Ballinacorr, Portadown, Co Armagh, N Ireland BT63 5RJ; Abbicoil Springs Ltd, Obin St, Portadown, Co Armagh, N Ireland (☎ 0762 333245)

GREY, Sir Anthony Dysart; 7 Bt (UK 1814); s of Capt Edward Elton Grey (d 1962); suc gf, Sir Robin Edward Dysart Grey, 6 Bt, 1974; *b* 19 Oct 1949; *Educ* Guildford GS Western Australia; *m* 1970, (m dis), Donna (museum curator), da of Donald Daniels, of Park Lane, W1; *Career* inspector for dept of industl affairs Govt of Western Australia; *Recreations* fishing, painting; *Style*— Sir Anthony Grey, Bt; 86 Ringsway Gardens, 38 Rings Park Rd, West Perth, Western Australia 6005

GREY, Dame Beryl Elizabeth; DBE (1988), CBE (1973); da of Arthur Ernest Groom (d 1983), and Annie Elizabeth, *née* Marshall (d 1952); *b* 11 June 1927; *Educ* Dame Alice Owen Professional Madeleine Sharp, Sadlers Wells Ballet Sch; *m* 15 July 1950, Dr Sven Gustav Svenson, s of Ernest Svenson (d 1967) of Heleneborg, Vadstena, Sweden; 1 s (Ingvar b 1954); *Career* danced Swan Lake at 15, Giselle at 16, Sleeping Beauty at 19, prima ballerina Sadlers Wells, later Royal Ballet 1941-57; first foreign guest Bolshoi Ballet Moscow 1957, Peking Ballet 1964; dir gen Arts Educnl Sch 1966-68, artistic dir London Festival Ballet 1968-79, chm Imperial Soc of Teachers of Dancing 1984-; int guest dancer; prodr Giselle with West Australian Ballet 1980, Sleeping Beauty with Royal Swedish Ballet Stockholm 1985, etc; pres Dance Cncl Wales, vice-pres Royal Acad of Dancing 1980-, vice-chm Dance Teachers Ben Soc, London Coll of Dance etc; Hon DMus Leicester 1970, Hon DLitt City of London Univ 1974; Hon DEd CNAA 1989, FRSA, FJSTD; *Books* Red Curtain Up, Through the Bamboo Curtain, Favourite Ballet Stories (ed); *Recreations* swimming, reading, playing piano, painting; *Clubs* Anglo-Belgian, Royal Thames YC; *Style*— Dame Beryl Grey, DBE, CBE; Fernhill, Forest Row, East Sussex RH18 5JE (☎ 0342 822539)

GREY, Maj Hon Jeremy Francis Alnwick; yr s of Baron Grey of Naunton (life Peer); *b* 1949; *Educ* Marlborough, RAC Cirencester; *m* 1973, Susan Elizabeth Louise, da of Duncan Richard Fraser, CBE, of Nairobi Kenya; 2 s (Barnaby b 1976, Sebastian b 1979); *Career* Maj (1982) 14/20 King's Hussars (Royal Armoured Corps); *Style*— Major the Hon Jeremy Grey; c/o Overbrook, Naunton, Glos

GREY, John Egerton; CB (1980); s of John Grey (d 1979), of 68 Abingdon Villas, London W8, and Nancy Augusta, *née* Nickalls (d 1984); *b* 8 Feb 1929; *Educ* Blundell's, BNC Oxford (MA, BCL); *m* 1961, Patricia, da of Col Walter Francis Hanna, MC, RE (d 1963); 2 adopted s; *Career* called to the Bar Inner Temple 1954, practised at Chancery Bar 1954-59; various posts as clerk Parly Off 1959-74, clerk asst and clerk of public bills House of Lords 1974-88; *Recreations* gardening, boating; *Clubs* Arts, West Mersea YC; *Style*— J E Grey, Esq, CB; 51 St Peter's Rd, West Mersea, Colchester, Essex CO5 8LL

GREY, Maj-Gen John St John; CB (1986); s of Maj Donald John Grey, RM (d 1942), and Doris Mary Grey, *née* Beavan; *b* 6 June 1934; *Educ* Christ's Hosp Sch, Royal Coll of Defence Studies, Army Staff Coll Camberley, US Marine Corps Cmd and Staff Coll, Nat Defence Coll; *m* 1958, Elisabeth Ann, da of late Frederick Charles Langley; 1 s (Angus Matthew St John b 1968), 1 da (Emelia St John b 1969); *Career* cmmnd 1952, Cdr Serv: Malta, Egypt, Cyprus 1955-58, Support CO Cmd 43 Commando RM 1962-64, Cruiser HMS Lion 1964-65, instr Army Sch of Infantry 1967-69, Rifle Co Cmd 41 Commando RM 1969-70, US Marine Corps 1970-71, directorate Naval Plan MOD 1971-74, CO 45 Commando RM 1976-79, mil sec and col Ops and Plans MOD 1979-84, maj-gen cmd Commando Forces 1984-87, Chief of Staff RM 1987-88, ret Oct 1988; Clerk Worshipful Co of Pewterers; *Recreations* sailing; *Clubs* Hurlingham, Army and Navy, RYA, RNSA, RWYC, Royal Marines Sailing (Commodore); *Style*— Maj-Gen John Grey; c/o Lloyds Bank Ltd, Teignmouth, Devon

GREY, Hon Jolyon Kenneth Alnwick; er s of Baron Grey of Naunton, GCMG, GCVO, OBE (Life Baron); *b* 4 June 1946; *Educ* Marlborough, Pembroke Coll Camb; *m* 1971, Sarah Jane, da of Lt-Col Samuel Brian Digby Hood, TD; 2 s; *Career* Bar Inner Temple 1968; *Style*— Hon Jolyon Grey; 36 Octavia St, London SW11

GREY, Lt-Col (James) Michael Harling; CBE (1973), TD (1949), JP (1968), DL (Lancs 1975); s of late sir John Grey, and late Emma, *née* Harling of Burnley; *b* 5 Feb 1916; *Educ* Wrekin; *m* 1, 1967, Ruth (d 1978), da of late Arthur Haighton, of Yorks; 1 step da m 2, 1983, Mary, da of late Ernest Gibbs, of Worcs; 3 step da ; *Career* formerly RA (TA); chm: Cotton & Allied Textiles Industrial Trg Bd 1967-82, indust ctee Br Textile Employment Assoc 1969-82; employer memb Cotton Bd and Textile Cncl 1958-70; *Recreations* travelling, reading; *Style*— Lt-Col Michael Grey, CBE, TD, JP, DL; Shay Cross, Wiswell, Blackburn, Lancs (☎ 0254 822 157)

GREY, Sir Paul Francis; KCMG (1963, CMG 1951); s of Col Arthur Grey, CIE; *b* 2 Dec 1908; *Educ* Charterhouse, Christ Church Oxford; *m* 1936, Agnes Mary, da of Richard Shireburn Weld-Blundell, of Ince-Blundell Hall, Lancs; 3 s; *Career* HM Dip Serv 1933-64: min Moscow 1951-53; ambass: Prague 1957-60, Berne 1960-64; Knight of Malta 1977; *Recreations* shooting, fishing; *Style*— Sir Paul Grey, KCMG; Holmwood House, Elstead, Godalming, Surrey GU8 6DB (☎ 0252 702397)

GREY, 6 Earl (UK 1806); Sir Richard Fleming George Charles Grey; 7 Bt (GB 1746); also Baron Grey of Howick (UK 1801) and Viscount Howick (UK 1806); s of

Albert Grey (ggs of Adm Hon George Grey, himself 4 s of 2 Earl Grey, who was PM 1830-34); suc 2 cous twice removed 1963; *b* 5 Mar 1939; *Educ* Hounslow Coll, Hammersmith Coll of Bldg; *m* 1, 1966 (m dis 1974), Margaret, da of Henry Bradford, of Ashburton; m 2, 1974, Stephanie, da of Donald Gaskell-Brown, of Newton Ferrers, Plymouth, and formerly w of Surgn-Cdr Neil Denham, RN; *Heir* bro, Philip Grey; *Career* pres Cost and Exec Accountants Assoc 1978; memb Liberal Pty; *Style*— The Rt Hon the Earl Grey; 40 Compton Ave, Mannamead, Plymouth, Devon

GREY, Robin Douglas; QC (1979); s of Francis Temple Grey (d 1941), and Eglantine, *née* Ellice; *b* 23 May 1931; *Educ* Eastbourne Coll, King's Coll London (LLB); *m* 8 Aug 1969, Borenice Anna, da of Dennis Wheatley (d 1985); 1 s (Julian Alexander b 2 May 1970), 1 da (Louise Katherine b 20 Aug 1973); *Career* Nat Serv Army 1950-51; barr Grey's Inn 1957; crown counsel in Aden 1959-63: acting attorney gen, acting reistrar gen, acting sr crown counsel; in practice SE circuit 1963-79, dep circuit judge 1977-, rec 1979-; memb Bar Cncl 1957, memb Soc Forensic Med 1976; *Recreations* tennis, golf, fishing; *Clubs* Hurlingham; *Style*— Robin Grey, Esq, QC; Dun Cottage, Hungerford, Berks (☎ 0488 835 78); Queen Elizabeth Bldg, London EC4Y 9BS (☎ 01 583 5766)

GREY DE RUTHYN, Barony of (E 1324); see Lubienski Bodenham, Count Charles

GREY EGERTON, Sir (Philip) John Caledon; 15 Bt (E 1617), of Egerton and Oulton, Cheshire; s of Sir Philip Reginald Le Belward Grey Egerton, 14 Bt (d 1962); *b* 19 Oct 1920; *Educ* Eton; *m* 1, 1951, Margaret Voase (d 1971), da of late Rowland Rank, of Aldwick, Place, Aldwick, W Sussex, and wid of Sqdn-Ldr Robert Ullman, RAF; m 2, 1986, Frances Mary, da of late Col Robert Maximillian Raincy-Robinson, of Broadmagne, Dorchester, Dorset, and wid of Sqdn-Ldr William Dudley Williams, DFC; *Heir* bro, Brian Balguy Le Belward Egerton; *Career* late Capt Welsh Gds; *Style*— Sir John Grey Egerton, Bt; Rylstone, Martinstown, Dorchester, Dorset DT2 9JR, (☎ 030588 332)

GREY OF NAUNTON, Baron (Life Peer UK 1968); Ralph Francis Alnwick Grey; GCMG (1964, KCMG 1959, CMG 1955), GCVO (1973, KCVO 1956), OBE (1951); s of Francis Arthur Grey (d 1917), an accountant in NZ, and Mary Wilkie, *née* Spence (d 1952); *b* 15 April 1910; *Educ* Wellington Coll NZ, Auckland Univ Coll, Pembroke Cambridge; *m* 1 Nov 1944, Esmé Mae, CStJ, da of Albert Victor Kerry Burcher, of NZ, and widow of Pilot Offr Kenneth Kirkcaldie, RAFVR; 2 s, 1 da; *Career* barr and slr NZ; Colonial Service Nigeria 1937, devpt sec 1952, sec to Govr-Gen and Cncl of Mins Nigeria 1954, chief sec Fedn of Nigeria 1955, dep govr-gen 1957-59; govr and C-in-C: British Guiana 1959-64, Bahamas 1964-68, Turks and Caicos Is 1965-68, N Ireland 1968-73; chm: Cwlth Devpt Corpn 1979-80, Central Cncl Royal Overseas League 1976-81 (pres 1981-); hon Bencher Inn of Ct of Ireland, hon Freeman City of Belfast and Borough of Lisburn, Freeman City of London; pres: Chartered Inst of Secs NI 1970-, Britain-Nigeria Assoc 1983-89, Overseas Serv Pensioners' Assoc 1983-; chllr New Univ of Ulster 1980-84, chllr Univ of Ulster 1984-; Hon LLD (Queen's Univ Belfast), DLitt (New Univ of Ulster), LLD (Nat Univ of Ireland), DSc (Univ of Ulster); GCStJ 1976; Lord Prior of the Order of St John 1988- (Kt Cdr of Commandery of Ards 1968-76, Bailiff of Egle 1975-87 Chancellor 1987-88); *Recreations* golf; *Clubs* Travellers'; *Style*— The Rt Hon the Lord Grey of Naunton, GCMG, GCVO, OBE; Overbrook, Naunton, Glos (☎ 045 15 263)

GRIBBLE, Dorothy-Rose Jessie; da of Lt Charles Herbert Gribble (ka 1917), and Dorothy Phyllis, *née* Milton (d 1978); *b* 5 July 1917; *Educ* Wycombe Abbey, UCL; *Career* dir and fndr Plantagenet Productions, hon dir Westridge Open Centre for Healing and The Arts; recitalist; *Books* And I am a Doggerel Bard; *plays*: Blood Will Out, The On The Cards Interludes; *Recreations* reading, walking, driving, theatre, printing; *Style*— Miss Dorothy-Rose Gribble; Westridge Open Centre, Highclere, nr Newbury, Royal Berkshire

GRIBBLE, Capt (Douglas) Ronald; OBE (1963); s of William George Gribble (d 1961), of Wilts, and Victoria Daisy Gregory (d 1968); *b* 5 May 1918; *Educ* Reading Sch Berks, Sir John Cass Coll London, cert as Master Mariner; *m* 1, 19 Sept 1946, Jean, da of Storrie Hope (d 1950), of Co Durham; 1 s (George Bruce b 1948); m 2, 23 June 1973, Vera Ursula, da of John Hatton (d 1970), of Hants; 1 step s (Michael Peter b 1947); *Career* apprenticed to Pacific Steam Navigation Co 1933, joined Asiatic Petroleum Co (Shell) after obtaining 2 Mate Cert 1939, served Shell Tankers at sea WWII, transferred ashore with Shell as Pilot/Mooring Master at Lutong, Sarawak 1945, promoted Marine Superintendent 1952, gen mangr Sarawak Shell 1955-67 (dir 1956-67); dir small local Co in Salisbury 1967-68, agent (local mangr) Land & Marine Ltd Nigeria 1968-72; operations mangr Lamnalco Ltd Kuwait 1972-75, rep Cheoy Lee Shipyards, Hong Kong 1975-85; Order of Sarawak (1965), Liveryman Worshipful Co of Mariners 1975, Freeman City of London 1975; *Recreations* gardening, reading, study of history of British Isles and Europe; *Style*— Capt Ronald Gribble, OBE; Fosseway, High St, Hinton St George, Somerset TA17 8SE (☎ 0460 72420)

GRIBBON, Angus John St George; s of Maj-Gen Nigel St George Gribbon, OBE, 99 Pump St, Orford, nr Woodbrige, Suffolk, and Rowan Mary, *née* McLeish; *b* 25 Dec 1951; *Educ* Rugby, New Coll Oxford (MA); *m* 15 May 1965, Mary-Anne, da of Hugh Wynwel Gamon, CBE, MC, of Black Charles Underriver, nr Sevenoaks, Kent; 1 s (Edward b 1981), 2 da (Mary-Clare b 1983, Caroline b 1985); *Career* Clifford Turner slrs 1974-79, slr Allied-Lyons plc 1979-; memb; Enterprise Agency of E Kent; *Recreations* sailing, skiing; *Style*— Angus Gribbon, Esq; Pedlam Brook, West Peckham, Maidstone, Kent ME18 SJS (☎ 0732 851732); Allied-Lyons plc, Allied House, 156 St John St, London EC1P 1AR (☎ 01 251 9911, fax 01 251 8040, telex 267605)

GRIBBON, Maj Gen Nigel St George; OBE (1960); s of Brig W H Gribbon (decd), CMG, CBE; *b* 6 Feb 1917; *Educ* Rugby, RMA Sandhurst; *m* 1943, Rowan Mary, *née* MacLiesh; 2 s, 1 da; *Career* Maj Gen cmmnd King's Own Royal Regt 1937, Iraq 1941, Western Desert 1942, Staff Coll Quetta 1943, Palestine 1946, Trieste 1947-48, Malaysia 1948-50, RAF Staff Coll 1952, Hong Kong 1953-54, BM 1 Para Bde 1946, cmd: 5 King's Own 1958-60, 161 Bde TA 1964-65, AMS War Office 1960-62, Canadian Nat Defence Coll 1965-66, staff of CDS MOD, BAOR 1967-69, ACOS NORTHAG 1967-69, ACOS (Intelligence) SHAPE 1970-72, ret; vice-pres, King's Own Royal Border Regt 1974-; md Partnerplan Public Affairs Ltd 1973-75, chm Sallingbury Ltd 1975-77 (md 1977-84, chm 1985), dep chm Sallingbury Casey Ltd (Saatchi & Saatchi Gp) 1985-87, dir Gatewood Engrs 1976-84, dir Chancellor Insurance Co Ltd 1986; memb: exec ctee British Atlantic Ctee 1977-, European-Atlantic Gp 1977-86; pres Canada-UK Chamber of Commerce 1981; co-chm Joint Ctee with Canadian Chamber of Commerce 1984-, chm Falkland Islands Tst 1982-; Freeman City of London, Liveryman Worshipful Co of Shipwrights 1982; *Recreations* sailing (sloop 'Dendre'), swimming, skiing; *Clubs* Army & Navy, Canada; *Style*— Maj Gen Nigel Gribbon, OBE; 99 Pump St, Orford, Woodbridge, Suffolk IP12 2IX (☎ 039 45 413)

GRIDLEY, 2 Baron (UK 1955); Arnold Hudson Gridley; s of 1 Baron, KBE (d 1965); *b* 26 May 1906; *Educ* Oundle; *m* 1948, Lesley Winifred, da of Leslie Wheen, of Shanghai; 1 s, 3 da; *Heir* s, Hon Richard Gridley; *Career* sits as Conservative in House of Lords; entered Colonial Civil Serv Malaya 1928, interned by Japanese in Changi Gaol 1941-45; WWII, actg dep comptroller Fedn Malaya 1956, ret 1957; memb Cncl Overseas Serv Pensions Assoc 1966-, memb Exec Ctee Overseas Serv Pensions Assoc 1966-, govt tstee Far East Fund 1973- (for POWs and Internees); life pres Centralised Audio Systems 1985, memb Parly delegation to BAOR 1979, visited Rhodesia during Lancaster House Conf, London 1980 and 1985; commendation WWII 1941-45, visit of HRH the Duke of Kent on special duty to Singapore & Malaya to honour Civilian War Dead of all Races, incl Br Overseas Civil Servants; *Clubs* Royal Overseas League; *Style*— The Rt Hon Lord Gridley; Coneygore, Stoke Trister, Wincanton, Somerset (☎ 0963 32209)

GRIDLEY, Hon Richard David Arnold; only s, and h of 2 Baron Gridley; *b* 22 August 1956; *Educ* Monkton Combe Sch, Portsmouth Poly; *m* 1980, Suzanne Elizabeth Ripper; 1 s (Carl b 1981), 1 da (Danielle b 1983); *Career* site mangr Costain Homes (Southern) Ltd; *Style*— The Hon Richard Gridley

GRIER, Anthony MacGregor; CMG (1963); s of Very Rev Roy MacGregor Grier, sometime rector and provost of St Ninian's Cathedral, Perth; *b* 12 April 1911; *Educ* St Edward's Sch Oxford, Exeter Coll Oxford; *m* 1946, Hon Patricia Mary Spens, *qv*; 2 s, 1 da; *Career* Colonial Admin Serv: Sierra Leone 1935-43, Colonial Off 1943-47, North Borneo (now Sabah, Malaysia) 1947-64 (under-sec 1956); gen mangr Redditch Devpt Corpn 1964-76, memb (C) Hereford and Worcester CC 1977-85; *Recreations* shooting, golf; *Clubs* E India and Sports, Royal Cwlth Soc; *Style*— Anthony Grier, Esq, CMG; Mulberry House, Abbots Morton, Worcester WR7 4NA (☎ 0386 792422)

GRIER, Hon Mrs (Patricia Mary); *née* Spens; er da of 1 Baron Spens, KBE, PC; *b* 15 July 1919; *Educ* Heathfield; *m* 1946, Anthony MacGregor, *qv*, s of Very Rev Roy Grier; 2 s (Richard, Francis), 1 da (Lynda); *Career* served WWII as Capt FANY SOE in Europe and Far East; past pres Hereford and Worcester Red Cross; *Recreations* golf, tennis; *Clubs* Special Forces; *Style*— The Hon Mrs Grier; Mulberry House, Abbots Morton, Worcester WR7 4NA (☎ 0386 792422)

GRIERSON, Lady Daphne Olive; *née* Lambart; da of 11 Earl of Cavan; *b* 22 Dec 1909; *Educ* Shrewsbury HS, LSE; *m* 1944, Kenneth (d 1976), s of Douglas Grierson, barrister, of Shirley, Warwicks; 1 s (William); *Career* painter; author; social worker; *Recreations* reading, needlework; *Style*— Lady Daphne Grierson; 24f Four Limes, Wheathampstead, Herts AL4 8PW Shropshire TF11 9EF

GRIERSON, Sir Michael John Bewes; 12 Bt (NS 1685), of Lag, Dumfriesshire; s of Lt-Col Alexander Grierson, RM (decd), 2 s of 9 Bt; suc kinsman, Sir Richard Grierson, 11 Bt (d 1987); *b* 24 July 1921; *Educ* St Edmund's Sch Canterbury; *m* 1971, Valerie Anne, da of late Russell Wright, of Gidea Park, Essex; 1 da (Sarah Anne b 1973); *Style*— Sir Michael Grierson, Bt; 71 Wyatt Park Rd, Streatham Hill, London SW2

GRIERSON, Robert McMorrine; s of Robert Grierson (d 1987), and Gertrude, *née* Warwick; *b* 4 May 1943; *Educ* Yewlands Sch; *m* 12 Oct 1968, Pamela Christine, da of Richard Prewett (d 1985); 1 s (John Robert McMorrine b 1980), 1 da (Heather Louise b 1976); *Career* CA Robert M Grierson & Co, dir Data Memories plc, Upperdale Ltd, Hawbrook Hldgs Ltd, E Marsden Fabrications Ltd; holder of Duke of Edinburgh's Gold Award; FCA; *Recreations* squash, football; *Style*— Robert M Grierson, Esq; 2 Croft Close, Whirlow, Sheffield S11 9RP (☎ 0742 361774); Moor Oaks Lodge, 6 Moor Oaks Rd, Sheffield SI0 1BX (☎ 0742 680357)

GRIEVE, Alan Thomas; s of Lewis Miller Grieve (d 1963), of Stanmore, Middx, and Doris Lilian, *née* Amner (d 1975); *b* 22 Jan 1928; *Educ* Aldenham, Trinity Hall Cambridge (MA, LLM); *m* 1, 1957 (m dis 1971), Anne, da of Dr Lawrence Dulake, of The White House, Blandford Road, Reigate, Surrey; 2 s (Charles b 1960, Ivan b 1962), 1 da (Amanda (Baroness Harlech) b 1958); m 2, 1971, Karen Louise, da of Michael de Sivrac Dunn, of Awliscombe House, Awliscombe, Honiton, Devon; 1 s (Thomas de Sivrac b 1973), 1 da (Lara b 1974); *Career* 2 Lt 14/20 Kings Hussars, Capt City of London Yeo TA; slr; sr ptnr Taylor Garrett; dir: Baggeridge Brick plc, Colibri Lighters Ltd, Reliance Resources Ltd, Stenham plc, Med Insurance Agency Ltd, St George's Hosp Ltd, United Wine Producers Ltd and other cos; chm Racehorse Owners Award; dir Brendon Care for the Elderly; tstee: British Racing Sch, The Jerwood Fndn, The Jerwood Award, Oakham Sch; Friend The Royal Coll of Physicians; memb Educnl Assets Bd; memb Law Soc; *Books* Purchase Tax (1958); *Recreations* skiing, racing, shooting; *Clubs* Boodle's, Aula, Asparagus; *Style*— Alan Grieve, Esq; Brimpton House, Brimpton, Reading, Berks (☎ 0734 71 2100); Taylor Garrett, 180 Fleet St, London EC4A 2NT (☎ 01 430 1122, fax 01 528 7145, telex 25516, car tel 0836 527369)

GRIEVE, (William) Percival; QC (1962); s of 2 Lt W Percy Grieve (ka Ypres 1915), of Kirkcudbrightshire and Argentina, and Dorothy Marie, *née* Hartley, who m 2, William Cunningham, of Monkseaton, Northumberland; *b* 25 Mar 1915, (posthumously); *Educ* privately, Trinity Hall Cambridge; *m* 1949, Evelyn, da of Cmdt Hubert Mijouain, of Paris, and Liliane, da of Sir George Roberts, 1 and last Bt (d 1950); 1 s (and 1 s decd), 1 da (decd); *Career* late Maj Middx Regt; barr Middle Temple 1938, barr Hong Kong 1960, bencher Middle Temple 1969, rec Northampton 1965-71, rec Crown Ct 1971; MP (Cons) Warwicks Solihull 1964-83, UK delgn Cncl of Europe (chm legal affrs ctee 1979-83) and WEU 1969-83; Officier de l'Ordre d'Adolphe de Nassau, Chev de l'Ordre de la Couronne de Chêne, Croix de Guerre avec Palmes Luxembourg 1945-46, Bronze Star USA 1945, Chev de la Légion d'Honneur France 1974, Cdr de l'Ordre de Mérite Luxembourg 1976, Offr de l'Ordre de la Couronne Belgium 1980; *Recreations* swimming, travel, theatre; *Clubs* Carlton, Hurlingham, RAC, Special Forces; *Style*— Percy Grieve, Esq, QC; 1 King's Bench Walk, Temple, London EC4 (☎ 01 353 8436); 32 Gunterstone Rd, London W14 (☎ 01 603 0376)

GRIEVE, Sir (Herbert) Ronald Robinson; s of Lt Gideon James Grieve (ka Paardeberg 1900); *b* 6 June 1898; *Educ* Sydney GS, Sydney Univ (MB, ChM); *m* 1, 1945, Florence Ross (d 1969), da of Francis Timpson; 1 s, 2 da; m 2, 1972, Margaret Du Vé; *Career* memb NSW Med Bd 1938-63, hon clinical asst in med Royal Prince Alfred Hosp Sydney 1941-47, chm Med Benefits Fund of Australia 1947-75; kt 1958;

see Debrett's Handbook of Australia and New Zealand for further details; *Style*— Sir Ronald Grieve; 113 Homer St, Earlwood, NSW 2206, Australia

GRIEVE, Hon Lord; William Robertson Grieve; VRD (1958); s of Robertson Grieve (ka 1917), of Glasgow; *b* 21 Oct 1917; *Educ* Glasgow Acad, Sedbergh, Glasgow Univ; *m* 1947, Lorna, da of Rear Adm Edward Benn, CB; 1 s, 1 da; *Career* late Lt Cdr RNVR; senator Coll of Justice Scotland (Lord of Session) 1972-88; advocate 1947, QC 1957, Sheriff Renfrew and Argyll 1964-72, judge of appeal Jersey & Guernsey 1971-72; chm govrs Fettes Tst; *Recreations* golf, painting; *Clubs* New (Edinburgh), Hon Co of Edinburgh Golfers; *Style*— The Hon Lord Grieve, VRD; 20 Belgrave Crescent, Edinburgh EH4 3AJ (☎ 031 332 7500)

GRIEVES, John Kerr; s of Thomas Grieves (d 1979), of Littlehampton, Sussex, and Annie, *née* Davis (d 1976); *b* 7 Nov 1935; *Educ* Kings Sch Worcester, Oxford Univ (MA), Harvard Business Sch; *m* 21 Oct 1961, Ann Gorell, da of Vincent Charles Harris (d 1982), of London; 1 s (Thomas b 11 Jan 1969), 1 da (Kate b 25 May 1964); *Career* with Pinsent and Co 1958-63, managing ptnr Freshfields 1979-85 (joined 1963); *Recreations* the arts, running; *Clubs* Athenaeum, Roehampton; *Style*— John Grieves, Esq; 7 Putney Park Ave, London SW15 5QN (☎ 01 876 1207); Grindall House, 25 Newgate St, London EC1A 7LH (☎ 01 606 6677, fax 01 248 3487, telex 889292)

GRIFFIN, Adm Sir Anthony Templer Frederick Griffith; GCB (1975, KCB 1971, CB 1967); s of late Col Forrester Metcalf Griffith Griffin, MC, and Beryl Alice Beatrix, *née* Down; *b* 24 Nov 1920; *Educ* RNC Dartmouth; *m* 1943, Rosemary Ann, da of late Vice Adm Harold Hickling, CB, CBE, DSO, of NZ; 2 s, 1 da; *Career* RN 1934-75, served WWII E Indies, Mediterranean, N Atlantic; Capt 1956, Rear Adm 1966, Vice Adm 1968, Adm 1971; Capt Ark Royal 1964-65, Controller of Navy 1971-75 (Flag Offr Plymouth 1969-71, 2 i/c Cmd Far East Fleet 1968-69); chm Br Shipbuilders 1975-80; vice-pres Wellington Coll 1980-, pres Royal Inst Naval Architects 1981-84, exec chm Br Maritime League 1982-87 (vice-pres) 1987-, chm Br Maritime Charitable Fndn 1982-; Hon Fell RINA; Rear Adm of the UK 1986-88 (Vice Adm 1988-); *Recreations* sailing; *Clubs* Army and Navy, Pratt's; *Style*— Adm Sir Anthony Griffin, GCB; Moat Cottage, The Drive, Bosham, Chichester, W Sussex PO18 8JG (☎ 0243 573373)

GRIFFIN, Charles Frederick; ERD (1975); s of Frederick James Griffin, JP (d 1947), of Newton Court, Monmouth, and Rosemary, *née* Hardy (d 1923); *b* 25 April 1918; *Educ* Bromsgrove, Royal Agric Coll Cirencester; *m* 30 May 1959, Iris, da of Evan Carne David, MC, TD, DL, JP; 1 s (Ralph (Capt Griffin) b 1963), 1 da (Wynona (Mrs Peter Hollom) b 1960); *Career* WW II serv: sr offr Welch Regt 1938-46, Nigeria Regt 1942-45; JP Gwent 1959, High Sheriff of Gwent 1975-76; memb: Royal Anthropological Inst, Royal Forestry Soc, country Landowners Assoc, Timber Growers Assoc; *Recreations* (formerly) hunting, shooting; *Clubs* Army & Navy; *Style*— Charles Griffin, Esq, ERD; Newton Court, Monmouth (☎ 0600 2992)

GRIFFIN, Col Edgar Allen; CMG (1965), OBE (1943), ED (1945); s of Gerald Cecil Griffin (d 1926), and Isabella Margaret Griffin, *née* Cocks (d 1947); *b* 18 Jan 1907; *Educ* Aust Mil Staff Coll; *m* 1936, Alethea Mary, da of Joseph Patrick Byrne; 2 s (Peter, Alan), 2 da (Alethea, Kerin); *Career* Australian Govt nominee to Cwlth War Graves Cmmn, ret from AMF 1947, civic appts: chief admin offr: Eastern Dist (Cairo) 1947-54, UK Dist (London) 1954-58; regnl dir: Southern regn (Rome) 1958-69, Northern Regn (Arras France) 1969-72; chm of govrs English Sch Rome 1962-63; *Style*— Col E A Griffin, CMG, OBE, ED; 9 Arley Close, Plas Newton, Chester CH2 1NW (☎ 0244 312510)

GRIFFIN, Lady Jane; *née* Bingham; da of 6 Earl of Lucan, MC (d 1964); *b* 1932; *Educ* Badminton Sch Bristol, UCL (MB, BS); *m* 1960, James D Griffin; 3 s, 1 da; *Style*— Lady Jane Griffin; 444 East Sixty-Sixth St, NY, NY 10021, USA

GRIFFIN, Sir John Bowes; QC (1938); only s of Sir Charles Griffin, QC (d 1962); *b* 19 April 1903; *Educ* Clongowes, Dublin Univ, Cambridge Univ (MA, LLD); *m* 1927, Eva Orrell (d 1977), da of John Mellifont Walsh, of Wexford; 2 da; m 2, 1984, Margaret Guthrie Lever, *née* Sinclair; *Career* called to the Bar Inner Temple 1926, admin offr Uganda 1927, registrar High Ct Uganda 1929, crown counsel Uganda 1933, attorney-gen Bahamas 1936, KC Bahamas 1938, slr-gen Palestine 1939, attorney-gen Hong Kong 1946, chief justice Uganda 1952, ret 1956; acting chief justice N Rhodesia 1957, speaker Uganda Legislative Cncl 1958-62 and Nat Assembly 1962-63, chm Public Serv Cmmn N Rhodesia 1963 and Zambia 1964-65, chm Constitutional Cncl N Rhodesia 1964, ret 1965; CStJ 1960, kt 1955; *Style*— Sir John Griffin, QC; 1 Marina Court, Tigne Sea Front, Sliema, Malta

GRIFFIN, Rear Adm Michael Harold; CB (1973); s of Henry William Griffin (d 1947), and Blanche, *nér Michael*; *b* 28 Jan 1921; *Educ* Plymouth Tech Coll; *m* 1947, Barbara Mary, da of Charles Eugene Brewer (d 1928); 2 da (Jennifer, Jane); *Career* cmmnd 1941, HMS Kent 1942, HM Submarines Trusty, Tactician, Tally Ho Alderney 1944-50, Admty 1950-52, HMS Eagle 1952-54, Staff C-in-C Ports 1954-57, HM Dockyard Rosyth 1957-60, 3 Sub Sqdn 1960-62, Capt 1962, HM Dockyard Chatham 1963-65, HMS St Vincent 1966-69, Cmdr Singapore 1969-71, MOD Bath 1972-77, ret 1977; CEng, FIMechE, FIMart, MBHI; *Recreations* yachting, horology; *Style*— Rear Adm Michael Griffin, CB; 48 Little Green, Alverstoke, Gosport, Hants (☎ 0705 583348)

GRIFFIN, Patrick Charles Lake; s of John Griffin, of Top Farm, Highclere, Newbury, Berks, and Helen Evelyn, da of Sir Henry Bashford, Hon Physician to King George VI, knighted for servs to med 1937; *b* 15 Sept 1948; *Educ* Leighton Park Sch, Birmingham Sch of Architecture, Aston Univ (BSc) ; *m* 8 Sept 1973, Linda Dorothy, da of Reginald Mitchell (d 1955), of Yapton, W Sussex; 1 s (Thomas b 1978), 1 da (Joanna b 1980); *Career* chartered architect; md Sutton Griffin Morgan plc (architects, planners, landscape architects, surveyors) 1973-; received Civic Tst Award 1977, Berkshire Environmental Awards 1981, 1983, 1984, 1985, 1986, 1987, 1988; RIBA Housing Award 1987; vice-chm Berks Soc of Architects 1988; ARIBA; *Recreations* cricket; *Style*— Patrick Griffin, Esq; Whitewood, The Mount, Highclere, Newbury, Berkshire (☎ 0635 253155); Sutton Griffin Morgan plc, Albion Hse, Oxford St, Newbury, Berks (☎ 0635 521100, fax 0635 44188)

GRIFFIN, Paul; s of Reginald Stuart Griffin, and Sylvia Mary, *née* Toyn; *b* 29 Dec 1955; *Educ* Magdalen Coll Oxford (MA, BCL); *m* 16 April 1983, Janet Mary, da of Cecil Sidney Turner; *Career* barr Grays Inn 1979; *Recreations* collecting furniture, art, books, wine, gardening, travel, music; *Style*— Paul Griffin, Esq; 2 Essex Ct, Temple London EC4Y 9AP (☎ 01 583 8381, fax 01 353 0998 telex 8812528 ADROIT G)

GRIFFIN, Paul; MBE (1961); s of Maj John Edwin Herman Griffin, MC (d 1963), of Chingford, Essex, and Gertrude Lilian, *née* Farbridge (d 1968); *b* 2 Mar 1922; *Educ* Framlingham Coll, St Catharine's Coll Cambridge (BA, MA); *m* 24 March 1946, Felicity Grace, da of Canon Howard Dobson (d 1984), of Huntingfield, Suffolk; 1 s (Jonathan b 1949), 1 da (Angela b 1946); *Career* cmmnd 6 Gurkha Rifles 1941, Adj Capt 3/6 Gurkha Rifles 1942, GSO III Special Force (Chindits) North West Frontier 1943, served Burma 1944, Maj GSO II 34 Indian Corps 1944, served Malaya, transferred Suffolk Regt, demob 1945; asst master and head English dept Uppingham 1949-55, princ Eng sch Cyprus 1956-60, headmaster Aldenham Sch 1962-74, princ Anglo World Language Centre Cambridge 1976-82; newsreader Cyprus Broadcasting Corpn 1957-60; govr: Northwood Coll, Edge Grove Sch, Beechwood Park Sch; memb: MENSA 1947 (tres 1948), ct Corpn Sons of Clergy 1973 (sr tres 1982); memb Soc Authors; *Books* collaborated in: How to Become Ridiculously Well-Read in One Evening (1985), How to Become Absurdly Well-Informed About the Famous and the Infamous (1987), The Dogsbody Papers (1988); *Recreations* literary competitions, sea angling, bridge; *Clubs* Army & Navy; *Style*— Paul Griffin, Esq, MBE; 1 Strickland Pl, Southwold, Suffolk IP18 6HN (☎ 0502 723709)

GRIFFITH, David Humphrey; s of Maj H W Griffith, MBE; *b* 17 Feb 1936; *Educ* Eton; *m* 1966, Philippa Claire, *née* Roberts; 1 s, 3 da; *Career* dir Greenall Whitley & Co Ltd 1964-, dir Dennis Ruabon Ltd 1973-; *Recreations* gardening, fishing, shooting, racing; *Clubs* Boodle's; *Style*— David Griffith, Esq; Garthmeilio, Llangwm, Corwen, Clwyd, N Wales (☎ 049 082 269)

GRIFFITH, John McIver; s of Edward Ernest Griffith (d 1974), and Mary Ann Fraser, *née* McIver; *b* 3 July 1932; *Educ* Shrewsbury; *m* 1976, Margaret Ann Allan, da of George A Rennie, of S Africa; 2 step s (Andrew Dawes b 1965, Nicholas Dawes b 1969), 1 da (Philippa Griffith b 1979), 1 step da (Caroline Dawes b 1962); *Career* Maj TA 5 Bn Kings Regt, 2 Lt East Lancs Regt served Middle East; dir: Bowring Servs Ltd 1985, C T Bowring & Co (Insur) 1977, Bowring Marine & Energy Ltd 1986; *Style*— John Griffith, Esq, TD; The Old Post Office, Elmdon, nr Saffron Walden, Essex (☎ 0763 838221); The Bowring Bldg, Tower Place, London EC3 (☎ 01 283 3100)

GRIFFITH, Kenneth; brought up by grandparents Ernest and Emily Griffith; *b* 12 Oct 1921; *Educ* Tenby Cncl Sch, Tenby Green Hill GS; *m* three times (all dis); 3 s (David, Jono, Huw), 2 da (Eva, Polly); *Career* actor, writer and film maker; films incl: A Touch of Churchill, A Touch of Hitler (life of Cecil Rhodes), Hang Out Your Brightest Colours (life of Michael Collins - this film was suppressed), The Man on the Rock (last six years of Napoleon's life), The Sun's Bright Child (life of Edmund Kean), The Public's Right to Know (investigation into suppression of Collins films), Curious Journey (investigation into cause of Irish Republicanism - also suppressed), Black as Hell, Thick as Grass (the S Wales Borderers in the Zulu War of 1879), The Most Valuable Englishman Ever (the life of Thomas Paine), Clive of India, The Light (life of David Ben Gurion), Life of Paul Kruger, Life of Jawaharlal Nehru, Zola Budd, The Untouchable; *Books* Thank God We Kept the Flag Flying (1974), Curious Journey (1982); *Recreations* travelling around the world; *Style*— Kenneth Griffith, Esq; 110 Englefield Rd, Islington, London N1 (☎ 01 226 9013)

GRIFFITH, (Edward) Michael Wynne; CBE (1987), DL (Clywd); s of Maj Humphrey Wynne Griffith, MBE (d 1986), and Phyllis Lilian Griffith, JP, *née* Theobalds; *b* 29 August 1933; *Educ* Eton, RAC; *m* 31 Oct 1959, Jill Grange, da of Maj D P G Moseley (d 1986), of Dorfold Cottage, Cheshire; 3 s (Edward James Wynne b 1964, Anthony David Wynne b 1966, Martyn b 1968, d 1969); *Career* memb: ARC 1973-82, Wales ctee chm Nat Tst, exec ctee and cncl advsy bd Nat West Bank 1974-, chm Clwyd Health Authy; High Sheriff Denbighshire 1969; *Clubs* Boodles; *Style*— Michael Griffith, Esq, CBE, DL; Greenfield, Trefnant, Denbigtih, Clywd (☎ 074 574 633)

GRIFFITH, Owen Glyn; CBE (1980, OBE 1969), MVO (1954); s of William Glyn Griffith, MBE (d 1960), and Glwadys May Picton, *née* Davies (d 1981); *b* 19 Jan 1922; *Educ* Oundle, Trinity Hall Cambridge; *m* 1 Feb 1949, Rosemary Elizabeth Cecil, da of Dr John Cecil St George Earl (d 1973); 2 s (David b 1955, Michael b 1957); *Career* cmmnd Welsh Gds 1941-43, serv Tunisia (wounded twice); Colonel Serv (later Overseas Colonial Serv) Uganda 1944-63: dist offr 1944-51, private sec to govr 1952-54, dist cmmr 1954-61, perm sec Miny of Commerce and Indust 1961-63; HM Dip Serv 1963-82: princ CRO 1963, first sec and head of chancery Khartoum Embassy 1965, first sec (commercial) Stockholm Embassy 1969, dep high cmmr Malawi 1973, inspectorate 1976, high cmmr Lesotho 1978; community advsr (civil def) Gerrards Cross, memb exec cncl Beaconsfield Cons Assoc; local rep Forces Help Soc and Lord Roberts Workshops; *Recreations* golf, fishing; *Clubs* Denham GC; *Style*— Owen Griffith, Esq, CBE, MVO; The Sundial, Marsham Way, Gerrard's Cross, Buckinghamshire SL9 8AD; Blaengwilym, Rhydwilym, Clynderwen, Dyfed SA66 7QH (☎ 0753 882 438)

GRIFFITHS *see also*: Norton-Griffiths

GRIFFITHS, Air Vice-Marshal Arthur; CB (1972), AFC (1964); s of Edward Griffiths (d 1960), of Saltney, Chester, and Elizabeth Griffiths; *b* 22 August 1922; *Educ* Hawarden GS; *m* 1950, Nancy Maud, da of Herbert Sumpter, of Wansford; 1 da; *Career* RAF 1940-77 (served in UK, Germany, Canada, Far East, Australia); dir Trident Safeguards Ltd 1985-; *Clubs* RAF; *Style*— Air Vice-Marshal Arthur Griffiths, CB, AFC; Water Lane House, Marholm Rd, Castor, Peterborough, Cambs (☎ 0733 380 742)

GRIFFITHS, Brian Arthur; s of James Griffiths (d 1986), and Constance Lizzie Griffiths (d 1977); *b* 28 Jan 1932; *Educ* Lawrence Sheriff GS, Rugby; *m* 6 Oct 1956, Stella, da of Robert Dunning (d 1970); 1 da (Christine Julia b 1963); *Career* slr; dir Spireglade Gp of Cos 1984-; *Recreations* travel, photography, wine; *Style*— Brian A Griffiths, Esq; 5 Greswolde Road, Solihull, West Midlands (☎ 021 704 1509); 5 Lower Temple Street, Birmingham B2 4JF (☎ 021 643 8075)

GRIFFITHS, His Hon Judge David John; s of John Griffiths (d 1936), and Anne Virgo, formerly Griffiths, *née* Jones (d 1967); *b* 18 Feb 1931; *Educ* St Dunstan's Coll; *m* 1, 1959, Joyce, da of Charles Gosling (d 1963); 3 s (John b 1961, Huw b 1963, Bryn b 1965), 1 da (Jane b 1960); m 2, 1972, Anita, da of William John Williams (d 1967); *Career* Royal Tank Regt, 5 Bn BAOR 1949-51, TA City of London Yeo 1951-56; slr Supreme Court 1957, own practise Bromley Kent 1961, acquires Harvey of Lewisham practise 1970, HM rec 1988 Circuit Judge 1984; hon slr Bromley Marriage Guidance Cncl 1969 vice-chm Law Legal Aid Area Ctee 1983-84 (memb 1976), appt Panel of Chm of Nat Insur Local Tbnls, chm Bromley Cncl of Voluntary Servs 1980-87; Freeman City of London 1982; *Recreations* riding, music (male voice); *Style*— His Hon

Judge David Griffiths

GRIFFITHS, Ven David Nigel; RD; s of late William Cross Griffiths, LDS; *b* 29 Oct 1927; *Educ* Cranbrook Sch, Worcester Coll Oxford, Lincoln Theol Coll; *m* 1953, Joan, *née* Fillingham; 2 s, 1 da; *Career* chaplain RNR, clerk in Holy Orders, ordained 1958, vice-chllr and librarian of Lincoln Cathedral 1967-73, rector of Windsor 1973-87, officiating chaplain to Houshold Cavalry 1973-87, chaplain to HM The Queen 1977-, rural dean of Maidenhead 1977-82 and 1985-87, hon canon of Christ Church Oxford 1983-87, archdeacon of Berkshire 1987-; FSA; *Recreations* serendipity; *Style*— The Ven, the Archdeacon of Berkshire, RD, FSA; 21 Wilderness Road, Earley, Reading, Berks RG6 2RU (☎ 0734 663459); Choristers' Mews, 1A Nettleham Road, Lincoln LN2 1RF (☎ 0522 512014)

GRIFFITHS, Sir Eldon Wylie; MP (C) Bury St Edmunds May 1964-; s of Thomas Herbert Wylie Griffiths, of Dorset and Edith May, *née* Jones; *b* 31 Mar 1989; *Educ* Ashton GS, Emmanuel Coll Cambridge, Yale Univ; *m* 1949, Sigrid Gante; 1 s (John), 1 da (Pamela); m 2, 1985, Elizabeth Marie Beatrix, da of Adriaan den Engelse (d 1985); *Career* former journalist; Parly sec Min of Housing and Local Govt 1970, Parly under-sec of state DOE and Min for Sport 1970-74, conslt Nat Police Fedn; Regents prof Univ of California Irvine; dir: Caparo Gp, Lynton Delancey Ptnrs, Support Systems USA; chm: Br-Iranian and Br-Polish Gps, Indo Br Assoc, Special Olympics (UK); Hon Freeman City of London, Hon Citizen Orange County California; *Recreations* swimming, tennis, exploring wilderness America; *Clubs* Carlton, Overseas League; *Style*— Sir Eldon Griffiths, MP; The Wallow, Great Barton, Bury St Edmunds, Suffolk; House of Commons, SW1

GRIFFITHS, Gareth Lloyd; s of Curwen Lloyd Griffiths (d 1982), of Penarth, S Glam, and Doris Ceinwen, *née* Hughes; *b* 28 Mar 1954; *Educ* Penarth GS, Jesus Coll Oxford (BA, MA), City Univ, Cncl of Legal Educn; *Career* Thomson Regnl Newspapers 1975-78, Liverpool Post and Echo 1978-79, Financial Times 1979-84, dir Shardwick Conslts 1986-; barr Gray's Inn 1986; memb Paddington and N Kensington Community Health Cncl 1984-86; memb: Bodleian Library Appeal Ctee, Hon Soc of Cymmrodorion, memb: Royal Inst of PA, Royal Inst of Int Affrs; *Books* A Study of Competition and the Opticians (d 1987); *Recreations* 19th century political and church history, walking; *Clubs* The Reform, Glamorganshire GC, London Welsh; *Style*— Gareth Griffiths, Esq; 21 Rutland Ct, Denmark Hill, London SE5; 2 St Donats House, Seaview Ct, Kymin Rd, Penarth, S Glamorgan; Shandwick Consultants Ltd, Dauntsey House, Fredericks Place, Old Jewry, London EC2 (☎ 01 726 4291)

GRIFFITHS, Howard; s of Bernard Griffiths (d 1984), and Olive, *née* Stokes (d 1982); *b* 20 Sept 1938; *Educ* Gowerton GS, LSE (MSc); *m* 27 July 1963, Dorothy, *née* Todd; 1 s (Andrew b 1968), 1 da (Emma b 1972); *Career* MOD: res offr 1963-69, princ army dept 1970-72, princ central staffs 1972-76, asst sec head civilian faculty Nat Def Coll 1976-78, asst sec procurement exec 1978-80, dep and cnsllr def UK delegation Mutual & Balanced Force Reduction Talks Vienna 1980-84, asst-sec offs mgmnt and budget 1984-86, head def arms control unit 1986-88, asst under sec (policy) 1986-; *Style*— Howard Griffiths, Esq; Ministry of Defence, Whitehall, London SW1A 2HB

GRIFFITHS, John Calvert; CMG (1983), QC (1972); s of Oswald Hardy Griffiths (d 1952), and Christina Flora Littlejohn; *b* 16 Jan 1931; *Educ* St Peter's Sch York, Emmanuel Coll Cambridge (BA, MA); *m* 17 May 1958, Elizabeth Jessamy Jean, eld da of Prof G P Crowden, OBE (d 1967); 3 da (Amanda b 1963, Anna b 1970, Alyson b 1973); *Career* Lt (RE) 1949-51; called to Bar Middle Temple 1959 (bencher 1983), Hong Kong Bar 1979, attorney gen of Hong Kong 1979-83, chm Hong Kong Law Reform Cmmn 1979-83, memb Ct Hong Kong Univ 1980-84; memb exec ctee Prince Philip Cambridge Scholarships 1980-84; patron Matilda Hosp Charity for Handicapped Children 1981-83; tres Bar Cncl 1987; memb exec ctee Gen Cncl of Bar 1967-71; memb senate Inns of Court & The Bar 1984-86, (exec ctee 1973-77), Cncl of Legal Educn 1983-; Nat Cncl of Social Service 1974-79; Gtr London CAB Exec Ctee 1978-79; *Recreations* fishing, first edns, gardening; *Clubs* Fly Fishers, Hurlingham, Hong Kong; *Style*— John Griffiths, CMG, QC; 1 Brick Court, Temple, London EC4 (☎ 01 583 0777, fax 01 583 9401, Group 3)

GRIFFITHS, John Charles; JP (Cardiff 1959); s of Sir Percival Griffiths, KBE, and Kathleen Wilkes (d 1979); *b* 19 April 1934; *Educ* Uppingham, Peterhouse Cambridge (MA); *m* 1, 1956, Ann; 4 s (Timothy b 1957, Christopher b 1958, Gavin b 1961, Jonathan b 1964); m 2, 1983, Carole Jane; 1 da (Emily b 1984); *Career* pres: Thompson Newspapers 1958-61, BBC 1961-64; exec dir: National Extension Coll 1964-67, PR Advsr Br Gas 1969-73; chm and md MSG PR Ltd 1973-78, Rodhales Ltd 1978-, contact PR Ltd 1981-85, The Arts Channel 1983-; dep gen mangr Press Assoc 1968-69; contested (Lib): Ludlow 1964, Wanstead & Woodford 1966, Bedfird (Feb & Oct) 1974; pres Lib Pty 1982-83; *Books* The Survivors (1964), Afghanistan (1967), Modern Iceland (1969), The Science of Winning Squash, Three Tomorrows, Afghanistan; Key to a Continent (1980), Flashpoint Afghanistan (1987); *Recreations* reading, talking, squash, music; *Clubs* RAC; *Style*— John Griffiths, Esq; Cefn Crug, Llangynidr, Brecon, Powys; The Arts Channel, PO Box 7, Ebbw vale, Gwent NP3 5YP (☎ 0495 306995, fax 0495 306995)

GRIFFITHS, John Francis Philpin; s of James Maldwyn Griffiths, of Hayes, Bromley, Kent, and Joan, *née* Philpin; *b* 16 Sept 1948; *Educ* St Dunstan's Coll London SE6, Clare Coll Cambridge (MA, DipArch); *m* 16 Sept 1972, Fiona Barbara, da of Lt-Cmdr Hugh Desmond Campbell Gibson, of Kilmelford, Argyll, Scotland; 1 s (Leo b 27 July 1980), 1 da (Anna b 16 Jan 1977); *Career* architect; Scarlett Burkett Assoc (Scarlett Burkett Griffiths 1986-) joined 1972, assoc 1975, ptnr 1978; chm: London Regn of Assoc of Conslt Architects 1988-, Architectural Assoc part III Examination Bd 1989; memb Architectural Assoc 1987-; Freeman City of London 1987, Liveryman Worshipful Co of Arbitrators 1987; RIBA 1974, FCIArb 1986, ACA 1985; *Recreations* reading, railway memoribilia, woodworking; *Style*— John Griffiths, Esq; Lynhurst, 98 Hayes Rd, Bromley, Kent BR2 9AB (☎ 01 460 6246); Scarlett Burkett Griffiths, 10-14 Macklin St, London WC2B 5NF (☎ 01 242 1374, fax 01 242 5108)

GRIFFITHS, John Greville; s of Orlando HG Griffiths (d 1961), and Florence, *née* Beck (d 1971); *b* 17 Sept 1935; *Educ* Dr Morgan's GS Bridgwater, Cambridge Univ (MA); *m* 1 Sept 1962, Ruth, da of Edwin A Claypole (d 1976); 1 da (Claire b 1966); *Career* Castrol: dir Europe 1975-, dep md 1988-; *Recreations* archaeology, historical res, travel; *Style*— John Griffiths, Esq; Jenners, Poulton, Cirencester, Glos GL7 5JE (☎ 028585 476); Castrol Ltd, Burmah House, Pipers Way, Swindon SN3 1RE (☎ 0793 512 712, fax 0793 512 640)

GRIFFITHS, John Henry Morgan; s of Sir Eldon Griffiths, MP, and Sigrid, *née* Gante; *b* 3 Dec 1953; *Educ* Rugby, Emmanuel Coll Cambridge Univ (BA); *Career* Lloyds Bank Int 1975-79 (seconded to Bank of London & SA 1975-77, int mgmnt London 1977-79); Samuel Montagu & Co Ltd 1979- (syndications mangr 1981-83, dir S M Inc and W Coast rep (USA) 1983-87, exec dir 1986-); Hon MA Cambridge Univ 1979; *Recreations* tennis, squash, shooting; *Clubs* San Francisco Bay, The Metropolitan; *Style*— John Griffiths, Esq; 6 West Mews, West Warwick Place, London SW1; Lynton Cottage, Ixworth Thorpe, Bury St Edmunds, Suffolk; Samuel Montagu & Co Ltd, 10 Lower Thames St, London EC3R 6AE (☎ 01 260 9450, fax 01 488 1630, telex 887213)

GRIFFITHS, John Pankhurst; s of William Bramwell Griffiths (d 1978), of Broadstairs, and Ethel Doris, *née* Pankhurst; *b* 27 Sept 1930; *Educ* Torquay GS, King George V Sch Southport, Sch of Architecture Manchester Univ (Dip Arch); *m* 1 Aug 1959, Helen Elizabeth, da of Leonard Ivor William Tasker (d 1976), of Bristol; 2 s (Jonathan b 1962, Matthew b 1963), 1 da (Janet b 1964); *Career* res architect N Nigeria (Maxwell Fry) 1956-58, staff architect Granada TV 1959, fndr and first dir Manchester Bldg Centre 1959-65, head of tech info Miny of Public Bldgs and Works (later DOE) 1965-77, fndr Bldg Conservation Assoc (now building Conservation Tst at Hampton Court Palace) 1977; Freeman Worshipful Co of Tylers and Bricklayers 1981; memb RIBA 1956; *Recreations* designing odd things, examining buildings, cooking on solid fuel Aga; *Style*— John Griffiths, Esq; Building Conservation Tst, Aptmt 39, Hampton Ct Palace, E Molesey, Surrey KT8 9BS (☎ 01 943 2277)

GRIFFITHS, Kenneth Ernest Oliver; s of Ernest Griffiths (d 1948), of Neston, S Wirral, and Constance Annie, *née* Oliver (d 1970); *b* 1 May 1909; *Educ* Merchant Taylors Crosby; *m* 26 June 1937, Joy Masters, da of Horace Rowland Hill (d 1968), of Petersfield, Hants; 2 s (Brian Oliver Hill b 1938, Robin Mark Hill b 1941), 1 da (Paula Louise Hill b 1944); *Career* fndr ptnr Griffiths & Armour consulting insurance brokers; *Recreations* travel, walking, bridge; *Clubs* Athenaeum, St Stephen's Constitutional, Athenaeum, Artist's, Racquet (Liverpool); *Style*— Kenneth Griffiths, Esq; Brook Hey, Willaston, S Wirral (☎ 051 327 4220); Drury House, 19 Water Street, Liverpool L2 0RL (☎ 051 236 5656)

GRIFFITHS, Mervyn Christopher; TD (1976); s of Rev Leonard Lewis Rees Griffiths, of Angle Cottage, Polecat Valley, Hindhead, Surrey, and Eileen Clarice, *née* Diffey; *b* 28 May 1936; *Educ* St George's Sch Windsor Castle, Uppingham, Corpus Christi Coll Cambridge (MA), Harvard Business Sch (PMD); *m* 27 April 1974, Barbara Marchant, da of Dr (Heneage) Marchant Kelsey, of Ramparts, Rudgwick, West Sussex; 1 step s (Mark Selway b 7 Feb 1964); *Career* 2 Lt 4/7 Royal Dragoon Gds 1954-56, Capt Queens Own Warwickshire & Worcestershire Yeo 1956-68; special constable Met Police 1973-76; asst mktg mangr W & T Avery Ltd 1959-65, PR exec McLeish Assoc 1965-66; Eurocard Int SA, Belgium: mktg mangr 1966-67, exec vice pres NY 1967-71, md London 1971-76; dir and dep chief gen mangr Alliance Bldg Soc 1976-85, dir dep chief gen mangr and sec Alliance & Leicester Bldg Soc 1985-; memb: Sussex TA Ctee, Isfield PCC, NSPCC Nat Centenary Appeal Ctee 1984; govr: Handcross Park Sch Haywards Heath, St Bede's Sch Eastbourne; FCIM 1975; *Recreations* gardening, travel; *Clubs* Cavalry & Guards; *Style*— Mervyn Griffiths, Esq, TD; The Old Hse, Isfield, nr Uckfield, E Sussex TN22 5XU (☎ 082 575 446); Alliance & Leicester Bldg Soc, 49 Park Lane, London W1 (☎ 01 629 6661, 0273 224 117, fax 0273 224 451, car tel 0836 503 208)

GRIFFITHS, Nigel; MP (L) Edinburgh South 1987-; s of Lionel Griffiths, of Edinburgh, and Elizabeth, *née* Murray; *b* 20 May 1955; *Educ* Hawick HS, Univ of Edinburgh (MA 1977), Moray House Coll of Educn; *m* 1979, Sally, da of Hugh McLaughlin, of Kilmarnock; *Career* joined Labour Party 1970, pres Edinburgh Univ L Club 1976-77; rights advsr Mental Handicap Pressure Gp 1979-87, City of Edinburgh District cncllr; chm: Housing ctee, Decentralisation ctee; memb: Edinburgh Festival ctee, Wester Hailes Sch Cncl 1980; *Books* Council Housing on the point of Collapse (1982), Welfare Rights Guide (1982, 83, 84, 85, 86), A Guide to DHSS Claims and Appeal (1983); *Recreations* travel, hill walking, rock climbing, architecture, politics; *Style*— Nigel Griffiths, Esq, MP; 39 Thirlestane Road, Edinburgh EH9 1AP (☎ 031 447 1947); c/o Trevose House, Newburn Street, London SE11; House of Commons, London SW1A 0AA (☎ 01 219 3442); Constituency Office, 93 Causewayside, Edinburgh (☎ 031 662 4520)

GRIFFITHS, Sir Percival Joseph; KBE (1963), CIE (1943); s of late J T Griffiths, of London; *b* 15 Jan 1899; *Educ* Central Fndn Sch, Peterhouse Cambridge; *m* 1, 1924, Kathleen Mary (d 1979), da of late T R Wilkes, of Kettering; 3 s; m 2, 1985, Helen Marie Shirley Smith; *Career* served WW I, 2 Lt RFC 1917-18; entered ICS 1922, memb Indian Legislative Assembly 1937-47, central organiser Nat War Front India 1942-44, hon publicity advsr Govt of India 1942-47, hon advsr to India, Pakistan and Burma Assoc 1947-63, pres 1963, advsr to Indian Tea Assoc and Pakistan Tea Assoc 1947-63; co dir; kt 1947; *Style*— Sir Percival Griffiths, KBE, CIE; St Christopher, Abbots Drive, Wentworth, Virginia Water, Surrey

GRIFFITHS, Peter Harry Steve; MP (C) Portsmouth North 1979-; s of the late W L Griffiths, of West Bromwich; *b* 24 May 1928; *Educ* West Bromwich GS, City of Leeds Trg Coll, London Univ, Birmingham Univ; *m* 1968, Christine Jeannette, *née* Rubery; 1 s (John Paul) 1 da; *Career* former: headmaster, sr lectr, pres Young Cons; alderman Smethwick Borough Cncl 1964-66 (memb 1955-64), MP (C) Smethwick 1964-66, contested (C) Portsmouth North Feb 1974; Parly advsr MOD Staff Assoc; *Recreations* motoring, camping; *Clubs* Cons, Sloane; *Style*— Peter Griffiths, Esq, MP; House of Commons, London SW1

GRIFFITHS, Prof (Allen) Phillips; s of John Phillips Griffiths (d 1941), of Cardiff, and Elsie Maud, *née* Jones (d 1975); *b* 11 June 1927; *Educ* Univ Coll Cardiff (BA), Univ Coll Oxford (BPhil); *m* 1, 6 June 1948, Margaret Phillips (d 1974), da of John Henry Joseph Lock (d 1974); 1 s (John Benedict Phillips b 1960), 1 da (Sarah Katharine Phillips b 1961); m 2, 21 April 1984, Vera Clare Phillips, da of Patrick Dunphy; *Career* Sgt Intelligence Corps 1945-48 (despatches); lectr: Univ of Wales 1954-56, Birkbeck Coll London 1956-65; pro-vice chllr Univ of Warwick 1970-76 (prof of philosophy 1965-), dir Royal Inst of Philosophy 1979-; fell Univ Coll Cardiff 1984-; Queens Jubilee Medal; memb Mind Assoc Aristotelian Soc 1955-; *Style*— Prof Phillips Griffiths; 133 Beechwood Ave, Coventry CB5 6FR (☎ 0203 715747); Univ of Warwick (☎ 0203 523320)

GRIFFITHS, Sir Reginald Ernest; CBE (1965); s of Arthur Griffiths; *b* 1910; *Educ* St Marylebone GS, London Univ (externally); *m* 1935, Jessica Broad (d 1987); 2 s; *Career* dir of establishments LCC 1952-57; jt sec: Police Cncl, Nat Jt Industl Cncls

(Local Authorities) 1957-72; memb Nat Industl Rels Ct 1972-74; kt 1973; *Recreations* social work (voluntary), golf, gardening; *Style*— Sir Reginald Griffiths, CBE; 10 Woolbrook Park, Sidmouth, Devon (☎ Sidmouth 4884)

GRIFFITHS, Robin John; s of David Gromwell Morgan Griffiths, and Elizabeth Hope, *née* Limbert; *b* 15 Dec 1942; *Educ* Bedford Sch, Notting Ham Univ (BA); *m* 6 Jan 1968, Esme Georgina (Gina), da of Willim Hunter (d 1967); 4 s (Mark David b 24 Sept 1971, Paul Robin b 6 Sept 1974, David James b 4 Aug 1977, Andrew William b 29 nov 1979); *Career* Phillips & Drew 1964-68, ptnr Grieveson Grant 1968-84 (formerly Carr Sebag, previously W1 Carr), sr exec James Capel 1986-; chm Soc of Tech Analysts; memb: Nippon Tech Analysts Assoc, Int Fedn Tech Analysts; author and fndr The Amateur Chartist Newsletter; sailed the Atlantic with Robin Knox Johnston setting a Br record at the time; memb Stock Exchange 1971, FIMBRA 1987; *Recreations* sailing; *Style*— Robin Griffiths, Esq; James Capel & Co, Capel House, PO Box 551, 6 Bevis Marks, London EC3A 73Q

GRIFFITHS, Roger; s of William Thomas Griffiths (d 1979), of Barry, S Wales, and Annie Evelyn, *née* Hill; *b* 25 Dec 1931; *Educ* Lancing, King's Coll Cambridge (BA, MA), New Coll Oxford (BA, MA, DipEd); *m* 2 April 1966, Diana, da of Capt John Frederick Beaufoy Brown, OBE, DSC, RN (d 1979), of Burgess Hill, Sussex; 3 da (Elizabeth b 1966, Helen b 1968, Caroline b 1970); *Career* asst master Charterhouse 1956-64, headmaster Hurstpierpoint Coll 1964-86; sec HMC 1986-, dep sec SHA 1986-; JP Mid-Sussex Bench 1976-86, memb mgmnt ctee of Pallant House Chichester 1987-; govr Mill Hill Sch 1987-, Tormead Sch Guildford 1987-, Prebendal Sch Chichester 1987-; Freeman City of London 1970, Renter Warden of the Wax Chandlers Co 1988 (Liveryman 1971-); *Recreations* music, theatre, bowls, gardening; *Clubs* East India, Devonshire Sport, Public Schools, Sussex; *Style*— Roger Griffiths, Esq; Hanbury Cottage, Cocking, Midhurst, W Sussex GU29 0HF (☎ 073081 3503); The Headmasters' Conference, 1 Russell House, Bepton Rd, Midhurst, W Sussex GU29 9NB (☎ 073081 5635)

GRIFFITHS, Roy Garrad; s of William James Griffiths (d 1972), and Emma, *née* Garrad (d 1987); *b* 2 July 1934; *Educ* Ealing Coll; *m* 1, 26 Feb 1955 (m dis 1979), Sheila Elizabeth, da of Robert William Gerrish; 2 s (John Charles Roy b 30 Dec 1959, Paul James b 28 Nov 1965), 1 da (Anne Elizabeth b 21 Oct 1962); m 2, 8 May 1980, Christine Lillian Mackenzie Ronhof Gronbech, *née* Boote; *Career* md Clares Engrg Ltd 1967, dir White Child and Beney plc 1972; Clares Refrigeration Ltd 1985; chm Clares Equipment Ltd 1978, chm and chief exec Clares Equipment Hldgs Ltd 1987; Freeman City of London, Liveryman Worshipful Co of Carman; patron: Bath Rugby Club, Theatre Royal Bath; vice pres Somerset CCC; *Recreations* antiques, theatre, art, watching rugby and cricket; *Clubs* City Livery, MCC Lord Taverners; *Style*— Roy Griffiths, Esq; Clares Equipment Holdings Ltd, Parkwood Estate, Wells, Somerset BA5 1UT (☎ 0749 73688, fax 0749 73688, car phone 0860 327624, telex 449751 ROLPOL G)

GRIFFITHS, Walter Lloyd; s of Joseph Ewance Griffiths (d 1974), and Josephine Mary, *née* Stokes (d 1972); *b* 24 June 1927; *m* 3 March 1962, Paula, da of Reginald Lord Hollebone (d 1953); 2 s (David b 13 Jan 1963, Mark b 23 Nov 1965, d 1969), 1 da (Julie b 24 March 1964); *Career* slr 1960; sr ptnr Burnand and Burnand Hove and Worthing 1970- (ptnr 1961-70); NP 1966; Freeman City of London 1982 (Guild memb 1984), Liveryman Worshipful Co of Loriners 1982; memb: Law Soc 1960, Provincial Notaries Soc 1966; *Recreations* study of social and domestic life in Victorian England, gardening, travel; *Clubs* City Livery; *Style*— Walter Griffiths, Esq; Jefferies House, Jefferies Lane, Goring-by-Sea, Worthing, W Sussex (☎ 0903 43599); Burnand and Burnand, 39 Church Rd, Hove, E Sussex BN3 2BU; 4 Aldsworth Parade, Goring-by-Sea, Worthing, W Sussex BN12 4UA (☎ 0273 734022; 0903 502155, fax 0273 778760; 0903 506731)

GRIFFITHS, Baron (Life Peer UK 1985) William Hugh Griffiths; MC (1944), PC (1980), QC (1964); only s of Sir Hugh Ernest Griffiths, CBE (d 1961), by his w, Doris Eirene, da of W H James; *b* 26 Sept 1923; *Educ* Charterhouse, St John's Coll Camb (MA, Hon Fell 1985); *m* 1949, Evelyn, da of Col A F Krefting; 1 s; 3 da; *Career* 1939-45 War as Capt WG; barr Inner Temple 1949, QC 1964; judge: High Ct of Justice (Queen's Bench Div) 1970-80, Nat Industl Relations Ct 1973-74; memb Advsy Cncl on Penal Reform 1967-70, chm Tbnl of Inquiry on Ronan Point 1968, vice-chm Parole Bd 1976-77, memb Chancellor's Law Reform Ctee 1976-, pres Senate of Inns of Court and the Bar 1982-; a lord justice of appeal 1980-85, a lord of appeal in ordinary 1985-; chm Security Cmmn 1985-; hon memb Canadian Bar Assoc 1981; hon fell: American Inst of Judicial Admin 1985 American Coll of Trail Lawyers 1988; hon LLD Wales 1987; kt 1971; *Clubs* Garrick, MCC; *Style*— The Rt Hon Lord Griffiths, MC, PC; c/o House of Lords, London SW1

GRIFFITHS, Winston James (Win); MP (Lab) Bridgend 1987-; MEP (Lab) S Wales 1979-; *b* 1943,Feb; *m* Elizabeth Ceri, *née* Gravell; 1 s, 1 da; *Career* teacher; *Style*— Win Griffiths, Esq, MEP; Tny Llon, John St, Y Graig, Cefn Cribwr, Mid Glam CF32 0AB

GRIFFITS, Peter Kinloch; s of Kinloch Griffits (d 1976), of Kidbrooke Lodge, Forest Row, and Christine, *née* Parratt (d 1981); *b* 27 Feb 1918; *Educ* City of London Sch, Open Univ (BA); *Career* served HM Forces WWII; chartered insurer; reader in the Anglican Communion; dep Area Plans North Planning Ctee Wealdon DC, chm Forest Row PC, pres Forest Row Scout Assoc, chm Forest Row Cons Assoc, pres League of Friends Queen Victoria Hosp, ed Forest Row Parish News, chm Forest Row Br Legion; FCII, Fell Victoria Coll of Music; *Recreations* dramatic art, golf; *Clubs* English Speaking Union; *Style*— Peter Griffits, Esq; Kidbrooke Lodge, Forest Row, E Sussex

GRIGG, Hon Anthony Ulick David Dundas; yr s of 1 Baron Altrincham, KCMG, KCVO, DSO, MC, PC (d 1955), and hp to Barony of bro, John Edward Poynder Grigg, *qv* (2 Baron, who disclaimed Peerage for life 1963); *b* 12 Jan 1934; *Educ* Eton, New Coll Oxford; *m* 1965, Eliane de Cassagne de Beaufort, da of the Marquis de Miramon; 2 s (Sebastian b 1965, Steven b 1969), 1 da (Casilda b 1967); *Career* late 2 Lt Grenadier Gds; *Style*— The Hon Anthony Grigg; 11 Horbury Mews, London W11 3NL (☎ 01 229 6005)

GRIGG, John Edward Poynder; s of 1 Baron Altrincham, KCMG, KCVO, DSO, MC, PC (d 1955), and Hon Joan Dickson-Poynder, da of 1 Baron Islington; disclaimed Barony for life 1963; *b* 15 April 1924; *Educ* Eton, New Coll Oxford; *m* 1958, Patricia, da of Harold Campbell, of Co Down; *Heir* bro, Hon Anthony Grigg; *Career* serv WWII, Lt Grenadier Gds; party candidate (C) Oldham W 1951 and 1955, with The Guardian 1960-70, pres Greenwich Cons Assoc to 1982 when joined SDP; journalist; ed National and English Review 1954-60; FRSL; *Books* Two Anglican Essays, The Young Lloyd George, Lloyd George: the People's Champion (Whitbread Award, 1943), 1943: The Victory That Never Was, Nancy Astor: Portrait of a Pioneer, Lloyd George: From Peace to War (Wolfson Award); *Style*— John Grigg, Esq; 32 Dartmouth Row, London SE10 (☎ 01 692 4973)

GRIGGS, (Frank) Douglas; s of Maj Frank Robertson Griggs, JP (d 1956), of Wirksworth, Derbyshire, and Katharine Emily Joan Griggs, *née* Legge (d 1951); *b* 11 Sept 1904; *Educ* Repton, Jesus Coll Cambridge (MA); *Career* timber importer Joseph Griggs & Co Ltd: dir 1939-69, chm 1970-83;; *Clubs* Leander, Henley-on-Thames; *Style*— Douglas Griggs, Esq; c/o Lloyd's Bank plc, Montpellier, Cheltenham, Glos GL50 1SH

GRIGGS, The Rt Rev Ian Macdonald; s of Donald Nicholason Griggs (d 1967), of Thaxted, Essex, and Agnes Elizabeth, *née* Brown; *b* 17 May 1928; *Educ* Brentwood Sch, Trinity Hall Cambridge (BA, MA), Westcott House Cambridge; *m* 29 Aug 1953, Patricia Margaret, da of Ernest Charles Medland Vernon-Browne (d 1974), of Lindfield, Sussex; 3 s (Alistair b 1954, Mark b and d 1957, Julian b 1964), 3 da (Clare b 1956, Helen b 1959, Hilary b 1962); *Career* Lt Essex Regt 1947-49; ordained deacon 1954, priest 1955; asst curate St Cuthbert, Portsmouth 1954-59; domestic chaplain Bp of Sheffield 1959-64; diocesan youth chaplain, Sheffield 1959-64; vicar of St Cuthbert, Firvale, Sheffield 1964-71; vicar of Kidderminster 1971-83; hon canon Worcs 1977-84; archdeacon of Ludlow 1984-87; suffragan bishop of Ludlow 1987-; *Recreations* mountaineering, hill-walking; *Clubs* Lansdowne; *Style*— The Rt Rev Ian Griggs; Bishop's House, Halford, Craven Arms, Shropshire SY7 9BT (☎ 0588 673571)

GRIGGS, Jeremy David; s of Celadon Augustine Griggs, of Elm Tree Farm, East Brent, Highbridge, Somerset, and Ethel Mary, *née* Anderson; *b* 5 Feb 1945; *Educ* St Edward's Sch Oxford, Magdalene Coll Cambridge (MA); *m* 1, 1971 (m dis 1982), Wendy Anne Russell, *née* Culham; 2 s (Christopher b 1972, Tom b 1974), 1 da (Beth b 1976); m 2, 7 Sept 1985, Patricia Ann (the actress Patricia Maynard) da of Thomas Maynard, of Southfields, London SW19; 2 step da (Hannah Waterman b 1975, Julia Waterman b 1979); *Career* barr Inner Temple 1968, memb Western circuit, asst rec 1985-, Bar's alternate rep CCBE 1983-; chm London Choral Soc 1986-; *Recreations* choral singing, birdwatching, photography; *Clubs* Groucho's; *Style*— Jeremy Griggs, Esq; the Old Vicarage, South Walsham, Nr Norwich, Norfolk NR13 6DQ (☎ 060 549 522); 24 Cholmeley Lodge, Cholmeley Park, Highgate, London N6 (☎ 01 340 2241); Lamb Bldg Temple, London EC4Y 7AS (☎ 01 353 6381, fax 01 583 1786)

GRIGGS, Patrick John Spear; s of John Garson Romeril Griggs (d 1987), of Jersey, CI, and Inez Frances, *née* Cole; *b* 9 August 1939; *Educ* Stowe, Tours Univ France, Law Soc Sch of Law London; *m* 4 April 1964, Marian Patricia, da of John Pryor Birch, of Mere, Wils; 3 s (Simon Richard b 1967, Edward John b 1969, William Robert b 1972); *Career* slr 1963; joined Ince and Co 1958: ptnr 1966, sr ptnr 1989; Stanford Rivers Parish Cncllr; Freeman City of London; *Books* Limitation of Liability for Maritime Claims (jtly, 1987); *Recreations* tennis, skiing, walking, cycling, hockey; *Clubs* Gresham; *Style*— Patrick Griggs, Esq; Ince & Co, Knollys Ho, 11 Byward St, London EC3 (☎ 01 623 2011, fax 01 623 3225, telex 8955043)

GRIGGS, Roy; s of Norman Edward Griggs, CBE, of 5 Gledhow Gardens London SW5, and Livia Lavinia, *née* Levi; *b* 26 April 1950; *Educ* Westminster, Bristol Univ (LLB); *m* 4 Jan 1975, Anita Gwendolyn, da of Humphrey Osmond Nunes (d 1972); 3 da (Flavia b 1979, Eleanor b 1982, Cordelia b 1986); *Career* slr: Norton Rose Botterell and Roche 1975-84 (seconded to Hong Kong off 1981-83), Cameron Markby 1984- (ptnr 1985); memb City of London Slr's Co; memb Law Soc; *Recreations* bridge, sailing, opera, skiing; *Clubs* Itchenor SC; *Style*— Roy Griggs, Esq; 230 Hammersmith Gr, London W6 (☎ 01 749 2532); Sceptre Crt, 40 Tower Hill, London EC3 (☎ 01 702 2345, fax 01 702 2303)

GRIGSON, Dr Caroline (Mrs Colin Banks); da of Geoffrey Edward Harvey Grigson (d 1985), of Broadtown, Wiltshire, and Frances Franklin, *née* Galt (d 1937); *b* 7 Mar 1935; *Educ* Dartington Hall Sch, UCL (BSc), Inst of Archaeology London (PhD); *m* 18 Sept 1961, Colin Harold Banks, s of William James Banks (d 1985), of Faversham, Kent; 1 s (Joseph Caxton b 1967), 1 da (Frances Jenny Harriet b 1964, d 1978); *Career* archaeozoologist; asst curator Odontologica Museum RCS 1973-87, Osman Hill curator 1987-; author of numerous scientific papers incl many on animal remains from archaeological sites in Br and the Near E; fndr memb cncl of the Int Cncl for Archaeozoology (ICAZ), former memb cncl Br Sch in Jerusalem; memb: cncl Br Inst in Amman, CBA Sci Ctee; co-organiser Fourth Int Conf in Archaeozoology Univ of London 1982, organizer Aims in Archaeology London Univ Inst of Archaeology 1985; former govr Kidbrooke Comprehensive Sch; FSA 1982; memb Prehistoric Soc, Quaternary Res Assoc, Assoc for Environmental Archaeology (AEA), Museums Assoc; *Books* co-ed: Ageing and Sexing Animal Bones from Archaeological Sites (1982), Animals and Archaeology (4 vols, 1983 & 1984); Colyer's Variations and Diseases of the Teeth of Animals (co-author, 1989); *Recreations* excavation, travelling, gardening; *Style*— Dr Caroline Grigson; Odontological Museum, Royal College of Surgeons, 35-43 Lincoln's Inn Fields, London WC2A 3PN (☎ 01 405 3474 ext 3020, fax 01 831 9438)

GRIGSON, Jane; *née* McIntire; da of George Shipley McIntire, CBE, of Wroughton, Swindon, Wilts, and Doris Mabel Frampton *née* Berkley (d 1988); *b* 13 Mar 1928; *Educ* Casterton Sch, Newnham Coll Cambridge (BA); 1 da (Sophie b 19 June 1959); m 11 March 1976, Geoffrey Edward Harvey Grigson, s of Canon William Shuckforth Grigson; *Career* cookery corr Observer Magazine 1968-; memb: Save Our Skyline, Avebury in Distress (supporter and contrib to preservation of Avebury); *Books* Of Crimes and Punishments (by Cesare Beccaria, translated 1964), Charcuterie and French Pork Cookery (1967), Good Things (1971), Fish Cookery (1973), The Mushroom Feast (1975), English Food (second edn 1977), Jane Grigson's Vegetable Book (1978), Jane Grigson's Fruit Book (1982); *Style*— Mrs Jane Grigson; Broad Town Farmhouse, Broad Town, Swindon, Wiltshire SN4 7RG (☎ 0793 732159); Trôo, 41800 Montoire-sur-le-Loir, France (☎ 54 72 50 84)

GRILLER, Prof Sidney Aaron; CBE (1951); s of Salter Griller (d 1932), and Hannah, *née* Green (d 1963); *b* 10 Jan 1911; *Educ* London Co Sch, RAM; *m* 16 Dec 1932, Honor Elizabeth, da of James Linton, JP (d 1953); 1 s (Patrick Arnold), 1 da (Catherine Henry); *Career* Sgt RAF, 1940-45; ldr Griller String Quarte 1924-63, lectr in music Univ of California Berkley 1950-63, head of string dept Royal Irish Acad of Music 1963-73, dir of chamber music RAM 1964-86, several world tours, tutor Menuhin Sch 1986-88; composed 20 string quartets dedicated to the Griller Quartet; Hon Dr York Univ; *Style*— Prof Sidney Griller, Esq, CBE; (☎ 01 937 7067)

GRILLS, Michael Geoffrey; *b* 23 Feb 1937; *Educ* Royal GS Lancaster, Merton Coll Oxford (MA); *m* 1969, Ann Margaret Irene; 2 da (Alison, Victoria); *Career* ptnr Crombies, slr York 1965-73, dist registrar York & Harrogate 1973-; rec of Crown Ct on NE circuit 1982-; *Recreations* tennis, music; *Style—* Michael Grills, Esq; Cobblestones, Skelton, York YO3 6XX (☎ 0904 470246)

GRIMA, Andrew Peter; s of John Grima (d 1946), and Leopolda, *née* Farnese (descendant of Pope Paul III); *b* 31 May 1921; *Educ* St Joseph's Coll Beulah Hill London, Nottingham Univ; *m* 1977, Joanne Jill, da of Capt Nigel Maugham-Brown, MC (d 1970); 1 s, 3 da; *Career* served WW II Burma (despatches); chm Andrew Grima Ltd; jewellery designer to HM The Queen; Liveryman Worshipful Co Goldsmiths, Freeman City of London; Duke of Edinburgh Prize for Elegant Design 1966, Queen's Award for Export 1966, 11 Diamond Int Prizes New York; *Recreations* squash, tennis, cooking; *Clubs* RAC; *Style—* Andrew Grima, Esq; c/o Royal Automobile Club, 89-91 Pall Mall, London SW1

GRIMA, George Peter; s of John Grima (d 1945), and Leopolda, *née* Farnese (d 1984); *b* 31 July 1929; *Educ* St Joseph's Coll Beulah Hill, Northern Poly London (Dip Arch); *m* 14 Dec 1978, Christina Mary, da of Col Leslie Wright TD, DL, of Bakewell, Derbyshire; *Career* Nat Serv RE 1955-57; ptnr with bro Godfrey in 'Grima' 1962-78, work inc: commercial centre Pomezia Rome 1970, ski resort Grimentz Val d'Anniviers Valais Switzerland 1972, jewellery shops for bro Andrew, London, Zurich, Sydney, worked with Raymond Erith on re-construction of 10, 11 and 12 Downing St 1960; Royal Acad exhibitor 1960; ARIBA; *Recreations* gardening, antiquarian books, skiing, tennis; *Style—* George Grima, Esq; 33 Watery Lane, Sherbourne, Warwick CV35 8AL (☎ 0926 624 794);

GRIME, Geoffrey John; s of Sqdn Ldr John Frederic Grime, DFC, of Blackpool, Lancs, and José Thompson, *née* Bennett; *b* 7 Feb 1947; *Educ* Sedbergh; *m* 19 June 1971, Margaret Joyce, da of Stanley Hamilton Russell, of St Helier Jersey; 1 s (Charles b 1975), 1 da (Caroline b 1973); *Career* CA 1969, joined Coopers & Lybrand 1969 (ptnr 1972-); hon tres: Br Heart Fndn Jersey until 1987, Jersey Arts Cncl until 1985, Jersey Church Schs Soc 1987-; Freeman City of London 1975, Worshipful Co of Musicians 1977; FCA 1969; *Recreations* veteran and vintage cars; *Clubs* Brooks's, Victoria (Jersey), United (Jersey) Muthaiga (Nairobi); *Style—* Geoffrey Grime, Esq; Pine Farm, Rue Du Douet, St Mary, Jersey, Channel Islands (☎ 0534 63840); LA Motte Chambers, St Helier Jersey, Channel Islands (☎ 0534 76777, fax 0534 78358, telex 4192231)

GRIME, Mark Stephen Eastburn; QC (1987); s of Roland Thompson, of Wilmslow, and Mary Diana, *née* Eastburn; *b* 16 Mar 1948; *Educ* Wrekin Coll, Trinity Coll Oxford (MA); *m* 29 July 1973, Christine, da of J H A Emck, of West Wittering, Sussex; 2 da (Eleanor b 1977, Isabel b 1981); *Career* barr Middle Temple 1970, Northern circuit 1970-, asst rec 1988-; chm Disciplinary Appeal Tbnl UMIST 1980-; *Recreations* antiquarian horology, sailing; *Style—* Stephen Grime, Esq, QC; Windlehurst Cottage, 147 Windlehurst Road, High Lane, Stockport, Cheshire SK6 8AG (☎ 061 427 2062); Deans Court Chambers, Cumberland House, Crown Square, Manchester M3 3HA (☎ 061 834 4097, fax 061 834 4805)

GRIMKE-DRAYTON, Lancelot Whishaw; s of Norman Drayton Grimke-Drayton (d 1962), of Cotleigh, Devon, and Audrey, *née* Whishaw; *b* 29 Sept 1923; *Educ* Merchant Taylors' St John's Coll Oxford (BA); *m* 1, 27 July 1946, Nancy Muriel, da of John M Hooper (d 1927), of Streatham; 2 s (William Whishaw b 1948, James Whishaw b 1950), 1 da (Joanna Mary b 1957); m 2, 27 Dec 1977, Roseanne Faith, da of Roland Fairbrass Richardson (d 1950), of Melbourne, Aust; *Career* personnel mangr ICI plc, ret 1982; *Recreations* fishing, golf; *Style—* Lancelot Grimke-Drayton, Esq; Lower Hampton, Malpas, Cheshire SY14 8EA (☎ 094 885 316)

GRIMLEY, Martyn Andrew; s of Ivor Trewartha Grimley, of Sale, Cheshire, and Shirley Elizabeth, *née* Vaughan; *b* 24 Jan 1963; *Educ* Sale GS, South Trafford Coll of Further Educn, Crewe & Alsager Coll of Higher Educn (BEd); *Career* teacher Banbury HS 1985, schmaster Dulwich Coll 1986-; England Hockey player; Champions Trophy Tournament 1985-88, Silver Medallist World Cup London 1986, Silver Medallist Euro Cup Moscow 1987, Gold Medallist Olympic Games Seoul 1988; *Recreations* reading, water sports, walking; *Style—* Martyn Grimley, Esq; Dulwich College, College Rd, Dulwich, London SE21 7LD (☎ 01 693 3601, fax 01 693 6319)

GRIMLEY EVANS, Prof John; s of Harry Walter Grimley Evans (d 1972), of Birmingham, and Violet Prenter, *née* Walker (d 1976); *b* 17 Sept 1936; *Educ* King Edward's Sch, St John's Coll Cambridge (MA, MD), Balliol Coll Oxford (MA, DM); *m* 25 March 1966, Corinne Jane, da of Leslie Bernard Cavender (d 1947), of Edenbridge; 2 s (Edmund, Piers), 1 da (Freya); *Career* res fell med unit Wellington NZ 1966-69, lectr London Sch of Hygiene and Tropical Med 1969-71, conslt physician Newcastle Health Authy 19 71-73, prof of med (geriatrics) Univ of Newcastle Upon Tyne 1973-84, prof of geriatric med Oxford Univ 1985- (fell Green Coll 1985-), ed Age and Ageing 1988-; memb Oxage Forum; FRSS 1970, FRCP 1976, FFCM 1980; *Books* Care of the Elderly (jtly, 1977), Advanced Geriatric Medicine (jtly, 1981-88); *Recreations* fly fishing, photography; *Clubs* RSM; *Style—* Prof John Grimley Evans; University Division of Geriatric Medicine, Radcliffe Infirmary, Oxford

GRIMOND, Hon Grizelda Jane; only da of Baron Grimond, PC, TD, by his w Laura, *née* Bonham Carter, *qqv*; *b* 1942; *Educ* St Paul's Girls' Sch, St Hugh's Coll Oxford; *Style—* The Hon Grizelda Grimond

GRIMOND, Baron (Life Peer UK 1983), of Firth, Co Orkney; Rt Hon Jo(seph); PC (1961), TD; s of Joseph Bowman Grimond, of St Andrew's, Fife, by his w, Helen Lydia Richardson; *b* 29 July 1913; *Educ* Eton, Balliol Coll Oxford (hon Fell 1984); *m* 1938, Hon Laura (*see* Grimond, Baroness); 2 s (and 1 s decd), 1 da; *Career* sits as Lib peer in House of Lords; served WWII: Maj, Fife and Forfar Yeo (despatches); barr Middle Temple 1937, contested (Lib) Shetland and Orkney 1945, personnel dir Euro Office UNRAA 1945-47, sec Nat Trust for Scotland 1947-49, MP (Lib) Orkney and Shetland 1950-83, chief Lib whip 1950, ldr of parly Lib Pty 1956-67; rector: Edinburgh Univ 1960-63, Aberdeen Univ 1969-72; tstee Manchester Guardian and Evening News Ltd 1967-83; chllr Kent Univ 1970-; ldr Parly Lib Pty May-July 1976; Chubb fellow Yale; Hon LLD: Edinburgh 1960, Aberdeen 1972, Birmingham; Hon DCL Kent 1970; Hon D Univ Stirling 1984; *Publications include* The Liberal Future (1959), The Common Welfare (1978), Memoirs (1979), A Personal Manifesto (1983); *Style—* The Rt Hon the Lord Grimond, PC, TD; Old Manse of Firth, Orkney (☎ 085 676 393)

GRIMOND, Hon John Jasper; er s of Baron Grimond, TD, PC, by his w, Laura, *née* Bonham Carter *qqv*; *b* 1946; *Educ* Eton, Balliol Coll Oxford, Harvard Univ (Nieman Fellow); *m* 1973, Kate, er da of Lt-Col Peter Fleming, OBE (d 1971), of Nettlebed, Henley-on-Thames; 3 da (Mary Jessie b 1976, Rose Clementine b 1979, Georgia Celia b 1983); *Career* The Economist: joined 1969, asst ed 1975-, Br ed 1976-79, American ed 1979-88, foreign ed 1989-; Harkness Fell 1974-75; *Books* The Economist Pocket Style Book (ed); *Style—* The Hon John Grimond; 49 Lansdowne Road, London W11 2LG

GRIMOND, Baroness; Hon Laura Miranda; da of Sir Maurice Bonham Carter, KCB, KCVO, by his w, Baroness Asquith of Yarnbury, DBE (d 1969, who was Lady Violet Bonham Carter, da of 1 Earl of Oxford and Asquith, KG, PC, by his 1 w; the Earl was formerly Lib PM 1908-16); *b* 13 Oct 1918; *m* 1938, Baron Grimond, *qv*; 2 s, 1 da (and 1 s decd); *Style—* The Rt Hon the Lady Grimond; 24 Priory Avenue, London W4 1TY; The Old Manse of Firth, Kirkwall, Orkney

GRIMOND, Hon Thomas Magnus; 2 and youngest s of Baron Grimond, PC, TD, and Laura Miranda, *née* Bonham Carter, *qqv*, of The Old Manse of Firth, Kirkwall, Orkney; *b* 13 June 1959; *Educ* Stromness Academy, Edinburgh Univ; *Career* journalist; *Recreations* mending things; *Style—* The Hon Thomas Grimond; c/o Investors Chronicle, Greystoke Place, Fetter Lane, London EC4A 1ND

GRIMSBY, Bishop of 1979-; Rt Rev David Tustin; s of John Trevelyan Tustin (d 1983), and Janet Reynolds, *née* Orton; *b* 12 Jan 1935; *Educ* Solihull Sch Magdalene Coll Cambridge (MA), Univ of Geneva; *m* 15 Aug 1964, Mary Elizabeth, da of Rev Prebendary John Moreton Glover (d 1979, Prebendary of Hereford Cathedral); 1 s (Nicholas b 1969), 1 da (Juliet b 1971); *Career* curate of Stafford 1960-63, asst gen sec C of E Cncl on Foreign Rels 1963-67; vicar: Wednesbury St Paul 1967-71, Tettenhall Regis 1971-79; rural dean of Trysull 1976-79, Bishop of Grimsby 1979; pres Anglican-Lutheran Soc, co-chm Anglican-Lutheran Int Continuation Ctee; *Recreations* travel, music, European languages; *Style—* The Rt Rev the Bishop of Grimsby; 43 Abbey Park Rd, Grimsby, S Humberside DN32 0HS (☎ 0472 358223)

GRIMSHAW, Maj Gen (Ewing) Henry Wrigley; CB (1965), CBE (1957, OBE 1954), DSO (1945); s of Lt-Col Ewing Wrigley Grimshaw (d 1916), and Geraldine Grimshaw; *b* 30 June 1911; *Educ* Brighton Coll, RMC Sandhurst; *m* 1943, Hilda Florence Agnes, da of Dr Allison (d 1942), of Coleraine, NI; 2 s (Ewing, Roland), 1 da (Hilary); *Career* joined Indian Army 1931, served war 1939-45, Western Desert, Burma, (despatches twice), transferred to The Royal Inniskilling Fus 1947, active service Malaya, Kenya, Cyprus, Suez (1956), GOC 44 Div (TA) and home counties dist 1962-65, Col The Royal Inniskilling Fus 1966-68, dep Col The Royal Irish Rangers 1968-73; *Style—* Maj-Gen Henry Grimshaw, CB, CBE, DSO; The Trellis Ho, Copford Green, Colchester CO6 1BZ

GRIMSHAW, Nicholas Thomas; s of Thomas Cecil Grimshaw, (d 1942), and Hannah Joan, *née* Dearsley; *b* 9 Oct 1939; *Educ* Wellington Coll Berkshire, Edinburgh Coll of Art, Architectural Assoc Sch (Dip AA); *m* 20 Oct 1972, Lavinia, da of John Russell, CBE, of New York; 2 da (Chloe b 1973, Isabel b 1977); *Career* chm Nicholas Grimshaw & Ptnrs Ltd Architects and industl designers; major projects incl: Channel Tunnel terminal for Br Waterloo, Camden Superstore for J Sainsbury HQ for BMW Bracknell, factory for Herman Miller Bath, Oxford Ice Rink, Gillingham Business Park for Grosvenor Devpts res centre for Rank Xerox, printing plant for Fin Times, ; major awards incl: RIBA Awards 1978 and 1980, Fin Times Award for Indusl Archtecture 1977, Structural Steel Design Awards 1969 and 1977, Civic Tst Award 1978, Architectural Design Award 1974, Business and Indust Award Certificate of Merit 1977, Euro Award for Steel Structure 1981; memb: AA 1965, RIBA 1967; FCSD 1969; *Books* Nicholas Grimshaw & Partners Ltd Product and Process; *Recreations* sailing, tennis, skiing; *Style—* Nicholas Grimshaw, Esq; Nicholas Grimshaw & Partners Ltd, 118-126 New Cavendish Street, London W1M 7FE (☎ 01 631 0869, fax 01 636 4866)

GRIMSHAW, Hon Mrs; Hon Shelagh Mary Margaret; *née* Milner; da of 1 Baron Milner, of Leeds, PC, MC, TD, (d 1967); *b* 1925; *m* 1948 (m dis 1965), Harry Barker Grimshaw; 1 s, 1 da; *Style—* The Hon Mrs Grimshaw; High Barn, Thorner, Yorks

GRIMSTON, Viscount; James Walter Grimston; s and h of 7 Earl of Verulam; *b* 6 Jan 1978; *Style—* Viscount Grimston

GRIMSTON, Hon (Cecil) Antony Sylvester; s of 1 Baron Grimston of Westbury (d 1979), and Sybil (d 1977), da of Sir Sigmund Neumann, 1 Bt; *b* 28 Feb 1927; *Educ* Eton, Magdalene Coll Cambridge (MA); *m* 1958, Dawn, da of Guy Janson, of Fair Hall, Southover, Lewes; 2 s; *Career* late Coldstream Gds; chartered surveyor, ptnr Strutt & Parker; FRSA, FRICS; *Recreations* shooting, sport; *Clubs* MCC, Naval & Military; *Style—* The Hon Antony Grimston; Wellingham Vane, nr Lewes, E Sussex (☎ Ringmer (0273) 812241)

GRIMSTON, Hon (Gerald) Charles Walter; 2 s of 2 Baron Grimston of Westbury and Hon June Ponsonby, da of 5 Baron de Mauley, JP; *b* 4 Sept 1953; *Educ* Eton, Exeter Univ; *m* 10 May 1980, Katherine Evelyn, da of Maj Rupert Berkeley Kettle, DL, of Leamington Spa; 1 s (Edward b 1985); 1 da (Lucy b 1982); *Career* Major Scots Gds 1973-83 (NI and Falklands); dir Grimston Scott Ltd 1985-; *Recreations* cricket, skiing, real tennis; *Clubs* Royal Automobile; *Style—* Maj the Hon Charles Grimston; c/o Midland Bank, 69 Pall Mall, SW1

GRIMSTON, Hon Michael John Harbottle; yst s of 1 Baron Grimston of Westbury (d 1979); *b* 5 Jan 1932; *Educ* Eton; *m* 1957 (m dis 1978), Julia Mary, 3 da of Sir George Werner Albu, 2 Bt; 2 s, 2 da; *Clubs* Turf; *Style—* Hon Michael Grimston; Penny Hill, Bryanston, S Africa

GRIMSTON, Neil Alexander; TD (1982); s of Flt Lt Victor Gordon Manners Grimston (d 1966), and Adeline Jean Margaret Esson; *b* 8 Sept 1947; *m* 19 July 1975, Berylanne, da of David McNaught, of Thames Ditton, Surrey; 1 s (Alexander b 1979), 1 da (Henrietta b 1984); *Career* Private HAC 1970 (vet memb 1971-), cmmnd 2 Lt TA RCT 1971, Lt 1972, Capt 1976, cmd indep unit with BAOR 1977-82, Capt RARO 1983-; with Hill Samuel 1967-70, discount broker Smith St Aubyn 1970-73, discount broker Page and Gwyther Gp 1973-77: Chemical Bank 1977-; vice pres and mangr world insur gp (Asia) 1982-84, head city ints gp 1985-87, dir Chemical Bank trustee Co 1987-88, vice pres (responsible for UK and Benelux Banks and Financial Insts) 1987-; memb cncl London Borough of Richmond Upon Thames 1971-74; vice-chm Twickenham Cons Assoc 1969-71, memb Lombard Assoc (city of London); Freeman City of London 1971, Liveryman Worshipful Co of Scriveners 1974; *Recreations* collecting prints, oriental rugs, wine drinking, photography; *Clubs* City Livery, Overseas Bankers, Singapore Cricket; *Style—* Neil A Grimston, Esq, TD; Willow, 29 D'Abernon Drive, Stoke D'Abernon, Cobham, Surrey KT11 3JE a(☎ 0932 64973);

Chemical Bank House, 180 Strand, London WC2R 1EX (☎ 01 380 5240, fax 01 380 5928, telex 264766)

GRIMSTON, Hon Robert (Robin) John Sylvester; er s and h of 2 Baron Robert Walter Sigismund (Lord Grimston of Westbury), The Old Rectory, Westwell, Burford, Oxfordshire, and June Mary, *née* Ponsonby; *b* 30 April 1951; *Educ* Eton, Reading Univ (BSc); *m* 1984, Emily Margaret, da of Maj John Evelyn Shirley, of Ormly Hall, Ramsey, IOM; *Career* Capt Royal Hussars (PWO) 1970-81; CA: Binder Hamlyn, Citicorp Scrimgeour Vickers Ltd; *Clubs* Cavalry and Guards; *Style*— The Hon Robin Grimston; 51 Alderbrook Rd, London SW12 8AD (☎ 01 673 4293)

GRIMSTON OF WESTBURY, 2 Baron (UK 1964); Sir Robert Walter Sigismund Grimston; 2 Bt (UK 1952); s of 1 Baron Grimston of Westbury, (d 1979, er s of Canon Hon Robert Grimston, 3 s of 2 Earl of Verulam), by his w Sybil (d 1977), da of Sir Sigmund Neumann, 1 Bt (later anglicised to Newman); *b* 14 June 1925; *Educ* Eton; *m* 21 June 1949, Hon June Mary Ponsonby, er da of 5 Baron de Mauley; 2 s, 1 da; *Heir* s, Hon Robert Grimston; *Career* former Lt Scots Gds, WWII served NW Europe; formerly in oil and publishing, Hinton Hill & Coles Agencies Ltd (now Stewart Gray's Inn Underwriting Agency Ltd) 1962-; dir: Hinton Hill & Coles 1962-83, Stewart Hughman Ltd 1983-86, River Clyde Hldgs Ltd 1986-88; chm Gray's Inn (Underwriting Agency) Ltd 1970-87; Freeman City of London, Liveryman Worshipful Co of Gold and Silver Wyre Drawers; *Clubs* Boodle's, City of London; *Style*— The Rt Hon the Lord Grimston of Westbury; The Old Rectory, Westwell, Burford, Oxon OX8 4JJ; Gray's Inn (Underwriting Agency) Ltd; 5 Devonshire Sq, Cutlers Gardens, London EC2M 4YD

GRIMSTONE, Gerald Edgar; s of Edgar Wilfred Grimstone (d 1986), and Dorothy Yvonne, *née* Martin; *b* 27 August 1949; *Educ* Whitgift Sch, Merton Coll Oxford (MA, MSc); *m* 23 June 1973, The Hon Janet Elizabeth Gudrun, da of 2 Baron Grantchester, CBE, QC; 1 s (Toby b 1975), 2 da (Jenny b 1979, Anna b 1982); *Career* Civil Serv 1972-86 latterly asst sec HM Treasy, dir J Henry Schroder Wagg & Co Ltd 1986; dep chm Wimbledon House Residents Assoc 1986-88; *Recreations* shooting, skiing, children; *Clubs* Athenaeum; *Style*— Gerald Grimstone, Esq; 103 Home Park Rd, London SW19 7HT (☎ 01 946 9402); J Henry Schroder Wagg & Co Ltd, 120 Cheapside, London EC2V 6DS (☎ 01 382 6000)

GRIMSTONE, Hon (Janet Elizabeth Gudrun); *née* Suenson-Taylor; da of Kenneth Bent Suenson-Taylor, 2 Baron Grantchester, CBE, QC, of Kingston, Surrey; *b* 26 June 1949; *Educ* Cheltenham Ladies Coll, St Hilda's Coll Oxford (MA); *m* 1973, Gerald Edgar Grimstone, s of Edgar Wilfred Grimstone, of Sanderstead (d 1986); 1 s (Toby b 1975), 2 da (Jenny b 1979, Anna b 1982); *Career* conservator of paintings; *Recreations* fishing, skiing; *Style*— The Hon Mrs Grimstone; 103 Home Park Rd, London SW19 7HT (☎ 01 946 9402)

GRIMTHORPE, Dowager Baroness; Angela; da of Edward Courage; *b* 6 Oct 1901; *m* 1945, as his 2 w, 3 Baron Grimthorpe, TD (d 1963); 1 s (Hon William Beckett, *qv*); *Style*— The Rt Hon Dowager Lady Grimthorpe; Cross House, Ampleforth, N Yorks

GRIMTHORPE, 4 Baron (UK 1886); Sir Christopher John Beckett; 8 Bt (UK 1813), OBE (1958), DL (N Yorks, formerly E Riding, 1969), patron of 1 living; s of 3 Baron, TD (d 1963), by his 1 w Mary; through his gf's sis, Maud, Lord Grimthorpe is 2 cous of 22 Baron Hastings; *b* 16 Sept 1915; *Educ* Eton; *m* 1954, Lady Elizabeth, CVO, *née* Lumley, da of 11 Earl of Scarbrough (*see* Grimthorpe, Baroness); 2 s, 1 da; *Heir* s, Hon Edward Beckett; *Career* Brig (ret) 9 Queen's Royal Lancers, Lt Col cmdg 1955-58, Col 9/12 Lancers 1973-77; Brig RAC HQ W Cmmd 1961-64, Dep Cdr Malta & Libya 1964-67; ADC to HM The Queen 1964-68; dir: Standard Bdcasting Corpn Canada (UK) Ltd 1972-83, Thirsk Racecourse Ltd 1972-, Yorkshire Post Newspapers 1973-85; *Clubs* Cavalry & Guards, Jockey; *Style*— The Rt Hon Lord Grimthorpe, OBE, DL; Westow Hall, York (☎ 065 381 225); 87 Dorset House, Gloucester Place, NW1 (☎ 01 486 4374)

GRIMTHORPE, Baroness; Lady Elizabeth; *née* Lumley; CVO (1983); da of the late 11 Earl of Scarbrough, KG, GCSI, GCIE, GCVO, PC, TD, and Katharine, *née* McEwen, DCVO; *b* 22 July 1925; *m* 1954, 4 Baron Grimthorpe, *qv*; 2 s, 1 da; *Career* appointed lady of the bedchamber to HM Queen Elizabeth The Queen Mother 1973; *Style*— The Rt Hon the Lady Grimthorpe, CVO; Westow Hall, York (☎ 065 381 225)

GRIMWADE, Sir Andrew Sheppard; CBE (1977); s of Frederick Sheppard Grimwade (d 1950), and Gwendolen Ada, *née* Carnegie; *b* 26 Nov 1930; *Educ* Melbourne C of E GS, Melbourne Univ (BSc), Oxford Univ (MA); *m* 1959, Barbara Gaerloch, da of John Bayley Darvall Kater; 1 s (Angus b 1968); *Career* chm: Aust Consolidated Industs Ltd 1977-82, Aust Arts Exhibition Corp 1976-77, Aust Govt Official Estabs Tst 1979-82, Victorian Govt Arts City Ctee 1985; md Carba Industs Ltd 1960-70, dept chm Art Fndn of Victoria; dir: Nat Aust Bank Ltd 1965-85, Pilkington ACI Ltd 1977-83, Alex Harvey Industs Ltd (NZ) 1977-83, ACI Int Ltd 1982-85, Cwlth Industl Gases Ltd, IBM Aust Ltd, Kemtron Ltd (chm), Nat Mutual Life Assoc of Aust Ltd, Nat Mutual Royal Bank Ltd, Sony (Aust) Pty Ltd; pres: Nat Gallery of Victoria 1976-, Walter of Eliza Hall Inst of Med Res 1978-; dep pres Australiana Fund 1978-82, memb: Aust Govt First Trade Mission to China 1973, Aust Govt Remuneration Tbnl 1974-82, Cncl for the Order of Aust, Felton Bequests' Ctee; tstee Victorian Arts Centre Tst; kt 1980; *Recreations* ski-ing, Autralian art, Santa Gertrudis Stud Cattle Breeding; *Clubs* Ski Club of Aust, Peninsular Golf, Royal Sydney GC (Melbourne); *Style*— Sir Andrew Grimwade, CBE; 8 Cole Court, Toorak, Victoria, Australia 3142; office: 500 Bourke St, Melbourne, Victoria, Australia 3000

GRIMWOOD, Nigel Manning; s of Maj Basil Joseph Grimwood, of Westhampnett, Sussex, and Kitty Nora, *née* Andrews (d 1986); *b* 10 Mar 1929; *Educ* King's Sch Ely, King's Coll London (LLB); *m* 3 Nov 1973, Diana Monica, da of Arthur Cecil Williams, of Surrey; 2 s (Toby b 1974, Hugo b 1985), 1 da (Lucy b 1976); *Career* slr 1952, personal asst to Sir Archibald Forbes 1956-58, ptnr Clifford-Turner 1958-71, dir of public cos 1971-86; ret to devote more time to charitable work, (particularly conservation); fndr with Dr Sir Norman Moore Bart the Countryside Renewal Tst 1986, fndr Ancient Tree Soc 1987; chm Edward Barnsley Workshop 1987; *Recreations* conservation; *Clubs* Travellers'; *Style*— Nigel Grimwood, Esq; Mayfield, Strettington, Chichester, W Sussex PO18 0LA (☎ 0243 773214)

GRINDON, Group Captain John Evelyn; CVO (1957), DSO (1945), AFC (1948); s of Thomas Edward Grindon (ka Ypres 1917), and Dora *née* Eastlake of Cornwall;; *b* 30 Sept 1917; *Educ* Dulwich, RAF Coll Cranwell; *Career* WWII 1939-45 Advanced Air Striking Force France BEF (no 150 sqdn), Bomber Cmd (Ft and Sqdn Cdr) No 5 Gp (nos 106, 630 and 617 sqdns) 1940-45, cmd The Queen's Flight 1953-56, Gp Capt 1956, ret 1959; dir/gen mangr in publishing/printing 1961-71; Met Police New Scotland Yard 1976-81; *Recreations* music, racing, ocean surf; *Clubs* RAF, Special Forces; *Style*— Gp Capt John Grindon CVO, DSO, AFC; Flat No 8, Ellis Gordon Ct, Newhaven, East Sussex BN9 9TB

GRINDROD, Most Rev John Basil Rowland; *see*: Brisbane, Archbishop of

GRINLING, Jasper Gibbons; CBE (1978); s of Lt-Col Anthony Gibbons Grinling, MBE, MC (d 1982), by his w Jean Dorothy Turing; *b* 29 Jan 1924; *Educ* Harrow, King's Coll Cambridge; *m* 1950, Gertrude Jane Moulsdale; 1 s, 2 da; *Career* served WWII 12 Lancers 1942-46, Capt; W & A Gilbey Ltd: joined 1947, dir 1952, md 1964; md IDV Ltd 1967; dir: N Br Distillery Co 1968-86, corporate affrs Grand Met Ltd 1981-85; trade relations Grand Met plc 1985-86; memb Cncl Scotch Whisky Assoc 1968-86, pres EEC Confedn des Industs Agricoles et Alimentaires 1976-80; The Apple and Pear Devpt Cncl 1986-; vineyard proprietor; Chev l'Ordre National du Mérite (France) 1983; FRSA, CBIM; *Books* The Annual Report (1987); *Recreations* gardening, jazz drumming, painting; *Style*— Jasper Grinling, Esq, CBE; 94D Kensington Church St, London W8 (☎ 01 221 5377); The Old Vicarage, Helions Bumpstead, nr Haverhill, Suffolk CB9 7AS (☎ 044 084 316)

GRINSTEAD, Sir Stanley Gordon; s of Ephraim Grinstead; *b* 17 June 1924; *Educ* Strodes Sch Egham; *m* 1955, Joyce Preston; 2 da; *Career* served WW II in RN; chm and gp chief exec Grand Met plc 1982-86 (dep chm 1980-82, md 1980-86, with Grand Met 1957-62 and 1964-86), dir Reed Int plc 1981-; tstee Fleet Air Arm Museum 1982-, Master Worshipful Co of Brewers' 1983-84; FCA, CBIM; kt 1986; *Recreations* gardening, cricket, racing, thoroughbred horse breeding; *Clubs* MCC, Surrey County Cricket; *Style*— Sir Stanley Grinstead; 18 Bolton Street, London W1Y 7PA

GRINSTED, William Angus; CBE (1960); s of John Grinsted; *b* 29 August 1904; *Educ* Annan Acad, Imperial Coll London; *m* 1942, Kathleen, da of Capt Alexander Mackenzie (d 1986); *Career* Sqdn Ldr RAFVR (E Africa) 1943-46; meteorologist, dep dir E Africa Met Serv 1934-51, dir West Indies Met Serv 1951-60; conslt: Decca Radar 1961-65, Plessey Co 1965-79; *Clubs* Royal Overseas League; *Style*— W A Grinsted, Esq, CBE; 92b High St, Lindfield, Haywards Heath, W Sussex RH16 2HP (☎ 044 47 4313)

GRINYER, Prof Peter Hugh; s of Sydney George Grinyer, of Foxton, Cambs, and Grace Elizabeth, *née* Formals (d 1988); *b* 3 Mar 1935; *Educ* East Ham GS, Balliol Coll Oxford (BA, MA), LSE (PhD); *m* 6 Sept 1958, Sylvia Joyce, da of William James Boraston, of Chadwell Heath, Essex; 2 s (Paul Andrew b 27 July 1961, Nigel James b 12 May 1964); *Career* sr mgmnt trainee Unilever Ltd 1957-59, personal asst to md (later mangr of prodn planning and stock control) E R Holloway Ltd 1959- 61, asst lectr (later lectr and sr lectr) Hendon Coll of Technol 1961-64, lectr (later sr lectr and reader) graduate business centre City Univ 1964-74, prof of business strategy City Univ Business Sch 1974-79; Univ of St Andrews: Esmee Fairbairn prof of econs 1979-85, vice princ 1985-87, actg princ 1986, actg chm dept of mgmnt 1987-; memb business and mgmnt studies sub-ctee UGC 1979-85; non- exec dir: John Brown plc 1984-86, Don & Low Holdgs (formerly Don Bros plc) 1985-, Ellis & Goldstein Hldgs plc 1987-88; fndr memb Glenrothes Enterprise Tst 1983-86; memb: Royal Econ Soc, Scottish Econ Soc, Acad of Mgmnt, MInstD; *Books* Corporate Models Today (with J Wooller, second edn 1978), From Private to Public (with G D Vaughan and S Birley 1977), Turnaround (with J C Spender, 1979), Sharpbenders (with D G Mayes and P McKiernan 1988); *Recreations* golf, mountain walking; *Clubs* Royal and Ancient GC; *Style*— Prof Peter Grinyer; Aberbrothock, 60 Buchanan Gdns, St Andrews, Fife KY16 9LX (☎ 0334 72966); University of St Andrews, Dept of Management, Kinnessburn, Kennedy Gdns, St Andrews, Fife KY16 9DJ (☎ 0334 76161)

GRISBROOKE, William Jardine; s of Joseph Henry Grisbrooke (d 1975), of Friern Barnet, Middx, and Lilian Maud, *née* Betts (d 1979); *b* 2 Feb 1932; *Educ* The Woodhouse Sch Finchley, Sidney Sussex Coll Cambridge (MA, BD); *m* 12 April 1955, Maureen, da of Albert Newton Tasker (d 1972), of Southport, Lancs; *Career* historian and theologian, res fell Inst for the Study of Worship & Religious Architecture Univ of Birmingham 1967-72, lectr in theol Univ of Birmingham 1972-83; lectr in liturgy: The Queen's Coll Birmingham 1972-80, St Mary's Coll Oscott Birmingham 1980-83; visiting lectr Pontifical Univ of Salamanca Spain 1974-80, visiting prof St George's Coll Jerusalem 1986-; FRHistS; *Publications* Anglican Liturgies of the Seventeenth and Eighteenth Centuries (1958), Spiritual Counsels of Father John of Kronstadt (1967, 1981); contributions to symposia: Dying, Death and Disposal (1970), A Dictionary of Liturgy and Worship (1972), The Oxford Dictionary of the Christian Church (1974), The Study of Liturgy (1978), A Dictionary of Christian Spirituality (1983), A New Dictionary of Liturgy and Worship (1986), Dizionario Patristico e di Antichità Cristiane (1985), The Unsealed Fountain: Essays in the Christian Spiritual Tradition (1987); many articles in journals and reviews; *Recreations* music, reading, winemaking, cooking, walking, archery; *Style*— W Jardine Grisbrooke, Esq; Jokers, Bailey St, Castle Acre, King's Lynn, Norfolk PE32 2AG

GRIST, Graham John; s of John Alfred Grist, and Oenone Florence Muriel Butler; *b* 25 Dec 1946; *Educ* Southgate GS Herts, Ch Ch Oxford (MA), London Business Sch (Sloan Fellow 1976); *m* 3 June 1970 (m dis 1984), Deirdre Penelope, da of Joseph Robert Williams, The Malt House, Upton on Severn, Worcestershire (d 1983); 1 s (Barnaby b 1972), 1 da (Natasha b 1975); *Career* IBM 1968-75, BICC 1977-80, fin dir Balfour Beatty Ltd 1981-86, dep chief exec Br Satellite Bdcasting Ltd 1987-; *Recreations* sailing, tennis, opera and music; *Clubs* United Oxford and Cambridge Univ; *Style*— Graham Grist, Esq; 49 Markham St, London SW3 3NR (☎ 01 351 1228); British Satellite Broadcasting Ltd, 70 Brompton Rd, London SW3 1EY (☎ 01 581 1166, fax 01 589 9479)

GRIST, Ian; MP (Cons) Cardiff Central 1983-; s of the late Basil William Grist, MBE, and the late Leila Helen; *b* 5 Dec 1938; *Educ* Repton, Jesus Coll Oxford; *m* 1966, Wendy Anne, JP, *née* White; 2 s; *Career* former plebiscite offr S Cameroons and stores mangr United Africa Co in Nigeria; info offr Wales Cons Central Office 1963-74, CRD 1970-74; MP (C) Cardiff N Feb 1974-83; chm Cons W Africa Ctee 1977-87, vice-chm Cons Clubs Assoc 1978-82, pps to Nicholas Edwards (sec of state Wales) 1979-81, parly under sec of state for Wales 1987-; *Style*— Ian Grist, Esq, MP; 126 Penylan Rd, Cardiff; House of Commons, London SW1

GRIST, Prof Norman Roy; s of Walter Reginald Grist (d 1970), of Rothbury, Northumberland, and Florence Goodwin, *née* Nadin (d 1983); *b* 9 Mar 1918; *Educ* Shawlands Acad Glasgow, Univ of Glasgow (BSc, MB ChB); *m* 27 Feb 1943, Mary Stewart, da of Alexander McAlister (d 1926), of Cupertino, California; *Career* Glasgow

Univ: lectr in virus diseases 1952-62, reader in viral epidemiology 1962-65, prof of infectious diseases 1965-83; regnl advsr in virology to Scottish Western Regnl Hosp Bd 1960-74, head regnl virus laboratory Ruchill Hosp Glasgow 1958-83; memb: expert advsy panel on virus diseases WHO 1967-, BRAB of DSAC; pres: Br Soc for the Study of Infection 1982-83, Soc for the Study of Infectious Diseases 1971-72; chm: advsy gp on epidemiological and other aspects of infection SHS Planning Cncl 1975-; memb: jt cmmn on vaccination and immunisation DHSS 1970-, Dangerous Pathogens Advsy Gp 1978-80; ctee memb Glasgow branch Scottish Ornithology Club 1984-, sec Glasgow Natural History Soc 1989- (cncl memb 1988-); MRCPEd 1950, FRCPEd 1958, MRCPath 1959, FRCPath 1967, MRCP (Glasgow) 1980, FRCP (Glasgow) 1983; memb: Soc Gen Microbiology, Assoc Clinical Pathology, Br Soc for the Study of Infection, Pathology Soc of GB and Ireland; Order Civ de Sanidad cat Encomienda Spain 1974, Bronze Medal Univ of Helsinki 1973; *Books* Diagnostic Methods in Clinical Virology (jtly, 3 edn 1979), Infections in Current Medical Practice (with Reid and Pinkerton, 1986), Diseases of Infection (jtly, 1988); *Recreations* music, natural history; *Clubs* Royal Scottish Automobile; *Style—* Prof Norman Grist; 5A Hyndland Ct, Glasgow G12 9NR (☎ 041 339 5242); Communicable Diseases Unit, Ruchill Hospital, Glasgow G20 9NB (☎ 041 946 7120, telex 041 946 7120)

GROBECKER, The Ven Geoffrey Frank; MBE (1959); s of Archibald Douglas Grobecker (d 1967), and Ethel Mary, *née* Lawrence (d 1955); *b* 25 Sept 1922; *Educ* St Paul's Sch, Queens' Coll Cambridge (MA), Ridley Hall Cambridge; *m* 1949, Audrey Kathleen, da of Sidney James Bessell (d 1961); 2 da (Anne b 1950, Heather b 1953); *Career* chaplain to the Forces 1952-77; sr chaplain RMA Sandhurst 1966-69; ACG 1972-77; hon chaplain to the Queen 1973-77; archdeacon of Lynn 1980-87; *Recreations* gardening, walking, bird-watching; *Clubs* Norfolk; *Style—* The Ven Geoffrey Grobecker, MBE; c/o Royal Bank of Scotland, 67 Lombard Street, London EC3P 3DL

GROBLER, Richard Victor; s of Harry Steyn Grobler (d 1970), and Edith Alice Grobler (d 1982); *b* 27 May 1936; *Educ* Diocesan Coll (Bishops) Cape Town, Univ of Cape Town (BA); *m* 1961, Julienne Nora Delacour, da of late Rev Canon Laurie Sheath; 1 s (Andrew b 1970), 3 da (Caroline b 1963, Rosemary b 1966, Elizabeth b 1975); *Career* barr Gray's Inn; dep clerk Centl Criminal Ct 1970-72, dep courts admin 1972-74; courts admin: Inner London Crown Ct 1974-77, Centl Criminal Ct 1977-79; dep circuit admin SE circuit 1979-84; dep sec of Cmmns Lord Chancellor's Dept 1984-; Liveryman Worshipful Co of Gold & Silver Wyre Drawers; *Recreations* gardening, swimming, golf; *Clubs* Temple Golf; *Style—* Richard Grobler, Esq; 26 Old Queen Street, London SW14 9HP (☎ 01 210 3479)

GROCHOLSKI, Count Alexander Luan; er s of Count Kazimierz Adam Grocholski, *qv*; *b* 30 August 1949; *Educ* French Lycée Lond, Study Centre for the History of the Fine and Decorative Arts London; *m* 1979, Bridget Caroline, da of Capt John Hamilton Fleming (d 1971); 1 da (Katherine Rose Mary b 1980); *Career* Phillips Son & Neale ceramics dept 1969-73; Sotheby's Valuation Dept 1973-78; Grocholski & Co Fine Art Valuers and Consultants 1978-; *Recreations* reading, walking, travel; *Clubs* Polish Hearth (London); *Style—* Count Alexander Grocholski; 287 Baalbec Road, London N5 1QN (☎ 01 226 8806)

GROCHOLSKI, Count Kazimierz Adam; yr s of Zdzislaw Henryk, Count Grocholski (d 1968), of Pietniczany and Poniatow (Poland), and Maria, *née* Countess Soltan; yr br and hp of Count Stanislas Gohdan Karol Grocholski, *qv*; *b* 21 Jan 1917; *Educ* Bielany Coll Warsaw Univ, LSE; *m* 1, 1946 (m dis 1969, annulled 1981), Elzbieta Zofia (d 1987), da of Count Jerzy Baworowski (d 1933); 2 s (Alexander, *qv* Jacek), 2 da (Ida, Thea); m 2, 15 March 1989, Madame Anna (Nita) Mueller, *née* Svertschkov; *Career* Pilot Offr Polish Air Force; external rels offr Union of Polish Craftsmen and Workers in GB; editorial sec Polish Emigre Weekly, programme asst BBC Polish Section; freelance journalist and writer; *Recreations* reading, music, theatre, travel, swimming; *Clubs* Polish Air Force, Polish Hearth; *Style—* Count Kazimir Grocholski; 111 The Ave, London W13 8JT (☎ 01 997 3560)

GROCHOLSKI, Count Stanislas Bohdan Karol; Head of the family;; s of Zdzislaw Henryk, Count Grocholski (d 1968), of Pietniczany and Poniatow, Poland, and Maria, *née* Countess Soltan (of an ancient Lithuanian-Ruthenian family of which Alexander Soltan, Treasurer and Court Marshal of the Gd Duchy of Lithuania, was a royal envoy to the courts of Europe in 15 cent); descendant of ancient Polish nobility of the Syrokomla clan known since 1347, who fought under their family banner at Grimwald against the Teutonic Knights in 1410, under the walls of Vienna against the Turks in 1683 and, after moving to Podolia in the 17 cent produce, among others, Martin, Palatine of Braclaw and Mikolaj, Govr of Podolia; gf Count Stanislaw Grocholski and his bro Count Tadeurz m Countesses Wanda and Zofia Zamoyska, while their sister Countess Maria m Prince Witold Czartoryski and as a widow entered the Carmelite Order; hereditary title of Count confirmed in Russia 1881; er br of Count Kazimierz Adam Grocholski, *qv*; *b* 4 Nov 1912; *Educ* Bielany Coll Warsaw Univ (MA), Warsaw Acad of Political and Social Studies; *m* 1980, Elisabeth Victoria Adelaide, da of Albert Edouard Jansenn (d 1966), Belgian Min of State, and wid of Count Thaddée Plater-Zyberk; *Heir* br, Count Kazimierz Adam Grocholski, *qv*; *Career* Offr Polish Forces, vice-consul Marseilles 1938-40, consul Dublin 1945-46, gen sec Fedn of Poles in Britain 1946-51, vice-pres Anglo-Polish Soc 1955-, foreign affairs ed The Polish Daily 1959-74; chm Veritas Foundation 1965-, vice-chm and Polish rep The Euro Movement 1953-, vice-chm Euro Liaison Gp 1970-; memb Catholic Union of Gt Britain 1972-; *Recreations* riding, tennis, swimming, travel; *Clubs* Special Forces, POSK (London); *Style—* The Count Grocholski; 111 The Avenue, London W13 8JT; Château de Valduc, 5990 Hamme-Mille, Belgium

GROCOTT, Bruce Joseph; MP (Lab) The Wrekin 1987; s of Reginald Grocott; *b* 1 Nov 1940; *Educ* Leicester Univ, Manchester Univ; *m* 1965, Sally Barbara, nee Ridgway; 2 s; *Career* lectr in politics 1965-74, television journalist and prodr Central Television 1979-87; MP (Lab) Lichfield and Tamworth 1974-79 CPPS to Min for Local Govt Planning 1975-76, Min of Agric 1976-78), currently dep shadow leader of the House and dep campaigns co-ordinator; *Clubs* Trench Labour; *Style—* Bruce Grocott, MP; House of Commons, London SW1A 0AA

GROGONO, James Lyon; s of Dr Eric Bernard Grogono, and Clare Anderton, *née* Jolly, JP; *b* 5 July 1937; *Educ* Oundle, London Hosp Medical Coll London Univ (MB BS); *m* 21 April 1972, Catherine Margaret, da of Dr Richard Bertram Morton, of 6 Hawk's Road, Hailsham, E Sussex; 1 s (Angus b 1974), 2 da (Emma b 1973, Dorothy b 1981); *Career* conslt surgeon Wycombe Health Dist, surgical tutor Royal Coll of Surgns of England; author; chm windsurfing ctee Royal Yalchting Assoc, vice-chm multihull ctee Iant Yacht Racing Union; FRCS, LRCP, DCH; *Books* Hydrofoil Sailing (1972), Icarus: The Boat the Flies (1987); *Recreations* sailing, windsurfing, sculling, skiing, skating, tennis; *Clubs* Aldeburgh YC, Chiltern Med Soc; *Style—* James Grogono, Esq; The Garden House, Riverside, Marlow, Bucks (☎ 06284 4261)

GRONHAUG, Arnold Conrad; s of James Gronhaug, MBE (d 1951), and Beatrice May, *née* Guppy (d 1983); *b* 26 Mar 1921; *Educ* Barry GS, Cardiff Tech Coll (Dip Electrical Engrg); *m* 28 March 1945, Patricia Grace, da of Douglas Leslie Smith (d 1963), of Brighton; 2 da (Anne b 1946, Jennifer b 1952); *Career* RNVR Electrical Offr 1941-46; Air Miny Works Directorate 1946-63 (dep chief engrg (AMWD) RAF Germany 1960-63), Miny of Public Bldg and Works 1963-73 (JSSC 1964-65, superintending engr HQ 1967-71, dir Def Works Overseas 1971-73), Property Servs Agency DOE 1973-81 (dir Social and Res Servs 1973-75, dir and under sec Mechanical & Electrical Engrg Servs 1975-81); memb Nominations Ctee Engrg Cncl 1983-, chm Membership Ctee IEE 1979-82 (memb 1975-82), Membership Advsr IEE Surrey 1984-, memb Qualifications Bd CIBSE 1981-87; Freeman City of London 1979, Liveryman Worshipful Co of Engrs 1984; CEng, FIEE 1964, FCIBSE 1976, Hon FCIBSE 1980; *Recreations* photography, music; *Style—* Arnold Gronhaug, Esq; 6 Pine Hill, Epsom, Surrey KT18 7BG (☎ 0372 721888)

GRONOW, Alun Gwilym; s of Ivor Austin Gronow (d 1951), and Kate Evelyn, *née* Worhite (d 1970); *b* 22 Oct 1931; *Educ* Dorking GS Surrey, Kings Coll London (BA); *m* 24 Dec 1978, Kathleen Margaret, da of Robert Stevenson Hodge, of Guildford, Surrey; *Career* 2 Lt RAOC 1952-54; teacher 1955-67, educn admin 1967-77, memb Local Authys Conditions of Serv Advsy Bd 1977-83, sec Assoc of Met Authys 1985- (memb 1983-); *Recreations* theatre, travel, bridge; *Clubs* Reform; *Style—* Alun Gronow, Esq; 7 Helford Walk, Woking, Surrey, GU21 3PL (☎ 048 62 20953); 35 Great Smith St, London SW1P 3BS (☎ 01 222 8100, fax 01 222 0878)

GRONOW, Dr Michael; s of Vivian (d 1970), and Mary Amelia, *née* Chappell; *b* 26 July 1937; *Educ* Cardiff HS, Univ Coll of S Wales (BSc), Trinity Coll Cambridge (PhD); *m* 20 Dec 1968, Janet Ruth, da of Guy Tomkins, of Ockley, Surrey; 1 s (Simon Richard b 19 March 1972), 1 da (Kathryn Louise b 26 Dec 1973); *Career* Univ of Cambridge: MRC res asst dept of radiotherapeutics 1963-65, demonstrator dept of chemistry 1962-65; res assoc dept of pharmacology Baylor Univ Houston Texas USA 1965-66, res assoc and demonstrator dept of biochemistry Univ of Oxford 1966-69, lectr dept of experimental pathology and cancer res Univ of Leeds 1969-75, permanent sr res fell cancer res unit Univ of York 1975-79; conslt PA Tech Centre Int 1979-80, head of biosciences PA Centre for Advanced Studies 1980-81, jt md and fndr Cambridge Life Scis plc 1981-88; memb: Biochemical Soc 1967, Br Assoc Cancer Res 1969; author of 49 pubns; *Recreations* music, photography, hockey, chess, wine; *Style—* Dr Michael Gronow; Cambridge Research Labs, 181A Huntingdon Rd, Cambridge CB3 0DJ (☎ 0223 277709, fax 0223 276444)

GROOM, Maj-Gen John Patrick; CB (1984), CBE (1975, MBE 1963); s of Samuel Douglas Groom (d 1975), and Gertrude Groom, *née* Clinton; *b* 9 Mar 1929; *Educ* King Charles Sch Kidderminster, Rugby, RMA Sandhurst, Staff Coll Camberley, Royal Coll Def Studies; *m* 1951, Jane Mary, da of Thomas Miskelly (d 1937); 3 da (Susan, Maryanne, Josephine); *Career* served N Africa, Egypt, UK, Aden, BAOR, Malaya, Singapore, Cyprus 1949-83 (despatched 1965); Col Cmdt Corps RE 1983, rep Col Cmdt 1986; dir gen The Guide Dogs for the Blind Assoc, chm GDBA (Trading Company) Ltd 1983; govr: Gordon Boys' Sch, Sandle Manor Sch; Liveryman Worshipful Co of Plumbers; FBIM, Fell Inst Plant Engrgs; *Recreations* sailing (Josumjay), ornothology, country pursuits; *Clubs* Royal Ocean Racing, Army & Navy, Royal Lymington YC; *Style—* Maj-Gen John Groom, CB, CBE; Withybed, All Saints Rd, Lymington, Hants (☎ 0590 75710); The Guide Dogs for the Blind Assoc, 9/10/11 Park St, Windsor, Berks SL4 1JR (☎ 0753 855711)

GROOM, Michael John; s of Thomas Rowland Groom (d 1984), of Wolverhampton, and Elizabeth Groom (d 1971); *b* 18 July 1942; *Educ* St Chad's GS Wolverhampton, Cotton Coll N Staffs; *m* 4 June 1966, Sheila Mary, da of Harold Cartwright, of Wolverhampton; 2 da (Nichola b 1971, Sally b 1975); *Career* Michael Groom & Co 1971-76 and 1981-, Tansley Witt 1976-80, Binder Hamlyn 1980-81, dir Professional Enterprise Gp, lectr mgmnt & legistlation; hon tres ICAEW (cncl memb 1975-); dep chm St Dominic's Ind Sch for Girls; Freeman Worshipful Co Of CAs; FCA 1964; *Books* Chartac Adminstration Manual (1975), ed 1975-81: Chartac Accounting Manual, Chartac Auditing Manual, Chartac Taxation Manual, Chartac Accounting and Auditing Model File; Financial Management in the Professional Office (1977), Cash Control in the Smaller Business (1978), Budgeting and Cash Management (1981); *Recreations* tennis, squash, photography, dog obedience training; *Clubs* Wolverhampton Lawn Tennis & Squash; *Style—* Michael Groom, Esq; 10 Clarendon St, Wolverhampton WV3 9PP (☎ 0902 773644)

GROOM, Air Marshal Sir Victor Emmanuel; KCVO (1953), KBE (1952, CBE 1945, OBE 1940), CB (1943), DFC (1918 and bar 1921); s of William Edwin Groom (d 1937), and Grace Mary, *née* Chapman; *b* 4 August 1898; *Educ* Alleyn's Sch; *m* 1, 1924, Maisie Monica (d 1961), da of Athelstan Maule (d 1909); 1 s (and 1 s decd); m 2, 1969, Muriel Constance, da of late Joseph Windsor, and widow of Capt G S Brown; *Career* Artists' Rifles 1916, 2 Lt West Yorks Regt 1917, transferred RFC 1917, RAF 1918-55, served WWI: France 1918, Palestine, Egypt, Turkey; Mesopotamia 1919-22; RAF Staff Coll 1928/9 (PSC); RAF in India 1929-34; served WWII: Gp Capt ops HQ Bomber Cmd, Gp Capt commanding RAF station Marham HQ Bomber Cmd (with 2 Wellington sqdns), Joint Planning Staff Office Whitehall, head of RAF section under COS to Supreme Allied Cdr planning invasion of Europe 1942-43, SASO 2nd Tactical Air Force 1943-45 (France, Belgium, Germany; despatches twice); AOA HQ Flying Training Command 1945-46; dir gen Manning Air Miny 1947-49, AOC 205 Gp (Egypt) 1949-51, C-in-C MEAF 1952, AOC-in-C Technical Training Cmd 1952-55, ret; *Recreations* gardening (roses); *Clubs* RAF; *Style—* Air Marshal Sir Victor Groom, KCVO, KBE, CB, DFC; 8 Somerville House, Manor Fields, Putney Hill, London SW15 3LX (☎ 01 788 1290)

GROSBERG, Prof Percy; s of Rev Gershon Grosberg (d 1970), of Johannesburg and Tel Aviv, and Pearl, *née* Ornstein (d 1986); *b* 5 April 1925; *Educ* Parktown Boys' HS Johannesburg, Univ of the Witwatersrand (BSc, MSc, PhD), Univ of Leeds ; *m* 5 Sept 1951, Queenie, da of Rabbi Dr Solomon Fisch (d 1985), of Leeds; 2 s (Jonathan b 25 Jan 1953, d 1980, David b 28 Jan 1957), 1 da (Gillian (Mrs Braunold) b 15 Aug 1955); *Career* sr res offr South African Wool Res Inst 1949-55; Univ of Leeds: lectr dept of textile indust 1955-61, res prof of textile engrg 1961-, head of dept of textile industr

1973-83 and 1987-; visiting prof Shenkar Coll of Textile Technol and Fashion Israel 1984; chm Leeds Friends of Bar-Ilan Univ Ramat-Fan Israel 1963-, rep of Chief Rabbi on Ct of Univ of Bradford; visiting expert for UNIDO to the Inst of Fibres and Forest Products Res Jerusalem 1969; Warner Meml Medal 1968, Textile Inst Medal 1972, hon fell Textile Inst 1988; MIMechE 1965, FTI 1966, Distinguished Serv Award Indian Inst of Technol Delhi 1986; *Books* An Introduction to Textile Mechanisms (1968), Structural Mechanics of Fibres, Yarns And Fabrics (1969), author of many papers in textile and other Scientific jls; *Style*— Prof Percy Grosberg; 2 Sandringham Crescent, Leeds LS17 8DF (☎ 0532 687478); 3 Shilo St, Tel Aviv 64688, Israel; Dept of Textile Industries, Univ of Leeds, Leeds LS2 9JT (☎ 0532 333703)

GROSS, John Jacob; s of Abraham and Muriel Gross; *b* 12 Mar 1935; *Educ* City of London Sch, Wadham Coll Oxford; *m* 1965, Miriam May; 1 s, 1 da; *Career* former asst lectr London Univ, fellow King's Coll Cambridge 1962-65, literary ed New Statesman 1973, ed TLS 1974-81, tstee Nat Portrait Gallery 1977-, dep chm George Weidenfeld & Nicolson Ltd 1982-; *Books* The Rise and Fall of the Man of Letters (1969, awarded Duff Cooper Meml Prize), Joyce (1971); *Style*— John Gross, Esq; 24a St Petersburgh Place, London W2; George Weidenfeld & Nicolson Ltd, 91 Clapham High St, London SW4 7TA

GROSS, Robert; *b* 16 August 1930; *Educ* Tulane Univ, New Orleans, Louisiana (BA); *m* 1952, Marilyn, da of Louis Heller (d 1956); 2 da; *Career* US Navy Public Relations Offr, served Pacific (Korean War) 1952-56; chm and chief exec Geers Gross; author; *Books* Boy and Girl (1981); *Recreations* tennis, travel; *Clubs* Brooks's, Hurlingham, Queen's; *Style*— Robert Gross, Esq; Geers Gross plc, 110 St Martin's Lane, London WC2N 4DY (☎ 01 734 1655); 20 Ormonde Gate, London SW3; 265 East 66th St, New York, NY 10021, USA

GROSSART, Angus McFarlane McLeod; s of William John White Grossart, JP (d 1980), and Mary Hay, *née* Gardiner; *b* 6 April 1937; *Educ* Glasgow Acad and Univ (LLD, MA, CA advocate); *m* 1978, Marion Gay Kerr Dodd; 1 da (Flure b 1982); *Career* md Noble Grossart (merchant bank) 1969-; chm Scottish Investmt Tst plc 1973-; dir include: Alexander & Alexander Servs Inc 1985-, American Tst plc 1973-, The Royal Bank of Scotland Gp plc 1985-, Hewden Stuart Plant plc; chm: Edinburgh Fund Managers plc 1983-, Globe Investmt Tst plc 1986, Tstee Nat Galleries of Scotland; *Recreations* golf, castle restoration, decorative arts; *Clubs* New (Edinburgh), Royal and Ancient St Andrews, Hon Co of Edinburgh Golfers; *Style*— Angus Grossart, Esq; 48 Queen St, Edinburgh EH2 3NR (☎ 031 226 7011, telex 72536)

GROSVENOR, Hon Hugh Richard; s of 4 Baron Ebury; *b* 1919; *Educ* Radley; *m* 1, 1939 (m dis 1952), Margaret, da of James Jacobs, of St Ives, Cornwall; 1 da (Margaret b 1947); m 2, 1955, Victoria, da of H Wright, of Newport, Salop; 1 s (William b 1959), 1 da (Rebecca b 1975); *Career* served WWII as Capt King's Shropshire LI; *Style*— The Hon Hugh Grosvenor; River Ridge, Courtlands Park, Carmarthen (☎ 0267 235610)

GROSVENOR, Hon Julian Francis Martin; s & h of 6th Baron Ebury by his 1 w; *b* 8 June 1959; *m* 15 April 1987, Danielle, 6 da of Theo Rossi, of Sydney, NSW, Australia; *Style*— The Hon Julian Grosvenor

GROSVENOR, Hon Laura Georgina Kiloran; *née* Grosvenor; reverted to maiden name by deed poll 1983; da (twin) of 5 Baron Ebury, DSO (d 1957), by 2 w, Hon Denise Yard-Buller (da of 3 Baron Churston); *b* 1946; *m* 1969, G R Mark Cross, only s of Geoffrey Cross, of Bray-on-Thames; *Style*— The Hon Laura Grosvenor; Bartons Lodge, Eversholt, Bletchley, Bucks (☎ 052 528 333) A333)

GROSVENOR, Hon Richard Alexander; s of 5 Baron Ebury, DSO, by his 2 w, Hon Denise Yarde-Buller (da of 3 Baron Churston); *b* 5 July 1946; *Educ* Milton Abbey, Perugia Univ, Montpelier Univ, Lyons Univ, Tours Univ, Munich Univ; *m* 1970 (m dis 1986), Gabriella, da of Dr Xavier Speckert; 1 s (Bendor; *Career* self-employed; *Style*— The Hon Richard Grosvenor; c/o Drummonds Bank, 49 Charing Cross, London SW1

GROSVENOR, Hon (Robert) Victor; s of 5 Baron Ebury (d 1957); *b* 1936; *Educ* Eton, Gordonstoun; *m* 1959, Caroline, da of Ronald Higham by his w Hon Barbara, *qv*; 2 da (Rachel b 1963, Virginia b 1965); *Career* late 2 Lt Life Gds; *Clubs* Puffins (Edin); *Style*— The Hon Victor Grosvenor; Bennetts, Grafton, Oxford OX8 2RY

GROSVENOR, Hon William Wellesley; s of 5 Baron Ebury, DSO, and his 2 w, Hon Denise Yarde-Buller (da of 3 Baron Churston); *b* 12 Sept 1942; *Educ* Eton, Perugia Univ, Trinity Oxford; *m* 1966, Ellen, da of late Dr Günter Seeliger, sometime Fed German ambass to Mexico; 1 s, 1 da; *Career* publicist; *Recreations* shooting, fishing, bridge, golf; *Clubs* Portland, Buck's; *Style*— The Hon William Grosvenor

GROTRIAN, Sir (Philip) Christian Brent; 3 Bt (UK 1934); s of Sqdn Ldr Robert Grotrian (decd), s of 1 Bt, by 1 w, Elizabeth, da of Maj Herbert Hardy-Wrigley (decd); hp of unc, Sir John Grotrian, 2 Bt (d 1984); *b* 26 Mar 1935; *Educ* Eton, Trinity Coll Toronto; *m* 1960, Anne Isabel, da of Robert Sieger Whyte, of Toronto; 1 s; *Style*— Sir Philip Grotrian, 3 Bt; 295 Glen Rd, Toronto, Ontario, Canada

GROTRIAN, John Stephen Martin; s of Col Frederick Stephen Brent Grotrian MC (d 1953), of Dumfries, Scotland, and Eileen Gertrude Deane (d 1974); *b* 16 Sept 1925; *Educ* Ampleforth; *m* 25 April 1953, Clodagh, da of Maj Richard Shaw de Courcy Bennett (d 1959), of Collingwood Lodge, Camberley; 1 s (Jeremy Brent b 1959), 2 da (Amanda b 1963, Emma b 1955); *Career* Capt Grenadier Guards 1944-49; dir various Advertising Agencies, mktg conslt 1985-, garden design conslt 1987-; *Recreations* shooting, gardening, skiing; *Clubs* Cavalry and Guards; *Style*— John Grotrian, Esq; Lake House, Lake, Salisbury, Wilts (☎ 09802 2138); 100 New Cavendish Street, London W1 (☎ 01637 7970)

GROTRIAN, Philip Timothy Adam Brent; s and h of Sir (Philip) Christian Brent Grotrian, Bt; *b* 9 April 1962; *Style*— Philip Grotrian Esq; c/o RR 3, Mansfield, Ontario LON 1MO, Canada

GROUND, (Reginald) Patrick; QC (1981), MP (C) Feltham and Heston 1983-; s of late Reginald Ground, and Ivy Elizabeth Grace, *née* Irving; *b* 9 August 1932; *Educ* Beckenham and Penge County GS, Lycée Guy Lussac Limoges, Selwyn Coll Cambridge (MA), Magdalen Coll Oxford, (MLitt), Inner Temple Scholar; *m* 1964, Caroline da of Col J F C Dugdale, of 5 St Leonards Terrace, London SW3; 3 s (Andrew b 1967, Richard b 1970, Thomas b 1974), 1 da (Elizabeth b 1969); *Career* Sub Lt RNVR Mediterranean Fleet 1955-56; pres Oxford Univ Cons Assoc 1958; memb Hammersmith Borough Cncl 1968-71; chm: ctees responsible for Health Social Servs 1969-71, Fulham Soc 1975; PPS to the Solicitor General 1987-; *Recreations* lawn tennis, sailing, travel; *Clubs* Carlton, Brooks's; *Style*— Patrick Ground, Esq, QC, MP; 13 Ranelagh Avenue, London SW6 3PJ; 8 New Square, Lincoln's Inn, WC2

GROUNDS, Stanley Paterson; CBE (1968); s of Thomas Grounds (d 1941), of 94 Buckley St, Footscray, Victoria, Aust, and Olivia Henrietta, *née* Anear (d 1954); *b* 25 Oct 1904; *Educ* Melbourne HS, Queen's Coll Univ of Melbourne (MA); *m* 20 Oct 1932, Freda Mary Gale, adopted da of William Humphrey Ransford (d 1915), of The Lodge, Farnham Royal, Bucks; 1 s (Roger b 1938), 1 da (Gillian (twin) b 1938); *Career* RAF 1940-45, Sqdn Ldr 19 Gp, Coastal Cmd, Air Miny; called to the Bar Middle Temple 1933, Chancery Bar 1934-40, asst charity cmmr 1946-58, sec Charity Cmmn 1958-60, charity cmmr 1960-69; *Recreations* other mens flowers, colour photography; *Clubs* Army and Navy; *Style*— Stanley Grounds, Esq, CBE; St Helena, 19 Bell Rd, Haslemere, Surrey GU27 3DQ (☎ 0428 51230)

GROUSE, Leonard David; s of Isaac Michael Grouse (d 1960); *b* 18 Sept 1930; *Educ* Bishopshalt Sch, LSE (BSc); *m* 1957, Jeannette Pauline, da of Leonard Thurgood (d 1944); 1 s, 1 da; *Career* HM Inspr of Taxes 1952-56; dir Noble Lowndes & Ptnrs Ltd 1964-65, md Gp Assurance Consultants 1965-71; dir: Stewart Wrightson Ltd 1971-77, Wigham Poland Hldgs 1977-81; md Leonard Grouse Associates Ltd; ATII, fell Pensions Mgmnt Inst; *Recreations* squash, chess, backgammon, reading, horse racing, crosswords; *Clubs* Savile, RAC; *Style*— Leonard Grouse, Esq; Highfield, Golf Side, Cheam, Surrey (☎ 01 642 1935)

GROUT, Noel Alfred Brian; s of Lt Noel Kenneth Grout, RNVR (d 1964), and Violet Mary, *née* Jolliff; *b* 8 August 1927; *Educ* Culford Sch Bury St Edmunds; *m* 12 April 1958, Cynthia Audrey (Thea), da of Leonard Marks (d 1975); 1 s (Simon Kenneth b 1964); *Career* Nat Serv S Lancs Regt and RAOC; later HAC; press offr Western Union Int, dir E K Monks Ltd 1963-72, chief exec Royal Masonic Benevolent Inst 1979- (asst sec 1972-78); Freeman: City of London 1979, Worshipful Co of Gold and Silver Wyre Drawers 1979; FBIM 1980; *Recreations* angling, bird watching, church architecture, walking; *Clubs* Royal Naval, Wig & Pen; *Style*— Noel A Grout, Esq; 61 Baston Rd, Hayes, Bromley, Kent BR2 7BS (☎ 01 462 3855); 20 Great Queen St, London WC2B 5BG (☎ 01 405 8341)

GROVE, Sir Charles Gerald; 5 Bt (UK 1874), of Ferne, Wilts; s of Walter Peel Grove (decd); suc bro, Sir Walter Grove, 4 Bt, 1974; *b* 10 Dec 1929; *Heir* bro, Harold Grove; *Style*— Sir Charles Grove, Bt; resident in USA

GROVE, Christopher John (Chris); s of Ronald Albert John Grove (d 1984), and Edna May, *née* Lazell; *b* 12 Dec 1947; *Educ* Manton House GS Goodmayes Essex, Thurrock Tech Coll Grays Essex; *m* 1 July 1972, Patricia Susan, da of Harold Charles Studholme, of South Ockendon, Essex; 2 s (Robert Allen b 2 Nov 1977, Jamie Oliver b 3 July 1979); *Career* gen mangr Rentmaster Ltd 1986-87, sales dir AI Int Ltd 1987-88, dir and ptnr Dickerson Tport Ltd; Nat Cricket Assoc: advanced coaching award, staff coach; *Recreations* coaching cricket, organising Youth Football; *Style*— Chris Grove, Esq; Dickerson Tport Ltd, Tomo Indust Estate, Stowmarket, Suffolk IP14 5AY (☎ 0449 615211, fax 0449 677733, car 0836 634900)

GROVE, (William) Dennis; s of William Grove (d 1968); *b* 23 July 1927; *Educ* Gowerton Sch, King's Coll London (BSc); *m* 1953, Audrey Irma, da of John Bernard Saxel (d 1961); 1 s, 1 da; *Career* Lt South Wales Borderers; overseas gen mangr Dunlop Gp 1968-70, chm and chief exec Sonoco UK Ltd and TPT Ltd 1970-85, chm NW Water 1985-; *Recreations* travel, golf; *Clubs* Bramall Park Golf; *Style*— Dennis Grove, Esq; Wilmslow, Cheshire

GROVE, Sir Edmund Frank; KCVO (1982, CVO 1974, MVO 4 Class 1963, MVO 5 Class 1953); s of Edmond Grove and Sarah Caroline, *née* Hunt; *b* 20 July 1920; *m* 1945, Grete Elisabet, da of Martinus Skou, of Denmark; 2 da; *Career* WWII RASC served M East; memb Royal Household 1946-82, chief accountant Privy Purse 1963-82, Sergeant-at-Arms to HM The Queen 1975-82, ret 1982; chevalier Order of Dannebrog (Denmark) 1974, offr Order of the Polar Star (Sweden) 1975, chevalier Légion d'Honneur (France) 1976; *Recreations* gardening; *Style*— Sir Edmund Grove, KCVO; Chapel Cottage, West Newton, Norfolk

GROVE, Harold Thomas; s of Walter Peel Grove (decd); hp of bro, Sir Charles Grove, 5 Bt; *b* 6 Dec 1930; *Style*— Harold Grove, Esq

GROVE, Rear-Adm John Scott; CB (1984), OBE (1964); s of late William George Grove, and late Frances Margaret Scott Grove; *b* 7 July 1927; *Educ* Dundee HS, St Andrews Univ (BSc); *m* 1950, Betty Anne Robinson; 1 s (Peter), 1 da (Diana, decd); *Career* RN 1948-85; qualified in submarines 1953, nuclear trg 1958-59, Cdr 1963, Capt 1970, Rear Adm 1980, first Sr Engr Offr HMS Dreadnought (first RN nuclear sub) 1960-64, RCDS 1974, CSO(E) to Flag Off Submarines 1975-77, Capt Fisgard 1977-79, Chief Strategic Systems Exec 1980-85, Chief Naval Engr Offr 1983-85, ret 1985; defence conslt Babcock Energy Ltd 1986-, non-exec dir Devonport Mgmnt Ltd 1987-; Liveryman (Ct Asst) Worshipful Co of Engrs; *Recreations* walking; *Clubs* Army and Navy, Royal Cwlth Soc; *Style*— Rear-Adm John Grove, CB, OBE; Maryfield, South Close, Wade Court, Havant, Hants PO9 2TD (☎ 0705 475116)

GROVE, Josceline Philip; s of Brig Geoffrey Reginald Grove (d 1972), and Barbara Constance, *née* Woodburn; *b* 8 Nov 1938; *Educ* Hurstpierpoint Coll, RMA Sandhurst; *m* 6 April 1975, Jennifer Clifton, da of Maj E A Calverty, qv, of Rose Cottage Farmhouse, Faygate Sussex; 1 s (decd), 2 da (Miranda Clifton b 1974, Venetia Mary b 1976); *Career* RMA Sandhurst 1957-58, cmnnd 1 Bn Cheshire Regt 1958, Lt 1960; TA QRR 1963-66, 4 Vol Bn RGJ Capt 1966-71; mgmnt trainee J & P Coats Patons & Baldwins 1963, C T Bowring & Co 1964-65, The Economist 1966, The Sunday Times 1967-70, J Walter Thompson 1970-73; Charles Barker 1974-83 (dir 1978-83), Grandfield Rork Collins Financial 1983- (md 1986-), exec sec Wider Share Ownership Cncl 1976-78; memb: City branch ctee BIM 1978-83, City Sponsor's GP - Tower Hamlets Ltd, Business in the Community 1986-87; Ct of Assistants, Worshipful Co of Bowyers; *Recreations* ocean racing, deer stalking, grand opera; *Clubs* Army & Navy; *Style*— Josceline Grove, Esq; 27 Cloncurry St, London SW6 6DR (☎ 01 736 1533); Fasnakyle, Cannich, Invernesshire (☎ 045 65 202); Grandfield Rork Collins Financial, Prestige House, 14-18 Holborn, London EC1N 2LE (☎ 01 242 2002)

GROVE, Norman Harold; MBE (1986); s of Francis Harold Grove (d 1944), of Kidderminster, and Lilian Grove, *née* Hodgetts (d 1963); *b* 29 Dec 1914; *Educ* Wrekin Coll Wellington; *m* 1940, Lesley Joan, da of Frank Harvey (d 1973), of Kidderminster; 1 s (Peter b 1946), 1 da (Lesley b 1943); *Career* dir: James Grove & Sons Ltd 1940- (chm 1944-), Harbury & Cradley Building Soc 1968-80; *Recreations* walking, travel, swimming, cricket; *Clubs* St Paul's; *Style*— Norman Grove, Esq; View Bank, Church Hill, Kinver, Stourbridge DY7 6HY (☎ 0384 877107); James Grove & Sons Ltd, PO Box 5, Stourbridge Road, Halesowen B63 3UW (telex 336921, fax 021 501 3905)

GROVE, Peter Hulbert; TD (1975 and bar 1982); s of James Hulbert Grove (d 1985), and Elfrida, *née* Golby (d 1976); *b* 24 July 1936; *Educ* Whitgift Sch; *m* 1, 3 Oct 1964 (m dis 1984), Mary Frances, da of Harry Ingledew Hopper (d 1972); 1 s (William b 1967), 2 da (Catherine b 1969, Victoria b 1971); m 2, 19 Oct 1984, Mary, da of Dr Harry Graham Dowler; *Career* joined HAC 1956, Nat Serv 15/19 Hussars 2 Lt 1958-60, resigned cmmn and rejoined HAC 1960, HAC recmmnd Lt 1964, Capt 1967; transfer: Queens Regt 1972, CVHQ RA 1977; Maj 1979, attached Staff of London Dist as SO2 (TA liason), ret 1986; Knox Cropper and Co: articled clerk 1952-58, rejoined after Nat Serv 1960, ptnr 1968, sr ptnr 1988; fin and gen purposes ctee of Royal Masonic Benevolent Inst 1987-, various mgmnt ctees of Royal Masonic Hosp 1976-86; special constable 1974-85, divnl offr in command of HAC Detachment of Met Special Constabulary 1984-85; Freeman City of London 1972, Liveryman Worshipful Co of Scriveners 1975; ACA, FCA; *Recreations* clock restoration, Co of Pikemen and Musketeers HAC, canals, narrow boats; *Clubs* HAC, City Livery XIX; *Style—* Peter Grove, Esq, TD; 121 Old Woking Rd, Woking GU22 8PF (☎ 09323 40620); Knox Cropper, 16 New Bridge St, London EC4V 6AX (☎ 01 583 8355, fax 01 583 2944)

GROVE-WHITE, Robin Bernard; s of Charles William Grove-White, of Amlwch, Gwynedd, and Mary, *née* Dobbs; (*see* Burke's Irish Family Records); *b* 17 Feb 1941; *Educ* Uppingham, Worcester Coll Oxford (BA); *m* 1970 (m dis 1974), Virginia Harriet, da of Christopher Ironside, OBE; 1 s (William b 1973); m 2, 1979, Helen Elisabeth, da of Sir Francis Graham Smith, of The Old Sch House, Henbury, Cheshire; 2 s (Simon b 1982, Francis b 1986), 1 da Ruth b 1980); *Career* freelance writer for TV, radio, press in US, Canada and UK 1963-71, asst sec Cncl for the Protection of Rural England 1972-80, (dir 1981-87), vice-chm Cncl for National Parks; research fell: Centre for Environmental Technology, Imperial Coll London 1987-; contributor to various publications including The Times, Guardian, New Scientist, Nature; *Recreations* reading, walking, cricket; *Style—* Robin Grove-White, Esq; 77 Chevening Rd, London NW6 6DA (☎ 969 7375); Centre for Environmental Technology, Imperial College, 48 Prince's Gardens, London SW7 1LU (☎ 01 589 5111) Protection of Rural Eng, 4 Hobart Place, London SW1 (☎ 01 235 9481)

GROVES, Brian Arthur; s of Alfred Edward Groves *qv*, and Winifred May, *née* Sheen, *qv*; *b* 3 July 1933; *Educ* Bishop Wordsworth Sch Salisbury; *m* 1 Aug 1955, Daphne Frances, da of Frederick Gale (d 1957); 2 da (Heather b 1956, Beverley, b 1957); *Career* journalist 1950-71, motoring ed, Daily Mail 1968-71, mktg dir Nissan UK Ltd 1975-83 (advtg and PR dir 1983-); *Recreations* golf, swimming, boating; *Style—* Brian Groves, Esq; Sarum, Mare Hill, Pulborough, W Sussex (☎ 07982 3464); Nissan House, Worthing, Sussex (☎ 0903 68561, car ☎ 0836 256242)

GROVES, Sir Charles Barnard; CBE (1968, OBE 1958); *b* 10 Mar 1915; *Educ* St Paul's Cathedral Choir Sch, Sutton Valence Sch, Royal Coll of Music; *m* 1948, Hilary Hermione Barchard; 1 s, 2 da; *Career* conductor; conductor BBC Northern Orchestra 1944-51, dir of Music Bournemouth Corpn and conductor Bournemouth Municipal Orchestra 1951-54, conductor Bournemouth Symphony Orchestra 1954-61, resident musical dir WNO 1961-63, musical dir and resident conductor Royal Liverpool Philharmonic Orchestra 1963-77, assoc conductor Royal Philharmonic Orchestra 1967-, music dir ENO 1977-80, pres Nat Youth Orchestra of Great Britain 1977-; pres and artistic advsr English Sinfonia 1980-, princ conductor Guildford Philharmonic Orchestra 1987-; FRCM, Hon RAM, Hon FTCL, CRNCM, Hon GSM, Hon DMus Liverpool, Hon DUniv Open, Hon DLit Salford ; kt 1973; *Style—* Sir Charles Groves, CBE; 12 Camden Sq, London NW1 9UY

GROVES, Capt Peter Leslie John; s of Lt-Col Leslie Herbert Selby Groves, OBE (d 1961), of Dorset (gs of Sir John Groves, of Weymouth, dir John Groves & Sons, brewers), and Dorothy Olive Josephine Gundry (d 1969); *b* 30 Dec 1925; *Educ* Eton; *m* 14 Dec 1956, Anthea Mary, da of Col Cuthbert Vaux, MC, TD (d 1960), of Richmond, N Yorks; 1 s (Michael b 1961), 2 da (Carol b 1958, Joanna b 1964); *Career* RMC Sandhurst 1945, cmmnd 1945, Adj 14/20 King's Hussars 1956-57, Adj Duke of Lancaster's Own Yeomanry TA 1952-55, instr Eaton Hall OCS 1957-58, temp Maj 1955 (ret 1960); exec Aspro-Nicholas 1961-70, sec Olympic Ski Appeal 1970-72, liaison offr SSAFA 1972-75, exec Help the Aged 1984-87; memb ctee Wessex Area Cons Assoc 1970-72; underwriting memb Lloyds 1971; MBIM 1984; *Recreations* shooting; *Clubs* Army and Navy; *Style—* Capt Peter Groves; The Old Rectory, Great Langton, Northallerton, N Yorks DL7 0TA (☎ 0609 748 681)

GROVES, Philip Denys Baker; DL (Co of Hertford 1989); s of Joseph Rupert Groves (d 1958), of Watford, Herts, and Eva Lilian, *née* Baker (d 1986); *b* 9 Jan 1928; *Educ* Watford GS, Poly Sch of Architecture; *m* 21 June 1952, Yvonne Joyce, da of George Chapman (d 1971), of Rickmansworth; 2 s (Mark b 29 April 1957, Michael b 23 Sept 1965), 1 da (Sarah b 27 May 1961); *Career* RAF 1946-48 serv: UK, Palestine, Egypt; chm Architects Co-Partnership 1980- (joined 1955, ptnr 1965); architect for educn and health care projects: UK Middle East, Far East, Caribbean; memb RIBA cncl 1962-81 (vice pres 1972-75 and 1978-80), memb bd of educn RIBA 1962-80 (chm 1974-75 and 1979-80), cncl memb ARCUK 1962-80 (chm 1971-74); chm: Univ of York Centre for 1978-81, chm CPD in Construction GP 1986-; memb Comite De Liason Des Architect du Marche Commun 1972-80, external examiner at several Schools of Architecture in UK and overseas; dir Herts C of C (chm 1985-88), chm Herts Community Tst 1988-; ARIBA 1955, FRIBA 1968, FRSA 1989; *Books* Design for Health Care (jtly, 1981); *Recreations* walking, reading, architecture; *Clubs* Reform; *Style—* Philip Groves, Esq, DL; The Dingle, Whisperwood, Loudwater, Rickmansworth, Hertfordshire WD3 4JU, (☎ 0923 775921); Architects Co Partnership, Northaw House, Potters Bar, Hertfordshire EN6 4PS, (☎ 0707 51141 fax 0707 52600 telex 27997 ACP SCP G)

GROVES, His Hon Judge Richard Bebb; TD (1966), RD (1979); s of George Thomas Groves (d 1965), and Margaret Anne Underhill, *née* Bebb; *b* 4 Oct 1933; *Educ* Bancroft's Sch Essex; *m* 1958, Eileen Patricia, da of Capt Graham Payne Farley (d 1942); 1 s (Christopher b 1963), 1 da (Caroline b 1961); *Career* Nat Serv 1952-54; TA 1954-70, Maj Intelligence Corps (TAVR) RNR 1970-83; Lt Cdr (SP) RNR PI Gp Nijmegen Medal Royal Netherlands League of Physical Culture 1965 and 1966; admitted slr 1960; ptnr: H J Smith & Co, Richard Groves & Co 1962-85; dep circuit judge 1978-80, rec the Crown Ct 1980-85, circuit judge 1985; *Recreations* watching sport, playing tennis, walking, reading; *Clubs* Colchester Garrison Offrs, Chelmsford; *Style—* His Hon Judge Groves

GROVES, Ronald Edward; CBE (1972); s of Joseph Rupert Groves (d 1958), of Watford, and Eva Lilian, *née* Baker (d 1986); *b* 2 Mar 1920; *Educ* Watford GS; *m* 16 Nov 1940, Beryl Doris Lydia, da of Frank William Collins (d 1940), of Watford; 2 s (Peter Warland b 1941, Richard Michael b 1958); 1 da (Mary Delia Margaret b 1945); *Career* RAF 1940-46, Flt Lt; seconded BOAC 1942, Capt 1943-46; pres Timber Trade Fedn 1969-71; chm: Meyer Int plc 1982-87, Int Timber plc 1976-87; pres Nat Cncl of Bldg Material Producers 1987-; chm: Nat Sawmilling Assoc 1966-67, W Herts Main Drainage Authy 1970-74; dir Nat Bldg Agency 1978-82, Business in the Community 1984-87; memb: EDC for Bldg 1982-86, Cncl of London C of C 1982-, LCCI London Regnl Affrs Ctee 1980-, London Regnl Cncl CBI 1983-87; cncllr Three Rivers Dist Cncl 1974- (chm 1977-78), Rickmansworth Urban DC 1950-74 (chm 1957-58, 1964-65, 1971-72); chm Watford GS 1980-; *Style—* Ronald Groves, Esq, CBE; 8 Pembroke Rd, Moor Park, Northwood, Middx HA6 2HR (☎ 09274 23187)

GROVES, Terry Randolph Alexander; s of Dr T A Groves (d 1976), of Slegaby-Beg, Quarterbridge Rd, Douglas, IOM, and Daphne Carine, *née* Pruddah (d 1961); *b* 9 August 1946; *Educ* Shrewsbury; *m* 2 Sept 1972, Janet Pauline Elaine, da of H J Partington, JP, of 10 Lumley Rd, Chester; 2 s (Thomas Charles Alexander b 5 Nov 1974, Timothy Simon Robert b 7 Aug 1977); *Career* exec property devpt co 1969-75, property mangr South African Mutual Life (Natal region) 1975-77, ptnr Cowley Groves & Co (esates agents, surveyors and valuers) IOM 1977-86; dir: Cresta Hldgs Ltd, Cresta Properties Ltd 1986-; bd memb Sun Alliance Ltd (IOM), chm Ramsey Golf links Ltd; memb: mgmnt ctee IOM Hospice Care Charity, appeals ctee IOM Cwlth Games Assoc; cncl memb (Cons) Chester City Cncl 1973-75; *Recreations* golf, tennis, gardening; *Clubs* Ramsey GC (currently vice-pres, capt 1984-85), Castletown GC, Executive (IOM); *Style—* Terry Groves, Esq; West Kella, Sulby Lezayre, Isle of Man (☎ 0624 897904); Peregrine House, Peel Rd, Douglas, Isle of Man (☎ 0624 73800, fax 0624 73827, car ☎ 0860 640502)

GRUBB, Lt-Col Alexander James Watkins; JP (Cheshire 1956), DL (1972); s of Col Alexander Henry Watkins Grubb, CMG, DSO, JP (d 1933), and Frances Marie, *née* Cox (d 1944); *b* 25 July 1909; *Educ* Wellington, RMA Woolwich; *m* 1, 1936, Margaret (d 1972), da of Richard Dale, of Malpas; 2 s (Alexander, Peter); m 2, 1973, Lois Keitha (d 1985), da of Keith Rowland Ritchie, of Launceston, Tasmania, and widow of Maj R F A David; m 3, Rowena Ball-Greene; *Career* served RA 1929-50 (GSO1 AA Gp Warrington 1949-50); chm Nantwich Divs Cons Assoc 1959-66, pres 1967-79; High Sheriff Cheshire 1972; chm: Cheshire Police Authy Complaints Ctee 1978-79, Runcorn Devpt Corpn Licensed Premises Ctee 1972-79; *Recreations* hunting, shooting, cricket; *Clubs* Army & Navy; *Style—* Lt-Col Alexander Grubb, JP, DL; Farley Court, Farley Hill, Berks RG7 1TT (☎ 0734 732380)

GRUBB, Ralph Ernest Watkins; DL (E Sussex 1977); s of Rev Ernest Watkins Grubb (d 1914), and Mary Pauline, *née* Bevan (d 1946); *b* 12 April 1911; *Educ* Wellington, Trinity Coll Cambridge (BA), Inner Temple; *m* 1944, Caroline Elizabeth Mabel, da of William Reierson Arbuthnot (d 1938); 1 s, 2 da (and 1 decd); *Career* Inns of Court Regt TA 1936-46; Maj, GS Intelligence Palestine 1945-46; barr Inner Temple; High Sheriff Sussex 1972-73, memb E Sussex CC 1954-74, vice-chm 1973-74; chm: Countryside Ctee 1969-74 Rye Harbour Nature Reserve 1969-80, Sussex County Playing Fields Assoc 1974-83, Plumpton Agricultural Coll 1966-69; memb Nat Tst Regnl Ctee Kent and E Sussex 1974-84 (vice-chm 1980); conservator Ashdown Forest 1958-74; FRICS; *Recreations* shooting, fishing, birdwatching; *Clubs* Farmers, Royal Cwlth Soc; *Style—* Ralph Grubb, Esq, DL; Mayes House, nr East Grinstead, Sussex (☎ 0342 810 597); Ottershatch, Beach St, Deal, Kent (☎ 0304 375533)

GRUBMAN, Wallace Karl; s of Samuel Grubman (d 1988), of Philadelphia, PA, USA, and Mildred, *née* Lippe (d 1985); *b* 12 Sept 1928; *Educ* Columbia Univ NY (BS), New York Univ (MS); *m* 29 July 1950, Ruth, da of Lewis Winer (d 1965); 3 s (James Wallace b 1954, d 1979, Steven Lee b 1956, Eric Peter b 1958); *Career* Nat Starch and Chem Corpn USA 1950-: corporate vice-pres 1971-75, gp vice-pres 1976-77, dir 1978-, pres and chief operating offr 1978-83, chm and chief exec offr 1983-85; dir: Utd Nat Bank NJ USA 1978-86 (conslt to bd 1986-), Unilever US 1981-86; dir and chemicals co-ordinator Unilever plc and Unilever NV 1986-; memb: engrg cncl Columbia Univ NY, chem engrg dept studies ctee Imperial Coll Sci and Technol, Royal Opera Covent Gdn, Royal Acad, American Friends Gp; patron Met Opera Lincoln Centre NY; memb American Inst Chem Engrs 1950, SCI 1978, FInstD 1986; *Recreations* sports, music; *Clubs* Wentworth GC, Mid Ocean Bermuda, SKY and Princeton NY; *Style—* Wallace Grubman, Esq; Unilever House, Blackfriars, London EC4P 4BQ (☎ 01 822 6895); Nat Starch and Chemical Corpn, Bridgewater, New Jersey 08807 (☎ 201 685 5161)

GRUFFYDD, Prof (Robert) Geraint; s of Moses Griffith (d 1973), of Menai Bridge, Gwynedd, and Ceridwen, *née* Ellis (d 1982); *b* 9 June 1928; *Educ* Ardwyn GS Aberystwyth, Gordonstoun, UCNW Bangor (BA), Jesus Coll Oxford (DPhil); *m* 1 Oct 1953, (Elizabeth) Eluned Gruffydd, da of John Roberts (d 1965), of Holyhead; 2 s (Rhun b 4 March 1961, Pyrs b 26 Nov 1963), 1 da (Sian b 14 Oct 1957); *Career* asst ed Univ of Wales Dictionary of the Welsh Language 1953-55, lectr in welsh UCNW Bangor 1955-70, prof of welsh language and literature Univ Coll of Wales Aberystwyth 1970-79, librarian Nat Library of Wales 1980-85, dir Centre for Advanced Welsh and Celtic Studies Univ of Wales 1985-; chm welsh language section Yr Academi Gymreig (Welsh Acad) 1986-; memb Hon Soc of Cymmrodorion (ed of Transactions 1989-); *Books* ed: Cerddi '73 (1973), Meistri'r Canrifoedd (1973), Bardos (1982), Cerddi Saunders Lewis (1986), Gair ar Waith (1988); *Recreations* meditating upon the uses of leisure; *Style—* Prof Geraint Gruffydd; Eirianfa, Caradog Rd, Aberystwyth, Dyfed (☎ 0970 623396); Centre for Advanced Welsh & Celtic Studies, The Old College, Aberystwyth, Dyfed (☎ 0970 624463)

GRUGEON, Sir John Drury; (DL Kent 1986); s of Drury Grugeon (d 1969), of Westfield Lodge, Broadstairs; *b* 20 Sept 1928; *Educ* Epsom GS, RMA Sandhurst; *m* 1955, (m dis 1986), Mary Patricia, da of Walter James Rickards (d 1957), of Hoath Farm, Canterbury; 1 s, 1 da; *Career* served The Buffs 1948-60, Capt, Regimental Adj (later Adj 5 Bn), served: Europe, Middle East, Far East; ldr Kent CC 1973-81 (elected 1967), chm policy ctee Assoc CCs 1978-80, vice-chm Assoc of CCs 1980-82; memb: Medway Ports Authy 1977-, Consultative Cncl Local Govt Fin; exec mangr Save & Prosper Gp Ltd (joined 1960); dir of Liverpool Nat Garden Festival 1982-83, chm Tunbridge Wells Health Authy, kt 1980; *Recreations* shooting, cricket; *Clubs* Carlton, MCC, Kent CCC; *Style—* Sir John Grugeon, DL; 2 Shrublands Ct, Sandrock Rd, Tunbridge Wells, Kent TW2 3PS (☎ 0892 31936)

GRUMBALL, Clive Roger; s of Frederick William Grumball (d 1988), and Joan Doreen, *née* Ottewell (d 1976); *b* 17 Dec 1946; *Educ* Sir Roger Manwood's Sch Sandwich Kent, Welbeck Coll Worksop Notts, RMA Sandhurst; *m* 20 Feb 1971 (m dis

1986), Jennifer, da of David James Springhall, of Wallingford, Oxon; 1 s (Ian Nigel Clive b 1974), 2 da (Kirsty Elizabeth b 15 April 1973, Karen Louise d 1973); *Career* 2 Lt RCS 1967-68; asst to md Gillett Bros Discount Co Ltd 1969-77, asst tres Amex Bank Ltd 1977-80; dir: Nordic Bank plc 1980-85, County Gp Ltd 1985-87, treasy Br and Cwlth Merchant Bank plc 1987-; *Books* Managing Interest Rate Risks (1987); *Recreations* horse riding, hockey; *Style—* Clive Grumball, Esq; 66 Cannon Street, London EC4N 6AE (☎ 01 248 0900, fax 01 248 0906, telex 884040)

GRUNBERG, Michael; s of Solomon Aaron Grunberg, and Greta, *née* Fox; *b* 23 Sept 1956; *Educ* City of London Sch, LSE (BSc); *Career* CA, ptnr Stoy Hayward 1985, dir Stoy Hayward Assocs 1985; chm steering ctee Comic Relief; MIMC 1986; *Recreations* squash, skiing, scuba diving; *Style—* Michael Grunberg, Esq; Stoy Hayward, 8 Baker Street, London W1M 1DA (☎ 01 486 5888, fax 01 487 3686, telex 267716 HORWAT G)

GRUNDY, Lady; Marie-Louise; da of Frederick Amaza Holder (d 1972), of Corsham, Wilts, and Ellen Mary, *née* Nation (d 1984), of Taunton, Somerset; *b* 30 Mar 1922; *Educ* Exeter Univ (BA) ; *m* 1975 (as his 2 w), Air Marshal Sir Edouard Grundy, KBE, CB (d 1987), s of Frederick Grundy (d 1924), of London; *Career* co dir; chm American Legacy Fndn Inc, tstee Florida Inst of Technol, co chm Winston Churchill Meml Fund; former pres: Rotary Inner Wheel Singapore, Business and Professional Womens Club; *Recreations* sailing (yacht 'Fresh Aire'), genealogy, travel, chess, bridge; *Clubs* Utd Oxford and Cambridge, IOD, American, St James's, RAF, Eau Gallie YC, Goodwood Race Course; *Style—* Lady Marie-Louise Grundy; 26 Basil Street London SW3 1AS

GRUNDY, Vincent Arthur; s of Cecil Frederick Grundy (d 1976), and Elizabeth Agnes, *née* Mason (d 1968); *b* 6 Dec 1931; *Educ* Worksop Coll; *m* 19 Oct 1957, Moira Patricia, da of George Barbour (d 1985); 1 da (Patricia b 1958); *Career* Nat Serv RE 1950-52; dir: Trafalgar House plc, John Brown plc; chm: Cementation Civil & Specialist Hldgs Ltd, Cementation Int Construction Hldgs Ltd, Cleveland Redpath Engrg Hldgs Ltd, Trafalgar House Offshore Ltd; md Trafalgar House Construction Hldgs Ltd; *Recreations* gardening, boating, shooting; *Clubs* Phyllis Court, Carlton; *Style—* Vincent Grundy, Esq; Trafalgar House plc, 1 Berkeley St, London W1A 1BY (☎ 01 499 9020, fax 01 355 4418, telex 921341)

GRYLLS, Brig (William) Edward Harvey; OBE (1945); er s of Maj (William) Edward John Grylls (d 1931), of Funtington Hall, nr Chichester, Sussex (*see* Burke's Landed Gentry, 18 Edn, vol II, 1969), and Helen Aline, *née* Combe (d 1941); *b* 11 July 1902; *Educ* Harrow, RMC Sandhurst; *m* 9 July 1929, Rachel Elizabeth (decd), o da of Brig-Gen Kempster Kenmure Knapp, CB, CMG (d 1948), of Brooke Lodge, Weedon, Northants; 1 s (William Michael John, *qv*), 1 da (Angela Mary Elizabeth b 18 June 1931, m Ronald Cathcart Roxburgh, *qv*); *Career* cmmnd 15/19 King's Royal Hussars 1923; Instructor Army Equitation Sch Weedon 1925-26; served: Tidworth, Egypt, India, NW Frontier, Mohmond War 1930-31, Shorncliffe, Tidworth, York 1934-38; instr RMC Sandhurst 1938-40, 2 i/c 15/19 King's Royal Hussars 1940, mission to USA to advise on tank design at Fort Knox 1941, dep dir armd fighting vehicles under Gen Montgomery 8 Army in Egypt 1942, served Sicily and Italy, returned to UK Dec 1943 with Gen Montgomery as dep dir armd fighting vehicles 21 Army Gp (serving from invasion of Normandy until surrender of Germany), Brig cmdg 'T' Force (involved in reparations and intelligence), cmdt Sch of Tank Technol 1951; ret 1954; memb Dorset CC 1955-72, judge Br Show Jumping Assoc 1949-76, chm Hampshire and W of England Utd Retriever Club, memb ctee Golden Retriever Club; *Clubs* Army and Navy, Royal Cruising; *Style—* Brig W E H Grylls, OBE; Winterbourne Zelston House, Blandford, Dorset

GRYLLS, (William) Michael John; MP (C) NW Surrey 1974-; s of Brig (William) Edward Harvey Grylls, OBE, *qv*, and Rachel Elizabeth, *née* Knapp; *b* 21 Feb 1934; *Educ* RNC Dartmouth, Paris Univ, Madrid Univ; *m* 1965, Sarah, da of Neville Montague Ford, *qv*; 1 s, 1 da; *Career* served RM 1952-55; contested (C) Fulham 1964 and 1966, memb GLC 1967-70, chm Further and Higher Educn 1968-70, memb Nat Youth Employment Cncl 1968-70, dep ldr ILEA 1969-70; MP (C) Chertsey 1970-1974, memb Select Ctee Overseas Devpt 1970-78; chm: Small Business Bureau 1979-, Cons Industry Ctee 1981- (vice-chm 1975-81); parly spokesman IOD 1979-; *Recreations* gardening, shooting, sailing, skiing; *Style—* Michael Grylls, Esq, MP; House of Commons, London SW1A 0AA (☎ 01 219 4193)

GUADACORTE, Marquis of; Don Rafael de Tramontana y Gayangos, Count of Casa Fuerte; s of Dr Rafael de Tramontana y Tramontana, Patrician of Messina (d 1964); gs of the Arabic author and scholar, Pasqual de Gayangos, who m an Englishwoman, Frances Revell, and who was k by a horsedrawn carriage and buried in Kensal Green cemetery; descendant of the noble family of Spain for whom the title of Marquis was created in 1690 and the title of Count in 1743; *b* 16 Mar 1947; *Educ* Areneros Madrid, Sherborne, License ès Sciences Econ Geneva; *Career* economist; chm Pasqual de Gayangos Arab-Hispanic Fndn, Carmona, Spain; memb Assoc of Hidalgos of Spain; Kt of Honour and Devotion SMO Malta, Kt of Justice Constantine Order of St George of Naples; *Recreations* horse-breeding, golf, polo, jogging, yachting; *Clubs* Royal Yacht Club of Gibraltar; *Style—* Marquis of Guadacorte, Count of Casa Fuerte; Felipe IV, 8 Madrid 14, Spain

GUASCHI, Francis Eugene; s of Gino Guaschi (d 1986), of Holborn EC1, and Catherine Bridget, *née* Smith (d 1982); *b* 5 April 1931; *Educ* St Marylebone GS; *m* 25 June 1960, Sylvia Rose, da of Douglas Jones Willesden (d 1959); 1 s (John b 27 Sept 1965), 1 da (Jane b 11 Aug 1967); *Career* Nat Serv 1955-57; asst gen mangr Mercantile and Gen Reinsur Co Ltd 1980-85, ptnr Bacon and Woodrow Consltg Actuaries 1985-; FIA; *Recreations* playing the piano, mathematics, computers; *Clubs* Actuaries; *Style—* Francis Guaschi, Esq; 18 Clements Rd, Chorleywood, Rickmansworth, Herts WD3 5JT (☎ 09278 2425); Messrs Bacon & Woodrow Consulting Actuaries, Empire House, St Martins-Le-Grand, London EC1A 4ED (☎ 01 600 2747, fax 01 726 6519, telex 8953206 BWLONG)

GUDENIAN, John; s of Mihran Gudenian (d 1921), of London, and Nevric *née* Mouradian (d 1941); *b* 27 April 1914; *Educ* Univ Coll Sch Hampstead, Hornsey Art Coll, St Martins Sch of Art; *m* 27 Aug 1955, Margaret, da of John Yateley (d 1984), of Newcastle; 2 da (Miranda Nevric b 1958, Christina Mary b 1961); *Career* WWII RAF UK N Africa Italy; theatrical and film designer and costumier: BJ Simmons & Co Ltd 1931-39, J Arthur Rank Films 1946-50, dir LH Nathan Ltd 1950-72, dir and conslt Bermans & Nathans Ltd 1972-87; involved in tennis, cricket, ex-serv activities, Br Legion; Freeman City of London; *Style—* John Gudenian, Esq

GUDKA, (Narendre) Naresh Zaverchand; s of Zaverchand Gosar, of Nairobi, Kenya, and Jiviben Zaverchand; *b* 13 Jan 1942; *Educ* Duke of Gloucester Sch Nairobi Kenya, Balham and Tooting Coll of Commerce London; *m* 1 April 1967, Catherine Elizabeth, da of Michael Charles (d 1951), of Kilkee, Co Clare, Eire; 2 da (Rita Claire b 13 Feb 1968, Michelle Christine b 11 Feb 1971); *Career* articled clerk Leslie Furneaux and Co 1961-66, qualified CA 1966, Peat Marwick McLintock 1967-68, J and A Scrimgeour and Co 1968-74, Banque Paribas Capital Markets Ltd 1974-82, Citicorp Scrimgeour Vickers and Co 1982-; FCA 1967, ASIA 1975, TSA 1975; *Recreations* keen on sports and gardening; *Clubs* MCC; *Style—* Mr Naresh Gudka, Esq; 2 Aston Ave, Kenton, Middx HA3 ODB (☎ 01 907 3226); Cottons Centre, Hay's Lane, London SE1 2QT (☎ 01 234 2145, fax 378 6208, telex 885171/886004)

GUERITZ, Rear-Adm Edward Findlay; CB (1971), OBE (1957), DSC (1942) and bar (1944); s of late Elton L Gueritz; *b* 8 Sept 1919; *Educ* Cheltenham; *m* 1947, Pamela Amanda Bernhardina, *née* Jeans; 1 s, 1 da; *Career* RN: 1939-45 War, Home, Mediterranean and Eastern Waters; Capt of Fleet Far East Fleet 1965-66, Dir of Defence Plans (Navy) 1967, dir Jt Warfare Staff MOD 1968, Admiral-Pres RN Coll Greenwich 1968-70, Cmdt Joint Warfare Establishment 1970-72, ret 1973; chief hon steward Westminster Abbey 1975-85, pres Society for Nautical Research 1975-; dir Royal United Services Inst for Defence Studies 1979-81 (dep dir and ed 1976-79, dir and ed-in-chief 1979-81); vice-chm The Marine Soc 1987-; *Publications* (jt ed) Ten Years of Terrorism, Will the Wells Run Dry, RUSI/Brassey's Defence Year Book (1978/79, 1980, 1981, 1982), Nuclear Attack/Civil Defence (1982); contributor: The Third World War (1978), The Second World War (1982), NATO's Maritime Strategy (1987); *Clubs* Army & Navy; *Style—* Rear-Adm Edward Gueritz, CB, OBE, DSC; 56 The Close, Salisbury, Wilts (☎ Salisbury 3649)

GUERNSEY, Lord; Charles Heneage Finch-Knightley; s and h of 11 Earl of Aylesford; *b* 27 Mar 1947; *Educ* Oundle, Trinity Coll Cambridge; *m* 1971, Penelope Anstice, da of Kenneth A G Crawley (d 1988), of London; 1 s (Hon Heneage James Daniel b 29 April 1985); 4 da (Hon Rachel Louise b 1974, Hon Kate Pamela b (twin) 1974, Hon Alexandra Rosemary b 1977, Hon Laura b 1982); *Recreations* shooting, archery, real tennis; *Style—* Lord Guernsey; Packington Hall, Meriden, nr Coventry, Warwicks CV7 7HF (☎ 0676 22274)

GUERRICO, Lady Moira Beatrice Forbes; da of 9 Earl of Granard; *b* 1951; *m* 1, 1971 (m dis 1975), HH Prince Charles Antoine Louis de Ligne de la Tremoille (who later m Princesse Aliette de Croy); m 2, 1978, José Guerrico; 1 s (Killian Arthur b 16 March 1987), 1 d (Shannon b 1983); *Style—* Lady Moira Guerrico; 17 Avenue de l'Annonciade, Monte Carlo, Monaco

GUEST, Albert Sidney; s of Thomas Albert Guest (d 1978); *b* 17 Nov 1934; *Educ* Sladen Kidderminster, Birmingham Univ; *m* 1962, Maureen, da of Frederick Corker (d 1961); 1 s, 1 da; *Career* 2/Lt Royal Army Pay Corpn; dir: Sheerloom Carpets 1977-81, (sales) Heckmondwike Carpets 1978-82; UK dir Besmer Carpets (UK) Ltd, Sub Besmer Germany 1982-: memb Inst of Marketing; *Recreations* golf, walking; *Clubs* Woodsome Hall GC (Huddersfield), Dubai Country (United Arab Emirates); *Style—* Albert Guest, Esq; 11 Fenay Crescent, Almondbury, Huddersfield, W Yorks (☎ 0484 532801)

GUEST, Dr Ann Hutchinson; da of Robert Hare Hutchinson (d 1975), of West Redding, Conn, USA, and Delia Farley, *née* Dana; *b* 3 Nov 1918; *Educ* private; *m* 20 Jan 1962, Ivor Forbes Guest, s of Cecil Marmaduke Guest (d 1954), of Bickley, Kent; *Career* dancer in a series of successful musicals New York 1942-50; dance notator: Ballet Jooss 1938-39, New York City Ballet 1948-61; fndr Dance Notation Bureau New York 1940 (dir 1941-61, hon pres 1961-), fndr memb Int Cncl Kinetography Laban (pres 1985), fndr and dir Language of Dance Centre 1967-; dance reconstructor: Cachucha (Royal Ballet, Ballet for All 1967, Vienna Staatsoper 1969), Pas de Six, La Vivaudière (Joffrey Ballet 1977, Sadler's Wells Royal Ballet 1982); Hon LHD Marygrove Coll Detroit Univ 1977, Hon DHum Ohio State Univ 1987; *Books* Labanotration (1953), Your Move (1983), Dance Notation (1984), Choreo-Graphics (1989); *Recreations* photography; *Style—* Dr Ann Hutchinson Guest; 17 Holland Pk, London W11 3TD (☎ 01 229 3780)

GUEST, Prof Anthony Gordon; CBE (1989), QC (1987); s of Gordon Walter Leslie Guest (d 1982), of Maidencombe, Devon, and Alice Marjorie, *née* Hooper; *b* 8 Feb 1930; *Educ* Colston's Sch Bristol, St John Coll Oxford (MA); *Career* Lt RA (reg army and TA) 1948-50; called to the Bar Gray's Inn 1955, dean Univ Coll Oxford 1963-64 (fell and praelector 1955-65), prof English Law Univ of London 1966-, reader Common Law Cncl of Legal Educn (Inns of Ct) 1967-80, fell Kings Coll London 1982-, bencher Grays Inn 1978-; memb Lord Chllr Law Reform Ctee 1963-84, UK del to UN Cmmn on Int Trade Law 1968-88; memb bd govrs Rugby Sch 1968-88; FCIarb 1986; *Books* Anson's Law of Contract (21-26 edns 1959-84), Chitty on Contracts (gen ed, 23-26 edns 1968-89), Benjamin's Sale of Good (gen ed, 1-3 edns 1974-86), The Law of Hire-Purchase (1966), Encyclopaedia of Consumer Credit (jt ed, 1975); *Clubs* Garrick; *Style—* Prof Anthony Guest, CBE, QC; 16 Trevor Place, London SW7 1LB (☎ 01 584 9260); Gray's Inn Chambers, Gray's Inn, London WC1 (☎ 01 405 7211)

GUEST, Hon Charles James; yst s of Maj 2 Viscount Wimborne, OBE (d 1967), and Lady Mabel Fox-Strangways, yr da of 6 Earl of Ilchester; *b* 10 July 1950; *Educ* Harrow, Sandhurst; *m* 1976, Simone, da of Patrick Whinney, of Guernsey; 2 s, 1 da; *Career* served 9/12 Royal Lancers 1973; Capt Royal Wessex Yeomanry; memb Int Stock Exchange 1986; with Cobbold Roach Ltd; *Recreations* shooting, fishing; *Clubs* Flyfishers', White's; *Style—* The Hon Charles Guest; Truckwell Manor Farm, Lydeard St Lawrence, Taunton, Somerset TA4 3PT (☎ 0984 56327)

GUEST, Hon David William Graham; er s (by 2 m) of Baron Guest, PC (Life Peer); *b* 18 Sept 1943; *Educ* Charterhouse Cambridge, Clare Coll Cambridge (BA); *Career* chartered accountant; *Style—* Hon David Guest; c/o Rt Hon Lord Guest, PC, 22 Lennox St, Edinburgh EH4 1QA

GUEST, Dr Douglas (Albert); CVO (1975); s of Harold Eastwood Guest (d 1948), of Henley-on-Thames, and Margaret Sarah, *née* Higgins; *b* 9 May 1916; *Educ* Reading Sch, RCM, King's Coll Cambridge (MA MusB); *m* 4 Dec 1941, Peggie Florentia, da of Thomas Falconer (d 1934), of Amberley, Glos; 2 da (Susan Jennifer b 1943, Penelope Anne b 1946); *Career* WWII Maj RA, (despatches Normandy 1944), gazetted Hon Maj RA 1945; dir music Uppingham 1945-50; organist: Salisbury Cathedral 1950-57, Worcester Cathedral 1957-63; conductor 3 Choirs Festival 1957-63, organist and master of choristers Westminster Abbey 1963-81, prof RCM 1963-81; examiner Royal Sch Music 1948-86; Mus D (Cantuar) 1981, MA Oxford by inc 1947; FRCM 1963, Hon RAM 1964, Hon FRCO 1966, FRSCM 1970; *Recreations* fly-fishing, golf; *Clubs*

Fly Fishers; *Style*— Dr Douglas Guest; The Gables, Minchinhampton, Glos GL6 9JE (☎ 0453 883191)

GUEST, Dr George Howell; CBE (1987); s of Ernest Joseph Guest (d 1966), and Gwendolen, *née* Brown (d 1965); *b* 9 Feb 1924; *Educ* Chester Cathedral Choir Sch, Kings Sch Chester, Saint John's Coll Cambridge (MA, MusB); *m* 31 Oct 1959, Nancy Mary, da of William Peters Talbot; 1 s (David b 26 June 1963), 1 da (Elizabeth b 11 Oct 1965); *Career* WW II RAF (France and India) 1942-46; organist and dir of Music St John's Coll Cambridge 1951-, lectr in Music Cambridge Univ 1956-82 (asst lectr 1953-56), examiner to Associated Bd of RSM 1959-, univ organist Cambridge 1973-, dir Arts Theatre Cambridge; concerts with St John's Coll Choir incl: USA, Canada, Japan, Australia, Western Europe, Philippines, S Africa; pres: Royal Coll of Organists 1978-80, Cathedral Organists Assoc 1980-82, Incorporated Assoc of Organists 1987-89; Mus D (Lambeth) 1977, hon Mus D (Univ of Wales) 1989, hon memb RAM, hon memb Gorsedd y Beirdd Eisteddfod Genedlaethol Cymru; fell Royal Coll of Organists 1942, FRSCM; *Recreations* Welsh language, Association football; *Clubs* Utd Oxford & Cambridge Univ, Clwb Ifor Bach (Cardiff); *Style*— Dr George Guest, CBE; 9 Gurney Way, Cambridge (☎ 0223 354932); Saint John's College, Cambridge (☎ 0223 338683)

GUEST, Ivor Forbes; s of Cecil Marmaduke Guest (d 1954); *b* 14 April 1920; *Educ* Lancing, Trinity Coll Cambridge; *m* 1962, Ann Hutchinson; *Career* slr, dance historian; sec Radcliffe Tst 1966-; chm Royal Acad of Dancing 1969-; *Books* Napoleon III in England, The Ballet of the Second Empire, The Romantic Ballet in Paris, The Romantic Ballet in England, Fanny Elssler, Jules Perrot, Gautier on Dance, The Dancer's Heritage, etc; *Clubs* Garrick, MCC; *Style*— Ivor Guest Esq; 17 Holland Park, London W11 3TD (☎ 01 229 3780)

GUEST, Hon (Christopher) John Graham; only s (by 1 m) of Baron Guest, PC (Life Peer) (d 1984); *b* 30 July 1929; *Educ* Eton, Clare Coll Cambridge (BA); *m* 1960, Myrna Dukes, MD, Chicago; 1 s (Christopher b 1967), 1 da (Amanda b 1964); *Career* AA Dipl, RIBA; *Clubs* Chelsea Arts; *Style*— The Hon John Guest; 19 Cheyne Row, London SW3 5HW

GUEST, Hon Julian John; 2 s of 2 Viscount Wimborne, OBE, JP, DL (d 1967); *b* 12 Oct 1945; *Educ* Stowe; *m* 1, 1970 (m dis 1978), Emma Jane Arlette, da of Cdr Archibald Gray, DSO, RN (ret), of Tilbridge, Gt Staughton, St Neots, Hunts; m 2, 1983, Jillian, da of late N S G Bannatine; *Style*— The Hon Julian Guest; 29 Bolton Gdns, London SW5

GUEST, Hon Simon Edward Graham; WS; s of Baron Guest, PC (Life Peer, d 1984), by his 2 w, Catherine Hotham (gda of Adm of the Fleet Sir Charles Hotham, GCB, GCVO, and cous of Lord Hotham); *b* 22 April 1949; *Educ* Charterhouse, Univ of Dundee; *m* 1977, Fiona, da of Robert Wilson Taylor Lamont (1976); 1 s, 1 da; *Career* solicitor; *Recreations* shooting, golf; *Clubs* New (Edinburgh), Hon Co of Edinburgh Golfers (Muirfield); *Style*— The Hon Simon Guest, WS; 40 Hope Terrace, Edinburgh EH9 2AR (☎ 031 447 4075; office 031 226 6703)

GUEST de SWARTE, Lindsey (Lyn); da of Alfred John de Swarte, of Stanmore, Mx, and Anne, *née* Yashvin; *b* 12 June 1941; *Educ* Rosa Bassett Sch, St Martins Sch of Art; *m* 1, 1958 (m dis 1970), Frank Colin Sutton-McCrae; 2 s, 2 da; m 2, 1970 (m dis 1983), Raymond Guest; 1 s,1 da; ptnr 1984, Catherine Gibb; *Career* publisher and managing ed Sportswoman 1984-86, dir Sportsworld International 1987, publisher and managing ed Sportscene 1988; freelance writer 1989-; elected Magazine Sportswriter of the Year 1988; life memb Nat Skating Assoc of GB (ice speed skating referee); helped found Women's Ice Hockey and League 1980, played for Streatham Strikers (league winners 1981) 1980-84; on Int Skating Union panel of Starters, referee Euro Youth Championships 1983; *Books* Women and Sport (1988); *Recreations* ice skating, reading, painting; *Clubs* Sports Writers Assoc of Gr Britain; *Style*— Ms Lyn Guest de Swarte; 21 Mount Earl Gdns, London SW16 (☎ 01 677 4985)

GUETERBOCK, Hon Mrs; Hon Cynthia Ella; *née* Foley; da of Eva Mary FitzHardinge, Baroness Berkeley (16 in line, d 1964), and Col Frank Wigram Foley, CBE, DSO (d 1949); hp of sis, Baroness Berkeley (17 in line); *b* 31 Jan 1909; *m* 4 Aug 1937, Brig Ernest Adolphus Leopold Gueterbock, RE (d 1984), yst s of Alfred Gueterbock, of Bowdon, Cheshire; 1 s (Anthony FitzHardinge Gueterbock b 20 Sept 1939); *Recreations* golf, bridge; *Clubs* Naval and Military; *Style*— The Hon Mrs Gueterbock; The Plough, Terrick, Aylesbury, Bucks

GUILD, Ivor Reginald; CBE (1985), WS; s of Col Arthur Marjoribanks Guild, DSO, TD, DL (decd), and Phyllis Eliza, *née* Cox; *b* 2 April 1924; *Educ* Cargilfield, Rugby, New Coll Oxford, Edinburgh Univ; *Career* procurator fiscal of Lyon Court 1961-, clerk to Abbey Court of Holyroodhouse 1970-79, baillie of Abbey Ct 1979-, chm Nat Museum of Antiquities Scotland 1981-86, ed Scottish Genealogist 1959-, Chancellor of dioceses of Edinburgh and St Andrew's; *Recreations* golf, genealogy; *Clubs* New (Edinburgh); *Style*— Ivor Guild, Esq, CBE, WS; 16 Charlotte Sq, Edinburgh EH2 4YS (☎ 031 225 8585; home 031 226 4882)

GUILD, Stuart Alexander; TD (1955), WS (1950); s of William John Guild (d 1958), of Belmont Gardens, Edinburgh, and Mary Margaret Morton Stuart (d 1968); *b* 25 Jan 1924; *Educ* Edinburgh Academy, George Watson's Coll, Queen's Univ Belfast, Edinburgh Univ (BL); *m* 21 Nov 1950, Fiona Catherine, da of Andrew Francis MacCulloch (d 1952); 1 s (David b 1952), 2 da (Cathleen b 1955, Lesley b 1960); *Career* RA, served UK 1942-44, Burma 1944-45, French Indo-China 1945-46, Malaya 1946-47, TA RA 1947-65; ptnr (now sr ptnr) Guild & Guild WS 1950; Notary Public memb The Company of Merchants of the City of Edinburgh (asst Master's Court) 1972-75, hon tres Army Cadet Force Assoc (Scotland) 1976-, cncl memb The Army Cadet Force Assoc 1976-; memb RA Cncl of Scotland 1985-; chm Scottish Smallbore Rifle Assoc 1986-88, memb Scottish Target Shooting Cncl 1986-88; govr Melville Coll Tst 1976-; chm Sandilands Memorial Tst 1985-; *Recreations* golf, target shooting, photography, collecting; *Clubs* Watsonian, Murrayfield GC, Edinburgh Academical; *Style*— Stuart Guild, Esq, TD, WS; 5 Rutland Square, Edinburgh, (☎ 031 229 5394)

GUILDFORD, 7 Bishop of 1983-; Rt Rev Michael Edgar Adie; s of Walter Granville Adie and Kate Emily, *née* Parish; *b* 22 Nov 1929; *Educ* Westminster, St John's Coll Oxford (MA); *m* 1957, Anne Devonald Roynon; 1 s, 3 da; *Career* former resident chaplain to Archbishop of Canterbury, vicar St Mark Sheffield 1960-69, rural dean of Hallam 1966-69, rector of Louth 1969-76, vicar of Morton with Hacconby 1976-83, archdeacon of Lincoln 1977-83; chm Gen Synod Bd of Educn and Nat Soc 1989-; *Style*— The Rt Rev the Lord Bishop of Guildford

GUILFORD, David John Scotchburn; s of Arthur Guilford, CBE (d 1975), of Banstead, and Nora Christine, *née* Snell (d 1987); *b* 4 Oct 1930; *Educ* Harrow, Christ's Coll Cambridge (MA); *Career* asst master Highfield Sch Liphook 1954-59, house master Eton Coll 1973-88 (asst master 1959-); winner of Eton Fives Amateur Championship Kinnaird Cup, govr Beaudesert Park Sch 1968-, hon sec Eton Fives Assoc 1961-69, vice pres Eton Fives Assoc 1975-; Liveryman Worshipful Co of Goldsmiths' 1978; *Recreations* sport, philately, contract, bridge; *Clubs* Hawks (Cambridge), MCC, Jesters; *Style*— David Guilford, Esq; 1 Gulliver's, Eton Coll, Windsor, Berks SL4 6DB (☎ 0753 865045)

GUILFORD, 9 Earl of (GB 1752); Edward Francis North; DL (Kent 1976); also Baron Guilford (E 1683); patron of three livings; s of Major Lord North (k accidentally 1940, himself er s of 8 Earl of Guilford), and Joan, da of Sir Merrik Burrell, 7 Bt, CBE; suc gf, 8 Earl; *b* 22 Sept 1933; *Educ* Eton; *m* 1956, Osyth Vere Napier, da of Cyril Leeston Smith; 1 s; *Heir* s, Lord North; *Style*— The Rt Hon the Earl of Guilford, DL; Waldershare Park, Dover, Kent (☎ 820244)

GUILFOYLE, Senator the Hon Dame Margaret Georgina Constance; *née* McCartney; DBE (1980); *b* 15 May 1926; *Educ* Australian National University; *m* 20 Nov 1952, S M L Guilfoyle; 1 s, 2 da; *Career* accountant; senator (Lib) for Vic 1971-87, formerly federal minister for finance; minister for educn, minister for social security; dir Victoria State Opera Bd; *Recreations* reading, theatre; *Clubs* Lyceum (Melbourne); *Style*— Senator the Hon Dame Margaret Guilfoyle; 21 Howard St, Kew, Vic 3101, Australia; Melbourne, Vic 3002, Australia

GUILLAUME, John; s of Reginald Guillaume (d 1953), and Isabel, *née* Turton (d 1980); *b* 9 May 1925; *Educ* Cheltenham; *m* 1975, Angela Rae, da of Norman Moffett; 1 s, 2 da; *Career* Fleet Air Arm, Eastern Fleet; slr, conslt (formely sr ptnr) Guillaume & Sons Slrs; master Worshipful Co of Solicitors of the City of London 1980-81; contrib Roving Commissions; *Recreations* cruising (yacht 'New Melody'), skiing, tennis, gardening, choral music; *Clubs* Carlton, Royal Cruising (Hon slr 1985-), Royal Lymington Yacht (vice-commodore 1987-); *Style*— John Guillaume, Esq,; c/o Guillaume & Sons Slrs, Dorchester House, Church St, Weybridge, Surrey (☎ 0932 840111, telex 929843, fax 0932 858092)

GUILLUM SCOTT, Lady; Muriel Elizabeth; da of late James R Ross, of Thornton Heath, Surrey; *m* 1939, Sir John Arthur Guillum Scott, TD (d 1983), s of Guy H Guillum Scott, of Kensington, London; 1 da; *Style*— Lady Guillum Scott; 5 North Close, St Martins Sq, Chichester, W Sussex

GUILOR, Ralph John; s of John Kenneth Guilor, and Ingeborg Elizabeth *née* Bambach; *b* 1 Jan 1955; *Educ* Dartford GS, Portsmouth Sch of Architecture; *m* 9 Sept 1979, Judith Elizabeth, da of Harold James Turner; 1 s (Edward Charles b 1985), 1 da (Rachel Elizabeth b 1983); *Career* architect; sr ptnr Guilor Petch Design Ptnrship, BArch, Dip Arch, RIBA; *Recreations* music, art, sport; *Style*— Ralph Guilor, Esq; c/o Barclays Bank, 1 Montpellier Exchange, Cheltenham, Glos; Suite 8, Bath Mews, 19 Bath Parade, Cheltenham, Glos (☎ 0242 521608)

GUINNESS, Sir Alec; CBE (1955); *b* 2 April 1914; *Educ* Pembroke Lodge Southbourne, Roborough Eastbourne; *m* 1938, Merula Silvia, da of M H Salaman; 1 s; *Career* RN Combined Ops WWII; actor; films incl: Oliver Twist, Kind Hearts and Coronets, The Lavender Hill Mob, The Bridge on the River Kwai (Best Actor of the Year Oscar 1957), Tunes of Glory, Laurence of Arabia, Star Wars, A Hanful of Dust, and more; Special Oscar for contribution to film 1979, Lawrence Olivier Award for Services to the Theatre 1989; recent roles incl (*plays*) The Old Country, A Walk in the Woods; (*television*) Tinker, Tailor, Soldier, Spy, Smiley's People, Monsignor Quixote; Hon Doctor of Fine Arts (Boston Coll), Hon DLitt Oxon; Kt 1959; *Books* Blessings in Disguise (1985); *Clubs* The Garrick, Athenaeum; *Style*— Sir Alec Guinness, CBE; c/o London Management, 235/241 Regent St, London W1

GUINNESS, Hon Catriona Rose; da of 2 Baron Moyne; *b* 1950; *Educ* Cranborne Chase and Winchester Co HS, LMH Oxford (MA); *Career* botanist and farm manager; *Style*— The Hon Catriona Guinness; Biddesden Farm, Andover, Hants

GUINNESS, Hon Desmond Walter; s of 2 Baron Moyne; *b* 1931; *Educ* Gordonstoun, Ch Ch Oxford; *m* 1, 1954 (m dis 1981), HSH Princess Marie-Gabrielle Sophie Joti Elisabeth Albertine Almeria, da of HSH Prince Albrecht Eberhard Karl Gero-Maria von Urach, Count of Wurttemberg; 1 s, 1 da; m 2, 1984 Penelope, da of Graham Cutherbertson; *Career* pres Irish Georgian Soc; Hon LLD Trinity Coll Dublin; *Books* Georgian Dublin (1979), Irish Houses and Castles (co-author, 1971) The White House (1980), Palladio, a Western Progress (co-author, 1976), Newport Restored (co-author, 1981); *Style*— The Hon Desmond Guinness; Leixlip Castle, Co Kildare

GUINNESS, (Cecil) Edward; CVO (1986); er s of John Cecil Guinness (d 1970, gs of Richard Samuel Guinness, whose great uncle Arthur was the founder of the family brewing firm), of Clarehaven, Parbold, nr Wigan, Lancs; *b* 1924; *Educ* Stowe, Univ of Belfast, Sch of Brewing Birmingham; *m* 1951, Elizabeth Mary Fossett, da of George Alan Thompson (d 1971), of Albrighton Hall, nr Wolverhampton; 3 da ; *Career* served WWII, Offr Cadet RA (invalided out); vice-chm Guinness Brewery Worldwide; dir: Guinness plc, Wolverhampton and Dudley Breweries 1964-87; chm Harp Lager; vice-pres Brewers' Soc (chm 1985-86); chm: governing body Dame Alice Owen's Sch Potters Bar, UK Tstees Duke of Edinburgh's Cwlth Study Cons 1971-86, Fulmer Parish Cncl, Licensed Trade Charities Tst; past pres and memb exec ctee Licensed Victuallers Nat Homes; Past Master Worshipful Co of Brewers; memb: governing body Lister Inst, dept tst Queen Elizabeth's Fndn for the Disabled; life memb Industl Soc; *Recreations* gardening, shooting, travel; *Style*— C Edward Guinness, Esq, CVO; Huyton Fold, Fulmer Village, Bucks (☎ 395 3179, office 01 965 7700)

GUINNESS, Lady Emma Lavinia; da of 3 Earl of Iveagh; *b* 7 Dec 1963; *Educ* Lincoln Coll, Oxford (BA, MPhil); *Style*— Lady Emma Guinness

GUINNESS, Hon Erskine Stuart Richard; s of 2 Baron Moyne; *b* 16 Jan 1953; *Educ* Winchester, Edinburgh Univ; *m* 26 April 1984, Louise Mary Elizabeth, o da of late Patrick Dillon-Malone; 1 s (Hector b 1986), 1 da (Molly b 1985); *Career* MFH Tedworth Hunt 1981-84, memb Wilts CC 1979-81, farmer, tstee Guinness Tst Housing Assoc, govr Chadacre Agric Inst 1982-88; *Recreations* bee-keeping, fishing, rare breeds; *Style*— The Hon Erskine Guinness

GUINNESS, Hon Mrs Diarmid; Felicity; da of Sir Andrew Hunter Carnwath, KCVO, *qv*; *b* 15 Nov 1942; *m* 1962, Hon Diarmid Edward Guinness (d 1977); 1 s, 3 da; *Style*— The Hon Mrs Diarmid Guinness; 2 Keats Grove, London NW3 2RT (☎ 01 435 5861)

GUINNESS, Hon Finn Benjamin; s of 2 Baron Moyne; *b* 26 August 1945; *Educ* Winchester, Ch Ch Oxford (MA), Inst of Animal Genetics Edinburgh U (PhD); *Career* biologist; former pres Arabian Horse Soc; *Style*— The Hon Finn Guinness; Biddesden

House, Andover, Hants

GUINNESS, Hon Fiona Evelyn; da of 2 Baron Moyne; *b* 26 June 1940; *Educ* Cranborne Chase, McGill Univ Canada; *Career* zoologist; joint author of publication Red Deer, Behaviour and Ecology of Two Sexes; *Style—* The Hon Fiona Guinness; Isle of Rhum, Inner Hebrides, Scotland

GUINNESS, Lt Cdr Sir Howard Christian Sheldon; VRD (1953); s of Edward Douglas Guinness, CBE (d 1983), by his 1 w, Martha Letière, *née* Sheldon; er bro of John Guinness, CB, *qv*; *b* 3 June 1932; *Educ* Eton; *m* 1958, Evadne, da of Capt Evan Gibbs, Coldstream Gds (n of 1 Baron Wraxall); 2 s (Christopher b 1963, Dominic b 1966), 1 da (Annabel b 1959); *Career* served RNR, Lt Cdr; joined S G Warburg & Co 1955, exec dir 1970-85; dir Haris & Sheldon GP 1960-81; dir and dep chm Youghal Carpets (Hldgs) 1972-80; chm N Hants Cons Assoc 1971-74; Wessex Cons Assoc: vice-chm 1974, chm 1975-78, tres 1978-81; dairy farmer, memb cncl English Guernsey Cattle Assoc 1963-72; kt 1981; *Clubs* White's; *Style—* Lt Cdr Sir Howard Guinness, VRD; The Manor House, Glanvilles Wootton, Sherborne, Dorset DT9 5QF

GUINNESS, James Edward Alexander Rundell; CBE (1986); s of Sir Arthur Guinness, KCMG, of Hawley Place, Hants; *b* 23 Sept 1924; *Educ* Eton, Oxford Univ; *m* 1953, Pauline, da of Vivien Mander; 1 s (Hugo), 4 da (Miranda, Sabrina, Anita (Hon Mrs Amshal Rothschild), Julia (Hon Mrs Michael Samuel)); *Career* Sub Lt RNVR; dir Guinness Peat Gp; chm Public Works Loan Bd; *Recreations* hunting, shooting, fishing; *Clubs* Brooks's, Pratt's, Roy Yacht Sqdn; *Style—* James Guinness, Esq, CBE; Coldpiece Farm, Mattingley, Basingstoke, Hampshire (☎ 073 326 292)

GUINNESS, John Ralph Sidney; CB (1985); s of Edward Douglas Guinness, CBE (d 1983), by his 1 w, Martha Letière, *née* Sheldon; yr bro of Sir Howard Guinness, *qv*; *b* 23 Dec 1935; *Educ* Rugby, Trinity Hall Cambridge; *m* 1967, Valerie, da of Roger North, JP (7 in descent from Roger North, KC, MP Dunwich, memoirist and yr bro of 1 Baron Guilford, whose descendants became Earls of Guilford), whose m was Grace, da of Gen Hon Sir Percy Feilding, KCB, 2 s of 7 Earl of Denbigh, PC); 1 s, 1 da (and 1 s decd); *Career* Overseas Devpt Inst 1961-62; joined FO 1962, econ relations dept 1962-63, third sec UK mission to UN NY 1963-64, seconded to UN Secretariat as special asst to Dep Under-Sec (later Under-Sec Econ and Social Affrs) 1964-66, FCO 1967-69, first sec (econ) High Cmmn Ottawa 1969-72, seconded to Central Policy Review Staff (Cabinet Off) 1972-75 and 1977-79, alternate UK rep to Law of the Sea Conf 1975-77; transferred to Domestic Civil Serv 1980; under-sec Dept of Energy 1980-83, dep sec 1983-; *Recreations* iconography; *Clubs* Brooks's, Beefsteak; *Style—* John Guinness, Esq, CB; Department of Energy, Thames House South, Millbank, London SW1P 4QJ (☎ 01 211 5444)

GUINNESS, Hon Jonathan Bryan; s and h of 2 Baron Moyne by his 1 w, Hon Diana, *née* Freeman Mitford (da of 2 Baron Redesdale and who subsequently m Sir Oswald Mosley, 6 Bt, *see* Mosley, Hon Lady); *b* 16 Mar 1930; *Educ* Eton (King's Scholar), Trinity Coll Oxford; *m* 1, 1951 (m dis 1963), Ingrid, da of Maj Guy Wyndham, MC (ggs of 1 Baron Leconfield), by his 2 w, Grethe; 2 s, 1 da (*see* Neidpath, Lord); m 2, 1964, Mrs Suzanne Phillips, da of H W D Lisney, of Gerona, Spain; 1 s, 1 da; *Career* dir: A Guinness Son & Co, Leopold Joseph & Sons; former Reuters journalist, chm Monday Club 1972-77; *Clubs* Carlton, Beefsteak, Ibstock Working Men's; *Style—* The Hon Jonathan Guinness; 17 Kensington Square, London W8; Osbaston Hall, Market Bosworth, Nuneaton; Ermita de San Sebastian, Cadaques, Gerona, Spain

GUINNESS, Kenelm Edward Lee; s and h of Sir Kenelm Guinness, 4 Bt; *b* 30 Jan 1962; *Educ* Embry-Riddle Aeronautical U (BSc); *Career* commercial pilot; *Style—* Kenelm Guinness, Esq; Rich Neck, Claiborne, Maryland 21624 USA (☎ 301 745 5079)

GUINNESS, Sir Kenelm Ernest Lee; 4 Bt (UK 1867); s of Kenelm Edward Lee Guinness, MBE, RNVR (decd), suc unc, Sir Algernon Guinness, 3 Bt, 1954; *b* 13 Dec 1928; *Educ* Eton, MIT (BSc); *m* 1961, Mrs Jane Nevin Dickson; 2 s; *Heir* s, Kenelm Edward Lee Guinness; *Career* late 2 Lt RHG; engr Int Bank for Reconstruction and Devpt (World Bank) 1954-75; ind consltg engr 1975-; *Clubs* Cavalry & Guards; *Style—* Sir Kenelm Guinness, Bt; Rich Neck, Claiborne, Maryland, 21624, USA (☎ 301 745 5079)

GUINNESS, Hon Kieran Arthur; 5 s of 2 Baron Moyne, *qv*; *b* 11 Feb 1949; *Educ* Winchester, Ch Ch Oxford; *m* 4 Nov 1983, Mrs Vivienne Halban, da of André-Jacques van Amerongen, DFC, MB, of Grafton House, Blisworth, Northants; 1 s (Malachy b 1986), 1 da (Kate b 1985); *Career* botanist; *Style—* The Hon Kieran Guinness; Knockmaroon House, Castleknock, Co Dublin

GUINNESS, Lady Louisa Jane; da of 3 Earl of Iveagh; *b* 20 Feb 1967; *Style—* Lady Louisa Guinness

GUINNESS, Hon Murtogh David; s of 1 Baron Moyne, DSO, TD, PC (assassinated in Cairo 1944); *b* 1913; *m* 1949, Nancy Vivian Laura, da of Cyril Edward Tarbolton (decd); *Style—* The Hon Murtogh Guinness; 117 E 80th St, New York, USA

GUINNESS, Hon Thomasin Margaret; da of 2 Baron Moyne; *b* 1947; *Educ* Cranborne Chase, Farnham Coll of Art; *Career* potter and painter; *Style—* The Hon Thomasin Guinness; Biddesdon House, Andover, Hants

GUINNESS, Timothy Whitmore Newton (Tim); s of Capt Eustace Guinness, DSC, RN, and Angela, *née* Hoare; *b* 20 June 1947; *Educ* Eton, Magdalene Cambridge (BSc), MIT (MSc); *m* 6 June 1974, Beverley Anne, da of George Mills, of Rotherfield, East Sussex; 2 s (Edward, Harry), 2 da (Mary, Katherine); *Career* Baring Bros & Co Ltd 1970-77, Guinness Mahon & Co 1977-87 (investmt dir 1982-87), md Guinness Flight Global Asset Mgmnt Ltd 1987-; *Recreations* sailing; *Clubs* City Univ, MCC, RYS; *Style—* Tim Guinness, Esq; 32 St Mary at Hill, London EC3P 3AJ (☎ 01 623 9333, fax 01 623 2760, telex 884035)

GUINNESS, William Loel Seymour; s of Gp Capt Loel Guinness, OBE (d 1988), and his 2 w, Lady Isabel Manners, yr da of 9 Duke of Rutland; bro of Marchioness of Dufferin and Ava, *qv*; *b* 28 Dec 1939; *Educ* Eton; *m* 1971, (Agnes Elizabeth) Lynn, da of Ian Day, of Brampton Ash, Northants; 2 s, 1 da; *Career* served Irish Gds 1959-61, Lieut; farmer; *Recreations* golf, skiing, tennis; *Clubs* White's, Pratt's; *Style—* William Guinness, Esq; 10 Bourne St, London SW1; Arthingworth Manor, Market Harborough, Leics

GUIREY, Prince Azamat; yr s of Prince Kadir Guirey (d 1953), and his 2 w, Vaguidé, *née* Sheretlock (d 1975); family descends from Genghis Khan and were Khans of the Crimea until conquered by Catherine the Great of Russia in 1783 and later recognized as Princes by several Imperial Ukases; *b* 14 August 1924; *Educ* Hotchkiss Sch, Yale Univ (BA); *m* 1, 10 Aug 1957 (m dis 1963), Princess Sylvia, da of Prince Serge Platonovitch Obolensky-Neledinsky-Meletzky; 2 s (Kadir Devlet b 1961, Adil Sagat b 1964), 1 da (Selima b 1960); m 2, 25 Aug 1971, Fredericka Ann, da of Frederick Sigrist, co-fndr with Sir Thomas Sopwith of Hawker Siddeley Gp Ltd (d 1956); 1 s (Caspian b 1972); *Career* associated with Young & Rubicam, advertising agency; formerly dir Weidenfeld Publishers; *Recreations* hunting, shooting, fishing, golf; *Clubs* White's, Garrick, Pratt's, Beefsteak, Kildare St (Dublin), Brook (NY); *Style—* Prince Azamat Guirey; Bakchisarai, Lyford Cay, Nassau, Bahamas, PO Box N969 (☎ 809 32 64506)

GUISE, Christopher James (Jamie); s of Sir Anselm Guise, 6 Bt (d 1970), and Nina Margaret Sophie, *née* Grant; hp of bro, Sir John Guise, 7 Bt, *qv*; *b* 10 July 1930; *Educ* Stowe; *m* 7 Nov 1969, Carole Hoskins, eld da of Jack Hoskins Master (d 1979), and Ruth Master, of Long Parrish, Hants; 1 s (Anselm b 1971), 1 da (Ruth b 1972); *Career* dir: Shenley Tst Servs Ltd, Winglaw Gp Ltd, Purchasing Mgmnt Servs Ltd, Justice (UK) Ltd, Pasta Galaore Ltd; *Recreations* golf, shooting, fishing, gardening; *Clubs* Turf, White's, MCC; *Style—* Jamie Guise, Esq; Easton Town Farm, Sherston, Malmesbury, Wilts

GUISE, George Robert John; s of George Wilfred Guise (d 1987); *b* 17 June 1943; *Educ* Ratcliffe Coll, Ch Ch Oxford, Hatfield Coll Durham; *m* 1972, Hilary Hope, da of Hastings Beck, of Cape Town (d 1973); 3 s; *Career* exec dir Consolidated Gold Fields 1981-86; special advsr on indust and sci PMS Policy Unit 1986-; *Recreations* shooting, music, physics; *Clubs* East India; *Style—* George Guise, Esq

GUISE, James Theodore (Louis); TD (1946); s of John Dougal Guise (d 1952), of 25 Kensington Gate, London W8, and Laura Lilian, *née* Buckland (d 1950); *b* 26 August 1910; *Educ* Winchester, Trinity Coll Oxford (MA); *m* 22 June 1940, Barbara, da of Alfred Jefferson Brett (d 1958), of Mark Ash, Abinger Common, Surrey; 1 s (Richard b 10 Sept 1941); *Career* 2 Lt City of London Yeo RHA 1939, Adj 10 Lt AA Trg Regt 1940-41, Maj RA 14 Army Burma 1942-45, instr in Gunnery 1944-45; slr 1935; sr ptnr Hunters Slrs Lincolns Inn 1968-69, dir Law Fire Insur 1955-65; gen cmmr of Income Tax 1957-67, first pres Holborn Law Soc 1967, chm Slrs Benevolent Assoc 1962, memb Lowtonian Soc; *Recreations* cricket, soccer, golf, skiing, tapestry work; *Clubs* MCC; *Style—* Louis Guise, Esq, TD; Greathed Manor, Lingfield, Surrey (☎ 0342 832884)

GUISE, Sir John; GCMG (1975), KBE (1975), MP (Ind) Papua New Guinea 1977-; *b* 1914; *Career* MHA Papua New Guinea 1964-67, speaker 1968-75, dep chief min and min for agric to 1975, govr-gen Papua New Guinea 1975-77; KStJ; *Style—* Sir John Guise, GCMG, KBE, MP; National Parliament, Port Moresby, Papua New Guinea

GUISE, Sir John Grant; 7 Bt (GB 1783), of Highnam Court, Glos; s of Sir Anselm Guise, 6 Bt, JP (d 1970), by his w Margaret, da of Sir James Grant, first and last Bt; *b* 15 Dec 1927; *Educ* Winchester, RMC Sandhurst; *Heir* bro, Christopher James Guise, *qv*; *Career* Capt 3 Hussars (ret 1959); Jockey Club official 1968-; patron of one living; *Clubs* Turf; *Style—* Sir John Guise, Bt; Elmore Court, Gloucester (☎ 0452 720293)

GULL, Sir Rupert William Cameron; 5 Bt (UK 1872); s of Sir Michael Swinnerton Cameron Gull, 4 Bt (d 1989), and his 1 w, Yvonne, *née* Heslop; *b* 14 July 1954; *Educ* Diocesan Coll Cape Town, Cape Town Univ; *m* 1980, Gillian Lee, da of Robert MacFarlaine; *Style—* Rupert Gull, Esq; 2 Harcourt Rd, Claremont 7700, Cape Town, S Africa

GULLIVER, James Gerald; s of William Frederick Gulliver and Mary Gulliver; *b* 17 August 1930; *Educ* Campbeltown GS, Glasgow Univ, Harvard Univ; *m* 1, 1958, Margaret Joan, *née* Cormack; 3 s, 2 da; m 2, 1977, Joanne, *née* Sims; *Career* Nat Serv RN; mgmnt conslt Urwick Orr & Ptnrs Ltd 1961-65; md Fine Fare (Hldgs) Ltd 1965-72 (chm 1967-72); chm: Argyll Gp plc, James Gulliver Assocs Ltd 1977-, Alpine Hldgs Ltd 1977-, Gulliver Foods Ltd 1978-, Argyll Foods 1979-, Gulliver Hotels Ltd 1978-, Amalgamated Distilled Products; dir: Concrete (Scotland) Ltd 1960-61, Assoc Br Foods Ltd, Manchester Utd Football Club plc 1979-; memb cncl IOD, vice pres Mktg Soc, memb PM's Enquiry into Beef Prices 1973; Liveryman Worshipful Co of Gardeners; Guardian Young Businessman of the Year 1972; FBIM, FRSA; *Recreations* skiing, sailing, music, motoring; *Clubs* Carlton, Royal Thames YC; *Style—* James Gulliver, Esq; 27 Seymour Walk, London SW10 9NE; Argyll Group plc, Argyll House, Millington Rd, Hayes, Middx UB3 4AY (☎ 01 848 3801, telex 924888)

GULLIVER, Pam (Pamela Mary); da of Wilfred Arthur Glasby (d 1972), and Ada, *née* Featam (d 1970); *b* 10 Nov 1942; *Educ* Chorleywood Coll, Reading Univ (BA), Open Univ; *m* 17 March 1962, William Albert (Bill) Gulliver, *qv*, s of Robert William Gulliver (d 1967); *Career* writer under pen names: Victoria Thirsk (fiction) books incl Besminster Calendar (1980), Mary Allerton-North (non-fiction) with numerous magazine articles published; dir: Int Tennis Servs 1981-, Anything Nostalgic 1983-, Leisurescope 1987-; served various charity ctees (often with husband); *Recreations* voluntary work, good food, history; *Style—* Mrs Pam Gulliver; The Neraldage, 35 North Ct Ave, Reading RG2 7HE (☎ 0734 871479)

GULLIVER, William (Bill) Albert; s of Robert William Gulliver (d 1967), and Irene May, *née* Shaw; *b* 27 Sept 1935; *Educ* Sherborne, Univ of Reading, Univ of Bristol; *m* 17 March 1962, Pamela Mary, *qv*, da of Wilfred Arthur Glasby (d 1972), of Yorkshire; *Career* farmed on family farm near Bath; currently md: Int Tennis Servs, Anything Nostalgic, Varves (a charity); prison visitor 1983-; memb: Reading C of C 1983-, mgmnt ctee The Keep; *Books* Scottish Verse (compiler 1989), numerous articles on prisom reform in nat and trade jnls; *Clubs* IOD, Berkshire Hash House Harriers; *Style—* Bill Gulliver, Esq; The Neraldage, 35 North Court Avenue, Reading RG2 7HE

GULLY, Hon Edward Thomas William; s and h of 4 Viscount Selby; *b* 21 Sept 1967; *Style—* The Hon Edward Gully

GULLY, Hon James Edward Hugh Grey; yr s of 3 Viscount Selby (d 1959); *b* 17 Mar 1945; *Educ* King's Sch, Canterbury; *m* 1971, Fiona Margaret, only da of Ian S Mackenzie, of Iona; 2 s; *Style—* Hon James Gully; Island of Shuna, Ardnaine, by Oban, Argyll, Scotland

GUMBEL, (Henry) Edward; OBE (1989); s of Gustav Ludwig Gumbel (d 1942); *b* 31 August 1913; *Educ* Univs of Zürich, Geneva, Heidelberg, Berlin, LSE; *m* 1946, Ellen, *née* Frank; 3 s, 2 da; *Career* barr Middle Temple; dir: Willis Faber plc and assoc cos 1956-83, Storebrand (UK) 1972-85, Teddington Inair Co (UK) 1983-, Allianz Legal Protection Co 1986-; chm: Allianz Int Inair Co 1980-88, Tokio (UK) 1980-88, Tokio Reinsur Co 1982-88, hon pres Willis Faber Zurich 1988-; vice-pres Chartered Insur Inst, chm British Insurance Law Assoc 1979 and 1980; author of numerous legal pubns; Commander's Cross of Order of Merit (German Federal Repbulic) 1984; *Recreations* tennis, skiing, walking, music, reading; *Style—* H Edward Gumbel, Esq,

OBE; Windybrae, The Highlands, E Horsley, Surrey; 15 Trinity Sq, London EC3P 3AX (☎ 01 481 7088)

GUMLEY, Frances Jane Miriah Katrina (Mrs A S Mason); da of Franc Stewart Gumley (d 1981), and Helen Teresa McNicholas (d 1987); *b* 28 Jan 1955; *Educ* St Benedicts Ealing, Newnham Coll Cambridge (MA); *m* Andrew Arthur Mason 2 July 1988; *Career* journalist, broadcaster, radio and television prodr; braille transcriber 1975, ed asst Catholic Herald 1975-76, staff reporter and literary ed 1976-79, ed Catholic Herald 1979-81, sr prodr religious broadcasting BBC 1981-88, series ed Channel 4 1988-89; Mistress of the Keys (Catholic Writers Guild) 1982-87; *Books* The Good Book (with Brian Redhead), The Christian Centuries (with Brian Redhead); *Recreations* embroidery, deep sea diving; *Style—* Miss Frances Gumley; c/o Mr & Mrs M J Mason, 3 Hurst Close, London NW11;

GUMLEY, Kenneth Louis; s of Lindsay Douglas Gumley, JP (d 1973); *b* 7 Oct 1932; *Educ* Fettes Coll; *m* 1959, Anne Hogg, da of Lt-Col Robert Hogg Forbes, OBE (d 1978); 1 s (John Lindsay Robert b 1967), 1 da (Sally Catherine b 1961); *Career* chartered surveyor, sr ptnr Gumley's Estate Agents Edinburgh; md: The Joint Properties Ltd, Gogar Park Curling Club Ltd; *Recreations* curling, sailing (yacht: 'Bandit of Lorne', westerly corsair); *Clubs* New (Edinburgh), Royal Forth YC, Royal Caledonian Curling; *Style—* Kenneth L Gumley, Esq; Almondfield, 18 Whitehouse Rd, Edinburgh EH4 6NN (☎ 031 336 4839)

GUMMER, Rt Hon John Selwyn; PC (1985), MP (C) Suffolk Coastal 1983-; s of Canon Selwyn Gummer, and Sybille, *née* Mason; *b* 26 Nov 1939; *Educ* King's Sch Rochester, Selwyn Coll Cambridge; *m* 1977, Penelope Jane, yr da of John P Gardner; 2 s, 2 da; *Career* dir Shandwick Publishing Co 1966-81; md EP Gp of Cos 1975-80; chm: Selwyn Sancroft Int 1976-81, Siemssen Hunter Ltd 1980 (dir 1973); memb Gen Synod C of E 1978-, guardian of the Shrine of Our Lady of Walsingham 1983-; MP (C): Lewisham W 1970-74, Eye Suffolk 1979-1983; additional vice-chm Cons Party 1972-74, PPS to Min of Agric 1972, govt whip 1981-83, under-sec of state Employment June-Oct 1983; min of state: Employment 1983-85, Agric Fisheries and Food 1985-; chm Cons Pty 1983-85; *Books* To Church with Enthusiasm (1969), The Permissive Society (1971), The Christian Calendar (1973), Faith in Politics (1987); *Recreations* reading, gardening, Victorian buildings; *Style—* The Rt Hon John Selwyn Gummer, MP; 25 Creffield Rd, London W5 (☎ 01 992 2271); Winston Grange, via Stowmarket, Suffolk (☎ 0728 860522)

GUMMER, Peter Selwyn; s of Rev Canon Selwyn Gummer, and Sybille, *née* Mason; *b* 24 August 1942; *Educ* Kings Sch Rochester, Selwyn Coll Cambridge (BA, MA); *m* 23 Oct 1982, Lucy Rachel, da of Antony Ponsonby Dudley-Hill (d 1969), of Sandle Manor, Fordingbridge, Hants; 3 da (Naomi b 10 Jan 1984, Chloe b 17 Nov 1985, Eleanor b 5 Aug 1988); *Career* Portsmouth and Sunderland Newspaper Gp 1964-65, Viyella Int 1965-66, Hodgkinson & Ptnrs 1966-67, Industl & Commercial Fin Corpn (part of 3i Gp) 1967-74, chm and chief exec Shandwick plc 1974-; memb: IOD, IPR, IOM; FRSA; *Recreations* opera, cricket, rugby; *Clubs* MCC, Hurlingham; *Style—* Peter Gummer, Esq; 4 Cottesmore Gdns, London W8 5PR; Shandwick plc, 61 Grosvenor St, London W1X 9DA, (☎ 01 408 2232, fax 01 493 3048, car phone 0836 283 313)

GUN-MUNRO, Sir Sydney Douglas; GCMG (1979), MBE (1957); s of Barclay and Marie Josephine Gun-Munro; *b* 29 Nov 1916; *Educ* Grenada Boys' Secdy Sch, King's Coll Hosp London; *m* 1943, Joan Benjamin; 2 s, 1 da; *Career* house surgn Horton EMS Hosp 1943, MO Lewisham Hosp 1943-46; dist MO Grenada 1946-49, surgn Gen Hosp St Vincent 1949-71, dist MO Bequia 1972-76, govr St Vincent 1977, govr-gen St Vincent and Grenadines 1979-85; FRCS 1985; kt 1977; *Style—* Sir Sydney Gun-Munro, GCMG, MBE; Bequia, St Vincent and the Grenadines, West Indies (☎ 83261)

GUNDILL, (James) Norman; s of Maj (Henry) James Gundill (d 1979), of Pontefract, and Marjorie, *née* Sainter (d 1967); *b* 29 Oct 1942; *Educ* Sedbergh, The Coll of Law; *m* 5 Sept 1967, Angela Dianne, da of John Massarella (d 1988), of Almholme Grange, Doncaster; *Career* admitted slr 1966; sr ptnr Carter Bentley & Gundill 1987- (asst slr 1966-68, ptnr 1968-); pres Wakefield Incorporated Law Soc 1984-85 (sec 1976-79); Pontefract Park Race Co Ltd: dir 1972-, sec 1973-, md 1977-, clerk of the course 1983; chm Northern Area Racecourse Assoc 1988- (sec 1977-88), dir The Racecourse Assoc Ltd 1977-; memb Law Soc 1967-; *Recreations* racing, gardening, cricket, squash, keeping fit; *Style—* J Norman Gundill, Esq; The Coach House, Kirk Smeaton, Pontefract, West Yorks WF8 3JS (☎ 0977 620649); 33 Ropergate, Pontefract, West Yorks WF8 1LE (☎ 0977 703224)

GUNDRY, Hon Mrs; Hon Caroline Anne Sabina; *née* Best; er da of 8 Baron Wynford, MBE; *b* 28 Mar 1942; *m* 1964, Edward Patrick Gundry; 1 s, 2 da; *Style—* Hon Mrs Gundry; 15 Genoa Ave, London SW15 (☎ 01 789 0390)

GUNDRY, Rev Canon Dudley William; s of Cecil Wood Gundry (d 1955), and Lucy, *née* Wright (d 1973); *b* 4 June 1916; *Educ* Sir Walter St John's Sch, King's Coll London (AKC, BD, MTh); *Career* curate St Matthew Surbiton 1939-44, lectr in the history of the religions Univ Coll of N Wales 1944-60, warden Neuadd Reichel Bangor 1947-60, dean Bangor Faculty of Theology 1956-60, prof of religious studies Univ of Ibadan 1960-63, canon residentiary and chllr Leicester Cathedral 1963-87, canon emeritus 1987-, rural dean Leicester 1966-74; co-fndr and hon sec Br Assoc for the History of the Religious 1954-60, memb C of E Gen Synod 1970-80, church affrs conslt and corr The Daily Telegraph 1978-86, chm Alderman Newton's Educnl Fndn 1977-, fndn govr Leicester GS 1981-; *Books* Religions: An Historical and Theological Study (1958), The Teacher and the World Religions (1968), Neil's Bible Companion (contrib 1959), Collins's Dictionary of the English Language (contrib 1979), The Synod of Westminster (1986); *Clubs* Athenaeum; *Style—* The Rev Canon D W Gundry; 28 Stoneygate Ct, Leicester LE2 2AH

GUNDRY, Maj Gerald Ashton; DSO (1944); s of Edward Pearkes Gundry, of Chilfrome, Maiden Newton, Dorchester, Dorset, and Marjorie Una, *née* Milne (d 1973); *b* 16 August 1911; *Educ* Eton; *m* 5 Jan 1937 (m dis 1948), Barbara Margaret, da of Lt-Col A J Wilson, DSO, of Mulsey Brnk, Malton, Yorks; m 2, 1948, Ferelith Patricia Clarke; 1 s (Robin b 6 March 1949), 1 da (Jane b 27 March 1956); *Career* cmmnd 16/5 The Queens Royal Lancers 1932, ret 1938, rejoined 1939; landowner; sec Duke of Beaufort's Hunt 1938-50, jt master 1951-85; *Style—* Maj Gerald Gundry, DSO; Clayfields, Shipton Moyne, Tetbury, Glos GL8 8QA

GUNLAKE, John Henry; CBE (1947); s of John Gunlake (d 1916), of 138 Upper Clapton Rd N16, and Alice, *née* Marriott (d 1943); *Educ* Grocers' Co's Sch, Epsom Coll; *Career* Miny of Shipping statistics and intelligence div 1943-47 (attended confs between Churchill, Roosevelt and combined Chiefs of Staff: Washington, Quebec, Cairo, Yalta); N Br and Mercantile Insur Co Ltd 1923-25, Guardian Life Assur Co Ltd 1927-34, sr ptnr R Watson & Sons consulting actuaries 1962-70 (joined 1935); hon consulting actuary to Royal UK Beneficent Assoc 1967-84; memb: ctee on econ and fin problems of the problems of the Provision for Old Age 1953-54, Cons Pty Policy Gp on public servants' pensions 1965-69, Cons Pty Policy Gp on the Fin of Soc Security 1964-65, Royal Cmmn on Doctors' and Dentists' Remuneration 1957-60, Permanent Review Body on Doctors' & Dentists' Remuneration 1962-70; FIA 1933 (cncl memb 1941-66, hon sec 1952-54, vice-pres 1956-59, pres 1960-62), FSS 1951, FIS 1952; *Books* Text-Book Premiums for Life Assurance and Annuities (1939), contrib Journal of the Institute of Actuaries; *Recreations* reading, music, working; *Clubs* Reform; *Style—* John Gunlake, Esq, CBE; 120 Clapham Common, Northside, London SW4 9SP (☎ 01 228 3008)

GUNN, Dr Alexander Derek Gower; OBE (1989); s of Col Alexander Joseph Gunn (d 1978), of West Bridgford, Nottingham, and Cassandra Valerie, *née* Hines (d 1978); *b* 27 August 1933; *Educ* William Hulme's GS Manchester, Univ of Sheffield; *m* 4 Jan 1956, Sheila Mary, da of Wilfred Gearey (d 1976), of Sale, Manchester; 1 s (Mark Alexander Gower b 25 Aug 1958), 1 da (Jessica Mary Cassandra b 21 April 1960); *Career* asst Gp Darbishire House Health Centre Manchester 1961-64, asst MO Univ Health Serv Sheffield 1964-67, dir Univ Health Serv Reading 1971- (dep dir 1967-71); temp advsr WHO Geneva 1982; Pres: Br Assoc Health Servs in Higher Educn (UK), Euro Union Sch and Univ Health Servs Assoc of Welfare Offrs in Higher Educn (UK), Reading Diabetic Assoc; med advsr Berks Red Cross Soc; former govr: Nat Bureau for Handicapped Students, Norlands Trg Coll for Nursery Nurses Hungerford Berks; med author ed and advsr to publishers; MRCS, LRCP, MRCGP, DPH, DObstRCOG; *Books* Priviledged Adolescent (1970), International Handbook of Medical Science (1974), Uprooting - Psycho - Social Problems of Overseas Students (1983), Oral Contraception - 30 Year History (1986); *Recreations* wining, dining, gardening, boating; *Style—* Dr Alexander D G Gunn, OBE; The Old Barn, School Lane, Wargrave, Berks RG10 8AA (☎ 073 522 2845); 23c South Snowdon Harbour, Portmadoc, N Wales; University Health Centre, 9 Northcourt Ave, Reading RG2 7HE (☎ 874551/2)

GUNN, Catherine Rachel; da of John Sinclair Gunn, of Callow, Derbys, and Rosemary Elizabeth, *née* Williams; *b* 28 May 1954; *Educ* St Swithuns Sch Winchester, Univ of Durham (BA), Univ of Edinburgh (Dip Business Admin); *Career* investmt analyst Rouch Remnant & Co 1976-78; fin writer: Investors Chronicle 1978-80, The Times 1980-81, freelance 1981-83; fin writer and dep ed Financial Weekly, fin writer and dep city ed Today 1986 (city ed 1987-); memb NUJ 1978-; *Recreations* reading, travel, scribbling, entertaining; *Clubs* Health Haven; *Style—* Miss Catherine Gunn; 70 Vauxhall Bridge Rd, London SW1 (☎ 01 630 1300, fax 01 630 6839)

GUNN, Prof Sir John Currie; CBE (1976); s of Richard Gunn, and Jane Blair Currie; *b* 13 Sept 1916; *Educ* Glasgow Acad, Glasgow Univ, St John's Coll Cambridge; *m* 1944, Betty Russum; 1 s; *Career* WWII researching for Admty; former applied mathematics lectr Manchester and London Univs; Cargill prof of natural pholosophy Glasgow Univ 1949-82 (head of dept 1973-82, emeritus prof 1982-); former memb: Sci Res Cncl, UGC; FRSE, FIMA, FInstP; *Style—* Prof Sir John Gunn, CBE; 32 Beaconsfield Rd, Glasgow G12 0NY (☎ 041 357 2001)

GUNN, John Humphrey; s of Francis Gunn, of Northwich, Cheshire, and Doris, *née* Curbishley; *b* 15 Jan 1942; *Educ* Sir John Deane's GS, Univ of Nottingham (BA); *m* 2 Oct 1965, Renate Sigrid, da of Alfred Boehme (d 1968), 3 da (Ingrid b 1966, Alison b 1968, Natalie b 1968); *Career* Barclays Bank 1964-68, Astley & Pearce Ltd 1968-79, formed EXCO plc 1979, Br & Cwlth Holdings plc 1985- (currently chm); non exec dir: Rank Houis McDougall plc 1987, Smith New Court plc 1986, Silvermines plc 1985; chm Barnham Broom plc Norfolk, co-fndr Inst of German, Austrian and Swiss Affairs Univ of Nottingham; *Recreations* golf, opera, skiing, walking, classical music; *Clubs* MCC, City of London; *Style—* John Gunn, Esq; British & Commonwealth Holdings plc, King's House, 36/37 King St, London EC2V 8BE (☎ 01 600 3000, fax 600 0734, telex 884095)

GUNN, Robert Norman; s of Donald MacFie Gunn (d 1930), and Margaret, *née* Pallister (d 1965); *b* 16 Dec 1925; *Educ* Royal HS Edinburgh, Worcester Coll Oxford (MA); *m* 1956, Joan, da of Fredrick Parry (d 1972); 1 da (Jane Victoria b 1961); *Career* Lt RAC 1944-47; chm Boots Co plc 1985- (vice-chm 1983-85, chief exec 1983-87, md industl div 1980-83, dir 1976-), dir Foseco plc 1984-; memb: bd of mgmnt Assoc Br Pharmaceutical Indust 1981-84 (vice-pres 1983-84), cncl CBI 1985-; PCFC 1989, CBIM 1983, FInstD 1985; *Style—* Robert Gunn, Esq; The Boots Company plc, Nottingham NG2 3AA (☎ 0602-506111)

GUNN, Thom(son) William; s of Herbert Smith Gunn; *b* 29 August 1929; *Educ* Univ Coll Sch Hampstead, Trinity Coll Cambridge (BA); *Career* poet; teacher Univ of California at Berkeley, assoc prof of English 1958-66, freelance for 10 years, visiting lectr in English 1976-; *Books of Poetry* Fighting Terms (1954), The Sense of Movement (1957), My Sad Captains (1961), Positives (with Ander Gunn, 1966), Touch (1967), Moly (1971), Jack Straw's Castle (1976), Selected Poems (1979), The Passages of Joy (1982); *Clubs* Mind Shaft (NY); *Style—* Thom Gunn, Esq; 1216 Cole St, San Francisco, Calif 94117, USA

GUNN, Sir William Archer; KBE (1961), CMG (1955), JP; s of late Walter Gunn; *b* 1 Feb 1914; *Educ* King's Sch Parramatta NSW; *m* 1939, Mary, nee Haydon; 1 s, 2 da; *Career* grazier and co dir; chm Int Wool Secretariat 1961-73, dir: Rothmans of Pall Mall (Aust) Ltd, Grazcos Co-Op Ltd, Clausen Steamship Co (Aust) Pty Ltd, Walter Reid & Co Ltd, Gunn Rural Mgmnt Pty Ltd; chm and md: Moline Pastoral Co Pty Ltd, Roper Valley Pty Ltd, Coolibah Pty Ltd, Mataranba Pty Ltd, Unibeef Australia Pty Ltd, Gunn Devpt Pty Ltd; *Style—* Sir William Gunn, KBE, CMG, JP; 98 Windermere Rd, Ascot, Qld 4007, Australia (☎ 268 2688); Wool Exchange, 69 Eagle St, Brisbane, Qld 4000 (☎ 21 4044)

GUNNING, Charles Theodore; CD (1964); s and h of Sir Robert Gunning, 8 Bt; *b* 19 June 1935; *Educ* Royal Roads Mil Coll BC, RN Engrg Coll, Tech Univ of Nova Scotia; *m* 1969 (m dis 1982), Sarah, da of Col Patrick Easton, of Tonbridge; 1 da; *Career* Lt Cdr RCN/Canadian Armed Forces 1952-80; engrg conslt; pres Ottawa Branch Royal Cwlth Soc 1975-78 and 1980-81, vice-chm Nat Cncl in Canada 1980-; Silver Jubilee Medal 1977; PEng; *Recreations* squash, rugby (refereeing), skiing; *Clubs* RMC of Canada, Ottawa Athletic, Royal Cwlth Soc; *Style—* Charles Gunning, Esq, CD; 2940 McCarthy Rd, Ottawa K1V 8K6, Ontario, Canada (☎ 613 737 2179)

GUNNING, Christopher; s of Alexis Lambertus Gunning (d 1962), of Cheltenham, London, and Janet Alice, *née* Bennett; *b* 5 August 1944; *Educ* Hendon Co GS,

Guildhall Sch of Music and Drama (ARCM, AGSM, BMus); *m* 17 June 1974, Annie Christine, da of Flt Lt Clifford William Cornwall Farrow (d 1985), of Bristol; 4 da (Olivia b 1975, Pollyanna b 1977, Verity b 1981, Chloe b 1985); *Career* composer; TV and film scores incl: Day of the Triffids 1981, Rogue Male 1975, Charlie Muffin 1979, Wilfred and Eileen 1981, Flame to the Phoenix 1982, East Lynne 1982, Children's Opera "Rainbow Planet" 1983, Rebel Angel 1987, Porterhouse Blue 1987 (BAFTA Award for the Best Original TV Music), Hercule Poirot 1989, Why the Whales Came 1988; composer dir PRS, fndr memb Assoc of Professional Composers; *Books* First Book of Flute Solos , Second Book of Flute Solos, Really Easy Flute Book, Really Easy Trumpet Book, Really Easy Horn Book (1987); *Recreations* sailing, walking, reading, horticulture, wine; *Style*— Christopher Gunning, Esq; The Old Rectory, Mill Lane, Monks Risborough, nr Aylesbury, Bucks HP17 9LG

GUNNING, John Edward Maitland; CBE (1960, OBE 1945); s of John Elgee Gunning of Manor House, Moneymore, Co Down; *b* 1904; *Educ* Harrow, Magdalene Coll Cambridge; *m* 1936, Enid Menhinick; 2 s; *Career* barr Gray's Inn 1933, sr asst judge advocate gen Far East 1965-70; *Style*— John Gunning, Esq, CBE; 31 Brunswick Ct, Regency St, London SW1

GUNNING, Sir Robert Charles; 8 Bt (GB 1778); s of Charles Archibald John Gunning (d 1910) (ggs of 6 Bt); suc kinsman, Brig-Gen Sir Charles Vere Gunning, 7 Bt, CB, CMG; *b* 2 Dec 1901; *Educ* St Paul's, Leeds Univ; *m* 1934, Helen Nancy, da of late Vice Adm Sir Theodore John Hallett, KBE, CB; 8 s, 2 da (and 1 da decd); *Heir* s, Lt-Cdr Charles Gunning, RCN; *Career* Lt RA (TA) Anti-Aircraft Cmd, Capt 1940; *Style*— Sir Robert Gunning, Bt; Box 802, Peace River, Alberta, Canada

GUNNINGHAM, John Robert; s of Howard James Gunningham (d 1974), and Zaida Zula (d 1946); *b* 26 Mar 1924; *Educ* Brentwood Sch, Oxford Univ (MA); *m* 22 July 1951, Philippa Anne, da of Brig Rev CEL Harris, of Church House, Sutton, Dover, Kent; 3 s (Robert b 1953, Paul b 1955, Charles b 1963); *Career* RCS 1942-47, 2 Lt 1944, T/Capt 1947; colonial serv and overseas civil serv Tanganyika E Africa 1951-61, dist cmmnr: Lushoto 1959, Manyoni 1960, Kahama 1960-61, slr 1965-; ptnr: Chestermans 1966-67, Ford Gunningham & Co 1967-89; memb Law Soc; *Clubs* Leander (Henley); *Style*— John Gunningham, Esq; Thuja, Bath Rd, Marlborough, Wilts (☎ 0672 52777); Kingsbury House, Marlborough, Wilts (☎ 0672 52265, fax 0672 54891)

GUNNINGHAM, Hon Mrs (Mary Cynthia Burke); *née* Roche; da of 4 Baron Fermoy and Ruth, Lady Fermoy, DCVO, OBE, JP; aunt of HRH The Princess of Wales; *b* 1934; *m* 1, 1954 (m dis 1966), Hon Anthony Berry, MP (later Hon Sir Anthony Berry, d 1984), 6 s of 1st Viscount Kemsley; m 2, 1973 (m dis 1980), Dennis Roche Geoghegan; m 3, 1981, Michael Robert Fearon Gunningham; *Style*— The Hon Mrs Gunningham; 40 Chester Terrace, Regent's Park, NW1; Broadfield Hall Farm, Broadfield, Buntingford, Herts

GUNSTON, Sir Richard Wellesley; 2 Bt (UK 1938); s of Maj Sir Derrick Wellesley Gunston, 1 Bt, MC (d 1985) and Evelyn, Lady Gunston; *b* 15 Mar 1924; *Educ* Harrow, Clare Coll Cambridge; *m* 1, 1947 (m dis 1956), Elizabeth Mary, da of Sir Arthur Colegate, MP; 1 da; m 2, 1959 (m dis), Joan Elizabeth Marie, da of Mrs Marie Walker, of Somerset West, Cape Province, S Africa; 1 s; m 3, 1962, Veronica Elizabeth Loyd, da of Maj Haines, and wid of Capt Vivian Loyd; *Heir* s, John Wellesley Gunston b 1962; *Career* Colonial Serv Nigeria, Nyasaland, Bechuanaland 1948-60; *Style*— Sir Richard Gunston, Bt

GUNTER, John Forsyth; s of Dr Herbert Charles Gunter (d 1959), and Charlotte Rose Scott, *née* Reid; *b* 31 Oct 1938; *Educ* Bryanston, Centl Sch of Art and Design; *m* 19 Dec 1969, Micheline, da of Col Maxwell S McKnight, of 520 N St S W, Washington DC; 2 da (Jessica b 4 June 1972, Nicolette b 16 Oct 1978); *Career* theatre designer; 28 prodns Royal Court Theatre 1965-66 incl: D H Lawrence Trilogy, Saved, The Contractor, The Philanthropist, West of Suez, Inadmissible Evidence; RSC: Juno and the Paycock, All's Well that Ends Well (produced on Broadway 1983), Mephisto 1986; National Theatre: Guys and Dolls (SWET Award Best Designer), The Rivals, The Beggar's Opera, Wild Honey (SWET Award Best Designer), The Government Inspector, Bay at Nice, Wreckedc Eggs; West End: Comedians, Stevie, The Old Country, Rose, Made in Bangkok, High Society, Mrs Klein, Secret Rapture; opera designs incl: The Greek Passion WNO, Faust ENO, Peter Grimes Teatro Colon Buenos Aries, The Meistersinger Cologne, Un Ballo in Masquera Sydney Opera House, The Turn of the Screw Munich, Macbeth Leeds, Simon Boccanegra for Sir Peter Hall Glyndebourne (also Albert Herring, La Traviata 1987, Fulstaff 1988), Porgy and Bess for Trevor Nunn Glyndebourne; FRSA 1982; *Style*— John Gunter, Esq; The National Theatre, South Bank (☎ 01 928 2033)

GUPWELL, Reginald John; s of Alfred John Gupwell (d 1936); *b* 21 Jan 1908; *Educ* King Edward's Sch Birmingham; *m* 1, 1938, Betty (d 1965), *née* Fraley; 1 s (Peter Hugh b 1946): m 2, 1969, Gene Gladys, *née* Hurford; *Career* Maj (England, Egypt, Iraq); chm A J Gupwell Ltd Shopfitters 1975-81 (dir 1936, md 1962-75); pres Nat Assoc of Shopfitters 1963-64; ret; *Recreations* golf, bridge, walking; *Clubs* Harbourne Golf, Edgbaston Priory, St Paul's; *Style*— Reginald Gupwell, Esq; 181 Court Oak Rd, Harborne, Birmingham B17 9AD

GURDEN, Sir Harold Edward; s of late Arthur William Gurden, and Ada Elizabeth, *née* Clewer, of Moseley, Birmingham; *m* 1, 1929, Lucy Isabella Izon (d 1976); 3 da; m 2, Elisabeth Joan Taylor; *Career* MP (C) Birmingham Selly Oak 1955-74; former chm: Ctee of Selection House of Commons, Cons Educn Ctee; chm Soc Dairy Technol; kt 1983; *Recreations* bridge, golf, numismatics; *Style*— Sir Harold Gurden; 20 Portland Rd, Oxford OX2 7EY (☎ 0865 58335)

GURDON, Brig Adam Brampton Douglas; CBE (1980, OBE 1973); elder s of Maj-Gen Edward Temple Leigh Gurdon, CB, CBE, MC (d 1959), of Suffolk, and Elizabeth Madeleine, *née* Wilson (d 1967); *b* 4 May 1931; *Educ* Rugby; *m* 30 Aug 1958, Gillian Margaret, da of Col Charles Newbigging Thomson (d 1987), of Dundee; 4 da (Miranda b 1960, Madeleine b 1962, Melanie b 1966, Mary Louise b 1968); *Career* cmmnd Black Watch 1950, Korean War 1953-53, Mau Mau Kenya 1953-55, Adj Berlin 1956-57, Cyprus 1958, cmmnd Regtl Depot Perth 1960, KAR Tanganyka and Zanzibar 1961-62, Staff Coll 1963, DAA & QMG Gurkha Bde 1964-66, UN Cyprus 1967, MOD Mil Ops 1968-72, GSO1 Eastern Dist 1973-76, Mil Ops 1976-79, (while at MOD became involved in Lancaster House Settlement on Rhodesia, formulated Cwlth Monitoring Force, went to Rhodesia as CoS to Maj-Gen Sir John Acland); RDCS 1981; Cabinet Office 1982-85; ret as Brig 1985; dir St Edmundsbury Cathedral Appeal 1986; *Recreations* shooting, fishing, gardening; *Clubs* Army and Navy (vice chm 1986); *Style*— Brig Adam Gurdon, CBE; Burgh House, Woodbridge, Suffolk (☎ 047335 273); Cathedral Office, Angle Hill, Bury St Edmunds, Suffolk (0284 64205)

GURNEY, David Quintin; s of Richard Quintin Gurney (d 1980), and Elisabeth Margaret, *née* Boughey (d 1985); *b* 6 Feb 1941; *Educ* Harrow, Cambridge Univ, Grenoble Univ; *m* 1965, Jacqueline McLeod, *née* Rawle; 1 s, 2 da; *Career* banker, local dir Barclays Bank Ltd Norwich 1988-; farmer, chm and dir Bawdeswell Farms Ltd, mangaging ptnr Breck Farms, dir Tudor Hall Ltd; pres Norfolk branch Br Red Cross Soc 1989-; *Recreations* field sports; *Clubs* Farmers', MCC, Norfolk; *Style*— David Gurney, Esq; Bawdeswell Hall, East Dereham, Norfolk (☎ 036 288 307); Barclays Bank plc, Regional Office, Bank Plain, Norwich (☎ 0603 660255)

GURNEY, John; s of Sir Eustace Gurney, JP (d 1927); *b* 3 July 1905; *Educ* Eton, New Coll Oxford; *m* 1932, Ann, da of Capt Frederick Ogilvy, RN (3 s of Sir Reginald Ogilvy, 10 Bt, JP, DL, by his w Hon Olivia, da of 9 Lord Kinnaird, KT, PC); 4 da (Priscilla, m Gregory Meath-Baker; Jean m Sir Patrick Mayhew, QC, MP, *qv*; Elizabeth Olivia, m Timothy Bristol; Christian m Maj Clive Forestier-Walker, *qv*) and 1 da decd (Elizabeth); *Career* served with Roy Norfolk Regt & W Africa Frontier Force 1939-43; JP Norfolk 1930-75; md Medici Soc 1935-, chm and md Walsingham Estate Co 1928-; *Recreations* photography; *Clubs* Norfolk (Norwich); *Style*— John Gurney, Esq; The Abbey, Walsingham, Norfolk

GURNEY, Dr Michael James Tyson; s of Norman James Stratton Gurney, of Highfield, Hillcourt Rd, Cheltenham, Glos, and Phyllis Anne May, *née* Tyson; *b* 8 Oct 1941; *Educ* Eastbourne Coll, The London Hosp Med Coll (MB, BS); *m* 22 July 1967, Margaret, da of Arthur Thomas Woodward (d 1976), of Leigh on Sea, Essex; 1 s (Adrian Michael b 1 Dec 1977), 2 da (Nicola b 29 Nov 1970, Philippa b 4 Feb 1973); *Career* surgical registrar Cheltenham Gen Hosp 1969-71, orthopaedic registrar Bristol Royal Infirmary 1971-72, princ in GP ptnrship 1973-; FRCS 1971; *Recreations* squash, tennis, skiing; *Clubs* The Escorts Squash Rackets; *Style*— Dr Michael Gurney; Potters End, Buxted, E Sussex TN32 4PU (☎ 082 581 3249); Ireby Grange, Cumbria; The Meads, Grange Rd, Uckfield, E Sussex (☎ 0825 5777)

GURNEY, Hon Mrs; (Diana) Miranda; *née* (Hovell-Thurlow-) Cumming-Bruce; da of 8 Baron Thurlow, KCMG; *b* 1954; *m* 1981, Michael (Mike) J Gurney, s of J C Gurney; 1 s (Mungo), 1 da (Rowan); *Style*— The Hon Mrs Gurney

GURNEY, Prof Oliver Robert; s of Robert Gurney (d 1950), of Bayworth Corner, Boars Hill, Oxford, and Sarah Gamzu, *née* Garstang, MBE (d 1973); *b* 28 Jan 1911; *Educ* Eton, New Coll Oxford (MA, DPhil); *m* 23 Aug 1957, Diane Hope Grazebrook, da of Rene Esencourt; *Career* Capt RA 1939-45, Bimbashi Sudan Def Force 1940-44; Shillito reader in assyriology Oxford 1946- (prof 1965-78), fell Magdalen Coll 1963, pres Br Inst of Archaeology at Ankara; Freeman City of Norwich; FBA 1959; *Books* The Hittites (latest edn 1981), Some Aspects of Hittite Religion (1977), The Middle Babylonian Legal and Economic Documents From (1983); *Recreations* golf; *Style*— Prof Oliver Gurney; Fir Tree House, Milton Lane, Steventon, Abingdon, Oxon OX13 6SA (☎ 0235 831 212)

GUROWSKA, Countess; Rosanna; only da of Maj 23 Knight of Kerry, 5 Bt, MC; *b* 5 Feb 1945; *m* 1964, 8 Count (Richard Melchior Beaumont) Gurowski (6 in descent from Raphael Gurowski, Chamberlain to Augustus III of Poland and who was cr Count by Letters Patent (1787) of Frederick William II of Prussia. The present Count Gurowski's mother was Angela, da of Peter Haig-Thomas by his w Lady Alexandra, *née* Agar, herself da of 4 Earl of Normanton); 2 da (Iona b 1967, Anya b 1970); *Style*— Countess Gurowska; North End House, Damerham, Fordingbridge, Hants (☎ 072 53 308)

GUTHE, Alexander Digby; s of Digby Ernest Guthe (d 1982), of Silton Hall, Thirsk, N Yorks, and Rosemary, *née* Reid; *b* 3 Jan 1966; *Educ* Haileybury, RAC Cirencester (Dip in Agric); *Career* exec corporate fin dept Greenwell Montagu Securities (London) 1987-88, dir West Hartlepool Steam Navigation Co Ltd (family co) 1989-; *Recreations* shooting, fishing, skiing; *Clubs* Schools; *Style*— Alexander Guthe, Esq; Silton Hall, Thirsk, N Yorks; 4 Church Sq, Hartlepool, Cleveland

GUTHRIE, Maj-Gen Charles Ronald Llewelyn; LVO (1977), OBE (1980); s of Ronald Dalglish Guthrie (d 1982), of 35 Egerton Cres, London SW3, and Nina, *née* Llewelyn (d 1987); *b* 17 Nov 1938; *Educ* Harrow, RMA Sandhurst; *m* 11 Sept 1971, Catherine, da of Lt-Col Claude Worrall, MVO, OBE (d 1973), of Bitham Hall, Avon Dassett, Warwicks; 2 s (David Charles b 21 Oct 1972, Andrew James b 3 Sept 1974); *Career* cmmnd Welsh Gds 1959, serv BAOR and Aden, 22 SAS Regt 1965-69, psc 1972, mil asst to Chief of Gen Staff MOD 1973-74, Bde Maj Household Div 1976-77, CO 1 Bn Welsh Gds serv Berlin and NI 1977-80, Col gen staff mil ops MOD 1980-82, cmd Br Forces New Hebrides 1980, 4 Armd Bde 1982-84, Chief of Staff 1 (Br) Corps 1984-86, GOC NE Dist cmd 2 Inf Div 1986-87, Col Cmdt Intelligence Corps, currently Asst Chief of the Gen Staff MOD; Freeman City of London, memb Worshipful Co of Painters and Stainers; *Recreations* tennis, skiing, travel; *Clubs* Whites; *Style*— Maj-Gen Charles Guthrie, LVO, OBE; Lloyds Bank, 79 Brompton Rd, London SW8 1LH

GUTHRIE, Giles Malcolm Welcome; s and h of Sir Malcolm Guthrie, 3 Bt; *b* 16 Oct 1972; *Style*— Giles Guthrie Esq

GUTHRIE, Sir Malcolm Connop; 3 Bt (UK 1936), of Brent Eleigh Hall, Co Suffolk; s of Sir Giles Guthrie, 2 Bt, OBE, DSC (d 1979), and Rhona, Lady Guthrie; *b* 16 Dec 1942; *Educ* Millfield; *m* 1967, Victoria, da of Douglas Willcock; 1 s, 1 da; *Heir* s, Giles Malcolm Welcome Guthrie b 16 Oct 1972; *Recreations* competitive shooting, deer stalking and hunting; *Style*— Sir Malcolm Guthrie, Bt; Brent Eleigh, Belbroughton, Stourbridge, Worcs DY9 0DW

GUTHRIE, Robert Isles Loftus (Robin); s of Dr W K C Guthrie (d 1981), and A M Guthrie; *b* 27 June 1937; *Educ* Clifton, Trinity Coll Cambridge (MA), Liverpool Univ (CertEd), LSE; *m* 1963, Sarah Julia, da of J Weltman, OBE; 2 s (Andrew b 1965, Thomas b 1970), 1 da (Clare b 1969); *Career* 2 Lt Queens Own Cameron Highlanders 1956-58; head Cambridge House South London 1962-69, schoolteacher Kennington Sch Brixton 1964-66, social devpt offr Peterborough Devpt Corpn 1969-75, asst dir social work serv DHSS 1975-79, dir Joseph Rowntree Meml Tst 1979-88; chief charity cmmr England and Wales 1988-; memb Arts Cncl GB 1979-81 and 1987-88, chm York Arts Assoc 1984-88; memb: cncl Regnl Arts Assoc 1985-88, cncl Univ of York 1980-, cncl Policy Studies Inst 1979-88; chief charity cmmr England and Wales 1988-; *Recreations* music (french horn), mountaineering, archaeology, travel; *Clubs* Utd Oxford and Cambridge Univ; *Style*— Robin Guthrie, Esq; Braeside, Acomb, York YO2 4EZ

GUTHRIE, Hon Sir Rutherford Campbell; CMG (1960); s of late Thomas Oliver

Guthrie; *b* 28 Nov 1899; *Educ* Melbourne C of E GS, Jesus Coll Cambridge (BA); *m* 1927, Rhona Mary, da of late Thomas McKellar; 1 s (and 1 decd); *Career* WWII 1939-45; served: N Africa, N Australia, wounded Alamein (MID); (MID); MLA Vic 1947-50, Min for Lands and for Soldier Settlement 1948-50, dir Phosphate Co-op Co, dir Perpetual Tstees and Executors; kt 1968; *Clubs* The Melbourne, Naval and Military (Melbourne), Leander (Henley on Thames), Ritt and Hawkes (Cambridge); *Style*— The Hon Sir Rutherford Guthrie, CMG; Jedburgh Cottage, Howey St, Gisborne, Vic 3437, Australia

GUTKIND, Fernand Albert (Ferdi); s of Felix Gutkind (d 1966), of Golders Green, London, and Sophie Camille, *née* Espir (d 1984); *b* 10 July 1924; *Educ* Aldenham, RAF, Sorbonne; *m* 16 March 1957, Honor, da of Charles Edward Blow (d 1983), of Old Coulsdon, Surrey; 2 s (Peter b 1958, Charles b 1961), 2 da (Sally b 1962, Diana b 1968); *Career* co dir; specialised in import/export essential oils and gums for the food indust; *Recreations* golf, bridge; *Clubs* Hendon GC, Harrow Bridge; *Style*— Ferdi Gutkind, Esq; 8 The Park, Golders Green, London NW11 7SU; F Gutkind & Co Ltd, 37/38 Chancery Lane, London WC2A 1EL (☎ 01 242 7642, telex 24465)

GUY, Diana; da of Charles Stanley Eade (d 1964), of Broadstairs, Kent, and Vera Dorothy, *née* Manwaring; *b* 27 Mar 1943; *Educ* Queen Anne's Sch Caversham, Lady Margaret Hall Oxford (MA); *m* 25 May 1968, (John) Robert Clare Guy, s of Wilfred Guy (d 1965), of Sydenham, London; 2 s (Jonathan b 1972, Matthew b 1975); *Career* admitted slr 1968, ptnr Theodore Goddard 1973-; chm: Law Soc's Slrs Euro Gp 1985, Law Soc's 1992 Working Pty 1988; memb City of London Slrs Co 1985; memb Law Soc 1968; *Books* The EEC and Intellectual Property (with G I F Leigh, 1981); *Recreations* reading, opera; *Style*— Mrs Diana Guy; 29 Ennerdale Rd, Kew Gdns, Richmond, Surrey TW9 3PE (☎ 01 948 3594); Theodore Goddard, 16 St Martin's-Le-Grand, London EC1A 4EJ (☎ 01 606 8855, fax 01 606 4390, telex 884678)

GUY, Cdr Percy (Denis); s of Henry Percival Guy (d 1953), of New Barnet, Herts, and Elsie Dorothy Angell (d 1972); of the same family as Thomas Guy fndr of Guy's Hospital; *b* 22 Oct 1919; *Educ* Shoreham GS; *m* 1 July 1947, Norma Kimber, da of Norman Frank Kimber (d 1978); 1 s (Jonathan b 1959); *Career* Sub Lt RNVR 1941, Lt RN, engrg specialisation 1946, serv Atlantic, Middle East, Far East, Med, East Africa; Cdr; sr ptnr consultancy practice; CEng, MIEE, FBIM, FIMC, FIIM, FMS, FInstD; *Recreations* sailing, horse riding including dressage and show jumping; *Clubs* Naval and Military, Royal Naval, Royal Albert YC, Infantry Saddle ; *Style*— Cdr Denis Guy; Rowan Hill, Perrymead, Bath BA2 5AY (☎ 0225 834015, fax 0225 836176)

GUY, Richard Perran; s of Rev Wilfred Guy (d 1965) of Newlands Park, London, and Winifred Margaret Guy, *née* Hardesty (d 1988); *b* 10 May 1936; *Educ* Kingswood Sch Bath, Wadham Coll Oxford (MA); *m* 26 Sept 1981, Deborah Ann, da of Kenneth Owen, of Hillside Farm, Adlestrop, Glos; 1 s (Benjamin b 1983), 1 da (Georgina b 1986); *Career* Nat Serv 2 Lt CRMP 1955-57; called to the Bar Inner Temple 1970; memb: Hon Soc Inner Temple; *Recreations* tennis, theatre, skiing; *Clubs* RAC; *Style*— Richard Guy, Esq; 108 Barnsbury Rd, London N1 0ES (☎ 01 278 7220); Brynbanc Farm, Cwmbach, Whitland, Dyfed (☎ 09 946 317); Queen Elizabeth Buildings, Temple, London EC4 (☎ 01 353 7181, fax 01 353 3929)

GUY, Gén Sir Roland Kelvin; GCB (1987, KCB 1980), CBE (1978, MBE 1955), DSO (1972); s of Lt-Col Norman Greenwood Guy; *b* 25 June 1928; *Educ* Wellington, RMA Sandhurst; *m* 1957, Deirdre, da of Brig P Graves-Morris, DSO, MC; 2 da (Gillian, Nicola); *Career* cmmnd KRRC 1948; Col GS HQ Near East Land Forces 1971, cmd 24 Airportable Bde 1972, RCDS 1975, princ staff offr to Chief of Def Staff 1976-78, chief of Staff HQ BAOR 1978-80, Col Cmdt Small Arms Sch Corps 1981-87, mil sec MOD 1980-83, Col Cmdt 1 Bn Royal Green Jackets 1981-86; rep Col Cmdt Royal Green Jackets 1985-86, Adj Gen MOD 1984-865, govr Royal Hosp Chelsea 1987; *Recreations* music, skiing; *Clubs* Army & Navy; *Style*— Gen Sir Roland Guy, KCB, GBE, DSO

GUYATT, Richard Gerald Talbot; CBE (1969); s of Thomas Guyatt (d 1924); *b* 8 May 1914; *Educ* Charterhouse; *m* 1941, Elizabeth Mary, da of Col Arthur Corsellis; 1 step da; *Career* prof of graphic design Royal Coll of Art 1948-78, rector 1978-81 (ret); *Style*— Richard Guyatt, Esq; Forge Cottage, Ham, nr Marlborough, Wilts (☎ 048 84 270)

GUYMER, Patricia Lesley; *née* Bidstrup; eld da of Clarence Leslie Bidstrup (d 1961), and Kathleen Helena (d 1968), *née* O'Brien; *b* 24 Oct 1916; *Educ* Kadina HS and Walford House Adelaide South Australia, Univ of Adelaide (MB BS, MD); *m* 18 Apr 1952, Ronald Frank Guymer (d 1977), s of Frank Guymer (d 1958); 1 step s (Anthony b 1930), 1 step da (Jill b 1932); *Career* AAMC 1942-45; acting hon asst physician Royal Adelaide Hosp 1942-45, MO UN Relief & Rehabilitation Admin Glyn Hughes Hosp 1945-46, asst dept res in industl med MRC 1947-58, clinical asst St Thomas's Hosp 1958-76; memb: sci sub-ctee on Poisonous Substances used in Agric & Food Storage 1956-58, Industl Injuries Advsy Cncl 1970-83, med appeal tbnls 1970-88, Indust Health Fndn Ctee, Chromium Chemicals environmental Health & Safety Ctee 1971-; examiner for Dipl in Indust Health Conjoint Bd and Dundee 1965-82; memb Cons Pty; Mayoress Royal Borough Kingston-upon-Thames 1959-60 and 1960-61; FRSM 1950; FRACP 1954, FRCP, FACOM 1958; *Books* Toxicity of Mercury and Its Compounds (1964); contrib: Cancer Progress (1960), Prevention of Cancer (1967), Chromium (1953), Clinical Aspects of Inhaled Particle (1972); *Recreations* theatre, ballet, music; *Style*— Mrs Patricia Guymer; 11 Sloane Terrace Mansions, Sloane Terrace, London SW1X 9DG (☎ 01 730 8720)

GWENLAN, Gareth; s of Charles Aneurin Gwenlan (d 1939), and Mary, *née* Francis (d 1980); *m* 1, 1962 (m dis); 1 s (Simon); m 2, 1986, Sarah Elizabeth, da of Peter Fanghanel; *Career* head of light entertainment BBC TV; prod and dir: Woodhouse Playhouse 1977, The Fall and Rise of Reginald Perrin 1978-80, Butterflies 1979-81, To The Manor Born 1978-81, Solo 1980, and approx 200 more programmes; *Recreations* dressage, eventing; *Clubs* Savage; *Style*— Gareth Gwenlan, Esq; Alderbourne Manor, Fulmer Lane, Gerrards Cross, Bucks; BBC TV Centre, Wood Lane, London W12 (☎ 01 743 8000)

GWILLIAM, Russell; s of Ernest Charles Gwilliam, of London SW16, and Jessie, *née* Mason; *b* 24 June 1931; *Educ* Mitcham Co GS For Boys, King's Coll London (BSc), Sch of Mil Survey Newbury, Victoria Univ Manchester (DipTP); *m* 24 Oct 1953, Gillian Lesley, da of Leslie Hunkin (d 1980), of Richmond, Surrey; 2 s (Miles b 1962, Nigel b 1970), 2 da (Lesley b 1958, Stephanie b 1960); *Career* HM Colonial Serv Sarawak: asst dir planning 1963-67, chief planning offr 1968-69; ptnr Peat Marwick & Ptnrs Canada 1973-74 (joined 1969), sr ptnr IBI Gp Canada 1974-83, sometime independent conslt UK, awarded Heywood Silver Medal for town & country planning; vice-pres Croydon Bowling Club Ltd; FRGS 1949, FRICS 1959, FRTPI 1963, MCIP 1975; *Recreations* reading, sport, travel; *Clubs* Royal Overseas League, Rugby Club of London; *Style*— Russell Gwilliam, Esq; Canon's End, 37 Canon's Hill, Old Coulsdon, Surrey CR3 1HB (☎ 0737 553 086)

GWILT, George David; s of Richard Lloyd Gwilt (d 1972); *b* 11 Nov 1927; *Educ* Sedbergh, St John's Coll Cambridge; *m* 1956, Ann Dalton, da of Arthur J Sylvester, of Connecticut, USA (d 1973); *Career* actuary; Standard Life Co 1949-: asst official 1956, asst actuary 1957, statistician 1962, mechanisation mangr 1964, systems mangr 1969, dep pensions mangr 1972, pensions actuary 1973, asst gen mangr and pensions mangr 1977, asst gen mangr (fin) 1978, gen mangr and actuary 1979; md and actuary 1985, ret 1988; dir: Hammerson Property Investmt and Devpt Corpn plc 1979-, Euro Assets Tst 1979-, Scottish Mortgage and Tst plc 1983; tstee TSB S Scotland 1966-83, pres Faculty of Actuaries 1981-83, memb Monopolies and Mergers Cmmn 1983-87; *Recreations* flute playing; *Clubs* RAF, New (Edinburgh); *Style*— George Gwilt, Esq; 39 Oxgangs Rd, Edinburgh (☎ 031 445 1266)

GWYN, Hon Mrs; (Clare); *née* Devlin; er da of Rt Hon Baron Devlin, PC (Life Peer); *b* 2 Mar 1940; *m* 1961, Julian Reginald Desgrand Jermy Gwyn, prof in history at Ottawa U, 3 s of Quintin P T J Gwyn, CD, of Thelwell House. Rosemere, Quebec (Vice-Pres & Dir Seagram Overseas Corpn), and gs of the Maj Reginald P J Gwyn (decd), of Stanfield Hall, Norfolk; 2 s (1 decd), 3 da; *Style*— Hon Mrs Gwyn; 484 Highland Ave, Ottawa, Ontario, Canada

GWYN, Philip Hamond Rhys; s of Brig Rhys Anthony Gwyn, OBE (d 1987), and Dorothy Eileen, *née* Macmillan; is a collateral branch of Gwyn of Stanfield Hall, Norfolk (sold 1920), who can trace their ancestry back to Hwfa ap Cynddelw, Chief of the First Noble Tribe of Wales (19th in descent from Cunedda *fl* 400 AD); *b* 18 August 1944; *Educ* Eton, Trinity Coll Camb (MA); *m* 1970, Susan Alice Margaret, da of Brig Derek Shuldham Schreiber, CVO (d 1972); 1 s (Hwfa b 1980), 3 da (Katherine b 1972, Anna b 1974, Christina b 1977); *Career* bar-at-law (Inner Temple 1968); chm Christie Gp plc, dir Alumasc Gp plc, SFV Communications Gp plc, etc; chm The Friends of Great Ormand St; *Recreations* sports, the arts; *Clubs* Brooks's; *Style*— Philip Gwyn, Esq; Dean House, Kilmeston, Alresford, Hants (☎ 096 279 287); 74 Ebury Street, London SW1 (☎ 01 730 7898); 2,4 & 6 York Street, London W1A 1BP (☎ 01 486 5974)

GWYNEDD, Viscount; David Richard Owen; s and h of 3 Earl Lloyd George of Dwyfor, *qv*; *b* 22 June 1951; *Educ* Eton; *m* 29 June 1985, Pamela Alexandra, o da of late Alexander Kleyff; 2 s (Hon William Alexander, Hon Frederick Owen b 15 Aug 1987); *Heir* s Hon William Alexander Lloyd George b 16 May 1986; *Career* Lloyd's broker; hon Adm Texas Navy; *Recreations* shooting; *Clubs* White's; *Style*— Viscount Gwynedd; Fulwood House, Longstock, Nr Stockbridge, Hants

GWYNN-JONES, Peter Llewellyn; s of Maj Jack Llewellyn Gwynn-Jones, of Kalk Bay, Cape Town, SA (d 1981); stepson and ward of Lt-Col Gavin David Young (d 1978), of Spring House, Long Burton, Dorset; *b* 12 Mar 1940; *Educ* Wellington, Trinity Coll Cambridge (MA); *Career* Bluemantle Pursuivant of Arms 1973-83, Lancaster Herald of Arms 1982-; House Comptroller College of Arms 1982; sec Harleian Soc 1982; *Recreations* local architecture, tropical forests, wildlife conservation, fishing; *Style*— Peter Gwynn-Jones, Esq; 79 Harcourt Terrace, London SW10 (☎ 01 373 5859); College of Arms, Queen Victoria St, London EC4 (☎ 01 248 0911)

GWYNNE, Derek Selby; OBE (1986); s of Samuel Frederick Gwynne (d 1975), and Margaret Marth, *née* Fayers (d 1973); *b* 17 June 1924; *Educ* Oxford Sch of Technol Art and Commerce; *m* 2 Sept 1950, Phyllis Gertrude, da of Joseph Edward Freeman (d 1955); 2 s (Derek b 1954, Robert b 1957), 1 da (Julie b 1951); *Career* md: Bentley Engrg Co Ltd 1975-88, Wildt Mellor Bromley Ltd 1983-88, Gwynne Assocs Ltd 1986; chm Br Textle Machinery Assoc, Leicester Engrg Trg Gp; Freeman City of London 1981, Liveryman Worshipful Co of Framework Kuitters 1981; FIProdE 1965, FRS 1987; *Style*— Derek Gwynne, Esq, OBE; 3 Firle Drive, Seaford, E Sussex (☎ 0323 891 563, home 0323 891 563)

GWYNNE-EVANS, David Gwynne; s of Sir Francis Loring, 4 Bt; *b* 1943; *Style*— David Gwynne-Evans, Esq

GWYNNE-EVANS, Monica, Lady; Monica Dalrymple; *née* Clinch; da of Douglas Clinch, of Durban; *m* 1946, Sir Ian William Gwynne-Evans, 3 Bt (d 1986); *Style*— Lady Gwynne-Evans; 57 Eastood Road, Dunkeld, Johannesburg, S Africa

GYNGELL, Bruce; *b* 8 July 1929; *m* 1957 (m dis), Ann Barr; 1 s, 2 da; m 2, 1986, Kathryn Rowan; 2 s; *Career* chief exec Nat Channel 9 Network Australia unitl 1969, md Seven Network 1969-72, dep chm and jt md ATV London 1972-75, fndr chm Australian Broadcasting Tbnl 1977-80, md TV-am (UK) 1984-; *Style*— Bruce Gyngell, Esq; TV-AM, Breakfast Television Centre, Hawley Crescent, London NW1 8EF (☎ 01 267 4300)

H

HABAKKUK, Sir John Hrothgar; s of Evan Guest Habakkuk; *b* 13 May 1915; *Educ* Barry Co Sch, St John's Coll Cambridge; *m* 1948, Mary Richards; 1 s, 3 da; *Career* lectr faculty of economics Cambridge Univ 1946-50, dir of studies in history and librarian Pembroke Coll Cambridge 1946-50 (fell 1938-50, hon fell 1973), Chichele Prof Econ History Oxford and fell All Souls 1950-67, princ Jesus Coll Oxford 1967-84, pres Univ Coll Swansea 1975-84, pro-vice-chllr Oxford Univ 1977-84 (vice-chllr) 1973-77); memb: advsy cncl Public Records 1958-70, SSRC 1967-71, Nat Libraries Ctee 1968-69, admin bd Int Assoc of Univs of UK 1975-84, Royal Cmmn on Historical Manuscripts 1978-; chm: Ctee of Vice-Chllrs and Principals of Univs of UK 1976-77, Oxfordshire Dist Health Authority 1981-84; former pres Royal Historical Soc; Hon DLitt: Wales 1971, Cambridge 1973, Pennsylvania 1975, Kent 1978; kt 1976; *Style*— Sir John Habakkuk; 28 Cunliffe Close, Oxford (☎ 0865 56583)

HABGOOD, Most Rev and Rt Hon John Stapylton; *see*: York, Archbishop of

HACKER, Alan Ray; OBE; s of Kenneth Ray Hacker, and Sybil Blanche, *née* Cogger; *b* 30 Sept 1938; *Educ* Dulwich, RAM; *m* 1, (m dis 1976), Karen Wynne, *née* Evans; m 2, 1977, Anna Maria, *née* Skoka; 3 da (Alcuin, Katy, Sophie); *Career* prof RAM, sr lectr York Univ, conductor/teacher Royal Northern Coll; composer of maj modern clarinet works dedicated to HM the Queen, revived Mozart bassett clarinet in the 1960's, pioneer of authentic classical performances in England, many first modern performances of classical works in the 1970's (Haydn to Mendlessohn), recent debut as operatic conductor; fndr: York early music festival (dir), York clarion band; memb of various arts Cncl Ctees, host Br Cncl; FRAM; *Books* Mozart's Clarinet concerto, Schumann's fantasy pieces (soirée stücke); *Recreations* cooking; *Style*— Alan Hacker, Esq, OBE; 7 Foxthorn Paddock, York YO1 5HJ (☎ 0904 410312); Haydn Rawstron Int Management, PO Box 654, London SE26 4DZ

HACKER, Richard Daniel; s of Samuel Hacker, of London, and Lilli Paula, *née* Eick; *b* 26 Mar 1954; *Educ* Haberdashers Aske's, Downing Coll Cambridge (MA), Universtté Libre De Bruxelles (Licencié Speciale En Droit Européen); *m* 25 March 1988, Sarah Anne, da of Richard Miller, of Bath; *Career* called to the Bar Lincoln's Inn 1977; Hardwicke Scholar 1977, Lincoln's Inn Student of the Year Prize 1977; *Recreations* travel, gastronomy, opera; *Style*— Richard Hacker, Esq; 12 Belsize Rd, London NW6 4RD; 3 Paper Buildings, Inner Temple, London EC4Y 7EU (☎ 01 353 3721, fax 01 353 3527)

HACKET PAIN, Maj Wyndham Jermyn; JP (Surrey 1964), DL (Surrey 1986); eld s of Lt Col Michell Wyndham Hacket Pain (d 1971), of Surrey, and Audrey Ernestine Jermyn, *née* Ford; *b* 27 Dec 1921; *Educ* Harrow, RMA Sandhurst; *m* 6 Dec 1949, Wenllian Kennard, o da of Sir Godfrey Llewellyn, 1 Bt, CB, CBE, MC, JP, DL (d 1986); 2 s (Nicholas Wyndham Llewellyn Hacket Pain b 1953, Simon Michell Hacket Pain b 1956); *Career* serv Grenadier Guards: Western Desert, Italy (Salerno landing), Palestine (despatches), Malaya 1941-52; dir: Lloyd's brokers, Laurence Philipps and Co, Anderson Finch Villiers and Co 1953-67; chm Michell and Jermyn Co Ltd 1968-; chm Woking Cons Assoc 1965-68, serv SE Area Exec Ctee, Area Asst Treas and serv on Central Bd of Finance 1973-74; elected SE Area rep Cncl of Nat Union 1969-74; chm Woking Bench 1979-87; chm Surrey Magistrates' Courts Ctee 1984-87; appointed memb of the Ct Univ of Surrey 1986-; *Recreations* shooting; *Clubs* Boodle's, Pratt's, City of London, MCC; *Style*— Major Wyndham Hacket Pain, JP, DL; Parkstone House, Ashwood Rd, Woking, Surrey (☎ 04862 60754); Dixton Lodge, Hadnock Rd, Monmouth (0600 6702); Michell and Jermyn Co Ltd, 1 Oriental Road, Woking, Surrey GU22 7AH (☎ 04862 20152, telex 859516 MERJER G)

HACKETT, Cyril Charles; s of Charles Edward, (d 1967), and Letitia Elizabeth, *née* Husband (d 1982); *b* 27 April 1924; *Educ* SW Essex Tech Coll; *m* 29 Dec 1946, Peck, da of Joseph Frederick (d 1983); 2 s (Peter Andrew b 1948, Paul Charles b 1960), 2 da (Gillian Letitia b 1950, Francesca Jane b 1958); *Career* dir: Chingford Masonic Hall Ltd, French Kier (London) Ltd; Freemen City of London; *Recreations* community, church, DIY; *Clubs* Thulby; *Style*— Cyril C Hackett, Esq; Pippins, Chelmsford Road, Hatfield Heath, Bishops Stortford, Herts CM22 7BD (☎ 0276 (STD) 730470)

HACKETT, John Charles Thomas; s of Thomas John Hackett of 31 Ventnor Rd, Sutton, Sy, and Doris, *née* Whitefoot (d 1978); *b* 4 Feb 1939; *Educ* Glyn GS Epsom, London Univ (LLB); *m* 27 Dec 1958, Patricia Margaret, da of Eric Ronald Clifford Tubb of 100 Kennel Lane, Fetcham, Sy; *Career* prodn planning mangr Rowntree Gp 1960-64, prodn controller Johnson's Wax 1964, commercial sec Heating and Ventilating Contractors Assoc 1964-70, sec Ctee of Assocs of Specialist Engrg Contractors 1968-79, dir Br Constructional Steelwork Assoc 1980-84 (dep dir 1970-79); dir gen Br Insur and Investmt Brokers Assoc 1984-; memb cncl CBI 1980-88; MInstD 1979, FBIM 1981; *Books* BCSA Members Contractual Handbook (1972, 1979); *Recreations* music, reading, walking, motoring; *Style*— John Hackett, Esq; 15 Downsway Close, Tadworth, Surrey KT20 5DR (☎ 0737 813024); The Br Insur and Investmt Brokers Assoc, Biiba House, 14 Bevis Marks, London EC3A 7NT (☎ 01 623 9043, fax 01 626 9676, telex 987321 Lloyds G)

HACKETT, Gen Sir John Winthrop; GCB (1967, KCB 1962, CB 1958), CBE (1953, MBE 1938), DSO and Bar (1942, 1945), MC (1941), DL (Glos 1982); s of Hon Sir John Winthrop Hackett, KCMG, MLC, of Perth, WA (d 1916), and Deborah Vernon (d 1932, having m 2, 1918, Ald Sir Frank Beaumont Moulden, Lord Mayor of Adelaide), 2 da of Frederick Slade Drake-Brockman, of Guildford, W Australia; *b* 5 Nov 1910; *Educ* Geelong GS, New Coll Oxford (MA, BLitt, hon fellow 1972); *m* 21 March 1942, Margaret, da of Joseph Frena (d 1953), of Graz, Austria. and widow of Friedrich Grossman 1 da and 2 adopted step da; *Career* 2 Lt 8 Hussars 1931, served Palestine 1936 (despatches), seconded Transjordan Frontier Force 1937-39 (despatches), Syria (wounded), Western Desert (wounded), Italy 1943 (despatches), OC 4 Parachute Bde Arnhem 1944 (wounded), Temp Lt-Col 1942, Brig 1943, OC Transjordan Frontier Force 1947, Dep QMG BAOR 1952, OC 20 Armd Bde 1954, Gen OC 7 Armd Div 1956, Maj-Gen 1957, Cmdt RMC of Science 1958-61, Gen OC Northern Ireland Cmd 1961-62, Dep Ch Imperial Gen Staff 1963-64, Dep Chief Gen Staff 1964-66, Gen 1966, C-in-C BAOR and Cdr Northern Army Gp in NATO 1966-68, ADC to HM The Queen 1967-68, ret; principal King's Coll London 1968-75; pres: UK Classical Assoc 1971, UK English Assoc 1974; visiting prof of classics King's Coll; Hon LLD: WA, Queen's U Belfast, Exeter; author; *Books Incl:* I Was A Stranger (1977), The Third World War (1978), The Untold Story (1982), The Profession of Arms (1983); *Recreations* music, wine, reading, travel, salmon and trout fishing; *Clubs* Cavalry and Guards, Carlton, United Oxford and Cambridge, White's; *Style*— Gen Sir John Hackett, GCB, CBE, DSO, MC, DL; Coberley Mill, nr Cheltenham, Glos GL53 9NH (☎ (024 287) 207)

HACKING, Hon (Leslie) Bruce; s of 2 Baron Hacking (d 1971); *b* 16 June 1940; *Educ* Eton; *m* 23 Sept 1967, Hon Fiona Margaret Noel-Paton, da of Baron Ferrier (Life Peer); 1 s, 1 da; *Career* apprenticed to Haberdashers' Co 1955, Liveryman 1962; Freeman City of London 1962; stockbroker; *Clubs* MCC; *Style*— The Hon Bruce Hacking; Burchetts, Lower Mousehill Lane, Milford, Surrey

HACKING, Daphne, Baroness; Daphne Violet; *née* Finnis; eld da of late Robert Finnis, of Kensington, W; *Educ* Priors Field, Godalming, and Paris; *m* 19 Feb 1936, 2 Baron Hacking (d 1971); 2 s (3 Baron, Hon Bruce Hacking), 2 da (Hon Mrs de Laszlo, Hon Mrs du Preez); *Style*— The Rt Hon Daphne, Lady Hacking

HACKING, 3 Baron (UK 1945); Sir Douglas David Hacking; 3 Bt (UK 1938); s of 2 Baron Hacking (d 1971); n of Hon Lady Waller *qv*; *b* 17 April 1938; *Educ* Charterhouse, Clare Coll Cambridge, (BA, MA); *m* 1, 31 July 1965 (m dis), (Rosemary) Anne (who m subsequently, 1982, Anthony Askew, of Highgate), da of Frank Penrose Forrest, FRCSE, of Lytchett Matravers, Dorset; 2 s (Hon Douglas Francis b 8 Aug 1968, Hon Daniel Robert b 27 May 1972), 1 da (Hon Belinda Anne b 1966); m 2, 1982, Dr Tessa Hunt, MB, MRCP, FFARCS, er da of Roland Hunt, CMG, of Whitchurch Hill, Reading, Berks; 2 s (Hon Alexander Roland Harry b 20 Jan 1984, Maxwell David Leo b 8 July 1987); *Heir* s, Hon Douglas Francis Hacking; *Career* Nat Serv RN 1956-58; Lt RNR (ret); sits as Independent peer in House of Lords; barr 1963-76, Harmsworth Maj Entrance Exhibition and Astbury Scholar; attorney New York State 1975, Simpson Thacher and Bartlellt, New York 1975-76; slr Supreme Court Eng & Wales 1977; ptnr Richards Butler; Freeman Worshipful Co of Merchant Taylors' City of London; *Clubs* MCC, Century (New York); *Style*— The Rt Hon the Lord Hacking; Richards Butler and Co, 5 Clifton St, London EC2A 4DQ (☎ 01 247 6555); 21 West Square, London SE11 4SN (☎ 01 735 4400)

HACKING, Hon Edgar Bolton; MBE (1942), TD (1950); yr s of 1 Baron Hacking, PC, OBE (d 1950); *b* 31 May 1912; *Educ* Charterhouse, Clare Coll Cambridge, London Hosp (MA, MB BS, BCh); *m* 1, 3 April 1943, (m dis 1950), Winifred Mary, da of John Christie Kelly; 2 da; m 2, 5 July 1950, Evangeline Grace, da of late Percy Burstal Shearing; 2 s, 1 da; *Career* served with RAMC as anaesthetic specialist; Maj 1940-45; sr resident anaesthetist London Hosp 1939; MO to Queen's Westminsters (TA) 1938-40; sr asst anaesthetist Groote Schuur Hosp; anaesthetist instr Cape Town U 1946-51 and Stellenbosch U 1958; fellow Assoc of Anaesthetists; MRCS, LRCP, FFARCS, DA; *Clubs* MCC and Western Province Sports; *Style*— The Hon Edgar Hacking, MBE, TD,; Leeming, Alice Rd, Claremont, Cape Town, South Africa (☎ 01027 21 774 4544)

HACKING, Hon Mrs (Fiona Margaret); *née* Noel-Paton; da of Baron Ferrier (Life Peer); *b* 1943; *m* 1967, Hon (Leslie) Bruce Hacking, *qv*; *Style*— The Hon Mrs Hacking; Burchett's, Lower Moushill Lane, Milford, Surrey

HACKNEY, Arthur; s of John Thomas (d 1971), of Stoke-on-Trent, and Annie, *née* Morris (d 1979); *b* 13 Mar 1925; *Educ* Burslem Sch of Art, RCA; *m* 14 Aug 1954, Mary Cecilia, ARCA, da of Ernest Baker (d 1946), of Coventry; 2 da (Rosalind b 27 Jul 1956, Clare b 17 May 1961); *Career* WWII RN, serv Western Approaches 1943-46; RCA travelling scholarship 1949; lectr then princ lectr head of dept W Surrey Coll of Art and Desgin 1949-85; work in pub collections inc: Bradford City Art Gallery, V & A, Ashmolean Gallery, Wellington Nat Gallery NZ, Nottingham Art Gallery, Keighley Art Gallery, Wakefield Art Gallery, Preston Art Gallery, Stoke-on-Trent Gallery, Kent Educn Ctee, Staffs Educn Ctee; memb Fine Art Bd CNAA 1975-78; RWS, RE, ARCA; *Clubs* Chelsea Arts; *Style*— Arthur Hackney, Esq; Woodhatches, Spoil Lane, Tongham, Farnham, Surrey (☎ 0252 23919)

HACKNEY, Dr Roderick Peter (Rod); s of William Hackney, and Rose, *née* Morris; *b* 3 Mar 1942; *Educ* John Bright's GS Llandudno, Sch of Architecture Manchester Univ (MA, BA, ARCH, PhD); *m* Christine (Tina); 1 s (Roan b 27 April 1982); *Career* job architect Expo 1967 monorail stations 1965-66, housing architect Libyan govt Tripoli 1967-68, asst to Arne Jacobson Copenhagen 1968-71, establish practice of Rod Hackney Architect in Macclesfield 1972, established a number of offices throughout the UK 1975-87, set up Castward Ltd building and devpt 1983; RIBA: elected nat memb to the cncl 1978, vice pres 1981-83, memb 3 man delgn to USSR under Anglo/Soviet Cultural Agreement 1984, chm The Times/RIBA Community Enterprise Scheme 1985-, pres 1987-; UIA: elected cncl for Gp 1 1981, memb ed bd Int Architect 1983 (Jl of Architect Theory and criticism 1988), vice pres 1985, pres 1988-; visiting prof UP6 Paris 1984, pres Young Architect World Forum Sofia 1985, pres Building Communities Int Community Architecture Conf 1986, special prof in architecture Nottingham Univ

1987; awards: first prize DOE Awards for Good Design in Housing 1975, first prize St Ann's Hospice Architectural Competition 1976, Prix Int d'Architecture de l'Institut National du Logement 1979, commended RICS and The Times Conservation Awards 1980, highly commended DOE Awards 1980, commended The Civic Tst Awards 1980, hon mention Sir Robert Matthews Award 1981, commended Civic Tst Awards 1981, pres' award Manchester Soc for Architects 1982, commended Otis Award 1982, Gold Medal Bulgarian Inst of Architects 1983, Gold Medal Young Architect of the Biennale Sofia 1983, award of commendation Civic Tst Awards 1984, Grand Medal of the Federation de Colegios de Arquitectas de la Republica Mexicana 1986, PA Award for Innovation in Building Design and Construction 1988; hon fell: American Inst of Architects 1988, Federacion de Colegias de Arquitectos de la Republica Mexicana 1988, Utd Architects of the Philippines 1988; chm of tstees Inner City Tst 1986, presented the case for Int Year of Shelter for the Homeless to all Pty Confs 1986, pres Snowdonia Nat Park Soc 1987, patron Llandudno Museum and Art Gallery 1988; ARIBA 1969, FIArb 1977, MCIOB 1987, FFB 1987, PRIBA 1987; *Recreations* photography, butterflies, travelling, walking, outdoor pursuits, looking at buildings, speaking at conferences; *Clubs* Commonwealth; *Style—* Dr Rod Hackney; St Peter's House, Windmill St, Macclesfield, Cheshire SK11 7HS (☎ 0625 31792, fax 0625 616929, car tel 0860 310833)

HADDINGTON, 13 Earl of (S 1619) John George Baillie-Hamilton; also Lord Binning (S 1613) and Lord Byres and Binning (S 1619); only s of 12 Earl (d 1986); *b* 21 Dec 1941; *Educ* Ampleforth, Trinity Coll Dublin, RAC Cirencester; *m* 1, 19 April 1975 (m dis 1981), Prudence Elizabeth, da of Andrew Rutherford Hayles, of Bowerchalke, Wilts; m 2, 8 Dec 1984, Susan Jane, da of John Heyworth, of Bradwell Grove, Burford, Oxon; 1 s (George Edmund Baldred, Lord Binning b 1985), 1 da (Lady Susan Moyra b 15 July 1988); *Heir* s, George Edmund Baldred, Lord Binning b 27 Dec 1985; *Career* farmer, horse breeder; *Recreations* beekeeping, exotic birds, field sports, photography, racing, ufology; *Clubs* Turf, New, Puffin's, Chelsea Arts; *Style—* The Rt Hon the Earl of Haddington; Mellerstain, Gordon, Berwicks TD3 6LG

HADDINGTON, Dowager Countess of; Sarah; da of late George William Cook, of Westmount, Montreal, Canada; *m* 10 Oct 1923, George Baillie-Hamilton, 12 Earl of Haddington (d 1986); *Style—* The Rt Hon Dowager Countess of Haddington; Tyninghame, Prestonkirk, E Lothian

HADDO, Earl of; Alexander George Gordon; s and h of 6 Marquess of Aberdeen, and Temair, *qv*; *b* 31 Mar 1955; *Educ* Harrow, Poly of Central London (Dip of Bldg Econs); *m* 30 May 1981, Joanna Clodagh, da of late Maj Ian George Henry Houldsworth, of Dallas Lodge, Forres, Moray; 2 s (George Ian Alastair, Hon Sam Dudley b 25 Oct 1985), 1 da (Lady Anna Katharine b 2 Sept 1988); *Heir* s, George Ian Alastair, Viscount Formartine b 4 May 1983; *Career* Devpt exec London and Edinburgh Tst plc 1986-, dir: Letinvest plc, Washington Devpts Ltd; landowner (10,000 acres); ARICS; *Recreations* sport, music, art; *Clubs* MCC, The Arts, London Scottish RFC; *Style—* Earl of Haddo; 22 Beauclerc Rd, London W6 0NS (☎ 01 748 4849); Estate Office, Haddo House, Aberdeen (☎ Tarvers 664); London and Edinburgh Trust plc, 243 Knightsbridge, London SW7 1DH (☎ 01 581 1322)

HADDON, Hon Mrs (Teresa Mary); da of 1 Viscount Head, GCMG, CBE, MC, PC (d 1983) and Dorothea, Viscountess Head, *qv*; *b* 20 June 1938; *m* 1972, Richard Deacon Haddon; 2 s, 1 da (twin); *Style—* The Hon Mrs Haddon; Ivydene, Hailey, Oxon OX8 5XD

HADDON, Brig Thomas; CBE (1961); s of Maj J T Haddon, DCM (d 1937); *b* 19 Feb 1913; *Educ* Hamilton Acad Lanarkshire, RMC Sandhurst; *m* 5 Sept 1939, Clodagh, 4 da of late Lt-Col Hon Bertrand Russell, DSO, s of Lord Russell of Killowen (Life Peer, d 1900) and bro of Baron Russell of Killowen (Life Peer d 1946); 3 s; *Career* 1 Bn Border Regt, WWII (staff Europe, Middle East), UK Cabinet Offices, Lt-Col 1955, Brig 1961, ADC to HM The Queen 1964-68, ret 1968; *Style—* Brig Thomas Haddon, CBE; Mole End, Hale House Lane, Churt Farnham, Surrey GU10 2JG (☎ 0428 713195l); Combe End, Hindhead, Surrey (☎ (042873 4931)

HADDON-CAVE, Charles Anthony; s of Sir Philip Haddon-Cave, KBE, CMG, *qv*, of The Old Farmhouse, Tackley, Oxford OX5 3AW, and Elizabeth, *née* Simpson; *b* 20 Mar 1956; *Educ* The King's Sch Canterbury, Pembroke Coll Cambridge (BA); *m* 2 Aug 1980, Amanda Charlotte, da of Timothy James Law, of Spire Hollen, Priorsfield Rd, Godalming, Surrey; 1 da (Alexandra b 11 Feb 1987); *Career* called to bar: Gray's Inn 1978, Hong Kong 1980; *Recreations* tennis, squash; *Clubs* RAC; *Style—* Charles Haddon-Cave, Esq; 65 Bromfelde Rd, Clapham Old Town, London SW4 6PP (☎ 01 622 2106); 2 Essex Court, Temple, London EC4Y 9AP (☎ 01 583 8381, fax 01 353 0998, telex 8812528)

HADDON-CAVE, Sir (Charles) Philip; KBE (1980), CMG (1973); s of Francis Macnamana Haddon-Cave; *b* 6 July 1925; *Educ* Tas Univ, King's Coll Cambridge; *m* 1948, Elizabeth Alice May, da of Frederick Alfred Simpson, 2 s, 1 da; *Career* joined Colonial Admin Service 1952; chief secretary Hong Kong 1981- (financial sec Hong Kong 1971-81); *Style—* Sir Philip Haddon-Cave, KBE, CMG; Government Secretariat, Hong Kong (☎ 95406); Victoria House, Hong Kong

HADEN, Harold John; s of Harold Stanley Haden (d 1979) and Eunice Escott *née* Wood (d 1962); *b* 14 Feb 1941; *Educ* Wrekin Coll, Hackley Sch, New York, (ESU Exchange Scholar), Birmingham Univ (LLB); *m* 4 April 1964, (Elizabeth) Jane da of George Noel de St Croix, MBE; 1 s (Rupert b 1974), 2 da (Rachel b 1967, Philippa b 1970); *Career* pupillage practice 1964-65, barr 1966-69, loss adjuster 1970-72, M & G 1973, currently legal dir and sec M & G Gp PLC; *Recreations* shooting, travel, theatre; *Style—* Harold Haden, Esq; M & G Limited, Three Quays, Tower Hill, London EC3R 6BQ (☎ 01 626 4588, fax 01 623 8615)

HADEN-GUEST, Hon Christopher; s and h of 4 Baron Haden-Guest; *b* 5 Feb 1948; *m* 1984, Jamie Lee Curtis, actress, eldest da of Tony Curtis, film actor; 1 da (Anne b 1986); *Career* actor; *Style—* The Hon Christopher Haden-Guest; 1242 South Camden Drive, Los Angeles, California 90035, USA; HC-64, Box 8018, Ketchum, Idaho 83340, USA

HADEN-GUEST, Dorothy, Baroness; Dorothy; da of Thomas Roseberry Good, late of Princeton, NJ; *m* 1968, as his 2 wife, 2 Baron Haden-Guest (d 1974); *Style—* The Rt Hon Dorothy, Lady Haden-Guest; 105 Bayard Lane, Princeton, New Jersey 08540, USA

HADEN-GUEST, Hon Hadley; da of 2 Baron Haden-Guest (d 1974); *b* 1949; *Style—* The Hon Hadley Haden-Guest; Apt A503, 250 Mercer Street, New York, NY 10012, USA

HADEN-GUEST, Hon Nicholas; 2 s of 4 Baron; *b* 5 May 1951; *m* 1980, Jill, da of Harry Demby; *Style—* The Hon Nicholas Haden-Guest; 119 East 60th Street, New York, NY 10021, USA

HADEN-GUEST, 4 Baron (UK 1950); Peter Haden Haden-Guest; yr s (by 2 m) of 1 Baron, MC (d 1960); suc half-brother as 4 Baron 1987; *b* 29 August 1913; *Educ* City of London Sch, New Coll Oxford (MA); *m* 1945, Jean Pauline, da of late Dr Albert George Hindes, of Waverly Pl, New York City, USA; 2 s (Hon Christopher, *qv*; Hon Nicholas, *qv*), 1 da (Hon Mrs (Elissa) Smith, *qv*); *Heir* s, Hon Christopher Haden-Guest, *qv*; *Career* Lt RCNVR 1939-45; United Nations Official 1946-72 (Chief of Editorial Control, UN HQ; Chief Editor UN Office, Geneva, and Chief of Repertory Editing Gp, UN HQ, New York); *Style—* The Rt Hon Lord Haden-Guest; 198 Old Stone Highway, East Hampton, New York 11937, USA

HADEN-TAYLOR, Anthony St John; s of Frank Pacey Haden-Taylor (d 1971), of Broughton House, Broughton Gifford, nr Melksham, Wilts, and Enid Christine Bousfield, *née* Bushnell; *b* 26 Mar 1948; *Educ* Kings Sch Sherborne; *Career* sr ptnr Int Mgmnt Consits SA 1970-82, chief exec Taylor Downs & Co 1987; Freeman City of London, Liveryman Worshipful Co of Basket Makers; *Recreations* polo, shooting; *Clubs* City Livery, Cirencester Polo; *Style—* Anthony Haden-Taylor, Esq; Bledisloe House, Coates, Cirencester, Glos, GL7 6NH (☎ 0285 770682); 114 New Bond St, London W1Y 9AB (☎ 01 493 2890, fax 01 491 1461, car tel 0836 711614)

HADFIELD, Antony; s of Thomas Henry Hadfield, and Edna Hadfield; *b* 9 Sept 1936; *Educ* Sheffield, Brighton, Middx Poly (BA); *m* 1959, Dorothy Fay, da of Charles Edwin Osman (d 1976); 1 s (Warren b 1966); *Career* design engr Plessey 1958-62, design and project engr Metal Industs Gp 1962-65, design engr CEGB 1965-67; sr engr and mangr Eastern Electricity 1967-77, area mangr Yorks Electricity 1977-79; dir of engrg Midlands Electricity 1979-85, dep chm and chief exec Northern Ireland Electricity 1985-; *Recreations* mountaineering, sailing; *Clubs* Royal North of Ireland YC; *Style—* Antony Hadfield, Esq; Northern Ireland Electricity, PO Box 2, Danesfort, 120 Malone Rd, Belfast BT9 5HT (☎ 0860 616535)

HADFIELD, (Ellis) Charles Raymond; CMG (1954); s of Alexander Charles Hadfield (d 1926); *b* 5 August 1909; *Educ* Blundell's, St Edmund Hall Oxford (MA); *m* 1945, Alice Mary Miller, da of Lt-Col Henry Smyth, DSO (d 1943), of Brook Cottage, S Cerney, Glos; 1 s, 1 da (and 1 s decd); *Career* dir pubns Centl Off of Info: dir pubns 1946-48, controller (overseas) 1948-62; dir David & Charles 1960-64; memb Br Waterways Bd 1963-66; author; Assoc CIT; *Books* British Canals: An Illustrated History (7 edn 1984), Afloat in America (with AM Hadfield 1979), William Jessop, Engineer (with AW Skempton, 1979), The Canal Age (2 edn 1981), World Canals: Inland Navigation Past and Present (1986), also a series, by regions, of the canals of Eng and Wales; *Recreations* writing, exploring canals; *Style—* Charles Hadfield, Esq, CMG; 13 Meadow Way, South Cerney, Cirencester, Glos GL7 6HY (☎ 0285 860422)

HADFIELD, James Irvine Havelock; s of Prof Geoffrey Hadfield (d 1970), of Ruperts Close, Henley-on-Thames, Oxon, and Sarah Victoria Eileen, *née* Irvine (d 1975); *b* 12 July 1930; *Educ* Radley, Brasenose Coll Oxford (BA), St Thomas' Hosp Med Sch (MA, BM, BCh, MCh); *m* 5 Jan 1957, Ann Pickernell, da of Dr G C Milner (d 1974), of 3 Church Row, Rye, Sussex; 1 s (Geoffrey Irvine Havelock b 10 Jan 1964), 2 da (Esme Victoria b 12 Sept 1960, Helen Sarah (twin)); *Career* St Thomas' Hosp 1955-57: house surgn, casualty offr, lectr Dept Anatomy; RAS St Thomas' Hosp Hysestile 1962, RSO Leicester Royal Infirmary 1962-64, surgical tutor Univ of Oxford 1964-66, first asst Nuffield Dept Surgery 1964-66, conslt surgn and urologist Bedford Gen Hosp 1966, surgical and clinical tutor N Bedfordshire 1968-78; examiner: pathology MRCS and LRCP 1971-77, surgery Univ of Cambridge 1974-84; Univ of Cambridge: pt/t departmental demonstrator Dept Anatomy, recognised teacher surgery 1974-, Arris and Gale lectr RCS 1975, conslt memb DMT 1979-84, chm med exec ctee Bedford Gen Hosp 1979-84; memb: Ed Bd Health Trends 1972-77, res and devpt ctee King Edwards Fund for London 1973-79; tstee Bedford Charity 1970-85, vice-chm estate ctee Harpur Tst 1980-85 (govt Harpur Tst 1970-85), pres Bedford Med Soc 1988; fell: Assoc Sports in Medicine, Assoc Surgns Pakistan: FSZ (London) memb Anatomical Soc GB, Ireland; boat club winner St Thomas' Hosp: sr fours, sr pairs, sr sculls, double sculls, United Hosps Regatta 1956 (15 races in 1 day); coach: Brasenose Coll 1951-80, St Thomas Hosp Boat Club 1955-70, Oriel Coll Eight 1975-80; vice-pres: Bedfords CC, Bedford RFC (qualified umpire ARA); memb ctee Bedford Regatta; Freeman City of London, Liveryman Worshipful Co of Fellmakers 1975-; FRCS, FRCSE 1960, FRSM, Fell Soc Clinical Anatomists, memb Assoc Urological Surgns; *Books* articles med jls on: Venous Thrombosis, Intravenous Feeding and Topics in Urology; *Recreations* shooting, fishing, watching rowing, sport in general, hates gardening; *Clubs* London Rowing, Leander, Henley-on-Thames, Vincents (Oxford); *Style—* James Hadfield, Esq; Baker's Barn, Stagsden West End, Bedford MK43 8SZ (☎ 02302 4514); Porthiddy Cottage, St Davids, North Pembrokeshire SA62 6OW (☎ 03483 345)

HADFIELD, John Charles Heywood; s of Heywood George Hadfield (d 1946), of Birmingham, and Hilda Hadfield, *née* Bragg (d 1959); *b* 16 June 1907; *Educ* Bradfield Coll; *m* 1, 1931, Phyllis Anna (d 1971), da of Capt Leonard McMullen, of West Mersea, Essex; 1 s (Jeremy d 1988); m 2, Elisabeth Joy Westendarp (d 1975); *Career* ed J M Dent & Sons 1935-42, books offr for Br Cncl in Middle East 1942-44, dir Nat Book League 1944-50, organiser Festival of Britain Book Exhibition 1951, dir Rainbird Publishing Gp 1965-80; *Books* Love on a Branch Line (1959), A Book of Beauty (ed, 1952), A Book of Delights (ed, 1954), A Book of Love, (ed, 1958), Shell Guide to England (ed, 1970), Shell Book of English Villages (ed, 1980), Everyman's Book of English Love (ed), The Saturday Book (1952-73), Poems (1980); *Recreations* gardening; *Clubs* Savile; *Style—* John Hadfield, Esq; 2 Quay St, Woodbridge, Suffolk (☎ 03943 7414); The Cupid Press, 2 Quay St, Woodbridge, Suffolk (☎ 03943 7414)

HADFIELD, John Peter Brookes; JP (1969), DL (1986); s of John William Claude Hadfield (d 1965), of Devon, and Edith Annie, *née* Brookes; *b* 9 Mar 1926; *Educ* Brighton GS, Sandhurst; *m* 1949, Iris, da of Frederick Arthur Brailsford (d 1947), of Chesterfield; 2 da (Vivienne b 1954, Sarah b 1957); *Career* mil serv 1943-47 Sandhurst, 2 Recce Regt, 25 Dragoons RAC Capt served Far East 14 Army India, Malaya, Singapore, Sumatra; joined Bass Ratcliffe & Gretton Ltd 1947, md Bass Mitchells and Butlers (Northern) Ltd 1966; dir: Mitchells and Butlers Ltd, Bass Marketing Ltd, Bass UK Ltd 1968; md Bass (South West) Ltd 1975; chm and md Bass North West Ltd 1976-86, vice-chm Bass North Ltd 1986 (ret March 1986); chm 1976-86: Bass Mitchells and Butlers (North West) Ltd, Bents Brewery Co Ltd,

Catterall and Swarbricks Brewery Ltd, Fred Anderton Ltd, Gartsides (Brookside Brewery) Ltd, Masseys Burnley Brewery Ltd, Park Hall Leisure; chm NW Regional Bd Br Inst of Mgmnt and Nat Cncl; memb: CBI National Cncl, NW Regional Cncl 1984; pres North Cheshire Branch BIM 1985; chm: Gtr Manchester Residuary Body, Trafford Park Devpt Corp; Mainkind Ltd, Gtr Manchester Property Tst; dir: Gtr Manchester Economic Devpt Cncl, Central Station Properties Ltd, Lloyds Bank plc (NW Region), Burtonwood Brewery plc, Petros Devpts Ltd, Prestbury Golf Club, Savoy Hotel (Blackpool) plc, Manchester Chamber of Commerce; Midland Hotel Crown Plaza Manchester, tstee The Hammond Sch Chester; patron Henshaws Soc for the Blind; memb Inst of Brewing; CBIM, FRSA; *Recreations* golf, shooting, gardening; *Clubs* St James's Manchester, Royal Lytham Golf, Prestbury Golf; *Style—* Peter Hadfield, Esq, JP, DL

HADFIELD, Hon Mrs; Hon Maureen; elder da of Baron Segal (Life Peer); *b* 15 Feb 1935; *Educ* St Anne's Coll, Oxford (MA); *m* 6 Dec 1956, Jeremy Hadfield, s of John Hadfield, of 2 Quay St, Woodbridge, Suffolk; 2 s; *Career* dir Economic Assocs 1969-76, economic advsr, Price Cmmn 1976-78; mgmnt conslt Pannellkerr Forster Associates 1985; chm International Consulting Economics Assoc 1986 ; *Recreations* sailing; *Clubs* Royal Harwich Yacht Club; *Style—* The Hon Mrs Hadfield; 19 Christchurch Hill, London NW3 1JY

HADFIELD, Maj (Robert) Michael; JP (Middx 1980); s of John William Claude Hadfield (d 1965), and Edith Anne, *née* Brookes; *b* 2 Sept 1928; *Educ* Brighton, RMA Sandhurst; *m* 29 Jan 1966, Helen Nancy, da of Rear Adm William Penrose Mark-Wardlaw, DSO (d 1952); 1 da (Rosemary Ann Elizabeth b 1972); *Career* cmmnd RA 1948 served: N Africa, Trieste, BAOR, Hong Kong; ret Major 1963; mangr gp public affrs Guinness plc (joined 1963, info offr Guinness Brewing 1971); MIPR, MInstM, FRSA; *Recreations* arts, reading, gardening; *Clubs* Savile, Denham GC, Royal Western YC; *Style—* Major Michael Hadfield, JP; Old Ashmead, Denham Village, S Bucks UB9 5BB; c/o Guinness plc, 39 Portman Square, London W1 (☎ 01 486-0288)

HADFIELD, Ronald; QPM (1989); s of George Hadfield (d 1975) of Oldham Lancs, and Phyliss Marjorie Hadfield (d 1983); *b* 15 July 1939; *Educ* Chadderton GS; *m* 1 April 1961, Anne Phylissia, da of Ernest Frederick Worrall, of Royton Lancs; 1 s (Neil Stuart b 25 April 1964), 1 da (Elaine Louise b 29 Dec 1962); *Career* Oldham Borough Police 1958-69 (Sgt 1965-67, Inspr 1967-69), Lancs Constabulary 1969-74 (Chief Inspr 1973), Greater Manchester Police 1974-81 (Supt 1975, Chief Supt 1980), Acting Dep Chief Constable Derbyshire 1984-86 (Asst Chief Constable 1981-84), Chief Constable Notts 1987- (Dep Chief Constable 1986-87); pres Notts Life Saving Assoc; memb: nat ctee Police Athletic Assoc, Notts branch St Johns Ambulance; *Recreations* golf; *Style—* Ronald Hadfield, Esq, QPM; Sherwood Lodge, Arnold Notts NG5 8PP (☎ 0602 670 999)

HADINGHAM, Reginald Edward Hawke (Buzzer); CBE (1988, OBE 1971), MC and bar (1944), TD; 2 s of Edward Wallace Hadingham (d 1973), and Ethel Irene Penelope (d 1936), 5 da of Sir William Gwynne-Evans, 1 Bt ; *b* 6 Dec 1915; *Educ* St Paul's; *m* 1940, Lois, da of Edward Pope, of Montreal, Canada; 2 da (Susan, Stephanie); *Career* 67 ATK TA RA, served UK, Iraq, N Africa, Italy, actg Lt-Col; non-exec chm Slazengers Ltd 1976-83 (joined 1933, Euro sales mangr 1936, export mangr 1949, sales dir 1952, joined bd 1952, md 1967, chm and md 1973); chm SPARKS (the Sportsman's Charity); dep chm Action Research for the Crippled Child; vice-pres PHAB (physically handicapped and able-bodied); sr memb and tres 1957-, Sette of Odd Volumes (a dining club founded in 1878); *Recreations* lawn tennis; *Clubs* All Eng Lawn Tennis, Queens LTC, Hurlingham, Lords Taverner; *Style—* Buzzer Hadingham, Esq, OBE, MC, TD; 118 Wimbledon Hill Rd, Wimbledon SW19 5QU (☎ 01 946 9611); All England Lawn Tennis Club (☎ 01 946 2244)

HADLEE, Richard John; MBE (1980); s of Walter Arnold, OBE, of Christchurch NZ, and Lilias Agnus; *b* 3 July 1951; *Educ* Christchurch Boys HS; *m* 1973, Karen Ann, da of Maurice Marsh; 2 s (Nicholas b 1981, Matthew b 1985); *Career* professional cricketer, writer, radio talkbacks, lay promotional activities; *Recreations* golf, watching videos; *Clubs* Jaycee; *Style—* Richard Hadlee Esq; 302 Highsted Rd, Christchurch, New Zealand (☎ 599861)

HADLEY, David Allen; s of Sydney Hadley (d 1980), and Gwendoline Alice, *née* Rodwell (d 1987); *b* 18 Feb 1936; *Educ* Wyggeston GS Leicester, Merton Coll Oxford (MA); *m* 1965, Veronica Ann, da of Stanley Hopkins, of Sussex; 1 s (Christopher b 1970); *Career* Miny of Agric 1959-75 (tres 1976-78), min of Agric 1979-, deputy sec Agricultural Commodities 1987-; *Recreations* music, gardening; *Style—* David Hadley, Esq; Miny of Agric, Whitehall Place, London SW1 (☎ 01 270 8109)

HADLEY, Graham Hunter; s of Albert Leonard Hadley (d 1973), and Lorna Elizabeth, *née* Hunter; *b* 12 April 1944; *Educ* Eltham Coll, Jesus Coll Cambridge (BA); *m* 1971, Lesley Mary Ann, da of Stanley Anthony Andrew Smith, of Kingston; 1 s (Andrew Hunter b 1978); *Career* Civil Serv; asst princ: Miny of Aviation 1966, Miny of Technology 1968, principal, Min of Aviation Supply 1971, Dept of Energy 1974; seconded to Civil Serv Cmmn 1976, asst sec Dept of Energy 1977, seconded to British Aerospace HQ Weybridge 1980, asst sec electricity div Dept of Energy 1981 (under sec 1983), seconded as bd sec CEGB 1983, permanent bd sec CEGB 1986-; bd memb designate Nat Power Co 1988; *Recreations* cricket, history of architecture, theatre; *Clubs* Royal Soc of Arts, Mandarins CC; *Style—* Graham Hadley, Esq; The Coach House, 14 Genoa Avenue, Putney, London SW15 (☎ 01 788 2698); CEGB, Sudbury House, 15 Newgate Street, London EC1 (☎ 01 634 5111)

HADLEY, (Jennifer) Katharine; da of John Hadley, of Codmanchester, and Theresa Monica, *née* Ward (d 1986); *b* 20 Mar 1946; *Educ* Huntingdon GS, Reading Univ; *m* 1 1977 (m dis 1980) Dr Charles Hope, s of Sir Archibald Hope; 1 s (Thomas b 4 April 1978); m2 Adrian Sington; 1s (Hugh b 11 March 1981), 1 da (Angelica b 24 Feb 1986); *Career* womans ed: The Sun 1973-81, asst ed Daily Express 1988 (womans ed 1981-), womans ed Sunday Mirror 1988; memb Network; *Recreations* needlepoint, collecting paintings, theatre, music; *Style—* Katharine Hadley; 39 Camberwell Grove, London SE5 (☎ 01 701 7581); Sunday Mirror, High Holborn, London (☎ 01 822 2094)

HADLEY, Lady Paulina Mary Louise; *née* Pepys; yr da of 6 Earl of Cottenham (d 1943), and Sybil Venetia, *née* Taylor (now Countess of Devon); *b* 14 June 1930; *Educ* Oxford Univ (MA 1956); *m* 1973, Denis Bernard Hadley; *Style—* Lady Paulina Hadley; White Hill House, Upham, Hants

HADOW, Sir Gordon; CMG (1953), OBE (1945); s of Rev Frank Burness Hadow (d 1941), of Woolton, Liverpool, by his wife Una Durrant; *b* 23 Sept 1908; *Educ* Marlborough, Trinity Coll Oxford; *m* 19 Oct 1946, Marie, da of Lionel Henry Moiser, of Coventry (d 1985); 2 s (Roger b 1947, Paul b 1950); *Career* entered colonial serv Gold Coast 1932, dep fin sec Tanganyika 1946, under-sec Gold Coast 1948, sec for civil serv 1949, sec to govr and exec cncl Gold Coast 1950, dep govr Gold Coast (now Ghana) 1954-57; kt 1956; *Clubs* Athenaeum; *Style—* Sir Gordon Hadow, CMG, OBE; Little Manor, Coat, Martock, Somerset

HADOW, Sir (Reginald) Michael; KCMG (1971, CMG 1962); s of Malcolm Macgregor Hadow (d 1921); *b* 17 August 1915; *Educ* Berkhamsted Sch, King's Coll Cambridge; *m* 1, 1943, Maria Anna Stefania Szemplinska; m 2, 1955, Dolores Frances, da of Alfred Fillibrow Main, of Mexico City; 1 step s, 1 step da; m 3, 1976, Daphne Madge Kerin, (d 1988, formerly w of late Hon Michael Sieff, CBE), da of Cyril Aaron Michael, of London; 1 steps; *Career* entered ICS 1937, IPS 1941-47, transferred FO 1948, private sec to Min of State 1949-52, head of chancery Mexico City 1952-54, cnsllr FO 1958, cnsllr Paris 1959-63, head of News Dept FO 1963-65, ambass to: Israel 1965-69, Argentine Republic 1969-72; ret; *Style—* Sir Michael Hadow, KCMG; Old Farm, Ashford Hill, Newbury, Berks RG15 8AX (☎ 063 523 335)

HADSLEY-CHAPLIN, (Edwin) Hadsley; s of Arthur Hadsley-Chaplin (d 1965), of Surrey, and Annie Violet Lewis (d 1983); *b* 27 August 1922; *Educ* Radnor House; *m* 1954, Margaret Mary, da of Robert Potter (d 1951); 2 s (Peter b 1957, Mark b 1961), 1 da (Anne b 1955); *Career* capt RE 1941-46; md Rowe Evans Investmt plc; chm: Beradin Hldgs Ltd 1982-, Beradin UK Ltd, Supara Investmt Ltd 1959, MP Evans and Co Ltd 1964, Jitra Rubber Plantations Ltd 1964, Rowe Evans Agencies Ltd 1971, Rowe White and Co Ltd 1973, Dimid Agencies Ltd 1975, Sungkai Hldgs plc 1978, Sungkai Estates Ltd 1978, Bertam Hldgs Ltd 1980, Rowe Evans (Indonesia) Ltd 1980, Bertam UK Ltd 1981, Lendu Hldgs plc 1983, Lendu UK Ltd 1983, Padang Senang Hldgs plc, Rembia Rubber plc; Beradin Rubber Ltd, Bertram Consolidated Rubber Co Ltd, Lendu Rubber Estates Ltd, Dimbula Valley Ceylon Tea Co 1971; memb Tropical Growers Assoc (chm 1973-74); FCIS; *Recreations* watching cricket, travel, model railways, theatre; *Clubs* Oriental, Gresham; *Style—* Hadsley Hadsley-Chaplin, Esq; Norton House, Gatton Road, Reigate, Surrey (☎ 0550 246217)

HAGAN, David Lloyd; s of William Hamill Hagan (d 1984), of Liverpool, and Miriam Dilys, *née* Lloyd; *b* 21 May 1946; *Educ* Merchant Taylors Sch Crosby, Emmanuel Coll Cambridge; *m* 5 Dec 1981, Anita Janet Shepstone, da of Lennart Pettersson, of Karlstad, Sweden; 2 s (Charles b 1 Nov 1982, Felix b 14 Mar 1987), 1 da (Isabel b 4 Aug 1984); *Career* chm and chief exec Marlon House Hldgs Ltd 1974-83, dir Med and Professional Softwear Ltd 1984-, chm David Hagan Ltd 1986-, md Tullett & Tokyo Equities Ltd 1986-; FCA 1970, ATII 1970, memb Stock Exchange; offshore powerboat racing Class II World Champion; *Recreations* offshore powerboat racing, boatbuilding; *Clubs* Royal Thames YC, Royal Motor YC, The South West Shingles YC (Vice cdr); *Style—* David Hagan, Esq; 46 Argyll Rd, London W8 (☎ 01 937 7060); Tullett & Tokyo Equities Ltd, 77 Gracechurch St, London EC3 (☎ 01 626 3741, fax 01 626 2236, car phone 0836 288 421, telex 941 3534)

HAGART-ALEXANDER, Claud; s and h of Sir Claud Hagart-Alexander, 3 Bt; *b* 5 Nov 1963; *Educ* Trinity Coll Glenalmond, Glasgow Univ (BSc (Eng) Hons); *Career* electronics and electrical engr; *Style—* Claud Hagart-Alexander Esq; c/o Coutts & Co, Adelaide Branch, 440 Strand, London WC2R 0QS; Devron-Hercules Inc, 500 Brook Bank Ave, N Vancouver Canada V7J 354 (tel: 604 980 3421)

HAGART-ALEXANDER, Sir Claud; 3 Bt (UK 1886), of Ballochmyle, Co Ayr; JP (1985); s of late Wilfred Archibald Alexander, 2 s of 2 Bt; suc gf 1945; additional surname Hagart recognised by decree of Lord Lyon 1948; Maj-Gen Sir Claud Alexander, 1 Bt, served in the Crimea and was MP for S Ayrshire (C) 1874-85; *b* 6 Jan 1927; *Educ* Sherborne, CCC Cambridge (BA); *m* 16 April 1959, Hilda Etain, yr da of late Miles Malcolm Acheson, of Ganges, BC, Canada; 2 s, 2 da; *Heir* s, Claud Hagart-Alexander, *qv*; *Career* vice-lord-lieut Ayr and Arran (Strathclyde Region) 1983-; memb Inst of Measurement and Control (MInstMC); *Clubs* New Club, Edinburgh; *Style—* Sir Claud Hagart-Alexander, Bt, DL, JP; Kingencleugh House, Mauchline, Ayrshire (☎ 0290 50217)

HAGDRUP, Alan; s of Sofus Vilhelm Hagdrup (d 1983), of Cheam; *b* 19 May 1932; *Educ* Epsom Coll, UCL; *m* 1958, Elizabeth, da of Lt-Col Harold Mason, OBE, TD (d 1960); 1 s, 2 da; *Career* dir: Hanson Tport Gp 1969-, Hanson plc 1974-; ptnr Goulden's (slrs) 1962-69; *Recreations* golf, skiing, bridge, music; *Clubs* Walton Heath Golf; *Style—* Alan Hagdrup, Esq; The Mill House, Dorking Road, Tadworth, Surrey (☎ 073 7814522)

HAGER, David Paul; s of Donald Charles Hager of Bournemouth, and Betty Kathleen, *née* Hewitt; *b* 7 Jan 1951; *Educ* Bournemouth Sch, Oxford Univ (MA); *m* 10 Sept 1951, Jeanette Carolyn, da of Alan Peter Hares of Chilbolton, Hants; 1 s (Tristram b 1984); *Career* investment advsr N M Rothschild and Sons Ltd 1972-74, ptnr in Investment Dept Bacon and Woodrow consulting actuaries 1976-85 (joined 1975), dir County Investment Mgmnt Ltd 1985-87 (dir County Gp Ltd 1986-87); ptnr Bacon and Woodrow 1987-; memb: FIA 1975, FPMI 1982; *Books* An Introduction to Institutional Investment (with AJ Frost, 1986), Debt Securities (with AJ Frost 1989) Pension Fund Investment (with CD Lever 1989); *Recreations* flying light aircraft; *Clubs* Oxford and Cambridge; *Style—* David Hager, Esq; Bacon and Woodrow, Empire House, St Martins Grand, London EC1A 4ED (☎ 01 600 2747, fax 01 726 6519)

HAGGART, Mary Elizabeth; OBE; s of John Neville Carpenter Scholes, and Margaret Elizabeth, *née* Hines; *b* 8 April 1924; *Educ* Wyggeston GS For Girls Leicester, Leicester Royal Infirmary and Children's Hosp (SRN), Guy's Hosp London (CMB Part 1), Royal Coll of Nursing London (Admin Cert); *m* 3 April 1983, most Rev Alastair Iain MacDonald Haggart; *Career* matron Dundee Royal Infirmary (matron designate Ninewells Hosp Dundee) 1964-68, chief nursing offr bd of mgmnt Dundee Gen Hosps and Ninewells and assoc hosps 1968-73, chief area nursing offr Tayside Health Bd 1973-83; pres Scottish Assoc of Nurse Admins 1973-77, chm Scottish Nat Bd for Nursing Midwifery and Health Visiting 1980-84; memb: Scottish Bd RCN 1965-70, Gen Nursing Cncl for Scotland 1966-70 and 1970-80, Standing Nursing and Midwifery Scottish 1971-74 (vice chm 1973-74), UK Central Cncl Nursing Midwifery and Health Visiting 1980-84, bd of mgmnt Carstairs State Hosp 1983-, Scottish Hosp Endowments Res Tst 1984-; memb RCN; *Recreations* walking, music, travel; *Clubs* Royal Cwlth Soc; *Style—* Mrs Mary Haggart, OBE; 19 Eglinton Cres, Edinburgh EH12 5BY (☎ 031 337 8948)

HAGGER, Jonathan Osborne; s of Cyril Francis Osborne Hagger (d 1957), of Loughton, Essex, and Norah Harrison, *née* Broadley (d 1981); *b* 3 Feb 1949; *Educ* Chigwell Sch; *m* 27 April 1974, (Carol) Anne, da of Alan David Luton, of Loughton,

Essex; 2 s (William b 1981, James b 1984); *Career* CA, Edward Moore & Sons (CAs) 1968-72, BUPA 1972-75, Willis Faber 1976-85, fin dir Bain Clarkson 1985-; Church Organist (deputize at King Charles the Martyr Tunbridge Wells); memb: The Nevill Tennis Club (Tunbridge Wells), Tunbridge Wells Civic Soc; ARCM 1968, FCA 1972; *Recreations* music, tennis; *Style—* Jonathan Hagger, Esq; 104 Warwick Park, Tunbridge Wells, Kent TN2 5EN (☎ 0892 29161); Bain Clarkson Ltd, 15 Minories, London EC3N 1NJ (☎ 01 481 3232)

HAGGETT, Prof Peter; s of Charles Frederick Haggett (d 1966), and Ethel Elizabeth Haines (d 1971); *b* 24 Jan 1933; *Educ* Dr Morgan's GS Somerset, St Catharine's Coll Cambridge (MA, PhD, ScD); *m* 28 July 1956, Brenda Mavis, da of Cyril Robert Woodley (d 1976); 2 s (Timothy b 1961, Andrew b 1965), 2 da (Sarah b 1960, Jacqueline b 1963); *Career* asst lectr UCL 1955-57, lectr Cambridge Univ 1957-66, prof of urban and regnl geography Bristol Univ 1966- (acting vice-chllr 1984-85); memb: SW Econ Planning Cncl, UGC 1985-89, Nat Radiological Protection Bd 1985-; Hon DSc York Canada 1983, Hon DSc Durham 1989, Hon LLD Bristol 1985; memb: Euro Acad 1988; *Books* Geography: A Modern Synthesis (1983); *Clubs* Utd Oxford and Cambridge Univ; *Style—* Prof Peter Haggett; 5 Tunbridge Close, Chew Magna, Avon (☎ 0272 332780); Dept of Geography, University of Bristol, Bristol BS8 1SS (☎ 0272 303751)

HAGUE, Prof Sir Douglas Chalmers; CBE (1978); s of Laurence Hague; *b* 20 Oct 1926; *Educ* Moseley GS, King Edward VI HS Birmingham, Birmingham Univ; *m* 1947 (m dis 1986), Brenda Elizabeth Fereday; 2 da; m2, 1986, Janet Mary Leach; *Career* economist (mgmnt prof, conslt, co dir); chm Manchester Industl Relations Soc, dep chm Price Cmmn and pres NW Operational Res Gp, rapporteur to IEA 1953-78 (ed gen 1981-86), reader political economy London Univ 1957, Newton Chambers prof of econs Sheffield Univ 1957-63, visiting prof of econ Duke Univ N Carolina USA 1960-61, head business studies dept Sheffield Univ 1962-63, prof applied econs Manchester Univ 1963-65, cncl memb Manchester Business Sch 1964, prof managerial econs 1965-81 (dep dir 1978-81); London Visiting prof 1981-; fell Templeton Coll Oxford 1981-; personal econ advsr to Rt Hon Margaret Thatcher 1967-79 (incl Gen Election 1979), advsr PM's Policy Unit 1979-83; chm Econ and Social Sci Res Cncl (ESRC) 1983-87; chm: Metapraxis Ltd 1984-, Oxford Strategy Network 1984-; kt 1981;; *Recreations* Manchester Utd supporter, organist of classical music (granted permission to play at Blenheim Palace); *Clubs* Athenaeum; *Style—* Prof Sir Douglas Hague, CBE; Templeton College, Oxford OX1 5NY

HAGUE, Paul Nicholas; s of Bernard Hague, and Annie Nichols; *b* 3 August 1947; *Educ* Belle Vue Boys GS, Hatfield Coll, Durham Univ (BA); *m* 1969, Alice Christine, da of Alf Tyreman; 1 s (Nicholas James b 1974), 1 da (Chrissie Anne b 1976); *Career* chm business & Market Research plc; *Books* The Industrial Market Research Handbook (1987), Do Your Own Market Research (1987); *Recreations* athletics; *Style—* Paul Hague, Esq; 13 Marple Hall Drive, Marple, Stockport SK6 6JN (☎ 061 427 7552); Business & Market Research, High Lane, Stockport SK6 8DX (☎ (0663) 65115)

HAHN, Prof Frank Horace; s of Dr Arnold Hahn; *b* 26 April 1925; *Educ* Bournemouth GS, LSE; *m* 1946, Dorothy Salter; *Career* formerly: reader in mathematical econs Univ of Birmingham, lectr in econs Cambridge Univ; prof of econs LSE 1967-72, prof of econs Cambridge Univ 1967-72 (fell Churchill Coll); pres: Econometic Soc 1968, Royal Econ Soc 1976-89; hon memb American Econ Assoc 1986, Foreign Assoc US Nat Acad of Scis 1988; Hon: DScoSci Birmingham 1983, DLitt UEA 1984, DSc London 1985, D Honoris Causa 1984; *Books* General Competitve Analysis (with K J Arrow), The Share of Wages in the National Income, Money and Inflation, Equilibrium and Macroeconomics 1984, Money Growth and Stability 1985; *Publications include* : General Competitive Analysis (jointly with K J Arrow), The Share of Wages in the National Income, Money and Inflation; *Style—* Prof Frank Hahn; 16 Adams Rd, Cambridge; Churchill College, Cambridge

HAIG, 2 Earl (UK 1919); George Alexander Eugene Douglas Haig; OBE (1965), DL (Roxburghshire, Ettrick & Lauderdale 1976); also Viscount Dawick, Baron Haig (both UK 1919) and thirtieth Laird of Bemersyde Chief of the Haig family; s of Field Marshal 1 Earl Haig, KT, GCB, OM, GCVO, KCIE (d 1928), by his w, Hon Dorothy, GCStJ (d 1939), 2 da of 3 Baron Vivian; *b* 15 Mar 1918; *Educ* Stowe, Ch Ch Oxford (MA); *m* 1, 19 July 1956 (m dis 1981), Adrienne Thérèse, da of Derrick Morley; 1 s, 2 da; m 2, 1981, Doña Geroloma Lopez y Royo di Taurisano; *Heir* s, Viscount Dawick; *Career* Capt Royal Scots Greys M East Force 1939-42, POW 1942-45, Maj on disbandment of Home Gd; sits as Conservative Peer in House of Lords; train bearer at Coronation of King George VI; painter (studied at Camberwell Sch Arts & Crafts, holds exhibitions at regular intervals); memb: Royal Fine Art Cmmn for Scotland 1958-61, Scottish Arts Cncl (chm art ctee 1969-76); tstee: National Galleries of Scotland 1963-73, Trustee of Scottish National War Memorial 1961-, President Border Area RBLS 1955-61, President Scottish Crafts Centre 1953-1974, Chairman Disablement Advisory Ctee SE Scotland 1960-73, Chairman Berwickshire Civic Society 1970-76, member Board of Directors Richard DeMarco gallery 1986-87, Scottish Nat War Memorial (chm bd of trustees 1983-); chm Offr's Assoc (Scottish Branch) 1977-87; President OA Scottish Branch 1987-, pres: Royal British Legion Scotland 1979-86 (nat chm 1963-66), The Earl Haig Fund Scotland 1979-86; vice-pres: Royal Blind Asylum, Scottish National Inst for War Blinded; DL Berwickshire 1953-76, vice-lieut Berwicks 1967-70; memb Royal Co of Archers (Queen's Body Guard for Scotland); FRSA; KStJ; *Recreations* fishing, shooting; *Clubs* New (Edinburgh), Cavalry & Guards; *Style—* The Rt Hon the Earl Haig, OBE, DL; Bemersyde, Melrose, Roxburghshire (☎ 083 52 2762)

HAIG, (Jean) Henrietta Rose; 2 da of Peter Haig Thomas and Lady Alexandra Agar (2 da of 4th Earl of Normanton, DL, by Lady Amy Byng, da of 4th Earl of Strafford, CB); *b* 20 Dec 1920; *m* 1, 12 Feb 1940, Sir Peter Greenwell, 3rd Bt, TD, DL (d 1978); 2 s (Sir Edward, 4th Bt; James), 1 da (Julia b 1946, m 1970 Alexander Trotter); m 2, 3 June 1985, Hugh Kenneth Haig, TD, only surv son of late Kenneth George Haig, MRCS, LRCP, of Gogarth, Llanidloes, Montgomeryshire; *Heir* Maj James Greenwell; *Career* landowner (2000 acres); *Recreations* fishing, shooting; *Style—* Mrs Hugh K Haig; Butley Abbey Farm, Woodbridge, Suffolk

HAIG, Lady (Elizabeth) Vivienne Thérèse; da of 2 Earl Haig, OBE; *b* 1 Mar 1959; *Educ* St George's Edinburgh, Bedales Sch, St Martin's Sch of Art; *Career* glass engraver; *Style—* Lady Vivienne Haig

HAIGH, (Austin) Anthony Francis; CMG (1954); s of Percy Barnes Haigh, ICS; *b* 29 August 1907; *Educ* Eton, King's Coll Cambridge; *m* 1, 1935 (m dis 1971), Gertrude, da of Frank Dodd; 2 s, 2 da; m 2, 1971, Eleanore, da of Tom H Bullimore and wid of J S Herbert; *Career* Foreign Serv, ret; dir Educn and Cultural and Scientific Affrs Cncl Europe 1962-68; *Books* A Ministry of Education for Europe (1970), Congress of Vienna to Common Market (1973), Cultural Diplomacy in Europe (1974); *Clubs* Leander; *Style—* Anthony Haigh, Esq, CMG; The Furnace, Crowhurst, nr Battle, E Sussex (☎ 042 483 279)

HAIGH, Dr Clement Percy; *b* 11 Jan 1920; *Educ* Univ of Leeds (BSc), Kings Coll Univ of London (PhD); *m* 8 June 1945, (Ruby) Patricia, *née* Hobdey; 3 s ((Julian) Robin David b 5 July 1950, (Stephen) Patrick Hobdey b 19 Nov 1957, Jeremy Rupert Michael b 6 June 1961); *Career* with Radiochem Centre Thorium Ltd 1943-49, med physicist Barrow Hosp Bristol 1949-56; CEGB: joined 1956, dir Berkeley Nuclear Labs 1959-73, dep dir gen Design and Construction Div Gloucester 1973-78; dir of res BNOC 1978-81, (conslt 1981-), dir S Western Industl Res 1981-86; distinguished lectr American Nuclear Soc San Francisco 1965, assessor Nuclear Safety Advsy Ctee 1972-76; memb: BBC W Advsy Cncl 1972-76, Mech Engrg and Machine Tools Requirements Bd 1972-76, Off-Shore Engrgy Technol Bd 1978-81, Nat Maritime Inst 1981-82; UK chm Joint UK/USSR Working Group on Problems of Electricity Supply 1974-78, chm programme steering ctee UK Off-Shore Steels Res Project 1981-87; CPhy, FInstP 1953, FRSA 1985; *Recreations* music; *Clubs* Savile, RAC; *Style—* Dr C P Haigh; Painswick, Old Sneed Pk, Bristol BS9 1RG (☎ 0272 68 2065); Duncombe, 121 Wetherby Rd, Harrogate, N Yorks

HAIGH, Maurice Francis; s of late William Haigh and Ceridwen Haigh; *b* 6 Sept 1929; *Educ* Repton; *Career* barr Gray's Inn 1955, recorder Crown Ct 1981-, chm Medical Appeal Tribunals; *Clubs* English Speaking Union; *Style—* Maurice Haigh, Esq; 83 Bridge St, Manchester M3 23F (☎ 061 832 4036)

HAIGH, (John) Randal; s of Fred Willoughby Haigh (d 1956), of Holmfirth, Yorks; *b* 12 Dec 1919; *Educ* King James's Sch Almondbury, St Catharine's Coll Cambridge (MA); *m* 1952, Zara Mary, da of W Ronald Martin (d 1970), of Coulsdon; 1 s, 1 da; *Career* served Lt, Middle East and Italy; dir Imperial Gp Ltd 1972-81 (sec 1968-74, investment advsr 1974-81); dir of pension fund; FIA; *Recreations* golf, walking, music, watching cricket and rugby football; *Clubs* MCC, HAC, Denham Golf; *Style—* Randal Haigh, Esq; Gable End, Spurgrove, Frieth, Henley-on-Thames, Oxon, RG9 6PB (☎ 0494 882335)

HAILES, Julia Persephone; da of Lt-Col John Martin Hunter Hailes, of Chiselborough House, Stoke-sub-Hamdon, Somerset, and Marianne Carlyon, *née* Coates; *b* 23 Sept 1961; *Educ* St Mary's Sch Calne Wilts; *Career* Leo Burnett Advty 1981-83; dir and co sec Sustainability Ltd; organiser: Green Consumer Week 1988, green kitchen stand Ideal Home Exhibition 1989; FRSA; *Books* Green Pages, The Business of Saving The World (1988), The Green Consumer Guide (1988); *Recreations* tennis, travel; *Style—* Miss Julia Hailes; 5 St Lawrence Terrace, London W10 5SU (☎ 01 968 9415); 1 Cambridge Rd, London SW13 0PE (☎ 01 878 8416, fax 01 878 5643)

HAILES, Leslie Sydney; s of Sydney Hailes (d 1979), and Hilda Hailes, *née* Turner (d 1974); *b* 14 June 1932; *m* 17 Dec 1955, Mary, da of Leonard Gomer (d 1976); 2 s (Stephen Christopher b 1956, Paul David b 1960), 1 da (Christine Lesley b 1962); *Career* md Robert Heyworth Gp Ltd 1977-, chm The Forum of Private Business 1979-; *Style—* Leslie S Hailes, Esq; 3 Saxfield Drive, Baguley Hall, Manchester (☎ (061) 998 5687); 2 Needham Ave, Chorlton-cum-Hardy, Manchester M21 2AA (telex 665185, fax 061860 7342)

HAILEY, Arthur; s of George Wellington Hailey and Elsie Mary Wright; *b* 5 April 1920; *Educ* Eng elementary schs; *m* 1, 1944 (m dis 1950), Joan Fishwick; 3 s; m 2, 1951, Sheila Dunlop; 1 s, 2 da; *Career* Pilot RAF 1939-47, Fl-Lt; emigrated to Canada 1947; various positions in ind and sales until becoming free lance writer 1956; author; *Books* Flight into Danger (with John Castle 1958), The Final Diagnosis (1959), Close-Up (collected plays 1960), In High Places (1962), Hotel (1965, film 1966), Airport (1968, film 1970), Wheels (1971, film 1978), The Moneychangers (1975, film 1976), Overload (1979), Strong Medicine (1984, film 1986); *Other films* Zero Hour (1956), Time Lock (1957), The Young Doctors (1961); *Clubs* Lyford Cay (Bahamas); *Style—* Arthur Hailey, Esq; Lyford Cay, PO Box N7776, Nassau, Bahamas; office: Seaway Authors Ltd, First Canadian Place - 6000, PO Box 130, Toronto, Ontario M5X 1A4, Canada

HAILSHAM, Viscountcy of (UK 1929); *see*: Hailsham of St Marylebone, Baron

HAILSHAM OF ST MARYLEBONE, Baron (Life Peer UK 1970); Quintin McGarel Hogg; KG (1988), CH (1974), PC (1956); s of 1 Viscount Hailsham (d 1950) by his 1 w Elizabeth, da of Judge Trimble Brown, of Nashville, Tennessee, and widow of Hon Archibald Marjoribanks (4 s of 1 Baron Tweedmouth); disclaimed both Viscountcy and Barony for life 1963; 1 cous of Sir John Hogg, TD, *qv*; *b* 9 Oct 1907; *Educ* Eton, Ch Ch Oxford; *m* 1, 1931 (m dis 1943), Natalie Antoinette (d 1987), da of Alan Sullivan, of Sheerland House, Pluckley, Kent; m 2, 1944, Mary Evelyn (d 1978), o da of Richard Martin, of Kensington; 2 s, 3 da; m 3, 1986, Deirdre, er da of Mrs Margaret Briscoe and late Capt Peter Shannon; *Heir* (to Viscountcy and Barony of Hailsham, UK cr respectively 1928 & 1929, only) s, Hon Douglas Hogg, MP; *Career* served WW II Rifle Bde; barrister 1932, QC 1953; MP (C) Oxford City 1938-58, St Marylebone 1963-70; first lord Admiralty 1956-57, min Educn 1957, lord pres of cncl 1957-59 and 1960-64, lord privy seal 1959-60, min Science and Technology 1959-64, ldr House of Lords 1960-63 (dep ldr 1957-60), lord chllr 1970-74 and 1979-88 (3 in precedence in Cabinet); chm Cons Pty Orgn 1957-59; rector Glasgow U 1959; editor Halsbury's Laws of England (4th edn) 1972-; fellow All Souls Oxford 1951-38 and 1962-; Hon DCL Oxford; FRS; *Style—* The Rt Hon the Lord Hailsham of St Marylebone, CH, PC; Corner House, Heathview Gdns, London SW15 (☎ 01 789 3954/788 2256)

HAINES, Dr Charles Ian; s of Col George Harris Haines, MC, RAMC (d 1974), and (Laura) Ailsa, *née* MacPhail (d 1979); *b* 15 Sept 1934; *Educ* Marlborough, St Mary's Hosp Med Sch and London Univ (MBBS); *m* 14 Sept 1963, Mollie Cynthia, da of James Reid Wheeler Reid (d 1973); 1 s (Rupert b 1967), 3 da (Alexandra b 1965, Ruth b 1971, Lucy b 1974); *Career* Surgn Lt RN 1960-63; princ in gen practice 1963-66, conslt paediatrician to Bromsgrove and Kidderminster Gen Hosps and Alexandra Hosp Redditch 1974-, sr clinical lectr dept of paediatrics Univ of Birmingham 1988-; pres League of Friends Scott Atkinson Child Devpt Centre Redditch, conslt memb Bromsgrove and Redditch DHA 1985-; FRCP 1984; *Recreations* gardening, golf, fishing, opera; *Clubs* Gentlemen of Worcs CC; *Style—* Dr Charles Haines; 34

Greenhill, Blackwell, Bromsgrove, Worcs B60 1BJ (☎ 021 445 1729); Alexandra Hospital, Woodrow Drive, Redditch, Worcs (☎ 0527 503030)

HAINES, Rev Dr Daniel Hugo; s of Dr Richard Wheeler Haines, of 54 Elm Grove, London SE15, and Ellen Stephanie, *née* Swift; *b* 16 Mar 1943; *Educ* Abbotsholme Sch Derbys, Guys Hosp Dental Sch Univ of London (BDS, LDS), London Hosp Med Coll Univ of London, Staff Coll Camberley; *m* 20 July 1968, Dr Hilary Margaret, da of Tudor Isaac, of 107 Alma Rd, Maesteg, Mid Glam; 2 s (Tudor b 1972, Gwyn b 1977), 1 da (Catherine b 1974); *Career* Univ of London Offrs Trg Corps 1962, Dental Offr 221 (Surrey) Field Ambulance RAMC (Capt) 1968, MO 217 (London) Gen Hosp RAMC (Maj) 1984; hon lectr in forensic dentistry London Hosp Med Coll 1968-75, med offr Govt of the Cayman Islands 1975-77, chief med offr Usutu Forests Swaziland 1977-80, sr med offr Govt of the Falkland Islands 1980-82, med and dental practitioner 1982-; ordained priest Southwark Cath 1984, hon curate St Catherine's Hatcham 1984-; Freeman City of London 1968, Liveryman Worshipful Soc of Apothecaries of London 1970; memb: BMA, BDA; FRSM, LRCP, MRCS, DRCOG; *Recreations* gardening, walking; *Style—* The Rev Dr Daniel Haines; 56 Vesta Rd, London SE4 2NH (☎ 01 635 0305); The Surgery, 29 Crossway Ct, Endwell Rd, London SE4 2NQ (☎ 01 639 0654)

HAINES, Hon Mrs; Hon Emma Charlotte; *née* Bancroft; o da of Baron Bancroft, GCB (Life Peer); *b* 1959; *Educ* Sheen Sixth Form Coll, Canterbury Coll of Art (MA); *m* 2 June 1984, Jeremy Guy Minton Haines, s of G D M Haines, of Uckfield, Sussex; 1 da (Phoebe b 1988); *Career* graphic designer; *Style—* The Hon Mrs Haines

HAINES, Joe (Joseph) Thomas William; s of Joseph and Elizabeth Haines; *b* 29 Jan 1928; *m* 1955, Irene Lambert; *Career* dir: Mirror Group Newspapers (1986), Scottish Daily Record and Sunday Mail Ltd, asst ed The Mirror, political ed Mirror Gp Newspapers 1984- chief leader writer Daily Mirror 1978-, feature writer 1977-78; political correspondent: The Sun 1964-68, Scottish Daily Mail 1960-64, The Bulletin (Glasgow) 1958-60 (parly correspondent 1954-58); chief press sec to Harold Wilson as PM 1969-70 & 1974-76 and when Leader Oppn 1970-74 (dep press sec 1969); chm Tonbridge & Malling Labour Party to 1981 when resigned; former memb Tonbridge UDC and Royal Cmmn on Legal Servs; *Books* The Politics of Power (1977), Malice in Wonderland (ed 1986), Maxwell (1986); *Style—* Joe Haines, Esq; 1 South Frith, London Rd, Southborough, Tunbridge Wells, Kent (☎ 0732 365919)

HAINING, Thomas Nivison; CMG (1982); s of late William Haining, of Ayrshire (d 1977), and Agnes Nivison Haining, *née* Williamson; *b* 15 Mar 1927; *Educ* Edinburgh Univ, Göttingen Univ; *m* 1955, Dorothy Patricia, da of late Leslie Robson and Mrs A D Robson, of Whitley Bay; 1 s (Nicholas); *Career* HM Foreign Serv 1952-82, ambassador consul gen to Mongolian People's Republic 1979-82, ret; conslt on int and personnel questions 1982-87; non res assoc dept of history Univ of Aberdeen 1988-; Freeman City of Rochester NY State 1972; FRGS; *Recreations* reading, historical travel studies, local historical studies, music golf; *Clubs* RAC; *Style—* Thomas Haining, Esq, CMG; Carseview, 7 The Banks, Brechin, Angus DD9 6JD (☎ 03562 2584)

HAINWORTH, Henry Charles; CMG (1961); s of Charles Samuel Hainworth (d 1957), and Emily Gertrude Irene *née* Laycock (d 1948); *b* 12 Sept 1914; *Educ* Blundells Sch, Sidney Sussex Coll Cambridge (BA); *m* 1944, Mary, da of Felix Basil Ady (d 1942); 2 da (Victoria, Daphne); *Career* HM Consular Serv Tokyo 1939, Br Min of Info New Delhi 1942-46, diplomatic posts in Tokyo, London, Bucharest, Paris, Cyprus, 1946-57, head of Atomic Energy and Disarmament Dept FO 1958-61, delgn sec for negotiations with EEC Brussels 1961-63, min cnsllr and HM consul-gen Br Embassy Vienna 1963-68, HM ambass Indonesia 1968-70, ambass and UK perm del to Disarmament Conference Geneva 1971-74; ret; *Books* A Collector's Dictionary (1980); *Recreations* reading, fishing; *Style—* Henry Hainworth, Esq, CMG; 23 Rivermead Court, Ranelagh Gardens, London SW6 3RU

HAIRE, Hon Christopher Peter; s of Baron Haire of Whiteabbey (Life Peer, d 1966); *b* 6 Feb 1951; *Educ* Michael Hall Sch Forest Row Sussex, Holland Park Sch W8; *Style—* The Hon Christopher Haire; 34 Elm Park Gdns, London SW10 (☎ 01 352 6846)

HAIRE, Hon Michael John Kemeny; s of Baron Haire of Whiteabbey (Life Peer, d 1966); *b* 19 Dec 1945; *Educ* St Paul's, UCL, Pennsylvania Univ; *Style—* The Hon Michael Haire; 34 Elm Park Gdns, SW10 (☎ 01 352 6846)

HAIRE OF WHITEABBEY, Baroness - Suzanne Elizabeth; da of Dr Eugene Kemeny, of London; *m* 1939, Baron Haire of Whiteabbey (Life Peer, d 1966); 2 s; *Style—* The Rt Hon Lady Haire of Whiteabbey; Lynford Hall, Mundford, Norfolk; Whiteabbey House, Belfast

HAITINK, Bernard; Hon KBE (1977); *b* 1929; *Career* artistic dir Concertgebouw Orchestra Amsterdam 1964-, artistic dir (and princ conductor) London Philharmonic Orchestra 1967-79, debut Royal Opera House 1977, musical dir Glyndebourne Opera 1978-, appointed musical dir Royal Opera House, Covent Garden 1986-; *Style—* Bernard Haitink, Esq, KBE; c/o Harold Holt Ltd, 31 Sinclair Rd, London W14

HAKEWILL SMITH, Lady Edith Margaret; *née* Nelson; eldest da of late Brig-Gen Herbert Nelson, DSO (d 26 May 1949), of Shovel, N Petherton, Somerset, by his wife Edith Frances Wright, da of late Richard Cory, of Langdon Court, Devon; *m* 1928, Maj-Gen Sir Edmund Hakewill Smith, KCVO, CB, CBE (d 15 April 1986); 1 da; *Style—* Lady Hakewill Smith; 28 Tennis Court Lane, Hampton Court Palace, East Molesey, Surrey

HALAHAN, (George Edward) Desmond; CBE (1976); s of Capt George Crosby Halahan (d 1929), of Eastwick, Chiddingfold, Surrey, and Bertha Beryl Constance, *née* Boyle (d 1966); *b* 13 April 1910; *Educ* Westminster Sch, Balliol Coll Oxford (MA); *m* 1 Aug 1942, Doreen, da of Harry Reed (d 1966), and Margaret Ellen *née* Clark, of Scunthorpe, Lincolnshire; 2 s (George Desmond Thomas b 1944, Richard John Crosby b 1946), 1 da (Frances Jane b 1950); *Career* steel plant mangr: Richard Thomas and Co Ltd 1935-45, Utd Steel Cos Ltd 1945-60, dir Tube Investmts Ltd 1965-67 (md Iron and Steel Div 1965-67), md Round Oak Steelworks 1967-76; fndr and first chm The Industl Steel Employers Assoc, chm Br Industl Steel Prodrs Assoc 1971-72; memb: Dept of Employment Industl Tbnl 1976-80, first Police Complaints Bd 1977-82; chm Black Country Museum Tst Ltd 1975-88; *Recreations* old clocks, gardening; *Clubs* Athenaeum, London Rowing; *Style—* Desmond Halahan, CBE; Sinton Court, Sinton Green, Hallow, Worcester WR2 6NP (☎ 0905 640206)

HALAS, John; OBE (1972); s of Victor Halas, and Bertha Halas; *b* 16 April 1912; *Educ* Acad of Arts Budapest, Institut De Beaux Arts Paris; *m* 1940, Joy Ethel, *née* Batchelor; 1 s (Paul b Feb 1949), 1 da (Vivien b July 1945); *Career* fndr: Halas & Batchelor Animation Studio 1940, Educnl Film Centre 1960, Gt Masters Ltd 1981; dir and prodr of over 2000 animated films incl: Animal Farm (first Euro animated feature film), Dilema (first computer generated film); winner of over 200 int awards, pres Br Fedn of Film Socs 1980-, hon pres Int Animated Film Assoc; Freeman San Francisco 1961; memb: BKSTS 1972, SFRCA 1988; *Recreations* arts, music, painting; *Style—* John Halas, Esq, OBE; 6 Holford Rd, Hampstead, London NW3 1AD (☎ 01 435 8674); 3-7 Kean St, London WC2B 4AT (☎ 01 836 5108, fax 01 836 5401, telex 269 496)

HALBERT, Trevor Anthony; s of Ronald Halbert, of Wirral, Cheshire, and Freda Mabel, *née* Impett; *b* 2 June 1952; *Educ* Kings Sch Chester, Selwyn Coll Cambridge (MA); *m* 30 May 1983, Elaine Elizabeth, JP, da of William Alan Richardson, of Wirral, Merseyside; 1 s (Matthew b 1985); *Career* 2 Lt 3 Bn RWF 1975-77; barr Inner Temple 1975, standing counsel to DOSS 1983- (Wales and Chester circuit); *Recreations* mountaineering, music; *Style—* Trevor Halbert, Esq; Sedan House, Stanley Place, Chester CH1 2LU (☎ 0244 48282, fax 0244 42336)

HALDANE, Yr of Gleneagles, Brodrick Vernon Chinnery; yr s of James Brodrick Chinnery-Haldane, JP (d 1941), and Katherine Annie, *née* Napier (d 1957); bro and hp of Alexander Chinnery Haldane of Gleneagles, *qv*; *b* 12 July 1912; *Educ* Lancing; *Career* WWII served 83 Battery Light Artillery RA; actor 1932-35; appeared with Sir Philip Ben Greet's Shakespearian theatre co; films incl: Two Hearts in Waltz Time, Happy, Murder in Monte Carlo; int soc photographer 1930-; exhibitions held in: Lausanne, Traquair House Innerleithen 1982, Edinburgh Festival 1987; contrib to numerous books, magazines and newspapers; *Style—* Brodrick Chinnery Haldane, Yr of Gleneagles; 56 India Street, Edinburgh EH3 6HD (☎ 031 225 5222)

HALDANE, James; er s of Herbert William Haldane (d 1957), dir of Royal Bank of Scotland, by his wife Helen Rachel (d 1965, aged 89), da of George Alston, of Craighead, Lanarkshire; *b* 14 May 1903; *Educ* Winchester, Magdalen Coll Oxford (BA); *m* 3 Oct 1939, Joanna Margaret, da of Col William Thorburn; 2 s (James Martin, *qv*, and Robert b 1952) 1 da (Angela b 1944, Mrs David J Cockshott, 1 da decd); *Career* chartered accountant 1929; ptnr: Lindsay Jamieson & Haldane 1930-70, Arthur Young McClelland Moores & Co 1970-74; co dir; *Recreations* golf; *Clubs* Naval & Military, New (Edinburgh), Hon Co of Edinburgh Golfers; *Style—* James Haldane of Gleneagles; The Old Schoolhouse, Gleneagles, Auchterarder, Perthshire PH3 1PJ (☎ Blackford 076 482 427);

HALDANE, (James) Martin; er s of James Haldane (*qv*); *b* 18 Sept 1941; *Educ* Winchester, Magdalen Oxford; *m* 5 Oct 1968, Petronella Victoria, da of Sir Peter Scarlett, KCMG, KCVO, *qv*; 1 s, 2 da; *Career* chartered accountant; ptnr Arthur Young 1970; chm: Scottish Philharmonic Soc 1978-1985, Scottish Chamber Orchestra 1981-1985; chm: Craighead Investmts plc 1982-; dir: Northern and Scottish Bd, Legal & Gen Assur Soc 1984-87, memb: Council Edinburgh Festival Soc 1985-, tstee D'Oyly Carte Opera Tst 1985-, memb Royal Co of Archers (Queen's Body Guard for Scotland); *Recreations* music, golf; *Clubs* Brooks's, New (Edinburgh); *Style—* J Martin Haldane of Gleneagles, Yr; Gleneagles, Auchterarder, Perthshire (☎ Blackford 388); 23 Northumberland St, Edinburgh (☎ 031 556 2924)

HALDANE OF GLENEAGLES, Capt Alexander Napier Chinnery; 27 Laird of Gleneagles; er s of James Brodrick Chinnery-Haldane, JP, 26 Laird of Gleneagles (d 1941), and Katherine Annie, *née* Napier (d 1957); bro of Brodrick Chinnery Haldane, Yr of Gleneagles, *qv*; family inherited the ancient barony of Gleneagles in 1918 by deed of entail on the death of 3 Earl of Camperdown; *b* 17 June 1907; *Educ* Harrow, Wadham Coll Oxford; *Career* WWII served Royal Scots, took part in evacuation of Dunkirk; *Style—* Alexander Chinnery Haldane of Gleneagles; Gleneagles, Auchterarder, Perthshire PH3 1PJ (☎ 0764 82 249/472)

HALDANE-STEVENSON, Rev (James) Patric; TD and bar; s of Graham Morton Stevenson (d 1939), of Llandaff, Glam (descended from 3 Haldane Laird of Airthrey, later Campus of Stirling Univ), and Jane Haldane, da of James Thomson, of Airdrie; *b* 17 Mar 1910; *Educ* King Edward's Sch Birmingham, St Catherine's Coll Oxford (BA, MA); *m* 1, 1938, (m dis 1967), Leila Mary, da of Arthur Flack; 2 s (Alan, Keith), 1 da (Janet); m 2, 1983, Mrs Joan Talbot Smith, o da of Lt Cdr C W Wilson, of Par, Cornwall; *Career* served British Regular Army 1946-55; Westminster Bank 1927-30, ordained Southwark 1935; rector: Hillington Norfolk (but on active service 1939-46), Anglican Church in Wongan Hills Australia 1956-59; vicar of N Balwyn Melbourne 1959-80, cmmr for Canon Law 1971-77; author, contrib to various books and journals, Aust corr Le Monde 1969-73; pres Cambrian Soc of ACT 1985-88; memb Celtic Cncl of Australia; *Books* In Our Tongues (1944), Religion and Leadership (1948), Crisanzio and Other Poems (1948), Beyond the Bridge (1973), The Backward Look (1976); *Recreations* riding; *Clubs* Athenaeum, Quorn Hunt, Melbourne, Naval and Military (Melbourne) ; *Style—* The Rev Patric Haldane-Stevenson, TD; c/o Coleg Mihangel Sant, Llandâf CF5 2YJ

HALE, Charles Martin; s of Charles Sydney Hale (d 1981), and Carmen, *née* de Mora; *b* 19 Jan 1936; *Educ* St Bernard's Sch NY, Culver Mil Acad, Stanford Univ (BSc), Harvard Business Sch (MBA); *m* 11 Feb 1967, Kaaren Alexis Hale; 2 da (Melissa b 18 May 1971, Amanda b 9 Nov 1976); *Career* SN: serv USS Union, Ensign i/c Boat Gp Div 1958, Lt 1960; gen ptnr Hirsch & Co London 1963-71, md and sr offr Europe AG Becker Inc 1971-83, gen ptnr Lehman Bros Kuhn Loeb Inc 1983-84, md and head of int div Donaldson Lufkin & Jenrette Securities Corpn 1984-; vice chm UK Assoc of NY Stock Exchange Membs (dep chm 1988-); memb: Harvard Business Sch Club of London, Stanford Univ Club of GB; *Recreations* tennis; *Clubs* Hurlingham, Annabel's; *Style—* Charles Hale, Esq; 33 Lyall Mews, London SW1 (☎ 01 245 9916); Donaldson, Lufkin & Jenrette Securities Corp, Jupiter House, Triton Ct, 14 Finsbury Sq, London EC2A 1BR (☎ 01 638 5822, fax 01 588 0120)

HALE, John Hampton; Dr John Hale, and Elsie Ledbrooke Coles; *b* 8 July 1924; *Educ* Eton, Magdalene Coll Cambridge (MA), Harvard Business Sch (hon fell); *m* 1, 1950, 1 s (Jonathan), 2 da (Susan, Anne); m 2, 1980, Nancy Ryrie Birks; *Career* Alcan Aluminium Ltd 1949-83: exec vice pres finance 1970-83, dir 1970-85, md Pearson plc 1983-86; dir: Pearson plc 1983-, Economist Newspaper Ltd 1984-, Bank of Montreal 1985-, SSMC Inc 1986-; lay memb Cncl Int Stock Exchange 1987-; *Recreations* skiing, fishing, shooting; *Clubs* Royal Thames YC, Mount Royal; *Style—* John Hale, Esq; Pearson plc, Millbank Tower, London SW1P 4QZ. (☎ 01 828 9020, telex 8953869).

HALE, Prof Sir John Rigby; *b* 17 Sept 1923; *Educ* Eastbourne Coll, and Jesus Coll Oxford (DLitt); *m* 1, 1952, Rosalind Williams; 1 s, 2 da; m 2, 1965, Sheila Haynes MacIvor, journalist; 1 s; *Career* prof of Italian History Univ Coll London 1970-; chm tstees Nat Gallery 1974-80 (tstee 1973-80), tstee V & A 1983-, tstee British Museum 1985-, chm Govt Art Collection Advsy Cncl 1982; author; FSA, FRHistS, FRSA, FBA; kt 1984; *Style—* Prof Sir John Hale; Department of History, University College, Gower St, London WC1 (☎ 01 387 7050)

HALE, (Mathew) Joseph Hovey; MC (1945), TD (1974); s of Mathew Roger Hale (d 1926), of Bognor Regis, and Grace Muriel, *née* Hovey (d 1962); *b* 14 Oct 1918; *Educ* St Johns Coll Hurstpierpoint; *m* 28 Jan 1950, Gwenda, da of Sidney Herbert Roberts (d 1972), of Worthing, W Sussex; 2 da (Sheila b 1950, Sally b 1955); *Career* WWII 1939-46, cmmnd RA 1939, served N African and Italian campaigns, Maj 1944; admitted slr 1947, in private practice; dir T R Beckett Ltd 1959-; chm: Beckett Newspapers Ltd 1967-, T R Beckett Ltd and subsid cos 1969-, Today Interiors Ltd 1976-; pt/t sec London Master Stevedares Assoc 1946-77; memb exec ctee Worthing Area Guild for Voluntary Serv 1974-, chm govrs Our Lady of Slow Sch Worthing 1984-; memb Law Soc 1947; *Recreations* golf, walking, gardening; *Clubs* Army and Navy; *Style—* Joseph Hale, Esq, MC, TD; Stortford, Little Drove, Steyning, W Sussex (☎ 0903 814 852), 1 Commercial Rd, Eastbourne, E Susex (☎ 0323 220 91)

HALE, Michael; s of Bertram Hale (d 1986), of Dudley, W Midlands, and Nellie, *née* Cartwright (d 1977); *b* 20 June 1942; *Educ* Sir Gilbert Claughton GS; *m* 19 June 1965, Maureen Janet, da of John Thomas Shipley (d 1978), of Dudley; 1 s (Stephen Michael b 26 Nov 1971), 1 da (Helen Louise b 20 Oct 1975); *Career* dir: Centl Mfrg & Trg Gp 1975-80, Caparo Industs plc 1980-83, Glynwed Distribution Ltd 1983-86; md GEI Int plc 1986-; FCMA 1969, ACIS 1971; *Recreations* tennis, walking; *Style—* Michael Hale, Esq; Lower House, 57A Norton Road, Stourbridge (☎ 0384 373789); GEI International plc, 42-44 West Street, Dunstable, Beds LU6 1TA (☎ 0582 601201, fax 0582 666930, telex 825261)

HALE, Norman Morgan; s of Thomas Norman Hale (d 1961), of Worcs, and Ada Emily, *née* Morgan (d 1969); *b* 28 June 1933; *Educ* Prince Henry's GS, St John's Coll Oxford (MA); *m* 1965, Sybil Jean, da of Stephen Leonard Maton (d 1974), of Glos; 1 s (Roger b 1966), 1 da (Alison b 1968); *Career* under sec (grade 3) in DHSS 1975-, Miny of Pensions and National Insurance 1955, asst sec at Assistance Bd 1966, Miny of Social Security 1966-70, Civil Service Dept 1970-72; head Mental Health Div 1978-82, head Medicines Div 1982-87; currently head: child health, maternity and prevention div (with AIDS unit); *Recreations* gardening, historical geography; *Style—* Norman Hale, Esq; DHSS, Elephant and Castle, London SE1 (☎ 01 407 5522)

HALE, Raymond; s of Tom Raymond Hale (d 1963), and Mary Jane *née* Higgin of Fleetwood; *b* 4 July 1936; *Educ* Baines GS Poulton-le-fylde; *m* 22 Aug 1956, Ann, da of George Elvidge of Thornton-Cleveleys; 1 s (Philip Raymond b 1963); *Career* RAF 1954-56; with Lancs CC 1952-61, Notts CC 1961-65, co tres Leics CC; tres: Leics Probation Serv, Magistrates Cts Serv , Leics & Rutland Police Authy, E Mids Area Museums Serv; vice chm Leics Guild of Physically Handicapped, tres Parkinson Disease Soc (Leics Branch); IPFA 1959, FCCA 1981; *Recreations* DIY, gardening, rugby, cricket; *Style—* Raymond Hale, Esq; County Hall, Glenfield, Leicester, LE3 8RB, (☎ 0533 316375, fax 0533 317820, telex 341478)

HALES, Christopher Atherstone; s of Lt Col Herbert Marwicke Atherstone Hales (d 1956), of Turweston, Bucks, and Mary, *née* Bell (d 1970); *b* 26 August 1931; *Educ* Wellingborough, HMS Worcester; *m* 17 May 1956, Barbara Mary, da of Edwin Arthur Ryan (d 1963), of London N18; 2 s (Julian b 1963, Adrian b 1966), 4 da (Katherine b 1958, Caroline b 1959, Antonia b 1961, Marie Louise b 1964); *Career* Merchant Navy, Blue Funnel Line: Midshipman 1949-52, 3 offr 1952-55, 2 offr 1955-58; Master Mariner 1957; called to the Bar Grays Inn 1960, articled Alsop Stevens and Co 1961-64, admitted slr 1964, asst slr Alsop Stevens and Co 1964, ptnr Holman Fenwick and Willan 1968-(asst slr 1965-67); Freeman City of London, Liveryman Master Mariners Co; memb Law Soc; *Recreations* concert and theatre going, history, following cricket; *Style—* Christopher Hales, Esq; Flat 4, 66 Gloucester St, London SW1V 4EF; Farthing Green, Elmdon, Saffron Walden, Essex; Holman Fenwick and Willan, Marlow House, Lloyds Ave, London EC3N 3AL (☎ 01 488 2300, fax 01 481 0316)

HALEWOOD, David Frank; s of Thomas Halewood (d 1972), and Winifred, *née* Spencer (d 1974); *b* 28 April 1933; *Educ* Walton Tech Coll, Burton Tech Coll; *m* 29 Sept 1958, Eleanor Ann, da of John Smith (d 1970), of Burton on Trent; 2 da (Jacqueline b 1961, Jayne b 1965); *Career* jt md Chamberlain Phipps plc 1985; chm and md Chamter Ltd 1985; dir: Plasilem (Vic) Australia, Tanner Chemical USA 1984, CP Italia Spa 1983; CEng, MIMechE, MIProdE; *Recreations* golf, walking; *Clubs* Charnwood Forest; *Style—* David Halewood, Esq; 3 Paterson Drive, Woodhouse Eaves, Loughborough, Leics LE12 8RL (☎ 0509 890784); Wanlip Road, Syston, Leics (☎ 0533 601757, 34485)

HALEY, Prof Keith Brian; s of Arthur Leslie Haley (d 1972), and Gladys Mary, *née* Robson (d 1957); *b* 17 Nov 1933; *Educ* King Edward VI GS Birmingham, Univ of Birmingham (BSc, PhD); *m* 2, April 1960, Diana Elizabeth Haley, JP, da of Albert Bottrell Mason (d 1981); 1 s (Alan John b 1962); *Career* operational res sci NCB 1957-59; Univ of Birmingham: lectr 1959, sr lectr 1963, prof operational res 1968, head of dept engrg prodn 1980; govr and tstee Bromsgrove Sch 1969-, pres Operational Res Soc 1982-83, vice pres Int Fedn of Operational Res Socs 1983- 86; FIMA 1968, FOR 1970, FIProdE 1982; *Books* Mathematical Programming for Business & Industry (1964), Operational Research in Search (1980), Operational Research in Fishing (1981), Operational Research 75 (1975), Operational Research 78 (1978); *Recreations* squash, bridge; *Style—* 22 Eymore Close, Selly Oak, Birmingham B29 4LB (☎ 021 475 331); School of Engineering Production, The University of Birmingham, Edgbaston, Birmingham B15 2TT (☎ 02 414 4542)

HALFORD, (James) Harold; s of James Henry Halford (d 1962), and Blanche Ida, *née* Cowling (d 1973); *b* 9 Jan 1923; *m* 4 Dec 1948, Norma; 1 s (Martin James b 28 Dec 1955), 1 da (Philippa Caroline (Mrs Gasson) b 19 Aug 1958); *Career* WWII 1942-45; cmmnd RE 1944 served: 210 Field Co (Holland, Belgium, Germany), HQ 30 Corps (Germany); Stirling Maynard and Ptnrs (formerly Maj E M Stirling): asst engr (later chief asst) 1946-55, ptnr 1955-75, sr ptnr 1975-86, conslt 1986-87, ret 1987; engrg advsr Nottingham Univ, former chm E Midlands ICE, pres Peterborough Rotary Club 1984; FICE 1954, MIHT 1954, MIWEM 1955, MConsE 1957, CEng; *Recreations* photography, wood turning, caravanning; *Clubs* Peterborough Rotary; *Style—* Harold Halford, Esq; Kirkby House, 94 Tinwell Road, Stamford, Lincs PE9 2SD (☎ 0780 54783)

HALFORD, Maj Gen Michael Charles Kirkpatrick; DSO (1946), OBE (1957, MBE 1943), DL (1975); s of Lt-Col Michael Francis Halford (d 1951), and Violet Margaret Halford, *née* Kirkpatrick (d 1940); *b* 28 Oct 1914; *Educ* Wellington, Trinity Coll Cambridge; *m* 1945, Pamela Joy, da of Norman Anthony Wright (d 1959); 3 s (David, Peter, Jeremy); *Career* served in Palestine 1936, France 1940, N Africa, Italy, France 1944-45, COS, GOC (Wessex) Div Dist 1964-67; *Recreations* golf, fishing; *Clubs* Army & Navy; *Style—* Maj Gen Michael Halford, DSO, OBE, DL

HALIFAX, Archdeacon of; *see*: Chesters, Ven Alan David

HALIFAX, 3 Earl of (UK 1944); Sir Charles Edward Peter Neil Wood; 7 Bt (GB 1784); DL (Humberside 1983); also Viscount Halifax (UK 1866), Baron Irwin (UK 1925); s of 2 Earl of Halifax (d 1980); *b* 14 Mar 1944; *Educ* Eton, Ch Ch Oxford; *m* 1976, Camilla, da of Charles Younger, of Gledswood, Melrose, Roxburghshire, and former w of Richard Eustace Parker Bowles; 1 s, 1 da (Lady Joanna b 1980); *Heir* s, Lord Irwin; *Career* dir Hambro's Bank; JP; High Steward of York Minster 1988; OStJ; *Style—* The Rt Hon the Earl of Halifax, DL; Garrowby, York YO4 1QD

HALIFAX, Ruth, Countess of - Ruth Alice Hannah Mary; da of late Rt Hon Neil James Archibald Primrose, MC, MP (ka 1917), 2 s of 5 Earl of Rosebery, and Lady Victoria Alice Louise Stanley (d 1927), da of 17 Earl of Derby; *b* 18 April 1916; *m* 1936, 2 Earl of Halifax (d 1980); 1 s (3 Earl), 2 da (Lady Caroline Feilden, Lady Susan Watson); *Style—* The Rt Hon Ruth, Countess of Halifax; Low House, Kirby Underdale, York; Alston Lodge, Stanley House, Newmarket, Suffolk

HALL, Adrian Charles; s of Alexander Stephenson Hall, of Boarstall Tower, Boarstall, Aylesbury, Bucks, and Edith Mary Partington, *née* Smith (d 1975); *b* 8 June 1945; *Educ* Dragon Sch Oxford, Eton, Mansfield Coll Oxford (MA); *m* 17 Oct 1981, Magdalena Mary, da of Maj Edward Lewis Fiteni, of Morpeth Mansions, Morpeth Terr, London SW1; 2 s (Richard b 27 June 1985, Edward (twin) b 27 June 1985), 1 da (Mary b 2 Dec 1982); *Career* asst slr Norton Rose (London) 1971-75, assoc barr/slr Borden & Elliot (Toronto) 1975-78, asst slr Allen & Overy 1978-82, sr legal mangr Standard Chartered Bank 1982-86, ptnr Turner Kenneth Brown slrs 1986-; memb: Law Soc of England and Wales 1971, Law Soc of Upper Canada 1977; memb Worshipful Co of Slrs; *Recreations* historic motor racing, field game; *Clubs* MCC, Historic Sports Car, Eton Ramblers, Raffles, Alfa Romeo Owners; *Style—* Adrian Hall, Esq; Turner Kenneth Brown, 100 Fetter Lane, London EC4A 1DD (☎ 01 242 6006, fax 01 242 3003, telex 297696)

HALL, Col Alan Edmund Matticot; TD (1975), DL (1985); s of Maj Edmund Hall (d 1983), of Helston, Cornwall, and Norah, *née* Carrick (d 1985); *b* 7 Oct 1935; *Educ* Emanuel Sch, Churches Coll Petersfield, The Grammar Sch Enfield; *m* 8 Feb 1958, Diane Mary, da of Robert William Keyte (d 1969), of Cliftonville; 1 s (James b 1968), 2 da (Amanda b 1959, Nicola b 1962); *Career* Nat Serv 1955-57, Territorial Serv Royal Mil Police 1961-82; Offr Commanding: 44 Parachute Bde Provost Co 1965-67, 253 Provost Co 1969-76; appt Hon Col Royal Mil Police TA 1977-82; ctee memb Greater London TAVRA: exec & fin, gen purpose & fin, HQ; md: Ind Coope East Anglia Ltd 1981-84, J & W Nicholson & Co 1984; dir of UK sales Löwenbräu Lager 1986-; former pres The Percheron Horse Soc, regnl chm The Wishing Well Appeal, pres NE London SSAFA & FHS, vice-pres Essex Boy Scout Assoc; DL Co of London, rep DL London Borough of Redbridge; Freeman City of London 1984, Liveryman Worshipful Co of Broderers; FBIM 1979; *Recreations* shooting, wood working, curry cooking; *Clubs* Wig and Pen; *Style—* Col Alan Hall, TD, DL; Pippins, Tye Green, Good Easter, Essex (☎ 024 531 280); The Brewery, High St, Romford, Essex CMI 4SH (☎ 0708 762 839, 0708 22743, fax 0708 33407, car tel 0860 339 900, telex 265657 LOBRAU)

HALL, Alan Vivian; s of Walter Hall (d 1963) of Hull and Vera, *née* Thompson (d 1978); *b* 5 April 1930; *Educ* Hull GS, Nottingham Univ (BSc); *m* 26 June 1954, June Kathleen, da of William Redvers Beck (d 1977), of Hull; 2 s (Richard Guy b 1958, Jonathan Charles b 1961); *Career* RAF 1948-50; Shell-Mex and BP Ltd 1961-72, investmt mangr Shell Int Petroleum Co Ltd 1973-, memb bd of tstees Coll Retirement Equities Fund (USA) 1978-; Freeman City of London 1979, Liveryman Worshipful Co of Actuaries 1979; AIA 1958, FSS 1962, AMSIA 1961, FPMI 1978; *Recreations* travel, golf; *Clubs* MCC, Burhill GC; *Style—* Alan Hall, Esq; Shell Centre, London SE1 7NA (☎ 01 934 6261, telex 919651)

HALL, Alfred Charles; CBE (1977, OBE 1966); s of Alfred Hall (d 1951); *b* 2 August 1917; *Educ* Oratory Sch and Open Univ; *m* 1946, Clara Georgievna, *née* Strunin, of Moscow; 5 s, 1 da; *Career* served WWII Intelligence Corps; HM Dip Serv; attached to embassies Cairo, Tehran, Moscow; first sec: India, Pakistan, Canada; cncllr: (info) Nigeria, Canberra; attached to Dept of Trade 1969-71, cncllr (econ and devpt) Nigeria 1972-75, dep high cmmr in S India 1975-77; grants offr Save the Children Fund 1979-82; *Recreations* gardening, journalism; *Clubs* Royal Cwlth, Royal Hort; *Style—* Alfred Hall Esq, CBE; White Cliff, St Margarets Bay, Kent (☎ 0304 852230)

HALL, Hon Mrs (Alison Elizabeth Vivienne); *née* Gridley; 2 da of 2 Baron Gridley; *b* 27 June 1953; *m* 1975, Michael John Hall; *Style—* The Hon Mrs Hall; c/o Rt Hon Lord Gridley, Coneygore, Stoke Trister, Wincanton, Somerset

HALL, Anthony Stewart (Tony); s of Albert Hall (d 1970), of Gillingham, Kent, and Dora Rose Ellen, *née* Rundle (d 1987); *b* 26 Oct 1945; *Educ* Gillingham GS, LSE (BSc); *m* 28 Dec 1968, Phoebe Katharine, da of John Leonard Souster; 1 s (Simon Anthony b 19 Dec 1973), 1 da (Katharine Phoebe b 17 May 1976); *Career* lectr mgmnt and orgn studies Nat Inst for Social Work Trg 1971-73, lectr social admin Bristol Univ 1971-78; dir Assoc of Br Adoption and Fostering Agencies 1978-80, dir and sec Br Agencies for Adoption and Fostering 1980-86, dir Central Cncl for Educn and Trg in Social Work 1986-; *Books* The Point of Entry: A Study of Client Reception in the Social Services (1974), Part-Time Social Work (with Phoebe Hall, 1980); *Recreations* photography, music, old films, genealogy, sport, stamps; *Style—* Tony Hall, Esq; 115 Babington Road, Streatham, London SW16 6AN (☎ 01 769 1504); Ccetsw, Derbyshire House, St Chads St, London WC1H 8AD (☎ 01 278 2455)

HALL, Sir Arnold Alexander; s of Robert Alexander Hall (d 1960), of Wirral, Cheshire, and Ellen Elizabeth, *née* Parkinson; *b* 23 April 1915; *Educ* Alsop HS, Clare Coll Cambridge (MA); *m* 29 Nov 1946, (Moira Constance) Dione, da of Rev J A Sykes, of Mugginton, Derby; 3 da (Caroline, Elizabeth, Veronica); *Career* Royal Aircraft Estab Farnborough: princ sci offr 1938-45, dir 1951-55; Hawker Siddeley Gp: dir 1955-86, vice chm 1963-67, md 1967-81, chm 1981-86, chm various subsidiary cos; md Bristol-Siddeley Engines 1959-63; dir: ICI, Lloyds Bank 1966-85, Lloyds Bank UK Mgmnt 1979-84, Phoenix Assur 1969-86, Rolls-Royce 1983-88; memb: Air Registration Bd 1963-73, Electricity Supply Res Cncl 1963-72, Advsy Cncl on Technol 1964-67, Defence Industs Cncl 1969-77, Industl Devpt Advsy Bd 1973-75; dep chm Engrg Industs Cncl 1975-; chm bd of tstees Sci Museum 1984-86; pro-chllr Warwick

Univ 1964-70, chllr Loughborough Univ of Technol 1980-89; hon fell Clare Coll Cambridge 1966; foreign assoc US Nat Acad of Engrg 1976-, hon memb American Soc of Mech Engrs 1981-, Hon Fell American Inst Aero Astronautics; Von Baumhauer Medallist of Royal Netherlands Aero Club 1959; Hambro Award for Businessman of the Year 1975; Gold Medal: Royal Aeronautical Soc 1962, Br Inst of Mgmnt 1982; Albert Medal Royal Soc of Art 1983; Freeman City of London 1988; FRS, FEng, Hon FAIAA, Hon FIMechE, Hon ACGI, Hon FIEE, Hon FRAeS kt 1954; *Recreations* sailing; *Style*— Sir Arnold Hall; Wakehams, Dorney, nr Windsor, Berks SL4 6QD (☎ 0753 64916); c/o Hawker Siddeley Group plc, 18 St James's Sq, London SW1 (☎ 01 930 6177)

HALL, Lt-Col Austin Patrick; TD (1970); s of Austin Percy Stuart Hall (d 1984), of Harrogate, Yorks, and Lily, *née* Melloy (d 1981); *b* 13 Mar 1932; *Educ* King James GS Knaresborough, Bradford Coll of Advanced Technol (DipEng); *m* 1957, Dorothy Hall, da of George Alfred Whitfield (d 1961), of Harrogate; 1 s (Richard), 2 da (Sarah, Fiona); *Career* Lt Col Engr and Tport Staff Corps RE (TA), Cmdt-Gen Legion of Frontiersmen of the Cwlth; chartered civil engr and builder, chief exec Bovis Civil Engrg 1974-81; dir: Bovis Ltd 1977-81, Soil & Rock Engrg Ltd; gp md Turriff Corpn plc 1981-84; non exec dir: ARC Properties Ltd; chm: The Bath & Portland Gp plc, ARC Building Ltd, ARC Homes Ltd, Dudley Coles Ltd, Dudley Coles (SW) Ltd, Bath & Portland Stone Ltd, Wansdyke Security Ltd; Freeman City of London, Liveryman Worshipful Co of Arbitrators; CEng, FICE, FCIOB, FCIArb, FFB, FIQA; *Recreations* golf, sailing, philately; *Clubs* IOD, Bath & County; *Style*— Lt-Col Austin Hall, TD; 12 Trossachs Drive, Bathampton, Bath, Avon BA2 6RP (☎ 0225 65957); ARC Building Ltd, Piccadilly House, Piccadilly, London Rd, Bath, Avon BA1 6PL (☎ 0225 445 891)

HALL, Sir Basil Brodribb; KCB (1976), MC (1944), TD; s of Alfred Brodribb Hall; *b* 2 Jan 1918; *Educ* Merchant Taylors', London Univ (LLB); *m* 1955, Jean Stafford, da of Edgar Frederick Gowland; 2 s, 1 da; *Career* Maj 27 Lancers and (post-war) Inns of Court Regt (TA), 12 Lancers France 1940, 27 Lancers UK 1940-44, Italy 1944-45; slr 1942, entered Treasy Slrs Dept 1946, HM procurator-gen & treasury slr 1975-80; chm Civil Serv Appeal Bd 1981-84 (former dep chm); legal advsr Broadcasting Complaints Cmmn 1981-, memb cncl Nat Army Museum 1981-, chm gen ctee Athenaeum 1983-86, memb Euro Cmmn of Human Rights 1985-; *Recreations* military history; *Clubs* Athenaeum; *Style*— Sir Basil Hall, KCB, MC, TD; Woodlands, 16 Danes Way, Oxshott, Surrey KT22 OLX (☎ 0372 842 032)

HALL, Brian Allan; s of Harold Hall, of Manchester, and Barbara Violet, *née* Jeffkins; *b* 15 August 1947; *Educ* Ashton-under-Lyne GS, Kings Coll London Univ (LLB); *m* 14 April 1973, Judith, da of Ronald Roberts, of Exeter; 1 s (Timothy b 29 Jan 1978), 1 da (Jenny b 11 May 1975); *Career* slr 1972; ptnr Leeds Smith 1976-; dep under sheriff Beds 1979-, Notary Public 1981-; sec Biggleswade Chamber of Trade; memb: Law Soc, Provincial Notaries Soc, Shrievalty Assoc, Under-Sheriffs Assoc; *Recreations* music, reading; *Clubs* John O'Gaunt GC; *Style*— Brian Hall, Esq; Lodge Cottage, Church La, Hemingford Grey, Huntingdon, Cambs (☎ 0480 68631); Leeds Smith Solicitors, 20 Hitchin St, Biggleswade, Beds (☎ 0767 315 040, fax 0767 316 573)

HALL, Dame Catherine Mary; DBE (1981, CBE 1967); da of Robert Hall, OBE (d 1955), and Florence Irene, *née* Turner (d 1975); *b* 19 Dec 1922; *Educ* Hunmanby Hall Sch for Girls, Filey; *Career* nursing; Gen Infirmary Leeds 1941-53, asst matron Middx Hosp 1954-56, gen sec Royal Coll of Nursing 1957-82; memb Gen Med Cncl 1979-; chm UK Centl Cncl for Nursing Midwifery and Health Visiting 1980-1985; pt/t memb: Cmmn on Industl Relations 1971-74, Br Regnl Bd (London and SE) 1975-77; Hon DLitt City Univ 1975; FRCN 1976; life vice pres Royal Coll of Nursing 1982; OStJ 1977; *Recreations* reading, gardening; *Style*— Dame Catherine Hall, DBE; Barnsfield, Barnsfield Lane, Buckfastleigh, Devon TQ11 0NP (☎ 0364 42504)

HALL, (Cecil) Charles; CB (1968); s of Frederick Harrington Hall, of Croydon Surrey, and Alice Hilditch; *b* 10 May 1907; *Educ* Beckenham GS, London U (PhD, MSc); *m* 1950, Margaret Rose, da of James George Nicoll, of Sanderstead, Surrey; *Career* res sci Civil Serv; dir Warren Spring Laboratory DTI 1964-68; *Recreations* gardening, plant breeding; *Clubs* Civil Service, Stevenage Rotary; *Style*— Dr Charles Hall, CB; Tanglewood, 17 Sollershott West, Letchworth, Herts SG6 3PU (☎ Letchworth 684339)

HALL, Christopher John; TD (1980); s of Maj Gordon Hamer Hall, of Watford, Herts, and Esme, *née* Gaunt; *b* 13 Oct 1947; *Educ* Watford GS, Corpus Christi Coll Cambridge (MA); *m* 31 Aug 1974, Susan Kathleen, *née* Renolds, da of Capt Sidney George Reynolds, of Watford, Herts; *Career* Cambridge Univ OTC 1966-69 (cmmnd 1968), 2 Lt (later Maj) 217 (London) FD Sqdn RE (V) 73 Engr Regt (V) 1969-80, Maj 2 i/c III Engr Regt (V) 1981-83 and 1986-88 (Trg Maj 1984-86); CA; chief accountant SE Labs (EMI) Ltd 1976-80, fin dir and co sec Metal and Pipeline Endurance Ltd (Amec plc Gp), fin dir Biggs Wall & Co Ltd 1987; gp fin dir and co sec Penspen Ltd 1988-; hon tres: Watford Operatic Soc 1976-86, St Neots and Dist Operatic Soc 1987-; FCA 1972; *Recreations* cruising on inland waterways; *Style*— Christopher Hall, Esq; 124 Station Rd, Tempsford, Sandy, Beds SG19 2AY (☎ 0767 40 952); 20 Grosvenor Place, London SW1X 7HP (☎ 01 235 4300, fax 01 235 5695, telex 27 515 Penspen G)

HALL, Christopher Myles; s of Gilbert Hall, of Gt Cutts Farmhouse, East Hyde, Beds, and Muriel *née* Filsell; *b* 21 July 1932; *Educ* Berkhamsted, New Coll Oxford (BA); *m* 24 March 1957 (m dis 1980), Jennifer Bevan, da of late Harold Keech, of Woodbury, Devon; 1 s (Gilbert), 1 da (Jessica); *Career* Nat Serv RA 1951-52; reporter one feature-writer Daily Express, sub-ed and ldr-writer Daily Mirror, feature and ldr-writer Daily Herald and Sun; special asst (info) to: Min of Overseas Devpt, Miny of Tport; chief info offr Miny of Tport, ed The Countryman 1981-; chm Ramblers Assoc 1987- (sec 1969-74, exec ctee 1982-), dir Cncl for Protection of England 1974-80, South Eastern Rambler 1974-82; chm Save The Broad St Line Ctee 1963-65, hon sec Chiltern Soc 1965-68, memb Common Land Forum 1984-86; NUJ 1959-; *Recreations* country walking; *Style*— Christopher Hall, Esq; Greyhounds, Sheep St, Burford OX8 4LS (☎ 099 382 2258); The Countryman, Sheep St, Burford OX8 4LH (☎ 099 382 2258)

HALL, Christopher Sandford; TD (1970), DL (East Sussex, 1986); s of Brig Geoffrey Sandford Hall, TD, DL (d 1975), and Christine, *née* March; *b* 9 Mar 1936; *Educ* Rugby, Trinity Coll Cambridge (MA); *m* 8 July 1967, Susanna Marion, da of Richard Harry Bott, of Benington Lordship, Stevenage, Herts; 3 s (David b 1968, Colin b 1970, Philip b 1973); *Career* Nat Serv 5 Royal Enniskillen Dragoon Gds 1954-56 (TAVR 1956- 70); admitted slr 1963, ptnr Cripps Harries Hall Tunbridge Wells 1964-; dir Mid Sussex and W Kent Water Cos; chm: A Burslem & Son Ltd, Br Equestrian Promotions Ltd, S Eng Agric Soc 1984-; tstee and govr Temple Grove Sch, memb cncl Br Horse Soc, steward Nat Hunt Ascot Folkestone and Plumpton; memb Law Soc; *Recreations* hunting, racing, farming; *Clubs* Cavalry & Guards; *Style*— Christopher Hall, Esq, TD, DL; Great Danegate, Eridge Green, Tunbridge Wells, Kent (☎ 089 275 385); 84 Calverley Rd, Tunbridge Wells (☎ 0892 515 121)

HALL, Colin; s of Arthur Graham Henry Hall, of Enfield, Middlesex, and Winifred Martha, *née* Gray (d 1979); *b* 23 April 1945; *Educ* Stationer's Company's Sch, Univ of Bristol (LLB); *m* 29 Sept 1973, Philippa Margaret, da of Hac Collinson, of Sway, Hants; 4 s (Nicholas Justin b 1976, Oliver Rupert b 1978, Giles Edward b 1981, Rupert Charles (twin) b 1981); *Career* HM Dip Serv 1966-68, Slaughter and May slrs 1969-(ptnr 1978); *Recreations* sailing, gardening, conservation; *Style*— Colin Hall, Esq; The Oast House, West End, Frensham, Surrey (☎ 025 125 3422); 35 Basinghall St, London EC2 (☎ 01 600 1200, fax 01 600 0289, telex 883986)

HALL, David; CBE (1983), QPM (1977); s of Arthur Thomas Hall (d 1974), of London, and Dorothy May, *née* Bryant (d 1965); *b* 29 Dec 1930; *Educ* Richmond and East Sheen GS for Boys; *m* 14 June 1952, Molly Patricia, da of Roland Knight (d 1981), of London; 2 s (Philip David b 20 Oct 1956, Nicholas Peter b 29 Nov 1958); *Career* joined Met Police 1950, supt 1965; staff offr to Col Eric St Johnstone, (chief inspr of Constabulary), asst chief constable Staffordshire 1970, (later dep chief constable), chief constable Humberside 1976-; memb St John Cncl; Freeman City of London 1987; CBIM 1987; *Recreations* music (playing the piano), gardening; *Clubs* Sloane; *Style*— David Hall, Esq, CBE, QPM; Humberside Police Headquarters, Queens Gardens, Kingston upon Hull HU1 3DJ (☎ 0482 26111, fax 0482 226 877)

HALL, David Bernard; s and h of Sir John Bernard Hall, 3 Bt, by his w Delia Mary (da of Lt-Col James Innes, DSO, by his 3 w, Evelyn (*see* Lady Joly de Lotbinière), gda of Hon William Dawnay, JP, DL, 6 s of 7 Viscount Downe); *b* 12 May 1961; *Educ* Eton, Univ of York; *Career* clerk Bank of America (Hamburg) 1980, sales United Biscuits 1985-; *Recreations* water skiing, marathon running, tennis; *Clubs* Lansdowne; *Style*— David Hall, Esq; Rose Cottage, Holly Lane, Haughton, Stafford

HALL, David Christopher; s of Sir Frederick Hall, 2 Bt (d 1949), and bro and h of Sir (Frederick) John (Frank) Hall, 3 Bt; *b* 30 Dec 1937; *m* 24 Nov 1962, Irene, da of William Duncan, of Kincorth, Aberdeen; 1 s, 1 da; *Career* joiner/cabinet maker 1962-79, woodwork teacher 1980-, antique restorer 1982-; *Style*— David Hall, Esq; Inverene, 368 Queens Rd, Aberdeen (☎ 0224 319766)

HALL, David John Lees; s of Herbert Vaughan Lees Hall (d 1974), of Tilneys, Hall Road, Rochford, Essex, and Nancy Dewar Hall (d 1989); *b* 19 Feb 1946; *Educ* Felsted, Univ of Nottingham (BSc); *m* 18 April 1972, Yvonne Pepita, da of Douglas Acock, of Westcliffe-on- Sea, Essex; 1 s (Christopher b 27 June 1974), 1 da (Katharine b 20 April 1982); *Career* chm Monometer Mfrg Co Ltd 1974- (dir 1967-); AMIIBF 1968 ; *Recreations* yachting, skiing, squash; *Clubs* Royal Ocean Racing, Royal Corinthian Yacht, Royal Burnham Yacht, Courtland Park Country, Ski of Great Britain; *Style*— David Hall, Esq; 1 Thorpe Bay Gdns, Thorpe Bay, Essex SS1 3NS (☎ 0702 582183); Monometer Manufacturing Co Ltd, Monometer House, Rectory Grove, Leigh-on-Sea, Essex (☎ 0702 72201, fax 0702 715112, telex 99381); car ☎ 0836 244979

HALL, David Nicholas; s of William Noel Hall (d 1981), of London, and Louisa Augusta, *née* Palmer; *b* 19 Nov 1933; *Educ* London Choir Sch, Carlisle & Gregson (Jimmy's), Sandhurst; *m* 28 Dec 1963, Harriet Mary Arden, da of William Lloyd McElwee, MC, TD (d 1978); 3 da (Susannah b 25 Feb 1965, Phillie b 13 April 1967, Christina b 17 Oct 1969); *Career* active serv Korean War 1953; cmmnd RE serv: Cyprus, Congo (Zaire), Ghana; instr RMA Sandhurst, Staff Coll, staff appt with engr-in-chief, Sqdn Cdr Scotland and Gibraltar, Kirkcudbright, CO RE Depot 1974-77, servs rep stores & clothing R & D Estab 1977-79, dep cdr manning & record off RE 1979-81, ret Lt-Col 1981; dir Fndn for Sci & Technol 1981-, liaison offr Learned Socs 1981-; hon tres Palestine Exploration Fund 1983-, chm expeditions ctee RGS 1985- (vice-pres 1984-87, hon foreign sec 1973-83), pres (first) The Desert Dining Club 1980, chm Young Explorers' Tst Screening 1983-; organiser and cdr Br Expedition to Air Mountains 1970; various camel journeys and scientific expeditions to arid regions; FICS, FRGS, FRSA; *Books* Expeditions (1977); *Recreations* exploration, fishing, music; *Clubs* Athenaeum; *Style*— David Hall, Esq; 3 Spencer Rd, London SW18 2SP (☎ 01 228 8476); 12 Upper Belgrave St, London SW1X 8BB

HALL, Denis Whitfield; CMG (1962); s of Henry Ruston Hall (d 1945), of Haslemere, Surrey, and Marie Gabrielle Hall (d 1960); *b* 26 August 1960; *Educ* Dover Coll, Wadham Coll Oxford (BA); *m* 12 Sept 1940, Barbara, da of Boys Carman; 2 s (Richard Whitfield b 1941, Nigel Rushton b 1945); *Career* Colonial Admin Serv: dist offr cadet 1935, dist offr 1937, dist cmmr 1946, personal asst to chief native cmmr 1948-51, sr dist cmmr 1955, provincial cmmr 1959; dep chm Sussex Church Campaign 1965-73; *Recreations* walking, reading, sailing; *Clubs* Oxford Univ YC; *Style*— Denis Hall, Esq, CMG; Martins Priory Close, Boxgrove, Chichester, Sussex PO18 OEA (☎ 0243 773 351)

HALL, Dr Derek Gordon; s of Gordon Ivor Hall (d 1986), of Dinas Powys, S Glam, and May Magaretta, *née* Horsey; *b* 17 April 1944; *Educ* Penarth Co Sch, UCL (BSc, PhD); *m* 1, 1967 (m dis 1971), Pauline Margaret Vivienne, *née* Coombe; 1 da (Samantha Kate b 1969); m 2, 6 Oct 1979, Susan Olga, da of Eric Eaton, of Cheltenham, Glos; 2 s (Guy Sebastian b 1968, Daniel Gordon b 1973); *Career* mgmnt consultancy div Arthur Andersen & Co 1970-76; J P Morgan 1976- vice pres 1978-87, sr vice pres 1987-; *Style*— Dr Derek Hall; J P Morgan Securities Ltd, PO Box 124, 30 Throgmorton St, London EC2N 2NT (☎ 01 600 7545, telex 895 4804/5)

HALL, Air Marshal Sir Donald Percy; KCB (1984, CB 1981), CBE (1975), AFC (1963); s of William Reckerby Hall, and Elsie Hall; *b* 11 Nov 1930; *Educ* Hull GS, RAF Coll; *m* 1953, Joyce, *née* Warburton; 2 da; *Career* AOC 38 Gp RAF 1980-83, dep CDS 1983-86, ret 1986; chm Marconi Def Systems 1987; FRAeS; *Style*— Sir Donald Hall; c/o Lloyds Bank, 6 Pall Mall, London SW1Y 5NH

HALL, Lady Dorothy Maud; da of late William Laurence Jones; *m* 22 June 1957, Sir Neville Reynolds Hall, 13 Bt (d 1978); *Style*— Dorothy, Lady Hall; Ash Cottage, Ash, Dartmouth, S Devon

HALL, Sir Douglas Basil; 14 Bt (NS 1687), of Dunglass, Haddingtonshire; KCMG (1959, CMG 1958), JP (Devon 1964); s of Capt Lionel Erskine Hall (d 1948); suc bro Sir Neville Hall, 13 Bt 1978; *b* 1 Feb 1909; *Educ* Radley, Keble Coll Oxford; *m* 25 April 1933, Rachel Marion, da of late Maj Ernest Gartside-Tippinge; 1 s, 2 da (and 1 s decd); *Heir* s, John Douglas Hoste Hall; *Career* entered HMOCS as a cadet N

Rhodesia 1930, dist offr 1932-50, sr dist offr 1950-53, provincial cmmr 1953, admin sec 1955-56, sec for Native Affrs 1956, govr and C-in-C of Somaliland Protectorate 1959-60; memb Police Authy for Devon and Cornwall 1971-79; *Style*— Sir Douglas Hall, Bt, KCMG; Barnford, Ringmore, Nr Kingsbridge, Devon (☎ 0548 81810401)

HALL, Lady; Elinor Claire; da of Paul Hirschorn, of New York, and previously w of Eric H Marks; *m* 13 Sept 1946, as his 2 w, Sir Noel Frederick Hall (d 1983); former princ: Henley Mgmnt Coll 1946-60, Brasenose Coll Oxford 1960-73; 1 s (Jonathan b 1952), 1 da (Louise b 1950); *Clubs* Huntercombe Golf; *Style*— Lady Hall; 1 Northfield End, Henley-on-Thames, Oxon (☎ 0491 573 265)

HALL, Rear Adm Geoffrey Penrose Dickinson; CB (1973), DSC (1943), DL (1982); s of Maj Arthur Kenrick Dickinson Hall (d 1945), of Legbourne Abbey, Louth, Lincs, and Phyllis Mary, *née* Penrose (d 1969); maternal gf Brig-Gen Cooper Penrose, CB, CMG, cmd RE Southern Cmd; maternal ggf Thomas Greene DD was sec of the Gen Synod of the Church of Ireland for 40 years; ggf Thomas Dickinson Hall was High Sheriff of Nottingham & Leicester, gf Frederick Dickinson Hall was rector of Manby and rural dean of Louthesk; *b* 19 July 1916; *Educ* Haileybury; *m* 1945, Mary Ogilvie, da of Henry George Carlisle (d 1954), of Ardlair, Heswall, Ches; 2 s (Nicholas, Adrian), 1 da (Virginia); *Career* Naval Offr 1934-75, cmd six of HM ships 1945-67, hydrographer of the Navy 1971-75, served in Atlantic, Iceland, W Africa, India, Burma & Far East 1939-45, hydrographic surveying in N and S Atlantic, Antarctic, Indian Ocean and NZ 1938-67, combined ops 1943-45, various appts within Admty and MOD 1954-75; landowner (6 acres); *Recreations* walking, wooding, writing, tennis, golf, dogs; *Clubs* Naval and Military, Royal Navy, Lincolnshire, Louth; *Style*— Rear Adm Geoffrey Hall, CB, DSC, DL; Manby Ho, Manby, Louth, Lincs LN11 8UF (☎ 0507 82777)

HALL, Prof Geoffrey Ronald; CBE (1985); s of Thomas Harold Hall, JP (d 1974), of Douglas, IOM; *b* 18 May 1928; *Educ* Douglas HS, Univ of Manchester (BSc); *m* 1950, Elizabeth, da of Thomas Day Sheldon (d 1951), of Manchester; 3 children; *Career* Colombo plan expert India 1956-58; prof (formerly reader) of nuclear technol Imperial Coll 1958-70, dir and prof Brighton Poly 1970-; pres Br Nuclear Energy Soc 1970; memb: cncl Engrg Cncl 1982-86; Sci and Engrg Res Cncl 1982-86, Nat Cncl for Vocational Qualification 1987-; *Recreations* travel, golf, caravanning; *Style*— Prof Geoffrey Hall, CBE; 1 Great Wilkins, Falmer, Brighton BN1 9QW; Brighton Polytechnic, Moulsecoomb, Brighton BN2 4AT (☎ 0273 693 655)

HALL, Hon Georgina Anne; yr da of 2 Viscount Hall; *b* 8 Jan 1953; *Educ* Godstowe Sch, Wycombe Abbey, Univ of Wales; *Style*— Hon Georgina Hall; c/o Rt Hon Viscount Hall, Belgrave Cottage, Upper Belgrave St, London SW1

HALL, Harold Percival; CMG (1963), MBE (1947); s of late Maj George Charles Hall; *b* 9 Sept 1913; *Educ* Portsmouth GS, Sandhurst; *m* 1939, Margery, da of Joseph Dickson; 3 s; *Career* Maj NWFP, Indian Army 1933-37 & 1940-43, Indian Political Serv 1937-40; Colonial Off 1947-66, asst under-sec 1966-73; *Recreations* gardening; *Style*— Harold Hall Esq, CMG, MBE; 77 Moss Lane, Pinner, Middx (☎ 01 866 1162)

HALL, Dr Ion Simson; s of Rev Dr John Hall, OBE (d 1944), of Edinburgh, and Isabella, *née* Stuart (d 1927); *b* 30 June 1896; *Educ* George Watson's Coll, Univ of Edinburgh (MB, ChB); *m* 14 April 1937, Kathleen Scott, da of Prof Robert Scott Troup, CMG, CIE (d 1939), of Oxford; *Career* RA 1915-18, Capt served France; surgn Royal Infirmary Edinburgh 1936-61, vice chm and chm S E Scotland Regnl Hosp Bd; FRCPEd, FRCSEd; *Books* Diseases of Nose, Throat and Ear (13 edn 1987); *Recreations* gardening; *Style*— Dr Ion S Hall

HALL, Joan Valerie; da of Robert Hall (d 1979), and Winifred Emily, *née* Umbers; *b* 31 August 1935; *Educ* Queen Margaret's Sch Escrick Park, Ashridge House of Citizenship; *Career* MP (C) Keighley 1970-74 (Feb), pps to MAFF Food 1972-74, fought Barnsley 1964 & 1966; memb cncl: Univ Coll Buckingham 1977-83, Central Tport User's Consultative Ctee 1981-86; CTUCC; *Style*— Miss Joan Hall; Mayfields, Darton Rd, Cawthorne, Barnsley, S Yorks S75 4HY (☎ 0226 790230)

HALL, John Anthony Sanderson; DFC (1944, bar 1945), QC (1967); s of Rt Hon William Glenvil Hall, MP (d 1962), of Heath Mansions, Hampstead, and Rachel Ida, *née* Sanderson (d 1950); *b* 25 Dec 1921; *Educ* Leighton Park Sch, Trinity Hall Cambridge (MA); *m* 1, 27 Oct 1945 (m dis 1974), Nora Ella, da of Arthur Ulrich Crowe (d 1941); 1 s (Jonathon Mark Glenvil b 1950) 2 da (Sally Anne b 1946, Pamela Mary b 1952); m 2, 10 July 1976, Elizabeth Mary, da of Richard Wells; *Career* called to the Bar Inner Temple 1948, bencher Inner Temple 1975, dep chm Hants QS 1967-72, rec Swindon 1971, rec Crown Ct 1972-78; memb: gen cncl of the Bar 1964- 68 and 1970-74, senate Inns of Ct 1966-68 and 1970-74; chm: UK delegn consultative ctee of European Bar & Law Socs 1978-79, govrs St Catherine's Sch Guildford 1972-87; memb Worshipful Co of Arbitrators; FCIArb 1982; *Recreations* fly fishing, book collecting; *Clubs* RAF, Garrick; *Style*— John Hall, Esq, DFC, QC; Swallows, Blewbury, OXON (☎ 0235 850511)

HALL, Sir John Bernard; 3 Bt (UK 1919), of Burton Park, Sussex; s of Lt-Col Sir Douglas Hall, 2 Bt, DSO (d 1962), and his 2 w, Nancie (who m 2, 1962, Col Peter J Bradford, DSO, MC, TD), o da of Col John Edward Mellor, CB, JP, DL; *b* 20 Mar 1932; *Educ* Eton, Trinity Coll Oxford (MA); *m* 19 Oct 1957, Delia Mary, da of Lt-Col James Innes, DSO (d 1949), and his 3 w, Evelyn (*see* Lady Joly de Lotbinière); 1 s, 2 da; *Heir* s, David Bernard Hall b 12 May 1961; *Career* Lt Royal Fus RARO; joined J Henry Schröder & Co (later J Henry Schröder Wagg & Co Ltd) 1955 (dir 1967-73), dir Bank of America Int 1974-82, vice-pres Bank of America NT & SA, 1982-, md European Brazilian Bank 1983- (dir 1976-); memb: exec ctee Anglo-Colombian Soc (former chm), exec cncl Brazilian C of C in Great Britain; former chm Assoc of British Consortium Banks; Liveryman Worshipful Co of Clothworkers (Warden 1987-); FCIB 1976, FRGS 1988; *Recreations* travel, fishing; *Clubs* Boodle's, Lansdowne, Overseas Bankers; *Style*— Sir John Hall, Bt; Penrose House, Patmore Heath, Albury, Ware, Herts SG11 2LT (☎ 027 974 255); Inver House, Lochinver, Lairg, Sutherland

HALL, John Douglas Hoste; s and h of Sir Douglas Hall, 14 Bt, KCMG, of Barnford, Ringmore, Kingsbridge, Devon; *b* 7 Jan 1945; *Educ* Dover Coll, Gonville and Caius Coll Cambridge, Univ of Southampton ; *m* 1972, Angela Margaret, da of George Keys, of 2 Barnsfield Lane, Buckfastleigh, S Devon; 2 s; *Career* poet; sr lectr Dartington Coll of Art; *Books of Poetry* Between the Cities, Days, Malo-Lactic Ferment, Couch Grass, Repressed Intimations, Meaning Insomnia; *Style*— John Hall, Esq; Brook Mill, Buckfastleigh, S Devon TQ11 0HL (☎ 0364 42985)

HALL, Sir (Frederick) John Frank; 3 Bt (UK 1923), of Grafham, co Surrey; s of Sir Frederick Henry Hall, 2 Bt (d 1949), and Olwen Irene, *née* Collis, who subsequently m Arthur Borland Porteous; *b* 14 August 1931; *Educ* Bryanston; *m* 1, 3 April 1956 (m dis 1960), Felicity Anne, da of late Edward Rivers-Fletcher, of Norwich; m 2, 3 June 1961 (m dis 1967), Patricia Ann, da of Douglas Atkinson (d 1973), of Carlisle; 2 da; re-m 9 Nov 1967, his 1 w, Felicity Anne; 2 da; *Heir* bro, David Christopher Hall; *Style*— Sir John Hall, Bt; Carradale, 29 Embercourt Rd, Thames Ditton, Surrey KT7 0LH (☎ 01 398 2801)

HALL, John Michael; s of Ernest Smith Hall (d 1964), of Solihull, West Midlands, and Joyce Kathleen, *née* Butler; *b* 30 Jan 1936; *Educ* Bloxham Sch; *m* 20 Oct 1962, Angela Phyllis, da of Ralph Dixon Coates, MBE, of Milford-on-Sea, Hampshire; 4 da (Katherine b and d 23 Jan 1964, Sophie b 6 Feb 1965, Lucy b 11 Nov 1967, Charlotte b 14 Nov 1969); *Career* Nat Serv 2 Lt RAPC 1959-61; CA, sr ptnr Halls CAs 1964-, non-exec dir Marley plc; chm mgmnt ctee Warren Pearl House (Cancer Home under Marie Curie Fndn), govr St Martins Sch Solihull; FCA 1959; *Recreations* vintage and classic cars, messing with boats; *Style*— John Hall, Esq; New Oxford House, 16 Waterloo Street, Birmingham (☎ 021 643 3451, fax 021 643 3859, car tel 0836 507716)

HALL, His Hon Judge Julian; s of Alexander Stephenson Hall, of Bucks, and Edith Mary Partington Hall, *née* Smith (d 1975); *b* 13 Jan 1939; *Educ* Eton, Christ Church Oxford (MA), Trinty Coll Dublin (LLB); *m* 1, 1968 (m dis 1988), Margaret Rosalind, *née* Perry; 1 s (Benjamin b 1971), 1 da (Rebecca b 1969); m 2, 11 March 1989, Ingrid C, *née* Lunt; *Career* industl res chemist 1961-63; called to the Bar Grays Inn 1966, practicing Northern Circuit 1966-86, rec Crown Ct 1982-86, prosecuting counsel Inland Revenue Northern Circuit 1985-86, Circuit Judge 1986-;; *Recreations* making music; *Clubs* Buxton Musical Soc, Music Camp; *Style*— His Honour Judge Julian Hall; c/o The Courts of Justice, Crown Square, Manchester M3 3FL (☎ 061 832 -8393)

HALL, Keith Rawlings; TD; s of Alfred Brodribb Hall (d 1974), of Surrey, and Elsie Hilda, *née* Banks; *b* 10 June 1928; *Educ* Clayesmore, King's Coll Cambrige (MA); *m* 1958, Susan (Shoonan) Rosemary Lee, da of Sir Algernon Arthur Guinness, 3 Bt, and former w of Samuel Charles Gillchrest (d 1954); 2 s (Simon b 1959, Mark b 1967), 2 da (Susan b 1960, Jennifer b 1963); *Career* Maj 2 i/c Inns of Court and City Yeo 1962; chief exec and dir Legal & General PMC Ltd 1986, chm Rich St Ltd; dir Warrington Festival Tst, vice chm Donnington Tst, exec ctee memb St Loyes Coll; *Recreations* hunting, music; *Clubs* Cavalry and Guards'; *Style*— Keith Hall, Esq, TD; Higher Hewood, South Chard, Somerset (☎ 0460 20235)

HALL, Prof Laurance David; s of Daniel William Hall, of Stevenage, and Elsie, *née* Beard; *b* 18 Mar 1938; *Educ* Leyton Co HS, Univ of Bristol (BSc, PhD); *m* 1 Aug 1962, (Winifred) Margaret, da of Henry Arthur Golding; 2 s (Dominic Courtney St John b 15 Dec 1971, Brecken Guy D'Arcy (twin) b 15 Dec 1971), 2 da (Gwendolen Judith Virginia b 21 May 1963, Juliet Katharine Olivia b 1 July 1964); *Career* post doctoral fell Univ of Ottawa 1962-63, prof of chemistry Univ of Br Columbia Vancouver Canada 1963-84, first holder Herchel Smith prof of medicinal chem Cambridge Univ Clinical Sch; FCIC 1974, FRS (Canada) 1982, CChem, FRSC 1985; *Recreations* wine-making, skiing, scientific research; *Clubs* Emmanuel Coll Cambridge; *Style*— Prof Laurance Hall; 22 Long Rd, Cambridge CB2 2QS (☎ 0223 336 805); Laboratory for Medicinal Chemistry, University Forvie Site, Cambridge CB2 2PZ (☎ 0223 336 805)

HALL, Leonard Graham; s of William Edwin Hall (d 1951), of Grimsby, and Nellie Alice, *née* Smith (d 1919); *b* 25 Feb 1917; *Educ* Humberstone Fndn Sch Cleethorpes, St John's Coll Cambridge (MA); *m* 1946, Betty, da of William James Minns (d 1939), of Grimsby; 2 s (William, John), 1 da (Rosalind); *Career* actuary; Clerical Med and Gen Life Assur Soc 1938- (dep gen mangr 1961-75, gen mangr 1975-82, non exec dir 1982-); dir: Lands Improvement Gp, Sumit plc; chm: Soc of Investmt Analysts 1969-71, Life Offices Assoc 1979-81; vice pres Inst of Actuaries 1970-73; Master Worshipful Co of Actuaries 1984-85; *Recreations* music, travel, golf; *Clubs* United Oxford and Cambridge, RAF, Northwood Golf; *Style*— Leonard Hall, Esq; Temple Bar, Green Lane, Northwood, Middlesex HA6 2UY; (☎ 09274 25942)

HALL, Viscountess Marie-Colette; da of Col Henri Bach; *m* 1974, as his 3 w, 2 Viscount Hall (d 1984); *Style*— The Rt Hon Viscountess Hall; Solvain, 41210 St Viatre, Loir et Cher, France; 18 Egerton Gdns, London SW3

HALL, Maj-Gen (Edward) Michael; CB (1970), MBE (1944), DL (Cornwall 1972); s of Brig Edward George Hall, CB, CIE (d 1968), by his w Elinor Brodrick, elder da of Col William Spiller Birdwood, IA, of Colmer, Modbury, S Devon; *b* 16 July 1915; *Educ* Sherborne, RMA Woolwich, Peterhouse Cambridge; *m* 4 Dec 1948, Nina Diana, da of Maj Valentine Goold McArthur, MC (d 1966); 3 s (Timothy b 1949, Jeremy b 1952, Robin b 1958); *Career* cmmnd RE 1935, COS Northern Command 1965-66, mil dep to Head of Def Sales 1966-70; Cdr and Cmmr St John's Ambulance Bde Cornwall 1971-81, KStJ 1981; High Sheriff Cornwall 1985-86; *Style*— Maj-Gen Michael Hall, CB, MBE, DL; Treworgey Manor, Liskeard, Cornwall (☎ 0579 42568)

HALL, Michael Robert; s of Robert Hall (d 1980), of Cheshire, and Hannah Hall; *b* 9 May 1942; *Educ* William Hulmes Manchester; *m* 1969, Irene Mavis, da of Percy Cuthbert Archer, of Cheshire; 1 s (Robert Anthony b 1973), 1 da (Kathryn Elizabeth b 1971); *Career* former gp fin dir Fine Art Devpts plc; dir: Selective Fin Servs Ltd 1987, Derby HS Ltd 1987, Heritage Brewery Museum 1987, Heritage Brewery Ltd 1985-87, W Hawley & Son Ltd 1987, Selective Tech Innovations Ltd 1988, Park Stationery Ltd 1988, Construction Cosmetics Ltd 1988; FCT, FCA, FCMA; *Recreations* squash, walking, sailing; *Clubs* Duffield Derbyshire; Stakis Regency International; *Style*— Michael Hall, Esq; Selective Financial Services Ltd, 102 Friar Gate, Derby

HALL, Peter Dudley; OBE (1980); s of Leonard Hall, of Sidmouth; *b* 13 Nov 1919; *Educ* Tiffins Sch, London Univ; *m* 1945, Eldwyth Gladys, da of John Marsden, of Malvern; 1 s, 1 da; *Career* chartered engr; former dir ICL, pres Br Computer Soc 1981-82, ret; *Recreations* tennis, golf, music; *Clubs* Athenaeum; *Style*— Peter Hall, Esq, OBE; Brendon Cottage, Henshaw Lane, Siddington, nr Macclesfield, Cheshire (☎ 026 04 363)

HALL, Prof Peter Geoffrey; s of Arthur Vickers Hall (d 1973), of Blackpool, and Bertha, *née* Keefe (d 1979); *b* 19 Mar 1932; *Educ* Blackpool GS, St Catharine's Coll Cambridge (MA, PhD); *m* 1, 7 Sept 1962 (m dis 1967), Carla Maria, da of Frank Wartenberg (d 1986); m 2, 13 Feb 1967, Magda, da of Antoni Mróz of Warsaw; *Career* asst lectr then lectr Birkbeck Coll Univ of London 1957-65, reader in geography LSE 1966-67, prof of geography Univ of Reading 1968-, visiting prof city and regnl planning Univ of California 1980-; memb various govt bodies inc SE Regnl Econ & Planning Cncl 1960-79; FBA 1983, FRGS; *Books* London 2000 (1963), The Containment of Urban England (1973), Europe 2000 (1977), Great Planning Disasters

(1980), High-Tech America (1986), Western Sunrise (1987), Cities of Tomorrow (1988), London 2001 (1988); *Recreations* walking; *Clubs* Athenaeum, RGS; *Style—* Prof Peter Hall; 5 Bedford Rd, London W4 1JD (☎ 01 994 5950); Dept of Geography, Univ of Reading, PO Box 227, Reading RG6 2AB (☎ 0734 318 736, fax 0734 755 865, telex 847813)

HALL, Sir Peter Reginald Frederick; KBE (1977, CBE 1963); s of Reginald Edward Arthur Hall, and Grace, *née* Pamment; *b* 22 Nov 1930; *Educ* Perse Sch Cambridge, St Catharine's Coll Cambridge (MA); *m* 1, 1956 (m dis 1965), Leslie Caron, the actress; 1 s, 1 da; m 2, 1965 (m dis 1981), Jacqueline Taylor; 1 s, 1 da; m 3, 1982, Maria Ewing, the mezzo-soprano; 1 da (Rebecca b 1982); *Career* dir: Oxford Playhouse 1954-55, Arts Theatre London 1955-57; fndr Int Playwrights' Theatre 1957; md RSC 1960-68 (created the RSC as a permanent ensemble, and opened the RSC's London home at the Aldwych Theatre); dir Nat Theatre of GB 1973-88; artistic dir Glyndebourne Festival Opera 1984-; assoc prof of drama Warwick Univ; memb Arts Cncl of GB 1969-72; hon doctorates: York, Reading, Liverpool, Leicester, Cornell USA; winner Tony Award 1967: for Pinter's Homecoming, 1981 for Shaffer's Amadeus; awarded Order des Arts et des Lettres; Sidney Edwards Award 1982 for Nat Theatre prodn of The Oresteia; has directed over sixty major prodns in London, Stratford-upon-Avon and New York, including 19 Shakespeare plays, and the premieres of plays by Samuel Beckett, Harold Pinter, Tennessee Williams, Edward Albee, Jean Anouiih, Peter Shaffer, John Mortimer, John Whiting, Alan Ayckbourn; has directed opera at Covent Garden, Sadler's Wells, Glyndebourne, the Metropolitan Opera, New York, and Bayreuth, and 8 films; *Productions include* Waiting for Godot 1955, Gigi 1956, Love's Labours Lost 1956, Cat on a Hot Tin Roof 1958, Twelfth Night 1958 & 1960, A Midsummer Night's Dream 1959 & 1963, Becket 1961, The Collection 1962, The Wars of the Roses 1964, The Homecoming 1965 & 1973, The Magic Flute 1966, Macbeth 1967 & 1982, A Delicate Balance 1969, Perfect Friday 1969, La Calisto 1970, Bedroom Farce 1977, Don Giovanni 1977, Cosii Fan Tutte 1978, The Cherry Orchard 1978, Betrayal 1978 & 1980, The Importance of Being Earnest 1982, Yonadab 1985, Carmen 1985 & 1986, Albert Herring 1985, Antony and Cleopatra 1988; *Books* The Wars of the Roses (with John Barton), adaptation of Ibsen's John Gabriel Borkman (with Inga-Stina Ewbank), adaptation of George Orwell's Animal Farm, Peter Hall's Diaries; *Clubs* Garrick, Athenaeum, RAC; *Style—* Sir Peter Hall, KBE; 33 Bramerton St, Chelsea, London SW3 5JS; National Theatre, South Bank, London SE1 9PX (☎ 01 928 2033, telex 297306 NATTRE G)

HALL, Prof Reginald; s of Reginald Peacock Hall (d 1969), of Berwick upon Tweed, and Maggie Watson (d 1980); *b* 1 Oct 1931; *Educ* Univ of Durham (BSc, MB BS, MD); *m* 1, 1956, Joan, *née* Patterson (d 1959); 1 da (Susan b 1958); m 2, 11 June 1960, Molly, da of Clifford Vincent Hill (d 1977), of Frinton-on-Sea; 2 s (John b 1963, Andrew (twin)b 1963), 2 da (Amanda b 1962, Stephanie b 1966); *Career* Harkness fell Cwlth Fund and clinical res fell in med Harvard Univ and Mass Gen Hosp 1960-61, hon lectr in med Univ of Newcastle upon Tyne 1965-67 (Wellcome sr res fell in clinical sci 1964-67), hon conslt physician Royal Victoria Infirmary 1966-79; prof of med: Univ of Newcastle upon Tyne 1970-79, Univ of Wales Coll of Med 1980-; MRCP 1959, FRCP 1970; *Books* Fundamentals of Clinical Endocrinology (1979), Wolfe Atlas of Endocrinology (1979); *Style—* Prof Reginald Hall; 37 Palace Rd, Llandaff, Cardiff CF5 2AG; 22 Grantbridge St, Islington, London N1; 11 Brundholme Gardens, Keswick, Cumbria (☎ 0222 567 689); Department of Medicine, University of Wales College of Medicine, Heath Park, Cardiff CF4 4XN (☎ 0222 755 944 ext 2307, fax 0222 762 208)

HALL, Richard Martin; s of James Livingston Hall (d 1976), of Seaton, Devon and Sybil, *née* Mycroft; *b* 8 July 1944; *Educ* Owen's Sch London, Balliol Coll Oxford (BA); *m* 2 Feb 1974, Caroline Jane, da of Gordon Ngaio Wright; *Career* Reckitt and Colman 1966-68, RHM Foods 1968-71, FGA Ltd 1971-76, Mettoy plc 1976-83; md FCO Ltd 1983-; *Recreations* golf, cricket; *Style—* Richard Hall, Esq; FCO Ltd, Eldon House, 1 Dorset St, London W1 (☎ 01 486 3836 fax 01 486 7092)

HALL, Richard Nicholas Congreve; s of Ernest Nicholas Hall, of Hales Hall, Market Drayton, Salop, by his w Frances Hope, yr da of late Col Francis Lane Congreve, DSO, MC, of Ditcheat, Somerset; *b* 27 April 1937; *Educ* Eton; *Career* chm and md Hall Engrg (Hldgs) Ltd; dir: BRC Steel Ltd, James Jackson & Co Ltd, Press Steel Industs Ltd, Stingray Investmts (Pty) Ltd, Shrewsbury Tool & Die Co Ltd, William Deakin & Co Ltd; *Style—* Richard Hall Esq; c/o Hall Engineering Ltd, 2 Lygon Place, SW1

HALL, Robin Alexander; s of Leslie Alexander Hall (d 1984), and Sheila Mary, *née* Martin; *b* 19 May 1948; *Educ* Highbury Co GS; *m* 25 March 1977, Hazel Ann, da of Ronald William George Maidman; 2 s (James Alexander b 1978, Richard William b 1983), 1 da (Emma Rebecca b 1980); *Career* CA; audit mangr Arthur Young & Co 1969-75, investmt exec Nat Enterprise Bd 1976-79, fin dir Insac Prods Ltd 1980-81, md CIN Venture Mangrs Ltd 1981-; non-exec dir: NVC Hldgs Ltd 1983-, Spectrum Gp plc 1983-, Citylink Gp plc 1983-, Gabicci plc 1984-, Barnes Thomson Mgmnt Ltd 1984-, Sema Gp plc 1985- Coloroll Gp plc 1985-, Quester Capital Mgmnt Ltd 1988-, Reedpack Ltd 1988-; FCA 1972; *Style—* Robin Hall, Esq; CIN Venture Mangrs Ltd, Hobart House, Grosvenor Place, London SW1X 7AD (☎ 01 245 6911)

HALL, Ronald; s of John Hall (d 1960), and Amy (d 1975); *b* 28 July 1934; *Educ* Dronfield GS, Pembroke Coll Cambridge (BA); *m* 1982, Christine; *Career* chief sub editor Topic Magazine 1962, co-fndr of Insight Team Sunday Times 1963 (Insight ed 1964-66, asst ed 1966-68, managing ed features 1969-77), ed Sunday Times Magazine 1978-81, jt dep ed Sunday Times 1981-82, ed Sunday Express Magazine 1982-86, associate ed London Daily News 1986-87; *Books* Scandal 1963, A Study of The Profumo Affair (jtly), The Strange Voyage of Donald Crowhurst (1970, with Nicholas Tomalin); *Recreations* chess, travel, building; *Style—* Ronald Hall, Esq; 13a Pond St, London NW3; (☎ 01-794 8849)

HALL, Simon Andrew Dalton; s of Peter Dalton Hall, CB, of Milton Keynes, Bucks, and Stella Iris, *née* Breen; *b* 6 Feb 1955; *Educ* Ampleforth, St Catharine's Coll Cambridge (MA), Coll of Law; *m* 26 Aug 1978, Teresa Ann, da of John Edmund Bartleet, of Great Tey, Colchester, Essex; 2 s (Teddy b 8 Dec 1980, Harry b 31 March 1983), 2 da (Rachal b 16 June 1979, Sophie b 18 March 1988); *Career* slr, articled clerk Freshfields 1977-79, seconded to Cravath Swaine & Moore 1983-84, Freshfields NY off 1984-85 (ptnr 1985); memb: Law Soc, Int Bar Assoc, City Slrs Co; *Books* Leasing Finance (jtly, Euromoney 1985); *Style—* Simon Hall, Esq; Freshfields, Grindall Ho, 25 Newgate St, London EC1A 7LH (☎ 01 606 6677, fax 01 248 3487/8/9, telex 889292)

HALL, Simon Robert Dawson; s of Wilfrid Dawson Hall (d 1984), and Elizabeth Helen, *née* Wheeler; *b* 24 April 1938; *Educ* Tonbridge, Univ Coll Oxford (MA); *m* 30 Dec 1961, Jennifer, da of Cecil Henley Harverson, of Tunbridge Wells; 2 s (Stephen b 1963, Andrew b 1964); *Career* Nat Serv 7 RTR 1956-58; TA: 21 SAS Regt 1958-61, Intelligence Corps (V) 1968-71; asst master Gordonstoun Sch 1961-65, jt headmaster Dunrobin Sch 1965-68, second master Haileybury 1976-79 (asst master 1969-79), headmaster Milton Abbey Sch 1979-87, warden Glenalmond Coll 1987; FRSA 1983; *Recreations* reading, music, motoring, sailing, hill-walking; *Style—* Simon Hall, Esq; The Warden's House, Glenalmond Coll, Glenalmond, Perth PH1 3RY (☎ 073 888 227)

HALL, Stephen Hargreaves; TD (1969); s of Walter Brian Hall (d 1987), and Marjorie Marian, *née* Hargreaves; *b* 30 April 1933; *Educ* Rugby, Christ's Coll Cambridge (MA); *m* 9 July 1960, Nuala, da of Edward James Walker Stanley (d 1985); 2 s (Niall James b 1962, Patrick Thomas b 1963), 1 da (Victoria Jane b 1974); *Career* Nat Serv 2 Lt KOYLI Korea 1951-53, Maj TA 1953-70; ptnr Ernst & Whinney 1962-; non exec dir: Yorks TV Hldgs plc 1986-, Yorks TV Ltd 1973-; High Sheriff of Humberside 1981-82, memb Cncl Univ of Hull 1972-84; FCA; *Recreations* fishing; *Clubs* City of London, Army and Navy; *Style—* Stephen H Hall, Esq, TD; 10 Douro Place, London W8 5PH (☎ 01 937 1778); Becket House, 1 Lambeth Palace Rd, London SE1 7EU (☎ 01 928 2000, fax 01 928 1345)

HALL, Prof the Rev Stuart George; s of George Edward Hall (d 1980), of London, and May Catherine, *née* Whale; *b* 7 June 1928; *Educ* Univ Coll Sch, New Coll Oxford (BA, MA, BD); *m* 9 April 1953, Brenda Mary, da of Walter McLaren Henderson, OBE (d 1975), of Glasgow; 2 s (Lindsay b 1954, Walter b 1965), 2 da (Nicola (Mrs Nicholson) b 1956), Edith b 1959); *Career* Nat Serv RA/RAEC (1947-48); ordained: deacon 1954, priest 1955; asst curate Newark-upon-Trent 1954-58, tutor The Queens Coll Birmingham 1958-62, lectr in theology Univ of Nottingham 1962-73 (sr lectr 1973, reader 1978), prof of ecclesiastical history King's Coll 1978-, ed Theologische Realenzyklopädie 1977-; memb: Studiorum Novi Testamenti Societas 1969, Academie Internationale de Science Religieuse 1983;; *Books* Melito of Sardis and Fragments (1979); *Recreations* gardening, choral music, bad golf; *Clubs* Golf House (Elie); *Style—* Prof the Rev Hall; 15 High St, Elie, Leven, Fife KY9 1BY (☎ 0333 330 216); King's College, London, Strand, London WC2R 2LS (☎ 01 836 5454, 01 673 5711)

HALL, Col Thomas Armitage; OBE (1966); o child of Athelstan Argyle Hall (d 1962), of Cricket St Thomas, Chard, Somerset; *b* 13 April 1989; *Educ* Eton; *m* 24 Feb 1954, Mariette, da of Sir (Roger) Antony Hornby (d 1987); 2 s (Edward b 1960, John b 1964), 4 da (Jane b 1955, Annabel b 1956, Lucy b 1960, Catherine (twin) b 1964); *Career* Hon Col Royal Hussars 1974-83; Hon Corps of Gentlemen-at-Arms 1980-; High Sheriff Oxon 1981; dir Lloyds Bank 1982-, chm Int Language Centres 1971-; *Recreations* skiing, shooting, travel; *Clubs* Cavalry and Guards; *Style—* Col Thomas Hall, OBE; Chiselhampton House, Stadhampton, Oxford (☎ 0865 890350); office: 1 Riding House St, London W1 (☎ 01 580 4351)

HALL, Dr Trevor Henry; JP (Leeds 1959); s of H Roxby Hall, of Wakefield; *b* 28 May 1910; *Educ* Wakefield Sch, Trinity Coll Cambridge, Univ of Leeds (MA, PhD); *m* 1, 1937, Dorothy (d 1973), da of A Keningley, of Nostell; 1 s, 1 da; m 2, 1977, Marguerite, wid of Dr R McMorris; 1 step s, 1 step da; *Career* sr ptnr V Stanley Walker & Son Chartered Surveyors, of Leeds, Wakefield, Rothwell, Morley and Bramhope 1945-82; dir and former pres Huddersfield Bldg Soc (now Yorkshire Bldg Soc) 1958-82, dir and former chm (Northern and Scottish bds) Legal & General Assur Soc 1962-82; chm Leeds dist ctee Nat Tst 1968-70, pres Leeds Library 1969-82; one of 300 invited fndr life members Cambridge Soc 1977; memb Oxford Univ Soc of Bibliophiles (lectr 1980 and 1982); Cecil Oldman Mem lectr in bibliography and textual criticism Univ of Leeds 1972; FSA, FRICS; *Books Incl:* The Testament of R W Hull (1945), The Strange Case of Edmund Gurney (1964), Stange Things (with Dr John Lorne Campbell, 1968), Sherlock Holmes, Ten Literary Studies (1969), Mathematical Recreations 1633: An Exercise in 17th Century Bibliography (1970), The Early Years of the Huddersfield Building Society (1974), Sherlock Holmes and his Creator (1978), Search for Harry Price (1978), The Strange Story of Ada Goodrich Freer (1979), Dorothy L Sayers: Nine Literary Studies (1980), The Leeds Library, A Check-List of Publications relating to its History from 1768 to 1977; *Style—* Dr Trevor Hall, JP; The Lodge, Selby, N Yorks YO8 0PW (☎ 703372)

HALL, Dr Vernon Frederick; CVO (1960); s of Cecil Septimus Hall, and Maud Mary, *née* Fuller; *b* 25 August 1904; *Educ* Haberdashers' Aske's, King's Coll London, King's Coll Hosp Med Sch; *m* 19 Jan 1935, Constance Marcia, da of Rev H T Cavell, rector of Woodford Green, London; 1 s (Desmond Lawrence b 1937), 2 da (Judith Margaret b 1939, Janet Elizabeth b 1943); *Career* WWII RAMC advsr in anaesthetics to SE Asia Cmd, late dir of anaesthetics Indian and Burma Cmd, Brig; fell King's Coll London, fndr memb Faculty of Anaesthetists RCS, pres Assoc of Anaesthetics of GB & Ireland; anaesthetist to HM The Queen for births of her four children, also HRH The Princess Margaret and HRH Duchess of Kent; vice-pres The Exmoor Soc; MRCS, LRCP, FFARCS; *Books* History of King's College Hospital Dental School, Scrapbook of Snowdonia; *Recreations* rugby, squash, tennis, riding; *Clubs* RAC; *Style—* Dr Vernon F Hall, CVO; 83A Foxgrove Rd, Beckenham, Kent BR3 2DA (☎ 01 650 2212)

HALL, Victor Edwin; s of Robert Arthur Victor James Hall (d 1978), of Selsey, Sussex, and Gladys *née* Fukes (d 1986); *b* 2 Mar 1948; *Educ* Chichester HS for Boys, Univ of Hull (LLB); *m* 11 May 1974, Rosemarie Berdina, da of Walter Raymond Jenkinson, of Stoneygate, Eaton Hill, Baslow, Derby; 2 s (Timothy James b 24 July 1981, Matthew Peter b 16 Feb 1984); *Career* barr Inner Temple 1971, tenancy in chambers 1972-, rec Crown Ct 1988 (asst rec 1983-); former memb Market Harborough Round Table 1981-88, vice chm E Farndon Parish Cncl 1987-(chm 1985-87); memb Inner Temple Soc; *Recreations* skiing, cooking, music, computer addict; *Style—* Victor Hall, Esq; 65/67 King Street, Leicester, LE1 6RP (☎ 0533 547710, fax 0533 470145, telex 0858 67459)

HALL, William; DFC (1944); s of Archibald Hall (d 1956), and Helen Macfadyen (d 1977); *b* 25 July 1919; *Educ* Paisley GS, Coll of Estate Mgmnt; *m* 1945, Margaret Semple, da of Robert Gibson (d 1965); 1 s (David b 1954), 3 da (Elinor b 1947, Elaine b 1951, Maureen b 1959); *Career* Pilot RAF Bomber Cmd 1939-45, served Europe, M East, Burma (despatches); memb: Lands Tbnl for Scotland 1971-, Lands Tbnl for England & Wales 1979-; sr ptnr R & W Hall (chartered surveyors) 1949-79, chm RICS in Scotland 1972; Hon Sheriff Paisley; *Recreations* golf; *Clubs* RAF; *Style—* William Hall, Esq; Windyridge, Brediland Road, Paisley PA2 9HF (☎ 050 581 3614)

HALL, Brig Sir William Henry; KBE (1968, CBE 1962), DSO (1942), ED; s of

William Hall (d 1944), of Edinburgh; *b* 6 Jan 1906; *Educ* Morgan Acad Dundee, Univ of Melbourne; *m* 1930, Irene Mary, da of William Hayes, of Chonmel, Co Tipperary; 1 s, 4 da; *Career* joined State Electricity Cmmn 1924, Maj RAA Mid E and S W Pacific WWII, Brig 1951, OC RAA 1951-57, comptroller of Stores State Electricity Cmmn Victoria 1957-70, Col RAA 8 Cmd 1967-; kt 1968; *see Debrett's Handbook of Australia and New Zealand for further details*; *Style—* Brig Sir William Hall, KBE, DSO, ED; Rosemont, 112 Kooyong Rd, Caulfield, Vic 3929, Australia; Montrose, Flinders, Vic 3929, Australia

HALL-SMITH, Martin Clive William; s of Sydney Patrick Hall-Smith, of 30 The Drive, Hove, Sussex, and Angela Wilma, *née* Hall; *b* 21 July 1948; *Educ* Eton, Univ of Edinburgh (LLB), Selwyn Coll Cambridge (MA); *m* 17 December 1983, Victoria Mary, da of John Sherwood Stephenson, of West Mews, Wylam, Northumberland; 2 da (Rose b 14 May 1985, Katharine b 21 April 1987); *Career* barr 1972, in practice 1973-; Freeman City of London 1978, Liveryman Worshipful Co of Loriners; *Recreations* music, skiing, walking, family life ; *Clubs* City Livery; *Style—* M C W Hall-Smith, Esq; Chichester House, 64 High St, Hurstpierpoint, W Sussex; Goldsmith Building, Temple, London EC4 (☎ 01 353 7881, fax 01 353 5319)

HALL-THOMPSON, Maj (Robert) Lloyd; ERD (1953), TD (1956), JP (1959); s of Col Rt Hon Samuel Herbert Hall-Thompson JP, DL, MP (d 1954); *b* 9 April 1920; *Educ* Campbell Coll Royal Sch; *m* 1948, Alison (Freda), *née* Leitch; 1 s, 1 da; *Career* served RA, Maj 1939-56; joined Unionist Party 1938, vice-pres Clifton Unionist Assoc (chm 1954-57), MP (U) Clifton 1969-73; memb (U) N Belfast NI Assembly 1973-75, (chief whip and ldr of Assembly 1974), memb (U) N Belfast NI Constitutional Convention 1975-76; dir of several companies; life govr and vice-chm Samaritan Hosp Mgmnt Ctee 1958-73, memb NI Hosps Authy, pres and tstee N Belfast Working Men's Club 1954-87, pres Irish Draught Horse Soc, sec Half Bred Horse Breeders Soc; freeman, chm of exec and mgmnt ctee and steward of Down Royal Corpn of Horse Breeders (incorp by Royal Charter 22nd Dec 1685 granted by King James II); *Recreations* horse riding, hunting, racing, eventing, show jumping, breeding, golf, reading; *Clubs* Ulster; *Style—* Maj Lloyd Hall-Thompson, ERD, TD, JP; Maymount, Ballylesson, Co Down, N Ireland

HALLADAY, Eric; s of The Rev Albert Raymond Halladay (d 1969), of Loversal, Yorks, and Helena Nicholson, *née* Renton; *b* 9 July 1930; *Educ* Durham Sch, St John's Coll Cambridge (BA, MA), Ripon Hall Oxford; *m* 1 Aug 1956, Margaret Leslie, da of Leslie Baster (d 1946), of Newcastle; 1 s (Richard b 1963), 2 da (Claire b 1962, Katharine b 1966); *Career* Nat Serv 2 Lt 5 Regt RHA 1948-50; Exeter Sch 1954-60 (sr history master 1956-60), sr lectr RMA Sandhurst 1960-64; Grey Coll Univ of Durham 1964-: sr tutor 1964-80, vice-master 1967-80, master 1980-; hon lectr in history; pres and chm Durham Regatta 1982-, sec Durham Branch Soldiers Sailors and Airmens Families Assoc 1976-, memb N Eastern TA, Volunteer Res Assoc 1978; *Books* The Buildings of Modern Africa (with DD Rooney, 1966), The Emergent Continent (1972); *Recreations* rowing, gardening; *Clubs* Leander (Henley-on-Thames); *Style—* Eric Halladay, Esq; The Master's House, Hollingside Lane, Durham (☎ 091 384 0049); The Coign, Corbridge, Northumberland (☎ 043 471 2838); Grey College, Durham (☎ 091 374 2961)

HALLAM, Edwin William Lewis; DFC (1945); s of Canon Henry James Brunsdon Hallam (d 1979), and Anita Muriel, *née* Lewis (d 1978); *b* 28 July 1923; *Educ* Demstone Coll Uttoxeter Staffs; *m* 14 Sept 1946, Barbara Mary, da of the late Wilfred Anthony; 3 da (Elizabeth b 1950, Judith b 1953, Catherine b 1958); *Career* WW11 1942-46, RAF aircrew 1942, cmmnd PO 1943, Fl Lt 1944, served 115 Sqdn Bomber Cmd (35 ops); slr 1948, sr ptnr Thatcher and Hallam Slrs Midsomer Morton Bath 1949-88; pres Somerset Law Soc 1982-83; chm Cheshire Home Timsbury, memb Royal Br Legion; memb Law Soc;; *Recreations* gardening, flying; *Clubs* RAF; *Style—* Edwin Hallam, Esq; Ragg House, Killmeasoon, nr Bath, Somerset (☎ 0761 32132); Island House, The Island, Midsomer Norton, nr Bath, Avon (☎ 0761 414646)

HALLAM, Bishop of (RC diocese est 1980), 1980-; Rt Rev Gerald Moverley; s of William Joseph Moverley (d 1973), and Irene Mary, *née* Dewhirst (d 1964); *b* 9 April 1922; *Educ* St Bede's GS Bradford, Ushaw Coll Durham, Angelicum Univ Rome (JCD); *Career* ordained priest 1946, sec to Bishop of Leeds 1946-51, chllr Diocese of Leeds 1957, domestic prelate to HH Pope Paul VI 1965, titular bishop of Tinisa in Proconsulari (aux bp of Leeds) 1968; *Style—* The Rt Rev the Bishop of Hallam; Quarters, Carsick Hill Way, Sheffield, S Yorks S10 3LT (☎ 0742 309101)

HALLAM, (John) Stuart; s of George Albert Hallam (d 1947), and Ada, *née* Leaworthy (d 1961); *b* 3 Mar 1921; *Educ* Giggleswick Sch; *m* 2 Sept 1950, Marjorie, da of George Beardmore (d 1983), of Newcastle under Lyme; 2 s (David John Antony b 1952, Simon Charles Richard b 1955); *Career* Sgt RAF 1942-46; CA; chief accountant Kirby & West Ltd 1949-54, fin controller High Speed Steel Alloys Ltd 1954-69, fin dir Cwlth Curtain Co Ltd 1970-81; *Recreations* music, (organist), bridge; *Style—* Stuart Hallam, Esq; 88 Glendyke Road, Liverpool L18 9TH (☎ 051 724 3901)

HALLCHURCH, David Thomas; TD; s of Walter William Hallchurch (d 1962), and Marjorie Pretoria Mary, *née* Cooper (d 1978); *b* 4 April 1929; *Educ* Bromsgrove, Trinity Coll Oxford (MA); *m* 1, 1954 (m dis 1972), Cherry, da of Basil Jagger (d 1980); 3 s (Nicholas b 1958, Nigel b 1960, Adrian b 1966); m 2, 1972, Susan Kathryn Mather Brennan, *née* Wilson; 2 step children (Myles b 1967, Kathryn b 1964); *Career* Maj Staffs Yeo (QORR) TA 1962; barr 1954, Lec Crown Ct 1980; puisne judge of the High Ct of Botswana 1986-88; chm Mental Health Review Tbnl for W Mids 1979-86; *Recreations* tennis, golf; *Clubs* Vincent's (Oxford); *Style—* David Hallchurch, Esq, TD; Neachley House, Tong, nr Shifnal, Shropshire (☎ 090722 3542)

HALLER, (Bernard) John Frederick; s of Bernard Haller (d 1961), of Sheffield, and Ellen Louise Norah, *née* Holmes; *b* 1 Jan 1922; *Educ* Central Secdy Sch Sheffield, Univ of London (BSc); *m* 24 July 1948, Nora Mary (Lew), da of Charles David Lewis, MBE, of Hope, Derbys; 1 s (Nicholas b 1955), 2 da (Sally b 1957, Katherine b 1961); *Career* Beds & Herts Regt 1942-43, Glider Pilot Regt 1943-47; GS master 1948-61; dir: Philip Harris Bilogical Ltd 1961-, Philip Harris Hldgs plc 1968-(md 1978-88, chm 1983-); involved in local charities incl St Giles Hospice; FIBiol 1974; *Recreations* swimming, running, hill walking, amateur art; *Style—* John Haller, Esq; 54 Tudor Hill, Sutton Coldfield, W Mids B73 6BH (☎ 021 3546036); Philip Harris Hldgs plc, Lynn La, Shenstone, Staffs (☎ 0543 480 077, fax 0543 481 091)

HALLETT *see also*: Hughes Hallett

HALLGARTEN, Anthony Bernard Richard; QC; s of (Siegfried) Salmon (Fritz) Hallgarten, of 20 Bracknell Gdns, London, and Friedel Liselotte, *née* Liebmann (d 1986); *b* 16 June 1937; *Educ* Merchant Taylors' Northwood, Downing Coll Cambridge (BA); *m* 16 Dec 1962, Katherine Anne, da of Kurt Borchard; 1 s (Joseph b 22 May 1970), 3 da (Ruth b 1 Feb 1965, Judy b 24 Oct 1966, Emily b 26 Oct 1972); *Career* Nat Serv Int Corps 1955-57; barr, jr counsel 1962-78, leading counsel 1978-; bencher Middle Temple, advocate and arbitrator in commercial matters, chm Ctee on Waybills Br Maritime Law Assoc; active in Soviet Jewry Movement; *Recreations* cricket, cycling, historical novels, visiting the Ariege; *Clubs* Garrick, MCC; *Style—* Anthony Hallgarten, Esq, QC; 3 Essex Court, Temple, EC4Y 9AL (☎ 01 583 9294, fax 01 583 1341, telex 893468)

HALLGARTEN, Dr Peter Alexander; s of Siegfried Salomon (Fritz) Hallgarten, and Friedel Liselotte, *née* Leibmann; *b* 29 Sept 1931; *Educ* Merchant Taylors, Univ of Zurich, Univ of London (PhD), Univ of Chicago; *m* 3 July 1960, Elaine, da of Sqdn Ldr Philip Braham, MBE; 2 s (Daniel Arthur b 1961, Simon Alfred b 1963), 1 da (Lisa Ann b 1966); *Career* chm Hallgarten Wines Ltd 1986- (joined 1958, md 1967); chm Wine and Spirit Assoc of GB and NI 1978-79; Liveryman Worshipful Co of Distillers 1968; FRSC, CChem; Chevalier Dans L'Ordre Du Merite Agricole France 1982; *Books* Liqueurs (special edn 1973), Guide To The Wines Of The Rhone (1979), French and Danish Spirits and Liqueurs (special edn 1983); *Recreations* golf, travel, music, theatre; *Style—* Dr Peter Hallgarten; 14 Antrim Grove, London NW3 4XR (☎ 01 722 1077); Dallow Rd, Luton, Beds LU1 1UR (☎ 0582 22538, fax 0582 23240)

HALLIDAY, David Ralph; s of Walter Henry Halliday (d 1976), and Isabel Kathleen, *née* Blagdon; *b* 28 Sept 1952; *Educ* Devonport HS, Selwyn Coll Cambridge (MA); *Career* pension fund actuary; ptnr Bacon and Woodrow 1987- (joined 1974), FIA 1979; *Recreations* reading, bridge, swimming, drinking; *Style—* David Halliday, Esq; 5 Sunnyside, Catford, London SE6 4UR; Bacon and Woodrow, Empire House, St Martins-Le-Srand, London EC1A 4ED (☎ 01 600 2747, fax 01 726 6519, telex 8953206 BWLON G)

HALLIDAY, Mrs John; (Mary) Elizabeth; MBE (1980), JP (1958); da of Maj William Edmond Logan Stewart, DSO, JP, DL (d 1964), of Llanfair House, Llandovery, Dyfed, and Mary Adela Morland, *née* Rice (d 1969); *b* 20 Feb 1909; *Educ* St Mary and St Anne Abbots Bromley, Harcombe House, Mrs Hoster's Secretarial Training Coll; *m* 4 Dec 1935, (Ruthven) John Wyllie Halliday, s of Richard William Ruthven Halliday (d 1943), of Weston Mark, Upton Grey, Basingstoke, Hants; 1 s (David b 1939 d (in a motor accident) 1983, leaving 1 s Stewart b 1970); *Career* Army Welfare Offr and WVS Canteen Organiser WWII; pres Llandovery Royal British Legion Women's Section 1958-; Borough Cncllr 1957-62; memb Governing Body of Church in Wales 1969-74; foundation memb Cncl of Coleg Elidyr Camphill Coll for Special Educn 1973-88; Gen Cmmr of Income Tax 1959-84; memb of cncl and exec Trinity Coll Carmarthen 1971-80; minister's rep Carmarthanshire Exec Cncl and FPC (NHS) 1958-82; *Recreations* gardening, music; *Style—* Mrs John Halliday, MBE, JP ; Llanfair House, Llandovery, Dyfed SA20 OYF (☎ 0550 20319)

HALLIDAY, Ian Francis; s of Michael Halliday; *b* 16 Nov 1927; *Educ* Lincoln Coll Oxford (MA); *m* 1952, Mary Busfield; 1 s, 2 da; *Career* chief exec Nat Enterprise Bd 1980, dir Lowndes Lambert Gp Ltd 1981-87, bd memb Port of London Authy 1984-; FCA; *Style—* Ian F Halliday, Esq; 40 Finthorpe Lane, Huddersfield HD5 8TU (☎ 0484 530311)

HALLIDAY, James Gordon Tollemache; s of Col Cecil Alexander Tollemache Halliday, OBE, DL (d 1982), and Lilias Rollo Maitland, *née* Fischer; *b* 10 Feb 1947; *Educ* Beaumont Coll, Trinity Coll Dublin (MA); *m* 19 Sept 1970, (Mary Margaret) Anne, da of Patrick Joseph MacNamara; 1 s (Patrick b 1978), 2 da (Louise b 1974, Anna b 1981); *Career* slr, John Laing 1969-71, Foster Wheeler 1971-73, ptnr Foreman Laws Hitchin 1977-; memb Law Soc 1977; *Recreations* tennis, cricket, skiing, music; *Clubs* MCC; *Style—* James Halliday, Esq ; Hillsbank House, Graveley, Herts (☎ 0438 355 477); Foreman Laws, 25 Bancroft, Hitchin Herts (☎ 0462 58 711, fax 0462 59 242)

HALLIDAY, Maj (Francis) Michael Joseph; s of Lt-Col Francis Spencer Halliday (d 1971), of Wimbledon, and Emily Elizabeth, *née* Burgess (d 1958); *b* 25 April 1915; *Educ* Imp Serv Coll, RMC Sandhurst; *m* 9 Oct 1941, Olive Norah, da of Rev Frank Irvine Pocock (d 1958); 2 s (John Michael b 1948, d 1979, James Alastair b 1956), 1 da (Jane Elizabeth b 1942); *Career* Army Offr 1935-68, cmmnd East Surrey Regt 1935, Cipher Offr Tientsin 1939-40, Staff Capt 2 Malaya Inf Bde Singapore 1940-42 (POW Singapore-Thailand 1942-45), served with regt in Greece, Somalia and UK, Garrison Cdr Derna 1950-51, served Egypt, BAOR, Aden, Bahrain and UK, ret as Maj 1968; *Recreations* gardening, beekeeping; *Style—* Maj Michael Halliday; Ducksmoor, Doccombe, Moretonhampstead, Devon TQ13 8ST (☎ 0647 40411)

HALLIDAY, Dr Norman Pryde; s of James Grieve Halliday (d 1962), of Tree House, Sandyford, Glasgow, and Jessie Thompson Hunter, *née* Pryde (d 1960); *b* 28 Feb 1932; *Educ* Woodside Glasgow, King's Coll London, King's Coll Hosp Med Sch London (MB, BS); *m* 25 Oct 1953, Eleanor, da of Alfred Walter Smith (d 1959), of Kingston-upon-Hull; 3 s (Allen Norman b 8 Sept 1955, Derek Clive b 17 March 1958, Jonathan Neil b 25 Aug 1960), 1 da (Susan Elaine b 17 March 1963); *Career* Nat Serv RAMC 1950-52; SRN 1955, qualified in med 1964; various hosp appts: King's Coll Hosp, New End Hosp, Queen Mary's Hosp Kent, Royal Hosp Wolverhampton, Medway Hosp; Civ Serv: 1970-(under sec 1977-) FRSM 1970, DCH, RCP, MRCS, LRCP; *Recreations* photography, sub-aqua diving, fashion, reading, DIY, cross-bow shooting; *Style—* Dr Norman Halliday; 12 Regalfield Close, Guildford, Surrey GU2 6YC (☎ 0483 236 267); Dept of Health, Alexander Fleming House, Elephant and Castle, London SE1 6BY (☎ 01 407 5522)

HALLIDAY, Col Peter Alexander Tollemache; OBE (1963); s of Alexander Tollemache Halliday, late Indian Police (d 1965), and Ethel Maud, *née* Gilbert (d 1969); descended from a yr son of John Delap Halliday (d 1794), of Castlemains, Kirkcudbright by his w Lady Jane Tollemache (1750-1802), da of 4 Earl of Dysart; sr line cr Baron Tollemache; *b* 8 Nov 1917; *Educ* Stonyhurst, RMC Sandhurst; *m* 22 July 1942, Sarah, da of Maj Philip Hamond, DSO, MC (d 1954), of Morston, Holt, Norfolk; 1 s (Stratford b 1954), 1 da (Charlotte b 1951); *Career* cmmnd 2 Lt Hampshire Regt 1937, served WWII, BEF 1939-40, SEAC 1945, AMA Ankara 1951-53, Malayan Operations 1953-54 (despatches), transfd Intelligence Corps 1958, GSO1 (Intelligence) Hong Kong 1960-62, Col (GS) on staff of Lord Mountbatten CDS 1962-64, dep sec Jt Intelligence Ctee 1964-67 (ret at own request 1967); *Recreations* fishing, messing about in boats; *Style—* Col Peter Halliday, OBE; The Cottage, Tighnabruaich, Argyll PA21 2EA (☎ 0700 811472)

HALLIDAY, Vice Adm Sir Roy William; KBE (1980), DSC (1944); *b* 27 June 1923; *Educ* William Ellis Sch, Univ Coll Sch; *m* 1945, Dorothy Joan Meech; *Career* joined RN 1941, serv WWII Fleet Air Arm (Fighter Pilot), Test Pilot Boscombe Down 1947-48, Naval Asst to Chief of Naval Information 1962-64, Cdr (Air) HMS Albion 1964-66, Capt 1966, Dep Dir Naval Air Warfare 1966-70, Capt D3 Far East Fleet and D6 Western Fleet 1971-73, Cdre (Intelligence) Def Intelligence Staff 1973-75, ADC to HM The Queen 1975, Cdre British Navy Staff Washington and Naval Attaché and UK nat liaison rep to SACLANT 1975-78, Dep CDS (Intelligence) 1978-81, dir-gen Intelligence 1981-84; *Clubs* Royal Navy; *Style*— Vice Adm Sir Roy Halliday, KBE, DSC; Willow Cottage, Bank, nr Lyndhurst, Hants.

HALLIDIE, Geoffrey Andrew; MBE (1942), TD (1945); s of Andrew Hallidie Smith Hallidie (d 1958), of Linton House, Linton, Cambridge, and Alice Maud Mary, *née* Deakin (d 1966); *b* 20 Nov 1904; *Educ* Radley, King's Coll Cambridge (MA); *m* 3 Aug 1929, (Marjorie) Zöe, da of Rev William Charles Eppstein (d 1928), of Lambourne Rectory, Abridge; 2 s (Mark b 5 May 1934, Nicholas b 8 Dec 1935); *Career* RE (TA) 1939, London Corps Troops Engrs 1939, Devon and Cornwall Engrs (TA), 1940, WO Demolition Greece 1941, Maj 27 Military Mission 1942, OC 297 Corps FD Park Co Western Desert and later Italy, WO 1945, demobbed 1946, TARO until retiring age; Ransomes and Rapier Ltd 1926-28 (Egypt Nag Harmadi Battage 1928-32), engr Guthries (sent to oil palm factory Malaga) 1934-38; farmer Suffolk 1945-65, Elvas Portugal 1965-88; sometime chm serv ctee Royal Br Legion (tres Bures branch); MICE 1931; *Recreations* rowing, swimming; *Clubs* Royal British Club (Lisbon); *Style*— Geoffrey Hallidie, Esq, MBE, TD; Quinta dos Passarinhos, Ribas de Cima, Bucelas 2760 Loures, Portugal (☎ 010 351 1985 5500)

HALLIFAX, Adm Sir David John; KCB (1983), KBE (1982); s of Vice Adm Ronald Hamilton Curzon Hallifax, CB, CBE, of Longcroft, Shedfield, Hants; *b* 3 Sept 1927; *Educ* Winchester; *m* 8 Dec 1962, Anne, da of Lt-Col John Matthew Blakiston-Houston (d 1984), of Beltrim Castle, Gortin, Co Tyrone; 2 s (Thomas b 1965, Matthew b 1967), 1 da (Louisa b 1964); *Career* joined RN 1945, Flag Offr 1 Flotilla 1978-80, COS to C-in-C Fleet 1980-82, Vice Adm and Dep Supreme Allied Cdr Atlantic 1982-84, Adm and cmdt RCDS 1986-87; constable and govr Windsor Castle 1988-;; *Recreations* sailing, woodwork, conchology, gardening; *Clubs* Royal Yacht Sqdn, Farmers', Pratt's, Pitt;; *Style*— Adm Sir David Hallifax, KCB, KBE; c/o Lloyds Bank, Winchester, Hants

HALLILEY, Alec Addison; OBE (1973, MBE 1945); s of William Alexander Fortescue Halliley (d 1912), of Ceylon, and Margaret Elizabeth, *née* Darling (d 1965); *b* 19 Jan 1912; *Educ* Christ's Hosp, RMA Sandhurst, St Andrew's Univ (MA); *m* 16 Aug 1943, Rosemary Constance Campbell, da of Sir Charles MacIver Grant Ogilvie, CSI, OBE; 3 s (Nicholas b 1944, Jan b 1945, Mark b 1952); *Career* regular soldier, British and Indian Armies 1933-48, Royal Garhwal Rifles 1937-47, served Malaya 1940-41, Staff Col Quetta 1941, Assam-Burma 1942, Brig Maj GHQ Indian Assam-Burma 1944-45, Sumatra 1945; Lt-Col Instructor Tactical Sch India, sr lectr late hd of dept RMA Sandhurst 1951-61; planning off Cwlth Rels Off (HM Dip Serv) 1961-67, 1 sec Br High Cmmn Rawalpindi/Islamabad 1967-72; ret 1974; *Recreations* gardening, travel, voluntary charitable work; *Clubs* Royal Cwlth Soc; *Style*— Alec Halliley, Esq, OBE; Church Farm House, Raydon, Ipswich, Suffolk IP7 5LW (☎ 0473 310405)

HALLINAN, Sir (Adrian) Lincoln; DL (Glam 1969); s of Sir Charles Hallinan, CBE (d 1981), of Cardiff, his 1 w, Theresa Doris, JP (d 1961), da of Frederick William Holman, of Knole Park, Almondsbury, nr Bristol; *b* 13 Nov 1922; *Educ* Downside; *m* 1955, Mary Alethea (*see* Parry Evans, Mary), da of Dr Evan Parry-Evans, JP; 2 s, 2 da; *Career* barr 1950, recorder 1972, stipendiary magistrate S Glam 1976; lord mayor Cardiff 1969-70; kt 1971; *Recreations* music, the arts; *Style*— Sir Lincoln Hallinan, DL

HALLINAN, Lady (Mary); *see*: Parry Evans, Mary

HALLISSEY, Michael; s of John Francis Hallissey, MBE (d 1986), and Mary, *née* Kendall; *b* 6 Mar 1943; *Educ* Royal GS Lancaster, Magdalen Coll Oxford (MA); *Career* CA Price Waterhouse 1964-: staff accountant 1964-68, asst mangr Melbourne 1969-70, mangr Milan 1970-71, sr mangr London 1971-74, audit ptnr London 1974-79, practise devpt ptnr UK 1979-81, strategic planning ptnr UK 1981-82, corp fin ptnr London 1982-85, head corp fin servs UK 1985-87, head strategic planning world firm 1987-88, dir strategy Price Waterhouse Europe 1988-; FCA 1968, FRSA; *Books* numerous articles on corporate strategy, strategic planning, mergers and acquisitions; *Recreations* politics, sailing, music, opera, good food; *Style*— Michael Hallissey, Esq; 49 Whitelands House, Cheltenham Terr, London SW3 4QX; Price Waterhouse, Southwark Towers, 32 London Bridge St, London SE1 9SY (☎ 01 407 8989, fax 01 378 0647, telex 884657)

HALLIWELL, Brian; s of Norman Halliwell (d 1980), of Preston, Lancs, and Emma, *née* Kay (d 1981); *b* 17 Dec 1930; *Educ* Preston GS, Centl London Poly Sch of Mgmnt (DMS); *m* 2 March 1957, Agnes, *née* Lee; *Career* RAOC 1949-51; HM Customs and Excise (princ 1969, asst sec 1973, dep accountant gen 1976, accountant and comptroller gen 1980-85), VAT conslt KPMG Peat Marwick McLintock 1985-, pres Customs Annuity and Benevolent Fund Inc 1985- (dir 1981-); FBIM 1985; *Recreations* chess, reading, sport; *Style*— B Halliwell, Esq; 3 Knollcroft, Ulster Ave, Shoeburyness, Southend-on-Sea SS3 9JY (☎ 0702 297 570); KPMG Peat Marwick Mc Lintock, PO Box 486, 1 Puddle Dock, Blackfriars, London EC4V 3PD (☎ 01 236 8000 ext 2926, fax 01 248 6552 (gp 3))

HALLIWELL, Thomas Morton; s of Rev Dr Thomas Halliwell (d 1982), of Pembrokshire, and Kathleen, *née* Morton; *b* 17 June 1945; *Educ* Marlborough, Coll of Law; *m* 11 April 1970, Susan Winifred, da of Maj F Fitt, of Mallorca; 1 s (Giles b 1973), 1 da (Rebecca b 1971); *Career* slr 1969, dist notary 1984, memb regnl duty slr ctee 1985; *Recreations* fishing, photography, ceramics, music; *Clubs* Law Society; *Style*— Thomas M Halliwell, Esq; Perrymead Dilwyn, Hereford (☎ 0544 318 514); Topaze, Anzere, Switzerland; The Old Merchants House, Leominster, Herefords (☎ (0568) 6333, fax 0568 4013)

HALLOWES, Odette Marie-Céline; GC (1946), MBE (1945); da of Sergeant Gaston Eugène Brailly (ka 1918), of Villers-sous-Ailly, Somme; *b* 28 April 1912; *Educ* Convent of Ste Thérèse Amiens, and privately; *m* 1, 1931, Roy Sansom (decd); 3 da; m 2, 1947 (m dis 1955), Capt Peter Morland Churchill, DSO (d 1972); m 3, 1956, Geoffrey Macleod Hallowes; *Career* Cdr FANY; vice-pres Mil Medallists League, fndr vice pres Women of the Year Luncheon, pres 282 (E Ham) Air Cadet Sqdn, memb ctee VC & GC Assoc, hon memb St Dunstan's ex POW Assoc; Légion d'Honneur 1950; *Recreations* reading, conversation, gardening; *Clubs* Naval and Military, Special Forces; *Style*— Mrs Geoffrey Hallowes, GC, MBE; 8 Eriswell Rd, Burwood Pk, Walton-on-Thames, Surrey

HALLSWORTH, Norris Edward; s of Norris Carl Hallsworth; *b* 9 Mar 1941; *Educ* Long Eaton GS; *m* 1964, Sylvia Christine, da of Leonard Smith; 2 s; *Career* chartered accountant; md Slack & Parr; various other gp dirships; *Clubs* Longcliffe Golf; *Style*— Norris Hallsworth Esq; 28 Shepshed Rd, Hathern, Loughborough, Leics

HALLWORTH, David Malcolm; s of Frank Hallworth (d 1961), of Mapperley, 34 Arthog Rd, Hale, Altrincham, Cheshire, and Irene Mildred, *née* Perry (d 1973); *b* 17 April 1930; *Educ* Shrewsbury, Oxford Univ (MA); *m* 16 May 1959, Joan Stewart, da of Leslie Arnold (d 1968), of Timperley, Altrincham, Cheshire; 3 da (Alison b 1961, Claire b 1963, Sarah b 1965); *Career* slr 1957; ptnr: Hall Brydon and Co Slrs Manchester 1959-79, Foysters slrs Manchester 1979-; former memb cncl Manchester Law Soc 1966-78 (hon tres 1976-78); Oxford half blue: for golf 1951 and 1952 (full blue 1953), for Eton fives 1953; memb: Law Soc 1957-, Manchester Law Soc 1960-; *Recreations* physical exercise, singing; *Clubs* Hale GC, Royal St Davids GC (Harlech), Bowdon Cricket Hockey and Squash, St James's (Manchester); *Style*— David Hallworth, Esq; Redcroft, Belmont Rd, Hale, Altrincham, Cheshire (☎ 061 928 2346); 34 Ty Canol, Harlech, Gwynedd, N Wales; Foysters, Harvester House, 37 Peter St, Manchester M2 5GB (☎ 061 228 3702, fax 061 835 2407)

HALPERN, Sir Ralph Mark; *b* 1938; *m* Joan, *née* Donkin, JP; 1 da; *Career* jnd Peter Robinson 1961, developed Top Shop chain 1968, chief exec Burton Retail and chm Peter Robinson and Top Shop 1977; chm and chief exec The Burton Group 1981; MInstD, CBIM; kt 1986 ; *Style*— Sir Ralph Halpern; c/o The Burton Group Ltd, 214 Oxford St, London W1 (☎ 01 636 8040)

HALPIN, William Richard Crozier; yr s of William Henry Halpin (d 1937), of Ford Lodge, Cavan, Ireland, and, Caroline Isabella Emma, da of Albert Hutton, JP, of Rockwood House, Swanlinbar, Co Cavan; *b* 28 June 1912; *Educ* Rugby, CCC Cambridge; *m* 25 Nov 1939, Hilary Alicia, da of Col Gilbert Henry Keighley-Bell, of Hurlingham Court, Putney, SW; 1 s, 2 da; *Career* chm Premier Consolidated Oilfields 1957-63, North Sea Oil Finders 1972-76, Albion 1974-80; dep chm: Fine Fare 1963-68, S & K Hldgs 1970-72; fin controller Assoc Br Foods 1963-68, md Knight Wegenstein 1968-70; dir Francis Industs 1972-83, Polly Peck 1983-; FCA; *Recreations* beagling; *Clubs* Carlton; *Style*— William Halpin, Esq; 11 Provost Rd, London NW3 4ST (☎ 01 722 4637)

HALSBURY, 3 Earl of (UK 1898); John Anthony Hardinge Giffard; also Baron Halsbury (UK 1885), and Viscount Tiverton (UK 1898); s of 2 Earl of Halsbury (d 1943; himself s of 1 Earl, lawyer, MP, solicitor-gen and lord chllr of three Conservative administrations), and Esmé Stewart Wallace (d 1973); *b* 4 June 1908; *Educ* Eton; *m* 1, 1 Oct 1930 (m dis 1936), Ismay Catherine, da of Lt-Col Lord Ninian Crichton-Stuart; 1 s; m 2, 12 Dec 1936, Elizabeth Adeline Faith (d 1983), da of Maj Harry Godley, DSO, and his w Elizabeth Mary (great niece of 3 Earl Annesley); 2 da; *Heir* s, Adam Edward Giffard (Viscount Tiverton, but does not use title); *Career* sits as Independent Peer in House of Lords; md Nat Research Dvpt Corpn 1949-59; memb DSIR Advisory cncl 1950-55; and SRC 1967-71; chm Science Museum Advsy Cncl 1951-65; first chllr Brunel Univ 1966, chm Meteorological Ctee 1970-82; memb: standing cmmn on Museums and Galleries 1960-76, MRC 1973-77, ctee of mangrs Royal Instn 1976-79; govr: LSE 1959-88, BBC 1960-62, UMIST 1966-; Hon DTech Brunel 1966, Hon DUniv Essex 1968; Hon FRSC, FEng, FRS; *Recreations* music, philosophy, mathematics; *Clubs* Athenaeum, RAC; *Style*— The Rt Hon the Earl of Halsbury, FRS; 4 Campden House, 29 Sheffield Terrace, London W8 7NE (☎ 01 727 3125)

HALSEY, Prof Albert Henry; s of William Thomas Halsey, and Ada, *née* Draper (d 1976); *b* 13 April 1923; *Educ* Kettering GS, LSE (BSc, PhD); *m* 12 April 1944, (Gertrude) Margaret, da of Herbert Arthur Littler (d 1979), of Winsford, Ches; 3 s (Robert William b 13 July 1958, David b 16 Feb 1966, Mark b 22 Dec 1967), 2 da ((Catherine) Ruth b 10 April 1955, Lisa Jane b 13 Oct 1964); *Career* RAF: Cadet Pilot 1942-45, Sgt 1945, Flt Sgt 1946-47; lectr in sociology Liverpool Univ 1952-54, sr lectr in Sociology Birmingham Univ 1954-62, dir Dept of Social and Admin Studies Oxford Univ 1962-, professorial fell Nuffield Coll Oxford 1962-, advsr to Sec of State for Educn 1964-66; hon DSSC Birmingham 1987, American Acad of Arts and Sciences 1988; *Books* Social Class and Educational Opportunity (with J E Floud and F M Martin 1956), Technical Change and Industrial Relations (with W H Scott et al), The Sociology of Education - A Trend Reports and Bibliography (with J E Floud 1958), Education, Economy and Society (with J E Floud and C A Anderson 1961), Ability and Educational Opportunity (1962), Power in Co-operatives (with G N Ostergaard 1965), Social Survey of the Civil Service (with Ivor Crewe 1966-68), The British Academics (with Martin Trow 1971), Trends in British Society Since 1900 (ed 1972), Educational Priority (ed 1972), Traditions of Social Policy (ed 1976), Power and Ideology in Education (with J Karabel 1977), Heredity and Enviroment (1977), Change in British Society (1978, 1981, 1986), Origins and Destinations (with A F Heath and J M Ridge 1980), Faith in the City (1985), British Social Trends Since 1900 (1988), English Ethical Socialism: from Thomas More to R H Tawney (1988); plus over 250 articles in various learned jls; *Recreations* gardening and squash; *Style*— Prof Albert Halsey; 28 Upland Park Rd, Oxford OX2 7RU (☎ 0865 58625); Nuffield College, Oxford, OX1 1NF (☎ 0865 270336)

HALSEY, Rt Rev Henry David; *see*: Carlisle, Bishop of

HALSEY, Rev Sir John Walter Brooke; 4 Bt (UK 1920); s of Sir Thomas Edgar Halsey, 3 Bt, DSO (d 1970); *b* 26 Dec 1933; *Educ* Eton, Magdalene Coll Cambridge; *Career* deacon 1961, priest 1962, Diocese of York, curate of Stocksbridge 1961-65, brother in Community of the Transfiguration 1965-; *Style*— The Reverend Brother John Halsey; Community of the Transfiguration, Manse Rd, Roslin, Midlothian

HALSEY, (James) Richard; s of James Henry Halsey, of Devon, and May Doris, *née* Hunt; *b* 19 July 1946; *Educ* St Albans Sch; *m* 6 Jan 1973, Maureen Claire, da of Trevor Henry Alfred Taylor, of Tedburn, St Mary, Devon; *Career* specialist antique dealer (early oak and walnut furniture and allied items), guest lectr on antiques and their devpt in the English home; former memb: Tedburn Village Hall Ctee, Tedburn Charity Ctee; former: parish cncllr for 10 years (chm 1984-86), sch govr London Colney; *Recreations* studying vernacular architecture, countryside; *Clubs* Veteran Car; *Style*— James R Halsey, Esq; Lower Cadham Farm, Jacobstowe, nr Okehampton, Devon (☎ 0837 85 288); Taylor-Halsey Antiques (☎ 0837 85 288)

HALSTEAD, Sir Ronald; CBE (1976); s of Richard Halstead, of Burton-in-Lonsdale, Lancs, and late Bessie, *née* Harrison; *b* 17 May 1927; *Educ* Lancaster Royal GS,

Queens' Coll Cambridge; *m* 1968, Yvonne Cecile (d 1978), da of Emile de Moncnaux (d 1970), of Australia; 2 s; *Career* chm Beecham Prods 1967-84, md (Consumer Prods) Beecham Gp plc 1973-84, chm and chief exec British Steel Corpn 1984-85 (non exec dir 1979-), dep chm Burmah Oil 1986-; cncl memb and exec ctee memb Food Mfrs Fedn Inc 1966-86 (pres 1974-76); cncl memb: CBI 1970-86, Univ of Buckingham 1973-, Univ of Reading 1978-, The Advertising Assoc 1973-81; chm: Knitting Economic Devpt Ctee (National Econ Devpt Off) 1978-, Nat Coll of Food Technol 1978-83; memb: Agric Res Cncl 1978-84, Monopolies & Mergers Cmmn Newspaper Panel 1980-, Industl Devpt Bd DTI 1983-; govr Ashridge Mgmnt Coll 1970- (vice-chm 1977-); tstee Inst of Econ Affrs 1980-; chm Bd for Food Studies Univ of Reading 1978-83; memb Priorities Bd for Res & Devpt in Agric & Food MAFF 1984-87; dir & hon tres Centre for Policy Studies 1984-; chm Ind Devpt Advsy Bd DTI 1985-, cncl memb Trade Policy Res Centre 1985-; Hon DSc: Reading 1982, Lancaster 1987, hon fell Queens' Coll Cambridge 1985; FBIM, FRSA, FRSC, FInstM (Hon 1982), FIGD, fell Mktg Soc, Hon FIFST; kt 1985; *Recreations* squash, racquets, skiing; *Clubs* Carlton, Lansdowne, Royal Thames Yacht, Hurlingham; *Style—* Sir Ronald Halstead, CBE; 37 Edwardes Sq, London W8 6HH (☎ 01 603 9010); Br Steel Corpn, 9 Albert Embankment, London SE1 7SN (☎ 01-735-7654, telex 916061)

HALSTED, Nicolas; s of Erik Jacob Halsted (d 1976), and Winifred Lena Henrietta, *née* Lever; *b* 24 Oct 1942; *Educ* Westminster, Wadham Coll Oxford (MA); *m* 23 Sep 1972, Clare June, da of Sir Douglas Henley, KCB, of Banstead, Surrey; 2 s (Benjamin b 1977, Laurence b 1984), 1 da (Alexandra b 1981); *Career* slr 1968; corporate legal advsr Reed Int plc 1983-; pres Amateur Fencing Assoc; memb Law Soc; *Recreations* fencing, tennis, theatre; *Style—* Nicolas Halsted, Esq

HALTON, Nicholas Allen; s of Eric Creighton Halton (ka 1941), of Carlisle, and Diana Mabel, *née* Carr (now Mrs Wilkinson); *b* 26 August 1940; *Educ* Marlborough, Emmanuel Coll Cambridge; *m* 1, 17 Sept 1966 (m dis 1981), Nicola Mary Wynne (d 1982), da of Gerald Mole (d 1971); 1 da (Candida b 27 Feb 1974); m 2, 21 Jan 1983 (m dis 1986), Diana Jane, *née* Hall; *Career* admitted slr 1966; ESSO Gp 1968-: legal advsr and co sec Esso Petroleum Co Ltd 1979-82, sr cncl Esso Europe inc 1982-86, gen cncl Esso Europe-Africa Servs Inc 1986-; memb Putney Soc, hon tres Putney Cons Assoc, memb Indust Tribunals 1977-87, exec tstee Petroleum and Mineral Law Educ Tst 1981-, chm Insolvency Practitioners Tribunal 1987-, cncl memb Section on Energy Law, Int Bar Assoc; memb Law Soc 1966; *Recreations* sport, walking, reading; *Clubs* Roehampton; *Style—* Nicholas Halton, Esq; 36 Granard Ave, Putney, London SW15; Esso House, Victoria St, London SW1 (☎01 834 6677, fax 01 245 3146)

HALUCH, (Stefan) James; s of Stefan L Haluch, and Elizabeth, *née* Wallace; *b* 9 Mar 1944; *Educ* St Mary's Acad Bathgate; *m* 25 May 1968, Joyce Vevers, da of late George S McClelland; 2 s (James b 1969, Eoin b 1974), 2 da (Helena b 1965, Shelagh b 1971); *Career* sales mangr (advtg) Scotsman Publns Ltd 1965-70, sr ptnr Athol Business Conslts 1970-75, md Athol Restaurants Ltd (Hoteliers) 1975-, chm Highland Coach Tour Hotels Ltd 1987-88, business and mktg conslt 1988-; vice chm Isle of Arran Tourist Bd 1983-86 (chm 1980-83), pres Isle of Arran License Trade Assoc 1983-86; former cncllr: Bathgate Town Cncl, W Lothian CC; memb Incorpn of Maltmen 1986, MBIM; *Recreations* music, travel; *Style—* James Haluch, Esq; 150 Easter Bankton, Livingston, West Lothian, Scotland EH54 9BW

HAMBLEDEN, Dowager Viscountess; Lady Patricia; *née* Herbert; DCVO (1953); da of 15 Earl of Pembroke and (12 Earl of) Montgomery, JP, DL (d 1960), by his w, Lady Beatrice Paget, CBE (yr da of Lord Alexander Paget and sis of 6 Marquess of Anglesey, GCVO); *b* 12 Nov 1904; *m* 26 Sept 1928, 3 Viscount Hambleden (d 1948, s of 2 Viscount by Lady Esther Gore, 3 da of 5 Earl of Arran); 3 s (4 Viscount, Hon Richard and Hon Philip Smith, *qqv*), 2 da (Hon Mrs Brand, Hon Mrs Townend, *qqv*); *Career* lady-in-waiting to HM The Queen (now HM Queen Elizabeth The Queen Mother) 1937-; JP 1961; *Style—* The Rt Hon the Dowager Viscountess Hambleden, DCVO; Hill House, Ewelme, Oxon (☎ 0491 39242)

HAMBLEDEN, 4 Viscount (UK 1891); William Herbert Smith; s of 3 Viscount (d 1948), and Lady Patricia Herbert (*see* Dowager Viscountess Hambleden); *b* 2 April 1930; *Educ* Eton; *m* 1955 (m dis 1988), Donna Maria Carmela Attolico di Adelfia, da of Conte Bernardo Attolico, of Rome; 5 s; *Heir* s, Hon William Henry Smith; *Style—* The Rt Hon the Viscount Hambleden; The Manor House, Hambleden, Henley-on-Thames, Oxon (☎ 0491 335)

HAMBLEN, Derek Ivens Archibald; CB (1978), OBE (1956); s of Maj Leonard Tom Hamblen (d 1966), and Ruth Mary Archibald (d 1983) ; *b* 28 Oct 1917; *Educ* St Lawrence Coll Ramsgate, St John's Coll Oxford (BA, MA); *m* 1950, Pauline Alison, da of Gen Sir William Morgan, GCB, DSO, MC (d 1977); 1 s (Nicholas), 1 da (Susan); *Career* serv WWII 1940-46 1 Army N Africa 1942-43, Maj GS AFHQ N Africa and Italy, GSOI Allied Cmd for Austria 1945-46, WO, MOD 1946-77, HQ Br Troops Egypt 1946-47; asst sec Off of UK High Cmmn in Aust 1951-55, seconded FO 1957-60, asst sec 1964-68, special advsr to NATO and SHAPE 1968-74, under sec 1974-77, ret; memb bd of govrs St Lawrence Coll 1977-; pres Old Lawrentian Soc 1984-86; FRSA 1987; *Recreations* cricket, hockey (represented Oxford v Cambridge 1940), golf, music, theatre; *Clubs* MCC, Vincent's (Oxford); *Style—* Derek Hamblen, Esq, CB, OBE; c/o Lloyds Bank, East Grinstead, West Sussex

HAMBLETON, Kenneth George; s of George William Hambleton (d 1972), of Chesterfield, Derbys, and Gertrude Ellen, *née* Brighouse (d 1981); *b* 15 Jan 1937; *Educ* Chesterfield GS, Queens' Coll Cambridge (MA); *m* 4 April 1959, Glenys Patricia, da of Horace Smith, of Hayling Island, Hants; 1 s (Neil b 1963), 1 da (Lindsey b 1965); *Career* res and devpt of semiconductor materials devices and applications Servs Electronics Res Lab Herts 1958-73, res and devpt on naval radars weapon systems and computers Admty Surface Weapons Establishment 1973-81 (dep dir 1981-82), dir strategic electronics MOD 1982-85, asst chief sci advsr MOD (responsible for advising on sci content of all def projects and long term res programmes) 1985-86 (dir gen Air Weapons and Electronic Systems), CEng, FIEE 1982; *Recreations* bridge, chess, music, computing, golf; *Clubs* Woking Bridge, Woking 41; *Style—* Kenneth Hambleton, Esq; Prospect House, 100 New Oxford St, London WC1A 1HE (☎ 01 632 6543, fax 01 632 3979)

HAMBLETON, Roy David; s of Harry Hambleton, of Macclesfield, and Minnie, *née* Henshall; *b* 29 August 1944; *Educ* King's Macclesfield, Univ of Manchester (BSc); *m* 13 Aug 1966, Carol, da of Charles Arnold, of Macclesfield; 1 s (Mark James), 1 da (Lucy-Jane); *Career* prodn and projecrs mgmnt Staveley Chems 1967-68, md Graesser Laboratories 1986-88 (chief engr until 1981, ops dir 1981-86), currently gen ops dir Nipa Laboratories Ltd; CBI rep on N Wales Tech Liaison Ctee for Waste Disposal, sec Pantymwyn Scout Troop; graduate memb IChem 1966; *Recreations* walking, running, football spectating; *Style—* Roy Hambleton, Esq; Greenheys, Cefn Bychan Rd, Pantymwyn, Mold, Clwyd (☎ 0352 740 206); NIPA Laboratories Ltd (Incl Graesser Laboratories Ltd) Sandycroft, Deeside, Clwyd (☎ 0244 520 777, fax 0244 537 216, telex 61128 GRSL G)

HAMBLIN, Frederick Thomas; CBE (1966); s of John Frederick Hamblin, of Ashwick, Kingswood, Bristol; *b* 14 Oct 1914; *Educ* Kingswood GS, Bristol Univ (BSc, PhD); *m* 1, 1939, Audrey (d 1965), da of John Lawrence, of Chedworth, Glos; 2 s, 1 da; m 2, 1966, Christa, da of Judge Ernst Schmidt, of Schloss Hilbringen, W Germany; 2 da; *Career* chm: ICI Deutschland 1962-70, ICI Switzerland 1968-70; Freeman City of London; FRIC, FCIS, FPI; *Recreations* sailing, archaeology; *Clubs* Athenaeum; *Style—* Frederick Hamblin, Esq, CBE; Hilbringen, Roedean Way, Brighton, Sussex (☎ 0273 603719)

HAMBLING, Gerald James; s of Ernest James Hambling (d 1965), and Elsie Maud, *née* Sedman (d 1971); *b* 14 June 1926; *Educ* Whitgift Middle Sch Croydon, Selhurst GS Thornton Heath Surrey; *m* 23 May 1954, Margaret, da of George Speakman (d 1945); 1 s (Robert b 31 July 1957), 1 da (Belinda b 18 Oct 1954); *Career* Coldstream Gds 1944-47; asst ed J Arthur Rank Two Cities Films 1947-50, sound ed: Herbert Wilcox Films 1950-54, Alexander The Great 1954, Freud - The Passion 1962, The Servant 1964, Pretty Polly 1966, Night of the Iguana 1966, Wuthering Heights 1970; film ed: Dry Rot 1955, The Whole Truth 1956, The Story of Esther Costello 1957, Sally's Irish Rogue 1958, Left Right and Centre 1959, The Bulldog Breed 1960, She'll Have to Go 1961, The Early Bird 1963, A Stitch in Time 1965, The Intelligence Men 1967, That Riviera Touch 1968, The Magnificent Two 1969, Roger Cherrill Ltd documentaries and commercials 1971-74, Bugsy Malone 1975, Moses - The Lawgiver 1976, Midnight Express 1977 (Br and Amercian Acad nomination), Fame 1979 (Br Acad Award and American Acad nominations, Br Guild of Film Eds award, American Eds Guild nomination), Heartaches 1980, Shoot the Moon 1981, Pink Floyd - The Wall 1982, Another Country 1983 (Br Acad nomination), Birdy 1984 (Br Guild of Eds award), Absolute Beginners 1985, Angel Heart 1986 (Br Guild of Eds nomination), Leonard VI 1987, Mississippi Burning 1988; memb: Br Guild of Film Eds 1966-, American Acad of Arts and Scis 1980-, American Cinema Eds Guild 1980-; *Recreations* horology, fishing, antiques, photography; *Style—* Gerald Hambling, Esq; Ramblers, Skirmett, nr Henley-on-Thames, Oxon RG9 6TG (☎ 049 163 316)

HAMBLING, Sir (Herbert) Hugh; 3 Bt (UK 1924); s of Sir (Herbert) Guy Musgrave Hambling, 2 Bt (d 1966), and Olive Margaret Gordon, *née* Carter (d 1969); *b* 3 August 1919; *Educ* Wixenford, Eton; *m* 23 Sept 1950, Ann Page, er da of Judge Hugo Edmund Oswald (d 1932), of Seattle, USA; 1 s; *Heir* s, (Herbert) Peter Hugh; *Career* RAF Training and Atlantic Ferry Cmd 1939-45; airline representative British Airways 1956-74, Royal Brunei Airlines 1975-; mangr Sir Guy Hambling & Son 1956-; *Clubs* Seattle Tennis; *Style—* Sir Hugh Hambling, Bt; Rookery Park, Yoxford, Suffolk (☎ 072 877 310); 1219 Evergreen Point Rd, Bellevue, Washington 98004, USA

HAMBLING, Maggi; da of Harry Leonard Hambling, of Wistaria House, Hadleigh, Suffolk, and Marjorie Rose, *née* Harris (d 1988); *b* 23 Oct 1945; *Educ* Hadleigh Hall Sch, Amberfield Sch, Ipswich Sch of Art, Camberwell Sch of Art (Dip A D Painting), Slade Sch of Fine Art (Higher Dip in Fine Art), Boise travel award NY 1969; *Career* first artist in residence Nat Gallery London 1980-81, works in public collections incl: Arts Cncl of GB, Birmingham City Art Gallery, Br Cncl, Br Museum, Christchurch Mansion Ipswich, Clare Coll Cambridge, Chelmsford and Essex Museum, Contemporary Art Soc, Eastern Arts Collection, Euro Parliament Collection, Fndn Du Musee De La Main Lausanne, GLC, Greene King Breweries, Gulbenkian Fndn, Haddo House Aberdeen, Harris Museum and Art Gallery Preston, HTV Bristol Imperial War Museum, Leics Educn Ctee, Minories Colchester, Morley Coll London, Nat Gallery, Nat Portrait Gallery, Petworth House, Rugby Museum, RAMC, Scottish Nat Gallery of Modern Art Edinburgh, Scottish Nat Portrait Gallery, Southampton Art Gallery, St Mary's Church Hadleigh Suffolk, St Mary's Coll Strawberry Hill London, St Mary's Hosp London, Tate Gallery, Unilever House London, Whitworth Art Gallery Manchester, William Morris Sch London; exhibited: Hadleigh Gallery Suffolk 1967, Morley Gallery London 1973, Warehouse Gallery London 1977, Nat Gallery London 1981, Nat Portrait Gallery London and Tour 1983, Serpentine Gallery London 1987, Richard Demarco Gallery Edinburgh 1988, Maclaurin Art Gallery Ayr 1988, Arnolfini Gallery Bristol and Tour 1988; *Clubs* Chelsea Arts; *Style—* Miss Maggi Hambling; 1 Broadminton Rd, London SW4 OLU, (☎ 01 720 4084)

HAMBLING, (Herbert) Peter Hugh; s and h of Sir (Herbert) Hugh Hambling, 3 Bt; *b* 6 Sept 1953; *Educ* Washington Univ (BSc), von Karman Inst for Fluid Dynamics (Dip), Yale Sch of Orgn and Mgmnt (Master Public & Private Mgmnt); *m* 8 Aug 1982, Jan Elizabeth, da of Stanton Willard Frederick, Jr, of Seattle, Washington; *Career* management consultant; *Recreations* flying (certified flight instr), sailing (yacht 'Boo Diggly'), skiing; *Clubs* Seattle Tennis, Corinthian Yacht (Seattle), Wings Aloft Flying, Felthorpe Flying; *Style—* Peter Hambling Esq; Rookery Park, Yoxford, Suffolk

HAMBRO, Jocelyn Olaf; MC (1944); eldest s of Ronald Olaf Hambro, JP, and Winifred, 5 da of Martin Ridley-Smith (ggs of Abel Smith, MP for Nottingham, consequently cousin to Lords Bicester and Carrington) by his 2 w (also his 1 w's sis), Cecilia, da of Henry Stuart, gs of 1 Marquess of Bute; *b* 7 Mar 1919; *Educ* Eton, Trinity Coll Cambridge; *m* 1, 28 March 1942, Ann Silvia (d 1972), da of Rowland Muir, of Binfield; 3 s (Rupert *qv*, Richard *qv*, James) m 2, 1976, Margaret Elisabeth (d 1983), da of late Frederick McConnel (she m 1, Lt-Col James Church, MC; m 2, 1954, 9 Duke of Roxburghe, who d 1974); m 3, 28 Jan 1988, Margaret Anne, formerly w of 7 Earl Fortescue, and da of Charles Michael Stratton; *Career* served WW II, Coldstream Gds; non-exec chm Charter Consolidated 1982- (dir 1965-); chm Hambros Ltd 1970-83 (pres 1983-); chm: Phoenix Assurance Co, The Hambros Tst, Hambros Investment Tst, HIT Securities, Hambros Diamond Investment Corpn, Hereditaments Ltd, Berkeley Hambro Property Co, Newmarket Estates & Property Co, Rosedimond Investment Tst, Waverton Property Co, Wiltons (St James's) Ltd; *Clubs* Jockey, White's, Pratt's; *Style—* Jocelyn Hambro, Esq, MC; Waverton House, Moreton-in-Marsh, Glos; 16 Victoria Rd, London W8 (☎ 01 937 4550/7573); Hambros, 41 Bishopsgate, London EC2P 2AA

HAMBRO, Peter Charles Percival; elder s of Lt-Col Everard Bingham Hambro, MBE (d 1971, ggs of Baron Hambro, cr a Danish Baron 1851, and founder of the Hambros as British bankers, by his 1 w), of Durrington House, Old Harlow, Essex; *b*

18 Jan 1945; *Educ* Eton, Université d'Aix-Marseille; *m* 1968, Karen Guinevere Gould, da of Capt George Brodrick, of Dunley Manor, Whitchurch, Hants; 3 s; *Career* md Smith St Aubyn & Co Hldgs to 1983; md Richco Bullion Ltd 1982-83; dir Mocatta & Goldsmid Ltd 1985-; dir City of Oxford Investment Tst; *Recreations* shooting, fishing, painting; *Clubs* Pratt's, White's; *Style*— Peter Hambro, Esq; 108 St George's Square, London SW1 (☎ 01 821 8400)

HAMBRO, (Alexander) Richard; s of Jocelyn Hambro, MC, *qv*; *b* 1 Oct 1946; *Educ* Eton; *m* 1, 1973 (m dis 1982), Hon Charlotte, da of Baron Soames, GCMG, GCVO, CH, CBE, PC, *qqv*; 1 da (Clementine, b 1976, bridesmaid to Lady Diana Spencer at her marriage to HRH The Prince of Wales 1981); m 2, 12 July 1984, Mrs Juliet Grana Mary Elizabeth da Maj Thomas and Lady Mary Harvey; *Style*— Richard Hambro Esq; 49 Egerton Crescent, SW3

HAMBRO, Rupert Nicholas; eldest s of Jocelyn Hambro, MC, *qv*, of Waverton House, Stow-on-the-Wold, Glos; *b* 27 June 1943; *Educ* Eton, Aix-en-Provence; *m* 1970, Mary, da of Francis Boyer; 1 s, 1 da; *Career* chm Hambros Bank 1983-86 (dir 1969-), dir Anglo American Corpn of SA 1981-; chm Assoc of Int Bond Dealers 1979-82; dir: Daily Telegraph plc 1986, Racecourse Hldgs Tst 1985-; Sedgwick Gp plc 1987-, Triton Europe plc; *Recreations* racing, shooting; *Clubs* White's, Portland, Jupiter Island; *Style*— Rupert Hambro, Esq; 42 Eaton Place, SW1 (01 235-5656), Jo Hambro & Company, 30 Queen Anne's Gate, London SW1N 9AL

HAMBURGER, Sir Sidney Cyril; CBE (1966), JP (Salford 1957, DL Greater Manchester 1981); s of Isidore Hamburger (d 1953); *b* 14 July 1914; *Educ* Salford GS; *m* 1940, Gertrude, da of Morris Sterling (d 1951); 3 s; *Career* cllr and alderman Salford City Cncl 1946-71, mayor Salford 1968-69; memb North Western Electricity Consultative Cncl 1953-70 (chm Manchester area ctee 1963-68, dep chm cncl 1968-70); chm: NE Manchester Hosp Mgmnt Ctee 1970-74, NW Regnl Health Authy 1973-82, North West ASH 1977-; life pres: Manchester Jewish Homes for the Aged 1965, Zionist Central Cncl 1976 (pres 1967-70 and 1974-75); pres: Jewish Day Centre for the Elderly, Jewish Rep Cncl 1962-65, Trades Advsy Cncl (national), Jt Israel Appeal, Labour Friends of Israel; memb: Manchester Univ Ct 1972-83, advsy bd Salvation Army 1983; govr King David Schs, pres Manchester ctee Bar-Ilan Univ Jerusalem, hon fell Bar-Ilan Univ 1979; Hon MA Salford 1979, Hon LLD Manchester 1983; Papal Award Cross Pro Ecclesia et Pontifice 1983; Supplementary Benefit Cmmn 1967-77, Bd of Gov Ben Gurion Univ 1979, chm: Age Concern/Salford 1984, Manchester Cncl for Soviet Jewry 1984, Greater Manchester Citizens Advice Bureau 1985, Bnei Brith Annual Award 1984; kt 1981; *Recreations* reading, public service, football; *Style*— Sir Sidney Hamburger, CBE, JP, DL; 26 New Hall Rd, Salford M7 0JU (☎ 061 834 5452)

HAMER, Marie Ella Marguerite; *née* Cordasco; da of Charles Merryl Humbert Cordasco (d 1974), of Montreal, Canada, and Ella Winifred Edith, *née* Woodhouse (d 1968); *b* 30 Sept 1922; *Educ* Convent Our Lady of Sion London, St Martin's Sch of Art, Grande Chaumiére Paris; *m* 27 July 1943 (m dis), Robert Sydney Dymock Maunsell, s of late Sydney Augustus Wray Maunsell, of Bath; 1 da (Penelope b 1948); m 2, 19 Aug 1955, John Richard, s of Capt Richard Lloyd Hamer, DSO, RN (d 1951), of Shropshire; 1 da (Alexandra b 1957); *Career* artist and potter, exhibitions incl: Durham, Chapel Hill, N Carolina, FO 1939-43, min of Economic Warfare 1943-45, with Allied Control Cmmn (Germany) 1946-47; *Recreations* opera, yoga, reading biography; *Style*— Mrs J R Hamer; Vicarage Cottage, Old Hunstanton, Norfolk PE36 6JS (☎ 04853 2918)

HAMER, Hon Sir Rupert James; KCMG (1982) ED; s of late H R Hamer; *b* 29 July 1916; *Educ* Melbourne GS, Geelong GS, Trinity Coll Melbourne Univ (LLM, Hon LLD); *m* 1944, April, da of N R Mackintosh; 2 s, 2 da; *Career* serv WWII AIF 1939-45, Tobruk, Alamein, New Guinea, NW Europe; MLC for East Yarra 1958-71, min for Immigration 1962-64 (Local Govt 1964-71), MLA for Kew Vic 1971-, chief sec and dep premier Vic 1971-72, premier 1972-81, tres and min for the Arts Vic 1972-79, min State Devpt Decentralisation and Tourism 1979-81; dir Charles Davis Ltd 1982-, dir Burns Philp Trustee Co Ltd; pres Victorian Coll of the Arts 1982-; chm Victoria State Opera 1982-; tstee Yarra Bend Park; fell: Trinity Coll, Australian Inst of Mgmnt; kt 1982; FAIM; *Recreations* tennis, walking, sailing, music; *Clubs* Naval and Military; *Style*— The Hon Sir Rupert Hamer, KCMG, ED; 39 Monomeath Ave, Canterbury, Vic 3126, Australia

HAMILL, Sir Patrick; QPM (1979); s of late Hugh Hamill; *b* 29 April 1930; *Educ* St Patrick's HS Dumbarton; *m* 1954, Nell Gillespie; 4 s, 1 da; *Career* Dunbartonshire Police 1950, City of Glasgow Police 1972 (asst chief constable), Strathclyde Police 1975, Royal Coll Def Studies 1976, chief constable Strathclyde Police 1977-85; bd of govrs: Scottish Police Coll 1977-85, St Aloysius Coll Glasgow 1983; pres Assoc of Chief Police Offrs (Scotland) 1982-83 (rep to INTERPOL 1977-81, hon sec 1983-85); chm: bd of mgmnt St Margaret Hospice Clydebank 1986-, bd of govrs St Andrew's Coll of Edcn Bearden 1987-88; OStJ 1977; kt 1984; *Recreations* walking, gardening, golf; *Style*— Sir Patrick Hamill, QPM

HAMILTON *see also*: Douglas-Hamilton, Stirling-Hamilton

HAMILTON, Duke of; *see*: Hamilton and Brandon

HAMILTON, Adrian Walter; QC (1973); s of Walter George Morrell Hamilton (d 1957), and Sybil Emily Hamilton, *née* Thomson (d 1972); *b* 11 Mar 1923; *Educ* Highgate, Balliol Coll Oxford (MA); *m* 1966, Jill Margaret Beverlie, da of Stanley Richard Brimblecombe, of Eastbourne; 2 da (Sarah b 1967, Philippa b 1970); *Career* Lt RNVR (Atlantic, Mediterranean, English Channel); barr Lincoln's Inn, Middle Temple and Inner Temple 1949, rec Crown Ct 1974, memb Senate and Inns of Court and the Bar 1976-82, (tres 1979-82), memb cncl of Legal Educn 1977-87, inspr Peek Foods Ltd 1977-81, bencher Lincoln's Inn 1979; *Recreations* golf, sailing, family; *Clubs* Garrick, Roehampton; *Style*— Adrian Hamilton, Esq, QC; 7 King's Bench Walk, Temple, London, EC4 (☎ 01 583 0404)

HAMILTON, Andrew; s of Peter Hamilton, of Sussex, and Susie, *née* Blackwell; *b* 15 Jan 1950; *Educ* Univ Coll Sch, Coll of Estate Mgmnt Reading Univ; *m* 23 July 1983, Fiona Ann, da of John Scott-Aide, of Perthshire; 1 s (Charles Scott-Aide b 1988); *Career* dir: John D Wood SA 1975-77, Haslemere Estates plc 1985-86, Ranleigh Devpts Ltd 1986-; md Culverin Hldgs Ltd 1986-; dir Opera 80; FRICS 1986; *Recreations* opera, conservation, shooting; *Clubs* RAC; *Style*— Andrew Hamilton, Esq; 82 Park St, Mayfair W1Y 3HQ (☎ 01 408 1188, fax 01 493 8042)

HAMILTON, Andrew Caradoc; s and h of Sir (Robert Charles) Richard Caradoc Hamilton, 9 Bt; *b* 23 Sept 1953; *Style*— Andrew Hamilton Esq; c/o The Old Rectory, Walton, Warwick CV35 9HX

HAMILTON, Lord (Claud) Anthony; s of 4 Duke of Abercorn (d 1979), and Dowager Duchess of Abercorn, GCVO, *qv*; *b* 8 July 1939; *Educ* Eton; *m* 17 April 1982, Catherine Janet, eldest da of Dennis Faulkner, CBE, of Ringhaddy House, Killinchy, Co Down; 1 s (Alexander James b 1987), 1 da (Anna Kathleen b 1983); *Career* Lt Irish Gds; Capt RARO Ulster Def Regt 1979-; *Clubs* Kildare St and University; *Style*— Lord Anthony Hamilton; Killyreagh, Tamlaght, Enniskillen, Co Fermanagh, N Ireland (☎ 0365 87 221)

HAMILTON, Hon Archie (Archibald) Gavin; MP (C) Epsom and Ewell 1978-; 2 s of 3 Baron Hamilton of Dalzell, GCVO, MC, JP; *b* 30 Dec 1941; *Educ* Eton; *m* 14 Dec 1968, Anne, da of late Cdr Trevelyan Napier, DSC, RN; 3 da; *Career* cncllr Kensington & Chelsea 1968-71; pps to Sec of State Energy 1979-81, pps to Sec of State Transport 1981-82, asst govt whip 1982-84, lord cmmnr to the Treasy 1984-86, parly Under Secretary of State (Defence Procurement) 1986-87, PPS to PM 1987-88, min of State (Armed Forces) 1988-; *Style*— The Hon Archibald Hamilton, MP; House of Commons, London SW1

HAMILTON, Arthur Campbell; QC (1982);; s of James Whitehead Hamilton (d 1954), of Glasgow, and Isabel Walker, *née* McConnell; *b* 10 June 1942; *Educ* Glasgow HS, Glasgow Univ, Worcester Coll Oxford (BA), Edinburgh Univ (LLB); *m* 12 Sept 1970, Christine Ann, da of Thomas Carlyle Croll, of St Andrews, Fife; 1 da (Miranda b 1975); *Career* advocate, memb Faculty of Advocates 1968; standing jr csl: Scot devt dept, 1975-78, Bd Inland Revenue (Sc) 1978-82; Advocate Depute 1982-85, judge of the Courts of Appeal of Jersey and Guernsey 1988-; *Recreations* hill walking, fishing; *Style*— Arthur Hamilton, Esq, QC; 8 Heriot Row, Edinburgh EN3 6HU (☎ 031 556 4663); Advocates Library, Parliament House, Edinburgh (☎ 031 226 5071, fax 031 225 3642)

HAMILTON, Baron Carl-Diedric Hugo Gustav; s of Baron Fredrik Adolf Hugo Johan Hamilton (d 1968), and Karin Odelstierna; *b* 7 August 1948; *Educ* Sigtuna Skolan, Stockholm Sch of Business; *m* 1976, Astrid Gudrun Ebba Charlotte, da of Erik Carleson (d 1959); 1 s (Carl-Johan b 1977), 2 da (Ebba b 1980, Louise b 1982); *Career* Capt Reserve Royal Swedish Lifeguards; dir Hambros Bank Ltd 1976-82; exec dir Enskilda Securities 1982-; *Style*— Baron Carl-Diedric Hamilton; 9 Queen Anne's Gdns, London W4 1TU (☎ 01 995 6768); Enskilda Securities, 26 Finsbury Square, London EC2A 1DS (☎ 01 638 3500, telex 8955951

HAMILTON, Donald Algernon William; s of Alfred Parke Hamilton and Annie, *née* Creswell; *b* 20 Jan 1910; *Educ* County HS Ilford Essex; *m* 2 June 1936, Hilda Eileen, da of Percy Arthur Foster, of Bexhill-on-Sea; 2 s (Anthony b 15 Sept 1939, David b 14 Jan 1941), 1 da (Patricia b 13 Sept 1942); *Career* princ: Bursham Nixon & Hamilton, Hamilton & Wilton (Bexhill); dir: Heal & Son Hldgs Ltd, Heal & Son Ltd, Heal Textil GMBH (W Germany), MP Harris Hldgs Ltd, Staples & Co Ltd, the Antiference Gp Ltd; memb Hartings Chess Club, bridge: South of England Campion (Paris) Bexhill Congress 1946; Freeman Worshipful Co of Cooks; FCA, ACIS; *Recreations* bridge, chess, computer chess; *Style*— Donald Hamilton, Esq; Hamilton & Wilton, 28 Wilton Rd, Bexhill-on-Sea, East Sussex (☎ 0424 430 300, fax 0424 430 086)

HAMILTON, Douglas Owens; s of Oswald Hamilton (d 1949), and Edith Florence Hamilton (d 1987); *b* 20 April 1931; *Educ* John Fisher Sch Purley Surrey, London Univ (LLB); *m* 15 Sept 1962, Judith Mary, da of Harold Arthur Benjamin Wood (d 1979); 3 s (Giles Alexander Douglas, Angus James Douglas, Benjamin Charles Douglas); *Career* sr ptnr Norton Rose Slrs 1982-(ptnr 1959, fin ptnr 1970-76, exec ptnr 1978-82); hon tres Br Maritime Charitable Fndn; Liveryman Worshipful Co of Shipwrights; memb: Law Soc 1955, Baltic Exchange 1970; *Recreations* tennis, golf, travelling; *Style*— Douglas O Hamilton, Esq; Kempson House, Camomile Street, London, EC3N 7AN (☎ 01 283 2434, fax 588 1181, telex 883652)

HAMILTON, (James) Dundas; CBE (1985); s of late Arthur Douglas Hamilton, and Jean Scott Hamilton; *b* 11 June 1919; *Educ* Rugby, Clare Coll Cambridge; *m* 1954, Linda Jean, da of late Sinclair Frank Ditcham; 2 da; *Career* Lt-Col RA, Europe and Far East 1939-46; memb Stock Exchange 1948- (cncl memb 1972-78, dep chm 1973-76), sr ptnr Feilding Newson-Smith & Co 1977-85; dep chm Br Invisible Exports Cncl 1976-86; chm: TSB Commercial Hldgs Ltd, Utd Dominions Tst Ltd, Wates City of London Properties plc; dir: TSB plc, LWT (Hldgs) plc, Archival Facsimiles Ltd, WIB Publications Ltd; memb: exec ctee City Communications Hons Centre 1977-87, advsy bd Royal Coll Def Studies 1980-87, govr Pasold Res Fund; parly candidate (Cons) East Ham North 1951; novelist and playwright; *Recreations* swimming, writing, golf, tennis; *Clubs* City of London, All England Lawn Tennis and Croquet, Hurlingham, Worplesdon GC; *Style*— Dundas Hamilton, Esq, CBE; 45 Melbury Court, London W8 6NH (☎ 01 602 3157)

HAMILTON, Eben William; QC (1981); s of Rev John Edmund Hamilton, MC (d 1981), of Edinburgh, and Hon Lilias Maclay (d 1966); *b* 12 June 1937; *Educ* Winchester, Trinity Coll Cambridge (MA); *m* 1985, Themy Rusi, da of Brig Rusi Bilimoria (d 1963), of Bellagio, Warden Rd, Bombay, India; *Career* 4/7 Royal Dragoon Gds 1955-57, Fife and Forfar Yeo Scottish Horse TA 1957-68; barr 1962, bencher Inner Temple 1985; *Clubs* Garrick; *Style*— Eben Hamilton, Esq, QC; 28 Pembroke Sq, London W8; Priests Island, Co Longford, Ireland; 1 New Sq, Lincoln's Inn, London WC2

HAMILTON, Sir Edward Sydney; 7 Bt (GB 1776), of Marlborough House, Hampshire, and 5 Bt (UK 1819), of Trebinshun House, Brecknockshire; s of Sir (Thomas) Sydney (Percival) Hamilton, 6 and 4 Bt (d 1966); *b* 14 April 1925; *Educ* Canford Sch; *Heir* none; *Career* RE 1943-47, 1st Royal Sussex Home Guard 1953-56; *Style*— Sir Edward Hamilton, Bt; The Cottage, East Lavant, nr Chichester, West Sussex PO18 OAL (☎ 0243 527414)

HAMILTON, Hon Evelyn William James; s of 3 Baron Holmpatrick; *b* 28 April 1961; *Style*— The Hon Evelyn Hamilton

HAMILTON, Francis Rowan Oldfield de Courcy; s of James Percival de Courcy Hamilton, of Brightwell Baldwin, Oxon, and Elizabeth Millicent, *née* Oldfield; *b* 11 Feb 1940; *Educ* Winchester, Christ Church Oxford (PPE); *m* 22 July 1972, Catherine Rae, da of Lt Cdr William Alastair Robertson, CBE, DSC, RN, of Garvald, East Lothian; 1 s (Thomas b 1983), 2 da (Antonia b 1977, Olivia b 1979); *Career* The Economist Intelligence Unit 1965-72 (dir Mexico Off from 1967), dir Samuel Montagu & Co Ltd 1978-86; on secondment sr advsr Int Finance Corpn Washington DC 1986-; *Clubs* Travellers'; *Style*— Francis de C Hamilton, Esq; 4610 Chesapeake St, NW Washington, DC 20016 (☎ 202 362 9525); 44 Moreton St, London SW1 (☎ 01 828 5018)

HAMILTON, Lady Claud; Genesta Mary; da of Cuthbert Eden Heath, OBE (d 1939), of Anstie Grange, Holmwood, Surrey; *b* 5 May 1899; *Educ* private; *m* 1, 1919 (m dis 1924), Arthur McNeill Farquhar (d 1964); 1 s, 1 da; m 2, 1924 (m dis 19-) Edward Caswell Long; m 3, 1946, Lord Claud David Hamilton (d 1968), 2 s of 3 Duke of Abercorn, KG, KP, PC; *Books* In the Wake of da Gama, Princes of Zinge, A Stone's Throw; *Clubs* Cavalry and Guards; *Style*— Lady Claud Hamilton; c/o Lloyds Bank, 39 Old Bond St, London W1

HAMILTON, (Alexander) Gordon Kelso; s of Arthur Hamilton Kelso Hamilton of Weybridge, Surrey and Elizabeth Evelyn, *née* Williams; *b* 27 August 1945; *Educ* Charterhouse, Pembroke Coll, Cambridge (MA); *m* 12 July 1980, France Elisabeth Mary Colette, da of Pierre Laurent Millet (ret ambass), of Paris, France, 1 s (Edward b 1984) 1 da (Georgina b 1986); *Career* CA, ptnr Mann Judd 1975-79; following merger ptnr Touche Ross & Co, 1979-; tstee Pembroke Coll, Cambridge (The Valence Mary (1997) Endowment fund), dir St George's Hill GC Ltd; FCA; *Recreations* golf; *Clubs* R & A, St George's Hill GC; *Style*— Gordon Hamilton, Esq ; Touche Ross & Co, Hill House, 1 Little New St, London, EC4A 3TR (☎ 01 353 8011, fax 01 583 8517)

HAMILTON, Capt (James Alexander) Hans; s of Cmdr George Cecil Hans Hamilton, CBE, RNVR (d 1960), of Somersby House, Lincs (*see* Burke's Irish Family Records, Hamilton, Co Leix), and Eva Marjorie, *née* Hornby (d 1972); *b* 28 April 1921; *Educ* Nautical Coll Pangbourne, RN Engrg Coll; *m* 20 Dec 1941, Patricia Adelaide, da of (Thomas Percival) Guy Lawes (d 1978), of Plymouth, Devon; 1 s (Gavin b 1950), 3 da (Gaye b 1944, Briony b 1947, Georgina b 1960); *Career* Capt RN served WWII, naval advr British High Commn Delhi 1969-71, dir Naval Engrg Trg, MOD 1971-73, ret 1973; Rank Orgn gen mangr Yacht Marina 1973-86, conslt marine leisure; CEng, FIMechE, MIMarE; *Recreations* field sports, fishing, yacht cruising; *Clubs* Royal Ocean Racing, Royal Naval Sailing Assocn, Royal Southern Yacht, Royal Bombay Yacht, Royal London Yacht, Island Sailing; *Style*— Capt J A Hans Hamilton, RN; 15 Queens Rd, Cowes, Isle of Wight PO31 8BQ (☎ 0983 298740)

HAMILTON, Hon Hans James David; s and h of 3 Baron Holmpatrick; *b* 15 Mar 1955; *m* 1984, Mrs G du Feu, eldest da of K J Harding, of Binisafua, Minorca; *Style*— The Hon Hans Hamilton

HAMILTON, Brig Hugh Gray Wybrants; CBE (1964, MBE 1945), DL (Northants 1977); s of Lt-Col Henry Wybrants Hamilton (d 1946), and Blanche Christina, *née* Baines (d 1963); *b* 16 May 1918; *Educ* Wellington, RMA Woolwich, Peterhouse Cambridge; *m* 1944, Claire, da of Henry Buxton (d 1965); 2 da; *Career* RE 1938-68; gen mangr Corby Devpt Corpn 1968-80; chm Forces Help Soc and Lord Roberts Workshops; *Recreations* riding, sailing, DIY; *Clubs* Army and Navy; *Style*— Brig Hugh Hamilton, CBE, DL; Covert House, E Haddon, Northants (☎ 0604 770488)

HAMILTON, (Robert) Ian; s of Robert Tough Hamilton (d 1951), and Daisy, *née* Mackay; *b* 24 Mar 1938; *Educ* Queen Elizabeth GS Darlington, Keble Coll Oxford (BA); *m* 1, 1963 (m dis 1979), Gisela Dietzel; 1 s (Matthew William b 1967); m 2, 1981, Ahdaf Soueif; 1 s (Robert b 1984); *Career* Nat Serv RAF 1956-58; poet and author; ed: The Review 1962-72, The New Review 1974-79; *Books* incl: The Visit (poems, 1970), A Poetry Chronicle (1973), The Little Magazines (1976), Robert Lowell: A Biography (1983), In Search of J D Salinger (1988), Fifty Poems (1988); *Style*— Ian Hamilton, Esq; 54 Queens Rd, London SW19 (☎ 01 946 0291)

HAMILTON, Ian Robertson; QC (Scotland 1980); s of John Harris Hamilton (d 1968), of Paisley, Renfrewshire, and Martha, *née* Robertson (d 1976); *Educ* John Neilson Sch Paisley, Allan Glens Sch Glasgow, Glasgow Univ (BL), Edinburgh Univ; *m* 1 and 2; 1 s, 2 da; m 3, 4 March 1974, Jeanette Patricia Mairi, da of Sqdn Ldr James Mitchell Watson Stewart, MBE (d 1966), of Dimbula, Ceylon; 1 s (Ian Stewart b 26 Oct 1975); *Career* RAFVR 1946-48; called to the Scottish Bar 1954, advocate depute 1964, state advocate Zambia 1966, hon sheriff Lanarkshire 1968, called to the Canadian Bar 1982, sheriff of Strathclyde and Kelvin 1984 (resigned to return to private practice); chm fndr Castlewood Printers Ltd 1954, fndr chm Watchway Tst for young offenders 1988;; *Books* No Stone Unturned (1956), The Tinkers of the World (1958); *Recreations* sailing, oyster growing; *Style*— Ian Hamilton, Esq, QC; Parliament House, Edinburgh (☎ 031 226 2881, car phone 086 0820869)

HAMILTON, Hon Ion Henry James; s of 3 Baron Holmpatrick; *b* 12 June 1956; *Style*— The Hon Ion Hamilton

HAMILTON, James; CBE (1979), MP (Lab) Motherwell North 1983-; s of late George Hamilton, of Baillieston, Lanarkshire; *b* 11 Mar 1918; *Educ* St Bridget's, St Mary's HS; *m* 1945, Agnes, da of Constantine McGhee; 1 s (and 1 s decd), 3 da; *Career* Reconnaissance Corps 1939-46, constructional engr, pres Constructional Engineering Union 1968-, former county cllr Lanarkshire, MP (Lab) Bothwell 1964-83, asst govt whip 1969-70, oppn whip 1970-74, Lord Commr of the Treasury 1974; vice-chamberlain HM Household 1974-1978, comptroller 1978-79; former chm PLP trade union gp, memb Select Ctee on Selection; *Style*— James Hamilton, Esq, CBE, MP; 12 Rosegreen Crescent, Bellshill, Lanarkshire (☎ 0698 2071)

HAMILTON, Sir James Arnot; KCB (1978, CB 1972), MBE (1952); *b* 2 May 1923; *Educ* Lasswade Sch, Edinburgh Univ (BSc); *m* 1947 (m dis), Christine Mary, da of Robert McKean of Glasgow; 3 s; *Career* Marine Aircraft Establishment 1943-52 (head of Flight Research 1948), Royal Aircraft Estab 1952, head of Projects Div 1964; dir Anglo-French Combat Aircraft Miny of Aviation 1965, dir-gen Concorde Miny of Technology 1966-70, dep sec Dept of Trade and Industry 1971-73, dep sec Cabinet Office 1973-76, permanent sec Dept of Education and Science 1976-83; dir: Hawker Siddeley Gp 1983-; Smiths Industries 1984-; Devonport Royal Dockyard 1987-; memb Advisory Bd, Brown & Root (UK) Ltd; Tstee Br Museum (Natural History) 1984-88; vice-chm of cncl Univ Coll London 1985-; vice-pres of cncl Reading Univ 1985-; *Clubs* Athenaeum; *Style*— Sir James Hamilton, KCB, MBE; Pentlands, 9 Cedar Rd, Farnborough, Hants (☎ 0252 543254)

HAMILTON, Marquess of; James Harold Charles Hamilton; s and h of 5 Duke of Abercorn; *b* 19 August 1969; *Heir* bro, Lord Nicholas Hamilton; *Career* Page of Honour to HM The Queen 1982-84; *Style*— Marquess of Hamilton

HAMILTON, Hon James Leslie; s and h of 3 Baron Hamilton of Dalzell, GCVO, MC; *b* 11 Feb 1938; *Educ* Eton; *m* 29 March 1967, (Ann Anastasia) Corinna Helena, da of Sir Pierson John Dixon, GCMG, CB (d 1965), and sis of Piers Dixon, *qv*; 4 s (Gavin b 8 Oct 1968, Robert b 29 July 1971, John b (twin) 29 July 1971, Benjamin b 5 Nov 1974); *Career* 2 Lt Coldstream Gds 1956-58; memb Stock Exchange 1967-80; dir Rowton Hotels plc 1978-85; govr Queen Elizabeth's Fndn for the Disabled 1978- (chm of appeals 1980-88, chm of executive 1989); vice-chm Surrey branch CLA 1986-89, chm 1989; Freeman of City of London, Liveryman of Worshipful Co of Drapers 1977; Farmer; *Recreations* shooting; *Clubs* Boodle's, Pratt's; *Style*— The Hon James Hamilton; Stockton House, Norton Shifnal, Shropshire (☎ 095 271 270); Betchworth House, Betchworth, Surrey RH3 7AE (☎ 073 784 3324)

HAMILTON, Jeremy Ian Macaulay (Jim); s of Zachary Macaulay Hamilton (d 1986), of Roe Downs House, Medstead, Alton, and Pamela Lucie, *née* Robson (d 1983); *b* 6 Jan 1944; *Educ* Canford Sch, Bristol Univ (LLB); *m* 12 Mar 1977, Janet Lorna Joanna, da of David Morrice Man (d 1957) of Alresford, Hants; 2 s (James b 1977, Kit b 1979), 1 da (Nina b 1981); *Career* solr Beaumont & Son 1969-70, asst co sec Tioxide plc 1970-73, ptnr Grieveson Grant and Co 1980-85 (joined 1973); dir Kleinwort Benson Ltd 1986-; church warden; memb: Law Soc 1970; *Recreations* salmon and trout fishing, wine; *Style*— Jim Hamilton, Esq; Kleinwort Benson Ltd, 20 Fenchurch Street, EC3P 3DS, (☎ 01 623 8000)

HAMILTON, Adm Sir John Graham; GBE (1966, KBE 1963, CBE 1958), CB (1960); s of Col Ernest Graham Hamilton, CMG, DSO, MC (d 1950); *b* 12 July 1910; *Educ* RNC Dartmouth; *m* 1938, Dorothy Nina, da of Col John Eamer Turner, CMG, DSO (d 1955), of Sandhurst, Surrey; *Career* joined RN 1924, serv WWII, Capt 1949, Dep Dir Radio Equipment 1950-51, cmd 5 Destroyer Sqdn 1952-53, Dir of Naval Ordnance 1954-56, cmd HMS Newfoundland 1956-58, Rear Adm 1958, Naval Sec to First Lord of the Admiralty 1958-60, Flag Offr Flotillas (Home) 1960-62, Vice Adm 1961, Flag Offr Naval Air Command 1962-64, Adm 1964, C-in-C Mediterranean and C-in-C Allied Forces Mediterranean 1964-67, ret 1967; nat pres Inst of Marketing 1972-75; *Recreations* walking, climbing, photography; *Style*— Adm Sir John Hamilton, GBE, CB; Chapel Barn, Abbotsbury, Weymouth, Dorset DT3 4LF (☎ 0305-871507)

HAMILTON, Loudon Pearson; CB (1987); s of Vernon Hamilton (d 1980), of Glasgow, and Jean Mair (d 1987); *b* 12 Jan 1932; *Educ* Hutchesons' GS Glasgow, Glasgow Univ (MA); *m* 15 Aug 1956, Anna Mackinnon, da of Hugh Young (d 1955), of Glasgow; 2 s (Hugh Vernon b 1958, Gavin Patrick b 1964); *Career* Nat Serv 2 Lt RA 1954-55; Dept of Agric (Scottish Off) 1960, priv sec to Parly Under Sec of State for Scotland 1963-64, first sec Agric Br Embassy Copenhagen 1966-70, asst sec Dept of Agric and Fisheries for Scotland 1973-79, princ estabs offr Scottish Off 1979- 84, sec Dept of Agric and Fisheries for Scotland 1984-; memb Agric and Food Res Cncl 1984-; *Recreations* hillwalking, bad bridge; *Clubs* Royal Cwlth Soc; *Style*— Loudon Hamilton, Esq, CB; DAFS Pentland House, Robbs Loan, Edinburgh EH14 1TW (☎ 031 556 8400)

HAMILTON, Dr Michael; OBE (1988); s of Dr Archibald Hamilton (d 1939), of Clifton End, Manningham Lane, Bradford, Yorks, and Silvia, *née* Wolf (d 1971); *b* 17 Feb 1923; *Educ* Bradford GS, Epsom Coll, St Mary's Hosp Med Sch, Univ of London (MB BS, MD); *m* 23 Nov 1946, Jane, da of Dr Edgar Bernard Argles (d 1955), of Amersham, Bucks; 2 s (David b 1948, Ian b 1951), 1 da (Susan b 1961); *Career* Flt Lt (later Sqdn ldr) RAFVR serv acting med specialist RAF Nocton Hall;house physician St Mary's Sector Hosps 1945-46, sr med registrar St Mary's Hosp 1949-52, sr med registrar RPMS Hammersmith Hosp 1952-56; Nuffield travelling res fell: Alfred Hosp Melbourne 1954, Univ of OTAGO Dunedin 1955; conslt physician Chelmsford Hosps 1956-81, hon conslt physician Mid Essex Health Authry 1981-; examiner in med: Univ of Glasgow, Royal Coll of Physicians; former memb: Chelmsford Hosp Mgmnt Ctee, NE Thames Regnl Hosp Bd, Essex Area Health Authy, Mid Essex Dist Health Authy; memb: Int Soc of Hypertension 1966, BMA 1945; MRCP 1946, FRCP 1966, Assoc of Physicians 1966; *Books* Anti-Hypertensive Therapy (jtly, 1966), The Hypertensive Patients (jtly, 1980); *Recreations* gardening, golf; *Style*— Dr Michael Hamilton, OBE; The Chestnuts, 148 Main Rd, Great Leighs, Essex CM3 1NP, (☎ 0245 361263)

HAMILTON, Sir Michael Aubrey; s of Rt Rev Eric Hamilton, KCVO, sometime Bp Suffragan of Shrewsbury, Registrar of the Most Noble Order of the Garter and Dean of Windsor, by his w Jessie, da of Sir Walter Cassels; *b* 5 July 1918; *Educ* Radley, Univ Coll Oxford; *m* 16 May 1947, Lavinia, da of Sir Charles Ponsonby, 1 Bt, TD; 1 s, 3 da; *Career* served WW II 1 Bn Coldstream Gds; MP (C): Wellingborough 1959-64, Salisbury 1965-83; asst govt whip 1961-62, lord commissioner Treasury 1962-64; UK rep UN Gen Assembly 1970, US Bicentennial Celebrations 1976; pps to Francis Pym (Foreign Sec) 1982-83; kt 1983; *Style*— Sir Michael Hamilton; Lordington House, Chichester, W Sussex (☎ 024 34 371717);

HAMILTON, Michael John; s of William E Hamilton (d 1985), of Guelph, Canada, and Jean I, *née* Clark; *b* 24 Oct 1939; *Educ* Univ of Western Ontario (BA), Oxford Univ (MA); *m* 20 Sept 1967, Irena, da of Albert Rudusons (d 1962); 1 s (Andrew), 3 da (Katharine, Anna, Nina); *Career* jt md Mfrs Hanover Ltd 1969-73; exec dir: First Boston Corpn Europe Ltd 1973-78, Blyth Eastman Dillon Inc 1978-79; euro advsy bd memb Nippon Telephone and Telegraph Inc 1986-, md Wallace Smith Tst Co Ltd 1980-; tstee St Margaret's Residential Estate; *Recreations* tennis, opera, cottage; *Clubs* City of London; *Style*— Michael Hamilton, Esq; Wallace, Smith Trust Co Ltd, 77 London Wall, London EC2 (☎ 01 638 6444, fax 01 588 6470)

HAMILTON, (Mostyn) Neil; MP (C) Tatton 1983-; s of Ronald Hamilton, of Southsea, Hants, and Norma, *née* Jones; *b* 9 Mar 1949; *Educ* Amman Valley GS,Univ Coll Aberystwyth (BSc, MSc), CCC (LLB); *m* 1983, (Mary) Christine, da of Dr Edward Theodore Holman, of Manaccan, Cornwall; *Career* barr Middle Temple 1978; dir IOD 1982-83; contested (C): Abertillery 1974, Bradford N 1979; *Books* The Facts of State Industry, UK/US Double Taxation Treaty; *Recreations* book collecting, music, silence, gardening; *Style*— Neil Hamilton, Esq, MP; House of Commons, London SW1A 0AA (☎ 01 219 4157)

HAMILTON, Nigel John Mawdesley; QC (1981); s of Archibald Dearman Hamilton, OBE, of 21 Briant's Piece, Hermitage, nr Newbury, Berks, and Joan Worsley, *née* Mawdesley; *b* 13 Jan 1938; *Educ* St Edward's Sch Oxford, Queens' Coll Cambridge (BA, MA); *m* 31 Aug 1963, Leone Morag Elizabeth, da of William Smith Gordon, CBE; 2 s (Andrew b 5 Oct 1966, William b 5 May 1970); *Career* Nat Serv RE 2 Lt; asst master: St Edward's Oxford 1961-65, King's Sch Canterbury 1963-65; barr Inner Temple 1965, Western circuit; *Recreations* fishing; *Clubs* Flyfishers'; *Style*— Nigel Hamilton, Esq, QC; St Johns' Chambers, Small St, Bristol, BS1 1DW (☎ 0272 213456, fax 0272 294 821); 1 Essex Ct, Temple, London EC4Y 9AR (☎ 01 583 7759, fax 01 363 8650)

HAMILTON, Sir Patrick George; 2 Bt (UK 1937), of Ilford, co Essex; s of Maj Sir (Collingwood) George Clements Hamilton, 1 Bt (d 1947), and Eleanor (d 1957), eld da of Henry Simon, of Manchester; *b* 17 Nov 1908; *Educ* Eton, Trinity Coll Oxford; *m* 17

Oct 1941, Winifred Mary Stone (Pix), CBE, MA, Cantab and an assoc of Newnham, fndr chm Disabled Living Fndn and of Winged Fellowship Tst, memb exec cncl Royal Assoc for Disablement and Rehabilitation (Radar), da of late Hammond B Jenkins, of Maddings, Hadstock; *Heir* none; *Career* md and later chm Tyresoles Ltd 1934-53; dir: Simon Engineering Ltd 1937-78, Propellor Production Miny of Aircraft Prodn 1941-43, Renold Ltd 1952-78, Lloyds Bank Ltd 1953-79, Possum Controls Ltd; chm Expanded Metal Co Ltd 1955-78; tstee: Eleanor Hamilton Educational Trust, Disabled Living Fndn, Charitable Tst, Sidbury Tst; *Clubs* Carlton; *Style*— Sir Patrick Hamilton, Bt; 21 Madingley Rd, Cambridge CB3 0EG (☎ 0223 351577)

HAMILTON, Peter Boris; *b* 17 Oct 1928; *Educ* Bedford Sch, St Andrews Univ, Harvard Univ (MBA); *m* 1953, Gwendolen Mary, *née* Clark; 1 s (Michael), 1 da (Susan); *Career* Pilot Offr RAF; chm and chief exec: Firth Cleveland Ltd 1977-79; GKN Engineering and Construction Services 1978-79; gp chief exec APV Holdings plc 1980-; *Recreations* sailing (sloop 'Moorea II'), skiing, photography, politics; *Clubs* Royal Yacht Sqdn, Royal Thames Yacht, Royal Southampton Yacht; *Style*— Peter Hamilton, Esq; 31 Chantry View Rd, Guildford, Surrey GU1 3XW (☎ 0483 65318); APV Holdings plc, APV House, Station Way, Crawley, West Sussex RH10 2QB (☎ 0293 27777, telex 87237)

HAMILTON, Maj Peter James Sidney; MBE (1953); s of Maj Frank Carr Hamilton (d 1946), late RGA, of Bishop's Stortford, Herts, and Alice Joan, *née* Trumper (d 1973); *b* 19 Nov 1917; *Educ* Bishop's Stortford Coll; *m* 1962, Patricia Douglas, da of Robert Hirst (d 1940), of Croydon; 2 s (Andrew, Hamish), 2 da (Rosamund, Penelope); *Career* served WW II N Africa, Palestine, Iraq, India, Burma, China, Malaya, Cyprus, attained rank of Maj; banker 1936-38; instructor Mons Officer Cadet School 1951-54, Cyprus 1957-60; security advsr to PM of S Rhodesia 1961-62; dir Chubb Security Services Ltd 1962-78; md Zeus Security Consultants Ltd 1978-83, dep chm Zeus Security Ltd 1980-83; md Peter Hamilton (Security Conslts) Ltd 1983-; twice chm American Soc for Industrial Security (Euro Chapter); hon fellow Inst of Professional Investigators, hon memb Br Security Industry Assoc, Assoc Memb Nat Supervisory Cncl for Intruder Alarms; FRSA, FIPI, FInstD; *Books* editor Handbook of Security; *Publications* Espionage Terrorism and Subversion in an Industrial Society (1968 and 1980), Computer Security (1972), Business Security (1980); The Adminstration of Corporate Security (1987); several works translated into Japanese, Finnish and Italian; *Recreations* country life, fishing; *Clubs* Athenaeum, Army and Navy; *Style*— Maj Peter Hamilton, MBE; 37-39 Eastcheap, London EC3M 1DT (☎ 01 623 9913)

HAMILTON, Sir (Robert Charles) Richard Caradoc; 9 Bt (NS 1646), of Silvertonhill, Lanarkshire; s of Sir Robert Hamilton, 8 Bt (d 1959), and Irene (d 1969), 2 da of Sir Charles Mordaunt, 10 Bt; *b* 8 Sept 1911; *Educ* Charterhouse, St Peter's Coll Oxford; *m* 16 April 1952, Elizabeth Vidal, da of Sir William Pell Barton, KCIE, CSI, formerly of Lower Lodge, Ardingly, Sussex; 1 s (Andrew), 3 da (Susanna b 1956, Sophie b 1964, Penelope b 1966); *Heir* s, Andrew Caradoc Hamilton; *Career* Intelligence Corps 1940-45; taught French and Drama at Ardingly Coll 1945-61; church warden Walton d'Eivile 1970-; Warwickshire Co Cncl Educn Ctee 1965-73; Govr Westham House Adult Educn Coll; memb Warwickshire CLA; plays acted at Margate, Dundee and Farnham Reps, five Shakespeare plays directed at the Minack Theatre; landowner (4000 acres); *Publications* Translation of A de Luze's La Magnifique Histoire du Jeu de Paume, Barcellon's Règles et Principes de Paume; *Recreations* real tennis, playwright; *Style*— Sir Richard Hamilton, Bt; The Old Rectory, Walton, Warwick CV35 9HX (☎ 0789 840460)

HAMILTON, His Hon Judge Richard Graham; s of Henry Augustus Rupert Hamilton (d 1970), and Frances Mary Graham, *née* Abercrombie; *b* 26 August 1932; *Educ* Charterhouse, Univ Coll Oxford (MA); *m* 16 April 1960, Patricia Craghill, da of Willian Newton Ashburner (d 1954); 1 s (William Graham b 1963), 1 da (Susan Elizabeth b 1965); *Career* recorder of Crown Court 1974, chllr of Diocese of Liverpool 1976; *Books* Foul Bills and Dagger Money (1979), All Jangle and Riot (1986), A Good Wigging (1988), *radio plays* Van Gogh in England (1981), Voices from Babylon (1983), A Longing for Dynamite (1984); *Recreations* reading, walking, films; *Clubs* Athenaeum, Liverpool; *Style*— His Hon Judge Hamilton

HAMILTON, Robert Abraham; CBE (1971); s of Isaac Hamilton (d 1955), of Annalong, Co Down; *b* 5 Feb 1909; *Educ* Royal Belfast Academical Inst, Queen's Univ Belfast (BSc, BAgr), Fitzwilliam Hall Cambridge (DipAgric), Imperial Coll of Tropical Agric; *m* 1935, Caroline Dorothea, da of Henry Adams (d 1934), of Belfast; 2 s; *Career* dir: Central Agric Control Board ICI Ltd 1944-58, Pharmaceutical Div ICI Ltd 1955-60, Billingham Div ICI Ltd 1958-64, Scottish Agric Industries Ltd 1959-64, W & HM Goulding Ltd 1964-71; dep chm Agric Div ICI Ltd 1964-71; chm: Plant Protection Ltd, Richardsons Fertilisers Ltd, Ulster Fertilisers Ltd 1964-71, Northern Ireland Agric Trust 1967-74, NI Tourist Board 1970-75, Pigs Marketing Board Investment Company 1971-77, Unipork Ltd 1976-78; pres Société Pour La Protection de L'Agriculture (Paris) 1967-71; snr pro-chllr Queen's Univ Belfast 1980-; Hon DSc Queen's Univ 1973; *Recreations* gardening, travelling; *Clubs* Ulster, Farmers'; *Style*— Robert Hamilton, Esq, CBE; 3 Rathbeg Ave, Coleraine, N Ireland BT51 3JL (☎ 0265 51956)

HAMILTON, Thomas Gottfried Louis; s of Louis Hamilton (d 1948), of 77 Ladbroke Grove, London W11, and Johanna Agnes Lucia, *née* Jahn (d 1956); *b* 29 Mar 1930; *Educ* The Kings Sch Canterbury, UCL (BA); *m* 23 March 1957, Georgina Vera, da of Hugh Millen Craig (d 1956), of 3 Rose Park East, Belfast; 1 s (Richard b 1964), 1 da (Julia b 1962); *Career* asst architect Bertram Carter 1956-58, Campbell-Jones & Ptnrs 1958-60, ptnr Hammett & Norton 1960-64, fndr ptnr McDonald Hamilton & Montefiore 1964-86 (dir 1986-); ctee memb Norland Conservation Soc; memb RIBA; *Recreations* painting, theatre, music, literature, winter sports; *Clubs* Arts; *Style*— Thomas Hamilton, Esq; 55 Addison Ave, London W11 4QU; Dorking Tye Cottage, Dorking Tye, Bures, Suffolk CO8 5JY; 102 Jermyn St, London SW1Y 6EE (☎ 01 930 3381, fax 01 839 1085)

HAMILTON, William Herbert; OBE (1979); s of Edward Hamilton (d 1973), and Margaret, *née* O'Brady Jones (d 1957); *b* 24 Jan 1924; *Educ* Trowbridge Boys' HS, Rutherford Tech Coll, South Shields Marine Sch; *m* 1950, Leonora, da of John Palmer Morrison (d 1967); 1 s (Richard), 2 da (Barbara, Kathleen); *Career* Hon 2 Lt Northumberland Fus 1946; md Gulf Oil (GB) Ltd 1979-81, vice-pres Gulf Oil Co (Eastern Hemisphere) 1981-83; ret; CEng; *Style*— William Hamilton, Esq, OBE

HAMILTON, Willie - William Winter; MP (Lab) Fife Central 1974-87; s of J Hamilton, of Philadelphia, Co Durham; *b* 26 June 1917; *Educ* Washington GS, & Alderman Smith GS both Co Durham, Sheffield Univ (BA, DipEd); *m* 1, 1944, Joan Callow (d 1968), of Cumberland; 1 s, 1 da; m 2, 1982, Mrs Margaret Cogle, of Newcastle-Upon-Tyne; *Career* serv WWII Middle East with RAF and Capt Pioneer Corps; joined Labour Pty 1936, contested (Lab) W Fife 1945, MP (Lab) W Fife 1950-74; chm House of Commons Estimates Ctee 1964-70, vice-chm PLP 1966-70, chm Rules & Procedure Ctee 1975-76 (vice-chm 1976-79), memb Public Accounts Ctee 1979-; MEP 1975-79; noted for anti-monarchy views; sponsered MP for COHSE former schoolmaster; *Books* My Queen and I (1975); *Recreations* Baiting Establishment and other Public Menaces; *Style*— Willie Hamilton Esq

HAMILTON AND BRANDON, 15 and 12 Duke of (S 1643, GB 1711); Angus Alan Douglas Douglas-Hamilton; also Earl of Arran (S 1389), Marquess of Douglas, Lord Abernethy and Jedburgh Forest (both S 1633), Marquess of Clydesdale, Earl of Arran and Cambridge, Lord Aven and Innerdale (all S 1643), Earl of Lanark, Lord Machansire and Polmont (both S 1661), Baron Dutton (GB 1711); Premier Duke in the Peerage of Scotland; Hereditary Keeper of Holyrood House; s of 14 and 11 Duke of Hamilton and Brandon, KT, GCVO, AFC, PC (d 1973), and Dowager, Duchess of Hamilton and Brandon, *qv*; *b* 13 Sept 1938; *Educ* Eton, Balliol Coll Oxford (MA); *m* 1, 1972 (m dis 1987), Sarah, da of Sir Walter Scott, 4 Bt; 2 s (Alexander b 1978, John b 1979), 2 da (Eleanor b 1973, Anne b 1976); m 2, 1988, Jillian, da of Noel Robertson, formerly w of (1) Martin Page, and (2) Edward Hulton; *Heir* s, Alexander, Marquess of Douglas and Clydesdale b 1978; *Career* Fl Lt RAF to 1967, flying instructor 1965, Instrument Rating Examiner 1966, sr commercial pilot's license 1968, test pilot Scottish Aviation 1971-72; KStJ and Prior Order of St John in Scotland 1975-83, hon memb Royal Scottish Pipers Soc, patron British Airways Pipe Band 1977, Hon Air Cdre No 2 (City of Edinburgh) Maritime HQ Unit RAuxAf 1982-; chm Hamilton & Kinneil Estates Ltd 1973; memb The Queen's Body Guard for Scotland (Royal Co of Archers); *Recreations* motorcycling, piping, Scottish history; *Clubs* New (Edinburgh), RAF; *Style*— His Grace the Duke of Hamilton and Brandon; Lennoxlove, Haddington, E Lothian (☎ 062 082 3720)

HAMILTON AND BRANDON, Dowager Duchess of; Lady Elizabeth Ivy; *née* Percy; OBE, DL; da of 8 Duke of Northumberland, KG, CBE, MVO (d 1930); *b* 25 May 1916; *m* 2 Dec 1937, 14 Duke of Hamilton and (11 of) Brandon, KT, GCVO, AFC, PC (d 1973); 5 s (including 15 Duke); *Style*— Her Grace the Dowager Duchess of Hamilton and Brandon, OBE, DL; North Port, Lennoxlove, Haddington, E Lothian (☎ 062 082 2478)

HAMILTON OF DALZELL, 3 Baron (UK 1886); John d'Henin Hamilton; GCVO (1987, KCVO 1981), MC (1945), JP (Guildford 1957); s of Maj Hon Leslie Hamilton, MVO, Coldstream Gds (ka 1914, bro of 2 Baron, KT, CVO, MC, who d 1952), and Amy, da of Col Horace Ricardo, CVO, Gren Gds, of Bramley Park, Surrey; *b* 1 May 1911; *Educ* Eton, Sandhurst; *m* 4 March 1935, Rosemary Olive, da of Hon Sir John Coke, KCVO (d 1957; 5 s of 2 Earl of Leicester, KG, JP, DL, by his 2 w, Hon Georgina Cavendish, da of 2 Baron Chesham), and Hon Dorothy Levy-Lawson, only child of 1 and last Viscount (and 2 Baron) Burnham, GCMG, CH; 2 s, 1 da; *Heir* s, Hon James Leslie Hamilton; *Career* Maj Coldstream Gds, served 1931-37 (Palestine 1936) and 1939-45 (NW Europe 1944-45); farmer; Lord-Lieut Surrey 1973-86 (vice-lt 1957-73, DL 1957); chm Ld Chllr's Ctee Legal Aid 1972-79; lord-in-waiting to HM The Queen 1968-81; *Style*— The Rt Hon the Lord Hamilton of Dalzell, GCVO, MC, JP; Garden Cottage, Snowdenham House, Bramley, Guildford, Surrey GU5 0DB (☎ 0483 892002)

HAMILTON-DALRYMPLE, Lady Anne-Louise Mary; *née* Keppel; da of 9 Earl of Albemarle, MC, and his 2 w, Dame Diana Grove, DBE (*see* Countess of Albemarle); *b* 17 Mar 1932; *m* 25 Sept 1954, Maj Sir Hew Fleetwood Hamilton-Dalrymple, 10 Bt, KCVO, *qv*; 4 s; *Style*— Lady Anne-Louise Hamilton-Dalrymple; Leuchie, North Berwick, East Lothian (☎ 0620 2903)

HAMILTON-DALRYMPLE, Sir Hew Fleetwood; 10 Bt (NS 1698), of North Berwick, Haddingtonshire; KCVO (1985, CVO 1974), JP (1987); s of Sir Hew Clifford Hamilton-Dalrymple, 9 Bt (d 1959), and Anne Dorothea Dyce Nicol, *née* Thorne (d 1979); *b* 9 April 1926; *Educ* Ampleforth; *m* 25 Sept 1954, Lady Anne-Louise Mary Keppel, *qv*; 4 s (Hew Richard, John James b 1957, Robert George b 1959, William Benedict b 1965); *Heir* s, Hew Richard Hamilton-Dalrymple; *Career* Maj Gren Gds, ret 1962; Lt Queen's Body Guard for Scotland (Royal Co of Archers), Adjt 1964-85; pres cncl Scottish & Newcastle Breweries 1988- (vice-chm 1983-86); dir Scottish American Investment Co 1967- (chm 1985-); DL East Lothian 1964-87; vice-lieut East Lothian 1973-87; Lord Lieutenant East Lothian 1987-; *Clubs* Cavalry and Guards'; *Style*— Sir Hew Hamilton-Dalrymple, Bt, KCVO, JP, DL; Leuchie, North Berwick, East Lothian (☎ 0620 2903)

HAMILTON-DALRYMPLE, Hew Richard; s and h of Sir Hew Hamilton-Dalrymple, 10 Bt; *b* 3 Sept 1955; *Educ* Ampleforth, Corpus Christi Coll Oxford (MA), Clare Hall Cambridge (MPhil), Birkbeck Coll London (MSc); *Career* Overseas Development Inst Fellowship Swaziland 1982-84, Peat Marwick Management Consultants 1984-; *Style*— Hew Dalrymple Esq; 1 Puddle Dock, London EC4 (☎ 01 236 8000)

HAMILTON-GRIERSON, Philip John; s of Philip Francis Hamilton Grierson (d 1963), of Edinburgh, and Margaret Bartholomew (d 1969); *b* 10 Oct 1932; *Educ* Rugby Sch, CCC Oxford (MA); *m* 1963, Pleasaunce Jill, da of Peter Gordon Cardew, of Somerset; 1 s (Philip b 1967), 2 da (Sophie b 1964, Katherine b 1966); *Career* pilot offr RAF (asst adjutant 207 AFS); sec to Lib Party 1962-65; dir: Gallaher Ltd 1978-88, dep chm Highlands and Islands Devpt Bd 1988-, chm Highland Hospice Ltd 1988-, dir: Cromarty Firth Port Authority 1989-; *Recreations* tennis, music, sailing; *Clubs* Highland; *Style*— Philip Hamilton-Grierson, Esq; Pitlundie, North Kessock, By Inverness 1V1 1XG (☎ 0463 73 392); Highland and Island Development Board, Bridge St, Inverness 1V1 1QR (☎ 0463 234 171)

HAMILTON-MOORE, Sophie Mary; da of Maj-Gen Claude Douglas Hamilton-Moore, CB, CMG, DSO (d 1928), and Jessie Gladys, *née* Chamberlain; *b* 14 July 1914; *Educ* Royal Sch for Daughters of Army Offrs; *Career* FANY 1937-38, ATS 1939-45; local govt offr CD 1964-67, boarding cattery prop 1968-81; boarding cattery offr Feline Advsy Bureau 1969-; *Books* Cattery Construction and Management (1972); *Recreations* reading, gardening, animal welfare; *Style*— Miss Sophie Hamilton-Moore; 1 Church Close, Orcheston, nr Salisbury, Wilts (☎ 0980 620251)

HAMILTON-RUSSELL, Hon Gustavus Michael Stucley; s and h of 10 Viscount Boyne, JP, DL; *b* 27 May 1965; *Educ* Harrow; *Clubs* Turf; *Style*— The Hon Gustavus

HAMILTON-RUSSELL, Col James Gustavus; MBE (1976); s of Maj Hon John Hamilton-Russell (ka 1943), and Lady Diana, *née* Legge (d 1970); *b* 11 Sept 1938; *Educ* Eton; *m* 30 Oct 1965, Alison Mary, da of Dr Sydney Haydn Heard, MBE, of Channel Islands; 2 s (Mark b 1969, Edward b 1969), 1 da (Julia b 1967); *Career* Col; cmmnd Royal Dragoons 1958; served Middle East, Far East, Europe 1958-78; mil asst to Dep Supreme Allied Cdr Europe Shape 1978-80; CO The Blues and Royals 1980-82; Cdr: Household Cavalry and Silver Stick-in-Waiting 1983-86, Br Contingent UN Force in Cyprus 1986-88, asst mil attaché Br Embassy Washington 1988-; *Recreations* shooting, fishing, travel, golf, music; *Clubs* Cavalry and Guards'; *Style—* Colonel James G Hamilton-Russell, MBE; The Brewhouse, Budmaston, Bridgnorth, Shropshire (☎ 0746 780094); British Defence Staff, British Embassy, Washington DC

HAMILTON-RUSSELL, Hon Richard Gustavus; DSO (1943, and bar 1944), LVO (4 Class 1977), DL (N Yorks 1973); 2 s of 9 Viscount Boyne, JP, DL; *b* 4 Feb 1909; *Educ* Eton, RMC Sandhurst; *m* 17 July 1939, Hon Pamela Cayzer (d 1987), da of 1 Baron Rotherwick; 2 s (Brian, Richard), 1 da (Veronica); *Career* served WWII N Africa & Italy (despatches 1945); Brig late 17/21 Lancers (Col 1957-65); memb HM's Body Guard of Hon Corps of Gentlemen at Arms 1956-79 (standard bearer 1977); High Sheriff Yorks 1968; *Clubs* Cavalry and Guards'; *Style—* Brig the Hon Richard Hamilton Russell, DSO LVO, DL; South Hill House, Cornbury Park, Charlbury, Oxfordshire OX7 3EU

HAMILTON-SMITH, Hon Timothy; s of late 2 Baron Colwyn; *b* 28 June 1944; *Educ* Cheltenham, Oxford Univ (MA); *m* 29 July 1967, Carolyn, da of Bernulf Llewelyn Hodge; 2 da; *Style—* The Hon Timothy Hamilton-Smith; 45 Third Ave, Claremont 7700, S Africa

HAMILTON-TEMPLE-BLACKWOOD, Lady Perdita Maureen; yr da of late 4 Marq of Dufferin and Ava (ka 1945); *b* 17 July 1934; *Career* racehorse breeder; *Style—* Lady Perdita Hamilton-Temple-Blackwood

HAMILTON-TURNER, William Allen; s of Claude Frederic Hamilton-Turner (d 1988), of Castletown, IOM, and Mary Eileen, *née* Allen; *b* 16 July 1947; *Educ* Eton; *m* 4 Dec 1976, Dulcie Jill, da of Herbert Secretan Procter, of Balla Salla, IOM; 1 s (Henry b 1978), 1 da (Lucy b 1980); *Career* Brown Shipley & Co Ltd 1966-74, Singer & Friedlander (IOM) Ltd 1974-80, md Rea Bros (IOM) Ltd 1980-; Hon ADC to HE The Lieut Govr of the Isle of Man; Freeman City of London, Liveryman Worshipful Co of Skinners; ACIB 1972; *Recreations* golf; *Clubs* MCC; *Style—* William Hamilton-Turner, Esq; Ballaquayle, Princes Rd, Douglas, IOM (☎ 0624 24063); 29 Athol St, Douglas, IOM (☎ 0624 29696, fax 0624 22039, telex 627752)

HAMILTON-WEDGWOOD, Kenneth Roy; s of Thomas Hamilton-Wedgwood (d 1978), of Rustington, W Sussex, and Elsie Maude, *née* Kershaw (d 1978); *b* 11 Dec 1931; *Educ* Warwick and Whitgift Schs; *m* 19 May 1973 (m dis 1979), Rita, da of George William Gransden, of Hyde Home Farm, East Hyde, Luton, Bedfordshire; *Career* conslt/tech author (electronics) Environmental Instrumentation Satellite Data Collection (Argos) Oceanography; Nat Serv RAF; SAC airborne wireless communciations early experimental decca navigator 1950-52; with Whessoe Ltd Darlington Co Durham, resident engr i/c instrumentation installation; data measurement and transmission system for Esso West London Terminal, bulk fuel storage 1960-67; with Ultra Electronics London 1968-69; Marine Electronics Ltd 1971-72; *Recreations* fully licensed radio amateur G3XKW, country walking, music, photography; *Style—* Kenneth Hamilton-Wedgwood, Esq; Rosedale, Redmoor, Bodmin, Cornwall PL30 5AR (☎ 0208 872608); Partech Electronics Ltd, Eleven Doors, Charlestown, St Austell, Cornwall PL25 3NN (☎ 0726 74856, telex 45362 G a/G PARTEK, fax 0726 68850)

HAMMENT, Hon Mrs (Tania Ann); *née* Campbell; eldest da of 6 Baron Stratheden and Campbell, *qv*; *b* 19 Sept 1960; *m* 1984, Paul Hamment; c/o The Rt Hon Lord Stratheden and Campbell, Ridgewood, MS 1064, Cooroy, Queensland 4563, Australia

HAMMER, James Dominic George; CB (1983); s of E A G Hammer and E L G Hammer; *b* 21 April 1929; *Educ* Dulwich, Corpus Christi Coll Cambridge; *m* 1955, Margaret Eileen Halse; two s 1 da; *Career* dep dir gen Health & Safety Exec, vice chm Camberwell Health Authy, pres Int Assoc of Labour Insprs; *Style—* James Hammer, Esq, CB; Health and Safety Executive, Baynards House, 1 Chepstow Place, London W2 4TF

HAMMER, Rev Canon Dr Raymond Jack; s of Mendel Paul Hammer (d 1968), and Lily, *née* Simons (d 1972); *b* 4 July 1920; *Educ* Liverpool Inst, Oxford Univ (BA, Dip Theol, MA), London Univ (BD, MTheol, PhD); *m* 23 July 1949, Vera Winifred, da of Charles Thomas Reed (d 1947), of Hayes, Middx; 2 da (Alison b 1954, Elizabeth b 1956); *Career* ordained: deacon 1943, priest 1944; sr tutor St John's Coll Durham 1946-49, lectr in theology Univ of Durham 1946-49; prof: Central Theological Coll Tokyo 1950-64, St Paul's Univ Tokyo 1954-64; chaplain Br Embassy Tokyo 1954-64, lectr The Queen's Coll Birmingham 1965-77; lectr dept of theology Univ of Birmingham 1965-77;dir: W Midlands Ministry Course 1971-76, Bible Reading Fellowship 1977-85; tutor Open Univ 1978-85; external examiner for London, Warwick, Southampton and Exeter Univs; canon St Michael's Cathedral Kobe Japan 1964-; sec Archbishops' Interfaith Conslts 1981-, tres Studiorum Novi Testamenti societas 1970-82; memb: SNTS, SOTS, SST; *Books* Japan's Religious Ferment, Commentary on Daniel, Oxford Dictionary of the Christian Church (contrib), Theological Word Book of the Bible; New Testament Editor Times Bible Atlas; contrib to: Shorter Books of the Apocrypha, Man and His Gods, Concise Dictionary of the Bible, Concise Dictionary of Christian Mission, World Religions; *Recreations* travel; *Clubs* Athenaeum, Sion Coll; *Style—* The Rev Canon Dr Raymond Hammer; 22 Midsummer Meadow, Inkberrow, Worcs WR7 4HD (☎ 0386 792 883)

HAMMERSLEY, Rear Adm Peter Gerald; CB (1982), OBE (1965); s of the late Capt Robert Stevens Hammersley, of Endon Stoke-on-Trent, and Norah, *née* Kirkham; *b* 18 May 1928; *Educ* Denstone Coll, RN Engrg Coll, RNC Coll Greenwich, Imperial Coll (DIC); *m* 1959, (Audrey) Cynthia Henderson, da of Pelham Bolton, of Wilmslow Cheshire; 1 s (Robert), 1 da (Daphne); *Career* RN 1946-82, First Engr Offr First Br Nuclear Submarine HMS Dreadnought 1960-64, Capt RN Engrg Coll 1978-80, CSO (Engrg) to C-in-C Fleet 1980-82; dir Br Marine Equipment Cncl 1985; chief exec Br Internal Combustion Engine Mfrs Assoc 1982-85; Master Worshipful Co of Engrs; *Recreations* walking, gardening; *Clubs* Army and Navy; *Style—* Rear Adm Peter Hammersley, CB, OBE; Wistaria Cottage, Linersh Wood, Bramley, nr Guildford, Surrey GU5 0EE (☎ 0483 898568); BMEC, 32/38 Leman St, London E1 8EW (☎ 01 488 0171)

HAMMERTON, His Hon Judge Rolf Eric; s of Eric Maurice Hammerton (d 1967), and Dorothea Alic, *née* Zander (d 1970); *b* 18 June 1926; *Educ* Brighton GS, Peterhouse Cambridge (MA, LLB); *m* 1953, Thelma Celéstine, da of Vernon Peters Appleyard (d 1955); 1 s (Alastair Rolf b 1960), 3 da (Veronica Lesley b 1954, Andrea Frances b 1956, Lorraine Hilary b 1958); *Career* Capt R Sussex Regt seconded RWAFF 1946-48; barr Inner Temple 1952, circuit judge 1972, contrib to Butterworth Co Ct Precedents; Philip Teichman Prizeman 1953; *Recreations* cooking; *Style—* His Hon Judge Hammerton; The Old Rectory, Falmer, nr Brighton BN1 9PG

HAMMETT, Sir Clifford James; s of late Frederick John Hammett; *b* 8 June 1917; *Educ* Woodbridge Sch; *m* 1946, Olive Beryl, da of Frank A Applebee; 4 s, 1 da; *Career* serv WWII 1 Punjab Regt (despatches), POW Siam Railway 1942-45; barr Middle Temple 1948, chief justice: Tonga 1956-68, Fiji 1967-72; acting govr-gen Fiji 1971; kt 1969; *Style—* Sir Clifford Hammett; c/o Lloyds Bank, 6 Pall Mall, London SW1

HAMMICK, Charles Cyril Willmott; s of Henry Alexander Hammick, OBE, MC (d 1968), and Mabel Emily, *née* Pilditch; gs of Sir Murray Hammick KCSI, CIE, govr of Madras, and of Sir Philip Pilditich, 1 Bt; *Educ* Sherborne; *m* 1, 1953 (m dis 1959), Mary Rose, da of Col W H Crichton, CIE (d 1983); 1 s (Piers b 1954), 1 da (Charlotte b 1956); m 2, 1960, Georgina, da of Maj-Gen G D G Heyman, CB, CBE (d 1961); 1 s (Thomas b 1963), 2 da (Kate b 1965, Rose b 1970); m 3, Carol Elspeth, da of Brig Richard Montagu Villiers, DSO, (d 1973) and formerly w of Gerald Charles Mordaunt; *Career* cmmnd Grenadier Gds 1946, Gds Parachute Battn Palestine 1946-48, Trucial Oman Scouts 1957-59, W Africa (Cameroons) 1963, ret Maj 1964; fndr Hammick's Bookshops 1968 (chm 1968-87), dir Assoc Book Publishers plc 1978-87; chm Cromwells Chocolatiers Ltd 1987; ACIS; *Recreations* riding, pedigree sheep farming; *Clubs* Garrick; *Style—* Charles Hammick, Esq; Higher Waterston Farm, Dorchester DT2 7SW (☎ 0305 848208); (fax 0305 848 894)

HAMMICK, Paul St Vincent; s and h of Sir Stephen George Hammick, 5 Bt; *b* 1 Jan 1955; *Educ* Sherborne; *m* 11 July 1984, Judith Mary, da of Ralph Ernest Reynolds, of Wareham, Dorset; *Style—* Paul Hammick Esq

HAMMICK, Sir Stephen George; 5 Bt (UK 1834); s of Sir George Frederick Hammick, 4 Bt (d 1964), and Mary Adeliza, *née* Welch-Thornton (d 1988); *b* 27 Dec 1926; *Educ* Stowe, RAC Cirencester; *m* 16 April 1953, Gillian Elizabeth, da of Maj Pierre Elliot Inchbald, MC (d 1959); 2 s (Paul b 1955, Jeremy b 1956), 1 da (Wendy b 1960); *Heir* s, Paul St Vincent Hammick; *Career* RN 1944-48, RAC Cirencester 1949-50, MFH Cattistock Hunt 1961 and 1962, CC Dorset 1958, farmer; high sheriff Dorset 1981; vice-chm Dorset CC, chm 1988; chm Cattistock Hunt; *Recreations* hunting, fishing, music; *Style—* Sir Stephen Hammick, Bt; Badgers, Wraxall, Dorchester, Dorset DT2 OHN (☎ 093583 343)

HAMMON, Michael Antony; s of Arthur Stanley Hammon (d 1985), of Leam Bank Farm, Wappenbury, Leamington Spa, and Mary Augusta, *née* Salter; *b* 5 Mar 1937; *Educ* Oundle; *m* 8 Oct 1966, Letitia Sara, da of Henry Leslie Johnson, of Offchurch Bury, Leamington Spa; 2 s (Charles b 1969, George b 1973), 2 da (Sara b 1970, Elizabeth b 1972); *Career* slr and farmer; memb: Warwick RDC 1965-70, Warwickshire CC 1967-81 (chm Fin Educn and Policy and Resources Ctees, ldr of cncl 1976-81); memb Coventry City Cncl 1987-; vice-chm Warwick, Leamington and Kenilworth Cons Assoc 1970-73; lawyer memb W Midlands Rent Assessment Panel 1982-86; press and PR offr Warwickshire Law Soc 1984-; dir: Edenhurst Court (Torquay) Ltd, H H Goddard Ltd, Eathorpe Hall Farms Ltd, Marath Devpts Ltd; *Recreations* gardening, photography; *Clubs* Naval and Military; *Style—* Michael Hammon, Esq; Eathorpe Hall, Leamington Spa CV33 9DF (☎ 0926 632755); Lloyd's Bank Chambers, 53 Corporation St, Coventry CV11GL (☎ 0203 27537)

HAMMOND, Col Catherine Elizabeth; CBE (1950); da of late Frank Ernest Rauleigh Eddolls; *b* 22 Dec 1909; *Educ* Lassington House Highworth, Chesterville Sch Cirencester; *m* 1, 1930, Albert Edward Haynes (decd); 1 s, 1 da; m 2, 1949, Aldwyn Hammond (d 1958), farmer and racehorse trainer; *Career* Col WRAC, dep dir HQ Eastern Command 1947-50, Hon Col 54 (E Anglian) Div/Dist WRAC (TA) 1964-68; chm WRAC Assoc Cncl 1966-70, life vice-pres WRAC Assoc 1971-; chm Highworth Branch RNLI 1971-; pres: Highworth Royal Br Legion (Women's Section) 1977-86, Highworth Amateur Dramatic Soc 1982-86; town mayor Highworth 1979-81 and 1984-85; 5 S St J 1986; *Recreations* racing, hockey; *Style—* Col Mrs Catherine Hammond, CBE; Red Down, Highworth, Wilts (☎ 0793 762331)

HAMMOND, Donald William; s of Capt Eric Gardiner Hammond, of Bollington, and Mabel Joyce, *née* Buck; *b* 5 Mar 1948; *Educ* King's Sch Macclesfield, Univ of Lancaster (BA), Manchester Business Sch (DBA); *m* 19 March 1982, Carole Isobel Hammond; *Career* Turner & Newall Ltd 1969-73, account exec Citibank NA 1974-76, Banco Hispano Americano Ltd 1976-86; dir: Edington plc 1986-, Henry Cooke Lumsden plc 1988-, Henry Cooke Gp plc 1988-, William Hammond Ltd (currently); chm various schs in Ealing 1978-86, chm fin and dep ldr London Borough of Ealing 1983-86 (cncllr 1978-86); FInstD, assoc MBA; *Recreations* riding, shooting, chess, reading science fiction; *Style—* Donald Hammond, Esq; The Butts, Smithy Lane, Gt Budworth, Ches; No 1 King St, Manchester (☎ 061 834 2535, fax 061 834 8650, car 0860 326948)

HAMMOND, Eric Albert Barratt; OBE (1977); s of Arthur Edgar Hammond (d 1963), and Gertrude May, *née* Barratt (d 1983); *b* 17 July 1929; *Educ* Corner Brook Sch Newfoundland; *m* 26 Sept 1953, Brenda Mary, da of George Edgeler; 2 s (Ivan b 1958, Shaun b 1961); *Career* Nat Serv REME 1950-52; EETPU: electrician 1952-64, exec cncllr 1964-84, gen sec 1984-; chm 5 N Fleet Scout Gp 1979-84; cncllr: Northfleet UDC 1960-63, Gravesend Borough Dist Cncl 1957-40; *Recreations* gardening, photography, watching rugby, reading; *Clubs* Gravesend Rugby; *Style—* Eric Hammond, Esq, OBE; EETPU, Hayes Ct, West Commond Rd, Hayes Bromley, Kent (☎ 01 462 7755)

HAMMOND, Frederick Alexander; s of Frederick Hammond (d 1976), and Alice Hammond (d 1980); *b* 8 July 1936; *Educ* Ashton GS, Manchester Univ (MSc); *m* 16 April 1960, Margaretta, da of Edward Thorpe (d 1974); 2 s (Nigel Derek b 1964, Nicholas Mark b 1965); *Career* sr ptnr The APC Int Gp; chm: Project Management Int plc, Rogers Chapman plc; *Recreations* golf, bridge, shooting; *Clubs* Brooks, Burhill, City Livery; *Style—* Frederick Hammond, Esq; 3 Ince Road, Burwood Park, Walton-on-Thames KT12 5BJ (☎ 0932 227686); The Lodge, Harmondsworth, West Drayton, Middx UB7 0LA (☎ 01 759 0966)

HAMMOND, Dame Joan; DBE (1974, CBE 1963, OBE 1953), CMG (1972); da of Samuel Hood Hammond (d 1963), of Sydney, and late Hilda May, *née* Blandford; *b* 24 May 1912; *Educ* Presbyterian Ladies' Coll Sydney, Sydney Conservatorium of Music; *Career* singer commencing Sydmey 1929 operatic debut Vienna 1939; head of vocal studies and vocal consit Victorian Coll of the Arts, bd of dirs Victorian State Opera, tstee Geelong Performing Arts Centre, memb Victorian Cncl for the Arts; Coronation Medal 1953; memb Australian Opera Cncl; GonDMus (WA); *Books* A Voice, A Life (1970); *Clubs* Royal Sydney Golf, RMYC (Poole); *Style—* Dame Joan Hammond, DBE, CMG; 46 Lansell Rd, Toorak, Victoria 3142, Australia

HAMMOND, (John) Martin; s of Rev Canon Thomas Chatterton Hammond (d 1981), Rector of Beckenham, and Joan *née* Cruse; *b* 15 Nov 1944; *Educ* Winchester, Balliol Coll Oxford; *m* 25 June 1974, Meredith Jane, da of Kenneth Wesley Shier of Ontario, Canada; 1 s (Thomas b 1976), 1 step da (Chantal b 1970); *Career* asst master St Paul's 1966-71, teacher Anargyrios Sch Spetsai Greece 1972-73, asst master Harrow 1973-74, hd of classics dept Eton 1974-80 (Master in College Eton 1980-84), headmaster City of London Sch 1984; memb Gen Advsy Cncl of the BBC; *Books* Homer: The Iliad, A New Prose Translation (1987); *Style—* Martin Hammond, Esq; City of London School, Queen Victoria St, London, EC4V 3AL, (☎ 01 489 0291)

HAMMOND, Michael Harry Frank; s of Cecil Edward Hammond (d 1963), and Kate Hammond, *née* Lovell (d 1984); *b* 5 June 1933; *Educ* Leatherhead Co Secdy Sch, Law Soc Sch of Law; *m* 21 Aug 1965, Jenny, da of Dr George Macdonald Campbell (d 1981); 2 s (Ralph b 1968, Richard b 1971), 1 da (Sara b 1966); *Career* slr; chief exec and town clerk Nottingham City Cncl 1973, dep town clerk Nottingham 1971-73, dep town clerk Newport Monmouthshire 1969-71; prosecuting slr Nottingham City Cncl 1963-66; election supervisor Rhodesia Independence Elections 1980; chm Assoc of Local Authy (chief exec 1984-85), vice pres Nottinghamshire Law Soc 1988-89, chief exec E Midlands branch Soc of Local Authy 1988- (former chm); Rhodesia Medal 1980-; Zimbabwe Independence Medal 1980; *Recreations* walking, gardening, any sport; *Style—* Michael Hammond, Esq; 41 Burlington Rd, Sherwood, Nottingham (☎ 0602 602 000); The Guildhall, Nottingham NG1 4BT (☎ 0602 483 501, telex 377459, fax 473246)

HAMMOND, Valerie June; *née* Amas; da of Stanley F Amas (d 1972), and Eileen M Amas; *b* 22 Oct 1942; *Educ* Pendergast GS, Open Univ (BA); *m* 1982, A Knighton Berry; *Career* dir of res Ashridge Mgmnt Coll 1980-, pres European Women's Mgmnt Devpt Network, policy memb trg agency Women and Trg Policy Gp; previously: project mangr Petroleum Indust Training Bd, Mobil Oil, Friden Ltd, Rank Screen Servs; *author*: Employment Potential: Issues in the Development of Women (with Ashridge team, 1980), The Computer in Personnel Work (with Edgar Wille, 1981), Tomorrow's Office Today (with David Birchall 1981), No barriers here? (1982), Practical approaches to Women's Management Development (1984), Current Research in Management (1985), Men and Women in Organisations (with Tom Boydell, 1985), and jl articles from research and conferences; *Style—* Ms Valerie Hammond; Ashridge Mgmnt Coll, Berkhamsted, Herts HP4 INS (☎ 044 284 3491, telex 826434 Aschcol G)

HAMMOND INNES, Ralph; CBE (1978); s of William Hammond Innes and Dora Beatrice, *née* Crisford; *b* 15 July 1913; *Educ* Cranbrook Sch; *m* 1937, Dorothy Mary, da of William Cape Lang; *Career* Maj RA WWII, served in ME; journalist Financial News 1934-40; author, landowner Hon DLitt Bristol Univ 1985:; *Books* (all made into films): The Lonely Skier (1947), The White South (1949), Campbells Kingdom (1952), The Mary Deare (1956), Levkas Man (1971), Golden Soak (1973); other books incl: The Last Voyage: Captain Cook's Lost Diary (1978), Solomons Seal (1980), The Black Tide (1982), High Stand (1985), Medusa (1988); non-fiction incl: Harvest of Journeys (1960), Scandinavia (with the eds of Life, 1963), Sea and Islands (1967), The Conquistadors (1969), Hammond Innes Introduces Australia (1971), Hammond Innes' East Anglia (1986); plays include: Campbells Kingdom (screenplay, 1957), The Story of Captain James Cook (TV play, 1975); *Clubs* Soc of Authors, PEN, Royal Yacht Sqdn, Royal Ocean Racing, Royal Cruising; *Style—* Ralph Hammond Innes, Esq, CBE; Ayres End, Kersey, Suffolk IP7 6EB

HAMMOND-MAUDE, Hon Mrs; Hon (Sonia Mary); *née* Peake; da of 1 Viscount Ingleby (d 1966); *b* 12 Dec 1924; *m* 1, 26 Oct 1946 (m dis 1958), David George Montagu Hay, GC, RN, later 12 Marquess of Tweeddale (d 1979); 3 s; m 2, 27 June 1966, Maj Michael William Vernon Hammond-Maude, JP, 5 Royal Inniskilling Dragoon Gds (ret); *Career* served WW II, WRNS; *Style—* The Hon Mrs Hammond-Maude; Mitton Cottage, Arncliffe, nr Skipton, N Yorks

HAMMOND-STROUD, Derek; OBE (1987); s of Herbert William Stroud (d 1951), of Stanmore, Middx, and Ethel Louise, *née* Elliott (d 1988); *b* 10 Jan 1926; *Educ* Salvatorian Coll Harrow, Trinity Coll of Music; *Career* RWAFF India, Burma 1944-47; concert and opera baritone, private study with Elena Gerhardt and Prof Gerhard Husch; Glyndebourne Festival Opera 1959-, ENO 1960-, Covent Garden Opera 1971-, Netherlands Opera 1976-87, Metropolitan Opera NY 1977-80, Teatro Colón Buenos Aires 1981, Munich State Opera 1983; Festivals: Edinburgh, Aldburgh, Vienna, Munich, Cheltenham, English Bach; concerts and recitals in Spain, Iceland, Denmark; recordings: EMI, RCA, Philipps, Célébre, Symposium Records; prof of singing RAM 1974-; Freeman City of London 1952; ISM 1971; Hon: RAM 1976, FTCL 1982; *Recreations* chess, study of philosophy; *Style—* Derek Hammond-Stroud, Esq, OBE; 18 Sutton Road, Muswell Hill, London N10 1HE (☎ 01 883 2120)

HAMOND; *see*: Harbord-Hamond

HAMP-HAMILTON, Mary Agnes; da of James Murdoch, JP (d 1960), of Torloisque, Drumchapel, Dunbartonshire, and Janet, *née* Gray (d 1979); *b* 28 Oct 1911; *Educ* Park Sch Glasgow, RADA; *m* 23 July 1935, William Henry, JP, s of William Henderson Hamp-Hamilton (d 1935); *Career* regnl organiser WVS W Perthshire 1956-58, dir PR WRVS Scotland 1958-74, chm Women of Scotland Luncheon 1958-; Serving Sis Order St John of Jerusalem; FSA (Scotland); *Recreations* gardening; *Style—* Mrs William Hamp-Hamilton; Glentye, Sheriffmuir, Dunblane, Perthshire FK15 0LN (☎ 0786 822 269)

HAMP-HAMILTON, William Henry; s of William Henderson Hamp-Hamilton (d 1935), of Spring Garden, Hamilton, Lanarks, and Margaret, *née* Lockhart (d 1939); *b* 14 Dec 1906; *Educ* Hamilton Academy; *m* 23 July 1935, Mary Agnes *qv*, eld da of James Murdoch, JP, of Drumchapel, Glasgow; *Career* Pilot Offr RAF/VR T 1939-42; advertisement mangr Scottish Daily Express 1928-39, gen-mangr Glasgow Observer 1943-52; publicity mangr: Anchor Line Ltd, Currie Line Ltd 1952-78; PR conslt 1978-; memb Scottish cncl 1945-65, exec and cncl memb The Advertising Assoc 1953-55, dir Glasgow C of C 1958-68; chm: Inst of Public Relations Scot 1962-63, Inst of Mkting Glasgow 1957-58; Advertising Assoc Mackintosh Medal Award 1959, govr Royal Scottish Academy of Music and Drama 1963-68; dir The Scottish Nat Orchestra 1963-68; FSA 1984, FInstM 1978, FIPR 1966; *Recreations* gardening, photography; *Clubs* Naval; *Style—* W H Hamp-Hamilton, Esq, JP; Sheriffmuir, Dunblane, Perthshire FK15 0LN

HAMPDEN, 6 Viscount (UK 1884); Anthony David Brand; DL (E Sussex 1986); s of 5 Viscount Hampden (d 1975), and Hon Imogen Rhys, da of 7 Baron Dynevor; *b* 7 May 1937; *Educ* Eton; *m* 27 Sept 1969 (m dis 1988), Cara Fiona, da of Capt Claud Proby, Irish Guards (d 1987), 2 s of Sir Richard Proby, 1 Bt, MC, JP, DL; 2 s (Hon Francis, Hon Jonathan Claud David Humphrey b 24 Aug 1975), 1 da (Hon Saracha Mary b 7 March 1973); *Heir* s, Hon Francis Anthony Brand b 17 Sept 1970; *Career* chm Emanuel Sch Governing Body 1985-; *Books* Henry and Eliza; *Clubs* White's; *Style—* The Rt Hon the Viscount Hampden, DL; Glynde Place, Glynde, Lewes, Sussex (☎ 079 159 337)

HAMPDEN, Imogen, Viscountess; Hon Imogen Alice; *née* Rhys; da of late 7 Baron Dynevor and Lady Margaret Child-Villiers, da of 7 Earl of Jersey; *b* 27 August 1903; *m* 14 July 1936, 5 Viscount Hampden (d 1975); 1 s (6 Viscount), 2 da (Hon Mrs Hodgson, Hon Mrs Chetwode); *Style—* The Rt Hon Imogen, Viscountess Hampden; Trevor House, Glynde, Lewes, Sussex

HAMPDEN, Leila, Viscountess; Leila Emily; only da of Lt-Col Frank Seely, JP, DL (d 1928, 3 s of Sir Charles Seely, 1 Bt), of Ramsdale Park, Notts; *b* 24 August 1900; *m* 26 July 1923, 4 Viscount Hampden, CMG (d 1965); 2 da (Lady Dacre, w of Hon William Douglas-Home; Hon Mrs Ogilvie Thompson) and 2 da decd; *Style—* The Rt Hon Leila, Viscountess Hampden; Mill Court, Alton, Hants (☎ 0420 23125)

HAMPEL, Ronald Claus; s of Karl Victor Hugo Hampel (d 1960), and Rutgard Emil Klothilde, *née* Hauck (d 1975); *b* 31 May 1932; *Educ* Canford Sch, CCC Cambridge (MA); *m* 11 May 1957, Jane Bristed, da of Cdr Wilfred Graham Hewson, RN, of Wellington, Som; 3 s (Andrew b 1960, Rupert b 1962, Peter b 1962), 1 da (Katharine b 1958); *Career* Nat Serv 2 Lt 3 RHA 1951-52; ICI 1955-: vice pres Americas 1973-77, gen mangr commercial gp 1977-80, chm paints div 1980-83, chm agrochemicals 1983-85, (dir 1985-); non-exec dir: Powell Duffryn plc 1984-, Commercial Union 1987-; memb Br N American Ctee 1986, bd memb American C of C 1988; CBIM 1985; *Recreations* skiing, tennis, golf; *Clubs* All England Lawn Tennis, MCC; *Style—* Ronald Hampel, Esq; ICI plc, ICI Group HQ, 9 Millbank, London SW1P 3JF (☎ 01 834 4444, fax 01 834 2042, telex 21324 ICI HQ G)

HAMPERL, John Frederick; s of Alois Hamperl (d 1987), of Watford, Herts, Copthorn, Sussex, and Fort George, Guernsey, and Pauline Wilhelmena, *née* Henne; *b* 6 April 1936; *Educ* Ardingly, Nat Coll of Food Technol London, Cassio Coll Watford; *m* 2 June 1963, Elaine Karen, da of Henry Holm (d 1979), of London; 1 s (Lawrence b 1965), 1 da (Karen b 1967); *Career* Nat Serv RASC 1955-57; Malaya and Singapore; dir: A Hamperl Ltd 1960-82, Porky Boy Products Ltd 1967-73, Alan Drew Ltd 1974-87 (chm 1987-); chm: Bushey and Oxhey Round Table 1970-71, Round Table Area 42 (The Chilterns) 1975-76, Fullerians Rugby Club 1982-85; memb: Herts RFU, Orders and Medals Research Soc; Freeman City of London, Liveryman Worshipful Co of Butchers 1959; *Recreations* vintage motor cars (especially Bentleys), rugby football, British Naval Medals; *Clubs* Durrant's, Bentley Drivers; *Style—* John Hamperl, Esq; Alan Drew Ltd, Caxton Way, Watford, Herts WD1 8TH (☎ 0923 817 933, fax 0923 37824, car tel 0860 414 520)

HAMPSHIRE, Margaret Grace; da of Dr Charles Herbert Hampshire, CMG (d 1955), of 12 Hyde Park St, London W1 and Grace Mary Hampshire, *née* Taylor (d 1954); *b* 7 Sept 1918; *Educ* Malvern Girls' Coll Worcs, Girton Coll Cambridge (BA, MA); *Career* admin civil servant BOT 1941-51, sr exec Courtaulds Ltd 1951-64, princ Cheltenham Ladies Coll 1964-79, bd of govrs UC Hosp London 1959-64; memb: St Marylebone Borough Cncl 1961-64, SW Regnl Hosp Bd 1967-70, Midlands Electricity Consultative Cncl 1973-80; govr: Berkhampstead Sch Cheltenham 1975-80, Alice Ottley Sch Worcester 1979-; county sec Gloucestershire Girl Guides 1980-85, chm Cheltenham Gen Hosp Intensive Care Tst 1982-85; reader in Diocese of Gloucesters (Parish) of Painswick and Shepscombe) 1987-; JP (Cheltenham) 1970-88; *Clubs* Royal Overseas League; *Style—* Miss Margaret Hampshire; Ringwood, 9 The Croft, Painswick, Glos GL6 6QP (☎ 0452 813468)

HAMPSHIRE, Sir Stuart Newton; s of G N Hampshire; *b* 1 Oct 1914; *Educ* Repton, Balliol Coll Oxford; *m* 1961, late Renée Ayer; *Career* served WW II; lectr in philosophy Univ Coll London 1947-50, fell New Coll Oxford 1950-55, domestic bursar and research fell All Souls' Coll 1955-60, Grote prof of philosophy mind and logic Univ of London 1960-63, prof of philosophy Princeton Univ USA 1963-70, warden Wadham Coll Oxford 1970-84; FBA; kt 1979; *Books* Spinoza (1951), Thought and Action (1959), Freedom of the Individual (1965), The Socialist Idea (1975), Two Theories of Morality (1977); *Style—* Sir Stuart Hampshire; Wadham College, Oxford

HAMPSHIRE, Susan; da of George Kenneth Hampshire (d 1964), and June Hampshire (d 1967); *b* 12 May 1942; *Educ* Hampshire Sch Knightsbridge; *m* 1, 1967 (m dis 1974), Pierre Julian Granier-Deferre; 1 s, 1 da (decd); m 2, 1981, Eddie Kulukundis, *qv*; s of George Elias Kulukundis (d 1978); *Career* actress; plays: Exprees Bongo, Follow That Girl, Fairy Tales Of New York, The Ginger Man, Past Imperfect, The Sleeping Prince, Peter Pan, The Taming of The Shrew, Romeo and Jeanette, As You Like It, Miss Julie, The Circle, Arms and The Man, Man and Superman, Tribades, An Audience Called Edward; films: During One Night, The Three Lives of Thomasina, Night Must Fall, The Flighting Prince of Donegal, Paris in August, Monte Carlo or Bust, Violent Enemy, David Copperfield, A Time For Loving, Living Free, Baffled, Malpertius, Neither The Sea Nor The Sand, Roses and Green Peppers, Bang; TV incl: The Forsythe Saga 1970, The First Churchills 1971, Variety Fair 1973, The Pallisers 1975, Dick Turpin 1980, Borchester Chronicles 1982, Learning (2 series); winner 3 Emmy Awards for Best Actress; Hon DLitt: London Univ 1984, St Andrews Univ 1986; *Books* Susan's Story, The Maternal Instinct, Lucy Jane at the Ballet, Trouble Free Gardening, Lucy Jane II; *Recreations* gardening, food, colour, water skiing; *Style—* Miss Susan Hampshire; c/o Midland Bank Ltd, 92 Kensington High St, London W8

HAMPSON, Bernard William; s of James William Hampson, of Theakston Hall Stud, Theakston, Bedale, North Yorks, and Nellie Hampson; *b* 1 Feb 1942; *m* 16 Sept 1965, Pamela Jean, da of Arnold Pearson, DSO, DFC, of 9 Helmesy Way, Northallerton,

North Yorks; 2 s (Simon b 1966, Jeremy b 1968), 1 da (Rebecca b 1970); *Career* chm and md Mavitta Hldgs Ltd, md John Evans and Assoc Ltd, dir Inbucon Mgmnt Conslts Ltd; *Recreations* racehorse owner (horse, Madraco, won William Hill Stewards Cup), golf, cricket; *Style*— Bernard Hampson, Esq; 32 Mearse Lane, Barnt Green, Birmingham B45 8HL (☎ 021 445 3849); Systems House, Great Hampton St, Birminghamn B18 6AO (☎ 021 236 5877)

HAMPSON, Christopher; s of Harold Ralph Hampson (d 1972), of Montreal, Canada, and Geraldine Mary, *née* Smith (d 1984); *b* 6 Sept 1931; *Educ* Ashbury Coll Ottawa Canada, McGill Univ Montreal Canada (BEng); *m* 18 Sept 1954, Joan Margaret Cassils, da of Lt-Col Arthur C Evans (d 1960), of Montreal; 2 s (Christopher Geoffrey b 1957, Harold Arthur b 1965), 3 da (Daphne Margaret (Mrs Kearns) b 1955, Sarah Anne (Mrs Claridge) b 1958, Aimée Joan Geraldine b 1966); *Career* CIL Inc Canada: vice pres and dir 1973-78, sr vice pres and dir 1982-82; md and chief exec offr ICI Aust Ltd 1984-87, exec dir ICI plc 1987-; memb chm's cncl Br Inst of Mgmnt; FBIM 1988; *Recreations* tennis, skiing; *Clubs* York (Toronto), Mount Royal (Montreal), Hurlingham; *Style*— 77 Kensington Court, London W8; Imperial Chemical Industries Plc, 9 Millbank, London SW1 (☎ 01 834 4444)

HAMPSON, Dr Keith; MP (C) Leeds North-West 1983-; s of Bert Hampson (d 1967), of Shildon, Co Durham; *b* 14 August 1943; *Educ* King James I GS Bishop Auckland, Bristol Univ, Harvard Univ (PhD); *m* 1975, Frances Pauline Einhorn (d 1975); m 2, 1979, Susan, da of John Cameron; *Career* former chm Bristol Univ Cons Assoc, PA to Rt Hon Edward Heath 1966, 1968 and 1970; history (American) lectr Edinburgh Univ 1968-74, MP (C) Ripon 1974-1983 (contested same at by-election July 1973), vice-chm Cons educn ctee 1975-79, vice-pres WEA 1979-, vice-chm Youthaid 1979-, PPS to Rt Hon Tom King as Min for Local Govt and Environmental Services 1979-83, PPS to Rt Hon Michael Heseltine Sec of State for Defence 1983-84; *Recreations* tennis, dancing, DIY; *Clubs* Carlton; *Style*— Dr Keith Hampson, MP; Pool Hall, Pool-in-Wharfedale, Leeds LS21

HAMPSON, Professor Norman; s of Frank Hampson (d 1967), and Elizabeth Jane, *née* Fazackerley (d 1946); *b* 8 April 1922; *Educ* Manchester GS, Univ Coll Oxford (MA), Univ of Paris (Docteur de l'Université); *m* 22 Apr 1948, Jacqueline Juliette Jeanne Marguerite, da of Charles Hector Gardin (d 1933); 2 da (Francoise b 1951, Michèle b 1955); *Career* RNVR (Lieut 1943) 1941-45; asst lectr then sr lectr Manchester Univ 1948-67, prof Univ of Newcastle 1967-74, prof Univ of York 1974-; FRHS 1970, FBA 1980; *Books* La Marine de l'An II (1959), A Social History of the French Revolution (1963), The Enlightenment (1968), The First European Revolution (1969), The Life and Opinions of Maximilien Robespierre (1974), A Concise History of the French Revolution (1975), Danton (1978), Will and Circumstance 1983, Prelude to Terror (1987); *Recreations* gardening; *Style*— Professor Norman Hampson; 305 Hull Road, York, YO1 3LB (☎ 0904 412 661)

HAMPSTEAD, Archdeacon of; *see*: Coogan, Ven Robert Arthur William

HAMPTON, Antony Barmore (Tony); TD (1955), DL (S Yorks 1971); s of Charles William Hampton (d 1958), of Hayling Island, and Winifrid Elizabeth, *née* Unwin (d 1950); *b* 6 Mar 1919; *Educ* Birkdale Sch Sheffield, Rydal Sch, Christ's Coll Cambridge (MA) ; *m* 14 Feb 1948, (Helen) Patricia, da of Alan Parker Lockwood, MC (d 1970, Coroner of Sheffield); 5 s (Charles, James, Marcus, David, Andrew); *Career* served IA 1941-46 (despatches), Maj TA 1947-54 RA; chm C and J Hampton 1958-72, merger with Ridgway, became chm Record-Ridgway Tools 1972-81; memb: Lloyds Bank Yorks Bd 1961 (chm 1972-83), Lloyds Bank UK Bd 1972-85, Black Horse Agencies 1982-85; pres Engrg Employers' Fedn 1980-82, tstee Engrg Employers' Fedn Ltd; chm Crucible Theatre Tst 1970-81; memb: Engrg Training Bd 1980-83, govt review Body Youth Serv 1981-82; cmmr Inland Revenue 1969-80; Hon Fell Sheffield Poly; Master Cutler of Hallamshire 1966-67; *Recreations* sailing, fishing; *Clubs* Little Ship, Hayling Island Sailing; *Style*— Tony Hampton, Esq, TD, DL; 20 Wittering Rd, Hayling Island, Hants PO11 9SP (☎ 0705 464361); Flat N, Rectory Chambers, Old Church St, London SW3 5DA (☎ 01 351 1719)

HAMPTON, Barry Charles; s of Charles Frederick Ernest Hampton, of Chippenham; and Elsie Ray, *née* Watkins; *b* 22 August 1937; *Educ* Chippenham GS, Bath Tech Coll; *m* 11 June 1966, Lesley May, da of Lesley Matterson Massey (d 1967), of Corsham; 1 da (Susan Jane b 26 April 1968); *Career* ptnr Harvey McGill & Hayes 1979-; ctee memb W Counties branch of CIArb (listed panel arbitrator), former chm SW branch Inst of Public Health Engrs, memb Rotary Int and Exeter C of C; memb: Royal Philatelic Soc London, Postal History Soc, Helvetia Philatelic Soc, Exmouth Stamp Club, Wessex Philatelic Fedn, Br Philatelic Fedn (lectr and judge); county timekeeper Amateur Swimming Assoc, fndr memb Chippenham Modern Pentathlon Club; Freeman: City of London 1987 Worshipful Co of Arbitrators 1987; C Eng, FIStructE 1965, FIWEM 1972 FCIArb 1974, MConsE, FFS 1985 ; *Recreations* postal history, philately, sea fishing; *Style*— Barry Hampton, Esq; 188 Exeter Rd, Exmouth, Devon EX8 3DZ (☎ 0395 279 513); c/o Harvey McGill & Hayes, Northernhay House, Northernhay Place, Exeter, Devon EX4 3RY (☎ 0392 525 31, fax 0392 791 24)

HAMPTON, 6 Baron (UK 1874); Sir Richard Humphrey Russell Pakington; 6 Bt (UK 1846); s of 5 Baron Hampton, OBE, FRIBA (d 1974), and Grace, da of Rt Hon Sir Albert Spicer, 1 Bt; *b* 25 May 1925; *Educ* Eton, Balliol Coll Oxford; *m* 25 Oct 1958, Jane, da of Thomas Arnott, OBE, TD, MB, ChB; 1 s, 2 da; *Heir* s, Hon John Pakington; *Career* Sub-Lt Fleet Air Arm, RNVR WW II; in advertising to 1958, CPRE Worcs 1958-71, with Tansley Witt and Co 1971-73; sits as a Liberal Democrat in House of Lords, Lib spokesman on NI 1977-87, pres South Worcestershire Lib Assoc 1978-88; *Books* The Pakingtons of Westwood (1975); *Style*— The Rt Hon Lord Hampton; Palace Farmhouse, Upton-upon-Severn, Worcs (☎ 068 46 2512)

HAMPTON, Roland Edgar Spillar; s of Arthur Creswell Hampton (d 1983), and Emily Frances, *née* Cummings (d 1955); *b* 25 Feb 1908; *Educ* Chorlton GS; *m* 17 Aug 1935, Phyllis Anna (d 1987), da of Julius Norden (d 1968); 1 s (Adrian Creswell b 24 Nov 1945), 1 da (Leonie Frances b 11 April 1939); *Career* md The Civic Co Ltd 1944-69, dir Cadogan Investmts 1949-69; fndr memb Worshipful Co of Tobacco Pipe Makers and Tobacco Blenders 1954 (Freeman 1961); *Style*— Roland Hampton, Esq; 27 Burleigh Ct, Western Pl, Worthing BN11 3LU (☎ 0903 200001)

HAMPTON, Surgn Rear Adm Trevor Richard Walker; CB (1988); s of Percy Ewart Erasmus Hampton (d 1952), of King's Lynn, Norfolk, and Violet Agnes, *née* Neave (d 1987); *b* 6 June 1930; *Educ* King Edward VII GS King's Lynn, Edinburgh Univ Sch of Medicine (MB ChB); *m* 1, 11 Aug 1952 (m dis 1976), (Celia) Rosemary, da of Stanley Day (d 1957), of Winchmore Hill; 3 da (Fiona, b 1956, Nicola b 1959, Judy b 1963); m 2, 12 Aug 1976, Jennifer Lily, da of Leonard R Bootle (d 1986), of Fillongley, Warwickshire; *Career* Surgn Lt RN 1955; serv: HMS Ganges, Harrier and Victorius; conslt physician RN Hosps: Plymouth, Haslar and Gibraltar; Surgn Cdr 1967, Surgn Capt 1977, Surgn Rear Adm 1984; med offr i/c RN Hosps: Gibraltar 1980-82, Plymouth 1982-84; Support Med Servs 1984-87, Operational Med Servs 1987-89; author of pubns on Waterhouse-Friderichsen Syndrome, inhalation injury, drowning and med screening; MRCPE 1964, FRCPE 1975; *Recreations* professional and amateur theatre, music, writing; *Style*— Surgn Rear Adm Trevor Hampton, CB; Coombe House, Latchley, nr Gunnislake, Cornwall PL18 9AX (☎ 0822 832419)

HAMSON, John Everard; s of Vincent Everard Hamson (d 1978), of Croydon, and Florence, *née* Reynolds (d 1979); *b* 3 April 1925; *Educ* Bromley County GS, Bedford Evening Inst; *m* 1, 1949, Mary, da of Capt George Thomas (d 1965), Beckenham; 2 da (Anna b 1958, Victoria b 1959); m 2, 1980, Cherry, da of Herbert Edwards, of Tenby; 1 s (Jack b 1983), 1 da (Rose b 1980); *Career* RAF (warrant offr) 1943-47; news reporter 1941-43, 1947-56, press and PR exec 1956- (Hamson and Hamson PR Conslts); *Recreations* bass trombone; *Clubs* Wig and Pen, Press (Birmingham); *Style*— John Hamson, Esq; 42 High Street, Bidford-on-Avon, Warwicks (☎ (0789) 773347)

HAMYLTON JONES, Keith; CMG (1979); s of G Jones, of Fairholm, Sussex; *b* 12 Oct 1924; *Educ* St Paul's, Balliol Coll Oxford; *m* 1953, Eira, da of B Morgan; 1 da; *Career* serv WWII Capt HM Welsh Gds (Italy, Germany and S France); HM For Serv 1949-: Warsaw, Lisbon, Manila, Montevideo, Rangoon; HM consul-gen to Katanga 1970-72; ambass: Costa Rica 1974-79, Honduras 1975-78, Nicaragua 1976-79; chm: (for Devon and Cornwall) Operation Raleigh 1983-85 (led their Int Expdn to Costa Rica 1985), Anglo-Costa Rican Soc 1983-88; memb Anglo-Central American Soc 1988; *Recreations* reading, writing (pen-name Peter Myllent); *Clubs* Chelsea Arts; *Style*— Keith Hamylton-Jones, Esq, CMG; Morval House, Morval, nr East Looe, Cornwall (☎ 050 36 2342)

HANAGAN, Patrick Sean; s of Maj John Thomas Frederick Hanagan, and Eva Helen, *née* Ross; *b* 9 August 1950; *Educ* Gordonstown, St Johns Coll Coolhurst, Univ of Hull, London Univ (BA); *Career* involved in int banking, econ advise and research Royal Bank of Scotland 1974-81, exec fin info servs Reuters 1981-84, co founding dir Enigma Systems Ltd 1984, fndr Business Enterprise Award 1979, Art Exhibition 1985; Freeman City of London 1978, Liveryman Worshipful Co of Needlemakers 1983; *Recreations* oil painting, piano, music and opera, books, travel, walking, woking, gardening; *Style*— Patrick Hanagan, Esq; 11 Welbeck St, London W1

HANBURY, Antony; s of 3 and yst s of Horace Hanbury, but yr s by Horace's 2 w Clara, da of Edward Matthew Howard, of Gosebrook House, Wolverhampton, Staffs; Horace was 3 s of Sir Thomas Hanbury, KCVO, who was seventh in descent from Philip Hanbury (b 1582), whose er bro John was ancestor of 1 Baron Sudeley. Philip and John's Hanbury ancestors were MPs for Worcester and Worcestershire in the fourteenth century; *b* 31 July 1922; *m* 1 Sept 1949, Elizabeth Anne (d 20 Sept 1982), sole da of Col Robert Edward Kennard Leatham, DSO; 1 s (Rupert b 1952: m 1979, Anne, da of Brig Alan and Hon Mrs Breitmeyer, *qv*), 2 da (Sarah b 1950, Jane b 1954); *Career* md Singer and Friedlander, to 1982 (remains as non-exec dir); *Style*— Antony Hanbury, Esq; c/o Singer and Friedlander plc, 21 New St, Bishopsgate, London EC2M 4HR (☎ 01 623 3000)

HANBURY, Benjamin John; s of Lt-Col Christopher Lionel Hanbury, MBE, TD, DL, JP, of Burnham, Bucks, and Lettice Mary Charrington (d 1980); *b* 19 Jan 1934; *Educ* Eton, Christ Church Oxford; *m* 8 May 1962, Verena Elizabeth Anne Kimmins, da of Capt Anthony Martin Hannam Kimmins, RN, OBE (d 1964); 4 s (James b 1964, Timothy b 1967, Simon b 1969, Marcus b 1972), 1 da (Lucinda b 1963); *Career* dir: Charrington and Co Ltd, The Brewers' Soc, Procrescent Ltd, Aldenham Sch Co, Aldenham Sch Enterprises Ltd, Temple Grove Sch Tst Ltd, Southover Manor Educnl Tst (1966) Ltd, The Medical Cncl on Alcoholism; *Recreations* skiing, shooting, gardening; *Style*— Benjamin J Hanbury, Esq; 8 Hans Str, London SW1X 0NJ; Cogans Piltdown, nr Uckfield, Sussex TN22 3XR; 30 Portland Place, London W1N 3DF

HANBURY, Lt-Col Christopher Lionel; MBE (1946), TD (1943), JP (Bucks 1956), DL (1956); yr s of Col Lionel Henry Hanbury, CMG, VD (d 1954), and Margaret Colmore (d 1949), da of Henry Christian Allhusen, of Stoke Court, Bucks; *b* 6 Mar 1905; *Educ* Eton, Christ Church Oxford; *m* 6 Oct 1932, Lettice Mary (d 8 May 1980), da of Arthur Finch Charrington (d 1922); 2 s, 1 da; *Career* serv WWII Royal Bucks Yeo (France, India and Burma), GSO (1) GHQ India, Maj 1940; High Sheriff Bucks 1954; *Recreations* field sports, bird watching; *Style*— Lt-Col Christopher Hanbury, MBE, TD, JP, DL; Juniper Hill, Burnham, Bucks SL1 8GA (☎ 062 86 3652)

HANBURY, Maj Christopher Osgood Philip; s of Sqdn Ldr Osgood Villiers Hanbury, DSO, DFC (ka 1943), and Cecil Patricia Thompson, *née* Harman; *b* 16 Feb 1944; *Educ* Millfield, RAC Cirencester; *m* 2 Dec 1969, Bridget Anne, da of Charles Francis Birch, (d 1974), of Southern Rhodesia; 2 s (Charles b 15 May 1986, George b 6 Nov 1987), 4 da (Zahra b 10 April 1971, Emma b 15 Jan1 973, Arabella b 13 Dec 1975, Jessica b 13 April 1979); *Career* Mons Offr Cadet Sch 1964, cmmnd Queens Royal Irish Hussars 1965; serv BAOR 1965, Hong Kong 1968-69, BAOR 1970-73, loan serv to Royal Brunei Malay Regt (Equerry to HM Sultan of Brunei) 1974-81; dir Dorchester Hotel 1985; memb Cirencester Polo Club Ctee; Brunei SLJ 1975, SNB and PHBS 1976, DPMB 1978; *Recreations* racing, polo, shooting; *Clubs* Cavalry and Guards, Cirencester Polo; *Style*— Maj Christopher Hanbury; Lovelocks House, Shefford Woodlands, Hungerford, Berks RG17 0PU (☎ 048839 558)

HANBURY, Evan Robert (Joss); s of Lt-Col James Robert Hanbury (d 1971), of Burley on the Hill, Oakham, Leics, and Sarah Margaret, *née* Birkin (d 1976); *Educ* Eton, RAC Cirencester; *m* 22 July 1974, Rosalind Jeannette, da of Derrick Alex Pease, of Britten Street, London SW3; 2 s (James b 1979, William b 1983), 1 da (Susanna b 1977); *Career* farmer; master of foxhounds of Cottesmore and Quorn; memb Rutland CC 1972-74; *Recreations* riding, gardening; *Style*— Evan Hanbury, Esq; Burley on the Hill, Oakham, Rutland (☎ 0572 2017)

HANBURY, Lt-Col Hanmer Cecil; LVO (1953), MC (1943), JP (Beds 1959), DL (Beds 1958); yr s of Sir Cecil Hanbury (d 1937) sometime Unionist MP for N Dorset (himself eld s of Sir Thomas Hanbury, KCVO, who in his turn was 8 in descent from Philip Hanbury (*b* 1582), whose er bro John was ancestor (5 generations) of 1 Baron Sudeley); *b* 5 Jan 1916; *Educ* Eton, RMC Sandhurst; *m* 4 July 1939, Prunella Kathleen Charlotte, o child of Air Cdre Thomas Charles Reginald Higgins, CB, CMG, JP, DL, of Turvey House; 1 s, 1 da; *Career* serv WWII Grenadier Gds NW Europe, N Africa, Italy, Maj 1948, Temp Lt-Col 1955-57, ret 1958; Lord-Lt Beds 1978- (High Sheriff

1965, Vice-Lord-Lt 1970), patron Br Red Cross Soc Beds 1978- (dep-pres 1972-78, dir 1959-71); pres St John's Cncl Beds 1979-, KStJ 1980; chm Beds, T and AVR Ctee 1970-78 and pres 1978-, pres E Anglia T and AVR 1980-86 (vice-pres 1978-80, vice-chm 1970-78 and 1986); *Recreations* most country pursuits; *Clubs* White's, Pratt's, Army and Navy; *Style*— Lt-Col H C Hanbury, LVO, MC, JP, DL; Turvey House, Turvey, Beds MK43 8EL (☎ 023 064 227); Villa Hanbury, La Mortola, Ventimiglia, Italy 18030

HANBURY, Sir John Capel; CBE (1969); s of Frederick Capel Hanbury (d 1957), by his w Muriel Hope, da of late John Franklin-Adams, of Mervel Hill, Godalming, Surrey; *b* 26 May 1908; *Educ* Downside, Trinity Coll Cambridge, London Univ; *m* 29 May 1935, Joan Terry, da of late Edward John Fussell, of Frinton-on-Sea, Essex ; 2 s (and 1 s decd), 1 da; *Career* memb Pharmacopoeia Cmmn 1948-73; pres Assoc of Br Pharmaceutical Indust 1950-52; chm Assoc of Br Chemical Mfrs 1961-63; chm Central Health Servs Cncl 1970-76; memb Thames Water Auth 1974-79; FRSC, FPS, Fellow UCL 1977; kt 1974; *Clubs* Utd Oxford and Cambridge Univs; *Style*— Sir John Hanbury, CBE; Amwellbury House, Great Amwell, Ware, Herts (☎ 0920 2108)

HANBURY, Leslie Francis; s of Capt Robert Francis Hanbury (d 1960), of Kirkcudbright, and Margaret Lucy Hanbury, *née* Scott (d 1966); *b* 23 Sept 1926; *Educ* Eton, Magdalene Coll Cambridge (MA); *m* 23 April 1966, Daphne Gillian, da of Lt-Gen Charles James Briggs, KCB, KCMG (d 1941), of Suffolk; 2 da (Anna b 1973, Lucy b 1976); *Career* agriculturist, serv Capt RASC (MT) 1945-48, Greece, Egypt; arable farmer, hill sheep and cattle 1968; *pubns incl*: Journal of Agric Sci (vol 68), various journals; memb of Inst of Agric Engrs; ctee memb Br Soc for Res in Agric, friend of Rothamsted Agric Experimental Station, tax cmmr; *Recreations* rural conservation, gardening; *Style*— Leslie F Hanbury, Esq; Manor Ho, Wickhambrook, nr Newmarket CB8 8XJ (☎ 0440 820 213)

HANBURY, Robert Edmund Scott; s of Capt Robert Francis Hanbury (d 1960), and Margaret Lucy, *née* Scott (d 1966); *b* 20 Mar 1925; *Educ* Eton, Scotland Coll of Agric; *m* 28 Oct 1961, Celia, da of Lt Col Gerald Ian Maitland-Heriot, MC, of SA; 1 s (Roland b 1964), 1 da (Melanie b 1967); *Career* serv W Seaforth Highlanders 1943-47; farmer, landowner; *Recreations* golf, shooting; *Style*— Robert Hanbury, Esq; Drumstinchall, Dalbeattie, Kirkcudbridgeshire, Scotland DG5 4PD

HANBURY-TENISON, Richard; JP (Gwent 1979); s of Maj G E F Tenison (d 1954), sometime Jt MFH Essex and Suffolk, of Lough Bawn, Co Monaghan, Ireland, by his w Ruth (da of John Capel Hanbury, JP, DL, who was n of 1 Baron Sudeley); *b* 3 Jan 1925; *Educ* Eton, Magdalen Coll Oxford; *m* 12 May 1955, Euphan Mary, JP, er da of Maj Arthur Wardlaw-Ramsay and Hon Mary, *née* Fraser, only da of 18 Lord Saltoun; 3 s (John b 1957, William b 1962, Capel b 1965), 2 da (Sarah b 1956, Laura b 1966); *Career* WWII Irish Gds NW Europe (wounded), Capt 1946; For Serv 1949-75; first sec: Vienna, Phnom Penh, Bucharest; cnsllr: Bonn, Brussels; head aviation and telecommunication dept FCO 1970-71, ret 1975; pres Monmouthshire (later Gwent) Rural Community Cncl 1959-67, chm Gwent Community Servs Cncl 1967-74 (pres 1975-), memb art ctee Nat Museum of Wales 1976- (1986 memb Court and Cncl 1979-, chm 1986), dir S Wales regnl bd Lloyds Bank 1980- (chm 1987-); DL Monmouthshire 1973, DL Gwent 1974, High Sheriff Gwent 1977, Lord Lt Gwent 1979-; Hon Col 3 Bn Royal Regt of Wales 1982-, pres TA and VR Assoc for Wales 1985-; CStJ 1980; *Recreations* shooting, fishing, conservation; *Clubs* Boodles, Kildare St Univ (Dublin); *Style*— Richard Hanbury-Tenison, Esq, JP; Clytha Park, Abergavenny, Gwent (☎ 0873 840 300); Lough Bawn, Co Monaghan, Ireland

HANBURY-TENISON, (Airling) Robin; OBE (1981); s of Maj Gerald Evan Farquhar Tenison (d 1954), of Co Monaghan Ireland, and Ruth Julia Marguerite, *née* Hanbury; *b* 7 May 1936; *Educ* Eton, Magdalen Coll Oxford (MA); *m* 1, 14 Jan 1959, Marika (d Oct 1982), cookery writer, da of Lt-Col John Montgomerie Hopkinson, of Garwyns Farm, Sussex; 1 s (Rupert b 1970), 1 da (Lucy b 1960); m 2, 1983, Louella Gage, da of Lt-Col George Torquil Gage Williams, of Menkee, Cornwall; 1 s (Merlin); *Career* farmer, author, explorer, pres Survival Int 1984 (chm 1969-84); *Books* The Rough and The Smooth (1969), A Question of Survival (1973), A Pattern of Peoples (1975), Mulu: The Rain Forest (1980), The Yanomami (1982), Worlds Apart (1984), White Horses Over France (1985), A Ride along the Great Wall (1987); *Recreations* travelling, conservation; *Clubs* Kildare Street and Univ (Dublin), Groucho; *Style*— Robin Hanbury-Tenison Esq, OBE; Maidenwell, Cardinham, Bodmin, Cornwall PL30 4DW (☎ 020 882 224)

HANBURY-TRACY, (Desmond) Andrew John; er s of Maj Claud Edward Frederick Hanbury-Tracy-Domvile, TD (d 1987), and his 1 w Veronica May (d 1985), da of Cyril Grant Cunard; hp of kinsman 7 Baron Sudeley, *qv*; *b* 30 Nov 1928; *Educ* Sherborne, RAC Cirencester; *m* 1, 22 June 1957 (m dis 1966), Jennifer Lynn, o da of Dr Richard Christie Hodges; 1 s (Nicholas Edward John b 13 Jan 1959); m 2, 4 April 1967 (m dis 19--), Lilian, da of late Nathaniel Laurie; 1 s (Timothy Christopher Claud b 25 March 1968); m 3, 28 July 1988, Mrs Margaret Cecilia White, da of late Alfred Henry Marmaduke Purse; 7 Gainsborough Drive, Sherborne, Dorset DT9 6DS

HANBURY-TRACY, Hon Mrs (Blanche Mary); *née* Arundell; da of 15 Baron Arundell of Wardour (d 1944); *b* 5 Dec 1908; *m* 11 Jan 1935 (m dis 1954), Ninian John Frederick Hanbury-Tracy (d 1971), gs of 4 Baron Sudeley; 1 da; *Style*— The Hon Mrs Blanche Hanbury-Tracy; Maude, 10 Haldane Rd, London SW6; Casita Blanca, Nerja, Malaga, Spain

HANCOCK, Cyril James; s of Herbert James Hancock (d 1958), and Lilian, *née* Smith; *b* 9 Nov 1931; *Educ* Univ of Durham (BSc); *m* 9 July 1955, (Jean) Helen Spence, da of Samuel Steel (d 1967); 2 da (Karen b 1961, Ann b 1963); *Career* princ conslt and divnl dir PE Conslt gp 1961-78, dir Binder Hamlyn Fry 1979-81; non-exec dir: William Tathan Ltd 1981-, Wrights and Dobson Bros 1981-84, Shackleton Engrg 1984-86; princ Cyril Hancock Assocs 1981-; FIProdE, FIMC, MIMechE; *Recreations* walking, veteran bicycles and cycling, vintage cars; *Clubs* Vintage Sports Car; *Style*— Cyril Hancock, Esq; Fairacre, Bellingdon, Chesham, Bucks HP5 2XU (☎ 024 029 243)

HANCOCK, Lt-Col Sir Cyril Percy; KCIE (1946, CIE 1941), OBE (1930), MC (1918); s of Maj Francis de Bercken Hancock, IA (d 1916), by his w Kathleen, da of late Corbet John Coventry, (ggs of 6 Earl of Coventry); *b* 18 Sept 1896; *Educ* Wellington, RMC Sandhurst; *m* 25 July 1925, Joyce (d 13 June 1982), da of late Frederick Reckitts Hemingway, ICS; 3 s, 1 da; *Career* served WWI with 114 Mahrattas, joined Indian Political Serv 1920, ret as Resident 1st class 1947; *Clubs* fndr memb of Cricket Club of India; *Style*— Lt-Col Sir Cyril Hancock, KCIE, OBE, MC; Woodhayes, Firgrove Rd, Yateley, Hants (☎ 0252 873240)

HANCOCK, James Harrison; s of John Hancock (d 1970), of 39 Rushley Drive, Dore, Sheffield, and late Winifred May, *née* Harrison; *b* 8 July 1918; *Educ* Westbourne PS Sheffield, Richmond Sch Yorks; *m* 1 May 1943, Audrey Helen, da of Frank Mason (d 1957), of Ivy Bank, Broomhill, Sheffield; 1 s (Michael b 8 May 1944), 1 da (Elizabeth b 8 Aug 1948); *Career* CA 1945, conslt Hancock & Ashford 1987- (ptnr 1945, sr ptnr 1960); pres: Sheffield Jr C of C 1956-57, Sheffield Chamber of Trade 1973-74; former memb: Sheffield No 3 Hosp mgmnt ctee, Sheffield Area Health Authy; Freeman Worshipful Co of Cutlers in Hallamshire; FCA; *Recreations* fishing, shooting, swimming, squash, travel; *Clubs* Sheffield, Naval and Military, Exchange; *Style*— James Hancock, Esq; The Moorings, 65 Newfield Lane, Dore, Sheffield S17 3DD (☎ 0742 361 011); 47, 5 Spinila Ct, Upper Gardens, St Julians, Malta GC (☎ 010 356 335 326); Hancock & Ashford, Nimrod House, 42 Kingfield Rd, Sheffield S11 9AG (☎ 0742 556 591)

HANCOCK, John Norman David; s of John Norman Hancock, of Evington, Leicester, and Eunice Elizabeth, *née* Sturges; *b* 4 Oct 1939; *Educ* Wyggeston GS for Boys, Leics Poly (HNC); *m* 31 Aug 1963, Patience Anne, da of Philip James Taylor, of Cropston, Leics; 1 s (Mark James b 1965), 1 d (Jane Elizabeth b 1968); *Career* heating engr 1966-71, private narrow fabric mfr 1971-, chm and chief exec Hanro Gp of Cos 1975-; memb: employment policy ctee CBI, Smaller Firms Cncl, regnl cncl, ctee Br Narrow Fabrics Assoc; FInstD 1983; *Recreations* golf, sailing, aviation; *Clubs* Leics and Rothley GCs, Salcombe YC; *Style*— John N D Hancock, Esq; Beech House, Stoughton, Leics LE2 2FH (☎ 712 426); Hancock & Roberts Ltd, Stadon Rd, Anstey, Leics LE7 7AY (☎ 0533 357 520, fax 0533 366 423, car tel 0836 612 4404, telex 341843)

HANCOCK, John Stuart; s of W J S Hancock; *b* 8 June 1941; *Educ* Dynevor Sch Swansea, Univ of Birmingham (BCom); *m* 1977, Marjorie Elizabeth; *Career* dep md and fin dir T T Pascoe Ltd; FCA; *Recreations* travel, walking, gardening, golf; *Style*— Stuart Hancock, Esq; Somercombe House, 109 Higher Lane, Langland, Swansea SA3 4PS; T T Pascoe Ltd, York Chambers, Swansea SA1 3NJ (☎ 0792 54135, telex Swansea 48145)

HANCOCK, Michael Anthony; s of Anthony Ilbert Hancock, (d 1954), of Bickley, Kent, and Eileen Mary, *née* King; *b* 11 Sept 1943; *Educ* Tonbridge; *m* 11 July 1967 (m dis 1975), Diana Margaret, da of Albert Edward Peter; 1 s (Froude), 2 da (Claire, Emma); *Career* Bank of England 1961-63, ptnr WN Middleton & Co and Stock Exchange memb 1969-75, chm and chief exec Chart Estates Ltd 1985-; *Recreations* vintage cars, fine wines, antique furniture; *Clubs* Wig and Pen, Kent Woolgrowers; *Style*— Michael Hancock, Esq; Crabbe Farm, Lenham, Heath, Kent (☎ 0622 858 320); Bourg de Borreze, Dordogne, France; Stone Barn, Court Lodge, Egerton, Kent (☎ 0233 76474)

HANCOCK, Maj-Gen Michael Stephen; CB (1972), MBE (1953); s of Rev William Hugh Mundy Hancock (d 1926); *b* 19 July 1917; *Educ* Marlborough, RMA Woolwich; *m* 1941, Constance Geraldine Margaret, da of Brig-Gen Robert Montgomery Ovens, CMG (d 1950), of Aughnagaddy House, Ramelton, Co Donegal; 1 s, 1 da; *Career* cmmnd Royal Signals 1937, Brig 1963, CCRSigs 1 Br Corps 1963-66, chief Current Operations SHAPE 1966-67, sec NATO Mil ctee 1967-68, Maj-Gen 1968, COS FARELF 1968-70, Vice QMG 1970-72; Col Cmdt Royal Signals 1970-77, chm Combined Cadet Force Assoc 1972-82; planning inspr DOE 1972-87; *Style*— Maj-Gen Michael Hancock, CB, MBE; Brakey Hill, Godstone, Surrey (☎ 0883 842273)

HANCOCK, Norman; CB (1976); s of Louis Everard Hancock (d 1945), of Stoke Flemming Devon, and Rose Violetta, *née* Bowden (d 1963); *b* 6 Mar 1916; *Educ* Plymouth GS, RN Coll (first class prof cert in naval arch); *m* 1940, Marie Eva, da of William Ernest Bow, of St Leonards, Warminster Rd, Bath; 2 s (Robin, Mark); *Career* naval architect, RCNC (Royal Corps of Naval Constructors) 1940-, AEW Haslar 1940, Naval Construction Dept Bath 1944, Constructer Cdr: Germany 1945, Japan 1945-46, Bikini 1946, Singapore 1949, Bath 1952; prof naval architecture RNC Greenwich 1957-62, asst dir Submarine Design and Construction 1963-69, dir naval construction as dir of warship design and project dir, Invincible, Broadsword and Brecon 1969-76; past memb cncl RINA; Liveryman Worshipful Co of Shipwrights; *Recreations* cabinet making, organ music, travel; *Style*— Norman Hancock Esq, CB; 41 Cranwells Park, Bath, Avon BA1 2YE (☎ 0225 26045)

HANCOCK, Dr Robert Peter Dawbney; s of Sqdn Ldr Francis William Hancock, of Studland, Dorset, and Daphne Mary, *née* Baguley; *b* 21 April 1944; *Educ* Rugby, Guy's Hosp Med Sch; *m* 2 July 1966, Sonia Rosemary, da of Cdr Henry Petre, RN; 3 s (Benjamin b 1974, Toby b 1974, Bertie b 1979), 1 da (Scarlett b 1981); *Career* RAMC 1967-73: Capt surgical specialist Mil Hosps: Millbank, Woolwich Aldenshott, Rinteln BAOR; Regtl MO 3 Bn LI, princ in private practice GP; memb private practice ctee BMA; hon clinical asst and gp ldr staff support gp ICRF Breast Unit Guy's Hosp 1985-88; vice-chm Dulwich Dyslexia Soc; FRCS;; *Recreations* tennis, skiing, sailing; *Style*— Dr Robert Hancock; Furdie House, 82 Sloane St, London SW1 9PA, (☎ 01 235 3002)

HANCOCK, Ronald Philip; s of Philip Henry Hancock (d 1953), and Ann, *née* Lioni (d 1980); *b* 9 August 1921; *Educ* Epsom Coll; *m* 1958, Stella Florence (d 1988), da of Arthur Howard Mathias CBE (d 1970); 2 s, 1 da; *Career* Lt RNVR, serv Atlantic and Pacific Oceans and with Coastal Forces in English Channel; memb Lloyd's, int insur conslt; farmer; forester; chm: Euro Risk Mgmnt Ltd 1972-77, A R M Int Ltd 1972-84, Leumi Insur Servs (UK) Ltd 1983-87; dep chm Bland Welch and Co Ltd 1955-70 (dir 1946-70); dir: De Falbe Halsey and Co (Hldgs) Ltd 1972-74, Int Risk Mgmnt Ltd 1972-77, American Risk Mgmnt Inc (USA) 1972-77, Med Insur Agency Ltd 1974-; memb cncl: Royal Med Fndn of Epsom Coll 1969-, Br Horse Soc 1980-87; chm Horse Driving Trials Ctee 1983-87; memb: Br Equestrian Fedn 1983-87; chm: Surrey PHAB (Physically Handicapped and Ablebodied) 1973-79, tstee PHAB 1979-; pt/t cmmr and memb Forestry Cmmn 1988-, cncl memb Riding for the Disabled Assoc 1989-; Freeman City of London, memb Worshipful Co of Carmen; *Recreations* ocean racing and cruising, hunting, horse driving trials; *Clubs* Royal Thames YC, Lloyd's YC; *Style*— Ronald Hancock, Esq; Hillside Farm, Shere Rd, West Horsley, Surrey (☎ 04865 2098)

HANCOCK, Stephen Clarence; s of Norman Harry Hancock, of Brynmore, West Parade, West Shore, Llandudno, Wales, and Jean Elaine, *née* Barlow; *b* 1 Nov 1955; *Educ* King Edward VI Lichfield Staffs, City of Stoke-On-Trent Sixthform Coll, Sheffield Univ (LLB); *Career* slr of the Supreme Ct 1980; ptnr Herbert Smith Slrs 1986- (articled clerk 1978-80, asst slr 1980-86); memb Worshipful Co of Slrs; *Recreations* golf; *Clubs* Lakeside Golf and Country (Staffs); *Style*— Stephen Hancock, Esq; 1 Willow End, Surbiton, Surrey; Watling House, 35 Cannon St, London EC4 (☎ 01 489 8000)

HANCOCK, Air Marshal Sir Valston Eldridge; KBE (1962, CBE 1953, OBE 1942), CB (1959), DFC (1945); s of Richard John Hancock (d 1946), and Olive Mary Laura Hancock, *née* Prior (d 1977); John Hancock, formerly of England, landed Perth 1830 pioneered pastoral indust in Pilbara; *b* 31 May 1907; *Educ* Hale Sch Perth, RMC Duntroon, RAF Staff Coll (psc), Imperial Def Coll (idc); *m* 1932, Joan Elizabeth, da of Col Arthur Graham Butler, DSO, ED (d 1949); 2 s (John, Richard), 1 da (Rosemary); *Career* head Jt Servs Staff UK 1955-57, Air OC Malaya 1957-59, Air OC Operational Cmd Australia 1959-61, Air Marshal 1961, Chief of Air Staff RAAF 1961-65, ret 1965; Cmmr Gen Aust Expo 1967, pres Royal Cwlth Soc WA 1975-80, chm Aust Def Assoc 1975-81, dir exec Air West 1973-83; dir Works and Buildings RAAF HO 1937-39; Co No 1 Bombing and Gunnery Sch 1939-41; dir Plans 1942-43; Dir Postings 1944, Co 71 Beaufort Bomber Wing New Guinea 1945; dir Air Staff Plans and Policy 1946-47; Cmdt RAAF Coll 1947-49; Dep Chief of the Air Staff 1951-52; Air Memb of the Air Bd for Personnel 1953-54; pres Royal Cwlth Soc WA Branch 1974-80, life patron Aust Def Assoc Independent' newspaper 1970-75; contributions to def journals WA; defence corr Sunday Independent newspaper 1970-75; contribs to def journals and circulars *see Debrett's Handbook of Australia and New Zealand for further details*; *Style*— Air Marshal Sir Valston Hancock, KBE, CB, DFC; 108a Victoria Ave, Dalkeith, W Australia 6009 (☎ Perth 386 3651)

HANCOX, Tony; s of Christopher Hancox (d 1957), of Nottingham, and Gwendoline, *née* Chapman (d 1975); *b* 1927; *Educ* Oxford Univ (BA, MA); *m* 1949, Doreen, da of Thomas Bertie Anthony (d 1972), of London; 1 s (George b 1959), 1 da (Alcina b 1958); *Career* memb: ct of govrs London Inst 1986, cncl of coll for Distributive Trades 1981, Assoc Templeton Coll Oxford 1983-85, Careers Advsy Bd Univ of London 1970-80, City of Westminster local employment ctee (dep chm 1969-72), cncl Assoc of Retail Distributors 1970-72, employers sides Retail Wages Councils, 1965-80, Steering Gp retail mktg degree Manchester Poly 1987, Nat Cncl Vocational Qualifications (supervisory and magmnt awards) 1987, chm Hancox Mgmnt Servs 1987, nat coordinator Nat Retail Trg Cncl 1987, retail mangr, (latterry in personnel mgmnt and trg 1952-87, faculty Euro Sch of Mgmnt Oxford 1987; moderator external exam Univ of Stirling 1986; capt Thames Rowing Club 1958, memb of English Eight Commonwealth Games (Bronze Medallist) 1958; FIPM (1975), FInst Trg and Devpt 1987; *Recreations* music, reading, writing, rowing; *Clubs* Leander, Athenaeum; *Style*— Tony Hancox, Esq; National Retail Training Council, Commonwealth House, 1-19 New Oxford St, London WC1A 1PA (☎ 01 404 4622, telex 922488 BUREAUG REF RCO, fax 01 242 0156)

HAND-BOWMAN, Denis; s of Elmer Leopold Baumann (d 1968), of Sussex, and Mable Lydia, *née* Woodcock (d 1969); *b* 25 Jan 1917; *Educ* Haberdasher's Askes, Guy's Hosp (LDS, RCS); *m* 18 Sept 1943, Margaret McQueen Hill, da of Dr John McArthur (d 1950, of Denaby; 1 s (Michael b 1951), 1 da (Wendy b 1955); *Career* Capt Army 3 Canadian Div serv Normandy Beach Gp and Europe; dental surgn; dir Estuary Labs Ltd for 25 years, formerly house surgn Royal Dental Hosp; *Recreations* golf, gardening, music, choral singing, reading; *Clubs* Life Memb Thorpe Bay YC, Nevill GC, 250; *Style*— Denis Hand-Bowman, Esq; Pippins, Old Lane, Crowborough Hill, Crowborough, E Sussex TN6 2AB (☎ 0892 663669)

HANDCOCK, John Eric; DL (Royal County of Berkshire 1986); s of Eric George Handcock (d 1979), and Gladys Ada Florence, *née* Prior, of Bolton Avenue, Windsor; *b* 7 Oct 1930; *Educ* Aldenham Sch, King's Coll London (LLB); *m* 1956, Joan Margaret, da of Wilfred Joseph Bigg, CMG (d 1983), of Swanage, Dorset; 2 s (David, Jonathan), 2 da (Sandra, Nicola); *Career* slr; sr ptnr Lovegrove and Durant of Windsor and Ascot 1966-; pres Berks, Bucks and Oxon Incorporated Law Soc 1979-80; dir Solrs' Benevolent Assoc 1981-; chm Berks Bucks and Oxon Professional Council 1981-82; govr St George's Choir Sch Windsor Castle 1975-; dep Capt lay stewards St George's Chapel Windsor Castle 1977-; tstee Prince Philip Tst for Windsor and Maidenhead 1978-; Citoyen d'Honneur de la Ville Royale de Dreux 1976; Hon Life Member River Thames Soc 1986; *Recreations* history, travel, wine, books; *Clubs* Law Society; *Style*— John E Handcock, Esq, DL; Red Deer House, Kingswood Rise, Englefield Green, Surrey (☎ 0784 34289); Lovegrove and Durant, 4 Park St, Windsor, Berks SL4 1JF (☎ 0753 851133, telex 849275 LOVDUR G)

HANDFORD, Peter Thomas; MBE (1945); s of Rev Hedley William Mountenay Handford (d 1928), Vicar of Four Elms, Edenbridge, Kent, and Helen Beatrice, *née* Crosse (d 1964); *b* 21 Mar 1919; *Educ* Christ's Hosp; *m* 12 May 1974, Helen Margaret; 2 da (Lyn Patricia (Mrs Hedges), Pamela Anne (Mrs Kucel) by previous m; *Career* WWII (Capt RA) serv incl 50th BFF and D Day landings 1939-46; sound recordist London Film Prodns 1936-39; after war worked with various film cos before becoming freelane; responsible for sound recording on more than 60 films inc: Room at the Top, Billy Liar, Out of Africa (won Academy (Oscar) and Bafta awards for sound track 1986), Murder on the Orient Express; prodr Sounds of the Steam Age on records (awarded Grand Prix du Disque, Paris 1964); memb Acad of Motion Picture Arts and Sciences 1986; *Books* The Sound of Railways (1980); *Recreations* gardening, sound recording, railway enthusiasm and travel, country pursuits; *Clubs* Academy of Motion Picture, Arts and Scis, Sloane; *Style*— Peter T Handford, Esq; Sandra Marsh Management, Post Box 37, Lee International Studios, Studios Road, Shepperton, Middx TW17 0QD (☎ 0932 568148, telex MOVIES G 929416)

HANDLEY; *see*: Davenport-Handley

HANDLEY, Dr Anthony James; s of Wing Cdr Austyn James Handley, RAF (d 1985), of W Mersea, Essex, and Beryl Janet, *née* Ashling (d 1982); *b* 22 June 1942; *Educ* Kimbolton Sch, King's Coll London, Westminster Hosp Med Sch (MB BS, MD); *m* 3 Dec 1966, Jennifer Ann, da of Noël Lindsay Ross Kane (d 1986), of Colchester, Essex; 1 s (Simon b 1973), 1 da (Juliette b 1971); *Career* Maj RAMC (TA) 1970-, chm inter-serv cadet rifle matches ctee; conslt physician NE Essex Health Authy 1974-, hon clinical tutor Charing Cross and Westminster Med Sch 1976-, clinical tutor dolches Colchester Postgrad Med Centre 1980-85; vice-pres and med advsr RLSS; county judge Essex amateur swimming assoc, MRCP 1968, FRCP 1985, memb Br Cardiac Soc 1984, FRSM 1985, memb Resuscitation Cncl 1986; *Books* Thoracic Medicine (contrib, ed Emerson 1981), Resuscitation and First Aid (ed 1986); *Recreations* swimming, squash, music (trombone player); *Style*— Dr J Anthony Handley; 40 Queens Rd, Colchester, Essex CO3 3PB (☎ 0206 562 642); 27 Oaks Drive, Colchester, Essex CO3 3PR (☎ 0206 573 253)

HANDLEY JONES, Susan Kathleen (Sue); da of Patrick John Dickinson (d 1984), of Surrey, and Christine Margaret Wells, *née* Weston; *b* 13 July 1955; *Educ* Malvern Girls Coll, Univ of Warwick (BA); *m* 10 Sept 1983, Nicholas, s of Anthony Handley Jones, of Bucks; *Career* recruitment specialist Badenach and Clark, pr consultancy work for Honewell, Philips, Telephone Rentals 1981-83, recruitment and personnel work 1977-81; *Clubs* Oriental; *Style*— Mrs Susan Handley Jones; Westwood House, Westwood, Southfleet, Kent (☎ 047 483 2156); Badenoch and Clark, 16 New Bridge St, London EC4V 6AU (☎ 01 583 0073, fax 01 353 3908)

HANDS, Hargrave Patrick; *b* 2 Feb 1921; *m* 19 Aug 1947, Daphne Mary; 1 s (Jeremy b 1951), 1 da (Rowena b 1954); *Career* artist and illustrator; considerable work in all fields of publishing and advertising world wide, regular contrib to newspaper magazines over past 30 years and pioneer of the realistic but decorative approach; specialist in anantomical, entomolgical, ornithological and horticultural illustration; awarded Grenfell Medal (RHS); *Recreations* music, golf; *Clubs* Flempton and SIA; *Style*— Hargrave Hands, Esq; Thatch End, Flempton, Suffolk IP28 6EG (☎ 0284 84467)

HANDS, Sydney Edward; TD (1946); s of William Hands (d 1958), of High Wycombe, and Mary Annie, (d 1943); *b* 4 June 1903; *Educ* Royal GS High Wycombe; *m* 21 Dec 1938, (Edith) Irene, da of Arthur William Head (d 1953); 1 s (Christopher b 1949), 2 da (Rosemary Irene b 1943, Venetia Mary b 1948); *Career* WWII, gazetted 1938 RAPC, Lt/Staff Paymaster CII, TA 1939, Capt 1939, Maj and Staff Paymaster class II 1941, Lt-Col and Staff Paymaster class I 1944, discharged with HonRank Lt Col 1945; W Hands and Son (est 1906): joined 1921, dir and sec 1935, md 1966, chm 1969-71, ret 1973; Old Wycombiesians RUFC: jt fndr 1929, Capt 1930-39, hon tres 1929-60, pres 1968-69; fndr H W Motor Cycle Club 1921; Royal Philatelic Soc London: hon tres 1949-67, vice-pres 1965-69, pres 1969-71, hon life memb 1973; High Wycombe Rotary Club: joined 1953-; tres 1955-68, pres 1968-69; Freeman Worshipful Co of Furniture Makers 1941 (life memb 1973); *Recreations* philately, gardening; *Style*— Lt-Col Sydney Hands, TD; 1 Brands Hill Ave, High Wycombe, Bucks HP13 5PZ (☎ 0494 25307)

HANDS, Terry; *b* 9 Jan 1941; *Educ* Birmingham Univ, trained at RADA; *m* 1, 1964 (m dis 1967), Josephine Barstow; m 2, 1974, (m dis 1980), Ludmila Mikael; 1 da (Marina); *Career* joined RSC 1966, artistic dir RSC's Theatreground (touring schs and community centres) 1966-68; dir The Merry Wives of Windsor for RSC 1968 (revived 1975/76), Pericles 1969, etc; dir Henry V, Henry IV Parts I and 2, and The Merry Wives of Windsor (all subsequently transferred to Aldwych) for centenary season at Stratford 1975; dir all 3 parts of Henry VI (1st time in entirety since Shakespeare's day), Stratford 1977 (jt winner Plays and Players Award for Best Prodn and SWET Award for Dir of the Year), and many other prodns at Stratford and Aldwych; dir Richard III for Comedie Francaise, Paris 1972 Twelfth Night 1976, and Othello for Paris Opera (televised in France 1978), etc; dir Parsifal for Royal Opera House 1979, As You Like It, Richard II and Richard III at Stratford 1980 (the latter two completing the entire Shakespeare history cycle, begun 1975, with Alan Howard in leading roles); dir Much Ado About Nothing, Stratford 1982, Cyrano de Bergerac (SWET Award for Best Dir, etc) Barbican 1983, Red Noses 1985, etc; *Style*— Terry Hands; 54 Onslow Gardens, Muswell Hill, London N10 (☎ 883 1545); Royal Shakespeare Company, Barbican Centre, Barbican, London EC2 (☎ 01 628 3351)

HANDSCOMBE, Richard Stanley; s of Stanley George Handscombe (d 1957), of Harrow, London, and Phoebe Blow; family traces ancestry back to hamlet of Hanscombe End, near Shillington, Bedfordshire—first published records 1222; *b* 31 Mar 1937; *Educ* Haberdasher's Askes Hampstead, Univ Coll London (BSc); *m* 1, 10 Sept 1960, Jennifer Anne, da of Beresford Paul (d 1986), of Minchinhampton; 3 da (Fiona b 1966, Sophie b 1968, Naomi b 1971); m 2, 30 May 1978, Maria Thersia, da of Jan Bakker, of Amsterdam; *Career* mangr: ICI 1958-62, Mars 1962-65, Bernard Matthews 1965-68, Urwick Orr and Ptnrs 1968-76; md: Urwick Int N Europe 1973-76, Kepner Tregoe N Europe 1976-80; managing ptnr Richard S Handscombe and Ptnr 1980-; lectr and dir int mangmt conf and courses; chm Br Business Assoc Netherlands 1976; FBIM; FInstD; FIMC; MIChemE; *Books* Bankers Management Handbook (ed in chief 1976), The Product Management Handbook (1988); contributions to Handbooks and circa 100 articles; *Recreations* skiing, gardening, fishing, writing; *Style*— Richard S Handscombe, Esq; 10 Gloucester Place, Windsor, Berks (☎ 0753 863 947)

HANDY, Prof Charles Brian; s of Ven Brian Leslie Handy, and Joan Kathleen Herbert, *née* Scott; *b* 25 July 1932; *Educ* Bromsgrove Sch, Oriel Coll Oxford (BA, MA), MIT (SM); *m* 5 Oct 1962, Elizabeth Ann, da of Lt-Col Rowland Fenwick Ellis Hill (d 1978), of Sliema, Malta; 1 s (Scott b 1968), 1 da (Kate b 1966); *Career* mktg exec Shell Int Petroleum Co Ltd 1956-65, economist Charter Consolidated Co Ltd 1965-66, int faculty fell MIT 1966-67, London Business Sch 1967- (prof 1978-), warden St George's House Windsor Castle 1977-81, writer and broadcaster 1981-; chm RSA 1986-88 (cncl memb 1983-); hon DLitt Bristol Poly 1988; *Books* Understanding Organizations (1983), Future of Work (1984), Gods of Management (1985), Understanding School (1986), Understanding Voluntary Organizations (1988), The Age of Unreason (1989); *Recreations* theatre, cooking, travel; *Style*— Prof Charles Handy; 73 Putney Hill, London SW15 3NT (☎ 01 788 1610); Old Hall Cottages, Bressingham, Dis, Norfolk; Le Bagnaie, Castellina in Chianti, Siena, Italy; London Business Sch, Susssex Place, Regent's Park, London NW1 (☎ 01 262 5050)

HANDYSIDE, Robert Graham; s of George Robinson Handyside (d 1966), of Gwent, and Marion Handyside, *née* Graham; *b* 1 August 1938; *Educ* Bassaleg GS; *m* 25 Feb 1963, Rhona Nancy; 1 s (Richard b 1968), 1 da (Julie b 1966); *Career* CA; chm: Argosy Fin & Co Ltd 1970, Argosy Fin and Guarantees Ltd 1970, Glenwood Securities Ltd 1975, Office & Factory Engrg and Servs Ltd 1982; *Recreations* golf; *Clubs* RAC, Cardiff and County (Cardiff); *Style*— Robert Handyside, Esq; The Mews, 4 Cathedral Rd, Cardiff CF1 9RF (☎ 0222 372331, telex 497132, fax 0222 222624)

HANFORD, John; s of Joseph Henry Hanford (d 1965), and Caroline English, *née* Smith (d 1967); *b* 10 Dec 1932; *Educ* St James Choir Sch Grimsby, Loughborough Univ (BSc); *m* 13 Aug 1960, Rita Katrina, da of Herbert Arthur (d 1964), 2 s (Timothy John b 1964, James Philip b 1966); *Career* md Pencol Engng Constls, Liveryman Worshipful Co of Engs 1985, FICE, MIWEM; *Clubs* St Stephens; *Style*— John Hanford, Esq; Kingscliffe, Pinner Hill, Pinner, Middx HA5 3XU (☎ 01 866 6824)

HANHAM, Prof Harold John (Harry); s of John Newman Hanham (d 1960), and Ellie, *née* Malone (d 1977); *b* 16 June 1928; *Educ* Mount Albert GS, Auckland Univ Coll (Univ of NZ, BA, MA), Selwyn Coll Cambridge (PhD); *m* 27 Jan 1973, Ruth Soulé, da of Prof Daniel I Arnon, of Univ of California; *Career* asst lectr (latterly sr lecturer) Univ of Manchester 1954-63, prof of politics Univ of Edinburgh 1963-68, prof of history Harvard Univ (also fell of Lowell House) 1968-73, prof of hist and political sci and dean sch of humanities social sci MIT 1973-85, hon prof of hist and vice-chllr Univ of Lancaster 1985-; memb Econ and Socl Res Cncl 1986-; memb Cncl for Mgmnt Educn and Devpt 1988- Guggenheim Fell 1972-73; Hon AM Harvard Univ 1968; FRHistS, FAAAS; *Books* Elections and Party Management (1959), The Nineteenth Century Constitution (1969), Scottish Nationalism (1969), Bibliography of British History 1851-1914 (1976 awarded John H Jenkins prize); *Clubs* UTD Oxford and Cambridge Univ, St Botolph (Boston); *Style—* Prof HJ Hanham; The Croft, Bailrigg Lane, Lancaster, LA1 4XP (☎ 0524 63454); University House, University of Lancaster, Lancaster, LA1 4YW (☎ 0524 65201 ext 203, fax 0524 63808, telex 65111 LANCUL G)

HANHAM, Sir Michael William; 12 Bt (E 1667), of Wimborne, Dorsetshire, DFC (1944); s of Patrick Hanham (d 1965), by his 1 w, Dulcie, *née* Daffarn formerly Hartley (d 1979); 3 s of Col Phelips Hanham, bro of Sir John Hanham, 9 Bt; *b* 31 Oct 1922; *Educ* Winchester; *m* 27 Feb 1954, Margaret Jane, da of Wing-Cdr Harold Thomas; 1 s, 1 da; *Heir* s, William Hanham; *Career* Flying Offr RAF Pathfinder Force 1944-45, Actg Flt Lt India 1946; with BOAC 1947-61; own garden furniture workshop 1963-74; running family estate at Wimborne 1974-; KASG; *Clubs* Pathfinder; *Style—* Sir Michael Hanham, Bt, DFC; Deans Court, Wimborne, Dorset

HANHAM, William John Edward; s and h of Sir Michael Hanham, 12 Bt, DFC; *b* 4 Sept 1957; *Educ* Winchester, Courtauld Inst of Art (BA); *Career* press offr Christie's; *Recreations* painting, beekeeping, chess; *Style—* William Hanham, Esq; 36 Lena Gdns, London W6 (☎ 01 602 0429)

HANKES-DRIELSMA, Claude Dunbar; *b* 8 Mar 1949; *Career* chm: mgmnt ctee Price Waterhouse and Ptnrs (London, New York, Hong Kong, Paris, Toronto, Zurich) 1983-89, The Export Fin Co Ltd 1983-, The Br Export-Fin Advsy Cncl 1981, Action Resource Centre 1986-; Robert Fleming and Co Ltd 1972-77 (dir 1974); Mfrs Hanover 1968-72; asstd Dr Fritz Leutwiler in his role as Independent Mediator between the South African Govt and Foreign Banks 1985, initiator of project sponsored by US Agency for Int Devpt to explore ways of asstg Developing Countries to improve liquidity and trade fin 1985; memb cncl of mgmnt Action Resource Centre 1983-86, governing cncl Business in the Community 1986-(memb pres's ctee 1988-), nat cncl Young Enterprise 1987-; chm Business in the Community Target Team Suport Gp on voluntary sector initiatives 1987-; memb Deanery Synod; Parochial Church Cncl; *Recreations* gardening, walking, skiing, reading; *Style—* Claude Hankes-Drielsma, Esq; Stanford Place, Faringdon, Oxon, England (☎ 0367 20547, fax 0367 22853)

HANKEY, Hon Alexander Maurice Alers; s of 2 Baron Hankey, KCMG, KCVO; *b* 18 August 1947; *Educ* Rugby, Trinity Coll Cambridge, MIT (PhD), MERU (MSCI); *m* 1970, Deborah, da of Myron Benson, of Mass, USA; *Career* Greenlaw Fell MIT 1969-71; Lindemann Fellowship 1972-73 (held at Stanford Linear Accelerator Centre); teacher of transcendental meditation 1973-; asst prof of physics Maharishi Int Univ US 1973-74 (associate prof 1974-75, prof 1975-1978); prof of physics Maharishi Euro Research Univ Switzerland and UK 1975-; govr of the Age of Enlightenment 1977-; Dean of Faculty Maharishi Int Academy UK 1985-86; co-dir Academy for the Science of Creative Intelligence, Massachusetts, 1978; Registrar Maharishi University of Natural Law, North of England Campus 1986-; Leverhulme Foundation Research Award 1986; (Teacher of Transcendental Meditation 1973, govr of the Age of Enlightment 1977); *Recreations* skiing, tennis, hiking; *Clubs* Queen's, Royal Tennis; *Style—* Dr the Hon Alexander Hankey; 5 Rowan Lane, Woodley Park, Skelmersdale, Lancs WN8 6TX (☎ 0695 28847)

HANKEY, Hon Christopher Alers; OBE (1958); s of 1 Baron Hankey, PC, GCB, GCMG, GCVO (d 1963); *b* 1911; *Educ* Rugby, Oxford Univ (MA), London Univ (BSc); *m* 1, 31 Oct 1945 (m dis 1957), Prudence May, da of Keith Brodribb; 1 da; m 2, 5 Sept 1958, Helen Christine, da of late Alexander John Cassavetti; 1 s; *Career* serv WWII, Maj RM; princ Miny of Overseas Devpt 1964-72, ret; exec Cncl for Tech Educn and Trg in Overseas Countries 1972-78; *Recreations* amateur artist; *Style—* The Hon Christopher Hankey, OBE; New Cottage, French Street, nr Westerham, Kent

HANKEY, Hon Donald Robin Alers; s of 2 Baron Hankey, KCMG, KCVO; *b* 12 June 1938; *Educ* Rugby, UCL; *m* 1, 1963 (m dis 1974), Margaretha Thorndahl; m 2, 1974, Eileen Désirée, da of Maj-Gen Stuart Hedley Molesworth Battye, CB; 2 da (Fiona, Beatrice); *Style—* The Hon Donald Hankey; 53 Woodfield Ave, London SW16 6ES

HANKEY, Hon Henry Arthur Alers; CMG (1959), CVO (1960); yst s of 1 Baron Hankey, GCB, GCMG, GCVO, PC (d 1963); *b* 1 Sept 1914; *Educ* Rugby, New Coll Oxford; *m* 1 Jan 1941, Vronwy, only da of late Rev Thomas Frederic Fisher, Rector of Stilton, Peterborough; 3 s (Christopher, Maurice, Peter), 1 da (Veronica); *Career* ambass to Panama 1966-69, under-sec FCO 1969-74; dir: Lloyds Bank International 1975-80, Autofagasta (Chili) and Bolivia Railway Co 1975-82; sec British North American Ctee 1981-85; *Clubs* Utd Univ; *Style—* Hon Henry Hankey, CMG, CVO; Hosey Croft, Westerham, Kent

HANKEY, 2 Baron (UK 1939); Robert Maurice Alers Hankey; KCMG (1955, CMG 1947), KCVO (1956); s of 1 Baron Hankey, GCB, GCMG, GCVO, PC, FRS, Secretary of Cabinet 1915-38, Chllr Duchy of Lancaster 1940 and Paymaster-Gen 1941-42 (d 1963); *b* 4 July 1905; *Educ* Rugby, New Coll Oxford, Bonn Univ, Sorbonne Paris; *m* 1, 27 Sept 1930, Frances Bevyl (d 1957), da of Walter Stuart-Menteth (4 s of Sir James Stuart-Menteth, 4 Bt); 2 s, 2 da; m 2, 2 Oct 1962, Joanna, da of Rev James Johnston Wright, late chaplain to Edinburgh Castle and asst St Giles Cathedral; *Heir* s, Hon Donald Hankey; *Career* sits as Independent Peer in House of Lords; FO 1927-65, served Berlin, Paris, London, Warsaw, Bucharest, Cairo, Teheran, Madrid, Budapest; ambass Stockholm 1954-60, perm UK delegate OEEC and OECD anc chm Econ Policy Ctee 1960-65; pres Anglo Swedish Soc 1970-78, vice-pres European Inst of Business Admin Fontainebleau (INSEAD) 1966-80; dir Alliance Bldg Soc to 1983; *Recreations* reading, skiing, tennis, golf; *Clubs* Royal Cwlth Soc; *Style—* The Rt Hon the Lord Hankey, KCMG, KCVO; Hethe House, Cowden, Edenbridge, Kent (☎ 034 286 538)

HANKINS, (Frederick) Geoffrey; s of Frederick Aubrey Hankins (d 1966), of Eltham, and Elizabeth, *née* Stockton (d 1957); *b* 9 Dec 1926; *Educ* St Dunstan's Coll; *m* 1951, Iris Esther, da of George Robert Perkins (d 1977), of Wotton-under-Edge; 2 da (Susan, Jane); *Career* served Army BAOR 1946-48; mgmnt trainee later mfrg mgmnt J Sainsbury 1949-55, gen mangr Allied Suppliers 1955-62, prodn dir Brains Food Prods 1962-69, Kraft Foods 1966-69; W L Miller and Sons Poole: gen mangr 1970-72, md 1972-82, chm 1975; Fitch Lovell plc: dir 1971-, chief exec 1982-, chm 1983-; dir: Blue cap Frozen Food Servs Ltdm Fitch & Son Ltd, Fitch Lovell nominees Ltd, Hedges Frozen Foods Ltd Jus-rol Ltd, L Noel & Sons Ltd, Lovell & Christmas (Canada) Inc, Newforge Foods Ltd, Parrish and Fenn Ltd, Robirch Ltd, Salaisons Le Vexin SA, Stocks Lovell Ltd, Trent Meat Co Ltd, W L Miller & Sons Ltd, FRSA; *Recreations* genealogy, antiques, practical pursuits; *Style—* Geoffrey Hankins, Esq; 51 Elms Ave, Parkstone, Poole, Dorset BH14 8EE; Fitch Lovell plc, 1 West Smithfield, London EC1A 9LA (☎ 01 248 6431, telex 887029 LOVELL)

HANKINS, Prof Harold Charles Arthur; s of Harold Arthur Hankins (d 1982), of Crewe, Cheshire, and Hilda Hankins (d 1959); *b* 18 Oct 1930; *Educ* Crewe GS, Univ of Manchester (BSc, PhD); *m* 23 July 1955, Kathleen, da of Alec Higginbottom (d 1983), of Glossop, Derbyshire; 3 s (Anthony b 22 Dec 1957, Matthew b 9 July 1961, Nicholas b 21 Dec 1962); *Career* asst chief engr Metropolitan Vickers Electrical Co Ltd 1955-68; UMIST: lectr in electrical engrg 1968-71, sr lectr in electrical engrg 1971-74, prof of communication engrg and dir of med engrg unit 1974-84, vice-princ 1979-81, dep princ 1981-82, acting princ 1982-84, princ 1984-; non-exec dir Thorn EMI Lighting Ltd 1979-85; chm NW centre ctee Inst of Electrical Engrs 1977-78 (memb NW centre ctee 1969-77); memb: bd of govrs Manchester Poly 1989-, Manchester Lit & Phil Soc 1983-; hon fell Manchester Poly 1984; CEng, FIEE 1975; *Recreations* hill walking, music, choral work; *Clubs* Athenaeum; *Style—* Prof Harold Hankins; Rosebank, Kidd Rd, Glossop, Derbyshire SK13 9PN (☎ 04574 3895); UMIST, P O Box 88, Manchester M60 1QD (☎ 061 236 3311, fax 061 228 7040, telex 666094)

HANKINS, Timothy Glyn; s of Maj Hankins, of Crittles Ct, and Eileen Molly Hankins; *b* 19 Mar 1944; *Educ* Monmouth Sch, City Univ (BSc); *m* 30 May 1970, Susan Rosalie, da of Richard Stanley Oke (d 1982), of Cornwall; 2 da (Lucy Sarah b 1972, Emma Louise b 1975); *Career* div dir Honeywell Info Systems 1972-76, mktg dir Avery Label Systems 1976-81, md Alpha-Numeric Systems Ltd 1981-86, chm Alpha-Numeric Systems plc 1986-, pres Alpha-Numeric Systems SA (Spain); ctee memb Automiatic Identification Advsy Orgn (AIM); MIOD; *Recreations* squash, wine collecting, shooting, skiing, water sports; *Clubs* Barnet RFC (vice-pres); *Style—* Timothy Hankins, Esq; Charlton Cottage, 18 Copperkins Lane, Chesham Bois, Bucks (☎ 0494 725 385); Alpha-Numeric Systems plc, Alpha-Numeric Hse (☎ 0628 810 180, fax 0628 810 157, car tel 0836 617 049)

HANKINSON, Alan; s of Robert Hankinson (d 1970), of Lancs, and Beatrice, *née* Nelson (d 1966); *b* 25 May 1926; *Educ* Bolton Sch, Oxford Univ (MA); *m* Dec 1952 (m dis 1984), Roberta Lorna, da of James Gibson (d 1977), of Bolton; 1 s (Robert James b 1958); *Career* news ed Nigerian Broadcasting Corpn 1953-58, journalist ITN London 1958-75; author; *Books* The First Tigers (1972), The Mountain Men (1977), Man of Wars (1985), A Century on the Crags (1988); *Recreations* rock climbing, reading, tennis, squash, chess, fell walking; *Clubs* Keswick Chess, Keswick Squash; *Style—* Alan Hankinson, Esq; 30 Skiddaw St, Keswick, Cumbria CA12 4BY; (☎ 0596 73746)

HANKINSON, David Kyrle; s of Ernle George Hankinson (d 1959), of Upper Richmond Rd, London and Hilda Muriel, *née* Sykes (d 1968); *b* 30 May 1928; *Educ* St Peter's Ct, RNC Dartmouth; *m* 1, 2 Aug 1958 (m dis 1965), Carolyn Anne, da of Capt Charles Keys, RN (d 1986), of Buckland Monachorum, Devon; 2 s (Mark b 1960, Piers b 1963); m 2, 3 Sept 1969, Lavinia Joan, da of Rt Hon Sit Alan Lascelles, GCB, GCVO, CMG, MC (d 1981), of Kensington Palace; *Career* sr in destroyers Home and Med Fleets 1945-59, specialised in gunnery 1955, Cdr 1962, cmd HMS Cambrian Near and Far East 1962-64, resigned 1966; portrait painter; *Recreations* landscape painting, walking and bldg stone walls; *Style—* David Hankinson, Esq; 12a Barkston Gdns, London SW5 0ER (☎ 01 370 4949)

HANKS, Capt Alfred Leonard; s of William Thomas (d 1941), da of Emma Berry (d 1943); *b* 25 Oct 1918; *Educ* Chipping Campden GS; *m* 13 April 1941, Kathleen May, da of Arthur John Catling (d 1976); 1 da (Judith Caroline b 1948); *Career* serv RA 1940-46, attached to Indian Army and serv in Far East (India and Burma); auctioneer and land agent - principal Tayler and Fletcher 1982, conslt 1982; *Recreations* all country sports; *Style—* Capt Leonard Hanks; High View, Lyneham, Oxford OX7 6QL (☎ 0993 830404); Tayler and Fletcher, Stow-on-the-Wold, Cheltenham, Glos GL54 1BL (☎ 0451 30383)

HANLEY, Howard Granville; CBE (1975); s of Frederick Thomas (d 1951), of Bournemouth, and Edith, *née* Hill (d 1949); *b* 27 July 1909; *Educ* St Bees Sch Cumberland; *m* 7 Oct 1939, Margaret, da of James Jeffrey (d 1957), of Kensington; 2 s (David, Paul); *Career* Maj RAMC, civilian conslt urologist to Army 1950-65; urologist St Peters Hosps 1945-65; conslt urologists: Italian Hosps 1948, St Luke's Hosp for Clergy 1948, Royal Hosp for Chelsea 1950-65; urologist: King Edward VII Hosp for Offrs 1950-68; dean Inst of Urology 1965-70 (chm and pres 1988), vice-pres RCS 1978-79 (dean basic scis 1971-76, Hunterian prof); visiting prof of urology: Univ of California, State Univ Ohio Columbus, Univ of Texas, Univ of New Orleans; hon fell American Coll of Surgns 1967; Freeman City of London, Liveryman Worshipful Co Apothecaries 1958; pres Br Assoc of Urologist Surgery 1972-74 (memb cncl); *Books* Recent Advances in Urology (1957); *Recreations* gardening; *Clubs* Athenaeum; *Style—* Howard Hanley, Esq, CBE; Brandon House, Northend Ave, London NW3 7HP

HANLEY, Jeremy James; MP (C) Richmond and Barnes 1983-; s of Jimmy Hanley (d 1970), and Dinah Sheridan, actress (now Mrs Jack Merivale); *b* 17 Nov 1945; *Educ* Rugby; *m* 1973, Verna, Viscountess Villiers, da of Kenneth Stott of Jersey; 2 s, 1 da; *Career* CA; contested (C) Lambeth Central (by-election) 1978 and 1979; vice-chm Cons Trade and Indust Ctee, memb House of Commons Select Ctee on Home Affairs, memb House of Commons Select Sub-Ctee on Race Relations and Immigration; PPS to the min of State at the Privy Council Off, the min for the Civil Serv and the Arts; Parly Advsr to the Inst of CAs in England and Wales; dep chm The Fin Trg Co; chm, Nikko Fraser Green Ltd (memb of IMRO); FCA, FCCA, FCIS; *Recreations* cookery, cricket, golf, chess, languages; *Style—* Jeremy Hanley, Esq, MP; House of Commons, London SW1A 0AA

HANLEY, Hon Lady (Lorna Margaret Dorothy); JP; da of Hon Claude Hope-Morley (d 1968), and sis of 3 Baron Hollenden; raised to rank of Baron's da 1977; *b* 1929; *m* 1957, Sir Michael Bowen Hanley, KCB, *qv*; 1 s (Peter b 1968), 1 da (Sarah b 1967); *Style—* The Hon Lady Hanley, JP; The Old Rectory, Brixton Deverill, Warminster, Wilts BA12 7EL

HANLEY, Sir Michael Bowen; KCB (1974); s of late Prof J A Hanley; *b* 24 Feb

1918; *Educ* Sedbergh Sch, Queen's Coll Oxford; *m* 1957, Hon Lorna Margaret Dorothy, *qv*; *Career* serv WWII; attached to MOD; *Style—* Sir Michael Hanley, KCB; Hatfield Way, St John's Rd, Haslemere, nr High Wycombe, Bucks HP15 7QS

HANLON, Lady Colleen; *née* Wellesley; da of late 4 Earl Cowley; *b* 1925; *m* 1945, Paul A Hanlon, MD, late Capt US Army; 5 s, 2 da; *Style—* Lady Colleen Hanlon; 543 Westmoreland av, Kingston, Pennsylvania, USA

HANMER, Lady Frances Jane; *née* Cole; da of 5 Earl of Enniskillen, CMG (d 1963), and Irene Frances *née* Miller Mundy; *b* 16 Dec 1914; *m* 1954, as his 2 w, Gp Capt Henry Ivan Hanmer, DFC, RAF, (d 1984) gggs of 2 Bt; 1 s (Thomas Edward decd); *Style—* Lady Frances Hanmer; 1 Church Way, Grendon, Northampton

HANMER, (Wyndham Richard) Guy; s and h of Sir John Wyndham Edward Hanmer, 8 Bt; *b* 27 Nov 1955; *Educ* Wellington; *m* 9 Aug 1986, Elizabeth, (*née* Taylor, of Frampton on Severn; *Career* Blues and Royals, ret 1981-; now farming; *Style—* Guy Hanmer, Esq; The Stables, Bettisfield Park, Whitchurch, Shropshire

HANMER, Sir John Wyndham Edward; 8 Bt (GB 1774), of Hanmer, Flintshire, JP (Clwyd 1971), DL (1978); s of Lt-Col Sir Edward Hanmer, 7 Bt (d 1977), by his 1 w, Aileen; *b* 27 Sept 1928; *Educ* Eton; *m* 1954, Audrey, da of Maj Arthur Congreve, of the same family (which held land in Staffs from *temp* Edward II) as William Congreve, the Restoration playwright; 2 s; *Heir* s, Wyndham Hanmer; *Career* Capt late The Royal Dragoons; landowner and farmer; dir Chester Race Co 1978, Ludlow Race Club Ltd 1980; high sheriff Clwyd 1977; *Recreations* shooting, racing; *Clubs* Army and Navy; *Style—* Sir John Hanmer, Bt, JP, DL; The Mere House, Hanmer, Whitchurch, Shropshire (☎ 094 874 383)

HANN, Air Vice-Marshal Derek William; s of Claude Tavener Hann (d 1974), of Williton, Somerset, and Ernestine Freda, *née* Bowerman; *b* 22 August 1935; *Educ* Dauntsey's Sch; *m* 1, 1958 (m dis), Jill Symonds; 1 s (Simon b 1961), 1 da (Carol b 1959); m 2, 1987, Sylvia Jean, da of Rev John Newton Holder, of Eastbourne; *Career* joined RAF 1954; served on 65, 201 and 203 Sqdns; OC No 42 Sqdn 1972-74; OC RAF St Mawgan 1977-79; dir Operational Requirements 2 (RAF) MOD 1981-84; chief of staff HQ No 18 Gp 1984-87; dir-gen RAF Personal Servs MOD 1987-; *Recreations* theatre, gardening, watching sport; *Style—* Air Vice-Marshal Derek Hann; Adastral House, Theobalds Road, London WC1X 8RU (☎ 01 430 7239)

HANNA, Herbert Frederick; s of Arthur F Hanna (d 1980), of Dublin; *b* 26 Oct 1934; *m* 12 Sept 1955, Vyvyenne, *née* Davis; 1 s (Arthur b 1958); *Career* gen mangr Basic System IBM Europe 1968-74, md ITT Consumer Prods and dir ITT Europe 1974-82; md: Dataport-Parcon (Unitech Sudsid) 1982-86, FKI Metamec Dereham Norfolk 1986-; memb Norfolk C of C, vice-chm Br Clock and Watchmakers Assoc; MBHI; *Recreations* rugby, cricket, boating; *Clubs* Middx Co RU, Middx CC, Norfolk Broads YC; *Style—* Herbert Hanna, Esq; Fairbourne, 27 Norwich Rd, Dereham, Norfolk (☎ 0362 698219); Bristol Gardens, London W9; Cowper Rd, Rathmines, Dublin; FKI Metamec, South Green, E Dereham, Norfolk (☎ 0362 692121, fax 0362 693022)

HANNA, (James) Rainey; s of James Hanna (d 1964), of Coleraine Rd, Portrush, Co Antrim, and Margaret, *née* Henry; *b* 30 May 1924; *Educ* Enniskillen Model Sch, Portora Royal Sch, Queen's Univ Belfast (LLB); *m* 30 March 1950, Kathleen Isobel, da of Francis Wright Hoey (d 1968), of Dyan House, Caledon, Co Tyrone; 2 s (Jonathan b 1953, Paul b 1956); *Career* RAF 1943-46, Fl Sgt, Air Gunner; slr; chm Local Tbnls 1955-, HM coroner 1956-; memb: Inc Law Soc of NI 1948, ctee of mgmnt Enniskillen Savings Bank 1960 (custodian tstee 1960); *Recreations* golf, music; *Clubs* Royal Cwlth Soc (life memb), Royal Overseas League, Fermanagh County, Enniskillen GC; *Style—* Rainey Hanna, Esq; Larage Ho, Ballinamallard, Co Fermanagh (☎ 0365 230 90); 25 Darling St, Enniskillen, NI (☎ 0365 22 009); Main St, Fivemiletown, Co Tyrone, NI (☎ 03655 212 34); 92 Lisburn Rd, Belfast, NI (☎ 0232 683 126)

HANNAH, David Stuart; s of Daniel Hannah, of Appleton, Warrington, and Phyllis, *née* Mottershead; *b* 1 Jan 1953; *Educ* Royal GS Lancaster, Liverpool Univ (LLB); *m* 26 March 1977, Joanne Alison, da of James Crichton, of Minchinhampton, Glos; 3 s (Daniel b 1981, Christopher b 1983, Michael b 1987), 1 da (Louise b 1979); *Career* slr 1977-; tutor in law of equity and trusts Liverpool Univ 1974-78; memb Legal and Area Ctee Chester; *Recreations* swimming, restoring classic cars; *Style—* David S Hannah, Esq; 1 Marlfield Rd, Grappenhall, Warrington WA4 2JT (☎ 0925 64974); 1 Victoria Rd, Stockton Heath, Warrington (☎ 0925 61354)

HANNAH, Gordon Marshall; s of Dr Daniel Marshall Hannah (d 1971 former Wing-Cdr), of Eccles, Manchester, and Kathleen Mary, *née* Schaap, JP; *b* 30 April 1940; *Educ* Ellesmere Coll Shropshire, Trinity Coll Cambridge (MA); *m* 14 March 1964, Carolyn Joyce, da of William Dancer, of Axminster, Devon; 2 da (Juliette b 29 June 1966, Vanessa b 8 Oct 1968); *Career* chief engr The Dredging & Construction Co Contractors 1972-76; ptnr: Brown Crozier & Wyatt Conslt Engrs 1976-79, Hannah Reed & Assocs, 1979-; cncl memb Inst of Civil Engrs 1982-85; past pres Rotary Club of Cambridge Rutherford; past chm: Cambridge Round Table, E Anglian Assoc of Inst of Civil Engrs; FICE 1981, MConsE 1982, FIHT 1983, FRSA 1986; *Recreations* golf, gliding, gardening, modelmaking; *Clubs* Gog Magog GC, Cambridge Univ Gliding; *Style—* Gordon Hannah, Esq; 1 Bunkers Hill, Girton, Cambridge (☎ 0223 276 399); Hannah Reed & Assocs, Telford Hse, Station Rd, Cambridge CB1 2JF (☎ 0223 68523, fax 0223 316 894, car tel 0860 533 523)

HANNAH, Prof Leslie; s of Arthur Hannah (d 1969), and Marie, *née* Lancashire; *b* 15 June 1947; *Educ* Manchester GS, St John's and Nuffield Colls Oxford (BA, MA, DPhil); *m* 29 Dec 1984, Nuala Barbara Zahedieh, da of Thomas Hockton, of Hove, Sussex; 1 s (Thomas b 1988), 2 step da (Sophie b 1977, Miranda b 1981); *Career* res fell St John's Coll Oxford 1969-73, lectr in econs Essex Univ 1973-75, lectr Cambridge Univ 1975-78 (fell Emmanuel Coll, fin tutor 1977-78); LSE: dir Business Hist Unit 1978-88, prof 1982-; res fell Centre for Econ Policy Res London 1984-, visiting prof Harvard Bus Sch 1984-85, assoc fellow Centre for Business Strategy London Business School, 1988-89, invited lectr at univs in USA Europe and Japan; dir NRG (UK) Hldgs and other co's, fndr memb London Econs Econs (specialist res conslt); referee/tstee for various res funding agencies, charities and jls; socl sci Res Cncl (UK) 1982-84, chm ed advsy bd Dictionary of Business Biography 1979-85, panel speaker Celebrity Speakers Int; memb Inst of Dirs; *Books* The Rise of the Corporate Economy (1976, 2 ed 1983, Japanese ed 1987), ed Management Strategy and Business Development (1976), Concentration in Modern Industry: Theory, Measurement and the UK Experience (co-author, 1977), Electricity Before Nationalisation (1977), Engineers, Managers and Politicians (1982), Entrepreneurs and the Social Sciences (1984), Inventing Retirement: The Development of Occupational Pensions in Britain (1986), Electricity Privatisation and the Area Boards: the Case for 12 (co-author, 1987), Pension Asset Management: An International Perspective (ed 1988); *Recreations* reading, walking, talking; *Style—* Prof Leslie Hannah; LSE, Houghton St, London WC2A 2AE (☎ 01 405 7686 ext 3110, fax 01 242 0392, telex 24655)

HANNAM, Eric James Stanley; s of Capt Frank Stanley Hannam (d 1943), and Margaret Ada, *née* Collens (d 1956); *b* 13 Nov 1919; *Educ* Reading Sch Berks; *m* 1953, Betty Sinclair, da of Herbert George Cheel, MBE; 1 s (Mark James b 1955), 2 da (Sarah Margaret b 1957, Judith Emma b 1959); *Career* Inns of Ct Regt TA 1938, 2 Lt Shropshire Yeomanry 1939, subsequently 76 (Shrop Yeo) Medium Regt RA, served with regt in Middle East and Italy 1942-46, demobbed Capt RA 1946, memb Regtl Ctee London 1946-; joined staff Nat Provincial Bank Ltd 1936 (subsequently Nat West Bank plc), ret as sr mangr in the West End of London 1979; exec dir Leopold Joseph and sons Ltd 1979-81; non exec dir: London and Provincial Shop Centre (Hldgs) plc 1980-87, Grillford Ltd Fine Art Printers Milton Keynes (chm 1982-); Freeman City of London; Worshipful Co of Broderers: Freeman 1965, Liveryman 1965, Warden 1986, Master 1987; FCIB; *Recreations* theatre, reading, fine arts, watching sport; *Clubs* Oriental; *Style—* Eric Hannam, Esq; 11 Oakhill Avenue, Pinner, Middx HA6 3DL (☎ 01 866 3444); Grillford Ltrd, 26 Peverel Drive, Granby, Bletchley, Milton Keynes MK1 1QZ (☎ 090 864 4123)

HANNAM, John Gordon; MP (C) Exeter 1970-; s of Thomas William Hannam (d 1955), and Selina, *née* Young (d 1986); *b* 2 August 1929; *Educ* Yeovil GS; *m* 1, 19 June 1956 (m dis 1981), Wendy, da of late Thomas Lamont Macartney, of Beckenham; 2 da (Amanda b 1961, Katie b 1976); m 2, 1983, Mrs Vanessa Wauchope, da of Wing Cdr Henry Albert Anson, RAF (d 1955; gs of 2 Earl of Lichfield); 1 step s, 3 step da; *Career* cmmnd 4 Royal Tank Regt 1947-48, 4 Bn Somerset LI (TA) 1949-51; md: Hotels & Restaurants Co 1952-61, Motels & Restaurants Co 1961-70; chm British Motels Fedn 1967-74, pres 1974-80; memb Cncl Br Travel Assoc 1968-69; PPS min Indust 1972-73, chief sec Treasy 1973-74; sec All-Pty Disablement Gp 1975-; chm: W Country Cons Backbench Ctee 1979-81, Cons Energy Ctee 1979-; capt: Lords and Commons Tennis Club 1975-, Lords and Commons Ski Club 1975-82; memb: govt advsy ctee on Transport for Disabled, cncl Action Res, Glyndebourne Festival Soc, bd Nat Theatre; pres Br Motels Fedn 1974-79; vice-pres Disabled Drivers' Assoc; dir Berkeley Exploration and Prodn plc; Hon MA Open Univ 1986; *Recreations* tennis (ex Somerset Singles Champion), skiing, sailing, music, singing, reading; *Clubs* All England Lawn Tennis, Royal Yacht Sqdn; *Style—* John Hannam, Esq, MP; 4 Thurleigh Rd, London SW12 8UG (☎ 01 673 5750); Pightel Cottage, Plymtree, Devon (☎ 088 47 332)

HANNAY, Sir David Hugh Alexander; KCMG (1986, CMG 1981); s of J G Hannay (d 1972), of Aston Tirrold nr Didcot Oxon, and E M Hannay (d 1986), *née* Lazarus; *b* 28 Sept 1935; *Educ* Winchester, New Coll Oxford; *m* 1961, Gillian Rosemary, da of H Rex (d 1962), of Exmouth, Devon; 4 s (Richard, Philip, Jonathan, Alexander); *Career* 2 Lt 8 Kings Royal Irish Hussars 1954-56; joined FCO 1959, Tehran 1960-61, oriental sec Kabul 1961-63, eastern dep FO 1963-65, 2 and 1 sec UK Delgn to the EC 1965-70, 1 sec UK Negotiating Team with the EC 1970-72, chef de cabinet to Sir Christopher Soames vice-pres of cmmn of EC Brussels 1973-77, head Energy Sci and Space Dept FCO 1977-79, head ME Dept FCO 1979, asst under-sec of state (Euro Community) FCO 1979-84, min Washington 1984-85, ambass and UK perm rep to Euro Community 1985-; *Recreations* travel, gardening; *Clubs* Travellers'; *Style—* Sir David Hannay, KCMG; Avenue Henri Pirenne 21, 1180 Brussels (☎ 345 76 04); Rond Point Schuman 6, 1040 Brussels (☎ 230 62 05)

HANNAY, Dr Patrick Wyatville; s of Harry Rivers Hannay (d 1933), and Helen Knapp (d 1978); *b* 15 Nov 1914; *Educ* Eastbourne Coll, Edinburgh Univ (MB, ChB); *m* 8 Aug 1945, Kathleen Ronaldson Logan, da of Alexander Shand Gordon, of Edinburgh (d 1936); 1 s (Keith b 1947), 1 da (Alison b 1950); *Career* Lt-Col RAMC, ME, India, Burma (despatches) 1939-45; conslt dermatologist Edinburgh Royal Infirmary 1948-74; sr lectr in dermatology Edinburgh Univ 1948-74; FRCPE; *Recreations* gardening, walking, photography; *Style—* Dr Patrick Hannay; 2 Deans Park, Dunkeld, Perthshire PH8 0JH (☎ 03502 530)

HANNAY OF KIRKDALE AND THAT ILK, Ramsay William Rainsford; s of Col Frederick Rainsford-Hannay, CMG, DSO, JP (d 1959), of Cardoness, Gatehouse-of-Fleet, Kirkcudbrightshire, and Dorothea Letitia May *née* Maxwell (d 1981); *b* 15 June 1911; *Educ* Winchester, Trinity Coll Cambridge (LLB); *m* 19 Sept 1936, Margaret, da of Sir William Wiseman 10 Bt (d 1962), of Content, Montego Bay, Jamaica; 1 s (David b 3 Jan 1939), 1 da (Jessica b 2 Sept 1937); *Career* serv WWII, cmmnd Highland Light Inf, serv with SOE in US and Europe, attached to Kings Liverpool Regt, demob as Maj; barr 1934, legal asst Bd of Trade 1937-64 (ret to look after family estates in Galloway); appointed hon sheriff subsititute, Stewartry of Kirkcudbright; appointed chief of Clan Hannay 1980, as Hannay of Kirkdale and That Ilk and relinquished the surname of Rainsford; *Recreations* shooting, fishing, sailing; *Clubs* New (Edinburgh), Royal Ocean Racing (London); *Style—* Ramsay of Kirkdale and That Ilk; Cardoness House, Gatehouse-of-Fleet, Kirkcudbrightshire (☎ 0557 24 207)

HANNEY, Douglas William John; s of Percy John Hanney, of Sidmouth, Devon, and Iris May, *née* Wright; *b* 9 May 1955; *Educ* Abingdon Sch; *m* 1 June 1982, Helen Anne, da of Donald Arthur Parkes, of Halesowen, W Midlands; 2 s (Jonathan b 16 June 1984, Mark b 18 April 1986); *Career* dir Baring Securities Ltd; *Recreations* horse racing, golf, flying; *Style—* Douglas Hanney, Esq; Hampton, Middx; Sidmouth, Devon; 1 Lloyds Chambers, 1 Portsoken St, London E1 (☎ 0860 818039)

HANNING, Hugh Peter James; s of John Rowland Hanning (d 1961), (kinsman of John Hanning Speke, who discovered source of the Nile), and Valentine Mary Bradshaw (d 1975), da of Mayor Barrow-in-Furness; *b* 5 Feb 1925; *Educ* Winchester, Univ Coll Oxford; *m* 11 Dec 1954, Caragh McClure Williams; 1 s (James b 1956); *Career* cmmnd RNVR WWII; former def corr The Observer and def conslt The Guardian, ed Royal United Servs Inst Jnl 1967-70, sec C of E Internat Ctee 1972-80, dir Br Atlantic Ctee (Govt financed) 3 times 1974-82, former advsr MOD and FO Disarmament Ctee (sent by FO to Biafra), vice pres Intermediate Technol Devpt Gp, UK dir Int Peace Acad NY, conslt (Africa) Int Inst for Strategic Studies; lectr and ctee memb Chatham House (RIIA); *books*: The Peaceful Uses of Military Forces, A Global Strategy for Britain, Peace: The Plain Man's Guide (1988); *Recreations* piano, golf, childrens' games; *Clubs* Army and Navy; *Style—* Hugh Hanning, Esq; 18 Montpelier Row, Blackheath, London SE3 0RL (☎ 01 852 4101)

HANNON, Lady Fiona Mary; *née* Graham; da of 7 Duke of Montrose and his 1 w

Isobel Veronica, *née* Sellar; *b* 1 Jan 1932; *Educ* North Foreland Lodge; *m* 10 Oct 1966, Peter Alexander O'Brien Hannon, s of Ven Gordon Hannon (d 1978); 2 da (Catherine b 1968, Veronica b 1971); *Style—* Lady Fiona Hannon; The Fort House, Dundooan, Coleraine, N Ireland BT52 2PX

HANRAHAN, Brian; s of Thomas Hanrahan, and Kathleen, *née* McInerney; *b* 22 Mar 1949; *Educ* St Ignatius Coll, Essex Univ (BA); *m* 4 Jan 1986, Honor Catherine, *née* Wilson; *Career* BBC: Far East corr 1983-85, Moscow corr 1986-89, foreign affrs corr 1989-; *Style—* Brian Hanrahan, Esq; c/o BBC TV Centre, Wood Lane, London W12 (☎ 01 743 8000)

HANRATTY, James Francis; OBE (1989); s of Dr James Joseph Hanratty (d 1968), of Huddersfield, and Elsie May, *née* Lycett (d 1987); *b* 27 July 1919; *Educ* Stonyhurst, Leeds Univ (MB, ChB); *m* 26 May 1945, (Mary) Irene Evangeline, da of Andrew Belton (d 1977); 4 s (James b 1946, John b 1949, Patrick b 1952, Peter b 1957), 1 da (Mary b 1947); *Career* Surgn Lt RNVR 1943-46 (despatches 1944); serv HMS Cam: Atlantic, Med, Normandy invasion; GP N Derbys 1946-78, med dir St Joseph's Hospice Hackney 1978-88 (chm); hon conslt physician Mildmay Hosp Shoreditch; lectr terminal illness: RAMC, USA 1981, Sorbonne 1983, Hong Kong 1984, Brussels 1987, Hague 1987; former pres Derbys branch BMA, memb Industl injuries Med Bd Chesterfield 1949-78, master Guild of Catholic Doctors Nottingham 1975-78, govr Stonyhurst Coll 1975-81, fndr memb of cncl and tstee Help the Hospices; MRCGP 1969, FRSM 1977; Knight of the Order of St Gregory the Great (Papal) 1988, Knight of the Order of the Holy Sepulchre of Jerusalem English Lieutenancy 1987; *Books* Control of Distressing Symptoms in the Dying Patient (1982); *Recreations* watching cricket, classical music; *Clubs* Naval, Hurlingham, Athenaeum; *Style—* Dr James Hanratty, OBE; 44 Westminster Gardens, Marsham St, London SW1P4JG (☎ 01 834 4660)

HANSCOMB, Hon Mrs (Elinor Ruth); *née* McNair; da of 1 Baron McNair, CBE, QC, LLD (d 1975); *b* 25 Feb 1924; *m* 24 March 1955, Raymond Hanscomb, MRCVS, s of William Hanscomb, of Chapel House, Overthorpe, Banbury, Oxon; 1 s (Benjamin Douglas b 30 Aug 1956), 1 adopted s (George Sebastian b 21 Dec 1965), 1 adopted da (Emma Frances Mary b April 1963); *Style—* The Hon Mrs Hanscomb; Powells End, Kempley, Dymock, Glos

HANSCOMBE, Philip Martin; s of Stanley William Hanscombe, MBE (d 1967), and Sylvia, *née* Gordon (d 1983); *b* 9 Jan 1930; *Educ* Giggleswick Sch, Univ of Liverpool (BA); *m* 17 Sept 1960, Margaret Winnifred, da of George Erskine (d 1981); 2 s (Jonathan b 1963, Nicholas b 1969, d 1973), 2 da (Philippa b 1964, Caroline b 1975); *Career* Nat Serv Corpl RE 1948-50; dir mktg Trend plc 1958-61; ICI Paints 1961-: mktg mangr 1965-72, dir 1972-; memb Inc Soc of Br Advertising; *Recreations* golf, tennis, badminton, bridge, reading; *Clubs* Denham GC; *Style—* Philip Hanscombe, Esq; ICI Paints, Wexham Rd, Slough, Berks (☎ 0753 877273, fax 0753 74195, telex 847683)

HANSEN, Hon Mrs (Elizabeth Joan); *née* Bradbury; only da (by 1 m) of 2 Baron Bradbury; *b* 17 Mar 1940; *m* 1965, Warren G Hansen, s of Joseph H Hansen, of Dallas, Texas, USA; 1 s, 1 da; *Style—* The Hon Mrs Hansen; 2 Sargent Place, Waxahachie, Texas, 75167

HANSEN, Dr Robert Emil Albert Saabye; s of Christian Matteus Hansen (d 1926), of Denmark, and Winifred Ethel Williams (d 1971); gd s of Prof Emil Christian Hansen who discovered method of yeast cultivation in 1885 at Carlsberg Laboratories Denmark; *b* 29 Sept 1916; *Educ* Lydney GS, Kings Coll Camb, London Hospital (MA, MB BChir, DPH, FFCM); *m* 16 Feb 1948, Olga Nina, da of John Fryer Glossop (d 1917) of Rio de Janeiro; 2 s (John Christian Saabye b 1949, Nicholas Robert Saabye b 1951), 1 da (Angela Nina Saabye b 1955 d, 1985); *Career* Capt (physician) RAMC 1942-47, serv Persian Gulf, Middle East, Italy, Austria; GP N Lancs, chm med bd MW and MO Stonyhurst Coll; MOH Gloucester 1959-62, Glos County Area 1962-74; med advsr RDC Assoc, DC Physician Cheltenham Health Dist 1974-76, SCM Control of Infection Glos Area Health Dist for Environmental Health; Mil Italy Star (1946), W Atlantic Star (1946) (VM 1946); *Recreations* gardening, farming; *Clubs* Country Gentlemans Assn; *Style—* Dr Robert Hansen; Copelands, Staunton, Gloucester GL19 3QA

HANSON, Sir Anthony (Leslie Oswald) Dominic Sean; 4 Bt (UK 1887), of Bryanston Sq, Co Middx; s of Sir Gerald Stanhope Hanson, 2 Bt (d 1946), and his 3 w Flora Libre, *née* Blennerhassett (d 1956); suc half-bro Sir Richard Leslie Reginald Hanson, 3 Bt, 1951; *b* 27 Nov 1934; *Educ* Hawtrey's, Gordonstoun, Exeter Univ (BEd); *m* 1964, Denise Jane, da of Richard S Rolph, of Stoke-sub-Hamdon, Somerset; 1 da (Charlotte b 1971); *Heir* none; *Career* servd RN; farming to 1967; teacher to 1983; owing to a serious motorcyle accident was brain damaged and now does very little; *Recreations* riding, avoiding rows with wife, reading, working for Amnesty Int and Greenpeace, talking; *Style—* Sir Anthony Hanson, Bt; Woodland Cottage, Woodland, Ashburton, Devon (☎ 0364 52711)

HANSON, Brian John Taylor; s of Benjamin John Hanson (d 1978), of Norwood Green, Middx, and Gwendoline Ada, *née* Taylor; *b* 23 Jan 1939; *Educ* Hounslow Coll, Law Soc Coll of Law; *m* 10 June 1972, Deborah Mary Hazel, da of Lt Col Richard Stewart Palliser Dawson, OBE, of Shrubbery Cottage, Stowting, Kent; 2 s (James b 1973, Crispin b 1982), 3 da (Sarah b 1975, Rebecca b 1979, Alice b 1986); *Career* slr ecclesiastical notary; slr 1963-65; slr church cmmnrs for Eng 1965-70, asst legal advsr Gen Synod of C of E 1970-74; Gen Synod (registrar 1980-) House of Bishops 1974-; registrar to the Convocation of Canterbury 1984-; memb legal advsy cmmn of the Gen Synod 1980-(sec 1970-86); Guardian Shrine of Our Lady of Walsingham 1984-, memb cncl: St Luke's Hosp for the clergy 1985-, The Ecclesiastical Law Soc 1987-; fell Woodward Corp 1987-, govr St Michaels Sch Burton Park 1987-, Bishops Nominee on Chichester Diocesan Synod 1987-; memb Law Soc 1963, Canon Law Soc of GB 1980, Ecclesiastical Law Assoc 1980-; *Books* The Opinions of the Legal Advisory Commission (ed 6 edn 1985), The Canons of the Church of England (ed 2 edn 1975, 4 edn 1986), Norwood Parish Church - A Short History (1970); *Recreations* the family, gardening, genealogy; *Clubs* RCS; *Style—* Brian Hanson, Esq; Daltons Farm, Bolney, W Sussex RH17 5PG (☎ 0444881 890); Church House, Deans Yard, London SW1 (☎ 01 222 9011)

HANSON, (John) Brook; s of Baron Hanson (Life Peer), and Geraldine, *née* Kaelin; does not use courtesy title of Hon; *b* 2 April 1964; *Educ* Hawtrey's, Pangbourne Coll; *Career* mgmnt trainee Babcock Power; investmt analyst and industl sales mangr Chin Tong, Hong Kong; corporate res James Capel, Japan; *Recreations* hunting, helicopter flying, golf; *Clubs* Brooks's, Royal Thames YC, The Brook (NY); *Style—* Brook Hanson, Esq; 65 Eaton Square, London SW1W 9BQ (☎ 01 235 8179)

HANSON, Christopher John; s of Laurence William Hanson (d 1966), of Oxford, and Carola Mary, *née* Hawes; *b* 20 April 1940; *Educ* The King's Sch Canterbury, Oxford (MA); *m* 26 May 1975, Jayne Gwenllian, da of Evan Morgan Lewis, of Maidstone; 1 s (David William b 1976), 1 da (Elizabeth Jane b 1979); *Career* slr; ptnr Lovell White Durrant; memb insolvency jt working pty Bar and Law Soc 1977-, vice-chm insolvency sub ctee City of London Slrs Co; *Style—* Christohper Hanson, Esq; The Shaw, Brasted Chart, nr Westerham, Kent (☎ 0959 63 763); Lovell White Durrant, 21 Holborn Viaduct, London EC1A 2DY (☎ 01 236 0066, fax 01 248 4212, telex 887122 LWD G)

HANSON, Derrick George; s of late John Henry Hanson; *b* 9 Feb 1927; *Educ* Waterloo GS, London Univ, Liverpool Univ; *m* 1 1951, Daphne Elizabeth (decd); 1 s, 2 da; 2 1974, Hazel Mary (decd); *Career* dir and gen mangr Martins Bank Trust Co 1968, Barclays Bank Tst Co 1969-76, chm Barclays Unicorn 1972-76, sr advsr (UK) Mfrs Hanover Tst Co 1977-79, pres Assoc of Banking Teachers 1977-, dir Midshires Building Soc, chm City of London and European Property Co Ltd, dir Phillips Fine Art Auctioneers, chm Moneyguide Ltd, dir Toye and Co Ltd, chm Christian Arts Tst, dir Albany Investmt Tst Ltd, memb of cncl Liverpool Univ 1981-84; dir: Br Leather Co Ltd, James Beattie plc; chm Key Fund Mgrs Ltd; hon fell City Univ Business Sch; *pubns*: Service Banking: The Arrival of the All-Purpose Bank (1982) (Sr Prize of Inst of Bankers for 'outstanding contribution to banking literature'), Moneyguide: The Handbood of Personal Finance (1980), Dictionary of Banking and Finance (1985). 1981-84; *Recreations* golf, gardening, hill-walking; *Clubs* RAC, Formby GC; *Style—* Derrick Hanson Esq; Tower Grange, Grange Lane, Formby, Liverpool (☎ Formby 74040)

HANSON, Baron (Life Peer UK 1983), of Edgerton, Co of W Yorks; Sir James Edward Hanson; s of Robert Hanson, CBE (d 1973), and Louisa Ann (Cis), *née* Rodgers; *b* 20 Jan 1922; *m* 1959, Geraldine, *née* Kaelin; 2 s, 1 step da; *Career* chm: Hanson Tst plc 1965-, Hanson Transport Gp Ltd 1965-; tstee Hanson Fellowship of Surgery, Oxford Univ; Fell Cancer Research Campaign; Liveryman Worshipful Co of Saddlers', Freeman City of London; FRSA, CBIM; Hon LLD Leeds 1984; kt 1976; *Clubs* Brooks's, Huddersfield Borough, The Brook (New York), Toronto; *Style—* The Rt Hon the Lord Hanson; 1 Grosvenor Place, London SW1X 7JH (☎ 01 245 1245, telex 917202)

HANSON, Sir (Charles) John; 3 Bt (UK 1918), of Fowey, Cornwall; s of Sir Charles Edwin Bourne Hanson, 2 Bt (d 1958); *b* 28 Feb 1919; *Educ* Eton, Clare Coll Cambridge; *m* 1, 1944 (m dis 1968), Patricia Helen, da of late Adm Sir (Eric James) Patrick Brind, GBE, KCB; 1 s, 1 da; m 2, 1968, Violet Helen, da of late Charles Ormonde Trew, and formerly wife of late Capt Philip Cecil Langdon Yorke, OBE, RN; *Heir* s, Charles Rupert Patrick Hanson; *Career* late Capt, The Duke of Cornwall's Light Inf; serv WWII; *Clubs* Army and Navy, MCC; *Style—* Sir John Hanson, Bt; Gunn House, Shelfanger, nr Diss, Norfolk

HANSON, John Gilbert; CBE (1979); s of Gilbert Fretwell Hanson (d 1981), and Gladys Margaret, *née* Kay; *b* 16 Nov 1938; *Educ* Manchester GS, Wadham Coll Oxford (MA); *m* 1962, Margaret, da of Edward Thomas Clark, MBE, of Oxfordshire; 3 da (Mark b 1966, Paul b 1967, James b 1971); *Career* WO 1961-63, Br Cncl: 1963 Madras India 1963-66, MECAS Lebanon 1966-68, Bahrain 1968-72, London 1972-75, Tehran Iran 1975-79, London 1979-82, RCDS 1983; Min (cultural affrs) British High Cmmn New Delhi 1984-88; dep dir gen Br Cncl 1988-; memb governing cncl Br Inst Persian Studies F; *Recreations* books, music, sailing, sport, travel; *Clubs* Athenaeum, MCC, Gymkhana (Madras); *Style—* John Hanson, Esq, CBE; c/o The British Council, 10 Spring Gardens, London SW1A 2BN (☎ 01 930 8466)

HANSON, Prof Philip; s of Eric Hugh Cecil Hanson (d 1942), of London, and Doris May, *née* Ward (d 1980); *b* 16 Dec 1936; *Educ* Highgate Sch, Jesus Coll Cambridge (MA), Birmingham Univ (PhD); *m* 22 Oct 1960, Evelyn, da of Sidney James Rogers (d 1968), of London; 2 s (Paul Edward b 1963, Nicholas James b 1972); *Career* Nat Serv Middx Regt and Intelligence Corps, Sgt mil interpreter (Russian); lectr in econs Univ of Exeter 1961-67, visiting prof of econs Univ of Michigan 1967-68; Univ of Birmingham 1968-: lectr, sr lectr, reader, currently prof of Soviet econs; first sec HM Embassy Moscow, sr res offr FCO 1971-72; visiting prof Univ of Michigan 1977, sr Mellon fell Harvard Univ 1986-87; conslt: Planecon Inc, Oxford Anamtica, Radio Liberty; ctee memb Birmingham Jazz 1978-83, memb E Europe Exec Birmingham C of C and Indust 1980-; MRIIA; *Books* Trade and Technology in Soviet-Western Relations (1981), The Comparative Economics of Research, Development & Innovation (with K Pavitt, 1987), Western Economic Statecraft in East-West Relations (1988); *Recreations* jazz, cricket; *Style—* Prof Philip Hanson; c/o Crees, University of Birmingham, Birmingham, B15 2TT, (☎ 021 414 6353 fax 021 414 6707)

HANSON, Richard William Durrant; TD (1969); s of William Gordon Hanson, OBE, and Dulce Durrant Hanson; *b* 11 August 1935; *Educ* Eton; *m* 23 June 1961, Elizabeth Deirdre Dewar, da of late Dr A D Frazer; 1 s (James b 1969), 2 da (Arabella b 1962, Georgina b 1963) ; *Career* 2 Lt 17/21 Lancers 1954-56, Maj Sherwood Rangers Yeo and Royal Yeo 1956-69; dir Hardys & Hansons plc Kimberley Brewery Nottingham 1962, md 1973, chm and md 1989; High Sheriff Nottinghamshire 1980-81; *Recreations* shooting, tennis; *Clubs* MCC; *Style—* Richard Hanson, Esq, TD; Budby Castle, Newark, Notts NG22 9EU (☎ 0623 822293); Hardys & Hansons plc, Kimberley Brewery, Nottingham NG1 2DN (☎ 0602 383611, fax 0602 459055)

HANSON, Hon Robert William; s of Baron Hanson (Life Peer); *b* 3 Oct 1960; *Educ* Eton, St Peter's Coll Oxford; *Career* with N M Rothschild Ltd; *Recreations* hunting, polo, helicopter flying, golf; *Clubs* White's, Brooks's, The Berkshire, Cirencester Polo, The Brook (NY); *Style—* The Hon Robert Hanson; Bice Chileconsult, Teatinos 220, Santiago, Chile

HANSON, (Charles) Rupert Patrick; s and h of Sir (Charles) John Hanson, 3 Bt; *b* 25 June 1945; *Educ* Eton, Central London Poly; *m* 1977, Wanda, da of Don Arturo Larrain, of Santiago, Chile; 1 s (Alexis b 1978); *Career* tech, legal and commercial translator 1977-; teacher of english as foreign language 1981-;; *Recreations* classical music, writing poetry, tennis; *Style—* Rupert Hanson, Esq; 125 Ditchling Rd, Brighton, E Sussex BN1 4SE (☎ 0273 697882)

HANSON-SMITH, Christopher John; s of Herbert Cecil Smith, CBE (d 1981), of Monmouth, and Jane Bell, *née* Blair (d 1983); *b* 24 Dec 1927; *Educ* Winchester, New Coll Oxford; *m* 16 April 1955, Jennifer Margery, da of John Douglas Latta, MC (d

1973), of Ayr; 1 s (Julian b 1962), 3 da (Jane b 1956, Louise b 1957, Gabrielle b 1964); *Career* Lt Royal Norfolk Regt, India, BAOR 1946-48; dist offr HMOCS Nigeria 1950-59; vice consul Spanish Guinea 1957; export salesman Br Celanese Ltd 1959-64; md Vine Fuels Ltd 1964-66; PR offr Nat Tst 1967-87 (conslt 1988-); lectr for NADFAS, ESU (USA); chm: Beatrix Potter Soc, Food and Farming (Norfolk); MIPR; medals: Rhodesia (1980), Zimbabwe Independence (1980); *Recreations* photography, walking, fishing, travel; *Clubs* Lansdowne, Naval and Military; *Style*— Christopher Hanson-Smith, Esq; Foxley Lodge, Derham, Norfolk NR20 4QJ; National Trust, 36 Queen Anne's Gate SW1 (☎ 01 222 9251)

HANWORTH, 2 Viscount (UK 1936); Sir David Bertram Pollock; 2 Bt (UK 1922); also Baron Hanworth (UK 1926); s of Charles Pollock (s of 1 Viscount Hanworth, KBE, PC, JP, who d 1936 and was 5 s of George Pollock, himself the 3 s of Rt Hon Sir Frederick Pollock, 1 Bt, PC; his lordship m Laura, da of Sir Thomas Salt, 1 Bt, sometime MP for Stafford, JP, DL, whose w, Emma, was great-niece of Cardinal Manning); *b* 1 August 1916; *Educ* Wellington, Trinity Coll Cambridge; *m* 27 April 1940, (Isolda) Rosamond, JP, DL, FSA da of Geoffrey Parker (3 s of Hon Cecil Parker, JP, by his w Rosamond, da of Most Rev Charles Longley, DD, sometime Archbishop of Canterbury); *Heir* s, Hon (David) Stephen (Geoffrey) Pollock; *Career* formerly independent, then SDP, now sits as Social and Lib Democratic peer in House of Lords; barr 1958; late Lt-Col RE; CEng, MIMechE, FIEE, FIQA, FRPS; author of books on colour photography; *Style*— The Rt Hon the Viscount Hanworth; Quoin Cottage, Shamley Green, Guildford, Surrey (☎ 0483 893 018)

HAPPOLD, Edmund; s of Prof Frank Charles Happold, of Three Roods, New Barnes Road, Arnside, Cumbria, and Margaret, *née* Smith (d 1988); *b* 8 Nov 1930; *Educ* Leeds GS, Bootham Sch York, Leeds Univ (BSc); *m* 21 Dec 1967, Evelyn Clare, da of Charles Matthews of Hayle, Cornwall; 2 s (Matthew b 1969, Thomas b 1971); *Career* site engr Sir Robert MacAlpine and Sons 1952-54, asst engr OVE Arup and Ptnrs (worked on Coventry Cathedral, Sydney Opera House) 1956-58, engr Severud Elstad and Kruger NY (Lincoln Centre Yale Ice Hockey 1958-60, exec ptnr (prev assoc, sr engr) OVE Arup and Ptnrs (projects inc: Conference Centres Riyadh of Mecca, Knightsbridge Cavalry Barracks, Br Embassy Rome, Centre Pompidou Paris, Mannheim Lattice Shell), 1960-76; sr ptnr Buro Happold (projects inc: Dip Club Riyadh, Munich Aviary, 58 degrees N Alberta 1976 and Prof bldg engr Univ of Bath 1976-; chm: advsy bd Const Indust Computer Assoc 1982-, Bldg Indust Cncl 1988-; awards: cultural centres in Hong Kong and High Wykeham, Green Giant Lambeth, Queen Award 1987, Guthrie Brown Medal (Theatre Royal Bath 1988-), 2 Oscar Faber Medals, Leslie Murray Medal: Memb: Design Cncl 1980-, Property Servs Agency DOE 1981-86, Advsy Ctee DOE 1988-; Freeman City of London, Worshipful Co of Carmen; hon DSc City Univ 1988; RDI, FEng, FICE, FIStructE (pres 1986-87), FCIOB, FHKIE, hon FRIBA, hon FCIBSE; *Books* contrib numerous tech papers to learned jnls; *Recreations* travel, family activities; *Clubs* Athenaeum; *Style*— Prof Edmund Happold; 4 Widcombe Terrace, Bath, Avon BA2 6AJ (☎ 0225 315 656); 32 Grosvenor St, London W1X 9FF; Buro Happold, Camden Hill, Lower Bristol Rd, Bath BA2 3DQ (☎ 0225 337510); Sch of Architecture and Building Engrg, Univ of Bath, Claverton Down, Bath (☎ 0225 826 622)

HARBERTON, 10 Viscount (I 1791); Thomas de Vautort Pomeroy; also Baron Harberton (I 1783); s of 8 Viscount Harberton, OBE (d 1956); suc bro, 9 Viscount, 1980; *b* 19 Oct 1910; *Educ* Eton; *m* 1, 1939 (m dis 1946), Nancy, da of C Penoyer, of San Francisco; m 2, 1950, Pauline (d 1971), da of Wilfred Baker, of Plymouth; m 3, 1978, Vilma (Wilhelmine), widow of Sir Alfred Butt, 1 Bt; *Heir* bro, Hon Robert Pomeroy; *Career* Lt-Col Welsh Gds (1931-41) and RAOC from 1941; *Clubs* Cavalry and Guards; *Style*— The Rt Hon The Viscount Harberton; c/o Barclays Bank, High Street Branch, St Peters Port, Guernsey CI

HARBISON, Air Vice-Marshal William; CB (1977), CBE (1965), AFC (1956); s of William Harbison, of Garvagh, NI; *b* 11 April 1922; *Educ* Ballymena Acad; *m* 1950, Helen, da of William Blaine Geneva, of Bloomington, Illinois; 2 s; *Career* cdr RAF Staff and air attaché Washington 1972-75, AOC HQ 11 Gp RAF 1975-77; vice-pres Br Aerospace, Washington DC 1979-; *Recreations* motoring; *Clubs* RAF, Army and Navy (Washington); *Style*— Air Vice-Marshal William Harbison, CB CBE, AFC; c/o Cox's and King's Branch of Lloyds Bank, 6 Pall Mall, London SW1

HARBORD, Richard Lewis; s of Lewis Walter Harbord, of Norwich, and Dorothy Florence, *née* Mobbs; *b* 30 April 1946; *Educ* Minchendon GS, Anglian Regnl Mgmnt Centre (M Phil), Henley Coll of Mgmnt (Phd); *m* 2 May 1970, Jenny Ann, da of Herbert John Berry (d 1988), of London; 3 s (Mark b 26 Aug 1971, Adam b 5 Oct 1975, Guy b 21 June 1984); *Career* chief exec London Borough of Richmond Upon Thames 1988- (dir of fin 1981-88), memb cncl Ratings and Valuation Assoc 1987-; memb ct Surrey Univ; hon tres: Richmond Crossroads, Windlesham PCC; memb IPFA 1967, memb IDPM 1968, FCCA 1981, FRVA 1982; *Recreations* family; *Style*— Richard Harbord, Esq; Gooserye, Cooper Rd, Windlesham, Surrey GU20 6EA; York House, Twickenham (☎ 01 891 1411 fax 01 891 7703)

HARBORD-HAMOND, Hon Charity Patricia; da of late 10 Baron Suffield; *b* 1917; *Style*— The Hon Charity Harbord-Hamond; c/o Woodnorton Grange, Dereham, Norfolk

HARBORD-HAMOND, Hon Charles Anthony Assheton; s and h of 11 Baron Suffield, MC; *b* 3 Dec 1953; *Educ* Eton; *m* 10 Sept 1983, Lucy Lennox Scrope, yr da of Cdr A S Hutchinson, of Lechlade, Glos; *Career* Capt Coldstream Gds 1972-79; md: temp equerry to HM The Queen 1977-79; Insur Broker, ACII; dir: Investmt Insur Int (mangrs) Ltd 1981-1985, Donner Underwriting Agencies Ltd, Lloyds 1985; OStJ; *Clubs* Pratts; *Style*— The Hon Charles Harbord-Hamond; 12b Albert Bridge Road, London SW11 4PY

HARBORD-HAMOND, Hon John Edward Richard; s of 11 Baron Suffield, MC and Elizabeth Eve, *née* Edgedale; *b* 10 July 1956; *Educ* Eton, Coll of Law; *m* 1983, Katharine Margaret Lucy Seymour, only da of Maj and Hon Mrs Raymond Seymour, of Bucklebury, Berks; 1 s (b 4 Feb 1989); *Career* memb Inner Temple; stockbroker; *Style*— The Hon John Harbord-Hamond; 9 Frere St, London SW11 2JA

HARBORD-HAMOND, Hon Penelope Mary; da of late 10 Baron Suffield; *b* 1915; *Style*— The Hon Penelope Harbord-Hamond; Walton House, Walton St, London SW3

HARBORD-HAMOND, Hon Robert Philip Morden; 3 s of 11 Baron Suffield, MC; *b* 10 Mar 1964; *Style*— The Hon Robert Harbord-Hamond; Wood Norton Grange, Dereham, Norfolk NR20 5BD

HARBOTTLE, Rev Anthony Hall Harrison; LVO (1984, MVO 1979); s of Alfred Charles Harbottle (d 1938), of Topsham, Devon, and Ellen Muriel, *née* Harrison (d 1955); *b* 3 Sept 1925; *Educ* Sherborne, Christ's Coll Cambridge (MA), Wycliffe Hall Oxford; *m* 1955, Gillian Mary, da of Hugh Goodenough (d 1975); 3 s (Charles, Jonathan, David), 1 da (Jane); *Career* serv WWII RM (Cpl) Holland, NW Germany; deacon 1952, priest 1953, asst curacies: Boxley 1952-54, St Peter-in-Thanet 1954-60; rector of Sandhurst with Newenden 1960-68, chaplain Royal Chapel Windsor Great Park 1968-81, rector of East Dean with Friston and Jevington 1981-, chaplain to: HM The Queen 1968-, County of Sussex, Royal Br Legion 1982-; FRES; *Recreations* butterflies and moths, nature conservancy, entomology, ornithology, philately, coins, treasury and bank notes, painting, cooking, lobstering; *Style*— The Rev Anthony Harbottle, LVO; The Rectory, East Dean, Eastbourne, E Sussex BN20 0DL (☎ 032 15 3266)

HARBOTTLE, (George) Laurence; s of George Harbottle, MC, of Newcastle upon Tyne, and Winifred Ellen, *née* Benson (d 1982); *b* 11 April 1924; *Educ* The Leys Sch Cambridge, Emmanuel Coll Cambridge (MA); *Career* cmmnd RA 1942, Capt and Adj 9 Field Regt RA 1945-47; sr ptnr Harbottle and Lewis 1955-; chm various theatre co's incl: Prospect Prodns Ltd, Royal Exchange Theatre Co Ltd, Cambridge Theatre Co Ltd; chm of govrs: Central Sch of Speech and Drama, ICA; former pres Theatrical Mgmnt Assoc; memb Arts Cncl 1976-78, vice chm Theatres Tst; memb: Law Soc, The Bookmen Soc; *Recreations* works of art, gardening; *Clubs* The Savile; *Style*— G Laurence Harbottle, Esq; Hanover Ho, Hanover Square, London W1R 0BE (☎ 01 629 7633, fax 01 493 0451, telex 22233 HARLEX)

HARBOTTLE, Brig Michael Neale; OBE; s of Capt Thomas Cecil Benfield Harbottle, RN (d 1968), and Kathleen Millicent, *née* Kent (d 1937); *b* 7 Feb 1917; *Educ* Marlborough, RMA Sandhurst, Staff Coll Pretoria SA (psc); *m* 1, 1 Aug 1940 (m dis 1972), Alison Jean, *née* Humfress; 1 s (Simon Neale b 2 April 1942), 1 da (Carolyn Daphne b 6 Nov 1946); m 2, 5 Aug 1972, Eirwen Helen, da of Hugh Llewlyn Jones (d 1962); *Career* cmmnd The Oxfordshire and Bucks Light Inf 1937, WWII serv UK and Italy (despatches), GSO2 instr UK Army Staff Coll 1945, GSO2 staff duties WO 1950-52, GSO1 43 Inf Div TA/SW Dist 1957-59, CO 1 Green Jackets Regt 1959-62, Security Cdr and Cdr Aden Garrison 1962-64, Co 129 Inf Bde TA 1964-66, COS UN Peacekeeping Force Cyprus 1966-68, ret 1968; chief security offr Sierra Leone Selection Tst 1969-71, VP Int Peace Acad 1970-73, visiting sr lectr Sch of Peace Studies Bradford Univ 1974-79; visiting prof: Univ of Cape Town SA 1976, Waterloo Univ 1979, Carleton Univ Canada 1979; hd of dept Vietnamese Section Br Cncl for Aid to Refugees 1979-80, gen sec World Disarmament Campaign (UK) 1980-82, fndr and dir London Centre for Int Peacebuilding 1983-, memb: Generals for Peace and Disarmament, RIAA; *Books* The Impartial Soldier (1970), Blue Berets (1971), The Thin Blue Line (co author 1974), The Knaves of Diamonds (1976), The Peacekeepers' Handbook (1978); *Recreations* cricket, tennis, hockey, golf; *Clubs* MCC; *Style*— Brig Michael Harbottle OBE; 9 West St, Chipping Norton, Oxon (☎ 0608 2335); London Centre for Int Peacebuilding, Wickham House, 10 Cleveland Way, London E1 4TR (☎ 01 790 2424, telex 932011 GEN FIN G)

HARCOURT-SMITH, Lt-Col Charles Simon; s of Simon Guisbert Harcourt-Smith (d 1982), of London, and Rosamund Hilda, *née* Miller (d 1987); *b* 11 Feb 1942; *Educ* Inst Auf Den Rosenberg Switzerland; *m* 10 July 1971, Sabrina Jane, da of Lt-Col Richard Harry Longland (d 1968), of IOW; 3 s (William b 1972, Alexander b 1974, Edward b 1977); *Career* Army Offr joined Life Gds 1962, promoted Lt-Col 1984, attended Staff Coll 1976, serv Germany, Libya, Far East, Middle East, Belgium, Holland, Army Helicoptor Pilot Far East 1966-68; *Recreations* shooting, fishing, sailing; *Clubs* Cavalry and Guards', Flyfishers, Bembridge Sailing; *Style*— Lt-Col Charles Harcourt-Smith; c/o Lloyds Bank, 6 Pall Mall SW1Y 5NH; MOD, Whitehall (☎ 218 6559)

HARCOURT-SMITH, Air Chief Marshal Sir David; GBE (1989), KCB (1984), DFC (1957); *b* 14 Oct 1931; *Educ* Felsted Sch, RAF Coll; *m* 1957, Mary, *née* Entwistle; 2 s, 1 da; *Career* cmmnd RAF 1952, served with 11, 8 and 54 Squadrons, Staff Coll 1962, OC 54 Sqdn 1963-65, Cmdt RAF Coll Cranwell 1978-80, Asst CAS (Operational Requirements) 1980-, Air Marshal 1984, Air Office Commanding-in-Chief RAF Support Cmmd 1984, Controller Aircraft (MOD PE) and memb Air Force Bd 1986, Air Chief Marshal, 1987; *Books* tennis, music, golf; *Recreations* RAF; *Style*— Air Chicl Marshal Sir David Harcourt-Smith, KCB, DFC; c/o Barclays Bank, Walters Ash, High Wycombe, Bucks

HARCUS, Rear Adm Ronald Albert; CB (1976); s of Henry Alexander Harcus (d 1966), and Edith Maud, *née* Brough; *b* 25 Oct 1921; *Educ* St Olave's GS, RNC Greenwich, Royal Coll of Def Studies; *m* 1946, Jean, da of Hubert Maxwell Heckman; 2 s, 2 da; *Career* RN ret, asst chief Fleet Support MOD 1974-76, md RWO (Marine Equipment) 1976-79; *Recreations* sailing, fishing, gardening; *Style*— Rear-Adm Ronald Harcus, CB; 2 Church Hill Close, Blackawton Devon TQ9 7BQ (☎ 080 421 574)

HARDAWAY, (Adolph) James; s of Lawrence Hardaway (d 1960), of the USA, and Grace Maria, *née* Habig (d 1977); *b* 12 Sept 1929; *Educ* Brown Univ USA (BA) ; *m* 6 Sept 1961, Sheila Ann; *Career* stockbroker; memb The Stock Exchange; chm: Whale Hardaway and Co, Ltd, stock and share brokers, Toroak Investmt and Fin Servs; Metropolitan London Gp; former memb Provincial Stock Exchange, Pacific Coast Stock Exchange, New York Stock Exchange; FID; FESU; *Recreations* tennis, literature, theatre, music, travel, fine art; *Clubs* English-Speaking Union London, Royal Torbay YC; *Style*— James Hardaway, Esq; c/o 5 Park Hill Rd, Torquay, Devon (☎ 0803 292441 and 293098, fax 0803 292615)

HARDCASTLE, Prof Jack Donald; s of Albert Fenton Hardcastle, and Bertha, *née* Ellison; *b* 3 April 1933; *Educ* St Batholomews GS Newbury, Emmanuel Coll Cambridge (BA, MB BChir, MA, MChir); *m* 18 Dec 1965, Rosemary, da of Col Cecil Hay-Shunker; 1 s (Philip b 3 May 1968), 1 da (Rachel b 19 June 1971); *Career* lectr and registrar London Hosp 1963-65, (sr registrar 1965-68, sr lectr 1968-70), sr registrar St Marks Hosp, prof and head of dept of surgery Queen's Med Centre Univ of Nottingham, Sir Authur Sims Cwlth Travelling Prof 1985, Mayne Guest Prof Univ of Queensland Aust 1987; chm Nottingham Ice Hockey Club (med advsr Br Ice Hockey Assoc); MRCP 1961, FRCS 1962, FRCP 1984; *Books* Isolated Organ Perfusion (jtly 1973) ; *Clubs* RSM; *Style*— Jack Hardcastle, Esq; Department of Surgery, University Hospital, Queen's Medical Centre, Nottingham NG7 2UH, (☎ 0602 701372)

HARDCASTLE, Leslie Jesse; OBE (1978); s of Francis Ernest Hardcastle, and Dorothy Alma, *née* Schofield; *b* 8 Dec 1926; *Educ* St Joseph's Coll Croydon; *m* 14 Sept 1968, (Vivienne Mansel) Wendy, da of Maj Trevor Richards (d 1968), of Red Tiles Farm, Fairwarp, Sussex; 2 s (Adam Alexander b 23 June 1972, Paul James b 3 Jan 1975); *Career* RN sick berth Br Pacific Fleet 1944-47; prodn Br Lion Film Studio

1943, admin Br Film Inst 1947, mangr Festival of Br Telekinema 1951, admin London Film Festival 1958-86, controller Nat Film Theatre 1968 (mangr 1952), creator Museum of Moving Image 1988, controller Br Film Inst South Bank (Nat Film Theatre and Museum of Moving Image) 1989; chm and pres Soho Soc, chm housing mgmnt Soho Housing Assoc; *Recreations* theatre, music, community work; *Style*— Leslie Hardcastle, Esq, OBE; 37 C Great Pulteney St, London W1 (☎ 01 437 5149); Woodlands Cottage, Nursery Lane, Fairwarp, Sussex (☎ 082 571 2887); NFT & Museum of Moving Image, South Bank Arts Complex, Waterloo SE1 (☎ 01 928 3535)

HARDEN, Dr Donald Benjamin; CBE (1969, OBE 1956); s of Rt Rev John Mason Harden, DD, LLD, MA (d 1931; Bishop of Tuam, Killala and Achonry 1927-31), and Constance Caroline, *née* Sparrow (d 1960); *b* 8 July 1901; *Educ* Kilkenny Coll, Westminster Sch, Trinity Coll Cambridge (BA, MA), Oxford Univ (MA); *m* 1, 1934, Cecil Ursula (d 1963), da of Rev James Adolphus Harriss (d 1919), vicar St Andrew's, Linton Rd, Oxford; 1 da (Georgina Boosey, *qv*); m 2, 1965, Dorothy May, da of Daniel Herbert McDonald (d 1960), accountant, of Whitehorse Rd, Box Hill, Victoria, Australia; *Career* classical scholar, archaeologist, museum dir; sr asst in humanity Aberdeen Univ 1924-26, Commonwealth Fund Fellow, Univ of Michigan 1926-28; asst keeper Dept of Antiquities, Ashmolean Museum Oxford 1929-45, keeper 1945-56; temp civil servant Miny of Supply and Miny of Prodn 1940-45, Leverhulme res fell 1953; dir The London Museum 1956-70, FSA (Gold Medallist 1977); Hon FBA 1987; ret; *Recreations* archaeology, history, history of glass; *Clubs* Athenaeum; *Style*— Dr Donald B. Harden, CBE; 12 St Andrew's Mansions, Dorset St, London W1H 3FD (☎ 01 935 5121)

HARDEN, Maj James Richard Edwards; DSO (1945), OBE (1983), MC (1944), JP (Armagh 1956, Caernarvonshire 1971), DL (Armagh 1946, Caernarvonshire 1968); s of James Edwards Harden (d 1945), and Letita Grace Campbell Connal (decd); *b* 12 Dec 1916; *Educ* Bedford Sch, RMC Sandhurst; *m* 1948, Ursula Joyce, da of Gerald Murray Strutt (d 1956); 1 s (David), 2 da (Theresa, Carolyn); *Career* landowner and farmer; MP (UU) Armagh 1948-54; High Sheriff Caernarvonshire 1971-72, chm regnl land drainage ctee Welsh Water Authy 1973-83; landowner (5000 acres); *Recreations* shooting; *Style*— Maj James Harden, DSO, OBE, MC, JP, DL; Nanhoran, Pwllheli, Gwynedd LL53 8DL (☎ 0758 83610)

HARDER, Ian Gray; s of Robert William Harder (d 1940), and Gladys Dorothy, *née* Mawby (d 1980); *b* 3 June 1931; *Educ* E Barnet GS, Southampton Univ (BSc), London Univ; *Career* corpl RAF 1953-55; head Economist Intelligence Unit, Economic and Financial Dept 1955-65; md New Ventures (Investmts) Ltd 1965-68; chm and md Maxwell Stamp Assocs Ltd 1968-; *Recreations* music, theatre, walking; *Style*— Ian G Harder, Esq; 5 Blake Road, New Southgate, London N11 2AD (☎ 01 368 6417); Maxwell Stamp Associates Ltd, 2 Hat and Mitre Court, St John St, London EC1M 4EL (☎ 01 251 0147, fax 01 251 0140)

HARDERS, Sir Clarence Waldemar; OBE (1969); s of E W Harders; *b* 1 Mar 1915; *Educ* Concordia Coll SA, Adelaide Univ; *m* 1947, Gladys, da of E Treasure; 1 s, 2 da; *Career* sec Dept of Attorney-Gen 1970-79, legal advsr Dept of Foreign Affairs 1979-80, slr Freehill Hollingdale and Page 1980-; kt 1977; *Style*— Sir Clarence Harders, OBE; 43 Stonehaven Crescent, Deakin, ACT 2600, Australia

HARDESTY, Hon Mrs (Rachel Henrietta); *née* Cunliffe; o da of 3 Baron Cunliffe, *qv*; *b* 14 Feb 1960; *Educ* N London Collegiate Sch, Felsted, Cambridge Univ (BA), Manchester Univ, Univ of Minnesota; *m* 1987, Roger David Hardesty, s of late R D Hardesty, of Belle Mead, New Jersey, USA; *Style*— The Hon Mrs Hardesty

HARDIE, Prof Alexander Merrie; s of Alexander Hardie (d 1930), of Aberdeen, and Margaret Elizabeth, *née* Begg (d 1961); *b* 10 Feb 1910; *Educ* Aberdeen GS, Aberdeen Univ (MA, BSc, PhD); *m* 3 July 1940, Phyllis Amy Isobel, da of Alexander Auld (d 1949), of Aberdeen; 1 s (Alexander b 1947), 1 da (Joyce b 1942); *Career* RAF Flt Lt 1939-41, Sqdn-Ldr 1941-45; radio res engr Metropolitan Vickers Electrical Co 1934-37 and 1945-51, princ lectr Aberdeen Univ 1951-63, pro vice chllr and a prof physics Bath Univ 1963-75; artist; paintings in various public galleries & private collections; ARWA 1967, RWA 1970, FIEE 1970; *Books* Elements of Feedback and Control (1964), various papers in journals; *Recreations* painting; *Clubs* Bristol Savages; *Style*— Prof A M Hardie; 49 Church St, Cromarty, Ross-Shire IV11 8XA (☎ 03817 394)

HARDIE, Andrew Rutherford; QC (1985); s of Andrew Rutherford Hardie, of 263 Ashley Terr, Alloa, and Elizabeth Currie, *née* Lowe; *b* 8 Jan 1946; *Educ* St Modan's HS Stirling, Edinburgh Univ (MA, LLB); *m* 16 July 1971, Catherine Storrar, da of David Currie Elgin, of Crescent Wood Rd, London; 2 s (Ewan b 1975, Niall b 1981), 1 da (Ruth b 1977); *Career* enrolled slr 1971, memb Faculty of Advocates 1973, advocate depute 1979-83, standing jr counsel City of Edinburgh DC 1983-85 (sr counsel 1987-); *Clubs* Caledonian (Edinburgh), Murrayfield GC; *Style*— Andrew Hardie, Esq, QC; 27 Hermitage Gdns, Edinburgh, EH10 6AZ (☎ 031 447 2917); Advocate Library, Parliament House, Edinburgh EH1 1RF (☎ 031 226 5071)

HARDIE, Sir Charles Edgar Mathewes; CBE (1963, OBE 1943); s of Dr Charles Frederick Hardie (d 1964), of Blyth, Notts; and Mrs R F Hardie, *née* Moore; *b* 10 Mar 1910; *Educ* Aldenham Sch; *m* 1, 1937, Dorothy Jean Hobson (d 1965); 1 s (Jeremy *qv*), 3 da; m 2, 1966 (m dis 1975) Angela, widow of Raymond Paul Richli, and da of George Street; m 3, 1975, Rosemary Margaret Harwood; *Career* serv WWII (Col); ptnr Dixon Wilson and Co 1934-81 (sr ptnr 1975-81); chm: White Fish Authority 1967-73, BOAC 1969-70, Br Printing Corpn 1969-76 (dir 1965-82), Fitch Lovell Ltd 1970-77; dir: Trusthouse Forte 1970- (dep chm 1983-), Royal Bank of Canada 1969-81, Hill Samuel Gp 1970-77; Legion of Merit (USA); FCA; kt 1970; *Recreations* bridge; *Clubs* Phyllis Court; *Style*— Sir Charles Hardie, CBE; The Old School House, Sturminster Newton, Dorset (☎ 0258 72983); 25 New St, Henley on Thames, Oxon RG92 2BP (☎ 0491 577944)

HARDIE, David; WS (1982); s of John Hardie, of Gourock, Renfrewshire, Scot, and Amy Alfreda, *née* Masey; *b* 17 Sept 1954; *Educ* Glasgow Acad, Greenock HS, Univ of Dundee (LLB); *m* 27 Feb 1981, Fiona Mairi, da of Dr Alexander Donaldson Willox, MBE, of W Lothian, Scot; 2 s (Iain b 1981, Stewart b 1984); *Career* NP 1979, ptnr Dundas & Wilson CS 1983; Law Soc of Scot, Int Bar Assoc; *Recreations* sailing, golf, swimming, cycling,; *Clubs* Royal Forth YC; *Style*— David Hardie, Esq; 25 Charlotte Sq, Edinburgh, EH2 4EZ, (☎ 031 225 1234, fax 031 225 5594, telex 72404)

HARDIE, Maj (John) Donald Morrison; OBE (1987); s of Capt John David Hardie (d 1949), and Gertrude Louise, *née* Morrison; *b* 27 Sept 1928; *Educ* Beckenham GS, St Andrews Univ (MA), Indiana Univ USA (MSc); *m* 9 Aug 1952, Sally Patricia, da of Thomas Whipple Connally (d 1928); 2 s (David b 1954, Robin b 1957), 1 da (Katharine b 1960); *Career* Lt 1 Bn Queen's Own Cameron Highlanders 1952-56, Maj TA Bn 1956-67; dir Wood and Hardie Ltd 1961-82; currently dir: Bute Fabrics Ltd, Woolward McCann Ltd, Corporate Risk and Ins Mgmnt Ltd; dir Scottish Div IOD 1980-; organised 'Yes' campaign in Scotland for EEC referendum 1975; session clerk Humbie Kirk 1960-; memb Scottish XI (hockey) 1950-53; *Recreations* golf, shooting; *Clubs* Hon Co of Edinburgh Golfers, Royal and Ancient GC (St Andrews), New (Edinburgh), Piedmont Driving, Peachtree GC (Atlanta); *Style*— Maj Donald Hardie, OBE; Chesterhill House, Humbie, E Lothian EH36 5PL (☎ 087 533 648); Inst of Directors, 13 Great Stuart Street, Edinburgh EH3 7TP (☎ 031 225 8101)

HARDIE, Douglas Fleming; CBE (1979), JP (1970); s of James Dunbar Hardie, JP, of 5 Invergowrie Drive, Dundee, and Frances Mary, *née* Fleming; *b* 26 May 1923; *Educ* Trinity Coll Glenalmond ; *m* 5 Sept 1945, Dorothy Alice, da of Frederick William Warner (d 1971), of 8 North Rd, Ponteland, Newcastle-upon-Tyne, Northumberland; 2 s (Michael b 1948, Christopher b 1954), 1 da (Hilary b 1947); *Career* Trooper 58 Trg Regt RAC 1941, cmmnd RMA Sandhurst 1942, 1 Fife and Forfar Yeomanry Flamethrowing Tank Regt NW Europe 1942-46 (despatches), Maj; chm and md Edward Parker and Co Ltd 1960-, dep chm Scottish Dvpt Agency 1978-; dir: H and A Scott (Hldgs) Ltd 1964-84 (chm 1984-85), Dayco Rubber (UK) Ltd 1956-86, Clydesdale Bank plc 1981-, The Alliance Tst plc 1982-, The Second Alliance Tst plc 1982-, Alliance Tst (Fin) Ltd 1982-, SECDEE Leasing 1982-, Alliance Tst (Nominees) Ltd 1982-, Grampian Television plc 1984-, A G Scott Textiles Ltd 1985-88; memb: CBI Grand Cncl London 1976-85, Scottish Econ Cncl 1977-, Cncl Winston Churchill Meml Tst 1985-; chm Dundee Forfar and Dist Sub assoc, pres Dundee Rotary Club 1967-68; vice-pres Fife and Forfar Yeomanry Regtl Assoc, deacon convener Nine Incorporated Trades of Dundee 1951-54; elder Dundee Parish church (St Mary's); vice-pres Fife & Forfar Yeomanry Regtl Assoc; chm Dundee Forfar & Dist Sub-Assoc Fife & Forfar Yeo; memb Cncl Winston Churchill Memorial Tst 1985; dir Prince's Scottish Youth Business Tst 1988; FRSA 1988; *Recreations* golf, fishing; *Clubs* Caledonian, Royal and Ancient GC, Blairgowrie GC, Panmure GC; *Style*— Douglas F Hardie, Esq, CBE, JP; 6 Norwood Terrace, West Park, Dundee DD2 1PB (☎ 0382 69107); Edward Parker and Co Ltd, Progress Works, Dundee DD1 1PD (☎ 0382 25865, fax 0382 29074, telex 76243 prefix message EP)

HARDIE, (Charles) Jeremy (Mawdesley); CBE (1983); s of Sir Charles Hardie, CBE *qv*; *b* 9 June 1938; *Educ* Winchester Coll, New Coll Oxford; *m* 1, 1962 (m dis 1976), Susan Chamberlain; 2 s, 2 da; m 2, 1978, Xandra, Countess of Gowrie, da of late Col Robert Albert Glanvill Bingley, CVO, DSO, OBE (d 1976); 1 da; *Career* Monopolies and Mergers Cmmn: memb 1976-, dep chm 1980-83; Nat Provident Inst: dir 1972-77, dep chm 1977-80, chm 1980-; dep chm Alexanders Discount Co (dir 1978-); dir: Unilever Pensions Investmt Mgmnt Ltd 1980-, Stockholders Investmt Tst 1979-, John Swire and Sons 1982-; ptnr Dixon Wilson and Co 1975-; chm Alexander Syndicate Mgmnt Ltd 1982-, memb local bd Bank of Scotland 1983-; Parly candidate (SDP) Norwich South 1983; memb Arts Cncl of GB 1984-; FCA; *Style*— Jeremy Hardie Esq, CBE; The Old Rectory, Netton, nr Cromer, Norfolk (☎ 026 376 765)

HARDIE, Miles Clayton; OBE (1988); s of Frederick Russell Hardie (d 1930), of London, and Estelle Mary Harwood, *née* Clarke (d 1929); *b* 27 Feb 1924; *Educ* Charterhouse, Oriel Coll Oxford (MA); *m* 1, 22 July 1949 (m dis 1974), Pauline, da of Prof Sir Wilfrid Edward Le Gros Clark (d 1971), of Oxford; 2 s (Philip b 1952, Roger b 1953); m 2, 21 Nov 1974 (m dis 1985), (Katherine) Mellissa Woelfel, da of the late James Edward Witcher, of USA; m 3, 20 April 1985, (Madeline) Elizabeth Spencer-Smith, da of the late Herbert Dudley Ash; *Career* WWII RAF Pilot 1943-46, debom Flt Lt; joined NHS 1949; sec: Victoria Hosp for Children Chelsea 1952-56, Bahrain Govt Med Dept 1956-58, joined King Edwards Hosp Fund for London 1958, dep dir King's Fund Centre 1963-66 (dir 1966-75), dir gen Int Hosp Fedn 1975-87; helped estab Br Hosps Export Cncl 1964 (hon sec and cncl memb); served: on various cncls and ctees incl: MIND, Mental Health Fndn, Centre for Policy on Ageing, Spinal Injuries Assoc, Volunteer Health Centre; advsr to WHO; memb Worshipful Co of Salters 1954, Hon Dr Admin Northland Open Univ Canada 1987; FHSM 1955; World Health Orgn Geneva Health for all Medal 1987; *Recreations* walking, gardening; *Style*— Miles Hardie, Esq, OBE; Tallow Cottage, Fishers Lane, Charlbury, Oxford OX7 3RX (☎ 0608 810088)

HARDIMAN, Michael John; s of Eric Walter Hardiman (d 1978), and Evelyn Winifred Galloway, *née* Fisher; *b* 11 Dec 1942; *Educ* Ardingly Coll, Univ of Aberdeen; *m* 15 Aug 1986, Francoise Anne-Marie, da of Andre Raufaste-Tistet, of Paris; 2 s (Andrew b 29 Aug 1987, Peter b 11 Dec 1988); *Career* asst mangr Harrods Tst Ltd 1970-73, special projects mangr Manex Ltd 1973-79, mktg mangr Hambros Bank Ltd 1979-84, corp servs mangr Societe Generale Merchant Bank plc 1984-87, sr mangr Int Corporate Fin Commercial Union Capital Ltd 1987-89, dir Translink Servs Ltd 1989-; hon tres Camberley Soc; Freeman City of London 1988; fndn fell Assoc Corp Treasurers; *Recreations* fly fishing; *Style*— Michael Hardiman, Esq; 37 Rosehill Ave, Horsell, Woking, Surrey GU21 4SD (☎ 04862 66 975); St Helen's, 1 Undershaft, London EC3P 3DZ (☎ 01 283 7500)

HARDING, (Robert John) Bob; s of John Henry Harding (d 1960), of Bideford, Devon, and Ethel, *née* Luxton; *b* 31 Oct 1923; *Educ* Bideford GS; *m* 24 Feb 1946, Dorothy Alice Harding, JP, da of Frederick George Holdsworth (d 1974); 1 s (David John b 16 Jan 1948), 1 da (Maureen Ann b 12 July 1953); *Career* RN and Combined Ops 1942-46; serv: Sicily, Italy, Normandy (D Day) Walcheron; Western Countries Bldg Soc: chief clerk 1946, asst sec 1954, sec 1970, dir 1980; W of Eng Bldg Soc: md 1985, ret 1986; cncl memb Bldg Socs Assoc 1983-86 (rep Wales and W of Eng Assoc of Bldg Socs) past chm regnl assoc; fndr memb Bideford Round Table and 41 Clubs, past pres: Bideford C of C, Bideford Rotary Club; pres Torridgeside RNA, fndn govr Bideford Coll, dir Torridge Trg Servs Ltd, bd memb Bideford Housing Soc; ACIS 1954, FCBSI 1948; *Recreations* cricket and golf; *Clubs* Bideford Rotary, North Devon CC; *Style*— Bob Harding, Esq; 17 Rectory Park, Bideford, N Devon EX39 3AJ (☎ 023 727 4199)

HARDING, Maj (George William) Cecil; s of Col George Harding, DSO, of Co Laois, Eire; *b* 12 July 1916; *Educ* Wellington, RMA; *m* 1947, Beatrice, da of Col Geoffrey Youl, MC, of Tasmania; 3 da; *Career* served RA (Europe, M East, Pacific) Maj, ret 1958; chm: Ewart New Northern plc 1977-86, Capital Gearing Tst plc 1963-; landowner (inherited from f) 1957-; *Recreations* travel; *Clubs* Naval and Military, Ulster (Belfast); *Style*— Maj Cecil Harding; Tulachnore, Pike of Rushall, Portlaoise, Eire (☎ 0502 35113); Capital Gearing Trust plc, 34 Upper Queen Street, Belfast BT1

6HG (☎ 0232 244001)

HARDING, Cherry Jacinta; da of James Albert Harding, of Homer, Much Wenlock, Shropshire, and Pauline Mary, *née* Temlett; *b* 2 June 1956; *Educ* The Canon Slade GS Bolton Lancs, King's Coll London (LLB); *Career* called to the Bar Gray's Inn 1978; in practice 1980-, main area of work, The Family Bar; *Recreations* theatre, cookery; *Style*— Miss Cherry Harding; 2 Paper Bldgs, Temple, London EC4 (☎ 01 353 0826)

HARDING, Christopher George Francis; s of Frank Harding, of Amersham; *b* 17 Oct 1939; *Educ* Merchant Taylors', Corpus Christi Coll Oxford; *m* 1, 1963, Susan Lilian; 1 s, 1 da; m 2, 1978, Françoise Marie, da of Christian Grouillé; *Career* md Hanson Transport Gp 1974-; non-exec dir: Hanson plc 1979-, British Nuclear Fuels plc 1984- (chm 1986-); *Recreations* tennis, travel, music, pocillory; *Clubs* Brooks's; Huddersfield Borough; *Style*— Christopher Harding, Esq; 180 Brompton Road, London SW3 1HF

HARDING, Derek William; s of William Arthur Harding (d 1972); *b* 16 Dec 1930; *Educ* Glendale GS London, Bristol Univ; *m* Daphne Sheila, *née* Cooke 1965; 1 s, 1 da; *Career* engr Pye Ltd 1954-56, sr physics master Thornbury GS Bristol 1956-60, sr lectr physical sci St Paul's Coll Cheltenham 1960-64, registrar sec Inst Metallurgists 1969-76, sec gen Br Computer Soc 1976-86; exec sec Royal Statistical Soc 1986-; *Recreations* music, sailing; *Style*— Derek Harding Esq; 16 Exeter Rd, Middlesex N14 5JY (☎ 01 368 1463)

HARDING, Edmund Rudge; s of Sir Harold John Boyer Harding, DSc, FEng, FICE (d 1986), of Topsham, Exeter, and Lady Sophie Helen Blair Harding, *née* Leighton; *b* 15 August 1930; *Educ* Bryanston Sch, Imperial Coll London (City and Guilds, BSc, ACGI); *m* 22 April 1961, Diana Joan, da of Selwyn Read (d 1981), of Edinburgh; 1 s (John Gavin Blair b 1964), 1 da (Amanda b 1962); *Career* Nat Serv in Royal Engineers (Capt in AER); chartered civil engineer (ret); now a potter; *Recreations* making things; *Style*— Edmund R Harding, Esq; The Old Chapel, Church Street, Semington, Trowbridge, Wilts BA14 6JR (☎ 0380 870 932)

HARDING, Dr Geoffrey Wright; s of Jack Harding, of Gravesend, Kent, and Ethel Florence, *née* Wilkinson; *b* 25 July 1932; *Educ* King's Coll London (LLB, AKC), Gen Electric Fndn Fellow Northwestern Univ Sch of Law Chicago (LLM), QMC London (PhD); *m* 7 Oct 1972, Margaret June, da of Eric Oscar Danger; 1 s (Peter James John b 1980), 1 da (Kate Joanna b 1978); *Career* Nat Srev RAF 1951-53; barr Gray's Inn 1957, asst sec Fedn Civil Engrg Contractors 1958-60, legal advsr Br Insur (Atomic Energy) Ctee 1960-63, exchange lawyer under Harvard Law Sch Prog Isham, Lincoln and Beale Attorneys Chicago 1963-64, asst slr Joynson Hicks 1965-67, ptnr Wilde Sapte 1967- (specialising in banking, competition and intellectual property law);p memb Bar and Law Soc Jt Working Pty on Banking Law; memb: Nat Autistic Soc, Kent Autistic Community Tst; Freeman City of London 1986, memb Guild of Freemen of City of London; memb Law Soc; *Books* Banking Act 1987-Current Law Annotated (1987), Encyclopedia of Competition Law (jt conslting ed, 1987); *Recreations* music, fell-walking, avoiding domestic DIY; *Style*— Dr Geoffrey Harding; Wilde Sapte, Queensbridge House, 60 Upper Thames St, London EC4V 3BD (☎ 01 236 3050, fax 01 236 9624, telex 887793)

HARDING, Lt-Col Henry Christian Ewart; MC (1945); s of Col George Harding, DSO (d 1957), of Tulach Nore, Leix, Eire, and Charlotte Hope, *née* Ewart (d 1934); *b* 8 Dec 1919; *Educ* Wellington, RMA Woolwich, Staff Coll Camberley; *m* 21 Nov 1958, Audrey Lennox, da of Maj Charles McNaughton Napier (d 1967), of Broadway, Worcs; 1 s (William b 1964), 2 da (Sarah b 1961, Susan b 1966); *Career* WWII cmmnd RA 1939 serv Sicly and Italy 1943-45; instr of gunner Sch of Artillery Larkhill 1945-47, Staff Coll Camberley 1948, regtl and staff UK and abroad 1949-65, GSO 1 head C in C secretariat M East Cmd 1965-67, superintendent Proof and Experimental Estab Eskmeals 1968-69, ret 1969; dir: Capital Gearing Tst Ltd 1969-(co sec 1976-), Capital Gearing Mgmnt Ltd; tst mangr Paris Smith Randall Slrs 1977-85; rep Kent Athletics 1939; dep chm New Forest Cons Assoc 1985-88; ACIS 1974; *Recreations* sailing, photography, travel; *Style*— Lt-Col Christian Harding, MC; Furzey Lodge, Furzey Lane, Beaulieu, Hants (☎ 0590 612 283)

HARDING, John Richard Vincent; s of William Henry Harding, (d 1981), and Winifred Elsie, *née* Brett; *b* 1 Sept 1939; *Educ* Enfield GS, Clare Coll Cambridge, (MA); *m* 30 March 1965 (m dis 1983), Janet Ann, da of Albert Norman Roué, of Kempston, Bedford; 2 da (Clare b 1966, Susan b 1968); *Career* asst mangr Martins Bank Ltd 1962-70, vice-pres and asst gen mangr Republic Nat Bank of Dallas London 1970-76, mangr rising to dep gen mangr Euro Bank Ltd 1977-85, gen mangr AK Int Bank 1985-; ACIB 1966; *Recreations* swimming, music, theatre, gardening, photography; *Style*— John Harding, Esq; 10 Finsbury Square, London EC2A 1HE (☎ 01 628 3844, fax 01 638 2037, telex 8955636)

HARDING, Paul Anthony; s of Norman John Harding, and Yvonne Mary, *née* Rees; *b* 6 Oct 1955; *Educ* Hardye's GS Dorchester Dorset; *m* 18 Aug 1979, Deborah Anne, da of Roy William George Harvey, of Farnham, Surrey; 1 s (Benjamin James); 1 da (Alison Jane); *Career* slr: NCB 1979-82, Forsyte Kerman 1982-84, Titmuss Sainer Webb 1984-86 (ptnr 1986-); memb Law Soc; *Style*— Paul A Harding, Esq; Esher, Surrey; Titmuss, Sainer & Webb, 2 Serjeants' Inn, London EC4Y 1LT (☎ 01 583 5353, fax 01 353 0683)

HARDING, Peter Leslie; s of Leslie O'Brien Harding (d 1977), and Muriel Ellen, *née* Money (d 1966); *b* 22 Sept 1926; *Educ* Rugby, King's Coll Cambridge; *m* 6 Nov 1954, Nina Doris, da of Charles Downing Barnard (d 1967); 1 s (David b 30 July 1959), 1 da (Caroline b 23 March 1956); *Career* Union Castle Line 1947-53, dir Alexr Howden & Co Ltd 1960-67 (joined 1953); Baltic Exchange Ltd: dir 1969-73 and 1975-83, chm 1981-83; chm JE Hyde & Co Ltd 1986-(ptnr 1968-86); Freeman City of London 1982, Liveryman Worshipful Co of Shipwrights 1984; FICS; *Recreations* gardening, fly-fishing; *Style*— Peter Harding, Esq; Martlets, Greenways, Walton-on-The-Hill, Surrey (☎ 0737 813766); Baltic Exchange Chambers, 14-20 St Marys Axe, London EC3P 3EQ (☎ 01 283 4266, fax 01 283 2968, telex 885991)

HARDING, Air Chief Marshal Sir Peter Robin; GCB (1988, KCB 1982, CB 1980); s of Peter Harding, and Elizabeth, *née* Clear; *b* 2 Dec 1933; *Educ* Chingford HS; *m* 1955, Sheila Rosemary, da of Albert May; 3 s (Simon, Timothy, Stephen), 1 da (Katherine); *Career* joined RAF 1952, pilot 12 Sqdn 1954-57, QFI and Flt Cdr, RAF Coll Cranwell 1957-60, pilot 1 Sqdn RAAF 1960-62, Staff Coll 1963, Air Secretary's Dept MOD 1964-66, OC 18 Sqdn Gutersloh and Acklington 1966-69, Jt Serv Staff Coll Latimer 1969-70, Def Policy Staff MOD 1970-71, dir Air Staff Briefing MOD 1971-74, station cdr RAF Bruggen 1974-76, dir of def policy MOD 1976-78, asst chief of staff (plans and policy) SHAPE 1978-80, AOC 11 Gp 1981-82, vice chief of air staff 1982-84, vice chief of def staff 1985, air offr cmdg-in-chief Strike Cmd and Cdr-in-Chief UK Air Forces 1985-88, chief of air staff 1988-; ADC to HM The Queen 1975-77, Air ADC to HM The Queen 1988; Upper Freeman Guild of Air Pilots and Navigators; contrib aritcles to professional jnls, magazines and books; FRAeS, CBIM 1983, FRSA 1988; *Recreations* pianoforte, bridge, walking, bird watching; *Clubs* RAF; *Style*— Air Chief Marshal Sir Peter Harding, GCB; c/o Lloyds Bank plc, 6 Pall Mall, London SW6

HARDING, Robert Alan; s of Alan Killoch Harding, of Farnham, Surrey, and Aileen Margaret, *née* McBride; *b* 6 Dec 1937; *Educ* Elmhurst Sch, Whitgift Sch, St Martins Sch of Art; *m* 1, 8 April 1961 (m dis 1972), (Elisabeth) Ann; 1 s (Rupert Gordon McBride b 16 April 1966), 1 da (Samantha Minou Kathleen (Mrs Haynes) b 13 June 1964); m 2, 6 Dec 1972, Dolores Brenda, da of Edward Warris Mantez (d 1969), of Ghana; 1 s (Robert Tony Nelson Mantez b 12 March 1974); *Career* dir William Sommerville & Son plc 1966-; Br Paper and Bd Indust Fedn: chm paper and bd trade custom ctee 1986-, chm 1992 working pty 1988-, vice-chm AMPW 1988- (chm 1986-88); dir Conservation Papers Ltd 1989-; life memb London Soc RFU Referees, referee RFU and Surrey RFU 1967-72; *Recreations* rugby football, painting, calligraphy; *Clubs* Westons; *Style*— Robert Harding, Esq; 2 Barham Rd, Croydon, Surrey CR2 6LD (☎ 01 688 5409); Dalmore Mill, Miltonbridge, Penicuik, Midlothian EH26 0NE (☎ 0968 72 214, fax 01 681 1176/0968 73 314, car tel 0860 327 723, telex 72451 SOMPEN G)

HARDING, Air Vice-Marshal Ross Philip; CBE (1968); s of late Philip James Harding, of Salisbury, and late Ellen Alice, *née* Mann; *b* 22 Jan 1921; *Educ* Bishop Wordsworth's Sch Salisbury, St Edmund Hall Oxford (MA); *m* 29 Mar 1948, (Laurie) Joy, da of late Edward James Gardner, of Salisbury; 3 s (Russell b 1950, Murray b 1957, Stuart b 1963); *Career* WWII serv no 41 Sqdn Fighter Cmd and 2 TAF 1943-45; RAF Staff Coll Andover 1951, ACAS (Ops) Air Miny 1952-54, CO No 96 Sqdn Germany 1955-58, dir staff RAF Staff Coll Andover 1958-60, CO Oxford Univ Air Sqdn 1960-62, dep chief Br Mil Mission Berlin 1963-65, sr dir staff (air) Jt Servs Staff Coll 1968-69, def and air attaché Moscow 1970-72, dir Personal Servs I MOD (Air) 1973, sr RAF memb RCDS 1974-76, ret 1976; head Airwork Ltd Oman 1976-78, def advsr House of Commons Select Ctee on Def 1979-83, chm selection bds Civil Serv 1979-, chm govrs Bishop Wordsworth's Sch; *Recreations* bridge, skiing; *Clubs* RAF; *Style*— Air Vice-Marshal Ross Harding, CBE; 8 Hadrian's Close, Lower Bemerton, Salisbury, Wilts (☎ 0722 336 075)

HARDING, His Honour Rowe; DL (W Glam 1970); s of Albert Harding (d 1940), of Swansea; *b* 10 Sept 1901; *Educ* Gowerton Co Sch, Pembroke Coll Cambridge (MA); *m* 1933, Elizabeth Adeline, da of John George (d 1963), of Hirwaun; 1 s, 1 da (and 1 s decd); *Career* circuit judge 1953-76; chm Swansea Porcelain Ltd 1976-; Hon LLD Wales; *Recreations* gardening, watching rugby and cricket; *Clubs* Swansea City and Co; *Style*— His Hon Rowe Harding, DL; The Old Rectory, Ilston, Gower, Swansea, W Glam (☎ 044 125 243)

HARDING, Sir Roy Pollard; CBE (1978); s of William Foster Norman Harding (d 1966), of Cornwall, and Phebe Emma, *née* Pollard (d 1978); *b* 3 Jan 1924; *Educ* Liskeard GS, King's Coll London (BSc, DPA, AKC); *m* 1948, Audrey Beryl, da of Arthur Wimble Larkin (d 1973), 2 s (Alan, Paul), 1 da (Hilary); *Career* educationalist Ballistics Res Sch and Coll Teaching 1950, educn admin in Wilts, Herts, Leics and Bucks 1951-84 (chief educn offr Bucks 1966-84), advsr CC Assoc 1972-74, Assoc of CC Cncl of Local Educn Authorities 1974-84, sec County Educn Offrs Soc 1973-76 (chm 1978-79), memb exec Soc of Educn Offrs 1974-79 (pres 1977-78, chm Int Ctee 1978-83, gen sec 1984-89), vice-chm Secdy Examinations Ctee 1983-86, chm Educn Policy Interchange Ctee 1979-88; memb: cncl Inst Mathematics and Applications 1983-88 (vice-pres 1986-88, fin ctee 1986-), Cncls and Educnl Press Ed Advsy Panel 1977-87, Educnl Mgmnt Info Exchange 1981-, Open Univ Cncl 1985- (chm bd for Educnl In-Service Trg 1983-87), Printing and Publishing Ind Trg Bd 1970-72, BBC Further Educn Advsy Ctee 1970-75, Burnham Ctee 1972-77, DES Local Authy Educnl Expenditure Gp 1976-84, Sec of State's Visiting Ctee, Cranfield Inst of Technol 1976-81, Teaching of Mathematics in Schs (Cockcroft) Ctee 1978-81; pres Br Educnl Equipment Assoc 1980-83; memb bd Nat Advsy Body for Higher Educn 1982-84; chm: Further Educn Staff Coll 1986-, Brunel Univ Educn Policy Centre Advsy Ctee 1986-; pres Br Assoc, Edn Section 1986-87, memb Higginson Ctee (A level) 1987-88, pres Nat Inst Adult & Continuing Educn 1988-, chm EMIS Ltd 1988-; Hon DUniv (Open); kt 1985; *Clubs* Royal Overseas; *Style*— Sir Roy Harding, CBE; 27 King Edward Ave, Aylesbury, Bucks HP21 7JE (☎ 0296 23006)

HARDING, Lady Sophie Helen Blair; *née* Leighton; *m* 1927, Sir Harold John Boyer Harding (d 1986); 2 s, 1 da; *Style*— Lady Harding; 37 Monmouth St, Topsham, Exeter, Devon (☎ 039 287 3281)

HARDING, Sir (George) William; KCMG (1983), CMG (1977, CVO 1972); s of Lt-Col George Richardson Harding, DSO, MBE (d 1976), and Grace Henley, *née* Darby; *b* 18 Jan 1927; *Educ* Aldenham, St John's Coll Cambridge; *m* 1955, Sheila Margaret Ormond, da of Maj John Ormond Riddel (d 1945), of Edinburgh; 4 s (Rupert, Simon, Martin, James); *Career* Lt Royal Marines 1945-48; entered Diplomatic Serv 1950, served Singapore, Burma, Paris, Santo Domingo, Mexico City, Paris; ambass Peru 1977-79, asst under-sec of state FCO 1979-81, ambass Brazil 1981-84, dep under-sec of state for Asia and the Americas FCO 1984-86; int advsr to bd and non-exec dir of Lloyds Bank plc 1988-) dir Lloyds Merchant Bank Hldgs Ltd 1988-; chm: First Spanish Investmt Tst plc 1988-, Thai-Euro Fund Ltd 1988-, govr Centre for Int Briefing Farmham Castle 1987-; memb: Cncl of Royal Inst of Int Affrs 1988-, Cncl of Royal Geographical Soc 1988-, Tbnl Cmmn 1987-; visiting fell Harvard Univ Center for Int Affs 1986; *Clubs* Garrick, Beefsteak, Leander; *Style*— Sir William Harding, KCMG, CVO; Shelley Ct, Tite St, Chelsea, London SW3 4JB, Lloyds Bank plc, 71 Lombard St, London EC3P 3BS

HARDING OF PETHERTON, 2 Baron (UK 1958); John Charles Harding; o s of Field Marshal 1 Baron Harding of Petherton, GCB, CBE, DSO, MC (d 1989), and Mary, *née* Rooke (d 1983); *b* 12 Feb 1928; *Educ* Marlborough, Worcester Coll Oxford; *m* 20 June 1966, Harriet, da of Maj-Gen James Hare, CB, DSO (d 1970); 2 s (Hon William Allan John, Hon David Richard John b 1978), 1 da (Hon Diana Mary b 1967); *Heir* s, Hon William Allan John Harding b 5 July 1969; *Career* Maj 11 Hussars, ret 1968; farmer; *Style*— The Rt Hon Lord Harding of Petherton; Lower Farm, Nether Compton, Sherborne, Dorset (☎ 0935 813140)

HARDING-DAVIES, Baroness, Vera Georgina; da of George Bates; *m* 1943, Rt Hon John Emerson Harding-Davies, MBE, PC, nominated Life Peer (Baron) 1979 but who d before Peerage cr; 1 s, 1 da; *Style*— Thr Rt Hon The Lady Harding-Davies; Sutton Villiage, nr Pulborough, West Sussex

HARDINGE, Hon Andrew Hartland; 2 s of 5 Viscount Hardinge (d 1984); br and hp of 6 Viscount Hardinge; *b* 7 Jan 1960; *Style*— The Hon Andrew Hardinge; c/o 5 Somerset Sq, London W14 8EE

HARDINGE, Hon Charles Alexander; s of 3 Baron Hardinge of Penshurst by 2 m; *b* 17 May 1967; *Style*— The Hon Charles Hardinge

HARDINGE, 6 Viscount (UK 1846); Charles Henry Nicholas Hardinge; s of 5 Viscount Hardinge (d 1984), and 1 w (m dis 1982), Zoe Ann (Mrs C M H Murray), da of Hartland de Montarville Molson, OBE, of Montreal, Senator of Canada; *b* 25 August 1956; *Educ* Upper Canada Coll, Trin Coll Sch, MaGill Univ; *m* 1985, Mrs Julie Therese Sillett, eldest da of Keith Sillett, of Sydney, Australia; 2 da (Hon Emilie Charlotte b 1986, Hon Olivia Margaux b 1989), and 1 step s (Matthew b 1982); *Heir* bro, Hon Andrew Hartland Hardinge, *qv*; *Career* Independant in House of Lords, mangr Private Banking, The Royal Bank of Canada; *Style*— The Rt Hon the Viscount Hardinge; 12 Strathbourne Rd, London SW17

HARDINGE, Hon Edward Frederick; s of 3 Baron Hardinge of Penshurst; *b* 25 Oct 1958; *Educ* Gordonstoun; *Style*— The Hon Edward Hardinge; Bracken Hill, 10 Penland Rd, Bexhill-on-Sea, E Sussex

HARDINGE, Viscountess Florence Elisabeth; *née* Baroness von Oppenheim; da of late Baron Harold von Oppenheim, of Cologne; *Educ* Fondation Nationale des Sciences Politique (Paris) & Université Paris II; *m* 1982, as his 2 w, 5 Viscount Hardinge; 1 da (Hon Georgia Victoria b 1984); *Recreations* shooting, skiing, music; *Style*— Rt Hon Florence Viscountess Hardinge; 5 Somerset Sq, London W14 8EE

HARDINGE, Hon Hugh Francis; s of 3 Baron Hardinge of Penshurst; *b* 9 April 1948; *Educ* Eton; *Style*— The Hon Hugh Hardinge; Hunts Barn, Mayfield, Sussex (☎ 2151)

HARDINGE, Margot, Viscountess; Margaret (Elizabeth Arnot); da of late Hugh Percy Fleming, of Wynyards, Rockcliffe, Ottawa; *m* 15 Sept 1928, 4 Viscount Hardinge, MBE (d 1979); 1 s (5 Viscount d 1984), 2 da (Hon Mrs Worsley, Hon Mrs Raymond); *Style*— Margaret, Viscountess Hardinge; 1523 Summerhill Ave, Montréal, Québec, Canada

HARDINGE, Hon Maximillian Evelyn; s of 5 Viscount Hardinge; *b* 19 Jan 1969; *Style*— The Hon Maximillian Hardinge; c/o 5 Somerset Sq, London W14 8EE

HARDINGE, Sir Robert Arnold; 7 Bt (UK 1801), of Lurran, Fermanagh; s of Sir Robert Hardinge, 6 Bt (d 1973); *b* 19 Dec 1914; *Heir* kinsman, 5 Viscount Hardinge; *Style*— Sir Robert Hardinge, Bt

HARDINGE OF PENSHURST, 3 Baron (UK 1910); George Edward Charles Hardinge; s of 2 Baron, GCB, GCVO, MC, PC (d 1960), and Helen, Baroness Hardinge of Penshurst (d 1979); *b* 31 Oct 1921; *Educ* Eton, RNC Dartmouth; *m* 1, 22 July 1944 (m dis 1962), Janet (d 1970), da of Lt-Col Francis Balfour, CIE, CVO, CBE, MC (n of 1 and 2 Earls of Balfour); 3 s; m 2, 1966, Mrs Margaret Trezise, da of William Jerrum; 1 s; *Heir* s, Hon Julian Hardinge; *Career* Lt Cdr RN ret; page of honour to HM 1933-38, train bearer at Coronation of George VI; 30 years as a professional publisher (Collins, Longmans, Macmillan); *Books* An Incompleat Angler (1976); *Clubs* Brooks's; *Style*— The Rt Hon Lord Hardinge of Penshurst; Bracken Hill, 10 Penland Road, Bexhill-on-Sea, E Sussex (☎ 0424 211866)

HARDMAN, Blaise Noel Anthony; s of Air Chief Marshal Sir Donald Hardman, GBE, KCB, DFC (d 1982), and Dorothy, *née* Ashcroft Thompson; *b* 24 Dec 1939; *Educ* Eton; *m* 1967, Caroline Marion, da of Sir Donald Cameron of Lochiel, KT, CVO, of Inverness-shire; 1 s (Thomas b 1977), 4 da (Jane b 1969, Annabel b 1971, Elizabeth b 1974, Rosanna b 1979); *Career* cmmnd 2 Lt HM forces 1959, served 13/18 Royal Hussars 1959-61, Malaya 1961, BAOR; joined Morgan Grenfell and Co Ltd 1962, (dir 1971, chm 1987); dir P and O Steam Navigation Co 1980-83; dir: Matthew Clark and Sons (Hldgs) 1982, Morgan Grenfell Gp plc 1985; *Recreations* gardening; *Clubs* Boodles; *Style*— Blaise Hardman, Esq; Farley House, Farley Chamberlayne, nr Romsey, Hants; Morgan Grenfell and Co Ltd, 23 Great Winchester St, London EC2 (☎ 01 588 4545)

HARDMAN, Lady; Dorothy; da of William Ashcroft Thompson, JP, of Larkenshaw, Chobham; *m* 1930, Air Chief Marshal Sir (James) Donald Innes Hardman, GBE, KCB, DFC (d 1982); 2 s, 1 da (*see* North, Sir Jonathan, 2 Bt); *Style*— Lady Hardman; Dolphin Cottage, St Cross Hill, Winchester, Hants

HARDMAN, Sir Fred; MBE (1942); s of Fred Hardman, KSLI (ka Hooge, Ypres 1915); *b* 26 Sept 1914; *Educ* Leverbridge, Muttenz Basle; *m* 1941, Ennis, da of Joseph Lawson (d 1971), of Warrington; 1 child; *Career* Acting Sqdn Ldr, served UK, Europe, SE Asia; Cons agent (Cannock) 1946-52, sr exec lectr PR Rentokil 1952-74; industl rels conslt; pres Coalbrookdale Royal Br Legion; chm: Cons Trade Unionists 1977-80, Nat Union of Cons Assocs 1981-82 (now vice pres); pres Cons Trade Unionists (West Midlands), vice-pres Wrekin Cons; memb bd Telford Devpt Corpn, chm Taws Printers (Telford); former ccncllr Staffs; kt 1982; *Clubs* St Stephen's Constitutional, Royal Overseas League; *Style*— Sir Fred Hardman, MBE; The Old Bakehouse, The Wharfage, Ironbridge TF8 7NH (☎ 0952 453423)

HARDMAN, Sir Henry; KCB (1962), CB (1956); s of Harry Hardman (d 1957); *b* 15 Dec 1905; *Educ* Manchester Central HS, Manchester Univ; *m* 1937, Helen Diana, da of late Robert Carr Bosanquet; 1 s, 2 da; *Career* economics tutor Leeds Univ 1934-45, entered Miny of Food 1940, dep head Br Food Mission to N America 1946-48, under-sec Miny of Food 1948-53, min UK delegation to NATO Paris 1953-54, dep sec Miny of Agric Fisheries and Food 1955-60, dep sec Miny of Aviation 1960, perm sec Miny of Aviation 1961-63, perm under-sec of State MOD 1963-66; memb Monopolies Cmmn 1967-70 (dep chm 1967-68), chm Covent Garden Market Authy 1967-75, govr and tstee Reserve Bank of Rhodesia 1967-79; chm Home-Grown Cereals Authy 1968-77; *Style*— Sir Henry Hardman, KCB; 9 Sussex Square, Brighton, East Sussex BN2 1FJ (☎ 0273 688904)

HARDWICK, Dr Donald; CBE (1980); *b* 1926; *Educ* Sheffield Univ (BMet, PhD); *m* 1950, Dorothy Mary; 2 s; *Career* chm: Steel Div Johnson and Firth Brown plc 1975-86, Firth Brown Castings Ltd,Firth Vickers Foundery Ltd, Glossop Superalloys Ltd, The Firth-Derihon Stampings Ltd; dir: Mitchell Somers Ltd 1974-, Johnson and Firth Brown plc; FIM; *Style*— Dr Donald Hardwick, CBE; Steel Divn, Johnson and Firth Brown plc, Southfield House, Sheffield S1 2AG

HARDWICK, Donald Hugh; s of Capt Donald Frederick Hardwick, MC (d 1967), of Purlands, Charing, Kent, and Adeline Marion, *née* Sulston (d 1966); *b* 28 Oct 1936; *Educ* St Edmund's Canterbury, Canterbury Coll of Art (Nat Dip in Design); *m* 29 Feb 1964, Kathleen, da of Alfred George Englefield (d 1959); 2 s (Leigh Hardwick b 22 Nov 1967, Giles Hardwick b 27 Oct 1968); *Career* Nat Serv REME attached to 4 Gds Bde BAOR 1956-58; advertising indust 1958-; dir: Appropriate Technol Ltd 1979-, Butler Borg Ltd 1986-; md Jogdean Ltd 1979-; *Style*— Donald Hardwick, Esq; St Margarets, Rochester, Kent (☎ 0634 402632); 4 Gee's Ct, Oxford St, London W1M 5HQ (☎ 01 408 2301, fax 01 408 0382, telex 267529)

HARDWICK, Mary Atkinson (Mollie); *née* Greenhalgh; da of Joseph Greenhalgh (d 1940), of Cheadle Hulme Cheshire, and Anne Frances Greenhalgh, *née* Atkinson (d 1959); *Educ* Manchester HS for Girls; *m* 1961, Michael Hardwick, s of George Drinkrow Hardwick, of Leeds, W Yorks; 1 s (Julian); *Career* announcer BBC North Region 1940-45, BBC (Radio) Drama Dept 1945-62; freelance author 1962-; FRSA; *Books* Stories from Dickens (1968), Emma, Lady Hamilton (1969), Mrs Dizzy (1972), Upstairs Downstairs: Sarah's Story (1973), The Years of Change (1974), The War to end Wars (1975), Mrs Bridges' Story (1975), The World of Upstairs Downstairs (1976), Alice in Wonderland (play, 1975), Beauty's Daughter (1976, Elizabeth Goudge Award for best historical romantic novel of year), The Duchess of Duke Street: The Way Up (1976), The Golden Years (1976), The World Keeps Turning (1977), Charlie is My Darling (1977), The Atkinson Heritage (1978), Thomas and Sarah (1978), Thomas and Sarah: Two for a Spin (1979), Lovers Meeting (1979), Sisters in Love (1979), Dove's Nest (1980), Willowwood (1980), Juliet Bravo 1 (1980), Juliet Bravo 2 (1980), Monday's Child (1981), Calling Juliet Bravo: New Arrivals (1981), I Remember Love (1982), The Shakespeare Girl (1983), By the Sword Divided (1983), The Merrymaid (1984), Girl with a Crystal Dove (1985), Malice Domesti (1986), Parson's Pleasure (1987), Uneaseful Death (1988) Blood Royal (1988), The Bandersnathch (1989); with Michael Hardwick: The Jolly Toper (1961), The Sherlock Holmes Companion (1962), Sherlock Holmes Investigates (1963), The Man Who Was Sherlock Holmes (1964), Four Sherlock Holmes plays (1964), The Charles Dickens Companion (1965), The World's Greatest Sea Mysteries (1967), Writers' Houses: a literary journey in England (1968), Alfred Deller: A Singularity of Voice (1968), Charles Dickens As They Saw Him (1969), The Game's Afoot (Sherlock Holmes Plays, 1969), Plays from Dickens (1970), Dickens' England (1970), The Private Life of Sherlock Homes (1970), Four More Sherlock Holmes Plays (1973), The Charles Dickens Encyclopedia (1973), The Bernard Shaw Companion (1973), The Charles Dickens Quiz Book (1974), The Upstairs Downstairs Omnibus (1975), The Gaslight Boy (1976), The Hound of the Baskervilles and Other Sherlock Holmes Plays (1982); numerous plays and scripts for radio and television; contributions to women's magazines; *Recreations* reading detective novels; *Style*— Mollie Hardwick; 2 Church St, Wye, Kent TN25 5BJ (☎ 0784 813051)

HARDWICK, Michael John Drinkrow; s of George Drinkrow Hardwick (d 1964), and Katharine Augusta, *née* Townend (d 1964); *b* 10 Sept 1924; *Educ* Leeds GS; *m* 1961, Mollie, da of Joseph Greenhalgh (d 1940), of Cheadle Hulme, Cheshire; 1 s (Julian); *Career* Indian Army 1943-47, Capt served in India and Japan; author and dramatist, reporter Morley Observer 1942-43; dir: NZ Nat Film Unit 1948-53, Freedom Newspaper NZ 1953-54, BBC Radio Drama Dept 1958-63; freelance author 1963-; FRSA; *Books* The Royal Visit to New Zealand (1954), Emigrant in Motley: letters of Charles Kean and Ellen Tree (1954), Seeing New Zealand (1955), Opportunity in New Zealand (ed with Baron Birkett, 1955), The Verdict of the Court (1960), Doctors on Trial (1961), The Plague and Fire of London (1966), The Worlds Greatest Air Mysteries (1970), The Discovery of Japan (1970), The Osprey Guide to Gilbert and Sullivan (1972), The Osprey Guide to Jane Austen (1973), A Literary Atlas and Gazetter of the British Isles (1973), The Osprey Guide to Oscar Wilde (1973), Upstairs Downstairs: Mr Hudson's Diaries (1973), Mr Bellamy's Story (1974), On with the Dance (1975), Endings and Beginnings (1975), The Osprey Guide to Anthony Trollope (1974), The Inheritors (1974), The Pallisers (abridger 1974), The Four Musketeers (abridger 1975), The Man Who Would be King (abridger 1976), The Cedar Tree (1976), The Cedar Tree: Autumn of an Age (1977), A Bough Breaks (1978), Regency Royal (1978), Prisoner of the Devil (1979), Regency Rake (1979), Regency Revenge (1980), Bergerac (1981), The Chinese Detective (1981), Regency Revels (1982), The Barchester Chronicles (1982), The Private Life of Dr Watson (1983), Sherlock Holmes: my life and crimes (1984), Last Tenko (1984), Complete Guide to Sherlock Holmes (1986), The Revenge of the Hound (1987); as John Drinkrow: The Vintage Operetta Book (1972), The Vintage Musical Comedy Book (1973); with Mollie Hardwick: The Jolly Toper (1961), The Sherlock Holmes Companion (1962), Sherlock Holmes Investigates (1963), The Man Who Was Sherlock Holmes (1964), Four Sherlock Holmes Plays (1964), The Charles Dickens Companion (1965), The World's Greatest Sea Mysteries (1967), Writers' Houses: a literary journey in England (1968), Alfred Deller: A Singularity of Voice (1968), Charles Dickens As They Saw Him (1969), Dicken's England (1970), The Private Life of Sherlock Holmes (1970), The Bernard Shaw Companion (1973), The Charles Dickens Encyclopaedia (1973), The Charles Dickens Quiz Book (1974), The Upstairs Downstairs Omnibus (1975), The Gaslight Boy (1976); plays: A Christmas Card (1975), Four Sherlock Holmes Plays (jtly, 1964), The Game's Afoot (jtly, 1969), Four More Sherlock Holmes Plays (jtly, 1973), The Hound of the Baskervilles and other Sherlock Holmes Plays (1982); author of many plays and scripts for tv and radio; *Recreations* listening to music, watching old films on television; *Style*— Michael Hardwick, Esq; 2 Church St, Wye, Kent TN25 5BJ (☎ 0233 813 051)

HARDWICKE, Countess of - Enid Munnick; *m* 1, Roy Boulting, the film producer and one half of the Boulting Bros; m 2, 1970, as his 2 w, 9 Earl of Hardwicke (d 1974); *Style*— The Rt Hon The Countess of Hardwicke

HARDWICKE, 10 Earl of (GB 1754); Joseph Philip Sebastian Yorke; also Baron Hardwicke (GB 1733) and Viscount Royston (GB 1754); s of Viscount Royston (d 1973, s and h of 9 Earl, who d 1974); *b* 3 Feb 1971; *Heir* kinsman, Richard Yorke; *Style*— The Rt Hon Earl of Hardwicke; 9 Fernshaw Rd, SW10

HARDY, David William; s of Brig John Herbert Hardy, CBE, MC (d 1969), of Lancaster, and (Amy) Doris, *née* Bacon (d 1982); *b* 14 July 1930; *Educ* Wellington Coll, Harvard Business Sch (AMP); *m* 11 Sept 1957, Rosemary Stratford, da of Sir Godfrey Ferdinando Stratford Collins, KCIE, CSI, OBE (d 1952); 1 s (Alexander David b 11 May 1968), 1 da (Sarah Elizabeth b 28 May 1964); *Career* 2 Lt 2 Royal Horse Artillery Germany 1953-54; dir: Funch Edye Co Inc 1960 (1954-64), Imperial Tobacco (vice pres Fin and Admin 1964-70), (finance) Tate and Lyle plc 1972-77, Ocean Transport and Trading plc 1977-83, Waterford Glass Gp plc 1984, Paragon Gp

Ltd 1984-88, Sturge Hldgs plc 1985, Aberfoyle Hldgs plc 1986; chm: Ocean Inchcape Ltd 1980-83, Globe Investmt Tst plc 1983- (dir 1976), London Park Hotels 1983-87, Docklands Light Railway 1984-87, Swan Hunter Ltd 1986-88, MGM Assurance 1986- (dir 1985), Leisuretime Int (non-exec) 1988-, Docklands Devpt Corpn (non-exec) 1988-, DTI Engrg Mkts Advsy Ctee (non-exec) 1988-; dep chm: London Regnl Tport 1984-87, The Agricultural Mortgage Corpn 1986 (dir 1973); secondment to HM Govt (co-ordinator of Industl Advsrs) 1970-72; memb NEDC for Agriculture 1970-72, memb export credits guarantees advsy cncl 1973-78, chm Economics and Social Affairs Ctee 1974-78, memb CBI Econs and Fiscal Ctee 1982-; memb cncl BIM 1974-79, co-opted cncl Inst CAs 1974-78, chm 100 Gp CAs and fin dirs 1986-88; FCA, FCIT, CBIM; *Recreations* flyfishing, shooting; *Clubs* Brooks's, MCC, HAC, The Parlour, The Philippics; *Style—* David Hardy, Esq; Globe Investment Trust plc, Electra House, Temple Place, London WC2R 3HP (☎ 01 836 7766, fax 01 836 4225, telex 24101)

HARDY, Hon Lady (Diana Joan); *née* Allsopp; da of 3 Baron Hindlip, OBE, JP, DL (d 1931), and Agatha (d 1962), da of John Thynne, DL (d 1918), who was 6 s of Rev Lord John Thynne, 3 s of 2 Marquess of Bath, KG (d 1837); *b* 1908; *m* 2 June 1930, Lt-Col Sir Rupert John Hardy, 4 Bt; 1 s, 1 da; *Style—* The Hon Lady Hardy; Gulliver's Lodge, Guilsborough, Northampton

HARDY, Graham John; s of William A Hardy (d 1976), and Lettie M, *née* Lovell (d 1984); *b* 5 Mar 1938; *Educ* Llandaff Cathedral Sch, Cathays HS, Welsh Sch Architecture Univ of Wales (BArch, ARIBA); *m* 7 Sept 1963, Sara Maureen, da of David Metcalfe Morgan, of Archer Road, Penarth; 1 s (Keiron b 1972), 2 da (Bridget b 1966, Elise b 1968); *Career* chartered architect; Prince of Wales Award 1984, St John Ev Church Grounds Cardiff; Prince of Wales Award 1984, Eglwysilian Church Mid Glam; Catnic UK Restoration Award 1981; first prize: competition for Inner Areas 1982, Prince of Wales' Ctee 1980, Civic Tst Commendation Victoria Place Newport 1980; architect and surveyor to the Fabric: Margam Abbey, Old Priory Caldey Abbey, St Illtyds Church Llantwit Major; architect to the Cathedral Parish of Llandaff; pres Rotary Club of Cardiff East; *Clubs* Rotary; *Style—* Graham J Hardy, Esq; Timbers, 6 Cefn Coed Road, Cyncoed, Cardiff CF2 6AQ (☎ 0222 752960); Graham J Hardy and Assoc, 6 Cefn Coed Rd, Cardiff CF2 6AQ

HARDY, Herbert Charles; s of Charles Hardy; *b* 13 Dec 1928; *Educ* Sandhurst; *m* 1960, Irene Burrows; 1 da; *Career* dir News Gp Newspapers Ltd 1969-78, md and chief exec News International Ltd 1976-78 (dir 1972-78), chief exec Evening Standard Co Ltd 1980-, md Associated Newspapers Ltd 1989-; *Style—* Herbert Hardy, Esq; 118 Fleet St, London EC4P 4DD (☎ 01 353 8000)

HARDY, Sir James Gilbert; OBE (1975); s of Tom Mayfield Hardy (d 1938), and Eileen Clara, *née* Ponder (d 1980); *b* 20 Nov 1932; *Educ* St Peter's Coll (Adelaide), SA Inst of Tech; *m* 1956, Anne, da of Ronald A Jackson (decd); 2 s (David, Richard); *Career* vintner and vingneron; chm of dirs Thomas Hardy and Sons Pty Ltd 1981- (sales rep 1953, dir and mangr Sydney Branch 1962, regnl dir Eastern Aust 1977); dir: S Aust Film Corpn 1981-, Advertiser Newspapers Ltd 1984-; pres Jubilee Sailing Ship Project 1981-, Capt S Aust Challenge for the defence of the America's Cup 1987; vice-pres Royal Blind Soc of NSW 1980-, bd of advice Rothmans Nat Sport Fndn 1985, memb Brisbane Olympic Ctee (1992) 1985; skipper America's Cup Challenger 1970, 1974, 1980, team advsr 1983; helmsman Aust Adm's Cup Team 1973, 1979; kt 1981; *Recreations* internat competitive sailing (owner Nyamba, Runaway), built 5 of own racing sailboats; *Clubs* Int Wine and Food Soc (London), Beefsteak (Sydney), Aust (Sydney), Tattersalls (Sydney), Royal Sydney Yacht Sqdn (Sydney), Brighton and Seacliff Yacht (S Aust), Canberra Yacht (Qld), Fort Worth Boat (USA); *Style—* Sir James Hardy, OBE; 7/10 Marine Parade, Manly East, NSW 2095, Australia (☎ 02 977 5560); Thomas Hardy and Sons Pty Ltd, 104 Bay Street, East Botany, NSW 2019, Australia (☎ 02 666 5855, telex AA70758)

HARDY, Brig (Arthur) John; CBE (1967), MBE (1953, TD); s of Henry Harrison Hardy, CBE (d 1958), of Cheltenham, Glos, and Edith Jocelyn, *née* Dugdale (d 1977); *b* 19 August 1918; *Educ* Rugby, BNC Oxford (MA); *m* 3 Dec 1946, Anne Primrose, da of Guy Sutton, of London; 2 da (Sarah Mary Anne b 1949, Katherine Harriet Louise b 1954); *Career* cmmnd KSLI 1939 (despatches 1946 and 1955); ADC to HM The Queen 1970-73; dep Col The Light Infantry 1968-78; cmd: 1 Bn KSLI 1958-60, Kenya Army and Br Army Trg Team Kenya 1964-66; dep dir Manning (Army) 1968-71, dir Equipment Mgmnt (Army) 1971-73, ret; *Style—* John Hardy, CBE, MBE, TD; Oates, Bepton, Midhurst, W Sussex GU29 0JB

HARDY, Maj-Gen John Campbell; CB (1985), LVO (1978); s of Gen Sir Campbell Hardy, KCB, CBE, DSO (d 1984); *b* 13 Oct 1933; *Educ* Sherborne Sch; *m* 1961, Jennifer Mary Kempton; 1 s, 1 da; *Career* joined RM 1952, 45 Commando 1954, HMS Superb 1956, Instr NCOs' Sch at Plymouth 1957, 42 Commando 1959, 43 Commando 1962, Adj Jt Serv Amphibious Warfare Centre 1964, Co Cdr 45 Commando 1965, student RAF Staff Coll Bracknell 1966, instr RNC Greenwich 1967, extra equerry to HRH Prince Philip 1968-69, staff offr in Dept of Cmdt Gen RM 1969, Rifle Co Cdr 41 Commando 1971, student NDC Latimer 1972, staff of CDS 1973, staff offr HQ Commando Forces 1975, CO RM Poole 1977, Col 1978, COS and asst def attaché Br Def Staff Washington 1979, ADC to HM The Queen 1981-82, Maj-Gen 1982, COS to Cmdt Gen RM 1982-84, dep chief of staff HQ AFNORTH 1984-87; dir Br Digestive Fndn 1987; *Recreations* current affairs, sailing; *Clubs* Army and Navy; *Style—* Maj-Gen John Hardy, CB, LVO; c/o National Westminster Bank, 51 The Strand, Walmer, Deal, Kent

HARDY, Laurence Carey; s of Herbert Ronald Hardy (d 1954); *b* 17 Nov 1929; *Educ* RNC Dartmouth; *m* 1953, Rebeka Ann; 1 s, 3 da; *Career* Lt RN serv Korea, Malaya; dir: Allied Leather Industs Ltd 1967-, Freshfield Lane Brickworks Ltd 1980-; High Sheriff E Sussex 1976; conservator Ashdown Forest 1977-; chm Haywards Heath Housing Soc Ltd 1987-; *Recreations* shooting, fishing, conservation, gardening; *Style—* Laurence Hardy, Esq; Latchetts Dane Hill, Haywards Heath, W Sussex RH17 7HQ (☎ 0825 790237); Freshfield Lane Brickworks Ltd, Dane Hill, Haywards Heath, W Sussex RH17 7HH (☎ 0825 790350)

HARDY, Peter; MP (Lab) Wentworth 1983-; s of Lawrence Hardy, of Wath-upon-Dearne; *b* 17 July 1931; *Educ* Wath-upon-Dearne GS, Westminster, Univ of Sheffield; *m* 1954, Margaret Anne, *née* Brookes; 1 s; *Career* MP (Lab) Rother Valley 1970-83; pps to: Sec of State for Environment 1974-76, For Sec 1976-79; vice-chm Cncl of Europe Socialist Gp, chm C of E Environment ctee sponsored by NACODS, ldr of Lab delegation to Cncl of Europe, chm Parly Lab Pty Energy Ctee; memb: Cncl RSPB, Central Exec Cncl NSPCC, Cncl of World Wildlife Fund UK; *Books* A Lifetime of Badgers (1975); *Style—* Peter Hardy, Esq, MP; 53 Sandygate, Wath-upon-Dearne, Rotherham, S Yorkshire (☎ 0709 874590)

HARDY, Richard Charles Chandos; s and h of Lt-Col Sir Rupert Hardy, 4 Bt *qv*; *b* 6 Feb 1945; *Educ* Eton; *m* 1972, Venetia, da of Simon Wingfield Digby, TD, DL, MP; 4 da; *Career* insurance broker; *Recreations* hunting, point-to-pointing, racing; *Clubs* Turf; *Style—* Richard Hardy Esq; Springfield House, Gillingham, Dorset

HARDY, Richard Harry Norman; s of Norman Hardy (d 1938), of Amersham, Bucks, and Gladys Marjorie, *née* Berneys (d 1951); *b* 8 Oct 1923; *Educ* Marlborough, Doncaster Tech Coll (HNC); *m* 30 April 1949, (Anne) Gwenda, da of Leonard Aspinall (d 1961); 2 s (James b 1953, Peter Miles b 1958), 1 da (Anthea Jane b 1950); *Career* apprenticeship locomotive engrg and mgmnt 1941-45; mangr engine depots LNER and BR 1949-55: Woodford Halse, Ipswich, Battersea, dist motive power supt (formerly asst) Stratford 1955-62; divnl gen mangr: Kings Cross 1963-68, Liverpool 1968-73; advsr engrg and res Br Railways Bd 1973-82; chm Steam Locomotive Operators Assoc; CEng, FIMechE; *Books* Steam in the Blood (1971), Railways in the Blood (1985); *Recreations* family and people, railways, writing, cricket, hunting, riding, dressage, gardening, photography; *Clubs* MCC; *Style—* Richard Hardy, Esq; Greenbank Hse, 20 South Rd, Amersham, Bucks HP6 5LU (☎ 0494 726 281)

HARDY, Robert Hugh; JP (Berkshire 1984); s of Rev Charles Sidney Hardy (d 1965), of Curfew House, Sandwich, Kent and Eva Meriel Violet, *née* Hodson; *b* 15 August 1932; *Educ* Winchester, Merton Coll Oxford (BA, MA); *m* 18 July 1970, Penelope Jean Maxwell, da of Robert Sherson (d 1982), of Ringwell House, Ditcheat, Somerset; 1 s (James b 1975), 1 da (Caroline b 1972); *Career* house master Eton Coll 1969-84 (asst master 1956-87), Headmaster Milton Abbey Sch 1987-; govr N Foreland Lodge 1984; *Recreations* walking, fishing, cricket, antique glass; *Style—* Robert Hardy, Esq, JP; The Headmaster's House, Milton Abbey, Blandford Forum, Dorset DT11 ODA (☎ 0258 880484); Dorcas Cottage, Bicknoller, Taunton, Somerset TA4 4EG (☎ 0258 880500)

HARDY, His Hon Judge; Robert James; s of James Frederick Hardy and Annie, *née* Higinbotham; *b* 12 July 1924; *Educ* Mostyn House, Wrekin, Univ Coll London (LLB); *m* 1951, Maureen Scott; 1 s, 1 da; *Career* barr 1950, circuit judge 1979-; *Style—* His Hon Judge Hardy; Smithy House, Sandlebridge, Little Warford, Cheshire SK9 7TY; Betlem, Mallorca

HARDY, Lady Robina; *née* Bookless; Robert Bookless; *m* 1937, Sir James Douglas Hardy, CBE (d 1986); 2 s; *Style—* Lady Hardy; c/o Midland Bank, Poultry and Princes St, London EC2

HARDY, Lt-Col Sir Rupert John; 4 Bt (UK 1876), of Dunstall Hall, Co Stafford; s of Sir Bertram Hardy, 3 Bt (d 1953), and Violet, da of Hon Sir Edward Chandos Leigh, KCB, KC, JP (2 s of 1 Baron Leigh); *b* 24 Oct 1902; *Educ* Eton, Trinity Hall Cambridge; *m* 2 June 1930, Hon Diana *née* Allsopp, *qv*; 1 s (Richard *qv*), 1 da (Mrs Robert Black *see* Baronetage b 1931); *Career* Lt-Col Life Gds, served WW II 8 Army in W Desert, Palestine, Syria, France; ret from Army 1948; rejoined as RARO 1952, Lt-Col Cmdg Household Cavalry 1952-56; *Recreations* hunting, shooting; *Clubs* Turf; *Style—* Lt-Col Sir Rupert Hardy, Bt; Gulliver's Lodge, Guilsborough, Northampton (☎ Guilsborough 375)

HARDY-ROBERTS, Brig Sir Geoffrey Paul; KCVO (1972), CB (1945), CBE (1944, OBE 1941), JP (W Sussex 1960), DL (W Sussex 1964); s of late Alfred Roberts; *b* 16 May 1907; *Educ* Eton, RMC Sandhurst; *m* 1945, Eldred, (d 1987) widow of Col John Ronald Macdonell, DSO (d 1944); *Career* regular cmmn 9 Lancers 1926-37, served WWII, Mid East, Sicily, Italy, NW Europe, Brig 1943; contested (C) Wimbledon 1945; sec-superintentent Middx Hosp 1946-67; master of HM's Household 1967-73, extra equerry to HM The Queen 1967-, memb W Sussex AHA 1974-81, dep chm King Edward VII Hosp Midhurst 1967-81; high sheriff Sussex 1965; Offr Legion of Merit (USA) 1945; *Style—* Brig Sir Geoffrey Hardy-Roberts, KCVO; The Garden Hse, Coates, Pulborough, W Sussex RH20 1ES (☎ 079 882 446)

HARDYMAN, Norman Trenchard; CB (1984); s of late Rev Arnold Victor Hardyman, and late Laura Hardyman; *b* 5 Jan 1930; *Educ* Clifton, Ch Ch Oxford; *m* 1961, Carol Rebecca Turner; 1 s, 1 da; *Career* princ Miny of Educn 1960 (asst princ 1955), private sec to Sec of State 1966-68, DES 1975-79 (asst sec 1968-75), under sec DHSS 1979-81, sec Univ Grants Ctee 1982-; *Style—* Norman Hardyman, Esq, CB; 16 Rushington Ave, Maidenhead, Berks (☎ 0628 24179); office: 14 Park Crescent, London W1N 4DH (☎ 01 636 7799)

HARE, Hon Alan Victor; MC (1942); s of 4 Earl of Listowel and Hon Freda, da of 2 Baron Derwent; *b* 14 Mar 1919; *Educ* Eton, New Coll Oxford (MA); *m* 1945, Jill, da of late Gordon North; 1 s (Alan b 1948), 1 da (Marcia b 1946); *Career* WWII Europe and Far East (MC); FCO 1947-61 (1 sec Br Embassy Athens 1957-60); dir: Pearson Longman 1975-82; chm Industl and Trade Fairs Hldgs 1979-82 (dep chm 1977-79); chm Financial Times Ltd 1978-83 (chief exec 1975-83); pres Soc Civile du Vignoble du Chateau Latour 1983- dir Economist Newspaper Ltd 1975-; (dep chm 1985-) dir English Nat Opera 1982-; tstee Reuters 1985-; *Recreations* music, walking, opera; *Clubs* White's; *Style—* The Hon Alan Hare, MC; Flat 12, 53 Rutland Gate, London SW7 (☎ 01 581 2184)

HARE, Ann, Lady; Barbara Mary Theodora (Ann); da of Joseph Arthur Walton; *m* 1960, as his 3 w, Maj Sir Ralph Hare, 4 Bt (d 1976); 1 da (Mary-Ann b 1961); *Style—* Ann, Lady Hare; Stow Bardolph, King's Lynn, Norfolk PE34 3HU

HARE, Christopher Peter; s of Reginald Charles Hare (d 1980), and Mary Euphemia, *née* Lefroy (d 1988); *b* 6 Nov 1947; *Educ* Dover Coll; *m* (Dorothy) Jane, da of Richard Gough Dowell, of Middleton-on-Sea, Sussex; 2 s (Nicholas Anthony b 28 May 1977, Julian Charles b 17 Nov 1981), 1 da (Rebecca Anne b 14 Feb 1975); *Career* John Dickenson & Co 1966-68; Lyon Trail Attenborough (formerly Lyon Lohr & Sly) 1968-85; dir Lyon Lohr Gp Servs 1979, gp admin 1979-85, dir Lyon Lohr Int 1980; dir Fenchurch Underwriting Agencies 1986 (joined 1985); memb Lloyds 1977-, chm City Forum 1983 (memb 1978, ctee memb 1980-83); govr Dover Coll 1982- (memb cncl and fin ctee 1982-), chm ctee Old Doverian Soc 1984- (memb 1975-); Freeman City London, Liveryman Worshipful Co of Merchant Taylors 1978; *Recreations* cricket, tennis, squash; *Clubs* MCC, RAC; *Style—* Chistopher Hare, Esq; 40 Doneraile St, London SW6 6EP (☎ 01 736 4218); Fenchurch Underwriting Agencies Ltd, Boundary House, 7 Jewry St, London EC3N 2EX (☎ 01 488 2388, fax 01 481 9467, telex 884442)

HARE, Christopher William Trelawny; s of Wing Cdr Bertram William Trelawny Hare (d 1959), of S Devon, and Violet Evelyn Seaforth, *née* Fisher; *b* 17 April 1935;

Educ Bundells, RAC; *m* 7 Aug 1965, Lavinia Frances, da of George Ronald Pigé Leschallas, of Kent; 3 s (Henry b 1966, Jonathan b 1968, James b 1971); *Career* farmer and landowner; *Recreations* fishing, shooting; *Style*— Christopher W T Hare, Esq; Henceford Farm, Black Dog, Crediton, Tiverton (☎ 860342)

HARE, David; s of Clifford Theodore Rippon and Agnes Cockburn Hare; *b* 5 June 1947; *Educ* Lancing, Jesus Coll Cambridge; *m* 1970 (m dis 1980), Margaret Matheson; 2 s, 1 da; *Career* playwright; *Plays* Slag (1970), The Great Exhibition (1972), Brassneck (with Howard Brenton 1973), Knuckle (1974), Teeth 'n' Smiles (1975), Fanshan (1975), Plenty (1978), A Map of the World (1983), Pravda (with Howard Brenton 1985), The Bay at Nice/Wrecked Eggs (1986), The Knife (opera with Nick Bicat and Time Rose Price 1987), The Secret Rapture (1988); *Films* Wetherby (written and dir 1985), Plenty (1985), Paris By Night (written and dir 1988), Strapless (written and dir 1988), *TV Plays* Licking Hitler (1978), Dreams of Leaving (1980), Saigon (1983); *Style*— David Hare, Esq; 33 Ladbroke Rd, London W11

HARE, Lady Diana; da of 5 Earl of Listowel, GCMG, PC; *b* 1965; *Style*— Lady Diana Hare

HARE, Diane Margaret; da of Rowland Hare, of Ecclesall, Sheffield, and Edna, *née* Jepson; *b* 9 Dec 1948; *Educ* Abbeydale Girl's GS Sheffield, St Anne's Coll Oxford (BA, MA); *Career* barr Middle Temple 1973; lectr Law Lanchester Poly Coventry 1972-74, Univ of Manchester (dir studies in accounting and law 1984-) 1974-, writer and speaker corpn insolvency commercial and co law; memb: res team Int Accounting Harmonization Network (and res cmmnd by Home Off), Justice; memb: legal Action Gp, Child Poverty Action Gp, Stockport Garrick Theatre; local preacher Stockport Methodist Church ; *Recreations* theatre, music, poetry, travelling; *Style*— Diane Hare; Faculty of Law, Univ of Manchester, Manchester M13 9PL (☎ 061 275 3560)

HARE, Hon Mrs Richard; Dora; da of late Mark Gordine, of St Petersburg, Russia; *m* 1936, Hon Richard Gilbert Hare, (d 1966 2 s 4 Earl of Listowel); *Career* FRBS; *Style*— The Hon Mrs Richard Hare; Dorich House, Kingston Vale, SW15

HARE, John Neville; s of late Capt Lancelot Geldart Hare, MC (D 1957), and Esther Maria, *née* Whales (d 1969); *b* 11 Dec 1934; *Educ* St Edward's Coll Oxford; *m* 17 Sept 1966, Pippa, da of Harding McGregor Dunnett, of Eliot Vale, Blackheath, London; 3 da (Charlotte b 1968, Henrietta b 1970, Emily b 1974); *Career* Lt Oxfordshire and Buckinghamshire LI Royal W Africa Frontier Force 1954-55; sr dist offr Colonial Serv Northern Nigeria 1957-64; dir Macmillan Educn Publishers 1966-74, author and conslt Hodder and Stoughton Publishers 1980-; *Books* (under pseudonym of Dan Fulani), Hijack (1979), No Condition is Permanent (1979), Sauna and the Bank Robbers (1980), Sauna, Secret Agent; Sauna to the Rescue (1981), Sauna and the Drug Pedlars (1988), God's Case No Appeal (1985), The Fight For Life (1986), The Price of Liberty (1987), No Telephone To Heaven (1985), The Power of Corruption (1986), Flight 800 (1986), Rhino's Horn (1988), Leopard's Coat (1989), Medicinal Pots of the Cham and Mwana Tribes (1985), Primary Hausa Course (1979); *Recreations* hunting, amateur dramatics (prodr Benenden Players), travel, writing; *Clubs* East India; *Style*— John Hare, Esq ; School Farm, Benenden, Kent (☎ 0580 240 755)

HARE, Prof (Frederick) Kenneth; CC (1987, OC 1978); s of Frederick Hare; *b* 5 Feb 1919; *Educ* Windsor GS, King's Coll London (BSc), Univ of Montreal (PhD); *m* 1, 1941 (m dis 1952), Suzanne Bates; 1 s; m 2, 1953, Helen Neilson, da of Alvin Morrill (d 1954), of Montreal; 1 s, 1 da; *Career* served WWII Flt Lt RCAFVR; geographer; prof in geography Univ of Toronto 1969-, provost Trinity Coll Univ Toronto 1979-86, chllr Trent Univ 1988-; FRSC; *Clubs* York (Toronto); *Style*— Prof F Kenneth Hare, CC; 301 Lakeshore Rd West, Oakville, Ontario, Canada L6K 1G2 (☎ 416 849 1374)

HARE, Philip Leigh; s of Edward Philip Leigh Hare (d 1954) and his 3 w, Lady Kathleen, *née* Stanhope (d 1971), da of 9 Earl of Harrington, and widow of Edward Morant, JP, of Brockenhurst Park, Hants; hp of cous, Sir Thomas Hare, 5 Bt, *qv*; *b* 13 Oct 1922; *m* 4 Nov 1950, Anne Lisle, 2 da of Maj Geoffrey Nicholson, CBE, MC; 1 s (Nicholas b 1955), 1 da (Louisa (twin) b 1955); *Style*— Philip Hare, Esq; The Nettings, Hook Norton, Oxon

HARE, (Thomas) Richard; *see*: Pontefract, Bishop of

HARE, Lady Rose Amanda; *née* Bligh; da (by 2 m) of 9 Earl of Darnley; *b* 1935; *m* 1961, Sir Thomas Hare, 5 Bt, *qv*; 2 da (Lucy b 1962, Elizabeth b 1964); *Style*— Lady Rose Hare; Stow Bardolph, King's Lynn, Norfolk PE34 3HU

HARE, (William) Rowan; CBE (1968), JP (Norwich 1961); s of Warren Hare (d 1969); *b* 9 April 1905; *Educ* Stamford Sch, CCC Oxford; *m* 1932, Dorothea Desiree (d 1981), da of Wilfrid E J La Fontaine Moda, of Istanbul; 2 s; *Career* chm J J Colman Ltd 1960-70, dir Reckitt and Colman 1960-70; pres Food Manufacturers Assoc 1965-68; Sheriff of Norwich 1979-80; tres UEA 1973-76; Hon DCL UEA 1977; *Recreations* cricket, music; *Clubs* Reform, MCC, Norfolk (Norwich); *Style*— Rowan Hare, Esq, CBE, JP; 9 Grove Road, Norwich NR1 3RQ

HARE, Sir Thomas; 5 Bt (UK 1818), of Stow Hall, Norfolk; s of Maj Sir Ralph Leigh Hare, 4 Bt (d 1976, an earlier Btcy in the family, dating from 1641, died out in 1764), and his 1 w, Doreen, da of Maj Sir Richard Bagge, DSO; *b* 27 July 1930; *Educ* Eton, Magdalene Coll Cambridge; *m* 1961, Lady Rose Amanda, *née* Bligh, *qv*; 2 da; *Heir* cous, Philip Leigh Hare, *qv*; *Career* Lt RARO Coldstream Gds; chartered surveyor, ARICS; landowner and farmer; *Clubs* RAC; *Style*— Sir Thomas Hare, Bt; Stow Bardolph, King's Lynn, Norfolk PE34 3HU

HARE, Hon Timothy Patrick; s of 5 Earl of Listowel, GCMG, PC; *b* 1966; *Style*— The Hon Timothy Hare

HARE DUKE, Michael Geoffrey; *see*: St Andrews, Dunkeld and Dunblane, Bishop of

HAREWOOD, 7 Earl of (UK 1812); George Henry Hubert (Lascelles); KBE (1986); also Baron Harewood (GB 1796) and Viscount Lascelles (UK 1812); s of 6 Earl of Harewood, KG, GCVO, DSO, TD (d 1947), and HRH Princess Mary (The Princess Royal), CI, GCVO, GBE, RRC, TD, CD (d 1965), only da of HM King George V, *see* Debretts Peerage, Royal family section; *b* 7 Feb 1923; *Educ* Eton, King's Coll Cambridge; *m* 1, 29 Sept 1949 (m dis 1967; she m 2, 1973, as his 2 w, Rt Hon Jeremy Thorpe), Maria Donata Nanetta Paulina Gustava Erwina Wilhelmina (Marion), o da of late Erwin Stein; 3 s (Viscount Lascelles b 1950, Hon James b 1953, Hon Robert b 1964); m 2, 31 July 1967, Patricia Elizabeth, o da of Charles Tuckwell, of Sydney, and former w of Athol Shmith; 1 s (Hon Mark b 1964); *Heir* s, Viscount Lascelles; *Career* Capt late Gren Guards, serv WWII (wounded, POW); ADC to Earl of Athlone 1945-46; ed Opera magazine 1950-53, asst to David Webster at The Royal Opera Covent Garden 1953-60; artistic dir: Leeds Festival 1956-74, Edinburgh Festival 1961-65, Adelaide Festival 1988; md ENO 1972-85, govr BBC 1985-87, pres Br Bd of Film Classification 1985-; pres Leeds United Football Club 1962-, Football Assoc 1963-72; chllr Univ of York 1963-67; Hon LLD Leeds 1959, Aberdeen 1966, Hon DMus Hull 1962, Janaček Medal 1978, Hon RAM 1983, Hon DLitt Bradford 1983, Hon Doctorate York Univ 1983, hon fell Kings Coll Cambridge 1984, hon memb Royal Northern Coll of Music 1984; Austrian Great Silver Medal of Honour 1959, Lebanese Order of the Cedar 1970; *Books* Kobbé's Complete Opera Book (ed), The Tongs and the Bones (memoirs 1981); *Recreations* shooting, watching cricket, football, films; *Style*— The Rt Hon The Earl of Harewood, KBE; Harewood House, Leeds, LS17 9LG

HARFORD, Anstice, Lady; Anstice Marion; yst da of Sir Alfred Ernest Tritton, 2 Bt (d 1939), and Agnetta Elspeth, *née* Campbell (d 1960); *b* 17 July 1909; *m* 9 April 1931, Lt-Col Sir George Arthur Harford, 2 Bt, OBE (d 1967); 2 s (Sir Timothy *qv*, Piers b 1937), 1 da (Mrs Jeremy Glyn *see* Peerage B Wolverton); *Style*— Anstice, Lady Harford; No 3 Sutton Manor Mews, Sutton Scotney, Winchester SO21 3JX (☎ 0962 760012)

HARFORD, Sir James Dundas; KBE (1956), CMG (1943); s of late Rev Dundas Harford; *b* 7 Jan 1899; *Educ* Repton, Balliol Coll Oxford; *m* 1, 1932, Countess Thelma, da of Count Albert Metaxa; 1 s; m 2, 1937, Lilias, da of Maj Archibald Campbell; 2 da; *Career* govr and c-in-c St Helena 1954-58; *Style*— Sir James Harford, KBE, CMG; Links Cottage, Rother Rd, Seaford, East Sussex (☎ 0323 892115)

HARFORD, Mark John; s and h of Sir Timothy Harford, 3 Bt; *b* 6 August 1964; *Style*— Mark Harford, Esq

HARFORD, Philip Hugh; er s of Mark William Harford (d 1969), of Horton Hall, Chipping Sodbury, and Little Sodbury Manor, Glos, and Elizabeth Ellen, da of late Brig-Gen Philip Leveson-Gower, CMG, DSO, DL, of Saltings, Yarmouth, IOW; gs of Hugh Wyndham Luttrell Harford (d 1920), who acquired Horton Hall; descended from William Harford, of Marshfield, Glos, living 1602 (*see* Burke's Landed Gentry, 18 edn, vol I, 1965); *b* 14 August 1946; *m* 11 June 1982, Willa, yr da of William Joseph Franklin, of North Lodge, Brill, Bucks; *Career* served LI; *Clubs* Royal Yacht Sqdn; *Style*— Philip Harford, Esq

HARFORD, Sir (John) Timothy; 3 Bt (UK 1934), of Falcondale, co Cardigan; s of Lt-Col Sir George Arthur Harford, 2 Bt, OBE (d 1967), and Lady Harford *qv*, *née* Anstice Marion Tritton; *b* 6 July 1932; *Educ* Harrow, Worcester Coll Oxford, Harvard Business Sch; *m* 12 May 1962, Carolyn Jane, o da of Brig Guy John de Wette Mullens, OBE (d 1981), of North House, Weyhill, Andover; 2 s (Mark b 1964, Simon b 1966), 1 da (Clare b 1963); *Career* dir Singer and Friedlander Ltd 1970-88, dep chm Wolseley-Group plc 1983-, dep chm Wesleyan and General Assur Soc 1987-; dir: Provincial Group plc, Kwiksave Group plc, Apricot Computers plc, Wagon Industries Holdings plc; *Clubs* Boodles; *Style*— Sir Timothy Harford, Bt; South House, South Littleton, Evesham, Worcs (☎ 0386 830478)

HARGRAVE, David Grant; s of (Frank) Edward Hargrave, of 7 Henllys Rd, Lyncoed, Cardiff, and Margaret Constance Mabel, *née* Grant; *b* 11 April 1951; *Educ* Howardian HS Cardiff, Univ of Birmingham (BCom, MSc); *m* 13 Dec 1969, Celia, da of Harry Hawksworth (d 1963); 1 s (Neil David b 30 July 1974), 1 da (Emma Louise b 17 June 1970); *Career* actuary Duncan C Fraser & Co (later William M Mercer Fraser Ltd) 1973-79, ptnr T G Authur Hargrave 1979-, non-exec dir Homeowner's Friendly Soc 1982-; sec and tres Birmingham Actuarial Soc 1979-81; Nat Assoc Pension Funds Ltd (W Midlands): tres 1982-85, sec 1985- 87, chm 1987-, govr Yew Tree Sch 1988-, FIA 1977; *Recreations* long distance running, swimming, windsurfing, rugby; *Style*— David Hargrave, Esq; 41 Calthorpe Rd, Edgbaston, Birmingham B15 1TS (☎ 021 456 3040, fax 021 456 3041)

HARGREAVES, Andrew Raikes; MP (C) Birmingham Hall Green 1987-; s of Col David William Hargreaves, and Judith Anne Hargreaves, *née* Currie; *b* 15 May 1955; *Educ* Eton Coll, St Edmund Hall Oxford (MA Hons); *m* 1978, Fiona Susan, da of Guy William Dottridge; 2 s (William b 1985, Thomas b 1986); *Career* former auctioneer and valuer Christies 1977-81; exec Hill Samuel 1981-85; asst dir Sawwa Int 1983-85, Schroders 1985-87; *Recreations* fishing, gardening, walking; *Clubs* Boodle's; *Style*— Andrew Hargreaves, Esq, MP; 245 Alcester Road South, Kings Heath, Birmingham B14 6DY; House of Commons, Westminster, London SW1 (☎ 01 219 3000)

HARGREAVES, Hon Mrs; Hon Angela; *née* Goschen; el da of late Hon Sir William Henry Goschen, and sis of 3 Viscount Goschen; raised to the rank of a Viscount's da, 1953; *b* 4 Sept 1897; *m* 1920 (m dis 1939), Lt-Col John Carne Hargreaves, Gren Gds; 2 s (David b 1926, George b 1931), 1 da (Mrs James Scott-Hopkins b 1924); *Style*— Hon Mrs Hargreaves; c/o Col D W Hargreaves, The Garden Cottage, Crowthorne, Berks

HARGREAVES, Maj (Edgar) Charles Stewart; s of Edgar Horace Hargreaves (d 1968), of Christchurch, NZ, and Ellen Margaret, *née* Stewart (d 1951); *b* 7 Sept 1917; *Educ* St Andrew's Coll Christchurch NZ; *m* 1, 19 Dec 1945 (m dis 1951), Betty, da of the late Duncan McFarlane, of NZ; 2 s (Guy b 22 March 1946, David b 21 Oct 1948); m 2, June 1952 (m dis 1955), Phyllis Kathleen Anderson; m 3, 14 Oct 1965, Valerie Dawn, da of Donald John Mackay (d 1968), of Berks; *Career* cmmnd Supplementary Reserve & Offrs, Royal Armoured Corps 1937, NZ Divnl Cavalry Regt 1939-40, North Irish Horse 1940, 2 Cmd 1941, 11 Special Air Serv Bn, 1 Parachute Bn 1941, VIII King's Royal Irish Hussars, Parachute Instr, special serv with SOE Eastern Euro 1942-43, (POW 1943) Intelligence Unit in Halmahera Gp 1945; Intelligence Servs 1956, private sec Govr of Trinidad and Tobago 1957-58, comptroller to Duke of Bedford 1958-60, bursar Heathfields Sch 1962-63, Queens Messenger 1963-76, opened Hatchlands Finishing Sch for Girls Surrey 1965, moved Finishing Sch to Scotland 1980, ret 1987; *Clubs* Cavalry & Guards, Special Forces, Highland; *Style*— Maj Charles Hargreaves; Aultmore House, Nethybridge, Innverness-shire PH25 3ED (☎ 06678 424)

HARGREAVES, David; s of Herbert Hargreaves (d 1959); *b* 3 June 1930; *Educ* Pocklington Sch; *m* 1978, Jill, da of Joseph Fuller (d 1977); 4 children; *Career* Lt E Yorks Regt, Malaya; chm: Hirst and Mallinson to 1980, Hestair plc and subsidiaries; FCA; *Recreations* sailing, golf, gardening, squash; *Clubs* Royal Ascot Squash, Foxhills Golf; *Style*— David Hargreaves Esq

HARGREAVES, Prof David Harold; s of Clifford Hargreaves (d 1977), and Marion, *née* Bradley (d 1961); *b* 31 August 1939; *Educ* Bolton Sch, Christ's Coll Cambridge (MA, PhD), Univ of Oxford (MA, DPhil); *Career* reader dept of educn Univ of Manchester 1964-79 (formerly lectr and sr lectr), reader educn Univ of Oxford 1979-84 (fell Jesus Coll), chief inspr ILEA 1984-88, prof of educn Univ of Cambridge

1988- (fell Wolfson Coll); FRSA 1984; *Books* Social Relations in a Secondary School (1967), Interpersonal Relations and Education (1972), Deviance in Classrooms (1975), The Challenge for the Comprehensive School (1982); *Recreations* opera; *Clubs* Athenaeum; *Style*— Prof David Hargreaves; Dept of Educn, Univ of Cambridge, 17 Trumpington St, Cambridge CB2 1QA (☎ 0223 332 888)

HARGREAVES, (Basil) John (Alexander); s of Capt Reginald C Hargreaves, of Surrey (d 1974), and Alison Jean, *née* Ogilvie-Grant (d 1970); *b* 7 April 1925; *Educ* Eton Coll; *m* 1, 1960 (m dis), Anne Belinda Stacey; 1 s (Charles b 1966); m 2, 3 April 1980, Barbara Anne Court; *Career* cmmnd Rifle Bde 1944, served NW Europe, Kenya , ret 1956 as Maj; joined IBM UK 1956, ret 1976; (dir 1966-76), chm Matrix Conslts; Christian Science Practitioner 1976-; memb OECD Ctee on Work and Educn, Date Protection Ctee; *Recreations* travel, reading, writing; *Clubs* Travellers; *Style*— John Hargreaves, Esq; Yew Arch, Dallington, Heathfield, E Sussex TN21 9NH (☎ 0435 830 224)

HARGREAVES, Prof John Desmond; s of Arthur Swire Hargreaves (d 1950), of Colne, Lancs, and Margaret Hilda, *née* Duckworth (d 1968); *b* 25 Jan 1924; *Educ* Ermysted's GS Skipton, Bootham, Manchester Univ (BA, MA); *m* 30 Sept 1950, Sheila Elizabeth, da of George Samuel Wilks (d 1960), of Stockton, Warwickshire; 2 s (Alastair b 1952, Nicholas b and d 1957), 2 da (Sara b 1953, Catherine b 1959); *Career* 2 Lt The Loyal Regt 1944, served Germany 1945, Malaya 1945-46, T/Capt 1946; asst lectr and lectr in history Manchester Univ 1948-52, sr lectr Fourah Bay Coll Sierra Leone 1952-54, lectr in history Univ of Aberdeen 1954-62 (Burnett-Fletcher prof of history 1962-85); visiting prof: Union Coll Schenectady NY 1960-61, Univ of Ibadan 1970-71; Hon DLitt Univ of Sierra Leone 1985; FRHistS 1963; *Books* Prelude to the Partition of West Africa (1963), West Africa Partitioned (two vols, 1974 and 1985), The End of Colonial Rule in West Africa (1979), Aberdeenshire to Africa (1981), Decolonisation in Africa (1988); *Recreations* hill walking, lawn tennis, theatre; *Style*— Prof John Hargreaves; Balcluain, 22 Raemoir Rd, Banchory, Kincardine AB3 3UJ (☎ 03302 2655)

HARGREAVES, Brig Kenneth; CBE (1956, MBE 1939), TD (1942), DL (W Yorks 1978); s of late Henry Hargreaves; *b* 23 Feb 1903; *Educ* Haileybury; *m* 1, 1958, Else Allen (d 1968); 1 s, 1 da (both adopted); m 2, 1969, Hon Margaret, *née* Lane Fox da 1 and last Baron Bingley (d 1947), w of Maj Charles Packe (ka 1944) and James Hunter (d 1957), *qv*; 2 step da (Mrs John Grove b 1941, Mrs Ian Gow b 1944); *Career* WWII Brig Cmdg 3 Indian AA Bde 1942-45; pres Chartered Inst of Secretaries 1956, chm BR Eastern Bd 1964-68; dir: Lloyds Bank 1965-73, Yorks Bank 1969-79; Lord-Lt: West Riding and City of York 1970-74, W Yorks 1974-78; hon pres Hargreaves Gp 1974-; dir: Sadler's Wells Tst 1969, ENO 1975-82, Opera North 1982-83 (pres Friends of Opera North 1983-88, currently patron); High Sheriff Yorks 1962-63, tstee York Minster 1970-, high steward Selby Abbey 1974-; Liveryman Worshipful Co of Clothworkers 1938 (Master 1969-70); Hon LLD Leeds Univ; KStJ 1970; *Style*— Brig Kenneth Hargreaves, CBE, TD, DL; Easby House, Great Ouseburn, N Yorks YO5 9RQ (☎ 0423 330548)

HARGREAVES, (Joseph) Kenneth; MP (C) Hyndburn 1983-; s of James and Mary Hargreaves; *b* 1 Mar 1939; *Educ* St Mary's Coll Blackburn, Manchester Coll of Commerce; *Career* ACIS; *Recreations* music, theatre, travel; *Style*— Ken Hargreaves, Esq, MP; House of Commons, London SW1

HARGREAVES, Michael Robert; s of Robert Hacking Hargreaves (d 1987), and Evaline, *née* Walsh; *b* 28 May 1942; *Educ* Lancing; *m* 17 Sept 1966 (m dis 1979), Gillian Patricia, da of Major Peter Duncan Morris, of France; 1 s (Richard b 19 April 1972), 1 da (Susanna b 25 Feb 1969); *Career* CA; McClelland Moores 1960-68, mangr Arthur Young 1968-73, Charterhouse Bank Ltd 1985- (joined 1973); non exec dir MEMEC 1981-; MICAS 1966; *Recreations* shooting, golf; *Clubs* Liphook GC; *Style*— Michael Hargreaves, Esq; 7 St Catherines Ct, The Avenue, Bedford Park, London W4 1UH (☎ 01 995 6894); Charterhouse Bank Ltd, 1 Paternoster Row, St Paul's, London EC4M 7DH (☎ 01 248 4000, fax 01 248 1998, telex 884276)

HARGREAVES, (Thomas) Peter; s of Arthur Hargreaves, of Lancs, and Phylis Mary, *née* Seymour (d 1987); *b* 24 Oct 1987; *Educ* Charney Hall Preparatory Sch, Shrewsbury Sch, Queen Elizabeths GS Blackburn; *m* 1958, Maureen Elizabeth, da of Francis Joseph Higginson (d 1985); 4 s (Arthur b 1959, Mark b 1960, Craig b 1966, Boyd b 1975); *Career* md dir: Enfield MFG Co Ltd, Hilden MFG Co Ltd, J B Smith and Co Ltd, Shilott plc; *Recreations* squash, pigeon racing; *Style*— Peter Hargreaves, Esq; 10 Royds Avenue, Hollins Lane, Accrington, Lancs BB5 2LE (☎ 0254 33462); Hilden MFG Co Ltd, Clifton Mill, Pickup St, Oswald Twistle, Accrington, Lancs (☎ 0254 391131, telex 635233 HILDEN G)

HARGREAVES, Richard Strachan; MC (1944); s of Col James Hargreaves, of Parkhill, Lyndhurst, Hants (d 1980), and Mary, *née* Barton (d 1975); *b* 26 Sept 1919; *Educ* Dauntsey's Sch West Lavington Wiltshire; *m* 9 Oct 1945, Kathleen Jenny, da of Herbert Truman Nightingale (d 1951), of Harnham, Salisbury, Wilts; 1 s (Timothy b 28 June 1952) 3 da (Joanna b 23 Oct 1947, Judy b 12 Dec 1949, Sally (twin) b 12 Dec 1949); *Career* 2 Lt Royal Fusiliers TA 1939, Capt 12 Bn Royal Fusiliers 1942, Capt and Adj Parachute Regt 1942, Maj and Co Cdr 4 Bn Parachute Regt 1943; overseas serv: N Africa, Italy, France, Greece and Palestine; staff coll 1944, Bde Maj 4 Br Div Greece 1945-46, demob 1946; Peter Merchant Ltd 1946-56 (exec dir 1952-56), Gallaher Ltd 1956-68 (exec dir 1965-68), exec dir Savoy Hotel Ltd 1968-84, chm Devenish plc 1980-86 (non exec dir 1986-); Westminster City Cncllr 1973-77, dep Lord Mayor Westminster 1977; Freeman City of London 1960, Liveryman Worshipful Co Tobacco Pipe Makers and Tobacco Blenders (Master 1976); *Recreations* shooting, sailing, skiing, theatre; *Style*— Richard Hargreaves, Esq, MC; Church Walk, Little Bredy, Dorchester, Dorset (☎ 030 83 356); J.A Devenish plc, Trinity St, Weymouth, Dorset (☎ 0305 761 111)

HARGROVES, Brig Sir (Robert) Louis; CBE (1965), DL (Staffs 1974); s of William Robert Hargroves (d 1946); *b* 10 Dec 1917; *Educ* St John's Coll Southsea; *m* 1940, Eileen Elizabeth, da of Lt-Col W M Anderson, CIE (d 1947); 4 da; *Career* served WWII, Sicily and Italy, Brig 1964, Col The Staffordshire Regt (The Prince of Wales') 1971-77; kt 1987;; *Recreations* field sports; *Style*— Brig Sir Louis Hargroves, CBE, DL; Hyde Cottage, Temple Guiting, Cheltenham, Glos GL54 5RT (☎ 04515 242)

HARINGTON, Gen Sir Charles Henry Pepys; GCB (1969, KCB 1964, CB 1961), CBE (1957, OBE 1953), DSO (1944), MC (1940); s of Col Hastings Harington (ka 1916), and Dorothy, da of Hon Walter Courtenay Pepys, (1914) 5 s of 1 Earl of Cottenham (Lord High Chllr of England 1836-41, and 1846-50); *b* 5 May 1910; *Educ* Malvern, Sandhurst; *m* 1942, Victoire Williams-Freeman; 1 s (Guy b 1946), 2 da (Louise b 1949, Clare (Mrs Julian Calder) b 1956); *Career* cmmnd Cheshire Regt 1930, served WW II NW Europe Co and Bn Cdr, CO 1 Para 1949, Cdr 49 Bde Kenya 1955, Cmdt Sch of Infantry 1958, GOC 3 Div 1959, Cmdt Army Staff Coll 1961, C-in-C Middle East Cmd 1963, DCGS 1966, Chief of Personnel and Logistics to the 3 Services 1968-71, ADC (Gen) to HM The Queen 1969-71; vice-pres Star and Garter Home; pres Hurlingham Club; *Style*— Gen Sir Charles Harington, GCB, CBE, DSO, MC; 19 Rivermead Court, London SW6

HARINGTON, David Richard; s of His Honour John Charles Dundas Harington, QC (decd), and Lavender Cecilia Harington (d 1982); hp of bro, Sir Nicholas Harington, 14 Bt *qv*; *b* 25 June 1944; *Educ* Westminster, Ch Ch Oxford; *m* 1983, Deborah Jane, da of Maurice William Catesby, MC, of Long Compton, Warks; 2 s (John b 1984, Christopher b 1986); *Style*— David Harington Esq; 7 Vale Grove, London W3 7QP (☎ 01 740 8382)

HARINGTON, Guy Charles; s of Gen Sir Charles Harington, GCB, CBE, DSO, MC, of London, and Victoire Marion, *née* Williams-Freeman; *b* 12 Dec 1946; *Educ* Malvern, Univ Coll Oxford (MA), Loughborough Univ of Technol (MSc); *m* 8 Sept 1984, Kay Elizabeth; 1 s (Charles Hasting b 1986), 1 da (Zara Elizabeth b 1988); *Career* with BP 1969-71, dir J Henry Schroder Wagg & Co Ltd 1985- (joined 1971); tres Central London Branch of Cystic Fibrosis Res Tst; *Recreations* swimming, skiing, music, reading; *Clubs* Hurlingham; *Style*— Guy Harington, Esq; 120 Cheapside, London EC2

HARINGTON, Kenneth Douglas Evelyn Herbert; s of His Honour Edward Harington, JP (d 1937; 3 s of Sir Richard Harington, 11 Bt, JP, DL), and Louisa Muriel, *née* Vernon; bro Vernon Harington *qv*; *b* 30 Sept 1911; *Educ* Stowe; *m* 1, 1 March 1939, Lady Cecilia Bowes-Lyon (d 1947), er da of 15 Earl of Strathmore and Kinghorne, JP, DL, bro of HM Queen Elizabeth The Queen Mother; 2 s (Michael b 9 Aug 1951, Jonathan b 14 March 1953); m 2, 28 July 1950, Maureen Helen, da of Brig-Gen Sir Robert McCalmont, KCVO, CBE, DSO; *Career* served WW II, NW Europe, Maj Coldstream Gds; barr 1952; met stipendiary magistrate 1967-84; hon attaché Br Legation Stockholm 1930-32; *Recreations* shooting, fishing, gardening; *Clubs* Cavalry and Guards; *Style*— Kenneth Harington, Esq; Orchard End, Upper Oddington, Moreton-in-Marsh, Glos (☎ 0451 30989)

HARINGTON, Sir Nicholas John; 14 Bt (E 1611), of Ridlington, Rutland; s of His Honour late John Charles Dundas Harington, QC (s of Sir Richard Harington, 12 Bt); suc uncle, Sir Richard Harington, 13 Bt, 1981; *b* 14 May 1942; *Educ* Eton, Ch Ch Oxford; *Heir* bro, David Richard Harington, *qv*; *Career* barr; joined Civil Service 1972; *Style*— Sir Nicholas Harington, Bt; The Ring o'Bells, Whitbourne, Worcester WR6 5RT

HARINGTON, (Edward Henry) Vernon; s of His Honour Edward Harington (d 1937; 3 s of Sir Richard Harington, 11 Bt, JP, DL), and Louisa Muriel, *née* Vernon (d 1963); bro of Kenneth Harington, *qv*; *b* 13 Sept 1907; *Educ* Eton; *m* 1, 1937 (m dis 1949), Mary, da of Louis Egerton (ka 1917, s of Sir Alfred Egerton, KCVO, CB, and Hon Mary, *née* Ormsby-Gore, er da of 2 Baron Harlech) and Jane, er surviving da of Rev Lord Victor Seymour (s of 5 Marquess of Hertford, GCB, PC, DL); 1 da (Mrs Sidney Whitteridge b 1941) and 1 da decd; m 2, 1950, Mary Johanna Jean, JP, da of late Lt-Col R Cox, MC; 2 da (Marie Louisa (Mrs Robin Pagan Taylor) b 1951, Susan (Mrs David Scott) b 1953); *Career* served WWII, Maj Coldstream Gds and in War Office; barr 1930; ps to Lord Chllr and dep serjeant-at-arms House of Lords 1934-40, served on Control Cmmn for Austria in the legal div 1945, asst sec to Lord Chllr for Commissions of the Peace 1945-46, a dep judge advocate 1946, AJAG 1955; dep chm Herefs QS 1969-71, recorder of Crown Ct 1972-74; cllr Malvern Hills Dist Cncl 1979-87; JP Herefs 1969-71; chm Hereford, Worcester, Warwicks and W Midlands Regnl Agric Wages Ctee; *Recreations* shooting, fishing; *Style*— Vernon Harington, Esq; Woodlands House, Whitbourne, Worcester (☎ Knightwick 21437)

HARKINS, His Hon Judge Gerard Francis Robert; s of Francis Murphy Harkins (d 1977) and Katherine *née* Hunt; *b* 13 July 1936; *Educ* Mount St Mary's Coll Spinkhill, King's Coll Univ of Durham, LDS (Dunelm) 1961; *Career* dental surgn in gen practice Yorks 1961-70; called to the Bar (Middle Temple) 1969, in practice NE circuit 1970-86; appointed circuit Judge 1986-; *Style*— His Hon Judge Harkins; c/o The Crown Court, Kenton Bar, Newcastle Upon Thames, (☎ 091 286 8901)

HARKNESS, Lt-Col Hon Douglas Scott; OC (1978), GM (1943), ED (1944), PC (Can 1957); s of William Harkness (d 1938); *b* 29 Mar 1903; *Educ* Alberta Univ (BA), Calgary Univ (LLD); *m* 1932, Frances Elisabeth, da of James Blair McMillan (d 1958); 1 s; *Career* Lt-Col RCA; teacher, farmer, formerly in oil business; Canadian politician: MP 1945-72, min of Agriculture 1957-60, min of Defence 1960-63; *Recreations* golf, reading, bridge; *Style*— Lt-Col Hon Douglas Harkness, OC, GM, ED, PC; 716 Imperial Way SW, Calgary, Alberta, Canada T2S 1N7 (☎ 403 243 0825)

HARKNESS, Ven James; OBE (1978), QHC (1982); s of James Harkness, of Dumfries, and Jane McMorn, *née* Thomson; *b* 20 Oct 1935; *Educ* Dumfries Acad, Univ of Edinburgh (MA); *m* 1960, Elizabeth Anne, da of George Tolmie (d 1959); 1 s (Paul b 1965), 1 da (Jane b 1962); *Career* DACG: NI 1974-75, 4 Div 1974-78; staff chaplain HQ BAOR 1978-80, asst chaplain gen Scotland 1980-81; sr chaplain: 1 (Br) Corps 1981-82, BAOR 1982-84; dep chaplain gen 1985-86, chaplain gen 1987-; OStJ 1988; *Clubs* New (hon memb, Edinburgh); *Style*— The Ven James Harkness, OBE, QHC, Chaplain General; MOD Chaplains (Army), Bagshot Park, Bagshot, Surrey GU19 5PL (☎ 0276 71717); c/o The Royal Bank of Scotland, Holt's Whitehall Branch, Kirkland House, Whitehall, London SW1

HARKNESS, Rear-Adm James Percy Knowles; CB (1971); s of Capt P Harkness, W Yorks Regt; *b* 28 Nov 1916; *m* 1949, Joan, da of Vice-Adm N Sulivan, CVO (decd); 2 da; *Career* Dir-Gen Naval Manpower 1970-72; *Style*— Rear-Adm James Harkness, CB

HARKNESS, John Leigh; OBE; s of Verney Harkness, OBE (d 1980), and Olivia Austin (d 1941); *b* 29 June 1918; *Educ* Whitgift; *m* 1947, Betty, *née* Moore; 2 s, 1 da; *Career* rose breeder; md R Harkness and Co 1960-77; vice-pres Royal Nat Rose Soc 1969-, sec Br Assoc of Rose Breeders 1973-85;; *Books* Roses (1978), The World's Favourite Roses (1979), The Makers of Heavenly Roses (1985); *Style*— John Harkness, Esq, OBE; 1 Bank Alley, Southwold, Suffolk (☎ 0502 722030)

HARKNESS, Capt Kenneth Lanyon; CBE (1963), DSC (1940); s of late Maj T R Harkness, RA, and late Mrs G A de Burgh; *b* 24 August 1900; *Educ* RNCs Osborne and Dartmouth, Cambridge; *m* 1, 1932, Joan Phyllis (d 1979), da of Maj Arthur N Lovell; 1 da; m 2, 1979, Mary Isabel, *née* Stroud; *Career* RN: COS C-in-C Portsmouth

1947, ret 1949; regnl dir Civil Def London Regn 1954-65; *Style*— Capt Kenneth Harkness, CBE, DSC, RN; Far Rockaway, Durford Wood, Petersfield, Hants GU31 5AW (☎ 0730 893173)

HARLAND, His Excellency (William) Bryce; s of Edward Dugard Harland (d 1939) and Annie Mcdonald Harland *née* Gordon (d 1965); *b* 11 Dec 1931; *Educ* Victoria Univ of Wellington, NZ (MA), Fletcher Sch of Law & Diplomacy Medford, USA (AM); *m* 1, 15 June 1957, (m dis 1977) Rosemary Anne *née* Gordon; 3 s (James b 1958, Michael b 1960 d 1978, David b 1962); m 2, 29 June 1979, (Margaret) Anne da of Andrew Blackburn, of Auckland NZ; 1 s (Thomas b 1981); *Career* joined NZ Foreign Serv 1953, third sec Singapore and Bangkok 1956-59, second sec NZ Mission to UN NY 1959-62, Dept External Affrs Wellington 1962-65, cnsllr NZ Embassy Washington 1965-69, Miny of Foreign Affrs Wellington NZ 1969-73, NZ ambass to China Peking 1973-75, asst sec Foreign Affrs NZ 1976-82, ambass and permananent rep to UN NY 1982-85, NZ high cmmr London 1985; chm Econ and Fin ctee UN General Assembly 1984; memb Worshipful Co of Butchers 1986, Freeman City of London 1987-; K St J 1985; *Recreations* history, music, walking; *Clubs* Broaks, East India, RAC; *Style*— Bryce Harland, Esq; New Zealand House, Haymarket, London, SW1, (☎ 930 8422)

HARLAND, (Henry Charles) Hector; s of the Rev Charles Joseph Harland (d 1950), of Nether Stowey, Somerset, and Amabel Georgina (d 1947), 2 da of Cdr Hon Henry Baillie-Hamilton, s 10 Earl of Haddington; *b* 27 June 1905; *Educ* Harrow; *m* 11 Oct 1938, Rachel Osgood, da of Maj Philip Hanbury (d 1955), of Updown House, Eastry, Kent; 2 da (Henrietta b 1941, Penelope b 1946); *Career* RMC Sandhust, joined Royal Scots 1925, WWII Maj 1942, Bde Maj Hong Kong 1941; (POW, despatches), cmd 8 Bn; Royal Scots; ret as Lt-Col 1948; controller of The Burn, Edzell under Dominion Student's Hall Tst 1948-76; memb Queen's Bodyguard for Scotland, The Royal Co of Archers; *Recreations* all field sports, trains gun dogs, field trail judge, shooting, fishing; *Style*— Lt-Col Henry Harland; Burn Garden House, Glenesk, Brechin, Angus (☎ 03564 579)

HARLAND, Air Marshal Sir Reginald Edward Wynyard; KBE (1974), CB (1972), AE; s of Charles Cecil Harland (d 1945); *b* 30 May 1920; *Educ* Stowe, Trinity Coll Cambridge; *m* 1942, Doreen, da of William Hugh Cowie Romanis (d 1972); 2 s, 2 da (and 1 s decd); *Career* joined RAF 1939, served W Med 1942-45, Gp Capt 1960, STSO HQ 3 Gp Bomber Cmd 1962-64, STSO HQ FEAF 1964-1966, Air Cdre 1965, Harrier project dir Miny Technol 1967-69, idc 1969, AOC 24 Gp 1970, Air Vice-Marshal 1970, AO i/c E Air Support Cmd 1972, Air Marshal 1973, AOC-in-C RAF Support Cmd 1973-77; tech dir W S Atkins and Ptnrs Epsom 1977-82, engrg and mgmnt conslt 1982-; parly candidate (Alliance) Bury St Edmunds 1983 and 1987; *Recreations* politics, bridge, chess,; *Clubs* RAF; *Style*— Air Marshal Sir Reginald E W Harland, KBE, CB, AE; 49 Crown St, Bury St Edmunds, Suffolk IP33 1QX (☎ 0284 763 078)

HARLECH, 6 Baron (UK 1876); Sir Francis David; s of 5 Baron Harlech, PC, KCMG (d 1985), and his 1 w Sylvia (d 1967), da of late Hugh Lloyd Thomas, CMG, CVO (*see* Peerage B Bellew); *b* 13 Mar 1954; *m* 1986, Amanda Jane, da of Alan T Grieve, of Brimpton House, Brimpton, Berks; 1 s (Jasset David Cody), 1 da (Tallulah Sylva b 16 May 1988); *Heir* s, Hon Jasset David Cody Ormsby-Gore b 1 July 1986; *Style*— The Rt Hon Lord Harlech; The Mount, Race Course Rd, Oswestry, Salop

HARLECH, Pamela, Lady; Pamela; *née* Colin; only da of Ralph Frederick Colin (d 1985), of NY; *b* 18 Dec 1934; *Educ* Smith Coll, Finch Coll; *m* 1969, as his 2 wife, 5 Baron Harlech, KCMG, PC (d 1985); 1 da (Hon Pandora b 19 April 1972); *Career* journalist/producer: tstee V & A; memb: South Bank Bd, Arts Cncl; Cncl of Assoc for Business Sponsorship of the Arts; chm Women's Playhouse Tst; *Books* Feast Without Fuss, Pamela Harlech's Complete Book of Cooking, Entertaining and Household Management, Vogue Book of Menus; *Style*— The Rt Hon Pamela, Lady Harlech; 14 Ladbroke Road, London W11 3NJ; Hinton Field, Hinton Charterhouse, Bath BA3 6AR

HARLEY, Basil Hubert; s of Mervyn Ruthven Harley (d 1973), of Stud Farm, Lamb Corner, Dedham, Essex, and Marion, *née* Parkinson (d 1973); *b* 17 July 1930; *Educ* Harrow, St John's Coll Oxford (MA); *m* 10 Oct 1959, Annette, da of Edgar Wolstan Bertram Handsley Milne-Redhead, ISO, TD, of Parkers, Bear St, Nayland, Suffolk; 3 da (Jane Elizabeth b 12 Oct 1960, Emma Katherine b 7 June 1962, Harriet Susanna b 15 May 1965); *Career* Nat Serv RA 1949-50, cmmnd 2 Lt 1949, 17 Trg Regt Oswestry 1949-50, TA Capt Queens Own Oxfords Hussars & Royal Bucks Yeo 1950-60; md Curwen Press Ltd 1964-82, dir: Curwen Prints Ltd 1970, Wedge Entomological Res Fndn US at Nat Museum Natural History Washington DC 1974-, chm and md Harley Books, natural history publishers (BH & A Harley Ltd) 1983-, cncl memb Essex Naturalists' Tst 1975-78, chm Wynken de Worde Soc 1975, exec ctee Nat Book League 1974-78; Liveryman Worshipful Co of Stationers & Newspaper Makers 1973-; fell of Linnean Soc 1955, fell Royal Entomological Soc 1981; *Books* The Curwen Press A Short History (1970); *Recreations* natural history, reading; *Clubs* Utd Oxford and Cambridge Univ, Double Crown; *Style*— Basil Harley, Esq; Martns, Great Horkesley, Colchester, Essex CO6 4AH (☎ 0206 271 216)

HARLEY, Christopher Charles; JP (1960), DL (1987); s of Maj John Ralph Henry Harley, JP, DL (d 1960), of Brampton Bryan, and Rachel Mary, *née* Gwyer (d 1967); *b* 31 Dec 1926; *Educ* Eton, Magdalene Coll Cambridge; *m* 2 April 1959, Susan Elizabeth, da of Sir Roderick Barclay, GCVO, KCMG, of Latimer, Bucks; 4 s (Edward b 1960, John b 1961, Adrian b 1965, Philip b 1969); *Career* Mech Engr to 1956, since when landowner, Brampton Bryan, Herefords; JP (1960), DL (1987), High Sheriff of Hereford and Worcs (1987-88); memb Nat Tst Severn Regnl Ctee 1968-; MIMechE; *Recreations* shooting, forestry; *Style*— Christopher Harley, Esq; Brampton Bryan Hall, Bucknell, Salop SY7 0DJ (☎ 05474 241)

HARLEY, David Adams Henry; s of Robert Harley (d 1965), 93 Wester Drylaw Avenue, Edinburgh, and Ann Crighton, *née* Henry; *b* 15 April 1930; *Educ* Boroughmuir Sr Sec Sch Edinburgh, James Gillespie Sch Edinburgh, Heriotwatt Coll Edinburgh (Bus Admin Cert); *m* 26 Sept 1953, Irene Helen, da of John Walker Blanch, of 69/2 Murrayburn Park, Edinburgh; 2 s (Douglas Robert b 1955, Gordon David b 1965), 2 da (Dorothy Helen b 1958, Joyce Walker b 1961); *Career* RAF Nat Serv Sr Aircraftsman and Equipment Asst 1948-50; stores clerk Hawkhill Bakeries 1950-52, cost clerk Ransomes Sims and Jefferies 1952-53, asst cost accountant Alder and Mackay 1953-58; Arthur Bell Distillers (formerly Arthur Bell and Sons Ltd): bond Mngr 1958-62, purchasing offr 1962-70, purchasing dir 1970-73, admin dir 1973-85, vice chm and Trade Rels dir 1985-; er Church Scotland 1964-, pres Perth toastmasters Club 1970-71, capt King James VI GC 1975-77, pres Licensed Victuallers Nat Homes 1986-87; companion memb Br Inst Innkeeping; *Recreations* golf, tennis; *Clubs* Blair Gowrie G.C, King James VI G.C, Gleneagles Hotel GC, Perth Lawn Tennis; *Style*— David Harley, Esq; Ellwyn, Craigie Knowes Rd, Perth PH2 0DG (☎ 0738 23 514); Arthur Bell Distillers, Scotch Whisky Distillers, Cherrybank, Perth PH2 0NG (☎ 0738 21 111, fax 0738 38 739, telex 76 275)

HARLEY, Paul Stuart; s of Brian Erskine Harley (d 1972), of Melbourne, Australia, and Elizabeth Ann Charlton, *née* Allan; *b* 20 June 1939; *Educ* St Lawrence Coll Kent, Univ Coll of N Staffs Keele (IEE PtIII); *m* 15 April 1963, Sally Ann, da of Eugene Prosser, of Wilts; 2 s (Nicholas b 1965), Adam b 1970), 1 da (Cherie-Ann b 1973); *Career* electrical engr, inventor of Welliwarma, md Wiltsavon Leisure Ltd 1984-86, tech and mktg conslt to various cos; *Recreations* choral singing, riding; *Style*— Paul S Harley, Esq; The Old Farmhouse, Milbourne, Malmesbury, Wilts SN16 9JA (☎ 0666 824107)

HARLEY, Sir Thomas Winlack; MBE (Military 1944), MC (1918) DL (Cheshire 1962); s of George Harley (d 1916), of The Elms, Upton, Wirral, Cheshire, and Annie, *née* MacWatty (d 1939); *b* 27 June 1895; *Educ* Birkenhead Sch, Eton; *m* 1924, Margaret Hilda (d 1981), da of late Canon Joseph Udell Bardsley; Vicar of Lancaster; 3 s (Ian, Michael, Christopher); *Career* served WW I 2 Lt 9 King's Own (Royal Lancaster) Regt, (despatches 1917), Maj (1918), France and Balklands 1915-19; memb Liverpool Reg Hosp Bd 1947 (chm 1960-69), memb Bd of Govrs Liverpool Teaching Hosps 1961, 21 years on Liverpool Cathedral Building Ctee 1969, cnslt lawyer; kt 1960; *Clubs* Royal Liverpool Golf, (Hon Life Memb); *Style*— Sir Thomas Harley, MBE, MC, DL; Hesketh Haven, Thornton Hough, Wirral, Cheshire L63 1JA (☎ 051 336 7932)

HARMAN, Harriet; MP (Lab) Peckham 1982-; da of John Bishop Harman and Anna Charlotte Malcolm Spicer; niece of Countess of Longford; *b* 20 July 1950; *Educ* St Paul's Girls Sch, York Univ; *m* Jack Dromey, Sec of SE Area TUC; 2 s, 1 da (Amy b 1987); *Career* lawyer; memb Nat Cncl Civil Liberties; MP 1982; *Style*— Ms Harriet Harman, MP; House of Commons, London SW1

HARMAN, Hon Mr Justice; Hon Sir Jeremiah LeRoy Harman; s of late Rt Hon Sir Charles Harman; *b* 13 April 1930; *Educ* Eton; *m* 1960 (m dis 1986), Erica, da of Hon Sir Maurice Bridgeman, KBE (d 1980, 3 s of 1 Viscount Bridgeman); 2 s (Charles Richard LeRoy b 1963, Toby John b 1967), 1 da (Sarah b 1962); m 2, 1987, Katharine, da of late Rt Hon Sir Eric Sachs; *Career* served Coldstream Gds and Para Regt 1948-51; barr 1954, QC 1968, barr Hong Kong 1978, Singapore Bar 1980, High Ct judge (Chancery) 1982-; kt 1982; *Recreations* fishing, bird watching; *Style*— The Hon Mr Justice Harman; The Royal Courts of Justice, The Strand, London WC2A 2LL

HARMAN, Michael Godfrey; s of John Richard Harman (d 1986), and Elsie, *née* Stokes (d 1960); *b* 30 Jan 1937; *Educ* Mercers Sch, Magdalen Coll, Oxford (BA); *m* 4 Sept 1971, Phyllis Eveline, da of John Henry North, of Thistlewood Farm, Sutton St James, Lincs; 1 s (Paul b 1972); *Career* chartered patent agent, european patent attorney; *Recreations* recreational mathematics; *Style*— Michael Harman, Esq; Holmwood, 37 Upper Park Rd, Camberley, Surrey GU15 2EG (☎ 0276 22985, telex 858902 BARON G, fax 0276 64091)

HARMAN, Robert Donald; QC (1974); s of late Herbert Donald Harman, MC; *b* 26 Sept 1928; *Educ* St Paul's, Magdalen Coll Oxford; *m* 1, 1960, Sarah (d 1965), *née* Cleverly; 2 s; m 2, 1968, Rosamond Geraldine, JP, da of late Cdr G Scott, RN; 2 da; *Career* barr Gray's Inn 1954, Bencher 1984; SE Circuit, treasy counsel Central Criminal Ct 1967-74, rec Crown Ct 1972-; judge Cts of Appeal Jersey and Guernsey 1986-; *Clubs* Garrick, Beefsteak, Pratt's; *Style*— Robert Harman, Esq, QC; 17 Pelham Cres, London SW7 (☎ 01 584 4304); 2 Harcourt Bldgs, Temple, London EC4 (☎ 01 353 2112)

HARMAR-NICHOLLS, Baron (Life Peer 1974), of Peterborough, Cambs; Sir Harmar Harmar-Nicholls; 1 Bt (1960), JP, MEP (EDG) Gtr Manchester S 1979-; s of Charles Nicholls; *b* 1 Nov 1912; *Educ* Q Mary's GS Walsall; *m* 1940, Dorothy, da of James Edwards; 2 da (Hon Mrs Alan Aspden b 1941, Hon Susan *qv*); *Career* takes Con Whip in House of Lords; MP (C) Peterborough 1950-74; pps to Asst Postmaster-Gen 1951-1955, parly sec Miny of Ag, Fish and Food 1955-57, parly sec Miny of Works 1957-60; chm Nicholls and Hennessy (Hotels) Ltd, Malvern Festival Theatre Tst Ltd; dir J and H Nicholls and Co, Radio Luxemburg (London) Ltd; Lloyd's underwriter; *Style*— The Rt Hon the Lord Harmar-Nicholls, JP, MEP; Abbeylands, Weston, Stafford (☎ 0889 252)

HARMAR-NICHOLLS, Hon Susan Frances Nicholls; da of Baron Harmar-Nicholls, JP, MEP (Life Peer and 1 Bt); *b* 23 Nov 1943; *Career* actress (Sue Nicholls); TV roles incl: Coronation Street (Audrey Roberts, *née* Potter), Crossroads, Rise and Fall of Reginald Perrin, Rent a Ghost, Up the Elephant, Village Hill; Royal Shakespeare Co, Broadway, In London Assurance; *Style*— The Hon Susan Harmar-Nicholls

HARMER, Sir (John) Dudley; OBE (1963), JP (Kent 1962); s of Ernest Harmer; *b* 27 July 1913; *Educ* Merchant Taylors' Sch, Wye Coll; *m* 1947, Erika Minder-Lanz, of Switzerland; 2 s; *Career* farmer; dep chm Kent Agric Exec Ctee 1964-72, tstee Kent Incorporated Soc for Promoting Experiments in Horticulture 1979-; chm: SE Area Cons Provincial Cncl 1966-71, E Kent Euro-Cons Cncl 1979-82 (pres 1982-); kt 1972; *Style*— Sir Dudley Harmer, OBE, JP; Stone Hill, Egerton, Ashford, Kent (☎ 023 376 241)

HARMER, Sir Frederic Evelyn; CMG (1945); s of late Sir Sidney Harmer, KBE; *b* 3 Nov 1905; *Educ* Eton, King's Cambridge; *m* 1, 1931, Barbara (d 1972), da of late Maj J Hamilton, JP, of Fyne Court, Bridgwater; 1 s, 3 da; m 2, 1973, Daphne Shelton Agar; *Career* with Treasy 1939-45, dep chm P and OSN Co 1957-70, govt dir BP 1953-70; kt 1968; *Style*— Sir Frederic Harmer, CMG; Tiggins Field, Kelsale, Saxmundham, Suffolk (☎ 3156)

HARMER, Robert James Andrew; s of Sir Frederic Harmer, CMG, of Suffolk, and Barbara Susan, *née* Hamilton (d 1972); *b* 4 Oct 1936; *Educ* Eton Coll, King's Coll Cambridge (MA) (Mech Sci Tripos part I); *m* 2 June 1962, Nichola Anne, da of Major Eric James Mather, MBE, of Argyll; 2 s (Andrew b 1964, Dominic b 1969), 1 da (Fiona b 1970); *Career* Lt RNR HM Subs; dir Overseas Containers Ltd 1975-85, chm F W Harmer (Hldgs) Ltd and F W Harmer (Engrg) Ltd 1982- (dir 1971-82); dir: MAT Transauto Ltd 1985-87, MAT Shipping Ltd 1987-, MAT Fleet Servs Ltd 1987-; *Recreations* sailing, fishing, opera; *Clubs* Lansdowne, Aldenburgh Yacht, Epee; *Style*— Robert J A Harmer, Esq; Yew Tre Holuse, Stratford St Mary, Colchester, Essex (☎ 0206 37 232); MAT Group Ltd, Arnold House, 36/41 Holywell Lane, London EC2P 2EQ

HARMOOD-BANNER, Sir George Knowles; 3 Bt (UK 1924); s of Sir Harmood Harmood-Banner, 2 Bt, JP (d 1950); *b* 9 Nov 1918; *Educ* Eton, Cambridge Univ; *m* 22 Dec 1947, Rosemary Jane, da of Col Maurice Lawrence Treston, CBE, FRCS, FRCOG, late IMS; 2 da (Susan b 1951, Gillian b 1953); *Heir* none; *Career* served WW II, Lt Royal Welch Fus 1942, attached to East African Engrs and SEAC, transferred RASC (India) 1945; *Style*— Sir George Harmood-Banner, Bt; c/o National Westminster Bank plc, Sloane Sq Branch, 14 Sloane Sq, London SW1W 8EQ

HARMSWORTH, Hon Camilla Patricia Caroline; da of 3 Viscount Rothermere; *b* 28 July 1964; *Style*— The Hon Camilla Harmsworth

HARMSWORTH, 2 Baron (UK 1939); Cecil Desmond Bernard Harmsworth; s of 1 Baron (d 1948); *b* 19 August 1903; *Educ* Eton, Ch Ch Oxford (MA); *m* 1926, Dorothy, da of Hon J C Heinlein, sometime State Senator of Ohio; 1 da (Hon Mrs Frank Phillips b 1928); *Heir* n, Thomas Harold Raymond Harmsworth; *Career* served Br Info Servs in NY 1940-46; formerly newspaperman and book publisher; painter, has exhibited in London, Paris, New York, Washington and Dallas 1933-; *Portraits include* Norman Douglas, Havelock Ellis, James Joyce, Sir Osbert Sitwell; *Style*— The Rt Hon the Lord Harmsworth; Lime Lodge, Egham, Surrey TW20 0ND (☎ Egham 32379)

HARMSWORTH, Elen, Lady; Elen; da of Nicolaj Billenstein, of Randers, Denmark; *m* 1925, Sir Hildebrand Alfred Beresford Harmsworth, 2 Bt (d 1977); *Style*— Elen, Lady Harmsworth; Aucassin, Le Vallon, St Clair, Le Lavandon, France

HARMSWORTH, Hon Esmond Vyvyan; s of 2 Viscount Rothermere by his 3 w Mary, Viscountess Rothermere, *qv*; *b* 18 June 1967; *Educ* Eton; *Style*— The Hon Esmond Harmsworth

HARMSWORTH, Hildebrand Esmond Miles; s and h of Sir Hildebrand Harold Harmsworth, 3 Bt; *b* 1 Sept 1964; *Educ* Dean Close Sch Cheltenham, Crewe and Alsager Coll; *Recreations* hockey, golf; *Style*— Hildebrand Harmsworth, Esq

HARMSWORTH, Sir Hildebrand Harold; 3 Bt (UK 1922), of Freshwater Grove, Parish of Shipley, Co Sussex; s of Sir Hildebrand Alfred Beresford, 2 Bt (d 1977); *b* 5 June 1931; *Educ* Harrow, Trinity Coll Dublin; *m* 1960, Gillian Andrea, da of William John Lewis, of Tetbury, Gloucs; 1 s (Hildebrand, *qv*), 2 da (Claire b 1961, Kirsten b 1963); *Style*— Sir Hildebrand Harmsworth, Bt; Ewlyn Villa, 42 Leckhampton Rd, Cheltenham, Gloucs

HARMSWORTH, Lady Jessamine Cécile Marjorie; *née* Gordon; da of 3 Marquis of Aberdeen and Temair; *b* 14 August 1910; *Educ* private; *m* 1937, Michael St John Harmsworth, TD, DL, Seaforth Highlanders (d 1981), nephew of Lords Northcliffe, Rothermere and Harmsworth; 2 s (Andrew b 1939, Peter b 1952), 4 da (Mrs Francis Pym b 1940, Mrs Petros Demitriades b 1946, Mrs Donald Sinclair b 1949, Mrs R MacLeod b 1951); *Career* chm County Multiple Sclerosis Soc; pres: Caithness County Music Ctee (former chm), County Children's League, County Save the Children Fund, Wick Choral Soc; vice-pres Nat Deaf Children's Soc (Highland region); dir County Red Cross 1968-85, (currently hon vice-pres and life memb receiving Badge of Honour for distinguished serv); BRCS Voluntary Med Service Medal 1983; *Recreations* music, singing, organist, grandmother to 22 grandchildren; *Style*— Lady Jessamine Harmsworth; Thrumster House, Caithness (☎ 095 585 262)

HARMSWORTH, Hon (Harold) Jonathan Esmond Vere; s and h of 3 Viscount Rothermere; *b* 3 Dec 1967; *Style*— The Hon Jonathan Harmsworth

HARMSWORTH, St John Bernard Vyvyan; s of Vyvyan Harmsworth, and Constance, *née* Catt; *b* 28 Nov 1912; *Educ* Harrow, New Coll Oxford; *m* 1937, Jane, da of Basil Boothby; 3 da; *Career* barr 1937, met magistrate 1961-; *Style*— St John Harmsworth Esq; 25 Whitelands, London SW3

HARMSWORTH, Thomas Harold Raymond; o s of Hon Eric Beauchamp Northcliffe Harmsworth (d 1988), and Hélène Marie, *née* Dehove (d 1962); n and h p of 2 Baron Harmsworth, *qv*; *b* 20 July 1939; *Educ* Eton, Christ Church Oxford; *m* 26 June 1971, Patricia Palmer, da of Michael Palmer Horsley; 2 s (Dominic b 18 Sept 1973, Timothy b 6 April 1979), 3 da (Philomena 10 Feb 1975, Abigail b 14 June 1977, Pollyanna b 8 Sept 1981); *Career* Nat Serv 2 Lt Royal Horse Gds 1957-59; in the City 1962-74, civil serv 1974-88, publisher 1988-; tstee Dr Johnson's House, Gough Square, London; *Style*— Thomas Harmsworth, Esq

HARMSWORTH BLUNT, Margaret, Lady; Margaret Hunam; da of William Redhead, of Carville Hall, Brentford; *m* 1, 1920 (m dis 1938), 2 Viscount Rothermere (d 1978); 1 s (3 Viscount), 2 da (Hon Lady Cooper-Key, Countess of Cromer, *qv*); m 2, Capt Thomas Hussey, RN (ret); m 3, 1947, as his 2 w, Sir John Blunt, 10 Bt (d 1969); *Style*— Margaret, Lady Harmsworth Blunt; The Old Mill, Mayfield, Sussex

HARNDEN, Arthur Baker; CB (1969), TD (1950); s of Cecil Henry Harnden (d 1962); *b* 6 Jan 1909; *Educ* various state schs, London Univ; *m* 1, 1935, Maisie Elizabeth Annie, nee Winterburn (d 1970); 1 s; m 2, 1971, Jean Kathleen, nee Wheeler; *Career* Lt-Col GSO1 WO; civil servant GPO, chartered engr dir London Telecommunications Region 1962-67 (sr dir ops 1967-69), ret 1969; chm Supplementary Benefits Appeal Tbnl, ret 1982; *Recreations* painting, pottery; *Style*— Arthur Harnden Esq, CB, TD; Comrie, Park St, Fairford, Glos GL7 4JL (☎ 0285 712805)

HARNDEN, Prof David Gilbert; s of William Alfred Harnden (d 1934), of London, and Anne McKenzie, *née* Wilson (d 1983); *b* 22 June 1932; *Educ* George Heriots Sch Edinburgh, Univ of Edinburgh (BSc, PhD); *m* 9 Jul 1955, Thora Margaret, da of Alexander Ralph Seatter (d 1945), of Burray, Orkney; 3 s (Ralph b 1957, Mark b 1960, Richard b 1965); *Career* lectr Univ of Edinburgh 1956-57, sci memb MRC Harwell and Edinburgh 1957-69, res fell Univ of Wisconsin USA 1963-64, prof of cancer studies Univ of Birmingham 1969-83, dir Paterson Inst for Cancer Res Manchester 1983-, prof of experimental oncology Univ of Manchester 1983-; chm Br Assoc Cancer Res 1984-87, pres Assoc Clinical Cytogenetectists 1985-88, chm ed bd Br Journal of Cancer; many papers on cytogenetics and cancer published in learned jls and books; memb exec ctee Cancer Res Campaign; FIBiol 1970, FRCPath 1983, FRSE 1983, hon MRCP 1987; *Recreations* sketching, a little gardening; *Style*— David Harnden, Esq; Tanglewood, Ladybrook Road, Bramhall, Stockport, Cheshire SK7 3NE (☎ 061 485 3214); Paterson Institute for Cancer Research, Christie Hospital and Holt Radium Institute, Wilmslow Road, Manchester M20 9BX (☎ 061 445 8123, fax 061 434 7728, telex 934999 TXLINKG)

HARNEY, Desmond Edward St Aubyn; OBE (1968); s of Edward Augustine St Aubyn Harney, KC, MP (d 1929), of London, and Kathleen, *née* Anderson (d 1973); *b* 14 Feb 1929; *Educ* Corby Sch Sunderland, Univ of Durham (BSc), Univ of Cambridge, SOAS, Univ of London; *m* 10 July 1954, Judith Geraldine, da of Daniel McCarthy Downing (d 1940), of Dublin; 1 s (Richard Tindle b 16 Oct 1958), 2 da (Geraldine Anne b 3 July 1955, Bridget Clare b 14 Sept 1957); *Career* Nat Serv Sgt 1947-49 serv Canal Zone (Suez) and Pakistan; ICI 1954-56, cnsllr Dip Serv Iran and Kenya 1956-74, dir Morgan Grenfell & Co Ltd 1974-87; non exec dir: London Brick plc 1981-85, Equatorial Bank plc 1986-, Middle East Conslts Ltd 1988-; chm Irano-British C of C 1976-79; cncl memb: Royal Soc For Asian Affrs 1987-, Br Inst of Persian Studies 1987-; chm Chelsea Cons Assoc 1986-, cncllr RBKC 1986-; *Recreations* photography, skiing, riding; *Clubs* Garrick; *Style*— Desmond Harney, Esq, OBE; 16 Stafford Terr, London W8 7BH (☎ 01 938 3291); Broadwater House, 31 Sherborne, Gloucestershire GL54 3DR; The Glassmill, Suite 13, 1 Battersea Bridge Rd, London SW11 3BG (☎ 01 924 2980, fax 01 924 2991)

HARNIMAN, John Phillip; OBE 1984; s of William Thomas Harniman (d 1941), and Maud Kate Florence, *née* Dyrenfurth (d 1939); *b* 7 May 1939; *Educ* Leyton CHS, Culham Coll (Dip Ed), London Univ (BA), Université de Paris; *m* 26 August 1961, Avryl da of Harold Hartley (d 1953), 1 s (Denzil b 20 Nov 1971), 1 da (Claire b 24 Dec 1968) ; *Career* teacher and lectr William Morris Sch Walthamstow and Ecole Normale Supérieure de St Cloud 1960-67; Br Cnc: Algeria 1967-70, asst dir personnel 1970-76, rep Singapore 1976-81, cultural attache Romania 1981-84, cultural cnsllr and rep for Belgium and Luxembourg 1984-87, dir of trg Br Cncl London 1988; *Recreations* music, reading, letter-writing, cats; *Clubs* Anglo-Belgian; *Style*— John Harniman, Esq, OBE; The British Council, 10 Spring Gdns, London SW1A 2BN (☎ 01 930 8466, fax 01 839 6347, telex 8952201)

HARPER, Lt-Col Alexander Forrest (Alec); DSO (1946); s of Lt-Col Alexander Forrest Harper (d 1972), of Littoncheney, Dorset, and Clare Rosamund, *née* Rowlandson; *b* 12 July 1910; *Educ* Blundells', RMC Sandhurst; *m* 18 Dec 1946, (Margaret Helen) Rosemary, da of Eric Hayward, of Dane St House, Chilham, Kent; 1 s (Alexander (Sandy) b 16 March 1947), 1 da (Caroline b 16 Sept 1950); *Career* Royal Deccan Horse IA 1931-44, Capt 1937, seconded cmdt Govr of Bengal's Bodyguard 1938-40, Maj 1942, 9 Gurkha Rifles 1944-47 (despatches 1944), Lt-Col 1944, Staff Coll Quetta 1947, ret 1948; jt md Bengal Distilleries Co Ltd 1948-55; hon sec Hurlingham Polo Assoc 1972-; memb: Indian Cavalry Offrs Assoc, 9 Gurkhas Offrs Assoc, ctee Cowdray Park Polo Club; *Recreations* polo, shooting, fishing, hunting; *Clubs* Cavalry and Guards, Shikar; *Style*— Lt-Col Alec Harper, DSO; Ambersham Farm, Midhurst, Sussex (☎ 079 85 254)

HARPER, Brig (Charles) Anthony des Noëttes; CBE (1969, OBE 1964); s of Dr Charles Harold Lefebvre Harper (d 1936), of Finchley; *b* 17 July 1916; *Educ* St Edward's Oxford; *m* 1947, Francesca Marie, da of Col Frank John Beecham (d 1945), of Cape Town; 1 da; *Career* WWII served: NW Europe, India, Malaya, Singapore, Germany; mil attaché Moscow 1966-68, cdr Br Forces Antwerp 1969-71, security advsr HQ CENTO (Turkey) 1971-74, MOD HQ Intelligence centre 1974-82; diplomat 1971-74, civil servant MOD 1974-82; memb Ashford Borough Cncl 1983- (ldr 1985-); *Clubs* Army and Navy; *Style*— Brig Anthony Harper, CBE; Venus House, The St, Appledore, Ashford, Kent TN26 2BU (☎ 023 383 375)

HARPER, Hon Mrs (Hazel Eleanor); da of Baron Woolley, CBE, DL (Life Peer); *b* 11 Dec 1938; *Educ* Malvern Girls Coll; *m* 1961, William David Harper, only s of William Richard Harper, OBE; 2 s, 1 da; *Career* SRN; pt/t night nursing supt; magistrate 1980-; *Recreations* golf, walking, family activities; *Clubs* Royal Liverpool GC; *Style*— The Hon Mrs Harper; Felsberg, Gerard Rd, West Kirby, Wirral (☎ 051 625 9840)

HARPER, Heather (Mrs Eduardo Benarroch); CBE; da of Hugh Harper, of Belfast, and Mary Eliza, *née* Robb; *b* 8 May 1930; *Educ* Ashleigh House Sch Belfast, Trinity Coll of Music (LTCL); *m* 19 May 1973, Eduardo J Benarroch, s of Hector A Benarroch, of Buenos Aires; *Career* soprano; leading int opera and concert singer 1954-, has sung at all major opera houses and with all major symphony orchs in the world; recent season incl: Japan, Hong Kong, Australia, New York, Geneva, Rome, Milan, Madrid, Vienna, Paris, Amsterdam, Los Angeles; soprano soloist first BBC Symphony Orch first Far East tour 1982; regular soloist: Covent Garden, New York Met, Teatro Colon Buenos Aires; notable performances incl: Elsa in Lohengrin (Bayreuth debut), Countess in The Marriage of Figaro, Deutsche Opera Berlin (conducted by Barenboim), Die Marschallin and Die Kaiserin by Richard Strauss; world premieres incl: Britten's War Requiem Coventry Cathedral 1962, Mrs Coyle in Britten's Owen Wingrave 1971, Tippett's Third Symphony 1972, Nadia in Tippett's The Icebreak Covent Garden 1975, Britten's Praise We Great Men 1985; recorded over 80 major works with all main recording cos in Britain and abroad; awards incl: Edison Award for Britten's Les Illuminations Grammy Nomination for Berg's Seven Early Songs, Grammy Award and Grand Prix du Pisque for Peter Grimes, Grammy Award Best Solo Recording for Ravel's Sheherazade 1984; prof of singing and conslt Royal Coll of Music 1985-, dir singing studies Britten-Pears Sch Snape, visiting lectr Royal Scottish Acad of Music, vice-pres N Ireland Youth Symphony Orch; Hon DMUS Queen's Uni Belfast 1964; hon RAM 1972, FTCL, FRCM 1988, RSA 1989; *Recreations* reading, biographies, gardening; *Style*— Miss Heather Harper, CBE; 20 Milverton Rd, London NW6 7AS; Virrey Olaguer y Feliu 3444-80; 1426 Buenos Aires, Argentina

HARPER, James Norman; s of His Hon Judge Norman Harper (d 1967), and Iris Irene, *née* Rawson; *b* 30 Dec 1932; *Educ* Marlborough, Magdalen Coll Oxford (BA); *m* 1956, Blanka Miroslava Eva, da of Miroslav Sigmund, of Henley on Thames; 1 s, 1 da; *Career* Lt RA (Nat Serv and TA for 3 years); barr Gray's Inn 1957, rec 1980; pres Northumberland Co Hockey Assoc 1982-; *Recreations* cricket, hockey; *Clubs* MCC; *Style*— James Harper, Esq; 59 Kenton Rd, Gosforth, Newcastle upon Tyne NE3 4NJ (☎ (091 285) 7611)

HARPER, Prof John Lander; s of John Hindley Harper, and Harriet Mary, *née* Archer; *b* 27 May 1925; *Educ* Lawrence Sheriff Sch Rugby, Magdalen Coll Oxford (MA, DPhil); *m* 8 Jan 1954, Borgny, da of Toralf Lero; 1 s (Jonathan b 24 Sept 1960), 2 da (Belinda b 19 Jan 1955, Claire b 20 Jan 1957); *Career* univ demonstrator dept of agric Oxford Univ 1948-60, prof of agric botany Univ of N Wales 1960-67 (prof of botany 1967-82), emeritus prof Univ of Wales 1982-; memb: Agric and Food Res Cncl 1980-, Natural Environment Res Cncl 1971-78 and 1987-, foreign assoc Nat Acad of Sci USA, Hon DSc Univ of Sussex 1984, FRS 1978 (memb cncl 1987-); *Books* Population Biology of Plants (1977), Ecology: Individuals, Populations and Communities (with M Begon and C Townsend, 1986); Population Biology of Plants (1977), Ecology: Individuals, Populations and Communities (with M Begon and C Townsend);

Recreations gardening; *Clubs* The Farmers; *Style*— Prof John Harper; Cae Groes, Glan-y-Coed Park, Dwygyfylchi, Penmaenmawr, Gwynedd LL34 6TL (☎ 0492 622362)

HARPER, John Mansfield; s of Thomas James Harper (d 1944), of Bucks, and May, *née* Charlton; *b* 17 July 1930; *Educ* Merchant Taylors, St John's Coll Oxford; *m* 1956, Berenice Honorine, da of Harold Haydon (d 1970), of Spain; 1 s (Neil Mansfield b 1960), 1 da (Ann Berenice b 1963); *Career* Civil Serv (Post Off) 1953-69, PO Telecommunications 1969-81, md inland div and bd memb Br Telecom 1981-83 (ret 1983); special advsr to the bd NEC Business Systems (UK) Ltd 1985-; CIEE, CBIM; *Recreations* reading, electronics, gardening, carpentry; *Style*— John Harper, Esq; 34 Longfield Drive, Amersham, Bucks HP6 5HE (☎ 020 43 5443); NEC Business Systems (UK) Ltd, 1 Victoria Rd, London W3 6UL (☎ 01 993 8111)

HARPER, Martin John; s of Frank Harper, of Welford-on-Avon; *b* 26 Mar 1925; *Educ* King Edward's GS Birmingham, LSE; *m* 1949, Stella, da of Francis Beavis, of Birkdale, Southport; 1 s, 2 da; *Career* merchant banker; dir: Keyser Ullmann 1971, London Interstate Bank 1980, Charterhouse Japhet 1980 (md 1984-), chm Charterhouse Japhet Credit 1983; Johnson Matthey Bankers 1984, Royal Scot Fin Gp 1986-; chm: Minories Fin 1986-88, examinations bd London C of C; *Recreations* reading, music, walking; *Clubs* Carlton, Overseas Bankers; *Style*— Martin Harper, Esq; 123 Minories, London EC3 (☎ 01 488 2671); 46a Priestlands Park Rd, Sidcup, Kent (☎ 01 300 1264)

HARPER, Peter Philip Dudley; s of William John Harper (d 1984), and Ida Bertha, *née* Evans (d 1948); *b* 4 Nov 1930; *Educ* Richmond and East Sheen GS, UCL (LLB); *m* 15 Jan 1955, Joyce, da of Sidney Thomas White (d 1967); 1 s (Robert b 1966), 1 da (Vivien b 1960); *Career* Nat Serv 2 Lt RASC, Temp Capt claims cmmn 1955-57; admitted slr 1954, ptnr Warmingtons & Hasties 1959-; Clerk to Worshipful Co of Woolmen 1970-75 (Liveryman 1975); memb Law Soc; *Style*— Peter P D Harper, Esq; 15 York Ave, East Sheen, London SW14 7LQ (☎ 01 876 4827); 3 John St, Grays Inn, London WCIN 2ES (☎ 01 242 3333, fax 01 405 6462, telex 22169)

HARPER, Rev Roger; s of Albert William Harper (d 1979), of Peel, IOM, and Joyce, *née* Griffiths; *b* 10 Jan 1943; *Educ* Merchant Taylors Crosby, Manchester Inst for Science and Technol (BSc); *m* 26 July 1966, Joan, da of John Worthington, of Freckleton, Lancs; 2 da (Charlotte b 1967, Camilla b 1969); *Career* CA; ordained priest 1988, in diocese of Sodor and Man, chm diocesan bd of fin 1984-; dir: Edenbrace Ltd 1985-, Manx Indust Tst 1973-, Westmorland Smoked Foods 1988-, FCA; *Recreations* drag hunting (IOM bloodhounds), sailing; *Style*— Rev Roger Haper; Ballahowin House, St Marks, Ballasalla, Isle of Man (☎ 0624 851251); 5th Floor, Victory House, Prospect Hill Douglas, Isle of Man (☎ 0624 24945, telex 629222, fax 24530)

HARPER, Prof (John) Ross; CBE (1986); s of Thomas Harper (d 1960), and Margaret Simpson, *née* Ross; *b* 20 Mar 1935; *Educ* Hutchesons' Boys' GS, Glasgow Univ (MA, LLB); *m* 26 Sept 1963, Ursula Helga Renate, da of Hans Gathman (d 1966), of Zimerstrasse, Darmstadt; 2 s (Robin b 1964, Michael b 1969), 1 da (Susan b 1966); *Career* slr Scotland; sr ptnr Ross Harper & Murphy; pres Law Soc of Scotland, pt/t prof of law Univ of Strathclyde, former pres Glasgow Bar Assoc, sec gen practice section Int Bar Assoc; temp Sheriff; hon sec Scottish Cons and Unionist Assoc; *Books* Practitioners' Guide to Criminal Procedure, A Guide to the Courts, The Glasgow Rape Case, Fingertip Guide to Criminal Law; *Recreations* angling, bridge, shooting; *Clubs* RSAC, Glasgow and Western; *Style*— Prof Ross Harper, CBE; 97 Springkell Avenue, Pollokshields, Glasgow (☎ 041 427 3223); 163 Ingram Street, Glasgow G1 1DQ (041 552 6343)

HARPER GOW, Sir (Leonard) Maxwell; MBE (1944); s of Capt Leonard Harper Gow (d 1965), and Eleanor Amelie Salvesen (d 1980); *b* 13 June 1918; *Educ* Rugby, CCC Cambridge; *m* 1944, Lillan Margaret, da of Aage Jul Kiaer (d 1931); 2 s (Maxwell, Leonard), 1 da (Karen); *Career* served war 1939-46, Maj RA 1 Commando Bde; shipowner; vice-chm Christian Salveson plc 1981- (dir 1952-, chm 1964-81); dir: The Royal Bank of Scotland plc 1965- (vice-chm 1981-85), The Royal Bank of Scotland Gp plc 1978-, Radio Forth Ltd 1973-, DFM Hldgs Ltd 1985, The Scottish Cncl Devpt and Indust 1972- (vice-pres 1985); memb cncl IOD, chm Scottish Widows' Fund and Life Assur Soc (past chm 1964-85), Edinburgh Investmt Tst plc 1965-85; memb: Queen's Body Guard for Scotland (The Royal Co of Archers), Lloyd's underwriter; Liveryman Worshipful Co of Shipwrights; chm Friends of the Queen's Hall Edinburgh 1980-85 (pres 1985); CBIM; kt 1985; *Recreations* hill farming, shooting, fishing; *Clubs* New (Edinburgh), Caledonian; *Style*— Sir Maxwell Harper Gow; Eventyr, Lyars Road, Longniddry, East Lothian EH32 0PT (☎ 0875 52142); 50 East Fettes Ave, Edinburgh EH4 1EQ (☎ 031 552 7101)

HARPHAM, Sir William; KBE (1966, OBE 1948), CMG (1953); s of William Harpham, of Grimsby (d 1932); *b* 3 Dec 1906; *Educ* Wintringham Secdy Sch Grimsby, Christ's Coll Cambridge; *m* 1943, Isabelle, da of Maurice Droz; 1 s, 1 da; *Career* HM Foreign Serv, ret 1967; dep to UK del to OEEC 1953-56, min Tokyo 1956-59, min (econ) Paris 1959-63, ambass to Bulgaria 1964-66; dir GB East Europe Centre 1967-80; *Clubs* RAC; *Style*— Sir William Harpham, KBE, CMG; 9 Kings Keep, Putney Hill, London SW15 6RA (☎ 01 788 1383)

HARPUR-CREWE, Charles Arthur Richard; DL (Derbyshire); s of Arthur William Jenney (d 1934), and Frances Caroline Julia Harpur Jenney, *née* Harpur-Crewe (d 1960); *b* 25 Feb 1921; *Educ* Bedford Sch and privately; *Career* High Sheriff of Derbyshire 1961; *Recreations* shooting, walking, racing; *Style*— Mr Harpur-Crewe, DL; Calke Abbey, Ticknall, Derby (☎ 03316 84 2245); Warstow Hall, Sheen, Buxton, Derbyshire

HARRAP, Robert Charles Henry; s of Robert Evan Harrap (d 1981), of Tunbridge Wells, and Gladys Mabel, *née* Webb (d 1972); *b* 2 Nov 1926; *Educ* Cranleigh, London Univ (LLB); *m* 30 March 1957, Anne Catherine, da of William Clark (d 1985), of Forest Row; 3 da (Claire b 1958, Judith b 1962, Elizabeth b 1966); *Career* admitted slr 1950, sr ptnr Berrymans 1979- (ptnr 1954-); memb Coleman St Ward Club; Freeman City of London 1948, Liveryman City of London Slrs Co 1972; memb Law Soc 1950; *Recreations* walking, music; *Style*— Robert Harrap, Esq; 69 Westhall Rd, Warlingham, Surrey CR3 9HG (☎ 08832 2582); Salisbury House, London Wall, London EC2M 5QN (☎ 01 638 2811, fax 01 920 0361, telex 892070)

HARRAP, Simon Richard; s of M W Harrap, of Marsh House, Bentley, and Cynthia Mary, *née* Darell; *b* 25 Mar 1941; *Educ* Harrow; *m* 24 May 1969, Diana, da of Ian Akers Douglas (d 1952); 1 s (Nicholas Guy 17 Oct 1971), 2 da (Louise Jane b 15 March 1975, Lara Sophie b 5 Jan 1979); *Career* Stewart Smith & Co 1960-71; dir: Stewart Wrightson N America Ltd 1971-83, Stewart Wrightson plc 1984-87, Willis Faber plc 1985-, Gibbs Hartley Cooper ltd 1988; *Style*— Simon Harrap, Esq; Gibbs Hartley Cooper Ltd, 27-33 Artillery Lane, London E1 7LP (☎ 01 247 5433)

HARRIES, Hon Mrs (Anne Marjorie); *née* Sidney; da (by 1 m) of 1 Visc De L'Isle, VC, KG, GCMG, GCVO, PC; descent King William IVs natural da Lady Sophia FitzClarence (d 1837) w 1 Baron De L'Isle and Dudley (d 1851); *b* 1947; *m* 1967, David Alexander Harries, s of Rear-Adm David Hugh Harries, CB, CBE; 2 s (David b 1970, James b 1972), 1 da (Alexandra b 1968); *Style*— The Hon Mrs Harries; Hayselden Manor, Sissinghurst, Kent

HARRIES, John Arthur Jones; CBE (1979); s of Tom Llewelyn Harries, MBE,JP (d 1971), of Pelroath, Llangain, Carmarthen, Dyfed, and the late Muriel, *née* Thomas; *b* 24 Nov 1923; *Educ* Queen Elizabeth GS Carmarthen, Royal Veterinary Coll London; *m* 1, Nov 1950, Hazel (d 1982), da of Alec F Richards (d 1937), of Johnstown, Carmarthen; 1 s (Fevan), 3 da (Gwyn, Wendy, Julie); m 2 Margaret Mair; 2 s (Paul, Martin), 1 da (Annea); *Career* qualified vet 1946, self employed practice Carmarthen 1946-82; fndr (later sec and pres) West Wales Vet Clinical Club 1950-; memb: cncl S Wales div Br Vet Assoc 1950-, cncl Br Vet Assoc 1966-86; memb: cncl Trinity Coll Carmarthen 1973-, Welsh Counties Ctee 1973-, cncl OU 1973, Nat Steering Gp Tech Vocational Educnl Initiative 1980-; chm ctee Local Educn Authorities 1986-87, dir Business & Technician Educn Cncl 1986-; vice chm Welsh Coll of Music and Drama, Cardiff 1976-, dir WNO Co 1981-87; memb: Carmarthenshire CC 1966-73 (ldr 1969-73), Assoc of CCs 1976-, cncl Int Union of Local Authorities 1981-, cncl of Euro Municipalities 1981-, Welsh Advsy Body 1984-; memb: Calvinistic Methodist and Deacon Moriah Chapel Llanstephan 1935-, cncl Nat Eisteddfod 1975-84, ct and cncl Cardiff Univ 1988-; pres Carmarthen Rotary Club 1982-83, admitted to the Druidical order of Gorsedd 1985; MRCVS 1946, memb Br Vet Assoc 1947; *Recreations* sailing, gardening; *Clubs* Rivertown YC, Nat Liberal; *Style*— Arthur Harries, Esq, CBE, JP; 1 Whitehall Place, London

HARRIES, Rt Rev Richard Douglas; *see*: Oxford, Bishop of

HARRIES, Roy Edward; s of John Benjamin Harries (d 1983), and Elizabeth Anne, *née* Twigg; *b* 15 Sept 1943; *Educ* Rhondda County GS; *m* 21 Jan 1973, Caryl Ann Harries, da of Thomas James Jones (d 1965); 1 s (Neil Edward b 1976), 1 da (Joannie Louise b 1978); *Career* ptnr Barlow Mendham & Co 1974-75, sr ptnr Harries Watkins & Co (ptnr 1975); ACA 1972, FCA 1979; *Recreations* chess, reading, twentieth century history, music; *Style*— Roy Harries, Esq; Teg Fan, 67, Coychurch Rd, Pencoed, Mid-Glam (☎ 0656 865 683); 85, Taff St, Pontypridd, Mid Glam (☎ 01443 402 627); 16, Coychurch Rd, Pencoed, Mid-Glam (☎ 0656 863 000)

HARRIMAN, Hon Mrs (Pamela Beryl); da of late 11 Baron Digby, KG, DSO, MC, TD; *b* 1920; *m* 1, 1939 (m dis 1946), Maj the Hon Randolph Frederick Edward Spencer-Churchill, MBE (d 1968, eld s is Rt Hon Sir Winston Churchill KG, PC, OM, CH, TD, DL (PM), and Baroness Spencer-Churchill (Life Peeress), *see* Peerage D of Marlborough), 1 s (Winston b 1940); m 2, 1960, Leland Hayward (d 1971); m 3, 1971, (William) Averell Harriman (d 1986); *Style*— The Hon Mrs Harriman; 3038 N Street NW, Washington DC, 20007, USA

HARRINGTON, Peter Roy; s of Clifford Roy Harrington, OBE, of Beeches, 33 Annings Lane, Burton Bradstock, Dorset, and Sylvia Abigail Bernadette, *née* Lilwall; *b* 3 Mar 1951; *Educ* St John's Sch Leatherhead; *m* 8 Nov 1980, Sally Anne, da of John Leslie Boyer, OBE, of Friars Lawn, Norwood Green Road, Southall, Middx; 2 s (Oliver Brendan b 4 Sept 1981, Joshua Edward b 3 May 1984), 1 da (Pandora Jane b 11 Sept 1987); *Career* slr 1977; ptnr 1978-: Kidd Rapinet, MacDonald Stacey; memb Royal Cwth Soc; *Recreations* tennis, squash, golf, music; *Style*— Peter Harrington, Esq; 14/15 Craven St, London, WC2N 5AD, (☎ 01 925 0303, fax 01 925 0334)

HARRINGTON, 11 Earl of (GB 1742); William Henry Leicester Stanhope; also Viscount Stanhope of Mahon, Baron Stanhope of Elvaston (both GB 1717), Baron Harrington (GB 1730), and Viscount Petersham (GB 1742); s of 10 Earl of Harrington, MC (d 1929, ggn of 4 Earl, inventor of the blend of snuff known as Petersham mixture, snuff being colour he used for his livery and equipage); suc kinsman, 7 and last Earl Stanhope, in the Viscountcy of Stanhope of Mahon and the Barony of Stanhope of Elvaston 1967; *b* 24 August 1922; *Educ* Eton; *m* 1, 1942 (m dis 1946), Eileen, da of Sir John Foley Grey, 8 Bt; 1 s (Viscount Petersham b 1940), 1 da (Lady Avena Maxwell b 1944); m 2, 1947 (m dis 1962), Anne, da of Maj Richard Chute, of Co Limerick; 1 s (Hon Steven b 1951), 2 da (Lady Trina b 1947, Lady Sarah Barry b 1951); m 3, 1964, Priscilla, da of Hon Archibald Cubitt (5 s of 2 Baron Ashcombe); 1 s (Hon John b 1965), 1 da; *Heir* s, Viscount Petersham; *Career* Capt RAC serv WWII; landowner; adopted Irish citizenship 1965; *Clubs* Kildare Street (Dublin); *Style*— The Rt Hon Earl of Harrington; Greenmount Stud, Patrickswell, Co Limerick, Ireland

HARRIS *see also*: Reader-Harris, Stuart-Harris, Sutherland Harris

HARRIS, Prof Sir Alan James; CBE (1968); s of Walter Harris; *b* 8 July 1916; *Educ* Owen's Sch Islington, Northampton Poly, London Univ (BSc); *m* 1948, Marie Thérèse, da of Prof Paul Delcourt (d 1976), of Paris; 2 s; *Career* WWII RE served NW Europe (despatches), Maj 1945; local govt engr 1933-40, sr ptnr (later conslt) Harris & Sutherland 1955-; memb Engrg Cncl 1982-85, prof of concrete structures Imperial Coll London 1973-81 (emeritus 1981-), chm Hydraulics Res Ltd 1981-, tstee Imperial War Museum 1983-; Ordre de Mérite (France) 1978, Croix de Guerre France 1945; FEng, FIStructE (pres 1978, gold medal 1984), FICE, MConsE; kt 1980; *Recreations* sailing; *Clubs* Itchenor SC; *Style*— Professor Sir Alan Harris, CBE; 128 Ashley Gdns, Thirleby Rd, London SW1P 1HL (☎ 01 834 6924)

HARRIS, Alan John Fraser; s of Sqdn Ldr Nigel Mayhe Wilfred Harris, of Longford, Duntisbourne Leer, nr Cirencester, Glos, and Marion Lawrence, *née* Little; *b* 7 Jan 1942; *Educ* Charterhouse, Univ of Toronto (unfinished); *m* 18 June 1966, Veronica Fraser, da of Malcolm Cardouff Calderwood (d 1985), of Eastbourne, E Sussex; 2 s (Malcolm b 3 July 1969, Rupert b 9 Feb 1971); *Career* investmt mangr Black Geoghegan and Till London 1960-66, Coopers and Lybrand Ltd Toronto 1966-68, Imperial Oil Ltd Toronto 1968-72, William Brandts Ltd London 1973-76, Lloyds Bank plc London 1976-85, Lloyds Merchant Bank Ltd London 1985-; asst tres East Chiltington PCC; Freeman City of London 1963, Liveryman Worshipful Co of Grocers 1977 (Freeman 1963); ACA 1965, FCA 1975; *Recreations* football (soccer), cricket, golf; *Clubs* Marylebone CC, Old Carthusian FC; *Style*— Alan Harris, Esq; The Old Sch, Novington Lane, E Chiltington, Lewes, E Sussex BN7 3AX (☎ 0273 890 141); Lloyds Investmt Mangrs Ltd, 82 Queen St, London EC4N 1SE (☎ 01 600 4500, fax

01 929 5542, telex 881 2696)

HARRIS, Sir Anthony Travers Kyrle; 2 Bt (UK 1953), of Chepping Wycombe, Bucks; s of Marshal of the RAF Sir Arthur Harris, 1 Bt, GCB, OBE, AFC and 1 w, Barbara, da of Lt-Col E W K Money, 85th Regt (KSLI); *b* 18 Mar 1918; *Educ* Oundle; *Career* WWII 1939-45 with auxiliary units, Queen Victoria's Rifles and Wilts Regt, ADC to GOC-in-C Eastern Cmd 1944; a reader for MGM 1951-52; subsequently work with antiques; *Recreations* music, horology; *Style—* Sir Anthony Harris, Bt; 33 Cheyne Ct, Flood St, London SW3

HARRIS, Cdr Antony John Temple; OBE (1963); s of George James Temple Harris (d 1929), and Eva Kenyon, *née* Green Wilkinson (d 1942); *b* 5 August 1915; *Educ* RNC Dartmouth, RNC Greenwich; *m* 25 April 1940, Doris (Deedee), da of Frank Dufford Drake (d 1981), of USA; 2 s (Michael b 1941, John b 1944); *Career* RN: Cadet 1933, Midshipman 1933-35, Home and Med Fleets, Sub Lt 1937-38, Home Fleet, Lt China 1938-40, coastal forces 1940-42 long anti submarine course 1942, escort trg W Isles 1942-43, Lt and Lt Cdr E Indies and Pacific 1944-45, Naval Staff Course 1946, torpedo course 1946, Home Fleet 1947, TAS Course instr 1948, Cdr Staffs of C-in-C Home Fleet 1949-51, Jt Servs Staff Course 1951-52, Admty 1952-54, E Indies 1954-55, NATO SSO Gallant USA 1958-60, NATO (Staff of C-in-C North Norway 1961-63, NATO (Staff of C-in-C and C-in-C HOME) 1964-65, ret 1965; naval staff author MOD 1966-74; field master Meon Valley Beagles 1969-74, Churchwarden St Nicholas Church Wickham 1965-72, memb Droxford RDC 1970-74; *Recreations* walking, beagling; *Style—* Cdr Anthony Harris, OBE, RN; Hawthorns, Park Place, Wickham, Hants PO17 5EZ (☎ 0329 832 204)

HARRIS, Basil Vivian; s of Henry William Harris (d 1984), of Bexhill on Sea, and Sarah May, *née* Edwards (d 1983); *b* 1 July 1921; *Educ* Watford GS; *m* 15 May 1943, Myra Winifred Mildred, da of William Abbott Newport (d 1943), of Harrow; *Career* WWII RAF 1943-46; GPO engrg (res) dept 1939-43 and 1946-63; FCO: Dip Wireless Serv 1963-71, dep chief engr communications div FCO 1971-79, (chief 1979-81), ret 1981; Civil Serv Cmmn 1981-87, ret; CEng, MIEE 1956; *Books* contrib numerous tech jls on communications; *Recreations* golf, photography, travel; *Clubs* Royal Eastbourne GC (formerly Capt); *Style—* Basil Harris, Esq; 13 Decoy Drive, Eastbourne, Sussex BN22 0AB (☎ 0323 505 819)

HARRIS, Brian Nicholas; s of Claude Harris (d 1976), and Dorothy, *née* Harris (d 1982); *b* 12 Dec 1931; *Educ* Coll of Estate Mgmnt, Univ of London; *m* 18 March 1961, Rosalyn Marion, da of Geoffrey Alfred Caines (d 1982); 2 da (Suzanne b 1961, Jennifer b 1965); *Career* chartered surveyor; chm: ptnrship of Richard Ellis 1984 (ptnr 1961), City Branch Royal CS 1984-85; vice-chm: RICS bldg surveying div 1976-77, RICS Continental Gp 1977-78; memb Cncl: London C of C 1985; *Recreations* flyfishing, gardening, golf; *Clubs* Carlton, Flyfishers; *Style—* Brian Harris, Esq; Grants Paddock, Grants Lane, Limpsfield, Surrey RH8 0RQ (☎ 0883 723215); Richard Ellis, 55 Old Broad St, London EC2M 1LP (☎ 01 256 6411, fax 01 256 8328)

HARRIS, Carol Ruth; *née* Leibson; da of Dr Michael Leibson, and Sylvia, *née* Schwartz; *b* 2 Feb 1943; *Educ* Central Fndn Girls Sch, Highbury Hill HS, London Univ (BSc); *m* 22 March 1964, Paul Harris, s of Sidney Harris, of Wanstead, London; *Career* conslt in personnel, mgmnt and image design 1986-; dir of personnel and admin Arts Cncl of GB 1979-86 (earlier posts in health serv, local govt, mgmnt consultancy and res), chm IPM Central London Gp, memb IPM nat ctees on Orgn and Manpower Planning and Public Serv, vice chm Alexandra Palace Action Gp; FIPM, MAIE; *Recreations* fencing, riding, collecting fans, Indian classical dance; *Style—* Mrs Carol Harris; 360 Alexandra Park Rd, London N22 4BD (☎ 01 889 6244)

HARRIS, Cecil Rhodes; s of Frederick William Harris (d 1954); *b* 4 May 1923; *Educ* Kingston GS; *m* 1946, Gwenyth, da of Hugh Llewelyn Evans (d 1956); 1 s, 2 da; *Career* aommercial Union Assur Co: asst gen mangr 1969-73, dep gen mangr and asst sec 1973-74, co sec 1974-78, dir 1975, exec dir 1976-, dep chief gen mangr 1980-82, chief exec 1982-85; dep chm Trade Indemnity plc 1986; FCIS, FSCA; *Recreations* Bible study; *Style—* Cecil Harris, Esq; Ashley, 35a Plough Lane, Purley, Surrey CR2 3QJ (☎ 01 668 2820)

HARRIS, Christopher John Ashford; s and h of Sir Jack (Wolfred) Ashford Harris, 2 Bt; *b* 26 August 1934; *m* 1957, Anna, da of F de Malmanche, of Auckland, NZ; 1 s, 2 da; *Style—* Christopher Harris Esq; 21 Anne St, Wadestown, Wellington, New Zealand

HARRIS, Rev Cyril Evans; JP (Beaconsfield 1976-); s of Arthur Frederick Harris (d 1982), of The Ridings, Angmering-on- Sea, Sussex, and Phillis, *née* Evans (d 1977); *b* 27 April 1930; *Educ* Cranleigh Sch, Eaton Hall Officer Cadet Sch, Lincoln Theol Coll, Central Sch for Arts and Crafts; *m* 29 May 1954, Heather Louise, da of George Frederick White; 3 s (Paul, Bruce, Martin), 2 da (Louise, Mary); *Career* Nat Serv 1948, cmmnd 2 Lt Essex Regt 1949, seconded Beds and Herts, served Greece 1949-50, Oxford and Bucks LI 1950; co mangr (theatrical supplies, TV, stage and screen) 1951-62, designer embroidery and costume; ordained: deacon 1963, priest 1964; curate and priest i/c Beaconsfield 1963-68, vicar St Giles Stoke Poges 1968-89; hon chaplain: Wexham Park Hosp 1987-, Educn Corps Wilton Park Beaconsfield, 4 Prince of Wales Offrs Assoc Gurkhas; chm: Stoke Poges First and Middle Schs, Stoke Common Tst; tstee Lord Hastings Tst, govr Oakdene Sch Beaconsfield; fndr memb: Round Table, Beaconsfield Advsy Centre; memb: RSPB, Nat Tst; *Books* Guide to the Work and Life of Thomas Gray, Historical Guide of St Giles Stoke Poges; *Recreations* squash, tennis, hockey, art (oils), walking; *Clubs* Cranleigh Hockey; *Style—* The Rev Cyril Harris, JP; The Vicarage, Park Rd, Stoke Poges, Bucks (☎ 02814 4177)

HARRIS, David Anthony; MP (C) St Ives 1983-, MEP (EDG) Cornwall and Plymouth 1979-84; s of Edgar Courtenay Harris (d 1980), and Betty Doreen Harris (d 1977); *b* 1 Nov 1937; *Educ* Mount Radford Sch Exeter; *m* 1962, Diana Joan, *née* Hansford; 1 s (Justin b 1966), 1 da (Rebecca b 1967); *Career* journalist with W Country newspapers before joining the Daily Telegraph 1961, political corr Daily Telegraph 1976-79; *Clubs* Farmers; *Style—* David Harris Esq, MP; Trewedna Farm, Perranwell, nr Truro, Cornwall (☎ 0872 863200)

HARRIS, David Keith; OBE (1987, MBE 1983), TD (1978); s of Edwin Harris (d 1974), of Epworth, Doncaster, and Mona Doreen, *née* Sleight; *b* 27 Jan 1945; *Educ* Worksop Coll, King's Coll London (LLB); *m* 25 Jan 1975, Veronica Mary, da of Arthur Vernon Harrison (d 1983), of Manor Farm, Finningley, Doncaster; *Career* Univ of London OTC 1963-67, cmmnd Royal Lincolnshire Regt TA 1967; served: 5R Anglian 1967-78, 7R Anglian 1978-80, SO2 G3 7 Field Force 1980-82, SO2 G3 49 Inf Bde 1982; cmd 7R Anglian 1984-87, dep cdr 49 Inf Bde 1987-; admitted slr 1969, sr ptnr Hayes Son & Richmond 1987-, co dir; parly candidate (Cons) for Bassetlaw Oct 1974 and May 1979; memb Law Soc 1967; *Recreations* shooting, gardening, good food and wine; *Clubs* East India; *Style—* Col David Harris, OBE, TD; Green Hill House, Haxey, Doncaster, S Yorks DN9 2JU (☎ 0427 752794); Hayes Son & Richmond, Ship Ct, Silver St, Gainsborough, Lincs DN21 2DN (☎ 0427 3831, fax 0427 311022, car 0836 298307)

HARRIS, David Michael; s of Maurice Harris, of Liverpool, and Doris, *née* Ellis; *b* 7 Feb 1943; *Educ* Liverpool Inst HS for Boys, Oxford Univ (BA, MA), Cambridge Univ (PhD); *m* 16 Aug 1970, Emma Lucia, da of Dr Italo Calma, of Liverpool; 2 s (Julian b 3 July 1974, Jeremy b 9 May 1977), 1 da (Anna b 10 May 1980); *Career* asst lectr in law Manchester Univ 1967-69, barr 1969, rec 1988- (asst rec 1984-88); *Books* Winfield & Jolowicz on Tort (co-ed, 1971), Supplement to Bingham's The Modern Cases on Negligence (co-ed, 1985); *Recreations* arts, travel, sport; *Style—* David M Harris, Esq; 20 Aldbourne Ave, Liverpool L25 6JE (☎ 051 722 2848); Peel House, 3rd Floor, Harrington St, Liverpool L2 9XN (☎ 051 236 0718, fax 051 255 1085)

HARRIS, (Walter) Frank; s of Walter Stanley Harris (d 1955), and Ellen, *née* Shackell; *b* 19 May 1920; *Educ* King Edward VI Sch Birmingham, Univ of Nottingham (BCom), Univ of SA Open Univ (BA); *m* 8 Aug 1941, Esther Blanche (Tessa), da of Harold Joe Hill; 2 s (Walter Douglas b 1945, Clive Richard b 1947), 2 da (Christine Mary Beatrice (Tina) b 1953, Sarah Elizabeth Frances b 1956); *Career* WWII RAFVR 1939-46, coastal cmd pilot, demob Flt Lt; Wood Bastow Nottingham 1948-49, Ford of Britain 1950-65, princ city offr and town clerk Newcastle upon Tyne 1965-69, dir Massey Ferguson 1969-71, fin dir Dunlop SA 1971-79, Dunlop Tyres 1980-81; parish and dist cncllr 1966-69; FCA, FCIS, FCMA; *Recreations* astrophysics, fell-walking, DIY; *Clubs* Reform, Beacon, Brunswick; *Style—* Frank Harris, Esq; Acomb High House, Northumbria NE46 4PH (☎ 0434 602844)

HARRIS, Geoffrey Ronald; s of Clarence Edgar Harris (d 1966); *b* 10 Sept 1926; *Educ* Whitgift; *m* 1953, Joan Lyn, da of George Jarvis; 2 s (Nigel David, Mark Stephen), 1 da (Sally Elizabeth); *Career* WWII Lt served Germany and India; insur broker; dir: Stewart Wrightson (Marine) 1965-, Codresa (Spain) 1973-, Stewart Wrightson Chile Ltd 1978-, Stewart Wrightson Cusur (Argentina) 1978-, Golding Stewart Wrightson 1985-; *Recreations* sport, travel; *Style—* Geoffrey Harris, Esq; Rookwood, Lower Park Rd, Chipstead, Surrey (☎ 073 75 53768); Golding Stewart Wrightson Ltd, 1 Camomile St, London EC3A 7HJ (☎ 01 623 7511, telex 8811181)

HARRIS, Geoffrey Thomas; CBE (1968); s of John Henry Harris (d 1937), of Lincoln; *b* 4 August 1917; *Educ* Lincoln Sch, Christ's Coll Cambridge (MA, PhD); *m* 1940, (Constance) Geraldine, da of Vernon Seymour White (d 1967), of Wallingford; 4 children; *Career* aa Jessop-Saville Ltd Sheffield 1967-73 (res and tech dir 1951-61), directeur relations techniques Creusot-Loire SA (France) 1973-82, consulting engr 1982-; pres Iron and Steel Inst 1972-73; FEng; *Recreations* music (organ); *Clubs* Athenaeum; *Style—* Dr Geoffrey T Harris, CBE; 103 Oak Tree Rd, Tilehurst, Reading, Berks RG3 6LA (☎ 0734 417506)

HARRIS, 6 Baron Harris (UK 1815); George Robert John Harris; s of 5 Baron Harris, CBE, MC (d 1984), and Dorothy Mary (d 1981), da of Rev John Crookes; *b* 17 April 1920; *Educ* Eton, Christ Church Oxford; *Career* Capt RA; *Style—* The Rt Hon the Lord Harris; Huntingfield, Faversham, Kent (☎ 0795 282)

HARRIS, Hugh Christopher Emlyn; s of T E Harris, CB, CBE, (d 1955), and M A Harris (d 1980); *b* 25 Mar 1936; *Educ* The Leys Sch, Trinity Coll Cambridge (MA); *m* 7 Sept 1968, Pamela Susan, da of R A Woollard (d 1980); 1 s (William b 1972), 1 da (Kate b 1970); *Career* Nat Serv Lt RA 1954-56; assoc dir Bank of England 1988- (chief of corporate servs 1984-88, joined 1959); dir: BE Services Ltd 1979-, Houblon Nominees 1988-, The Securities Mgmnt Tst Ltd 1988-; dir Solefield Sch Educnl Tst Ltd, church warden St Margaret's Lothbury, memb Cncl Business in the Community; ACIB; *Recreations* rugby, tennis; *Style—* Hugh Harris, Esq; Bank of England, London EC2R 8AH (☎ 01 601 3131)

HARRIS, Hugh Martin West; JP (Surrey 1961, Sussex 1971); s of Sir Sidney West Harris, CB, CVO (d 1962), of Wimbledon, and Emily Mary, *née* Wilson (d 1940); *b* 12 May 1919; *Educ* Marlborough, Queen's Coll Oxford (MA); *m* 1, 1947, Ann (d 1967), da of E A A Varnish, OBE, of Wimbledon; 1 s, 3 da; m 2, 1967 (m dis), Isobel, da of Alexander Macdonald, of Lanarks; m 3, 1971, Jean Chisholm-Batten, da of E M Taberman, of Jersey; *Career* WWII serv The Queen's Royal Regt Ceylon, India, Paiforce Burma: Lt-Col cmd 5 Bn Queen's Royal Regt TA 1956-59; joined Broad & Co Ltd 1946 (md 1965, chm 1974), dep chm Sandell Perkins plc 1975-81; memb W Sussex CC 1981-85; *Recreations* local affairs, golf; *Clubs* Naval and Military, RAC; *Style—* Lt-Col Hugh Harris, JP; 4 Sumners College Rd, Ardingly, W Sussex RH17 6SA (☎ 0444 892506)

HARRIS, Iain Grant Nicolson; *b* 17 Mar 1946; *Educ* George Heriot's Sch Edinburgh, Univ of Aberdeen (MA); *m* 8 Aug 1969, Jane Petrie, *née* Robertson; 1 s (Grant b 1975), 1 da (Rochelle b 1980); *Career* sales promotion mangr RMC Gp 1968-73; dir: Parker PR Assocs Ltd 1973-80, Shandwick Conslts Ltd 1980-82, Good Rels City Ltd 1982-85; chm: Lombard Communications plc 1985-, Wolfe Lombard Ltd 1985-, Lombard Communications Inc (USA) 1987-; pres: Windsor Soc for Mentally Handicapped Children and Adults, Windsor Talking Newspaper; tstee New Windsor Community Assoc, vice pres Royal Windsor Rose and Horticultural Soc; Mayor Royal Borough of Windsor and Maidenhead 1976-78 (borough cncllr 1970-79); Freeman City of London 1982; *Recreations* gardening supervision, travel; *Style—* Iain Harris, Esq; Chanonry, St Leonard's Hill, Windsor, Berks SL4 4AT (☎ 0753 863452); Lombard Communications plc, 127 Cheapside, London EC2V 6BT (☎ 01 600 0064, fax 01 600 7406)

HARRIS, Lt-Gen Sir Ian Cecil; KBE (1967, CBE 1958), CB (1962), DSO (1945); s of late J W A Harris; *b* 7 July 1910; *Educ* Portora Royal Sch Enniskillin, RMC Sandhurst; *m* 1945, Anne-Marie Desmotreux; 2 s; *Career* 2 Lt Ulster Rifles 1930, WWII served NW Europe and Burma (despatches), Lt-Col 1952, Brig 1958, Maj-Gen 1960, GOC Singapore Base Dist 1960-62, chief of staff Contingency Planning SHAPE 1963-66, Lt-Gen 1966, GOC NI 1966-69, ret; owner Victor Stud, memb of family partnership and mangr Ballykisteen Stud Tipperary, chm Irish Bloodstock Breeders Assoc 1977-; *Style—* Lt-Gen Sir Ian Harris, KBE, CB, DSO; Acraboy House, Monard, Co Tipperary, Ireland (☎ 052 51564)

HARRIS, Irene; da of Sydney Harris (d 1971), film prodr, and Kitty Harris (d 1963); *b* 11 May 1948; *Educ* Wessex Gdns and Whitefields Secdy Sch; *Career* special events dir UN, admin Women of the Year Luncheon, convener Women of Tomorrow Awards, fndr pres Network; *Recreations* films, charity work; *Clubs* The Belfry, IOD, Network;

Style— Ms Irene Harris; 25 Park Rd, London NW1

HARRIS, Air Cdre Irene Joyce; CB (1983), RRC (1976); da of Robert John Harris (d 1963), and Annie Martha, *née* Breed (d 1967); *b* 26 Sept 1926; *Educ* Southgate Co Sch, Charing Cross Hosp (SRN), The London and Queen Mary's Maternity Home Sch (SCM); *Career* Princess Mary's RAF Nursing Serv 1950-84; served UK, Singapore, Germany, Cyprus; Gp Capt HQ RAF SC princ matron PMRAFNS 1978, Gp Capt MOD, dep dir PMRAFNS Mar-Sept 1981, dir Nursing Servs (RAF) and matron-in-chief PMRAFNS and Queen's Hon Nursing Sister 1981-84, ret; *Recreations* travel, wildlife; *Clubs* RAF; *Style*— Air Cdre Joy Harris, CB, RRC; Evdhimou, 51 Station Rd, Haddenham, Ely, Cambs CB6 3XD (☎ 0353 741149)

HARRIS, Sir Jack Wolfred Ashford; 2 Bt (UK 1932), of Bethnal Green, London; s of Rt Hon Sir Percy Harris, 1 Bt, PC, DL (d 1952); *b* 23 July 1906, ; *Educ* Shrewsbury, Trinity Hall Cambridge; *m* 1933, Patricia, da of Arthur Penman, of NSW; 2 s, 1 da; *Heir* s, Christopher John Ashford Harris; *Career* chm Bing Harris & Co NZ 1935-; past pres Wellington C of C; *Recreations* reading, gardening, swimming, writing; *Clubs* Wellington, Northern; *Style*— Sir Jack Harris, Bt; Flat 12, Quarterdeck, Carabella st, Kirribilli, NSW, Aust; Te Rama, Waikanae, New Zealand (☎ 5001)

HARRIS, John Charles; DL (S Yorks 1986); s of Sir Charles Joseph William Harris (d 1986), and Lady Emily Kyle Harris; *b* 25 April 1936; *Educ* Dulwich, Clare Coll Cambridge (BA, MA, LLB, LLM); *m* 1 April 1961, Alison Beryl, da of Dr Kenneth Reginald Sturley; 1 s (Edward John Charles b 15 June 1968), 1 da (Susan Alison b 16 Sept 1966) ; *Career* Nat Serv cmmnd Intelligence Corps 1954-56; slr 1966, with UK AEA (seconded to OECD) 1959-63, Poole Borough Cncl 1963-67, dep town clerk Bournemouth CC 1971-73 (offr 1967-73); S Yorks CC 1973-86: co sec 1973-83, chief exec and co clerk 1983-86, non-exec dir S Yorks Passenger Tport Exec, sec to Lord-Lieut S Yorks; conslt, public sector advsr and recruitment conslt PA Conslt Gp, admin Eng Camerata, freelance corr on public affrs; memb exec cncl Soc of Local Authorities (chief exec 1984-86), nat chm Soc of Co Secretaries 1983 vice chm and sec Friends of Opera North 1978-87 (Opera North cncl memb 1979-88 and devpt ctee memb 1987-), ctee memb Ackworth gp Riding for the Disabled Assoc 1976-, hon PR offr S Yorks and Humberside region RDA 1983- (memb RDA Nat Pubns ctee 1988-), fndr memb and sec Barnsley Rotary club 1976-79; Freeman City of London 1957; FRSA 1984; *Recreations* family, friends, riding, opera, music, theatre, foreign travel; *Style*— John Harris, Esq, DL; Long Lane Close, High Ackworth, Pontefract, Yorkshire, WF7 7EY (☎ 0977 795 450); 13-19 St Paul's St, Leeds, Yorkshire LS1 2JG (☎ 0532 424 220, fax 0532 424 297)

HARRIS, John Eric; s of Jack Harris (d 1982), of Ilford, Essex, and Freda, *née* Jacobs (d 1979); *b* 29 April 1932; *Educ* Slough GS, Plaistow GS; *m* 15 June 1958, Helene Hinda (d 1985), da of Aaron Coren (d 1960), of 19 Morton Way, Southgate, London N14; 1 s (Daniel Bruce b 1960), 1 da (Allyson b 1961); *Career* chm: Alba plc 1987, Harvard Int 1980-87, Bush Radio plc, Satellite Technol Systems Ltd; md Harris Overseas Ltd 1963-82, chm and tstee Helene Harris Meml Tst promoting res into ovarian cancer; dir Alba France SA; *Recreations* reading, bridge, golf, theatre, opera; *Clubs* Les Ambassadeurs; *Style*— John Harris, Esq; Arranmore, 19 Totteridge Village, London N20 8PN (☎ 01 446 3300); Harvard House, 14-16 Thames Rd, Barking, Essex OHX 1GII (☎ 01 594 5533, car tel 0034 214 309)

HARRIS, His Hon Judge John Percival Harris; DSC (1945), QC (1974); s of Thomas Percival Harris (d 1981), of Ebbor Hall, Somerset; *b* 16 Feb 1925; *Educ* Wells Cathedral Sch, Pembroke Coll Cambridge (BA); *m* 1959, Janet Valerie, da of Archibald William Douglas, of Jersey, CI; 1 s, 2 da; *Career* Sub Lt RNVR 1943-46, serv: Western Approaches, Far East, China, Japan; barr Middle Temple 1949 (master of the bench 1970), rec of Crown Ct 1972-80, circuit judge 1980-, dep sr Judge of the Ct of the Sovereign Base Area Cyprus; *Recreations* golf, reading, Victorian paintings; *Clubs* Woking GC, Rye, GC, The Royal St Goerge's GC; *Style*— His Hon Judge Harris, DSC, QC; Tudor Ct, Fairmile Park Rd, Cobham, Surrey KT11 2PP (☎ 0932 64756)

HARRIS, John Robert; TEM (1945); s of Maj Alfred Harris, CBE, DSO, and Rosa Alfreda, *née* Alderson; *b* 5 June 1919; *Educ* Harrow, Architectural Assoc Sch of Architecture (AA Dip); *m* 10 June 1950, Gillian, da of Col C W D Rowe, CB, MBE, TD, JP, DL (d 1954), of Peterborough; 1 s (Mark b 27 Sept 1952), 1 da (Georgina b 7 Aug 1956); *Career* active serv and TA 1939-45, Lt RE Hong Kong 1940-41, (POW of Japanese 1941-45); memb: Br Army Aid Gp China 1943-45, Hong Kong Resistance 1942-45; architect; fndr and sr ptnr J R Harris Partnership 1949- (fndr and sr ptnr assoc firms in Brunei, Dubai, Hong Kong, Oman, Qatar); projects won in int competition: State Hosp Qatar 1953, New Dubai Hosp 1976, Corniche Devpt and traffic intersection Dubai 1978, HQ for Min of Social Affrs and Lab Oman 1979, Tuen Mun Hosp Hong Kong 1981; int assessment Rulers off Devpt Dubai 1985, architect and planner Zhuhai New Town Econ Zone Peoples Republic of China 1984; major UK works incl: Stoke Mandeville Hosp 1983, Wellesley House and St Peters Ct Sch re-devpt 1975; major overseas works incl: Int Trade Centre (40 storey) Dubai 1982, Br Embassy chancery offs and ambassador's residence Abu Dhabi 1982, Univ Teaching Hosp Maiduguri Nigeria 1982, dept stores 1973-83 (Antwerp, Brussels, Lille, Paris, Strasbourg); FRIBA 1949, memb Survey Club 1960 (pres 1968), HKIA 1982, FRSA 1982; Membre de l'Ordre des Architects Francais 1978; *Books* John R Harris Architects (jtly 1984); *Recreations* arthitecture, sketching, boats ("Dream Lady"); *Clubs* Athenaeum, Royal Thames YC; *Style*— John Harris, Esq; 24 Devonshire Place, London W1N 2BX (☎ 01 935 9353, fax 01 935 5709)

HARRIS, Joseph Hugh; JP (Penrith, 1971), DL (1984); s of John Frederick Harris; *b* 3 June 1932; *Educ* Harrow, RAC Cirencester (DipAg); *m* 1957, Anne, da of Brig L H McRobert (d 1981); 3 s; *Career* Lt 11 Hussars PAO; chm Cumbrian Newspapers Ltd 1987- (formerly dir); farmer landowner, sr steward Royal Agric Soc 1960-77, memb Miny of Agric Northern Regnl Panel 1977-83, hon dir Royal Show 1978-82; chm dir Grasmere Sports 1977, chm govrs Aysgarth Sch 1975-, high sheriff Cumbria 1976-77, dep pres RASE 1987-;; *Recreations* shooting and field sports; *Style*— Joseph Harris Esq, JP, DL; Brackenburgh, Calthwaite, Penrith, Cumbria, CA11 9PW (☎ 076 885 253)

HARRIS, Leslie George; MBE (1972); s of William George Harris (d 1935), of Birmingham, of Florence Ann, *née* Deakin (d 1943); *b* 20 June 1905; *Educ* Birmingham Central Secdy Sch; *m* 1942, Edith Mary, da of Frederick Wood (d 1975); 2 s (Andrew b 1944, Richard b 1945), 1 da (Geraldine b 1951); *Career* fndr chm L G Harris & Co Ltd Stoke Prior, chm L G Harris & Co (SA Pty) Ltd; chm: L G Harris and Co (E Africa) Ltd 1964-, Harris (Ceylon) Ltd 1968-, Harris Brushes (Far East) Ltd 1984-, Margery Fry Meml Tst (hostels for ex-prisoners, chm 1963-72, pres 1972-); life govr Birmingham Univ 1972-; chm Mgmnt Res Gps (Midlands) 1960-62, fndr chm Avoncroft Museum of Bldgs 1963-79, (vice-pres 1979-), tstee Fircroft Coll Birmingham 1966-; *Recreations* golf, forestry, music; *Clubs* Blackwell; *Style*— Leslie G Harris, Esq, MBE; Ridge End, Hanbury, Worcs (☎ 052 784 359); L G Harris and Co Ltd, Stoke Prior, Worcs (☎ 0527 575441)

HARRIS, Hon Mrs (Linda Carol); *née* Bellow; yr da of Baron Bellwin, JP (Life Peer); *b* 1956; *m* 1976 (m dis 1988), Leslie Harris; *Style*— The Hon Mrs Harris; 46 Oakdene Drive, Leeds 17

HARRIS, Lyndon Goodwin; s of late Sydney Ernest Harris, of Halesowen, and late Mary Elsie, *née* Tilley; *b* 25 July 1928; *Educ* Halesowen GS, Birmingham Coll of Art, Slade Sch of Fine Art, Univ of London Inst of Educn (ATD), Courtauld Inst; *Career* works exhibited at: Paris Salon (gold medal in painting, hon mention in etching), RA, RSA, RBA, RGI, NEAC; works in permanent collections incl: Govt Art Collection, UCL, Birmingham and Midland Inst; works reproduced: Young Artists of Promise (Studio), The Artist (Masters of Water Colour and their Techniques), Royal Inst of Painters in Water Colours History and Membership List 1831-1981; scholarships: Leverhulme, Pilkington, Slade; Slade Anatomy Prizeman; memb: RI 1958, RSW 1952, RWA 1947; *Recreations* music (organ and pianoforte), cycling; *Style*— Lyndon Harris, Esq

HARRIS, Prof Martin Best; s of William Best Harris (d 1987), of Plymouth, and Betty Evelyn, *née* Martin; *b* 28 June 1944; *Educ* Devonport HS for Boys Plymouth, Queen's Coll Cambridge (BA, MA), Univ of London (PhD); *m* 10 Sept 1966, Barbara Mary, da of Joseph Daniels (d 1971); 2 s (Robert b 1 July 1968, Paul b 13 June 1970); *Career* lectr in french linguistics Univ of Leicester 1967-72; Univ of Salford: sr lectr in french linguistics 1972-76, prof of romance linguistics 1976-87, dean social science and arts 1978-81, pro vice cnllr 1981-87; vice chllr Univ of Essex 1987-, author of numerous books and articles on the romance languages; govr Colchester Sixth Form Coll; memb UGC 1983-87 (chm NI sub-ctee 1984-), cncl memb Philological Soc; *Books* Evolution of French Syntax (1978), The Romance Verb (with N Vincent, 1983), The Romance Languages (with N Vincent, 1988); *Recreations* walking, gardening, wine; *Style*— Prof Martin Harris; University of Essex, Wivenhoe Park, Colchester, Essex, CO4 3SQ (☎ 0206 872000, fax 0206 869493)

HARRIS, (Maurice) Martin; s of Sidney Simon Harris, and Mignonette, *née* Jonas; *b* 29 Dec 1927; *m* 1, 21 June 1951, Betty (d 1981), da of Morris Rei (d 1967); 1 s (Philip Anthony b 15 Sept 1953), 1 da (Louise b 19 March 1955); m 2, 9 March 1983, June Marlene; *Career* Gaumont Br News 1942-53, cmmnd photographer with army in British W Africa 1947-49, started own film prodn co 1953, made over 40 films for Rank Film Distributors; exclusive film rights: Melbourne Olympics 1956, Investiture of Prince of Wales 1969; made feature film A Prince for Wales (incl first public interview with HRH The Prince of Wales); MRPS, MBKS; *Style*— Martin Harris, Esq; 14 Haywood Close, Pinner, Middx HA5 3LO (☎ 01 866 9466)

HARRIS, Martin Richard; s of Col T B Harris, DSO (d 1965), of Bexhill-on-Sea, Sussex, and Phyllis Margaret, *née* Goode (d 1972); bro Oliver Harris, *qv*; family members of Drapers' Co since 1760; *b* 30 August 1922; *Educ* Wellington Coll, Trinity Hall Cambridge; *m* 1952, Diana Moira, da of R W Gandar Dower (d 1967), of 15 Ennismore Gdns, London SW1; 4 s (Andrew, Colin, Thomas, Peter); *Career* WWII Capt RE serv Middle East and Italy 1941-46; CA; Price Waterhouse & Co 1946-74 (ptnr 1956-74), dir gen of the City Panel on Take-overs and Mergers 1974-77; dir: Reckitt and Colman 1977-82 (dep chm 1979-82), NatWest Bank 1977-, Nat West Investmt Bank 1977-, Inmos Int 1980-84, Equity and Law Life Assur Soc 1981- (dep chm 1983-87), The De La Rue Co 1981-, Westland 1981-85, TR Industl and Gen Tst 1983-88; chm The Nineteen Twenty-Eight Investmt Tst 1984-86; govr QMC London 1979-, memb cncl RCM 1985-; memb ct: The Worshipful Co of Drapers 1978- (master 1987-88), Co of CAs 1972- (master 1983-84); FCA, FRCM US Silver Star 1945; *Recreations* music, antique furniture and china, philately; *Clubs* Carlton, MCC, Pilgrims; *Style*— Martin Harris Esq; 29 Belvedere Grove, Wimbledon, London SW19 7RQ (☎ 01 946 0951); Equitable House, 48 King William St, London EC4R 9DJ (☎ 01 623 0532)

HARRIS, Michael Abraham Philip; s of Louis Harris (d 1974), of 7 Clarendon Ct, Clarendon Rd, Southsea, Hants, and Rebecca, *née* Peter; *b* 14 Mar 1937; *Educ* Portsmouth GS, Queen's Coll Oxford (MA); *m* 11 Aug 1963, Sylvia Freda, da of Joshua Berman (d 1969), of Grove Rd South, Southsea, Hants; 2 s (David, Jonathan), 1 da (Claire); *Career* slr 1965; tstee and hon slr Portsmouth and Southsea Hebrew Soc; memb: Law Soc, Hants Inc Law Soc 1965-; *Recreations* all sport (especially cricket and soccer), bridge, classical music; *Clubs* Old Portmuthian; *Style*— Michael A P Harris, Esq; 16 Burbridge Grove, Southsea, Hants, PO4 9RR (☎ 0705 825 129); 106 Victoria Road North, Portsmouth, Hants, PO5 1QG (☎ 0705 828 611, fax 0705 736 978)

HARRIS, Capt Michael George Temple; s of Cdr Antony John Temple Harris, OBE, RN of Wickham, Hants, and Doris, *née* Drake; *b* 5 July 1941; *Educ* Pangbourne, RNC Dartmouth; *m* 17 Oct 1970, (Caroline) Katrina, da of Gp Capt Patrick George Chichester, OBE, RAF (d 1983), of Hayne Manor, Stowford, Devon; 3 da (Tamsin b 1971, Rebecca b 1973, Emily b 1979); *Career* Sub Lt RN 1961, Lt 1963, Cdr 1975, Capt 1980, Rear Adm 1989; served: home, Med, submarines, Canada, long TAS course, submarine CO's Course, North Pole 1976, staff of flag offr submarines 1977-79, Capt HMS Cardiff 1980-82, Falklands Campaign, Capt 3 Submarine Sqdn 1982-85, central staff MOD 1985-87, Capt HMS Ark Royal 1987-89; FRGS 1978, FNI 1988; *Recreations* fishing, reading, bellringing; *Clubs* Naval and Military; *Style*— Capt Michael Harris, RN; c/o Naval Secretary, Ministry of Defence, Spring Gardens, Whitehall, London SW1A 2BE

HARRIS, Oliver Birkbeck; s of Col T B Harris, DSO, RE (d 1965), of Bexhill-on-Sea, Sussex, and Phyllis Margaret, *née* Goode (d 1972); bro Martin Harris, *qv*; *b* 28 Feb 1929; *Educ* Wellington Coll; *m* 20 Aug 1966, Caroline Mary, da of Lt Col J Y B Sharpe, RA, of Godalming, Surrey; 2 s (John b 1967, Robert b 1972), 1 da (Felicity b 1968); *Career* Nat Serv cmmnd 2 Lt RE 1952-54; ptnr Rowley Pemberton Roberts 1959-69, sec Baring Bros & Co Ltd and dir various subsid cos 1969-85; dir Nat Heritage Meml Fund 1988- (dep dir 1985-88), assoc memb Lloyds 1965 (memb 1968), memb ctee of mgmnt Abbotstone Agric Property Unit Tst 1975-; FCA, AMSIA; *Recreations* philately, gardening, history; *Clubs* City of London, Army and Navy, MCC; *Style*— Oliver Harris, Esq; Eden House, Winkworth Hill, Godalming, Surrey

(☎ 048 632 236); Nat Heritage Memorial Fund, 10 St James's St, London SW1A 1EF (☎ 01 930 0963, fax 01 930 0968)

HARRIS, Paul Haydn Beverley; s of Michael James Harris, and Vivien Diana, *née* Hoyland; *b* 4 Sept 1945; *Educ* Emanuel Sch, The Univ of Kent at Canterbury (BA); *m* 27 Oct 1979, Amanda Helen, da of late Arthur Robert Charles Stiby, TD, JP; 1 s (Kit b 1988); *Career* broadcaster and writer; radio and TV newsreader and presenter 1973-86, BBC staff 1970-80, freelance 1980-, currently specialising in prodn of commercial educnl and med videos and films; memb local RNLI ctee, widely involved in charity fund-raising in S of England; *Recreations* cricket, carriage driving, writing, fine art, ceramics; *Clubs* Hants CCC; *Style—* Paul Harris, Esq; Mile Tree House, Crawley, Winchester, Hampshire SO21 2QF (☎ 0962 885916)

HARRIS, Paul Ratliff; OBE (1980); s of Maurice Harris, of Bexhill; *b* 31 August 1913; *Educ* Gresham's; *m* 1946, Barbara, da of Lyn Albrecht, of Melbourne; 3 s, 1 da; *Career* Lt-Col SE Asia Cmd, HQ Supreme Allied Cmmd; chm MP Harris Hldgs (ret); *Recreations* golf, sailing, vintage cars; *Clubs* Naval, IOD; *Style—* Paul Harris, Esq, OBE; Island House, South St, Lewes, E Sussex BN7 2BS (☎ 0273 471 683)

HARRIS, Prof Peter Charles; s of David Jonathan Valentine Harris (d 1987), and Nellie Dean, *née* Blakemore (d 1986); *b* 26 May 1923; *Educ* St Olave's and St Saviours GS, King's Coll Hosp London (MB BS, MD, PhD); *m* 24 Jan 1952 (m dis 1982), Felicity Margaret, da of Prof Hamilton Hartridge (d 1977); 2 da (Sophie b 1956, Libbie b 1964); *Career* Simon Marks prof of cardiology Univ of London, physician Nat Heart Hosp 1966-88; Freeman City of: La Paz 1966, Winnipeg 1986; FRCP 1964; *Books* The Human Pulmonary Circulation (with D Heath, 1986); *Recreations* painting, music; *Style—* Prof Peter Harris; 42 Great Percy St, London WC1; Cannaregio 4627, Venezia (☎ 01 278 2911)

HARRIS, Gp Capt Peter Langridge; CBE (1988), AE (1961 and clasp 1971), DL (Greater London 1986); s of Arthur Langridge Harris (d 1975), of Eastbourne, and Doris Mabel, *née* Offen (d 1978); *b* 6 Sept 1929; *Educ* St Edward's Sch Oxford, Birmingham Univ (BSc); *m* 29 Dec 1955, (Yvonne) Patricia, da of Arthur James Stone, DSM (d 1986), of Southsea; 2 da (Sally b 1960, Philippa b 1962); *Career* FARVR 1947-60, RAuxAF 1960-88, Gp Capt 1983, inspr 1983-88, ADC to HM The Queen 1984-88, vice chm (air) TA & VR Assoc for Greater London 1988-; chartered engr; Elliott Bros (London) Ltd 1952-55, Decca Navigator Co Ltd 1955-59, Elliott-Automation GEC plc 1959-; FIEE 1976; *Recreations* travel, gardening; *Clubs* RAF; *Style—* Gp Capt Peter L Harris, CBE, AE, DL; 10 Dolphin Court, St Helen's Parade, Southsea, Hants (☎ 0705 817602); Marconi Defence Systems Ltd, Elstree Way, Borehamwood, Herts WD6 1RX (☎ 01 906 6633, telex 22777)

HARRIS, Sir Philip Charles; s of Charles William Harris, and Ruth Ellen, *née* Ward; *b* 15 Sept 1942; *Educ* Streatham GS; *m* 1960, Pauline Norma, da of Bertie William Chumley (d 1968); 3 s, 1 da; *Career* chm Harris Queensway plc 1964 (chief exec 1987); non exec dir Fisons plc 1986; memb: Br Showjumping Assoc, cncl of govrs Utd Med and Dental Schs of St Guys and St Thomas's Hosps 1984, Ct of Patrons RGOG 1984; govr Nat Hosp for Nervous Diseases 1985; Hambro Business Man of the Year 1983; kt 1985; *Recreations* showjumping, cricket; *Style—* Philip Harris, Esq; Harris Queensway plc, Harris House, 76 High St, Orpington, Kent BL6 0LX (☎ 0689 36977)

HARRIS, Philip James; s of Philip John Harris, of Avenue Diecelles, Montreal, Canada, and Violet Edna May, *née* Fretwell; *b* 4 Oct 1936; *Educ* Northampton Sch of Art, Watford Coll of Technol; *m* 1, 20 April 1959 (m dis 1977), Audrey Mary, da of Richard Stanley Flawn (d 1968), of The Old Manor, Irthlingborough, Northants; 1 s (Philip Julian b 1964), 1 da (Susan Mary (Mrs Goodwin) b 1967); m 2, 15 March 1980, Esther Elizabeth, da of James Buchanan (d 1982), of Blunham, Beds; *Career* Parachute Regt 1955-58 active serv: Cyprus, Eoka Campaign, Suez; chief exec Reporter Newspapers Kent 1977-79, dir and gen mangr Middx Co Press 1979-83; currently md: B Lansdown & Sons Trowbridge 1983-, Wessex Newspapers Bath 1987-; pres SW Fedn Newspaper Owners, vice pres Newsvendors Benevolent Inst; memb: Patrons Club, W Wilts Cons Assoc; memb IOD 1985, FBIM 1983, MIIM 1979, memb Inst of Printing 1981; *Recreations* horse racing, polo, rowing (all spectator); *Clubs* Leander, Bath and County, Guards Polo, Cirencester Polo; *Style—* Philip Harris, Esq; 18 Palairet Close, Bradford-on-Avon, Wiltshire (☎ 02 216 4223); Principal Office, Wessex Newspapers, Westgate St, Bath BA1 1EW (☎ 0225 444 044, fax 0225 446 495, car tel 0836 260 788)

HARRIS, Phillip; s of Simon Harris (d 1970), and Sarah Leah *née* Horowts (d 1984); *b* 28 Mar 1922; *Educ* Royal HS Edinburgh, Univ of Edinburgh; *m* 7 Nov 1949, Sheelagh Shena, da of Harry Coutts (d 1977); 1 s (Harvey b 14 May 1953), 1 da (Frances b 27 Oct 1950); *Career* Capt RAMC 1945-48; Univ of Edinburgh: sr conslt neurosurgeon dept of clinical neurosciences, sr lectr dept of surgical neurology, lectr dept of linguistics; visiting prof in univs worldwide; pres Br Cervical Spine Assoc, sr del Br Neurosurgeons to the World Fedn of Neurological Surgery, pres Scottish Sports Assoc for the Disabled, dir and tstee Scottish Tst For the Physically Disabled, hon memb Scottish Paraplegic Assoc, cncl memb Thistle Fndn Scotland, memb Med Appeals Tbnl Scotland; ed Paraplegia (the int jl of the spine); LRCP Edinburgh, LRCS Edinburgh, LRFP Glasgow, LRCS Glasgow, FRCS Edinburgh, FRCP Edinburgh, FRCS Glasgow;; *Books* Head Injuries (ed 1971), Epilepsy (ed 1974), Spine (ed 1987); *Recreations* sport, music, art, travel; *Clubs* New (Edinburgh), Edinburgh Univ, Royal Scottish Automobile (Glasgow); *Style—* Phillip Harris, Esq; 4/5 Fettes Rise, Edinburgh EH4 1QH (☎ 031 552 8900); Murray Field Hospital, Corstorphine, Edinburgh (☎ 031 334 0363); Royal College of Surgeons, Nicolson Street, Edinburgh (☎ 031 668 2557)

HARRIS, The Ven Reginald (Brian); s of Reginald George Harris (d 1985), of Kent, and Ruby C Harris; *b* 14 August 1934; *Educ* Eltham Coll, Christs's Coll Cambridge (MA), Ridley Hall Cambridge; *m* 1959, Anne Patricia, da of George Frederick Hughes (d 1986); 1 s (Nigel b 1962), 1 da (Celia b 1963); *Career* archdeacon of Manchester 1980-, canon residentiary of Manchester Cathedral 1980-, sub-dean 1986-; curate of Wednesbury 1959-61, curate of Uttoxeter 1961-64, vicar of St Peter Bury 1964-70, vicar and rural dean of Walmsley 1970-80; *Recreations* long distance walking, painting; *Style—* The Ven the Archdeacon of Manchester; 4 Victoria Avenue, Eccles, Manchester M30 9HA (☎ 061 707 6444)

HARRIS, Richard Leslie; s of William Leslie Freer Harris (d 1956), of Romsley Worcs, and Lucy Penelope Harris (d 1976); *b* 31 Mar 1927; *Educ* Shrewsbury; *m* 1955, Jane, da of Herbert Charles Oxenhad, of Rhvallt, St Asaph; 2 s; *Career* stockbroker and CA; ptnr Harris Allday Lea and Brooks; memb: Stock Exchange 1961, Stock Exchange Cncl; chm: Midlands and Western Stock Exchange 1969, Feoffees Old Swinford Hosp Sch; Freeman City of London; *Clubs* Birmingham; *Style—* Richard Harris, Esq; 23 Farlands Rd, Old Swinford, Stourbridge, W Midlands DY8 2DD (☎ 0384 5760); Harris, Allday, Lea and Brooks, Stock Exchange Buildings, 33 Great Charles St, Queensway, Birmingham B3 3JN (☎ 021 233 1222)

HARRIS, Richard Travis; 2 son of Douglas Harris (d 1964), and Emmeline, *née* Travis; *b* 15 April 1919; *Educ* Charterhouse, RMA Woolwich; *m* 1, 1941 (m dis 1953), June Constance, *née* Rundle; 2 da; m 2, 1953, Margaret Sophia Nye, *née* Aron; 1 s, 1 da; *Career* joined Royal Signals 1939, France 1940, W Desert 1941-43, Italy 1943, Staff Coll 1944, instr Sch of Inf 1944-45, BAOR 1945-46, Sudan Def Force 1947-50, ret Lt-Col 1950; md Rediffusion (Nigeria) Ltd 1951-54, dep gen mangr Assoc Rediffusion Ltd 1954-57, md Coates & Co (Plymouth) Ltd 1957-63, md Dollond & Aitchison Gp Ltd 1964-70, chm and md Dollond & Aitchison Gp Ltd 1970-78 (dir 1964-86), dep chm Gallaher Ltd 1978-84 (dir 1970-87), dir Burton Gp plc 1984-; chm: IOD 1982-85, (vice-pres 1985-); Wilder Share Ownership Cncl 1988-; govr Royal Shakespeare Theatre, memb cncl Birmingham Univ; *Recreations* flyfishing, theatre; *Clubs* Athenaeum, Royal Western YC; *Style—* Richard Harris, Esq; 21 Lucy's Mill, Mill Lane, Stratford-upon-Avon, Warwicks CV37 6DE (☎ 0789 299631)

HARRIS, Sir Ronald Montague Joseph; KCVO (1960, MVO 1943), CB (1956); only s of Rev Joseph Montague Harris by his w Edith Annesley, 4 da of George Forbes Malcolmson, whose w Catherine Annesley was paternal gda of Sir Henry Austen, JP, DL; Sir Henry's maternal grandmother was Hon Helen Thompson, da of 1 Baron Haversham (cr 1696) by his w Lady Frances Annesley (da of 1 Earl of Anglesey of the 1661 creation); *b* 6 May 1913; *Educ* Harrow, Trinity Coll Oxford; *m* 1, 1939, Margaret Julia (d 1955), eldest da of John Robert Wharton; 1 s (Jocelin), 3 da (Imogen, Celia, Olivia); m 2, 1957, Marjorie, widow of Julian Tryon and da of Sir Harry Verney, 4 Bt, DSO, by his w Lady Rachel, *née* Bruce, da of 9 Earl of Elgin and Kincardine; 1 step s (decd), 1 step da (Edith); *Career* Civil Serv 1936, Burma Off 1936-39, War Cabinet Secretariat 1939-44, India Offr 1944-46, private sec to sec of state for India and Burma 1946-47, Treasy 1949-52, Cabinet Off 1952-55, perm cmmr Crown Lands 1955, second Crown Estate cmmr 1956-60, third sec HM Treasy 1960-64, sec Church Cmmrs for England 1964-68, first Church Estates cmmr 1969-82, chm Central Bd of Fin 1978-82; dir General Accident Fire and Life Assur Corpn 1970-84; govr and vice-chm Yehudi Menuhin Sch; *Books* Memory-soft the Air (recollections of life and service with Cabinet, Crown and Church) (1987); *Clubs* Boodles; *Style—* Sir Ronald Harris, KCVO, CB; Slyfield Farm House, Stoke D'Abernon, Cobham, Surrey

HARRIS, Rosemary Jeanne; da of Marshal of the RAF Sir Arthur Harris, 1 Bt, GCB, OBE, AFC (d 1984), and Barbara Daisy Kyrle (d 1986), da of Lt-Col E W K Money, KSLI; gf and gt-uncs were the famous ten Fighting Battyes chronicled by Younghusband's Story of the Guides and by Evelyn Battye in her book The Fighting Ten; *b* 20 Feb 1923; *Educ* privately, Thorneloe Sch Weymouth, Chelsea Sch of Art, Dept of Technol Courtauld Inst; *Career* author of fiction, thrillers and children's books; picture restorer 1949, reviewer of children's books for The Times 1970-73; *Books* plays: Peronik (1976), The Unknown Enchantment (1981); books: The Summer-House (1956), Voyage to Cythera (1958), Venus with Sparrows (1961), All My Enemies (1967), The Nice Girl's Story (1968), A Wicked Pack of Cards (1969), The Double Snare (1975), Three Candles for the Dark (1976); for children: Moon in the Cloud (won Carnegie Medal for 1968), The Shadow on the Sun (1970), The Seal-Singing (1971), The Child in the Bamboo Grove (1971), The Bright and Morning Star (1972), The King's White Elephant (1973), The Lotus and the Grail (1974), The Flying Ship (1974), The Little Dog of Fo (1976), I Want to be a Fish (1977), A Quest for Orion (1978), Beauty and the Beast (1979), Greenfinger House (1979), Tower of the Stars (1980), The Enchanted Horse (1981), Janni's Stork (1982), Zed (1982), Heidi (adapted 1983), Summers of the Wild Rose (1987), Love and the Merry-go-Round (ed poetry anthology, 1988); *Recreations* music, reading, gardening; *Style—* Miss Rosemary Harris; c/o A P Watt Ltd, Literary Agents, 20 John St, London WC1N 2DL

HARRIS, Rosina Mary; da of Alfred Harris, DSO, CBE (d 1976); *b* 30 May 1921; *Educ* Oxford (BCL, MA); *Career* WWII serv with American Ambulance Corps in the UK; slr; sr ptnr Joynson-Hicks 1977-86; dep chm of Blundell-Permoglaze Hldgs 1981-86; Queen's Silver Jubilee Medal; *Recreations* riding, opera, theatre; *Style—* Miss Rosina Harris; 23 Devonshire Place, London W1 (☎ 01 935 6041)

HARRIS, Hon Mrs (Thelma Eirene); *née* Kitson; da of 2 Baron Airedale, JP; *b* 1902; *m* 1923, Noel Gordon Harris (d 1963), s of Sir Alexander Harris, KCMG, CB, CVO); 1 s (James b 1933, who assumed the additional forename of Mallet, m Primrose, da of late Sir Philip du Cros, 2 Bt, by 1 w Dita, da of Sir Claude Mallet, CMG; 3 da (Mrs Edward Griffith b 1924, Mrs Michael Johnson b 1926, Mrs James Arnot b 1931); *Style—* The Hon Mrs Harris; 28 Lyttleton Court, Lyttleton Road, London N2 0EB

HARRIS, William Barclay; QC (1961); s of William Cecil Harris (d 1942), and Rhoda Mary, *née* Barclay (d 1961); landed gentry family formerly of Westcotes; *b* 25 Nov 1911; *Educ* Harrow, Trinity Coll Cambridge (MA); *m* 1937, Elizabeth Hermione, da of Capt Sir Clive Milnes-Coates, 2 Bt, OBE, JP, and Lady Celia, *née* Crewe-Milnes, JP (da of 1 and last Marquess of Crewe, KG); 1 s (Jonathan), 2 da (Jessica, Hermione); *Career* WWII 1940-45 Coldstream Gds served: N Africa, Italy, Germany (despatches), demob Maj; barr Inner Temple 1937; chm Rowton Hotels 1965-83; Church cmmr 1966-82, chm Redundant Churches Ctee 1972-82, chm Georgian Gp 1985; Liveryman Worshipful Co Merchant Taylors; *Recreations* shooting; *Clubs* Brooks's, Athenaeum, MCC; *Style—* William Harris Esq, QC; Moatlands, East Grinstead, West Sussex (☎ 0342 810228); 29 Barkston Gdns, London SW5 (☎ 01 373 8793)

HARRIS, William Cecil; s of Richard Cecil Harris (d 1928), and Florence Maud, *née* Fisher (1969); *b* 3 Dec 1913; *Educ* William Hulmes Sch Manchester; *m* 1940, Florence Annie, da of James Henry Tidswell (d 1942); 1 s; *Career* WWII served Flt Lt Burma (BAFSEA); insur exec; dep chm Phoenix Gp 1979-84 (chief gen mangr 1969-78); pres Chartered Insur Inst 1972-73, chm Br Insur Assoc 1976; Master Worshipful Co of Insurers 1979-81; *Recreations* golf, forestry; *Clubs* City of London, Pilgrims; *Style—* William Harris, Esq; Hardbarrow Copse, Threals Lane, W Chiltington, Pulborough (☎ 079 83 2300); Apartment 146, 3 Whithall Court, SW1A 2EL (☎ 01 930 8859)

HARRIS, Sir William Gordon; KBE (1969), CB (1963); s of Capt James Whyte Harris, RNR (d 1952); *b* 10 June 1912; *Educ* Liverpool Coll, Sidney Sussex Coll Cambridge (MA); *m* 1938, Margaret Emily, da of John Steel Harvie (d 1951); 3 s, 1 da; *Career* civil engr; joined Admty 1937, civil engr-in-chief Admiralty 1959, dir-gen Navy Works Admty 1960-63; dir-gen: of Works Miny of Public Bldgs and Works 1963-65, highways Miny of Tport (later Environment) 1965-73; ptnr Peter Fraenkel &

Ptnrs 1973-78; chief Br del: Perm Int Assoc of Navigation Congresses 1969-85 (vice-pres 1976-79), Perm Int Assoc of Road Congresses 1970-73; Hon Seabee (US Navy) 1961, Decoration for Distinguished Civilian Serv (US Army) 1985; pres: Inst of Civil Engrs 1974-75, Smeatonian Soc of Civil Engrs 1983-84; chm: Construction Indust Manpower Bd 1976-80, B & CE Holiday Mgmnt Co 1978-87, Dover Harbour Bd 1980-83; dir Br Sch of Osteopathy 1982-; Hon DSc City Univ 1977; FEng, FICE; *Recreations* gardening, walking, music, 10 grandchildren; *Style—* Sir William Harris, KBE, CB; 3 Rofant Rd, Northwood, Middx HA6 3BD (☎ 092 74 25899)

HARRIS OF GREENWICH, Baron (Life Peer UK 1974); John Henry Harris; s of Alfred Harris; *b* 5 April 1930; *Educ* Pinner GS; *m* 1, 1952 (m dis 1982), Patricia, da of George Alstrom; 1 s (Hon Francis b 1961), 1 da (Hon Deborah b 1958) 1 da; m 2, 1983, Angela, da of Joseph Arthur Smith; *Career* sits as SDP Peer in House of Lords; PA to ldr of oppn (Rt Hon Hugh Gaitskell) 1959, dir of publicity Labour Pty 1962-64; special asst to: Foreign Sec 1964-66, Home Sec 1966-67; chllr Exchequer 1967-70, min of state Home Off 1974-79; pres Nat Assoc of Sr Probation Offrs, chm Parole Bd England and Wales 1979-82; political corrt The Economist 1970-74; *Style—* The Rt Hon the Lord Harris of Greenwich; House of Lords, London SW1

HARRIS OF HIGH CROSS, Baron (Life Peer UK 1979); Ralph Harris; s of William Henry Harris (d 1954); *b* 10 Dec 1924; *Educ* Tottenham GS, Queens' Coll Cambridge; *m* 1949, Jose Pauline, da of Roger Fredrick Jeffery (d 1975); 1 s (Hon Julian Paul), 1 da (and 1 s decd); *Career* sits as Independent Peer in Lords; contested (C): Kirkcaldy 1951, Edinburgh 1955; ldr writer Glasgow Herald 1956, lectr in political economy St Andrews Univ 1949-56, gen dir Inst of Econ Affrs 1957-87 (chm 1987-); memb cncl Univ of Buckingham; dir Churchill Press; tstee: Ross McWhirter Fndn, Wincott Fndn, Centre for Research into Communist Econs; *Books* Politics Without Prejudice, End of Government, Challenge of a Radical Reactionary, No Minister!; *Style—* The Rt Hon the Lord Harris of High Cross; 2 Lord North St, London SW1 (☎ 01 799 3745); 4 Walmar Close, Beech Hill, Hadley Wood, Barnet, Herts (☎ 01 449 6212)

HARRISON, Anthony Augustus Bertie; s of Capt Augustus Bertie Harrison (d 1930), of 41 Cornwallis Rd, Holloway, London N7, and Dorothy Rosina, *née* Schafe-Harrissen (d 1980); *b* 4 June 1920; *Educ* Highgate Sch, Cambridge Univ; *m* 1, 29 March 1959 (m dis 1970), Marie, *née* McKenna-Lewis; 1 da (Antonia Michelle b 11 Dec 1961); m 2, 26 March 1971, Veronica Lesley, da of Capt Norman Hack, of 67 Kent View Rd, Vange, Essex; *Career* enlisted RAC 1939, cmmnd 1940, appointed Capt in Field Western Desert Egypt 1942, demob 1946; chm: Harrison & Willis Ltd 1958-83, HW Task Force 1982-85, Peats Investmts Ltd 1978-82; dir: Forrest Harrison Orgn 1950-53, Mervyn Hughes & Co 1953-58, Esquire Catering Co Ltd 1983-; vice pres Variety Club of GB 1976-82, ctee memb Save the Family Appeal 1982-, govr Royal Masonic Hosp; JP 1977-85; Freeman City of London 1980, memb Worshipful Co of Painter Stainers Co Hon Citizen Arizona USA 1982; FBIM 1965, FIAA 1968, MIEC 1963, FRPS 1962, FInst D 1965; *Recreations* sailing, music; *Clubs* City Livery, Royal Temple YC, Coda (sec 1987-); *Style—* Anthony Harrison, Esq; 29 Thamespoint, Fairways, Teddington TW11 9PP (☎ 01 977 9473); 214 Piccadilly, London W1 (☎ 01 734 9695)

HARRISON, Lt-Col Antony Roy; TD (1946), DL (1947); s of Ernest Charlton Harrison (d 1951), of Hill Crest, Whittington Rd, Worcester; *b* 17 June 1905; *Educ* King's Sch Worcester; *m* 1932, Margaret Lovell, da of Sidney Charles Harrison, of Birmingham; 3 s, 1 da; *Career* Lt-Col 1943, cmd 61 Inf Divn Battle Sch 1943, cmd 1 Worcs Regt 1944, cmd 8 Worcs Regt 1945, served NW Europe (despatches 1944); slr 1928; hon slr to Worcs CCC 1947-84 (hon life memb 1984); *Recreations* fishing, shooting, golf; *Clubs* Royal and Ancient GC; *Style—* Lt-Col A R Harrison, TD, DL; Lobden, Upper Colwall, nr Malvern, Worcs (☎ 0684 40590)

HARRISON, (Alastair) Brian Clarke; DL (Essex 1980); s of late Brig E Harrison, of Melbourne; *b* 3 Oct 1921; *Educ* Geelong GS, Trinity Coll Cambridge; *m* 1952, Elizabeth Hood Hardie, of NSW; 1 s, 1 da; *Career* Capt AIF; farmer; MP (C) Maldon 1955-74, PPS to: Min State Colonial Off 1955-56, Sec State for War 1956-58; min Agric 1958-60; visited US on Ford Fndn English Speaking Union fellowship 1957; former memb: One Nation Gp, Cwlth Parly Delgn to Kenya, Somalia and Aden 1960; reported on Br Pacific Territories for colonial sec 1965; organiser (with Univ of W Australia) of expeditions to Nepal studying human physiology 1980-84; High Sheriff Essex 1979; *Publications*: (with others) The cumulative effect of High altitude on Motor performance, A comparison between causasian visitors and native highlanders (1985), Entrainment of respiratory frequency to exercise rhythm during hypoxia (1987); *Books* The cumulative effect of High Altitude on Motor Performance, A Comparison Between Caucasian Visitors and Native Highlanders (1985), Entrainment of Respiratory Frequency to Excercise Rhythm During Hypoxia (1987); *Clubs* Pratt's, Melbourne, Weld (Perth); *Style—* Brian Harrison, Esq, DL; Green Farm House, Copford, Colchester, Essex; Mundethana, Orchid Valley, Kojonup, W Australia

HARRISON, Brian Fraser; s of James Fraser Harrison, county ct judge (d 1971); *b* 6 Sept 1918; *Educ* St Christopher's Sch, Liverpool Coll for Boys; *m* 1939, Constance Kathleen Fraser, da of John Edward Bennion (d 1962); 1 s; *Career* WWII RASC (TA) served, Gold Coast and Br West Africa; slr, ptnr Mace & Jones 1948-83, memb Lord Chllr's Circuit Advsy Ctee (Liverpool) 1972-81; professional mil artist 1983-; author; *Books* Advocacy at Petty Sessions, A Business of Your Own, A Business of Your Own Today, Work of a Magistrate, How to Select Your Professional Advisers - And Get the Best Out of Them, How to Make More Money as a Freelance Bookkeeper, How to Be a Successful Outside Caterer, How to Make Money as a Neighbourhood Handyman, How to Get What You Really Want Out of Life; *Recreations* art, writing, walking; *Style—* Brian Fraser Harrison, Esq; Peddars Cottage, The Street, Hessett, Bury St Edmunds IP30 9AX (☎ 0359 70409)

HARRISON, Christopher John; s of John Forth Harrison (d 1947), of Manchester, and Margaret Heywood, *née* Ham; *b* 20 August 1934; *Educ* St Edwards Sch Oxford; *m* 15 July 1961, Daphne Gwen, da of Trevor Spickett Roberts (d 1985), of Cardiff; 2 s (Robert, James); *Career* Price Waterhouse & Co 1958-61; ptnr: Richard Leyshon & Co 1961-64, Brown Harrison Weare & Co (formerly Longdon Griffiths Griffin & Co 1964-); pres Cardiff Caledonian Sec 1973-74 (sec 1964-73); FCA 1958; *Recreations* golf; *Clubs* Glamorganshire GC, Rotary; *Style—* Christopher Harrison, Esq; Machrihanish, 16 Clinton Rd, Penarth CF6 2JB (☎ 0222 708 978); Brown Harrison Weare & Co, Midland Bank Chambers, 97-100 Bute St, Cardiff CF1 6PP (☎ 0222 480 167)

HARRISON, Claude William; s of Harold Harrison (d 1976), and Florence Mildred, *née* Ireton (d 1986); *b* 31 Mar 1922; *Educ* Hutton GS, Harris Art Sch Preston, Liverpool City Sch of Art, RCA (ARCA); *m* 1 March 1947, Audrey, da of Arthur John Johnson (d 1964); 1 s (Tobias b 1950); *Career* WWII RAF 1942-47; serv: India, Burma, China; painter of conversation pieces, portraits, figure compositions; exhibitions: RA, London, Florida, NY, Chicago; RSPP 1961; *Books* The Portrait Painters Handbook (1968), Book of Tobit (1970); *Recreations* walking and reading; *Style—* Claude Harrison, Esq; Barrow Wife, Cartmel Fell, Grange over Sands, Cumbria LA11 6NZ (☎ 053 95 31323)

HARRISON, Sir (Robert) Colin; 4 Bt (UK 1922), of Eaglescliffe, Co Durham; s of late Sir John Fowler Harrison, 2 Bt, and Kathleen Lady Harrison, *qv*; suc bro, Sir (John) Wyndham Harrison, 3 Bt 1955; *b* 25 May 1938; *Educ* Radley, St John's Coll Cambridge; *m* 1963, Maureen Marie, da of E Leonard Chiverton, of Garth Corner, Vivers Place, Kirkbymoorside, Yorks; 1 s, 2 da (Rachel b 1966, Claire b 1974); *Heir* s, John Wyndham Fowler Harrison b 14 Dec 1972; *Career* Nat Serv cmmnd 5 Royal Northumberland Fusiliers 1957-59; chm Young Master Printers Nat Ctee 1972-73; *Style—* Sir Colin Harrison, Bt; The Grange, Rosedale Abbey, Pickering, N Yorks YO18 8RD (☎ 075 15 329)

HARRISON, David; s of Harold David Harrison (d 1987), of Exeter, Devon, and Lavinia, *née* Wilson; *b* 3 May 1930; *Educ* Bede Sch Sunderland, Clacton Co HS, Selwyn Coll Cambridge (BA, PhD, MA, ScD); *m* 11 Aug 1962, Sheila Rachel, da of Denis Richardson Debes, of Little Budworth, Ches; 2 s (Michael b 1963, Tony b 1966, d 1986), 1 da (Sarah b 1965); *Career* Nat Serv 2 Lt REME 1949; Cambridge Univ: lectr 1956-79, fell Selwyn Coll 1957- (sr tutor 1967-79), chm bd of tstees Homerton Coll 1979-; visiting prof Delaware Univ USA 1967and Sydney Univ Aust 1976; vice chllr: Keele Univ 1979-84, Exeter Univ 1984-; chm UCCA 1984-; FEng 1 FRSC, FRIC 1961, FIChemE 1968, FRSA 1985; *Books* Fluidised Particles (with J F Davidson, 1963), Fluidization (with J F Davidson and R Cliff, second edn 1985); *Recreations* music, tennis, hill walking, good food; *Clubs* Athenaeum, Fdn House (Stoke-on-Trent); *Style—* Dr David Harrison; Redcot, Streatham Dr, Exeter; 7 Gough Way, Cambridge; University of Exeter, Northcote House, The Queen's Drive, Exeter (☎ 0392 263 000, fax 0392 263 108, telex 42894 EXUNIV G)

HARRISON, David Richard; s of Richard Frankland Harrison (d 1973), and Muriel Eileen (d 1963), *née* Wilson; *b* 3 June 1932; *Educ* Clayesmore Sch Blandford Dorset; *m* 12 Sept 1959, Diana, da of Gerald Clay Megson (d 1982); 1 s (Richard b 31 Aug 1964), 1 da (Caroline b 8 Sept 1966); *Career* CA 1957; sec: Oldham C of C and Indust 1971, sec Oldham branch RNLI 1961; FCA 1962; *Recreations* golf, contract bridge; *Style—* David Harrison, Esq; 6 Beech Hill Rd, Grasscroft, Oldham, Lancs OL4 4DR (☎ 04577 3151); 8 Clydesdale St, Oldham, Lancs OL8 1BT (☎ 061 624 2482)

HARRISON, David Roger; s of John Charles Rowles Harrison, and Muriel Florence, *née* Hubbard; *b* 14 June 1942; *Educ* Wellingborough Sch; *m* 9 Sept 1965, Veronica Jean, da of Peter Kirkby, DFM; 1 s (Robert David b 6 Sept 1976), 3 da (Claire Veronica b 17 May 1968. Charlotte Jane b 13 March 1970, Bryony Jean b 1 Jan 1974); *Career* dir Duplex Plastics Ltd 1969-74; md: RC Harrison Ltd 1980-88 (dir 1973-88), Nylacast Systems Ltd 1982-; dir WMI Ltd Hong Kong 1987-, non-exec dir Kanoria Alkalis & Plastics Ltd Delhi India 1988-; chm Keyham Utd Charities 1972-80; Freeman City of Leicester 1964; *Recreations* motor sport, skiing, swimming; *Clubs* Vintage Sports Car; *Style—* David Harrison, Esq; The Old Rectory, Hungarton, Leicester (☎ 053 750 639); Nylacast Systems Ltd, Brighton Rd, Leicester (☎ 0533 764 048)

HARRISON, Denis Byrne; s of Arthur Harrison (d 1939), and Priscilla, *née* Byrne (d 1973); *b* 11 July 1917; *Educ* Birkenhead Sch, Liverpool Univ (LLM); *m* 1956, Alice Marion, da of Hedley Vickers (d 1952); *Career* WWII Capt RA 1939-46, served in Europe and Middle East; slr 1939; town clerk and chief exec Sheffield 1966-74, local cmmr (ombudsman) 1974-81, vice-chm Cmmn for Local Admin 1975-81, pro chllr Sheffield Univ 1980-82; *Recreations* golf, walking, reading, music; *Style—* Denis Harrison, Esq; 2 Leicester Close, Henley-on-Thames, Oxon RG9 2LD

HARRISON, Sir Ernest Thomas; OBE (1972); s of Ernest Horace Harrison by his w Gertrude Rebecca Gibbons; *b* 11 May 1926; *Educ* Trinity GS London; *m* 1960, Janie (Phyllis Brenda) Knight; 3 s, 2 da; *Career* CA (Harker Holloway & Co), Nat Savings Movement 1964-76; chm: Racal Electronics plc 1966 (joined 1951, dir 1958, dep md 1961, chief exec), Chubb and Sons 1984-, Decca 1980- (and chief exec, acquired by Racal 1980); former cncl memb Electronics Engrg Assoc and Nat Electronics Cncl; memb Worshipful Co of Scriveners'; Capt of Industry (Livingston Industl and Commercial Assoc Edinburgh) 1980, Hambro Businessman of the Year 1981, Aims of Industry Nat Free Enterprise Award 1982, Br Enterprise Award for Racal 1982; Hon DSc Cranfield Inst of Technol, Hon DUniv Surrey, Hon DSc City Univ, Hon DUniv Edinburgh; memb RSA, FCA, CompIERE, CompIEE; kt 1981; *Recreations* horse racing (owner), gardening, wild life, all sports (particularly soccer); *Style—* Sir Ernest Harrison, OBE; Mackenzies, Tilford, nr Farnham, Surrey; Racal Electronics plc, Western Rd, Bracknell, Berks

HARRISON, Sir Francis (Frank) Alexander Lyle; MBE (1943), QC (NI), DL (Co Down 1973); s of Rev Alexander Lyle Harrison; *b* 19 Mar 1910; *Educ* Campbell Coll Belfast, Trinity Coll Dublin; *m* 1940, Norah Patricia Rea; 2 da; *Career* barr NI 1937, bencher Inn of Ct NI 1961, pres Lands Tbnl NI 1964-; fndr memb NI Assoc of Mental Health 1959, chm Glendhu Children's Hostel 1969-81, cmmr Local Govt Boundaries NI 1971-72 and 1983-84, cmmr Dist Electoral Areas 1984; kt 1974; *Style—* Sir Frank Harrison, MBE, QC, DL; Ballydorn Hill, Killinchy, Newtownards, Co Down, NI (☎ 0238 541 250);

HARRISON, Sir Geoffrey Wedgwood; GCMG (1968, KCMG 1955, CMG 1949), KCVO (1961); s of Lt Cdr Thomas Edmund Harrison, RN (d 1914); *b* 18 July 1908; *Educ* Winchester, King's Coll Cambridge (BA); *m* 1936, Amy Katherine, da of Rt Hon Sir Robert Clive, GCMG, PC (d 1948); 3 s, 1 da; *Career* entered FO 1932, ambassador: Brazil 1956-58, Iran 1958-63, USSR 1965-68; dep under-sec of state FO 1963-65 (asst under-sec 1951-56); memb W Sussex CC 1970-77;; *Recreations* music, gardening; *Style—* Sir Geoffrey Harrison, GCMG, KCVO; Westwood, Mannings Heath, nr Horsham, Sussex (☎ 0403 40 409)

HARRISON, Gerald Stanley; s of Arthur Guiton Harrison, CBE (d 1976), of Jersey, and Noella Alice, *née* Laurens; *b* 5 May 1938; *Educ* Victoria Coll Jersey, Exeter Coll Oxford (MA); *m* 22 May 1961, Gillian Mary (d 1986), da of Michael Hubert Horris, of 15 Chilbury Gardens, Owermoigne, nr Dorchester, Dorset; 1 da (Catherine b 11 Sept 1964); *Career* dir Overseas Trading Corp (1939) Ltd Jersey 1972-87 (mktg mangr

1962-72); Capt Jersey Cwlth Games Team 1958, Half Blue Athletics (Oxford) 1959; memb ctee Jersey Cancer Relief; *Recreations* lawn bowls, swimming, gardening, travel; *Style—* Gerald Harrison, Esq; La Conchiere, La Rocque, Jersey (☎ 0534 534 19)

HARRISON, (James) Graham; s of Col Alfred Marshal Langton Harrison, CBE, MC (d 1986) of West Malvern, Worcs, and Violet, *née* Robinson (d 1988); *b* 3 July 1930; *Educ* The Elms Colwall Worcs, Bishop Cotton Sch Simla India, Geelong GS Victoria Aust, Uppingham; *m* 26 July 1958, June Eveline, da of Robert Eustace Taylor (d 1958), of Woodford Wells, Essex; 2 s (Robert b 1962, Nicholas b 1973), 1 da (Sarah (Mrs Moloney) b 1959); *Career* Nat Serv 2 Lt RHA 1954-56; TA: L/Bdr HAC 1956-59, Capt S Nottingham Hussars 1959-64; articled Wright & Westhead 1948-54, qualified CA 1954, Price Waterhouse 1956-59, Chamberlain & Merchant 1959-64, sole practitioner: Sacker & Harrison Bournemouth 1964-70, Bicker & Co 1970-84, Thornton Baker 1985; fndr Harrison & Co 1986-; dir Wessex Bldg Soc 1986- (dep chm 1987); chm: Wessex branch Inst of Taxation 1978-80, courses ctee S Soc of CAs 1979-82; tres St Saviours PCC 1984- (sec 1974-79, churchwarden 1979-84), FCA 1954, ATII 1963; *Books* Handbook on Taxation of Land (1982), Taxation of Income Arising From Furnished Lettings (1985); *Recreations* sport, music; *Clubs* Lanz Sportz Centre; *Style—* Graham Harrison, Esq; 45 Littledown Ave, Queens Park, Bournemouth, BH7 7AX (☎ 0202 33540); Rowland House, Hinton Rd, Bournemouth, BH1 2EG (☎ 0202 294 162, fax 0202 295 546)

HARRISON, Harry Cyril; CBE (1982); s of late Richard Harrison, and Elsie May; *b* 1 Mar 1920; *m* 1945, Joyce, da of Samuel Nicholls; 1 s (Geoffrey), 1 da (June); *Career* served Worcester Regt 1940-46 (despatches); chm: Simon Engrg plc 1982- (chief exec 1970-82), Warman Int Ltd, Simon Engrg plc, Dudley Business Venture, Dudley Zoo Dvpt Tst; dir: Simon US Corpn, Barclays Bank (Manchester local bd), John Folkes Hefo plc (non-exec); memb: CBI cncl London, 10D Manchester Branch Ctee, Engrg Industs Cncl, Ct of Univ of Manchester, Ct of Govrs Univ of Manchester Inst of Science and Technol; FRSA, MIBF, CBIM; *Recreations* golf, reading, travelling, swimming; *Style—* Harry Harrison Esq, CBE; Tudor Lodge, Redlake Drive, Pedmore, Stourbridge, W Midlands DY9 0RX; Simon Engineering plc, Bird Hall Lane, Cheadle Heath, Stockport, Cheshire (☎ 061 428 3600)

HARRISON, Maj-Gen Ian Stewart; CB; s of Capt Leslie George Harrison (d 1930), and Evelyn Simpson, *née* Christie (d 1980); *b* 25 May 1919; *Educ* St Albans Sch; *m* 5 Dec 1942, Winfred (Wynne) Raikes, da of George Vose Stavert, of Endmoor, Kendal, Westmorland; 1 s (David Raikes Stewart 11 June 1947), 1 da (Jenifer Anne b 15 April 1949); *Career* cmmnd RM 1937; serv at sea 1939-45: Norway, M East, Sicily, BAOR; student staff coll Camberley 1948, HQ 3 Commando Bde 1949-51, dir staff coll Camberley 1953-55, cmdt signal sch RM 1959-61, staff of cmdt gen RM 1962-63, chief instr Jt Warfare Estab 1963-65, CO RM barracks Eastney 1966-67, Br def staff Washington DC 1967-68, chief of staff RM 1968-70; dir gen Br Food Export Cncl 1970-78, Br Conslts Bureau 1978-88; fndr tstee Br Sch of Brussels 1969-, chm Chicester Festivities 1982-; ADC to HM The Queen 1966-67, Capt of Deal Castle 1980-; FBIM; *Recreations* golf, real tennis, sailing; *Clubs* Royal Yacht Squadron, Army and Navy, Royal St George's Golf; *Style—* Maj-Gen Ian Harrison, CB; Manor Cottage, Runcton, Chicester, W Sussex PO20 6PU (☎ 0243 785 480)

HARRISON, John; s of John Henry Jordan, of Grantham, Lincs, and Margaret, *née* Harrison; *b* 20 Feb 1944; *Educ* Silverdale Secdy Modern Sch, Sheffield Tech Coll,; *m* 13 July 1968, Vivien Ann Eveline, da of Frederick Charles Hardisty (d 1988), of Brighton; 1 s (Mark b 31 July 1976); *Career* asst electrician to chief engr Harold Fielding 1961-63, lighting designer Theatre Projects Ltd 1964-68, prodn mangr and tech dir ENO 1968-74, theatre conslt John Wyckham Assocs 1975-76, tech dir: WNO 1976-88, Vancouver Opera (Canada) 1984-88, Royal Opera House Covent Garden 1989-; md Cardiff Theatrical Servs Ltd 1984-88; memb: Assoc of Br Theatre Technicians 1968, Soc of Br Theatre Designers 1964, Soc of Br Lighting Designers 1964, IOD 1987; *Recreations* travel, gardening; *Style—* John Harrison, Esq; 6 Summerswood Close, Kenley Lane, Kenley, Surrey CR2 5DR; Royal Opera House, Covent Garden, London WC2E 9DD (☎ 01 240 1200, fax 01 836 1762, telex 27988 COVGAR G)

HARRISON, John; s of Kenneth Ridley Harrison (d 1960), of Stockton on Tees, and Margaret, *née* Calvert; *b* 12 Nov 1944; *Educ* Grangefield GS, Sheffield Univ (BA); *m* 4 June 1969, Patricia Alice Bridget, da of Dr Harry Raymond Alban (d 1974), of London; 1 s (Joseph b 1979), 2 da (Rachel b 1971, Philippa b 1973); *Career* articled clerk Coopers & Lybrand 1966-70, Tillotson corporate planner 1970-72, ptnr Touche Ross 1981- (mgmnt conslt 1972-) dir Granta Radio Ltd; FCA 1969, FIMC 1973; *Recreations* skiing, sailing, shooting; *Clubs* Royal Harwich Yorks; *Style—* John Harrison, Esq; Goodwin Manor, Swaffham Prior, Cambridge (☎ 0638 742 850); Touche Ross, Hill House, 1 Little New St, London EC4A 3TR (☎ 01 936 3000, fax 01 583 8517, telex 884739 TRLNDN G)

HARRISON, Surgn Vice Adm Sir John (Albert Bews); KBE (1981); s of Albert William Harrison (d 1959), of Dover, Kent and Lilian Eda *née* Bews (d 1973); *b* 20 May 1921; *Educ* St Bartholomew's Hosp; *m* 1943, Jane Harris; 2 s; *Career* RN Medical Service 1947-83: after service with RMs and at sea served in RN Hosps Plymouth, Hong Kong, Chatham, Malta and Haslar; advsr in radiology to Med Dir-Gen Navy 1967-76, dep med dir-gen and dir Medical Personnel and Logistics 1975-77, dean Naval Medicine and Surgn Rear Adm in charge of Inst of Naval Medicine 1977-80, QHP 1976-83, med dir-gen Navy and Surgn Vice Adm 1980-83; memb MRC Decompression Sickness Panel, former memb Cncl for Medical Postgraduate Educn of England and Wales; pres Rad Section RSM 1984-85; pres Med Soc London 1985-86; FRCP, FRCR, DMRD; CStJ 1983 (OStJ 1975); *Recreations* various Radiology articles in Med press; *Clubs* RSM, MCC; *Style—* Sir John Harrison, KBE; Alexandra Cottage, Swanmore, Hants SO3 2PB

HARRISON, John Clive; LVO (1971); s of Sir Geoffrey Wedgwood Harrison GCMG, KCVO, and Amy Katherine, *née* Clive; *b* 12 July 1937; *Educ* Winchester Coll, Jesus Coll Oxford (BA); *m* 1967, Jennifer Heather, da of Cdr John Courtney Evered Burston, OBE, RN (d 1970); 1 s (James b 1968), 2 da (Carolyn b 1970, Sarah b 1972); *Career* dip serv offr, cnsllr hd of Chancery Lagos 1981-84, hd of Consular Dept FCO; *Recreations* gardening, golf, tennis; *Clubs* Mannings Heath GC; *Style—* John Harrison, Esq, LVO; Foreign and Commonwealth Office, King Charles St, London SW1 (☎ 01 270 4100)

HARRISON, Col John George; OBE (1975), TD (1960), DL (1973); s of James Harrison (d 1960); *b* 15 Mar 1920; *Educ* Bridgens GS, St Luke's and Loughborough Colls; *m* 1946, Mona Patricia, da of Onslow Francis Froud (d 1950); 1 s, 2 da; *Career* served WWII with Indian Ing, cmd Devon (1 RV) (TA) 1961-64, Dep Cdr 130 Inf Bde (TA) 1965-67, Territorial Col SW District 1967-68, Cmdt Devon ACF 1970-75; TD 1960, OBE 1975, DL (Devon 1973); *Clubs* Exeter Golf and Country; *Style—* Col John Harrison, OBE, TD, DL; Ivy Cottage, 36 Buckerell Ave, Exeter, Devon EX2 4RD (☎ 0392 74959)

HARRISON, Julian Pitman Hyde; s of Lt-Col Jim Willoughby Hyde Harrison, MC (d 1958), and Sylvia Hayward, *née* Pitman (d 1956); *b* 21 August 1929; *Educ* Bryanston, Magdalen Coll Oxford (MA); *m* 23 Jan 1965, June Selby, da of Herbert Saysell Colwill (d 1959); 1 s (James b 10 July 1967), 1 da (Sarah b 23 Aug 1965); *Career* memb Lloyds 1957-, underwriter T R Mountain and others 1970-; chm: H Pitman (Underwriting) Ltd 1986-, A R Mountain & Son Ltd 1988-; cncllr Camden Borough (Cons) 1968-71 and 1978-86; contested (C) Stoke-on-Trent (Central) 1959 and 1964; Liveryman Merchant Taylor's Co 1956; *Recreations* chess, reading, maintaining a country house; *Clubs* Carlton, City of London; *Style—* Julian Harrison, Esq; Danemore Park, Speldhurst, Kent TN3 OJP (☎ 0892 862 829); 37 Gayton Road, London NW3 1VB; A R Mountain & Son Ltd, Lloyds, London EC3M 7HL (☎ 01 623 7100, ext 3153)

HARRISON, Lady Kathleen; *née* Livingston; da of Robert Livingston, of The Gables, Eaglescliffe, co Durham; *m* 29 April 1930, Sir (John) Fowler Harrison, 2 Bt (d 1947); 2 s (Sir (John) Wyndham, 3 Bt d 1953, Sir (Robert) Colin *qv*), 1 da (Mrs Paul Standing); *Style—* Kathleen, Lady Harrison; Bonnie Banks, Sproxton, Helmsley, York YO6 5BJ (☎ 0439 70598)

HARRISON, Kenneth Arthur; TD (1965); s of Arthur Reginald Harrison (d 1969), and Agnes, *née* Hutcheson (d 1963); *b* 4 July 1930; *Educ* Denstone Coll Staffs, Manchester Univ; *m* 12 Sept 1953, Christine Mary, da of Joseph Herrod; 2 s (Anthony b 1955, Peter b 1960); *Career* chm: Harrison Industries plc 1971- (sr engr 1951-61, building design conslt 1961-65, md (engrg) 1965-70), Bostwick Doors (UK) Ltd (subsid; Queen's Award for Export 1980); *Recreations* tennis, parachuting, business, golf, garden design; *Clubs* St James's (Manchester and London); *Style—* Kenneth Harrison, Esq, TD; White Cottage, Oldfield Rd, Altrincham, Cheshire; Shippon, Moelfre, Anglesey; Chesaux-Dessous, St Cergues, Switzerland; Bostwick Doors (UK) Ltd, Stockport, Cheshire (telex 667724)

HARRISON, Kenneth Cecil; OBE (1980, MBE (Mil) 1946); s of Thomas Harrison (d 1947), of Hyde, Cheshire, and Annie, *née* Wood (d 1976); *b* 29 April 1915; *Educ* Hyde GS Cheshire, Coll of Technol Manchester; *m* 26 Aug 1941, Doris, da of Frank Taylor (d 1927), of Hyde, Cheshire; 2 s (David John b 25 Aug 1945, Timothy Michael b 28 Aug 1948); *Career* WWII served: South Lancs Regt 1940-42, offr cadet RMC 1942, 2 Lt West Yorks Regt 1942, Lt East Yorks Regt 50 Div Western Desert 1942, platoon cdr Sicily Landing 1943, Capt 1943, Maj 1944, company cdr D-Day landing (wounded) 1944, Normandy and Arnhem 1944, Italy and Austria 1945; demob bd Maj 1946; borough librarian: Hyde and Glossop 1939, Hove 1947, Eastbourne 1950, Hendon 1958; city librarian Westminster 1961-80, chief exec Cwlth Library Assoc 1980-83, conslt librarian Ranfurly Library Serv 1983-; vice pres City of Westminster Arts Cncl 1980-(hon sec 1965-80), govr Westminster Coll 1962-80, pres Paddington Soc 1982-; memb Rotary Club: Hyde 1939-47, Hove 1947-50, Eastbourne 1950-58 (pres 1957-58), Hendon 1958-61; memb past Rotarians Club of Eastbourne and dist 1986-, memb Eastbourne Local History Soc 1987-; fell Library Assoc 1932-(pres 1973); memb Cwlth Library Assoc (pres 1972-75); First Class Order of the Lion of Finland 1976; *Books* Public Libraries Today (1963), Facts at your Fingertips (2 edn 1966), British Public Library Buildings (1966), Libraries in Britain (1968), Libraries in Scandanavia (2 edn 1969), The Library and the Community (3 edn 1977), First Steps in Librarianship (3 edn 1980); Public relations for librarians (2 edn, 1982), Public library buildings 1975-83 (ed 1987); *Recreations* reading, writing, travel, wine-bibbing, crosswords, cricket, zoo visiting; *Clubs* MCC, Royal Cwlth Soc, Surrey CCC, Sussex CCC; *Style—* K C Harrison, Esq, OBE; 5 Tavistock, Devonshire Place, Eastbourne, East Sussex BN21 4AG (☎ 0323 26747)

HARRISON, (George) Michael Antony; CBE (1980); s of George Harrison and Kathleen Harrison; *b* 7 April 1925; *Educ* Manchester GS, Brasenose Coll Oxford (MA); *m* 1951, Pauline, *née* Roberts; 2 s, 1 da; *Career* chief educn offr City of Sheffield 1967-85, educn systems conslt 1985-; memb Engrg Cncl 1982-87 1985-;; *Style—* Michael Harrison, Esq, CBE; (☎ 0742 553783)

HARRISON, Sir Michael James Harwood; 2 Bt (UK 1961); s of Col Sir Harwood Harrison, 1 Bt, TD (d 1980), MP (C) Eye 1951-79, of Little Manor, Woodbridge, Suffolk and Peggy Alberta Mary, *née* Stenhouse; *b* 28 Mar 1936; *Educ* Rugby; *m* 1967, Louise, da of Edward Buxton Clive (d 1975), of Swanmore Lodge, Swanmore, Hants; 2 s (Edwin b 1981, Tristan b 1986), 2 da (Davina b 1968, Priscilla b 1971); *Heir* s, Edwin Michael Harwood Harrison b 29 May 1981; *Career* nat serv 17/21 Lancers 1955-56; Lloyd's insurance broker 1958-; chm: Leggett Porter and Howard Ltd 1981-, L P H Pitman Ltd 1987-; dir of private cos 1980-; memb cncl Sail Training Assoc 1968-; freeman City of London 1964-, master Mercers' Co 1986 (liveryman 1967), vice-pres Assoc of Combined Youth Clubs 1983-; chm management ctee Assoc of Combined Youth Clubs 1987-; *Recreations* sailing (yacht 'Falcon'), skiing, riding (horse and bicycle), Daily Telegraph crossword; *Clubs* Boodle's, MCC, Royal Harwich Yacht; *Style—* Sir Michael Harrison, Bt; 35 Paulton's Sq, London SW3 (☎ 01 352 1760); c/o L P H Pitman Ltd, St Michael's Alley, off Cornhill, London EC3 (☎ 01 283 7345)

HARRISON, Patrick Kennard; CBE (1982); s of Richard Harrison Mice (d 1969), and Sheila Griffin; *b* 8 July 1928; *Educ* Lord Williams's Sch Thame, Downing Coll Cambridge (BA); *m* 1955, Mary Wilson, da of Capt Guybon Chesney Castell Damant, CBE, RN (d 1963); 1 da (Cordelia b 1966); *Career* with Dept of Health for Scotland 1953, ps to Departmental Sec and Parly Under Secs of State Scottish/Off 1958-60; princ Scottish Devpt Dept and Regnl Devpt Div Scottish Off 1960-68; RIBA (sec 1968-87); *Recreations* gardening; *Clubs* Reform, New (Edinburgh); *Style—* Patrick Harrison, Esq, CBE; 63 Princess Road, London NW1 8JS (☎ 01 722 8508); Upper Stewarton, Eddleston, Peebles

HARRISON, Prof Sir Richard (John); s of late Geoffrey Arthur Harrison, and Theodora Beatrice Mary West; *b* 8 Oct 1920; *Educ* Oundle, Gonville and Caius Coll Cambridge (MA, MD), St Bart's; *m* Barbara (d 1988), da of James Fuller, of Neston, Cheshire; *Career* prof of anatomy Cambridge Univ 1968-82 (later emeritus), fell

Downing Coll Cambridge 1968-82 (hon fell 1982); chm: Farm Animal Welfare Cncl 1979-, Bd of Tstees Br Museum (natural history) 1984-; pres Int Fedn of Assocs of Anatomists 1985-87; Hon DSc Glasgow 1948; FRS 1973; kt 1984; *Books* Handbook of Marine Mammals (vols I-IV (1981), Research on Dolphins (1986), Whales, Dolphins and Porpoises (1988); *Recreations* gardening; *Clubs* Garrick; *Style—* Prof Sir Richard Harrison; The Beeches, 8 Woodlands Rd, Great Shelford, Cambridgeshire CB2 5LW (☎ 0223 843287)

HARRISON, (Desmond) Roger Wingate; s of Maj-Gen Desmond Harrison, CB, DSO; *b* 9 April 1933; *Educ* Rugby, Worcester Coll Oxford (MA), Harvard; *m* 1965, Victoria, MVO, da of Rear Adm J Lee Barber; 4 da; *Career* dir: The Observer, Capital Radio, London Weekend TV; dir Duke of York's Theatre, govr Sadlers Wells Theatre; *Recreations* fishing, shooting; *Clubs* Cavalry and Guards; *Style—* Roger Harrison Esq; 35 Argyll Rd, London, W8 (☎ 01 937 2770)

HARRISON, Tony; s of Harry Ashton Harrison (d 1980), and Florence Horner, *née* Wilkinson (d 1976); *b* 30 April 1937; *Educ* Leeds GS, Univ of Leeds (BA); *Career* poet and dramatist; pres Classical Assoc 1988, FRSL; *Books* Earthworks (1964), Aikin Mata (1965), Newcastle is Peru (1969), The Loiners (1970), The Misanthrope (1973), Phaedra Britannica (1975), The Passion (1977), Bow Down (1977), From The School of Eloquence (1978), Continuous (1981), A Kumquat for John Keats (1981), US Martial (1981), The Oresteia (1981), Selected Poems (1984), The Mysteries (1985), Dramatic Verse 1973-85 (1985), The Fire-Gap (1985), Theatre Works 1973-85 (1986), Selected Poems (augmented edn 1987), The Trackers of Oxyrhynchus (performed ancient stadium of Delphi 1988); dir: The Oresteia (Channel 4 1982), The Big H (BBC 1984), The Mysteries (Channel 4 1985), Yan Tan Tethera (Channel 4 1986), Loving Memory (BBC 1986), (Channel 4 1987 Royal television Soc Award); *Style—* Tony Harrison, Esq; c/o Peters Fraser & Dunlop, 5th Floor, The Chambers, Chelsea Harbour, Lots Rd, London SW10 OXF (☎ 01 376 7676, fax 01 352 7356)

HARRISON, Rt Hon Walter; PC (1977), JP (W Riding Yorks 1962), MP (Lab) Wakefield 1964-; s of Henry Harrison, of Dewsbury; *b* 2 Jan 1921; *Educ* Dewsbury Tech and Art Coll; *m* 1948, Enid Coleman; 1 s, 1 da; *Career* dep chief oppn whip 1979- (and 1970-74), dep ch govt whip (treasurer HM Household) 1974-79, ld commissioner Treasury 1968-70, asst govt whip 1966-68; JP 1962, MP 1964, PC 1977; *Style—* The Rt Hon Walter Harrison, JP, MP; House of Commons, SW1 (☎ 01 219 3000)

HARRISON, Walter Paul; s of Walter Harrison, of Morecambe, and Margaret Hildred, *née* Buttery; *b* 19 Mar 1955; *Educ* Skerton Co Boys Sch Lancaster, Preston Poly (OND, HNC), Leicester Poly (BA, Dip Arch); *Career* Cassidy & Ashton Partnership Preston 1973-75, W E Moore & Sons Leicester 1978-79 (ptnr and dir 1987), Robert Davis John West Assocs Staines 1981-88, assoc 1986, ptnr local off Robert Davis John West & Assoc Crawley 1988-; RIBA, ARCUK; *Recreations* squash, badminton, cars, horse riding; *Clubs* Coptherne Country, Crawley; *Style—* Paul Harrison, Esq; Denholme, Crawley Rd, Horsham, West Sussex (☎ 0403 62224); Robert Davies John West & Associates, Buxton House, 2 East Park, Crawley RH10 6AS (☎ 0293 541581/2, fax 0293 548104, telex 877565 ROSWAG)

HARRISON, William Robert (Bill); s of William Eric Harrison, and Catherine Frances, *née* Dyson; *b* 5 Oct 1948; *Educ* George Dixon GS Birmingham, LSE (BSc, MSc) ; *m* 18 July 1970, Jacqueline Ann, da of Marwood Eric Brown, of Birmingham; 1 s (Nicholas David b 1977), 1 da (Charlotte Ann b 1976); *Career* md Shearson Lehman Hutton Inc, formerly dir J Henry Schroder Wagg & Co Ltd; *Recreations* soccer, cricket, music, gardening; *Style—* Bill Harrison; 1 Broadgate, London EC2 (☎ 01 601 0011)

HARROD, Maj-Gen Lionel Alexander Digby; OBE; s of Frank Henry Harrod, CBE (d 1958), of Coventry, and Charlotte Beatrice Emmeline Harrod (d 1981); *b* 7 Sept 1924; *Educ* Bromsgrove; *m* 2 Feb 1952, (Anne) Priscilla Stormont, da of Charles Cobden Stormont Gibbs (d 1969); 1 s (David b 1955), 2 da (Elinor b 1953, Catherine b 1959); *Career* Grenadier Gds 1943-63, Staff Coll 1955, Bde Maj 19 Bde 1956-58, GSO 2 SD2 WO 1961-63, 2 I/C 1 Bn The Welch Regt 1964-66, Co 1 Bn The Welch Regt 1966-69, Br Liaison Staff Washington 1969-70, def and mil attaché (Col) Baghdad 1971, Col Staff Duties HQ UKLF 1972, chief (Brig) BRIX MLS 1974-76, ACOS Intelligence SHAPE 1976-79, Col The Royal Regt of Wales 1977-82, inspr of Army Recruiting 1979-89; vice chm N Dorset Cons Assoc, chm Marnhull Br NDCA, pres Marnhull Br Legion, ctee Mil Commentator Circle, active in Peace Through NATO and Br Atlantic Ctee; *Recreations* fishing, current affairs; *Clubs* Pratt's, Army and Navy, MCC, Pilgrim's, European Atlantic Gp; *Style—* Maj-Gen Lionel Harrod, OBE; The Grange, Marnhull, Dorset DT10 1PS (☎ 0258 820 256)

HARROD, Lady (Wilhelmine Margaret Eve); *née* Cresswell; da of Capt Francis Joseph (Joe) Cresswell (ka 1914), and Barbara, *née* ffolkes, wid of Gen Sir Peter Strickland, KCB; *b* 1 Dec 1911; *Educ* Langford Grove Maldon Essex; *m* 8 Jan 1938, Sir Roy Forbes Harrod (d 1978), s of Henry Harrod; 2 s (Henry b 1939, Dominick b 1940); *Career* involved in conservation countryside and bldgs; memb: Georgian Gp, Oxford Preservation Tst, Cncl Protection Rural Eng, Regnl Ctee Nat Tst, Historic Churches Preservation Tst, Norfolk Churches Tst (fndr and pres), various diocesan ctees; Hon DCL UEA 1989; fndr Norfolk Churches Tst; *Books* Shell Guide to Norfolk (jtly 1957), The Norfolk Guide (1988); *Recreations* gardening; *Clubs* The Norfolk (Norwich); *Style—* Lady Harrod; The Old Rectory, Holt, Norfolk NR25 6RY (☎ 0263 712 204)

HARROLD, Leslie Percy; s of Harry Hodge Harrold (d 1980), and Ivy Helen Harrold (d 1966); *b* 7 April 1921; *Educ* Bournemouth GS; *m* 1, 17 Dec 1951, Jean (d 4 Aug 1962), da of John Paterson (d 1960), of Barrow-in-Furness; 2 s (Murray b 1952, Roger b 1961); m 2, 3 May 1964, Gisela (d 21 March 1986), da of Ewalt Uhlenburch (d 1980), of Recklinghausen, W Germany; *Career* chartered accountant (princ); chm Value Holidays and Travel Ltd; dir: Asco Consultants UK Ltd; commercial dir Vickers Ltd London 1946-64; finance dir Vickers-Zimmer AG Frankfurt (W Germany) 1964-72; Gascoigne-Sudstall GmbH Bavaria Geschäfts führer 1972-75; Shaw-Leonard Inc, Jeddah, admin vice-pres 1975-79; FCA, FCMA; *Recreations* golf, swimming; *Clubs* Inst of Directors, Rotary, Wig and Pen; *Style—* Leslie Harrold, Esq; 984 Garrat Lane, Tooting, London SW17 0ND (☎ 01 767 4460)

HARROLD, Timothy John (Tim); s of Col W G Harrold (d 1969), and Christine Russell, *née* Kilburn Scott; *b* 12 May 1938; *Educ* Bryanston, Lausanne Univ Switzerland, Pembroke Coll Cambridge (MA); *m* 9 Sept 1967, Gillian Doris, da of Leslie Albert Cruttenden; 3 s (Simon Timothy b 14 March 1970, Michael Stephen b 24 March 1971, James Andrew b 15 Sept 1976), 1 da (Katherine b 2 Sept 1973); *Career* with ICI 1960-69, mktg dir Polydor Ltd London 1970-74, exec vice-pres Phonodisc Inc NY 1974-75; pres: Polygram Inc Montreal 1975-81, Polydor Int Hamburg 1981-83; exec vice-pres Polygram Int London 1983- (chm Polygram Classics, Decca Int); *Recreations* skiing; *Style—* Tim Harrold, Esq; Dunstanburgh, Downside Rd, Guildford, Surrey (☎ 0483 648 76); Polygram Int, 30 Berkeley Sq, London (☎ 01 493 8800, car tel 0836 236 822)

HARROP, Sir Peter John; KCB (1984, CB 1980); s of Gilbert Harrop (d 1971), and Frances May, *née* Dewhirst; *b* 18 Mar 1926; *Educ* King Edward VII Sch Lytham, Peterhouse Cambridge (MA); *m* 1975, Margaret Joan, da of E U E Elliott-Binns; 2 s (Andrew b 1976, Nicholas b 1978); *Career* Sub Lt RNVR 1946-48; asst princ: Miny of Town and Country Planning 1949, Miny of Housing and Local Govt 1951, DOE 1970; regnl dir and chm Yorks and Humberside Econ Planning Bd 1971-73, HM Treasy 1973-76, Cabinet Off 1979-80, second perm sec DOE 1981-86; chm UK ctee Euro Year of the Environment 1987, chm Nat Bus Co 1988, non exec dir Nat Home Loans plc; managing tstee Municipal Mutual Insur Ltd, tstee Br Museum; *Recreations* sailing, golf; *Clubs* United Oxford and Cambridge, Roehampton; *Style—* Sir Peter Harrop, KCB; 19 Berwyn Road, Richmond, Surrey TW10

HARROWBY, 7 Earl of (UK 1809); Dudley Danvers Granville Coutts Ryder; TD (1953); also Baron Harrowby (GB 1776) and Viscount Sandon (UK 1809); er s of 6 Earl of Harrowby (d 1987), and Lady Helena Blanche, *née* Coventry (d 1974), sis of 10 Earl of Coventry; *b* 20 Dec 1922; *Educ* Eton; *m* 14 June 1949, Jeannette Rosalthé, yr da of Capt Peter Johnston-Saint (d 1974); 1 s, 1 da (Lady Frances Rundall, *qv*); *Heir* s, Viscount Sandon, *qv*; *Career* served WW II with 59 Inf Div, 5 Para Bde in NW Europe (wounded); India and Java (political offr) 56 Armoured Div 1941-45; Lt-Col RA cmdg 254 (City of London) Field Regt RA (TA) 1962-64; dep chm Nat Westminster Bank plc 1971-87 (dir 1968); chm: Int Westminster Bank plc 1977-87, Nat Westminster Investment Bank 1986-87; dep chm Coutts & Co 1970- (md 1949); chm Dowty Gp plc 1986-; dir Saudi Int Bank 1980-82 and 1985-87; chm Nat Biological Standards Bd 1973-88; memb: Trilateral Cmmn 1980-, Ctee of Management Inst of Psychiatry 1953-73 (chm 1965-73), Bd of Govrs: Bethlem Royal and Maudsley (Postgraduate Teaching) Hosps 1955-73 (chm 1965-73), Univ of Keele 1956-68, Lord Chancellor's Advisory Investment Ctee for Ct of Protection 1965-77, Advisory Investment Ctee for Public Tstee 1974-77, Psychiatry Research Tst (tstee) 1982-, Institut Internationale d'Etudes Bancaires 1977-87, Kensington Borough Cncl 1950-65 (chm Gp Ctee 1957-59), Kensington and Chelsea Borough Cncl 1965-71 (chm Finance Ctee 1968-71); govr Atlantic Inst of Int Affairs 1983-88; hon tres: Staffs Soc 1947-51, exec ctee London Area Conservative Assoc 1949-50; hon tres: Family Welfare Assoc 1951-65, S Kensington Conservative Assoc 1953-56, Central Cncl for Care of Cripples 1953-60; dir Dinorwic Slate Quarries Co Ltd 1951-69; mangr Fulham and Kensington Hosp Gp 1953-56; gen commr for Income Tax 1954-71; dir: Nat Provincial Bank 1961-69, UKPI 1955-86 (dep chm 1956-64), Olympic Gp 1968-73 (chm 1971-73), Powell Dyffryn Gp 1976-86 (chm 1981-86), Sheepbridge Engineering Ltd 1977-79; chm: Orion Bank 1979-81, Bentley Engineering Co Ltd 1983-86; CBIM, MRIIA, Hon Fell Royal Coll of Psychiatrists; *Style—* The Rt Hon Earl of Harrowby; Sandon Hall, Stafford (☎ 08897 338); 5 Tregunter Road, London SW10 9LS (☎ 01 373 9276); Burnt Norton, Chipping Campden, Glos (☎ 0386 840 358)

HARSTON, Julian John Robert Clive; s of Col Clive Harston, of Surrey, and Kathleen Mary, *née* Grace; *b* 20 Oct 1942; *Educ* The King's Sch Canterbury, Univ of London (BSc); *m* 1966, Karen Howard Oake, da of Col T E Longfield (ka 1941); 1 s (Alexander b 1978); *Career* mangr Br Tourist Authy Copenhagen and Vancouver 1965-71; FO 1971; 1 sec/consul Hanoi 1973-74, 1 sec Blantyre 1975-79, 1 sec Lisbon 1982-84; Cnsllr Harare 1984-88; *Recreations* travel, photography, Switzerland; *Clubs* East India, RAC, Gremio Literario (Lisbon), Harare Club; *Style—* Julian Harston, Esq; c/o 33 Rosemont Rd, Richmond, Surrey; Foreign and Cwlth Office

HART; *see*: Turton-Hart

HART, Anelay Colton Wright; s of Anelay Thomas Bayston Hart, of Orchard Close, Alne, York (d 1971), and Phyllis Marian, *née* Wright (d 1981); *b* 6 Mar 1934; *Educ* Stamford Sch, King's Coll London (LLB); *m* 22 March 1979, Margaret Gardner; *Career* slr, ptnr Appleby, Hope & Matthews 1963-; memb RSPCA Cncl 1969- (hon tres 1974-81, chm 1981-83, 1985-86, 1988-89, vice-chm 1983-84, 1986-88); Queen Victoria Silver Medal 1984; advsy dir World Soc for the Protection of Animals 1982-; pres Rotary Club of South Bank and Eston 1972-83; memb Law Soc; *Recreations* walking; *Clubs* Royal Overseas League; *Style—* Anelay Hart, Esq; Chequers, High St, Normanby, Middlesbrough, Cleveland TS6 OLD; 35 35 High St, Normanby, Middlesbrough, Cleveland TS6 OLE (☎ 0642 440444, fax 0642 440 342)

HART, Anthony John; JP (1977), DSC (1945); s of Cecil Victor Hart (d 1982), and Kate Winifred Hart (d 1971); *b* 27 Dec 1923; *Educ* Dauntsey's Sch; *m* 1947, Penelope, da of George Philip Morris (d 1971); 1 s (Colin), 1 da (Sally); *Career* Lt RNVR serving in RN 1942-46, Atlantic, English Channel, Med; Chartered Loss Adjuster; chm and md Cunningham Hart and Co Ltd (sr ptnr 1972-87, ret), pres Chartered Inst of Loss Adjusters 1970-71; govr Dauntsey's Sch; Alderman City of London 1977-84, master Worshipful Co of Broderers 1975-76; *Recreations* golf; *Clubs* City Livery, Richmond Golf; *Style—* Anthony Hart, Esq, DSC, JP; 7 Dickens Close, Petersham, Surrey (☎ 01 948 0587)

HART, Sir Byrne; CBE (1968), MC; s of F McD Hart; *b* 6 Oct 1895; *Educ* Southport Sch, Brisbane GS; *m* 1922, Margaret, da of D Cramond; 2 s; *Career* accountant; former chm Utah Mining Australia Ltd, chm Castlemaine Perkins Ltd; kt 1974; *Style—* Sir Byrne Hart, CBE, MC; City Mutual Bldg, 307 Queen St, Brisbane, Qld 4000, Australia

HART, (Christopher) Charles Dudley; s of late Rev Canon Charles Dudley Hart; *b* 15 Dec 1913; *Educ* St Edward's Oxford; *m* 1946, Meryl Pera, *née* Wardle; 2 da; *Career* slr (ret snr ptnr); pres: Notts Law Soc 1964, Mental Health Tribunals; chm of govrs Lilley and Stone Sch Newark until 1980 (ret); *Recreations* travel, ornithology, photography; *Style—* Charles Hart, Esq; The Burnt House, South Collingham, Newark, Notts (☎ 0636 092238)

HART, Dr (Francis) Dudley; s of Rev Canon Charles Dudley Hart (d 1952), of Southwell Cathedral, and Kate Evelyn, *née* Bowden (d 1961); *b* 4 Oct 1909; *Educ* Grosvenor Sch Nottingham, Univ of Edinburgh (MB, ChB, MD); *m* 18 Dec 1944, Mary Josephine (Maureen), da of Luke Tully (d 1956), of Carrigaline, Co Cork, Ireland; 1 s (Paul b 1950), 2 da (Elizabeth b 1946, Clare b 1948); *Career* Maj (med specialist) and Lt-Col i/c Med Div RAMC 1942-46, civilian conslt physician Army 1972-74; house surgn: Royal Hosp for Sick Children Edinburgh 1933, Paddington Green Children's Hosp 1934; house physician Brompton Hosp 1937, med registrar Royal Northern Hosp 1935-37 (house physician 1935); currently consulting physician: Westminster Hosp (conslt physician and physician i/c rheumatism clinic 1946-74, med registrar 1939-42), Hosp St John and St Elizabeth St John's Wood London; former: memb and vice-chm ctee Review of Medicines, pres Heberden Soc (rheumatism res and educn); chm ctee Tst Educn and Res Therapeutics, memb exec ctee Arthritis and Rheumatism Cncl; Freeman City of London 1956, Liveryman Worshipful Co Apothecaries 1956; hon memb French Italian American Australian Rheum Socs, MRCP 1937, FRCP 1949 hon FRSM; *Books* Frenchs Index of Differential Diagnosis (ed 10-12 edns 1973-85), Drug Treatment of Rheumatic Diseases (3 edns 1978-87), Overcoming Arthritis (1981), Practical Problems in Rheumatology (1983), Colour Atlas of Rheumatology (1987), Clinical Rheumatology Illustrated (1987); *Recreations* walking, schnorkling; *Style—* Dr Dudley Hart; 19 Ranulf Rd, London NW2 2BT (☎ 01 794 2525); 24 Harmont House, 20 Harley St, London W1N 1AN (☎ 01 935 4252)

HART, Frank Thomas; JP; s of Samuel Black Hart (d 1968), of Gravesend Kent, and Ada Frances Laura, *née* Knight (d 1965); *b* 9 Nov 1911; *Educ* Gravesend Sheerness Tech Schs, Regent St Poly, Open Univ (BA); *m* 1938, Evelyn Brenda, da of William Edward Deakin (d 1933), of Leek, Staffs; 3 s (Michael, Philip, John); *Career* sec Buchanan Hosp St Leonard's-on-Sea 1935-42, sec Central London Ophthalmic Hosp 1942-45, sec supt Princess Louise Children's Hosp 1945-48, supt Royal Infirmary Sheffield 1948-52, house govr Charing Cross Hosp 1952-73, hosp dir Zambia Med Aid Soc Lusaka Zambia 1973-75; JP: Gore Div Middx 1954-67, Dorking Surrey 1967-77, Hastings E Sussex 1977-; *Recreations* cricket, rugby football, bowls, reading; *Style—* Frank Hart, Esq, JP; St Alban, 11 The Mount, St Leonards on Sea, Hastings (☎ 0424 425559)

HART, Garry Richard Rushby; s of Dennis George Hart (d 1984), and Evelyn Mary, *née* Rushby; *b* 29 June 1940; *Educ* Northgate GS Ipswich, UCL (LLB); *m* 1, 24 March 1966 (m dis 1986), Paula Lesley, da of Leslie Shepherd; 2 s (Alexander, Jonathan), 1 da (Katey); m 2, 1986, Valerie Elen Mary, da of Finlaw Cledwyn Wilson Davies; *Career* slr; ptnr Herbert Smith 1970- (head property dept 1988-); Freeman City of London, Liveryman Worshipful Co of Slrs; memb Law Soc 1966; *Recreations* farming, travel; *Clubs* Carlton; *Style—* Garry Hart, Esq; 36 Alwyne Road, London N1; Watling House, 35/7 Cannon St, London EC4 (☎ 01 489 8000, fax 01 329 0426, telex 886633)

HART, Prof Herbert Lionel Adolphus; QC (1984); s of Simeon Hart (d 1954), and Rose, *née* Samson (d 1954); *b* 18 July 1907; *Educ* Bradford GS, New Coll Oxford (MA); *m* 1941, Jenifer Margaret, da of Sir John Fischer Williams, CBE, KC (d 1947), of Lamledra, Gorran Haven, Cornwall; 3 s (Adam, Charles, Jacob), 1 da (Joanna); *Career* barr; Oxford Univ: fell and tutor in philosophy New Coll 1946-53, prof of jurisprudence 1953-69, princ Brasenose Coll 1973-78; FBA; *Books* Causation In The Law, The Concept of Law, Essays on Bentham, Punishment and Responsibility, Essays in Jurisprudence and Philosophy, Law Liberty and Morality; *Recreations* bicycling; *Style—* Prof Herbert Hart, QC; 11 Manor Place, Oxford (☎ 0865 242402); UC Oxford (☎ 0865 276602)

HART, K Mortimer; s of Frank Mortimer (d 1969), and Minnie Anna, *née* Houlson (d 1968); *b* 24 Mar 1914; *Educ* Redland Hill House Sch Bristol; *m* 7 Dec 1946, Shirley, da of Percy Burkinshaw, of Wakefield and Sheffield; 1 da (Catherine Jane Mortimer b 23 June 1955); *Career* WWII RAF Volunteer Reserve 1940-45, seconded Indian Air Force 1942-45; chartered surveyor and town planner; sr planning inspr: Miny of Housing, local govt, Welsh Off; surveyor and town planning conslt; chm Conwy Valley Civic Soc 1976-82; ARICS 1935, MRTPI 1945; *Books* Conwy Valley and the Lands of History (1988); *Recreations* formerly swimming, photography; *Clubs* Royal Cwlth Soc; *Style—* K Mortimer Hart, Esq; Pen Rhiw, Rowen, Conwy, Gwynedd LL32 8TR (☎ 0492 650 343)

HART, Keith; s of Joseph Henry Hart (d 1986), of Bermuda, and Mildred, *née* Birch; *b* 3 Mar 1944; *Educ* Thornton GS, St George's GS Bermuda, Warwick Acad Bermuda; *m* 1 (m dis 1971); 1 s (Keith b 10 Nov 1967), 1 da (Alison (twin) b 10 Nov 1967); m 2, 23 June 1974, Linda Susan, da of Baldo P Castelli; *Career* pres and md Hart Advtg Ltd Hamilton Bermuda, pres Bermuda Technol Int and Island TV; previously involved with: Bermuda Broadcasting Co Ltd, Investors Overseas Servs, American Int Ltd; memb: Commemorative Collectors Soc, Br-Bermuda Soc, Ephemera Soc, Universal Autograph Collectors Club, The Magic Circle, Advertising and Publicity Assoc of Bermuda, Civil & Mil No 726 Freemasons Lodge, St Andrews No 270 Royal Arch Chapter, Bermuda Musical and Dramatic Soc; *Recreations* antique collecting, travelling, conjuring, photography; *Style—* Keith Hart, Esq; P O Box HM 2229, Hamilton HM JX, Bermuda

HART, Michael Christopher Campbell; QC (1987); s of Raymond David Campbell Hart, and Penelope Mary, *née* Ellis; *b* 7 May 1948; *Educ* Winchester, Magdalen Coll Oxford (MA, BCL); *m* 12 Aug 1972, Melanie Jane, da of Richard Hugh Sandiford; 2 da (Jessie (b 3 Oct 1973, Zoe b 13 Dec 1974); *Career* fell All Soul's Coll Oxford 1970, barr Gray's Inn 1970; *Style—* Michael Hart, Esq, QC; 2 New Sq, Lincoln's Inn, London WC2A 3RU (☎ 01 242 6201, fax 01 831 8102, telex 264815 NEWSQ G)

HART, Michael John; s of Ernest Stanley Granville Hart (d 1982), of Theydon Bois, Essex, and Wilhelmine Patricia, *née* McClurg (d 1972); *b* 26 Dec 1932; *Educ* LSE (BSc); *m* 30 May 1964, (Ann) Sheila, da of William Severy Conrad Decker (d 1965), of Loughton, Essex; 1 s (Samuel b 19 Jan 1977), 1 da (Susan b 23 May 1975); *Career* Nat Serv RAF 1950-52; jt mangr Foreign and Colonial Investmt Tst 1969-, dep chm Foreign and Colonial Mgmnt 1986-; ACIS 1956; *Recreations* cricket, gardening, reading biographies; *Style—* Michael Hart, Esq; Springs, Water End, Ashdon, Essex (☎ 079 984 259); 1 Laurence Pountney Hill, London, EC4 (☎ 01 623 4680)

HART, Peter Dorney; s of Sydney Charles Hart (d 1974), of Fulham and Croydon, and Florence Jane, *née* Dorney; *b* 24 June 1925; *Educ* Dulwich, The Polytechnic Regent St; *m* 18 March 1958, Paulette Olga, da of Julian Pearmain (d 1971), of Hayes, Kent; *Career* RE 1943-48, Capt attached to Indian Army 1945-48, RARO 1949-75; sr ptnr Walfords Chartered Quantity Surveyors 1987- (joined 1950, ptnr 1967, jt sr ptnr 1982); dir Surveyors Pubns 1984-; memb Nat Jt Consultative Ctee for Bldg 1978-86, memb bd Coll of Estate Mgmnt Reading 1985-, vice-chm RICS Quantity Surveyor's Divnl cncl 1987-; tstee: Douglas Haig Memorial Homes 1978-, Housing Assoc for Offrs Families 1988-; hon sec Surrey & North Sussex Beagles 1979-; pres The Surveyors' Club 1988; Freeman City of London 1977; Liveryman: Worshipful Co of Chartered Surveyors 1977, Worshipful Co of Carpenters 1984; ARICS 1953, FRICS 1965; *Recreations* beagling, archaeology, local history; *Clubs* Athenaeum; *Style—* Peter Hart, Esq; The Coach House, 50 Lovelace Rd, Surbiton, Surrey KT6 6ND (☎ 01 399 8423); Walfords, 7/9 St James's St, London SW1A 1EN (☎ 01 930 4293, fax 01 839 2962)

HART, Philip; s of Jacob Hart, (d 1973), of Cape Town S Africa, and Rosa, *née* Suitkin (d 1979); *b* 5 Oct 1939; *Educ* South African Coll Sch, Coll of Law London; *m* 3 May 1960, Anita, da of Percy Bub (d 1982); 1 s (Gaon Leslie b 17 Oct 1965), 1 da (Shana b 31 Oct 1961); *Career* slr, fndr (sr ptnr) Hart Fortgang 1961; *Recreations* hiking, skiing; *Style—* Philip Hart, Esq; Princess House, 50 Eastcastle St, London W1A 4BY (☎ 01 436 3300, fax 255 3066, telex 8956086)

HART, Capt Raymond; CBE (1963), DSO (1945), DSC (1941, Bar 1943); s of Herbert Harry Hart (d 1955), of Bassett, Southampton, and Daisy Gladys, *née* Warn (d 1968); *b* 24 June 1913; *Educ* King Edward VI Sch Southampton, Naval Staff Coll, Jt Servs Staff Coll; *m* 16 June 1945, Margaret (Peggy) Evanson, da of Capt Samuel Barbour Duffin (d 1959), of Danesfort, Belfast; 2 s (Ian b 1950, Peter b 1956), 1 da (Nicola b 1952); *Career* RN 1937-63: WWII, HMS Hasty 2 destroyer flotilla 1939-42, i/c HMS Vidette 1942-44, i/c HMS Havelock 1944, i/c sr offr HMS Conn 1944-45 (despatches 1944), 1 Lt HMS Vanguard Royal Cruise to S Africa 1947, promoted Cdr 1947, promoted Capt 1954, Liaison Offr CINC Allied Forces Southern Europe 1954-56, Capt i/c HMS Undine 6 Frigate Sqdn 1957-58, dep dir plans div Admiralty 1958-60, Cdre naval drafting 1960-62, ret RN 1963; Br Cwlth Shipping Co 1963-72, nautical dir (later fleet mangr) Cayzer Irvine & Co 1972-; memb bd Br Cwlth 1966, ret 1976; vice-pres Seaman's Hosp Sco 1983, memb cncl Marine Soc 1964-89, memb cncl Missions to Seamen 1965; FRIN 1970, FNI 1966; Offr Order of Merit Republic of Italy 1958; *Recreations* golf, swimming, gardening; *Clubs* RN Club of 1765 and 1785, Liphook Golf; *Style—* Capt Raymond Hart, CBE, DSO, DSC; Three Firs Cottage, Bramshott Chase, Hindhead, Surrey

HART, Timothy Guy Collins; s of Dr Robert John Collins Hart (Lt-Col RAMC), of Budleigh, Salterton, Devon, and Mary Winifred, *née* Sawday; *b* 31 August 1953; *Educ* The Kings Sch Canterbury, Oxford Poly; *m* 2 Aug 1980, Judith Charlotte, da of Brig Bernard Cyril Elgood, MBE, of Pauntley, Glos; 2 s (Thomas b 1982, Nicholas b 1985), 1 da (Jennifer b 1988) ; *Career* Arthur Young 1974-83, Prudential Assur 1983-85, Phildrew Ventures Advisers 1985-; ACA 1980; *Recreations* tennis, golf, skiing; *Style—* Timothy Hart, Esq; Herberts Hole Cottage, Ballinger, Gt Missenden, Bucks HP16 0RR; Phildrew Ventures, Triton Ct, 14 Finsbury Sq, London EC2A 1PD (☎ 01 628 6366, fax 01 638 2817)

HART, William Stephen; s of John Edward Cecil Hart (d 1980), and Evelyn Lucy, *née* Bateman; *b* 10 Dec 1955; *Educ* The Cathedral Sch Bristol, Univ of Exeter (LLB); *m* 14 July 1976, Jill, da of John Edwin Vaughan (d 1978); *Career* barr Middle Temple 1979-, practising in Bristol; *Recreations* riding, sport, photography, ornithology; *Style—* William Hart, Esq; Albion Chambers, Broad Street, Bristol BS1 1DR (☎ 0272 272144)

HART DYKE, Sir David William; 10 Bt (E 1677), of Horeham, Sussex; s of Sir Derek Hart Dyke, 9 Bt (d 1987); 2 Bt m Anne, da and heir of Percival Hart of Lullingstone Castle, 5 Bt unsuccessfully claimed the Barony of Brayes of which he was a co heir through the Harts 1836; *b* 5 Jan 1955; *Heir* Uncle (Oliver) Guy Hart b 1928; *Style—* Sir David Hart Dyke, Bt; 28 King St West, Apt B14, Stoney Creek, Ontario, Canada

HART DYKE, Trevor; DSO 1944, DL (Derbys 1981); er s of Col Percyvall Hart Dyke, DSO (whose gf Thomas was 2 s of Sir Percival Hart Dyke, 5 Bt); *b* 19 Feb 1905; *Educ* Marlborough; *m* 1, 1933 (m dis 1965), Eileen Joyce, er da of John Niblock-Stuart, of Nairobi; 1 s (Terence b 1934), 1 da (Jennifer (Mrs Vaudrey) b 1939); 2, 1965, Mary Eliot, da of J A Roberts and widow of Maj D E Lockwood; *Career* Brig Queen's Royal Regt, serv WWII, Gibraltar, NW Europe, SE Asia;; *Style—* Brig Trevor Hart Dyke, DSO, DL; Clough House, Bamford, Derbys

HART OF SOUTH LANARK, Baroness (Life Peer 1988), of Lanark, Co Lanark; Judith Constance Mary Hart; DBE (1979), PC (1967); da of Harry and Lily Ridehalgh; *b* 18 Sept 1924; *Educ* Clitheroe Royal GS, LSE (BA); *m* 1946, Anthony Bernard Hart; 2 s; *Career* contested (Lab): Bournemouth West 1951, Aberdeen South 1955; MP (Lab): Lanark 1959-1983, Clydesdale 1983-87; jt parly under-sec Scotland 1964-66, min of state Cwlth Off 1966-67, min Social Security 1967-68, paymaster-gen with seat in Cabinet 1968-69, min Overseas Devpt 1969-70 (1974-75 and 1977-79), front bench oppn spokesman Overseas Aid 1979-80; memb: Lab Party NEC 1969-83 (chm 1981-82, vice-chm 1980-81), Lab Party-TUC liaison ctee to 1982-83 (chm Industl Policy Sub-Ctee until 1983); hon fell Inst of Devpt Studies Univ of Sussex 1984; *Books* Aids and Liberation; *Recreations* gardening; *Style—* The Rt Hon Baroness Hart of South Lanark, DBE, PC; 3 Ennerdale Rd, Kew Gdns, Richmond, Surrey (☎ 01 948 1989);

HART-DAVIS, Sir Rupert Charles; s of Richard Vaughan Hart-Davis and Sybil Cooper (the actress, and sister of Rt Hon Sir Alfred Duff Cooper, GCMG, DSO, 1 Viscount Norwich, da of Sir Alfred Cooper, FRCS, and Lady Agnes, *née* Duff, 4 of da 5 Earl of Fife and sister of 1 Duke of Fife; *b* 28 August 1907; *Educ* Eton, Balliol Coll Oxford; *m* 1, 1929 (m dis), Dame Peggy Ashcroft *qv*; m 2, 1933 (m dis), Catherine Comfort Borden-Turner; 2 s (Duff b 1936, Adam b 1943), 1 da (Lady Silsoe *qv*); m 3, 1964, Winifred Ruth (d 1967), da of C H Ware and widow of Oliver Simon; m 4, 1968, June, née Clifford, widow of David Williams; *Career* editor, author, publisher; dir Rupert Hart-Davis Ltd (which he founded) 1946-68 (former dir Jonathan Cape Ltd), vice-pres ctee of London Library 1971- (former chm); kt 1967; *Books* Hugh Walpole: a biography 1952, The Arms of Time: a memoir 1979; has edited letters of: Oscar Wilde, Max Beerbohm, The Lyttelton Hart-Davis Letters and Siegfried Sassoon Diaries 1920-22; *Style—* Sir Rupert Hart-Davis; The Old Rectory, Marske-in-Swaledale, Richmond, N Yorks

HART-LEVERTON, Colin Allen; QC (1979); s of Morris Hart-Leverton, of London; *b* 10 May 1936; *Educ* Stowe; *Career* barr Middle Temple 1957, dep circuit judge 1975, attorney-at-law Turks and Caicos Islands 1976, Crown Ct recorder 1979; occasional Radio and TV Broadcasts in UK and USA; AInstT 1957; *Recreations* table tennis, jazz; *Style—* Colin Hart-Leverton, Esq, QC; 10 King's Bench Walk, London EC4Y 7EB (☎ 01 353 2501)

HARTE, Geoffrey Charles; s of Charles Fredrick Harte (d 1982); *b* 16 Sept 1923; *Educ* Plympton GS; *m* 1950, Moira, da of James Kennedy (d 1958); 1 s; *Career* engr; pres J and S Marine Ltd; non exec dir Cray Electronics Hldgs plc; *Recreations* music, photography, books, boats; *Clubs* IOD; *Style—* Geoffrey Harte, Esq; Combers Week, Harracott, Barnstaple, N Devon (☎ 0271 85448)

HARTE, John Denis; MBE (1981); s of Frank Harry Roach Harte (d 1980), and Beatrice Mary, *née* de Looze (d 1971); *b* 14 Mar 1926; *Educ* Clapham Secdy Sch; *m* 23 Feb 1952 (m dis 1983), (Kathleen) Joan, da of Percy Joseph Cater (d 1971), of Farnborough Park, Kent; 2 s (Jeremy Mark b 30 Nov 1960, Joby John b 30 Jan 1982), 1 da (Judith Anne b 15 July 1955); m 2, 25 April 1983, Jane Nicholson, da of John Kennedy; 1 step da (Joanna Louise b 26 July 1973); *Career* slr 1952, ptnr Goodwin Harte & Co Harrow; Notary Public; legal advsr St Marylebone CAB 1958-87; chm mgmnt ctee: Westminster CAB 1980-85, Elstree CAB 1981-86; memb Law Soc; *Style—* John Harte, Esq, MBE; The Grotto, Yanwath, Penrith, Cumbria (☎ 0768 63288); 221/225 Station Rd, Harrow, Middlesex (☎ 01 427 8361, fax 01 861 3069)

HARTE, Dr Michael John; s of Harold Edward Harte, of Sussex, and Marjorie Irene, *née* Scaife; *b* 15 August 1936; *Educ* Charterhouse, Trinity Coll Cambridge (BA), Univ Coll London (Dip Biochemical Engr, PhD); *m* 1, 1962 (m dis); m 2, 1975, Mrs Mary Claire Preston, da of D J Hogan (d 1972); 4 step-da (Caroline b 1962, Emma b 1964, Abigail and Lucy b 1966); *Career* chm NATO Budget Ctees 1981-83; asst under sec (Dockyard Planning Team) MOD 1985; asst under sec (personnel) (air) MOD 1987; *Recreations* wine, walking, weeding; *Style—* Dr Michael Harte; Greenman Farm, Wadhurst, Sussex TN5 6LE (☎ 0892 88 3292); Adastral House, Theobalds Rd WC1X 8RU

HARTIG, Hon Mrs Linda; *née* Nivison; er da of 3 Baron Glendyne; *b* 23 Oct 1954; *m* 1976, Dr Count Nikolaus Hartig; 1 s; 1 da; *Style—* The Hon Mrs Hartig; Heuberggasse 9, A-1170 Vienna, Austria

HARTILL, (Edward) Theodore; s of Clement Augustus Hartill, of Shropshire, and Florence Margarita, *née* Ford; *b* 23 Jan 1943; *Educ* Priory Sch for Boys Shrewsbury, Coll of Estate Mgmnt London Univ (BSc Estate Mgmnt); *m* 1975, Gillian Ruth, da of Harold Todd (d 1963); 4 s (Jeremy b 1969, Richard b 1972, Andrew b 1977, Giles b 1981); *Career* joined messrs Burd and Evans Land Agents, Shrewsbury 1963; Estates Dept Legal and Gen Assurance Soc 1964-73; Property Investmt Dept Guardian Royal Exchange Assurance Gp 1973-85; The City Surveyor, Corporation of London 1985-; vis lectr in Law of Town Planning and Compulsory Purchase, Hammersmith and West London Coll of Advanced Business Studies 1968-78;Memb of British Schs Exploring Soc FRICS; Liveryman Worshipful Company of Chartered Surveyors 1985-; *Recreations* travel, hill walking, cinema, family; *Style—* E T Hartill Esq; 215 Sheen Lane, East Sheen, London SW14 8LE (☎ 01 878 4494); The City Surveyor, City Surveyor's Dept, Corporation of London, PO Box 270, Guildhall, London EC2P 2EJ (☎ 01 606 3030, telex 265608 LONDON G, fax 01 260 1119)

HARTINGTON, Marquess of; Peregrine Andrew Morny Cavendish; s and h of 11 Duke of Devonshire, MC, PC, and Hon Deborah (Debo) Freeman-Mitford (sis of Nancy, Jessica and Unity Mitford, (*see* Treuhaft, Hon Mrs, and Hon Lady Mosley), da of 2 Baron Redesdale; *b* 27 April 1944; *Educ* Eton, Exeter Coll Oxford; *m* 28 June 1967, Amanda Carmen, da of late Cdr Edward Gavin Heywood-Lonsdale, RN; 1 s, 2 da (Lady Celina Imogen b 1971, Lady Jasmine Nancy b 1973); *Heir* Earl of Burlington b 1969; *Style—* Marquess of Hartington; Beamsley Hall, Skipton, N Yorks BD23 6HD (☎ 075 671 410/424)

HARTLAND, Robert Arthur; s of William Thomas Hartland (d 1956), of Croydon, and Alice Jane, *née* Woodman (d 1958); *b* 13 May 1926; *Educ* Whitgift Middle Sch; *m* 17 July 1948, Jean Beryl Helen, da of Arthur Robert Flindell (d 1984), of London; 1 s (Neil b 1953); *Career* RE 1944-48; Sir Frederick Snow & Ptnrs (formerly Frederick Snow & Ptnrs): articled pupil 1948, assoc 1960, ptnr 1965, sr ptnr 1984; Constantine Gold Medal Manchester Soc of Engrs 1978; Freeman: City of London 1977, Worshipful Co of Constructors 1977, Worshipful Co of Engrs 1985; CEng 1952, FICE 1965, MConsE 1967, Inst of Demolition Engrs (pres 1983 and 1984), The Concrete Soc (sr vice pres 1988); *Books* Design of Precast Concrete (1975); *Recreations* hill walking, gardening; *Clubs* IOD, Arts; *Style—* Robert Hartland, Esq; West Winds, Hazelwood Lane, Chipstead, Surrey CR3 3QZ (☎ 07375 53939); Ross House, 144 Southwark St, London SE1 0SZ (☎ 01 928 5688, fax 01 928 1774, telex 917478 SNOMEN G)

HARTLAND-SWANN, Julian Dana Nimmo; s of Prof John Hartland-Swann (d 1961), and Kenlis, *née* Taylour (d 1957); *b* 18 Feb 1936; *Educ* Stowe, Lincoln Coll Oxford (BA); *m* 22 Oct 1960, Ann Deirdre, da of Lt Cdr Robert Green, DSO, of St Helier, Shotley Gate, nr Ipswich; 1 s (Piers b 1961), 1 da (Justina b 1963);; *Career* Nat Serv RA 1955-57; Dip Serv 1960-; 3 sec Bangkok Embassy 1961-65, 1 sec FO 1965-68, head of external dept Br Mil Govt Berlin 1968-71, 1 sec and head of chancery Vienna 1971-74, FCO 1975-77, cnsllr 1977, ambass to Mongolian People's Republic 1977-79, cnsllr and head of chancery Brussels 1979-83, head of SE Asian dept FCO 1983- 85, consul gen Frankfurt 1986; *Recreations* French food, sailing, restoring ruins; *Style—* Julian Hartland-Swann, Esq; c/o Foreign and Commonwealth Office, London SW1A 2AH

HARTLEY, Arthur Coulton; CIE (1945), OBE (1943); s of John Aspinall Hartley (d 1940), of Worsley, Lancs, and Jennie Hartley (d 1968); *b* 24 Mar 1906; *Educ* Cowley GS, Manchester Univ (BA), Balliol Coll Oxford; *m* 1943, Mrs Cecilie Leslie; 1 s (John); *Career* Indian Civil Service 1929, asst magistrate and subdivisional offr Sirajganj Bengal 1929-32. settlement offr Rangpur Bengal 1932-37, ps to govr of Bengal 1938-40, district magistrate Howrah 1940-43, controller of rationing Calcutta 1943-45, dir gen civil supplies (food) Bengal 1945-47; ret; mangr: Parry (India) 1950-53, Atomic Energy Authy 1953-71; *Recreations* hill walking, painting; *Style—* Arthur Hartley Esq, CIE, OBE; 12 Grange Rd, Lewes, E Sussex (☎ 0273 471194)

HARTLEY, Charles William Stewart; CBE (1959); s of Dr Arthur Conning Hartley,TD, FRCS(E) (d 1919), and Margaret, *née* Stewart (d 1945); g nephew of Sir Charles Augustus Hartley, KCMG, FRSE, the Victorian Engr; *b* 5 Oct 1911; *Educ* Wellington Coll, Peterhouse Cambridge (BA, DipAgricSc, MA), Imperial Coll of Tropical Agric (AICTA); *m* 16 Dec 1936, Marie Zoyla, da of Major J D Lenegan, MBE (d 1957); 1 s (William Denis b 1953), 3 da (Margaret b 1940, Doreen Mary b 1941, Lilias Ann b 1955); *Career* Lt Straits Settlement Vol Force Malayan Campaign 1941-42, POW Singapore and Thailand 1942-45; Agric Offr Malaya 1935-47, offr i/c Central Experiment Station, Serdang 1947-48, sr Agronomist 1948-51, dir W African Inst for Oil Palm Research 1955-63; Independent Conslt in Tropical Agric 1964-82; *Books* The Oil Palm (1967, 3 edn 1988), A Biography of Sir Charles Hartley, Civil Engineer: The Father of the Danube (1988); *Recreations* gardening, walking; *Clubs* East India; *Style—* Charles W S Hartley, CBE; Three Gables, Amberley, Stroud, Glos GL5 5AH (☎ 045 387 2538)

HARTLEY, Air Marshal Sir Christopher Harold; KCB (1963, CB 1961), CBE (1957, OBE 1949), DFC (1945), AFC (1944); s of Brig-Gen Harold Hartley, GCVO, CH, CBE, MC, FRS (d 1972); *b* 31 Jan 1913; *Educ* Eton, Balliol Coll Oxford, King's Coll Cambridge; *m* 1, 1937 (m dis 1943), Anne Sitwell; m 2, 1944, Margaret Watson; 2 s; *Career* joined RAFVR 1938, served WWII, Gp Capt 1952, Air Cdre 1958, AOC 12 Gp Fighter Cmd 1959, Air Vice-Marshal 1960, asst chief Air Staff (Operational Requirements) Air Miny 1961-63, Air Marshal 1963, dep chief Air Staff 1963-66, controller of Aircraft Miny of Aviation 1966, ret 1970; dir Westland Aircraft Ltd 1971-83, dep chm British Hovercraft Corpn 1979-83 (chm 1974-79); export consultant; *Recreations* fishing; *Clubs* Travellers', Flyfishers'; *Style—* Air Marshal Sir Christopher Hartley, KCB, CBE, DFC, AFC; c/o Marex (Whitehall) Associates, Whitehall House, 41 Whitehall, London SW1; c/o Barclays Bank, Bank Plain, Norwich, Norfolk

HARTLEY, Christopher Ian James; s of C J Hartley (d 1987), and Rosemary Pamela Metcalf, *née* Horne; *b* 10 August 1961; *Educ* St Edward's Sch Oxford, Bristol Univ (BSc); *Career* business mangr; ICI Fire Chemicals (ICI C and P Ltd) 1985-86, ICI Australia 1988-; Bristol Univ Red (rowing rep level); *Style—* Christopher I J Hartley, Esq; Greenhayes, Grove Hill, Dedham, Colchester, Essex; c/o ICI Australia, Melbourne, Australia

HARTLEY, David Fielding; s of Robert Maude Hartley (d 1980), of Hebden Bridge, Yorks, and Sheila Ellen, *née* Crabtree (d 1977); *b* 14 Sept 1937; *Educ* Rydal Sch, Clare Coll Cambridge (MA, PhD); *m* 23 April 1960, Joanna Mary, da of John Stanley Bolton (d 1988), of Halifax; 1 s (Timothy b 1965), 2 da (Caroline (Mrs Eatough) b 1963, Rosalind b 1968); *Career* Univ of Cambridge: lectr mathematical laboratory 1967-70 (sr asst in res 1964-65, asst dir of res 1966-67) jr res fell Churchill Coll 1964-67, dir computing serv 1970-, fell Darwin Coll 1969-86, fell Clare Coll 1987-; dir: Lynxvale Ltd, Cad Centre Ltd, Cambridge Control Ltd; chm and dir NAG Ltd; memb: Computer Bd for Univs and Res Cncls 1979-83, PM's Info Technol Advsy Panel 1981-86, BBC Sci Consultative GP 1984-87, vice-pres Br Computer Soc; Freeman City of London 1988, Co of Info Technologists 1988; FBCS 1967; Medal of Merits Nicholas Copernicus Univ Poland 1984; *Style—* Dr David Hartley; 26 Girton Rd, Cambridge (☎ 0223 276 975); Univ of Cambridge, Computer Laboratory, New Museums Site, Pembroke St, Cambridge (☎ 0223 334 703)

HARTLEY, Sir Frank; CBE (1970); s of Robinson King Hartley (d 1916), and Mary, *née* Holt (d 1959); *b* 5 Jan 1911; *Educ* Nelson Municipal Secondary Sch, Sch of Pharmacy London Univ, UC London, Birkbeck Coll London (PhD); *m* 1937, Lydia May England; 2 s; *Career* dean Sch of Pharmacy London Univ 1962-76, vice-chllr London Univ 1976-78; chm Br Pharmacopoeia Cmmn 1970-80, vice-chm Medicines Cmmn 1974-83; chm: cmmrs Lambeth Southwark and Lewisham Health Area 1979-80, Consortium of Charing Cross and Westminster Medical Schs 1981-84; hon FRCP (London) 1979, hon FRCS (London) 1980, hon DSc Warwick 1978, hon LLD Strathclyde 1980, hon LLD London 1987; Charter Gold Medal Royal Pharmaceutical Soc of GB 1974; FPS, FRSC; kt 1977; *Recreations* reading; *Clubs* Athenaeum, Savage; *Style—* Sir Frank Hartley, CBE; 24 Old School Close, St Mary's Mead, Merton Park, London SW19 3HY

HARTLEY, Prof Frank Robinson; s of Sir Frank Hartley, CBE, of Old School Close, Merton Park, London SW19 3HY, and Lydia May, *née* England; *b* 29 Jan 1942; *Educ* King's Coll Sch Wimbledon, Magdalen Coll Oxford (MA DPhil DSc); *m* 12 Dec 1964, Valerie, da of George Peel (d 1984), of Silksworth, Co Durham, and Watchfield, Oxon; 3 da (Susan b 1967, Judith b 1971, Elizabeth b 1974); *Career* res fell div of protein chem CSIRO (Aust) 1966-69, ICI res fell and tutor in chem UCL 1969-70, lectr chem Univ of Southampton 1970-75, princ and dean RMCS 1982- (prof chem 1975-82); special advsr to PM on Euro fighter aircraft 1988; memb Oxon Soc of Rugby Football Referees; FRSC 1977, FRSA 1988; *Books* Chemistry of Platinum and Palladium (1973), Elements of Organometallic Chemistry (1974), Solution Equilibria (1980), Supported Metal Complexes (1985), Chemistry of the Metal-Carbon Bond (vol 1 1983, vol 2 1984, vol 3 1985, vol 4 1987); *Recreations* rugby refereeing, swimming, cliff walking, reading, gardening, squash; *Clubs* Shrivenham, IOD; *Style—* Prof Frank Hartley; Royal Military College of Science, Shrivenham, Swindon, Wilts, SN6 8LA (☎ 0793 785 436, fax 0793 783 878, telex 265871 REG WJJ110)

HARTLEY, Rev Godfrey; s of Isaac Hartley, and Hannah, *née* Lowther; *b* 26 August 1937; *Educ* Clare Hall Sch, Manchester Univ, Cuddesdon Coll Oxford; *m* 17 Aug 1963, Maureen Ruth, da of Norman Harding Goldsworth, of Nottingham; 2 s (António b 1965, Richard b 1974); *Career* Nat Serv RAF 1956-58; chaplain: RNR 1973-, Fleets Representative Ships Building (Clyde); ordained: deacon 1964, priest 1965; curate St Giles Balderton Diocese of Southwell 1964-67, port chaplain Missions to Seamen rector St George Beira Mozambique 1968-73, sr chaplain and sec for Scotland Missions to Seamen 1974-, priest i/c St Gabriel's Govan 1974-; memb: SSC, Sea Care; Freeman City of Glasgow 1979; memb Incorporation of Coopers of Glasgow 1979; *Recreations* skiing, photography, painting, reading; *Clubs* Army and Navy, Naval, Ski Club of GB, Glasgow Press, Bearsden Ski; *Style—* The Rev Godfrey Hartley; 121 Southbrae Drive, Jordanhill, Glasgow G13 1TU (☎ 041 954 7968); The Missions To Seamen Scotland, St Gabriel's, 40 Greenfield St, Glasgow G13 1TU (☎ 041 445 3361)

HARTLEY, Roger Anderson; s of John Herbert Hartley (d 1975), of Clevedon House, Ranmoor, Sheffield, and Hilda Mary, *née* Sowerby (d 1987); *b* 28 May 1942; *Educ* Shrewsbury, St Catharine's Coll Cambridge (MA); *m* 1, 4 Oct 1969 (m dis 1981), Roslynne Mary, *née* Vincent-Jones; 1 s (Peter Anderson b 16 July 1974), 1 da (Sarah Catharine b 26 April 1977); m 2, 9 July 1984, Tina Elizabeth, da of Jack Alderson, of Woodthorpe, York; *Career* slr 1970; vice-pres: Malton and Norton Operatic Soc, Malton Agric Soc, Ryedale Show; slr to Malton Town Cncl, memb Rydale DC 1979-83, clerk to Fearnsides and Stephensons Charities 1970-84; memb: Law Soc, Yorks Law Soc; *Recreations* boating, walking, music; *Style—* Roger Hartley, Esq; Melrose, Sandsend, Whitby, N Yorks YO21 3SZ (☎ 0947 83250); 13 Yorkersgate, Malton, N Yorks YO17 0AA (☎ 0653 693101/2)

HARTOP, Barry; s of Philip William Hartop (d 1954), of Lowestoft, and Constance Winifred Hartop; *b* 15 August 1942; *Educ* Lowestoft GS, Durham Univ (BSc); *m* 30 July 1965, Sandra, da of Alan Walter Swan (d 1976), Lowestoft; 1 s (James), 1 da (Anna); *Career* mgmnt trainee Unilever, prodn mangr Lever Bros, Unilever Res Div (Euro Operational Res Rotterdam), head Euro devpt and application centre Utrecht, chm and md Lever Indust UK; *Style—* Barry Hartop, Esq; Field Cottage, The

Ridgeway, Guildford, Surrey (☎ 0483 577617); Lever House, St James Rd, Kingston-upon-Thames, Surrey (☎ 01 541 5577)

HARTSHORNE, (Bertram) Kerrich; s of Bertram Charles Hartshorne (d 1949), of Alexandria, Egypt, and Beatrice Mabel, *née* Spencer (d 1974); *b* 24 Nov 1923; *Educ* Charterhouse, Clare Coll Cambridge (MA), Birmingham Univ (MSc); *m* 27 Sept 1952, Jean Irving, da of Oswald Irving Bell (d 1946), of Dumfries; 3 s (David b 1954, Christopher b 1955, James b 1965), 1 da (Pamela b 1958); *Career* WWII RE 1942-47, cmmnd 1943, active serv with Royal Bombay Sappers and Miners in India, Burma and Indo-China (despatches 1946), commanded: field sqdn 1945, depot bn 1946-47; cnslt Sir William Halcrow & Ptnrs civil engrs 1984-(joined firm 1949, assoc 1969-73, ptnr 1973-), dir Halcrow Fox & Assocs 1977-83; chm: Halcrow Surveys 1982-84, Sir William Halcrow & Ptnrs Scotland 1983-84; sr ptnr The Hartshorne Ptnrship 1985-; involved with many major projects incl: Volta River Project Ghana 1950-60, Pangani River Basin and Nym Dam Tanzania 1961-68, Orange Fish Tunnel 1963-64, military and civil devpt projects Sultanate of Oman 1973-79; FICE 1968, FInsHE 1970, memb ACE 1973; *Books* Transport Survey of the Territories of Papua and New Guinea (1971); *Recreations* sailing, landscape gardening, travelling; *Style—* Kerrich Hartshorne, Esq; Mill House, Irongray, Dumfries DG2 9SQ (☎ 038773 417); The Hartshorne Partnership, Oakwood Farm, Irongray, Dumfries DG2 9SQ (☎ 038773 493)

HARTWELL, Sir Brodrick William Charles Elwin; 5 Bt (UK 1805), of Dale Hall, Essex; s of Sir Brodrick Hartwell, 4 Bt (d 1948), and his 2 w, Joan; *b* 7 August 1909; *Educ* Bedford Sch; *m* 1, 1937 (m dis 1950), Marie, da of Simon Mullins; 1 s; m 2, 1951, Mary, MBE, da of J Church; (1 s, 1 da both decd); *Heir* s, Francis Antony Charles Peter Hartwell, *qv*; *Career* served RAF 1928-29, Army 1931-48 (Capt Leics Regt); *Style—* Sir Brodrick Hartwell, Bt; 50 High St, Lavendon, nr Olney, Bucks (☎ 0234 712619)

HARTWELL, Edward George; s of Edward Hartwell (d 1978); *b* 29 April 1922; *Educ* Poole GS, Reading Sch; *m* 1943, Kathleen Joan, da of Harold Reginald Montague (d 1959); 1 child; *Career* served WWII 1942-46 RN, Allied landings in Italy and Russian Convoys; consulting engr to the automotive and allied industries; memb mgmnt ctee Poole Engrg Industrial Trg Centre; past dir Hunts Groups of Cos; operating dir Hunts Engrg (Crankshafts) Ltd 1962-82; past chm of Dorset and Hants Ctee of the Engrg Employers Fedn 1982; CEng, MIMechE; *Recreations* walking, swimming, industrial archaeology; *Style—* Edward Hartwell, Esq; 12 Herm Rd, Parkstone, Poole, Dorset BH12 4LE

HARTWELL, Eric; CBE (1983); s of Alfred Hartwell (d 1932), of Holmleigh, West Parade, Worthing, Sussex, and Edyth Maud, *née* Brunning (d 1980); *b* 10 August 1915; *Educ* Mall Sch Twickenham, Worthing HS; *m* 1, 1937 (m dis 1951), Gladys Rose, *née* Bennett; 1 s (Anthony Charles b Jan 1939), 1 da (Susan b Jan 1946); m 2, 14 June 1952, Dorothy Maud, da of late Harold Mowbray, MM, of Edgware, Middx; 1 s (Keith Alan b Sept 1958), 1 da (Janine Erica b June 1956); *Career* served WW II with RE 1940-46 (QMSI); chief exec Trusthouse Forte plc 1978-83 (vice-chm 1972-), chm Br Hotels Restaurants and Caterers Assoc 1981-84; memb cncl CBI 1972-87 (memb finance and gen purposes ctee and chm fin sub-ctee 1980-87), fndr memb LV Catering Educnl Tst; vice-chm Thames Heritage Tst 1983-87, memb Inner Magic Circle; Freeman of City of London, Liveryman of Worshipful Co of Upholders; CBIM, FHCIMA, FRSA, MIMC; *Recreations* yachting (yacht 'Kandora'), painting, photography, golf, magic; *Clubs* Thames Motor Yacht, South Herts Golf, Terenure Country, Inner Magic Circle; *Style—* Eric Hartwell, Esq, CBE; Tall Trees, 129 Totteridge Lane, London N20 8NS (☎ 01 445 2321); Trusthouse Forte plc, 166 High Holborn, London WC1V 6TT

HARTWELL, Francis Anthony Charles Peter; s and h of Sir Brodrick William Charles Elwin Hartwell, 5 Bt, *qv*; *b* 1 June 1940; *Educ* Thames Nautical Trg Coll, HMS Worcester, Cadet RNR, Univ of Southampton (Sch of Navigation)-Master Mariner; *m* 26 Oct 1968, Barbara Phyllis Rae, da of Henry Rae Green (d 1985), of Sydney, Aust; 1 s (Timothy b 1970); *Career* P and OSNCo/Inchcape Gp 1958-69 and 1972-75, Chief Offr/Cadet trg Offr, Mate/master, OCL (London) 1969-71, Cargo Supt, 1975-, Overseas Managerial Services for marine and port ops contracts, pt/t ind marine and cargo surveyor; nominated surveyor for Lloyd's Agency (Port Moresby) and The Salvage Assoc 1981-86; Port Advsy ctee 1981-82, memb Arbitration Tbnl 1982-83 and 1985 for Papua New Guinea Govt; gen mangr Marine Services-Port and Agency-WA Liner Agencies; Fed of Aust Underwater Instructors (FAUI), MCIT, MRIN; *Recreations* scuba diving, water skiing, photography, reading, philately; *Clubs* Master Mariners (Southampton), Old Worcester's Assoc; *Style—* Francis Hartwell, Esq; c/o Barclays Bank, 11 High St, Olney, Bucks

HARTWELL, Baron (Life Peer UK 1968), of Peterborough Court in the City of London; Hon (William) Michael Berry; MBE (1945), TD; 2 s of 1 Viscount Camrose; hp to bro, 2 Viscount; *b* 18 May 1911; *Educ* Eton, Ch Ch Oxford; *m* 1936, Lady Pamela, *née* Smith (d 1982), yr da of 1 Earl of Birkenhead; 2 s (Hon Adrian b 1937, Hon Nicholas b 1942), 2 da (Hon Harriet b 1944, Hon Eleanor b 1950); *Career* served WW II, Lt-Col 1944; dir Daily Telegraph plc; tstee Reuters, ed Sunday Mail (Glasgow) 1934-35, managing ed Financial Times 1937-39, chm Amalgamated Press Ltd 1954-59; chm and ed-in-chief Daily Telegraph 1954-87, Sunday Telegraph 1961-87; *Clubs* White's, Royal Yacht Sqdn, Beefsteak; *Style—* The Rt Hon Lord Hartwell, MBE, TD; Oving House, Whitchurch, Aylesbury, Bucks (☎ 0296 641307); 18 Cowley St, London SW1 (☎ 01 222 4673)

HARTY, Bernard Peter; s of William Harty (d 1975), and Eileen Nora, *née* Canavan; *b* 1 May 1943; *Educ* St Richard's Coll Droitwich, Ullathorne GS Coventry; *m* 12 Aug 1965, Glenys Elaine, da of Ernest Simpson (d 1969); 1 da (Sarah Jane b 1970); *Career* accountant Coventry City Cncl 1961-69; forward budget planning offr Derbys County Cncl 1969-72; chief accountant Bradford City Cncl 1972-73; chief finance offr Bradford Met Dist Cncl 1972-73; City Tres Oxon County Cncl 1976-83; Chamberlain of London City of London Corp 1983-; chm Fndn for Information Technol in Local Govt, govr Oxford Poly; Liveryman Worshipful Co of Tallow Chandlers, Freeman Worshipful Co of Information Technologists; IPFA, MBCS; Chmn Foundation for Information Technol in Local Govt, non ex dir Chelsea Bldg Soc; memb: The Worshipful Co of Tallow Chandlers, Co Information Technologists, The Nat Tst; *Recreations* Nat Tst, music cricket; *Style—* Bernard Harty, Esq; Chamberlain of London, Guildhall, London EC2P 2EJ (☎ 01 260 1300)

HARVEY, Alan Frederick Ronald; OBE (1970); s of Edward Frederick Harvey (d 1966), and Alice Sophia, *née* Cocks (d 1963); *b* 15 Dec 1919; *Educ* Tottenham GS; *m* 28 July 1946, Joan Barbara, da of Arthur Stanley Tuckey (d 1976), of Barnes; 1 s (Ian b 16 March 1952); *Career* RAF 1940-45: RAF station Amman 1940, Br Embassy Ankara 1942, Br Embassy Paris 1945; Air Miny 1946-49; Dip Serv; FO 1949-52, vice-consul Turin 1953-55; second sec: Rome 1956, Tokyo 1957-59; consul (info) Chicago 1959-62, FO 1963-65; first sec (commercial): Belgrade 1965-67, Tokyo 1967-72; commercial cnsllr: Milan 1973-74, Rome 1975-76; consul-gen Perth 1976-78; *Recreations* golf, gardening; *Clubs* Royal Cwlth Soc, Civil Serv, Windwhistle GC, Squash and Country; *Style—* Alan Harvey, Esq, OBE; Ken Hill House, Cricket St Thomas Chard, Somerset TA20 4DE

HARVEY, (Sir) Charles Richard Musgrave; 3 Bt (UK 1933), of Threadneedle St, City of London; does not use title; s of Sir Richard Musgrave Harvey, 2 Bt (d 1978), and Frances, *née* Lawford (d 1986); *b* 7 April 1937; *Educ* Marlborough, Pembroke Coll Cambridge; *m* 1967, Celia Vivien, da of George Henry Hodson; 1 s, 1 da (Tamara b 1977); *Heir* s, Paul Richard Harvey b 2 June 1971; *Career* fell Inst of Development Studies Sussex Univ; *Style—* Charles Harvey, Esq; 33 Preston Park Avenue, Brighton, Sussex BN1 6XA; IDS, University of Sussex, Brighton BN1 9RE (☎ 0273 606261, telex 877159 RR HOVE IDS)

HARVEY, Dr David Robert; s of Cyril Francis Harvey (d 1971), of Orpington, Kent, and Margarita, *née* Cardew-Smith (d 1986); *b* 7 Dec 1936; *Educ* Dulwich, Guy's Hosp Med Sch (MB, BS 1960); *Career* held jr appointments in paediatrics at Guy's Hosp, Gt Ormond St and Hammersmith Hosp; conslt paediatrician: Queen Charlotte's Maternity Hosp 1970-, St Charles Hosp 1971-, St Mary's Hosp 1986-; hon sec: Neonatal Soc 1974-79, British Paediatric Soc 1979-84, British Assoc for Perinatal Paediatrics 1983-86; dir: Terrence Higgins Tst 1983-88, Radio Lollipop; Freeman of City of London (Worshipful Co of Apothecaries); MRCP 1963, FRCP 1976; *Books* articles on general and neonatal paediatrics and child health, A New Life (1979), New Parents (1988); *Recreations* opera, learning Chinese, using word processor; *Style—* Dr David Harvey; 2 Lord Napier Place, Upper Mall, London W6 9UB (☎ 01 748 7900); Queen Charlotte's and Chelsea Hospital, Goldhawk Road, London W6 OXG (☎ 01 740 3918)

HARVEY, David Stanley; s of Stanley Joseph Harvey (d 1964), and Edna Nancy May, *née* Harvey; *b* 2 August 1952; *Educ* Gresham's Sch Holt; *m* 3 April 1981, Kerry Louise, da of David Owen; 2 s (James b 1978, Tavis b 1982), 1 da (Lucy b 1986); *Career* slr; memb Law Soc; *Recreations* sailing, swimming; *Style—* David S Harvey, Esq; Driftwood, 22 Bedford Road, St Ives, Cornwall (☎ 0736 796710); Poldho, High Street, St Ives, Cornwall (☎ 0736 795618)

HARVEY, Hon Guy Alan Vere; s of Baron Harvey of Prestbury (Life Peer); *b* 1947; *Educ* Eton, Neuchâtel Univ Switzerland; *m* 1977 (m dis) Margaret C B, da of Lewis Robertson, of The Blair, Blairlogie, Stirling; 4 children; *Career* incorporated surveyor, dir Northcote Valuations Ltd; *Style—* The Hon Guy Harvey; c/o Mrs J A Harvey, 42 Ennismore Gardens, London SW7

HARVEY, Ian Alexander; s of Dr Alexander Harvey (d 1987), and Mona, *née* Anderson; *b* 2 Feb 1945; *Educ* Cardiff HS, Cambridge Univ (MA), Harvard Business Sch (MBA); *m* 21 Nov 1976, Dr DeAnne, da of Prof Marvin Julius, of Ames, Iowa, USA; 1 s (Ross b 1980), 1 da (Megan b 1979); *Career* apprentice mech engr Vickers Ltd 1963-69, project engr Laporte Industs 1969-73, sr loan offr World Bank 1975-82, ptnr Logan Assocs Inc 1984-85, chief exec Br Technol Gp 1985-; memb: res and prodn ctee CBI, sci and industl ctee Br Assoc for Advancement of Sci; CBIM 1987; *Recreations* piano, skiing, sailing, windsurfing; *Style—* Ian Harvey, Esq; Tanglewood, Cobham Road, Fetcham, Surrey KT22 9SJ (☎ 0372 54010); British Technology Group, 101 Newington Causeway, London SE1 6BU (☎ 01 403 6666, fax 01 403 7586, car 0860 515229, telex 894397)

HARVEY, Jane Margaret; da of Dr William James Harvey, of The Hirsel, Coldstream, Berkwicks, and Ann Margaret, *née* Shaw; *b* 10 June 1958; *Educ* St Mary's Covent Longridge Towers Berwick-upon-Tweed, Univ of Edinburgh (Bsc, Dip MBA); *m* 28 June 1986, Timothy Ernest Myer, s of Henry Ernest Myer, of 86 Deacons Hill Rd, Elstree, Herts; *Career* res analyst: McKinsey and Co Inc 1982-84, The Mac Gp 1984-85; mktg mangr One to One 1985-86, account dir Shandwick Communications 1986-88, jt md Harrington Communications; *Style—* Ms Jane Harvey; 44 Burtonhole Lane, London NW7 1AL (☎ 01 959 3475)

HARVEY, John Charles Tolmie; s of John St Clair Harvey (d 1959), and Carol May, *née* Tolmie (d 1960); *b* 10 Sept 1937; *Educ* Harrow, Clare Coll Cambridge (MA); *m* 16 June 1961 (m dis), (Irene Margaret) Rosamund, *née* Gillespie; 1 s (John James Russell b 10 March 1975), 3 da (Julia Carol b 22 June 1962, Mary Elizabeth b 20 July 1964, Kate Sally b 19 June 1972); *Career* Nat Serv 2 Lt 4 Queen's Royal Lancers 1956-58; Lt Royal Gloucestershire Hussars TA; int trade dir Harveys of Bristol; pres Bristol Children's Help Soc, memb Soc of Merchant Venturers, former pres Grateful Soc; chm Harrow Assoc; Freeman; City of Bristol, City of London; memb Worshipful Co of Vintners; *Recreations* racing, fishing; *Clubs* Army and Navy, Clifton; *Style—* John Harvey, Esq; 1 Miles Rd, Clfton, Bristol BS8 2JN (☎ 0272 738874); John Harvey & Sons Ltd, 12 Denmark St, Bristol BS1 4DD (☎ 0272 836161, fax 0272 833878, telex 44100)

HARVEY, Hon John Wynn; s of 1 Baron Harvey of Tasburgh, GCMG, GCVO, CB (d 1968), and hp of bro, 2 Baron *qv*; *b* 4 Nov 1923; *Educ* Eton, Westminster, Cambridge Univ; *m* 1950, Elena Marie-Teresa, da of Giambattista, Marchese Curtopassi (d 1945); 2 s (Charles b 1951, Robert b 1953), 1 da (Antonella); *Career* served WW II, with infantry (POW Italy); farmer; *Books* Within and Without (1960), Beside the Sea (1966), Diplomatic Diaries of Oliver Harvey (1972); *Style—* The Hon John Harvey; Coed-y-Maen, Meifod, Powys

HARVEY, Prof Jonathan Dean; s of Gerald Harvey, and Noelle Heron, *née* Dean (d 1969); *b* 3 May 1939; *Educ* St Michael's Coll Tenbury, Repton, St John's Coll Cambridge (MA, DMus), Glasgow Univ (PhD); *m* 24 Sept 1960, Rosaleen Marie, da of Daniel Barry (d 1949); 1 s (Dominic b 3 May 1967), 1 da (Anna Maria b 13 Jan 1964); *Career* composer; lectr Southampton Univ 1964-77, Harkness fell Princeton Univ 1969-70, reader Sussex Univ 1977-80 (prof of music 1980-); works performed at many festivals and int centres; compositions: Persephone Dream (for orchestra 1972), Inner Light (trilogy, for performers and tape 1973-77), Smiling Immortal (for chamber orchestra 1977), String Quartet (1977), Veils and Melodies (for tapes 1978), Magnificant and Nunc Dimitis (for choir and organ 1978), Album (for wind quintet 1978), Hymn (for choir and orchestra 1979), Be(com)ing (for clarinet and piano 1979), Concelebration (instrumental 1979 and 1981), Mortuos Plango Vivos Voco (for tape

1980), Passion and Resurrection (church opera 1981), Resurrection (for double chorus and organ 1981), Whom ye Adore (for orchestra 1981), Bhakti (for 15 instruments and tape 1982), Easter Orisons (for chamber orchestra 1983), The Path of Devotion (for choir and orchestra 1983), Nachtlied (for soprano piano and tape 1984), Gong-Ring (for ensemble with electronics 1984), Song Offerings (for soprano and players 1985), Madonna of Winter and Spring (for orchestra synthesizers and electronics 1986), Lightness and Weight (for tuba and orchestra 1986), Forms of Emptiness (for choir 1986), Tendril (for ensemble 1987); Timepieces (for orchestra 1987), From Silence (for soprano, 6 instruments and tape 1988), Valley of Aosta (for 13 players 1988); *Books* The Music of Stockhausen (1975); *Recreations* tennis, meditation; *Style*— Prof Jonathan Harvey; 35 Houndean Rise, Lewes, Sussex BN7 1EQ (☎ 0273 471 241)

HARVEY, Lady Julia Helen; 3 da of 10 Duke of Northumberland, KG, GCVO, TD, PC, JP (d 1988); *b* 12 Nov 1950; *m* 1983, Nicholas Robert Craig Harvey, s of Andrew John Craig Harvey, of Lainston House, Sparsholt, Hants; c/o Lainston House, Sparsholt, Hants

HARVEY, Lawrence M; s of Charles Harry Harvey, and Queenie, *née* Schryber; *b* 19 Sept 1951; *Educ* UCS, UCL (LLB); *m* 14 Oct 1982, Marian, da of Philip Rosenblatt (d 1974), of London; 1 s (Daniel Philip b 13 July 1985), 1 da (Rebecca Louise b 10 June 1987); *Career* dir Anglo-Continental Gp and Wesser Homes Gp 1974-78, md Harvey Gp 1978-87; md Metfield Estates 1987-; cm supporting ctee for Nat Assoc Mentally Handicapped Children 1972-78, prison visitor 1974-82; Freeman City of London 1982, Liveryman Worshipful Co of Glovers 1982; MIOD; *Recreations* bridge, golf, theatre; *Clubs* City Livery; *Style*— Lawrence Harvey, Esq; 305 Ballards Lane, London N12

HARVEY, (Graham) Lionel; s of C and BMH Harvey (d 1980), of 36 Westway, Stoneleigh, Epsom, Surrey; *b* 29 August 1936; *Educ* Reading Sch, Queen's Coll Oxford (MA); *m* 1 (m dis 1980), J Harvey; 4 s (Philip b 1962, Robert b 1966, James b 1967, Jonathan 1971), 5 da (Carolyn b 1963, Jane b 1964, Samantha b 1965, Katherine b 1970, Victoria b 1972); m 2, 25 Sept 1981, Rosemary Joyce, da of RJ Harvey, of Keynsham; *Career* planning mangr GE (USA) 1966-69, corporate planning dir Lex Serv plc 1978 - (corporate planning mangr 1969-78); chm of several local PTA'S; memb CBI Econ Ctee; *Recreations* cycling, walking, food and wine; *Style*— Lional Harvey, Esq; Lex Service plc, 17 Connaught Place, London W2 2EL (☎ 01 723 1212)

HARVEY, Lady Mary Katherine; *née* Coke; da of 4 Earl of Leicester (d 1949), and Marion, da of Col Hon Walter Trefusis, CB (3 s of 19 Baron Clinton by his w, Lady Elizabeth Kerr, da of 6 Marquess of Lothian); *b* 7 Mar 1920; *m* 1940, Maj Thomas Harvey, CVO, DSO, *qv*; 1 s (David b 1941), 2 da (Mrs Nicholas Raison b 1943, Mrs Richard Hambro b 1947); *Career* woman of the bedchamber to HM Queen Elizabeth The Queen Mother 1961-63; *Style*— Lady Mary Harvey; Warham House, Warham, Wells-next-the-Sea, Norfolk (☎ 0328 710457)

HARVEY, Michael; s of Owen Harvey (d 1961), of Bishop's Waltham, Hants, and Amy Marie Elise, *née* Wood; *b* 12 April 1934; *Educ* Winchester, Oriel Oxford (MA); *m* 1 Oct 1970, Susan (d 1988), da of Hans Schaffner-Buerli, of Baden, Switzerland; 1 da (Deborah Ann b 1973); *Career* Nat Serv Rifleman KRRC, 2 Lt Royal Hampshire Regt 1952-54; Shell Cos (Indonesia, Argentina, Switzerland, France, Nigeria, The Netherlands) 1957-86, Royal gp tres Dutch Shell Gp of Cos London 1986-; ACIS; *Style*— Michael Harvey, Esq; 12 Melton Court, Old Brompton Rd, London SW7 3JQ; Shell International Petroleum Co Ltd, Shell Centre, London SE1 7NA (☎ 01 934 4064, fax 01 934 8060, telex 919651)

HARVEY, Michael Anthony; s of Edgar Charles Harvey (d 1975), of Dorking, Surrey, and Evelyn May, *née* Klein (d 1976); *b* 22 August 1921; *Educ* Bryanston, Selly Oak Coll Woodbrooke Birmingham, Wimbledon Sch of Art (Intermediate Exam in Art and Crafts, Nat Dip in Design); *m* 30 Oct 1965 (m dis 1973), (Anne) Jennifer; 1 s (Anthony b 1966); *Career* Friends' Ambulance Unit 1940-42, Fishing Fleet 1942-43, MN 1943-55, awarded Africa Star 1945; teacher: Royal Alexandra and Albert Schs Reigate 1957-59, Ewell Castle Sch Surrey 1959-64, Tollington Park Sch 1965-69, Ct Lodge Sch Horley 1970-76; exhibited paintings: Qantas Gallery 1964, Royal Acad 1965, Fine Arts Gallery London 1967, John Whibley Gallery 1969-70, Rutland Gallery 1970-71, Royal Inst of Oil Painters, Royal Soc of Br Artists, Royal Inst of Oil Painters Australia 1977, Silver Longboat Exhibition Portsmouth and Oslo 1988; awarded Linton Prize for Painting 1972, art critic Surrey Mirror Gp of Newspapers 1973-80, art corr Croydon Advertiser Gp 1975-78; memb: Chichester Art Soc, Reigate Soc of Artists; tutor and memb Bognor Regis Art Soc; life memb Int Assoc of Art 1970, FRSA 1972, cncl memb Soc of Graphic Fine Art 1980-; *Recreations* sailing; *Clubs* Royal Soc of Arts; *Style*— Michael Harvey, Esq; 15 Waterloo Sq, Bognor Regis W Sussex (☎ 0243 863 732)

HARVEY, Michael Llewellyn Tucker; QC (1982); s of Rev Victor Llewellyn Tucker Harvey, of Suffolk, and Pauline, *née* Wybrow; *b* 22 May 1943; *Educ* St John's Sch Leatherhead, Christ's Coll Cambridge (BA, LLB, MA); *m* 2 Sept 1972, Denise Madeleine, da of Leonard Walter Neary, of London; 1 s (Julian b 19 June 1976), 1 da (Alexandra b 30 June 1973); *Career* barr Gray's Inn 1966, Recorder 1986; *Books* Damages in Halsbury's Laws of England (jt contrib, 4 edn 1975); *Recreations* shooting, golf; *Clubs* Athenaeum, Hawks (Cambridge); *Style*— Michael Harvey, Esq, QC; 2 Crown Office Row, Temple, London EC4Y 7HJ (☎ 01 353 9337, fax 01 583 0589, telex 8954005 TWOCOR G)

HARVEY, Prof Paul Dean Adshead; s of John Dean Monroe Harvey (d 1978), and Gwendolen Mabel Darlington, *née* Adshead; *b* 7 May 1930; *Educ* Bishop Field Coll St John's Newfoundland, Warwick Sch, St John's Coll Oxford (BA, MA, DPhil); *m* 6 July 1968, Yvonne, da of Howard Leonard Crossman (d 1965); *Career* asst archivist Warwick Co Record Off 1954-56, asst keeper dept of manuscripts Br Museum 1957-66, sr lectr dept of history Southampton Univ 1970-78 (lectr 1966-70), prof of medieval history Durham Univ 1978-85 (emeritus prof 1985-); gen ed: Southampton Records Series 1966-78, Portsmouth Record Series 1969-; vice-pres Surtees Soc 1978-, memb Advsy Cncl on Public Records 1984-, hon fell Portsmouth Poly 1987; FRHistS 1961, FSA 1963; *Books* The Printed Maps of Warwickshire 1576-1900 (with H Thorpe 1959), A Medieval Oxfordshire Village: Cuxham 1240-1400 (1965), Manorial Records of Cuxham Oxfordshire 1200-1359 (ed, 1976), The History of Topographical Maps (1980), The Peasant Land Market in England (ed, 1984), Manorial Records (1984), Local Maps and Plans from Medieval England (ed with R A Skelton, 1986); contrib to: Victoria History of Oxfordshire Vol 10 (1972), History of Cartography Vol 1 (1987), Agricultural History Review, Economic History Review, Past and Present; *Recreations* Br topography; *Style*— Prof Paul Harvey; Lyndhurst, Farnley Hey Road, Durham DH1 4EA (☎ 091 386 9396)

HARVEY, Peter; CB (1980); s of George Leonard Hunton Harvey (d 1948), and Helen Mary, *née* Williams (d 1973); *b* 23 April 1922; *Educ* King Edward VI HS Birmingham, St John's Coll Oxford (MA, BCL); *m* 1950, Mary Vivienne, da of John Osborne Goss (d 1971); 1 s (Roderick), 1 da (Vivienne); *Career* RAF 1942-45; barr Lincoln's Inn 1948, legal asst Home Off 1948, princ asst legal advsr Home Off 1971-77, legal advsr Dept of Educn and Sci 1977-83, conslt Legal Advsr's Branch Home Off 1983-86, asst to Speaker's Counsel House of Commons 1986-; *Publications* contributor to 3rd and 4th editions of Halsbury's Laws of England; *Recreations* walking, history; *Style*— Peter Harvey, Esq, CB; Mannamead, Old Ave, Weybridge, Surrey KT13 0PS (☎ 0932 845133)

HARVEY, Peter Martin Seaver; s of George Edward Harvey (d 1960); *b* 16 July 1927; *Educ* St John's Coll, Hurstpierpoint Coll of Estate Mgmnt; *m* 1962, Maureen Richardson, da of Dr Arthur Gray (d 1979); 1 s, 1 da; *Career* Capt India and Malaya; md Herring Son and Daw (chartered surveyors) 1976-79 (ptnr-dir 1964-75); FRICS; *Recreations* shooting, fly-fishing, squash; *Clubs* Army and Navy; *Style*— Peter Harvey, Esq; Flat 5, 26/28 Sackville St, London W1 (☎ 01 734 8155); Kempson House, Whitchurch, Bucks (☎ 0296 641 205)

HARVEY, Hon Philip William Vere; s of Baron Harvey of Prestbury (Life Peer), and Jacqueline Anne, *née* Dunnet; *b* 4 Mar 1942; *Educ* Eton, Geneva Univ; *Career* insur broker; md Harvey and Boyd Ltd; *Recreations* skiing; *Style*— The Hon Philip Harvey

HARVEY, Richard Charles; s of Cyril Joseph Harvey (d 1988), and Elsa, *née* Syer (d 1977); *b* 5 Sept 1935; *Educ* Caterham Sch, Merton Coll Oxford (MA); *m* 22 Sept 1962, Susan Rae, da of Bernard Sidney Keeling, of Southwold, Suffolk; 1 s (Ben 29 Aug 1967), 1 da (Sarah b 4 June 1965); *Career* Nat Serv 2 Lt RASC; ptnr Slaughter and May 1969-; Liveryman Worshipful Co of Solicitors; memb Law Soc (cncl memb 1980, chm trg ctee 1986-); *Recreations* golf, skiing, fly fishing, tennis; *Clubs* Hurlingham, Royal Wimbledon GC, Leander; *Style*— Richard Harvey, Esq

HARVEY, Robert Lambart; MP (C) Clwyd South-West 1983-; *b* 21 August 1953; *Educ* Eton, Christ Church Oxford; *Career* contested (C): Caernarvon Oct 1974, Merioneth 1979; memb: NUJ, Bow Gp; BBC broadcaster, asst ed *The Economist*; *Style*— Robert Harvey, Esq, MP; House of Commons, London SW1

HARVEY, Maj Thomas Cockayne; CVO (1951), DSO (1944); s of Col John Harvey, DSO, whose mother, Rosa, was 6 da of Adm Hon Keith Stewart, CB (2 s of 8 Earl of Galloway) by Mary Fitzroy (paternally ggda of 3 Duke of Grafton and maternally gda of 4 Duke of Richmond); *b* 22 August 1918; *Educ* Radley, Balliol Coll Oxford; *m* 1940, Lady Mary Katherine, *qv*; 1 s, 2 da; *Career* joined Scots Gds 1938, serv Norway 1940, Italy 1944; private sec to HM The Queen 1946-51; extra gentleman usher to HM King George VI 1951-52, to HM The Queen 1952-; regnl dir Lloyds Bank 1980-85; *Recreations* golf, shooting; *Clubs* White's, Beefsteak; *Style*— Maj Thomas Harvey, CVO, DSO; Warham House, Warham, Wells-next-the-Sea, Norfolk (☎ 0328 710 457)

HARVEY OF PRESTBURY, Baron (Life Peer UK 1971); Arthur Vere Harvey; CBE (1942); s of Arthur Harvey; *b* 31 Jan 1906; *Educ* Framlingham Coll; *m* 1, 1940 (m dis 1954), Jacqueline, da of W Dunnett; 2 s (Hon Philip *qv*, Hon Guy *qv*); m 2, 1955 (m dis 1975), Hilary (d 1975), da of David Charles and formerly w of Lt-Col Brian Robertson Williams; m 3, 1978, Carol, da of late Austin Cassar-Torregiani; *Career* Air Cdre RAuxAF; served RAF 1925-30, Flying Instructor; dir Far East Aviation Co and Far East Flying Training Sch 1930-35; advsr to S Chinese AF and Sqdn Ldr AAF, served WW II France (despatches 2); MP (C) Macclesfield 1945-71, chm 1922 Ctee 1966-70; dir Tradewinds Airways; FRAeS; Hon DSc Salford; Order of Orange Nassau; kt 1957; *Clubs* Royal Yacht Sqdn, Buck's, RAF; *Style*— The Rt Hon the Lord Harvey of Prestbury, CBE; The Cedars, Kappara Rd, San Gwann, Malta GC

HARVEY OF TASBURGH, 2 Baron (UK 1954); Sir Peter Charles Oliver Harvey; 5 Bt (UK 1868); s of 1 Baron, GCMG, GCVO, CB, Ambass France 1948-54 (d 1968), and Maud, da of Arthur Williams-Wynn (gn of Sir Watkin Williams-Wynn, 4 Bt; *b* 28 Jan 1921; *Educ* Eton, Trin Coll Cambridge; *m* 1957, Penelope, yr da of Lt-Col Sir William Makins, 3 Bt; 2 da (Hon Juliet b 1958, Hon Miranda b 1960); *Heir* bro, Hon John Harvey *qv*; *Career* served WWII RA N Africa and Italy; chartered accountant investment consultant Brown Shipley and Co 1978-81; formerly with Bank of England, Lloyd's Bank Int Ltd, English Transcontinental Ltd; *Clubs* Brooks's; *Style*— The Rt Hon the Lord Harvey of Tasburgh; Crownick Woods, Restronguet, Mylor, Falmouth, Cornwall TR11 5ST

HARVEY-JAMIESON, Lt-Col Harvey Morro; OBE (1969), TD, DL (Edinburgh 1968); assumed surname of Harvey-Jamieson by authority of Lord Lyon; s of Maj Alexander Harvey Morro Jamieson, OBE (d 1945, great-nephew of Sir George Harvey, PRSA), and Isobel (d 1954), da of Maj-Gen Sir Robert Murdoch Smith, KCMG ; *b* 9 Dec 1908; *Educ* Edinburgh Acad, RMC Sandhurst, Edinburgh Univ; *m* 1936, Frances, da of Col Julian Yorke Hayter Ridout, DSO (d 1951); 3 s; *Career* cmmnd 1 Bn KOSB 1928, Capt 1938, Maj RA (TA) 1939, Lt-Col 1943, memb Royal Co of Archers (Queen's Body Guard for Scotland) 1934-; sec The Co of Merchants of the City of Edinburgh 1946-71; WS, memb of Ctee of Conveyancing Legislation and Practice 1964-66 appointed by sec of state of Scotland; *Books* numerous articles in yachting and legal periodicals; *Clubs* Royal Forth Yacht, Royal Lymington Yacht; *Style*— Lt-Col Harvey Harvey-Jamieson, OBE, TD, DL; Walhampton Cottage, Walhampton, Lymington, Hants SO41 5SB (☎ 0590 74589)

HARVEY-JONES, Sir John Henry; MBE (1952); s of Mervyn Harvey-Jones, OBE, and Eileen Harvey-Jones; *b* 16 April 1924; *Educ* Tormore Sch Deal, RNC Dartmouth,; *m* 1947, Mary Evelyn Atcheson, er da of E F Bignell and Mrs E Atcheson; 1 da; *Career* served in RN 1937-56, naval intelligence, qualifying as German and Russian interpreter; joined ICI 1956, dir 1973-, dep chm 1978-81, chm ICI 1982-87; dep chm HOC Div, chm ICI Petrochemicals Div; former chm Phillips-Imperial Petroleum, memb NE Dvpt Bd 1971-73; dir: Carrington Viyella Ltd 1974-79 and 1981-82, Reed Int plc 1975-84; non-exec dir Grand Metropolitan plc 1983-; vice-pres Industrial Participation Assoc 1983, memb cncl British-Malaysian Soc 1983-; vice-chm: Policy Studies Inst 1980-85, BIM 1980-; hon vice-pres Inst of Marketing 1982-; pres Conseil Européen des Fédération de l'Industrie Chimique (CEFIC) 1984- (vice-pres CEFIC 1982-84); tstee: Science Museum 1983-; Police Fndn; chm of Tstees Police Foundation 1984-; hon fell Royal Soc of Chemistry 1985, hon fell Inst of Chemical Engrs 1985; Hon LLD Univ of Manchester 1985, DUniv Surrey 1985, Hon DSc Bradford 1986, Leicester 1986, Hon LLD Liverpool 1986, Cambridge 1987; vice-pres Hearing and Speech Tst

1985-: chancellor Univ of Bradford 1986-; Cdr's Cross Order of Merit of Fed Republic of Germany 1985; kt 1985; *Books* Making it Happen (1988); *Clubs* Athenaeum; *Style—* Sir John Harvey-Jones, MBE; Parallax Enterprises, PO Box 18, Ross-on-Wye, Herefordshire HR9 7TL

HARVEY-KELLY, (Hugh) Denis; s of Lt-Col Charles Hamilton Grant Harvey-Kelly, DSO (d 1982), of Clonhugh, Mullingar, and Sybil Mary *née* Nuttall (d 1980); paternal (Kelly) lineage listed in Burke's Irish Family Records; *b* 5 Mar 1932; *Educ* Wellington, RMA Sandhurst; *m* 20 June 1964, Jennifer Rosemary, da of John Elton-Phillips (d 1943); 1 da (Sarah b 1971); *Career* Capt 8 RI Hussars Germany Aden 1949-57; Vickers da Costa Stockbrokers London 1958-84, Dudgeon & Sons Stockbrokers Dublin; dir: Investmt Bank of Ireland 1968-85, Marlborough Prodns plc 1985-; chm: Ovidstone Bloodstock 1984-, Dolormore plc 1985-87; master of Foxhounds Westmeath Hunt 1979-83; *Recreations* hunting, shooting, fishing; *Clubs* Kildare St University; *Style—* Denis Harvey-Kelly, Esq; The Old Glebe, Newcastle, Co Dublin (☎ 0001 589862); 185 Old Brompton Rd, London SW5 (☎ 3701098, fax Dublin 589368)

HARVIE, Alida Gwendolen Rosemary; *née* Brittain; da of Sir Harry Brittain, KBE, CMG (d 1974), and Dame Alida Luisa Brittain, *née* Harvey (d 1943); *b* 23 June 1910; *Educ* St George's Sch Harpenden, Hanover Germany; *m* 3 Oct 1950, Maj John Keith Harvie (d 1971), s of John Walter Harvie (d 1939); *Career* Staff Offr Army Educnl Corps (home cmd), Snr Cdr (Maj) ATS 1943-46, memb Kensington BC and London Co Cncl 1949-54; WHO 1947-48, LCC lectr 1949-57; Fund raising for tree replacement 1977-87; *Books* Those Glittering Years (1980 biography of Sir Harry Brittain), The Rationed Years (1982), The Sundial Years (1984 biography of J K Harvie), The Doom-Laden Years (1985); *Recreations* reading, history study, history research, classical music; *Clubs* Royal Overseas League London; *Style—* Mrs John Harvie; 15 Brackens Way, Martello Road Sth, Poole, Dorset (☎ 0202 700734)

HARVIE-WATT, Sir George Steven; 1 Bt (UK 1945), of Bathgate, Co Linlithgow, TD and 3 Bars (1942), QC (KC 1945); s of James McDougal Watt, of Woodlands House, Armadale, W Lothian, and Jessie Harvie; *b* 23 August 1903; *Educ* George Watson's Coll Edinburgh, Glasgow Univ, Edinburgh Univ; *m* 1932, Jane, da of Paymaster-Capt Archibald Taylor, OBE, RN; 2 s, 1 da; *Heir* s, James Harvie-Watt *qv*; *Career* cmmnd RE (TA) 1924, Bt-Maj 1935, Lt-Col 1938, Brig 1941, Hon Col 566 LAA Regt 1949-62; ADC to King George VI 1948-52, ADC to HM The Queen 1952-58; barr Inner Temple 1930; MP (U) Keighley 1931-35, Richmond (Surrey) 1937-59; parly sec to Rt Hon Winston Churchill when PM 1941-45; DL Surrey 1942, Greater London 1966-78, JP London 1944-56; pres Consolidated Gold Fields Ltd 1973-80 (chm 1960-69), dir Clydesdale Bank Ltd and other cos; hon freeman City of London; memb Royal Co of Archers (Queen's Body Guard for Scotland); FRSA; *Books* Most of My Life (1980); *Clubs* Caledonian; *Style—* Sir George Harvie-Watt, Bt, TD, QC; Sea Tangle, Earlsferry, Fife KY9 1AD (☎ 0333 330506)

HARVIE-WATT, James; s and h of Sir George Harvie-Watt, 1 Bt, TD, QC *qv*; *b* 25 August 1940; *Educ* Eton, Ch Ch Oxford (MA); *m* 28 May 1966, Roseline, da of Baron Louis de Chollet (d 1972), of Fribourg, Switzerland; 1 s (Mark b 19 Aug 1969), 1 da (Isabelle b 19 March 1967); *Career* Lt London Scottish (TA) 1959-67; with Coopers and Lybrand 1962-70; exec British Electric Traction Co Ltd and dir of subsid cos 1970-78; md Wembley Stadium Ltd 1973-78; memb: exec ctee London Tourist Bd 1977-80, Sports Cncl 1980-88 (vice-chm 1985-88); chm Crystal Palace Nat Sports Centre 1984-88; memb of mgmt ctee: The Nat Coaching Fndn 1984-88, The Nat Water Sports Centre Holme Pierrepont 1985-88; memb: Sports Cncl enquiries into Financing of Athletics in UK 1983, Karate 1986, Cncl NPFA 1985-; OStJ 1964, memb London Cncl of the Order 1975-84; FCA 1975 (ACA 1965), FRSA 1978; *Recreations* tennis, golf, shooting, photography, philately; *Clubs* White's, Pratt's, Sunningdale, Queen's (vice-chm 1987-); *Style—* James Harvie-Watt, Esq; 15 Somerset Sq, London W14 8EE (☎ 01 602 6944)

HARVINGTON, Baron (Life Peer UK 1974); Robert Grant Grant-Ferris; AE (1942), PC (1971); s of Dr Robert Grant-Ferris; *b* 30 Dec 1907; *Educ* Douai; *m* 1930, Florence, da of Maj William De Vine, MC; 1 s, 1 da; *Career* Wing Cdr Auxiliary (now Royal) AF WW II Europe, Malta, Egypt, India; barr 1937; MP (C) N St Pancras 1937-45 and Nantwich 1955-74; dep speaker House of Commons 1970-74; KStJ; kt 1969; *Recreations* golf, motor yachting; *Clubs* Carlton, Royal Thames Yacht, RAF, Royal and Ancient Golf, MCC, Royal Yacht Sqdn; *Style—* The Rt Hon Lord Harvington, AE, PC; La Vieille Maison, The Bulwarks, St Aubin, Jersey, CI

HARWOOD, (Basil) Antony; QC (1971); s of Basil Harwood (d 1949), of Olveston Glos, and Mabel Ada, *née* Jennings (d 1974); *b* 25 June 1903; *Educ* Charterhouse, Oxford (MA); *m* 1929, Enid, da of Philip Grove (d 1901), of Leamington Warwicks; 2 s (Christopher, Giles); *Career* served WWII, City of London Police War Reserve 1939-40, Miny of Food (Southern Div) rising to dep divnl food offr 1940-42, cmmnd from Emergency Reserve 2/Lt RASC 1942, overseas service in Italy included 6 Br Armd Div Tport, transferred after illness to JAG Staff, dep judge advocate 1945, Maj; barr Inner Temple 1927, prosecuting counsel to PO on Western circuit 1948-50, master of the Supreme Ct (Queen's Bench Div) 1950-70, sr master and Queen's remembrancer 1966-70; pre Medico-Legal Soc 1967-69; Liveryman Worshipful Co of Loriners; *Books* Circuit Ghosts: A Western Circuit Miscellany (1980); *Recreations* fencing (rep Oxford v Cambridge Epee 1925), mountaineering, music (cello), chess; *Clubs* Royal Automobile, Epee (hon memb); *Style—* Antony Harwood, Esq, QC; Fernhill House, Almondsbury, Bristol BS12 4LX

HARWOOD, Hon Mrs (Elizabeth Margaret); *née* Leonard; da of Baron Leonard, OBE (Life Peer, d 1983); *b* 1946; *Educ* Univ of Wales (LLB); *m* 1963, Michael Harwood, of The Hague, Netherlands; *Style—* The Hon Mrs Harwood

HARWOOD, Lady Felicity Ann; *née* Attlee; 2 da of Rt Hon Clement Attlee, 1 Earl Attlee, KG, OM, CH, PC (d 1967; PM 1945-51); *b* 22 August 1925; *Educ* St Felix Sch Southwold, Rachel McMillan Trg Coll Deptford; *m* 1955, (John) Keith Harwood, OBE, *qv*; 1 s (Richard b 1963), 3 da (Penelope b 1956, Joanna b 1958, Sally b 1960); *Career* teacher; headmistress New Gregorys Sch Beaconsfield 1972-74; memb Beaconsfield Ctee, Schs/rep Save The Children Fund; *Recreations* bridge, gardening, reading, travel; *Style—* Lady Felicity Harwood; Whinbury, 6 Hogback Wood Rd, Beaconsfield, Bucks HP9 1JR (☎ 04946 3284)

HARWOOD, Giles Francis; s of Basil Antony Harwood, QC, qv, and Enid Arundel, *née* Grove; *b* 31 Jan 1934; *Educ* Douai Sch, Christ Church Oxford (BA, MA); *m* 1, 5 Jan 1963 (m dis 1979), Ursula Mary, da of Norman Humphrey, OBE (d 1965), of Exeter; 3 s (Francis, Dominic, Nicholas), 2 da (Monica, Bridget); m 2, 31 March 1983, Diana Mary, da of Gerald Cuthbert Galahad Roe (d 1957), of Birkdale; *Career* Nat Serv 2 Lt RA 1956-58, Asst Akj/BHQ Troop Cdr Sch of Anti-Aircraft Artillery and Guided Weapons Manorbier (TA) HAC G Battery 1959-66, Veteran Co 1966-88; barr Inner Temple 1956, in practice London and Western circuit 1959-70, sr State Counsel Kenya 1970-73, First Parly Counsel Kenya 1973-75, legal advsr St Vincent & The Grenadines 1976-78, chief parly draftsman Malawi 1978-83, chief justice Tonga 1983-85, pt/t chm Social Security Appeal Tbnls 1986, chm Registered Homes Tbnl 1987, law revision cmmr Grenada 1988; ACIArb 1985; *Books* Odgers' Principles of Pleading and Practice (17-20 edns, 1960-71); *Recreations* music, travel; *Clubs* Nairobi; *Style—* Giles Harwood, Esq; Fernhill House, Almondsbury, Bristol BS12 4LX (☎ 0454 616 755)

HARWOOD, Gillian Margaret; da of Herbert Norton Harwood, of Kyrenia, Cyprus, and Margaret, *née* Gadsby; *b* 29 Nov 1942; *Educ* Farrington Girls' Sch, Institut Britanique Paris; 2 da, (Hester Lallen b 4 April 1974, Flossie Allen b 28 Nov 1975); *Career* worked with: Mather & Crowther Ltd 1962-64, WGBH TV Boston USA 1964-66, CBC News London 1966-68; involved in antique selling, BBC drama and gardening business 1968-73, having babies 1973-75, converting redundant industrial buildings into managed workspace for small and growing firms; md: Omnibus Workspace Ltd, Forum Workspace Chichester, The Old Needlemakers Lewes, Tideway Yard Mortlake; opened The Depot Winebar Mortlake 1986; winner Options/TSB Tst Co Women Mean Business Award 1988; *Recreations* gardening, breeding Staffordshire Bull Terriers; *Style—* Miss Gillian M Harwood; 35 Gorst Road, London, SW11; Podmore's Farm, Tillington, Petworth, Sussex; 12 Flitcroft St, London, WC2 (☎ 01 836 7580, fax 379 4671)

HARWOOD, (John) Keith; OBE (1985); s of Col George Edward Harwood, IA (d 1967), of Putney, and Patricia Mary, *née* Beardsall (d 1970); *b* 30 Sept 1926; *Educ* Canford Sch Dorset; *m* 1, 1948 (m dis 1954), Nicolette (d 1962), da of Frank Popplewell, OBE, of Wonersh; 1 da; m 2, 1955, Lady Felicity, *qv*, da of 1 Earl Attlee, KG, OM, CH, FRS (d 1967); 1 s, 3 da; *Career* Capt Black Watch (RHR), served India 1943-48; Hon Artillery Co Inf Bn 1950-56; chm Export Buying Offices Assoc 1979-88; vice-pres R H Macy (USA) Corporate Buying 1982- (md UK and Ireland 1964-); memb: Inst of Export 1965, N American Advsy Gp BOTB/DTI 1980-; patron Roy Masonic Hosp 1972, memb mgmnt ctee CAB Bucks; Freeman City of London 1984, Liveryman of the Glovers' Co 1985; FBIM 1968; *Recreations* shooting, sailing, gardening, cricket, cooking; *Clubs* Pilgrims of GB, Knotty Green Cricket (pres), Beaconsfield Rugby, IOD, Rugby (London), Probus (Beaconsfield), Emeritus (Bucks); *Style—* Keith Harwood, Esq, OBE; Whinbury, 6 Hogback Wood Rd, Beaconsfield, Bucks HP9 1JR (☎ 04946 3248); R H Macy Corporate Buying, Elsley House, 24/30 Great Titchfield St, London W1P 8BB (☎ 01 637 0122, telex 27564 MACYLN G)

HARWOOD, Ronald; s of Isaac Horwitz (d 1950), and Isobel, *née* Pepper (d 1985); *b* 9 Nov 1934; *Educ* Sea Point Boys' HS Capetown, Royal Acad of Dramatic Art; *m* 1959, Natasha, da of William Charles Riehle, MBE (d 1979); 1 s (Antony), 2 da (Deborah, Alexandra); *Career* actor 1953-60; writer 1960-; artistic dir Cheltenham Festival of Literature 1975; presenter: Kaleidoscope BBC 1973, Read All About It BBC TV 1978-79; wrote and presented All The World's A Stage for BBC-TV; chm Writers Guild of GB 1969; memb Lit Panel Arts Cncl of GB 1973-78; Visitor in Theatre, Balliol Coll Oxford 1986; FRSL; *TV plays include* The Barber of Stamford Hill (1960), Private Potter (1961), The Guests (1972), adapted several Roald Dahl's Tales of the Unexpected for TV 1979-80, Breakthrough at Reykjavik (1987); *Screenplays include* A High Wind in Jamaica (1965), One Day in the Life of Ivan Denisovich (1971), Evita Péron (1981), The Dresser (1983), The Doctor and the Devils (1985), Mandela (1987); *Books* All the Same Shadows (1961), The Guilt Merchants (1963), The Girl in Melanie Klein (1969), Articles of Faith (1973), The Genoa Ferry (1976), Cesar and Augusta (1978); short stories: One Interior Day (adventures in the film trade 1978), New Stories 3 (1978); biography: Sir Donald Wolfit, CBE - his life and work in the unfashionable theatre (1971); essays: A Night at the Theatre (ed, 1983), The Ages of Gielgud (1984)Dear Alec (1989), Ivanov (from Chekov) (1989); *others* All The World's A Stage (1984), Mandela (1987); *plays* Country Matters (1969), The Ordeal of Gilbert Pinfold (from Evelyn Waugh, 1977), A Family (1978), The Dresser (New Standard Drama Award, Drama Critics Award, 1986), After the Lions (1982), Tramway Road (1984), The Deliberate Death of a Polish Priest (1985), Interpreters (1985), J J Farr (1987); *Musical Libretto* The Good Companions (1974); *Recreations* tennis, cricket; *Clubs* Garrick, MCC; *Style—* Ronald Harwood, Esq; c/o Judy Daish Associates, 83 Eastbourne Mews, London W2 6LQ

HARWOOD-LITTLE, Major Mark Guy; s of Lt-Col Cuthbert Joseph Harwood-Little (d 1963), of Chichester, and Barbara Fox, *née* Dodgson (d 1962); *b* 30 Oct 1924; *Educ* Wellington Coll, Peterhouse Cambridge (Mech Science Tripos MA); *m* 10 Dec 1949, Josephine Mary, da of Maj Aidan Staples (d 1942); 1 s (David b 1955), 1 da (Philippa b 1952); *Career* Maj RE 1942-60, served India, BAOR; psc; Lucas Industries 1960-78; dir Ironbridge Gorge Museum Devpt Tst 1978-; Upper Severn Navigation Tst 1980-; FRSA; *Recreations* sailing, industl archaeology; *Style—* Major Mark G Harwood-Little; The Old Rectory, Stapleton, Dorrington, Shrewsbury SY5 7EF (☎ 074 373 220); Ironbridge Gorge Museum Development Trust, Ironbridge, Telford TF8 (☎ 095 245 3522)

HARWOOD-SMART, Philip Mervyn Harwood; s of Harold Leslie Harwood Smart (d 1976), of High Point, Cuckfield, Sussex, and Moira Veronica, *née* Scanlon (d 1986); *b* 1 Oct 1944; *Educ* Eastbourne Coll, Univ of Lancaster (BA); *m* Juliet Marion Frances, da of Keith Mackay Campbell, of West Bagborough, Somerset; 2 da (Venetia Louise b 14 June 1977, Davina Brietzcke b 17 Feb 1980); *Career* 4/5 Bn KORR Lancaster (TA) 1964-67, cmmnd 1965, memb HAC 1986-; admitted slr 1971, assoc ptnr Herbert Smith & Co 1973-75, asst slr Farrer & Co 1977-80, ptnr Ashurst Morris Crisp 1984-; hon sec Old Eastbournian Assoc 1970; memb: Sussex Archaeological Soc, Sussex Record Soc, Royal Archaeological Inst Alresford Agricultural Soc; Freeman: City of London 1973, Worshipful Co of Solicitors 1973; *Books* The History of Jevington (1962, second edn 1972); *Recreations* heraldry, genealogy; *Clubs* Carlton, Coleman Street Ward, Henley Royal Regatta; *Style—* Philip Harwood-Smart, Esq; Thimble Hall, Owslebury, Winchester, Hants; Broadgate House, 7 Eldon St, London EC2 (☎ 01 247 7666, fax 01 377 5659, telex 8870670)

HASELGROVE, Dennis Cliff; CB (1963); s of Harry Haselgrove (d 1956), of Chingford, and Gladys, *née* Self; *b* 18 August 1914; *Educ* Uppingham, King's Coll Cambridge (MA); *m* 1941, Evelyn, *née* Johnston; 1 s; *Career* under-sec Miny of

Transport 1957-71, Dept of Environment 1971-75, ret; FSA; *Recreations* archaeology, local history, philately, travel; *Style*— Dennis Haselgrove, Esq, CB; 10 Church Gate, London SW6 (☎ 01 736 5213)

HASELHURST, Alan Gordon Barraclough; MP (C) Saffron Walden 1977-; s of John Haselhurst and Alyse, *née* Barraclough; *b* 23 June 1937; *Educ* Cheltenham, Oriel Coll Oxford; *m* 1977, Angela, da of John Bailey; 2 s, 1 da; *Career* MP (C) Middleton and Prestwich 1970-74, pps to Sec of State Educn 1979-81; chm of Trustees, Community Projects Foundation 1986-; *Recreations* music, gardening, watching cricket; *Style*— Alan Haselhurst, Esq, MP; House of Commons, London SW1

HASELTINE, Barry Albert; s of Albert Edward Haseltine (d 1974), of 53 Clarence Rd, Horsham, Sussex, and Lillian Sarah Louise, *née* Payne; *b* 17 June 1933; *Educ* Collyers Sch Horsham, Imperial Coll London (BSc, DIC); *m* 6 July 1956, Sylvia Ethel, da of Arthur George Jones (d 1975), of Gloucester; 1 s (Richard Barry b 16 Feb 1963), 1 da (Susan Jane b 8 March 1966); *Career* Flying Offr RAF 1955-57; ptnr Jenkins and Potter Consulting Engrs 1967-; chm: Euro Cmmns Code and Practice Ctee for Masonry, several Br Standards Inst Ctees, Int Standards Orgn Ctee; FEng, FICE, FIStructE, MConsE, FICERAM, FCGI; *Books* Bricks and Brickwork (1974), Handbook to BS5628: Part 1 (1980); *Recreations* gardening, golf, skiing; *Clubs* RAF, Copthorne GC (Sussex); *Style*— Barry Haseltine, Esq; Jenkins and Potter, 12-15 Great Turnstile, London WC1V 7HN (☎ 01 242 8711, fax 01 404 0742, telex 21120 ref 2060)

HASKARD, Sir Cosmo Dugal Patrick Thomas; KCMG (1965, CMG 1960), MBE (1945); s of Brig-Gen John McDougall Haskard, CMG, DSO (d 1967), and Alicia Isabel, *née* Hutchins (d 1960); *b* 25 Nov 1916; *Educ* Cheltenham, RMC Sandhurst, Pembroke Coll Cambridge; *m* 3 Aug 1957, Phillada, da of Sir Robert Christopher Stafford Stanley, KBE, CMG (d 1981); 1 s (Julian Dominic Stanley b 1962); *Career* served WW II, Maj 1944; entered Colonial Service (Tanganyika) 1940, Nyasaland 1946, memb Nyasaland Mozambique Boundary Cmmn 1951-52, provincial cmmr Nyasaland 1955, acting sec for African Affairs 1957-58, sec for Labour and Social Dvpt 1961, sec for Local Govt 1962, sec for Natural Resources 1963, Govr and C-in-C Falklands Islands and high cmmr for British Antarctic Territory 1964-70; trustee Beit Trust 1976-; *Style*— Sir Cosmo Haskard, KCMG, MBE; Tragariff, Bantry, Co Cork, Ireland

HASKELL, (Donald) Keith; CVO (1979); s of Lt Donald Eric Haskell, RN, of Southsea, Hants, and Beatrice Mary, *née* Blair (d 1985); *b* 9 May 1939; *Educ* Portsmouth GS, St Catharine's Coll Cambridge (BA, MA); *m* 7 Feb 1966, Maria Luisa Soeiro, da of Dr Augusto Tito de Morais (d 1981); 3 s (Donald Mark b and d 1972, Jonathan b 1974, Paul b 1976), 3 da (Lysa b 1970, Anne-Marie b 1979, one other unnamed b and d 1969); *Career* HM Dip Serv 1961-: language student MECAS Shemlan Lebanon (1961-62 and 1968-69), 3rd sec Br Embassy Baghdad Iraq 1962-66, 2nd sec F O London 1966-68, 1st sec and consul Br Embassy Benghazi Libya 1969-70, 1st sec Br Embassy Tripoli Libya 1970-72, 1st sec FCO London 1972-75, chargé d'affaires and consul-gen Br Embassy Santiage Chile, cnsllr and consul-gen Br Embassy Dubai UAE 1978-81, head Nuclear Energy Dept FCO London 1981-83, head ME Dept FCO London 1983-84, cnsllr Br Embassy Bonn W Germany 1985-88-; seconded to indust 1988-; target rifle shooting half blue 1960-61, shot for Hampshire Eng and GB on various occasions; *Recreations* target shooting, squash, tennis, skiing, wine & food; *Clubs* Hawks (Cambridge); *Style*— Keith Haskell, Esq, CVO; Vosper Thornycroft (UK) Ltd, Victoria Rd, Woolston, Southampton SO9 5GR (☎ 0703 422 849, fax 0703 421 539, telex 47682)

HASLAM, Rear Adm Sir David William; KBE (1984, OBE 1964), CB (1979); s of Gerald Haigh Haslam and Gladys, *née* Finley; *b* 26 June 1923; *Educ* Bromsgrove; *Career* Hydrographer of the Navy 1975-85; pres Directing Ctee, Int Hydrographic Bureau, Monaco 1985-; *Style*— Rear Adm Sir David Haslam, KBE, CB; Palais Saint James, 5 Avenue Princesse Alice, Monte Carlo MC 98000, Principaute de Monaco

HASLAM, (William) Geoffrey; OBE (1985), DFC (1944); yr s of William Haslam (d 1938), and Hilda Irene, *née* Tarn (d 1972); *b* 11 Oct 1914; *Educ* New Coll and Ashville Coll Harrogate; *m* 1940, Valda Patricia, da of Norman Adamson (d 1956); 2 s, 1 da; *Career* chief exec Prudential Assurance Co 1974-79, dep chm 1980-84; chm British Insurance Assoc 1977-79; *Recreations* golf, reading; *Clubs* City of London, MCC, RAF; *Style*— Geoffrey Haslam, Esq, OBE, DFC; 6 Ashbourne Rd, London W5 3ED (☎ 01 997 8164)

HASLAM, John; LVO; s of William Haslam; *b* 17 June 1931; *Educ* King George V GS Southport, Liverpool Univ; *m* 1953, Jean Anne, *née* Capstick; 2 s; *Career* joined BBC 1955, mangr BBC Radio Outside Broadcasts 1974-81; asst press sec to HM The Queen 1981-88 (dep press Sec 1988-); *Recreations* fell-walking, reading, music, Times crossword; *Style*— John Haslam, Esq, LVO; 4 The Old Barracks, Kensington Palace, London W8 4PU

HASLAM, Hon Mrs (Judith); *née* Browne; da of 4 Baron Oranmore and Browne; *b* 23 Sept 1934; *m* 1958, (Ralph) Michael Haslam, s of William Heywood Haslam, OBE (d 1981); 2 s, 1 da; *Style*— The Hon Mrs Haslam; Cairngill, Dalbeattie, Kirkudbrightshire, Scotland

HASLAM, Sir Robert; s of Percy Haslam (d 1971); *b* 4 Feb 1923; *Educ* Bolton Sch, Birmingham Univ (BSc); *m* 1947, Joyce, da of Frederick Quinn (d 1937); 2 children; *Career* dep chm ICI plc 1980-83; chm: Tate and Lyle plc 1983-86, Br Steel Corpn 1983-86, British Coal Sept 1986-; dir Bank of Eng 1985-, FIMinE, Advisory dir of dir of Unilever plc Sept 1986-; Hon: DTech Brunel Univ 1987, DEng Birmingham Univ 1987; kt 1985; *Recreations* golf, travel; *Clubs* Brooks's, Athenaeum, Wentworth; *Style*— Sir Robert Haslam; British Coal, Hobart House, Grosvenor Place, London SW1X 7AE (☎ 01 235 2020)

HASLAM, Simon Mark; s of Peter Haigh Haslam, of Derby, and Elizabeth Anne, *née* Gallimore; *b* 29 May 1957; *Educ* Ecclesbourne Sch Duffield Derbys, Magdalen Coll Oxford (BA, MA); *m* 15 May 1982, Catherine Nina (Kate), da of Capt Robert Kenneth Alcock, CBE, RN, of Brantham Court, Suffolk; 1 s (Thomas b 9 July 1987), 1 da (Eleanor b (twin) 9 July 1987); *Career* CA; Spicer & Oppenheim (formerly Spicer & Pegler): student accountant 1978, mangr 1984, ptnr 1986; memb: Cons Assoc Welwyn Hatfield, St Francis Church Welwyn Gdn City; ACA (1981); *Recreations* classical music, reading, walking the dog; *Style*— Simon Haslam, Esq; 11A Guessens Rd, Welwyn Garden City, Herts AL8 6QW (☎ 0707 325 117); Spicer & Oppenheim, Friary Ct, 65 Crutched Friars, London EC3N 2NP (☎ 01 480 7766, fax 01 480 6958, telex 884257 ESANO G)

HASLUCK, Dame Alexandra Margaret Martin; AD (1978); da of John William Darker (d 1925), and Margaret Darker (d 1962); *b* 26 August 1908; *Educ* Perth Coll, Univ of WA (BA); *m* 1932, Rt Hon Sir Paul Hasluck, KG, GCMG, GCVO, *qv*; 1 s (and 1 decd); *Career* historian and author of 13 books; nat pres: Girl Guides Assoc 1969-74, Aust Red Cross Soc 1969-74; vice-pres Nat Trust (WA) 1966; DStJ 1971; *Style*— Dame Alexandra Hasluck, AD; 2 Adams Rd, Dalkeith, W Australia 6009

HASLUCK, Rt Hon Sir Paul Meernaa Caedwalla; KG (1979), GCMG (1969), GCVO (1970), PC (1966); s of E M C Hasluck (d 1971), and P E Hasluck (d 1956); *b* 1 April 1905; *Educ* Perth Modern Sch, Univ of Western Australia (MA); *m* 1932, Dame Alexandra Margaret Martin, *née* Darker, *qv*; 1 s (and 1 decd); *Career* journalist 1922-38, univ lectr 1938-40, Australian Foreign Serv 1941-47, official war historian, MP (Lib) for Curtin WA 1949-69, cabinet minister 1951-69, min for Territories 1951-63, min for Defence 1963-64, min for External Affairs 1963-69, govr-gen Australia 1969-74; author; FASSA, FAHA, FRAHS; KStJ 1969; *Recreations* book collecting, recorded music, the Australian Bush; *Clubs* Weld (Perth), Claremont Football; *Style*— Rt Hon Sir Paul Hasluck, KG, GCMG GCVO, PC; 2 Adams Rd, Dalkeith, Western Australia 6009

HASSALL, Tom Grafton; s of William Owen Hassall, of The Manor House, Wheatley, Oxford, and Averil Grafton, *née* Beaves; *b* 3 Dec 1943; *Educ* Dragon Sch, Lord William's GS Thame, Corpus Christi Coll Oxford (BA); *m* 2 Sept 1967, Angela Rosaleen, da of Capt Oliver Goldsmith (d 1944), of Thirsk; 3 s (Oliver b 28 Nov 1968, Nicholas b 30 April 1970, Edward b 10 July 1972); *Career* asst local ed Victoria County History of Oxford 1966-67, dir Oxford Archaeological Excavation Ctee 1967-73, dir Oxford (formerly Oxfordshire) Archaeological Unit 1973-85, fell St Cross Coll Oxford (emeritus fell 1988-), assoc staff tutor dept for external studies Oxford Univ 1978-85, sec Royal Cmmn on the Historical Monuments of England 1986-; tstee Oxford Preservation Tst 1973-, chm Standing Conf of Archaeological Unit Mangrs 1980-83, pres Cncl for Br Archaeology 1983-86, chm Br Archaeological Awards 1983-87, pres Oxfordshire Architectural and Historical Soc 1984-; Freeman City of Chester 1973; FSA 1971, MIFA 1985; *Books* Oxford, The Buried City (1987); *Recreations* gardening; *Style*— Tom Hassall, Esq; The Manor House, Wheatley, Oxford OX9 1XX (☎ 08677 4428); The Little Cottage, Cley-Next-The-Sea, Holt, Norfolk; The Royal Commission on the Historical Mounuments of England, Fortress House, 23 Savile Row, London W1X 2JQ (☎ 01 734 9847)

HASSAN, Sir Joshua Abraham; GBE (1987, CBE 1957), KCMG (1985), LVO (1954), QC (Gibraltar 1961), JP (Gibraltar 1949); s of late Abraham M Hassan; *b* 21 August 1915; *Educ* Line Wall Coll Gibraltar; *m* 1, 1945 (m dis 1969), Daniela, *née* Salazar; 2 da; m 2, 1969, Marcelle, *née* Bensimon; 2 da; *Career* barr Mid Temple 1939; dep coroner for Gibraltar 1941-64, mayor of Gibraltar 1945-50 and 1953-69, MEC and MLC Gibraltar 1950-64, ch memb 1958-64, ldr of Oppn House of Assembly 1969-72, chief minister of Gibraltar 1964-69 and 1972-87, hon bencher Mid Temple 1983-; Hon LLD Hull Univ; kt 1963; *Clubs* United Oxford and Cambridge University, Royal Gibraltar Yacht; *Style*— Sir Joshua Hassan, GBE, KCMG, LVO, QC, JP; 11-18 Europa Rd, Gibraltar (☎ 010 350 77295); chambers: 57 Line Wall Rd, Gibraltar (☎ 010 350 79000)

HASSELL, Michael Patrick; s of Maj Albert Marmaduke Hassel, MC, Croix de Guerre, of Mayfield House, Clench, nr Marlborough, Wilts, and Gertrude, *née* Loeser (d 1973); *b* 2 August 1942; *Educ* Whitgift Sch, Clare Coll Camb (MA), Oriel Coll Oxford (DPhil); *m* 1, 7 Oct 1966 (m dis), Glynis Mary Ethel, da of John Everett; 2 s (Adrian Michael b 6 Feb 1971, David Charles b 2 April 1973); m 2, Victoria Anne, da of Reginald Taylor (d 1984); 1 s (James Mark b 10 June 1986), 1 da (Kate Helen b 18 April 1988); *Career* Imperial Coll London: lectr dept of zoology and applied entomology 1970-75, reader in insect ecology dept of zoology and applied entomology 1975-79, prof of insect ecology dept of pure and applied biology 1979-, dep head of dept pure and applied biology 1984, dir of Silwood Park 1988-; FRS 1986; *Books* The Dynamics of Competition and Predation (1976), The Dynamics of Arthropod and Predator-Prey Systems (1978); *Recreations* walking, natural history, croquet; *Style*— Prof Michael Hassell; 2 Oaklea Cottages, Osbourne La, Warfield, Berks RG12 6EB (☎ 0344 52155); Imp Coll at Silwood Park, Dept of Pure & Applied Biology, Ascot, Berks SL5 7PY (☎ 0990 23911, fax 0990 20094)

HASSETT, Gen Sir Francis George; AC (1975), KBE (1976, CBE 1966, OBE 1945), CB (1969), DSO (1953), MVO (1954); s of John Francis Hassett (d 1946), and Alice May Hassett (d 1969); *b* 11 April 1918; *Educ* Canterbury HS, RMC Duntroon; *m* 1946, Margaret Hallie Spencer, da of Dr Alfred John Cecil Spencer Roberts (d 1939); 2 s, 2 da; *Career* dep CGS Australia 1964-66, head Aust Jt Servs Staff London 1966-67, extra gentleman usher to HM The Queen 1966-68, GOC Northern Cmd 1968-70, Vice Chief of Gen Staff Aust 1971-73, Chief of General Staff 1973-75, Lt-Gen 1975, chief of Defence Force Staff, chm Chiefs of Staff 1975-77, ret; *see Debrett's Handbook of Australia and New Zealand for further details*; *Clubs* Commonwealth; *Style*— Gen Sir Francis Hassett, AC, KBE, CB, DSO, MVO; 42 Mugga Way, Red Hill, ACT 2603, Australia (☎ 95 8035)

HASTIE-SMITH, Richard Maybury; CB (1984); s of Engr-Cdr D Hastie-Smith and H I Hastie-Smith; *b* 13 Oct 1931; *Educ* Cranleigh Sch, Magdalene Coll Cambridge (MA); *m* 1956, Bridget Noel Cox; 1 s, 2 da; *Career* entered Civil Service (War Office) 1955-: priv sec to perm under-sec 1957, asst priv sec to sec of State 1958, princ 1960, asst pte sec to sec of State for Defence 1965, priv sec to min of Defence (Equipment) 1968, asst sec 1969, RCDS 1974, under-sec MOD 1975, Cabinet Office 1979-81, dep under-sec of State MOD 1981-; *Style*— Richard Hastie-Smith, Esq, CB; 18 York Avenue, East Sheen, London SW14 (☎ 01 876 4597)

HASTILOW, Michael Alexander; s of Cyril A F Hastilow, CBE (d 1975); *b* 21 Sept 1923; *Educ* Mill Hill, Birmingham Univ; *m* 1953, Sheila Mary, da of Maj J J Barker, RCS (d 1947); 1 s, 2 da; *Career* dir Glynwed Ltd 1969-81; pres Br Non-Ferrous Metals Fedn 1979-80; chm Nat Home Improvement Cncl 1980-81; memb: Construction Exports Advsy Bd 1975-78, Cmmn for New Towns 1978-86, EDC for Bldg 1980-82; *Recreations* railways, cricket; *Clubs* Old Millhillians, RAC; *Style*— Michael Hastilow, Esq; The Mount, 3 Kendal End Rd, Rednal, Birmingham B45 8PX (☎ 021 445 2007)

HASTINGS; *see*: Abney-Hastings

HASTINGS, Christine Anne; da of Peter Edwards Hastings, and Anne Fauvel, *née* Picot; *b* 15 Feb 1956; *Educ* Whyteleafe GS; *m* 5 May 1985 (m dis 1988), Lawrie Lewis; *Career* dir: Pact Ltd (PR Consultancy) 1980-86, Biss Lancaster plc 1986-88;

managing ptnr Quadrangle Mktg Servs Ltd 1988-; *Style*— Miss Christine Hastings; Quadrangle Marketing Services, 180 Wardour St, London W1V 3AA (☎ 01 287 2262, fax 01 439 1537, telex 894767)

HASTINGS, 22 Baron (E 1290); Sir Edward Delaval Henry Astley; 12 Bt (E 1660); s of 21 Baron (d 1956), and Lady Marguerite Nevill, da of 3 Marquess of Abergavenny; *b* 14 April 1912; *Educ* Eton, abroad; *m* 1954, Catherine, yr da of Capt Harold Virgo Hinton, and formerly w of Vernon Coats; 2 s, 1 da; *Heir* s, Hon Delaval Astley; *Career* Maj Coldstream Gds ret; patron of seven livings; lord-in-waiting to HM The Queen 1961-62, jt parly sec Min Housing and Local Govt 1962-64; former farmer S Rhodesia (now Zimbabwe); pres: British-Italian Soc 1972-, Br Epilepsy Assoc 1965-; govr: Br Inst Florence, Royal Ballet; grand offr Order of Merit (Italy); *Clubs* Brooks's, Army and Navy; *Style*— The Lord Hastings; Seaton Delaval Hall, Northumberland (☎ 091 237 0786); Fulmodeston Hall, Fakenham, Norfolk (☎ 032 877 231)

HASTINGS, Hon Mrs (Eileen Ellen); *née* Wise; da of Baron Wise (d 1968), and Kate Elizabeth, (*née* Sturgeon; *b* 28 Sept 1916; *m* 1940, Sqdn Ldr Gerald Edmund Hastings; s of Alfred Philip Hastings (d 1984); 3 da (Tanera, Eileen, Bridget); *Style*— The Hon Mrs Hastings; Bridge Cottage, Rousdon Lymeregis, Dorset (☎ 029 743433)

HASTINGS, Hon Lady; Elizabeth Anne Marie Gabrielle; *née* FitzAlan-Howard; yr da of 2 and last Viscount FitzAlan of Derwent, OBE (d 1962), and Joyce Elizabeth, now Countess Fitzwilliam, *qv*; *b* 26 Jan 1934; *m* 1, 17 Jan 1952 (m dis 1960), Sir Vivyan Naylor-Leyland, 3 Bt; 1 s; m 2, 1975, Sir Stephen Lewis Edmonstone Hastings, MC, *qv*; *Career* MPhil, egyptologist; hon research asst dept of Egyptology Univ Coll London; Jt Master Fitzwilliam Hounds; *Style*— The Hon Lady Hastings; Milton, Peterborough, Cambridgeshire (☎ 0733 380780)

HASTINGS, George Frederick; s of J Maurice Hastings (d 1965), of Rainthorpe Hall, and Rosemary Crane Hastings (d 1983); *b* 17 June 1932; *Educ* Eton, Christ Church Oxford (MA); *m* 1, 17 April 1965 (m dis 1974), Alys, da of Viggo Kihl (d 1969), of Canada; 1 s (Magnus b 1968), 1 da (Sophie b 1966); m 2, 7 Oct 1983, Melissa, da of Peter Cuyler Walker, of Washington DC; 1 s (Samuel b 1984); *Career* Nat Serv Pilot Offr RAF 245 Day Fighter Sqdn 1950-52; called to the Bar Inner Temple 1972; Parish Cncl 1976-86; *Recreations* writing, shooting, sylviculture; *Clubs* Brooks's, Norfolk; *Style*— George Hastings, Esq; Rainthorpe Hall, Tasburgh, Norfolk NR15 1RQ (☎ 0508 470 618)

HASTINGS, Max Macdonald; s of Douglas Macdonald Hastings (d 1982), and Anne Scott-James (Lady Lancaster); *b* 28 Dec 1945; *Educ* Charterhouse (scholar), Univ Coll Oxford (exhibitioner); *m* 1972, Patricia Mary, da of Tom Edmondson, of Leics; 2 s (Charles b 1973, Harry b 1983), 1 da (Charlotte b 1977); *Career* author, journalist and broadcaster; reporter London Evening Standard 1965-70, fell World Press Inst St Paul USA 1967-68, reporter BBC TV 1970-73, ed Evening Standard Londoner's Diary 1976-77; columnist/contributor: Evening Standard, Daily Express, Sunday Times 1973-86; ed The Daily Telegraph 1986-; *Books* The Fire This Time (1968), The Struggle for Civil Rights in Northern Ireland (1970), The King's Champion (1976), Hero of Entebbe (1979), Bomber Command (1979, Somerset Maugham Prize), Das Reich (1981), The Battle for the Falklands (with Simon Jenkins, 1983; Yorkshire Post Book of the Year Prize), Overlord: D-Day and The Battle for Normandy (1984, - Yorkshire Post Book of the Year Prize), Victory in Europe (1985), The Oxford Book of Military Anecdotes (ed, 1985), The Korean War (1987); *Recreations* shooting, fishing; *Clubs* Brooks's, Beefsteak, Saintsbury; *Style*— Max Hastings, Esq; Guilsborough Lodge, Northamptonshire, 32 Chepstow Court, London W11; The Daily Telegraph, South Quay Plaza, London E14 9SR (☎ 01 538 5000)

HASTINGS, Lt-Col Robin Hood William Stewart; DSO and bar (1944, 1945), OBE (1946), MC (1943); s of Hon Osmond Hastings (d 1933; 2 s of 13 Earl of Huntingdon), and Mary Caroline Campbell, *née* Tarratt (d 1955); hp to cous, 15 Earl of Huntingdon; *b* 16 Jan 1917; *Educ* Stowe, Ch Ch Oxford (MA); *m* 25 May 1950, Jean Suzanne, da of Henry Palethorpe, of Stone Manor, Chaddesley Corbett, Worcs, and formerly w of John Ronald Christopher Holbech; 1 da (Lucinda Ileene b 15 July 1955 m Michael Waterhouse); 1 s); *Career* serv WWII 1939-46, cmmnd Rifle Brigade 1939, cmd 6 Bn The Green Howards 1943-44 and 2 Bn KRRC 1944, GSO 11 Armd Div 1945, cmd 1 Rifle Bde 1945-46 (despatches 2); chm British Bloodstock Agency Ltd 1968-86; *Books* The Rifle Brigade 1939-45, Without Reserve (1986); *Recreations* hunting, shooting, fishing; *Clubs* White's; *Style*— Lt-Col Robin Hastings, DSO, OBE, MC; The Malt House, Bramdean, Alresford, Hampshire S024 0LN (☎ 096 279 243)

HASTINGS, Lady Selina Shirley; da of 15 Earl of Huntingdon by his 2 w, Margaret Lane; *b* 5 Mar 1945; *Educ* St Paul's Girls' Sch, St Hugh's Coll Oxford (MA); *Career* journalist; literary ed Harper's and Queen; *Books* Sir Gawain and the Green Knight, Sir Gawain and the Loathly Lady, Nancy Mitford a Biography; *Style*— Lady Selina Hastings; c/o Rogers, Coleridge & White, 20 Powis Mews, London W11

HASTINGS, Sir Stephen Lewis Edmonstone; MC (1944); s of Lewis Aloysius Macdonald Hastings, MC (d 1966), and Meriel, *née* Edmonstone (d 1971); *b* 4 May 1921; *Educ* Eton, RMC Sandhurst; *m* 1, 1948 (m dis 1971), Harriet Mary Elizabeth, da of late Col Julian Latham Tomlin, CBE, DSO; 1 s (Neil), 1 da (Carola); m 2, 1975, Hon Elizabeth Anne Marie Gabrielle, *qv*; *Career* serv Scots Gds 1939-48: 2 Bn Western Desert 1941-43 (despatches), SAS Regt 1943; later serv with: Special Forces in Italy, Br Troops in Austria; Foreign Off 1948, Br Legation Helsinki and Embassy Paris 1952-58, first sec Political Off Middle East Forces 1959-60; MP (C) Mid-Bedfordshire 1960-1983; dir of various cos; chm: BMSS Ltd, Br Field Sports Soc 1982-88; thoroughbred breeder Milton Park Stud; kt 1983; *Publications* The Murder of TSR2 (1966); *Recreations* field sports, painting; *Clubs* White's, Buck's, Pratt's; *Style*— Sir Stephen Hastings, MC; Milton Hall, Peterborough (☎ 0733 380 780); 12a Ennismore Gardens, London SW7 (☎ 01 589 6494)

HASTINGS-BASS, William Edward Robin Hood; s of Capt Peter Hastings-Bass (assumed additional name Bass 1954, d 1964), and Priscilla (b 1920, m 1947, dir Newbury Race Course, memb Jockey Club), da of Capt Sir Malcolm Bullock, 1 Bt, MBE, and Lady Victoria Stanley (da of 17 Earl of Derby); through paternal gf (Hon Aubrey Hastings, 3 s of 13 Earl of Huntingdon) he is next in line to that Earldom after Lt-Col Robin Hastings, *qv*; *b* 30 Jan 1948; *Educ* Winchester, Trin Cambridge; *Style*— William Hastings-Bass, Esq; Wells Head House, Kingsclere, Newbury, Berks

HASTWELL, Vincent Edward; s of Dennis Edward Hastwell (d 1972), and Monica Dorothy Grace, *née* Lawson-White (d 1971); *b* 9 May 1943; *Educ* Chichester HS for Boys, Architectural Assoc Sch of Architecture (AA Dipl); *m* 7 Oct 1968, Lynne, da of Douglas Richardson (d 1986), of Bersted, Sussex; 1 s (Leon Alastair b 1971), 1 da (Anya Victoria b 1978); *Career* ptnr Hastwell Associates Chartered Architects 1977-; joint first prize Millbank competition 1977 for Crown Estates; RIBA 1972; *Recreations* walking, music, collecting vintage guitars; *Clubs* Architectural Assoc; *Style*— Vincent Hastwell, Esq; Old Nags Head Cottage, Horsham Road, Homwood, nr Dorking, Surrey RH5 4ED; 11-13 Sheen Road, Richmond, Surrey TW9 1AD (☎ 01 940 8096)

HASWELL, Charles Kenneth; s of Charles John Roderick Haswell (d 1936), of London, and Marion Etta, *née* Miles; *b* 3 Dec 1913; *Educ* St Paul's, King's Coll London (BSc); *m* 5 Sept 1939, Genevieve, da of Lennox Bywater (d 1942), of London; 1 s (Charles Christopher Miles); *Career* London Passenger Tport Bd 1936-40, ptnr Sir William Halcrow & Ptnrs 1941-64; fndr and sr ptnr: Charles Haswell & Ptnrs 1964-, Charles Haswell & Ptnrs (Far East) 1972-, Charles Haswell Consits PTE Ltd 1983-; responsible for the design and construction of a wide range of civil engrg works; Awards: Telford Prize, Frederick Palmer Prize, Halcrow Premium, David Hislop Award; author of numerous pubns on and lectr in tunnels and contract matters; arbitrator ICE 1964; memb: Br Standards Ctee on concrete aggregates, ICE piling ctee, jt ctee on the revision of ICE conditions of contract, ICE ctee on training in civil engrg, ICE arbitration advsy bd; chm ICE ctee on arbitration procedure; FICE, FIStructE, FSE, MConsE; *Recreations* golf; *Clubs* Athenaeum, RAC; *Style*— Charles Haswell, Esq; Magnolia Cottage, 403 Upper Richmond Road, London SW15 5QW (☎ 01 876 3003); 99 Gt Russell Street, London WC1B 3LA (☎ 01 580 2412, fax 01 631 4602, telex 299544)

HASWELL, (Anthony) James Darley; OBE (1985); s of Brig Chetwynd Henry Haswell, CIE (d 1956), and Dorothy Edith, *née* Berry (d 1976); *b* 4 August 1922; *Educ* Winchester, St John's Coll Cambridge (MA); *m* 6 July 1957, Angela Mary, da of Guy Blondel Murphy (d 1949), of Harrow, Middx; 3 s (Timothy b 1958, Jonathan b 1960, Jeremy (twin) b 1960), 1 da (Kate b 1965); *Career* cmmnd DCLI (TA) 1951, Capt Army Legal Servs Staff List (now Army Legal Corps) 1952, Capt Legal Staff MELF 1953-55, Temp Maj 1956, Maj 1960, DADALS HQLF 1965-67, Lt-Col 1967, ADALS NELF Cyprus 1968-71, CO HQ Army Legal Aid 1971-73, Legal Offr Army Legal Aid BAOR 1974-80, Army Legal Aid Aldershot 1980-81, ret 1981; admitted slr of Supreme Ct 1949, legal dept RAC 1949, asst slr Reginald Rogers & Co Helston 1950-51, first Insur Ombudsman 1981-89; chm and playing memb Insur Orchestral Soc; Freeman City of London, Liveryman Worshipful Co Insurers 1987; *Books* Insurance Ombudsman Annual Reports (1981-88); *Recreations* music, theatre, painting, woodwork; *Style*— James Haswell, Esq, OBE; 31 Chipstead St, London SW6 3SR (☎ 01 736 1163)

HASZARD, (Jacinth) Rodney; JP (1974); s of Col Gerald Fenwick Haszard, CBE, DSC, DL, JP (d 1967), of Milford Hall, Stafford, and Dyonese Rosamund, *née* Levett; *b* 24 Oct 1933; *Educ* RNC Dartmouth; *m* 28 Oct 1980, Anna Serena, da of Paul Henry Hawkins (d 1984), of Chetwynd Knoll, Newport, Shropshire; 1 step s (Charles Roarie Scarisbrick), 1 step da (Arabella Domenica Scarisbrick); *Career* Kings Shropshire LI: Platoon Cdr 1 Bn BAOR 1952-55, Platoon Cdr Mau Mau rebellion Kenya 1955-56, Mortar Arabian Peninsula Dhala battle of Jebel Jihaf 1957, ADC to HE Govr and C in C Tanganyika 1959-60; Adj Herford LI 1960-65, Co Cdr 3 Bn LI Plymouth, Malaya 1965-67, Trg Maj 5 Bn LI (TA) 1968-71; regnl sec CLA 1971-78, agent to tstees of the Earl of Lichfield 1978-; underwriting memb Lloyds 1976; gen cmmr of Income Tax 1985-88; High Sheriff of Staffordshire 1978; *Recreations* shooting, fishing, aboriculture; *Style*— Maj Rodney Haszard; Barwhinnock, Twynholm, Kirkcudbright; (☎ 0557 6212); Yeld Bank Farm, Knightley, Stafford (☎ 0785 74682); Lichfield Est Off, Walton Bank Farm, Eccleshall, Stafford (☎ 0785 282659)

HATCH, Barbara Helen Mary; *née* Bird; da of Col Austin Carlos Bird (d 1937), and Agnes Mary, *née* Coates (d 1961); descended from Capt Carlos who helped King Charles II escape by hiding in the oak tree; *b* 2 Jan 1916; *Educ* Royal Sch Bath; *m* 28 March 1936, Philip George, s of George Washington Hatch (d 1955); 1 s (Peter b 1938), 2 da (Diana b 1937, Barbara b 1942); *Career* artist, exhibitions at Henley and Farnham 1987; *Recreations* gardening; *Style*— Mrs Barbara Hatch; Little Chesters, Eversley, Hants G27 0PJ (☎ 0734 732371)

HATCH, David Edwin; s of Rev Raymond Harold Hatch (d 1967), and Winifred Edith May, *née* Brookes (d 1987); *b* 7 May 1939; *Educ* St Johns Leatherhead, Queens' Coll Cambridge (MA, DipEd); *m* 1964, Ann Elizabeth, da of Christopher Martin (d 1945); 2 s (Christopher b 1967, Richard b 1970), 1 da (Penelope b 1965); *Career* co-starred with John Cleese, Graham Chapman, Bill Oddie and Tim Brooke Taylor in Cambridge Footlights Revue "Cambridge Circus" 1963; actor, writer BBC "I'm Sorry I'll Read That Again"; Radio Light Entertainment 1965, exec producer Programme Devpt 1971, Radio Network ed Manchester 1978, head of Radio Light Entertainment 1978, controller Radio 2 1980, controller Radio 4 1983, dir of Programmes 1986-87, md Network Radio BBC 1987-, vice-chm BBC Enterprises Ltd, memb Bd of Mgmnt The Services Sound and Vision Corpn; FRSA; *Recreations* Bruegel Jigsaws, family, laughing; *Clubs* Reform; *Style*— David Hatch, Esq; The Windmill, Ray's Hill, Chesham, Bucks HP5 2UJ; Broadcasting House, Langham Place, London W1A 1AA (☎ 01 927 5460)

HATCH, John Vaughan; s of Brian Hatch, of Rippingale, Lincs, and Eileen Mabel, *née* Woodmansey; *b* 25 May 1949; *Educ* Worksop Coll, Mansfield Coll Oxford (MA), St Anthony's Coll Oxford (MPhil); *m* 30 June 1973, Sally Margaret, da of Geoffrey William Randle Brownscombe (d 1950), of Hove, Sussex; 2 da (Rebecca b 1978, Amber b 1982); *Career* mgmnt conslt Deloitte Haskins & Sells 1973-82, dep dir of Investmt Water Authorities Superannuation Fund 1982-84, md Venture Link (Hldgs) Ltd 1984-87, chm and md Venture Link Investors Ltd 1987-; non exec dir: Century Publishing Co Ltd 1982-85, Century Hutchinson Ltd 1985-; chm Electricity Consumers' Cncl 1984-, non exec dir Nat Grid Co Advsy Bd; memb: Nat Consumer Cncl 1980-86, Gen Optical Cncl 1984-88; ccncllr Oxfordshire 1973-77; former capt and chm Blewbury and Upton Cricket Club; Freeman City of London 1985, Memb Worshipful Co of Info Technologists 1989; ACMA (1980); *Books* Controlling Nationalised Industries (with John Redwood 1982), Value For Money Audits (with John Redwood 1981); *Recreations* cricket, bridge; *Clubs* City of London, Lansdowne; *Style*— John Hatch, Esq; Rose Cottage, High St, Upton, Nr Didcot, Oxfordshire (☎ 0235 850 671); Tectonic Place, Holyport Rd, Maidenhead, Berks (☎ 0628 771 050, fax 0628 770 392)

HATCH OF LUSBY, Baron (Life Peer UK 1978); John Charles Hatch; s of John James Hatch; *b* 1 Nov 1917; *Educ* Keighley Boys' GS, Sidney Sussex Coll Cambridge; *Career* sits as Labour Peer in House of Lords; journalist (on New Statesman), broadcaster, author, lecturer; national organiser ILP 1944-48, head Cwlth Dept Lab

Pty HQ 1954-61, first dir Inst of Human Relations Zambia Univ to 1982, dir emeritus Inter-Univ African Studies Programme Houston Texas; Hon DLitt St Thomas Univ Houston 1981; *Books* A History of Post-War Africa, Africa Emergent, Two African Statesmen; *Recreations* cricket, music; *Clubs* MCC and Royal Cwlth Soc; *Style*— The Rt Hon the Lord Hatch of Lusby; House of Lords, London, SW1A 0PW (☎ 01 219 5353)

HATCHARD, Frederick Harry; s of Francis Joseph (d 1960), and May Evelyn, *née* Tyler (d 1982); *b* 22 April 1923; *Educ* Yardley GS, Birmingham Univ; *m* 22 Oct 1955, Patricia Evelyn, da of Frederick Edward Egerton (d 1955), of Sutton Coldfield; 2 s (Simon b 1959, Michael b 1962); *Career* pilot RAF 1942-46, RAFVR 1950-55; admitted slr 1958; justices clerk: Sutton Coldfield 1963-67, Walsall 1967-81; stipendary magistrate Birmingham 1981-; *Recreations* sport, gardening; *Style*— Frederick Hatchard, Esq; 3b Manor Rd, Streetly, Sutton Coldfield, W Midlands

HATCHER, Mark; s of Peter Thomas Hatcher, of 71 Eastwick Drive, Great Bookham, nr Leatherhead, Surrey, and Joan Beatrice, *née* Crisp; *b* 16 Oct 1954; *Educ* Sutton Valence Sch Kent, Exeter Coll Oxford (BA, MA); *m* 9 July 1988, Clare Helen, eld da of Prof Clifford Hugh Lawrence, 11 Durham Rd, London SW20; *Career* barr Middle Temple 1978 (ad eundem Lincoln's Inn), private practice 1978-80, legal asst Law Cmmn 1980-83, Dept legal and sr legal asst legislation gp Lord Chancellor's 1980-88, grade 6 (legal) cts and legal servs gp 1988; mgmnt conslt Deloitte Haskins & Sells 1989-; memb Greenwich Soc (conservation); memb Gen Cncl of Bar; *Recreations* windsurfing, second-hand books, cooking; *Style*— Mark Hatcher, Esq; 37 Ashburnham Grove, Greenwich, London SE10 8UL (☎ 01 691 7191); Deloitte Haskins & Sells, Mgmnt Consultancy Div, PO Box 198, Hillgate Hse, 26 Old Bailey, London EC4M 7PL (☎ 01 248 3913, fax 01 248 1368, telex 8955899 DHSHHG)

HATCHETT, Alan George; CBE (1987); s of Ralph Hatchett (d 1929); *b* 3 Oct 1924; *Educ* William Ellis Sch Hampstead; *m* 1960, Margaret Kathlyn, da of Albert Victor Brockhurst; 1 child; *Career* dir: The Australia Japan Container Line, Federal Steam Navigation Co, P and O Lines, The Peninsular and Oriental Steam Navigation Co; dep chm Overseas Containers Ltd 1983-, jt md (fleet mgmnt) 1983-; *Recreations* gardening, fishing; *Clubs* Oriental; *Style*— Alan Hatchett, Esq, CBE; St Ronans, Wonersh Park, Wonersh, Surrey; Overseas Containers Ltd, Beagle House, Braham St, London E1 8EP (☎ 01 488 1313)

HATHAWAY, Derek Charles; *Career* chm: Dartmouth Investments, Ashby Leisure Products, Combat Engineering, Energy Machine Tools, Lawton Pressings; *Style*— Derek Hathaway, Esq; Dartmouth Investments Ltd, Bilston Trading Estate, Oxford St, Bilston, Staffs

HATHERLEY, John; s of Harold Norman Hatherley (d Margate S Africa 1986), and Hester Van Heerden (d 1972); *b* 18 Oct 1926; *Educ* Christian Bros Coll Boksburg (S Africa), Univ of Cape Town (MA), Univ of Witwatersand (BA); *m* 5 Jan 1955, Gertruida Johanna, da of Jacobus Mattys-Botha; 1 s (Peter b 1957), 1 da (Anita b 1956); *Career* accountant Gearings Water Boring and Equipment Co Ltd 1950-51; assoc memb Chartered Inst of Secs 1953; teacher Charterhouse King's Coll Sch Wimbledon, head of Econ and Politics Dept Purley HS and Wimbledon Coll; memb: exec ctee, Econ Research Cncl, Econ and Social Science Research Assoc, London Lib Exec and Policy Panel 1974-86; pres Sutton Educn Assoc; prospective parly candidate (Lib) Carshalton (Sutton) 1975-83, London Lib Party Exec and Policy Panel 1974-83; *Recreations* esoteric philosophy, new economics, economic reform (especially as regards taxation, inner city decay), education reform, freelance writing (mostly economics, Maltese politics); *Clubs* Gladstone; *Style*— John Hatherley, Esq; 16 Brighton Rd, Coulsdon, Surrey CR3 2BA (☎ 01 668 4038)

HATHERTON, 8 Baron (UK 1835) Edward Charles Littleton; only s of Mervyn Cecil Littleton (d 1970), gs of 3 Baron, by his w, Margaret Ann, da of Frank Sheehy; *b* 24 May 1950; *m* 1974, Hilda Maria Robert, of San Jose, Costa Rica; 1 s (Hon Thomas); 1 da (Hon Melissa Ann b 1975); *Heir* s, Hon Thomas Edward, b 1977; *Style*— Rt Hon Lord Hatherton

HATHORN, Eric Anthony; s of James Hathorn, of Edinburgh; *b* 18 June 1929; *Educ* Wellington, Merton Coll Oxford; *m* 1966, Hon Jean Rosemary *qv*, da of Lord Evans, GCVO (d 1963); 2 s, 1 da; *Career* 2 Lt Gren Gds; with ICI 1952-68, joined L Messel and Co (Stockbrokers) 1968, ptnr: Beardsley Bishop Escombe 1973-83, Henderson Crosthwaite 1983-; *Recreations* travel, theatre, opera, gardening; *Clubs* City University; *Style*— Eric Hathorn, Esq; 51 Netherhall Gdns, London NW3 (☎ 01 794 6892); Henderson Crosthwaite Ltd, 32 St Mary-at-Hill, London EC3 (☎ 01 283 8577)

HATHORN, Hon Mrs (Jean Rosemary); *née* Evans; da of 1 and last Baron Evans, GCVO (d 1963); *b* 14 April 1934; *m* 1966, Eric Anthony Hathorn, *qv*; 2 s, 1 da; *Style*— The Hon Mrs Hathorn; 51 Netherhall Gdns, London NW3 (☎ 01 794 6892)

HATT-COOK, Mark Edward; RD (and Bar); s of Lt-Col John Edward Hatt-Cook, MC, of The Courtyard, Stoke Farthing, Broadchalke, Salisbury, Wilts, and Lavender Helen, *née* Covernton; *b* 18 Dec 1942; *Educ* Bradfield; *m* 18 Oct 1969, Susan Georgina, da of Lt-Col Ronald John Henry Kaulback, OBE, of Altbough, Hoarwithy, Hereford; 2 da (Catherine Emma b 13 Aug 1974, Georgina Alice b 13 June 1977); *Career* cmmd RMR 1963; attached: 45 Commando S Arabia 1963 (active serv), 42 Commando Malaysia 1969, 41 Commando N Ireland 1970; qualified Arctic survival instr 1980, TAVR staff course Camberley 1981, promoted Maj 1 Sept 1982, USMC staff course Quantico 1984, 2 i/c RMR City of London 1987; serv articles with Hunters and with Bichoffs, asst slr Deacons Hong Kong, ptnr Wilsons Salisbury; regnl Br Olympic Ctee 1988, Freedom City of London 1981; memb Law Soc; *Recreations* shooting, skiing; *Style*— Mark Hatt-Cook, Esq, RD; Mascalls, Broadchalke, Salisbury, Wilts (☎ 0722 780 480); Steynings House, Salisbury, Wilts (☎ 0722 412 979, fax 0722 411 500, telex 265871 MONREF G 74 NFL 3011)

HATTERSLEY, Lt Cdr Charles William; s of Maj J S Hattersley, of 17 Conference Way, Colkirk, Fakenham, Norfolk, *née* Howard; *b* 22 Mar 1949; *Educ* Marlborough, Durham Univ (BA), Guildford Coll of Law; *m* 30 July 1988, Rebecca Jane, da of Capt David Vernon Smith, of Guildford, Surrey; *Career* Britannia RN Coll Dartmouth 1971-72, Seaman Offr HMS Ark Royal 1972-73, Navigating Offr HMS Olympus 1973-74, 4 i/c HMS Courageous 1974-76; 3 i/c: HMS Walrus 1976-77, and HMS Conqueror 1977-79, 2 i/c HMS Opportune 1979-81; memb: Jt Servs team to Phabrang 21000 peak India, Jt Servs team to Manaslu North 24000 Nepal, Jt Servs team to North face of Everest reached 27,200 feet; Capt 4 Bn Devonshire & Dorset Regt First Rifle Volunteers TA Exeter, (2 i/c of Company 1988-); articled clerk Holman Fenwick, London 1985-87, qualified slr 1988, maritime lawyer Middleton Potts London 1988-; lectr Royal Geographical Soc and Alpine Club, played for Naval and Military Club in Bath Cup London; Liveryman Worshipful Co of Skinners 1981; FRGS, MNI; *Recreations* mountaineering, skiing, squash, golf; *Clubs* Naval & Military, Alpine; *Style*— Lt Cdr Charles Hattersley; 97 Howard Rd, Westbury Plc, Bristol BS6 7UX (☎ 0272 245421); Middleton Potts, 3 Cloth St, Long Lane, London EC1A 7LD (☎ 01 600 2333, fax 01 600 0108, telex 928357 MIDLEX G)

HATTERSLEY, Prof (William) Martin; s of Col Sidney Martin Hattersley, MC (d 1943), and Vera, *née* Blackbourn (d 1962); *b* 31 Mar 1928; *Educ* Marlborough, Univ of London (BSc); *m* 1, 1 Sept 1950 (m dis 1982), Shena Mary, da of Sydney Drummond Anderson (d 1961); 3 da (Susan b 1955, Clare b 1956, Diana b 1957); m 2, 1 Oct 1982, May Ling, da of Wee Bin Chye (d 1949); *Career* probationary 2 Lt RM 1946, Lt RM 1948, resigned cmmn 1950, elected memb HAC 1988; Gerald Eve & Co (chartered surveyors): improver 1950-54, tech asst 1954-58, ptnr 1958, responsible for all overseas assignments 1962-86, responsible for Brussels Off 1975-83; chief resident valuation offr Kuala Lumpur Municipal Cncl 1959-61, prof and head of centre for studies in property valuation and mgmnt City Univ; memb: Lavant Valley Decorative and Fine Arts Soc, Emsworth Maritime and Historical Tst, Solent Protection Soc, Chichester Canal Soc; friend of Chichester Festival Theatre; pres: BSc Estate Mgmnt Club 1970, Rating Surveyors' Assoc 1978; Freeman City of London 1950; Liveryman: Worshipful Co of Skinners 1963, Worshipful Co of Chartered Surveyors 1977; FRICS 1963, FISM 1968, FSVA 1971, memb FIABCI 1973, FRVA 1986, FIABCI Medaille d'Honor for Leadership of Professional Standards Ctee (France 1986); *Books* Chapter: Valuation Priniciples into Practice (1988); *Recreations* sailing; *Clubs* Carlton, Naval and Military, City Livery; *Style*— Prof Martin Hattersley; 4 Roundhouse Meadow, Emsworth, Hants PO10 8BD (☎ 0243 375 664); 17 Osprey Quay, Emsworth, Hants PO10 8BZ; City Univ, Northampton Sq, London EC1V 0HB (☎ 01 253 4399, ext 3950, fax 01 250 0837)

HATTERSLEY, Rt Hon Roy Sydney George; PC (1975), MP (Lab) Birmingham Sparkbrook 1964-; s of late Frederick Hattersley by his w Enid (Lord Mayor Sheffield 1981-); *b* 28 Dec 1932; *Educ* Sheffield City GS, Hull Univ; *m* 1956, Molly (Edith Mary, headmistress Creighton Sch London, formerly ctee chm Headmistresses' Assoc and pres Secondary Heads Assoc, asst educn offr in charge of teaching staff ILEA 1982-), da of Michael Loughran; *Career* journalist; exec Health Serv and memb Sheffield City Cncl; PPS to Min of Pensions and Nat Insurance 1964-67, jt parly sec Employment 1967-69, min of defence for admin 1969-70; Lab spokesman: defence 1972, Educn and Science 1972-74; min of state FCO 1974-76, prices and consumer protection sec 1976-79; chief oppn spokesman on: Environment 1979-80, Home Affairs 1981-83, Treasy and Econ Affairs 1983-87, Home Affairs 1987-; stood in Lab leadership and dep leadership elections, elected dep ldr Oct 1983-; named columnist of the year 1982 by Granada TV's *What the Papers Say*; re-elected to shadow cabinet and appointed chief oppn spokesman Treasury and Econ Affrs 1983-; *Style*— The Rt Hon Roy Hattersley, MP; 14 Gayfere St, London SW1P 3HP (☎ 01 222 1309)

HATTON, Christopher John Bower; s of Alan Herbert Hatton (d 1960); *b* 5 Mar 1933; *Educ* Charterhouse; *m* 1962, Alison Myfanwy, da of Robert Faulkner Armitage (d 1982); 3 children; *Career* slr 1956; chm: Greenall Whitley plc (brewers), Crane Property Devpt; dir: Nat West Bank (north regional bd), Sun Alliance Assurance Co (Chester branch bd); *Style*— Christopher Hatton, Esq; Robert Davies and Co, Solicitors, PO Box 1, 21 Bold St, Warrington, Cheshire (☎ 0925 50161)

HATTRELL, Michael Walter; s of (Walter) Stanley Hattrell (d 1977), of The Limes, Brancaster, Norfolk, and Pauline Gertrude, *née* Herbert; *b* 1 May 1934; *Educ* Ampleforth , Trinity Coll Cambridge (MA); *m* 2 Sept 1967, Charmian Adele, da of Louis Larth, of Brimpsfield, Glos; 2 da (Samantha b 1968, Victoria b 1971); *Career* Nat Serv cmmnd Green Howards, serv Canal Zone and Cyprus 1952-54; architect ptnr WS Hattrell & Ptnrs 1961-75, currently in practice as Michael Hattrell & Assoc 1975-; works incl: St Andrews Shared Church Slough 1970, works for house of Stanley Kubrick in St Alban's 1977, works at Brocket Hall Herts 1985-89; hon sec: Chilterns Cricket League, Soc of Int Christian Artists; Freeman City of London, Liveryman Worshipful Co Coach Makers and Coach Harness Makers; FRIBA; *Recreations* cricket, golf; *Style*— Michael Hattrell, Esq; Priory Cottage, Stomp Rd, Burnham, Bucks (☎ 06286 5030); 29 Trott St, London SW11 3DS (☎ 01 228 1672)

HATTY, Sir Cyril James; s of James Hatty; *b* 22 Dec 1908; *Educ* Westminster City Sch; *m* 1937, Doris Evelyn Stewart; 2 s; *Career* dep dir O and M Div UK Treasury to 1947; MP for Bulawayo, S Rhodesia 1950-62 (min of Treasury 1954-62, min of Mines 1956-62); min of finance Bophuthatswana 1979-82; FCIS, FCMA; kt 1963; *Style*— Sir Cyril Hatty; Merton Park, Norton, Zimbabwe

HAVARD, Dr John David Jayne; CBE (1989); s of Dr Arthur William Havard, MB, BS (d 1964), and Ursula Vernon Jayne, *née* Humphrey; *b* 5 May 1924; *Educ* Malvern, Jesus Coll Cambridge (MA, MD, LLM), Middx Hosp Med Sch; *m* 1, 1950 (m dis 1982), Margaret Lucy, da of Albert Collis, OBE (d 1963), of Wimbledon; 2 s, 1 da; m 2, 1982, Anne Audrey, da of Rear-Adm Lawrence Boutwood, CB (d 1982), of Tideford, Cornwall; *Career* Actg Sqdn Ldr RAF Medical Service 1950-52 (Nat Serv); barr Middle Temple; house physician Professorial Medical Unit Middx Hosp 1950, GP Lowestoft 1952-58, sec E Suffolk LMC 1956-58; BMA staff 1958-, sec BMA 1979-; dep chm Staff Side Whitley Cncl (Health Servs); chm science ctee Int Driver Behaviour Research Assoc, pres British Academy of Forensic Sciences 1985, sec/tres Commonwealth Medical Assoc 1986-; MRCP; *Books* Detection of Secret Homicide (Cambridge Studies in Criminology Vol XI 1960), chapters in several books on legal medicine, alcohol, drugs etc; *Recreations* Bach Choir, English countryside; *Clubs* Oxford and Cambridge, Achilles; *Style*— Dr John Havard, CBE; 1 Wilton Sq, London N1 3DL (☎ 01 359 2802); BMA, Tavistock Square, London WC1H 9JP (telex 265929, fax 388 2544)

HAVARD-EVANS, Samuel James; OBE (1971), JP; s of David Lewis Evans (d 1961); *b* 10 April 1904; *Educ* Emlyn GS, St John's Coll Florida, Gray's Inn; *Career* Sqdn Ldr RAF; legal adviser Records Office RAF Gloucester, barr Gray's Inn 1931, dep chm Carmarthenshire Quarter Sessions 1955-71; chm: Agric Land Trib (Wales), Medical Appeal Tribunal (Wales); acted as dep county court judge 1952-71, dep recorder, dep circuit judge 1971-79; pres Carmarthen Rotary Club 1955; vice-pres: Carmarthenshire Antiquarian Soc, Carmarthen Care Soc; welfare offr Carmarthen RAF Assoc for 40 years; fndr Coomb Cheshire Home (pres 1978-); chm W Wales Magistrates' Assoc 1957- (former memb nat cncl); *Style*— Samuel Havard-Evans, Esq, OBE, JP

HAVELOCK, Sir Wilfrid Bowen; s of Rev E W Havelock (d 1916), and F H Bowen; *b* 14 April 1912; *Educ* ISC Windsor; *m* 1, 1938 (m dis 1967), Mrs Muriel Elizabeth Pershouse, *née* Vincent; 1 s; m 2, 1972, Mrs Patricia Mumford; *Career* served in 3/4 African Rifles 1940-42; MLC Kenya 1948-63 (min Local Govt, Health and Lands 1954-62, min Agric and Animal Husbandry 1962-63); dep chm Kenya Agric Fin Corpn 1964-84; memb Nat Irrigation Bd Kenya 1974-79; dir Bamburi Portland Cement Co 1974-86; dir: Baobab Farm Ltd Bamburi 1974-, African Fund for Endangered Wildlife Ltd (Kenya); memb Hotels and Restaurant Authy 1975-82; chm Kenya Assoc of Hotelkeepers and Caterers 1973-76; kt 1963; *Clubs* Muthaiga Country (Nairobi), Fellow Royal Commonwealth Soc London, Nairobi, Mombasa; *Style*— Sir Wilfrid Havelock; Limuru Rd, Muthaiga, PO Box 30181, Nairobi, Kenya (☎ 749806)

HAVELOCK-ALLAN, Sir Anthony James Allan; 4 Bt (UK 1858), of Lucknow; s of Allan Havelock-Allan (2 s of Sir Henry Havelock-Allan, 1 Bt, VC, GCB, MP, DL and his w Lady Alice Moreton, da of 2 Earl of Ducie), and Annie Julia, da of Sir William Chaytor, 3 Bt; suc bro, Sir Henry Ralph Moreton Havelock-Allan, 3 Bt, 1975; *b* 28 Feb 1905; *Educ* Charterhouse, Switzerland; *m* 1, 12 April 1939 (m dis 1952), (Babette) Valerie Louise (the film actress Valerie Hobson; she m 2, 1954, John Dennis Profumo, CBE), da of late Cdr Robert Gordon Hobson, RN; 2 s; m 2, 1979, Maria Theresa Consuela (Sara), da of late Don Carlos Ruiz de Villafranca (formerly Spanish ambass to Chile and Brazil); *Heir* s, Simon Anthony Henry Havelock-Allan b 6 May 1944; *Career* film producer; formerly produced quota films for Paramount, produced for Pinebrook Ltd and Two Cities Films 1938-40, assoc producer to Noel Coward 1941, with David Lean and Ronald Neame formed Cineguild 1942, producer, assoc producer and in charge of production for Cineguild 1942-47, formed Constellation Films 1949, formed with Lord Brabourne and Maj David Angel Br Home Entertainment (first co to attempt to introduce pay TV by cable) 1962; chm British Film Academy 1952, govr Br Film Inst (memb Inst's Production Ctee) 1958-65, chm Council of Soc of Film and Television Arts (now BAFTA) 1962 and 1963; *Style*— Sir Anthony Havelock-Allan, Bt; c/o Messrs Gorrie Whitson and Sons, 9 Cavendish Sq, London W1

HAVELOCK-ALLAN, Simon Anthony Henry; s and h of Sir Anthony Havelock-Allan, 4 Bt; *b* 6 May 1944; *Style*— Simon Havelock-Allan, Esq

HAVERS, Christopher Anthony Gore; s of Antony Cecil Oldfield Havers, of Berks, and Barbara Harrison Havers; *b* 30 April 1950; *Educ* Repton, Trinity Coll Dublin (BA); *m* 6 May 1978, Christine Mary, da of Kevin Patrick Moore, of Coventry; 2 s (Timothy b 1981, Patrick b 1984), 1 da (Rosie b 1988); *Career* barr Inner Temple 1975; dir: Through Tport Mutual Services Ltd 1985, West of Eng Ship Owners Insur Services 1987; *Recreations* shooting, sailing, farming; *Style*— Christopher A G Havers, Esq; West of England Services, International House, 1 St Katharine's Way, London E1 9UE

HAVERS, Baron (Life Peer 1987), of St Edmundsbury, Co Suffolk; (Robert) Michael Oldfield; PC (1977), QC (1964); s of Sir Cecil Havers, sometime High Ct judge, by his w Enid, da of William Oldfield Snelling, JP, of Norwich; *b* 10 Mar 1923; *Educ* Westminster, Corpus Christi Coll Cambridge; *m* 1949, Carol Elizabeth, da of Stuart Lay, of London; 2 s; *Career* barr Inner Temple 1948, dep chm W Suffolk QS 1961-65 (chm 1965-71); rec: Dover 1962-68, Norwich 1968-71, Crown Ct 1972; slr gen 1972-74, shadow attorney gen and legal advsy to shadow cabinet 1974-79, attorney gen 1979-87, Lord Chllr July-Oct 1987; chllr: Diocese of St Edmundsbury and Ipswich 1965-73, Diocese of Ely 1969-73; MP (C) Wimbledon 1970-87; hon fell Corpus Christi Coll Cambridge 1988; kt 1972; *Clubs* Garrick, Pratts; *Style*— The Rt Hon Lord Havers, PC, QC; 5 King's Bench Walk, Temple, London EC4 (☎ 01 353 4713); White Shutters, Ousden, Newmarket, Suffolk (☎ 063 879 267)

HAVERS, Hon Nigel; s of Baron Havers, *qv*; *b* 6 Nov 1950; *m* 1974 (m dis 1989), Carolyn Gillian, da of Vincent Cox; 1 da (Katharine b 1977); *Career* actor: The Glittering Prizes, Nicholas Nickleby, Horseman; TV: A Horseman Riding By, Upstairs Downstairs, Nancy Astor, Strangers and Brothers, Don't Wait Up; films: Chariots of Fire, A Passage to India, Burke and Wills, The Whistle Blower, Empire of the Sun, Farewell to the King; *Recreations* keeping fit, reading, gardening; *Clubs* Garrick; *Style*— The Hon Nigel Havers; 143 Ramsden Road, London SW12

HAVERS, Hon Philip; s of Baron Havers (Life Peer); *Style*— David Buck Esq; 74 Cadogan Terrace, London SW1

HAVERY, Richard Orbell; QC (1950); s of Joseph Horton Havery, of London, and Constance Eleanor, *née* Orbell (d 1987); *b* 7 Feb 1934; *Educ* St Paul's, Magdalen Coll Oxford (BA, MA); *Career* barr, rec of Crown Ct 1986, asst rec 1982, joint ed of Kemp and Kemp The Quantum of Damages (3 ed) 1967; *Recreations* music, croquet, steam locomotives; *Clubs* Garrick, Hurlingham; *Style*— Richard Havery, Esq, QC; 11 Alderney Street, SW1; Gray's Inn Chambers, Gray's Inn London WC1R 5JA (☎ 01 405 7211, fax 01 405 2084)

HAVILAND, Christopher Philip; s of late Col Philip Haviland Haviland, OBE, and Molly Gwendoline Parker, *née* Butt; *b* 9 Feb 1940; *Educ* Trinity Coll Dublin (MA, LLB); *m* 1970, Catherine Margaret Joan, da of George Ernest Swanson, of Colinton, Lothian; 2 s (Philip Julian Swanson b 27 Jan 1972, Adrian Christopher Clemow (twin) b 27 Jan 1972), 1 da (Fiona Mary Katharine b 30 June 1975); *Career* merchant banker; dir: N M Rothschild & Sons (CI) Ltd 1975-81, N M Rothschild & Sons Ltd 1976-81, Barclays Merchant Bank Ltd 1981-86, Barclays de Zoete Wedd Ltd 1986-, Barclays Bank regnl dir 1987-, Korea Merchant Banking Corpn 1987-, Barclays Tst & Banking (Japan) Ltd 1987-, Seibu Barclays Finance Ltd 1987-; *Recreations* swimming, tennis, walking; *Style*— Christopher Haviland, Esq; 54 Lombard Street, London EC3P 3AH (☎ 01 626 1567)

HAVILAND, Julian Arthur Charles; er s of Maj Leonard Proby Haviland (d 1971, Indian Cavalry), by his w, Helen Dorothea (d 1972), only da of Sir Charles Fergusson, 7 Bt, GCB, GCMG, DSO, MVO; *b* 8 June 1930; *Educ* Eton, Magdalene Cambridge; *m* Sept 1959, Caroline Victoria, yst da of late George Freland Barbour, PhD, by his w Hon Helen Victoria, da of 8 Lord Polwarth; 3 s (Peter b 1961, Charles b 1964, Richard b 1967); *Career* political ed The Times 1981-85 (suc Fred Emery, who became home ed), political ed ITN to 1981, has worked for: Surrey Advertiser, Evening Standard, Daily Telegraph; *Style*— Julian Haviland, Esq; Cator Rd, London SE26 (☎ 01 778 4428)

HAVILLE, Robert William; s of James Haville (d 1983), and Eileen Haville; *b* 27 July 1955; *Educ* Marlborough GS, Lancaster Univ (BA), Bradford Univ (MBA); *m* 18 Oct 1980, Hazel Dawn, da of George Burke, of London; 1 s (James b 1988), 1 da (Rosalind b 1986); *Career* fin analyst Kimberley Clark 1976-77; investmt analyst: McAnally Montgomery 1978-81, James Capel 1982-87, Morgan Stanley 1988-; Business Graduates Assoc; *Style*— Robert Haville, Esq; Morgan Stanley International, Kingsley House, 1A Wimpole St, London W1 (☎ 01 709 3000)

HAW, Jonathan Stopford; s of Denis Stopford Haw (d 1979), of Sidcup, Kent, and Elisabeth Mary Dorothy, *née* Mack; *b* 16 Mar 1945; *Educ* Radley, Keble Coll Oxford (MA); *m* 20 Dec 1969, Héléne Lucie, da of Louis Lacuve, Chevalier de L'Ordre National du Merité, of Perpignan, France; 1 s (Alexander b 1973), 1 da (Katherine b 1976); *Career* slr; Slaughter and May: ptnr 1977-, resident ptnr New York 1984-87 (first ptnr 1984); ctee memb Bassishaw Ward Club London; memb int governing cncl Juvenile Diabetes Fndn; Freeman City of London 1970, Liveryman Armourers and Brasiers Co, Freeman City of London Slrs Co; memb: Law Soc, Int Bar Assoc; *Recreations* tennis, reading, wine; *Clubs* Leander; *Style*— Jonathan S Haw, Esq; Goldhill House, East Garston, Newbury, Berks (☎ 0488 39 265); 27 St Paul's Place, Islington, London N1; 35 Basinghall St, London EC2V 5DB (☎ 01 600 1200, fax 01 600 0289, 01 726 0038, telex 883486/888926)

HAWARDEN, 8 Viscount (I 1793); Sir Robert Leslie Eustace Maude; 10 Bt (I 1705); also Baron de Montalt (I 1785); s of 7 Viscount (d 1958), by his w Marion (da of Albert Wright, whose w Margaretta was sis of 20 Baron FitzWalter); *b* 26 Mar 1926; *Educ* Winchester, Christ Church Oxford; *m* 1957, Susannah, da of Maj Charles Gardner (gggs of 1 Baron Gardner); 2 s, 1 da; *Heir* s, Hon Connan Maude; *Career* served Coldstream Gds 1945-46; landowner and farmer; *Style*— The Rt Hon the Viscount Hawarden; Wingham Court, Canterbury, Kent CT3 1BB (☎ 0227 720222)

HAWES RICHARDS, Derek; s of Arthur Hawes Richards (d 1971), and Eva Evelyn, *née* Small (d 1987); *b* 2 Feb 1933; *Educ* South Devon Technical Coll Torquay; *m* 29 Aug 1959, Hazel Anne, da of Victor Maddison, of Kent; 2 da (Lisa b 1966, Sophie b 1973); *Career* CA, FRIBA; cncllr Kent County Cncl 1985-, pres C of C 1988-; *Recreations* cricket, snooker, music, reading; *Style*— Derek Hawes Richards, Esq; Hop Press Oast, Mascalls Court Road, Paddock Wood, Kent TN12 6NB; 4 St Johns Road, Tunbridge Wells, Kent (☎ 0892 38777, fax 0892 49849)

HAWKE, Hon Edward George; s and h of 10 Baron Hawke, *qv*; *b* 25 Jan 1950; *Educ* Eton; *Style*— The Hon Edward Hawke; c/o The Rt Hon Lord Hawke, Old Mill House, Cuddington, Northwich, Cheshire

HAWKE, Ina, Lady; Ina Mary Faure Hawke; *née* Faure Walker; er da of Henry Faure Walker (d 1940), of Highly Manor, Balcombe, Sussex and Edith Ina, *née* Bartholomew (d 1940); *m* 1 Nov 1934, 9 Baron Hawke (d 1985); 7 da (who include the w of Nicholas Scott, MP, *qv*); *Style*— The Rt Hon Ina, Lady Hawke; Faygate Place, Faygate, Sussex

HAWKE, Hon Julia Georgette; yst da of 10 Baron Hawke; *b* 1 Jan 1960; *Style*— The Hon Julia Hawke; c/o The Rt Hon Lord Hawke, Old Mill House, Cuddington, Northwich, Cheshire

HAWKE, Cdr Michael George Richard; s of Peter Kenneth Nöel Hawke (d 1979), and Mary Olivia, *née* Wilson; *b* 29 Oct 1940; *Educ* RNC; *m* 20 July 1971, Juliet Beaumont Fullerton, da of Cdr Leslie George Wilson, OBE, of Dunbartonshire; 1 s (Simon Andrew b 1977), 2 da (Harriet b 1973, Catherine b 1974); *Career* joined BRNC Dartmouth 1959, apptd to HMS Loch Alvie 9 Frigate Sqdn, joined HMS Dolphin 1962 (subs), HMS Ocelot 1963-64, CO HMS Oberon 1972-73, memb C in C Fleet Staff (CTF 345) 1973-75, OC NUSCOT 1978, CO HMS Repulse 1981-84, Cdr HMS Dryad 1987-89; staff Comnasouth Izmir 1989-; chm Nautical Inst Scot Branch 1979, fell Nautical Inst 1988-;; *Recreations* sailing, walking, music, shooting, fishing, model making; *Style*— Cdr Michael G R Hawke; Yew Tree House, Nicholashayne, Wellington, Somerset TA21 9QY (☎ 0884 40302); Comnasouth Staff Izmir

HAWKE, 10 Baron (GB 1776); (Julian Stanhope) Theodore; s of 8 Baron Hawke (d 1939), and Frances Alice, *née* Wilmer (d 1959); suc bro, 9 Baron Hawke (d 1985); *b* 19 Oct 1904; *Educ* Eton, King's Coll Cambridge (MA); *m* 1, 17 Feb 1933 (m dis 1946), (Angela Margaret) Griselda (d 1984), o da of Capt Edmund William Bury (d 1918); 2 da; m 2, 22 May 1947, Georgette Margaret, o da of George Davidson, of 73 Eaton Sq, London; 1 s, 3 da; *Heir* s, Hon Edward George, *qv*; *Career* Wing Cdr AAF 1945, West Africa; with Manchester textile firm 1926-69; dir Glazebrook Steel Ltd 1932-69; *Recreations* golf, gardening, shooting; *Style*— The Rt Hon the Lord Hawke; The Old Mill House, Cuddington, Northwich, Cheshire (☎ 0606 882248)

HAWKEN, Lewis Dudley; CB (1983); s of Richard and Doris May Evelyn Hawken; *b* 23 August 1931; *Educ* Harrow County Sch for Boys, Lincoln Coll Oxford (MA); *m* 1954, Bridget Mary Gamble; 2 s, 1 da; *Career* dep chm Bd of Customs and Excise 1980-; *Style*— Lewis Hawken, Esq, CB; 19 Eastcote Rd, Ruislip, Middx

HAWKER, Christopher Henry Acton; MBE (1972); s of Lt Col (Albert) Henry Hawker, CMG, OBE, of Bowling Green Farm, Cottered, nr Buntingford, Herts, and Margaret Janet Olivia Hawker (d 1980); *b* 6 Dec 1945; *Educ* Kenton Coll Nairobi Kenya, Haileybury, RMA Sandhurst, Exeter Coll Oxford; *m* 29 July 1977, (m dis 1988), (Sarah) Jane, da of Prof GIC Ingram, of Staple Lees, Hastingleigh, Ashford, Kent; 1 s (Nicholas b 24 Aug 1982), 1 da (Kate b 23 Jan 1985); *Career* cmmnd Royal Green Jackets 1966, 1 Bn Berlin 1966-67, 1 and 3 Bn 1970-75, Adj 3 Bn 1973-75, ret 1975; co-founding dir Ridgeway Int Ltd (int freight forwarders) 1975-; *Recreations* sailing, skiing, squash, tennis, walking; *Clubs* Army and Navy, Vincents (Oxford); *Style*— Christopher Hawker, Esq, MBE; c/o Ridgeway International Ltd, 69 High Street, Wallingford, Oxon OX10 0BX, (☎ 0491 39780, fax 0491 39765, telex 847994)

HAWKER, Sir (Frank) Cyril; s of Frank Charley Hawker (d 1946); *b* 21 July 1900; *Educ* City of London Sch; *m* 1931, Marjorie Ann, da of Thomas Henry Pearce (d 1943); 3 da; *Career* joined Bank of England 1920, dep chief cashier 1944-48, chief accountant 1948-53, advsr to govr 1953-54, exec dir 1954-62; chm: Standard Bank Ltd 1962-74, Bank of W Africa 1965-74, Standard and Chartered Banking Gp Ltd 1970-74; dep chm Midland and Int Banks 1964-72, vice-pres Nat Playing Fields Assoc; High Sheriff Co of London 1963; chm Minor Counties Cricket Assoc; pres MCC 1970-71; kt 1958; *Recreations* cricket, soccer, fives (Eton), billiards, snooker, real tennis; *Clubs* MCC, Athenaeum; *Style*— Sir Cyril Hawker; Hadlow Lodge, Burgh Hill, Etchingham, E Sussex TN19 7PE (☎ 058 086 341)

HAWKER, Rt Rev Dennis Gascoyne; s of Robert Stephen Hawker, of Ashtead Surrey (d 1983), and Amelia Caroline, *née* Gascoyne (d 1984); *b* 8 Feb 1921; *Educ* Addey and Stanhope GS London, Queens' Coll Cambridge (MA), Cuddesdon Theological Coll Oxford; *m* Margaret Hamilton, da of Robert Henderson, of Brockley SE14 (d 1980); 1 s (Martin Robert b 1946), 1 da (Alison Margaret b 1954); *Career* Major Royal Marines 1940-46; curate SS Mary and Eanswythe Folkestone 1950-55, vicar St Mark S Norwood 1955-60, St Hughs missioner Diocese of Lincoln 1960-65, vicar SS Mary and James Gt Grimsby 1965-72, bishop of Grantham 1972-87; *Recreations* walking, gardening, naval and military history; *Clubs* Army and Navy; *Style—* The Rt Rev D G Hawker; Pickwick Cottage, Hall Close, Heacham, nr Kings Lynn, Norfolk PE31 7JT (☎ 0485 70450)

HAWKER, Geoffrey Fort; TD; *b* 20 Dec 1929; *Educ* London Univ (BSc); *m* ;2 da; *Career* chartered civil engr 1956; called to the Bar Grays Inn 1970, in practice as conslt and arbitrator; pres Soc of Construction Arbitrators 1986-89; Liveryman: Worshipful Co of Arbitrators, Worshipful Co of Engrs; CEng, FEng, FICE, FIEI, FIStructE, MSocIS (France), MConsE, FCIArb; *Books* A Guide to Commercial Arbitration under the 1979 Act (with R Gibson-Jarvis 1980), The ICE Arbitration Practice (with Uff and Timms 1986); *Style—* Geoffrey Hawker, Esq, TD; 3 Temple Gardens, Temple, London EC4Y 9AU (☎ 01 353 0832, fax 01 353 4929)

HAWKER, (Albert) Henry; CMG (1964), OBE (1960); s of Harry John Hawker (d 1948), of Cheltenham and Gladys Amy, *née* Webb (d 1973); *b* 31 Oct 1911; *Educ* Pate's Sch Cheltenham; *m* 1944, Margaret Janet Olivia, da of Theodore John Chichester Acton, ICS (d 1969), of Brackley, Northants; 2 s; *Career* served WWII, Bde Maj 12 Bde 1941-43, Staff Coll Camberley 1943-44, Lt-Col MA to CGS India 1944-46, RARO Lt-Col The Gordon Highlanders 1946-61; HMOS: joined 1946, served in Palestine 1946-48, N Rhodesia 1948-52, Zanzibar 1952-64 (devpt sec, admin sec, perm sec in Miny of Fin, Prime Minister's Office, Vice-Pres's Office, Pres's Office) ret 1964; dir: Thomson Regnl Newspapers Ltd 1965-69, The Times Ltd, The Sunday Times Ltd 1968-69, The Thomson Orgn 1969-76; Gold Cross Royal Order of George I of Greece 1948, Brilliant Star of Zanzibar 1957; *Recreations* gardening, sailing (cdre Zanzibar Sailing Club 1955 and 1961); *Clubs* Royal Cwlth Soc, Royal Yachting Assoc; *Style—* Henry Hawker, Esq, CMG, OBE; Bowling Green Farm, Cottered, nr Buntingford, Herts (☎ 076 381 234)

HAWKES, Michael John; s of Wilfred Arthur Hawkes (d 1968), and Anne Maria Hawkes (d 1966); *b* 7 May 1929; *Educ* Bedford Sch, New Coll Oxford (MA); *m* 1, 7 Dec 1957 (m dis 1973), Gillian Mary, *née* Watts; 2 s (James b 1964, Jason Michael b 1967), 2 da (Louise b 1963, Laura b 1966); m 2, 10 July 1973, Elizabeth Anne, *née* Gurton; *Career* banker; chm: Kleinwort Benson Gp (former chm Kleinwort Benson Ltd), Sharps Pixley Ltd; *Recreations* walking, gardening; *Style—* Michael Hawkes, Esq; Brookfield House, Burghfield Common, Berks (☎ 073 529 2912); Kleinwort Benson Ltd, PO Box 560, 20 Fenchurch St, London EC3P 3DB (☎ 01 623 8000, telex 888531)

HAWKES, (Henry) William; s of William Neville Hawkes, of Honington, Warwicks, and Marjorie Elsie, *née* Jackson; *b* 4 Dec 1939; *Educ* Uppingham, Cambridge Univ (MA, Dip Arch); *m* 22 Oct 1966, Hester Elizabeth, da of David Foster Gretton (d 1967); 3 da (Harriet b 1967, Polly b 1969, Olivia b 1972); *Career* architect, dir Stoneleigh Abbey Preservation Tst 1980-; chm Coventry Diocesan Advsy Ctee 1986-; tstee Coventry and Warwickshire Historic Churches Tst 1986-; Georgian Gp Exec Ctee 1985-; publications on 18th C Gothic Revival; *Recreations* hand printing, cycling, architectural history; *Style—* William Hawkes, Esq; 20 Broad Street, Stratford upon Avon, Warwickshire (☎ 0789 66415); Hawkes and Cave, 1 Old Town, Stratford upon Avon, Warwickshire (☎ 0789 298877)

HAWKESBURY, Viscount; Luke Marmaduke Peter Savile Foljambe; s and h of 5 Earl of Liverpool; *b* 25 Mar 1972; *Style—* Viscount Hawkesbury; The Grange Farm, Exton, Oakham, Rutland LE15 8BN

HAWKESWORTH, John Stanley; s of Lt-Gen Sir John Ledlie Inglis Hawkesworth, KBE, CB, DSO (d 1945), and Lady Helen Jane, *née* McNaughton (d 1962); *b* 7 Dec 1920; *Educ* Rugby, Queen's Coll Oxford (BA); *m* 10 April 1943, Hyacinthe Nairne Marteine, da of Maj Gen Philip Saxon George Gregson-Ellis, CB (d 1956); 1 s (Philip b 2 Oct 1978); *Career* WWII Capt Grenadier Gds served France, Belgium, Holland, Germany 1941-46; entered film indust 1946 as asst to Vincent Kords (London Films); art dir: The Third man (1949), Sound Barrier (1952), The Heart of the Matter (1953); writer/producer: Rowlandson's England (1956), Tiger Bay (1959); for tv: creator/ producer/writer: The Goldrobbers (LWT 1967), Upstairs Downstairs (LWT 1970-75), The Duchess of Duke St (BBC 1976-77), Danger UXB (Euston Films 1979), The Flame Trees of Thika (Euston Films 1981), QED (CBS 1982), The Tale of Beatrix Potter (BBC 1983), Oscar (BBC 1985), By The Sword Divided (1983-85); writer/ developer The Adventures and the Return of Sherlock Holmes (Granada 1984-88); developer Campion (BBC 1989), co- creator Chelworth (BBC 1989); chm Rutland branch Mental Health Fndn, pres Rutland and Leics branch Grenadier Guards Assoc; awards incl: BAFTA, Writers Guild GB, Emmy (US), Critics Circle (US), Peabody Award Univ of Georgia; *Books* Upstairs, Downstairs (1972), In My Lady's Chamber (1973); *Recreations* hunting, tennis, gardening; *Style—* J S Hawkesworth, Esq; Fishponds House, Knossington, Oakham, Rutland LE15 8LX (☎ 066 477 339); Flat 2, 24 Cottesmore Gardens, London W8; Consolidated Productions Ltd, 5 Jubilee Place, London SW3 3DT (☎ 01 376 5151, fax 01 225 2890)

HAWKESWORTH, Rex; s of Christopher Gilbert Hawkesworth (d 1963), and Queenie Victoria; *b* 8 Sept 1939; *Educ* Portsmouth Northern GS; *m* 25 Oct 1961, Pauline Mary; 2 da (Ruth b 1962, Lee b 1965); *Career* architect; freelance 1972-, specialist in private houses and estates in S Hampshire; articles on building, architecture and environment in nat and local magazines and newspapers; *Recreations* athletics coaching; *Clubs* Atlanta, Fareham Ladies Ath; *Style—* Rex Hawkesworth, Esq; 4 Rampart Gdns, Hilsea, Portsmouth, Hants (☎ 0705 662330)

HAWKESWORTH, (Thomas) Simon Ashwell; QC (1982); s of Charles Peter Elmhirst Hawkesworth, and Felicity *née* Ashwell; *b* 15 Nov 1943; *Educ* Rugby, Queen's Coll Oxford (MA); *m* 1970 (m dis 1989), Jennifer, da of Dr Thomas Lewis (d 1944); 2 s (Thomas b 1973, Edward b 1978); *Career* barr 1967, apptd rec of the Crown Ct 1982; *Style—* Simon Hawkesworth, Esq, QC; Tanner Beck House, Staverley, Knaresborough, N Yorks HG5 9LD (☎ 0423 340 604); 2 Harcourt Bldgs, Temple, London EC47 9DB

HAWKINGS, Christopher Robert; s of Reginald Hawkings (d 1983), and Molly Hawkings (d 1988); *b* 24 August 1937; *Educ* Berkhampsted Sch; *m* 25 April 1965, Sandra, da of James Kerr (d 1984); 2 s (Simon b 18 Dec 1965, Timothy b 25 Nov 1971), 1 da (Caroline b 18 Dec 1965); *Career* Phillips Auctioneers: joined 1957, md 1972, dep chm 1989; FIAScot; *Style—* Christopher Hawkings, Esq; Phillips Auctioneers, 7 Blenheim St, London W1Y 0AS (☎ 01 629 6602, fax 01 629 8876)

HAWKINGS, Sir (Francis) Geoffrey; s of Harry Wilfred Hawkings, of Lymington, Hants, and Louise Hawkings; *b* 13 August 1913; *Educ* Wellington, New Coll Oxford (MA); *m* 1940, Margaret Mary, da of Alexander Wilson, OBE, MD, DL; 1 s, 1 da; *Career* serv WWII Lancs Fusiliers (TA); joined Textile Machinery Makers Ltd 1950, dir 1959, md 1961; memb Courts of Govrs Manchester Univ 1964-79; pres Engineering Employers' Fedn 1978-80; dir Stone Platt Ind Ltd 1962 (md 1967, chm 1974-80); dir Chloride Gp Ltd 1975; dep chm 1976; chm 1977-79; dir Alliance Invst Tst Ltd 1976-81; kt 1978; *Style—* Sir Geoffrey Hawkings; Lovington House, Alresford, Hants SO24 0RD (☎ 096 278 371)

HAWKINGS, Patrick Stanley; s of late Stanley Albert Hawkings, and late Edith Laura Hawkings; *b* 5 May 1914; *Educ* Laxton Sch Oundle; *m* 4 June 1945, Sylvia Hilda, *née* Chamberlain; *Career* WWII (Maj) serv Middle E and BAOR 1939-46; ptnr: Wood Albery and Co 1948-74, Baker Rooke 1974-80; dir London and Associated Investment Tst plc 1974-; former dir Cordova Land Co, Land Australian Gen Exploration Co; Freeman City of London; FCA; *Style—* Patrick Hawkings, Esq; 3 Red Lodge Gardens, Graemesdyke Rd, Berkhamsted, Hertfordshire HP4 3LW (☎ 04427 75744)

HAWKINS, Prof Anthony Donald; s of Kenneth St David Hawkins, and Marjorie, *née* Jackson; *b* 25 Mar 1942; *Educ* Poole GS, Univ of Bristol (BSc, PhD); *m* 31 July 1966, Susan Mary; 1 s (David Andrew b 23 Feb 1973); *Career* dir of Fisheries Res Scotland 1987-, chief scientific offr Scottish Office 1987-, hon prof Univ of Aberdeen 1987; FRSE 1988; *Recreations* whippet racing; *Style—* Prof Anthony Hawkins; Kincraig, Blairs, nr Aberdeen (☎ 0224 868984); Marine Laboratory, PO Box 101, Victoria Road, Torry, Aberdeen (☎ 0224 876544, fax 0224 879156, telex 73587)

HAWKINS, Sir Arthur Ernest; s of Rev Harry Robert Hawkins (d 1942); *b* 10 June 1913; *Educ* The Blue Sch Wells, Gt Yarmouth GS, London Univ (BSc); *m* 1939, Laura Judith Tallent, da of Albert Draper (d 1956); 1 s, 2 da; *Career* memb CEGB 1970- (chm 1972-77), memb Nuclear Power Advsy Bd 1973-; kt 1976; *Recreations* fell walking, swimming; *Clubs* The Hurlingham; *Style—* Sir Arthur Hawkins; 61 Rowan Rd, Brook Green, London W6 7DT (☎ 01 603 2849)

HAWKINS, Blanche, Lady; (Marjorie) Blanche; da of A E Hampden-Smithers, of Springs, Transvaal; *m* 1920, Sir Villiers Geoffrey Caesar Hawkins, 6 Bt (d 1955); *Style—* Blanche, Lady Hawkins; 187 Lynnwood Rd, Brooklyn, Pretoria, Transvaal, S Africa

HAWKINS, Christopher James; MP (C) High Peak 1983-; *b* 26 Nov 1937; *Educ* Bristol GS, Bristol Univ; *Career* Courtaulds Ltd 1959-66; sr lecturer economics Southampton Univ 1966-1985; *Style—* Christopher Hawkins, Esq, MP; House of Commons, London SW1

HAWKINS, Dave; s of George Vincent, of London, and Irene Lavina, *née* Mallett; *b* 22 Dec 1948; *Educ* St Bonaventure's GS, York Univ (BA); *m* 4 June 1978, Chris da of Leslie George Rodgers, of London; 2 s (Elliott Alexander b 1981, Bradley Wade b 1987), 1 da (Cassie Louise b 1982); *Career* Benton & Bowles Advertising Agency 1970-73, Ogilvy & Mather 1973-83 (dir 1982-83), exec dir McCann Erickson 1983-85; fndr Beard Hawkins Direct 1985-; memb: MRS 1974, Mktg Soc 1984, IOD 1984; *Clubs* The Rugby; *Style—* Dave Hawkins, Esq; Beard & Hawkins Direct, Southbank House, Black Prince Rd, London SE1 7SJ (☎ 01 587 0166, fax 01 587 1589, car telephone 0836 344 066, telex 295555 LSPG)

HAWKINS, Air Vice-Marshal Desmond Ernest; CB (1971), CBE (1967), DFC and Bar (1942); s of Ernest Hawkins (d 1957); *b* 27 Dec 1919; *Educ* Bancroft Sch Essex; *m* 1947, Joan Audrey, da of James Munro (d 1936); 1 s, 1 step s; *Career* joined RAF 1938, served WW II, Gp Capt 1961, Air Cdre 1966, Air Vice-Marshal 1969, dir-gen Personal Services (RAF) MOD 1971-74, ret; md Services Kinema Corporation 1974-80; *Recreations* sailing (yacht 'Barada'); *Clubs* Royal Lymington Yacht, Cruising Assoc, RAF Sailing Assoc; *Style—* Air Vice-Marshal Desmond Hawkins, CB, CBE, DFC and Bar; c/o Barclays Bank, 21 High St, Lymington, Hants

HAWKINS, Prof Eric William; CBE (1973); s of James Edward Hawkins (d 1958), of West Kirby, Wirral, and *née* Clarie Hawkins (d 1973); *b* 8 Jan 1915; *Educ* Liverpool Inst, Trinity Hall Cambridge; *m* 12 Aug 1938, Ellen Marie Baunsgaard, da of Prof Peder Thygesen (d 1955), of Copenhagen; 1 s (John b 1947), 1 da (Anne b 1939); *Career* WWII 1940-46 offr 1 Bn Loyal Regt served: N Africa (wounded), Anzio beachhead (despatches), Adj 1944-45; headmaster: Oldershaw GS Wallasey 1949-53, Calday Grange GS West Kirby Cheshire 1953-65; prof language educn and dir language teaching centre Univ of York 1967-79 (reader in educn 1965-67, emeritus prof 1979-), hon prof Univ Coll of Wales Aberystwyth 1985; memb: Nat Advsy and Educn Ctee (Plowden Ctee) 1963-67, Nat Ctee for Cwlth Immigrants 1965-68, Ctee of Inquiry Educn of Children of Ethnic Minorities 1979-81; FIL 1973; Commandeur dans l'Ordre des Palmes Académiques France 1985; *Books* Modern Languages in the Curriculum (second edn 1987), Awareness of Language - An Introduction (second edn 1987); *Recreations* cello, walking; *Clubs* Royal Cwlth; *Style—* Prof Eric Hawkins, CBE

HAWKINS, Howard Caesar; s and h of Sir Humphry Villiers Caesar Hawkins, 7 Bt; *b* 17 Nov 1956; *Style—* Howard Hawkins, Esq

HAWKINS, Sir Humphry Villiers Caesar; 7 Bt (GB 1778); s of Sir Villiers Geoffrey Caesar Hawkins, 6 Bt (d 1955); *b* 10 August 1923; *Educ* Hilton Coll, Witwatersrand Univ (MB, ChB); *m* 1952, Anita, da of Charles H Funkey; 2 s, 3 da; *Heir* s, Howard Hawkins; *Career* European War 1942-45 with 6 S African Armoured Div; medical practitioner; *Clubs* Johannesburg County; *Style—* Sir Humphry Hawkins, Bt; 41 Hume Rd, Dunkeld, Johannesburg, S Africa

HAWKINS, Keith John; *b* 19 Nov 1947; *m* 23 April 1977, Linda Claire; 1 s (Richard b 1979), 1 da (Philippa b 1982); *Career* slr; ptnr Dutton Gregory & Williams; memb Law Soc 1974; *Style—* Keith Hawkins, Esq; 29 Hocombe Wood Rd, Chandlersford, Hants (☎ 0703 261026); Dutton Gregory and Williams, 96 Winchester Rd, Hants (☎ 0703 267222, TELEX 477921 DGWLAW G, fax 0703 251436)

HAWKINS, Louis; s of Edgar Ernest, of Harrow, Middlesex, and Winifred Elizabeth, *née* Stevens; *b* 19 August 1945; *Educ* Chandos Secdy Mod Stanmore, Willesden Tech Coll, The Poly of Central London (Dip Arch); *m* 20 Aug 1966, Patricia Anne, da of Douglas Herbert Jarvis (d 1976), of Godstone, Surrey; 1 s (Joseph b 1983), 1 da (Harriet b 1980); *Career* architect, chm Devon Branch of the Assoc of Conslts, vice-chm govrs Upottery C P Sch 1986-88; chm ACA Quality Assurance Working Pty 1988; ARIBA; *Recreations* photography, fell walking, music; *Style—* Louis Hawkins, Esq; Stoneburrow Cottage, Rawridge, Upottery, Honiton, Devon EX14 9PY (☎ 0404 86 533); The Louis Hawkins Practice, Chartered Architects, School House, Old School House Ct, High St, Honiton, Devon EX14 8PD (☎ 0404 45528/9)

HAWKINS, Michael Richard; OBE (1987); s of William Hawkins, MM (d 1987), of

Minehead, Somerset, and Winifred May, *née* Strawbridge (d 1985); *b* 27 Nov 1927; *Educ* Minehead GS; *m* 1, 20 May 1950 (m dis 1977), Doreen, *née* Went; 2 s (Malcolm b 1951, Lyndsay b 1953); m 2, 4 Feb 1978, Judith Carole, da of Leslie Fauxton Yelland, of Newquay; *Career* borough engr Torquay 1965-68, dir tech servs Torbay 1968-74, co engr and planning offr Devon 1974-; pres: Inst of Municipal Engrs 1982-83, Co Surveyors Soc 1987-88; chm: Nat Ctee reporting on cause and remedies of alkali silica reaction in concrete, Br Nat Ctee of PIARC, Civil Engrg Consultative Ctee Exeter Coll; hon memb Dartmoo4r Rescue Serv; Freeman City of London, Liveryman Worshipful Co of Paviors; FICE 1981, FIStructE 1962, MRTPI 1963, FIHT 1969, FRS 1986; *Books* Devon Roads (1988); *Recreations* walking, collecting antique maps; *Clubs* RAC; *Style*— Michael Hawkins, Esq, OBE; County Hall, Exeter, Devon (☎ 0392 272 149, fax 0392 272 135, car tel 0836 275 076, telex 42467)

HAWKINS, Sir Paul Lancelot; TD (1945); s of Lance G Hawkins (d 1947) and Mrs Hawkins (*née* Peile); *b* 7 August 1912; *Educ* Cheltenham; *m* 1, 1937, E Joan Snow (d 1984); 2 s, 1 da; m 2, 1985, Tina A Daniels; *Career* served Royal Norfolk Regt (TA) 1933-45 (POW Germany 1940-45); chartered surveyor 1933, having joined family firm 1930; co cncllr Norfolk 1949-70, alderman 1968-70, MP (C) SW Norfolk 1964-87, asst govt whip 1970-71, lord cmmr of Treasury (govt whip) 1971-73, vice-chamberlain of HM Household 1973-74; memb: select ctee House of Commons Services 1976-87, Delgn to WEU and Cncl Europe 1976-87; chm Agric Ctee Council of Europe 1985-87; kt 1982; *Recreations* gardening, travel; *Clubs* Carlton; *Style*— Sir Paul Hawkins, TD; Stables, Downham Market, Norfolk

HAWKINS, Peter John; s of Derek Gilbert, of Ariége, France, and Harriet Joanne, *née* Mercier; *b* 20 June 1944; *Educ* private tutors, Hawtreys, Eton, Oxford (MA); *Career* dir Christies 1973-87, md Christies Monaco (Monte Carlo) sale room 1987-; Freeman City of London, Liveryman Worshipful Co of Gunmakers; *Recreations* shooting, foxhunting, fishing, driving, collectors' cars, skiing, skindiving, ballooning (hot air), collecting antiques, travel, art; *Clubs* Turf, Carlton House Terrace; *Style*— Peter Hawkins, Esq; 20 Ennismore Gdns, London SW7 (☎ 01 839 9060); Caroline Cottages, Hull Farm, Chipping Norton, Oxon; 22 Avenue de la Costa, 98000 Monte-Carlo; 8 King St, St James's, London SW1 (☎ 01 839 9060); Christie's (Monaco) SAM, Park Palace, 98000 Monte-Carlo (☎ 93 251 933, fax 93 503 864, telex 489 287)

HAWKINS, Richard Graeme; QC (1984); s of Denis William Hawkins, of Frinton-on-Sea Essex, and Norah Mary Hawkins, *née* Beckingsale; *b* 23 Feb 1941; *Educ* Hendon County Sch, Univ Coll London (LLB); *m* 1969, Anne Elizabeth, da of Dr Glyn Charles Edwards, of Bournemouth Hants; 1 s (Benjamin b 1975), 1 da (Victoria b 1972); *Career* barr Gray's Inn, South Eastern Circuit; recorder of Crown Ct 1985; *Recreations* sailing; *Clubs* Royal Corinthian Yacht; *Style*— Richard Hawkins, Esq, QC; 3 Temple Gardens, London EC4 (☎ 01 353 3533)

HAWKINS, Capt Richard Henry; s of Maj H Hawkins, OBE (d 1930), of Everdon Hall, Daventry, Northants, and Dorothy Kathleen, *née* Hanmer (d 1957); *b* 1 Sept 1922; *Educ* Stowe, RMC Sandhurst; *m* 12 April 1944 (m dis 1964), Elizabeth Heather, da of Maj Robert Stafford, MC (d 1959), of Elvaston Place, SW7; 1 s (Anthony Richard b 1 Oct 1946), 1 da (Anne Elizabeth b 29 July 1949); *Career* 4 Bn Coldstreams Gds 1942-46; handicapper under jockey club rules of racing and nat hunt rules 1947-59, currently steward Warwick and Towcester; memb: Arrows CC, I Zingari; jt master Grafton Hounds 1953-54 and 1961-85; former memb: R H Hawkins XI, Bucks and Guards Club; *Recreations* hunting, cricket; *Clubs* Farmers, Forty, MCC; *Style*— Capt Richard Hawkins; Everdon Hall, Daventry, Northants NN11 6BG, (☎ 032 7367 207)

HAWKINS, Richard Ingpen Shayle; s of Vice Adm Sir Raymond Hawkins, KCB (d 1987), and Rosalind Constance Lucy, *née* Warren; *b* 20 June 1944; *Educ* Bedford Sch; *m* 26 July 1969, Amanda Louise, da of Rear Adm E F Gueritz, CB, OBE, DSC, *qv*, of Salisbury, Wilts; 2 s (William b 1973, George b 1976); *Career* cmmnd 2 Lt RM 1963, Lt 42 Commando Far East 1964-65, 43 Commando UK 1965-66, 45 Commando Aden and UK 1967-69, Capt 40 Commando Far East 1970-71, GSO3 HQ Commando Forces 1971-73, Adj RMR Tyne 1973-75, Army Staff Coll Camberley 1976, Co Cdr 45 Commando UK, Maj Instr Sch of Inf 1978-80, GSO2 Dept of Capt Gen RM MOD 1980-82, ret 1982; dir: Burgoyne Alford Ltd 1983-85, Richard Longstaff (insur) Ltd 1985-; pres Bedwyn and Dist Royal Br Legion; *Recreations* sailing, field sports; *Clubs* Royal Yacht Sqdn; *Style*— Richard Hawkins, Esq; The Old Forge, Upton, Andover, Hants SP11 OJS (☎ 026 476 269)

HAWKINS, Lady; Virginia Anne Noel; da of Gp Capt Noel Heath; *b* 31 Dec 1925; *Educ* Ascham Sch Sydney, Frensham Mittagong Australia; *m* 1947, Maj Sir Michael Hawkins, KCVO, MBE (d 1977; private sec to HRH The Duke of Gloucester), s of Lancelot Hawkins, of Bilney Hall, Norfolk; 1 da; *Recreations* gardening, reading; *Style*— Lady Hawkins; 37 Rumbold Rd, London SW6 (☎ 01 736 3701)

HAWKS, Lady Kara Virginia Louisa; *née* King-Tenison; da of 10 Earl of Kingston (d 1948); *b* 1938; *m* 1964 (m dis 1974), Anthony John Conroy Hawks, MB, BS, DCH; 1 da; *Style*— Lady Kara Hawks; White Gates, Old Romsey Rd, Cadnam, Southampton

HAWKSEY, Brian Foran; s of Joseph Osmund Hawksey (d 1979), of Manchester, and Mary Susan, *née* Foran (d 1981); *b* 22 August 1932; *Educ* St Bede's Coll Manchester, Douai Sch Woolhampton; *m* 19 June 1965, (Patricia) Anne, da of Patrick Maginnis, of Bognor Regis, W Sussex; *Career* materials mangr Smiths Indust Ltd 1973-77, dep dir of trg Purchasing Economics Ltd 1977-79, ptnr Brian Hawksey & Assoc 1979-80, purchasing devpt & trg mangr Thorn-EMI plc 1981-86; sr conslt Purchasing Materials Mgmnt Servs 1986-; FInstPS, MBIM; *Recreations* music, photography; *Style*— Brian Hawksey, Esq; Tall Trees, Egypt Lane, Farnham Common, Bucks SL2 3LD (☎ 02814 2698); Purchasing & Materials Management Services, PO Box 4, Lytham, Lytham St Annes Lancs FY8 2EL (☎ 02814 2698)

HAWKSLEY, (Phillip) Warren; *b* 10 Mar 1943; *Educ* Denstone Coll Uttoxeter; *m* 2 da; *Career* Lloyd's Bank clerk, memb Shropshire CC 1970-81, memb W Mercia Police Authority 1977-81, contested (C) Wolverhampton NE Feb and Oct 1974; MP (C) The Wrekin 1979-87; company dir; *Style*— Warren Hawksley, Esq; Whitehall, Church Street, Broseley, Shropshire

HAWLEY, Sir Donald Frederick; KCMG (1978, CMG 1970), MBE (1955); s of Frederick George Hawley (d 1973), of Little Gaddesden, Herts; *b* 22 May 1921; *Educ* Radley, New Coll Oxford (MA); *m* 1964, Ruth Morwenna Graham, da of Rev Peter Graham Howes (d 1964), of Charmouth, Dorset; 1 s, 3 da; *Career* served WW II Capt (RA); barr Inner Temple 1951; Sudan Govt and Sudan Judiciary 1944-55; Dip Serv 1956-81: ambass Muscat 1971-75, asst under-sec of state 1975-77, Br high cmmr Malaysia 1977-81; chm The Centre for Br Teachers 1987-; dir Ewbank & ptnrs 1981-, chm Ewbank Preece Ltd 1982-86, (special advsr 1986-); memb London Advsy ctee Hong Kong and Shanghai Banking Corpn 1981-; pres of Cncl Reading Univ; vice-pres Anglo-Omani Soc 1981-, chm Br Malaysian Soc 1983-; *Books* Handbook for Registrars of Marriage and Ministers of Religion (Sudan Govt, 1963), Courtesies in the Trucial States (1965), The Trucial States (1971), Oman and its Renaissance (1977), Courtesies in the Gulf Area (1978), Debrett's Manners and Correct Form in the Middle East (1984); *Recreations* tennis, golf, travel; *Clubs* Travellers', Beefsteak; *Style*— Sir Donald Hawley, KCMG, MBE; Little Cheverell House, nr Devizes, Wilts (☎ 0380 813 322)

HAWLEY, James Appleton; TD (1968); s of John James Hawley (d 1968), of Longdon Green, Staffs, and Ethel Mary Hawley JP; *b* 28 Mar 1937; *Educ* Uppingham, St Edmund Hall Oxford (MA); *m* 8 April 1961, Susan Anne Marie, da of Alan Edward Stott, JP, DL, of Henley-on-Thames; 1 s (Charles John b 1965), 2 da (Catherine Marie b 1963, Jane Rachel b 1968); *Career* 2 Lt S Staffs Regt 1955-57, Nat Serv Cyprus, TA 2 Lt to Maj Staffs Yeo 1957-69; barr Middle Temple 1961; chm and md: John James Hawley Ltd 1961-, J W Wilkinson & Co Ltd 1970-; dir: A D 2 Ltd 1986-, Stafford Railway Bldg Soc 1985-; bd memb TSB Bank plc West Midlands Bd 1985-; High Sheriff Staffs 1976-77, chm Walsall Soc for Blind 1979-; Freeman City of London 1987, Liveryman Worshipful Co of Saddlers 1988; *Recreations* fishing, shooting; *Clubs* Utd Oxford & Cambridge; *Style*— James Hawley, Esq, TD, JP, DL; John James Hawley (SW) Ltd, Lichfield Rd, Walsall, West Midlands WS4 2HX (☎ 0922 25641, fax 0922 720163, telex 335056 JJHWAL G)

HAWLEY, Peter Edward; s of Albert Edward Hawley (d 1962), of Leicester, and Winifred, *née* Skinner; *b* 20 July 1938; *Educ* Wyggeston Sch, Magdalene Coll Cambridge (MA, LLB); *m* 19 Sept 1964, (Mary) Tanya, da of John Ounsted, of Appletree Cottage, Woodgreen Common, Fordingbridge, Hants; 1 da (Sasha Louise b 26 Aug 1967); *Career* Nat Serv 1957-59 basic trg Lancs Fusiliers 1957, RAEC 1957, Sgt attached 9 Gurka Inf Johore Malaya 1957-59; admitted slr 1967; Walker Martineau: articled clerk 1964-67, asst slr 1967-69, ptnr 1970-, managing ptnr 1983-; hon tres Magdalene Coll Assoc 1975-87 (hon sec 1970-75), hon tres Whitchurch-on-Thames Swimming Assoc 1980-; Freeman City of London 1989, memb Worshipful Co of Slrs 1988; MIOD 1984; *Recreations* finding shade in hot climates; *Clubs* Gresham; *Style*— Peter Hawley, Esq; Whitchurch House, Whitchurch on Thames, Reading; 55/57 Gloucester Road, London SW7; Walker Martineau, 64 Queen Street, London EC4 (☎ 01 236 4232, fax 01 236 2525, tlx 28843)

HAWORTH, Christopher; s and h of Sir Philip Haworth, Bt, *qv*, Cheshire, and Joan Helen, *née* Clark; ggf (Sir Arthur Addlington Haworth) Liberal MP; *b* 6 Nov 1951; *Educ* Rugby Sch, Reading Univ (BSc); *Career* dir Dunlin Devpt Ltd 1987; chm Chelsea Harmonic Soc 1987; ARICS; *Recreations* shooting, fishing, skiing, squash, singing; *Clubs* Ski of GB, RAC, Lansdowne; *Style*— Christopher Haworth, Esq; 11 Mossbury Road, London SW11 2PA (☎ 01 350 2941); Coordinated Land and Estates, 19 Hertford St, London W1Y 1BB (☎ 01 493 3821)

HAWORTH, Hon Mrs (Hester Josephine Anne); *née* Freeman-Grenville; yr da of Lady Kinloss; *b* 9 May 1960; *m* 2 June 1984, Peter Haworth, s of Arnold FC Haworth, of Ganthorpe, York; 3 s (Joseph Anthony b 1985, David Arnold b 1987, Christopher b 1989); *Career* cordon bleu cook; *Style*— Hon Mrs Peter Haworth; The Laurels, Tholthorpe, Yorks YO6 2JN

HAWORTH, Lionel; OBE (1958); s of John Bertram Haworth (d 1953), of Trooilaps Pan, Via Upington, Cape, SA, and Anna Sophia, *née* Ackerman (d 1916); *b* 4 August 1912; *Educ* Rondebosch Boys HS Cape Town SA, Univ of Cape Town (BSc); *m* 1 Dec 1956, Joan Irene, da of Wilfred Bertram Bradbury, of Whitchurch, Shrops; 1 s (John Andrew), 1 da (Erica Jane); *Career* graduate apprentice Assoc Equipment Co 1934; Rolls Royce Ltd: designer 1936, asst chief designer 1944, dep chief designer 1951, chief designer (civil engines) 1954, chief engr (turboprops) 1962; Bristol Siddeley Engines Ltd: chief design conslt 1963, chief designer 1964, dir of design Aero Div Rolls Royce Ltd 1968-77; Br Gold Medal for Aeronautics 1971; RDI 1976; fndr and sr ptnr Lionel Haworth & Assocs 1977; FRS 1971, F Eng 1976, GI Mech E 1936, FIMechE 1954, FRAeS 1959; *Recreations* sailing, walking; *Clubs* Bristol Scientific, Trent Valley Sailing, Is Cruising (Salcombe); *Style*— Lionel Haworth, Esq, OBE; 10 Hazelwood Road, Sneyd Park, Bristol, BS9 1PX (☎ 0272 683032)

HAWORTH, Michael Goodier; CBE (1965), DSC and Bar; s of Frank Abraham Haworth (d 1931); *b* 25 Jan 1914; *Educ* RNC Dartmouth; *m* 1, 1943 (m dis 1973) Cynthia Noble; 2 da; m 2, 1976, Fenella Evelyn, *née* Forsyth-Grant, former w of Air Chief Marshal Sir Francis Fogarty (d 1970); *Career* Capt RN; serv WWII, cmd HMS Aisne 1951-52, ADNI Admiralty 1952-55 cmd HMS Diamond 1956-57, plans and policy SHAPE 1958-59, DOD Admiralty 1960-61, dep dir NATO Def Coll 1962-65; *Recreations* gardening, cricket; *Style*— Michael Haworth Esq, CBE, DSC and Bar; 4 Burford Lea, Elstead, Godalming, Surrey GU8 6HT (☎ 0252 702212)

HAWORTH, Sir Philip; 3 Bt (UK 1911), of Dunham Massey, Co Cheshire; s of Sir Geoffrey Haworth, 2 Bt (d 1987); *b* 17 Jan 1927; *Educ* Reading Univ (BSc); *m* 1951, Joan Helen, da of Stanley Percival Clark (decd), of Ipswich; 4 s, 1 da; *Heir* s Christopher b 1951, *qv*; *Career* Agriculture; *Recreations* music; *Clubs* Farmers; *Style*— Sir Philip Haworth, Bt; Free Green Farm, Over Peover, Knutsford, Cheshire

HAWORTH, (John) Vernon (Stewart); s of Lt Richard Haworth (d 1957), and Irene, *née* Holt (d 1961); *b* 24 Feb 1928; *Educ* Ackworth Sch, Leeds Univ (B Com); *m* 11 April 1953, Heather Margaret, da of Lt-Col James Barker (d 1971); 2 s (John b 1954, Richard b 1961), 1 da (Sarah b 1957); *Career* master printer; served RN 1946-48; chm of dirs Japa Paper Products Ltd (joined bd 1955); *Recreations* golf, sailing; *Style*— Vernon Haworth, Esq; 23 Park Lane, Leeds LS28 2EX (☎ 0532 663980); Laneside Mills, Churwell, Morley, Leeds LS27 7NP (☎ 0532 532661)

HAWORTH, Lady; Winifred; da of William Wright Senior (decd); *m* 1929, Sir William Crawford Haworth (sometime memb Aust Cwlth Parliament; d 1984), s of Edward Haworth (decd), and Jessie, *née* Crawford (decd); *Style*— Lady Haworth; 25 Grange Road, Toorak, Vic 3142, Australia (☎ 241 7055)

HAWS, Edward Thomas; s of Edward Haws (d 1983), and Phyllis Annie, *née* Thomas; *b* 19 Jan 1927; *Educ* Southend-on-Sea HS, St John's Coll Cambridge (MA); *m* 26 Aug 1950, Moira Jane, da of John Forbes (d 1957), of Pitlochry, Scotland; 2 s (Gordon b 1951, Tony b 1958), 1 da (Linda b 1954); *Career* Sir Alexander Gibb & Ptnrs 1947-63: res engr Meig Dana, res engr Atiamuri Power Project, engr i/t Tongariro River Power Devpt; John Malvern & Co Ltd 1963-78: dir Soil Mechanics Lyd, md Engrg &

Resources Conslts; Rendel Palmer & Tritton 1978-: dir (chm, md, dir of 4 assoc cos); chm Br Nat Ctee on Large Dams 1986-89, chm Br Hydromechanics Res Assoc 1978-81, chm Ctee on the Environment of Int Cmmn on Large Dams 1981-, author of numerous technical papers; FICE 1952-62, FIPENZ 1959; *Recreations* golf, walking, music; *Style*— Edward Haws, Esq; Rendel Palmer & Tritton, 61 Southwark St, London SE1 1SA (☎ 01 928 8999, fax 01 928 5566, telex 919 553 RENDEL G)

HAWSER, Anthony Greairey; s of His Honour Judge Lewis Hawser, QC, and Phyllis, *née* Greatrex, JP; *b* 23 May 1946; *Educ* Westminster Sch, Christ Church Coll Oxford (MA), The Coll of Law; *m* 1, 5 March 1970 (m dis 1981), Anna Maria, da of Dugan Chapman; m 2, 1 March 1984, Carol Ann, da of Philip Correll (d 1980), of Westchester NY; 1 da (Eloise Elizabeth b 1985), 1 step s (Matthew Alexander b 1976); *Career* barr Inner Temple 1970-71; md The Reject Shop plc 1973-; *Recreations* tennis, skiing, ballet; *Clubs* Turf, Queens, Sunningdale; *Style*— Anthony Hawser, Esq; 15 Townmead Road, London SW6 (☎ 01 736 7474, fax 01 731 5409, telex 914177)

HAWSER, His Honour Judge; (Cyril) Lewis Hawser; QC (1959); s of Abraham Hawser, MBE (d 1966), and Sarah, *née* Corne (d 1970); *b* 5 Oct 1916; *Educ* Cardiff HS, Balliol Oxford (MA), Williams Law Scholar; *m* 1940, Phyllis, da of Herbert Greatrex (d 1962); 1 s (Anthony b 1942), 1 da (Gillian b 1942); *Career* barr 1938, QC 1959; recorder Salisbury 1967-69; Portsmouth 1969-71; Crown Court recorder 1972-78; circuit judge 1978-, sr official referee 1985- (official referee 1978-85); memb cncl and vice-chm ctee justice; *Publications* (Report) Case of James Hanratty; *Recreations* tennis, chess, reading; *Style*— His Hon Judge Hawser, QC; 39 Eaton Sq, SW1 (☎ 01 235 6566)

HAWTHORNE, James Burns; CBE (1982); s of Thomas Hawthorne (d 1980), of Belfast, and Florence Mary Kathleen Hawthorne, *née* Burns (d 1977); *b* 27 Mar 1930; *Educ* Methodist Coll Belfast, Queen's Univ, Stranmillis Coll Belfast (BA); *m* 1958, Sarah Patricia, da of Thomas Allan King (d 1975); 1 s (Patrick), 2 da (Fiona, Deirdre); *Career* joined BBC 1960, Schools prodr i/c NI, chief asst BBC NI 1969-70, controller Television Hong Kong 1970-72, dir Broadcasting Hong Kong 1972-77; controller BBC NI 1978-87; media conslt James Hawthorne Assocs 1988-, memb Fair Employment Agency NI 1987-; NI Cncl for Educnl Devpt 1980-85; chm Health Promotion Agency 1988-, memb accreditation Panel Hong Kong Acad for Performing Arts 1988-, gave 1988 Listener lecture; hon LLD Queens Univ Belfast 1988, FRTS 1988; Winston Churchill Fellowship 1968; Royal Television Soc (Cyril Bennett) Award 1986; *Books* Two Centuries of Irish History (ed, 1967), Reporting Violence from Northern Ireland (1981); *Recreations* music, angling; *Clubs* BBC; *Style*— Dr James Hawthorne, CBE; 5 Tarawood, Cultra, Holywood, Co Down, N Ireland BT18 0HS (☎ 02317 5570, fax 02317 7749)

HAWTHORNE, Nigel Barnard; CBE (1987); s of Dr Charles Barnard Hawthorne (d 1969), of Coventry, and Agnes Rosemary Rice (d 1982); *b* 5 April 1929; *Educ* Christian Brothers' Coll, Cape Town and Univ of Cape Town; *Career* actor and writer; Privates on Parade (1976/77), Uncle Vanya Hampstead, The Magistrate National Theatre (1986), Hapgood (1988); TV: Yes (Prime) Minister, Barchester Chronicles, Mapp and Lucia; Hon (MA) Sheffield Univ 1987; *Recreations* writing, gardening; *Style*— Nigel Hawthorne, Esq, CBE; c/o Ken McReddie, 91 Regent St, London W1R 7TV

HAWTHORNE, Dr William McMullan; s of Thomas Hawthorne (d 1980), of Ireland, and Florence, *née* Burns (d 1977); *b* 27 Mar 1930; *Educ* Methodist Coll Belfast, Stranmillis Coll Belfast, Univ of London, Queen's Univ Belfast (BSc, PhD); *m* 18 Dec 1957, Isobel Irene, da of Hamilton Donaldson (d 1976); 2 s (Michael Laurence Forsythe b 7 Jan 1959, Julian Thomas Hedley b 5 Dec 1969); *Career* sr lectr Mathematics Stranmillis Coll Belfast 1963-75, conslt to African and Caribbean educn systems, sr res fell Mathematics educn Univ of Ibadan 1975-79, inventor HMX Ciphersystem; currently dir Gelosia Ltd Norwich; *Books* author num books on Mathematics incl: Mathematics for West Cameroon Schools (1966), Mathematics for Nigerian Schools (1980), Continuing Mathematics (1982); *Recreations* angling, boating; *Style*— Dr William Hawthorne; Kenmare, Bramerton Rd, Surlingham, Norwich NR14 7DE (☎ 05088 249); Gelosia Ltd, 17/19 St Georges St, Norwich NR3 1AB (☎ 0603 617506, fax 0603 664083)

HAWTHORNE, Prof Sir William Rede; CBE (1959); s of William Hawthorne, MInstCE and Elizabeth Hawthorne; *b* 22 May 1913,Newcastle-upon-Tyne,; *Educ* Westminster (Govr 1956-76), Trinity Coll Cambridge (MA, ScD), MIT USA (ScD); *m* 1939, Barbara Runkle, of Cambridge Mass; 1 s, 2 da; *Career* devpt engr Babcock and Wilcox 1937-39; scientific offr: Royal Aircraft Est 1940-44, seconded to Sir Frank Whittle Power Jets Ltd, developed combustion chambers for first jet engine 1940-41; Br Air Cmmn Washington USA 1944-45; dep dir Engine Research Miny of Supply London 1945-46, George Westinghouse prof of mech engrg MIT 1948-51 (assoc prof 1946-48, Jerome C Hunsaker prof of aeronautical engrg 1955-56, visiting Inst prof 1962-63), Hopkinson and ICI prof of applied thermodynamics Cambridge Univ 1951-80 (head Engrg Dept 1968-73, master Churchill Coll 1968-83); dir: Dracone Devpts 1958-, Cummins Engine Co Inc 1974-; chm: Home Office Scientific Advsy Cncl 1967-76, Def Scientific Advsy Cncl 1969-71, Advsy Cncl on Energy Conservation 1974-79; former memb: Electricity Supply Research Cncl, Energy Cmmn, Cmmn on Energy and Environment; tstee Winston Churchill Fndn of USA 1968-; has published numerous papers on fluid mechanics, aero-engines, flames and energy in scientific and technical journals; *Publications include* Aerodynamics of Compressors and Turbines (ed, Vol X), Design and Performance of Gas Turbine Power Plants (co-ed, Vol XI), High Speed Aerodynamics and Jet Propulsion; FRS (vice-pres 1969-70 and 1979-81), FEng, FIMechE, Hon FRAeS, Hon FAIAA, Hon DEng Sheffield Univ 1976; Hon DSc: Salford Univ 1980, Strathclyde Univ 1981, Bath Univ 1981, Oxford Univ 1982; Hon DEng Liverpool Univ 1982, Hon DSc Univ of Sussex 1984, Hon FRSE 1983, fell Imperial Coll of Science and Technology 1983; kt 1970; *Clubs* Athenaeum, Pentacle (Cambridge); *Style*— Prof Sir William Hawthorne, CBE; Churchill College, Cambridge CB3 0DS (☎ 0223 61 200); 19 Chauncy St, Cambridge, Massachusetts 02138, USA

HAWTHORNE LEWIS, Lady; Geraldine Susan Maud; da of Prof James Edward Geoffrey de Montmorency (d 1934), and Maud (d 1973), 3 da of Maj-Gen J de Havilland; *Educ* Blackheath HS, Cheltenham Ladies Coll, UCL; *m* 1957, as his 2 w, Sir William Hawthorne Lewis, KCSI, KCIE (d 1970), govr of Orissa 1941-46, s of William Crompton Lewis (d 1928) sometime dir of Public Instruction, UP India; *Career* librarian of Univ of London Inst of Education 1925-57; awarded UNESCO Travelling Fellowship 1952; FLA; *Recreations* travel, reading, gardening; *Clubs* English Speaking Union; *Style*— Lady Hawthorne Lewis; The Bridge House, Wilton, nr Salisbury, Wilts SP2 0BG (☎ 0722 742233)

HAWTON, Lady; Hilda; *née* Cawley; *m* 1935, Sir John Hawton, KCB, sometime Perm Sec Miny of Health (where he did much to build up the NHS) and sometime chm British Waterways Bd (d 1982); 1 da; *Style*— Lady Hawton; Melbury House, Melbury Terrace, NW1

HAWTREY, Stephen Charles; CB (1966); s of Edmond Hawtrey (d 1942); *b* 8 July 1907; *Educ* Eton, Trinity Cambridge (MA); *m* 1934, Leila (d 1982), da of Lt-Col Wilmot Blomefield (d 1926); 2 s, 1 da; *Career* clerk of the Journals House of Commons 1958-72; *Style*— Stephen Hawtrey, Esq; 52 New St, Henley-on-Thames, Oxon (☎ 0491 574521)

HAY; *see*: Dalrymple-Hay

HAY, Alexander Douglas; s of Lt-Col George Harold Hay, DSO (d 1967), of Duns Castle, Duns, Berwickshire, and Patricia Mary, *née* Hugonin; *b* 2 August 1948; *Educ* Rugby, Edinburgh Univ (BSc); *m* 20 Jan 1973, Aline Mary, da of Robert Rankine Macdougall; 1 s (Robert Alexander b 29 July 1976), 1 da (Caroline Laura b 9 July 1978); *Career* ptnr Greaves West & Ayre Chartered Accountants Berwick upon Tweed 1978- (joined 1975); chm: Scottish Episcopal Church Widows & Orphans Fund Corpn Ltd 1980, Berwickshire Dist Scout Cncl; vice chm Roxburgh & Berwickshire Cons & Unionist Assoc; MICAS 1975; *Recreations* golf; *Clubs* hon Co Edinburgh Golfers; *Style*— Alexander Hay, Esq; Duns Castle, Duns, Berwickwhire (☎ 0361 83211); 1/3 Sandgate, Berwick upon Tweed, TD15 1EW (☎ 0289 306688)

HAY, Lord Andrew Arthur George; s of 12 Marquis of Tweeddale, GC (d 1979); *b* 1959,(twin); *Educ* Fettes, RAC Cirencester; *m* 6 Sept 1986 Rosanna Meryl, *née* Booth; *Career* Chartered Surveyor for Knight Frank and Rutley; *Recreations* avoiding wheel clamps and over zealous traffic wardens; *Style*— Lord Andrew Hay; 21 Martindale Rd, London SW12

HAY, Andrew MacKenzie; CBE (1968); s of Ewen James MacKenzie Hay (d 1961), and Bertine Louise Vavasseur, *née* Buxton; *b* 9 April 1928; *Educ* Blundells, St John's Coll Cambridge (BA, MA); *m* 30 July 1977, Catherine, da of Cdr Horace Newman, US Navy (d 1975); *Career* Inteligence Corps and RAEC 1946-48, demob 1948; commodity exec London and Colombo Ceylon 1950-54, pres and chief exec offr Calvert Vavasseur Co Inc NYC 1962-78 (vice pres 1954-61), merchant banking exec NY 1979-81, int trade conslt Portland Oregon 1982- (also HM hon consul at Portland); pres: Br American C of C 1966-68, American Assoc if Exporters and Importers NYC 1977-79; bd memb and tstee Winston Churchill Fndn of US 1970-75, exec dir Pacific NW Int Trade Assoc 1986-; memb advsy ctee of tech innovation US Nat Acad of Sci; *Books* A Century of Coconuts (1972); *Recreations* photography, food and wine, books; *Clubs* Arlington, University; *Style*— Andrew Hay, Esq, CBE; 3515, SW Council Crest Drive, Portland, Oregon 97201; 5595 Norwester, Oceansill, Oregon 97134 (☎ 503 224 5163, 503 227 5669)

HAY, Anthony Michael; s of Norman Leslie Stephen Hay (d 1979), and Joan Agnes Eileen, *née* Watson; *b* 17 Sept 1986; *Educ* St Paul's Sch West Kensington; *m* 26 Nov 1969, Gayle Dales-Howarth; 1 s (Julian b 1970), 2 da (Francesca b 1969, Victoria b 1973); *Career* chm Norman Hay plc 1983-(dir Norman Hay Ltd 1963-83); *Recreations* cricket, tennis; *Style*— Anthony Hay, Esq; Mossat Farm, Gracious Pond, Chobham, Surrey; Norman Hay plc, Bath Rd, Harmondsworth, West Drayton, Middx UB7 0BU (☎ 01 759 1911, fax 01 897 3060, telex 933036)

HAY, Sir Arthur Thomas Erroll; 10 Bt (NS 1663), of Park, Wigtownshire; s of Sir Lewis John Erroll Hay, 9 Bt (d 1923); *b* 13 April 1909; *Educ* Fettes Coll Edinburgh, Liverpool Univ (Dip Arch) 1935; *m* 1, 1935 (m dis 1942), Hertha Hedwig Paula Louise, da of Ludwig Stölzle (decd), of Nagelberg, Austria, and widow of Walter Biheller; 1 s; m 2, 1943, Mrs Rosemary Anne Weymouth, da of Vice-Adm Aubrey Lambert (decd); *Heir* s, John Hay; *Career* WWII serv RE 1939-45, 2 Lt 1943, Lt 1944; retired civil servant; ARIBA, ISO; *Style*— Sir Arthur Hay, Bt; c/o Lloyds Bank, Castle St, Farnham, Surrey

HAY, Lady Atalanta Rose; da of 15 Earl of Kinnoull; *b* 25 Sept 1974; *Style*— Lady Atalanta Hay; 15 Carlyle Sq, London SW3

HAY, David John MacKenzie; s of Ian Gordon McHattie Hay, of Inverness, and Ishbel Jean Hay, *née* MacKenzie; *b* 30 June 1952; *Educ* Inverness Royal Acad, Univ of Edinburgh (MA), Magdalene Coll Cambridge (MA LLM); *Career* barr Inner Temple 1977, managing ed Atkin's Encyclopaedia of Ct Forms 1984-85, ed R & D 1985-86, managing ed Electronic forms publishing 1986-88; memb The Barley Players, ctee memb Cons Assoc; *Recreations* music, enjoying the countryside, reading, trains; *Clubs* Savage; *Style*— David Hay, Esq; The Cottage, School Lane, Barley, nr Royston, Herts SG8 8JZ (☎ 076384 8110); Butterworth Law Publishers Ltd, 88 Kingsway London WC2B 6AB (☎ 01 405 6900, fax 01 405 1332, telex 95678)

HAY, Sir David Osborne; CBE (1962), DSO (1945); s of late H A Hay, of Barwon Heads, Victoria; *b* 29 Nov 1916; *Educ* Geelong GS, Oxford Univ, Melbourne Univ; *m* 1944, Alison Marion Parker, da of late A P Adams, of Nagambie, Victoria; 2 s; *Career* high cmmr Canada 1961-63, Aust ambass to UN New York 1963-65, administrator Territory of Papua and New Guinea 1967-70, sec Dept External Territories 1970-73, Defence Force ombudsman 1973-76, sec Dept of Aboriginal Affairs 1977-80; kt 1979; *Style*— Sir David Hay, CBE, DSO; 10 Hotham Cres, Deakin, ACT 2600, Australia

HAY, Elizabeth Joyce (Jocelyn); *née* Board; da of William George Board (d 1951), and Olive Price Jones (d 1962); *b* 30 July 1927; *Educ* Open Univ (BA); *m* 26 Aug 1950, William Andrew Hunter Hay, TD, s of Sheriff J C E Hay, CBE, MC, TD, DL (d 1975); 2 da (Penelope Jill b 1960, Rosemary b 1961); *Career* freelance journalist and broadcaster 1954-83: Forces Broadcasting Serv Womans' Hour BBC Radio 2 and 4, head of press and PR dept Girl Guides Assoc, Cwlth HQ 1973-78, fndr London Media Workshops 1978-, fndr and chm Voice of the Listener 1983-; examiner CAM Dip in Non-Commercial PR; *Recreations* gardening, bee-keeping; *Style*— Mrs Jocelyn Hay; 101 Kings Dr, Gravesend, Kent, (☎ 0474 564676)

HAY, Lord Hamish David Montagu; s of 12 Marquess of Tweeddale, GC (d 1979); *b* 1959,(twin); *Educ* Fettes, Wadham Coll Oxford (BA Botany), Kings Coll Hosp Medical Sch (MB, BS London); *Career* Doctor; *Style*— Lord Hamish Hay; c/o Lord Andrew Hay, 21 Martindale Road, Balham London SW12

HAY, Ian Wood; s of John William Hay (d 1977), of Harwich, Essex, and Winifred May, *née* Fox (d 1975); *b* 25 Jan 1940; *Educ* Colchester Sch of Art (NDD), RCA; *m* 26 March 1968, Teresa Mary, da of Stanislav Antoni Sliski, of Harwich, Essex; 2 s (James b 1978, Rupert b 1982); *Career* visiting lectr: St Martins Sch of Art 1963-77,

Norwich Sch of Art 1971-75; sr lectr in drawing Sch of Art Colchester Inst 1988-, award RCA prize for landscape painting 1963; known for pastel paintings of London and The Thames; many one man and group shows in Essex and London in The Minories and Phoenix Art Gall, works in pte and public collections incl: Guildhall Art Gall, Sheffield Art Gall, Doncaster City Art Gall, Univ of Essex; memb Colchester Art Soc; ARCA (1963); *Recreations* travel; *Style—* Ian Hay, Esq; 32 Tall Trees, Mile End, Colchester, Essex CO4 5DU (☎ 0206 852 510)

HAY, Lady Iona Charlotte; da of 15 Earl of Kinnoull; *b* 15 Oct 1967; *Style—* Lady Iona Hay; 15 Carlyle Sq, London SW3

HAY, John Erroll Audley; s and h of Sir Arthur Hay, 10 Bt; *b* 3 Dec 1935; *Educ* Gordonstoun, St Andrew's Univ (MA); *Style—* John Hay, Esq; c/o National Westminster Bank, Fitzroy Sq, London W1

HAY, Lady Marioth Christina; resumed use of maiden name Hay 1971; da of Lt-Col Lord Edward Hay, DL, (3 s of 10 Marquess of Tweeddale, KT, DL) by his 1 w, Violet, da of Maj Cameron Barclay; sis of 12 Marquess of Tweeddale; raised to rank of a Marquess's da 1970; *b* 1 Sept 1918; *m* 1, 1940 (m dis 1954), Lt-Col George Trotter (2 s of Col Algernon Trotter, DSO, MVO, JP, DL, by Lady Edith Montgomerie, yr da of 15 Earl of Eglinton and Winton); 2 s (Richard b 1941, m Marian Campbell; Edward b 1943, m Jemima Mills), 1 da (Bridget Mary b 1944, m John Ellwood); m 2, 1954, as his 2 w, Sqdn Ldr Sir Gifford Fox, 2 and last Bt (d 1959); m 3, 1963 (m dis 1971), Sir John James, KCVO, CB; *Style—* Lady Marioth Hay; Forbes Lodge, Gifford, East Lothian (☎ 062 081 212)

HAY, Lady Melissa Ann; el da of 15th Earl of Kinnoull; *b* 25 Sept 1964; *Educ* Heathfield, Manchester Coll Oxford; *Recreations* scuba diving, tennis, squash; *Style—* Lady Melissa Hay; 15 Carlyle Sq, SW3

HAY, Lady Olga; *see*: Maitland, Lady Olga

HAY, Peter Laurence; s of Norman Leslie Stephen Hay (d 1979); *b* 7 Mar 1950; *Educ* St Paul's, Brunel Univ; *m* 19 July 1985, Perdita Sarah Amanda Lucie Rogers; *Career* dir: Norman Hay plc, Borough Plating Ltd, Montgomery Plating Co Ltd, Armourrote Surface Treatments Ltd, Techniplate Ltd, Plasticraft Ltd; *Recreations* flying helicopters; *Clubs* Lamborghini Club UK (chm); *Style—* Peter Hay, Esq; Windlesham Grange, Kennel Lane, Windlesham, Surrey GU20 6AA (☎ 0276 72 980); Norman Hay plc, Bath Rd, Harmondsworth, West Drayton, Middx UB7 0BU (☎ 01 759 1911, telex 933036 HAYNOR G, fax 01 897 3060)

HAY, Richard; s of Prof Denys Hay, of Edinburgh, and Sarah Gwyneth Hay, *née* Morley; *b* 4 May 1942; *Educ* George Watson's Coll Edinburgh, Balliol Coll Oxford; *m* 1969, Miriam Marguerite Alvin, da of Charles Arthur England (d 1975); 2 s (Jonathan b 1971, Timothy b 1973); *Career* dir gen Personnel and Admin Euro Cmmn Brussels 1986-; *Style—* Richard Hay, Esq; 200 Rue de la Loi, 1049 Brussels, Belgium (☎ 235 1111)

HAY, Maj-Gen Robert Arthur; CB (1970), MBE (1946); s of Eric Alexander Hay and Vera Eileen, *née* Whitehead; *b* 9 April 1920; *Educ* Brighton GS, Melbourne Victoria; *m* 1944, Endrée Patricia, da of Sir Patrick McGovern, CBE; 2 s, 1 da; *Career* Lt-Col 1945, Col 1955, Col GS HQ Eastern Cmd, military attaché Washington DC 1956, dir Admin Planning AHQ Canberra 1959, defence rep Singapore and Malaya 1962, Brig 1964, IDC London 1965, dir Military Ops and Plans 1966, Dep Chief of Gen Staff AHQ1967-69; Cdr: Aust Forces Vietnam 1969, First Aust Div 1970; Chief Military Planning Off SEATO 1971-73, Cmdt RMC Duntroon 1973-77, ret; pres Veterans Tennis Assoc of Aust 1981-, sec Aust Cncl of Professions 1978-86, exec offr Aust Cncl for Pubns acquired for Devpt 1982-87; *Recreations* tennis, golf; *Clubs* Melbourne Cricket, Cwlth and Royal Canberra Golf (Canberra), Tanglin (Singapore); *Style—* Maj-Gen Robert Hay, CB, MBE; 5 Borrowdale St, Red Hill, ACT 2603, Australia

HAY, Robin William Patrick Hamilton; s of William Reginald Hay (d 1975), of Nottingham, and (Mary Constance) Dora, *née* Bray; *b* 1 Nov 1939; *Educ* Eltham, Selwyn Coll Cambridge (MA, LLB); *m* 18 April 1969, Lady Olga Maitland, *qv*, er da of 17 Earl of Lauderdale; 2 s (Alastair b 18 Aug 1972, Fergus b 22 April 1981), 1 da (Camilla b 25 June 1975); *Career* barr Inner Temple 1964, rec of Crown Ct 1985; ILEA candidate (Cons) Islington S and Finsbury 1986; *Recreations* gastronomy, church tasting, choral singing; *Style—* Robin Hay, Esq; 21 Cloudesley St, London N1 (☎ 01 837 9212); Mill Farm, Wighton, Norfolk; Goldsmith Bldgs, Temple, London EC4Y 7BL (☎ 01 353 7881, fax 01 353 5319)

HAY, Sir Ronald Nelson; 11 Bt (s 1703), of Alderston; yr s of late Frederick Howard Hay (d 1934), and May Elizabeth, *née* Tomlinson; suc bro Sir Frederick Baden Powell Hay, 10 Bt 1985; *b* 9 July 1910; *m* 1940, Rita, da of John Munyard; 1 s, 1 da (Pamela Rosemary b 1945); *Heir* s, Ronald Frederick Hamilton Hay, b 1941; *Style—* Sir Ronald Hay, Bt

HAY-DRUMMOND, Lady Betty Mary Seton; *née* Montgomerie; da of late 16 Earl of Eglinton and Winton by 1 w, Lady Beatrice Dalrymple, da of 11 Earl of Stair; *b* 1912; *m* 1933, Capt George Vane Hay-Drummond, ggs of Lt-Col the Hon Charles Hay-Drummond (s of 11 Earl of Kinnoull); 1 s, 1 da; *Style—* Lady Betty Hay-Drummond; Vane House, 1 The Glebe, Dunning, Perthshire

HAYCRAFT, Anna Margaret; da of John Richard Alfred Lindholm (d 1960), and Gladys Irene Alexandra, *née* Griffith; *b* 9 Sept 1932; *Educ* Bangor County GS for Girls, Liverpool Art Coll; *m* 1956, Colin Berry Haycroft, *qv*, s of Maj William Church Stacpoole Haycraft, MC (d 1929); 5 s (William, Joshua d 1978, Thomas, Oliver, Arthur), 2 da (Rosalind d 1970, Sarah); *Career* writer; dir G Duckworth and Co Ltd 1975; *Books* The Sin Eater (Welsh Arts Cncl Award, 1977), The Birds of the Air (1980), The 27 Kingdon (Booker Prize nomination 1982), The Other Side of the Fire (1983), Unexplained Laughter (1985); The Clothes in The Wardrobe (1987), The Skeleton in the Cupboard (1988), weekly column Home Life in Spectator; *Style—* Anna Haycraft; 22 Gloucester Cres, London NW1 (☎ 01 485 7408)

HAYCRAFT, Colin Berry; s of Maj William Church Stacpoole Haycraft, MC and bar (ka 1929), and Olive Lillian Esmée Haycraft, *née* King (d 1976); *b* 12 Jan 1929; *Educ* Wellington Coll (open scholar and foundationer), The Queen's Coll Oxford (open classical scholar MA); *m* 1956, Anna Margaret, *qv*, (pseudo Alice Thomas Ellis, novelist), da of John Alfred Lindholm (d 1961); 5 s (William, Joshua d 1959, Thomas, Oliver, Arthur), 2 da (Rosalind d 1970, Sarah); *Career* on staff Daily Mirror Newspapers Ltd 1955-, editorial staff Observer 1959-; dir: Weidenfeld and Nicolson, Ltd Weidenfeld (Publishers) Ltd 1962-; jt md Gerald Duckworth and Co Ltd 1968, (chm and md 1971-); *Recreations* real tennis; *Clubs* Vincents, Jesters, Queen's, Beefsteak; *Style—* Colin Haycraft, Esq; 22 Gloucester Cres, London NW1 (☎ 01 485 7408); Gerald Duckworth and Co Ltd, The Old Piano Factory, 43 Gloucester Cres, London NW1 (☎ 01 485 3484)

HAYCRAFT, John Bernard; s of Bernard Gottfried Haycraft, of Bucks, and Diana Margery, *née* Brockwell; *b* 1 Sept 1942; *Educ* Eversley Sch Southwold, Marlborough Coll; *m* 1, 1 Oct 1966, Marie Luize, da of Bryan Hervey Talbot, of Runcorn, Ches; 3 s (Alexander Richard b 1969, Oliver Talbot b 1972, Simon Hervey b 1973); m 2, 7 May 1982, Paula Celeste, da of Franco C Vegnuti, of Rowington, Warks; 1 s (Thomas Julian b 1984), 1 da (Jessica Celeste b 1987); *Career* fine art auctioneer and valuer; regnl dir Phillips 1981-; *Recreations* gardening, hockey; *Clubs* Warwick Hockey; *Style—* John Haycraft, Esq; 7 Church Lane, Snitterfield, Stratford-upon-Avon, Warks (☎ 0789 731400); Phillips, The Old House, Station Rd, Knowle, Solihull, W Midlands B93 0HT

HAYCRAFT, John Stacpoole; CBE (1981); s of Maj William Stacpoole Haycraft, MC (d 1929), and Olive Lillian, *née* King (d 1978); *b* 11 Dec 1926; *Educ* Wellington, Jesus Coll Oxford (MA), Yale; *m* 17 Oct 1953, Brita Elisabeth, da of Gösta Langenfelt (d 1965), of Stockholm; 2 s (Richard b 1959, James b 1964), 1 da (Katinka b 1957); *Career* Guardsman Coldstream Gds 1945, 2 Lt Queen's Regt 1945, Lt 8 Pungabis 1946, Lt East Surrey Regt 1947; fndr: Academia Britannica 1953, Int Language Centre 1959, Int Teacher Trg Inst 1962, Int House 1964, English Teaching Theatre 1969, English Language Servs Int Ltd 1974; founded schs: Cordoba 1953, London 1959, Algiers 1963, Tripoli 1965, Rome 1967, Osaka 1968, Paris 1969; ARELS 1962; *Books* Babel in Spain (1958), Getting on in English (1964), Babel in London (1965), Choosing your English (1972), Introduction to English Language Teaching (1978), Italian Labyrinth (1985), In Search of the French Revolution (1989); *Recreations* tennis, swimming, chess, reading; *Clubs* Canning; *Style—* John Haycraft, Esq, CBE; 79 Lee Rd, London SE3 (☎ 01 852 5495); International Ho, 106 Piccadilly, London W1 (☎ 01 499 0177, fax 01 495 0284, telex 918162 INTHSE G)

HAYDAY, Sir Frederick; CBE (1963); s of late Arthur Hayday, sometime MP for W Notts; *b* 26 June 1912; *Career* national industrial offr National Union of General and Municipal Workers 1946-71; General Cncl TUC: memb 1950-72, chm 1962-63, vice-chm 1964-69; memb Police Complaints Bd 1977-; kt 1969; *Style—* Sir Frederick Hayday, CBE; 42 West Drive, Cheam, Surrey (☎ 01 642 8928)

HAYDAY, Terence John (Terry); s of John Alfred Hayday (d 1978), and Annie Dorothy, *née* Tebby; *b* 23 June 1947; *Educ* Hampton GS, Univ of Sussex (BA); *m* 9 June 1973, Susan Pamela, da of Gordon Grenville Dean; 2 s (Nicholas b 1977, Christopher b 1979). 1 da (Annabel b 1987); *Career* Lloyd's broker Leslie & Godwin Ltd 1965-67, Lloyd's underwriting asst R W Sturge & Co 1967-69, reinsur underwriter Slater Walker Insur Co Ltd 1972-76, dir Holmes Kingsley Carritt Ltd (now Holmes Hayday) Underwriting Agencies Ltd 1976-79 (dep Lloyd's underwriter), underwriter Lloyd's Syndicate 694 1980-; chm Holmes Hayday (Underwriting Agencies) Ltd 1988- (md 1980-88), non-exec dir Newman & Stuchbery Ltd 1988-; ctee memb Insur Inst of London, chm and memb various sub ctees at Lloyd's; FCII 1976; *Recreations* sailing, rugby, theatre, literature; *Clubs* Lloyd's YC, Twickenham YC, Haywards Heath RFC; *Style—* Terry Hayday, Esq; Suite 643, Lloyd's, 1 Lime St, London, EC3M 7DQ (☎ 01 623 8317, fax 01 623 8254)

HAYDEN, (William) Bill Joseph; CBE (1976); s of George Hayden (d 1977), of Brentwood, Essex, and Mary Ann Overhead; *b* 19 Jan 1929; *Educ* Romford Tech Coll; *m* 1954, Mavis, da of Redvers Ballard (d 1957), of Elm Park Essex; 2 s (Christopher, Andrew), 2 da (Elisabeth, Tracey); *Career* dir: Ford Netherlands 1970-81, Ford Britain 1972-; vice-pres mfrg Ford of Europe 1974-, corporate vice-pres Ford US 1974-; *Recreations* golf, gardening, soccer; *Clubs* Thorndon Park Golf; *Style—* Bill Hayden Esq, CBE; Warley, Brentwood, Essex (☎ 0277 252213, telex 995311 FORDCO G)

HAYDON, Prof Denis Arthur; s of Ernest George Haydon (d 1967), and Grace Violet, *née* Wildman (d 1980); *b* 21 Feb 1930; *Educ* Dartford GS, King's Coll London (BSc, PhD), Cambridge Univ (MA, ScD); *m* 1, 3 May 1958 (m dis 1986), (Anne) Primrose, da of late Hector William Wayman; 2 s (Keith Fawcitt b 18 Jan 1961, Daniel Thomas b 10 June 1965), 1 da (Rosalind Jane b 4 Sept 1967); m2, 6 Feb 1987, Dr Ann Juliet Bateman, da of P H Simon (d 1985); *Career* ICI res fellowship Imp Coll London 1956-58; Univ of Cambridge: asst dir of res dept of Colloid Sci 1959-70, asst dir of res dept of Physiology 1970-74, reader in surface and membrane biophysics 1974-80, prof of membrane biophysics 1980-; Trinity Hall Cambridge: fell 1965-, tutor for natural sciences 1973-74 (dir of studies 1965-78, asst tutor 1968-73), vice master 1978-82; writer of various res papers on surface chemistry and membrane biophysics in Proceeedings of Royal Soc, J Physiology, Trans Faraday Soc; awarded medal Royal Soc of Chemistry 1976; memb: Cambridge Philosophical Soc, Physiological Soc, Royal Soc of Chemistry; FRS 1975; *Books* An Introduction to the Principle of Surface Chemistry (with R Aveyard); *Recreations* sailing, music; *Style—* Prof Denis Haydon; Lower Farm, Wicken Bonhunt, Saffron, Walden, Essex CB11 3UG (☎ 0799 40989); Physilogical Laboratory, Univ of Cambridge, Downing St, Cambridge CB2 3EG (☎ 0223 333832)

HAYDON, Francis Edmund Walter; s of Surgn Capt Walter Turner Haydon (d 1954), of E Sheen, and Maria Christina, *née* De La Hoyde (d 1978); *b* 23 Dec 1928; *Educ* Downside Sch, Magdalen Coll Oxford (BA); *m* 1959, Isabel Dorothy, da of William Archibald Kitchin (d 1962), of Jersey; 2 s (Walter John b 1960, Peter William b 1962); 2 da (Margaret Ann b 1967, Philippa Jane b 1970); *Career* joined FCO 1955; second sec HM Embassy: Benghazi 1959-62, Beirut 1962-64; first sec: Br High Cmmn Blantyre 1969-72, Br Embassy Ankara 1978-81; cnsllr For and Cwlth Off 1982-87; ret; *Recreations* cricket, lawn tennis, enjoying ecclesiastical architecture, countryside; *Style—* Francis Haydon, Esq; Le Picachon, Trinity, Jersey, C1 (☎ 0534 61331)

HAYDON, Hon Mrs (Kathleen Mary); *née* Seely; da of 1 Baron Mottistone, CB, CMG, DSO, TD (d 1947); *b* 1907; *m* 1946, (Clement) Maxwell Winton Haydon; *Style—* The Hon Mrs Haydon; Paddock Hill, Lymington, Hants

HAYDON, Sir Robin - Walter Robert (Robin); KCMG (1980, CMG 1970); s of Walter Haydon (d 1946), and Evelyn Louise, *née* Thom; *b* 29 May 1920; *Educ* Dover GS; *m* 1941, Joan (d 1988), da of Col Reginald Tewson (d 1948); 1 s (decd), 1 da (decd); *Career* WWII served: France India Burma; head news dept FO 1967-71, high cmmr Malawi 1971-73), chief press sec 10 Downing Street 1973-74, high commissioner Malta 1974-76, ambass to Republic of Ireland 1976-80, ret; dir: Imperial Gp 1980-84; Imperial Tobacco 1984-88; govr: English-Speaking Union 1980-86 and 1987, Dover GS; memb: Tobacco Advsy Cncl 1988-, Reviewing Ctee on Export of Works of Art 1984-87; *Recreations* tennis, walking, swimming; *Clubs* Travellers';

Style— Sir Robin Haydon, KCMG; c/o Lloyds Bank, Cox's and King's Branch, 6 Pall Mall, London SW1

HAYEK, Maj Anthony George; DL (Staffs 1971); s of Gustav Hayek (d 1924); *b* 6 August 1920; *Educ* AKAD Gymnasium Vienna, Ecole Supérieure de Commerce Lausanne, Keele Univ; *m* 1972 (m dis 1985), Nicola Jane, da of Prof Walter Simon (decd); 3 s (Max b 1975, Thomas b 1976, Benjamin b 1978); *Career* Maj RAOC and Indian Army; company advsr; dir: Mangood Ltd 1973, Railweight Ltd 1979, Chronos Richardson Ltd 1983, Thermica Ltd 1988, Keele Univ Science Park 1984; former hon tres Univ of Keele, now tstee of its Devpt Tst; CEng, CBIM; *Recreations* shooting, beagling, travel; *Style*— Maj Anthony Hayek, DL; The Spinney, Butterton, Newcastle, Staffs ST5 4DT (☎ 0782 619001)

HAYES, Chief Constable Brian; QPM (1985), Order of St John (Brother) (1987); s of James Hayes (d 1984), and Jessie, *née* Spratt; *b* 25 Jan 1940; *Educ* Plaistow County GS, Sheffield Univ (BA); *m* 1960, Priscilla (*née* Bishop); 1 s (Steven b 1962), 3 da (Priscilla b 1962, Jacqueline b 1963, Emma b 1975); *Career* Metropolitan Police 1959-77; seconded Northern Ireland 1971-72; Police Advsr Mexico 1975/76, Colombia 1977; Br Police Rep EEC 1976-77; asst Chief Constable Surrey Constabulary 1977-81; dep Chief Constable Wiltshire Constabulary 1981-82; Nat Sec Police Athletic Assoc 1984-88 (chm 1989-); vice pres Union Sportive des Pahiers d'Europe (VSPE) 1986-; Police Long Service and Good Conduct Medal 1981; *Recreations* martial arts, sailing, running; *Style*— Chief Constable Brian Hayes, QPM; Surrey Constabulary, Mount Browne, Sandy Lane, Guildford, Surrey GU3 1HG (☎ Guildford 571212)

HAYES, Sir Brian David; GCB (1988, CB 1976, KCB 1980); s of Charles Wilfred Hayes (d 1958); *b* 5 May 1929; *Educ* Norwich Sch, Corpus Christi Coll Cambridge (MA, PhD); *m* 1958, Audrey, da of Edward Mortimer Jenkins (d 1973); 1 s (Edward b 1963), 1 da (Catherine b 1962); *Career* 2 Lt RASC Home Cmd 1948-49; civil servant; MAFF 1979-83, perm sec Dept of Indust 1983, jt perm sec DTI 1983-85 (perm sec 1985-); *Recreations* reading, watching cricket; *Style*— Sir Brian Hayes, GCB; Department of Trade and Industry, 1 Victoria St, London SW1 (☎ 01 215 4436)

HAYES, (Francis) Brian; s of Col Pierse Francis Hayes, OBE, RE, of The Apple House, 2 Davis Close, Marlow, and Sheila Mary, *née* O'Brien; *b* 22 April 1942; *Educ* Downside, Worcester Coll Oxford (BA); *m* 18 May 1968, Lesley Anne, da of Oliver Roy Holcroft (d 1984), of Endon Hall, Pershore, Worcs; 8 s (William b 1969, Alexander b 1970, Oliver b 1974, Toby b 1977, Benedict b 1979, Damian b 1981, Matthew b 1985, Theodore b 1987), 1 da (Rebecca b 1972); *Career* CA; memb of governing bd Coopers & Lybrand 1988- (joined 1964, ptnr 1971); tstee Cyclotron Tst 1984-; memb Historic Houses Assoc; memb ICAEW 1967; *Books* UK Taxation Implications International Trade (1985); *Recreations* shooting, riding; *Style*— Brian Hayes, Esq; Holt Castle, Holt Heath, Worcester WR6 6NJ (☎ 0905 621065); Coopers & Lybrand, Plumtree Court, London EC4 (☎ 01 583 5000, fax 01 822 8278)

HAYES, Sir Claude James; KCMG (1974, CMG 1969); s of James Benjamin Fidge Hayes (d 1951); *b* 23 Mar 1912; *Educ* Ardingly, St Edmund Hall Oxford (MA, MLitt), Sorbonne Univ Paris, New Coll Oxford; *m* 1940, Joan, da of Edward McCarthy Fitt (d 1974); 2 s (Peter, Robert), 1 da (Rosemary); *Career* Lt-Col BEF 1939 N Africa, Sicily, Italy, combined operations NW Europe; civil service cmmr 1949, HM Treasury 1957-64, princ fin offr Ministry of Overseas Devpt 1965-68, chm Crown Agents for Oversea Govts and Administrations 1968-74; vice-chm E D Sassoon Banking Co Ltd 1968-72; interim cmmr for W Indies 1968-85; *Recreations* garden maintenance and betterment, old oak furniture, Georgian domestic chattels, Wealden timber houses; *Style*— Sir Claude Hayes, KCMG; Prinkham, Chiddingstone Hoath, Kent (☎ 034 286 335)

HAYES, David Nelson; s of Peter Nelson Hayes, of 249 Norwich Rd, Fakenham, Norfolk, and Gwyneth Harper, *née* Jones; *b* 11 Feb 1943; *Educ* The Leys Sch Cambridge, Sidney Sussex Coll Cambridge Univ; *m* 1, 7 Feb 1970 (m dis 1981), Wendy Vanessa, da of William Herbert Nowell, of 24 The Warren, Old Catton, Norwich, Norfolk; 2 da (Melissa b 1973, Sarah b 1977); m 2, 11 Sept 1981, Susan Lee, da of Henry Robins Cook (d 1980); 3 step s (Timothy b 1971, Nicholas b 1973, Benjamin b 1977); *Career* slr 1967, legal memb Mental Health Review Tbnl 1986; pres: W Norfolk and King's Law Soc 1987-88, Fakenham Day Centre for Physically Handicapped 1981-; chm Fakenham and Dist Care Attendant Scheme 1983-; *Recreations* gardening and walking; *Style*— David Hayes, Esq; Green Farm House, Little Snoring, Fakenham, Norfolk NR21 OHU (☎ 0328 7772); Hayes and Storr, 18 Market Place, Fakenham, Norfolk NR21 9BH (☎ 0328 3231, fax 0328 55455)

HAYES, Francis Edward Sutherland; s of Raymond Stanley Hayes, JP (d 1956), of Bryngarw, Brynmenyn, Bridgend, and Gladys Vera, *née* Keating (d 1981); *b* 14 May 1930; *Educ* Wycliffe Coll Stonehouse Gloucester, Jesus Coll Cambridge; *m* 26 April 1958, (Nesta) Suzanne, da of Maj Sir William Reardon-Smith Bt, RA, of Rhode Farm, Romansleigh, South Molton, N Devon; 1 s (Patrick b 5 Nov 1961), 3 da (Thira b 5 April 1960, Elizabeth b 27 July 1964, Philippa b 21 Sept 1966); *Career* Nat Serv Sub Lt RNR 1950-52; chm Gresswell Valves Ltd 1977-, dir AB Electronic Products Gp plc 1982-, dep chm Wales regnl bd TSB Eng & Wales 1987- (dir 1984), dir Bruno Electrical Ltd 1983, chm The Br Valve Mfrs Assoc 1984; fell The Woodard Corpn 1973-, chm of govrs The Cathedral Sch Llandaff Cardiff 1985-; High Sheriff S Glamorgan 1977-78; gen cmmr Inland Revenue 1976-; Freeman: City of London 1966, Worshipful Co of Farriers 1966; *Recreations* music, sailing, shooting; *Clubs* Cardiff & County, Naval; *Style*— Francis Hayes, Esq; Llansannor House, Cowbridge, South Glamorgan CF6 7RW (☎ 044 63 5453); New Worcester Works, Elkington St, Birmingham B6 4SL (☎ 021 359 2052, fax 021 359 5938, telex 337114)

HAYES, Jeremy Joseph James (Jerry); MP (Cons) Harlow 1983-; s of Joseph B Hayes and Daye Julia Hayes, of Theydon Mount, Essex; *b* 20 April 1953; *Educ* Oratory Sch, London Univ (LLB); *m* 22 Sept 1979, Alison Gail, da of Frederick John Mansfield (d 1985), of Epping, Essex; 1 s (Lawrence Frederick b 1986), 1 da (Francesca Julia b 1984); *Career* barr at law, practising on S Eastern Circuit; memb select ctee on Social Services; jt sec Backbench Cons Health Ctee; hon dir State Leadership Fndn; Freeman of City of London, memb Worshipful Co of Fletchers and Worshipful Co of Watermen and Lightermen; *Clubs* Carlton; *Style*— Jerry Hayes, Esq, MP; House of Commons, London SW1A 0AA (☎ 01 219 6349)

HAYES, Vice Adm Sir John Osler Chattock; KCB (1967, CB 1964), OBE (1945); s of Maj Lionel Chattock Hayes, RAMC (d 1962); *b* 9 May 1913; *Educ* RNC Dartmouth; *m* 1939, Hon Rosalind Mary, *qv*, da of 2 and last Viscount Finlay; 2 s (Colin b 1943, Malcolm b 1951), 1 da (Griselda b 1954); *Career* entered RN 1927; served WWII, Atlantic, Far East (HMS Repulse), Arctic Convoys, Malta; Naval Sec to First Lord of Admiralty 1962-64, Flag Offr 2 i/c Western Fleet 1964-66, Flag Offr Scotland and N Ireland 1966-68; pres King George's Fund for Sailors (Scotland) 1968-79; memb Queen's Body Guard for Scotland 1969-; dep chm Gordonstoun Sch 1970-86; chm Cromarty Firth Port Authy 1974-77; HM Lord-Lt of Ross and Cromarty, Skye and Lochalsh 1977-88; *Recreations* walking, music, writing; *Style*— Vice Adm Sir John Hayes, KCB, OBE,; Wemyss House, Niss, Tain, Ross and Cromarty (☎ 086 285 212)

HAYES, John Philip; CB (1984); s of Harry Hayes (decd), and G E Hayes, *née* Hallsworth (decd); *b* 1924; *Educ* Cranleigh Sch, CCC Oxford; *m* 1956, Susan Elizabeth, da of Sir Percivale Liesching, GCMG, KCB, KCVO; 1 s, 1 da; *Career* WWII RAFVR 1943-46; political and economic planning 1950-53, OEEC 1953-58, Int Bank For Reconstruction and Devpt 1958-64, head economic devpt div OECD 1964-67, dir world economy div (economic planning staff) Miny of Overseas Devpt 1967-69; dep dir gen econ planning Miny of Overseas Devpt and Overseas Devpt Admin 1969-71; dir econ program dept (later economic analysis and projections dept) Int Bank for Reconstruction and Devpt 1971-73; dir trade and finance div Cwlth Secretariat 1973-75, asst undersec of state (econs) FCO 1975-84; sr fell Trade Policy Reseach Centre 1984-; *Books* Economic Effects of Sanctions on Southern Africa (1987); *Recreations* music, travel; *Style*— J P Hayes, Esq, CB; 51 Enfield Rd, Brentford, Middx TW8 9PA (☎ 01 568 7590)

HAYES, Dr John Trevor; CBE (1986); s of Leslie Thomas Hayes (d 1976), of London, and Gwendoline, *née* Griffiths (d 1976); *b* 21 Jan 1929; *Educ* Ardingly Coll Sussex, Keble Coll Oxford (MA), Courtauld Inst of Art London Univ (PhD), Inst of Fine arts NY; *Career* dir London Museum 1970-74 (asst keeper 1954-70), dir Nat Portrait Gallery 1974-; visiting prof in history of art Yale Univ 1969; Hon fell Keble Coll Oxford; FSA 1975; *Books* The Drawings of Thomas Gainsborough (1970), Gainsborough as Printmaker (1971), Rowlandson Watercolours and Drawings (1972), Gainsborough Paintings and Drawings (1975), The Art of Graham Sutherland (1980), The Landscape Paintings of Thomas Gainsborough (1982); *Recreations* music, walking, gardening, travel; *Clubs* Beefsteak, Garrick, Arts; *Style*— Dr John Hayes; National Portrait Gallery, 2 St Martin's Place, London WC2H OHE (☎ 01 930 1552, fax 01 930 9123)

HAYES, (Michael) Richard Lloyd; DL (Dyfed 1963); s of R S Hayes, JP (d 1957), of Brynmenyn, nr Bridgend, Glamorgan, and Gladys Vera Haynes, *née* Keating, (d 1981); *b* 26 Mar 1921; *Educ* Cheltenham Coll, RNCs Pangbourne, Dartmouth, Keyham and Manadon; *m* 1943, Cynthia Kathleen, da of Spencer Shelley (d 1942), of Huntley Court, Huntley, Glos; 3 da (Sylvia b 1942, Patsy b 1948, Wendy b 1950); *Career* Lt Cdr RN, HMS Jamaica, Arctic convoys; HMS Mauritius in European waters (despatches 1944); fndr chm Richard Hayes Investments Ltd 1965-84; High Sheriff Pembrokeshire 1963; DL Dyfed 1962; cmdt St John Ambulance Bde and Inspectorate Ctee for Wales 1980-; Liveryman Worshipful Co Shipwrights 1956; chm Prince of Wales Dry Dock Co 1965-69; dir Excelsior Ropes Ltd 1965-67; pres of the St John Cncl for Pembrokeshire 1985- (chm 1969-79); FIMechE, FRINA, FIMarE, CEng; KStJ (1982); *Recreations* shooting, fishing, sailing; *Clubs* Royal Yacht Squadron, Royal Thames Yacht, East India and Devonshire Sports and Public Schools; *Style*— Richard Hayes Esq, DL; Four Ashes, Cosheston, Pembroke Dock, Dyfed SA72 4TX (☎ 0646 682670); 4 Iverna Gdns, London W8 (☎ 01 937 3322)

HAYES, Hon Lady (Rosalind Mary); da of 2 and last Viscount Finlay (d 1945), and Beatrice Marion Hall (d 1942); *b* 27 Dec 1914; *m* 1939, Vice-Adm Sir John Osler Chattock Hayes, KCB, OBE, *qv*; 2 s (Colin b 1943, Malcolm b 1951), 1 da (Griselda b 1954); *Recreations* houses, walking, gardening, music; *Style*— The Hon Lady Hayes; Wemyss House, Nigg, by Tain, Ross and Cromarty (☎ 086 285 212)

HAYES, Hon Mrs (Sarah); da of 2 Baron Maclay, KBE (d 1969); *b* 1937; *m* 1968, David Richard Hayes, s of Eric Gerald Hayes (d 1958); *Style*— The Hon Mrs Hayes; Muir of Knock, Pityoulish, Aviemore, Inverness-shire

HAYES, Dr William; s of Robert Hayes (d 1986), and Eileen, *née* Tobin (d 1985); *b* 12 Nov 1930; *Educ* Univ Coll Dublin (BSc, PhD), Univ of Oxford (MA, DPhil); *m* 28 Aug 1962, Joan Mary, da of John Ferriss (d 1986); 2 s (Robert b 1973, Stephen b 1974), 1 da (Julia b 1970); *Career* 1851 overseas scholar 1955-57 and offical fell and tutor in physics St Johns Coll Oxford 1960-67, sr fell American Nat Sci Fndn Purdue Univ USA 1963-64, visiting prof Univ of Illinois USA 1971, princ bursar St Johns Coll Oxford 1977-87, dir and head Clarendon Laboratory Oxford 1985-87, pres St Johns Coll Oxford 1987-; hon DSc Nat Univ of Ireland 1988; *Books* Scattering of Light by Crystals (with R Loudon, 1978), Defects and Defect Processes in Non-Metallic Solids (with A M Stoneham, 1985); *Recreations* walking, reading, listening to music; *Clubs* Utd Oxford and Cambridge; *Style*— Dr William Hayes; President's Lodgings, St John's Coll, Oxford (☎ 0865 277 424); St John's Coll, Oxford (☎ 0865 277 419)

HAYGARTH, (Edward James) Anthony; s of Edward Haygarth (d 1961), and Sarah Agnes, *née* McGill (d 1949); *b* 28 Mar 1931; *Educ* Birkenhead Sch, Liverpool Univ (BCom); *m* 29 Oct 1957, Catherine Patricia, da of Henry William Carpenter (d 1953); 1 s (Edward b 1972); *Career* Nat Serv pilot offr RAF 1956-58; dir Combined English Stores Gr plc 1972-87; FCA; *Recreations* tennis; *Clubs* Cumberland LTC, Hampstead CC; *Style*— Anthony Haygarth, Esq

HAYGARTH-JACKSON, Angela Ray; OBE (1984); da of Harold Haygarth-Jackson, MC (d 1972), and Frieda, *née* Barraclough (d 1979); *b* 25 July 1929; *Educ* Cheltenham Ladies' Coll, Univ of Manchester (BSc, MSc); *Career* mangr Information Servs Section, ICI Pharmaceuticals 1956-86 (Information Science Consultant 1986-); pres Inst of Information Scientists 1983-84; chm Editorial Bd of Journal of Documentation 1984-; chm Royal Soc of Chemistry Secondary Services Mgmnt Ctee 1983-; memb: Royal Society Scientific Information Ctee 1978-, Br Library advsy cncl 1981-86; external examiner Univ of Sheffield, Dept of Information Studies 1983-87; memb UK delegation to advice the People's Republic of China on library and information matters 1984; author of many papers on information science and lectures in UK and overseas; FI Inf Sc; *Recreations* travel, bridge, gardening, DIY, photography, original tapestry; *Style*— Miss Angela Haygarth-Jackson, OBE; ICI Pharmaceuticals, Aldesley Park, Macclesfield, Cheshire SK10 4TG

HAYHOE, Rt Hon Sir Barney (Bernard) John; PC (1985), MP (C) Brentford and Isleworth 1983-; s of Frank and Catherine Hayhoe; *b* 8 August 1925; *Educ* Borough Poly; *m* 1962, Anne Gascoigne Thornton; 2 s, 1 da; *Career* MP (C): Heston and Isleworth 1970-74, Hounslow Brentford and Isleworth 1974-1983; CRD 1965-70, pps to Lord Pres and Ldr of the Commons 1972-74, additional oppn spokesman

Employment 1974-79; parly under-sec Def (Army) 1979-81; min of state: CSD 1981, Treasy 1981-85, min for Health 1985-86; kt 1987; *Style*— The Rt Hon Sir Barney Hayhoe, MP; 20 Wool Rd, London SW20 0HW (☎ 01 947 0037)

HAYHURST-FRANCE, Christopher; s of Capt George Frederick Hayhurst-France, DSO, MC (d 1940), and Joyce Lilian, *née* Le Fleming (d 1961); *b* 6 Feb 1927; *Educ* Durham Sch, Coll of Estate Mgmnt; *m* 6 Sept 1956, Suzanne, da of Howard Spackman Ferris (d 1973), of Swindon; 2 s (David b 1957, Jonathan b 1960), 2 da (Sarah b 1959, Rachel b 1965); *Career* RM 1945 (invalided out), Lt 3 Glos Bn HG 1952-56; chartered surveyor, auctioneer, valuer; ptnr Moore Allen & Innocent Lechlade 1954-87 (currently conslt); pres Centl Assoc Agric Valuers 1975-76, dir Stroud Building Soc 1970-, chm Stroud & Swindon Building Soc 1986-, sec Berners Estate Co Faringdon 1988-; vice-pres Oxfordshire Fedn Young Farmers Clubs, memb Faringdon Rotary Club; FRICS 1951, FAAV 1956; *Recreations* gardening; *Clubs* Farmers; *Style*— Christopher Hayhurst-France, Esq; 9 Orchard Hill, Faringdon, Oxon SN7 7EH (☎ 0367 20433); Moore Allen & Innocent, Lechlade, Glos GL7 3AJ (☎ 0367 52541)

HAYKLAN, Stephen Paul; s of Michael Bernard Hayklan, and Marjorie Elizabeth Hayklan, *née* Cochrane; *b* 19 April 1934; *Educ* Christ's Hospital; *m* 1959, Barbara Anne, da of Richard Kingston Bayes (d 1975); 1 s (Guyon), 1 da (Sofia); *Career* chm and chief exec Wiggins Gp plc 1981-, chm Abingdon Gp of Cos 1970; fell Incorp Soc of Valuer and Auctioneers; *Recreations* sailing, shooting; *Clubs* Naval and Military; *Style*— Stephen Hayklan, Esq; 18 Rutland Gate, London SW7 1BB (☎ 01 589 3082)

HAYLEY, Dr Thomas Theodore Steiger; s of Otto Johannes Steiger (d 1945), and Constance Mary Steiger, *née* Hayley (d 1971); *b* 4 Oct 1913; *Educ* Clifton, Univ of Cambridge (MA), Univ of Oxford (MA), Univ of London (PhD); *m* 7 Sept 1946, Audrey, da of Sir Keith Cantlie, CIE (d 1977); 3 s (Keith b 1952, Clive b 1957, Robin b 1962), 2 da (Ann b 1954, Emma b 1973); *Career* field work in social anthropology among Lango Tribe Uganda 1936 and in Brahmaputa Valley of Assam 1947-50; Indian Civil Serv: dep cmmr, sec to the Govt of Assam in the depts under the PM 1938-50; psychoanalyst; memb Br Psychoanalytical Soc 1956- (chm and vice-pres 1969-72); editor: Int Journal of Psycho-Analysis 1978-, Int Review of Psychoanalysis 1978-; *Publications*: The Anatomy of Lango Religion and Groups (monograph), Ritual Pollution and Social Structure in Hindu Assam (PhD Thesis); *Style*— Thomas T S Hayley, Esq; Old East Haxted, Edenbridge, Kent TN8 6PT (☎ 0732 862276); 5 Upper Wimpole St, London W1M 7TD (☎ 01 935 9305); 63 New Cavendish St, London W1M (☎ 01 580 5625)

HAYMAN, Louise Ann (Mrs Reade); da of His Hon Judge John Hayman, of Alton, Hants, and Jane, *née* Davison; *b* 13 Feb 1956; *Educ* St Paul's Girls Sch, Girton Coll Cambridge (BA); *m* 23 June 1984, Dr (Evelyn) Patrick Edgeworth Reade, s of Maj Arthur Reade (d 1971), of Jersey; 1 s (Orlando b 1988), 1 da (Zenobe b 1987); *Career* slr, asst mangr Hampstead Theatre 1979-80, slr Herbert Smith & Co 1980-83, legal advsr Thames TV plc 1983-88 (exec asst to md 1988-); memb Religious Soc of Friends (Quakers); memb: Law Soc, Copinger Soc of Copyright Lawyers; *Recreations* collecting, music, tennis, family and friends, surviving; *Style*— Ms Louise Hayman; Thames Television plc, 306 Euston Road, London NW1 3BB (☎ 01 387 9494, fax 0273 494860)

HAYMAN, Sir Peter Telford; KCMG (1971, CMG 1963), CVO (1965), MBE (1945); s of Charles Henry Telford Hayman (d 1950), of The Manor House, Brackley, Northants; *b* 14 June 1914; *Educ* Stowe, Worcester Coll Oxford; *m* 1942, Rosemary Eardley, da of Lt-Col Wilmot Blomefield, OBE, RE (d 1926, yst s of Sir Thomas Wilmot Peregrine Blomefield, 4 Bt); 1 s (Christopher b 1947), 1 da (Virginia b 1944); *Career* WWII Maj Rifle Bde 1942-45; entered Home Office 1937, Miny of Home Security 1939-41, asst sec MOD 1950, cnsllr UK Delegation to NATO, transferred FO 1954, cnsllr Belgrade 1955-58, info advsr to govr of Malta 1958-59, cnsllr Baghdad 1959-61, dir-gen Br Info Servs NY 1961-64, min and dep cmdt Br Mil Govt Berlin 1964-66, asst under-sec of State Foreign Office 1966-69, dep under-sec of State 1969-70, high cmmr Canada 1970-74, ret; *Recreations* fishing, travel; *Clubs* MCC; *Style*— Sir Peter Hayman, KCMG, CVO, MBE; Uxmore House, Checkendon, Oxon (☎ 0491 680 658)

HAYMAN, Prof Walter Kurt; s of Prof Franz Samuel Hayman (d 1947), of Oxford, and Ruth Matilde Therese, *née* Hensel (d 1979); *b* 6 Jan 1926; *Educ* Gordonstoun, St John's Coll Cambridge (BA, MA); *m* 20 Sept 1947, Margaret Riley, da of Thomas William Crann (d 1978), of 48 Hawthorn Terr, New Earswick, York; 3 da (Daphne Ruth b 1949, Anne Carolyn b 1951, Gillian Sheila b 1956); *Career* lectr Univ of Newcastle 1947, fell St John's Coll Cambridge 1947-50; Univ of Exeter (formerly Univ Coll Exeter): lectr in mathematics 1947-53, reader in mathematics 1953-56; Imp Coll London: first prof of pure mathematics 1956-85, dean of Royal Coll of Sci 1978-81; pt/t prof Univ of York 1985-; fndr with Mrs Hayman Br Mathematic Olympiad; memb: cncl of RS 1962-63, Finnish Acad of Arts and Scis 1978, Bavarian Acad 1982, Accademia Dei Lincei (Rome) 1985, London Mathematic Soc, Cambridge Philosophical Soc, Soc Protection of Sci and Learning (memb cncl); Hon DSc Exeter 1981 and Birmingham 1985; FRS 1956, FIC 1989; *Books* Mulitvalent Functions (1958), Merumorphic Functions (1964), Research Problems in Function Theory (1967), Subharmonic Functions (with PB Kennedy 1976); *Recreations* music, travel, television; *Style*— Prof W K Hayman; 24 Fulford Park, Fulford, York YO1 QE (☎ 0904 37713); 3 Lancaster Cottages, Goathland, Whitby, N Yorks YO22 5NQ (☎ 0947 86319); Dept of Maths, Univ of York, Heslington, York YO1 5DD (☎ 0904 433 076)

HAYMAN, Rev Canon William Samuel; s of William Henry Hayman (d 1918), of Leckford Hants, and Louise Charlotte Hayman, *née* Meyer (d 1950); *b* 3 June 1903; *Educ* Merchants Taylors' Sch London, St John's Coll Oxford (MA); *m* 1930, Rosemary Prideaux, da of Humphrey Gostwyck Metcalfe (d 1942), of Felixkirk, Yorks; 1 s (Andrew), 1 da (Angela); *Career* clerk in Holy Orders, rector of Cheam 1938-72, rural dean of Beddington 1955-60, archdeacon of Lewisham 1960-72, chaplain to HM The Queen 1961-73, canon emeritus of Southwark; *Recreations* fly-fishing, music, photography; *Style*— Canon William Samuel Hayman; 8 Black Jack Mews, Black Jack St, Cirencester, Glos GL7 2AA (☎ 0285 655024)

HAYMAN-JOYCE, James Leslie; s of Maj Thomas F Hayman-Joyce, RA (d 1946), and B C Hayman-Joyce; *b* 12 May 1945; *Educ* Radley, RAC; *m* 3 March 1973, Charlotte Alexandra Mary, da of J P Crump, DFC, of Cold Aston, Gloucs; 2 s (Thomas b 1981, Simon b 1983); *Career* qualified chartered surveyor, ptnr Blinkhorn & Co 1983, dir Sandoes Nationwide Anglia Estate Agents 1988-; FRICS 1970; *Style*— James Hayman-Joyce, Esq; Bakers Farmhouse, Barton-on-the-Heath, Moreton-in-Marsh, Gloucs GL56 0PN (☎ 0608 74 291); 22 High St, Moreton-in-Marsh, Gloucs (☎ 0608 50564)

HAYNES, Edwin William George; CB (1971); s of Frederick William George Haynes (d 1934), and Lilian May, *née* Armstrong (d 1950); *b* 10 Dec 1911; *Educ* London Univ (BA, LLM); *m* 1942, Dorothy Kathleen; 1 s (Andrew), 1 da (Kathleen); *Career* barr Lincoln's Inn; civil servant, under sec DTI; ret; *Recreations* books, gardens; *Clubs* Civil Service; *Style*— Edwin Haynes, Esq, CB; 92 Malmains Way, Beckenham, Kent (☎ 01 650 0224)

HAYNES, (David) Francis; MP (L) Ashfield 1979-; *b* 8 Mar 1926; *Career* NUM sponsored (and former branch official), memb: Nottinghamshire CC 1965-, Select Ctee on Parly Cmmn for Admin 1979-; *Style*— Frank Haynes Esq, MP; House of Commons, London SW1

HAYNES, John Harold; *b* 25 Mar 1938; *Educ* Sutton Valence Sch Kent; *m* Annette Constance; 3 s (John b 1967, Marc b 1968, Christopher b 1972); *Career* wrote and published first book 1956, ret from RAF as Fl-Lt 1967 to take up full-time publishing, having founded J H Haynes and Co 1960; chm and ch exec Haynes Publishing Gp plc; dir: J H Haynes and Co Ltd 1960-, Haynes Pubns Inc (USA) 1984, GT Foulis and Co Ltd 1977-, Haynes Devpts Ltd 1979-, J H Haynes (Overseas) Ltd 1979-, John H Haynes Devpts Inc (USA) 1979-, Oxford Illustrated Press Ltd 1981-, Gentry Books Ltd, Camway Autographics Ltd 1984-; *Recreations* cycling, walking, veteran and vintage cars, reading; *Clubs* Southern Milestone Motor (pres), Guild of Motoring Writers; *Style*— John Haynes Esq; Sparkford, Somerset BA22 7TT (☎ 0963 40635, telex 46212); 861 Lawrence Drive, Newbury Park, Ca 91320 USA (☎ 818 889 5400, telex 0236662406)

HAYNES, Lady; Kathleen Norris; da of William Greenhalgh, of Blandford, Dorset; *m* 1930, Sir George Ernest Haynes, CBE (d 1983, dir National Cncl of Social Service 1940-67); 2 da; *Style*— Lady Haynes; 103 Richmond Hill Court, Richmond, Surrey (☎ 01 940 6304)

HAYNES, Michael John; s of Ronald John Haynes, of Bucks, and Barbara marion, *née* Paine; *b* 15 Jan 1956; *Educ* Highgate Public Sch, Univ of Leicester (LLB), Cncl of Legal Educn; *m* 17 May 1980, Caroline Alma, da of William Edmonds, of North Kensington; *Career* called to the Bar Gray's Inn 1979, practice from D Medhurst Chambers London; *Recreations* wine, karate, photography; *Clubs* Int Food and Wine Soc; *Style*— Michael Haynes, Esq; Top Floor, 4 Brick Ct, Temple, London EC4 (☎ 01 353 1492, fax 01 583 8645)

HAYNES, Hon Mrs (Penelope Margaret); *née* Gilbey; da of 10 Baron Vaux of Harrowden; *b* 1942; *m* 1965, John Charles Haynes; 2 s, 2 da; *Style*— The Hon Mrs Haynes; Evelith Mill, Shifnal, Salop

HAYNES, The Very Rev Peter; s of Francis Harold Stanley Haynes (d 1978), of Bristol, and Winifred Annie, *née* Ravenhill (d 1970); *b* 24 April 1925; *Educ* St Brendans Coll Clifton, Selwyn Coll Cambridge (MA), Cuddesdon Coll Oxford; *m* 1952, Ruth, da of Dr Charles Edward Stainthorpe (d 1971), of Newcastle-upon-Tyne; 2 s (Richard b 1953, Michael b 1956); *Career* RAF coastal cmd 1943-47, Barclays Bank 1941-43, ordained Deacon York Minister 1952; asst curate: Stokesley 1952-54, Hessle 1954-58; vicar St John's Drypool Hull 1958-63; bishops chaplain for youth; asst dir of religious educn Dioc Bath and Wells 1963-70; vicar of Glastonbury 1970-74, archdeacon of Wells 1974-82, dean of Hereford 1982-; *Recreations* sailing, model engineering; *Style*— The Very Rev the Dean of Hereford; The Deanery, The Cloisters, Hereford HR1 2NG (☎ 0432 59880)

HAYNES, (Frank) Richard; s of Frank Sydney Haynes (d 1964), and Ethel Lulu, *née* Winfield (d 1963), gf William Haynes, master clockmaker, installed clock in St Paul's Cathedral and in many other churches and public bldgs; *b* 8 Dec 1936; *Educ* Cheltenham; *m* 7 Feb 1959, Patricia Saunders, da of Dr James Bryn Saunders Morgan (d 1987); 2 s (Michael b 1960, David b 1963), 1 da (Kathryn b 1967); *Career* jeweller; chm and md John D Eaton Ltd 1967- (dir 1960, md 1964); memb Royal Hort Soc Orchid Ctee 1985-, Br Orchid Cncl Judge 1986; *Recreations* orchid growing and breeding, golf, badminton; *Style*— Richard Haynes, Esq; Esseburne, 272 Broadway, Derby DE3 1BN (☎ 0332 557491); 4 Main Centre, Derby DE1 2PE (☎ 0332 44884)

HAYNES, Richard Stainthorpe; s of The Very Rev Peter Haynes (Dean of Hereford), of The Deanery, Hereford, and Ruth, *née* Stainthorpe; *b* 17 June 1953; *Educ* Wells Cathedral Sch, Ealing Business Sch (BA, Dip MRS); *m* 2 June 1979, Penelope Jane, da of Robert Oliver Prentice, MC, of Ipswich; 1 s (Robert Alexander b 1987), 1 da (Sophie Elizabeth b 1984); *Career* Shell UK Oil: mgmnt trainee 1971-73, sponsored business studies student 1973-77, advertising exec 1977-78; mktg devpt mangr/int mktg Fisons Ltd 1978-83, mktg conslt Gwyn-Thomas Assocs Ltd 1983-85, unit tst mktg mangr TSB tst Co Ltd 1985-88, mktg communications mangr TSB Gp plc 1985-88, investmt mktg dir Abbey Life Gp plc 1988-; MInstM; *Recreations* classical guitar, hill walking, choral music, organic gardening; *Style*— Richard Haynes, Esq; Abbey Life Gp plc, 80 Holdenhurst Rd, Bournemouth BH8 8AL (☎ 0202 292 373)

HAYNES, Roger John; s of Thomas William (d 1974), of Haslemere, Surrey, and Phyllis, *née* Turner; *b* 26 April 1937; *Educ* Trinity Sch Croydon; *m* 20 March 1964, (Marr) Caroline, da of late Maurice Nitsch, of Guildford; 2 s (John Charles, Will Benedict); *Career* sr ptnr Brewers CA's; dir County Sound plc, hon treas Surrey Cncl Order of St John; *Recreations* music, golf, reading, gardening, people; *Clubs* County (Guildford); *Style*— Roger Haynes, Esq; Onslow Bridge Chambers, Bridge St, Guildford, Surrey GU1 4RA (☎ 0483 302 200, fax 0483 301 232)

HAYNES-DIXON; *see*: Godden, Rumer

HAYR, Air Marshal Sir Kenneth William; KCB (1988, CB 1982), CBE (1976), AFC (1963 and bar 1972); s of Kenneth James Maxwell Hayr, of Auckland NZ, and Jeannie Templeton Hayr, *née* Crozier; *b* 13 April 1935; *Educ* Auckland GS, RAF Coll Cranwell; *m* 1961, Joyce (d 1987), da of T Gardner (d 1954); 3 s (Simon, James, Richard); *Career* RAF Offr, Fighter Pilot 1957-71, Offr cmdg RAF Binbrook 1974-76, Inspr of Flight Safety 1976-79, Asst Chief of Air Staff (Ops) 1981-82, Air Offr cmdg No 11 Gp 1982-85, Cdr Br Forces Cyprus and Admin of the Sovereign Base Areas 1985-88, Dep CinC Strike Cmd/Cos UKAIR 1988-; *Recreations* tennis, golf, windsurfing, skiing, parachuting; *Clubs* RAF; *Style*— Air Marshal Sir Kenneth Hayr, KCB, CBE, AFC; Headquarters Strike Command, Royal Air Force, High Wycombe, Bucks HP14 4UE (☎ 0494 461461 ext 2603/2604)

HAYTER, Alison, Baroness; (Margaret) Alison; da of J G Pickard, of Leicester; *m* 1949, as his 2 w, 2 Baron Hayter (d 1967); *Career* sculptress, exhibitor Royal Academy; *Style*— The Rt Hon Alison, Lady Hayter; 31 Iverna Gdns, Kensington, W8

(☎ 01 937 6860)

HAYTER, (John) David Henzell; s of Lt-Col Herbert Roche Hayter, DSO (d 1952), and Elsie Helen Evelyn Winterton, *née* Pidcock-Henzell (d 1978); *b* 2 Oct 1921; *Educ* Marlborough, Clare Coll Cambridge (MA); *m* 17 April 1948, Mary Vivien, da of late Richard Vyvyan Mansell, OBE; 3 da (Vivien Helen (Mrs Cassel), Rosemary Margaret (Mrs Walker), Susan Carolyn (Lady Muir-Mackenzie); *Career* Univ of Cambridge Air Sqdn, joined RAF, pilot Canada 1942-43, cmmnd Pilot Offr, instr Fleet Air Arm RAF Station Kingston Ontario Canada, returned UK 1945, instr RAF Little Rissington and RAF Turnhill, demobbed; Rootes Gp Motor Manufacturing 1946, purchased farm at Methuen Castle Perthshire 1953, sold Castle and Farm 1981, purchased Hollington Estate Highclere Newbury Berks 1982 (sold 1989); involved with political and church affrs, agric orgns; *Recreations* shooting, yachting; *Clubs* Royal Perth Golfing Soc, Royal Solent YC; *Style*— David Hayter, Esq; Kinghams, Highclere, Newbury, Berks RG15 9SB (☎ 0635 253 251)

HAYTER, Hon Mrs (Deborah Gervaise); *née* Maude; da of Baron Maude of Stratford-upon-Avon (Life Peer); *b* 1948; *Educ* Bristol Univ (BA); *m* 1973, Paul David Grenville Hayter (chief clerk House of Lords); 2 s (William b 1978, Giles b 1981), 1 da (Arabella b 1984); *Style*— The Hon Mrs Hayter; Williamscot, nr Banbury, Oxon

HAYTER, Dianne; JP (Inner London 1976); da of Flt Lt Alec Bristow Hayter (d 1972), and Nancy, *née* Evans (d 1959); *b* 7 Sept 1949; *Educ* Penrhos Coll, Aylesbury HS, Trevelyan Coll Univ of Durham (BA); *Career* res asst Gen & Municipal Workers Union 1970-72; res offr: Euro Trade Union Confedn Brussels 1973, Trade Union Advsy Ctee to OECD Paris 1973-74; gen sec Fabian Soc 1976-82 (asst gen sec 1974-76), journalist Channel 4's A Week in Politics 1982-83, dir Alcohol Concern 1983-; memb: Lon Lab Pty Exec 1976-82, Lab Pty Nat Constitutional Ctee 1987-, NCVO exec ctee, Fabian Soc exec ctee 1986-, Royal Cmmn on Criminal Procedure 1978-81; *Style*— Ms Dianne Hayter, JP; Alcohol Concern, 305 Grays Inn Rd, London, WC1X 8QF (☎ 01 833 3471)

HAYTER, 3 Baron (UK 1927); Sir George Charles Hayter Chubb; 3 Bt (UK 1909), KCVO (1977), CBE (1976); s of 2 Baron (d 1967), by his 1 w Mary; *b* 25 April 1911; *Educ* Leys Sch, Trinity Coll Cambridge; *m* 1940, Elizabeth Anne Hayter, MBE, da of Thomas Rumbold (ggs of Sir Thomas Rumbold, 1 Bt); 3 s, 1 da; *Heir* s, Hon George Chubb; *Career* chm Chubb and Son's Lock and Safe Co 1957-81 (md 1941-57); dir Charles Early and Marriott (Witney) Ltd 1952-83; pres Royal Warrant Holders Assoc 1967; dep chm House of Lords 1982-; govr King Edward's Hosp Fund for London 1983-86 (chm mgmnt ctee 1965-82); *Style*— The Rt Hon the Lord Hayter, KCVO, CBE; Ashtead House, Ashtead, Surrey (☎ 03722 73476)

HAYTER, Sir William Goodenough; KCMG (1953, CMG 1948); s of Sir William Goodenough Hayter, KBE (d 1924); *b* 1 August 1906; *Educ* Winchester, New Coll Oxford; *m* 1938, Iris Marie, da of Lt-Col C H Grey (formerly Hoare), DSO (d 1955); 1 da; *Career* entered FO 1930, asst under-sec of State 1948-49, min Paris 1949-53, ambass to USSR 1953-56, dep under-sec of State FO 1957-58; warden New Coll Oxford 1958-76, tstee Br Museum 1960-69; fell Winchester Coll 1958-76, hon fell New Coll Oxford 1976; *Books* The Diplomacy of the Great Powers (1961), The Kremlin and the Embassy (1966), Russia and the World (1970), William of Wykeham (1970), A Double Life (autobiography, 1974), Spooner (1977); *Style*— Sir William Hayter, KCMG; Bassetts House, Stanton St John, Oxford (☎ 086 735 598)

HAYTON, Philip John; s of Rev Austin Hayton, of Great Yarmouth, Norfolk, and Jennie Margaret Violet, *née* Errington; *b* 2 Nov 1947; *Educ* Fyling Hall Sch, Robin Hood's Bay Yorks; *m* 22 Dec 1972, Thelma Susan, da of James Gant; 1 s (James b 1980), 1 da (Julia Elizabeth b 1988); *Career* various jobs incl: teacher in Jordan, foundry worker, lavatory assembler, valet, doughnut salesman; pirate radio disc jockey and advtg salesman 1967-, reporter and prodr BBC Radio Leeds 1968-71; BBC TV 1971: reporter and presenter Look North Leeds 1971-74, nat news reporter (covering: Belfast, Beirut, Iranian Revolution, Uganda War, Cod War, Rhodesia War) 1974-80, S Africa corr (also covering Argentina during Folklands War) 1980-83, reporter and newscaster (One, Six and Nine O'Clock News); sidesman Fingest Village Church; *Recreations* sailing, theatre, walking, restaurants; *Style*— Philip Hayton, Esq; BBC TV, Television Centre, Wood Lane, London W12 7RJ (☎ 01 579 7771)

HAYTON, Thomas Sutton; s of John Thomas Hayton (d 1955), of Tollgarth, Scotforth Rd, Lancaster, and Ethel Annie, *née* Sutton (d 1965); *b* 15 Sept 1921; *Educ* Lancaster Royal GS; *m* 23 Sept 1965, Veronica Anne, da of Bernard Ignatius Hughes (d 1979), of Lancaster; 1 s (John Peter b 1973), 2 da (Anne Catherine b 1968, Elizabeth Marie b 1969); *Career* Lt RN Home Waters and Middle East 1941-46; slr; ptnr: J T Hayton and Sons Slrs 1948-70, Hayton and Hallam Slrs 1970-85; sr ptnr Hayton, Middleton and Wilson Slrs 1985-; Lancaster city cncllr 1949-80, mayor of Lancaster 1957-58, Lancashire co cncllr 1950-52 and 1967-76; *Recreations* walking, motoring, gardening; *Clubs* Lancaster Cons; *Style*— Thomas Hayton, Esq; St Kitts, 116 Newlands Rd, Lancaster (☎ 0524 66318); 31-35 Sun St, Lancaster (☎ 0524 62985)

HAYWARD, Sir Anthony William Byrd; s of Eric Hayward (d 1964), of Dane St House, Chilham, nr Canterbury, and Barbara Olive Hayward, *née* Bird (d 1976); *b* 29 June 1927; *Educ* Stowe, Christ Church Oxford; *m* 1955, Jenifer Susan, da of Dr Francis Howard McCay (d 1985), MD DTMH; 2 s, (Simon, Charles) 2 da (Charlotte, Emma); *Career* temp Sub-Lt RNVR 1945-48, served in Scotland, SE Asia, Persian Gulf; family business in India 1948-57, dir Shaw Wallace and Co India 1957-78 (chm and md 1970-78), md Guthrie Berhad Singapore 1978-81, pres and chief exec offr private investmt co for Asia (PICA) SA 1982-84, dir of various cos; kt 1978; *Recreations* shooting, fishing, golf, photography; *Clubs* Boodles, Oriental, Rye GC; *Style*— Sir Anthony Hayward; Dane St House, Chilham, near Canterbury, Kent (☎ 0227 730221)

HAYWARD, Barry Charles; s of Peter Alfred Edward Hayward, of 3 Glossop Close, E Cowes, Isle of Wight, and Muriel Hilda, *née* Gillard; *b* 30 July 1953; *Educ* Carisbrooke GS, London Univ (LLB); *m* 21 April 1979, Christine, da of Albert George Glenister, of Ashford, Middx; 1 s (Colin Charles b 1982), 1 da (Verity Jane b 1985); *Career* Messrs Owen White & Catlin Slrs Feltham: articles 1976-78, asst slr 1978-82, ptnr 1982-85; ptnr Hayward Ptnr Slrs 1985-; memb Law Soc 1976; *Recreations* swimming, gardening; *Style*— Barry Hayward, Esq; 28 Inglewood Avenue, Heatherside, Camberley, Surrey (☎ 0276 62 921); 265 Yorktown Rd, College Town, Camberley, Surrey (☎ 0276 32 543, fax 0276 33 194)

HAYWARD, Christopher Timothy Esmond; s of Tom Christopher Hayward, CBE, DL (d 1975), and Sybil Lisette, *née* Grainger-Brunt; *b* 13 Sept 1940; *Educ* Eton, Corpus Christi Coll Cambridge (MA); *m* 9 June 1964 (m dis 1976), Charmian Rosalind, da of Derek Leaf (d 1943); 1 s (Derek Christopher b 1967), 1 da (Chloe Amanda b 1969); *Career* qualified CA 1965, ptnr Peat Marwick Mitchell and Co 1977 (joined 1962), sen ptnr corporate recovery Peat Marwick McLintock 1987; ICAEW 1966, FCA; *Recreations* shooting, tennis; *Clubs* Bucks, MCC; *Style*— Timothy Hayward, Esq; 10 Bishop's Mansions, Bishop's Park Rd, Lonodn SW6 6DZ (☎ 01 736 5226); 1 Puddle Dock, Blackfriars, London EC4 3PD (☎ 01 236 8000, fax 01 248 1790, telex 8811541 PMM LON G)

HAYWARD, Lady; Elsie Darnell; da of Charles George; *m* 1972, as his 2 w, Sir Charles William Hayward, CBE (d 1983), sometime chm and jt md Firth Cleveland Ltd; 1 step s; *Style*— Lady Hayward; 16 Grosvenor Place, London SW1X 7HH

HAYWARD, Leslie Roy; s of George Ralph Hayward (d 1971), of Bengeo, Herts, and Maud Rose, *née* Thompson (d 1973); *b* 29 Jan 1928; *Educ* Tottenham Tech Coll; *m* 1, 4 Aug 1951 (m dis 1970), (Meriel) Ann, da of Maj George Cramp Bond (d 1970), of Hawthorns Bath Rd, Taplow, Bucks; m 2, 11 June 1977, Rosemary Anne, da of George Lawrence Hart (d 1963), of 57 Mandrake Rd, London SW17; *Career* fndr Ariel Plastics gp 1962 which grew into a notable orgn with depots in Glasgow, Wakefield, Birmingham, Hertford and Alton; chm of parent bd until ret 1984; *Recreations* motor racing, off-shore sailing, vintage car restoration, architecture, skiing; *Style*— Leslie Hayward, Esq; Lawrence House, Monkwood, Nr Alresford, Hants SO24 0HB (☎ 0962 772468, car telephone 0836 273 779)

HAYWARD, Mark Reece; s of Walter Hayward, of Redbourn, Herts, and Rosalie Gordon, *née* Richards; *b* 27 Nov 1959; *Educ* Ellesmere Coll Shropshire; *Career* Central Selling Orgn De Beers 1978-79, H M Diplomatic Serv 1979, apptd to Lord Carrington's private office 1981-82, theatre mgmnt 1982-, apptd theatre mangr for Phantom of the Opera March 1988; involved with Variety Club of Gt Britain; *Recreations* swimming, squash; *Style*— Mark Hayward, Esq; 92A Clarendon Rd, Holland Park, London, W11 (☎ 01 727 6010); Her Majesty's Theatre, Haymarket, London, SW1Y 4QL

HAYWARD, Lady Patricia Mary; *née* Stopford; eldest da of 7 Earl of Courtown (d 1957), and Cicely Mary, *née* Birch; *b* 1 Feb 1906; *m* 26 May 1934, Maurice John Hayward, Malayan Civil Service (ret), s of Sir Maurice Henry Weston Hayward, KCSI; 1 s, 3 da; *Style*— Lady Patricia Hayward; White Hart House, Haddenham, Aylesbury, Bucks (☎ 0844 291474)

HAYWARD, Peter Allan; s of Peter Hayward (d 1953), and Anne, *née* Jackson (d 1975); *b* 27 Mar 1932; *Educ* Haileybury, Trinity Coll Cambridge, (BA, MA) ; *m* 13 March 1954, Elizabeth Layton, da of John Layton Smith (d 1976); 1 da (Pandora b 1962); *Career* Lt Royal Artillery 1952; called to the Bar Lincoln's Inn 1958 (Cassell Scholar), practised at Patent Bar 1958-68, lectr UCL 1959-60, fell and tutor in jurisprudence St Peter's Coll, Oxford 1968- (ed of reports of patent cases 1970-74), memb Gen Bd of faculties Oxford Univ 1980-85; memb Holborn Borough Cncl 1962-66; *Books* Annual Survey of Commonwealth Law (contrib on succession and monopolies) 1970-73, Hayward's Patent Cases 1600-1883 (11 vols, (1988); *Style*— Peter Hayward, Esq; St Peter's College, Oxford, OX1 2DL (☎ 0865 278885)

HAYWARD, Sir Richard Arthur; CBE (1966); s of late Richard Bolton Hayward, and Jessie Emmeline Elisabeth; *b* 14 Mar 1910; *Educ* Catford Central Sch; *m* 1936, Ethel Wheatcroft; 1 s, 1 da; *Career* dep gen sec Union of Post Office Workers 1951 (asst sec 1947), sec gen Civil Service National Whitley Cncl 1956-66; chm: Supplementary Benefits Cmmn 1966-69, NHS Staff Cmmn 1972-75, New Towns Staff Cmmn 1976-77; memb: Post Office Bd 1969-71, Civil Service Security Appeals Panel 1967-82, Home Office Advsy Panel on Security (Immigration Act 1972) 1972-81, Parole Bd for England and Wales 1975-79, Solicitors Disciplinary Tbnl 1975-82; freedom City of London 1980; chm Civil Service Sports Cncl 1968-1973, vice life pres 1973-; pres Civil Service: Cricket Assoc, Civil Sevice FA; vice life pres of Nat Assoc of Young Cricketers, pres of Assoc of Kent Cricket Clubs 1970-84; life vice-pres 1984; kt (1969); *Recreations* sport, history of Southwark; *Style*— Sir Richard Hayward, CBE; 10 Birchwood Ave, Southborough, Tunbridge Wells, Kent (☎ (0892) 29134)

HAYWARD, Richard Wellesley; s of Harold Joseph Hayward, MC, and Olive Mary, *née* Stanley (d 1988); *b* 4 August 1928; *Educ* Colston's Sch Bristol, Brixton Sch of Bldg (now S Bank Poly); *m* 14 June 1952, Jill Patricia, da of Wing Cdr Arthur Leslie Grice (ka), of Hatch End, Middlesex; 1 da (Jenny (Mrs Spivey) b 29 July 1958); *Career* sr ptnr Burrell Hayward and Budd 1974-80; memb gen cncl RICS 1971-79, chm RICS (Central London Branch) 1979-80, dir and sec School Mistresses and Governesses Benevolent Inst 1980-; memb The Clapham Soc; Freeman City of London 1977; memb Worshipful Co of Tallow Chandlers 1978, Worshipful Co of Chartered Surveyors 1977-87; ARICS 1954, FRICS 1965; *Recreations* reading, walking the dog, Georgian and Victorian glass; *Style*— Richard Hayward, Esq; Flat 3, 23 West Side, Clapham Common, London SW4 9AN (☎ 01 228 5232); SGBI Office, Queen Mary House, Manor Park Rd, Chislehurst, Kent BR7 5PY (☎ 01 468 7997)

HAYWARD, Robert Antony; MP (C) Kingswood 1987; s of Ralph Hayward, of Swinford Farm, Eynsham, Oxon, and Mary Patricia, *née* Franklin; *b* 11 Mar 1949; *Educ* Maidenhead GS, Rhodesia Univ (BSc); *m* 1981, Gillian Mary, da of Raymond Icke (d 1985); *Career* vice-chm Nat Young Cons 1976-77, City cllr Coventry 1976-78; memb Select Ctee on Energy 1983-85; MP (C) Kingswood 1983-87, pps Parly Under Sec of State Trade and Ind 1985-87, miny for Indust 1986-87, and to Sec of State for Transport 1987-; *Recreations* rugby referee; *Style*— Robert Hayward, Esq, MP; House of Commons, London SW1; 2 Bracey Drive, Downend, Bristol B516 2UG

HAYWARD, Maj-Gen (George) Victor; s of George Harold Hayward (d 1971), of Stratford-on-Avon, and Daisy, *née* Ball (d 1975); *b* 21 June 1918; *Educ* Blundell's, Birmingham Univ (BSc); *m* 18 July 1953, Gay Benson, da of Hamilton Barrett Goulding, MB, BCh (d 1947), of Dublin; 1 s (Stephen George Hamilton b 1954), 1 da (Victoria Clare b 1956); *Career* sr planning inspr DOE; served WWII 1939-45, cmmnd 1940, transf to REME 1942, GSO1 REME Training Centre 1958, cdr REME 2nd Div 1960, asst mil sec WO 1962, Col RARDE, Fort Halstead 1963, CO 38 Central Workshop 1965, Dep Cmdt Technical Gp REME 1966, Cmdt REME Trg Centre 1969, Cmdt Technical Gp REME 1971-73, ret; Col Cmdt REME 1973-78; CEng, FICE, FIMechE, FBIM; *Recreations* sailing, skiing, shooting; *Clubs* Army and Navy; *Style*— Maj Gen Victor Hayward; Chart Cottage, Chartwell, Westerham, Kent TN16 1PT (☎ 0732 866253)

HAYWARD SMITH, Rodger; QC (1988); s of Frederick Ernest Smith, of Ingatetone Essex, and Heather Hayward, *née* Rodgers; *b* 25 Feb 1943; *Educ* Brentwood Sch

Essex, St Edmund Hall Oxford (MA); *m* 4 Jan 1975, (Gillian) Sheila, *née* Johnson; 1 s (Richard b 1976, 1 da (Jane b 1978); *Career* barr Gray's Inn 1967, rec of Crown Ct 1986 (asst rec 1981-86); memb Legal Aid Ctee of Law Soc 1983-; *Recreations* rambling, music, theatre; *Style—* Rodger Hayward Smith, Esq, QC; 1 King's Bench Walk, Temple, London, EC4Y 7DB (☎ 01 583 6266)

HAYWOOD, Bryan; s of Arthur Haywood; *b* 1 May 1939; *Educ* King Edward VII Sch Leics; *m* (m dis); 1 s (Timothy); *Career* certified accountant, dir: Balfour Kilpatrick Ltd 1975-, Balfour Kilpatrick Int Ltd UK, Kilpatrick Gp of Cos; FBIM; *Recreations* country life; *Clubs* St James's, Institute of Directors; *Style—* Bryan Haywood, Esq; 35 Kent Road, East Molesey, Surrey (☎ 01 979 9714); Balfour Kilpatrick Ltd, PO Box 47, Kelvin House, London Rd, Wallington, Surrey SM6 7EH (☎ 01 669 4477, telex 25144)

HAYWOOD, Christopher Warren; s of Oliver Pilling Haywood, JP, FCA (d 1973), of Bolton, and Audrey Lillian Openshaw, *née* Warren; *b* 17 Nov 1945; *Educ* St Bees Cumbria; *m* 27 March 1981, Julie Anne, da of Peter Orrell Kirkpatrick, of 139 Turton Road, Tottington, Bury; 4 s (Charles Alexander b 1973, Edward Christopher b 1982, Michael Henry b 1983, Oliver Peter b 1985), 1 da (Katie Victoria b 1971); *Career* accountant to the Duke of Norfolk, pres Bolton Soc of Chartered Accountants 1974; chm Bolton Club 1985-87; tres Bolton Lads Club 1973-; dir: Ladybridge Developments Ltd 1983-, Victor New Homes Ltd 1979-, City Gate Registrars Ltd 1987, Forshaw Watson Holdings Ltd 1986-; memb cncl Bolton Chamber of Commerce and Industry 1984-(dep pres 1988) ; ptnr Kevan Pilling and Co Chartered Accountants; FCA, FBIM, ATII; *Recreations* golf, skiing, family pursuits; *Clubs* Bolton Golf, The Bolton, Markland Hill LTC, Windermere Motorboat Racing; *Style—* Christopher Haywood, Esq; Elsinore, 32 Albert Rd, Heaton, Bolton BL1 5HF (☎ 0204 42958); Acresfield House, Exchange St, Bolton (☎ 0204 22611, fax 0204 35210)

HAYWOOD, Janette; da of Ronald Haywood, of Borehamwood, Herts, and Evelyn, *née* Jefferson; *b* 22 May 1952; *Educ* Copthall Mill Hill, Univ Coll Cardiff (LLB), UCL (LLM), Coll of Law; *m* 2 July 1988, Jonathan Michael, s of John Anderson, JP, and Rosamund, *née* Baines Lake, Chideock, Dorset; *Career* called to the Bar Middle Temple 1977; memb Family Law Bar Assoc; *Recreations* travel, interior design, theatre; *Style—* Miss Janette Haywood; 53 Ennismore Gardens, Knightsbridge, London SW7; 9 Holland Park Mansions, Holland Park Gardens, London W14 (☎ 01 371 6827); 1 Essex Ct, Temple, London EC4 (☎ 01 583 7759, fax 01 353 8620)

HAYWOOD, John (Barry); s of Bernard Haywood (d 1986), of Macclesfield, Cheshire, and Joyce Haywood, *née* Walker; *b* 18 Sept 1945; *Educ* King's GS Macclesfield, Leeds Polytechnic; *m* 11 May 1968, Ann, da of George Gosling (d 1986), of Macclesfield, Cheshire; 2 da (Melanie b 1968, Kirstyn b 1971); *Career* mgmnt conslt and co dir; fndr and chm IMO Gp 1976; dir: IMO Gp Ltd, IMO Ltd, IMO (Fin Servs) Ltd; chief conslt Algerian Miny of Water Resources 1977-78, Algerian Miny of Oil 1978-79; memb: MBIM 1977, AIL 1977, MIEx 1977, FInstD 1977, FIMC 1981; *Recreations* international travel, french/german language; *Clubs* IOD London; *Style—* Barry Haywood, Esq; 5 Daisybank Drive, Congleton CW12 1LS; IMO Group Ltd, 13-15 Kingsway, Altrincham WA14 1PN (☎ 061 941 7017)

HAYWOOD, Roger; s of Maj George Haywood, of Norwich, and Ethel Florence, *née* Reynolds; *b* 24 July 1939; *Educ* Westcliff Sch Westcliff-on-Sea; *m* 30 June 1962, Sandra Leonora, da of George Yenson (d 1972); 2 s (Ian b 1965, Mark b 1966), 2 da (Sarah b 1963, Laura b 1971); *Career* mktg positions with Dunlop Dexios and in various advtg agencies, Euro PR mangr Air Products 1971-75, md Haywood Hood & Assocs Ltd 1975-78, md Tibbenham Gp 1981, chm Roger Haywood Assocs Ltd 1982-; chm int ctee Inst PR; vice chm: Inst Mktg, PR Consults Assoc; Freeman City of London, memb Worshipful Co of Marketors; FCIM, ABC, FCAM, FIPR; *Books* All about PR (1985); *Recreations* music, classic cars; *Style—* Roger Haywood, Esq; 103 St Georges Square Mews, London SW1 (☎ 01 931 9250); Keswick Mill Norwich, Norfolk; Roger Haywood Assocs Ltd, 7 Eccleston Street, London SW1 (☎ 01 823 4125, car tel 0860 343015, fax 730 5300)

HAZELL, Ven Frederick Roy; s of John Murdoch Hazell (d 1978), and Ruth Hazell, *née* Topping (d 1960); *b* 12 August 1930; *Educ* Hutton GS, Fitzwilliam Coll Cambridge, Cuddesdon Coll Oxford (MA); *m* 1956, Gwendoline Edna, da of Percival Vare (d 1975); 1 steps (Dr James William Douglas Armstrong b 1945); *Career* vicar of Marlpool Derbyshire 1959-63; chaplain Univ of West Indies 1963-66; vicar of Holy Saviour Croydon 1968-84, rural dean of Croydon 1972-78; archdeacon of Croydon 1978-; *Recreations* listening to music, swimming, history; *Style—* The Ven, The Archdeacon of Croydon;; 246 Pampisford Road, South Croydon CR2 6DD (☎ 01 688 2943); St Matthew's House, 100 George Street, Croydon CR0 1PE (☎ 01 681 5496)

HAZELL, Quinton; CBE (1978, MBE 1961), DL (Warwicks 1982); s of Thomas Arthur Hazell (d 1962), of Colwyn Bay, N Wales; *b* 14 Dec 1920; *Educ* Manchester GS; *m* 1942, Morwenna Parry-Jones; 1 s; *Career* served WWII RA; chm and md Quinton Hazell Hldgs 1946-73, chm Supra Gp 1973-82, non-exec chm F and C Enterprise Tst plc 1981-86; dir: Edward Jones (Contractors) Ltd 1962-74, Phoenix Assurance 1968-86, For and Colonial Investmt Tst 1978-, Winterbottom Tst 1978-82, Hawker-Siddeley 1979-; non-exec dir: Banro Inds plc 1985-88, F and C Mgmnt Ltd 1985-86; chm: W Midlands Econ Planning Cncl 1971-77, Aerospace Engrg plc 1986-; FIMI; *Style—* Quinton Hazell, Esq, CBE, DL,; Wootton Paddox, Leek Wootton, Warwick CV35 7QX (☎ 0926 50704)

HAZLEHURST, Ernest (Raymond); s of George Hazlehurst (d 1934), and Florence Emily Oakes (d 1986); *b* 15 Oct 1924; *Educ* Highfield Sch Liverpool; *m* 1962, Dorothy Wendy (*née* Wright); *Career* chm: Finance Houses Assoc 1986, UAPT Infolink plc 1986, dep chm North West Securities Ltd 1986 (chief exec 1980-86), dir Chester City Tport 1986; *Clubs* Atheneum (Liverpool), City (Chester); *Style—* Raymond Hazlehurst, Esq; North West Securities Ltd, North West House, City Road, Chester (telex 312067, fax 0244 316684)

HAZLEHURST, (Charles) Patrick; DL (1987); s of Capt Charles Arthur Cheshyre Hazlehurst (d 1953), and Evangeline Vere Eben, *née* Edwards (d 1980); *b* 2 April 1924; *Educ* Wellington; *m* 30 Sept 1965, Annsybella Sarah Penelope, da of Brig Archer Francis Lawrence Clive, DSO, MC, DL, of Perrystone, Ross-on-Wye, Herefords; 1 s (Charles Dominic b 1966), 1 da (Annsybella Emma Lucinda b 1969); *Career* joined 60 Rifles 1942, cmmnd 1943, serv Italy 1944-45, N Africa Tripoli 1946, ADC to Lt-Gen Sir Evelyn Barker 1946-48 (when GOC(-in-C) in Palestine 1946-47 and GOC(-in-C) Eastern Cmd, Hounslow 1947-48), Capt 1948 (ret 1949); fndr Woodcemair Ltd (bldg prods) 1952 (md 1952-64, chm 1965-71), chm Torvale Gp Ltd (inc Woodcemair Ltd) 1972-; High Sheriff Hereford and Worcester 1985-86; *Recreations* shooting, fishing, field trials (labradors, retrievers); *Clubs* Boodles', Flyfishers, Royal Greenjackets; *Style—* Capt Patrick Hazlehurst; Broomy Ct, Llandinabo, Hereford HR2 8JB (☎ 0981 540215); Torvale Gp Ltd, Pembridge, Leominster, Herefordshire (☎ 05447 262, fax 05447 426, telex 35265)

HAZLEMAN, Dr Brian Leslie; s of Eric Edward Hazleman (d 1981), of Reading, Berks, and Gladys Marjorie, *née* Wells; *b* 4 Mar 1942; *Educ* Leighton Park Sch Reading, The London Hosp London Univ (MB, BS), Cambridge Univ (MA); *m* 29 Jan 1972, Ruth Margaret, da of Douglas Eynon, of Bristol; 3 da (Anna b 1973, Christina b 1976, Sarah b 1983); *Career* house physician and surgn London Hosp 1966-67 (registrar rheumatology 1968-69, registrar medicine 1969-71), sr registrar medicine and rheumatology Radcliffe Infirmary Oxford and Nuffield Orthopaedic Hosp 1971-73, conslt physician Addenbrookes Hosp Cambridge and Newmarket Hosp 1973-, hon conslt Strangeways Res Lab Cambridge 1973-, dir rheumatology res unit Cambridge 1975-, assoc lectr Cambridge Univ 1975- (fell CCC 1982); memb ed bd: Br Journal Rheumatology, Journal of Orthopaedic Rheumatology and Sports Medicine and Soft Tissue Trauma; Begley Prize RCS 1965, Margaret Holyrode Prize Heberden Soc 1975-; FRCP; *Books* The Sclera and Systemic Disorders (1976), Rheumatoid Arthritis Pathology and Pharmacology (1976); *Recreations* sailing, photography, travel; *Clubs* Royal Harwich (Suffolk); *Style—* Dr Brian L Hazleman; Church End House, Weston Colville, Cambs CB1 5PE (☎ 0223 290 543); Dept of Rheumatology, Addenbrokes Hospital, Hills Road, Cambridge (☎ 0223 217457)

HAZLERIGG, 2 Baron (UK 1945); Sir Arthur Grey; 14 Bt (E 1622), MC (1945), JP (Leics 1946), DL (1946); s of 1 Baron (d 1949); *b* 24 Feb 1910; *Educ* Eton, Trinity Coll Cambridge; *m* 1945, Patricia (d 1972), da of John Pullar, of Natal, S Africa; 1 s, 2 da; *Heir* s, Hon Arthur Hazlerigg; *Career* served WW II Maj RA (TA) and Leics Yeo; FRICS; *Recreations* golf; *Clubs* Army and Navy, MCC; *Style—* The Rt Hon the Lord Hazlerigg, MC, JP, DL; Noseley Hall, Billesdon, Leicester LE7 9EH (☎ 053 775 322)

HAZLERIGG, Hon Arthur Grey; s and h of 2 Baron Hazlerigg, MC; *b* 5 May 1951; *m* 1986, Laura, eld d of Sir William Dugdale, 2 Bt; 1 s (Arthur William Grey b 13 May 1987) ; *Clubs* Leicester Tiger Old Players, MCC; *Style—* The Hon Arthur Hazlerigg; The Chapel House, Noseley, Billesdon, Leics LE7 9HE (☎ 053 755 606)

HAZLERIGG, Hon Robert Maynard; yst s of 1 Baron Hazlerigg (d 1949); *b* 21 July 1916; *Educ* Eton, Trinity Coll Cambridge (BA); *m* 9 Jan 1942, Rose, da of Charles Cox; 2 da; *Career* Major RA (TA); ARICS; farmer; *Clubs* Oriental; *Style—* The Hon Robert Hazlerigg; Cottonsfield Farm, Three Gates, Billesdon, Leicester (☎ 053 755 382)

HAZLERIGG, Hon Thomas Heron; 2 s of 1 Baron Hazlerigg (d 1949), and Dorothy Rachel, *née* Buxton (d 1972); *b* 17 Jan 1914; *Educ* Eton, Trinity Coll Cambridge (BA); *m* 1, 28 March 1942 (m dis 1956), Audrey Cecil, da of late Maj Cecil Robert Bates, DSO, MC; 2 s; m 2, 31 Jan 1957 (m dis 1974), Doussa da of Fahmy Bey Wissa, of Ramleh, Egypt, formerly w of Maj Harold Stanley Cayzer; m 3, 1978, Anne Frances Roden, da of Capt Roden Henry Victor Buxton, RN, of Rodwell House, Loddon, Norfolk; *Career* Maj Leics Yeo, formerly Flying-Offr RAF Reserve; banker; *Recreations* skiing, Cresta Run, golf, shooting; *Clubs* White's, Pratt's, MCC; *Style—* The Hon Thomas Hazlerigg; Caflida, Klosters, Switzerland

HAZLEWOOD, Gerry (Gerald) Alan; OBE (1986); s of Reginald Hazlewood, of Okanagan Centre, BC, Canada, and Lilian May, *née* Lofts; *b* 25 July 1939; *Educ* Royal GS, High Wycombe; *m* 6 Sept 1961, Toni Gay, da of Sqdn Ldr Edward John Lisle, of Mundaring, Western Australia; 1 s (Daniel b 1979), 2 da (Christine b 1967, Helen b 1965); *Career* chm Westwood Engineering Ltd 1986- (dir 1967-86); *Recreations* golf; *Style—* Gerry Hazlewood, OBE; Midland bank Plc, City Centre, Old Town St, Plymouth PL1 1DD; Westwood Engineering Ltd, Bell Close, Newnham Industrial Estate, Plympton, Plymouth PL7 4JH (car ☎ 0836 502067)

HAZLEWOOD, Maurice Charles; s of Alfred Ernest Hazlewood (d 1981), of Liverpool, and Laura, *née* Hughes (d 1972); *b* 16 Oct 1927; *Educ* Liverpool Coll, Liverpool Univ (BSc), St Peter's Hall Oxford; *m* 6 Aug 1955, Morfydd Elizabeth, da of John Rowlands (d 1972), of Rhyl; 1 s (Richard b 1960), 1 da (Mary b 1959); *Career* called to the Bar Gray's Inn 1952, practised Northern Circuit; joined Royal Dutch Shell Gp 1958, head of chemical licensing and legal Div Shell Int Chemical Co Ltd 1961-68 (gen mangr Chemicals New York 1969-74), pres N American Plant Breeders Inc 1972-74; vice-pres Masterflex Rubber Corpn, Sureflex Rubber Co 1972-74, Akzona Inc New York 1974-76; (conslt 1976-79); practised in Temple 1979-85; memb Police Complaints Authy 1985-88; *Recreations* gardening, viticulture (memb English Vineyards Assoc), cricket; *Clubs* MCC; *Style—* Maurice Hazlewood, Esq; Whitethorne, Chapel Rd, Limpsfield Common, Oxted, Surrey RH8 0SX (☎ 088 372 2345)

HAZZARD, (Lawrence) Gordon; s of Frederick Hazzard, and Minnie; *b* 1925,Birmingham; *Educ* Waverley GS Birmingham; *m* 1, 1956 (m dis), Margery Elizabeth Charles; 1 da (Clare); m 2 1985, Miyuki Sedohara; *Career* served WW 2, RAF 1943-47; gp md MK Elec Hldgs to 1980; dep chm, then chm Grosvenor Gp plc 1981-86; chm Wigfalls plc 1981-88; chm Waingate Insurance Ltd 1985-88; chm HB Electronic Components plc 1983-85; dir Electropatent Ltd 1982-86; chm Toby Lane Ltd 1984-; chm Gordon Hazzard Ltd Anglo Japanese Bus Advsrs 1988-, past Cncl memb CBI, past bd memb ASTA, past vice-chm EIEMA, past dep pres Br Electrical and Allied Mfrs' Assoc; past pres London Handel Festival; memb Industrial Policy Ctee of CBI; FID, CBIM; *Recreations* music; *Clubs* Oriental, RAC; *Style—* Gordon Hazzard, Esq; 5 Balfour Place, London W1Y 5RG (☎ 01 408 0626, fax 01 629 8105)

HEAD, His Honour Judge Adrian Herbert; s of His Honour Judge George Herbert Head (d 1927), of The Lodge, Acomb, York, and Geraldine Maria, *née* Pipon (d 1959); *b* 4 Dec 1923; *Educ* RNC Dartmouth (invalided polio), privately, Magdalen Coll Oxford (BA, MA), Student Hon Soc of Gray's Inn; *m* 22 July 1947, Ann Pamela, da of John Stanning (d 1928), of Engoshura Farm, Nakuru, Kenya; 3 s (Henry b 1948, Christoher b 1954, David b 1955); *Career* called to the Bar Gray's Inn 1947, subs ad eundem Inner Temple; chm Norfolk Lavender Ltd and Chilvers & Son (1874) Ltd 1958-71, chm Agricultural Land Tribunals (SE Region) 1971, dep chm Middx Quarter Sessions 1971, circuit judge 1972-, memb Law Advsy Bd Univ of E Anglia 1979-, co-fndr and sr tstee Norfolk Family Conciliation Serv 1983-, pres West Norfolk and Fenland Marriage Guidance Cncl 1984-; reader for the C of E 1961-; Hon D of Civil Law Univ of East Anglia 1987; *Books* The Seven Words and the Civilian (1946, awarded the Tredegar Meml Lectureship RSL 1948), Essays by Divers Hands (contrib 1953), Safety Afloat (trans from Dutch 1965), McCleary's County Ct Forms (contrib 1979), Poems in

Praise (first edn 1982), Butterworths County Ct Precedents and Pleadings (devised and gen ed 1985, consulting ed and contrib 1985), Poems in Praise (second edn 1987); *Recreations* writing, painting, sailing, trees; *Clubs* Norfolk, RNSA, Cruising Assoc, St Katharine Haven YC; *Style—* His Honour Judge Adrian Head; Overy Staithe, King's Lynn, Norfolk PE31 8TG (☎ 0328 738312); 5 Raymond Bldgs, Gray's Inn, London WC1 5BP (☎ 01 405 7146)

HEAD, Audrey M; da of Eric Burton Head (d 1969), of Guildford, Surrey, and Kathleen Irene (d 1978); *b* 21 Jan 1924; *Educ* St Catherine's Sch, Bramley; *Career* md Hill Samuel Unit Tst Mangrs 1976-86 (dir 1973-86); dir: Hill Samuel Investmt Mgmnt 1974-86, Hill Samuel Life Assurance 1983-86; chm Unit Tst Assoc 1983-85; Trades Union Unit Tst Mangr (dir 1986-); memb: Monopolies and Mergers Commn 1986-; chm of governing body St Catherine's Sch Bramley 1988- (govr 1979-); govr Cranleigh Sch 1988-; Silver Jubilee Medal 1977; *Recreations* golf, gardening; *Clubs* Sloane; *Style—* Ms Audrey Head; West Chantry, 4 Clifford Manor Rd, Guildford, Surrey GU4 8AG

HEAD, Eric Howard; TD (1968); s of Thomas Howard Head (d 1953), of Sussex, and Jane, *née* Baxter (d 1963); *b* 6 Dec 1919; *Educ* Brighton Coll; *m* 18 June 1949, Carol Elizabeth, da of Walter Bridgwood Batkin (d 1977), of Hertfordshire; 3 da (Victoria, Erica, Joanna); *Career* private KOYLS, 2/lt Royal Sussex Regt, Maj 6/19 Hyderabad Regt Indian Army 1940-46, Lt-Col APIS (TA) 1952-67; CA: ptnr 1950, sr ptnr 1980-85, ret 1985; dir: Astral Computer Servs Ltd 1980, R L Glove Underwriting Agency 1985; memb: Worshipful Co of Honers, Worshipful Co of Chartered Accountants; master Tower Ward Club 1984-85, pres Bishopsgate Ward Club 1986-87; memb: IOD, Guild of Freemen, Royal Soc of St George; assoc memb Lloyd's 1954-; *Recreations* golf, foreign travel; *Clubs* City of London, City Livery, Haywards Heath Golf, St Enodoc Golf; *Style—* Eric H Head, Esq, TD; Russell's Farmhouse, St Georges Lane, Hurstpierpoint, E Sussex BN6 9QX (☎ 0273 833174); Fairwinds, Trebetherick, Cornwall

HEAD, Major Sir Francis David Somerville; 5 Bt (UK 1838); s of Sir Robert Pollock Somerville Head, 4 Bt (d 1924), and Grace Margaret, *née* Robertson (d 1967); *b* 17 Oct 1916; *Educ* Eton, Peterhouse Cambridge; *m* 1, 11 Feb 1950 (m dis 1965), Susan Patricia, da of late Arthur Douglas Ramsay, OBE; 1 s, 1 da; m 2, 25 Jan 1967, Penelope Marion Acheson, yr da of late Wilfrid Archibald Alexander; *Heir* s, Richard Douglas Somerville Head, *qv*; *Career* Maj (ret) Queen's Own Cameron Highlanders; served WW II (wounded, POW); *Clubs* Naval and Military; *Style—* Major Sir Francis Head, Bt; 63 Chantry View Rd, Guildford, Surrey GU1 3XU

HEAD, 2 Viscount (UK 1960); Richard Antony Head; s of 1 Viscount Head, GCMG, CBE, MC, PC (d 1983), MP (C) for Carshalton 1945-60, Sec of State for War 1951-56, Minister of Def 1956-57, first high cmmr to Fedn of Nigeria 1960-63, high cmmr to Fedn of Malaysia 1963-66, and Lady Dorothea Louise (d 1987), da of 9 Earl of Shaftesbury; *b* 27 Feb 1937; *Educ* Eton, RMA Sandhurst; *m* 1974, Alicia Brigid, da of Julian John William Salmond, of The Old Manor Farmhouse, Didmarton, Badminton, Avon; 2 s (Hon Henry Julian b 30 March 1980, Hon George Richard b 20 July 1982), 1 da (Hon Sarah Georgiana b 26 Nov 1984); *Heir* s, Hon Henry Head; *Career* served Life Guards 1957-66, Capt ret; trainer of racehorses 1968-83; *Recreations* sailing, golf; *Clubs* White's, Cavalry and Guards'; *Style—* The Rt Hon the Viscount Head; Throope Manor, Bishopstone, Salisbury, Wilts (☎ 072 277 318)

HEAD, Richard Douglas Somerville; s and h of Sir Francis David Somerville Head, 5 Bt; *b* 16 Jan 1951; *Educ* Eton, Magdalene Coll Cambridge, Bristol (Art Coll) Poly; *Career* gardener, the Royal Hort Soc Wisley Garden; *Recreations* music, painting, drawing, skiing; *Style—* Richard Head, Esq; 69 High Rd, Byfleet, Weybridge, Surrey KT14 7QN

HEAD, Sarah Daphne (Sally); da of Richard George Head, of Lavalow, Sithney Green, Helston, Cornwall, and Daphne Grace, *née* Henderson; *b* 20 Feb 1951; *Educ* Ancaster House Sussex, St Maurs Convent Weybridge; *m* 25 Sept 1975 (m dis 1987), Francis Vincent Keating, s of Bryan Keating; *Career* Sally Head Poetry Corner Radio London 1969, story of Warner Bros (Europe) 1972-75, script ed BBC and Thames TV 1976-84; prodr BBC Drama 1984-88: First Born, Marksman, Life and Loves of a She Devil, Breaking Up, The Detective, Inside Out; *Recreations* gardening sailing, theatre, pubs; *Clubs* Helford River Sailing, Stand-on-the-Green Sailing; *Style—* Miss Sally Head; 1 Hearne Road, Stand-on-the-Green, London WL1

HEAD, Hon Simon Andrew; s of 1 Viscount Head, GCMG, CBE, MC, PC (d 1983), and Dorothea, Viscountess Head, *qv*; *b* 1944; *Educ* Eton, Christ Church Oxford, Berkeley Univ Calif; *Career* asst ed Far Eastern Economic Review in Hong Kong 1966-67, correspondent in S E Asia for Financial Times 1970-72, New York correspondent New Statesman 1974-76; contributor on for affairs New York Review of Books 1973-; contested S Dorset (SDP-Lib) 1983; *Style—* The Hon Simon Head; 155 Cranmer Court, Sloane Ave, London SW3

HEADFORT, 6 Marquess of (I 1800); Sir Thomas Geoffrey Charles Michael Taylour; 9 Bt (I 1704); also Baron Headfort (I 1760), Viscount Headfort (I 1762), Earl of Bective (I 1766), and Baron Kenlis (UK 1831, which sits as); s of 5 Marquess, TD (d 1960), by his w Elsie, widow of Sir Rupert Clarke, 2 Bt, and da of James Tucker; *b* 20 Jan 1932; *Educ* Stowe, Christ's Coll Cambridge Univ (MA); *m* 1, 1958 (m dis 1969), Hon Elizabeth Nall-Cain, da of 2 Baron Brocket; 1 s, 2 da; m 2, 1972, Virginia, da of Mr Justice Nable, of Manila; *Heir* s, Earl of Bective; *Career* 2 Lt Life Gds 1950, actg PO RAFVR 1952; holds Commercial Pilot's Licence; Freeman Guild of Air Pilots and Air Navigators; dir Bective Electrical Co 1953, sales mangr and chief pilot Lancashire Aircraft Co 1959; Lloyd's Underwriter; Inspector Royal Hong Kong Aux Police 1977; FRICS, FCIArb, MIAUI; *Style—* The Most Hon The Marquess of Headfort; 1425 Figueroa St, Paco, Manila, Philippines (☎ 5220218, 593829, telex 64792 HORT PN); Affix Ltd, Room 601 Kam Chung Bldg, 54 Jaffe Road, Wanchai, Hong Kong (☎ 5 286011/2); Ellerslie Manor, Crosby, IOM (☎ Marown 851521)

HEADLEY, 7 Baron (I 1979); Sir Charles Rowland Allanson-Winn; 7 and 13 Bt (GB 1776, of Warley; E 1660, of Nostell); s of 5 Baron by his 1 w Teresa, *née* Johnson; suc bro, 6 Baron, 1969; *b* 19 May 1902; *Educ* Bedford Sch; *m* 1927, Hilda, da of Thomas Thorpe; 1 s, 3 da; *Heir* s, Hon John Allanson-Winn; *Style—* The Rt Hon Lord Headley; 'Dreys', 7 Silverwood, West Chiltington, West Sussex RH20 2NG (☎ West Chiltington 3083)

HEADLEY, Edith, Baroness; Edith Jane; yst da of late Rev George Dods, DD, minister of the parish of Barr, Ayrshire; *m* 18 Aug 1936, 6 Baron Headley (d 1969); *Recreations* travelling, gardening; *Clubs* RSAC, New Cavendish (London); *Style—* The Rt Hon Edith, Lady Headley; Haworth House, Turnberry, Ayr (☎ 065 53 342)

HEADLEY, (William) Robert; s of William James Headley (d 1982), of Desford, Leicestershire, and Alice Mary, *née* Horspool (d 1977); *b* 8 April 1922; *Educ* Hammersmith Sch, Architectural Assoc Sch of Architecture (Dip Arch); *m* 1, 18 Aug 1946, Margaret Elizabeth Vining, *née* Harris; 2 da (Jennifer b 1948, Carolyn b 1950), 1 s (Nigel b 1955); m 2, 27 May 1978, Anne Julia, da of Maj Richard Clive Strachey, MC (d 1980); 1 step da (Francesca b 1954), 1 step s (Dominic b 1959); *Career* architect: dep chief architect Western Region BR 1947-55 (responsible for modernisation programme incl Plymouth and Banbury), chief architect Midland Region BR 1955-63 (programme responsible for all architectural bldgs incl electrification programme from London to Manchester and Liverpool); maj new stations: Coventry, Piccadilly Manchester, Stafford; GMW Ptnership Chartered Architects: ptnr 1963-68, sr ptnr 1968- (maj projects incl New Covent Garden Market, New College and HQ RMA Sandhurst, Coll of Science Shrivenham, responsible for overall mgmnt of practices in UK, Hong Kong, Singapore, Saudi Arabia; FRIBA, HKIA; *Recreations* music, cricket; *Clubs* MCC, Arts, Oriental, Roehampton; *Style—* W Robert Headley, Esq; 7 Lansdowne Walk, London W11 3LN (☎ 01 727 6197); Funtington Lodge, Funtington, W Sussex PO18 9GL (☎ 0243 575 205); GMW Partnership, PO Box 1613, 239 Kensington High St, London W8 6SL (☎ 01 937 8020, telex 28566, fax 01 937 5815)

HEADLY, Derek; CMG (1957); s of Lawrence Compton Headly (d 1957), of Woodhouse Eaves, and Violet Ethelwyn Tabberer (d 1965); *b* 27 April 1908; *Educ* Repton Sch, Corpus Christi Coll Cambridge (BA); *m* 1946, (m dis 1967), Joyce Katherine, da of Eric Freeman; 1 s (Nicholas), 1 da (Victoria); *Career* mil service: SOE, Force 136, Malaya 1944-45, Maj (despatches), Br Mil Admin Malaya, sr civil affrs offr Trengganu 1945-46, Lt-Col; Malayan Civil Serv 1931-38, served in Trengganu, Muar, Pekan, seconded Palestine Mandate 1938-44, HMOCS: Malaya 1946-49, N Borneo 1949-53, Malaya Br advsr, Kelantan 1953-57, ret 1957; dir Vipan and Headly 1957-67, Midlands Sec Ind Schs Careers Orgn 1967-77; OStJ 1957; *Recreations* mountain walking, gardening; *Clubs* Special Forces; *Style—* Derek Headly, Esq, CMG; Rooftree Cottage, Hoby, Melton Mowbray, Leics (☎ 066 475214)

HEADY, Donald Edward; s of Albert Edward Heady (d 1957), of London, and Edith, *née* Hunt (d 1984); *b* 28 Sept 1933; *Educ* Southend-on-Sea HS for Boys (FCA); *m* 22 Sept 1956, Doreen Joan, da of Albert Sharpe (d 1969), of Essex; *Career* CA, ptnr Donald Heady and Co; pres South Essex Soc of CA's 1980-81; memb: cncl The Inst of CA's in England and Wales 1981-, Accounting Standards Ctee of the Consultative Ctee of Accountancy Bodies 1982-85; Freeman City of London, Liveryman Worshipful Co of CA's in England and Wales 1978-; FCA 1958, ATII 1962; *Recreations* swimming, playing piano and organ; *Style—* Donald Heady, Esq; 2 Great Lawn, Ongar, Essex CM5 0AA (☎ 0277 362905); 87 Western Rd, Romford, Essex RM1 3LX (☎ 0708 730101, fax 0708 44728)

HEAL, Anthony Standerwick; s of Sir Ambrose Heal (d 1959), of Beaconsfield, and Lady Edith Florence Digby, *née* Todhunter (d 1946); *b* 23 Feb 1907; *Educ* Leighton Park Sch Reading; *m* 1941, Theodora, da of William Henry Griffin (d 1924), of Cornwall; 2 s (Ambrose b 1942, Oliver Standerwick b 1949); *Career* chm Heal and Son Ltd (later Heal and Son Hldgs Ltd) 1952-81; Master Furniture Makers Guild (now Worshipful Company of Furniture Makers) 1959-60; memb: Cncl of Industl Design (now Design Cncl) 1959-67, cncl City and Guilds of London Inst 1969-81; pres Design and Industries Assoc 1965; Rose of Finland 1970; Chevalier (first class); Order of Dannebrog 1974; *Recreations* vintage cars and steam engines; *Clubs* Vintage Sports Car; *Style—* Anthony Heal, Esq; Baylins Farm, Knotty Green, Beaconsfield, Bucks HP9 2TN

HEALD, Lady; Daphne Constance; *née* Price; CBE (1976); da of Montague Price; *b* 1904; *Educ* Private; *m* 1929, as his 2 w, Rt Hon Sir Lionel Heald, PC, QC, JP, sometime MP Chertsey and attorney-gen (d 1981); 2 s, 1 da; *Career* Connected with many voluntary organizations; Dame OStJ; *Recreations* gardening; *Style—* Lady Heald, CBE; Chilworth Manor, Guildford, Surrey (☎ 0483 61414)

HEALD, Mervyn; QC (1970); s of Rt Hon Sir Lionel Frederick Heald, PC, QC, MP (d 1982), and Daphne Constance Heald, CBE; *b* 12 April 1930; *Educ* Eton, Magdalene Coll Cambridge; *m* 1954, Clarissa, da of Harold Bowen; 1 s, 3 da; *Career* barr Middle Temple 1954, bencher 1978, cmmr Social Security 1988-; *Recreations* country pursuits; *Style—* Mervyn Heald Esq, QC; Headfoldswood, Loxwood, Sussex; 1 Crown Office Row, London EC4

HEALD, Oliver; s of John Anthony Heald, of Folkestone, and Joyce, *née* Pemberton; *b* 15 Dec 1954; *Educ* Reading Sch, Pembroke Coll Cambridge (MA), Coll of Law; *m* 18 Aug 1979, Christine Janice Heald, da of Eric Arthur Whittle (d 1980), of Eastbourne; 1 s (William b 1987), 1 da (Sarah b 1985); *Career* called to the Bar Middle Temple 1977, SE Ciruit; memb area legal aid ctee Law Soc, Herts sponsor Mental Health Fndn, emergency plans community advsr; former chm N Herts Cons Assoc, parly cand (C) Southwark and Bermansey 1987; memb Bar Cncl and Hon Soc of Middle Temple; *Recreations* travel, gardening, sports; *Clubs* St Stephens Constitutional, Cambridgeshire County Farmers; *Style—* Oliver Heald, Esq; The Acacias, 9 The Green, Royston, Herts SG8 7AD (☎ 0763 47640); Fenners Chambers, 5 Gresham Rd, Cambridge (☎ 0223 68761)

HEALD, Owen Hubert; s of Henry Claypole Heald (d 1974), and Lilian May, *née* Cranness (d 1974); *b* 17 Jan 1925; *Educ* Westcliff HS; *m* 8 Nov 1947, Georgina Ruth, da of George Warman (d 1969); 1 da (Carole b 1949); *Career* oil indust exec Shell Petroleum Co Ltd and subsidiary cos 1949-85, vice-pres Shell Int Trading Co 1975-76, dir Shell UK Ltd 1979-84; bd memb The Oil and Pipeline Agency 1985- (chm 1988); *Recreations* sailing, golf; *Clubs* Thames Estuary Yacht; *Style—* Owen Heald, Esq; 6 Wyatts Drive, Thorpe Bay, Essex SS1 3DH (☎ 0702 68226); The Oil and Pipeline Agency, 35/38 Portman Square, London W1H 0EU (☎ 01 935 2585)

HEALD, His Hon Judge; Thomas Routledge; *b* 19 August 1923; *m* 1950, Jean Campbell; 2 s, 2 da; *Career* barr Middle Temple 1948; prosecuting cncl to Inland Revenue Midland Circuit 1965-70; dep chm: Lindsey QS 1965-71, Notts QS 1969-71; circuit judge 1970-; memb Matrimonial Causes Rule Ctee to 1983; pres Cncl of HM's Circuit Judges 1988 (sec 1984-85); memb cncl Nottingham Univ 1975-; *Style—* His Hon Judge Heald; Rebbur House, Nicker Hill, Keyworth, Nottingham NG12 5ED

HEALD, Timothy Villiers; s of Col Villiers Archer John Heald, CVO, DSO, MBE, MC (d 1972), of Wilts, and Catherine Eleanor Jean, *née* Vaughan; *b* 28 Jan 1944; *Educ* Sherborne, Balliol Coll Oxford (MA); *m* 1968, Alison Martina, da of Norman Alexander Leslie, of Bucks; 2 s (Alexander b 1971, Tristram b 1977), 2 da (Emma b 1970, Lucy b 1973); *Career* writer Sunday Times Atticus Column 1965-67, features ed: 'Town' Magazine 1967, Daily Express 1967-72; assoc editor: 'Weekend' Magazine Toronto 1977-78, 'Simon Bognor' Mystery novels 1973- (televised by Thames), Networks (1983), Class Distinctions (1984), Red Herrings (1985), The Character of Cricket (1986), Brought to Book (1988); ed The Newest London Spy; thriller reviewer The Times; contributor to various newspapers and magazines; *Recreations* real tennis, spectator sports, lunch; *Clubs* MCC, Crime Writers Assoc (chm 1987-88), PEN (int co-ordinator, writers-in-prison ctee 1986-); *Style*— Timothy Heald Esq; 305 Sheen Rd, Richmond-upon-Thames TW10 5AW (☎ 01 878 2478)

HEALEY, Rt Hon Denis Winston; CH (1979), MBE (1945), PC (1964), MP (L) Leeds E 1955-; s of William Healey, of Keighley, Yorks; *b* 30 August 1917; *Educ* Bradford G S, Balliol Coll Oxford; *m* 1945, Edna May, da of Edward Edmunds, of Coleford, Glos; 1 s, 2 da; *Career* int sec Lab Pty 1946-52, memb Parly Ctee Lab Party 1959, MP (L) Leeds S E 1952-55, sec state Def 1964-70, oppn spokesman Foreign and Commonwealth Affrs 1971, shadow chllr 1972-74, chllr of Exchequer 1974-79; dep ldr Lab Pty 1981-Oct 1983, shadow sec Foreign and Commonwealth Affrs 1981-87 ; former exec memb Fabian Soc; Hon DLitt Bradford 1983; Hon Fell Balliol Coll Oxford 1980; Grand Cross Order of Merit Germany 1979; *Books* The Curtain Falls (1951), New Fabian Essays (1952), Neutralism (1955), Fabian International Essays (1956), A Neutral Belt in Europe (1958), NATO and American Security (1959), The Race Against the H Bomb (1960), Labour Britain and the World (1963), Healey's Eye (photographs, 1980), Labour and a World Society (1985), Beyond Nuclear Deterrence (1986); *Style*— The Rt Hon Denis Healey, CH, MBE, MP; House of Commons, London SW1

HEALING, Hon Mrs (Elisabeth Mary Lionel Margaret); da of 16 Baron Petre (d 1915); *b* 1915,(posthumous); *m* 1935, Robert Peter Healing; 1 s, 2 da; *Style*— The Hon Mrs Healing; The Priory, Kemerton, Glos

HEALY, Maurice Eugene; s of Thomas Shine Healy (d 1961), and Emily Mary, *née* O'Mahoney (d 1980); *b* 27 Nov 1933; *Educ* Downside, Peterhouse Cambridge (BA); *m* 20 Dec 1958, Jose Barbara Speller, da of John Edward Dewdney (d 1971); 3 da (Kate b 1961, d 1977, Lulu b 1963, Jessica b 1964); *Career* Nat Serv 2 Lt RA 1954-56; asst princ Bd of Trade 1956-60, Consumers Assoc 1960-76; Which?: ed-in-chief and head of ed div 1973-76, project offr, dep ed, ed (Motoring Which, Handyman Which); dir Nat Consumer Cncl 1987-(joined 1977); memb Highgate Primary Sch Soc, chm Highgate Wood Sch 1982-86 (govr 1976-86, soc memb); *Recreations* jazz, Irish music, gardening, walking; *Style*— Maurice Healy, Esq; 15 Onslow Gdns, Muswell Hill, London N10 3JT (☎ 01 883 8955); National Consumer Council, 20 Grosvenor Gdns, London SW1W 0DH (☎ 01 730 3469)

HEANEY, Henry Joseph; s of Michael Heaney (d 1951), of Newry, Co Down, and late Sarah, *née* Fox; *b* 2 Jan 1935; *Educ* Abbey GS Newry Ireland, Queen's Univ Belfast (BA, MA); *m* 19 March 1976, Mary Elizabeth, da of Desmond Moloney, of Dublin; *Career* asst librarian Queen's Univ Belfast 1959-63, librarian Magee Univ Coll Londonderry 1963-69, dep librarian New Univ of Ulster Coleraine 1967-69, asst sec Standing Conf of Nat and Univ Libraries 1969-72, librarian Queen's Univ Belfast 1972-74, librarian and dir sch of librarianship Univ Coll Dublin 1975-78, Univ librarian and keeper of the Hunterian Books and Manuscripts Univ of Glasgow 1978-; chm: working gp on library cooperation Nat Library of Scotland, advsy ctee Scottish Sci Library Users; tstee Nat Library of Scotland, vice pres Scottish Library Assoc; sec advsy ctee on res collections Standing Conf of Nat and Univ libraries, memb ctee of univ and libraries, section Int Fedn of Library Assoc; ALA 1962, FLA 1967; *Books* World Guide to Abbreviations of International Organisations 8th ed (1988); *Clubs* XIII (Glasgow); *Style*— Henry Heaney, Esq; 50A Sherbrooke Ave, Glasgow G41 4SB (☎ 041 427 1518); Glasgow Univ Library, Hillhead Street, Glasgow G12 8QE (☎ 041 330 4283)

HEANEY, John Bryan; s of Brig George Frederick Heaney (d 1983), and Doreen Marguerite, *née* Hammersley-Smith; *b* 26 Feb 1931; *Educ* Marlborough Coll, Christs Coll Cambridge (MA); *m* 19 Nov 1956, Catherine Ann, da of Lt Cdr Eliot Phillip Rayleigh Haller, RNVR (ka 1940); 1 s (Quintin John b 1957), 1 da (Alison Mary b 1959); *Career* cmmnd RE 1950, surveyor on first land based expedition to South Georgia, Falkland Islands 1951-52; led expdn to Gough Island S Atlantic 1955-56; Shell Int Petroleum Cos 1956-79, fndr and chief exec Saxon Oil plc 1980-85, chm Waveney Apple Growers Ltd; *Clubs* IOD; *Style*— John Heaney, Esq; Oldhouse Farm, Wakes Colne, Colchester, Essex CO6 2DR (☎ 07875 2329, fax 07875 4313)

HEANEY, Leonard Martin; CMG (1958); s of Alexander John Heaney (d 1936), and Lilian, *née* Davies; *b* 28 Nov 1906; *Educ* Bristol GS, Oriel Coll Oxford (BA); *m* 1947, Kathleen Edith Mary, da of Robert Lewis Chapman (d 1940); *Career* mil serv Ethiopia, Burma 1940-45, Major sr provincial cmmnr Tanganyika (Colonial Admin Serv); *Recreations* golf; *Style*— Leonard Heaney Esq, CMG; 9 Salcombe Court, Salcombe Hill Road, Sidmouth, Devon

HEAP, Peter William; CMG (1987); s of Roger Heap (d 1966), and Dora Heap, *née* Hosier; *b* 13 April 1935; *Educ* Bristol Cathedral Sch, Merton Coll Oxford (BA); *m* 1, 1960; 2 s (Alan, Derek), 2 da (Angela, Jane); m 2, 1977, Dorrit Breitenstein; 1 step s (Robert), 3 step da (Suzanne, Marina, Katania); *Career* Br high cmmnr Nassau Bahamas 1983-, former posts HM Dip Serv in Dublin, Ottawa, Colombo, New York, Caracas, FCO London; *Clubs* Royal Cwlth Soc, Lyford Cay (Nassau); *Style*— Peter Heap Esq, CMG; Br High Cmmn, PO Box N7516, Nassau, Bahamas; 22 Ormonde Rd, London SW14

HEAPS, Christopher Seymour; s of Capt Christopher Robert Milner Heaps, TD (d 1962), and Peggy Margaret Catherine, *née* Mill (d 1984); *b* 15 Nov 1942; *Educ* Dorking GS, Univ of Exeter (LLB); *m* 14 March 1970, Ann Mary, da of Capt Peter Frederick Dudley Mays, of Dorking; 2 da (Grace b 1973, Elizabeth b 1975); *Career* slr 1967-; ptnr Jaques & Lewis (formerly Jaques & Co) 1971-; pres Holborn Law Soc 1983-84, cncl memb Law Soc 1985-; memb: TUC for London 1981-84, London Regnl Passengers Ctee 1984-(dep chm 1985-), advsy panel Railway Heritage Tst 1985-; chm Dorking Round Table 1978-79, pres Dorking Deepdene Rotary Club 1986-87, tstee Harrowlands Appeal (Dorking Hosp), govr Parson's Mead Sch Ashtead; Liveryman: Worshipful Co of Curriers 1976, Worshipful Co of Coachmakers and Coach Harness Makers 1985; MCIT 1988; *Books* London Transport Railways Album (1978), Western Region in the 1960's (1981), This is Southern Region Central Division (1982), B R Diary 1968-1977 (1988); *Recreations* transport and transport history; *Style*— Christopher Heaps, Esq; Pinecroft, Ridgeway Rd, Dorking, Surrey RH4 3AP (☎ 0306 881752); 33 Wendron St, Helston, Cornwall; 2 South Square, Gray's Inn, London WC1R 5HR (☎ 01 242 9755, fax 01 405 4464, telex 27938)

HEARD, Peter Graham; CB (1987); s of Sidney Horwood Heard (d 1959), of Devon, and Doris Winifred, MBE, *née* Gale (d 1982); *b* 22 Dec 1929; *Educ* Exmouth GS, Coll of Estate Mgmnt, FRICS; *m* 1953, Ethne Jean, da of Denys Stanley Thomas (d 1956), of Devon; 2 da (Tessa Jane b 1956, Julie Ann b 1957); *Career* chartered surveyor, dep chief valuer Valuation Office Bd of Inland Revenue 1983-89, joined 1950; served in: Exeter, Kidderminster, Dudley Leeds; district valuer Croydon 1971, superintending valuer head Office 1973-, asst sec Somerset House 1975, superintendent valuer Midlands 1978, asst chief valuer Head Office 1978; *Recreations* cricket, golf, theatre, countryside, walking the dog; *Clubs* MCC, Civil Service; *Style*— Peter Heard, Esq, CB; Romany Cottage, High St, Lindfield, Sussex (☎ 044 47 2095); Chief Valuers Office, New Court, Carey St, London (☎ 01 831 6111)

HEARLEY, Timothy Michael; s of Maurice James Goodwin Hearley, CBE (d 1975); *b* 10 Mar 1942; *Educ* Malvern, Oxford Univ (MA); *m* 1966, Pauline Muriel, *née* Dunn; 3 s (Philip Michael b 1967, James Paul b 1970, Richard Matthew b 1973); *Career* memb of Stock Exchange; chm: The Beaver Gp Ltd, CH Industrials plc, Garden Wines Ltd, Rolfe and Nolan Computer Services plc, Aston Martin Tickford Ltd; dir: Chackmore Management Services Ltd, Oceanic Commercial Hldgs Ltd, Protea Commercial Properties Ltd, Quantum Investments Ltd, Securitex Investments Ltd, memb Soc of Investment Analysts; *Recreations* tennis, piano, ballet, theatre; *Clubs* Reform; *Style*— Timothy Hearley, Esq; Rush Leys, 4 Birds Hill Rise, Oxshott, Surrey (☎ Oxshott 037 284 2506); CH Industrials plc, 33 Cavendish Sq, London W1M 9HF (☎ 01 491 7860, telex 266498)

HEARN, Clive Lennard; s of Lennard Clarence Hearn (d 1981), of London, and Doris Susannah, *née* Goodwin (d 1977); *b* 8 July 1926; *Educ* Collegiate Sch London; *m* 1 Sept 1951, Audrey Elizabeth, da of Capt Edward John Smith (d 1972), of London; 2 s (Andrew b 1956, Jonathan b 1967), 1 da (Karen b 1953); *Career* CA; dir: Alfred Booth and Co Ltd 1965-81, Hazel Heath Homes Ltd 1984, Maulden Homes Ltd 1988; tres Cuffley Free Church 1960-81; govr: Stormont Sch Potters Bar 1962-, Lochinver House Sch Potters Bar 1966-; dir George Carter Ltd 1962-; *Recreations* cricket, football; *Clubs* Reform, Hove, MCC, Sussex CCC; *Style*— Clive Hearn, Esq; 15 The Ridgeway, Cuffley, Potters Bar, Herts EN6 4AY (☎ 0707 873084); 30 Market Place, Hitchin, Herts SG5 1DT (☎ 0462 37117/8)

HEARN, Rear Adm Frank Wright; CB (1976); s of John Henry Hearn, BSc (d 1975), of Kent, and Elsie Gertrude Hearn, *née* Price (d 1951); *b* 1 Oct 1919; *Educ* Abbotsholme Sch Derbyshire; *m* 1, 1947, Ann Cynthia Wood (decd), da of Edward Wood, CB, of London; 2 da (Katherine Ann b 1948, Mary Elizabeth b 1952); m 2, 1965, Ann Christina, da of Frederick Augustos St Clair Miller, of Essex; *Career* joined RN 1937, HMS Hood 1937-39, served war 1939-45 in various HM Ships Atlantic, Mediterranean, East Indies; staff C-in-C Home Fleet 1951-53; sec Flag Offr Submarines 1954-56; sec Dir Naval Intelligence 1958-60; HMS Tiger 1960-62; Fleet Supply Offr Western Fleet 1962-64; asst Chief Personnel and Logistics 1974-76 as Rear Adm; *Recreations* golf, tennis, gardening, wine making; *Clubs* Royal Commonwealth, Goodwood Golf; *Style*— Rear Adm Frank Hearn, CB; Hurstbrook Cottage, Hollybank Lane, Emsworth, Hants (☎ 0243 372149)

HEARN, Hon Mrs; Hon Kathleen Gertrude; *née* O'Grady; only child of 6 Viscount Guillamore (d 1927); *b* 21 April 1914; *m* 1945, Capt Geoffrey Hearn, Somersetshire LI; 1 s; *Career* late Junior Com ATS; *Style*— Hon Mrs Hearn; Badgers Mount, Bottle Square Lane, Radnage, Bucks

HEARNE, Graham James; s of Frank Hearne and Emily, *née* Shakespeare; *b* 23 Nov 1937; *Educ* George Dixon GS Birmingham; *m* 1961, Carol Jean, *née* Brown; 1 s, 3 da; *Career* slr 1959, practised law in UK and USA 1959-67; exec Industl Reorgn Corpn 1967-70, exec dir N M Rothschild and Sons Ltd 1970-77, fin dir Courtaulds 1977-81, chief exec Tricentrol 1981-83, gp md Carless Capel and Leonard plc 1983-84, chief exec Enterprise Oil plc 1984-; *Clubs* Reform, MCC; *Style*— Graham Hearne Esq; 8 Church Row, London NW3 6UT (☎ 01 794 4987); One Hook Lane, Bosham, Chichester, W Sussex PO18 8EY (☎ 0243 572351); Enterprise Oil plc, 5 Strand, London WC2N 5HR (☎ 01 930 1212, telex 9850611)

HEARSE, Prof David James; s of James Read Hearse (d 1974), of Holt, Wilts, and Irene Annetta, *née* Nokes (d 1982); *b* 3 July 1943; *Educ* John Willmott GS, Univ of Wales (BSc, PhD, DSc); *Career* instr in pharmacology New York Univ Med Centre 1968-70, res fell Br Heart Fndn Imperial Coll London 1970-76, hon sr lectr St Thomas' Hosp Med Sch 1976-86, prof of cardio vascular biochemistry United Med and Dental Schs Guys Hosp and St Thomas' Hosp; dir cardiovascular res The Rayne Inst St Thomas Hosp; author of 6 books and over 400 scientific papers in areas of res into heart disease; Fell of American Coll of Cardiology 1980; memb: Royal Soc Med, Br Cardiac Soc; *Recreations* furniture, house restoration, photography, carpentry; *Clubs* Royal Soc of Medicine; *Style*— Prof David Hearse; Cardiovascular Res, Rayne Inst, St Thomas' Hosp, London SE1 (☎ 01 928 9292 ext 2990)

HEARSEY, David Glen; s of Leonard Walter Hearsey (d 1985), of London, and Gwenda Kathleen, *née* Taylor; *b* 7 Feb 1948; *Educ* Willesdon Coll of Tech; *m* 23 Dec 1972, Roxie Anne, da of Norman Geoffrey Davies (d 1973), of London; 1 s (Lee James b 26 Sept 1979), 1 da (Sophie Jane b 28 Sept 1976); *Career* fndr David Glen Assocs (consulting Engrs) 1969 (ptnr 1970, sr ptnr 1980-), sr ptnr Glen Leasing 1981-86; conslt engr in respect of over 300 major construction projects worldwide; memb Con Assoc; Freeman City of London 1973, Liveryman Worshipful Co of Plumbers; MRSH 1970, MIP 1972, TEng CEI 1972, AMI Mun BM 1979, MSAME 1980; *Recreations* offshore sailing, skiing, shooting, golf, squash, tennis, chess, fishing; *Clubs* City Livery; *Style*— David Hearsey, Esq; David Glen Assocs Consulting Engineers, Times House, Station Approach, Ruislip, Middx HA4 8LE (☎ 0895 638007, fax 0895 679121, car 0836 289266, telex 945922)

HEARST, Stephen; CBE (1979); s of Dr Emanuel Hirschtritt (d 1962), of Harley St, London, and Claire Hearst (d 1980); *b* 6 Oct 1919; *Educ* Rainer Gymnasium Vienna, Vienna Univ Med Faculty, Reading Univ, Brasenose Coll Oxford (MA); *m* 17 July 1948, Lisbeth Edith, da of Dr Ludwig Neumann (d 1979), of Haifa, Israel; 1 s (David Andrew b 1954), 1 da (Daniela Carol (Mrs Pountney) b 1951); *Career* joined Pioneer Corps 1940, Corporal home serv 1940-42, cmmnd 1943, served N Africa 1943, beach landing bde 5 Army Salerno Landing 1943, posted Allied Mil Govt 1944 (served Florence, Bologna and Piacenza), Capt 1945, camp cmdt POW camps Palestine 1945, demob 1946; BBC TV: newsreel writer 1952, trainee prodr 1952-53, writer for Richard Dimbleby documentaries 1953-55, documentary writer and prodr 1955-64, exec prodr arts programmes 1965-67, head of arts features 1967-71; controller BBC Radio 3 1972-78, controller future policy gp BBC 1978-82, special advsr to Dir-Gen BBC 1982-86, dir Orsino Prodns 1980-; visiting fell Inst for the Advanced Study of the Humanities Edinburgh Univ 1988; memb BAFTA, FRSA 1980; *Books* 2000 Million Poor (1965), The Third Age of Broadcasting (jtly 1984); *Recreations* reading, gardening, swimming, golf; *Style*— Stephen Hearst, Esq, CBE; The British Academy of Film and Television Arts, 195 Piccadilly, London SW1

HEARTH, John Dennis Miles; CBE (1983); s of Cyril Howard Hearth, MC (d 1973), of Leicester, and Pauline Kathleen, *née* O'Flanagan; *b* 8 April 1929; *Educ* The King's Sch Canterbury, Brasenose Coll Oxford (MA); *m* 1959, Pamela Anne, da of Arthur Gilbert Bryant, MC (d 1966), of Speldhurst, Kent; 2 s (Jonathan, Dominic); *Career* Nat Serv Intelligence Corps 1947-49; Admin Offr (Overseas Civil Serv) Br Solomon Islands Protectorate 1953-60, ed Fairplay Shipping Journal Fairplay Pubns Ltd 1961-66, special asst to chm The Cunard Steamship Co Ltd 1966-67 (gp planning advsr 1967-68, jt ventures dir 1970, corporate planning dir 1971), chief exec Royal Agric Soc of England 1972-89 (chm rural enterprise unit 1988-), tstee RAC Rural Tst (village homes for village people) 1988-, memb Rural and Agric Affrs Advsy Ctee 1988-; memb of ct Univ of Warwick 1985- (tres-designate 1989-); CBIM; *Recreations* golf, theatre, travel, history; *Clubs* Farmers', Anglo-Belgian; *Style*— John D M Hearth Esq, CBE; Bayard's, Fenny Compton, Nr Leamington Spa, Warwicks CV33 0XY; Royal Agric Soc of England, NAC, Stoneleigh, Kenilworth, Warwicks CV8 2LZ (☎ 0203 696969, telex 31697)

HEASLIP, Rear Adm Richard George; CB (1987); s of Eric Arthur Heaslip, and Vera Margaret Heaslip, *née* Bailey (d 1986); *b* 30 April 1932; *Educ* Chichester HS, RN Coll Dartmouth; *m* 1959, Lorna Jean, da of Alfred D Grayston (d 1976), of Canada; 3 s (Edmund b 1960, Christopher b 1964, Paul b 1966), 1 da (Lorna b 1960); *Career* Capt second submarine sqdn 1975-76, CO HMS Conqueror 1971-72, exec offr of first RNM nuclear submarine HMS Dreadnought 1965-67, CO HMS Sea Devil 1961-62; NATO Defence Coll Rome 1979-80; dir of Defence Policy MOD 1982-84; asst Chief of Staff Operations SHAPE 1984; Flag Offr Submarines and NATO COMSUBEASTLANT 1984-87; dir gen English Speaking Union 1987-; ADC (1984); chm RN Football Assoc 1977-84; pres London Submarine Old Comrades Assoc 1987; *Recreations* walking, music; *Style*— Rear Adm Richard Heaslip, CB; South Winds, Wallis Rd, Waterlooville, Hants (☎ 0705 241679); Dartmouth House, Charles St, London W1 (☎ 01 493 3328)

HEATH, Andrew Robert; only s of Capt Robert Arthur Heath, MC (d 1943), and Lady Marjorie Mary Winifrede, *née* Feilding, 4 da of 9 Earl of Denbigh and Desmond; *b* 1926; *m* 1, 1953 (m dis 1966), Sarah Joanna Evelyn Helen (b 1930, d 1970), third and youngest da of Earl of Stockton; m 2, 1966, Judith Clare Silver; 1 s (William b 1966), 1 da (Rachel b 1968); *Style*— Andrew Heath Esq; George's Plot, Church Road, Abbot's Leigh, Bristol

HEATH, Prof Bernard Oliver; OBE (1980); s of Bernard Ernest Heath (d 1951), and Ethel May, *née* Sweeting (1981); *b* 8 Mar 1925; *Educ* Bemrose Sch, Derby Sch, Univ Coll Nottingham (BSc), Imperial Coll of Sci and Technol (DIC); *m* 1948, Ethel, da of Sidney Riley (d 1954); 1 s (Robert, b 1951); *Career* Panavia; dir Systems Engrg (Warton) 1969-81, div tech dir 1978-81; divnl dir Advanced Engrg Br Aerospace Warton Div 1981-84; chm SBAC Tech Bd 1980-82 (memb 1975-84); prof Br Aerospace integrated chair in aeronautical engrg Salford U 1983-; CEng, FRAeS; *Recreations* military history, history of transport; *Style*— Prof Bernard Heath, OBE; Dept of Aeronautical and Mechanical Engineering, Univ of Salford, Salford M5 7QD

HEATH, Catherine Judith; da of Samuel Michael Hirsch (d 1976), and Anna, *née* de Boer (d 1980); *b* 17 Nov 1924; *Educ* Hendon Co Sch, St Hilda's Coll Oxford (MA); *m* 19 July 1947 (m dis 1977), Dennis Heath, s of Frederick Heath (d 1958); 1 s (David b 1955), 1 da (Anne b 1953); *Career* novelist, theatre criticism: Plays Int; *Books* Stone Walls (1973), The Vulture (1974), Joseph and the Goths (1975), Lady on the Burning Deck (1978), Behaving Badly (1984, TV adaptation 1989); *Recreations* theatre, conversation, walking; *Clubs* PEN, Soc of Authors, Oxford and Cambridge; *Style*— Mrs Catherine Heath; 17 Penarth Ct, Devonshire Avenue, Sutton, Surrey SM2 5LA (☎ 01 661 0213)

HEATH, Christopher John; s of Sir Lewis Macclesfield Heath (d 1954), of Kenya, and Lady Katherine Margaret, *née* Lonergan (d 1984); *b* 26 Sept 1946; *Educ* Ampleforth Coll; *m* 14 June 1979, Margaret Joan, da of Col Richard Arthur Wiggin, TD, JP, DL (d 1977); 1 s (William Henry Christopher b 29 April 1983); *Career* ICI 1964-, George Henderson & Co 1969-75, ptnr Henderson Crosthwaite & Co 1975-84; md Baring Securities Ltd 1984-, (dir numerous subsidaries), dir Baring Brothers & Co Ltd; memb nat appeals ctee Cancer Res Campaign, Save the Children Fund; memb Stock Exchange 1976-; *Recreations* horse racing, fishing; *Clubs* Turf, Flyfishers; *Style*— Christopher Heath, Esq; 8 Scarsdale Villas, London W8 6PR; Baring Securities Ltd, 1st Floor Lloyds Chambers, 1 Portsoken St, London E1 8DF (☎ 01 621 1500, fax 01 623 1873)

HEATH, David Arthur; s of Richard Arthur Heath, of Chesterfield, and Gladys Heath; *b* 6 Sept 1946; *Educ* Chesterfield Boys GS, Glos Coll of Art and Design (Dip Arch); *m* 27 June 1973, Angela Mary, da of late James Joseph Niall Hardy, of Chesterfield; 2 s (Richard b 1978, John b 1980); *Career* architect; ptnr Heath Avery Ptnrship 1980-; dir Heath (Properties) Ltd 1986; Cheltenham Civic Award 1987 (commendations 1986, 1987); *Recreations* motor racing, music, reading; *Style*— David Heath, Esq; 11A The Verneys, Old Bath Rd, Cheltenham, Glos (☎ 0242 42066); 17 Imperial Square, Cheltenham, Glos (☎ 0242 529169, fax C 224069)

HEATH, David William St John; CBE (1989); s of Eric William Heath of Street, Somerset and Pamela Joan *née* Bennett; *b* 16 Mar 1954; *Educ* Millfield Sch, St John's Coll Oxford (MA), The City Univ; *m* 15 May 1987, Caroline Marie Therese da of Harry Page Netherton, of Alicante, Spain; 1 da (Bethany b 31 March 1988); *Career* optician; memb: Somerset CC 1985 (ldr 1985), nat exec Lib Pty 1986-87; FADO 1978; *Recreations* rugby football, cricket, pig-breeding; *Clubs* Nat Lib; *Style*— David Heath, CBE, Esq; 34, The Yard, Witham Friary, Nr Frome, Somerset (☎ 074 985 458); County Hall, Taunton, Somerset (☎ 0823 255 023, 255963, fax 0823 255 258, telex 46682)

HEATH, Edward (Peter); OBE (1947); s of Edward Lindsay Heath (d 1957), of Guildford, and Elizabeth Wright (d 1960); gggf pioneered artificial teeth; *b* 6 May 1914; *Educ* St Lawrence Coll Ramsgate; *m* 1953, Eleanor Christian, da of Edwart Francis Peck (d 1949); 1 s (David b 1961), 3 da (Jane b 1955, Pamela b 1956, Jocelyn b 1957); *Career* joined Borneo Co Thailand 1934 (interned 1941-45), asst gen mangr Borneo Co Bangkok 1952-62 (asst mangr 1945-51), md Borneo Co London 1963-67; md Inchcape & Co Ltd 1967-75, (dep chm 1975-79), dir: Mann Egerton & Co Ltd 1973-79, Dodwell & Co Ltd 1974-79, Inchcape Far East 1972-79; chm Toyota GB 1978-79; Order of Orange Nassau 1947, Order of White Elephant 1963, Johore Coronation Medal 1961; *Recreations* hunting, gardening; *Clubs* Boodles; *Style*— Peter Heath, Esq; Cooks Place, Albury, Guildford, Surrey GU5 9BJ (☎ 048641 2698)

HEATH, Rt Hon Edward Richard George; MBE (1946), PC (1955), MP (C) Bexley Sidcup 1974-; s of late William George Heath and his 1 w Edith Annie, *née* Pantony; the family has been traced back in a continuous male line to one William Heath, of Cliston in Blackawton, Devon (d 1546); Mr Heath's f was a builder, his gf a railwayman, his ggf a merchant seaman, his gggf a coastguard, his ggggf a mariner; *b* 9 July 1916; *Educ* Chatham House Sch Ramsgate, Balliol Coll Oxford ; *Career* served WWII RA (Maj 1945, despatches); Lt-Col cmdg 2 Regt HAC (TA) 1947-51; Master Gunner within the Tower of London, 1951-54; admin civil service 1946-47, worked in journalism and merchant banking 1947-50; MP (C) Bexley 1950-74, oppn leader 1965-70 and 1974-75, PM 1970-74; asst oppn whip 1951, lord cmmr Treasury 1951, jt dep chief whip 1952, dep chief whip 1953-55, parly sec Treasy and govt chief whip 1955-59, min Labour 1959-60, lord privy seal with FO responsibilities (negotiating UK entry EEC) 1960-63, sec state Indust, Trade, Regnl Devpt and pres BOT 1963-64; memb of Ind Cmmn on Int Devpt Issues (the Brandt Cmmn 1977-80 Advisory Ctee), chm IRIS 1981-83; chm LSO Tst 1963-70 (memb 1974-), vice-pres Bach Choir 1970-, pres EEC Youth Orch 1977-, hon memb LSO 1974-; lectures: Godkin at Harvard 1968, Cyril Foster Meml Oxford 1965, Montagu Burton Leeds 1976, Edge Princeton 1976, Romanes Oxford 1976, Ishizaka Japan 1979, Felix Neubergh Gothenburg 1979, 10 STC Communication London 1980, Noel Buxton Univ of Essex 1980, Alastair Buchan Meml London 1980; Hoover Univ of Strathclyde 1980; Stanton Griffs Disting, Cornell Univ 1981; Edwin Stevens, RSM, 1981; William Temple, York 1981; City of London, Chartered Insce Inst 1982; John Findley Green, Westminster Coll, Missouri 1982; Mizuno, Tokyo, 1982; ITT European, Brussels, 1982; Bruce Meml, Keele Univ 1982; Gaitskell, Univ of Nottingham 1983; Trinity Univ, San Antonio 1983; lect to mark opening Michael Fowler Centre, Wellington, NZ 1983; Bridge Meml, Guildhall, 1984; David R Calhoun Jr Meml Washington Univ, St Louis 1984; Corbishley Meml RSA 1984; John Rogers Meml Llandudno 1985; George Woodcock, Univ of Leicester 1985; Royal Inst of Int Affairs, Chatham House 1985; Int Peace Lecture, Univ of Manchester 1985; London Business Sch Lecture, Regent's Park 150 Anniversary of the Tamworth Manifesto 1985; 4 Annual John F Kennedy Mem Lectr, Oxford 1986; Employment Inst, Josiah Mason Lectr, Birmingham 1986; The Netherlands Inst for Int Relations 1986; Address to both Houses of the Swiss Parliament, Zurich 1986; Lothian Fndn Lectr 1987, Maitland, Edward Boyle Meml Lectr, Sir John Keswick Meml Lectr; visiting Chubb Fell Yale 1975, Montgomery Fell Dartmouth Coll 1980; Hon DCL Oxford, DTech Bradford, DCL Kent; Hon Doctorate Sorbonne; hon fell Balliol Coll Oxford; Nuffield Coll Oxford, Inst of Devpt Studies at Univ of Sussex; hon FRCM, FRCO and Fell Royal Canadian Coll of Organists, Hon DL Westminster Coll Fulton Missouri; Liveryman Worshipful Co of Goldsmiths, Hon Freeman Musicians' Co; *Books* One Nation: A Tory Approach to Social Problems (co-author 1950), Old World, New Horizons (1970), Sailing-A Course of My Life (1975), Music-A Joy for Life (1976), Travels-People and Places in My Life (1977), Carols-The Joy of Christmas (1977) music - chm London Symphony Orch Tst 1963-70, 1971 conducted Orch in Elgar's 'Cockaigne' Overture at its gala concert in the Royal Festival Hall, London, has since conducted the Orch in London, Cologne and Bonn, also conducted Liverpool Philharmonic Orch, Bournemouth Symphony Orch, the English Chamber Orch, the Thames Chamber Orch and the Sarum Chamber Orch, Berlin Philharmonic Orch, Chicago Symphony Orch, Philadelphia Symphony Orch, Cleveland Symphony Orch, the Minneapolis Symphony orch, the Grand Teton Festival, the Jerusalem Symphony Orch, The Shanghai Philharmonic Orch, the Beijing Central Symphony Orch, the Swiss-Italian Radio Television Symphony Orch and the Zurich Chamber Orch, was instrumental in founding the European Community Youth Orch of which he is pres, and conducted it on its 1978 Easter tour and 1978, 1979 and 1980 Summer tours of Europe. He has also conducted at the World festival of Youth Orchs in Aberdeen in 1977 and 1978, (Freiherr Von Stein Fndn Prize; Charlemagne Prize 1963, Estes J Kefauver Prize 1971; Stresseman Gold Medal 1971; Gold Medal of City of Paris, 1978; World Humanity Award 1980; Gold Medal European Parl); sailing (bought ocean racer 'Morning Cloud' 1969, won Sydney to Hobart race 1969, Capt British team Admiral's Cup 1971 and 1979, Capt British team Sardinia Cup 1980), (winner Sydney to Hobart Ocean Race 1969); *Recreations* music, sailing; *Clubs* Royal Yacht Sqdn, Buck's, Carlton, St Stephen's; *Style*— The Rt Hon Edward Heath, MBE, MP; House of Commons, London SW1A 0AA

HEATH, Lady Emma Cathleen; da of 12 Marquess of Queensberry by his 1 w; *b* 13 Sept 1956; *Educ* Middlesex Poly (BA), RCA (MA); *Career* painter; *Style*— Lady Emma Heath

HEATH, Dr Gordon William; s of Frederick William Heath (b 1971), and Edith Mary, *née* Nelder; *b* 7 Dec 1926; *Educ* Thornbury GS, Durham Univ (BSc), London Univ (PhD, CBiol); *m* 2 Aug 1952, Margaret Patricia, da of Aloyisus Benjamen Cole (d 1951); 1 s (William b 1964), 3 da (Clare b 1955, Sarah b 1960, Helen b 1963); *Career* res scientist (biologist) Rothamstead Experimental Stn 1952-54, 1959-65, Colonial Services (Nyavaland) 1956-59, sr princ sec and offr Natural Environment Res Cncl 1965-78, biol conslt Heath and Ptnrs 1978-; memb Lib Pty Cncl 1982 (nat exec 1984) with Euro Affrs main political interest; vice chm Lib Pty Agric Panel, Govrs Plymouth Poly, chm Devon and Cornwall Lib Pty 1984-87; *Books* Marine Environment Research (ed 1980-86), contributor of numerous sci papers in entomology, soil science and marine biology; books incl: Principles of Agricultural Entomology (with C A Edwards 1964), Future of Man (with J Ebling 1972); *Style*— Dr Gordon W Heath; Taviton Mill House, Tavistock, Devon (☎ (0822) 613560)

HEATH, (Dennis) Ivan (Ewart); s of Joseph Henry Heath (d 1952), of Southend-on-Sea, and Elsie Anne, *née* Moore (d 1943); *b* 20 Nov 1915; *Educ* Sir George Monoux GS, Chelsea Coll of Tech Sci; *m* 16 oct 1939, da of Albert Henry Wakeling (d 1945), of Leigh-on-Sea; *Career* WWII RAF 1941-44: AC2, LAC, PO 1942, Flying Offr 1943, Flt-Lt 1944, Sqdn Ldr 1944; md Perivan Press Ltd 1938, memb Lloyds 1963, jt gp md Williams Lea Gp Ltd 1964-74 (dep gp md 1974-78), ret 1978; hon tres Printers Pension Corp; Freeman City of London, Liveryman Worshipful Co of Stationers and Newspaper Makers; MInstD 1944; *Recreations* golf; *Clubs* RAF Piccadilly; *Style*— Mr

Heath; Acres Gate, 18 Woodsie, Leigh-on-Sea, Essex SS9 4QU (☎ 0702 525 645)

HEATH, John Moore; CMG (1976); s of Philip George Heath (d 1977), and Olga, *née* Sinclair (d 1986); *b* 9 May 1922; *Educ* Shrewsbury Sch, Merton Coll Oxford (MA); *m* 1952, Patricia Bibby; 1 s (Philip), 1 da (Diana); *Career* HM Forces 1942-45, Capt, Inns of Ct Regt (despatches); HM Dip Serv 1950-82: Br consul-gen Chicago 1976-79, HM ambass Chile 1980-82; dir-gen Hispanic and Luso Brazilian Cncl (Canning House) 1982-87; *Recreations* book collecting, walking, Mexican philately; *Clubs* Naval and Military; *Style*— John Heath, Esq, CMG; 6 Cavendish Cres, Bath BA1 2UG, Avon (☎ 0225 21181)

HEATH, Sir Mark Evelyn; KCVO (1980), CMG (1980); s of Capt John Moore Heath, RN and Hilary Grace Stuart nee Salter; *b* 22 May 1927; *Educ* Marlborough, Queens' Cambridge; *m* 1954, Margaret Alice, da of Sir Lawrence Bragg, OBE, MC, CH (d 1971); 2 s, 1 da; *Career* RNV(S)R 1945-49; HM Dip Serv 1950-85, Br ambass to Vatican 1982-85 (upgraded from representation as min which rank held from 1980), inspr FCO 1978-80, head W African Dept FCO and ambass Chad 1975-78, on secondment to Cabinet Office 1974-75, dep head UK Delgn to OECD 1971-74, formerly served, Jakarta, Copenhagen, Sofia, Ottawa ; dir protocol Hong Kong Govt 1985-88; Chm Friends of the Anglican Centre, Rome; *Clubs* Athenaeum, Nikaian; *Style*— Sir Mark Heath; Drummonds Branch, Royal Bank of Scotland, 49 Charing Cross, London SW1A 2DX

HEATH, Air Marshal Sir Maurice Lionel; KBE (1962, OBE 1946), CB (1957), CVO (1978), DL (West Sussex 1977); s of late H Lionel Heath (princ Mayo Sch of Arts, Lahore, India) and Maggie, *née* Forsyth; *b* 12 August 1909; *Educ* Sutton Valence Sch, RAF Coll Cranwell; *m* 1938, Kathleen Mary (d 1988), da of Boaler Gibson, of Bourne Lincs; 1 s (James), 1 da (Julia); *Career* joined RAF 1927, served in Nos 16 and 28 Sqdns 1929-32, specialist armament duties 1933-43, OC Bomber Station 5 Gp Bomber Cmd 1944-45 (despatches), dep to Dir Gen Armament Air Miny 1946-48, CO Central Gunnery Sch 1948-49, sr Air Liaison Offr Wellington NZ 1950-52, CO Bomber Cmd Bombing Sch 1952-53, Air Cdre 1953, idc 1954; Dir Gen Plans Air Miny 1955, Dep Air Sec 1955-57; Air V-Marshal 1956, Cdr Br Forces Arabian Peninsula 1957-59, Cmdt RAF Staff Coll Bracknell 1959-62, Air Marshal 1962, COS Allied Air Forces Central Europe 1962-65, ret 1965; chief hon steward Westminster Abbey 1964-74; Gentleman Usher to HM the Queen 1966-79, Extra Gentleman Usher 1979-; dir Boyd and Boyd Estate Agents 1971-76; memb Cncl Offrs Pension Soc 1974-83; King's Coll Hosp appeal dir 1977-79, appeal conslt Voluntary Res Tst King's Coll Hosp and Med Sch 1979-84; private agent Henderson Fin Mgmnt 1980-88; *Recreations* sailing, golf, gardening, travel; *Clubs* RAF, W Sussex Golf, Sussex; *Style*— Air Marshal Sir Maurice Heath, KBE, CB, CVO, DL; Heronscroft, Rambledown Lane, W Chiltington, Pulborough, W Sussex RH20 2NW (☎ 079 83 2131)

HEATH, (Bryan) Michael; s of (George) Bryan Stevens Heath, of Buckingham, and Euphemia, *née* Wilson; *b* 16 June 1944; *Educ* Keswick Sch, Manchester Univ (BSc); *m* 4 Dec 1976, Patricia Jane Margaret, da of Francis Johnston, of Bedford; 1 da (Jane Mary Felicity b 1979); *Career* analyst Esso Petroleum 1965-67, ptnr Arthur Andersen and Co 1977 (joined 1967); *Style*— Michael Heath, Esq; Putney, London SW15; Olney, Bucks; Arthur Andersen & Co, 2 Arundel St, London WC2R 3LT (☎ 01 438 3316, fax 01 831 1133, telex 8812711)

HEATH, Michael Robert; s of George Ernest Heath (d 1988), and Kathleen Mary *née* Van Der Pant (d 1980); *b* 9 Nov 1937; *Educ* Fernden Sch, Hurstpierpoint Coll; *m* 1, 1967 (m dis 1986), Judith Susan Heath; 3 s (Benjamin Elliot b 29 Nov 1968, Oliver Gideon b 30 April 1970, Samuel Barnaby b 1 Aug 1971); m2, 1 Sept 1987, Lucinda Rosslyn Heath da of Frank Arnold Instone of Tunbridge Wells;; *Career* md Smith New Court plc; memb stock exchange; *Recreations* skiing, windsurfing, sub-aqua; *Style*— Michael Heath, Esq; Chetwynd House, 24 St Swithins Lane, London EC4N 8AE (☎ 01 626 1544)

HEATH, Samuel Bonython; s of Denis William Heath (d 1983), of S Aust; *b* 11 Feb 1938; *Educ* Rugby; *m* 1981, Bobbi, da of Thomas Cruickshanks; 3 children; *Career* Nat Service RAF; chm and md Samuel Heath and Sons plc 1970- (jt md 1963-70); *Recreations* travel, languages, jazz; *Style*— Samuel Heath Esq; Churchill Glebe, Churchill, Spetchley, nr Worcester (☎ 090 565 640)

HEATH-STUBBS, John Francis Alexander; OBE (1989); s of Francis Heath-Stubbs (d 1938), and Edith Louise Sara, *née* Marr (d 1972); *b* 9 July 1918; *Educ* Bembridge Sch, Worcester Coll for the Blind, Queen's Coll Oxford (BA, MA); *Career* english master The Hall Sch Hampstead 1944, ed asst Hutchinsons 1944-45, Gregory fell in poetry Univ of Leeds 1952-55, visiting prof in english Univ of Ann Arbor Michigan 1960-61, lectr in english Coll of St Mark & St John Chelsea 1962-72, non-stipendary lectr Merton Coll Oxford 1972-; Queen's Medal for Poetry 1973; memb: English Assoc, Folklore Soc, Poetry Soc, Omar Khayyan Soc (pres 1989-90); FRSL; *Style*— John Heath-Stubbs, Esq, OBE; 35 Sutherland Place, London W2 5BZ

HEATHCOAT-AMORY, Hon Mrs (Angela Jane); *née* Borwick); eldest da of 4 Baron Borwick, MC, *qv*; *b* 12 July 1955; *Educ* St David's Convent; *m* 1988, Charles William Heathcoat-Amory, 2 s of Sir William Heathcoat-Amory, 5 Bt, DSO (d 1982); *Career* trainer of competition horses; *Style*— The Hon Mrs Heathcoat-Amory; Pound House, Krowstone, South Molton, Devon

HEATHCOAT-AMORY, David Philip; MP (C) Wells 1983-; s of Brig Roderick Heathcoat Amory, and Sonia Heathcoat Amory; *b* 21 Mar 1949; *Educ* Eton, Christ Church Oxford (MA); *m* 1978, Linda Adams; 2 s, 1 da; *Career* CA, asst fin dir Br Technol Gp 1980-83; contested (C) Brent S 1979, PPS to Home Sec 1987-88, asst whip; FCA; *Recreations* walking, talking; *Style*— David Heathcoat-Amory, Esq, MP; House of Commons, London SW1

HEATHCOAT-AMORY, Sir Ian; 6 Bt (UK 1874), of Knightshayes Court, Tiverton, Devon; JP, DL (Devon 1981); s of Sir William Heathcoat-Amory, 5 Bt, DSO (d 1982), by his w Margaret, da of Col Sir Arthur Doyle, 4 Bt, JP (d 1948); *b* 3 Feb 1942; *Educ* Eton; *m* 1972, Frances Louise, da of Jocelyn Francis Brian Pomeroy (gggs of 4 Viscount Harberton); 4 s; *Heir* s, William Francis Heathcoat-Amory b 19 July 1975; *Style*— Sir Ian Heathcoat-Amory, Bt, JP, DL; Calverleigh Court, Tiverton, Devon

HEATHCOAT-AMORY, Hon Mrs; Hon Margaret Irene Gaenor; JP (1968); da of 8 Baron Howard de Walden (d 1945); *b* 2 June 1919; *Educ* Benenden; *m* 1938, Richard Frank, s of Lt Col Harry William Ludovic Heathcoat-Amory (d 1945); 1 s, 2 da; *Career* parly candidate (Lab) contested Taunton 1964 and 1966; *Style*— The Hon Mrs Heathcoat-Amory, JP; 78 Elm Park Rd, London SW3 (☎ 01 352 2318)

HEATHCOAT-AMORY, Margaret, Lady; Margaret Isabella Dorothy Evelyn; yr da of Sir Arthur Doyle, 4 Bt, JP, sometime ADC to Prince Edward of Saxe Weimar, by his w Joyce, da of Hon Greville Howard (himself 2 s of 17 Earl of Suffolk and (10 of) Berkshire); *b* 1907; *Educ* privately; *m* 1933, Lt-Col Sir William Heathcoat-Amory, 5 Bt, DSO (d 1982), sometime memb Queen's Bodyguard of Hon Corps of Gentlemen-at-Arms; 2 s (6 Bt, Ian), 2 da (Mrs Peter Sichel, Mrs David Cavender); *Style*— Margaret, Lady Heathcoat-Amory; 14 Pomeroy Rd, Tiverton, Devon (☎ 0884 254033)

HEATHCOAT-AMORY, Michael FitzGerald; only s of Maj Edgar Heathcoat-Amory (gs of Sir John Heathcoat-Amory, 1 Bt, JP, DL) by his w Sonia, da of Capt Edward Conyngham Denison, MVO, RN (whose f Henry was s of 1 Baron Londesborough by his 2 w, and half-bro of 1 Earl of Londesborough); *b* 2 Oct 1941; *Educ* Eton, Christ Church Oxford; *m* 1, 1965 (m dis 1970), Harriet Mary Sheila, da of Lt-Gen Sir Archibald Nye, GCSI, GCMG, GCIE, KCB, KBE, MC (d 1967); 1 s (Edward); m 2, 1975, Arabella, da of late Raimund von Hofmannstahl, and formerly w of Piers de Westenholz; 2 da (Lucy, Jessica); *Career* dir: Harraps Ltd, The River Plate and General Investmt Tst plc; farmer; chm London and Devonshire Tst; High Sheriff of Devon 1985-86; *Clubs* Bucks, Pratts; *Style*— Michael Heathcoat-Amory, Esq; Chevithorne Barton, Tiverton, Devon; 2 Montrose Ct, London SW

HEATHCOAT-AMORY, Brig Roderick; MC; s of Sir Ian Murray Heathcoat-Amory; *b* 30 Jan 1907; *Educ* Eton; *m* 1947, Sonia Myrtle, da of late Cdre E C Denison; 1 s, 1 da (and 2 step children); *Career* Brig; served: Palestine, Syria, N Africa, Italy, NW Europe; High Sheriff Yorks 1971; *Recreations* outdoor sports; *Clubs* Cavalry and Guards; *Style*— Brig Roderick Heathcoat-Amory, MC; Allington Grange, nr Chippenham, Wilts SN14 6LW (☎ 0249 658 013)

HEATHCOTE, Brig Sir Gilbert Simon; 9 Bt (GB 1733), CBE (Mil 1964, MBE 1945); s of Lt-Col Robert E M Heathcote, DSO (d 1969), of Manton Hall, Rutland (he was gggs of Sir Gilbert Heathcote, 3 Bt, MP, who was gs of Sir Gilbert Heathcote, 1 Bt, one of the originators of the Bank of England and Lord Mayor of London 1711, also bro of Samuel, ancestor of Heathcote, Bt of Hursley) and Edith Millicent Heathcote (d 1977); suc kinsman, 3 Earl of Ancaster, 8 Bt, KCVO, TD, JP, DL, who d 1983; *b* 21 Sept 1913; *Educ* Eton; *m* 1, 1939 (m dis 1984), Patricia Margaret, da of Brig James Leslie, MC, of Sway, Hants; 1 s, 1 da; m 2, Ann Mellor, widow of Brig J F C Mellor, DSO, OBE; *Heir* s, Mark Simon Robert Heathcote, *qv*; *Career* 2 Lt RA 1933, served WW II NW Europe, Lt-Col 1953, Brig 1960, COS Mid E Cmd 1962-64, Brig RA Scottish Cmd 1964-66, ret 1966; *Recreations* sailing, skiing, equitation; *Clubs* Army and Navy, Royal Yacht Squadron, Royal Cruising; *Style*— Brig Sir Gilbert S Heathcote, Bt, CBE; The Coach House, Tillington, nr Petworth, Sussex

HEATHCOTE, Mark Simon Robert; OBE (1988); s and h of Brig Sir Gilbert Simon Heathcote, 9 Bt, CBE, *qv*, and Patricia Margaret Lady Heathcote, *née* Leslie *qv*; *b* 1 Mar 1941; *Educ* Eton, Magdalene Coll Cambridge (BA); *m* 1976, Susan, da of Lt Col George Ashley, of Torquay (d 1963); 2 s (Alastair b 1977, Nicholas b 1979); *Career* Peninsular and Orient Steamship Co 1963-70; Dip Serv; 1 sec: Athens, Buenos Aires; *Recreations* water sports; *Style*— Mark Heathcote, Esq; c/o Upton Dean, Upton, nr Andover, Hants; Foreign and Commonwealth Office, London SW1

HEATHCOTE, Sir Michael Perryman; 11 Bt (GB 1733); s of Sir Leonard Vyvyan Heathcote, 10 Bt (d 1963); in remainder to the Earldom of Macclesfield; *b* 7 August 1927; *Educ* Winchester, Clare Cambridge; *m* 2 June 1956, Victoria, da of Cdr James Edward Rickards Wilford, RD, RNR, of Ackland Cottage, Shirley Holms, Lymington, Hants; 2 s, 1 da; *Heir* s, Timothy Heathcote; *Career* 2 Lt 9 Lancers; farmer; *Style*— Sir Michael Heathcote, Bt; Warborne Farm, Boldre, Lymington, Hants (☎ Lymington 73478); Carie and Carwhin, Lawers, by Aberfeldy, Perthshire

HEATHCOTE, Michael Ryley; s of Col Lewis Heathcote, DL (d 1975), of York; *b* 23 Sept 1934; *Educ* Felsted; *m* 1961, Sally, da of Gilbert Burton (d 1975), of Brough, E Yorks; 4 children; *Career* corporate financier; former dir: Allied Plant Gp plc, Allied Residential plc, London and Foreign Investmt Tst plc; chm Humberside Industl Tst Ltd and Wightwood Industs Ltd; *Recreations* cricket; *Clubs* MCC, Farmers', Lloyds; *Style*— Michael Heathcote, Esq; Westgate House, North Cave, E Yorks HU15 2NJ (☎ 043 02 2481)

HEATHCOTE, Timothy Gilbert; s and h of Sir Michael Perryman Heathcote, 11 Bt; *b* 25 May 1957; *Style*— Timothy Heathcote Esq

HEATHER, Kenneth Thomas; s of Capt Thomas William Heather, MC (d 1968), and Marjorie, *née* Williams (d 1977); *b* 29 May 1921; *Educ* Uppingham, Jesus Coll Cambridge (BA, MA); *m* 12 June 1954, (Constance) Olive, da of James Findlay (d 1968); 1 s (Peter b 1958), 1 da (Kaeren b 1960); *Career* WWII serv: temp actg Sub Lt (Special Branch) RNVR 1942, trg HMS Victory, temp Sub Lt (Special Branch) RNVR 1942-43, HMS Belfast Russian Convoys NW Approachers, HMS Faulkner (8 Destroyer Flotilla) 1943, Salerno an Anzio landings Invasion of Sicily, HMS Grenville (25 Destroyer Flotilla) 1944, DDay Landings, Br Pacific Fleet land posting Sydney and Hong Kong 1945-46, demobbed 1947; GEC Res Laboratories Wembley 1947-49 (responsible for first radio tv link London to Birmingham), asst mangr special projects GEC Head Off 1950-60, sales mangr Elliott Automation & Tally Ltd 1960-71; Pragma Ltd: dir 1971-79, chm and md 1979-88, ret and sold co 1988; Freeman City of London, Liveryman Worshipful Co of Playing Card Makers; MIEE, CEng 1960, MBIM 1965; *Recreations* DIY, rambling; *Clubs* Naval; *Style*— Kenneth Heather, Esq; 33 Westbury Road, Northwood, Middx (☎ 09274 23474)

HEATHER, Stanley Frank; CBE (1980); s of Charles Heather (d 1954), of Ilford, Essex, and Jessie, *née* Powney (d 1953); *b* 8 Jan 1917; *Educ* privately, Downhills Sch, London Univ; *m* 11 March 1946, Janet Roxburgh (Bunty), da of William Adams, (d 1951) of 2 Croft Park, Craigie, Perth, Scotland; 1 s (Gerald Roxburgh b Jan 1949), 1 da (Gillean Alison Elsie b Aug 1951); *Career* WWII 1939-45, cmmnd RAC 1941, served Burma and India; slr 1959; in private practice Horsham 1959-63; legal advsr City of London Police Force 1974-80, comptroller and city slr Corpn of London 1974-80 (dep comptroller 1968-74, asst slr 1963-68); as comptroller was hon slr to: Museum of London, City Arts Tst, City, Educnl Tsts Fund, City Archaeological Tst Fund, Sir WM Coxon Tst Fund, William Lambe Charity (tstee), Sir John Langham Tst Fund, The Wilson Tst, Leonidas Alcibiades Oldfield Charity, The City Almshouse Charities; attorney and gen counsel to City of London (Arizona) Corpn; Freeman: City of London (1965), Liveryman Worshipful Co of Slrs 1965; Hon Liveryman Worshipful Co: of Clothworkers, of Engrs 1983; FRSA 1981; *Recreations* golf, fishing; *Clubs* City Livery, Guildhall; *Style*— S F Heather, Esq, CBE; Kinnoull, 14 Morrell Avenue, Horsham, West Sussex RH12 4DD (☎ 0403 60 109)

HEATLEY, Norman George; OBE (1978); s of Maj Thomas George Heatley (d 1957), of Marton Place, Woodbridge, Suffolk, and Grace Alice, *née* Symonds (d 1958); *b* 10 Jan 1911; *Educ* Tonbridge, Cambridge Univ (MA, PhD); *m* 18 Dec 1944, Mercy Irene, da of Geoffrey Bing (d 1952), of Rockport, Craigavad, Co Down; 3 s (Christopher George b 23 Jan 1950, Geoffrey Piers b 1952 d 1955, Jonathan Patrickb 13 Feb 1956), 2 da (Rose b 5 Feb 1948, Tamsin b 6 Sept 1957); *Career* res biochemist Sir Wm Dunn Sch of Pathology Oxford 1936-78; worked on: micro methods, penicillin (with W H Florey), microbial problems, secretin, pancreozymin; Nuffield res fell Lincoln Coll Oxford 1950-79, Hon Fell Lincoln Coll 1982; *Recreations* gardening, gadgetry, sailing; *Style—* Norman Heatley, Esq, OBE; 12 Oxford Road, Old Marston, Oxford OX3 0PQ (☎ 0865 248588)

HEATLY, Peter; CBE (1971), DL (1984); s of Robert Heatly (d 1968), and Margaret Ann, *née* Sproull (d 1955); *b* 9 May 1924; *Educ* Leith Acad, Edinburgh Univ (BSc); *m* 1, 1948 (m dis), Jean Robertha Johnston; da of William B Hermiston; 2 s (Peter b 19 55, Robert b 1958), 2 da (Ann b 1949, Jane b 1951); m 2, Mae Calder; *Career* civil engr - dir Peter Heatly & Co Ltd 1958-; chm: Scottish Sports Cncl 1975-87, Cwlth Games Fedn 1982- (Cwlth Diving Champion: 1950, 1954, 1958), Scottish Exhibition Centre 1984-; *Clubs* New (Edinburgh); *Style—* Peter Heatly Esq, CBE, DL; Lanrig, Balerno, Edinburgh EH14 7AJ (☎ 031 449 3998); 45 Castle St, Edinburgh (☎ 031 225 2299)

HEATON; *see*: Henniker-Heaton

HEATON, Maj Basil Hugh Philips; s of Cdr Hugh Edward Heaton JP, DL (d 1964), and Gwendoline Margaret, *née* Philips, CBE, TD (d 1979); *b* 23 Dec 1923; *Educ* Shrewsbury, Queen's Univ Belfast; *m* 1, 30 June 1958, Bronwyn, (d 1978), da of BCH Poole (d 1971), of Sydney NSW; 3 da (Sara Margaret b 28 April 1956, Julia Mary b 2 Aug 1959, Victoria Bronwyn b 5 July 1971, d 1979); m 2, 22 Nov 1979, Jennifer, da of Sir Francis Williams, of Denbigh; *Career* WWII cmmnd RA 1943, served BLA (landed on D Day); serv: Japan, Hong Kong, Malaya, Korea 1951-53; Staff Coll 1956, ret 1965; landowner and dairy farmer; chm and pres: Flintshire NFU, Flintshire CLA; High Sheriff Flintshire 1971; *Books* A Short History of Rhual (1987); *Recreations* shooting, fishing; *Clubs* Naval & Military; *Style—* Maj Basil Heaton, MBE; Rhual, Mold, Clywd CH7 5DB (☎ 0352 700457)

HEATON, Very Rev Eric William; s of late Robert William Heaton, and late Ella Mabel, *née* Brear; *b* 15 Oct 1920; *Educ* Ermysted's Skipton, Christ's Coll Cambridge (MA); *m* 1951, Rachel Mary, da of late Rev Charles Harold Dodd, CH, FBA; 2 s (Jeremy Paul William b 1952, Nicholas Giles b 1968), 2 da (Anne Caroline b 1954, Josephine Charlotte b 1960); *Career* dean of Ch Ch Oxford 1979-, pro-vice-chllr Oxford Univ 1984-; hon fell: Champlain Coll Univ of Trent Ontario Canada 1973-, St John's Coll Oxford 1979, Christ's Coll Cambridge 1983; *Publications* His Servants the Prophets (1949), The Old Testament Prophets (1958, 1977), The Book of Daniel (1956), Everday Life in Old Testament Times (1956), Commentary of the Sunday Lessons (1959), The Hebrew Kingdoms (1968), Solomon's New Men (1974); *Style—* The Very Rev Eric Heaton; The Deanery, Christ Church, Oxford OX1 1DP (☎ 0865 276162, office: 0865 276161)

HEATON, Lady Jane; *née* Butler; da of 6 Marquess of Ormonde, CVO, MC (d 1971); *b* 1925; *m* 1945 (m dis 1952), Lt Peter Heaton, RNVR; 1 s; *Style—* Lady Jane Heaton; La Chapelle St Jean, La Garde Freinet, Var, France

HEATON, Naomi Claire Helen; *née* Jarrett; da of Dr Boaz Antony Jarrett, of 43 Strand on the Green, Chiswick, London, and Patricia Evelyn *née* White; *b* 11 Sept 1955; *Educ* Walthamstow Hall Sch for Girls, St Hilda's Coll Oxford (BA); *m* 18 March 1988, Mark Frederick Heaton, s of Peter Heaton (d 1964), of Ampney St Mary Manor, Ampney St Mary, Cirencester, Gloucs; *Career* graduate trainee Leo Burnett Advertising 1977-82, appt main bd Saatchi & Saatchi Advertising 1984 (joined 1982), main bd dir Young & Rubicam 1985-86; estab: Manor Properties 1986-, The Frederick Co Ltd 1988-, Lowerfield Rentals Ltd (property rental co) 1989-; memb Ampney St Mary Parish Cncl; *Recreations* skiing, horse racing; *Clubs* Boodles; *Style—* Mrs Mark Heaton; 18 Salisbury Place, London W1 (☎ 01 935 5016); Manor Farm, Ampney St Mary, Cirencester, Gloucs (☎ 0285 85 321)

HEATON, (Ralph) Neville; CB (1951); s of Ernest Heaton (d 1951), of Greenford Middx, and (Gertrude Lilian) Dorothy, *née* Lavelle (d 1973); *b* 4 June 1912; *Educ* Westminster Sch, Ch Ch Oxford (BA, MA); *m* 1939, Cecily Margaret, da late of Dr George Herbert Alabaster, MD, FRCS, of Queenstown, S Africa; 3 s (Nicholas, Martin, Stephen), 1 da (Priscilla); *Career* civil servant; dep sec: Miny of Educn 1954-61 (under sec 1946-53), Miny of Tport 1961-68, Dept of Econ Affrs 1968-69, Miny of Housing and Local Govt 1969-70, DOE 1971-72, ret; Cwlth Fund fell 1951-52; *Style—* Neville Heaton Esq, CB; Rossmore, 38 Manor Park Ave, Princes Risborough, Bucks HP17 9AS

HEATON, Noel Thomas; *Educ* Manchester Coll of Technol; *m* 1, 1946, Sheila Mary, *née* McAndry; 1 da; m 2, 1983, Maria, *née* Kukulska; *Career* dir mktg: Wickman Machine Tools Ltd UK 1970-79 (USA 1976-82, France 1976-82, John Brown Machine Tool Div 1980-82), conslt Telford Devpt Corpn 1982-; *Recreations* special constabulary (div cmdt Warwicks, ret); *Style—* Noel Heaton Esq; 21 Convent Close, Kenilworth, Warwicks CV8 2FQ (☎ 0926 53598)

HEATON, Stuart Michael; s of Arthur Heaton (d 1965); *b* 29 May 1924; *Educ* Ledbury GS Herefords; *Career* WWII, Flt Lt Bomber Cmd 1944-45; dir Alfred Herbert India Ltd 1947-58, chm and md Ciro plc (joined 1964); *Recreations* having nothing to do; *Clubs* Oriental; *Style—* Stuart Heaton, Esq; 6 Daleham Gdns, Hampstead, London NW3 5DA (☎ 01 794 0893); Ciro Pearls Ltd, 178 Regent St, London W1R 6AS (☎ 01 734 7631)

HEATON WATSON, Richard Barrie; s of Kenneth Walter Heaton Watson, (d 1981), of Albufeira, Portugal, and Jean Alexandra, *née* Harvey (d 1958); *b* 29 April 1945; *Educ* Harrow, Queen's Univ Belfast (BA), Cambridge Univ (PGCE); *m* 29 July 1978, Caroline Ann, da of Leonard Cyril Mckane, MBE, *qv*, of Ampney St Peter, Glos; 1 s (Dominic b 1982), 2 da (Lucy b 1979, Fenella b 1987); *Career* head of dept Charterhouse 1975-84, housemaster Weekites 1985-; GA (1971); *Recreations* antiques, theatre, skiing; *Clubs* 1900, Golf Soc of GB; *Style—* Richard Heaton Watson, Esq; 20 Bywater St, London SW3 4XD; Brooke Hall, Charterhouse, Godalming, Surrey GU7 2DX (☎ 0483 426808)

HEATON-ARMSTRONG, Anthony Eustace John; s of William Henry Dunamace Heaton-Armstrong, of 1 Blandys Lane, Upper Basildon, Nr Pangbourne, Berks, and Idonea, *née* Chance; *b* 27 Sept 1950; *Educ* Ampleforth Coll, Bristol Univ (LLB); *m* 1, 10 Feb 1973 (m dis 1977), Susan *née* Allnutt; m2, 20 May 1982, Anne Frances, da of Ethel Robigo of The Lodge, Kings Walden, Hitchin, Herts; 1 s (John William b 15 Feb 1983), 2 da (Eleanor b 8 May 1985, Celestine b 3 Sept 1988); *Career* barr practice 1973-; memb of 'Justice', tstee Aldo Tst, former chm Nat Assoc of Prison Visitors; *Recreations* gardening, the countryside; *Clubs* Garrick; *Style—* Anthony Heaton-Armstrong, Esq; 3 Paper Buildings, Temple, London EC4 (☎ 01 353 6208)

HEATON-ARMSTRONG, Bridget Almina Suzanne; MBE (1988); da of Sir John Heaton-Armstrong (d 1967), of 46 Carlisle Mansions, Carlisle Place, SW1, and Suzanne Laura, *née* Bechet de Balan; *b* 9 August 1920; *Career* L/72 voluntary aid detachment Br Red Cross Soc; hosp nurse: Red Cross 1939-42, St Bart's Hosp 1942-44; organiser hosp car serv 1944-46, Cmdt L/72 1944-48, awarded Def Medal 1939-43; sec Victoria League for Cwlth Friendship 1948-53, pa Earl Marshal's Office 1953, awarded Queen Elizabeth II Coronation Medal 1953, asst home sec Royal UK Benevolent Assoc 1957-62, int sec nat Assoc of Youth Clubs 1964-70, advsr Citizen Advice Bureau 1972-80; chm Kensington and Chelsea Arthritus Care, res asst radio therapy dept Royal Marsden Hosp, life govr and memb Royal UK Benevolent Assoc, key memb Cancerlink Wimbledon branch; *Style—* Miss Bridget Heaton-Armstrong

HEATON-WARD, Dr (William) Alan; s of 2 Lt Ralph Heaton-Ward (d 1921), of Durham City, and Mabel, *née* Orton (d 1964); *b* 19 Dec 1919; *Educ* Queen Elizabeth's Hosp Clifton Bristol, Univ of Bristol (MB, ChB, DPM); *m* 28 March 1945, Christine Edith, da of Maj David Fraser, RHA, DSO, MC (d 1943), of Nairn, Scotland; 2 da (Nicola (Mrs Kennedy), Lindsay (Mrs Maldini)); *Career* Local Def Volunteers and HG 1940-41, surgn/Lt-Cdr and neuropsychiatrist Nore Cmd RNVR 1946-48; dep med supt Hortham/Brentry Hosp Gp Bristol 1950-54, clinical teacher in mental health Univ of Bristol 1954-78; Stoke Park Hosp Gp Bristol: med supt 1954-61, hon conslt 1978-; Lord Chllr's med visitor Ct of Protection 1978, Blake Marsh lectr RCPsych 1976, Burden Res gold medal and prize 1978; Br Cncl visiting lectr Portugal 1971, vice pres RCPsych 1976-78, pres Br Soc for Study of Mental Subnormality 1978-79, vice pres Fortune Centre Riding for the Disabled 1980-; memb: advsy cncl Radio Bristol 1985-88, Police Liaison ctee 1988-; FRCPsych 1971; memb: Bristol Medico-Legal Soc, Bristol Medico-Chirurgical Soc, BMA; hon memb American Assoc of Physician Analysts 1978; *Books* Notes on Mental Deficiency (3 edn 1955), Mental Subnormality (4 edn 1975), Left Behind (1978), Mental Handicap (jtly 1984); *Recreations* following all forms of sport, asking "Why", gardening; *Clubs* Bristol Savages, Bristol FC; *Style—* Dr Alan Heaton-Ward; Flat 2, 38 Apsley Rd, Clifton, Bristol BS8 2SS (☎ 0272 738971)

HEAVENER, Rt Rev Robert William; s of Joseph Heavener and Maria Heavener; *b* 28 Feb 1906; *Educ* Trinity Coll Dublin (MA); *m* 1936, Ada Marjorie, da of Rev Chancellor Thomas Dagg; 1 s, 1 da; *Career* ordained 1929, archdeacon of Clogher 1968-73, bishop of Clogher 1973-80, ret; *Style—* The Rt Rev Robert Heavener; c/o The See House, Thornfield, Fivemiletown, Co Tyrone (☎ Fivemiletown 265)

HEBBLETHWAITE, Harold; s of late John Hebblethwaite, and late Mary, *née* Backhouse; *b* 14 June 1914; *m* 27 April 1940, Kathleen, da of late Bernard Bray; 1 s (Neil b 1945); 1 da (Kay b 1942); *Career* CA 1940-; chm: Rockingham Gp 1959-, Wincro Gp 1966-, RDB Freight Lines Gp 1966-, Burgon & Ball Ltd 1971-82; cncllr City of Sheffield 1955: ldr Cons gp 1963, alderman 1966, ldr of cncl 1968-69, Lord Mayor 1971-72; ldr Cons gp S Yorks CC 1974, ret from local politics 1977; JP 1966 (Sheffield Bench); FCA 1940, ACIS 1938; *Recreations* gardening, travel; *Style—* Harold Hebblethwaite, Esq; Beaucrest, Newfield Lane, Dore, Sheffield S17 3DD (☎ 0742 363928); Belmayne House, Clarkehouse Road, Sheffield (☎ 0742 664518, fax 0742 683842)

HEBBLETHWAITE, Richard Jeremy; TD; s of Lt-Col Roger Vavasour Hebblethwaite, MC (d 1976); *b* 5 Dec 1933; *Educ* Wellington, Nottingham Univ; *m* 1, 1966, Sara Elizabeth, da of James Stucker Offutt; 2 children; m 2, 1988, Josceline Mary Morley-Fletcher, da of Sir Harry Phillimore, OBE; *Career* Nat Serv 2 LT 2 RHA; Capt TA; dir Save & Prosper Gp 1969-87 (fin and mktg advsr 1987-); memb: organising ctee Mktg Investmt Bd 1985-86, Norman Fowlers Pension Advsy Gp 1986-87, Occupational Pensions Bd 1987-; FCA; *Recreations* sailing, gardening, golf; *Clubs* City, New (Edinburgh); *Style—* Jeremy Hebblethwaite, Esq, TD; 89 Cornwall Gardens, London SW7 4AX

HEBER-PERCY, Algernon Eustace Hugh; DL (Shropshire 1986); s of Brig Algernon George William Heber-Percy, DSO (d 1961), of Hodnet Hall, and Daphne Wilma Kenyon, *née* Parker Bowles; *b* 2 Jan 1944; *Educ* Harrow; *m* 6 July 1966, Hon Margaret Jane, *née* Lever, yst da of 3 Viscount Leverhulme, KG, TD; 1 s ((Algernon) Thomas Lever b 29 Jan 1984), 3 da (Emily Jane b 19 Feb 1969, Lucy Ann b 29 Dec 1970, Sophie Daphne b 22 Jan 1979); *Career* Lt Grenadier Gds 1962-66; farmer; vice-chm ctee Mercian region Nat Tst; chm Prince's and Royal Jubilee Tst for Shropshire; memb ctee Walker Tst; chm Pynes and Lyneal Tst; memb Historic Houses Gardens Ctee; Fell Woodard Schs; High Sheriff of Shropshire 1987; *Recreations* gardening, shooting, fishing ; *Clubs* Cavalry and Guards'; *Style—* Algernon Heber-Percy, Esq, DL; Hodnet Hall, Hodnet, Market Drayton, Shropshire TF9 3NN (☎ 063 084 202)

HEBER-PERCY, Lady Dorothy; *née* Lygon; 4 and yst da of 7 Earl Beauchamp (d 1938); *b* 22 Feb 1912; *m* 1985, as his 2 w, Robert Vernon Heber-Percy (d 1987), 4 and yst s of Maj Algernon Heber-Percy, JP, DL (d 1911), of Hodnet Hall, Salop; *Career* late section offr WAAF; *Style—* Lady Dorothy Heber-Percy; Lime Tree Cottage, 7 Coach Lane, Faringdon, Oxford SN7 8AB

HEBER-PERCY, Hon Mrs (Margaret Jane); *née* Lever; DL (Shropshire 1986); da of 3 Viscount Leverhulme, KG, TD; *b* 1947; *m* 1966, Algernon Eustace Hugh Heber-Percy; 1 s, 3 da; *Heir* Allgernon Thomas Lever, b Jan 1984; *Career* (AEHH) Harrow; Lt Grenadier Gds; High Sheriff 1987; memb regnl ctee Nat Tst; chm Shropshire Ctee Royal Jubilee Tsts; *Recreations* gardening, shooting, fishing; *Clubs* Guards and Cavalry; *Style—* The Hon Mrs Heber-Percy; Hodnet Hall, Market Drayton, Shropshire

HECKENDORN, Hon Mrs (Roselle Sarah); *née* Bruce-Gardyne; o da of Baron Bruce-Gardyne (Life Peer); *b* 7 Dec 1959; *Educ* St Paul's Girls' Sch, Durham Univ; *m* 26 Sept 1978, David Heckendorn, o s of C H Heckendorn, of Beaux Arts Village, Washington, USA; *Style—* The Hon Mrs Heckendorn; 13 Kelso Place, London W8

HECKS, Malcolm; s of Ronald Frederick Hecks, of Chippenham, Wilts, and Ivy, *née* Rose (d 1962); *b* 5 Dec 1942; *Educ* Chippenham GS, Univ of Bath (BSc, BArch); *m* 12 Aug 1967, Donna Leslie, da of Robert Leslie Pratt, of Cape Town, SA; 1 s (Oliver Lewis Ledoux b 1978), 1 da (Alexandra Sophie Ivy b 1975); *Career* conslt architect; sr ptnr Malcolm Hecks Assocs Godalming Surrey 1970-; designed World Wildlife HQ Bldg

Godalming 1982; FRIBA 1971, MBIM 1978, FFAS 1985; *Recreations* music, theatre, travel, films, history of art and architecture, ecology; *Style—* Malcolm Hecks, Esq; Nat West Bank plc, Syon Lane Corner, Gt West Road, Isleworth, Middx TW7 5NR; The Tower, 145/147 High Street, Godalming, Surrey GU7 1AF (☎ 04868 27466, fax 04868 24335)

HECTOR, Gordon Matthews; CMG (1966), CBE (1961, OBE 1955); s of George Pittendrigh Hector (d 1962), of 51 Forest Rd, Aberdeen, and Helen Elizabeth, *née* Matthews (d 1963); *b* 9 June 1918; *Educ* St Mary's Sch Melrose, Edinburgh Acad, Lincoln Coll Oxford (MA); *m* 28 Aug 1954, Mary Forrest, da of Robert Gray (d 1933); 1 s (Alistair b 5 Oct 1955), 2 da (Jean b 30 April 1957, Katy b 12 Oct 1961); *Career* cmmnd RASC 1939, served with East Africa Forces 1940-45; dist offr Kenya 1946, asst sec 1950, sec to road authy 1951, sec to Govr of Seychelles 1952, actg govr 1953, dep res cmmr and govt sec Basutoland 1956, dep Br Govt rep Lesotho 1965; dep sec Aberdeen Univ 1976 (clerk to Univ ct 1967-76), sec assembly cncl of gen, memb assembly Church of Scotland 1980-85; chm: West End Community Cncl Edinburgh Dist, Victoria League for Cwlth Friendship Scotland; vice-pres The St Andrew Soc Edinburgh; Burgess of Guild City of Aberdeen 1979; fell Cwlth Fund 1939; *Recreations* town and country walking, railways, grandchildren; *Clubs* New Club Edinburgh, Royal Overseas League, Vincents Oxford; *Style—* Gordon Hector, Esq, CMG, CBE; 18 Magdala Crescent, Edinburgh EH12 5BD

HECTOR, Col (Ralph) Melville; CBE (1963); s of Thomas Walker Hector (d 1952), and Ethel Melville Burnet, *née* Craigie (d 1968); *b* 24 July 1913; *Educ* Glenamond Coll, Aberdeen Univ (MB, ChB, DMRD); *m* 11 July 1942, Joan, da of Jonathan Philip Brazier (d 1963); 1 s (decd), 1 da; *Career* serv RAMC 1939-74; ret with rank of Col, War Serv inc France and Belgium with BEF 1939- 1940, France and Germany 1944-45, mostly with Field Ambulance or as DADMS various formations; post war serv in Malaya and Ceylon as OC 25 Indian CCS, 48 Indian Gen Hosp and BMH Colombo; 1948 began career in diagnostic Radiology serving in UK, USA, Singapore and Ghana; final appt as conslt radiologist Cambridge Mil Hosp Aldershot; *Recreations* fishing, shooting, woodland stalking; *Clubs* Army and Navy; *Style—* Col Melville Hector; Lyndhurst, Waverley Ave, Fleet, Hants GU13 8NW; The Firs, Rosehall, Sutherland, Scotland IV27 4BD

HEDDLE, (Bentley) John; MP (C) Mid-Staffordshire 1983-; s of Oliver Heddle and late Lilian Heddle; *b* 15 Sept 1943; *Educ* Bishop's Stortford Coll, Coll of Estate Mgmnt (London Univ); *m* 1, 1964, (m dis 1984), Judith, da of Dr Richard Robinson; 2 s, 2 da; m 2 1986, Janet Mary, da of John Stokes; 1 da; *Career* contested (C) Gateshead W Feb 1974, Bolton E Oct 1974; MP (C) Lichfield and Tamworth 1979-83; sec Cons parly media ctee; chm: Cons parly environment ctee 1983- (jt sec 1979-83), chm Bow Gp Environment Ctee 1980-; underwriting memb Lloyd's 1974; conslt ptnr Elliott, Son and Boyton (chartered surveyors) 1980-; dir: Giffard Securities Ltd, Cornhill Investmts Ltd and other companies; vice-pres Bldg Socs Assoc; Freeman City of London; chm Cons Pty nat local govt advsy ctee; memb nat union exec of Cons Pty; FCIArb, FRSA, Hon FIAS, FRVA, FInstD; *Publications* The Way Through the Woods (1973), A New Lease of Life - a solution to Rent Control (1975), St Cuthbert's Village - an Urban Disaster (1976), The Great Rate Debate (1980), No Waiting? - a Solution to the Hospital Waiting List Problem (1982); *Recreations* politics, reading music, cricket, relaxing with family; *Clubs* Carlton; *Style—* John Heddle, Esq, MP; Old College House, 15 Dam Street, Lichfield, Staffs; 15 Lowndes Close, Belgravia, London SW1

HEDDY, Brian Huleatt; s of William Reginald Huleatt Heddy, MD (d 1972), and Ruby, *née* Norton-Taylor (d 1974); *b* 8 June 1916; *Educ* St Paul's, Pembroke Coll Oxford; *m* 1, 1940, Barbara (d 1965); 2 s (Julian b 1941, Martin b 1950), 1 da (Celia b 1943); m 2, 1966, Ruth (d 1967); m 3, 1969, Horatia Clare, da of Aubrey Leo Kennedy, MC (1965); *Career* cmmnd 75 Highland Fd Regt RA, served France 1940, W Africa 1943 WO (SOE), France 1944-45, Capt (Temp); barr Grays Inn 1943; H M Dip Serv: Brussels 1946, Denver 1948, FO 1952, Tel Aviv 1953, UK Delgn ECSC Luxembourg 1955, FO 1959, cnsllr 1963, HM consul-gen Lourenco Marques 1963-65, head of nationality and consular dept Cwlth Off 1966-67, head of migration and visa dept FCO 1968-71, HM consul-gen Durban 1971-76, ret 1976; *Recreations* travel, reading; *Clubs* East India, Devonshire, sports and public schools, MCC; *Style—* Brian Heddy, Esq; Wynyards, Winsham, nr Chard, Somerset (☎ 046 030 260)

HEDGECOE, Prof John; s of William Alec Hedgecoe (d 1983), of Priory Farm, Lt Dunmow, Essex, and Kathleen Alice, *née* Don (d 1981); *b* 24 Mar 1937; *Educ* Gulval Village Sch, Guildford Sch of Art, Epsom Sch of Art, Ruskin Coll Oxford, RCA (Dr RCA); *m* 3 Oct 1959, Julia, da of Sidney Mardon (d 1971), of Bishops-Stortford, Herts; 2 s (Sebastian John b 1961, Auberon Henry b 1968), 1 da (Imogen Dolly Alice b 1964); *Career* Nat Serv RAF SAC 1955-56; staff photographer Queen Magazine 1957-72; freelance: Sunday Times and Observer 1960-70, most int magazines 1958-; RCA: fndr photography sch 1965, head dept and reader in photography 1965-74, fell 1973, chm of photography 1975, fndr audio/visual dept 1980, fnd holgraphy unit 1982, managing tstee 1983; portrait of HM The Queen for Br and Aust postage stamps 1966, photographer The Arts Multi-Projection Br Exhibition Expo Japan Show 1970, visiting prof Norwegian Nat TV Sch Oslo 1985; dir: John Hedgecoe Ltd 1965-, Perennial Pictures Ltd 1980; md Lion & Unicorn Press Ltd 1986; illustrator of numerous books 1958-, contributor to numerous radio broadcasts; TV: Tonight (Aust) 1967, Folio (Anglia) 1980, eight programmes on photography (Channel Four) 1983 (repeated 1984), Winners (Channel Four) 1984, Light and Form US Cable TV 1985; exhibitions: London, Sydney, Toronto, Edinburgh, Venice and Prague; collections: V & A, Museum Art Gallery of Ontario, Nat Portrait Gallery, Citibank London, Henry Moore Fndn, Museum of Modern Art NY, Leeds City Art Gallery; govr W Surrey Coll of Art 1975- (memb acad advsy bd 1975-), memb photographic bd CNAA 1976-78, acad govr Richmond Coll London; FRSA; *Books* Henry Moore (1968, prize best art book world-wide 1969), Kevin Crossley-Holland book of Norfolk Poems (jtly 1970), Photography, Material and Methods (jtly 1971-74 edns), Henry Moore Energy in Space (1973), The Book of Photography (1976), Handbook of Photographic Techniques (1977, 2 edn 1982), The Art of Colour Photography (1978), Possession (1978), The Pocket Book of Photography (1979), Introductory Photography Course (1979), Master Classes in Photography: Children and Child Portraiture (1980), Poems of Thomas Hardy (illustrated 1981), Poems of Robert Burns (illustrated), The Book of Advanced Photography (1982), What a Picture! (1983), The Photographer's Work Book (1983), Aesthetics of Nude Photography (1984), The Workbook of Photo Techniques (1984), The Workbook of Darkroom Techniques (1984), Pocket Book of Travel and Holiday Photography (1986), Henry Moore: his ideas inspirations and life as an artist (1986), The Three Dimensional Pop-up Photography Book (with A L Rowse, 1986), Shakespeares Land (1986), Photographers Manual of Creative Ideas (1986), Portrait Photography (with A L Rowse, 1987), Rowse's Cornwall (1987), Practical Book of Landscape Photography (1988), Hedgecoe on Photography (1988); *Recreations* sculpture, building, gardening; *Style—* Prof John Hedgecoe; Royal College of Art, Kensington Gore, London SW7

HEDGES, Lady; Barbara Mary; da of late Capt Bernard Ward, OBE, RN, of Chilworth; *b* 17 Jan 1910; *Educ* privately, Winchester Sch for Girls; *m* 1, 1940, Lt-Cdr Richard Scobell Palairet, RN (d 1953); m 2, 1957, Sir John Hedges, CBE (d 1983), s of Maj Francis Reade Hedges, of Wallingford Castle, Berks; *Career* pres Sir John and Lady Hedges Extension Appeal Fund for John Masefield Cheshire Home; voluntary work; *Recreations* gardening, the arts; *Style—* Lady Hedges; The Coach House, Castle St, Wallingford, Oxon OX10 8DL (☎ (0491) 36217)

HEDGES, Dennis Mitchell; CBE (1962); s of George Mitchell Hedges (d 1950), of Georgeham, N Devon, and Nora, *née* Ingram (d 1980); *b* 29 Nov 1917; *Educ* Felsted, Lausanne Univ, St Catharine's Coll Cambridge (MA); *m* 2 Jan 1951, Margaret Janet, da of Bertram Francis Borland Belcham (d 1963), of Westcliff-on-Sea, Essex; 2 s (Nicholas b 1953, Jonathan b 1958); *Career* Colonial Admin Serv; dist cmmr and prov cmmr Sierra Leone 1940-59; chief sec Br Guiana (now Guyana) 1959-61; chm bd of govrs Hordle House Sch Milford-on-Sea; FRCS 1946; *Recreations* golf; *Clubs* Royal Cwlth Soc; *Style—* Dennis M Hedges, CBE; Forshem, Elvetham Road, Fleet, Hampshire (☎ 0252 616271)

HEDGES, George Arthur; s of George Arthur Hedges (d 1942), of Enfield, Middx, and Leah Anna, *née* Ferguson (d 1986); *b* 5 April 1936; *Educ* Mill Hill, Northern Poly Holloway Road; *m* 30 Jan 1980, Sheena, da of Robert McLelland Craig (d 1986), of Gwynedd, N Wales; *Career* CA; private practice; ARIBA; *Recreations* water sports; *Clubs* Cheyne (life memb), Mombasa, Victoria Craig-y-Don Llandudno; *Style—* George A Hedges, Esq; c/o Lloyd Chambers, Reform Street, Llandudno, Gwynedd, N Wales (☎ 0492 79444)

HEDGES, Neil Francis; s of Kenneth Francis Chevalier, of Walmer, Kent, and Peggy, *née* Best; *b* 12 Dec 1956; *Educ* Watford Boys' GS, Univ of Sheffield (BA); *m* 19 Sept 1981, Katherine Anne, da of Trevor Noel Louis, of Bushey Heath, Herts; 1 da (Frances b 13 Feb 1986); *Career* md Valin Pollen Ltd 1988- (asst md 1985, account exec 1980); *Recreations* music, cinema, walking, family; *Style—* Neil Hedges, Esq; 7 Nicholas Rd, Elstree, Herts (☎ 01 207 5559); Valin Pollen Ltd, 18 Grosvenor Gardens, London SW1H 0DH (☎ 01 730 3456, fax 01 730 7445, telex 296846)

HEDLEY, Prof Anthony Johnson; s of Thomas Johnson Hedley (d 1977), of Yealmpton, Plymouth, Devon, and Winifred, *née* Duncan; *b* 8 April 1941; *Educ* Rydal Sch Colwyn Bay, Univ of Aberdeen (MB, ChB, MD), Univ of Edinburgh (Dip Soc Med); *m* 2 Aug 1967, Elizabeth-Anne, da of William Henry Walsh; *Career* Aberdeen Univ OTC 1960-63; res fell dept of therapeutics and pharmacology Univ of Aberdeen 1968-69 (Philipps and Garden fell 1986-68), hon asst dept of pharmacology and therapeutics Univ of Dundee 1969-73, fell community med Scottish Health Serv 1973-74, lectr community med Univ of Aberdeen 1974-76, sr lectr community health Univ of Nottingham 1976-83, Henry Mechan prof and head dept of community med Univ of Glasgow 1984-88 (titular prof and mechan prof- designate 1983-84), prof of community med Univ of Hong Kong 1988-, memb: Thyroid Club, Soc for Social Med, Nottingham Medico Chirurgical Soc, Hong Kong Med Assoc, Burton Joyce Preservation Soc, Cathay Camera Club; Hon MD Khon Kaen Univ Thailand 1983, FFCM 1981, FRCP (Edin) 1981, FRCP (Glas) 1985 FRCP (Lond) 1987; *Clubs* Freelancers (Nottingham), Rydal Veterans (Colwyn Bay), Aberdeen Boat Hong Kong; *Style—* Prof Anthony Hedley; 39 Foxhill Rd, Burton Joyce, Notts NG14 5DB (☎ 0602 31 2558); Flat 8 Block 2, Tam Towers, 25 Shawan Dr, Pokfulam, Hong Kong (☎ 5 819 4708); Department of Community Medicine (☎ 5 8199 280, fax 852 5 479 907)

HEDLEY, Mark; s of Peter Hedley, of Windsor and Eve, *née* Morley; *b* 23 August 1946; *Educ* Framlingham Coll Univ of Liverpool (LLB); *m* 14 April 1973, Erica Rosemary, da of John Capel Britton, of Crowborough; 3 s (Michael b 1975, Steven b 1981, Peter b 1982), 1 da (Anna b 1978); *Career* barr Grays Inn 1969, recorder of Crown ct 1988; reader C of E, chm Liverpool Diocesan Assoc of Readers; *Recreations* cricket, railways; *Style—* Mark Hedley, Esq; 55 Everton Rd, Liverpool 2 (☎ 051 227 1081, fax 051 236 1120, car telephone NIA, telex NIA)

HEDLEY, Dr Ronald Henderson; CB (1986); s of Henry Armstrong Hedley (d 1970), of Scarborough, Yorks, and Margaret, *née* Hopper (d 1950); *b* 2 Nov 1928; *Educ* Durham Johnston Sch, Univ of Durham Kings Coll (BSc, PhD), Univ of Newcastle Upon Tyne (DSc); *m* 28 Feb 1957, Valmai Mary, da of Roy Griffith (d 1971), of Taihape, NZ; 1 s (Iain b 18 June 1960); *Career* cmmnd RA 1953-55; Br Museum Natural History: sr and princ scientific offr, dep keeper of zoology 1955-71, dep dir 1971-76, dir 1976-88; nat res fell NZ 1960-61; and memb cncl Fresh Water Biol Assoc 1972-76, tstee Percy Sladen Meml Fund 1972-77, pres Br Soc of Protozoa 1975-78, memb cncl & govr Marine Biology Assoc 1976-, vice-pres Zoological Soc of London 1980-85 (Hon sec 1977-80); cncl memb: Royal Albert Hall 1982-88, Nat Tst 1986-88; FZS 1960, FIBiol 1970, FRSA 1988; *Books* Foraminifera Vols 1-3 (1974-78), Atlas of Testate Amoebae (1980), tech papers on biology & cytology of protozoa (1958-80); *Recreations* horology, horticulture, humour; *Style—* Dr Ronald Hedley, CB; 25 Ashburn Place, London SW7 4LR

HEDLEY-DENT, Maj Ronald Peter; er s of Lt-Col William Edward Hedley-Dent (d 1980), of Shortflatt Tower, Belsay, Northumberland, and Renée Maude (d 1978), er da of Sir Arthur Philip du Cros, 1 Bt; descended from William Hedley, Mayor of Newcastle 1778, whose s William m Anne, sis and eventual heiress of John Dent, of Shortflatt Tower, which was inherited by their gs William Dent Hedley (later William Dent Dent) 1831; the additional surname and arms of Hedley were re-assumed in 1926 (*see* Burke's Landed Gentry, 18 edn, Vol III, 1972); *b* 29 June 1921; *Educ* Eton; *m* 24 June 1964, Nancy, da of Bryant H Dixon, of Rockaway Valley, Boonton, New Jersey, USA; 1 adopted da (Octavia b 23 Sept 1967); *Career* served in Welsh Gds 1941-62, ret as Maj; Northern Insp of Courses for the Jockey Club 1964-86; chm: Belsay Parish Cncl, Northern Branch Mental Health Fndn; High Sheriff of Northumberland 1974-75; *Recreations* travellintg, horseracing, farming, gardening; *Style—* Major Ronald Hedley-Dent; Shortflatt Tower, Belsay, Newcastle-upon-Tyne NE20 OHD (☎ 066 181 609)

HEDLEY-MILLER, Dame Mary Elizabeth; DCVO (1989), CB (1983); da of late J W Ashe; *b* 5 Sept 1923; *Educ* Queen's Sch Chester, St Hugh's Coll Oxford (MA); *m*

1950, Roger Latham Hedley-Miller; 1 s, 2 da; *Career* under-sec HM Treasy 1973-83, ceremonial offr Cabinet Off 1983-88; *Style*— Dame Mary Hedley-Miller, DCVO, CB; 108 Higher Drive, Purley, Surrey

HEDLEY-MILLER, Rosalind; da of Roger Latham Hedley-Miller, of 108 Higher Drive, Purley, Surrey, and Dame Mary Elizabeth, *née* Ashe, DCVO, CB; *b* 25 Nov 1954; *Educ* St Pauls's Girls Sch, St Hugh's Coll Oxford (MA), Harvard Univ; *Career* investmt dept J Henry Schroder Wagg & Co Ltd 1977-79; Kleinwort Benson Ltd: corporate fin dept 1979-, dir 1987-; non-exec dir Bejam Gp plc 1987-88; *Recreations* chamber music, orchestra, singing, bridge, tennis; *Style*— Miss Rosalind Hedley-Miller; 11 Manchuria Rd, London SW11 6AF; 20 Fenchurch St, London EC3P 3DB (☎ 01 623 8000, fax 01 623 5535)

HEEKS, Alan David; s of Leonard Frank Heeks, and Peggy Eileen, *née* Lawless; *b* 20 August 1948; *Educ* Reading Sch, Balliol Coll Oxford, Harvard Business Sch (MBA); *m* 7 Aug 1971, Ruth Frances, da of Arthur Stone; 2 da (Elinor b 1977, Frances b 1979); *Career* brand mangr Proctor & Gamble 1969-73, mangr mktg and new prods Hygena Kitchens 1976-78, dir mktg and sales: Chloride Standby Systems 1978-81, Redland Roof Tiles 1981-83; md: Redland Prismo 1983-86 Caradon Twyfords Ltd 1986- (exec dir Caradon plc); dir Nat Home Improvement Cncl 1986-; FInstM; *Recreations* design, the arts, steam railways, walking; *Style*— Alan Heeks, Esq; 9 Hockley Cottages, Twyford, Winchester, Hants, SO21 1PJ, Caradon Plc, 30 St John's Road, Woking, Surrey, GU21 1SA (☎ 04862 30821, fax 04862 28864, telex 859975)

HEELIS, Robert McRae; s of Robert Loraine Heelis (d 1971), of Mickledore, West Bridgford, Notts, and Susannah Heelis; *b* 20 June 1930; *Educ* Repton, Nottingham Univ (LLB); *m* 1, 23 July 1955 (m dis 1965), Elizabeth Isobelle, *née* Radford; m 2, 20 Dec 1968, Patricia Margaret, *née* Fletcher; 2 s (Robert Alexander Piers b 2 Dec 1970, Toby Edward Loraine b 12 May 1973), 1 da (Sarah Caroline Hillier); *Career* Nat Serv 2 Lt 1953-55, Capt Leics and Derbys Yeo 1955-68, memb E Midland T & AFA cncl; slr 1953; ptnr Taylor Simpson & Mosley, Derby and Nottingham; sec Derby & Derbyshire Disabled Soldiers Settlement, cncllr Derby Borough Cncl 1967-70; Under Sheriff Derbyshire 1980-; *Recreations* shooting, vintage car racing; *Clubs* County Derby, VSCC, BOC; *Style*— Robert Heelis, Esq; Shaw House, Melbourne, Derby (☎ 0332 863827); 35 St Mary's Gate, Derby (☎ 0332 372311)

HEENAN, Maurice; CMG (1966), QC (Hong Kong 1962); s of David Donnoghue Heenan (d 1942), and Anne, *née* Frame (d 1976); *b* 8 Oct 1912; *Educ* Ashburton Coll, Canterbury Coll, NZ Univ (LLB); *m* 1951, Claire (Klara Gabriela Stephanie), da of Emil Ciho (d 1975), of Trencin, Bratislava, Czechoslovakia; 2 da (Ingrid (Mrs Ogden H Hammond III), Karen (Mrs Juan Herrick Pujol) ; *Career* Maj 2 NZEF, active serv: W Desert, Libya, Cyrenaica and Italy; (despatches) 1940-45; barr and slr of Supreme Ct of NZ 1932-40, crown counsel Palestine 1946-48, slr-gen Hong Kong 1961, HM's attorney gen Hong Kong (ex-officio MEC and MLC) 1961-66, dep-dir gen legal div (Off of Legal Affrs) Offs of Sec-Gen UN NY 1966-73; gen-counsel UN Relief and Works Agency for Palestine Refugees in Near East 1973-77; *Recreations* rugby, squash, tennis, skiing, golf; *Clubs* New Canaan Country, Hong Kong; *Style*— Maurice Heenan, Esq, CMG, QC; Plane Trees, West Rd, New Canaan, Connecticut 06840, USA (☎ 203 966 8677)

HEEPS, William (Bill); known as Bill; s of William Headrick Heeps (d 1980), and Margaret, *née* Munro (d 1978); *b* 4 Dec 1929; *Educ* Graeme HS Falkirk; *m* 1, 1956, Anne Robertson Paton (d 1974); 2 da (Elaine b 1958, Donna b 1961); m 2, 1983, Jennifer Rosemary, da of Jack Evans, of Herts; 1 step da (Sarah-Jane, name changed to Heeps by deed poll); *Career* reporter Falkirk Mail 1943-52, reporter/sports sub-ed Daily Record (Kemsley Newspapers) 1952-54, joined editorial staff of Evening Dispatch (later Evening News and Dispatch) of Scotsman Pubns Ltd 1954 (asst ed 1962), asst to md Belfast Telegraph 1965-66, ed Middlesbrough Evening Gazette 1966-68; md: Celtic Newspapers 1968-72, Teesside 1972-75, Evening Post (Luton) and Evening Echo (Watford) 1975-77, Thomson Magazines 1977-80, Thomson Data 1980-82; chm and chief exec Thomson Regnl Newspapers 1984- (ed dir 1982-83, md and ed-in-chief 1983-84); memb bd Int Thomson Orgn 1984-; elder of Church of Scotland; dir: Thomson Regnl Newspapers Ltd, Chester Chronicle and Assoc Newspapers Ltd, Teeside Communications Ltd, Belfast Telegraph Newpapers Ltd, Aberdeen Jls Ltd, The Scotsman Pubns Ltd, Thomson Int Press Consultancy Ltd, The Thomson Orgn plc, Thomson Television Ltd, Thomson Free Newspapers Ltd; chm Royal Caledonian Schs; pres Newspaper Soc; tstee The Thomson Fndn; FBIM; *Recreations* golf, badminton; *Clubs* Caledonian; *Style*— Bill Heeps Esq; Jollivers, Longcroft Lane, Felden, Hemel Hempstead, Herts (☎ 0442 53524); Hannay House, 39 Clarendon Rd, Watford, Herts WD1 1JA (☎ 0923 55588, telex 915054)

HEESOM, Tom Michael Anthony; s of Dr A H B Heesom (d 1955), of Redhill, Surrey, and Gwendoline Mary Aeesom; *b* 26 Feb 1937; *Educ* Marlborough, Guys Hosp; *m* 23 March 1966, Willo Elizabeth, da of Dr W H Murby, of Toronto, Canada; *Career* gen dental surgn private practice, visiting conslt in preventive dentistry State of Qatar 1979-82; chm Pankey Assoc (UK) 1985; BOA, fell Int Coll Dentists 1988; LDS, BDS.FRCS. MRCS; *Recreations* vintage cars, walking, travel, music, gardening; *Style*— Tom Heesom, Esq; The Old Bothy, Norwood Hill, Horley, Surrey RH6 OHP (☎ 0293 862622); The Wall House, Yorke Rd, Reigate, Surrey RH2 9HG (☎ 0737 247424)

HEFFER, Eric Samuel; MP (Lab) Liverpool Walton 1964-; s of William Heffer, and Annie, *née* Nicholls; *b* 12 Jan 1922; *Educ* Longmore Sr Sch Hertford; *m* 1945, Doris Murray; *Career* served WWII RAF; Lab front bench spokesman industl relations 1970-72, min state Dept Industry 1974-75, memb Lab NEC 1975- (chm orgn sub-ctee to Nov 1982), chm of Lab Pty 1983-84, memb shadow cabinet and oppn front bench spokesman: Euro and Community Affrs (incl responsibility for planning UK withdrawal from EEC in event of Lab electoral victory) 1981-1983, housing and construction Nov 1983-; vice-pres League Against Cruel Sports; pamphlets incl Democratic Socialism, Why You should vote Labour, Forward to Socialism; former columnist The Times, New Statesman, Tribune, Liverpool Daily Post & Echo; contrib to numerous foreign and br newspapers and jls; *Books* Class Struggle in Parliament, Labours Future - Socialist or SDP Mark II; *Style*— Eric Heffer Esq, MP; House of Commons, London SW1

HEFFER, John N M; s of late Sidney Heffer; *b* 8 Jan 1919; *Educ* Leys Sch Cambridge; *m* 1944, Margaret, *née* Moore; 3 s; *Career* bookseller and stationer, dep chm W Heffer and Sons Ltd; *Recreations* sailing, gardening, shooting; *Style*— John Heffer, Esq; Solway, Drayton, Cambridge (Crafts Hill 80628)

HEFFERNAN, John Francis; *b* 1 Sept 1927; *Educ* Gunnersbury GS, London Univ (BCom); *m* 19 July 1952, Veronica, da of Dr John Laing, of 7 Corfton Rd, Ealing; 2 da (Maureen, Catherine); *Career* Daily Express (later Evening Standard) 1939-45, chm and princ proprietor City Press Newspaper 1965-75; city ed: Yorkshire Post 1986-, United Provincial Newspapers Ltd 1965-; vice pres Free Trade Leaque; hon sec: Assoc Regnl City Eds, Yorks and Humberside Devpt Assoc London Ctee; barr Inner Temple 1954; Memb Ct Worshipful Co of Basketmakers; *Clubs* City Livery; *Style*— John Heffernan, Esq; 1 Fern Dene, Ealing, London W13 8AN; United Newspapers, 23-27 Tudor St, London EC4Y 0HR (☎ 01 353 3424, fax 01 353 7796)

HEFFERNAN, Patrick Benedict; s of Dr Daniel Anthony Heffernan, of Sutton, Surrey, and Margaret, *née* Donovan; *b* 17 Mar 1948; *Educ* Wimbledon Coll, Jesus Coll Cambridge (MA); *m* 5 May 1973, Elizabeth, da of Robert Essery (d 1966), of Huddersfield and Melbourne; 1 s (Thomas b 1984), 1 da (Miranda b 1987); *Career* slr 1974, ptnr Clyde & Co 1988-; *Recreations* times crossword, sport, reading; *Style*— Patrick Heffernan, Esq; 9 Victoria Rd, London N22 (☎ 01 888 0349); Clyde & Co, 51 Eastcheap, London EC3M 1JP (☎ 01 623 1244, fax 01 623 5427, telex 884886)

HEFFLER, Lady Tara Francesca; *née* Fitz-Clarence; er da (by 1 m) of 7 Earl of Munster, and Louise Marguerite Diane Delvigne; descended from William Duke of Clarence (later King William IV) and Dorothy Jordan; *b* 6 August 1952; *m* 1979, Ross Jean Heffler, s of Dr Leon Heffler (d 1983); 1 s (Leo Edward Michael b 1985); 1 da (Alexandra Louise b 1982); *Career* mangr Sotheby Fine Art Auctioneers; *Recreations* family, travelling, the arts; *Style*— Lady Tara Heffler; 146 Ramsden Rd, London SW12 8RE (☎ 01 673 4017)

HEGGS, Geoffrey Ellis; s of George Heggs, MBE (d 1972), of Guernsey, and Winifred Grace Ellis (d 1974); *b* 23 Oct 1928; *Educ* Elizabeth Coll Guernsey, London Univ (LLB), Yale Univ (LLM); *m* 28 March 1953, (Reneé Fanny) Madeleine, da of Emilio Calderan, (d 1940) of London; 2 s (Christopher b 1957, Oliver b 1964), 1 da (Caroline b 1960); *Career* slr 1952, asst sec to The Law Soc 1956-58, practised as a slr in London 1958-77, chm of Industl Tbnls 1977-, rec Crown Ct (SE circuit) 1983-; Freedom of the City of London; memb: City of London Slrs Co, Law Soc; *Recreations* military history, music, painting; *Style*— Geoffrey Heggs, Esq; 93 Ebury Bridge Rd, London SW1W 8RE (☎ 01 730 9361)

HEGINBOTHAM, Stafford; s of Stafford Heginbotham, of Oldham; *b* 12 Sept 1933; *Educ* Greenhill GS Oldham; *m* 1963, Lorna, da of Alfred Silverwood, of Leeds; 2 s (Simon b 1965, James b 1967); *Career* served RAF; chm and md Tebro Toys Ltd 1966-, chm Bradford AFC 1965-73; dir: Carlton Diecasters 1976-80, Douglas Plastics 1976-80; *Recreations* racing (racehorses 'Cutler Heights', 'Tebro Teddy'), golf, int travel; *Style*— Stafford Heginbotham Esq; The Pastures, Tong Village, Bradford, W Yorks (☎ 0532 853661)

HEILBRON, Hilary Nora Burstein; *née* Burstein; QC (1987); da of Dr Nathaniel Burstein, of London, and Hon Dame Rose Heilbron, DBE, *qv*; *b* 2 Jan 1949; *Educ* Huyton Coll, LMH Oxford (MA); *Career* barr Gray's Inn 1971; *Style*— Miss Hilary Heilbron, QC; 1 Brick Court, Temple, London EC4Y 9BY (☎ 01 583 0777)

HEILBRON, Hon Mrs Justice; Hon Dame Rose; DBE (1974); da of late Max and Nellie Heilbron; *b* 19 August 1914; *Educ* Belvedere Sch, Liverpool Univ (LLB); *m* 1945, Dr Nathaniel Burstein; 1 da; *Career* Lord Justice Holker Scholar Gray's Inn 1936, barr Gray's Inn 1939, QC 1949, bencher 1968, recorder and hon recorder of Burnley 1972-74, memb Bar Cncl 1973-74, joined Northern Circuit (ldr 1973-74), judge of the High Court of Justice Family Division 1974-88, chm Home Sec's advsy gp on Law of Rape 1975-, hon fell Lady Margaret Hall Oxford 1976, presiding judge 1979-82, tres Gray's Inn 1985; Hon LLD Liverpool 1975, Warwick 1978, Manchester 1980; Hon Col WRAC(TA); LLM; *Style*— The Hon Dame Rose Heilbron, DBE; Royal Courts of Justice, Strand, London WC2A 2LL

HEIM, Most Rev Archbishop Bruno Bernard; s of Bernhard Heim and Elisabeth Studer; *b* 5 Mar 1911; *Educ* St Thomas Aquinas, Gregorian and Fribourg Univs (PhD, BD, DCL), Papal Acad of Diplomacy; *Career* ordained priest 1938; chief chaplain for Italian and Polish mil internees in Switzerland 1943-45; served as attaché and sec at Paris Nunciature under Nuncio Roncalli (later Pope John XXIII); also served: Austria, Germany; Archbishop of Xanthus; Apostolic Delegate to Scandinavia 1961-69, Pro Nuncio (ambass of Holy See) to Finland 1966-69, Pro Nuncio to Egypt 1969-73 and pres of Caritas Egypt 1973-82; Apostolic Delegate to GB 1973-82, Pro Nuncio to UK 1982-85; heraldic artist (designed coat of arms of Popes John XXIII, Paul VI, John Paul I and John Paul II); author of heraldic works; memb: Cncl Swiss Heraldic Soc, Heraldry Socs of London and Scotland, and others; patron Cambridge Univ Heraldic and Genealogical Soc; laureate of Fr Acad; memb: Cncl Int Heraldic Acad; hon memb: Accademia Archeologica Italiana, Real Acad de la Historia Madrid; honours include: Grand Cross Orders of Malta, the Finnish Lion, St Mauritius and Lazarus, Bailiff Grand Cross Constantinian Order of St George, Kt of Hon Teutonic Order, OStJ; *Recreations* cooking, gardening, heraldry,; *Clubs* Atheneum; *Style*— The Most Rev Bruno Heim; Zehnderweg 31, CH-4600 Olten, Switzerland

HEIMANN, Hon Mrs (Diana Hester); *née* Macleod; da of Baroness Macleod of Borve (Life Baroness); *b* 1944; *m* 1968, David Heimann; 3 s; *Style*— The Hon Mrs Heimann; Hertfordshire House, Coleshill, Bucks

HEIN, (Paul Joseph) Raymond; QC (Mauritius 1976); s of Sir Raymond Hein, QC (d 1983), and Lady Hein, *née* Marcelle Piat (d 1981); *b* 23 Jan 1929; *Educ* Royal Coll Mauritius, Wadham Coll Oxford (MA); *m* 1962, (Amélie Sybille) Marie Josée, da of E Jacques Harel (d 1962); 2 s (b 1965 and 1969); *Career* barr Mid Temple 1955, Mauritius 1955; municipal cncllr Port Louis 1956-69, mayor Port Louis 1963; chm Mauritius Bar Cncl 1973 (memb 1972-73); dir: Mauritius Commercial Bank Ltd, New Mauritius Dock Co Ltd, Union SE Co Ltd, Constance and La Gaieté SE Co Ltd, Harel Frères Ltd, Beau Plan SE Co Ltd, Bel Air St Félix Co Ltd, Promotion and Devpt Co Ltd; *Recreations* reading, hunting; *Clubs* Mauritius Turf, Mauritius Gymkhana; *Style*— Raymond Hein, Esq, QC; Floreal, Mauritius (☎ 861782); chambers: Cathedral Sq, Port Louis, Mauritius (☎ 20327/081044)

HEINEY, Paul; *see*: Ms Libby Purves

HEININGER, Patrick; s of John Jacob Heininger, of Pittsburgh, Pennsylvania, and Catherine Ann, *née* Gaffney (d 1944); *b* 22 June 1942; *Educ* Georgetown Univ Washington DC (LLM, JD), American Univ Washington DC (BA); *m* 10 Oct 1987, Caroline, da of Eric Atack, of Essex; *Career* barr: dist of Columbia 1967, New York 1971; lawyer Debevoise & Pimpton New York 1969-71, lectr and advsr Univ of Nairobi/Govt of Kenya 1971-73, legal advsr fin World Bank Washington DC 1973-82, dir Baring Bros Ltd 1982-; *Books* Liability of US Banks for Deposits Placed in Their Foreign Branches, Law & Policy in International Business (1979); *Recreations* tennis, squash, chamber music; *Style—* Patrick Heininger, Esq; 18 Clarendon St, London, SW1V 4RD (☎ 01 828 5034); Sweetslade Farm, nr Bourton-on-the-Water, Glos, GL54 3BL; Baring Bros & Co Ltd, 8 Bishopsgate, London, EC2N 4AE (☎ 01 283 8833, fax 01 283 2633, telex 883622)

HEISER, Sir Terence Michael; KCB 1987 (CB 1984); s of David and Daisy Heiser; *b* 24 May 1932; *Educ* Windsor Co Boys' Sch Berks, Birkbeck Coll Univ of London (BA); *m* 1957, Kathleen Mary Waddle; 1 s, 2 da; *Career* served RAF 1950-52; joined Civil Serv 1949, served with Colonial Office, Miny of Works, Miny of Housing and Local Govt; perm sec DOE 1985-; *Style—* Sir Terence Heiser, KCB

HELE, Sir Ivor Henry Thomas; CBE (1969, OBE 1954); s of A Hele; *b* 13 June 1912; *Educ* Prince Alfred Coll Adelaide; *m* 1957, May E, da of A E Weatherly; *Career* served Intelligence Sect AIF 1940, official war artist WW II, and Korea 1952; oil painter and draughtsman; kt 1983; *Style—* Sir Ivor Hele, CBE; Aldinga, S Australia 5173

HELEY, Richard William; s of Wilfred Charles Heley, of Shaw, Newbury, Berks, and Joyce, *née* Chalker; *b* 9 Oct 1948; *Educ* Forest Sch, Univ of Wales (BA), Univ of Sussex; *m* 7 Sept 1974, Barbara Alessandra, da of Alexander Kirk Kidd, Banbury Rd, Oxford; 1 s (Adam Frederick Peter b 1983), 1 da (Lara Alessandra Cornelia Constantina b 1985); *Career* int fin dept Phillips & Drew 1969-74, dir corporate fin dept Hill Samuel & Co Ltd 1974-86, head of corporate fin Barclays de Zoete Wedd Ltd 1986-; ASIA; *Books* Profit Forecasting (1981); *Recreations* riding; *Style—* Richard Heley, Esq; Hope Villa, 1 Wallace Rd, London N1 2PG (☎ 01 226 8698); Barclays De Zoete Wedd Ltd, Ebbgate House, Swan Lane, London EC42 3TS (☎ 01 623 2323, fax 01 929 3846)

HELLER, Michael Aron; s of Simon Heller, of Harrogate Yorks, and Nettie, *née* Gordon; *b* 15 July 1936; *Educ* Harrogate GS, St Catharine's Coll Cambridge (MA); *m* 1965, Morven, da of Dr Julius Livingstone; 2 s (John b 1966, Andrew b 1968), 1 da (Nicola b 1981); *Career* chm: London and Assoc Investmt Tst plc, Bisichi Mining plc, Electronic Data Processing plc; non-exec dir Utd Biscuits (Hldgs) plc; FCA; *Recreations* collecting modern British paintings; *Clubs* RAC; *Style—* Michael Heller, Esq; Stationers Hall Court, 30/32 Ludgate Hill, London EC4M 7ND

HELLER, Robert Gordon Barry; s of late Norman Joseph Heller, and Helen, *née* Flatto; *b* 10 June 1932; *Educ* Christ's Hosp, Jesus Coll Cambridge (BA); *m* 8 Jan 1955, Lois Ruth, da of Michael Malnick; 1 s (Matthew Jonathan b 1960), 3 da (Jane Charlotte b 1962, Kate Elizabeth b 1965, Rachel Pearl b 1972); *Career* 2 Lt RASC 1950-52; industl corr (later diary ed and US corr) Fin Times 1955-63, business ed Observer 1963-65, ed (later ed in chief and editorial dir) Mgmnt Today 1965-87, editorial dir Haymarket Publishing 1978-85, ed in chief Finance Magazine 1987-; chm: Graduate Gp, Heller Arts; dir: Angela Flowers Gallery 1970-, Sterling Publishing plc 1985, Reginald Watts Assocs, The Mgmnt Exchange, Business Newsletters; *Books* Superman, Can you Trust your Bank? (with Norris Willatt), The European Revenge (with Norris Willatt), The Naked Investor, The Common Millionaire, The Once and Future Manager, The Business of Winning, The Business of Success, The Naked Market, The Pocket Manager, The New Naked Manager, The State of Industry, The Supermanagers, The Supermarketers, The Age of the Common Millionaire, The Unique Success Proposition, The Decision Makers, The Best of Robert Heller; *Recreations* modern art, food and wine, books, music, exercise; *Style—* Robert Heller, Esq; Angela Flowers Gallery, 199 Richmond Road, London E8 (☎ 01 985 3333)

HELLIKER, Adam Andrew Alexander; s of Maurice William Helliker, DFC, AFC (d 1984), and Jane Olivia, *née* Blunt; *b* 13 Sept 1958; *Educ* King's Sch Bruton, Somerset Coll of Arts & Technol; *Career* reporter: Western Times Co Ltd 1978-81, Daily Mail 1981-86; dep diary ed: Daily Mail 1986-, Mail on Sunday 1988; contrib to several nat magazines; Freeman: City of London 1989, Worshipful Co of Wheelwrights 1989; FRGS; *Books* The Debrett Season (ed 1981), The English Season (contrib 1988); *Recreations* shooting, book collecting, idle gossip; *Clubs* City Livery, St James's, Wig & Pen, RAC; *Style—* Adam Helliker, Esq; 1 Sandilands Rd, London SW6 2BD (☎ 01 736 9388); Coombe Hill House, Keinton, Mandeville, Somerset; Daily Mail, Tudor St, London EC4 (☎ 01 353 7045)

HELLINGS, Brian Aliol; s of Robert Aliol Hellings (d 1984), of Falmouth, Cornwall, and Phyllis Selena, *née* Ferris (d 1987); *b* 12 Jan 1936; *Educ* Truro Cath Sch; *m* 23 May 1959, Ann, da of Edward Robert Rule (d 1961); 3 s (Mark Robert Aliol b 6 Oct 1962, James Edward Aliol b 16 May 1970, Charles Mathew Aliol b 9 Sept 1978), 3 da (Caroline Gail b 21 June 1961, Joanne Elizabeth b 24 April 1964, Sarah Victoria b 9 Sept 1978); *Career* articled Lodge & Winter 1953-59, audit clerk Deloitte Plender Griffiths & Co 1959-61, dir PB Cow & Co Ltd 1967-68 (fin comptroller and co sec 1961-68); sr dir responsible for fin Hanson plc 1988- (fin comptroller 1968, fin dir 1973); FCA (1959); *Recreations* fishing, gardening, reading; *Style—* Brian Hellings, Esq; Riverlands, W River Rd, Rumson, NJ 07760, USA (☎ 201 842 7005); 2 Third Street, Rumson, NJ, USA (☎ 201 549 7058, fax 201 549 7058, telex 132222, car tel 201 715 9742)

HELLINGS, Gen Sir Peter William Cradock; KCB (1970, CB 1966), DSC (1940), MC, (1942), DL (Devon 1973); s of Stanley Hellings (d 1922), and Nora Hellings; *b* 6 Sept 1916; *Educ* RNC Pangbourne; *m* 1941, Zoya, da of Col Samuel Bassett, CBE; 1 s (decd), 1 da; *Career* joined RM 1935, Co Cdr 40 Commando 1942, Cdr 41 and 42 Commandos 1945-46, Bde Maj 3 Commando Bde Malaya 1949-51, joined Directing Staff Marine Corps Schs Qunatico USA 1954, Cdr 40 Commando 1958, Bdr Cdr 3 Commando Bde 1959, Col RM 1960, idc 1962, Dep Dir Jt Warfare Staff 1963, COS to Cmdt-Gen RM 1964, Maj-Gen cmdg Portsmouth Gp RM 1967-68, Cmdt-Gen RM 1968-71, Lt-Gen 1968, Gen 1970; Col Cmdt RM 1977-79, Rep Col Cmdt 1979-80; *Style—* Gen Sir Peter Hellings, KCB, DSC, MC, DL

HELLINIKAKIS, Capt George John; JP (1980); s of John Michael Hellinikakis (d 1979), of Sitia, Crete, Greece, and Claire, *née* Mauroleon (d 1966); *b* 2 Feb 1930; *Educ* Greek Gymnasium, Navy Sch; *m* 29 Aug 1953, Yvonne Alice, da of Charles Richard Barraclough ICS (d 1964); 2 s (John George b 1954, Nicolas George b 1962); *Career* Capt served Navy till 1960; marine conslt, Unitor Gp of Cos 1960-; *Recreations* sailing, walking; *Clubs* American, Nat Lib, Marine, Master Mariners, Marine Engineers, Propeller (USA); *Style—* Capt George Hellinikakis, JP; 48 Brackley Square, Woodford Green, Essex IG8 7LL (☎ 01 504 0874); Unitor Ships Service Ltd, 3 High Street, Rickmansworth, Herts WD3 1SW (☎ 0923 777 484)

HELME, Hon Mirabel Jane; *née* Guinness; da of 2 Baron Moyne; *b* 1956; *Educ* Cranborne Chase and E Anglia Univ (BA); *m* 10 August 1984, Patrick Ian Helme, interior designer; 1 da (Alice Mirabel b 1987); *Career* equestrienne; *Books* Biddesden Cookery (1987); *Style—* The Hon Mirabel Helme; Mount Orleans, Collingbourne Ducis, Marlborough, Wilts

HELMORE, Charles Patrick; s of Patrick Helmore, of Crumlin Lodge, Inverin, Co Galway, Ireland, and Mary, *née* Hull; *b* 26 May 1951; *Educ* Eton, Magdalene Coll Cambridge (MA), Insead Fontainebleau (MBA); *m* 16 May 1981, Rachel, da of Bertram Aykroyd (d 1983), of Treyford Manor, Sussex; 2 s (Max b 1984, Caspar b 1987); *Career* barr Middle Temple practiced 1973-75, Jardine Matheson Co Ltd 1975-78, Paine Webber Mitchell Hutchins 1979-82, dir Foreign & Colonial Mgmnt 1982-; *Recreations* fishing, shooting, reading; *Style—* Charles Helmore, Esq; Wyndham Cottage, Rogate, nr Petersfield, Hants; 1 Laurence Pountney Hill, London EC4 (☎ 01 623 4680, fax 01 626 4947, telex 886197)

HELMORE, Roy Lionel; CBE (1980); s of Lionel John Helmore (d 1972), and Ellen, *née* Gibbins (d 1983); *b* 8 June 1926; *Educ* Montrose Acad, Edinburgh Univ (BSc), Cambridge Univ (MA); *m* 5 April 1969, Margaret Lilian, da of Ernest Martin (d 1971); *Career* various lectr posts electrical engrg 1949-57, head of dept electrical engrg & sci Exeter Tech Coll 1957-61; princ: St Albans Coll 1961-77, Cambridgeshire Coll of Arts & Technol 1977-86; fell Hughes Hall Cambridge Univ 1982-; clerk Heydon Parish Cncl 1986-, JP St Albans 1964-78, vice-chm Technician Educn Cncl 1973-79, memb Manpower Servs Cmmn 1974-82, pres Assoc of Princs of Tech Insts 1972-73 (hon sec 1968-71), chm of cncl Assoc of Colls for Further & Higher Educn 1987-88; hon memb City and Guilds of London Inst 1987; FIEE, FBIM; *Books* CCAT A Brief History (1989); *Recreations* gardening, watercolours, opera; *Style—* Roy Helmore, Esq, CBE; 83 Chishill Rd, Heydon, Royston, Herts SG8 8PN (☎ 0763 838 570)

HELSBY, George; s of George Isaac Helsby (d 1948); *b* 9 Dec 1941; *Educ* Ellergreen HS; *m* 1964, Joyce, da of Thomas Walls (d 1984); 2 da; *Career* formerly chm and chief exec Burnett and Hallamshire Hldgs plc, chm and chief exec Columbus Hldgs Ltd; *Recreations* music, philosophy; *Clubs* Clubs Int; *Style—* George Helsby Esq

HELSBY, Hon Nigel Charles; s of Baron Helsby (Life Peer d 1978), by his w Wilmett Mary (who m 2, Rex Hines), da of William Granville Maddison (d 1953), of Durham; *b* 26 July 1941; *Educ* Wellington, Keble Coll Oxford (MA); *m* 1969, Sylvia Rosena, da of Ronald Brown, of Burnham-on-Crouch; 2 da (Rebecca, Genevieve); *Career* electronics engr; mangr electronics centre, Univ of Essex 1977-87, dir Radiocode Clocks Ltd 1983-; *Style—* The Hon Nigel Helsby; Abbots Wood, The Street, Salcott-cum-Virley, Maldon, Essex CM9 8HW (☎ 0621 860416); Radiocode Clocks Ltd, Radiocode House, Kernick Rd, Penryn Cornwall TR10 9LY (☎ 0326 76007)

HELSBY, Richard John Stephens (Rick); s of John Michael Helsby (d 1972), and Margaret Stella, *née* Andrews; *b* 10 Jan 1949; *Educ* Magdalen Coll Sch Oxford, Warwick Univ (BA), Oxford Univ (Dip Ed); *m* 27 July 1968, Kathryn Diana, da of Robert Alan Langford, of Abingdon, Oxford; 3 s (James b 1968, Nathan b 1972, William b 1986); *Career* HM inspr of Taxes Oxford 1972-78, sr inspr of Taxes Inland Revenue Enquiry Branch 1978-84, sr tax mangr Deloitte Haskins & Sells 1984-87, ptnr Tax Investigators Serv Gp 1987-; *Books* Trouble with the Taxman (1985), Offshore Survival (with Jim McMahon, Bernard McCarthy 1988);; *Recreations* squash, football, theatre, cinema, snooker; *Style—* Rick Helsby, Esq; 44 Tredegar Sq, Bow, London E3 5AE (☎ 01 981 1422); Deloitte Haskins & Sells, 128 Queen Victoria St, London EC4P 4JX (☎ 01 248 3913, fax 01 248 3623, telex 894941)

HELVIN, Marie; da of Hugh Lee Helvin, of Honolulu, Hawaii, USA, and Linda S Helvin; *b* 13 August 1952; *m* 1975 (m dis 1985), David Bailey, *qv*; *Career* model; commenced career in Tokoyo; modelled for: (designers) St Laurent, Armani, Valentino, Lagerfeld, Calvin Klein, (photographers) Lategan, Lartique, Helmut Newton, David Bailey; presenter of Frocks on the Box (with Murial Gray, ITV series); author of articles for: The Independent, The Sunday Telegraph, Time Out; cncl memb Aids Crisis Tst; patron: Foster Parents Plan, Frontliners; *Books* Catwalk - The Art of Model Style (1985); *Style—* Miss Marie Helvin; The Pier House, Strand-on-the-Green, Chiswick, London W4 3NN (☎ 01 994 1404, fax 01 994 9606, telex 267486)

HELY-HUTCHINSON, Hon Mark; yr s of late 7 Earl of Donoughmore; *b* 19 May 1934; *Educ* Eton, Magdalen Coll Oxford (BSc, MA), MIT USA (SM); *m* 1962, (Rosita) Margaret, yr da of late Dr Robert Rowan Woods, of Dublin; 2 s, 1 da; *Career* 2 Lt Irish Gds; joined Arthur Guinness Gp 1958, md Guinness Ireland 1975-82; chief exec Bank of Ireland 1983- (dir 1975); *Style—* The Hon Mark Hely-Hutchinson; Larch Hill, Santry, Co Dublin, Ireland (☎ 428718)

HELY-HUTCHINSON, Hon Nicholas David; 3 s of 8 Earl of Donoughmore, *qv*; *b* 30 April 1955; *Educ* Harrow; *m* 1982, Fiona Margaret MacIntyre, da of late Maj W R Watson; 1 s (Seamus David b 1987), 1 da (Flora Clare b 1984); *Clubs* Beefsteak, Chelsea Arts; *Style—* The Hon Nicholas Hely-Hutchinson; c/o The Rt Hon the Earl of Donoughmore, The Manor House, Bampton, Oxon OX8 2LQ

HELY-HUTCHINSON, Hon Ralph Charles; 4 and youngest s of 8 Earl of Donoughmore; *b* 16 Dec 1961; *Educ* Eton; *Style—* The Hon Ralph Hely-Hutchinson; 8 Kensington Palace Gdns, London W8

HELY-HUTCHINSON, Hon Timothy Mark; 2 s of 8 Earl of Donoughmore; *b* 26 Oct 1953; *Educ* Eton, Oxford; *Career* md Macdonald and Co Ltd (Publishers) 1982-86, Headline Book Publishing plc 1986-; *Clubs* Groucho; *Style—* The Hon Timothy Hely-Hutchinson; 2 Redan St, London W14 0AD

HEMANS, Simon Nicholas Peter; CVO (1983); s of Brig P R Hemans, CBE, of Hants, and M E, *née* Melsome; *b* 19 Sept 1940; *Educ* Sherborne, LSE (BSc); *m* 1970, Ursula Martha, da of Herr Werner Naef (d 1972); 3 s (Alexander b 1967, Oliver b 1974, Anthony (twin) b 1974), 1 da (Jennifer b 1972); *Career* FO 1964, Br Embassy Moscow 1966-68; dep cmmr Anguilla 1969, FCO 1969-71, UK Mission to UN NY 1971-75, Br Embassy Budapest 1975-79, asst head Southern African Dept FCO 1979-81, dep high cmmr Nairobi 1981-84, cnsllr and head of chancery Moscow 1985-87, appt head of Soviet Dept FCO 1987-; *Recreations* travel, ballet, opera; *Style—* Simon Hemans, CVO; c/o Soviet Dept, FCO, King Charles St, London SW1A 2AH (☎ 01 270 2115)

HEMINGFORD, 3 Baron (UK 1943); (Dennis) Nicholas Herbert; s of 2 Baron Hemingford (d 1982), and Elizabeth McClare, *née* Clark (d 1979); *b* 25 July 1934; *Educ* Oundle, Clare Coll Cambridge (MA); *m* 8 Nov 1958, Jennifer Mary Toresen, o da of

Frederick William Bailey (d 1986), of Harrogate; 1 s, 3 da (Hon Elizabeth b 1963, Hon Caroline b 1964, Hon Alice b 1968); *Heir* s, Hon Christopher Herbert b 1973; *Career* journalist Reuters London and Washington DC 1956-61; joined The Times 1961: asst Washington correspondent 1961-65, Middle East correspondent 1965-68, dep features ed 1968-70; ed Cambridge Evening News 1970-74, editorial dir Westminster Press 1974-, pres Guild of British Newspaper Editors 1980-81 (vice-pres 1979-80); hon sec Assoc of British Editors 1985-; memb East Anglia Regnl Ctee, Nat Tst; pres Huntingdonshire Family History Soc, govr Bell Educnl Tst; Liveryman of the Grocers' Co; *Recreations* destructive gardening, Victorian military history, genealogy; *Clubs* City Livery, Royal Commonwealth Soc; *Style*— The Rt Hon the Lord Hemingford; The Old Rectory, Hemingford Abbots, Huntingdon, Cambs PE18 9AN (☎ 0480 66234); Westminster Press Ltd, 8-16 Great New Street, London EC4P 4ER (☎ 01 353 1030)

HEMINGWAY, Peter; *b* 19 Jan 1926; *m* 1952, June; *Career* ptnr John Gordon Walton and Co 1959-62, joined Leeds Perm Bldg Soc as sec 1962, (dir and chief gen mangr 1982-87); hon sec Yorks and N Western Assoc of Bldg Socs 1970-82; (chm 1984-86); memb cncl: Bldg Socs Assoc 1981-87, Chartered Bldg Socs Inst 1982-87; vice-pres Northern Assoc of Bldg Socs; local dir (Leeds) Royal Insur (UK) Ltd 1983-; FCA; *Recreations* travel, motor racing, music, gardening; *Style*— Peter Hemingway, Esq; Old Barn Cottage, Kearby, nr Wetherby, Yorks (☎ 0532 886380)

HEMMING, Alice Louisa; OBE (1974); da of William Arthur Weaver (d 1958), of Penticton, Br Columbia, and Alice Louisa, *née* Chorley (d 1964); *b* 18 Sept 1907; *Educ* Vancouver HS, Univ of Br Columbia (BA); *m* 5 March 1931, (Henry) Harold Hemming, OBE, MC, s of Henry Keane Simmons Hemming, of Charlottestown, Prince Edward Island, Canada; 1 s (John b 5 Jan 1935), 1 da (Louisa b 13 Dec 1931); *Career* journalist Vancouver Sun 1928-30, columnist Vancouver Province 1940-44, broadcaster 1940-43, info offr Nat Film Bd of Canada 1943-44, Marquis of Donegall Sunday Despatch 1937-41, ed advsr Municipal Jl 1948-68, dir Municipal Gp; pres Cwlth Countries League 1948-, vice-pres Women's Cncl; memb: Br American Assocs, Cncl Canadian Univs Socs, Ctee 'Woodstock', Hampstead Old People's Housing Tst, Canadian Ctee of London House (for overseas graduates), Jt Cwlth Socs cncl; govr CCLA Ed Ctee; *Recreations* dancing, entertaining for charities; *Style*— Mrs Alice Hemming, OBE; 35 Elsworthy Rd, London NW3 3BT (☎ 01 722 6619); The Municipal Journal, 178-202 Great Portland St, London W1

HEMMING, Dr John Henry; s of Lt-Col Henry Harold Hemming, OBE, MC (d 1977), of London, and Alice Louisa, OBE, *née* Weaver; *b* 5 Jan 1935; *Educ* Eton, McGill Univ, Oxford Univ (MA, DLitt); *m* 19 Jan 1979, Sukie Mary, da of Brig Michael J Babington-Smith, CBE (d 1984); 1 s (Henry Sebastian b 1979), 1 da (Beatrice Margaret Louisa b 1981); *Career* charity dir RGS 1975-; publisher: jt chm Hemming Publishing Ltd (formerly Municipal Journal Ltd) 1976- (dir 1962, dep chm 1967-76); jt chm Municipal Gp Ltd 1976-; chm: Brintex Ltd 1979- (md 1962-71), Newman Books Ltd 1979-; dir and sec RGS 1975-; ldr Maraca Rainforest Project Brazil 1987-89; fndr, tstee and sponsor Survival Int; memb cncl/ctee: Lepra, Anglo-Brazilian Soc, Geographical Club, L S B Leakey Tst, Gilchrist Educnl Tst, Cncl for Nat Academic Awards, Cncl of Br Geography; hon corresponding memb Academia Nacional de Historia Venezuela; Freeman Worshipful Co of Stationers and Newspapermakers; Hon DLitt Warwick 1989; Mungo Park Medal of RGS (Scot) 1988; Orden de Mérito (Peru) 1987; *Books* The Conquest of the Incas (1970), Tribes of the Amazon Basin in Brazil (1973), Red Gold (1978), The Search for El Dorado (1978), Machu Picchu (1981), Monuments of the Incas (1982), Change in the Amazon Basin (1985), Amazon Frontier (1987), Maracá (1988); *Books Incl:* The Conquest of the Incas, Red Gold, The Search for El Dorado, Amazon Frontier; *Recreations* writing, travel; *Clubs* Travellers', Beefsteak, Geographical; *Style*— Dr John Hemming; 10 Edwardes Sq, London W8 6HE (☎ 01 602 6697); 178-202 Great Portland Street, London W1N 6NH (☎ 01 637 2400, 01 589 0648, fax 01 631 0360, telex 262568 MUNBEX G)

HEMMING, Lindy; da of Alan Hemming (d 1983), of Crug-y-Bar, Llanwrda, Dyfed, and Jean, *née* Alexander; *b* 21 August 1948; *Educ* RADA; Bob Starrett; 1 s (Daniel Grace b 16 Nov 1974), 1 da (Alexandra Grace b 30 Jan 1969); *Career* costume designer in theatre, tv and film 1972-; Hampstead Theatre Club 1974-79: Abigail's Pary, Ecstasy, The Elephant Man, Uncle Vanya, Clouds; RSC 1978-84: Juno and the Paycock, Mother Courage, All's Well That Ends Well; National Theatre Co: Death of a Salesman, Schweyk in the Second World war, Pravda, A View from the Bridge, A Small Family Business, Waiting for Godot; West End theatre: Donkeys Years, Brighton Beach Memoirs; film and tv: Wetherby, 84 Charing Cross Rd, Abigail's Party, My Beautiful Laundrette, High Hopes, Meantime, Porterhouse Blue, Queen of Hearts; memb Soc Br THeatre Designers; *Recreations* cycling, walking, eating, drinking coffee, watching people; *Style*— Ms Lindy Hemming; 8 Bewdley St, London N1 1HB (☎01 607 6107)

HEMMINGS, Edward Ernest; s of Edward Hemmings and Dorothy Phyllis Hemmings; *b* 20 Feb 1949; *Educ* Campion HS; *m* 1971, Christine Mary; 2 s (Thomas, James); *Career* professional cricketer, starter 1965; *Style*— Edward Hemmings, Esq; Nottinghamshire CCC; Trent Bridge, Nottingham (☎ 821525)

HEMPHILL, Hon Dr (Pamela); *née* Rhodes; da of Baron Rhodes, KG, DFC*, PC, DL, and Anne, da of John Henry Bradbury; *b* 1 May 1927; *Educ* university (PhD); *m* 1953 (m dis 1969), Walter Leaman Hemphill, s of late Wesley Hemphill; 2 da; *Style*— The Hon Dr Hemphill; Cheyney, Pennsylvania 19319, USA

HEMPHILL, 5 Baron (UK 1906); Peter Patrick Fitzroy Martyn Martyn-Hemphill; assumed the additional surname of Martyn by deed poll of 1959; s of 4 Baron (d 1957); *b* 5 Sept 1928; *Educ* Downside, Brasenose Coll Oxford (MA); *m* 1952, Olivia, da of Major Robert Ruttledge, MC, of Co Mayo, and sis of Lady Edward FitzRoy (herself da-in-law of 10 Duke of Grafton); 1 s, 2 da; *Heir* s, Hon Charles Martyn-Hemphill; *Career* chm Racing Control Ctee, former sr steward Turf Club, memb Irish Nat Hunt Steeplechase Ctee; Cross of Order of Merit, Order of Malta; *Clubs* White's, RIYC, Irish Cruising, RLAC, County (Galway); *Style*— The Rt Hon the Lord Hemphill; Raford House, Kiltulla, Co Galway, Ireland

HEMPSALL, (William) John; MBE (1969); s of Fred Hempsall (d 1970), and Ethel, *née* Barton (d 1960); *b* 5 July 1912; *Educ* Sloane Sch Chelsea, Chelsea Art Sch, Chelsea Poly; *m* 1, 9 Sept 1939, (m dis), Eunice Anne, da of late John Robinson ; 1 s (William b 1941); m 2, 23 June 1948, Agnes Kathleen, da of Thos Charles Wathes, of Hurley, Warks; 2 da (Susan b 1950, Elizabeth b 1952); *Career* worked Epsom UDC 1935-37, Middx Co Engrs Dept 1937-40, Admty E-in-C's Dept Dover and Chatham 1940-43, Air Ministry Works Directorate 1943-47, St Marylebone BC 1947-49, Camberwell BC 1949-51; Uganda PWD and Miny of Works 1951-69, asst engr Sir Frederick Snow and Ptnrs London 1969-71, Crown Agents 1971-74; engr Ghana, RE Nigeria; sr conslt CE Acid Plant N Wales 1977-78; sr res engr mangr Zaire Airports Contract 1975-77, Chemico Ltd 1977; conslt CE Acid Plant N Wales 1977-78; sr res engr Belfast Airport (Aldergrove) NI 1977-80; ret 1980; CEng, FICE, FIHT; *Recreations* reading, writing, art, DIY; *Style*— John Hempsall, MBE; Cote House, Burton Street, Marnhull, Sturminster Newton, Dorset DT10 1PP (☎ 0258 820 484)

HEMSLEY, Hon Mrs (Gwenllian Ellen); *née* James; eldest da of 4 Baron Northbourne; *b* 9 Sept 1929; *m* 1, 14 June 1952 (m annulled 1960), Michael Hugh Rose, 3 s of late Rt Rev Alfred Carey Wollaston Rose, Bishop of Dover; m 2, 9 Nov 1960, Thomas Jeffrey Hemsley, s of Sydney William Hemsley, of Hugglescote, Leics; 3 s; *Style*— The Hon Mrs Hemsley; 10 Denewood Rd, Highgate, London N6

HEMSLEY, Henry Neville (Harry); DL (Leics); s of Neville Hemsley (d 1948), of Jersey, CI, and Mary Florence Eliza, *née* Farran (d 1968); *b* 27 Nov 1922; *Educ* Sherborne, Cambridge (MA); *m* 26 Feb 1949, Margaret Ruth, da of Hon William Borthwick (d 1956); 2 s (John Neville b 1956, Oliver Charles b 1960), 2 da (Patricia Mary b 1964, Clare Margaret b 1953); *Career* Lt (E) Temp RN 1942-46; farmer 1961-; chm Rutland Magistrates Ct 1987-; memb: bd of vistors Ashwell Prison 1969-, LRC Ashwell Prison Circa 1975-; former chm Local NAVSS, nat mgmnt ctee NAVSS 1982-87, former cdre Rutland SC; *Recreations* shooting, bridge; *Style*— Henry Hemsley, Esq, DL; Langham Lodge, Oakham, Rutland LE15 7HZ (☎ 0572 2912)

HEMSLEY, Michael John; s of Reginald James Hemsley (d 1968), and Therese Elizabeth (d 1987); *b* 9 Mar 1940; *Career* slr,fndr and princ Hemsleys Slrs, Chester; *Style*— Michael J Hemsley, Esq; "Spring Villa", Liverpool Road, Chester (☎ 0244 371125); Upper Northgate, Chester (☎ 0244 382400, fax 0244 372335)

HEMSLEY, Thomas Jeffrey; s of Sydney William Hemsley (d 1986), of Little Eversden, Cambs, and Kathleen Annie, *née* Deacon (d 1976); *b* 12 April 1927; *Educ* Ashby-de-la-Zouch Boys GS, Brasenose Coll Oxford (MA); *m* 9 Nov 1960, Hon Gwenllian Ellen James, *qv*, s of Walter Ernest Christopher James, 4 Baron Northbourne (d 1982), of Northbourne Ct, Deal, Kent; 3 s (William b 1962, Matthew b 1963, Michael b 1965); *Career* PO RAF 1948-50; vicar choral St Paul's Cathedral 1950-51, opera debut Mermaid Theatre 1951, Glyndebourne Festival Opera debut 1953 (first of many appearances until 1983), princ baritone Opernhaus Zurich 1963-67; freelance singer 1967-: Covent Garden, ENO, Scottish Opera, WNO, Kent Opera, Glyndebourne Festival, Edinburgh Festival, Bayreuth Festival (1968-70) soloist for many orchestras throughout Europe; teacher: Royal Northern Coll of Music, Royal Danish Acad of Music, Britten-Pears Sch, etc; TV masterclasses: Denmark 1971, BBC TV 1976; opera prodr: RNCM, Dallas Public Opera, Kent Opera; jury memb at many singing competitions, Cramm lectr Glasgow univ 1976; Hon RAM (1974), Hon FTCL 1988; memb: ISM 1953, Equity 1953; *Recreations* gardening, mountain walking ; *Clubs* Garrick; *Style*— Thomas Hemsley, Esq; 10 Denewood Rd, London N6 4AJ (☎ 01 348 3397)

HEMSTED, Dr Edmund Henry; s of Edmund Spencer Hemsted, and Evelyn Mary, *née* Stawell-Brown; *b* 16 August 1914; *Educ* Bryanston, Jesus Coll Cambridge (BA, MB, Bch, DCP); *m* 4 Jan 1943, Joyce, da of Sir Arthur Thewell, KB, CBE, of Jamaica (d 1966); 1 s (Peter b 1945 (d 1966)), 2 da (Carlotta b 1943, Louise b 1947); *Career* conslt pathologist, ret 1979; FRCPath; publishes articles (jointly) on Histology, Haematology and Immunology; *Style*— Dr Edmund H Hemsted

HENDER, (John) Derrik; CBE (1986), DL (West Midlands 1973); s of Jesse Peter Hender (d 1944), and Jennie Williams (d 1965); *b* 15 Nov 1926; *Educ* Gt Yarmouth GS; *m* 1949, Kathleen, da of Frederick William Brown (d 1945); 1 da (Annette); *Career* dep tres: Newcastle-upon-Lyme BC 1957, Wolverhampton MBC 1961; city tres City of Coventry 1964, chief exec and town clerk City of Coventry 1969, chief exec W Midlands CC 1973-86, public sector conslt 1986-; *Style*— J D Hender Esq, CBE, DL; 5 Cringleford Chase, Cringleford, Norwich NR4 7RS

HENDERSON, (James Stewart) Barry; s of James Henderson, CBE; *b* 29 April 1936; *Educ* Lathallan Sch, Stowe; *m* 1961, Janet; 2 s; *Career* info offr Scottish Cons Cent Off 1966-70; Parly candidate (Cons): Edinburgh E 1966, E Dunbartonshire 1970; MP (Cons): E Dunbartonshire Feb-Oct 1974, Fife E 1979-83, NE Fife 1983-87; Scottish Cons backbench ctee 1983; memb: select ctee for Scottish Affrs 1979-87, cncl of Parly Info Technol Ctee 1980-87, Commons Chm's Panel 1981-83; Treasy PPS 1984-87; MBCS; *Style*— Barry Henderson, Esq; 43c South St, St Andrews, Fife, Scotland

HENDERSON, Charles Edward; s of David Henderson (d 1972), and Georgiana Leggatt, *née* Mackie; *b* 19 Sept 1939; *Educ* Charterhouse, Univ of Cambridge; *m* 1966, Rachel, da of Dr A S Hall, of Bucks; 1 s (Luke b 1971), 1 da (Catherine b 1970); *Career* asst investmt sec Equity and Law Life Assur Soc Ltd 1966-70; princ Export Credits Ctee Dept DTI, Dept Energy 1971-75 (asst sec Dept Energy 1976-82), head Atomic Energy Div 1982-84, head Oil Div 1984-85, princ estab and fin offr 1985-88, head Off of Arts and Libraries 1989-; FIA; *Recreations* music (listening and playing), golf, reading, mountain walking; *Style*— Charles Henderson, Esq; 33 Fairfax Rd, London W4 1EN (☎ 01 994 1345); Office of Arts & Libraries, Horse Guards Rd, London SW1P 3AL

HENDERSON, (George) Clifford McLaren; s of Robert McLaren Henderson (d 1962); *b* 7 Feb 1938; *Educ* Bembridge Sch IOW; *Career* dir: Frank Partridge 1973-77, Stair and Co (New York) 1977-79; antiques conslt 1979-88, exec dir Partridge Fine Arts Ltd 1988; *Recreations* music, swimming, theatre, bridge; *Style*— Clifford Henderson, Esq; 23 Lochmore House, Ebury St, London SW1W 9JX (☎ 01 730 2725)

HENDERSON, David Alexander; s of George Alexander Henderson (d 1973), of Edinburgh, and Jessie, *née* Wilson; *b* 16 Sept 1944; *Educ* Broughton HS; *m* 5 April 1970, (Constance) Mary, da of Adam Renton (d 1986), of Edinburgh; 1 s (Bryan b 1973), 1 da (Dayne b 1977); *Career* audit mangr Scott Mancrieff Thomson-Sheills 1969-71; gen mangr Scottish Equitable Life 1987- (asst gen mangr 1984-87, chief asst 1979-84, accountant 1974-79, asst accountant 1971-74); FCCA 1968; *Recreations* golf, rugby; *Clubs* Warsonian, Moronhall Golf; *Style*— David Henderson, Esq; 28 St Andrew Square, Edinburgh (☎ 031 556 9101)

HENDERSON, Denys Hartley; *b* 11 Oct 1932; *Educ* Univ of Aberdeen (MA, LLB); *m* m, 2 da; *Career* slr; dir: ICI plc 1987-; non-exec dir: Dalgety plc 1981-87, Barclays Bank plc 1983-, Barclays plc 1985-, Barclays Int Ltd 1985-87; chm Stock Exchange Listed Cos Advsy Ctee; memb: Ct of Govrs Henley Mgmnt Coll, Presidents Ctee CBI, Br Malaysian Soc, Advsy Cncl of The Prince's Youth Business Tst, NY Stock

Exchange Listed Co Advsy Ctee, Opportunity Japan Campaign Ctee, Appeal Cncl, Winston Churchill Memb Tst, Save the Children Fund; tstee British Museum (Natural History); memb Law Soc of Scotland; FRSA, CBIM, FInstM; DUniv Brunel 1987, Hon LLD Aberdeen 1987; *Recreations* family life, swimming, reading, travel, minimal gardening, unskilled but enjoyable golf; *Clubs* Royal Automobile; *Style*— Denys H Henderson, Esq; Imperial Chemical Industries plc;, Imperial Chemical House, Millbank, London SW1P 3JF (☎ 01 834 4444)

HENDERSON, Douglas John; MP (Lab) Newcastle upon Tyne North 1978-; s of John Henderson, and Joan, *née* Bryson; *b* 9 May 1949; *Educ* Waid Acad, Central Coll Glasgow, Univ of Strathclyde (BA Econ); *m* 1974, Janet Margaret, da of Robert Graham (d 1984), of Scotland; 1 s (Keir John b 1986); *Career* apprentice Rolls Royce Glasgow 1966-68; Trade Union organisor (GMWU later GMB) 1973-87; memb Exec Scottish Cncl Lab Pty 1979-87 (chm 1984-85); memb NEDO Sector Working Pty 1981-84, industry spokesperson for Lab Pty; *Recreations* athletics, mountaineering; *Clubs* Lemington Labour, Newburn Memorial, Dinnington, Cambuslang Harriers, Elswick Harriers, Desperados Climbing; *Style*— Doug Henderson, Esq, MP; Ossian, 4 Parkside, Throckley, Newcastle upon Tyne NE15 9AX (☎ 091 267 2427); House of Commons (☎ 01 219 5017)

HENDERSON, Douglas Lindsay; s of Capt Arthur Henderson, of Sydney, Australia, and Sheila Lindsay, *née* Russel; *b* 17 Dec 1947; *Educ* Univ of New England USA (BA), Univ of NSW Australia (MBA, PhD); *m* 20 Jan 1970, Marilyn Gail, da of Ronald Clifford (d 1982), of Sydney, Australia; 3 s (Angus Arthur Lindsay b 1975, Duncan Ronald Alan b 1978, Stuart b 1987); *Career* lectr Univ of NSW Australia 1972-74; vice pres Bank of America NT and SA 1973-83, first vice pres and dir Swiss Bank Corpn 1983-89; memb Graduate Business Assoc, AIB; *Clubs* Royal Overseas League; *Style*— Douglas Henderson, Esq; 99 Gresham Street, London EC2 (☎ 01 606 4000)

HENDERSON, Edward Firth; CMG (1972); s of Andrew Edward Firth Henderson (d 1959), of Bristol, and Ann DeCourcy (d 1919); *b* 12 Dec 1917; *Educ* Clifton, Brasenose Coll Oxford; *m* 1960, Jocelyn, da of late Leonard Nenk; 2 da (Anna, Lucy); *Career* Br Army 1939-48, Maj, seconded to Arab Legion 1945-47; Iraq Petroleum Co 1948 (rep: Trucial States and Oman 1949-52, Bahrain and Oman 1952-56); seconded to For Serv 1959, served in Bahrain, Jerusalem and London 1959; political agent Qatar 1969, ambass Qatar 1971, ret 1974; specialist in history of Gulf Centre for Documentation and Research in Abu Dhabi 1976; dir cncl Arab-Br Understanding in London 1981-82; chm American Educnl Tst Washington DC 1982-83, returned to Centre for Documentation 1983-; *Clubs* Travellers; *Style*— Edward Henderson, Esq, CMG; PO Box 2841, Abu Dhabi, UAE; 4 Purcell Close, Tewin Wood, Herts AL6 0NN; Centre for Documentation and Research, PO Box 2380, Abu Dhabi

HENDERSON, Eleanora Anderson; da of Maj David Anderson Spence (d 1922), of Montrose, and Eleanora Ramsay, *née* Borrie; *b* 21 June 1917; *Educ* St Georges Sch Edinburgh, Edinburgh Coll of Art (DA); *m* 12 March 1944, David Hope Henderson, s of Lt Col the Hon Philip Henderson, (d 1939); 2 s (Philip b 1947, Ian b 1949); *Career* artist; SSA Carnegie Award Postgraduate Scholarship 1940; exhibited: SSA, RA, RSA, RSPA, Dumfries Art Soc, Castle Douglas Kirkudbright; several solo shows London and Scotland; elected professional memb Soc of Scottish Artists 1941; *Recreations* art, golf, Scottish dancing; *Style*— Mrs Eleanora Henderson; Achie Farm, New Galloway, Kirkcudbrightshire, Scotland

HENDERSON, Hon Mrs (Elizabeth Frances); *née* May; o da of 1 Baron May, KBE (d 1946), and Lily Julia, *née* Strauss (d 1955); *b* 29 June 1907; *m* 10 June 1955, George Leonard Brunton Henderson, MRCVS, s of late Edward Joseph Henderson; 2 s; *Career* served WW II as Flt Capt ATA (award for valuable service in the air 1945); *Style*— The Hon Mrs Henderson; Oak Lodge, Oak Hill Grove, Surbiton, Surrey KT6 6DS

HENDERSON, Hon Mrs Flora Elizabeth; *née* Hewitt; da of 8 Viscount Lifford; *b* 1947; *m* 1965 (m dis 1975), Edward Bell Henderson; 2 da (Samantha b 1967, Amanda b 1971); *Style*— The Hon Mrs Flora Henderson

HENDERSON, Giles Ian; s of Charles David Henderson (d 1980), of Henfield, Sussex, and Joan, *née* Firmin; *b* 20 April 1942; *Educ* Michaelhouse Natal SA, Witwatersrand Univ SA (BA), Magdalen Coll Oxford (MA, BCL); *m* 21 Aug 1971, Lynne, da of Charles William Fyfield, OBE, of Alnmouth, Northumberland; 2 s (Mark b 1974, Simon b 1975), 1 da (Clare b 1978); *Career* admitted slr 1970, ptnr Slaughter and May 1975-; ; *Recreations* sport, music; *Style*— Giles Henderson, Esq; Slaughter and May, 35 Basinghall St, London EC2V 5DB (☎ 01 600 1200, fax 01 726 0038, 01 600 0289, telex 883486)

HENDERSON, Sir Guy Wilmot McLintock; s of late Arthur James Henderson, of Maidenhead, Berks; *b* 13 July 1897; *Educ* Blundell's, Wanganui Coll Sch New Zealand, Trinity Coll Cambridge (BA, LLB); *m* 1930, (Doris Mary) Ann Elizabeth (d 1980), da of late Cdr George Dring-Campion, RN; 2 s, 1 da; *Career* served WWI France, Lt RFA; barr Inner Temple 1923, magistrate Bahamas 1932-37, crown counsel Tanganyika 1937-40, legal draftsman Nigeria 1940-45, slr-gen Singapore 1946-48, attorney-gen Uganda 1948-51, QC Uganda 1949, chief justice Bahamas 1951-60, ret Colonial Serv 1960; barr Bahamas Bar 1960, private practice Bahamas 1960-; kt 1956; *Clubs* Lyford Cay (Bahamas); *Style*— Sir Guy Henderson; PO Box N 7776, Lyford Cay, Nassau, Bahamas (☎ 64084)

HENDERSON, Ian Ramsay; s of David Hope Henderson (d 1977), of Achie Farm, New Galloway, Kirkcudbrightshire, and Eleanora Anderson, *née* Spence; *b* 21 June 1917; *Educ* Eton, Univ of Edinburgh (MA, LLB); *m* 28 Oct 1978, Virginia Theresa, da of Lt-Col John E B Freeman (d 1986), of Buxhall Vale, Buxhall, Stowmarket, Suffolk; 3 s (Alexander b 1982, Charles b 1984, George b 1987); *Career* Peat Marwick Mitchell & Co 1972-76, Morgan Grenfell & Co 1977-82; dir: Wardley Marine Int Investmt Mgmnt Ltd 1982 (md 1985), Wardley Investment Mgmnt Servs Int Ltd 1987-; ACA 1984, FCA 1989; *Recreations* golf, tennis, windsurfing; *Clubs* Brook's, St James's; *Style*— Ian Henderson, Esq; 20 Westbourne Park Road, London W2 5PH; 99 Bishopsgate, London EC2P 2LA

HENDERSON, Dr James Ewart; CVO; s of Rev James Ewart Henderson (d 1968), of Trinity Manse, Beith, Ayrshire, and Agnes Mary, *née* Crawford (d 1957); *b* 29 May 1923; *Educ* Univ of Glasgow, Univ of Edinburgh (MA, DSc); *m* 1, 20 Aug 1949, Alice Joan, da of Horace James Hewlitt (d 1958), of Herts; 1 da (Joanna b 1956); m 2, 17 Jan 1966, Nancy Maude; 2 s (Jamie b 1966, Crawford b 1969),; *Career* scientist, operational res and admin (res air rockets and guns) MAP 1943-44, hon cmmn RAFVR 1944-46, operational res air attacks in Belgium, Holland and Germany, 2 TAF 1944-45, experimental res: fighter armament RAF APC Germany 1945-46, fighter and bomber capability also use of radar and radio aids Fighter Cmd 1946-49 (subsequently Centl Fighter Estab 1949-52), weapons effects and capability Air Miny 1952-54; AWRE 1955, Air Miny 1955-58, asst scientific advsr (ops) Air Miny 1958-63, dep chief scientist (RAF) MOD 1963-69, chief scientist (RAF) and memb Air Force Bd 1969-73; aviation conslt Hawker Siddeley Aviation Ltd 1973-77, fin conslt Charles Stapleton and Co Ltd 1973-78, freelance operational res and mgmnt conslt 1974-78, dir Lewis Security Systems Ltd 1976-77, sci advsr Br Aerospace 1978-82, chm TIB Netherlands 1982-86, chm and md Mastiff Electronic Systems Ltd 1985- (dir Security Systems Ltd 1977-82, md 1982-84, pres and chief exec (US) 1982-); pres Air League 1987- (memb cncl 1979-80, chm 1981-87); tech papers on operational capability of aircraft and weapons 1949-73, UK Manual on Blast Effects of Nuclear Weapons (1955); *Recreations* sailing, golf, opera; *Clubs* Naval and Military, Royal Scottish Automobile, Royal Western Yacht, Moor Park Golf, New Zealand Golf; *Style*— Dr James E Henderson, Esq; Mastiff Electronic Systems Ltd, Little Mead, Cranleigh, Surrey (☎ 0483 272097, telex 859307 MASTIF G, fax 0483 276728)

HENDERSON, Hon James Harold; s and h of 3 Baron Faringdon; *b* 14 July 1961; *m* 1986, Lucinda, yr da of Desmond Hanson, of Knipton, nr Grantham, Lincs; *Style*— The Hon James Henderson

HENDERSON, Sir James Thyne; KBE (1959), CMG (1952); s of Sir Thomas Henderson (d 1951); *b* 18 Jan 1901; *Educ* Sedbergh, Queen's Coll Oxford; *m* 1929, Karen Margrethe, da of R P Hansen, of Denmark; 1 s, 4 da; *Career* entered FO 1925, consul-gen Houston 1949-53, min Iceland 1953-56, ambass Bolivia 1956-60, ret; chm Cwlth Inst Scotland 1963-73; *Style*— Sir James Henderson, KBE, CMG; 43/14 Gillespie Crescent, Edinburgh EH10 4HY (☎ 031 229 8191)

HENDERSON, John Crombie; s of Maj Morrice Pitcairn Henderson, TD; *b* 8 April 1939; *Educ* Uppingham; *m* 1968, Marylou Susan, da of Maj-Gen Sir Francis de Guingand, KBE, CB, DSO (d 1979); 2 da; *Career* Lt Black Watch 1959-63; memb Stock Exchange 1969, chief exec Capel-Cure Myers Capital Mgmnt Ltd 1988- (joined 1964),; *Recreations* shooting, fishing, golf; *Clubs* Turf, Berkshire GC; *Style*— John Henderson, Esq; 125 Abbotsbury Rd, London W14 8EP

HENDERSON, John Ronald; CVO (1986), OBE (1985, MBE 1944), DL (Berks); s of late Maj R H W Henderson, and Marjorie, *née* Garrard ; *b* 6 May 1920; *Educ* Eton, Univ of Cambridge; *m* 1, 1949, Katherine Sarah (d 1972), da of late Maj-Gen Beckwith- Smith; 2 s, 1 da; m 2, 1976, Catherine, *née* Christian; 1 step s, 2 step da;; *Career* chm: Updown Investmt Tst, Racecourse Hldgs Tst, Henderson Admin Gp; dir Howard De Walden Estates; vice Ld-Lt of Berks 1979-; *Recreations* racing, shooting, hunting; *Clubs* White's; *Style*— John Henderson Esq, CVO, OBE, DL; West Woodhay House, Newbury, Berks (☎ 048 84 271); 3/4 Balfour Place, London W1 (☎ 01 629 4861)

HENDERSON, John Wilson; OBE (1978); s of Frederick James Henderson (d 1977), and Bertha May, *née* Wilson; *b* 8 July 1935; *Educ* Perse Sch Cambridge, Luton Coll of Technol; *m* 1963, Vivienne, da of Ronald Cedric Parker (d 1969); 1 s (David John Charles b 1967), 1 da (Sarah Jayne b 1970); *Career* dir: George Kent (Malaysia) BHD 1963-78, George Kent (Singapore) Pte Ltd 1965-78, Kent Precision Engrg Pte Ltd 1964-78, George Kent Int Ltd 1979-86, Brown Boveri Kent (E Asia) Pte Ltd 1980-87, Kent Belgium SA 1983-87, Compteurs Kent SA 1983-87, Kent Meters Ltd 1985-; *Clubs* Penang (Malaysia); *Style*— John Henderson, Esq, OBE; April Cottage, West Wickham, Cambridge CB1 6SB (☎ 022 029 243); Kent Meters Ltd, Pondwicks Road, Luton, Bedfordshire (☎ 402020, telex 825367, fax 36657)

HENDERSON, Hon Launcelot Dinadan James; er s of Baron Henderson of Brompton (Life Peer), and Susan Mary, *née* Dartford; *b* 20 Nov 1951; *Educ* Westminster, Balliol Coll Oxford; *m* 1989, Elaine Elizabeth, er da of Kenneth Frank Webb, of Dringhouses, York; *Career* barr Lincoln's Inn 1977; appointed standing jr counsel Chancery to the Inland Revenue 1987; fell All Souls Coll Oxford 1974-81 and 1982-; *Style*— The Hon Launcelot Henderson; 17 Carlisle Road, London NW6 6TL

HENDERSON, Mark Ian; s of Ian Sidney Campbell Henderson (d 1954), and Patricia Joyce, *née* Muers; *b* 10 April 1947; *Educ* Stowe, CLP Business Studies BA (Hons); *m* 1970, Ann, da of Albert Edwin Reed (d 1982); 1 s (James b 1978), 1 da (Johanna b 1976); *Career* md RCB Int 1987-; dir: Hill Samuel Pensions Investmt Mgmnt 1981-87 (md 1986-87), Mpalanganga Estates (Malawi) 1983-, Hill Samuel Asset Mgmnt 1984-87, Hill Samuel Investmt Mgmnt 1985-87 (formerly American Distributors plc), Sapphire Petroleum plc 1985-88; Freeman City of London; memb Lloyd's; ASIA, Assoc London Oil Analysists Gp; *Publications* numerous articles on investmt mgmnt; *Recreations* running, music, scuba diving; *Clubs* Carlton; *Style*— Mark Henderson, Esq; 39 Winsham Grove, London SW11 6NB (☎ 01 228 9880); RCB Int Ltd, Int House, 1 St Katharines Way, London E1 9UN (☎ 01 481 2506)

HENDERSON, Hon Mary Sophia; da of Baron Henderson of Brompton (Life Peer), and Susan Mary, *née* Dartford; *b* 1965; *Style*— The Hon Mary Henderson; 16 Pelham St, London SW7 2NG

HENDERSON, Michael John Glidden; s of William Glidden Henderson (d 1946), and Aileen Judith, *née* Malloy; *b* 19 August 1938; *Educ* St Benedict's Sch Ealing; *m* 29 Sept 1965, Stephanie Maria, da of John Dyer, of Hampton Court, Surrey; 4 s (Nicholas b 1966, Simon b 1968, Angus b 1972, Giles b 1976); *Career* chief exec Cookson Gp plc; dir: Cookson Overseas Ltd, Cookson Investmts Ltd, Cookson America Inc, Cookson (Europe) SA, Cookson Hong Kong Ltd, Cookson India, Cookson Australia Pty Ltd, LIG Canada Inc, Spinnaker Insur Co Ltd Gibraltar, Mainsail Insur Co Ltd Bermuda, Guiness Mahon Hldgs Plc; FCA 1961; *Recreations* tennis, cricket; *Style*— Michael Henderson, Esq; Langdale, Woodland Drive, East Horsley, Surrey (☎ 048 65 3844); Cookson Group plc, 14 Gresham St, London EC2V 7AT (☎ 01 606 4400, fax 01 606 2851, telex 884141)

HENDERSON, Sir (John) Nicholas; GCMG (1977, KCMG 1972, CMG 1965); s of Prof Sir Hubert Henderson; *b* 1 April 1919; *Educ* Stowe, Hertford Coll Oxford; *m* 1951, Mary Barber, *née* Cawadias; 1 da (Alexandra m 1978 Viscount (Henry Dermot Ponsonby) Moore, *qv*); *Career* private sec to Foreign Sec 1963-65, min Madrid 1965-69; ambass: Poland 1969-72, W Germany 1972-75, France 1975-79, USA (Washington) 1979-82; dir: M and G Reinsurance 1982-, Foreign and Colonial Investmt Tst plc 1982; Hambros plc 1983-, Tarmac plc 1983-, F and C Eurotrust plc 1984-; chm: Channel Tunnel Gp 1985-86, Fuel Tech NV; Lord Warden of the Stannaries, Keeper of the Privy Seal of the Duchy of Cornwall, vice chm of the Prince of Wales cncl 1985-, tstee Nat Gallery 1985-; hon fell Hertford Coll Oxford 1975, hon DCL

Oxford; *Books* Prince Eugen of Savoy (biography), The Birth of NATO (1982), The Private Office (1984), Channels and Tunnels (1987); *Recreations* gardening; *Clubs* Brooks's, Garrick, Beefsteak; *Style*— Sir Nicholas Henderson, GCMG; 6 Fairholt St, London SW7 1EG (☎ 01 589 4291); School House, Combe, Newbury, Berks (☎ 480 84 330); Hambros plc, 41 Tower Hill, London EC3N 4HA (☎ 01 480 5000, telex 883851)

HENDERSON, Adm Sir Nigel Stuart; GBE (1968, OBE 1944), KCB (1962, CB 1959), DL (Kirkcudbrightshire 1973); s of Lt-Col Selby Herriott Henderson (d 1935); *b* 1 August 1909; *Educ* Cheltenham; *m* 1939, Catherine Mary, *née* Maitland; 1 s, 2 da; *Career* RN 1927, served WW II, Cdr 1942, Capt 1948, Rear Adm 1957, Vice Adm 1960, Adm 1963, chm mil ctee NATO 1968-71, ret 1971; Rear Adm of UK 1973-76, Vice Adm of UK and Lt of the Admty 1976-79; pres Royal Br Legion Scotland 1974-80; *Style*— Adm Sir Nigel Henderson, GBE, KCB, DL; Hensol, Mossdale, Castle Douglas, Kirkcudbrightshire, Scotland (☎ 064 45 207)

HENDERSON, Oscar William James; OBE (1984), DL (Belfast 1977); s of Cdr Oscar Henderson, CVO, CBE, DSO (d 1969); bro of Robert B Henderson, *qv*; *b* 17 August 1924; *Educ* Brackenber House Belfast, Bradfield; *m* 1949, Rachel Primrose, da of Col John Vincent Forrest, CMG, of Belfast; 3 da; *Career* served WW II NW Europe, Capt Irish Gds 1942-47; chm Century Newspapers Ltd (publishers of The Newsletter, estab 1737, UK's oldest daily morning newspaper); dir: Ulster TV Ltd, Ulster Sheltered Employment Ltd and others; FBIM; *Recreations* gardening, fishing; *Clubs* Ulster Reform (Belfast); *Style*— Oscar W J Henderson, Esq, OBE, DL; Glenalmond, Quarry Rd, Belfast BT4 2NQ (☎ 0232 63145)

HENDERSON, Philip William Alexander; s of Edgar Stuart Henderson (d 1974), of Bournemouth, Hants, and Dora Amelia, *née* Sizer (d 1956); *b* 3 April 1939; *Educ* Aldenham; *m* 29 June 1963, Patricia Elizabeth, da of Albert Edgar Civati (d 1976), of Wallington, Surrey; 1 da (Claire Annette b 1 April 1965, d 10 Jan 1972); *Career* articled clerk Viney Price and Goodyear 1956-61; stockbroking analyst: Vickers da Costa 1961-67, Laurence Keens Gardner 1967; ptnr James Capel and Co 1967-73, fndr Candean Ltd 1973-76, ptnr Henderson Crosthwaite 1976-80, gp exec Strategy Dalgety plc 1980-82, dep int mangr Merchant Navy Offrs Pension Fund 1982-, int mangr Ensign Tst 1985-; dir: Banque Bruxelles Lambert 1987-, Charles Heidsieck SA 1986-, Meghraj Gp 1981-, Clydesdale Investmt Tst 1987-, Ensign Tst 1986-, India Fund 1986-, Abtrust Hldgs 1988-; Chm: Filmtrax 1987-, Merchant Navy Inv Mgt 1985-; Organiser: Vamps Ball June 1985, Golddiggers Ball June 1987, Sweethearts Ball 1989, Ensign Prize RCA 1988, Ensign Prize RCA 1988-89; *Recreations* charity work, popular music 1900-69; *Clubs* City of London; *Style*— Philip Henderson, Esq; Fishing Cottage, Powermill Lane, Battle, E Sussex; 30 Finsbury Circus, London EC2 (☎ 01 588 6000, fax 01 588 1224, telex 888607)

HENDERSON, Hon Richard Crosbie Aitken; yr s of Baron Henderson of Brompton, KCB (Life Peer), and Susan Mary, *née* Dartford; *b* 27 Mar 1957; *Educ* Westminster, Magdalen Coll Oxford (MA, DPhil), Univ of Nottingham (Dip Th); *m* 1985, Anita Julia, da of Antony Gerald Stroud Whiting; *Style*— The Hon Richard Henderson; 16 Pelham St, London SW7 2NG

HENDERSON, Robert Alistair; s of Robert Evelyn Henderson (himself er bro of Rt Hon Sir Nevile Henderson, GCMG, PC (d 1942), Ambass to Germany 1937-39 and eld s of Robert Henderson, of Sedgwick Park, nr Horsham) and Beatrice (d 1980), o da of Sir William Clerke, 11 Bt (d 1930); R A Henderson is bro of 7 Earl Fortescue's first wife and 2 cous of 2 Baron St Just; *b* 4 Nov 1917; *Educ* Eton, Magdalene Cambridge; *m* 1947, Bridget Elizabeth, only da of Col John Lowther, CBE, DSO, MC, TD, DL (yr bro of Sir Charles Lowther, 4 Bt) and Hon Lilah White (er da of 3 Baron Annaly); 2 s (Robert b 1948, James b 1955), 1 da (Emma b 1950); *Career* served WW II, Capt 60 Rifles (KRRC); chm: Kleinwort Benson Lonsdale plc 1978-, Kleinwort Benson 1975-83, Kleinwort Benson Inc 1971-83, Kleinwort Benson (Tstees) Ltd 1975-83, Cross Investmt Tst 1969-; pres Klescan Investmts 1971-83; dir: Inchcape plc 1967-, Hamilton Oil (GB) plc 1973-; dep chm: Cadbury Schweppes plc 1977-83, Hamilton Bros Oil and Gas Ltd 1981-, BA plc 1985-; memb BA 1981-; former pres Equitable Life Assur Soc; *Clubs* Brooks's, White's; *Style*— Robert Henderson, Esq; 7 Royal Ave, London SW3 4QE (☎ 01 730 1104); North Ecchinswell Farm, Ecchinswell, nr Newbury, Berks RG15 8UJ (☎ 063 523 244); Kleinwort Benson Lonsdale plc, 20 Fenchurch St, London EC3P 3DB (☎ 01 623 8000), N Ecclinaswell Farm, Newbury, Berks

HENDERSON, Robert Brumwell; CBE (1979); s of Cdr Oscar Henderson, CVO, CBE, DSO, RN (d 1969); bro of Oscar W J Henderson, *qv*; *b* 28 July 1929; *Educ* Brackenber House Sch Belfast, Bradfield, Trinity Coll Dublin (MA); *m* 1970, Patricia Ann, da of Mathew Davison, of Belfast; 2 da; *Career* journalist 1951-59; dir: ITN 1964-68, Ind TV Pubns 1968-87; chm: Ulster TV 1983- (md 1959-, dep chm 1977-83), Laganside Ltd 1987-; chm: Cinema and TV Benevolent Fund NI, Cncl of the Royal TV Soc 1982-84; pres: Assocs of Ulster Drama Festivals 1983-, Northern Ireland C of C and Indust 1979-80; memb cncl Inst of Dirs 1972-; DLitt Ulster 1982; *Books* Midnight Oil (1961), A Television First (1977), Amusing (1984); *Recreations* reading, theatre, cinema, golf; *Clubs* Naval and Military, Royal County Down Golf, Malone Golf; *Style*— Robert Brumwell Henderson, Esq, CBE; (☎ 0232 328122); 8 Crabtree Rd, Ballynahinch, Co Down, N Ireland BT24 8RH

HENDERSON, Dr Robert Gregory; CBE (1947); s of late George Henderson, of Smithfield, Clatt, Aberdeenshire; *b* 1902; *Educ* Univ of Aberdeen (MB, ChB, MD, DPH); *Career* conslt physician and Surgn-Capt late RNVR; princ asst med offr Centl Staff Dept Pub Health Dept LCC 1937-39, divisional med offr Miny of Health Emergency Med Serv 1939-40; designed and made the Henderson Respirator (first iron lung) 1933, supt Southern Hosp Dartford Kent 1940-60; *Style*— Dr Robert Henderson, CBE; The Mill House, Brenchley, Tonbridge, Kent TN12 7NS (☎ 089 272 2052)

HENDERSON, Hon Roderic Harold Dalzell; granted title rank and precedence of a Baron's son 1935; s of Lt-Col Hon Harold Greenwood Henderson, CVO, MP (d 1922), and Lady Violet Dalzell, da of 14 Earl of Carnwath (d 1956); bro of 2 Baron Faringdon; *b* 3 Mar 1909; *Educ* Eton, Pembroke Coll Cambridge; *Career* hon attaché: Br Legation Stockholm 1932-33, HM Embassy Uruguay; civil attaché and private sec: HM Embassy Buenos Aires 1943-46, Stockholm 1946, Rome 1946, ret; dir Ellis Meml Boston Mass; *Recreations* swimming; *Style*— The Hon Roderic Henderson; 565 Tuckerman Ave, Middletown, Rhode Island 02840, USA (☎ 401 846 9358); 100 Alhambra Pl, W Palm Beach, Florida, USA 33405

HENDERSON, Roger Anthony; QC (1980); s of Dr Peter Wallace Henderson (d 1984), and Dr Stella Dolores, *née* Morton; *b* 21 April 1943; *Educ* Radley, St Catharines Coll Cambridge; *m* 1968, Catherine Margaret, da of Claude Williams; 3 da (Camilla, Antonia, Venetia); *Career* barr 1964, rec 1983; pres Br Acad of Forensic Sci 1986, chm public affrs ctee of the Bar 1989; *Recreations* fly fishing, shooting; *Style*— R A Henderson, Esq, QC; 9 Brunswick Gdns, London W8 (☎ 01 727 3980); 2 Harcourt Bldgs, Temple, London EC4 (☎ 01 583 9020, telex 8956788 HARKEN G, fax 5832686)

HENDERSON, Roy Galbraith; CBE (1970); s of Rev Dr Alexander Roy Henderson (d 1951); *b* 4 July 1899; *Educ* Nottingham HS, RAM; *m* 1926, Bertha Collin, *née* Smyth; 3 children; *Career* baritone; debut Queens Hall London 1925, Glyndebourne from opening night 1934-39, Covent Garden and concert platform (performed recitals at first two Edinburgh Festivals); conductor Choral Socs: Huddersfield 1932-39, Nottingham 1936-53, Bournemouth 1942-52; int competition adjudicator in Holland, Spain and Switzerland, private teacher of singing, prof of singing RAM 1940-75 (ret 1985); master of classics Holland and Canada 1985; FRAM; *Recreations* watching cricket, trout fishing, gardening, DIY; *Clubs* MCC; *Style*— Roy Henderson Esq, CBE; 90 Burbage Rd, London SE24 9HE (☎ 01 274 9004)

HENDERSON, Sir William MacGregor; s of William Simpson Henderson (d 1948); *b* 17 July 1913; *Educ* George Watson's Coll Edinburgh, Edinburgh Univ (BSc, DSc); *m* 1941, Alys Beryl, da of Dick Owen Cyril Goodridge (d 1932); 4 s; *Career* asst Dept of Med Royal Veterinary Coll Edinburgh 1936-38, memb sci staff Animal Virus Res Inst Pirbright 1939-55 and 1955-56; dir: Pan-American Foot and Mouth Disease Centre Rio De Janiero 1957-65, ARC Inst for Res on Animal Diseases Compton 1967-72 (dep dir 1966-67); sec Agric Res Cncl 1972-78, chm Genetic Manipulation Advsy Gp 1979-81; memb Sci Cncl Celltech Ltd 1980-82 (bd of dirs 1982-84); bd of dir Wellcome Biotechnology Ltd 1983-; pres Zoological Soc of London 1984-, Royal Assoc of Br Dairy Farmers 1985-87; FRS, FRSE; kt 1976; *Clubs* Athenaeum, New (Edinburgh); *Style*— Sir William Henderson; Yarnton Cottage, Streatley, Berks (☎ 0491 872162)

HENDERSON-STEWART, Sir David James; 2 Bt (UK 1957), of Callumshill, Co Perth; s of Sir James Henderson-Stewart, 1 Bt, MP (d 1961); *b* 3 July 1941; *Educ* Eton, Trinity Coll Oxford; *m* 1972, Anne, da of Count Serge de Pahlen; 3 s; *Heir* s, David Henderson-Stewart b 2 Feb 1973; *Clubs* Travellers'; *Style*— Sir David Henderson-Stewart, Bt; 3 Chepstow Crescent, London W11 (☎ 01 221 6255)

HENDRIE, Prof Gerald Mills; s of James Harold Hendrie (d 1981), and Florence Mary, *née* MacPherson (d 1968); *b* 28 Oct 1935; *Educ* Framlingham Coll Suffolk, RCM, Selwyn Coll Cambridge (MA, MusB, PhD); *m* 1, 11 July 1962, Dr Dinah Florence Barsham (d 1985); 2 s (Piers Edward b 13 May 1968, Dorian Mills b 15 Sept 1969); m 2, 15 Feb 1986, Dr Lynette (Lynne) Anne Maddern; *Career* dir of music Hometon Coll Cambridge 1962-63, lectr in history of music Univ of Manchester 1963-67, prof and chm Dept of Music Univ of Victoria Canada 1967-69, reader in music (later prof) Open Univ 1969-, dir of studies in music St John's Coll Cambridge 1981-84, visiting fell in music Univ of Western Australia 1985; active as organist and harpsichordist; memb cncl Handel Inst; FRSA 1981, FRCO, ARCM; *Recreations* windsurfing, reading; *Style*— Prof Gerald Hendrie; The Garth, 17 The Ave, Dallington, Northampton NN5 7AJ; Dept of Music, Faculty of Arts, The Open University, Walton Hall, Milton Keynes MK7 6AA (☎ 0908 653 280)

HENDRY, Prof Arnold William; s of George Hendry (d 1953), of Buckie, and Mary, *née* Grassick (d 1921); *b* 10 Sept 1921; *Educ* Buckie HS, Univ of Aberdeen (BSc, PhD, DSc); *m* 1, 27 June 1946, Sheila Mary Cameron (d 1966), da of William Nicol Roberts (d 1962); 2 s (George b 1953, Eric b 1958, d 1978), 1 da (Margaret b 1948); m 2, 28 Dec 1968, Elizabeth Lois Alice, da of Harry R G Inglis (d 1939); *Career* civil engr Sir William Arrol & Co 1941-43, lectr Univ of Aberdeen 1943-49, reader King's Coll London 1949-51, prof civil engrg, Univ of Khartoum 1951-57, prof bldg sci Univ of Liverpool 1957-63, prof civil engrg Univ of Edinburgh 1964-88, prof emeritus; memb cncl The Cockburn Assoc Edinburgh 1978-87, pres Scottish Assoc for Public Tport; FInstCE, FIStructE, FRSA, FRSE; *Recreations* reading, walking, travel, DIY; *Style*— Prof Arnold Hendry; 146/6 Whitehouse Loan, Edinburgh EH9 2AN (☎ 031 447 0368); Dept of Civil Engineering, The King's Buildings, Edinburgh EH9 3JL (☎ 031 667 1081)

HENDRY, Prof David Forbes; s of Robert Ernest Hendry, of 12 Craigdarroch Drive, Contin, RossShire, Scotland, and Catherine Elizabeth, *née* Mackenzie; *b* 6 Mar 1944; *Educ* Glasgow HS, Univ of Aberdeen (MA), LSE (MSc, PhD); *m* 7 Oct 1966, Evelyn Rosemary, da of Rev John Vass (d 1974), of Aberdeen; 1 da (Vivien Louise b 1977); *Career* prof of econs: LSE 1977-81 (lectr 1969-73, reader 1973-77), Univ of Oxford 1982-; visiting prof: Yale Univ 1975, Univ of California Berkeley 1976, Catholic Univ of Louvain-la-Neuve 1980, UC San Diego 1981; special advsr House of Commons select ctee on the Treasy and Civil Serv 1979-80, memb Academic Panel of HM Treasy 1976-; hon LLD Aberdeen 1987; fell Econometric Soc 1976, FBA 1987; *Books* Econometrics and Quantitative Economics (with K F Wallis, 1984); *Recreations* squash, cricket; *Style*— Prof David F Hendry; 26 Northmoor Road, Oxford OX2 6UR (☎ 0865 515588); Nuffield College, Oxford OX1 1NF (☎ 0865 278587, fax 0865 278 621)

HENDRY, Hon Mrs; Hon Elspeth Mariot; da of 1 Baron Ironside, GCB, CMG, DSO (d 1959, former Field Marshal); *b* 8 Jan 1917; *m* 1941, Capt Andrew Gilbert Hendry, Black Watch (Royal Highland Regt), s of Andrew Hendry, slr, of Dundee; 3 s; *Career* regnl cllr Tayside Region 1973-; *Recreations* tennis, gardening, travelling; *Clubs* New Cavendish; *Style*— The Hon Mrs Hendry; Kerbet House, Kinnettles, nr Forfar, Angus (☎ 030 782 286)

HENDY, Hon Mrs (Mary Jemima); *née* Best; da of 6 Baron Wynford, DSO (d 1940), and Hon Eva Napier, da of 2 Baron Napier of Magdala; *b* 1912; *m* 1944, John Hendy; 2 s; *Style*— The Hon Mrs Hendy; 1 Portherras Cross, Pendeen, Penzance, Cornwall

HENEAGE, Peter Edward Findlay; DL (Lincs 1979); s of Lt-Col Sir Arthur Pelham Heneage, DSO, DL (d 1971), and Anne, *née* Findlay (d 1982); *b* 5 Feb 1923; *Educ* Eton, Univ of Edinburgh; *m* 5 March 1949, Jean Georgiana Ethel, o da of Hon William Sholto Douglas (d 1932, 4 s of 19 Earl of Morton); 3 s (Thomas b 24 May 1950, Charles b 7 Nov 1952, Robert b 25 June 1956), 1 da (Katherine b 23 April 1960); *Career* served WWII RHA in NW Europe (wounded, despatches); Derbyshire Yeo 1950-58, ret as Maj; farmer; dir: Benskins Brewery Ltd 1958-63, Sanders & Co Ltd 1963-70, Pidcock Ltd 1965-70; chm Waldgrain Ltd 1976-88; chm Lincs Branch CLA 1979-82, former chm Gainsborough Constituency Cons Pty; chm: Educ Ctee Lincs CC 1979-80, fin and dep ldr Lincs CC 1981-85; High Sheriff of Lincs 1982; chm Nat Jt

Cncl Manual Workers' Wages 1982-83; *Recreations* country pursuits; *Clubs* Cavalry and Guards'; *Style—* Peter Heneage, Esq, DL; North Carlton Old Hall, Lincoln LN1 2RR (☎ 0522 730262)

HENHAM, His Hon Judge; John Alfred Henham; s of Alfred and Daisy Henham; *b* 8 Sept 1924; *m* 1946, Suzanne Jeanne Octavie Ghislaine *née* Pinchart (d 1972); 2 s; *Career* stipendiary magistrate 1975-83, rec 1979, circuit judge 1983-; *Style—* His Hon Judge Henham; Crown Court, Castle St, Sheffield 3 8LW (☎ 0742 737511)

HENLEY, Sir Douglas Owen; KCB (1973, CB 1970); *b* 5 April 1919; *Educ* Beckenham County Sch, LSE (BSc); *m* 1942, June Muriel, da of Thomas Ibbetson; 4 da; *Career* served WW II Queen's Own Royal W Kent Regt, N Africa, Italy, Greece (despatches twice); joined Treasy 1946, asst then dep under-sec Dept of Econ Affrs 1964-69, second perm sec Treasy 1972-76, comptroller and auditor-gen 1976-81; advsr to Deloitte Haskins and Sells (accountants) 1982-; Hon LLD Bath 1981; memb of Cncl, Girls Public Day Sch Tst 1981-, govr Alleyn's Coll of God's Gift Dulwich 1981-; *Style—* Sir Douglas Henley, KCB; Walwood House, Park Rd, Banstead, Surrey (☎ 0737 352626)

HENLEY, Rear Adm Sir Joseph Charles Cameron; KCVO (1963), CB (1962); s of Vice Adm Joseph Charles Walrond Henley, CB (d 1968); *b* 24 April 1909; *Educ* Sherborne; *m* 1, 1934 (m dis 1965), Daphne Ruth Wykeham; 1 s, 3 da; m 2, 1966, Mrs Patricia A Sharp, MBE; *Career* joined RN 1927, served WW II, Capt 1951, Naval Attaché Washington 1956-57, Rear Adm 1960, Flag Offr Royal Yacht, extra equerry to HM the Queen 1962-65, ret; *Clubs* Royal Yacht Sqdn, Royal Sydney Golf; *Style—* Rear Adm Sir Joseph Henley, KCVO, CB; 11A Hopewood Gdns, Darling Point, Sydney, NSW 2027, Australia (☎ 32 1068)

HENLEY, Michael Cameron; s of Vice-Adm Joseph Charles Walrond Henley, CB (d 1968), of Kent, and Esme Gordon Henley (d 1968), da of Col A S Cameron, VC CB; *b* 7 Dec 1914; *Educ* Radley, RMA Woolwich; *m* 9 June 1945, Margaret Rosemary, da of Major Albert Collum Brooks, RE (d 1955); 3 s (Robert b 1946, Charles b 1949, Philip b 1950); *Career* Capt RA 1934-45 served India, UK, Tunisia (wounded 1943), ret owing to wounds 1945; chartered surveyor 1946-64, dir of three public property cos, mangr own property 1971-; *Recreations* shooting, fishing, golf; *Clubs* United Service; *Style—* Michael Henley, Esq; Clonyard Farm, Southwick, Dumfries, Scotland (☎ 038 778 664)

HENLEY, Col Michael George Howard; CBE (1957); s of The Rev Edward Cornish Henley (d 1956), and Margaret Cara Wilkinson (d 1971); *b* 29 April 1910; *Educ* Radley, RMC Sandhurst, Staff Coll Camberley; *m* 1, 15 March 1938, Clare Marjorie, da of Brig D M Sole, DSO (d 1954); 2 da (Serena b 1941, Philippa b 1943); m 2, 11 Feb 1950, Esther Virginia, da of Atkin Lee Marsh (d 1954); 1 da (Harriet b 1954); *Career* cmmnd Kings Regt 1930-62, KAR and Somaliland Camel Corps 1933-38; served: Normandy landing in France, Belgium, Holland, Germany 1944-45; Col i/c admin Malta 1956-59; memb World Wildlife Fund 1964-75; *Recreations* horses, natural history, music, reading; *Style—* Col Michael G H Henley, CBE; Rookery House, Lower Seagry, nr Chippenham, Wiltshire

HENLEY, Nancy, Baroness; Nancy Mary; da of Stanley Walton, of The Hill, Gisland, Carlisle; *m* 1949 (m dis 1975), as his 2 w, 7 Baron Henley (d 1977); *Style—* Nancy, Lady Henley; 29 Somerset St, Kingsdown, Bristol 2

HENLEY, 8 Baron (I 1799); Oliver Michael Robert Eden; also (and sits as) Baron Northington (UK 1885); s of 7 Baron (d 1977) by his 2 w Nancy, da of S Walton, of Gilsland, Cumbria; *b* 22 Nov 1953; *Educ* Dragon Sch Oxford, Clifton, Durham; *m* 11 Oct 1984, Caroline Patricia, da of A G Sharp, of Mackney, Oxon; 1 s (John Michael Oliver b 1988); *Heir* s, Hon John Michael Oliver Eden b 30 June 1988; *Career* sits as Cons in House of Lords; barr Middle Temple 1977; memb Cumbria CC 1986-, chm Penrith and The Border Cons Assoc 1987-; Lord in Waiting 1989-; *Clubs* Brooks's, Pratt's; *Style—* The Rt Hon the Lord Henley; Scaleby Castle, Carlisle, Cumbria

HENLEY, Cdr Robert Stephen; OBE (1969), DSC (1942); s of Capt Charles Beauclerk Henley, RIM (d 1945), and Nellie Barbara, *née* Stranack (d 1962); *b* 4 July 1917; *Educ* Nautical Coll Pangbourne; *m* 31 July 1940, (Cecile) Noreen Sheila, da of Eric Hudson (d 1968); 4 s (Nigel b 1942, Timothy b 1945, Basil b 1953, Jonathan b 1956); *Career* RN; Cadet 1935, Lt 1940 qualified as Pilot, Lt Cdr 1944, Cdr 1955, Naval Attaché Madrid 1966-69; mangr Container Tport Int 1970-72; Amphibious Container Leasing Ltd: fndr 1972, md 1972-88, chm 1988-; MBIM 1970; *Recreations* riding; *Clubs* Naval and Military; *Style—* Cdr Robert Henley, OBE, DSC; Eden Lodge, West Liss, Hampshire (☎ 0730 892 325); Amphibious Container Leasing Ltd, Farnham Rd, West Liss, Hants (☎ 0730 892 611, fax 0730 894 352, telex 86576)

HENN, Alan Wesley; s of Thomas Wesley Henn; *b* 24 Sept 1930; *Educ* Uppingham; *m* 1956, Anne Whishaw, *née* Webb; 1 s, 2 da; *Career* Lt RA; past chm Nat Assoc of Goldsmiths; chm: TA Henn and Son Ltd and assoc cos, Beacon Broadcasting Co Ltd (W Midland ILR Station); dep chm Birmingham Midshires Bldg Soc; chm Jewellers of GB and Ireland Ltd; *Recreations* shooting, fishing; *Style—* Alan Henn, Esq; Rudge Hall, Pattingham, nr Wolverhampton (☎ 0902 700667);

HENN, Brig Francis Robert; CBE (1972); s of Col William Francis Henn, CBE, MVO (d 1964), of Paradise House, Ennis, Co Clare, Ireland, and Geraldine Frances Jane, *née* Stacpoole-Mahon dgda 14 Baron Inchiquin (d 1981); *b* 20 Nov 1920; *Educ* Aldenham, RMC Sandhurst; *m* 2 March 1957, Monica Traill, da of Brig Charles Cooper Russell, MC, of Hurlingham, London; 1 da (Frances Jane, b 1959); *Career* Regular Army 1939-75; 2 Lt Gloucs Regt 1939, France and Belgium 1940, Reconnaissance Corps 1941-46, NW Europe 1944-45, 11 Hussars (Prince Albert's Own) 1946, HQ Rhine Army 1947-48, Liaison Staff Norwegian Bde Germany 1949-50, psc 1951, Mil Sec's Branch WO 1952-54, Malayan Emergency 1954-56 (despatches), jssc 1959, Mil Ops Directorate War Off 1961-63, Def Operations Staff MOD 1963-65, Directing Staff Aust Army Staff Coll 1966-68, Head of Staff of the Chief of Def Staff MOD 1969-72, COS, Brig and Cdr Br Contingent UN Force in Cyprus 1972-74, ret 1975; special advsr House of Commons Foreign Affrs Ctee 1980-83; *Recreations* sailing, country pursuits; *Clubs* Army and Navy; *Style—* Brig Francis Henn, CBE; Royal Oak House, Stoke Trister, Wincanton, Somerset BA9 9PL (☎ 0963 33036)

HENNESSY; *see*: Pope-Hennessy

HENNESSY, Helen Julia; da of Frank Arthur Conway, and Joan Dorothy, *née* Shearman; *b* 7 Oct 1955; *Educ* Southend HS for Girls; *m* 2, 31 May 1987, James Edward Davis; *Career* chief housing offr Borough of Broxbourne 1980-86, mgmnt conslt specialising in interpersonal and mgmnt training 1986-, private practice as a qualified psychosynthesis cnsllr; MIH; *Recreations* husband, home, friends, studying alternative medicine, psychology, philosophy; *Clubs* Network; *Style—* Mrs Helen Hennessy; 46 Peel Rd, London E18 2LG (☎ 01 505 7850)

HENNESSY, Sir James Patrick Ivan; KBE (1982, OBE 1968, MBE 1959), CMG (1975); s of Richard Hennessy, DSO, MC; *b* 26 Sept 1923; *Educ* Bedford Sch, Sidney Sussex Coll Cambridge, LSE; *m* 1947, Patricia, da of Wing Cdr F Unwin, OBE; 1 s (decd), 5 da; *Career* served RA 1942, seconded to IA (Adj) 1944, Battery Cdr 6 Indian FD Regt 1945; joined Colonial Admin Serv 1948; appts incl: dist offr Basutoland 1948, judicial cmmr 1953, jt sec Constitutional Cmmn 1957-59, sec to Exec Cncl 1960, seconded to Br High Cmmr's Off Pretoria 1961-63, electoral cmmr 1963, perm sec Miny of Local Govt, Housing and Social Welfare 1964, min Home Affrs and Internal Security and MLC 1965, sec External Affrs and memb PM's Off 1966, ret; joined Dip Serv 1968; appts incl: chargé d'affaires Montevideo 1971-72, high cmmr to Uganda and non-res ambass to Rwanda 1973-76, consul-gen Cape Town 1977-79, govr and C-in-C Belize 1980-81, ret 1982; HM chief inspr of Prisons for Eng and Wales 1982-87 (memb Parole bd 1988-); *Clubs* Naval and Military, Royal Cwlth Soc; *Style—* Sir James Hennessy, KBE, CMG; 901 Hood House, Dolphin Square, London SW1

HENNIKER, Adrian Chandos; s and h of Brig Sir Mark Chandos Auberon Henniker, 8 Bt, CBE, DSO, MC; *b* 18 Oct 1946; *Educ* Marlborough; *m* 1971, Ann, da of Stuart Britton, of Malvern House, Fairwater Rd, Llandaff, Cardiff; 2 da (twins); *Style—* Adrian Henniker, Esq; Llwyndu, Abergavenny, Gwent

HENNIKER, 8 Baron (I 1800); Sir John Patrick Edward Chandos Henniker; 9 Bt (GB 1765), KCMG (1965, CMG 1956), CVO (1960), MC (1945); also Baron Hartismere (UK 1866); s of 7 Baron Henniker (d 1980), and Molly (d 1953), da of Sir Robert Burnet, KCVO, MD; *b* 19 Feb 1916; *Educ* Stowe, Trinity Coll Cambridge (MA); *m* 1, 18 Dec 1946, (Margaret) Osla (d 1974), da of James Benning, of Montreal; 2 s, 1 da; m 2, 1976, Mrs Julia Poland, da of George Mason, of Kew; *Heir* s, Hon Mark Henniker-Major; *Career* serv WWII Rifle Bde, Maj, mil mission to Yugoslav Partisans; For Serv 1938-68: ambass Jordan 1960-62, ambass Denmark 1962-66, asst under-sec FO 1967-68; dir-gen Br Cncl 1968-72; dir Wates Fndn 1972-78; tstee City Parochial Fndn 1973-, govr Cripplegate Fndn 1979-; memb Parole Bd 1979-83; memb Mental Health Review Tbnl (Broadmoor); dep chm Toynbee Hall 1980-87 (memb cncl 1978-87, vice-pres 1987-), pres Rainer Fndn, (chm Intermediate Treatment Fund 1985-); chm: Suffolk Rural Housing Assoc, Suffolk Community Alcohol Servs 1983-; pres Community Cncl for Suffolk, vice pres Suffolk Tst for Nature Conservation; pres Suffolk and N Essex Br Inst of Mgmnt 1985-88; govr Stowe Sch 1982; lay canon St Edwards Bury Cathedral 1986; DL (Suffolk 1988), pres Suffolk Agric Assoc 1989; *Clubs* Special Forces; *Style—* The Rt Hon the Lord Henniker, KCMG, CVO, MC; The Red House, Thornham Magna, Eye, Suffolk (☎ 037 983 336)

HENNIKER, Brig Sir Mark Chandos Auberon; 8 Bt (UK 1813), CBE (1953, OBE 1944), DSO (1944), MC (1933), DL (Gwent 1963); s of late Frederick Chandos Henniker (d 1953, ggs of 1 Bt); suc cous, Lt-Col Sir Robert John Aldeborough, MC (d 1958); *b* 23 Jan 1906; *Educ* Marlborough, RMA Woolwich, King's Coll Cambridge; *m* 1945, Kathleen Denys, da of John Anderson (d 1930), and Mrs John Anderson, of Pilgrim's Way, Farnham, Surrey; 1 s, 1 da; *Heir* s, Adrian Chandos Henniker; *Career* served RE 1925-58: Mohmand Ops 1933, WWII 1939-45 France, N Africa, Sicily (wounded), Italy and NW Europe, Malaya 1952-54 (despatches), Suez 1956 (despatches), ret Brig 1958; worked in industry 1959-62, self-employed in oil business 1963-77; *Books* Memoir of a Junior Officer (1951), Red Shadow over Malaya (1955), An Image of War (1987); *Recreations* appropriate to age and rank; *Clubs* Athenaeum; *Style—* Brig Sir Mark Henniker, Bt, CBE, DSO, MC, DL; 27 Western Rd, Abergavenny, Gwent, NP7 7AB

HENNIKER HEATON, Lady; Margaret Patricia; da of late Lt Percy Wright, Canadian Mounted Rifles; *m* 1948, as his 2 w, Wing-Cdr Sir (John Victor) Peregrine Henniker Heaton, 3 Bt (d 1971); *Style—* Lady Henniker Heaton; c/o Mrs I J S Mann, 10 The Street, Hoole Bank, Hoole Village, Chester

HENNIKER HEATON, Sir Yvo Robert; 4 Bt (UK 1912); s of Wing-Cdr Sir (John Victor) Peregrine Henniker Heaton, 3 Bt (d 1971); *b* 24 April 1954; *m* 1978, Freda, da of B Jones; *Heir* 1 cous, John Lindsey Henniker Heaton; *Style—* Sir Yvo Henniker-Heaton, Bt; 6 Lord Nelson St, Sneinton, Nottingham

HENNIKER-HEATON, (John) Lindsey; eld s of Clement Algernon Henniker-Heaton, CBE (d 1983; 3 s of late Sir John Henniker-Heaton, 2 Bt), and (Marjorie) Peggy, da of W E Speight, of Bournemouth; hp of 1 cous, Sir Yvo Henniker-Heaton, 4 Bt; *b* 19 June 1946; *Educ* Wellington, Emmanuel Coll Cambridge (MA); *m* 1970, Elisabeth Gladwell; 2 s (James b 1974, Robert b 1978); *Career* Br Aircraft Corpn 1964-74, RTZ Gp 1974-; CEng, FIMechE, MBIM; *Style—* Lindsey Henniker-Heaton, Esq; Northwoods House, Northwoods, Winterbourne, Bristol BS17 1RS (☎ 0454 775002)

HENNIKER-MAJOR, Hon Charles John Giles; 2 s of 8 Baron Henniker, KCMG, CVO, MC; *b* 1949; *Educ* Stowe; *m* 1980, Mrs Sally D M Kemp, da of Donald Newby, of Halesworth, Suffolk; 1 s (Thomas Charles John b 1982), 2 da (Osla Mary b 1981, Ruth Felicity b 1985); *Style—* The Hon Charles Henniker-Major; Great Chilton Farm, Ferryhill, Co Durham DL17 OJY

HENNIKER-MAJOR, Hon Mark Ian Philip Chandos; s and h of 8 Baron Henniker, KCMG, CVO, MC, by his w, Margaret Osla Benning (d 1974); *b* 29 Sept 1947; *Educ* Eton, Trinity Coll Cambridge (MA), UCL (LLM); *m* 1973, Mrs Lesley Antoinette Masterton-Smith, da of Wing Cdr G W Foskett, of Spitchwick Farm, Poundsgate, Newton Abbot, Devon; 2 s (Frederick John Chandos b 1983, Edward George Major b 1985), 3 da (Jessica b 1977, Josephine b 1979, Harriet b 1981); *Career* slr; co-fndr (1982) and ptnr Henniker-Major and Co of Ipswich, Felixstowe, Needham Market and Dovercourt/Harwich; dir: Foxwest Ltd, Anglia Business Conslts Ltd, Medvei John and Co; memb: Harwich Harbour Bd, CLA Suffolk; memb: Royal Aeronautical Soc, Br Insur Law Assoc, Law Soc; FCIArb; *Recreations* squash, chess, bridge; *Clubs* Ipswich and Suffolk, MCC; *Style—* The Hon Mark Henniker-Major; c/o Henniker-Major and Co, 1 and 3 Upper Brook St, Ipswich, Suffolk IP4 1EG (☎ 0473 212681, telex 98221, fax 0473 215118)

HENNIKER-MAJOR, Hon Richard Arthur Otway; s of 7 Baron Henniker (d 1980); *b* 1917; *Educ* Stowe, Magdalene Coll Cambridge (BA); *m* 1946, Nancy Pauline, da of late Sir John Armitage Stainton, KCB, KBE, QC; 2 s, 1 da; *Career* served WW II, Lt RA (POW); slr 1948; *Style—* The Hon Richard Henniker-Major; 13 Market Cross Place, Aldeburgh, Suffolk

HENNING, Kathleen Ann (Kathy); da of Robert Albert Henning, and Glenys Doreen, *née* Jones; *b* 26 April 1956; *Educ* Falmouth HS; *Career* creative mangr Mary

Quant Cosmetics 1978-83, gp product devpt mangr and now product devpt dir Rimmel Int 1983-; *Clubs* Network; *Style*— Ms Kathleen Henning; 135 Gloucester Terr, London W2 2DY (☎ 01 402 4857); 17 Cavendish Square, London W1M 0ME (☎ 01 637 1621, fax 01 409 0930)

HENNING, Matthew Clive Cunningham; s of Matthew Henning (d 1982), of Co Londonderry, and Olivia Mary, *née* Cunningham; *b* 4 Jan 1934; *Educ* St Andrew's Coll Dublin, Coll of Architecture Oxford (Dip Arch); *m* 27 Sept 1972, Vivien Margaret, da of David Earnest Walker (d 1971), of Armagh; 1 s (Daniel Clive Walker b 1978), 1 da (Kate Louise b 1982); *Career* conslt architecture in private practice, formerly princ architecture for the Southern Educn and Library Bd (1972-78); *Recreations* golf; *Clubs* County (Armagh), City (Armagh), Portadown Golf, Tandragee Golf, Bushfoot Golf; *Style*— Matthew Henning, Esq; The Roost, Ridgeway Park, S Portadown, Co Armagh (☎ 0762 331489); Bawnmore, Castlerock, Coleraine, Co Londonderry; Clive Henning Architects, 17 Bridge St, Portadown, Co Armagh (☎ 0762 338811)

HENRICK, Ernest John; DFM (1945); s of Ernest Alfred, DCM, MM (d 1977), of London, and Mary, *née* Taylor (d 1978); *b* 10 May 1924; *Educ* Borough Poly; *m* 10 Nov 1945, Elizabeth Rose, da of Albert Edward McKenzie (d 1967), of London; 1 s (John Christopher b 13 March 1947), 1 da (Christine Mary Rose b 11 April 1950); *Career* WWII RAF 1942-46, Sgt Pilot 1943, 601 Sqdn (Spitfires) Italy 1944, Fl Sgt 1944, cmmnd Pilot Offr 1945, 253 Sqdn 1945, 91 Sqdn Duxford 1946, Flying Offr 1945, demob 1946; Sulzer Bros (UK) Ltd: mangr Manchester branch 1956, UK branch 1964, dir 1969-84, ret 1984; Freeman City of London, memb Worshipful Co of Fan Makers; CEng, MIEE 1956, MIMechE 1960, FCIBS 1956; *Recreations* golf, gardening; *Clubs* Livery, Wig and Pen, Hindhead GC; *Style*— Ernest Henrick, Esq, DFM; Pine Hurst, Headley Hill Rd, Headley Bordon, Hants GU35 8DX (☎ 0428 713630)

HENRIKSEN, Bent; OBE (1983); *b* 20 Mar 1938; *Educ* Handelsskole Horsens Denmark, Forsvarets Gymnasium Copenhagen, Copenhagen Business Sch, Holbeck Denmark, Manchester Business Sch Imede Lausanne Switzerland; *m* 12 Oct 1963, Hanne; 2 s (Troels b 1964, Rasmus b 1975), 1 da (Mette b 1966); *Career* Nat Serv Danish Army 1958-60, UN Army Force ME 1961-62; vice pres Elmwood Sensors Inc Providenc USA 1971-83, md Elmwood Sensors Ltd 1974-83, chief exec TSL Gp plc Wallsend-on-Tyne 1983-87, vice pres Europe Victor Corpn RI USA, chm Pharma Nord (UK) Ltd, vice chm Newcastle Poly Prods Ltd; govr Newcastle upon Tyne Poly, chm export ctee Tyne & Wear C of C; FInst 1975, FRSA 1982; *Recreations* riding, badminton; *Style*— Bent Henriksen, Esq, OBE; Spital Hall, Mitford, Morpeth, Northumberland NE61 3PN (☎ 0670 518667)

HENRIQUES, Lady; Marjory Brunhilda; *née* Burrows; *m* 1938, Sir Cyril Henriques, QC (d 1982), sometime pres Ct of Appeal Jamaica; 2 da; *Style*— Lady Henriques; Caribocho Rios Aptmts Ltd, Apt 111 Ocho Rios, St Ann, Jamaica (☎ 0974 5003)

HENRY, Hon Mrs (Christian) Alison; da of The Rt Hon Lord Hughes, CBE, PC, and The Rt Hon Lady Hughes, *née* Gordon; *b* 2 Mar 1952; *Educ* Dundee HS, Univ of Strathclyde (BSc); *m* 1973, Allan Cameron Cassells, s of Allan Douglas Henry, of Hamilton; 1 s (Graham b 1984), 2 da (Gillian b 1977, Elaine b 1980); *Career* md Comrie (Dispensary) Ltd; *Style*— The Hon Mrs Henry; Tigh-an-Lios, The Ross, Comrie, Perthshire (☎ 0764 70864); Comrie (Dispensary) Ltd, Drummond St, Comrie (☎ 0764 70210)

HENRY, Brian Glynn; s of Emrys Glynn Henry (d 1979), of Berks, and Edith, *née* Jones (d 1982); *b* 5 Feb 1926; *Educ* Stowe, Trinity Coll Cambridge (MA); *m* 1, 10 June 1950, Elizabeth Jean, da of Ernest Victor Craig (d 1977); 1 s (Julian b 1959), 3 da (Susan b 1951, Louise b 1953, Deborah b 1959); m 2, 30 June 1982, Jan Barney; *Career* Lt RNVR Home Fleet and Far East 1943-47; former co dir, Southern TV 1961-81, Remploy 1982-85, Wadlow Grosvenor 1982-84, Riviera TV 1982-84; (memb Western Orchestral Soc 1977-82, chm Oxford Playhouse 1988); *Books* TV Advertising in Britain; The First 30 Years (1986); *Recreations* walking, photography, cycling; *Clubs* Buck's, Special Forces; *Style*— Brian G Henry, Esq; Bere House, Pangbourne, Berks RG8 8HT (☎ 073 57 3676)

HENRY, Sir Denis Aynsley; OBE (1962), QC (Grenada 1968); s of Ferdinand Henry; *b* 3 Feb 1917; *Educ* Grenada Boys' Sch, King's Coll London (LLB); *m* 1966, Kathleen Carol Sheppard; 2 s, 3 da; *Career* barr Inner Temple 1939; MLC Grenada 1952-65, sen in First Parl of Assoc State of Grenada 1966-67; chm Granada Banana Co-op Soc 1953-76; *Style*— Sir Denis Henry, OBE, QC; Mount Parnassus, St George's, Grenada, West Indies (☎ 2370)

HENRY, (Ernest James) Gordon; s of Ernest Elston Henry (d 1948), of Glasgow, and Dolina Campbell, *née* Smith (d 1944); *b* 16 June 1919; *Educ* Bellahuston Acad Glasgow; *m* 2 Sept 1950, Marion Frew Allan (Myra), da of William Bell Allan (d 1963), of Glasgow; 3 da (Jane, Pamela, Sally); *Career* RASC 1939-40, No 5 Commando 1940-46; md Matthews Wrightson & Co Ltd London 1964; chm: Stewart Wrightson plc 1977-81, Adam & Co plc 1983-, New Scotland Insur Gp plc 1986-, Ind Insur Co plc 1986-, London & Erskine Estate Ltd 1987-; hon vice chm Kilmacolm Cons Assoc; FCIB; *Recreations* writing, golf, gardening; *Clubs* Western (Glasgow), R&A (St Andrews), Western Gailes Golf; *Style*— Gordon Henry, Esq; Rannoch, Gryffe Rd, Kilmacolm, Scotland (☎ 050 587 3382); Johnstone Ct, North St, St Andrews, Scotland; Adam & Co plc, 22 Charlotte Sq, Edinburgh (☎ 031 225 8484, fax 01 225 5136, telex 72182)

HENRY, Hugh William; s of Glynn Henry (d 1979), of Berks, and Edith, *née* Jones (d 1981); *b* 25 May 1929; *Educ* Stowe; *m* 1957, Pauline Anne, da of Gp Capt George Richard Melville Clifford (d 1970), of Herts; 2 s (Peter b 1961, Rupert b 1965); *Career* joined Scottish TV 1957 (head of sales 1963-85, appointment bd 1969, ret 1988), chm and chief exec Airtime Int 1985-88; fndr New North Mktg 1988; *Recreations* gardening, books, water-colour painting, fly fishing; *Style*— Hugh Henry, Esq; Mill Farm, Wennington, Lancaster LA2 8NU (☎ 0468 21722); New North Marketing, Storey House, White Cross, Lancashire LA1 4XQ (☎ 0524 39911, fax 841 098, telex 65187)

HENRY, Sir James Holmes; 2 Bt (UK 1923), CMG (1960), MC (1944), TD (1950), QC (Tanganyika 1953, Cyprus 1957); s of Rt Hon Sir Denis Stanislaus Henry, 1 Bt (d 1925), 1 Lord Chief Justice of NI, and Violet (d 1966), da of Rt Hon Hugh Holmes (former Lord Justice, Court of Appeal Ireland); *b* 22 Sept 1911; *Educ* Mount St Mary's Coll Chesterfield, Downside, UCL; *m* 1, 1941 (m dis 1948), Susan Mary Blackwell; m 2, 1949, Christina Hilary, da of Sir Hugh Oliver Holmes, KBE, CMG, MC, QC, and wid of Lt-Cdr Christopher Hayward Wells, RN; 3 da; *Heir* nephew, Patrick Denis Henry; *Career* served WW II (wounded), Capt London Irish Rifles (Royal Ulster Rifles); barr Inner Temple 1934, crown counsel Tanganyika 1946, legal draftsman 1949, slr-gen 1952, attorney-gen Cyprus 1956; memb Foreign Compensation Cmmn 1960-83 (chm 1977-83), ret; *Clubs* Travellers', Royal Cwlth Soc; *Style*— Sir James Henry, Bt, CMG, MC, TD, QC; Kandy Lodge, 18 Ormond Ave, Hampton-on-Thames, Middx

HENRY, Hon Mrs; Hon (Helen) Judith; *née* Somers-Cocks; yr da of 7 Baron Somers (d 1953), and Benita, *née* Sabin (d 1950); *b* 1901; *m* 1, 1949, T Everett Malen (d 1961); m 2, 1965, Earl G Henry (d 1979); *Style*— The Hon Mrs Henry; 445 Wawona St, Apt 326, San Francisco, California 94116, USA (☎ 0415 666 9298)

HENRY, Richard Charles; TD (1976); s of John Richard Henry, OBE, JP, of Hilltop Cottage, Hopgoods Green, Bucklebury, Berks, and Blanche Catherine, *née* Barrett; *b* 26 Feb 1941; *Educ* Sherborne; *m* 15 April 1976, Judy Ann, da of Roger Massey (d 1974), of Stock, Essex; 1 s (Charles b 1977), 3 da (Belinda b 1979, Jane b 1979, Margaret b 1983); *Career* Capt HAC (TA) 1961-76, memb Ct HAC since 1975; articled clerk Deloittes 1960-67, various jobs in indust 1967-78, Coopers & Lybrand Assoc 1978-84, fin dir Press Assoc 1989 (joined 1984); dir: Universal News Servs 1986, Tellex Monitors 1988; Freeman City of London 1986, memb Worshipful Co of Barbers 1989; FCA 1966; *Recreations* TA, bridge, fishing; *Clubs* Army and Navy, Muthaiga; *Style*— Richard Henry, Esq, TD; Bailiffs Farmhouse, Ibworth, Basingstoke, Hants RG26 5TJ (☎ 0256 850 270); The Press Assoc, 85 Fleet St, London EC4P 4BE

HENSMAN, Hon Mrs ((Mary) Sheila); *née* Wakefield; da of 1 Baron Wakefield of Kendal (d 1983), and Rowena Doris, *née* Lewis (d 1981); *b* 29 April 1922; *Educ* Francis Holland Sch, Downe House Newbury; *m* 6 July 1945, Brig Richard Frank Bradshaw Hensman, CBE (d 1988), s of Capt Melvill Hensman, DSO, RN (d 1967), of South Hay House, Bordon, Hants; 1 s (Peter Richard Wavell b 30 Aug 1948), 1 da (Suzannah Mary b 9 Feb 1953); *Career* dir: Battlefields (Hldgs) Ltd, Shapland & Petter Hldgs Ltd, Lake District Estates Co Ltd, Ullswater Navigation & Transit Co Ltd, Ravenglass & Eskdale Railway Co Ltd, Nat Caravan Cncl Ltd; pres DHO Ski Club 1975-80, Ladies Ski Club 1987-; vice-pres Cumbria Tourist Bd; *Recreations* skiing, walking, gardening; *Clubs* Lansdowne, Ski Club of Great Britain; *Style*— The Hon Mrs Hensman; Lindum Holme, Stricklandgate, Kendal, Cumbria LA9 4QG (☎ 0539 25093)

HENSON, Brian David; s of James Maury Henson, of New York and London, and Jane Anne Nebel Henson; *b* 3 Nov 1963; *Educ* Phillips Acad Andover USA, Univ of Colorado USA; *Career* film dir, puppeteer, animatronics performance co-ordinator and conslt: special effects technician and performer The Great Muppet Caper 1981 and The Muppets Take Manhattan 1983, performer of Jack Pumpkinhead in Return to Oz 1984, princ performer and performer co-ordinator Labyrinth 1984-85, princ performer Little Shop of Horrors 1986, princ performance co-ordinator Storyteller (TV series) 1987, dir Mother Goose Stories (TV) 1988, princ performer Jim Henson Presents: Living with Dinosaurs and Monster Maker (TV) 1988; memb: SAG, AFTRA, Equity (UK), ACTT, DGA; *Recreations* skiing, squash, cars, dogs, travelling, fashion; *Style*— Brian Henson, Esq; 1b Downshire Hill, London NW3 (☎ 01 431 2818)

HENTON, Roger Gordon; s of (William) Gordon Henton, of Lincoln, and Pamela, *née* Evans (d 1983); *b* 2 April 1940; *Educ* Bedford Sch; *m* 15 June 1966, Susan Eleanor, da of John Richmond Edwards: 1 s (Thomas b 1972), 1 da (Isabel b 1970); *Career* Streets & Co CAs Lincoln 1969-64, Coopers & Lybrand Geneva 1965-67, PA to md AAH Plc Lincoln 1968-72, dir Camamile Assocs Lincoln 1973-77, fndr and sr ptnr Henton & Plycke CAs Leeds 1978-; ACA 1964, FCA; *Recreations* squash, golf; *Clubs* RAC, Scarcroft GC; *Style*— Roger Henton, Esq; 12 York Place, Leeds, West Yorks (☎ 0532 457553, fax 0532 420474, car tel 0836 742200)

HEPBURN, (Bryan) Audley St John; CMG (1962); s of late A F St John Hepburn, and Marie, *née* Thomas; *b* 24 Feb 1911; *Educ* Cornwall Coll Jamaica; *m* 5 Oct 1940, Sybil Isabel, da of H V Myers (d 1952), of Jamaica; 2 da (Patricia, Judith); *Career* asst sec Jamaica 1944, princ asst sec Sarawak 1947 (devpt sec 1951, fin sec 1958-63); chm: Sarawak Devpt Fin Corp 1958-63, Sarawak Electricty Corpn 1958-63; dir: Malayan Airways 1959-63, Borneo Airways 1959-63; dep chm: Malaysian Tariff Advsy Bd 1963-65, Miny of Overseas Devpt 1966-73; *Recreations* golf; *Clubs* Royal Overseas League, Haywards Heath GC; *Style*— Audley Hepburn, Esq, CMG; 27 Dumbrells Court, Northend, Ditchling, Sussex (☎ 07918 5064)

HEPBURN, Gavin Andrew Harley; s of John Harley Hepburn, JP (d 1966), of Kirkcaldy, and Lena Champbell, *née* Ritchie; *b* 6 Dec 1937; *Educ* Loretto Sch Musselburgh, Dundee Tech Coll; *m* 28 Sept 1966, Anne Margaret, da of James Mitchell, Girvan, Ayrshire; 2 s (Alastair b 11 March 1968, David b 3 Feb 1976), 1 da (Katherine b 8 July 1967); *Career* md: Fife Forge Co Ltd 1973 (co sec 1966), Fife Indmar plc 1981 (chm 1981, dir 1988); dir: Robert Taylor Hldgs 1981-88, Brumtons plc Musselburgh 1983-86, Smith Anderson Ltd Leslie 1986-, Scotfresh Ltd Eyemouth 1987-; pres Kirkaldy Jr C of C 1963, dir Kirkaldy C of C 1976-80; memb: Scot Cncl CBI 1976-82, Scot Cncl Devpt & Indust 1982-86; chm Forth Ports Authy 1980-86, dir Glenrothes Devpt Corpn 1984-, tstee Scot Hosps Tst 1985-; memb Incorporation of Hammermen (Edinburgh); ACMA, ACIS; *Recreations* fishing, golf, bridge, curling; *Clubs* New (Edinburgh), Elie Golf House; *Style*— Gavin Hepburn, Esq; 22 Mansion Ho Rd, Edinburgh EH9 2JD (☎ 031 667 7767); Fife Indmar plc, Smeaton Rd, Kirkcaldy, Fife (☎ 0592 533 88, fax 0592 549 88, car tel 0836 702 526, telex 72378)

HEPBURN, (James) Michael Harley; s of John Harley Hepburn, JP (d 1966), of Kirkcaldy, Fife; *b* 7 July 1934; *Educ* Loretto Sch; *m* 1953, Ethne Margaret Forbes, da of Dr Percival Binnington (d 1944), of Hull; 3 da; *Career* served Lt 1 Royal Scots Korea 1952-53; dir: Fife Indmar plc 1969-, The Girls Sch Co 1970-82; chm and md William Paton Ltd 1985; dir: Scottish Music Info Centre 1985-, Paton Hldgs Ltd 1985-; MInstMSM, MinstD; *Recreations* skiing, marathon running, hill walking, choral singing; *Style*— Michael Hepburn, Esq; Upper Gavelmoss, Lochwinnoch, Renfrewshire (☎ 0505 843071); William Paton Ltd, Johnstone Mill, High St, Johnstone, Renfrewshire (☎ 0505 216333, telex 777841)

HEPBURN, Surgn Rear Adm (Nicol) Sinclair; CB (1971), CBE (1968); s of John Primrose Hepburn (d 1960), of Edinburgh, and Susan Hepburn (d 1957); *b* 2 Feb 1913; *Educ* Broughton Sch, Univ of Edinburgh (MB, ChB), Univ of London (DPH), Soc of Apothecaries (DIH); *m* 1939, Dorothy, da of David Robert Blackwood (d 1945), of Edinburgh; 2 s (David, Donald); *Career* RN 1935- incl war-time serv in S Atlantic and Far East; Naval MO of Health: Portsmouth Cmd 1959, Malta 1962; dep to Med Dir-Gen of the Navy 1966, MO i/c RN Hosp Haslar 1969, ret 1972; barr Grays Inn; CStJ

1971; *Style*— Surgn Rear Adm Sinclair Hepburn, CB, CBE; Mallows, Chilbolton Ave, Winchester SO22 5HD

HEPBURNE SCOTT, Hon Francis Michael; MC; raised to rank of Baron's son 1945; 2 s of Capt Hon Walter Thomas Hepburne Scott (eldest s of 9 Baron Polwarth, decd); bro of 10 Baron Polwarth, TD; *b* 1920; *Educ* Eton, King's Coll Cambridge; *m* 1946, Marjorie Hamilton, da of Horatio John Ross; 2 s, 1 da; *Career* sometime Maj, Lothians and Border Horse; conslt to Smiths Gore Chartered Surveyors; farmer; FRICS; *Style*— The Hon Francis Hepburne Scott; Newhouse, Lilliesleaf, Melrose, Roxburghs (☎ 083 57 307)

HEPHER, Michael Leslie; s of Leslie and Edna Hepher; *b* 17 Jan 1944; *Educ* Kingston GS; *m* 1971, Janice Morton; 1 s (Daniel b 1980); 2 da (Kelly b 1973, Erin b 1975); *Career* chm and md Abbey Life Gp plc 1980-; FIA, FCIA, ASA, FLIA; *Recreations* tennis, reading; *Style*— Michael Hepher, Esq; Abbey Life Group plc, 80 Holdenhurst Rd, Bournemouth BH8 8AL (☎ 0202 292373)

HEPPEL, Peter John Merrick; s of John Edward Thomas Heppel (d 1964), of Romford, Essex, and Ida Florence, *née* Ford (d 1983); *b* 31 Mar 1948; *Educ* Royal Liberty Sch Romford Essex, Univ of Hull (LLB), UCL (LLM); *m* 20 Sept 1980, Janice da of John Coulton, of Southport, Merseyside; 2 s (Edward b 1981, William b 1986), 2 da (Charlotte b 1979, Indea b 1982); *Career* barr Middle Temple 1970, practising NE circuit 1972-, rec 1988-; *Recreations* family, music, reading; *Clubs* Sloane; *Style*— Peter Heppel, Esq; Warriston, Parkfield Ave, N Ferriry, Humberside HU14 3AL (☎ 0482 631657); 2 Harcourt Bldgs, Temple, London EC4 (☎ 01 353 1394); Wilberforce Chambers, 171 High St Hull HU1 1NE (☎ 0482 631657)

HEPPELL, Thomas Strachan; CB (1986); s of Leslie Thomas Davidson Heppell, and Doris Abbey, *née* Potts; *b* 15 August 1935; *Educ* Acklam Hall GS Middlesborough, Queen's Coll Oxford (BA); *m* 1963, Felicity Ann, da of Lt-Col Richard Bernard Rice (ka 1943); 2 s (Jeremy Strachan b 1965, Martin Richard b 1967); *Career* asst princ Nat Assistance Bd 1958, (princ 1963); DHSS asst sec 1973, under sec 1979, dep sec 1983; *Recreations* gardening, travelling; *Style*— Strachan Heppell, CB; Lloyds Bank, 6 Holborn Circus EC1N 2HP; Department of Health, Richmond House, Whitehall, SW1

HEPPER, Anthony Evelyn; s of Lt-Col John E Hepper (d 1967), and Rosalind, *née* Bowker; *b* 16 Jan 1923; *Educ* Wellington, Loughborough Coll; *m* 1970, Jonquil Francesca; *Career* served RE (N Africa, Sicily, Italy, France, Belgium, Holland, Norway, Palestine, Egypt), Maj; dir: Cape Industries plc 1968-; chm: Lamont and Partners plc; Hyde Sails Ltd 1984-; CEng, FIMechE; *Recreations* golf; *Clubs* Boodle's; *Style*— A E Hepper, Esq; 70 Eaton Place, London SW1X 8AT (☎ 01 235 7518);

HEPPLE, Keith Michael; s of Peter David Hepple (d 1982), and Patricia Mary, *née* Heppel (now Mrs Fitzsimmons); *b* 31 July 1965; *Educ* Knavesmire Secdy Modern Sch York, York Coll of Arts and Technol (Dip Fashion), Trent Poly of Art and Design (BA); *Career* styled Benettons winter 1985/86 collection 1985, fashion asst to Debbi Mason at the launch of Br Elle Magazine 1985, finalist Smirnoff UK Fashion awards 1986, Paris corr to Thom O'Dwyer Fashion Weekly 1986-87, illustration cmmn for Warehouse 1987, conslt to John Partridge menswear 1987, lectr Trent Poly 1987, dep fashion ed Fashion Weekly 1987 (DR magazine 1988), author of articles for various fashion magazines; *Recreations* swimming, reading, books; *Clubs* The Daisy Chain (Brixton); *Style*— Keith Hepple, Esq; International Thomson Business Publishing, 100 Avenue Rd, London NW3 (☎ 01 965 6611 ext 2238, fax 01 722 4920, telex 299973 ITP LN G)

HEPPLESTON, Dr (John) Dennis; s of Alfred Styal Cheshire (d 1953), and Edith, *née* Clough (d 1960); *b* 16 Dec 1919; *Educ* Manchester GS, Manchester Univ (MBChB, Dip in Pathology); *m* 30 March 1949, Hilda Joan, da of Percy Hulme (d 1969), of Nantwich Cheshire; 2 da (Jane b 1951, Susan b 1954); *Career* sr conslt pathologist Crewe Area Health Authy 1954-84, asst lectr in pathology Manchester Univ; memb: BMA, Pathological Soc of GB and NI; fell Royal Coll of Pathology; *Recreations* ONC Electrical and Electronic Engrg, sailing, car restoring; *Style*— Dr Dennis Heppleston; Glynwood, 108 Crewe Rd, Nantwich, Cheshirue CW5 6JS (☎ 0270 625691)

HEPTONSTALL, Cyril Philip; s of Lt-Col Robert Allatt Heptonstall (d 1969), and Mary Aline, *née* Dixon (d 1969); *b* 7 July 1924; *Educ* Tonbridge, St John's Coll Cambridge (MA, LLM); *m* 24 April 1954, Cora Arline Mary, da of Ernest Henry Smith (d 1971); 1 s (Hugh b 1956), 2 da (Julia b 1955, Anna b 1959); *Career* RAFVR 1943-46, Flying Offr (pilot); slr 1951; practised at bar 1956- 59; practising slr 1959-; *Recreations* fishing, shooting, photography; *Style*— Cyril Heptonstall, Esq; Martins, Howden, nr Goole, N Humberside DN14 7ER (☎ 0430 430519); 11/13 Gladstone Terrace, Goole, N Humberside DN14 5AH (☎ 0405 5661, fax 0405 4201, telex 57579) F

HEPWORTH, David; s of Ernest Hepworth (d 1981), of Ossett, Yorkshire, and Sarah Marjorie, *née* Rollinson; *b* 27 July 1950; *Educ* Queen Elizabeth GS Wakefield, Trent Park Coll of Educn Barnet Herts (BEd); *m* 5 Sept 1979, Alyson, da of Ronald Elliott, of Hove, Sussex; 1 s (Henry b 1987), 1 da (Clare b 1982); *Career* freelance journalist 1975-79, ed Smash Hits 1980-82, ed Just Seventeen 1983-85, editorial dir Emap Metro 1984-, presenter BBC TV Whistle Test 1980-86; Periodical Publishers' Assoc: Ed of the Year 1985, Writer of the Year 1988; *Recreations* books, tennis, music; *Style*— David Hepworth, Esq; 48 The Mall, London N14 6LN (☎ 01 882 5963); 42 Great Portland St, London W1 (☎ 01 436 5430, fax 01 631 0781)

HEPWORTH, Rear Adm David; CB (1976); s of Alfred Ernest Hepworth (d 1966), and Minnie Louisa Catherine Bennet (formerly Tanner), *née* Bowden (d 1939); *b* 6 June 1923; *Educ* Banbury GS; *m* 1, 1946 (m dis 1974), Brenda June, da of Herbert Valentine Case (d 1962); 1 da (Nicola Gaye b 1949); m 2, 1975, Eileen Mary, da of William Robert Henderson Robson (d 1969); *Career* entered RN as boy telegraphist 1939, serv: Atlantic, Mediterraean and E Indies 1939-44, cmmnd 1944, submarines 1945-50, CO HMS Tudor, HMS Thorough, HMS Truncheon 1950-58; snr offr submarines Londonderry 1959-61, CO HMS Ashanti 1961-64; JSSC 1964, dep dir undersea warfare MOD 1964-67, Imperial Def Coll 1967; CO HMS Ajax and Capt 2 Far East Destroyer Sqdn 1968-69, dir Naval Warfare MOD 1971-73; Br naval advsr to Imperial Iranian Navy 1973-76, retd Rear Adm 1974; Naval advsr to Int Mil Services Ltd 1976-83; *Recreations* home and family; *Style*— Rear Adm Hepworth, CB; Darville House, Lower Heyford, Oxon (☎ 0869 47460)

HERBECQ, Sir John Edward; KCB (1977); s of Joseph Edward and Rosina Elizabeth Herbecq; *b* 29 May 1922; *Educ* Chichester HS for Boys; *m* 1947, Pamela Filby; 1 da; *Career* joined Colonial Off 1939; private sec to chm UKAEA 1960-62, asst sec Treasy 1964; Civil Serv Dept: asst sec 1968, under-sec 1970, dep sec 1973, 2 perm sec 1975-81; Church cmmr 1982-; *Style*— Sir John Herbecq, KCB; Maryland, Ledgers Meadow, Cuckfield, Haywards Heath, W Sussex RH17 5EW (☎ 0444 413387)

HERBERT, Hon Alice Christine Emma; da of 3 and youngest da of 3 Baron Hemingford; *b* 4 May 1968; *Educ* Perse Sch for Girls Cambridge; *Style*— The Hon Alice Herbert

HERBERT, Anthony James; s of Maj Kenneth Faulkner Herbert, MBE, of Park Rd, Nursing Home, Winchester, and Kathleen Ellis, *née* Robertson ; *b* 28 Mar 1940; *Educ* Eton, King's Coll Cambridge (MA); *m* 4 May 1968, Lowell, da of George M Pelton, of Nova Scotia, Canada; (Dominic b 9 April 1971, Daniel b 21 Feb 1973), 1 da (Julia b 21 March 1978); *Career* admitted slr 1965; ptnr Allen & Overy 1970- (asst slr 1965-69); memb Law Soc 1965, City of London Law Soc, IBA; *Recreations* painting, tennis, skiing; *Clubs* Roehampton; *Style*— Anthony Herbert, Esq; 16 Woodborough Rd, London SW15 6PZ (☎ 01 788 7042); c/o Allen Overy, 9 Cheapside, London EC2V 6AD (☎ 01 248 9898, fax 01 236 2192, telex 8812801)

HERBERT, Arthur James (Jim); CBE (1982); s of Arthur Stephens Herbert (d 1959), of Middx, and Ethel Mary Ferguson (d 1954), of Tasmania; *b* 24 Oct 1918; *Educ* Sydney C of E GS, Merchant Taylors' Sch and Pembroke Coll, Cambridge (MA); *m* 1948, Pamela Mary, da of Capt John Gyde Heaven (d 1923), of Bristol; 1 s (Richard b 1949), 3 da (Caroline b 1951, Nicola b 1955, Linda b 1958); *Career* serv WWII Maj RE (granted rank of Hon Maj on demob) (despatches), chm Herbert & Sons Ltd; dir: Swift Scale Co Ltd, Lion Electronics Ltd, Meatex Ltd; pres Nat Fed Scale & Weighing Machine mfrs 1966-68 and 1982-84; memb Engr Employers Fed Policy Ctee 1982-84 and Mgmnt Bd 1981-89, pres E Anglian Engr Employers Assoc 1980-82 and 1986-88; chm Bury St Edmunds Constit Cons Assoc 1972-80 (pres 1980-86),chm Suffolk & SE Cambs Euro Constit Cons Assoc 1987-89, pres S Suffolk Constit Con Assoc 1987-89; Freeman City of London; *Recreations* gardening; *Clubs* Hawks, Cambridge, East India Sports, MCC; *Style*— Jim Herbert, Esq, CBE; 18 Rookwood Way, Haverhill, Suffolk CB9 8PD (☎ 0440 703551, telex 817931 HERBRT G, fax 0440 62048)

HERBERT, Austin Godfrey Vivian; s of John George Herbert (d 1947), of 202 Ross Rd, Hereford, and Alice Susanah, *née* Blackford (d 1927); *b* 30 April 1907; *Educ* Hereford HS, Leicester Coll of Technol, Birmingham Commercial Coll; *m* 14 Nov 1953, Joan, da of Archibald Howard Osborne, MBE (d 1964); 1 da (Alison Sybil b 29 March 1957); *Career* Herefordshire Regt TA 1924-29, RAFVR 1939-45, Fighter Cmd 1939-41, SE Asia Cmd 1941-45, Sqdn Ldr; serv: Malaysia, Java, Aust, Sri Lanka, India; chief fin offr Tamworth DC 1928-31, clerk of the cncl Ross-on-Wye Dist cncl 1932-35, chief exec C B Buxton Ltd London 1935-39, co sec Bakelite Ltd 1945-65, dir of admin BXL (now part of BP) 1965-69, dir of courses and sr lectr S W London Coll 1969-77, business conslt 1977-; past pres and cncl memb Inst of Chartered Secretaries and Administrators, memb cncl (former chm) Corpn of Secretaries 1955-70, sr vice-pres ICSA Registrars Gp 1961-, memb exec ctee Chemical Industs Assoc 1967-69, cnsllr Second Careers for RN Offrs 1971-81, memb Industl Tbnl Panel 1973-80; involved with Penn Parish Church; Freeman: City of London 1961, Worshipful Co of Scriveners 1961; FCIS 1938, FBIM 1959, FAIA 1964; *author of*: various books on company secretarial practice, off admin, mgmnt and law and procedure of meetings; *Clubs* The Naval, Mansfield Law; *Style*— Austin Herbert, Esq; 19 Hogback Wood Rd, Beaconsfield, Bucks HP9 1JR (☎ 0494 674650)

HERBERT, Barry; s of Harold John Herbert (d 1985), of N Humberside, and Gladys Irene Everitt, *née* Wade; *b* 13 April 1938; *Educ* Beverley GS; *m* 3 Sept 1966, Margaret Avril, da of Norman Nicholson MBE (d 1962), of Humerside; 1 s (Christopher John b 1974), 1 da (Julia Anne b 1972); *Career* jt md Atlas Caravan Co Ltd 1978-; FCCA; DMS; MInstM; *Recreations* traction engine, organ restoration; *Clubs* Nat Traction Engine Tst, Leeds and Dist Traction Engine; *Style*— Barry Herbert, Esq; Owl Hill, 29 Old Village Rd, Little Weighton, East Yorks HU20 3US (☎ 0482 844337); Atlas Caravan Co Ltd, Wykeland Ind Estate, Wiltshire Rd, Hull, North Humberside HU4 6PH (☎ 0482 562101)

HERBERT, Hon Caroline Mary Louise; 2 da of 3 Baron Hemingford; *b* 4 Oct 1964; *Educ* Perse Sch for Girls Cambridge, Liverpool Poly, Lancaster Univ (BEd); *Career* sch teacher (primary); *Recreations* reading, sewing, outdoor activities; *Style*— The Hon Caroline Herbert; The Old Rectory, Hemingford Abbots, Huntingdon, Cambs

HERBERT, Hon Christopher Dennis Charles; only s and h of 3 Baron Hemingford; *b* 4 July 1973; *Educ* King's Coll Choir Sch Cambridge, Oundle; *Recreations* cricket, rugby; *Style*— The Hon Christopher Herbert

HERBERT, Hon David Alexander Reginald; s of 15 Earl of Pembroke and Montgomery, MVO (d 1960); *b* 1908; *Educ* Eton; *Career* serv WWII Lt RNVR; *Style*— The Hon David Herbert; Box 2304, Tangier (Socco)

HERBERT, David Passmore; s of late A H Herbert; *b* 11 Jan 1935; *Educ* The Leys Sch, Queens' Coll Cambridge; *m* 1966, Rosemary Elaine, *née* Bawtree; 2 s; *Career* slr; ptnr Messrs Triggs Turner and Co 1962-71, gp sec and slr Davies and Newman Gp of Cos 1971-78; dir: Davies and Newman Hldgs plc 1978-, Dan-Smedvig Ltd 1979-, Davies's Educnl Servs Ltd 1982-, Dan-Smedvig Supply Ships Ltd 1983-; Dan-Air Servs Ltd 1978-; dep chm Davies and Newman Hldgs plc 1985-; *Recreations* sailing, gardening, reading; *Clubs* Utd Oxford and Cambridge Univ; *Style*— David D Herbert, Esq; Meadowfold, South Rd, Liphook, Hants GU30 7HS (☎ 0428 722029); Davies and Newman Holdings plc, New City Court, 20 St Thomas St, London SE1 9RJ (☎ 01 378 6464 telex 888973 fax 01 403 2010)

HERBERT, Lady Diana Mary; da of 16 Earl of Pembroke and Montgomery, CVO (d 1969) and Lady Mary Dorothea Hope, da of 1 Marquess of Linlithgow; *Style*— Lady Diana Herbert; The Old Rectory, Wilton, Salisbury, Wilts SP2 0HT

HERBERT, Edward David; *b* 1 July 1958; *Educ* Bryanston, Lancaster Univ (BSc); *m* 1985, Diana Christine, eld da of Cedric Shore; 1 s (David Andrew b 1988), 1 da (Joy Sarah b 1986); *Career* ACMA; *Style*— Edward Herbert, Esq; c/o The Rt Hon the Earl of Powis, Marrington Hall, Chirbury, Powys

HERBERT, Elizabeth Anne Morse; da of late Lt-Col HG Herbert, and late Elizabeth Vera *née* Morse; *b* 9 Feb 1948; *Educ* St Swithons Sch Winchester; *Career* res mangr Kuoni Travel E Africa 1969-81, various foots in PR and Mktg 1981-, dir ABS Communications; MIPR 1984; *Style*— Miss Elizabeth Herbert; 47 Westmoreland Terrace, London SWN 4AQ (☎ 01 630 9349); Willow Cottage, Broads Green, Gt Waltham, Essex CMS LDX (☎ 0245 360 746);14 Kinnerton Place South, Kinnerton St, London SW1X 8EH (☎ 01 245 6262, fax 01 235 3916)

HERBERT, Hon Geordie - George Reginald Oliver Molyneux; s and h of Lord

Porchester (s and h of 6 Earl of Carnarvon); *b* 10 Nov 1956; *Educ* St John's Coll Oxford (BA); *Career* a page of honour to HM the Queen 1969-73; computer conslt and horticulturalist 1979-87; formerly with GEC, computer conslt; pa to Hon Peter Morrison, MP (dep chm of Cons Pty) 1986-87; *Style—* Lord Porchester

HERBERT, Hon Harry - Henry Malcolm; yr s of 7 Earl of Carnarvon; *b* 1959; *Educ* Eton; *Career* md HMH Mgmnt, Bloodstock Mgmnt Co, dir Hogg Rosinson Agric; *Recreations* golf, tennis; *Style—* The Hon Harry Herbert

HERBERT, John Anthony; s of Rev Canon Frank Selwood Herbert (d 1978), of Nuneaton, Warks, and Joan Mary Walcot Herbert, *née* Burton (d 1976); *b* 10 Sept 1939; *Educ* Dean Close Sch, Cheltenham and Exeter Univ; *m* 2 Aug 1962, Michelle, da of Nigel Forbes Dennis, of Malta; 2 da (Rebecca b 1964, Tamsin b 1968); *Career* over 250 films and documentaries to credit, on archaeological, mil trg and historical subjects (clients inc Saudi Arabian TV, MOD, oil indust), ed Quaryat Al fau (1981) and Al Rabadhah (1984), books of archaeological excavations, contrib illustrated London News on Arabian archaeology; photo exhibs London and Paris 1986; FRGS; *Recreations* France, english wine growing, sailing; *Clubs* The Anglo-Arab Assoc, The Georgian Gp, The Historic Houses Assoc, English Vineyards Assoc; *Style—* John A Herbert, Esq; Much Hadham Hall, Much Hadham, Herts SG10 6BZ (☎ 0279 842663)

HERBERT, Lynn Kathryn Wightman; *née* Herbert; da of Robert French Herbert, of Glasgow, and Margaret Hepburn, *née* Wightman; *b* 24 Dec 1957; *Educ* Hutchesons' Girls' GS, Glasgow Univ (LLB); *Career* slr, notary public; ptnr Smith and Grant Levin 1983-; *Recreations* golf, skiing, reading; *Clubs* Lundin Ladies GC, Leven Golfing Soc; *Style—* Ms Lynn Herbert

HERBERT, Martin Geoffrey Greenham; s of Geoffrey Basil Herbert (d 1974), and Alice Margery *née* Greenham; *b* 9 Dec 1946; *Educ* Rugby, Balliol Coll Oxford (BA); *m* 10 June 1981, Alicia Malka, da of Dr Benjamin Abraham Jolles (d 1985); 1 s (Edward b 1987), 2 da (Susannah b 1982, Katharine b 1985); *Career* slr 1971, ptnr Clifford Chance (formerly Coward Chance) 1977-; *Recreations* sailing, tree planting; *Clubs* Royal Fowey YC, Royal Harwich YC; *Style—* Martin Herbert, Esq; 23 Alwyne Road, London, N1; The Gables, East Bergholt, Suffolk; Clifford Chance, Royex House, Aldermanbury Sq, London, EC2V 7LD (☎ 01 600 0808, fax 01 726 8561, telex 8959991)

HERBERT, Hon Mrs Mervyn; Mary Elizabeth; da of J E Willard (former US Ambassador to Madrid); *m* 1921, Hon Mervyn Robert Howard Molyneux Herbert (3 s of 4 Earl of Carnarvon and who died 1929); 1 s, 2 da; *Style—* The Hon Mrs Mervyn Herbert; 25 Eaton Sq, London SW1

HERBERT, (Sydney) Mervyn; er s of Sydney B Herbert (d 1951), of Sandown IOW, and Ruth, *née* Smith; *b* 23 April 1912; *Educ* Ryde Sch; *m* 13 May 1937, Barbara, da of Walter H Findon (d 1950), of Sandown, IOW; 2 da;; *Career* Br Embassy Lisbon 1941-44, civilian advsr Supreme HQ AEF 1944-45, head euro dept MOI 1945-46, head euro info dept FO 1947; provincial journalist 1931-36, Morning Post 1937, foreign ed New Chronicle 1948-55, md Dickens Press 1956-63, chm Frank L Crane Ltd 1964-89, dir Lloyd's of London Press 1969-, chm Carlton Berry Co 1980-; govr and tstee Mermaid Theatre 1961-82; Freeman City of London 1969, Liveryman Worshipful Co Stationers & Newspapermakers; memb Inst Journalists 1931; *Books* Britain's Health (1938), The Stansted Black Book(1966); *Recreations* fishing; *Clubs* Travellers', City Livery; *Style—* S Mervyn Herbert; Brook House, Great Dunmow, Essex CM6 3PQ (☎ 0371 2684); 5/15 Cromer St, Grays Inn Rd, London WC1H 8LS (☎ 01 837 3330, fax 01 837 0917)

HERBERT, Michael; s of W R Herbert (d 1982), of Kent, and Eileen, *née* McKee; *b* 16 August 1933; *Educ* King's Sch Canterbury, St Edmund Hall Oxford (MA); *m* 1967, Anna Vibeke, da of Christian Madsen (d 1971), of Denmark; *Career* Nat Serv in RHA Germany 1956-58 2 Lt; CA; chief exec: Tussaud Gp, Madam Tussauds Ltd, Chessington World of Adventures Ltd, Warwick Castle Ltd, Wookey Hole Caves Ltd; FCA; *Recreations* walking, cricket, speaking Danish; *Clubs* Travellers', Hurlingham, MCC, Kent CC; *Style—* Michael Herbert, Esq; 14 Eaton Place, London SW1X 8AE (☎ 01 935 6861, fax 01 935 8906); Knudsseje, 9352 Dybvad, Denmark;

HERBERT, Hon Michael Clive; 2 s of 7 Earl of Powis, *qv*; *b* 22 August 1954; *Educ* Wellington, Christ's Coll Camb (MA), London Business Sch (MSc); *m* 1978, Susan Mary, da of Guy Baker (d 1982), of Welshpool, Powys; 2 s (Thomas Guy Clive b 1981, Mark Philip Clive b 1983), 1 da (Joanna Frances Clare b 1987); *Style—* The Hon Michael Herbert; Wicken Hall, Wicken, Ely, Cambs CB7 5XT

HERBERT, Hon Oliver Hayley Dennis; yst s of 1 Baron Hemingford, KBE, PC (d 1947); *b* 14 August 1919; *Educ* Oundle, Wadham Coll Oxford; *m* 1976 (m annulled), Rosemary Muriel, da of Rev Canon Roland Bate; *Career* formerly Maj Queen's Royal Regt, attached Indian Army; former tres and exec ctee memb Anglican Soc; *Style—* The Hon Oliver Herbert

HERBERT, Adm Sir Peter Geoffrey Marshall; KCB (1982), OBE (1969); s of A G S and Herbert P K M Herbert; *b* 28 Feb 1929; *Educ* Dunchurch Hall, RN Coll Darmouth; *m* 1953, Ann Maureen, *née* McKeown, 1 s, 1 da; *Career* served in submarines 1949-63, Cdr Nuclear Submarine HMS Valiant 1963-68, Capt appts 1966-76, cmd HMS Blake 1974-75, Dep Chief Polaris Exec 1976-78, Flag Offr Carriers and Amphibious Ships 1978-79, dir gen Naval Manpower and Trg 1980-81, Flag Offr Submarines and Cdr Sub Area E Atlantic 1981-83, Adm 1983, vice-chief of Def Staff (Personnel and Logistics) 1983-85; non-exec dir Radamec Gp 1985-, chm SSAFA Cncl, def conslt, chm sub Museum, memb exec ctee White Ensign Assoc; CBIM, MINucE; *Recreations* golf, swimming, woodwork, gardening; *Clubs* Army and Navy; *Style—* Adm Sir Peter Herbert, KCB, OBE; Dolphin Sq, London SW1

HERBERT, Hon Peter James; 3 s of 7 Earl of Powis, *qv*; *b* 26 Dec 1955; *Educ* Wellington; *m* 1978, Terri, yr da of Sean McBride, of Callan, Co Kilkenny; 1 s (Oliver George Laurie b 1983), 2 da (Sophie Louise Mary b 1980, Lucy Alison Julia b 1988); *Style—* The Hon Peter Herbert; Wade Tower, Wade Ct, Havant, Hants

HERBERT, Wally; s of Capt Walter William Herbert, RAPC (d 1972), and Helen, *née* Manton (d 1982); *b* 24 Oct 1934; *m* 24 Dec 1969, Marie Rita, da of Prof Charles McGaughey (d 1982); 2 da (Kari b 17 Sept 1970, Pascale b 30 March 1978); *Career* RE 1950-54; trained as surveyor Sch of Mil Survey, serv in Egypt 1953-54; surveyor Falklands Islands Dependencies Survey based at Hope Bay Antarctica 1955-58, hitch hiked 15,000 miles Montivideo Uruguay to UK 1958-59, expeditions to Lapland and Spitzbergen 1960, surveyor with NZ Antarctic Expdn based at Scott Base McMurdo Sound 1960-62; ldr Expdn NW Greenland (retracing route of Dr Frederick Cook) 1967-68, ldr Br Trans-Arctic Expdn (first surface crossing of Arctic Ocean from Alaska via N Pole to Spitzbergen a 3,800 mile journey with dog teams which took 16 mths to complete) 1968-69, ldr Expdnt to NW Greenland (travelling over 4,000 miles with Eskimos) 1971-73, ldr winter expdn to Lapland 1974, ldr Br N Polar Expdn (attempting to circumnavigate Greenland with dog teams and Eskimo skin boat) 1977-80, ldr Expdn to NW Greenland 1980, conducted feasibility study for an Explorers Museum at Sir Francis Drake's house (Buckland Abbey) 1981-84; writing and filming biog of Adm Robert E Perry 1985-88, filming in NW Greenland 1987 with second visit to N Pole 1987; total time spent in polar regions 13 yrs, total distance travelled by dog sledges and in open boats in polar regions over 25,000 miles; Polar medal (1962, Clasp 1969) awarded for Antarctic and Arctic exploration, Livingstone Gold Medal RGS (Scot) 1969, Founders Gold Medal RGS 1970, City of Paris Medal 1983, French Geog Soc Medal 1983, Explorers Medal 1985, Finn Ronne Award 1985; hon memb Br Schs Exploring Soc, hon pres World Expeditionary Assoc; FRGS; *Books* A World of Men (1968), Across the top of the World (1969), The Last Great Journey on Earth (1971), Polar Deserts (1971), Eskimos (1976), North Pole (1978), Hunters of the Polar North (1982), The Noose of Laurels (1989)); *Recreations* painting; *Clubs* Lansdowne, Explorers; *Style—* Wally Herbert, Esq; c/o Royal Geographical Soc, 1 Kensington Gore, London SW7 2AR

HERBERT, Lord; William Alexander Sidney Herbert; s and h of 17 Earl of Pembroke and Montgomery; *b* 18 May 1978; *Style—* Lord Herbert

HERBERT-JONES, Hugo Jarrett; CMG (1973), OBE (1963); s of Capt H Herbert-Jones (d 1923), of Llanrwst, Denbighshire, and Dora Jarrett, *née* Rowlands, MBE (d 1974); *b* 11 Mar 1922; *Educ* Bryanston, Worcester Coll Oxford (BA); *m* 1954, Margaret, da of Rev J P Veall (d 1971), of Eastbourne; 1 s (Nicholas), 2 da (Sarah, Siân); *Career* served Welsh Gds 1941-46, (wounded NW Europe 1944), Maj; HM Foreign later Dip Serv 1947-79; dir int affrs CBI 1979-87; *Recreations* sailing, golf, shooting, music, spectator sports; *Clubs* Garrick, MCC, London Welsh RFC, Aldeburgh YC, Aldeburgh GC; *Style—* Hugo Herbert-Jones, Esq, CMG, OBE; Priors Hill, Aldeburgh, Suffolk IP15 5ET (☎ 072 885 3335); 408 Nelson House, Dolphin Sq, SW1V 3LX (☎ 01 821 1183)

HERBERTSON, (Robert) Ian; s of Robert Hopkirk Herbertson (d 1969), and Winifred Rose, *née* Rawlinson; *b* 30 Dec 1953; *Educ* Selhurst GS, Birkbeck Coll London (BA); *m* 22 March 1985, Joanna Hazel North, da of Reginald Bernard North, of Gwent, Wales; 1 da (Rebecca Elizabeth b 1987); *Career* system analyst Crown Agents for Overseas Govt and Admin 1979-85; Bank of Eng: sr systems analyst 1985-88, audit div 1988-; dir The Claridge Press 1987; memb: Aristotelian Soc 1982-, Royal Inst of Philosophy 1980-, ctee Ct of Electors Birbeck Coll 1987-, Convocation Univ of London 1984; CDipAF 1985, FIAP 1986; *Recreations* philosophy, literature, astronomy; *Clubs* Challoner; *Style—* Ian Herbertson, Esq; 21 Euston St, Huntingdon, Cambs (☎ 0480 55601); 15 Dovercourt Ave, Thornton Heath, Surrey (☎ 01 684 9218); Bank of England, Threadneedle St, London (☎ 01 601 4210)

HERBISON, Rt Hon Margaret McCrorie; *née* McCrorie; PC (1964); *b* 11 Mar 1907; *Educ* Bellshill Acad, Glasgow Univ; *Career* MP (Lab) N Lanark 1945-70, jt parly under-sec Scottish Off 1950-51, chm Lab Pty 1957, min Pensions and Nat Insur 1964-66, min Social Security 1966-67, former memb NEC; lord high cmmr to Gen Assembly of Church of Scotland 1970-71, memb Royal Cmmn on Standards of Conduct in Public Life 1974-; Scots Woman of Year 1970; Hon LLD Glasgow; *Style—* The Rt Hon Margaret Herbison; 8 Mornay Way, Shotts, Lanarks ML7 4EG (☎ 0501 21944)

HERCHENRODER, Lady; Marie Charlotte Paule; *née* Genève de St Jean; da of Augustin Emil Henri Genève de St Jean and Suzanne Berthe, *née* de la Haye Duponsel; *b* 22 Sept 1904; *m* 1923, Sir Francis Herchenroder, QC (d 1982; sometime asst legal advsr Cwlth Off); 2 da (Paula, Cecile); *Style—* Lady Herchenroder; 11 Pelham Court, London SW3 (☎ 01 584 3937)

HERD, (James) Peter; MBE (1946), WS (1949); s of Maj Walter Herd, MC (d 1951), of Kirkcaldy, Fife, and Sigrid, *née* Russell Johnston (d 1972); *b* 18 May 1920; *Educ* Edinburgh Acad, St Andrews Univ, Edinburgh Univ; *m* 5 Aug 1943, Marjory Phimister, da of James Mitchell (d 1961), of Aberdeen; 3 s (Michael b 1945, David b 1949, Malcolm b 1955), 2 da (Katherine b 1947, Penelope b 1959); *Career* Maj The Black Watch (RHR) 1939-46, serv in UK and SE Asia; ptnr Beveridge Herd & Sandilands 1951-, local dir Royal Insur Gp 1952-, tstee Kirkcaldy & Dist Tstee Savings Bank 1952-83, Notary Public 1952; dir Kirkcaldy Abbeyfield Soc; Hon Sheriff Kirkcaldy; *Recreations* curling, gardening; *Clubs* New (Kirkcaldy); *Style—* Peter Herd, Esq, MBE, WS; Nether Strathore, Thornton, Fife KY1 4DY (☎ 0592 773 863); 1 East Fergus Place, Kirkcaldy, Fife KY1 4DY (☎ 0592 261 616)

HERD, Hon Mrs (Sheelagh Margaret); *née* Monckton; eld da of 12 Viscount Galway; *b* 1945; *m* 1967, William Arthur Herd; *Style—* The Hon Mrs Herd; 726 Galloway Crescent, London, Ontario N6J 2Y7, Canada

HERDMAN, John (Mark) Ambrose; LVO (1979); s of Cdr Claudius Alexander Herdman, DL, RN, of Braewood, Sion Mills, Strabane, 10 Tyrone, N I, and Joan Dalrymple, *née* Tennant (d 1937); *b* 26 April 1932; *Educ* St Edward's Sch Oxford, Dublin Univ (BA, MA), Queen's Coll Oxford; *m* 29 June 1963, Elizabeth Anne, da of Rupert McLintock Dillon (d 1972), of Dublin; 1 s (Patrick b 1969), 2 da (Deirdre b 1966, Bridget b 1970); *Career* HMOCS Kenya 1954-64 (ret dist cmmr W Pokot); FCO (formerly Cwlth Rels Off): London 1964-65, MECAS Lebanon 1965-66, 1 sec (devpt) Amman 1966-68, FCO 1969-71, 1 sec (devpt) Lusaka 1971-74, head of chancery Jedda 1974-76, FCO 1976-78, 1 sec (aid and commercial) Lilongwe 1978-81, FCO 1981-83, dep govr Bermuda 1983-86, govr Br Virgin Is 1986-; *Recreations* golf, fishing, philately; *Clubs* Ebury Court (London); *Style—* Mark Herdman, Esq, LVO; Government House, Tortola, British Virgin Islands (☎ 49 43400); c/o FCO (Tortola), King Charles St, London SW1A 2AH

HEREFORD, Dean of; *see*: Haynes, The Very Rev Peter

HEREFORD, 102 Bishop (cr 676) 1974-; Rt Rev John Richard Gordon Eastaugh; s of Gordon Eastaugh; *b* 11 Mar 1920; *Educ* Leeds Univ; *m* 1963, Bridget, da of Sir Hugh Chance, CBE (bro of Sir Robert Chance, 3 Bt); 2 s, 1 da; *Career* curate 1944, vicar St Peter's Eaton Sq 1967-74, archdeacon Middx 1966-74, sub-prelate Order St John 1978-; patron 64 livings, the 3 Canonries, the Archdeaconries of Hereford and Ludlow, and the Prebends of his Cathedral; *Style—* The Rt Rev the Lord Bishop of Hereford; The Bishop's House, The Palace, Hereford (☎ 0432 271355)

HEREFORD, 18 Viscount (E 1550); Sir Robert Milo Leicester Devereux; 15 Bt (E 1611); Premier Viscount in the Peerage of England; s of Hon Robert Godfrey de Bohun Devereux (d 1934, s of 17 Viscount) and Audrey, who m, as her 2 husb, 7 Earl of Lisburne; suc gf 1952; *b* 4 Nov 1932; *Educ* Eton; *m* 1969, Susan Mary, only child of Maj Maurice Godley, of Sevenoaks; 2 s (Hon Charles, Hon Edward Mark de Breteuil b 1977); *Heir* s, Hon Charles Robin de Bohun Devereux b 11 Aug 1975; *Style*— The Rt Hon the Viscount Hereford; Lyford Cay Club, PO Box N-7776, Nassau, Providence, Bahamas

HERINCX, (Raymond Frederick) Raimund; s of Florent Herincx (d 1974) and Marie Therese Lucia, *née* Cheal; *b* 23 August 1927; *Educ* St Mary Abbot's Kensington, Thames Valley GS Twickenham, Univ of London; *m* 27 March 1954, (Margaret Jean) aka Astra Blair, da of Lt-Col Douglas Waugh; 1 s (Gareth James) 2 da (Nicole Elaine, Gemma Marelen); *Career* Educn Offr Household Cavalry 1946-48; memb Royal Opera House Chorus 1949-53, joined Welsh Nat Opera 1956, joined Met Opera House (NY) 1976; prof of voice RAM 1970-77, sr voice teacher NE of Scotland Music Sch 1979-, lectr Univ Coll Cardiff 1984-87; voice therapist 1979-, music critic 1987-; fndr: Quinville Tst (for Handicapped Children), Sadler's Wells Soc; fndr memb Assoc of Artists Against Aids; world record for no of operatic roles and concert works sung (468); int music awards opera medal 1968, Hon RAM 1971; *Recreations* wine & its history, vine & plant breeding; *Style*— Raimund Herincx, Esq; 54 Regents Park Rd, London NW1 7SX (☎ 01 586 7841); Monks' Vineyard, Larkbarrow, East Compton, Pilotn, Shepton Mallet, Somerset (☎ 0749 4462)

HERMON-TAYLOR, Prof John; s of Hermon Taylor, of Bosham, W Sussex, and Mearie Amelie, *née* Pearson (d 1981); *b* 16 Oct 1936; *Educ* Harrow, St John's Coll Cambridge, (BA, MB, BChir, MChir), The London Hosp Med Coll; *m* 18 Sept 1971, Eleanor Ann, da of Dr Willard S Pheteplace (d 1985), of Davenport, Iowa, USA; 1 s (Peter Maxwell b 1979), 1 da (Amy Caroline b 1975); *Career* various NHS and Univ trg posts in surgery 1963-68, MRC travelling fell in gastrointestinal physiology Mayo Clinic USA 1968-69, reader in surgery The London Hosp Med Coll 1971-76 (sr lectr 1970-71), prof and chm of surgery St George's Hosp Med Sch 1976-, author of numerous scientific and med res articles; memb: cncl Assoc of Surgeons of GB and Ireland 1980-83, clinical panel The Wellcome Tst 1985-88, cncl Action Res for the Crippled Child 1988; The Times Newspaper/Barclays Bank Innovator of the Year Award 1988; Hallet Prize (1988); FRCS 1963, memb Biochem Soc; *Recreations* sailing, shooting; *Clubs* Royal Thames YC; *Style*— Prof John Hermon-Taylor; 11 Parkside Ave, Wimbledon, London SW19 5ES (☎ 01 946 0557); Dept of Surgery, St George's Hosp Medical Sch, London SW17 ORE (☎ 01 767 7631, fax 01 767 4696)

HERON, (John) Brian; s of John Henry Heron (d 1944), of Leeds, and Dorothy, *née* Hinton; *b* 22 Jan 1933; *Educ* Manchester GS, St Catharine's Coll Cambridge (MA); *m* 7 Sept 1968, Margaret, da of Harvey Jessop (d 1965), of Heywood; 1 s (John Michael b 16 Nov 1972), 1 da (Joanne Elizabeth b 29 July 1970); *Career* dir: TBA Indust Products Ltd 1969, Duglass Fibres 1969; chief exec and dep chm TBA 1968-; chm: TBA (Pty) Australia 1986-, Moor Plastics Ltd 1988-, Telford Rubber Processors Ltd 1986-, Fratherm GMBH 1987-; vice-pres Bentley-Harris Inc 1988-; chm Textilver SA 1988-; dir Manchester Sci Park; govr: UMISJ (memb court and cncl), Rochdale Employer Network; chm Indust Scis Gp UMISJ; *Recreations* sailing, motoring; *Clubs* Cambridge Univ Cruising, Oxford and Cambridge Sailing Soc, Royal Yachting Assoc, Hollingworth Lake Sailing; *Style*— Brian Heron, Esq; Cleggswood Heys Farm, Hollingworth Lake, Littleborough, Lancs (☎ 0706 73292); TBA Industrial Products Ltd, Rochdale, Lancs (☎ 0706 47422, fax 0706 354295, telex 63174)

HERON, Sir Conrad Frederick; KCB (1974, CB 1969), OBE (1953); s of Richard Foster Heron, of South Shields, and Ida Fredrika Heron; *b* 21 Feb 1916; *Educ* South Shields HS, Trinity Hall Cambridge; *m* 1948, Envye Linnéa, da of Hermann Gustafsson, of Sweden; 2 da; *Career* entered Min of Labour 1938, dep chm Cmmn on Indust Relations 1971-72, perm sec Dept of Employment 1973-76, ret; *Style*— Sir Conrad Heron, KCB, OBE; Old Orchards, West Lydford, Somerton, Somerset (☎ 096 324 387)

HERON, Michael Gilbert (Mike); s of Gilbert Thwaites (d 1962), and Olive Lilian, *née* Steele; *b* 22 Oct 1934; *Educ* St Josephs' Acad Blackheath, New Coll Oxford (MA); *m* 16 Aug 1958, Celia Veronica Mary, da of Capt Clarence Hunter (d 1960); 2 s (Jonathan, Damian), 2 da (Louise, Annette); *Career* Lt RA 1953-55; dir BOCM Silcock 1971-76, chm Batchelors Foods Ltd 1976-82, dep co-ordinator food and drinks co-ordination Unilever 1982-86, main bd dir Unilever plc and NV 1986-; Food and Drink Fedn: memb exec ctee, memb cncl, chm food policy res ctee; memb Armed Forces Pay Review Bd 1981 and 1982; *Recreations* very keen sportsman in the past, now a viewer; *Style*— Mike Heron, Esq; Paradise Cottage, Paradise Lane, Bucklebury, Berks RG7 6NU (☎ 0734 712 228); Flat 2, 17 Cranley Gdns, London SW7 3BD (☎ 01 244 7253); Unilever plc, Unilever House, Blackfriars, London EC4P 4BQ (☎ 01 822 6616, fax 01 822 5970, car 0860 340275, telex 28395 Unil G)

HERON, Robert; CVO (1988); s of James Riddick Heron (d 1959), and Sophie Lockhart, *née* Leathem (d 1956); *b* 12 Oct 1927; *Educ* King Edward's Sch Birmingham, St Catharine's Coll Cambridge (MA); *m* 8 Aug 1953, Patricia Mary, da of Frank Robert Pennell (d 1945); 2 s (Andrew, Neil), 1 da (Susan); *Career* 6/7 Bn The Black Watch (RHR) TA, ret to RARO; housemaster 1953-59: Strathallan Sch, Christ Coll Brecon; headmaster King James 1 Sch IOW 1962-65; ATV London 1965-69: head educnl broadcasting (responsible for TV series in sciences, languages, soc-documentaries, and leisure interests), del Europe Broadcasting Union (Paris, Stockholm, Basle, Rome), programme dir EVR Partnership (CBS USA, ICI GB, Ciba Giegy UK) 1970, md EVR Enterprises Ltd 1976, Dir Duke of Edinburgh's Award 1978-87; currently: special projects dir Blue Arrow America's Cup Challenge, hon advsr Outward Bound Tst, conslt Br Int Ostomy Support Assoc; Freeman City of London 1981; FRGS 1988; *Clubs* Army and Navy, ISC (Cowes), Port Pendennis, Hawks (Cambridge), Achilles (Oxford and Cambridge); *Style*— Robert Heron, ESQ, CVO; The Oast House, Ingleden Park, Tenterden, Kent

HERON-MAXWELL, Geraldine, Lady; D(orothy) Geraldine E(mma); yr da of late Claud Paget Mellor, of Victoria, BC; *m* 1942, Sir Patrick Heron-Maxwell, 9 Bt (d 1982); 3 s (Nigel M, 10 Bt *qv*, Colin, Paul); *Style*— Geraldine, Lady Heron-Maxwell; 9 Cowslip Hill, Letchworth, Herts

HERON-MAXWELL, Sir Nigel Mellor; 10 Bt (NS 1683), of Springkell, Dumfriesshire; s of Sir Patrick Ivor Heron-Maxwell, 9 Bt (d 1982), sr male rep of the Maxwells of Pollock and the Clydesdale Maxwells; *b* 30 Jan 1944; *Educ* Milton Abbey; *m* 1972, Mary Elizabeth Angela, da of W Ewing, of Co Donegal; 1 s, 1 da (Claire Louise b 1977); *Heir* s, David Mellor Heron-Maxwell b 22 May 1975; *Career* navigation apprentice London and Overseas Freighters Ltd 1961-65, navigation offr Royal Fleet Aux Service 1966-76, flying instr 1976-80; commercial pilot 1980-83; asst data controller Smith Kline and French Res Ltd 1983-85, programmer/analyst Smith Kline and French Laboratories Ltd 1985-; *Style*— Sir Nigel Heron-Maxwell, Bt; 105 Codicote Rd, Welwyn, Herts AL6 9TY (☎ 0438 820387); Smith Kline and French Laboratories Ltd, Mundells, Welwyn Garden City, Herts AL7 1EY (☎ 0707 325111)

HERRIDGE, Geoffrey Howard; CMG (1962); s of Edward Herridge (d 1940), of Eckington, Worcs, and Mary Elizabeth, *née* Welford (d 1954); *b* 22 Feb 1904; *Educ* Crypt Sch Gloucester, St John's Coll Cambridge (MA); *m* 1935, Dorothy Elvira, da of Arthur White Millar Tod (d 1949); 2 s (Charles, Michael), 2 da (Christina, Elizabeth); *Career* chm: Iraq Petroleum Co Ltd and assoc cos 1965-70 (gen mangr in ME 1947-51, exec dir 1953-57, md 1957-63, dep chm 1963-65), Petroleum Ind Trg Bd 1967-70; memb London Ctee Ottoman Bank 1964-79; *Clubs* Oriental; *Style*— Geoffrey Herridge Esq, CMG; Flint, Sidlesham Common, Chichester, Sussex (☎ 024 356 357)

HERRIES, Sir Michael Alexander Robert Young; OBE (1968), MC (1945), DL (Dumfries and Galloway 1983); s of Lt-Col William Dobree Young-Herries, and Ruth Mary, *née* Thrupp; *b* 28 Feb 1923; *Educ* Eton, Trinity Coll Cambridge; *m* 1949, Elizabeth Hilary Russell, *née* Smith; 2 s, 1 da (Julia); *Career* served KOSB 1942-47; joined Jardine Matheson and Co 1948 (chm and md 1963-70), chm Royal Bank of Scotland 1976- (dir 1972-, vice-chm 1974-75, dep chm 1975-76), dep chm: Williams and Glyn's Bank 1978-85, dir Scottish Widows' Fund and Life Assur Soc 1974-; memb Royal Co of Archers 1973-; kt 1975; *Style*— Sir Michael Herries, OBE, MC, DL; c/o Royal Bank of Scotland plc, 42 St Andrew Sq, Edinburgh EH2 2YE (☎ 031 556 8555); Spottes, Castle Douglas, Stewartry of Kirkcudbright, Scotland (☎ 055 666 202); 30 Heriot Row, Edinburgh (☎ 031 226 2711); Flat 14, Lochmore House, Cundy St, London SW1W 9JX (☎ 01 730 1119)

HERRIES OF TERREGLES, Lady (14 holder of S Lordship 1490); Lady Anne Elizabeth; *née* Fitzalan-Howard; eldest da of 16 Duke of Norfolk, KG, GCVO, GBE, TD, PC (d 1975, when the Dukedom and all other honours save the Lordship passed to his kinsman, 17 Duke, *qv*; the late Duke's mother was Lady Herries of Terregles *suo jure* following the death of her f, the 11 Lord), and Lavinia, Duchess of Norfolk (*qv*); *b* 12 June 1938; *m* 1985, as his 2 w, (Michael) Colin Cowdrey, CBE, *qv*; *Heir* sis, Lady Mary Mumford, *qv*; *Career* racehorse trainer; *Style*— The Rt Hon Lady Herries of Terregles; Angmering Park, Littlehampton, West Sussex (☎ 090 674 421)

HERRIN, John Edward; CBE (1985); s of Harold John Herrin (d 1974), of Humecourt, Hythe, Kent, and Gertrude Mary MacDermot; *b* 15 Sept 1930; *Educ* Bancrofts Sch, Rugby Coll of Technol (CEng); *m* 4 April 1959, Heather Yeoman, da of Leslie Kirkpatrick Reid, JP (d 1980), of Mill House, Hale, Cheshire; 1 s (Jeremy b 1970), 2 da (Johanna b 1961, Caroline b 1962); *Career* Lt Cdr RNR 1953-55; chm Welwyn Electronics Ltd 1972; md: Roy Worcester plc 1975-83, Crystalate Hldgs plc 1983-85: dep chm Crystalate 1988- (chief exec 1985-88); pres Euro Electronics Component Mfrs Assoc 1986-88; memb: cncl of Electronic Component Indust Fedn (chm 1981-82), Nedo Electronics SG; chm N Regnl Cncl for Sport and Recreation 1982-84, Freeman City of London, Liveryman Worshipful Co of Scientific Instrument Makers (Jr Warden 1988-89); FIEE; *Recreations* sailing, shooting, fishing; *Clubs* East India, MCC; *Style*— John Herrin, Esq, CBE; Petteridge Oast, Matfield, Kent TN12 7LX; Crystalate Holdings plc, Wharf House, Medway Wharf Road, Tonbridge, Kent TN9 1RE (☎ 0732 361414)

HERRING, Timothy Stephen; s of Cdr Philip Maurice Herring, RNVR (d 1982), and Flora Pepita Herring (d 1985); *b* 25 May 1936; *Educ* Bishops Stortford Coll; *m* 22 April 1960, Cathleen Elizabeth, da of Thomas Stephen Nevin (d 1972); 2 s (Stephen Ashley b 26 Nov 1960, Andrew Philip b 15 March 1963); *Career* Lamson Engrg 1956-66; proprietor: Julie's Restaurant 1969-, Portobello Hotel 1970-, Ark Restaurant USA 1983-; yachtsman, winner: Britannia Cup, Queens Cup, Queen Victoria Cup; Freeman City of London 1961, memb Worshipful Co of Blacksmiths 1961; *Recreations* yachting; *Clubs* Royal Burnham YC, Royal Thames YC; *Style*— Timothy Herring, Esq; 127 Elgin Crescent, London W11 (☎ 01 727 2776); Quaycote, Burnham-on-Crouch, Essex

HERRINGTON, Air Vice-Marshal Walter John; CB (1982); s of Maj Henry Herrington, MBE, MM, (d 1975), of Winchester, Hants, and Daisy Restall, *née* Gardiner (d 1974); *b* 18 May 1928; *Educ* Woking GS Woking, RAF Coll Cranwell; *m* 1958, Joyce Maureen, da of Walter Cherryman (d 1970), of Ealing; 2 s (Martin, Simon); *Career* RAF, Air Vice-Marshal, Def Attache Paris, SDS Air RCDS, dir Serv Intelligence MOD ret 1982; aviation advsr Int Mil Serv, memb Cncl Tavra; *Recreations* walking, reading, military history; *Clubs* RAF; *Style*— Air Vice-Marshal John Herrington, CB; c/o Lloyds Bank plc, Camberley, Surrey (☎ 22308); International Military Services, 4 Abbey Orchard St, London SW1P 2JJ (☎ 01 222 8090)

HERRON, Very Rev Andrew; s of John Todd Herron, and Mary Skinner, *née* Hunter; *b* 29 Sept 1909; *Educ* Glasgow Albert Road Acad, Glasgow Univ (MA, BD, LLB); *m* 26 Dec 1935, Joanna Fraser (Queenie), da of David Neill (d 1914), of Forfar; 4 da (Ann b 1938, Lorna b 1940, Eleanor Isobel b 1942, Muriel b 1944); *Career* ordained min Church of Scotland 1934; min: Linwood 1936-40, Houston and Killellan 1940-59, clerk to Presbytery of Glasgow 1959-81, moderator Gen Assembly of Church of Scotland 1971-72 (covener: Dept of Publications 1959-69, Business Ctee 1972-76), special lectr in practical theol Univ of Glasgow 1968-85 (Baird lectr 1985); Hon DD Univ of St Andrews 1975, Hon LLD Univ of Strathclyde 1983; *Books* Record Apart (1974), Guide to the General Assembly (1976), Guide to Congregational Affairs (1979), Guide to Presbytery (1982), Kirk by Divine Right (1985), Guide to the Ministry (1987), Guide to Ministerial Income (1987); *Style*— The Very Rev Andrew Herron, DD, LLD; 36 Darnley Rd, Glasgow G41 4NE (☎ 041 423 6422)

HERRON, Anthony Gavin; TD (1972); s of Gavin Bessell Herron, of The Wilderness, Maresfield Park, Sussex, and Irene Dorothy, *née* Peel (d 1986); *b* 10 April 1934; *Educ* Canford Sch, LSE (BSc); *m* 5 July 1958, Gray, da of Henry Francis Gray (d 1987); 1 s (Angus b 1966), 1 da (Tracy b 1964); *Career* ptnr Touche Ross and Co 1966- (currently i/c Corporate Fin Gp; seconded to Postal Servs as dir of Postal Fin and Corporate Planning 1974-76, dir Expamet Int 1974-; past tres and vice-pres HAC; FCA; *Recreations* golf, swimming, walking, antiques; *Clubs* RAC; *Style*— Anthony Herron, Esq, TD; Hill House, 1 Little New St, London EC4A 3TR; (☎ 01 353 8011, telex 884739 TRLNDNG)

HERSCHEL-SHORLAND, John; s of Christopher William Shorland (d 1982), and Eileen Dorothea, *née* Herschel (d 1980); descendant of Sir William and Sir John Herschel pioneers of science and astronomy; *b* 23 May 1935; *Educ* Wellington, UCL (BSc); *m* 19 Sept 1959, Christian Esther Flowerdew, da of John Noel Mason Ashplant

Nicholls, OBE, KPM (d 1987); 1 s (William b 1966), 2 da (Amanda b 1961, Catherine b 1962); *Career* with Rolls Royce 1960-86 (latterly exec mangr Ind Gas Turbine Div); *Recreations* photography, sailing, music, real tennis; *Style—* John Herschel-Shorland, Esq

HERSCHELL, Baroness; Lady Heather Margaret Mary; *née* Legge; da of late 8 Earl of Dartmouth; *b* 1925; *m* 1948, 3 Baron Herschell, *qv*; *Style—* The Rt Hon the Lady Herschell; Westfield House, Ardington, Wantage, Berks

HERSCHELL, 3 Baron (UK 1886); Rognvald Richard Farrer; s of 2 Baron, GCVO (d 1929), and Vera (d 1961), da of Sir Arthur Nicolson, 10 Bt; *b* 13 Sept 1923; *Educ* Eton; *m* 1 May 1948, Lady Heather Mary Margaret Legge, o da of 8th Earl of Dartmouth; 1 da; *Heir* none; *Career* page of hon to King George V, King Edward VIII and King George V; late Capt Coldstream Gds; *Style—* The Rt Hon the Lord Herschell; Westfield House, Ardington, Wantage, Oxfordshire (☎ 0235 833224)

HERSEY, Hon Mrs (Katherine Viola); *née* James; da of 4 Baron Northbourne; *b* 1940; *m* 1963, John Wharton Hersey; 3 s; *Style—* The Hon Mrs Hersey; Thorneyburn, Old Rectory, Tarset, Northumberland

HERSHAM, Gary; s of W S Hersham, of London, and Anne Deborah *née* Reicher (d 1987); *b* 30 April 1953; *Educ* Imperial Coll of Sci and Technol (BSc); *m* 15 Sept 1981, Aida, da of Naim Dellal; 1 s (Alexander b 1986), 1 da (Gabriella b 1982); *Career* md estate agent,; ARCS; *Recreations* shooting, skiing, skydiving; *Style—* Gary Hersham, Esq; c/o 1 Cadogan St, London SW3 2PP

HERTFORD, 8 Marquess of (GB 1793); Hugh Edward Conway Seymour; DL (Warwicks 1959); also Lord Conway, Baron Conway of Ragley (E 1703), Baron Conway of Killultagh (I 1712), Viscount Beauchamp, Earl of Hertford (both GB 1750), and Earl of Yarmouth (GB 1793); patron of 3 livings; s of Brig-Gen Lord Henry Seymour, DSO (2 s of 6 Marquess) and Lady Helen Grosvenor (da of 1 Duke of Westminster); *b* 29 Mar 1930; *Educ* Eton; *m* 1956, Comtesse Pamela Thérèse Louise de Caraman-Chimay, da of Lt-Col Prince Alphonse de Chimay, TD (d 1973), by his w, Brenda (d 1985), da of Lord Ernest Hamilton (7 s of 1 Duke of Abercorn); 1 s, 3 da; *Heir* s, Earl of Yarmouth; *Career* late Lt Gren Gds; Hertford PRs Ltd; estate mangr and prop of Ragley Hall; *Clubs* White's, Pratt's, Turf; *Style—* The Most Hon the Marquess of Hertford; Ragley Hall, Alcester, Warwicks (☎ 0789 762455)

HERTFORD, Bishop of; Rt Rev Kenneth Harold Pillar; s of Arthur Harold Pillar (d 1974), of Plymouth, and Dorothy Mary, *née* Towillis (d 1924); *b* 10 Oct 1924; *Educ* Devonport HS, Queen's Coll Cambridge, Ridley Hall Cambridge (MA); *m* 1955, Margaret Elizabeth, da of David Morgan Davies (d 1943), of Blackburn; 1 s (Stephen b 1961), 3 da (Helen b 1957, Sarah b 1959, Rachel b 1963); *Career* Sub Lt RNVR 1943-46; made deacon 1950, ordained priest 1951; curate Childwall Parish Church Liverpool 1950-53; chaplain Lee Abbey N Devon 1953-57; vicar St Paul's Beckenham 1957-62; vicar St Mary Bredin Canterbury 1962-65, Warden Lee Abbey N Devon 1965-70, vicar of Waltham Abbey Essex 1970-82; bishop of Hertford 1982; *Recreations* walking, travel, washing up; *Style—* The Rt Rev the Bishop of Hertford; Hertford House, Abbey Mill Lane, St Albans, Herts AL3 4HE (☎ St Albans 66420)

HERTZOG, Dr (Christopher) Barry; s of Dr William Hertzog, of Ramsey, Cambs, and Elfreda; *b* 21 August 1939; *Educ* Uppingham Sch, Cambridge (MA, PhD); *m* 21 Aug 1963, Dr Jeanne Lovell, da of William Brough (d 1939); 3 da (Sophia b 1964, Zoë b 1967, Justine b 1969); *Career* snr lectr in law Surrey CC 1974-; md Vale Royal Abbey now Vale Royal Abbey plc 1982; *Recreations* flying, skiing, tennis, photography, travel, archaeology; *Clubs* IOD, Naval, RAC, Aircraft Owners' and Pilots' Assoc, Jaguar Drivers'; *Style—* Dr Barry Hertzog; Vale Royal, Whitegate, Northwich, Cheshire CW8 2BA (☎ 0606 889313, telex 666985 JRG-G, fax 0606 783662, car tel 0836 599235)

HERVEY, Rear Adm John Bethell; CB (1982), OBE (1970); s of Capt Maurice William Bethell Hervey, RN (d 1965), of Lee Common Bucks, and Joan Hanbury (d 1975); f served in both World Wars and was in HMS Ocean at the Dardanelles and in HMS Colossus at Jutland; *b* 14 May 1928; *Educ* Marlborough; *m* 1950, Audrey Elizabeth, da of Leonard Mallett Mote (d 1947), of Colombo; 2 s (Nicholas, Jonathan), 1 da (Katrina); *Career* RN 1946, specialized in submarines 1950, nuclear submarines 1968, cmd appts: HMS Miner VI 1956, HMS Aeneas 1956-57, HMS Ambush 1959-62, HMS Oracle 1962-64, Sixth Submarine Div 1964-66, HMS Cavalier 1966-67, HMS Warspite 1968-69, Second Submarine Sqdn 1973-75, HMS Kent 1975-76; Staff appts: Course offr RN Petty Offrs Leadership Sch 1957-59, Submarine Staff Offr to Canadian Maritime Cdr Halifax Nova Scotia 1964-66, Flotilla Operations Offr to Flag Offr Submarines 1970-71, Def Operational Requirements Staff 1971-73, Dep Chief Allied Staff to: C-in-C Channel, C-in-C E Atlantic 1976-80, Hon ADC to HM the Queen 1979, Cdr Br Navy Staff and Br Naval Attaché Washington; UK Nat Liaison Rep to Saclant 1980-82, Rear Adm 1980, ret; marketing vice-pres Western Hemisphere MEL 1982-86, Independant Naval Conslt 1986-; *Recreations* walking, talking, reading; *Clubs* Army and Navy, Royal Navy of 1765 and 1785, Anchorites (pres 1988); *Style—* Rear Adm John Hervey, CB, OBE; c/o Nat Westminster Bank, 26 Haymarket, London SW1Y 4ER

HERVEY, Lord (Frederick William Charles) Nicholas Wentworth; s of 6 Marquess of Bristol (d 1985), and his 2 w, Lady Anne Juliet Dorothea Maud Fitzwilliam (da of 8 Earl Fitzwilliam); hp of half-bro, 7 Marquess of Bristol; *b* 26 Nov 1961; *Educ* Eton, Yale; *Career* pres and fndr: Rockingham Club, and Woodhouse Ltd; vice-chllr and memb Grand Cncl of Monarchist League (fndr and pres of its Youth Assoc); tstee, Yale Club of GB; vice-pres: ESU Appeals Ctee, ESU Eastern Regn; *Recreations* skiing, swimming, golf; *Clubs* Turf, Brooks's, CLA, The Pundits Soc of Yale Univ; *Style—* Lord Nicholas Hervey; 128 Pavilion Road, London SW1X 0AX (☎ 01 245 0906)

HERVEY-BATHURST, Sir Frederick Peter Methuen; 6 Bt (UK 1818), of Lainston, Hants; s of Maj Sir Frederick Edward William Hervey-Bathurst, 5 Bt, DSO (d 1956); *b* 26 Jan 1903; *Educ* Eton; *m* 1, 1933 (m dis 1956), Maureen Gladys Diana, da of Charles Gordon (d 1957), of Boveridge Park, Salisbury; 1 s, 1 da; m 2, 1958, Cornelia, da of late Frederic White Shepard, of New York, USA, and widow of Dr John Lawrence Riker, of Rumson, NJ, USA; *Heir* s, Frederick Hervey-Bathurst; *Career* former: Capt Grenadier Gds, estate agent; ret; *Recreations* sailing, flying, climbing; *Clubs* Cavalry and Guards, Royal Ocean Racing; *Style—* Sir Frederick Hervey-Bathurst, Bt; Bellevue Avenue, Rumson, New Jersey 07760, USA (☎ 842 0791)

HERVEY-BATHURST, (Frederick) John Charles Gordon; s and h of Sir Frederick Peter Methuen Hervey-Bathurst, 6 Bt; *b* 23 April 1934; *Educ* Eton, Trinity Coll Cambridge; *m* 1957, Caroline Myrtle, da of Sir William Randle Starkey, 2 Bt; 1 s, 2 da (*see* Portal, Sir Jonathan, Bt, and Colthurst, Sir Richard, Bt); *Career* Lt Gren Gds (Reserve); dir Lazard Bros and Co Ltd; *Style—* John Hervey-Bathurst Esq; Somborne Park, King's Somborne, Hants (☎ 079 47 322); Lazard Bros and Co Ltd, 21 Moorfields, London EC2P 2HT (☎ 01 588 2721)

HERVEY-BATHURST, Hon Mrs (Sarah Rachel); *née* Peake; 2 da of 2 Viscount Ingleby, of Northallerton, Yorks, *qv*; *b* 27 Nov 1958; *Educ* Queensgate, UCL; *m* 25 Sept 1982, James Felton Somers Hervey-Bathurst , er s of Maj Benjamin Hervey-Bathurst, OBE, DL (half-bro of Sir Frederick Hervey-Bathurst, 6 Bt); 1 da (Imogen b 1986); *Recreations* reading; *Style—* The Hon Mrs Hervey-Bathurst; Eastnor Castle, Ledbury, Herefordshire (☎ 0531 3318)

HERWALD, Basil Mark Jonathan; s of Samuel Herwald, and Enid, *née* Brodie; *b* 27 July 1953; *Educ* Salford GS, Queens' Coll Cambridge (MA); *Career* slr, ptnr Herwald Seddon; city cncllr 1980-86; chm: Salford Victims Support Scheme Festival 200 (Manchester Jewry Bicentennial Commn), Pendleton Coll Govrs, Meadley Pk Sch; memb LS Lowry Centenary Festival Ctee; *Recreations* painting, etching, rambling, avoiding Coronation St; *Style—* Basil Herwald, Esq; Herwald Seddon, Solicitors, 306 Gt Cheetham St E, Salford, Lancs (☎ 061 792 2770)

HERZBERG, Charles Francis; s of Franz Herzberg (d 1971), of Hundith Hill, Cockermouth, Cumbria, and Marie Louise, *née* Oppenheimer (d 1986); *b* 26 Jan 1924; *Educ* SHL Sigtuna Sweden, Fettes Coll Edinburgh, Cambridge Univ (MA); *m* 10 March 1956, Ann Linette, da of Lt-Cdr (Keith) Robin Hoare, DSO, DSC; 1 s ((Francis) Robin b 18 Dec 1956), 2 da ((Elizabeth) Jane b 21 Jan 1961, Victoria Ann b 15 July 1964); *Career* industl conslt; dir commercial Plastics 1955-66, dir Robin Willey (Utd Gas) 1966-70, md Churchill Gears (TI GP) 1970-72, regnl industl dir DTI Northern region 1972-75; dir: industl planning Northern Engrg Industs plc 1975-88, Northern Investors Co Ltd, Newcastle upon Tyne Poly Prods Ltd; pres elect Tyne & Wear C of C; memb: Northern Cncl CBI, Northern Ctee IOD; govr Newcastle upon Tyne Poly; CEng, FIMechE, MIGasE; *Recreations* shooting; *Clubs* East India, Public Schools; *Style—* Charles Herzberg, Esq

HESELTINE, Rt Hon Michael Ray Dibdin; PC (1979), MP (C) Henley 1974-; s of Col R D Heseltine; *b* 21 Mar 1933; *Educ* Shrewsbury, Pembroke Coll Oxford; *m* 1962, Anne Harding Williams; 1 s, 2 da; *Career* Nat Serv Welsh Gds; contested (C): Gower 1959, Coventry N 1964; MP (C) Tavistock 1966-74; oppn spokesman Tport 1969, parly sec Miny Tport June-Oct 1970, parly under-sec Environment 1970-72, min Aerospace and Shipping (DTI) 1972-74, oppn spokesman Indust 1974-76, Environment 1976-79, sec Environment 1979-83, sec of state for Def 1983-86; dir Bow Pubns 1961-65, chm Haymarket Press 1966-70; Assoc Cons Clubs 1978, Nat YCs 1982-83 (vice-pres 1978); *Books* Where There's A Will (1987); *Style—* The Rt Hon Michael Heseltine, MP; Thenford House, Banbury, Oxon

HESELTINE, Richard Mark Horsley; s of late Edwin Oswald Heseltine, and Penelope Horsley, *née* Robinson; *b* 3 Oct 1945; *Educ* Dragon, Winchester, New Coll Oxford (MA), Wharton Sch, Univ of Pennsylvania (USA); *m* 1976, Joanna Elisabeth, da of Ronald C Symonds, CB, of London; 2 da (Catherine b 1978, Emma b 1981); *Career* corporate fin dept Morgan Grenfell 1969-71; exec Croda Int plc 1971-80; dir Croda Int plc 1981-; cncllr London Borough of Islington (SDP); *Recreations* yacht racing; *Clubs* Reform, Oxford and Cambridge Sailing Soc; *Style—* Richard Heseltine, Esq; 29 Gibson Square, London N1 (☎ 01 359 0702); Passage House, The Quay, Dittisham, nr Dartmouth, S Devon; Croda International plc, 168 High Holborn, London WC1 (☎ 01 836 7777)

HESELTINE, Sir William Frederick Payne; KCB (1986, CB 1978), GCVO, (1988, KCVO 1981, CVO 1969, MVO 1961), PC (1986), AC (1988); s of Henry William Heseltine (d 1984), of Fremantle, W Australia, and Louise Mary Gwythyr, *née* Payne (d 1966); *b* 17 July 1930; *Educ* Christ Church GS Claremont, Univ of Western Australia (BA); *m* 1, Ann (d 1957), da of L Turner, of Melbourne; m 2, 1959, Audrey Margaret, da of late Stanley Nolan, of Sydney; 1 s (John b 1964), 1 da (Sophy b 1961); *Career* Aust Civil Serv, PM's Dept Canberra 1951-62: private sec to PM of Aust (Sir Robert Menzies) 1955-59; asst fed dir Lib Pty of Aust 1962-64; asst press sec to HM The Queen 1960-61 and 1965-67 (press sec 1967-72), asst private sec 1972-77, dep private sec to HM The Queen 1977-86, private sec 1986-; *Clubs* Boodle's, Press, BAFTA; *Style—* The Rt Hon Sir William Heseltine, GCVO, KCB, AC; The Old Stables, Kensington Palace, London W8 4PU

HESKETH, (Claude Robert) Blair; s of Maj Claude Walter Hesketh (d 1964), and Antoinette Roberta, *née* Bull; *b* 15 Jan 1939; *Educ* Stowe; *m* 10 April 1974, Margaret Isabel, da of Col Hubert Bromley Watkins, DSO (d 1984); 1 s (Rollo b 1975), 1 da (Arabella b 1977); *Career* dir Hill Samuel Australia Ltd 1969-78, md Hill Samuel Pacific Ltd 1978-84, dir Hill Samuel Bank Ltd 1984-; govr Cheam Sch; FCA 1962; *Recreations* music, shooting, racing, golf; *Clubs* Turf; *Style—* Blair Hesketh, Esq; The Close, Odiham, Hants (☎ 0256 703746); 19 St James's Sq, London SW1 (☎ 01 628 8011, fax 01 839 5910)

HESKETH, Dowager Baroness; Christian Mary; OBE (1984); da of Sir John McEwen, 1 Bt, JP, DL, and Bridget, da of Rt Hon Sir Francis Lindley, GCMG, CB, CBE, and Hon Etheldreda Fraser (3 da of 13 Lord Lovat); *b* 17 July 1929; *Educ* John Watson's Sch, St Mary's Convent Ascot; *m* 22 Nov 1949, 2 Baron Hesketh, DL (d 1955); 3 s (incl 3 Baron); *Career* county organiser WRVS 1952-83; chm Daventry Cons Assoc 1964-74; memb Arts Cncl 1960-63; High Sheriff Northants 1981; Hon LLD Leicester 1982; *Books* Tartans (1961), The Country Home Cookery Book (co-author with Elisabeth Luard and Laura Blond) (1985); *Style—* The Rt Hon the Dowager Lady Hesketh; 20a Tregunter Rd, London SW10 (☎ 01 373 9821); Pomfret Lodge, Towcester, Northants (☎ 0327 50526)

HESKETH, Baroness; Hon Claire Georgina; *née* Watson; eldest da of 3 Baron Manton; *b* 7 Feb 1952; *m* 1977, 3 Baron Hesketh *qv*; 1 s, 2 da; *Style—* The Rt Hon the Lady Hesketh; Easton Neston, Towcester, Northants (☎ 0327 50969)

HESKETH, Lady Mary Constance; *née* Lumley; OBE (1974) DStJ; da of eld 11 Earl of Scarborough, KG, GCSI, GCIE, GCVO, TD, PC (d 1969), and Katharine Isobel, DCVO, da of Robert McEwen, of Marchmont and Bardrochat; *b* 20 April 1923; *m* 23 Aug 1952, Col Roger Fleetwood Hesketh, OBE, TD, *qv*; 1 s, 2 da (1 da decd); *Style—* Lady Mary Hesketh, OBE; Meols Hall, Southport, Lancs (☎ 0704 28171)

HESKETH, 3 Baron (UK 1935); Sir Thomas Alexander Fermor-Hesketh; 10 Bt (GB 1761); s of 2 Baron Hesketh (d 1955), and Dowager Lady Hesketh, *qv*; *b* 28 Oct 1950; *Educ* Ampleforth; *m* 1977, Hon Claire *qv*, da of 3 Baron Manton; 1 s, 2 da; *Heir*

s, b 13 Oct 1988; *Career* under sec of state for the environment 1989-; *Clubs* Turf, White's; *Style*— The Rt Hon the Lord Hesketh; Easton Neston, Towcester, Northants (☎ 0327 50445; office 50969, telex 311667)

HESLOP, Colin Bernard; s of Air Vice-Marshal Herbert William Heslop, CB, OBE (d 1976), of Sonning-on-Thames, Berks, and Phyllis Bletsoe, *née* Brown; *b* 16 Sept 1943; *Educ* Millfield; *m* 6 May 1967, Penelope, da of Arthur Huw Stow (d 1973), of Shoreham By Sea, Sussex; 2 s (Durran Bernard b 25 Aug 1968, Gordon Piers b 29 Feb 1972); *Career* trainee Thornton Baker 1960-64; accountant: Landau Morley & Scott 1965-66, James Cowper 1967, Michael Beckett Ltd 1968; co sec: St Swithins Hldgs 1969-77, Cascom Ltd 1978; sr ptnr CB Heslop Co 1979-, chm Thatcham C of C, W Berks Trg Consortium; former pres and chm Thatcham Rotary and Round Table Clubs; FCA; *Recreations* motor boating; *Clubs* RYA; *Style*— Colin Heslop, Esq; C B Heslop & Co, 1 High St, Thatcham, Newbury, Berks, RG13 4JG (☎ 0635 68202, 68880, telex 849125)

HESSAYON, Dr David Gerald; s of Jack Hessayon (d 1958), and Lena Hessayon (d 1933); *b* 13 Feb 1928; *Educ* Leeds Univ, Manchester Univ; *m* 1951, Joan Parker, da of Weeden T Gray, of USA; 2 da; *Career* chm: Pan Britannica Industs 1972-, Turbair 1970-, Br Agrochemicals Assoc 1980-81; dir Tennants Consolidated 1982-; Guild of Freeman of the City of London, memb Worshipful Co of Gardeners; *Books* The House Plant Expert, The Rose Expert, The Tree and Shrub Expert, The Armchair Book of the Garden, The Flower Expert, The Lawn Expert, The Vegetable Expert, The Indoor Plant Spotter, The Garden Expert, The Home Expert, The Gold Plated House Plant Expert, Rose Jotter, Hosue Plant Jotter, Vegetable Jotter; *Recreations* Times crossword, American folk music; *Clubs* London Press; *Style*— Dr David Hessayon; Hilgay, Mill Lane, Broxbourne, Herts EN10 7AX (☎ 0992 463490); PBI Ltd, Britannica House, Waltham Cross, Herts EN8 7DY (☎ 0992 23691, telex 23957 fax 0992 26452)

HESSE AND THE RHINE, HRH The Princess of; Hon Margaret Campbell; *née* Geddes; o da of 1 Baron Geddes, PC, GCMG, KCB, TD (d 1954), and Isabella Gamble, *née* Ross (d 1962); *b* 18 Mar 1913,Dublin,; *m* 17 Nov 1937, HRH Prince Louis (Ludwig) Hermann Alexander Chlodwig of Hesse and the Rhine (b 1908, d 1968), whose mother, elder brother, sister-in-law and two nephews were killed in an aircrash 1937. Prince Louis' aunt, on his f's side, Alexandra, m Emperor Nicholas II and was murdered at Ekaterinburg 1918. Another aunt, Victoria, m 1 Marquess of Milford Haven and was mother of late 1 Earl Mountbatten of Burma, and also gm of HRH Prince Philip, Duke of Edinburgh. His paternal gm was Princess Alice, 2 da of Queen Victoria; 1 adopted s (Moritz, Prince and Landgrave of Hesse b 1926); *Style*— HRH The Princess of Hesse and the Rhine; Schloss Wolfsgarten, 6070 Langen, Hessen, W Germany

HESTER, Canon John Frear; s of William Hester (d 1978), and Frances Mary, *née* Frear (d 1964); *b* 21 Jan 1927; *Educ* West Hartlepool GS, St Edmund Hall Oxford (MA), Cuddesdon Coll Oxford; *m* 1959, Elizabeth Margaret, da of late Sir Eric Riches, of Rutland Gate, London; 3 s (Robert b 1963, James b 1965, Alexander b 1971); *Career* clerk in holy orders, rector of Soho 1963-75, vicar of Brighton 1975-85, chaplain to HM The Queen 1984-, canon residentiary and precentor of Chichester Cathedral 1985-; chm Chichester Diocesan Overseas Cncl 1985-; *Books* Soho Is My Parish (1970); *Recreations* travel (real and imaginary), theatre, soccer; *Style*— The Rev Canon John Hester; The Residentiary, Canon Lane, Chichester PO19 1PX (☎ 0243 782961)

HETHERINGTON, Anthony Richard; s of Richard Ernest Hetherington, of Hants, and Charlotte Alice Annie, *née* Miller; *b* 6 Nov 1940; *Educ* Preston Manor Sch, Law Soc Sch of Law; *m* 1, 19 June 1965, Jacqueline, da of Auguste Théophile Duteil, of Paris; 2 s (David Anthony St Clare b 1967, Julian Anthony St John b 1968), 2 da (Sarah Jane and Joanna Mary b 1967); m 2, 14 Feb 1977, Hazel Mary, da of George Gorman (decd), of Hamps; *Career* slr; Cmmr for Oaths; dep Registrar of the High Ct of County Cout 1975-; Freeman City of London, Liveryman Worshipful Co of Arbitrators 1981; sec The Pulmerston Forts Soc 1986-; FCIArb; *Recreations* mucis, fly fishing, shooting, military history, travel, book, dogs; *Clubs* Fly Fishers; *Style*— Anthony R Hetherington, Esq; Folly House, The Crescent, Alverstoke, Hants; 10 Stokesway, Stoke Rd, Gosport, Hants

HETHERINGTON, Sir Arthur Ford; DSC (1944); s of Sir Roger Gaskell Hetherington, CB, OBE (d 1952), and Honoria, *née* Ford; *b* 12 July 1911; *Educ* Highgate Sch, Trinity Coll Cambridge (BA); *m* 1937, Margaret Lacey; 1 s, 1 da; *Career* serv WWII RNVR; chm: Southern Gas Bd 1961-64 (dep chm 1956-61), E Midlands Gas Bd 1964-66, Br Gas Corpn (formerly Gas Cncl) 1972-76 (memb 1967, dep chm 1967-72); kt 1974; *Clubs* Athenaeum, Royal Southampton Yacht; *Style*— Sir Arthur Hetherington, DSC; 32 Connaught Sq, London W2 (☎ 01 723 3128)

HETHERINGTON, Rear Adm Derick Henry Fellowes; CB (1961), DSC (1941), Bar to DSC (1944), 2nd Bar to DSC (1945); s of Cdr Henry Reginald Hetherington, RD, RNR (d 1926), and Hilda, *née* Fellowes (d 1963); *b* 27 June 1911; *Educ* St Neots Hants, RNC Dartmouth; *m* 1942, Josephine Mary, da of Sir Leonard Vavasour, Bt (d 1961); 2 s (Andrew d 1952, Mark), 3 da (Virginia, Teresa, Dinah); *Career* Cadet and Midshipman HMS Barham and HMS Effingham 1928-31, Sub Lt and Lt HMS Leander 1933-35, HMS Anthony 1935-37, HMS Wildfire 1937-39, HMS Kimberley, Home Fleet Red Sea Med 1939-41, HMS Windsor Harwich Force 1942-43, Lt Cdr HMS Lookout Med 1943-45, Cdr 1945 HMS Royal Arthur 1946-48, HMS Cheviot 1948-49, Capt 1950, chief staff offr Canal Zone 1951-53, sr Br naval offr Ceylon 1954-55, Capt (D) 4 Destroyer Sqdn HMS Agincourt 1956-57, dir Naval Trg 1958, Rear Adm Flag Offr Malta 1959-61, ret 1961; Croix de Guerre (1945); domestic bursar and fell Merton Coll Oxford 1961-76, emeritus fell; ret 1976; *Style*— Rear Adm Derick Hetherington, CB, DSC; Magpie Cottage, Christmas Common, Oxford OX9 5HR

HETHERINGTON, Lt-Col John David; s of Howard Walklett Hetherington (d 1977), of Berks, and Doris Amy. *née* Dowling; *b* 28 Feb 1934; *Educ* H and IS Coll, Eaton Hall, Def Serv Staff Coll India;; *Career* 2 Lt The Sherwood Foresters 1953 served: BAOR, Far E, India, Cyprus; Lt Col OIC The Worcestershire and Sherwood Foresters Rgt 1972-74, ret 1979; memb county ctee TAVRA Derbyshire 1984-, memb ctee ABF Derbyshire 1984-; vice chm and tech del The Midlands Driving Trials Gp 1984-; dep pres The Sherwood Foresters Assoc 1985; memb ctee Royal Windsor House Show 1986- memb BBC Radio Derby Advsy Cncl 1989-; OStJ Derbyshire: cdr 1986-88, cmmr 1987-88; land owner; *Recreations* competition carriage driving, ornithology; *Style*— Lt-Col John D Hetherington; The Stud Farm, Byrkley, Rangemore, Burton upon Trent, Staffordshire (☎ 0283 712368)

HETHERINGTON, Sir Thomas Chalmers; KCB (1979), CBE (1970), TD, QC (1978); s of W Hetherington; *b* 1926; *Educ* Rugby, Christ Church Oxford; *m* 1953, June Catliff; 4 da; *Career* barr 1952, bencher 1978; former dep Treasy slr; dir of Public Prosecutions 1977-87; *Style*— Sir Thomas Hetherington, KCB, CBE, TD, QC; 4-12 Queen Anne's Gate, London SW1H 9AZ (☎ 01 213 5337)

HETZEL, Phyllis Bertha Mabel; *née* Myson; da of Stanley Myson and Bertha Short; *b* 10 June 1918; *Educ* Wimbledon HS, Newnham Coll Cambridge (MA); *m* 1, 1941, John James (d 1961); 1 da; m 2, 1974 (m dis 1983), as his 3 w, Baron Bowden, *qv*; m 3, 1985, Ralph Dorn Hetzel, JR; *Career* Dept of Ind 1941-75 (asst under-sec of state 1972), pres Lucy Cavendish Coll Cambridge 1979-84; memb: Local Govt Boundary Cmmn for England 1977-81; W Midlands Ctee Nat Tst 1976-82; Monopolies and Mergers Cmmn 1975-78; Cambridge Univ Cncl of Senate and Fin bd 1983-84; Bd of American Friends of Cambridge Univ Inc; Cwlth Fund fell 1957-58; *Clubs* United Oxford and Cambridge Univ; *Style*— Mrs Ralph Dorn Hetzel, Jr; 18 Trafalgar Rd, Cambridge CB4 1EU (☎ (0223) 69878); 4411 Gloria Avenue, Encino, California 91436, USA (☎ (818 990) 5224)

HEUVEL, Christopher John; s of Desmond John Heuvel, of Lower Earley, and Joan Margaret, *née* Hooper; *b* 22 Oct 1953; *Educ* Douai Sch Woolhampton, Univ of Newcastle-upon-Tyne (BArch), Poly of Central London (Dip TP); *m* 7 March 1986, Diana Crystal, da of James William Joseph Collis (d 1981), of Ipswich, Suffolk; 1 s (Benjamin b 1985), 1 da (Beatrice b 1986); *Career* architect, princ one-man private practice; planning conslt; lectr environmental sci Norwich City Coll; *Recreations* fine art, film, photography, writing, travel; *Clubs* RIBA; *Style*— Christopher J Heuvel, Esq; 39 Riverside Rd, Norwich NR1 1SR (☎ 0603 629746); 9 Earlham Rd, Norwich NR2 3AA (☎ 0603 629746)

HEWARD, Air Chief Marshal Sir Anthony Wilkinson; KCB (1972, CB 1968), OBE (1952), DFC and Bar, AFC; s of late Col E J Heward; *b* 1 July 1918; *m* 1944, Clare Myfanwy, da of Maj-Gen C B Wainright, CB (decd); 1 s, 1 da; *Career* Gp Capt RAF 1956, Air Cdre 1963, Air Vice-Marshal 1966, Dep Cmdr RAF Germany 1966-69, AOA Air Support Cmmd 1969-70, Air Marshal 1970, COS RAF Strike Cmd 1970-72, AOC 18 (Maritime) Gp 1972-73, Air memb for supply and orgn MOD 1973-76, Air Chief Marshal 1974, ret 1976; CC Wilts 1981-; *Clubs* RAF, Flyfishers'; *Style*— Air Chief Marshal Sir Anthony Heward, KCB, OBE, DFC and Bar, AFC; Home Close, Donhead St Mary, nr Shaftesbury, Dorset (☎ 066 283 339)

HEWARD, Edmund Rawlings; CB (1984); s of Rev Thomas Brown Heward (decd), and Kathleen Amy Rachel Rawlings; *b* 19 August 1912; *Educ* Repton, Trinity Coll Cambridge; *m* 1945, Constance Mary Sandiford, da of George Bertram Crossley, OBE (decd); *Career* serv WWII, 1940-46 RA, Maj; slr 1937, ptnr Rose, Johnson and Hicks 1946; chief master of the Supreme Ct (Chancery Div) 1980-85 (master 1959-79); *Books* inc: Guide to Chancery Practice (1962), Matthew Hale (1972), Lord Mansfield (1979), Chancery Practice (1983), Chancery Orders (1986); *Style*— Edmund Heward Esq, CB; 36a Dartmouth Row, Greenwich SE10 8AW (☎ 01 692 3525)

HEWAT, Hon; Hon Mrs Victoria Esmé; *née* Erskine; only da of Lt-Cdr 6 Baron Erskine, RNVR (d 1957), and sis of 16 Earl of Buchan and 7 Baron Erskine; *b* 3 Jan 1897; *m* 1932, A/Cdr Harry Aitken Hewat, CBE, RAF, who d 1970; *Style*— The Hon Mrs Hewat; 34 Brynaston Sq, London W1

HEWETSON, Sir Christopher Raynor; TD (1967), DL (1986); s of Harry Raynor Hewetson, and Emma Hewetson; *b* 26 Dec 1929; *Educ* Sedbergh, Peterhouse Cambridge (MA); *m* 1962, Alison May Downie; 2 s, 1 da; *Career* slr 1956, ptnr Lace Mawer Slrs 1961-; memb cncl Law Soc 1966-87, pres Liverpool Law Soc 1976, pres Law Soc 1983 (vice-pres 1982); kt 1984; *Style*— Sir Christopher Hewetson, TD, DL; 24c Westcliffe Rd, Birkdale, Southport, Merseyside PR8 2BU (☎ 0704 67179)

HEWETT, Sir John George; 5 Bt (UK 1813), of Nether Seale, Leics, MC (1919); s of Sir Harald George Hewett, 4 Bt (d 1949); *b* 23 Oct 1895; *Educ* Cheltenham; *m* 1926, Yuilleen Maude (d 1980), da of late Samuel Frederick Smithson, of Lauriston, Camberley, Surrey; 2 s; *Heir* s, Peter Hewett; *Career* British East Africa during European War 1914-18 as Capt King's African Rifles; *Style*— Sir John Hewett, Bt, MC

HEWETT, Kenneth Arthur John; s of Arthur Charles Frederick Hewett (d 1961); *b* 17 April 1921; *Educ* Westminster City Sch; *m* 1945, Jean Rosaline, *née* Nye; 1 s, 1 da; *Career* co dir shipping, jt md and vice-chm Davies Turner and Co Ltd, dir Davies Turner Motors Ltd, Manchester Int Terminal Ltd; cncl memb Inst of Freight Forwarders Ltd; *Recreations* golf, music, swimming; *Clubs* E India, Devonshire (Eastbourne); *Style*— Kenneth Hewett, Esq; 41 St James Rd, Mitcham, Surrey (☎ 01 640 7268)

HEWETT, Peter John Smithson; MM; s and h of Sir John George Hewett, 5 Bt, MC; *b* 27 June 1931; *Educ* Bradfield, Jesus Coll Cambridge; *m* 1958, Jennifer Ann Cooper, da of E T Jones, OBE, of Nairobi, Kenya; 2 s, 1 da; *Career* barr Gray's Inn 1954; practising advocate Kenya; *Recreations* windsurfing; *Clubs* Muthaiga Country, Naivasha Yacht; *Style*— Peter Hewett, Esq, MM; P O Box 40763, Nairobi, Kenya

HEWETT, Richard William; s of Brig W G Hewett, OBE, MC (d 1976); *b* 22 Oct 1923; *Educ* Wellington Coll; *m* 1954, Rosemary, da of B E Cridland, MC, TD (d 1979); 2 da (Vanessa, Virginia); *Career* serv WWII Army, Europe, Far East, Maj; regular offr to 1962; dir Reader's Digest Assoc Ltd UK (joined 1962), aux vice-pres, dir Int Ops Readers Digest Assoc Inc NY USA; *Recreations* fishing, tennis; *Clubs* Bucks, Annabels; *Style*— Richard Hewett, Esq; 78 Walton St, London SW3 2HH; Reader's Digest Assoc Ltd, 25 Berkeley Sq, London W1X 6AB (☎ 01 629 8144), Chappagna House, (Roaring Brook Road) Chappagnq, New York 10514

HEWISH, Prof Antony; s of Ernest William Hewish (d 1975), and Francis Grace Lanyon, *née* Pinch (d 1970); *b* 11 May 1924; *Educ* King's Coll Taunton, Gonville and Caius Coll Cambridge (MA, PhD); *m* 19 Aug 1950, Marjorie Elizabeth Catherine, da of Edgar Richards (d 1954); 1 s (Nicholas b 1956), 1 da (Jennifer b 1954); *Career* RAE Farnborough 1943-46; Cambridge Univ: res fell Gonville and Caius Coll 1952-54, asst dir of res 1954-62, lectr in physics 1962-69, reader 1969-71; prof of radioastronomy 1971-, dir Mullard Radio Astronomy Observatory 1982-87, fell Churchill Coll 1962-; discovered pulsars (with S J Bell-Burnell) 1967; Nobel Prize for Physics (with M Ryle) 1974, Hughes Medal Royal Soc 1974-; prof of astronomy Royal Inst 1977-81; govr Knight's Templar Sch Baldock, churchwarden Kingston Parish Church Cambridge; Hon DSc: Leicester 1976, Exeter 1977, Manchester 1989; FRS 1968, foreign hon memb American Acad of Arts and Scis, foreign fell Indian Nat Sci Academy 1982; *Recreations* sailing, gardening; *Style*— Prof Antony Hewish ; Pryor's Cottage, Field Rd, Kingston,

Cambridge CB3 7NQ (☎ 0223 262 657); Cavendish Laboratory, Madingley Road, Cambridge CB3 0HE (☎ 0223 337 296)

HEWITT, Hon Mrs (Diana Marie Faith); raised to the rank of a Baron's da 1948; da of late Hon Edward Crofton (s of late 5 Baron Crofton); *b* 1927; *m* 1, 1949, Cdr Hugh May, RN; 1 s, 1 da; m 2, 1963, Cdr Edward Michael George Hewitt, RN; 1 s, 1 da; *Style*— The Hon Mrs Hewitt; Flat H, 63 Drayton Gdns, SW10

HEWITT, Edwin John; s of Sydney Hewitt (d 1968); *b* 14 April 1934; *Educ* Berkhamsted; *m* 1957, Jennefer Judy, née Oakley; 3 c; *Career* dir and joint gen mangr Co-operative Bank plc; dir: FC Finance Ltd, Centenary Finance (Glasgow) Ltd, Crowngap Ltd; FCA; *Recreations* riding, music, chess; *Style*— Edwin Hewitt, Esq; Co-operative Bank plc, PO Box 101, 1 Balloon Street, Manchester M60 4ET; Tudor Lodge, Lyme Green, nr Macclesfield, Cheshire (☎ Sutton 2209)

HEWITT, Gillian Beresford; da of Hilary Max Torry (d 1987), of Cheshire, and Margaret Beresford, *née* Theaker; *b* 20 June 1946; *Educ* Birkenhead HS, Brighton Coll of Art; *m* 7 April 1970, Richard Frank, s of Frank Lambert Hewitt; 1 da (Emma b 1978); *Career* dir Austin Reed Ltd 1983-; *Recreations* travel, literature, art; *Clubs* Arts; *Style*— Mrs Gillian Hewitt; 10 St Paul's Place, London N1 2QE (☎ 01 226 3125); Austin Reed, 103-113 Regent St, London W1 (☎ 7346789)

HEWITT, His Hon Judge Harold; s of George Trueman Hewitt (d 1958), and Bertha Lillian Hewitt, *née* Teasdale (d 1984); *b* 14 Mar 1917; *Educ* King James I GS Bishop Auckland; *m* 1946, Doris Mary; 2 s (Christopher, Timothy); *Career* circuit judge 1980-; *Clubs* Carlton; *Style*— His Hon Judge Harold Hewitt; Longmeadows, Etherley, Bishop Auckland, Co Durham

HEWITT, Harry Ronald; s of Charles William Hewitt (d 1951), and Florence Mary, *née* Kelsey; *b* 12 April 1920; *Educ* City of Leeds HS, Leeds Coll of Technol, London Univ (BSc); *m* 1954, Rosemary Olive, *née* Hiscock; 2 s, 1 da; *Career* chartered chemist, chartered engr; works mangr Imperial Smelting Corpn (now RTZ) 1947-58; joined Johnson Matthey plc 1959-84, gp md and chief exec 1976-1983, chm 1983-84, ret; FEng, MIChemE; *Recreations* music, golf, tennis, skiing; *Style*— Harry Hewitt, Esq; 6 Loom Lane, Radlett, Herts (☎ 0923 855 243)

HEWITT, Sir (Cyrus) Lenox (Simson); OBE (1963); s of the late Cyrus Lenox Hewitt, and Ella Louise Hewitt; *b* 7 May 1917; *Educ* Scotch Coll Melbourne, Melbourne Univ (BCom); *m* 1943, Alison Hope, da of Dr R J Tillyard; 1 s, 3 da; *Career* sec to PM's Dept 1968-71, Dept of the Environment, Aborigines and the Arts 1971-72, Dept of Minerals and Energy 1972-75; chm: Qantas Airways Ltd 1975-80, Q H Tours Ltd 1975-80; dir Santos 1981-82, non exec dir Ansett Tport Industs Ltd 1982-; dir: Aberfoyle Ltd 1982-, Airship Ind plc 1983-, Short Bros (Australia) Pty Ltd 1981-, Austmark Int Ltd 1983-, Qintex Australia Ltd 1985-, Mirage Mgmnt 1986-, Universal Telelasters Securities Ltd 1986-, Br Midland Airways Pty Ltd 1986-, Qintex America Ltd 1987, Fortis Pacific Aviation Ltd 1987, Qintex Ltd 1987, Amalgamated TV Servs Pty Ltd 1988-; chm State Rail Authy of NSW 1985-88; memb Judicial Cmmn of NSW 1986-; kt 1971; *see Debrett's Handbook of Australia and New Zealand for further details*; *Style*— Sir Lenox Hewitt, OBE; 9 Torres St, Red Hill, Canberra, ACT 2603, Australia (☎ 01 328 6513)

HEWITT, Marguerite, Lady; Marguerite; da of Charles Burgess, of Deepdene, Filey; *m* 1940, Maj Sir Joseph Hewitt, 2 Bt (d 1973); *Style*— Marguerite, Lady Hewitt; Lebberston Hall, nr Scarborough

HEWITT, Michael Earling; s of Herbert Erland Hewitt (d 1938), and Dorothy Amelia, *née* Morris; *b* 28 Mar 1936; *Educ* Christ's Hosp, Merton Coll Oxford (MA), London Univ (BSc); *m* 10 Aug 1961, Elizabeth Mary Hughes, da of Maj Arnold James Batchelor (d 1956); 1 s (Thomas b 1970), 1 da Joanna b 1974); *Career* Gunner RA 1955-57; Bank of England: joined 1961, seconded econ advsr Govt Bermuda 1970-74, asst advsr oil 1974-76, fin forecaster 1976-78, advsr fin insts 1981-83 (asst advsr 1979-81), head fin supervision gen div 1984-87, head fin and indust area 1987-88, sr advsr fin and indust 1988-; memb: EEC Central Bank Gp Experts Money Supply 1976-78, Br Invisible Exports Cncl 1987-, Dearing Ctee on Making of Accounting Standards 1988, City Advsy Panel City Univ Business Sch 1988-; chm: City EEC Ctee 1987-, OECD Gp Experts Securities Mkts 1988-; assoc memb Soc Investment Analysts 1979-; *Recreations* chess, travel, wine; *Style*— Michael Hewitt, Esq; Bank of England, Threadneedle St, London EC2R 8AH (☎ 01 601 4657, fax 601 4830, telex 885001)

HEWITT, Sir Nicholas Charles Joseph; 3 Bt (UK 1921); s of Maj Sir Joseph Hewitt, 2 Bt (d 1973); *b* 12 Nov 1947; *m* 1969, Pamela Margaret, da of Geoffrey J M Hunt, TD, of Scalby, Scarborough; 2 s, 1 da; *Heir* s, Charles Edward James Hewitt b 15 Nov 1970; *Style*— Sir Nicholas Hewitt, Bt; Colswayn House, Huttons Ambo, York

HEWITT, Patricia Hope; da of Sir (Cyrus) Lenox Simson Hewitt, OBE *qv*, of Sydney, Aust, and (Alison) Hope Hewitt; *b* 2 Dec 1948; *Educ* Girls GS Canberra, Aust Nat Univ Canberra, Newnham Coll Cambridge (MA), Sydney (AMusA); *m* 1, 8 Aug 1970 (m dis 1978), (David) Julian Gibson Watt, s of Baron Gibson-Watt, *qv*; m 2, 17 Dec 1981, William Jack Birtles, s of William George Birtles (d 1976), of Shepperton, Middx; 1 s (Nicholas b 1988), 1 da (Alexandra b 1986); *Career* gen sec NCCL 1974-83, policy coordinator to Ldr of the Opposition 1988-89 (press and broadcasting sec 1983-88), sr res fell Inst for Public Policy Res 1989; assoc Newnham Coll Cambridge, bd memb bd Int League for Human Rights; memb Sec of State's Advsy Ctee on the Employment of Women 1977-83, Parly candidate Leicester East 1983; *Books* The Abuse of Power: Civil Liberties in the United Kingdom (1983); *Recreations* gardening, music, theatre, cooking; *Style*— Ms Patricia Hewitt; 21 Rochester Sq, London NW1 9SA (☎ 01 267 2567); Leader of the Opposition's Office, House of Commons, London SW1 (☎ 01 219 4151)

HEWITT, Peter McGregor; OBE (1967); s of Douglas McGregor Hewitt (d 1984), and Audrey Vera, *née* Walker; *b* 6 Oct 1929; *Educ* De Aston Sch Market Rasen Lincs, Keble Coll Oxford (MA); *m* 23 June 1962, Joyce Marie, da of Robert J Gavin (d 1982); 2 da (Clare Katherine b 1963, Sarah b 1965); *Career* Army 1947-49; HM Overseas Civil Serv 1952-64: Malaya, N Borneo; Dip Serv 1964-71: FO, Shanghai, Canberra; Home Serv 1971-, regnl dir E Midlands DOE and Dept of Tport 1984-; *Recreations* cricket, gardening, music; *Clubs* Royal Cwlth Soc; *Style*— Peter Hewitt, Esq, OBE; Dept of the Environment & Transport, Cranbrook House, Cranbrook St, Nottingham NG1 1EY (☎ 0602 476121)

HEWITT, Esq Thomas; s of Thomas Hewitt (d 1981), and Helen Graham; *b* 10 June 1950; *Educ* Central Sch Jarrow, S Shields Marine and Tech Coll, Gateshead Tech; *Career* engr, energy conservation, civil servant, DoE/Property Servs Agency; chm Friends of Tarrow Hall; *Recreations* gardening, crosswords, genealogy, DIY, tstee St Pauls Jarrow devpt tst, reading; *Style*— Thomas Hewitt, Esq; 65 Underwood Grove, Northburn Grange, Cramlington NE23 9UT (☎ 0610 731848); Dept of Environment, 133 Jesmond Rd, Newcastle (☎ 091 2810372)

HEWLETT, Hon (John) Richard; s of Baron Hewlett (Life Peer d 1979); *b* 1955; *Educ* Oundle, Bath Acad of Art; *Style*— The Hon Richard Hewlett

HEWLETT, Hon Thomas Anthony; s of Baron Hewlett (Life Peer d 1979); *b* 1952; *Educ* Oundle, Magdalene Cambridge; *m* 1980, Jane Elizabeth, da of B Dawson, of Aldeburgh, Suffolk; 1 da; *Style*— The Hon Thomas Hewlett

HEWSON, Michael John; s of George Alfred Hewson (d 1959), of Portsmouth, and Marjorie Phyllis, *née* Hall; *b* 17 Mar 1944; *Educ* Southern GS Portsmouth; *m* 21 July 1970, Sharland Elisabeth, da of Frank Templeman, of Grimsby; 1 s (Martin Philip b 1970); *Career* Nationwide Anglia Bldg Soc: branch mangr Oxford 1982-85 (Northampton 1976-81, Boston Lincs 1973-75), regnl mangr S E London 1988- (Surrey 1987, S E 1986); FCBSI 1973, MBIM 1973; *Recreations* mountaineering, rock climbing; *Style*— Michael Hewson, Esq; 9 Widmore Rd, Bromley, Kent BR1 1RP (☎ 01 464 0929)

HEWSON, Roy Gregory; s of Alfred Bertram Hewson, ISM (d 1981), of London, and Rosa Elder, *née* Eggleton (d 1964); *b* 27 August 1930; *Educ* East Barnet GS, City of London Coll; *m* 16 April 1955, Pamela Noreen, da of Lawson Hartley Birch (d 1960), of Leek, Staffordshire; 1 s (Paul b 1961), 2 da (Claire b 1958, Nicola b 1970); *Career* Nat Serv RAF 1952-54; mgmnt trainee GEC Ltd 1946-52, sec Britannia Bldg Soc 1985- (joined 1954, exec appt 1965-); pres local branch CBSI; FCBSI 1963, FCIS 1973; *Recreations* walking, swimming, gardening; *Clubs* Rotary; *Style*— Roy Hewson, Esq; Bank House, Bagnall, Stoke-On-Trent, Staffs ST9 9JR (☎ 0782 502 727); Newton House, P.O.Box No 20, Leek, Staffs ST13 5RG (☎ 0538 399 399, fax 0538 399 149)

HEXHAM AND NEWCASTLE, Bishop of 1974-; Rt Rev Hugh Lindsay; s of William Stanley Lindsay (d 1966), and Mary Ann, *née* Warren (d 1958); *b* 20 June 1927; *Educ* St Cuthbert's Coll Ushaw Durham; *Career* RAF 1945-48; priest 1953, asst diocesan sec Hexham and Newcastle 1953-59; asst priest: St Lawrence Newcastle 1953-54, St Matthew Ponteland 1954-59, diocesan sec 1959-60, auxiliary bishop of Hexham & Newcastle 1969-74; *Recreations* walking; *Style*— The Rt Rev the Bishop of Hexham and Newcastle; Bishop's House, East Denton Hall, 800 West Road, Newcastle upon Tyne NE5 2BJ (☎ 091 228 0003)

HEY, Prof John Denis; s of George Brian Hey, of Adlington, Cheshire, and Elizabeth Hamilton, *née* Burns; *b* 26 Sept 1944; *Educ* Manchester GS, Univ of Cambridge (BA), Univ of Edinburgh (MSc); *m* 18 Oct 1968, Marlene Robertson, da of Thomas Bissett (d 1958), of Perth; 1 s (Thomas 1981), 2 da (Clare b 1979, Rebecca b 1984); *Career* econometrician Hoare & Co Stockbrokers 1968-69; lectr in econs: Durham Univ 1969-73, Univ of St Andrews 1974-75; prof of econs and statistics Univ of York 1984- (lectr in socl and econ statistics 1975-81, sr lectr 1981-84), ed Economic Journal 1986-, co-dir centre for Experimental Econs 1986-, author of articles for numerous jls; memb: RES, AEA; *Books* Statistics in Economics (1974), Uncertainty in Microeconomics (1979), Britain in Context (1979), Economics in Disequilibrium (1981), Data in Doubt (1984); *Recreations* squash, walking, eating; *Style*— Prof John Hey; 49 Monkgate, York, N Yorks (☎ 0904 621 333); Dept of Economics Related Studies, Univ of York, Heslington, York, N Yorks YO1 5DD (☎ 0904 433 786, fax 0904 433 433, telex 57933)

HEYCOCK, Hon Clayton Rees; s of Baron Heycock (Life Peer); *b* 1941; *Style*— The Hon Clayton Heycock; 6 Tanygroes Place, Tailbach, Port Talbot, W Glam

HEYCOCK, Baron (Life Peer UK 1967); Llewellyn Heycock; CBE (1959), JP (Glam 1949, Port Talbot), DL (Glam 1963); s of William Heycock (d 1970), of Port Talbot; *b* 12 August 1905; *Educ* Eastern Elementary Sch; *m* 1930, Elizabeth Olive, da of Emmanuel Rees; 1 s (and 1 s decd); *Career* memb NUR 1919; former engine driver; elected Glam CC 1937 (sec Labour gp 1941-73, chm 1962-63), ldr W Glam Cncl 1973-77; fndr memb and chm: Welsh Jt Educn Ctee, School Museum Serv for Wales; fndr memb advsy ctee for Educn in Wales under 1944 Butler Act, original memb Cncl of Wales 1949-54, memb ct and cncl Univ of Wales; exec memb: Assoc of Educn Ctees for England Wales and CI and IOM (pres 1964-65), Assoc of Divisional Exec Educn for England and Wales (pres 1954-55 and 1965-66), Local Authorities Assoc for England and Wales; pres: Aberavon RFC, Welsh Youth Rugby Union, Coleg Harlech; vice-pres Nat Theatre Co for Wales; bard Nat Eisteddfod 1963; sword bearer for HM The Queen at Investiture of HRH Prince of Wales; Kt of Mark Twain Soc of America; Hon LLD Wales 1963; CStJ; *Recreations* rugby football (Aberavon Rugby Club); *Style*— The Rt Hon the Lord Heycock, CBE, JP, DL; 1 Llewellyn Close, Taibach, Port Talbot, W Glam SA13 2TY (☎ 0639 882565)

HEYGATE, Sir George Lloyd; 5 Bt (UK 1831); s of Sir John Edward Nourse Heygate, 4 Bt (d 1976); *b* 28 Oct 1936; *Educ* Repton, Trin Cambridge; *m* 1960, Hildegard Mathilde, da of August Anton Kleinjohann, of Wildstrasse 69, Duisburg, Germany; 2 twin da (Joanna b 1977, Catherine b 1977); *Heir* bro, Richard Heygate; *Career* slr 1965; *Style*— Sir George Heygate, Bt; Willow Grange, Wissett, Halesworth, Suffolk

HEYGATE, Richard Gage; s of Sir John Edward Nourse Heygate, 4 Bt (d 1976), and hp of bro, Sir George Lloyd Heygate, 5 Bt; *b* 30 Jan 1940; *Educ* Repton, Balliol Oxford; *m* 1968 (m dis 1972), Carol Rosemary, da of late Cdr Richard Michell, RN, of Leith House, Amberley, Sussex; *Style*— Richard Heygate, Esq

HEYGATE, (Arthur) Robert; JP, DL (Northants 1983); s of Arthur Robert Heygate (d 1963), and Frances Amelia Heygate (d 1958), of Stone House, Bugbrooke; descendant of Thomas Heygate, of Highgate, Essex and Hayes, Middx, who was given land in Northants ; *b* 15 Mar 1914; *Educ* Oakham Sch; *m* 1940, Phyllis Mary, da of Rev John Foster Williams; 1 s (Robert), 1 da (Rosemary); *Career* landowner, farmer, flour miller; *Recreations* shooting; *Style*— A Robert Heygate, Esq, JP, DL; Lichborough Hall, Towcester, Northants NN12 8JF (0327 830240); Bugbrooke Mills, Northampton NN7 3QH (☎ 0604 830381)

HEYHOE FLINT, Rachael; *née* Heyhoe; MBE (1971); da of Geoffrey Heyhoe (d 1972), of Penn, Wolverhampton, and Roma Kathleen, *née* Crocker (d 1978); Heyhoe is an Anglo-Saxon farming name derived from Hey Mow; *b* 11 June 1939; *Educ* Wolverhampton Girls' HS, Dartford Coll of Physical Educn (Dip Phys Ed); *m* 1 Nov 1971, Derrick Flint, s of Benjamin Flint, of Underwood, Notts; 1 s (Benjamin b 8 June 1974); *Career* Women's Cricket Int England 1960-63, Capt 1966-77, scoredc 179 v

Australia (Oval) 1976 (world record score for England, fourth highest score by woman in test); Women's Hockey Int England 1964; journalist; Guild of Professional Toastmasters Best After Dinner Speaker 1972; *Books* Fair Play, History of Womens Cricket (1976), Heyhoe (autobiography 1978); *Recreations* golf, squash; *Clubs* Staffs GC, Wig and Pen, Sportwriters Assoc, La Manga (Spain), Patshull Pk Golf and Country (Wolverhampton); *Style—* Mrs Rachael Heyhoe Flint, MBE: Danescroft, Wergs Rd, Tettenhall, Wolverhampton, Staffs (☎ 0902 752103)

HEYLIN, Angela Christine Mary (Mrs Maurice Minzly); da of Bernard Heylin (d 1985), and Ruth Victoria Heylin; *b* 17 Sept 1943; *Educ* Apsley GS, Watford Coll; *m* 13 March 1971, Maurice Minzly, s of Salem Minzly (d 1974); 1 s (James b 1982); *Career* dir FJ Lyons; Charles Barker Lyons: dir 1976, jt md 1980, chief exec 1984; dir Charles Barker Gp 1984; chief exec: Charles Watney & Powell 1986, Charles Traverse Healy 1987; chm and chief exec Charles Public Rels 1988; tstee Int Fndn for PR Studies 1987, FInstM 1987, FIPR 1987 vice chm PRCA 1984; *Recreations* theatre, piano, entertaining; *Style—* Miss Angela Heylin; 46 St Augustine's Rd, London NW1 9RN (☎ 01 485 4815); Charles Barker Public Relations, 30 Farringdon St, London EC4A 4EA (☎ 01 634 1011, fax 01 236 0170, car tel 860 318 205, telex 883588/ 887928)

HEYMAN, Sir Horace William; *b* 13 Mar 1912; *Educ* Ackworth Sch, Darmstadt Univ, Birmingham Univ (BSc); *m* 1, 1939 (m dis); 1 s (Timothy), 1 da (Helen Thompson); m 2, 1966, Dorothy Forster Atkinson; *Career* chm English Industl Estates Corpn 1970-77; pres Northumbria Tourist Bd 1983-86, govr Newcastle-on-Tyne Poly 1974-86, (vice-chm 1983-86, hon fell 1985); dir various UK and European engrg and travel cos; FIEE, FRSA, CEng; kt 1976; *Style—* Sir Horace Heyman; 20 Whitburn Hall, Whitburn, Sunderland SR6 7JQ (☎ 091 5294957)

HEYMANN, Bernard; s of Joseph Heymann (d 1954) and Luise Irene Heymann (d 1977); *b* 19 Jan 1937; *Educ* Quintin Sch London, Univ of Durham (BA); *m* 10 Sept 1966, Anne Catherine Valentine, da of Melville Elphinstone Thomson; 1 s (Gavin Marcus b 29 May 1970), 1 da (Anne Belinda (Mrs Lindy) 29 July 1968; *Career* dir: Ledpold Joseph & Sons Ltd 1985-1988 conslt (1976-85), Highland Forest Products plc 1948-88, Localisation of Indust 1986, Tilner Delvaux Ltd 1987-; FCA, FBIM; *Recreations* gardening; *Clubs* Old Quintinian; *Style—* Bernard Heymann, Esq; 5 Ranulf Rd, London NW2 2BT (☎ 01 435 9375); 11 Jerusalem Passage, St John's Sq, London EC1V 4JB (☎ 01 490 3464, fax 01 250 1874)

HEYNES, David Gordon; s of Gordon Albert Arthur Heynes; *b* 17 April 1945; *Educ* Charterhouse; *m* 1968, Jennifer Jane, *née* Dreyer; 2 s, 1 da; *Career* CA, Hill Samuel and Co Ltd 1969-71, chief exec Park Place Investmts Ltd 198l (dir 1972-); *Recreations* shooting and motor racing; *Style—* David Heynes, Esq; Newton Lodge, Buckland, Faringdon, Oxfordshire 036787 225

HEYWOOD, Francis Melville; s of Bernard Oliver Francis Heywood (d 1960), Bishop of Southwell, Hull & Ely, and Maude Marion, *née* Lempriere (d 1957); *b* 1 Oct 1908; *Educ* Haileybury, Gonville and Caius Coll Cambridge (BA, MA); *m* 28 Dec 1937, Dorothea Kathleen (d 1983), da of Sir Basil Edgar Mayhew, KBE (d 1966), of Felthorpe Hall, Norwich; 1 s (Simon b 1945, d 1985), 2 da (Susan, Janion) 1 s adopted (Michael b 1940); *Career* asst master Haileybury Coll 1931-35, fell asst tutor and praelector Trinity Hall Cambridge 1935-39, Master of Marlborough Coll 1939-52, Warden of Lord Mayor Treloar Coll 1952-69; *Books* A Load of New Rubbish (1985); *Recreations* formerly: cricket, rugby, squash, gardening, now walking; *Style—* F M Heywood, Esq; 30 The Bayle, Folkestone, Kent (☎ 0303 52366)

HEYWOOD, Geoffrey; MBE (Mil 1945), JP (Liverpool 1962); s of Edgar Heywood (d 1972), of Blackpool, and Annie, *née* Dawson (d 1960); *b* 7 April 1916; *Educ* Arnold Sch Blackpool, Open Univ; *m* 1941, Joan Corinna, da of Edward Lumley (d 1984), of Lancs; 1 s (Edward), 1 da (Corinna); *Career* WWII RA N Africa, Italy, Greece; cmmnd 1941, Maj 1944; (despatches twice); consulting actuary; joined Duncan C Fraser and Co (Consulting Actuaries) 1946- (sr ptnr 1952-86); pres Manchester Actuarial Soc 1951-53; chm: Assoc of Consulting Actuaries 1959-62, Int Assoc of Consulting Actuaries 1968-72; pres Inst of Actuaries 1972-74 (vice-pres 1964-67); memb Page Ctee to review Nat Savings; dir Mersey Docks and Harbour Co 1971-85 (dep chm 1974-85); memb Nat Bus Co 1978-85; dir: Liverpool Bd Barclays Bank 1972-86, Barclays Bank Tst Co (1967-86), Univs Superannuation Scheme (1974-86); govr Birkenhead Sch 1977-83; fndr Master Actuaries Co 1979; Liveryman Worshipful Co of Clockmakers; FIA, FFA, FRAS; *Books* contrib to Jnl of the Inst of Actuaries; *Recreations* golf, antiquarian horology, fishing; *Clubs* Army and Navy, RAC; *Style—* Geoffrey Heywood, Esq; Drayton, Croft Drive East, Caldy Wirral (☎ 051 625 6707); Mercury Ct, Tithebarn St, Liverpool (☎ 051 227 1530)

HEYWOOD, Keith Alban; s of John Alban Heywood (d 1955), and Kittie Elizabeth, *née* Rennie; *b* 7 Oct 1948; *Educ* The Royal Masonic Sch; *m* 26 Aug 1968, Vivien, da of Alan Irwin (d 1979); 1 s (Jason b 1972), 1 da (Kirsten b 1970); *Career* CA; Crane Christmas & Co 1965-, ptnr Jeffreys Ubysz and Co 1975, slr practitioner Heywood & Co 1982, ptnr Brett Jenkins & Ptnrs 1987, fin conslt 1988; former sec Old Masonians Assoc; FCA; *Recreations* printing, shooting, walking; *Clubs* Silverstone Racing; *Style—* Keith Heywood, Esq; 10 Green End St, Aston Clinton, Aylesbury, Bucks P22 5JE (☎ 0296 630114)

HEYWOOD, Peter; s and h of Sir Oliver Kerr Heywood, 5 Bt; *b* 10 Dec 1947; *Educ* Bryanston, Oxford Univ; *m* 1970, Jacqueline Anne, da of Sir Robert Frederick Hunt, CBE, *qv*; 2 da; *Career* account director; *Style—* Peter Heywood, Esq; 64 Newbridge Rd, Weston, Bath, Avon BA1 3LA

HEYWOOD, Hon Mrs (Rosalind Louise Balfour); *née* Bruce; er da of 3 Baron Aberdare, GBE (d 1957); *b* 11 Nov 1923; *m* 25 Sept 1956, Benjamin Coote Heywood, s of late Col Henry Frank Heywood, MC; 2 da; *Career* served 1943-46 WRNS; *Style—* The Hon Mrs Heywood; 1 Elm Park Rd, SW3 6BD (☎ 01 352 0429)

HEYWOOD-LONSDALE, Hon Mrs (Jean Helen); *née* Rollo; da of 12 Lord Rollo; *b* 2 Dec 1926; *m* 1952, Lt-Col Robert Heywood-Lonsdale, MBE, MC, DL, Gren Gds (s of John H-L, DSO, OBE, TD, JP, sometime MFH The Bicester, and Hon Helen Annesley, 3 da of 11 Viscount Valentia); 1 s, 3 da; *Style—* The Hon Mrs Heywood-Lonsdale; Mount Farm, Churchill, Oxon

HEYWOOD-LONSDALE, Lt-Col Robert Henry; MBE (1952), MC (1945), DL; s of Col John Pemberton Heywood-Lonsdale, DSO, OBE, TD (d 1944), of Poundon, Bicester, Oxon (*see* Burke's Landed Gentry, 18 Edn Vol i), and Hon Helen Annesley (d 1965), da of 11 Viscount Valentia; *b* 18 Dec 1919; *Educ* Eton; *m* 7 Oct 1952, Hon Jean Helen, da of Maj 12 Lord Rollo (d 1947); 1 s (Thomas b 1953, Peter b and d 1956), 3 da (Jane b 1957, Clare b 1961, Emma b 1962); *Career* Gren Gds 1938-55, Capt 1942, Maj 1943, Royal Wilts Yeo 1961-67; served NW Europe, Palestine, Malaya, Egypt; High Sheriff Wilts 1975, DL Wilts 1972 and Oxfordshire 1983; *Recreations* country pursuits; *Clubs* Boodles, Pratts; *Style—* Lt-Col Robert H Heywood-Lonsdale, MBE, MC, DL; Mount Farm, Churchill, Oxon (☎ 060 871 316)

HEYWORTH, James David; s of James Heyworth, of Read nr Burnley, and Margaret, *née* Myerscough; *b* 18 July 1950; *Educ* St Mary's Coll Blackburn, London Univ (LLB); *m* 1, 26 July 1975 (m dis), Margaret Helen; 1 s (James Edward Watson b 1977); m 2, 23 Dec 1982, Hayden Boethman; 1 s (Christopher David b 1983); *Career* slr; ptnr Donald Race and Newton; *Recreations* shooting, farming, working gun dogs; *Style—* James Heyworth, Esq; Harwes Farm, Black Lane Ends, Colne, Lancaster (☎ 0282 864383); 59 Albert Rd, Colne (☎ 0282 864500, fax 0282 869579)

HEYWORTH, John; s of Lt Col Reginald Francis Heyworth (ka 1941), and Hon Moyra, *née* Marjoribanks, da of 3 Baron Tweedmouth; *b* 21 August 1925; *Educ* Eton; *m* 10 June 1950, Susan Elizabeth, da of Sir John Henry Burder, ED, of Burford, Oxford; 1 s (Reginald b 1961), 3 da (Caroline b 1952, Jane b 1953, Joanna b 1957); *Career* Royal Dragoons NW Europe 1943-47; farmer and owner of Wild Life Park; High Sheriff Oxon 1962; *Style—* John Heyworth, Esq; Bradwell Grove, Burford, Oxford, (☎ 099 382 3154, 2200/3006)

HEYWORTH, Baroness; Lois; da of Stevenson Dunlop, of Woodstock, Ontario, Canada; *m* 1924, 1 and last Baron Heyworth (d 1974); *Style—* The Rt Hon the Lady Heyworth; 20 Sussex Sq, London W2

HEZLET, Vice-Adm Sir Arthur Richard; KBE (1964), CB (1961), DSO and Bar (1944, 1945), DSC (1941); s of Maj-Gen Robert Knox Hezlet, CB, CBE, DSO (d 1963); *b* 7 April 1914; *Educ* RNC Dartmouth, RNC Greenwich; *m* 1948, Anne Joan Patricia, *née* Clark; 2 adopted da; *Career* served WW II submarines, dir RN Staff Coll Greenwich 1956-57, Rear-Adm 1959, Flag Offr Submarines 1959-61, Flag Offr Scotland and NI 1961-64, Vice-Adm 1962, ret 1964; area pres Royal Br Legion NI, a vice pres RNLI; *Books* The Submarine and Sea Power (1967), Aircraft and Sea Power (1970), Electron and Sea Power (1975), The B Specials (1972); *Clubs* Army and Navy, Royal Ocean Racing; *Style—* Vice-Adm Sir Arthur Hezlet, KBE, CB, DSO, DSC; Bovagh House, Aghadowey, Co Londonderry, N Ireland BT51 4AU (☎ 0265 868 206)

HIBBARD, Prof Bryan Montague; s of Montague Reginald (d 1972), of Norfolk, and Muriel Irene, *née* Wilson; *b* 24 April 1926; *Educ* Queen Elizabeth's Sch Barnet, St Bartholomews Hosp Med Coll and Univ of London (MB, BS, MD), Univ of Liverpool (PhD); *m* 30 July 1955, Elizabeth Donald, da of Dr James Campbell Grassie (d 1976), of Aberdeen; *Career* sr lectr Univ of Liverpool 1963-73, prof and head of dept of obstetrics and gynaecology Univ of Wales Coll of Med 1973-; memb advsy sub ctee in obstetrics and gynaecology Welsh Office 1974-, assessor confidential enquiries into maternal deaths DHSS 1980-; memb: Ctee on Safety of Meds 1980-84, maternity servs advsy ctee DHSS 1980-85, ctee gynaecological cytology DHSS 1983, S Glamorgan Health Authy 1983-88, cncl RCOG 1982-88; pres Welsh Obstetric and Gynaecological Soc 1985-86, Meds Commn 1986-, chm Jt Standing Advsy Ctee on Obstetric Anaesthesia 1988-, chm Jt Standing Advsy Ctee RCOG and Royal Coll of Midwives 1988-; FRCOG 1965 (memb 1956); *Books* Principles of Obstetrics (1988), The Obstetric Forceps (1988); *Recreations* eighteenth century glass, fell walking, coarse gardening; *Clubs* RSM; *Style—* Prof Bryan Hibbard; The Clock Hse, Cathedral Close, Llandaff, Cardiff CF5 2ED (☎ 0222 564 565); Dept of Obstetrics & Gynaecology, Univ of Wales Coll of Medicine, Health Park, Cardiff CF4 4XN (☎ 0222 755 944)

HIBBERT, Alan Ashton; s of Joseph Hibbert (d 1952), and Bertha Hibbert, *née* Ashton (d 1967); *b* 24 Mar 1922; *Educ* Audenshaw GS, Manchester Univ; *Career* serv WWII Maj RASC; admitted slr 1948; prosecutor War Crimes Tribunal, Singapore; pres Assoc of County Ct add Dist Registrars 1983-84, memb County Ct Rules Ctee 1968-74; *Recreations* motor sports; *Style—* Alan A Hibbert, Esq; 14 Westbrook Avenue, Ravenshead, Nottingham (☎ 0623 794221); All High Court and County Courts, Nottinghamshire and Derbyshire, Nottingham County Court (☎ 0602 5983956)

HIBBERT, Christopher; MC (1945); s of Canon H V Hibbert (d 1980); *b* 5 Mar 1924; *Educ* Radley, Oriel Coll Oxford (MA); *m* 1948, Susan, da of Rayner Piggford (d 1978); 2 s (James, Tom), 1 da (Kate); *Career* Capt London Irish Rifles Italy 1944-45; ptnr firm of land agents and auctioneers 1948-59; author 1959-; won Heinemann Award for Literature 1962; FRSL, FRGS; *Books Incl:* The Destruction of Lord Raglan (1961), Corunna (1961), Benito Mussolini (1962), The Battle of Arnhem (1962), The Court at Windsor (1964), The Roots of Evil (1964), Agincourt (1965), Garibaldi and his Enemies (1966), The Making of Charles Dickens (1967), The Grand Tour (1969), London: Biography of a City (1969), The Dragon Wakes: China and the West (1970), The Personal History of Samuel Johnson (1971), George IV (2 vols 1972, 1973), The Rise and Fall of the House of Medici (1974), Edward VII (1976), The Great Mutiny: India 1857 (1978), The French Revolution (1980), Rome: Biography of a City (1985), The English: A Social History (1986), The Grand Tour (1987), Venice: The Biography of a City (1988), The Encyclopaedia of Oxford (ed 1988); *Recreations* cooking, gardening, travel; *Clubs* Army and Navy, Garrick; *Style—* Christopher Hibbert, Esq, MC; 6 Albion Place, West Street, Henley-on-Thames, Oxfordshire

HIBBERT, (Caroline) Maria; da of Sir John Lucas-Tooth, 2 Bt, *qv* ; *b* 12 May 1956; *Educ* St Paul's Girls' Sch, Oxford Poly (BA); *m* 19 April 1980, William John Hibbert, s of Sir Reginald Hibbert, KCMG, of Machynlleth, Powis; 2 da (Cosima Mary b 1984, Clover Frances b 1988); *Career* dir Capel-Cure Myers Capital Mgmnt; *Style—* Mrs Maria Hibbert; 39 Lancaster Road, London W11 (☎ 01 727 2807); 65 Holborn Viaduct, London EC1 (☎ 01 236 5080)

HIBBERT, Sir Reginald Alfred; GCMG (1981, KCMG 1979, CMG 1966); s of Alfred Hibbert, of Sawbridgeworth; *b* 21 Feb 1922; *Educ* Queen Elizabeth's Sch Barnet, Worcester Coll Oxford; *m* 1949, Ann Alun, da of His Honour Sir Alan Pugh (d 1971), of Dunsfold, Surrey; 2 s, 1 da; *Career* served WWII, SOE and 4 Hussars (Albania and Italy); FO 1946-, served: Bucharest, Vienna, Guatemala, Ankara, Brussels; chargé d'affaires Ulaan Bator (Mongolian People's Republic) 1964-66, res fell Leeds Univ 1966-67, Political Advsr's Office Singapore 1967-69, political advsr to C-in-C Far East 1970-71, min Bonn 1972-75, asst under-sec state FCO 1975-76, dep under-sec 1976-79, ambass France 1979-82, ret 1982; dir Ditchley Fndn 1982-87; visiting fell Nuffield Coll Oxford 1984-88; *Clubs* Reform; *Style—* Sir Reginald Hibbert, GCMG; Frondeg, Pennal, Machynlleth, Powys SY20 9JX (☎ 065 475 220)

HIBBERT-HINGSTON, Andrew Donovan Huntly; s of Col Alan T Hingston (d

1973); *b* 9 Sept 1926; *Educ* Clifton, Queens' Coll Cambridge; *m* 1952, Evelyn Valery, da of Maj-Gen Hugh Brownlow Hibbert, DSO; 2 s (Mark b 1953, James b 1960), 1 da (Teresa b 1956); *Career* engr, dir The Rom River Co Ltd 1963-85; *Recreations* country pursuits; *Style*— Andrew Hibbert-Hingston, Esq; Kilsall Hall, Shifnal, Salop TF11 8PL

HIBBITT, Brian Leslie; s of Edgar Bennett Hibbitt (d 1977), and Kathleen Marion, *née* Groom (d 1965); *b* 15 July 1938; *Educ* SW Essex County Tech Sch, London Coll of Printing; *m* 1963, Jill Mavis, da of Albert Henry Oakley (d 1983); 2 s (Timothy John b 1964, Andrew James b 1968); *Career* md Greenaway Harrison Ltd 1984-, dir P C Richardson Ltd, chm SSB Corporate Communications Ltd; grantee of Royal Warrants as Printer to HM The Queen, HRH The Duke of Edinburgh, HM Queen Elizabeth The Queen Mother; chm of Br Printing Industs Fedn Industl Rels Ctee SE Region 1986-; *Recreations* local affairs, gardening, theatre; *Style*— Brian L Hibbitt, Esq; Tharance House, Priors Wood, Crowthorne, Berkshire RG11 6BZ (☎ 0344 772215); Greenaway House, 132 Commercial St, London E1 6NF (☎ 01 247 4343, telex 883016, fax 01 247 8426

HIBBITT, Dr Kenneth George; s of Reginald Ennever Hibbitt (d 1967), of Bristol, Avon, and Helen Grace, *née* Millard (d 1974); *b* 12 Sept 1928; *Educ* St Brendans Coll Berkley Sq Bristol, Univ of Bristol Sch of Veterinary Sci (BVSc), Univ of Bristol Dept of Physiology (PhD); *m* 1 Sept 1962, Helen Teresa, da of Alfred Henry James Bown, OBE (d 1957), of Sunderland; 1 s (Richard b 12 Feb 1969), 1 da (Wendy b 20 May 1967); *Career* gen vet practise 1954-57, res and lectr dept of physiology Bristol Univ 1957-62; Inst for Res on Animal Diseases Compton Newbury Berks: dep head of biochem 1962-72, head of dept of immunology and parisitology 1972-85, head of div of immunopathology 1985-88, ret 1988; memb: governing body schs of S Helen and S Katharine Abingdon Oxon, St Helens Tst Abingdon Oxon; recent chm Steventon branch Wantage Constituency Cons Assoc; MRCVS 1954, memb: Br Vet Assoc 1954,Biochem Soc 1962, AVTRW 1964; *Books* Production Disease in Farm Animals (co ed with Payne and Sansom 1973); *Recreations* walking, gardening, music, theatre; *Clubs* Farmers, Veterinary Res London; *Style*— Dr Kenneth Hibbitt; Whitecleave House, Burrington, Umberleigh, North Devon EX37 9JN (☎ 07693 468)

HICHENS, Antony Peverell; RD; s of Lt-Cdr Robert Peverell Hichens, DSO and bar, (DSC and two bars, RNVR), and Catherine Gilbert Enys; *b* 10 Sept 1936; *Educ* Stowe, Magdalen Coll Oxford, Univ of Pennsylvania; *m* 1963, Sczerina Neomi, da of Dr F T J Hobday; 1 da; *Career* called to the Bar Inner Temple, dep md Redland Ltd 1979 (fin dir 1972), md fin Consolidated Gold Fields plc 1981 (md 1984); chm: Caradon plc 1987; *Recreations* travel, boats, wine; *Clubs* Naval and Military; *Style*— Antony Hichens, Esq; Slape Manor, Netherbury, Nr Bridport, Dorset (☎ 0308 882323); Consolidated Gold Fields plc, 31 Charles II St, London SW1 (☎ 01 930 6200)

HICKEY, Sir Justin; s of Hon Sir Simon Hickey, MLC (d 1958), and Hilda Ellen, *née* Dacey (d 1963); *b* 5 April 1925; *Educ* De La Salle Coll; *m* 1964, Barbara Standish, da of Robert Adams Thayer; 1 s, 4 da; *Career* chm Accident Insur Mutual Ltd 1968, and of thirty two cos and family tsts; chm Queensland Sci and Technol 1984; fell Australian Inst of Mgmnt 1984; landowner (110 acres); FRS; kt 1979; *Recreations* yachting (MV Lady Barbara); *Clubs* Royal Motor Yacht; *Style*— Sir Justin Hickey; Bartinon, 20 Marseille Court, Sorrento, Qld 4217, Australia; Suite 24, 35 Orchid Av, Surfers Paradise 4217, Australia Telex AA44519

HICKMAN, Alan John; s of William Ralph Hickman, of Kent, and Mabel Ethel, *née* Johnson; *b* 10 Mar 1946; *Educ* Hayes Sch Kent (various engrg qualifications); *m* 1 July 1970 (m dis 1988), Leone, da of Donald Andrewartha, of Devon; 1 s (Scott John b 1976), 1 da (Carly Caroline b 1973); *Career* workstudy engr Osram GEC Ltd; work study offr: London Borough of Bromley, Sevenoaks Dist Cncl; work study team ldr Buckinghamshire CC, mgmnt servs offr Thames Valley Police (HQ Oxon), Force Organisation method offr Devon and Cornwall Constabulary (HQ Exeter); MIMS; *Recreations* raquet sport, literature, art, theatre, architecture; *Style*— Alan J Hickman, Esq; 110 Wonford Street, Exeter, Devon EX2 5DE (☎ 0392 210259)

HICKMAN, Frederick; QPM (1985); s of John Harry Hickman (d 1955), and Lucy Maria, *née* Bloomer (d 1982); *b* 2 Nov 1926; *Educ* Rowley Regis Central GS; *m* 1, 2 June 1951, Doreen Mary (d 1955), da of Wilfred Millington, of Halesowen, W Midlands; m 2, 28 June 1958, Joy Maureen, da of John Aubrey Jones (d 1965); 1 s (Steven b 4 June 1961), 1 da (Sharon b 10 March 1960); *Career* RCS 1945-48, serv UK and Germany, Worcestershire Constabulary 1948-67; West Mercia Constabulary 1967-85 positions incl: detective supt Ops and dep 4 Dist (Midland) Regnl Crime Squad 1970-76, detective chief supt co-ordinator 4 Dist (Midland) Regnl Crime Squad 1976-82, i/c West Mercia Constabulary Force Inspectorate and Systems Devpt Depts 1982-85; civil servant 1985-; *Recreations* shooting, historic building restoration, travel; *Style*— Frederick Hickman, Esq, QPM; Thatch Cottage, Danes Green, Claines, Worcester

HICKMAN, Sir (Richard) Glenn; 4 Bt (UK 1903), of Wightwick, Tettenhall, Staffordshire; s of Sir Alfred Howard Whitby Hickman, 3 Bt (d 1979), and Margaret Doris, *née* Kempson; *b* 12 April 1949; *Educ* Eton; *m* 1981, Heather Mary Elizabeth, er da of Dr James Moffett (d 1982), of Westlecot Manor, Swindon, and Dr Gwendoline Moffett (d 1975); 1 s (Charles Patrick Alfred b 1983), 1 da (Elizabeth Margaret Ruth b 1985); *Heir* s, Charles; *Clubs* Turf; *Style*— Sir Glenn Hickman, Bt; 13 Gorst Rd, Wandsworth Common, London SW11

HICKMAN, John Kyrle; CMG (1977); s of John Barlow Hickman (d 1932), and Joan Hickman, of Cirencester Glos; *b* 3 July 1927; *Educ* Tonbridge Sch, Cambridge Univ (BA); *m* 1956, Jennifer, da of Reginald Kendall Love (d 1976); 2 s (Matthew, Andrew), 1 da (Catherine); *Career* HM Forces 1948-50 2 Lt RA, asst princ WO 1950; CRO 1958, first sec Wellington 1959, CRO 1962, FCO 1964, first sec Madrid 1966, cnsllr 1967, consul-gen Bilbao 1967, dep High Cmmr Singapore head SW Pacific Dept FCO 1971, cnsllr Dublin 1974 (chargé d'affaires 1976), HM ambass Quito 1977-80, attached to Inchape Gp plc 1981-82, HM ambass Santiago 1982-1987; Tstee of New Theatre Royal, Portsmouth; business conslt; dir Anatonda (Sth America) Inc 1988; *Books* The Enchanted Islands: The Galapagos Discovered (1985); *Recreations* golf, tennis, skiing, history; *Clubs* Garrick (London), Los Leones GC (Santiago), Prince of Wales (Santiago); *Style*— J K Hickman, Esq, CMG; 3 Weltje Rd, London W6 9TG (☎ 01 846 9475)

HICKMAN, Margaret, Lady; Margaret; da of Leonard Kempson, of Potters Bar, Middx; *m* 1, Denis Thatcher; m 2, 1948, Sir (Alfred) Howard Whitby Hickman, 3 Bt (d 1979); 1 s (Sir Glenn Hickman, 4 Bt, *qv*); *Style*— Margaret, Lady Hickman; Twin Cottage, Batlers Green, Radlett, Herts

HICKMAN, His Hon Judge Michael Ranulf; s of John Owen Hickman (d 1949), and Nancy Viola, *née* Barlow (d 1963); *b* 2 Oct 1922; *Educ* Wellington, Trinity Hall Cambridge (MA); *m* 1943, Diana, da of Col Derek Charles Houghton Richardson (d 1975); 1 s (Peter), 1 da (Susan); *Career* Flt Lt RAFVR 1940-46, serv in Atlantic and SE Asia Coastal Cmd; barr Middle Temple 1949; dep chm Hertfordshire Quarter Sessions 1965-72, rec 1972-74, circuit judge 1974-; *Recreations* shooting, fishing, gundog trg; *Style*— His Hon Judge Michael Hickman; The Acorn, Bovingdon, Herts (☎ Hemel Hempstead 832226); St Albans Crown Ct, (☎ St Albans 34481)

HICKMAN, Beryl, Lady; Nancy Beryl; da of Capt Trevor George Morse-Evans, MA (d 1972); *m* 1940, as his 2 w, Sir Alfred Edward Hickman, 2 Bt (d 1947); *Style*— Beryl, Lady Hickman; Charringworth Court, Winchcombe, Glos

HICKMAN, Patrick Nelson; s of Maj Sir Alfred Edward Hickman, 2 Bt (d 1947); *b* 13 Mar 1921; *Educ* Nautical Coll Pangbourne; *m* 1, 1944 (m dis 1950), Mary Lena, da of Capt J A D Perrins; 1 s, 1 da; m 2, 1953 (Margaret) Gail, da of Col C R St Aubyn, of Paris, France; 1 s, 1 da; *Career* Flt Lt RAFVR (ret); Freeman City of London, Liveryman Worshipful Co of Fishmongers; *Recreations* farming; *Clubs* White's; *Style*— Patrick Nelson Hickman, Esq; 65 Onslow Gdns, London SW7; Hale Park, Fordingbridge, Hants

HICKMAN, Peter Leslie Victor; OBE (1983); *Career* ret Br Aerospace 1988; currently European Conslt, SPAR Aerospace Ltd (Canada); *Clubs* Naval and Military; *Style*— Peter Hickman Esq, OBE; Nottingham Farm, Cottered, Buntingford, Herts SG9 9PU (☎ 076 381 308; fax 076 381 431)

HICKMAN, Roger Christopher; s of Joseph Green Hickman (d 1986), of Blakedown, nr Kidderminster, and Mary Elizabeth, *née* Richardson; *b* 21 Oct 1938; *Educ* Bilton Grange Rugby, Malvern Coll; *m* 1969, Margaret Isabel, da of Leslie Hackett, of Worcs; 1 s (David Christopher b 1970); *Career* chm of the South Staffs Gp Ltd 1985-; *Recreations* motor racing; *Style*— Roger Hickman, Esq; Birch Hollow, Ct Farm Way, Churchill, Worcs DY10 3LZ; South Staffs Gp Ltd, New Rd, Dudley, Worcs (☎ 0384 455121)

HICKMOTT, Sqdn-Ldr Maurice Ernest John; DFC (1955); s of Arthur John Hickmott, and Winifred Violet *née* Wood (d 1986); *b* 11 July 1924; *Educ* Windsor GS and in USA; *m* 10 Sept 1952, Joan Mackrell; 2 s (Paul J M b 1953, Simon J B b 1959), 1 da (Jane E M b 1956); *Career* Sqdn-Ldr RAF UK and Far East 1946-71; conslt Pilot Trg Equipment; Freeman City of London 1964, Liveryman Guild of Air Pilots and Navigators 1964, fell Royal Aeronautical Soc 1984; *Recreations* tennis, swimming, cricket, golf; *Clubs* RAF, City of London Liverymen; *Style*— Sqdn-Ldr Maurice Hickmott, DFC; 39 Hawkhurst Way, Bexhill, Sussex TN39 3SG (☎ 0424 345 88)

HICKS; *see*: Steele, Tommy

HICKS, Charles Antony; s of Peter Rivers Hicks, OBE, of Kent, and Felicity Hicks, *née* Hughes; *b* 31 July 1946; *Educ* Marlborough, Clare Coll Cambridge (MA); *m* 1, 1969, Jennifer Joy (*née* Boydell); 1 s (James b 1972), 1 da (Emma b 1974); m 2, 1980, Virginia Helen Juliana, da of Col John Robert Guy Stanton, of Derbyshire; 1 s (Oliver b 1981), 2 da (Camilla b 1983, Sophia b 1985); *Career* ptnr Wedlake Bell (slr) 1972, non exec dir Platignum plc 1982, ward clerk of Walbrook 1975; *Clubs* Boodles; *Style*— Charles Hicks, Esq; 26 Lonsdale Square, London N1 1EW (☎ 01 607 4602); 16 Bedford Street, covent Garden, London WC2E 9HF (☎ 01 379 7266, telex 25256, fax 01 836 6117)

HICKS, David Nightingale; s of Herbert Hicks (d 1940), of The Hamlet, Coggeshall, Essex, and Iris Elsie, *née* Platten; *b* 25 Mar 1929; *Educ* Charterhouse, Central Sch of Art and Design; *m* 1960, Lady Pamela Carmen Louise, *qv*, yr da of the late Earl Mountbatten of Burma, KG, OM, DSO; 1 s (Ashley Louis David b 1963), 2 da (Edwina Victoria Louise b 1961, India Amanda Caroline, b 1967, bridesmaid to Lady Diana Spencer at her marriage to HRH The Prince of Wales 1981); *Career* interior and product designer; author; *Books Incl:* David Hicks on Decoration (1966), David Hicks on Living - with Taste (1968), David Hicks on Decoration - with Fabrics (1971), David Hicks Garden Design (1982); *Recreations* gardening, riding, shooting; *Style*— David Hicks Esq; The Grove, Brightwell Baldwin, Oxon; Albany, Piccadilly, London W1; David Hicks International, 101 Jermyn St, London SW1Y 6EE (☎ 01 627 4400, telex 8812724 FALCON G)

HICKS, His Hon Judge John Charles; QC (1980); s of Charles Hicks (d 1963), and Marjorie Jane Hicks, *née* Bazeley (d 1980); *b* 4 Mar 1928; *Educ* Maldon Road Primary Sch Witham Essex, King Edward VI GS Chelmsford, King Edward VI GS Totnes, London Univ (LLB, LLM); *m* 1957, (Elizabeth) Mary, da of Rev John Barnabas Jennings (d 1979); 1 s (David, decd), 1 da (Elizabeth); *Career* Nat Serv RA (Gunner) 1946-48; slr 1952-66, ptnr Messrs Burchells 1954-65; Methodist Missionary Soc (Caribbean) 1965-66; barr 1966-88, rec Western Circuit 1978-88, circuit judge 1988; *Recreations* music, theatre, opera, squash racquets; *Style*— His Hon Judge John Hicks, QC; Flat 3, 17 Montagu Square, London W1H 1RD L(☎ 01 935 6008)

HICKS, Prof Sir John Richard; s of Edward Hicks, of Leamington Spa, Warwicks; *b* 8 April 1904; *Educ* Clifton Coll and Balliol Coll Oxford; *m* 1935, Ursula Kathleen (univ lectr in Public Finance Oxford 1947-63, Fellow Linacre Coll 1963-66), da of W F Webb, of Dublin; *Career* prof of political economy Manchester Univ 1938-46, fellow Nuffield Coll Oxford 1946-52, Drummond Prof of political economy, Oxford Univ 1952-65, fell All Souls Coll Oxford 1952-71, joint Nobel Prize for Economics 1972; hon fell: Gonville and Caius Coll Cambridge 1971 (former fell), LSE 1969; FBA; kt 1964; *Style*— Prof Sir John Hicks; All Souls College, Oxford

HICKS, Martin Leslie Arther; s of Sgt William James Hicks (d 1968), of St Albans, Herts, and Elizabeth, *née* White; *b* 23 Dec 1953; *Educ* Bedford Sch, (BA, LLB); *m* 7 July 1984, Peta Alexandra, da of Capt Michael Stuart Hughes, MN (d 1982), of Wheatheampstead, Herts; *Career* barr Inner Temple 1977, memb David Dethridee's Chambers 1980-, Aldun Property Co Ltd 1984-, Sec Oakbrave Ltd 1988-; memb Civic Soc 1985; Memb Hon Soc of Inner Temple 1977; *Recreations* squash, skiing, seafood; *Style*— Martin Hicks, Esq; 12 Old Sq, Lincoln's Inn, London WC2 3T8 (☎ 01 242 4289, fax 01 831 6736)

HICKS, Maureen Patricia; MP (C) Wolverhampton North East 1987-; da of Ronald Cutler, of Bucks, and Norah, *née* O'Neill; *b* 23 Feb 1948; *Educ* Ashley Secondary Sch, Brockenhurst GS, Furzedown Coll of Educn London; *m* 1973, Keith Henwood Hicks, s of Thomas Henwood Hicks, of Australia; 1 s (Marcus b 1979), 1 da (Lydia b 1982); *Career* teacher; asst Area Educn Offr 1974-75, Marks and Spencer Mgmnt 1970-74; dir Stratford Motor Museum 1975-83 (conslt/dir 1983-); educn select ctee memb and sec House of Commons Backbench Tourism Ctee 1987-; Stratford District Cncllr 1979-84; *Recreations* amateur dramatics, golf, travel; *Clubs* Royal Overseas; *Style*— Mrs Maureen Hicks, MP; c/o House of Commons, London SW1

HICKS, Maj Gen (William) Michael (Ellis); CB (1983), OBE (1969); s of Gp Capt William Charles Hicks, AFC (d 1939), and Nellie Kilbourne Kay (d 1970); *b* 2 June 1928; *Educ* Eton, RMA Sandhurst; *m* 1950, Jean Hilary, da of Brig William Edmonstone Duncan, CVO, DSO, MC (d 1970); 3 s (William, Peter, Alistair); *Career* Army Offr, cmmnd 1948, attended Staff Coll 1958; GSO1 MOI 1967-70, CO 1 Bn Coldstream Guards 1970-72, attended RCDS 1973, cmd 4 Guards Armd Bde 1974-75, BGS Trg HQ UKLF 1976-78, GOC NW Dist 1980-83, ret 1983; sec RCDS 1983-; *Recreations* golf, gardening; *Style*— Maj Gen Michael Hicks, CB, OBE; c/o Cox and Kings, 6 Pall Mall, London SW1; Seaford Ho, 37 Belgrave Sq, London SW1X 8NS (☎ 01 235 1091)

HICKS, Michael Frank; s of Frank Henry Hicks (d 1985), and Annie Elizabeth Lydia, *née* Beeson (d 1988); *b* 11 Mar 1935; *Educ* Fairlop Secdy HS Hainault, Dane Secdy Modern Ilford; *m* 19 Sept 1959, Veronica Constance, da of Frederick Edwin Martin; 2 da (Corinne Veronica b 14 May 1962, Anne Christine b 15 April 1964); *Career* Nat Serv RAF 1953-55, serv Aden; stockbroker: HE Goodison 1948-56, Blount 1956-59; ptnr Simon and Coates 1959-80, equity ptnr Statham Duff Stoop 1980-86, dir Prudential Bache Capital Funding 1986-; chm Stock Exchange 20 Over Cricket League; memb IOD; *Recreations* golf; *Clubs* Stoke by Nayland; *Style*— Michael F Hicks, Esq; Spring Hill, Stoke by Nayland, Suffolk (☎ 020 637 321); Prudential Bache Capital Funding, 9 Devonshire Square, London EC2 (☎ 01 220 7252)

HICKS, Lady Pamela (Carmen Louise); *née* Mountbatten; yr da of 1 Earl Mountbatten of Burma, KG, GCB, OM, GCSI, GCIE, GCVO, DSO, PC, FRS (assas 1979); sister of Countess Mountbatten of Burma, *qv*; *b* 19 April 1929; *m* 13 Jan 1960, David Nightingale Hicks, *qv*; 1 s, 2 da; *Career* bridesmaid to HRH The Princess Elizabeth at her marriage 1947; lady-in-waiting to HM The Queen on her tour of Aust and NZ 1953-54; *Style*— Lady Pamela Hicks; Albany, Piccadilly, London W1 (☎ 01 734 3183); The Grove, Brightwell Baldwin, Oxon (☎ 0491 35353)

HICKS, Philip; s of Brig Philip Hugh Whitby Hicks, CBE, DSO, MC (d 1967), and Patty, *née* Fanshawe (d 1985); *b* 11 Oct 1928; *Educ* Winchester, RMA Sandhurst, Royal Acad Schs (Dip RAS); *m* 22 July 1952, Jill, da of Maj Jack Tweed (d 1979); 1 s (David b 1971), 1 da (Nicola b 1960); *Career* Irish Gds 1946-47, 2 Lt Royal Warwicks Regt 1948-49; pt/t teacher various art schs 1960-85, concentrated full time on painting 1986-; solo exhibitions incl: Camden Arts Centre 1971, Richard Demarco Gall Edinburgh 1971, Robert Self Gall London 1971, Imperial War Museum 1975, Galerie VFCU Antwerp 1977-79, Battersea Arts Centre 1977, Gallery 22 Dublin 1980, New Art Centre (London) 1980-82, Galleri Engstrom Stockholm 1985, Gallery 10 London 1986, Bohun Gall Henley 1986; mixed exhibitions incl: Tate Gallery London 1976, Mall Galleries London 1980, Israel Mus Jerusalem 1980-81, Serpentine Gall London 1982; works in pub collections incl: Tate Gall, Comtemporary Art Soc, V & A, Imp War Mus; Br Cncl award 1977; also performs professionally as a jazz pianist; hon sec and memb cncl Artists Gen Benevolent Inst; *Recreations* music; *Clubs* Cheslea Arts; *Style*— Philip Hicks, Esq; 15 Cleveland Rd, London SW13 OAA (☎ 01 876 7889)

HICKS, Robert Adrian; MP (C) South-East Cornwall 1983-; s of W H Hicks of Horrabridge, Devon; *b* 18 Jan 1938; *Educ* Queen Elizabeth GS, Univ Coll London, Exeter Univ; *m* 1962, Maria, da of Robert Gwyther of Plympton, Devon; 2 da; *Career* nat vice-chm Young Cons 1964-66, tech coll lectr 1964-1970, contested (C) Aberavon 1966, MP (C) Bodmin (formerly held by Libs) 1970-74 and 1974-1983; chm Horticultural Ctee 1971-73, asst govt whip 1973-74, memb Select Ctee on European Secdy Legislation 1973-; vice-chm: Cons Pty Agric Ctee 1971-73 and 1974-81, Cons Pty European Affrs Ctee 1979-81; chm: Westcountry Cons Membs Ctee 1977-78 (sec 1970-73), chm UK branch Parly Assoc for Euro-Arab Co-operation 1983-; tres Cons Pty Middle East Cncl 1979-; Parly advsr Br Hotels Restaurants and Caterers Assoc 1974-, Milk Mktg Bd 1985-; *Clubs* MCC; *Style*— Robert Hicks, Esq, MP; Little Court, St Ive, Liskeard, Cornwall

HICKS BEACH, Hon David Seymour; s of 2 Earl St Aldwyn, PC, GBE, TD, JP, DL; *b* 1955; *Educ* Eton, Royal Agricultural Coll Cirencester; *Career* a page of honour to HM The Queen 1969-71, agriculture; *Recreations* natural history, fishing, shooting, travel; *Clubs* Royal Agricultural Soc of England; *Style*— The Hon David Hicks Beach; Williamstrip Park, Cirencester, Glos GL7 5AT

HICKS BEACH, Hon Peter Hugh; s of 2 Earl St Aldwyn, PC, GBE, TD, JP, DL; *b* 1952; *Style*— The Hon Peter Hicks Beach; The Moors, Coln St Aldwyns, Cirencester, Glos

HICKSON, Joan Bogle (Mrs Eric Butler); OBE 1987; da of Harold Alfred Squire Hickson, and Edith Mary, *née* Bogle; *b* 5 August 1906; *Educ* Castle Hall Sch Northampton, Castle Bar Sch London, Oldfeld Sch Swanage; *m* 29 Oct 1933, Eric Norman, s of Thomas Harrison Butler (d 1945), of Leamington Spa; 1 s (Nicholas Andrew Mark b 24 May 1936), 1 da (Caroline Margaret Julia b 3 May 1939); *Career* actress, trained RADA; debut His Wife's Children 1927, first London appearance The Tragic Muse 1928; appeared in num plays incl: Appointment with Death, See How They Run, The Guinea Pig, A Day in the Life of Joe Egg, Forget-me-not-Lane, Bedroom Farce (won Miss Hickson a Tony award in NY; made many films incl: The Guinea Pig, The Magic Box, Seven Days to Noon; num tv appearances incl 9 adaptations of Agatha Christie novels in which she played Miss Marple 1984-87; hon MA (Leicester) 1988; *Recreations* reading; *Style*— Miss Joan Hickson, OBE; c/o Fraser & Dunlop Ltd, 91 Regent Street, London W1R 8RU (☎ 01 734 7311)

HICKSON, Peter Hanam; s of Capt Keneth Roy Hickson, CBE, AFC, RN, of 4A Hollow Lane, Hayling Island, Hants, and Mary, *née* Hilary; *b* 31 Oct 1949; *Educ* Churchers Coll, Southampton Univ (BSc); *m* 2 Oct 1976, Janet Fay, da of Thomas Robinson, of 37 Goodman Cres, London SW2; 1 s ((Philip) Guy Hanam b 1981), 1 da (Ella Jocelyn b 1985); *Career* drilling engr: Burmah Oil Co 1971-74, Chevron Petroleum 1974-75; Houlder Offshore Ltd: asst ops mangr 1976-77, devpt mangr 1978-80, gen mangr 1980-82, md 1982-; memb Exec Ctee Hayling Island Sailing Club 1978-79 (gen Ctee 1974-77); *Recreations* sailing, food, wine, squash, jogging; *Clubs* Hayling Island Sailing, St Katherines YC; *Style*— Peter Hickson, Esq; 59 Lafone St, London EC3 (☎ 01 357 6001, fax 01 357 7437, telex 884801)

HIDE, Prof Raymond; s of Stephen Hide (d 1940), and Rose Edna, *née* Cartlidge; *b* 17 May 1929; *Educ* Percy Jackson GS, Manchester Univ (BSc), Cambridge Univ (PhD, ScD); *m* 1958, (Phyllis) Ann, da of Gerald James William Licence (d 1946); 1 s (Stephen), 2 da (Julia, Kathryn); *Career* res assoc in astrophysics Univ of Chicago 1953-54, sr res fellow Atomic Energy Estab Harwell 1954-57, physics lectr Univ of Durham 1957-61, prof of Geophysics and Physics MIT 1961-67, head geophysical fluid dynamics laboratory UK Meteorological Off 1967-; visiting prof dept of meteorology Reading Univ 1970-, dept of mathematics UCL 1970-82; Adrian fell Univ of Leicester 1980-83 (Hon DSc 1983), fell Jesus Coll Oxford 1983-, Gresham prof of astronomy Gresham Coll City of London 1985-; pres: Royal Meteorological Soc 1975-76, Euro Geophysical Soc 1982-84 (hon fell 1988), Royal Astronomical Soc 1983-85; fell American Acad of Arts and Sciences 1964, FRS 1971; *Style*— Prof Raymond Hide; Meteorological Office (Met 021), Bracknell, Berks RG12 2SZ (☎ 0344 420242, 2592)

HIDER, Dr Calvin Fraser; *b* 29 May 1930; *Educ* George Watsons Coll, Edinburgh Univ (MB, CLB); *m* 16 Jan 1959, Jean Margaret Douglas (d 1988); da of Prof N Dott CBE; 3 da (Jacqueline b 1960, Katherine b 1962, Susan b 1965); *Career* RNR 1955-64, Surgn Lt Cdr; sr conslt anaesthetist-cardiothoracic unit Edinburgh 1964; FFARCS Eng; *Recreations* fishing, riding, shooting, breeding Jacob sheep, sailing, Ocean Yacht Masters cert BOT; *Clubs* Sloane; *Style*— Dr Calvin Hider, Esq; Marchwell Cottage, Penicuik, Mid Lothian (☎ 0968 72680); Royal Infirmary, Edinburgh (☎ 031 229 2477)

HIGGIN, Capt William Bendyshe; s of Major Walter Wynnefield Higgin, DL (d 1971), of Cheshire, and Olive, *née* Earle (d 1978); *b* 14 Feb 1922; *Educ* Gresham's Sch Holt, Royal Agric Coll; *m* 26 March 1947, Mary Patricia, da of Capt George Lee-Morris (d 1983), of Cheshire; 2 s (Mark b 1954, Jonathan b 1956), 1 da (Gail b 1947); *Career* WWII co cdr 5/10 Baluch Regt IA 1941, ADC to GOC N India 1943-44, invalided out 1946; landowner in: Cheshire, Shropshire, Clwyd, Anglesey; *Recreations* game shooting; *Clubs* Sind; *Style*— Capt William Higgin; Mellus Manaw, Bodederk, Anglesey; Bryn Celyn, Glascoed Abergele, Clwyd

HIGGINS, Dr Andrew James; s of Edward James Higgins (d 1966), and Gabrielle Joy Higgins, *née* Kelland; *b* 7 Dec 1948; *Educ* St Michael's Coll, Royal Veterinary Coll, Univ of London (BVetMed, PhD), Centre for Tropical Veterinary Med Univ of Edinburgh (MSc); *m* 19 Dec 1981, Nicola Lynn, da of Peter Rex Eliot (d 1980); 1 s (Benjamin b 1982), 2 da (Amelia b 1984, Joanna b 1986); *Career* cmmnd RAVC 1973, Capt, served Dhofar War 1974; veterinary offr HM The Sultan of Oman 1975-76, veterinary advsr The Wellcome Fndn 1977-82, conslt Food and Agric Orgn of the UN 1981- vet advsr Animal Health Tst 1988-; memb cncl Soc for the Protection of Animals in North Africa (vice chm 1987-); memb: Conservation and Welfare Ctee, Zoological Soc of London 1987-, cncl BR Equine Veterinary Assoc 1984- (hon sec 1984-88, vice-chm 1986-), Editorial Advsy Bds Equine Veterinary Journal, Br Veterinary Journal; hon veterinary advsr to Jockey Club 1988-; winner of Equine Veterinary Journal Open Award 1986, Ciba-Geigy prize for res in animal health 1985, awarded Univ of London Laurel 1971; MRCVS; *Books* An Anatomy of Veterinary Europe (contrib 1972), The Camel in Health and Disease (ed & contrib 1986), many papers in scientific and general publications and communications to learned societies; *Recreations* skiing, riding, opera, camels; *Clubs* Buck's; *Style*— Dr Andrew Higgins; Lanwades Hall, Kennett, Newmarket, Suffolk CB8 7PN (☎ 0638 750448); Animal Health Tst, PO Box 5, Newmarket, Suffolk CB8 7DW (☎ 0638 661111, telex 818418 ANHLTH G, fax 0638 665789)

HIGGINS, (John) Christopher; s of Sidney James Higgins (d 1958), of Surbiton, Surrey, and Margaret Eileen, *née* Dealtrey (d 1973); *b* 9 July 1932; *Educ* King George V Sch Southport, Gonville and Caius Coll, Cambridge (BA, MA), Bedford Coll London (MSc), Birbeck Coll London (BSc), Univ of Bradford (PhD); *m* 24 Sept 1960, Margaret Edna, da of William John Howells, of 17 Rookwood Close, Llandaff, Cardiff; 3 s (Peter John b 1962, David Richard b 1964, Mark Robert b 1969); *Career* short serv cmmn RAF 1953-56; conslt Metra Gp 1964-67, dir econ planning and res IPC Newspapers Ltd 1967-70, prof mgmnt sci 1970-89, dir Mgmnt Centre Bradford Univ 1972-89, non-exec dir Amos Hinton & Sons plc 1980-84; tstee Wool Fndn; memb: BIM Regnl Bd, DTI Regnl Industl Devpt Bd, CS Scientific Advsrs Branch Air Miny 1962-64, various govt ctees 1976-89; CBIM 1982, FIEE 1981; *Books* Last Two Strategic and Operational Planning Systems, Computer Based Planning Systems; *Recreations* music, fellwalking, bridge; *Clubs* Royal Over-Seas League; *Style*— Prof Christopher Higgins; 36 Station Rd, Baildon, Shipley, W Yorks (☎ 0273 592836); Management Centre, Univ of Bradford, Emm Lane, Bradford BD9 4JL (☎ 0274 542299)

HIGGINS, Sir Christopher Thomas; s of Thomas Higgins (d 1964), and Florence Maud, *née* Wilkinson (d 1966); *b* 14 Jan 1914; *Educ* West Kensington Central Sch, London Univ; *m* 1936, Constance Joan, da of Walter Herbert Beck (d 1951); 1 s, 1 da (Geoffrey b 1944, Jacqueline b 1939); *Career* serv WWII Lt RA; Acton Borough Cncl 1945-64, Mayor 1957; memb: Middx Co Cncl 1952-55 and 1958-64, GLC 1964-67, Hemel Hempstead Devpt Corpn 1947-52, Bracknell Devpt Corpn 1965-68; chm: Peterborough Devpt Corpn 1968-81, North Thames Gas Consumers' Cncl 1969-79; kt 1977; *Style*— Sir Christopher Higgins; Coronation Cottage, Wood End, Little Horwood, Milton Keynes, Bucks MK17 0PE (☎ 029 671 2636)

HIGGINS, John Dalby; s of Frank Edward John Higgins, of Clifftop, Burlington Rd, Swanage, Dorset, and Edith Florence, *née* Dalby (d 1986); *b* 7 Jan 1934; *Educ* KCS Wimbledon, Worcester Coll Oxford (BA); *m* 3 Sept 1977, Linda Irene, da of Edward Sidney Christmas (d 1983); *Career* Nat Serv PO RAF; Fin Times: features ed 1962-64, arts ed 1963-69, literary ed 1966-69; The Times: arts ed 1970-88, chief opera critic 1988-, obituaries ed 1988-; memb: Ctee Royal Literary Fund 1969-, Advertising Ctee Musicians' Benevolent Fund 1985-; Goldene Verdienstzeichen des Landes Salzburg Austria 1985, Chevalier de l'Ordre des Arts et des Lettres France 1973, Ehrenkreuz für Kunst und Wissenschaft (first Class) Austria 1977; *Books* Travels in the Balkans (1970), The Making of An Opera (1977), Glyndebourne: A Celebration (ed 1984), British Theatre Design 1978- 88 (contrib 1989); *Recreations* claret, watching Chelsea FC; *Clubs* Garrick; *Style*— John Higgins, Esq; The Times, Virginia St, London E1 9BD (☎ 01 782 5868, telex 262141)

HIGGINS, Prof Peter Matthew; OBE (1986); s of Peter Joseph Higgins (d 1952), of Stamford Hill, London, and Margaret Higgins, *née* De Lacey (d 1981); *b* 18 June 1923; *Educ* St Ignatius Coll London, UCL, UCH (MB, BS) ; *m* 27 Sept 1952, Jean Margaret Lindsay, da of Capt Dr John Currie, DSO (d 1932), of Darlington; 3 s (Nicholas b 1954, Anthony b 1956, David b 1958), 1 da (Jane b 1959); *Career* Capt RAMC 1948-49; asst med registrar UCH (house physician med unit 1947 and 1950, res med offr 1951-52); princ in gen practice: Rugeley Staffs 1954-65, Castle Vale Birmingham 1966-67, Thamesmead London 1968-88; Prof in gen practice Guys Hosp Med Sch

1974-88 (sr lectr 1968-73); vice chm SE Thames RHA 1976- (memb 1974-), chm Thamesmead Family Serv Unit (memb Nat Cncl of Family Serv Units) 1983-; memb: Attendance Allowance Bd 1971-74, standing med advsy ctee DHSS 1970-74; tstee: Thamesmead Community Assoc, Tst Thamesmead; vice chm of govrs Linacre Centre for Study of Med Ethics; FRSM 1950, FRCP, FRCGP; *Recreations* reading, music, squash; *Style—* Prof Peter Higgins, OBE; Wallings, Heathfield Lane, Chislehurst, Kent BR7 6AH (☎ 01 467 2756)

HIGGINS, Rt Hon Terence Langley; PC (1979),DL (W Sussex 1988), MP (Cons Worthing 1964-); s of Reginald Higgins; *b* 18 Jan 1928; *Educ* Alleyn's Sch Dulwich, Gonville and Caius Coll Cambridge (MA); *m* 1961, Prof Rosalyn, *née* Cohen; 1 s, 1 da; *Career* fin sec to Treasy 1971-74 (Min State 1970-72), oppn spokesman Treasy and Econ Affrs 1974 (and 1966-70), Trade 1974-76; chm: Cons Parly Sports Ctee 1979-81, Tport 1979-, House of Commons Liaison Ctee 1983-, Treasy and Civil Serv Select Ctee 1983- (memb 1980-); memb: Pub Accounts Cmmn 1983-, Cncl Inst of Advanced Motorists; govr Dulwich Coll 1978-; NZ Shipping Co 1948-55, Unilever 1959-64; dir: Warne Wright Gp 1976-84, Lex Serv Gp 1980-; former memb Br Olympic Athletics Team (1948, 1952), lectr on econ principles Yale, pres Cambridge Union Soc 1958; *Style—* The Rt Hon Terence Higgins, DL, MP; House of Commons London SW1

HIGGINS, Rear Adm William Alleyne; CB (1985), CBE (1980); s of Cdr Henry Gray Higgins, DSO, RN (d 1977), of Dauntsey Salisbury, and Lilian Anne Higgins, *née* Leete (d 1980); *b* 18 May 1928; *Educ* Wellington Coll; *m* 1963, Wiltraud, da of Josef Hiebaum (d 1968), of Innsbruck Austria; 2 s (Charles, David), 1 da (Selina); *Career* joined RN 1945, promoted Rear Adm 1982, Last Flag Offr Medway and Port Adm Chatham 1982-83, Dir Gen Naval Personal Servs 1983-86; *Recreations* rock climbing, mountaineering; *Style—* Rear Adm William Higgins, CBE, CB

HIGGS, Air Vice-Marshal Barry; CBE (1981); s of Percy Harold Higgs (d 1973), of Hitcham, Ipswich, Suffolk and Ethel Eliza, *née* Elliot; *b* 22 August 1934; *Educ* Finchley Co GS; *m* 30 March 1957, Sylvia May, da of Harry Wilks; 2 s (David Stanford b 1958, Andrew Barry b 1959); *Career* 1955-70 served with Sqdn nos: 207, 115, 138, 49, 51; RAF Staff Coll 1968, Directorate of Forward Policy RAF 1971-73, Nat Def Coll 1974, cmd 39 (PR) Sqdn 1975-77, Asst Dir Def Policy 1978-79, cmd RAF Finningley 1979-81, Royal Coll of Def Studies 1982, Dep Dir of Intelligence 1983-85, Asst Chief of Def Staff (overseas) 1985-87; dir Gen Fertiliser Mfrs Assoc 1987-; *Recreations* sailing (cruising), bridge, gardening, theatre; *Clubs* RAF; *Style—* Air Vice-Marshal Barry Higgs, CBE; 33 Parsonage St, Cambridge, CB5 8DN (☎ 0223 63062); FMA Ltd Greenhill House, 90-93 Cowcross St, London EC1 6BH (☎ 01 251 6001, fax 01 490 1413, telex 94012856=TFMAG)

HIGGS, Brian James; QC (1974); s of James Percival Higgs (d 1984), of Brentwood, and Kathleen Anne, *née* Sullivan; *b* 24 Feb 1930; *Educ* Wrekin Coll, London Univ; *m* 1, 1953 (m dis), Jean Cameron Dumerton; 2 s (Jeremy b 1963, Jonathan b 1963), 3 da (Antonia b 1955, Nicola b 1962, Juliet b 1969), m 2, Vivienne Mary, da of Vivian Oliver Johnson of Essex; 1 s (Julian b 1982); *Career* serv RA 1948-50, cmmnd; barr Grays Inn 1955, bencher 1986, rec Crown Ct 1974; *Recreations* gardening, golf, wine, chess, bridge; *Clubs* Thorndon Park Golf; *Style—* Brian Higgs, Esq, QC; Butt Hatch House, Dunmow Road, Fyfield, Essex (☎ 0277 85509); 9 Kings Bench Walk, Temple, London EC4 (☎ 01 353 5638)

HIGGS, Derek Alan; s of Alan Edward Higgs (d 1979), and Freda Gwendoline, *née* Hope (d 1984); *b* 3 April 1944; *Educ* Solihull Sch, Univ of Bristol (BA); *m* 1970, Julia Mary, da of Robert T Arguile, of Leics; 2 s (Oliver b 1975, Rowley b 1980), 1 da (Josephine b 1976); *Career* dir S G Warburg Gp plc, head of corporate fin S G Warburg and Co Ltd; FCA; *Style—* Derek Higgs, Esq; 4 Upper Addison Gdns, London W14; 2 Finsbury Ave, London EC2 (☎ 01 860 1090)

HIGGS, John Walter Yeoman; s of Walter Frank Higgs (d 1961); *b* 1 Sept 1923; *Educ* Oundle, Emmanuel Coll Cambridge; *m* 1948, Elizabeth Patricia; 2 da; *Career* Univ of Reading 1948-57, Univ of Oxford 1958-73, fell Exeter Coll Oxford 1963-73; Food and Agriculture Orgn of UN 1970-74; memb Prince of Wales's Cncl 1979-, sec and keeper of the records Duchy of Cornwall 1981-; FSA; *Recreations* fishing, shooting; *Clubs* Brooks's, Farmers', Leander; *Style—* John Higgs, Esq; Arkleton, Langholm, Dumfries (☎ 054 17 247); Duchy of Cornwall, 10 Buckingham Gate, London SW1E 6LA (☎ 01 828 3550 834 7346)

HIGGS, Roger Junior; JP (1971); s of Roger Higgs (d 1948), of Caversham, Reading, and Joyce Kearle Rich Higgs, *née* Maggs; *b* 8 Mar 1932; *Educ* St Edward's Sch Oxford, Harper Adams Agric Coll; *m* 7 Feb 1953, Daphne Jean, da of Robert Victor Gray (d 1968), of Knebworth, Herts; 1 s (Timothy b 1955), 2 da (Janferie b 1954, Sarah b 1957); *Career* farmer; gen cmmnr of Income Tax 1974, govr Nat Soc For Epilepsy 1985, dir NSE Enterprises Ltd (later chm) 1986, dir Chiltern Hospital 1987; *Recreations* sailing, travel; *Clubs* Rotary, Royal Southampton YC; *Style—* Roger Higgs, Esq; Quarrendon Farm, Amersham, Bucks HP7 0JT

HIGHAM, Hon Mrs; Hon Barbara Constance; da of 3 Viscount Hampden, GCVO, KCB, CMG (d 1958); *b* 1907; *m* 1934, Ronald Harry Higham (d 1966); 1 s, 1 da (*see* Grosvenor, Hon Mrs Victor); *Style—* The Hon Mrs Higham; Flat 6, 212 Old Brompton Rd, London SW5

HIGHAM, Lt-Col John Bernard; s of Lt Col Bernard Higham (d 1944), and Florence, *née* Parsons (d 1941); *b* 20 Jan 1915; *Educ* Epsom Coll, RMA Woolwich, Jesus Coll Cambridge (MA); *m* 8 April 1950, Sheila, da of James Courthope Wood (d 1949); *Career* cmmnd RE, serv WO, GHQ India, Embarkation Cmdt Karachi, dir of Tranportation Army HQ Australia; psc, jssc 1935-55; schoolmaster and coll lectr; Liveryman Worshipful Co of Coach Makers and Harness Makers; *Books* Army Movements 1939-45 (1955, with E A Knighton), Theoretical Mechanics (1975, with G S Light); *Clubs* RORC; *Style—* Lt-Col John B Higham, Esq; 16 Castle Meadow, Sible Hedingham CO9 3PZ (☎ 0787 60587)

HIGHAM, Rear Adm Philip Roger Canning; CB (1972); s of Edward John George Higham (d 1958), of Bristol, and Ethel Agatha Higham (d 1972); *b* 9 June 1920; *Educ* Royal Naval Coll Dartmouth; *m* 1942, Pamela Bracton, da of Gerald Bracton Edwards, (d 1971), of Lancashire; 2 s (David b 1944, Nicholas b 1947); *Career* midshipman 1938, sub lt 1940, gunnery offr 1944, PSC 1948, experimental dept HMS Excellent 1951-52, cdr 1953, Trials cdr RAE Aberpurth 1954-55, jssc 1956, experimental cdr HMS Excellent 1957-59, admlty (DTWP) 1961, Capt 1961, naval attaché Middle East 1962-64, idc 1965 dep chief Polaris Exec 1966-68; commodore-in-charge, Hong Kong 1968-70, rear adm 1970, asst chief of Naval Staff (operational requirements) 1970-72, ret 1973; dir HMS Belfast Tst 1973-78, keeper HMS Belfast (Imperial War Museum) 1978-83; Portsmouth Naval Base Property Tst 1986-; *Recreations* gardening; *Clubs* Naval and Military; *Style—* Rear Adm Philip Higham, CB; Apple Tree Farm, Prinsted, Emsworth, Hampshire (☎ 0243 372195)

HIGHAM, William Michael; s of Thomas Ashworth Higham (d 1959), and Doris Bertha Rowsell Brakspear; *b* 21 Nov 1928; *Educ* Stowe; *m* 1953, Gillian Mary, *née* Higham, da of John Sharp Higham (d 1980); 3 s (Christopher, Richard, Paul), 2 da (Elizabeth, Judith); *Career* chm and md Highams Ltd 1975-83; *Recreations* tennis, swimming, golf; *Style—* William Higham, Esq; Norcliffe Lodge, Styal, Wilmslow, Cheshire (☎ 0625 525149) SK9 4LH

HIGHETT, Hon Mrs (Jean Mary); *née* Montagu; da (by 1 m) of 3 Baron Swaythling, OBE; *b* 1927; *m* 1951, Lintorn Trevor Highett, MC; 1 s, 2 da; *Style—* The Hon Mrs Highett; 2A Gore St, SW7

HIGHFIELD, (William) Barry; s of Alfred Highfield (d 1978), of Sevenoaks, Kent and Eileen Margaret, *née* Leavey; *b* 22 May 1934; *Educ* Tonbridge, Brooksby Hall Leics; *m* 8 Feb 1980, Rosemary Helen, da of Lt Cdr Ian Nagle Douglas Cox, DSC, RN; 1 s (David b 1965), 1 da (Jane b 1963); *Career* Nat Serv RAF 1952-54; farmer intensive livestock Kent and Sussex 1959-76; mangr Albany Life Assur 1980-, dir Hurstdens Ltd (gen insur brokers); memb Life Assur Assoc; *Recreations* golf; *Clubs* Sloane, Tavistock GC; *Style—* Barry Highfield, Esq; 2nd Floor, Sycamore House, 88 Coombe Rd, New Malden, Surrey KT3 4QS (☎ 01 942 7806)

HIGHMORE, Neil Sinclair; s of John Sinclair Highmore, Maj (ret), of Rookdykes, Corse, by Huntly, Aberdeenshire, and Margaret Boyes Highmore *née* Sinclair (d 1974); *b* 27 May 1948; *Educ* Broughton Secdy Sch, Edinburgh Art Coll/Heriot Watt Univ (BArch); *Career* ptnr in arch practice Patience and Highmore, former chm of Borders Arch Gp; RIBA, ARIAS; *Recreations* squash, gardening, angling; *Style—* Neil Highmore, Esq; Tighcarr, St Ronans Terrace, Innerleithen, Peeblesshire (☎ 0896 830128); Quadrant, 17 Bernard St, Edinburgh EH6 6PW (☎ 031 555 0644)

HIGNETT, John Michael; TD (1967); s of Lt Col John Derrick Hignett, DL, JP, of East Langton Grange, Market Harborough, Leics, and Alice Gwencoline, *née* Manners (d 1965); *b* 29 Sept 1928; *Educ* Stowe, Trinity Coll Cambridge (BA, MA); *m* 23 April 1960, Mary Beatrice Mella, da of Osborne Risk Burchnall (d 1970), of The Manor House Aston Flamville, Leics; 2 s (Rupert b 1967, Edward b 1971), 1 da (Charlotte b 1969); *Career* Queens Own Warwicks and Worcs Yeo 1952-64; Bass plc 1952-84: dir Bass UK 1970-81, vice-chm Charrington & Co Ltd 1981-84 (md 1975-81); chm London Brewers Soc 1970-84; High Sheriff of Leicester 1976, JP 1980; memb ctee Leics and Rutland Army Benevolent Fund, tstee Fernie Hunt (chm supporters assoc), woodman of Arden; Memb Ct Worshipful Co of Brewers 1977-84; memb Inst Brewing; *Recreations* foxhunting, fishing, shooting; *Clubs* Boodles, St James'; *Style—* Michael Hignett, Esq, TD, JP; Clipston Court, Market Harborough, Leics LE16 7RU (☎ 085 880 230)

HIGNETT, John Mulock; s of Reginald Arthur Hignett (d 1975), of Bermuda, and Marjorie Sarah Louise Hignett; *b* 9 Mar 1934; *Educ* Harrow, Magdalene Coll Cambridge; *m* 5 Aug 1961, (Anne) Marijke Inge, da of Rudolf-Jeorje de Boer (d 1988), of Amsterdam; 1 s (Martin b 26 Nov 1962), 1 da (Karin b 4 March 1965); *Career* Lazard Bros 1963-: mangr issues dept 1971, dir 1972, head corporate fin 1980-81, on secondment 1981-84, md 1984-88; non-exec dir: DEK Printing Machines, Carless Capel and Leonard unitl 1981; dir-gen: Panel on Takeovers and Mergers 1981-84, CSI 1983-84 (first time these two posts have been held by one person); fin dir Glaxo Hldgs plc 1988-; boxing blue 1955 (capt 1956); FCA 1961; *Recreations* growing orchids; *Clubs* MCC, Hawks (Cambridge); *Style—* John M Hignett Esq; Glaxo Holdings plc, 61 Curzon St, London W1Y 7PA (☎ 01 493 4060)

HIGTON, Dennis John; s of John William Higton (d 1966), of Surrey, and Lillian Harriet, *née* Mann (d 1932); *b* 15 July 1921; *Educ* Guildford Tech Sch, RAE Farnborough Tech Sch (CEng); *m* 1945, Joy Merrifield, da of William Merrifield Pickett (d 1964), of Wilts; 1 s (Peter William b 1962), 1 da (Priscilla Margaret b 1949); *Career* engrg student apprentice RAE 1938-42, aerodynamic flight res RAE 1942-52, fighter and naval aircraft flight testing A and AEE 1953-66, def staff Washington DC USA 1966-70, asst dir Aircraft Prodn 1972-75, dir gen (under sec) MOD (PE) 1976-81; conslt to aviation indust and dir 1981-; bd chm Civil Serv Cmmn 1981-; chm S Wilts and Salisbury NSPCC 1982-; FIMech, FRAes; *Recreations* sailing, skiing, painting, bee keeping; *Style—* Dennis Higton, Esq; Jasmine Cottage, Rollestone Rd, Shrewton, Salisbury, Wilts SP3 4HG (☎ 0980 620276)

HILARY, David Henry Jephson; s of Robert Jephson Hilary (d 1937), and Nita Margaret Macmahon, *née* Mahon (d 1972); *b* 3 May 1932; *Educ* King's Coll Cambridge (MA); *m* 22 June 1957, Phoebe, da of John James Buchanan (d 1983); 2 s (John b 1964, Henry b 1968), 2 da (Miriam b 1967, Rachel b 1970); *Career* RA 1953-54; Home Office 1956-87, Cabinet Office 1967-69 and 1981-83; asst under-sec of state 1975-87, receiver for Met Police Dist 1987-; *Recreations* cricket, bridge, family pursuits; *Clubs* RAC, MCC; *Style—* David Hilary, Esq; c/o New Scotland Yard, Broadway, London SW1

HILDESLEY, Michael Edmund; s of Paul Francis Glynn Hildesley, and Mary, *née* Morgan; *b* 16 Oct 1948; *Educ* Sherborne, Trinity Coll Oxford (MA); *m* 1972, Judith Carol, da of George Michael Pistor, of USA; 3 s (Robert b 1980, David b 1982, Charles b 1982); *Career* merchant banker; dir Morgan Grenfell and Co Ltd 1984-; *Style—* Michael Hildesley, Esq; 23 Gt Winchester Street, London EC2P 2AX (☎ 01 588 4545)

HILDRETH, Henry (Jan) Hamilton Crossley; s of Maj Gen Sir John Hildreth, KBE, and Joan Elsie Hallett, *née* Hamilton (d 1975); gf Alfred H J Hamilton, of Dibden Manor, descended from Hugh H, s of Sir James H who went to Ireland 1616, and hence of Hamiltons who arrived England mid 10 century, see H and Abercorn in Burkes P and B and Irish FR; *b* 1 Dec 1932; *Educ* Wellington Coll, The Queen's Coll Oxford (MA); *m* 1958, Wendy Moira Marjorie, da of Arthur Harold Clough, CMG (d 1967), of Penn, Bucks; 2 s (Gerald, Gavin), 1 da (Frances); *Career* Nat Serv 1952-53, 2 Lt RA, TA 44 Para Bde; memb Baltic Exchange 1956; Royal Dutch Shell Gp Philippines and London 1957, Kleinwort Benson Ltd 1963, dir and asst chief exec John Laing and Son Ltd 1972, exec dir Minster Tst Ltd, non-exec dir Monument Oil and Gas plc 1984-88; chm: Sea Catch plc 1987-, Carroll Securities Ltd 1986-, Scallop Kings plc; dir numerous cos, ind conslt; memb NEDO 1965- (memb of 3 EDC's), memb bd London Tport 1968, memb cncl The Spastics Soc 1980-, dir Contact A Family 1980-; govr: Wellington Coll 1974, Eagle House Sch 1986-; chm Wimbledon Cons Assoc 1986-89; memb: cncl Br Exec Serv Overseas, IOD (dir gen 1975-78), ctee GBA

1978-86, cncl ISIS 1979-82 (life) Industl Soc (ctee 1973-83), Accounting Standard advsy ctee 1976-79; *Recreations* running, watermills, gardening, photography; *Clubs* Athenaeum, Vincent's (Oxford), Thames Hare and Hounds, The Political Economy, Achilles; *Style*— Jan Hildreth, Esq; 50 Ridgway Place, Wimbledon SW19 4SW (☎ 01 946 0243); The Mill, Ponsworthy, Newton Abbot, Devon; Minster House, Arthur St, London EC4 R9HB (☎ 01 623 1050)

HILDRETH, Maj-Gen Sir (Harold) John Crossley; KBE (1964, CBE 1952, OBE 1945); s of Lt-Col Harold Crossley Hildreth, DSO, OBE (d 1936); *b* 12 June 1908; *Educ* Wellington Coll, RMA Woolwich; *m* 1950, Mary, MBE, da of George Wroe; 2 s, 3 da; *Career* 2 Lt RA 1928, Capt RAOC 1935, served WW II, Col 1943, Brig 1958, DOS BAOR 1957-59, Inspr RAOC 1959-61, Maj- Gen 1961, DOS WO 1961-64, ret; Col Cmdt RAOC 1963-70; md: Army Kinema Corpn 1965-69, The Services Kinema Corpn 1969-75; chm Gtr London branch SS and AFA 1977-; *Style*— Maj-Gen Sir John Hildreth, KBE; 59 Latymer Court, London W6 (☎ 01 748 3107); 56 The Cottages, North St, Emsworth, Hants (☎ Emsworth (024 34) 3466)

HILDYARD, Hon Mrs (Aislinn Mary Katharine); *née* Morris; JP; eldest da of 2 Baron Morris (d 1975), and Lady Salmon (da of Lt-Col David Maitland-Makgill-Crichton); *b* 22 April 1934; *m* 1954, Capt Angus Jeremy Christopher Hildyard, DL, *qv*; 1 s, 1 da; *Style*— The Hon Mrs Hildyard, JP; Goxhill Hall, Goxhill, Barrow-upon-Humber, South Humberside DN19 7LZ (☎ 0469 30121)

HILDYARD, Capt Angus Jeremy Christopher; DL (1977); s of Maj Donald Maxwell Dunlop (d 1963), and Noel Florence Dora, *née* Hildyard (who m 2, Col Alexander Bainbridge Craddock, CIE, OBE, and d 1963); changed surname by Deed Poll from Dunlop to mother's maiden name Hildyard 1945; sr co-heir of the Barony of Le Scrope of Masham through his grandmother, as sr descendant of Catherina d'Arcy, w of Sir Robert Hildyard, 3 Bt; *b* 15 Feb 1928; *Educ* Charterhouse, RMA Sandhurst; *m* 1954, Hon Aislinn Mary Katharine, *née* Morris, *see* Hon Mrs Hildyard; 1 s, 1 da; *Career* Adj 17 Trg Regt Staff Capt RA 2 Inf Divn, ret 1960; High Sheriff of Humberside 1978-79; chm Georgian Soc for E Yorks; gen cmmr Income Tax; vice-chm Yorks Ctee Historic Houses Assoc; memb exec ctee Yorks Tourist Bd; pres Humberside Victims Support Scheme; *Recreations* gardening, classical architecture; *Style*— Captain Angus Hildyard, DL; Goxhill Hall, Goxhill, Barrow-upon-Humber, South Humberside DN19 7LZ (☎ 0469 30121)

HILDYARD, Sir David Henry Thoroton; KCMG (1975, CMG 1966), DFC (1943); s of His Hon Gerard Momsby Thoroton Hildyard, QC, DL (d 1956), of Flintham Hall Newark, and Sybil Hamilton Hoare (d 1978); *b* 4 May 1916; *Educ* Eton, Ch Ch Oxford; *m* 1947, Millicent, da of Sir Edward Baron (d 1962) and widow of Wing Cdr R M Longmore; 1 s (Robert b 1952), 1 da (Marianna b 1955); *Career* served WWII RAF; joined Foreign Serv 1948, cnsllr Mexico 1960-65, head of econ rels dept; FO 1965, min and alternate UK delegate to UN 1968, ambass Chile 1970-73, ambass and perm rep to UN (Geneva) 1973-76; dir Lombard Odier Int Portfolio Mgmnt 1980; *Clubs* Garrick, Reform, Hurlingham; *Style*— Sir David Hildyard, KCMG, DFC; 97 Onslow Sq, London SW7 (☎ 01 584 2110)

HILDYARD, Myles Thoroton; MBE, MC, TD, JP, DL; s of His Hon G M T Hildyard KC, (d 1956), of Flintham Hall, Newark, and Sybil, *née* Hamilton Hoare (d 1978) ; *b* 31 Dec 1914; *Educ* Eton, Magdalene Coll Cambridge; *Career* farmer and landowner, md Newfield Farm Ltd; pres Thoroton Soc of Notts and of CPRE, vice chm Nat Tst Eastern Midlands Region; landowner, farmer and local historian; lord of manor of Flintham and Screveton Notts, patron of living of Flintham; *Clubs* Brooks; *Style*— Myles T Hildyard, MBE, MC, TD, DL, JP; Flintham Hall, Newark, (☎ 063 525 214)

HILEY, Carole Shirley; da of George Quastel (d 1976), of London, and Golda Gertrude Quastel (d 1982); *b* 25 August 1931; *Educ* Colwyn Bay Secdy Sch North Wales; *m* 1, 17 Aug 1952 (m dis 1972), Stanley S Cowan, s of William Cowan (d 1958); 1 s (Simon Anthony b 1955), 1 da (Suzanne b 1956); m 2, 6 June 1975, Ronald H Hiley, s of Charles Henry Hiley (d 1941); *Career* professional childcare; fndr and md: Beck Kindergartens Ltd 1959-80, Kindergartens for Commerce Ltd 1966-80, Our Childrens World Ltd, Childrens World Ltd 1980, World of Children Ltd 1980-; *Recreations* children, gardening; *Clubs* Network, Phylis Court Henley; *Style*— Mrs Carole S Hiley; Pankridge Manor, Bledlow Ridge, Buckinghamshire HP14 4AE (☎ 024 027 521 and 305); 10 Lincoln Park Business Centre, Cressex, High Wycombe, Bucks HP12 3RD (☎ 0494 215051)

HILEY, Peter Haviland; s of Sir (Ernest) Haviland Hiley, KBE (d 1943), of Cambridge, and Brenda Lee, *née* Lord (d 1961); *b* 19 Feb 1921; *Educ* Eton, Grenoble Univ; *m* 21 May 1955, (Isabel) Susan, da of Herbert George Hope, MBE (d 1956), of Blackmoor, Hants; 1 s (William b 1960); *Career* WWII Intelligence Corps 1941-45; Br Cncl 1945-49, joined Laurence Olivier Prodns Ltd 1949; current dir: Wheelshare Ltd (formerly Laurence Olivier Prodns Ltd), St James's Players Ltd, Old Vic Tst Ltd, Central Sch of Speech and Drama, Sheppee Hldgs Ltd; govr Petersfield Comprehensive Sch 1965-, gen cmmr Income Tax 1966-; *Recreations* theatre, sightseeing; *Style*— Peter Hiley, Esq; Byways, Steep, Petersfield, Hants GU32 1AD; 102 Valiant House, Vicarage Crescent, London SW11 3LX

HILEY, Hon Sir Thomas Alfred; KBE (1966); s of William Hiley (d 1944), and Maria, *née* Savage (d 1960); *b* 25 Nov 1905; *Educ* Brisbane GS, Queensland Univ (MCom); *m* 1929, Marjory Joyce, da of Louis Jarrott (d 1952); 2 s; *Career* CA 1925-65, MLA Qld 1944-66, pres ICEAW in Aust 1946-47; min of Crown 1957-65 incl: tres and min for Housing Qld 1957, dep premier Qld 1965; *Recreations* cricket, shooting, fishing; *Clubs* Queensland (Brisbane); *Style*— The Hon Sir Thomas Hiley, KBE; Illawong, 39 The Esplanade, Tewantin, Qld 4565, Australia

HILL, Prof Alan Geoffrey; s of Thomas Murton Hill (d 1988) of London, and Alice Marian, *née* Nunn (d 1988); *b* 12 Dec 1931; *Educ* Dulwich, St Andrews Univ (MA), Merton Coll Oxford (BLitt); *m* 9 Sept 1960, Margaret Vincent, da of Cuthbert Vincent Rutherford (d 1959), of Caterham; 3 da (Alison b 1961, Juliet b 1964, Diana b 1967); *Career* English lectr Exeter Univ 1958-62, lectr St Andrews Univ 1962-68, sr English lectr Dundee Univ 1968-80, visiting English prof Saskatchewan Univ 1973-74; prof English language and lit Royal Holloway Coll Univ of London 1980-; Warton lectr Br Acad 1986; tstee Dove Cottage and the Wordsworth Library Grasmere 1969-; *Books* gen ed and princ contrib to The Letters of William and Dorothy Wordsworth (8 vols 1967-)-; ed John Henry Newman Loss and Gain (1986), Wordworth's Grand Design (1987); *Clubs* Savile; *Style*— Prof G Alan Hill; Dept of English, Royal Holloway & Bedford New Coll, Egham Hill , Egham, Surrey TW20 0EX (☎ 0784 34455)

HILL, Alan John Wills; CBE (1972); s of William Wills Hill (d 1974), of London, and May Francis Victoria, *née* Dixon (d 1962); *b* 12 August 1912; *Educ* Wyggeston GS Leicester, Jesus Coll Cambridge (MA); *m* 1939, Enid, Adela, da of Frederick Malin (d 1915), of Leicester; 2 s (Stephen, David), 1 da (Carolyn); *Career* RAF 1940-45, Sqdn Ldr Europe; publisher; dir William Heinemann Ltd 1956-79, chm and md Heinemann Educn Books Ltd 1961-79, md Heinemann Gp 1972-79; hon public rels offr, the Prehistoric Soc 1988-; fell King's Coll London; *Books* In Pursuit of Publishing (1988), and many articles in jnls; *Recreations* swimming, mountain walking; *Clubs* Athenaeum, Garrick, RAF, PEN; *Style*— Alan Hill, Esq, CBE; 56 Northway, London NW11 6PA (☎ 01 455 8388); New Ho, Rosthwaite, Borrowdale, Cumbria (☎ 059 684 687); Heinemann, Halley Ct, Jordan Hill, Oxford OX2 8EJ (☎ 0865 311 366, telex 837292)

HILL, Alastair Malcolm; QC (1982); s of Sir Ian George Wilson Hill, CBE, TD (d 1982); *b* 12 May 1936; *Educ* Trinity Coll Glenalmond, Keble Coll Oxford (BA); *m* 1969 (m dis 1977), Elizabeth Maria Innes; 2 children; *Career* barr Gray's Inn 1961; recorder Crown Ct SE circuit 1982-; *Recreations* flyfishing, collecting watercolours and prints, opera; *Style*— Alastair Hill Esq, QC; New Court, Temple, London EC4Y 9BE (☎ 01 583 6166)

HILL, (George) Andrew; s of Cdr George Walter Hill (d 1974), of Orlestone Grange, Ashford, Kent, and Kathleen Mary Kynaston, *née* Jacques (d 1986); *b* 15 April 1939; *Educ* Winchester, Christ Church Oxford (MA); *m* 17 June 1972, Margaret Mary Katherine, da of Harold Arthur Armstrong While, MBE, TD (d 1983); 1 s (Timothy Trigger b 5 May 1976), 1 da (Lucy Kynaston b 14 Dec 1974); *Career* slr 1966, sr ptnr Le Brasseur and Monier Williams 1987- (former asst slr and ptnr); ctee memb Holborn Law Soc 1985-; Freeman City of London 1986, Liveryman Worshipful Co of Co of Tin Plate Workers 1986 (clerk 1980-88); *Recreations* golf, gardening, wine and watercolours; *Clubs* City Livery, Royal Wimbledon and Trevose GC's; *Style*— Andrew Hill, Esq; 235 Sheen Lane, London SW14 8LE (☎ 01 876 2055); 71 Lincolns Inn Fields, London WC2A 3JF (☎ 01 405 6195)

HILL, Lady Anne Catherine Dorothy; *née* Gathorne-Hardy; da of 3 Earl of Cranbrook (d 1915), and Lady Dorothy Montagu Boyle, da of 7 Earl of Glasgow; *b* 12 Oct 1911; *m* 1938, George Heywood Hill; 2 da (Harriet, Lucy); *Style*— Lady Anne Hill; Snape Priory, Saxmundham, Suffolk

HILL, 8 Viscount (UK 1842); Sir Antony Rowland Clegg-Hill; 10 Bt (GB 1727); also Baron Hill of Almarez and of Hardwick (UK 1816); strictly speaking the full title of the Viscountcy is: Viscount Hill of Hawkstone and of Hardwick; s of 7 Viscount Hill (d 1974, fourth in descent from John, er bro of 1 Viscount, who commanded Adam's Brigade in the Battle of Waterloo, was second in command of the Army of Occupation (of France) 1815-18 and was C-in-C 1828-42) by his 1 w Elisabeth, *née* Smyth-Osbourne (d 1967); *b* 19 Mar 1931; *Educ* Kelly Coll, RMA Sandhurst; *m* 1963 (m dis 1976), Juanita, da of John Pertwee, of Surrey;; *Heir* cous, Peter Clegg-Hill; *Career* late Capt RA; has freedom of Shrewsbury; *Style*— The Rt Hon Viscount Hill; c/o House of Lords, SW1

HILL, Sir Austin Bradford; CBE (1951); s of Sir Leonard Erskine Hill (d 1952); *b* 8 July 1897; *Educ* Chigwell Sch Essex, UCL (PhD, DSc); *m* 1923, Florence Maud, *née* Salmon (d 1980); 2 s, 1 da; *Career* serv WWI Fl Sub Lt RNAS; London Sch of Hygiene and Tropical Med London Univ: reader in epidemiology and vital statistics 1933-45, prof of med statistics 1945-61, dean 1955-57; hon dir statistical res unit MRC 1945-61; author of pubns on health res; Hon DSC Oxford 1963, Hon MD Edinburgh 1968; FRS 1954; kt 1961; *Style*— Sir Austin Hill, CBE; April Cottage, Lower Hopton, Nesscliffe, Shrops SY4 1DL (☎ 074 381 231)

HILL, Brian; DL (Lancs 1977); *b* 16 Oct 1930; *Educ* Wigan GS, Univ of Manchester (LLB); *m* 3 July 1954, Barbara, *née* Hickson; 1 da; *Career* slr 1953, asst slr Manchester Corpn 1953-56; Lancs CC: sr slr and second dep clerk 1956-74, dep clerk 1974-76, chief exec and clerk 1977-; clerk of Lancs Lieutenancy 1977-, Co electoral returning offr 1977-; sec: Lancs Advsy Ctee 1977-, Lord Chllr's Advsy Ctee on Gen Cmmrs of Income Tax 1977-, Lancs Probation and After Care Ctee 1977-; chm: Local Govt Legal Soc 1970-71, Soc of Co Secretaries 1976-77, NW branch SOLACE 1985; sr vice chm Assoc of Co Chief Execs 1988-89, advsr to ACC policy ctee 1987-; co sec Lancs Enterprises Ltd 1982-, memb MSC Area Manpower Bd 1983-86, sec Lancs ctee Royal Jubilee and Prince's Tsts 1985-; clerk to ct Royal Northern Coll of Music 1977-, memb ct Univ of Lancaster 1977-; vice pres Lancs Youth Clubs Assoc 1977-, memb Preston Select Vestry 1977-; hon degree Royal Northern Coll of Music 1979; FRSA 1983, CBIM 1987; *Recreations* music; *Clubs* Royal Overseas League; *Style*— Brian Hill, Esq, DL; Lancashire CC, PO Box 78, County Hall, Preston PR1 8XJ (☎ 0772 263350, fax 0772 263506)

HILL, Sir Brian John; s of Gerald A Hill, OBE (d 1974); *b* 19 Dec 1932; *Educ* Stowe, Cambridge Univ (MA); *m* 1959, Janet Joyce, da of Alfred S Newman, OBE; 3 children; *Career* served Lt Army (Nat Service); gp md Higgs and Hill Ltd 1972-83, chm and chief exec Higgs and Hill plc 1983-; dir Bldg Centre 1981-85; memb: advsy bd of Property Services Agency 1981-86, memb Lazard Property Unit Tst 1982-, Lancs and Yorks Property Mgmnt Ltd 1985-, Palmerston Property Devlp's plc 1985-, Grainhurst Properties Ltd 1985-; dir Property Servs Agency 1986-88; chm Vauxhall Coll of Bldg and Further Educn 1976-86, pres London Regn of Bldg Trade Employer's Confed NFBTE 1981-82; chm: Nat Contractors Gp 1983-84, Chartered Inst of Bldg 1984- (pres 1987-88), Great Ormond St Hosp Bldg Ctee; govr Great Ormond Street Hosp for Sick Children; FCIOA, PPCIOB, FRICS, hon FInStruckE; *Recreations* travelling, tennis and gardening; *Clubs* RAC; *Style*— Sir Brian Hill; Barrow House, The Warren, Kingswood, Surrey; Higgs and Hill plc, Crown House, Kingston Rd, New Malden, Surrey KT3 3ST (☎ 01 942 8921)

HILL, Brian Lionel; s of Lionel Hill (d 1965); *b* 21 Dec 1935; *Educ* Hornchurch GS; *m* 1960, Julia Mary, *née* Woolford; 1 s (Simon), 1 da (Penelope); *Career* engaged in fin and industl mgmnt; gp tres Meggitt Hldgs plc; dir: Columbia Controls Inc USA, General Connectors Corpn USA, Room Ready Ltd; FCA; *Recreations* pretending to be a farmer; *Style*— Brian Hill, Esq; Meggitt Holdings plc, 4 West Street, Wimborne, Dorset BH21 1JN (☎ 0202 880105, telex 417133); Middle Farm, Hogshaw, Bucks (☎ 029 667 665)

HILL, Molly, Viscountess; Catherine Mary (Molly); da of Dr Rowland Venables Lloyd-Williams, of Maiford, Denbigh; *m* 1942, as his 2 w, 7 Viscount Hill (d 1974); *Style*— The Rt Hon Molly, Viscountess Hill

HILL, Charles (Mark) Roper; s of Charles Guy Roper Hill, MC (d 1977), of Lathom, Lancs, and Ethel Wilma, *née* Fair; *b* 28 Oct 1943; *Educ* Marlborough; *m* 6 Aug 1982, Judith Mary, da of John Clancy, of Ormskirk; 1 s (James b 1983), 1 da (Emily b 1986);

Career slr 1967, clerk to cmmrs of income tax 1971, NP 1977; tstee Ormskirk Postgrad Med Tst; memb Law Soc 1967; *Recreations* golf, fell walking, gardening; *Clubs* Ormskirk GC, Liverpool Ramblers AFC; *Style*— Mark Hill, Esq; Dickinson Parker Hill & Son, 22 Derby St, Ormskirk, Lancs L39 2BZ (☎ 0695 742 01)

HILL, Rev Canon Christopher; s of Leonard Hill, of Kinver, Staffs, and Frances Vera, *née* Bullock; *b* 10 Oct 1945; *Educ* Sebright Sch Worcs, King's Coll London (BD, MTh, AKC); *m* 21 Dec 1976, Hilary Ann, da of Geoffrey James Whitehouse, of Brewood, Staffs; 3 s (Vivian b 1978, Adrian b 1982, Edmund b 1983), 1 da (Felicity b 1980); *Career* ordained Lichfield Cathedral: deacon 1969, priest 1970; asst curate: St Michael's Tividale Diocese of Lichfield 1969-73, St Nicholas Codsall 1973-74; asst chaplain to Archbishop of Canterbury for foreign rels 1974-81, co-sec Anglican-RC Int Cmmn 1974-81 and 1983-, sec Anglican-Lutheran Euro Cmmn 1981-82, canon of Canterbury Cathedral 1982-, sec for ecumenical affrs to Archbishop of Canterbury 1982-, chaplain to HM the Queen 1987-; *Recreations* reading, walking, eating and drinking, classical music; *Clubs* Athenaeum, Nikaean Guestmaster; *Style*— The Rev Canon Christopher Hill; 3 Lambeth Palace Cottages, London SE1 7JX (☎ 01 928 8282); Lambeth Palace, London SE1 7LB (☎ 01 928 4880, fax 01 261 9836, telex 915 365 LTHPL)

HILL, David Beatty; s of Frederick Charles Hill (d 1964), and Jane Elizabeth Garlick (d 1934); *b* 5 Nov 1918; *m* 29 March 1952, Patricia, da of Thomas Walsh (d 1982), of Cornel House, Manor Park, Chislehurst, Kent; 2 da (Stevanne, Nikki); *Career* WWII, RN 1939-40, special opns 1940-44, Fleet Air Arm 1944-45; asst ed Kentish Times 1946; ed: Ford Times 1946, European Esquire 1951; asst ed Daily Sketch 1953, ed Weekend 1956; ed-in-chief and md: Harmsworth Publications 1958, Weekend Publications 1958, Harmsworth Press 1977; dir Associated Newspapers 1979; hon citizen New Orleans USA 1969; Freeman City of London 1967, Liveryman Worshipful Co Stationers and Newspaper Makers; *Books* The Cat Race (1952); *Recreations* golf, indolence as a fine art; *Clubs* Special Forces; *Style*— D Beatty Hill, Esq; Hill Ct, Manor Park, Chislehurst, Kent

HILL, David Layland; s of James Duncan Hill (d 1979), of Huddersfield, and Margaret, *née* Sykes; *b* 8 May 1935; *Educ* Bradford GS; *m* 1958, Pauline, da of Jack Steel (d 1976), of Huddersfield; 1 s (Michael b 1961); *Career* RAPC 1956-62, Lt in Singapore 1960-62; CA, sr ptnr Wheawill and Sudworth, former pres of Huddersfield Soc of CAs 1985; FCA (1959); *Recreations* golf; *Clubs* Woodsome Hall; *Style*— David Hill; 24 Dean Brook Road, Armitage Bridge, Huddersfield, West Yorkshire HD4 7PB (☎ 0484 666770); 35 Westage, Huddersfield, West Yorkshire HD1 1PA (☎ 0484 23691, fax (0484) 518803)

HILL, David Roderick; s of Desmond D'Artrey Hill, of Beaconsfield, Bucks, and Margaret Angela Ellis, *née* Hughes; *b* 28 Feb 1952; *Educ* Merchant Taylors; *m* 6 April 1988, Jane Frances, da of Jack Collins, of Canterbury, Kent; *Career* violin maker; Freeman: City of London, Worshipful Co of Musicians 1973-; *Recreations* fishing, shooting, art, music; *Style*— David Hill, Esq; Havenfields, Gt Missenden, Bucks HP16 9LS (☎ 02406 3655)

HILL, Duncan James Stanier; s of Maj Harold James Hill, of Cosford Grange, Shifnal, Shropshire, and Sheila, *née* Hughes; *b* 16 Mar 1956; *Educ* Shrewsbury, Magdalene Coll Cambridge (MA); *Career* md George Hill Industs Ltd 1987-; *Recreations* hunting, three day eventing; *Style*— Duncan Hill, Esq; 1 Bank Steps, Bridgnorth, Shropshire, (☎ 07462 2497); George Hill Industries Ltd, Halesfield 21, Telford, Shropshire, (☎ 0952 586460, fax 0952 581522, telex 35881 GRANGE)

HILL, Dame Elizabeth Mary; DBE (1976); *b* 24 Oct 1900; *Educ* Univ and King's Colls, London Univ, (BA, PhD, MA); *m* 1984, Stojan J Veljković; *Career* slavonic specialist Min of Info; univ lectr in slavonic 1936-48, prof of slavonic studies Univ of Cambridge 1948-68, Andrew Mellon prof of slavic languages and literatures Pittsburgh Univ 1968-70; fell UCL, Girton Coll Cambridge; Hon LittD East Anglia 1978; *Style*— Dame Elizabeth Hill, DBE; 10 Croft Gardens, Cambridge

HILL, Air Cmdt Dame Felicity Barbara; DBE (1966, OBE 1954); da of late Edwin Frederick Hill, and Frances Ada, *née* Cocke; *b* 12 Dec 1915; *Educ* St Margaret's Sch Folkestone; *Career* joined WAAF 1939, cmmnd 1940, Inspr of WRAF 1956-59, OC RAF Hawkinge 1959-60, OC RAF Spitalgate 1960-65, dir of the WRAF 1966-69; Hon ADC to the Queen 1966-69; *Clubs* RAF; *Style*— Air Cmdt Dame Felicity Hill, DBE; Worcester Cottage, Mews Lane, Winchester, Hants

HILL, George Raymond; s of George Mark, and Jill Hill; *b* 25 Sept 1925; *Educ* St Dunstan's Coll London; *m* 1948, Sophie, *née* Gibert; 2 da; *Career* Lt RM 1943-46; Distillers Co Ltd (Industl Gp) 1952-66, BP Chems Ltd 1967-69, chief exec Br Tport Hotels Ltd 1970-76 (chm 1974-76), dir Bass plc 1976-84 (memb exec ctee); chm: Bass UK Ltd 1978-80, Howard Machinery plc 1984-85, Channel Tunnel Nat Tourism Working Pty 1986-, Crest Hotels Investmt Ltd 1982-, Sims Catering plc 1984-87, Liquor Licensing Ctee (Br Tourist Authy); dir Chester Int Hotel plc 1987-, Ashford Int Hotel plc 1988-; memb Br Tourist Authy Bd 1982-; FCA, FCIT, FHCIMA, FRSA 1980; *Recreations* music, theatre, works of art, country life; *Clubs* RAC; *Style*— George Hill, Esq; 23 Sheffield Terrace, W8 (☎ 01 727 3986); The Paddocks, Chedworth, Gloucestershire

HILL, Graham Starforth; s of Capt Harold Victor John Hill (d 1955), of Alresford, Hants; *b* 22 June 1927; *Educ* Dragon Sch Oxford, Winchester, St John's Coll Oxford; *m* 1952 (m dis), Margaret Elise, da of Charles Ambler (d 1952), of Itchen Abbas, Hants; 1 s, 1 da; *Career* Flying Offr RAF Fighter Cmd UK 1948-50; barr Gray's Inn 1951, crown counsel Colonial Legal Serv Singapore 1953-56,;slr 1961, ptnr (later sr ptnr) Rodyk and Davidson Advocates and Slrs Singapore 1957-76; chm Guinness Mahon & Co Ltd 1979-83 (dir 1977-79); conslt to: Frere Cholmeley 1984, Rodyk & Davidson (Singapore) 1985-; pres Law Soc of Singapore 1970-74; chm London City Ballet Tst 1981-82; tstee: Southwark Cathedral Devpt Tst Fund 1980-84, Royal Opera House Tst 1982-85; Cavaliere della Solidarieta 1975, Commendatore al Merito 1977-; memb cncl Royal Opera House; *Recreations* music, Italy; *Clubs* Garrick, Turf (Singapore), Costa Smeralda YC (Italy); *Style*— Graham Hill, Esq; 10 St Thomas St, Winchester, Hants SO23 9HE (☎ 0962 54146); Casa Claudia, 07020 Porto Cervo, Italy (☎ 0789 92317)

HILL, Gregory John Summers; s of Frederick John Hill (d 1987), and Margaret May, *née* Greenwood ; *b* 5 May 1949; *Educ* Weston-super-Mare GS for Boys, Exeter Coll Oxford (MA, BCL); *m* 10 Sept 1977, Anne Gillian, da of William Spencer Barrett of Clifton, Bristol; 1 s (Richard b 1982), 1 da (Alison b 1985); *Career* barr Lincoln's Inn 1972, practising barr 1973-; *Books* Securities for Advances: Encyclopaedia of Banking Law (jtly 1982-) (jtly 1982-); *Style*— Gregory Hill, Esq; 17 Old Buildings, Lincoln's Inn, London WC2A 3UP (☎ 01 405 9653, fax 01 405 5032)

HILL, Harold James; s of Arthur Frederick Hill (d 1952); *b* 18 May 1920; *Educ* Wolverhampton GS; *m* 1949, Sheila Gwendolen, da of Hughes Alfred Thomas (d 1966); 2 children; *Career* chm George Hill Industs Ltd, dir Beacon Broadcasting Ltd; *Style*— H James Hill, Esq; Cosford Grange, Shifnal, Shrops (☎ 090 722 2501); George Hill Industries Ltd, Halesfield 21, Telford, Shropshire TF7 4PA (☎ 0952 588088, fax 0952 581522, telex 35881)

HILL, Ian Frederick Donald; JP (1978); s of Frederick Donald Banks Hill (d 1952); *b* 14 May 1928; *Educ* Shrewsbury; *m* 1955, Marlene Elizabeth, da of Norman Vincent Rushton (d 1971); 2 children; *Career* ptnr Arthur Young and Co 1958-88, chm Kwik Save Group plc 1973-, dir Park Food Gp plc 1983-; FCA, CBIM; *Recreations* golf; *Clubs* Royal Birkdale Golf; *Style*— Ian Hill Esq, JP; 22 Hastings Rd, Southport, Merseyside PR8 2LW (☎ 0704 68398)

HILL, His Hon Judge Ian Starforth; QC (1969); s of Capt Harold Victor John Hill (d 1967), and Helen Dora, *née* Starforth; *b* 30 Sept 1921; *Educ* Dragon Sch, Shrewsbury, Brasenose Coll Oxford (MA); *m* 1, 1950 (m dis), Bridget Mary Footner; 1 s (David b 1951), 2 da (Jane b 1953, Juliet b 1956); m 2, 1982, Greta Grimshaw; m 3, Wendy Elizabeth Stavert; *Career* Capt Indian Army 1940-45, India, Africa, Italy (despatches); dep chm IOW Quarter Sessions 1968-71, rec Crown Ct 1972-74, memb Parole Bd 1983-84; *Recreations* gardening, games, amateur theatre; *Clubs* Hampshire; *Style*— His Hon Judge Ian Hill, QC; Tulls Hill, Preston, Candover, Hants RG25 2EW

HILL, (Stanley) James Allen; MP (C) Southampton Test 1979-; s of James Hill and Mrs Florence Cynthia Hill, of Southampton; *b* 21 Dec 1926; *Educ* Regent's Park Sch, North Wales Naval Coll, Southampton Univ; *m* 1958, Ruby Evelyn, da of Ross Albert Ralph of Clanfield Farm, Basingstoke; 2 s, 3 da; *Career* Royal Fleet Aux 1941-46, served 11 yrs on BOAC flying staff, sr ptnr firm of Estate Agents; memb: UN Assoc, Southampton City Cncl 1966-; MP (C) Southampton Test 1970-Oct 1974, sec Cons backbench ctee on housing and construction 1971-73, memb select ctee on expenditure 1972-73, UK memb Euro Parl Strasbourg 1972-75 (chm regnl policy and tport ctee 1973-75, govt whip to Cncl of Europe and WEU), memb select ctees: Europ Legislation 1979-83, Industry and Trade 1979-83;; *Clubs* St Stephen's Constitutional, Carlton; *Style*— James Hill, Esq, MP; c/o House of Commons, London SW1, Gunfield Lodge, Melchet Pk, Plaitford, Hants

HILL, Sir James Frederick; 4 Bt (UK 1916), of Bradford; s of Sir James Hill, 3 Bt (d 1976); *b* 5 Dec 1943; *Educ* Wrekin Coll Bradford Univ; *m* 1966, Sandra Elizabeth, da of J C Ingram, of Ilkley; 1 s, 3 da; *Heir* s, James Laurence Ingram Hill b 22 Sept 1973; *Career* exec chm Sir James Hill and Sons Ltd; dir: Yorks Bldg Soc, Br Rail Eastern Region; *Recreations* tennis, golf; *Clubs* RAC, Bradford, Ilkley; *Style*— Sir James Hill, Bt; Roseville, Moor Lane, Menston, Ilkley, W Yorks LS29 6AP (☎ 0943 74624); Sir James Hill and Sons Ltd, Melbourne Mills, Dalton Lane, Keighley, W Yorks BD21 4LQ (☎ 0535 662831, telex 51105)

HILL, Jeremy Adrian; s of Lt-Col Cecil Vivian Hill (d 1978); *b* 16 Jan 1940; *Educ* Eton, Ch Ch Oxford; *m* 1965, Virginia Ann, da of Maj Gordon Darwin Wilmot; 3 s; *Career* dir: J Henry Schroder Wagg and Co, Korea Europe Fund plc; *Recreations* tennis, shooting; *Style*— Jeremy Hill, Esq; Peyton Hall, Bures, Suffolk; J Henry Schroder Wagg and Co Ltd, 120 Cheapside, London EC2V 6DS (☎ 01 382 6000, telex 885029)

HILL, Hon John; s of Baron Hill of Luton, PC (Life Peer); *b* 29 June 1945; *Educ* Epsom Coll, Cambridge Univ (MA), Univ of NSW; *m* 1974, Dawn Kay, da of Ian Hamilton Lance, of West Pennant Hills, NSW Aust; 2 s (Simon b 1975, Charles b 1977), 1 da (Melanie b 1979); *Career* system studies offr Aust Safeguards Office 1981-; *Recreations* amateur theatre; *Clubs* Sydney Journalists; *Style*— The Hon John Hill; 1 Oatley Park Ave, Oatley, NSW 2223 (☎ 02 570 6052; Australian Safeguards Office, PO Box KX 261, Kings Cross, NSW 2011 (☎ 02 358 6255)

HILL, John Andrew Patrick; CBE (1978); s of Henry Wilfred Hill and Beatrice Rose, *née* Smith; *b* 8 Feb 1936; *Educ* Ealing Tech Coll, MECAS; *m* 1960, Barbara Anne, da of Maj Frederick Joseph Knifton (d 1965); 2 s (Andrew, Timothy), 1 da (Philippa); *Career* served RAF 1954-56; banker; Br Bank of the ME 1956-78, asst gen mangr Hongkong and Shanghai Banking Corpn Hong Kong 1979-82, chief exec offr The Hongkong and Shanghai Banking Corpn Singapore 1982-; chm: Hongkong Bank Tstee (Singapore) Ltd, Wayfoong Mortgage and Fin (S) Ltd, advsy bd Salvation Army Singapore; dep chm Commercial Discount Co Ltd; dir:Banking Computer Services Pte Ltd, Concord Leasing (Asia) Pte Ltd, Hotel Marco Polo Singapore, Ocean Properties Pte Ltd, Reinsurance Mgmnt Corpn of Asia Pte Ltd, Rediffusion (Singapore) Pt Ltd; memb: NZ Insur Co, investmt advsy ctee Singapore C of C; govr Utd World Coll of South East Asia; memb Lloyds; FInstD; *Recreations* organ playing, travel, photography, fishing; *Clubs* Oriental, Hongkong, Royal Coll of Organists; *Style*— John Hill Esq, CBE; Hawkwood Manor, Sible Hedingham, Essex; The Hongkong and Shanghai Banking Corporation, Ocean Building, 10 Collyer Quay, Singapore (☎ 224 41272, telex RS 21258 HSBC)

HILL, John Edward Bernard; s of Capt Robert William Hill (ka 1917), and Majorie Jane Lloyd-Jones, *née* Scott-Miller (d 1981); *b* 13 Nov 1912; *Educ* Charterhouse, Merton Coll Oxford (MA); *m* 7 July 1944, Edith wid Cdr RAE Luard, RNVR, and da of John Maxwell (d 1940), of Cove, Dumbartonshire; 1 da adopted (Linda (Mrs KRB Jackson) b 7 March 1943); *Career* cmmnd RA (TA) 1938, air observation post Pilot RA WO 1942 (wounded Tunisia 1943), specially employed WO 1944, invalided out 1945; barr Inner Temple 1938, farmer in Suffolk 1946-; memb CLA exec 1957-59 and 1977-82; MP (C) South Norfolk 1955-74, govt whip and lord cmmr of Treasy 1959-64, memb Cncl of Europe and WEU 1970-72, MEP 1973-74; memb: E Suffolk and Suffolk Rivers Bd 1952-62, governing body Charterhouse Sch, exec ctee GBA 1966-83, govr Suttons Hosp in Charterhouse 1966-, cncl UEA 1975-82; *Clubs* Garrick, Farmers; *Style*— JEB Hill, Esq; Watermill Farm, Wenhaston, Halesworth, Suffolk IP19 9BY, (☎ 050 270 207)

HILL, Sir John Maxwell; CBE (1969), DFC (1945), QPM; s of late L S M Hill, of Plymouth; *b* 25 Mar 1914; *Educ* Plymouth Coll; *m* 1939, Marjorie Louisa Reynolds; 1 s, 1 da; *Career* served WW II Flying Offr Bomber Cmd RAFVR; HM Inspector of Constabulary 1965-66; asst cmmr: admin and ops 1966-68, personnel and trg Met Police 1968-71; dep cmmr 1971-72, chief inspr of Constabulary Home Office 1972-75; *Recreations* golf, walking; *Clubs* RAC, RAF; *Style*— Sir John Hill, CBE, DFC, QPM; 23 Beacon Way, Banstead, Surrey (☎ 073 73 52771)

HILL, Sir John McGregor; s of John Campbell Hill (d 1982); *b* 21 Feb 1921; *Educ* King's Coll London, St John's Coll Cambridge; *m* 1947, Nora Eileen, *née* Hellett; 2 s, 1 da; *Career* Fl Lt RAF 1941; UKAEA: joined 1950, memb prodn 1964-67, chm 1967-81; memb: advsy cncl on Technol 1968-70, Nuclear Power Advsy Bd 1973-81, Energy Cmmn 1977-79; chm: Br Nuclear Fuels Ltd 1971-83 (hon pres 1983-86), Amersham Int plc 1975-88, Aurora Hldgs 1984-88, Rea Bros Ltd 1987-; FRS, FInstP, FIChemE, FInstE, FEng; Chevalier de la Légion d'Honneur; kt 1969; *Recreations* golf, gardening; *Clubs* East India; *Style—* Sir John Hill; Dominic House, Sudbrook Lane, Richmond, Surrey TW10 7AT (☎ 01 940 7221)

HILL, John Michael; s of Stanley Hill, of Oxshott, Surrey, and Ellen May, *née* Rose; *b* 28 August 1944; *Educ* St Dunstans Coll Catford, Jesus Coll Cambridge (MA); *m* 25 Jan 1973, (Jean) Shirley, da of Van Jakub Spyra (d 1979) of Cheadle; 1 s (Jeffrey), 1 da (Nicola); *Career* R Watson & Sons Consulting Actuaries 1970-74 (ptnr 1974) FIA 1971, FPMI 1981; *Recreations* music, keeping fit; *Style—* John Hill, Esq; 4 Underhill Park Rd, Reigate, Surrey RH2 9LX (☎ 0737 249 473); R Watson & Sons, Watson House, Reigate, Surrey RH2 9PQ (☎ 0737 241 144, fax 0737 241 496, telex 946070)

HILL, Julian; s of Harold Brian Cunningham Hill (d 1980), and Elise Magdalen, *née* Jeppe (d 1971); *b* 9 August 1932; *Educ* Eastbourne Coll; *m* 20 March 1956, (Ruth) Monica, da of late Paul Sekvens Toll, of 10 Villagatan, Stockholm; 2 s (Rowland b 1956, Michael b 1960), 1 da (Anne-Louise b 1963); *Career* Nat Serv 2 Lt 22 Cheshire Regt 1952-54; dir various cos operating UK and overseas for Unilever 1954-77, chm and md Scanhill Ltd & Julian Hill Ltd 1977-; commercial advsr UN 1977-; Freeman City of London 1982, Liveryman Worshipful Co of Marketors 1984; FBIM, MInstM; *Recreations* sailing, skiing, cricket, opera; *Clubs* MCC, Naval & Military; *Style—* Julian Hill, Esq; Huntsland Cottage, Huntsland Lane, Crawley Down, Sussex RH10 4HB (☎ 0342 712 286); Julian Hill Ltd, 26 Wilfred St, Westminster, London SW1E 6PL (☎ 01 828 7494, fax 01 630 9256, telex 8950933 TEAPOT)

HILL, Kenneth George; s of George Bertram Hill (d 1982), and Ethel Dora, *née* Gibbs; *b* 11 June 1932; *m* 20 April 1968, Diana Sylvia Mary, da of Richard Harold Piper, TD (d 1977), of Weir Courtney, Lingfield, Surrey; 1 da (Sophie Diana Alexandra b 11 Feb 1969); *Career* King's Troop RHA 1950-52; Mullens and Co Stockbrokers 1952-86, Bank of England 1986-87; hon tres E Sussex branch of Distressed Gentlefolks Aid Assoc, The Old Surrey & Burstow Foxhounds; ctee memb Sussex Co Playing Field Assoc, govr Moira House Sch Eastbourne; Freeman Worshipful Co of Loriners; *Recreations* country sports; *Style—* Kenneth Hill, Esq; Ducklys Holt, West Hoathly, Sussex

HILL, Lewis; s of Maurice Hill (d 1942), and Nettie, *née* Friedberg; *b* 19 July 1915; *Educ* St Pauls; *m* 28 Aug 1955, Caryll Edwina, da of Leonard Samuel Davis-Marks (d 1980); 2 da (Lesley Jane, Stephanie Lynn); *Career* cmmnd RASC 1940, served 8 Army Western Desert, Capt 1942, Maj 1944, served 21 Army Gp in invasion of Europe, OC Amphibious Unit Force 135; chm and md: L Hill (Veneers) Ltd, L Hill (Plastics) Ltd, Dykes & Co Ltd; Furniture Trade Benevolent Assoc (FTBA): pres London area 1967, nat pres 1979, chm exec ctee 1983-86, hon vice pres and tstee 1986; Freeman: City of London 1953, Worshipful Co of Furniture Makers 1953 (Liveryman 1979); *Recreations* travel, bridge, sport; *Style—* Lewis Hill, Esq; 85 Brunner Rd, London E1Y 7NW (☎ 01 521 8801, fax 01 521 7809, telex 8951263)

HILL, Lady; Lorna; da of J F Wheelan and B E Wheelan; *b* 1 Mar 1925; *Educ* Aberdeen Univ (MB, ChB, MD, DPM, FRCPsych); *m* 1962, as his 2 w, Prof Sir (John) Denis Nelson Hill, MB, BS, FRCP, FRCPsych, DPM (d 1982), s of Col Hill, Orleton Manor, Salop; Prof Psychiatry London Univ Inst of Psychiatry 1966-79; 1 s (Richard b 1963), 1 da (Annabel b 1968); *Career* conslt psychiatrist Kings Coll Hospital 1958-, hon conslt Maudsley Hosp; *Recreations* reading, painting, walking; *Style—* Lady Hill; Orleton Manor, nr Ludlow, Salop; 71 Cottenham Park Rd, Wimbledon, London SW20 0DR (☎ 01 946 6663); Kings Coll Hospital, Denmark Hill, London SE5

HILL, Marcus Tufton; s of Lt-Col the Hon George Chenevix Hill (d 1963; bro of 6 Baron Sandys) and Hon Patricia, *née* Tufton (d 1979), da of 2 Baron Hothfield by 1 w, Lady Irene, *née* Hastings (da of 13 Earl of Huntingdon); hp of cous, 7 Baron Sandys; *b* 13 Mar 1931; *Educ* Eton, St John's Coll Cambridge; *m* 1980, as her 2 husb, Margaret, da of late Maj G L St Aubrey Davies; *Career* commercial pilot; *Style—* Marcus Hill, Esq; More House, More, Bishop's Castle, Shropshire SY9 5HH

HILL, Marjory, Lady; Marjory; JP; da of late Frank Croft, of Brocka, Lindale, Grange-over-Sands; *m* 1930, Sir James Hill, 3 Bt (d 1976); *Style—* Marjory, Lady Hill; Brea House, Trebetherick, Wadebridge, Cornwall

HILL, Michael William; s of Geoffrey William Hill (d 1961), of Cadewell Park, Torquay, and Dorothy, *née* Ursell (d 1973); *b* 27 July 1928; *Educ* King Henry VIII Sch Coventry, Nottingham HS, Lincoln Coll Oxford (MA, BSc); *m* 1, 1957, Elma Jack, *née* Forrest (d 1967); 1 s (Alastair Geoffrey Frank b 1961), 1 da (Sally Ann b 1959); m 2, 1969, Barbara Joy, *née* Youngman; *Career* Sgt/instr RAEC 1947-49; res scientist Laporte Chems Ltd 1953-56, res and prodn mangr Morgan Crucible Gp 1956-64, asst keeper Br Museum 1964-68; dir: Nat Reference Library of Sci and Invention 1968-73, Sci Reference Library Br Library 1973-86; assoc dir sci technol and industry Br Library 1986-88, jt series ed Butterworths Guides to Info Sources; UK del to CEC Working Parties on Patents and on Info for Indust 1973-78; memb UK Chemical Info Serv Bd 1974-77, advsy ctee for Scottish Sci Reference Library 1983-88, vice pres Int Assoc of Technol Univ Libraries 1976-81; chm: ASLIB cncl 1979-81, Circle of State Librarians 1977-79, pres Int Fedn for Infro and Documentation 1984-; FRSA, MRSC, FIInfSci; *Books* Patent Documentation (with Wittmann and Schiffels, 1975), Michael Hill on Science Invention and Information (1988); *Clubs* United Oxford & Cambridge; *Style—* Michael Hill, Esq; Jesters, 137 Burdon La, Cheam, Surrey SM2 7DB (☎ 01 642 2418)

HILL, Reginald John Tower; er s of Lt-Col Francis Tower Hill (d 1974), of Holfield Grange, Essex, and Judith Mary, *née* Newall (d 1986); gs of Reginald Duke Hill, JP, DL (d 1922), who acquired Holfield Grange through his marriage to Flora, *née* Tower, widow of Osgood Beauchamp Hanbury (d 1889), whose family had owned it since the 18 century (*see* Burke's Landed Gentry, 18 edn, Vol I, 1965); *b* 25 Jan 1925; *Educ* Harrow; *m* 1, 30 April 1953, Anne Horsman (d 1980), da of Maj Vivian Horsman Bailey, MC, of Collyweston Manor, Stamford, Lincs; 1 s (Christopher Francis Edward b 12 May 1955), 1 da (Caroline Anne (Mrs Everard) b 19 March 1957); m 2, 25 Sept 1985, Jennifer Ann, da of Cdr E J Tamlyn, RN, and widow of William R C Quilter; *Career* Lt The Rifle Bde 1943-48; landowner and farmer; past ctee memb: Parish Cncl, PCC, Essex Club, E Essex Hunt Club, E Anglian Friesian Breeders Club; Jockey Club Point-to-Point Course Inspector 1956-; *Recreations* shooting, fishing, racing; *Clubs* Cavalry and Guards'; *Style—* Reginald Hill, Esq; Holfield Grange, Coggeshall, Essex (☎ 0376 61409)

HILL, Sir Richard George Rowley; 10 Bt (I 1779) of Brook Hall, Londonderry; MBE (1974); s of Sir George Alfred Rowley Hill, 9 Bt (d 1985); *b* 18 Dec 1925; *Educ* Clayesmore Sch, Glasgow Univ; *m* 1, 1954, Angela Mary (d 1974), da of Lt-Col Stanley Herbert Gallon (d 1986), of Berwick-on-Tweed; m 2, 1975 (m dis 1985), Zoreen Joy MacPherson, da of late Norman Warburton Tippett, of Kirkland, Berwick-on-Tweed, and widow of Andrew David Wilson Marshall, KOSB; 2 da; m 3, 1986, Elizabeth Margaret, *née* Tarbitt, widow of Laurence Sage, RNVR/FAA; *Career* Maj KOSB (ret); *Style—* Sir Richard Hill Esq, Bt, MBE; 21 Station Approach, Great Missenden, Bucks HP16 9AZ (☎ 02406 5536)

HILL, Rear Adm (John) Richard; s of Stanley Hill (d 1963), of Standlake, Oxon, and May, *née* Henshaw (d 1969); *b* 25 Mar 1929; *Educ* RNC Dartmouth, King's Coll London; *m* 21 July 1956, Patricia Anne, da of (Leslie) Edward Sales, of Upwey, Dorset; 1 s (Nigel b 1959), 2 da (Anna b 1960, Penelope b 1960); *Career* Naval Offr (Navigation Specialist) HM ships to 1962, MOD, Flag Offr Admty Interview Bd 1981-83, ret 1983; under tresr The Hon Soc of The Middle Temple 1983-; ed The Naval Review 1983-; *Books* The Royal Navy Today and Tomorrow (1981), Anti-Submarine Warfare (1984), British Seapower in the 1980s (1985), Maritime Strategy for Medium Powers (1986), Air Defence at Sea (1988); Arms Control at Sea 1988, articles incl: Survival, Navy Int, Naval Forces, NATO's 16 Nations, Brassey's Annual, Defence and Diplomacy, World Survey, The Naval Review; *Recreations* amateur theatre, crumbly cricket; *Clubs* Royal Cwlth Soc; *Style—* Rear Adm Richard Hill; Cornhill House, Bishop's Waltham, Southampton, Hants; Carpmael Building, Temple, London EC4Y 9AT; Treasury Office, Middle Temple, London EC4Y AT (☎ 01 353 4355, fax 01 583 3220)

HILL, Richard Kenneth; TD (1972); s of Lt Col Peter Kenneth Hill, TD (d 1988), of 248 Thorpe Rd, Longthorpe, Peterborough, and Sylvia Mary Jephson, *née* Widdowson; *b* 20 April 1941; *Educ* Oakham Sch; *m* 29 April 1967, Pip Mary, da of Bernard Shiptman, of Belton, nr Grantham, Lincolnshire; 1 s (Timothy Kenneth b 6 Sept 1969), 1 da (Zoë Louise b 31 Dec 1971); *Career* TA Served: 8 Bn Sherwood Foresters, 5/8 Bn Sherwood Foresters, 4/5 Bn Northamptonshire Regt, 5 (volunteer) Bn Royal Anglican Regt, Major 1970 served as OC HQ at Peterborough; slr 1964, sr ptnr Wyman & Abbott Peterborough; fndr vice pres of Rotary Club of the Ortons, chm Cambridgeshire TAVR Assoc, pres Peterborough branch of Northants Regtl Comrades Assoc; memb Law Soc; *Recreations* gardening, field sports; *Clubs* Royal Overseas League; *Style—* Richard Hill, Esq, TD; Cherry Orton Farm, Orton Waterville, Peterborough (☎ 0733 231495); 35 Priestgate, Peterborough PE1 1JR (☎ 0733 64131)

HILL, Hon Robert; s of Baron Hill of Luton, PC (Life Peer); *b* 1938; *Educ* Epsom Coll, Harper Adams Agric Coll; *m* 1960, Ann, da of E Williamson, of Southampton; issue; *Career* agric; gp sec NFU; *Style—* The Hon Robert Hill; 33 Meadow View, Dunvant, Swansea, W Glam SA2 7UZ

HILL, (Arthur) Robin Ian; s of late Capt Lord (Arthur) Francis Hill, Greys Reserve (yr s of late 6 Marq of Downshire) and hp of unc, 7 Marquess; *b* 10 May 1929; *Educ* Eton; *m* 1957, Hon Juliet Mary, *see* Hon Mrs Hill (d 1986); 2 s (Nicholas b 1959, Anthony b 1961), 1 da (Georgina b 1964); *Career* 2 Lt Royal Scots Greys; CA; *Recreations* tennis, golf, shooting; *Clubs* White's; *Style—* Robin Hill Esq; Clifton Castle, Ripon, N Yorks (☎ 0765 89326); 60 Cheniston Gdns, London W8 (☎ 01 937 5978)

HILL, Col (Edward) Roderick; DSO (1944), JP (1955); s of Capt Roderick Tickell Hill, RA (d 1907), and Gwendolene, *née* Lewis (d 1954); *b* 9 June 1904; *Educ* Winchester, Magdalen Coll Oxford (MA); *m* 10 April 1934, Rachel, da of Ellis Hicks Beach (d 1943), of Witcombe Park, North Gloucester; 1 s (Michael), 1 da (Caroline); *Career* cmmnd Coldstream Gds 1926, Col 1952, ret; High Sheriff of Monmonthshire 1956 (DL, Vice Lt and Lt 1964-74), Ld-Lt Gwent 1974-79; KStJ 1969; Dutch Order of Orange Nassau 1945; *Clubs* Cavalry and Guards; *Style—* Col Roderick Hill, DSO, JP; Manor Farm Cottage, Stamford in the Vale, Faringdon, Oxon (☎ 0367 8926)

HILL, Rosalind Margaret; da of Brian Percival Hill, and Joan Barbara Warren, *née* Rollinson; *b* 18 April 1955; *Educ* St Margaret's Convent Sussex, Univ of Exeter (BA); *Career* Ernst & Whinney 1977, J Henry Schroder Wagg & Co Limited 1986, dir corporate fin P & P plc 1988-; memb Home Farm Tst; ACA 1981; *Recreations* skiing, riding, the arts; *Style—* Miss Rosalind Hill; Hamilton House, 1 Temple Ave, London EC4Y OHA ☎ (01 3534212, fax 01 353 2105, tlx 926604)

HILL, Hon Mrs (Rosamund Shirley); da of Baron Crowther-Hunt (Life Peer); *b* 1950; *m* 1978, John Christopher Hill; issue; *Style—* Hon Mrs Hill; 104 Ridgeway, Weston Favell, Northampton

HILL, Roy Thomas; s of John Thomas Hill DSM (d 1977), of Bury St Edmunds, Suffolk, and Lucy Clara; *b* 4 Jan 1935; *Educ* Culford Sch Suffolk; *m* 12 March 1963, Ann Elizabeth, da of Arthur Chambers, 1 s (Stephen b 1964), 2 da (Sharon b 1967, Paul b 1970); *Career* United Dominions Tst plc, Credit Investigators 1959-66, R T Hill and Co CAs 1966-67, sr ptnr Clayton and Brewill CAs 1967-; chm Bridgeway Fin Ltd, Argonaut Securities Ltd, W Bridgford 41 Club; fin dir S Notts Trg Agency Ltd, tres 3 W Bridgford Friary Scout Gp; FCA 1958, FCMA 1961; *Recreations* golf, 1/2 marathon running; *Clubs* 41, Ruddington Graner GC; *Style—* Roy Hill, Esq; Bridgeway House, 308 Loughborough Rd, W Bridgford, Nottingham (☎ 0602 503044); Cawley House, 149-153 Canal St, Nottingham (☎ 0602 503044)

HILL, Stanley Arthur; s of John Henry Hill (d 1976), and Edith Muriel, *née* Matthews (d 1985); *b* 22 May 1935; *Educ* Townsend C of E St Albans; *m* 9 July 1960, Elizabeth Scott (Betty), da of James McKay, of Forsyte Shades, Canford Cliffs, Poole, Dorset; 2 da (Elizabeth Scott b 19 Feb 1962, Catherine McKay b 11 Nov 1964); *Career* Nat Serv RMP 1953-55, served M East; md: Coopers Hldgs Ltd, Coopers Metal Hldgs Ltd, Coopers (Metals) Ltd, United Ferrous Supplies, Marple & Gillott Ltd, Coopers Wednesbury; Swindon Car and Commercials, Gloucs Steel Stock, dir: Coopers Non Ferrous Ltd, Cooper Barnes Metal Ltd, Norton Barrow Hldgs Ltd, Norton Barrow Metals Ltd, Coopers Robinson Metals Ltd, Cooper Friswell Ltd; bd memb nat cncl Br Scrap Fedn, memb ctee Mid-West Scrap Assoc, chm Br Scrap Fedn Exporters Ctee, Bp vice-pres BIR Ctee; ctee memb: 1986 Indust Year, Lechlade Soc; capt Burford GC 1973-74; MIOD 1967-; *Recreations* cricket, golf; *Clubs* Burford GC, Parkstone GC, Swindon GC; *Style—* Stanley Hill, Esq; The Butts, Bryworth Lane, Lechlade,

Gloucestershire (☎ 0367 52598); Bridge House, Gipsy Lane, Swindon, Wilts SN2 6DZ (☎ 0793 32111, fax 0793 614 214, car tel 0836 597 483, telex 44251)

HILL, Stephen; s of Vincent Wolstenholme Hill (d 1959), of Edenfield, Lancs, and Ruth Emily Hill; *b* 27 Oct 1937; *Educ* Bury GS; *m* 21 Sept 1963, Elaine Margaret, da of Horace Sheldon (d 1979), of Tottington; 1 s (Richard b 1972), 2 da (Alison b 1965, Elizabeth b 1968); *Career* ptnr Grundy Middleton & Co CAs 1963-69; ptnr Hill Eckersley & Co 1969-; govr Bury GS, former memb Radcliffe Round Table-; FCA 1960; *Recreations* golf, walking, skiing, working; *Clubs* Bury GSOB, Rossendale GC; *Style—* Stephen Hill, Esq; Wyvern, 935 Walmersley Rd, Bury, Lancs BL9 5LL (☎ 061 764 5931); Hill Eckersley & Co, Chartered Accountants, 62 Chorley New Rd, Bolton BL1 4BY (☎ 0204 22113)

HILL, Hon Mrs (Wendy Helen); *née* Fitzherbert; yst da of 14 Baron Stafford (d 1986), and Morag Nada, The Lady Stafford, *née* Campbell; *b* 28 April 1961; *Educ* Convent of the Sacred Heart Woldingham; *m* 1983, Jeremy John Maurice Hill, eld s of Lt-Col Colin Hill (d 1985), of Coley Court, Coley, East Harptree, Bristol, 2 s (Thomas b 1985, Nicholas b 1987); *Recreations* skiing, tennis, swimming; *Style—* The Hon Mrs Hill; 66 Scarsdale Villas, London W8 6PP (☎ 01 937 6828)

HILL, Prof William George; s of William Hill (d 1984), of Hemel Hempstead, Herts, and Margaret Paterson, *née* Hamilton (d 1987); *b* 7 August 1940; *Educ* St Albans Sch, Wye Coll Univ of London (BSc), Univ of California Davis (MS), Iowa State Univ, Univ of Edinburgh (PhD, DSc); *m* 1 July 1971, (Christine) Rosemary, da of John Walter Austin, of Kingskerswell, Devon; 1 s (Alastair b 1977), 2 da (Louise b 1973, Rachel b 1974); *Career* prof of animal genetics Univ of Edinburgh 1983- (lectr 1965-74, reader 1974-83); visiting prof and visiting res assoc: Univ of Minnesota 1966, Iowa State Univ 1967-78, N Carolina State Univ 1979 and 1985; memb: Sci Study Gp Meat and Livestock Cmmn 1969-72, Directors Advsy Gp AFRC Animals Res Grant Bd 1986-, AFRC Animal Breeding Res Orgn 1983-87, AFRC Inst of Animal Physiology and Genetics Res 1987-; FRSE 1979, FRS 1985; *Books* Benchmark Papers on Quantitative Genetics (1984); *Recreations* farming, bridge; *Clubs* Farmers; *Style—* Prof William Hill; 4 Gordon Terr, Edinburgh EH16 5QH (☎ 031 667 3680); Institute of Animal Genetics, University of Edinburgh, West Mains Rd Edinburgh EH9 3JN (☎ 031 667 1081 extn 3505, fax 01 668 3861, telex 727 442)

HILL, Hon Mrs (Yvonne Aletta); da of late 2 Baron de Villiers; *b* 1913; *Educ* LMH Oxford; *m* 1939, James Kenneth Hill; 3 s, 1 da; *Style—* The Hon Mrs Hill; Edgehill, 22 Wynhdorn Ave, Buderim, Queensland, Australia

HILL OF LUTON, Baron (Life Peer UK 1963); Charles Hill; PC (1955); s of Charles Hill and Florence Cook, of London; *b* 15 Jan 1904; *Educ* St Olave's Sch, Trinity Coll Cambridge (LLD), London Hosp (MD, DPH); *m* 1931, Marion Spencer, da of M Wallace, of Halifax; 2 s, 3 da; *Career* sits as Independent peer in House of Lords; dep MOH Oxford, sec BMA 1944-50, MP (Lib and C) Luton 1950-63, PMG 1955-57, chllr Duchy Lancaster 1957-61, min Housing and Local Govt and Welsh Affrs 1961-62; chm: ITA 1963-67, govrs of BBC 1967-72, Abbey Nat Bldg Soc 1976-78; former pres World Medical Assoc; chm Chest, Heart and Stroke Assoc 1974-83, vice-pres 1983-; *Clubs* Reform; *Style—* The Rt Hon the Lord Hill of Luton, PC; 9 Borodale, Kirkwick Ave, Harpenden, Herts (☎ (058 27) 64288)

HILL-NORTON, Rear Adm the Hon Nicholas John; s of Baron Hill-Norton, GCB (Life Peer); *b* 1939; *Educ* Marlborough Coll, RNC Dartmouth; *m* 1966, Ann Jennifer, da of Vice-Adm Dennis Mason, CB, CVO; 2 s (Simon b 1967, Tom b 1975), 1 da (Claudia b 1969); *Career* RN, Capt HMS Invincible 1983-84, Flag Offr Gibraltar 1987; *Style—* Rear Admiral The Hon Nicholas Hill-Norton; Newton Valence, Hants

HILL-NORTON, Baron (Life Peer UK 1978); Peter John; GCB (1970, KCB 1967, CB 1964); s of Capt Martin John Norton (d 1928); *b* 8 Feb 1915; *Educ* RNCs Dartmouth and Greenwich; *m* 1936, Margaret, da of Carl Adolph Linstow (d 1947); 1 s, 1 da; *Career* Independent peer in House of Lords; RN 1932, served WW II Arctic Convoys and N W Approaches; Capt 1953, Rear Adm 1962, asst ch Naval Staff 1962-64, flag offr 2 in cmd Far East Fleet 1964-66, Vice Adm 1965, dep ch Defence Staff (Personnel and Logistics) 1966-67, Second Sea Lord 1967, vice ch Naval Staff 1967-68, Adm 1968, C-in-C UK Forces Far East 1969-70, ch Naval Staff and First Sea Lord 1970-71, Adm of the Fleet 1971, ch Defence Staff 1971-74, chm NATO Mil Ctee 1974-77; memb steering ctee for Volunteer Home Def Force 1983; pres Br Maritime League; vice-pres Royal United Services Inst; *Books* No Soft Options (1978), Sea Power (1982); *Recreations* gardening, shooting; *Clubs* Army and Navy, Royal Thames Yacht; *Style—* Adm of the Fleet the Rt Hon the Lord Hill-Norton, GCB; Cass Cottage, Hyde, Fordingbridge, Hants (☎ (0425) 52392)

HILL-SMITH, His Hon Judge Derek Edward; VRD; s of Charles George Hill-Smith (d 1942), and Ivy Down (d 1985); gf A R W Smith - entrepreneur and importer of silks and fine cloth from Far East last century; *b* 21 Oct 1922; *Educ* Sherborne, Trinity Coll Oxford; *m* 1950, Marjorie Joanna, da of His Hon Judge Montague L Berryman, QC (d 1974), of Essex; 1 s (Alexander b 1955), 1 da (Nicola b 1958); *Career* RNVR 1942-46, served in Atlantic 1942, cmmnd 1943, fighter direction offr 1943, attack on Tirpitz 1944, Normandy landings May 1944, FDO Flagship SE Asia, cmmnd 1945 Relief of Singapore, Lt-Cdr RNR; in business 1947-50, taught classics 1950-54; barr Inner Temple 1954; chm Kent Quarter Sessions 1970, recorder 1971; circuit judge 1972-87; *Recreations* theatre, tennis, sailing, painting, restoring Old Masters; *Clubs* Bar Yacht, Garrick; *Style—* His Hon Derek Hill-Smith; c/o National Westminster Bank, 7 North St, Bishops Stortford, Herts; Crown and County Courts in London and Home Counties

HILL-TREVOR, Hon Nevill Edward; JP (Berwyn Div 1971), DL (Denbighshire, now Clwyd 1965); s of 3 Baron Trevor (d 1950); *b* 1931; *m* 1963, Deborah, da of late W T B Jowitt, of Killinghall, Harrogate; 2 da; *Career* Flying Offr RAF (ret), ADC to C-in-C Fighter Cmd 1958-59, ADC to Chief of Air Staff 1959-61; High Sheriff Denbighshire 1965-66; joint master: Border Counties (NW) Otter Hounds 1950-59, Sir W W Wynn's Foxhounds 1970-78; *Style—* The Hon Nevill Hill-Trevor, JP, DL; Plas Lledrod, Llansilin, Clwyd

HILL-WOOD, Sir David Basil; 3 Bt (UK 1921); s of Sir Basil Samuel Hill Hill-Wood, 2 Bt (d 1954), by his w, *see* Hon Lady Hill-Wood; *b* 12 Nov 1926; *Educ* Eton; *m* 1970, Jennifer Anne McKenzie Stratmann (assumed surname, Stratmann, by deed poll 1960), da of Peter McKenzie Strang (Japanese POW, presumed d 1943); 2 s, 1 da; *Heir* s, Samuel Thomas Hill-Wood b 24 Aug 1971; *Career* Lt Grenadier Gds (Palestine) 1945-48; Morgan Grenfell 1948-55; ptnr Myers and Co stockbrokers 1955, sr ptnr 1971-74; dir: Capel Cure Myers 1974-77, Guinness Mahon and Co 1977-; High Sheriff Berks 1982-83; former pres Victoria FA (Aust), Aust rep on FA 1977;; *Recreations* tennis, farming; *Clubs* White's, Melbourne (Australia); *Style—* Sir David Hill-Wood, Bt; Dacre Farm, Farley Hill, Reading, Berks (☎ (0734) 733185); 58 Cathcart Rd, London SW10 (☎ 01 352 0389); Guinness Mahon and Co Ltd, 32 St Mary at Hill, London EC3P 3AJ (☎ 01 623 9333)

HILL-WOOD, Hon Lady - Hon Joan Louisa; *née* Brand; da of 3 Viscount Hampden, GCVO, KCB, CMG (d 1958); *b* 1904; *m* 1925, Capt Sir Basil Samuel Hill Hill-Wood, 2 Bt (d 1954); 1 s (David, 3 Bt *qv*), 1 da; *Style—* The Hon Lady Hill-Wood; Knipton Lodge, Grantham, Lincs (☎ (047 682) 226)

HILLABY, John; s of Albert Ewart Hillaby (d 1967), and Mabel, *née* Colyer (d 1977); *b* 24 July 1917; *Educ* Woodhouse Grove Sch Leeds Yorks; *m* 1, 1940 (m dis 1966), Eleanor, *née* Riley; 2 da (Susan b 1947, Felicity b 1949); m 2, 1966, Thelma, *née* Gordon (d 1972); m 3, 1981, Kathleen (formerly Mrs Burton); *Career* WWII RA Field Gunner 1939-44, served briefly in France; author, journalist, TV and radio presenter, long distance walker; local journalism up to 1939, magazine contrib and bdcaster 1944, zoological corr Manchester Guardian 1949, euro sci writer New York Times 1951-, biological conslt New Scientist 1953; former dir Univs Fedn for Animal Welfare, fndr pres Backpackers Club; travelled on foot through parts of: boreal Canada, Eastern USA, central and N Eastern Africa (incl Zaire, Ituri Forest and Mountains of the Moon Ruwenzoni), Sudan, Tanzania; three months foot safari with camels to Lake Rudolf; walked from; Lands End to John O'Groats, The Hague to Nice via the Alps, Provence to Tuscany, Athens to Mt Olympus via the Pindus Mountains; Woodward lectr Yale 1973; radio and TV series incl; Men of the North, Expedition South, Alpine Venture, Hillaby Walks, Globetrotter etc; fell Scientific Zoological Soc of London; *Books* Within The Streams (1949), Nature and Man (1960), Journey to the Jade Sea (1964), Journey Through Britain (1968), Journey Through Europe (1972), Journey Through Love (1976), Journey Home (1983), John Hillaby's Yorkshire (1986), John Hillaby's London (1987), Walking in Britain (1988); *Recreations* rectification of mis-spent youth by reading, slight academic instruction and observant travel; *Clubs* Savage; *Style—* John Hillaby, Esq; London & Yorks; c/o Constable Publisher, 10 Orange St, London WC2

HILLAND, Robert James McNally; s of Richard McNally Hilland (d 1978), of Scotland, and Grace McClymont, *née* Blackwell; *b* 31 July 1939; *Educ* Stranraer HS, Univ of Strathclyde (BA), Jordanhill Coll of Educn (DCE); *Career* merchant banker; dir: Charterhouse Devpt Capital Ltd 1985, Charterhouse Devpt Ltd 1985, Nat Commercial and Glyns Ltd 1986, Royal Bank Devpt Ltd 1986, Scottish Allied Investors Ltd 1982-, Kirkby Centl Gp Ltd 1984, NW Independent Hosps Ltd 1987, Dean Smith Garages Ltd 1987; memb Scottish Venture Capital Forum; *Recreations* shooting, fishing, golf, theatre; *Clubs* St James, Mere Golf Country; *Style—* Robert Hilland, Esq; 24 Heriot Row, Edinburgh EH3 6EN (☎ (031 225) 6699); Auchencloy Cottage, Stoneykirk, Stranraer, Wigtownshire (☎ 077682367); Charterhouse Capital Ltd, 26 St Andrews Square, Edinburgh EH2 1AF (☎031 556 2555, fax 031 557 2900, car 0836 605637)

HILLARY, Sir Edmund P; KBE (1953); s of Percival Augustus Hillary, of Remuera, Auckland, New Zealand; *b* 20 July 1919; *Educ* Auckland G S, Auckland Univ Coll; *m* 1953, Louise Mary Rose (d 1975); 1 s, 2 da (and 1 da decd); *Career* served WW II with RNZAF; explorer, author, lectr; memb: Br Mount Everest Expdn (reached summit with Sherpa Tensing) 1953, Cwlth Antarctic Expdn 1957-58; leader Himalayan Sch House Expdn 1963; pres NZ Voluntary Service Abroad; dir: Field Educn Enterprises of Australasia Pty Ltd; consult to Sears Roebuck and Co (USA); *Style—* Sir Edmund Hillary, KBE; 278a Remuera Rd, Auckland, New Zealand

HILLEARY, Hon Mrs (Fiona Mary); yst da of 3 Baron Burton, *qv*, and his 1 w, Elizabeth Ursula Forster, *née* Wise; *b* 31 Oct 1957; *Educ* West Heath Sevenoaks; *m* 1982, Alasdair Malcolm Douglas Macleod Hilleary, eldest s of Maj Ruaraidh Hilleary, of Logie Farm, Glen Ferness, Nairn, and Edinbaine, Isle of Skye; 2 da (Flora Elizabeth Macleod b 1985, Rosannagh Catriona b 1988); *Recreations* riding, stalking; *Style—* The Hon Mrs Hilleary; Fettes House, Redcastle, Muir of Ord, Ross-shire

HILLEARY, Hon Mrs (Grace Janet Mary); *née* Best; eldest da of 6 Baron Wynford, DSO (d 1940), and Hon Eva Napier, da of 2 Baron Napier of Magdala; *b* 27 August 1907; *m* 12 Nov 1930, Edward Kenneth Macleod Hilleary, MVO, 2 s of Maj Edward Langdale Hilleary, OBE, TD, DL; 3 da; *Style—* The Hon Mrs Hilleary; Nettlebed House, Droxford, Hants

HILLER, Robin John Cecil; s of Cecil Bernard Hiller (d 1966) and Esmé Leonora Patience Hiller, *née* Hughes; *b* 31 Oct 1933; *Educ* Epsom Coll; *m* 17 June 1961, Ann Margaret, da of Edwin Walter Booth, of Limpsfield, Oxted; 1 s (Mark Andrew Robin b 1962), 1 da (Alison Claire b 1963); *Career* Lt RNR Nat Serv; CA Annan Dexter to BDO Binder Hamlyn 1961-87; memb: Livery Co of Glovers, Royal Surgical Aid Soc, King Edward VII Fund grant ctee; Freeman Worshipful Co of Glovers;; *Recreations* charitable work, skiing, golf; *Clubs* Reform, City of London, Naval; *Style—* Robin John Cecil Hiller, Esq; Bydown, 73 Blue House Lane, Limpsfield, Oxted, Surrey RH8 OAP; H J Symons Investments and Services Ltd, 22 Alie Street, London E1 8DH

HILLER, Dame Wendy; DBE (1975, OBE 1971); da of Frank Watkin, and Marie Hiller; *b* 1912; *Educ* Winceby House Bexhill; *m* 1937, Ronald Gow; 1 s, 1 da; *Career* actress; plays inc: Love on the Dole (Garrick London and Shubert NY), Twelfth Night (war factory tour), Tess of the d'Urbervilles (Picadilly), The Heiress (Biltmore NY) 1948, Old Vic Season 1955-56, Aspern Papers (NY) 1962, The Wings of the Dove (Lyric) 1963, The Sacred Flame 1967, Crown Matrimonial (Haymarket); John Gabriel Baskman (National) 1975, The Importance of Being Earnest (Royalty) 1987, Driving Miss Daisy (Apollo) 1988; *films incl:* Pygmalion, Sons and Lovers, A Man for all Seasons, David Copperfield, Murder on the Orient Express, The Elephant Man; *Style—* Dame Wendy Hiller, DBE; c/o ICM, 388 Oxford St, London

HILLERY, Dr Patrick John; s of Dr Michael Joseph Hillery, and Ellen McMahon; *b* 2 May 1923; *Educ* Nat Sch Miltown Malbay, Rockwell Coll Cashel, UC Dublin (BSc, MB, BCh, BAO); *m* 1955, Mary Beatrice Finnegan (MD); 1 s (John), 1 da (Vivienne); *Career* worked in Gen Children's Tuberculosis and Psychiatric Hosp 1955-57 (memb Health Cncl), MO Miltown Malbay Dispensary Dist 1957-59, coroner for West Clare 1958-59, memb Dáil Éireann Clare 1951-73; min for: Educn 1959-65, Industry and Commerce 1965-66, Lab 1966-69, Foreign Affrs 1969-72; vice-pres Cmmn of the Euro Communities with special responsibility for Social Affrs 1973-76; pres Ireland 1976, re-elected 1983; memb Royal Irish Acady; LLD: Nat Univ of I, Univ of Dublin; Univ of melbourne; hon fell: RCSI RCSI (faculty of dentistry), All India Inst of Medical Sciences, RCPI, RCGP, PSI; hon life memb Irish Medical Assoc;; *Style—* Dr Patrick Hillery; Áras an Uachtaráin, Phoenix Park, Dublin 8

HILLHOUSE, (Robert) Russell; s of Robert Hillhouse, of Newton Mearns, Glasgow, and Jean Russell; *b* 23 April 1938; *Educ* Hutchesons' GS Glasgow, Glasgow Univ (MA); *m* 4 June 1966, Alison Janet, da of Barclay Stewart Fraser, of Edinburgh; 2 da (Catriona b 1967, Susanna b 1969); *Career* entered Home Civil Serv; so asst prine educn dept 1962, princ 1966, treasy 1971, asst sec 1974, home and health dept 1977, princ fin offr 1980, undersec educn dept 1985, sec educn dept 1987, perm under sec of state 1988;; *Recreations* making music; *Style*— Russell Hillhouse, Esq; c/o St Andrews house, Regent Rd, Edinburgh

HILLIARD, Spenser Rodney; s of Alfred Hilliard (d 1982), of 62 Water Lane, London, and Kathleen Claribelle Hilliard; *b* 14 Mar 1952; *Educ* City of London Sch, Queen Mary Coll, Univ of London (LLB), Inns of Cts School of Law; *Career* bar Middle Temple 1975, practising barr; memb Hon Soc of Middle Temple; *Recreations* wine; *Style*— Spenser Hilliard, Esq; Lamb Building, Temple, London EC4Y 7AS (☎ 01 353 0774, fax 01 353 0535, telex 265871 MONREF G INK 3025)

HILLINGDON, Baroness; Phoebe Maxwell; da of late Capt Mervyn James Hamilton, of Cornacassa, Monaghan, by his w, Hildred (da of Hon Bernard Ward, CB, 4 s of 3 Viscount Bangor); *b* 25 June 1918; *m* 1, Lt-Cdr John Sholto Fitzpatrick Cooke, CBE, RNVR; m 2, John Cooper; m 3, as his 2 wife, 4 Baron Hillingdon (d 1978); *Style*— The Rt Hon the Lady Hillingdon; Shalom Hall, Layer Breton, Colchester, Essex

HILLMAN, Arthur Joseph; MBE (1987), TD (1946), JP (1961); s of Arthur Lionel Hillman, JP (d 1958); *b* 21 Feb 1917; *Educ* Stonyhurst; *m* 1943, Marjorie Pamela, da of Howard Frederick Smith (d 1939); 5 children; *Career* serv WWII, France 1939-40, Middle East 1941-42, Maj; md Hillman Douglas Ltd 1934-69, chm Hillman Newby Ltd 1969-78, govr BUPA Ltd 1981-86; *Recreations* golf; *Clubs* Blackwell Golf; *Style*— Arthur Hillman Esq, MBE, TD, JP; Keys Cottage, Lower Bentley, Bromsgrove, Worcs

HILLMAN, Ellis Simon; s of David Hillman (d 1974) of, 91 Priory Rd, West Hampstead, London NW6, and Annie, *née* Roland (d 1967); *b* 17 Nov 1928; *Educ* York House Sch, Univ Coll Sch, Chelsea Coll of Science and Technol (BSc); *m* 10 Dec 1973, Louise, da of Jack Shalom (d 1980), of 9 Barlow Moor Court, Manchester; 1 s (Eli Yaakov b May 1974); *Career* ground wireless mechanic RAF 1947-49, instr Empire Radio Sch RAF Debden 1948-49; scientific tech offr: Soil Mechanics Ltd 1955, NCB field of investigation gp 1956-59, secondary sch teacher 1960-64, admin offr Architectural Assoc 1964-69, lectr Kilburn Poly 1969-70; NE London Poly: sr lectr 1970-73, princ lectr in environmental studies 1973-, (head of Int Off 1981-85); princ lectr Sch of Architecture, Sch of Ind Studies 1985-; elected to: LCC Norwood 1958, GLC, ILEA Hackney 1964-81; chm: London Subterranean Survey Assoc 1968-, GLC Arts and Recreation ctee 1977-81, Further and Higher Educn Ctee ILEA 1977-81, (vice chm 1980-81); cncllr Colindale Barnet 1986-, govr Imperial Coll of Science and Technol 1973-; memb: Lee Valley Regnl Park Authy 1973-81, sports cncl 1975-81, Water Space Amenity Cmmn 1977-80, Inland Waterways Amenity Advisy Cncl 1977-80; govr: Museum of London 1973-82, archaeology ctee Museum of London 1980-; pres Lewis Carroll Soc; FRSA; *Books* Essays in Local Government Enterprise (3 vols 1964-67), Towards a Wider Use (1976), London Under London (with John Murray 1985); *Style*— Ellis Hillman, Esq; 29 Haslemere Ave, London NW4 2PU (☎ 01 202 7792); North East London Poly (☎ 01 590 7722 ext 3239)

HILLMAN, Prof John Richard; s of Robert Hillman, 20 Beechwood Ave, Farnborough, Orpington, Kent, and Emily Irene Hillman; *b* 21 July 1944; *Educ* Chislehurst and Sidcup GS, University Coll of Wales (BSc, PhD); *m* 23 Sept 1967, Sandra Kathleen, da of George Palmer, 16 Alton Rd, Luton, Beds; 2 s (Robert George b 1968, Edmund John b 1969); *Career* Univ of Nottingham: asst lectr 1968-69, lectr 1969-71 of physiology and environmental studies; Univ of Glasgow: lectr botany 1971-77, sr lectr 1977-80, reader 1986-82, prof 1982-86; visiting prof: Univ of Dundee 1986-, Univ of Strathclyde 1986-, Univ of Edinburgh 1988-; dir Scottish Crop Res Inst 1986-; FIBiol, CBiol 1985, FLS 1982, FBIM 1987, FRSE 1985; *Books* ed: Isolation of Plant Growth Substances (1978), Biosynthesis and Metabolism of Plant Hormones (with A Crozier 1984), Biochemistry of Plant Cell Walls (with CT Brett 1985), papers in scientific journals and books on plant physiology and plant biochemistry; *Recreations* landscaping, building, renovations, horology, reading; *Clubs* Farmers; *Style*— Prof John Hillman; 11 The Logan, Liff, Dundee DD2 5PJ (☎ 0382 580 105); Scottish Crop Res Inst, Invergowrie, Dundee DD2 5DA (☎ 0382 562 731, fax 0382 562 426, telex 265871 MONREF G Quote Ref NQQOO3)

HILLS, Barrington William; s of William George (d 1967), of Upton on Severn Worcs, and Phyllis, *née* Biddle; *b* 2 April 1937; *Educ* Ribston Hall Gloucester, St Mary's Convent, Newmarket, Mr Whittaker's Worcester; *m* 1, 21 Nov 1959, (m dis 1977), Maureen, da of late Patrick Newson; 3 s (John b 1960, Michael b 1963, Richard b 1963); m2, 1 Sept 1977, Penelope Elizabeth May, da of John Richard Woodhouse, of Roehoe Lodge, Widmerpool, Notts 2 s (Charles b 1978, George b 1983); *Career* Nat Serv King's Troop RHA, racehorse trainer 1969-; won: Prix de L'Arc de Triomphe, Budweiser Irish Derby, 2000 Guineas Newmarket, 1000 Guineas Newmarket; second place Epsom Derby three times; held open day at Manton Stables for Charity 1987; *Recreations* hunting, shooting, golf; *Clubs* Turf; *Style*— Barrington W Hills, Esq; Manton House, Marlborough, Wilts SN8 1PN (☎ 0672 54871); BW Hills Southbank Ltd, Manton House Estate, Marlborough, Wilts SN8 1PN (☎ 0672 54901, fax 0672 54907, car telephone 0836 203 641, telex 44322)

HILLS, Hon Mrs (Brenda); *née* Stallard; da of Baron Stallard (Life Peer); *b* 1949; *m* 1972 (m dis 1987) Colin Hills, of Kentish Town, London; 2 da (Claire, Kerry); *Style*— The Hon Mrs Hills

HILLS, Air Vice-Marshal David Graeme Muspratt; CB (1985), OBE (1965); s of Arthur Ernest Hills (d 1958), of Frant Middleton-on-Sea Sussex and Muriel Steinman Fisher (d 1958); *b* 28 Feb 1925; *Educ* Epsom Coll, Middx Hosp Medical Sch (MB, BS), London Univ; *m* 1960, Hilary Enid Mary, da of The Rev Raymond Morgan Jones, of Pine Lodge Liss Forest Hants; 2 s (Nigel, Robin), 1 da (Julia); *Career* RAF Air Vice-Marshal Korea, Far East, ME, Germany; dep dir-gen RAF Med Servs 1979-83, Hon Surgn to HM 1981, dir-gen Med Policy and Plans 1983-85; CStJ 1980; QHS 1980-85; MFCM, DPH, AFOM; *Recreations* music, painting, gardening, golf; *Clubs* RAF, Royal St Georges; *Style*— Air Vice-Marshal David Hills, CB, OBE; Heather House, Lingfield, Surrey RH7 6EF

HILLS, David Henry; s of Henry Stanford Hills (d 1945), and Marjorie Vera Lily Constable; *b* 9 July 1933; *Educ* Varndean Sch Brighton; Univ of Nottingham (BA); *m* 1957, Jean Helen, *née* Nichols; 1 s (Simon b 1962); 2 da (Susan b 1959, Jacqueline b 1960); *Career* MOD 1956-67, NBPI 1967-70; Nat Industrial Rels Ct 1971-73; dir of mktg, Defence Sales Orgn MOD 1979-82, dir Economic and Logistic Intelligence MOD 1982-88, dir gen of Intelligence MOD 1988-; *Recreations* gardening; *Clubs* Royal Cwlth Soc; *Style*— David Hills, Esq; Ministry of Defence, Main Building, Whitehall, Londn SW1A 2HB

HILLS, Lady Rosemary Ethel; *née* Baring; da of 2 Earl of Cromer, GCB, GCIE, GCVO, PC (d 1953) and Lady Ruby Elliot, da of 4 Earl of Minto; *b* 1908; *m* 1932, Lt-Col John David Hills, MC (d 1976), former headmaster of Bradfield Coll; 1 s (John), 2 da (Jean (*see* Hon Christopher Willoughby) and Margaret); *Career* FRGS; *Recreations* mountaineering; *Style*— Lady Rosemary Hills; House by the Dyke, Chirk, Wrexham, Denbighshire

HILLYER, John Selby; OBE (1975); s of Stanley Gordon Hillyer, OBE (d 1965), of Sussex, and Margaret, *née* Selby; *b* 14 Feb 1925; *Educ* Stowe, Trinity Coll, Oxford (MA); *m* 2 June 1951, Elizabeth Ann, da of Sinclair Jeavons Thyne, CBE, of Tasmania; 1 s (James b 1952), 2 da (Sarah b 1955, Caroline b 1958); *Career* Lt Coldstream Gds; barr Inner Temple 1949; ptnr Hill Vellacott, CA 1954-88; sr ptnr Chantrey Vellacett; master worshipful Co of Fanmakers 1969; chm Dr Barnardo's 1970; dir T H White Ltd 1954-, dir Vanguard Tst Managers Ltd; Master Worshipful Co of Fanmakers 1969;; *Recreations* gardening, Barnardo's; *Clubs* Royal Automobile; *Style*— John S Hillyer, Esq; Copden House, Biddenden, Kent; Russell Sq House, 10-12 Russell Sq, London WC1 (☎ 01 436 3666)

HILMY, Hon Mrs (Mary Trevor); *née* Bruce; yr da of Baron Bruce of Donington (Life Peer); *b* 1945; *m* 1968, Shuhada Hilmy; *Style*— The Hon Mrs Hilmy

HILSUM, Prof Cyril; s of Benjamin Hilsum, and Ada Hilsum; *b* 17 May 1925; *Educ* Raines GS, UCL (BSc, PhD); *m* 16 Aug 1947, Betty (d 1987), da of Herbert Cooper; 2 da (Karen b 1954, Lindsey b 1958); *Career* Admty HQ 1945-47, Admty Res Laboratory 1947-50, Servs Electronics Res Laboratory 1950-64, RSRE 1964-83, dir of res GEC plc 1983-, visiting prof of physics UCL; foreign assoc US Nat Acad, FRS, FEng, FInst P, FIEE; *Books* Semiconducting III - V Compounds (1961), Handbook of Semiconductors (1984); *Recreations* tennis, chess; *Style*— Prof Cyril Hilsum; Hirst Research Centre, GEC, East Lane, Wembley, Middx HA9 7PP (☎ 01 908 9006)

HILTON, Bernard Carter; s of Clifford Hilton (d 1948); *b* 24 August 1921; *Educ* Rugby Coll of Engineering Technology; *m* 1, 1949, Betty Doreen; 1 da (Erica); m 2, 1976, Margaret Cynthia, *née* Edwards; *Career* former chm constructional and special products div Aurora Hldgs Ltd 1976; chm engrg div Firth Cleveland Ltd; vice-chm and chief exec AI Welders Ltd 1978-85; CEng, FBIM, FIMC, MIEE; *Recreations* lecturing, travel, reading; *Clubs* Reform; *Style*— Bernard Hilton, Esq; 18 The Glen, Sheffield S10 3FN (☎ (0742) 663188)

HILTON, (Wilfrid) Graham; s of Harry Hilton, and Doris Hilton *née* Dawson; *b* 18 May 1937; *Educ* Manchester GS, St John's Coll Oxford (BA); *m* 17 Sept 1966, Hilary, da of Rev Charles Frederick Jones; 1 s (Jonathan b 1974), 1 da (Sunita Claire b 1971); *Career* slr and in private practice 1965-; dep coroner High Peak Dist 1979-, dir Sports and Leisure Foods Ltd 1974-; chm Stockport Harriers and AC 1984-; *Recreations* sport, athletics, marathon running, squash, bird watching; *Clubs* Stockport Warriers, AC, RSPB; *Style*— W G Hilton, Esq; Beacom Villa, Compstall, Stockport SK6 5JZ (☎ 061 427 2519); Pricketts, 32 Union Rd, New Mills, Stockport SK12 3EU (☎ 0663 43367)

HILTON, Anthony Victor; s of Maj Raymond W Hilton (d 1975), of Huntly, Aberdeenshire, and Miriam, *née* Kydd; *b* 26 August 1946; *Educ* Woodhouse Grove Sch Bradford Yorks, Aberdeen Univ (MA); *m* 1, 30 March 1969 (m dis 1973); 1 s (Steven b 1970); m 2, Cyndy Miles 2 s (Michael b 1985, Peter b 1987); *Career* The Times 1982-83, city ed Evening Standard 1984- Employee Reports (1978), City within a State (1988); *Clubs* Lansdowne; *Style*— Anthony Victor Hilton, Esq; Evening Standard, City Office, Temple House, Temple Ave, London EC4 (☎ 01 938 6000)

HILTON, (Alan) John Howard; s of Alan Howard Hilton, (d 1986), of Bowdon, and Barbara Mary Campbell, *née* Chambers, (d 1958); *b* 21 August 1942; *Educ* Haileybury, Manchester Univ (LLB); *m* 21 Dec 1978, Nicola Mary, da of Percy Harold Bayley (d 1977), of Brighton; 1 s (Felix b 24 Dec 1983); *Career* barr 1963, in practice 1964-; recorder 1985; *Books* Fish Cookery (1981), Opera Today (1985); *Recreations* opera, conjuring, 19 century females in oils, cooking; *Style*— John Hilton, Esq; 21 Durand Gardens, London SW9 (☎ 01 735 1359); Queen Elizabeth Building, Temple EC4 (☎ 01 583 5766)

HILTON, Nicholas David; s of John David Hilton, of Wyndsway, Woodside Hill, Chalfont Heights Gerrards Cross, Bucks SL9 9TF, and Dorothy Gwendoline, *née* Eastham; *b* 27 June 1952; *Educ* Marlborough; *m* 14 July 1984, Vanessa Jane, da of Brig W John Reed of Frensham, Surrey; *Career* CA 1974; ptnr Moore Stephens 1979-; chm London Accountants' Trg Discussion Gp; memb ICEAW, FCA 1979; *Recreations* hockey, golf, skiing, mah jong, entertaining; *Clubs* Richmond GC, Richmond Hockey, Cygnets Hockey; *Style*— Nicholas Hilton, Esq; St Pauls House, Warwick Lane, London EC4 P 4BN (☎ 01 248 4499, fax 01 248 3408, telex 884610)

HILTON, Col Peter; MC (1942 and two bars 1943 and 1944), JP (Derbyshire, 1967); er s of Maj-Gen R Hilton, DSO, MC, DFC, and Phyllis Martha, *née* Woodin; *b* 30 June 1919; *Educ* Malvern, RMA Woolwich, Staff College Camberley; *m* 1942, Winifred, da of Ernest Smith; 1 s (and 1 s decd); *Career* served WW II RA, France, N Africa, Italy, Greece; Lord-Lt and custos rotulorum Derbys 1978- (DL 1972, High Sheriff 1970-71); conslt James Smith (Scotland Nurseries) Ltd; Hon Col Derbys ACF 1972-77, pres: TA and VRA E Midlands 1978, Derbys Rural Community Cncl, Derbys Br Heart Fndn, St John Cncl Derbys, Derbys Imperial Veterans, 8 Army Veterans, Dunkirk Veterans, Normandy Veterans, RSPCA Derby and District; KStJ, FRHS; *Style*— Col Peter Hilton, MC**, JP; c/o James Smith (Scotland Nurseries) Ltd, Tansley, Matlock, Derbys DE4 5GF (☎ 0629 3036); Alton Manor, Idridgehay, Derbys (☎ 062 982 2435)

HILTON, (Annie) Winifred; da of Ernest Herbert Smith (d 1965), of Matlock, Derbyshire, and Annie, *née* Wilkes-Green (1972); the Smith family of Tansley have lived at Scotland House and owned the old firm of James Smith Scotland Nurseries Ltd for 307 years, they hold the Royal Warrant as nurserymen to HM The Queen; *b* 26 July 1919; *Educ* Matlock Modern Sch, Trinity Coll London, The Nat Training Coll of Domestic Science London, Associate of Trinity Coll London; *m* 8 Jan 1942, Col Peter Hilton, MC, KSTJ, JP, Lord Lt of Derbyshire, s of Maj Gen Richard Hilton, DSO, MC, DFC (d 1982), of Tysoe, Warwickshire; 2 s (Andrew Peter b 1945, James Richard Woodin b 1947 (decd));; *Career* war service WAAF 1940-45 (special duties branch, radar codes and cyphers section offr), county pres St John Ambulance 1978-; chm of many centenary appeals for Derbyshire from 1967-; pres East Midlands Home and Leisure Safety Ctee 1978-; patron League of Friends Derbyshire Hosp for Women 1970-87 (pres League of Friends Derbyshire Royal Infirmary 1980-); Arthritis and Rheumatism Cncl nat gold badge 1985; British Heart Foundation nat gold award 1978 (co chm 1974-78, co vice pres 1978-); pres WRVS assoc Derbyshire 1987; Royal British Legion Womens Section national golden award 1987 (nat vice pres 1985, county chm 1977-); pres Wirkoworth, Birmingham and Micklover branches; memb: Nat Cncl (NSPCC) Nat Certificate of Appreciation 1982 (chm Derby Mid West Derbyshire 1967-); Derbyshire Civil Guides Co Award 1977 (chm house ctee 1979-); chm of the directors James Smith Scotland Nurseries Ltd; Tansley Matlock Derbyshire 1965-86 (dir 1940-86); memb: Derbyshire war Pensions Ctee 1973- co SSAFA ctee 1950-; Womens Voluntary Service co organiser 1973-86 medal and 2 bars; Certificate of Merit for distinguished achievement 1961; *Recreations* walking, gardening, heraldry; *Clubs* St John Ambulance London; *Style—* Winifred A Hilton; Alton Manor, Idridgehay, Derbyshire (☎ Wirksworth 2435)

HIMSWORTH, Sir Harold Percival; KCB (1952); s of Arnold Himsworth (d 1960); *b* 19 May 1905; *Educ* Almondbury GS, UCL, Univ Coll Hosp London (MD); *m* 1932, Charlotte Gray; 2 s; *Career* prof of med London Univ 1939-49; dep chm MRC 1967-68 (memb 1948-49, sec 1949-68); *Clubs* Athenaeum; *Style—* Sir Harold Himsworth, KCB; 13 Hamilton Terrace, London NW8 (☎ 01 286 6996)

HINCHCLIFFE, Peter Robert Mossom; CMG (1987), CVO (1979); s of Herbert Peter Hinchliffe (d 1978), and Jeannie Wilson, MD (d 1973); *b* 9 April 1937; *Educ* Radley, Trinity Coll Dublin (MA); *m* 1965, Archbold Harriet, da of Hugh Edward Siddall, of Dublin; 3 da (Fiona b 1967, Sally b 1969, Clare b 1972); *Career* military service W Yorks Regt 1955-57, 2 Lt (Suez Campaign 1956), HMOCS Aden, political offr 1961-67; acting dep high cmmr 1967; joined FCO 1969, first sec UK mission to UN 1971-74, first sec and head of chancery Kuwait 1974-76, asst head of Science and Technology Dept and Central and Southern African Dept 1976-78, counsellor and dep high cmmr Dar es Salaam 1978-81, consul gen Dubai, UAE 1981-85, head of Information Dept FCO 1985-87; HM ambassador Kuwait 1987; *Recreations* golf, tennis; *Clubs* East India, Royal Co Down Golf; *Style—* Peter Hinchcliffe, Esq, CMG, CVO; 7 Cranley Gardens, Muswell Hill, London N10 3AA (☎ 01 444 8561); British Embassy, PO Box SAFAT 2, Kuwait 13001

HINCHLIFF, Stephen; CBE (1976); s of Gordon Henry Hinchliff (d 1976), and Winifred, *née* Ellis (d 1955); *b* 11 July 1926; *Educ* Almondbury GS Huddersfield, Boulevard Nautical Coll Hull, Huddersfield Coll of Tech (Dip Mech Engrg), Cranfield Inst of Tech (MSc); *m* 1, 1951 (m dis 1987), Margaret Arrundale Crossland; 1 s, 1 da; m 2, 1987, Ann Fiona Maudsley; *Career* cadet and deck offr MN 1943-48; production engr Dowty Auto Units Ltd Cheltenham 1953, chief production engr Dowty Seals Ltd: chief producn engr 1953, works mangr 1954, production mangr 1956, dir 1958, dep md 1966, md 1967; dep chm Dowty Gp Ltd 1972 (dir 1968); md Dowty Gp Industrial Divn 1973-76; chm and md Dexion Gp 1976-; dir: Dacorum Enterprise Agency, Business in the Community; memb of court Cranfield Inst of Technology; CEng, FIMechE, FIProdE, CBIM, FRSA; *Recreations* squash, badminton, tennis, fishing; *Style—* Stephen Hinchliff, Esq, CBE; Bowmore Farm, Hawridge Common, nr Chesham, Bucks HP5 2UH (☎ 024029 237)

HINCHLIFFE, David Martin; MP (Lab) Wakefield 1987-; s of Robert Victor Hinchliffe (d 1982), of Wakefield, and Muriel, *née* Preston (d 1987); *b* 14 Oct 1948; *Educ* Catherdral Secdy Mod Sch Wakefield, Wakefield Tech & Art Coll, Leeds Poly, Banford Univ (MA), Hudderfield Poly (Cert Fd); *m* 17 July 1982, Julia, da of Harry North, of Mold Clwyd; 1 s (Robert b 10 Oct 1985), 1 da (Rebecca b 24 May 1988); *Career* princ social worker Leeds Social Servs dept 1974-79, social work tutor Kirklees Cncl 1980-87; cncllr: Wakefield City Cncl 1971-74, Wakefield DC 1978-88; former vice pres: Wakefield and Dist Trades Cncl, Wakefield Constituency Lab Pty; vice pres Wakefield Trinity RLFC; *Recreations* rugby league, football, Wakefield Trinity RLFC; *Style—* David Hinchliffe, Esq; 21 King Street, Wakefield, W Yorks (☎ 0924 290134)

HINCHLIFFE, Ralph Eric; s of Lawrence Hinchliffe (d 1974); *b* 30 Jan 1931; *Educ* Royds Hall Grammar; *m* 1957, Jean Lesley, da of Vernon Rawlings (d 1978), of Huddersfield; 3 children; *Career* Corpl Royal Pay Corps (nat service); ptnr Smith and Garton CAS Huddersfield 1957-69; chm Heywood William Gp plc 1981-(joined 1969); FCA, FCMA;; *Recreations* all sports; *Clubs* Woodsome Hall Golf, Yorkshire County Cricket, Liverpool Football; *Style—* Ralph Hinchliffe Esq; Bank House, New Mill, Huddersfield, W Yorks HD7 8HU (☎ (0484) 682104); Heywood Williams Group plc, Bayhall, Birkby, Huddersfield, W Yorks (☎ (0484) 20581)

HINCHLIFFE, Stephen Leonard; s of William Leonard (d 1974), and Ilse, *née* Sparer; *b* 2 Jan 1950; *m* 14 July 1973, Marjorie, da of Eric Wood (d 1971); 1 s (James b 1975), 1 da (Julia b 1978); *Career* accountant Sheffield Twist Drill, Trent Regnl Hosp Bd; chm and chief exec: Wade Gp of Co's Ltd, James Wilkes plc; FBIM, FSMM;; *Recreations* helicopter flying, golf, motoring, shooting; *Clubs* Dore & Totley GC; *Style—* Stephen L Hinchliffe, Esq; Beauchief Hall, Beauchief, Sheffield (☎ 0742 670076/620062, fax 0742 666276, car tel 0836 521521)

HINCKLEY, Gilbert Clive; OBE (1988); s of Capt Gilbert Percy (d 1972), of Hinckley, and Dorothy Kate, *née* Bown; *b* 6 July 1937; *Educ* The Leys Sch, Clare Coll Cambridge (MA); *m* 1 (m dis 1977), Jane Susan, *née* Bourne; 1 da (Hannah Jane b 1979); m 2, 21 Aug 1981, Karen Ann, da of Gerald Wilson; *Career* 2 Lt pack tport RASC 1957-58, TA 1959-64 Lt Queens Own Yorks Yeo; Hinckley Gp of Assoc Cos: gp dir 1962-, jt chief exec 1976-82, chm Flogates div, dep chm KSR int div, gp md 1982-; chm of Derbyshire cncl Order of St John, memb of ct Cutlers Co Hallamshire; FIOD, Fell Inst Br Foundrymen, memb Inst of Metals; *Recreations* game shooting, fishing, hunting; *Clubs* Cavalry & Guards; *Style—* Gilbert Hinckley, Esq, OBE; Amber House, Kelstedge, Amber Valley, Derbyshire S45 0EA;The Hinckley Group of Assoc Companies, Abbey Lane Beauchief, Sheffield S722RA (☎ 0742 369 011, fax 0742 364 775, telex 54496)

HIND, Andrew Charles; s of John William Hind (d 1986), of Grayshott, and Evelyn May, *née* Sidford (d 1986); *b* 10 July 1943; *Educ* Sutton County GS; *m* 27 Dec 1969, Janet Margaret, da of Norman William George Scullard (d 1983), of Hove; 1 s (Duncan William b 1976), 3 da (Joanna Scullard b 1973, Annalee Scullard b 1975, Suzanne Catherine b 1985); *Career* Lovell and Rupert Curtis Ltd (advertising): joined 1966, dir 1974, md 1984, chm and md 1987; MIPA; cmmnd FIOD; *Clubs* Naval and Military; *Style—* Andrew Hind, Esq; Cranley Cottage, Guildford, Surrey (☎ 0483 32120); 26 King St, Covent Garden, London WC2E 8JD (☎ 01 836 1522, fax 01 836 5166, telex 261000)

HIND, John; s of WO George Hind, of 2 Woodlands Ave, Wheatley Hill, Co Durham, and Marjorie, *née* Terry; *b* 6 August 1954; *Educ* AJ Dawson GS, Newcastle upon Tyne Poly (BA), RCA (MA); *Career* Vogue Magazine: art ed 1980-85, art dir 1985-; memb D & ADA 1982-; *Style—* John Hind, Esq; 28 Park Road, Chiswick, London W4 3HN (☎ 01 994 2583); Condenast Pubns, 1 Hanover Sq, London W1 (☎ 01 499 9080)

HIND, Rev Canon John William; s of Harold Hind, and Joan Mary, *née* Kemp (d 1976); *b* 19 June 1945; *Educ* Watford GS, Univ of Leeds (BA); *m* 16 April 1966, Janet Helen, da of David Hamilton Burns McLintock; 3 s (Dominic b 1967, Jonathan b 1969, Philip b 1971); *Career* asst master Leeds Modern Sch 1966-69, asst lectr King Alfred's Coll Winchester 1969-70, student Cuddesdon Theol Coll Oxford 1970-72; asst curate: St John the Baptist Church Catford Southend, Downham Team Ministry Doicese of Southwark 1972-76; vicar Christ Church Forest Hill Diocese of Southwark 1976-82, p-in-c St Paul's Forest Hill 1981-82, princ Chichester Theol Coll 1982-, Bursalis prebendary and residentiary canon Chichester Cathedral 1982-; *Books* contrib to Stepping Stones (ed Baxter1987), Church, Kingdom, World (ed Limouris 1986), Working for the Kingdom (ed Fuller & Vaughan 1986); *Recreations* judo, languages; *Style—* The Rev Canon John Hind; The Theological College, Chichester, West Sussex PO19 1SG (☎ 0243 783369)

HIND, Kenneth Harvard; MP (C) West Lancashire 1983-; *b* 15 Sept 1949; *Educ* Woodhouse Grove Sch, Bradford Yorks, Leeds Univ; *m* Patricia Anne *née* Millar; 1 s, 1 da; *Career* barr 1973 Gray's Inn 1973, practising barr Leeds until 1983; pps: Lord Trefgarne MOD 1986-87, John Cope Min DOE 1987-; *Recreations* sailing, skiing; *Clubs* vice pres Headingley RUFC, Ormskirk Agric; *Style—* Kenneth Hind, Esq, MP; House of Commons, London SW1

HINDE, David Richard; s of Walter Stanley Hinde (d 1952), and Marjorie Jewell Grieg, *née* Butcher (d 1970); *b* 16 August 1938; *Educ* Marlborough, Cambridge Univ (Law Degree); *m* 1963, Rosemary Jill, da of Malcolm Hartree Young (d 1965); 3 da (Sasha Karen b 1966, Rachel Olivia b 1968, Anna-Louise b 1972); *Career* asst slr Slaughter and May 1961-69; exec dir: Wallace Bros Gp 1969-77, Wardley Ltd 1977-81, Samuel Montagu and Co Ltd 1981-; *Recreations* skiing, gardening, travel; *Clubs* MCC, City of London; *Style—* David Hinde, Esq; Flat 2, 17 Clarendon Rd, London W11; The Glebe House, Great Gaddesden, Hemel Hempstead, Hertfordshire HP1 3BY; Samuel Montagu and Co Ltd, 10 Lower Thames Street, London EC3R 4AE (☎ 01 260 9699, fax 623 5512, 887213)

HINDE, Keith Stevens Gleave; TD (1969); s of Wing Cdr Sydney Arthur Hinde, OBE, DL (d 1977), of W Mersea, Essex and Guinevere Waneeta Ashore, *née* Gleave (d 1974); *b* 4 Oct 1934; *Educ* Colchester Royal GS, Corpus Christi Coll Cambridge (MA); *m* 8 May 1965, Gillian Myfanwy, da of William Godfrey Morgan (d 1955), of Coventry; 1 s (Edward Morgan Stevens b 1976); *Career* 2 Lt RA 1953-55, Battery Capt Suffolk & Norfolk Yeo 1955-67, Maj Suffolk/Cambs Regt (S and NY) 1967-69; slr 1961, ptnr Pothecary & Barratt; tstee: Stretham Engine Tst, Suffolk & Norfolk Yeo Tst; cncl memb and hon slr King George's Fund for Sailors; Liveryman Worshipful Co of Slrs 1966 (Clerk 1969-76, Master 1988), Clerk Worshipful Co Cutlers 1975-; *Books* Steam in the Fens (1974); *Recreations* history (local and general), country pursuits; *Clubs* Utd Oxford & Cambridge; *Style—* Keith Hinde, Esq; Denny House, Waterbeach, Cambs (☎ 0223 860895); Pothecary & Barratt, Talbot House, Talbot Court, Gracechurch St, London EC3 (☎ 01 623 7520)

HINDLE, Timothy Simon; s of Edwin Frederick Branwell Hindle (d 1969), and Joan Marjorie, *née* Pearson; *b* 7 June 1946; *Educ* Shrewsbury, Worcester Coll Oxford (MA), Heriot Watt Univ Edinburgh (Postgrad Dip Fin Studies); *m* 11 June 1975, Ellian Lea, da of Eli Aciman, of Istanbul; 1 s (Alexis b 1982), 1 da (Alara b 1979); *Career* dep ed The Banker 1978; The Economist: banking corr 1980, fin ed 1983, world business ed 1985; ed EuroBusiness 1988; voluntary serv overseas Dacca Bangladesh 1968-69; *Books* Pocket Banker (1984); *Recreations* reading novels, cinema, water skiing; *Style—* Timothy Hindle, Esq; 22 Royal Crescent, Holland Park, London W11 (☎ 01 602 2601); EuroBusiness, 61 Old St, London EC1 (☎ 01 490 2115, fax 01 253 9994)

HINDLEY-SMITH, David Dury; CBE (1972); s of Dr James Dury Hinley-Smith (d 1974 physician), of 45 Welbeck St, London W1, and Mary Ethel Josephine HS, *née* McMaster (d 1953); Hindley-Smith collections of impressionist paintings in FitzWilliam and Ashmolean Museum presented by gu Frank; *b* 20 Feb 1916; *Educ* Uppingham Sch, King's Coll Cambridge (MA);; *m* Dorothy Westwood (d 1987), da of Arthur Collins (financial adviser to the H of Commons), of Baston Manor, Hayes, Kent; 2 stepda (Sarah Jane b 1936, Amanda Mary b 1937); *Career* served Artists Rifles 1939, cmmnd Royal Fusiliers 1940; liason offr: Gen Leclere 1942, Gén de Gaulle's first admin 1944, actg Col; vice chm Surrey Assoc of Youth Clubs 1950-70 (vice-pres 1970-), exec chm Nat Assoc of Youth Clubs 1970-74 (vice-pres 1974-); chm Sembal Tst 1972-81, vice-pres Suffolk Assoc of Youth 1984- (chm 1982-84), hon memb BDA 1975, hon FDSRCSE 1977, hon FDSRCS 1980, Cecil Peace Prize 1958; *Recreations* gardening, cooking; *Clubs* Royal Soc of Medicine; *Style—* David Hindley-Smith, CBE; The Ark House, Whepstead, Bury St Edmunds, Suffolk, IP29 4UB (☎ Horringer 351)

HINDLIP, 5 Baron (UK 1886); Sir Henry Richard Allsopp; 5 Bt (UK 1880), JP (Wilts 1957), DL (1956); s of 3 Baron Hindlip, OBE, JP, DL, by his w Agatha (herself da of John Thynne, who was in his turn 6 s of Rev Lord John Thynne, 3 s of 2 Marquess of Bath); suc er bro (4 Baron) 1966; *b* 1 July 1912; *Educ* Eton, Sandhurst; *m* 1939, Cecily, da of Lt-Col Malcolm Borwick, DSO (nephew of 1 Baron Borwick and sometime Joint Master of the Pytchley); 2 s, 1 da; *Heir* s, Hon Charles Allsopp; *Career* 2 Lt Coldstream Gds 1932, Maj 1941, ret 1948, served WW II NW Europe; *Clubs* White's, Pratt's, Turf; *Style—* The Rt Hon the Lord Hindlip, JP, DL; Tytherton House, East Tytherton, Chippenham, Wilts

HINDS, Joan Patricia Dobson; da of Ernest Ivor Dobson, and Muriel Augusta, *née* Rees; *b* 4 Mar 1950; *Educ* Bible Coll of Wales, Girls GS Neath, Univ of London (BA), Univ of Wales, London Business Sch (Sloan Fell); *m* 28 Sept 1974, Dr Charles Johnston, s of Dr Sydney Johnston Hinds; *Career* dep hosp sec The London Hosp 1975-76, dep house govr Moorfields Eye Hosp 1976-81, sec NHS National Staff Ctee, Admin and Clerical Staff (DHSS princ) 1981-84; mgmnt conslt Hay MSL 1985-86, fundraiser Advance in Medicine 1987-; *Recreations* opera, ballet, theatre, skiing, gardening, husband-minding; *Clubs* Network, The Blizard; *Style—* Mrs Joan Hinds; 38 Langton Way, Blackheath, London SE3 (☎ 01 853 0955); The London Hospital Medical Coll, Turner St, London E1 2AD (☎ 01 377 7471, telex 893750, fax 01 377

7677)

HINDS, Ralph William Gore; s of Lt-Col Walter Augustus Gore Hinds, MC (d 1975), of Bournemouth; and Honoria Mary, *née* Quinn (d 1965); *b* 27 April 1925; *Educ* Cheltenham, Sandhurst; *m* 1, 23 Feb 1952, Barbara Diana, da of late John Sidey, of Bournemouth; 1 s (Nigel b 1955), 1 da (Hilary b 1958); m 2, 29 April 1982, Judith Margaret, da of William Henry Williams (d 1962), of Devon; *Career* served WW II 1943-46, Lt 1 Royal Dragoons; slr 1950-, sr ptnr Walker Hinds Bournemouth; *Recreations* jazz music, philately; *Style—* Ralph W G Hinds, Esq; Cliff Lodge, 5 Boscombe, Overcliffe Drive, Bournemouth BH5 1JB (☎ 0202 303397); 878 Christchurch Rd, Pokesdown, Bournemouth BH7 6DJ (☎ 0202 417122)

HINDS, William James; MBE (1969), JP; s of Ben Hinds; *b* 9 Sept 1910; *Educ* Queen Elizabeth's GS Carmarthen, Pibwrlwyd Farm Inst, Univ Coll of Wales; *m* 1938, Gwendolen, da of Thomas Harries; *Career* farmer; memb: S Wales Milk Marketing Bd 1952-1962 and 1965-83, cncl Royal Welsh Agric Soc 1983- (pres 1987), ct of govrs Univ Coll Wales Aberystwyth, memb S W Wales River Authy, High Sheriff Dyfed 1981-82; FRAGS; *Recreations* fishing, rugby; *Style—* William Hinds Esq, MBE, JP; Danyrallt, Abergorlech Rd, Carmarthen, Dyfed SA32 7AY (☎ 0267 88233)

HINDSON, William Stanley; CMG (1962); s of William Abner Lucas Hindson, of Darlington, Durham, and Mary Jane, *née* Richmond; *b* 11 Jan 1920; *Educ* Darlington GS, Coatham Sch Redcar, Constantine Tech Coll Middlesbrough, London Univ (BSc);; *m* 1, 1944 Mary Study (d 1961); 1 s (William Richard Forster b 1948), 1 da (Rosemary Ann Allen b 1946); m 2, 11 Jan 1965, Catherine Berthe Leikine of Paris, France; 1 s (William Alexander Joseph b 1966); *Career* devpt engr Dorman Long (steel) Ltd 1946 (steel plant mangr 1945-46); chief engr and md: Metallurgical Equipment Export Co Ltd 1956-57, Indian Steelworkers Construction Co Ltd 1962-69; dir: Anglo German Bosphorus Bridge Consortium, Br Bridge Builders Consortium 1969-71; md Humphreys & Glasgow Ltd 1972-74 (dir of engrg 1971-72), engrg and metallurgical conslt 1975-88; FIMechE, MIM; *Recreations* chess, philately, history; *Style—* William Hindson, Esq, CMG; 36 Eresby House, 19 Rutland Gate, London SW7 1BG (☎ 01 589 3194)

HINE, Ivon Francis Milton; s of John Knox Hine (d 1943), and Lavinia Suie, *née* Milton (d 1971); *b* 11 Nov 1920; *Educ* Queen's Coll Taunton; *m* 22 Oct 1955, Elizabeth, da of Philip Arthur Barclay Cherry (d 1964); 2 s (John Philip b 1957, Richard Henry b 1959), 1 da (Catherine Symons b 1961); *Career* WWII Sqdn Ldr RAF served SEAC 1941-46; slr 1947, sr ptnr Hine Stonehouse and Barrington, NP 1959, Cmmr for Oaths 1959; chm Devon and Cornwall Rent Assessment Ctee and Rent Tbnl; former pres: Cornwall Co Squash Rackets Assoc (former chm and tres), Cornwall Golf Union; played cricket for Cornwall 1948-55; *Recreations* golf, breeding budgerigars, diocesan ctees; *Style—* Ivon Hine, Esq; Hopelands, Chaple Amble, nr Wadebridge PL27 6EU (☎ 020 881 4246); 8/10 Berkeley Vale, Falmouth TR11 3PL (☎ 0326 316655, fax 0326 313448)

HINE, Air Chief Marshal Sir Patrick (Paddy) Bardon; GCB (1989, KCB 1983); s of Eric Graham Hine (d 1971) and Cecile Grace Hine (*née* Shilippe) (d 1971); *b* 14 July 1932; *Educ* Peter Symonds Sch Winchester; *m* 1956, Jill Adèle, da of James Charles Gardner (d 1984); 3 s (Nicholas b 1962, Andrew b 1966, Jeremy b 1969); *Career* joined RAF 1952, memb Black Arrows aerobatic team 1957-59, cmd RAF Wildenrath 1974-75, dir P/R RAF 1975-77, SASO HQ RAF Germany 1979, ACAS (Policy) MOD 1979-83, Air Marshal 1983, C-in-C RAF Germany and Cdr Second Allied Tactical Air Force 1983-85, ACAS (Policy) MOD 1979-83 in rank of Air Vice-Marshal; Vice CDS 1985 in rank of air chief Marshal; fRAeS, CBIM;; *Recreations* golf, skiing, fell walking, photography, military history; *Clubs* RAF, Brokenhurst Manor Golf; *Style—* Air Marshal Sir Patrick Hine, KCB; c/o MOD, Whitehall, London SW1 (☎ 01 218 7576

HINE, Royston Graeme; s of Graeme Douglas Hine, of Purley Way, Pangbourne, Berkshire, and Verena Morella, *née* Belt; *b* 10 May 1943; *Educ* Pangbourne Sch, Reading Tech Coll, Distributive Trades Coll; *m* 14 Dec 1961, Heather Eileen, da of Bernard Frank Brown; 1 s (Stephen John), 4 da (Linda Anne, Caroline Anne, Sarah Anne, Barbara Anne); *Career* Colebrook & Hedges, controller Keymarkets Ltd 1969-72, assoc dir Asda Stores Ltd 1972-78, dir Borthwick plc 1978-86; currently dir: Hine Meats Ltd, Scobie of Junor Ltd; fndr memb Meat Forum, vice-pres Butchers and Drovers Charitable Inst; Freeman City of London 1979, Liveryman Worshipful Co of Butchers 1980; fell Inst of Meat 1986 (former chm); *Recreations* shooting, snooker, tennis; *Clubs* City Livery; *Style—* Royston Hine, Esq; Summertrees, 48A Allcroft Rd, Reading RG1 5HN (☎ 0734 874 498); 10 Whitchurch Rd, Pangbourne, Berks RG8 7BP (☎ 07357 2063, 0753 686 126, fax 0753 685 144, car tel 0860 207 899)

HINE-HAYCOCK, Brig William; DL (1981); s of Archibald Leslie Hine-Haycock (d 1949), of Ceylon and Devon, and Alexa Maud, *née* Petherick (d 1962); *b* 26 Nov 1917; *Educ* Banstead Hall Surrey, Canford Sch Dorset, RMC (PSA); *m* 1 Nov 1947, Deborah Eve Felicity, da of Brig Eric Fairweather Harrison, of Melbourne and Flinders, Victoria; 1 s (Gerald b 1951), 2 da (Rozanthe b 1949, Daphne b 1954); *Career* RMC Sandhurst 1936-37, cmmnd Duke of Cornwalls LI 1938, BEF France and Belgium (despatches), Western Desert and Syria 1941-42 (despatches), India and Burma 1942-43, New Guinea and Australia 1943-44, Burma 1944, Staff Coll Quetta 1945, cmd 1 Bn Som and Cornwall LI, AMS to GOC iC Southern Cmd 1962-63, Col LI Brigade 1964-67, mil attaché Br Embassy Madrid 1969; ret 1970; Freeman of Shrewsbuty 1982; FRPSL; *Books* Posted in Gibraltar (1978); *Recreations* most country sports, philately and preservation of the countryside; *Clubs* MCC, Army and Navy, Dart and Royal Gibraltar Yacht; *Style—* Brig William Hine-Haycock, DL; Hay Hill, Totnes, Devon (☎ 0803 862080); Kittery Quay, Kingswear Devon

HINES, Sir (Colin) Joseph; OBE (1973); s of J Hines; *b* 16 Feb 1919; *Educ* All Saints' Coll Bathurst; *m* 1942, Jean, da of A Wilson; 2 s; *Career* pres Returned Services League NSW 1971-, dep nat pres RSL of Australia 1974-; kt 1976; *Style—* Sir Colin Hines, OBE; The Meadows, Lyndhurst, NSW 2741, Australia

HINGSTON; *see*: Hibbert-Hingston

HINKS, Frank Peter; s of Henry John Hinks, of Stamford, Lincs, and Patricia May, *née* Adams; *b* 8 July 1950; *Educ* Bromley GS, St Catherine's Coll Oxford, (BA, BCL MA);; *m* 31 July 1982, Susan Mary, da of Col John Arthur Haire, of Bickley, Kent; 3 s (Julius b 1984, Alexander b 1985, Benjamin b 1987); *Career* barr Lincoln's Inn 1973, Chancery Bar 1974-; memb: Shoreham PCC, Pastoral Ctee, Shoreham Players; Freeman Worhsipful Co of Innholders 1988;; *Recreations* poetry, gardening, collecting jugs; *Style—* Frank Hinks, Esq; The Old Vicarage, Shoreham, Sevenoaks, Kent (☎ 095 92 4480); 13 Old Sq, Lincoln's Inn, London WC2 (☎ 01 242 6105, fax 01 405 4004)

HINSLEY, Prof Sir Francis Harry; OBE 1946,; s of Thomas Henry Hinsley (d 1956), and Emma Hinsley, *née* Adey (d 1980); *b* 26 Nov 1918; *Educ* Queen Mary's GS Walsall, St John's Coll Cambridge MA; *m* 1946, Hilary Brett, da of Herbert Francis Brett (d 1952); 2 s (Charles b 1947, Hugo b 1950), 1 da (Clarissa b 1954); *Career* HM FO (war serv) 1939-46; Univ of Cambridge: research fell St John's Coll 1944-50, U tidpr St John's Coll 1956-63, Univ lectr of History 1949-65, reader in history of int relations 1965-67, prof history of int relations 1969-83, vice chancellor 1981-83, chm faculty bd of history 1970-72; FBA 1981, kt 1985; *Clubs* Oxford and Cambridge United Univ; *Style—* Prof Sir Francis Hinsley; Master's Lodge, St John Coll, Cambridge CB1 1TP (☎ Cambridge 338635)

HINTON, Prof Denys James; s of James Charles Hinton (d 1966), of Reading, and Nell Beatrice, *née* Shord (d 1964); *b* 12 April 1921; *Educ* Reading Sch, Architectural Assoc Sch of Architecture London (AAdip Hons, MSc); *m* 1, June 1947, Daphne; 1 da (Sarah b 1952); m 2, March 1971, Lynette Payne, *née* Pattinson,; *Career* architect, fndr of architectural practice Hinton Brown Langstove in Warwick, dir Birmingham Sch of Architecture 1964-72, emeritus prof of architecture Aston Univ Birmingham; (head of dept of architectural planning and urban studies 1972-81); chm: Redditch New Town Devpt Corpn 1978-85, Architects Registration Cncl of UK 1983-86; *Recreations* travel, watercolours; *Style—* Professor Denys Hinton; 45 Park Hill, Moseley, Birmingham B13 8DR (☎ 021 449 9909, 021 449 1032)

HINTON, Michael Herbert; s of Walter Leonard Hinton (d 1979), of Thorpe Bay, Essex, and Freda Millicent Lillian, *née* Crowe; *b* 10 Nov 1934; *Educ* Ardingly; *m* 1, 4 April 1955 (m dis 1982), Sarah, da of Oliver Gordon Sunderland, DL (d 1967); 1 s (Timothy b 1964), 2 da (Catherine b 1956, Jennifer b 1960); m 2, 5 Nov 1984, Jane Margaret, da of Arthur Crichton Howell; *Career* CA; ptnr Griffin & ptnrs; Alderman City of London 1970-81, Sheriff City of London 1977-78, Ct of Common Cncl 1968-70; Freeman: City of London, Co of Watermen & Lightermen of the River Thames; Liveryman and Master; Worshipful Co of Farmers 1981-82, Wheelwrights Co; Liveryman of Arbitrators Co, memb Parish Clerks Co; JP, FCA, FRSA, FICM, FFA, ACInsARB; *Recreations* cricket assoc, football, travel, collecting; *Clubs* Farmers, MCC, City Livery (pres 1976); *Style—* Michael Hinton, Esq, JP;; 9E Brechin Place, London SW7 4GB; Quags, Lower Oddington, Glouc; Practise 38 Grosvenor Gdns, London SW1W OEB (☎ 01 730 6171, fax 01 730 7165, telex 940 13870 Grifg)

HINTON, Nicholas John; CBE (1985); s of the Rev Canon John Percy Hinton, of Wiltshire, and Josephine Eleanor Hinton (d 1971); *b* 15 Mar 1942; *Educ* Marlborough, Selwyn Coll Cambridge (MA); *m* 1971, Deborah Mary, da of The Hon Douglas Vivian (d 1974); 1 da (Josephine Mary b 1984); *Career* dir: Nat Assoc for the Care and Resettlement of Offenders 1973-77, Nat Cncl for Voluntary Orgns 1977-84; dir gen The Save The Children Fund 1984-; *Recreations* music; *Style—* Nicholas J Hinton, Esq; 12 Maunsel Street, London SW1P 2QL (☎ 01 828 3965); Mary Datchelor House, Grove Lane, London SE5 8RD (☎ 01 703 5400, fax 703 2278 (G3)

HINTON, Russell Fletcher; TD (1968); s of Arthur Russell Hinton (d 1974), of Middlesbrough, and Muriel Isabel, *née* Fletcher; *b* 22 July 1931; *Educ* Uppingham, Keble Coll Oxford (MA); *m* 13 May 1961, Patricia Anne, da of Terence Edward Maguire, of Nottingham; 3 da (Claire b 1962, Elizabeth b 1963, Ruth b 1966); *Career* Maj REME, DAA and QMG 151 Inf Bde (TA), Maj Green Howards mangr Consumer Res Agric Div ICI plc 1955-72, dir Amos Hinton and Sons plc 1972-84; chm Scarborough Health Authy 1986-; MIPM 1988; *Recreations* beagling, beekeeping, riding; *Style—* Russell Hinton, Esq, TD; Croft House, Sowerby, Thirsk, N Yorks (☎ 0845 22514); Toutvent Bas, 24580 Rouffignac, France; Scarborough Hospital, Scalby Rd, Scarborough (☎ 0723 386 111)

HINTON COOK, Gavin; s of Ronald Edward William Cook, and Gwendolin Bessie Hinton; *b* 9 April 1947; *Educ* Kingsbury GS, Architectural Assoc Sch of Architecture (AA Dip); *m* 11 Sept 1971, Janine Dewar, da of Wing Cdr William Charles Ramsay (d 1979); *Career* chartered architect: WF Johnson and Assoc, Melvin and Lansley, London Borough of Lambeth; Philip mercer RIBA; project architect Milton Keynes Devpt Corp 1976-79 (chief architect 1979-85, completed 2400 houses and co-ordinated Energy World at MK); md Orchard Design 1985- (39 current design projects, complete site development, engrg and total integration managed); lectr architectural studies Birmingham Univ; awards: Arch Design Mag, Beit of Brit Arch, Design Award Commendation, RIBA S Region Energy Award; ARIBA; *Recreations* sailing, squash, cycling, marathon running; *Style—* Gavin Hinton Cook, Esq; The Orchard, Mentmore, Leighton Buzzard, Beds LU7 0QE; Orchard Design Studio, Mentmore, Leighton Buzzard, Beds LU7 0QF

HINWOOD-ZEIDLER, Kathleen Mary (Kay); da of Lt Robert Wylie, MC, RA (d 1941), of 43 Rodway Rd, Bromley, Kent, and Maimie Emilie, *née* Malling (d 1981); *b* 26 Nov 1920; *Educ* Stratford House Sch Bickley Kent; *m* 26 July 1941, George Yorke (d 1960), s of late Frederick Hinwood, of Malmesbury, Wilts; 1 s (Peter Wylie b 17 May 1946), 1 da (Georgina Mary (Mrs Fowkes) b 18 April 1942); m 2, 17 Feb 1966, Lt Cdr Douglas Louis Zeidler (d 1967); *Career* ambulance driver CD 1939-41; studied art: studio of Edouard MacAvoy Paris 1937, London, privately with Sonia Mervyn, City and Guilds, final studies with Kratochwil Kathleen Brown Studios Chelsea; exhibitions: RP, RBA, ROI, NEAC, SWA, Pastel Soc, UA; paintings in private collections: England, France, Spain, Canada, USA, Australia; Award for Pastel, Pastel exhibition Mall Galleries 1986 (UA exhibition 1984); memb: Pastel Soc, United Soc of Artists, Fedn Br Artists; signs work K Hinwood; *Recreations* reading, writing, photography; *Clubs* Chelsea Arts; *Style—* Mrs Kay Hinwood

HIPKIN, Hubert (Raymond); s of Hubert John Hipkin (d 1969), of The Limes, Stickford, Boston, Lincolnshire, and Mary Hannah Hipkin, *née* Truman (d 1967); *b* 17 Oct 1928; *Educ* King Edward VI GS Spilsby, Univ of Sheffield (ARIBA); *m* 26 March 1958, Janet Ann, da of Sydney Bacon (d 1973); 3 s (Gregory b 1959 (decd), Robert b 1961, Michael b 1963); *Career* sr ptnr and fndr Architectural Practice 1969-; fell of Melton Mowbray Town Estate 1980-; town warden Melton Mowbray Town Estate 1977-80; govr: Melton Mowbray Coll of FE, Ferneley High Sch, Melton Mowbray; ARIBA; *Recreations* golf, game shooting, foreign travel; *Style—* Raymond Hipkin, Esq; Waverley House, The Park, Melton Mowbray, Leicestershire (☎ 63208); 44 Asfordby Road, Melton Mowbray, Leicestershire (☎ 63288)

HIPPISLEY-COX, Peter Denzil John; s of Col Sir Geoffrey Hippisley-Cox (d 1954); *b* 22 May 1921; *Educ* Stowe, Trinity Coll Cambridge (MA); *m* 1956, Frieda Marion; 2 da; *Career* served WWII Fl-Lt (Signals) Europe; slr and parly agent; chm Equity and

Law Life Assur Soc plc 1977-85; Master Worshipful Co of Drapers 1983-84; *Recreations* music; *Clubs* Carlton; *Style—* Peter Hippisley-Cox, Esq; 48D Whistlers Ave, London SW11 3TS; Dyson Bell and Company, 15 Great College St, Westminster, SW1P 3RX (☎ 01 222 9458)

HIPWOOD, Lady Camilla Diana; da of 15 Earl of Westmorland; *b* 26 Dec 1957; *m* 27 Sept 1985, Howard J Hipwood; 1 s (Sebastian John b 1988), 1 da (Rosanna Charlotte b 1986); *Style—* Lady Camilla Hipwood; Burnt Ash Cottage, Hyde, Chalford, Glos

HIPWOOD, Julian Brian; s of Brian John Hipwood, of Thame, Oxon and Marion Barbara Sharpe, *née* Brice; *b* 23 July 1946; *Educ* Kohat Sch Pakistan, St George's Sch Amberley, Stroud Tech Stroud; *m* 1, 11 Oct 1969 (m dis 1980), Zofia Krystina, da of Col Przemyflaw Kazimerz Kaminski, Polish Army (d 1985); 1 s (Tristan Julian b 28 Feb 1976), 1 da (Accalia Colette b 14 March 1971); m 2, 1 April 1980, Patricia Anne Secunda, da of Maj Neal Lane McRoberts, US Army (d 1966), of The Old Hall, Ashwell, Leics; *Career* professional polo player 1964, England capt 1971-76 and 1978-88; captained England to win the Coronation Cup: against Mexico 1979, USA 1988; only player to have won World Cup in five consecutive years (1980-84), twice Br Open Winner, twice French Open winner, once US Open winner; ctee memb Cowdray Park Polo Club; *Recreations* racing and breeding of thoroughbreds; *Style—* Julian Hipwood, Esq; Lychgate Cottage, Easebourne, Mid Hurst, West Sussex (☎ 073 081 3293); 12665 Shady Pines Ct, West Palm Beach, Florida 33414 USA (☎ 407 793 1327)

HIRD, Thora (Mrs Scott); OBE; da of James Henry Hird (d 1946), and Mary Jane, *née* Mayor (d 1942); *b* 28 May 1911; *m* 3 May 1937, James Scott, s of James Scott (d 1942); 1 da (Janette (Mrs Radenmaekers) b 14 Dec 1938); *Career* actress of stage and screen; theatre starred in: The Queen Came By (Duke of Yorks) 1949, Tobacco Road (Playhouse) 1951, The Happy Family (Duchess) 1951, The Same Sky (Duke of Yorks) 1952, The Troublemakers (The Strand) 1952, The Love Match (Palace) 1953, TV Comedy series: Meet the Wife, In Loving Memory, Hallelusah, Last of the Summer Wine; TV drama series: First Lady, Flesh and Blood, Romeo and Juliet, Cream Cracker Under The Setee; presenter Praise Be BBC TV; has appeared in numerous Br Films; fndr The Thora Hird Charitable Tst; *Books* Scene and Hird (autobiog 1976); *Style—* Miss Thora Hird; c/o Felix de Wolfe, Manfield House, 376/378 The Strand, London WC2R OLR (☎ 01 379 5769)

HIRSCH, Prof Sir Peter Bernhard; s of Ismar Hirsch; *b* 16 Jan 1925; *Educ* Sloane Sch Chelsea, St Catharine's Coll Cambridge (MA, PhD); *m* 1959, Mabel Anne, *née* Stephens, wid of James Kellar; 1 step s, 1 step da; *Career* reader in physics Cambridge 1964-66, fell St Edmund Hall Oxford 1966-, Isaac Wolfson prof of metallurgy Oxford 1966-; pt/t chm Atomic Energy Authy 1982-84; hon fell: RMS, Christ's Coll Cambridge 1978 (fell 1960-66), St Catharine's Coll Cambridge 1983, Imperial Coll 1988-; Hon DSc: Newcastle, City Univ, Northwestern, E Anglia; FRS; kt 1975; *Style—* Prof Sir Peter Hirsch; 104A Lonsdale Rd, Oxford; Dept of Metallurgy and Science of Materials, University of Oxford, Parks Rd, Oxford OX1 3PH (☎ 0865 273737)

HIRSHFIELD, Baron (Life Peer UK 1967); Desmond Barel Hirshfield; s of Leopold Hirshfield; *b* 17 May 1913; *Educ* City of London Sch, Birkbeck Coll London; *m* 1951, Bronia, da of Joseph Eisen, of Tel Aviv; *Career* jt sr ptnr Stoy Horwath and Co (CA) 1975-82, pres Horwath and Horwath int 1978-84, Int pres Horwath and Horwath Int 1984-85; chm Horwath and Horwath (UK)1967-85; fndr chm Trades Union Unit Tst Managers Ltd 1961-83 and chm TUUT Charitable Trust 1961-83; chm: Norwood Charitable Trust 1971-83, Norwood Fndn 1971-83; dep chm MLH Consultants 1973-83, memb Top Salaries Review Body 1976-84; dir: Woodmond Securities, Ralmond Securities, Ralwood Securities, Fieldwood Securities; govr LSE; pres Br Assoc Hotel Accountants 1971-83; tres UK Ctee UNICEF 1975-83 and 1986-; FCA; *Recreations* painting, drawing and travelling; *Style—* The Rt Hon the Lord Hirshfield; 8 Baker St, London W1M 1DA (☎ 01 486 5888) 44 Imperial Court, Prince Albert Rd, London NW8 7PT (☎ 01 586 4486)

HIRST, Alan Frank; s of Frank Leonard Hirst, CBE (d 1961); *b* 9 Dec 1922; *Educ* Epsom Coll; *m* 1944, Jenny Clarissa; 4 children; *Career* CA, chm and jt md Dairy Produce Packers Ltd 1964-76, md RHM Gen Prodeucts Ltd 1976-82, ret; Liveryman Worshipful Co of CAs; FCA; *Recreations* gardening; *Clubs* RNVR; *Style—* Alan Hirst, Esq; The Old School House, Chipstable, Taunton, Somerset (☎ 0984 23721)

HIRST, Christopher Halliwell; s of John Kenneth, of Oulston Close, Hutton Buscel, nr Scarborough, Yorks, and Marian Harrison, *née* Smith; *b* 27 May 1947; *Educ* Merchant Taylors, Trinity Hall Cambridge (MA); *m* 1, 12 Aug 1972 (m dis 1985), (Moira) Cecilia, da of Arthur Tienken, of Minneapolis, USA; 1 s (William b 1974), 1 da (Elizabeth b 1976); m 2, 28 March 1987, Sara Louise, da of Arthur James Petherick, of Bodmin, Cornwall; 1 da (Victoria b 1988); *Career* trainee exec Bank of London & S America Chile 1969-71, asst master Radley Coll 1972-85 (housemaster 1978-85), headmaster Kelly Coll Tavistock 1985-; *Recreations* antiquarian, literary, sporting; *Clubs* East India, Free Foresters, Jesters, MCC; *Style—* Christopher Hirst, Esq; Headmaster's House, Kelly Coll, Tavistock, Devon PL19 0HZ (☎ 0822 616 677); Kelly Coll, Tavistock (☎ 0822 613 005)

HIRST, David Brian Addis; s of Harold Rupert Hirst, CBE of Seaview, IOW, and Maureen, *née* Doherty; *b* 31 August 1938; *Educ* St George's Coll Weybridge; *m* 20 Dec 1969, Honoria (Nora) Bernadette, da of Dr P W Kent, OBE, of Roundwood, County Wicklow, Ireland; 2 s (Richard b 15 June 1973, Michael b 28 Nov 1977), 2 da (Patricia b 30 Sept 1971, Anthea b 4 May 1976); *Career* Coopers & Lybrand: articled 1956, ptnr 1970, ptnr i/c Cardiff Off 1970-83, ptnr i/c East Region 1983-, memb governing bd 1988-; FCA 1972; KSG 1984, KHS 1985; *Recreations* sailing, golf; *Clubs* Royal Cwlth Soc, Northampton and County; *Style—* David Hirst, Esq; Home Farm House, Rectory Lane, Orlingbury, Kettering NN14 1JH (☎ 0933 678 250); Coopers & Lybrand, Oriel House, 55 Sheep St, Northampton NN1 2NF (☎ 0604 230 770, fax 0604 238 001)

HIRST, Hon Mr Justice; Hon Sir David Cozens-Hardy Hirst; er s of Thomas William Hirst (d 1965), of West Lodge, Aylsham, Norfolk, and Margaret Joy, *née* Cozens-Hardy (niece of 1 Baron Cozens-Hardy) (d 1984); *b* 31 July 1925; *Educ* Eton, Trinity Coll Cambridge; *m* 1951, Pamela Elizabeth Molesworth, da of Col Temple Percy Molesworth Bevan, MC, of London (s of Hon Charlotte Molesworth, 2 da of 8 Viscount Molesworth); 3 s, 2 da; *Career* served WW II, RA and Intelligence Corps, Capt 1946; barr Inner Temple 1951, QC 1965; memb: Lord Chllr's Law Reform Ctee 1966-80, Cncl on Tbnls 1966-80, Ctee to Review Defamation Act, Supreme Ct Rule Ctee 1984-; chm of the Bar 1978-79 (vice-chm 1977-78); High Ct judge (Queen's Bench) 1982; kt 1982; *Recreations* shooting, theatre and opera, growing vegetables; *Clubs* Boodle's, MCC; *Style—* The Hon Mr Justice Hirst; Royal Courts of Justice, Strand, London WC2

HIRST, Hubert John; s of John Hirst (d 1983), of Oldham, and Elsie, *née* Makin; 1857 ggf (John Hirst) purchased Oldham Chronicle; *b* 24 Jan 1940; *Educ* Hulme GS Oldham, Manchester Coll of Sci and Technology (AMCST); *m* 1965, Kay Bradbury, da of James Gwylfa Roberts (d 1966); 2 s (Nigel b 1969, Roger b 1971); *Career* chm Hirst Kidd and Rennie Ltd 1985 (dir 1965, md 1983);; *Recreations* photography, walking, rotary, good food; *Style—* Hubert J Hirst, Esq; 21 Tandle Hill Rd, Royton, Oldham OL2 5UU; Hirst, Kidd-Rennie Ltd, PO Box 47, 172 Union St, Oldham OL1 1EQ (☎ 061 633 2121)

HIRST, Jonathan William ; s of Sir David Cozens-Hardy Hirst, *qv*, and Pamela Elizabeth Molesworth, *née* Bevan; *b* 2 July 1953; *Educ* Eton, Trinity Coll Cambridge (MA); *m* 20 July 1974, Fiona Christine Mary, da of Dr Peter Anthony Tyser; *Career* barr Inner Temple 1975, SE circuit; memb gen cncl of the Bar 1986; *Recreations* shooting, gardening, music; *Clubs* Boodle's; *Style—* Jonathan Hirst, Esq; 1 Brick Court, Temple, London EC4Y 9BY (☎ 01 583 0777)

HIRST, Michael William; s of John Melville Hirst (d 1969), and Christina Binning Hirst, of Milngavie; *b* 2 Jan 1946; *Educ* Glasgow Acad, Glasgow Univ (LLB), Univ of Iceland; *m* 1972, Naomi Ferguson, da of Robert Morgan Wilson (d 1977); 1 s, 2 da; *Career* ptnr Peat Marwick Mitchell and Co Chartered Accountants to 1983, conslt to Peat Marwick Mitchell and Co 1983-, ptnr Garrigue Hirst & Assocs 1987-, dir Struthers Advertising Gp 1988-; MP (C) Strathkelvin and Bearsden 1983-87; vice chm Scottish Conservative Party 1987; govr The Queen's College 1988-; *Recreations* golf, hill walking, theatre, skiing; *Clubs* Carlton, Western (Glasgow); *Style—* Michael Hirst Esq; Enderley, Milngavie, Glasgow

HIRST, Prof Paul Heywood; s of Herbert Hirst (d 1971), of Huddersfield, and Winifred, *née* Michelbacher; *b* 10 Nov 1927; *Educ* Huddersfield Coll, Trinity Coll Cambridge (BA, MA), Univ of London (Dip), Christ Church Oxford (MA); *Career* lectr and tutor dept of educn Oxford Univ 1955-58, lectr in philosophy of educn Univ of London Inst of Educn 1959-65; prof of educn: Kings Coll London 1965-71, Cambridge Univ 1971-88 (fell Woolfson Coll 1971-); visiting prof Univ of: BC, Malawi, Otago, Melbourne, Puerto Rico, Sydney; CNAA: vice chm ctee for educn 1975-81, chm res ctee 1988-; memb: cncl Royal Inst of Philosophy 1972-, educn sub-ctee UGC 1974-80, Ctee for Enquiry into the Educn of Children from Ethnic Minorities (Lord Swann Ctee) 1981-85; *Books* Knowledge and the Curriculum (1974), Moral Education in a Secular Society (1974), Education and its Foundation Disciplines (1983), Initial Teacher Training and the Role of the School (jtly 1988); *Recreations* music (especially opera); *Clubs* Athenaeum; *Style—* Prof Paul Hirst; 63 Norwich St, Cambridge CB2 1ND (☎ 0223 350697); Department of Education, University of Cambridge, 17 Trumpington St, Cambridge CB2 1QA (☎ 0223 332882)

HISCOCK, Robert Heath; s of Frederick Heath Hiscock (d 1963), of Highfields 257 Singlewell Rd, Gravesend Kent and Edith Rose, *née* Turnbull (d 1984); *b* 18 August 1920; *Educ* Kings Sch Rochester, London Univ (LLB);; *m* 2 July 1947, Mrs (Kathleen) Patricia Tong, da of Herbert Septimus Humphreys of Powers Ct, 25 The Avenue, Gravesend, Kent (d 1952); 1 s (Robert Grigor b 1948), 1 da (Catherine Patricia (Mrs Leadbetter) b 1952), 1 step s (Michael Ronald Tong b 1943); *Career* Sgt HG; slr 1944, ptnr Tolhurst & Hiscock 1948 and successor The Martin Tolhurst Ptnrship 1970-; Notary Public; memb Gravesend Historical Soc, Kent Archaelogical Soc, Gravesend Cons Assoc, Law Soc; FSA; *Books* contrib Archaeologia Cantiana; *Recreations* gardening, walking; *Style—* Robert Hiscock, Esq; 10 Old Road East, Gravesend, Kent (☎ 0474 567 378); 7 Wrotham Rd, Gravesend, Kent DA11 OPD (☎ 0474 325 531, fax 0474 560 771)

HISCOX, Lady Julia Elizabeth; *née* Meade; 3 da of 6 Earl of Clanwilliam, *qv*; *b* 31 Dec 1953; *m* 12 Oct 1985, Robert R S Hiscox, o son of Ralph Hiscox (d 1970), CBE, Netherton Grove, London SW10; 1 s (b 1987); *Style—* Lady Julia Hiscox

HISKEY, Rex Arthur; s of Harry Charles Hiskey, and Gwynneth, *née* Bush; *b* 9 Mar 1947; *Educ* Birmingham Univ (LLB); *m* 2 Oct 1971, Christine Elizabeth, da of Maurice Henry Cobbold; 1 s (Thomas b 1981), 1 da (Florence b 1986); *Career* slr private practice hldg various local appts, ptnr Hayes & Storr; *Style—* Rex A Hiskey, Esq; Chancery Lane, Wells-next-the-Sea, Norfolk (☎ 0328 710210, fax 0328 711261)

HISLOP, Ian; s of late David Atholl Hislop, and Helen Hislop; *b* 13 July 1960; *Educ* Ardingly Coll Sussex, Magdalen Coll Oxford (BA); *m* 16 April 1988, Victoria, *née* Hamson; *Career* scriptwriter Spitting Image 1984-, columnist The Listener 1985, ed Private Eye 1986-; regular contrib and book reviewer and contrib to various newspapers and magazines, writer and broadcaster for radio and tv; *Books* Gnome of the Rose (ed 1987), Secret Diary of a Lord Gnome (1985), Battle of Britain (1987), Heir of Sorrows (co-writer, 1988); *Style—* Ian Hislop, Esq; Private Eye, 6 Carlisle St, London W1V 5RG

HISLOP, John Leslie; MC (1944); s of Maj Arthur Fowler Hislop (d 1918), of Castle Park, Preston Pans, and Janet Grace, *née* Wilson (d 1940); *b* 12 Dec 1911; *Educ* Wellington Coll, RMC Sandhurst; *m* 6 Oct 1945, Jean Christian, da of William Albert Bankier, of Nonsuch, Calne; 2 s (Ian b 1948, Andrew b 1951); *Career* 1939-45 War: 98 Field Rgt RA (Surrey, Sussex, Yeomanry), 21 Anti-Tank Regt (Dunkirk), 'Phantoms' and SAS (NW Europe, 1944); breeding and racing horses; bred and owned (with Mrs Hislop) Brigadier Gerard, winner of 17 races from 18 starts, inc The Two Thousand Guineas, King George VI and Queen Elizabeth Stakes, Eclipse Stakes, Middle Park Stakes, Champion Stakes (twice); leading amateur rider on the flat 1938, 1939 and 1946-56; 3 in Grand Nat on Kami 1947; racing corr The Observer 1946-52, md The Br Racehorse 1949-80; *Books* Far From a Gentleman, Anything But A Soldier, Steeple Chasing, The Turf (Britain in Pictures);; *Recreations* reading, gardening; *Clubs* Jockey, White's; *Style—* John Hislop, Esq, MC; Regal Lodge, Exning, Newmarket, Suffolk CB8 7EN (☎ (0638) 77255)

HISLOP, John Samuel; s of Andrew James Hislop (d 1978), of Colwyn Bay, and Miriam, *née* Davies; *b* 18 April 1932; *Educ* Abergele GS; *m* 1967, Enid, da of Edward Roberts Rhyl (d 1964); 2 s (Mark b 1959, Timothy b 1964); *Career* FICA; *Recreations* farming, theatre, opera, charity fund-raising; *Clubs* Royal Overseas; *Style—* John Hislop, Esq; Geinas House, Bodfari, Clwyd (☎ 0745 75219); 17 Clwyd St, Rhyl Clwyd (☎ 0745 343118)

HISTON, John Robert; s of Robert Histon (d 1986), of Cheshire, and Elizabeth

Histon, *née* Eshelby; *b* 16 August 1938; *Educ* Wellington Boys Sch, Altrinchan GS, Manchester Univ; *m* 1966, Susan Alicia, da of William Ronald Missett, of Cheshire; 2 da (Samantha Charlotte b 1967, Sophie Fleur b 1970); *Career* chartered architect; snr ptnr Covell Mattews Histon Partnership; dir: Corell Matthews Partnership, Marthal Investmts; RIBA (1972), FCIArb (1984); *Recreations* sailing, offshire racing, carriage driving; *Clubs* Royal Thames Yacht, Pwllhell Sailing, Irish Sea Offshore Racing Assocn, Cheshire Carriage Driving; *Style*— John Histon, Esq;; The Hermitage, Holmes-Chapel, Cheshire CW4 8DP (☎ (0477) 33130); 20 Kennedy Street, Manchester M2 4BS (☎ (061 236) 9000, fax (061 228) 1515)

HITCH, Brian; CMG (1985), CVO (1980); s of Richard Souter Hitch (d 1986), of Wisbech, Cambridge, and Gladys Evelyn, *née* Harley; *b* 2 June 1932; *Educ* Wisbech GS, Magdalene Coll Cambridge (BA, MA); *m* 4 Sept 1954, Margaret (Margot) Kathleen, 2 da (Susan Jennifer Magdalene b 1956, Caroline Margaret b 1959); *Career* diplomat FO 1955-; lang student, second (formerly third) sec Tokyo 1955-61, Far Eastern dept FO 1961-62, first (formerly second) sec Havana 1962-64, language student first sec Athens 1965-68, head of chancery Tokyo 1968-72, asst head Southern European Dept FCO 1972-73 head (formerly dep head) Marine and Transport dept FCO 1973-75, cncllr: (Bonn Gp) Bonn 1975-77, cncllr and consul-gen Algiers 1977- 80, consul-gen Munich 1980-84, minister Tokyo 1984-87, high cmmr Malta 1988-; LRAM 1949. FRCO 1950; *Recreations* music; *Clubs* VOCUC; *Style*— Brian Hitch, Esq; British High Commission, 7 St Annes's St, Floriana, Malta GC (☎ 2331348, telex MW 1249)

HITCHCOCK, Dr Anthony; s of Dr Ronald Hitchcock (d 1976), of Bishops Waltham, Hants, and Hilda *née* Gould; *b* 26 June 1929; *Educ* Bedales Petersfield Hants, Manchester GS, Trinity Coll Cambridge (BA, PhD), Univ of Chicago; *m* 6 June 1953, Audrey Ellen, da of William Ashworth, of Hartshill, Stoke on Trent; 1 s (Pier J O b 1957), 2 da (Rowena J I b 1959, Elfrida I A b 1963); *Career* UKAEA (Risley, Harwell, Windscale, Winfrith) 1953-67, hd of safety and transportation, transport and road res laboratory 1967-76 and 1979-; DOE 1976-79; C Phys 1959, MCIT 1976; *Books* Nuclear Reactor Control (1960); *Recreations* Bridge; *Style*— Dr Anthony Hitchcock; Seal point, Comeragh Close, Golf Club Road, Woking Surrey GU22 0LZ (☎ 04862 5219); TRRL Crowthorne, Berks RG11 6AU (☎ 0744 770024)

HITCHCOCK, Geoffrey Lionel Henry; CBE (1975, OBE 1957); s of Maj Frank Bridge Hitchcock, MC (d 1968), of Bay Lodge, Danbury, Essex, and Mildred Sloane Stanley (d 1973); *b* 10 Sept 1915; *Educ* The Oratory Sch, Hertford Coll Oxford; *m* 1950, Rosemary Eva, da of Albert de las Casas (d 1947), of The Beeches, Washfield, Tiverton, Devon; 2 s (Jeremy, Roger), 1 da (Rosamund); *Career* cmmnd 2 Bn London Rifle Bde 1939, served with East African Forces (Africa and SE Asia) 1940-46, ret temp Maj; joined British Cncl 1939 (rejoined 1946), liaison offr Germany 1950-54; Br Cncl rep: Austria 1954-59, Yugoslavia 1961-67; controller Home Div 1970-73; Br Cncl rep France and cultural cnsllr Br Embassy Paris 1973-76, ret; *Recreations* racing, gardening; *Clubs* Travellers'; *Style*— Geoffrey Hitchcock, Esq, CBE; The Old Post, Shipton-under-Wychwood, Oxon (☎ 0993 831474)

HITCHCOCK, (Manfred) Witgar Sweetlove; s of Manfred Cooper Hitchcock (d 1957), of The Mill House, Bures, Suffolk, and Margaret, *née* Sweetlove, MBE (d 1987); *b* 7 June 1923; *Educ* Gresham's Sch Norfolk, St Catherine's Coll Cambridge (MA); *Career* scientific staff ARC 1944-47; C Hitchcock Ltd (animal feed mfrs): joined 1947, dir 1952, chm and jt md 1957-68, chm and md 1968-; tres Bures Victory Hall 1955-62, former tres and chm Bures and Dist Agric Club, ctee memb Bures and Dist Local History and Natural Soc; assoc memb Inst of Commercial and Agric Merchants 1948;; *Recreations* tennis, walking, travel, reading, researching family history; *Style*— Witgar Hitchcock, Esq

HITCHING, His Honour Judge Alan Norman; s of Norman Henry Samuel Hitching (d 1987), and Grace Ellen, *née* Bellchamber; *b* 5 Jan 1941; *Educ* Forest Sch Snaresbrook, Ch Ch Oxford (MA BCL); *m* 1967, Hilda Muriel, da of Arthur William King (d 1984); 2 s (Malcolm b 1972, Robert b 1977), 1 da (Isabel b 1969); *Career* barr Temple 1964, Recorder 1985-87, Circuit Judge 1987-; *Style*— His Honour Judge Alan Hitching; 9 Monkhams Drive, Woodford Green, Essex

HITCHINGS, Russell Walter; s of Walter Hitchings (d 1956), and Gladys Magdelin, *née* Bell; *b* 22 Mar 1922; *Educ* Rutlish Sch, RMC Sandhurst; *m* 1, 1941 (m dis 1956), Joan Kathleen Hughes (d 1980); 1 s (Derek Russell b 1947, d 1979); 2 da (Janet Kathleen b 1943, Ann Kathleen b 1948); m 2, 1956 (m dis 1961), Olga Dubska (d 1975); m 3, 24 Jan 1963, Betty Jean, JP, da of Keith Robinson (d 1978); 1 da (Julia Betty b 1964); *Career* TA Middx Yeo 1939, Cadet RMC Sandhurst 1942-43, Royal Tank Regt 1943-46; organiser Liberal Pty Orgn 1946-50, gen mangr Pilot Travel Ltd 1950-51, exec Eldridge and Co Ltd 1951-53; H J Symons (agencies) Ltd: dir 1953-55, md 1955, managing ptnr; H J Symons Gp of Cos: chm and chief exec 1960, exec and pres 1987, ret 1988; forestry owner, underwriting memb Lloyd's, memb Liberal Pty; Freeman City of London 1969, memb Worshipful Co of Blacksmiths; FCIB 1955; *Recreations* sailing, gardening; *Clubs* Royal Thames YC, Royal Ocean Racing, Lloyd's YC, City Livery; *Style*— Russell Hitchings, Esq; The Mount, South Godstone, Surrey RH9 8SD (☎ 0342 892176, 893488)

HITCHMAN, Frank Hendrick; s of Sir (Edwin) Alan Hitchman, KCB (d 1980), of London, and Katharine Mumford, *née* Hendrick; *b* 21 July 1941; *Educ* Westminster Sch, Univ of St Andrews (BSc); *Career* Coopers & Lybrand 1964-69, Samuel Montagu & Co Ltd 1970-73, Sedgwick Gp plc 1973-: sec 1980-85, dir E W Payne Co Ltd 1985-; FCA 1978; *Recreations* opera, travel, collecting; *Style*— Frank Hitchman, Esq; 9 West Warwick Place, London SW1V 2DL (☎ 01 821 1695); Upper End, Chaddleworth, Newbury, Berks RG16 0EA; Aldgate House, 33 Aldgate High St, London EC3N 1AJ (☎ 01 623 8080, fax 01 3750361, telex 6952031)

HITCHON, George Michael; s of Alfred Clifford Hitchon (d 1987), and Beatrice Helen, *née* Daniels (d 1982); *b* 26 Nov 1944; *Educ* King Edward's Five Ways Sch, Newent Sch, Univ of Nottingham (MSc); *Career* horticulturist at W of Scotland Agric Coll 1969-; dir Ayrshire Arts Festival 1983-, pres Kyle and Carrick Civic Soc 1981-; *Recreations* music, conservation, architectural history, curling; *Clubs* Auchincruive Curling; *Style*— George M Hitchon, Esq; West of Scotland Agric Coll, Auchincruive, Ayr KA6 5HN (☎ 0292 520331)

HIVES, Hon David Benjamin; s of 1 Baron Hives, CH, MBE (d 1965); *b* 1931; *Educ* Repton; *m* 1954, Shirley, da of late Harold Walker, of Duffield, Derbys; 1 s, 2 da; *Career* Gp Capt RAF (retd); air attaché The Hague 1976-78, cdr RAF Hong Kong 1981-83; *Recreations* fishing, shooting, skiing; *Style*— The Hon David Hives; Cumberhill House, Duffield, Derbys DE6 4HA

HIVES, Hon Mrs; Dinah; *née* Wilson-North; da of F Wilson-North, of Walcott, Norfolk; *b* 13 Dec 1928; *m* 1956, Hon Peter Anthony Hives (d 1974); 1 s, 3 da; *Style*— The Hon Mrs Peter Hives; Harmer Garry, Harmer Green Lane, Welwyn, Herts

HIVES, Hon Michael Bruce; s of 1 Baron Hives, CH, MBE (d 1965); *b* 1926; *Educ* Repton; *m* 1951, Janet Rosemary, da of late W E Gee, of Lynngarth, Duffield, Derby; 2 s, 1 da; *Style*— The Hon Michael Hives; Fairfield, The Pastures, Duffield, Derbys

HOARE, Capt (Edward Melvill) Brodie; DSC (1944); s of Joseph Brodie Hoare (d 1962), of Meole Brace Hall, Shrewsbury, and Gwendolen Margaret, *née* Melvill; *b* 18 Dec 1918; *Educ* RNC Dartmouth; *m* 20 Dec 1951, Nancy Beatrix, da of Maj John Edward Mountague Bradish-Ellames (d 1984), of Manor House, Little Marlow, Bucks, and 9 West Eaton Place, London, SW1; 2 s (Antony b 1953, Mark b 1957), 1 da (Caroline b 1955); *Career* RN 1932-69; WWII, served Home Waters and Pacific 1939-45, Cdr 1952, Jt Planning Staff MOD 1954-57, asst sec COS Ctee MOD 1959-61, Capt 1960, Queen's Harbourmaster Gilbraltar 1961-63, chief of staff to C-in-C Portsmouth 1965-67, Cdre def intelligence staff MOD 1967-69; ADC to HM The Queen 1968-69; dir Br Shippers' Cncl 1970-79, pres Soc of Shipping Execs 1980-87; underwriting memb of Lloyd's 1973-; *Recreations* country living, music; *Clubs* Army and Navy; *Style*— Capt Brodie Hoare, DSC, RN; Velhurst Farm, Alfold, Cranleigh, Surrey (☎ 0403 752 224)

HOARE, Prof Charles Antony Richard; s of Henry Samuel Malortie Hoare, of 54 Copers Cope Rd, Beckenham, Kent, and Marjorie Francs, *née* Villiers; *b* 11 Jan 1934; *Educ* King's Sch Canterbury, Merton Coll Oxford (MA), Moscow State Univ; *m* 13 Jan 1962, Jill, da of John Pym, of Foxwold, Brasted Chart, Westerham, Kent; 2 s (Thomas b 1964, Matthew b 1967, d 1981), 1 da (Joanna b 1965); *Career* Nat Serv RN 1956-8, Lt RNR 1958; Elliot Bros Ltd 1960-69: programmer, chief engr, tech mangr, chief scientist; prof computer sci Queen's Univ Belfast 1969-77, prof computation Oxford Univ 1977-; Turing Award 1980, Faraday Medal 1985; Hon DSc: Univ Southern Calif (1979), Univ Warwick (1985), Univ Pennsylvania (1986), Queen's Univ Belfast (1987); Soc Stran Accad dei Lincei 1988, DFBCS 1978, FRS 1982; *Books* Structured Programming (1972), Communicating Sequential Processes (1985), Essays in Computing Science (1988); *Recreations* reading, walking, swimming, music; *Style*— Prof C A R Hoare; 22 Chalfont Rd, Oxford OX2 6TH (☎ 0865 58933); Computing Laboratory, 8-11 Keble Rd, Oxford OX1 3QD (☎ 0865 273 841, fax 0865 273 839)

HOARE, Lady Christina Alice; *née* McDonnell; only da of 8 Earl of Antrim, KBE, JP, DL (d 1977), and Angela Christina, *née* Sykes (d 1984); *b* 18 Sept 1938; *Educ* Les Oiseaux Convent, Slade Sch of Art (Dip of Fine Arts); *m* 23 Jan 1963, Joseph Andrew Christopher Hoare, *qv*, s of Sir Reginald Hoare, KCMG (d 1954); 1 s (Charles William Reginald b 1966), 2 da (Jane Alice Patience b 1963, Lucy Mary Christina b 1968); *Career* artist; fndr Christian art centre 1988; memb Lloyd's 1979-; *Recreations* painting, meeting friends; *Clubs* Arts; *Style*— Lady Christina Hoare; Hartridge Manor Farm, Cranbrook, Kent TN17 2NA

HOARE, David John; s of Sir Peter William Hoare, 7 Bt (d 1973), and hp of bro, Sir Peter Richard David Hoare, 8 Bt; *b* 8 Oct 1935; *Educ* Eton; *m* 1, 1965, Mary Vanessa, yr da of Peter Cardew, of Westhanger, Cleeve, Bristol, 1 s (Simon b 1967); m 2, 1984, Virginia Victoria Labes, da of Michael Menzies, of Long Island, NY.; *Career* banker and farmer; ptnr in family co, C Hoare and Co; *Recreations* fishing, shooting, skiing; *Style*— David Hoare, Esq; 21 Kelso Place, London W8 (☎ 01 937 9925); Luscombe Castle, Dawlish, Devon; C Hoare and Co, 37 Fleet St, London EC4P 4DQ (☎ 01 353 4522)

HOARE, Ernest George; *b* 9 June 1927; *Educ* Saltash GS; *m* 1950, Nancy Beatrice; 3 s; *Career* md J and F Pool (Hldgs) Ltd 1970-83, chm 1983-87; dir: Western Motor Hldgs 1980-84, Western Enterprise Fund 1982-84, Cornwall Hospitals Independent Trust 1979-; memb Industl Tbnls Panel 1976-; chm Cornwall Gp CBI 1984-85; FCA; memb South West Industl Devpt Bd 1986-; chm Cornwall and Devon Area Manpower Bd 1986-; govr Cornwall Coll 1984-; cons CI Gp plc 1987-88; cnsllr DTI Enterprise 1988-; *Recreations* gardening, ctee work; *Clubs* Royal Thames YC; *Style*— Ernest Hoare Esq; 51 Pendarves Rd, Camborne, Cornwall (☎ 0209 714332)

HOARE, Hon Mrs (Frances Evelyn); *née* Hogg; da of Baron Hailsham of St Marylebone (Life Peer); *b* 1949; *Educ* St Paul's Girls' Sch, Homerton Teacher Training Coll Cambridge; *m* 1970, Richard Quintin Hoare; 2 s, 1 da; *Style*— The Hon Mrs Hoare; 1 Logan Pla, London W8

HOARE, Henry Cadogan; s of Henry Peregrine Rennie Hoare (d 1981), and Lady Beatrix Lilian Ethel Cadogan (*see* Lady Beatrix Fanshawe); *b* 23 Nov 1931; *Educ* Eton, Trinity Coll Cambridge (BA); *m* 1, 30 May 1959 (m dis 1970), Pamela Saxon, da of late Col G F Bunbury, OBE; 2 s (Timothy b 1960, Nicholas b 1964), 1 da (Arabella b 1968); m 2, 16 June 1977, Caromy Maxwell Macdonald, da of Robert Jenkins, CBE, JP; *Career* dir Nat Mutual Life 1985, chm C Hoare & Co 1988 (managing ptnr 1959); *Style*— Henry Hoare, Esq

HOARE, John Michael; s of Leslie Frank Hoare (d 1976), of Leatherhead, and Gladys, *née* Mepham; *b* 23 Oct 1932; *Educ* Raynes Park GS, Christ's Coll Cambridge (BA); *m* 3 Aug 1963, Brita Gertrud, da of Gustav Hjalte (d 1978), of Falkenberg, Sweden; 1 s (Nicholas b 1968), 1 da (Katherine b 1966); *Career* Nat Serv 2 Lt RA 1951-52; asst sec Utd Bristol Hosps 1960-62, house govr St Stephen's Hosps 1963-65, asst clerk of govrs St Thomas's Hosp 1965-67, admin Northwick Park Hosp Gp 1967-73, regnl gen mangr Wessex RHA 1984-(regnl admin 1973-84); memb Inst Health Serv Mgmnt 1960-; *Recreations* reading, music, walking, squash; *Style*— John Hoare, Esq; 24 Clansentum Rd, Winchester SO23 9QE

HOARE, Joseph Andrew Christopher; s of Sir Reginald Hervey Hoare, KCMG (d 1954), and Lucy Joan (d 1971), da of William George Frederick Cavendish-Bentinck, JP, and sis of 8 and 9 Dukes of Portland; *b* 23 Mar 1925; *Educ* Eton, Balliol Coll Oxford (MA); *m* 23 Jan 1963, Lady Christina Alice McDonnell, *qv*, da of 13 Earl of Antrim, KBE (d 1977); 1 s, 2 da; *Career* Fl Offr RAF Regt 1946-47; Fl Offr 604 Sqdn R AUX AF 1951-57; dir Canadian Overseas Packaging Industs 1962-; memb Stock Exchange 1957-77, underwriting memb Lloyd's 1985; chm Assoc of Chartered and Tech Analysts 1970-73; farmer 1972-;; *Clubs* Brooks's; *Style*— Joseph Hoare, Esq; Hartridge Manor Farm, Cranbrook, Kent TN17 2NA

HOARE, Kenneth Ninian; MBE (1977); s of Capt Frank Edgar Hoare, RAOC (d 1958), and Mabel Elizabeth, *née* Powell (d 1987); *b* 4 Mar 1916; *Educ* Cardiff HS, Jesus Coll Oxford (MA); *m* 1, 18 June 1940 (m dis 1970), Marion Gertrude, da of Rev

Dr Frederick Augustus Morland Spencer, of Oxford; 2 da (Gillian Sheila (Mrs Button) b 1947, Celia Jennifer (Mrs Reading) b 1952); m 2, 17 June 1971, Daphne Josephine, da of Donald Elstob Lubbock (d 1979), of Leatherhead, Surrey; *Career* cmmnd RA 1938, SO (intelligence) 1939-40, invalided 1940; dir admin Res Assoc for the Paper & Bd and Printing & Packaging Indust UK 1945-79, sec gen Int Assoc of Res Insts for Graphic Arts Indust Switzerland 1965-; Liveryman Worshipful Co of Stationers 1977; FInstD; *Books* Graphic Arts Research (1972, 1973, 1984); *Recreations* reading, travel, gardening; *Clubs* IOD, Oxford Union; *Style*— Kennneth Hoare, Esq, MBE; Fetcham Pk, Leatherhead, Surrey; Old Bell Cottage, Ferring, W Sussex

HOARE, Laura, Lady; Laura Ray; o da of Sir John Esplen, 1 Bt, KBE (d 1930); *m* 10 July 1929, Sir Peter William Hoare, 7 Bt (d 1973); 2 s; *Style*— Laura, Lady Hoare; Luscombe Castle, Dawlish, Devon

HOARE, Michael Rollo; s of Rollo Hoare (d 1983), of Dogmersfield, and Elizabeth, *née* Charrington; *b* 8 Mar 1944; *Educ* Eton, New Coll Oxford; *m* 1, 1965 (m dis 1978), Penelope, da of Sir Charles Mander, 3 Bt, *qv* ; 2 da (Venetia b 1965, Fiona b 1969); m 2, 1981, Caroline Jane, da of Derek Abele; 1 s (Rollo b 1987), 1 da (Isabella b 1985); *Career* memb Stock Exchange 1977-81, managing ptnr C Hoare & Co 1982-; govr RAM 1984-; *Recreations* hunting, skiing, singing, gardening; *Clubs* Brooks's; *Style*— Michael Hoare, Esq; C Hoare & Co, 37 Fleet St, London EC4P 4DQ

HOARE, Sir Peter Richard David; 8 Bt (GB 1786); s of Sir Peter William Hoare, 7 Bt (d 1973), of Luscombe Castle, Dawlish, Devon; *b* 22 Mar 1932; *Educ* Eton; *m* 1961 (m dis 1967), Jane, da of late Daniel Orme, m 2, 1978 (m dis 1982), Katrin Alexa, da of late Erwin Bernstiel, m 3, 1983, Angela Francesca de la Sierra, da of Fidel Fernando Ayarza, of Santiago, Chile; *Heir* bro, David John Hoare; *Career* co dir; *Clubs* Royal Automobile; *Style*— Sir Peter Hoare, Bt; c/o Crèdit Andorrà, Av Princep Benlloch 19, Andorra La Vella, Principality of Andorra

HOARE, Quintin Vincent; OBE (1944); s of Maj Vincent Robertson Hoare (ka 1915), and Elspeth Florence, *née* Hogg (d 1965); *b* 21 June 1907; *Educ* Eton, Oriel Coll Oxford; *m* 1, 2 May 1936 (m dis 1948), Lucy Florence, da of Very Rev Gordon Selwyn, Dean of Winchester; 3 s ((Benjamin) Quintin b 1938, Gavin Quintin b 1940 (d 1986), Richard Quintin (Tigger) b 1943); m 2, Rosemary, da of Lt-Col Charles Hezlet, DSO (d 1965); 2 s (David Quintin b 1954, d 1981, Nicholas Quintin b 1956), 1 da (Belinda Rosemary Cash b 1958); *Career* 2 Rangers TA 1933-36, 8 KRRC 1939-45, AA and QMG (formerly SO) 6 Armed Div 1940-45; sr ptnr C Hoare & Co (joined 1928, managing ptnr 1935); *Recreations* golf, bridge; *Clubs* White's, Portland, Royal St George's Golf, Royal Cinque Ports Golf, Rye Golf; *Style*— Quintin Hoare, Esq, OBE; Stuart House, Delf St, Sandwich, Kent (☎ 0304 612 133); 37 Fleet St, London EC4 (☎ 01 353 4522)

HOARE, Richard Quintin; s of Quintin Vincent Hoare, OBE, and Lucy Florence, *née* Selwyn; *b* 30 Jan 1943; *Educ* Eton; *m* 19 Oct 1970, Hon Frances Evelyn Hogg, da of Lord Hailsham of St Marylebone, KG; 2 s (Alexander b 1973, Charles b 1976), 1 da (Elizabeth b 1978); *Career* HAC 1 RHA 1963-68, Home Serv Force HAC Detachment 1985-88; chm Bulldog Securities Ltd 1986 (dir 1964); dir: William Weston Gallery Ltd 1986, Yelverton Investmts plc 1986; managing ptnr Hoare & Co Bankers 1969; govr Westminster Med Sch 1972-76, memb African Med Res Fndn 1977-84, vice-pres Winchester & Dist MacMillan Servs Appeal; memb BBA; *Recreations* travel, walking, stalking; *Clubs* White's; *Style*— Richard Hoare, Esq; Tangier House, Wootton St Lawrence, Basingstoke, Hants RG23 8PH (☎ 0256 780 240); 67 Victoria Rd, London W8 (☎ 01 376 2440); 37 Fleet St, London EC4 P4DG (☎ 01 353 4522, fax 01 353 4521, telex 24622)

HOARE, Col Ronald John; CBE (1947); *b* 31 August 1913; *Educ* St Paul's; *m* 1948, Anne Louise, da of late Ronald Deterding, of Kelling Hall, Holt, Norfolk; 1 s, 2 da; *Career* Col RA, ret; chm: RJH Gp Ltd, Maranello Concessionaires Ltd, Frien Investmts Ltd, Franco Britannic Autos Ltd, Chute Ltd, Weber UK Ltd, Weber Concessionaires Ltd; *Recreations* shooting; *Clubs* Boodle's, Cavalry and Guard's; *Style*— Col Ronald Hoare, CBE; 4 Leyton Conyers, Martello Park, Canford Cliffs, Poole, Dorset BH13 7BA (☎ 0202 709022)

HOARE, Sarah, Lady; Sarah Lindsay; *née* Herald; o child of Robert Irwin Herald (d 1956), of Glengyle, Belfast, and Alma May, *née* Sinanian (d 1969); *Educ* Ashleigh House Belfast; *m* 1, James Henry Bamber (d 1978); m 2, 24 March 1984 (m dis 1986), as his 3 w, Sir Frederick Alfred Hoare, 1 and last Bt (d 1986); *Recreations* music, sailing; *Style*— Sarah, Lady Hoare; 82 Eaton Place, London SW1

HOARE, Sir Timothy Edward Charles; 8 Bt (I 1784); s of Sir Edward O'Bryen Hoare, 7 Bt (d 1969); *b* 11 Nov 1934; *Educ* Radley, Worcester Coll Oxford (MA), London Univ (MA); *m* 1969, Felicity Anne, da of Peter Boddington; 1 s, 2 da (twins Louisa Hope and Kate Annabella b 1972); *Heir* s Charles James Hoare b 15 March 1971; *Career* dir Career Plan Ltd, New Metals and Chems Ltd, memb: Gen Synod of C of E 1970-; Chadwick Cmmn on Church and State; Crown Appointments 1987; supporter Arsenal FC; dir World Vision of Br, govr Canford Sch; Fell Linnean Soc, FZS; *Recreations* music, literature, natural history; *Clubs* MCC; *Style*— Sir Timothy Hoare, Bt; 10 Belitha Villas, London N1 (☎ 01 607 7359)

HOBAN, (Brian) Michael Stanislaus; s of Capt Richard Aloysius Hoban, of Georgetown, British Guiana (d 1930); *b* 7 Oct 1921; *Educ* Charterhouse, Univ Coll Oxford (MA); *m* 1947, Jasmine Jane, da of Jasper Cyril Homes, MC, of Charterhouse, Godalming (d 1978); 1 s, 1 da (and 1 da decd); *Career* Capt Westminster Dragoons, 2 Co London Yeomanry served NW Europe 1944-45 (despatches), Capt Northamptonshire Yeo 1950-59; asst master: Uppingham Sch 1949-52, Shrewsbury Sch 1952-59; headmaster: St Edmund's Sch Canterbury 1960-64, Bradfield Coll 1964-71, Harrow 1971-81; hon tres HMC 1975-80 (hon assoc memb 1981-); govr: Wellington Coll 1981-, St Edmund's Sch Canterbury 1974-, St Margaret's Sch Bushey 1974; Sometime memb of central advsy bd RAF Coll, Cranwell; pt/t chm of various Civil Serv selection bds 1982-; JP Berks 1967-71; *Books* Jesu Parvule (with Donald Swann); *Recreations* music, reading, walking, golf; *Clubs* Vincent's, East India and Sports, Devonshire and Public Schools; *Style*— Michael Hoban, Esq; Upcot, Wantage Rd, Streatley, Berks RG8 9LD (☎ 0491 873 419)

HOBART, Caroline, Lady; Caroline Fleur; yr da of Col Henry Monckton Vatcher, MC, of Valeran, St Brelade's, Jersey (d 1954), and Beryl Methwold, *née* Walrond; *m* 1, 22 Feb 1955, as his 3 w, 11 Duke of Leeds (d 1963); m 2, 30 March 1968 (m dis 1975), Peter Hendrik Peregrine Hoos; m 3, 1975, as his 2 w, Lt Cdr Sir Robert Hampden Hobart, 3 Bt (d 1988); *Career* artist (paints under name of Caroline Leeds); *Style*— Caroline, Lady Hobart; 42 Egerton Gardens, London SW3 2BZ

HOBART, Sir John Vere; 4 Bt (UK 1914); s of Sir Robert Hampden Hobart, 3 Bt (d 1988), and his 1 w Sylvia, *née* Argo (d 1965); gggs of 3 Earl of Buckinghamshire and h p to kinsman 10 Earl; *b* 9 April 1945; *m* 1980, Kate, o da of late George Henry Iddles, of Cowes, Isle of Wight; 2 s (George Hampden, James Henry Miles b 1986); *Heir* s, George Hampden Hobart b 10 June 1982; *Career* restaurateur; *Style*— John Hobart, Esq; Shore End, Queen's Road, Cowes, Isle of Wight

HOBART, Leonard Frederick; s of Leonard Francis Hobart, of Clacton, Essex, and Margaret Kate, *née* Wilkinson; *b* 2 Mar 1926; *Educ* William Ellis Sch London, Regent St Poly (Dip Arch); *m* 19 Oct 1947, Ida Evelyn, da of Carlo Rasmussen, of Kolding, Denmark (d 1977); 2 s (Martin Leonard b 1949, Colin Frederick b 1952); *Career* Army 1944-47; architect; sr ptnr Culpin Ptnrship; Freeman City of London 1987, Liveryman Worshipful Co of Glaziers & Painters of Glass 1989; FRIBA, FCIArb; *Recreations* travel; *Clubs* Danish; *Style*— Leonard Hobart, Esq; 68 Galley Lane, Barnet, Herts ENS 4AL (☎ 01 449 0344); Culpin Partnership, Hogarth House, Paradise Rd, Richmond, Surrey TWA 1SE (☎ 01 948 4281, fax 01 948 5102)

HOBBS, Lady Clare Charlotte Rosemary; *née* Finch-Knightley; da of 11 Earl of Aylesford; *b* 13 Sept 1959; *m* 1985, James Remington Hobbs; *Style*— Lady Clare Hobbs; 10 Trevor St, London SW1

HOBBS, Edward Cullen; s of Charles Hobbs (d 1958), of 7 Railway Terrace, Ilkley, Yorks, and Gertrude Louisa, *née* Cullen (d 1960); *b* 25 Oct 1905; *Educ* Ilkley GS; *m* 29 Sept 1932, Ida Mary, da of Ralph Gozney (d 1915), of Shireoaks, Worksop, Notts; 2 s (John Peter, Richard Gozney), 2 da (Gillian Mary (Mrs Fraser), Margaret (Mrs Evans)); *Career* WWII Air Raid Warden; articled to N Williamson & Co Chartered Accountants 1923; FCA 1928, ACIS 1927; *Recreations* gardening, reading; *Style*— Edward Hobbs, Esq; 5 Trafalgar Crescent, Bridlington, N Humberside (☎ 0262 675747); Exchange St, Retford, Notts (☎ 0777 703623)

HOBBS, Herbert Harry; CB (1956), CVO (1972); s of Bertie Hobbs (d 1952), and Agnes Dora, *née* Clarke (d 1961); *b* 7 Nov 1912; *Educ* Bedford Sch, Oxford Univ; *m* 1937, Joan Hazel (d 1979), da of Arthur Timmins (d 1955); 2 s (Gerald, Richard), 1 da (Averil); *Career* civil servant 1935-72: WO 1935-63; Miny of Public Bldgs and Works (later incorporated into DOE; dir of Ancient Monuments and Historic Bldgs; USA Medal of Freedom with Bronze Palm 1946; *Recreations* music; *Style*— Harold Hobbs, Esq, CB, CVO; 9 Hemp Garden, Minehead, Somerset (☎ 0643 5350)

HOBBS, (William) James; s of Stanley Hobbs (d 1960), of Glos, and Emmeline Mary Badham (d 1948); *b* 7 April 1910; *Educ* Wellingborough; *m* 3 Feb 1937, Doris Kathleen (d 1986), da of Louis John Simmonds (d 1916), of Som; 1 s (Michael b 1946); *Career* enlisted TA 1938, RA 80 Regt HAA to 1941, RAFVR 1943-45 (fl offr), UK Theatre of Operations; civil engr to Berkshire CC 1946-73; *Recreations* fishing, gardening, walking; *Clubs* MCC, Forty; *Style*— James Hobbs, Esq; River Cottage, Lower Slaughter, nr Cheltenham, Gloucestershire (☎ 0451 20693)

HOBBS, John (Jack) Michael; TD (2 bars); s of Alfred Robert Hobbs (d 1982), and Vera Mary, *née* Selwood; father founded family business in 1927 (Hobbs Hldgs Ltd); *b* 27 Mar 1936; *Educ* The Downs Sch Somerset, Allhallows Sch Devon; *m* 4 April 1964, Jea Irene, da of Charles Harris (d 1944); 2 s (Richard John b 1965, Graham Michael b 1967); *Career* Nat Serv 2 Lt Somerset LI Cyprus 1956-58; TAVR RE 1960, 111 Engr Regt (V) 1960-78 (specialist unit), quarry advsr to Army 1978-82, Home Def Force SW Dist 1983- (Maj); dir: Hobbs Quarries 1960-81, Llanwern Slag 1962-87, Wimpey Hobbs Ltd 1982-; dep chm Hobbs Hldgs Ltd 1981-, chm Hobbs (Cornelly) Ltd 1980-86; chm: West of England branch Inst of Quarrying 1983-84, cncl Inst of Quarrying (Int) 1987-88, SW section Fedn of Civil Engrg Contractors 1985-86, safety panel Br Aggregate Construction Materials Industs 1987-; FIQ, FIHT, MIAT, MITD; *Recreations* golf; *Style*— Jack Hobbs, Esq, TD; Wimpey Hobbs Ltd, 4 High St, Nailsea, Avon BS19 1BW (☎ 0272 858151)

HOBBS, Hon Mrs (Julia Elizabeth Heather); *née* Hamilton; da of 13 Lord Belhaven and Stenton; *b* 1956; *m* 1, 1975, Richard Newbury; m 2, 1979, Stephen Hobbs; *Style*— The Hon Mrs Hobbs

HOBBS, Ven Keith; s of Percival Frank Hobbs (d 1962), and Gwennyth Mary Jenkins (d 1988); *b* 3 Mar 1925; *Educ* St Olave's GS, Exeter Coll Oxford (MA), Wells Theological Coll; *m* 1950, Mary, da of Louis Lingg Ruderman (d 1981); 2 s (Jonathan b 1955 (d 1960), Robin b 1956); 1 da (Anne b 1953 (d 1988)); *Career* DSO Min of Supply 1945-46, Instr Branch RN (Lt Cdr) 1946-56; curate: Clewer St Stephen 1958-60, Soho St Anne 1960-62, St Stephen S Kensington 1962-78; lectr and counselling coordinator Borough Road Coll 1964-77; actg gen sec Church Union 1977-78, chaplain to Bishop of Chichester 1978-81, archdeacon of Chichester 1981-; *Style*— The Ven the Archdeacon of Chichester; 4 Canon Lane, Chichester, W Sussex PO19 1PX (☎ 0234 784260)

HOBBS, Maj-Gen Michael Frederick; CBE (1982, OBE 1979, MBE 1975); s of Brig Godfrey Pennington Hobbs (d 1985), and Elizabeth Constance Mary, *née* Gathorne Hardy (d 1952); *b* 28 Feb 1937; *Educ* Eton; *m* 1967, Tessa Mary, da of Gerald Innes Churchill, of Oxon; 1 s (William b 1978), 2 da (Elizabeth b 1969, Victoria b 1970); *Career* served Gren Gds 1956-80, directing staff, staff coll 1974-77; MOD 1980-82; cdr 39 Infantry Bde 1982-84; dir of PR (Army 1984-85; GOC 4 Armoured Div 1985-87 (ret 1987); dir of Duke of Edinburgh's Award Scheme 1988-; *Recreations* field sports, horticulture; *Clubs* Army and Navy, MCC; *Style*— Maj Gen Michael Hobbs, CBE; The Red House, Kirby Cane, Bungay, Suffolk NR35 2HW; The Duke of Edinburgh's Award Scheme, 5 Prince of Wales Terrace, Kensington, London W8 5PG

HOBBS, Peter Thomas Goddard; s of Reginald Stanley Hobbs, BEM (d 1970), of Gloucester, and Phyllis Gwendoline, *née* Goddard; *b* 19 Mar 1938; *Educ* Crypt Sch Gloucester, Exeter Coll Oxford (MA); *m* Victoria Christabel, da of Rev Alan Matheson (d 1988), of Clifton Campville, Staffs; 1 da (Katherine b 1971); *Career* Nat Serv 2 Lt RASC 1957-59; Capt RCT TA 1959-68; ICI Ltd 1962-79 (final position jt personnel mangr Mond Div), gp personnel dir Wellcome Fndn and Wellcome plc 1979-; Chemical Industs Assoc 1979-: memb employment offr bd, chm trg ctee; dep chm Pharmaceuticals and Fine Chemicals Jt Industl Cncl, dir Employment Conditions Abroad Ltd 1984-, vice pres Int Inst of Personnel Mgmnt 1987-89, dir Roffey Park Inst 1989, tstee Learning from Experience Tst; FIPM 1979; *Recreations* history, topography, theatre, opera; *Clubs* United Oxford and Cambridge; *Style*— Peter Hobbs, Esq; Wellcome Foundation Ltd, Wellcome Building, 183 Euston Rd, London NW12BP (☎ 01 387 447, fax 01 388 5462, telex 8951486)

HOBBS, Ronald William; s of William Matthew Hobbs (d 1976), of Nailsea, Somerset, and Florence Harriet Martha, *née* Holder (d 1988); *b* 18 Oct 1923; *Educ*

Cotham GS, Univ of Bristol (BSc); *m* 5 June 1948, (Beatrice) May, da of Albert Hilling (d 1966), of Broadstairs, Kent; 1 s (Malcolm b 20 Nov 1951), 1 da (Marilyn b 9 May 1954); *Career* Royal Aircraft Estab 1943-46, jr engr Oscar Faber and ptnrs 1946-48, Ove Arup and ptnrs 1948- (ptnr 1961), Arup Assoc 1963- (fndr ptnr, chm 1981-84), Ove Arup Partnership 1969- (fndr dir, co chm 1984-), memb of awards panel of ARCUK 1970-, rep of ACE on Jt Contracts Tbnl 1979-, memb of cncl of Assoc of Consulting Engrs 1982-83 and 1985-87; past chm: S Bucks Lib party, Iver Parish Cncl; FICE 1985, FISTructE 1981; *Recreations* bridge, gardening, history, 18th century porcelain; *Style*— Ronald Hobbs, Esq; Ove Arup Partnership, 13 Fitzroy St, London W1P 6BQ (☎ 01 636 1531, fax 01 580 3924, telex 295341 OVARPART G)

HOBDAY, Sir Gordon Ivan; s of Alexander Thomas Hobday (d 1971), and Frances Cassandra, *née* Meads; *b* 1 Feb 1916; *Educ* Long Eaton GS, Univ Coll Nottingham (BSc, PhD, LLD); *m* 1940, Margaret Jean Joule; 1 da; *Career* chm: Boots Co Ltd 1972-82, Central Independent TV (covers E and W Midlands franchise area) 1981-85; dir Lloyds Bank 1981-86 (also chm N and E Regnl Bd); Lord-Lieut Notts 1983-, DL 1981-83; chllr Nottingham Univ 1979- (pres of cncl 1973-82); FRSC; kt 1979; *Style*— Sir Gordon Hobday; c/o Lloyds Bank, St James's St, Nottingham NG1 6FD (☎ 0602 42501)

HOBDAY, Thomas Lyrian; TD (1960), JP (Liverpool 1968), DL (Merseyside 1973); s of Thomas Owen Francis Hobday (d 1927), of Amlwch, Anglesey, and Elizabeth, *née* Denman (d 1937); *b* 22 Jan 1920; *Educ* Holt GS Liverpool, Liverpool Univ (MB, ChB, DPH, DPA), Inner Temple, Barrister-at-law; *Career* WWII 1939-46, army: cmmnd in Intelligence Corps, served in Norway, Africa, and Europe 1939-46; TA: Capt RAMC 1957, Lt-Col CO 126 Field Ambulance 1962, Col Co 208 General Hosp 1966; princ med offr Health Dept Liverpool 1957-64, travelling fell World Health Orgn (India) 1960, sr lectr in Epidemiology Univ of Liverpool 1964-85; conslt: Liverpool Health Authy, Merseyside Regl Health Authy 1974-85; QHP 1967-70; Contested Huyton 1966, memb Liverpool City Cncl 1966-73; chm: Fire Brigade, Civic Undertakings, Health and Educn ctees; memb Merseyside cc 1974-86, chief whip Cons pty; *Recreations* reading and swimming; *Clubs* Athenaeum (Liverpool); *Style*— T L Hobday, Esq, TD, JP, DL; 8 Princes Park Mansions, Toxteth, Liverpool, Merseyside L8 3SA, (☎ 051 727 2297)

HOBHOUSE, Sir Charles Chisholm; TD; s of Sir Reginald Hobhouse, 5 Bt, JP (d 1947), y s of Sir Charles P Hobhouse, 3 Bt, who was nephew of Sir John Cam Hobhouse, a leading Whig politician, created Lord Broughton 1851, who was, in his youth, friend of Lord Byron; *b* 7 Dec 1906; *Educ* Eton; *m* 1, 1946, Mary (d 1955), da of John Park, of Northumberland; m 2, 1959, Jo (Elspeth Jean), da of Thomas Spinney, of Morocco; 1 s (b 1962); *Heir* s, Charles J S Hobhouse; *Career* former stockbroker; farmer; late Hon Col N Somerset Yeo; *Recreations* hunting, shooting; *Clubs* Brooks's, City of London; *Style*— Sir Charles Hobhouse, Bt, TD; The Manor, Monkton Farleigh, Bradford-on-Avon, Wilts (☎ 0225 858558)

HOBHOUSE, Charles John Spinney; s and h of Sir Charles Hobhouse, 6 Bt, by his 2 w; *b* 27 Oct 1962; *Style*— Charles Hobhouse Esq; The Manor, Monkton Farleigh, Bradford-on-Avon, Wilts

HOBHOUSE, (Mary) Hermione; MBE (1981); da of Sir Arthur Lawrence Hobhouse, JP (d 1965), of Somerset, and Konradin Huth Jackson (d 1965); *b* 2 Feb 1934; *Educ* Cheltenham Ladies' Coll, Lady Margaret Hall Oxford (MA); *m* 1958, Henry Trevenen Davidson Graham, s of W Murray Graham (d 1956), of Cairo; 1 s (Francis Henry b 1960), 1 da (Harriet Konradin b 1964); *Career* writer, conservationist, freelance journalist 1960-76, sec Victorian Soc 1976-82, gen ed 1983; *Books* Survey of London (RCHM(E) Thomas Cubitt: Master Builder (1971), Lost London (1971), Prince Albert: His Life and Work (1983); *Recreations* gardening, looking at buildings of all periods; *Clubs* Reform; *Style*— Miss Hermione Hobhouse, MBE; 61 St Dunstan's Road, Hammersmith, London W6 8RE; Survey of London, Royal Commission on Historical Monuments (England) Newlands House, Berners Street, London W1 (☎ 01 631 5065)

HOBHOUSE, Hon Mr Justice; Sir John Stewart; 2 s of Sir John Hobhouse, MC, JP (d 1961), and Catherine, yr da of Henry Stewart-Brown (3 cous of Sir William Brown, 2 Bt); Sir John was gn of 1 and last Baron Hobhouse; *b* 31 Jan 1932; *Educ* Eton, Ch Ch Oxford (BA, BCL); *m* 1959, Susannah Sybil Caroline, o da of Sir Ashton Wentworth Roskill, QC; 2 s (William b 1963, Sebastian s b 1964), 1 da (Charlotte b 1961); *Career* barr 1955, practising at Commercial Bar to 1982, QC 1973, High Court Judge (Queen's Bench Div) 1982-; chm Cncl of Legal Educn 1986-; kt 1982; *Style*— The Hon Mr Justice Hobhouse; Royal Courts of Justice, Strand WC2 (☎ 01 936 6000)

HOBLER, Air Vice-Marshal John Forde; CB (1958), CBE (1945); s of Louis Edward Hobler (d 1950), of Rockhampton, Queensland, and Minnie Alma, *née* Forde (d 1942); *b* 26 August 1907; *Educ* Rockhampton GS Rockhampton Queensland; *m* 12 Aug 1939, Dorothy Evelyn Diana, da of Basil John Edmondes Haines (d 1965), of Wilsford House, Wilsford, Wilts; 2 s (Roger b 1942, Charles b 1948), 1 da (Sue b 1941); *Career* RAF 1933, 32 Sqdn 1933, 100 Sqdn 1933-37, instr 9 FTS 1938, Sqdn-Cdr 2 Sqdn Cosford 1939, Sqdn-Ldr 142 Sqdn France AASF 1939-40, wounded (staff duties) 1940-42, CO Raf Lossiemouth 1942-45 (4 times mentioned in despatches) staff coll 1945-48 (psa), Air Miny (Plans) 1948-50, CO RAF Habbanya Iraq 1950-52, HQ Flying Trg Cmd 1952-53, dir of personal servs Air Miny 1953-56, AOA MEAF 1956-58, AOC 25 Gp 1958-61, AOA FEAF 1961-63, ret 1963, former dir of several co's; fndr memb Rockhampton Aero Club, fndr of what is now Rockhampton Airport; FRGS 1960; *Clubs* United Services Brisbane, RAF Escaping Soc; *Style*— Air Vice-Marshal John Hobler, CB, CBE; Unit P8, The Domain Country Club, Ashmore, Queensland 4214, Aust (☎ 075 393 349)

HOBLEY, Brian; s of William Hobley (d 1959), and Harriet Hobson (d 1976); *b* 25 June 1930; *Educ* Univ of Leicester (BA); *m* 1953, Florence Elisabeth, da of John Parkes (d 1976); 1 s (Paul), 1 da (Toni); *Career* chief urban archaeologist City of London 1973-; chm Standing Ctee Archaeological Unit Mangrs, joint sec: The British Archaeologists and Developers Liaison Gp; City of London Archaeological Tst; dir: Citydig Ltd (Trading Co of City of London Archaeological Tst), Inst of Field Archaeologists (hon tres); FSA, AMA, MBIM, MIFA; *Books* Waterfront Archaeology in Britain and Northern Europe (1981, jt ed), Roman Urban Defences in the West (1983, jt ed), Roman Urban Topography in Britain and the Western Empire (1985, jt ed), The Rebirth of Towns in the West AD 700-1050 (jt ed 1988), Roman and Saxon London: a reappraisal (1986); reports in many learned journals; *Recreations* music, gardening, chess; *Style*— Brian Hobley, Esq; 21 St Martins Rd, Finham, Coventry (☎ 0203 411 068); Dept of Archaeology Museum of London, London Wall, London EC2Y 5HN (☎ 01 600 3699)

HOBLEY, Denis Harry; s of John Wilson Hobley of Bolton, Cumbria, and Ethel Anne, *née* Dixon; *b* 6 Feb 1931; *Educ* King George V GS Southport; *m* 1 April 1957, June, da of Barnard Windle (d 1982); 3 s (Philip b 12 Jan 1961, David b 11 Oct 1962, Keith b 25 Oct 1964); *Career* Nat Serv RAPC 1953-55; qualified CA 1953, sr ptnr Lithgow Nelson and Co 1985- (joined 1948); pres Liverpool Soc CAs 1986-87, memb: ctee many local charities, Methodist Ch (on dist, circuit and local ctees); FICA; *Style*— Denis Hobley, Esq; 11 Silverthorne Drive, Southport, Lancs (☎ 0704 25274); 399 Lord St, Southport, Lancs (☎ 0704 31888, fax 0704 48343)

HOBMAN, David Burton; CBE (1983); s of Joseph Burton Hobman (d 1953), and Daisy Lucy, *née* Adler (d 1961); *b* 8 June 1927; *Educ* Univ Coll Sch, Blundell's; *m* 1954, Erica, da of Hugh Irwin (d 1954); 1 s (Anthony), 1 da (Lucy); *Career* community work Forest of Dean 1954-56, Br Cncl for Aid to Refugees 1957, Nat Cncl of Social Service 1958-67, visiting lectr in social admin Nat Inst for Social Work 1967, dir Social Work Advsy Service 1968-70; dir Age Concern England 1970-87; visiting prof Sch of Social Work McGill Univ Montreal 1977, memb: BBC/ITA Appeals Advsy Cncl 1965-69, Steering Ctee Enquiry into Homelessness Nat Assistance Bd 1967-68; Advsy Cncl Nat Corpn for Care of Old People 1970-74; Metrication Bd 1974-80, Lord Goodman's Ctee Reviewing Law and Charity 1975-76, Family Housing Assoc 1969-70; conslt UN Div of Social Affairs 1968-69; observer White House Congress on Ageing 1971-; pres Int Fedn on Ageing 1977-80, 1983-87 (vice-pres 1974-77); memb: Personal Social Services Cncl 1978-80, exec ctee Nat Cncl of Vol Orgns 1981-83, Anchor Housing 1982-85; special advsr Br Delgn to World Assembly on Ageing 1982; prod Getting On (Central tv) 1987, exec sec Charities Effectiveness Review Tst 1986-; govr: Cardinal Newman Comprehensive Sch Hove 1971-76 (chm), Volunteer Centre 1975-79; KSG 1977; *Books* A Guide to Voluntary Service (1964, 2nd edn 1967), Who Cares (1971), The Social Challenge of Ageing (1978), The Impact of Ageing (1981), and numerous papers and broadcasts; *Recreations* travel, caravanning, reading, writing; *Clubs* Reform; *Style*— David Hobman Esq, CBE; Robinswood, George's Lane, Storrington, Pulborough, W Sussex RH20 3JH (☎ 090 66 2987)

HOBSON, Anthony Robert Alwyn; s of Geoffrey Dudley Hobson, MVO (d 1949), of 11 Chelsea Park Gardens, London SW3, and Gertrude Adelaide, *née* Vaughan; *b* 5 Sept 1921; *Educ* Eton, New Coll Oxford (MA); *m* 4 Dec 1959, (Elena Pauline) Tanya (d 1988), da of Igor Pavlovich Vinogradoff (d 1987), of 10 Gower St, London W1; 1 s (William b 1963), 2 da (Emma b 1960, Charlotte b 1970); *Career* WWII Scots Gds 1941-46, Capt Italy 1943-46 (despatches); dir Sotheby & Co 1949-71 (assoc 1971-77), Sandars reader in bibliography Univ of Cambridge 1974-75, Franklin Jasper Walls lectr Pierpont Morgan Library NY 1979 (hon fell 1983-), visiting fell All Souls Coll Oxford 1982-83; pres: Assoc Internationale de Bibliophile 1985-, Bibliographical Soc 1977-79, hon pres Edinburgh Bibliographical Soc 1971-; tstee: Eton Coll Collections Tst 1977-, Lambeth Palace Library 1984-; Socio Straniero Accademia Veneta 1987-; Freeman City of London, Liveryman Worshipful Co of Clothworkers; Cavaliere Al Merito della Republica Italiana; *Books* French and Italian Collectors and their Findings (1953), Great Libraries (1970), Apollo and Pegasus (1975), Humanists and Bookbinders (1989); *Recreations* travel, opera, visiting libraries founded before 1800; *Clubs* Brooks's, Roxburghe; *Style*— Anthony Hobson, Esq; The Glebe Hse, Whitsbury, Fordingbridge, Hampshire SP6 3QB (☎ 072 53 221)

HOBSON, (Alfred) Collingwood; MC (1944); s of Alfred Allen Hobson (d 1954), of Stonecroft, Woodcote, Epsom and Mary Ann Denton, *née* Collingwood; *b* 2 Mar 1917; *Educ* Marlborough, Munich Univ; *m* 7 Sept 1946, Priscilla Ruth, yst da of Maj Harry Grant Thorold (d 1946), of Cranford Hall, Kettering; 3 da (Penelope (Mrs Hedley Lewis) b 1948, Caroline (Mrs Dunant) b 1951, Diana (Mrs Elliott) b 1952); *Career* former Army Offr, served Eagle Troop RHA Europe (despatches), ret Maj; slr; late sr ptnr Druces & Attlee; *Recreations* field sports, golf, skiing; *Clubs* Boodle's; *Style*— Collingwood Hobson, Esq, MC; Birkholme Manor, Corby Glen, Grantham, Lincolnshire NG33 4LF (☎ 047 684 500)

HOBSON, Sir Harold; CBE (1971); s of Jacob Hobson; *b* 4 August 1904; *Educ* Univ of Sheffield (LittD), Oriel Coll Oxford (MA, hon fellow 1974); *m* 1, 1935, Gladys Bessie Johns (d 1979); 1 da; m 2, 1981, Nancy Penhale; *Career* special writer The Sunday Times 1976- (drama critic 1947-76), author; Chevalier of The Legion of Honour; kt 1977; *Books* Devil in Woodford Wells, French Theatre, Indirect Journey, Theatre in Britain; *Recreations* cricket, reading seventeenth century French literature; *Clubs* Lasserre (Paris); *Style*— Sir Harold Hobson, CBE; Nyton House, Westergate, Chichester, W Sussex

HOBSON, Valerie Babette Louise (Mrs John Profumo); da of late Robert Gordon Hobson, and late Violet, *née* Hamilton-Willoughby; *b* 14 April 1917; *Educ* St Augustine's Priory London, RADA; *m* 1, 1939 (m dis 1952), Anthony James Allan Havelock-Allan, now Sir Anthony Havelock-Allan, 4 Bt; 2 s (Simon, Mark); m 2, 1954, John Profumo, CBE, *qv*; 1 s (David); *Career* stage, television and film actress; *Recreations* painting, reading, writing; *Style*— Miss Valerie Hobson/Mrs John Profumo

HOCHFELDER, Harry Christopher Walter; s of Isidor Hochfelder (d 1941), of Oderberg, Czechoslovakia, and Emma, *née* Heller (d 1942); *b* 20 Dec 1914; *Educ* Gymnasium GS Saaz Bohemia, Univ Prague, Univ Erlangen (PhD); *m* 2 Oct 1948, Dagmar Carol Ann, da of Rudolf Slajch (d 1954), of Prague; 1 s (Henry b 1955), 1 da (Sonia b 1952); *Career* military service 1941-47, SOE Istanbul 1942-44, Control Commission for Germany 1945-47, (Capt); career in Civil Service: Control Commission for Germany 1947-52, Dept of Trade and Industry 1952-75, princ assist sec as head of Overseas Projects Gp 1973-74; dir Renis Commodities Ltd 1975-77; many contributions to quarterly Sudetenland, Munich; *Recreations* walking, swimming; *Clubs* Civil Service; *Style*— Harry C W Hochfelder, Esq; 67 Woodhall Gate, Pinner, Middlesex HA5 4TZ (☎ 01 428 0459)

HOCKADAY, Sir Arthur Patrick; KCB (1978, CB 1975), CMG (1969); s of (William) Ronald Hockaday (d 1974), of Plymouth, and Marian Camilla Hockaday (d 1988); *b* 17 Mar 1926; *Educ* Merchant Taylors', St John's Coll Oxford; *m* 1955, Peggy, da of Hector Wilfred Prince, of Portsmouth; *Career* private sec to successive mins and secs of state MOD 1962-65, NATO Int Staff 1965-69, asst sec-gen Defence Planning and Policy 1967-69, asst under-sec state MOD 1969-72, under-sec Cabinet Off 1972-73, dep under-sec MOD 1973-76, second perm under-sec state MOD 1976-82; sec and dir-gen Cwlth War Graves Cmmn 1982-; *Books* contrib: Ethics and Nuclear Deterrence (1982), The Strategic Defence Initiative, New Hope or New Peril? (1985), Ethics and European Security (1986); *Recreations* fell-walking; *Clubs* Naval and

Military, Civil Service; *Style—* Sir Arthur Hockaday, KCB, CMG; Commonwealth War Graves Commission, Maidenhead, Berks SL6 7DX (☎ 0628 34221)

HOCKING, Dr (Frederick) Denison (Maurice); s of Rev Almund Trevosso Hocking (d 1936), and Gertrude Vernon Mary, *née* Parkinson (d 1955); *b* 28 Feb 1899; *Educ* Leyton HS, City and Guilds Tech Coll Finsbury, Middx Hosp (MB, BS, MSc, FRSC, FRSH, MIBiol); *m* 1, 14 June 1927, Amy Gladys, da of Thomas Coucher (d 1936), of Marylebone, London; 2 da (Elizabeth b 1932, Jennifer b 1936); m 2, 4 June 1967, Kathleen, da of Dr Gerald O'Donnell (d 1972), of Redruth; *Career* conslt Pathologist and Forest Scientist, asst Pathologist Westminster Hosp 1926-34, conslt Pathologist Royal Cornwall Infirmary and SW Regional Hosp Bd 1934-64; Cornwall Co Pathologist 1941-85, actg dir Public Health Laboratory Service 1952-64; *Recreations* retired golf, sailing; *Clubs* Assoc Memb Nat Liberal; *Style—* Dr Denison Hocking; Strathaven, Sea Rd, Carlyon Bay, St Austell (☎ 0726 2470)

HOCKLEY, Rev Canon Raymond Alan; s of Henry Hockley (d 1957), and Doris *née* Stonehouse (d 1987); *b* 18 Sept 1929; *Educ* Firth Park Sch, Royal Acad of Music (BMus), Westcott House Cambridge (MA); *Career* curate St Augustine's Sheffield 1958-61, p-in-c Holy Trinity Wicker Sheffield 1961-63, chaplain Westcott House Cambridge 1963-68, fell chaplain and dir of music Emmanuel Coll Cambridge 1968-76, canon residentiary precentor and chamberlain York Minster 1976-; prize for best piece of Br Chamber Music (String Quartet) 1954, Oratorio, Suite for Orchestra, articles for learned journals; LRAM; *Recreations* cooking; *Clubs* Yorkshire; *Style—* The Rev Canon Raymond Hockley; 2 Minster Court, York (☎ 0904 624965); Dean and Chapter of York (☎ 0904 642526)

HOCKNEY, David; s of Kenneth and Laura Hockney; *b* 9 July 1937; *Educ* Bradford GS, Bradford Sch of Art, RCA; *Career* artist, photographer, costume and set designer (opera); one-man shows inc: Kasmin Ltd London 1963, 1965, 1966, 1968, 1969, 1970, 1972, Alan Gallery New York 1964-67, Louvre Paris 1974, Knoeuller Gallery 1979, 1981, 1982, 1986, Tate 1986, Hayward Gallery 1983, 1985; Exhibn photographs Hayward Gall 1983; designer: The Rake's Progress Glyndebourne 1975, The Magic Flute 1978, costumes and sets for Met Opera N York 1980; ARA; *Books* The Glue Guitar (1977), China Diary (1982), Hockney Paints the Stage (1983); *Style—* David Hockney, Esq, ARA; 7506 Santa Monica Boulevard, Los Angeles, California 90048

HOCKNEY, Michael Brett; s of Stanley Waller Hockney, of St Annes on Sea, Lancashire, and Jean, *née* Duston; *b* 29 July 1949; *Educ* King Edward VII Sch Lytham, Manchester Univ, London Sch of Economics; *m* 30 July 1983, Elizabeth Anne (Dr Elizabeth Hockney), da of Bruce James Cryer, of Richmond, Surrey; *Career* md Butterfield Day Devito Hockney 1987-, dir and memb exec ctee of Boase Massimi Pollitt 1980-87; vice-chm Berkeley Square Ball Charity Cttee 1986-; memb cncl of Royal School of Church Music 1986-; organist and Choir Master All Saints Church London SW14 1976-; FInstM, FIPA, FBIM; *Recreations* church music, 18 century English porcelain; *Clubs* IOD; *Style—* Michael B Hockney, Esq; 64 East Sheen Avenue, London SW14 (☎ 01 876 4391); Butterfield Day Devito Hockney Ltd, 47 Marylebone Lane, London W1 (☎ 01 224 3000)

HODDER, James Gordon; s of Arthur Sylvester Hodder (d 1974); *b* 14 Jan 1920; *Educ* Hardyes Sch Dorchester, London Univ; *m* 1950, Eileen Margaret, da of Thomas John Scott; 2 s; *Career* slr 1948; Gibson and Weldon 1948-50, Powers Samas Accounting Machines Ltd 1950-52, Marsh and Baxter Ltd 1952-57; vice-chm Metal Box Ltd 1979- (entered 1957, asst sec 1964, sec 1970, dir 1972); *Recreations* music, reading, cricket, swimming, walking, theatre; *Clubs* MCC, Wig and Pen; *Style—* James Hodder Esq; 7 South Drive, Wokingham, Berks (☎ 0734 780246)

HODDER-WILLIAMS, (John) Christopher Glazebrook; s of Capt Ralph Hodder-Williams, MC (d 1960), and Marjorie, *née* Glazebrook (d 1970); *b* 25 August 1926; *Educ* Eton; *m* Nov 1967, Deirdre, da of Wilfred Matthew (d 1988); 1 s (Simon), 1 da (Petra); *Career* RCS 1945-48, PA to Maj-Gen C M F White; novelist and songwriter; wrote over 70 songs for TV 1955-57; *Books* Chain Reaction, Final Approach, Turbulence, The Higher They Fly, The Main Experiment, The Egg Shaped Thing, Fistful of Digits, Ninety-Eight Point Four, Panic O'Clock, Cowards' Paradise, The Prayer Machine, The Silent Voice, The Thinktank That Leaked, The Chromosome; TV plays: The Ship That Couldn't Stop, The Higher They Fly (from the novel); *Recreations* flying, music; *Style—* Christopher Hodder-Williams, Esq; 19 Erpingham Rd, Putney, London SW15 1BE

HODDER-WILLIAMS, Mark; s of Paul Hodder-Williams, OBE, TD, of Somerset, and Felicity Blagden (d 1986); *b* 24 Mar 1939; *Educ* Rugby Sch, Oxford Univ (MA); *m* 1961, Janette Elspeth, da of Harry Archibald Cochran (d 1980), of Kent; 3 s (Andrew b 1963, James b 1964, Peter b 1968), 1 da (Susanna b 1969); *Career* Book publisher; dir: Hodder and Stoughton Hldgs Ltd; *Recreations* golf, skiing, gardening, music; *Clubs* Vincents (Oxford), Wildernesse (Sevenoaks); *Style—* Mark Hodder-Williams, Esq; 38 Greenhill Road, Otford, Sevenoaks, Kent TN14 5RS; Hodder and Stoughton Ltd, Mill Road, Dunton Green, Sevenoaks, Kent TN13 2YA

HODDER-WILLIAMS, Lt-Col Paul; OBE (1945), TD; s of Very Rev Frank Garfield Hodder-Williams (d 1960), Dean of Manchester, and Sara Myfanwy Nicholson (d 1970); *b* 29 Jan 1910; *Educ* Rugby, Gonville and Caius Coll Cambridge (MA); *m* 1936, Felicity (d 1986), da of Rt Rev Claude Martin Blagden (d 1952), Bishop of Peterborough; 2 s (Mark b 1939, Richard b 1943), 2 da (Susan b 1937, Mary Anna b 1949); *Career* joined HAC 1938, served with HAC (Maj 1942), then 99th (London Welsh) HAA Regt RA (Lt-Col cmdg 1942-45); conslt Hodder and Stoughton Ltd 1975- (joined Hodder and Stoughton Ltd 1931, dir 1936, chm 1961-75); chm The Lancet Ltd 1961-77; *Recreations* growing vegetables; *Clubs* Hawkes (Cambridge), Royal Cwlth; *Style—* Lt-Col Paul Hodder-Williams, OBE, TD; Court House, Exford, Somerset (☎ 064 383 268)

HODGART, Alan William; s of William George Hodgart, of Australia, and Hilda Murial Herschel, *née* Hester; *b* 19 July 1940; *Educ* Univ of Melbourne (Econ, MA), Univ of Cambridge; *Career* mgmnt conslt Cortis Powell Ltd (UK) 1967-76, md DHS Conslts Ltd 1976-83, dep managing ptnr Deloitte Haskins & Sells (Australia) 1983-84 (dir int strategy NY 1984-88), md Spicers Conslts Gp Ltd (UK) 1988-; *Books* The Economics of European Imperialism (1978); *Recreations* literature, 19 cent music, walking; *Clubs* Athenaeum, Princeton Univ; *Style—* Alan Hodgart Esq; 29 Micklethwaite Rd, London SW6 1QD (☎ 01 385 4548); Spicers Conslt Gp Ltd, 13 Bruton St, London W1 (☎ 01 480 7766)

HODGE, James William; s of William Hodge, of Edinburgh, and Catherine, *née* Carden (d 1977); *b* 24 Dec 1943; *Educ* Holy Cross Acad Edinburgh, Univ of Edinburgh (MA); *m* 20 June 1970, Frances Margaret, da of Michael Coyne, of Liverpool; 3 da (Catherine b 1973, Fiona b 1975, Claire b 1979); *Career* Cwlth Office 1966, 2 Sec Br Embassy Tokyo 1970-72 (3 sec 1967-69), FCO 1972-75, 1 sec BHC Layes 1975-78, FCO 1978-81, Cnsllr (commercial) Tokyo 1982-86 (1 Sec 1981-82); Cnsllr and Head of Chancery Br Embassy Copenhagen 1986-; AIL 1988; *Recreations* books, tennis, Scandinavian studies; *Clubs* Travellers', MCC; *Style—* James Hodge, Esq; c/o Foreign and Commonwealth Office (Copenhagen), King Charles St, London SW1A 2AH

HODGE, Sir John Rowland; 2 Bt (UK 1921), MBE (1940); s of Sir Rowland Hodge, 1 Bt (d 1950); *b* 1 May 1913; *Educ* Wrekin Coll, and Switzerland; *m* 1, 1936 (m dis 1939), Peggy Ann, da of Sydney Raymond Kent; m 2, 1939 (m dis 1961), Joan, da of late Sydney Foster Wilson; 3 da; m 3, 1962 (m dis 1967), Jean Wood Anderson, da of late Cdr W E Buchanan, of Edinburgh; m 4, 1967, Vivien, da of Alfred Knightley, of Norwood; 1 s, 1 da; *Heir* s, Andrew Rowland Hodge b 4 Dec 1968; *Career* formerly Lt Cdr RNVR, formerly Lt Oxfordshire and Bucks LI, WWII 1939-40; *Clubs* British Racing Drivers, Naval, Royal Malta Yacht, Royal Yachting Assoc, Cruising Assoc; *Style—* Sir John Hodge, Bt, MBE; A16 Sutherland Drive, Gunton Park, Lowestoft, Suffolk NR32 4LP; Casa Toro, St Andrews, Malta (☎ 37583)

HODGE, Sir Julian Stephen Alfred; s of Alfred Hodge, and Jane, *née* Simocks; *b* 15 Oct 1904; *Educ* Cardiff Tech Coll; *m* 31 Dec 1951, Moira, da of John Oswald Thomas (d 1983); 2 s (Robert b 24 April 1955, Jonathan b 3 April 1958), 1 da (Jane b 2 June 1953); *Career* founded Hodge & Co Accountants 1941, chm and md Hodge Gp 1963-75 (exec chm 1975-78), chm Avana Gp Ltd 1973-81, fndr and chm Bank of Wales 1971-85, chm Bank of Wales (Jersey) Ltd 1974-87, dir Bank of Wales (IOM) Ltd 1974-85; former chm: Julian S Hodge & Co Ltd, Gwent Enterprises Ltd, Hodge Fin Ltd, Hodge Life Assur Ltd, Carlyle Tst Ltd; dir: Standard Chartered Bank 1973-75, Channel Islands Conslts Ltd 1968-89; fndr: Jane Hodge Fndn 1962, Sir Julian Hodge Charitable Tst 1964; chm Aberfan Disaster Fund, cncl memb UWIST (tres 1968-76, dep pres 1976-81, pres 1981-88), tstee Welsh Sports Tst; memb: industl project sub ctee Welsh Econ Cncl 1965-68, Welsh Cncl 1968-79, fndn fund ctee Univ of Surrey, Duke of Edinburgh Conf 1974, Prince of Wales Ctee; pres S Glamorgan Dist St Johns Ambulance Bde; former govr All Hallows (Cranmore Hall) Sch Tst Ltd; KStJ (1977, CStJ 1972); Hon LLD Univ of Wales 1971; FCCA 1930, FTII 1941, FRSA; K St Gregory 1978 (Papal); kt 1970; *Books* Paradox of Financial Preservation (1959); *Recreations* golf, gardening, reading, walking; *Clubs* Victoria (St Helier), La Moye Golf (Jersey); *Style—* Sir Julian Hodge; Clos Des Suex, Mont De Coin, St Aubin, St Brelade, Jersey, Channel Islands

HODGE, Malcolm; s of Bertram William Hodge (d 1985), and Edith Olive, *née* Wilks (d 1968); *b* 5 August 1935; *Educ* Kings Coll Taunton; *m* 1968, Tyler, da of Henry Tyler; 1 s (James b 1971), 1 da (Emma Olivia b 1975); *Career* Lt 1 Bn Devonshire Regt Kenya; md chevron Int Oil Co 1978-85, dir Chevron Oil Service Co 1985-87, chm Chevron Oil Service Co Ltd Pension Tstees 1985-87; *Recreations* gardening, sailing, golf; *Clubs* Chichester Yacht; *Style—* Malcolm Hodge, Esq; Great Thorndean House, Warninglid, Sussex

HODGE, Ronald Jacob; s of Jacob Hodge (d 1964); *b* 16 May 1926; *Educ* Wycliffe Coll Stonehouse, New Coll Oxford (MA); *m* 1956, Pauline Phyllis Beale; 3 da (Nicola, Alison, Virginia); *Career* Lt Middx Regt; chm Emhart Int Ltd; dir of other cos in same gp in UK, USA, France, Germany, Japan, Sweden, Denmark, Finland, Australia, Spain 1971-86, chm BSA Guns Ltd 1986- FRSA 1985; *Recreations* golf, music, horticulture; *Clubs* Edgbaston Golf; *Style—* Ronald Hodge, Esq; Park Mount, 259 Bristol Rd, Birmingham B5 7SR (☎ 021 472 0683)

HODGES, Anthony; s of John Humphrey Hodges (d 1950), and Emma, *née* Fadil (d 1984); *b* 3 Oct 1947; *Educ* Harrow, Oriel Coll Oxford; *m* 4 Oct 1975, Deborah June, da of Maj Arthur Wright, REME, of Cheam, Surrey; *Career* dir Benton & Bowles Advertising Agency 1978 (1970-83), fndr Tony Hodges & Ptnrs 1983; MIPA; *Recreations* tennis, fly-fishing, wine collecting; *Style—* Anthony Hodges, Esq; Honeysuckle Cottage, 31 Henning St, London SW11 (☎ 01 585 2116) Tony Hodges & Partners Ltd, Inner Court, 48 Old Church St, London SW3 5BY (☎ 01 351 4477, fax 01 351 2231, car tel 0860 713656)

HODGES, David Reginald Eyles; s of Edward Reginald George Hodges, of Dolphin Sq, London SW1, and Irene Muriel, *née* Turner; *b* 26 August 1942; *Educ* Mickleburgh; *m* 19 Dec 1969, Yolande Wadih (d 1988), da of Joseph Yuha (d 1975), of San Pedro Sula, Honduras; 1 s (Crispin James David b 1973); *Career* memb of Lloyds; dir Cayzer Steel Bowater Int Ltd 1975-86; dir and chm Ridgelawn Assocs Ltd 1986-; conslt J H Davies (Underwriting Agency) Ltd 1986-; *Recreations* sailing, travel, skiing; *Clubs* Turf; *Style—* David Hodges, Esq; c/o Messrs C Hoare and Co, 37 Fleet St, London EC4; 18 Mansell St, London E1 8AA (☎ 01 481 4455 or 01 821 0179)

HODGES, Air Chief Marshal Sir Lewis MacDonald; KCB (1968, CB 1963), CBE (1958), DSO and bar (1944, 1945), DFC and bar (1962, 1943); s of Arthur MacDonald Hodges (d 1940); *b* 1 Mar 1918; *Educ* St Paul's Sch London, RAF Coll Cranwell; *m* 1950, Elisabeth Mary, da of Geoffrey Blackett, MC (d 1977); 2 s; *Career* joined RAF 1937, serv WWII Bomber Cmd, SE East Asia, Gp Capt 1957, Air Cdre 1961, Air Vice-Marshal 1963, asst ch Air Staff (Ops) MOD 1965-68, AOC-in-C Air Support Cmd 1968-70, air memb Personnel Air Force Bd 1970-73, Air Chief Marshal 1971, dep C-in-C AFCENT 1973-76, Air ADC to HM The Queen 1973-76, ret; govr British United Provident Assoc 1973-85; dir Pilkington Bros plc (Optical Div) 1979-83; chm of govrs Duke of Kent Sch 1979-86; chm RAF Benevolent Fund Educn Ctee 1979-86; pres: RAF Escaping Soc 1979-, RAF Assoc 1981-84; Croix de Guerre (Fr) 1944, Légion d'Honneur (Fr) 1948 pres: Special Forces Club 1982-86, Old Pauline Club 1985-87, RAF Club 1985-; *Clubs* RAF, Special Forces; *Style—* Air Chief Marshal Sir Lewis Hodges, KCB, CBE, DSO, DFC; Allens House, Plaxtol, nr Sevenoaks, Kent

HODGES, Mark Willie; s of William Henry Hodges (d 1924), of Newport, Monmouthshire, and Eva, *née* Smith (d 1964); *b* 20 Oct 1923; *Educ* Cowbridge GS, Jesus Coll Oxford (MA); *m* 11 May 1948, Glenna Marion, da of Alfred Leopold Peacock (d 1979), of Oxford; 1 s (Timothy b 1965), 1 da (Tessa b 1957); *Career* WWII Sub Lt RNVR 1942-45; lectr Univ of Sheffield 1950-54, Dept of Scientific and Industl Res 1954-56, asst scientific attaché Br Embassy Washington 1956-61, Off of the Min for Sci 1961-64, sec Royal Cmmn on Med Educn 1965-68, asst sec Dept of Educn and Sci 1968-79 (arts and libraries branch 1977-79); head Off of Arts and Libraries 1982-84 (joined 1979, under sec 1982, dep sec 1983); memb: South Bank Theatre bd 1982- (chm 1984-), cncl Royal Albert Hall 1983- cncl and mgmnt ctee Eastern Assoc 1986-; *Recreations* woodwork, computer programming, listening to music; *Clubs* Athenaeum,

United Oxford and Cambridge; *Style*— Mark Hodges, Esq; The Corner Cottage, Church Way, Little Stukeley, Cambs PE17 5BQ (☎ 0480 59266)

HODGES, Hon Mrs (Naomi Katharine); *née* Lloyd; da of Baron Lloyd of Hampstead (Life Peer), and Ruth Emma Cecilia, da of late Carl Tulla; *b* 5 Nov 1946; *Educ* Arts Educational School, West London Institute of Higher Education; *m* 1967, Peter Campbell Hodge, s of Donovan Hodges; 1 s (Benjamin b 1974), 1 da (Katharine b 1971); *Career* primary sch teacher; *Style*— The Hon Mrs Hodges; 3 Cleveland Rd, Barnes, London SW13

HODGKIN, Sir Alan Lloyd; OM (1973), KBE (1972); s of George Lloyd Hodgkin (d 1918); *b* 5 Feb 1914; *Educ* Gresham's Sch Holt, Trinity Coll Cambridge (MA, ScD); *m* 1944, Marion de Kay, da of Francis Peyton Rous (d 1970); 1 s, 3 da; *Career* scientific offr working on radar for Air Miny and Miny of Aircraft Prodn 1939-45, lectr then asst dir of res Cambridge Univ 1945-52; Foulerton res prof Royal Soc 1952-69, J F Plummer prof of biophysics Cambridge Univ 1970-81, pres Royal Soc 1970-75, chllr Leicester Univ 1971-85, master Trinity Coll Cambridge 1978-84 (fell 1936-78 and 1984-); jt winner Nobel Prize for Medicine or Physiology 1963; FRS; *Recreations* travel, ornithology, fishing; *Style*— Sir Alan Hodgkin, OM, KBE; 18 Panton St, Cambridge CB2 1HP (☎ 0223 352707); Physiological Laboratory, Cambridge (☎ 0223 64131)

HODGKIN, Prof Dorothy Mary; OM (1965); da of John Winter Crowfoot, CBE (d 1959); *b* 1910; *Educ* Sir John Leman Sch Beccles, Somerville Coll Oxford; *m* 1937, Thomas Lionel Hodgkin (d 1982), s of Robert Howard Hodgkin (d 1951), sometime provost Queen's Coll Oxford; 2 s, 1 da; *Career* official fell and tutor in Natural Science at Somerville Coll Oxford; lect and demonstrator Oxford 1946-56, reader 1956-60, Wolfson res prof of the Royal Soc 1960-77, emeritus prof Oxford 1977-; chllr Bristol Univ 1970-88; Nobel Laureate in Chemistry 1964; FRS; *Recreations* archaeology, children; *Style*— Prof Dorothy Hodgkin, OM; Crab Mill, Ilmington, Shipston-on-Stour, Warwicks CV36 4LE (☎ 060 882 233); Laboratory of Chemical Crystallography, 9 Parks Rd, Oxford (☎ 0865 270833)

HODGKIN, Hon Mrs (Katharine Mary); da of 1 and last Viscount Hewart (d 1964); *b* 1907; *m* 1929, Eliot Hodgkin; 1 s, 1 da; *Style*— The Hon Mrs Hodgkin; Shelley's Hare Hatch, Twyford, Berks

HODGKINS, David John; s of Rev Harold Hodgkins and Elsie Hodgkins, of Rhos-on-Sea, Clwyd; *b* 13 Mar 1934; *Educ* Buxton Coll, Peterhouse Cambridge (MA); *m* 6 July 1963, Sheila; 2 s (James b 1964, Andrew b 1967); *Career* Miny of Labour 1956-64, Tresy 1965-68, Dept of Employment 1969-84, Health & Safety Exec 1984 (dir of Safety Policy 1984-); *Clubs* Royal Cwlth Soc; *Style*— David Hodgkins, Esq; Four Winds, Batchelors Way, Amersham, Bucks HP7 9AJ (☎ 0494 725207); Baynards House, Chepstow Place, London W2 (01 243 6370)

HODGKINSON, Air Chief Marshal Sir (William) Derek; KCB (1971, CB 1969), CBE (1960), DFC (1941), AFC (1942); s of late Ernest Nicholls Hodgkinson; *b* 27 Dec 1917; *Educ* Repton; *m* 1939, Nancy Heather Goodwin; 1 s, 1 da; *Career* joined RAF 1936, serv WWII (POW 1942-45), Gp Capt 1958, ADC to HM The Queen 1959-63, Air Cdre 1963, SASO RAF Training Cmmd 1969, Air Marshal 1970, C-in-C Near East Air Force 1970-73, Air Sec 1973-76, Air Chief Marshal 1974, ret 1976; pres Regular Forces Employment Assoc 1982-86 (chm 1980-82); *Recreations* fishing, cricket; *Clubs* RAF, MCC; *Style*— Air Chief Marshal Sir Derek Hodgkinson, KCB, CBE, DFC, AFC; Frenchmoor Lodge, West Tytherley, Salisbury, Wilts SP5 1NU

HODGKINSON, Paul Richard; s of Peter George Hodgkinson, DL (d 1986), of St Georges House, Lincoln, and Gwyneth Anne, *née* Evans (d 1984); *b* 9 Mar 1956; *Educ* Lincoln GS, Oxford Poly (BA, DipArch); *m* 13 Oct 1984, Catherine Ann, da of George Giangrande, of New Vernon, New Jersey, USA; *Career* Shepherd Ipstein & Hunter 1975-76, Capital and Counties plc 1979-81, Simons Design Conslts 1981-86, chm and chief exec Simons Gp Ltd 1986-; gp chm Lincs CBI, tstee Harding House Arts Tst; RIBA 1980, IOD, RSA 1986, ARCUK; *Recreations* squash, cricket, reading, golf, walking, food, opera, skiing; *Style*— Paul Hodgkinson, Esq; Simons Gp Ltd, Outer Circle Rd, Lincoln (☎ 0522 513 505, fax 0522 513 520, telex 563 74)

HODGKINSON, (Claude) Peter; s of Claude Harold Hodgkinson, of Stoke-on-Trent, and Gweneth Mary, *née* Cupit; *b* 26 June 1943; *Educ* Ratcliffe Coll Leicester, Manchester Univ (BA); *m* 27 Nov 1974, Julie Margaret Wesley Thompson, of Birmingham; 1 s (Oliver b 1976), 1 da (Sophie b 1982); *Career* dir: Hanley Econ Bldg Soc 1972-, Naybro Stone (Stoke-on-Trent) Ltd 1972-, A G (Plaster) Ltd 1978-, William Boulton Gp plc 1983-, Rose Vale Cement Tile Co Ltd 1984-, Cauldon Gp plc 1987-; FCA 1968; *Recreations* golf, squash; *Clubs* British Pottery Manufacturers Fedn, Trentham Golf; *Style*— Peter Hodgkinson, Esq; Holly Cottage, Maer, Newcastle, Staffs ST5 5EF (☎ 0782 680255); A G (Plaster) Ltd, Unit 19, Reddicap Trading Estate, Coleshill Rd, Sutton Coldfield, W Midlands (☎ 021 329 2874)

HODGSON, Alfreda Rose; da of Alfred Hodgson (d 1979), and Rose *née* McAllister; *b* 7 June 1940; *Educ* Levenshulme HS, Northern Sch of Music Manchester, Graduate Northern Sch of Music; *m* 21 Dec 1963, Paul Frederick Blissett, s of Arthur John Blissett (d 1955); 2 da (Alison Ruth b 1968, Rosemary Anne b 1972); *Career* concert singer (contralto), concert debut with Royal Liverpool Philharmonic Orch 1964, Covent Garden debut 1983; has performed with major orchestras throughout the world with: Klemperer, Horpenstein, Boult, Barbirolli, Abbado Britten, Colin Davis, Haitink, Rattle, Mazel; Kathleen Ferrier Meml Scholarship 1964, Sir Charles Santley Meml Gift Worshipful Company of Musicians 1985; hon fell Northern Sch of Music 1972; LRAM; *Style*— Ms Alfreda Hodgson; 16 St Marys Rd, Prestwich, Manchester M25 5AP (☎ 061 773 1541)

HODGSON, Gordon Hewett; s of John Lawrence Hodgson (d 1936), and Alice Joan, *née* Wickham (d 1966); *b* 21 Jan 1929; *Educ* Oundle, UCL (LLB); *m* 1958, Pauline Audrey, da of William George Gray (d 1979), of Pinner; 2 s (John, William); *Career* Nat Serv RAEC 1947-49; barr Middle Temple 1953, pte practise SE circuit 1954-83, asst boundary cmmr 1976-83, ass rec 1979-83; Master of the Supreme Court 1983-; memb ctee Bentham Club 1987; *Recreations* sailing (yacht Shardik), enjoying Tuscany; *Clubs* East India, Royal Corinthian, Bar Yacht; *Style*— Gordon Hodgson, Esq; Royal Cts of Justice, Strand, London WC1A 2LL (☎ 01 936 6131)

HODGSON, Hon Mrs (Jean Margaret); *née* Brand; er da of 5 Viscount Hampden and sister of 6 Viscount; *b* 19 August 1938; *m* 1976, as his 2 w, Robert John Hodgson, only s of John Hodgson; 1 s (Thomas Edward b 1981); *Style*— The Hon Mrs Hodgson; 2 St Hilda's Rd, London Sw13 9JQ (☎ 01 748 9689)

HODGSON, Kenneth; s of Joseph Hodgson (d 1982), and Margaret May, *née* Johnston; *b* 18 Nov 1950; *Educ* St Cuthbert's GS Newcastle, Newcastle Univ; *m* 30 July 1971, Judith Helen, da of Matthew Docherty Brown (d 1986); 2 s (Timothy b 1975, Nicholas b 1977); *Career* chm Caldaire Hldgs Ltd 1986-; md W Riding Automobile Co Ltd 1984-; vice-chm W Yorks Metro-Nat Ltd 1984-, dir: Yorks Woollen District Co Ltd 1984-, Sheffield and District Transport Co Ltd 1987-, United Automobile Services Co Ltd 1987-, United Automobile Enterprises Ltd 1987-; *Recreations* theatre, swimming; *Style*— Kenneth Hodgson, Esq; Tanglewood, 91 Leeds Rd, Bramhope, W Yorks; 24 Barnsley Rd, Wakefield WF1 5JX

HODGSON, Sir Maurice Arthur Eric; s of Walter Hodgson and Amy Walker; *b* 21 Oct 1919; *Educ* Bradford GS, Merton Coll Oxford (MA, BSc, hon fellow 1979); *m* 1945, Norma Fawcett; 1 s, 1 da; *Career* chm: ICI 1978-82 (joined 1942, dep chm 1972-78), BHS 1982-87; non-exec dir Storehouse plc 1985-; nominated memb of cncl of Lloyd's 1987-; chm: Civil Justice Review Advsy Ctee 1985-88; Dunlop Hldgs plc 1984 (resigned 1984 non-exec dir 1982-83), Imperial Chemicals Insur Ltd 1972-78; memb: Int Cncl Salk Inst 1978-, cncl CBI 1978-82, court Bradford Univ 1979-, int advsy ctee, Chase Manhattan Bank 1980-83, presidents ctee The Advertising Assoc 1978-, Euro advsy cncl Air Products and Chemicals Inc 1982-84, int advsy bd AMAX Inc 1982-85; govr London Graduate Sch Business Studies 1978-87; visiting fell Sch of Business and Organisational Studies Lancaster Univ 1970-; pres Merton Soc 1986-89; Hon DTech Univ of Bradford; Hon FUMIST, Hon DUniv Heriot-Watt, Hon DSc Loughborough; Messel Medal Soc of Chemical Indust 1980, George E Davis Medal IChemE 1982; FEng, FIChemE, CChem; FRSC; kt 1979; *Recreations* horse-racing, swimming; *Clubs* RAC; *Style*— Sir Maurice Hodgson; c/o BHS, Marylebone House, 129-137 Marylebone Rd, London NW1 5QD (☎ 01 262 3288, telex 261209)

HODGSON, Michael Patrick Sanford (Mick); s of Arthur Geoffrey Sanford Hodgson, MBE, of Geerings, Warnham, Horsham, W Sussex, and Sheila Beatrice, *née* Sheppard; *b* 19 April 1946; *Educ* Eton, London Univ (BSc); *m* 21 Jan 1977, Gytha Margaret Kerr, da of Gerald Lawrence Clarke, of Chesterley, Swanage; 2 s (Benjamin Gerald Sanford b 21 Jan 1978, Roger Geoffrey Sanford b 25 Nov 1983), 1 da (Erica Sarah b 21 Feb 1980); *Career* ptnr Edward Erdman Surveyors 1977-; chm Warnham Parish Cncl; Freeman City of London 1968, Liveryman Worshipful Co Vintners 1973; ARICS 1969; *Recreations* skiing; *Style*— Michael Hodgson, Esq; Old Manor, Warnham, Horsham, West Sussex RH12 3SN (☎ 0403 65069); 6 Grosvenor St, London W1 (☎ 01 629 8191, fax 01 409 2757, telex 28169)

HODGSON, Patricia Anne; da of Harold Hodgson, of Brentwood, Essex, and Lilian Mary, *née* Smith; *b* 19 Jan 1947; *Educ* Brentwood Co High, Newham Coll Cambridge (MA); *m* 23 July 1979, George Edward Donaldson, s of Edward George Donaldson, of Donington-le-Heath, Leics; 1 s; *Career* with Cons Res Dept 1968-70, prodr for Open Univ BBC 1970 (specialising in history and philosophy), freelance journalist and broadcaster in UK and USA, worked on Today and Tonight; TV series incl English Urban History 1978, Conflict in Modern Europe 1980, Rome in the Age of Augustus 1981; BBC: with secretariat 1982-83 the Dep Sec 1983-85, the Sec 1985-87, dir BARB 1987-, head policy and planning unit 1987-; chm Bow Gp 1975-76, ed Crossbow 1976-80, memb London Electricity Consultative Cncl 1981-83; memb Royal TV Soc (RTS) 1986, LRAM 1968; *Recreations* quietness; *Style*— Miss Patricia Hodgson; BBC Broadcasting House, Portland Place, London W1 (☎ 01 927 4974, fax 01 436 0393, telex 265 781)

HODGSON, Peter Gerald Pearson; s of Thomas William Hodgson, of Elloughton, North Humberside, and Edna, *née* Pearson; *b* 13 July 1934; *Educ* Reade Sch Yorks, Hull Univ (BSc), Imperial Coll London (DIC); *m* 30 Sept 1956, Noreen, da of Albert James Warnes, of Byfleet, Surrey; 2 s (Michael Charles Peter b 1966, John Paul Richard b 1967); *Career* chm and chief exec Petrocon Gp plc 1963-88 (chm: Petrocon Gp plc 1988-), chm Richards Gp plc 1988-; MICHEME (1965), FINSTPET (1968); *Recreations* golf, horse racing (owner); *Clubs* MCCm RAC; *Style*— Peter Hodgson, Esq; Richards Group plc, Phoenix Works, Leicester LE4 6FY (☎ 0533 661 521, fax 0533 666 369, telex 341433)

HODGSON, Peter John Dixon; OBE (1979); s of John Dixon Hodgson, of Manaton, Launceston, Cornwall, and Dorothy Blanche, *née* Saunders; *b* 21 Mar 1947; *Educ* Charterhouse; *m* 18 July 1970, Cecilia Anne, da of Brig Arnold de Lerisson Cazenove, CBE, DSO, MVO (d 1969); 2 s (James b 1973, Timothy b 1975), 1 da (Charlotte b 1977); *Career* CA; chm fin ctee Red Cross Cornwall, hon tres western provincial area Nat Union of Cons and Unionist Assocs; FCA 1970; *Recreations* gardening, fishing; *Style*— Peter Hodgson, Esq, OBE; Langore House, Langore, Launceston, Cornwall PL15 8LD (☎ 0566 2880); John D Hodgson, 12 Southgate St, Launceston, Cornwall PL15 9DP (☎ 0566 2177)

HODGSON, (Adam) Robin; s of Thomas Edward Highton Hodgson, CB (d 1985), and Emily Catherine, *née* Hodgson; *b* 20 Mar 1937; *Educ* William Ellis Sch London, Worcester Coll Oxford (MA); *m* 1962, Elizabeth Maureen Linda, da of Vernon Gordon Fitzell Bovenizer, CMG, of Cambridge; 1 s (Harvey b 1971), 2 da (Kate b 1968, Amy b 1972); *Career* admitted slr 1964, asst slr LCC and GLC 1964-66, snr asst slr Oxfordshire CC 1966-71, asst clerk Northamptonshire CC 1972-74, dep Co Sec East Sussex CC 1974-77, dep chief exec and clerk Essex CC 1977-85, chief exec Hampshire CC 1985-; *Recreations* music, drama, geology; *Clubs* Law Soc; *Style*— Robin Hodgson, Esq; Tara, Dean Lane, Winchester S022 5RA (☎ 0962 62119); The Castle, Winchester SO23 8UJ (☎ 0962 841841)

HODGSON, Robin Granville; s of Henry Edward Hodgson, of Astley Abbotts, Bridgnorth Shropshire, and Natalie Beatrice, *née* Davidson; *b* 25 April 1942; *Educ* Shrewsbury, Oxford Univ (BA), Wharton Sch Univ of Pennsylvania (MBA) ; *m* 8 May 1982, Fiona Ferelith, da of Keith Storr Allom; 3 s (Barnaby Peter Granville b 1986, James Maxwell Gower (twin) b & d 1986, Toby Henry Storr b 1988); *Career* Lt 4 Bn Kings Shrops LI TA 1960-64; md Granville & Co investmt bankers 1972-, chm Nasdim 1979-85, dir Securities & Invest Bd 1985-; memb West Midland Indust Devpt Bd 1988-; tres Cons Party West Midlands Area 1987-, MP (Cons), Walsall North 1976-79, tstee Friend of Shrewsbury Sch; Liveryman Goldsmiths Co ; *Style*— Robin Hodgson, Esq; Astley Abbotts, Bridgnorth, Shropshire (☎ 074 623 122); 12 Scarsdale Villas, London W8 (☎ 01 937 2964); Granville & Co, Lovat Lane, London EC3R 8BP (☎ 01 621 1212, fax 01 929 4954, telex 8814 884 GVILCO G)

HODGSON, Stuart Henry; s of Henry Stockdale Hodgson, and Edith, *née* Vickers; *b* 16 April 1935; *Educ* Lancaster Royal GS, Ermysteds Sch Skipton; *m* 7 Jan 1959, (Doreen) June, da of Lawrence Packham (d 1985), of Bolton-le-Sands, Lancs; 2 da (Linzi Jane Bridson b 19 April 1959, Amanda b 11 Sept 1961); *Career* Nat Serv RAF

1953-55; press photographer Westminster Press, advertisement mangr Utd Newspapers (Lancaster), pharmaceutical mktg Lederle Laboratories London, founded Porton Gp of Cos 1970 (currently chm and princ shareholder); bd chm St Martins in the Field Enterprises Ltd; City cncllr Scotforth ward Lancaster City 1964-69; memb IPA; *Recreations* motor sport (historic racing), tennis, golf; *Style*— Stuart Hodgson, Esq; The Old Coach House, 11 Princes Rd, Weybridge, Surrey, (☎ 0932 843816); Chiltlee Manor Chase, Liphook, Hants GU30 7AZ (☎ 0428 724248, fax 0428 725276, car phone 0836 595 277)

HODGSON, Col Terence Harold Henry (Terry); DSO (1945), MC (1944), TD (1953), DL (Westmorland 1959); s of Michael Cecil Lewthwaite Hodgson (d 1958), of Grange-over-Sands, and Hilda, *née* Cleary (d 1962); *b* 10 Dec 1916; *Educ* Kendal Sch, 167 Officer Training Unit, Aldershot; *m* 1, 12 Aug 1942 (m dis 1969), Joan, *née* Servant (d 1974); 3 s (Peter b 9 Dec 1947, Michael b 12 Dec 1948, Richard b 3 Jan 1953), 3 da (Caroline b Nov 1946, Victoria b 1950, Elizabeth); m2, 11 April 1977, Doreen Jacqueline, *née* Pollitt Brunzell (d 1987); m3, Sept 1987, Elizabeth, *née* Robinson; *Career* Border Regt 1939, cmmnd 1940, served 2 Bn, 7 Bn, and 9 Bn, in Eng, Ceylon, India and Burma, 4 Bn Border Regt TA 1945 (Cmd 1950-53), dep cdr Col 126 Inf Brigade TA (Hon Col 1959), King's Own Royal Border Regt 1976-82, Hon Col Cumbria Cadet Force 1982-85; princ Michael CL Hodgson Auctioneers 1950-88 dir Cartmel Steeplechased Ltd (after 1950-88); memb: Cumberland Westmorland TA Assoc, NW Eng and IOM TAVR Assoc; chm Cumbria Army Benevolent Fund Ctee 1984, memb Kendal Almshouses Ctee (former chm) former pres Cumbria & Westmorland Rugby Union; Vice Lord Lieut of Cumbria 1983-; FSVA, FRSH; *Recreations* shooting, horse racing, work; *Style*— Col Terry Hodgson, DSO, MC, TD, DL; School House, Winster, Windermere LA23 3NP (☎ 09662 0539); Michael G Hodgson, 10 Highgate, Kendal LA9 4SX (☎ 0539 21375, fax 0539 20303)

HODGSON, Ven Thomas Richard Burnham; s of Richard Shillito Hodgson (d 1949), of Kendal, Westmorland, and Marion Thomasena Bertram, *née* Marshall (d 1974); *b* 17 August 1926; *Educ* Heversham GS, London Univ, London Coll of Divinity (BD, ALCD); *m* 1952, Margaret Esther, da of Evan Makinson, (d 1964), of Cumberland; 1 s (Richard Nicholas b 1954), 1 da (Rachel Margaret b 1957); *Career* ordained: deacon 1952, priest 1953; curate: Crosthwaite 1952-55, Stanwix 1955-59; vicar St Nicholas Whitehaven 1959-65, rector of Aikton 1965-67, vicar of Raughton Head 1967-73, domestic chaplain to Bishop of Carlisle 1967-73, dir of ordinands 1970-74, surrogate 1962-, hon canon of Carlisle 1972-, vicar of Grange-over-Sands 1972-79, rural dean of Windermere 1976-79, archdeacon West Cumberland 1979-, vicar of Mosser 1979-83; memb: of General Synod of Church of England 1983-, Central Bd of Finance C of E, Carlisle Diocesan Bd of Finance; *Recreations* meteorology, geology, listening to music, vegetable gardening; *Style*— The Ven the Archdeacon of West Cumberland; Moorside, 50 Stainburn Road, Workington, Cumbria CA14 1SN (☎ 0900 66190)

HODIN, Prof (Josef) Paul; s of Edward David Hodin (d 1942), of Prague, and Rosa Rachel, *née* Klug; *b* 17 August 1905; *Educ* Kleinseitner Realschule and Neustädter Realgymnasium Prague, Charles Univ Prague, Dresden Art Acad, College de France Paris, Courtauld Inst London; *m* 1, (m dis), Birgit, *née* Akesson, of Stockholm; m 2, 22 May 1944, Doris Pamela, da of George W Simms, of Kuala Lumpur and Cornwall; 1 s (Michael b 1946), 1 da (Annabelle b 1948); *Career* author, art historian and critic; press attaché to Norwegian Govt London 1944-45; dir of studies and librarian ICA London 1949-54; hon memb editorial cncl Journal of Aesthetics and Art Criticism Cleveland 1955, memb exec ctee editorial consultative ctee Br Soc of Aesthetics 1960-, pres Br section Int Assoc of Art Critics 1974-75, memb Int PEN; co ed: Prisme des Arts Paris 1956-59, Quadrum Brussels 1956-66; int dir: Relations Studio Int, Journal of Modern Art London 1965-75; first int prize for art criticism Biennale Venice 1954; Hon LLD Prague Univ, Hon PhD Uppsala Univ 1969, Hon Prof Austria; DSM first class Czechoslovakia 1947, Cavaliere Ufficiale Italy 1956, St Olav Medal Norway 1958, Cdr Order of Merit Italy 1966, Grand Cross Order of Merit Austria 1968, Order of Merit first class Germany 1969, Silver Cross of Merit Vienna 1972, Grand Cross of the Order of Merit West Germany 1986; *Books* Monographs on Sven Erixson (1940), Ernst Josephson (1942), Edvard Munch (1948), Isaac Grünewald (1949), Art and Criticism (1944), J A Comenius and Our Time (1944), The Dilemma of Being Modern (1956), Henry Moore (1956), Ben Nicholson (1957), Barbara Hepworth (1961), Lynn Chadwick (1961), Alan Reynolds (1962), Bekenntnis zu Kokoschka (1963), Edvard Munch, Der Genius des Nordens (1963), Kokoschka The Artist and His Work (1966), Der Maler Walter Kern (1966), The Painter Ruszkowski (1967), Bernard Leach A Potter's Work (1967), Kokoschka Sein Leben, seine Zeit (1968), Kafka und Goethe (1968), Giacomo Manzu (1969), Emilio Greco His Life and Work (1970), Die Brühlsche Terrasse, Ein Künstler Roman (1970), The Painter Alfred Manessier (1971), Kokoschka, The Psychography of an Artist (1971), Edvard Munch (1972), Modern Art and the Modern Mind (1972), Bernard Stern, Paintings and Drawings (1972), Hilde Goldschmidt (1973), Ludwig Meidner (1973), Paul Berger-Bergner (1974), Die Leute von Elverdingen, Erzählung (1974), Kokoschka and Hellas (1976), Alfred Aberdam (1977), John Milne (1977), Else Meidner (1978), Elisabeth Frink (1981), Douglas Portway (1981), Franz Luby (1981), Mary Newcomb (1984), Dieses Mütterchen hat Krallen, Die Geschichte einer Prager Jugend (1986), FK Gotsch (1986), Verlorene Existenzen, Erzählungen (1987), Der Künstler Jan Brazda (1989); *Recreations* travel, reading; *Clubs* Athenaeum, Arts; *Style*— Prof Paul Hodin; 12 Eton Ave, London NW3 3EH (☎ 01 794 3609)

HODKINSON, James Clifford; s of John Eric Thomas Hodkinson (d 1985), of 53 Arnold Rd, Westmoor, Ferndown, Dorset, and Edith Lilian, *née* Lord; *b* 21 April 1944; *Educ* Salesian Coll Farnborough Hants; *m* 8 Feb 1968, Janet Patricia, da of George William Lee (d 1941); 1 da (Justine b 30 April 1970); *Career* trainee mangr F W Woolworth 1962-71; B & Q plc: mangr Bournemouth Store 1971-74, sales mangr south 1974-79, ops dir 1979-84, ops and personnel dir 1984-86, md 1986-; Princes Youth Business Tst: chm young entrepreneurs section, dep chm southern regnl bd, memb bd nat appeal steering ctee advsy cncl; dir Nat Home Improvement Cncl; FInstD, CBIM; *Recreations* golf, shooting; *Style*— James Hodkinson, Esq; B & Q plc, Portswood House, Hampshire Corporate Park, Chandlers Ford Eastleigh SO5 3YX (☎ 0703 256 256, fax 0703 256 030)

HODSON, Hon (Charles) Christopher Philip; s of Baron Hodson, MC, PC (Life Peer, d 1984); *b* 1922; *m* 1953, Rose (d 1986), da of Sir Charles Markham, 2 Bt; 1 s, 3 da; *Style*— The Hon Christopher Hodson; Stoney Hall, Hannington, Hants

HODSON, Daniel Houghton; s of Henry Vincent Hodson, of 105 Lexham Gdns, London, and Margaret Elizabeth, *née* Honey; *b* 11 Mar 1944; *Educ* Eton, Merton Coll Oxford (MA); *m* 22 Feb 1979, Diana Mary, da of Christopher Breen Ryde, of Middleton-on-Sea, W Sussex; 2 da (Susannah Fleur b 1980, Emma Katharine b 1982); *Career* Chase Manhattan Bank NA 1965-73, Edward Bates & Sons Ltd 1973-76 (dir 1974-76), gp fin dir Unigate plc 1981-87 (gp tres 1976-81), pres Unigate Inc 1986-87, dir Girobank plc 1986-, chm Davidson Pearce Gp plc 1988 (chief exec 1987-88); pt/t bd memb Post Office Corpn, exec ed Corporate Fin and Treasy Mgmnt 1984-, chm Assoc of Corporate Treasurers 1984-86; chm Fulham Carnival 1979-81, govr The Yehudi Menuhin Sch 1984-; memb Worshipful Co Mercers 1965; FCT 1978; *Books* Businessman's Guide to the Foreign Exchange Market (jtly); *Recreations* music, travel, skiing, gardening; *Clubs* Brooks's; *Style*— Daniel Hodson, Esq; Treyford Manor, Midhurst, W Sussex GU29 OLD (☎ 073 085 436); Post Office Corpn, Grosvenor Place, London SW1 (☎ 01 235 8000)

HODSON, Denys Fraser; CBE (1982); s of Rev Harold Victor Hodson, MC (d 1977), of Gloucestershire, and Marguerite Edmée, *née* Ritchie; *b* 23 May 1928; *Educ* Marlborough, Trinity Coll Oxford (MA); *m* 1954, Julie Compton, da of Harold Goodwin (d 1984), of Warwicks; 1 s (Nicolas b 1965), 1 da (Lucy b 1963); *Career* dir arts and recreation Thamesdown Borough Cncl 1970; chm Southern Arts Assoc 1975-81 and 1985-87, cncl of Regional Arts Assoc 1976-81, dir Oxford Playhouse Co 1974-86, govr Br Film Inst 1976-87, memb Arts Cncl GB 1987-; *Recreations* arts, fishing, bird watching; *Style*— Denys Hodson, Esq; Manor Farm House, Fairford, Gloucestershire GL7 4AR (☎ 0285 712642); Arts and Recreation Gp, Civic Office, Euclid Street, Swindon, Wiltshire SN1 2JH (☎ 0793 26161, ext 3101)

HODSON, Geoffrey Allan; s of Capt Allan C Hodson, and Hylda, *née* Taylor; *b* 26 Nov 1947; *Educ* Emmanuel Coll Cambridge Univ (MA), Harvard Business Sch (MBA); *m* 29 July 1972, Bridget Elizabeth, da of Cyril D Deans (d 1987); 1 s (James b 1978), 1 da (Sarah Louise b 1975); *Career* ICI 1970-72, conslt McKinsey & Co 1974-76, asst chief of staff Triad Hldg Corpn 1976-78, vice-pres Bankers Tst Int Ltd 1978-82, md head of int mergers and acquisitions Merrill Lynch Int & Co 1982-; *Recreations* photography, ornithology, railways, rowing; *Style*— Geoffrey Hodson, Esq; Kilmory, Guildford Road, Cranleigh, Surrey GU6 8LT (☎ 0483 276200); Merrill Lynch International & Co, Ropemaker Place, 25 Ropemaker Street, London EC2Y 9LY (☎ 01 867 4865)

HODSON, Sir Michael Robin Adderley; 6 Bt (I 1787), of Holybrooke House, Wicklow; s of Maj Sir Edmond Adair Hodson, 5 Bt, DSO (d 1972); *b* 5 Mar 1932; *Educ* Eton; *m* 1, 16 Dec 1963 (m dis 1978), Katrin Alexa, da of late Erwin Bernstiel, of St Andrew's House, St Andrew's Major, Dinas Powis, Glam; 3 da; m 2, 1978, Catherine, da of John Henry Seymour; *Heir* bro, Patrick Hodson; *Career* Capt (ret) Scots Gds; *Style*— Sir Michael Hodson, Bt; The White House, Awbridge, Romsey, Hants

HODSON, Patrick Richard; s of Maj Sir Edmond Adair Hodson, 5 Bt, DSO (d 1972), and hp of bro, Sir Michael Robin Adderley Hodson, 6 Bt; *b* 27 Nov 1934; *Educ* Eton; *m* 1961, June, da of H M Shepherd-Cross, of The Old Rectory, Brandsby, Yorks; 3 s; *Career* Capt (ret) Rifle Bde; *Style*— Patrick Hodson, Esq; Shipton Slade Farm, Woodstock, Oxford

HODSON, William Francis; s of William H Hodson (d 1961); *b* 9 July 1921; *Educ* King George V Sch Southport; *m* Nancy, *née* Partington; 1 s, 1 da; *Career* Maj Royal Glos Hussars (TA) 1939-40, Adjt Manchester Regt 1941-45, Gen Staff Offr 1945-46, Kent Yeomanry (TA) 1947-58, dir Smith, Kline and French Laboratories Ltd 1957-, memb Bd of Welwyn Garden City Dvpt Corp and memb of Cmmn for New Towns 1963-77, memb NW Thames Regional Health Authority 1973-; memb cncl of St Mary's Hospital Medical Sch; *Recreations* golf; *Clubs* Army and Navy; *Style*— William Hodson, Esq; Dormy Pool, 167 Saxmundham Rd, Aldeburgh, Herts (☎ 072 885 2623; 16 Bryanston Mews West, London W1H 7FR (☎ 01 429 3626)

HODSON-PRESSINGER, Selwyn Philip; s of Thomas Hodson-Pressinger (d 1961), and Pamela, *née* Howard Snow, who m 1973 as 3 w 14 Lord Torphichen (d 1975); *b* 9 Dec 1954; *Educ* Ludgrove, Downside, Aix-en-Provence Univ; *Career* mgmnt conslt, MBIM; *Recreations* history, deer-stalking; *Clubs* Turf; *Style*— Selwyn P Hodson-Pressinger, Esq; 16 Moore St-eet, Chelsea, London SW3 (☎ 01 603 3014)

HOFF, Harry Summerfield (pseudenym: William Cooper); s of Ernest Hoff (d 1960), of Crewe, and Edith Annie, *née* Summerfield (d 1979); *b* 4 August 1910; *Educ* Crewe Co Secdy Sch, Christs Coll Cambridge (BSc); *m* 3 Jan 1951, Joyce Barbara (d 1988), da of William Frederick Harris, of Bristol; 2 da (Louisa b 1953, Catherine b 1955); *Career* Sqdn Ldr RAFVR 1940-46; writer (as William Cooper); asst cmmr Civil Serv Cmmn 1945-58; personnel conslt: UKAEA 1958-72, CEGB 1958-72, Commn of Euro Communities 1972-73; asst dir Civil Serv Selection Bd 1973-75, memb Bd of Crown Agents 1975-77, personnel advsr Millbank Tech Serv 1955-77; adjunct prof of Eng Lit Syracuse Univ London Centre 1977-; Fell Royal Soc of Lit, Int PEN; *Books* (as H S Hoff): Trina (1934), Réha (1935), Lisa (1937), Three Marriages (1946); (as William Cooper): Scenes From Provincial Life (1950), The Struggles of Albert Woods (1952), The Ever-Interesting Topic (1953), Disquiet and Peace (1956), Young People (1958), C P Snow (Br Cncl Bibliographic Series, Writers and Their Work no 115) (1959), Prince Genji (a play 1960), Scenes from Married Life (1961), Memoirs of a New Man (1966), You Want The Right Frame of Reference (1971), Shall We Ever Know (1971), Love on The Coast (1973), You're Not Alone (1976), Scenes From Metropolitan Life (1982), Scenes From Later Life (1983); *Recreations* swimming; *Clubs* Savile; *Style*— Harry Hoff, Esq; 22 Kenilworth Ct, Lower Richmond Rd, London SW15 1EW (☎ 01 788 8326)

HOFFBRAND, Prof (Allan) Victor; s of Philip Hoffbrand (d 1959), of Bradford, Yorks, and Minnie, *née* Freedman; *b* 14 Oct 1935; *Educ* Bradford GS, The Queen's Coll Oxford (MA, DM), London Hosp (BM, BCh); *m* 3 Nov 1963, (Irene) Jill, da of Michael Mellows, of Wembley Pk, Middx; 2 s (Philip b 11 May 1967, David b 12 July 1970), 1 da (Caroline b 21 March 1966); *Career* jr hosp doctor London Hosp 1960-62, registrar and res fell Royal Postgrad Med Sch 1962-66, lectr in haematology St Bart's Hosp 1966-67, MRC res scholar Tufts Univ Boston 1967-80, lectr and sr lectr in haematology Royal Postgrad Med Sch 1968-74, prof of haematology Royal Free Sch of Med 1974-; hon FRCP (Ed) 1986, FRCP 1976, FRCPath 1980, DSc 1987; *Books* Essential Haematology (jtly, first edn 1980, second edn 1984), Clinical Haematology (1987), Sandoz Atlas: Clinical Haematology (jtly 1988), Postgraduate Haematology (jt ed 3 edn 1989), Recent Advances in Haematology (ed 5 edn 1988), Clinics in Haemotology (ed 1986); *Recreations* squash, chess, bridge, antiques, music; *Style*—

Prof Victor Hoffbrand; 57 Camden Sq, London NW1 9XE (☎ 01 485 6984); Department of Haematology; Royal Free Hosp, London NW3 2QG (☎ 794 0500 ext 3258)

HOFFMAN, George Henry; s of George Hoffman, of Pennsylvania, and Anna Cecilia, *née* Hojnowski; *b* 30 Oct 1939; *Educ* Columbia Univ (MA), Cornell Univ (BA); *m* 1961, Pauline Margaret, da of Gilbert R Lewis, of London; 1 s (Philip b 1968), 2 da (Erika b 1962, Bridgit b 1965); *Career* chm and chief exec Hoffman Assocs Ltd, non exec dir ISS Serrisystem UK; dir American C of C UK 1984-, chm Euro Affairs Ctee 1986-; *Recreations* tennis, skiing, photography; *Clubs* Les Ambassadeurs, Gravetye, Annabels; *Style*— George Hoffman; Hoffman Assocs Ltd, Asphalte House, Palace St, London SW1E 5HS (☎ 01 834 9091, fax 01 828 8191); Ranvers House, The Haven, Billingshurst, W Sussex RH14 9BS (☎ 040 372 2860)

HOFFMAN, Mark; s of Dr Mark Hoffman (d 1975), of USA; *b* 14 Dec 1938; *Educ* Harvard Coll (AB), Trinity Coll Cambridge (MA), Harvard Business Sch (MBA); *m* 1968, Mary Jo, da of John C Pyles of Washington DC, USA; 3 s (Nicholas b 1969, John b 1972, James b 1978); *Career* East African Common Services Orgn/MIT (Africa/USA) 1964-66, World Banks Int Finance Corpn (Washington) 1966-68, Olympic Investment Gp (Paris) 1968-69. dir: Hambros Bank (UK) 1970-74, Millipore Corpn (USA) 1975-, George Weston Ltd 1975- (Canada), Guinness Peat Gp plc (UK) 1982-84, LAC Minerals (Canada) 1984-86; chm Int Financial Markets Trading Ltd (UK) 1984-,; *Style*— Mark Hoffman, Esq; 21 Campden Hill Square, London W8; 1 Finsbury Avenue, London EC2M 2PA; Estabrook Woods, Concord, Mass, USA

HOFFMAN, Michael Richard; s of Sydney William Hoffman, of Letchworth, Herts, and Ethel Margaret Hoffman (d 1978); *b* 31 Oct 1939; *Educ* Hitchin GS, Bristol Univ (BSc); *m* 1, 1963, Margaret Edith; 1 da (Rachel); m 2, 1982, Helen Judith; *Career* chm Perkins Engines Ltd, pres farm and industl machinery div Massey Ferguson Toronto; chief exec: Thames Water 1988-, Airship Industries Ltd 1987-88 (dep chm 1989-); md Babcock Int plc 1983-87; dep chm Cosworth Engrg Ltd 1988-; memb: Monopolies & Mergers Cmmn 1988-, cncl Brunel Univ 1984; BOTB; *Recreations* shooting, squash, tennis; *Clubs* RAC, Reform, MCC; *Style*— Michael Hoffman, Esq; 43 De Vere Gardens, London W8 5AW (☎ 01 581 4612); St Marks Mews, Leamington Spa, Warwicks CV32 6EJ (☎ 0926 429643); Cleveland House, St James's Sq, London SW1Y 4LN (☎ 01 930 9766)

HOFFMAN, Paul Maxim Laurence; s of Gerard Hoffman (d 1985), of Ottawa, Canada, and Laura, *née* Vtein; *b* 29 July 1942; *Educ* Roundham Boys Sch, Sheffield Univ (LLB); *m* 19 March 1967 (m dis), Pamela Judith, da of Julius Werthemer, (d 1976), of Bradford; 3 s (Oliver b 1970, Simon b 1971, Adam b 1974); *Career* barr Lincoln Inn 1964, standing prosecuting counsel Inland Revenue NE Circuit 1983-, recorder 1985-; *Recreations* music, gardening, walking; *Style*— Paul Hoffman, Esq; 25 Park Square, Leeds (☎ 0532 665498)

HOFFMAN, Thomas; s of Dirk Hoffman (d 1986), of Cambridge, and Marie-Luise, *née* Leyser; *b* 9 August 1945; *Educ* The Leys Sch Cambridge, Univ of Exeter (LLB); *m* June 1971, Verena Hoffman; 1 s (Alexander b 1975); *Career* CA; Spicer & Oppenheim 1963-70, Arthur Andersen & Co 1970-71, Williams & Glyn's Bank Ltd 1971-76, Hill Samuel & Co Ltd 1976-78, dir capital mkts Lloyds Bank Int Ltd 1978-84, dep md dir Fuji Int Fin Ltd 1984-; ed The Bracton Law Journal 1968; estab British Univs Rowing Championships 1968, hon tres Ward of Cordwainer Club London 1985-; Freeman City of London (memb The Guild of Freeman), Liveryman Worshipful Co of Tylers & Bricklayers; Fell Royal Cwlth Soc 1964, memb Japan Soc 1988; FCA 1971; *Publications* The Inter-Universities Race Re-Considered (1967), Accounting in the EEC (with Patrick Browning, 1973), Yen Financing (1987), The Euroyen Bond Market & Swap Transactions (1987); *Recreations* gardening, tennis, opera, 17th century choral music, ballet, collecting books on rowing; *Clubs* United Wards, City Livery, Royal Cwlth Soc; *Style*— Thomas Hoffman, Esq; Old Curteis, Biddenden, Ashford, Kent; 72 Gainsford St, Tower Bridge Sq, London SE1; 101 Moorgate, London EC2

HOGAN, Brian; s of late Thomas Hogan, and Margaret Mary, *née* Murray (d 1958); *b* 4 May 1932; *Educ* St Mary's GS Darlington, Univ of Manchester (LLB); *m* 10 Aug 1957, Pauline, da of Walter Cox (d 1950); 1 s (Christopher Paul b 1964), 1 da (Catherine Margaret Mary Alice b 1966); *Career* barr Gray's Inn; prof of common law Univ of Leeds 1967-, pro-vice chllr Univ of Leeds 1981-83, lectr Univ of Nottingham 1956-67, ed Criminal Law Review 1966-73; visiting prof: Univ of Adelaide 1960, Villanova Univ 1962-63, Law Reform Cmmn of Canada 1975, Dalhousie Univ 1978-79, Vanderbilt Univ 1984; *Books* Smith and Hogan Criminal Law 6 edns (ed), Smith and Hogan Cases and Materials on Criminal Law 3 edns (ed); *Recreations* DIY, reading, music; *Style*— Prof Brian Hogan; 11 Lady Wood Rd, Leeds LS8 2QF (☎ 0532 658045); Faculty of Law, Univ of Leeds, Leeds LS2 9JT (☎ 0532 335014; telex 556473, UNILDS G, fax 0532 420090)

HOGAN, Fursa Francis; s of James Edmund (d 1961), and Frances Jane Pope (d 1986); *b* 1 Jan 1931; *Educ* Xaviers's Dublin, Trinity Coll Dublin; *m* 4 May 1954, Arlette Mary, da of James Grew, of Shrewsbury Rd, Dublin; 3 da (Mandy b 1954, Doon b 1957, Kate b 1964); *Career* chm and ptnr The Manchester Tobacco Co; *Recreations* golf, tennis, swimming; *Clubs* RAC; *Style*— Fursa Hogan, Esq; 42 St Lawrence Quay, Salford Quays, Port of Manchester M5 4XT; Manchester Tobacco Co, Ludgate Hill, Manchester M4 4DA (car ☎ 0860 629243)

HOGAN, Air Vice-Marshal Henry Algernon Vickers; CB (1955), DFC (1940); s of Lt-Col E M A Hogan (d 1971), and Isabel O A, *née* Johnstone (d 1928); *b* 25 Oct 1909; *Educ* Malvern Coll, RAF Coll Cranwell, RAF Staff Coll; *m* 15 April 1939, (Margaret) Venetia, da of Vice Adm Wilfred Tomkinson CB, MVO (d 1970), of Stert House, nr Devizes, Wilts; 1 s ((John) Michael b 1943), 1 da (Sarah Venetia Mary b 1940); *Career* cmmnd 1930 Fighter Sqdns including Fleet Airarm, Flying Instr; long range flight 1938; cmd 501 Sqdn Battle of Britain 1940, USA Staff and Liaison Duties 1941-43, chief instr Empire Flying Sch RAF Hallowington 1944, Staff Coll 1946, Commanded 19 Flts on formation at Cranwell later becoming established with RAF College 1945, Air Miny 1947-48, SPSO Middle East Air Force 1949-51, cmd: RAF Wattisham 1951-52, Northern Sector 1953-54, 81 Gp Fighter Cmd 1954-55, 83 Gp 2nd TAF Germany 1955-58, SASO Flying Trg Cmnd 1958-62, ret 1962; regnl dir Civil Def Midlands 1964-68; USA Legion of Merit (Offr) 1945; *Recreations* field sports; *Clubs* RAF; *Style*— Air Vice-Marshal Henry Hogan, CB, DFC; Sugar Hill, Bickley, nr Tenbury Wells, Worcs WR15 8LU (☎ 058 479 432)

HOGAN, Michael Henry; s of late James Joseph Hogan and late Edith Mary Hogan; *b* 31 May 1927; *Educ* Ushaw Coll Durham, LSE; *m* 1, 1953, Nina Spillane (d 1974); 1 s (Dominic b 1957), 3 da (Elizabeth b 1959, Anne b 1959, Sarah b 1962); m 2, 1980, Mrs Mollie Rosemarie Burtwell, da of Leslie John Buckland, of Surrey; 1 step-s (Simon b 1965), 1 step-da (Joanna b 1961); *Career* chief probation inspector HO 1970-80; sec Gaming Bd for GB 1980-86, memb Gaming Bd for GB 1986-; *Recreations* golf; *Style*— Michael Hogan, Esq; Yew Tree Cottage, The Street, Capel, Surrey RH5 5LD (☎ 0306 711523)

HOGAN, Thomas Patrick; s of Daniel Hogan (d 1920); *b* 4 August 1908; *Educ* Mount St Joseph Coll, Univ Coll Dublin; *m* 1949, Mary Joan, *née* Bourke; 5 children; *Career* chm: Plessey Ireland, Mica and Micanite, Mallow Industries, Pye Ireland, hon consul-gen Iceland; Order of Falcon (Iceland); FIEE; *Recreations* golf, sailing; *Clubs* Royal Irish Yacht, Portmarnock Golf; *Style*— Thomas Hogan, Esq; Monkstown Castle, Co Dublin, Ireland (☎ 0001 808103)

HOGARTH, (Arthur) Paul; s of Arthur Hogarth (d 1966), of Kendal, Cumbria, and Janet, *née* Bownass; *b* 4 Oct 1917; *Educ* St Agnes Sch, Manchester Coll of Art, St Martin's Sch of Art London, Royal Coll of Art (PhD 1971); *m* 1, 1940, Doreen (d 1948), da of Albert Courtman, of Alderley Edge, Ches; m 2, 1949, Phyllis, *née* Pamplin (d 1962); 1 s (Toby Graham Hogarth b 1 Aug 1960); m 3, 2 Feb 1963, Patricia Morgan Graham, *née* Douthwaite (d 1981); *Career* painter in watercolours, illustrator, author and printmaker, author: Looking at China (1955), Creative Pencil Drawing (1964, 1981), Artists on Horseback (1972- USA only), Drawing Architecture (1973, 1980), Arthur Boyd Houghton (1982), Artist as Reporter (1986); illustrated books in collaboration with authors notably: Brendan Behan's Island (with Brendan Behan, 1962) Majorca Observed (with Robert Graves, 1965), Graham Greene Country (with Graham Greene, 1986), The Mediterranean Shore (with Lawrence Durrell, 1988); sr tutor Faculty Graphic Art RCA 1964-71, cmmnd by Imperial War Museum to depict Berlin Wall 1981, drawings, watercolours and prints in permanent collections of the Fitzwilliam Museum, Whitworth Gallery, Univ of Manchester, City Art Gallery Manchester, Victoria and Albert Museum, Library of Congress (Washington USA), Boston Public Library (USA), Yale Centre of Br Art (USA); Francis Williams Award for Best Literary Illustration (1982), Yorkshire Post Award for best art book (1986); memb library ctee Royal Acad of Arts (memb cncl 1979-80 and 1986-88) rep of Royal Acad of Arts Copywright Cncl/Ctee HM Govt, hon pres Assoc of illustrators; memb: ARA (1974), RA (1984), RDI (1979), RE (1988), Fell CSD (1964); *Clubs* Reform; *Style*— Paul Hogarth, Esq; c/o Tessa Sayle, 11 Jubilee Place, London SW3 (☎ 01 823 3883)

HOGARTH, Peter Laurence; s of Michael Hogarth, of Perranaworthal, and Joyce, *née* Ponder; *b* 10 July 1949; *Educ* Haileybury; *m* 15 July 1972, Margaret Rosemary, da of Alexander Sidney Alison; 1 s (Ian b 30 Jan 1982), 2 da (Rosemary b 6 June 1983, Juliet b 25 April 1988); *Career* CA 1972; Peat Marwick McLintock 1967-88, Societe Generale Strauss Turnbull Securities 1988-; Liveryman Worshipful Co Joiners and Ceilers 1978; *Recreations* golf, bridge, chess, cooking; *Style*— Peter Hogarth, Esq; 164 Court Lane, Dulwich, London SE21 7Ed (☎ 01 693 4011); Societe Generale Strauss Turnbull Securities Ltd, 3 Moorgate Place, London EC2R 6HR (☎ 01 638 5699, fax 01 588 1437, telex 883204)

HOGBIN, Walter; p of Walter Clifford John Hogbin (d 1969), and Mary, *née* Roberts; *b* 21 Dec 1937; *Educ* Kent Coll Canterbury, Queen's Coll Cambridge (MA, CEng); *m* 1968, Geraldine Anne-Marie, da of Gerald Castley; 2 s (Justin Walter b 1970, Mark Walter b 1972); *Career* dir Taylor Woodrow plc, chm/md Taylor woodrow Int Ltd; memb Advsy Cncl - ECGD; memb Overseas Projects Bd; vice-chm Export Gp Construciton Industry; *Recreations* golf, tennis, gardening; *Style*— Walter Hogbin, Esq; Taylor Woodrow International Ltd, Western Avenue, London W5 1EU (☎ 01 997 6641, telex 23502 TAYINT G, fax 01 991 3117)

HOGG, Sir Arthur Ramsay; MBE (1945); 7 Bt, (UK 1846), of Upper Grosvenor Street, Co Middlesex; s of Ernest Charles Hogg (d 1907), and Lucy (d 1924) da of late William Felton Peel, of Alexandria, Egypt; suc cous, Sir Kenneth Weir Hogg, OBE, 6 Bt (d 1985); *b* 24 Oct 1896; *Educ* Sherborne, Ch Ch Oxford (MA); *m* 1924, Mary Aileen Hester Lee (d 1980), da of late P H Lee Evans; 3 s, (Michael, Mark, Simon), 1 da (Anthea); *Heir* s, Michael David, *qv*; *Career* WWI, Capt Royal W Kent Regt (twice wounded), WW II, Major (Gen List); *Style*— Sir Arthur Hogg, Bt; 27 Elgin Rd, Bournemouth, Dorset (☎ 0202 763287)

HOGG, Lady; Barbara Elisabeth; yr da of late Capt Arden Franklyn, of New Place, Shedfield, Hants, and 33 Bryanston Sq, W1; *m* 1, 2 June 1936, Brig Viscount Garmoyle, DSO, late Rifle Bde (ka 1942); m 2, 28 Oct 1948 Sir John Nicholson Hogg, TD; 1s, 1 da; *Style*— Lady Hogg; The Red House, Shedfield, Southampton, Hants

HOGG, Hon Douglas Martin; MP (C) Grantham 1979-; s of Baron Hailsham of St Marylebone KG, PC (Life Peer 1970; suc as 2 Visc Hailsham 1950, disclaimed Viscountcy 1963); h to Viscountcy of Hailsham; *b* 5 Feb 1945; *Educ* Eton, Ch Ch Oxford; *m* 6 June 1968, Hon Sarah Elizabeth Mary, *qv*, da of Lord Boyd- Carpenter, PC (Life Peer); 1 s (Quintin b 12 Oct 1973), 1 da (Charlotte b 26 Aug 1970); *Career* pres Oxford Union 1965; barr Lincoln's Inn 1968; pps to Leon Brittan (chief sec to Treasury) 1982-83, asst govt whip 1983-84; parly under sec Home Office 1986-; *Style*— The Hon Douglas Hogg, MP; House of Commons, London SW1A 0AA; Kettlethorpe Hall, Lincs LN1 2LD

HOGG, Vice Adm Sir Ian Leslie Trower; KCB (1968, CB 1964), DSC and Bar (1941, 1944); s of Col John M T Hogg (d 1955); *b* 30 May 1911; *Educ* Cheltenham Coll; *m* 1945, Mary Gwynneth Jean, da of Col Cecil W Marsden, MC (d 1973); 2 s; *Career* joined RN 1929, served WWII, Capt 1953, Cdre Cyprus 1960-62, Rear Adm 1963, Flag Offr Medway and Adm Supt HM Dockyard Chatham 1963-66, Vice Adm 1966, Defence Services Sec 1966-67, Vice CDS MOD 1967-70, ret; Comptroller Royal Soc of St George 1971-74; dir Richard Unwin Int Ltd 1975-87; FRSA; *Recreations* golf, china restoring; *Clubs* Naval; *Style*— Vice Adm Sir Ian Hogg, KCB, DSC; 32 Westbridge Road, London SW11 (☎ 01 223 5770)

HOGG, James Dalby; s of Sir James Cecil Hogg, KCVO (d 1973), of 2 Upper Harley St, London NW1, and Lady Hogg; *b* 9 July 1937; *Educ* Eton; *m* 19 Aug 1964, Joan, da of Richard Blackledge; 2 s (James b 1965, Samuel b 1966); *Career* reporter: Bolton Evening News 1960-64, Morning Telegraph Sheffield 1964-65, BBC Manchester 1965-66, BBC Leeds 1967-69, 24 Hours BBC London 1970-72, Nationwide 1972-83, Newsnight 1983-; writer and presenter numerous documentaries; *Recreations* keeping animals, reading, jazz, trying to play piano; *Clubs* The Count Basie Soc; *Style*— James Hogg, Esq; Forge House, Therfield, Royston, Herts SH8 9QA (☎ 076 387 280); BBC TV, Television Centre, London W12 7RJ (☎ 01 743 8000)

HOGG, Hon James Richard Martin; s of Baron Hailsham of St Marylebone, KG, PC (Life Peer; disclaimed Viscountcy of Hailsham 1963); *b* 25 Mar 1951; *Educ* Eton, Ch Ch Oxford; *m* Dorothy Clare, da of Maurice, and Dorothy Raffael; *Career* Capt Gren Gds, ret; shipping, md Simplex Turbulo Co Ltd; *Recreations* climbing, skiing, sailing; *Style—* The Hon James Hogg; 67 Victoria Road, London W8 5RH

HOGG, John Goldsborough; s of F G Hogg (d 1969); *b* 21 Jan 1925; *Educ* Harrow, Trinity Coll Cambridge; *m* 1955, Hon Sarah Edith, *qv* yst da of 1 Baron Noel-Buxton, PC, (d 1948); 2 da; *Career* Lloyd's Insurance Broker 1947-85; dep chm Hogg Robinson Gp 1979-85;; *Recreations* golf, shooting, fishing, skiing, flying; *Clubs* Boodle's; *Style—* John Hogg Esq; Old Broad Oak, Brenchley, Kent (☎ 089 272 2318); Hogg Robinson Group plc, Lloyds Chambers, 1 Portsoken St, London E1 8DF (☎ 01 480 4000; telex 884633)

HOGG, Sir John Nicholson; TD (1946); s of Sir Malcolm Hogg (d 1948, yr bro of 1 Viscount Hailsham and sometime dep chm Bombay Chamber of Commerce, banker and memb Viceroy's Legislative Cncl in India), and Lorna, da Sir Frank Beaman, sometime High Court Judge Bombay; 1 cous of Lord Hailsham of St Marylebone, *qv*; *b* 4 Oct 1912; *Educ* Eton, Balliol Coll Oxford; *m* 1948, Elisabeth, yr da of Capt Henry Arden Franklyn (d 1960), of Shedfield, Hants, and widow of Brig Viscount Garmoyle (who d 1942, of wounds received in action); 1 s (Malcolm b 1949), 1 da (Susan b 1954); *Career* served WWII KRRC (Greece, Crete, Western Desert, Tunisia, NW Europe); joined Glyn Mills and Co (which later became Williams and Glyn's Bank) 1934, md Glyn Mills and Co 1950-70 (dep chm 1963-68, chm 1968-70) dep chm Williams and Glyns Bank plc 1970-83; fell Eton Coll 1951-70, memb Cwlth War Graves Cmmn 1958-64, sheriff County of London 1960, chm ECGD's Advsy Cncl 1962-67, dep chm Gallaher Ltd 1964-78, tstee Imperial War Graves Endowment Fund 1965-87, chm Abu Dhabi Investmt Bd 1967-75, dir Royal Bank of Scotland Gp 1970-82, chm Banque Francaise de Crédit Int 1972-83, dir Prudential Corpn Ltd 1964-85; pres Eton Ramblers; hon tres Inst Child Health; kt 1963-; *Style—* Sir John Hogg, TD; The Red House, Shedfield, Southampton SO3 2HN (☎ 0329 832121)

HOGG, Hon Katharine Amelia; da of Baron Hailsham of St Marylebone (Life Peer; disclaimed Viscountcy of Hailsham 1963), and Lady Hailsham, *née* Martin (d 1978); *b* 18 Oct 1962; *Educ* Roedean Sch, St Peter's Coll Oxford U (BA); *Career* publishing (with Michael Joseph); *Style—* The Hon Katharine Hogg; 79 Church Rd, Richmond, Surrey (☎ 01 940 1456); Michael Joseph Ltd, 44 Bedford Square, London WC1 (☎ 01 323 3200

HOGG, Michael David; s and h of Sir Arthur Ramsay Hogg, 7 Bt, MBE, and Mary Aileen Hester Lee (d 1980), da of late Philip Herbert Lee Evans; *b* 19 August 1925; *Educ* Sherborne, Ch Ch Oxford; *m* 21 Jan 1956, Elizabeth Anne Thérèse, el da of Sir Terence Edmond Patrick Falkiner, 8 Bt (d 1987), 3 s; *Career* WWII 1943-45 as Capt Gren Gds; journalist; The Daily Telegraph 1951-87 (asst ed 1976); letters ed Peterborough 1986-87 (ed 1971-79, arts ed 1979-86); *Style—* Michael Hogg, Esq; 19 Woodlands Rd Barnes, London SW13

HOGG, Norman; MP (Lab) Cumbernauld and Kilsyth 1983-; *b* 12 Mar 1938; *Educ* Ruthrieston Secdy Sch; *m* 1964, Elizabeth McCall Christie; *Career* dist offr Nat and Local Govt Offrs Assoc 1967-69, memb Transport Users' Consultative Ctee for Scotland 1977-79; sec Trade Unions' Ctee for the Electricity Supply Industry 1978-79; MP (Lab) E Dunbartonshire 1979-83, memb select ctee Scottish Affrs 1979-82, Scottish Lab whip 1982-83, Lab dep chief whip 1983-87; Appointed Opposition Front Bench Spokesman-Scottish Affairs; *Style—* Norman Hogg, Esq, MP; House of Commons, London SW1A 0AA (☎ 01 219 5095)

HOGG, Rear Adm Peter Beauchamp; CB (1980); s of Beauchamp Hogg (d 1964), of Hungerford, Berks, and Sybil, *née* Medley (d 1967); *b* 9 Nov 1924; *Educ* Bradfield; *m* 1951, Gabriel Argentine, da of Argentine Francis Alington (d 1977), of Dorset; 2 s (Christopher b 1954, Gavin b 1960), 2 da (Catherine b 1956, Annabel b 1962); *Career* RN (engrg branch) 1943-80; final appt as Rear Adm 1977-80, def advsr Br High Cmmn Canberra and head of Br Def Liaison Staff; appeal sec and bursar i/c bldg modernisation Winchester Coll 1980-88; *Recreations* woodwork, furniture repairs, walking, gardening; *Style—* Rear Adm Peter Hogg, CB; c/o National Westminster Bank, 14 Old Town St, Plymouth PL1 1DG

HOGG, Rear Adm Robin Ivor Trower; s of Dudley William Bruce Trower Hogg and Lillian Nancy Hogg; *b* 25 Sept 1932; *Educ* New Beacon Sevenoaks, Bedford Sch; *m* 1, 1958, Susan Bridget Beryl, da of Adm Sir Guy Grantham, GCB, CBE, DSO; 2 s, 2 da; m 2, 1970, Angela Sarah Patricia, da of Brig Rudolph Kirwan, CBE, DSO; *Career* RCDS 1977, RN Presentation Team 1978, Capt First Frigate Sqdn 1979-81, dir Naval Operational Requirements 1981-84, Rear Adm 1984, Flag Offr First Flotilla 1984-86, chief of staff to GNC Fleet 1986-87; *Recreations* private life; *Style—* Rear Adm Robin Hogg; c/o Coutts & Co, 440 Strand, London WC2 0QS

HOGG, Hon Mrs (Sarah Edith Noel); *née* Noel-Buxton; yst da of 1 Baron Noel-Buxton, PC (d 1948); *b* 23 Jan 1928; *m* 2 June 1955, John Goldsborough Hogg, *qv*; 2 da; *Style—* The Hon Mrs Hogg; 11 Mallord Street, London SW3

HOGG, Hon Mrs (Sarah Elizabeth Mary); *née* Boyd-Carpenter; yr da of Baron Boyd-Carpenter, PC, DL (Life Peer); *b* 14 May 1946; *Educ* St Mary's Convent Ascot, Lady Margaret Hall Oxford; *m* 6 June 1968, Hon Douglas Hogg, MP, *qv*; 1 s, 1 da; *Career* Economist Newspaper 1968-82; economics editor Sunday Times 1981-82; presenter and economics editor Channel 4 News 1982-; Wincott Fndn Financial Journalist of 1985; dir London Broadcasting Co; govr, Centre for Economic Policy Research 1985-; asst ed, business and fin ed The Independent 1986-; IDS, Hon MA Open Univ 1987; *Style—* The Hon Mrs Hogg; The Independent, 40 City Road, London EC2 (☎ 01 253 1222, fax 01 608 1205)

HOGGART, Dr (Herbert) Richard; s of Tom Longfellow Hoggart and Adeline Hoggart; *b* 24 Sept 1918; *Educ* schs in Leeds, Leeds Univ (MA, LittD); *m* 1942, Mary Holt France; 2 s, 1 da; *Career* served WWII RA; staff tutor and sr staff tutor Univ Coll Hull 1946-59, sr lectr in English Leicester Univ 1959-62, prof of English Birmingham Univ 1962-73 (dir Centre for Contemporary Cultural Studies 1964-73), visiting fell Inst of Dvpt Studies Sussex Univ 1975, warden Goldsmith's Coll London Univ 1976-84; visiting prof Rochester Univ (NY) 1956-57; hon prof E Anglia Univ 1984-, Reith lecturer 1971; memb: British Cncl Br Books Overseas Ctee 1959-64, BBC Gen Advsy Cncl 1959-60 and 1964-, Pilkington Ctee on Broadcasting 1960-62, culture advsr ctee of UK Nat Cmmn for UNESCO (asst dir-gen UNESCO 1970-75), Arts Cncl 1976-81 (chm drama panel 1977-80, vice-chm 1980-81), ed bd New Universities Quarterly; chm: advsy cncl for Adult and Continuing Educn 1977-83, European Museum of the Year Award Ctee 1977-, Statesman and Nation Publishing Co 1978-81 (publishers New Statesman), Nat Broadcasting Res Unit 1981-; govr Royal Shakespeare Theatre until 1988; pres Br Assoc Former UN Civil Servants 1979-86; hon DLitt OU 1973, hon D-ès-L Univ Bordeaux 1975, hon DUniv Surrey 1981, hon LLD Cncl for National Academic Awards 1982, hon LLD York Univ (Toronto), hon DLitt (Leicester Univ), hon DLitt (Hull Unvi); hon fell Sheffield Poly 1983, hon DUniv East Anglia 1986, hon Des L Paris 1987; *Books* The Uses of Literacy (1957), various works on W H Auden, Speaking to Each Other (1970), Only Connect (1972), An Idea and Its Servants (1978), An English Temper (1982), An Idea of Europe (with Douglas Johnson, 1987), A Local Habitation (1988); *Style—* Dr Richard Hoggart; Mortonsfield, Beavers Hill, Farnham, Surrey GU8 7DF (☎ 0252 715740)

HOGGART, Simon David; s of Dr (Herbert) Richard Hoggart, *qv*, of Farnham, Surrey, and Mary Holt, *née* France; *b* 26 May 1946; *Educ* Hymers Coll Hull, Wyggeston GS Leicester, King's Coll Cambridge (MA); *m* 9 Jul 1983, Alyson Clare, da of Cdr Donald Louis Corner, RN, of Rusper, Sussex; 1 s (Richard b 1988), 1 da (Amy b 1986); *Career* political corr The Guardian 1973-81 (reporter 1968-71, NI corr 1971-73), US corr The Observer 1985- (reporter 1981-85), political corr Punch 1979-85; author books incl: The Pact (with Alistair Michie 1978), Michael Foot: A Portrait (with David Leigh 1981), On The House (1981), Back On The House (1982), House of Ill Fame (1985), House of Cards (ed 1988); *Recreations* reading, writing, travel; *Style—* Simon Hoggart, Esq; The Observer, Chelsea Bridge House, Queenstown Road, London SW8 (☎ 01 627 0700)

HOGGE, Maj-Gen Arthur Michael Lancelot; CB (1979); s of Lt-Col Arthur Herbert Fountaine Hogge (d 1940), and Kathleen Mary, *née* Hare (d 1951); *b* 4 August 1925; *Educ* Wellington Coll, Brasenose Coll Oxford; *m* 1952, Gunilla Jeane, da of William Henry Earley (d 1956); 2 s (Jonathan b 1954, Andrew b 1956); *Career* Army 1944-80, cmmnd The Queen's Own Hussars 1965-67 UK and Aden; Brig dir of Operational Requirements 1972-74; Maj Gen, dir gen fighting vehicles and engr equipment (DGFVE) 1974-77, dep master gen of Ordnance (DMGO) 1977-80; gen mangr Regular Forces Employment Assoc 1981-87; *Recreations* horticulture, sailing; *Style—* Maj-Gen Michael Hogge, CB; c/o Lloyds Bank, 120-124 High Street, Dorking, Surrey

HOGGE, Philip Arthur Fountain; s of Arthur Henry Hogge (d 1952), and Margaret Julia, *née* Large; *b* 2 Sept 1941; *Educ* Blundell's Sch, Devon, CAT Hamble; *m* 3 Oct 1964, Joyce Ann, da of Herbert Vassall Southby, of Vancouver, Canada; 2 s (Gavin b 1965, Giles b 1972), 1 da (Alice b 1968); *Career* pilot: BOAC 1962, Capt 1975, flt trg mangr: 707 1978, 747 1981; mangr flt crew 747 1986, chief pilot 747 1988; Liveryman of The Guild of Air Navigators; Freeman City of London; *Recreations* gardening, boats; *Style—* Philip A F Hogge, Esq; Magdalen House, Wharfe Lane, Henley-on-Thames, Oxon RG9 2LL; A311 TBA, British Airways, PO Box 10, Heathrow Airport, Hounslow, Middx TW6 2JA (☎ 01 562 5285)

HOGGETT, Prof Brenda Marjorie; da of Cecil Frederick Hale (d 1958), and Marjorie, *née* Godfrey (d 1981); *b* 31 Jan 1945; *Educ* Richmond (Yorks) HS for Girls, Girton Coll Cambridge (MA); *m* 1968, Anthony John Christopher Hoggett, QC, s of Christopher Hoggett, of Grimsby; 1 da (Julia b 1973); *Career* barr Gray's Inn 1969; asst lectr Univ of Manchester 1966, lectr 1968, snr lectr 1976, reader 1981-, prof of law 1986-89; law cmmr 1984-, asst rec 1984-, managing tstee Nuffield Fndn 1987-, prof of law King's Coll London 1989-; memb Cncl of Tribunals 1980-84, jt gen ed Journal of Social Welfare Law 1978-84; *Books* Mental Health Law (1976, 2 edn 1984), Parents and Children (1977, 3 edn 1987 with D S Pearl), The Family Law and Society - Cases and Materials (1983, 2 edn 1987 with S Atkins), Women and the Law (1984); many contribs to legal texts and periodicals; *Recreations* domesticity, drama; *Style—* Prof Brenda Hoggett; Law Commission, Conquest House, 37/38 John St London WC1N 2BQ

HOGWOOD, Christopher Jarvis Haley; CBE (1989); s of Haley Evelyn Hogwood (d 1982), of Saffron Walden Essex, and Marion Constance Higgott; *b* 10 Sept 1941; *Educ* Nottingham HS, Skinners Sch Tunbridge Wells, Cambridge Univ (MA), Charles Univ Prague; *Career* musician, musicologist, conductor and writer; dir The Academy of Ancient Music; author and ed: Faber Music, Thames and Hudson, OUP; artistic dir Handel and Haydn Soc, Boston USA, music dir St Paul Chamber Orchestra Minnesota; *Books* Music at Court (1977), The Trio Sonata BBC (1979), Haydn's Visits to England (co-ed Richard Lucke 1980), Music in Eighteenth Century England (1983), Handel (1984); *Style—* Christopher Hogwood, Esq, CBE; 2 Claremont, Hills Rd, Cambridge (☎ 0223 63975)

HOHLER, Gerald Arthur; s of Sir Thomas Hohler, KCMG, CB, of Fawkham Manor, Kent, and Cynthia Violet, da of W H Astell, of Woodbury Hall, Cambs; *b* 1923,july; *Educ* Eton, Trinity Coll Cambridge, RAC Cirencester; *m* 1953, Margaret Cynthia, da of Maj Sir Dennis Stucley, 5 Bt, of Hartland Abbey, N Devon; 1 s (Edward b 1958), 2 da (Henrietta b 1955, Lucinda (Mrs Newby) b 1960); *Career* Lt Coldstream Gds 1943, served in Normandy and N Europe; *Clubs* Pratt's; *Style—* Gerald A Hohler, Esq; Trent Manor, nr Sherborne, Dorset DT9 4SL; 7 Montrose Villas, Chiswick Mall, London W6 9TT

HOING, Roy Coote; s of Albert Edward Hoing (d 1978), and Vera Rubina, *née* Coote; *b* 1 June 1935; *Educ* Royal GS High Wycombe; *m* 25 June 1960, Gay Yvonne, da of Roland Kenneth Hatchett (d 1985); 1 s (Adrian Clive b 30 Jan 1967), 2 da (Frances Elizabeth b 25 April 1965, Laura Louise b (twin) 30 Jan 1967); *Career* Lt RAPC 1959, served Singapore; CA; ptnr Nash Broad (formerly Waller Broad) Chartered Accountants 1965-; Nat Tres Assoc of Ex Tablers Clubs 1982-88; FCA 1958; *Recreations* badminton, British butterflies; *Clubs* MCC; *Style—* Roy Hoing, Esq; Coachmans, Whielden Street, Old Amersham, Bucks (☎ 0494 726937); Nash Broad, 42 Upper Berkeley St, London W1 (☎ 01 723 7293)

HOLBECH, Geoffrey Victor Leigh; 2 s of Ronald Herbert Acland Holbech, OBE, JP (d 1956), of Farnborough Hall, and Catherine Emma, yst da of Sir Leigh Hoskyns, 11 Bt; descended from Ambrose Holbech, of Mollington, Oxfordshire, whose son, also Ambrose, acquired Farnborough in the 17 century (*see* Burke's Landed Gentry, 18 edn, vol 1, 1965); *b* 12 Nov 1918; *Educ* Stowe; *m* 1, 16 Nov 1940 (m dis 1944), Clara Joan, da of Gustav Eckard; m 2, 22 April 1950, Elizabeth Ariana, er da of Capt Lionel George Everson Harrisson, of Caynham Cottage, nr Ludlow, Shropshire; 2 s, 2 da; *Style—* Geoffrey Holbech, Esq; Farnborough Hall, Banbury, Oxon (☎ 029 589 202)

HOLBEN, Terence Henry Seymour; s of Henry George Seymour Holben, and Ivy Blanche, *née* Blomfield; *b* 4 Mar 1937; *Educ* Mark House Sch, S W Essex Technical Coll, London Coll of Printing; *m* 7 Oct 1961, June Elizabeth, da of Alan John Elliot, of

Uckfield, Sussex; 2 s (Matthew Seymour b 1966, Simon Lee b 1969); *Career* Royal Navy 1955-57; art dir advertising companies: McCann Erickson 1960-66, Graham and Gillies 1967-77; creative dir Ogilvy and Mather 1977- (dir 1983-); *Recreations* rowing, wife and two sons; *Style—* Terence H S Holben, Esq; Oakwood, 19 London Rd, Stanford Rivers, Essex

HOLBORN, Thomas; *b* 5 Sept 1936; *Educ* London Sch of Econ (BSc); *m* 1960, Maureen, 1 s (Neil b 1969); *Career* chm (md to 1982) Tobler Suchard (now Jacobs Suchard Ltd) 1982-; *Style—* Thomas Holborn, Esq; Old Pond House, Upper Dean, Huntingdon, Cambs PE18 0ND; c/o Tobler Suchard Ltd, Miller Rd, Bedford (☎ 0234 55141)

HOLBOROW, Christopher Adrian; TD (1969); s of Rev Canon George Holborow (d 1966), of Northants, and Barbara Stella, *née* Watson (d 1971); *b* 24 Dec 1926; *Educ* Repton, Gonville and Caius Coll Cambridge (MA, MD), Middx Hosp; *m* 1, 1960, Wanda Margaret (d 1982), da of John Douglas Nickels (d 1963), of Bridgnorth; 1 s (John b 1967), 2 da (Caroline b 1961, Emma b 1963); m 2, 1984, Caroline Ann, da of Edward Percy Woollcombe, OBE (d 1975), of Somerset; *Career* Maj RAMC (RARO) City of London FD Regt RA TA 1955-80, served Germany 1953-55; conslt surgn Westminster Hosp and Westminster Childrens Hosp 1964-85; chm Cwlth Soc for the Deaf 1984- (med advsr 1964-84); JP 1978-82; Cdr Order of The Republic of The Gambia 1984; *Recreations* fishing, shooting, travel; *Clubs* Army and Navy; *Style—* Christopher Holborow, Esq; Witham House, Witham Friary, Frome, Somerset (☎ 074 985 340); 152 Harley St, London W1N 1HH (☎ 01 935 2477)

HOLBOROW, Geoffrey Jermyn; OBE (1979); yst s of Rev Canon George Holborow (d 1966), and Barbara Stella, *née* Watson (d 1971); *b* 17 Sept 1929; *Educ* Repton, RMA Sandhurst, Emmanuel Coll Cambridge (MA); *m* 8 Aug 1959, Lady Mary Christina, JP, DStJ, da of 8 Earl of Courtown, OBE (d 1976), of Marfield House, Gorey, Co Wexford; 1 s (Crispin b 1963), 1 da (Katharine b 1961); *Career* jt sr ptnr Stratton and Holborow, Chartered Surveyors; vice-pres Chartered Land Agents Soc 1969, pres Land Agency Division RICS 1976, memb gen cncl RICS 1970-83; High Sheriff of Cornwall 1977; govr RAC Cirencester 1976-88; chm Assoc of Cornish Boys' Clubs 1965-83; *Recreations* gardening; *Style—* Geoffrey Holborow, Esq, OBE; Ladock House, Ladock, Truro, Cornwall (☎ 0726 88224);

HOLBOROW, Prof (Eric) John; s of Albert Edward Ratcliffe Holborow (d 1923), and Marian, *née* Crutchley (d 1966); *b* 30 Mar 1918; *Educ* Epsom Coll, Clare Coll Cambridge (MA, MD), St Bartholomew's Hosp; *m* March 1943, Cicely Mary, da of Arthur Taylor Foister (d 1961); 2 s (Jonathan b 1943, Paul b 1948), 1 da (Margaret Mary b 1950); *Career* Maj RAMC 1939-43, served Egypt; emeritus prof of immunopathology and hon conslt immunologist London Hosp Med Coll; chm Smithline Fndn Tstees; dir MRC Rheumatism Res Unit 1974; FRCP, FRCPath; *Books* Autoimmunity and Disease (co author with L E Glynn 1965), An ABC of Modern Immunology (1968), Immunology in Medicine (1981); *Recreations* local history; *Style—* Prof John Holborow; The Old Rectory, Fingest, Henley-on-Thames, Oxon

HOLBOROW, Lady Mary Christina; *née* Stopford; JP (1970); da (by 1 m) of 8 Earl of Courtown, OBE , DL, TD (d 1976); *b* 19 Sept 1936; *m* 8 Aug 1959, Geoffrey Jermyn Holborow, OBE, s of Rev Canon George Holborow (d 1966); 1 s, 1 da; *Career* memb SW Water Authy 1980-, regnl bd memb Tstee Savings Bank 1981-, chm Cornwall ctee, Rural Devpt Cmmn, cmmr St John's Ambulance Bde Cornwall 1982-87; DStJ; *Style—* Lady Mary Holborow, JP; Ladock House, Ladock, Truro, Cornwall (☎ 0726 882274)

HOLBROOK, David; s of Kenneth Redvers Holbrook (d 1968), of Norwich, and Elsie Eleanor Holbrook (d 1956); *b* 9 Jan 1923; *Educ* City of Norwich Sch, Downing Coll Cambridge (BA, MA); *m* 23 April 1949, (Frances Margaret) Margot, da of Charles Davies-Jones (d 1938), of Bedwas, Wales; 2 s (Jonathan b 1956, Thomas b 1966), 2 da (Susan (Suki) b 1950, Kate b 1953); *Career* Lt E Riding Yeomantry RAC 1942-45, serv Normandy Invasion and NW Europe; asst ed Bureau of Current Affrs 1947-52, tutor Bassingbourn Village Coll Cambridge 1954-61, fell Kings Coll Cambridge 1961-65, sr Leverhulme res fell 1965, writer in res Dartington Hall 1971-73, fell and dir eng studies Downing Coll 1981-88 (asst dir 1973-75), Hooker visiting Prof MacMaster Univ Hamilton Ontario 1984, emeritus fell Downing Coll 1988-, sr Leverhulme Res Fell 1988-; Arts Cncl Writers Grant: 1968, 1976, 1980; pubns incl: Selected Poems (1980), Flesh Wounds (1966), A Play of Passion (1977), Nothing Larger Than Life (1987), Worlds Apart (1988), English for Maturity (1961), English for the Rejected (1964), Education and Philosophical Anthropology (1987), Gustav Mahler and the Courage to Be (1975), Sylvia Plath, Poetry and Existence (1976), Lost Bearings in English Poetry (1977), Images of Woman in Literature (1989); memb editorial bd Universities Quarterly 1978-86, pres Forum for Educnl Therapy 1988-; *Recreations* oil painting, foreign travel, cooking, gardening; *Style—* David Holbrook, Esq; Denmore Lodge, Brunswick Gardens, Cambridge, CB5 8DQ (☎ 0223 315 081); Downing Coll, Cambridge (☎ 0223 334 800)

HOLCROFT, Charles Anthony Culcheth; s and h of Sir Peter George Culcheth Holcroft, 3 Bt; *b* 22 Oct 1959; *Style—* Charles Holcroft, Esq

HOLCROFT, Sir Peter George Culcheth; 3 Bt (UK 1921), JP (Shropshire 1976); s of Sir Reginald Culcheth Holcroft, 2 Bt, TD (d 1978), and his 1 w, Mary Frances, *née* Swire (d 1963); *b* 29 April 1931; *Educ* Eton; *m* 21 July 1956 (m dis 1987), Rosemary Rachel, yr da of late Capt George Nevill Deas, 8 Hussars; 3 s, 1 da; *Heir* s, Charles Anthony Culcheth Holcroft; *Career* High Sheriff of Shropshire 1969; *Style—* Sir Peter Holcroft, Bt, JP; Berrington, Shrewsbury

HOLDEN, Brian Peter John; s of Sir George Holden, 3 Bt (d 1976), and hp of n, Sir John Holden, 4 Bt; *b* 12 April 1944; *m* 1984, Bernadette Anne Lopez, da of George Gerard O'Malley; *Style—* Brian Holden, Esq

HOLDEN, Sir David Charles Beresford; KBE (1972), CB (1963), ERD (1954); s of Oswald Addenbrooke Holden (ka 1917), and Ella Mary Beresford (d 1960); *b* 26 July 1915; *Educ* Rossall, King's Coll Cambridge (MA); *m* 1948, Elizabeth Jean, da of Arthur Norman Odling, OBE (d 1975); 1 s, 1 da; *Career* served WWII RA, BEF 1939-40, India, Burma 1942-45; temp Maj; NI Civil Serv 1937-76: sec Miny of Fin 1970-76, head Civil Serv 1970-76, dir Ulster Office London 1976-77; *Clubs* Oriental; *Style—* Sir David Holden, KBE, CB, ERD; Falcons, Wilsford Cum Lake, Amesbury, Salisbury, Wilts SP4 7BL (☎ 0980 22493)

HOLDEN, His Hon Judge Derek; s of Frederic Holden, of Sussex, and Audrey Lilian Holden (d 1985); *b* 7 July 1935; *Educ* Cromwell House, Staines GS; *m* 1961, Dorien Elizabeth, da Henry Douglas Bell, of Sunningdale; 2 s (Derek Grant b 1968, Derek Clark b 1970); *Career* Lt East Surrey Regt 1953-56; ptnr Derek Holden and Co (slrs) 1966-82; rec Crown Ct 1980-84, circuit judge 1984-,; *Recreations* sailing, rowing, photography, music; *Clubs* Leander, Royal Solent YC, Remenham, Staines Boat, Burway Rowing, Eton Excelsior Rowing; *Style—* His Hon Judge Derek Holden; c/o Court Administrator, Sessions House, Ewell Rd, Surbiton SY

HOLDEN, Hon Donna Diana; da of 2 and last Baron Holden (d 1951); *b* 1916; *Style—* The Hon Donna Holden; Hadeigh Court, Stanley Rd, Babbacombe, Torquay

HOLDEN, Sir Edward; 6 Bt (UK 1893), of Oakworth House, Keighley, Yorks; s of Sir Isaac Holden, 5 Bt (d 1962); *b* 8 Oct 1916; *Educ* Leys Sch, Christ's Coll Cambridge, St Thomas's Hosp (MRCS, LRCP); *m* 17 Oct 1942, Frances Joan, da of John Spark, JP, of Ludlow, Stockton-on-Tees; 2 adopted s; *Heir* bro, Paul Holden; *Career* conslt anaesthetist Darton and Northallerton Gp Hosp 1957-74; FFARCS; *Clubs* Farmers'; *Style—* Sir Edward Holden, Bt; Moorstones, Riverbury Lane, Osmotherley, Northallerton DL6 3BG

HOLDEN, Dr Harold Benjamin; s of Reginald Holden (d 1979), and Frances Hilda, *née* Haslett (d 1983); Haslett family built and manned the first lifeboats on the Sussex coast (circa 1880-1910); *b* 2 June 1930; *Educ* Highgate, Charing Cross Hosp Med Sch Univ of London (MB BS); *m* 1, Nov 1963, Ann, da of Archibald Sinclair, of Cardiff; 2 s (Andrew b 1964, Michael b 1970), 1 da (Sarah b 1966); m 2, March 1979, Lydia, da of Dr Ronals James, of Toronto, Canada; 2 s (Benjamin b 1978, Robin b 1979); *Career* surgn, dir ENT Unit Charing Cross and Westminster Hosp Med Sch Univ of London, previously postgraduate dean Charing Cross Hosp Med Sch; fell Harvard Univ; FRCS; *Recreations* yachting, flying, golf; *Clubs* Royal Southampton YC, British Med Pilots Assoc, St Georges Hill GC; *Style—* Dr Harold B Holden; Yew Tree Cottage, Hyde, Fordingbridge, Hants (☎ 0425 52564); 128 Harley St, London W1N 1AH (☎ 01 486 9400)

HOLDEN, Sir John David; 4 Bt (UK 1919), of The Firs, Leigh, Lancaster; s of late David George Holden (eldest s of Sir George Holden, 3 Bt); suc gf 1976; *b* 16 Dec 1968; *m* 29 Aug 1987, Suzanne, *née* Cummings; *Heir* unc, Brian Holden; *Style—* Sir John Holden, Bt; 32 Rowntree Ave, York

HOLDEN, Maj-Gen John Reid; CB (1965), CBE (1960, OBE 1953), DSO 1941; s of late John Holden; *b* 8 Jan 1913; *Educ* Hamilton Acad, Glasgow Univ, RMC Sandhurst; *m* 1939, Rosemarie Florence (d 1980), da of late William Henry de Vere Pennefather, of Carlow; 1 da; *Career* 2 Lt RTC 1937, Adj 7 RTR 1940-41 (despatches), Bde Maj 32 Army Tank Bde 1942 (POW), GSO1, GHQ Far ELF Singapore 1951-52, CO 3 RTR BAOR 1954-57, AAG WO 1958, cdr 7 Armd Bde Gp BAOR 1958-61, Royal Naval War Coll 1961, chief of mission Br Cdrs-in-Chief Mission to the Soviet Forces in Germany 1961-63, GOC 43 (Wessex) Div Dist 1963-65, dir RAC 1965-68, ret 1968, Col Cmdt RTR 1965-68, Hon Col The Queen's Own Lowland Yeomanry RAC, T&AVR 1972-75; *Recreations* books, gardening; *Style—* Maj-Gen John Holden, CB, CBE, DSO; c/o Royal Bank of Scotland, Kirkland Ho, Whitehall, London SW1

HOLDEN, Lady; Mabel; da of Harry Morgan, of Cwt Blethyn, Usk, and Ethel, *née* Jones; *m* 1941, Sir Michael Holden, CBE, ED (d 1982), sometime Chief Justice Rivers State, Nigeria; 2 s, 1 da; *Style—* Lady Holden; 3 Rushton Rd, Wilbarston, Market, Harborough (☎ 0536 771100)

HOLDEN, Patrick Brian; s of Reginald John Holden, of East Hampshire, and Winifred Isabel; *b* 16 June 1937; *Educ* All Hallows Sch, St Catharine's Coll Cambridge (BA, MA); *m* 1972, Jennifer Ruth, da of Francis Meddings (d 1985); *Career* served Royal Hampshire Regt 1955-57, seconded 1 Ghana Regt RWAFF; sec Fine Fare Gp 1960-69 (legal and property dir 1965-69); Pye of Cambridge 1969-74, dir Pye Telecom 1972-74; sec New Town Assoc 1974-75, dir and sec Oriel Foods Gp 1975-81; gp sec Fisons plc 1981-83, chm Steak Away Foods Ltd 1982-; FCIS, FBIM; *Recreations* bridge, walking; *Clubs* Naval and Military; *Style—* Patrick Holden, Esq; The Old School House, Lower Green, Tewin, Welwyn, Herts AL6 0LD (☎ 043 871 7573)

HOLDEN, Paul; s of Sir Isaac Holden, 5 Bt (d 1962), and hp of bro, Sir Edward Holden, 6 Bt; *b* 1923; *m* 1950, Vivien Mary, da of late Hedley Broxholme Oldham, of Allesley, Coventry; 1 s, 2 da; *Career* software and quality mgmnt, ret; tstee Understanding Disabilities Educatnl Tst; *Recreations* cine and video photography; *Clubs* Lions, Surrey Border Film Makers; *Style—* Paul Holden, Esq; Glenside, Rowhills, Heath End, Farnham, Surrey

HOLDEN, Robert David; s of Major Hobert Robert Holden, MC (d 1987), of Sibdon Castle Craven Arms, Shropshire, and Lady Elizabeth, *née* Herbert; *b* 14 Jan 1956; *Educ* Eton; *m* 18 June 1988, Susan Emily Frances, *née* Rowley, 7 Bt, *qv*; *Career* chm Robert Holden Ltd 1978-, Fine Arts Courses Ltd 1985-; patron of the living of Sibdon; *Clubs* Army & Navy; *Style—* Robert Holden, Esq; Sibdon Castle Craven Arms Salop; 34 Nevern Place, London SW5; 15 Savile Row, London W1 (☎ 01 437 6010)

HOLDEN, William John; s of James Alfred Holden, and Elsie Sophia, *née* Hinson (d 1979); *b* 7 August 1933; *Educ* Kings Sch Worcester, Aston Univ; *m* 17 July 1954, Cleone Winifred, da of Frank Henry Hodges, of Droitwich; 2 s (Jeremy b 1956, Simon b 1959), 1 da (Andree b 1961); *Career* engr; fndr and chm Holden Hydroman plc 1969-87; chm Holden Heat plc 1987-; FPRI; *Recreations* yachtsman, skiing; *Clubs* Sloanes; *Style—* William J Holden, Esq; The Old Rectory, Suckley, Worcester WR6 5DF (☎ 08864 337); Holden Heat plc, Court Farm Trading Estate, Bishops Frome, Worcester (☎ 08853 634)

HOLDEN-BROWN, Sir Derrick; *b* 14 Feb 1923; *Educ* Westcliff; *m* 1950, Patricia Mary Ross Mackenzie; 1 s, 1 da; *Career* WWII Lt RNVR; CA 1948; vice-chm Allied Breweries 1975-82 (dir 1967, fin dir 1972); vice-chm Sun Alliance and London Insurance Co 1977-, chm Allied-Lyons (beer, wine and spirits gp) 1982-; chm: White Ensign Assoc Ltd 1987-, Portsmouth Naval Heritage Tst 1989-; memb: Brewers' Soc 1978-80, Alcohol Educn and Res Cncl 1982-; kt 1979; *Recreations* sailing (yacht 'Aqualeo of Lymington'); *Clubs* Boodle's, Royal Yacht Squadron; *Style—* Sir Derrick Holden-Brown; Copse House, De La Warr Rd, Milford-on-Sea, Hants (☎ 059 069 2247); Allied-Lyons plc, Allied House, 156 St John St, London EC1P 1AR (☎ 01 253 9911; telex 267605)

HOLDER, Sir (John) Henry; 4 Bt (UK 1898), of Pitmaston, Moseley, Worcs; s of Sir John Eric Duncan Holder, 3 Bt; *b* 12 Mar 1928; *Educ* Eton, Birmingham Univ (Dip Malting and Brewing); *m* 10 Sept 1960, Catharine Harrison, da of Leonard Baker (d 1973); 2 s (Nigel John Charles and Hugo Richard (twins) b 1962), 1 da (Bridget Georgina b 1964); *Heir* s, Nigel John Charles b 1962; *Career* prodn dir and head brewer Elgood and Son Ltd (Wisbech) 1975-; chm E Anglian Section Incorporated Brewers' Guild 1981-83; dip memb Inst of Brewing; *Recreations* sailing; *Clubs* Ouse

Amateur SC; *Style*— Sir Henry Holder, Bt; 47 St Pauls Rd, Walton Highway, Wisbech, Cambs PE14 7DN

HOLDER, Maj Nicholas Paul; TD (1982); s of Air Marshal Sir Paul Holder, KBE, CB, DSO, DFC, *qv*, of Innisfree, Bramshott Chase, Hindhead, Surrey, and Lady Mary Elizabeth, *née* Kidd; *b* 10 Nov 1942; *Educ* Sherborne; *Career* Royal Scots Greys (2 Dragoons) 1963-71, Royal Scots Dragoon Gds Res of Offrs 1971-82; Inns of Ct and City Yeo; currently exec dir Fuji Int Fin (merchant banking subsid of Fuji Bank Tokyo); *Recreations* skiing, tennis; *Clubs* Bucks; *Style*— Maj Nicholas Holder, TD; 92 Settrington Rd, London SW6 3BA (☎ 01 736 0072); Fuji International Finance Ltd, 101 Moorgate, London EC2 (☎ 01 588 74 62)

HOLDER, Nigel John Charles; s and h of Sir John Henry Holder, 4 Bt; *b* 6 May 1962; *Style*— Nigel Holder, Esq; 47 St Paul's Road, Walton Highway, Wisbech, Cambs PE14 7DN

HOLDER, Air Marshal Sir Paul Davie; KBE (1965), CB (1964), DSO (1942), DFC (1941); s of Hugh John Holder (d 1961); *b* 2 Sept 1911; *Educ* Bristol Univ (MSc, PhD), Univ of Illinois USA (Robert Blair Fell); *m* 1941, Mary Elizabeth Kidd; 2 s; *Career* cmmnd RAF 1936, CO No 218 Sqdn Bomber Cmd 1942, Admin Staff Coll Henley-on-Thames 1949, IDC 1956, AOC Singapore 1957, AOC Hong Kong 1958-59, ACAS (Trg) Air Miny 1960-63, AOC No 25 Gp Flying Trg Cmd; AOC-in-C Coastal Cmd, Cdr Maritime Air E Atlantic and Cdr Maritime Air Channel Cmd 1965-68, ret; memb Waverley Dist Cncl 1976-83; FRAeS; *Clubs* RAF; *Style*— Air Marshal Sir Paul Holder, KBE, CB, DSO, DFC; Innisfree, Bramshott Chase, Hindhead, Surrey GU26 6DG (☎ 042 873 4579)

HOLDERNESS, Martin William; s and h of Sir Richard William Holderness, 3 Bt; *b* 24 May 1957; *Style*— Martin Holderness Esq

HOLDERNESS, Baron (Life Peer UK 1979); Hon Richard Frederick Wood; PC (1959), DL (Yorks E Riding 1967); 3 s of 1 Earl of Halifax, KG, OM, GCSI, GCMG, GCIE, TD, PC, sometime Viceroy of India and Foreign Sec (d 1959), and Lady Dorothy Onslow, CI, DCVO, JP, DGStJ, yr da of 4 Earl of Onslow; unc of present (3) Earl of Halifax, 1 cous of 6 Earl of Onslow,; *b* 5 Oct 1920; *Educ* Eton, New Coll Oxford; *m* 15 April 1947, Diana, o da of late Col Edward Orlando Kellett, DSO, MP (ka 1943; whose widow, Myrtle, m as her 2 husb Hon William McGowan, 2 s of 1 Baron McGowan); 1 s (Edward), 1 da (Emma, m Sir Nicholas Brooksbank, 3 Bt, *qv*); *Career* sits as Conservative peer in House of Lords; served WWII, Middle East, Lt KRRC 1943, ret severely wounded, Hon Col 4 Bn Royal Green Jackets TAVR; MP (C) Bridlington 1950-79, parly sec to min Pensions and NI 1955-58; parly sec to: Min Labour 1958-59, Min Power 1959-63, Min Pensions and Nat Insur 1963-64, Min Overseas Devpt 1970-74; chm Disablement Servs Authy 1987-; dir Hargreaves Gp 1974-86; Hon LLD: Sheffield 1962, Leeds 1978, Hull 1982; *Recreations* gardening, travel, shooting; *Style*— The Rt Hon Lord Holderness, PC, DL; House of Lords, London SW1; Flat Top House, Bishop Wilton, York YO4 1RY (☎ 075 96 266); 65 Collines de Guerrevieille, 83120 Ste Maxime, France

HOLDERNESS, Sir Richard William; 3 Bt (UK 1920), of Tadworth, Surrey; s of Sir Ernest William Elsmie, 2 Bt, CBE (d 1968); *b* 30 Nov 1927; *Educ* Corpus Christi Coll Oxford; *m* 1953, Pamela, da of Eric Chapman, CBE (d 1985); 2 s, 1 da; *Heir* s, Martin Holderness; *Career* ret as dist offr HM Overseas Civil Serv 1954; dir Whiteheads (estate agents and surveyors) 1967-86; FRICS 1976; *Recreations* golf, gardening; *Clubs* East India; *Style*— Sir Richard Holderness, Bt; Bramfold Ct, Nutbourne, nr Pulborough, W Sussex

HOLDGATE, Dr Martin Wyatt; CB (1978); s of Francis Wyatt Holdgate, JP (d 1981), of Lancs, and Lois Marjorie, *née* Bebbington; *b* 14 Jan 1931; *Educ* Arnold Sch Blackpool, Queens' Coll Cambridge, (BA, MA, PhD 1955); *m* 2 April 1963, Elizabeth Mary, *née* Dickason; 1 s (Nicholas Michael David b 1965); 1 step s (Martin Robert Arnold Weil b 1956); *Career* res fell Queens' Coll Cambridge 1955-56, sr scientist and jt-ldr Gough Island Scientific Survey 1955-56, lectr in zoology Univ of Manchester 1956-57, Durham Coll Univ of Durham 1957-60, ldr Royal Soc expdn to Southern Chile 1958-59; asst dir of res Scott Polar Res Inst Cambridge 1960-63, sr biologist Br Antarctic Survey 1963-66, dep dir The Nature Conservancy 1966-70; dir Central Unit on Environmental Pollution Dept of the Environment 1970-74; Inst of Terrestrial Ecology Natural Environment Res Cncl 1974-76, dir gen of res (and dep sec) Dept of the Environment and Dept of Tport 1976-83, dep sec (Environment Protection) and chief enviroment scientist Dept of the Environment 1983-88, chief scientific advsr Dept of Tport 1983-88; dir gen Int Union for Conservation of Nature and Natural Resources (The World Conservation Union) 1988; UNEP 500 Award 1988, UNEP Silver Medal 1983, Bruce Medal Royal Soc Edinburgh 1964; CBiol, FIBiol; *Books* Mountains in the Sea (1958), Antarctic Ecology (ed 1970), A Perspective of Enviromental Pollution (1979), The World Environment 1972-82 (jt ed 1982); numerous papers in biological and environmental journals and works on Antarctic; *Recreations* hill walking, local history, natural history; *Clubs* Athenaeum; *Style*— Dr Martin Holdgate, CB; International Union for Conservation of Nature and Natural Resources, Avenue du Mont-Blanc, CH-1196, Gland, Switzerland

HOLDING, Malcolm Alexander; s of Adam Anderson Holding (d 1962), of Edinburgh, and Mary Lillian, *née* Golding; *b* 11 May 1932; *Educ* King Henry VIII Sch Coventry; *m* 28 Dec 1955, Pamela Eve, da of late Jack Hampshire; 2 da (Alison b 18 Aug 1959, Penelope b 14 Feb 1962); *Career* 2 Lt RCS 1951-53; Dip Serv: FO 1953-55, MECAS 1956-57, third sec commercial Br Embassy Tunis 1957-60, second sec commercial Br Embassy Khartoum 1960-64, second sec commercial (later first sec) Br Embassy Cairo 1964-66, Consul Bari 1968-69, FCO 1970-72, first sec Br Dep High Cmmn Madras 1972-74, FCO 1975-78, cnsllr 1978, Nat Def Coll Canada 1978-79, commercial cnsllr Br Embassy Rome 1979-81; Br consul gen: Edmonton 1981-85, Naples 1986; Commendatore dell'Ordine del Merito Italy 1980; *Recreations* sailing, skiing, travel, pottering; *Clubs* Rotary; *Style*— Malcolm Holding, Esq; Foreign and Commonwealth Office, London SW1A 2AH; British Consulate General, Via Crispi 122, I-80122 Naples Italy (☎ 39 81 663511)

HOLDSWORTH, Albert Edward; QC (1969); s of Albert Edward Holdsworth (d 1943), and Catherine Sarah, *née* Walton (d 1967); *b* 10 April 1909; *Educ* Sir George Monoux Sch Walthamstow, Gonville and Caius Coll Cambridge (MA); *m* 1, 1941, Barbara Frances (d 1968), da of Ernest Henry Reeves (d 1923); 1 s (Richard); m 2, 1970, Brianne Evelyn Frances, da of Arthur James Lock (d 1978); 2 s (Mark b 1971, Dominic b 1973); *Career* journalist Financial News 1932-33, special corr World Econ Conf 1933, political corr (later London ed) Yorkshire Post 1933-46, broadcast for BBC on current topics 1935-56; barr Middle Temple 1936; Party candidate (cons) Ipswich 1951; moved resolution in favour of UK entry into EEC Cons Conf Llandudno 1962; dep chm SW Metropolitan Mental Health Tribunal 1962-65, circuit judge, ret; *Publications* Forward Together, an Outline of an Idea for a Common Social Inspiration (1983); *Recreations* reading, theatre; *Clubs* Reform; *Style*— His Hon A E Holdsworth, QC; 2 Middle Temple Lane, Temple, London EC4Y 9AA (☎ 01 353 7926); Sutton Gate, Sutton, Pulborough, West Sussex RH20 1PN (☎ 07987 230)

HOLDSWORTH, Lt Cdr Arthur John Arundell; CVO (1980), OBE (1962), RN (ret); eld s of Frederick John Cropper Holdsworth, JP, DL, sometime Mayor of Totnes and Master of the Dart Vale Harriers (whose maternal grandmother was Hon Margaret, da of 1 Baron Denman); *b* 31 Mar 1915; *Educ* RNC Dartmouth; *m* 1940, Barbara Lucy Ussher, da of Lt-Col William Acton, DSO; 1 s (Nicholas b 1942), 1 da (Jane b 1945); *Career* served WWII at sea (despatches), Asst naval attaché Warsaw 1947-49; Br Jt Servs Mission Washington DC 1950-51, Naval Staff Germany 1954-56, Flag Lt to Admty Bd 1956-65; gentleman usher to HM The Queen 1967-85 (extra gentleman usher 1985-); steward Newton Abbot Racecourse 1967-85; dep pres Devon Branch BRCS 1971-85 (patron 1985-); vice Lord Lt Devon 1982- (DL 1973, High Sheriff 1976-77); *Recreations* shooting, fishing; *Style*— Lt Cdr John Holdsworth, CVO, OBE, RN; Holbeam Mill, Ogwell, nr Newton Abbot, Devon (☎ 0626 65547)

HOLDSWORTH, Nicholas John William Arthur; s of Lt Cdr (Arthur) John Arundell Holdsworth, CVO, OBE, of Newton Abbot, S Devon, *qv*, and Barbara Lucy Ussher, *née* Acton; *b* 10 May 1942; *Educ* Winchester Coll; *m* 17 Sept 1966, Susan Antonia, da of Charles Anthony Fradgley, of Combe Florey, Somerset; 2 s (Ben b 1968, Sam b 1970); *Career* RB 1960-64; account exec Charles Hobson and Grey 1964-69, account mangr Lintas 1969-70, account dir Charles Barker Gp 1970-85 (dir Charles Barker City 1982-85), dir Dewe Rogerson 1985-; hon sec Weyfarers CC; *Recreations* cricket, horse racing; *Clubs* MCC, Hurlingham; *Style*— Nicholas Holdsworth, Esq; 32 Carmalt Gardens, Putney, London SW15 (☎ 01 788 1240); Dewe Rogerson Ltd, 3 1/2 London Wall Buildings, London Wall, EC2M 5SY (☎ 01 638 9571, fax 01 628 3444, telex 883610)

HOLDSWORTH, Sir (George) Trevor; s of William Holdsworth; *b* 29 May 1927; *Educ* Hanson GS Bradford, Keighley GS Yorkshire; *m* 1951, Patricia June Ridler; 3 s; *Career* Rawling Greaves and Mitchell 1944-51, Bowater Corpn Ltd 1952-63; joined Guest, Keen and Nettlefolds plc as dep chief accountant 1963, rising to dep chm 1974, md and dep chm 1977, gp chm 1980-; dir: Thorn-EMI plc 1977-87, Midland Bank plc 1979-; chm Allied Colloids Gp plc 1983-; vice-pres: Engrg Employers' Fedn 1980-, Ironbridge Gorge Museum Devpt Tst 1981-, BIM 1982- (vice-chm 1978-80, chm 1980-82, vice-pres 1982-); chm Brighton Festival Tst 1982 (tstee 1980-); dep chm Advsy Bd of Inst of Occupational Health 1980; tstee: Anglo-German Fdn for the Study of Industl Soc 1980-, Royal Opera House Tst 1981-; memb of cncl: CBI 1974- (and Steering Gp on Unemployment 1982-, Special Programmes Unit 1982-, and chm Tax Reform Working Party 1984-); dep pres CBI 1987; memb: bd of govrs Ashridge Mgmnt Coll 1978-, Engrg Industries' Cncl 1980- (chm 1985-), Overseas Panel of Duke of Edinburgh's Award 1980-, Ct of Br Shippers' Cncl 1981-, British-N America Ctee 1981-, Cncl of Royal Inst of Int Affrs 1983-, Int cncl of INSEAD 1985-; memb Worshipful Co of CAs 1977-; Hon DTech Loughborough 1981, Hon DSc Aston 1982, Hon DEng Bradford 1983; CAs Founding Socs' Centenary Award 1983; FCA; kt 1981; *Recreations* music, theatre; *Style*— Sir Trevor Holdsworth; 7 Cleveland Row, London SW1A 1DB (☎ 01 930 2424, telex 24911)

HOLE, Rev Canon Derek Norman; s of Frank Edwin Hole (d 1987), of Durban, 11 Widley Lane, Crownhill, Plymouth, Devon PL6 5JS, and Ella Evelyn, *née* Thomas; *b* 5 Dec 1933; *Educ* Public Central Sch Plymouth, Lincoln Theol Coll; *Career* ordained (Leicester Cath): deacon 1960, priest 1961; asst curate St Mary Magdalen Knighton Leicester 1960-62, domestic chaplain to Archbishop of Cape Town 1962-64, asst curate St Nicholas Kenilworth Warwicks 1964-67, rector St Mary the Virgin Burton Latimer Kettering Northants 1967-73, vicar St James the Greater Leicester 1973-, hon canon Leicester Cathedral 1983-, rural dean Christianity South 1983-, chaplain Leicester HS 1983-, chaplain to HM The Queen 1985-, The Chaplain to the High Sheriffs of Leicestershire 1980-85 and 1987; chm House of Clergy, vice pres Diocesan Synod, memb Bishop's Cncl 1986-, govr Alderman Newton's Sch Leicester 1976-82, tstee Leicester Church Charities 1983-, pres Leicester Rotary Club 1987-88; memb: Leicester Charity Orgn Soc 1983-, Victorian Soc 1986-; *Recreations* music, walking, reading biographies and victorian history; *Clubs* The Leicestershire; *Style*— The Rev Canon Derek Hole; St James The Greater Vicarage, 216 London Rd, Leicester LE2 1NE (☎ 0533 542 111)

HOLEY, Brian; s of Clifford Holey (d 1966), of Harrogate, and Lillian Agnes, *née* Chappell (d 1982); *b* 29 Sept 1928; *Educ* Ripon GS; *m* 10 Sept 1955, Joanne, da of George Henry Plews, of Norton, Cleveland; 1 s (Adrian b 1959); *Career* CA; ptnr Brough Holey & Peel 1953-55, sr ptnr Holey & Co 1955-, chm Ashworth Fin Ltd 1959-72 (dir 1955-59), chm Templey Homes Ltd 1964-82, ptnr Dickenson Keighley & Co Harrowgate 1975-78, fin advsr Entergold Gp of Cos 1977-86; FCA 1951, FTII 1964; *Recreations* working, walking, music, theatre; *Style*— Brian Holey, Esq; Sheringham, Hornbeam Crescent, Harrogate, N Yorks; White Gates, Sedbusk, Hawes, N Yorks; Stuart House, 15/17 North Pk Rd, Harrogate, HG1 5PD (☎ 0423 66086)

HOLFORD, Francis Lindsay; s of Lindsay Tillestone Holford (d 1971), and Kathleen Swain (d 1942); *b* 1 April 1937; *Educ* Collyers Sch Sussex; *m* 1963, Jennifer Jane, da of Frederick Ferdinand Wolff, CBE; 2 s (Michael b 1964, John b 1973), 3 da (Clare b 1965, Catherine b 1967, Anna b 1969); *Career* chm and md Rudolf Wolff and Co Ltd (Metals and Commodities Futures and Options Traders); memb cncl Assoc of Futures Brokers and Dealers Ltd; *Recreations* walking, reading, music; *Clubs* Gresham; *Style*— Francis Holford, Esq; Winton, 46 London Rd, Guildford, Surrey GU1 2AL (☎ 0483 69167); 2nd Floor, D Section, Plantation House, 31-35 Fenchurch St, London EC3M 3DX (☎ 01 626 8765, telex 885034, fax 01 626 3939)

HOLFORD, Rear Adm Frank Douglas; CB (1969), DSC (1944); s of Charles Frederick Holford, DSO, OBE (d 1949), and Ursula Isobel, *née* Corbett (d 1963); *b* 28 June 1916; *Educ* RNC Dartmouth; *m* 1942, Sybil Priscilla, da of Cdr Sir Edward Robert Micklem (d 1952); 2 s (Michael, Mark); *Career* served WWII in Far East, Mediterranean, Atlantic, Offr RN, Dir Gen Naval Manpower 1967-70; served HM Ships: Hood, Wolverine, Kent, Anson, Sheffield, Triumph; Rear Adm 1967, ret 1970; *Style*— Rear Adm Frank Douglas Holford, CB, DSC; Little Down Cottage, Church Rd,

Shedfield, Hampshire SO3 2HY (☎ 0329 832295)

HOLFORD-WALKER, (Alan) Fionn; OBE (1987); s of Major Allen Holford-Walker (d 1948), and Joan Barrington Moody (d 1958); *b* 5 Feb 1922; *Educ* Nautical Coll Pangbourne, Gonville and Caius Coll Cambridge (BA, MA); *m* 18 Feb 1950, Megan, da of Edward Vaughan Llewenan (d 1953), of N Wales; 1 s (Edward Alan b 1954), 1 da (Sian Fiona b 1952); *Career* Lt Westminster Dragoons 1942-44; dist cmmr Kenya HM Overseas Civil Serv 1944-64; nat sec Cncl for the Protection of Rural England 1966-87; vice chm Tree Cncl 1978-86; *Recreations* countryside conservation; *Clubs* Lansdowne; *Style*— Fionn Holford-Walker, Esq, OBE; Dolphins, Hayes Lane, Slinfold, W Sussex

HOLLAMBY, Edward Ernest; OBE (1970); s of Edward Thomas Hollamby (d 1979), of Kent, and Ethel May Kingdom; *b* 8 Jan 1921; *Educ* Sch of Arts and Crafts Hammersmith, London Univ (Dip Town Planning and Civic Design); *m* 1941, Doris Isabel, da of William John Parker, of London; 1 s (Andrew b 1953), 2 da (Marsha b 1946, Jillian b 1948); *Career* Royal Marine Engrs Far East 1941-46; architect/designer/town planner; sr architect London CC 1949-62; dir of architecture and town planning London Borough of Lambeth 1969-81 (borough architect 1962-69), chief architect/planner London Docklands Devpt Corpn 1981-85 (conslt 1985-); projects incl: Erith Township Kent (Thamesmead prototype), Brixton town centre, relocation Covent Garden Market, Isle of Dogs, London Dockland, Wapping and Limehouse; works incl conservation of historic bldgs: Brandon Est, Kennington Brixton Rec Centre, Lambeth housing, Christopher Wren and Burlington Schs Hammersmith; numerous design awards including 2 DOE bronze medals; memb: Historic Bldgs Cncl for Eng 1971-83, RIBA cncl 1961-70 (hon tres 1967-70), London advsy ctee English Heritage 1986-; FRSA; Hon Ass Landscape Institute; *Books* Docklands Heritage - A Study in Conservation and Regeneration in London Docklands (1987); *Recreations* travel, music, theatre, opera, gardening; *Clubs* Arts; *Style*— Edward Hollamby, Esq, OBE; Red House, Red House Lane, Upton, Bexleyheath, Kent (☎ 01 303 8808)

HOLLAND, Anthony Delano Rokeby; s of late H D Holland; *b* 20 Feb 1929; *Educ* Harrow; *m* 1973, Anne Patricia Russell, da of Russell Lang, CBE; 1 da; *Career* former Lt Coldstream Gds, served Palestine; exec chm: The Lincroft Kilgour Group plc 1974-88, chm The Holland & Sherry Gp Ltd; pres Assoc of Wholesale Woollen Merchants; *Recreations* hunting, tennis, golf; *Clubs* MCC, Sunningdale GC; *Style*— Anthony D R Holland, Esq; Windlesham Manor, Windlesham, Surrey (☎ 0276 72373); 7 Savile Row, London W1X 1AF (☎ 01 437 0404)

HOLLAND, Brian Arthur; s of George Leigh Holland, of Cumbria, and Hilda Holland, MBE, *née* Hogg; *b* 14 June 1935; *Educ* Manchester GS, Univ of Manchester (LLB); *m* 1964, Sally, da of late Gordon W Edwards, of East Sussex; 1 s (Andrew David b 1966), 1 da (Alison Mary b 1969); *Career* admitted slr 1961; head civil litigation div Post Off Slrs Off 1977-79 (dir litigation and prosecution dept 1979-81), slr to the Post Off 1981-;; *Recreations* scouting, photography, studying railways, sketching, gardening; *Style*— Brian Holland, Esq; 23 Grasmere Rd, Purley, Surrey (☎ 01 660 0479); Post Office Solicitors Office, Impact House, 2 Edridge Rd, Croydon, Surrey CR9 1PJ (☎ 01 681 9011, telex 927405 POSOLG)

HOLLAND, Christopher John; QC (1978); s of Frank Holland (d 1979), of Leeds, and Winifred Mary Holland (d 1983); *b* 1 June 1937; *Educ* Leeds GS, Emmanuel Coll Cambridge (MA, LLB); *m* 1967, Jill Iona; 1 s (Charles), 1 da (Victoria); *Career* bencher Inner Temple 1985; vice-chm Ctee of Inquiry into the Outbreak of Legionnaires' Disease at Stafford 1985; *Clubs* Utd Oxford and Cambridge Univ; *Style*— Christopher Holland, Esq, QC; Pearl Chambers, 22 East Parade, Leeds LS1 5BU (☎ Leeds 452702); 6 Pump Court, Temple, London EC4Y 7AR (☎ 01 583 6013)

HOLLAND, (Robert) Einion; s of Robert Ellis Holland, and Bene, *née* Williams; *b* 23 April 1927; *Educ* Univ Coll North Wales Bangor (BSc); *m* 1955, Eryl Haf (d 1988); 1 s (Gareth), 2 da (Sian, Eluned); *Career* chm: Pearl Group plc 1986-; Pearl Assurance plc 1983- (joined 1953, dir 1953, chief gen mangr 1977-83; dir: Aviation and General Insurance Co Ltd 1973-, British Rail Property Board 1987-, Crawley Warren Group plc, New London Properties Ltd 1984-, Pearl Assurance (Unit Funds) Ltd 1975-, Queens Ice Skating Ltd 1984-. FIA; *Recreations* golf, Welsh literature; *Style*— Einion Holland, Esq; 55 Corkscrew Hill, West Wickham, Kent BR4 9BA (☎ 01 777 1861); 252 High Holborn, London WC1V 7EB (☎ 01 405 8441, telex 296350 Pearl G)

HOLLAND, Elisabeth, Lady; Elisabeth Hilda Margaret; only child of Thomas Francis Vaughan Prickard, CVO, JP, by his w Margaret, *née* Raikes, niece through her mother of 1st Baron Parmoor; *m* 1937, Sir Jim Sothern Holland, 2 Bt, TD (d 1981); 2 da; *Style*— Elisabeth, Lady Holland; Dderw, Rhayader, Powys LD6 5EY (☎ 0597 810226)

HOLLAND, Frank Robert Dacre; s of Ernest Albert Holland (d 1975); *b* 24 Mar 1924; *Educ* Whitgift; *m* 1948, Margaret Lindsay, da of John Aird (d 1926); 1 da; *Career* Capt 4 Hussars Italy 1944-47; chm: C E Heath plc, Lloyd's Insur broker and underwriters 1973-83; dir: Br Aviation Insur Co 1973-85, Trade Indemnity Co 1973-87, Greyhound Corpn USA 1974-85; Freeman Worshipful Co of Insurers, Worshipful Co of Glass Sellers; *Recreations* travel, gardening; *Clubs* Oriental, Cavalry and Guards'; *Style*— Frank Holland, Esq; Moatside, 68 Ashley Rd, Walton-on-Thames, Surrey (☎ 0932 227 591)

HOLLAND, Frank Walter; MBE (1979); s of Walter James Holland (d 1952), of Linton Lodge, 34 Pelham Rd and Hillside, Gravesend, and Clara Daisy, *née* Kirby (d 1947); *b* 29 April 1910; *Educ* Deal Sch Kent, Ardingly Coll Sussex, Bth Rugby, Kings Coll London; *Career* reserved in electricity supply, instructor ATC cadets No 7 Radio Sch RAF London 1943-44; Allen & Son Electrical Contractors Gravesend 1927-29, Gravesend Corpn Electricity Supply 1930-31, 5 year apprenticeship Br Thomson-Houston Co Ltd Rugby 1931-36, installation engr RCA Photophone Ltd 1936-38, consumers' engr Central London Electricity Ltd 1938-42, maintenance engr Miny of Works London 1942-44, sales engr developing radio frequency heating Redifon Ltd (Rediffusion) 1944-55, importer of pianos into Vancouver BC from England 1955-58, exporter of pianos from Danemann & Co, gen exporting DW Mortlock & Co; fndr (1963) Br Piano Museum Educnl Charitable Tst with Dept Educn & Sci 1966, fndr Player Piano Gp; memb Brentford C of C 1959; memb: Cinema Organ Soc, Theatre Organ Club, Music Box Soc GB, Museums Assoc, Int Cncl Museums, Nat Heritage, Eng Heritage, Assoc Industl Museums Gtr London Industl Archaeology Soc; hon memb: Hounslow Cncl Arts, Gesellschaft für selsbstspielende Musikinstrumente EV; fell Inst of Musical Instrument Technol; Music Box Soc Int Award; Liveryman Worshipful Co Musicians 1962; FIMIT; author of various articles incl Drying Billets for Broomheads with Radio Frequency for Br Communications & Electronics, and for British Columbia Lumberman, 1955; *Recreations* tennis, swimming, boating, fishing, music; *Clubs* City Livery; *Style*— Frank Holland, Esq, MBE; Musical Museum, 368 High St, St Georges Church, Brentford TW8 OBD (☎ 01 560 8108)

HOLLAND, Geoffrey; CB (1984); s of late Frank Holland, CBE, and Elsie Freda, *née* Smith; *b* 9 May 1938; *Educ* Merchant Taylors', St John's Coll Oxford (MA); *m* 1964, Carol Ann, da of Sidney Challen (d 1982); *Career* joined Miny of Labour 1961, asst private sec 1964-65, princ private sec to Sec of State for Employment 1971-72; Manpower Servs Cmmn: head of Planning 1973, dir of Special Programmes 1977, conslt Industl Ctee C of E Bd of Social Responsibility 1980-, second perm sec 1986, dir Manpower Servs Cmmn 1981-; *Recreations* journeying, opera, exercising the dog; *Clubs* East India; *Style*— Geoffrey Holland, Esq, CB; Manpower Services Commission, Moorfoot, Sheffield S1 4PQ

HOLLAND, Sir Guy Hope; 3 Bt (UK 1917), of Westwell Manor, Oxford; yr s of Sir (Alfred Reginald) Sothern Holland, 1 Bt, JP (d 1948), and Stretta Aimee, *née* Price (d 1949); suc er bro, Sir Jim Sothern Holland, 2 Bt, TD, 1981; descended from the Holland family of Pendleton, Lancashire, as recorded at the College of Arms; *b* 19 July 1918; *Educ* privately, Christ Church Coll Oxford; *m* 12 May 1945, Joan Marianne, da of late Capt Herbert Edmund Street, 20 Hussars; 2 da (Davina, Georgiana); *Heir* none; *Career* late Capt Royal Scots Greys; farmer; art dealer; *Recreations* hunting, shooting, gardening, travel; *Clubs* Boodle's, Pratt's; *Style*— Sir Guy Holland, Bt; Sheepbridge Hill Barn, Eastleach, Cirencester, Glos GL7 3PS (☎ 036 785 296)

HOLLAND, John Anthony; s of Maj John Holland, of Cornerways, Southella Rd, Yelverton, Devon, and Dorothy Rita, *née* George; *b* 9 Nov 1938; *Educ* Ratcliffe Coll Leics, Nottingham Univ (LLB); *m* 1 June 1963, Kathleen Margaret (Kay), da of John Smellie Anderson (d 1978); 3 s (Andrew John Anderson, Christopher Iain Anderson, Nicholas Alexander Anderson); *Career* admitted slr 1962, ptnr Foot & Bowden Plymouth, chm Social Security Appeals Tbnl; memb Marre Ctee; Law Soc: elected to cncl 1976, dep vice pres 1988; govr Plymouth Coll 1979-, chm regnl advsy cncl BBC SW 1984-87; pres: Plymouth Law Soc 1986, Cornwall Law Soc 1988; memb Law Soc 1962; *Books* Principles of Registered Land Conveyancing (1968), Landlord and Tenant (1970); *Recreations* opera, travel, sailing; *Clubs* Royal Western YC of England; *Style*— Anthony Holland, Esq; 46 Thornhill Way, Mannamead, Plymouth PL3 5NP (☎ 0752 220 529); 66 Andrewes House, Barbican, London EC2Y 8AY (☎ 01 638 5044); 70/76 North Hill, Plymouth, Devon Pl4 8HH (☎ 0752 663 416, fax 0752 671 802, telex 45223)

HOLLAND, Sir John Clifton Vaughan; AC (1988); s of Thomas Holland, and Mabel Ruth Elizabeth Holland; *b* 21 June 1914; *Educ* Frankston HS, Queen's Coll Melbourne (BCE); *m* 1942, Emily Joan, da of John Atkinson; 3 s, 1 da; *Career* WWII 1939-45, served RAE & Z Special Force ME and SW Pacific, Lt-Col; jr engr BP 1936-39, construction engr BP Aust 1946-49, fndr John Holland (Constructions) Pty Ltd 1949 (md 1949-73, chm 1949-81); chm: Process Plant Construction Pty Ltd 1949-82, John Holland Hldgs Ltd 1963-86; dir: T & G Life Soc 1972-82, Aust and NZ Banking Gp 1976-81; fndn fell The Aust Acad of Technological Sciences and Engrg, bd memb Royal Melbourne Hosp 1963-79, chm Victorian div Outward Bound 1964-77 (nat chm 1973-74), cncllr Inst of Public Affairs 1980-, memb Rhodes Scholar Selection Ctee 1970-73, fell Queen's Coll 1978-, fndn pres Aust Fedn of Civil Contractors (life memb 1971); chm: Matthew Flinders Bi-Centenary Cncl 1973-75, La Trobe Centenary Commemoration Cncl 1975-76, Economic Consultative Advsy Gp to the Treasurer 1975-81, History Advsy Cncl of Victoria 1975-83, Loch Ard Centenary Commemoration Ctee 1976-78; memb Centenary Test Co-ordinating Ctee 1976-77, dir Winston Churchill Memorial Tst 1976-82 (Victorian chm 1977-82, life memb 1982), Victorian chm The Queen Elizabeth II Silver Jubilee Tst for Young Australians 1977-80 (nat chm 1981-88), govr Corps of Cmmrs (Victoria) Ltd 1978- (vice chm 1986-), dir Child Accident prevention Fndn of Aust 1979-81, chm citizen's cncl Victoria's 150 Anniversary Celebrations 1979-82, dir and Victorian chm Australian Bicentennial Celebrations 1980-82, chm Victorian ctee for the Anzac Awards 1982-, dep chm Melbourne Univ Engrg Sch Centenary Fndn 1982-, vice pres English Speaking Union 1982-, memb Baker Med Res Unit 1982-, chm Nat Construction Indust Conf Organising Ctee 1982-, memb Construction Indust Res Bd 1982-, pres Stroke Res Fndn 1983-; chm steering ctee Victorian 150 Anniversary Celebrations 1984-85; Awards: Peter Nicoll Russell Memorial Medal 1974, Kernot Memorial Medal 1976, Total Community Devpt Award 1982, Consulting Engrs Advancement Soc of Aust Medal 1984; construction projects incl: Jindabyne Pumping Station in Snowy Mountains, Westgate Bridge, Tasman Bridge Restoration, New Parliament House; *Recreations* golf, music, gardening, cricket; *Clubs* Australian (Melbourne), Naval & Military, Royal Melbourne GC, Frankston GC, Flinders GC; *Style*— Sir John Holland; Georges Rd, Flinders, Victoria 3929, Australia

HOLLAND, John Lewis; s of George James Holland (d 1988), of Notts, and Esther, *née* Swindell; *b* 23 May 1937; *Educ* Nottingham Technical GS; *m* 1958, Maureen Ann, da of Leonard Adams (d 1973), of Notts; 1 s (Jeremy b 1965), 1 da (Lesley b 1959); *Career* reporter Nottingham Evening News 1954, sports ed Aldershot News Gp 1956, sub ed Bristol Evening Post 1964, ed West Bridgford and Clifton Standard 1966, dep sports ed Birmingham Evening Mail 1972; ed: Sandwell Evening Mail 1979 (gen mangr 1981), The Birmingham Post 1984-, Birmingham Post and Evening Mail 1986- (dir circulation and promotions); dir Birmingham convention and visitor bureau; *Recreations* sport (playing squash), gardening, DIY, horses; *Style*— John Holland, Esq; Windgarth, Lynn Lane, Shenstone, Lichfield (☎ 021 236 3366); 5 Maistrali II, Protaras, Cyprus; Birmingham Post and Mail Ltd, 28 Colmore Circus, Birmingham B46 AX

HOLLAND, Sir Kenneth Lawrence; CBE (1971), QFSM (1974); s of Percy Lawrence Holland (d 1966), of Colwyn Bay, Wales; *b* 20 Sept 1918; *Educ* Whitcliffe Mount GS Yorks; *m* 1941, Pauline Keith, da of George Mansfield (d 1925), of Oldham; 2 s, 1 da; *Career* entered fire serv Lancs 1937; chief fire offr: Bristol 1960-67, W Riding Yorks 1967-72; HM chief inspr of Fire Servs 1972-80; dir Gent Ltd Leicester 1981-; chm: Fire Services Central Examinations Bd 1978-84, Loss Prevention Certification Bd 1985-; tstee Fire Services Res and Trg Tst 1983-; hon tres Poole Arts Fedn (Friends of the Poole Arts Centre 1985-); OStJ 1964; pres Assoc Structure Fire Protection Contractors and Manufacturers; memb BS2 Bd, chm BSI Multitechnics cncl 1984-; kt 1981; *Recreations* motor sport, the arts (especially theatre); *Clubs* St John House, Royal Overseas League; *Style*— Sir Kenneth Holland, CBE, QFSM

HOLLAND, Hon Mrs; Hon Peggy Margaret Catharine; *née* Edmondson; da of Rev

2 Baron Sandford, DSC, and Catherine Mary, da of late Rev Oswald Andrew Hunt; *b* 7 Nov 1947; *Educ* Downe House Newbury, Trinity Coll Dublin (Dip Social Studies), Bristol Univ (Cert in Applied Social Studies); *m* 1977, Charles Alan Simon Holland, s of Francis Holland; 1 s (Hereward b 1984), 2 da (Hannah b 1979, Venetia b 1981); *Career* social worker; ILEA Sch Health Serv 1969-72, psychiatric social worker Friern Barnet Hosp 1973-75, sr social worker Child Abuse Unit (Reading) 1977-79; gp ldr Reading Parents Anonymous 1980-83; garden designer 1983-; book-seller 1987-; *Recreations* music, art, swimming, gardening; *Style—* The Hon Mrs Holland; Barncroft, Brightwell-cum-Sotwell, Wallingford, Oxon OX10 0RJ

HOLLAND, Peter Rodney James; s of Arthur Giles Stewart Holland (d 1981), and Elizabeth Hamilton, *née* Simpson; *b* 31 July 1944; *Educ* St Edmunds Canterbury, Univ Coll Oxford (MA); *m* 16 May 1975, Susan Elizabeth, da of Frederick Roger Okeby (d 1987); 1 s (William), 1 da (Philippa); *Career* slr 1968, ptnr Allen and Overy 1972-; chm law ctee Law Soc 1983-87; *Recreations* skiing, outdoor activities; *Clubs* Combined Oxford and Cambridge Univs;; *Style—* Peter Holland, Esq; Long Sutton, Basingstoke, Hants; Allen and Overy, 9 Cheapside, London EC2V 6AD (☎ 01 248 9898, fax 01 236 2192, telex 8812801)

HOLLAND, Sir Philip Welsby; s of late John Holland, of Middlewich, Cheshire; *b* 14 Mar 1917; *Educ* Sir John Deane's Sch, Northwich; *m* 1943, Josephine Alma, da of Arthur Hudson, of Plymouth; 1 s; *Career* RAF 1936-46, cmmnd Electrical Engrg Branch 1943; memb Cncl Kensington 1955-59, fndr memb Cons Cwlth Cncl; MP: Acton 1959-64, Nottinghamshire (Carlton) 1966-83; PPS to: Min of Pensions and Nat Insur 1961-62, Chief Sec to Treasy 1962-64, Min for Aerospace 1970-72, Min for Trade and Indust 1972-74; personnel conslt Standard Telephones and Cables until 1981; MP (C) Gedling 1983-87; kt 1983; *Books* The Quango Explosion (1978), Quango Quango Quango (1979), The Governance of Quango (1981), Quelling the Quango (1982), Lobby Fodder (1988); *Style—* Sir Philip Holland; 53 Pymers Mead, West Dulwich, London SE21 8NH

HOLLAND, Robert Matthew Crowder; s of Maj Charles Matthew Holland (d 1959), and Roberta Violet, *née* Crowder, JP; *b* 18 May 1948; *Educ* St Philip's GS Birmingham, Birmingham Art Coll, Oxford Poly Sch of Architecture; *m* 22 Sept 1973, Phillipa Madeleine, da of Wilfred Tracy (d 1980); 2 s (Matthew, Thomas), 1 da (Elizabeth); *Career* bd dir CG Smedley & Assocs Ltd Advertising Agency 1978- (jr account exec 1969); memb cncl Birmingham Publicity Assoc (chm 1987-88); memb Edgbaston Archery and Lawn Tennis Soc, hon sec and hon trophies sec Warwicks Lawn Tennis Assoc; *Recreations* tennis, swimming, photography, reading; *Style—* Robert Holland, Esq; CG Smedley & Assocs Ltd, Royton House, George Rd, Edgbaston, Birmingham B15 1PD (☎ 021 454 6666, fax 021 454 7577)

HOLLAND, Dr Stuart Kingsley; MP (Lab) Vauxhall 1983-; s of Frederick and Mary Holland; *b* 25 Mar 1940; *Educ* Christ's Hosp, Missouri Univ, Balliol Oxford, St Antony's Oxford; *m* 1976, Jenny Lennard; 1 da, 1 s; *Career* memb Tribune Gp Labour MPs 1979-, Campaign Gp Labour MPs 1982-; EC asst Cabinet Office 1966-67, PA to PM 1967-68, res fell Centre for Contemporary Euro Studies Sussex Univ 1968-71; visiting fell: Sussex Euro Res Centre 1979-, Brookings Inst Washington DC 1970; govr Int Devpt Studies 1987- (assoc 1974-); memb cncl Inst for Workers' Control 1974-; memb Labour NEC 1972- (joined party 1962); exec memb: Labour Coordinating Ctee 1978-81, Euro Nuclear Disarmament Campaign 1980-82; memb Lambeth Community Rels Cncl, MP (Lab) Lambeth Vauxhall 1979-83, oppn front bench spokesman: Overseas Devpt and Cooperation Nov 1983-, Treasy and Economic Affairs 1987; *Style—* Stuart Holland Esq, MP; House of Commons, London SW1 (☎ 01 733 5829)

HOLLAND, Rt Rev Thomas; DSC (1944); s of late John Holland of Southport; *b* 11 June 1908; *Educ* Upholland Coll Wigan, Pontifical English Coll Valladolid Spain (PhD), Pont Gregorian Univ Rome (DD); *Career* ordained Roman Catholic priest 1933; former prof English Colls Valladoid, Spain and Lisbon, Portugal; Coadjutor Bishop of Portsmouth 1960-64, Bishop of Salford 1964-83, apostolic administrator Salford 1983-84; Hon DLitt Salford; *Recreations* poetry, music, sailing, cricket; *Style—* The Rt Rev Thomas Holland, DSC; c/o Wardley Hall, Worsley, Manchester M28 5ND

HOLLAND-HIBBERT, Hon Diana; MBE (1946); da of 4 Viscount Knutsford (d 1976); *b* 1914; *Career* Sr Cdr ATS, 1939-45 War; *Style—* The Hon Diana Holland-Hibbert; Munden, Watford, Herts (☎ 0923 672002)

HOLLAND-HIBBERT, Hon Henry Thurstan; er s and h of 6 Viscount Knutsford, *qv*; *b* 6 April 1959; *Educ* Eton, RAC Cirencester; *m* 1988, Katherine, da of Sir John Bruce Woolacott Ropner, 2 Bt; *Career* Lt Coldstream Guards; *Style—* The Hon Henry Holland-Hibbert; 7 Walham Grove, London SW6

HOLLAND-MARTIN, Robert (Robin) George; s of Cyril Holland-Martin (d 1983), and Rosa, *née* Chadwyck-Healey; *b* 6 July 1939; *Educ* Eton; *m* 1976, Dominique, da of Maurice Fromaget; 2 da; *Career* with Cazenove and Co 1960-74 (ptnr 1968-74), fin dir Paterson Products Ltd 1976-86, conslt Newmarket Venture Capital plc 1982-; dir Henderson Admin Gp plc 1983-; memb: cncl Metropolitan Hospital-Sunday Fund 1963- (chm of cncl 1977-), Homeopathic Tst 1970- (vice-chm 1975-) advsy cncl V & A Museum 1972-83, ctee Assocs of V & A 1976-85 (chm 1981-85), visiting ctee Royal Coll of Art 1982- (chm 1984-); tstee V & A Museum 1983-85; hon dep tres Cons and Unionist Pty 1979-82; tstee Blackie Fndn Tst 1971- (chm 1987-); *Clubs* White's, RAC; *Style—* Robin Holland-Martin, Esq; 18 Tite St, London SW3 4HZ (☎ 01 352 7871)

HOLLAND-MARTIN, Dame Rosamund Mary; DBE (1983, OBE 1948), DL (Hereford & Worcester); da of Charles Harry St John Hornby (d 1946), and Cicely Rachel Emily, *née* Barclay (d 1971); *b* 26 June 1914; *m* 1951, Adm Sir Deric (Douglas Eric) Holland-Martin, GCB, DSO, DSC (d 1977), s of Robert Holland-Martin (d 1944), of Overbury Ct, Tewkesbury; 1 s (Benjamin), 1 da (Emma); *Career* chm NSPCC 1969-88; govr Malvern Coll; pres: Sea Cadets, Friends of Worcester Cathedral; *Recreations* photography, needlework, collecting; *Style—* Lady Holland-Martin, DBE, DL; Bell's Castle, Kemerton, Tewkesbury, Glos GL20 7JW

HOLLENDEN, 3 Baron (UK 1912); Gordon Hope Hope-Morley; o s of Hon Claude Hope-Morley (d 1968, yr s of 1 Baron), and Lady Dorothy Edith Isabel Hobart-Hampden-Mercer-Henderson (d 1972), da of 7 Earl of Buckinghamshire; suc unc 1977; *b* 8 Jan 1914; *Educ* Eton; *m* 27 Oct 1945, Sonja, da of late Thorolf Sundt, of Bergen, Norway; 3 s; *Heir* s, Hon Ian Hampden Hope-Morley; *Career* served Black Watch 1939-45, Maj; alderman City of London 1954-58, former chm I and R Morley Ltd, ret; *Clubs* Brooks's, Beefsteak; *Style—* The Rt Hon the Lord Hollenden; Hall Place, Leigh, Tonbridge, Kent (☎ 0732 832255)

HOLLENDEN, Anne, Baroness; Violet Norris; da of Alfred Leverton, of Peterborough; *m* 1, Dr Frank Howitt, CVO (decd); m 2, 1963, as his 3 wife, 2 Baron Hollenden (d 1977); *Style—* The Rt Hon Anne, Lady Hollenden; Valley Farm, Duntisbourne Hill, nr Cirencester

HOLLICK, Clive Richard; s of Leslie George and Olive Mary, *née* Scruton; *b* 20 May 1945; *Educ* Taunton's Sch Southampton, Univ of Nottingham (BA); *m* 1977, Susan Mary, *née* Woodford; 3 da; *Career* md MAI plc; dir subsids and other cos; *Recreations* reading, theatre, cinema, tennis, countryside; *Clubs* RAC; *Style—* Clive Hollick, Esq; c/o MAI plc, 8 Montague Close, London SE1 (☎ 01 407 7624)

HOLLICK, Peter Nugent; s of Dr Cyril Leslie Hollick, of Seaton, Devon, and Grace Helena, *née* Gibbins; *b* 23 Feb 1949; *Educ* Wycliffe Coll, Birmingham Univ (LLB), Inns of Court Sch of Law, Brunel Univ (MEd); *Career* princ lectr Windsor and Maidenhead Coll 1983-85, hd of dept of business studies and humanities Dunstable Coll 1985-; chm Beds Fedn Professional Assoc of Teachers, sec NW Met Regnl Assoc for Mgmnt Devpt, S Mids rep tertiary educn ctee Professional Assoc of Teachers, moderator Business and Technician Educn Cncl (former sr examiner AEB); memb Hon Soc of the Middle Temple 1969, FCollP 1985; *Recreations* tennis, squash, cycling, photography, travel; *Style—* Peter Hollick, Esq; 1 Carlisle Close, Dunstable, Beds LU6 3PH; Dunstable Coll, Kingsway, Dunstable, Beds LU5 4HG (☎ 0582 696451)

HOLLIDAY, (Peter) David; s of Leslie John Holliday, *qv* of Berkhamsted, and Kathleen Joan Marjorie, *née* Stacey; *b* 20 July 1947; *Educ* Brixton Sch of Bldg, London Business Sch; *m* 1972, Diana Patricia, da of Philip Shirley Christian Aldred, of Surrey; 1 s (Michael Stuart b 1978), 2 da (Rebecca Louise b 1976, Amanda Alice b 1982); *Career* dir John Laing plc 1984-88; chm: Laing Homes 1983-88, Super-Homes 1983-88, John Laing Homes Inc (California) 1985-88; vice pres House Builders Fedn 1988; Freeman: City of London 1987, Worshipful Co of Plaisterers; MCIB, MBIM; *Recreations* sailing, golf; *Clubs* Royal Southern YC, Poole Harbour YC, Woburn GC; *Style—* David Holliday, Esq; Dundry, Water End Rd, Potten End, Berkhamsted, Herts HP4 2SG (☎ 04427 5466)

HOLLIDAY, Prof Frederick George Thomas; CBE (1975), DL (County Durham 1985); s of Alfred Charles Holliday, of Scotland, and Margaret, *née* Reynolds; *b* 22 Sept 1935; *Educ* Bromsgrove Co HS, Sheffield Univ (BSc, DSc); *m* 1957, Philippa Mary, da of Charles Davidson (d 1985), of Dunning, Scotland; 1 s (Richard John b 1964), 1 da (Helen Kirstin b 1961); *Career* devpt cmmn fisheries res student Aberdeen 1956-58; sci offr Marine Lab Aberdeen 1958-61; lectr in zoology Univ of Aberdeen 1961-66, prof and head of dept of biology Univ of Stirling 1967-75, dep princ Univ of Stirling 1972-73, acting princ/vice-chllr Univ of Stirling 1973-75, prof of zoology Univ of Aberdeen 1975-79, vice-chllr and warden Univ of Durham 1980-; vice-pres Scottish Wildlife Tst 1980-; Nature Conservancy Cncl 1975-80 (chm 1977-80); tstee The Nat Heritage Meml Fund 1980-; non-exec bd memb Shell UK Ltd 1980-, BR Eastern Region Bd 1983- (chm 1986-); chm of the ind review of Disposal of Radioactive Waste at Sea 1984; tstee The Scottish Civic Tst 1984-87; bd memb: Northern Investors Ltd 1984-, Lloyds Bank Northern Regnl Bd 1985- (chm 1986-), Leverhulme Tst Res Awards advsy ctee 1978- (chm 1977-); FRSE; *Recreations* hill walking, vegetable gardening; *Clubs* Royal Cwlth Soc; *Style—* Prof Frederick Holliday, CBE, DL; Old Shire Hall, Old Elvet, Durham DH1 3HP (☎ 091 3742000); Univ of Durham, Old Shire Hall, Durham DH1 3HP (☎ 091 3742000, fax 091 3743740)

HOLLIDAY, Hon Mrs (Jane); *née* Sinclair; yr da of 2 Baron Sinclair of Cleeve, OBE (d 1985); *b* 13 July 1955; *Educ* Sherborne Sch for Girls; *m* 1982, Robert Anthony John Holliday, s of R F Holliday, of Dragon Hall, Tattenhall, Chester; 1 s (James b 1984); 1 da (Fiona b 1987); *Style—* The Hon Mrs Holliday; Hill Close, Llangathen, Carmarthen, Dyfed SA32 8QE

HOLLIDAY, Leslie John; s of John Holliday (d 1976), and Elsie May, *née* Hutchinson (d 1985); *b* 9 Jan 1921; *Educ* St John's Whitby; *m* 1943, Kathleen Joan Marjorie, da of Ernest Stacey (d 1963); 2 s (David b 1947, Philip b 1950); *Heir* OLLIDAY Peter David; *Career* radio offr Merchant Navy 1940-45, Atlantic, Mediterranean and Indian Ocean; mgmnt conslt 1985-; non-exec dir: Decan Kelly Gp plc 1985, Robert M Douglas Hldgs plc 1986; chm and chief exec John Laing plc 1982-85; chm: Nat Contractors Gp, Nat Fed of Building Trades Employers 1976-77, Laing Homes Ltd 1978-81, Super Homes Ltd 1979-81, Laing Mgmnt Contracting Ltd 1980-81, John Laing Construction Ltd 1980-84, John Laing Int Ltd 1981-82; Prince Philip Medal 1982; FCIOB, CBIM; *Recreations* golf; *Clubs* Porters Park Berkhamsted; *Style—* Leslie Holliday, Esq; The White House, Frithsden Copse, Berkhamsted, Herts (☎ 04427 72563, fax 04427 74312)

HOLLIDAY, Hon Mrs; Hon (Celia) Mary; *née* Bethell; da of 5 Baron Westbury, MC; *b* 5 Mar 1955; *m* 1980, L Brook Holliday; 1 da (b 10 Nov 1983); *Style—* The Hon Mrs Holliday; Mount St John, Felixkirk, Thirsk, N Yorks

HOLLIDGE, Ronald; *b* 28 Jan 1944; *m* 11 March 1967, Diana Margaret Rae, *née* Hermon; 1 s (Simon John b 1972), 1 da (Julie Ann b 1969); *Career* sr mangr Mincing Lane branch Lloyds Bank plc 1981-84 (various positions within Lloyds Bank plc 1963-81), md Lloyds Devpt Capital Ltd 1984-; ACIB 1969; *Recreations* rugby football, squash, theatre, reading; *Clubs* Cornhill, Harvard, RAC ; *Style—* Ronald Hollidge, Esq

HOLLIMAN, (Henry) Raymond; s of Henry William Holliman (d 1964), of Croydon, Surrey, and Florence, *née* Oven (d 1978); *Educ* Croydon Coll; *m* 3 June 1964, Hazel Elsie, da of Bertram Higgs (d 1966); 2 s (Carl Henry b 20 May 1966, James Edward b 13 May 1973); *Career* Nat Serv REME E Africa; landowner and estate agent; princ of Couriers Estate Agent (SE London estab 1912); md Professional Publication (printers & publishers) 1964-; *Recreations* classic car meetings, golf, numismatist; *Clubs* Jaguar Drivers; *Style—* Raymond Holliman, Esq; 4 & 6 Station Rd, South Norwood, London SE25 5AJ (☎ 01 653 6333, fax 01 688 7041)

HOLLINGBERY, Michael John; s of George Henry Hollingbery (d 1958), and Mary Orovida Hammond (d 1984); *b* 16 April 1933; *Educ* Rossall; *m* 1962, Karen Jane, da of Edward Wells (d 1971); 2 s, 1 da; *Career* dir: Woolworth Hldgs plc, Wilson (Connolly) Holdings plc, Hewetson plc; pres Humberside Youth Assoc, govr Queen Margaret's Sch (Escrick); CBIM 1975; *Recreations* fishing, shooting; *Clubs* Brooks; *Style—* Michael Hollingbery, Esq; Joby, Bishop Burton, Nr Beverley, N Humberside HU17 8QA

HOLLINGS, Hon Mr Justice; Sir (Alfred) Kenneth; MC (1944); s of Alfred Holdsworth Hollings (d 1941); *b* 12 June 1918; *Educ* Leys Sch Cambridge, Clare Coll Cambridge (MA); *m* 1949, Harriet Evelyn Isabella, da of W J C Fishbourne, OBE, of Brussels; 1 s, 1 da; *Career* served WWII, Africa, Sicily and Italy, Maj RA (Shropshire

Yeo); barr Middle Temple 1947, QC 1966, recorder of Bolton 1968, county ct judge (Circuit 5) 1968-71, master of the bench Middle Temple 1971, judge of the High Court of Justice (Family Div) 1971-, presiding judge of the Northern Circuit 1975-78; kt 1971; *Clubs* Garrick, Hurlingham, Tennis and Racquets (Manchester); *Style—* Hon Mr Justice, Hollings, MC; Royal Courts of Justice, Strand, London WC2

HOLLINGS, Rev Michael Richard; MC (1943); s of Lt Cdr Richard Eustace Hollings, RN, and Agnes Mary, *née* Hamilton-Dalrymple; *b* 30 Dec 1921; *Educ* Beaumont Coll, St Catherine's Soc Oxford (MA), St Catherine's Sandhurst, Beda Coll Rome; *Career* ordained Rome 1950, asst priest St Patrick's Soho Square London 1950-54, chaplain Westminster Cathedral 1954-58, asst chaplain London Univ 1958-59, chaplain to RCs at Oxford Univ 1959-70; parish priest: St Anselm's Southall Middx 1970-78, St Mary of the Angels Bayswater London 1978-; religious advsr: ATV 1958-59, Rediffusion 1958-68, Thames Television 1968, advsr Prison Christian Fellowship 1983-; memb: Nat Catholic Radio and TV Cmmn 1968, Westminster Diocesan Schs Cmmn 1970-, Southall C of C 1971-78, Oxford and Cambridge Catholic Educn Bd 1971-78; exec Cncl of Christians and Jews 1971-79 and 1984-, lay memb Press Cncl 1969-75; memb: Nat Conf of Priests Standing Ctee 1974-76, Rampton Ctee 1979-81, Swann Ctee 1981-84; exec: Ealing Community Relations Cncl 1973-76, Notting Hill Social Cncl 1980-; chm N Kensington Action GP 1980-81, memb bd Christian Aid 1984-87; chaplain: SMOM 1957, Nat Cncl of Lay Apostolate 1970-74, Catholic Inst of Int Relations 1971-80; *Books* Hey, You! (1955), Purple Times (1957), Chaplaincraft (1963), The One Who Listens (1971), The Pastoral Care of Homosexuals (1971), It's Me, O Lord (1972), Day by Day (1972), The Shake of his Hand (1973), Restoring the Streets (1974), I Will be There (1975), You Must Be Joking, Lord (1975), The Catholic Prayer Book (1976), Alive to Death (1976), Living Priesthood (1977), His People's Way of Talking (1978), As Was His Custom (1979), St Thérèse of Lisieux (1981), Hearts not Garments (1982), Chaplet of Mary (1982), Path to Contemplation (1983), Go in Peace (1984), Christ Died at Notting Hill (1985), Athirst for God (1985), Prayers before and after Bereavement (1986), By Love Alone (1986), Prayers for the Depressed (1986), You are not Alone (1988); *Recreations* reading, walking, people; *Style—* The Rev Michael Hollings, MC; St Mary of the Angels, Moorhouse Rd, Bayswater, London W2 5DJ (☎ 01 229 0487)

HOLLINGSWORTH, Elizabeth; da of Justin Brooke (d 1963), of Suffolk, and Doris Lascelles Brooke, *née* Mead (d 1981); *b* 20 Dec 1922; *Educ* Bedales Sch, Newnham Coll Cambridge (MA); *m* 11 June 1949 (m dis 1977), John Brian, s of John Herbert Hollingsworth (d 1957), of Sussex; 1 s (John Christopher b 1955), 3 da (Elizabeth Mary b 1950, Rosamund Anna b 1953, Alice Camilla b 1957); *Career* dir (and co sec): Justin Brooke Ltd (now Clapton Hallfarms Ltd) 1954- (chm 1977-87), Landowners Ltd 1970-76; cnsllr 1962-87, chm Bury St Edmunds Branch of Nat Farmers Union 1985-87; churchwarden of St Andrew's Stowmarket 1980-87; *Style—* Mrs John B Hollingsworth; 27 Northgate St, Bury St Edmunds, Suffolk; Clapton Hall Farms Ltd, Wickham Brook, Newmarket, Suffolk

HOLLINGWORTH, John Harold; s of Harold Hollingworth (d 1978), of Birmingham, and Lilian Mary, *née* Harris (d 1982); *b* 11 July 1930; *Educ* King Edward's Sch Birmingham; *m* 1967 (m dis 1986), Susan Barbara, da of J H Walters (d 1984), of Isle of Man; *Career* MP (C) Birmingham All Saints 1959-64; chm Elmdon Tst (Stress Charity); govr Cambridge Symphony Orchestra Tst Ltd; dir Cambridge Connection Ltd (Support for young musicians); dir Thaxted Festival Fndn Ltd (Music Festival); *Recreations* walking, map reading, talking; *Clubs* Lansdowne; *Style—* John Hollingworth, Esq; Easingwell House, Little London, Berden, Bishops Stortford, Herts; Lloyds Bank, Sidney St, Cambridge (☎ 0279 78567)

HOLLINS, Rear Adm Hubert Walter Elphinstone; CB (1974); s of Lt-Col Walter Thorne Hollins (d 1956), and Ellen Murray, *née* Rigg (d 1974); *b* 8 June 1923; *Educ* Stubbington House, RNC Dartmouth; *m* 11 May 1963, Jillian Mary, da of Donald McAlpin, of Victoria, Australia; 1 s (Rupert Patrick b 1964), 1 da (Rachel Jane b 1965); *Career* Royal Navy 1940-76; in command HM Ships: Petard, Dundas, Antrim; flag offr Gibraltar, com Gib Med and Port Admiral Gibraltar 1972-74; Adm Cmdg Reserves 1974-76; gen mangr Middle East Navigation Aids Serv 1977-84; marine conslt 1984-; FBIM, MNI; *Recreations* fishing, gardening; *Clubs* RNVR YC; *Style—* Rear Adm Hubert W E Hollins, CB; Roselands, The Avenue, Bucklebury, Berks (☎ 0734 744 551)

HOLLINSHEAD, Darren; s of Kenneth Hollinshead, and Jean, *née* Baker; *b* 20 Jan 1967; *Educ* Regis Sch of Tettenhall Wolverhampton, Coll of Insur Sevenoaks Kent; *Career* working for fathers insurance broking empire KGJ Insurance Servs Ltd 1985-87, returned to family business 1988-; memb Wolverhampton Insur Inst; ACII; *Recreations* skiing, squash, swimming, tennis; *Clubs* Club 64 (Birmingham); *Style—* Darren Hollinshead, Esq; St Johns Ct, Bridgnorth, Shropshire; Maythorn Gdns, Tettenhall, Wolverhampton (☎ 0902 743030); KGJ Insurance Servs, 26 Mount Pleasant, Bilston, W Mids (☎ 0902 44491)

HOLLIS, Hon Mr Justice; Hon Sir Anthony Barnard; s of Henry Lewis Hollis; *b* 11 May 1927; *Educ* Tonbridge, St Peter's Hall Oxford; *m* 1956, Pauline Mary, *née* Skuce; 1 step da; *Career* barr Gray's Inn 1951, QC 1969, chm Family Law Bar Assoc 1974-76, Crown Court rec 1976-82, High Court judge 1982-; kt 1982; *Style—* The Hon Mr Justice Hollis; Royal Courts of Justice, Strand, London WC2

HOLLIS, Anthony John; s of Henry Clifford Hollis (d 1946), of Finchley, London, and Dora Elizabeth, *née* Mason (d 1957); *b* 31 Oct 1930; *Educ* King Edward VI GS Totnes; *m* 22 Oct 1960, Margaret Joyce da of Percy Herbert Dennis (d 1979), of Radlett, Herts; 2 s (Richard b 1962, David b 1964), 2 da (Elizabeth b 1966, Catherine b 1969); *Career* Nat Serv 1953-55 RAPC, 2 Lt 1954, Lt and Pmr; CA, Hope Agar 1961-88 (sr ptnr 1978), Kidsons 1988-; tstee Finchley Charities, sec Old Totnesian Soc, tres Radlett United Free church; Freeman City of London, 1966, Liveryman Worshipful Co Fanmakers 1976; ACA 1953, FCA 1964; *Recreations* gardening; *Style—* Anthony Hollis, Esq; Kidsons, Russell Square House, 10/11 Russell Square, London WCB 5AE (☎ 0923 856106)

HOLLIS, Arthur Norman; OBE (1985), DFC (1943); s of Egerton Clark Hollis (d 1967), of Eastbourne, Sussex, and Vera Lina, *née* Leigh (d 1944); *b* 11 August 1922; *Educ* Dulwich Coll; *m* 2 Dec 1944, Elizabeth, da of Reginald Chase Edmunds (d 1986), of Westwell, nr Ashford, Kent; 1 s (Richard b 1953), 2 da (Jennifer b 1945, Sylvia b 1949); *Career* RAFVR 1941-46; Pilot Offr 1942, Flt-Offr 1943, Flt-Lt 1943, Sqdn Ldr 1945-46; memb HAC 1978; CA; ptnr: Limebeer & Co 1953-75, Russell Limebeer 1975-88; sr ptnr based in City of London specialising in countries of W Europe; dir various cos, memb mgmnt ctee Yehudi Menuhin Sch 1964, govr Live Music Now 1977, offr of various Cons Assoc; chm: Ashford constituency 1980-83, Kent East Euro constituency 1985-88; chm Westwell Parish Cncl 1976-79; Master Worshipful Co of Woolmen 1982-83; FCA 1958, FRSA 1983; *Recreations* travel, shooting, country pursuits; *Clubs* Travellers, City of London, United and Cecil, City Livery; *Style—* Arthur Hollis, Esq, OBE, DFC; Court Lodge, Westwell, nr Ashford, Kent TN25 4JX (☎ 023 371 2555)

HOLLIS, Eric Arthur; s of Arthur Thomas Hollis (d 1963), and May Annie, *née* Martin (d 1975); *b* 6 June 1918; *Educ* Addey and Stanhope; *m* 11 Nov 1944, Joan Helena, da of Alfred Gore (d 1946); 1 s (Keith b 1951), 1 da (Patricia b 1947); *Career* Army serv Africa, Italy, France 1939-45; accountant; dir: Securicor Group plc 1958, Security Servs plc 1974-, Metal Closures Gp plc; chm London Hotels Ltd; FCCA, FCT; *Recreations* golf, fishing; *Clubs* Arun YC; *Style—* Eric Hollis, Esq; Sutton Park House, 15 Carshalton Rd, Sutton, Surrey SM1 4LE (☎ 01 770 7000)

HOLLIS, John Charles; s of Charles Henry Hollis, and Audrey Cynthia, *née* Davis; *b* 16 June 1953; *Educ* Latymer Upper Sch, Univ of Bristol (BSc); *m* 22 July 1978, Clara Sian, da of Trevor Clement Tranter; 3 da (Emma b 1980, Lisa b 1981, Amy b 1983); *Career* joined Arthur Andersen 1974: ptnr Andersen Consulting 1985, appointed i/c Worldwide Financial Planning and Reporting Consulting Function 1985, appointed i/c UK Consumer Servs Consulting Gp 1988; FCA, IMA; *Books* Disappearing Financial Systems (1988), The Torturing and Dismembering of the Finance Function (1988); *Recreations* music, sports, interior design; *Clubs* RAC; *Style—* John Hollis, Esq; Andersen Consulting, 2 Arundel St, London WC2R 3LT (☎ 01 438 3832)

HOLLIS, John Denzil; s of Christopher Hollis (d 1977), of Mells, Somerset, and Margaret Madeleine, *née* King (d 1984); *b* 9 May 1931; *Educ* Stonyhurst Coll, Trinity Coll Oxford (BA, MA); *m* 21 April 1960, Pauline Lorraine, da of Julian Janvrin (d 1988); of Vancouver, Canada; 1 s (Charles b 1962), 1 da (Katharine b 1961); *Career* Nat Serv cmmnd RB, active serv Kenya 1953-55, 2 i/c London RB Rangers TA 1955-66; Minnesota Mining and Mfrg Co 1955-59, staff of Stock Exchange Cncl 1959-76 (head of Centl Settlement Servs 1967-71, head of Public Relations 1971-76); advsr to: govt of Kuwait 1976-81; Eurokuwaiti Investmt Co 1981-85, dir of info Dewe Rogerson and Co Ltd 1985-; *Style—* John Hollis, Esq; 26 Westwood Rd, Barnes SW13 0LA (☎ 01 876 2027); 3 London Wall Bldgs, London Wall (☎ 01 638 9571)

HOLLIS, Malcolm Richard Arthur; s of Arthur Edwin Hollis (d 1970), of 57 Hartwood Rd, Southport, Merseyside, and Esmé Muriel, *née* Pettit; *b* 17 Mar 1944; *Educ* King George V GS Southport, Univ of South Wales and Monmouth, Univ of London (BSc); *m* 11 Sept 1965, Andea Joan, da of Sqdn Ldr John Edward Fuller, of Challows, The Martlets, W Chiltington; 2 s (Richard b 1969, Gavin b 1976), 1 da (Tricia b 1970); *Career* chartered surveyor; ptnr Best Gapp & Ptnrs 1969, princ Malcolm Hollis Assoc 1972-80, ptnr Baxter Payne & Lepper (inc Malcolm Hollis Assocs) 1980- (dep chm 1986-88), Surveyor to the Fabric Worshipful Co Skinners 1982-, mangr professional servs Nationwide Anglia Estate Agents 1987-, memb cncl RICS Bldg Surveyors 1988-; cncllr London Borough Lambeth 1977-81; govr Woodmansterne Sch 1978-81 (chm 1979-81); over 50 appearances on TV and radio 1984-; fell dept construction mgmnt Univ of Reading 1988; Freeman City of London 1983, Liveryman Worshipful Co Chartered Surveyors 1982; FSVA 1969, FIAS 1969, FRICS 1970, ACIARB 1974; *Books* Surveying Buildings (1 edn 1983, 2 edn 1986, 3 edn 1989), Householders Action Guide (1984), Model Survey Reports (1 edn 1985, 2 edn 1989), Surveying for Dilapidations (1988); *Recreations* writing, photography, skiing, thinking; *Clubs* Hurlingham, Ski of GB; *Style—* Malcolm Hollis, Esq; 6 Rydal Rd, London SW16 1QN (☎ 01 769 5092); 108 Rochester Row, London SW1P 1JP (☎ 01 828 9010, fax 01 630 0321, car tel 0860 350304, telex 916513)

HOLLIS, Dr Patricia Lesley; da of H L G Wells, of Norwich, and (Queenie) Rossalyn, *née* Clayforth; *b* 24 May 1941; *Educ* Plympton GS, Cambridge Univ (BA, MA), Univ of California (Berkeley), Columbia Univ NY, Nuffield Coll Oxford (MA, DPhil); *m* 18 Sept 1965, (James) Martin Hollis, s of (Hugh) Mark Noel Hollis, of Oxted, Surrey; 2 s (Simon b 1969, Matthew b 1971); *Career* Harkness Fell 1962-64, Nuffield Scholar 1964-67, sr lectr (formerly lectr) modern history UEA 1967-89, dean sch of english and american studies UEA 1988-; cncllr Norwich City 1968- (ldr 1983-88); memb: East Anglia Economic Planning Cncl 1975-79, Regnl Health Authy 1979-83, BBC Regnl Advsy Ctee 1979-83, Norfolk CC 1981-85; dir Radio Broadland 1983; Parly cand Gt Yarmouth 1974 and 1979; nat cmmr English Heritage 1988-, memb Press Cncl 1989-; FRHistS; *Books* The Pauper Press (1970), Class and Class Conflict 1815-50 (1973), Women in Public 1850-1900 (1979), Pressure from Without (1974), Ladies Elect: Women in English Local Govt 1865-1914 (1987); *Recreations* boating on the broads, domesticity; *Style—* Dr Patricia Hollis; 30 Park Lane, Norwich (☎ 0603 621990); Sch of Eng and American Studies Univ of E Anglia, Norwich (☎ 0603 56161)

HOLLIS, Richard George; s of George Edward Hollis (d 1981); *b* 19 Nov 1934; *Educ* Bancroft's Sch Essex; *m* 1967, Belinda Jacqueline, *née* Rose; 2 da; *Career* Nat Serv, ret Capt; fin dir HP Bulmer Hldgs plc 1967-88, non exec dir Chloride Alcad Ltd (Chloride Gp) 1977-82; memb Consumers Ctees for GB and England and Wales 1979-84, non exec dir Alfred Preedy and Sons plc 1985-88; FCA; *Recreations* fishing, music; *Clubs* Flyfishers'; *Style—* Richard Hollis, Esq; The Leys, Aston, Kingsland, Leominster, Herefordshire HR6 9PU (☎ 056 881 411)

HOLLOM, Sir Jasper Quintus; KBE (1975); s of Arthur Hollom (d 1954); *b* 16 Dec 1917; *Educ* King's Sch Bruton Somerset; *m* 1954, Patricia Elizabeth Mary Ellis; *Career* Bank of Eng: entered 1936, dep chief cashier 1956-62, chief cashier 1962-66, exec dir 1966-70, non exec dir 1980-84, dep govr 1970-80; chm: Cncl for Securities Industs 1985-86, Panel on Takeovers and Mergers 1980-87; non exec dir: BAT Industs plc 1980-87, Portals Hldgs plc 1980-88; chm Eagle Star Gp 1985-87; *Style—* Sir Jasper Hollom, KBE; High Wood, Selborne, Hants (☎ 042 050 317)

HOLLOWAY, Hon Sir Barry Blyth; KBE (1984, CBE 1974), MP Papua New Guinea; s of Archibald and Betty Holloway; *b* 26 Sept 1934; *Educ* Launceston Church GS Tasmania, Sch of Pacific Admin Sydney, Univ of Papua New Guinea; *m* 1974, Ikini Aikel; 3 s, 4 da; *Career* min for educn Papua New Guinea 1982-; knighted for services to politics and government; *Style—* The Hon Sir Barry Holloway, KBE; c/o PO Box 6361, Boroko, Papua New Guinea

HOLLOWAY, David Richard; s of William Edwyn Holloway (d 1952), and Margaret Boyd, *née* Schleselman (d 1979); *b* 3 June 1924; *Educ* Westminster, Birkbeck Coll London, Magdalen Coll Oxford; *m* 8 March 1952, Sylvia (Sally) Eileen, da of Douglas Arthur Gray; 2 s (Mark b 1954, Paul b 1956), 1 da (Pippa b 1958); *Career* RAF 1942, navigator 1944, served Middle East, Aden, Ceylon, India, PO 1945, sr welfare offr 2nd Indian Gp 1946; reporter: Middx Co Times 1940-41, Daily Sketch 1941-42, Daily Mirror 1949; News Chronicle: reporter and ldr writer 1950-53, asst literary ed 1953-58, book page ed 1958-60; lit ed Daily Telegraph 1968-88 (dep literary ed 1960-68); chm: Soc of Bookmen 1968-71, Booker Prize Judges 1969; registrar Royal Literary Fund 1981-; *Books* John Galsworthy (1968), Lewis and Clark on the Crossing of America (1971), Derby Day (1975), Playing The Empire (1979), Nothing So Became Them (with Michael Geare, 1987); *Clubs* Reform; *Style*— David Holloway, Esq; 95 Lonsdale Rd, London SW13 9DA (☎ 01 748 3711)

HOLLOWAY, Frank; s of late Frank Holloway; *b* 20 Oct 1924; *Educ* Burnage HS Manchester; *m* 1949, Elizabeth, *née* Beattie; 3 da; *Career* various sr fin appts in The Utd Steel Companies and later British Steel Corpn 1949-72; md: supplies and prodn control British Steel Corpn 1973-76, finance and supplies 1976-80, supplies and tport and bd memb 1978-; chm British Steel Corpn (Chemicals) Ltd; FCA, FBIM; *Recreations* cricket, collecting books; *Style*— Frank Holloway, Esq; 11 Copperfield Way, Chislehurst, Kent (☎ 01 467 9559); BSC, Supplies and Transport Div, 9 Albert Embankment, London SE1 7SN (☎ 01 735 7654; telex 916061)

HOLLOWAY, Laurence (Laurie); s of Marcus Holloway (d 1979), of Oldham, Lancs, and Annie, *née* Gillespie; *b* 31 Mar 1938; *Educ* Oldham GS; *m* 1, 31 March 1956, Julia Planck, da of Rufus Macdonald (d 1975), of Rothesay, Isle of Bute; 1 da (Karon b 1957); m 2, 16 June 1965, Marian Montgomery, the singer, da of Forrest Marion Runnels (d 1966), of Atlanta Georgia; 1 da (Abigail b 1967); *Career* pianist, composer, arranger; studio musician 1959-69, musical dir for tv; composer: A Dream of Alice (BBC TV), pop preludes, etc; musical dir: Engelbert Humperdinck 1969-74, Dame Edna Everage 1987; pianist for Judy Garland and Liza Minelli (London Paladium) 1964; composer TV signature tunes (Blind Date, etc); *Recreations* golf, music; *Clubs* MCC, Wig and Pen, Temple GC; *Style*— Laurie Holloway, Esq; Elgin, Fishery Rd, Bray-on-Thames, Berkshire (☎ 0628 24613)

HOLLOWAY, Michael Derek; s of Sir Henry Thomas Holloway (d 1951), of W Lavington Manor, Devizes, Wilts, and Brucine Mildenhall, *née* Pimm; *b* 18 Mar 1915; *Educ* Marlborough, Cambridge Univ (BA); *m* 1, 4 Oct 1947 (m dis), Muriel Marie Elizabeth, da of William Ernest Keames (d 1981), of Kenton Harrow; 2 da (Jacqueline b 1949, Gillian b 1953); m 2, 2 Dec 1978, Estelle Margaret, da of Arthur Stuart Voivell (d 1931), of Cheltenham, Glos; *Career* WWII Capt RA 1940-45, Normandy, Belgium, Holland, Germany; asst surveyor of lands Admty 1946-47, estate and farm mangr 1947-51, farmed estate lands after father's death 1951 until ret Sept 1987; breeder and exhibitor of cattle, sheep and pigs, winner Reserve Supreme Championship Smithfield Show 1955 and 1956; *Recreations* fishing; *Clubs* Royal Overseas League; *Style*— Michael Holloway, Esq; Oriel House, Bollands Hill, Seend, Melksham, Wilts (☎ 038 082 318)

HOLLOWAY, Peter Henry Charles; s of Maj Frederick Charles Holloway, MC, and Kathleen Winifred, *née* Seear; *b* 12 August 1943; *Educ* Aldenham; *m* 1, March 1966 (m dis 1983), Patricia, *née* Monk; 2 s (Simon b 21 Feb 1970, Peter b 12 July 1971), 1 da (Penelope b 31 May 1968); m 2, 9 May 1984, Margaret Yvonne; 2 s (Frederick b 19 May 1984, Edward b 22 April 1987); *Career* dealer Joseph Sebag 1963-68, dir Slater Walker (Bahamas) 1968-71, Eurobond trader Samuel Montagu 1971-73, Eurobond mangr Banque Nationale de Paris 1973-74, mangr dealing ops Samuel Montagu 1974-79, int gilt sales mangr Laing & Cruickshank 1979-83, ptnr Wedd Durlacher Mordaunt & Co 1983-86; dir: Barclays de Zoete Wedd (Securities) 1986-, Barclays de Zoete Wedd Hldgs 1987-; md Barclays de Zoete Wedd Equity Trading & Global Princ Risk 1988-; memb ctee Stock Exchange mkts; *Recreations* squash, swimming, walking; *Clubs* Gresham; *Style*— Peter Holloway, Esq; 523 Ben Jonson House, Barbican, London EC2Y 8DL; Churchgate Barn, Wood Dalling, Norfolk NR11 6SN; Ebbgate House, 2 Swan Lane, London EC4R 3TS (☎ 01 623 2323, fax 01 626 1753, telex 888221)

HOLLOWAY, Reginald Eric; CMG (1984); s of late Ernest and Beatrice Holloway; *b* 22 June 1932; *Educ* St Luke's Brighton; *m* 1958, Anne Penelope, da of late Robert Walter, and Doris Lilian Pawley; 1 da; *Career* RAF 1953-55; apprentice reporter 1947-53, journalist in Britain and E Africa 1955-61, press off Tanganyika Govt 1961-63, dir Info Br Guyana 1964-67, Info dept FCO 1967-69 (Anguilla 1969), 2 later 1 sec chancery in Malta 1970-72, E African Dept FCO 1972-74, consul and head of Chancery Kathmandu 1974-77, asst head S Asian Dept FCO 1977-79 (cnsllr 1979, inspr 1979-81), consul-gen Toronto 1981-85, sr Br trade cmmr Hong Kong 1985-; *Style*— Reg Holloway, Esq, CMG; British Trade Commission, PO Box 528, Hong Kong; c/o Foreign and Commonwealth Office, London SW1A 2AH

HOLLOWS, Peter Twist; s of Samuel Hollows (d 1976), of Ribble Lodge, Lytham, Lancs, and Elizabeth, *née* Twist (d 1959); *b* 9 June 1921; *Educ* Silcoates Sch; *m* 19 Sept 1949, Joan Hurst, da of Arthur Smith (d 1965), of Cringles, Embsay, Skipton, Yorkshire ; 1 s (Jeremy b 1953), 1 da (Anne b 1951); *Career* RAF Coastal Cmd 1941-46 (despatches for work on airborne radar); stockbroker; memb: Manchester Stock Exchange 1948 (chm 1971-80), Manchester Stock Exchange Ctee 1966-80, Northern Stock Exchange Cncl 1971-73, Ctee of the Northern Unit of the Stock Exchange 1973-79; chm: Northern Stock Exchange 1972-73, Northern Unit of the Stock Exchange 1973-76; memb Cncl of the Stock Exchange 1973-79; presently conslt to Bell Houldsworth Fairmount Ltd; tres property div Methodist Church 1967-; memb: fin bd Methodist Church 1969-, bd of tstees for Methodist Church Purposes 1972-; *Recreations* travel, horticulture, classical music, cricket, rugby union; *Clubs* Rotary (pres Manchester) 1963-64; Lancashire CC, Flyde RUFC; *Style*— Peter Hollows, Esq; 174 St Annes Rd East, St Annes-on-Sea, Lancs FY9 3HP (☎ 0253 722783); Bell Houldsworth Ltd, PO Box 329, Fountain Ct, 68 Fountain St, Manchester M60 2QL (☎ 061 228 2228)

HOLM, Hon Mrs (Rosetta Mancroft); *née* Samuel; da of 1 Baron Mancroft (d 1942); *b* 1918; *m* 1, 1947, Alfred John Bostock Hill (d 1959, late puisne judge Malaya); m 2, 1966, Dr Cai Christian Holm (d 1983); *Style*— The Hon Mrs Holm; 12 Eaton Place, London SW1

HOLMAN, Lady; Adeline Betty; da of Sir Gilbert Fox, 1 Bt (d 1925); *b* 18 July 1906; *Educ* Heathfield Ascot; *m* 1, 1929 (m dis 1939), Capt Basil Allfrey; 2 s; m 2, 1940, as his 2 w, Sir Adrian Holman, KBE, CMG, MC (d 1947); *Recreations* waterfowl collecting, gardening; *Style*— Lady Holman; Bohunt Manor, Liphook, Hants

HOLMAN, Barry William; s of Ronald Cecil Holman, of Loughton, Essex, and Irene Winifred; *b* 7 July 1949; *Educ* Coopers Co GS; *m* 17 Aug 1974, Christine, da of Norman Thomas Richards; *Career* CA; own practice B W Holman & Co, Newman Harris & Co, Silver Altman & Co, Lewis Bloom, Macnair Mason; FCA; *Recreations* golf, horse riding, clay pigeon shooting, motor boat cruising, music, chess; *Clubs* ICAEW, Penton Hook YC; *Style*— Barry W Holman, Esq; Brook House, Ongar Rd, Abridge, Essex RM4 1UH (☎ 0037 881 3079); 309 High Rd, Loughton, Essex IG10 1AH (☎ 01 508 9228)

HOLMAN, Christopher Boot; s of Alexander Mc Arthur Holman (d 1979), of Hyes, Rudgwick, Sussex, and The Hon Margery Amy, *née* Boot (d 1987); *b* 8 Feb 1926; *Educ* Loretto Sch, Cirencester Agric Coll; *m* The Hon Elizabeth Winifred Ponsonby, da of The Lord de Mauley (d 1962), of Langford House, Lechlade, Glos; 4 da (Sarah Charlotte, Serena jane, Alice Eljiva, Catherine Rose); *Career* 1 Lt Royal Horse Gds 1944-47; Lloyds broker, (underwriting name 1951-); farmer; High Sherrif (Waves) 1986-87;; *Recreations* shooting, hunting, fishing; *Clubs* Boodles; *Style*— Christopher Holman, Esq

HOLMAN, David McArthur; s of Alexander McArthur Holman (d 1979), of Springland, Millbrook, Jersey, CI, and The Hon Margery Amy, *née* Boot (d 1987); *b* 11 Dec 1928; *Educ* Rugby; *m* 1, 1951 (m dis 1964), Felicity Frances, da of Capt Richard Donovan, CBE, RN (d 1956); 1 s (Mark Richard b 1957); m 2, 1966, Valerie Brythonig Pryor; 2 s (Michael Jesse b 1967, Andrew Mc Arthur b 1968); *Career* Lt RHG 1948-49; chm and md: John Holman & Sons Ltd 1953-, David Holman & Co 1971-; chm Phyllis Holman Richards Adoption Soc 1970-; memb Lloyds 1954; *Recreations* shooting, fishing, hunting; *Clubs* Cavalry & Guards, City of London; *Style*— David Holman, Esq; John Holman & Sons Ltd, Minster House, Arthur St, London EC4 (☎ 01 929 4037)

HOLMAN, Lady Diana Elizabeth Virginia Sydney; *née* Baird; da of 12 Earl of Kintore, *qv*; *b* 22 June 1937; *m* 20 July 1957, John Francis Holman, OBE, eld s of Alexander McArthur Holman, of Springland, Millbrook, Jersey, CI; 2 s, 2 da; *Style*— Lady Diana Holman; Rickarton House, Stonehaven, Kincardineshire (☎ 0569 63236); 6 St Luke's St, London SW3 (☎ 01 352 1475)

HOLMAN, Hon Mrs; Hon Elizabeth Marjorie; *née* Plumb; er da of Baron Plumb (Life Peer), *qv*; *b* 1948; *m* 1, 1971 (m dis), Robin Arbuthnot; m 2, 1982, Maj Anthony Holman; 2 s (Thomas Henry b 1984, Charles Anthony b 1986); *Style*— The Hon Mrs Holman; 6B United Mansions, Shuifai Terrace, Hong Kong

HOLMAN, (Edward) James; s of Edward Theodore Holman, of Manaccan, Cornwall, and Mary Megan, *née* Morris, MBE; *b* 21 August 1947; *Educ* Dauntsey's, Exeter Coll Oxford (BA, MA); *m* 14 Jul 1979, Fiona Elisabeth, da of Ronald Cathcart Roxburgh, of Wiggenhall St Mary, King's Lynn, Norfolk; 1 s (Edward b 1988) 1 da (Charlotte b 1984); *Career* called to the Bar Middle Temple 1971, memb Western circuit in practice 1971-; a legal assessor UK Central Cncl for Nursing Midwifery and Health Visiting 1983-, sec Family Law Bar Assoc 1988-; memb: cncl RYA 1980-83, 1984-87 and 1988-, ctee RORC; *Recreations* sailing, skiing, music; *Clubs* RYS, RORC; *Style*— James Holman, Esq; 58 Grove Park, Camberwell, London SE5 8LG (☎ 01 274 0340); Queen Elizabeth Building, Temple, London EC4Y 9BS (☎ 01 583 7837, fax 01 353 5422)

HOLMAN, Hon Mrs (Elizabeth) Winifred; *née* Ponsonby; da of 5 Baron de Mauley (d 1962), and Elgiva, da of Hon Cosparick Thomas Dundas (himself yr bro of 3rd Earl, later 1st Marquess of Zetland), b 1928; *b* 1928; *m* 1950, Christopher Boot Holman, s of Alexander MacArthur Holman (d 1979), and Margery Amy, da of 1 Lord Trent; 4 da; *Style*— The Hon Mrs Holman; Sheilbridge, Acharacle, Argyll (☎ 096 785 258); Foxcote, Shipston-on-Stour, Warwicks (☎ 060 882 240)

HOLME, Richard Gordon; CBE (1983); s of J R Holme (1940), and E M Holme, *née* Eggleton; *b* 27 May 1936; *Educ* St Johns Coll Oxford (MA); *m* 1958, Kay Mary, da of Vincent Powell; 2 s (Richard Vincent b 1966, John Gordon (twins) b 1965), 2 da (Nicola Ann b 1959, Penelope Jane b 1962); *Career* chm Constitutional Reform Centre 1984-, dir Avi Hldgs 1987-, sec Parly Democracy Tst 1979-, pres Lib Pty 1981; *Recreations* reading, walking, opera; *Clubs* Reform; *Style*— Richard Holme, Esq, CBE; 60 Chandos Place, London WC2

HOLMER, Paul Cecil Henry; CMG (1973); s of Bernard Cecil Holmer (d 1980), of Emsworth Hants, and Mimi Claudine, *née* Braudé (d 1978); *b* 19 Oct 1923; *Educ* King's Sch Canterbury, Balliol Coll Oxford (MA); *m* 1946, Irene Nora, da of Orlando Lenox Beater, DFC (d 1964), of Ardley, Oxford; 2 s (Felix, Thomas), 2 da (Sarah, Juliet); *Career* serv Army 1942-46, Lt RA, (took part in D-Day assault on Normandy and NW Europe Campaign 1944-45); Colonial Off 1947-49; H Dip Serv 1949-83; serv FO Singapore, Moscow, Berlin, Abidjan, Brussels, Bucharest; head security dept FCO 1969-72, ambassador Ivory Coast, Upper Volta and Niger 1972-75, min UK dep perm rep on North Atlantic Cncl (Brussels) 1976-79, ambassador Romania 1979-83, ret 1983; memb Civil Serv Selection Bd 1956, dir African Devpt Fund 1973-75; *Recreations* reading, walking; *Clubs* Royal Cwlth Soc; *Style*— Paul Holmer, Esq, CMG; Wincott House, Whichford, Shipston-on-Stour, Warwicks (☎ 060 884 609)

HOLMES, Alan Wilson Jackson; s of Luke Jackson Holmes (d 1979); *b* 13 Sept 1945; *Educ* Portora Royal Sch Enniskillen, Cambridge Univ; *m* 1970, Frances-Maria, *née* Kadwell; 3 s, 1 da; *Career* dir Courage (Central) Ltd 1973-81, chm Courage (Scotland) Ltd 1979-81, dir Courage Ltd 1982-;; *Recreations* golf, theatre; *Clubs* Royal and Ancient GC, Huntercombe GC; *Style*— Alan Holmes, Esq; Courage Ltd, Anchor Terr, Southwark Bridge, London SE1 9HS; The Copse, Ockham Rd South, East Horsley, Surrey (☎ 04865 2396)

HOLMES, Andrew Jeremy; MBE (1987); s of Donald George Holmes (d 1986), of Uxbridge, Middx, and Janet Mary, *née* Hider; *b* 15 Oct 1959; *Educ* Latymer Upper, West London Inst (BA); *m* 18 Aug 1984, Pamela Anne, da of Derek Kent, of Portsmouth; 1 da (Aimée Elizabeth b 14 Nov 1987); *Career* oarsman; Olympic Games 1984 Gold Medallist coxed fours; Cwlth Games 1986: Gold Medallist coxed fours, Gold Medallist coxless pairs; World Championships 1986, Gold Medallist coxless pairs; World Championships 1987: Gold Medallist coxless pairs, Silver Medallist coxed pairs; Olympic Games 1988: Gold Medallist coxless pairs, Bronze Medallist coxed pairs; holder 2 World records, winner 9 Henley Medals; *Recreations* classical music, antiques, interior design; *Clubs* Leander; *Style*— Andrew Holmes, Esq, MBE; Melfort Ave, Thornton Heath, Surrey CR4 7RH (☎ 01 684 0318, car tel 0836 527 469)

HOLMES, Anthony; CBE (1982); s of Herbert Holmes (d 1959), and Jessie, *née* Caffrey (d 1973); *b* 4 Sept 1931; *Educ* Calday Grange GS Wirral; *m* 1954, Sheila Frances, da of William Povall (d 1986); *Career* Sgt RAOC 1950-52; joined HM Customs and Exile 1949, transferred to Passport Off 1955; dep chief and passport offr

1977, chief passport offr 1980, head Passport Off; *Recreations* golf; *Clubs* Royal Liverpool GC, Cowdray Park GC; *Style—* Anthony Holmes, Esq, CBE; Passport Department, Clive House, Petty France, London SW1H 9HD (☎ 01 271 3000)

HOLMES, Brian; s of Albert Holmes (d 1966), of Folkestone, Kent, and Gertrude Maude, *née* Atkinson (d 1972); *b* 25 April 1920; *Educ* Salt HS Shipley, UCL (BSc), Univ of London Inst of Educn (PhD); *m* 1, 1945 (m dis 1971), Mary Isabel, *née* Refoy; 2 s (Nicholas Paul b 1947, Andrew Brian b 1950); m 2, 1971, Margaret Hon Yin Wong; 1 da (Ruth Lin Wong b 1972); *Career* WW11 Flt Lt RAFVR served radar, CO RAF AMEStations in Middle East 1941-45; physics master: St Clement Danes 1946-51, Kings Coll Sch Wimbledon 1949-51, lectr Univ of Durham 1951-53; Univ of London Inst of Educn: asst ed World Year Book of Educn 1953, lectr 1959, sr lectr 1963, reader 1964, prof 1975, prof of comparative educn and head dept 1975-85, pro-dir 1983-85, Charter fell dean and prof of educn Coll of Preceptors 1979-, dean faculty of educn Univ of London 1981-85; ed Educn Today; conslt: UNESCO, Int Bureau of Educn Geneva, OECD, Br Cncl, foreign govts; sr fellowship Japan Soc for Promotion of Sci 1987-88, vis lectr Nat Sci Cncl Republic of China 1988; vis prof: USA, Canadian and Japanese Univs; pres: Br Int and Comparative Educn Soc 1971, Comparative Educn Soc in Europe 1973-77 (sec tres 1961-73); chm World Congress Comparative Educn Socs 1974-77; annual professional visits USSR 1960-87; *Books* American Criticisms of American Education (1957), Problems in Education (1965), Educational Policy and the Mission Schools (ed 1967), Comparative Education through the Literature (with T Bristow 1968), Diversity and Unity in Education (ed 1980), International Guide to Educational Systems (1979), Comparative Education (1981), Equality and Freedom in Education (ed 1985), The Curriculum (with M McLean 1989); incl numerous (1007) articles in int periodicals; *Recreations* collecting antique clocks; *Clubs* Roy Cwlth Soc; *Style—* Prof Brian Holmes; 4 Sandwell Mansions, West End Lane, London NW6 1XL (☎ 01 794 3835); Univ of London, Inst of Educn, 20 Bedford Way, London WC1H OAL (☎ 01 636 1500)

HOLMES, Brian Archibald James; s of Archibald Love Holmes, MBE, TD, of Ebor House, Troon, Ayrshire, Scotland, and May Eileen Buchanan, *née* Smith (d 1962); *b* 4 Dec 1941; *Educ* Loretto Sch, Glasgow Tech Coll; *m* 31 March 1967, Jacoba (Cobi), da of Leendert Muller (d 1974), of Terneuzen, Holland; 1 s (Archie b 1970), 2 da (Johanna b 1969, Eileen b 1973); *Style—* Brian Holmes, Esq; Woodside, Benenden, Cranbrook, Kent (☎ 0580 240606)

HOLMES, David; CB (1985); s of George Archibald Holmes (d 1962), of Doncaster, and Annie, *née* Hill (d 1979); *b* 6 Mar 1935; *Educ* Doncaster GS, Christ Church Oxford (MA); *m* 1963, Ann, da of late John Chillingworth, of London; 1 s (Matthew b 1970), 2 da (Joanne b 1965, Elise b 1972); *Career* asst princ Miny of Tsport and Civil Aviation 1957, princ HM Treasy 1965-68, princ private sec to Min of Tport 1968-70, asst sec DOE 1970, under sec 1976, dep sec Dept of Tport 1982-; *Style—* David Holmes, Esq, CB; Department of Transport, 2 Marsham St, London SW1P 3EB

HOLMES, Dr George Arthur; s of John Holmes (d 1949), of Aberystwyth, and Margaret, *née* Thomas (d 1977); *b* 22 April 1927; *Educ* Ardwyn Co Sch Aberystwyth, Univ Coll of Wales, St John's Coll Cambridge (MA, PhD); *m* 19 Dec 1953, (Evelyn) Anne, da of Dr John William Klein (d 1973), of Wimbledon; 2 s (Peter b 1955, d 1968, Nicholas b 1963), 2 da (Susan b 1957, Catherine (twin) b 1957); *Career* fell St John's Coll Cambridge 1951-54, tutor St Catherine's Soc Oxford 1954-62, fell and tutor St Catherine's Coll Oxford 1962- (vice-master 1969-71); memb Inst for Advanced Study Princeton 1967-68, delegate Oxford Univ Press 1982-, chm Victoria Co History Ctee of Inst of Historical Res 1978-; FBA 1985; *Books* The Estates of the Higher Nobility in 14th Century England (1957), The Later Middle Ages (1962), The Florentine Enlightenment 1400-50 (1969), Europe: Hierarchy and Revolt 1320-1450 (1975), The Good Parliament (1975), Dante (1980), Florence, Rome and the Origins of the Rennaissance (1986), The Oxford Illustrated History of Medieval Europe (ed 1988); *Style—* Dr George Holmes; Highmoor House, Bampton, Oxon (☎ 0993 850 408); St Catherine's College, Oxford (☎ 0865 271 720)

HOLMES, George Dennis; CB (1979); s of James Henry Holmes (d 1960), of Gwynedd N Wales, and Florence Jones (d 1978); *b* 9 Nov 1926; *Educ* John Bright's Sch Llandudno, Univ of Wales (BSc, DSc); *m* 1953, Sheila Rosemary, da of George Henry Woodger (d 1949), of Surrey; 3 da (Carolyn, Deborah, Nicola); *Career* dir gen Forestry Cmmn 1977-86; chm Scottish Council for Spastics 1986-, memb E Board of Bank of Scotland 1987, FRSE; *Recreations* sailing, swimming, photography, fishing; *Clubs* Royal Cwlth Soc; *Style—* George Holmes, Esq, CB; 7 Cammo Rd, Edinburgh EH4 8EF (☎ (031 339) 7474)

HOLMES, Hugh; MBE (1947); s of Sir Hugh Oliver Holmes, KBE, CMG, MC (d 1955), and Rose, *née* Falls (d 1971); *Educ* Charterhouse, RMC Sandhurst; *m* 23 June 1945, Marguerite Blanche, da of Hans Rudolph de Jenner (d 1960), of Switzerland; 1 s (Hugh b 1946), 2 da (Carolyn b 1947, Kathryn b 1951); *Career* cmmnd Royal Northumberland Fusiliers 1936, served Palestine and Egypt, ADC to Govr of Cyprus 1938-39, WWII serv Western Desert 1939-42 (POW), WO 1945-46, Staff Coll 1946-47, Br Army staff plans 1947-48, Gibraltar 1949-51, WO 1951-53 and 1956-58, KAR 1954-55, resigned 1958; joined BSA Co Rhodesia 1958 (transferred London 1964), personnel conslt Charter Consolidated Ltd 1965-77, dir Charter Consolidated Subsids 1965-77, wine trader 1977-86; memb cncl Br Cwlth Ex Serv League;; *Recreations* golf; *Clubs* Naval and Military; *Style—* Hugh Holmes, Esq, MBE; 45 High Street, Malmesbury, Wilts

HOLMES, Sir Maurice Andrew; s of Rev A T Holmes (d 1942); *b* 28 July 1911; *Educ* Felsted; *m* 1935, Joyce Esther Hicks; *Career* WWII serv RASC (despatches); barr Gray's Inn 1948; chm Tilling Gp 1960-65; chm London Tport Bd 1965-69; circuit admin SE circuit 1969-74; govr Felsted Sch; kt 1969; *Style—* Sir Maurice Holmes; The Limes, Felsted, nr Dunmow, Essex (☎ 0371 820352)

HOLMES À COURT, (Michael) Robert Hamilton; s of Peter Worsley Holmes à Court (d 1966, s of Hon Henry Holmes à Court, bro of 3 and 4 Barons Heytesbury) and, Ethnée Celia, da of H Cumming, of Rhodesia, now Zimbabwe; Robert is 2 cous of 6 Baron Heytesbury; *b* 27 July 1937; *Educ* Michaelhouse Natal, Univ of W Australia (LLB); *m* 1966, Janet Lee (BSc), da of F H Ranford, of Perth, W Australia; 3 s (Peter Michael Hamilton b 1968, Simon Antony b 1972, Paul William b 1973), 1 da (Catherine Elizabeth b 1969); *Career* barr and slr WA 1965; chm and chief exec Associated Communications Corpn plc 1982-, chm Bell Gp of Cos (Australia); *Style—* Robert Holmes à Court, Esq; 22 The Esplanade, Peppermint Grove, Western Australia 6011

HOLMES À COURT, Hon Sarah Camilla; da of 6 Baron Heytesbury; *b* 1965; *Style—* The Hon Sarah Holmes à Court

HOLMES-WALKER, Dr (William) Anthony; ERD (1971); s of Lt-Col William Roger Holmes Walker, TD, RA (d 1967), of South Corner, Duncton, N Petworth, Sussex, and Katharine Grace, *née* Foote (d 1988); *b* 26 Jan 1926; *Educ* Westminster, Queens Univ Belfast (BSc, PhD), Imperial Coll London (DIC); *m* 26 July 1952, Marie-Anne, da of Willy Eugene Russ (d 1959), of Villa Eugenie, 43 Evole, Neuchâtel, Switzerland; 2 da (Antonia b 1954, Katharine b 1957); *Career* RE Belfast 1944, Lt 1945, Capt RE 1946, serv Middle East; Lt-Col AER/TAVR 1960 (Maj 1956); tech offr ICI Ltd 1954-59, head of plastics R & D Metal Box Co Ltd 1959-66, prof of polymer sci & technol Brunel Univ 1966-74, dir Br Plastics Fedn 1974-81, visiting prof City Univ 1981-83, sec gen Euro Brewers Trade Assoc 1983-88, dir of industl liaison Reading Univ 1988-; memb Round Table Hemel Hempstead 1955-66, pres Villars Visitors Ski Club 1955-74; Freeman City of London 1951, memb ct Worshipful Co of Skinners (Master 1980-81), Liveryman Worshipful Co of Horners; churchwarden St John's Boxmoor 1966-72; FRSC 1966, FPRI 1969, FIM 1972; *Books* Polymer Conversion (1975); *Recreations* skiing, golf, music, genealogy; *Style—* Dr Anthony Holmes-Walker, ERD; Blue Cedars, Sheethanger Lane, Felden, Boxmoor, Herts HP3 0BG (☎ 0442 53117); The University of Reading, Palmer Building, Whiteknights, Reading RG6 2AH (☎ 0734 318978, fax 0734 314404, telex 847813)

HOLMPATRICK, 3 Baron (UK 1897); James Hans Hamilton; s of 2 Baron Holmpatrick, DSO, MC (d 1942), and Lady Edina Hope, formerly w of Sir Thomas Ainsworth, 2 Bt, and da of 4 Marquess Conyngham; *b* 29 Nov 1928; *Educ* Eton; *m* 1954, Anne, da of Cdr Ernest Brass, RN (ret), of Haverfordwest; 3 s; *Heir* s, Hon Hans Hamilton; *Career* late Lt 16/5 Lancers; *Style—* The Rt Hon Lord Holmpatrick; Tara Beg, Dunsany, Co Meath, Eire (☎ 0462 5138)

HOLROYD, (William) Arthur Hepworth; s of Rev Harry Holroyd (d 1970), and Annie Dodgshun Holroyd; *b* 15 Sept 1938; *Educ* Kingswood Sch Bath, Trinity Hall Cambridge (MA), Manchester Univ (Dip Soc Admin); *m* 24 June 1967, Hilary; 3 s (Mark b 1968, Simon b 1970, Christopher b 1974); *Career* hosp sec: Crewe Mem Hosp 1963-65, Wycombe Gen Hosp 1965-67; seconded Dept Health 1967-69, dep gp sec Blackpool HMC 1969-72, regnl manpower offr Leeds RHB 1972-74, dist admin York Health Dist 1974-82, regnl admin Yorks RHA 1982-85, dist gen mangr Durham Health Authy 1985-; memb: NHS Nat Staff Ctee 1973-82, Gen Nursing Cncl 1978-83, English Nat Bd Nursing Midwifery and Health Visiting 1980-87, NHS Trg Authy 1988-; ed Hosp Traffic and Supply Problems 1969; FHSM 1972; *Recreations* classical music, walking, visiting Shetland Isles; *Style—* Arthur Holroyd, Esq; 3 Dunelm Court, South St, Durham; Durham Health Authority, Lanchester Rd, Durham (☎ 091 386 4911)

HOLROYD, Air Marshal Sir Frank Martyn; KBE (1989), CB (1985); s of George Lumb Holroyd (d 1987), and Winifred Hetty, *née* Ford; *b* 30 August 1935; *Educ* Southend-On-Sea GS; *m* 1 Feb 1958, Veronica Christine, da of Arthur George Booth (d 1984); 2 s (Martyn Paul b 26 Jan 1959, Myles Justin b 9 Nov 1966), 1 da (Bryony Jane 4 June 1961); *Career* RAF (initially Nat Serv cmmn) 1956, appt fighter stations RAF Leconfield and RAF Leeming, RAF Tech Coll Henlow, blind landing experimental unit RAE Bedford 1960-63, Cranfield Inst Technol (MSc, Sqdn Ldr) 1963-65, HQ Fighter Cmd 1965-67, OC electrical engrg sqdn RAF Changi Singapore 1967-69, Wing Cdr Staff Coll RAF Bracknell 1970, MOD 1970-72, OC engrg wing RAF Brize Norton 1972, Gp Capt 1974, station cdr No 1 Radio Sch RAF Locking 1974-76, sr engrg offr HQ 38 Gp 1976, Air Cdre dir aircraft engrg MOD 1977, RCDS 1981, Air Vice Marshal dir gen strategic electronic engrg (former dir weapons and support engrg) MOD, (PE) 1982, air offr engrg HQ Strike Cmd 1986, Air Marshal chief engr RAF 1988; memb: BBC Tech Advsy Bd, Advsy Cncl RMCS, ct Cranfield Inst Technol; CEng, FRAeS, FIEE; *Recreations* gardening, competitive sports; *Clubs* RAF; *Style—* Air Marshal Sir Frank Holroyd, KBE, CB; MOD, Neville House, Page St, London (☎ 01 218 5999, car tel 0836 775 332)

HOLROYD, Michael de Courcy Fraser; CBE (1989); s of Basil de Courcy Fraser Holroyd, of Surrey, and Ulla, *née* Hall; *b* 27 August 1935; *Educ* Eton; *m* 1982, Margaret, da of John Frederick Drabble, QC (d 1983), of Suffolk; *Career* biographer; chm: Soc of Authors 1973-74, Nat Book League 1976-78; pres English PEN 1985-88; *Books* Lytton Strachey (1967-68), Augustus John (1974-75), Bernard Shaw (1988-89); *Recreations* listening to music and stories, watching people dance; *Style—* Michael Holroyd, Esq, CBE; 85 St Mark's Rd, London W10 (☎ 01 960 4891)

HOLROYD, Lady Sheila Mary; da of late 4 Earl Cairns; *b* 1905; *m* 1930, Maj Charles Ivor Patrick Holroyd, late Rifle Bde; 2 s, 3 da; *Style—* Lady Sheila Holroyd; Providence Cottage, Chute Cadley, Andover, Hants

HOLT, Christopher Robert Vesey; CVO (1976), VRD (1952); s of Vice Adm Reginald Vesey Holt, CB, DSO, MVO (d 1957), and Evelyn Constance, *née* Day (d 1978); *b* 17 Oct 1915; *Educ* Eton; *m* 1 June 1945, Margaret Jane Venetia, da of Sir Michael Albert James Malcolm, 10 Bt (d 1976); 1 s (Nicholas James b 1947), 1 da (Ianthe Evelyn b 1950); *Career* WWII serv RN, ret as Lt-Cdr 1957; memb London Stock Exchange 1938-82, ret; ptnr James Capel & Co 1938- (sr ptnr 1968-70, chm 1970-75, dir 1975-76); cncl memb King George's fund for Sailors 1982-87, hon tres Hampshire and IOW Naturalist's Tst 1985-; *Recreations* wildlife, painting; *Clubs* Boodles, Lansdowne; *Style—* Christopher R V Holt, Esq, CVO, VRD; Westbury Manor, West Meon, Petersfield, Hants GU32 1ND

HOLT, Prof James Clarke; s of Herbert Holt (d 1980), of Bradford, Yorks, and Eunice Holt, BEM, *née* Clarke (d 1974); *b* 26 April 1922; *Educ* Bradford, Queen's Coll Oxford, Merton Coll Oxford (MA, D Phil); *m* 3 July 1950, (Alice Catherine) Elizabeth, da of David Suley (d 1962), of Bingley, Yorks; 1 s (Edmund b 7 Oct 1954); *Career* RA 1942-45, Capt 1943; prof of medieval history Univ of Nottingham 1962-66 (lectr 1949-62), dean of faculty of letters and social scis Univ of Reading 1972-76 (prof of history 1966-78); Cambridge: prof of medieval history 1978-88, professorial fell Emmanuel Coll 1978-81, master Fitzwilliam Coll 1981-88; pres: Royal Historical Soc 1980-84, Lincoln Record Soc 1987-; vice pres: Selden Soc 1978-88, Br Acad 1987-89; chm of cncl Pipe Roll Soc 1976-, memb advsy cncl on public records 1974-81; Hon DLitt Univ of Reading 1984; Fell: BA Acad 1978, Royal Historical Soc 1954; Encomienda de la Orden del Merito Civil 1988; *Recreations* music, mountaineering, fly-fishing; *Clubs* Utd Oxford and Cambridge, Nat Liberal, Wayfarers (Liverpool); *Style—* Prof James Holt; 5 Holben close, Barton, Cambridgeshire CB3 7AQ (☎ 0223 263074); Fitzwilliam College, Cambridge CB3 0DG (☎ 0223 332041)

HOLT, Sir James Richard; KBE (1977, CBE 1972); s of Albert Edward Holt; *b* 24 Dec 1912; *Educ* Bishop Vesey's GS Sutton Coldfield; *m* 1974 (m dis 1984), Jennifer

May, da of Gp Capt P D Squires; 1 adopted s, 1 adopted da; *Career* interned Bangkok 1942-45; md Sinobrit Ltd 1957- (dir 1946-56, company name formerly Sino-British Ltd)); tstee and memb exec ctee Asian Inst of Technol 1977-; *Style—* Sir James Holt, KBE; 71 Belwell Lane, Four Oaks, Sutton Coldfield, West Midlands B74 4TS (☎ 021 308 0932); Sinobrit Ltd, GPO Box 307, Bangkok 10501, Thailand

HOLT, Rear Adm John Bayley; CB (1969), DL (Surrey 1981); s of Arthur Holt, and Gertrude, *née* Bayley; *b* 1 June 1912; *Educ* William Hulme GS Manchester, Manchester Univ; *m* 1940, Olga Creake; 3 da; *Career* RN; dir-gen Aircraft (Naval) 1967-70; dir: Premmit Assocs, Premmit Engrg Servs, Elint Engrg; FIEE; *Style—* Rear Adm John Holt, CB, DL; Rowley Cottage, Thursley, Godalming, Surrey (☎ 0252 702140)

HOLT, John Frederick; s of Edward Basil Holt (d 1984), and Monica, *née* Taylor; *b* 7 Oct 1947; *Educ* Ampleforth, Univ of Bristol (LLB); *m* 26 Sept 1970, Stephanie Ann, da of Peter Watson, of Belaugh, Norfolk; 3 s (Samuel John b 16 June 1973, Benjamin Alexander b 2 Sept 1974, Edward Daniel b 11 Oct 1980); *Career* called to the Bar Lincoln's Inn 1970, Co Ct Rules Ctee 1981-85, asst rec 1988; *Recreations* cricket, restoring vintage motor cars; *Clubs* Twinstead CC; *Style—* John Holt, Esq; 53 North Hill, Colchester, Essex (☎ 0206 572 756, fax 0206 562 447)

HOLT, Dr John Michael; s of Frank Holt (d 1977), and Constance Cora, *née* Walton; *b* 8 Mar 1935; *Educ* St Peter's Sch York, Univ of St Andrews (MB ChB, MD), Queen's Univ Oxtario Canada (MSc), Oxford Univ (MA); *m* 27 June 1959, Sheila Margaret, da of William Hood Morton (d 1968), of Harrogate; 1 s (Timothy b 8 May 1964), 3 da (Jane b 27 May 1960, Sally b 13 July 1962, Lucy b 30 July 1968); *Career* res fell dept of med and biochemistry Queens Univ Ontario Canada 1961-63, registrar lectr and med tutor Nuffield dept of med Radcliffe Infirmary Oxford 1963-74, dir of clinical studies Univ of Oxford 1972-77, conslt physician 1969-, fell Linacre Coll 1970-, chm med staff Oxford 1983-85; memb: Ctee on Safety of Medicine 1978-86, Oxford RHA 1984-88, gen bd of faculties Univ of Oxford 1987-; examiner Univs of Oxford, London, Glasgow, Hong Kong; Liveryman Hall of Apothecaries, Freeman City of London; FRCP London 1974; *Recreations* sailing; *Clubs* Utd Oxford and Cambridge, Royal Cornwall YC; *Style—* Dr John Holt; Old Whitehill, Tackley, Oxon OX5 3AB; 23 Banbury Road, Oxford OX2 6NX; John Radcliffe Hosp, Headington, Oxford OX3 9DU (☎ 0865 817348, 0865 515036)

HOLT, (Stanley) John; s of Frederick Holt (d 1949), of Toot-Hill, nr Chipping Ongar, Essex, and May, *née* Abblett (d 1984); *b* 27 Sept 1931; *Educ* Chipping Ongar, Walthamstow; *m* 6 Aug 1959, Anne, da of Richard Catherall (d 1943); 3 da (Sarah b 30 May 1960, Ruth b 15 July 1962, Rachel b 13 April 1966); *Career* Nat Serv RAMC 1953-55; chm Isodan UK Ltd 1975- (formerly with: Rentokil Labs, Pilkington's Tiles, Bayer AG W Germany); hon sec Portsoken Ward Club; memb: Utd Ward Club, Royal Soc of St George, cncl City Livery Club, Fellowship of Clerks; former chm Lunchtime Comment Club; Freeman City of London 1983, Liveryman Worshipful Co of Marketors 1983, Clerk Worshipful Co of Environmental Cleaners 1986; MInstM, MBIM, MIEx, FInstD; *Recreations* showering; *Clubs* Wig and Pen, City Livery; *Style—* John Holt, Esq; Whitethorns, Rannoch Rd, Crowborough, E Sussex TN6 1RA (☎ 0892 655 780); 102 Marlyn Lodge, Portsoken St, London E1 8RB; 55b Colebrook Rd, Royal Tunbridge Wells, Kent TN4 9DP (☎ 0892 5448 22, fax 0892 515 811, telex 878736)

HOLT, Lady; Margaret; da of T S Lupton, formerly of Runswick, Cheadle Hulme, Cheshire; *m* 1931, Sir Edward Holt, 2 Bt (d 1968, when the title became ext); *Style—* Lady Holt

HOLT, Richard Anthony Appleby; s of Frederick Appleby Holt, OBE (d 1980) and Rae Vera Franz, *née* Hutchinson; *b* 11 Mar 1920; *Educ* Harrow, Kings Coll Cambridge; *m* 6 Oct 1945, Daphne Vivien, da of Vice Adm Frank Henderson Pegram, CB, DSO (d 1944); 3 s (Christopher Appleby b 1947, Richard Frederick b 1956, Edward b 1960), 2 da (Harriet b 1949, Alice b 1954); *Career* Serv KRRC 1940-46, demob Maj; slr 1949; dir Hutchinson Ltd 1952-80 (chm 1959, md 1978), chm Hutchinson Publishing 1965-80, dir Constable Publishing 1968-; govr Harrow 1952-82 (chm governing body 1971-80); ctee memb all England Lawn Tennis Club 1959-82; Liveryman Worshipful Co of Slrs 1960; *Clubs* All England Lawn Tennis, MCC; *Style—* Richard Holt, Esq; 55 Queens Gate Mews, London SW7 5QN (☎ 01 589 8469)

HOLT, (James) Richard; MP (C) Langbaurgh 1983-; *b* 2 August 1931; *Educ* Wembley County GS, Hendon and Harrow Tech Colls; *m* 1959, Mary June Leathers; 1 s, 1 da; *Career* RN seaman; contested (C) Brent S Feb 1974, memb Wycombe Boro Cncl 1976-; FIPM, MBIM; *Style—* Richard Holt, Esq, MP; House of Commons, London SW1

HOLT, Sarah Caroline; da of Brian Alfred Holt (d 1984), and Joan Patricia, *née* Burrell; *b* 25 Jan 1954; *Educ* Wycombe Abbey Sch, Girton Coll Cambridge (MA); *m* 18 Jan 1986, John Nicholas Sharman, s of Brig-Gen Ronald Llewellyn Sharman, RAMC (d 1974), 1 s (Thomas b 1988); *Career* slr; ptnr Norton Rose (specialising in shipping and aviation fin); *Recreations* history, music, aviation; *Style—* Miss Sarah Holt; Norton Rose, Kempson House, Camomile Street, London EC3A 7AN (☎ 01 283 2434, fax 01 588 1181, telex 883652)

HOLT, Thelma Mary Bernadette; da of David Holt (d 1941), and Ellan, *née* Finnagh Doyle (d 1969); *b* 4 Jan 1933; *Educ* St Anne's Coll for Girls, RADA; *m* 1, 31 March 1957 (m dis), Patrick Graucob; m 2, 6 Oct 1968 (m dis), David Pressman; *Career* actress 1955-68, jt art dir Open Space Theatre 1968-77, art dir Round House Theatre 1977-83, exec prodr Theatre of Comedy 1983-85, head of touring and commercial exploitation Nat Theatre 1985-88, exec prodr Peter Hall Co 1988; head: Int Theatre 89, Nat Theatre 1989-; Observer award for Special Achievement in Theatre 1987; dir: Vanessa Redgrave Entreprises Ltd, Theatre Investmt Fund Ltd, Citizens' Theatre Glasgow, Petard Prodns Ltd; memb cncl RADA; *Style—* Miss Thelma Holt; c/o Nat Theatre of GB, Upper Ground, South Bank, London SE1 9PX (☎ 01 928 2033, fax 01 836 9832/620 1197)

HOLT, Vesey Martin Edward; DL (Shropshire 1986); s of Martin Drummond Vesey Holt (d 1956), of Mount Mascal, Bexley, Kent (d 1956), and Lady Phyllis Hedworth Camilla Herbert, sister of 5 and 6 Earls of Powis (d 1972); direct decendant of Lord Clive (Clive of India); *b* 28 Mar 1927; *Educ* Radley, RAC Cirencester; *m* 1955, Elizabeth Jane, da of John Geoffrey Sanger, of Prattenden, Bury, West Sussex; 1 s (Peter), 1 da (Amanda); *Career* farmer; ccncllr Shropshire 1968-74 and 1977-, govr Wrekin Coll 1968-, memb Shropshire Valuation Panel 1970- (dep chm 1984-), pres Shropshire CCC 1973-, pres Minor Counties Cricket Assoc 1983-; memb Agric Land Tbnl 1975-; High Sheriff Shropshire 1981, pres Wrekin Cons Assoc 1983-; *Recreations* shooting, cricket; *Clubs* Brooks's, MCC; *Style—* Vesey Holt, Esq, DL; Orleton Hall, Wellington, Telford, Shropshire (☎ 0952 242780); 42 Stanford Rd, London W8 (☎ 01 937 4970)

HOLT-WILSON, Peter John; s of Maj John Holt-Wilson (d 1963), of Snape Hill House, Rickinghall, Diss, Norfolk, and Violet Bailey, *née* Traill (d 1976); *b* 30 June 1924; *Educ* Radley; *m* 1, 18 Dec 1957 (m dis 1973) Pauline Glover; 1 s, 2 d; m 2, 26 March 1973, Sarah Maxine, da of Arthur Tite (d 1984), of 48 Westbourne Terr, London; 1 s, 1 da; 2 s (Timothy David b 1959, Benjamin John b 1974), 3 da (Philippa Jane Pauline b 1960, Joanna Helen b 1966, Sophie Maxine b 1976); *Career* Sgt Rifle Bde 1942-47, serv Italy and N W Europe; suc Redgrave Estate 1964, sold 1971; owner Bibury Trout Farm; *Recreations* shooting, country life; *Style—* Peter Holt-Wilson, Esq; Redgrave, Diss, Norfolk IP22 1RR (☎ 0397 898 241 and 0379 898 934)

HOLTBY, Very Rev Robert Tinsley; s of William Holtby (d 1972), of Dalton, Thirsk, N Yorks, and Elsie, *née* Horsfield (d 1959); *b* 25 Feb 1921; *Educ* Scarborough Coll, St Edmund Hall Oxford (MA, BD), King's Coll Cambridge; *m* 22 Nov 1947, Mary, da of Rt Rev Eric Graham, Bishop of Brechin (d 1964), of Forbes Court, Broughty Ferry, Dundee; 1 s (David b 1953), 2 da (Veronica b 1948, Caroline b 1951); *Career* ordained 1946, curate Pocklington Yorks 1946-48, chaplain to the Forces Catterick and Singapore 1948-52; chaplain and asst master: Malvern Coll 1952-54, St Edward's Sch Oxford 1954-59; canon residentiary Carlisle Cathedral and diocesan dir of educn 1959-67, gen sec Nat Soc for Religious Educn 1967-77, sec Schools Cncl C of E 1967-74, gen sec C of E Bd of Educn 1974-77, dean of Chichester 1977-; chm Cumberland Cncl of Social Serv 1962-67, memb Cumberland and Carlisle Educn Ctees, chaplain to High Sheriff of Cumberland; author of biographies educnl and historical works; *Recreations* music, historical work; *Clubs* Utd Oxford and Cambridge, Sussex; *Style—* The Very Rev the Dean of Chichester; The Deanery, Chichester, W Sussex PO19 1PX (☎ 0243 783286); 4 Hutton Hall, Huttons Ambo, York, N Yorks YO6 7HW

HOLTON, Michael; s of George Arnold Holton (d 1950), of Hampstead Garden Suburb, and Ethel Maud, *née* Fountain (d 1976); *b* 30 Sept 1927; *Educ* Finchley Co GS, LSE (BSc); *m* 1, 14 July 1951 (m dis 1987), Daphne Elizabeth, da of Charles Stanley Bache (d 1950), of Gloucester; 1 s (Philip b 1960), 2 da (Alison b 1954, Rosemary b 1957); m 2, 11 April 1987, Joan Catherine, da of George Frederick Hickman (d 1984); *Career* Nat Serv RAF 1946-48; Civil Serv: Miny of Food 1949-54, Air Miny 1955-60, MOD 1961-68 and 1976-87, ret asst sec 1987; sec: Countryside Cmmn for Scotland 1968-70, Scottish ctee Euro Conservation Year 1970, tres Carnegie UK Tst 1971-75, hon memb Royal Soc for Nature Conservation 1988- (cncl memb 1976-), hon memb RAF Mountaineering Assoc 1952-54, (organised RAF Himalayan Expedition 1954-55), memb Br Mountaineering Cncl 1955-59; dir Cairngorm Chairlift Co 1973-; FRGS 1952-68, FRSGS 1971-; *Books* RAF Mountain Rescue Training Handbook (1953); *Clubs* Athenaeum, Alpine, Himalayan (Bombay); *Style—* Michael Holton, Esq; 4 Ludlow Way, Hampstead Garden Suburb, London N2 0LA (☎ 01 444 8582)

HOMAN, (Lawrence) Hugh Adair; s of Lawrence William Nicholson Homan (d 1981), of Harpenden, Herts, and Mary Graves, *née* Adair; *b* 26 June 1945; *Educ* Sherborne, Worcester Coll Oxford (MA); *m* 19 June 1971, Lyn Claudine, da of Lt Cdr Hubert John Douglas Hamilton (d 1975), of Deal, Kent; 1 s (Alexander b 1973), 1 da (Oliva b 1975); *Career* asst slr Allen & Overy 1968-73, ptnr Berwin Leighton 1975-; memb Law Soc; *Recreations* sailing, golf; *Style—* Hugh Homan, Esq; Chantry Drift, Gedgrave Rd, Orford, Suffolk; 21 Crescent Grove, London SW4; Berwin Leighton, Adelaide Ho, London Bridge, London EC4R 9HA (☎ 01 623 3144, fax 01 623 4416, telex 88642)

HOMAN, Hon Mrs (Mary Graham); *née* Buckley; da of 2 Baron Wrenbury (d 1940), and Helen Malise, *née* Graham; *b* 30 May 1929; *m* 8 April 1961, John Richard Seymour Homan, CBE, yr s of late Capt Charles Edward Homan, Elder Bro of Trin House; 1 s (Robert b 1964), 2 da (Frances b 1967, Rosalind b 1969); *Style—* The Hon Mrs Homan; 30 High St, Ticehurst, Sussex

HOMAN, Dr Roger Edward; s of Edward Alfred Homan, of Brighton, and Olive Florence, *née* Dent (d 1988); *b* 25 June 1944; *Educ* Varndean GS Brighton, Univ of Sussex (BA), Univ of Lancaster (PhD), LSE (MSc); *m* 4 Sept 1982, Caroline, da of Michael Arthur Baker, of Alfriston, East Sussex;; *Career* lectr religious studies Brighton Coll Educn 1971-73 (lectr educn 1973-76), princ lectr educn Brighton Poly 1985- (lectr 1976-); memb: ctee Barcombe Mills Preservation Soc, Prayer Book Soc (former nat vice-chm), Victorian Soc, Br Educnl Res Assoc; *Recreations* gardening, church music, chapel hunting, poetry; *Style—* Dr Roger Homan; Crink View, Barcombe Mills, East Sussex (☎ 0273 400 238); Brighton Poly, Falmer, East Sussex (☎ 0273 606 622)

HOMAN, Rear Adm Thomas (Tom) Buckhurst; CB (1978); s of Arthur Buckhurst Homan (d 1965), of Kent, and Gertrude, *née* Lindsay (d 1973); *b* 9 April 1921; *Educ* Maidstone GS; *m* 1945, Christine Oliver, da of Waldemar Oliver (d 1982), of Suffolk; 1 da (Teresa Caroline b 1950); *Career* cadet RN 1939, serv WWII, dir naval offr appts (S) 1971-73, Capt HMS Pembroke 1973-74, Rear Adm 1974, dir gen Naval Personnel Servs 1974-78; sub tres Inner Temple 1978-85; *Recreations* reading, painting, theatre; *Clubs* Army and Navy, Garrick; *Style—* Rear Adm Tom Homan, CB; 602 Hood House, Dolphin Square, London SW1V 3NJ (☎ 01 798 8434)

HOME, Anna Margaret; da of James Douglas Home, and Janet Mary, *née* Wheeler (d 1975); *b* 13 Jan 1938; *Educ* Convent of Our Lady St Leonards-on-Sea Sussex, St Anne's Coll Oxford (MA); *Career* BBC Radio 1960-64, exec prodr Children's Drama Unit 1970-81 BBC TV (prodn positions 1964-70), dep dir programmes (formerly controller of programmes) TVS 1981-86, head of children's dept BBC TV 1986-; FRTS; *Recreations* reading, theatre, gardening, cooking; *Style—* Miss Anna Home; BBC TV Centre, Wood Lane, London W12 (☎ 01 576 1875)

HOME, Sir David George; 13 Bt (NS 1671), of Blackadder, co Berwick; s of Sir John Home, 12 Bt (d 1938), and Hon Gwendolina Hyacinth Roma Mostyn (d 1960), sis of 7 Baron Vaux of Harrowden (d 1935); *b* 21 Jan 1904; *Educ* Harrow, Jesus Coll Cambridge; *m* 1933, Sheila, da of late Mervyn Campbell Stephen; 2 s (John b 1936, d 1988, Patrick b 1941), 2 da (Hermione b 1934, Anne b 1942, d 1986); *Heir* gs, William Dundas Home b 19 Feb 1968; *Career* Maj late Argyll and Sutherland Highlanders, memb Queen's Body Gd for Scotland (Royal Co of Archers); claims dormant Scottish Earldom of Dunbar (cr 1607); *Clubs* Brooks's, New (Edinburgh), Royal and Ancient (St Andrews); *Style—* Sir David Home, Bt; Winterfield, North Berwick, East Lothian EH39 4LY (☎ 0620 2962)

HOME OF THE HIRSEL, Baron (Life Peer UK 1974); Alexander Frederick

Douglas-Home; KT (1962), PC (1951), DL (Lanarks 1960); s of 13 Earl of Home, KT, TD, JP, DL (d 1951) and Lady Lilian Lambton, da of 4 Earl of Durham; suc as 14 Earl of Home (S 1605), and also to titles Lord Home (S 1473), Lord Dunglass (S 1605, previously his title by courtesy), Baron Douglas (UK 1875); having disclaimed these peerages for life on becoming PM in 1963, he was created a life peer in 1974; *b* 2 July 1903; *Educ* Eton, Christ Church Coll Oxford; *m* 1936, Elizabeth, da of Very Rev Cyril Alington, DD (sometime Dean of Durham and Lord Home of the Hirsel's headmaster at Eton), by his w Hon Hester Lyttelton, da of 4 Baron Lyttelton; 1 s, 3 da; *Heir* (to all titles except Life Barony), s Hon David Douglas-Home (styled Lord Dunglass 1951-63); *Career* sits as Cons in House of Lords; Maj Lanark Yeo (TA Reserve), Brig Royal Co Archers (Queen's Body Gd for Scotland); MP (C) Lanark 1931-45 and 1950-51, Kinross and W Perth 1963-74; pps to: chllr Exchequer 1936-37, PM (Neville Chamberlain) 1937-40; jt under-sec of state for affrs May-July 1945, min State Scottish Off 1951-55, sec State Cwlth Rels 1955-60 (Lord pres Cncl Jan-Sept 1957 and Oct 1959-July 1960), ldr House of Lords 1957-60, for sec 1960-63, PM 1963-64, ldr oppn 1964-65, for sec 1970-74; chllr Order of Thistle 1973-, 1 chllr Heriot-Watt Univ 1966-77, hon pres NATO Cncl 1974, pres Peace Through NATO; grand master Primrose League 1966, pres MCC 1966-67; Freedom of Edinburgh 1969, memb NFU 1964; *Clubs* Travellers', Carlton, Buck's, I Zingari (govr); *Style*— The Rt Hon Lord Home of the Hirsel, KT, PC, DL; The Hirsel, Coldstream, Berwicks (☎ 2345); Castlemains, Douglas, Lanarks (☎ 241); 28 Drayton Ct, Drayton Gardens, London SW10 9RH (☎ 01 373 4704); c/o House of Lords, London SW1

HOME ROBERTSON, John David; MP (Lab) East Lothian 1983-; s of Lt-Col John Wallace Robertson TD, JP, DL (d 1979), and Helen Margaret (d 1987), eld da of Lt-Col David Milne-Home (assumed additional name of Home by Scottish licence 1933); *b* 5 Dec 1948; *Educ* Ampleforth, West of Scotland Agric Coll; *m* 1977, Catherine Jean, da of Alex Brewster, of Glamis, Angus; 2 s (Alexander b 1979, Patrick b 1981); *Career* farmer; memb: NUPE, TSSA, Berwickshire Dist Cncl 1974-78, Borders Health Bd 1975-78; MP (Lab) Berwick and East Lothian (by-election) Oct 1978-83, memb Select Ctee Scottish Affrs 1979-83, chm Scottish Gp of Lab MPs 1983, Scottish Labour whip 1983-84; oppn spokesman: on Agric 1984-87, in Scotland 1987-; *Clubs* Prestonpans Labour, East Lothian Labour, Haddington Labour; *Style*— John Home Robertson, Esq, MP; Paxton House, Berwick-on-Tweed; House of Commons, London SW1 (☎ 01 219 4135)

HOMER, Ronald Frederick; Dr; s of George Frederick Alexander Homer (d 1976), and Evelyn Partridge, *née* Chillington (d 1984); *b* 15 April 1926; *Educ* Dudley GS, Birmingham Univ (BSc, PhD); *m* 1950, Audrey, *née* Adcock; 2 s (Richard b 1954, Peter b 1956); *Career* res chemist ICI 1948-59, gp mangr Nat Res Devpt Corpn 1959-81, divnl dir Br Technol Gp 1981-82; conslt and writer on pewter and pewtering; ed Journal of the Pewter Soc 1984-, pres The Pewter Soc 1975-77; Leverhulme Tst Grant for Res on Pewtering 1983-85; Freeman of the City of London 1981, Liveryman Worshipful Co of Pewterers 1982 (archivist 1988-); *Books* Five Centuries of Base Metal Spoons (1975), Provincial Pewterers (with DW Hall, 1985), numerous articles and part works on pewter; *Recreations* gardening, DIY; *Style*— Dr Ronald Homer; Gorse Croft, West Hill Rd, West Hill, Ottery St Mary, Devon EX11 1TU

HONAN, John Patric; s of Patrick William Honan (d 1971); *b* 26 July 1923; *Educ* Xaverian Coll London, Emmanuel Coll Cambridge; *m* 1 (m dis); 2 da; m 2, 1977, Margaret Stella, *née* Cracknell (d 1987); *Career* mktg mangr Izal Overseas Ltd 1960, mktg dir Horton Cleaning Prods 1966-74, md Southon-Horton Laboratories Ltd 1976-83, gen mangr Horton Hygiene Co 1983-86; ret; *Recreations* horticulture, music; *Clubs* Inst of Dirs; *Style*— John Honan, Esq

HONE, Barry Nathaniel; s of Capt Thomas Nathaniel Hone, OBE (d 1946), of Bosbury House, nr Ledbury, Herefords, and Mary Eveline, *née* Byass (d 1982); *b* 15 Sept 1931; *Educ* Winchester; *m* 30 Sept 1955, Eva Agnarsdotter, da of Agnar August Hall (d 1969), of Alvesta, Sweden; 1 s (Rupert b 1966), 1 da (Joanna b 1963); *Career* rifleman 60 Rifles 1950, 2 Lt KSLI 1950 and 4 (Uganda) KAR 1951-52, 4 Bn Shrops LI TA 1952-62 (Maj 1958-62); dir Bosbury House Nurseries Ltd 1952-63, farmer and landowner Glentromie Invernesshire 1964-75, dir Graphic Systems Int Ltd 1976-77, dir employment dept The Offrs Assoc 1988- (recruitment conslt 1979-88); pres Kingussie Sheepdog Trials Assoc, sec West Grampian Deer Mgmnt Soc, chm Kingussie Cons and Unionist Assoc; *Recreations* shooting, fishing; *Clubs* Boodles, Army and Navy; *Style*— Barry Hone, Esq; 19 Bywater St, London SW3 4XD; Glentromie Lodge, By Kingussie, Invernesshire (☎ 01 584 3159); The Officers Association, 48 Pall Mall, London SW1 (☎ 01 930 0125)

HONE, Maj-Gen Sir (Herbert) Ralph; KCMG (1951), KBE (1946, CBE 1943), MC (1918), TD (1946); s of Herbert Hone (d 1950); *b* 3 May 1896; *Educ* Varndean GS Brighton, London Univ (LLB); *m* 1, 1918 (m dis 1945), Elizabeth Daisy Matthews; 1 s, 1 da; m 2, 1945, Sybil Mary, JP, da of A Collins (d 1941) and wid of Wing Cdr Geoffrey Simond (d 1942); 1 s; *Career* served WWI, Capt 1916, served WWII M East and S E Asia (despatches twice), Brig 1941, Maj-Gen 1943; barr Middle Temple 1924, registrar High Ct Zanzibar 1925-27, res magistrate Zanzibar 1927-28, crown counsel Tanganyika 1929-32; attorney-gen: Gibraltar 1933-36 (QC 1934), Uganda 1937-40 (QC 1938); sec-gen to govr-gen of Malaya 1946, dep cmmr-gen for colonial affrs SE Asia 1948-49, govr and C-in-C N Borneo 1949-54, ret 1954; head Legal Div Cwlth Rels Off 1954-61; resumed practice at Bar 1961; constitutional advsr: Bahamas Govt, Kenya Conf 1962, S Arabian Govt 1965, Bermuda Govt 1966; memb Chapter-Gen Order St John 1955-; GCStJ 1973; *Clubs* Athenaeun, Royal Cwlth Soc; *Style*— Maj-Gen Sir Ralph Hone, KCMG, KBE, MC TD; 1 Paper Buildings, Temple, London EC4 (☎ 01 583 7355); 56 Kenilworth Court, Lower Richmond Rd, London SW15 (☎ 01 788 3367)

HONEY, Peter John; s of Gordon Harold, and Kathleen June; *b* 5 June 1955; *Educ* Peter Symonds Sch, Winchester, Bristol Univ (BA, DipArch); *Career* architect; *Style*— Peter Honey, Esq; 4 Elmgrove Rd, Weybridge, Surrey KT13 8NZ

HONEY, Bill - (Bill) William Andrew; *b* 19 Dec 1938; *Educ* Eastbourne GS; *m* 1963, Maureen, *née* McGrane; 2 s, 1 da; *Career* sr ptnr Honey Barrett & Co (and assoc cos), WA Honey & Co, Cornfield Secretarial; dir: Investmt Matters Ltd, Money Matters Ltd, assoc cos, Cornfield Fin and Mgmnt Ltd, Eastbourne and Dist C of C, Eastbourne and Dist Managing Agency Ltd, Eastbourne and Dist Enterprise Agency Ltd, Honey Barrett and Co, Ocklynge Estates Ltd, Clipper Hotels Ltd, Hotel L'Horizon Ltd; memb: nat cncl CBI 1982-87, E Sussex CC 1977-81; chm E Sussex Family Practitioners' Ctee; Freeman City of London; FCA, FCIS, ATII, FCIArb, FBIM; *Recreations* family, home life; *Clubs* City Livery; *Style*— Bill Honey, Esq; Appledown, Old Willingdon Rd, Friston, E Dean, Eastbourne, E Sussex (☎ 0323 42022); Honeysuckle Cottage, Hill Bottom, Worth Matravers, Swanage, Dorset; business: 55 Gildredge Rd, Eastbourne, E Sussex BN21 4SF (☎ 0323 412 277)

HONEYBORNE, Dr Christopher Henry Bruce; s of Henry Thomas Honeyborne, of Romsey, Hants, and Lily Margaret, *née* Fox; *b* 5 Dec 1940; *Educ* Cambridgeshire HS for Boys, St Catharine's Coll Cambridge (MA, DipAgSci), Univ of Reading (PhD); *m* 12 Oct 1968, (Anne) Veronica, da of Stephen Sullivan, of Guernsey; 1 s (James b 1970), 2 da (Clare b 1975, Katharine b 1986); *Career* res demonstrator Univ of Reading 1964-68, res scientist ARC Univ of Bristol 1968-70, mangr Cuprinol Ltd 1971-72, sr mangr Lazard Bros & Co Ltd 1972-77 (seconded to Dalgety Ltd 1976-77), Banque Paribas 1977- (dep gen mangr London branch 1977-86, chief exec Quilter Goodison Co Ltd 1986-88); dir: Cartier Ltd 1979-, Finotel plc 1983-, Modern Vitalcall Ltd 1983-; chm Lynne Stern Assocs 1987; vice chm Wokingham & N Somerset Constituency Cons Assoc; memb Inst Biology; *Recreations* gardening, shooting, tennis, viewing art; *Clubs* City of London, The Arts, United & Cecil, Overseas Bankers; *Style*— Dr Christopher Honeyborne; Ashwick Court, Oakhill, Bath BA3 5BE (☎ 0749 840219); Martins Cottage, Hovingham, York YO6 4LA; Cartier Ltd, 175-176 New Bond St, London W1Y 0QA (☎ 0836 250674, fax 01 355 3011, telex 264441)

HONEYCOMBE, (Ronald) Gordon; s of Gordon Samuel Honeycombe (d 1957), and Dorothy Louise Reid, *née* Fraser (d 1965); all the Honeycombes in the world (approx 350) are related, being descended from Matthew Honeycombe, of St Cleer, Cornwall, who died in 1728, the earliest Honeycombe is documented as John de Honyacombe of Calstock, Cornwall 1327; *b* 27 Sept 1936; *Educ* Edinburgh Acad, Univ Coll Oxford (MA); *Career* announcer Radio Hong Kong 1956-57; actor: Tomorrow's Audience 1961-62, RSC 1962-63, That was the Week That Was 1964; newscaster: ITN 1965-77, TV-am 1984-89; TV presenter: A Family Tree, Brass-Rubbing (1973), Something Special (1978), Family History (1979); TV narrator: Arthur C Clarke's Mysterious World (1980), A Shred of Evidence (1984); appeared in films: The Commuter, Ransom, The Medusa Touch, The Fourth Protocol; appeared in plays: Playback 625 (1970), Paradise Lost (1975), Noye's Fludde (1978), and in various TV plays, charity and variety shows; writer, author and playwright; TV plays: The Golden Vision (1968), Time and Again (1974), The Thirteenth Day of Christmas (1985); Radio plays: Paradise Lost (1975), Lancelot and Guinevere (1976); Royal Gala performances: God Save the Queen! (1977), A King shall have a Kingdom (1977); musicals: The Princess and the Goblins (1976), Waltz of my Heart (1980); stage plays: The Miracles (1960), The Redemption (1963), Paradise Lost (1975), Lancelot and Guinevere (1980); *Books* Neither the Sea Nor the Sand (1969), Dragon under the Hill (1972), Adam's Tale (1974), Red Watch (1976), Nagasaki 1945 (1981), The Edge of Heaven (1981), Royal Wedding (1981), The Murders of the Black Museum (1982), The Year of the Princes (1982), Selfridges (1984), Official Celebration of the Royal Wedding (1986); *Recreations* brass-rubbing, bridge, crosswords; *Clubs* Eccentric; *Style*— Gordon Honeycombe, Esq; c/o Jon Roseman Associates, 103 Charing Cross Rd, London WC2H 0DT (☎ 01 439 8245)

HONNYWILL, Godfrey Coleridge; s of John Honnywill (d 1984), of Tunbridge Wells, and Mary Rosalind, *née* Gair; ggggs of Samuel Taylor Coleridge; *b* 14 Mar 1934; *Educ* Sherborne; *m* 1962, Helen Newbery, da of Dudley Searle Freeman (d 1978), of Chiddingstone, Kent; 3 s (Charles b 1963, Thomas b 1965, David b 1967), 1 da (Alice (twin) b 1967); *Career* slr 1957; dir Crown Chemical Co (Hldgs) Ltd 1972-86; pres: Kent Law Soc 1974, Tunbridge Wells Law Soc 1980; memb Law Soc; *Recreations* travel, gardening; *Style*— Godfrey Honnywill, Esq; The Timberyard, Lamberhurst, Kent TN3 8DT (☎ 0892 890417); The Priory, Tunbridge Wells, Kent (☎ 0892 510222, fax 0892 510333)

HONYWOOD, Sir Filmer Courtenay William; 11 Bt (E 1660), of Evington, Kent; s of Col Sir William Wynne Honywood, 10 Bt, MC (d 1982), and Maud, yr da of William Hodgson-Wilson, of Hexgrave Park, Southwell, Notts; *b* 20 May 1930; *Educ* Downside, RMA Sandhurst, RAC Cirencester (MRAC Dip); *m* 1956, Elizabeth Margaret Mary Cynthia, 2 da of late Sir Alastair George Lionel Joseph Miller, 6 Bt; 2 s (Rupert Anthony b 1957, Simon Joseph b 1958), 2 da (Mary Caroline b 1961, Judith Mary Frances b 1964); *Heir* s, Rupert Honywood; *Career* 3 Carabiniers (Prince of Wales's Dragoon Gds); asst surveyor MAFF Maidstone 1966-73, surveyor Cockermouth Cumbria 1973-74, sr lands offr SE regn Central Electricity Generating Bd 1974-78 (regnl surveyor and valuer 1978-88); FRICS; *Style*— Sir Filmer Honywood, Bt; Greenway Forstal Farmhouse, Hollingbourne, Maidstone, Kent ME17 1QA (☎ 062 780 418)

HONYWOOD, Rupert Anthony Pagan; s and h of Sir Filmer Honywood, 11 Bt; *b* 2 Mar 1957; *Educ* Downside; *Career* conslt proprietor of Honeywood Business Consultancy Servs; *Style*— Rupert Honywood, Esq; 185 Primrose Lane, Shirley Oaks Village, Croydon, Surrey (☎ 01654 9040)

HOOD *see also*: Fuller-Acland-Hood

HOOD, 7 Viscount (GB 1796); Sir Alexander Lambert Hood; 7 Bt (GB 1778); also Baron Hood (I 1782 and GB 1795); s of Rear Adm Hon Horace Hood, KCB (never invested due to death at Jutland 1916), MVO, DSO; suc bro, 6 Viscount 1981; Lord Hood is sixth in descent from 1 Viscount, the naval hero who captured Corsica 1793; *b* 11 Mar 1914; *Educ* RNC Dartmouth, Trinity Coll Cambridge (MA), Harvard Business Sch (MBA); *m* 1957, Diana Maud, CVO (1957, LVO 1952; *b* 1920; asst press sec to George VI 1947-52 (HM The Queen 1952-57), eldest da of Hon George Lyttelton (sometime asst master at Eton, 2 s of 8 Viscount Cobham, and yr bro of 9 Viscount), sister-in-law of two former house masters at Eton (Peter Lawrence and Robert Bourne), and sis of Humphrey Lyttelton, the jazz musician and journalist; 3 s; *Heir* s, Hon Henry Hood; *Career* Lt Cdr RNVR WWII; former chm: Continental and Industl Tst, Tanganyika Concessions Ltd; chm Petrofina (UK) 1982- (dir 1958-); dir: J Henry Schroder Wagg 1957-75, George Wimpey 1957-, Elbar (chm until 1983), Tanks Consolidated Investmts (chm 1976-83), Union Minière SA Belgium, Abbott Laboratories Inc; former part-time memb Br Waterways Bd; *Clubs* Brooks's; *Style*— The Rt Hon Viscount Hood; 67 Chelsea Sq, London SW3 (☎ 01 352 4952); Loders Ct, Bridport, Dorset (☎ 0308 22983)

HOOD, Hon Anthony Nelson; s of 4 Viscount Bridport; *b* 7 Jan 1983, in Lausanne, Switzerland; *Style*— The Hon Anthony Hood

HOOD, (Hilary) David Richard; s of Maj Hilary Ollyett Dupuis Hood, RA (d 1982), and Nicandra Lorraine Reid, *née* Sampson; *b* 6 Feb 1955; *Educ* Dragon Sch Oxford, Radley, Millfield, King's Coll London (LLB); *Career* barr Inner Temple 1980; *Clubs*

Wig & Pen, RAC, Berkeley; *Style*— David Hood, Esq; 90 Overstrand Mansions, Prince of Wales Drive, London SW11 4EU, (☎ 01 622 7415), 1 Gray's Inn Square, London WCIR 5AG, (☎ 01 404 5416, fax 01 405 9942)

HOOD, Eric Cochran; s of Harold Cochran Jellico Hood, of Scotland, and Catherine Cown Hood; *b* 2 Sept 1946; *Educ* Paisley GS, Paisley Coll of Technol (Bronze Medal, Full Tech City and Guilds Cotton Spinning), Outward Bound Sch Scotland; *m* 24 April 1979, Denise, da of Sidney Chapman, of Beds; 1 s (James William b 1976), 1 da (Carolyn Ann b 1986); *Career* dir Blue Arrow (UK) plc 1973, Flexglen Ltd 1976; previously with Marks and Spencer, Smith and Nephew, Coats Viyella; *Recreations* walking, music, reading, cooking; *Clubs* County Constitutional; *Style*— Eric Hood, Esq; 128 Clarence Rd, St Albans, Herts (☎ 0727 54094); Blue Arrow House, Camp Rd, St Albans, Herts AL1 5UA (☎ 0727 66266, fax (0727) 38064)

HOOD, Hon Lady; Hon Ferelith Rosemary Florence; *née* Kenworthy; da of 10 Baron Strabolgi (d 1953), and his 1 w, Doris, *née* Whitley-Thomson, *qv*; *b* 31 May 1918; *Educ* Queen's Gate Sch London; *m* 30 April 1946, Sir Harold Joseph Hood, 2 Bt, TD, 2 s (John b 1952, Basil b 1955, also 1 s decd), 2 da (Josepha b 1953, Margaret b 1965); *Style*— The Hon Lady Hood; 31 Avenue Rd, St John's Wood, London NW8 (☎ 01 722 9088)

HOOD, Sir Harold Joseph; 2 Bt (UK 1922), of Wimbledon, Co Surrey, TD; s of Sir Joseph Hood, 1 Bt (d 1931); *b* 23 Jan 1916; *Educ* Downside; *m* 1946, Hon Ferelith Kenworthy, *see* Hon Lady Hood; 2 s, 2 da (and 1 s decd); *Heir* s, John Hood; *Career* 2 Lt 58 Middx Bn RE (AA) (TA) 1939, Lt RA 1941; ed The Catholic Who's Who 1952 edn, circulation dir Universe 1953-60, managing ed The Catholic Directory 1959-60, circulation dir Catholic Herald 1961-87; KCSG 1979, GCSG 1986, Kt of Sovereign Mil Order of Malta; *Clubs* Royal Automobile, MCC, Challoner; *Style*— Sir Harold Hood, Bt, TD; 31 Avenue Rd, St John's Wood, London NW8 6BS (☎ 01 722 9088, office: 01 588 3101)

HOOD, Hon Henry Lyttelton Alexander; s and h of 7 Viscount Hood; *b* 19 Mar 1958; *Style*— The Hon Henry Hood; 67 Chelsea Sq, SW3 (☎ 01 352 4952)

HOOD, Hon James Francis Touzalin; 3 s of 7 Viscount Hood; *b* 15 Mar 1962; *Educ* Eton; *Style*— The Hon James Hood; 67 Chelsea Sq, SW3 (☎ 01 352 4952)

HOOD, John Joseph Harold; s and h of Sir Harold Joseph Hood, 2 Bt, TD; *b* 27 August 1952; *Style*— John Hood Esq

HOOD, Hon John Samuel; 2 s of 7 Viscount Hood; *b* 16 Oct 1959; *Educ* Eton, Univ of NSW (BEng); *m* 1982, Melissa Bell; 1 da (Gemma Kathryn); *Career* civil engr; *Clubs* Brooks's; *Style*— The Hon John Hood; 72 Thurleigh Rd, London SW12

HOOD, Prof Neil; s of Andrew Hood (d 1984), of Wishaw, Lanarks, and Elizabeth Taylor, *née* Carruthers; *b* 10 August 1943; *Educ* Wishaw HS, Univ of Glasgow (MA, MLitt); *m* 24 Aug 1966, Anna Watson, da of Alexander Clark, of Lesmahagow, Lanarks; 1 s (Cameron 1970), 1 da (Annette b 1967); *Career* res fell and lectr Scottish Coll of Textiles 1966-68, lectr and sr lectr Paisley Coll of Technol 1968-78, prof of business policy Univ of Strathclyde 1979-, assoc dean/dean Strathclyde Business Sch Univ of Strathclyde 1982-87, dir (located in Scotland) Scottish Devpt Agency Scottish Off 1987-89 (dir employment and special initiatives 1989-); visiting appts: Univ of Texas Dallas 1981, Stockholm Sch of Econs 1982-87, Euro Inst for Advanced Study in Mgmnt Brussels 1986; non exec dir: Eurosiot Meat (Hldgs) Ltd 1981-86, Prestwick Hldgs plc 1986-87; investmt advsr Castleforth Fund Mangrs Ltd 1984-88, dir Scottish Devpt Fin Ltd 1984-; advsr and conslt to: Scottish Devpt Agency 1977-87, sec of State for Scotland 1980-87, DTI 1981-83, indust and employment ctee ESRC 1985-87; bd memb Irvine Devpt Corpn 1985-87, dir Lanarks Industl Field Exec Ltd 1984-86; conslt to: Int Fin Corpn Worldbank 1981-83, UN Centre of Transnat Corpns 1982-83, ILO 1984-85; FRSE 1987; *Books* Chrysler UK - A Corporation in Transition (with S Young, 1977), The Economics of Multinational Enterprise (with S Young, 1979), Multinationals in Retreat: The Scottish Experience (with S Young, 1982), Multinational Investment Strategies in the British Isles (with S Young, 1983), Industry Policy and the Scottish Economy (co ed with S Young, 1984), Foreign Multinationals and the British Economy (with S Young and J Hamill, 1988), Strategies in Global Competition (co ed with J E Vahlne, 1988); *Recreations* gardening, walking, reading; *Clubs* RAC, Glasgow; *Style*— Prof Neil Hood; Teviot, 12 Carlisle Rd, Hamilton ML3 7OB (☎ 0698 424870); Scottish Development Agency, 120 Bothwell St, Glasgow; University of Strathclyde, 193 Cathedral St, Glasgow (☎ 041 248 2700, 041 552 4400, fax 041 221 5129, car 0860 203495, telex 777600)

HOOD, Hon Peregrine Alexander Nelson; s and h of 4 Viscount Bridport; *b* 30 August 1974; *Style*— The Hon Peregrine Hood

HOOD, Roger Grahame; s of Ronald Hugo Frederick Hood, of Aldridge, West Midlands, and Phyllis Eileen, *née* Murphy; *b* 12 June 1936; *Educ* King Edward's Sch Five Ways Birmingham, LSE (BSc), Downing Coll Cambridge (PhD); *m* 1, 15 June 1963 (m dis 1985), Barbara, da of Donald Waldo Smith (d 1979), of Washington, Illinois; 1 da (Catharine b 1964); m 2, 5 Oct 1985, Nancy Colquitt, da of Maj John Heyward Lynah (d 1984), of Charleston, S Carolina; 2 step da (Clare b 1964, Zoe b 1969); *Career* res offr LSE 1961-63, lectr social admin Univ of Durham 1963-67, asst dir of res inst of criminology Univ of Cambridge 1967-73, fell Clare Hall Cambridge 1969-73, reader in criminology Univ of Oxford 1973, fell All Souls Coll Oxford 1973-; Sellin-Glueck Award for Int Contributions to Criminology 1986; memb: Parole Bd 1973, SSRC Ctee on Soc Sci and Law 1975-79, Judicial Studies Bd 1979-85, Department Ctee to review the Parole System 1987-88; pres Br Soc of Criminology 1986-; *Books* Sentencing in Magistrates Courts (1962), Borstal Re-Assessed (1965), Key Issues in Criminology (with Richard Sparks, 1970), Sentencing the Motoring Offender (1972), Crime, Criminology and Public Policy - Essays in Honour of Sir Leon Redziuowicz (ed, 1974); A History of English Criminal Law - Vol 5, The Emergence of Penal Policy (with Sir Leon Radzinowicz, 1986); *Recreations* cooking; *Style*— Dr Roger Hood; 63 Iffley Rd, Oxford OX4 1EF (☎ 0865 246084); All Souls Coll, Oxford OX4 1EF (☎ 0865 279347/274448)

HOOD, Stephen John; s of Leslie Gilbert Hood, of Canberra, Australia, and Margaret, *née* Vinnicombe; *b* 12 Feb 1947; *Educ* Brisbane Boys Coll, Univ of Queensland, Univ of London (LLM); *m* 1 Oct 1971, Maya, da of Leon Togonal (d 1984), of Paris; 4 s (Ludovic b 1973, William b 1974, Roderick b 1978, Frederick b 1980), 1 da (Victoria b 1985); *Career* ptnr Clifford Chance (formerly Coward Chance) 1978- (asst slr 1974-78), sr res ptnr Coward Chance Hong Kong 1981-86; chm: London Young Slrs Gp, Law Soc 1979 and 1980, sr branch Br-Aust Soc 1978-80, Royal Cwlth Soc in Hong Kong 1983-86, fin law sub ctee Law Soc Hong Kong 1984-86, exec ctee Sir Robert Menzies Meml Tst 1988-; Br bd memb Euro Assoc for Chinese Law 1988-; cncl memb: Royal Cwlth Soc 1987-, Britain Aust Soc 1981-; Freeman City of London 1987; *Books* Equity Joint Ventures in The People's Republic of China (co-author 1985, second edn 1987), Technology Transfer in The People's Republic of China (1985, second edn 1988); *Recreations* skiing, gardening, reading; *Style*— Stephen Hood, Esq; Royex House, Aldermanbury Sq, London EC2 (☎ 01 600 0808)

HOOK, Hon Mrs; (Edith Deirdre); *née* Handcock; da of late 7 Baron Castlemaine; *b* 1936; *m* 1, 1957 (m dis 1974), Keith Moss, BEM; 1 s; m 2, 1975, Terence Hook; *Style*— The Hon Mrs Hook

HOOK, Margaret; da of late Robert Barr, of Shadwell House, Yorks, and Edith Midgley; *b* 7 May 1918; *Educ* Calder Girls' Sch Seascale Cumberland, Univ of Leeds; *m* 12 July 1947, Sheriff William Thomson Hook, QC, s of late Peter Hook; 1 s (Christian b 1952); *Career* Jr Cdr ATS 1942-46, Staff Coll G3 staff duties Scottish Cdr 1943-45, War Off Educn 1945-46; dir: Barr and Wallace Arnold Tst plc, TSB plc Scotland, Scottish C of C 1980-83, Scottish Ballet 1983-84, Oswalds Hotels Ltd 1987-; chm: Sibbald Travel, Arts and Indust Ctee Scotland 1973-78, Edinburgh IOD 1982-84; pres Assoc of Br Travel Agents 1977-80; memb Nat Econ Devpt Cncl Hotel and Caterers 1978; CBIM; memb Panel of Value Added Tax Tbnls for Scotland; Lazo de Dama of the Order of Isabel la Catolica Spain; *Style*— Mrs William Hook; 10 Moray Place, Edinburgh EH3 6DT (☎ 031 225 5401); Kildavannan, Isle of Bute (☎ 0700 2455)

HOOK, Rt Rev Dr Ross Sydney; MC (1946); s of Sydney Frank Hook (d 1959), of Cambridge, and Laura Harriet Hook (d 1973); *b* 19 Feb 1917; *Educ* Christ's Hosp, Peterhouse Cambridge (BA, MA); *m* 26 Aug 1948, Ruth Leslie, da of Rev Herman Masterman Biddell (d 1946), of Sandown, IOW; 1 s (Philip b 1950), 1 da (Deborah b 1956); *Career* chaplain RNVR 1943-46, 44 RM Commando 1943, Holding Commando 1943-44, 2 Commando Bde 1944-46; curate Milton 1941-43, chaplain Ridley Hall Cambridge 1946-48, select preacher Cambridge Univ 1948; rector: Chorlton-cum-Hardy Manchester 1948-52, St Luke's Chelsea 1952-61; rural dean 1952-61; chaplain: Chelsea Hosp for Women 1953-61, St Luke's Hosp 1955-61; canon residentiary Rochester 1961-65; examining chaplain to: Bishop of Rochester 1961-69, Bishop of Grantham 1965-72, Bishop of Lincoln 1965-72; dean of Stamford 1971-72, prebendary Lincoln Cathedral 1965-72, bishop of Bradford 1972-80 (memb House of Lords 1975-80), chief of staff Archbishop of Canterbury 1980-84, asst bishop Canterbury 1980-; Freeman City of London 1981; Hon DLitt Univ of Bradford 1981; *Style*— The Rt Rev Dr Ross Hook, MC; Mill Rock, Newchurch, Romney Marsh, Kent TN29 0DN (☎ 0303 873 115)

HOOK, Susan Mary (Sue); da of Charles Ronald Bodger (d 1982), of Dorset, and Joan Bodger, *née* Ricketts; *b* 12 June 1944; *Educ* Totton County GS, Winchester Coll of Art and Design (Intermediate Dip), Univ of Reading (BA); *m* 1977, Michael William, s of William George Hook, of Herts; *Career* ed dir Purnell Publishers Ltd 1982-83, md Colourmaster Ltd 1984-85, publishing dir (childrens books) Century Hutchinson Ltd 1985-86, publishing conslt (freelance) 1987-; *Recreations* gardening, tennis, painting, music (lapsed violinist), cooking, reading, sculling; *Style*— Mrs Sue Hook; Summer Cottage, Lurgashall, Petworth, West Sussex (☎ 042878 743)

HOOKE, Lt Cdr Michael Richard Douglas; RN; s of Douglas Thomas Howard Hooke (d 1970), and Edith Mary Margaret, *née* Bisgood (d 1985); *b* 31 May 1929; *Educ* Ladycross Seaford, Ampleforth, RNC Greenwich; *m* 1, 11 April 1953 (m dis), Susan Lilian, da of Edward Morland; 3 s (Richard b 11 March 1954, Thomas b 8 Feb 1956, Benjamin b 2 Sept 1958), 1 da (Sophia b 16 Jan 1960); m 2, 16 Oct 1974, Valerie Diana, da of Thomas Baildon Oerton; *Career* joined RN 1946, french interpreter 1954, torpedo specialist 1956, i/c HMS Crofton 1958-60, Army Staff Coll Camberley 1960, sr Offr Ops, Persian Gulf 1963-65, liaison offr Def Intelligence Agency USA 1965-68, early retirement 1969; dir St James Advertising 1972-74, ptnr Travers Healey Lyons 1974-76, chm MSG PR 1976-79, PR conslt 1979-85; memb Forest of Dean DC; *Recreations* gardening, sailing; *Style*— Lt Cdr Michael Hooke, RN; Crookes, Newent, Gloucs (☎ 0531 821188)

HOOKER, David Symonds; s of Cdr John Joseph Symonds Hooker, RN, and Pamela Bowring, *née* Toms; *b* 9 Oct 1942; *Educ* Radley Coll, Magdalene Coll Cambridge (MA), Royal Sch of Mines (MSc); *m* 16 Jan 1965, (Catharine) Sandra, da of Maurice Hilary Thornely Hodgson (d 1986); 2 s (Benjamin b 1969, Joshua b 1979), 1 da (Samantha b 1966); *Career* Pennzoil Co 1965-73, Edward Bates & Sons Ltd 1973-75; md: Candecca Resources plc 1978-82, Plascom Ltd 1982-85, Hurricane Int Ltd 1985-87, Aberdeen Petroleum plc 1987-; *Style*— David Hooker, Esq; 29 Smith Terrace, London SW3 4DH and Ardura, Isle of Mull; Office: 40 George St, London W1H 5RE

HOOKER, Dr Michael Ayerst; s of Albert Ayerst Hooker, of Broomsleigh Park, Seal Chart, Kent, and late Marjorie Mitchell, *née* Gunson (d 1981); *b* 22 Jan 1923; *Educ* Marlborough, St Edmund Hall Oxford (MA), Univ of the Witwatersrand (PhD); *Career* HG 1940, Oxford Univ Sr Trg Corps 1941 ACF TARO 1942-48; memb Br Cncl 1945-47, sch master 1947-51, WELLS Organisations in NZ and UK 1951-53, involved with visual aids and PR 1953-59; md: Hooker Craigmyle & Co Ltd 1959-72 (first UK institutional fund-raising conslts), Michael Hooker and Assoc & Ltd 1972-79 (has helped to raise some £70 million for good causes); chief exec govr Truman and Knightley Educnl Tst 1981-87, exec dir the Jerwood Award 1987-; chm Fedn of Cons Students 1944, parly candidate (C) Coventry East 1955, various offs Cwlth Cncl 1955-60; memb advsy ctee on charitable fund raising Nat Cncl of Social Service 1971-73, memb working pty on Methodist Boarding Schs 1971-72; tstee: Ross McWhirter Fndn 1976-, Dicey Tst 1978-, Jerwood Oakham Fndn 1981-, Police Convalescence and Rehabilitation Tst 1985-; govr Oakham Sch 1971-83, jt chm Friends of Friends 1986-; *Books* The Charitable Status of Independent Schools (with C P Hill, 1969), School Development Programmes (1969), Counter Measures to Guard Against Loss of Charitable Status (1977); *Recreations* food and drink; *Clubs* Carlton, Royal Cwlth Soc; *Style*— Dr Michael Hooker; 4 Leinster Sq, Bayswater, London W24 PL (☎ 01 229 5483)

HOOKER, Prof Morna Dorothy; d of Percy Francis Hooker (d 1975), of High Salvington, Sussex, and Lily, *née* Riley; *b* 19 May 1931; *Educ* Univ of Bristol (BA, MA), Univ of Manchester (PhD); *m* 30 March 1978, Rev Dr (Walter) David Stacey, s of Walter Stacey (d 1957); *Career* res fell Univ of Durham 1959-61, lectr in New Testament Kings Coll London 1961-71; Univ of Oxford: lectr in theology 1970-76, fell of Linacre Coll 1970-76, lectr in theology Keble Coll 1972-76; Lady Margaret's prof of divinity Univ of Cambridge 1976-, fell Robinson Coll Cambridge 1977-; hon fell: Linacre

Coll Oxford 1980, Kings Coll 1979; pres Studiorm Novi Testamenti Societas 1988-89 (memb 1959-); *Books* Jesus & The Servant (1959), The Son of Man in Mark (1967), What about The New Testament (ed 1979), Pauline Pieces (1979), Studying The New Testament (1979), The Message of Mark (1983), Continuity and Discontinuity (1986), Paul & Paulinism (ed 1982); *Recreations* molinology, music, walking; *Style—* Prof Morna Hooker; The Divinity Sch, St John's St, Cambridge CB2 1TW (☎ 0223 332 598)

HOOKER, Ronald George; CBE (1985); s of Alfred George Hooker (d 1956), and Gertrude, *née* Lane (d 1950); *b* 6 August 1921; *Educ* Mitcham GS, Wimbledon Tech Coll, London Univ; *m* 26 June 1954, Eve, *née* Pigott; 1 s (Jonathan), 1 da (Jane); *Career* Philips Electrical Ltd 1938-50, special asst to Sir Norman Kipping Fedn of Brit Industry 1948-50, Brush Gp 1950-60, 600 Gp 1960-65, Rolls Royce (1971) 1971-73; chm: Co-ordinated Land and Estates Ltd, Mgmnt and Business Servs Ltd, Radyne Ltd, Thos Storey (Engrs) Ltd, Warner Howard Gp plc; dir: Airship Industs Ltd, Argunex Ltd, Computing Devices Hldgs Ltd, GEI Int plc, Gothic Crellon Ltd, Hambros Industl Mgmnt Ltd, The Top Mgmnt Partnership Ltd; Freeman of the City of London, memb Worshipful Co of Coachmakers' and Coach Harness Makers; hon fell mfrg Engr (USA), fndr memb Engrg Cncl, memb Court of Cranfield Coll of Technol, former pres Engrg Employers' Fedn, F Eng Hon Life fell IPE, CBIM, FRSA; *Recreations* gardening, music, reading, travel; *Clubs* Athenaeum, City of London, Lansdowne; *Style—* Ronald Hooker, Esq, CBE; Loxborough House, Bledlow Ridge, nr High Wycombe, Bucks HP14 4AA; 6 Tufton Ct, Tufton St, London; Hambros Bank, 41 Tower Hill, London EC3N 4HA (☎ 01 490 5000)

HOOKINS, Donald Henry; s of Henry Arthur Hookins (d 1922), and Lucy Helen, *née* Messenger (d 1978); *b* 19 Mar 1923; *Educ* locally in Henley and Reading; *m* 31 Jan 1951, Renée, da of James John Shefford; 2 da (Sara b 1955, Louise b 1959); *Career* Royal Berks Regt 1942-46; chm Gen Decorating Supplies Ltd 1961-; pres Henley and District Chamber of Trade, former chm and pres YMCA Henley Area 1973-, chm Br Heart Foundation Henley area 1985-, pres Henley Boys FC 1972-; *Recreations* charity work, amateur painter, fishing; *Clubs* Phyllis Ct; *Style—* Donald Hookins, Esq; Ferry Cottage, Marlow Rd, Henley-on-Thames, Oxon RG9 3AX; 7/9 Boulton Rd, Reading (☎ 0734 875266)

HOOKWAY, Sir Harry Thurston; s of William Hookway (d 1982); *b* 23 July 1921; *Educ* Trinity Sch of John Whitgift, London Univ (BSc, PhD); *m* 1956, Barbara, da of Oliver Butler; 1 s, 1 da; *Career* Dept Scientific and Industl Res 1949-65 (head info div 1964-65), asst under-sec DES 1969-73, dep chm and chief exec Br Library Bd 1973-84, pres Inst Info Scientists 1973-76, dir Arundel Castle Tstees 1976-, chm UNESCO Int Advsy Ctee on Documentation Libraries and Archives, govr Br Inst of Recorded Sound 1981-83, memb Royal Cmmn on Historical Monuments (Eng) 1981-88, pres Library Assoc 1985, chm LA Publishing Ltd 1986-89; pro-chllr Loughborough Univ 1987-; hon fell: Inst of Info Science, Library Assoc; Hon LLD Sheffield 1976, DLitt Loughborough 1980; kt 1978; *Style—* Sir Harry Hookway; 35 Goldstone Crescent, Hove, E Sussex

HOOLAHAN, Anthony Terence; QC (1973); s of Gerald Hoolahan (d 1961), and Doris Miriam Valentina, *née* Jackson; *b* 26 July 1925; *Educ* Dorset House Sussex, Framlingham Coll Suffolk, Lincoln Coll Oxford (MA); *m* 1949, Dorothy Veronica, da of Osmund Connochie (d 1963); 1 s (Mark b 1956), 1 da (Catriona b 1961); *Career* Sub Lt RNVR 1944, barr 1949, rec of the Crown Ct 1976-, bencher Inner Temple 1980, Social Security Cmmr 1986, barr NI 1980, QC NI 1980; *Recreations* swimming; *Clubs* RAC; *Style—* Anthony Hoolahan, Esq, QC; 83-86 Farringdon St, London EC4A 4BC (☎ 01 353 5145)

HOOLE, Sir Arthur Hugh; KB (1985); s of Hugh Francis Hoole (d 1947), of Surrey, and Gladys Emily, *née* Baker (d 1975); *b* 14 Jan 1924; *Educ* Sutton County Sch, Emmanuel Coll Cambridge (MA, LLM); *m* 1945, Eleanor Mary, da of Frank Washington Hobbs (d 1931), of Surrey; 2 s (Philip b 1955, John b 1957), 2 da (Margaret b 1957, Elizabeth b 1961); *Career* Flying Offr RAFVR; slr 1951, chm govrs Coll of Law 1983-, pres Law Soc 1984-85, memb Criminal Injuries Compensation Bd 1985-; govr 1987-; St Johns Sch Leatherhead, Sutton Manor HS; *Recreations* cricket, reading, music; *Clubs* RAC; *Style—* Sir Arthur Hoole, KB; Yew Tree House, St Nicholas Hill, Leatherhead, Surrey; 64 High St, Epsom, Surrey

HOOLE-LOWSLEY-WILLIAMS, Hon Mrs; Olivia; *née* Bootle-Wilbraham; da of late 6 Baron Skelmersdale and Ann, da of Percy Quilter (s of 1 Bt); *b* 1938; *m* 1961 (m dis 1975), Anthony John Hoole-Lowsley-Williams; 3 s (Richard Edward b 1962, Hugh Sebastian b 1964, Benjamin Christopher b 1968); *Style—* The Hon Mrs Hoole-Lowsley-Williams; 46 Haldane Road, Fulham, London SW6

HOOLEY, Paul James; (JP); s of James Henry Hooley, of Bedford, and Vera Margory, *née* Foot; *b* 25 August 1941; *Educ* Ewell HS; *m* 4 Jan 1964, Helen Frances, da of Keith Richardson, of Bedford; 2 s (Simon b 1966, Benjamin b 1975), 1 da (Susan b 1964); *Career* chm and md Newnorth Burt Ltd, dir Bedford Bldg Soc; Mayor N Beds 1978-79 (dep mayor 1977-78), chm Amenities Ctee 1983-87; pres Kempston Cons Assoc; pres: Riding for Disabled Bedford, Multiple Sclerosis Soc Bedford, St Raphael Assoc for Disabled Bedford; patron Cancer Relief Bedford; freeman City of London; FInstD; *Recreations* freemasonry, golf, local history, charitable work; *Clubs* Bedford; *Style—* Paul J Hooley, Esq, JP; 29 Elstow Rd, Kempston, Bedford (☎ 0234 851688); Newnorth House, College St, Kempston, Bedford (☎ 0234 41111)

HOOPER, Baroness (Life Peeress UK 1985); Gloria Hooper; da of Frederick Hooper of Sparrow Grove, Shawford, Hants (d 1977), and Frances, *née* Maloney (d 1984); *b* 25 May 1939; *Educ* Southampton Univ (BA); *Career* slr 1973, ptnr Taylor & Humbert 1974-85; MEP (C) Liverpool 1979-84; govt whip House of Lords 1985-87, parly under-sec of state Dept Educn and Science 1987-88, parly under-sec of state Dept of Energy 1988-; *Style—* The Rt Hon Baroness Hooper; House of Lords, Westminster, London SW1

HOOPER, John Edward; s of William John Henry Hooper, and Noëlle Patricia Terese, *née* Lang (d 1979); *b* 17 July 1950; *Educ* St Benedict's Abbey London, St Catharine's Coll Cambridge (BA); *m* 19 July 1980, Hon Lucinda Mary, da of 2 Baron Mountevans (d 1974); *Career* reporter BBC current affrs 1971-73, dip corr Ind Radio News 1973-74, corr Cyprus BBC, Guardian and Economist 1974-76; Guardian: corr Spain and Portugal 1976-79, reporter 1979-81, asst news ed 1981-84, energy and trade corr 1984-88; presenter Twenty Four Hours BBC World Service 1984-88, corr Spain and N Africa Guardian and Observer 1988-; winner Allen Lane award best first work of history or lit 1986; memb Soc of Authors; *Books* The Spaniards: a portrait of the new Spain (1986 and 1987), translated Los Espanoles de Hoy (Javier Vergara 1987); *Recreations* reading and travelling without having to write about it afterwards; *Style—* John Hooper, Esq; A/206-7 Calle Apolonio Morales 6, Madrid 28036, Spain (☎ 341 250 9748); c/o Agence France Presse, Paseo de Recoletos 18, Madrid 28001 Spain (☎ 341 275 3149, telex Spain 22335)

HOOPER, Sir Leonard James; KCMG (1967, CMG 1962), CBE 1951; s of James Edmund Hooper (d 1938), and Grace Lena Hooper (d 1968); *b* 23 July 1914; *Educ* Alleyn's Sch Dulwich, Worcester Coll Oxford; *m* 1, 1951 (m dis 1978), Ena Mary Osborn; m 2, 1978, Mary Kathleen Horwood, *née* Weeks; *Career* dir Govt Communications HQ 1965-73 (joined 1938); idc 1953, dep sec Cabinet Off 1973-78, ret; *Style—* Sir Leonard J Hooper, KCMG, CBE; 9 Vittoria Walk, Cheltenham, Glos GL50 1TL (☎ 0242 511007)

HOOPER, Sir Robin William John; KCMG (1968, CMG 1954), DSO (1943), DFC (1943); s of Col John Charles Hooper, DSO, King's Shrops LI (d 1954), of Harewell, Faversham, Kent; *b* 26 July 1914; *Educ* Charterhouse, Queen's Coll Oxford; *m* 1941, Constance Mildred Ayshford (d 1986), da of Lt-Col Gilbert Ayshford Sanford, DSO, DL, 3 Carabiniers (d 1961), of Triley Ct, Abergavenny; 3 s; *Career* RAFVR Bomber Cmd and special duties 1940-44, ret Wing Cdr; entered FO 1938, cnsllr Baghdad 1953-56, head perm under-sec's dept FO 1956-60, asst sec-gen (political) NATO 1960-66; ambass: Tunisia 1966-67, South Yemen 1967-68; dep sec Cabinet Off 1968-71, ambass Greece 1971-74, ret; memb NATO Appeals Bd 1977-85, dir Benguela Railway Co 1976-84; Croix de Guerre 1944, Chev Léigion d'Honneur 1945; *Recreations* music, gardening, field sports; *Clubs* Travellers', Pratt's; *Style—* Sir Robin Hooper, KCMG, DSO, DFC; Brook House, Egerton, nr Ashford, Kent TN27 9AP

HOOPER, William John; s of William Guy Hooper (d 1981), of Wolverhampton, and Ruth, *née* Dutton; *b* 20 Oct 1931; *Educ* Wolverhampton GS; *m* 31 Aug 1958, Marguerite Elaine, da of Arthur McLachrie (d 1969), of Wolverhampton; 1 da (Emma Jane Louise b 1967); *Career* CA; dep chm and fin dir Banro Industs plc 1973-88, chm The Abbeygate Gp Ltd 1989-; *Recreations* golf, gardening, family, overseas travel; *Style—* John Hooper, Esq; Lullington Court, Lullington, South Derbyshire DE12 8EJ

HOOS, Hon Mrs; Hon Sarah Marie Adelaide; *née* Cust; only surv da of 5 Baron Brownlow; *b* 3 Jan 1906; *m* 1930, Edward Jan Hoos (d 1962); 1 s, 1 da; *Style—* Hon Mrs Hoos; The Wooden House, Manton, Oakham, Leics

HOOSON, Baron (Life Peer UK 1979); (Hugh) Emlyn Hooson; QC (1960); s of Hugh Hooson, of Denbigh; *b* 26 Mar 1925; *Educ* Denbigh GS, Univ Coll of Wales; *m* 1950, Shirley Margaret Wynne, da of Sir George Hamer, CBE, of Powys;; *Career* sits as Lib peer in House of Lords; barr Gray's Inn 1949, dep chm Merioneth QS 1960-67 (chm 1967-71), dep chm Flintshire QS 1960-71, rec Merthyr Tydfil 1971 and Swansea 1971, rec Crown Ct 1972-, ldr Wales & Chester circuit 1971-74, bencher Gray's Inn 1968 (vice-tres 1985, tres 1986); non exec dir of Laura Ashley Hldgs Ltd 1985-; MP (Lib) Montgomeryshire 1962-79, ldr Welsh Lib Pty 1966-79, vice-chm Political Ctee Atlantic Assembly 1976-79, vice-pres Peace Through NATO 1985-, pres Llangollen Int Eisteddfod 1987-; hon professional fell Univ Coll of Wales 1971-; farmer; *Style—* The Rt Hon the Lord Hooson, QC; Summerfield, Llanidloes, Powys (☎ 055 12 2298); 1 Dr Johnson's Bldgs, Temple, London EC4 (☎ 01 353 9328): Sedan Ho, Stanley Place, Chester (☎ 0244 20480)

HOPCROFT, George William; s of Frederick Hopcroft (d 1952), and Dorothy Gertrude, *née* Bourne (d 1972); *b* 30 Sept 1927; *Educ* Chiswick GS, London Univ (BSc), Brasenose Coll Oxford, Insead Fontainebleau; *m* 31 March 1951, Audrey Joan, da of James Rodd (d 1963); 3 s (Terry b 1954, David 1956, Martin b 1958), 1 da (Geraldine b 1960); *Career* sr underwriter Export Credits Guarantee Dept 1946-53 (1957-65), asst UK Trade Cmmr Madras 1953-57, FCO 1965; first sec: (commericial) Amman 1965-69, (econ) Bonn 1969-71, (commerical) Kuala Lumpur 1971-75, FCO London 1975-77; cnsllr Br Embassy Bangkok 1977-81, fndr memb Export and Overseas Advsr Panel (EOTAP) 1982, affrs advsr Govt of Belize 1982-83, underwriter Lloyd's 1981-, cnslt on Int Affrs 1981-; vice pres Thames Valley Harriers (ex Civil Serv 880 yds champ), tres Hook Heath Residents Assoc; *Recreations* leisure and circumnavigation, athletics, serendipity; *Clubs* Royal and Commonwealth, Yvonne Arnaud Theatre, British (Bangkok); *Style—* George Hopcroft, Esq; Efrogs, Pond Rd, Hook Heath, Woking, Surrey GU22 0JT (☎ 048 62 5121)

HOPE, Alan; JP (1962); George Edward Hope, of Sutton Coldfields, W Midlands, and Vera, *née* Emms; *b* 5 Jan 1933; *Educ* George Dixon GS; *m* 1960, Marilyn Margaret, da of Douglas Dawson; 1 s (Philip b 1961), 1 da (Caroline b 1973); *Career* Nat Serv RAF 1952-54; trained in printing ind chm of several cos in the printing ind and aluminium fabrication; Cons cncllr: Birmingham City Cncl 1962-74, W Midlands Co Cncl 1974- (chm: trading standards ctee 1978-79, fin ctee 1979-80; ldr 1980-81, ldr cons oppn gp 1982-); chm Gen Servs Ctee AMA 1979-81, chm NMCU 1980-81, chm LACOTS 1980-81; magistrate 1974, chm Perry Barry Constituency Cons Assoc 1989-; govr: Birmingham Univ, Aston Univ; memb IBA Birmingham Advsy Ctee; *Clubs* Birmingham, Royal Commonwealth; *Style—* Councillor Alan Hope, Esq, JP; 7 Rosemary Drive, Little Aston Park, Streetly, Sutton Coldfield, West Midlands (☎ 021 353 3011); Renault Printing Co Ltd, Factory Centre, College Rd, Birmingham B44 8BS (☎ 356 0331)

HOPE, Bryan; s of Edward Sydney Hope (d 1959); *b* 27 July 1930; *m* 1964, Julia Anne, da of Aubrey Tearle, of Eaton Bray, Beds; 2 da; *Career* pres: Reed Worldwide Exhibitions, Cahners Exposition Gp; chm: Ind and Trade Fairs Hldgs Ltd, Reed Exhibitions, Reed Confs, United Exhibition Services Ltd; dir: Reed Publishing Ltd, Reed Publishing USA, Int Exhibition Servs Ltd, Cahners Exhibitions Ltd, Business Press Int, Cahners Publishing Co, Reed Asian Publishing (Pte Ltd), Int Wine and Spirit Competition Ltd; vice-pres Periodical Publishers Assoc (chm 1980-83), tres Wine Guild of the United Kingdom 1984-85; tstee: Nat Motor Museum, Reed Telepublishing Ltd; *Recreations* fly fishing, vegetable gardening; *Clubs* RAC; *Style—* Bryan Hope, Esq; 58 Chapelfields, Charterhouse Rd, Godalming, Surrey GU7 2BX (☎ 048 68 25640); Reed Worldwide Exhibitions, 999 Summer St, Stamford, Conneticut 06905 USA (☎ 0101 203 964 0000)

HOPE, (James Arthur) David; QC (Scotland 1978); s of Arthur Henry Cecil Hope OBE, TD, WS (d 1986), of Edinburgh, and Muriel Ann Neilson, *née* Collie; *b* 27 June 1938; *Educ* Edinburgh Acad, Rugby Sch, St John's Coll Cambridge (BA, MA), Univ of Edinburgh (LLB); *m* 11 Apr 1966, (Katharine) Mary da of William Mark Kerr, WS (d 1985), of Edinburgh; 2 s (William b 1969, James (twin) b 1969), 1 da (Lucy b 1971); *Career* cmmnd Seaforth Highlanders 1957, Lt 1959; admitted Faculty of Advocates

1965, standing jr counsel in Scotland to Bd of Inland Revenue 1974-78, advocate depute 1978-82, chm Med Appeal Tbnls 1985-86, legal chm Pensions Appeal Tbnl 1985-86; memb: Scottish Ctee on Law of Arbitration 1986-; elected dean of Faculty of Advocates 1986; hon memb Canadian Bar Assoc 1987; *Books* Gloag and Henderson's Introduction to the Law of Scotland (jt ed 7 edn 1968, asst ed 8 edn 1980 and 9 edn 1987), Armour on Valuation for Rating (jt ed: 4 edn 1971, 5 edn 1985); *Clubs* New (Edinburgh); *Style*— David Hope, Esq, QC; Advocates Library, Parliament House, Edinburgh ED1 1RF (☎ 031 226 5071, fax 031 225 3642)

HOPE, Hon Mrs (Diana Lyall); *née* Mackie; da of Baron Mackie of Benshie (Life Peer); *b* 1946; *m* 1968, John Carlyle Hope; 4 da; *Style*— The Hon Mrs Hope; 3 St Bernard Cres, Edinburgh

HOPE, Emma Mary Constance; da of Capt John David Hope, of Poundhill Cottage, Bletchingly, Surrey, and Margaret Daphne, *née* Boutwood; *b* 11 July 1962; *Educ* Reigate Co Sch for Girls, Sevenoaks Sch, Cordwainers Coll (SIAD Dip) ; *Career* owner Emma Hope's Shoes 1987-, designer for Laura Ashley, Betty Jackson, Jean Muir; 5 Design Cncl Awards for Footwear 1987-88, Martini Style Award 1988, Harpers and Queens Awards for Excellence 1988; memb: Local C of C, Chartered Soc of Designers 1984-; *Books* 2 articles for Design Magazine, Salvatore Ferragamo, A review of his exhibition at the V & A (1988), Shoe Design: Tiptoeing into Industry - Review of College Shows (1988); *Recreations* shopping, gardening, exploring, writing letters, museums, riding; *Clubs* Tandridge GC; *Style*— Miss Emma Hope; EMMA HOPE'S SHOES, 33 Amwell St, London EC1R 1UR (☎ 01 833 2367, fax 01 833 1796)

HOPE, Sir John Carl Alexander; 18 Bt (NS 1628), of Craighall, Co Fife; s of Gp Capt Sir Archibald Philip Hope, OBE, DFC, AE (d 1987), and Ruth (d 1986), da of Carl R Davis; *b* 10 June 1939; *Educ* Eton; *m* 1968, Merle Pringle, da of Robert Douglas, of Southside, Holbrook, Ipswich; 1 s, 1 da (Natasha Anne b 1971); *Heir* s, Alexander Archibald Douglas b 16 March 1969; *Style*— Sir John Hope, Bt; 10 Furlong Rd, London N7 8LS (☎ 01 607 4553)

HOPE, Hon Jonathan Charles; yr s of 1 Baron Glendevon, PC; *b* 23 April 1952; *Educ* Eton; *Style*— The Hon Jonathan Hope; 20 Roland Gdns, London SW7

HOPE, Hon Julian John Somerset; er s and h of 1 Baron Glendevon, PC; *b* 6 Mar 1950; *Educ* Eton, Christ Church Oxford; *Career* operatic prodr; resident prodr Welsh National Opera 1973-75; assoc prodr Glyndebourne Festival 1974-81; prodns incl: San Francisco Opera, Wexford and Edinburgh Festivals; *Recreations* tennis, cinema, travel; *Style*— The Hon Julian Hope; 17 Wetherby Gdns, London SW5

HOPE, Michael Richard; s of Hon Richard Hope, OBE (yst s of 1 Baron Rankeillour), and Helen (da of Alfred Charlemagne Lambart, gs of 7 Earl of Cavan); hp of cous, 4 Baron Rankeillour; *b* 21 Oct 1940; *Educ* Downside; *m* 1964, Elizabeth, da of Col Francis Fuller, Rajputana Rifles; 1 s, 2 da; *Style*— Michael Hope, Esq; Barningham Hall, Bury St Edmunds, Suffolk

HOPE, Sir (Charles) Peter; KCMG (1972, CMG 1956), TD (1945); s of George Leonard Nelson Hope (d 1973); *b* 29 May 1912; *Educ* Oratory Sch Reading, London Univ, Cambridge Univ (BSc, DSc); *m* 1936, Hazel Mary, da of George Turner (d 1920); 3 s; *Career* served WWII RA (TA), Maj; entered WO 1938, transferred FO 1946, cnsllr Bonn 1953-56, head news dept FO 1956-59, min Madrid 1959-62, consul-gen Houston USA 1963-64, alternate delegate to UN 1965-67, ambass Mexico 1968-72, ret; memb Acad Int Law 1970; pres Br Assoc SMOM 1983-89, bailiff Grand Cross SMOM; Grand Cross of the Aztec Eagle, Grand Offr Merito Melitense; KStJ 1985; *Recreations* shooting, fishing; *Clubs* White's, Army and Navy; *Style*— Sir Peter Hope, KCMG, TD; North End House, Heyshott, Midhurst, Sussex (☎ 073 081 3877)

HOPE, (Edward Rowland) Peter; s of Edward Leach Hope (d 1929), of Bolton, and May, *née* Aspinall (d 1968); *b* 12 May 1928; *Educ* Bolton Co GS, Univ of Edinburgh (MA), Univ of Manchester (LLB); *m* 3 April 1959, Adeline Diana, da of Thomas Howarth Clarke; 3 da (Sarah b 7 Jan 1962, Janet (twin) b 7 Jan 1962, Victoria b 15 Oct 1963); *Career* served RA 1950-52, cmmnd 2 Lt 1951, 2 Lt TA 1953; slr of the Supreme Ct 1956, ptnr Porter Hope and Knipe, ret 1988, conslt 1988; pt/t chm Industl Tbnl 1975, registrar Dep Co Ct 1985; chm Bolton and Dist Civic Tst, memb and former pres Bolton Rotary Club, sec Mrs Lums Charity, tstee Queen St Mission; memb: The Law Soc, Bolton Inc Law Soc; *Recreations* golf, fell walking, sailing; *Style*— Peter Hope, Esq; Bodnant, 18 Regent Rd, Bolton, Lancashire BL6 4DJ; Rose Lea, Outgate, Ambleside, Cumbria (☎ 0204 40693); 22 Bowkers Row, Bolton, Lancashire; 58 Market St, Westhoughton, Bolton, Lancashire (☎ 0204 386001, fax 0204 364168, telex 635109 CHAMCOMG)

HOPE, Sir Robert Holms-Kerr; 3 Bt (UK 1932), of Kinnettles, Co Angus; s of Sir Harry Hope, 1 Bt (d 1959); suc bro, Sir James Hope, 2 Bt, MM 1979; *b* 12 April 1900; *m* 1928, Margaret Eleanor, da of Very Rev Marshall Lang, DD, of The Manse, Whittingehame, East Lothian; *Heir* none; *Style*— Sir Robert Hope, Bt; Old Bridge House, Broxmouth, Dunbar, East Lothian

HOPE, William Arthur; s of Peter Dorian Hope, and Elsie Mercy Thompson; *b* 6 Dec 1945; *Educ* Walpole GS; *m* 21 Sept 1968, Brenda June, da of Wilfred Leslie Charles Bond; 1 s (David b 1976), 1 da (Natalie b 1973); *Career* CA 1970, chm Trilion plc 1983-87 (dir all subsidiary cos 1983-87); FICA; *Recreations* sailing, tennis, soccer; *Clubs* Groucho; *Style*— William Hope, Esq; Bois Cottage, Bridle Lane, Loudwater, Rickmansworth, Herts WD3 4JA

HOPE-DUNBAR, Sir David; 8 Bt (NS 1664), of Baldoon; o s of Maj Sir Basil Douglas Hope-Dunbar, 7 Bt (d 1961), and Edith Maud Maclaren, *née* Cross; *b* 13 July 1941; *Educ* Eton, RAC Cirencester; *m* 1971, Kathleen Ruth, yr da of late J Timothy Kenrick, of Birmingham; 1 s, 2 da; *Heir* s, Charles Hope-Dunbar b 5 March 1975; *Career* chartered surveyor; ARICS; *Recreations* fishing, tennis, shooting; *Style*— Sir David Hope-Dunbar, Bt; Banks Hse, Kirkcudbright (☎ 0557 30424)

HOPE-DUNBAR, Edith, Lady; Edith Maude Maclaren; da of late Malcolm Cross; *m* 1940, as his 2 wife, Maj Sir Basil Douglas Hope-Dunbar, 7 Bt (d 1961); *Style*— Edith, Lady Hope-Dunbar; Crofthead Cottage, by Kirkcudbright

HOPE-FALKNER, Patrick Miles; s of Robert E Hope-Falkner, and Diana, *née* Hazlerigg (d 1977); *b* 1 Dec 1949; *Educ* Wellington; *m* 17 June 1972, Wendy Margaret, da of Jack Douglas Mallinson (d 1966); 2 s (Timothy Douglas b 1980, James Edward b 1982); *Career* articles 1968-73, admitted slr 1973, Freshfields 1973-84, Lazard Brothers & Co Ltd 1985-; dir: Lazard Investors Ltd 1985-, Lazard Brothers & Co (Jersey) Ltd 1985-; memb Law Soc; *Clubs* Brooks; *Style*— Patrick Hope-Falkner, Esq; Lazard Bros & Co Ltd, 21 Moorfields, London EC2 P2HT (☎ 01 588 2721)

HOPE-MASON, David Gordon; s of Gordon Nisbett Hope-Mason (d 1987), and Gunnel Anna, *née* Schele; *b* 11 June 1940; *Educ* Haileybury, ISC; *m* 1, 15 June 1962 (m dis 1981), Maralyn Florence, da of Royce Gordon Martland, of St Brelades, Jersey, CI; 1 s (Justin b 1968), 1 da (Amanda b 1966); m 2, 9 May 1981; *Career* chm and md Lockwood Press Ltd, jt md Mkt Intellingence Ltd; govr Marlborough House Sch Hawkhurst Kent 1978-88; Liveryman Worshipful Co of Fruiterers 1973 (Master 1989); FIFP 1978; *Recreations* golf, skiing, computing; *Clubs* RAC, Royal Wimbledon GC; *Style*— David Hope-Mason, Esq; 23 Hazlewell Rd, London SW15 6LT (☎ 01 789 8608); Lockwood Press Ltd, Market Towers, London SW8 5NN (☎ 01 622 6677, fax 01 720 2047, telex 915149)

HOPE-MORLEY, Hon Andrew James Sundt; s of 3 Baron Hollenden; *b* 16 Sept 1952; *Educ* Eton; *Style*— The Hon Andrew Hope-Morley

HOPE-MORLEY, Hon Ian Hampden; s and h of 3 Baron Hollenden, *qv*; *b* 23 Oct 1946; *Educ* Eton; *m* 1972, Béatrice Saulnier, da of Baron Pierre d'Anchald, of Paris; 1 s (Edward b 9 April 1981), 1 da (Juliette b 1974); *Style*— The Hon Ian Hope-Morley; 26 Clarendon Rd, London W11 3AB

HOPE-MORLEY, Hon Robin Gordon; s of 3 Baron Hollenden; *b* 9 June 1949; *Educ* Brickwall, Northiam; *Career* owner and dir London Phone Co Ltd; *Recreations* tennis, snooker; *Clubs* Brooks's, MCC; *Style*— The Hon Robin Hope-Morley; Flat 2, 159 Ebury St, London SW1

HOPE-WALLACE, (Dorothy) Jaqueline; CBE (1958); da of Charles Nugent Hope-Wallace (d 1953), s of John Hope-Wallace, of Featherstone Castle, Northumberland; *b* 29 May 1909; *Educ* LMH Oxford; *Career* civil servant; under sec 1959-69, memb bd Corby Dvpt Corpn 1970-80; chm: Nat Corpn for the Care of Old People 1978-80, British Inst for Recorded Sound 1974-75, Friends Univ Coll Hospital 1973-84; *Recreations* arts, travel, gardening; *Style*— Miss Jacqueline Hope-Wallace, CBE; 17 Ashley Ct, Morpeth Terrace, London SW1 (☎ 01 834 8822); Whitegate, Alciston, Polegate, Sussex

HOPETOUN, Earl of; Andrew Victor Arthur Charles Hope; eldest s and h of 4 Marquess of Linlithgow, *qv*; *b* 22 May 1969; *Educ* Eton; *Career* Page of Honour to HM Queen Elizabeth The Queen Mother 1984-86; styled Viscount Aithrie 1969-87; *Style*— Earl of Hopetoun; c/o Hopetoun House, South Queensferry, West Lothian EH30 9SL

HOPKIN, Sir (William Aylsham) Bryan; CBE (1961); s of William Hopkin; *b* 7 Dec 1914; *Educ* Barry Co Sch, St John's Coll Cambridge, Univ of Manchester ; *m* 1938, Renée Ricour; 2 s; *Career* joined Miny Health 1938; dir Nat Inst of Econ and Social Res 1952-57, sec Cncl on Prices Productivity and Incomes 1957-58, dep dir econ dept Treasy 1958-65, Mauritius 1965, ODM 1966, dir-gen econ planning 1967-69, dir-gen Dept of Econ Affrs 1969; Treasy: dep chief econ advsr 1970-72, chief econ advsr and head govt econ serv 1974-77; prof of econs Univ Coll Cardiff 1972-82; memb Cwlth Devpt Corpn 1972-74, chm MSC Wales 1978-79; hon fell St John's Coll Cambridge 1982, hon prof Univ Coll Swansea 1988; kt 1971; *Style*— Sir Bryan Hopkin, CBE; Aberthin House, Aberthin, Cowbridge, S Glamorgan (☎ 044 63 2303)

HOPKIN, Nicholas Buxton; s of Dr Geoffry Buxton Hopkin, of Littleton, Winchester, and Harriet, *née* Moxon; *b* 31 Mar 1944; *Educ* George Watson's Coll Edinburgh (MB, ChB), Univ of Edinburgh (DLO); *m* 30 Aug 1966, Jennifer Margaret Bruce, da of Lt John MacPherson Ainslie, RN (ka 1944); 1 s (Tobias b 1976), 3 da (Lucy b 1967, Rosalind b 1970, Penelope b 1972); *Career* RN 1965-82, ret in rank of Surgn Cdr; conslt in otorhinolaryngology; formerly hon snr registrar head and neck unit Royal Marsden Hosp 1979-80, currently conslt ENT Surgn W Dorset Health Authy; FRCS (RCS England); *Recreations* travel, board-sailing, gardening; *Style*— Nicholas Hopkin, Esq; The Old Vicarage, Sydling St Nicholas, Dorchester, Dorset DT2 9PB; West Dorset Hospital, Dorchester (☎ 251150 ext 4205)

HOPKIN, Raymond John; s of Hywel Raymond Hopkin (d 1970), of Farnborough, Hants, and Violette Madge Lorraine, *née* Lethaby; *b* 13 July 1944; *Educ* Farnborough GS, Imperial Coll London Univ (BSc, ARCS); *m* 24 Nov 1967, Jeanette Graham, da of Robert William Clark, of Sanquhar, Dumfriesshire; *Career* Equity & Law Life Assur Soc plc 1966-, dep gen mangr Equity & Law Assocs 1988-, chm insur servs devpt ctee BT 1988-; MMS 1975; *Recreations* bridge, golf, all music, Paradores, working; *Clubs* Phyllis Court (Henley-on-Thames); *Style*— Raymond Hopkin, Esq; Crawfordjohn, Upper Warren Ave, Caversham Heights, Reading RG4 7EB (☎ 0734 461 403); Equity & Law House, Amersham Rd, High Wycombe, Bucks HP13 5AL (☎ 0494 463 463, fax 0494 461 989, car tel 0836 293 142, telex 83385)

HOPKINS; *see*: Scott-Hopkins

HOPKINS, (Philip) Anthony; CBE (1987); s of Richard Arthur Hopkins (d 1981), and Muriel Annie Yeates; *b* 31 Dec 1937; *Educ* Cowbridge GS, Royal Acad of Dramatic Art; *m* 1, 1968 (m dis 1972), Petronilla; 1 da (Abigail b 1968); m 2, 1973, Jennifer Ann, da of Ronald Arthur Lynton; *Career* actor; first joined Nat Theatre 1965, first film The Lion in Winter 1968, Broadway debut Equus 1974; lived and worked (American films and television) in USA 1975-84, returned to England 1984; films incl: The Lion in Winter 1967, The Looking Glass War 1968, Hamlet 1969, When Eight Bells Toll 1969, A Doll's House 1972, The Girl from Petrovka 1973, Juggernaut 1974, A Bridge Too Far 1976, Audrey Rose 1976, International Velvet 1977, Magic 1978, The Elephant Man 1979, The Bounty (Captain Bligh) 1983; tv credits incl: A Heritage and Its History (ATV 1968), A Company of Five (ATV 1968), The Three Sisters (BBC TV 1969), The Peasants Revolt (ITV 1969), Dickens (BBC 1970), Danton (BBC 1970), The Poet Game (BBC 1970), Decision to Burn (Yorkshire 1970), War and Peace (BBC 1971, 1972), Cuculus Canorus (BBC 1972), Lloyd George (BBC 1972), QB VII (ABC 1973), Find Me (BBC 1973), A Childhood Friend (BBC 1974), Possessions (Granada 1974), All Creatures Great and Small (NBC TV 1974), The Arcata Promise (Yorkshire 1974), Dark Victory (NBC 1975), The Lindbergh Kidnapping Case (NBC 1975, Emmy award), Victory at Entebbe (ABC 1976), Kean (BBC 1978), The Voyage of the Mayflower (CBS 1979), The Bunker (CBS 1980, Emmy award), Peter and Paul (CBS 1980), Othello (BBC 1981), Little Eyolf (BBC 1981), The Hunchback of Notre Dame (CBS 1981), A Married Man (LWT Channel 4 1982), Strangers and Brothers (BBC 1983), The Arch of Triumph (CBS 1984), Mussolini and I (RAI Italy 1984), Hollywood Wives (ABC 1984), Guilty Conscience (CBS 1984), The Good Father (LWT Channel 4 1985); stage credits incl: A Flea in Her Ear, The Three Sisters, Dance of Death (Nat Theatre 1967), The Architect and The Emperor of Assyria, A Woman Killed with Kindness, Coriolanus (Nat Theatre 1971), The Taming of the Shrew (Chichester Festival Theatre 1972), Macbeth (Nat

Theatre 1972), Equus (Plymouth Theatre NY 1974 and 1975, Huntington Hartford Theatre LA 1977), The Tempest (The Mark Taper Forum Theatre LA 1979), Old Times (Roundabout Theatre NY 1983), The Lonely Road (Old Vic Theatre London 1985), Pravda (Nat Theatre 1985), King Lear (1986), Antony and Cleopatra (1987); *Recreations* piano; *Style*— Anthony Hopkins, Esq, CBE

HOPKINS, Antony; CBE (1976); *b* 21 Mar 1921; *Educ* Berkhamstead Sch, Royal Coll Music; *m* Feb 1947, Alison; *Career* freelance composer of incidental music incl: Oedipus Rex (Old Vic 1945), Antony and Cleopatra (1945, 1953), Moby Dick (BBC 1947), The Oresteia (BBC 1956), twelve programmes on insects (BBC); films incl: Pickwick Papers, Decameron Nights, Billy Budd; operas incl: Lady Rohesia (1948), Three's Company (1953), Dr Musikus; other works incl John and the Magic Music Man (1975, which won Grand Prix at Besancon Film Festival 1976); conducter nearly all maj orchestras: UK, Hong Kong, Adelaide, Belgrade, Tokyo; pres numerous music clubs; medal of hon City of Tokyo 1973; doctorate Stirling Univ, fell Robinson Coll; hon RAM, fell RCM; *Books* Talking About Symphonies (1961), Talking About Concertos (1964), Music All Around Me (1967), Lucy and Peterkin (1968), Music Face to Face (with A Previn, 1971), Talking About Sonatas (1971), Downbeat Music Guide (1977), Understanding Music (1979), The Nine Symphonies of Beethoven (1981), Songs for Swinging Golfers (1981), Sounds of Music (1982) Beating Time (1982), Pathway to Music (1983), Musicamusings (1983), The Concertgoer's Companion (1984), The Concertgoer's Companion Vol 2 (1986); *Recreations* golf, motor sport; *Style*— Antony Hopkins, Esq, CBE; Woodyard Cottage, Ashridge, Berkhampstead, Herts (☎ 0442 842 257)

HOPKINS, David Rex Eugène; s of Frank Victor Densham Hopkins, of Somerset, and Vera Muriel Eugènie, *née* Wimhurst; *b* 29 June 1930; *Educ* Worthing HS for Boys, Christ Church Oxford (MA); *m* 1955, Brenda Joyce, da of Cecil Thomas Phillips (d 1940), of London, and Irene Newcomb, *née* Briggs; 2 s (Mark b 1957, Jeremy b 1962), 2 da (Ruth b 1955 d 1985, Sarah b 1960); *Career* cmmn RA 1952 Korea; asst princ WO 1953 (princ 1957), MoD 1964, asst sec 1967, HO 1969-70, Royal Coll of Def Studies 1971, dir HQ Security 1975, Defence Equipment Secretariat 1982, fin cnsllr UK delgn to NATO 1981; dir of Quality Assur (admin) 1983-; *Recreations* church work, archaeological digging, fell-walking, military history; *Style*— David Hopkins, Esq; 16 Hitherwood Drive, London SE19 1XB (☎ 01 670 7504)

HOPKINS, Capt David Sime Borrough; s of Thomas Wilfred Hopkins (d 1961), of Moorallerton Hall, Leeds, and Gladys Lilian Muir, *née* Douty (d 1955); *b* 24 Nov 1924; *Educ* Bradfield; *m* 26 Nov 1955, Jennifer Isabel, da of Sir John Cameron, of Cowsby Hall, Thirsk, N Yorks; 2 s (Stephen Borrough b 1956, Nicholas Martin b 1959), 2 da (Catherine Virginia b 1961, Sophie Anne b 1966); *Career* Capt KRRC 1943-47 NW Europe, Capt Yorks Hussars (TA) 1947-56; slr 1950; *Recreations* shooting, gardening; *Clubs* Brooks's; *Style*— Capt David Hopkins; Galphay Manor, Ripon, N Yorks (☎ 076 583 205)

HOPKINS, Adm Frank Henry Edward; KCB (1964, CB 1961), DSO (1942), DSC (1941), DL (Devon 1982); s of E F L Hopkins, of Glencairn, St Columb, Cornwall, and Sybil Mary Walrond; *b* 23 June 1910; *Educ* Stubbington House, Pangbourne Nautical Coll; *m* 1, 1939, Lois Barbara (d 1986), da of J R Cook, of Cheam, Surrey; m 2, 1987, Georgianna Priest; *Career* joined RN as Cadet 1927, served WWII (despatches), Med, E Atlantic and Pacific; served Korean War (despatches), Capt 1950, Cdr HMS Ark Royal 1956-58, Cdr RNC Dartmouth 1958-60, Rear Adm 1960, Flag Offr Flying Trg 1960-62, Vice Adm 1962, Flag Offr Aircraft Carriers 1962-63, Lord Cmmr Admty dep chief Naval Staff and 5 Sea Lord 1963-64, Dep Chief Naval Staff MOD 1964-66, Adm 1966, C-in-C Portsmouth 1966-67, ret; American Legion of Merit 1948, Cdr Order of Sword (Sweden) 1954; *Recreations* sailing, golf; *Clubs* Naval and Military, Royal Yacht Sqdn, Royal Naval Sailing Assoc, Britannia YC; *Style*— Adm Sir Frank Hopkins, KCB, DSO, DSC, DL; Kingswear Court Lodge, Kingswear, Dartmouth, S Devon TQ6 0DX (☎ 080 425 247)

HOPKINS, Ian William; s of Keith Burne Hopkins, of Reigate, Surrey, and Laura Mary, *née* Dowie; *b* 23 April 1947; *Educ* Trinity Sch of John Whitgift; *m* 6 March 1971, Valerie Joan Frances, da of Ralph Hughes, of Horsham, Sussex; 1 s (Guy), 1 da (Kirsty); *Career* Arthur Young McClelland Moores & Co 1965-71, Citicorp Leasing Int Inc 1971-72, London Multinational Bank Ltd and Chemical Bank Int Ltd 1973-82, Charterhouse Japhet plc 1982-86, fin dir Baring Brothers & Co Ltd 1986-; FCA 1970, MICAS 1970; *Recreations* tennis, sailing, choral music; *Clubs* Riverside Racquets; *Style*— Ian Hopkins, Esq; 48 Glebe Rd, Barnes, London SW13 0ED (☎ 01 878 2227); Baring Brothers & Co Ltd, 8 Bishopsgate, London EC2N 4AE (☎ 01 283 8833 fax 01 283 2633, telex 883622)

HOPKINS, John Seddon; s of Alan Hopkins (d 1931), of Christchurch, NZ, and Adeline Mary, *née* Oates; *b* 4 Mar 1930; *Educ* St Bartholomew's Hosp London Univ (MB, BS); *m* 26 Nov 1960, Carmel Rosemary, da of John Patrick McEvoy, of Tipperary; 2 s (Michael b 1963, Christopher b 1969), 3 da (Caroline b 1961, Louise (twin) b 1961, Rosalind (twin) b 1969); *Career* Capt RAMC Europe and Korea 1954-56; sr conslt orthopaedic surgn: Harlow Wood Orthopaedic, Mansfield and Newark Gen Hosp; clinical tutor Univ of Nottingham 1966; FRCS; *Recreations* theatre, travel, literary persuits; *Clubs* New Bone; *Style*— John Hopkins, Esq; Northwood House, 15 North Park, Mansfield, Notts NG18 4PA (☎ 0623 25166)

HOPKINS, (Richard) Julian; s of Richard Robert Hopkins, CBE, of Harpenden, Herts, and Grace Hilda, *née* Hatfield (d 1973); *b* 12 Oct 1940; *Educ* Bedford Sch; *m* 1, 1961 (m dis 1969), Jennifer, *née* Hawkesworth; 1 s (Justin b 1962), 1 da (Julia b 1963); m 2, 6 Aug 1971, Maureen Mary, da of Norman George Hoye (d 1977), of London; 1 s (Benjamin b 1976); *Career* asst mangr London Palladium 1964-66, centl servs mangr BBC 1966-70, admin and fin offr RSPCA 1972-78 (exec dir RSPCA 1978-82), gen mangr Charity Christmas Card Cncl 1982-83, fin dir War on Want 1984-88, nat dir CARE Britain 1988-; fndr and ctee memb Manor Theatre Gp W Sussex, dir and exec ctee memb World Soc for Protection of Animals 1977-83, memb farm animal welfare cncl Miny of Agric 1979-83; FBIM 1976; *Recreations* music, particularly opera, theatre, travel; *Style*— J Hopkins, Esq; 22 Falmouth Rd, London SE1 (☎ 01 407 1446); CARE Britain, 34-38 Southampton St, London WC2E 7HE (☎ 01 379 5247, fax 01 379 0543, telex 267239 CARE G)

HOPKINS, Rowland Rhys; s of David Verdun Hopkins, of Rugby, Warks, and Phyllis, *née* Dyson; *b* 19 Dec 1948; *Educ* Lawrence Sheriff Sch Rugby, UCL (LLB); *m* 12 Dec 1987, Elizabeth Ann, da of Ronald Williams (d 1980), of Church Stretton, Shrops; *Career* barr; memb Gen Synod CoE 1985-, chm House of Laity of Birmingham Diocesan Synod CoE 1988-; *Recreations* skiing, fell walking; *Style*— Rowland Hopkins, Esq; 108 Stanmore Rd, Edgbaston, Birmingham B16 0SX (☎ 021 429 8793); Victoria Chambers, 177 Corporation St, Birmingham B4 6RG (☎ 021 236 9900)

HOPKINS, Thomas Price; s of Evan Thomas Hopkins, JP (d 1934), of Cowbridge, Glam, and Mary Baker, *née* Price (d 1920); *b* 20 Jan 1915; *Educ* New Coll Harrogate, Dean Close Sch Cheltenham, Welsh Nat Sch of Medicine; *m* 9 Jan 1941, Bertha Estelle, da of Richard Jones (d 1935), of Bridgend, Glam; 2 s (Jonathan b 1952, Timothy b 1953); *Career* served WWII 1939-45; MO RAF, fighter sqdns W Derwent, Normandy and Belgium; gp MO Holland and Germany, sqdn ldr, sr MO RAF Gatow, Berlin 1940-46; conslt orthopaedic surgn Neath Gen Hospital 1954-79; *Recreations* rugby football, hockey, sailing; *Clubs* Mumbles Sailing; *Style*— Thomas P Hopkins, Esq; Bryn Wern, Northway, Bishopston, Swansea SA3 3JN (☎ 044 128 2629)

HOPKINSON, Rev Alfred Stephan; s of Ven John Henry Hopkinson (d 1960), of Cumbria, and Evelyn Mary, *née* Fountaine (d 1952); *b* 14 June 1908; *Educ* St Edward's Sch Oxford, Wadham Coll Oxford (MA); *m* 31 Dec 1935, Anne Cicely, da of Sir Walter Morley Fletcher, KBE, CB, (d 1933), of Kensington; 2 s (Barnabas b 1939, Simon b 1947), 4 da (Jennifer b 1937, Selina b 1941, Lucy b 1943, Elizabeth b 1945); *Career* cncllr and chaplain Winchester Coll; formerly Preb St Pauls Cathedral London, vicar St Mary Woolnoth, gen dir Industrial Christian Fellowship; anglican advsr to ATV, chaplain RNVR; *Recreations* gardening, travel; *Style*— The Rev Alfred S Hopkinson; Duke's Watch, 2 St Swithun St, Winchester (☎ 0962 69532); Winchester College, Winchester

HOPKINSON, Ven Barnabas John (Barney); s of Preb Alfred Stephan Hopkinson, of Dukes Watch, 2 St Swithun's Rd, Winchester, and Anne Cicely, *née* Fletcher (d 1988); *b* 11 May 1939; *Educ* Emmanuel Sch, Trinity Coll Cambridge (MA), Geneva Univ (Certificat d'Etudes Oecumeniques), Lincoln Theol Coll; *m* 27 July 1968, Esme Faith, da of Rev Cecil Wilson Gibbons (d 1985), of Cambridge; 3 da (Rachel b 1969, Sarah b 1971, Clare b 1974); *Career* asst curate: Langley 1965-67, Great St Mary's Cambridge 1967-70; asst chaplain Charterhouse 1970-75, team vicar Marlborough 1976-81 (rural dean 1977-81), rector Wimborne Minster 1981-86, canon Salisbury Cathedral 1983-, rural dean Wimborne 1985-86, archdeacon of Sarum 1986-, priest i/c Stratford-sub-Castle 1987-; *Recreations* walking, climbing, gardening; *Style*— The Ven the Archdeacon of Sarum; Russell House, Stratford-sub-Castle, Salisbury, Wilts SP1 3LG (☎ 0722 28756)

HOPKINSON, David Hugh Laing; CBE (1986), RD (1975), DL (1987); *b* 14 August 1926; *Educ* Wellington, Merton Coll Oxford (BA); *m* 1951, Prudence Margaret Holmes; 2 s (Adrian b 1953, Christopher b 1957), 2 da (Rosalind b 1955, Katherine b 1961); *Career* Lt Cmdr RNVR 1944-65; clerk House of Commons 1949-59, chief exec M & G Gp 1963-87, Church Cmmn 1973-; chm Harrisons and Gosfield plc, dep chm English China Clays plc, dir Wolverhampton and Dudley Breweries Merchants Tst; govr: Sherborne, Wellington; hon fell St Anne's Coll Oxford; *Recreations* travel, opera; *Clubs* Brooks's; *Style*— David Hopkinson, Esq, CBE, RD, DL, BA; St John's Priory, Poling, Arundel, W Sussex BN18 9PS (☎ 0903 882393)

HOPKINSON, Giles; s of Rev Arthur John Hopkinson, CIE (d 1953), of N Yorks, and Eleanor, *née* Richardson; *b* 20 Nov 1931; *Educ* Marlborough, Univ of Leeds (BSc); *m* 1956, Eleanor Jean, da of Leonard Harper Riddell (d 1984), of N Yorks; 3 da (Alison b 1958, Jane b 1959, Erica b 1962); *Career* E and J Richardson Ltd 1956, Forestal Land Timber and Rly's Co Ltd 1957, Civil Service 1958, scientific offr Dept of Scientific and Industl Res (DSIR), princ Miny of Tport 1964, asst sec 1971, under sec DoE 1976, dir London region property servs agency DoE 1983-; *Recreations* music, landscape gardening; *Clubs* Royal Cwlth Society; *Style*— Giles Hopkinson, Esq; St Christopher House, Southwark St, London SE1 (☎ 01 921 4897)

HOPKINSON, Maj-Gen John Charles Oswald Rooke; CB (1984); s of Lt-Col John Oliver Hopkinson, and Aileen Disney, *née* Rooke; *b* 31 July 1931; *Educ* Stonyhurst Coll, RMA Sandhurst; *m* 1956, Sarah Elizabeth, da of Maj-Gen (Matthew Herbert) Patrick Sayers, OBE; 3 s, 1 da; *Career* CO 1 Bn Queen's Own Highlanders 1972-74 (despatches), Dep Cdr 2 Armd Div and Cdr Osnabrück Garrison 1977-78, student RCDS 1979, dir Operational Requirements 3 (Army) 1980-82, COS HQ Allied Forces Northern Europe 1982-84, Col Queen's Own Highlanders 1983-; dir Br Field Sports Soc 1984-; *Recreations* shooting, fishing, sailing; *Clubs* Army and Navy; *Style*— Maj-Gen John Hopkinson, CB; Bigsweir, Gloucestershire; 59 Kennington Rd, London SE1 (☎ 01 928 4742)

HOPKINSON, Hon Nicholas Henry Eno; s (by 1 m) and h of 1 Baron Colyton, CMG, PC; *b* 18 Jan 1932; *Educ* Eton, Trinity Coll Cambridge; *m* 1957, Fiona Margaret, da of Sir (Thomas) Torquil Alphonso Munro, 5 Bt; 2 s; *Career* engr and farmer; *Style*— The Hon Nicholas Hopkinson; The Gardens House, Lindertis, Kirriemuir, Angus DD8 5NU (☎ 057 53 222)

HOPKINSON, Sir (Henry) Thomas; CBE (1967); s of Ven John Henry Hopkinson (d 1957), Archdeacon of Westmorland, and Evelyn Mary, *née* Fountaine; *b* 19 April 1905; *Educ* St Edward's Sch Oxford, Pembroke Coll Oxford (MA, hon fell 1978); *m* 1, Antonia White; 1 da, 1 step da; m 2, Gerti Deutsch; 2 da; m 3, 1953, Dorothy Vernon, wid of Hugh Kingsmill; *Career* author, journalist; ed: Picture Post 1940-50, Lilliput 1941-46; features ed News Chronicle 1954-56, ed Drum Magazine (S Africa) 1958-61, dir for Africa Int Press Inst (i/c trg of African journalists) 1963-66, sr fell Press Studies Sussex Univ 1967-69, visiting prof journalism Minnesota Univ USA 1968-69, dir centre of journalism studies Univ Coll Cardiff 1971-75 (hon professorial fell 1978); kt 1978; *Books* The Transitory Venus (short stories, 1946), The Lady and the Cut-Throat (short stories, 1958), In the Fiery Continent (1962), South Africa (1964), Much Silence: the life and work of Meher Baba (with Dorothy Hopkinson, 1974), Of This Our Time (autobiography, vol 1, 1982), Under the Tropic (vol 2, 1984), Shady City (novel 1987); *Style*— Sir Tom Hopkinson, CBE; 26 Boulter St, St Clement's, Oxford OX4 1AX

HOPKIRK, (Margaret) Joyce; *née* Nicholson; da of late Walter Nicholson, of Newcastle, and late Veronica, *née* Keelan; *b* 2 Mar 1937; *Educ* Middle Street Secdy Sch Newcastle; *m* 1, 1964, Peter Hopkirk; 1 da (Victoria b 11 April 1966); m 2, 9 Aug 1974, William James (Bill) Lear, s of Maj Cyril James Lear (d 1988), of Newick, Sussex; 1 s (Nicholas b 22 Nov 1975); *Career* women's ed (launch) Sun Newspapers 1969, ed (launch) Br Cosmopolitian 1970, asst ed Daily Mirror 1972-78, women's ed Sunday Times 1986, ed dir (launch) Br Elle 1987, ed She Magazine 1987-; *Style*— Mrs Joyce Hopkirk; Piccotts End, Hemel Hempstead, Herts (☎ 01 439 5339); National Magazines, Broadwick St, London W1

HOPPER, Andrew Christopher Graham; s of Hugh Christopher Hopper (d 1959), of Glamorgan, and Doreen Adele Harper (d 1976); *b* 1 Oct 1948; *Educ* Monkton Combe Sch Bath; *m* 6 Sept 1980, Rosamund Heather, da of Robert Nigel Towers, of Tiverton, Devon; *Career* admitted slr 1972, ptnr Adams and Black Cardiff 1972, (sr ptnr 1982), HM dep coroner for S Glamorgan 1977-83 (retained to represent the Law Soc in disciplinary investigations and proceedings 1980-, retained by continuing educn dept of the Law Soc to lecture on ethics and conduct 1986-), conslt Cartwrights with Adams and Black 1988; *Recreations* claret, badminton; *Clubs* East India; *Style*— Andrew C G Hopper, Esq; Talygarn House, Talygarn, Pontyclun, Mid Glam CF7 9JT; 36 West Bute St, Cardiff CF1 5UA (☎ 0443 237788, fax 0443 237410)

HOPPER, Brian Barnes; *b* 10 Jan 1926; *Educ* King George V Sch Southport, Univ of Liverpool (BEng); *m* 1952, Mavis Priscilla; 1 s, 2 da; *Career* formerly civil engr Shell-Mex and BP Ltd, CEGB and consulting engrs; projects mangr Unilever Ltd 1965-80, gen mangr Chester Waterworks Co 1980-; MICE, CEng, FBIM, MIWES, MRSH; *Recreations* golf, tennis, badminton; *Clubs* Eaton GC, Chester Lawn Tennis; *Style*— Brian Hopper, Esq

HOPPER, Lt-Col Patrick Desmond Leo; s of Brig Charles Reginald Leo Hopper (d 1959), and Daphne Elise, *née* Williams (d 1987); *b* 22 Nov 1930; *Educ* Monkton Combe Sch, RMA Sandhurst; *m* 28 March 1959, Gemma Felicity Bevan, da of Brig James Bevan Brown (d 1962); 1 s (Jonathan b 1962), 1 da (Joanna b 1960); *Career* cmmnd Suffolk Regt 1951, Platoon Cdr Malaya (despatches) 1951-53, servd 3 Para 1953-57 (took part in Suez Op), Adj 1 Suffolk 1958-59, cmd 5 Bn Royal Anglian Regt 1973-75, Asst Adj-Gen Rhine Army 1975-78; ret from Regular Army 1978; sec East Anglia TA and VR Assoc 1986- (dep sec 1979-86), Dep Hon Col TA (Essex) Royal Anglian Regt 1987-; *Recreations* fly fishing, sailing; *Clubs* Army and Navy; *Style*— Lt-Col Patrick D L Hopper; St Crispins, Radwinter, Saffron Walden, Essex CB10 2TH (☎ 079 987 205); East Anglia TAVRA, 250 Springfield Rd, Chelmsford, Essex CM2 6BU (☎ 0245 354262)

HOPPER, William Joseph; s of late Isaac Vance Hopper, and Jennie Josephine Black; *b* 9 August 1929; *Educ* Queen's Park Secdy Sch, Univ of Glasgow (BA); *m* 1959, Melisa; 1 da (Catherine b 1971); *Career* Flying Offr RAF; fin analyst W R Grace and Co New York 1956-59, London off mangr H Hentz and Co (memb NY Stock Exchange) 1960-66, gen mangr S G Warburg and Co Ltd 1966-69; dir: Hill Samuel and Co Ltd 1969-74, Morgan Grenfell and Co Ltd 1975-79; advsr Morgan Grenfell 1979-; dir: Wharf Resources Ltd (Calgary) 1984-, Manchester Ship Canal Co 1985-; fndr chm (now memb exec ctee) Inst for Fiscal Studies, tres Action Resource Centre 1985-; MEP (C) Greater Manchester W 1979-84; *Recreations* listening to music (records), gardening; *Clubs* St James's (Manchester); *Style*— William Hopper, Esq; 23 Great Winchester St, London EC2 (☎ 01 588 4545, telex 8953511)

HOPSON, David Joseph; s of Geoffrey Paul Hopson (d 1980), of Merryways, Newbury, and Nora Winifred, *née* Camp (d 1968); *b* 26 Feb 1929; *Educ* St Bartholomews GS Newbury; *m* 1 June 1957, Susan, da of Horace Caleb George Buckingham (d 1965); 2 s (Jonathan Joseph b 13 March 1960, Christopher Ian b 9 April 1963); *Career* RN 1946-49; chm: Camp Hopson 1966 (dir 1961), Newbury Bldg Soc 1986- (dir 1963); *Recreations* fly fishing; *Clubs* Fly Fishing, Winnowing, Twenty; *Style*— David Hopson, Esq; The Vineyard, Gdn Close Lane, Newbury, Berks; Camp Hopson & Co Ltd, 6-12 Northbrook St, Newbury, Berks RG13 1DN (☎ 0635 523 523, fax 0635 529 009)

HOPWOOD, Prof Anthony George; s of George Hopwood (d 1986), of Stoke-on-Trent, and Violet, *née* Simpson (d 1986); *b* 18 May 1944; *Educ* Hanley HS, LSE (BSc), Univ of Chicago (MBA, PhD); *m* 31 Aug 1967, Caryl, da of John H Davies (d 1981), of Ton Pentre, Mid Glam; 2 s (Mark J b 1971, Justin D b 1974); *Career* lectr in mgmnt accounting Manchester Business Sch 1970-73, sr staff Admin Staff Coll Henley-on-Thames 1973-75, visiting prof of mgmnt European Inst for Advanced Studies Mgmnt Brussels 1972-, professorial fell Oxford Centre for mgmnt studies 1976-78, ICA prof of accounting and fin reporting London Business Sch 1978-85, visiting distinguished prof of accounting Pennsylvania State Univ 1983-88, Arthur Young prof of int accounting and financial mgmnt LSE 1985-; pres Euro Accounting Assoc 1977-79 and 1987-88, American Accounting Assoc distinguished int lectr 1981, John V Ratcliffe Meml lectr Univ of NSW 1988; memb: mgmnt and industl rels ctee SSRC 1975-79; *Books* An Accounting System and Managerial Behaviour (1973), Accounting and Human Behaviour (1974), Essays in British Accounting Research (with M Bromwich, 1981), Auditing Research (with M Bromwich and J Shaw, 1982), Accounting Standard Setting: An International Perspective (with M Bromwich, 1983), European Contributions to Accounting Research (with H Schreuder, 1984), Issues in Public Sector Accounting (with C Tomkins, 1984), Research and Current Issues in Management Accounting (with M Bromwich, 1986), Acccounting from the Outside (1989), Internationa Pressures for Accounting Change (1989); *Style*— Prof Anthony Hopwood; Dept of Accounting and Fin, London Sch of Econs and Political Sci, Houghton St, London, WC2A 2AE (☎ 01 405 7686, telex 24655 BLPES G)

HOPWOOD, Prof David Alan; s of Herbert Hopwood (d 1963), of Lymm, Cheshire, and Dora, *née* Grant (d 1972); *b* 19 August 1933; *Educ* Purbrook Park Co HS Hants, Lymm GS Cheshire, Univ of Cambridge (MA, PhD), Glasgow Univ (DSc); *m* 15 Sept 1962, Joyce Lilian, da of Isaac Bloom (d 1964), of Hove, Sussex; 2 s (Nicholas Duncan b 1964, John Andrew b 1965), 1 da (Rebecca Jane b 1967); *Career* John Stothert bye-fell Magdalene Coll Cambridge 1956-58, univ demonstrator and asst lectr in botany Cambridge Univ 1957-61, res fell St John's Coll Cambridge 1958-61, lectr in genetics Univ of Glasgow 1961-68, John Innes prof genetics UEA and head genetics dept John Innes Inst 1968-; hon prof Chinese Acad Med Sciences (Insts of Microbiology and Plant Physiology) 1987; memb: Genetical Soc of GB 1957 (pres 1984-87), Euro Molecular Biology Orgn 1984, Academia Europaea 1988; hon memb Spanish Microbiological Soc 1985, for fell Indian Nat Sci Acad 1987; *Recreations* fishing, gardening; *Style*— Prof David Hopwood; 244 Unthank Rd, Norwich NR2 2AH (☎ 0603 53488); John Innes Inst, Colney Lane, Norwich NR4 7UH (☎ 0603 52571, fax 0603 56844, telex 975122)

HORAM, John Rhodes; s of Sydney Horam, of Preston, Lancs; *b* 7 Mar 1939; *Educ* Silcoates Sch Wakefield, St Catharine's Coll Cambridge; *m* 1, 1977, Iris Crawley; m 2, 1987, Judith Jackson; *Career* former fin journalist: Financial Times, The Economist; contested (Lab) Folkestone and Hythe 1966, MP (Lab 1970-81, SDP 1981-83) Gateshead West; parly under-sec tport 1976-79, oppn spokesman econ affrs 1979-81, SDP econ spokesman 1981-83; joined Cons Pty Feb 1987; md: Commodities Res Unit Ltd 1983-87 (jt md 1968-70), CRU Hldgs Ltd 1988-; *Style*— John Horam, Esq; 6 Bovingdon Rd, London SW6 2AP

HORDEN, Prof John Robert Backhouse; s of Henry Robert Horden (d 1950), of Warwicks, and Ethel Edith, *née* Backhouse (d 1970); *Educ* Christ Church Oxford, Pembroke Coll Cambridge, Heidelberg, Sorbonne, Lincoln's Inn; *m* 10 Jan 1948, Aileen Mary, da of Col Walter John Douglas, TD (d 1949), of Warwicks and S Wales; 1 s (Peregrine b 1955); *Career* former: tutor and lectr Christ Church Oxford, dir inst of bibliography and textual criticism Leeds Univ, Centre for Bibliographical Studies Stirling Univ; Cecil Oldman Meml lectr 1971, Marc Fitch Prize 1979, devised new academic discipline of publishing studies Leeds Univ 1972, initiated first Br degree in PR Stirling Univ 1987; Golf: represented England, Warwicks, Oxford, Cambridge and Br Univs; hon degree Doctor of Humane Letters Indiana State Univ 1974; FSA, FRSL; *Books* Francis Quarles A Bibliography (1953), Quarles' Hosanna and Threnodes (1960), English and Continental Emblem Books (22 vols 1968-74), Everyday Life in Seventeenth Century England (1974), John Freeth (1985); *Recreations* golf, music, painting; *Clubs* Athenaeum; *Style*— Prof John Horden; Centre for Bibliographical Studies, University of Stirling, Stirling FK9 4LA (☎ 0786 73171 ext 2362)

HORDER, Dr John Plaistowe; CBE (1980, OBE 1971); s of Gerald Morley Horder (d 1939), and Emma Ruth, *née* Plaistowe (d 1971); *b* 9 Dec 1919; *Educ* Lancing, Univ Coll Oxford (BA, MA), London Hosp Med Coll (BM, BCh); *m* 20 Jan 1940, Elizabeth June, da of Maurice Wilson (d 1924); 2 s (Timothy John b 1943, William Morley b 1950), 2 da (Annabelle Mary b 1945, Josephine Elizabeth b 1953); *Career* GP London 1951-81, conslt to expert ctee World Health Orgn 1960-61, travelling fell 1964 and 1984, Jephcott visiting prof Univ of Nottingham; RCGP: pres 1979-82, chm educn ctee 1967-70, John Hunt fell 1973-76, Woltson prof France and Belgium; RSM: pres section of gp, hon fell 1982, vice pres 1987-89; visiting fell King Edward's Hosp Fund 1983-86, visiting prof Royal Free Hosp Med Sch 1983-; Hon MD Free Univ Amsterdam 1985, hon memb The Canadian Coll of Family Practice 1981, hon fell Green Coll Oxford 1988-, FRCGP 1970, FRCP 1972, FRCPsych 1980, FRCP (Ed) 1981; *Books* The Future General Practitioner (jtly and ed 1972), 14 Prince's Gate (jtly 1987); *Recreations* playing the piano, painting water-colours; *Style*— Dr John Horder, CBE; 98 Regent's Pk Rd, London NW1 (☎ 01 722 3804); The Royal Free Hosp Med Sch, Pond St, London NW3 (☎ 01 794 0500 ext 4294)

HORDER, 2 Baron (UK 1933); Sir Thomas Mervyn Horder; 2 Bt (UK 1923); s of 1 Baron Horder, GCVO, DL (d 1955); *b* 8 Dec 1910; *Educ* Winchester, Trinity Coll Cambridge; *m* 6 July 1946 (m dis 1957), Mary Ross, yr da of Dr William Scott McDougall, of Wallington, Surrey; *Heir* none; *Career* served WWII, RAF Fighter Cmd, Air HQ India and SEAC, Wing Cdr RAFVR; chm Gerald Duckworth and Co 1948-70; *Books* The Little Genius - a Memoir of the first Lord Horder (1966), Six Betjeman Songs (1967), On Their Own - Shipwrecks and Survivals (1988), Seven Shakespeare Songs (1988); *Style*— The Rt Hon Lord Horder; c/o Gerald Duckworth and Co, 43 Gloucester Cres, London NW1 7DY

HORDERN, Maj John Richard; s of Rev Richard Lynch Hordern (d 1969), and Nancy Letitia, *née* Travis; *b* 20 Jan 1941; *Educ* Hurstpierpoint Coll, RMA Sandhurst; *Career* army career 1959-85, Royal Regt of Fus, served Hong Kong, BAOR, Aden, Canada, UN Cyprus, Ireland; emergency planning offr W Oxfordshire Dist Cncl 1985-86; regnl organiser (West) Royal Cwlth Soc for the Blind; MBIM; *Style*— Maj John Hordern; 42 Cooper Rd, Westbury-on-Trym, Bristol, Avon B59 3RA (☎ 0272 629652)

HORDERN, Sir Michael Murray; CBE (1972); s of Capt Edward Hordern, CIE, RIN; *b* 3 Oct 1911; *Educ* Brighton Coll; *m* 1943, Grace Eveline, da of Dudley Mortimer; 1 da; *Career* served Nat Serv RNVR, Atlantic, Med, Indian and Pacific Oceans, Lt Cdr; actor; hon fell Queen Mary Coll London Univ; Hon DLitt: Exeter Univ 1985, Warwick Univ 1987: kt 1982; *Recreations* fishing; *Clubs* Garrick, Flyfishers'; *Style*— Sir Michael Hordern, CBE

HORDERN, Peter Maudslay; MP (C) Horsham 1983-; s of C H Hordern, MBE; *b* 18 April 1929; *Educ* Geelong GS Australia, Ch Ch Oxford; *m* 1964, Susan Chataway; 2 s, 1 da; *Career* former memb London Stock Exchange; dir: Alliance Investmt Co, Petrofina (UK) and Atlas Electric and Gen Tst; MP (C): Horsham 1964-74, Horsham and Crawley 1974-83; *Style*— Peter Hordern, Esq, MP; 55 Cadogan St, London SW3

HORE, Anthony Richard Benedict; MBE (1975); s of Henry Herbert Hore, JP (d 1965), of Holmsley Lodge, Burley, Hants, and Alma, *née* Kellner (d 1976); *b* 21 Mar 1926; *Educ* Cheltenham Coll, Magdalene Coll Cambridge (MA); *m* 17 Feb 1953, Marigold Eileen Desmond, da of Maj-Gen Walter Reginald Paul, CBE (d 1953), of Firhill, Totland Bay, IOW; 1 da (Victoria Philippa Caroline b 1954); *Career* London C of C 1951-67 (head, overseas dept 1964-67); chief exec East Euro Trade Cncl 1967-86; Silver Nedal of the Order of Merit of the Polish People's Republic (1984), Star Order with Golden Wreath of the Hungarian People's Republic (1986); *Recreations* music, gardening, sailing; *Style*— Anthony Hore, Esq, MBE; Lane End, Hookley Lane, Elstead, Surrey GU8 6JE (☎ 0252 703 328)

HORLICK, Vice Adm Sir Ted Edwin John; KBE (1981); s of late Edwin William Horlick; *b* 1925; *Educ* Bedford Modern Sch, RN Engineering Coll; *m* 1953, Jean Margaret, da of Herbert Covington; 4 s; *Career* Vice Adm 1979, Chief Naval Engr Offr 1979-83, dir-gen ships MOD (Navy) 1979-83, ret; FEng,FIMechE, MIMarE; *Recreations* golf, gardening; *Clubs* Army and Navy; *Style*— Vice Adm Sir Ted Horlick, KBE; 33 Church St, Weston, Bath BA1 4BU

HORLICK, James Cunliffe William; s and h of Sir John James Macdonald Horlick, 5 Bt; *b* 19 Nov 1956; *Educ* Eton; *m* 1985 Fiona Rosalie, *née* McLaren; 1 s (Alexander b 1987); *Career* co dir; *Clubs* Beefsteak; *Style*— James Horlick, Esq; Merlin House, 79 St James's Drive, London SW17 7RP; 31 Clareville St, London SW7

HORLICK, Sir John James Macdonald; 5 Bt (UK 1914), of Cowley Manor, co Gloucester; s of Lt-Col Sir James Nockells Horlick, 4 Bt, OBE, MC, (d 1972); *b* 9 April 1922; *Educ* Eton, Babson Inst of Business Admin Wellesley Hills Mass USA; *m* 1948, June, da of Douglas Cory-Wright, CBE; 1 s, 2 da; *Heir* s, James Cunliffe William Horlick; *Career* served WWII, Coldstream Gds, Capt; dep chm Horlicks Ltd 1968-72, ptnr Tournaig Farming Co 1973-, chm Highland Fish Farmers 1978-85; *Recreations* military history, model soldiers; *Clubs* Beefsteak; *Style*— Sir John Horlick, Bt; Tournaig, Poolewe, Achnasheen, Ross-shire (☎ 044 586 250); Howberry Lane Cottage, Nuffield, nr Nettlebed, Oxon (☎ 0491 641454)

HORLOCK, Henry Wimburn Sudell; s of Rev Dr Henry Darell Sudell Horlock, DD (d 1953), and Mary Haliburton, *née* Laurie (d 1953); *b* 19 July 1915; *Educ* Pembroke Coll Oxford (MA); *m* 21 July 1960, Jeannetta Robin, da of Frederick Wilfred Tanner,

JP (d 1958), of The Towers, Farnham Royal, Bucks; *Career* WWII Army 1939-42; civil serv 1942-60; fndr and dir Stepping Stone Sch 1962-87, memb Ct of Common Cncl 1969-, Sheriff City of London 1972-73, dep Ward of Farrington Within 1978-; chm: City of London Sheriffs' Soc 1985-, West Ham Park Ctee 1979-82, Police Ctee 1987-; memb: Farringdon Ward Club 1970- (pres 1978-79), Utd Wards Club 1972- (pres 1980-81), City Livery Club 1969- (pres 1981-82), Guild of Freemen 1972- (Master 1986-87), Royal Soc of St George (City of London branch) 1972- (vice chm 1988-89); Freeman City of London 1937-; Liveryman Worshipful Co of: Saddlers 1937 (Master 1976-77), Parish Clerks 1966 (Master 1981-82), Fletchers 1977, Gardeners 1980; Cdr Order of Merit Federal Repub of Germany 1972, Cdr Nat Order of Aztec Eagle of Mexico 1973, Cdr Du Wissam Aloulite of Morocco 1987; *Recreations* travel, country persuits; *Clubs* Athenaeum, Guildhall, City Livery; *Style—* Wimburn Horlock, Esq; Copse Hill House, Lower Slaughter, Glos GL54 2HZ (☎ 0451 20276); 97 Defoe House, Barbican, London EC2Y 8DN (☎ 01 588 1602)

HORLOCK, Dr John Harold; s of Harold Edgar Horlock (d 1971), of Tonbridge, Kent, and Olive Margaret Horlock (d 1989); *b* 19 April 1928; *Educ* Edmonton Latymer Sch, St John's Coll Cambridge (MA, PhD, ScD); *m* 8 June 1953, Sheila Joy, da of Percy Kendolph Stutely (d 1980), of Hordle, Hants; 1 s (Timothy John b 4 Jan 1958), 2 da (Alison Ruth (Mrs Heap) b 20 April 1955, Jane Margaret (Mrs Spencer) b 28 Nov 1961); *Career* design engr with Rolls Royce 1949-51; res fell St John's Coll Cambridge 1954-57; prof of mechanical engrg Univ of Liverpool 1958-67, prof of engrg Cambridge Univ 1967-74; Vice-Chllr: Salford Univ 1974-80, Open Univ 1981-; dir SRC turbomachinery laboratory Cambridge Univ 1971-74, memb SRC 1974-77, chm ARC 1979-80; dir: BL Technol Ltd 1979-87, Br Engine Insur Ltd 1979-86, Open Univ Educnl Enterprises Ltd; memb Engrg Cncl 1982-84, vice-pres Royal Soc 1982-84; chm Advsy Ctee on Safety of Nuclear Installations 1984-; Hon DSc Salford 1981, Hon DSc Univ of E Asia 1985, Hon DEng Liverpool 1987; FRS 1976, FEng 1977, CBIM 1985, FIMechE, FRAeS; *Books* Axial Flow Compressors (1958), Axial Flow Turbines (1967), Actuator Disc Theory (1978), Cogeneration (1987) ; *Recreations* music, golf; *Clubs* Athenaeum, MCC; *Style—* Dr John Horlock; The Open University, Walton Hall, Walton, Milton Keynes, Bucks MK7 6AA (☎ 0908 274066)

HORN, Hon Mrs (Angela Ierne Evelyn Dixon); *née* Dixon; da of late 1 Baron Glentoran; *b* 1907; *m* 1, 1929, Lt Cdr Peter Ross, RN (ka 1940), eldest s of Una Mary, Baroness de Ros, 26 holder of the peerage (d 1956) 2 da (incl late Georgina Angela, Baroness de Ros, *see* de Ros, 28 Baron); m 2, 1943 Lt Col Trevor Langdale Horn, MC, 16/5 Lancers (d 1966); 1 da (June Victoria Langdale b 1946); *Style—* The Hon Mrs Horn; Luckington Court, Chippenham, Wilts

HORN, Prof Gabriel; s of Abraham Horn (d 1946), of Birmingham, and Anne, *née* Grill (d 1976); *b* 9 Dec 1927; *Educ* Univ of Birmingham (BSc, MB ChB, MD), Univ of Cambridge (MA, ScD); *m* 1, 29 Nov 1952 (m dis 1979), Hon Anne Loveday Dean, da of Baron Soper (Life Peer), *qv*, of London; 2 s (Nigel b 1954, Andrew b 1960), 2 da (Amanda b 1958, Melissa b 1962); m 2, 30 Aug 1980, Priscilla, da of Edwin Victor Barrett (d 1976), of Cape Town; *Career* educn branch RAF 1947-49; Univ of Cambridge: demonstrator and lectr in anatomy 1956-72, reader in neubiology 1972-74, prof of zoology 1978, head dept of zoology 1979, fell King's Coll 1962-74 and 1978; visiting prof Univ of California Berkeley USA 1963, visiting prof of zoology Makerere Univ Coll Uganda 1966, prof of anatomy and head of dept Univ of Bristol 1974-77, distinguished visiting prof Univ of Alberta 1988, visiting Miller prof Univ of California Berkeley 1989; memb: biological scis advsy panel and ctee Scientific Res Cncl 1970-75, res ctee Mental Health Fndn 1973-78, advsy bd Inst of Animal Physiology Cambridge 1980-85; pubns in various scientific journals; FRS 1986, FInst Biology 1978; *Books* Memory, Imprinting and the Brain (1985); *Recreations* riding, cycling, walking, listening to music, wine and conversation; *Style—* Prof Gabriel Horn; Jack of Clubs Barn, Fen Rd, Lode, Cambridgeshire CB5 9HE (☎ 0223 812 229), Univ of Cambridge, Department of Zoology, Downing St, Cambridge CB2 3EJ (☎ 0223 336 601, fax 0223 336 676, telex 81240 CAMSPL G)

HORN, Dr George; s of George Horn, MM (d 1937), of 5 Endcliffe Vale Ave, Sheffield, and Theodora, *née* Mason (d 1977); *b* 10 April 1928; *Educ* King Edward VII Sheffield, Univ of Sheffield (BSc, PhD, DSc); *m* 28 July 1951, Doreen, da of Edward Nash (d 1971), of Sheffield; 2 s (Christopher b 30 Oct 1954, Nicholas b 18 Jan 1957); *Career* 2 Lt 19 Air Formation Signal Regt Royal Signals 1948-49; res engr GEC atomic energy div 1955-58, head of thermodynamics section CEGB Marchwood Engrg Laboratories 1958-65, head of engrg div GEGB Berkeley Nuclear Laboraties 1965-70, dep chm Ireland Alloys (Hldgs) Ltd 1983 (gp tech dir 1970-89); author of over 40 scientific and tech papers; chm advsy ctee dept of chemical engrg and fuel technol Univ of Sheffield 1989-; FInst E 1963, CEng 1968, MIMechE 1968, MInstMet 1975, AIME 1984; *Recreations* cricket, swimming, skiing; *Style—* Dr George Horn; 10 Fountain Craig, 1010 Gt Western Rd, Glasgow G12 0NR (☎ 041 334 1635); Ireland Alloys (Hldgs) Ltd, P O Box 18, Hamilton, Scotland ML3 0EL (☎ 0698 822 246, fax 0698 825 167)

HORN, Hon Mrs (Mary Clare); *née* Douglas-Scott-Montagu; da of 2 Baron Montagu of Beaulieu, KCIE, CSI (d 1929); *b* 9 June 1928; *m* 1, 1953 (m dis 1968), David Bethune, Viscount Garnock (later 15 Earl of Lindsay); 1 s (Viscount Garnock, *qv*), 1 da (Lady Caroline Wrey, *qv*); m 2, 1979, Timothy Charles Austin Horn; *Style—* The Hon Mrs Horn; Chapel House, Builth Wells, Powys (☎ 098 23 236)

HORNAK, Lady Patricia Sybil; *née* Douglas; da of 11 Marquess of Queensberry (d 1954); *b* 1918; *m* 1, 1938 (m dis 1950), Capt Count John Gerard de Bendern; 1 s, 2 da; m 2, 1954 (m dis 1960), Herman Hornak; 2 s; *Style—* Lady Patricia Hornak; 36 St James's Rd, Tunbridge Wells, Kent

HORNALL, Capt Robert William; DFC (1945); s of Archibald Hornall (d 1945), of Hamilton, Scotland, and Constance, *née* Troughton (d 1974); *b* 3 Nov 1922; *Educ* Hamilton Acad, Univ of Southampton; *m* 6 July 1945, Betty, da of Capt Sydney Arthur Farrow (d 1936), of Canvey Island, Essex; *Career* RAF 1940, awarded Wing's Moose Jaw Canada 1942, Fighter Cmd 1 Sqdn Acklington, Biggin Hill, Lympne, Martlesham Heath 1942-44, 245 Sqdn 2 TAF France, Belgium, Holland, Fl-Cdr 184 Sqdn 2 TAF Holland, Germany 1944-45, instr Ops Trg Unit 1945-46, demob 1946; Fl-Capt African routes Hunting-Clan 1947-55, sr vice-pres M East Airlines 1957-64 (ops mangr 1955-57), master air pilot 1965; bd of dirs SITA 1958-64, memb tech ctee IATA 1959-64, special prod support exec Hawker Siddeley Aviation 1964-80, Br Aerospace 1980-86; tstee Amersham CC; memb; Amersham Soc, Thames & Chiltern C of C; Freeman City of London 1978, Liveryman Worshipful Co of Air Pilots and Air Navigators 1978; *Recreations* golf, rugby, racing, cricket; *Clubs* Bucks Co Rugby, Middx Co CC, RAF; *Style—* Capt Robert Hornall, DFC; 27 Whielden St, Old Amersham, Bucks HP7 OHU (☎ 0494 724728); Troika Consortium Ltd, 56 Abbey Gdns, London NW8 9AT (☎ 01 625 4597, fax 01 372 6056, telex 295528 FOSTAS G)

HORNBY, Derrick Richard; s of Richard Wittingham Hornby (d 1964); *b* 11 Jan 1926; *Educ* Southampton; *m* 1948, June, da of Nathaniel Steele (d 1963); *Career* md Edenvale (Express Dairy) 1968; chm: Carrington Viyella 1980, Spillers Foods Ltd 1973; *Recreations* golf, salmon fishing; *Clubs* Wentworth, Nat Sporting; *Style—* Derrick Hornby, Esq; 26a Shawfield St, Chelsea, London SW3 (☎ 01 352 6862)

HORNBY, John Fleet; s of John Fleet Hornby, of Cumbria, and Marion, *née* Charnley (d 1981); *b* 23 Dec 1945; *Educ* Dowdales Sch; *m* 1976, Elizabeth, da of John Chorley, of Cumbria; 1 s (Paul b 1978); *Career* dir: James Fisher and Sons plc 1981-, Shamrock Shipping Co Ltd 1981-, Thomas Jack Shipping Ltd 1981, Westfield Shipping Co Ltd 1982; Onesimus Dorey (shipowners) Ltd (Guernsey) 1983-, Venisol Shipping Corpn 1984-, COE Metcalf Shipping Ltd 1984, Alexanders Ptnrs (shipbrokers) Ltd 1986-, Anchorage Ferrying Servs Ltd 1986-, Project Shipping Services Ltd 1987-; *Recreations* walking, gardening, travel; *Clubs* Royal Overseas; *Style—* John Hornby, Esq; Hillside, Guards Rd, Lindal, nr Ulverston, Cumbria LA12 0TN (☎ 0229 65614); Fisher House, Barrow-in-Furness, Cumbria LA14 1HR (☎ 0229 22323, telex 65163, fax 0229 36761)

HORNBY, Richard Phipps; el s of Rt Rev Hugh Leyester Hornby, MC (d 1965), sometime Suffragan Bp of Hulme (whose maternal grandmother Vere was da of Robert Gosling, DL, of Botley's Park Surrey, by Robert's w Georgina, da of Rt Hon John Sullivan and Lady Henrietta Hobart, 2 da of 3 Earl of Buckinghamshire), and Katherine Rebecca May (d 1979); *b* 20 June 1922; *Educ* Winchester, Trinity Coll Oxford (MA); *m* 1951, Stella, da of William Lionel Hichens, of North Aston Hall, Oxon; 3 s (John b 1954, Patrick b 1958, Simon b 1960), 1 da (Juliet b 1956); *Career* served WWII KRRC; asst master (history) Eton 1948-50; contested (C) Walthamstow W 1955 and 1956; MP (C) Tonbridge 1956-74, pps to Duncan Sandys 1959-63, parly under-sec CRO and Cwlth Off 1963-64; with Unilever 1951-52; dir: J Walter Thompson 1974-81 (joined 1952), Cadbury Schweppes plc 1982-, McCorquodale plc 1982-; chm Halifax Bldg Soc 1983- (vice-chm 1981-83, dir 1976-); former memb: gen advsy cncl BBC, exec ctee Br Cncl; *Recreations* most country pursuits, shooting, fishing, deer-stalking, hill walking, bird watching; *Clubs* Brooks's; *Style—* Richard Hornby, Esq; 10 Hereford Sq, London SW7

HORNBY, Sir Simon Michael; er s of Michael Charles St John Hornby (d 1987), of Pusey House, Faringdon, and Nicolette Joan, *née* Ward (d 1988); *b* 29 Dec 1934; *Educ* Eton, New Coll Oxford; *m* 15 June 1968, (Ann) Sheran, da of Peter Victor Ferdinand Cazalet, of Fairlawne, Shipbourne, Kent; *Career* 2 Lt Grenadier Gds 1953-55; joined W H Smith 1958: merchandise dir 1968, retail dir 1974, retail md 1977, gp chief exec 1978, chm 1982; dir: Pearson plc 1978, Lloyds Bank plc 1988; memb: RSA Cncl 1985-, exec ctee Nat Tst 1966- (property ctee 1979-86, cncl 1976-); tstee British Museum 1975-85; chm: Nat Book League 1978-80, Design Cncl 1986-; Freeman and Liveryman Worshipful Co of Goldsmiths 1955-; FBIM, FRSA; kt 1988; *Recreations* golf, gardening, music; *Clubs* Garrick; *Style—* Sir Simon Hornby; Lake House, Pusey, Faringdon, Oxon SN7 8QB; 8 Ennismore Gdns, London SW7 1NL; office, Strand House, 7 Holbein Place, London SW1W 8NR (☎ 01 730 1200; fax 01 730 1200 ext 5563, telex 887777 WHS G

HORNBY PRIESTNALL, Cdr (Thomas) Keith; VRD (1963 and Clasp 1975); s of Rev Thomas Hornby Priestnall (d 1956), and Norah Hayward (d 1961); *b* 22 June 1925; *Educ* Burton Sch, Univ of Nottingham; *m* 2 Sept 1982, Gillian Christine, da of Police Supt William Edward Thomas Hinckley (d 1977), of Staffords; 1 da (Daniella b 1959); *Career* Cdr RNR, served WWII Midget Subs (X Craft); md and chm Salesprint and Display Ltd and Salesprint Temple Gp Ltd 1963-83, chm Peel House Publicity 1983-; vice-pres: E Midland Areas C of C, Allied Brewery Traders Assoc; dir: Brewery Traders Pubns Ltd, Brewing and Distilling Int, Peel House Promotional Prods Ltd; assoc dir DCL Advertising; memb Inst of Brewing; *Recreations* riding, bird watching, sailing; *Clubs* Naval and Military, Army and Navy, The Burton, Inst of Dirs; *Style—* Cdr Keith Hornby Priestnall, VRD; The Old Rectory, Kedleston, Derbys (☎ 0332 841515); Peel House, Burton-upon-Trent, Staffs (☎ 0283 66784)

HORNE, Alistair Allan; s of late Sir (James) Allan Horne, and Auriol Camilla, *née* Hay; *b* 9 Nov 1925; *Educ* Jesus Coll Cambridge (MA), Le Rosey Switzerland, Millbrook USA; *m* 1953 (m dis 1982), Renira Margaret, da of Adm Sir Geoffrey Hawkins, KBE, CB, MVO, DSC; 3 da; m 2, 1987, Sheelin Ryan Eccles; *Career* served RAF 1939-44, Coldstream Gds 1944-47, Capt attached to Intelligence Serv (ME); for corr Daily Telegraph 1952-55; founded Alistair Horne Res Fellowship in Modern History St Antony's Coll Oxford 1969 (supernumerary fell 1978-88, hon fell 1988-), fell Woodrow Wilson Centre Washington DC, USA 1980-81; memb: Mgmnt Ctee Royal Literary Fund 1969-, Franco-Br Cncl 1979-, ctee of mgmnt Soc of Authors 1979-81; tstee Imperial War Museum 1975-82; FRSL; *Publications* Back into Power (1955), The Land is Bright (1958), Canada and the Canadians (1961), The Price of Glory: Verdun 1916 (1962, Hawthornden Prize 1963), The Fall of Paris: The Siege and the Commune 1870-71 (1965), To Lose a Battle: France 1940 (1969), Death of a Generation (1970), The Terrible Year: The Paris Commune (1971), Small Earthquake in Chile (1972), A Savage War of Peace: Algeria 1954-62 (1972), Yorkshire Post Book of the Year Prize 1978, Wolfson Literary Award 1978, Napoleon Master of Europe 1805-07 (1979), The French Army and Politics 1870-1970 (1984), Macmillan 1894-1956, Vol I (1988), and contributions to a number of books and various periodicals; *Recreations* skiing, gardening, painting, travel; *Clubs* Garrick, Beefsteak; *Style—* Alistair Horne, Esq; 21 St Petersburgh Place, London W2

HORNE, Christopher Frederic; s of Frederic Thomas Horne, of Herts, and Madeleine Horne; *b* 25 June 1945; *Educ* Watford, Eton; *m* 12 Jan 1974 (m dis) Anne Margaret, da of George Henry Woodfield (d 1984); 1 s (Richard b 1979); *Career* CA, private practice Christopher Horne and Co 1969-88 (merged with Murrays May 1988); chm Highway Planning Ctee; Parly candidate: (C) Manchester 1974, Meriden 1974; memb London Borough of Hammersmith 1968-71; *Recreations* cricket, football, steam locomotives, bridge; *Clubs* MCC, Naval; *Style—* Christopher Horne, Esq; P O Box 296, Hemel Hempstead, Herts HP3 9RP

HORNE, Christopher Malcolm; s of Gerald Fitzlait Horne (d 1970), and Dora, *née* Hartley; *b* 14 June 1941; *Educ* King Edward VI Chelmsford; *m* 12 Sept 1964, Christine Ann, da of Reginald Arthur Fradley (d 1985); 2 s (Darren James b 7 Feb 1968, Alec Gerald b 20 Jan 1970); *Career* Coutts & Co 1958-: assoc dir 1980-89, head personnel 1980-88, sec of Bank 1988-, sr assoc dir 1989-; memb Vines Rochester URC; MIPM 1970, MInstD; *Recreations* golf, gardening, interest in most sports; *Clubs* Rochester & Cobham Park GC; *Style*— Christopher Horne, Esq; Silver Birches, 151 Maidstone Rd, Chatham, Kent ME4 6JE (☎ 0634 47594); Coutts & Co, 440 Strand, London WC2R 0QS (☎ 01 379 6262)

HORNE, David Oliver; s of Herbert Oliver Horne, MBE (d 1946), and Edith Marion, *née* Sellers (d 1963); *b* 7 Mar 1932; *Educ* Fettes; *m* 6 June 1959, Joyce Heather, da of Lt-Col Gordon Bryson Kynoch, CBE, TD, of Skara Brae, Broomhill Rd, Keith, Banffshire, Scotland; 2 s (Richard b 24 July 1962, Douglas b 9 April 1970), 2 da (Angela b 23 May 1960, Susan b 2 June 1965); *Career* dir: S G Warburg & Co Ltd 1966-70, Williams & Glyns Bank 1970-78 Lloyds Bank Int 1978-85; chm and chief exec Lloyds Merchant Bank 1988- (md 1985-87); FCA 1958; *Recreations* golf; *Style*— David Horne, Esq; Four Winds, 5 The Gdns, Esher, Surrey (☎ 0372 63510); 40-66 Queen Victoria St, London EC4P 4EL (☎ 01 248 2244, fax 01 329 6057, car 0860 344882, telex 926291)

HORNE, Frederic Thomas; s of Lionel E Horne, JP (d 1953), of Gloucs, and Hilda Marsh, *née* Vaughan (d 1970); *b* 21 Mar 1917; *Educ* Chipping Campden GS; *m* 1944, Madeline, *née* Hatton; 2 s, 2 da; *Career* RAFVR 1939-55; slr 1938, memb Lord Chancellors Advsy Ctee on Legal Aid; co-ed The Supreme Ct Practice 1988, contrib Atkins Ct Forms (14 edn), ed Cordery on slrs (8 edn); chief Taxing Master of the Supreme Ct 1983-; *Recreations* archaeology, cricket, grandchildren; *Clubs* MCC; *Style*— Frederic Horne, Esq; Dunstall, Quickley Lane, Chorleywood, Herts

HORNE, Geoffrey Norman; s of Albert Edward Horne (d 1982), of Berks, and Doris Irene, *née* Blackman; *b* 7 Feb 1941; *Educ* Slough GS, Open Univ (BA); *m* 1, 1967 (m dis 1977), Barbara Ann Mary; 1 s (Rupert b 1971); m 2, 1980, Davina Dorothy, da of David Lockwood London, of Dyfed; 2 s (Edward b 1984, Richard b 1986); *Career* advertising; sr writer: CDP 1973-74, Davidson Pearce Berry and Spottiswoode 1974-77, Saatchi and Saatch 1985-88; creative dir KMP Partnership 1977-84, head creative gp Grandfield Rork Collins 1984-85; bd dir: KMP Partnership 1978-84, Grandfield Rork Collins 1984-85, Saatchi and Saatchi 1985; over 50 advertising awards incl: Br Advertising Press Awards, D and AD Assoc Awards, NY One Show, Br Advertising TV Awards, The Creative Circle; MIPA, MCAM; *Recreations* cooking, reading, travel; *Style*— Geoffrey Horne, Esq; Pine Ridge, 46 Altwood Rd, Maidenhead, Berks

HORNE, Sir (Alan) Gray Antony; 3 Bt (UK 1929), of Shackleford, Surrey; s of Antony Edgar Alan Horne (d 1954); only s of 2 Bt, Sir Alan Edgar Horne, MC, who died 1984), and Valentine Antonia, da of Valentine Dudensing, of Thenon, Dordogne, France and 55 East 57th St, New York City; *b* 11 July 1948; *Heir* none; *Style*— Sir Gray Horne, Bt; Château du Basty, Thenon, Dordogne, France

HORNE, Mark John Fraser; s of Maj Ian Hunter Horne, of Kelso, Roxburghshire, and Honor Nancy, *née* Humphries; *b* 5 August 1948; *Educ* The Oratory Sch, Heriot-Watt Univ Edinburgh; *m* 20 May 1976, Elizabeth Mary, da of Lt-Col Gwyn William Morgan-Jones (d 1964), of Tetbury, Gloucs; 1 s (Archie b 1985); *Career* owner of General Printing Co, previously dir M W Marshall (Int Money Brokers); *Recreations* racing (steward), tobogganing, shooting, fishing; *Clubs* White's, St Moritz Tobogganing; *Style*— Mark J F Horne, Esq; Laundry Farm, Adbury, nr Newbury, Berks; 55 Flood St, Chelsea, London SW3; Midleton Estate, Guildford, Surrey

HORNE, Dr Nigel William; s of Eric Charles Henry Horne (d 1963), and late Edith Margaret, *née* Boyd; *b* 13 Sept 1940; *Educ* Lower Sch of John Lyon Harrow, Univ of Bristol (BSc), Univ of Cambridge (PhD); *m* 30 Oct 1965, Jennifer Ann, da of William Henry Holton (d 1988); 1 s (Peter b 1970), 2 da (Catherine b 1967, Joanna b 1973); *Career* dir and gen mangr GEC Telecommunications Ltd 1976-81, md GEC Info Systems Ltd 1981-83; dir: corporate devpt STC plc 1983-, Abingworth plc 1985-; chm infor technol advsy bd DTI 1988-, memb esprit advsy bd Euro Cmmn; Freeman City of London, memb Guild of Info Technologists; FIIM 1979, FENG 1982, FIEE 1984, FRSA 1983; *Recreations* piano, music, gardening; *Clubs* Utd Oxford and Cambridge; *Style*— Dr Nigel Horne; STC plc, 10 Maltravers St, London WC2R 3HA (☎ 01 836 8055, car tel 0836 220011)

HORNER, (William) Noel (Arthur); s of William Arthur Horner, MBE (d 1984), of Derbys, and Kitty Barbara, *née* Tonkin; *b* 25 Dec 1942; *Educ* various GS's, Univ of Manchester (LLB); *m* 25 March 1967, Margaret Jean, da of Wilfred Teed Tayler (d 1978), of Exeter, Devon; 1 s (Julian b 1970), 3 da (Sally b 1968, Anna b 1978, Natasha b 1980); *Career* slr 1969; ptnr: Amery Parkes and Co London 1969-72, Chellews St Ives 1973-77; princ Noel Horner 1977-; chllr Diocese of Damaraland-in-exile 1977-81; represented families of 2 deceased lifeboatmen at Penlee Lifeboat Enquiry 1983; ind Parly candidate St Ives 1983; *Recreations* music, history; *Clubs* Wig and Pen; *Style*— Noel Horner, Esq; c/o 73 Lemon St, Truro, Cornwall TR1 2PN (☎ 0872 71305)

HORNER, Stephen John; s of Harold Wallington Horner (d 1966), and Edith Harriet, *née* Spencer (d 1984); *b* 11 May 1944; *Educ* Radley; *m* 1968, Susanne Helen, da of John Basil Hancock (d 1983), 2 s (Simon Wallington b 1971, Edward John b 1975); *Career* fin dir: Agar Cross & Co Ltd 1977-80, dir Westland Helicopters 1980-84, mangr aerospace div Midland Bank plc 1984-88, chief exec London Bridge Aviation 1988-; FCA, FBIM; *Recreations* fishing, farming, genealogy; *Clubs* Thames Rowing; *Style*— Stephen Horner Esq; Old Woodhayne Farm, Bishopswood, nr Chard, Somerset (☎ 046 034 342);

HORNSBY, Alan Kenneth; s of Harold Ernest Hornsby (d 1984), and Clarice Winifred Wilson (d 1979); *b* 17 Oct 1929; *Educ* Buckhurst Hill County HS; *m* 3 April 1954, Audrey Constance, da of Joseph Lister Brown (d 1967); 3 s (Trevor b 1957, Neil b 1958, Paul b 1961), 2 da (Julie b 1961, Alison b 1963); *Career* fin dir Smiths Industs plc 1976-; FICA, fell Inst of Treasurers; *Recreations* tennis, golf; *Clubs* West Herts Tennis, West Herts GC; *Style*— Alan Hornsby, Esq; Smiths Industries plc, 765 Finchley Rd, Childs Hill, Finchley, London NW11 8DS (☎ 01 458 3232, telex 925761)

HORNSBY, Dr Bevé; da of Lt Leonard William Hodges, RNAS (d 1917); *b* 13 Sept 1915; *Educ* St Felix Sch Southwold Suffolk, Univ of London (MSc, PhD), Univ Coll N Wales (M Ed); *m* 1, 14 July 1939, Capt Jack Myddleton Hornsby (d 1975), s of Maj Frederick Myddleton Hornsby, CBE (d 1931), of Millfield, Stoke D'Abernon, Surrey; 3 s (Michael b 1942, Peter b 1943, Christopher b 1948), 1 da (Julie b 1947); m 2, 21 Dec 1976 (m dis 1986), John Hillyard Tennyson Barley; *Career* ambulance driver FANY and Mechanised Tport Corps 1939-42, Pilot Civil Air Gd 1938-39; head of speech therapy clinic Kingston 1969-71, head of remedial teaching St Thomas's Hosp 1970-71, teacher World Blind Clinic St Bart's Hosp 1969-71, head dyslexia dept St Barts Hosp 1971-80, dir Hornsby Centre for Learning Difficulties 1980-, princ Hornsby House Sch 1987-; govr All Farthing Primary Sch Wandsworth, memb Wandsworth Common Mgmnt Ctee; hon fell: Coll of Speech Therapist 1988, Br Dyslexia Assoc 1987; MCST, ABPSS 1983; *Books* Alpha to Omega - The A to Z of Teaching Reading, Writing and Spelling (1974), Alpha to Omega Flash Cards (1975), Overcoming Dyslexia (1984), Before Alpha - A Pre-Reading Programme for the Under-Fives (1989), Alpha to Omega Fun Book (1989); *Recreations* riding, sailing, golf, reading, walking, theatre, music; *Clubs* Royal Wimbledon GC; *Style*— Dr Bevé Hornsby; 39 Ovington St, London SW3 2JA (☎ 01 584 4799); The Hornsby Centre, 71 Wandsworth Common Westside, London SW18 2ED (☎ 01 871 2691/1092, fax 01 924 1668)

HORNSBY, Lady Elizabeth Anne Mary (Rufus); *née* Isaacs; da of 2 Marquess of Reading, GCMG, CBE, MC, TD, PC, QC, and Hon Eva Mond, CBE, JP, da of 1 Baron Melchett; *b* 11 Oct 1921; *m* 1945, Maj Derek Hornsby (d 1971), s of Maj Frank Hornsby (d 1935), and Hon Muriel Strutt, yst da of 2 Baron Belper, JP, DL; 2 s (Richard, Gerald m 1980 Maria Lara; 1 s Simon b 1983, 1 da Rachael b 1982; David Julian m 1975 Julie Ann Witford; 3 s (Alexander b 1977, Samuel b 1985 Michael b 1987); *Career* Jr Cdr ATS WWII; *Style*— Lady Elizabeth Hornsby; Flat K, 19 Warwick Sq, London SW1 (☎ 01 821 7051)

HORNSBY, Timothy Richard; s of Harker William Hornsby (d 1973), and Agnes Nora Phillips; *b* 22 Sept 1940; *Educ* Bradfield, Ch Ch Oxford (MA); *m* 1971, Charmian Rosemary, da of Frederick Cleland Newton, of Weybridge; 1 s (Adrian b 1978), 1 da (Gabrielle b 1975); *Career* res lectr Christ Church Oxford 1964-65, HM Treasy 1971-73, dir ancient monuments historic bldgs and rural affrs DoE 1983-; *Recreations* skiing; *Clubs* Athenaeum; *Style*— Timothy Hornsby, Esq; Dept of Environment, 2 Marsham St, London SW1 (☎ 01 212 4025)

HORNYOLD, Antony Frederick; Marchese (of the Habsburg cr, and of the Papal cr) di Gandolfi (Emperor Charles V 1529, Pope Leo XIII 1895), Duca di Gandolfi (Pope Leo XIII 1899); s of Ralph Gandolfi-Hornyold (d 1938), s of Thomas Gandolfi-Hornyold, cr *Marchese* Gandolfi by Pope Leo XIII 1895 and *Duca* 1899, Thomas being in his turn s of John Vincent Gandolfi-Hornyold (12 *Marchese* di Gandolfi, of the cr of Emperor Charles V of 1529, according to Ruvigny), whose mother Teresa was sis of Thomas Hornyold, then sr male rep of the old Hornyold recusant family (Teresa and Thomas's aunt by marriage was Mrs Fitzherbert, whom George IV, when Prince of Wales, m in contravention of the Royal Marriages Act); *b* 20 June 1931; *Educ* Ampleforth, Trinity Coll Cambridge; *Heir* bro, Simon Hornyold (b 11 Feb 1933, educ Ampleforth, residence: 271 Sandycombe Rd, Richmond, Surrey); *Career* For Off 1957-67 (1 sec Rawalpindi 1966-67), MOD 1967-; Kt of SMO Malta; *Style*— Antony Hornyold, Esq; Blackmore House, Hanley Swan, Worcester WR8 0ES (☎ 0684 310202)

HORNYOLD-STRICKLAND, Angela Mary; *née* Engleheart; DL (1988); da of Francis Henry Arnold Engleheart (d 1963), and Filumena Mary, *née* Mayne (d 1983); *b* 31 May 1928; *Educ* New Hall Convent, St Mary's Convent Ascot; *m* 20 Jan 1951, Lt Cdr Thomas HenryHornyold-Strickland, RN, 7 Count della Catena (d 1983), s of Henry Hornyold-Strickland (d 1975), of Kendal, Cumbria; 4 s (Henry b 1951, Robert b 1954, John b 1956, Edward b 1960), 2 da (Clare b 1953, Alice b 1959); *Career* pres: Br Red Cross Soc Westmorland 1972-74, Cumbria 1974-; vice pres Cumbria Assoc of Boys' Clubs 1975-; DL Cumbria 1988; *Clubs* Naval and Military; *Style*— Mrs Thomas Hornyold-Strickland (Dowager Countess della Catena), DL; Sizergh Castle, Kendal, Cumbria (☎ 05395 60285)

HORNYOLD-STRICKLAND, 8 Count Della Catena (Malta 1745) Henry Charles; s of Lt Cdr Thomas Henry Hornyold-Strickland, DSC, RN, 7 Count della Catena (d 1983), of Sizergh Castle, Kendal, Cumbria, and Angela Mary, *née* Engleheart; *b* 15 Dec 1951; *Educ* Ampleforth, Exeter Coll Oxford (BA), INSEAD Fontainebleau (MBA); *m* 1979, Claudine Thérèse, da of Clovis Poumirau, of Etche Churia, Av Des Piballes, Hossegor 40200, France; 2 s (Hugo b 1979, Thomas b 1985); *Career* ind mgmnt conslt 1984-; former mgmnt conslt Arthur D Little Ltd (1977-84), product support planning engr Rolls Royce Ltd (1973-76); dir: Allied Newspapers Ltd (Malta) 1988, Progress Press (Malta) 1988; Kt of Honour and Devotion SMOM 1977; *Style*— Henry Hornyold-Strickland, Esq (Count della Catena); 56 Ladbroke Rd, London W11 3NW (☎ 01 229 1949); Sizergh Castle, Kendal, Cumbria LA8 8AE (☎ 05395 60285)

HORRELL, John Ray; CBE (1979), TD (1960), DL (Hunts and Peterborough 1973); s of Harry Ray Horrell (d 1963), of Westwood, Peterborough, and Phyllis Mary, *née* Whittome; *b* 8 Mar 1929; *Educ* Wellingborough Sch; *m* 26 March 1951, Mary Elizabeth (Betty) Noëlle, da of Arthur Thomas Dickinson (d 1984), of Northorpe Hall, nr Gainsborough; 1 s (Peter Geoffrey Ray b 23 Feb 1952), 1 da (Judith Carolyn (Mrs Drewer) b 23 April 1954); *Career* Maj TA (ret); farmer; dir: Horrell's Farmers Ltd, Horrell's Dairies Ltd; memb Cambs (formerly Huntingdon and Peterborough) CC 1965- (chm 1971-77); chm: ACC 1981-83, E E Anglia TAVR Assoc 1986-, E of England Agric Soc 1984-87; memb Peterborough New Town Devpt Corpn 1969-, md East Anglia RHA Health Authy 1986-; FRSA; *Recreations* country pursuits; *Clubs* Farmers'; *Style*— John Horrell, Esq; The Grove, Longthorpe, Peterborough, Cambs PE3 6LZ (☎ 0733 262618)

HORRELL, Roger William; CMG (1988), OBE (1974); s of William John Horrell (d 1980), and Dorice Enid, *née* Young; *b* 9 July 1935; *Educ* Shebbear Coll, Exeter Coll Oxford (MA); *m* Nov 1970 (m dis 1975), Patricia Mildred Eileen Smith, *née* Binns; 1 s (Oliver b 1972), 1 da (Melissa b 1973); *Career* Nat Serv Devonshire Regt 1953-55; Overseas Civil Serv Kenya 1959-64; Dip serv: FCO 1964, econ offr Dubai 1965-67, FCO 1967-70, Kampala 1970-73, FCO 1973-76, Lusaka 1976-80, cnsllr FCO 1980-; *Recreations* walking, bridge, reading, cricket spectator; *Clubs* Reform; *Style*— Roger Horrell, Esq, CMG, OBE; c/o FCO, King Charles St, London SW1 (☎ 01 270 3000)

HORROCKS, Peter Leslie; s of Arthur Edward Leslie Horrocks, of Beaconsfield, Bucks, and Phillis Margaret Chiene, *née* Bartholomew; *b* 31 Jan 1955; *Educ* Winchester, Trinity Hall Cambridge (MA); *Career* barr Middle Temple 1977 and Lincoln's Inn 1987, in private practice 1978-; cncl memb: the Sherlock Holmes soc of London, 1984-87, Royal Stuart Soc 1987-; Freeman City of London 1982; FRAS 1984; *Recreations* travel, real tennis, cricket, Sherlock Holmes, opera, collecting books, dancing the minuet; *Clubs* MCC, Roy Tennis Court; *Style*— Peter Horrocks, Esq; 22 Old Buildings, Lincoln's Inn, London WC2A 3UJ (☎ 01 831 0222, car tel 0860 536 073, fax 01 831 2239, telex 883500 CICERO G)

HORROCKS, Raymond; CBE (1983); s of Cecil Horrocks (d 1933), and Elsie Horrocks; *b* 9 Jan 1930; *Educ* Bolton Municipal Secdy Sch, Wigan Technical Coll, Univ of Liverpool; *m* 1953, Pamela Florence, *née* Russell; 3 da (Susan, Lynn, Raina); *Career* HM Forces Army Intelligence Corps 1948-50; mgmnt trainee Textile Indust (Bolton and Manchester) 1950-51, sales rep Proctor and Gamble 1951-52, merchandiser Marks and Spencer 1953-58, buying controller Littlewoods Mail Order Stores 1958-63, mangr Ford Motor Co 1968-72 (depot mangr replacement parts 1963, mangr warranty and customer rels 1964, mangr car supply 1965, divnl mangr engine and special equipment operations 1966), regnl dir (Europe and ME) Materials Handling Gp 1972-77, chm and chief exec BL Cars Ltd 1981-82 (dep md 1977-78, chm and md Austin Morris Ltd 1978-80, md BL Cars 1980-81, bd of dirs BL Cars Ltd 1981-); chm: Unipart Gp Ltd 1981-86, Jaguar Cars Hldgs Ltd 1982-84; chm and chief exec ARG Hldgs Ltd 1981-, dir Nuffield Servs Ltd 1982-; non-exec dir: The Caravan Club 1983-, Jaguar plc 1984-85, Image Interiors (Wessex) Ltd 1985-; memb: CBI Cncl 1981-86, CBI Europe Ctee 1985-86; tstee Br Motor Ind Heritage Tst 1983-; chm: Exide Europe 1986-, Owen Ball Ltd 1987-; FIMI, CBIM, FRSA; *Recreations* fly fishing, steam trains, gardening, caravanning; *Style*— Ray Horrocks, Esq, CBE; Far End, Riverview Rd, Pangbourne, Reading, Berks RG8 7AU; BL plc, 106 Oxford Rd, Uxbridge, Middlesex UB8 1EH (☎ 0895 51177, telex 264654)

HORROX, Alan Stuart; s of Stanley Horrox, and Gudrun Horrox; *b* 3 Jan 1947; *Educ* St Johns Leatherhead, Christ Coll Cambridge ; *m* Viveka Britt Inger, da of Torsten Nyberg, of Fdllinge, Sweden; 2 da (Anna Helga b 1981, Katarina b 1983); *Career* prodr-dir: childrens' progs BBC, educn progs, dramas and documentaries Thames TV (cncllr children's and educn dept 1986-); televised work incl: Our People, Small World, Accidental Death of an Anarchist, A Foreign Body, Voices in the Dark, The Belle of Amherst, Rose, The Gemini Factor, Catherine; The Thief, Young Charlie Chaplin, Cora, Brief Lives; Int Emmy 1987, Special Jury Award at the San Francisco Film Festival 1988, Special Prize for fiction at the Prix Europa 1988; memb BAFTA; *Style*— Alan S Horrox, Esq; Thames TV, 149 Tottenham Ct Rd, London W1 (☎ 01 387 9494)

HORSBRUGH-PORTER, Sir John Simon; 4 Bt (UK 1902), of Merrion Sq, City and Co of Dublin; s of Col Sir Andrew Marshall Horsbrugh-Porter, DSO, 3 Bt (d 1986); *b* 18 Dec 1938; *Educ* Winchester, Trinity Coll Cambridge; *m* 18 July 1964, Lavinia Rose, 2 da of Ralph Meredyth Turton, of Kildale Hall, Whitby; 1 s (Andrew), 2 da (Anna b 1965, Zoe b 1967); *Heir* s, Andrew Alexander Marshall b 1971; *Career* served Nat Serv, 2 Lt 12 Lancers (Germany and Cyprus) 1957-59; schoolmaster; *Recreations* hunting, gliding, music, literature; *Style*— Sir John Horsbrugh-Porter, Bt; Bowers Croft, Coleshill, Amersham, Bucks HP7 SLO (☎ 024 03 4596)

HORSBRUGH-PORTER, Mary, Lady (Annette) Mary; *née* Browne-Clayton; o da of Brig-Gen Robert Clayton Browne-Clayton, DSO; *b* 28 April 1908; *Educ* Cheltenham Ladies Coll; *m* 21 April 1933, Col Sir Andrew Marshall Horsbrugh-Porter, 3 Bt, DSO and Bar (d 1986); 1 s (Sir John Simon, 4 Bt, b 1938), 2 da (Susan b 1936, Caroline Elaine, b 1940); *Recreations* gardening, writing; *Style*— Mary, Lady Horsbrugh-Porter; Lime Close, Lower Park St, Stow-on-the-Wold, Gloucs

HORSEMAN, Richard; s of Edwin Victor Horseman (d 1963), and Helen Horseman (d 1964); *b* 2 Nov 1929; *Educ* Alcester GS (NDA, CDA); *m* 20 March 1954, Heather, da of Eric Winter, JP (d 1987); 4 da (Jane b 1955, Elizabeth b 1956, Dorothy b 1958, Wendy b 1961); *Career* experimental offr Agric Res Cncl 1964-66, mangr SW area Fisons Gp 1966-78, md Int Furniture Agencies 1979-; Malaya Medal 1954; *Recreations* fishing, wine tasting, travel; *Style*— Richard Horseman, Esq; Glebe Hse, Aller, Langport, Somerset TA10 0QW; International Furniture Agencies (☎ 0836 512309, telex 46529, fax 0823 259526)

HORSEY, Gordon; s of Edgar William Horsey, MBE, and Henrietta Victoria Horsey; *b* 20 July 1926; *Educ* Magnus GS, St Catharine's Coll Cambridge (BA, LLB); *m* 8 June 1951, Jean Mary, da of Harold Favill; 1 da (Rebecca Jane b 12 Dec 1957); *Career* WWII Naval Airman RN 1944-45, Capt RE 1946-48; slr in private practice 1953-70; registrar: Coventry County Ct 1971-73, Leicester County Ct 1973-, rec Crown Ct 1978-84; memb Law Soc; *Recreations* fly fishing; *Style*— Gordon Horsey, Esq; 23 The Ridgeway, Rothley, Leics LE7 7LE (☎ 0533 302545)

HORSFALL, Edward John Wright; s and h of Sir John Musgrave Horsfall, MC, TD, 3 Bt; *b* 17 Dec 1940; *Educ* Uppingham; *m* 1965, Rosemary, da of Frank N King, of East Morton, Keighley; 3 s; *Style*— Edward Horsfall Esq; Long Thatch, Uffington, Faringdon, Oxon SN7 7RP

HORSFALL, Sir John Musgrave; 3 Bt (UK 1909), MC (1946), TD (1949, and clasp 1951), JP (N Yorks 1959); s of Sir (John) Donald Horsfall, 2 Bt (d 1975); *b* 26 August 1915; *Educ* Uppingham; *m* 1940, Cassandra Nora Bernardine, da of late George Wright, of Brinkworth Hall, Elvington, York; 2 s, 1 da; *Heir* s, Edward Horsfall; *Career* late Maj Duke of Wellington's (W Riding) Regt, served 1939-45 War in Burma (MC); Lloyds underwriter; *Style*— Sir John Horsfall, Bt, MC, TD, JP; Greenfield House, Embsay, Skipton, N Yorks (☎ Skipton 4560)

HORSFIELD, Maj-Gen David Ralph; OBE; s of Maj Ralph Beecroft Horsfield (d 1966), and Morah Susan Stuart, *née* Baynes (d 1980); *b* 17 Dec 1916; *Educ* Oundle, RMA Woolwich, Univ of Cambridge (MA); *m* 1948, Sheelah Patricia Royal, da of Thomas George Royal Eagan (d 1970); 2 s (Crispin b 1952, Hugo b 1955), 2 da (Antonia b 1954, Claudia b 1957); *Career* cmmnd Royal Signals 1936, WWII served in Egypt, Burma, Assam, India; cmd Burma Corps Signals 1942, instr Staff Coll Quetta 1944-45, cmd 2 Indian Airborne div Signals 1946-47, instr RMA Sandhurst 1950-53 (co cmd to HM King Hussein of Jordan), cmd 2 div Signal Regt 1956-59, princ Army Staff Offr MoD Malaya 1959-61, dir Telecommunications (army) 1966-68, ADC to HM The Queen 1968-69, dep Communications and Electronics Supreme HQ Allied Powers Europe 1968-69, Maj-Gen 1969, chief Signal Offr BAOR 1969-72 (ret); dir Rollalong Ltd 1965-76, assoc consit PA Mgmnt Consits 1972-87; vice-pres Nat Ski Fdn; MIOD; *Recreations* house and garden, skiing, (Br Champion 1949); *Clubs* Ski Club of Great Britain, Hawks; *Style*— Maj Gen David Horsfield, OBE; Southill House, Cranmore, Shepton Mallet, Somerset BA4 4QS (☎ 074 988 395)

HORSFIELD, Dr Dorothy; da of Cyril Gordon Horsfield (d 1968), and Mabel, *née* Berry (d 1981); *b* 24 Nov 1932; *Educ* Crossley and Porter Sch Halifax, Royal Free Hosp Sch of Med London (MBBS); *Career* sr house offr pathology Royal Free Hosp 1960-61, registrar clinical pathology Guy's Hosp 1963-66, lectr chemical pathology Nat Hosp for Nervous Diseases 1963-73, sr registrar chemical pathology Hammersmith Hosp 1976-77, conslt chemical pathology Barnsley Dist Gen Hosp 1978-; memb: conservation projects The Countryside Cmmn, York County Stand York Racecourse, Country Landowners Assoc, Yorks Agric Soc, NFU; MRCS, LRCP, FRSM 1963, ACP 1967, BMA 1979, FRC Path 1984; *Recreations* organic and compassionate farming, needlework, race meetings, music; *Style*— Dr Dorothy Horsfield; Holly Farm, New Brighton, Birdsedge, Huddersfield, W Yorkshire (☎ 0484 606 561); Dept of Chemical Pathology, Barnsley District General Hospital, Barnsley, S Yorkshire (☎ 0226 730 000)

HORSFIELD, (Thomas Norman) Roger; TD (1970, and two clasps 1976, 1982); s of Norman Horsfield (d 1968); *b* 21 Feb 1936; *Educ* Barrow GS, Univ of Manchester; *m* 1962, Ann, da of James William Evans, Wolverhampton; 1 s, 1 da; *Career* md Ayrton Saunders (Midland) Ltd; vice-pres and hon tres PATA; MIDPM, MPS, FBIM 1984 1984;; *Recreations* shooting; *Clubs* RAC, English XX Bisley; *Style*— Roger Horsfield, Esq, TD; 31 Fields Drive, Sandbach, Cheshire CW11 9EX; Ayrton Saunders (Midland) Ltd, Wilson Rd, Huyton, Liverpool L36 6AH

HORSFORD, Alan Arthur; s of Arthur Henry Horsford, and Winifred; *b* 31 May 1927; *Educ* Holt Sch, Univ of Liverpool (BA); *m* 1957, Enid Maureen, *née* Baker; 1 s (Jeffrey Alan b 1958), 1 da (Margaret Claire b 1963); *Career* gp chief exec Royal Insur Hldg plc 1985-89 (dir 1979); gen mangr Royal Insur Canada 1974-79; dep chm Assoc of Br Insurers 1985-88; *Style*— Alan Horsford, Esq; Royal Insurance plc, 1 Cornhill, London EC3V 3QR (☎ 01 283 4300, telex 8955701, fax 01 623 5282)

HORSFORD, Cyril Edward Sheehan; CVO (1984); s of Cyril Arthur Bennett Horsford (d 1953), of 24 Harley St, London W1, and Edith Louise, *née* Sayers (d 1987); *b* 13 Mar 1929; *Educ* Marlborough, Clare Coll Cambridge (MA); *m* 31 Aug 1957, Susan Frances, da of Francis Randall Hugh Bolton (d 1937), of London; 1 s (Simon b 1958); *Career* 2 Lt RA 1948-49; barr Inner Temple 1953, clerk of arraigns Centl Criminal Ct Old Bailey 1954-56, sr asst Inner London Sessions 1956-68, dep asst registrar of Criminal Appeals 1968-74, dep clerk of Privy Cncl 1974-89; vice pres Medico Legal Soc of London 1988; dir Int Inst of Space Law 1961-72, Andrew G Haley Award for contrib to Space Law (Warsaw) 1964; Freeman City of London 1970; FBIS 1973; *Books* Assize and Quarter Sessions Handbook (1958); contrib: 4 edn Halsbury's Laws of England, Journal of Criminal Law, Criminal Law Review, Solicitors Journal; *Recreations* amateur theatre, flyfishing; *Style*— Cyril Horsford, Esq, CVO; 32 Prairie St, London SW8 3PP (☎ 01 622 5984)

HORSFORD, Maj-Gen Derek Gordon Thomond; CBE (1962, MBE 1953), DSO (1944, and bar 1945); s of Capt Harry Thomond Horsford (d 1963), of Crowborough, and Violet Edith, *née* Inglis (d 1989); *b* 7 Feb 1917; *Educ* Clifton Coll, RMC Sandhurst; *m* 1948, Sheila Louise Russell, da of Capt Norman Stuart Crawford; 1 s (Ian b 1948), 1 step s (George b 1939), 2 step da (Joanna b 1942, Gail b 1945); *Career* cmmnd 8 Gurkha Rifles 1937, Cdr 4/1 Gurkha Rifles Burma 1944-45 (Lt Col), instr Staff Coll 1950-52, GSO1 2 Inf Div 1955-56, Cdr 1 Bn The Kings Regt 1957-59, AAG AG2 WO 1959-60 (Col), Cdr 24 Inf Bde Gp 1960-62 (Brig), IDC 1963, Brig Gen Staff HQ BAOR 1964-66, GOC 50 (Northumbrian) Div/Dist 1966-67 (Maj-Gen), GOC Yorks Dist 1967-68, GOC 17 Div Malaya Dist 1969-70, Dep Cdr Land Forces Hong Kong 1970-71, Col The Kings Regt 1965-70, Col The Gurkha Tport Regt 1973-78; ret 1972 (Maj-Gen); tst dir RCN Devpt tst 1972-75, sec League of Rememberance 1978-; *Recreations* travel; *Clubs* Army And Navy; *Style*— Maj-Gen Derek Horsford, CBE, DSO

HORSHAM, Archdeacon of; *see* Filby, The Ven William Charles Leonard

HORSHAM, Bishop of 1975-; Rt Rev Ivor Colin Docker; s of Col Philip Docker, OBE, TD, DL (d 1965), and Doris Gwendoline, *née* Whitehill (d 1975); *b* 3 Dec 1925; *Educ* King Edwards HS Birmingham, Univ of Birmingham (BA), St Catherine's Coll Oxford (MA); *m* 1950, Thelma Mary, da of John William Upton (d 1974); 1 s (Stephen b 1957), 1 da (Susan b 1953); *Career* vicar of Midhurst 1959-64; vicar and rural dean: Seaford 1964-71, Eastbourne 1971-75; chm C of E Nat Cncl of Soc Aid 1987-; *Recreations* photography, travel; *Style*— The Rt Rev the Bishop of Horsham; Bishop's Lodge, Worth, Crawley, W Sussex RH10 4RT (☎ 0293 883051)

HORSLEY, Very Rev Alan Avery; s of Reginald James Horsley, of Staffs, and Edith Irene, *née* Allen; *b* 13 May 1936; *Educ* Worcester Royal GS, Northampton GS, St Chad's Coll Durham (BA), The Queen's Coll at Birmingham Birmingham Univ, Pacific Western Univ (MA, PhD); *Career* curate: Daventry 1960-63, St Giles Reading 1963-64, St Paul Wokingham 1964-66; vicar St Andrew Yeadon 1966-71, Rector Heyford with Stowe-Nine-Churches 1971-78, rural Dean Daventry 1976-78, vicar Oakham with Hambleton and Egleton 1978-86 (with Braunston and Brooke from 1980-), non-residentiary canon Peterborough 1979-86, Canon Emeritus 1986-, vicar Lanteglos-by-Fowey 1986-88, provost of St Andrew's Cathedral Inverness 1988-; *Style*— The Very Rev Dr Alan Avery; The Cathedral Rectory, 15 Ardross St, Inverness IV3 5NS (☎ 0463 233535)

HORSLEY, Lady Angela Leslie; *née* Courtenay; da of late 16 Earl of Devon; *b* 1918; *m* 1947, Harold Cecil Moreton Horsley, MBE, Malayan Civil Service (ret) (d 1969); 2 s; *Style*— Lady Angela Horsley; Marwood House, Offwell, Honiton, Devon EX14 9RW

HORSLEY, Christopher Peter Beresford; s of Air Marshall Sir Peter Horsley, KBE, LVO, AFC, and Lady (Phyllis) Horsley; *b* 12 August 1944; *Educ* Wellington, Inst of Science & Technol Univ of Manchester (BSc); *m* 18 June 1973, Simone Jane, da of James Wood, MBE; 1 s (James Peter b 1976), 3 da (Kate Louise b 1974, Joanna Marie b 1980, Camilla b 1985); *Career* RAFVR 1965-68; euro mktg mangr Bell Helicopter 1970-74, md Aerogulf Dubai 1975-78; chm: Arabian Aviation Corpn Bahrain 1979-86, RCR Int Ltd 1986-; advsr Br Aerospace plc 1989; chm Tangmere Flight Spitfire Mk X1; *Recreations* ski-ing, fishing, flying; *Clubs* Oriental, RAF; *Style*— Christopher Horsley, Esq; RCR Int Ltd, RCR House, Segensworth West, Hants PO15 5TD

HORSLEY, (George) Nicholas (Seward); s of Alec Stewart Horsley, of Hessle, E Yorks, and Ida Susan Seward; *b* 21 April 1934; *Educ* Keswick GS, Bootham Sch York, Univ of Oxford (BA); *m* 1, 1958 (m dis 1975), Valerie, *née* Edwards; 2 s, 1 da; m 2, 1975, Sabita, *née* Sarkar; *Career* chm Northern Foods plc; chm BBC Industl and Consultative Ctee 1981-83; pres Dairy Trade Fedn 1975-77 and 1980-85; *Recreations* classical music, reading, watching cricket, keen bridge player, memb CND; *Style*— Nicholas Horsley Esq; Welton Lodge, 2 Dale Rd, Welton, nr Brough, E Yorks (☎ 0482 668341); 30 Clarges St, London W1; Northern Foods plc, Beverley House, St Stephens Sq, Hull, E Yorks HU1 3XG (☎ 0482 25432, telex 597149 NFOODS G)

HORSLEY, Air Marshal Sir (Beresford) Peter (Torrington); KCB (1974), CBE (1964), LVO (1956), AFC (1945); s of late Capt Arthur Beresford Horsley, CBE; *b* 26 Mar 1921; *Educ* Wellington; *m* 1, 1943 (m dis 1976), Phyllis Conrad Phinney; 1 s, 1 da; m 2, 1976, Ann MacKinnon, da of Gareth Crwys-Williams; 2 step s, 2 step da; *Career* joined RAF 1940, serv 2 TAF and Fighter Cmds; equerry to Princess Elizabeth and to the Duke of Edinburgh 1949-52, equerry to HM The Queen 1952-53, equerry to the Duke of Edinburgh 1953-56; Asst CAS (Ops) 1968-70, AOC No 1 Bomber Gp 1971-73, Dep C-in-C Strike Cmd 1973-75, ret 1975; (chm: ML Hldgs plc, Nat Printing Ink Co Ltd; dir: ML Aviation Co Ltd, Ml Aerospace and Def Ltd, ML Wallop Def Systems Ltd, IDS Aircraft Ltd, Horsley Hldgs Ltd, RCR Int Ltd; pres Yorkshire Skiing Ltd, Memb Honeywell Advsy cncl ; *Books* Journal of a Stamp Collector; *Style—* Air Marshal Sir Peter Horsley, KCB, CBE, LVO, AFC; c/o Barclays Bank Ltd, High St, Newmarket

HORSLEY-BERESFORD, Hon Mrs William - Ida Kaye; *m* 1941, as his 4 w, Hon William Arthur de la Poer Horsley-Beresford (d 1949), yst s of 3 Baron Decies d 1983; 1 s, 1 da; *Style—* The Hon Mrs William Horsley-Beresford; 53 Overstrand Mansions, Prince of Wales Drive, SW11

HORT, Andrew Edwin Fenton; s and h of Sir James Fenton Hort, 8 Bt; *b* 15 Nov 1954; *Style—* Andrew Hort, Esq

HORT, Sir James Fenton; 8 Bt (GB 1767), of Castle Strange, Middx; s of Sir Fenton George Hort, 7 Bt (d 1960), and Gwendolene (d 1983), da of late Sir Walter Alcock, MVO; *b* 6 Sept 1926; *Educ* Marlborough, Trinity Coll Cambridge (BA, MB, BChir); *m* 1951, Joan Mary, da of late Edward Peat, of Swallownest, Sheffield; 2 s, 2 da; *Heir* s, Andrew Hort; *Career* medical dir A H Robins Co Ltd; *Style—* Sir James Hort, Bt; Poundgate Lodge, Uckfield Rd, Crowborough, Sussex (☎ 089 26 4470; office, 0293 560161)

HORTON, Clive Fielding; s of Frank Fielding Horton (d 1970), and Hilda Elizabeth, *née* Powell (d 1983); *b* 3 July 1931; *Educ* Dover Coll; *m* 4 April 1959, Wendy Bradley, da of Henry Jordan (d 1983), of Maidstone; 3 da (Jane b 1963, Susan b 1963, Katie b 1966); *Career* cmmnd RA 1954, serv Malaya 1955-56; qualified CA 1954, ptnr DaySmith and Hunter 1958, pres SE Soc of CAs 1972-73, memb cncl ICAEW 1973-77, sr ptnr DaySmith and Hunter 1979-; hon tres Kent Assoc for the Blind, cncl memb Maidstone Hospice Appeal; *Recreations* golf; *Clubs* Royal St Georges GC, Bearsted GC (Capt 1974); *Style—* Clive Horton Esq; 14 Conway Rd, Maidstone, Kent ME16 0HD (☎ 0622 53695); Day Smith and Hunter, Star House, Maidstone, Kent ME14 1LT (☎ 0622 690666)

HORTON, Hon Mrs (Fiona Catherine); *née* Peake; da of 2 Viscount Ingleby; *b* 24 Jan 1955; *Educ* St Mary's Sch Wantage, Univ of Bristol (BA Hons); *m* 23 July 1977, (Gavin) Tobias Alexander Winterbottom Horton, s of Alistair Winterbottom, of Manor Farm House, Brill, Aylesbury and n of Lord Winterbottom; 2 s (George, b 1983, Thomas b 1985), 2 da (Alice b 1978, Violet b 1980); *Career* on editorial staff Antique Collectors Magazine 1976-77; *Recreations* tennis, reading; *Style—* The Hon Mrs Horton; Whorlton Cottage, Swainby, Northallerton, N Yorks DL6 3ER (☎ 0642 700213); 12 Vicarage Gdns, London W8 4AH (☎ 01 229 3871)

HORTON, Mark Anthony; s of Robert Anthony Horton, DFC, of Glanville, Tedburn, St Mary, Exeter, and Hélène, *née* Dubois; *b* 30 Sept 1953; *Educ* Blundells, Univ of Birmingham (LLB); *m* 20 Dec 1986, Madeleine, da of Edward Hunter Curry, of Flat 56, Yola II, Marbella; 1 s (James Anthony b 1987); *Career* called to the Bar 1976, Albion Chambers S Bristol 1977-83, St Johns Chambers Bristol 1983-88; *Recreations* tennis, football; *Style—* Mark Horton, Esq; St Johns Chambers, Small St, Bristol (☎ 0272 213456, fax 294 821)

HORTON, Matthew Bethell; s of Albert Leslie Horton, of Tunbridge Wells, Kent, and Gladys Rose Ellen, *née* Harding; *b* 23 Sept 1946; *Educ* Sevenoaks, Trinity Hall Cambridge (MA, LLM); *m* 1, 22 May 1972 (m dis 1983), Liliane, da of Henri Boleslawski, of Nice, France; 1 s (Jerome b 1971), 1 da (Vanessa b 1973); *Career* barr Middle Temple 1969; private practise specialising in: commercial property law, local govt law, admin law, parly law; memb: ctee Admin Law Bar Assoc, Admin Law Ctee Justice, Ctee Parly Bar Mess, Ctee Jt Planning Law Conf; *Recreations* tennis, skiing, windsurfing; *Style—* Matthew Horton, Esq; 2 Mitre Court Bldgs, Temple, London EC4Y 7BX (☎ 01 583 1380, fax 01 353 7772, car tel 0860 366 529, telex 28916 REDBAG G)

HORTON, Robert Baynes; s of W H Horton (d 1969), of Pangbourne; *b* 18 August 1939; *Educ* Kings Sch Canterbury, Univ of St Andrews (BSc), MIT (SM); *m* 1962, Sally Doreen, da of Edward Wells (d 1971), of Beverley, E Yorks; 1 s, 1 da; *Career* joined BP Co Ltd 1957, gen mangr BP Tanker Co 1975-76 and corporate planning BP 1976-79, md and chief exec BP Chemicals Int 1980-83, md BP plc 1983-86 and 1988- (dep chm 1989-), chm Standard Oil Ohio 1986-88; non-exec dir: ICL plc 1982-84, Pilkington Bros 1985-86, Emerson Electric 1987-; pres Chemical Industs Assoc 1982-84, memb SERC 1985-86, vice chm BIM 1985-; memb: Univ Funding Cncl 1989-, Bd of MIT 1987-, Case Western Reserve Univ 1987-, Cleveland Orchestra 1987-; govr Kings Sch Canterbury 1983-, chm Tate Gallery Fndn 1988-; Hon LLD Dundee 1987; *Recreations* opera, shooting; *Clubs* Carlton, Leander, Union (Cleveland, Ohio); *Style—* Robert Horton, Esq; BP plc, Britannic House, Moor Lane, London EC2Y 9BU (☎ 01 920 8000, telex 888811)

HORTON, Hon Mrs (Susan Elizabeth); da of Baron Donovan (Life Peer, d 1971); *b* 1936; *m* 1960 (m dis 1984), Gerard Francis Horton; issue; *Style—* The Hon Mrs Horton; 27 Weemla Rd, Northbridge, NSW, Australia

HORTON, Toby (Gavin Tobias Alexander); Lord of the Manor of Horton; yr s of Alistair Winterbottom, of Bucks, and Maria Kersti; *b* 18 Feb 1947; *Educ* Westminster, Ch Ch Oxford (MA); *m* 1977, Hon Fiona Catherine Peake, da of 2 Viscount Ingleby; 2 s (George William Arthur b 1983, Thomas Henry Ralph b 1985), 2 da (Alice Emily Rose b 1978, Violet Constance Lily b 1980); *Career* md Radio Tees 1979-83; dir and head of corporate fin dept Minster Tst Ltd 1984-; parly candidate (C) Sedgefield 1983; chm Fndn for Def Studies, vice-chm Families for Defence; vice-pres: Langbaurgh Cons Assoc, Yorks and Northern Branches Nat Soc of Cons and Unionist Agents; FBIM; *Books* Going to Market: New Polity for the Farming Industry (1985); Programme for Reform: a New Agenda for Broadcasting (1987); *Recreations* broadcasting, country pursuits; *Clubs* Buck's, Northern Counties (Newcastle); *Style—* Toby Horton, Esq; Whorlton Cottage, Swainby, Northerllerton, N Yorkshire DL6 3ER (☎ 0642 700213); office, Minster House, Arthur Street, London EC4R 9BH (☎ 01 623 1050, telex 01 623 1471)

HORTON-FAWKES, (George) Nicholas Le Gendre; er s of Maj Le Gendre George Willia Horton-Fawkes, OBE, DL (d 1982), and Sylvia, *née* Duckworth (whose paternal grand mother was Hon Edina Campbell, sis of 2nd and 3rd Barons Stratheden and Campbell, and whose father's 1 cous was Gerald Duckworth, the half-bro of Virginia Woolf); *b* 20 Sept 1925; *Educ* Eton, Trinity Coll Cambridge; *m* 1954, Audrey, da of Welles Bosworth, of Marietta, Seine-et-Oise, France; 3 s (Francis b 1955, William b 1957, John b 1963); *Style—* Nicholas Horton-Fawkes, Esq; Farnley Hall, Otley, W Yorks (☎ 0943 462198)

HORWOOD-SMART, John; s of late William Ogilvy Smart, and late Mabel Louisa Horwood; *b* 21 Oct 1924; *Educ* City of London Sch, Christ's Coll Cambridge (MA); *m* 3 Jan 1948, Sylvia, da of William Young Nutt (d 1926), of Cambridge; 1 s (Adrian Piers b 25 Sept 1953), 1 da (Rosamund (Mrs Blackford) b 21 Sept 1951); *Career* WWII Capt Intelligence Corps in SW Pacific and SE Asia; admitted slr 1951, NP; hon fell Robinson Coll Cambridge, chm Anglo American Rels Ctee RAF Meldenhall Suffolk 1967-72; memb: Law Soc (former pres Cambridge and Dist), Prov Notary Soc; *Style—* John Horwood-Smart, Esq; Rutland Cottage, Cheveley, Newmarket (☎ 0638 730 236); Lushington House, Newmarket, Suffolk (☎ 0638 663571)

HOSFORD-TANNER, (Joseph) Michael; s of late Dr Hubert Hosford-Tanner, of London SW1, and Betty, *née* Bryce; *b* 8 August 1951; *Educ* Midleton Coll, Trinity Coll Dublin (BA, LLB); *Career* called to the Bar Inner Temple 1974, legal assessor Farriers Registration Cncl 1985; *Recreations* horses, cricket, travel; *Clubs* Chelsea Arts, Kildare Street and University; *Style—* Michael Hosford-Tanner, Esq; Queen Elizabeth Building, Temple, London EC4Y 9BS (☎ 01 583 7837, fax 01 353 5422)

HOSKER, Gerald Albery; CB (1987); s of Leslie Reece Hosker (d 1971), and Constance, *née* Hubbard; *b* 28 July 1933; *Educ* Berkhamstead Sch; *m* 1956, Rachel Victoria Beatrice, da of Cdr Clifford Victor Middleton, RINVR (ret); 1 s (Jonathan Edward George b 1961), 1 da (Helen Bridget b 1958); *Career* admitted slr 1956, assoc Faculty of Secretaries and Admins 1964, legal asst Treasy Slrs Dept 1960; Treasy: snr legal asst 1966, asst slr 1973, princ asst slr 1980, dep 1982, slr DTI 1987-; FRSA (1964); *Clubs* Royal Cwlth Soc; *Style—* Gerald Hosker, Esq, CB, FRSA

HOSKIN, Ernest Jabez; s of Jabez Edmund Hoskin (d 1957), of Elmside Hse, Elmside, Exeter, and Eva Maud, *née* Anstey; *b* 15 Sept 1920; *Educ* Heles Sch Exeter; *m* 14 Nov 1946, (Hilda) Joyce, da of William Arthur Mawhinney (d 1936), of Torquay and Belfast; 1 s (Peter b 17 Sept 1948); *Career* Gunner 163-55 LAA Regt TA 1939, serv: France, Norway, Ceylon, cmmnd 1 Punjab Regt IA 1943, Lt 1944, Capt (Adj) 1944, Actg Maj 1945, served India and Burma, demob 1946; City Treasurer's Off Exeter 1938-49, sr inspr HM Customs and Excise 1949-79 (represented UK at customs and indirect taxation ctees of EEC 1974-79); led EEC delgn (indirect taxation) to Andean GP 1979-80 to promote a common market between: Peru, Bolivia, Ecuador, Colombia, Venezuela; registrar Vat Tbnls for the UK 1980-83, vat conslt Deloitte Haskins & Sells 1983-, managing conslt ed Vat Intelligence 1985-; Freeman City of London 1980, memb Worshipful Co of Blacksmiths 1980; FTII 1986; *Books* Community Law and UK Vat (1988), Appealing to a Vat Tribunal (1989); *Recreations* gardening, genealogy, golf; *Style—* Ernest Hoskin, Esq; Woodhayes, 76A The Ave, Beckenham, Kent BR3 2ES (☎ 01 650 8530)

HOSKING, Barbara Nancy; OBE (1985); William Henry Hosking (d 1963), and Ada Kathleen, *née* Murrish (d 1951); *b* 4 Nov 1926; *Educ* West Cornwall Sch for Girls, Hillcroft Coll; *Career* Civil Serv 1965-77, press offr 10 Downing St 1970-72, private sec to Parly Secs Cabinet Off 1973-75; controller info servs IBA 1977-86, former pres Media Soc, occasional broadcaster and writer, conslt Yorkshire TV; jt vice chm Nat Cncl of Voluntary Organisations; FRSA 1984; FRTS 1988; *Recreations* opera, Lieder, watching politics; *Clubs* Reform; *Style—* Miss Barbara Hosking, OBE; 8 Highgate Spinney, Crescent Rd, London N8 8AR (☎ 01 340 1853); Yorkshire Television, 32 Bedford Row, London WC1R 4HE (☎ 01 242 1666)

HOSKING, Eric; OBE (1977); s of Albert Hosking (d 1945), of London, and Margaret Helen Steggall (d 1975); *b* 2 Oct 1909; *Educ* Stationers' Company London; *m* 1939, Dorothy, da of Harry Sleigh (d 1959), of London; 2 s (Robin, David), 1 da (Margaret); *Career* self employed; *Publications incl:* Intimate Sketches from Bird Life (1940), The Art of Bird Photography (1944), Birds of the Day (1944), Birds of the Night (1945), More Birds of the Day (1946), The Swallow (1946), Masterpieces of Bird Photography (1947), Birds in Action (1949), Birds Fighting (1955), Bird Photography as a Hobby (1961), Nesting Birds, Eggs and Fledglings (1967), An Eye for a Bird (autobiography 1970), Wildlife Photography (1973), Minsmere (1977), Birds of Britain (1979), Eric Hosking's Birds (1979), Eric Hosking's Owls (1982), Eric Hosking's Waders (1983), Eric Hosking's Seabirds (1983), Eric Hosking's Wildfowl (1985), Antarctic Wildlife (1982), Just a Lark (1984), An Encyclopedia of Bible Animals (1986), Which Bird (1986), Eric Hosking's Birds of Prey (1987), illustrator of many books on natural history; *Recreations* travel, music, reading; *Style—* Eric Hosking, Esq, OBE; 20 Crouch Hall Rd, London N8 8HX (☎ 01 340 7703)

HOSKING, Prof Geoffrey Alan; s of Stuart William Stegall Hosking, of 7 Conway Rd, Maidstone, Kent, and Jean Ross, *née* Smillie; *b* 28 April 1942; *Educ* Maidstone GS, King's Coll Cambridge (BA), Moscow State Univ, St Anthony's Coll Oxford, Univ of Cambridge (MA, PhD); *m* 19 Dec 1970, Anne Lloyd Hirst; 2 da (Katya b 1974, Janet b 1978); *Career* lectr Univ of Essex: dept of govt 1966-71, dept of history 1972-76, reader dept of history 1976-80 and 1981-84; visiting prof: dept of political sci Univ of Wisconsin USA 1971-72, Slavisches inst Univ of Cologne 1980-81; prof of russian history sch of Slavonic and E European studies Univ of London 1984-; memb: Cncl of Writers and Scholars Int 1985-, cncl Keston Coll 1987-, East-West ctee Br Cncl of Churches 1988-, bd of govrs Camden Sch for Girls 1988-, Br Univs Assoc for Soviet and E Euro Studies; *Books* The Russian Constitutional Experiment: Government & Duma 1907-14 (1973), Beyond Socialist Realism: Soviet Fiction since Ivan Denisovich (1980), A History of The Soviet Union (1985); *Recreations* walking, music, chess; *Style—* Prof Geoffrey Hosking; Sch of Slavonic & E Euro Studies, Univ of London, Senate House, Malet St, London WC1E 7NU (☎ 01 637 4934 ext 4064)

HOSKINS, Arthur Henry James; CBE; s of Alfred George Hoskins; *b* 14 Jan 1923; *m* 1949, Margaret Lilian Rose, da of Albert Davis (d 1959); 1 child; *Career* certified accountant, chartered sec; *Recreations* reading, walking; *Style—* Arthur Hoskins, Esq, CBE; 2 Acorn Close, Chislehurst, Kent BR7 6LD (☎ 01 467 0755)

HOSKINS, Stanley William; s of William Edward Hoskins (d 1953), and Rose, *née* Beatrice (d 1984); *b* 18 Oct 1913; *Educ* Latimer Upper Sch, Acton Poly; *m* Dorothy Emma Daisy, da of Louis Frederick Howard (d 1917); 1 da (Teresa Dorothy); *Career* TA Capt 2 Middx Aux Bomb Disposal Unit 1946; Bell Punch Co: chief tool draughtsman 1937-39, prodn engr 1939-41, chief draughtsman 1941-42, mechanical supt 1942-45; devpt engr Firestone Tyre & Rubber Co 1945-46, tech mangr Fluid Control GB Ltd 1945-50, md IV Pressure Controllers Ltd 1950-76; Freeman City of London 1961, Liverman Worshipful Co of Feltmakers; CEng, MIMechE, FIProdE,

FIARB, assoc RIMA, MIBE; *Clubs* City Livery; *Style*— Stanley Hoskins, Esq

HOSKYNS, Sir Benedict Leigh; 16 Bt (E 1676), of Harewood, Herefords; 3 s of Rev Sir Edwyn Clement Hoskyns, 13 Bt, MC, DD (d 1937), and Mary Trym, *née* Budden; suc bro, Sir John Chevallier Hoskyns, 15 Bt, 1956; *b* 27 May 1928; *Educ* Haileybury, Corpus Christi Cambridge (MB, BChir), London Hosp; *m* 19 Sept 1953, Ann, da of Harry Wilkinson, of London; 2 s, 2 da; *Heir* s, Dr Edwyn Wren Hoskyns; *Career* Capt RAMC (ret); in general practice 1958-; DObstRCOG 1958; *Style*— Sir Benedict Hoskyns, Bt; Harewood, Great Oakley, nr Harwich, Essex (☎ Ramsay 880341)

HOSKYNS, Edwyn Wren; s and h of Sir Benedict Leigh Hoskyns, 16 Bt; *b* 4 Feb 1956; *Educ* Nottingham Univ Med Sch (BM, BS); *Career* sr chorister King's Coll Cambridge 1969; *Style*— Edwyn Hoskyns Esq

HOSKYNS, Sir John Austin Hungerford Leigh; s of Lt-Col Chandos Benedict Arden Hoskyns (d of wounds after def of Calais 1940; gs of Rev Sir John Hoskyns, 9 Bt, JP), and Joyce Austin, *née* Taylor; *b* 23 August 1927; *Educ* Winchester; *m* 1956, Miranda Jane Marie, o da of Tom Mott, of W Bergholt, Essex; 2 s (Barnaby b 1959, Benedict b 1963), 1 da (Tamasine b 1961); *Career* Capt Rifle Bde; IBM (UK) 1957-64, fndr John Hoskyns and Co (later part of Hoskyns Gp, of which chm and md 1964-75), head of PM's Policy Unit 1979-82, special advsr sec state for Tport 1982, non-exec dir ICL 1982-84, dir-gen IOD 1984-89; dir: AGB Research 1983-89, Pergaman AGB plc 1989-, Clerical Med and Gen Life Assur Soc 1983-, McKechnie 1983-; Ferranti Int Signal; kt 1982;; *Style*— Sir John Hoskyns; 83 Clapham Common West Side, London SW4 (☎ 01 228 9505); Windrush, Gt Waldingfield, Sudbury, Suffolk (☎ 07878, 210419)

HOSKYNS, Hon Mrs (Katharine Margaret); da of Baron Kaldor (Life Peer); *b* 1937; *m* 1958, Anthony Hungerford Hoskyns, s of Sir Chandos Wren Hoskyns, 14 Bt (ka 1945); 1 s, 2 da; *Style*— The Hon Mrs Hoskyns; 25 Hamilton Gdns, NW8

HOSKYNS, Mary, Lady; Mary Trym; da of late Edwin Budden, of Macclesfield; *m* 1922, the Rev Sir Edwyn Clement Hoskyns, MC, 13 Bt (d 1937); *Career* MA 1922, former Res fell of Newnham Coll Cambridge; *Style*— Mary, Lady Hoskyns; 25 Hamilton Gdns, NW8

HOSKYNS-ABRAHALL, (Anthony David) Wren; s of Rt Rev Anthony Leigh Egerton-Hoskyns-Abrahall (d 1982), former bishop of Lancaster, and Margaret Ada, *née* Storey; *b* 19 May 1943; *Educ* St Johns Sch Leatherhead, Britannia RNC Dartmouth, London Graduate Sch of Business Studies; *m* 23 April 1965, Phyllis Penrose, da of Rear Adm Willian Penrose Mark-Wardlaw, DSO, DSC, ADC; 1 s (Mark b 22 July 1966) 1 da (Sarah b 18 April 1971); *Career* RNC Dartmouth 1961-63, HMS Tiger 1962-63, RN Trg then Staff Offr Ops Kenya Navy 1966-68, HMS Chichester 1969-70, HMS Rapid (1970), HMS Malcolm 1970-71, Flag Lt to FOSNI 1972-72; dir: Portsmouth & Sunderland Newspaper plc 1973-1977, Debenhams plc 1978-1982, Prontaprint 1982-; memb Southwark Diocesan Synod, ed Barnes In Common; cncllr Fareham BC 1974-76; HCIM 1979; *Recreations* fishing; *Style*— Wren Hoskyns-Abrahall, Esq; 20 Grange Road, Barnes, London SW13 9RE (☎ 01 748 8455); 60 Wandsworth High St, London SW18 4lD (☎ 01 870 7672, fax 01 870 0056)

HOSTOMBE, Roger Eric; s of Eric Rudolf Hostombe, of Sheffield, and Irene Baxter; *b* 22 Dec 1942; *Educ* Sedbergh; *m* 20 Sept 1975, Susan Mary, da of Frank Ian Cobb, of Sheffield; 4 da (Clare b 1976, Natalie b 1979, Annabel b 1982, Lucinda b 1982); *Career* CA 1968, exec chm R Hostombe Ltd 1975-; underwriter Lloyds 1975-; regnl cncllr CBI Yorkshire and Humberside branch 1981-87; *Recreations* tennis, squash, skiing, gardening; *Clubs* The Sheffield, Annabels; *Style*— Roger E Hostombe, Esq; Fullwood Hall, Sheffield, Yorks S10 4PA (☎ 0742 302148); R Hostombe Ltd, Minalloy House, Regent St, Sheffield S1 3NJ (☎ 0742 724324, telex 54213, fax 0742 729550)

HOTCHKIN, Neil Stafford; TD (1946), DL (1954); s of Col Stafford Vere Hotchkin, MC, DL, (d 1953), of The Manor Hse, Woodhall Spa, Lincs, and Dorothy Robinson, *née* Arnold, (d 1962); *b* 4 Feb 1914; *Educ* Eton, Trinity Coll Cambridge (BA); *m* 27 Feb 1954, Sallie, da of Hugh Sudell Bloomer (d 1964), of Gt Coates, Grimsby; 1 s (David Stafford b 3 Aug 1959), 1 da (Sarah Nicola b 1 Aug 1961); *Career* serv Territorial 60th Field Regt RA 1938 (Capt 1940, Maj 1942), regt transfd to Chindits 1943, cmd 88 column in Burma 1944; memb London Stock Exchange 1938, pres English Golf Union 1972, patron Lincolnshire Union of Golf Clubs 1985; pres Woodhall Spa: cricket, football, golf and cons clubs; hon sec Euro Golf Assoc 1980-87 (pres-elect 1988-89); played cricket for Lincolnshire, Middlesex, Eton, and Cambridge Univ; *Recreations* golf; *Clubs* R and A; *Style*— Neil Hotchkin, Esq, TD, DL; (☎ 0526 52127)

HOTHAM, Capt (John) David (Durand); s of John Beaumont Hotham (d 1924), and Gladys Mary, *née* Wilson (d 1972); *b* 5 August 1917; *Educ* Eton, New Coll Oxford (BA); *m* 11 Dec 1954, Marianne, da of Col Louis Pollak (d 1941), of Austria; *Career* Capt ret, serv M East, Italy, (Africa Star and Italian Campaign Medal); journalist and writer; corr The Times: Saigon 1956-57; Turkey 1958-66, Bonn 1966-69; *Books* The Turks (1972), Britain and Europe: stay in or pull out? (1975); *Recreations* music, golf, languages; *Clubs* New (Edinburgh); *Style*— Capt David Hotham; Milne Graden, Coldstream, Scotland (☎ 0289 82245)

HOTHAM, 8 Baron (I 1797); Sir Henry Durand Hotham; 18 Bt (E 1662), DL (Humberside 1981); 3 s of 7 Baron Hotham, CBE (d 1967), and Lady Letitia Cecil, da of 5 Marquess of Exeter; *b* 3 May 1940; *Educ* Eton; *m* 1972, Alexandra, 2 da of Maj Andrew Charles Stirling Home Drummond Moray; 2 s (Hon William, Hon George b 1974) 1 da (Hon Elizabeth b 1976); *Heir* s, Hon William Beaumont Hotham b 13 Oct 1972; *Career* former Lt Gren Gds; patron of 1 living; ADC to Gov Tasmania 1963-66; *Style*— The Rt Hon Lord Hotham, DL; Scorborough Hall, Driffield, Yorks; Dalton Hall, Dalton Holme, Beverley, Yorks

HOTHAM, Hon Jocelyne Mary Emma; da of 6 Baron Hotham (d 1923); *b* 1908; *Style*— The Hon Jocelyne Hotham; Bridge Cottage, Brookside, Hovingham, York

HOTHAM, Dowager Baroness; Lady Letitia Sibell Winifred; *née* Cecil; da of late 5 Marquess of Exeter, KG, CMG, TD and Hon Myra, *née* Orde-Powlett, da of 4 Baron Bolton, and Lady Algitha Lumley, da of 9 Earl of Scarbrough; *b* 1903; *m* 1937, 7 Baron Hotham (d 1967); 6 s (incl 8 Baron; 3 are decd); *Career* lady-in-waiting to HRH the Duchess of Gloucester 1935-37; *Style*— The Rt Hon The Dowager Lady Hotham; The School House, Dalton Holme, Beverley, Yorks

HOTHAM, Martin Patrick; only s of Lt-Cdr The Hon David Hotham, DSC, RN (d 1962, bro of 7 Baron Hotham), and Aileen, *née* Coates; *b* 17 August 1941; *Educ* Stowe; *m* 2 Oct 1965, Erica Antoinette, da of Lt-Col Brian Maxwell Strang (d 1971), of N Wales; 2 s (Charles Beaumont David b 1969, Henry Ralph b 1974 d 1986), 2 da (Sophia Henrietta b 1967, Amelia Oriana Philadelphia b 1971); *Career* slr; *Recreations* shooting, racing, reading; *Clubs* Ipswich and Suffolk; *Style*— Martin Hotham, Esq; The Old Rectory, Drinkstone, Bury St Edmunds, Suffolk (☎ Beyton 70834); 32 Lloyds Ave, Ipswich, Suffolk (☎ Ipswich 213311, telex 98620, fax Ipswich 57739)

HOTHAM, Hon Nicholas Charles Frederick; s of 7 Baron Hotham, CBE (d 1967); *b* 1947; *Educ* Eton; *m* 1974, Jane Brydon, of Thurley Beck Farm, Harwood Dale, Scarborough, Yorks; *Style*— The Hon Nicholas Hotham

HOTHAM, Maj Hon Peter; s of Capt Henry Edward Hotham (d 1912), and bro of 7 Baron (d 1967); *b* 1904; *Educ* Winchester, RMC; *m* 1934, Margaret, da of Col Sir Robert Williams-Wynn, 9 Bt, KCB, DSO, TD (d 1951); 1 s, 2 da; *Career* Capt KOYLI 1936, Maj 1941, ret 1947; raised to the rank of a Baron's son 1924; *Clubs* Buck's; *Style*— Maj The Hon Peter Hotham; Plas Newydd, Glascoed, Abergele, N Wales

HOTHAM, Hon Peter William; s of 7 Baron Hotham, CBE (d 1967); *b* 1944; *Educ* Eton, Ch Ch Oxford; *m* 1978, Deborah S, da of late G Macdonald-Brown, of Rose Cottage, Campsall, Doncaster; 1 s (b 1982), 1 da (b 1979); *Style*— The Hon Peter Hotham

HOTHFIELD, 5 Baron (UK 1881); Lt-Col Sir George William Anthony Tufton; 6 Bt (UK 1851), TD, DL (Herts 1962); s of Hon Charles Henry Tufton, CMG (d 1923, 3 s of 1 Baron Hothfield), and Stella, da of Sir George Faudel-Phillips, 1 Bt, GCIE; suc 1 cous, 4 Baron Hothfield 1986; *b* 28 Oct 1904; *Educ* Eton, Hertford Coll Oxford; *m* 3 Dec 1936, Evelyn Margarette, eldest da of Eustace Mordaunt (bro of Sir Henry Mordaunt, 12 Bt); 2 s (Anthony b 1939, Nicholas b 1946), 1 da (Jennifer (Mrs Edward Raikes); *Heir* s, Hon Anthony Charles Sackville Tufton b 21 Oct 1939; *Career* underwriting memb Lloyd's; *Style*— Lt-Col The Rt Hon Lord Hothfield, TD, DL; The Garden House, 11A High St, Barkway, Royston, Herts ((☎ 076 384 266)

HOUFE, Simon Richard; s of Eric Alfred Scholefield Houfe, and Kathleen, *née* Richardson (d 1983); *b* 13 Sept 1942; *Educ* Stowe, Italy; *Career* journalist and biographer; on staff V and A Museum 1963-65, working on art collection in Italy 1965, ed The Antique Collector 1970-74, antiques corr Homes and Gardens 1976-87, memb, projects ctee Nat Art Collections Fund 1974-80; *Books* Old Bedfordshire (1975), The Birth of The Studio, 1893-1895 (1976), The Dalziel Family, Engravers and Illustrators (1978), The Dictionary of British Illustrators and Caricaturists, 1800-1914 (1978), Sir Albert Richardon - The Professor (1980), John Leech and The Victorian Scene (1984); contrib to: Apollo, Antiquarian Book Monthly Review, Country Life, A La Carte, Bedfordshire Magazine; wrote chapter on antiques official programme book for Britain's entry to the EEC 1972; *Recreations* collecting; *Style*— Simon R Houfe, Esq; Avenue Hse, Ampthill, Beds MK45 2EH (☎ 0525 402115)

HOUGH, George Hubert; CBE (1965); s of late Wilfrid Hough; *b* 21 Oct 1921; *Educ* Winsford Verdin GS Cheshire, King's Coll London (PhD); *m* 1943, Hazel Ayrton, da of late Kenneth Russell; 1 s, 2 da; *Career* md Hawker Siddeley Dynamics Ltd 1977-78; memb: British Aerospace Bd, BAC guided weapons div bd 1977-; chm and chief exec Br Smelter Constructions Ltd 1978-80, dir Programmed Neuro Cybernetics (UK Ltd) 1979-84, chm Forthstar Ltd 1980-; dir: Landis & Gyr UK 1978-84, Leigh Instruments Ltd (Canada); chm: Magnetic Components Ltd 1986-, Abasec Ltd 1988-; *Books* The Anatomy of Major Projects (with P Morris); *Recreations* shooting, golf, dinghy sailing; *Clubs* St James's; *Style*— George H Hough, Esq, CBE; Trelyon, Rock, Wadebridge, Cornwall (☎ 020 886 3454); 112 Andrewes House, Barbican, London (☎ 01 628 2580;

HOUGH, Prof James Richard; s of George Hough, of Brighton, Sussex, and Eileen Isobel, *née* Donovan; *b* 2 August 1937; *Educ* Xaverian Coll Brighton, Brighton GS, Univ of Keele (BA), Univ of London (MSc), Univ of Leicester (PhD); *m* 31 Aug 1968, Jane Louise, da of Vernon Blake Vincent (d 1982); 2 s (Steven David b 1972, Richard Martin b 1974), 1 da (Catherine Theresa b 1978); *Career* exec Lloyd's Underwriters 1953-65, sr lectr econ Huddersfield Poly 1971-72; Univ of Loughborough: lectr 1972-77, snr lectr 1977-84, reader 1984-85, dean of educn and humanities 1985-88, prof 1988-; conslt on econs of educn for: World Bank UNESCO, IIEP, The Br Cncl, TETOC; *Books* A Study of School Costs (1981), The French Economy (1982), Educational Policy (1984), Education and the National Economy (1987); *Recreations* walking, tennis, cycling, historical biography; *Style*— Prof James R Hough; Loughborough University, Loughborough, Leics LE11 3TU (☎ 0509 222752)

HOUGH, Richard; s of G S Hough (d 1970), of Brighton, and Margaret, *née* Esilman (d 1974); *b* 15 May 1922; *Educ* Frensham Heights; *m* 1, 17 July 1943 (m dis 1980), Helen Charlotte Woodyatt; 4 da (Sarah, Alexandra, Deborah, Bryony); m 2, 7 June 1980, Julie Marie (Judy) Taylor, MBE; *Career* Fl Lt RAF Pilot Fighter Cmd 1941-46; book publishing: mangr Bodley Head 1947-55, dir Hamish Hamilton 1955-70 (dir, fndr and md Hamish Hamilton Children's Books Ltd and Elm Tree Books); freelance writer 1955-; cncl memb and vice-pres Navy Records Soc 1970-82, cncl memb auxiliary hosps ctee King Edward VII's Hosp Fund 1970-84 (chm 1975-80); *Books* The Fleet that had to Die (1958), Admirals in Collision (1959), The Potemkin Mutiny (1960), The Hunting of Force Z (1963), Dreadnought (1964), The Big Battleship (1966), First Sea Lord: an authorised life of Admiral Lord Fisher (1969), The Blind Horn's Hate (1971), Captain Bligh and Mr Christian (1972, Daily Express Best Book of the Sea Award); Louis and Victoria: the first Mountbattens (1974), One Boy's War: per astra ad ardua (1975), Advice to a Grand-daughter (Queen Victoria's letters, ed 1975), The Great Admirals (1977), The Murder of Captain James Cook (1979), Man o' War (1979), Nelson (1980), Mountbatten: Hero of Our Time (1980), The Great War at Sea: 1914-1918 (1983), Edwina, Countess Mountbatten of Burma (1983), Former Naval Person: Churchill and the Wars at Sea (1985), The Ace of Clubs: a History of the Garrick (1986), The Longest Battle; the War at Sea 1939-45 (1986); *Clubs* Garrick, Beefsteak, MCC; *Style*— Richard Hough, Esq; 31 Meadowbank, Primrose Hill Road, London NW3 1AY (☎ 01 722 5663)

HOUGHAM, John William; s of William George Hougham, of Ash, Canterbury, Kent, and Emily Jane, *née* Smith; *b* 18 Jan 1937; *Educ* Sir Roger Manwood's Sandwich Kent, Univ of Leeds (BA); *m* 26 Aug 1961, Peggy Edith, da of Ernest Grove (d 1972), of Hales Owen, Worcs; 1 s (Simon b 1967), 1 da (Elizabeth b 1965); *Career* Royal Regt of Artillery 1955-57 (2 Lt 1956), TA 1957-60 (Lt 1959); dir industl rels Ford Espana SA Valencia Spain 1976-80, dir indust rels mfrg Ford of Europe Inc 1982-86, exec dir for personnel Ford Motor Company Ltd 1986-; memb: cncl CRAC, CBI's Employment Policy Ctee, Engrg Indust Trg Bd, IPM'S Ctee on Equal Opportunities; FIPM 1980, CBIM 1986; *Recreations* walking, collecting books on Kent, fishing; *Style*— John Hougham, Esq; Ford Motor Co Ltd, Warley, Brentwood, Essex CM13 3BW (☎ 0277 253 000, fax 0277 262 066)

HOUGHTON, Dr John Theodore; CBE (1983); s of Sidney Maurice Houghton (d 1987), of Abingdon, and Miriam, *née* Yarwood (d 1974); *b* 30 Dec 1931; *Educ* Rhyl GS, Jesus Coll Oxford (MA, DPhil); *m* 1, 1962, Margaret Edith (d 1986), da of Neville Broughton, of Colne, Lancs; 1 s (Peter b 1966), 1 da (Janet b 1964); m 2, 1988, Sheila, da of Sydney Thompson, of Bradford, Yorks; *Career* res fell Royal Aircraft Estab, lectr in atmospheric physics Oxford 1948 (reader 1962, prof 1976), official fell and tutor in physics Jesus Coll Oxford 1960-73 (prof fell 1973, hon fell 1983), visiting prof Univ of California LA 1969; developed the: Selective Chopper Radiometer (for the Nimbus 4 and 5 satellites), Pressure Modulator Radiometer (flown on Nimbus 6) 1975, Stratospheric and Mesopheric Sounder (flown on Nimbus 7) 1978; FRS, FInstP, FRMetS (pres 1976-78); Darton Prize (RMS) 1954, Buchan Prize (RMS) 1966, Charles Chree Medal of the Inst of Physics 1979; fell Optical Soc of America; memb: American Meteorological Soc, American Geophysical Union; chm Jt Scientific Ctee for World Climate Res Programmes 1981-84, vice-pres World Meteorological Orgn 1987-; *Books* Infra Red Physics (with S D Smith 1966), The Physics of Atmospheres (1977, 2nd ed 1986), Remote Sensing of Atmospheres (with F W Taylor and C D Rodgers 1984), The Global Climate (ed 1984), Does God Play Dice? (1988); *Style—* Dr John Houghton, CBE; Director-General, Meteorological Office, London Rd, Bracknell, Berks RG12 2SZ

HOUGHTON, Maj-Gen Robert Dyer; CB (1962), OBE (1947), MC (1942), DL (1977); s of John Mayo Houghton, of Sarum, Dawlish, Devon (d 1947), and Lucy Evelyn, *née* Trotman (d 1973); *b* 7 Mar 1912; *Educ* Haileybury; *m* 1940, Dorothy Uladh, da of late Maj-Gen R W S Lyons, IMS; 2 s (John, Neill), 1 da (Lucy); *Career* RM Offr 1930-64, Maj-Gen 1961, chief of Amphibious Warfare 1961; ADC to HM The Queen 1959-; Col Cmdt RM 1973-75; gen sec Royal Utd Kingdom Beneficient Assoc 1968-78; *Recreations* gardening, model engrg; *Clubs* Army and Navy; *Style—* Maj-Gen Robert Houghton, CB, OBE, MC, DL; Vert House, Whitesmith, nr Lewes (☎ 0825 872451)

HOUGHTON OF SOWERBY, Baron (Life Peer UK 1974); Arthur Leslie Noel Douglas Houghton; CH (1967), PC (1964); s of John Houghton, of Long Eaton, Derbys; *b* 11 August 1898; *m* 1939, Vera, da of John Travis, of Southall; *Career* takes Lab Whip in House of Lords; sec Inland Revenue Staff Fedn 1922-60, MP (Lab) Sowerby 1949-74, chllr Duchy of Lancaster 1964-66, min without portfolio 1966-67, chm PLP 1967-74; broadcaster BBC 1941-64, LCC Alderman 1947-49; memb: Gen Cncl TUC 1952-60, Royal Cmmn on Standards of Conduct in Public Life; chm: Teachers' Pay Inquiry, Ctee on Finances of Political Parties, Ctee on Security of Cabinet Papers 1974-76, Ctee for Reform of Animal Experiments; vice-pres: RSPCA 1978-82, Bldg Socs Assoc, League Against Cruel Sports; *Clubs* Reform; *Style—* The Rt Hon the Lord Houghton of Sowerby, CH, PC; Becks Cottage, Whitehill Lane, Bletchingley, Redhill, Surrey (☎ 0883 843340 3340); 110 Marsham Court, London SW1 (☎ 01 834 0602)

HOUISON CRAUFURD, Hon Mrs (Caroline Helen); *née* Berry; da of 2 Viscount Kemsley; *b* 1942; *m* 1965, John Peter Houison Craufurd of Craufurdland and Braehead; 2 s, 1 da; *Style—* The Hon Mrs Houison Craufurd; Craufurdland Castle, Kilmarnock, Ayrshire

HOULDSWORTH, Sir (Harold) Basil; 2 Bt (UK 1956), of Heckmondwike, West Riding of Yorkshire; s of Sir Hubert Stanley Houldsworth, 1 Bt, QC (d 1956), and Hilda Frances, *née* Clegg; *b* 21 July 1922; *Educ* Heckmondwike GS, Leeds Sch of Medicine; *m* 24 Sept 1946, Norah Clifford, da of Arthur Halmshaw; 1 da; *Heir* none; *Career* conslt anaesthetist Barnsley Hosps 1954-87; MRCS, LRCP 1946, DA Eng 1951, FFA, RCS Eng 1953; *Style—* Sir Basil Houldsworth, Bt; Shadwell House, Lundhill Rd, Wombwell, nr Barnsley, Yorks (☎ 0226 753191)

HOULDSWORTH, Margaret, Lady; Margaret May; *née* Laurie; 4 da of Cecil Emilius Laurie, JP (d 1919; 3 s of Rev Sir Emilius Laurie, 3 Bt), and Helen Janet Douglas, *née* Campbell (d 1919); *b* 13 May 1908; *m* 30 April 1934, Lt-Col Sir Reginald Douglas Henry Houldsworth, 4 Bt, OBE, TD, DL (d 1989); 1 s, 2 da; *Style—* Margaret, Lady Houldsworth; Kirkbride, Maybole, Ayrshire (☎ 065 54 202)

HOULDSWORTH, Sir Richard Thomas Reginald; 5 Bt (UK 1887), of Reddish, Manchester, Co Lancaster, and Coodham, Symington, Ayrshire; s of Sir Reginald Douglas Henry Houldsworth, 4 Bt, OBE, TD (d 1989), and Margaret May, *née* Laurie; *b* 2 August 1947; *Educ* Bredon Sch Tewkesbury; *m* 1970, Jane, o da of Alistair Orr, of Sydehead, Beith, Ayrshire; 2 s (Simon Richard Henry, a son b 1975); *Heir* s, Simon Richard Henry Houldsworth b 1970; *Style—* Sir Richard Houldsworth, Bt; The Giruam Lodge, Blairquhan, Straiton, Ayrshire

HOULTON, (Arthur) Conrad Leighton; s of Arthur John Houlton (d 1951), of Marlborough Ave, Hessle, E Yorks, and Florence, *née* Thompson (d 1939); *b* 22 June 1908; *Educ* Hymers Coll Hull, Emmanual Coll Cambridge, St Bartholomew's Hosp Medical Coll London (MA Cantab, MA Oxon, MB BChir, DO, DOMS); *m* 12 June 1939, Edna Mary, da of Charles Pidsley (d 1956), of London; 3 s (John Leighton b 1944, Peter Godfrey b 1946, Michael Richard b 1947); *Career* opthalmic surgn Oxford Eye Hosp 1938-73 (asst surgn 1938-42), clinical lectr in opthalmology Univ of Oxford; chm Oxford div BMA 1963, pres Oxford Med Soc 1966, vice-pres and memb of cncl of section of opthalmology Royal Soc of Medicine, memb prevention of blindness Ctee RNIB; MRCS, LRCP; *Clubs* Royal Soc of Medicine; *Style—* Arthur Houlton, Esq; 1 Berrow Ct, Gardens Walk, Upton upon Severn, Worcs WR8 0JP (☎ 068 46 43407)

HOUNSFIELD, Sir Godfrey Newbold; CBE (1976); s of Thomas Hounsfield; *b* 28 August 1919; *Educ* Magnus GS Newark, City Coll London; *Career* sr staff scientist central Res laboratories of Thorn EMI Hayes Middx; kt 1981; *Style—* Sir Godfrey Hounsfield, CBE; South Airfield Farm, Winthorpe, nr Newark, Notts

HOUSDEN, Norman Charles Nelson; s of Charles Frederick Webb Housden (d 1950); *b* 1 Jan 1919; *Educ* Loughton; *m* 1940, Marjorie Violet, *née* Meeson; 1 da; *Career* CA, chm Arlington Motor Hldgs 1955-85; *Recreations* boating (MV Velia), aircraft (Beechcraft Baron 58); *Style—* Norman Housden, Esq; White Heron, Fort George, St Peter Port, Guernsey, CI

HOUSE, Lt-Gen Sir David George; GCB (1977, KCB 1975), KCVO (1985), CBE (1967, OBE 1964), MC (1944); s of A G House; *b* 8 August 1922; *Educ* Regent's Park Sch London; *m* 1947, Sheila Betty Darwin; 2 da; *Career* serv WWII Italy KRRC, dep mil sec MOD 1969-71, Maj-Gen 1971, COS HQ BAOR 1971-73, Lt-Gen 1973, dir of inf MOD 1973-75, GOC and Dir (Ops) NI 1975-77, ret; Col Cmdt: Small Arms Sch Corps 1974-77, The Light Div 1974-77; gentleman usher of the Black Rod House of Lords 1978-85; regnl dir Lloyds Bank Yorks and Humberside Regn 1985; *Style—* Lt-Gen Sir David House, GCB, KCVO, CBE, MC; Dormer Lodge, Aldborough, nr Boroughbridge, N Yorks YO5 9EP

HOUSE, Dr John Peter Humphry; s of (Arthur) Humphry House (d 1955), and Madeline Edith, *née* Church (d 1978); *b* 19 April 1945; *Educ* Westminster, New Coll Oxford (BA), Courtauld Inst of Art London Univ (MA), Univ of London (PhD); *m* 31 Aug 1968, Jill Elaine, da of Ernest Sackville Turner, OBE, of Kew, Surrey; 2 s (Adam b 1973, Joseph b 1975); *Career* lectr: UEA 1969-76, UCL 1976-80, Courtauld Inst of Art Univ of London 1980-87; Slade prof of fine art Univ of Oxford 1986-87, reader Courtauld Inst of Art Univ of London 1987-, awarded Br Acad Res Readership 1988-; organiser Impressionism exhibition Royal Acad of Arts 1974; co-organiser: Post-Impressionism exhibition Royal Acad of Arts 1979-80, Renoir exhibition Arts Cncl of GB 1985; *Books* Monet (1976, enlarged ed 1981), Monet; Nature into Art (1986), Impressionist and Post-Impressionist Masterpieces: The Courtauld Collection (co-author, 1987); *Recreations* secondhand bookshops; *Style—* Dr John House; Courtauld Inst of Art, Univ of London, 20 Portman Sq, London W1H OBE (☎ 01 935 9292)

HOUSEMAN, Alexander Randolph; CBE (1984); s of Capt Alexander William Houseman (d 1962), and Elizabeth Maud, *née* Randolph (d 1986); *b* 9 May 1920; *Educ* Stockport GS, Stockport Coll; *m* 1942, Betty Edith, da of Alfred G Norrington (d 1976); 1 da; *Career* apprenticed Crossley Motors Ltd and Fairey Aviation, prodn engr Ford Motor Co (aero engines) Ltd 1940-43, Saunders-Roe Ltd 1943-48, gen works mangr 1948-54, conslt (later dir, md and dep chm) P-E Int 1954-81; chm: W Canning Ltd 1975-80, NEDO EDC Gauge and Tool Indust 1978-85; dir: P-E Consulting Gp Ltd 1968-81, Record Ridgway Ltd 1978-81, dir and depty chm British Rail Engrg Ltd 1979-; memb: cncl Inst of Mgmnt Conslts 1968-80, Industl Advsy Panel of Fellowship of Engrg 1980-; FEng, FIMechE, FIProdE (pres 1983-84), FIMC, CBIM, FRSA, life memb SME (USA), Hon Memb IIE (USA);; *Recreations* DIY, walking, sailing, photography; *Clubs* Caledonian, RAYC; *Style—* Alexander Houseman, Esq, CBE; 11 Kings Ave, Ealing, London W5 2SJ (☎ 01 997 3936)

HOUSLEY, Michael John Vernon; s of Ronald Housley, of Gorgys, High Rd, Chigwell, Essex, and Josephine Milne Housley (d 1988); *b* 15 Mar 1934; *Educ* Coopers' Company's Sch, King's Coll London; *m* 10 Sept 1960, Helen Russell, da of Rex Ransom (d 1970), of 20 Blakehall Cres, London E11; 3 s (Russell b 15 March 1964, Richard b 12 March 1967, Matthew b 8 Oct 1970), 1 da (Catherine b 30 May 1962); *Career* Nat Serv RN 1954-56; dir Scott North & Co Ltd 1964-66 (joined as trnee 1956), sr ptnr Housley Heath & Co 1966-76; md: Hambro Housley Heath Ltd 1977-79, Michael Housley Ltd (insur broker) 1980-; memb Lloyds; gp scout ldr 1956, asst Co Cmmnr (Int) Essex 1984-; govr: Coopers Co and Coburn Educn Fdn, Coopers' Co Sch; Freeman City of London, Liveryman Worshipful Co of Coopers (memb Ct of Assts and tres), Liveryman Worshipful Co of Insurers; ACII 1960; *Recreations* walking, sailing, music; *Clubs* City of London; East India; *Style—* MJV Housley, Esq; 4 Burnt House, Pudding Lane, Chigwell, Essex 1G7 6BY (☎ 01 500 3544); Barclays Bank Chambers, 99-101 Commercial St, London E1 6BG (☎ 01 247 3202, fax 01 375 1664, car phone 0836 230818, 0836 246 705, telex 265871 MONREF G Quote SJJ029 in First Line

HOUSSEMAYNE DU BOULAY, Sir Roger William; KCVO (1982, CVO 1972), CMG (1975); s of Capt Charles Houssemayne du Boulay, RN; *b* 30 Mar 1922; *Educ* Winchester, Univ of Oxford; *m* 1957, Elizabeth, da of late Brig Francis Wyville Home, and Molly, Lady Pile, *qv*; 1 da, 2 step s; *Career* serv WWII, RAFVR Fl Lt, Pilot; serv in Colonial Service in Nigeria, joined For Off 1959, Washington 1960-64, FO 1964-67; dir Asian Devpt Bank (Manila) 1969-71 (alternate dir 1967-69), cnsllr and head chancery Paris 1971-73, resident cmmr New Hebrides 1973-75, Vice-Marshal Dip Corps 1975-82; *Recreations* bellringing, riding, gardening; *Clubs* Boodles; *Style—* Sir Roger Houssemayne du Boulay, KCVO, CMG; Anstey House, nr Buntingford, Herts

HOUSTON, Hon Mrs (Averil); *née* Vivian; JP (Herts); da of late 3 Baron Swansea, DSO, MVO, and Hon Winifred, *née* Hamilton, da of 1 Baron Holm Patrick, PC, and Lady Victoria, *née* Wellesley, sis of 3 and 4 Dukes of Wellington; *b* 1930; *m* 1953, Alexander William Houston; 2 s, 1 da; *Style—* The Hon Mrs Houston, JP; The Little House, Datchworth, Knebworth, Herts SG3 6ST

HOUSTON, Maj-Gen David; CBE (1975, OBE 1972); s of late David Houston, and Christina Charleson, *née* Dunnett; *b* 24 Feb 1929; *Educ* Latymer Upper Sch; *m* 1959, Jancis Veronica Burn; 2 s; *Career* cmmnd Royal Irish Fus 1949; HQ UKLF 1979-80, pres Regular Cmmns Bd 1980-83, Col Queen's Lancs Regt 1983-; Hons Col Manchester & Salford Univ OTC 1985; *Style—* Maj-Gen David Houston, CBE; c/o Bank of Scotland, Bonar Bridge, Sutherland IV24 3EB

HOUSTON, Dr James Caldwell; CBE (1982); s of David Houston (d 1955), and Minnie Walker Caldwell (d 1973); *b* 18 Feb 1917; *Educ* Mill Hill, Guy's Hosp Med Sch (MD); *m* 1946, Dr Thelma Cromarty, da of Prof John Cruickshank, CBE (d 1966), of Aberdeen; 4 s (Kenneth, Brian, Alan, Andrew); *Career* dean: Guy's Hosp Med and Dental Schs 1965-82, United Med and Dental Schs of Guy's and St Thomas's Hosps 1982-84; emeritus conslt physician Guy's Hosp, dir Clerical Med and Gen Life Assur Soc 1964-87, vice-pres Med Def Union 1970-; FRCP; *Recreations* golf, gardening; *Clubs* Addington GC; *Style—* Dr J Caldwell Houston, CBE; Discovery Cottage, St Katharine-by-the-Tower, London E1 9UG (☎ 01 481 8912); Cockhill Farm, Detling, Maidstone, Kent (☎ 0634 31395); Keats House, Guy's Hospital, SE1 9RT (☎ 01 407 7600)

HOUSTOUN, Lt-Col Andrew Beatty; OBE (1983), MC (1946), DL (Angus 1971); s of William McAulay Houstoun (d 1936), of Sachel Ct, Alfod, Surrey and Isobel Parke Irvine, *née* Beatty (d 1978); *b* 15 Oct 1922; *Educ* Harrow; *m* 14 Aug 1953, Mary Elizabeth, da of late Sir Douglas L Spencer-Nairn; 4 s (William, David, Alexander, Neil); *Career* Army 1941-56, 1 Royal Dragoons 1943-56, ret Maj 1956; joined Fife and Forfar Yeo Scottish Horse TA 1958, CO 1962-65, ret Lt-Col (& Brevet Col) 1965; farmer and landowner 1956-; memb Angus CC 1966-75 (vice chm educn ctee), vice pres Scottish Landowner's Assoc 1983- (convener 1979-82), Scottish memb Euro Landowner's Orgn 1976-86, chllr's assessor Dundee Univ 1981-; Vice Lord Lt Angus 1987; *Recreations* country sports, gardening; *Clubs* Royal Perth Golfing Soc; *Style—* Lt-Col Andrew Houstoun, OBE, MC, DL; Lintrathen Lodge, Kirriemuir Angus DD8 5JJ (☎ 057 56 228)

HOUSTOUN-BOSWALL, Sir (Thomas) Alford; 8 Bt (UK 1836); s of Sir Thomas Houstoun-Boswall, 7 Bt (d 1982), by his 1 w (*see* Houstoun-Boswall, Margaret, Lady); *b* 23 May 1947; *m* 1971, Eliana Michele, da of Dr John Pearse, of NY; 1 s, 1 da (Julia Glencora b 1979); *Heir* s, Alexander Alford Houstoun-Boswall b 16 Sept 1972; *Style—*

Sir Alford Houstoun-Boswall, Bt; 22 Edwardes Sq, London W8 (☎ 01 602 6763); 11 East 73rd St, New York City, NY 10021, USA (☎ 212 517 8057)

HOUSTOUN-BOSWALL, Margaret, Lady; Margaret; da of George Bullen-Smith, of Squirrels, Arlington, E Sussex; *m* 1945 (m dis 1970), as his 1 w, Sir Thomas Houstoun-Boswall, 7 Bt (d 1982); 1 s (Sir Alford H-B, 8 Bt, *qv*), 1 da (Georgina, m Alan Moore); *Career* Eastbourne Boro cllr 1976-; licentiate Guildhall Sch of Music; *Style*— Margaret, Lady Houstoun-Boswall; 8 College Rd, Eastbourne, E Sussex (☎ 0323 32664)

HOVELL-THURLOW-CUMMING-BRUCE; *see*: Cumming-Bruce

HOVELL-THURLOW-CUMMING-BRUCE, Hon Roualeyn Robert; s and h of 8 Baron Thurlow, KCMG, *qv*; *b* 13 April 1952; *Educ* Milton Abbey; *m* 5 May 1980, Bridget Anne Julia, o da of (Hugh) Bruce Ismay Cheape, TD, of Sth Lodge, Craignure, Isle of Mull, Argyll; 1 s (Nicholas Edward b 1986), 1 da (Tessa Iona Bridget b 1987); *Clubs* Pratt's; *Style*— The Hon Roualeyn Hovell-Thurlow-Cumming-Bruce; 22 Hanover Sq, London W1R 0JL (☎ 01 493 6040, telex 23858)

HOW, Denzil Robert Onslow; s of Robert Boothby How, of St Andrews and Virginia, *née* Hughes-Onslow; *b* 3 August 1944; *Educ* Eton, Trinity Coll Cambridge; *m* 1968 (m dis 1985), Sarah, da of John Collins, of Tusmore Park, Bicester; 4 da (Nicola b 1970, Antonia b 1975, Francesca b 1978, Georgina b 1981); *Career* chm: Rediweld Hldgs 1972-, Mazer Wine Shippers plc 1985; dir: Mid Anglia Radio plc 1984-;; *Recreations* stalking, shooting, skiing, golf, tennis, racing; *Clubs* Pitt (Cambridge), White's; *Style*— Denzil How, Esq; 23 Ladbroke Sq, London W11

HOW, Sir Friston Charles; CB (1948); s of Charles Friston How; *b* 17 Sept 1897; *Educ* Co HS Leyton, Univ of London (BSc); *m* 1932, Ann Stewart Hunter; *Career* served WWI RM; barr Middle Temple 1927; joined Civil Serv 1920, under-sec Miny of Supply 1946-53, sec Atomic Energy Off 1954-59; memb: Air Tport Advsy Cncl 1960-61, Air Transport Licensing Bd 1960-70; kt 1958; *Style*— Sir Friston How, CB; Praesmohr Residential Home, Birse, Aboyne, Aberdeenshire AB3 5BP

HOW, Peter Cecil; s of Cecil How, of Lower Way, Upper Longdon, Rugeley, Staffs, and Dora, *née* Marshall (d 1960); *b* 27 June 1931; *Educ* Oundle, Open Univ (BA); *m* 21 Sept 1951, Jane, da of Thomas Erickson (d 1936); 2 s (Neil b 1952, Adam b 1954); *Career* dir Forggatt and Prior Ltd 1955-63; chm: How Gp Ltd and assoc cos 1974-86 (dir 1963, chm How Gp plc 1986-), Hansgross Estates plc 1986-, H and V Welfare Ltd; pres: How Gp Inc 1982-, Genie Climatique Int 1986-88; memb CBI W Mids regnl cncl 1979-85; memb Worshipful Co of Fan Makers 1975; *Recreations* travel, theatre, opera, music; *Clubs* E India, City Livery; *Style*— Peter How, Esq; 11 The Regents, Norfolk Rd, Edgbaston, Birmingham B15 3PP (☎ 021 454 4777); 5211 Everwood Run, Sarasota, Florida 34235, USA; How Group plc, Intersection House, West Bromwich, W Midlands B70 6RX (☎ 021 500 5000, fax 021 500 5159, telex 338449 HOWMID G)

HOW, Ronald Mervyn; s of Mervyn Darvell How (d 1973), of Bucks, and Kathleen Dorothy, *née* Honour; *b* 24 Dec 1927; *Educ* general schooling; *m* 30 June 1951, Brenda, da of Harold Brown (d 1976), of Herts; 1 s (David b 1953), 1 da (Margaret b 1956); *Career* RAF AC1 1946-47; farmer; dir of British Poultry Fedn and Br Turkey Fedn 1978; tres: Br Turkey Fedn 1984-88, Chesham Rotary 1983-; pres Chesham Rotary 1981; ctee memb: Hawridge Commons Pres Soc 1970-, League of Friends Amersham and Chesham Hosps 1979-; *Recreations* tennis, computer programming, photography; *Clubs* Chesham Rotary, Amersham Photographic Soc; *Style*— Ronald How, Esq; Woodlands Cottage, The Vale, Chesham, Bucks (☎ 0494 782434); Woodlands Farm, The Vale, Chesham, Bucks (☎ 0494 783737)

HOWARD; *see*: Fitzalan Howard *or* Fitzalan-Howard

HOWARD, Hon Mrs Henry; Adèle le Bourgois Chapin; *née* Alsop; da of late Reese Denny Alsop, of New York City, USA; *b* 5 Nov 1914; *Educ* Bennington Coll (BA); *m* 1937, Lt-Col the Hon Henry Anthony Camillo Howard, CMG, Coldstream Gds (d 1977), 5 s of 1 Baron Howard of Penrith, GCB, GCMG, CVO (d 1939); 4 da (and 1 da decd); *Career* admin St Kitts and Nevis Anguilla; *Recreations* carriege driving; *Style*— The Hon Mrs Henry Howard; Bushby House, Greystoke, Penrith, Cumberland (☎ 085 33 302)

HOWARD, Hon Andrew Barnaby; s (twin, by 1 w) of 4 Baron Strathcona and Mount Royal; *b* 1963; *Style*— The Hon Andrew Howard

HOWARD, Anthony John; s of Peter Dunsmore Howard (d 1965, former Capt Eng Rugby Team), of Hill Farm, Brent Eleigh, Sudbury, Suffolk, and Doris Emily, *née* Metaxas (former winner Wimbledon Ladies Doubles); *b* 31 Dec 1937; *Educ* Cheam Sch, Eton, Trinity Coll Oxford; *m* 12 Oct 1963, Elisabeth Ann, da of Capt Roddie Casement, OBE, RN (d 1987); 1 s (Tom), 2 da (Katie, Emma); *Career* film res/prodr/dir for TV; 2000 films and progs for TV incl: Greece - The Hidden War, A Passage to Britain, A Full Life, Dick Barton - Special Agent, Country Ways, Every Night Something Awful; *Books* five books published on The English Countryside; *Recreations* walking, talking, reading, wood clearing; *Style*— Anthony Howard, Esq; Drove Cottage, Newbridge, nr Cadnam, Southampton, Hants, SO4 2NW (☎ 0703 813 233); TVS, TV Centre, Northam, Southampton, Hants (☎ 0703 834 139)

HOWARD, Anthony Michell; s of late Canon Guy Howard, and Janet Rymer Howard; *b* 12 Feb 1934; *Educ* Westminster, Ch Ch Oxford; *m* 1965, Carol Anne Gaynor; *Career* formerly with Manchester Guardian, Sunday Times; ed The New Statesman 1972-78 (asst ed 1970-72, political corr 1961-64), ed The Listener 1979-81, dep ed The Observer 1981- (corr in Washington 1966-69, political columnist 1971-72); *Books include* The Condensed Crossman Diaries (ed, 1979), RAB: The Life of R A Butler (1987); *Style*— Anthony Howard, Esq; 17 Addison Ave, London W11 4QS (☎ 01 603 3749)

HOWARD, Hon Barnaby John; 2 s of 3 Baron Strathcona and Mount Royal (d 1959), and Hon Diana, *née* Loder (d 1985), da of 1 Baron Wakehurst; *b* 23 Nov 1925; *Educ* Eton, Trinity Coll Cambridge (MA), Harvard Univ; *m* 1, 19 Jan 1952 (m dis 1967), Elizabeth, yr da of Frank McConnell Mayfield, of St Louis, Missouri, USA; 1 s, 2 da; m 2, 1970, Mrs F N H Bishop, da of late Ambrose Chambers, of NY, USA; *Career* serv WWII Sub Lt RNVR (Air branch); cmmr S Rhodesian Forestry Cmmn 1957-63, chm Canadian American Investmt and Mgmnt Servs Ltd (Halifax NS Canada), gen ptnr Claflin Capital Mgmnt Inc (Boston Mass USA), dir Celtic Trust Ltd (Tortola, BVI); *Clubs* Brooks's, Queen's, Mill Reef (Antigua); *Style*— The Hon Barnaby Howard; Pinebrook Rd, RR 2, Bedford, New York 10506, USA (☎ 914 234 3528); St Ann's Bay, Englishtown, Nova Scotia B0C 1H0, Canada (☎ 909 929 2829)

HOWARD, Hon Caroline Anne; da (by 1 m) of 4 Baron Strathcona and Mount Royal; *b* 1959; *Style*— The Hon Caroline Howard

HOWARD, Lady Carolyn Bridget Dacre; da of late 11 Earl of Carlisle; *b* 1919; *Career* Subaltern ATS, transfd to FANY Ambulance Corps 1939-45; *Style*— Lady Carolyn Howard; 16 Brunswick Rd, Penrith, Cumbria

HOWARD, Hon Cecil John Arthur; 2 s of 19 Earl of Suffolk (ka 1917); *b* 24 June 1908; *Educ* Eton; *m* 1939, Frances Drake (former Hollywood film actress), da of late Edwin Morgan Dean, of Newcastle-upon-Tyne and Toronto; *Career* former Lt RTC; *Style*— Hon Cecil Howard; 1511 Summit Ridge Drive, Beverly Hills, Ca, USA

HOWARD, (Thomas) Charles Francis; LVO (1968); s of Brig Thomas Farquharson Ker Howard, DSO (d 1962), of Southampton, and Anne Cuningham, *née* Scott; *b* 5 Mar 1937; *Educ* Winchester, Sandhurst; *m* 16 July 1969, Mary Henrietta, da of Capt Hugh Dixon, DSC, RN (d 1960), of S Devon; 2 da (Jane b 1970, Philippa b 1971); *Career* 1 Queen's Dragoon Gds 1957-65, Equerry to HM The Queen 1965-68, ret Hon Maj 1968; trainee in insur indust 1968-73, dir HA Outwaite 1973-; *Recreations* gardening, silviculture, shooting; *Clubs* Army and Navy; *Style*— Charles Howard, Esq; Brunton House, Collingbourne Kingston, Marlborough, Wilts SN8 3SE (☎ 026 485 243); H A Outhwaite & Co Ltd, Regent House, 235 Regent St, London W1R 7AG (☎ 01 409 1630, fax 01 495 0267)

HOWARD, Hon David Francis; 3 s of 2 Baron Howard of Penrith; *b* 29 May 1949; *Educ* Ampleforth Univ of Oxford; *m* 1981, Diana, da of late John S Radway, by Judith (subsequently 2 w of Lt-Col Esmond Baring, OBE (gs of 4 Baron Ashburtom) and since 1965 2 w of 3 Marquess of Linlithgow (d 1987); Diana was formerly w of Timothy L B Davis; 2 da (Rachel b 1982, Alice b 1983, Olivia b 1986, Frances b 1988); *Style*— The Hon David Howard

HOWARD, David Howarth Seymour; s and h of Sir (Hamilton) Edward de Coucey Howard, 2 Bt, GBE, *qv*; *b* 29 Dec 1945; *Educ* Radley, Worcester Coll Oxford (MA); *m* 6 June 1968, Valerie Picton, o da of late Derek Weatherly Crosse, of Chase House, Callis Court Rd, Broadstairs; 2 s, 2 da; *Career* Alderman City of London, Common Councilman City of London 1972-86; cllr London Borough of Sutton 1974-78; memb Stock Exchange; *Style*— David Howard, Esq; 18 Finsbury Circus, London EC2

HOWARD, Cdr David Mowbray Algernon; s of Hon John Anthony Frederick Charles Howard (d 1971, s of 5 Earl of Effingham); hp of 6 Earl of Effingham; *b* 29 April 1939; *Educ* Fettes Coll; *m* 1964 (m dis 1975), Anne Mary, da of Harrison Sayer (d 1980), of Cambridge; 1 s (Edward b 1971); *Career* Offr RN, MOD London; *Recreations* squash, cricket, fishing; *Style*— Cdr David M A Howard, RN; Byways, South Harting, Petersfield, Hants GU31 5PH (☎ home: 0730 825211; office: 01 218 6516)

HOWARD, David Sanctuary; s of H Howard (d 1979); *b* 22 Jan 1928; *Educ* Stowe; *m* 1, 1952, Elizabeth, da of late Adm Sir Dudley North, GCVO; 1 s (Thomas), 3 da (Philippa, Sophie, Joanna); m 2, 1974, Anna-Maria, da of late Dante Bocci; *Career* co dir 1960-73, dir Heirloom and Howard Ltd 1973-; FSA; *Books* Armorial Porcelain (1974), China for the West (1978); *Clubs* Oriental; *Style*— David Howard, Esq; 1 Hay Hill, London W1 (☎ 01 493 5868)

HOWARD, Dennis; VRD (1965, and bars 1975, 1985); s of Henry Thomas Howard (d 1938), and Henrietta, *née* Sturley (d 1969); *b* 24 Mar 1927; *Educ* Hymers Coll Hull, Univ Coll Hull, Univ of London (BSc); *m* 10 July 1948, Hilda Mary, da of John Douglas Beeson (d 1931); 1 s (John Nigel b 1959), 2 da (Lorraine Alison b 1956, Lesley Ann b 1963); *Career* cmmnd RN 1945-50, RNR 1951-88, ret Lt Cdr; HM Colonial Serv (Overseas Civil Serv) admin offr Western regn of Nigeria 1953-61; slr in private practice 1964-, pt/t lectr in law Univ of Hull 1964-77; chm: Yorkshire Rent Assessment Ctee 1972-, Social Security Appeal Tbnl Hull 1978-, Med Appeals Tbnl Leeds 1987-; memb Law Soc 1964, FFA 1982; *Style*— Dennis Howard, Esq, VRD; The White Hse, Middleton-on-the-Wolds, Driffield, E Yorks (☎ 037781 578)

HOWARD, Hon Donald Alexander Euan; s (by 1 m) and h of 4 Baron Strathcona and Mount Royal; *b* 24 June 1961; *Educ* Hawtrey, Gordonstoun; *Career* Lt RN; *Recreations* steam boats, sailing, shooting; *Clubs* Fishmongers; *Style*— The Hon D Alex Howard

HOWARD, Hon Edmund Bernard Carlo; CMG (1969), MVO (1961); s of 1 Baron Howard of Penrith, GCB, GCMG, CVO (d 1939); *b* 8 Sept 1909; *Educ* Downside, Newman Sch USA, New Coll Oxford; *m* 1936, Cécile Henriette, da of Charles Geoffroy-Dechaume, of Valmondois, France; 3 s, 1 da (and 1 da decd); *Career* serv WWII KRRC (Italy), ret Maj; barr Middle Temple 1932, sec to tstees and mangrs of Stock Exchange 1937-39; joined Dip Serv, Second sec (info) Rome 1947-51, FO 1951-53, first sec Madrid 1953-57, head of chancery Bogota 1957-59, FO 1960, consul-gen San Marino and consul Florence 1960-61, cnsllr Rome 1961-65, consul-gen Genoa 1965-69, ret; Cdr Order of Merit Italy, 1973; *Books* Genoa, History and Art in an Old Seaport (1971); *Recreations* travel, gardening, walking; *Style*— The Hon Edmund Howard; Jerome Cottage, Marlow Common, Bucks SL7 2QR (☎ 062 84 2129)

HOWARD, Sir (Hamilton) Edward (de Coucey); 2 Bt (UK 1955), of Great Rissington, Co Gloucester; GBE (1972); s of Sir (Harold Walter) Seymour Howard, 1 Bt, Lord Mayor of London 1954 (d 1956); *b* 29 Oct 1915; *Educ* Le Rosey, Radley, Worcester Coll Oxford; *m* 1943, Elizabeth Howarth, da of Maj Percy H Ludlow (d 1968); 2 s; *Heir* s, David Howard; *Career* serv WWII Flt Lt RAF (despatches); memb of Stock Exchange London 1946, sr ptnr of the firm of Charles Stanley and Co (stockbrokers); chm: Eucryl 1946-71, LRC Int Ltd 1971-82; Alderman City of London 1963, Sheriff City of London 1966, Lord Mayor of London 1971-72, HM Lt City of London 1976; master of the Gardeners' Co 1961; KStJ 1972; *Recreations* gardening; *Clubs* City of London, City Livery, United Wards; *Style*— Sir Edward Howard, Bt, GBE; Courtlands, Bishops Walk, Shirley Hills, Surrey CR0 5BA (☎ 01 656 4444); Charles Stanley and Co, Stockbrokers, Garden House, 18 Finsbury Sq, London EC2M 7BL (☎ 01 638 5717)

HOWARD, Elizabeth Jane; da of David Liddon Howard (d 1962), and Katharine Margaret Somervell (d 1975); *b* 26 Mar 1923; *m* 1941, Peter Markham Scott, s of Capt Robert Falcon Scott; 1 da (Nicola); m 2, James Douglas-Henry; m 3, Kingsley Amis; *Career* novelist, playwright 14 TV plays; *Books* The Beautiful Visit (1950), The Long View (1956), The Sea Change (1959), After Julius (1965), Something in Disguise (1969), Odd Girl Out (1972), Getting It Right (1982); book of short stories Mr Wrong (1975); *Recreations* gardening, cooking, reading, music; *Style*— Miss Elizabeth Howard; c/o Jonathan Clowes, 22 Prince Albert Rd, London NW1

HOWARD, Hon Emma Laura Louise; da (twin, by 1 m) of 4 Baron Strathcona and Mount Royal; *b* 1963; *Style*— The Hon Emma Howard

HOWARD, Francis Alick; *b* 6 Mar 1922; *Career* WWII 1940-46, demob Sgt 1946; comedian and entertainer; worked in the London docks; started bottom of the bill in music-hall 1946, moved on to radio series Variety Bandbox; films: The Ladykillers, The Great St Trinians' Train Robbery, Carry on Doctor, Up Pompeii; theatre: Bottom in a Midsummers Nights Dream (Old Vic), A Funny Thing Happened on the way to the Forum; TV incl: Frankie Howerd Show, Frankie and Bruce Show, Francis Howerd's Tittertime; worldwide appearances for HM Forces Entertainment; *Recreations* theatre, walking, travelling, reading, music; *Style—* Francis Howard, Esq, OBE; c/o Tessa Le Bars Management, 18 Queen Anne St, London W1H 9LB (☎ 01 636 3191, fax 01 436 0229)

HOWARD, Francis John Adrian; s of Ewen Storrs Howard (d 1979), of Cape Town, S Africa, and Cynthia Beatrice, *née* Wallace; *b* 11 July 1935; *Educ* Michaelhouse, Natal SA, Univ of Natal SA; *m* 1961, Lynette, da of late John Ashford Mader, of S Africa; 2 s; *Career* dir: The Diamond Trading Co 1973-75, Beralt Tin and Wolfram Ltd 1977-86, Cape Industs plc 1977-86, Charter Consolidated plc 1978-87, Anderson Strathclyde Ltd 1980-87, Howard Perry Assocs Ltd 1987-, Nestor-BNA plc 1987-, Stream Resources Ltd 1988-, Hawtal Whiting plc 1988-; *Recreations* gardening, shooting, skiing; *Clubs* Country, Rand, Johannesburg, Boodles; *Style—* Francis Howard, Esq; 26 Chesson Rd, London W14 9QX (☎ 01 381 1814); Howard Perry Assocs Ltd, 16 John St, London WC1N 2DL (☎ 01 831 5560)

HOWARD, (Cecil) Geoffrey; s of Arthur Cecil Howard (d 1965), of Tankerton, Kent, and Bessie, *née* Quinn (d 1919); *b* 14 Feb 1909; *Educ* St Christoper's Sch Letchworth Herts, Alleynes's Stevenage Herts; *m* 11 May 1935, Nora, da of Robert Alexander Le Plastrier (d 1947), of Bromley, Kent; 4 da (Frances b 7 March 1939, Joy b 25 Feb 1941, Ursula b 20 July 1946, Rosalind b 26 June 1948); *Career* 500 (Co of Kent) Sqdn Roy Auxiliary Air Force 1938-40, cmmnd RAF 1940, serv air rescue 1940-45; Martins Bank 1926-39; asst sec Surrey CCC 1946-48, sec Lancs CCC 1949-64, sec Surrey CCC 1965-75; mangr MCC tours: India, Pakistan and Ceylon 1951-52, Aust and NZ 1954-55, Pakistan 1955-56; hon tres Minor Counties Cricket Assoc 1975-84; UK agent: Bd of Control for Cricket in Pakistan 1952-70, Bd of control for Cricket in India 1956-62; former Kent rugby player and Middx cricketer; memb Inst of Bankers; *Recreations* cricket, rugby football, dry stone-walling, gardening, reading; *Clubs* MCC, Surrey CCC (pres 1989), Lancs CCC; *Style—* Geoffrey Howard, Esq; The Barn, Windsoredge, Nailsworth, Gloucs

HOWARD, Greville Patrick Charles; s of Col Henry Redvers Greville Howard (d 1978), and Patience Nichol (d 1987); *b* 22 April 1941; *Educ* Eton; *m* 1, 4 March 1978 (decd); m 2, 20 Nov 1981, Mary Cortlandt, da of Robert Veitch Culverwell, of Chippenham, Wilts; 2 s (Thomas b 1983, Charles b 1986), 1 da (Annabel b 1984); *Career* landowner; chm and md The Keep Trust plc, dir Harvey and Thomson plc; *Recreations* hunting, tennis; *Style—* Greville P C Howard, Esq; Castle Rising, Kings Lynn, Norfolk

HOWARD, Hon Henry Francis Geoffrey; s of Baron Howard of Henderskelfe (d 1984); *b* 1950; *Style—* The Hon Henry Howard

HOWARD, Dr James Griffiths; s of Joseph Griffiths Howard (d 1973), and Kathleen Mildred (d 1984); *b* 25 Sept 1927; *Educ* Raynes Park GS, Middx Hosp Med Sch, Univ of London (MB, BS, PhD, MD) ; *m* 14 July 1951, Opal St Clair, da of John Harman Echalaz (d 1947); 1 s (Roger St Clair b 1956, d 1984), 2 da (Flavia Rosamund b 1954, Charmian Isabel b 1958); *Career* reader depts of zoology and surgical sci Univ of Edinburgh 1958-69; The Wellcome Res Laboratories 1969-86, dir biomedical res, head biological res div and head experimental immunobiology, asst dir The Wellcome Tst 1986-; FIBiol 1981, FRS 1984; *Recreations* fine arts, music, hillwalking, cooking ; *Style—* Dr James Howard; The Wellcome Trust, 1 Park Sq West, London NW1 4LJ (☎ 01 486 4902)

HOWARD, Jane Alison; da of Mr Eric George Bullough, of Blackpool, Lancs, and Doreen Ruth, *née* Towers, of Thornton Cleveleys, Lancs; *b* 6 Feb 1956; *Educ* Blackpool Collegiate GS, LSE (BSc), Leeds Poly (post grad mgmnt dip); *m* 1981 (m dis 1988), John G V Howard, s of Graham Howard, of Worthing, Sussex; *Career* mgmnt trainee NHS 1978-79, dir Hospitality Servs AMI 1979-80, exec dir (later mktg dir) Kingsway Rowland (Saatchi & Saatchi's PR Agency) 1982-89; won HCITB Travelling Scholarship Award 1979; involved in Cancerlink and Action on Addiction, memb London Regn CBI; MHCIMA, MCFA; *Recreations* riding; *Clubs* RAC; *Style—* Mrs Jane Howard; 67-69 Whitfield St, London W1P 5RL (☎ 01 436 4060, fax 01 255 2131)

HOWARD, Lady Jane Mary; *née* Waldegrave; resumed use of former married name, Lady Jane Howard, 1979; da of 12 Earl Waldegrave; *b* 1934; *m* 1, 1954 (m dis 1977), Donald Euan Palmer Howard, 4 Baron Strathcona and Mount Royal; 2 s, 4 da; m 2 (m dis 1979), Duncan McIntosh, OBE, AFC; *Career* guide, lectr, dir Specialtours Ltd; *Style—* Lady Jane Howard; 17 Durand Gdns, London SW9 0PS (☎ 01 582 9052)

HOWARD, Hon Mrs (Jean Margaret); *née* Parnell; da of 6 Baron Congleton (d 1932); *b* 4 June 1922; *m* 1952, as his 2 w, Frederick Henry, DSO, MC, s of Capt William Gilbert Howard, CBE, RN; 3 s (1 s decd), 1 da; *Career* hill farmer; *Style—* The Hon Mrs Howard; Isle of Ulva, Ulva Ferry, Mull, Argyll PA73 6LZ (☎ 068 85 243)

HOWARD, John Francis; s of William George Howard (d 1938), of London, and Frances Jane, *née* McLaren (d 1981); *b* 22 Oct 1918; *Educ* Merchant Taylors', King's Coll London Univ (LLB); *m* 17 July 1948, Phyllis Morecroft, da of Bernard Horsford Heaver, MBE; 2 s (Charles John b 4 Aug 1949, Peter William Heaver b 8 Aug 1952), 1 da (Mary Catherine b 23 May 1960); *Career* WWII RA: Militiaman 1939-40, Lt 1940-42, Pilot Offr to Fl Lt RAF (Pilot Fighter Cmd and 2 Tactical Air Force UK and Europe) 1942-46; Barr Grays Inn 1949; GKN plc: gp sec 1960-73, dir, 1973-78, memb mgmnt ctee UK and overseas; dir Birmingham Broadcasting Ltd 1973-; chm: St John's Ambulance, New Forest Centre 1980-86; Freeman: City of London, City of Glasgow; Liveryman Worshipful Co of Coopers (memb Ct 1979, Master 1986); FCIS; *Recreations* gardening (rose growing), photography; *Clubs* RAF, City Livery, Royal Lymington YC; *Style—* John Howard, Esq; Camera Principalis, The Old Deanery, 125 The Close, Salisbury, Wilts SP1 2EY (☎ 0722 332 129)

HOWARD, John Philip; s and h of Sir William Howard Lawson, 5 Bt; assumed by Royal Licence surname and arms of Howard 1962; *b* 6 June 1934; *m* 1960, Jean Veronica, da of late Col John Evelyn Marsh, DSO, OBE; 2 s (Philip William b 1961, m, 1988 Cara Margaret, 1 da; The Hon Martin Browne Thomas John b 1963), 1 da (Julia Frances b 1964)); *Style—* John Howard, Esq; Corby Castle, Carlisle

HOWARD, Hon Jonathan Alan; s of 3 Baron Strathcona and Mount Royal (d 1959), and Hon Diana Evelyn, *née* Loder, da of 1 Baron Wakehurst; *b* 15 Nov 1933; *Educ* Eton, Trinity Coll Cambridge, Royal Inst of Tech Stockholm, Stockholm Univ; *m* 1, 1956 (m dis 1969), Hon Brigid Mary, *née* Westenra, da of 6 Baron Rossmore; 2 da; m 2, 1970, Cecilia Philipson; 1 s; *Career* former 2 Lt Coldstream Gds, Argyll and Sutherland Highlanders (TA); memb Nat Assoc of Swedish Architects; *Style—* The Hon Jonathan Howard; Frihetsvaegen 56, Jaerfaella, Sweden

HOWARD, (James) Ken; s of Frank Howard (d 1974), of Mousehole, Cornwall, and Elizabeth Crawford, *née* Meikle (d 1987); *b* 26 Dec 1932; *Educ* Kilburn GS, Hornsey Coll of Art, Royal Coll of Art (ARCA); *m* 31 March 1961 (m dis 1974), Margaret Ann, da of Philip Popham, of Ickenham, Middx; *Career* Nat Serv RM 1953-55; artist; Br Cncl Scholarhship Florence 1958-59, taught at various London Art Schs 1959-73, official artist Imp War Museum NI 1978; painted for Br Army: NI, Germany, Cyprus, Hong Kong, Brunei, Nepal, Belize, Norway, Lebanon; one man exhibitions: Plymouth Art Centre 1955, John Whibley Gallery 1966-68, New Grafton Gallery 1971-, Oscar J Peter Johnson 1986-, Jersey 1980, Hong Kong 1979, Nicosia 1982, Delhi 1983; works purchased by: Plymouth Art Gallery, Imp War Musuem, Guildhall Art Gallery, Ulster Museum, Nat Army Museum, Southern Art Gallery, HNC Art Gallery, Sheffield Art Gallery; portraits incl: Gerald Durrell, Gen Sir Martin Farndale; cmmns for: Drapers Co, Haberdashers Co, States of Jersey, HQ Br Army of the Rhine, HM Forces in Cyprus, The Stock Exchange, Lloyds of London, Royal Hosp Chelsea, Banque Paribas; Hon RBA 1988, Hon ROI 1988; NEAC 1962, RWA 1981, RWS 1983, ARA 1983; *Books* The War Artists (1986); *Style—* Ken Howard, Esq; 8 South Bolton Gdns, London SW5 0DH (☎ 01 373 2912); St Clements Hall, Paul Lane, Mousehole, Cornwall TR19 6TR (☎ 0737 731596)

HOWARD, Lady Leonora Stanley; *née* Baldwin; da of late 1 Earl Baldwin of Bewdley (Rt Hon Sir Stanley Baldwin, KG, MP, PM), and Dame Lucy Baldwin, GBE, *née* Ridsdale; *b* 1896; *m* 1922, Capt The Hon Sir Arthur Jared Palmer Howard, KBE, CVO (d 1971), s of Margaret Charlotte, Baroness Strathcona and Mount Royal (2 in line); 2 s, 2 da (*see* Hon Mrs Langley G H Russell); *Style—* Lady Leonora Howard; 8 Sandwich St, St Pancras, London WC1

HOWARD, Margaret; da of John Bernard Howard (d 1969), and Ellen Corwenna, *née* Roberts; *b* 29 Mar 1938; *Educ* St Mary's Convent Rhyl, St Teresa's Convent Sunbury-On-Thames, Guildhall School of Music and Drama (LGSM), Univ of Indiana USA; *Career* BBC announcer 1966-69, reporter: World This Weekend 1971-74, Pick of the Week 1974-; memb: LRAM; *Books* Margaret Howard's Pick of the Week (1984), Court Jesting (1986); *Recreations* riding, wine tasting; *Style—* Miss Margaret Howard; Broadcasting House, London W1 (☎ 01 580 4468)

HOWARD, Michael; QC (1982), MP (C) Folkestone and Hythe 1983-; s of late Bernard Howard, and Hilda Howard; *b* 7 July 1941; *Educ* Llanelli GS, Peterhouse Cambridge; *m* 1975, Sandra Clare, da of Wing Cdr Saville Paul; 1 s, 1 da, 1 step-s; *Career* pres Cambridge Union 1962, called to the Bar Inner Temple 1964, chm Bow Gp 1970; contested (C) Liverpool Edge Hill 1966 and 1970, chm Coningsby Club 1972-73; memb: Cons Gp for Europe, Euro Movement exec ctee 1970-73; pps to Slr-Gen 1984-85, parly under-sec of state for Consumer and Corporate Affrs 1985-87, min for Local Govt 1987-88; min for Water and Planning 1988-; *Recreations* watching sport, reading; *Clubs* Carlton; *Style—* Michael Howard, Esq, QC, MP; House of Commons, London SW1

HOWARD, Hon Michael Edmund; 2 s of 2nd Baron Howard of Penrith; *b* 19 April 1947; *Educ* Ampleforth; *Style—* The Hon Michael Howard

HOWARD, Sir Michael Eliot; CBE (1977), MC (1943); s of Geoffrey Eliot Howard (d 1956), of Dorset, and Edith Julia Emma Edinger (d 1977); *b* 29 Nov 1922; *Educ* Wellington, Christ Church Oxford (MA, DLitt); *Career* serv Italian theatre with 2 & 3 Bns Coldstream Gds (Capt) 1943-45; prof war studies King's coll London 1963-68, Chichele prof history of war Oxford 1977-80, pres Int Inst of Strategic Studies, Regius prof Modern History Univ of Oxford 1980-, prof of history Yale Univ 1989-; *Books* The Franco-Prussian War (1961), Grand Strategy, Vol IV in UK Official History of World War II (1972), The Continental Commitment (1972), War in European History (1976); *Recreations* music; *Clubs* Athenaeum, Garrick; *Style—* Sir Michael Howard, CBE, MC; The Old Farm, Eastbury, Newbury, Berks RG16 7JN

HOWARD, Hon (Anthony) Michael Geoffrey; yst s of Baron Howard of Henderskelfe (d 1984); *b* 18 May 1958; *m* 1985, (Linda) Louise, yr da of Alexander McGrady, of Broughty Ferry, Angus; 2 da (Arabella Blanche Geneviève b 1986, Grania Alexandra Louise b 1988); *Style—* The Hon Anthony Howard; Leyfield Farm, Coneysthorpe, York YO6 7DF

HOWARD, Michael Jonathan; s of Alec Howard (d 1972); *b* 20 Mar 1927; *Educ* Bradfield Coll, Queen's Coll Oxford; *m* 1953, Susan Mai, da of George Francis Pitt-Lewis; 2 s; *Career* chm and md Thames Case Ltd 1967-83, dir Br Fibreboard Packaging Assoc 1983-86, sec Assoc Euro Solid Fibreboard Case Mfrs 1983-; FCA, FCMA; *Recreations* riding (principally hunting), squash, music; *Clubs* Naval; *Style—* Michael Howard, Esq; Purleigh Lodge, Purleigh, Essex (☎ home 0621 828 287; office 01 434 3851)

HOWARD, Hon Nicholas Paul Geoffrey; s of Baron Howard of Henderskelfe (d 1984); *b* 1952; *Educ* Eton, Univ of Oxford; *m* 1983, Amanda Kate Victoria, only da of Derek Nimmo, actor, of Kensington; *Style—* The Hon Nicholas Howard

HOWARD, Peter Reuben; s of Edward Reuben Howard (d 1966), of Battersea, and Ellen Ruth, *née* Carpenter (d 1979); *b* 18 Feb 1922; *Educ* Sir Walter St John's Sch, Univ of London (BSc, PhD); *m* 1945, Betty, da of Eakson Lee Morris (d 1972), of Norwich; 1 da (Suzanne); *Career* dir-gen CEGB transmission and tech servs div 1977-85, vice-pres IEE 1982-85, private conslt 1985-, dir ERA Technol Ltd 1985-; FEng, ; *Recreations* general engineering, photography, gardening; *Clubs* Worshipful Co of Engrs; *Style—* Dr Peter R Howard; The Old Thatch, Blackmoor, Liss, Hants GU33 6BZ (☎ 042 03 3642)

HOWARD, Hon Philip Charles Wentworth; s of 12 Earl of Carlisle; *b* 1963; *Style—* The Hon Philip Howard; Naworth Castle, Brampton, Cumbria

HOWARD, Hon Philip Esmé; s and h of 2 Baron Howard of Penrith, *qv*; *b* 1 May 1945; *Educ* Ampleforth, Ch Ch Oxford; *m* 1969, Sarah, da of late Barclay Walker; 1 s (Thomas Philip b 1974, Michael Barclay b 1984), 2 da (Natasha Mary b 1970, Laura Isabella b 1976); *Style—* The Hon Philip Howard; 45 Erpingham Rd, London SW15 (☎ 01 789 7604)

HOWARD, Philip Nicholas Charles; s of Peter Dunsmore Howard (d 1965), and Doris Emily Metaxa; *b* 2 Nov 1933; *Educ* Eton, Trinity Coll Oxford (MA); *m* 1959,

Myrtle Janet Mary, da of Sir Reginald Houldsworth, *qv*; 2 s, 1 da; *Career* Nat Serv Lt Black Watch; newspaper reporter and columnist; Glasgow Herald 1959-64, literary ed The Times 1978- (joined 1964), London ed Verbatim 1977-; author; FRSL; *Books* The Black Watch (1968), The Royal Palaces (1970), London's River (1975), New Words for Old (1977), The British Monarchy (1977), Weasel Words (1978), Words Fail Me (1980), A Word in Your Ear (1983), The State of the Language (1984), We Thundered Out, 200 Years of The Times 1785-1985 (1985), Winged Words (1988), Word-Watching (1988); *Recreations* reading, walking, talking; *Style*— Philip Howard, Esq; Flat 1, 47 Ladbroke Grove, London W11 (☎ 01 727 1077)

HOWARD, Robin Jared Stanley; CBE (1976); s of late Hon Sir Arthur Howard, KBE, CVO, DL, and Lady Lorna Howard; *b* 17 May 1924; *Educ* Trinity Coll Cambridge (MA); *Career* Scots Gds 1943-45; called to the Bar; ran refugee dept UN 1956, hon advsr for World Fedn of UN Assocs; dir gen and chm Contemp Dance Tst (formed 1966); chm Acad Indian Dance; *Recreations* contemporary dance, art; *Clubs* Garrick, MCC; *Style*— Robin Howard, Esq, CBE; 7 Sandwich Street, London WC1H 9PL; The Place, 17 Dukes Rd, London WC1H 9AB (☎ 01 387 0161 x 204)

HOWARD, Ronald John Frederick; s of Frederick Percial Howard (d 1947), and Lydia Mary Howard (d 1976); *b* 1 Sept 1921; *Educ* Whitgift Middle Sch; *m* 1, 1944, (Syliva) Betty (d 1974); m 2, 25 Sept 1976, (Ann) Veronica, da of Ward Turner Nicholson (d 1967); *Career* Metal Industs Ltd 1947-67 (dir 1959-67), dep gen mangr AEI/GEC 1967-68; chief exec dir: Plantation Hldgs Ltd 1969-78, Phicom plc 1978-81 (chm 1981-84); non exec dir: Cambridge Electronic Industs plc 1980-, Fothergill and Harvey plc 1973-87; dir: Cynanamid-Fothergill Ltd 1981-87, Infrared Assocs Inc 1985-88; fndr memb of bd and dep chm Chiltern Radio plc 1980-; chm: The Rank Phicom Video Gp Ltd 1981-84, Technol Mgmnt Servs Ltd 1981-, Baird UK Hldgs Ltd 1982-, Silver Chalice Prodns Int Ltd (Bermuda) and Silver Chalice Prodns Ltd 1983-86, Reflex Hldgs Ltd 1986-88, Commtel Consumer Electronics plc 1987-88, Synoptics Ltd 1988-; vice chm Spectros Int plc (now Kratos Gp plc) 1984-; Master Worshipful Co of Scientific Instrument Makers 1987-; FInstnl 1981, CBIM 1984; *Recreations* sailing, photography; *Clubs* City of London, Savile, Royal Thames YC; *Style*— Ronald Howard, Esq; 49 Beaumont St, London W1N 1RE (☎ 01 935 6355); Springwood House, Ickwell Green, Beds SG18 9EE (☎ 076 727 348); Technology Management Services Ltd, 4th floor, 43 Aldwych, London WC2B 4DA (☎ 01 379 3513, car tel 0860 367 290)

HOWARD, Hon Simon Bartholomew Geoffrey; s of Baron Howard of Henderskelfe (d 1984); *b* 26 Jan 1956; *Educ* Eton, RAC Cirencester, Study Centre for Fine and Decorative Arts; *m* 1983, Annette Marie, Countess Compton, er da of Charles Antony Russell Smallwood, and formerly 2 w (m dis 1977), of Earl Compton (now 7 Marquess of Northampton); *Career* chm of estate co; landowner (10,000 acres); chm: Yorkshire regnl HHA; *Recreations* photography, wine, country sports; *Style*— The Hon Simon Howard; Castle Howard, York (☎ 065 384 333)

HOWARD, Terence; s of Thomas James Howard (d 1979), of Eastbourne, and Nora Emily, *née* Moore; *b* 31 Oct 1939; *Educ* St Pauls; *m* 1, 22 Aug 1969 (m dis), Venetia, da of Gordon Smith Cuninghame (d 1965); 2 s (Charles b 1974, Thomas b 1982), 2 da (Tara b 1964, Scarlett b 1973); m 2, 13 July 1983, Belinda Elizabeth, da of David Charlton Humphreys; *Career* chm: Cuninghame Howard Ltd 1979-89, Nowlan Howard Ltd 1989; exec creative dir Ayer Barker 1984-88; creator and writer TV series The Other Arf 1979-83; *Recreations* photography, tennis; *Clubs* Groucho; *Style*— Terence Howard, Esq; 1 Shalcomb St, London SW10, (☎ 01 352 2126); 10 Bateman St, London W1, (☎ 01 439 1515)

HOWARD, Hon William John; 4 s of 2 Baron Howard of Penrith; *b* 30 May 1953; *Educ* Ampleforth; *Career* concert pianist (debut at Wigmore Hall Dec 1981); *Style*— The Hon William Howard

HOWARD, William McLaren; QC (1964); s of William George Howard (d 1938), and Frances Jane Howard, *née* McLaren (d 1980); *b* 27 Jan 1921; *Educ* Merchant Taylors'; *Career* judge advocate of the Fleet 1973-86, barr, rec; memb Hong Kong Bar; *Clubs* Garrick, Royal Hong Kong Jockey; *Style*— William M Howard, Esq, QC; The Red House, Holkham, Wells Next the Sea, Norfolk NR23 1RG; 1201 Prince's Bldg, Central Hong Kong

HOWARD DE WALDEN, 9 Baron (E 1597); John Osmael Scott-Ellis; TD; also Baron Seaford (UK 1826); s of 8 Baron Howard de Walden (d 1946, gs of 1 Baron Seaford, whose w Elizabeth was gda of 4 Earl of Bristol (Lord Bristol's f's mother was maternal gda of 3 Earl of Suffolk, who also held the Barony of Howard de Walden) and Margherita Van Raalte CBE, da of Charles van Raalte, JP; *b* 27 Nov 1912; *Educ* Eton, Magdalene Coll Cambridge; *m* 1, 1934, Countess Irene Harrach (d 1975), yst da of Count Hans Albrecht Harrach, of Munich (of a Mediatised Sovereign House of the Holy Roman Empire; the title of Baron Harrach was conferred by Ferdinand I 1552 (and under the Hungarian crown 1563) and the title of Count Harrach was cr by Emperor Ferdinand II 1627); 4 da; m 2, 1978, Gillian, da of Cyril Buckley and formerly w of 17 Viscount Mountgarret; *Heir* all 4 da as coheiresses: Hon Mrs Czernin, Hon Mrs Buchan of Auchmacoy, Hon Mrs White, Hon Mrs Acloque; *Career* Maj Westminster Dragoons (TA); dir Howard de Walden Estates Ltd; *Clubs* Jockey (sr steward 1957, 1964, 1976), Turf, Whites; *Style*— The Rt Hon the Lord Howard de Walden, TD; Avington Manor, Hungerford, Berks (☎ 0488 58229); Flat K, 90 Eaton Sq, London SW1 (☎ 01 235 7127)

HOWARD OF PENRITH, 2 Baron (UK 1930); Francis Philip Howard; DL (Glos 1960); 2 s of 1 Baron Howard of Penrith, GCB, GCMG, CVO (d 1939, 4 s of Henry Howard, n of 12 Duke of Norfolk), by his w Lady Isabella Giustiniani-Bandini, da of 8 Earl of Newburgh, Duca di Mondragone and Prince Giustiniani Bandini; *b* 5 Oct 1905; *Educ* Downside, Trinity Coll Cambridge; *m* 1 July 1944, Anne, da of John Beaumont Hotham (fifth in descent from Sir Beaumont Hotham, 7 Bt and f of 8, 9, 11 & 12 Bts, the last two being also 1 & 2 Barons Hotham); 4 s; *Heir* s, Hon Philip Howard; *Career* serv WWII, Capt RA (wounded); barr Middle Temple 1931; *Style*— The Rt Hon the Lord Howard of Penrith; Dean Farm, Coln St Aldwyns, Glos

HOWARD-DOBSON, Gen Sir Patrick John; GCB (1979, KCB 1974, CB 1973); s of Canon Howard Dobson; *b* 12 August 1921; *Educ* King's Coll Choir Sch, Framlingham Coll; *m* 1946, Barbara Mills; 2 s, 1 da; *Career* joined 7 Queen's Own Hussars 1941; served: Egypt, Burma, M East, Italy, Germany; CO The Queen's Own Hussars 1963-65, CO 20 Armd Bde 1965-67, COS Far East Cmd 1969-71, cmdt Staff Coll Camberley 1972-74, mil sec 1974-76, QMG 1977-79, Vice CDS Personnel and Logistics 1979-81, ret; ADC Gen to HM The Queen 1978-81, Col Cmdt Army Catering Corps 1976-82; Nat Pres Royal Br Legion 1981-87; *Recreations* sailing, golf; *Clubs* Cavalry and Guards, Royal Cruising, Senior Golfers Soc; *Style*— Gen Sir Patrick Howard-Dobson, GCB; 1 Drury Park, Snape, Saxmundham, Suffolk IP17 1TA

HOWARD-HARRISON, Anthony; *b* 29 Mar 1946; *Educ* privately (Dip Child Psychology, Cert Residential Social Work); *m* (m dis); *Career* landowner; chm two sch governing bodies apptd by by Devon CC 1974-85; voluntary social worker with the elderly and drug-related problems; chm Howard-Harrison Charitable Tst 1985-, fndr Cloudsleigh Nursing Hospice 1984-, princ Ward House Sch Devon for Maladjusted and Handicapped Children 1974-78; memb: Br Psychological Soc, Assoc of Workers with Maladjusted, Plymouth Gen Hosp League Ctee, Plymouth and dist Leukemia Fund, St Luke's Hospice, Age Concern, Nat Fund for Research into Crippling Diseases (former chm), Moorhaven Hosp League of Friends; supporter: Broadbeach House Ctee, Dhaka Brit Airways Orphanage Bangladesh, Starlight Fndn, Third World Volunteer; *Recreations* private pilot flying, rough shooting, antique collecting, foreign travel, eating good food constantly; *Clubs* Royal Western Yacht; *Style*— A Howard-Harrison, Esq; Thorn Park Mews, Thorn Pk, Mannamead, Plymouth PL3 4TG BZ (☎ (☎ 0752 660811)

HOWARD-HIGGINS, Capt Bruce Arthur; s of Arthur Edward Howard-Higgins (d 1979), of Imperial Coll Field Station, Sunninghill, Berks, and Madeleine Agnes, *née* Stanley-Smith; *b* 31 May 1940; *Educ* Allhallows Sch; *m* 17 Aug 1966 Maureen Mary (Mo), da of Desmond Milton Whitehouse, TD, of Clifford Chambers, Nr Stratford-Upon-Avon, Warwicks; 2 s (Charles Milton, James Milton); *Career* Lt (previously 2 Lt) Army Air Corps 1965-71; served: UK, Germany, The Gulf; pilot; BEA (viscount aircraft) 1971-77; BA: Boeing 707 1978-80 (also qualified as flight engr), Boeing 737 1981-83; seconded Air Mauritius 1984-86; pilot British Airways 1986- (B 737 1986-88 and B 757 1989); memb: Gt Chesterford Assoc, Gt Chesterford PCC, local Game conservancy branch; hon sec E Anglia branch Army Air Corps Assoc; *Recreations* shooting, skiing, motoring, gourmet; *Style*— Capt Bruce Howard-Higgins; c/o British Airways, P O Box 10, London Heathrow Airport, Hounslow TW6 2JA, (☎ 01 759 5511)

HOWARD-JOHNSTON, Rear Adm Clarence Dinsmore; CB (1955), DSO (1942), DSC (1940); s of John Howard-Johnston, of Nice, Alpes Maritimes, France (d 1913), and Dorothy Florence Baird (m 2, 1914, Comte Pierre du Brueil St Germain, d 1971); his ancestor John Howard Johnston left sch prematurely in order to fight as a Drummer Boy for the North in American Civil War, subsequently entered Dartmouth Coll, USA, an engr, built Peruvian railroad through Andes; Silver Mine owner Casapalca, Peru; *b* 13 Oct 1903; *Educ* Royal Naval Colls Osbourne & Dartmouth; *m* 1928, Esmé (m dis 1940), yst da of late Philip John FitzGibbon of Poona India; m 2, 1941 (m dis 1954), Lady Alexandra Henrietta Louisa Haig, da of 1st Earl Haig; 2 s, 1 da; m 3, 1955, Lise Rita Paulette, da of Paul César Helleu (d 1927); *Career* dir of studies Royal Hellenic Naval War Coll Athens 1938-40, dir Anti-U-Boat Div Naval Staff Admty 1943-45, Anti-Submarine Specialist to Cabinet Anti-U-Boat Meetings (under presidency of PM) 1943-45, cmd Cruiser HMS Bermuda, unit of Occupation Forces of Japan 1946-47, NA Paris 1947-50, Naval ADC to HM the Queen 1952; Cmdr: Order of Phoenix of Greece (1940), American Legion of Merit (1945); *Recreations* fishing, pisciculture, hill walking, gardening; *Clubs* White's, Naval & Military, Royal Yacht Squadron (naval member), Jockey (Paris); *Style*— Rear Admiral Howard-Johnston, CB, DSO, DSC; 5 Avenue Jomini, 1004 Lausanne, 45 Rue Emile Ménier, 75116 Paris

HOWARD-SMITH, Hon Mrs (Patricia Ann); da of 1 Baron Lambury (d 1967); *b* 1929; *m* 1951 (m dis 1968) Capt Morfryn James Howard-Smith, RN; 1 s, 1 da; *Style*— The Hon Mrs Howard-Smith; c/o Jose Villalonga 52 Bis, El Terreno, Palma de Mallorca

HOWARD-VYSE, Lt-Gen Sir Edward Dacre; KBE (1962, CBE 1955), CB (1958), MC (1941), DL (N Yorks 1974); s of Lt-Col Cecil Howard-Vyse, JP (d 1935), of Langton Hall, Malton,d and Ethel Maud Elsmie, *née* Hast (d 1946); *b* 27 Nov 1905; *Educ* Wellington, RMA; *m* 1940, Mary Bridget, er da of Col Hon Claude Henry Comaraich Willoughby, CVO (d 1932); 2 s, 1 da; *Career* memb Br Olympic Equestrian Team 1936; 2 Lt RA 1925, Lt-Col 1941, served with BEF in Fr 1939-40, MEF 1941-44, cmd 1 RHA CMF 1944-45, Brig 1949, CRA 7 armd div BAOR 1951-53, cmdt Sch of Artillery 1953, Maj-Gen Artillery NAG 1956-58, Maj-Gen 1957, dir RA WO 1959-61, Lt-Gen 1961, GOC-in-C Western Cmd 1961-64, ret 1964; Col Cmdt: RA 1962-70, RHA 1968-70; vice pres ACF Assoc 1974-(chm 1964-73), vice-pres Nat Artillery Assoc 1965-; DL East Riding and Kingston upon Hull 1964, vice-lt 1968-74; *Recreations* country pursuits; *Clubs* Army and Navy; *Style*— Lt-Gen Sir Edward Howard-Vyse, KBE, CB, MC, DL; Langton House, Malton, North Yorks

HOWARTH, Alan Thomas; MP (C) Stratford-on-Avon 1983-, CBE (1982); *b* 11 June 1944; *Educ* Rugby, King's Coll Cambridge; *m* 1967 Gillian Martha, da of Arthur Chance, of Dublin; 2 s, 2 da; *Career* former head chm's off CCO (PS to Rt Hon William Whitelaw and Rt Hon Lord Thorneycroft as Pty chm), dir Cons Record Dept 1979-81, vice-chm Pty orgn 1980-81, PPS to Dr Rhodes Boyson NI Off 1985-86, PPS to Dr Boyson, Dept Environment 1986-87, appointed asst govr whip 1987; Lord Cmmr of the Treasy 1989; *Books* Changing Charity (1984), Monty At Close Quarters (1985), Save Our Schools (1987), Arts: The Way Ahead (co-writer); *Recreations* books, travel, arts, running; *Style*— Alan Howarth, Esq, CBE, MP; House of Commons, London SW1

HOWARTH, (James) Gerald (Douglas); MP (C) Cannock and Burntwood 1983-; s of late James Howarth, of Berks, and Mary Howarth; *b* 12 Sept 1947; *Educ* Bloxham Sch Banbury, Southampton Univ; *m* 1973, Elizabeth; 2 s, 1 da; *Career* gen sec Soc for Individual Freedom 1969-71; Bank of America Int 1971-76, European Arab Bank 1976-81, Standard Chartered Bank plc 1981-83 (Loan Syndication Mangr); conslt to Astra Hldgs plc, Standard Chartered Bank plc, Trade Indemnity plc; memb Hounslow Borough Cncl 1982-83; parly private sec to Michael Spicer MP Dept of Energy 1987-, Hon Sec Cons Parliamentary Aviation Ctee 1983-87, fell Indust and Parly Tst; *Recreations* flying (Britannia Airways Parliamentary Pilot of the Year 1988), walking, DIY; *Style*— Gerald Howarth, Esq, MP; House of Commons, London SW1

HOWARTH, John Knight; s of Reginald Howarth, and Eleanor, *née* Knight; *b* 2 July 1914; *Educ* Royds Hall GS Huddersfield, Huddersfield Tech Coll of Commerce, RAF Coll of Aircraft Engrg, Hull Nautical Coll; *m* 3 Dec 1938, Elizabeth, da of Wilfred Wagstaff (d 1965), of 48 Beaumont Pk Rd, Huddersfield; 1 s (Richard Wagstaff b 1940); *Career* RAF 1941-42, seconded as internal auditor to Standard Aeor Shadow Factory Coventry 1942-45; trainee accountant Gen Accident Insur Co 1930-37, self employed as insur broker and commercial accountant 1937-45, dairy and beef farmer 1945-; chm: Malton RDC 1971-73, Ryedale Local Cncls Assoc 1973-; gen tax cmmr; churchwarden 1976-, chm Sheriff Hutton Parish Cncl, tres N Yorks Playing Fields Assoc, chm York Sea Cadet Unit; Member Co of Merchant Adventurers of City of York; FCCA 1946; *Books* History of Sheriff Hutton Castle (1949); *Recreations* sailing; *Clubs* Farmers' Club (London), Yorkshire, Whitby YC; *Style*— John Howarth, Esq; Castle Farm, Sheriff Hutton, York YO6 1PT (☎ 03477 341)

HOWAT, Prof Henry Taylor; CBE (1971); s of Adam Howat, (d 1917), of Pittenweem, Fife, and Henrietta, *née* Taylor (d 1955); *b* 16 May 1911; *Educ* Cameron Public Sch Madras, Coll St Andrews, St Andrews Univ (MB ChB, MD); *m* 29 June 1940; 2 s (John Michael Taylor b 18 April 1945, Andrew Alexander Taylor b 12 Feb 1952), 1 da (Henrietta Mary Taylor b 23 July 1948) ; *Career* WWII cmmnd RAMC 1940-46; regtl MO UK, physician specialist MEF and Br Liberation Army, Lt-Col i/c med div BAOR, demob Hon Lt-Col 1946; Manchester Royal Infirmary: chief asst to med unit 1945-46 (previously 1936-38 and 1939-40), res MO 1938-40 (physician Ancoats Hosp Manchester), physician 1948-76, i/c dept gastroenterology 1962-76; Univ of Manchester: reader (formerly lectr) in med 1969-72, prof gastroenterology 1972-76 (currently emeritus); chm Med Exec Ctee Utd Manchester Hosps 1968-73, chm faculty of med Univ of Manchester 1968-72, first pres Euro Pancreatic Club 1965; pres: Br Soc Gastroenterology 1968-69, Assoc of Physicians of GB and Ireland 1975-76, Pancreatic Soc of GB and Ireland 1978-79; Manchester Man of the Year 1973; Hon MD and medallist Faculty of Med Univ of Louvain Belgium 1945, Hon medallist JE Purkyne Czechoslovak Med Soc 1968, Hon MSc Manchester Univ 1975, Hon Dip and Medallion Hungarian Gastroenterological Soc 1988; FRCP (London) 1948, FRCP (Edin) 1965; *Books* The Exocrine Pancreas (co-ed 1979); *Recreations* golf; *Clubs* Athenaeum, Royal and Ancient GC; *Style*— Prof Henry T Howat, CBE; 3 Brookdale Rise, 1 Hilton Rd, Bramhall, Cheshire; 40 High St, Pittenweem, Fife

HOWAT, James Thom; s of William Howat (d 1964), of Glasgow, and Jean Shanks Carswell Howat, *née* Thom (d 1966); *b* 31 July 1926; *Educ* Glasgow HS, Dumfries Acad; *m* 1955, Christine Cowper, da of Charles Gordon (d 1973), of Scotland; 1 s (Russell b 1956), 3 da (Vyvian b 1958, Carole, b 1960, Linda b 1963); *Career* CA; dir Stanley P Morrison Ltd 1951, chm 1971-; dir: Morrisons Bowmore Distillery Ltd, Morrisons Glengarioch Distillery Ltd, Tannochside Bonding Co Ltd, Rob Royal Distillers Ltd, TA McClelland Ltd, The Spring burn Whisky Co Ltd, Doune Products Ltd, Laigh Woodston Farm Ltd; FID; *Recreations* history, literature, music, golf, bridge; *Clubs* Caledonian, Royal Scottish Automobile, Glasgow GC, Buchanan Castle GC, Prestwick GC; *Style*— James Howat, Esq; 14 Montrose Gdns, Milngavie, Glasgow G62 8NQ (☎ 041 956 2010); Stanley P Morrison Ltd, Springburn Bond, Carlisle St, Glasgow G21 1EQ (☎ 041 558 9011, telex 778340, fax 041 558 9010)

HOWDEN, Tim (Timothy Simon); s of Phillip Alexander Howden (d 1970), Irene Maud, *née* Thomas (d 1985); *b* 2 April 1937; *Educ* Tonbridge; *m* 20 Sept 1958 (m dis), Penelope Mary, *née* Wilmott; 2 s (Chalres b 6 April 1959, Dominic b 12 Oct 1965), 1 da (Joanna b 4 April 1961); *Career* Nat Serv 2 Lt RA 1955-57; Reckitt and colman 1959-73: sales mangr industl floor care UK 1959-62, gen mangr inudstl floor care France 1962-64, mktg mangr (later dep md) Germany 1964-70, dir Euro div 1970-73; Ranks Hovis McDougall (dir cereals div 1973-75), md RHM foods 1975-81, chm bakery div 1981-85, gp planning dir 1985-86, dep md 1987-; *Recreations* tennis, skiing, diving; *Clubs* Annabel's, Naval and Military; *Style*— Tim Howden, Esq; RHM plc, Alma Rd, Windsor, Berks SL4 3ST (☎ 0753 857123, fax 0753 846537, telex 847314)

HOWE, Charles Keith; s of Henry Beauclerk Howe (d 1948); *b* 11 Mar 1935; *Educ* Lancing, Trinity Hall Cambridge; *m* 1960, Carole, da of Alma Thomas Absalom, of Copthorne, Sussex; 1 s, 2 da; *Career* jt md Crystalate Hldgs 1978-83 (chief exec 1983-85), dir C H Resources Ltd 1985-; *Recreations* cricket; *Clubs* MCC; *Style*— Charles Howe Esq; Billhurst, Lingfield Common, Lingfield, Surrey (☎ 0342 832848)

HOWE, Prof Christopher Barry; s of Charles Roderick Howe, and Patricia, *née* Creden; *b* 3 Nov 1937; *Educ* William Ellis Sch Highgate London, St Catharine's Coll Cambridge (BA, MA), London Univ (PhD); *m* 2 Dec 1967, Patricia Anne, da of LG Giles; 1 s (Roderick Giles b 1972), 1 da (Emma Claire b 1968); *Career* econ directorate Fed Br Industs 1961-63, res fell and lectr SOAS, reader in econs of asia London Univ 1972-(prof 1979-), head Contemporary China Inst 1972-78; memb Hong Kong Univ and Poly Grants Ctee 1974, UGC 1979-84; *Books* Employment and Economic Growth in Urban China (1971), Wage Patterns and Wage Policies in Modern China (1973), China's Economy: A Basic Guide (1978), Shanghai (1980), Foundations of the Chinese Planned Economy (1989); *Recreations* walking, swimming, cycling, antiquarian books, France, music, photography; *Style*— Prof Christopher Howe; 12 Highgate Ave, London N6; Rue Maurice Lithaire, Arromanches, Normandy, France; School of Oriental & African Studies, Thornaaugh St, Russell Sq, London WC14 0XG (☎ 01 637 2388)

HOWE, Lady (Elspeth); JP (Inner London 1964-); *b* 8 Feb 1932; *Educ* Bath HS, Wycombe Abbey Sch, LSE (BSc); *m* Aug 1953, The Rt Hon Sir Geoffrey Howe, QC, MP, *qv*; 1 s (Alexander b 1959), 2 da (Caroline b 1955, Amanda (twin) b 1959); *Career* sec to princ of Architectural Assoc's Sch of Architecture 1952-55, dep chm Equal Opportunities Cmmn Manchester (chm legal ctee) 1975-79; chm Inner London Juvenile Cts: Southwark 1970-80, Greenwich 1980-83, Lambeth 1983-86, Wandsworth 1987-; non exec dir: Kingfisher (Hldgs) plc (formerly Woolworth Hldgs plc) 1987-, United Biscuits (Holdings) Ltd 1988-; pres Peckham Settlement 1976-, Fedn of Recruitment and Employment Servs 1980-; chm Business in the Community Women's Econ Decpt Initiative 1988-, NACRO working pty on fine enforcement 1980-81, NACRO drugs advsy gp 1988-; vice pres Pre School Playgroups Assoc 1978-83; memb: Lord Chllr's Advsy Ctee on Legal Aid 1971-75, Parole Bd For England and Wales 1972-75; contrib articles: The Times, Financial Times, Guardian, New Society; *Style*— Lady Howe, JP; 1 Carlton Gardens, London, SW1

HOWE, 7 Earl (UK 1821); Frederick Richard Penn Curzon; also Baron Howe of Langar (GB 1788), Baron Curzon of Penn (GB 1794) and Viscount Curzon of Penn (UK 1802); s of Cdr (Chambré) George William Penn Curzon, RN (d 1976), and Enid Jane Victoria, da of late Malcolm Mackenzie Fergusson; suc cous, 6 Earl Howe, CBE (d 1984); *b* 29 Jan 1951; *Educ* Rugby, Christ Church Oxford (MA); *m* 1983, Elizabeth Helen, elder da of Capt Burleigh Edward St Lawrence Stuart, of Ickford, Bucks; 1 da (Lady Anna Elizabeth b 19 Jan 1987); *Heir* cous Charles Mark Penn Curzon (b 1967); *Career* banker; dir: Adam & Co plc 1987-, Provident Life Assoc Ltd 1988-; pres: Nat Soc for Epilepsy, RNLI (Chilterns Branch), South Bucks Assoc for The Disabled, CPRE (Penn Country Branch); govr: King William IV Naval Fndn, Milton's Cottage Tst; hon tres The Trident Tst; *Recreations* words and music; *Style*— The Rt Hon the Earl Howe; Penn House, Amersham, Bucks HP7 0PS

HOWE, Prof Geoffrey Leslie; TD 1962 (bars 1969, 1974); s of Leo Leslie John Howe (d 1934), of Maidenhead, Berks, and Ada Blanche, *née* Partridge (d 1973); *b* 22 May 1924; *Educ* Royal Dental, Middx Hosp (LDS, RCS), Univ of Durham (MDS), Royal Coll of Surgns in Ireland; *m* 8 April 1948, Heather Patricia Joan, *née* Hambly; 1 s (Timothy John b 31 May 1958); *Career* dental offr RADC 1946-49, Col RADC (V) 1972-75, Col RARO 1973-(hon Col Cmdt RADC 1975-); prof oral surgery Univs of Durham and Newcastle-upon-Tyne 1959-67, prof oral surgery Royal Dental Hosp London Sch of Dental Surgery 1967-78 (dean 1973-78), prof Univ of Hong Kong 1978-84 (fndr Dean of Dentistry 1978-83); prof of oral surgery Jordan Univ of Sci and Technol 1986- (dean faculty of dentistry 1988-); vice-pres Br Dental Assoc 1979-(chm cncl 1973-78, vice chm 1971-73), memb cncl RCS 1977-78; OStJ: Liveryman Worshipful Co of Apothecaries Soc, Int Freeman New Orleans USA, Freeman Louisville USA; hon fell: Philippine Coll of Oral and Maxillo Facial Surgns 1979, Acad of Dentistry Int (USA) 1982; Fell Int Coll of Dentists, hon memb American Dental Assoc, LRCP, MRCS 1954, FDSRCS 1955, MDS 1961, FFD RCSI 1964,; *Books* Extraction of Teeth (1980), Minor Orsal Surgery (1985), Local Anaethesia in Dentistry (with F I H Whitehead 1981); *Recreations* sailing, reading, music, club life; *Clubs* Savage, Hong Kong, Royal Hong Kong YC; *Style*— Prof Geoffrey Howe, TD; 70 Croham Manor Rd, S Croydon, Surrey CR3 7BF (☎ 01 686 0941); Villa 2-1, Marina de Casares, Sabinillas, Manilva, Andalucia, Spain; Flat 7B, Block 11, Southern Housing, Yarmook Univ, Irbid, Jordan; Univ of Science and Technology, Irbid, Jordan (☎ 010962 2 295 111 ext 2087, fax 010962 2 295 123, telex 55545 JUST JO)

HOWE, Rt Hon Sir (Richard Edward) Geoffrey; PC (1972), QC (1965), MP (C) E Surrey 1974-; er s of B Howe; *b* 20 Dec 1926; *Educ* Winchester, Trinity Hall Cambridge; *m* 1953, Elspeth Rosamund Morton Shand, JP, *qv*, da of Philip Shand; 1 s, 2 da ; *Career* barr 1952; chm Bow Gp 1955, fought (C) Aberavon 1955 and 1959; memb Gen Bar Cncl 1957-61; md Crossbow 1957-60 (ed 1960-62); memb Cncl of Justice 1963-70; MP (C): Bebington 1964-66, Reigate 1970-74; oppn front bench spokesman Labour and Social Servs 1965-66, dep chm Glamorgan QS 1966-70, slr-gen 1970-72, min Trade and Consumer Affrs 1972-74; oppn front bench spokesman: Social Servs 1974-75, Treasy and Econ Affrs 1975-79; chllr Exchequer 1979-1983, lord cmmr Treasy 1979-83, chm IMF policy-making Interim Ctee 1982-1983; ldr team of policy gps preparing Cons gen election manifesto 1982-83; sec state Foreign and Cwlth affrs 1983-; *Style*— The Rt Hon Sir Geoffrey Howe, QC, MP; c/o Barclays Bank, Cavendish Sq Branch, 4 Vere St, London W1

HOWE, Gordon James; s of Frank Ernest Howe (d 1979), of Colchester, Essex, and Jessie Smith, *née* Withycombe (d 1953); *b* 6 Jan 1932; *Educ* Royal Liberty Sch Romford Essex; *m* 28 April 1957, Dawn Angela, da of Albert Edward Diver (d 1969), of Banstead, Surrey; 1 s (Duncan b 1962, d 1964), 1 da (Fiona b 1966); *Career* RA 1954-56, Lt 1955; qualified CA 1954; Arthur Young: ptnr 1961, memb exec ctee 1977, chm Arthur Young Europe 1984, memb int cncl 1984; memb Int Mind Matter Charity; tres: Young Minds Charity, The Child Psychotherapy Tst; chm Centenany Conf Ctee ICAEW; FCA 1964; *Recreations* swimming, travel philately; *Clubs* RAC; *Style*— Gordon Howe, Esq; 31 Queen' Gate Gdns, London SW7 5RR (☎ 01 581 1637); Rolls Hse, 7 Rolls Bldgs, Fetter Lane, London EC4A 1NH (☎ 01 831 7130, fax 01 405 2147, telex 888604)

HOWE, John Francis; OBE (1974); s of Frank Howe, OBE, of Devon, and Marjorie Alice, *née* Hubball; *b* 29 Jan 1944; *Educ* Shrewsbury, Balliol Coll Oxford (MA); *m* 1981, Angela Ephrosini, da of Charalamboles Nicolaides (d 1973), of Alicante and London; 1 da (Alexandra b 1983), 1 step da (Caroline b 1973); *Career* civil serv: asst princ MOD 1967 (princ 1972), civil advsr GOC N I 1972-73, private sec to perm under sec MOD 1975-78 (asst sec 1979), seconded FCO, cnsllr UK Delgn to NATO 1981-84, head Def Arms Control Unit 1985-86, private sec to Sec of State for Def 1986-87, asst under-sec of State (personnel and logistics) 1987-; *Books* International Security and Arms Control Mickiewicz of Kolkowicz (ed); *Recreations* travel, gardening; *Style*— John Howe, Esq, OBE; Ministry of Defence, Main Building, Whitehall SW1 (☎ 01 218 2762)

HOWE, Air Vice-Marshal John Frederick George; CB (1985), CBE (1980, AFC 1961); *b* 26 Mar 1930; *Educ* St Andrew's Coll Grahamstown S Africa; *m* 1961, Annabelle Gowing; 3 da; *Career* Cmdt-Gen RAF Regt and dir-gen Security (RAF) 1983-85, ret; American DFC 1951, Air Medal 1951; *Style*— Air Vice-Marshal J F G Howe, CB, CBE; c/o Barclays Bank plc, Oceanic House, 1 Cockspur St, London SW1; c/o Ministry of Defence, Whitehall, London SW1

HOWE, The Rt Rev John William Alexander; s of Frederic Arthur (d 1979), and Elsie, *née* Garner (d 1975); *b* 14 July 1920; *Educ* Westcliff HS (Essex), St Chad's Coll, Durham Univ (BA, MA, BD); *Career* ord 1943, dioc of York, curate All Saints' Scarborough 1943-46; chaplain Adisadel Coll Ghana 1946-50; vice-princ Edinburgh Theological Coll Scotland 1950-55; consecrated Bp of dioc of Saint Andrews, Dunkeld and Dunblane 1955, Bp 1955-69; exec offr of the Anglican Communion 1969; first sec gen of Anglican Consultative Cncl 1971-82 (first research fell 1983-85, 1985 ret); asst Bp Dioc of Ripon 1985-; sec Lambeth Conf 1978; hon degrees: STD General Theological Seminary, New York USA 1974, DD Lambeth 1978; *Books* Highways and Hedges: Anglicanism and the Universal Church (1985), various articles; presentation essays: Authy in The Anglican Communion; *Clubs* Royal Cwlth Soc; *Style*— The Rt Rev John Howe; 31 Scotton Drive, Knaresborough, N Yorks HG5 9HG (☎ 0423 866224)

HOWE, Dr Martin; s of Leslie Wistow Howe (d 1979), and Dorothy Vernon, *née* Taylor-Farrell; *b* 9 Dec 1936; *Educ* High Storrs GS, Leeds Univ (BCom, PhD); *m* 1959, Anne Cicely, da of Ernest Lawrenson, of Parbold; 3 s (Graeme Neil b 1963, Andrew b 1965, Robert b 1968); *Career* sr lectr (formerly asst lectr and lectr) of Sheffield 1960-72; sr econ advsr Monopolies Mergers Cmmn 1973-77, and Off of Fair Trading 1977-80; asst sec Off of Fair Trading, and Dept of Fair Trading 1980-84, under sec dir competition policy div Off of Fair Trading 1984-;; *Books* Equity Issues and The London Capital Market (with A J Merrett and GD Newbould, 1967) ; *Recreations* theatre, amateur dramatics, cricket, gardening; *Style*— Dr Martin Howe; Office of Fair Trading, Field House, Breams Buildings, London EC4A 1PR

HOWELL, Rt Hon David Arthur Russell; PC (1979), MP (C) Guildford 1966-; s of Col A H E Howell, DSO, TD, DL (d 1980), and his w, Beryl; *b* 18 Jan 1936; *Educ*

Eton, King's Coll Cambridge (MA); *m* 1967, Davina, da of Maj David Wallace (ka 1944); 1 s, 2 da; *Career* serv Coldstream Gds 1954-56, 2 Lt; worked in econ section Treasy 1959-60; ldr writer Daily Telegraph 1960-64; chm Bow Gp 1961-62, ed Crossbow 1962-64; dir Cons Political Centre 1964-66; contested (C) Dudley 1964; lord cmmr Treasy 1970-71, parly sec CSD 1970-72, parly under-sec Employment 1971-72, NI March-Nov 1972, min state NI 1972-74, Energy 1974, sec state Energy 1979-81, sec Transport 1981-83; chm House of Commons Foreign Affairs Ctee 1988-; dir Savory Mills Ltd; *Publications* A New Style of Government (1970), Time to Move On (1976), Freedom and Capital (1981), Blind Victory (1986); *Recreations* tennis, golf, writing, DIY; *Clubs* Buck's, Carlton; *Style—* The Rt Hon David Howell, MP; House of Commons, London SW1

HOWELL, Rt Hon Denis Herbert; PC (1976), MP (Lab) Birmingham, Small Heath 1961-; s of Herbert and Bertha Howell; *b* 4 Sept 1923; *Educ* Gower St Sch, Handsworth GS; *m* 1955, Brenda Marjorie, da of Stephen Willson; 3 s, 1 da; *Career* MP (Lab): All Saints 1955-59, Small Heath 1961-; jt parly under-sec DES 1964-69, min for Sport (1969-70); min state Housing and Local Govt, oppn spokesman Local Govt and Sport 1970-74, min state Environment 1974-79, oppn front bench spokesman Environment 1979-83, Home Affrs 1983-84; memb Nat Exec 1982-83, chm Labour Movement for Europe, Puer European Movement pres APEX 1971-83; former football league referee and memb Birmingham City Cncl; silver medal Olympic Order 1981; vice-pres Central Ctree of Physical Recreation; dir Wembley Stadium Ltd; Birmingham Cable Authy, Denis Howell PR; soccer referee Pelham 1969; *Recreations* sport, music, theatre; *Clubs* Reform, MCC, Warwickshire CC, Birmingham Press; *Style—* The Rt Hon Denis Howell, MP; 33 Moor Green Lane, Moseley, Birmingham B13 8NE

HOWELL, Air Vice-Marshal Evelyn Michael Thomas; CBE (1961); s of Sir Evelyn Berkeley Howell (d 1971), of Cambridge, and Laetitia Cecilia Campbell (d 1978); *b* 11 Sept 1913; *Educ* Downside, RAF Coll Cranwell; *m* 1937, Helen Joan, da of Brig William Moring Hayes (d 1960); 1 s (Michael), 3 da (Jennifer, Mary, Philippa); m 2, 1972, Rosemary, da of Ian Alexander Cram, of Warwick; 1 s (Rupert b 1975), 1 da (Caroline b 1977); *Career* RAF cmmnd 1934, Dir Air Armament Res & Dvpt 1960-62, Cmdt RAF Tech Coll Henlow 1962-65, Sr Air Staff Offr Tech Trg Cmd 1966-67, ret 1967; Aircraft Indust 1967-79; landowner (7 acres); *Recreations* gardening, conservation; *Clubs* RAF; *Style—* Air Vice-Marshal E M T Howell, CBE; Bank Farm, Lorton, Cockermouth CA13 0RQ (☎ Lorton 617)

HOWELL, Prof John Bernard Lloyd (Jack); s of David John Howell (d 1978), of Ynystawe Swansea, and Hilda Mary, *née* Hill (d 1943); *b* 1 August 1926; *Educ* Swansea GS, Middx Hosp Med Sch and Univ of London (BSc, MB BS, PhD); *m* 12 July 1952, Heather Joan, da of Lawrence Victor Rolfe (d 1939); 2 s (David b 1955, Peter b 1959), 1 da (Gillian b 1953); *Career* Nat Serv RAMC, Lt 1952, Capt 1953; Univ of Manchester: sr lectr and hon physician 1960-66, conslt physician and sr lectr 1966-69; Univ of Southampton: fndn prof of med 1969-, dean faculty of med 1978-83; memb GMC 1978-83, pres Thoracic Soc 1988-89, pres elect BMA; chm Southampton & S W Hampshire Dist Health Authy 1983-; FRCP 1966, Hon FACP 1982; Hon Life Memb Canadian Thoracic Soc 1978; *Books* Breathlessness (1966); *Recreations* DIY, wine; *Style—* Prof Jack Howell, Esq; The Coach House, Bassett Wood Drive, Southampton SO2 3PT (☎ 0703 768878); Medicine I, Southampton General Hospital, Centre Block, Southampton (☎ 0703 777222)

HOWELL, Kathleen Ludlow (Paddy); *née* Tucker; yr da of Cyril Ludlow Tucker (d 1988), of Whitchurch, S Glam, and Doris May, *née* Richards; *b* 30 April 1924; *Educ* Emmanuel Sch Swansea, HS Cardiff, Sch of Physiotherapy Cardiff Royal Infirmary; *m* 20 Dec 1947, Brian Pain (d 1979), s of E G Howell (d 1947), of Whitchurch, Cardiff; 1 s (Mark Edmund b 1951), 1 da (Julia Wynne b 1956); *Career* chartered physiotherapist; Miny of Pensions 1945-48; private practice 1948-51; MCSP; *Recreations* painting, gardening, fine arts, music; *Style—* Mrs Kathleen L Howell; Garreg Lwyd, Station Rd, Llanishen, Cardiff, South Glamorgan CF4 5UU (☎ 0222 753704)

HOWELL, Lisbeth Edna; da of Frederick Baynes, of Altrincham, and Jessica Edna, *née* Winrow; *b* 23 Mar 1951; *Educ* Blackburn House Liverpool, Univ of Bristol (BA); *m* 1 da (Alexandra Baynes Proniewicz b 1984); *Career* head of news Border TV Carlisle (previously dep dir of programmes); *Recreations* reading; *Style—* Ms Lisbeth Howell; The Nook, Moatside, Brampton, Cumbria (☎ 069 77 3689); Border Television plc, Harraby, Carlisle CA1 3NT (☎ 0228 25 101, fax 0228 41 384)

HOWELL, Maj-Gen Lloyd; CBE (1972); s of Thomas Idris Howell, (d 1987) and Anne Howell, (d 1964); *b* 28 Dec 1923; *Educ* Barry GS, UCW (BSc); *m* 1, 14 Feb 1945, Hazel (d 1974), da of Frank Edward Barker, (d 1963); 5 s (Rhodri b 1945, d 1979, Geraint b 1948, Ceri b 1952, Dewi b 1956, Alwyn b 1959), 3 da (Carys b 1949, Eirlys b 1951, Sara b 1954); m 2 19 April 1975, Elizabeth June Buchanan Husband, da of Archibald John Buchanan Atkinson (d 1966); *Career* Capt: regtl and staff appts RA 1943-47, Instr RMA Sandhurst RAEC 1949-53, staff course RMCS 1953-54; Maj: TSO 2 Trials Estab RA 1954-57, SO 2 Educn Div HQ BAOR 1957-59, long GW Course RMCS 1959-60; Lt Col: DS RMCS 1960-64, SEO Army Apprentices Coll 1964-67, headmaster and cmdt Duke of York's Royal Mil Sch 1967-72 (Col 1970); Col Educn MOD 19'2-74, Brig: Chief Educn Offr UK Land Forces 1974-76; Maj-Gen: Dir of Army Educn 1976-80, Col Cmdt RAEC 1982-86; conslt tech educn dept UCW 1980-86; dir Bldy Trades Exhibitions Ltd 1980-; memb: cncl City and Guilds of London Inst 1976-, ct of govrs UCW 1980-88; govr several schs 1980-; fell Univ Coll Cardiff 1981-; Hon MA Open Univ 1980; MRAES 1963-80; *Recreations* golf, gardening; *Clubs* A & N; *Style—* Maj-Gen Lloyd Howell, CBE

HOWELL, Michael John; s of Jack Howell, and Emmie Mary Elizabeth Howell; *b* 9 June 1939; *Educ* Strodes, King's Coll London (LLB), Chigaco Univ (JD), Cape Town Univ; *m* 14 May 1966, Caroline Sarah Eifiona, da of Charles Herbert Gray; 2 da (Juliet b 1967, Lucy b 1973); *Career* admitted slr 1966; Clifford Chance (formerly Clifford-Turner): joined 1964-, ptnr 1969-; Underwarden 1988-89, Liveryman Worshipful of Coopers, Freeman Worshipful Co of Slrs; memb: Law Soc, Int Bar Assoc; assoc memb Chartered Inst of Patent Agents; *Clubs* City Livery; *Style—* Michael Howell, Esq; Wood Cottage, Dome Hill Park, London SE26 6SP (☎ 01 778 9763); Clifford Chance, Bow Bells House, Bread St, London EC4M 9BQ (☎ 01 600 0808, fax 01 956 0199, telex 887 847 LEGIS G)

HOWELL, Michael William Davis; s of Air Vice-Marshal Evelyn Thomas Howell, of Bank Farm, Lorton, Cumbria, and Helen Joan, (*née* Hayes) (d 1976); *b* 11 June 1947; *Educ* Charterhouse, Trinity Coll Cambridge, INSEAD and Harvard Business Sch (MBA 1976); *m* 1975, Susan Wanda, da of Andrew Adie, (d 1986); 1 s (William b 1982); *Career* vice-pres: Corporate Strategy Cummins Engine Co Inc 1984-, (Europe 1981-83), BL Truck & Bus Div 1969-74; *Recreations* aviation, sailing, motorcycling, singing; *Clubs* Royal Automobile; *Style—* Michael Howell, Esq; c/o Bank of Scotland, 38 Threadneedle St, EC2P 2EH; Box 3005, Columbus In 47202 USA

HOWELL, Paul Frederic; MEP (EDG) Norfolk 1979-; s of Ralph Frederic Howell, MP, of Wendling Grange, Dereham, Norfolk, by his w Margaret Ellene; *b* 17 Jan 1951; *Educ* Gresham's, St Edmund Hall Oxford; *m* 23 May 1987, Johanna, *née* Turnbull; *Recreations* hunting, adventures; *Clubs* Farmers', Carlton; *Style—* Paul Howell Esq, MEP; The White House Farm, Bradenham Rd, Scarning, E Dereham, Norfolk NR20 3EY (☎ 036 287 239)

HOWELL, Paul Philip; CMG (1964), OBE (1955); s of Brig-Gen Philip Howell, CMG (ka 1916), and Rosalind Upcher, *née* Buxton (d 1968); *b* 13 Feb 1917; *Educ* Westminster, Trinity Coll Cambridge (MA, PhD), Christ Church Oxford (MA, DPhil); *m* 1949, Bridgit Mary Radclyffe, da of Geoffrey Dundas Luard (d 1955), of Buckland Newton Place, Dorset; 2 s (Philip Luard b 1955, James Christopher Francis b 1960), 2 da (Rosalind Sabrina b 1951, Clare Lucinda b 1953); *Career* Sudan Political Serv 1938-55, Uganda Govt 1955-61; head of ME Devpt Div Beirut (FO, later Miny of Overseas Devpt) 1961-69; fell and dir of Devpt Studies Wolfson Coll Cambridge 1969-83, emeritus fell 1983; *Books* Nuer Law (1954), The Jonglei Canal; Impact and Opportunity (ed 1988); *Recreations* fishing, country pursuits; *Clubs* Royal Cwlth Soc, Norfolk (Norwich); *Style—* Paul P Howell Esq, CMG, OBE; Burfield Hall, Wymondham, Norfolk NR18 9SJ (☎ 0953 603389)

HOWELL, Ralph Frederic; MP (C) North Norfolk 1970-; s of Walter Howell of Dereham, Norfolk; *b* 25 May 1923; *Educ* Diss GS; *m* 1950, Margaret, da of Walter Bone of Gressenhall; 2 s, 1 da; *Career* RAF 1941-46, farmer, memb: Lloyd's, Mitford and Launditch RDC 1961-74; former local chm NFU, contested (C) N Norfolk seat 1966, memb Euro Parl 1974-79, former chm Cons backbench ctee agric and employment, memb Select Ctee on the Treasy and Civil Serv 1981-87, memb Cncl of Europe 1981-84 and 1987-; *Clubs* Carlton, Farmers'; *Style—* Ralph Howell Esq, MP; Wendling Grange, Wendling, Dereham, Norfolk (☎ 036 287 247)

HOWELL, Robert; s of Jim Howell, of Chesterfield, Derbys, and Gladys Mary, *née* Clayworth; *b* 18 April 1950; *Educ* Brunts' GS Mansfield, Univ of Manchester (BA); *m* 21 Sept 1984, Kathleen Mary, da of Richard John Rabey, of St Merryn, Cornwall; 1 s (Richard b 1987), 1 da (Nicola b 1984); *Career* asst tres Blue Circle Industs plc 1979-85, tres Tesco plc 1986-; ACMA 1979, MCT 1984; *Recreations* squash, various sports, fine wine; *Clubs* N London Squash, Intrepid Football; *Style—* Robert Howell, Esq; 51 Landrock Rd, Crouch End, London N8 9HR (☎ 01 348 2198); New Tesco House, Delamare Rd, Chesthunt, Herts EN8 9SL (☎ 0992 32222 extn 3257, fax 0992 35883)

HOWELL, Dr Tudor Morgan; s of David John Howell; *b* 24 May 1924; *Educ* West Monmouth Sch, Cambridge Univ; *m* 1953, Sara Margaret Janey, da of Rev Geoffrey Earle Raven; 2 s, 1 da; *Career* formerly temp Sub-Lt RNVR; med practitioner; High Sheriff of Powys 1980; *Recreations* gardening; *Style—* Dr Tudor Howell; Ynyswen, Trefeglwys, Newtown, Powys (☎ 055 16 633)

HOWELL WILLIAMS, Peter; s of Rev Robert Howell Williams (d 1978), and Ellen Gwladys Howell Williams; *b* 22 June 1926; *Educ* Rydal Sch N Wales, Downing Coll Cambridge (MA, LLB); *m* 6 July 1954, Fiona Elizabeth, da of John Craig (d 1930); 1 s (Craig b 14 Sept 1957), 2 da (Rachel b 5 April 1955, Sian b 9 March 1960); *Career* mine sweepers RNVR 1944-47; slr admitted 1953, pres Law Soc Liverpool 1980-81, chm Rent Assessment and Mental Health Tribr, sr ptnr Bell Lamb & Joynson Liverpool; Parly candidate 1964 and 1966, cncllr Wallasey Borough 1955-64; chm Civic Soc Merseyside 1966-71, Everyman Theatre Liverpool; nat chm The Abbeyfield Soc; memb Law Soc and Slrs Benevolent Assoc; *Books* Liverpolitana (1971), A Gentleman's Calling (1980); *Recreations* antiquarian books, conservation, golf; *Clubs* Athenaeum Liverpool (pres 1980), Athenaeum London; *Style—* Peter Howell Williams, Esq

HOWELLS, Dr Gwyn; CB (1979); s of Albert Henry (d 1978), and Ruth Winifred, *née* Horton (d 1965); *b* 13 May 1918; *Educ* UC Sch Hampstead, Barts' London Univ, (MD, BS); *m* 1942, Simone, da of Carl Gordon Maufe (d 1940); 2 s (Robin, Lynden), 2 da (Barbara, Sheridan); *Career* dir gen of health Australia 1973-83; chm: Medical Res Cncl of Australia 1973-83; Health Insur Cmmn Australia 1976-78, Cocklear Pty Ltd 1983-; dir Nucleos Ltd 1983-; FRCP, FRACP; *Recreations* squash racquets, tennis, reading; *Clubs* Cwlth (Canberra), Nat Press (Canberra); *Style—* Dr Gwyn Howells, Esq, CB; 23 Beauchamp St, Deakin ACT 2600 Australia (☎ 812575)

HOWELLS, Michael Sandbrook; s of Bemjamin George Howells (d 1971), of Pembroke Dock, and Blodwen, *née* Francis (d 1978); *b* 29 May 1939; *Educ* Cheltenham, Univ Coll London; *m* 18 Jun 1966, Pamela Vivian, da of Gordon Harry Francis, Clandon, Surrey; 2 s (Luke b 1970, Toby b 1972); *Career* slr 1966, ptnr Price and Kelway Slrs 1971 (sr ptnr 1980); HM Coroner Pembrokeshire 1980; memb: Cncl of Law Soc 1983, Cncl of Coroners Soc of England and Wales 1986; pres Milford Haven Civic Soc, vice chm Torch Theatre Milford Haven; *Recreations* bee-keeping, messing about in boats; *Clubs* RAC, Waterloo, Milford Haven, Neyland Yacht; *Style—* Michael Howells, Esq; Glenowen, Mastlebridge, Milford Haven, Pembrokeshire SA73 1QS (☎ 0646 600 208); Price and Kelway, 17 Hamilton Terrace, Milford Haven, Pembrokeshire SA73 3JA (☎ 06462 5311, fax 06462 5848)

HOWELLS, Roger Alan; s of Lt Col G E Howells, OBE, of Fleet, Hampshire, and Cecilia Doris May, *née* Pope; *b* 30 Oct 1943; *Educ* Farnborough GS; *m* 18 June 1982, (Edome) Rowena, da of John Raymond Sharpe, of Earl Soham, Suffolk; 1 s (Christian Peter George b 1985) 1 da (Lucinda Chloe b 1983); *Career* Lt HAC 1968-74; dir: Howells Rawlings & Ward Ltd (independant fin advsrs) 1972-, Howells & Bingham Ltd (registered insur brokers) 1980-; memb Lloyds; Freeman City of London 1978, Liveryman Worshipful Co of Makers of Playing Cards 1979; ACII 1969; *Recreations* tennis, golf, shooting, fishing; *Clubs* Hurlingham, Berkshire & Royal Wimbledon Golf; *Style—* Roger Howells, Esq; 17 Nicosia Rd, London SW18 3RN (☎ 01 874 0299); 29 Bunhill Row, London EC1Y 8NE (☎ 01 638 8693, fax 01 638 1177)

HOWELLS, Roger Godfrey; s of Godfrey Frank Howells, of Bridgend, and Hilda, *née* Rogers; *b* 21 Oct 1954; *Educ* Bridgend Boys GS; *m* 20 March 1978 (m dis 1985), Susan Jean; *Career* CA; ptnr Cavells 1985-; dir Mutual Accountants Professional Indemnity Co Ltd, tutor Prince of Wales Business Initiative; ACA 1978; *Recreations* fishing, swimming, golf; *Style—* Roger Howells, Esq; Ross Cottage, Northwick Rd, Pilning, Bristol (☎ 04545 2438); Bridge House, 7-9 Church Rd, Lawrence Hill, Bristol

(☎ 0272 558 414, fax 0272 558 407)

HOWERD, Frankie; *see*: Howard, Francis Alick

HOWES, Prof Christopher Kingston; s of Leonard Arthur Howes, OBE, of Norfolk, and Marion Amy, *née* Bussey; *b* 30 Jan 1942; *Educ* Gresham's, LSE, Coll of Estate Mgmnt (BSc), Univ of Reading (MPhil); *m* 1967, Elfride Clare, da of Gordon Edward Cunliffe (d 1987), of Sussex; 2 s (Robert b 1976, Michael b 1977), 2 da (Catherine b 1973, Rosalind b 1975 (decd); *Career* GLC Planning & Valuation Depts 1965-67; ptnr (later sr ptnr) Chartered Surveyors & Planning Conslts 1967-79; dep dir Land Economy Directorate DOE 1979-80 (dir Land Economy 1981-84); dir Land and Property 1985-; visiting lectr Univs of London, E Anglia (sr visiting fell 1973), Cambridge, Reading and Aberdeen 1966-, visiting prof UCL 1985-; memb Norwich Cncl 1970-74, magistrate for Norfolk 1973-79, memb Ct of Advsrs St Paul's Cathedral 1980-, steward and hon surveyor to Dean and Chapter Norwich Cathedral 1972-79, memb: policy review ctee Royal Inst of Chartered Surveyors (planning & devpt divnl cncl memb) 1984-; *Books* Value Maps: Aspects of Land and Property Values (1980), Economic Regeneration (1988), Urban Revitalization (1988); contributor to many books and articles in learned journals; *Recreations* music, art, sailing, fly fishing; *Clubs* Athenaeum, Norfolk (Norwich), Aldeburgh Yacht; *Style*— Prof Christopher Howes; Highfield House, Woldingham, Surrey; Roudham Lodge, Roudham, Norfolk; Department of the Environment, 2 Marsham St, London SW1P 3EB (☎ 01 212 4994)

HOWICK OF GLENDALE, 2 Baron (UK 1960); Charles Evelyn Baring; s of 1 Baron Howick of Glendale, KG, GCMG, KCVO (d 1973; formerly Hon Sir Evelyn Baring, sometime govr Kenya and yst s of 1 Earl of Cromer), and Lady Mary Grey, da of 5 Earl Grey; *b* 30 Dec 1937; *Educ* Eton, New Coll Oxford; *m* 1964, Clare, yr da of Col Cyril Darby, MC, of Kemerton Court, Tewkesbury; 1 s, 3 da (Hon Rachel Monica b 1967, Hon Jessica Mary Clare b 1969, Hon Alice Olivia b 1971); *Heir* s, Hon David Evelyn Charles Baring b 26 March 1975; *Career* md Baring Bros & Co 1969-82; dir London Life Assoc 1972-82; dir Northern Rock Building Soc 1988-; memb exec ctee Nat Art Collections Fund 1973-88; *Style*— The Rt Hon Lord Howick of Glendale; Howick, Alnwick, Northumberland NE66 2LB (☎ 066 577 624); 42 Bedford Gdns, London W8 (☎ 01 221 0880)

HOWICK OF GLENDALE, Mary, Baroness; Lady Mary Cecil Grey; da of 5 Earl Grey (d 1963); *b* 1907; *m* 1935, 1 Baron Howick of Glendale, KG, GCMG, KCVO (d 1973); 1 s (2 Baron), 2 da (Hon Lady Wakefield, Hon Mrs Gibbs); *Style*— The Rt Hon Mary, Lady Howick of Glendale; Howick, Alnwick, Northumberland

HOWIE, Hon Alisoun Mary Kyle; da of Baron Howie of Troon; *b* 2 April 1959; *Style*— The Hon Alisoun Howie; c/o 34 Temple Fortune Lane, London NW11

HOWIE, Hon Angus; s of Baron Howie of Troon; *b* 20 May 1963; *Style*— The Hon Angus Howie; c/o 34 Temple Fortune Lane, London NW11

HOWIE, Prof Archibald; s of Robert Howie, and Margaret Marshall, *née* McDonald (d 1971); *b* 8 Mar 1934; *Educ* Kirkcaldy HS, Univ of Edinburgh (BSc), California Inst of Technol (MS), Univ of Cambridge (PhD); *m* 15 Aug 1964, Melva Jean, da of Ernest Scott (d 1959), of Tynemouth, Devon; 1 s (David Robert b 9 Oct 1965, d 1986), 1 da (Helena Margaret b 14 July 1971); *Career* prof of physics Univ of Cambridge; pres Royal Microscopical Soc 1984-86; Hon FRMS 1978; FRS 1978; *Recreations* winemaking, gardening; *Style*— Prof Archibald Howie; 194 Huntingdon Rd, Cambridge CB3 0LB (☎ 0223 276131); Cavendish Lab, Madingley Rd, Cambridge CB3 0HE (☎ 0223 337334, fax 0223 63263, telex 81292)

HOWIE, Sir James William; s of James Milne Howie (d 1958); *b* 31 Dec 1907; *Educ* Robert Gordon's Coll Aberdeen, Aberdeen Univ (MD); *m* 1935, Isabella Winifred Mitchell; 2 s, 1 da; *Career* WWII serv RAMC Nigeria and WO; prof of bacteriology Glasgow Univ 1951-63; med dir Public Health Laboratory Serv 1963-73; QHP 1965-68; pres: Royal Coll of Pathologists 1966-69, BMA 1969-70 (Gold Medal 1984); LLD Aberdeen 1969; FRCP, FRCPGlas, FRCPEd, FRCPath; Hon ARCVS; kt 1969; *Books* Portraits From Memory (by Br Med Journal); *Recreations* golf, music, writing; *Style*— Sir James Howie; 34 Redford Ave, Edinburgh, Scotland EH13 0BU (☎ 031 441 3910)

HOWIE, Prof John Mackintosh; s of Rev David Yuille Howie, of Aberdeen, and Janet Macdonald, *née* Mackintosh; *b* 23 May 1936; *Educ* Robert Gordon's Coll Aberdeen, Univ of Aberdeen (MA, DSc), Balliol Coll Oxford (DPhil); *m* 5 Aug 1960, Dorothy Joyce Mitchell, da of Alfred James Miller, OBE (d 1980) of Aberdeen; 2 da (Anne b 1961, Katharine b 1963); *Career* asst in maths Univ of Aberdeen 1958-59, asst then lectr in maths Glasgow Univ 1961-67, sr lectr in maths Univ of Stirling 1967-70, Regius prof of maths Univ of St Andrews 1970- (dean Faculty of Sci 1976-79); visiting appts: Tulane Univ 1964-65, Univ of Western Aust 1968, State Univ of NY at Buffalo 1969 & 1970, Monash Univ 1979, Northern Illinois Univ 1988; chm: Scot Central Ctee on Mathematics 1975-81, Dundee Coll of Educn 1983-87; memb ctee to Review Examinations (The Dunning Ctee) 1975-77, vice-pres London Mathematical Soc 1984-86; FRSE 1971; *Books* An Introduction to Semigroup Theory (1976), and author of articles for various mathematical jls; *Recreations* music, gardening; *Style*— Prof John M Howie ; Longacre, 19 Strathkinness High Rd, St Andrews, Fife KY16 9UA (☎ 0334 74103); Mathematical Institute, University of St Andrews, N Haugh, St Andrews, Fife KY16 9SS (☎ 0334 76161)

HOWIE, Hon Mrs (Kathleen Whalley); *née* Smith; MBE (1946); da of late 1 Baron Colwyn; *m* 1945, Robert Cullen Howie; *Style*— The Hon Mrs Howie, MBE; Paul's Place, Coombe Lane, Sway, Lymington, Hants SO41 6BP (☎ 0590 74550)

HOWIE, Prof Robert Andrew; s of Robert Howie (d 1959), of Rectory Farm, Emberton, Olney, Bucks, and Ruby, *née* Highet (d 1943); *b* 4 June 1923; *Educ* Bedford Sch, Trinity Coll Cambridge (MA, PhD, ScD); *m* 28 June 1952, (Honor) Eugenie, da of Robert Price Taylor, of Cardiff; 2 s (Robert Tremayne b 1956, Timothy Andrew b 1958); *Career* WWII 1941-46: Edinburgh Air Sqdn 1941-42, Pilots Wings and cmmn 1943, invalided out 1946 Flt Lt; asst lectr/lectr in geology Manchester Univ 1953-62; King's Coll London: reader in geology 1962-70, fell 1980, prof of mineralogy 1970-85; London Univ: Lyell prof of geology Royal Holloway and Bedford New Coll 1985-87, emeritus prof of mineralogy 1987-; London Univ: Senate 1974, ct 1984, chm academic cncl 1983-87; memb: Cwlth Scholarships Cmmn; Mineralogical Soc: sec 1965, ed Mineralogical Abstracts 1966-, pres 1978-80, managing tstee 1977-87; Geological Soc: vice-pres 1973-75, Murchison Medal 1976; *Books* Rock Forming Minerals (1962-63, 5 vols with W A Deer & J Z Zussman), An Introduction to the Rock Forming Minerals (1966); *Recreations* mineral collecting, writing abstracts; *Clubs* Geological Society; *Style*— Prof Robert Howie; Department of Geology, Royal Holloway & Bedford New College, Egham, Surrey, TW20 0EX (☎ 0784 34455)

HOWIE OF TROON, Baron (Life Peer UK 1978); William Howie; s of Peter Howie; *b* 2 Mar 1924; *Educ* Marr Coll Troon, Royal Tech Coll Glasgow; *m* 1951, Mairi, da of John Sanderson; 2 s, 2 da; *Career* civil engr, journalist and publisher; MP (Lab) Luton 1963-70, asst whip 1964-66, lord cmmr Treasy 1966-67, comptroller HM Household 1967-68, vice-chm PLP 1968-70; gen mangr Thos Telford Ltd; memb cncl City Univ 1968-; pro-chllr City Univ 1984-;FICE; FRSA; *Style*— Rt Hon Lord Howie of Troon; 34 Temple Fortune Lane, London NW11 (☎ 01 455 0492)

HOWITT, Miriam; *née* Cooper; da of Charles Brodie Cooper (d 1978), of Broad House, Cumbria, and Lydia, *née* Peltzer (d 1984); *b* 1 Feb 1929; *Educ* St Leonard's Sch, St Andrews, Architectural Assoc Sch of Architecture (Dip Arch); *m* 8 Oct 1958, David Alan Howitt, s of Claude Elborne Howitt (d 1964), of Nottingham; 3 s (Nicholas b 1960, Mark b 1962, Paul b 1963), 1 da (Philipa b 1959); *Career* architect and designer; private practice with husband, work incl: airports, hotels, showrooms, offices, schools, clubs; awards: Crown Inn Hotel Ampney Crucis Design Competition 1975; Br Design in Japan Lighting 1988, former govr London Coll of Furniture; Freedom to trade as citizen of City of London by virtue of birth on island of St Helena; RIBA 1953, FCSD 1976 (formerly vice-pres, memb of cncl, examiner, chm of examiners); *Books* One Room Living (1972, Japanese edn 1979); *Recreations* pottery, skiing, fell walking; *Style*— Mrs David Howitt; 33 Roehampton Gate, London SW15 5JR (☎ 01 878 0520, 01 878 0054)

HOWITT, Victor Charles; s of Sqdn Ldr Ronald Charles Howitt, DFC, of Flat 43, Rock Gdns, Bognor Regis, Sussex, and Ruby Frances Howitt (d 1976); *b* 13 July 1935; *m* 1, Dec 1956 (m dis 1977), Mary, da of Charles Langridge (d 1955); 2 s (Peter Charles b 28 Sept 1961, Stephen Jarvis Boughton b 7 Nov 1965), 1 da (Allison Mary b 13 Sept 1958); m 2, 17 June 1978, Elizabeth Anne (Betty), da of Charles Anthony Reghelini (d 1966); *Career* Nat Serv drill instr RAF 1953-55; articled CA 1951, trainee mangr 1952, locum dispensing optician (do) R W Bradshaw 1960 (trainee do 1956), dir Wigmores 1968, regnl md London and Home Counties, D & A Int 1974 (memb devpt team 1973); md 1982: Wigmores Ltd, Theodore Hamblin Ltd, Hamblin Wigmores Ltd; observer to bd D & A Gp Ltd 1983, dir D & A Gp UK 1985-, dir D & A Gp Operations; cncl memb: Gen Optical Cncl (companies ctee), Fedn of Ophthalmic & Dispensing Opticians 1984-86, Guild of Br Dispensing Opticians 1981-84; vice chm Abbey Park Resident Assoc 1986-87; Freeman 1988: City of London, Worshipful Co of Spectacle Makers; FBDO 1961; *Recreations* photography, reading, gardening, old houses, travel, collecting cranberry glass and stamps; *Style*— Victor Howitt, Esq; On Spec, 46 Hither Green Lane, Bordesley, Near Redditch, N Worcs B98 9BW (☎ 0527 63568); Dollond & Aitchison Gp (UK) plc, 1323 Coventry Rd, Yardley, Birmingham (☎ 021 706 6133, fax 021 708 1520, car phone 0836 729181, telex 339435)

HOWKINS, John Anthony; s of Col Ashby (Tim) Howkins (d 1977), and Lesley Stops; *b* 3 August 1945; *Educ* Rugby, Keele Univ (BA), Architectural Assoc (AA Dip); *m* 1, 1971, Jill, da of Ian Liddington; m 2, 1977, Annabel, da of John Whittet; *Career* exec dir Int Inst of Communications 1984-; mktg mangr Lever Bros 1968-70, TV ed Time Out 1971-74, jt fndr TV4 Conf 1971, dir Whittet Books 1976-84, chm Pool video Graz Austria 1976, ed Vision, chm London Int Film Sch 1970-84; memb Interim Action Ctee on the Film Indust, Dept of Trade and Indust 1980-85; exec ed Nat Electronics Review 1981-; memb Exec Ctee Broadcasting Res Unit 1981-, TV columnist Illustrated London News 1981-83; vice-chm New Media Assoc of Ind Producers 1984-85; specialist advsr Select Ctee on Euro Communities, House of Lords 1985; memb Br Screen Advsy Cncl (BSAC) (BSAC) Dept of Trade & Indust 1985-; *Books* Understanding Television (1977), Mass Communications in China (1982), New Technologies, New Policies (1982), Satellites International (1987); *Style*— John Howkins, Esq; 14 Balliol Rd, London W10 (☎ 01 960 4023)

HOWL, Oliver Brian; s of Maj Clifford Howl (d 1962), of Maycroft, Ash Hill, Wolverhampton, and Doris, *née* Savill (d 1985); *b* 8 Oct 1922; *Educ* Shrewsbury, St John's Coll Cambridge (MA); *m* 16 July 1956, Dr Elizabeth Mary Caroline, da of Dr Sidney Campbell Dyke, of Wolverhampton; 1 s (Oliver Jonathan b 1958), 1 da (Julia Caroline b 1956); *Career* WWII Actg Sub Lt (E) RNVR 1943-46, Lt (E) RN 1946, served Med and Home Fleet; Lee Howl & Co Ltd (pump mfrs): mgmnt trainee 1947-48, jr mangr 1946-49, jt md 1956-62, sole md 1963-80, chm 1972-79; chm APE Lee Howl Ltd 1980-81; lectr in physics RMA Sandhurst 1948-49; dir: Bailey & Mackey Ltd 1963-87, Swiftfire Engrg Ltd 1979-, Villiers Ltd 1986-; pres West Bromwich West Cons and Unionist Assoc, tstee Ironbridge Gorge Museum Tst Ltd, fixture sec Greenflies Cricket Club, memb Tettenhall Wood PCC; income tax cmmr1986-; AMIMechE 1953, MIMechE 1972, CEng 1972; *Recreations* mountaineering, cricket, squash, beagling, rambling; *Clubs* Naval; *Style*— Oliver Howl, Esq; 1 Merridgale Grove, Wolverhampton (☎ 0902 27708)

HOWLAND, Lord; Andrew Ian Henry Russell; s and h of Marquess of Tavistock; *b* 30 Mar 1962; *Educ* Harrow, Harvard (BA); *Recreations* racing, shooting; *Style*— Lord Howland; 7 Fairlawns, Dullingham Rd, Newmarket CB8 9JS; Tattersalls, Terrace House, Newmarket, Suffolk

HOWLAND JACKSON, Anthony Geoffrey Clive; s of Arthur Geoffrey Howland Jackson, and Pamela Foote *née* Wauton; *b* 25 May 1941; *Educ* Sherborne; *m* 15 June 1963, Susan Ellen, da of Geoffrey Hickson, (d 1984); 1 s (James Geoffrey b 10 Feb 1965), 2 da (Anna Kate b 10 July 1968, Louisa Jane b 13 May 1971); *Career* md: Clarkson Puckle: 1979-87, Bain Clarksons 1987; exec dir Gill & Duffus plc 1983-87; dep chm and md Hogg Robinson & Gardner Mountain plc 1987-; Freeman City of London, Liveryman Worshipful Co of Insurers; *Recreations* shooting, cricket, racing; *Clubs* Turf, City of London; *Style*— A G C Howland Jackson, Esq; Marks Gate, Fordham, Colchester, Essex CO6 3NR (☎ 0206 240 420); Lloyds Chambers, No 1 Portsoken St, London E1 8DF (☎ 01 480 4000 fax 01 480 4007, tlx 884 633

HOWLETT, Anthony Douglas; RD (1971); s of Ernest Robert Howlett (d 1968), of Lincs, and Catherine, *née* Broughton, of Lincs; *b* 30 Dec 1924; *Educ* King's Sch Rochester, Wellingborough, King's Sch Grantham, Trinity Coll Cambridge (MA, LLB); *m* 1952, Alfreda Dorothy, da of Arthur William Pearce (d 1976), of Sussex; *Career* serv WWII RNVR 1942-46; RNVS 1951-60, RNR 1940-75, Lt Cdr 1968; called to the Bar Gray's Inn 1950, joined Govt Legal Serv 1951, i/c Export Credit Guarantee Branch 1972-75, i/c Merchant Shipping Branch 1975-81; UK del: London Diplomatic Conf on Limitation of Liability for Maritime Claims 1976, Geneve Diplomatic Conf on Multi- Modal Tport 1980; memb Enfield Health Authy 1987-; Remembrancer of the City of London 1981-86, Freeman City of London 1981, Liveryman Worshipful Co of Scriveners 1981-; memb Catenian Assoc 1987, fndr memb the Sherlock Holmes Soc (chm 1960-63 and 1986-); Order of King Abdul Aziz (II) Saudi Arabia 1981, Order of Oman (III) 1982, Cdr Order of Orange-Nassau Netherlands 1982, Offr Legion d'Honneur France 1984, Order of the Lion of Malawi 1985, Order of Qatar 1985; OStJ; *Books* numerous articles on Conan Doyle and Holmesiana; *Recreations* sailing, book browsing, Sherlock Holmes, opera, photography, foreign travel; *Clubs* Naval, City Livery; *Style—* Anthony Howlett, Esq, RD; Rivendell, 37 Links Side, Enfield, Middx EN2 7QZ (☎ 01 363 5802)

HOWLETT, Gen Sir Geoffrey Hugh Whitby; KBE (1984, OBE 1972), MC (1952); s of Brig Bernard Howlett, DSO (ka 1943) and Joan, *née* Whitby; *b* 5 Feb 1930; *Educ* Wellington, RMA Sandhurst; *m* 1955, Elizabeth Anne, da of Sqdn Ldr Leonard Aspinal; 1 s, 2 da; *Career* cmmnd Queen's Own Royal West Kent Regt 1950, transfd Parachute Regt 1959, Mil Asst to C-in-C North (Oslo) 1969-71, cmd 2 Para 1971-73, RCDS 1973-75, cmd 16 Para Bde 1975-77, dir Army Recruiting 1977-79, GOC 1 Armoured Div (Lower Saxony, W Germany) 1979-82, Cmdt RMA Sandhurst 1982-83, GOC SE Dist 1983-85; C-in-C Allied Forces Northern Europe (Oslo) 1986-89; Col Cmdt: Army Catering Corps 1981-89, The Parachute Regt 1983-; bd memb Serv Sound and Vision Corp 1989-; tstee Cheshire Fndn 1988-, pres Straggbrs of Asia Cricket Club 1989-; *Recreations* cricket, shooting; *Clubs* Naval & Military, MCC; *Style—* Gen Sir Geoffrey Howlett, KBE, MC; c/o Lloyds Bank, Tonbridge, Kent

HOWLETT, Air Vice-Marshal Neville Stanley; CB (1982); s of Stanley Herbert Howlett (d 1981), and Ethel Shirley Pritchard (d 1934); *b* 17 April 1927; *Educ* Liverpool Inst HS, Peterhouse Cambridge; *m* 1952, Sylvia, da of James Foster (d 1982), of Lins; 1 s (Michael), 1 da (Gillian); *Career* RAF pilot trg 1945-47, 32 and 64 (Fighter) Sqdns 1948-56, RAF Staff Coll Course 1957, Sqdn Cdr 229 (Fighter) OCU 1958-59, took part in London-Paris Air Race 1959, Staff Offr HQ Fighter Cmd 1959-61, OC Flying Wing RAF Coltishall 1961-63, RAF Coll of Air Warfare Course 1963, Staff Offr HQ Allied Forces Northern Europe 1964-66, OC Admin Wing RAF St Mawgan 1966-67, directing staff RAF Staff Coll 1967-69, Station Cdr RAF Leuchars 1970-72, Royal Coll of Def Studies Course 1972, Dir of Operations (Air Defence and Overseas) MOD 1973-74, Air Attache Washington DC 1975-77, Dir Mgmnt Support of Intelligence MOD 1978-80, Dir Gen RAF Personal Servs MOD 1980-82, ret; memb: Lord Chllrs Panel of Indep Inquiry Insprs 1982-, Pensions Appeal Tbnl 1988-, Homes Ctee Officers' Assoc 1982-; vice-pres RAF Assoc 1984-; *Recreations* golf, fishing; *Clubs* RAF, Phyllis Ct (Henley-on-Thames), Huntercombe GC; *Style—* Air Vice-Marshal Neville Howlett, CB; Bolney Trevor Drive, Lower Shiplake, Oxon RG9 3PG (☎ 073 522 3773)

HOWLING, Richard John; s of Cecil Baden Howling, of Dorset, and Florence Irene Crowther, *née* Firth; *b* 22 August 1932; *Educ* Repton; *m* 4 April 1959, Shirley Maureen, da of Clifford Jackson (d 1964), of Lancs; 2 s (Rex b 1961, Philip b 1962), 1 da (Sally b 1964); *Career* Sub-Lt RNVR 1956-58 Pacific, Malaya; vice-chm The Mediscus Gp Inc, chm Mediscus Int Ltd & Mediscus Products Ltd 1977-, ptnr Bird Potter & Co CAs 1961-68, dir Peter Robinson Ltd 1968-71, asst to fin dir Carreras Rothmans 1971-72; dir Rednor Ltd (and other subsidiaries) 1972-74, chm Actus Hldgs Ltd 1988-; former chm: Wessex Export Club 1985-87, Dorset Indust Year Educn/ Indust Ctee 1986; memb Dorset Indust Matters Ctee 1987-; memb: S West Regnl Cncl CBI 1985-, Fin & Econ Ctee (small firms) CBI 1985-, Mktg & Consumer Affrs Ctee CBI 1987-, vice chm Dorset Co Gp CBI 1986-; former memb: Engrg Industs Assoc Nat Cncl 1985-87, Small firms Cncl CBI 1985-87, Royal Warrant Holder as Organ Blower Mfr to HM The Queen (Watkins & Watson Ltd, a subsidiary of the Lingard Gp) 1981-87; govr The Porbeck Sch 1988-; FCA, FRSA; *Recreations* sailing, tennis, golf, reading, photography, walking; *Clubs* Royal Motor YC, Royal Overseas League, Poole Harbour YC; *Style—* Richard Howling, Esq; Roakham, Old Coastguard Rd, Sandbanks, Poole (☎ 0202 708976); Estepona, Spain; 10 Westminster Rd, Wareham, Dorset (☎ 09295 6311, telex 418496 MEDISC G, fax 09295 3967)

HOWMAN, Alastair Clive Ross; MBE (1967); s of Brig ross Cosens Howman, CIE, OBE (d 1976), and Cecil Isabel Howman, of Pitlochry, Perthshire; *b* 8 July 1931; *Educ* Winchester, RMA Sandhurst; *m* 1, 22 May 1957, Elizabeth Ann, da of Admiral Sir Richard Symonds-Tayler, KBE, CB (d 1971); 1 s (Charles Richard Ross b 1960), 1 da (Rosemary Ann Ross b 1962); m 2, 4 April 1980, Penny Lindsay, da of James Rankin; *Career* cmmnd The Argyll and Sutherland Highlanders 1952; serv: UK 1952-53, Guiana 1953-54, UK & BAOR (Berlin 1954-56), Cyprus 1958 (Co Cdr), BAOR 1960-62, serv as GSO 3 in HQ 1 Div; Staff Coll Camberley 1963, Malaya and Borneo (Co Cdr) 1964, GSO 2 Army Trg Directorate MOD 1965-66, Aden (Co Cdr) 1967; dir Trade Coates Ltd 1963; joined Manbré & Garton 1969, mktg dir Manbré Sugars 1972, joined Tate & Lyle 1976, md Gen Sugar Traders Ltd, Lochore & Ferguson Ltd 1979; established partnership Alastair Howman Agencies 1981; md: Craigtoun Meadows Ltd, Auchnahyle Farm & Crafts Ltd 1981; *Recreations* co sports, fly tying, tapestry; *Clubs* Royal Perth Golfing Soc; *Style—* Alastair C R Howman, MBE; Auchnahyle, Pitlochry, Perthshire (☎ 0796 2318)

HOWMAN, Keith Cecil Ross; s of Brig Ross Howman, CIE, OBE (d 1977), and Cecil Isobel, *née* Elles; *b* 14 July 1935; *Educ* Winchester; *m* 8 Sept 1962, (Margaret) Jean Bruce, da of Ian Walker (d 1981); 1 s (Colin b 1968), 1 da (Susan b 1965); *Career* serv 1 Bn Argyll and Sutherland Highlanders Cyprus 1958-59; chm and md Trade Coaters Ltd 1966-; dir: Trade Coaters (Tradec) Ltd, Trade Coaters (Tradec) Ltd, Trade Coaters (Roofing) Ltd, Preseal Prefelt Ltd, Trade Coaters (Fabrication) Ltd, Auchnahyle Farm & Crafts Ltd, Ballechin Pheasantries Ltd, A B Incubators Ltd, Explorasia Ltd; chm World Pheasant Assoc (int conservation charity) 1985-; *Recreations* fishing, shooting, travel in Asia; *Style—* Keith Howman, Esq; Ashmere, Felix Lane, Shepperton, Middx (☎ 0932 225445); Trade Coaters Ltd, 34 Mead Lane, Chertsey, Surrey (☎ 09325 66591)

HOWSON, John Robert; s of Charles Howson (d 1981), and Grace Kershaw; *b* 9 June 1947; *Educ* Meols Cop HS, Southport Lancs; *m* 15 June 1968, Glenys Susan, da of Kenneth George Turk, of Hampton Fields, Glos; 1 s (Adam b 1969), 1 da (Rebecca b 1972); *Career* retail mangr; founding chm Grafton Centre Retail Assoc Cambridge 1984-85, pres Portsmouth District Retail and Commercial Assoc 1986-87, vice-pres SE Hants C of C and Indust 1987; memb Cambridge RFC 1984-85; *Recreations* golf, rugby union, early classic music; *Clubs* Cambridge Business and Prof, Royal Naval Club, Royal Albert YC; *Style—* John R Howson, Esq; C & A, North Row, London; 86 Wicklands Ave, Saltdean, Brighton, E Sussex

HOWSON, Roger Clive; s of Percy Clive Howson, of Leics, and Doris Clara Langham (d 1987); *b* 12 Mar 1943; *Educ* Gateway GS Leicester, King's Coll London (LLB); *m* 21 March 1968, Valerie Ann; 1 s (Daniel b 1972), 1 da (Nichola b 1969); *Career* slr 1967; Buckley Investmts Ltd - dir and chief exec 1985; dir and jt chief exec Rosehough plc and subsidiaries; *Recreations* rugby, cricket, golf; *Clubs* Oriental, Vipers RFC, Lutterworth Golf, Leics CC; *Style—* Roger Howson, Esq; 4 Spring Close, Lutterworth, Leics LE17 4DD (☎ 04555 2130); Rosehaugh plc, 53-55 Queen Anne St, London SW1M 0LJ (☎ 01 486 7100)

HOY, David Forrest; s of Peter Harold Hoy, of Bromley, Kent, and Helena Muriel, *née* Blackshaw; *b* 7 April 1946; *Educ* Leeds GS Yorks, Merchant Taylors Sch Crosby Lancs; *m* 11 Sept 1971, Angela, da of John Piddock; 1 da (Susanne Mary b 4 April 1976); *Career* asst internal auditor Dunlop Co Ltd 1964-67, accountant Redwood Press Ltd 1967-68, gen mangr Guinness Superlatives Ltd 1974-76 (co accountant 1968-74), md Guinness Publishing Ltd 1976-; FCCA 1971; *Recreations* skiing, photography, philately; *Style—* David Hoy, Esq; 71 The Park, St Albans, Herts AL1 4RX; Guinness Publishing Ltd, 33 London Rd, Enfield, Middx EN2 6DJ (☎ 01 367 4567, fax 01 367 5912, car tel 0836 277076, telex 23573)

HOY, Hon Ian Richard; s of Baron Hoy (Life Peer d 1976), and Lady Hoy, *née* Nancy Hamlyn Rae McArthur; *b* 9 Mar 1945; *Educ* George Heriot's Sch, Edinburgh; *Career* memb Lothian Regnl Cncl 1982-86; *Style—* The Hon Ian Hoy; 77 Orchard Road, Edinburgh EH4 2EX (☎ (031 332) 5765)

HOY, Baroness; Nancy Hamlyn Rae; da of John McArthur; *m* 1942, Baron Hoy, PC (Life Peer d 1976); 1 s (Hon Ian Hoy); *Style—* The Rt Hon the Lady Hoy; 77 Orchard Rd, Edinburgh EH4 2EX (☎ (031 332) 5765)

HOYER MILLAR, Hon Alastair James Harold; s of 1 Baron Inchyra, GCMG, CVO; *b* 13 Nov 1936; *Educ* Eton; *m* 1974, Virginia Margaret Diana, da of William Perine Macauley; 1 s, 1 da; *Career* late Scots Gds; *Style—* The Hon Alastair Hoyer Millar; 16 Pembridge Villas, London W11

HOYER MILLAR, Gurth Christian; s of Edward George Hoyer Millar, and Phyllis Edith Amy Wace (d 1956); *b* 13 Dec 1929; *Educ* Harrow, Oxford, Michigan Univ (LLM); *m* 17 March 1956, Jane Taylor, da of Harold John Aldington; 2 s (Christian b 1959, Luke b 1962), 1 da (Eliza b 1965); *Career* cmmnd Malaya 1949-50, cmmnd Reserve Bn SAS 1950-58; barr Middle Temple; main bd dir J Sainsbury plc: distribution 1966-, devpt 1974-; non-exec dir: Hudson Bay Co of Canada 1976-, P&O Steam Navigation Co 1980-;chm: Homebase Ltd 1979-, J Sainsbury (Properties) Ltd 1988-, Bonhams 1988-; *Style—* Gurth C Hoyer Miller, Esq; 27 Trevor Place, London SW7 1LD (☎ 01 584 3883); J Sainsbury Ltd, Stamford House, Stamford Street, London SE1 9LL (☎ 01 921 6785, telex 264241); car telephone 0836 242659

HOYER MILLAR, Hon Robert Charles Reneke; s and h of 1 Baron Inchyra, GCMG, CVO, and (Anna Judith) Elizabeth, da of Jonkheer Reneke de Marees van Swinderen (formerly Netherlands min in London); *b* 4 April 1935; *Educ* Eton, New Coll Oxford; *m* 1961, Fiona Mary, da of Edmund C R Sheffield (d 1977), of Normanby Park, Scunthorpe, Lincs; 1 s, 2 da; *Career* late Scots Gds; banker; local dir Barclays Bank Newcastle upon Tyne 1967-75, regnl gen mangr Barclays Bank 1976-81, dep chm Barclays Bank Tst Co Ltd 1982-85; gen mangr Barclays Bank plc 1985-87; dir UK Fin Servs 1987-88; sec gen Br Bankers Assoc and Ctee of London and Scottish Banks 1988-; *Clubs* White's; *Style—* The Hon Robert Hoyer Millar; Rookley Manor, Kings Somborne, Stockbridge, Hants (☎ 0794 388319); British Bankers Assoc, 10 Lombard St, London EC3V 9EL (☎ 01 626 1567)

HOYES, Dr Thomas; s of Fred Hoyes, and Margaret Elizabeth Hoyes; *b* 19 Nov 1935; *Educ* Queen Elizabeths GS Alford Lincs, Downing Coll Cambridge (BA, MA, PhD); *m* 27 Aug 1960, Amy Joan, da of Harry Bew Wood (d 1973), of Skegness, Lincolnshire; 2 da (Rebecca b 1963, Charlotte b 1966); *Career* conslt Hallam Bracket Chartered Surveyors Nottingham 1983-88 (ptnr 1963-83), prof of land mgmnt Univ of Reading 1983-88 (hd of dept 1986-88), memb Lands Tbnl 1989; pres Cambridge Univ Land Soc 1973, govr Nottingham HS for Girls 1976-82; Liveryman Worshipful Co of Chartered Surveyors 1980; ARICS 1964, FRICS 1969; memb: Rating Surveyors Assoc 1968, gen cncl RICS 1982-85 (pres planning and devpt div 1983-84); *Recreations* adapting houses, gardening; *Clubs* Farmers; *Style—* Dr Thomas Hoyes; c/o The Lands Tribunal, 48-49 Chancery Lane, London WC2A 1JR (☎ 01 936 7200)

HOYLE, (Eric) Douglas Harvey; JP (1958), MP (Lab, Warrington North 1983-); s of late William Hoyle, and Leah Ellen Hoyle; *b* 17 Feb 1930; *Educ* Adlington Sch, Horwich and Bolton Tech Colls; *m* 1953, Pauline, da of William Spencer; 1 s (Lindsay); *Career* sales engr; Parly candidate (Lab) Clitheroe 1964, MP (Lab): Nelson and Colne Oct 1974-79 (contested same 1970 and Feb 1974), Warrington (bye-election) July 1981-1983; memb Manchester Regnl Hosp Bd 1968-74, pres ASTMS 1985-87 (memb 1958, vice pres 1981-85), jt pres MSF 19880, memb Lab Pty Nat Exec Ctee 1978-82 and 1983-85, chm NEC Home Policy Ctee 1983, chm Lab Parly Pty trade and indust ctee 1987-, memb House of Commons trade and indust select ctee 1985-; *Style—* Douglas Hoyle, Esq, JP, MP; 30 Ashfield Road, Anderton, Nr Chorley, Lancs

HOYLE, Prof Sir Fred; s of Benjamin Hoyle; *b* 24 June 1915; *Educ* Bingley GS, Emmanuel Coll Cambridge (MA); *m* 1939, Barbara Clark; 1 s, 1 da; *Career* FRS 1957; fell St John's Coll Cambridge 1939-72, research in radar Admty 1940-45, Plumian prof of astronomy and experimental philosophy Cambridge Univ 1958-72, prof of astronomy Royal Inst 1969-72, Andrew D White prof-at-large Cornell Univ USA 1972-78, hon research prof Manchester Univ 1972-; fndr and dir Inst of Theoretical Astronomy Cambridge Univ 1967-72; foreign memb American Philosophical Soc 1980; hon memb: Mark Twain Soc 1978, Royal Irish Acad in the Section of Sci 1977; kt 1972; *Publications include* Man in the Universe (1966), From Stonehenge to Modern Cosmology (1973), Nicholas Copernicus (1973), The Relation of Physics and Cosmology (1973), Astronomy and Cosmology (1975), Ten Faces of the Universe (1977), On Stonhenge (1977), Energy or Extinction (1977), The Intelligent Universe (1983); with N C Wickramasinghe: Lifecloud (1978), Diseases from Space (1979), Space Travellers: The Bringers of Life (1981); *Novels include* The Black Cloud (1957), Ossian's Ride (1959), October the First is Too Late (1966), Element 79 (1967); with G Hoyle: Fifth Planet (1963), Rockets in Ursa Major (1969), Seven Steps to the Sun (1970), The Molecule Men (1971), The Inferno (1973), Into Deepest Space (1974), The Incandescent Ones (1977), The Westminster Disaster (1978), Comet Halley (1985); *Style—* Prof Sir Fred Hoyle; c/o The Royal Society, 6 Carlton House Terrace, London SW1Y 5AG

HOYOS, Hon Sir (Fabriciano) Alexander; s of Emigdio and Adelina Hoyos, of Peru; *b* 5 July 1912; *Educ* Harrison Coll, Codrington Coll, Durham Univ (MA); *m* 1, 1940, Kathleen Carmen (d 1970); 3 s, 1 da; m 2, 1973, Gladys Louise; *Career* leader-writer of Daily Advocate 1937-43, correspondent The Times London 1937-65; history teacher Barbados and Trinidad 1943-72; moderator and lectr Carribean History Survey Course Cave Hill University WI 1963-70; memb: Barbados Christian Cncl 1976-, Constitution Review Cmmn 1977-78, Privy Cncl for Barbados 1977-; Queen's Silver Jubilee Medal 1977; kt 1979; *Style*— Hon Sir Alexander Hoyos; Beachy Crest, Belair Cross Rd, St Philip, Barbados (☎ 36323)

HUBBARD, (Richard) David (Cairns); s of John Cairns Hubbard, of 6 Orchard Way, Esher, Surrey, and Gertrude Emille, *née* Faure (d 1967); *b* 14 May 1936; *Educ* Tonbridge; *m* 7 Feb 1964, Hannah Neale, da of Arthur Gilbert Dennison (d 1988); 3 da (Katie-Jane b 1966, Juliet b 1970, Nicola b 1973); *Career* Nat Serv 2 Lt RA; Peat Marwick Mitchell & Co 1957-64; fin dir: Cape Industs plc 1972-74, Bache and Co (London) Ltd 1974-76; chm Powell Duffryn plc 1986- (fin dir 1976-85); memb cncl Cancer Research Campaign 1981- (chm nat fin ctee 1986-, dep chm exec ctee 1985-), tres Berkshire GC 1981-; Freeman City of London, Liveryman Worshipful Co of Skinnets; FCA 1961; *Recreations* golf, skiing; *Clubs* Berks GC; *Style*— David Hubbard, Esq; Meadowcroft, Windlesham, Surrey GU20 6BJ (☎ 0276 721 98); Powell Duffryn House, London Rd, Bracknell, Berks RG12 2AQ (☎ 0344 531 01, fax 0344 505 99)

HUBBARD, Hon Frances Linden; da of 5 Baron Addington; *b* 26 July 1962; *Style*— The Hon Frances Hubbard

HUBBARD, Jack; s of Arthur Fredrick Hubbard (d 1984), and Alice Mary, *née* Fairman (d 1985); *b* 11 Oct 1932; *Educ* Rochester Tech Sch, Univ of Cardiff (BSc); *m* 11 Sept 1960, Christine Lilian, da of Francis Held (d 1985); 2 s (Andrew b 14 June 1961, Peter b 30 Oct 1964); *Career* Nat Serv RAF 1953-55; Reed Int: Central Engrg 1956-57, head engrg res 1967-69, PA to dep chm 1969-71, md Timperley engrg 1971-73, divnl chief exec 1973-87; chief exec Medway Packaging Ncb Sweden 1987-; involved in church activities; Liveryman Worshipful Co of Horners; MIEE, MIMechE; *Recreations* rambling; *Style*— Jack Hubbard, Esq; Medway Packaging, New Hythe Lane, Larkfield, Maidstone, Kent ME2 6SH (☎ 0622 717 179, fax 0622 76360, car tel 0836 231 274, telex 965131)

HUBBARD, Jack Ernest; s of Frederick Ernest (d 1953), and Violet Frances, *née* Kerridge (d 1987); *b* 15 July 1925; *Educ* Braintree; *m* 6 Jan 1954, Cecily Susan, da of Cecil Mott Bowles (d 1985); 1 da (Susan Louise b 1969); *Career* sportsman; E of England Scrambles Champion, Jersey Sand Racing Champion; competed many int events in France, Holland, Ireland, Belgium; *Recreations* rifle shooting; *Clubs* Braintree (MC, LCC), Rifle; *Style*— Jack E Hubbard, Esq; Hunters Roost, Church Rd, Bradwell, Braintree, Essex CM7 8EP (☎ 0376 62782); 135 High St, Aldeburgh, Suffolk

HUBBARD, John Michael; s of Leslie Leon Basil Hubbard, of W Midlands, and late Hilda Louise; *b* 21 April 1943; *Educ* Tudor Grange GS Solihull; *m* 7 Sept 1969, Rosemary, da of Leslie Meeks, of Solihulll; 2 s (James, Michael); *Career* CA; princ J Hubbard & Co; dir: Froude Engrg Ltd 1977-80, Worcester and Hereford Area C of C Trg Ltd 1985-87; FCA;; *Style*— John M Hubbard, Esq; Cotsford, Old Malvern Rd, Powick, Worcester WR2 4RX (☎ 0905 830057)

HUBBARD, Hon Mrs (Julia Elizabeth); *née* Callaghan; yr da of Baron Callaghan of Cardiff, KG, PC (Life Peer), *qv*; *b* 1942; *m* 1967, Ian Hamilton Hubbard; 3 s (Tobin James Hamilton b 1970, Tom Ian b 1975, Sam Jonathan b 1976), 1 da (Joanna Jane b 1971); *Style*— The Hon Mrs Hubbard; Nettleslack Farm, Lowick Green, Cumbria

HUBBARD, Leslie Antony Marcus; s of Gerald Jabez Hubbard, and Blanche Ivy May, *née* Turner ; *b* 24 Jan 1936; *Educ* East Barnet GS, Northampton Coll of Advanced Technol (now City Univ); *m* 28 Sept 1958, Barbara, da of Leslie Norman Lunn (d 1988); 1 s (Geoffrey b 1961), 2 da (Julia b 1959, Carol b 1964); *Career* RAF 1958-63: sr optician RAF Hosp Halton 1958-60, sr optician RAF Hosp Changi Singapore 1960-63; optometrist 1963- (own practise High Wycombe 1966-); former chm Bucks local optical ctee, memb Oxford local optical ctee, chm (former sec) Assoc of Optometrists Middle Thames Branch, memb Rotary club of High Wycombe (chm int serv ctee), chm Spectacle Makers Soc; Freeman City of London 1980, Liveryman Worshipful Co of Spectacle Makers 1981; FBCO 1980 (fndr fell); *Recreations* rambling, skiing; *Clubs* City Livery, Comrades (Wallingford); *Style*— Leslie Hubbard, Esq; Lima, 5 Beaconsfield Ave, High Wycombe, Bucks (☎ 0494 28 107); 55 West Wycombe Rd, High Wycombe, Bucks (☎ 0494 33 110)

HUBBARD, Michael Joseph; QC (1985); s of Joseph Thomas Hubbard, of Sussex, and Gwendoline Phyllis, *née* Bird (d 1957); *b* 16 June 1942; *Educ* Lancing Coll; *m* 1967, Ruth Ann, da of John Logan, of Hants; 5 s (Mark b 1968, Duncan b 1970, Lucian b 1972, Angus b 1974, Quinten b 1976); *Career* slr 1966-72, barr Grays Inn 1972, joined Western Circuit; prosecuting counsel to Inland Revenue Western Circuit 1983-85; rec Crown Ct 1984; *Recreations* sailing; *Style*— Michael Hubbard, QC; Bartons, Stoughton, Chichester, Sussex; 1 Paper Buildings, Temple, London

HUBBARD, Hon Michael Walter Leslie; s of 5 Baron Addington (d 1982); hp of bro, 6 Baron Addington, *qv*; *b* 6 July 1965; *Style*— The Hon Michael Hubbard

HUBBARD, Lady Miriam; *née* Fitzalan-Howard; da of 3 Baron Howard of Glossop, MBE, and Baroness Beaumont, OBE; sis of 17 Duke of Norfolk, *qv*; *b* 12 Dec 1924; *m* 19 April 1952, Lt-Cdr Theodore Bernard Peregrine Hubbard, RN (ret), er s of late Theodore Stephen Hubbard; 2 s, 3 da; *Recreations* walking and dogs; *Style*— Lady Miriam Hubbard; Thurston Croft, Bury St Edmunds, Suffolk

HUBBARD, Hon Sally Anne; da of 5 Baron Addington; *b* 19 Oct 1966; *Style*— The Hon Sally Hubbard

HUBBARD-MILES, Peter Charles; CBE (1981); s of Charles Hubbard (d 1927) and Ruth Agnes, *née* Lewis and later Miles (d 1974); *b* 9 May 1927; *Educ* Lewis' Sch Pengam; *m* 1948, Pamela, da of Sidney Wilkins (d 1958); 2 s, 3 da; *Career* serv RAF 1945-48; self-employed in retail and serv indust; contested (C) Aberavon Feb 1974; MP (C) Bridgend 1985-87; *Recreations* theatre; *Style*— Peter Hubbard-Miles, Esq, CBE

HUBBARD-RYLAND, Dr (Primrose) Anne; da of Benjamin John Hubbard, of London, and Sylvia Constance Kay; inventors of the 'Kay Loom'; *b* 17 Jan 1939; *Educ* Univ of London, Univ of Liverpool; *m* 1, 16 July 1966, David Andrew Ryland, s of C Ryland, CBE, of Sussex; m 2, 4 June 1986, Paul John Starmer, s of Albert Edward Starmer (d 1982), of Northants; *Career* house physician Whittington Hosp London 1971-72, house surgn Northampton General Hosp 1973; dir Elizabethan Lace Co Ltd 1987; RCS; LRCP; *Books* Condition of Geriatric Patients on Admission to Hospital (dental), Gerontologia Clinic (1973), Dental Care of the Elderly (Nursing Times 1977); *Recreations* needlework, keep-fit, church choir; *Clubs* British Sub-Aqua; *Style*— Dr Anne Hubbard-Ryland; The Chapel House, Greens Norton, Northants NN12 8BS (☎ 0327 53663)

HUCK, William Simpson; s of William Cecil Huck (d 1977), of Preston, Lancs, and Florence Ellen Davey, *née* Simpson (d 1982); *b* 24 June 1927; *Educ* Sedbergh; *m* 20 Aug 1955, Barbara Marion, da of Thomas Harold Berry (d 1943), of Chipping, Lancs; 2 s (Simon William John b 1958, Richard Anthony b 1959), 1 da (Kathryn Nancy b 1962); *Career* slr; pt/t chm Rent Tbnl and Rent Assessment Ctees (NW Area) 1965-75; chm Harris Charity Preston, tres Preston Grasshoppers RFC 1952-69 and sec 1969-71; pres:Preston Cricket and Hockey Club (Preston Sports Club) 1981-87, Preston Incorporated Law Soc 1985-86; *Recreations* cricket, rugby, shooting, gardening; *Style*— William S Huck, Esq; Broughton Lodge, Broughton, Preston PR3 5JE (☎ 0772 862711); 3 Ribblesdale Place, Preston PR1 3NA (☎ 0772 54048)

HUCKFIELD, Leslie John; MEP (L) Merseyside East 1984-; s of Ernest Leslie and Suvla Huckfield; *b* 7 April 1942; *Educ* Prince Henry's GS Evesham, Keble Coll Oxford, Univ of Birmingham; *Career* contested (Lab) Warwick and Leamington 1966; MP (Lab) Nuneaton March 1967-83; PPS to Min of Public Bldgs and Works 1968-70, parly under-sec Ind 1976-79, oppn front bench spokesman Ind 1979-81; memb: Lab NEC 1978-82, Lab W Midlands Regnl Exec Ctee 1978-82; political sec Nat Union Lab and Socialist Clubs 1979-82; former chm Lab Tport Gp 1974-76; ind advsr Cmmn of Tport Gp 1975-76; MEP for Merseyside East 1984-; pres Worcs Fedn of Young Socialists 1962-64; memb: Birmingham Regnl Hosp Bd 1970-72, Political Ctee Co-op Retail Soc 1981-; advertising mangr Tribune Pubns Ltd; *Publications* various newspaper and periodical articles; *Recreations* running marathons; *Style*— Les Huckfield, Esq, MEP; PO Box 200, Wigan, Lancashire WN5 0LU

HUCKIN, P(eter) Hugh; s of Albert Edward Huckin, OBE (d 1983), and Margaret, *née* Harris; *b* 17 Oct 1930; *Educ* Harrisons Coll Barbados, Haileybury ISC, Royal Sch of Mines London Univ (BSc); *m* 5 Sept 1955, Anne Margaret, da of James Duncan Webster (d 1964); 2 da (Jennifer b 1960, Elizabeth b 1963); *Career* RCS Lt 1950-53; petroleum engr: Shell Int Holland and Columbia 1956-62, Texaco Trinidad 1962-63; chief petroleum engr: Itaq Petroleum Co 1964-73, ARCO 1973-75; md REMI (UK) Ltd 1975-76, chm and md Welldrill Gp Ltd 1977-; *Recreations* work, garden, boats; *Style*— P Hugh Huckin, Esq; Haywards, Headley, Bordon, Hants GU35 8PX (☎ 0428 712224); Welldrill Ltd, Queen Anne House, Bagshot, Surrey GU19 5AT (☎ 0276 76666)

HUCKLE, Sir (Henry) George; OBE (1969); s of George Henry and Lucy Huckle; *b* 9 Jan 1914; *Educ* Latymer Sch, Oxford Univ; *m* 1, 1935, L Steel (d 1947); 1 s; m 2, 1949, Mrs Millicent Mary Hunter; 1 da, 1 step da; *Career* serv WWII bomber pilot (POW); Shell Gp 1945-70, md Shellstar Ltd 1965-70, ret; chm: Agric Trg Bd 1970-80, Home-Grown Cereals Authy 1977-83, Extrans Tech Servs Ltd 1980-; kt 1977; *Recreations* competition bridge, gardening, horse eventing follower, golf; *Clubs* Farmers'; *Style*— Sir George Huckle, OBE; Icknield House, Saxonhurst, Downton, Wilts

HUDDIE, Sir David Patrick; s of James Huddie, farmer (d 1936); *b* 12 Mar 1916; *Educ* Mountjoy Sch Dublin, Trinity Coll Dublin (MA); *m* 1941, Wilhelmina Betty, da of Dr John Booth (d 1940), of Cork; 3 s; *Career* engr; md aero engine div Rolls-Royce Ltd 1965-70, chm Rolls-Royce Aero Engines Inc 1968-70; sr res fell Imp Coll London 1971-80 (hon fell 1981); Hon ScD Dublin; FIQA, FIMechE, FEng; kt 1968; *Recreations* music, reading, gardening; *Clubs* Athenaeum; *Style*— Sir David Huddie; The Croft, Butts Rd, Bakewell, Derbys (☎ 062 981 3330)

HUDLESTON, Air Chief Marshal Sir Edmund Cuthbert; GCB (1963, KCB 1958, CB 1945), CBE (1943); s of Ven Cuthbert Hudleston (d 1944), Archdeacon of Perth, and Julia Marguerite, *née* Philips; *b* 30 Dec 1908; *Educ* Guildford Sch W Australia, RAF Coll Cranwell; *m* 1, 24 July 1936, Nancy (d 1980), da of Boyde Davis, of Rose Bay, Sydney, NSW; 1 s, 1 da; m 2, 1981, Brenda, da of A Whalley, of Darwen; *Career* joined RAF 1927, serv UK until 1933, India NWFP (despatches), RAF Staff Coll 1938, lent to Turkish Govt 1939-40, serv WWII Middle E and N Africa, Sicily, Italy 1941-43, (despatches 3 times), Gp Capt 1942, Air Cdr 1943, Sr Air SO Med Allied Tactical Air Forces 1943-44, AOC No 84 Gp 2 TAF Western Front 1944, IDC 1946, head UK Mil Delgn to Western Union Mil Staff Ctee 1948-50, AOC No 1 Gp Bomber Cmd 1950-51, dep COS Supreme HQ Allied Cmd Europe 1951-53, AOC No 3 Gp Bomber Cmd 1953-56, RAF instr IDC 1956-57, vice-chief of Air Staff 1957-62, Air Marshal 1958, Air Chief Marshal 1961, AOC-in-C Tport Cmd 1962-63, Air Cdr Allied Air Forces Central Europe 1964-67 and C-in-C Allied Forces Central Europe 1964-65; Air ADC to HM The Queen 1962-67, ret; dir Pilkington Bros (optical div) 1971-79; Cdr Legion of Merit (USA) 1944, Kt Cdr Order of Orange Nassau (Netherlands) 1945, Cdr Order of Couronne, Croix de Guerre (Belgium) 1945, Offr Legion of Honour 1956 and Croix de Guerre (France) 1957; *Recreations* cricket, squash, tennis, shooting; *Clubs* RAF; *Style*— Air Chief Marshal Sir Edmund Hudleston, GCB, CBE; 156 Marine Court, St Leonards-on-Sea, East Sussex TN38 0DZ

HUDLESTON, James Wallace; s of Wilfrid Andrew Hudleston, of Cyprus, and Barbara Jeanne, *née* Robotham;; *b* 14 July 1952; *Educ* Falcon Coll Essexvale Rhodesia; *m* 30 May 1979, Perronelle Jane, *née* Le Marchant; 1 s (Hugh Edward b 1983), 1 da (Tamara Avril b 1980); *Career* financier; dir: The Hutton John Co Ltd, Albemarle & Bond Hldgs plc, London & American Mining plc,; *Recreations* shooting, sailing, travel; *Clubs* Royal London YC; *Style*— James Hudleston, Esq; 252 Clapham Rd, London SW9 OP2 (☎ 01 735 2532); 45 Bloomsbury Sq, London WC1A 2RA (☎ 01 242 5544, fax 01 405 0977)

HUDSON, Mrs Jonathan - (Princess) Anna; *née* Obolensky; da of Prince Sergei Dimitrievitch Obolensky (of the Russian princely family descended from Mikhail Vsevolodovitch, Prince of Tchernigov (d 1368), 11 in descent from Rurik, founder of the Russian monarchy) and Patricia Olive, *née* Blake; *b* 2 Oct 1952,Windsor,; *m* 26 Feb 1981, as his 2 wife, Jonathan Philip Hudson (b 19 Jan 1945, stockbroker), son of Philip Alexander Hudson and Loveday Catherine, *née* Gibbs; *Style*— Mrs Jonathan Hudson; 11a Beauchamp Road, London SW11

HUDSON, Brian Paige; s of Sir Edmund Hudson (d 1978), of Edinburgh, and Lady Bodil Catherina, *née* Boschen; *b* 29 May 1945; *Educ* Marlborough, King's Coll Cambridge (MA); *m* 16 Jan 1971, Elisabeth Francoise, da of Jacques Cochemé (d 1971), of Rome; 2 da (Elodie b 16 Dec 1971, Emeline b 16 Sept 1973); *Career* princ HM Treasy 1970-76 (asst princ 1966-69, private sec to head of Treasy 1969-70), sec Wilson ctee on fin insts 1976-78; Den Norske Creditbank plc (formerly Nordic Bank): sr mangr 1978-79, assoc dir 1979-80, dep md 1981-88, md and chief exec 1989-;

Style— Brian Hudson, Esq; 92 Oakley St, Chelsea, London SW3 (☎ 01 352 5265); Edifici Bon Sol, Arinsal, Andorra; Den Norske Creditbank plc, 20 St Dunstan's Hill, London EC3R 2HY (☎ 01 621 1111)

HUDSON, Hon Mrs; Hon Carola; *née* Browne; er da of 6 Baron Kilmaine, CBE (d 1978); *b* 17 May 1932; *m* 30 April 1960, John Michael Carlyon Lowry Hudson, o s of late Herbert Hudson, of Gwavas, Tikokino, Hawkes Bay, NZ; 2 s, 1 da; *Style*— The Hon Mrs Hudson; Gwavas Station, Tikokino, Hawkes Bay, NZ

HUDSON, Lady Cathleen Blanche Lily; *née* Eliot; da of 6 Earl of St Germans, MC, and Lady Blanche Somerset, da of 9 Duke of Beaufort; through Lady Blanche she is co-heiress (with Samantha Cope and Alexandra Peyronel, *qqv*) to the Baronies of Botetourt and Herbert, which went into abeyance on the death of 10 Duke of Beaufort, KG, GCVO, PC (d 1984); *b* 29 July 1921; *m* 1, 1946 (m dis 1956), John Seyfried, of Kensington, RHG; 1 s, 1 da; m 2, 1957, Sir Havelock Hudson, *qv*; 1 s, 1 da; *Career* antique dealer; *Recreations* bridge; *Style*— Lady Cathleen Hudson; The Old Rectory, Stanford Dingley, Berks (☎ 0734 744346)

HUDSON, Christopher John; s of John Augustus Hudson, of The Holt, Benenden, Kent, and Margaret Gwendolen, *née* Hunt; *b* 29 Sept 1946; *Educ* The King's Sch Canterbury, Jesus Coll Cambridge (MA); *m* 10 March 1978, (Margaret), Kirsty, da of Alexander Drummond McLeod, of The Garden House, Ticehurst, Sussex; 1 s (Rowland Alexander b 1983); *Career* ed Faber & Faber 1968-70, literary ed The Spectator 1971-73, Harkness Fell 1975-77, columnist The Evening Standard 1985-88 (ed writer 1978-81, literary ed 1982-85) memb Soc of Authors (PEN); *Books* Overlord (filmed 1975), The Final Act (1979), Insider Out (1981), The Killing Fields (1984), Colombo Heat (1986); *Style*— Christopher Hudson, Esq; 64 Westbourne Park Rd, London W2 5PJ (☎ 01 229 8586); Northcliffe House, 2 Derry St, London W18

HUDSON, David Norman; s of Sir Edmund Peder Hudson (d 1978), of Edinburgh; *b* 29 May 1945; *Educ* Marlborough, Balliol Coll Oxford; *m* 1967, Rosemary McMahon, *née* Turner; 1 s (Stephen b 1969), 2 da (Isobel b 1971, Sarah b 1976); *Career* merchant banker, dir Samuel Montagu & Co Ltd 1974-81, asst gen mangr Arlabank 1981-84; ptnr and head of corporate Fin, James Capel & Co 1984-87; dep chm and chief exec Henry Ansbacher & Co Ltd 1987-; *Recreations* natural history, bridge, opera; *Style*— David Hudson, Esq; Hare Hatch House, Hare Hatch, Reading, Berks (☎ 073 522 2360)

HUDSON, Eric; s of John Wilden Hudson (d 1976), of W Yorks, and Ethel, *née* Burton (d 1981); *b* 31 August 1927; *Educ* GS in Yorks and Lancs; *m* 24 June 1954, Matilda Y D (Biddy), da of Robert Francis Hutchison (d 1948), of Callander, Perthshire, Scotland; 1 s (Ian R B b 1958), 1 da (Mary C B b 1956); *Career* CA 1949, in practice 1958-, cncl memb Inst of CAs in England and Wales 1985-; lay preacher, memb various Methodist Church Ctees, chm Nat Children's Home Cleveland Ctee 1984-87; vice chm Teesside Stockton Cons Assoc 1972-74, tres Local Ecumenical Church 1988-; FCA ; *Recreations* armchair cricket, walking, theatre; *Clubs* Lansdowne; *Style*— Eric Hudson, Esq; 22 Tunstall Ave, Hartlepool, Cleveland TS26 8NF (☎ 0429 231286); 114 Borough Road, Middlesborough, Cleveland TS1 2ES (☎ 0642 242365)

HUDSON, Francis Edward; TD; s of Edward Hudson (d 1945), of Bridge House, Harewood; *b* 10 June 1912; *Educ* Rugby; *m* 1944, Masha Violet, da of Col Murray Muirhead-Murray, DSO (d 1968); 1 s, 1 da; *Career* former Maj M East; former chm Yorkshire Post Newspapers (dep chm 1958, ret 1983), chm Doncaster Newspapers (ret 1981); dir United Newspapers (ret 1983); high sheriff N Yorks 1981; *Recreations* fishing, shooting; *Style*— Francis Hudson, Esq, TD; Winterfield House, Hornby, Bedale, Yorks DL8 1NN (☎ (0748) 811619)

HUDSON, Prof George; s of George Hudson (d 1956), of Edenfield, and Edith Hannah, *née* Bennett (d 1956); *b* 10 August 1924; *Educ* Edenfield C of E Sch, Bury GS, Univ of Manchester (BSc, MB ChB, MSc), Univ of Bristol (MD, DSc); *m* 14 April 1955, Mary Patricia (d 1977), da of Frank Hibbert (d 1929), of Chester; 1 da (Elisabeth b 1961); *Career* Capt RAMC 1951-53, unit MO Green Howards Army Operational Res Gp; house offr Manchester Royal Infirmary 1949-50; Univ of Bristol: demonstrator in anatomy 1950-51, lectr (later reader) in anatomy 1953-68, preclinical dean 1963-68; visiting prof (Fulbright Award) Univ of Minnesota 1959-60; Univ of Sheffield: admin dean 1968-83, hon clinical lectr in haematology 1968-75, prof of experimental haematology 1975-, head of dept of haematology 1981-, postgraduate dean 1984-88, regnl postgraduate dean 1988-; hon conslt in haematology Sheffield Health Authy 1969-, chm Conf of Deans of prov Med Schs 1980-82; memb: Sheffield Regnl Hosp Bd 1970-74, Sheffield Health Authy 1974-84, Cncl for Med postgraduate Educn for England and Wales 1980-83; chm ethical ctee Northern Gen Hosp 1985-; lay reader C of E 1953-; MRCPath 1970, FRCPath 1975, MRCP 1984, FRCP 1988; *Recreations* badminton, cavies, garden; *Style*— Prof George Hudson; The Medical School, Beech Hill Rd, Sheffield S10 2RX, (☎ 0742 721747)

HUDSON, Gillian Grace; da of Brian Hudson (d 1985), of E Grinstead, Sussex, and Grace Iris, *née* Hill; *b* 23 Mar 1955; *Educ* Univ of Sussex (BA); *Career* pres offr Eng Tourist Bd 1978-81, ed Home and County Magazine 1981-83, dep ed then ed Fitness Magazine 1984-85, ed Cook's Weekly 1986, dep ed then ed Company Magazine 1987-; BSME 1981, NUJ; *Recreations* cycling, reading, windsurfing, travel, walking, swimming; *Clubs* Groucho's; *Style*— Ms Gillian Hudson; Company Magazine, National Magazine House, 72 Broadwick St, London W1V 2BP (☎ 01 439 5000, fax 01 437 6886, telex 263879 NATMAG G)

HUDSON, Dr Harold Gaunt; s of Edwin Gaunt Hudson (d 1963), and Gertrude Elizabeth, *née* Jackson (d 1963); *b* 21 Feb 1912; *Educ* Repton, Clare Coll Cambridge (MA, PhD, DipAgric); *m* 7 June 1937, Doreen, da of Albert George Belben; 1 da (Ann b 14 April 1942); *Career* offr Norfolk War Agric Ctee 1939-45, lectr agric Univ of Cambridge 1945-47, farmer 1947-83; Alderman Norfolk CC (vice-chm); chm: Educn ctee Wymondham UDC 1963-72, South Norfolk DC, Shuttleworth Agric Coll, Norfolk Coll Agric, Norfolk Coll Arts and Technol, Norwich Sch; govr Gresham Sch, tax cmmr and chm South Norfolk, memb cncl Royal Vetinary Coll, co pres Norfolk Young Farmers; pres: Norfolk Lawn Tennis Assoc, Norfolk Bamdinton Assoc; Silver Jubilee Medal 1977; Fell Royal Statistical Soc 1946, FRAgS 1975 (chm); *Recreations* tennis, bridge, sailing; *Clubs* Farmers; *Style*— Dr Harold Hudson; St Marys, Vicar St, Wymondham, Norfolk NR18 ORJ (☎ 0953 603277)

HUDSON, Sir Havelock Henry Trevor; s of Savile Ernest Hudson (d 1952); *b* 4 Jan 1919; *Educ* Rugby; *m* 1, 1944 (m dis 1956), Elizabeth, da of Brig W Home; 2 s; m 2, Lady Cathleen, *qv*, da of 6 Earl of St Germans; 1 s, 1 da; *Career* serv WWII Europe; Lloyd's underwriter 1952-; chm Lloyd's 1975-77 (dep chm 1969-73); memb Bd of Govrs: Pangbourne Coll 1976, Bradfield Coll 1978-; pres City of London Outward Bound Assoc 1979-; kt 1977; *Recreations* shooting, bridge; *Clubs* Boodle's; *Style*— Sir Havelock Hudson; The Old Rectory, Stanford Dingley, Berks (☎ 0734 744346)

HUDSON, Ian; s of Donald Pryce Hudson, of Hoylake, Wirral, Cheshire, and Emily Grandison, *née* Campbell (d 1969); *b* 27 April 1930; *Educ* Worksop Coll Notts, St Andrews Univ (BSc); *m* 4 Sept 1965, Vivien Halliwell, da of Walter Marsden; 2 s (Andrew James b 28 July 1966, John Michael b 25 July 1968), 1 da (Joanne b 29 Dec 1971); *Career* Nat Serv RA 1952-54; dyestuffs div ICI 1954-60, Allied Colloids Ltd 1960-65, dir annd princ BTI Chemicals Ltd 1966-71; various stockbroking roles in Jersey 1974-84 with: Kemp-Gee & Co, Sheppards & Chase, Laurie Milbank; investmt dir Morgan Grenfell (Jersey) Ltd 1984-88; memb Jersey branch IOD (ctee memb 1987-); *Recreations* golf; *Clubs* Royal and Ancient GC, La Moye GC; *Style*— Ian Hudson, esq; Rosemount, Royte des Genets, St Brelade, Jersey (☎ 0534 42560)

HUDSON, James Ralph; CBE (1976); s of William Shand Hudson (d 1967), and Ethel, *née* Summerskill (d 1953); *b* 15 Feb 1916; *Educ* King's Sch Canterbury, London Univ Middx Hosp Med Sch (MB BS); *m* 29 June 1946, Margaret May Hunter, da of Paul Eugene Oulpe (d 1986); 2 s (James b 1949, Andrew b 1956), 2 da (Ann b 1948, Sarah b 1953); *Career* WWII RAFVR 1942-46: Flying Offr 1942-43, Flt Lt 1943-44, Sqdn Ldr 1944-46; civil conslt in ophthalmology to RAF 1970-82; ophthalmic surgn; res MO Tindal House Hosp Aylesbury 1939-42 (sr res offr 1949), house surgn Moorfields Eye Hosp; conslt ophthalmic surgn: W Middx Hosp 1950-56, Mount Vernon Hosp 1953-59, Moorfields Eye Hosp 1956-81, Guy's Hosp 1963-76; hon ophthalmic surgn: Hosp St John and St Elizabeth 1953-, King Edward VII Hosp for Offrs 1970-86; hon consulting surgn Moorfields Eye Hosp 1981-, conslt advsr in ophthalmology DHSS 1969-82; teacher: Inst of Ophthalmology Univ of London 1961-81, Guy's Hosp 1964-76; examiner: dip ophthalmology of exam bd of England 1960-65, memb ct of examiners RCS 1966-72; memb Soc Francaise d'Ophtal 1950, membre délégué étranger 1970-, UK rep Union Européene des Médecins Spécialistes ophthalmology section 1973- (pres 1982-86); hon steward Westminster Abbey 1972-; Freeman City of London, Liveryman Worshipful Co of Apothecaries 1953; DOMS, FRCS, LRCP, FCOphth, FRACO (Hon), FRSM, memb Ophthal Soc UK 1948- (hon sec 1956-58, vice-pres 1969-71, pres 1982-84), memb Faculty Ophthalmologists 1950- (memb cncl 1960-81, hon sec 1960-70, vice-pres 1970-74, pres 1974-77), memb Pilgrims of GB; *Recreations* motoring, travel; *Clubs* Garrick; *Style*— James Hudson, Esq, CBE; Flat 2, 17 Montagu Sq, London W1H 1RD (☎ 01 487 2680); 8 Upper Wimpole St, London W1M 7TD (☎ 01 935 5038)

HUDSON, Lady Jane Catherine; *née* Leslie Melville; da of 14 Earl of Leven and Melville; *b* 5 May 1956; *m* 1977, Philip Mark Gurney Hudson; 2 da (Katherine b 1983, Susanna b 1986); *Style*— Lady Jane Hudson; Southcott Lodge, Pewsey, Wilts

HUDSON, John Richard; s of Arthur Richard Hudson (d 1978), and Beryl Dorothy, *née* Brett; *b* 3 Sept 1944; *Educ* Ryde GS Ryde IOW, Thames Poly (HNC); *m* 12 Aug 1976, Kathleen Mary (Kate), da of David Thomas Heckscher (d 1950), of Aust; *Career* recording engr and md Mayfair Recording Studios London, recorded more than 159 top ten records (studio voted top Br Recording Studio 1986); Grammy Award (USA) 1984, nominated for Br Acad Award 1985; Grammy Award Certificate for work on Tina Turner Live in Europe 1988; dai ry farmer; APRS;; *Recreations* skiing, dairy farming, video filming & editing; *Style*— John Hudson, Esq; 18 Lyndhurst Rd, London NW3 5NL; Millers Ct, Birtsmorton nr Malvern, Worcs WR13 6AP(☎ 01 586 7746); Mayfair Recording Studios, 11A Sharpleshall St, London NW1 8YN (☎ 01 5867746, fax 01 586 9721)

HUDSON, Kathleen Mary (Kate); da of David Thomas Hecksher (d 1950), of Ipswich, Queensland, Aust, and Eileen Mary, *née* Downs; *b* 16 August 1944; *Educ* St Brigidines Coll Scarborough, Queensland Aust; *m* 1, (m dis 1969), Raymond Douglas Geitz; m 2, 12 Aug 1976, John Richard Hudson; *Career* telephonist Queensland Newspapers 1966-68, sec Leeds Music Sydney Aust 1968-73, pa Martin Coulter Music 1974-76, sec to fin dir Chrysalis Records London 1976-77, owner and md Mayfair Recording Studios 1977- (won Top Br Recording Studio 1986), owner Millers Ct Birtsmorton Commercial Dairy Farm; APRS; *Recreations* skiing, dairy farming; *Style*— Mrs Kate Hudson; 18 Lyndhurst Rd, London NW3 5NL (☎ 01 586 7746); Millers Ct, Birtsmorton, Nr Malvern, Worcs WR13 6AP; Mayfair Recording Studios, 11A Sharpleshall St, London NW3 5NL (☎ 01 586 7746, fax 01 586 9721)

HUDSON, Kathryn Jane; da of Col Leslie Eric Hudson, OBE of, 365 Perth Rd, Dundee, Scotland, and Jacqueline Elizabeth Packard, *née* Bell; *b* 13 Feb 1959; *Educ* Bristol Univ (LLB); *Career* called to the Bar Middle Temple 1981, tenant Chambers of Stewart Black 1983; awarded: Blackstone Entrance Exhibition 1978, Blackstone Pupillage 1983, Benefactors Law Scholarship 1983; co-opted memb The Young Barrister's Ctee; memb Hon Soc of Middle Temple 1978-; *Recreations* music, antiques, travel, the arts generally; *Style*— Miss Kathryn Hudson; 14 Gray's Inn Square, Gray's Inn, London WC1R 5JP (☎ 01 242 0858, fax 01 242 5434)

HUDSON, Prof Liam; s of Cyril Hudson (d 1985), and Kathleen Maud, *née* Shesgreen; *b* 20 July 1933; *Educ* Whitgift Sch, Oxford Univ (MA), Cambridge Univ (PhD); *m* 1, 8 Aug 1955 (m dis 1965), (Wendy) Elizabeth, da of Douglas Ward (d 1956); m 2, July 1985 (Claribel Violet) Bernadine, da of Bernard Louis Jacot de Boinod (d 1977); 3 s (Dominic b 1958, William b 1966, George b 1967), 2 da (Lucie b 1960, d 1965, Annabel b 1967); *Career* Nat Serv, 2 Lt RA 1952-54; fell King's Coll Cambridge 1966-68, prof educnl scis Edinburgh Univ 1968-77, memb Inst Advanced Study Princeton NJ 1974-75, prof psychology Brunel Univ 1977-87; Br Psychological Soc; *Books* Contrary Imaginations (1966), Frames of Mind (1968), The Cult of the Fact (1972), Human Beings (1975), The Nympholepts (1977), Bodies of Knowledge (1982), Night Life (1985); *Recreations* painting, photography, making things; *Style*— Prof Liam Hudson; 34 North Park, Gerrards Cross, Bucks (☎ 0753 886 281); Balas Copartnership, 34 North Park, Gerrards Cross, Bucks (☎ 0753 886 281)

HUDSON, Manley O (Jr); s of Judge Manley O Hudson (d 1960), of Cambridge, Mass, and Janet A Hudson, *née* Aldrich; *b* 25 June 1932; *Educ* Middx Sch Concord Mass, Harvard (AB), Harvard Law Sch (LLB); *m* 1 July 1971, Olivia, da of Count Olivier d'Ormesson, of Ormesson-sur-Marne, France; *Career* sec to Justice Reed Supremek Ct of the US 1956-57, ptnr Cleary Gottlieb Steen & Hamilton 1968- (assoc 1958-68); memb Cncl on Foreign Relations; memb: Assoc of the Bar NY City, NY Co Lawyers Assoc, NY State Bar Assoc, American Bar Assoc, American Soc of Int Law, Union Internationale des Avocats; *Clubs* Century Assoc, Knickerbocker (New York); *Style*— Manley O Hudson, Esq; Cleary Gottlieb, Steen & Hamilton, Winchester Ho, 77

London Wall, London EC2N 1DA (☎ 01 638 5291, fax 01 600 1698)

HUDSON, Martin Arthur; s of Philip Alexander Hudson (d 1986), of Sussex, and Loveday Catherine, *née* Gibbs (d 1988); *b* 22 Jan 1947; *Educ* Eton; *m* 1975, Primrose Pearl, da of The Hon Hugh de Beauchamp Lawson Johnston; 4 s (Hugh b 1977, Mark b 1978, Ian b 1979, Christopher b 1981); *Career* CA 1971; fin dir Houlder Offshore Ltd 1975-79 (non exec dir 1979-87), chm The Finsbury Secretariat Ltd 1983-; *Recreations* shooting, sailing, exercising 4 sons; *Clubs* Boodles; *Style—* Martin Hudson,Esq; 7 Grove Pk Gdns, London W4 3RY (☎ 01 994 0245); First Floor, 262 Regent St, London W1R 5DA (☎ 01 631 0181)

HUDSON, (Anthony) Maxwell; s of Peter John Hudson, CB, of Haslemere, Surrey, and Joan Howard, *née* Fitzgerald; *b* 12 April 1955; *Educ* St Paul's, New Coll Oxford (MA); *Career* slr 1980, ptnr Frere Cholmeley 1987; *Recreations* wine and food, squash; *Clubs* Utd Oxford and Cambridge Univ; *Style—* Maxwell Hudson, Esq; Willow Ct, Willow Place, London SW1; 28 Lincoln's Inn Fields, London WC2 (☎ 01 405 7878, fax 01 405 9056, telex 27623)

HUDSON, Norman Barrie; s of William Hudson, of Coventry, and Lottie Mary Hudson; *b* 21 June 1937; *Educ* King Henry VIII Sch Coventry, Univ of Sheffield (BA), UCL (MSc); *m* 1963, Hazel, da of Frederick Cotterill (d 1965); 2 s (Richard b 1965, Mark b 1974), 1 da (Jane b 1966); *Career* econ advsr; Civil Serv: head of SE Asia Div 1974, asst sec Overseas Devpt 1977, under sec Princ Estabs Offr 1981, under sec Africa 1986; *Recreations* watching football and cricket, theatre, reading; *Style—* Barrie Hudson, Esq; The Galleons, Sallows Shaw, Sole Street, Cobham, Kent DA13 9BP; Overseas Devpt Administration, Eland House, Stag Place, London SW1

HUDSON, Lt-Gen Sir Peter; KCB (1977), CBE (1970, MBE 1965), DL (Berks 1984); s of Capt William Hudson (d 1964); *b* 14 Sept 1923; *Educ* Wellingborough, Jesus Coll Cambridge; *m* 1949, Susan Anne, da of Maj Vernon Cyprian Knollys (d 1973); 1 da, 1 adopted s, 1 adopted da; *Career* cmmnd Rifle Bde 1944, served Mau Mau and Malaya Campaigns (despatches 2), CO 3RGJ 1966-67; GOC E Dist 1973-74, COS Allied Forces N Europe 1975-77, Dep C-in-C UKLF 1977-80; Col Cmdt Light Div 1977-80, Inspr-Gen TAVR 1978-80; sec-gen Order St John 1981-88; Lt HM Tower of London 1986-89; chm: Green Jackets Club 1977-85, Rifle Brigade Museum Tstees 1979-85, Royal Sch Bath 1981-88 (gour 1976), Rifle Bde Club and Assoc 1979-85, cncl TAVR Assoc 1981-; memb: gen advsy cncl BBC 1981-84, cncl Bradfield Coll 1983-; KStJ 1981; Hon Col Southampton UOTC 1979-85; pres RFA 1984; Hon Col 5RGJ 1985; FBIM; *Recreations* travel, wildlife, watching most games and sports; *Clubs* Naval and Military, MCC, IZ, Greenjackets; *Style—* Lt-Gen Sir Peter Hudson, KCB, CBE, DL; Little Orchard, Frilsham, Newbury, Berks (☎ 0635 201266)

HUDSON, Peter John; CB (1978); s of John Hudson (d 1948), of London, and Kate, *née* Tree, (d 1961); *b* 29 Sept 1919; *Educ* Tollington Sch, Birkbeck Coll London; *m* 1954, Joan Howard, da of Archibald FitzGerald (d 1973), of Kent; 1 s (Max), 1 da (Valerie); *Career* WWII RN 1940-46, Lt RNVR, serv N Atlantic and Med, Air Miny 1947, head Air Staff Secretariat 1958-61, Imperial Def 1962; under sec Cabinet Off 1969-72, dep under sec of state: Air 1975-76 and, Fin and Budget 1976-79; *Recreations* gardening, reading, golf; *Clubs* RAF, Liphook GC; *Style—* Peter Hudson, Esq, CB; Folly Hill, Haslemere, Surrey GU27 2EY (☎ 2078)

HUDSON, Brig Reginald Eustace Hamilton; DSO (1945); s of Edwin Hamilton Hudson (d 1951), of Rajpore, Budleigh Salterton, S Devon, and Grace Isobel, *née* Vaughan (d 1964) ; *b* 23 August 1904; *Educ* Haileybury, RMA Woolwich; *m* 1, 3 Oct 1930 (Gladys Mary) Maureen (d 1960), da of Capt Benjamin Henry Jones, CBE, RIM (d 1950), of Folkestone; m 2, 7 July 1962 Winifred Florence Isabel Vallentin, wid of Brig Claude Max Vallentin, MC, and da of Lt Col Evelyn Fountaine Villiers, CMG, DSO (d 1955); *Career* cmmnd RA 1924, served in field, mountain and medium artillery units (UK and India) 1924-31, ADC to GOC Peshawar dist and in NWF campaign 1929-32, Asst-Adj Field Bde RA (UK) 1932-34, Instr RMA Woolwich 1935-38, student Staff Coll 1939, BM RA 4 Div BEF 1940 (incl Dunkirk evacuation), Instr Staff Coll 1941, CO Field Regt RA 1942-45 (inc BLA 1944-45), CRA 2 Div (Malaya and India 1945-47, Staff appt WO 1947-48, Cmd S Malaya 1949-50, Cmd AA Bde and 2 i/c AA Gp (UK) 1951-55, Cmd RA Depot and Woolwich Garrison 1955-57; (des 1945, 1949, 1950); adc HM the Queen 1955-57; ret 1957; sec RA Inst Woolwich 1958-61, chm Ctee of Vol Welfare Work (BAOR) 1961-64; memb PCCs 1964-72; *Recreations* cricket, hockey, rackets, tennis, rugby; *Clubs* MCC, Free Foresters, IZ; *Style—* Brig Reginald Hudson, DSO; 38 Saffrons Ct, Compton Place Rd, Eastbourne, East Sussex BN21 1DX (☎ 0323 29601)

HUDSON, Prof Robert Francis; s of John Frederick Hudson (d 1966), and Ethel Lizzie, *née* Oldfield (d 1968); *b* 15 Dec 1922; *Educ* Brigs GS Lincs, Imperial Coll London (BSc, PhD, ARCS, DIC); *m* 3 Aug 1945, Monica Ashton, da of Charles Ashton Stray; 1 s (John Martin Edward b 1949), 2 da (Sarah Elizabeth b 1952, Mary Alexandra b 1952); *Career* asst lectr Imp Coll 1945-47, conslt Wolsey Leicester 1945-50, lectr QMC London 1947-59, gp dir CERI Geneva 1960-66; prof (organic chemistry) Univ of Kent 1966-85 (emeritus 1985-); visiting prof: Rochester USA 1970, Bersen 1971, Cnrs Thiairs Paris 1973, Calsary 1975, Mainz 1979, Queens Ontario 1983; memb: Chem Soc Cncl 1967-71, Perkin Cncl (RSC) 1980-83, Dalton Cncl (RSC) 1973-77; FRSC, FRS; *Clubs* Athenaeum; *Style—* Prof Robert Hudson; 37 Puckle Lane, Canterbury, Kent (☎ 0227 61340); Univ of Kent, Canterbury

HUDSON, Thomas Charles; CBE (1975); s of Thomas Bingant Hudson (d 1972), and Elsie Elizabeth, *née* Harris (d 1973); *b* 23 Jan 1915; *Educ* Middleton HS Nova Scotia; *m* 1, 1944 (m dis 1973), Lois Alma Johnson, da of Crawford Johnson (d 1977), of Montreal; 2 s (Ronald b 1947, Peter b 1965), 1 da (Margo b 1951); m 2, 1986, Susan Gillian Van Kan, da of Albert William G 1969); *Career* serv WWII RCNVR (Lt) 1940-45; Nightingale Haymen & Co (CAs) 1935-40, sales rep IBM Canada 1946-51, md IBM London 1954-65 (sales mangr 1951-54), dir Plessey Co 1969-76, (fin dir 1967), chm JCL 1971-79 (dir 1968), chm INFA Communications 1975-; cllr for Enfield GLC 1970-73, Farming in Devon 1979-; CA Canada; *Recreations* tennis, golf, skiing, gardening; *Clubs* Carlton, American; *Style—* Thomas Hudson, Esq, CBE; Hele Farm, North Bovey, Devon TQ13 8RW (☎ 0647 40249)

HUEBNER, Michael Denis; s of Dr Denis William Huebner, of Yarm, Cleveland, and Mary Irene Hargraves, *née* Jackson (d 1971); *b* 3 Sept 1941; *Educ* Rugby, St John's Coll Oxford (BA); *m* 18 Sept 1965, Wendy Ann, da of Brig Peter Crosthwaite, of Hove, Sussex; 1 s (Robin b 1971), 1 da (Clare b 1975); *Career* barr Gray's Inn 1965; Lord Chllrs Dept 1966: seconded Law Offrs Dept 1968-70, asst slr 1978, under sec 1985, circuit admin North Eastern Circuit 1985-88, princ estab and fin offr 1988-; *Recreations* looking at pictures, architecture; *Style—* Michael Huebner, Esq; Lord Chancellor's Dept, Trevelyan Ho, Great Peter St, London SW1P 2BY (☎ 01 210 8519)

HUGGETT, Brian George Charles; MBE (1978); s of George William Huggett (d 1983), and Annie May, *née* Flower; *b* 18 Nov 1936; *m* 1962, Winifred, da of Griffith Hughes (d 1979); 2 da (Yvonne b 1968, Sandra b 1973); *Career* int professional golfer; 18 major wins incl: Dunlop Masters, PGA Match Play Champion, PGA Stroke Champion, Vardan Trophy winner, Welsh Nat Champion, second and third Br Open, Dutch Open, German Open, Portuguese Open, Algarve Open, Singapore Int; Ryder Cup player (6 appearances, former capt), Capt GB twice, World Cup player (9 appearances); golf course designer; dir:; *Recreations* following sport generally; *Clubs* MCC, Royal Porthcawl GC, Lords Taverners; *Style—* Brian Huggett, Esq; 'Cherry Orchard', Weston-under-Penyard, Ross-on-Wye, Herefordshire HR9 7PH (☎ (0989) 62634)

HUGGETT, Monica Elizabeth; da of Victor Lewis Huggett (d 1983), of Epsom, and Monica Germaine, *née* May; *b* 16 May 1953; *Educ* Green Sch for Girls, Isleworth, Royal Acad of Music London; *Career* ldr Amsterdam Baroque Orchestra 1979-87, ldr/dir The Hanover Bond 1983-86 (recordings incl Beethoven Symphonies), memb Trio Sonnerie with Sarah Cunningham and Mitzi Meyerson, signed Virgin Classics 1988; other recordings incl Bach sonatas with Ton Koopman, Vivaldi concertos with The Academy of Ancient Music; memb Musicians Union; *Recreations* gardening, motor cycling, non-business travel; *Style—* Ms Monica Huggett; c/o Francesca McManus, 71 Priory Rd, Kew Gardens, Surrey, TW9 3DH (☎ 01 940 7086)

HUGGINS, Sir Alan Armstrong; s of William Armstrong Huggins (d 1938); *b* 15 May 1921; *Educ* Radley, Sidney Sussex Coll Cambridge (MA); *m* 1, 1950 (m dis), Catherine Davidson, da of David Dick (d 1929); 2 s, 1 da; m 2, 1985, Elizabeth Low, da of Dr Christopher William Lumley Dodd (d 1973); *Career* serv WWII Admiralty; barr Lincoln's Inn 1947, resident magistrate Uganda 1951-53; Hong Kong: stipendiary magistrate 1953-58, dist judge 1958-65, Puisne judge 1965-76, justice of appeal 1976-80, vice-pres Ct of Appeal 1980-87; justice of appeal: Gibraltar 1988, Br Antarctica 1988, Br Indian Ocean Territory 1988, Falkland Islands 1988; hon life govr British and Foreign Bible Soc, hon life memb American Bible Soc, Anglican reader; kt 1980; *Recreations* boating, archery, amateur theatre, tapestry, forestry; *Clubs* Royal Over-Seas League; *Style—* Sir Alan Huggins; Widdicombe Lodge, Widdicombe, Kingsbridge, Devon TQ7 2EF

HUGGINS, Hon Haoli Elizabeth Jane; da of 2 Viscount Malvern (d 1978); *b* 1953; *Style—* The Hon Haoli Huggins

HUGGINS, Hon (Martin) James; s of 1 Viscount Malvern, CH, KCMG, FRCS (d 1971), hp to newphew 3 Viscount Malvern; *b* 13 Jan 1928; *Educ* Hilton Coll, Natal; *Career* farmer; *Style—* The Hon James Huggins

HUGGINS, Hon Mrs; (Jean Audrey); *née* Wigg; da of Baron Wigg, PC; *b* 1932; *m* 1955, Andrew Huggins; *Style—* The Hon Mrs Huggins; Bryn-y-Mot, Nant-y-Camar Rd, Craig-y-Don, Llandudno

HUGGINS, Hon Michael Patrick John; s of 2 Viscount Malvern (d 1978); *b* 1946; *Style—* The Hon Michael Huggins; c/o PO Box AP 50, Salisbury Airport, Zimbabwe

HUGH SMITH, Andrew Colin; s of Lt-Cdr Colin Hugh Smith, RN (d 1975); *b* 6 Sept 1931; *Educ* Ampleforth, Trinity Coll Cambridge; *m* 1964, Venetia, da of Lt-Col Peter Flower, of The Old Manse, Broughton, Stockbridge, Hants; 2 s; *Career* barr 1957, memb Stock Exchange 1970, sr ptnr Capel-Cure Myers 1979-; memb: Cncl of Stock Exchange, Cncl's Property and Fin Ctee; *Recreations* reading, shooting, fishing, gardening; *Clubs* Brooks's, Pratt's; *Style—* Andrew Hugh Smith, Esq; Capel-Cure Myers, 65 Holborn Viaduct, London EC1A 2EU (☎ 01 236 5080, telex 886653); The Old Rectory, Grendon Underwood, Aylesbury, Bucks (☎ 029 677 200)

HUGH SMITH, Col Henry Owen; LVO (1976); s of Lt-Cdr Colin Edward Hugh Smith (d 1975), and Hon Elizabeth Dulcie, *née* Hotham (d 1969), sister of 7 Baron Hotham ; *b* 19 June 1937; *Educ* Ampleforth, Magdalene Coll Cambridge (BA); *Career* cmmnd RHG (The Blues) 1957, The Blues and Royals 1969; serv: Cyprus, Germany and N I (wounded), Egypt, Hong Kong, Kenya; Equerry to HRH the Duke of Edinburgh 1974-76; cmd The Blues and Royals 1978-80; GSO MOD 1980-83; Middle E and Hong Kong 1983-85; MOD 1985-87; def advsr to Br High Cmmr Nairobi Kenya 1987-; *Recreations* sailing, wild life, photography, music; *Clubs* Boodle's, Pratt's, Royal Yacht Sqdn; *Style—* Col Henry Hugh Smith, LVO; c/o National Westminster Bank plc, 1 Prince's St, London EC2P 2AH

HUGH-JONES, Dr Kenneth; s of Evan Bonnor Hugh-Jones, CB (d 1978), and Elsie Muriel, *née* Iggulden (d 1950); *b* 21 Dec 1923; *Educ* Uppingham, St Mary's Hosp, Univ of London (MB BS, MD); *m* m 1 1955, Denise(d 1986), da of Dr George Edward Hull (d 1965); 2 s (Simon b 1956, George b 1958), 2 da (Catherine, b 1963, Sarah b 1965); m 2 1987, Ruth Theodora, wid of Richard Purdon Heppel, CMG, da of Dr Horatio Matthews (d 1970); *Career* conslt paediatrician: Westminster Childrens Hosp, St Albans City Hosp; special interest in treating children with genetic diseases by bone marrow transplantation; FRCP, FRSM; *Style—* Dr Kenneth Hugh-Jones; The Heath, Redbourn, Herts AL3 7BZ (☎ 058 285 2347)

HUGH-JONES, Sir Wynn Normington; LVO (1961); s of Huw Hugh-Jones (d 1937), and May, *née* Normington (d 1979); *b* 1 Nov 1923; *Educ* Ludlow, Selwyn Coll Cambridge (MA); 1 s, 2 da; *Career* RAF 1943-46, Foreign Serv 1947-73; serv FO: Jeddah, Paris, Conakry, Rome (head of chancery), FCO, Elizabethville (now Lumbumbashi); cnsllr and head of chancery Ottawa 1968-70, FCO 1971, Lord President's Off 1971, Cabinet Off 1972-73; dir-gen English Speaking Union 1973-77; sec-gen Lib Pty 1977-83, hon jt tres Lib Pty 1984-87, vice-chm Eur-Atlantic Gp 1986-, govr Queen Elizabeth Fndn for the Disabled 1985-; FBIM; kt 1984; *Recreations* golf, gardening; *Clubs* Nat Lib; *Style—* Sir Wynn Hugh-Jones, LVO; Fosse House, Avebury, Wilts; 203 Duncan House, Dolphin Square, London SW1

HUGHES, Allan Berkeley Valentine; s of Capt Allan Gibson Hughes (d 1938), of Shrewsbury, and Kathleen Louise, *née* Paget (d 1973); *b* 27 Feb 1933; *Educ* Wellington; *m* 24 April 1964, (Gina) Ann, da of Alan Maconochie Stephen (d 1975), of St Brelades, Jersey; 2 s (Rupert b 18 April 1966, Oliver b 8 Aug 1968); *Career* Nat Serv 1951-53 (2 Lt QOH 1952-53), Lt Queen's Own Worcs Hussars 1953-57; admitted slr 1959, sr ptnr Payne Hicks Beach 1989- (ptnr 1960-89); chm: Iris Fund for Prevention of Blindness, cncl govrs Heathfield Sch; memb Law Soc; *Recreations* gardening, shooting; *Clubs* Buck's, The Justinians; *Style—* Allan Hughes, Esq; Siddington Mill, Cirencester, Glocs GL7 6EU; 10 Abbots House, St Mary Abbots

Terr, London; Payne Hicks Beach, 10 New Sq, Lincoln's Inn WC2A 3QG (☎ 01 242 6041)

HUGHES, Andrew Anderson; s of Alexander Hughes (d 1917), of Fife, and Euphemia Elder Anderson Hughes (d 1947); *b* 27 Dec 1915; *Educ* Waid Acad, St Andrews Univ, Marburg Univ, Emmanuel Coll Cambridge (MA); *m* 1, 1944 (m dis), Dorothy Murdoch; m 2, 1946, Margaret Dorothy Aikman, of Edinburgh; *Career* Colonial Admin Serv 1939-46, private sec to Govr Gold Coast 1940-42; home Civil Admin 1946-69; under sec Scottish Off 1964; md Crudens Ltd 1969-71; dir: Grampian Hldgs 1971-85, memb (non exec) Cairngorm Chairlift Co 1980-83; memb: Central Arbitration Ctee 1977-83, Scottish Tourist Bd (vice-chm 1969-81); chm Scottish Crafts Consultative Ctee 1979-85; dir non exec Gilmour and Dean Hldgs plc 1979-87; memb of Court Heriot Watt Univ (chm Building and Estates Ctee) 1981-; Hon DUniv Heriot-Watt 1988; *Recreations* golf, gardening; *Clubs* New (Edinburgh), Bruntsfield Links Golfing Soc; *Style—* Andrew Hughes, Esq; 9 Palmerston Rd, Edinburgh EH9 1TL (☎ 031 667 2353)

HUGHES, Anthony; s of Francis James Hughes (d 1983), and Mabel, *née* Hall; *b* 23 June 1938; *Educ* King Edward's Sch Birmingham; *m* 22 Sept 1973, Gillian Rose, da of Roger Hamilton Aitken, TD, of Birmingham; *Career* CA 1962-, sr ptnr J W Scrivens & Co 1967-; champion: Br Eton Fives nine times (a record) 1968-75, Br Rugby Fives Veterans 1986 and 1987; FICA; *Recreations* Eton Fives, travel; *Clubs* Edgbaston Priory; *Style—* Anthony Hughes, Esq; Imperial Hse, 350 Bournville La, Bournville, Birmingham, B30 1QZ (☎ 021 478 1431)

HUGHES, Maj-Gen Basil Perronet; CB (1954), CBE (1944); s of Rev E B A Hughes (d 1942), and Isabel, *née* Thompson; *b* 13 Jan 1903; *Educ* Eton, RMA Woolwich; *m* 1932, Joan Marion, da Lt Col Frank Worthington; 2 s (Edward, Nigel); *Career* cmmnd RFA 1923, Staff coll 1935-36, Directing Staff Staff Coll 1940, serv India 1926-36, Mohmand 1933, WWII 1 Div DEF AA Cmd 21AGp BLA (despatches); Hon Col: 2 Bn Mobile Def corps, 571 LAA Regt (9 Bn Middx Regt DCO) RA TA; ADC to HM the Queen 1952-54, GOC 4 Anti-Aircraft Gp 1954, Maj-Gen RA (AA) WO 1955-58, ret; comptroller RA Inst 1958-73; *Recreations* flying, sailing; *Clubs* Leander; *Style—* Maj-Gen Basil Hughes, CB, CBE; St Nicholas Close, Stour Row, Shaftesbury, Dorset

HUGHES, Brian Thomas; s of late Thomas Hughes; *b* 3 May 1937; *Educ* St Joseph's Coll, Glasgow Univ; *m* 1962, Maureen Duignan, *née* Smyth; 3 s; *Career* dir and md Ranco Motors Ltd 1969-73; dir: St Andrews Golf Hotel Ltd 1973-, Tedvox Ltd 1978-, Crusoe Hotels Ltd 1979-; *Recreations* golf, skiing; *Clubs* Murrayfield GC, Edinburgh, New GC, St Andrews; *Style—* Brian Hughes Esq; St Andrews Golf Hotel Ltd, St Andrews Golf Hotel, 40 The Scores, St Andrews, Fife

HUGHES, Christopher Wyndham; s of Dr John Philip Wyndham Hughes (d 1981), of Marsh Lock House, Henley-on-Thames, Oxfordshire, and Christine, *née* Jolley (d 1947); *b* 22 Nov 1941; *Educ* Manchester GS, King Edward's Sch Birmingham, UCL (LLB); *m* 31 Dec 1966, Gail, da of Percival Eric Ward (d 1957), of Cricklewood, London; 3 s (Christian Wyndham b 29 Feb 1968, Marcus Wyndham (twin) b 1968, Dominic Wyndham b 20 June 1974); *Career* slr 1966; articled clerk and slr until 1970 then ptnr Wragge & Co Birmingham 1970, Notary Public; memb cncl Birmingham Law soc 1977- (jt hon sec 1977-84, vice pres 1988-); memb and later chm of Solihull ctee of Cancer Res Campaign 1972-85, bd memb of Severn Trent Water Authy 1982-84, fndn govr of the schs of King Edward VI Birmingham 1984-; memb: Law Soc 1966, Birmingham Law Soc 1966, The Provincial Notaries Soc 1979-; *Recreations* travel theatre, sport, languages, old buildings; *Clubs* Warwickshire CCC; *Style—* Christopher Hughes, Esq; Cuttle Pool Farm, Cuttle Pool Lane, Knowle, Solihull, W Midlands B93 0AP (☎ 056477 2611); Wragge & Co, Bank House, 8 Cherry St, Birmingham B2 5JY (☎ 021 632 4131, fax 021 643 2417, telex 338728 WRAGGE G)

HUGHES, Hon Mrs (Claudia Madeleine); *née* Ackner; da of Baron Ackner, PC (Life Peer), *qv*; *Educ* Roedean, Girton Coll Cambridge (BA); *m* 1978, Iain Hughes; *Career* barr Middle Temple 1977; *Style—* The Hon Mrs Hughes

HUGHES, Capt David Brian Reginald; s of William Reginald Noel Hughes, of Capstan House, Tower St, Old Portsmouth, and Doris Margaret, *née* Attwool; *b* 23 Feb 1945; *Educ* Plymouth Coll, King Edward's Sch Bath, Kingswood Sch Bath, RN Engrg Coll Manadon (BSc); *m* 28 Sept 1974, Jacqueline Lynda (Jacky), da of Douglas Roy Charles Couch, of Waltham Chase; 1 s (Richard b 1980), 1 da (Sarah b 1978); *Career* joined RN 1963; serv: HMS Lynx, HMS Manxman, HMS Fearless, HMS Andromeda; Lt Cdr 1977, HM Yacht Britannia 1977-79, Cdr 1981, sr offr HMS Manchester 1981-83, Jt Servs Def Coll 1984, dir of naval ops and trade naval staff MOD 1984-87, dep chief SO (engrg) to Flag Offr Portsmouth 1987-89, Capt 1989 supt ships Rosyth; CEng 1970, MIMechE 1974, FIMarE 1975; *Recreations* sailing; *Style—* Capt David Hughes; 50 High St, Old Portsmouth, Hants (☎ 0705 738572); Superintendent Ships, HM Naval Base, Rosyth, fife (☎ 0383 418330)

HUGHES, Sir David Collingwood; 14 Bt (GB 1773), of East Bergholt, Suffolk; s of Sir Richard Edgar Hughes, 13 Bt (d 1970), and Angela Lilian Adelaide, *née* Pell (d 1967); *b* 29 Dec 1936; *Educ* Oundle, Magdalene Coll Cambridge (MA); *m* 14 March 1964, Rosemary Ann, MA, LLM, da of Rev John Pain, of Framfield Vicarage, Uckfield, Sussex; 4 s (Thomas b 1966, Timothy b 1968, Benjamin b 1969, Anthony b 1972); *Heir* s, Thomas Collingwood Hughes b 16 Feb 1966; *Career* heraldic sculptor, md Louis Lejeune Ltd 1978-; *Recreations* fishing; *Clubs* Flyfishers, Cambridge County; *Style—* Sir David Hughes, Bt; The Berristead, Wilburton, Ely, Cambs (☎ 0353 740770)

HUGHES, David John; s of Glynn Hughes (d 1985), and Gwyneth Mary, *née* Jenkins; *b* 19 Mar 1955; *Educ* Wolverhampton GS, Jesus Coll Oxford (MA); *m* 4 Sept 1987, Linda Anne, da of Thomas Hunt, of Wolverhampton; 1 s (Richard b 1987); *Career* asst slr: Nabarro Nathanson 1980-82, Slaughter and May 1982-85; ptnr Pinsent & Co 1987- (asst slr 1985-87); memb Law Soc; *Recreations* music, theatre; *Style—* David Hughes, Esq; Post and Mail House, 26 Colmore Circus, Birmingham B4 6BH (☎ 021 200 1050, fax 021 200 1040)

HUGHES, Hon Sir Davis; s of F Hughes; *b* 1910; *Educ* Launceston H S Tas; *m* 1940, Joan P, da of P Johnson; 1 s, 2 da; *Career* MLA NSW (Country Party) for Armidale 1950-53 and 1956-65, former ldr NSW Country Party, min for Public Works 1965-73, agent-gen for NSW in London 1973-78, chm Brambles Crouch Ltd 1980; kt 1975; *Style—* The Hon Sir Davis Hughes; 11 Sutherland Cres, Darling Point, NSW 2027, Australia

HUGHES, Air Vice-Marshal (Frederick) Desmond; CB (1972), CBE (1961), DSO (1945), DFC (and 2 bars 1941-43), AFC (1954), DL (Lincolnshire 1983); s of Frederick Cairns Hughes (d 1952), of Co Down, and Emily Hilda Kathleen, *née* Hunter (d 1977); *b* 6 June 1919; *Educ* Campbell Coll Belfast, Pembroke Coll Cambridge (MA); *m* 1941, Pamela Denton, da of Julius Harrison (d 1963), of Herts; 3 s (Patrick, Peter (decd), Michael); *Career* RAF 1939-74; WWII, Battle of Britain 1940; Night Fighters 1940-45: UK Med, France, Germany; directing staff RAF Staff Coll Bracknell 1954-56, personal staff offr to Chief of Air Staff 1956-58, cmd RAF Station Geilenkirchen 1959-61; dir Air Staff Plans MOD 1962-64, air offr cmd 18 Gp 1968-70, AOC and Cmdt RAF Coll Cranwell 1970-72, dep cdr Br Forces Cyprus 1972-74; ADC to HM The Queen 1963; *Recreations* fishing, shooting, dinghy sailing, music; *Clubs* RAF; *Style—* Air Vice-Marshal Desmond Hughes CB, CBE, DSO, DFC, AFC, DL; c/o Midland Bank plc, Sleaford, Lincs

HUGHES, Dr (Thomas) Eames; CBE (1961); s of late Henry Hughes, of Llanfairfechan; *b* 1908; *Educ* Friars Sch Bangor, Jesus Coll Oxford (BA); *m* 1933, Ada Marguerite, da of Arthur Evans, of Liverpool; *Career* colonial audit serv in Nigeria, N Rhodesia, Br Somaliland, London and Gibraltar 1931-43; colonial admin serv 1944-46, Labour and Welfare Off and sec Resettlement Bd Gibraltar; joined Malayan Civil Serv 1946; sec for Social Welfare, Singapore 1948-50; princ asst sec Federal Secretariat Malaya 1950-51, sec to memb for Health 1951-54, chief Social Welfare Off 1954-55, pres of Kuala Lumpur Municipal Cncl 1955, sec to Min of Educn 1955-59, permanent sec Min of Educn 1959-62; chm of Singapore Social Welfare Cncl 1947 and 1949-50 and of Official Panel Nat Jt Cncl for Teachers, Malaya, 1959-62, memb of cncls and cts Univs of Malaya and Singapore 1959-63, ret from Malayan Civil Serv 1963, exec dir Singapore Int C of C 1965-76, hon sec of jt Standing Ctee of C of C and Indust Singapore; pres Singapore Cricket Club 1972-75, vice-pres Wales Int 1973-, hon LLD Malaya 1963; *Books* Tangled Worlds, the story of Maria Hertogh (1980); *Clubs* Royal Cwlth Soc; *Style—* Dr T Eames Hughes, CBE; Cynlas, Llanfairfechan, Gwynedd LL33 0AU (☎ 0248 680 789)

HUGHES, Rev Dr Edward Marshall; s of Edward William Hughes (d 1940), of Kent, and Mabel Frances, *née* Faggetter (d 1947); *b* 11 Nov 1913; *Educ* City of London Sch, King's Coll London, Cuddesdon Coll Oxford (MTh, PhD, AKC); *Career* warden St Peter's Coll Jamaica 1952-61, fell St Augustine's Coll Canterbury 1961-65; vicar of Dover 1971-84, chaplain to HM The Queen 1973-83, hon chaplain of the county assoc Men of Kent and Kentish Men 1979- (of which his father was a fndr memb 1897); *Recreations* gardening, exercising the dogs, computing; *Style—* The Rev Dr Edward Hughes; Woodlands, Sandwich Road, Woodnesborough, Sandwich, Kent CT13 0LZ (☎ 0304 617098)

HUGHES, Prof Sir Edward Stuart Reginald; CBE (1971); s of Reginald Hawkins Hughes (d 1966), and Annie Grace, *née* Langford (d 1964); *b* 4 July 1919; *Educ* Melbourne C of E GS, Melbourne Univ; *m* 1944, Alison, da of A D Lelean; 2 s, 2 da; *Career* prof dept of surgery Monash Univ Alfred Hosp 1973-84, pres Royal Australasian Coll of Surgns 1975-78, conslt surgn to Aust Army 1976-82; first chm Sir Robert Menzies Fndn for Health, Fitness and Physical Achievement 1979-; emeritus prof Monash Univ 1984; Hon LLD Monash Univ; kt 1977; *Books* numerous books on gastro-enterology; *Clubs* Melbourne, MCC, Victoria Racing; *Style—* Prof Sir Edward Hughes, CBE; Suite 20, Cabrini Medical Centre, Isabella St, Malvern 3144 (☎ 509 4155)

HUGHES, George; s of Peter Hughes; *b* 4 May 1937; *Educ* Liverpool Collegiate, Gonville and Caius Cambridge (MA), Harvard Business Sch (MBA); *m* 1963, Janet; 2 s (David b 1964, Edward b 1966); *Career* ski instr 1959; banker Paris 1960; IBM London 1960-69 (strategy dvpt mangr 1968-69), merchant banking London 1969-70; chm and chief exec Hughes Int Ltd 1970-, Willowbrook World Wide Ltd 1971-, Castle Hughes Gp Ltd 1975-; chm Derbyshire Co Cricket Club 1976-77; memb Test and Co Cricket Bd; landowner; *Recreations* cattle farming, historic bldgs, shooting, soccer, tennis, squash; *Clubs* Carlton; *Style—* George Hughes, Esq; Hampton Court Castle, Leominster, Herefs HR6 OPN (☎ (056 884) 261, telex Hughes G 35655)

HUGHES, Wing Cdr Gordon Edward; DSO, DFC (and bar), AEA; s of late Arthur Joseph Hughes, OBE, of Pages, Chigwell Row, Essex, and late Emma Elsie, *née* Grimwade; *b* 4 May 1918; *Educ* Kelly Coll Tavintach Devon, City and Guilds Coll, Imperial Coll London; *m* 5 July 1947, Elizabeth Jane, da of late Frank Kestrel Webb, of Constanzia, SA; 3 s (David Arthur b 26 July 1948, Sebastian Graham Francis b 30 March 1952, Richard Gordon Kelson b 4 May 1954); *Career* London Univ Air Sqdn 1937, joined RAF 1939, trg RAF Cranwell 1939, trained as armaments offr Manby Lincs 1940, 608A Sqdn Thornaby, pilot (Spitfires) 1 photographic reconnaissance unit Benson Oxfordshire 1941, 336 Wing Photographic reconnaissance unit Italy (Mosquitoes) 1943, photographic duties 34 Wing Brussels 1944, shot down Germany 1945 (in hosp 1945-46), air cdr ATC Glasgow (Convalesence 1947, station cdr Turnhouse Scotland 1947, demob 1947; joined 601 Sqdn (Vampires and Meteors) whilst test pilot for Kelvin Hughes Ltd, joined Kelvin Ltd sales and test pilot 1950, left firm to farm 1958; rep RAF Benevolent Fund Cyprus; RAgs, RHS, RAFA; *Recreations* gardening, farming, books; *Clubs* Royal Aero, English Speaking Union; *Style—* Wing Cdr Gordon Hughes, DSO, DFC, AEA; Lemba, Paphos, Cyprus (☎ 010 357 61 061 41154, fax 010 357 61 061 33358, telex 6427 COLOR CY)

HUGHES, Hon Harri Cledwyn; o s of Baron Cledwyn of Penrhos, CH, PC (Life Peer), *qv*; *b* 16 Mar 1955; *Educ* Holyhead Comprehensive, Davies's Tutorial London, Hammersmith and W London Coll; *m* 14 June 1986, Jennifer Meryl, da of R P Hughes, of Coedlys, Valley, Anglesey; 2 da (Anna Myra Jane b 12 June 1987, Sara Ellen b 20 Jan 1989); *Career* surveyor; *Recreations* water skiing, sailing, golf, photography; *Clubs* London Welsh Assoc; *Style—* The Hon Harri Cledwyn Hughes; 23 Lydford Road, Willesden Green, London NW2 5QY (☎ 01 451 5137); Penmorfa, Trearddur Bay, Anglesey, Gwynedd (☎ 0407 860 544)

HUGHES, Howard; s of Charles William Hughes (d 1969), of W Kirby, Ches, and Ethel May, *née* Howard; *b* 4 Mar 1938; *Educ* Rydal Sch; *m* 1, 20 June 1964, Joy Margaret Pilmore-Bedford (d 1984), da of Charles Francis Pilmore-Bedford (d 1966), of Keston, Kent; 2 s (Quentin b 1969, Edward b 1971), 1 da (Charlotte b 1974); m 2, 2 April 1988, Christine Margaret da of Walter George Miles, of Tunbridge Wells, Kent; *Career* articled Bryce Hammer & Co Liverpool 1955-60, Price Waterhouse London: joined 1960, ptnr 1970-, memb policy ctee 1979-, dir London Off 1982-85, managing ptnr (UK) 1985, md Europe 1988-, memb World Bd 1988-; cncl memb Royal London Soc for Blind; FCA 1960; *Recreations* golf, music; *Clubs* Carlton, Wildernesse GC; *Style—* Howard Hughes, Esq; Witham, Woodland Rise, Seal, nr Sevenoaks, Kent TN15 0HZ (☎ 0732 61161), Price Waterhouse, Southwark Towers, 32 London Bridge

St, London SE1 9SY (☎ 01 407 8989, fax 01 378 0647, telex 884657/8)

HUGHES, Sir Jack William; s of George William Hughes and Isabel Hughes, of Maidstone, Kent; *b* 26 Sept 1916; *Educ* Maidstone GS, London Univ (BSc); *m* 1939, Marie-Theresa (d 1987), da of Graham Parmley Thompson; *Career* Special Duties Branch RAF 1940-46, demobilised Sqdn Ldr; jt sr ptnr Jones Lang Wootton 1949-76, conslt Jones Lang Wootton Int Real Estate Advsrs 1976-86; chm Bracknell Devpt Corpn 1971-82; dir Housing Corpn (1974) Ltd 1974-78; dir: South Bank Estates 1960-, URPT 1961-86, Public Property Companies, MEPC 1971-86, Brighton Marina Co (rep Brighton Corpn) 1974-86, BR Property Bd 1976-86, BR Investmt Co 1981-83, TR Property Investmt Tst 1982-, Property and Reversionary Investmt 1982-86; chm Property Advsry Gp DOE 1978-82; memb: ctee Mercantile Credit Gp Property Div, ctee of mgmnt Charities Property Unit Tst 1967-74, Advsy Gp to DOE on Commercial Property 1974-78, DOE Working Pty on Housing Tenure 1976-77; chm South Hill Park Arts Centre Tst 1972-79; tstee New Towns Pensions Fund 1975-82; Freeman City of London, Liveryman Worshipful Co of Painter Stainers Guild 1960-; FRSA, FRICS; kt 1980; *Publications* (jtly) Town and Country Planning Act 1949 (RICS), The Land Problem: a fresh approach (chm RICS ctee); *Recreations* golf, travel, reading; *Style*— Sir Jack Hughes; Challoners, The Green, Rottingdean, East Sussex

HUGHES, Hon Janet Margaret; da of Baron Hughes, CBE, PC (Life Peer 1961), of The Stables, Ross, Comrie, Perthshire PH6 2JU, and Lady Hughes *née* Gordon; *b* 21 Feb 1956; *Educ* Dundee HS, Edinburgh Univ (BSc); *Career* princ teacher computer studies Forfar Acad 1984-; *Recreations* hockey, squash; *Style*— The Hon Janet Hughes; Alltan, Tulloes, by Forfar, Angus (☎ 030 781 792)

HUGHES, (Hugh) Ken(neth); DFC; s of Thomas William Hughes (d 1951), and Louisa Maud, *née* Bond (d 1982); *b* 20 Feb 1920; *Educ* John Ruskin Sch Croydon; *m* 1, 14 July 1945, Joan Frances; 3 da (Philippa b 1947, Nicola b 1950, Penelope b 1951); m 2, 28 Feb 1987, Jane Elizabeth; 1 step s (Benjamin Edwards b 1980); *Career* learnt to fly No 19 E&RFTS Gatwick 1938, RAF 1939-45, serving Nos 79, 87, 3 Sqdns in UK, N Africa, Italy, Belgium, Holland, Germany; fighter tactics instr Milfield 1943, airline pilot 1946; started Aerocontracts Ltd 1947; currently chm Scoba Gp; *Recreations* flying; *Clubs* RAF, IOD, Annabel's; *Style*— Ken Hughes, Esq, DFC; c/o Gatwick House, Horley, Surrey RH6 9SU (☎ 0293 771133, telex 87116, fax 0293 774658)

HUGHES, Leonard Walter; s of Walter Hughes (d 1986), and Gwendoline May, *née* McNaught; *b* 22 June 1928; *Educ* King Edwards GS Birmingham; *m* 1956, Diane Sybil, da of Edward James Drinkwater; 1 s (Michael David b 1961), 3 da (Carol Ann b 1957, Penelope Jayne b 1959, Kate Rebecca b 1961); *Career* dir: CT Bowring & Co Ltd, RIAS Insur Servs Ltd, RACIB Ltd, Pay Book Engrg Ltd, Bowring Professional Indemnity (Scotland) Ltd, Key Edge Ltd; ex dir; various Bowring subsidiaries, Mathews Mulcahy & Sutherland Ltd, TL Dallas & Co Ltd; chm Bowring Macalaster & Senior Ltd, dep chief exec Bowring UK Ltd; FCII; *Recreations* golf, fishing, walking, music, sailing; *Clubs* RAC, Copt Heath GC, Dunbar GC, South Caernarvonshire YC; *Style*— Leonard Hughes, Esq; 104 Seddon House, Barbican, London; 14 Strathearn Place, Edinburgh; office: (☎ 01 283 3100, 031 226 6012)

HUGHES, Prof Leslie Ernest; s of Charles Joseph Hughes (d 1975), of Parramatta, NSW, and Vera Dorothy, *née* Raines (d 1984); *b* 12 August 1932; *Educ* Parramatta HS, Sydney Univ (MB BS); *m* 19 Dec 1955, Marian, da of James Edwin Castle (d 1956), of Sydney, NSW; 2 s (Graeme b 1964, Stephen b 1971), 2 da (Bronwyn b 1957, Gillian b 1960); *Career* reader in surgery Queensland Univ 1964-71, Eleanor Roosevelt Int Cancer Fell Roswell Park Memorial Inst Buffalo NY 1969-70, prof of surgery Univ of Wales Coll of Medicine 1971-; visiting prof Albany Univ NY, Hong Kong Benares, Sydney, Melbourne, Brisbane; FRCS (Eng) 1959, FRACS 1959, DS (Queensland) 1974; *Books* Benign Disorders of the Breast (1988); *Recreations* music, walking; *Style*— Prof Leslie Hughes; Dept of Surgery, Univ of Wales, Coll of Medicine, Heath Park, Cardiff CF4 4XN

HUGHES, Dr Louis; s of Richard Hughes (d 1962), and Anne, *née* Green (d 1958); *b* 10 Mar 1932; *Educ* Holyhead County Sch, Univ Coll Cardiff, Welsh Nat Sch of Med (MB, BCh, DObst); *m* 26 June 1959, Margaret Caroline Mary, da of Thomas Cyril Wootton, of Newport, Gwent; 1 s (Christopher b 1964), 1 da (Deborah b 1960); *Career* Capt RAMC (TA) 1964; pt/t MO (infertility): Royal Free Hosp 1972-, Queen Charlotte & Chelsea Hosp 1979-; conslt (infertility) Margaret Pyke Centre 1979-; memb mgmnt ctee Int Wine & Food Soc (chm 1982-86), chm Childless Tst 1980-83; Freeman City of London 1975, memb Worshipful Co of Apothecaries 1974; RCOG, FRSM, MBMA, memb Br Fertility Soc, Br Andrology Soc, memb American Fertility Soc; *Books* numerous papers on infertility, Monographs on Wine; *Recreations* golf, wine and food, cricket, book collecting; *Clubs* MCC, Savile, Saintsbury, Denham GC; *Style*— Dr Louis Hughes; Beechwood, Burton's Lane, Chalfont St Giles, Bucks HP8 4BA (☎ 02404 2297); 99 Harley St, London W1 (☎ 01 935 9004)

HUGHES, (William) Mark; s of Prof Edward Hughes, of Durham Univ (d 1965); *b* 18 Dec 1932; *Educ* Shincliffe Sch, Durham Sch, Balliol Coll Oxford (PhD); *m* 1958, Jennifer Mary, da of Dr G H Boobyer; 1 s, 2 da; *Career* res fell Newcastle 1958-60, staff tutor Manchester Univ (Extra-Mural Dept), lectr Durham Univ 1964-70, MP (Lab) Durham 1970-87, (did not seek re-election); memb Select Ctee on Expenditure 1970-74 and on Parly Cmmn 1970-75, PPS to Chief Sec to Treasy 1974-75, MEP 1975-79 when vice-chm Agric Ctee and chm Fisheries Sub-Ctee (both 1977-79), memb Delgn to Cncl of Europe Consultative Assembly and WEU 1974-75; vice-chm Exec Ctee Br Cncl 1978- (memb 1974-); oppn front bench spokesman Agric, Fish and Food 1981-; memb Gen Advsy Cncl BBC 1976-; hon vice-pres Br Veterinary Assoc 1976-; memb Durham RDC 1968-70; *Style*— Dr Mark Hughes; Grimsdyke, Vicarage Rd, Potten End, Berkhamsted, Herts (☎ 044 27 73083)

HUGHES, Melvyn; s of Evan Llewellyn Hughes, of Newcastle upon Tyne, and Irene Kathleen, *née* Spires; *b* 18 Nov 1950; *Educ* Royal GS Newcastle upon Tyne, St Catherine's Coll Oxford (MA); *m* 6 July 1974, Diane, da of Percival Moffett (d 1987); 1 s (Richard b 2 Nov 1983), 1 da (Alexandra b 28 Oct 1980); *Career* ptnr Slaughter and May 1983- (asst slr 1976-83, articled clerk 1974-76); Freeman City of London, memb: City of London Slrs, Law Soc; *Recreations* reading, cars, sport; *Style*— Melvyn Hughes, Esq; Little Steading, Godden, Green, Sevenoaks, Kent TN15 0JS (☎ 0732 61 610); Slaughter and May, 35 Basinghall St, London EC2V 5DB (☎ 01 600 1200, fax 01 726 0038/01 600 0289)

HUGHES, (Thomas) Merfyn; s of John Medwyn Hughes, of Beaumaris, Anglesey, and Jane Blodwen, *née* Roberts; *b* 8 April 1949; *Educ* Rydal Sch Colwyn Bay, Liverpool Univ (LLB); *m* 16 April 1977, Patricia Joan, da of John Edmund Talbot (d 1982), of Brentwood, Essex; 2 s (Thomas Jenkin Edmund b 14 Sep 1982, Joshua Edward Talbot b 7 Dec 1987), 1 da (Caitlin Mary b 19 Feb 1980); *Career* barr Inner Temple 1971, practising Wales and Chester circuit, asst recorder 1987; former pty candidate (Lab) Caernarfon; *Recreations* sailing, rugby; *Clubs* Royal Anglesey Yacht; *Style*— Merfyn Hughes, Esq; Plas Llanfaes, Beaumaris, Anglesey; 3 Stamford Court, Vicars Cross, Chester (☎ 0244 323 886); 40 King St Chester

HUGHES, Michael; s of Leonard Hughes, of Clwyd and Gwyneth Mair, *née* Edwards; *b* 26 Feb 1951; *Educ* Rhyl GS, Manchester Univ (BA), LSE (MSc); *m* 11 Feb 1978, Jane Ann, da of Percival Frederick Gosham, (d 1977) of Ipswich; 2 da (Sophie b 1979, Harriet b 1981); *Career* economist BP Pension Fund 1973-75, chief economist and ptnr de Zoete and Bevan 1976-86, dir Barclays de Zoete Wedd Ltd; BZW: Capital Markets 1986, exec dir Gilts Ltd 1986-, dir Research Ltd 1989-, md Strategy 1989-; chm Great Bentley Flower Show; patron and chm fin ctee Cncl, for Advancement of Communication with Deaf People; AMSIA 1977; *Recreations* horses; *Clubs* Gresham, National Liberal; *Style*— Michael Hughes, Esq; Ebbgate House, 2 Swan Lane, London, EC4R 3TS (☎ 01 623 2323, fax 01 626 1753, telex 888221)

HUGHES, Michael John; s of Frank Miller Hughes, of Sussex, and Jean Mary, *née* Allford, MBE; *b* 20 Nov 1949; *Educ* Collyers Sch Horsham, Oxford Poly (BSc); *m* 1977, Elizabeth Charlotte Margaret Mary Antoinette Marie-Therese, da of Maj Leslie William Hutchins (d 1968), of Norwich; 2 da (Sophie b 1979, Caroline b 1982); *Career* gen mangr Anglia TV Ltd 1984, exec dir: Anglia TV Gp plc 1986, Anglia TV Ltd 1986; asst gp chief exec Anglia TV Gp plc 1988-, dir: Ind Broadcasting Telethon Tst 1987, Anglia TV Telethon Tst 1987; *Recreations* tennis, squash, saxophone; *Style*— Michael Hughes, Esq; 6 Whitehouse Gardens, Poringland, Norwich, Norfolk (☎ 05086 4548); Anglia Television, Anglia House, Norwich (☎ 0603 615151, telex 97424, fax 0603 631032)

HUGHES, Nerys (Mrs Turley); da of Roger Edward Kerfoot Hughes (d 1974), of Rhyl, N Wales, and Annie Myfanwy, *née* Roberts; *Educ* Howells Sch Denbigh, Ross Bruford Coll; *m* 13 May 1972, (James) Patrick Turley, s of James Turley (d 1983), of Wednesbury, Staffs; 1 s (Ben b 1974), 1 da (Mari-Claire b 1978); *Career* actress; theatre work incl: BBC Rep Co, RSC, English Stage Co Royal Court; tv series incl: Diary of a Young Man, Liver Birds, District Nurse, Alphabet Zoo (children's tv); PYE Female Comedy Star Award 1974, Varity Club TV Actress of the Year 1984; vice-pres Nat Children's Home; *Recreations* gardening, reading; *Style*— Miss Nerys Hughes (Mrs Turley); c/o Barry Burnett Organisation, Suite 42/43, Grafton House, 2/3 Golden Sq, London W1 (☎ 01 437 7048/9, fax 01 437 1098)

HUGHES, (Robert) Peredur; s of Rev Robert Hughes (d 1938), of Coedlys, Valley, Anglesey, and Sidney, *née* Williams (d 1947); *b* 2 August 1916; *Educ* Holyhead GS, Univ Coll of Wales Aberystwyth (LLB); *m* 1946, Myra, da of John Bellis (d 1967), of Coedlys, Valley, Anglesey; 1 s (Robert Philip Hughes b 1947), 1 da (Jennifer Meryl Hughes b 1955); *Career* slr; serv Inns of Ct Regt on Western Front; clerk to cmmrs of taxes for Isle of Anglesey 1950-, sec of Ld Chllrs Advsy Ctee for appointment of cmmrs for income tax 1950-, dep coroner for Isle of Anglesey 1957-77, clerk of justices for Isle of Anglesey 1960-85; *Recreations* cricket, sailing; *Style*— Peredur Hughes, Esq; Coedlys, Valley, Anglesey, Gwynedd (☎ 740267); Stanley House, Hollyhead, Anglesey (☎ 2301)

HUGHES, (David Evan) Peter; s of Evan Gwilliam Forrest-Hughes, OBE (d 1983); *b* 27 April 1932; *Educ* St Paul's, St John's Coll Oxford (MA); *m* 8 Sept 1956, Iris, *née* Jenkins; *Career* Nat Serv 2 Lt 5 Regt RHA 1954-56; second master (later head of sci) Shrewsbury 1956-80, headmaster St Peter's Sch York 1980-84, head of sci Westminster 1984-, dir Leverhulme Understanding Sci Project 1989-; *Style*— Peter Hughes, Esq; 14 Barton St, London SW1P 3NE (☎ 01 222 0868); Westminster Sch, 17 Dean's Yard, London SW1P 3PB (☎ 01 222 2831)

HUGHES, Philip Arthur Booley; CBE (1982); s of Lelsie Booley Hughes, and Elizabeth Alice, *née* Whyte; *b* 30 Jan 1936; *Educ* Bedford Sch, Cambridge Univ (BA); *m* 21 Aug 1964, Psiche Maria Anna Claudia, da of Bertino Bertini (d 1971); 2 step da (Pauline b 1952, Carole b 1954), 2 da (Francesca b 1966, Simona b 1968); *Career* engr Shell Int Petroleum Co 1957-61, computer conslt Scicon (formerly CEIR) 1961-69; chm Logics plc 1972- co-fndr chm and md 1969-72); also artist with exhibitions: (with Beryl Bainbridge) Monks Gallery, Sussex 1972, contemporary Br Painting Madrid 1983, contemporary painters Ridgeway Gallery Swindon 1986; one man exhibitions: Parkway Focus Gallery London 1976, Angela Flowers Gallery London 1977, Gallery Cance Manguin Vaucluse 1979 and 1985, Francis Kyle Gallery London 1979, 1982, 1984, 1987; *Style*— Philip Hughes, Esq, CBE; c/o Logica plc, 64 Newman St, London W1

HUGHES, (William) Reginald Noel (Reggie); s of Rank George Hughess (d 1956), of Harare, Zimbabwe, and Annie May, *née* Locke (d 1963); *b* 14 Dec 1913; *Educ* Prince Edward Sch Harare, Esplanade House Sch Southsea, Royal Dockyard Sch HM Dockyard Portsmouth, Royal Naval Coll Greenwich; *m* 23 July 1936, (Doris) Margaret, da of Cdr Harry Maxwell Attwool, RN (d 1949), of Emsworth, Hants; 2 s (David (Capt Hughes RN) b 1945, Peter (Cdr Hughes RN) b 1950), 2 da (Annette (Mrs Newton) b 1942, Mary (Mrs Bernier) b 1946); *Career* constructor Sub Lt HM Dockyard Chatham 1933, RNC Greenwich 1934-37, Lt 1935, Admty London 1937, HM Dockyard Chatham 1938-40, constructor Admty Bath 1940-44, constructor Cdr Staff of C-in-C Home Fleet 1944-47, HM Dockyard Hong Kong 1947-51, Admty Bath 1951-54, chief constructor HM Dockyard Devonport 1954-58, Admty Bath 1958-61, asst dir Naval construction 1961 Admty repair mangr Malta 1961-64, mangr construction dept HM Dockyard Portsmouth 1964-67, dep dir Dockyards Admty Bath 1967-70, gen mangr HM Dockyard Chatham 1970 -73, ret 1973; FRINA 1938, C Eng; *Recreations* sailing, foreign travel, photography; *Clubs* Little Ship, Royal Naval, Royal Albert YC, Royal Naval Sailing Assoc; *Style*— W R N Hughes, Esq; Capstan House, Tower St, Old Portsmouth, Hants PO1 2JR (☎ 0705 812 997)

HUGHES, Richard; s of Lt Walter Cyril Hughes, RA (d 1947), of Cardiff, and Emily, *née* Palfrey (d 1941); *b* 15 April 1938; *Educ* Cardiff HS, Eaton Hall Offr Cadet Sch, Mons Offr Cadet Sch, Queens' Coll Cambridge (MA, LLM), Coll of Law Guildford Surrey; *m* 11 June 1963, Marie Elizabeth, da of William Rieb (d 1972), of Somerset West, Cape, SA; 1 s (David b 31 March 1964); *Career* cmmnd 2 Lt The Welch Regt 1958, serving Cyprus (GSM) and Libya 1958-59; legal advsr: Royal Insur Gp 1963-65, S African Mutual Life Assur Soc 1965-66;, slr of the Supreme Ct 1969-89, sr ptnr Sprake and Hughes 1982- (ptnr in private practice 1969-89); literary critic and reviewer The Cape Times 1964-66; memb: Law Soc, Norfolk and Norwich Law Soc;

Recreations travel, walking, reading, music; *Style*— Richard Hughes, Esq; Apple Acre, Low Rd, Norton Subcourse, nr Norwich, Norfolk NR14 6SA (☎ 050 846 316); Sprake and Hughes, Solicitors, 16 Broad St, Bungay, Suffolk

HUGHES, Robert; MP (Lab) Aberdeen N 1970-; *b* 3 Jan 1932; *Educ* Robert Gordon's Coll Aberdeen, Benoni HS Transvaal, Pietermaritzburg Tech; *m* 1957, Ina (*née* Miller); 2 s, 3 da; *Career* contested N Angus and Mearns 1959; formerly: engrg apprentice in SA and draughtsman in Aberdeen; memb: Aberdeen Town Cncl, Gen Med Cncl; chm: Aberdeen City Labour Pty, Aberdeen CND, Anti-Apartheid Movement, S Africa Ctee Movement for Colonial Freedom; memb Scottish Poverty Action Gp, parly under-sec Scottish Off 1974-75; oppn front bench spokesman: Transport 1981-83, Agric Nov 1983-; *Style*— Robert Hughes, Esq, MP; House of Commons, London SW1

HUGHES, Robert Charles; s of Clifford Gibson Hughes, of Walton-On-The-Hill, Surrey, and Elizabeth Joan, *née* Goodwin; *b* 20 Jan 1949; *Educ* Westminster, Emmanuel Coll Cambridge (MA); *m* 23 June 1973, Cynthia Rosemary (Cindy), da of Lionel Edward Charles Kirby-Turner (d 1986), of Guildford, Surrey; 3 da (Zoe b 1975, Emma b 1976, Sophie b 1980); *Career* Ernst & Whinney (formerly Barton Mayhew & Co): joined 1970, ptnr London 1978-81, ptnr Dubai UAE 1981-86, London 1986-; FCA; *Recreations* golf, squash, puzzles; *Clubs* Sutton Tennis and Squash; *Style*— Robert Hughes, Esq; Crazes, Heather Close, Kingswood, Surrey KT20 6NY (☎ 0737 832 256); Ernst & Whinney, Becket House, 1 Lambeth Palace Rd, London, SE1 7EU (☎ 01 928 2000, fax 01 928 1345, telex 885224)

HUGHES, Robert Gurth; MP (C) Harrow West 1987; s of Gurth Martin Hughes, and Rosemary Dorothy, *née* Brown; *b* 14 July 1951; *Educ* Spring Grove GS, Harrow Coll of Technol; *m* 1986, Sandra Kathleen, da of James Vaughan; 2 da (Catherine b 1987, Elizabeth b 1988); *Career* BBC TV news picture ed until 1987; PPS to Rt Hon Edward Heath MP 1988-; *Recreations* watching cricket, listening to music, photography; *Clubs* St Stephens & Constitutional, Harrow Borough Football; *Style*— Robert G Hughes, Esq; c/o House of Commons SW1A 0AA (☎ 01 219 6854)

HUGHES, Rodger Grant; s of Eric Hughes, of Rhyl, Clwyd, and Doreen, *née* Barnes; *b* 24 August 1948; *Educ* Rhyl GS, Queens' Coll Cambridge (MA); *m* 9 June 1973, Joan Clare, da of James Barker; 2 s (Marcus b 9 July 1979, Oliver b 2 Feb 1983); *Career* Price Waterhouse: joined 1970, ptnr 1982-, ptnr i/c ind business gp 1988-; FCA 1973; *Style*— Rodger Hughes, Esq; Timbers, 3 Dempster Close, Long Ditton, Surrey; Price Waterhouse, Southwark Towers, 32 London Bridge St, London SE1 9SY (☎ 01 407 8989, fax 01 407 0545, telex 884657)

HUGHES, Ronald Frederick (Ron); s of Harry Frederick James Hughes (d 1964), of Beccles, Suffolk, and Violet Kate, *née* Terry; *b* 21 Oct 1927; *Educ* Birmingham Central Tech Coll, Bradford Coll of Technol; *m* 21 Dec 1957, Cecilia Patricia, da of Maurice Nunis (d 1957), of Sereemban, Malaysia; 2 s (Anthony b 1959, John b 1968), 1 da (Lesley -Ann b 1958); *Career* engrg cadet RE 1946, cmmnd RE 1950, SORE 3 Design HQ Malaya Cmd 1950, garrison engr Centl Malaya 1951, engr offr 22 SAS (Malayan Scouts) 1952, Adj CRE S Malaya 1953, SORE 3 Resources HQ Northern Cmd (UK) 1954; res asst BISRA 1954-55, civil engr (later md) HW Evans & Co Malayan 1955-59, civil engr WO Chessington 1959-63, works Gp Singapore 1963-66, area offr MPBW Malaya 1966-69, princ civil engr PO works MPBW 1969-76, area offr PSA Birmingham 1977-79, asst dir (later dir) civil engrg PSA 1979-87, conslt Mott MacDonald Conslt Engrs 1987-; memb: Standing Ctee for Structural Safety 1983-87, cncl Construction Indust res and info Assoc 1983-87, Parly Maritime Gp 1986-, cncl Steel Construction Inst 1986-88; govt del Permanent Int Assoc of Navigation Congresses 1983-, dir Construction Indust Computing Assoc 1982-87; FICE 1962 (memb bd Maritime Gp 1983), FIStructE 1987, MSIS (Fr) 1987; *Recreations* golf, squash, music, photography; *Clubs* Effingham (Surrey); *Style*— Ronald Hughes, Esq; 9A The Street, West Horsley, Leatherhead, Surrey KT24 6AY (☎ 04 865 2182); Mott, MacDonald, Consulting Engineers, St Anne House, 20- 26 Wellesley Road, Croydon CR9 2UL (☎ 01 686 5041, fax 01 681 5706, telex 917 241)

HUGHES, Royston John; MP (Lab) Newport 1966-83 and Newport East 1983-; s of late John Hughes (coal miner), of Pontllanfraith, Mon; *b* 1925 June; *Educ* Pontllanfraith County GS, Ruskin Coll Oxford; *m* 1957, Florence Marion, da of John Appleyard of Scarborough; 3 da; *Career* official TGWU 1959-66, memb Coventry City Cncl and sec Coventry Borough Lab Pty 1962-66; MP (Lab) Newport 1966-1983 and Newport East 1983-; chm: PLP Sports Gp 1974-84, Welsh Lab Gp 1975-76, PLP Steel Gp 1975-86, Welsh Grant Ctee 1982-84, Speaker's Panel 1982-84, Ctee of Selection 1982-84, front bench spokesman Welsh Affairs 1984-88; *Style*— Roy Hughes, Esq, MP; 34 St Kingsmark Avenue, Chepstow, Gwent

HUGHES, Sean Francis; MP (Lab) Knowsley South 1983-; s of Francis and Mary Hughes; *b* 8 May 1946; *Educ* Liverpool Univ (BA), Manchester Univ (MA); *m* 1984, Patricia Cunliffe; 1 da (Charlotte b 24 Oct 1988); *Career* history teacher 1970-83; contested (Lab) Crosby Feb 1974, opposition def spokesman 1987-; *Style*— Sean Hughes, Esq, MP; 150 Tarbock Rd, Huyton, Merseyside L36 5TJ

HUGHES, Prof Sean Patrick Francis; s of Dr Patrick Joseph Hughes, and Kathleen Ethel, *née* Biggs; *b* 2 Dec 1941; *Educ* Downside, St Mary's Hosp Med Sch and Univ of London (MB BS, MS); *m* 22 Jan 1972, Dr Felicity Mary Anderson; 1 s (John Patrick b 3 Feb 1977), 2 da (Sara Jane b 28 Nov 1972, Emily Anne b 25 July 1974); *Career* med offr Save the Children Fund Nigeria, sr registrar in orthopaedics The Middx Hosp and Royal Nat Orthopaedic Hosp London, res fell Mayo Clinic USA, sr lectr/hon conslt orthopaedic surgn Royal Postgraduate Med Sch Hammersmith Hosp London, prof and head dept orthopaedic surgery Univ of Edinburgh, hon conslt orthopaedic surgn Royal Infirmary Edinburgh and Princess Margaret Rose Orthopaedic Hosp Edinbrugh, hon civilian Orthopaedic conslt to RN; memb: cncl RCS Edinburgh, cncl Br Orthopaedic Assoc, ed bd Jnl of Bone and Jt Surgery, ed bd Jnl of RCS Edinburgh; Fell Br Orthopaedic Assoc; FRSM; *Books* The Basis and Practice of Orthopaedics, Astons Short Textbook of Orthopaedics and Traumatology (4 edn), Orthopaedics: The Principles and Practice of Musculoskeletal Surgery; *Recreations* sailing, golf, lying in the sun; *Style*— Prof Sean Hughes; 9 Corrennie Gardens, Edinburgh EH10 6DG (☎ 031 44 1443); Univ Dept of Orthopaedic Surgery, Princess Margaret Rose Orthopaedic Hosp, Fairmilehead, Edinburgh EH10 7ED (☎ 031 445 4123)

HUGHES, Simon Henry Ward; MP (Lib) Southwark and Bermandsey 1983-; s of James Henry Annesley Hughes (d 1976) and Sylvia Hughes (*née* Ward); *b* 17 May 1951; *Educ* Christ Coll Brecon Wales, Selwyn Coll Cambridge (MA), Inns of Court Sch of Law, Coll of Europe Bruges; *Career* barr, MP (Lib) Southwark and Bermondsey Feb-May 1983 and June 1983-; Lib Parly spokesman for the Environment July 1983- Jan'87, and Jun'87; Alliance spokesman Jan-June 1987; *Style*— Simon Hughes, Esq, MP; 6 Lynton Rd, Bermondsey, London SE1; House of Commons, London SW1 (☎ 01 219 6256)

HUGHES, Stephen Skipsey; MEP (Durham 1984); *b* 19 August 1952; *Educ* St Bede's Sch Lanchester, Newcastle Poly; *m* (m dis), Cynthia, 1 s, 2 da (twins); *Career* local govt offr; memb GMBATU; *Style*— S. S Hughes, Esq; Room 4/74, County Hall, Durham DH1 5UR (☎ 091 384 9371, fax 091 386 0958)

HUGHES, Sir Trevor Poulton; KCB (1982, CB 1974); s of late Rev John Hughes and Mary Grace, *née* Hughes; *b* 28 Sept 1925; *Educ* Ruthin Sch; *m* 1, 1950 (m dis), Mary Walwyn; 2 s; m 2, 1978, Barbara June Davison; *Career* serv RE, Capt 1945-48; former local govt engr; Miny of Transport 1961-62; Miny of Housing and Local Govt, Engrg Inspectorate 1962-70; dep chief engr 1970-71, dir 1971-72 and dir gen water engrg DOE 1972-74, dep sec: DOE 1974-77, Dept Transport 1977-80; perm sec Welsh Off 1980-85; vice-chm Public Works and Municipal Servs Congress Cncl 1975-; a vice-pres ICE 1984-86; memb Br Waterways Bd 1985-88; chm B & C E Holiday mgmnt Co 1987-; Hon FIPHE; Hon FInstWPC; CEng, FICE, FIWES; *Style*— Sir Trevor Hughes, KCB; Clearwell, 13 Brambleton Ave, Farnham, Surrey GU9 8RA (☎ 0252 714246)

HUGHES, William; CB (1952); William Hughes (d 1971), of Herts, and Daisy Constance, *née* Davis (d 1940); *b* 21 August 1910; *Educ* Bishop's Stortford Coll, Magdalen Coll Oxford (MA); *m* 1941, Ilse Erna, da of Emil Plöhs (d 1948), of Aš, Czechoslovakia; 1 s (William), 1 da (Helga); *Career* under sec BOT 1948 (asst princ 1933, princ 1938, asst sec 1942), sec Monopolies Cmmn 1952-55, dep-sec Bd of Trade 1963-71; ret 1971; *Recreations* music, walking, formerly rowing; *Clubs* Reform, Leander; *Style*— William Hughes, Esq, CB; 250 Trinity Road, London SW18 (☎ 01 870 3652); Page's, Wood End, Widdington, Saffron Walden, Essex (☎ 0799 40896)

HUGHES, Baron (Life Peer UK 1961); William Hughes; CBE (1965, OBE 1942), PC (1970), DL (Dundee 1960); s of Joseph Hughes (d 1962), and Margaret Ann, *née* Stott (d 1971); *b* 22 Jan 1911; *Educ* Balfour Street Public Sch Dundee, Dundee Tech, St Andrews Univ (hon LLD); *m* 1951, Christian Clacher, da of James Gordon; 2 da (Christian, Janet) stood for Parl (Lab) E Perthshire 1945 and 1950; lord provost of Dundee and HM Lieut City of Dundee 1954-60, JP (Dundee) 1943-76; jt parly under sec of state Scotland 1964-69, min State Scotland 1969-70 and 1974-75; chm: Glenrothes Devpt Corpn 1960-64, E 1975-, Scottish Assoc Mental Health 1975, Royal Cmmn on Legal Services in Scotland 1976-80; dir: Beckman RIIC 1975-, Smithline Instruments Ltd 1984-, Comrie (Dispensary) Ltd 1976-; memb: cncl of Europe and Western Euro Union 1976-87, North of Scotland Hydro-Elec Bd 1960-64 ; *Recreations* gardening, travel; *Clubs* Sloane; *Style*— The Rt Hon the Lord Hughes, CBE, PC, DL; The Stables, Ross, Comrie, Perthshire PH6 2JU (☎ 0764 70557); House of Lords (☎ 01 219 3207)

HUGHES-HALLETT, Michael Wyndham Norton; s of Lt-Col James Hughes-Hallett (d 1981), and Marjorie Eliza, *née* Collard; *b* 10 Nov 1926; *Educ* Eton; *m* 19 Oct 1948, Penelope Anne, da of Capt Sydney Fairbairn, MC (d 1943); 2 s (James b 1949, Thomas b 1954), 1 da (Lucy b 1952); *Career* WWII Lt Scots Gds 1943-46; pupil to res land agent Sandringham Estate, res agent to OV Watney Esq, res agent and factor to Lord Dulverton and W Highland Woodlands Co, agent and sec Batsford Fndn; FRICS 1966; *Recreations* hunting, shooting, painting; *Clubs* Army & Navy, MCC; *Style*— Michael Hughes-Hallett, Esq; The Old Rectory, Barton on the Heath, Moreton-in-Marsh (☎ 0608 74349); Batsford Estate Office, Moreton in Marsh (☎ 0608 50722)

HUGHES-MORGAN, His Hon Judge; Sir David John; 3 Bt (UK 1925), of Penally, Pembroke; CB (Mil 1983), CBE (Mil 1973, MBE Mil 1959); s of Sir John Vernon Hughes-Morgan, 2 Bt (d 1969); *b* 11 Oct 1925; *Educ* RNC Dartmouth; *m* 1959, Isabel Jean Blacklock Gellatly Milne, da of John Milne Lindsay (d 1969), of Annan, Dumfriesshire; 3 s; *Heir* s, Parry Hughes-Morgan; *Career* Sub Lt RN, ret 1946; slr 1950; cmmnd Army Legal Servs 1955, Brig Legal HQ UKLF 1976-78, dir Army Legal Servs BAOR 1978-80, dir Army Legal Servs (Maj Gen) MOD 1980-84; rec SE circuit 1983-86, circuit judge 1986-; *Style*— His Hon Judge Sir David Hughes-Morgan, Bt, CB, CBE; c/o National Westminster Bank Ltd, 1 High St, Bromley, Kent BR1 1LL

HUGHES-MORGAN, Ian Parry David; s and h of Sir David John Hughes-Morgan, 3 Bt, CB, CBE; *b* 22 Feb 1960; *Style*— Ian Hughes-Morgan Esq

HUGHES-ONSLOW, James Andrew; s of Andrew George Hughes-Onslow (d 1979), and Betty Lee, half-sister of Lord Rossmore; gs of Capt Oliver Hughes-Onslow (d 1971), of Ayrshire, first cous of actress Jane How; *b* 27 August 1945; *Educ* Castle Park Dublin, Eton; *m* 1982, Christina Louise, da of Peter Henry Hay, bro of Sir David Hay, of Australia; 1 s (Andrew b 1985), 1 da (Fiona b 1988); *Career* sub ed and feature writer The Field 1968-70, reporter Sunday Telegraph 1970-71, Daily Express 1971-73, columnist: The Spectator 1974-75, What's On in London 1976-82, columnist and feature writer, London Evening Standard 1983-; articles and reviews in: Punch, The Times, The Field, Books and Bookmen, Business Traveller, The Spectator Tatler Country Times, Southside, The Illustrated London News, Country Living, The Melbourne Age, Sydney Morning Herald; *Recreations* travel; *Clubs* Boodle's; *Style*— James Hughes-Onslow, Esq; 42 Knatchbull Rd, Camberwell, London SE5 9QY (☎ 01 274 9347); The Evening Standard, 2 Derry St, London W8 5EE (☎ 01 938 8000)

HUGHES-RECKITT, John Brian; s of Col Brian Holland Hughes-Reckitt, TD (d 1970), of Sproughton Hall, Ipswich, Suffolk, and Nancie Hughes-Reckitt (d 1979); *b* 16 Jan 1930; *Educ* Shrewsbury; *Career* Nat Serv 10 Royal Hussars (PWO) 1948-50; wine merchant Block Grey Block Ltd (London) 1950-72; hon tres Pedro Youth Club Hackney 1960-; memb Worshipful Co of Vintners; *Recreations* gardening, tennis, skiing; *Clubs* Cavalry and Guards'; *Style*— John Hughes-Reckitt, Esq; Pinswell Plantation, Colesbourne, Cheltenham, Glos GL53 (☎ 024287 340); 32 Iffley Rd, London W60PA (☎ 01 741 1979)

HUGHES-WAKE-WALKER; *see*: Wake-Walker

HUGHESDON, Charles Frederick; AFC (1943); *b* 10 Dec 1909; *Educ* Raine's GS; *m* 1937, Florence Elizabeth (the actress Florence Desmond), wid of Capt Tom Campbell Black; 1 child; *Career* chm: Stewart Smith Gp of Cos, Stewart Wrightson Gp of Cos until ret 1976, Tradewinds Helicopters Ltd, Charles Street Co; former chm and dir Tradewinds Airways Ltd; dir: Headington Brokers Ltd, Aeronautical Tst Ltd; hon tres Royal Aeronautical Soc 1969-85; FRAeS; *Recreations* horse riding, shooting, water skiing, yachting, flying helicopters; *Clubs* RAF, Royal Thames YC; *Style*— Charles Hughesdon, Esq, AFC; Dunsborough Park, Ripley, Surrey (☎ 0483 225366)

HUGHFF, Victor William; s of William Scott Hughff (d 1974), and Alice Doris, *née* Kerry; *b* 30 May 1931; *Educ* City of Norwich; *m* 1955, Grace Margaret; 1 s (David), 1 da (Joanna); *Career* insur exec; chief gen mangr Norwich Union Insur Gp 1984-89; dir 1981-89: Norwich Union Life Insur Soc, Norwich Union Fire Insur Soc Ltd, Scottish Union & Nat Insur Co, Maritime Insur Co Ltd, Norwich Union Hldgs plc, Norwich Gen Tst Ltd, Castle Fin Ltd, Norwich Union (Servs) Ltd; dir Norwich Winterthur Hldgs Ltd 1984-89; er Utd Reform Church; FIA, CBIM; *Recreations* tennis, badminton; *Style*— Victor Hughff, Esq; 18 Hilly Plantation, Thorpe St Andrew, Norwich NR7 0JN (☎ 0603 34517); office: Norwich Union Insurance Gp, Surrey St, Norwich NR1 3NG (☎ 0603 622200, telex 97388)

HUGILL, John; QC (1976); s of John Alfred Hugill (d 1950), and Alice, *née* Clarke (d 1982); *b* 11 August 1930; *Educ* Fettes Coll, Trinity Hall Cambridge (MA); *m* 1956, Patricia Elizabeth, Stanley Welton (d 1966), of Cheshire; 2 da (Gail b 1962, Rebecca b 1968); *Career* RA 1949-50 2 Lt, Capt RA (T); barr 1954, asst rec Bolton 1971, rec 1972, bencher Middle Temple 1984; memb Senate of the Inns of Ct and the Bar 1984-86; memb Gen Cncl of the Bar 1987-; chm: Darryn Clare Inquiry 1979, Stanley Royd Inquiry 1985; *Recreations* sailing; *Style*— John Hugill, Esq, QC; 2 Old Bank St, Manchester M2 7PF (☎ 061 832 3791, car 0836 584211)

HUGO, Lt-Col Sir John Mandeville; KCVO (1969, CVO 1959), OBE (1947); s of R M Hugo (d 1921), and Marion, *née* Dickins (d 1942); *b* 1 July 1899; *Educ* Marlborough, RMA Woolwich; *m* 1952, Joan Winifred Hill; 2 da (Nicola-Jane, Tessa); *Career* WWI 2 Lt RFA 1917, appointed to RHA 1922 serv WWII with 7 Light Cavalry (India), Lt-Col; cmd: Bombay Body Guard 1937-38, Bengal Body Guard 1938-39; mil sec to govr Bengal 1939-40 and 1946-47; asst ceremonial sec Cwlth Relations Office 1948-52, ceremonial and protocol sec 1952-69; gentleman usher to HM The Queen 1952-69, extra gentleman usher 1969-; *Clubs* Army and Navy; *Style*— Lt-Col Sir John Hugo, KCVO, OBE; Hilltop House, Vines Cross, Heathfield, E Sussex (☎ 04353 2562)

HUHNE, Christopher Murray Paul; s of Peter Ivor Paul Huhne, and Margaret Ann Gladstone, *née* Murray; *b* 2 July 1954; *Educ* Westminster, Sorbonne, Magdalen Coll Oxford (BA); *m* 19 May 1984, Vicky, da of Nicholas Courmoulis (d 1987); 1 s (Nicholas b 1985), 2 step da (Georgia b 1976, Alexandra b 1979); *Career* freelance journalist 1975-76, graduate trainee Liverpool Daily Post 1976-77, Brussels corr The Economist 1977-80, econs ed The Guardian 1984- (econs led-writer 1980-84), author of various articles in academic journals; parly candidate (SDP-Lib Alliance) Reading E 1983, Oxford W and Abingdon 1987; Freeman City of Osqka Japan 1985; memb: Royal Econ Soc, NUJ; *Books* Debt and Danger: The World Financial Crisis (with Lord Lever, 1985); *Recreations* cinema, gardening, family; *Style*— Christopher Huhne, Esq; 57 Lyndihurst Grove, London SE15 5AH (☎ 01 703 0332); The Guardian, Farringdon Road, London EC1R 3ER (☎ 01 239 9601, fax 01 837 2114)

HULBERT-POWELL, Hon Mrs; Philippa Catherine; *née* St Aubyn; da of late 3 Baron St Levan and Hon Clementina, *née* Nicolson, da of 1 Baron Carnock; n of late Harold Nicolson, the writer, and 1 cous of Nigel Nicolson, the biographer; *b* 19 June 1922; *Educ* LSE; *m* 1948, Evelyn Charles Lacy Hulbert-Powell (d 1985), Lt Queen's Own Royal Regt (d 1985), only s of Rev Canon Charles Lacy Hulbert-Powell (d 1959), of Cambridge; 2 s, 3 da; *Recreations* gardening; *Style*— The Hon Mrs Hulbert-Powell; Park Farm, Rotherfield Lane, Mayfield, Sussex (☎ 0435 873222)

HULKES, Arthur Sackville; OBE; s of Horace William Hulkes (d 1945), of Hornchurch, Essex, and Amelia Jane, *née* Northcott (d 1943); *b* 12 Oct 1904; *Educ* Borough Poly London, Law Soc Sch; *m* 28 Dec 1927, May Haylock, *née* Jacobs, MBE; 1 s (Geoffrey Athur), 1 da (Diana May); *Career* admitted slr 1929, lectr (real and personal property, conveyancing, wills and tsts, constitutional laws) LLC Evening Inst Hugh Myddleton Sch 1936-40, asst dir Min of Supply 1941-47, civil defence co-ordinator 1943-44; chm Appeal Tbnl NHS 1951-75; memb: American Bar Conf Washington 1960-, Second Cmwlth and Empire Law Conf Ottawa 1960, E Anglia Law Conf 1962; memb fin and sch ctees Essex Divnl Educn Serv, chm Hornchurch Urban DC 1943-44 (memb 1939-51), sec and pres Essex Fedn of Ratepayers Assoc 1947-53, fndr chm and agent Hornchurch Divnl Cons Assoc 1945, fndr memb Friends of Historic Essex 1954-; memb Law Soc 1929-, pres Mid Essex Provincial Law Soc 1962 (memb 1957-); *Recreations* gardening, travel, reading; *Style*— Arthur Hulkes, Esq, OBE; 79 Parkstone Ave, Hornchurch, Essex RM11 3LT (☎ 040 24 467 02); 135 High St, Hornchurch, Essex RM11 3YJ (☎ 040 24 467 04, fax 040 24 760 18, telex 995758 SACHL G)

HULL, Prof Derek; s of William Hull (d 1974), of Blackpool, and Nellie, *née* Hayes (d 1958); *b* 8 August 1931; *Educ* Baines GS Poulton-Le-Fylde, Univ of Wales (BSc, PhD, DSc); *m* 5 Aug 1953, Pauline, da of Norman Scott (d 1950), of Halifax; 1 s (Andrew b 1956), 4 da (Sian b 1958, Karen b 1961, Beverley b 1965, Alison b 1967); *Career* section ldr AERE Harwell 1956-60; Univ of Liverpool: lectr 1960-62, sr Lectr 1962-64, prof 1964-84, dean of engrg 1971-74, pro-vice chllr 1983-84; Goldsmiths prof Univ of Cambridge 1984-; hon DTech Tampere Univ Finland 1987; FIM 1966, FPRI 1978, FEng 1986; *Books* Introduction to Dislocations, An Introduction to Composite Materials; *Recreations* golf, fell walking, music; *Clubs* Gog Magog Golf, Heswall Golf; *Style*— Prof Derek Hull; 1 Chaucer Close, Cambridge CB2 2TS; Dept of Materials Science and Metallurgy, Univ of Cambridge, Pembroke St, Cambridge CB2 3QZ (☎ 0223 334 305, fax 0223 334 748)

HULL, Bishop of 1981; Rt Rev Donald George Snelgrove; TD (1973); s of William Henry Snelgrove (d 1956), of London and Plymouth, and Beatrice, *née* Upshall; *b* 21 April 1925; *Educ* Christ's Coll Finchley, Devonport HS, Queens' Coll Cambridge (MA); *m* 1949, Sylvia May, da of Charles Lowe (d 1962), of Derbyshire; 1 s (John b 1956), 1 da (Elizabeth b 1957); *Career* Sub Lt RNVR UK and Far East 1943-46; Royal Army Chaplains Dept 1960-74; ordained St Paul's Cathedral 1950; curate: St Thomas Oakwood 1950-53, St Anselm Hatch End 1953-56, vicar: Dronfield Derbyshire 1956-62, Hessle 1963-70; rural dean of Kingston upon Hull 1966-70, canon and prebendary of York 1969-81, archdeacon of the E Riding 1970-81, rector of Cherry Burton 1970-78; dir: Central Bd of Fin of C of E 1975-, Ecclesiastical Insur Gp 1978-, Church Schs Co Ltd 1981-, E Coast Flats Ltd 1978-, Yorks TV Telethon Tst Ltd 1987-; *Style*— The Rt Rev the Bishop of Hull; Hullen House, Woodfield Lane, Hessle HU13 0ES (☎ 0482 649019)

HULL, Howard Antony; s of Michael Dias Hull (d 1982), and Phyllis Fairchild, *née* Proctor; *b* 26 Nov 1953; *Educ* Christ's Hospital Horsham, St Peter's Coll Oxford (MA); *m* 2 Aug 1977, Janet Elizabeth, da of Thomas Edward Lacy, of Lancs; *Career* schoolmaster Gordonstown 1976-79, charity fund-raising and devpt conslt 1980-, sr ptnr The Support Gp 1985-88, dir China Challenge Ltd 1986-, dir devpt acad of St Martin in the Fields; tstee Portland Sculpture Tst; memb London Sketch Club; FRGS, MICFM; *Recreations* painting, kora music, the outdoors; *Clubs* Lansdowne; *Style*— Howard A Hull, Esq; 2 New Erringham Farm, Mill Hill, Shoreham-by-Sea, W Sussex BN4 5FA (☎ 0273 465650)

HULL, John Folliott Charles; s of Sir Hubert Hull, CBE (d 1976), and Judith, *née* Stokes (d 1937); *b* 21 Oct 1925; *Educ* Downside, Jesus Coll Cambridge (MA); *m* 1951, Rosemarie Kathleen, da of Col Herbert Waring (d 1961); 1 s (Jonathan), 3 da (Judith-Rose, Charlotte, Victoria); *Career* Capt RA 1944-48, served with RIA 1945-48; barr Inner Temple 1952; dir: J Henry Schroder Wagg & Co Ltd 1961-72 (md 1961-72, dep chm 1974-77, chm 1977-83), Schroders plc 1969-72, 1974-85 (dep chm 1977-), Lucas Industs plc 1975-, Legal & Gen Assur Soc 1976-79, Legal & Gen Gp plc 1979-; chm City Co Law Ctee 1976-79, dep chm Land Securities plc 1976-; memb cncl Manchester Business Sch 1974-86, lay memb Stock Exchange 1983-84; dep chm City Panel on Take-overs and Mergers 1987- (dir-gen 1972-74); *Recreations* reading political history, 19th century novelists; *Clubs* MCC; *Style*— John Hull, Esq; 33 Edwardes Square, London W8 6HH (☎ 01 603 0715); Little Norton, Norton sub Hamdon, Stoke sub Hamdon, Somerset (☎ 093 588 465); J Henry Schroder Wagg & Co Ltd, 120 Cheapside, London EC2V 6DS (☎ 01 382 6000, telex 885029)

HULL, John Grove; QC (1983); s of Tom Edward Orridge Hull (d 1957), and Marjorie Ethel Whitaker, *née* Dinsley; *b* 21 August 1931; *Educ* Rugby, King's Coll Cambridge (MA, LLB); *m* 1961, Gillian Ann, da of Leslie Fawcett Stemp (d 1968); 2 da (Katharine b 1965, Caroline b 1968); *Career* Nat Serv in RE 1954-56, 2 Lt; barr 1958; rec 1983; *Recreations* gardening, English literature; *Style*— John Hull, Esq, QC; Ravenshoe, 16 High Trees Rd, Reigate, Surrey RH2 7ES (☎ (07372) 45181); Lamb Building, Temple, EC4Y 7AS (☎ 01 353 6381/2)

HULL, Hon Mrs (Patricia Ann); da of Baron Carron (Life Peer, d 1969); *b* 1945; *m* 1970, Victor Albert Hull and has issue; *Style*— The Hon Mrs Hull; 16-18 Hatton Garden, London EC1

HULL, Fld Marsh Sir Richard Amyatt; KG (1980), GCB (1961, KCB 1956, CB 1945), DSO (1943); s of Maj-Gen Sir Amyatt Hull, KCB; *b* 7 May 1907; *Educ* Charterhouse, Trinity Coll Cambridge; *m* 1934, Antoinette de Rougemont; 1 s, 2 da; *Career* 17/21 Lancers 1928, GOC Br Troops Egypt 1954-56, C-in-C FELF 1958-61, CIGS 1961-64 (dep 1956-58), CGS MOD 1964-65, CDS 1965-67; constable Tower of London 1970-75, former pres Army Benevolent Fund, Col Cmdt RAC 1968-71, ADC Gen to HM The Queen 1961-64; dir Whitbread & Co 1967-76; Lord-Lt Devon 1978-82 (DL 1973), High Sheriff 1975; Hon LLD Exeter 1965; *Recreations* fishing; *Clubs* Cavalry and Guards'; *Style*— Fld Marsh Sir Richard Hull, KG, GCB, DSO; Beacon Downe, Pinhoe, Exeter

HULLAND, Cdr Scott; s of Frederick Scott Hulland, of Duffield, Derbys, and Ethel Vera Hulland (d 1973); *b* 13 Mar 1948; *Educ* Derby Sch, RN Engrg Coll (BSc), RNC Greenwich (MSc); *m* 16 Sept 1978, Deborah Margaret, da of Angus McKerrow Baird (d 1984), of Saltash Cornwall; *Career* RN Offr engrg specialization, currently serving in the procurement exec of the MoD; CEng, MIMechE, MINucE; *Recreations* gardening, singing, stamp collecting; *Style*— Cdr Scott Hulland

HULME, Hon Sir Alan Shallcross; KBE (1971); s of late Thomas Shallcross Hulme; *b* 14 Feb 1907; *Educ* North Sydney Boys' HS; *m* 1938, Jean, da of late Robert John Archibald; 2 s, 1 da; *Career* MHR (Lib) for Petrie Qld 1949-61 and 1963-72, min of Supply 1958-61, postmaster-gen 1963-72, vice-pres Exec Cncl 1966-72; FCA; *Style*— The Hon Sir Alan Hulme, KBE; Highland Rd, Eudlo, Qld 4554, Australia

HULME, Geoffrey Gordon; CB (1984); s of Alfred Hulme and Jessie Hulme; *b* 8 Mar 1931; *Educ* Kings Sch Macclesfield, Corpus Christi Coll Oxford (MA); *m* 1951, Shirley Leigh, da of Herbert Cumberlidge (d 1980); 1 s (Andrew), 1 da (Alison); *Career* DHSS: jr min 1953, under sec 1974, dep sec and princ fin offr 1981-86; dir Public Expedition Policy Unit 1986-; *Recreations* usual things, collecting edible fungi; *Clubs* Royal Automobile; *Style*— Geoffrey Hulme, Esq, CB; 163A Kensington Park Rd, London SE11; Stone Farm, Little Cornard, Sudbury, Suffolk; Public Finance Fndn, 3 Robert St, London WC2

HULME, John; s of Arthur Hulme (d 1971), of Macclesfield, Cheshire, and Edith, *née* Bullock (d 1962); *b* 12 May 1933; *Educ* King's Sch Macclesfield, King's Coll Cambridge (BA, CertEd, MA); *m* 25 May 1957, Susanne, da of Dr Philipp Schwarz (d 1963), of Berlin, Germany; 1 s (Peter b 1965), 3 da (Caroline b 1958, Elizabeth b 1960, Nicola b 1962); *Career* Sqdn Ldr RAF Educ Branch 1957-72 (UK, Germany, Cyprus); asst educn offr London Boroughs of Barnet and Harrow 1972-88; writer, German interpreter and translator; *Books* Mörder Guss Reims (1981), Les Oeuvres Complètes de Lord Charles (1984), Die Gesammelten Werke des Lord Charles (1984 and 1985), Guillaume Chèquespierre (1985), 1789 and All That (1988); *Recreations* travel, languages, writing, food and wine, squash, chess; *Style*— John Hulme, Esq; 27 Devereux Drive, Watford, Herts (☎ 0923 34560)

HULSE, Edward Jeremy Westrow; s and h of Sir (Hamilton) Westrow Hulse, 9 Bt; *b* 22 Nov 1932; *Educ* Eton; *m* 1957, Verity Ann, da of William Pilkington, of Ivywell, Routes des Issues, St John, Jersey; 1 s, 1 da; *Career* late Capt Scots Gds, High Sheriff of Hants 1978; *Style*— Edward Hulse, Esq, DL; Breamore House, nr Fordingbridge, Hants (☎ 0725 22233)

HULSE, Richard Arthur Samuel; 2 s of Sir Westrow Hulse, 9 Bt; *b* 22 Mar 1936; *Educ* Eton; *m* 1963, Caroline Susan Joan, da of Sir George Tapps-Gervis Meyrick, 6 Bt, MC; 1 s (George Richard b 1967), 1 da (Frances Jacintha Caroline b 1968); *Career* 2 Lt Scots Guards Nat Serv in Germany; exec dir Robert Barrow Ltd 1980, dir Bain Dawes (Int) Ltd 1973-80, chm Willmead Ltd; *Recreations* gardening, backgammon, racing; *Clubs* White's; *Style*— Richard Hulse, Esq; Sherfield Mill, Sherfield English, nr Romsey, Hants (☎ 0794 22536)

HULSE, Sir (Hamilton) Westrow; 9 Bt (GB 1739), of Lincoln's Inn Fields; o s of Sir Hamilton John Hulse, 8 Bt (d 1931), and Estelle, *née* Campbell (d 1933); the 1 Bt was physician to Queen Anne, and to Kings George I and George II; *b* 20 June 1909; *Educ* Eton, Christ Church Oxford; *m* 1, 7 Jan 1932 (m dis 1937), Philippa Mabel, yr da of late Arthur James Taylor, of Strensham Court, Worcs; 2 s; m 2, 3 June 1938, Ambrosine Nellie Orr (d 1940), o da of late Capt Herbert Stanley Orr Wilson, RHA, of Dunardagh, Blackrock, co Dublin; m 3, 23 Oct 1945 (m dis 1954), Dorothy, da of late William Durran, and widow of James Anderson McKay Hamilton; m 4, 8 July 1954, Lucy Elizabeth Smitheyt, da of Col George Redesdale Brooker Spain, CMG, TD, FSA; *Heir* s, Edward Jeremy Westrow Hulse, *qv*; *Career* Wing Cdr RAF Vol Reserve, serv WWII (despatches); barr Inner Temple 1932; *Clubs* Carlton, Leander; *Style*— Sir Westrow Hulse, Bt; Breamore, Hants (☎ 0725 22773)

HULTON, Sir Geoffrey Alan; 4 Bt (UK 1905), JP (Lancs 1955), DL (Greater Manchester 1974); s of Sir Roger Braddyll Hulton, 3 Bt (d 1956), and Hon Marjorie Evelyn Louise (d 1970), da of late 6 Viscount Mountmorres; *b* 21 Jan 1920; *Educ* Marlborough; *m* 1945, Mary Patricia, da of P A de Vere Reynolds, of Farnborough, Hants; *Heir* none; *Career* Capt RM (ret), Far East 1941-45 (POW); owner of Hulton Park Estate, pres Bolton West Constituency Cons Assoc, vice-pres Lancs Co Cricket Club, memb Country Landowners' Assoc Lancs (former vice-pres); Kt Cdr Order St Gregory The Great, Kt Cdr with Star Order of Holy Sepulchre; *Clubs* Lansdowne, Royal Overseas League, Spanish, Victory; *Style*— Sir Geoffrey Hulton, Bt, JP, DL; The Cottage, Hulton Park, Over Hulton, Bolton BL5 1BE (☎ 0204 651324)

HUM, Christopher Owen; s of Norman Charles Hum (d 1950), and Muriel Kathleen, *née* Hines; *b* 27 Jan 1946; *Educ* Berkhamsted Sch, Pembroke Coll Cambridge (MA), Univ of Hong Kong; *m* 31 Oct 1970, Julia Mary, da of Sir Hugh Park *qv*, of London and Cornwall; 1 s (Jonathan b 1976), 1 da (Olivia b 1974); *Career* joined FCO 1967; serv: Hong Kong 1968-70, Peking 1971-73, off of UK perm rep to the EEC Brussels 1973-75, FCO 1975-79, Peking 1979-81, Paris 1981-83; asst head Hong Kong Dept FCO 1983-85 (cnsllr 1985), dep head Falkland Islands Dept FCO 1985-86, head Hong Kong Dept FCO 1986-, cnsllr and head of chancery UK Mission to the UN NYC 1989-; *Recreations* music (piano, viola), walking; *Style*— Christopher Hum, Esq; c/o Foreign and Commonwealth Office, King Charles Street, London SW1A 2AH

HUMBLE, James Kenneth; s of Joseph Humble, and Alice, *née* Rhodes; *b* 8 May 1936; *m* 1962, Freda, da of George Frederick Holden, OBE (d 1964); 3 da (Josephine Clare b 1964, Rebecca Jane b 1965, Sarah Louise b 1966); *Career* dir: Metrician Bd 1978-80, chief Trading Standards Croydon 1967-73, Supt Metrology, Nigeria 1962-66, dir Nat Metrological Coordinating Unit 1980-88, asst dir Off of Fair Trading 1973-78, chief exec Local Authy Body on Trading Standards 1980-; memb: Methven Ctee 1976, Eden Ctee 1987, Cars Ctee 1984-; chm Euro Ctee Experts 1976-, prof Rugby League 1958-62; DMS, DCA, FITSA; *Recreations* golf, bridge, opera; *Style*— James Humble, Esq; 153 Upperselsdon Rd, Croydon, Surrey (☎ 01 657 6170); PO Box 6, Token House, Croydon (☎ 01 688 1996)

HUMBLET, Hon Mrs; Christian Florance; *née* Irby; da of 7 Baron Boston (d 1958); *b* 1921; *m* 1947, Etienne Humblet (d 1971); *Style*— The Hon Mrs Humblet; St Kevin's, 50 Gladesville Rd, Hunters fHill, Sydney, N S W, 2110, Australia

HUME, Sir Alan Blyth; CB (1963); s of Walter Alan Hume (d 1937); *b* 5 Jan 1913; *Educ* George Heriot's Sch Edinburgh, Edinburgh Univ (MA); *m* 1943, Marion Morton, da of William Garrett, QC; 1 s, 1 da; *Career* Scottish Off 1936-: asst under-sec of state Scottish Office 1959-62, under-sec Miny of Public Buildings and Works 1963-64, sec Scottish Devpt Dept 1965-73; chm: Ancient Monuments Bd Scotland 1973-81, Edinburgh New Town Conservation Ctee 1975-; kt 1973; *Recreations* golf, fishing; *Clubs* New (Edinburgh), English-Speaking Union; *Style*— Sir Alan Hume, CB; 12 Oswald Rd, Edinburgh, Scotland EH9 2HJ (☎ 031 667 2440)

HUME, Cardinal (George) Basil; *see*: Westminster, Archbishop of (RC)

HUME, Lady Catherine Mary Clementina; *née* Heathcote-Drummond-Willoughby; da of 2 Earl of Ancaster, GCVO, TD; co-heiress to Barony of niece, Baroness Willoughby de Eresby, *qv*; *b* 25 Sept 1906; *m* 1, 1935 (m dis 1947), John St Maur Ramsden (assassinated in Malaya 1948), s of Sir John Ramsden, 6 Bt; 1 da; m 2, 1948, Charles Wedderburn Hume (d 1974); *Style*— Lady Catherine Hume; Hunting Ridge Farm, 2670 Ridge Rd, Charlottesville, Va 22901, USA

HUME, James Douglas Howden; CBE (1983); s of James Howden Hume (d 1981), and Kathleen Douglas, *née* MacFarlane (d 1973); *b* 4 May 1928; *Educ* Loretto Musselburgh, Royal Tech Coll Glasgow Univ (BSc, CEng), Strathclyde Univ (LLD); *m* 1950, June Katharine, da of Sir Frank Spencer Spriggs, KBE (d 1969); 1 s (Duncan), 2 da (Evelyn, Clare); *Career* chm Howden Gp 1988 (dir 1957, md 1963, dep chm and md 1973); Primard Ltd 1989-; FIMechE; *Recreations* sailing; *Clubs* Royal Northern and Clyde YC, Royal Thames YC, Western; *Style*— J D H Hume, Esq, CBE; Drimard, 22 E Lennox Dr, Helensburgh, Dunbartonshire G84 9JD (☎ 0436 72395); Primard Ltd, 22 East Lennox Drive, Helensburgh, Dunbartonshire G84 9JD (☎ 0436 751 32)

HUME, John; MP (SDLP) Foyle 1983-, MEP Socialist Group (EP) NI 1979-; *b* 18 Jan 1937; *Educ* St Columb's Coll, Nat Univ of Ireland; *m* 1951, Patricia Hone, 2 s, 2 da; *Career* pres Irish League of Credit Unions 1964-69; Derry civil rights leader 1968-70, Ind Stormont MP 1969-72; Elected NI Assembly 1973, NI Convention 1975-76, special advsr to EEC Cmmr Burke 1977-79, memb New Ireland Forum 1983-84, memb Irish Tport and Gen Workers Union; fndr memb SDLP (dep ldr 1970-79, ldr 1979-); sponsor: Irish Anti-Apartheid Movement, Europeans for Nuclear Disarmament; Hon Docs Univ of Massachusetts 1985-, Catholic Univ of America 1986-, St Josephs University Philadelphia 1986-; assoc fell Center for Int Affrs Harvard 1976, res fell European studies Trinity Coll Dublin 1976-77; *Books* John Hume - Statesman of the Troubles (1985); *Style*— John Hume, Esq, MP, MEP; 6 West End Park, Derry, Northern Ireland

HUME, Brig Richard Trevor Pierce; s of Capt Trevor Hume (d 1968), of Ongar, Essex, and Sybil Clare, *née* Lacy (d 1960); *b* 5 May 1934; *Educ* Ampleforth, RMA Sandhurst; *m* 1, 25 April 1962 (m dis), Gillian, da of Cdr Hodson, RN (d 1962); 1 da (Deirdre b 1963); m 2, 29 April 1971, Jane, da of Sir Eric Tansley, CMG, of London; 2 step s, 1 step da; *Career* cmmnd Irish Gds 1954; served: Middle East, Far East, Europe, USA, Canada, Falklands, UK, NI; cmd: 1 Bn Irish Gds 1974-77, Irish Gds Regt 1979-81, 2 Inf Bde 1982-84 Fortress Gibraltar 1984-86, ret 1987; bursar St Catherine's Sch 1987-; res govr and constable Dover Caslte Dep Lord Warden Cinque Ports 1981-84; *Clubs* Army and Navy; *Style*— Brig Richard Hume; Little Orchard, Blackheath, Guildford, Surrey GU4 8QY (☎ 0483 892216); St Catherine's School, Bramley, Guildford, Surrey GU5 0DF (☎ 0483 892562)

HUME-WILLIAMS, Lady; Frances Mary; da of Edmond Arthur Hudson Groom, OBE, of Warham, Wells, Norfolk; *b* 4 Jan 1911; *m* 1949, as his 2 w, Sir Roy Ellis Hume-Williams, 2 and last Bt (d 1980), s of Rt Hon Sir William Ellis Hume-Williams, KBE, KC; *Recreations* flower arranging, gardening; *Style*— Lady Hume-Williams; Ardlui, The Highlands, East Horsley, Leatherhead, Surrey

HUMFREY, Lady Emma Mary Helener; *née* French; 3 da of 3 Earl of Ypres by his 1 w Maureen; *b* 8 Dec 1958; *Educ* private tutor; *m* 1980, Charles Geoffrey, s of Charles Michael Humfrey, of Alderney; 1 s (Charles b 1986); *Recreations* racing, riding; *Style*— Lady Emma Humfrey; Stow Bedon Hall, Attleborough, Norfolk

HUMM, Roger Frederick; s of Leonard Edward Humm, MBE (d 1964), and Gladys, *née* Prevotat (d 1986); *b* 7 Mar 1937; *Educ* Hampton Sch, Sheffield Univ (BA); *m* 1966 (m dis), Marion Frances, *née* Czechman; *Career* md Ford Motor Co Ltd 1986- (dir 1980-); Liveryman Worshipful Co of Carmen; FIMI, CBIM, FID, FRSA; *Recreations* golf, scuba diving, writing, Harlequins, RAC; *Clubs* Variety of GB, Lord's Taverners; *Style*— Roger F Humm, Esq; c/o Ford Motor Co Ltd, Eagle Way, Warley, Brentwood, Essex CM13 3BW (☎ 0277 253000)

HUMMEL, Dr Frederick Cornelius; s of Cornelius Hummel OBE (d 1972), and Caroline, *née* Riefler (d 1973); *b* 28 April 1915; *Educ* Humanistisches Gymnasium St Stephan Ausburg, Wadham Coll Oxford (MA, DPhil, BSc); *m* 1, 25 Jan 1941 (m dis 1961), Agnes Kathleen, *née* Rushforth; 1 s (Antony b 1941); m 2, 1961, Florina Rosemary Silvia, da of William George Hollyer; 3 da (Anna b 1961, Silvia b 1963, Julia b 1964); *Career* Sgt and Lt KAR E African Forces 1939-43; dist forestry offr Uganda 1938-39 and 1943-45, mensuration offr Forestry Cmn GB 1946-61, co dir Mexican Nat Forest Inventory 1961-66, controller mgmnt servs Forestry Cmmn 1966-68, cmmnr harvesting and mktg Forestry Cmmn 1968-73, hd forestry divn Cmmn of the Euro Communities 1973-80; ind conslt 1980-; Dr hc Univ of Munich 1978; Fell Inst Chartered Forestry 1982; *Books* Forest Policy - A Contribution to Resource Development (ed 1984), Biomass Forestry in Europe - A Strategy for the Future (ed, 1988); *Recreations* travelling off the beaten track; *Style*— Dr Frederick Hummel; 8 The Ridgeway, Guildford, Surrey GU1 2DG (☎ 0483 572 383)

HUMPHERY-SMITH, Cecil Raymond Julian; s of Frederick Humphery-Smith, MBE (d 1979); *b* 29 Oct 1928; *Educ* St John's Hurstpierpoint, London Univ Sch of Hygiene and Tropical Medicine, Parma, Kent Univ; *m* 1951, Alice Elizabeth Gwendoline, da of late Charles Thomas Cogle, formerly chief inspr of Mines, Kenya Colony; 1 s, 5 da; *Career* mangr consumer servs dept H J Heinz Co 1955-60, conslt De Rica Sp A 1961-72, md Achievements Ltd 1961-81 (chm 1981); princ and tstee Inst of Heraldic and Genealogical Studies, ed Family History 1961-; lectr extra mural studies: London Univ 1951-, Kent 1964-; visiting prof: Univ Minho 1970-72, ISSC; cncl memb: Heraldry Soc 1953-, Manorial Soc of GB 1979-; memb Domesday Nat Ctee 1984-85; kt of Obedience, Sov Mil Order Malta 1968, memb cncl Sub-Priory B Adrian Fortescue 1981-87; Freeman and Liveryman Worshipful Co of Broderers and Scriveners (hon historian); fell: Soc of Antiquaries, Heraldry Society, Society of Genealogists; Academician l'Académie Internationale d'Héraldique (1976), Confédération Internationale des Sciences Généalogique (vice pres 1980-86, pres 1986-); Lord of the Manor of St John, Cardbrook and others; et al Héraldique 1986-; UNESCO, ISSC; *Books* The Colour of Heraldry (co author), General Armory Two, Heraldry in Canterbury Cathedral, Anglo-Norman Armory (2 vols), An Atlas and Index of Parish Registers, A Genealogist's Bibliography, Our Family History, Introducing Family History, Hugh Revel, etc; *Recreations* writing sonnets, walking, listening to good music; *Clubs* Challoner; Royal British, Lisbon; *Style*— Cecil Humphery-Smith, Esq; Alcroft Grange, Hackington, Canterbury, Kent CT2 9NN (☎ 462308); Fazarga, Moita-Fatima, 2495 Portugal

HUMPHREY, Albert S; s of Prof Albert Swartsendruber Humphrey, and Margaret Elizabeth Tomlinson, *née* Benton; *b* 2 June 1926; *Educ* Univ of Illinois (BSC), MIT (MSC), Harvard Sch of Business Admin (MBA); *m* 1, 6 Oct 1957 (m dis 1970), Virginia, da of Norman Potter (d 1976), of Cambridge, Mass; 2 s (Albert b 9 July 1959, Jonathon Benton Cantwell b 29 May 1962), 2 da (Virginia b 13 Sept 1960, Heidi b 10 Oct 1963); m 2, 20 Oct 1983, Mynam Alice Octaaf, da of Willy Petrus de Baere, of Lokeren, Belgium; 1 da (Stephania b 20 Sept 1986), 1 step s (Jonas Willems b 29 Aug 1955), 1 step da (Roosie Willems b 27 April 1952); *Career* staff engr Esso Standard Oil Co New Jersey 1948, chief of chemical and protective gp Office of the Chief Chemical Offr US Army Chemical Corp Washington DC 1952, asst to the pres Penberthy Instrument Co Seattle 1955, chief of product planning Boeing Airplane Co Seattle 1956, mangr value analysis programme small aircraft div GE Boston 1960, mangr of R & D planning P R Mallcry & Co Inc Indianapolis 1961, head of mgmnt audit Gen Dynamics San Diego 1963, dir Int Exec Seminar in Business Planning Stanford Res Inst California and consult NASA Off of Advanced Res and Technol Washington 1965, chief exec Business Planning and Devpt Kansas City 1969; currently chm and chief exec Business Planning and Devpt Inc (London); dir: Acquisition Re-Cycle Ltd (London), Sanbros Ltd (London), Candle Int Ltd (Huntingdon), Imperial Screen Systems Ltd (Birmingham) Tower Lysprodukter a/s (Oslo Norway) Petros Petrochemische Anwendumgssysteme GmbH (Nurnberg Germany), Russell Homes plc, Light Industry Ltd (London), Friborgh Instruments plc; faculty memb: Extension Sch for Adult Educn Univ of Washington, US Naval Reserve Offrs Trg Sch; visiting prof Sch of Business and Mgmnt Newcastle Poly; assoc Blackwood Hodge Mgmnt Centre Nene Coll Northampton; memb English Speaking Union; frequent contrib to various business and mgmnt pubns; MInstM; memb: IOD, American Inst of Chemical Engrs, Harvard Alumni, MIT Alumni Assoc, Univ of Illinois Alumni Assoc; *Recreations* public service, seminars, lectures, writing, skiing, windsurfing, water skiing; *Clubs* East India Devonshire Sports and Public Schools, Harward (Boston); *Style*— Albert Humphrey, Esq; 32 Jellicoe House, 4 Osnaburgh St, London NW1 3WA (☎ 01 388 1838, fax 01 388 7030); 4030 Charlotte St, Kansas City, Missouri 64110, USA (☎ 816 753 0495); Sportloan 6 W 22, 9100 Lockeren, Belgium (☎ 3291 488 666)

HUMPHREY, (Frank) Basil; CB (1975); s of John Hartley Humphrey (d 1961), and Alice Maud, *née* Broadbent (d 1975); *b* 21 Sept 1918; *Educ* Brentwood Sch, St Catharine's Coll Cambridge (MA),; *m* 1947, Ollga, da of Frantisek Cerny (d 1946), of Trencín, of Czechoslovakia; 2 s (Nicholas, Igor); *Career* served RA 1939-45, Adj 23 Mountain Regt and DAAG 4 Corps India and Burma; barr Middle Temple, memb parly counsel 1967-80; *Recreations* gardening, mountain walking, music; *Style*— Basil Humphrey, Esq, CB; 1a The Ave, Chichester, W Sussex PO19 4PZ (☎ 0243 778783)

HUMPHREY OF DINNET, (James Malcolm) Marcus; s of Lt Col James McGivern Humphrey, MC (d 1979), and Violet Joan, da of Col Sir Malcolm Barclay-Harvey of Dinnet, Govr of S Aust 1939-44 and for many years MP for Kincardine and W Aberdeenshire; *b* 1 May 1938; *Educ* Eton, ChCh Oxford (MA); *m* 15 Oct 1963, Sabrina Margaret, da of Lt Cdr Thomas Edward Pooley, RN (retd); 2 s (Edward b 1965, Simon b 1978), 2 da (Tania b 1966, Natasha b 1972); *Career* chartered surveyor; mangr own property; chm N of Scotland Bd Eagle Star Gp 1971-; memb: NFU of Scotland HQ Cncl 1968-73, Grampian Regnl Cncl 1974- (chm of fin 1974-78); Parly candidate (C) N Aberdeen 1966; chm of fin Aberdeen CC 1973-75, Grand Master Mason of Scotland 1983-88, memb Queens Bodyguard for Scotland 1969-,

FRICS, OStJ (1970); *Recreations* fishing, shooting, photography, philately; *Clubs* Boodle's, Royal Northern and Univ (Aberdeen); *Style*— Marcus Humphrey of Dinnet; Dinnet, Aboyne, Aberdeenshire; Estate Office, Dinnet, Aboyne AB3 5LL (☎ 0339 85341)

HUMPHREYS, Anthony John (Tony); s of Henry Rees Humphreys, OBE (d 1970), and Mary Gladys, *née* Marsh (d 1983); *b* 17 May 1937; *Educ* Uppingham, Glasgow Univ (BSc); *m* 11 April 1964, Susan Wyndham, da of Dr David W Evans, of Half Inn House, Frankby Green, Frankby, Wirral; 1 s (Timothy Rees b 1970), 2 da (Nikola Jane b 1965, Samantha b 1968); *Career* Lt (E) RNR 1959-67; dir Tport Engrg of Clitheroe Ltd 1981-86; md: Homer Grantham 1972-75, Atkinsons of Clitheroe Ltd 1975-81, RBPR Ltd Manchester 1981-84, JH Carruthers and Co Ltd E Kilbride 1985-88, Tidlo Croft Ltd Shepton Mallet 1988-; FIMechE; *Clubs* Burnham & Berrow GC; *Style*— Tony Humphreys, Esq; Yaffles, Norville Lane, Cheddar, Somerset (☎ 0934 743243); Tidlo Croft Ltd, Charlton Trading Estate, Shepton Mallet, Somerset BA4 5QE (☎ 0749 4321, fax 0749 5117, telex 444132 BARMAC G)

HUMPHREYS, Lt-Col Charles Andrew; MC; s of Brig Gen G Humphreys, CB, CMG, DSO (d 1943), and Lady Emily, *née* Nugent, da of 10 Earl of Westmeath; *b* 9 April 1922; *Educ* Downside Sch; *m* 21 Feb 1952, Phyllida Mary Delia, da of Capt Harold Pearce, RA (ka 1943); 3 s (Jasper Mark, Martin Charles, Toby James); *Career* cmmnd KRRC 1942, served 2 bn KRRC 1943-47, ADC to GOC 7 Armd Div 1948-49, Staff Coll Camberley 1951 (psc), Bde Maj 169 Greenjacket Bde (TA) 1955-56, 1 Bn KRRC 1957-60, Staff (GS02) HQ Afnorth (Oslo) 1961-63, Bde Adj Royal Greenjackets 1964-66, CO Oxfordshire and Bucks Lt (TA) 1967-68; Defence Attaché Helsinki 1969-71, ret 1975; sec cncl for Voluntary Serv 1976-82, Br Heart Fndn (Salisbury) 1986-89;; *Recreations* fishing, shooting; *Clubs* Army and Navy; MCC; *Style*— Lt-Col C A Humphreys, MC; Berwick House, Berwick St James, Salisbury, Wiltshire (☎ 0722 790212)

HUMPHREYS, (David) Colin; CMG (1977); s of Charles Roland Lloyd Humphreys (d 1982), and Bethia Joan, *née* Bowie (d 1980); *b* 23 April 1925; *Educ* Eton, King's Coll Cambridge (MA); *m* 1952, Jill Allison, da of James Cranmer (d 1963); 2 s (David, Martin), 1 da (Camilla); *Career* Army Lt, UK and India 1943-46, civil servant Air Miny 1949, private sec to Sec of State for Air 1959-60; def cnsllr: UK Del to NATO 1960-63, Air Force Dept 1963-69; Student Imperial Defence Coll 1970, dir Defence Policy Staff 1971-72, asst sec gen (Defence Planning and Policy) NATO 1972-76, asst under sec (Naval Staff) 1977-79, deputy under sec (Air) 1979-84, dir of devpt RIIA 1985-86; *Clubs* RAF, Wentworth; *Style*— Colin Humphreys Esq, CMG; Rivendell, North Drive, Virginia Water, Surrey GU25 4NQ (☎ 099 04 2130)

HUMPHREYS, Hon Mrs Ella Zia; *née* Grimston; da of 1 Lord Grimston of Westbury (d 1979), and Sybyl Rose (d 1977), da of Sir Sigmund Neumann, 1 Bt; *b* 4 May 1937; *m* 1972, Humphrey K Humphreys (d 1984); 1 da (Catherine Sybella b 1977); *Style*— The Hon Mrs Humphreys; Ferne Park Cottage, Berwick St John, Shaftesbury, Dorset (☎ 074 788 767)

HUMPHREYS, Hon Mrs Honor; *née* Byng; da of 10 Viscount Torrington (d 1961); *b* 1912; *m* 1937 (m dis 1951), Lisle Marles Humphreys; *Style*— The Hon Mrs Honor Humphreys; 26 Swan Court, London SW7

HUMPHREYS, Sir (Raymond Evelyn) Myles; JP, DL (Belfast); s of Raymond and May Humphreys; *b* 24 Mar 1925; *Educ* Skegoneil Primary Sch, Londonderry HS, Belfast Royal Acad; *m* 1 1963, Joan Tate (d 1979); 2 s (Ian, Mark); m 2, 1987, Sheila McFarland; *Career* res engr NI Road Tport Bd 1946-48, Ulster Tport Authy 1948-55, tport mangr Nestle's Food Prod (NI) Ltd 1955-59, dist tport offr St John Ambulance Bde 1946-66; memb: Belfast City Cncl 1964-81, NI Tport Hldg Co 1968-74, Nat Planning and Town Planning Cncl 1970-81 (chm 1976-77), NI Tourist Bd 1973-80, City Cncl Town Planning and Environmental Health Ctee 1973-75, NI Housing Exec 1975-78, May Ctee of Inquiry into UK Prison Servs 1978-79, bd of Abbey Nat Building Soc 1981- (chm advsy bd NI 1981-); dir: Walter Alexander (Belfast) Ltd 1959-, Quick Service Stations Ltd 1971-86, Bowring Martin 1978-88; chm: Belfast Corpn Housing Ctee 1966-69, NI Railways Co Ltd 1967-, Ulster Tourist Devpt Assoc 1968-78, City Cncl Planning Ctee 1973-75, Fin and Gen Purposes Ctee Belfast 1978-80, NI Police Authy 1976-86, Belfast Marathon Ltd 1981-85; Belfast Harbour cmmr 1979-; High Sheriff Belfast 1969, Lord Mayor 1975-77 (dep lord mayor 1970); senator Jr Chamber Int, NI rep Motability Int; pres: NI Polio Fellowship 1977-, City of Belfast Youth Orchestra 1980-; memb exec and former pres NI C of C and Indust, pres BIM (Belfast branch) 1983-; former pres Belfast Junior C of C; past chm: bd of mgmnt Dunlambert Secondary Sch, bd of visitors to HM Prison Belfast; memb: senate Queen's Univ Belfast 1975-77, ct Univ of Ulster 1985-; tstee Ulster Folk and Tport Museum 1976-81; memb cncl Queen's Silver Jubilee Appeal, dir Ulster Orchestra Soc 1980; Freeman City of London 1976; OStJ; FCIT, CBIM; kt 1977; *Clubs* Lansdowne (London); *Style*— Sir Myles Humphreys, JP, DL; Mylestone, 23 Massey Avenue, Belfast BT42 2JT (☎ Belfast 761166)

HUMPHREYS, Nigel Craven; s of Gordon Stephen Humphreys (d 1985), of The Drive, Godalming, Surrey, and Joan Olive, *née* Mudditt; *b* 15 Mar 1938; *Educ* Sherborne, New Coll Oxford (MA); *m* 29 Sept 1962, Jennie Mam, da of Maj Adrian Hugh Lovegrove, of West End House, Over Station, Somerset; 2 da (Julia b 1964, Annabella b 1966); *Career* RB 1956-58, cmmnd 1957, seconded to 3 Bn King's African Rifles Kenya; 1961-71: Courtaulds Ltd, Andrews & Ptnrs, Chaucer Estates Ltd; md Mitropa Gp Brussels 1971-77; Tyzack & Ptnrs Ltd: conslt 1977, ptnr 1978-84, managing ptnr 1984-85, chm (Far East) 1985-; chm govrs The Old Ride Sch 1988-; Vol Serv Housing Soc 1966-68, Cherwell Housing Tst 1968-71; Freeman City of London, Liveryman Worshipful Co of Glovers 1985; *Recreations* opera, shooting, distant uninhabited places; *Clubs* Boodles, Royal Green Jackets; *Style*— Nigel Humphreys, Esq; The Malt House, Chilton, Oxon OX11 0RZ (☎ 0235 834 409); 10 Hallam St, London W1N 6DJ (☎ 01 580 2924, fax 01 631 5317)

HUMPHREYS, Sir Olliver William; CBE (1957); s of late Rev J Willis Humphreys, of Bath; *b* 4 Sept 1902; *Educ* Caterham Sch, UCL (BSc); *m* 1933, Muriel Mary (d 1985), da of Charles John Hawkins, of Harrow; *Career* joined scientific staff GEC Res Laboratories 1925, dir 1951-60; dir GEC 1953, vice-chm GEC Ltd 1963-67; pres: Inst of Physics 1956-58, Inst of Electrical Engrs 1964-65; fndr chm Conf of the Electronics Indust 1963-67; fell UCL 1963; kt 1968; *Style*— Sir Olliver Humphreys, CBE; The Victoria Hotel, Sidmouth, Devon EX10 8RY

HUMPHREYS, Lt-Col Robert Benjamin; DL (Co Durham 1969); s of John Humphreys, of Castle House, Usk; *b* 14 Nov 1914; *Educ* Aldenham, Sandhurst; *m* 1942, Lorna Egremont, da of Douglas Hann, of Cascade House, Penpedaireol; 1 s, 1 da; *Career* gazetted Durham LI 1935, Lt-Col 1956, ret 1961; regtl sec Durham LI 1962-79; High Sheriff Co Durham 1981; *Recreations* hunting, gardening, entomology; *Clubs* Army and Navy, Durham County; *Style*— Lt-Col Robert Humphreys, DL; Peppermires Cottage, Brancepeth, Co Durham (☎ Durham 3780389)

HUMPHREYS, Col Thomas Victor; OBE (1958); s of Thomas Victor Humphreys (ka 1942), of Ballycastle, Co Antrim, and Anne Breakley Douglas (d 1967); *b* 26 May 1922; *Educ* Ballycastle HS Antrim, The Queens Univ of Belfast (MB BCh, BAO); *m* 18 Oct 1969, Elisabeth Penrose, da of Rev John Alfred Clarence Rogers (d 1984), vicar of Hindhead, Surrey; *Career* res hosp appts in med and surgery 1946-52, MO and second sec of legation HBM Legation Bucharest 1952-55, MO and first sec HBM Embassy Moscow 1955-57, surgn Royal Mail Line 1958-62; RAMC: entered 1963, Lt-Col 1969, Actg Col 1970, local col 1977, Col Staff 1980: sr specialist Army Community and Occupational Med 1980, regtl MO 2 Coldstream Gds and later Queens Dragoon Gds; SMO: (UK) SHAPE Belgium 1971-74, HQ Allied Forces N Europe Oslo Norway 1974-77; CO Br Mil Hosp: Munster BAOR 1977-79, ADMS Berlin and CO BMH 1979-82; Cdr Army Med Servs: HQ Western Dist UK 1982-86, HQ London Dist Horse Gds 1986-87, ret 1987; pres emeritus Berlin Int Med Soc 1981, Cdr Order of Polonia Restituta (govt in exile); OStJ 1981 (serving brother 1962); Lord of the Manor of Postcombe; *Publications*: articles in various professional medical jls on Medicine and Surgery in Easter Europe, various historical articles on European Monarchies (particularly the Habsburgs); *Recreations* european history, languages, genealogy, heraldry and all the vanished pomps of yesterday; *Style*— Col Victor Humphreys, OBE; Powderham House, Powderham, nr Exeter EX6 8JJ (☎ 0626 890 536)

HUMPHRIES, David Ernest; s of Ernest Augustus Humphries (d 1954), of Sussex, and Kathleen Humphries, *née* Keating (d 1986); *b* 3 Feb 1937; *Educ* Brighton Coll, Corpus Christi Coll Oxford; *m* 1959, Wendy Rosemary, da of Thomas James Cook (d 1982), of Sussex; 1 s (Charles b 1969), 1 da (Sarah b 1965); *Career* RAE (Farnborough) 1961-81: materials dept 1961-66, avionics dept 1966-74, supt inertial navigation div 1974, supt weapon aiming systems Div, supt flight systems dept 1975, head of systems assessment dept 1978-81; dir gen future projects Air Systems Controllerate MOD (PE) 1981-83, chief scientist RAF, dir gen res (C Sector) 1983-85, dir gen of res and technol Controllerate of Estab Res and Nuclear 1985-86, (asst chief scientific advsr projects and res); *Recreations* music, pipe organ (building and playing), reading; *Style*— David Humphries, Esq; 18 The Mount, Malton, North Yorks YO17 0ND (☎ 0653 693679); Miny of Defence, Main Building, Whitehall

HUMPHRIES, His Hon Judge; Gerard William; s of John Alfred Humphries (d 1980), and Marie Frances, *née* Whitwell (d 1980); *b* 13 Dec 1928; *Educ* St Bede's Coll Manchester, Manchester Univ (LLB); *m* 1957, Margaret Valerie, da of William Woodburn Gelderd (d 1975), of Cumbria; 4 s (Stephen b 1961, Paul b 1962, David b 1966, Bernard b 1971), 1 da (Frances b 1967); *Career* Flying Offr RAF 1950-52; barr 1952-80, circuit judge 1980; Knight of the Holy Sepulchre (Vatican) 1986; *Recreations* tennis, gardening, music, sailing, golf, computers, caravanning; *Clubs* Lansdowne, Northern LT (Manchester); *Style*— His Hon Judge Humphries; Crown Ct, Crown Square, Manchester

HUMPHRIES, Peter John William; s of William Humphries, of Stratford, London, and Eileen Ethel Stevens, *née* Scannel; *b* 15 June 1935; *Educ* Stratford GS; *m* 18 June 1955, Kay, da of late Enoch Fowler, of Liverpool; 2 s (Peter b 1956, Kevin b 1964); *Career* served RAF 1952-59, Far East Air Force Cmd 3609 Sqdn; ex automotive engr and tport mgmnt Miny of Tsport GLC, and Surrey CC; princ engr Avon CC; fndr memb Inst of Municipal Tport; dir Bristol Packers (American Football Club); FBIM, MIRTE, MInstTA, MIMT; *Recreations* golf, rugby, american football, pub dominoes, putting the world to rights; *Clubs* Fosseyway Golf, Rosslyn Park FC, Bristol Packers AFC; *Style*— Peter Humphries, Esq; Nelson House, Pensford, Avon BS18 4AH; Avon County Council, County Transport, Sandy Park Rd, Brislington, Bristol

HUMPHRYS, (Arthur) Francis Walter; OBE (1959, MBE 1945); s of Lt-Col Sir Francis Henry Humphrys, GCMG, GCVO, KBE, CIE (d 1971), and Lady Humphrys DBE, *née* Deane; *b* 20 Oct 1909; *Educ* Winchester, Ch Ch Oxford; *m* 1942, Lady (Eugénie) Pamela, *qv*, da of Field Marshal 1 Earl Wavell, GCB, GCSI, GCIE, CMG, MC (d 1950); 2 s (Francis b 1944, Owen b 1946), 1 da (Cecilia b 1950); *Career* Maj The Central India Horse, Egypt, Libya, Eritrea, Abyssinia, Persia, Italy, Macedonia; Lt-Col, mil sec to Viceroy of India; with Royal Dutch Shell Gp of Cos in London, India and Pakistan; *Clubs* Army and Navy; *Style*— Francis Humphrys, Esq, OBE; Marston Meysey Grange, nr Cricklade, Wilts (☎ 028 581 239)

HUMPHRYS, John Desmond; s of George Edward, and Winifred May (d 1988); *b* 17 August 1943; *m* 05/09/64; 1 s (Christopher b 30 April 1967), 1 da (Catherine b 21 July 1969); *Career* BBC TV news foreign corr in USA and SA 1970-80, dip corr 1980-81, TV news presenter 1981-86, presenter of Today 1986-; cncl memb Save the Children Fund;; *Recreations* failed farmer; *Style*— John Humphrys, Esq; BBC, Broadcasting House, London W1A 1AA (☎ 01 741 1097)

HUMPHRYS, Lady (Eugénie) Pamela; *née* Wavell; da of 1 Earl Wavell, GCB, GCSI, GCIE, CMG, MC (d 1950); *b* 1918; *m* 1942, (Arthur) Francis Walter Humphrys, OBE, *qv*, s of Lt-Col Sir Francis Humphrys, GCMG, GCVO, KBE, CIE; 2 s, 1 da; *Style*— Lady Pamela Humphrys; Marston Meysey Grange, nr Cricklade, Wilts (☎ 028 581 239)

HUNNICUTT, (Virginia) Gayle; da of Col S Hunnicutt, of Fort Worth, Texas, and Mary Virginia, *née* Dickenson; *b* 6 Feb 1943; *Educ* Pascal HS, UCLA (BA); *m* 1, 1968 (m dis 1974), David H Hemmings; 1 s (Nolan); m 2, 1 Sept 1978, Simon David Jenkins, s of Rev David Jenkins, of London; 1 s (Edward); *Career* actress; theatre: A Ride Across Lake Constanner 1974, Twelth Night 1975, The Tempest 1976, The Admiral Crighton 1977, A Woman of No Importance 1978, Hedda Gables 1978, Peter Pan 1979, Macbeth 1980, Uncle Clanya 1980, The Philadelphia Story 1981, The Miss Firecracks Contest 1982, Exit The King 1983, The Doctors Dilemma 1984, So Long On Lonely Street 1985, The Big Knife 1987; film: New Face in Hell 1967, Eye of the Cat and The Little Sisters 1968, Running Scared 1971, Scorpio 1972, L'Homne Sans Visage 1974, The Spiral Staircase 1976, One in Paris 1977, Dream Lovers 1985, Target 1986, Silence Like Glass 1988; Television: Man and Boy 1971, The Golden Bowl 1972, The Riping Seed 1973, Fall of Eagles 1974, The Ambandors 1975, The Martian Chronicles 1978, A Man Called Intrepid 1979, Fantomas 1980, Taxi 1982, The First Modern Olympics 1984, Sherlock Holmes 1985, Privilege 1986, Dream West 1987; memb bd of tstees The Theatre Tst, hon memb BFI 1980; memb: Acad of

Motion Pictures Arts & Scis 1979, Br Theatre Assoc 1982; *Books* Health and Beauty in Motherhood (1984); *Recreations* travel; *Style—* Miss Gayle Hunnicutt; 174 Regents Park Rd, London NW1, (☎ 01 722 4022, car phone 0860 417578)

HUNNISETT, Dr Roy Frank; s of Rrank Hunnisett, of Bexhill-on-Sea (d 1967), and Alice, *née* Budden (d 1979); *b* 26 Feb 1928; *Educ* Bexhill GS, New Coll Oxford (MA, DPhil); *m* 7 Aug 1954, Edith Margaret, *née* Evans; *Career* pt/t lectr New Coll Oxford 1957-63, Pub Record Off 1953-88; FRHistS 1961, FSA 1975; *Books* The Medieval Coroners' Rolls (1960), The Medieval Coroner (1961), Bedfordshire Coroners' Rolls (1961), Calendar of Nottinghamshire Coroners' Inquests 1485-1558 (1969), Indexing for Editors (1972), Editing Records for Publication (1977), Wiltshire Coroners' Bills 1752-1796 (1981), Sussex Coroners' Inquests 1485-1558 (1985); *Recreations* music, cricket; *Style—* Dr Roy Hunnisett; 23 Byron Gardens, Sutton, Surrey SM1 3QG (☎ 01 661 2618)

HUNSDON OF HUNSDON; *see*: Aldenham

HUNSWORTH, John Alfred; s of Fred Sheard Hunsworth (d 1970), of 43 Sandfield Rd, Thornton Heath, Surrey, and Lillian Margaret, *née* Wetmon (d 1972); *b* 23 Dec 1921; *Educ* Selhurst GS, LSE (BCom); *m* 20 Oct 1972, Phyllis Blodwen Sparshatt, da of Dr Philip Hughes (d 1952); *Career* WWII, enlisted Royal Fus 1941, RMC Camberley 1941-42, cmmnd E Surrey Regt 1942, transferred to Indian Army, serv 8 Bn 2 Punjab Regt 1942-45 (Lt 1942, Capt 1944), repatriated E Surrey Regt 1945-46, demobbed as Capt 1946; dep ed The Bankers Magazine 1948-54, dir Banking Info Serv (an arm of London and Scottish Clearing Banks) 1954-81, ret 1981; elder Sanderstead Utd Reform Church; Freeman City of London 1977; *Recreations* gardening, walking three basset hounds, world travel, philately, occasional journalistic writing; *Clubs* Reform, Royal Overseas League, Surrey CCC; *Style—* John Hunsworth, Esq; 29 West Hill, Sanderstead, South Croydon, Surrey (☎ 01 657 2585)

HUNT, Alannah Elizabeth; da of Humphrey Cecil Bowbeer Hunt (d 1965), of Curry Rivel, of Somerset, and Molly Daphne Albury, *née* Hill (d 1979); *b* 22 Mar 1949; *Educ* Millfield Taunton Tech Coll Somerset; *Career* selection conslt Webb Whitley Assoc Ltd 1975-82, dir Overseas Link Ltd 1982-84, head of exec selection Price Waterhouse 1984-, author of various articles on recruitment and selection; MBIM 1982, MPIM 1986, MIMC 1987; *Recreations* tennis, theatre, gardening; *Style—* Miss Alannah Hunt

HUNT, Bernard Andrew Paul; s of Sir Joseph (Anthony) Hunt (d 1982), and Hilde, *née* Pollitzer; *b* 24 Mar 1944; *Educ* Oundle, Magdalene Coll Cambridge (MA); *m* 1973, Florence, da of Alan White, of W Sussex; 1 s (Andrew b 1977), 1 da (Susanna b 1975); *Career* architect, ptnr Hunt Thompson Assocs 1969-; *Recreations* cinema, theatre, reading, skiing; *Style—* Bernard Hunt, Esq; 34 Fitzroy Road, London NW1; 79 Parkway, London NW1 (☎ 01 485 8555, fax 01 485 1232)

HUNT, Hon Christopher Godfrey Evill; s of Baron Hunt of Fawley, CBE (Life Peer d 1987); *b* 1947; *Educ* London Univ (MA, MB BS); MRCS, LRCP, DObSt, RCOG; *m* 1979, Carol, *née* McDermott; 2 da; *Style—* Dr the Hon Christopher Hunt; 4455 West 2nd Avenue, Vancouver, Br Columbia V6R 1K6, Canada

HUNT, David James Fletcher; MBE (1973), MP (C) Wirral West 1983-; s of Alan Hunt, OBE; *b* 21 May 1942; *Educ* Liverpool Coll, Montpellier Univ, Bristol Univ, Guildford Coll of Law; *m* 1973, Patricia Margery, *née* Orchard; 2 s, 2 da; *Career* slr, conslt Stanley Wasbrough and Co 1965-, ptnr Stanleys and Simpson North 1977-; contested Bristol S 1970, Kingswood 1974; vice-chm Nat Union Cons and Unionist Assocs 1974-76; chm: YC Nat Advsy Ctee 1972-73, Cons Gp for Europe 1981-82; vice-chm Parly Youth Lobby 1978-80, pres Br Youth Cncl 1978-81 (chm 1971-74); PPS to: Trade Sec 1979-81, Defence Sec 1981; jr Cons whip 1981-83, a lord cmmr of the Treasy (govt whip) 1983-84, MP (C) Wirral 1976-1983, vice-chm Cons Party 1983-85, Parly under sec of state Dept of Energy 1984-87, dep government chief whip 1987-; tres HM Household 1987-; *Clubs* Hurlingham; *Style—* David Hunt Esq, MBE, MP; 2 St Margaret's Rd, Hoylake, Wirral L47 1HX (☎ 051 632 4033); 14 Cowley St, SW1 (☎ 01 222 7149); House of Commons, SW1A 0AA (☎ 01 219 3400)

HUNT, David Roderic Notley; QC (1987); s of Dr Geoffrey Notley Hunt (d 1982), of Pembury, Kent, and Deborah Katharine Rosamund, *née* Clapham; *b* 22 June 1947; *Educ* Charterhouse, Trinity Coll Cambridge (MA); *m* 27 April 1974, Alison Connell, da of Lt-Col Arthur George Jelf (d 1958); 2 s (Thomas b 8 Feb 1976, Robert b 20 Feb 1979); *Career* barr Gray's Inn 1969, asst rec; *Recreations* sailing, golf, skiing; *Clubs* Bewl Valley SC, Nevill GC; *Style—* David Hunt, Esq, QC; Queen Elizabeth Building, Temple, London EC4 (☎ 01 936 3131, fax 01 353 1937, telex 8951414)

HUNT, Sir David Wathen Stather; KCMG (1963, CMG 1959), OBE (1943); s of Rev Canon Bernard Hunt (d 1967), of Norwich, and Elizabeth, *née* Milner; *b* 25 Sept 1913; *Educ* St Lawrence Coll Ramsgate, Wadham Coll Oxford; *m* 1, 1948 (m dis 1967), Pamela Muriel, da of late Nicholas Medawar; 2 s; m 2, 1968, Iro, da of John Myrianthousis; *Career* fell Magdalen Coll Oxford 1937; WWII Welch Regt Middle East, Balkans, N Africa, Sicily, Italy; Col Gen Staff Allied Force HQ 1945-46, Hon Col 1947; joined CRO 1947, private sec to PM 1950-52, dep UK high cmmr Pakistan 1954-62 (asst under-sec 1959), dep British high cmmr Lagos 1960-62; high cmmr: Kampala 1962-65, Cyprus 1965-66, Nigeria 1967-69; ambass Brazil 1969-73; chm govrs Cwlth Inst 1974-84; memb appts cmmn Press Cncl 1977-82, dir Observer 1982, visiting prof of int relations Edinburgh Univ 1980; winner of TV Mastermind title 1977 and Mastermind Champions title 1982; pres Soc for Promotion of Hellenic Studies 1986-; US Bronze Star 1945; Grand Cross Order of Southern Cross Brazil 1985; *Publications* A Don at War (1966), On The Spot (1975), Footprints in Cyprus (ed, 1982), Gothic Art and the Renaissance in Cyprus (1987), Caterina Cornard, Queen of Cyprus (ed 1989); *Clubs* Athenaeum, Beefsteak; *Style—* Sir David Hunt, KCMG, OBE; Old Place, Lindfield, W Sussex RH16 2HU (☎ 044 47 2298)

HUNT, Cdr (Arthur) Douglas; RD (1948 and bar 1966), RNR; s of Dr Arthur Douglas Hunt (d 1952, Capt RAMC), of Park Grange, Duffield Rd, Derby, and Mabel Sharpe, *née* Thomas; *b* 27 Sept 1919; *Educ* Derby GS, Brighton Coll, Nautical Coll, Pangbourne, Southampton Coll of Nautical Studies (Masters Foreign Going Cert of Competency); *m* 16 May 1942, Margaret Alison, da of Ernest William Sutcliffe (d 1947), of Carr Field, Carr Head Lane, Poulton-Le-Fylde, Lancs; 1 s (Christopher Douglas), 1 da (Jennifer Jane); *Career* RNR: Midshipman to Sub Lt 1939-42, Lt 1942-50, Lt Cdr 1950-56, Cdr 1956; MN (Union Castle Line) 1937-39, RN 1939-46, MN (Cunard Line) 1946-56, marine supt Cunard Line Southampton 1956-67, nautical surveyor and examiner of masters and mates 1977-83; sec RAF YC Hamble Hants 1968-70, chm Bursledon & Warsash Regatta Ctee 1970-73; Freeman City of London 1965, memb Hon Co of Master Mariners; *Recreations* sailing; *Clubs* Southampton Master Mariners (Capt 1977), Royal Southern YC, Hamble; *Style—* Cdr Douglas Hunt, RD, RNR; "Westward", Salterns Lane, Old Bursledon, Southampton, Hants SO3 8DH (☎ 042 121 2316)

HUNT, Dr Eric Millman; s of Arthur Millman Hunt (d 1951), and Irene Olive Cordwell (d 1981); *b* 30 April 1923; *Educ* Marling Sch Stroud, Univ of Leeds (BSc, PhD), UCL (Dip Chem Eng); *m* 1, 14 Dec 1951 (m dis 1971), Eve Sangster; 1 s (Trevor b 1959), 1 da (Cynthia b 1962); m 2, 15 July 1974, Phyllis Mary Charteris, da of Capt James Charteris Burleigh (d 1954); 1 s (Andrew b 1975), 1 da (Katrina b 1977); *Career* chief exec Akzo Chemicals Ltd 1967-81, chm Thomas Swan & Co Ltd 1982-; tres Plastics and Rubber Inst 1983- (chm 1981-83); chm N W Wimbledon Res Assoc 1982-88; Freeman City of London 1965, Liveryman Worshipful Co of Horners 1965 (clerk 1982-); FRSC, FIChemE, FPRI, FIOD; *Style—* Dr Eric Hunt; 37 Drax Avenue, Wimbledon, London SW20 (☎ 01 946 9767); 11 Hobart Place, London SW1 (☎ 01 245 9555, fax 01 823 1379)

HUNT, Lady; Esmé Jeanne; *née* Langston; da of Albert Edward Langston; *b* 31 August 1931; *m* 1960, as his 2 w, Sir Joseph Hunt, MBE (d 1982), chm Hymatic Engrg Co; 2 s, 2 da; *Recreations* reading, walking, gardening, music; *Style—* Lady Hunt; Field House, Huntington Lane, Ashford Carbonell, Ludlow, Shrops SY8 4DG

HUNT, (John) Frederick; s of Arthur Hunt (d 1942), and Beatrice, *née* May (d 1981); *b* 21 Oct 1925; *Educ* Scunthorpe GS, Queens Univ Belfast; *m* 17 Feb 1947, Maria, da of Ernesto Semenzato (d 1969); *Career* RA 1943-45, Intelligence Corps 1945-47, RAPC, Lt 1950-55; ptnr Stephenson Smart and Co Chartered Accoutants Peterborough 1965-; tres Cambridgeshire Assoc of Youth Clubs 1975-81, clerk Peterborough Almshouses Tst 1988; FCA 1950, ATII 1960, ACIArb 1989; *Recreations* travel, opera, bowls; *Clubs* City and Counties (Peterborough); *Style—* Frederick Hunt, Esq; 29 Audley Gate, Peterborough PE3 6PG (☎ 0733 262 900); Queen St Chambers, Peterborough PE1 1PB (☎ 0733 432 75, fax 0733 557 157)

HUNT, Geoffrey Harman; s of Alan Harman Hunt, of Devizes Castle, Devizes, and Alma Joan Spence, *née* Anderson; *b* 14 Oct 1955; *Educ* High Wycombe, Royal GS, Exeter Univ (LLB); *Career* slr 1980, ptnr Cardales 1981-86, co slr Vickers plc 1986-88, co exec Fitch Lovell plc 1988-; memb Law Soc; *Recreations* hockey, tennis, skiing; *Style—* Geoffrey Hunt, Esq; 130 Wymering Mansions, Wymering Rd, London W9 2NF (☎ 01 286 7057); Fitch Lovell plc, Market House, 85 Cowcross St, London EC1M 6LL (☎ 01 250 1559, fax 01 250 3334)

HUNT, (Henry) Holman; CBE (1988); s of Henry Hunt (d 1951); *b* 13 May 1924; *Educ* Queen's Park Sch Glasgow, Glasgow Univ; *m* 1954, Sonja, nee Blom; 1 s, 2 da; *Career* mgmnt conslt, md PA Computers and Telecommunications 1976-83, bd dir PA Consulting Servs Ltd (formerly PA Mgmnt Conslts Ltd) 1970-83, memb Monopolies and Mergers 'Cmmn 1980- (dep chm 1985-); pres Inst of Mgmnt Conslts 1974-75; *Recreations* music, reading, walking, travel, photography, gardening; *Clubs* Caledonian; *Style—* Holman Hunt Esq; 28 The Ridings, Epsom, Surrey KT18 5JJ (☎ Epsom 20974); office: New Court, 48 Carey St, London WC2A 2JT (☎ 01 324 1446)

HUNT, (Patrick) James; QC (1987); s of Thomas Ronald Clifford Hunt, and Doreen Gwyneth Katarina, *née* Granville-George; *b* 26 Jan 1943; *Educ* Ashby de la Zouch Boys GS, Keble Coll Oxford (MA); *m* 20 July 1969, Susan Jennifer, da of Noel Allen Goodhead, of Swadlincote; 1 s (Thomas Miles Benjamin b 1973), 3 da (Victoria Katharine b 1971, Suzanna Elisabeth b 1980, Alexandra Emily b 1982); *Career* barr; recorder of the Crown Ct 1982; *Recreations* singing, stonework; *Clubs* Northants County; *Style—* James Hunt, QC; Easton Hall, Easton on the Hill, Stamford, Lincs PE9 3LL; 1 King's Bench Walk, Temple, London EC4 (☎ 01 353 8436)

HUNT, John Beresford; s of Alfred Stanley Hunt (d 1984), of Ilminster, Somerset, and Elma Nellie, *née* Stacey (d 1983); *b* 22 Mar 1935; *Educ* Taunton Sch; *m* 19 Sept 1964, Patricia Ann, da of William Hillier Taylor (d 1968), of Corsham, Wilts; 1 s (Charles Beresford b 13 Aug 1965), 1 da (Victoria Mary b 17 Oct 1967); *Career* Nat Serv cmmnd 1957-59, Som LI TA 1962-68 (Capt 1963); sr ptnr Albert Goodman & Co 1979- (ptnr 1962-79); chm Soc of CA 1982, pres SW Soc of CA 1988; Som Assoc for the Blind, memb Taunton Ct Leet; FICA 1957; *Recreations* tennis, golf; *Clubs* Taunton Rotary; *Style—* John Hunt, Esq; Perris, Hatch Beauchamp, Taunton, Somerset TA3 6TH (☎ 0823 480 383); Messrs Albert Goodman & Co, Mary Street House, Mary Street, Taunton, Somerset (☎ 0823 286 096, fax 0823 286 096)

HUNT, John Edward Francis; s of Thomas Francis Hunt, of 5 Rectory Close, Stock, Ingatestone, Essex, and Norah Margaret, *née* Camps; *b* 25 April 1938; *Educ* Marlborough, Queens Coll Oxford (MA); *m* 1 May 1965, Annabel Gillian, da of Cdr Bradwell Talbot Turner, CVO, DSO, OBE, RN, ret, of 44 St John's Rd, Writtle, Chelmsford, Essex; 2 s (Mark b 1967, Justin b 1972), 2 da (Tamara b 1969, Fenella b 1977); *Career* admitted slr 1962, ptnr Hunt & Hunt 1965-; formerly: vestry clerk St Michaels Cornhill with St Peter le Poer and St Benet Fink in City of London, clerk to Cornhill Ward; memb glebe ctee Diocese of Chelmsford, churchwarden St Peter's South Hanningfield; Freeman City of London 1967; memb Law Soc; *Recreations* reading, tennis, music, browsing; *Style—* John Hunt, Esq ; Hunt & Hunt, Lambourne House, 7 Western Rd, Romford, Essex CM3 8YW (☎ 0708 764 433, fax 0708 762 915)

HUNT, Baron (Life Peer UK 1966); Sir (Henry Cecil) John Hunt; KG (1979), CBE (1945), DSO (1944); s of Capt Cecil Edwin Hunt, MC (d 1914), and Ethel Helen, *née* Crookshank; *b* 22 June 1910; *Educ* Marlborough, Sandhurst; *m* 3 Sept 1936, Joy, da of Dr Mowbray-Green; 4 da (Sally, Susan, Prudence, Jennifer); *Career* sits as SLD Peer in House of Lords; ldr Br Expedition to Mt Everest 1952-53; Cmd 11 KRRC in Italy and Middle East 1943-44 and 11 Indian Inf Brigade in Italy and Greece 1944-46; post-war as GSO, ALF Centl Europe, Planning Staff MELF, HQ (1) Br Corps, Asst Cmdt Staff Coll 1953-55, Cdr 168 Inf Bde TA 1955-56; rector Aberdeen Univ 1963-66; memb Royal Common on Press 1973-77; chm: Inquiry into Police in NI 1969, Parole Bd England and Wales 1967-73, Intermediate Treatment Ctee 1980-85; pres: Alpine Club and Climbers' Club, Br Mountaineering Cncl, Nat Ski Fedn, Nat Assoc of Probation Offrs, Cncl for Volunteers Overseas, Rainer Fndn; pres: RGS 1977-80, cncl Nat Parks 1980-86; hon degree: Aberdeen, Durham, London, Leeds, City, Sheffield; kt 1953; *Style—* The Rt Hon the Lord Hunt, KG, CBE, DSO; Highway Cottage, Aston, Henley-on-Thames, Oxon

HUNT, John Leonard; MP (C) Ravensbourne 1983-); s of William John Hunt (d 1968), of Keston, Kent, and Dora Maud Hunt; *b* 27 Oct 1929; *Educ* Dulwich; *Career* memb Bromley Borough Cncl 1953-65 (alderman 1961-65, mayor 1964), memb London Stock Exchange 1958-69; Parly candidate (C) Lewisham South 1959; MP (C): Bromley

1964-1974, Ravensbourne 1974-83; memb: gen advsy cncl BBC 1975-87, select ctee on Home Affrs 1979-87, select (chm's panel 1980-); jt chm Indo-British Parly Gp, memb UK delgn to Cncl of Europe and Western Euro Union 1988-; *Style*— John Hunt Esq, MP; House of Commons, London, SW1

HUNT, Dr John Leslie; OBE (1987); s of Leslie Hunt (d 1963), of Christchurch, NZ, and Helen, *née* Clarke (d 1971); *b* 24 Jan 1924; *Educ* Christs Coll Christchurch NZ, Canterbury Univ Coll, Otago Univ Med Sch Dunedin New Zealand (MB ChB); *Career* med registrar Guy's Hosp London 1955-56, med advsr and mangr Med Dept Br Drug Houses Ltd London 1957-60, lately princ (formerly sr) med offr Dept of Health London; fndn ed Prescribers Journal 1961-89, fndn ed Health Trends 1969-89, ed Annual Report on the State of Public Health 1962-88; ctee memb Australia and NZ Med and Dental Assoc; ed in chief of occasional official reports on health, and medicinal and social concerns for DHSS 1960-88; MRCP 1972, FFCM (formerly MFCM) 1979; *Recreations* philology, reading, writing, travel; *Style*— Dr John Hunt, OBE; 109 Northcote Rd, Battersea, London SW11 6PN (☎ 01 350 2234);

HUNT, John Maitland; s of Richard Herbert Alexander Hunt (d 1978), and Eileen Mary Isabelle, *née* Witt; *b* 4 Mar 1932; *Educ* Radley, Wadham Coll Oxford (MA, BLitt); *m* 26 July 1969, Sarah, da of Lt-Gen Sir Derek Lang, KCB, DSO, MC, of W Lothian; 2 s (Jonathan Alexander b 1971, Richard Martin b 1973); *Career* asst master and sixth form tutor Stowe Sch 1958-70, headmaster Roedean Sch 1971-84; FRGS; *Recreations* estate management, writing, travel; *Clubs* Royal Cwlth Soc; *Style*— John Hunt, Esq; Logie, Dunfermline, Fife KY12 8QN

HUNT, Jonathan Charles Vivian; OBE (1983), TD (1977, clasp 1983), DL (S Yorks 1981); s of Col George Vivian Hunt, OBE, TD (d 1979), of The Lodge, Woodvale Rd, Sheffield and Sylvia Ann, *née* Tyzack (d 1985); *b* 6 Mar 1943; *Educ* Stowe; *m* 17 July 1971, Susan Aline, eld da of Francis Rawdon Crozier, of Thospell House, Wickham Market, Woodbridge, Suffolk; 2 s (James b 14 Sept 1973, Edward 6 June 1976); *Career* TA serv; cmmnd Queens Own Yorks Yeo 1963, transferred B (Sherwood Rangers Yeo) Sqdn Royal Yeo (OC 1975-78), cmd Royal Yeo 1979-82, Dep Cdr 49 Inf Bde 1983-87, Project Offr Fast Track (new TA compact commissioning course) 1987-, Col TA RMA Sandhurst 1988-; sr ptnr Wakesmith & Co Slrs Sheffield 1988- (ptnr 1967); chm: Sheffield Enterprise Agency Ltd 1986-, Rotherham Rural Div SSAFA; Law Soc 1966; *Recreations* sailing, walking, TA; *Clubs* Sheffield, Cavalry and Guards'; *Style*— Jonathan C V Hunt, Esq, OBE, TD, DL

HUNT, Hon Jonathan Philip Henderson; s of Baron Hunt of Fawley, CBE, (Life Peer d 1987); *b* 1947; *Educ* Charterhouse, Pembroke Coll Oxford (MA, BM, BCh), St Thomas' Hosp; *m* 1977, Monika, da of Dr Herbert Kuhlmann, of Schloss Urstein, Salzburg, Austria; 3 da; *Career* physician; *Style*— Dr the Hon Jonathan Hunt; 29 South Terrace, London SW7

HUNT, Brig Kenneth; OBE (1955) MC (1943); s of John Hunt (d 1952), and Elizabeth, *née* Sills (d 1974); *b* 26 May 1914; *Educ* Chatham House Sch Ramsgate, Army Staff Coll Camberley, IDC; *m* 28 Jan 1939, Mary Mabel, da of Charles Crickett (d 1962); 2 s (Timothy John Leigh b 30 July 1949, Jeremy Peter b 25 Sept 1950), 1 da (Sarah Elizabeth b and d 1948); *Career* cmmnd RA 1940, serv AFrica, Italy, Austria with HAC, 1 RHA and 2 RHA 1942-46, Brevet Lt-Col 1955, CO 40 FD Regt 1958-60, Brig and CRA 51 Highland Div 1961-63, dep standing gp rep NATO Cncl 1964-66, resigned 1967; specialist advsr House of Commons Def Ctee 1971-84, dir Br Atlantic Ctee 1978-81; visiting prof: Fletcher Sch of Law Cambridge Mass 1975, Univ of Surrey 1978-86, Univ of Southern Calif 1979; res assoc Inst for Peace and Security Tokyo 1979-88, vice pres Int Inst for Strategic Studies 1988 (dep dir 1967-77); Freeman City of London 1977; Hon Dr political sci Korea Univ S Korea 1977; Order of the Rising Sun (3rd Class) Japan 1984; *Books* The Third World War (jtly, 1978), Europe in the Western Alliance (ed 1988); *Recreations* fly fishing; *Clubs* Army & Navy; *Style*— Brig Kenneth Hunt, OBE, MC; 22 The Green, Ewell, Epsom, Surrey KT17 3JN (☎ 01 393 7906); Int Inst for Strategic Studies, 23 Tavistock St, London WC2E 7NQ (☎ 01 379 7676)

HUNT, Hon Martin John; s of The Rt Hon The Lord Hunt of Tanworth and The Hon Magdalen Mary Hunt (d 1971), da of 1 Baron Robinson; *b* 19 Nov 1962; *Educ* Worth Abbey, The City Univ; *Career* commodity broker, fund mangr Adam, Harding Lueux (asset mangmt) Ltd dir Futures Mgmnt Ltd 1985-; *Recreations* skiing, motor racing, photography, shooting; *Style*— The Hon Martin Hunt; 24 Burnthwaite Rd, London SW6 5BE (☎ 01 381 4988); c/o Adam, Harding and Lueux (Asset Management) Ltd, 109 Jermyn St, London SW1Y 6HA (☎ 01 925 0282)

HUNT, Maurice William; s of Maurice Hunt (d 1987), of London, and Helen, *née* Andrews; *b* 30 August 1936; *Educ* Selhurst GS Croydon Surrey, LSE (BSc); *m* 27 Aug 1960, Jean Mary, da of Herbert Ellis (d 1940); 1 s (Neil b 1965), 1 da (Claire b 1966); *Career* Nat Serv RAF 1955-57; ANZ Bank London 1953-66, Joint Iron Cncl 1967, Bd of Trade DTI 1968-84, RCDS 1982, sec and exec dir ops CBI 1984-; AIB; *Clubs* RAC; *Style*— Maurice Hunt, Esq; 24 Fairford Close, Haywards Heath West Sussex (☎ 0444 452 916); Centre Point, New Oxford St, London WC1A IDU (☎ 01 379 7400, fax 01 240 1578, telex 21332)

HUNT, Hon Michael Anthony; s of Baron Hunt of Tanworth, GCB, and Hon Magdalen, da of 1 Baron Robinson; *b* 1942; *m* 1963, Rosemary Ann, da of late Col Theodore Ernle Longridge, OBE; *Style*— The Hon Michael Hunt; 86 Foxhill, Olney, Bucks, MK46 5HF

HUNT, Michael Ralph; s of Benjamin William Hunt (d 1975), and Marjorie Alice, *née* Atkinson; *b* 8 Jan 1939; *Educ* Haberdashers' Aske's, Bristol Univ (BSc), Bristol Univ (PhD); *m* 8 June 1962, Catherine Claire, da of Sidney Jules Block (d 1974); 2 s (Graham b 1966, Stephen b 1968); *Career* postdoctoral fellowship - Nat Res Cncl, Ottawa Canada 1963-65, scientific off Central Electricity Res Laboratories 1965-70; Akzo Salt Chemical Div Holland: various positions 1970-81, res and devpt dir 1981-82, dir of chloralkali products 1982-86; md Akzo Chemicals Ltd 1986-; memb CBI SE cncl 1987-, memb CEFIC sector gp gen ctee 1982-86; *Books* 6 Scientific Papers, 1 Patent; *Recreations* music, art, sport, skiing, tennis; *Style*— Dr Michael Hunt; 1 Fife Way, Great Bookham, Surrey KT23 3PH (☎ 0372 58616); AKZO Chemicals Ltd, 1-5 Queens Rd, Hersham, Walton-on-Thames, Surrey KT12 5NL (☎ 0932 247891, fax 0932 231204, telex 21997)

HUNT, Adm Sir Nicholas John Streynsham; GCB (1987), (KCB (1985), LVO (1961)); s of Brig and Mrs J M Hunt; *b* 7 Nov 1930; *Educ* BRNC Dartmouth; *m* 1966, Meriel Eve Givan; 2 s, 1 da; *Career* exec offr HMS Ark Royal 1969-71, RCDS 1974, dir of Naval Plans 1976-78, Flag Offr 2 Flotilla 1980-81, dir-gen Naval Manpower and Training 1981-83, Flag Offr Scotland and NI 1983-85, C-in-C Fleet and Allied C-in-C Channel and C-in-C E Atlantic Area 1985-87; former asst private sec to HRH Princess Marina, Duchess of Kent 1987-89; dep md (Orgn and Devpt) Eurotunnel; pres Royal Navy Club (1765 and 1785), cmmnr Cwlth War Graves Cmmn, vice-pres English Speaking Union of Malta, CBIM; *Clubs* Boodle's, Woodroffes; *Style*— Adm Sir Nicholas Hunt, GCB, LVO; c/o Boodles, St James's, London

HUNT, (David) Peter; s of Rev Charles Christopher Hunt (d 1987), of Neasham, Co Durham, and Edna, *née* Clarke; *b* 25 April 1951; *Educ* Grangefield GS Stockton, Keble Coll Oxford (MA); *m* 1 June 1984, Cherryl Janet, da of Alexander Hubert Nicholson, of Pinner, Middx; 2 s (James b 1985, Nicholas b 1987); *Career* called to the Bar Gray's Inn 1974; memb Bar Cncl 1981-84, jr NE circuit 1982; *Books* Distribution of Matrimonial Assets on Divorce (1982); *Recreations* watching cricket, running; *Style*— Peter Hunt, Esq; 25 Dunstarn Dr, Adel, Leeds LS16 8EH (☎ 0532 611 041); 25 Park Square, Leeds LS1 2PW (☎ 0532 451 841, fax 0532 420 194)

HUNT, Sir Rex Masterman; CMG (1980); s of Henry William (d 1982), of Burnham, Bucks, and Ivy Hunt; *b* 29 June 1926; *Educ* Coatham Sch, St Peter's Coll Oxford; *m* 1951, Mavis Amanda, da of George A Buckland; 1 s, 1 da; *Career* RAF 1944-48; Overseas Civil Service 1951: dist cmmr Uganda 1962, CRO 1963-64, first sec Kuching (Sarawak) 1964-65, Jesselton (Sabah) 1965-67, Brunei 1967, first sec (economic) Ankara 1968-70, first sec and head of chancery Jakarta 1970-72, M East dept FCO 1972-74; cnsllr: Saigon 1974-75, Kuala Lumpur 1976-77; dep high cmmr 1977-79, high cmmr Br Antarctic Territory 1980-85; govr and C-in-C Falkland Islands 1980-82, temporarily forced to evacuate Islands owing to Argentinian invasion in April 1982, returned June 1982 as civil cmmr (Govr 1985); pres Falkland Islands Assoc, vice pres World Ship Tst; chm Falkland Islands Fndn; Hon Air Cdre RAuxAF; kt 1982; *Recreations* golf, flying, fishing; *Clubs* Royal Commonwealth Soc; *Style*— Sir Rex Hunt, CMG; c/o FCO, London SW1

HUNT, Richard Bruce; s of late Percy Thompson Hunt; *b* 15 Dec 1927; *Educ* Christ's Hosp; *m* 1972, Ulrike Dorothea, *née* Schmidt; 2 da; *Career* shipbroker, fell Inst of Chartered Shipbrokers 1955, md R B Hunt and Ptrs Ltd 1966-, chm Euro-Gulf Mgmnt (UK) Ltd; dir Baltic Exchange 1977-80 (re-elected 1981, chm 1985-87); govr Christ's Hosp 1980-, Liveryman Worshipful Co of Shipwrights 1980; *Recreations* golf, skiing; *Clubs* MCC, Royal Lymington Yacht, Royal Wimbledon Golf; *Style*— Richard Hunt, Esq; Baltic Exchange Chambers, 14-20 St Mary Axe, London EC3P 3EQ

HUNT, Sir Robert Frederick; CBE (1974), DL (Glos 1977); s of Arthur Hunt, of Cheltenham; *b* 11 May 1918; *Educ* Pates G S Cheltenham, N Glos Tech Coll; *m* 1947, Joy (d 1984), da of Charles Harding; 4 da (Jacqueline m Peter Heywood, *qv*); m 2, 1987, Joyce Baigent, da of Otto Leiske; *Career* WWII RAF RAF Trg Cmd; joined Dowty Equipment as apprentice 1935; Dowty Gp: dir 1956-86, dep chm 1959-86, dep chm 1959-75, chief exec 1975-83, chm 1975-86; dir: Dowty Equipment of Canada 1949-86 (pres 1954-76, chm 1973-86), BL 1980-88 (dep chm 1982-88), Eagle Star Insur 1980-88, Dellfield Ltd 1983-86, Charter Consolidated 1983-; chm: gp mgmnt ctee Cheltenham Hosp 1959-74, Glos AHA 1974-81; Hon DSc Bath, Hon FRAes; FEng, FCASI; kt 1979; *Style*— Sir Robert Hunt, CBE, DL; Maple House, Withington, Glos GL5A 4DA (☎ 0242 89344)

HUNT, Lady Rowena; *née* Montagu-Stuart-Wortley-Mackenzie; yr da of 4 Earl of Wharncliffe (d 1987), and Dowager Countess of Wharncliffe, *qv*; *b* 14 June 1961; *m* 1986, John Hunt, s of Dr H G Hunt, of Greenwich; *Style*— Lady Rowena Hunt; Minety House, Minety, nr Malmesbury, Wilts

HUNT, Terry; s of Thomas John Hund (d 1976) of Taunton, Som and marie Louise, *née* Potter; *b* 8 August 1943; *Educ* Huish's GS Taunton; *m* 7 Jan 1967, Wendy Graeme, da of Dr Aldwyn Morgan George MC of Perranwell Cornwall; 1 s (Philip Benjamin (Ben) b 1968), 1 da (Nicola Jane b 1969); *Career* in hosp admin: Tone Vale Hosp 1963-65, NE Som Hosps 1965-67, Winchester Hosps 1967-69, Lincoln Co Hosp 1969-70; hosp soc Wycombe Gen Hosp 1970-73, dep gr sec Hillingdon Hosps 1973-74, area gen admin Kensington & Chelsea & Westminster AHA (T) 1974-76, dis admin NW Kensington & Chelsea and Westminster 1976-82, dist admin Paddington & N Kensington Health Authy 1982-84; admin and gen mangr NE Thames Regnl Health Authy 1984-; memb : Twyford & Dist Round Table 1975-84 (chm 1980-81, pres 1988), ctee Reading Town Regatta 1983- (tres 1984-86); memb Inst of Health Serv Mgmnt; *Recreations* sculling, rowing, cycling; *Style*— Terry Hunt, Esq; 36 Old Bath Road, Charvil, Reading, Berks (☎ 0734 341 062); 40 Eastbourne Terrace, London W2 (☎ 01 262 8011 ext 2037, fax 01 723 6623)

HUNT OF TANWORTH, Baron (Life Peer UK 1980), of Stratford-upon-Avon; John Joseph Benedict; GCB (1977, KCB 1973, CB 1968); s of Maj Arthur L Hunt, MC (d 1959), of Hale House, Churt, Surrey, and Daphne Hunt (d 1956); *b* 23 Oct 1919; *Educ* Downside, Magdalene Coll Cambridge; *m* 1, 1941, Hon Magdalen Mary (d 1971), da of 1 Baron Robinson (d 1952); 2 s (Hon Michael, *qv*, Hon Martin b 1962), 1 da (Hon Mrs H Gill b 1947); m 2, 1973, Madeleine Frances, da of Sir William Hume, CMG, and wid of Sir John Charles, KCB; *Career* RNVR 1940; Dominions Off 1946, attached off of high cmmr for UK in Ceylon 1948-50, memb directing staff IDC 1951-52, off of high cmmr for UK in Canada 1953-56, private sec to sec of Cabinet 1956-58, private sec to perm sec to Treasy and head of Civil Serv 1957-58, CRO 1958-60, Cabinet Off 1960-62, HM Treasy 1962, under-sec 1965-67, dep-sec 1968, first Civil Serv cmmr and dep sec CSD 1968-71, HM Treasy 1971, second perm sec Cabinet Off 1972, sec Cabinet 1973-79; chm Banque Nationale de Paris 1980-, dir IBM UK 1980-, advsy dir Unilever 1980-; chm: Disaster Emergency Ctee 1981-, govt inquiry into cable expansion and broadcasting policy 1982, Ditchley Fndn 1983-, Tablet Publishing Co 1984-, Prudential Corpn 1985- (dir 1980-, dep chm 1982-85, chm 1985); hon fell Magdalene Coll Cambridge; *Style*— The Rt Hon the Lord Hunt of Tanworth, GCB; 8 Wool Rd, Wimbledon, London SW20 (☎ 01 947 7640)

HUNTER, Hon Alan Marshall; s of Baron Hunter of Newington, MBE, *qv*; *b* 1946; *m* 1971, Elizabeth Goodall; *Style*— The Hon Alan Hunter; 31 Hillcrest Avenue, Nether Poppleton, York

HUNTER, Sir Alexander Albert; KBE (1976); s of Alexander Hunter, KSG; *b* 21 May 1920; *Educ* St John's Coll Belize, Regis Coll Denver USA, Queen's Univ Kingston Canada; *m* 1947, Araceli; 1 s, 2 da; *Career* served WWII RAF; joined James Brodie and Co 1947, co sec 1948, dir 1952-61, conslt 1975-82; Belize: MLA (PUP) 1961, min of Natural Resources Commerce and Industry 1961, MHR (PUP) 1965, min of Natural Resources and Trade 1965-69, min of Trade and Industry 1969-74; speaker of the House of Represenatives of Belize 1974-79; rep of and conslt to: Auschutz

Overseas Corp (Petroleum) Denver Colorado 1975-82, Pecten Belize Co (Shell Oil) Houston Texas 1982-; *Style—* Sir Alexander Hunter, KBE; 6 St Matthew St, Caribbean Shores, Belize City, Belize (☎ 44482)

HUNTER, Alexander Dudgeon; s of Ellis Dudgeon Hunter (d 1964), Monkscroft, Dunbar; *b* 5 Sept 1920; *Educ* Merchiston Castle Edinburgh, Heriot-Watt Univ Edinburgh; *m* 1944, Iris Patricia, da of William Grieve Reid Findlay (d 1963), of Felbrigg, Dunbar; *Career* chm, md and head brewer Belhaven Brewery Co Ltd 1972-82, dir Belhaven Brewery Gp 1972-82; brewing conslt 1983; *Recreations* swimming, gardening; *Clubs* Merchistonian, Scottish Wayfarers, Dunbar S and RFC; *Style—* Alexander Hunter, Esq; Monkscroft, Dunbar, East Lothian (☎ 0368 63309)

HUNTER, Andrew Robert Frederick; MP (C) Basingstoke 1983-; s of Sqdn Ldr Roger Hunter, DFC, of Winchester, and Winifred Mary, *née* Nelson; *b* 8 Jan 1943; *Educ* St George's Sch Harpenden, Durham Univ, Jesus Coll Cambridge; *m* 1972, Janet, da of Samuel Bourne, of Gloucester; 1 s, 1 da; *Career* Maj TAVR (resigned 1984); in indust 1969, asst master Harrow Sch 1971-83; Parly candidate (C) Southampton Itchen 1979, Sec Cons Environment Ctee 1984-85, memb Agric Select Ctee 1985, PPS to Lord Elton Min of State DOE 1985-86, memb Environment Select Ctee 1986-, vice chm Cons Agric Ctee 1987-, fndr chm Parly Br/Bophuthatswana Gp 1987-, memb CLA Agric Ctee 1986-; vice-pres: Nat Prayer Book Soc 1987-, NFU, Br Field Sports Soc (chm falconry ctee 1988); Order of Polonia Restituta; *Recreations* field sports, cricket, military history, toy soldiers; *Clubs* MCC; *Style—* Andrew Hunter, Esq, MP; House of Commons, London SW1A OAA (☎ 01 219 5216)

HUNTER, Brig (John) Antony; DSO (1944), OBE (1955, MBE 1943), MC 1942; s of Maj Gen Sir Alan Hunter, KCVO, CB, CMG, DSO, MC (d 1942), and Hon Joan, *née* Adderley, da of 5 Baron Norton; *b* 12 Sept 1914; *Educ* Stowe, RMC Sandhurst; *m* 1, 14 Feb 1944 (m dis 1971), Dauphine Laetitia Janet Colquhoun (d 1979), da of Nicholas Conyngham Simons Bosanquet (d 1955); 1 s (Antony b 1945), 1 da (Sarah (Mrs Ellson) b 1947); m 2, 1971 Carole da of Dr David Reid Milligan (d 1985); *Career* cmmnd 60 Rifles 1934, regtl serv 1945-49: Ireland, Burma, Egypt; GSO3 (later GSO2) intelligence GHQ Middle East 1940-41, Co Cdr 1 KRRC Western Desert and Libya 1941-42, Bde Maj 4 Armd Bde El Alamein 1942, Staff Coll Haifa 1942-43, GSO2 ops HQ 13 Corps invasion of Sicily 1943, DSD Staff Coll Camberley 1943-44, CO 8 Bn The Rifle Bde Normandy to Germany 1944-45, GSO1 HQ 21 Army Gp Germany 1945-46, chief instr New Coll Sandhurst 1947-50, Jt Servs Staff Coll 1951, GSO1 6 Armd Div Germany 1952-55, CO 1 Bn Bedfordshire and Hertfordshire Regt 1955-57, Col GS Middle East ops WO Whitehall 1957-59, cdr 11 Inf Bde Gp Germany 1960, ret 1960; Union Castle Line: 2 i/c Southampton 1960-63, directing staff Admin Staff Coll Henley 1963-64, area dir Southampton 1964-77 (also dir: Union Castle Line, Cayzer Irving & Co, London & Southampton Stevedoring Co); regnl dir Lloyds Bank Salisbury region 1974-85, dir Red Funnel Gp 1977-85 (chm Vectis Tport Co), pres Ocean Sound Hldgs plc (dir 1984-), dir Southampton C of C 1966-75 (pres 1972-73); Freeman: City of London 1983, Worshipful Co of Bowyers 1983; FIOD 1966-85, MBIM 1966-77, MCIT 1966-77; *Recreations* fishing, shooting, archery, skiing; *Style—* Brig Antony Hunter, DSO, OBE, MC; Ocean Sound Hldgs plc, Fareham, Hants PO15 5PA

HUNTER, Doreen Eleanor Maude; *née* Hunter; da of James Wylie Hunter, of 9 Larch Hill Avenue, Craigavad, Holywood, Co Down, and Maude Elizabeth, *née* Warnock; *b* 14 Feb 1940; *Educ* Richmond Lodge Sch Belfast, Queen's Univ Belfast (BA), Reading Univ (Dip Ed); *Career* headmistress: Princess Gardens Sch Belfast 1982-87, Hunterhouse Coll Belfast 1987-; govr Rockport Prep Sch Co Down 1987-, chm ptnrship NI Boarding Schs and Colls 1987-; dir NI Railways 1987-; memb SHA 1982-; *Recreations* gardening, golf; *Clubs* Royal Belfast GC; *Style—* Miss Doreen Hunter; Hunterhouse Coll, Finaghy, Belfast BT10 0LE (☎ 0232 612293/612 588)

HUNTER, Geoffrey Martin; s of Albert Hunter, of Chester-le-Street, Co Durham, and Mary, *née* Martin; *b* 4 Jan 1956; *Educ* Chester-le-Street GS, Univ of Newcastle-upon-Tyne (LLB); *Career* called to the Bar Gray's Inn 1979, in practice NE circuit; *Recreations* motor sport, hot-air ballooning, ornithology; *Style—* G M Hunter, Esq; 73 Westgate Rd, Newcastle-upon-tyne NE1 1SQ, (☎ 091 261 4407, 091 232 9785, fax 091 222 1845)

HUNTER, Sir Ian Bruce Hope; MBE (1945); s of William O Hunter; *b* 2 April 1919; *Educ* Fettes Coll, Edinburgh; *m* 1, 1949, Susan (d 1977), da of late Brig Alec Gaudie Russell; 4 da (Eugenie, Josephine, Serena, Catherine); m 2, 1984, Marie Sadie, da of Charles Golden, and widow of Sir Keith Showering (d 1982); 4 step-s, 2 step-da; *Career* dir numerous music festivals in UK and Int: Edinburgh 1950-55, Bath 1948-68, London 1962-80, Brighton 1967-83; dir gen Cwlth Arts' Festival 1965; dir Harold Holt Ltd; chm: London Festival Ballet Trust 1984-; Musicians Benevolent Fund 1987-; RCM 1984, FRSA (chm 1981-83); kt 1983; *Clubs* Garrick; *Style—* Sir Ian Hunter, MBE; Harold Holt Ltd, 31 Sinclair Rd, London W14

HUNTER, Hon Ian Thorburn; s of Baron Hunter of Newington, MBE, *qv*; *b* 1951; *m* 1974, Angela Hill; *Style—* The Hon Ian Hunter; 27 Affleck Gdns, Monikie, by Dundee

HUNTER, Hon Mrs (Iona Hélöise); da of Baron Tanlaw (Life Peer); *b* 1960; *m* 1978, Stephen P Hunter; *Style—* The Hon Mrs Hunter

HUNTER, (Mary) Irene; *née* Durlacher; MBE (1956); da of Cyril Charles Henry Durlacher (d 1968), and Glady Caroline, *née* Armstrong (d 1946); *b* 29 Sept 1919; *Educ* Caledonia Sch Sussex, Queen Anne's Sch Reading; *m* 1, 16 Oct 1956, Jean Francois Clouët des Pesruches Campagnon de la Liberation, OBE, MC (d 1957), s of Col Jean Clouët des Pesruches (d 1945); m 2, 13 Aug 1964, Antony Noel Hunter, MBE (d 1967), s of Noel Hunter (d 1954); *Career* WWII SOE served India and China 1941-45; Imperial Airways publicity dept 1937-41; PA: Jack Hylton 1946-47, Stuart Advtg 1947-49, HM Serv in Luxemborg, UN NY and Paris (Sir Gladwyn Jebb, now Lord Gladwyn in latter two posts) 1949-56, Baroness Jackson (Barbara Ward) 1968-81, Lord Gladwyn 1968-; memb Cncl Int Inst for Environment and Devpt; *Recreations* horse racing, cooking; *Style—* Mrs Irene Hunter; 21 Smith Terrace, London SW3 4DL (☎ 01 352 3289)

HUNTER, John Murray; CB (1980), MC (1943); s of Rev John Mercer Hunter (d 1968), of Fife, and Frances Margaret, *née* Martin (d 1953); *b* 10 Nov 1920; *Educ* Kirkcaldy HS, Fettes Coll, Clare Coll Cambridge (BA); *m* 1948, Margaret Mary Phyllis, da of Stanley Cursiter, CBE (d 1976); 2 s (Andrew, David), 3 da (Frances, Sunniva, Caroline); *Career* served Army 1941-45: W Desert, N Africa, Italy, Capt The Rifle Brigade; Rugby Football Cambridge 1946, Scotland 1947; Dip Serv: consul gen Buenos Aires 1969-71, head of Latin America Dept FCO 1971-73; cmmnr for admin and finance Forestry cmmn 1976-1981; Scottish tourist guide; chm Edinburgh W End Community Cncl 1983-86; *Recreations* music, curling; *Clubs* Scottish Tourist Guides Assoc, Nat Tst for Scotland, Hawks; *Style—* Murray Hunter, Esq, CB, MC; 21 Glencairn Cres, Edinburgh EH12 5BT (☎ 031 337 8785)

HUNTER, John Starkey; CBE (1976); s of Capt Bentley Moore Hunter, RAMC (ka 1917), and Gladys Maud, *née* Starkey (d 1961); *b* 7 April 1916; *Educ* Berkhamstead, Magdalen Coll Oxford (MA, BSc); *m* 1940, Iris Perrine Diana, da of Maj Percy Douglas Saxton MC (d 1950); 1 s (Michael b 1943); *Career* dir Distillers Co Ltd 1964-67; md BP Chemicals Int Ltd 1973-76, dir BP Trading Co Ltd 1973-76, ret; non-exec dir: Scott Bader Co Ltd 1979-81, Assoc Br Industs 1980-88; pres Chemical Industs Assoc 1974-76; *Style—* John Hunter Esq, CBE; Apt 29, The Mansion, Albury, Guildford, Surrey GU5 9BB (☎ 048 641 3296)

HUNTER, Keith Robert; OBE (1981); s of Robert Ernest Williamson Hunter (d 1967), of Hull, and Winifred Mary, *née* Bradshaw; *b* 29 May 1936; *Educ* Hymers Coll Hull, Magdalen Coll Oxford (MA), SOAS, Inst of Educ Univ of London; *m* 21 Dec 1959 (m dis 1989), Ann Patricia, da of Fredrick Fuller, of Eastbourne; 1 s (James b 1965), 2 da (Alisoun b 1961, Euphan b 1963); *Career* Nat Serv RAEC 1954-56; Br Cncl 1960-: Cambodia 1960-64, London 1964-66, Hong Kong 1967-69, Malaysia 1970-74, Algeria 1975-78, China 1979-82, controller Arts Div london 1985-; *Recreations* music; *Style—* Keith Hunter, Esq, OBE; The British Council, 11 Portland Place, London W1N 4EJ (☎ 01 389 3044)

HUNTER, (James) Martin Hugh; s of Colin Boorer Garrett Hunter (d 1950), of IOW, and Barbara Anne Crawford, *née* Cavendish (d 1962); *b* 23 Mar 1937; *Educ* Shrewsbury, Pembroke Coll Cambridge (MA); *m* 21 Jan 1972, Linda Mary, da of Francis Kenneth Ernest Gamble (1971); *Career* admitted slr 1963, ptnr Freshfields 1967- (asst slr 1963); Freeman: City of London, Worshipful Co of Arbitrators, City of London Slrs Co, Worshipful Co of Spectacle Makers; memb Law Soc; FCIArb; *Books* Law & Practice of International Commercial Arbitration (with Alan Redfern 1986); ed: Arbitration Title, Butterworths Encyclopedia of Forms & Precedents; *Recreations* cruising under sail, golf; *Clubs* Royal Cruising, Sunningdale Golf; *Style—* Martin Hunter, Esq; Freshfields, Grindall House, 25 Newgate St, London EC1A 7LH (☎ 01 606 6677, fax 01 248 2435, telex 884 242)

HUNTER, Muir Vane Skerrett; QC (1965); s of Hugh Stewart Hunter (d 1980), and Bluebell Matilda, *née* Williams (d 1980); *b* 19 August 1913; *Educ* Westminster, Ch Ch Oxford (MA); *m* 1, 29 July 1939, Dorothea Verstone (d 1986), 1 da (Camilla b 7 April 1947); m 2, 4 July 1986, Gillian Victoria Joyce Petrie; *Career* WWII serv: enlisted RTR 1940, cmmnd 2 Lt RMA Sandhurst 1941, 2 Royal Gloucestershire Hussars, transferred 7 KOYLI (renamed 149 Regt RAC) 1941, Capt (Bde IO) 50 Indian Tank Bde India 1941, Staff Capt (GSO 3) Gen Staff Intelligence GHQ New Delhi 1942, Lt-Col (GSO 1) War and Legislative Depts Govt of India New Delhi (judge of anti-corruption tbnl Lahore and Karachi) 1943, ret 1945, demobbed with rank of Hon Lt-Col 1946; Master of Bench Gray's Inn 1975 (called to Bar 1938); fndr-chm N Kensington Neighbourhood Law Centre 1970, memb exec and cncl Justice 1961-88, memb and int observer Amnesty Int, int observer Int Cmmn of Jurists; memb ctees DTI: advsy ctee on Draft EEC Bankruptcy Convention 1973-76, Insolvency Law Review Ctee 1977-82; govr RSC 1980-, memb cncl Royal Shakespeare Theatre Tst 1970-; memb Gen Cncl of the Bar, MRI; *Books* Williams on Bankruptcy (later Williams & Muir Hunter on Bankruptcy, ed 1948, 1958, 1968, 1979), Muir Hunter on Personal Insolvency (sr author 1988), Kerr on Receivers and Administrators (supervising ed 1989); *Recreations* travel, theatre, music; *Clubs* Hurlingham, Union (Oxford); *Style—* Muir Hunter, Esq, QC; 43 Church Rd, Barnes, London SW13 9HQ (☎ 01 748 6693); The Stable Ho, Donhead St Andrew, Shaftesury, Dorset SP7 8EB (☎ 0747 88 779); 3 Paper Bldgs, Temple, London EC4Y 7EU (☎ 01 353 3721)

HUNTER, Dame Pamela; *née* Greenwell; DBE (1981); da of Col Thomas George Greenwell, TD, JP, DL (d 1967), of Whitburn Hall, Co Durham, and Mabel Winifred, *née* Catcheside (d 1967); *b* 3 Oct 1919; *Educ* Westonbirt Sch, Eastbourne Sch of Domestic Economy; *m* 1942, Gordon Lovegrove Hunter, s of Sir Summers Hunter, JP (d 1963), of Jesmond, Newcastle upon Tyne; 1 s (Mark), 1 da (Victoria); *Career* served WRNS 1942-45; memb: Northumbrian Water Authy 1973-77, Berwick-upon-Tweed Boro Cncl 1973-83; chm: Northern Area Cons Women's Advsy Ctee 1972-75 (vice-chm 1969-72), Cons Women's Nat Advsy Ctee 1978-81 (vice-chm 1974-75); vice-pres Nat Union of Cons and Unionist Assoc 1985- (memb exec ctee 1971-88, vice chm 1981-84, chm 1984-85); vice-pres local ctees: Nat Soc of Prevention of Cruelty to Children, RNLI; elected Chatton Parish Cncl 1987;; *Recreations* politics, antiques, the garden, crosswords; *Clubs* Lansdowne; *Style—* Dame Pamela Hunter, DBE; The Coach House, Chatton, Alnwick, Northumberland NE66 5PY (☎ 066 85259)

HUNTER, Peter Basil; s of Harry Norman Hunter, and Martha Rose, *née* Lloyd-Jones; *b* 19 Oct 1938; *Educ* Kingswood Sch Bath, Oxford Sch of Arch (Dip Arch); *Career* architect, ptnr Shepheard Epstein and Hunter 1962, involvement with: Univ of Lancaster, local authy housing, inner city devpt such as Salford Quays Manchester and Laganside Belfast; former Civic Tst Assessor; memb RIBA, FSAI; *Recreations* music; *Style—* Peter Hunter, Esq; 33 Centre Point House, St Giles High St, London WC2H 8LW (☎ 01 497 9448); Shepheard Epstein and Hunter, 14-22 Banton St, London W1V 1LB 01 734 0111, fax 01 434 2690)

HUNTER, Peter Duncan; s of Thomas H D Hunter, of Kirriemuir, Angus, and Dr Margaret, *née* Macnaughton; *b* 25 July 1956; *Educ* Strathallan, Downing Coll Cambridge (MA), Lincoln Coll Oxford; *Career* master: Gordonstoun 1979-85, Lawrenceville New Jersey 1983-84, Harrow 1985-; *Recreations* golf, fencing, furniture restoration; *Style—* Peter Hunter, Esq; 80 Great King St, Edinburgh (☎ 031 556 4989); The Park, Harrow on the Hill, Middx (☎ 01 864 6894)

HUNTER, Philip Brown; TD (1949); s of Charles Edward Hunter (d 1956), of Heswall Wirral, and Marion, *née* Harper (d 1960); *b* 30 May 1909; *Educ* Birkenhead Sch, London Univ (LLB); *m* 1 May 1937, Joyce Mary, da of John Holt (d 1969), of Hoylake, Wirral; 2 s (Charles b 1946, James b 1949), 2 da (Philippa b 1938, Katharine b 1955); *Career* WWII 1939-45: cmmnd TARA 1939 (Capt 1941, Maj 1942) served India and Burma; ptnr Laces & Co slrs 1946-60, chm Cammell Laird 1966-70 (dir 1949-70), chm John Holt & Co (Liverpool) Ltd 1967-71 (dir 1957-71), dir Guardian Assur 1967-69, dir Guardian Royal Exchange 1969-79; memb Law Soc; *Recreations* sailing, gardening; *Clubs* Caledonian; *Style—* Philip Hunter, Esq, TD; Bryn Hyfryd, Holywell, Clwyd; Greystones, Trearddur Bay, Holyhead, Anglesey

HUNTER, Hon Robert Douglas; s of Baron Hunter of Newington, MBE, *qv*; *b* 1945; *m* 1969, Marion Mckenzie; *Style—* The Hon Robert Hunter; 2 Lindsay Ave, Cheadle

Hulme, Cheshire, SK8 7BQ

HUNTER, William Hill; CBE (1971), JP (1970), DL (1987); s of Robert Dalglish Hunter (d 1942), of Ayrshire, and Margaret Walker, *née* Hill (d 1977); *b* 5 Nov 1916; *Educ* Cumnock Acad; *m* 22 March 1947, Kathleen, da of William Alfred Cole (d 1966), of Cardiff; 2 s (John b 1950, Robert b 1953); *Career* Private RASC 1940, cmmnd RA 1941, Severn Fixed Defences 1941-44, Staff Capt Middle East with Br Mil Govt Cyrenaica 1944-46; CA 1940; ptnr McLay McAlister and McGibbon Glasgow 1946-; dir: Abbey Nat Building Soc scottish advsy bd 1966-86, City of Glasgow Friendly Soc 1966- (pres 1980-), J and G Grant Glenfarclas Distillery 1966-, CBI Scottish Cncl 1978-84; pres: Renfrew West and Inverclyde Cons and Unionist Assoc 1972-, Scottish Young Unionist Assoc 1958-60, Scottish Unionist Assoc 1964-65; Parly candidate (Unionist) South Ayrshire 1959 and 1964; chm: Salvation Army Advsy Bd in Strathclyde 1982-, Salvation Army Housing Assoc Scotland Ltd; hon tres Quarrier's Homes 1972-; deacon convener The Trades House of Glasgow 1986-87; *Recreations* gardening, golf, swimming, music; *Clubs* The Western (Glasgow), The Royal Scottish Automobile (Glasgow); *Style*— William Hill Hunter, Esq, CBE, JP, DL; Armitage, Kilmacolm (☎ 050 587 2444); McLay McAlister and McGibbon CA, 53 Bothwell Street, Glasgow G2 6TF (☎ 041 221 6516)

HUNTER GORDON, Christopher Neil (Kit); s of Lt-Col Patrick Hunter Gordon CBE, MC, JP, DL (d 1978), of Ballindou, Beauly, Inverness, and Valerie Margaret Frances, *née* Ziani de Ferranti; *b* 8 June 1958; *Educ* Ampleforth, Trinity Hall Cambridge (MA); *m* 29 Sept 1984, Georgina Mary, da of Capt Owen Buckingham Varney, of Hill House, Dedham, Essex; 1 s (Sam William b 5 March 1988); *Career* J Rothschild Hldgs plc, md Aurit Services 1983-85, dir Comcap plc 1986, jt md and co-fndr The Summit Gp plc 1985-, alt dir Atlantic Computers plc 1987-89; *Recreations* painting, architectural design, skiing, windsurfing; *Clubs* Brook's, Chelsea Arts, Utd Oxford and Cambridge Univs; *Style*— Kit Hunter Gordon, Esq; 31 Alexander St, London W2 5NU (☎ 01 229 7566); The Summit Group plc, 49 Pall Mall, London SW1Y 5JG (☎ 01 930 7682, fax 01 935 3576, car tel 0860 518281, telex 296816)

HUNTER GORDON, John Hugh; s of late Maj P Hunter Gordon, MC, DL; *b* 7 June 1942; *Educ* Eton, St Andrews Univ, Univ of Geneva; *m* 1966, Jillian Margaret, *née* Fox-Carlyon; 3 children; *Career* md: Ferranti Offshore Systems Ltd 1974-88, TRW-Ferranti Subsea Ltd 1977-88, Ferranti Industl Electronics Ltd 1986-88, Murray-Johnstone Europe Ltd 1988-; dir: Cairngorm Chairlift Co Ltd 1966, Ferranti ORE Inc 1982-88; *Clubs* Highland; *Style*— John Hugh Hunter Gordon, Esq; Highfield House, Kirknewton, Midlothian (☎ 0506 881489)

HUNTER GORDON, Nigel; s of Maj Patrick Hunter Gordon, MC (d 1978), of Ballindour House, Beauly, Inverness-shire, and Valerie Margaret France, *née* Ziami de Ferranti; *b* 2 Sept 1947; *Educ* Ampleforth, St Andrews Univ (MA); *m* 16 April 1977, Linda Anne, da of Brendan Robert Magill, of Eastbourne; 2 s (Kim b 23 March 1981, Bret b 19 March 1983); *Career* trained as CA Coopers & Lybrand 1970-76, James C Pringle & Co CA Inverness 1977-79, tax ptnr Ernst & Whinney 1983 (joined 1979); Highland Area rep on Tax Practices ctee, chm Highland Area Tax ctee; ACA 1977, FCA 1975, ATII 1979; *Recreations* skiing, windsurfing; *Clubs* Highland; *Style*— Nigel Hunter Gordon, Esq; Killearnan House, Muir of Ord, Ross-shire (☎ 0463 870002); Ernst & Whinney, Moray House, 16 Bank St, Inverness (☎ 0463 237581, fax 0463 226098, telex 75561)

HUNTER JONES, Col Hugh Edward; CBE (1980), MC (1942), TD (1946), JP (Essex 1965), DL (1961); s of Stanley Hunter Jones, of Marden Ash House, Ongar, Essex (d 1961); *b* 20 July 1915; *Educ* Rugby, Corpus Christi Coll Cambridge (MA); *m* 1947, Sheila Kathleen, da of Alfred Dickinson (d 1952), of The Lodge, Lanchester; 3 s (Nigel, Patrick, Nicholas), 1 da (Sarah); *Career* served Essex Yeo (CO 1959-62) 1938-43 MEF (Staff Coll Haifa 1943), staff appts in Italy and Germany 1944-46, dep cdr RA 54 Div 1964-67 (cdr 1967), Actg Brig; dir Charrington & Co until 1976, chm Hotel and Catering Indust Trg Bd 1973-85;pres Br Inst of Innkeeping 1981-85; Master Worshipful Co of Merchant Taylors 1976-77; chm E Anglian TAVR Assoc 1976-80; ADC to HM The Queen 1966-70; High Sheriff Essex 1963-64;; *Recreations* country pursuits; *Clubs* Cavalry and Guards; *Style*— Col Hugh Hunter Jones, CBE, MC, TD, JP, DL; Church Farm, Langham, Colchester, Essex CO4 5PS (☎ 0206 322181)

HUNTER OF HUNTERSTON, Neil Aylmer; formerly Neil Aylmer Kennedy-Cochran-Patrick, officially recognised by the Lord Lyon in the name of Hunter of Hunterston 1969; 29 laird of Hunterston; recognised as chief of Clan Hunter by Lord Lyon 1983; s of William John Charles Kennedy-Cochran-Patrick, DSO, MC (k in airplane accident 1933), and Natalie Bertha, *née* Tanner (d 1966); *b* 5 May 1926; *Educ* Eton, Ridley Coll Ontario Canada, Trinity Coll Cambridge, Sorbonne; *m* 1952, Sonia Isabelle Jane, da of late Brig Dennis Walter Furlong, DSO, OBE, MC; 6 s (Charles b 1954 *qv*, Robert b 1955, Nigel b 1957, John (twin) b 1957, Angus b 1960, Richard b 1962), 1 da (Pauline b 1953); *Heir* s, Charles Dennis Hunter yr of Hunterston; *Career* served WWII RNVR; silver medallist (yachting) Olympic Games 1956; memb Royal Co of Archers (Queen's Body Guard for Scotland); OStJ; *Recreations* sailing, skiing, shooting, fishing; *Clubs* Royal Yacht Sqdn; *Style*— Hunter of Hunterston; Tour d'Escas, La Massana, Principat d'Andorra (☎ 010 33 628 35029, telex 590301 AB Hunter 301 AND)

HUNTER OF HUNTERSTON, YOUNGER, Charles Dennis; s and h of Hunter of Hunterston, *qv*; *b* 16 Feb 1954; *Educ* Eton, RAC Cirencester; *m* 1979, Joanna, da of Alistair Malcolm Morison Scottish Law Lord as Lord Morison, QC, of Edinburgh; 1 s (Ruaraidh b 1983); *Career* co dir; admin Clan Hunter Assoc; FRGS; *Recreations* sailing, shooting; *Clubs* Royal Yacht Sqdn, New (Edinburgh); *Style*— Charles Hunter of Hunterston, yr; Hunterston Castle, West Kilbride, Ayrshire, KA23 9QL; (telex 778373 HUNTER G); office: Central Cottage, PO Box 4, Hunterston Castle, West Kilbride, Ayrshire KA23 9QL (☎ (0294) 823077)

HUNTER OF NEWINGTON, Baron (Life Peer UK 1978); Robert Brockie Hunter; MBE (1945); s of late Robert Marshall Hunter, of Edinburgh; *b* 14 July 1915; *Educ* George Watson's Coll, Univ of Edinburgh (MB, ChB); *m* 1940, Kathleen Margaret, da of James Wilkie Douglas, master painter, of Perth; 3 s (Hon Robert, *qv*, Hon Alan, *qv*), 1 da (Hon Mrs Edward b 1948); *Career* WWII Lt-Col RAMC NW Europe and Egypt, personal physician to Field-Marshal Montogomery 1944-45; prof materia medica pharmacology and therapeutics: Univ of St Andrews 1948-67 (dean Faculty of Med 1958-62), Univ of Dundee 1967-68; vice-chllr and princ Univ of Birmingham 1968-81; memb; Advsy Ctee on Med Res (Scotland) 1955-60, GMC 1962-68, Clinical Res Bd MRC 1960-64, Miny of Health Ctee on Safety of Drugs 1963-68, W Midlands RHA 1974-80, Mgmnt ctee King Edward's Hosp Fund for London 1980-84; chm: Clinical Trials Sub-Ctee UGC 1964-68, Med Sub-Ctee UGC 1966-68, Med Advsy Ctee of Ctee of Vice-Chllrs and Princs, DHSS Working Pty on Med Admins in Health Serv 1970-72, DHSS Ind Sci Ctee on Smoking and Health 1973-80; advsr to Imp Tobacco 1981-83; memb: House of Lords Select Ctee on Sci and Technol 1980-87, House of Lords Ctee on Euro Communities (sub-ctee C); DL 1975; Hon LLD: Dundee, Birmingham; Hon DSc Aston; FRCP 1962, FRCPE, F Inst Biol, FACP, FFCM, FRSE; kt 1977; *Recreations* fishing; *Clubs* Oriental; *Style*— The Rt Hon the Lord Hunter of Newington, MBE, TD; 3 Oakdene Drive, Barnt Green, Birmingham B45 8LQ (☎ 021 445 2636)

HUNTER SMART, (William) Norman; s of William Hunter Smart (d 1960), and Margaret Thorburn, *née* Inglis (d 1966); *b* 25 May 1921; *Educ* George Watson's Coll Edinburgh; *m* 1, 9 Feb 1948 (d 1974), Bridget Beryl, da of Dr Edward Philip Andreae (d 1975); 4 s (Alastair, Charles, James, Ian); m 2, 3 Dec 1977, Sheila Smith, da of Graham Mushet Speirs (d 1965), 1 step s (Robin); *Career* RAC Trg Centre 1941-42, cmmnd 1 Lothians and Border Horse 1943, 2 Lt Warwickshire Yeomanry, Capt (Adj)1944; (despatches); serv: M East 1943, UK 1945, Germany 1946; CA 1948, ptnr Hays Akers and Hays 1950-86, sr ptnr Hays Allan 1984-86 (ret), dir C J Sims Ltd 1963-, chm Charterhouse Devpt Capital Fund Ltd 1987-; memb: The Gaming Bd of GB 1985-, Scottish Legal Aid Bd 1987-; pres Inst of CAs of Scotland 1978-79, chm Assoc of CAs London 1970-72, pres London Watsonian Club 1975-; *Recreations* gardening; *Clubs* The Caledonian; *Style*— Norman Hunter Smart, Esq; Lauriel House, Knowle Lane, Cranleigh, Surrey GU6 8JW (☎ 0483 273513)

HUNTER STEVENS, Michel; s of Aubrey Hunter Stevens, of Norfolk, and Odette Denise Nichols, *née* Malter, whose f was advsr to King of the Belgians on constitutional law; *b* 24 April 1946; *Educ* King's Sch Ely; *m* (m dis); 1 s (Marcus Hunter b 1974), 1 da (Philippa Rachel b 1976); *Career* qual CA 1974; with Tansley Witt and Co 1974-76, joined Price Waterhouse and Co Brussels 1976-77; Hunter Stevens CAs; *Recreations* skiing, tennis, walking, tree planting, music, racing; *Clubs* Chelsea; *Style*— Michel Hunter Stevens, Esq; Linden House, Abbots Ripton, Cambs PE17 2LJ (☎ 04873 365); 3 The Quay, St Ives, Cambridgeshire PE17 4BR (☎ 0480 67567)

HUNTER-BLAIR, Sir Edward Thomas; 8 Bt (GB 1786), of Dunskey; s of Sir James Hunter-Blair, 7 Bt (d 1985), and Jean Galloway MacIntyre (d 1953); *b* 15 Dec 1920; *Educ* Eton, Univ of Paris, Balliol Coll Oxford (BA); *m* 21 April 1956, Norma (d 1972), er da of Walter S Harris (d 1983), of Bradford, Yorks; 1 adopted s (Alan Walter b 1961), 1 adopted da (Helen Cecilia b 1963); *Heir* bro, James Hunter-Blair b 18 March 1926; *Career* serv WWII 1939-41 with KOYLI, discharged; temp civil servant Miny of Info 1941-43; journalist London Evening News (asst foreign ed) 1944-49; mangr and dir own co in Yorks 1950-63, landowner and forester SW Scotland 1964-; memb Kirkcudbright CC 1970-71; memb Scottish Countryside Activities Cncl; Timber Growers UK SW Scotland ctee; *Books* Scotland Sings, a Story of Me (poems and autobiog, 1981), A Future Time, with an Earlier Life (poems, autobiog and prophesy), A Mission in Life (philosophy, religion, autobiog, poems, 1987); *Recreations* gardening, hill-walking; *Clubs* Western Meeting (Ayr), Royal Overseas League; *Style*— Sir Edward T Hunter-Blair, Bt; Parton House, Castle Douglas, Kirkcudbrightshire DG7 3NB (☎ 064 47 234)

HUNTER-TOD, Air Marshal Sir John Hunter; KBE (1971, OBE 1956), CB (1969); s of Hunter Finlay Tod (d 1923), of 11 Upper Wimpole St, London, and Yvonne Grace, *née* Rendall (who m 2, Cdr A P N Thorowgood, DSO, and d 1981); *b* 21 April 1917; *Educ* Marlborough, Trinity Coll Cambridge (MA), Coll of Aeronautics Cranfield (DCAe); *m* 12 Dec 1959, (Gwenith Ruth) Anne, da of late Thomas Chaffer Howard; 1 s (James Fredrik b 3 Dec 1960); *Career* cmmnd RAF 1940; served in night fighters Fighter Cmd and Middle E; HQME staff 1942; Actg Wing Cdr 1944; Air Miny 1945-46; Coll of Aeronautics Cranfield 1946-48; Guided Weapons Dept Royal Aircraft Estab 1949-55; HQ Fighter Cmd 1955-57; Br Jt Servs Mission, Washington DC (as Gp Capt) 1957-60; dep dir radio Air Miny 1960-62; Air Cdre 1963; dir guided weapons (Air), Min of Aviation 1962-65; Air Offr Engrg, RAF Germany 1965-67; AOC No 24 Gp RAF 1967-70; Air Vice-Marshal 1968; head of engrg and dir-gen of Engrg RAF 1970-73; Air Marshal 1971; ret 1973; memb ctee Sunninghill Cons Assoc; chm Ascot branch RNLI; CEng, Hon DSc Cranfield Inst of Technol 1974; *Recreations* gardening; *Clubs* RAF; *Style*— Air Marshal Sir John Hunter, KBE, CB; 21 Ridge Hill, Dartmouth, Devon TQ6 9PE (☎ 08043 3130)

HUNTING, (Lindsay) Clive; s of Gerald Lindsay Hunting (d 1966), and Ruth, *née* Pyman (d 1972); *b* 22 Dec 1925; *Educ* Loretto, Trinity Hall Cambridge (MA); *m* 4 Oct 1952, Shelagh Mary Pamela, da of Capt A N V Hill-Lowe; 1 s (Peter), 1 da (Deborah); *Career* RN 1944-47; Hunting Gp of Cos: joined 1950, dir 1952, vice-chm 1962, chm 1975-; chm Hunting Petroleum Servs plc 1975-85; pres: Br Independent Air Tport Assoc 1960-62, Fedn Internationale de Transporte Aerien Privée 1961-63, Air Educn and Recreation Orgn 1970, Soc of Br Aerospace Cos Ltd 1985-86 (previously tres and cncl memb); chm Air League 1968-71; memb ct Cranfield Inst of Technol 1980-, cdre Royal London YC; Nile Gold Medal for Aerospace Educn 1982; Freeman City of London 1982, former Master Worshipful Co of Coachmakers Coach Harness Makers; CBIM 1980, CRAeS 1983, FRSA 1984; *Recreations* fishing, yachting, bird watching; *Clubs* Royal Yacht Sqdn, Royal London YC; *Style*— Clive Hunting, Esq; April Cottage, Alderbourne Lane, Fulmer, Slough SL3 6JB; The Hunting Gp of Cos, 8th Floor, Bowater House East, 68 Knightsbridge, London SW1X 7LT (☎ 01 589 6383, fax 01 581 0842, telex 8952636)

HUNTINGDON, Bishop of 1980-; Rt Rev (William) Gordon Roe; s of William Henry Roe (d 1965), and Dorothy Myrtle, *née* Hayman (d 1975); *b* 5 Jan 1932; *Educ* Bournemouth Sch, Jesus Coll Oxford, St Stephen's House Oxford (MA, DPhil, DipTh); *m* 1953, Mary Primrose, da of Nils Arthur Efram Andreén (d 1973); 2 s (Patrick b 1957, Michael b 1964), 2 da (Helen b 1955, Rachel b 1959); *Career* RAEC Sjt Instr; vicar St Oswald's Durham and rural dean of Durham 1974-80, hon canon of Durham 1979-80, vice-princ St Chad's Coll Durham 1969-74, priest i-c St Michael's Abingdon 1961-69, asst curate St Peter's Bournemouth 1958-61, bishop of Huntingdon 1980-; *Books* Lamennais and England (1966), J B Dykes, Priest and Musician (with Arthur Hutchings, 1976); *Recreations* French literature, painting; *Style*— The Rt Rev the Bishop of Huntingdon; Powcher's Hall, Ely, Cambs CB7 4DL (☎ 0353 2137)

HUNTINGDON, 15 Earl of (E 1529); (Francis) John Clarence Westenra Plantagenet Hastings; s of 14 Earl of Huntingdon (d 1939), and Maud (d 1953), da of Sir Samuel Wilson; *b* 30 Jan 1901; *Educ* Eton, Christ Church Oxford; *m* 1, 1925 (m dis 1943), as her 1 husb (*see* Lord Milford), Cristina (d 1953), da of Marchese Casati by his 1 w, the celebrated Marchesa of Augustus John's portrait, 1 da (Lady Moorea Black b 1928); m 2, 1944, Margaret, JP, *qv* da of Harry Lane, of Vernham Dean, Andover, and formerly w of Bryan Wallace, 2 da 9 Lady Selina b 1945, Lady Caroline Shackleton *qv*); *Heir* first cous, Lt-Col Robin Hastings, DSO, OBE, MC; *Career* serv WWII, 2 Lt TA, RHG; artist (studied under the Mexican social realist painter Diego Rivera); exhibitions in London, Paris, Chicago, San Francisco; prof Camberwell Sch Arts and Crafts 1938, Central Sch of Arts and Crafts London; parly sec to Mr Atlee 1941-5 dep controller Civil Def, Andover Rural Dist Cncl 1941-45, and parly sec to min of Agric and Fisheries July 1945-Nov 1950; chm (subsequently pres) of ctee Soc of Mural Painters 1951-58, pres Solent Protection Soc 1958-68; *Books* The Golden Octopus, Commonsense about India; *Style*— The Rt Hon the Earl of Huntingdon; Blackbridge House, Beaulieu, Hants (☎ 0590 612305)

HUNTINGDON, Countess of; Margaret; da of late H G Lane; *b* 23 June 1907; *Educ* St Stephen's Coll Folkestone, St Hugh's Coll Oxford (MA); *m* 1, 1934 (m dis 1939), Bryan, s of Edgar Wallace; m 2, 1944, 15 Earl of Huntingdon *qv*; 2 da; *Career* novelist, biographer, journalist (as Margaret Lane); pres: Women's Press Club 1958-60, Dickens Fellowship 1959-61 and 1970, Johnson Soc 1971, Bronte Soc 1975-82, Jane Austen Soc; *Books* Faith, Hope, No Charity (Prix Femina-Vie Heureuse), Edgar Wallace: the Biography of a Phenomenon, Walk into My Parlour, Where Helen Lies, The Tale of Beatrix Potter, The Brontë Story, A Crown of Convolvulus, A Calabash of Diamonds, Life with Ionides, A Night at Sea, A Smell of Burning, Purely for Pleasure, The Day of the Feast, Frances Wright and the Great Experiment, Samuel Johnson and His World, Flora Thompson, The Magic Years of Beatrix Potter, (ed) Flora Thompson's A Country Calendar and other writings, The Drug-Like Bronte Dream; *Style*— The Rt Hon the Countess of Huntingdon; Blackbridge House, Beaulieu, Hants SO42 7YE

HUNTINGFIELD, 6 Baron (I 1796); Sir Gerard Charles Arcedeckne Vanneck; 7 Bt (GB 1751); s of 5 Baron Huntingfield, KCMG, JP (d 1969), and his 1 w Margaret Eleanor, *née* Crosby (d 1943); *b* 29 May 1915; *Educ* Stowe, Trinity Coll Cambridge; *m* 27 Oct 1941, Janetta Lois, er da of Capt Reginald Hugh Errington, RN (ret); 1 s, 2 da (Hon Sara Binney b 1944, Hon Mrs Darell-Brown b 1946, Hon Mrs Bacon b 1954), (1 da decd); *Heir* s, Hon Joshua Vanneck; *Career* serv WWII Flt Sgt RAFVR; UN Secretariat 1946-75; *Style*— The Rt Hon Lord Huntingfield; Rue du Sacre du Printemps 4, CH 1815 Clarens, Switzerland (☎ 021 964 67 28)

HUNTINGFORD, Donald Roy; s of Roy Huntingford (d 1951); *b* 3 June 1920; *m* 1945, Joan, da of Frederick George Wingrove; 3 children; *Career* CA; chm: Clark Whitehill 1982-85, Waltham Forest Housing Assoc Ltd; Croix de Guerre 1943; *Style*— Donald Huntingford, Esq; 4 Woodstock Rd, Walthamstow, London E17 4BJ

HUNTINGTON, Keith Graham; s of Nathianiel Huntington (Capt MN, d 1964), of 17 Pine View Drive, Heswall, Cheshire and late Christina Louise, *née* Griffiths; *b* 22 Sept 1943; *Educ* Wirral GS Cheshire, Nat Coll of Heating Ventilation and Fan Engrg London, Liverpool Coll of Building; *m* 19 Aug 1967, Helen, da of John George McKay (d 1973), of 15 Eccleston Ave, Chester; 2 da (Georgina Louise b 14 April 1974, Nicola Jayne b 11 Dec 1975); *Career* sr heating and ventilation engr Husband & Co Consltg Engrs 1971-72, section ldr Edward A Pearce & Ptnrs Consltg Engrs Sheffield 1972-77, sr ptnr Edward A Pearce & Assocs 1984- (assoc ptnr 1977-80, ptnr 1980-84); FCIBSE, MConsE, MASHRAE; *Recreations* squash; *Clubs* Abbeydale Squash (Sheffield); *Style*— Keith Huntington, Esq; 35 Old Hay Close, Dore, Sheffield S17 3GP (☎ 0742 368156); Granby Croft, Matlock St, Bakewell, Derbys DE4 1ET (☎ 0742 671188, fax 0742 671133); 6 Marlborough Rd, Sheffield S10 1DB (☎ 062981 3449)

HUNTINGTON-WHITELEY, Sir Hugo Baldwin; 3 Bt (UK 1918), of Grimley, Worcester, DL (Worcs 1972); s of Capt Sir Maurice Huntington-Whiteley *qv*, 2 Bt, RN (d 1975), and Lady (Pamela) Margaret (d 1976), da of 1 Earl Baldwin of Bewdley, KG, PC; *b* 31 Mar 1924; *Educ* Eton; *m* 1959, Jean Marie Ramsay, JP (1973), DStJ, da of late Arthur Francis Ramsay Bock; 2 da (Sophie Elizabeth (Mrs Zdatny) b 1964, Charlotte Anne b 1965); *Heir* bro, (John) Miles Huntington-Whiteley; *Career* RN 1942-47; FCA; ptnr Price Waterhouse 1963-83; memb Ct of Assts Goldsmiths' Co; High Sheriff of Worcs 1971; *Recreations* music and travel; *Clubs* Brooks's; *Style*— Sir Hugo Huntington-Whiteley, Bt, DL; Ripple Hall, Tewkesbury, Glos (☎ 068 46 2431)

HUNTINGTON-WHITELEY, (John) Miles; VRD (two clasps); s of Capt Sir Maurice Huntington-Whiteley, 2 Bt (d 1975, hp of bro, Sir Hugo Huntington-Whiteley, 3 Bt *qv*), and Lady Pamela Margaret, *née* Baldwin (d 1976); *b* 18 July 1929; *Educ* Eton, Trinity Coll Cambridge; *m* 1960, HIllH Countess Victoria Adelheid Clementine Luise, da of late HIllH Count Friedrich Wolfgang zu Castell-Rüdenhausen (ka 1940) *see* Debretts Peerage, Royal family section; 1 s (Leopold Maurice b 1965), 2 da (Alice Louise Esther Margot b 1961, m 1985, Charles Percy Sewell, 3 s of the late Maj Geoffrey Richard Michael Sewell by his wife Joan, 3 da of Sir Watkin William-Wynn 8 Bt; Beatrice Irene Helen Victoria b 1962); *Career* Lt Cdr RNR; int investmt portfolio mangr James Capel and Co; *Recreations* applied and fine arts, music, the paranormal; *Clubs* Naval; *Style*— Miles Huntington-Whiteley, Esq, VRD; 6 Matheson Road, London W14 8SW (☎ 01 602 8484); James Capel and Co, James Capel House, 6 Bevis Marks, London EC3A 7JQ (☎ 01 621 0011)

HUNTLY, 13 Marquess of (S 1599) Granville Charles Gomer Gordon; Premier Marquess of Scotland, also Earl of Aboyne, Lord Gordon of Strathavon and Glenlivet (both S 1660), and Baron Meldrum of Morven (UK 1815); s of 12 Marquess of Huntly (d 1987), and his 1 w, Hon Pamela, *née* Berry, da of 1 Viscount Kemsley; *b* 4 Feb 1944; *Educ* Gordonstoun; *m* 1972, Jane Elizabeth Angela, da of late Lt-Col Alistair Gibb and Hon Yoskyl, *née* Pearson, da of 2 Viscount Cowdray, DL; 1 s, 2 da (Lady Amy b 1975, Lady Lucy b 1979); *Heir* s, Earl of Aboyne, *qv*; *Style*— The Most Hon The Marquess of Huntly; Aboyne Castle, Aberdeenshire (☎ 0339 2118)

HUNTLY, Pamela, Marchioness of; Hon (Mary) Pamela; *née* Berry; da of 1 Viscount Kemsley, GBE (d 1968); *b* 1918; *m* 1941 (m dis 1965), 12 Marquess of Huntly; 1 s (13 Marquess of Huntly), 1 da (Lady Lemina Lawson-Johnston); *Style*— Pamela, Marchioness of Huntly; 80 Old Church St, London SW3

HUNTON CARTER, Lt Col (James) Anthony; OBE (1943); s of Arthur Hunton Carter (d 1961), and Winifred Ida, *née* Macmeikan (d 1947); *b* 12 Dec 1914; *Educ* Wells House Malvern Wells, Sedbergh Sch Yorks; *m* 14 Oct 1942, Mae Paulsen, da of John Christian Paulsen (d 1960), of Cape Town, SA; 1 s (Robert b 1952), 2 da (Susan b 1947, Jane b 1948); *Career* cmmnd King's Own Royal Regt 1937; serv: Palestine, Egypt, Libya, Tripolitania, Agleria, Sicily, Italy, France, Belgium, Holland, Germany; promoted Lt-Col 1943, ret 1948; author; dir and md Ward Blenkinsop and Co Ltd (later chm); *Books* Maintenance in the Field; *Recreations* shooting, wood turning; *Style*— Lt-Col Hunton Carter, OBE; Casa Pelicanos, Colina Del Sol 62A, Calpe, Alicante, Spain

HUNTSMAN, Peter William; s of William Huntsman (d 1970), and Lydia Irene, *née* Clegg (d 1982); *b* 11 August 1935; *Educ* Hymers Coll Hull, Coll of Estate Mgmnt London Univ (BSc), Cornell Univ USA; *m* 1, 30 Dec 1961 (m dis 1984), Janet Mary, da of William Albert Bell; 1 s (Mark William b 1965), 1 da (Fiona Mary b 1963); m 2, 21 June 1984, Cicely Eleanor Waymont, da of Robert Tamblin; *Career* MAFF: asst land cmmr 1961-66, sr asst land cmmr 1966-69, princ surveyor 1971-81; Kellogg Fndn Fellowship USA 1969-70, princ Coll of Estate Mgmnt Reading 1981-; Freeman: City of London, Worshipful Co of Chartered Surveyors; FRICS 1963, FAAV 1987; *Books* Walmsleys Rural Estate Management (contrib 1978); *Recreations* golf, bridge, reading; *Clubs* Athenaeum, Farmers, Phyllis Ct (Henley); *Style*— Peter Huntsman, Esq; Coachmans Cottage, Bulmershe Rd, Reading; 3 Greystones, Burlington Rd, Swanage (☎ 0734 67426); Coll of Estate Mgmnt, Whiteknights, Reading (☎ 0734 861101, fax 0734 755344)

HUNWICKS, Trevor Alec; s of Alec Alfred Hunwicks, of Maldon, Essex, and Jean Hunwicks, *née* Brazier; *b* 22 Sept 1943; *Educ* Chistlehurst and Sidcup GS; *m* 14 Dec 1968, Zara, da of Peter John Harris, of Isle of Wight; 1 s (William George b 7 Oct 1974), 1 da (Victoria Louise b 21 August 1971); *Career* Nationwide Anglia Building Soc (formerly Anglia Building Soc) 1968-: branch mangr 1968, dep London mangr 1970, London mangr 1971, London regnl mangr 1975, asst gen mangr mktg 1984, gen mangr mktg 1985, gen mangr corporate planning 1987-; MInstM 1971, FCBSI 1977, FBIM 1986; *Recreations* theatre, music, painting, tennis; *Clubs* RAC, Wig and Pen; *Style*— Trevor Hunwicks, Esq; The Old Barn, Ecton, Northampton, NN6 0QB (☎ 0604 406203); Nationwide Anglia Building Society, Chesterfield House, Bloomsbury Way, London WC1V 6PW (☎ 01 242 8822, car tel 0860 524 720)

HURD, Rt Hon Douglas Richard; CBE (1974), PC (1980), MP (C) Witney 1983-; eld s of Baron Hurd, sometime MP Newbury and agric corr The Times (Life Peer d 1966, himself er s of Sir Percy Hurd, sometime MP Frome and Devizes, ed Canadian Gazette and London ed Montreal Star; Sir Percy was er bro of Sir Archibald Hurd, also a journalist (Daily Telegraph) and formerly chm Shipping World Co); *b* 8 Mar 1930; *Educ* Eton, Trinity Coll Cambridge; *m* 1, 1960 (m dis 1982), Tatiana Elizabeth Michelle, da of A C Benedict Eyre, MBE, of West Burton House, Bury, Sussex, Evelyn; 3 s; m 2, 1982, Judy, 2 da of Sidney Smart, of Oak Ash, Chaddleworth, Berks; 1 s (Philip Arthur b 1983), 1 da (Jessica Stephanie b 1985); *Career* Dip Serv 1952-66 (Peking, UK Mission to UN, Rome, also ps to perm under-sec FO); CRD 1966-68 (head Foreign Affrs Section 1968); MP (C) Mid Oxon Feb 1974-1983, private sec to Rt Hon Edward Heath as ldr of Oppn 1968-70, political sec to PM 1970-74, oppn spokesman Foreign Affrs (with special responsibility for EEC) 1976-79; min of state: FCO 1979-1983, Home Office 1983-84;Sec of State for NI 1984-85; Home Sec 1985-; visiting fell Nuffield Coll Oxford 1978; *Books* The Arrow War (1967), Truth Game (1972), Vote to Kill (1975), An End to Promises (1979); with Andrew Osmond: Send Him Victorious (1968), The Smile on The Face of the Tiger (1969); Scotch on the Rocks (1971), War Without Frontiers (1982); Palace of Enchantments (co-author with Stephen Lamport 1985); *Clubs* Beefsteak; *Style*— The Rt Hon Douglas Hurd, CBE, MP; c/o House of Commons, London SW1

HURD, Hon Stephen Anthony; JP (Wilts 1969); yr s of Baron Hurd (Life Peer; d 1966), and Stephanie Frances, *née* Corner (d 1985); bro Rt Hon Douglas Hurd *qv*; *b* 6 April 1933; *Educ* Winchester, Magdalene Coll Cambridge (BA, Dip Agric, MA); *m* 30 June 1973, Pepita Lilian, da of Lt-Col Walter Hingston, OBE, of The Old Vicarage, Ramsbury, Marlborough, Wilts; 2 s (William b 1976, Christopher b 1977); *Career* farmer; dir: North Wilts Cereals Ltd 1970-85, Gp Cereals Ltd 1970- 84, W of England Farmers Ltd 1968- (chm 1988-), W of England Building Soc (formerly Ramsbury Building Soc) 1973-; tstee Duchess of Somerset Hosp Froxfield Wilts; chm Marlborough Petty Sessional Divn 1987-; *Style*— The Hon Stephen Hurd; Brown's Farm, Marlborough, Wilts SW8 4ND

HURDLE, Michael William Frederick; s of Maurice Frederick Hurdle, of Burton-on-Trent, and Mary Murielle Morton Wilson; *b* 3 June 1941; *Educ* Uppingham, Keele Univ (BA); *m* 1983, Jean Alicia, da of Frederick Ernest Savage (d 1975), of Burton-on-Trent; *Career* chm and md Marston Thompson and Evershed plc (Brewers); *Recreations* shooting, fishing, golf, tennis, horseracing; *Clubs* The Burton, Lloyds; *Style*— Michael Hurdle, Esq; Lower Stock Lane Farm, Marchington Woodlands, Uttoxeter, Staffs; Marston's plc, PO Box 26, Shobnall Rd, Burton-on-Trent DE14 2BW

HURLE-HOBBS, Glenys Rosemary; ISO (1982); da of Leonard Jeffrey Hembry (d 1966), and Olive May, *née* Deere (d 1977); *b* 15 Mar 1922; *Educ* Altrincham Girls HS, King's Coll London (BA, AKC); *Career* CS 1946-82; cncllr Arun DC 1985 (vice-chm); memb Housing and Community Care Ctee; chm: Arundel Cons Women's Ctee 1987; Admin Arundel Festival Soc 1983-85; dir overseas visitors and info studies div COI 1978-82; *Recreations* travel, opera, bridge, conservation; *Clubs* Univ Womens; *Style*— Mrs Glenys Hurle-Hobbs, ISO; Bumble Cottage, Houghton, Arundel, W Sussex BN18 9LN (☎ 0798 831509)

HURLEY, David Desmond; s of Frederick Desmond Hurley (d 1978), of Dublin, and Edith Duff Hurley (d 1976), of Toronto; *b* 8 August 1930; *Educ* Fettes Coll Edinburgh; *m* 1955, Mary Cecil, da of William Moore, OBE, TD (d 1950); 2 s (Guy, Giles), 5 da (Caroline, Susanna, Alexandra, Sarah, Nikola); *Career* chm: Irish Exporters Assoc 1969-70, Visionhire Ltd 1978, Dorking Cons Assoc 1980-83; md Electronic Rentals Gp plc 1982-88, dir: Teljoy Hldgs Ltd SA, Langdon and Sons Ltd Ireland; pres Mole Valley Cons Assoc 1983-86, memb Cons Bd of Fin 1985-, govr The Mgmnt Coll Henley 1986-88; *Recreations* sailing (sea muffin), gardening; *Clubs* Royal Irish YC, Kobe Regatta and Athletic; *Style*— David Hurley, Esq; Ballydaheen, Portsalon, Co Donegal, Ireland

HURLEY, George Nevill; s of John Everard Hurley (d 1962), of Hawks Hill, Chobham, Surrey, and Mary, *née* Marchant; *b* 21 May 1939; *Educ* Eton; *m* 8 June 1964, Ann Elizabeth, da of J Dickinson (d 1982), of Ilford, Essex; 2 s (Andrew b 5 Oct 1971, Jonathan b 17 Sept 1975); *Career* Nat Serv 1958-60: RB 1958-59, cmmnd KSLI 1959-60; TA serv: Queen's Westminsters (later Queen's Royal Rifles) 1960-63; shipbroker; McGregor Gow & Hotland 1961-62, Elder Smith & Co Ltd 1962-63,

Eldersmith Goldsbrough Mort Aust 1963-66 (London 1966-81), mangr (chartering) Elders IXL Ltd 1981-83, dir: Elders Chartering Ltd 1983, Baltic Exchange Ltd 1983-88, Minerva Marine Hong Kong 1983-, Rimpacific Shipping (London) Ltd 1985-; *Recreations* shooting, gardening, music; *Style*— George Hurley, Esq; Elders Chartering Ltd, 40 Dukes Place, London EC3A 5BX (☎ 01 626 9811, fax 01 929 4849, car tel 0860 306 044, telex 885 608)

HURLEY, Sir John Garling; CBE (1959), JP; s of John Hurley, MLA (d 1911); *b* 2 Oct 1906; *Educ* Sydney Tech HS; *m* 1, 1929, Alice Edith (decd), da of John Saunders (d 1931); 3 da; m 2, 1975, Desolie Richardson; *Career* md Berlei Utd Ltd 1948-69, former chm William Adams Ltd, memb Tech and Further Educn Advsy Cncl of NSW 1958-76, memb Indust Design Cncl of Aust 1958-76, former chm Museum of Applied Arts and Scis NSW, dir Royal North Hosp 1969-76; kt 1967; *see Debrett's Handbook of Australia and New Zealand for further details*; *Style*— Sir John Hurley, CBE, JP; 12 Locksley St, Killara, NSW 2071, Australia

HURN, Hon Mrs (Phillida Ann); da of late 9 Baron Walpole (d 1989); *b* 18 Jan 1950; *Educ* Abbots Hill Sch for Girls, Norwich HS for Girls; *m* 1, 1973 (m dis 1981), Clive Grainger Morgan-Evans; 2 s (Edward Evans b 1973, Daniel Evans b 1977); m 2, 1983, Antony Hurn, of Chop Lodge, Twyford, Norfolk; *Career* schools horses and rides in three-day horse trials; organiser BHS Horse trials at Wolterton Hall in Norfolk each July; *Recreations* keen supporter of Norwich City FC; *Style*— The Hon Mrs Hurn; Beck Farm, Calthorpe, Norwich NR11 7NG

HURN, Stanley Noel; s of Leonard Frederick Hurn (d 1973), of Colchester, and Kathleen Alice, *née* Frost (d 1984); *b* 24 Dec 1943; *Educ* Colchester Royal GS, Univ of Hull (BSc); *Career* mangr Standard Chartered Bank 1968-78, assoc Orion Royal Bank Ltd 1978-82, dir Samuel Montagu & Co Ltd 1985-; ACIB; *Style*— Stanley Hurn, Esq; 35 Durand Gardens, London SW9 0PS (☎ 01 735 8965); Samuel Montagu & Co Ltd, 10 Lower Thames St, London EC3R 6AE (☎ 01 260 9200)

HURRELL, Sir Anthony Gerald; KCVO (1986), CMG (1984); s of late William and Florence Hurrell; *b* 18 Feb 1927; *Educ* Norwich Sch, St Catharine's Coll Cambridge; *m* 1951, Jean Wyatt; 2 da; *Career* RAEC 1948-50, Miny of Labour 1950-53, Miny of Educn 1953-64, Miny of Overseas Devpt 1964, fell Center for Int Affairs Harvard 1969-70, head of SE Asia devpt div Bangkok 1972-74; under-sec: Int Div ODM 1974-75, central policy review staff cabinet Off 1976, Duchy of Lancaster 1977, Asia and Oceans Div ODA 1978-83, Int Div ODA 1983; ambass to Nepal 1983-86; *Style*— Sir Anthony Hurrell, KCVO, CMG; Lapwings, Dunwich, Saxmundham, Suffolk IP17 3DR

HURRELL, Air Vice-Marshal Frederick Charles; CB (1986), OBE (1970); s of Alexander John Hurrell (Lt d 1933), and Maria Del Carmen, *née* Di Biedma (d 1968); *b* 24 April 1928; *Educ* Royal Masonic Schs Bushey, St Mary's Hosp Med Sch and London Univ (MB BS); *m* 7 Oct 1950, Jay Ruby, da of Hugh Gordon Jarvis (d 1975); 5 da (Caroline b 1951, Rosemary b 1953, Katherine b 1956, Alexandra b 1959, Anne b 1960); *Career* cmmd RAF (med branch): Flying Offr 1953, sr med offr on flying stations in UK Aust and Far East 1954-67 (Flt Lt 1954, Acting Sqdn Ldr 1954, Sqdn Ldr 1959, Wing Cdr 1965), various jr staff appts 1967-74, Gp Capt and dep dir (aviation med 1974-77, staff offr (aerospace med) Br Def Staff Washington 1978-80, Air Cdre and OC Princess Alexandra Hosp RAF Wroughton 1980-82, dir of health and res 1982-84, Air Vice-Marshal and princ med offr RAF Strike Cmd 1984-86, dir gen med servs 1986-88, ret 1988; dir of appeals RAF Benelovent Fund 1988-; FRSM 1986, FRAeS 1987; CStJ 1986; *Recreations* photography, gardening, golf; *Clubs* RAF, Sports Club of London; *Style*— Air Vice-Marshal Frederick Hurrell, CB, OBE; Hale House, 4 Upper Hale Rd, Farnham, Surrey GU9 0NJ (☎ 0252 714 190); RAF Benevolent Fund, 67 Portland Place, London W1N 4AR (☎ 01 636 2654, fax 01 580 8343 ext 201)

HURST, Lady Barbara; *née* Lindsay; da of late 27 Earl of Crawford and 10 of Balcarres, KT, PC, and Constance, da of Sir Henry Carstairs Pelly, 3 Bt, MP; *b* 1915; *m* 1939, Col Richard Lumley Hurst, Royal Sussex Regt TA, barr (d 1962), s of Sir Cecil James Barrington Hurst, GCMG, KCB; 1 s (Robert b 1945), 3 da (Mrs Hugh Gilroy b 1940, Cecilia b 1944, *see Alastair Goodland, MP, Mrs Donald Corbett*); *Style*— Lady Barbara Hurst; Porters Farm, Rusper, Horsham, W Sussex RH12 4QA (☎ 029 384 593)

HURST, (Francis) John Embleton; s of Rev Canon Frank Hurst (d 1972), and Margaret Annie, *née* Embleton (d 1953); *b* 27 Dec 1920; *Educ* Sedbergh, Magdalen Coll Oxford (MA); *m* 1, 1947, Gwenda Josephine Whitty (d 1966), da of Alfred Norman-Jones, of Wellington NZ; m 2, 1968, Teresa Anne, da of Peter O'Doherty (decd), of Co Clare; 1 s (Peter b 1969), 1 da (Roisin b 1971); *Career* cmmnd RAC 1942 with 4/7 Royal Dragoon Gds, 8 Kings Royal Irish Hussars, instr RAC OCTU Sandhurst, served M East, N Africa, UK Capt; dep librarian 1958-65, librarian Trinity Coll Dublin 1965-67, librarian New Univ Ulster 1967-84; pres Library Assoc of Ireland 1972-74 (hon fell); former memb: Library Cncl Dublin, Library Advsy Cncl of NI, bd of library and info studies Queen's Univ Belfast, bd of Arts Cncl NI; occasional broadcaster and contrib to various periodicals; ALA, FLAI; *Recreations* ornithology, gardening; *Clubs* Kildare Street, Univ Dublin; *Style*— John Hurst, Esq; 72 Ballywillan Rd, Portrush, Co Antrim BT56 8JN N Ireland (☎ 0265 823209)

HURST, John George; s of John George Hurst, DSc (d 1972), of Artist's Cottage, Findon, Sussex; *b* 15 Mar 1926; *Educ* Steyning GS, RMA Sandhurst; *m* 1954, Angela Mary Ellen, da of Claude James Marsall (d 1958), of Butts Mead, Brockenhurst; 4 s; *Career* served 8 King's Royal Inf Hussars (NW Europe, Palestine, Korea), ret Maj; md S I Coolers Ltd, dir S I Group plc; memb of IOD; *Recreations* golf, tennis, equestrian activity, swimming, driving; *Clubs* Cavalry and Guards; *Style*— John Hurst Esq; 122 Cambridge St, Pimlico, London SW1 (☎ office 01 686 4651)

HURST, Kevin Anthony; s of Bertram Victor Hurst, of Manchester, and Anne, *née* Manning; *b* 17 June 1941; *Educ* Xaverian Coll Manchester; *m* 26 Dec 1964, Shirley Edna, da of Arthur Welsh (d 1987), of Warley, W Midlands; 2 da (Annette b 1965, Gillian b 1968); *Career* chief exec Nottingham Imperial Building Soc; dir Nottingham Imperial BS 1982; FCBSI; *Recreations* squash; *Clubs* Nottingham Squash Racquets; *Style*— Kevin Hurst, Esq; Ridgeway, 122 Bramcote Lane, Wollaton, Nottingham (☎ 0602 282193); Nottingham Imperial Building Society, Imperial Building, 29 Bridgford Rd, W Bridgford, Nottingham (☎ 0602 817220)

HURST, Paul Anthony (Tony); s of John William Hurst (d 1985), and Mildred Grace, *née* Smith (d 1984); *b* 19 July 1934; *Educ* Lancaster Royal GS; *m* 9 Nov 1957, Barbara, da of Robert Croft Woodhouse, of Seaford, E Sussex; 2 s (Simon Jeremy b 1958, Timothy Paul b 1962), 1 da (Samantha Lee b 1976); *Career* chem and res chem: Lansil Ltd 1951-57, Gen Foods (Canada) Ltd 1957-60; trg offr personnel mangr: Nairn-Williamson Ltd 1960-69, Velmar Textiles Ltd 1960-69; gp personnel mangr Aerialite Ltd 1969-70, personnel mangr Knowles Electronic Inc 1970-74, mgmnt conslt Russell Ewbank & Ptnrs 1974; dir and ptnr: Barnet Keel Int 1974-, Peter Dye Assocs 1974-; FIPM, MBIM, MIIM, MIMC; *Style*— Tony Hurst, Esq; 4 Chyngton Place, Seaford, E Sussex BN25 4HQ (☎ 0323 899539); Peter Dye Assocs, The Old Vicarage, Chiddingley, E Sussex BN8 6HE (☎ 0825 872703, fax 0825 872704)

HURST, Peter Thomas; s of Thomas Lyon Hurst (d 1981), of Cheshire, and Norah Mary, *née* Delaney (d 1977); *b* 27 Oct 1942; *Educ* Stonyhurst, Univ of London (LLB); *m* 1968, Diane, da of Ian George Irvine, of Cheshire; 1 s (Charles b 1975), 2 da (Elizabeth b 1970, Catherine b 1972); *Career* slr of Supreme Ct 1967; ptnr: Hurst and Walker Slrs Liverpool 1967-77, Gair Roberts Hurst and Walker Slrs Liverpool 1977-81; chm Liverpool Young Slrs Gp 1979, NW Young Slrs Conf 1980; master Supreme Ct 1981-; *Books* Butterworths Costs Service (1986), Costs in Criminal Cases, Slrs' Remuneration, Cordery on Slrs (8 ed 1988 contrib); *Style*— Peter Hurst, Esq; Ivy Lodge, Hitchen Hatch Lane, Sevenoaks, Kent TN13 3AT; Supreme Ct Taxing Office, Royal Cts of Justice, Strand, London WC2

HURST, Dr Robert; CBE (1973, GM 1944); s of Percy Cecil Hurst (d 1960), of Nelson, NZ, and Margery, *née* Whitwell (d 1957); *b* 3 Jan 1915; *Educ* Nelson Coll NZ, Canterbury Univ NZ (BSc, MSc), Cambridge Univ (PhD); *m* 28 Sept 1946, Rachael Jeanette, da of Charles Edward Marsh (d 1951), of Bexhill, Sussex; 3 s (Jonathan b 31 July 1949, Charles Edward b 8 Aug 1953, Nicholas Robert b 5 May 1956); *Career* demonstrator chemistry dept Canterbury Univ NZ 1938-39, experimental offr (bomb disposal res) HQ Miny of Supply 1940-45, gp ldr Transuranic Elements Gp Aere Harwell 1954-55, project ldr Homogenous Reactor Project Aere Harwell 1956-57, chief chemist res and devpt branch industl gp UKAEA 1957-58, dir Downreay experimental reactor estb UKAEA 1958-63, dir Br Ship Res Assoc 1963-77; JP (Caithness 1959-63); FRSC 1960-, companion RINA 1963-; *Books* Progress in Nuclear Engineering (ed 1957); *Recreations* gardening, sailing; *Clubs* Athenaeum, Parkstone; *Style*— Dr Robert Hurst, CBE, GM; 15 Elms Ave, Parkstone, Poole, Dorset BH14 8EE (☎ 0202 733 109)

HURST-BROWN, Alan Dudley; s of Kenneth Hurst-Brown (d 1971), of Williamsburg, Virginia, and Dorothy Joan, *née* Pinhey (d 1957); *b* 27 Dec 1920; *Educ* Dragon, Wellington ; *m* 9 Aug 1947, June Marcella, da of Cdr John Garrett Wood, RN (d 1982), of Aldeburgh, Suffolk; 2 s (David b 1949, Nigel b 1951), 2 da (Marcella b 1954, Lucy b 1962); *Career* WWII Private Royal Berks Regt 1939-40, Lt The Rifle Bde 1940-46 (POW Italy and Germany 1941-45); sr ptnr Read Hurst-Brown (Stockbrokers 1963-75 (ptnr 1949), sr ptnr Rowe & Pitman stockbrokers 1979-82 ptnr 1975), ret 1982; non exec dir: Kingfisher plc 1982-, Hambros Investmt Tst plc 1982-; non-exec chm Whitburgh Investmt Ltd 1982-; Freeman City of London 1952, Liveryman Co of Merchant Taylors 1952; *Recreations* fishing, golf, gardening; *Clubs* Boodle's; *Style*— Alan Hurst-Brown, Esq; The Mill House, Itchen abbas, Winchester, Hants SO21 1BJ (☎ 096278 433)

HURST-BROWN, Christopher Nigel; s of Alan Dudley Hurst-Brown, of Hants, and June Marcella, *née* Wood; *b* 11 July 1951; *Educ* Wellington, Bristol Univ (BSc); *m* 1976, Candida Madeleine, da of Arthur George Bernard Drabble, of Surrey; 2 da (Annabella, Tania); *Career* dir Hill Samuel Investmt Mgmnt 1984-86, md Lloyds Merchant Bank Ltd 1986-, chm Lloyds Investmt Mangrs Ltd 1986-; *Recreations* golf, tennis, shooting, fishing; *Clubs* Berks GC; *Style*— Nigel Hurst-Brown, Esq; The Old Bakery, Rotherwick, nr Basingstoke, Hants (☎ 0256 72 2572); Lloyds Investment Managers Ltd, Elizabeth House, 9-11 Bush Lane, London EC4P 4LN (☎ 01 500 4500, fax 01 623 1288, telex 8812696)

HURSTHOUSE, Roderick Henry; s of Henry Walter Hursthouse, of Portwey Close, Weymouth, and Joan, *née* Hanger; *b* 18 Nov 1952; *Educ* Broadway Sch, Coll of Law Guildford; *m* 19 April 1980, Joan, da of Thomas Emanuel Heath, of Hodge Hill, Birmingham; 2 s (Jonathan Roderick b 1982, Alexander James b 1984), 1 da (Bryony Jane b 1986); *Career* slr 1979-; fell Inst of Legal Execs 1978; *Recreations* shooting, swimming, arts, fishing; *Clubs* Royal Dorset YC; *Style*— Roderick Hursthouse, Esq; Rookside, Winters Close, Portesham, nr Weymouth, Dorset; 71 Fortuneswell Portland (☎ 0305 823111, fax 0305 820211), car (☎ 0836 249633)

HURT, John Vincent; s of The Rev Father Arnould Herbert Hurt, and Phylis, *née* Massey (d 1975); *b* 22 Jan 1940; *Educ* Lincoln Sch, St Martins Sch of Art, RADA; *m* 1984, Donna Lynn, da of Don Wesley Laurence (d 1986), of Texas USA; *Career* actor, films: A Man for All Seasons (1966), 10 Rillington Place (1970), The Shout (1977), Midnight Express (1977) (Oscar nom, Br Acad Award), Alien (1978), Elephant Man (1980) (Oscar nom, Br Acad Award), Champions (1983), Nineteen Eight Four (1984), The Hit (1984); TV: The Naked Civil Servant (1975) (Br Acad Award, best actor TV), I Claudius (1976), Crime and Punishment (1977), King Lear (Fool) (with Olivier, 1982); theatre: Little Malcolm and His Struggle Against The Eunuchs (1966), Belchers Luck (1966), Caretaker (1971), Travesties (1973); *Recreations* cricket, conservation activity; *Clubs* MCC, TVRF; *Style*— John Hurt, Esq; Mt Kenya Game Ranch, PO Box 288, Nanyuki, Kenya; c/o Julian Belfrage Assts, 60 St James' St, London SW1 (☎ 01 491 4400)

HURT, (Seymour Henry) Michael Le Fowne; s of Capt Henry Albert Le Fowne Hurt CMG (d 1969), of Castern Hall, nr Ashbourne, Derbyshire, and Mabel Alleyne, *née* Jessop (d 1964); *b* 27 Oct 1919; *Educ* Eton, Magdalene Coll Cambridge; *m* 1, 1945 (m dis 1959), Veronica Wigham; 2 s (Nicholas b 1948, Charles b 1952), 1 da (Cassandra b 1955); m 2, 1959, Cynthia Margaret Kemp, *née* Henry, da of Col Vivian Henry CB, JP, of Oakfield, Hay-on-Wye, Herefordshire (d 1929); *Career* WWII Lt RNVR 1940-45; FO 1945-46; career at Lloyd's; active Derbyshire Fedn of Boys' Clubs, chm Dovedale House Youth Trg Centre 1970-85; *Recreations* fishing, shooting; *Clubs* Boodle's, Pratt's; *Style*— Michael Hurt, Esq; Castern Hall, Ashbourne, Derbyshire

HURWICH, (Bertram) David; s of Dr Jack Hurwich (d 1945), of Leicester, and Priscilla Evelyn, *née* Thomas (d 1977); *b* 26 July 1937; *Educ* Epsom Coll Elland GS Yorks; *Career* CA, fin conslt Théatre de Complicité; hon tres: Inst for Study and Treatment of Delinquency, Friends of Richmond Orange Tree Theatre; author on Taxation, Accountancy, Artistic and Travel subjects; memb Assoc Inst of Taxation (1964), FCA 1965; *Recreations* theatre, the arts, skiing, francophilia, crosswords; *Style*— David Hurwich, Esq; 26 Fir Lodge, 3 Gipsy Lane, Barnes SW15 (☎ 01 878 6795)

HURWITZ, Emanuel Henry; CBE (1978); s of Isaac Hurwitz (d 1951), of 84 Bethune Rd, London N16, and Sarah Gabrilowitz (d 1966); *b* 7 May 1919; *Educ* RAM; *m* 3 Aug 1948, Kathleen Ethel, and Reginald Samuel Crome, of Onslowe House, William St, Slough, Bucks; 1 s (Michael b 1949), 1 da (Jacqueline b 1942); *Career* musician band RAMC, concerts in: Eng, Ireland, Egypt, Palestine, Syria, Lebanon, Iraq, Iran, Germany, Italy; Ldr: Hurwitz String Quartet 1946-52, (Goldsborough Orch 1947-57), Melos Ensemble of London 1956-74, London String Trio 1952-68, London Pianoforte Quartet 1952-68, English Chamber Orch 1957-69 New Philarmonia Orch 1969-71, Aeolian String Quartet 1970-81; prof RAM 1968-, visiting lectr Royal Scottish Acad of Music and Drama 1987-; recordings incl: Brandenburg Concerti, Handel Concerto Grossi, Schubert Octet, Beethoven Septet, Trout Quintet, Mozart & Brahms Clarinet Quintets, Complete Haydn String Quartets, Ravel, Debussy, Beethoven, etc; Gold Medal Worshipful Co of Musicians 1967; FRAM 1961; memb: Inc Soc of Musicians 1958, Euro String Teachers Assoc 1982; *Recreations* old violins and bows, swimming, walking - music of other instruments; *Style—* Emanuel Hurwitz, Esq, CBE; 25 Dollis Ave, London N3 1DA (☎ 01 346 3936)

HUSBAND, Lady; Eileen Margaret; *née* Howill; da of late Henry Nowill, of Sheffield; *b* 3 April 1906; *m* 1932, Sir (Henry) Charles Husband, CBE (d 1983, sr ptnr Husband and Co, Consulting Engrs); 2 s, 2 da; *Style—* Lady Husband; Okenhold, School Green Lane, Sheffield S10 4GP

HUSKINSON, (George) Nicholas Nevil; s of Thomas Leonard Bousfield Huskinson (d 1974), of Triscombe Ho, Triscombe, Taunton, Somerset, and Helen Margaret, *née* Hales (d 1983); *b* 7 Dec 1948; *Educ* Eton, King's Coll Cambridge (MA); *m* 20 Dec 1972, Pennant Elfrida Lascelles, *née* Iremonger, da of Thomas Lascelles Isa Shandon Valiant Iremonger, of Milbourne Manor, Malmesbury, Wilts; 2 s (Thomas b 1978, Charles b 1981); *Career* called to the Bar Grays Inn 1971, practising barr 1971-; memb Local Govt and Planning Bar Assoc; *Books* Woodfall's Law of Landlord and Tenant (twenty eight edn, ass ed 1978); *Recreations* cooking, walking, wine and food; *Clubs* Beefsteak, MCC; *Style—* Nicholas Huskinson, Esq; 34 Cheyne Row, Chelsea, London SW3 5Hl (☎ 01 352 6866); 4-5 Gray's Inn Sq, Gray's Inn, London WC1R 5AY (☎ 01 404 5252, fax 01 242 7803, telex GRALAW 8953743)

HUSKISSON, Dr Edward Cameron; s of Edward William Huskisson, of Northwood, middx, and Elinor Margot, *née* Gibson; *b* 7 April 1939; *Educ* Eastbourne Coll, King's Coll London and Westminster Hosp (BSc, MB BS, MD); *m* 1 s (Ian b 1971), 1 da (Anna b 1974); *Career* conslt physician St Bartholomew's Hosp London, conslt rheumatologist King Edward V11 Hosp for Offrs London; memb: BMA, RSM; MRCS, LRCP 1964, MRCP 1967, FRCP 1980; *Books* Joint Disease All The Arthropathies (fourth edn 1988); *Style—* Dr Edward Huskisson; 14A Milford House, 7 Queen Anne St, London W1M 9FD, (☎ 01 636 4278)

HUSKISSON, Robert Andrews; CBE (1979); s of Edward Huskisson (d 1964), and Catherine Mary, *née* Downing (d 1964), of Buckhurst Hill; *b* 2 April 1923; *Educ* Merchant Taylors', St Edmund Hall Oxford; *m* 1969, Alice Marian Swaffin, da of William John Tuck; 2 step da; *Career* dep chief exec Shaw Savill and Albion Co Ltd 1971-72; pres: Br Shipping Fedn 1971-72, Int Shipping Fedn 1969-73; dep chm and tres Lloyd's Register of Shipping 1972-73 (chm 1973-83); chm: Hotel and Catering Ctee 1975-79, Marine Technol Mgmnt Ctee SRC; dir: Smit Int Gp (UK) Ltd 1973-87, Lloyd's of London Press Ltd 1983-, Harland and Wolff 1983-87, Chatham Historic Dockyard Tst 1984-; *Recreations* golf; *Clubs* Thorndon Park GC, Vincent's (Oxford); *Style—* Robert Huskisson, Esq, CBE; Lanterns, 3 Luppitt Close, Hutton Mount, Brentwood, Essex

HUSS, Lawrence John; s of Laurence Leslie Huss; *b* 16 Mar 1926; *Educ* Stirling HS, Univ of Glasgow (BSc, CEng, MICE); *m* 1952, Rita; 2 children; *Career* Flying Offr RAF, served UK and Germany; sub-agent Holloway Bros (London) Ltd 1948-57; construction mangr: Shepherds Ltd York 1957-63, Clugston Constructions Ltd 1963-68; md Appleby Slag Co Ltd 1968-; *Recreations* golf, fishing; *Style—* Lawrence Huss Esq; Dunluce, 26 Town Hill Broughton, Brigg, S Humberside DN20 OHD (☎ Brigg 53424)

HUSSEY, Anthony Laurence; s of Robert Edward Hussey (d 1947), and Veronica Antonia Maria, *née* Connolly; *b* 13 June 1937; *Educ* Beaumont Coll Old Windsor Berks; *m* Lorna Mary, da of James Cedric Ball; 2 s (Paul Alexander James b 20 April 1973, Charles Peter Anthony b 21 Feb 1975); *Career* Nat Serv 1 Bn Queens Royal Regt, 1 Bn Royal Sussex Regt served in Korea and Gibraltar 1956-58; dir Connolly Bros Ltd (Royal Warrant Holder on co behalf); Freeman City of London, Liveryman Worshipful Co of Furniture Makers; *Recreations* skiing, classic rallying, reading; *Clubs* Kanbahar Ski, RAC; *Style—* Anthony Hussey, Esq; 1 Pelhams Close, Esher, Surrey (☎ 78 66178); Connoly Bros (Curriers) Ltd, Wandle Bank, Wimbledon SW19 1DW (☎ 01 543 4611, fax 01 543 7455, car tel 0836 731 176, telex 27495)

HUSSEY, Marmaduke James; s of E R J Hussey, CMG (d 1958); *b* 29 August 1923; *Educ* Rugby, Trinity Coll Oxford; *m* 1959, Lady Susan Katharine, *qv*; 1 s, 1 da; *Career* Lt Grenadier Gds 1942-45; joined Assoc Newspapers 1949 (dir 1964), md Harmsworth Pubns 1967-70, md and chief exec Times Newspapers Ltd 1971-80 when owned by Lord Thomson; dir: Thomson Orgn 1971-80, Times Newspapers Ltd 1982-86, Colonial Mutual Life Assur (Br Bd) 1982-, MK Electric Gp 1982-88, William Collins plc 1985-89; Rhodes tstee 1972-; chm: Royal Marsden Hosp 1985-, BBC 1986-; memb: Govt Working Pty on Artificial Limbs and Appliance Centres in England 1984-86, Br Cncl 1982-, Mgmnt Ctee, King Edward's Hosp Fund for London 1987-; hon fell Trinity Coll Oxford 1989; *Clubs* Brooks's; *Style—* Marmaduke Hussey, Esq; Waldegrave House, Chewton Mendip, nr Bath, Somerset (☎ 076 121 289); BBC Broadcasting House, Portland Place, London W1A 1AA (☎ 01 580 4468)

HUSSEY, Richard Alban; s of Sydney Frederick George Hussey (d 1949), and Doris Catherine Ellen, *née* Baker (d 1983); *b* 20 Mar 1940; *Educ* Colfe's GS; *m* 1967, Kay Frances, da of Albert Edward Povey England; 1 s (Paul Nicholas b 1977); 1 da (Erin Elizabeth b 1970); *Career* dir: Weidenfeld and Nicolson Ltd 1970, Weidenfeld (publishers) Ltd 1986; *Recreations* cricket and rugby football; *Clubs* Old Colfeians Rugby and Cricket, played rugby for Kent on 5 occasions; *Style—* Richard Hussey; Weidenfeld and Nicolson, 91 Clapham High St, London SW4 (☎ 01 622 9933)

HUSSEY, Lady Susan Katharine; *née* Waldegrave; DCVO (1984, CVO 1971); 5 da of 12 Earl Waldegrave, KG, GCVO; *b* 1 May 1939; *m* 25 April 1959, Marmaduke James Hussey, *qv*; 1 s (James Arthur b 1961, Page of Honour to HM The Queen 1975-76), 1 da (Katharine Elizabeth (Lady Brooke) b 1964); *Career* woman of the bedchamber to HM The Queen 1960-; *Style—* Lady Susan Hussey, DCVO; Flat 15, 45-47 Courtfield Road, London SW7 (☎ 01 370 1414); Waldegrave House, Chewton Mendip, nr Bath, Somerset (☎ (076 121) 289)

HUSTLER, John Randolph; s of William Mostyn Collingwood Hustler (d 1976), and Angela Joan, *née* Hanson (d 1983); *b* 21 August 1946; *Educ* Eton; *m* 23 Sept 1978, Elizabeth Mary, da of Andrew George Hughes-Onslow (d 1979), 2 s (Charles b 1982, Frederick b 1986), 1 da (Willa b 1983); *Career* CA; ptnr Peat Marwick McLintock 1983- (joined 1969); FCA 1965; *Recreations* golf, gardening; *Clubs* Boodles; *Style—* John Hustler, Esq; Ripsley House, Liphook, Hants GU30 7JH (☎ 0428 722 223); 1 Puddle Dock, Blackfriars, London EC4V 3PD (☎ 01 236 8000, fax 01 583 1938, telex 8811541)

HUSTON, Lady Margot Lavinia; da of 6 Marquess of Cholmondeley, GCVO, MC; *b* 1950; *m* 1978, (Walter) Anthony Huston, only s of John Huston film dir (d 1987); 2 s (Mathew, b 1979, Jack b 1982), 1 da (Laura b 1981); *Style—* Lady Margot Huston; Las Caletas, Puerto Vallarta, Mexico

HUTCHINS, Brig Peter Edward; s of Edward Stanley Hutchins (d 1976), and Afreda Beryl, *née* Newton-Davey (d 1985); *b* 11 Feb 1919; *Educ* St Dunstans Coll London, UCL; *m* 1, 15 July 1944 (m dis), Cynthia Margaret, da of Gilbert Gaul Gross (d 1944), of Essex; 2 s (Jeremy b 1946, Miles b 1948), 1 da (Georgina b 1958); m 2, 28 July 1984, Barbara Patience, da of Frederick Dillon-Edwards (d 1952), of Bucks; *Career* WWII cmmnd RCS 1940, regtl cmmn 1944, eventually Brig GS MOD, ret 1970; attended Slade Sch of Fine Art 1937-39 (Alfred Rich Open Scholarship 1987, Slade Scholar 1938-39), princ CS 1971, md London Press Centre 1971-88, memb and dir Int Press Centre 1971-88; chm and dir Greston Sch 1968-75, chm Armed Forces Art Soc 1973-; FRSA, FBIM F; *Recreations* painting, boats, gardening; *Clubs* Army and Navy, Press; *Style—* Brig Peter E Hutchins; 6 Yew Tree Court, Goring-on-Thames, Oxfordsshire RG8 9HF (☎ 0491 874091)

HUTCHINSON, Rear Adm Christopher Haynes; CB (1961), DSO (1940), OBE (1946); s of late Rev Canon Frederick William Hutchinson; *b* 13 Mar 1906; *Educ* Lydgate House Prep Sch Hunstanton, RNC Osborne, RNC Dartmouth; *m* 1941, Nancy Marguerite, *née* Coppinger; *Career* Naval Cadet RNC Osborne 1919, served mainly in Submarines, serv WWII, cmd submarine Truant which sank German cruiser Karlsruhe 9 April 1940, submarine base Malta 1942 (despatches), Staff Offr Br Pacific Fleet 1945, qualified RN Staff Coll 1946 and Jt Serv Staff Coll (Directing Staff), cmd 3 Submarine Flotilla 1950-52, Sr Naval Advsr to UK High Cmmr Australia 1952-54, Capt RNC Greenwich 1954-56, Cdre 1 Class, Chief of Staff Far East Station 1956-59, Dir-Gen Personal Servs and Offr Appts 1959-61; ret 1962; *Style—* Rear Admiral Christopher Hutchinson, CB, DSO, OBE; Pipits Hill, Avington, nr Winchester, Hants, SO21 1DE, (☎ 096 278 363)

HUTCHINSON, Frederick; MBE (1945); s of William Hutchinson (d 1950), and Margaret, *née* Kitching (d 1968); *b* 5 Dec 1915; *Educ* St Bede's Coll Manchester; *m* 5 Sept 1942, Edith, da of Arthur Nield (d 1953), of Oldham; 3 s (Stephen b 1957, Michael b 1947, Nicholas b 1954), 1 da (Denise Stephanie b 1945); *Career* TA 1938, UK and NW Europe Maj DAA and QMG 21 Army Gp 1939-46 (despatches twice) non exec dir: Shiloh plc 1970-, Shiloh Spinners Ltd 1980-; sales dir Shiloh plc 1970-81, sales mngr Elk Mill/Royton Spg Co Ltd 1954-70, mangr Shiloh Mills 1949-54, asst mangr Park and Sandy Lane Mills 1948-49; *Recreations* golf; *Style—* Frederick Hutchinson, Esq, MBE; 37 Broadway, Royton, Oldham OL2 5DD (☎ 061 626 4847)

HUTCHINSON, George Peter; CBE (1984); s of Robert Hutchinson (d 1976), and Eleanor Heath; *b* 12 Dec 1926; *Educ* St Bees Sch Cumbria, Durham Univ (BSc); *m* 7 June 1958, Audrey, da of late WOA Dodds; 1 s (Robert b 1959), 1 da (Katherine b 1962); *Career* chartered surveyor and land agent, sr ptnr J M Clark & Ptnrs, dir Newcastle & Gateshead Water Co; Co Cncllr 1983-, ldr Cons gp Northumberland CC (chm educn ctee 1988-), dir Newcastle Int Airport, memb Northumberland DHA, chm Slaley Parish cncl; FRICS, CAAU; *Recreations* gardening, travel; *Clubs* Northern Counties (Newcastle), Farmers; *Style—* George Hutchinson, Esq; Low House, Hexham, Northumberland (☎ 0434 73 237); 5 Henotes, Hexham, Northumberland (☎ 0434 602 301)

HUTCHINSON, Hon Mrs Georgiana Ann; da of late 5 Baron Crofton; *b* 1955; *m* Brent Hutchinson; 1 da; *Style—* The Hon Mrs Hutchinson

HUTCHINSON, (Edward) Graham; s of Roger Hutchinson (d 1971), of Southport, Merseyside, and Katharine Norma, *née* Robinson (d 1984); *b* 11 Jan 1940; *Educ* Bryanston, King's Coll Cambridge (MA), Europ Inst of Business Admin Fontainebleau France (MBA); *m* 7 Nov 1970, Diana Fair, da of William Fair Milligan, of Heswall, Wirral, Merseyside; 1 s (Mark b 1974), 2 da (Camilla b 1972, Christina b 1977); *Career* md Dan-Air Servs Ltd 1981-; dir: Davies and Newman Hldgs plc 1980-, Bowater Europe 1977-80; dir and chief exec Neptun Int Hldg AG; *Recreations* leisure travel, music, family; *Clubs* Leander; *Style—* Graham Hutchinson, Esq; Silver Birches, Startins Lane, Cookham Dean, Berks SL6 9TS; Dan-Air Services Ltd, New City Court, 20 St Thomas St, London SE1 9RJ (☎ 01 378 6464, telex 888973, fax 01 403 2010)

HUTCHINSON, Isabella Juliet (Judy); DL (1985); da of Capt George Thomas Hutchinson (d 1948), and Isabella Rose, *née* Wolryche-Whitmore (d 1920); *b* 6 Dec 1916; *Educ* private; *Career* joined FANY 1935, ATS 1939-45, served AFHQ Italy, i/c Field Marshal Alexander's Intelligence War Room 1944-45 (later political intelligence); farmed Oxfordshire 1946-; private sec to: Lady Slim wife of Field Marshal Viscount Slim Govr Gen Aust 1953-54, Lady Haipes wife of Lord Haipes Govr Gen WI 1957-58; govr Utd Oxford Hosps 1965-73, trustee Nuffield Dominions Tst 1973, govr English Speaking Union 1975-81, London HO for Overseas Graduates 1974-, Fairbridge Drake See 1954-, vice chm Oxfordshire Red Cross 1961- (sometime vice pres), chm Oxfordshire Historic Churches Preservation Tst 1981-; High Sheriff Oxfordshire 1984-85, FRGS; *Recreations* travel, country pursuits; *Style—* Miss Judy Hutchinson, DL; Sarsden Glebe, Churchill, Oxford;

HUTCHINSON, (John) Maxwell; s of Frank Maxwell Hutchinson (d 1977), and Elizabeth Ross Muir, *née* Wright (d 1987); *b* 3 Dec 1948; *Educ* Scott Sutherland Sch of Architecture Aberdeen (Dip Arch), Architectural Assoc Sch of Architecture London; *Career* fndr Hutchinson & Ptnrs Architects Ltd 1972 (chm 1987-), chm Permarock Prods Ltd Loughborough 1985-; RIBA: memb cncl 1978-, chm energy policy ctee 1986-, sr vice-pres 1988-89, pres 1989-; vice- pres Industl Bldg Bureau 1988-; chm: Property Discussion Gp City Branch Ctee BIM 1985-88, London Branch Elgar Soc 1986-; assoc memb PRS 1988; Freeman City of London 1980, memb Ct of Assistance Worshipful Co of Chartered Architects 1988; RIBA, FBIM, FRSA; *Recreations* composing, recording, playing the guitar loudly, music of Edward Elgar, opera, ballet, theatre, riding, running, Rutland; *Clubs* Athenaeum; *Style*— Maxwell Hutchinson, Esq; 29 Pied Bull Court, Galen Place, London WC1; Cobblers Cottage, Empingham, Rutland; Hutchinson & Ptnrs, 201 St John St, London EC1

HUTCHINSON, Hon Nicholas St John; s of Baron Hutchinson of Lullington, QC (Life Peer); *b* 3 May 1946; *Style*— The Hon Nicholas Hutchinson

HUTCHINSON, Patricia Margaret; CMG (1981), CBE (1982); da of Francis Bernard Hutchinson (d 1982), and Margaret Evelyn Hutchinson (d 1980); *b* 18 June 1926; *Educ* abroad, St Paul's Girls Sch London, Somerville Coll Oxford; *Career* HM Dip Serv: FCO 1948-50, 3 sec Bucharest 1950-52, FCO 1952-55, 2 then 1 sec Berne 1955-58, 1 sec (commercial) Washington 1958-61, FCO 1961-64, 1 sec Lima 1964-67, dep vice-rep to Cncl of Europe 1967-69; cncllr: Stockholm 1969-72, UK Perm Delgn to OECD 1973-75; consul gen Geneva 1975-80, ambass Montevideo 1980-83, consul gen Barcelona 1983-86; pres Somerville ASM 1988-; *Recreations* travel, reading, music; *Clubs* Oxford and Cambridge; *Style*— Miss Patricia Hutchinson, CMG, CBE; c/o Nat Westminster Bank plc, 6 Tothill St, London SW1

HUTCHINSON, (George) Peter; CBE (1984); s of late Robert Hutchinson, and Eleanor Heath, *née* Moffitt; *b* 12 Dec 1926; *Educ* St Bees Sch Cumbria, Durham Univ (BSc); *m* 7 June 1958, Audrey, da of late W O A Dodds; 1 s (Robert b 1959), 1 da (Katherine b 1962); *Career* chartered surveyor and land agent; sr ptnr J M Clark & Ptnrs; dir: Newcastle and Gateshead Water Co, Newcastle Int Airport; memb Northumberland CC 1973-, ldr Cons gp 1985-, chm Educ Ctee 1988-; chm Northern Area Cons Cncl 1981-84; FRICS; *Recreations* gardening, travel; *Clubs* Northern Counties (Newcastle-upon-Tyne), Farmers'; *Style*— Peter Hutchinson, Esq, CBE; Low House, Hexham, Northumberland (☎ 043 473 237); J M Clark & Ptnrs, 5 Hencotes, Hexham, Northumberland (☎ 0434 602301)

HUTCHINSON, His Hon Judge Richard Hampson; s of John Riley Hutchinson (d 1958), of Leeds, and May, *née* Hampson (d 1959); *b* 31 August 1927; *Educ* Hull Univ Coll (LLB), St Bede's GS Bradford; *m* 1954, Nancy Mary, da of John William Jones Warrington (d 1983); 2 s (Christopher, Damian), 3 da (Paula, Hilary, Marie-Louise); *Career* Nat Service 1949-51, Flying Offr RAF; barr Gray's Inn 1949, practised NE Circuit 1949-74; recorder: Rotherham 1971, Crown Ct 1972-74; circuit judge 1974-; *Recreations* reading, conversation; *Style*— His Hon Judge Hutchinson; Crown Court, Lincoln

HUTCHINSON OF LULLINGTON, Baron (Life Peer UK 1978); Jeremy Nicolas Hutchinson; QC (1961); o s of St John Hutchinson, KC (d 1943), and Mary, o da of Sir Hugh Barnes, KCSI, KCVO; *b* 28 Mar 1915; *Educ* Stowe, Magdalen Coll Oxford (MA); *m* 1, 1940 (m dis 1966), Dame Peggy Ashcroft, DBE, the actress *qv*; 1 s (Hon Nicholas St John, *qv*), 1 da (Hon Eliza b 14 June 1941); m 2, 1966, June Osborn; *Career* served WW II RNVR; barr 1939, recorder Bath 1962-72, Crown Court 1972-76; sat as Labour Peer in Lords till 1981/82 when joined SDP; vice-chm Arts Cncl 1977-79, chm Tstees Tate Gallery 1980-84 (tstee 1977-); prof of law RA 1988; tstee Chantrey Bequest 1987; *Clubs* MCC; *Style*— The Rt Hon Lord Hutchinson of Lullington, QC; House of Lords, Westminster SW1

HUTCHISON, David Alan; MBE (1976); s of Hector Donald Hutchison (d 1948), of Amberley Gardens, Bush Hill Park, Enfield, Middx, and Winifred, *née* Middlehurst (d 1986); *b* 13 Jan 1937; *Educ* Royal Masonic Sch Bushey Herts, Bartlett Sch of Architecture Univ Coll London (BA); *m* 3 April 1961 (sep 1984), Helen Elizabeth, da of Arthur George Penn (d 1981), of High St Pembury, Tunbridge Wells, Kent; 2 s (Michael b 1 Nov 1963, Peter b 24 Dec 1966), 2 da (Gillian b 21 Jan 1962, Christine b 9 Aug 1965); *Career* architect, worked with Powell & Moya 1960-64, chm HLM (formerly Hutchison Locke & Monk) 1988- (fndr ptnr 1964), architect for major public sector cmmns in health and civic authys 1964-88; health projects (hosps) incl: Bournemouth, Cheltenham, Ealing, Whipps Cross, Lister, Sheffield Northern Gen, Medway, St James Dublin; civic projects: Surrey Heath Borough Cncl, Broxbourne Borough Cncl, Daventry Dist Cncl, Colchester Borough Cncl, Waltham Forest Cncl, Macclesfield Cncl Offices, cmmns for Reading and Surrey Univs; winner: int competition (architecture) Paisley Civic Centre 1964, 6 Civic Tst awards DOE Good Housing Award, RIBA Architecture, Redland Roof Tile Award; nat seat on cncl RIBA 1987, assessor Civic Tst; Freeman: City of London 1977, Worshipful Co of Constructors 1977, Worshipful Co of Arbitrators 1987; RIBA, ARIAS, FIA, FFB, AInst(Hosp)E, FRSA 1989; *Recreations* amateur theatre, local amenity soc; *Clubs* Camberley Soc (chm), Farnborough and RAE Operatic Soc, Camms Productions; *Style*— David Hutchison, Esq, MBE; 43 London Road, Camberley, Surrey GU15 3UG (☎ 0276 27419); Lone Pines, North Road, Bathwick, Bath, Avon BA2 6JB (☎ 0225 66915); HLM Architects Ltd, Rayleigh House, 2 Richmond Hill, Richmond, Surrey, TW10 6QX (☎ 01 948 3136, fax 01 940 0160, car tel 0836 774264, telex 892410)

HUTCHISON, Geordie Oliphant; s of Lt Col R G O Hutchison (d 1934), and R G, *née* Black (d 1985); *b* 11 June 1934; *Educ* Eton; *m* 1964, Virginia, da of Flt Lt Barbezat (d 1943); 2 s (James b 1966, Timothy b 1967), 1 da (Victoria b 1970); *Career* Lt RNVR 1957; md Calders and Grandidge Ltd 1974-; cmmr Forestry Cmmn 1981-; chm: Meyer Timberframe Ltd 1985-, PDM Ltd 1987-; *Recreations* golf, shooting, skiing; *Clubs* Royal and Ancient GC; *Style*— Geordie Hutchison, Esq; Bank of Scotland, Haymarket, Swallowfield House, Welby, Grantham, Lincolnshire; Calders and Grandidge Ltd, London Road, Boston, Lincolnshire (☎ 0205 66660, telex 378267, fax 0205 52592)

HUTCHISON, Lt-Cdr Sir (George) Ian Clark; DL (Edinburgh 1958); s of Sir George A Clark Hutchison, KC, MP (d 1928); *b* 4 Jan 1903; *Educ* Edinburgh Acad, RNC Osborne, RNC Dartmouth; *m* 1926, Sheena Campbell (d 1966); 1 da; *Career* joined RN 1916, ret 1931, recalled 1939, served Naval Ordnance Inspection Dept 1939-43; MP (U) Edinburgh (West) 1941-59; memb Royal Co of Archers (Queen's Body Gd for Scotland); kt 1954; *Style*— Lt-Cdr Sir Ian Hutchison, DL; 16 Wester Coates Gdns, Edinburgh, Scotland EH12 5LT (☎ 031 337 4888)

HUTCHISON, Sir (William) Kenneth; CBE (1954); s of William Hutchison; *b* 30 Oct 1903; *Educ* Edinburgh Academy, CCC Oxford; *m* 1929, Dorothea Marion Eva Bluett; 1 da; *Career* joined staff of Gas Light and Coke Co 1926, asst dir Hydrogen Production Air Ministry 1940, dir Compressed Gas 1943-45 (md 1947), chm SE Gas Bd 1948-59, dep chm Gas Cncl 1960-66; pres National Soc for Clean Air 1969-71; FRS, REng, FIChem; kt 1962; *Style*— Sir Kenneth Hutchison, CBE; 2 Arlington Rd, Twickenham, Middx TW1 2BG (☎ 01 892 1685)

HUTCHISON, Sir Peter; 2 Bt (UK 1939), of Thurle, Streatley, Co Berks; s of Sir Robert Hutchison, 1 Bt, MD, FRCP (d 1960), of Thurle Grange, Streatley-on-Thames, nr Reading, and Laetitia Norah, *née* Ede (d 1963); *b* 27 Sept 1907; *Educ* Marlborough, Lincoln Coll Oxford (MA); *m* 16 July 1949, Mary-Grace, da of Very Rev Algernon Giles Seymour (d 1933, Rector and Provost of St Mary's Cathedral, Glasgow); 2 s (Robert, Mark b 1960), 2 da (Elspeth b 1950, Alison b 1951); *Heir* s, Robert Hutchison, *qv*; *Career* Flt Lt RAFVR 1941-45, intelligence offr photographic reconaissance unit (PRU); admitted slr 1932; asst slr; Warwicks CC 1934-36, E Suffolk CC 1936-47; dep clerk of the peace of the CC E Suffolk 1947-70, clerk of the peace and county slr E Suffolk CC 1970-72; memb Suffolk Coastal Dist Cncl 1973-83; chm govrs Orwell Park Prep Sch Nacton nr Ipswich 1974-86; *Recreations* gardening, reading; *Clubs* Ipswich and Suffolk (Ipswich); Sir Peter Hutchison

HUTCHISON, Sir Peter Craft; 2 Bt (UK 1956), of Rossie, Co Perth; s of Sir James Riley Holt Hutchison, 1 Bt, DSO, TD (d 1979), and Anne, Lady Hutchison (d 1988), *qv*; *b* 5 June 1935; *Educ* Eton, Magdalene Coll Cambridge (BA); *m* 1966, Virginia, da of John Millar Colville, of Gribloch, Kippen, Stirlingshire; 1 s; *Heir* s, James Colville Hutchison b 7 Oct 1967; *Career* former Lt Royal Scots Greys; chm Hutchison and Craft Ltd, dir Stakis plc and other cos; bd memb Scottish Tourist Bd 1981-87, chm of tstees Royal Botanic Garden Edinburgh, bd memb Br Waterways Bd 1987-; *Style*— Sir Peter Hutchison, Bt; Milton House, Milton, by Dumbarton

HUTCHISON, Robert; s and h of Sir Peter Hutchison, 2 Bt, *qv*; *b* 25 May 1954; *Educ* Marlborough; *m* 7 Feb 1987, Anne Margaret, er da of Sir Michael Thomas, 11 Bt, *qv*; 1 s (Hugo Thomas Alexander b 16 April 1988); *Career* withk J and A Scrimgeour Ltd 1973-78, financial adviser 1978-; *Recreations* tennis, watching association football, travelling, golf; *Clubs* Lansdowne; *Style*— Robert Hutchison, Esq; 40 Averill St, London W6 8EB

HUTCHISON, Sidney Charles; CVO (1977, LVO 1967); s of Henry Hutchison (d 1979), and Augusta Rose, *née* Timmons (d 1912); *b* 26 Mar 1912; *Educ* Holloway Sch London, London Univ (Dip History of Art); *m* 1937, Nancy Arnold (d 1985), da of Alfred Brindley (d 1962); *Career* Lt Cdr RNVR 1939-45; joined staff RA 1929, organist and choirmaster St Matthews Westminster 1933-37, lectr history of art Univ of London 1957-67, librarian RA 1949-68, sec RA 1968-82; govr Holloway Sch 1969-81; gen cmmr of Taxes 1972-87; tstee Chantrey Bequest 1982; sec: EA Abbey Memorial Tst Fndn 1960-87, Incorporated EA Abbey Scholarships 1965-, E Vincent Harris Fndn 1970-87, BR Inst Fnd 1968-82; pres Southgate Soc of Arts 1983-, hon archivist RAA, memb ICOM, FRSA, FSA, FMA, FAAA; Offr Polonia Restituta (1971), Chevalier Belgian Order of the Crown 1972, Grand Decoration of Honour (silver) Austria 1972, Cavaliere Ufficiale al Merito della Republica Italiana 1980; *Recreations* music, travel; *Clubs* Athenaeum, Arts; *Style*— Sidney Hutchison, Esq; 60 Belmont Close, Mount Pleasant, Cockfosters, Herts EN4 9LT (☎ 01 449 9821); Royal Academy of Arts, Piccadilly, London W1V 0DS (☎ 01 439 7438), telex 21812 RAARTS-G)

HUTCHISON, Prof William McPhee; s of William Hutchinson (d 1956), of 18 Merryvale Ave, Giffnock, Glasgow, and Anne, *née* McPhee (d 1962); *b* 2 July 1924; *Educ* Eastwood HS, Glasgow Univ (BSc, PhD), Strathclyde Univ (DSc); *m* 15 March 1963, Rev Ella Duncan, da of James McLaughland, of 29 Fairway, Bearsden, Glasgow; 2 s (Bruce b 1964, Leslie b 1966); *Career* Strathclyde Univ 1952-: asst lectr 1952-53, lectr 1953-68, sr lectr 1969-71, prof parasitology 1971-86, res prof 1986-; Fencing Blue Glasgow Univ Athletic Club 1949, Scottish Epée Open Champion 1949, Ford Epée Cup 1949, Capt and Champion Glasgow Univ Fencing Club 1949-51; elder Church of Scotland; FIBiol 1971, CBiol 1971, FRSE 1973, FLS 1974; *Recreations* gardening, woodwork, writing, music; *Style*— Prof William Hutchison; 597 Kilmarnock Rd, Newlands, Glasgow G43 2TH (☎ 041 637 488); Biology Division, University of Strathclyde, Glasgow G1 1XW (☎ 041 552 4400)

HUTLEY, Peter William; s of William Hutley, of Garden Cottage, Wintershall, Bramley, Surrey and Dorothy Violet, *née* Abbott; *b* 24 Dec 1926; *Educ* East Barnet Sch, Coll of Estate Mgmnt; *m* 19 June 1954, Ann Mary Morris, da of Thomas Morris Cox (d 1974), of Penny Pot Cottage, Cobham, Surrey; 2 s (Nicholas Peter b 1959, Edward Thomas b 1962), 2 da (Charlotte Ann b 1956, Henrietta Frances Mary b 1965); *Career* Capt (temp) RE, Br Mil Mission to Burma 1945-48; sr ptnr Pepper Angliss and Yarwood 1951-76, dep chm and md Property Growth Assurance Co Ltd 1968-76; chm: Shenley Tst Ltd 1973-76, Hutley Holdings plc 1976, Northbourne Developments Pty Ltd 1983, Peter Hutley Investments Pty Ltd 1967, Hutley Rural Property Trust 1983, Pitt Street Securities Pty Ltd 1983; OStJ; FRICS; *Clubs* Bucks, Royal Thames Yacht; *Style*— Peter Hutley, Esq; Wintershall, Bramley, Surrey GU5 0LR (☎ 0483 892167, fax 0483 898709, telex 859442 WINHUT, car ☎ 0836 591269)

HUTSON, Sir Francis Challenor; CBE (1960); s of Francis Hutson, of Barbados; *b* 13 Sept 1895; *Educ* Harrison Coll Barbados, Derby Tech Coll; *m* 1, 1925, Muriel Allen Simpkin (d 1945); 2 s, 1 da; m 2, 1947, Edith Doris Howell; *Career* served WW I RN; sr ptnr D M Simpson and Co (Consulting Engrs) 1943-70; MLC Barbados 1947-62, MEC Barbados 1958-61, PC Barbados 1961-70; kt 1963; *Style*— Sir Francis Hutson, CBE; Fleetwood, Erdiston Hill, St Michael, Barbados (☎ 0101 429 3905)

HUTSON, Maurice Arthur; s of William Arthur Hutson (d 1980), of S Yorkshire, and Ivy, *née* Roberts; *b* 27 Jan 1934; *Educ* Gainsborough Technical Coll, Leeds Coll of Technology; *m* 1959, Janet, da of Arthur Edward Parkin, of S Yorkshire; 2 s (Mark Andrew b 1961, Jonathan Peter b 1970), 1 da (Helen Claire b 1963); *Career* chartered engr; devpt engr Tarmac Roadstone Ltd 1963-71, (production and engrg mangr 1965, staff offr 1970); chm and md: Seaham Harbour Dock Co 1971-81 (dir 1981-), Mahcon Construction (Services) Ltd 1972-, Transport and Aggregates Ltd 1972-81, Wath Quarries Ltd 1977, Allerton Engrg Ltd 1983-, Naylor Sportscars Ltd 1986-, Hutson Motor Company Ltd 1986-; dir: Neocast Ltd 1980-, The Sundial Hotel Ltd Northallerton N Yorks, The Seaham Harbour Dock Co; CEng, MIMechE, MIProdE, FIQ; *Recreations* motor sport, travel and walking, gardening; *Clubs* Rotary (Stokesley), 41 Club (Gisborough); *Style*— Maurice Hutson, Esq; South Hambledon, Morton Carr Lane, Nunthorpe, nr Middlesbrough, Cleveland TS7 0JU (☎ 0642 315077); Allerton Engineering Ltd, Romanby Road Works, Northallerton, N Yorks DL7 8NG (☎ 0609 774471/2, telex 58102 ALLFAB, fax 0609 780364)

HUTSON, Thomas Guybon; TD (1966); s of Guybon John Hutson (d 1963), of Kensington Mansons, and Diana Chisholm, *née* Davidson (d 1972); *b* 17 April 1931; *Educ* Morrison's Acad Crieff, St Paul's Sch Hammersmith; *m* 9 May 1959, (Ann) Rosemary, da of Arthur Cranfield Coltman (d 1981), of Westheath Close, Hampstead; 1 s (Charles b 1960), 3 da (Catherine b 1962, Anna b 1964, Fiona b 1970); *Career* Nat Serv: Private Gordon Highlanders 1949, cmmnd 2 Lt 1950, served Highland Bde Trg

Centre, Fort George and Cameron Barracks Inverness 1951, 2 Lt 1 Bn London Scottish (TA) 1951, ret as Maj 1967; joined Bank of England 1948 (and after War Serv 1951), seconded Libya to establish Central Bank Tripoli 1957, mangr exchange control dept Nat Bank Libya 1958, returned Bank of England 1959, Tozer Kemsley & Millbourn 1960 (who founded Int Factors), md Int Factors 1978- (dir 1967), pres Int Factors Gp 1985-87, chm Assoc Br Factors 1987-89; memb cncl E Sussex Employers Network 1988-; FICM, FRPSL, memb Caledonian Soc London; *Books* Management of Trade Credit (1968); *Recreations* tennis, bridge, chess, opera, hill walking, philately, travel; *Style*— Thomas Hutson, Esq, TD; Ditchling Ct, Ditchling, Sussex BN6 8SP (☎ 07918 3558); Int Factors Ltd, Sovereign House, Queens Rd, Brighton, Sussex (☎ 0273 21211, fax 0273 771501, telex 87382)

HUTT, Rev David Handley; s of Frank Handley Hutt, and Evelyn Violet Catherine, *née* Faarup; *b* 24 August 1938; *Educ* Brentwood, RMA Sandhurst, King's Coll London (AKC); *Career* Regular Army 1957-64; ordained: deacon 1969, priest 1970; curate: Bedford Park London 1969-70, St Matthew Westminster 1970-73; priest vicar and succentor Southwark Cath 1973-78, sr chaplain King's Coll Taunton 1978-82; vicar: St Alban and St Patrick Birmingham 1982-86, All Saints' St Marlebone 1986-; *Recreations* gardening, cooking, music, theatre; *Clubs* Athenaeum; *Style*— The Rev David Hutt; All Saints Vicarage, 7 Margaret St, London W1N 8JQ (☎ 01 636 1788)

HUTT, Peter Morrice; s of Sqdn Ldr Harry Morrice Hutt, of Caversham, Reading, Berks, and Joan Ethel Ludlaw, *née* Whitmore; *b* 15 April 1945; *Educ* Leighton Park Sch, Southampton Univ (LLB); *m* 23 March 1974, Cynthia Anne, da of John Gauntlett Gubb (d 1988), of Ultenhage, SA; 1 s (Stephen b 1977) ; *Career* admitted slr 1969, ptnr Brain & Brain 1973-, Notary Public 1978; Rotherfield Peppard: chm Parish Cncl 1987-, lay chm All Saints parochial church cncl 1986-, tstee Releif in Need Charity, tstee Mem/Hall, clerk Polehampton Charities Twyford, former memb Caversham Round Table; Law Soc 1967, slr Benevolent Assoc 1969, Provincial Notaries Soc 1978; *Recreations* music, walking, gardening, tennis; *Style*— Peter Hutt, Esq; Rushton House, Church Lane, Rotherfield Peppard, Henley-on-Thames RG9 5JR (☎ 049 17 335); Brain & Brain, Addington House, 73 London St, Reading RG1 4QB (☎ 0734 581 441, fax 0734 597 875, telex 847645)

HUTTON, Alan Brian; s of Leslie Edward Hutton (d 1981), of Leeds, Yorks, and Annie Nora, *née* Browne; *b* 12 April 1937; *Educ* King Edward V GS,; *m* 27 Aug 1965, Brenda, da of Francis Laidler; 1 da (Kate Frances b 29 July 1966); *Career* md: HS Hutton & Sons 1959-75, LR Sarrom Ltd 1975-86; own business Salford Meat Products Ltd 1987-; Freeman: City of London 1983, The Worshipful Co of Butchers 1982; *Recreations* soccer, horse racing, rugby league, cricket; *Style*— Alan Hutton, Esq; c/o CR Barron (Markets) Ltd, 207 Central Meat Markets, Smithfield, London EC1A 9LH; (☎ 0744 819478, fax 0744 819511)

HUTTON, Alasdair Henry; MBE (1986), TD (1977), MEP (EDG) S Scotland 1979-; s of Alexander Hutton (d 1954), and Margaret Elizabeth, *née* Henderson; *b* 19 May 1940; *Educ* Gatehouse of Fleet Sch Dollar Academy, Brisbane State HS Australia; *m* 1975, Deirdre Mary, da of Kenneth Alexander Hume Cassels, of Wimbish Green, Essex; 2 s (Thomas b 1978, Nicholas b 1982); *Career* journalist and broadcaster; EDG spokesman on: regnl policy in the Euro Parl 1983-87, budgetary control 1987-; tstee Community Service Volunteers 1985-; 2 i/c 15 Scottish (Volunteer) Bn The Parachute Regt 1979-86; memb Queens Body Gd for Scotland, Royal Co of Archers 1987-; life memb John Buchan Soc, patron Volonteurop, elder Church of Scotland 1985-; *Style*— Alasdair Hutton, Esq, MBE, TD, MEP; 34 Woodmarket, Kelso TD5 7AX (☎ 0573 24369)

HUTTON, Brian Gerald; s of James Hutton (d 1977), of Barrow-in-Furness, Cumbria, and Nora Hutton (d 1984); *b* 1 Nov 1933; *Educ* Barrow GS, Nottingham Univ (BA), UCL (Dip in Archive Admin); *m* 23 May 1958, Serena Quartermaine, da of Charles Ernest May (d 1976), of Kingston Blount, Oxon; 1 s (Patrick James b 1964), 1 da (Katherine Mary b 1961); *Career* Nat Serv RN, Jt Servs Sch Linguists 1955-57; asst archivist Herts Co Record Off 1959-60; 1960-74: asst keeper and dep dir Public Record Office NI, administrator Ulster Historical Fndn, lectr archive admin Queen's Univ Belfast, princ tres div NI Civ Serv; sec and dep library Scotland 1974-88, archives conslt 1988-; cmmnd Kentucky Colonel for Services to Archives 1982; *Recreations* walking in lake district, visiting art galleries, listening to music; *Clubs* Royal Commonwealth Soc, New (Edinburgh); *Style*— Brian Hutton, Esq; Elma Cottage, The Green, Kingston Blount, Oxon OX9 4SE (☎ 0844 54 173); 9 Wilton Rd, Edinburgh EH16 5NX (☎ 031 667 2145)

HUTTON, His Hon Judge Gabriel Bruce; s of late Robert Crompton Hutton, of Gloucs, and late Elfreda, *née* Bruce; fourth successive generation of judges living in Gloucs; *b* 27 August 1932; *Educ* Marlborough, Trinity Coll Cambridge (BA); *m* 1965, Deborah Leigh, da of Vivian Leigh Windus (d 1950), of Sussex; 1 s (Alexander b 1972), 2 da (Joanna b 1966, Tamsin b 1968); *Career* barr Inner Temple 1956, dep chm Glos Quarter Sessions 1971, rec order Crown Ct 1972-78, circuit judge 1978, liason judge for Gloucs and designated judge for Gloucester Crown Ct 1987; *Recreations* hunting (chm Berkeley), boating, shooting; *Style*— His Hon Judge Hutton; Chestal, Dursley, Gloucs (☎ 0453 3285)

HUTTON, Hon Mrs (Jacqueline Patricia); *née* Grant of Grant; da (by 1 m) of 5 Baron Strathspey; *b* 1942; *m* 1966, Malcolm Usheen Lingen Hutton; *Style*— The Hon Mrs Hutton; Kinsley, Banchory, Kincardineshire

HUTTON, John Christopher; s of John Francis Hutton, of Cranmer Ct, Llandaff, Cardiff, and Elizabeth Margery Ethel, *née* Pugh; *b* 7 June 1937; *Educ* Kingswood Sch Bath, Ch Ch Oxford (MA); *m* 5 Aug 1963, Elizabeth Ann, da of Prof Eric Evans (d 1967); 2 da (Catrin b 1965, Bethan b 1968); *Career* Nat Serv RA Cyprus 1956-58; methods engr Tube Investmts 1963-64 (grad trainee 1961-63); Bristol and West Bldg Soc: PA to gen mangr 1964-67, res mangr 1967-76, asst gen mangr mktg and res 1976-86 (corporate info and analysis 1986-88), conslt fin mktg 1988-; conslt Money Which? 1971-, chm housing fin panel Bldg Socs Assoc 1973-84 (memb 1967-), co-chm tech sub-ctee of jt advsy ctee on mortgage fin Br Socs Assoc 1973-82; memb NEDO housing strategy ctee 1975-77 (construction industs jt forecasting ctee 1978-), ldr Netherlands res gp BSA 1979; memb: cncl sub-ctee on reserves and liquidity BSA 1981, fin advertising sub-ctee Advertising Standards Authy 1982; dir: Bristol Bldgs Preservation Tst Ltd 1984-, Wildscreen Tst Ltd 1987-, Bristol & West Personal Pensions Ltd 1988-; FSS 1968, assoc IMS 1968, memb Chartered Bldg Socs Inst; author of many articles for the Nat Press; *Recreations* antiques, wine, countryside, journalism; *Style*— John Hutton, Esq; Ferns Hill, Kingsweston Rd, Bristol BS11 0UX (☎ 0272 824 324); Wyevern, Aberedw, Builth Wells, Powys LD2 2UN

HUTTON, Sir Leonard; s of Henry Hutton (d 1947); *b* 23 June 1916; *Educ* Littlemoor Sch Pudsey; *m* 1939, Dorothy Mary Dennis; 2 s; *Career* served WW II with RA and APTC; professional cricketer, captained England: v India 1952, v Australia 1953 and 1954, v Pakistan 1954; kt 1956; *Style*— Sir Leonard Hutton; 1 Coombe Neville, Warren Rd, Kingston-on-Thames, Surrey KT2 7HW (☎ 01 942 0604)

HUTTON, Matthew Charles Arthur; s of Capt Ronald David Hutton, MC (d 1984), of Langley Grange, Loddon, Norfolk, and Rhodanthe Winnaretta, *née* Leeds; *b* 10 Sept 1953; *Educ* Eton, Ch Ch Oxford (BA 1975); *m* 6 Oct 1984, Anne Elizabeth Caroline, da of Leslie James Leppard, DFC, of Cobb Cottage, Dalwood, Axminster, Devon; 1 s (David b 1988), 1 da (Victoria b 1986); *Career* tax conslt, ptnr Daynes Hill & Perks (Slrs) Norwich 1987-89, govr St Felix Sch Southwold 1987; AInstT 1980; *Recreations* family life, country pursuits; *Clubs* MCC, Norfolk (Norwich); *Style*— Matthew Hutton, Esq; Abbot's House, 25 White Hart St, Aylsham, Norfolk NR11 6HG (☎ 0263 734634)

HUTTON, (Hubert) Robin; s of Kenneth Douglas Hutton, of 41 The Retreat, Princes Risborough, Bucks, and Dorothy, *née* de Wilde; *b* 22 April 1933; *Educ* Merchant Taylors', Peterhouse Cambridge (MA); *m* 1, 25 June 1956 (m dis 1967), Valerie, *née* Riseborough; 1 s (Andrew b 1958), 1 da (Sarah b 1960); m 2, 3 May 1969, Deborah, *née* Berkeley; 2 step da (Susan b 1957, Linda b 1959); *Career* Royal Tank Regt 1951-53; asst gen mangr Finance Corpn for Industry Ltd 1956-61, dir Hambros Bank Ltd 1961-70, special advsr HM Govt 1970-73, dir of Fin Insts Commission of Euro Communities 1973-78, exec dir SG Warburg and Co Ltd 1978-82; dir gen: Accepting Houses Ctee, Issuing Houses Assoc 1982-87, Br Merchant Banking and Securities Houses Assoc 1988-; non exec dir: Assoc Book Publishers 1982-87, Northern Rock Building Soc; dir Investmt Mgmnt Regulatory Organisation Ltd; memb: exec ctee Br Bankers Assoc, cncl Foreign Bondholders; chm: English National Advsy Ctee on Telecommunications, Londonclear Ltd; *Recreations* skiing, cricket, gardening, travel; *Clubs* MCC; *Style*— Robin Hutton, Esq; Church Farm, Athelington, nr Eye, Suffolk (☎ 072 876 361); 6 Frederick's Place, London EC2R 8BT (☎ 01 796 3606, fax 01 796 4345)

HUTTON, Lady; Virginia Jacomyn; JP; da of late Sir George Young, 4 Bt, MVO; *b* 1911; *Educ* England, Abroad; *m* 1936, Sir Noel Kilpatrick Hutton, CGB, QC (sometime First Parly Counsel; d 1984), s of William Hutton (d 1933); 2 s, 2 da; *Style*— Lady Hutton, JP; 8 Wyndham Way, Oxford OX2 8DF

HUTTON, Maj Gen Walter Morland; CB (1964), CBE (1960), DSO (1943), MC (1936), Bar (1942); s of Walter Charles Stritch Hutton (d 1953), and Amy Mary, *née* Newton (d 1950); *b* 5 May 1912; *Educ* Allhallows Sch, Parkstone Sch, RMC Sandhurst, Staff Coll, Imperial Defence Coll; *m* 1945, Peronelle Marie Stella, da of Cecil Arthur Stewart Luxmoore-Ball (d 1963); 2 s (David, Anthony), 1 da (Gillian); *Career* cmmnd 2 Lieut RTC 1932, served in England, Egypt and Palestine 1936, 1 Class Army Interpreter in Arabic 1937, served in WW II cmdg: 5 RTR in Western Desert, Alamein and N Africa, 40 RTR in Italy; Cmdt Sandhurst 1944-45, cmdg Specialized Armour Devpt Unit 1946-47, Br Liason Offr Kentucky and Virginia USA 1947-49, Instr Staff Coll Camberley 1949-51, Col 1953, Brig 1955, BGS Arab Legion Jordan 1953-56, Imperial Defence Coll 1957, Dep Cdr (Land) BFAP (Aden) 1957-59, Dir of Admin Plans War Off 1959-60, Memb Jt Planning Staff 1959-60, Maj Gen 1961-64, Dir Gen Fighting Vehicles War Off 1961-64, Sr Army Directing Staff Imperial Defence Coll 1964-66, ret; home bursar Jesus Coll Oxford 1966 (fell 1967, MA 1967), examiner Military History Oxford 1968-69, memb bd of govrs Utd Oxford Hosps 1969-72; *Recreations* reading, chess; *Style*— Maj Gen Walter Hutton, CB, CBE, DSO, MC; c/o Royal Bank of Scotland, 2 Old Town Street, Plymouth, Devon PL1 1DP

HUXLEY, Sir Andrew Fielding; OM (1983); s of Leonard Huxley (2 s of T H Huxley, the scientist and humanist), and his 2 w Rosalind, *née* Bruce; half-bro of Sir Julian Huxley, the biologist, and Aldous Huxley, the novelist; *b* 22 Nov 1917; *Educ* University Coll Sch Westminster, Trinity Coll Cambridge; *m* 1947, Jocelyn Richenda Gammell, JP, da of Michael Pease (whose paternal grandmother was Susanna, da of Joseph Fry, of the Bristol Quaker family of cocoa manufacturers, and 1 cous of Sir Theodore Fry, 1 Bt), and his w Hon Helen, *née* Wedgwood, JP, eldest da of 1 Baron Wedgwood; 1 s (Stewart Leonard b 1949), 5 da (Janet b 1948, Camilla b 1952, Eleanor b 1959, Henrietta b 1960, Clare b 1962); *Career* operational research for Anti-Aircraft Cmd and Admty WWII; fell Trinity Coll Cambridge 1941-60, dir of studies 1952-60; demonstrator physiology dept Cambridge 1946-50, asst dir of research 1951-59, reader in experimental biophysics 1959-60; Jodrell prof of physiology and head of dept UCL 1960-69, Fullerian prof of physiology and comparative anatomy Royal Inst+1967-73, Royal Soc research prof in Univ of London 1969-83, emeritus prof of physiology 1983; Cecil H and Ida Green visiting prof Univ of BC 1980; pres Royal Society 1980-85; (FRS 1955, memb cncl 1960-62 and 1977-79); master of Trinity Coll Cambridge 1984-; chm British Nat Ctee for Physiological Sciences 1979-80, memb ARC 1977-81; pres British Assoc for Advancement of Science 1976-77; tstee: British Museum (Natural History) 1981-, Science Museum 1984-88; memb Nature Conservancy Cncl 1985-87; hon memb Royal Inst (1981), Royal Irish Acad (1986), Japan Acad of Science (1988); Hon Fell: Inst of Biology, Darwin Coll Cambridge, Royal Soc of Canada, Royal Soc of Edinburgh, Univ Coll London, Imperial Coll, Fellowship of Engineering, Queen Mary Coll, Trinity Coll Cambridge; foreign assoc Nat Acad Sci USA; pres Int Union of Physiological Sciences 1986-; Nobel Laureate in Physiology or Medicine 1963, Copley Medal Royal Society 1973; Hon Dr of 20 Univs; kt 1974; *Books* Reflections on Muscle (1980); *Recreations* walking, designing scientific instruments; *Clubs* Oxford and Cambridge; *Style*— Sir Andrew Huxley, OM; The Master's Lodge, Trinity Coll, Cambridge CB2 1TQ (☎ 0223 338412)

HUXLEY, Col Colin Wylde; s of Brig Christopher Huxley, CBE (d 1965), of London, and Esmée, *née* Ritchie; *b* 21 April 1928; *Educ* Bradfield Coll, RMA Sandhurst; *m* 29 March 1958, Alison Barbour, da of George James Harris, MC (d 1958), of York; 1 s (Henry b 1962), 1 da (Annabel b 1960); *Career* cmmnd KOYLI 1948; served: Malaya, Germany, Aden, Cyprus, Berlin; instr RMA Sandhurst 1958-61, Staff GHQ FARELF Singapore 1961-63, MOD 1965-66, instr Sch of Infantry 1968-69, cmd LI Depot Shrewsbury 1969-72, AAG Light Div Winchester 1972-75, defence advsr Br High Cmmn Nicosia 1976-79, Col Army HQ UKLF Wilton 1980-83, Dep Col LI (Yorks) 1980-85; trust dir Treloar Tst 1983-; govr Priors Field Sch Godalming 1983-; *Recreations* pictures, picture framing, tennis, golf; *Clubs* Army and Navy; *Style*— Col Colin W Huxley; Brook Lodge, Old Alresford, Hampshire (☎ 0962 732582); Treloar

Trust, Froyle, Alton, Hampshire (☎ 0420 22442)

HUXLEY, Elspeth Josceline; CBE (1962); *née* Grant; da of Maj Josceline Grant (d 1947), of Njoro, Kenya, and Hon Eleanor, *née* Grosvenor (d 1977); *b* 23 July 1907; *Educ* Univ of Reading; *m* 1931, Gervas Huxley (d 1971), s of Dr Henry Huxley; 1 s (Charles); *Career* writer; author of 35 books, including biography, fiction, travel, autobiography; also free-lance radio journalist; most of these books relate to Africa, many to Kenya, her childhood home; two were EMI semi-fictional autobiographical The Flame Trees of Thika (TV Series) and The Mottled Lizard; Out in The Midday Sun (semi-travel, semi-autobiographical); *Recreations* resting, gossip; *Style—* Mrs Elspeth Huxley, CBE; Green End, Oaksey, Malmesbury, Wiltshire (☎ 06667 252)

HUXLEY, Sir Leonard George Holden; KBE (1964); s of George Hamborough Huxley (d 1944), and Lilian Sarah Huxley (d 1946); *b* 29 May 1902; *Educ* The Hutchins Sch Tas, Univ of Tas, New Coll Oxford (MA, DPhil); *m* 1929, Ella Mary Child, da of Rev Frederick G Copeland (d 1935); 1 s; *Career* princ scientific offr Telecommunications Res Estab Miny of Aircraft Prodn 1940-46, reader in electromagnetism Birmingham Univ 1946-49, elder prof of physics Adelaide Univ 1949-60, vice-chllr Australian Nat Univ 1960-67 (ret); *see Debrett's Handbook of Australia and New Zealand for further details*; *Style—* Sir Leonard Huxley, KBE; 19 Glasgow Place, Hughes, Canberra, ACT 2605, Australia (☎ 062 81 5560)

HUXLEY, Prof Paul; s of Ernest William Huxley, of Derby, and Winifred Mary Huxley; *b* 12 May 1938; *Educ* Harrow Sch of Art, Royal Academy Sch; *m* Sept 1957 (m dis 1972), Margaret Doris, da of James Perryman; 2 s (Mark b 1961, Nelson b 1963); *Career* artist, prof painting RCA 1986-; group exhibitions incl: Whitechapel Gallery London 1964, Marlborough Gerson New York 1965, Galerie Milano Milan 1965, Pittsburgh Int Carnegie Inst Pittsburgh 1967, UCLA Art Galleries Los Angeles 1968, Tate Gallery London 1968, Museum of Modern Art New York 1968, Museum am Ostwall Hanover 1969, Walker Art Gallery Liverpool 1973, Hayward Gallery London 1974, Royal Acad London 1977, Museo Municipal Madrid 1983, RCA London 1988, Mappin Art Gallery Sheffield 1988; solo exhibitions at galleries incl: Rowan Gallery London, Kornblee Gallery New York, Galleria da Emenda Lisbon, Forum Kunst Rotweil; cmmnd by London Tport to design 22 ceramic murals for King's Cross Underground Station 1984; works exhibited in public collections world-wide incl: Albright-Knox Gallery Buffalo New York, Art Gallery of NSW Aust, Leeds City Art Gallery, V & A Museum, Whitworth Art Gallery Manchester, Stuyvesant Fndn Holland, Ulster Museum Belfast, Art Gallery of Ontario Toronto, Centro Cultural Arte Contemporanes Mexico; memb: ctee Serpentine Gallery 1971-74, arts panel Arts Cncl GB 1972-76; tstee Tate Gallery 1975-82: ARA 1987; *Books* Exhibition Road - Painters at The Royal College of Art (1988); *Style—* Prof Paul Huxley; 29 St Albans Ave, London W4 5LL (☎ 01 994 5111); Royal College of Art, Kensington Gore, London SW7 2EV (☎ 01 584 5020)

HUXTABLE, Gen Sir Charles Richard; KCB (1984, CB 1982), CBE (1976, OBE 1972, MBE 1961); s of Capt W R Huxtable; *b* 22 July 1931; *Educ* Wellington Coll, RMA Sandhurst; *m* 31 March 1959, Mary, da of late Brig J H C Lawlor; 3 da; *Career* Col Cmdt The King's Div, Col Duke of Wellington's Regt 1982-; Dir Army Staff Duties MOD 1982-83, Cdr Training and Arms Directors 1983-86, Quartermaster General 1986-88, Cdr in Chief UK Land Forces 1988-; *Clubs* Army and Navy; *Style—* Gen Sir Charles Huxtable, KCB, CBE, ADC Gen; c/o Lloyds Bank, 23 High Street, Teddington, Middlesex TW11 8EX

HUYSHE, Lt-Col Patrick Vere; s of Rear Admiral Edgar Bocquet Swan, CBE (d 1951), and Edith Ellen, *née* Hyushe (d 1962); changed name to Huyshe by deed poll 1951, received Royal Licence to Bear Arms of Huyshe 1975; descended through mother from Richard De Hywis, of Lod Hywis, Somerset living in reign of King John, Henry Huysh purchased Sand 1560-61, rebuilt 1592-94 by Rowland Huyshe; Lord of the Manor of Clyst Hydon, Devon; *b* 21 August 1918; *Educ* Bradfield, RMA Woolwich, Emmanuel Coll Cambridge (BA); *m* 17 June 1946, (Sylvia) Margaret, da of Alfred Basil Reece (d 1963), of Westward Ho!, Devon; 2 s (Roger b 1946, Alan b 1956), 2 da (Stella b 1950, Tessa b 1953); *Career* cmmnd RE 1938, Lt-Col; France 1940, Italy 1944, NW Europe 1945, Malaya 1949-51 (despatches 1950), ret 1962; schoolmaster 1962-; *Recreations* golf, formerly cross-country running, heraldry; *Style—* Lt-Col Patrick Huyshe; Sand, Sidbury, Sidmouth, Devon (☎ 03957 230); Exeter School, Exeter (☎ 0392 78512); St David's Coll, Exeter (☎ 0392 36708)

HYAM, His Hon Judge Michael Joshua; s of Isaac Joseph Hyam (d 1972), of Sussex, and Rachel Hyam; *b* 18 April 1938; *Educ* Westminster Sch, Cambridge Univ (MA); *m* 1968, Diana, da of Rupert Vernon Mortimer, of Yorks; 3 s; *Career* barr SE circuit 1962-84, recorder of Crown Ct 1983-84, circuit judge; memb: cncl of Legal Educn 1980-85, Ethical Ctee of Cromwell Hosp 1983-; govr of Dulwich Coll Prep Sch 1986-; *Recreations* book collecting, cricket, gardening; *Clubs* Garrick, Norfolk, MCC; *Style—* His Hon Judge Hyam; Combined Court, Norwich

HYATALI, Sir Isaac Emanuel; TC (1974); s of Joseph Hyatali (d 1938), and Esther Hyatali (d 1930); *b* 21 Nov 1917; *Educ* Naparima Coll Trinidad, Cncl of Legal Educn Gray's Inn London; *m* 1943, Audrey Monica, da of Stanislaus Joseph (d 1971), and Emily Joseph; 2 s, 1 da; *Career* Civil Service 1939-44; barr Gray's Inn 1947; chm: Arima Rent Assessment Bd 1953-59, Agric Rent Bd Eastern Counties 1953-59, bd of inquiry Telephone Trade Dispute 1958, bd of inquiry Cement Trade Dispute 1959, Wages Cncl 1958-59, Oil and Water Bd 1959-62; judge Supreme Court Trinidad and Tobago 1959-62, justice of appeal 1962-72, pres Indust Court 1965-72, chief justice and pres of the Court of Appeal Trinidad and Tobago 1972-83, justice of appeal Seychelles Republic 1983-86; chm: Election and Boundaries Cmmn 1983-, American Life and Gen Insur Co Ltd 1983-, Constitution Cmmn 1987; conslt Hyatali & Co (attorneys at law), memb cncl of mgmnt Br Inst of Int and Comparative Law 1982-, arbitrator and umpire of Int Civil Aviation Orgn 1980-; memb World Assoc of Judges; kt 1973; *Clubs* Royal Cwlth Soc Port of Spain Rotary, Union, Union Park Turf; *Style—* Sir Isaac Hyatali, TC; 8 Pomme Rose Ave, Cascade, St Ann's, Republic of Trinidad and Tobago (☎ 62 43049); chambers: 63 Edward St Port of Spain (☎ 623 4007), Salvatori Bldg, Frederick St, Port of Spain, Repub of Trinadad and Tobago (☎ 623 8733)

HYATT, Peter Robin; s of Maj Arthur John Roach Hyatt (d 1987), of 9 Kevan Drive, Send, nr Woking, Surrey, and Molly, *née* Newman (d 1983); *b* 12 May 1947; *Educ* Cheltenham; *m* 1 (m dis 1984), Julie Ann, *née* Cox; 1 s (Ralph James Roach b 1978), 1 da (Gabriella b 1975); m 2, 15 Jan 1988, Jenny Countenay, da of Rt Rev John Bernard Taylor (Bishop of St Albans), *qv*; *Career* gp mangr Coopers and Lybrand 1964-80, div ptnr Neville Russell 1987- (sr mangr 1980-82, ptnr 1983-); dir: Care and Counsel, South American Missionary Soc, Caring for Life Properties plc; ACA 1971, FCA 1978; *Recreations* squash, golf, walking, watching cricket, rugby, running a pathfinder group; *Style—* Peter Hyatt, Esq; 3 Alderley Ct, Chesham Rd, Berkhamsted, Herts HP4 3AD (☎ 0442 873 191); Neville Russell, 246 Bishopsgate, London EC2 4PB (☎ 01 377 1000)

HYDE, Lt-Col (John) Anthony Wakeman; s of Lt-Col George Leslie Hyde, OBE (d 1978), of Ottershaw, Surrey, and Marjorie, *née* Halward (d 1961); *b* 19 Sept 1931; *Educ* Sherborne Sch; *m* 12 Jan 1957, Felicity Anne, da of Maj James Leighton Breeds (d 1974), of Selsey, Sussex and Ngaturi, NZ; 1 s (James b 1959), 1 da (Lucy b 1963); *Career* cmmnd The Royal Sussex Regt 1952, Staff Coll Camberley 1962, HQ Land Forces Persian Gulf 1963-64, Co Cdr I R Sussex 1965-66, US Army Cmd & Gen Staff Coll (USACGSC) Leavenworth 1967, HQ Mobile Cmd Canada 1968-69, 2 i/c I RRF 1970-71, HQ DINF and HQUKLF 1972-77; ret 1978; ptnr (with wife) Bratton Antiques 1976-; *Recreations* goats, gardening; *Clubs* Army & Navy; *Style—* Lt-Col Anthony Hyde; Bratton Antiques, Market Place, Westbury, Wiltshire BA13 3DE (☎ 0373 823 021)

HYDE, Michael Clarendon; s of Arthur Victor Hyde, MC (d 1944), of Coram St, London, and Winifred Florence, *née* Downton (d 1963); *b* 3 Sept 1923; *Educ* St John's Coll London; *m* 1, 3 Nov 1943, Irene Patricia, da of John Galliven (d 1943); 2 s (Nicholas b 1948, Philip b 1952); m 2, 14 April 1975, Shirley Audrey, da of George Mann, of Willoughby Close, Gt Barford, Beds; *Career* ed and publisher Chemical Insight 1972-, md Hyde Chemical Publications Ltd 1977-; ed: Chemical Age 1958-71, Leather Trades Review 1956-58; *Recreations* swimming, fell-walking, music, literature; *Clubs* Wig and Pen, IOD, Chemists', New York; *Style—* Michael Hyde, Esq; 6a West Grove, Greenwich, London SE10 8QT (☎ 01 691 6151, telex 297761, fax 01 692 7692); 12 Climping Ct, Rackham Rd, Rustington (☎ 0903 783 749)

HYDE, (Harford) Montgomery; s of James Johnstone Hyde, JP (d 1945), of Belfast, and Isobel Greenfield, *née* Montgomery (d 1966); ggs of James Johnstone, fndr and proprietor of The Standard Newspaper, cous of Henry James, OM, American novelist and critic; *b* 14 August 1907; *Educ* Sedbergh, Queen's Univ Belfast (DLitt), Magdalen Coll Oxford (MA); *m* 1, 1939 (m dis 1952), Dorothy Mabel Brayshaw, eldest da of Dr Murray Crofts; m 2, 1955 (m dis 1966), Mary Eleanor, da of Col L G Fischer, IMS; m 3, 1966, Rosalind Roberts, yst da of Cdr James Francis William Dimond, RN (d 1941); *Career* barr and author; Intelligence Corps 1940-45, Lt-Col Legal Offr, Allied Cmmn for Austria 1944-45; asst ed Law Reports 1946-47; legal advsr Br Lion Film Corpn 1947-49; MP (U) N Belfast 1950-59; UK delegate Cncl of Europe Assembly Strasbourg 1952-55; prof of history and political science Univ of the Punjab Lahore 1959-61; author of over 50 books, mostly biography, criminology and sociology, leading authority on life and works of Oscar Wilde; memb Royal Irish Acad; fell RAF Museum Leverhulme 1971-75; FRSL, FRHS; *Recreations* criminology, classical music, travel; *Clubs* Garrick, Beefsteak, Grolier (New York); *Style—* Dr H Montgomery Hyde; Westwell House, Tenterden, Kent TN30 6TT (☎ Tenterden 3189)

HYDE, Norman Vincent; s of Sidney Hyde, of Herts (d 1960), and Nellie, *née* Otter; *b* 28 April 1927; *Educ* Hitchin GS, UCL (BA); *m* 5 Sept 1953, Patricia Townsend, da of John Townsend Barker, JP, of Herts; 2 s (Jeremy b 1954, Christopher b 1955), 2 da (Theresa b 1959, Carolyn b 1963); *Career* RM 1944-47, Lt Corpl; architect self employed 1958-89, dep chm PSD 1987; chm: N Herts Licensing Ctee 1987, Betting and Gaming Ctee 1987; JP 1970, tax cmmr 1972 (chm 1984), memb Lord Chllrs Advsy Ctee 1984; ARIBA, FRSA; *Recreations* restoring antique furniture, reading, DIY; *Style—* Norman V Hyde, Esq; Windmill Hill House, Hitchin, Herts (☎ 0462 59617, fax 0462 54290, car ☎ 0860 350177)

HYDE PARKER, Sir Richard William; 12 Bt (E 1681); s of Sir William Stephen Hyde Parker, 11 Bt (d 1951); *b* 5 April 1937; *Educ* Millfield, RAC Cirencester; *m* 1972, Jean, da of late Sir Lindores Leslie, 9 Bt; 1 s (William), 3 da (twins Beata and Margaret b 1973, Lucy b 1975); *Heir* s, William John b 10 June 1983; *Style—* Sir Richard Hyde Parker, Bt; Melford Hall, Long Melford, Suffolk

HYDE SMITH, Cdr Bryan Edmund; s of Capt Richard Edmund Hyde Smith, RN (d 1972), of Cambridge, and Brenda Coralie, *née* Browne; *b* 18 August 1930; *Educ* Britannia RNC Dartmouth; *m* 3 Dec 1959, Fradzlon Sa'adon; 2 s (Karim b 1960, Malek b 1968), 1 da (Noraini b 1962); *Career* RN 1944-58, Royal Malaysian Navy 1958-72, (despatches 1965), ret Cdr 1972; cmd RMN ships and shore establishments; farmer on family estate in Cambridgeshire; KMN (Malayasia) 1968; *Recreations* naval history, philately, solving Daily Telegraph crossword; *Style—* Cdr Bryan Hyde Smith; The Grange, Great Wilbraham, Cambridge CB1 5JN (☎ 0223 880319)

HYDE-THOMSON, Paul Cater; DL (Leicestershire 1986); s of Robert Hyde Hyde-Thomson (d 1970), of London, and Joan Perronet, *née* Sells (d 1972); *b* 17 Mar 1927; *Educ* Harrow, Ch Ch Oxford (MA); *m* 26 Oct 1950, Zoë Caroline Georgia, da of Robin Regis d'Erlanger, MC (d 1934); 1 s (Henry b 1954), 4 da (Catherine b 1952, Philippa b 1956, Eleanor b 1960, Lucy b 1971); *Career* Capt Oxon and Bucks LI; chm Ibstock Johnsen plc 1961- (dir 1951-); dir: McKechnie plc, TR Property Investmt Tst plc, T R Hldgs Ltd; pres Nat Cncl of Bldg Material Producers 1981-83; chm Blaby Cons Assoc; High Sheriff Leics 1965, memb Leics CC 1961-70; FCA 1954; *Recreations* music, art, travel, gardening; *Style—* Paul Hyde-Thomson, Esq, DL; The Stable House, North Kilworth, Lutterworth, Leics LE17 6JE (☎ 0858 880581); Flat 91, 55 Ebury St, London SW1 (☎ 01 730 5270); office: Ibstock Johnsen plc, Lutterworth House, Lutterworth, Leics LE17 4PS (☎ 04555 3071, fax 04555 3182, telex 341010)

HYDON, Kenneth John; s of John Thomas Hydon (d 1966); *b* 3 Nov 1944; *Educ* Humphrey Perkins; *m* 1966, Sylvia Sheila; 2 children; *Career* fin dir: Racal Telecom plc, Orbital Mobile Communications (Hldgs) Ltd; *Recreations* badminton, sailing; *Style—* Kenneth Hydon, Esq

HYETT, Dr Anthony Roy; s of Sydney Charles Hyett (d 1962), and Gertrude, *née* Warbis; *b* 27 July 1928; *Educ* Univ of London , Queen Mary Coll and London Hosp (BSc, MB,BS, MRCS, LRCPS); *m* 6 Nov 1956, Doreen Margaret (d 1977), da of William Frederick Hudson (d 1978), of Essex; 4 s (Simon b 1961, Andrew b 1964, Peter b 1969, James b 1971); *Career* med practitioner; princ in gen practice 1964-, dermatologist Queen Mary's Hospital Sidcup and Lewisham Hospital; Treasy MO later local MO to Civil Serv 1971-, visiting MO to Bromley Health Authy 1983-; dep med dir William R Warner and Co 1960-64, Freeman City of London 1970, memb Guild of Freeman London 1971; bereavement cnsllr Keston PCC; *Recreations* sailing, riding, theatre, music, literature; *Style—* Dr Anthony Hyett; The Old Manor, Plaxdale Green,

Stansted, Sevenoaks, Kent; 10 Highland Rd, Bromley, Kent (☎ 01 460 2368)

HYLAND, (Henry) Stanley; s of Harry Hugh Hyland (d 1943), and Annie, *née* Rhodes (d 1974); *b* 26 Jan 1914; *Educ* Bradford GS, Birkbeck Coll, London Univ (BA); *m* 20 April 1940, Nora, da of Harold Hopkinson (d 1968); 2 s (Jeremy b 1944, Henry b 1951); *Career* WWII Lieut (spl branch) RNVR 1940-46; librarian Br Scientific Instruments Res Assoc 1946-47, res librarian House of Commons 1947- 51; BBC: successively news sub ed, reporter, programme orgnsr, producer (radio), producer (tv), chief asst Current Affrs Gp (tv) 1951-70; fndr dir Hyvision Ltd 1970-; chm Gt Bardfield Historical Soc 1977-87; *Books* Curiosities from Parliament (1955), Who Goes Hang (1958), Green Grow the Tresses-O (1965), Top Bloody Secret (1969); *Style—* Stanley Hyland, Esq; Cage Cottage, Great Bardfield, Braintree, Essex CM7 4ST (☎ 0371 810 413); Hyvision Ltd, 43 Earlham St, Covent Gdns, London WC2H 9LD (☎ 01 836 6938/9)

HYLTON, 5 Baron (UK 1866); Sir Raymond Hervey Jolliffe; 5 Bt (UK 1821), DL (Somerset 1975); s of Lt-Col 4 Baron Hylton (d 1967, whose mother was Lady Alice Hervey, da of 3 Marquess of Bristol) and Lady Perdita Asquith (sis of 2 Earl of Oxford and Asquith and gda of 1 Earl, better known as HH Asquith, the Lib PM, by his 1 w); *b* 13 June 1932; *Educ* Eton, Trin Oxford (MA); *m* 1966, Joanna, da of Andrew de Bertodano, himself eldest s of 8 Marques de Moral (cr by King Charles III of Spain 1765), by Andrew's m Lady Sylvia Savile (3 da of late 6 Earl of Mexborough, and sis of Lady Agnes Eyston and Lady Sarah Cumming-Bruce); 4 s (Hon William, Hon Andrew b 1969, Hon Alexander b 1973, Hon John b 1977), 1 da (Hon Emily b 1975); *Heir* s, Hon William Jolliffe; *Career* Lt Coldstream Gds Reserve; asst priv sec to Govr-Gen Canada 1960-62; previously chm: Catholic Housing Aid Soc, Nat Federation of Housing Associations, Housing Assoc Charitable Tst, Help the Aged Housing Tst; pres SW Regn Nat Soc Mentally Handicapped Children, Hugh of Witham Foundation; govr Ammerdown Study Center, tstee Acorn Christian Healing Tst, fndr memb Mendip and Wansdyke Local Enterprise Gp; Hon Tres Project on Human Rights and Responsibilities in Britain and Ireland; ARICS; *Style—* The Rt Hon the Lord Hylton, DL; Ammerdown, Radstock, Bath

HYLTON-FOSTER, Baroness (Life Peer UK 1965); Hon Audrey Pellew; *née* Clifton-Brown; da of 1 and last Viscount Ruffside, PC, DL (d 1958); *b* 19 May 1908; *Educ* St George's Ascot; *m* 1931, Rt Hon Sir Harry Hylton-Foster, QC, MP, speaker House of Commons 1959-65 (d 1965), s of Harry Braustyn Hylton-Foster; *Career* dir Chelsea div London Branch BRCS 1950-60, pres London Branch British Red Cross 1960-83, appointed to Nat BRCS HQ consultative panel 1984: pres Prevention of Blindness Research Fund 1965-76; memb cncl BRCS 1967-80; convenor Cross Bench Peers 1974-; *Recreations* fishing, gardening; *Style—* The Rt Hon the Baroness Hylton-Foster; 54 Cranmer Court, Whitehead Grove, London SW3 3HW (☎ 01 584 2889); The Coach House, Tanhurst, Leith Hill, Holmbury St Mary, Dorking, Surrey RH5 6LU (☎ 0306 711975)

HYMAN, Howard Jonathan; s of Joe Hyman, of Lukyns, Ewhurst, Surrey, and Corrine Irene, *née* Abrahams; *b* 23 Oct 1949; *Educ* Bedales Sch, Manchester Univ (BA); *m* 21 Sept 1972, Anne Moira, da of Capt Harry Sowden, of 3 Goodwood, Owler Park Rd, Middleton, Ilkley, Yorks; 2 s (Daniel b 1977, Sam b 1979), 1 da (Hannah 1982); *Career* ptnr i/c privatisation servs dept Price Waterhouse 1987- (ptnr 1984-, specialist advsr on privatisation HM Treasy 1984-87; FCA; *Recreations* walking, classical music, cricket, gardening; *Clubs* Reform, MCC; *Style—* Howard Hyman, Esq; 30 Sheen Common Dr, Richmond, Surrey (☎ 01 878 2618); Price Waterhouse, Southwark Towers, 32 London Bridge St, London SE1 9SY (☎ 01 334 2048, 01 407 8989, fax 01 403 0733, telex 884657/8)

HYMAN, Hon Mrs (Laura Alice); *née* Boyd; da of 6 Baron Kilmarnock, MBE (d 1975); *b* 10 June 1934; *Educ* Langford Grove, Barcombe Mills nr Lewes; *m* 1962, (Robert) Anthony Hyman; 2 s, 1 da; *Style—* The Hon Mrs Hyman; 38a Downshire Hill, Hampstead, London NW3 (01 794 4529)

HYNES, Dermott Francis; s of John Joseph Hynes (d 1975), of Kilrickle, Loughrea, Co Galway, Republic of Ireland, and Mary, *née* Byrnes (d 1926); *b* 2 July 1924; *Educ* St Columb's Coll Derry NI, London Univ (LLB, LLM); *m* 2 Jan 1952, Theresa, da of Joseph Jordan, JP (d 1950); 2 s (Shane Joseph b 24 April 1954, Eamonn Francis b 21 March 1956); *Career* called to the Bar Inner Temple; govr St Gregory's Sch Ealing; *Recreations* reading, fishing; *Clubs* Nat Liberal, Irish; *Style—* Dermott Hynes, Esq; 61 Castlebar Park, Ealing, London W5 1BA (☎ 01 997 0197); 9 Kings Bench Walk, Tempe, London EC4 (☎ 01 353 9564)

HYPHER, David Charles; s of Harold Eldric Hypher, MBE (d 1971), of Byfleet, Surrey, and Marcia Evelyn, *née* Spalding; *b* 24 July 1941; *Educ* Weybridge Tech Coll; *m* 1, March 1966 (m dis 1971), Jenifer da of Robert Ingle; 2 da; m 2, 17 July 1978, Pamela Alison, da of Peter Rowland Craddock; 2 da (Nicola, Emma); *Career* stockbroker 1958-82; dir: MIM Ltd (Britannia Asset Mgmnt) 1983-, MIM Britannia Unit Tst Managers Ltd 1984-, various MIM Britannia (offshore) Jersey Fund Cos 1985-; tstee and govr Rydes Hill Sch Guildford; memb Stock Exchange 1972-83, ASIA 1965-; *Recreations* collecting antiques and cars; *Style—* David Hypher, Esq; Comptons Farmhouse, Frog Grove Lane, Wood St Village, nr Guildford, Surrey (☎ 0483 234938); 8 La Fustera, Benisa, Allicante, Spain; c/o MIM Ltd, 11 Devonshire Sq, London EC2 (☎ 01 626 3434)

HYPHER, Terence Joseph; s of Dr Noel Charles Hypher (d 1979), of Slough, Berks, and Winifreda Mary, *née* Filmer; *b* 24 Mar 1932; *Educ* St Edmund's Coll Ware Herts, Nat Univ of Ireland (MB, BCh, BAO); *m* 2 Jan, Valerie Jane, da of Henry Percy Walker (d 1961); 3 s (Austen b 1965, Duncan b 1966, Marcus b 1967); *Career* ophthalmic surgn; asst surgn St John Ophthalmic Hosp Jerusalem 1965-66, lectr Ophthamology Univ of Liverpool 1974-79, hon sr registrar St Paul's Eye Hosp Liverpool 1974-79, conslt ophthamologist West Glamorgan Health Authy 1979-88; FRCS, FCOphth, DO; (Edinburgh); OStJ 1969; *Recreations* music, literature, art; *Style—* Terence Hypher, Esq; 46 Hendrefoilan Rd, Sketty, Swansea SA2 9LT

HYTNER, Benet Alan; QC (1970); s of Maurice Hytner (d 1978), of Manchester, and Sarah, *née* Goldberg (d 1978); *b* 29 Dec 1927; *Educ* Manchester GS, Trinity Hall Cambridge (MA); *m* 19 Dec 1954 (m dis), Joyce *qy*, da of Maj Bernard Myers (d 1979), of Manchester; 3 s (Nicolas b 1956, Richard b 1959, James b 1964), 1 da (Jennifer b 1958); *Career* Nat Serv Lt RASC 1949-51; called to the Bar Middle Temple 1952, rec Crown Ct 1970-, bencher 1977-, judge of appeal Isle of Man 1980-, ldr Northern Circuit 1984-88; memb: Gen Cncl of the Bar 1969-73 and 1984-88, Senate of Inns of Ct and Bar 1977-81; *Recreations* walking, reading, theatre; *Clubs* MCC; *Style—* Benet Hytner, Esq; 5 Essex Court Temple, London EC4Y 9AH; 25 Byrom St, Manchester M3 4PF

HYTNER, Joyce Anita; da of Bernard Myers (d 1979), of Altrincham Cheshire, and Vera Myers, *née* Classick (d 1974); *b* 9 Dec 1935; *Educ* Withington Girls' Sch Manchester; *m* 19 Dec 1954 (m dis 1980), Benet Hytner, QC *qv*; 3 s (Nicholas b 1956, Richard b 1959, James b 1964), 1 da (Jennifer b 1958); *Career* mangr external rels Granada Television; *Recreations* theatre, music; *Style—* Mrs Joyce Hytner; 1A Shepherd Market, London W1Y 7HS (☎ 01 491 0312); Granada Television, 36 Golden Square, London W1R 4AH (☎ 01 734 8080)

I

IBBOTT, Alec; CBE (1988); s of Francis Joseph Ibbott (d 1976), of Croydon, Surrey, and Madge Winifred, *née* Graham (d 1976); *b* 14 Oct 1930; *Educ* Selhurst GS Croydon; *m* 4 April 1964, Margaret Elizabeth, da of Rev Ernest Alfred Brown (d 1968), of Sompting, Sussex; 1 s (Jonathan b 1971), 1 da (Elizabeth b 1969); *Career* Nat Serv Intelligence Corps 1949-51; FO joined 1949, ed FO list 1951, studied at MECAS (Middle East Centre for Arab Studies) 1955-56, second sec and vice conul Br Embassy Rabat 1956 , FO 1960, second sec (inf) Br Embassy Tripoli 1961, second sec Br Embassy Benghazi 1961, first sec (inf) Br Embassy Khartoum 1965, FCO 1967, asst political agent Dubai 1971; first sec, head of Chancery and consul Br Embassy Dubai 1971 and Abu Dhabi 1972; first sec and head of chancery Br High Cmmn Nicosia 1973, first sec FCO 1975, first sec and head of chancery Br Embassy Caracas 1977, consul and head of chancery Br Embassy Khartoum 1979, cnsllr seconded to Int Mil Serv Ltd 1982, HM ambass and consul gen Monrovia 1985, currently Br high commr Banjul-; *Books* Professionalism: Problems and Prospects in Liberia (1986), One Hundred Years of English Law in the Gambia: Whither Gambian Law (1988); *Recreations* reading, walking, bird watching, scottish dancing; *Style—* Alec Ibbott, Esq, CBE; c/o FCO (Banjul), King Charles St, London SW1A 2AH, (☎ 95133, 95134, 95778 (off), 96025 (Banjul res))

IBBS, Sir Robin (John Robert); o s of late Prof T L Ibbs, MC and Marjorie, *née* Bell; *b* 21 April 1926; *Educ* Toronto Univ, Trin Coll Camb (MA); *m* 1952, Iris Barbara, da of late S Hall; 1 da; *Career* barr Lincoln's Inn; memb Cncl Chemical Industries Assocs 1982-; Head CPRS Cabinet Office 1980-82 (seconded from ICI, of which dir 1976-, having joined 1952, returned to ICI April 1982), govt advsr on efficiency in public service 1983-; kt 1982; *Style—* Sir Robin Ibbs; c/o Cabinet Office, 70 Whitehall, SW1

IDDESLEIGH, Dowager Countess of; Elizabeth; da of late Frederic Sawrey Archibald Lowndes, of 9 Barton St, Westminster, SW1; *m* 1930, 3 Earl of Iddesleigh (d 1970); 2 s (4 Earl, Hon Edward Northcote), 2 da (Lady Catherine Northcote; Lady Hilda Swan, w of York Herald); *Style—* The Rt Hon the Dowager Countess of Iddesleigh; Iddesleigh, Pynes, Exeter EX5 5EF

IDDESLEIGH, 4 Earl of (UK 1885); Sir Stafford Henry Northcote; 11 Bt (E 1641), DL (Devon 1979); also Viscount St Cyres (UK 1885); s of 3 Earl of Iddesleigh (d 1970, gs of 1 Earl, better known as Sir Stafford Northcote, a confidant of Gladstone in his youth and of Disraeli in maturity); *b* 14 July 1932; *Educ* Downside; *m* 1955, Maria Luisa (Mima) Alvarez-Builla y Urquijo, Condesa del Real Agrado (Spain CR of 1771), DL (Devon 1987), da of Don Gonzalo Alvarez-Builla y Alvera and Maria Luisa, Viscountess Exmouth; 1 s, 1 da; *Heir* s, Viscount St Cyres; *Career* late 2 Lt Irish Gds; chm S W TSB 1981-83, trustee of England and Wales TSB 1983-86, chm S W regnion TSB 1983-; dir: Westward TV 1981-82, Television South West 1982-, TSB Group plc 1987-, United Dominions Trust Ltd 1983-87, TSB Commercial Holdings Ltd 1987-; *Recreations* shooting; *Clubs* Army & Navy; *Style—* The Rt Hon the Earl of Iddesleigh, DL; Shillands House, Upton-Pyne-Hill, Exeter, Devon EX5 5EB (☎ 0392) 58916)

IDDON, Michael Ian; s of Harold Edgar (d 1971), and Edna Iddon, *née* McTear (d 1981); *b* 18 Oct 1938; *Educ* Arnold Sch Blackpool, Harris Technical Coll Preston; *m* 1963, Rhona, da of Robert Paul (d 1972), of Chorley; 2 s (Michael James b 1965, David Robert b 1966), 1 da (Katherine Michelle b 1971); *Career* chm & jt md Iddon Bros Ltd 1971; dir engr & Marine Applications Ltd 1980; ex-dir RAPRA Technology Ltd 1985; CEng, MIMechE, FPRI; *Recreations* fishing, golf, historic cars, stamps; *Clubs* Shaw Hill Golf & Country (Chorley), Royal Overseas League (London); *Style—* Michael Iddon, Esq; The Crest 2 Kingsway, Penwortham, Preston, Lancs PR1 0AP (☎ 0772 742416); Iddon Bros Ltd, Quin Street, Leyland PR5 1TB (☎ 0772 421258)

IEVERS, Rear Adm John Augustine; CB (1962), OBE (1945); s of Eyre Francis Ievers (d 1958), of Kent, and Catherine Lilian, *née* Macbeth (d 1941); *b* 2 Dec 1912; *Educ* RNC Dartmouth; *m* 1937, Peggy Garth, da of James Marshall, of Lancs; 1 s (Michael b 1948), 2 da (Carolyn b 1938, Maxine b 1945); *Career* joined RN 1926, served WWII in HMS Glasgow (Norwegian Campaign) and HMS Hermes (Indian Ocean and Ceylon); Capt 1951, cmmnd HMS Burgmead Bay (American and West Indies); RN Air Station Lossiemouth 1952-54, Dep Dir Air Warfare 1954-57, Capt Air Mediterranean 1957-60, promoted Rear Adm 1960, dep controller Aircraft, min of Aviation 1960-64; *Recreations* golf; *Style—* Rear Adm John Ievers, CB, OBE; 3 Hollywood Court, Hollywood Lane, Lymington, Hants (☎ Lym 77268)

IKERRIN, Viscount; David James Theobald Somerset Butler; s and h of 9 Earl of Carrick; *b* 9 Jan 1953; *Educ* Downside; *m* 1975, Philippa, da of Wing Cdr L V Craxton, RAF; 3 s (Hon Arion Thomas Piers Hamilton, Hon Piers Edmund Theobald Lismalyn b 1979, Hon Lindsay Simon Turville Somerset b (twin) 1979); *Heir* s, Hon Arion Thomas Piers Hamilton Butler b 1 Sept 1975; *Style—* Viscount Ikerrin

ILCHESTER, 9 Earl of (GB 1756) Maurice Vivian de Touffreville Fox-Strangways; Lord Ilchester of Ilchester, Somerset, and Baron Strangways of Woodford Strangways (GB 1741), and Baron Ilchester and Stavordale of Redlynch (GB 1747); s of 8 Earl of Ilchester (d 1970), and Laure Georgine Emilie, *née* Mazaraki; the 1 Earl was unc of Charles James Fox and brother of 1 Lord Holland; from 1889 Holland House reverted to the Earls of Ilchester before being bombed in WW II; it is now a Youth Hostel; *b* 1 April 1920; *Educ* Kingsbridge Sch; *m* 1941, Diana Mary Elizabeth , da of George Frederick Simpson, of Cassington, Oxford; *Heir* bro, Hon Raymond Fox-Strangways, *qv*; *Career* served RAF 1936-76, ret Gp Capt; dir Nottingham Bldg Soc 1982- (vice-chm 1985-87), exec dir Biggin Hill News Ltd, Bromley Borough News Ltd, County Border News Ltd 1983-, dir of other cos; pres SE Area RAF Assoc 1978-, vice-chm Biggin Hill Airport Consultative Ctee 1976-86, chm Govs Cannock Sch 1978-, memb House of Lords Select Ctee on Science and Technology 1984-; chartered engr; memb RAeS, Fell Inst of Nuclear Engrs (pres 1983-85), Freeman City of London; Liveryman Guild of Air Pilots and Air Navigators; FBIM, FIOD, FRSA; *Recreations* outdoor activities, passive enjoyment of the arts; *Clubs* Brooks's, RAF; *Style—* The Rt Hon the Earl of Ilchester; Farley Mill, Westerham, Kent

ILEY, Geoffrey Norman; s of (Henry) Norman Iley (d 1975), of Stratford-upon-Avon, and Winifield Lalla, *née* Bowman (d 1988); *b* 24 Sept 1928; *Educ* Oakham Sch, London Univ (BSc), Birmingham Univ; *Career* asst gen mangr MG Car Co Abingdon 1955-58, prodn mangr Morris Motors Ltd Cowley 1958-61, dep to dir of supplies Br Motor Corpn 1961-65 (dir prodn, paint, trim, assembly 1965-68), md Triplex Safety Glass Co Birmingham 1968-72, md Pilkington ACI Ltd Australia 1972-77, dir Pilkington plc 1977-; Freeman City of London 1984, Liveryman Worshipful Co of Spectaclemakers 1986; FBIM, CEng, MIMechE, MI Prod E; *Recreations* golf, walking, motoring, theatre, reading; *Clubs* Australian, Melbourne; *Style—* Geoffrey Iley, Esq; Pilkington plc, Prescot Road, St Helens, Merseyside WA10 3TT (☎ 0744 28 882, fax 0744 30 577, telex 627 441)

ILIFFE, Hon Mrs William; Christine Marie; da of Alfred Baton Baker, of Hastings, Sussex; *m* 1940, Hon William Henry Richard Iliffe (d 1959); 2 s; *Style—* The Hon Mrs William Iliffe; Church Cottage, Aldworth, Reading, Berks; 11 Evelyn Gardens, London SW7 3BE

ILIFFE, 2 Baron (UK 1933); Edward Langton Iliffe; s of 1 Baron Iliffe, GBE (d 1960), and Charlotte, *née* Gilding (d 1972); *b* 25 Jan 1908; *Educ* Sherborne, Clare Coll Cambridge; *m* 8 Dec 1938, Renée (dep pres London Branch Br Red Cross Soc), da of René Merandon du Plessis, of Chamarel, Mauritius; *Heir* n, Robert Iliffe; *Career* 1939-45 war with RAFVR (despatches), vice-chm Birmingham Post and Mail Ltd 1957-74, former chm Coventry Evening Telegraph Cambridge News; trustee Shakespeare's Birthplace, High Sheriff Berks 1957, Hon Freeman City of Coventry; *Clubs* Brooks's, Carlton, Royal Yacht Squadron; *Style—* The Rt Hon the Lord Iliffe; 38 St James's Place, London SW1 (☎ 01 493 1938); Basildon Park, Lower Basildon, nr Reading, Berks RG8 9NR (☎ Pangbourne 073 57 4409)

ILIFFE, Robert Peter Richard; s of Hon William Henry Richard Iliffe (d 1959; yr s of 1 Baron Iliffe, GBE); hp of uncle, 2 Baron Iliffe; *b* 22 Nov 1944; *Educ* Eton, Ch Ch Oxford; *m* 1966, Rosemary Anne, da of Cdr Arthur Grey Skipwith, RN; 3 s, 1 da; *Career* chm: BPM Hldgs 1982- (dep chm 1980-82), The Birmingham Post & Mail Ltd 1978-, West Midlands Press Ltd, Coventry Newspapers Ltd, British Transfer Printing Co Ltd, Cambridge Newspapers Ltd, dir T Dillon & Co Ltd, Birmingham Boat Shows Ltd; memb cncl Royal Agric Soc of England ; *Style—* Robert Iliffe, Esq; The Old Rectory, Ashow, Kenilworth, Warwickshire CV8 2LE

ILLINGWORTH, Sir Charles Frederick William; CBE (1946); s of John Illingworth (d 1939), and Edith Mary Boys (d 1922); *b* 8 May 1899; *Educ* Halifax GS, Edinburgh Univ (MB BCh); *m* 1929, Eleanor Mary (d 1971), da of Samuel Bennett, of Whitchurch, Hants (d 1938); 4 s (Michael, Geoffrey, Robert, James); *Career* 2 Lt RAF WWI; regius prof of surgery Glasgow Univ 1939-64, emeritus 1964-; hon surgeon to HM The Queen in Scotland 1961-65, (extra surgeon 1965-); Hon LLD: Glasgow, Leeds, Hon DSC: Sheffield, Belfast; Hon FRCS: Eng, Ireland; Hon FACS; Hon FRCPS: Canada, Glasgow; Hon FCSG (SA); FRCSE; kt 1961; *Style—* Sir Charles Illingworth, CBE; 57 Winton Drive, Glasgow G12 0QB (☎ 041 339 3759)

ILLINGWORTH, Dr David Gordon; CVO (1987, LVO 1980); s of Sir Cyril Gordon Illingworth (d 1959), and Grace Margaret; *b* 22 Dec 1921; *Educ* George Watson's Coll, Univ of Edinburgh (MD, MBChB); *m* 1946, Lesley Anderson, da of George Beagrie (d 1937), of Peterhead; 2 s (Lawrence, Stephen), 1 da (Susan); *Career* Surgn Lieut RNVR 1944-46, served in Atlantic and Northern Waters (2 Escort Group); various medical appts Edinburgh Northern Hosps 1947-80, travelling fell Nuffield Fndn 1966, surgn apothecary HM Household Palace of Holyrood House 1970-87, sr lectr Dept of Rehabilitation Studies Univ of Edinburgh 1975-80; FRCP; *Publications* papers in learned jls on cancer diagnosis and preventive medicine; *Recreations* golf, gardening; *Clubs* Univ of Edinburgh Staff, Bruntsfield Links Golfing Society; *Style—* Dr David Illingworth, CVO; 19 Napier Rd, Edinburgh EH10 5AZ (☎ 031 229 8102)

ILLINGWORTH, Hon Mrs (Katherine Elliott); da of Baron Foot (Life Peer); *b* 1937; *m* 1, 1955, David Stavely Gordon; 2 s, 1 da; m 2, David Illingworth (d 1976); 1 s; *Style—* The Hon Mrs Illingworth; 36 Albert Park Place, Montpelier, Bristol

ILLINGWORTH, Lady Margaret Cynthia; *née* Lindsay; da of late 27 Earl of Crawford and 10 of Balcarres, KT, PC, and Constance, da of Sir Henry Carstairs Pelly, MP, 3 Bt; *b* 27 June 1902; *m* 1928, Lt-Col Henry Cyril Harker Illingworth, MC, JP (d 1979), King's Royal Rifle Corps (Offr of Order of Crown of Roumania); *Career* ARRC; *Style—* Lady Margaret Illingworth; Headon Lodge, Brompton-by-Sawdon, Scarborough, Yorks (☎ 0723 85328)

ILLOVY, Denis; s of Gustav Illovy (d 1944), and Otilie (d 1944); *b* 20 Nov 1922; *Educ* Tower House Bucks; *m* 15 Nov 1961, Adele Rose; 1 s (Mark Gustav b 1965), 1 da (Gaynor Andrea b 1962); *Career* RAF 1944-45 (UK); md Tyremasters Ltd 1960; pres: Retread Manufacturers Assoc 1966-68, BIPAVER (Int Fed of Tyre Trade Assocs) 1971-74; *Recreations* riding, swimming, skiing, literature; *Clubs* Royal London Yacht, Cowes, IOW, Carleton; *Style—* Denis Illovy, Esq; Cliffhanger, The Maples, Bonchurch, IOW PO38 1NR; 40 Medina Road, Cowes, IOW PO31 7LP (telex 869334)

IMAIZUMI, Yokichi; s of Tokujiro Imaizumi, and Chiyoko Imaizumi; *b* 22 Feb 1928;

Educ Tokyo Univ of Commerce Japan, Univ of Chicago USA; *m* Toyoko Imaizumi; 1 s (Junri b 1963), 1 da (Mariko, now Mrs Watanabe); *Career* Mitsubishi Bank Tokyo 1952, dir Japan Int Bank London 1971-72, dep chief mangr int div Mitsubishi Bank London 1973-74, dir and gen mangr Japan Int Bank London 1975-76, dep chief mangr business div Mitsubishi Bank Tokyo 1977, asst chief mangr Credito Italiano Spa Tokyo Branch, advsr Int HQ The Nikko Securities Co Ltd Tokyo 1986, advsr The Nikko Securities Co (Europe) Ltd London 1986-87, md The Nikko Bank (UK) plc 1987-; *Recreations* golf, reading; *Clubs* Overseas Bankers, Highgate GC; *Style*— Yokichi Imaizumi; 17 Godliman Street, London EC4V 5BD (☎ 01 528 7070, fax 01 528 7077, telex 928703)

IMBERT, Sir Peter Michael; QPM (1980); s of William Henry Imbert, and Frances May, *née* Hodge (d 1985); *b* 27 April 1933; *Educ* Harvey GS Folkestone Kent, Holborn Coll of Law; *m* 1956, Iris Rosina, da of Christopher Thomas Charles Dove (d 1984), of London; 1 s (Simon), 2 da (Elaine, Sally); *Career* joined Metropolitan Police 1953-76, detective chief supt; asst and dep constable Surrey Constabulary 1976-79, chief constable Thames Valley Police 1979-85, cmmr Met Police 1987- (dep cmmr 1985-87); *Recreations* golf, gardening; *Style*— Sir Peter Imbert, QPM; New Scotland Yard, London SW1H 0BG (☎ 01 230 1212)

IMBERT-TERRY, Georgina Lady; Georgina; *née* Massie-Taylor; yr da of Maj Gerald Massie-Taylor, of Limassol, Cyprus; *m* 1979, as his 2 w, Sir Andrew Henry Bouhier Imbert-Terry, 4 Bt (d 1985); *Style*— Georgina, Lady Imbert-Terry

IMBERT-TERRY, Sir Michael Edward Stanley; 5 Bt (UK 1917); s of Maj Sir Edward Henry Bouhier Imbert-Terry, MC, 3 Bt (d 1978) and Lady Sackville, *née* Garton, of Knole, Kent; suc bro, Sir Andrew Imbert-Terry, 4 Bt (d 1985); *b* 18 April 1950; *Educ* Cranleigh; *m* 1975, Frances, 3 da of Peter Scott (d 1978), of Ealing; 2 s (Brychan b 1975, Jack b 1985); 2 da (Song b 1973, Bryony b 1980); *Heir* s, Brychan Edward; *Style*— Sir Michael Imbert-Terry, Bt; Little Hennowe, St Ewe, St Austell, Cornwall (☎ 0726 843893)

IMESON, Michael David; s of Terence Imeson, of Allerton, Bradford, Yorks, and Marian, *née* Glasby; *b* 26 Oct 1955; *Educ* Hanson GS Bradford, Univ of Bradford (BSc), LSE (MMPhil); *Career* ed Export Times 1983-84; reporter: The Times Diary 1986, London Daily News 1987; ed Headway Pubns 1987-89; *Recreations* running, photography, travel; *Style*— Michael Imeson, Esq; 17-18 Westbourne St, London W2 (☎ 01 402 1508); Gtr London House, Hampstead Rd, London NW1 (☎ 01 377 4633, fax 01 383 7486)

IMPEY, John Edward; s of Capt L A Impey; *b* 4 Mar 1931; *Educ* Eton; *m* 1, 1959 (m dis 1981), Patricia, *née* Creery; 1 s, 2 da; m 2, 1985, Antonia, da of 0 J G McMullen; *Career* Nat Serv Coldstream Guards; dir County Bank Ltd 1967-79, vice chm Capper Neill plc 1979-1983; exec Williams de Broe 1983; MICAS; *Recreations* winter sports, country pursuits; *Style*— John Impey, Esq; 5 Ladbroke Walk, London W11

IMRAY, Colin Henry; CMG (1983); s of Henry Gibbon Imray (d 1936), and Frances Olive, *née* Badman; *b* 21 Sept 1933; *Educ* Highgate and Hotchkiss USA, Balliol Coll Oxford; *m* 1957, Shirley Margaret, da of Ernest Matthews (d 1972); 1 s (Christopher), 3 da (Frances, Elizabeth, Alison); *Career* Nat Serv 2 Lt Seaforth Highlanders (Royal W African Force) 1952-54; Cwlth Relations Off 1957, third (later second) sec UK High Cmmn Canberra 1958-61, first sec Nairobi 1963-66, Br Trade Cmmn Montreal 1970-73; cnsllr Head of Chancery, consul gen Islamabad 1973-77; Royal Coll of Def Studies 1977; commercial cnsllr Tel Aviv 1977-80; dep high cmmr Bombay 1980-84, dep chief clerk and chief inspr FCO 1984-85, Br high cmmr to the Utd Rep of Tanzania 1986-; *Recreations* travel, walking; *Clubs* Travellers', Royal Cwlth Soc; *Style*— Colin Imray Esq, CMG; c/o FCO Heads of Mission, King Charles St, London SW1A 2AH; British High Commission, PO Box 9200, Dar Es Salaam, Tanzania (☎ 296017, telex 41004)

INCE, David Henry Gason; DFC; s of Maj Douglas Edward Ince, MC (d 1966), and Isobel, *née* Warren (d 1976), of Devonshire Lodge, Copthorne, Sussex; *b* 23 Mar 1921; *Educ* Cheltenham, Glasgow Univ (BSc); *m* 1954, Anne, da of Archer Robert Burton, CBE, of The Causey, Westgate, Old Town, Bridlington, Yorks; 2 da (Virginia b 1955, Rosalind b 1964); *Career* div mangr guided weapons div Elliott Bros (London) Ltd 1958-60, asst gen mangr Elliott Flight Automation Ltd 1960-65; md: Bryans Aeroquipment Ltd (former sales dir) 1965-70, LSM Controls and Seltronic Gp 1968-70; gp dir Gascoigne Gp Ltd 1971-82; ptnr Dynamic Relations 1983-; *Recreations* gliding, writing, woodworking, gardening; *Style*— David Ince Esq, DFC; Church Cottage, Church Lane, Easton, Winchester, Hants SO21 1EH (☎ Itchen Abbas 096 278 372)

INCE, Nigel Valentine; s of Norman Sedgwick Ince, MC (d 1962), and Angela Isobel, *née* Yorke (d 1984); *b* 18 April 1930; *Educ* Cheltenham, Radley; *m* 15 Aug 1959, Pamela Mary, da of Herbert Crewe Horobin (d 1959); 1 s (Robin Charles Crewe b 1969), 2 da (Camilla Jane b 1962, Sarah Elizabeth b 1964); *Career* dir: ABC Travel Guides 1975, ABC Int 1984, General & Executive Travel Ltd 1985; *Recreations* shooting, photography; *Style*— Nigel Ince, Esq; ABC International, Church St, Dunstable, Beds (☎ 0582 600111, telex 81268, fax 0582 695214)

INCH, Sir John Ritchie; CVO (1969), CBE (1958), QPM (1961); s of James Inch (d 1973); *b* 14 May 1911; *Educ* Hamilton Academy, Glasgow Univ (MA, LLB); *m* 1941, Anne Ferguson Shaw; 1 s, 2 da; *Career* chief constable: Dunfermline City Police 1943, combined Fife Constabulary 1949, Edinburgh City Police 1955-75; OStJ 1964; kt 1972; *Recreations* shooting, fishing, golf; *Clubs* Royal Scots (Edinburgh); *Style*— Sir John Inch, CVO, CBE, QPM; Fairways, 192 Whitehouse Rd, Barnton, Edinburgh EH4 6DA (☎ 031 336 3558)

INCHBALD, Denis John Elliot; s of Rev Christopher Chantrey Elliot Inchbald, CF (d 1976), and Olivia Jane, *née* Mills (d 1975); *b* 9 May 1923; *Educ* Oswestry Sch, Jesus Coll Cambridge; *m* 1955, Jacqueline Hazel, *née* Jones; *Career* Lt RNVR; head of publicity Br Industs Fair 1954-56; dir PR Foote Cone & Belding Ltd 1959-68, chm and md Welbeck PR Ltd 1968-84, chm Welbeck PR 1985-88; independent PR consult 1988-; pres Inst PR 1969-70, chm PRCA 1975-78; *Recreations* reading, gardening, photography, travel; *Clubs* Reform, Naval, MCC; *Style*— Denis Inchbald, Esq; 10 Shardeloes, Amersham, Bucks HP7 0RL (☎ 0494 726781)

INCHBALD, Michael John Chantrey; s of Geoffrey H E Inchbald (d 1982), and Rosemary Evelyn, *née* Ilbert (d 1958); *b* 8 Mar 1920; *Educ* Sherborne, Architectural Assoc Sch of Architecture; *m* m 1, 1955 (m dis 1964), Jacqueline Bromley; 1 s (Courtenay b 1958), 1 da (Charlotte b 1960); m 2, 1964 (m dis 1969), Eunice Haymes; *Career* designer; co fndr Inchbald Sch of Design; dir Michael Inchbald Ltd 1953-; FCSD; *Recreations* works of art, travel; *Style*— Michael Inchbald, Esq; Stanley House, 10 Milner St, London SW3 2PU (☎ 01 584 8832)

INCHBALD, Stephen Charles Elliot; s of Ralph Mordaunt Elliot Inchbald, da of Gertrude Elizabeth, *née* Ferres; *b* 16 Dec 1940; *Educ* Downside; *m* 16 Dec 1968, Elizabeth Mary, da of Bryan Frank Pocock (d 1979); 2 s (Charles b 1972, Alexander b 1974), 1 da (Louise b 1978); *Career* chartered surveyor, autioneer and estate agent, md TSB Property Servs Ltd 1988; FIOD, FRICS; *Recreations* shooting, gardening, travel; *Clubs* IOD, Beaconsfield Golf; *Style*— Stephen C E Inchbald, Esq; West Riding, Bottom Lane, Seer Green, Beaconsfield, Buckinghamshire (☎ 04946 2527); Raffety Buckland & Co Ltd, 30 High St, High Wycombe, Bucks (☎ 0494 21 234, fax 0494 36 362, telex 83544)

INCHCAPE, 3 Earl of (UK 1929); Kenneth James William Mackay; also Baron Inchcape (UK 1911), Viscount Inchcape (UK 1924), and Viscount Glenapp (UK 1929); s of 2 Earl of Inchcape (d 1939), and his 1 w, Joan (d 1933), da of Rt Hon John Francis Moriarty, Lord Justice of Appeal in Ireland; *b* 27 Dec 1917; *Educ* Eton, Trinity Coll Cambridge (MA); *m* 1, 12 Feb 1941 (m dis 1954), Aline Thorn, da of Sir Richard Arthur Pease, 2 Bt, and widow of Patrick Claude Hannay, FO AAF; 2 s (Viscount Glenapp, *qv*, Hon James b 1947), 1 da (Lady Lucinda b 1941); m 2, 13 Feb 1965, Caroline Cholmeley, da of Cholmeley Harrison, of Emo Court, Co Leix; 2 s (Hon Shane b 1972, Hon Ivan b 1976), and 1 adopted s (Anthony b 1967); *Heir* s, Viscount Glenapp; *Career* served WWII Maj 12 Royal Lancers, 27 Lancers (Europe); chm and chief exec Inchcape plc 1958-83 (now life pres); chm P&O Steam Navigation Co 1973-83 (chief exec 1978-81); former dir: Standard Chartered Bank Ltd, Guardian Royal Exchange, Nat Provincial Bank, Burmah Oil, British Petroleum; dir BAII plc; pres Cwlth Soc for the Deaf; pres Gen Cncl British Shipping 1976-77; Freeman and Lieut City of London; Prime Warden: Shipwrights' Co 1967, Fishmongers' Co 1977-78; *Recreations* field sports, farming; *Clubs* White's, Cavalry and Guards', Brooks's, Buck's, Oriental, City; *Style*— The Rt Hon The Earl of Inchcape; Addington Manor, Addington, Bucks MK18 2JR (☎ 029 671 4545); Forneth House, Blairgowrie, Perthshire

INCHIQUIN, 18 Baron (I 1543); Sir Conor Myles John O'Brien; 10 Bt (I 1686); s of Hon (Fionn) Myles Maryons O'Brien (youngest s of late 15 Baron Inchiquin); suc unc, 17 Baron Inchiquin, 1982; Lord Inchiquin is 13 in descent from the 3 s of 1 Baron Inchiquin, the latter being cr Earl of Thomond for life; The descendants of the eldest s of the 1 Baron held the Marquessate of Thomond 1800-55; The O'Briens descend from Brian Boroimhe, Prince of Thomond and High King of Ireland in 1002, who was k at the moment of victory against the Danes in the Battle of Clontarf 1014; *b* 17 July 1943; *Educ* Eton; *m* 1988, Helen O'Farrell, da of Gerald Fitzgerald Farrell, of Newton Forbes, Co Langford; *Heir* father's 1 cous, Maj Murrough O'Brien; *Career* late Capt 14/20 King's Hussars; *Clubs* Kildare Street and University Club (Dublin); *Style*— The Rt Hon the Lord Inchiquin; Thomond House, Dromoland, Newmarket-on-Fergus, Co Clare, Eire (☎ 061 71304)

INCHIQUIN, Baroness; Vera Maud; da of Rev Clifton Samuel Winter; *m* 1945, Maj 17 Baron Inchiquin (d 1982); *Style*— The Rt Hon The Lady Inchiquin; Winton House, Dawlish, Devon; Hanway Lodge, Richards Castle, Ludlow, Salop

INCHYRA, 1 Baron (UK 1961); Frederick Robert Hoyer Millar; GCMG (1956, KCMG 1949, CMG 1939), CVO 1938; s of late Robert Hoyer Millar; *b* 6 June 1900; *Educ* Wellington, New Coll Oxford; *m* 1931, Elizabeth, da of late Jonkheer Reneke de Marees van Swinderen, formerly Netherlands min in London; 2 s, 2 da; *Heir* s, Hon Robert Hoyer Millar; *Career* hon attaché Brussels 1922, Diplomatic Service 1923, third sec Berlin 1923, Paris 1924, second Sec FO 1928, Cairo 1930, first Sec FO 1935, asst private sec to sec state Foreign Affrs 1934-38, first sec Washington 1939, acting cnsllr 1941, sec Br Civil Secretariat Washington 1943, cnsllr FO 1944, min Washington 1948; UK deputy NATO Cncl 1950, UK perm rep thereon 1952; high cmmr FDR 1953-55, ambass Bonn 1955-56; perm under-sec state Foreign Affairs, FO 1957-61; King of Arms of Order of St Michael and St George 1961-75; *Clubs* Boodle's, Turf, New (Edinburgh), Metropolitan (Washington); *Style*— The Rt Hon the Lord Inchyra, GCMG, CVO; Inchyra House, Glencarse, Perthshire

IND, Jack Kenneth; s of Rev William Price Ind (d 1956), of Harlington, Beds, and Doris Maud, *née* Cavell; *b* 20 Jan 1935; *Educ* Marlborough St John's Coll Oxford (MA), London Univ Inst of Educ; *m* 2 Sept 1964, Elizabeth Olive, da of Edwin Gordon Toombs (d 1956), of Wokingham, Berks; 2 s (Mark b 1967, Hugh b 1969), 2 da (Rebecca b 1965, Katharine b 1972); *Career* Nat Serv 2 Lt RA 1953-55; asst master: Wellingborough Sch 1960-63, Tonbridge Sch 1963-81 (house master 1970-81); headmaster Dover Coll 1981-; memb: Headmasters Conf governing body Gt Walstead Sch W Sussex, Jt Assoc of Classics Teachers 1960, reader of C of E 1963-; *Recreations* music, team sports; *Clubs* Public Schools; *Style*— Jack K Ind, Esq; Headmasters House, Dover Coll, Dover, Kent, CT17 9RH (☎ 0304 205 905); Dover Coll, Dover, Kent, CT17 9RH (☎ 0304 205 969)

INFIELD, Paul Louis; s of Gordon Mark Infield, of 23 Alexandra Ct, Maida Vale, London, and Roda Molca, *née* Lincoln; *b* 1 July 1957; *Educ* Haberdashers' Aske's, The Peddie Sch Hightstown New Jersey USA, Univ of Sheffield (LLB); *m* 6 Feb 1987, Catharine Grace, da of Ancrum Francis Evans, of Harpley House, Clifton on Teme, Worcs, 1 s (Samuel b 1988); *Career* called to the Bar Inner Temple 1980; memb Bd of Deps of Br Jews; Freeman City of London 1979, Liveryman Worshipful Co of Plaisterers 1979; *Recreations* photography, running; *Clubs* RAC; *Style*— Paul Infield, Esq; 9A Eccleston Sq, London SW1V 1NP (☎ 01 828 2704); 9 Kings Bench Walk, Temple, London EC4Y 7DX (☎ 01 353 7202, 01 353 3909, fax 01 583 2030)

ING, Dr Brian Stuart; s of Denis Wilfred Ing, of 53 Boundstone Lane, Lancing, Sussex, and Christine Joyce Elenor, *née* Austin; *b* 23 August 1947; *Educ* Steyning, Sidney Sussex Coll Cambridge (BA, MA), Cavendish Lab Cambridge (PhD); *m* 5 Sept 1970, Ann Maureen Elaine, da of Reginald Ambrose Bennidict Lambert (d 1977); 1 s (James b 1981), 2 da (Julie-Ann b 1972, Victoria b 1974); *Career* Inter Bank Res Organisation, Anglia Water Authy, Scicon, manging conslt Arthur Young 1977-82, gp mangr CACI 1983-85, dir Clark Whitehill Conslts 1985-87, assoc ptnr Clark Whitehill 1987-; FCCA, FIMC; *Style*— Dr Brian Ing; 24 Woodcock Close, Impington, Cambridge CB4 4LD (☎ 0223 234 291); Clark Whitehill Consultants, 25 New Street Square, London EC4A 3LN (☎ 01 353 1577, fax 01 583 1720, telex 887422)

ING, David Newson; MBE (1986); s of Gilbert Newson Ing (d 1975), of Hull, E Yorks, and Edith Mary, *née* Adamson (d 1982); *b* 30 May 1934; *Educ* Pocklington Sch York; *m* 15 Sept 1962, Penelope Ann, da of Basil Charles William Hart, of Cranleigh, Surrey; 2 s (Richard b 1965, William b 1967); *Career* Nat Serv cmmnd RAF 1957-59

(Sword of Honour); slr 1957; sr ptnr Downs Slrs Dorking 1985- (joined 1961, ptnr 1963); lay chm Dorking Deanery Synod 1970-73; chm: mgmnt ctee Dorking and Dist CAB 1966-85, Surrey Bldg Soc 1981- (dir 1969-); hon slr Fire Servs Nat Benevolent Fund 1975-, The Lutyens Tst 1984-; Master Worshipful Co of Woolmen 1988-89 (Liveryman 1967-); memb Law Soc; *Recreations* reading, walking, gardening, cricket, theatre, opera; *Clubs* The Law Soc, MCC; *Style—* David N Ing, Esq, MBE; Ravenspur, Sutton Place, Abinger Hammer, Dorking, Surrey RH5 6RN (☎ 0306 730260); 156 High Street, Dorking, Surrey RH4 1BQ (☎ 0306 880110, fax 0306 76577, car tel 0836 209240, telex 859905 DOWNS G)

ING, Simon Burton; JP (1979); s of Cyril Henry Ing (d 1977); *b* 23 May 1938; *Educ* St Edward's Sch, Imperial Coll London; *m* 1962, Hazel Diana, da of Leonard Clare (d 1971); 1 s (Jason, b 1972), 1 da (Sophie b 1974); *Career* ptnr Coopers & Lybrand, vice chm King's Lynn Festival 1979-, chm govrs Beeston Hall Sch 1982-; Freeman City of London 1984; FCA; *Recreations* golf, swimming, gardening; *Clubs* IOD; *Style—* Simon Ing, Esq, JP; 15 King Street, King's Lynn, Norfolk PE30 1ET (☎ 0553 774810); office: 11 King St, King's Lynn, Norfolk PE30 1ET (☎ 0553 761316, telex 817843, fax 0553 766454)

INGAMELLS, John Anderson Stuart; s of George Harry Ingamells (d 1988), and Gladys Lucy, *née* Rollett (d 1979); *b* 12 Nov 1934; *Educ* Hastings and Eastbourne GS, Cambridge Univ (BA); *m* 30 May 1964, Hazel, da of George William Wilson (d 1985); 2 da (Ann b 1965, Clare b 1969); *Career* 2 Lt RASC 1956-58, serv Cyprus; art asst York City Art Gallery 1959-63, asst keeper Nat Museum of Wales Cardiff 1963-67, curator York City Art Gallery 1967-77, dir Wallace Collection 1978- (asst to dir 1977-78); catalogues of pictures produced incl: Wallace Collection vol 1 1985, vol II 1986, The English Episcopal Portrait 1981, The Davies Collection of French Art 1967; articles in: The Burlington Magazine, Apollo The Walpole Soc, Journal of Aesthetics, La Revue du Louvre; tstee Dulwich Picture Gallery 1988, cncl memb, Paul Mellon Centre for Studies in Br Art London; FRSA 1988; *Style—* John Ingamells, Esq; The Wallace Collection, Hertford House, Manchester Square, London W1M 6BN (☎ 01 935 0687)

INGE, Lt-Gen Sir Peter Anthony; KCB (1988); s of Raymond Inge, and Grace Maud Caroline, *née* Du Rose (d 1962); *b* 5 August 1935; *Educ* Summer Fields, Wrekin Coll RMA Sandhurst; *m* 26 Nov 1960, Letitia Marion, da of Trevor Thornton Berry (d 1967), of Swinithwaite Hall, Leyburn, N Yorks; 2 da (Antonia b 17 May 1962, Verity b 12 Oct 1965); *Career* cmmnd Green Howards 1954, served Hong Kong, Malaya, Germany, Libya and N Ireland, ADC to GOC 4 Div 1960-61, Adj 1 Green Howards 1963-64, student Staff Coll 1966, MOD 1967-69, Co Cdr 1 Green Howards 1969-70, student JSSC 1971, BM 11 Armd Bde 1972, Instructor Staff Coll 1973-74, CO 1 Green Howards 1974-76, Cmdt Junior Div Staff Coll 1977-79, Cdr Task Force C/4 Armd Bde 1980-81, Chief of Staff HQ1 (BR) Corps 1982-83, GOC NE Dist/2 Inf DN 1984-86, DGLP (A) MOD 1986-87, cmd 1 (Br) Corps 1987-, Col The Green Howards 1982, Col Cmdt RMP 1987, APTC 1988; *Recreations* cricket, walking, music, reading (especially military history); *Style—* Lt Gen Sir Peter Inge, KCB; c/o Barclays Bank, Leyburn, N Yorks; HQ, 1st (British) Corps, BFPO 39

INGE-INNES-LILLINGSTON, George David; CBE (1986), (Staffs 1969); s of Cdr Hugh William Innes-Lillingston, RN (d 1953); *b* 13 Nov 1923; *Educ* Stowe, Merton Coll Oxford (MA); *m* 1, 1946, Alison Mary (d 1947), da of late Rev Canon Frederick Green; 1 da; m 2, 1955, Elizabeth Violet Grizel, da of Lt-Gen Sir William Montgomerie Thomson, KCMG, CB, MC (d 1963); 2 s, 1 da; *Career* served WWII Lt Cdr RNR; memb Agric Land Tbnl 1962-72; chm: N Birmingham & Dist Hosps 1968-74, Agric and Horticulture Ctee British Standards Instn 1980-86, (Midland Regional) Sail Training Assoc 1983-; dir Lands Improvement Gp of Companies 1983-; crown estate cmmr 1974-; pres: Staffs Agric Soc 1970-71, Country Landowners Assoc 1979-81 (chm 1977-79, pres Staffs Branch 1983-); High Sheriff Staffs 1966; JP 1967-75; FRAgS (1986); *Recreations* growing trees, yachting; *Clubs* Boodle's, Royal Thames Yacht, Royal Highland Yacht, Farmers'; *Style—* George Inge-Innes-Lillingston, Esq, CBE, DL; Thorpe Hall, Thorpe Constantine, Tamworth, Staffs (☎ 0827 830224/5)

INGHAM, Bernard; s of Garnet Ingham (d 1974), of Hebden Bridge, W Yorks; *b* 21 June 1932; *Educ* Hebden Bridge GS; *m* 1956, Nancy Hilda, da of Ernest Hoyle (d 1944), of Halifax, W Yorks; 1 s; *Career* journalist: Hebden Bridge Times 1948-52, The Yorkshire Post and Yorkshire Evening Post 1952-59, The Yorkshire Post (northern industl correspondent) 1959-62, The Guardian 1962-67; civil servant: press advsr Nat Bd for Prices and Incomes 1967-68, head info dept Employment and Productivity 1968-72, dir of info Dept of Employment 1973, dir of info Dept of Energy 1974-78, under-sec (energy conservation div) Dept of Energy 1978-79, chief press sec to Prime Minister 1979-; *Recreations* walking, gardening, reading; *Style—* Bernard Ingham, Esq; 10 Downing St, London SW1

INGHAM, Maj (Francis) Roger; TD (and bar); s of Maj Joshua Lister Ingham (d 1963), of Wighill Park, Tadcaster, Yorks, and Violet Warburton, *née* Warburton-Lee (d 1980), (*see* Burke's Landed Gentry, 1952 edn); *b* 18 May 1914; *Educ* Eton RAC Cirencester; *m* 26 June 1943, Edna Maud, da of Frederick Hynde Fox, JP, DL, (d 1988) of Inglewood, Ledsham, Wirral, Cheshire; 1 s (Philip William b 1947), 1 da (Sarah Jane b 1944); *Career* 2 Lt Queens Own Yorkshire Dragoons 1935, Maj 1942, served in WWII in Palestine, Syria and Western Desert (ret 1956); dir Ingham's Thornhill Collieries Ltd 1937-47 (nationalised 1947); dir and chm: Croft & Blackburn Ltd, Harold Nickols Ltd, Kirkstall Finance Ltd 1947-80; High Sheriff Yorks 1956; chm cncl Order of St John for S and W Yorks 1966-80; KStJ 1976, FLAS; *Recreations* lawn tennis, shooting, skiing; *Clubs* Naval and Military; *Style—* Maj Roger Ingham, TD; Bellwood Hall, Ripon, N Yorks (☎ 0765 2005)

INGILBY, Diana, Lady; Diana; da of Brig-Gen Sir George Lethbridge Colvin, CB, CMG, DSO (d 1962); *m* 1948, Maj Sir Joslan William Vivian Ingilby, 5 Bt (d 1974); 1 s, 2 da; *Career* rural dist cncllr Nidderdale RDC to 1973; dist cncllr Harrogate Borough Cncl 1973-86 (hon alderman 1986); *Style—* Diana, Lady Ingilby; Ripley Castle, Ripley, Harrogate, N Yorks HG3 3AY (☎ 0423 770186)

INGILBY, Sir Thomas Colvin William; 6 Bt (UK 1866), of Ripley Castle, Yorkshire; s of Maj Sir Joslan William Vivian Ingilby, 5 Bt, JP, DL (d 1974); *b* 17 July 1955; *Educ* Eton, RAC Cirencester (MRAC); *m* 25 Feb 1984, Emma Clare Roebuck, da of Maj Richard R Thompson, of Whinfield, Strensall, York; 2 s (James b 1985, Joslan b 1986), 1 da (Eleanor Jane Pamela b 1989); *Heir* s, James William Francis b 15 June 1985; *Career* teacher Springvale Sch Rhodesia 1973-74; asst land agent: Stephenson & Son York 1978-80, Strutt and Parker Harrogate 1981-83; mangr Ripley Castle Estates 1983-; lecture tours USA 1978 and 1979; int hon citizen New Orleans 1979; tstee Cathedral Camps (reg charity) 1983; pres: Harrogate and Dist Talking Newspaper 1978-, Nidd Valley Evening NADFAS 1986-, Harrogate Gilbert and Sullivan Soc 1987-, Nidderdale Amateur Cricket League 1979-; govr Ashville Coll Harrogate 1985-; fndr and co-ordinator Nat Stately Home Hotline (a stately home and museum neighbourhood watch scheme) 1988; ARICS, FAAV; landowner (1800 acres); *Recreations* cricket, tennis, walking, historical research, reading; *Style—* Sir Thomas Ingilby, Bt; Ripley Castle, Ripley, nr Harrogate, N Yorks HG3 3AY (☎ 0423 770053, 0423 770053; work: 0423 770152)

INGLEBY, 2 Viscount (UK 1956); Martin Raymond Peake; s of 1 Viscount Ingleby (d 1966), and Joan, Viscountess Ingleby, *qv*; *b* 31 May 1926; *Educ* Eton, Trinity Coll Oxford; *m* 1952, Susan, da of Capt Henderson Landale, of Ewell Manor, W Farleigh, Kent; 1s (decd) 4 da; *Heir* none; *Career* late Lt Coldstream Gds; barr Inner Temple 1956; dir Hargreaves Gp Ltd 1960-80, CC N Riding Yorks 1964-67; landowner; *Recreations* forestry; *Style—* The Rt Hon the Viscount Ingleby; Snilesworth, Northallerton, N Yorks DL6 3QD; Flat 1, 61 Onslow Sq, London SW7 3LS

INGLEFIELD; *see*: Crompton-Inglefield

INGLEFIELD, David Gilbert Charles; s of Sir Gilbert Inglefield, GBE, TD, of 6 Rutland House, Marloes Rd, London, and Barbara, *née* Thompson; *b* 19 Nov 1934; *Educ* Eton, Trinity Coll Cambridge (MA); *m* 31 Oct 1970, Jean Mary, MBE, da of Col Sir Alan Gomme-Duncan, MC (d 1963), of Dunbarney Bridge of Earn, Perthshire; 1 s (Charles b 1977), 1 da (Mary b 1974); *Career* Nat Serv 1953-55, 2 Lt 12 Royal Lancers serv: Malaya BAOR; Price Forbes & Co 1958-60, The De La Rue Co 1961-65, dir Inglefield Gp Ltd 1965-80, appeals dir the Police Fndn 1981-; memb overseas ctee Save the Children Fund 1969-80, chm Prevention of Blindness Res Fund 1969-72, Trustee Order of Malta Homes Tst 1975-, Master Aldersgate Ward Club 1977-78; memb Chapter-Gen OstJ 1979-, Sheriff City of London 1980-81, memb Ct of Assts Worshipful Co of Haberdashers; OStJ 1973, Sovereign and Mil Order of Merit 1978, Order of Gorkha Dakshina Bahu (Nepal) Class III 1980, Order of King Abdul Aziz (Saudi Arabia) 1981; *Recreations* travel, shooting, military history; *Clubs* Boodles; *Style—* David Inglefield, Esq; 38 Kew Green, Richmond, Surrey TW9 3BH; The Police Foundation, 314-316 Vauxhall Bridge Road, London SW1V 1AA

INGLEFIELD, Sir Gilbert Samuel; GBE (1968), TD; s of Adm Sir Frederick Inglefield, KCB; *b* 13 Mar 1909; *Educ* Eton, Trinity Coll Cambridge; *m* 1933, Laura Barbara Frances, CStJ, da of Capt Gilbert Thompson, of the Connaught Rangers; 2 s, 1 da; *Career* served WWII Sherwood Foresters (France, Far East); Br Cncl: asst rep Egypt 1946-49, London 1949-56; chm Barbican Ctee 1963-66, Ld Mayor London 1967-68 (alderman Aldersgate Ward 1959-79, Sheriff 1963-64), one of HM's Lieuts City of London, chm City Arts Tst 1968-76, chllr Order St John of Jerusalem 1969-78, dep kt princ Imperial Soc Kts Bachelor 1972-, govr Fedn Br Artists 1972-; Master: Haberdashers' Co 1972, Musicians' Co 1974; former DL Beds 1973, trustee LSO, govr Royal Shakespeare Theatre, memb Redundant Churches Fund, asst Painter Stainers' Co; former: church cmmr for Eng, memb Royal Fine Arts Cmmn, tstee London Festival Ballet Tst; former provincial grand master Beds Freemasons; GCStJ; Hon: FLCM, GSM, RBA; Hon DSc City Univ 1967; ARIBA, AADipl, FRSA; kt 1965; *Clubs* Athenaeum; *Style—* Sir Gilbert Inglefield, GBE, TD; 6 Rutland House, Marloes Rd, London W8 5LE (☎ 01 937 3458)

INGLEFIELD, Timothy John Urquhart (Tim); s of William John Inglefield, DFC, of Dorset, and Mabel Dorothy Chattel; *b* 3 Nov 1946; *Educ* Harrow, Imperial Coll London (BSc); *m* 1975, Felicity Mary, da of Sqdn Ldr Edward Lawrence McMullen, MBE (ret); 2 da (Theresa b 1978, Kirstin b 1981); *Career* merchant banker; dep md Lloyds Devpt Capital Ltd, dir Lloyds Merchant Bank; dir Microbiologicals Ltd, Richard Lloyd Ltd; FCA; *Recreations* sailing, Normandy fish restaurants; *Style—* Tim Inglefield, Esq; 19 Hillside Road, Penn, Bucks HP10 8JJ; Lloyds Merchant Bank Ltd, 40/66 Queen Victoria Street, London EC4P 4EL

INGLEFIELD-WATSON, Lt-Col Sir John Forbes; 5 Bt (UK 1895); s of Sir Derrick William Inglefield-Watson, 4 Bt (d 1987), by his 1 w, Margrett Georgina (now Mrs Savill), da of Col Thomas Stokes George Hugh Robertson Aikman, CB; *b* 16 May 1926; *Educ* Eton; *Heir* 2 cous Simon Conran Hamilton Watson b 11 Aug 1939; *Career* RE 1945-81: cmmnd 1946; ret 1981, Lt-Col; *Recreations* philately, football refereeing (FA staff referee instr 1978-); *Style—* Lt-Col Sir John Inglefield-Watson, Bt; The Ross, Hamilton, Lanarkshire, ML3 7UF (☎ 0698 283734)

INGLEFIELD-WATSON, Lady; Therese; *née* Bodon; late Prof Charles Bodon, of Budapest; *m* 1946 (as his 2 w), Sir Derrick Inglefield-Watson, 4 Bt (d 1987); *Style—* Lady Inglefield-Watson; Ringshill House, Wouldham, nr Rochester, Kent ME1 3RB (☎ 0634 61514)

INGLEWOOD, 1 Baron (UK 1964); William Morgan (Fletcher-)Vane; TD, DL (Westmorland 1946, Cumbria 1974); assumed name Fletcher-Vane 1931; s of Col Hon William Vane, JP, DL, yst bro of 9 Baron Barnard, and Lady Katharine Pakenham, da of 4 Earl of Longford; *b* 12 April 1909; *Educ* Charterhouse, Trinity Coll Cambridge (MA, DipAgr); *m* 1949, Mary (d 1982), da of Maj Sir Richard Proby, 1 Bt, MC (d 1977); 2 s; *Heir* s, Hon Richard (Fletcher-)Vane; *Career* served WWII, Europe (despatches Dunkirk 1940), Middle East (El Alamein), Lt-Col Durham LI; sits as Conservative Peer in House of Lords; MP (C) Westmorland 1945-64, jt parly sec Min Pensions and Nat Insurance 1958-60, parly sec Agric 1960-62; ldr of UK delegation to World Food Congress (Washington) 1963; chartered surveyor; dir Spooner Industries 1963-80 (chm 1976-80); chm Anglo-German Assoc; *Clubs* Travellers'; *Style—* The Rt Hon the Lord Inglewood, TD, DL; Hutton-in-the-Forest, Penrith, Cumbria CA11 9TH (☎ 085 34 207); 21 Stack House, Cundy St, Ebury St, London SW1 (☎ 01 730 1559)

INGLIS, Sir Brian Scott; AC; s of late E S Inglis; *b* 3 Jan 1924; *Educ* Geelong C of E GS, Trinity Coll Melbourne Univ; *m* 1953, Leila, da of E V Butler; 3 da; *Career* served WWII, Flying Offr RAAF, 453 Sqdn 1942-45; dir and general mfrg mangr Ford Motor Co 1963-70 (first Aust mangr), dir Ford Motor Co of Aust Ltd 1970-81 (vice-pres 1981-83); chm: Ford Asia Pacific Inc 1983-84, Ford Motor Co of Aust 1981-85; dir dep chm Amcor Ltd; chm: Newment Holdings, The Centre for Molecular Biology and Med Monash Univ, Aerospace Technologies of Aust, Scalzo Automotive Res; memb cncl Trinity Coll Melbourne Univ; Kernot Medal Faculty of Engrg Univ of Melbourne, James N Kirby Medal ProdE 1979; *Style—* Sir Brian Inglis, AC; 10 Bowley Ave, Balwyn, Vic 3103, Australia

INGLIS, Brian St John; s of Sir Claude Cavendish Inglis (d 1974), and Vera Margaret St John (d 1972), elder da of late John Redmond Blood, of Malahide, Co Dublin; *b* 31 July 1916; *Educ* Shrewsbury, Magdalen Coll Oxford (BA), Trinity Coll Dublin (PhD); *m* 1958 (m dis), Ruth Langdon; 1 s (Neil), 1 da (Diana); *Career* Sqdn Ldr Coastal Cmd RAF 1944-45; ed Spectator 1959-62; writer and presenter What the Papers Say 1956-, All our Yesterdays 1962-73; *Books* The Story of Ireland (1956), West Briton (1962), Fringe Medicine (1964), Abdication (1967), Poverty and the Industrial Revolution (1971), Roger Casement (1973), The Forbidden Game (1975), The Opium War (1976), Natural and Supernatural (1977), Natural Medicine (1978), The Diseases of Civilisation (1981), Science and Parascience (1984), The Paranormal (1985), The Hidden Power (1986), The Unknown Guest (1987), The Power of Dreams (1987); *Style—* Brian Inglis, Esq; Garden Flat, 23 Lambolle Rd, London NW3 4HS (☎ 01 794 0297)

INGLIS, George Bruton; s of Cecil George Inglis (d 1968), and Ethel Mabel, *née* Till (d 1987); *Educ* Winchester Coll, Pembroke Coll Oxford (MA); *m* 16 Nov 1968, Patricia Mary, da of Archibald Christian Forbes (d 1967); 3 s (James b 1970, Robert b 1972, Jonathan b 1974); *Career* sr ptnr Slaughter and May 1986- (jt ptnr 1966-86); govr Royal Marsden Hosp; memb Law Soc; *Recreations* gardening; *Style—* George Inglis, Esq; 35 Basinghall St, London EC2V 5DB (☎ 01 600 1200)

INGLIS, Lt-Col John Charles; s of Maj Harold John Inglis, DSO, MC (d 1967), of Llansantffraed House, Bwlch, Brecon, and Elsie, *née* Tower (d 1958); *b* 18 Mar 1925; *Educ* Winchester; *m* 16 May 1959, Rosaleen Marjory Florinda, da of Capt Hubert Henry de Burgh, DSO, RN (d 1960), of Oldtown, NAAS, Co Kildare, Ireland; 2 s (Charles b 1965, James b 1968); *Career* joined RAC 1943, cmmnd Grenar Guards 1944, 2 Lt 4 Tank Bn NW Europe campaign 1945, transferred 15/19 The Kings Royal Hussars Palestine campaign 1945, Capt Malaya campaign 1951 and 1954-57, Maj NI 1958, Staff Coll 1959, Lt-Col 1967, CO 15/19 The Kings Royal Hussars 1968-70, ret 1972; net field sec The Salmon and Trout Assoc 1972-86, regnl sec Game Conservancy Cncl 1988; *Recreations* shooting, fishing; *Clubs* Farmers; *Style—* Lt-Col John Inglis; Hope Bowdler Hall, Church, Stretton, Shropshire (☎ 0694 722 041)

INGLIS, (James Craufuird) Roger; WS; s of Lt-Col John Inglis (d 1967); *b* 2 June 1925; *Educ* Winchester, Cambridge, Edinburgh Univ; *m* 1952, Phoebe Aeonie, da of Edward Mackenzie Murray-Buchanan; 2 s, 4 da; *Career* ptnr Shepherd & Wedderburn WS 1976-; chm: British Assets Trust plc 1978- (dir 1957-78), Investors Capital Tst plc 1985-; dir: Assets Trust plc 1988, Scottish Provident Instn for Mutual Life Assurance 1962-, Royal Bank of Scotland plc 1967-; *Recreations* golf; *Clubs* Royal & Ancient Golf (St Andrews), Army and Navy, New (Edinburgh), Hon Co of Edinburgh Golfers; *Style—* Roger Inglis, Esq, WS; Inglisfield, Gifford, East Lothian (☎ 062 081 339); office: 16 Charlotte Sq, Edinburgh (☎ 031 225 8585)

INGLIS OF GLENCORSE, Sir Roderick John; 10 Bt (NS 1703), of Glencorse, Midlothian (formerly Mackenzie of Gairloch, Ross-shire); s of Sir Maxwell Ian Hector Inglis, 9 Bt (d 1974); *b* 25 Jan 1936; *Educ* Winchester, Edinburgh Univ (MB ChB); *m* 1, 1960 (m dis 1975), Rachel Evelyn, da of Lt-Col N M Morris, of Dowdstown, Ardee, co Louth; 2 s (Ian b 1965, and Alexander (twin) b 1965, and 1 s decd), 1 da (Amanda b 1963); m 2, 1975 (m dis 1977), Geraldine, da of R H Kirk, of Thaxted, Essex; 1 da (Harriet b 1976); m 3, 1986, Marilyn, da of A L Irwin, of Glasgow; 1 s (Harry b 1986); *Heir* s, Ian Richard Inglis of Glencorse, yr, b 1965; *Clubs* Country (Pietermaritzberg); *Style—* Sir Roderick Inglis of Glencorse, Bt; 18 Cordwalles Rd, Pietersmaritzburg, Natal, S Africa

INGLIS-JONES, Nigel John; QC (1982); s of Maj John Alfred Inglis-Jones (d 1977), and Hermione, *née* Vivian (d 1958); *b* 7 May 1935; *Educ* Eton, Trinity Coll Oxford (BA); *m* 1, 1965, Lenette (d 1986), o da of Lt Col Sir Walter Bromley-Davenport, of Cheshire; 2 s (James b 1968, Valentine b 1972), 2 da (Imogen b 1966, Cressida b 1967); m 2, 1987, Ursula Jane Drury, y da of the late Captain G D and Mrs Culverwell (now Lady Pile), of Sussex; *Career* served as Ensign (Nat Serv) with Grenadier Gds 1953-55; rec of the Crown Ct 1977; bencher Inner Temple 1981; *Recreations* fishing, gardening; *Clubs* MCC; *Style—* Nigel Inglis-Jones, Esq, QC; 4 Sheen Common Drive, Richmond, Surrey TW10 5BN (☎ 01 878 1320); Lamb Building, Temple, London EC4Y 7AS (☎ 01 353 6381)

INGMAN, David Charles; s of Charles Ingman (d 1983), of Torquay, and Muriel, *née* Bevan (d 1974); *b* 22 Mar 1928; *Educ* London Univ (BSc), Durham Univ (MSc); *m* 29 Dec 1951, Joan Elizabeth Ingman; 2 da (Heather b 26 Dec 1953, Suzanne b 20 July 1957); *Career* ICI 1949-85: works mangr Polyolefines Wilton 1972-75, dir for prodn and engrg 1975-78, res dir 1978, dep chm plastics div 1978, gp dir plastics and petrochemical div 1981-85; dir Engrg Servs Ltd 1975-78, alternative dir ACCI Ltd S Africa 1978-82, non exec dir Negretti-Zambra 1979-81, chm and chief exec Bestobell plc 1985-86, chm Br Waterways Bd 1987-; memb Nationalised Industs Chm's Gp 1987-; *Recreations* golf, painting, gardening, travel; *Style—* David Ingman, Esq; British Waterways Board, Melbury House, Melbury Terrace, London NW1 6JX (☎ 01 725 8010, fax 01 402 0168, car tel 0836 521 163)

INGOLD, Prof (Cecil) Terence; CMG (1970); s of Edwin George Ingold (d 1951), of Surrey, and Gertrude, *née* Boardman (d 1954); *b* 3 July 1905; *Educ* Bangor Co Down GS, Queen's Univ Belfast (BSc, PhD, DSc); *m* 1933, Leonora Mary, da of James Heggie Kemp (d 1950), of Cheshire; 1 s (Timothy), 3 da (Joan, Patsy, Bridget); *Career* lectr: Univ of Reading 1930-37, UC Leicester 1937-44; prof of botany Birkbeck Coll London Univ 1944-72; *Books* Spore Discharge in Land Plants (1939), The Biology of Fungi (fifth edn 1984), Fungal Spores, Their Liberation and Dispersal (1971); *Recreations* walking; *Style—* Prof Terence Ingold, CMG; 11 Buckner's Close, Benson, Oxford (☎ 0491 38240)

INGRAM, Dr David John Edward; s of John Evans Ingram (d 1967), of Ships Lantern, Bexhill-on-Sea, and Marie Florence, *née* Weller (d 1965); *b* 6 April 1927; *Educ* King's Coll Sch Wimbledon, New Coll Oxford, Clarendon Lab Oxford (MA, DPhil, DSc); *m* 4 July 1952, (Ruth) Geraldine Grace, da of Donald McNair (d 1975), of The Old Grammar School, Cirencester, Glos; 3 s (Jonathan b 1953, Bruce b 1960, Marion b 1956); *Career* lectr and reader Dept of Electronics Univ of Southampton 1952-59, dep vice chllr Univ of Keele 1964 and 1968-71, prof and head of physics Univ of Keele 1959-73, princ Chelsea Coll Univ of London 1973-80, vice chllr Univ of Kent 1980-; memb Enterprise Agency of E Kent; chm: Chaucer Hosp Community Advsy Bd, Kent Co Consultative Ctee for Industry Year 1986; vice chm Canterbury-Reims Twinning Assoc, pres Kent Fedn of Amenity Socs 1986-87; hon DSc: Univ of Clermont-Ferrand 1960, Univ of Keele 1983; fell Chelsea Coll Univ of London; FInstP, FCS; *Books* Spectroscopy at Radio and Microwave frequencies (1955, 2 ed 1967), Free Radicals as Studied by Electron Spin Resonance (1958), Biological and Biochemical Applications of Electron Spin Resonance (1969), Radiation and Quantum Physics (1973), Radio and Microwave Spectroscopy (1976); *Recreations* sailing, DIY; *Clubs* Athenaeum; *Style—* Dr David J E Ingram; 22 Ethelbert Rd, Canterbury, Kent CT1 3NE (☎ 0227 65855); The Registry, The University, Canterbury, Kent CT2 7NZ (☎ 0227 764 000, fax 0227 451 684, telex 965449)

INGRAM, David Vernon; s of (Harold) Vernon Ingram, OBE, TD (Col RAMC, d 1980), of Ferndown, Dorset, and Bessie Mary, *née* Montauban; *b* 13 Nov 1939; *Educ* Rugby, St Johns Coll Cambridge, Middx Hosp Med Sch (MA, MB, BChir), Royal Coll of Surgns London; *m* 13 May 1967, Stella Mary, da of (Alan) Howard Cornes (d 1974), of Stockton Brook, Staffs; 1 s (Matthew b 1969), 2 da (Harriet b 1970, Catherine b 1972); *Career* sr resident offr Moorfields Eye Hosp London 1969-70, sr ophthalmic registrar St George's Hosp London 1970-73; conslt ophthalmic surgn: Sussex Eye Hosp Brighton 1973-, Cuckfield and Crawley Health Dist 1973-; pres Brighton and Sussex Medico Chirurgical Soc 1988; Liveryman Worshipful Soc of Apothecaries of London 1970, Freeman City of London 1971; FRCS 1969, FRSM 1971, FCOphth 1988; *Recreations* yacht cruising, photography, DIY; *Clubs* Cruising Assoc; *Style—* David Ingram, Esq; 4 Tongdean Rd, Hove, E Sussex BN3 6QB (☎ 0273 552 305); Sussex Eye Hosp, Eastern Rd, Brighton (☎ 0273 606 124)

INGRAM, Sir James Herbert Charles; 4 Bt (UK 1893), of Swineshead Abbey, Lincolnshire; s of (Herbert) Robin Ingram (d 1979, only s of Sir Herbert Ingram, 3 Bt, who d 1980), by his first w, Shiela, only da of late Charles Peczenik; *b* 6 May 1966; *Educ* Eton, Cardiff Univ; *Heir* half bro, Nicholas Ingram *qv*; *Recreations* golf, shooting, skiing, tennis; *Style—* Sir James Ingram, Bt; 8 Pitt St, London W8 4NX (☎ 01 937 8287)

INGRAM, Dame Kathleen Annie; *see*: Raven, Dame Kathleen Annie

INGRAM, Michael Warren; JP (1949), DL (Glos 1978), OBE (1986); 2 s of Sir Herbert Ingram, 2 Bt (d 1957); *b* 20 June 1917; *Educ* Winchester, Balliol Coll Oxford; *m* 1944, Auriol Blanche, da of Lt-Gen Sir Arthur Francis Smith, KCB, KBE, DSO, MC (d 1978, whose mother was Lady Blanche Keith Falconer, herself 2 da of 8 Earl of Kintore) and Hon Lady Smith (da of 1 Baron Somerleyton); 1 s, 3 da; *Career* dir Ashcroft Electronics Ltd; chm National Star Centre for Disabled Youth; *Recreations* tennis, golf, shooting, collecting English watercolours; *Clubs* Lansdowne; *Style—* Michael Ingram, Esq, OBE, JP, DL; The Manor House, South Cerney, Cirencester, Glos (☎ 0285 861902)

INGRAM, Nicholas David; s of (Herbert) Robin Ingram (d 1979, only s of Sir Herbert Ingram, 3 Bt, who d 1980), by his 2 w, Sallie Willoughby, da of Frank Hilary Minoprio; hp of half-bro, Sir James Ingram, 4 Bt; *b* 12 June 1975; *Style—* Nicholas Ingram Esq; Southridge House, nr Streatley, Berks RG8 9SJ

INGRAM, Paul; s of John Granville Ingram, (d 1971), of Manchester, and Sybil, *née* Johnson; *b* 20 Sept 1934; *Educ* Manchester Central HS, Univ of Nottingham (BSc); *m* 10 Aug 1957 (m dis 1988), Jennifer Gillian, da of Eric Morgan (d 1978), of Castletown, IOM; 1 s (David) Mark b 3 Aug 1960), 1 da (Susan Elizabeth b 2 July 1959); *Career* conservation offr and gp conservation offr Govt of the Fedn of Rhodesia and Nyasaland 1956-63, advsy offr Nat Agric Serv 1965-88; MAFF: memb long term policy planning unit 1969-72, chief agric offr 1986-87, dir farm and countryside serv and commercial dir 1987-88; head agric servs dept Barclays Bank plc 1988-; *Recreations* sailing; *Clubs* Farmers, Civil Service; *Style—* Paul Ingram, Esq; Barclays Bank plc, Juxon House, St Pauls Churchyard, London EC4M 8EH (☎ 01 248 9155)

INGRAM, William Eugene (Bill); s of Jack Lorrimer Ingram (d 1987), of Doncaster, and Marie Doreen, *née* Lejeune; *b* 8 July 1943; *Educ* GS; *m* 22 Aug 1969, Judith Alison, da of Edward Patterson Thompson (d 1983); 4 s (Stuart b 1971, Andrew b 1972, Duncan b 1974, Ross b 1977); *Career* chm Cenwick Electronics Ltd 1974; *Recreations* badminton, sailing, cruising, swimming, gardening; *Style—* William Ingram, Esq; Riverside House, South Brink, Wisbech, Cambs PE14 0RJ (☎ 0945 583427); Anglia Components, Burdett Rd, Wisbech, Cambs PE13 2PS, UK (☎ 0945 63281, fax 0945 588844, telex 32630), (car ☎ 0860 625943)

INGRAMS, Hon Caspar David; s and h of Baroness Darcy de Knayth; *b* 5 Jan 1962; *Style—* The Hon Caspar Ingrams

INGRAMS, Hon Catriona; da of Baroness Darcy de Knayth; *b* 1963; *Style—* The Hon Catriona Ingrams

INGRAMS, Leonard Victor; OBE (1980); s of Leonard St Clair Ingrams, OBE (d 1953), and Victoria Susan Beatrice, *née* Reid; *b* 1 Sept 1941; *Educ* Stonyhurst, Munich Univ, Corpus Christi Oxford (MA); *m* 19 Sept 1964, Rosalind Ann, da of Antony Ross Moore, CMG of Tonchbridge, Brill; 1 s (Rupert b 23 Aug 1967), 3 da (Lucy b 3 Dec 1965, Elizabeth b 9 Feb 1971, Catherine b 30 Nov 1976); *Career* Bros 1967, Eurofinance 1968-69, mangr and dir London Multinat Bank 1970-73, md Baring Bros 1975-81 (mangr 1973-74), chief advsr to the govr Saudi Arabian Monetary Agency 1981-84 (sr advsr 1975-79); dir: Robert Fleming Hldgs Ltd, Robert Fleming & Co Ltd, Robert Fleming Int Investmt Mgmnt; contribs to the Oxyrhynchus Papyri (various vols), Bond Portfolio Mgmnt (1989); *Recreations* music, gardening; *Clubs* Beefsteak; *Style—* Leonard Ingrams, Esq, OBE; 25 Copthall Ave, London EC2 (☎ 01 638 5858, fax 588 7219); Garsington Manor, Garsington, Oxford OX9 9DH

INGRAMS, Hon Miranda; da of Baroness Darcy de Knayth; *b* 1960; *Style—* The Hon Miranda Ingrams

INGRAMS, Richard Reid; s of Leonard St Clair Ingrams (s of Rev William Smith Ingrams, MA), and Victoria Susan Beatrice, da of Sir James Reid, 1 Bt, GCVO, KCB, MD, LLD, who was successively physician to Queen Victoria, to King Edward VII and to King George V; *see also* Darcy de Knayth, Baroness; *b* 19 August 1937; *Educ* Shrewsbury, Univ Coll Oxford; *m* 1962, Mary Joan Morgan; 1 s, 1 da (and 1 s decd); *Career* editor Private Eye 1963-86; *Style—* Richard Ingrams Esq; Forge House, Aldworth, Reading, Berks

INGREY-SENN, Ronald Charles; s of Charles Senn (d 1938), of Westcliff-on-Sea, Essex, and Florence May, *née* Henderson (d 1975); *b* 24 Dec 1920; *Educ* Fairfax High Sch Westcliff-on-Sea, Univ of Leeds (MB, ChB, DMJ, DPM); *m* 29 April 1944, (Louisa) Jean, da of Alexander Algar Ingrey; 1 s (Andrew b 1947), 1 da (Annette b 1951); *Career* RAF Med Branch 1940-46; gen med practice NHS 1957-69, Med Civil Serv 1969; Home Off: asst under sec 1981, Dir of Prison med Serv 1981-83 (dep dir 1976-81); conslt psychiatrist memb Parole Bd of England & Wales 1985-; cmmr Mental Health Act 1983-85, memb Rotary, co dir St John Ambulance Herts; CStJ; Freeman City of London, Liveryman Worshipful Soc of Apothecaries; FRCPsych, memb Medico-Legal Soc London 1969; *Recreations* water colour, calligraphy; *Style*— Dr Ronald Ingrey-Senn; 26 Battlefield Rd, St Albans, Herts (☎ 0727 60785)

INGROW, Baron (Life Peer UK 1982), of Keighley, in the Co of West Yorkshire; John Aked Taylor; OBE (1960), TD (1951), JP (Keighley, Yorks, 1949), DL (W Yorks, formerly West Riding, 1971); s of Percy Taylor, of Knowle Spring House, Keighley, and Gladys, *née* Broster (who m 2, Sir Donald Horsfall, 2 Bt); *b* 15 August 1917; *Educ* Shrewsbury; *m* 1949, Barbara Mary, da of Percy Wright Stirk; 2 da; *Career* served WW II Duke of Wellington's Regt and Royal Signals (Norway, Middle East, Sicily, NW Europe, Far East), Maj; memb Keighley Town Cncl 1946-67, mayor Keighley 1956-57; chm: Educn Ctee 1949-61, Finance Ctee 1961-67, Keighley Cons Assoc 1952-56 and 1957-67; gen cmmr Income Tax 1965; chm: Yorks Area Nat Union Cons and Unionist Assocs 1966-71, exec ctee Nat Union Cons and Unionist Assocs 1971-76; Ld Lieut W Yorks 1985- (Vice Ld Lieut 1976-85); chm Yorks W Cons European Constituency Cncl 1978-84, chm and md Timothy Taylor & Co Ltd; pres Nat Union of Cons and Unionist Assocs 1982-83; hon tres Magistrates' Assoc 1976-86 (memb Cncl 1957-86); kt 1972; *Style*— The Rt Hon Lord Ingrow, OBE, TD; Fieldhead, Keighley, W Yorks (☎ 0535 603895)

INKIN, Geoffrey David; OBE (1974, MBE 1971), DL (Gwent 1983); s of Noel David Inkin (d 1983), of Cardiff, and Evelyn Margaret Inkin; *b* 2 Oct 1934; *Educ* Dean Close Sch, RMA Sandhurst, RAC Cirencester; *m* 1961, Susan Elizabeth, da of Lt Col Laurence Stewart Sheldon (d 1988), of East Coker; 3 s (Piers b 1965, Charles b 1967, Edmund b 1971); *Career* cmmnd Royal Welch Fusiliers 1955-74, Malaya 1956-57, Cyprus 1958-59 (despatches), cmd 1 Bn 1972-74; parly candidate (C) Ebbw Vale 1977-79, memb Gwent CC 1977-83, chm Cwmbran Devpt Corpn 1983-87 (memb bd Welsh Devpt Agency 1984-87; High Sheriff of Gwent 1987, chm Land Authority for Wales 1986-, and Cardiff Bay Devpt Corpn 1987-; cncl memb UWIST 1987-88, memb ct Univ Coll of Wales of Cardiff 1988-; *Clubs* Brooks's, Cardiff and County, Ebbw Vale Cons; *Style*— Geoffrey Inkin, Esq, OBE, DL; Court St Lawrence, Llangovan, Monmouth NP5 4BT (☎ 0291 690 279)

INMAN, Edward Oliver; s of John Inman, of Cumnor, Oxford, and Peggy Florence, *née* Beard; *b* 12 August 1948; *Educ* King's Coll Sch Wimbledon, Gonville and Caius Coll Cambridge (BA), Sch of Slavonic and E European Studies London (MA); *m* 1, 3 April 1971 (m dis 1982), Elizabeth Heather Winifred, da of Ian Douglas Balmaclellan, of Scotland; 1 s (James 29 Dec 1974), 1 da (Louise b 10 Nov 1977); m 2, 27 June 1984, Sherida Lesley, da of Jack Brooks Sturton, of Biddenham, Bedford; 1 da (Isabel b 20 Aug 1986), 2 step da (Rachel b 23 Aug 1978, Harriet b 2 April 1980); *Career* Imp War Museum: joined as res asst dept of documents 1972, asst keeper and principal asst to dep dir 1974, keeper dept of exhibits (Duxford) 1976, keeper of Duxford Airfield 1978 (dir 1988); *Style*— Edward Inman, Esq; Willow Way Cottages, 11 North End, Meldreth, Royston, Herts SG8 6NR (☎ 0763 61533); Imperial War Museum, Duxford Airfield, Cambridge CB2 4QR (☎ 0223 833963, fax 0223 837267)

INMAN, (John) Michael; JP; s of Rev John Phillips Inman, of Coniston Cumbria, and Agnes, *née* Tyson; *b* 20 May 1941; *Educ* Durham Sch, Univ of Reading (Dip Rural Educn), Open Univ (BA); *m* Kathleen Barbara, da of James Arthur Davenport, of Cheddleton, Staffs; 1 da (Vanessa b 1984); *Career* teacher Westwood HS Leek Staffs; pres Nat Assoc of Schoolmasters Union of Woman Teachers 1986-87; landowner; *Recreations* farming; *Style*— Michael Inman, Esq, JP; c/o Westwood HS, Leek, Staffs (☎ 0538 385737)

INMAN, Col Roger; OBE (1945), MBE (1944, TD 1945, JP (1954); s of Samuel Marsden Inman (d 1951), and Ethel Violet Inman (d 1975); *b* 18 April 1915; *Educ* King Edward VII Sch Sheffield; *m* 1939, Christine Lucas, da of Lt-Col Joseph Rodgers (d 1970); 2 s (Christopher, Paul); *Career* served WW II with RA & Gen Staff Western Desert, ME, Italy, Hon Col Sheffield Artillery Volunteers 1964-70; jt md Harrison Fisher Gp 1950-, gen cmmnr of Income Tax 1969, vice chm Yorks & Humberside TAVRA 1973-80; chm: Sheffield City Bench 1974-80, Doncaster Div of Sheffield 1975-; vice ld-lt of S Yorks 1981-; *Clubs* Army & Navy, Sheffield, Hallamshire Golf; *Style*— Col Roger Inman, OBE, TD, JP; Flat 1, 15 Whitworth Rd, Sheffield S10 3HD; Eye Witness Works, Milton St, Sheffield S3 7WJ (☎ 0742 26521)

INMAN, Stephen Eric; s of John Eric Inman (d 1978), and Vera Alice, *née* Willis (d 1985); *b* 14 Oct 1935; *Educ* All Saints Sch Bloxham, St Thomas's Hosp Med Sch London Univ (MB, BS); *m* 1 July 1961, Ione Elizabeth Jill, da of Maurice Scott Murdoch (d 1963); 2 s (Paul b 1966, Dominic b 1973), 1 da (Nicola b 1962); *Career* resident med offr: Queen Charlotte's Hosp 1965-66, Chelsea Hosp for Women 1966-67; lectr St Thomas's Hosp 1968-70; sr registrar St Thomas's Hosp 1970-74; conslt obstetrician and gynaecologist W Surrey/NE Hants Health Dist 1974; chm Divn of Obstetrics, Gynaecology and Paediatrics at Frimley Park Hosp; memb Hosp Conslts & Specialists Assoc 1974; FRCOG 1981; *Recreations* sailing, swimming, squash, tennis; *Clubs* Royal Aldershot Officers'; *Style*— Stephen E Inman, Esq; Folly Hill House, Farnham, Surrey (☎ 0252 713389)

INMAN, Prof William Howard Wallace; s of Wallace Mills Inman (d 1971), and Maude Mary, *née* Andrews (d 1973); *b* 1 August 1929; *Educ* Ampleforth, Caius Coll Cambridge (MA); *m* 21 July 1962, June Evelyn, da of Stewart Arthur Maggs (d 1970), of Doncaster; 3 da (Stella b 1955 (adopted), Rosemary b 1963, Charlotte b 1966); *Career* prof of Pharmacoepidemiology of Southampton 1985-; med advsr ICI Ltd Pharmaceuticals Div 1959-64, princ med offr DHSS Ctee on Safety of Medicines 1964-80, dir Drug Safety Res Unit 1980-; author of Monitoring for Drug Safety (1980), editor of Prescription-Event Monitoring News, advsr to drug regulatory agencies & pharmaceutical industry worldwide; FRCP, FFCM; *Recreations* fishing, gardening; *Style*— Prof William Inman; Southcroft House, Botley, Southampton (☎ 0703 600263); Drug Safety Research Unit, Bursledon, Southampton

INNERDALE, John Hamilton; JP; s of Hamilton Inverdale (d 1982), of Eastbourne, E Sussex, and Margaret, *née* Cameron (d 1981); *b* 11 Feb 1933; *Educ* Manchester Univ, Cheadle Hulme Sch (BA, DipArch); *m* 22 Aug 1959, Diana Grace, da of Sidney Herbert Mould (d 1982), of E Dean, E Sussex; 3 s (Jonathan Hamilton, James Cameron, Michael John); *Career* CA; dir: Careform Ltd, Triumph Build Ltd; ARIBA 1960, FRIBA 1967; *Recreations* tennis, mountaineering, beekeeping, painting, sailing; *Style*— John Innerdale, Esq, JP; 15 Denton Rd, Eastbourne, E Sussex (☎ 0323 326 00); Wordsworth House, Sockbridge, Cumbria (☎ 0768 68322); Innerdale Hudson & Butland, Chartered Architects, 25 Lushington Rd, Eastbourne (☎ 0323 410421, fax 0323 410621)

INNES, Andrew Ross; s of Sir Andrew Lockhurst Innes, KBE, CB, QC (d 1960), and Irene Campbell, *née* Ross (d 1970); *b* 3 Mar 1944; *Educ* Eaton House PS, Pierrepont House Sch Farnham; *m* 22 June 1968, Sheila Maire, da of Drian Grazier Phips McKenzie, of Worcester; 1 s (Jamies Lockhart b 25 April 1973), 1 da (Penny Alexandra b 24 May 1971); *Career* Stockbroker 1963-75; bldg contractor 1975-; memb local village Hall ctee; *Recreations* gardening, tv; *Style*— Andrew Innes, Esq; Easter Calzeat House, Broughton, Biggar ML12 6HQ (☎ 08994 359)

INNES, Christian, Lady; (Elizabeth) Christian; eldest da of Lt-Col Charles Henry Watson, DSO, IMS (d 1954), of Cheltenham, Glos; *Educ* Cheltenham Ladies Coll, Royal Sch Bath; *m* 27 May 1961, as his 2 w, Lt-Col Sir (Ronald Gordon) Berowald Innes of Balvenie, 16 Bt (d 1988); *Career* WWII WRNS 1942-46, served SEAC (under Lord Louis Mountbatten; sec to the late Clifford Ellis (fndr and princ Bath Acad of Art) 1946-53, sec to Prof of Educn Makerere Coll Uganda 1958-61; sole propr (former ptnr) Berowald Innes, Handweaver and Heraldic Embroiderer 1988-; *Style*— Christian, Lady Innes; The Loom House, Aultgowrie, Muir of Ord, Ross-shire IV6 7XA

INNES, David Charles Kenneth Gordon; s and h of Sir Charles Innes of Coxton, 11 Bt; *b* 17 April 1940; *Educ* Haileybury, London Univ; *m* 1969, Marjorie Alison, da of Ernest W Parker; 1 s, 1 da; *Career* ACGI; *Style*— David Innes Esq; 28 Wadham Close, Shepperton, Middx

INNES, Frank (Francis) Lumsden Farquharson; s of Robert Alexander Innes (d 1932), and Barbara Mennie Gilchrist (d 1962); *b* 26 July 1919; *Educ* Aberdeen GS, Aberdeen Univ (MB, ChB, FRCS); *m* 1, 1944, Grace Isobel Grant; 2 s (Graham Gilchrist b 1945, Richard Francis b 1953); m 2, 1969, Wanda Mary, da of Alexander Dow (d 1953); 1 s (James Robert b 1972), 1 da (Catherine Mary b 1971); *Career* conslt Plastic Surgeon; MO RAF 1942-47, Sqdn-Ldr 1942-47; sr registrar Royal Hosp for Sick Children 1954-59, Nuffield dept of Plastic Surgery Oxford 1954-59, E Anglian Regnl Health Authy 1959-84, ret; *Recreations* golf; *Style*— Frank L F Innes, Esq; 2B Camberley Rd, Norwich, Norfolk NR4 6SJ (☎ Norwich 0603 54637)

INNES, Gordon; s of John William Innes (d 1952), of Sunderland, and Ethel Simmonds Innes (d 1955); *b* 22 Mar 1927; *Educ* Bede GS Sunderland, Sunderland Poly, Sheffield Univ, Manchester Business Sch; *m* Gwendoline, da of Bertram Harrold Williams (d 1986), of Maidenhead; *Career* engrg mangr Vickers Ltd, engrg dir Churchill Gears Machines Ltd 1957-68, technical dir Jones Cranes Ltd 1968-70, sr conslt Gordon Innes Assocs 1970-87; past pres Letchworth Howard Rotary Club; *Recreations* invention, cycling; *Style*— Gordon Innes, Esq; Garth Lodge, 29 Pasture Rd, Letchworth, Herts SG6 3LR

INNES, (Alexander) Guy Berowald; s and h of Sir Peter Innes of Balvenie, 17 Bt, *qv*; *b* 4 May 1960; *Educ* Queen Mary Coll Basingstoke; *m* 1986, Sara-Jane, da of Dennis Busher, of Cowbridge, S Glamorgan; *Career* financial conslt; *Style*— Guy Innes, Esq; 97 Wilton Road, Upper Shirley, Southampton SO1 5JH

INNES, Lt-Col James; s of Lt-Col James Archibald Innes, DSO (d 1948), and Lady Barbara, *née* Lowther (d 1979); *b* 7 June 1915; *Educ* Eton; *m* 14 Jan 1941, Hon (Veronica Wenefryde) Nefertari, da of Capt the Hon Richard Bethell (d 1929); 2 s (James R, Peter D), 1 da (Elizabeth M (Mrs Nicholl); *Career* 2 Lt Coldstream Gds 1935, served France and Germany 1935-45 (despatches twice), Capt 1945 (temp Lt-Col), ret with hon Lt-Col 1949; chm of tstees John Innes Fndn 1961-, vice chm John Innes Inst 1961-, dir and chm Univ Life Assur Soc, memb of ct VEA 1969-, vice pres Br Olympic Assoc 1980- (tres 1964-80); JP: Berks 1955-73, Inner London 1973-74; Liveryman Clothworkers Co 1936 (memb ct 1971, Master (excused serv) 1983-84); memb Royal Inst GB, memb London Stock Exchange 1955-80; *Recreations* gardening, game shooting; *Clubs* Turf, All England Lawn Tennis and Croquet; *Style*— Lt-Col James Innes; 25 Beaufort Close, London SW15 3TL (☎ 01 785 6614)

INNES, Lady Lucy Buchan; *née* Sinclair; da of late 18 Earl of Caithness; *b* 1902; *m* 1928, Sir Thomas Innes of Learney, GCVO, LLD (d 1971); 2 s, 1 da; *Style*— Lady Lucy Innes; The Laigh Riggs, Torphins, Aberdeenshire

INNES, Peter David; s of Lt-Col James Innes of 25 Beaufort Close, Putney, and Hon Veronica Winefryde Nefertari, *née* Bethell; *b* 25 August 1952; *Educ* Eton; *m* 9 Aug 1980, Carolyn Ann Darley, da of Julian Blackwell of Ossefield, Appleton, Oxford; 1 s (James b 1982) 2 da (Clemmie b 1984, Laura b 1987); *Career* Coldstream Gds 1972-78; Capt 1976; Steward Ayr and Musselburgh; *Recreations* hunting, racing, shooting, fishing, gardening,; *Clubs* Cavalry & Guards; *Style*— Peter Innes, Esq; Boon House, Lauder, Berwickshire TD2 6SB

INNES, Sheila Miriam; da of Dr James McGregor Innes, of Purton Court, Farnham Royal, Bucks, and Nora Elizabeth Amelia, *née* Wacks; *b* 25 Jan 1931; *Educ* Talbot Heath Sch Bournemouth, Lady Margaret Hall Oxford (MA); *Career* prodr BBC Radio World Serv 1955-61; BBC TV: prodr family programmes 1961-65, exec prodr Further Educn TV 1973-77, head BBC Continuing Educn TV 1977-84, controller BBC Educnl Broadcasting 1984-87; chief exec The Open College 1987-; memb: gen bd Alcoholics Anonymous 1980-83, bd of govrs Centre for Info on Language Teaching and Res 1981-84, Cncl for Educnl Technol 1984-86, cncl Open Univ 1984-87, City & Guilds of London Inst; chm: Br Gas Trg Awards 1989-, BTEC Product Devpt Ctee 1989-; pres (educn section) Br Assoc for the Advancement of Science 1989-; memb RTS 1984, CBIM 1987, FRSA 1987, FITD 1987; *Books* numerous articles in educn jls; *Recreations* music (classical & jazz), swimming, photography, travel, languages, country pursuits; *Clubs* Reform; *Style*— Miss Sheila Innes; The Knowle, Seer Green Lane, Jordans, Bucks HP9 2ST (☎ 02407 4575); The Open College, 101 Wigmore St, London W1H 9AA (☎ 01 935 8088, fax 01 935 0415, telex 24483 OCOLGE G)

INNES, Simon Alexander; s of Brian Stanley Innes, of London, and Felicity, *née* McNair-Wilson; *b* 10 Dec 1958; *Educ* St Christopher Sch, Univ of Warwick (LLB); *m* 14 July 1984, Emma Jane, da of Malcolm McIndoe; 1 s (Jack b 1988), 1 da (Harriet b 1987); *Career* RA Woolwich 1977-78, RMA Sandhurst Queen's Royal Irish Hussars 1978-79; barr Middle Temple, ed Readers Digest 1987-88, co dir (Consumer Legal Servs) 1988-; chm Holland Park Harriers; memb: Hon Soc Middle Temple, Royal United Serv Inst, Inst of Strategic Studies; *Books* The Middle East Wars 1949-80 (1984); *Recreations* racing, skiing, hunting; *Style*— Simon Innes, Esq; 2 Royal Crescent Mews, Kensington, London W11 (☎ 01 376 1050); Consumer Legal Serv, London House, Kensington, London W8 4PF

INNES, Hon Mrs (Veronica Wenefryde Nefertari); *née* Bethell; da of Hon Richard Bethell (d 1929), and Evelyn Lucia Milicent, *née* Hutton (d 1956); sis of 4 and 5 Barons Westbury; *b* 15 July 1917; *m* 1941, Lt-Col James Innes, Coldstream Gds, s of Lt-Col James Innes, DSO (d 1948), by Lady Barbara Lowther, da of 6 Earl of Lonsdale, OBE, JP, DL; 2 s, 1 da; *Style*— The Hon Mrs Innes; 25 Beaufort Close,

London SW15 3TL (☎ 01 785 6614)

INNES, Lt Col William Alexander Disney; JP (Banffshire 1964), DL (Banffshire 1959); Capt James William Guy Innes, CBE, RN, DL (d 1939), and Anna Orrok Stronach Sheila Foster Forbes (d 1949); *b* 19 April 1910; *Educ* Marlborough; *m* 1939, Mary Alison, da of Francis Burnett-Stuart (d 1949); 2 s (Michael, Jonathan); *Career* 2 Lt Gordon Highlanders 1930, served in 1939-45 war SE Asia (POW Malaya & Siam 1942-45), Temp Maj 1941, Maj 1946, Temp Lt Col 1951, ret 1952; vice Lord Lieut Banffshire 1971-87; *Recreations* gardening; *Style*— Lt Col William Innes, JP, DL; Heath Cottage Aberlour, Banffshire AB3 9ED (☎ 034 05 266)

INNES OF BALVENIE, Sir Peter Alexander Berowald; 17 Bt (NS 1628), of Balvenie, Banffshire; s of Lt-Col Sir Berowald Innes of Balvenie, 16 Bt (d 1988), and his 1 w Elizabeth Haughton, *née* Fayle (d 1958); *b* 6 Jan 1937; *Educ* Prince of Wales Sch Nairobi, Bristol Univ (BSc); *m* 18 July 1959, Julia Mary, yr da of late Alfred Stoyell Levesley, of Burlington Road, Bristol; 2 s (Alexander Guy Berowald b 1960, Alastair John Peter b 1965), 1 da (Fiona Julie b 1963); *Heir* s, Alexander Guy Berowald Innes, *qv*; *Career* conslt civil engr; ptnr Scott Wilson Kirkpatrick & Ptnrs; FICE; *Recreations* travel, pointers; The Wheel House, Nations Hill, Kings Worthy, Winchester SO23 7QY

INNES OF COXTON, Sir Charles Kenneth Gordon; 11 Bt (NS 1686), of Coxton, Co Moray; placed on Official Roll of Baronets 1973; s of Maj (Sir) Charles Gordon Deverell Innes, *de jure* 10 Bt (d 1953); *b* 28 Jan 1910; *Educ* Haileybury; *m* 1936, Margaret Colquhoun Lockhart, da of Frederick Charles Lockhart Robertson, and gda of late Sir James Colquhoun of Luss, 5 Bt; 1 s, 1 da; *Heir* s, David Charles Kenneth Gordon Innes, *qv*; *Career* WWII, RA, Capt Ayrshire Yeomanry; *Style*— Sir Charles Innes of Coxton, Bt; October Cottage, Haslemere, Surrey GU27 2LF

INNES OF EDINGIGHT, Malcolm Rognvald; CVO (1981), WS (1964); Baron of Yeochrie (territorial); s of late Sir Thomas Innes of Learney, GCVO, and Lady Lucy Buchan, da of 18 Earl of Caithness; *b* 25 May 1938; *Educ* The Edinburgh Acad, Edinburgh Univ (MA, LLB); *m* 1963, Joan, da of Thomas D Hay, of Edinburgh; 3 s; *Career* Lord Lyon King of Arms 1981- (Falkland Pursuivant Extraordinary 1957, Carrick Pursuivant 1958-71, Marchmont Herald 1971-81); sec to Order of Thistle 1981-; pres Heraldry Soc Scotland; KStJ 1982; FSA (Scot); Grand Offr Merit SMO Malta; memb Royal Co of Archers (Queen's Body Guard for Scotland); *Clubs* Puffin's, New (Edinburgh); *Style*— Malcolm Innes of Edingight, CVO, Lord Lyon King of Arms; 35 Inverleith Row, Edinburgh EH3 5QH (☎ 031 552 4924); Edingight House, Banffshire (☎ 046 686 270)

INNES-KER, Lord Robert (Robin) Anthony; 2 s of 9 Duke of Roxburghe (d 1974); *b* 28 May 1959; *Educ* Gordonstoun; *Career* short service cmmn Royal Horse Gds/ Dragoons (Blues & Royals): 2 Lt 1979-81, Lt 1981-, cmd Blues and Royals detachment in Falkland Islands 1982 (despatches); *Recreations* fishing, hunting, shooting and all ball games; *Clubs* Turf; *Style*— Lord Robert Innes-Ker; 46 Elm Park Gardens, London SW10

INNES-WILKIN, David; s of Charles Wilkin (d 1978), and Louisa Jane, *née* Innes; *b* 1 May 1946; *Educ* Lowestoft GS, Liverpool Univ Sch of Architecture (BArch 1969, Master of Civil Design 1970); *m* 1, 10 April 1968, Beryl; 2 s (Dylan b 1972, Matthew b 1974), 1 da (Thomasine b 1971); m 2, 25 April 1987, Sarah, da of Rev Prof Peter Runham Ackroyd, *qv*; *Career* chartered architect, princ Innes-Wilkins Assocs, chm of SW Housing Assoc 1986-87; pioneered tenant participation in new housing estate designed 1979-; memb: RIBA Regnl Ctee, Community Architecture Gp 1983; visiting lectr: Liverpool, Cardiff, Manchester, Bristol, Int Congress of Architects; design awards: Royal Town Planning Inst Commendation 1983, Housing Centre Tst Jubilee Award for Good Design in Housing 1983, Times/RIBA Community Enterprise Awards 1986/87 (three), Cuba — Universal Home Ownership (Roof 1987), Shelter and Cities (UK Individual Paper, selected for the Int Congress of Architects 1987), Community Schools (Paper Pub, by Educn Research Unit 1972); *Publications* A Common Language (The Architects Jl 1984), Among The Grass-Roots (RIBA Jl 1983), Cuba Universal Home Ownership (Roof 1987), Shelter and Cities (UK Individual Paper, selected for the Int Congress of Architects 1987), Community Schools (Paper Pub, by Educn Research Unit 1972); *Recreations* offshore sailing, music, writing, walking; *Clubs* The Clifton (Bristol); *Style*— David Innes-Wilkin, Esq; Regent Chambers, 24 Regent St, Clifton, Bristol BS1 4HB

INNISS, Sir Clifford de Lisle; s of Archibald de Lisle Inniss (d 1957), and Lelia Emmaline, *née* Springer (d 1963); *b* 26 Oct 1910; *Educ* Harrison Coll Barbados, Queen's Coll Oxford (BA, BCL); *Career* barr Middle Temple 1935, KC Tanganyika 1950, QC Trinidad and Tobago 1953; legal draftsman: Barbados 1938, Tanganyika 1947; slr-gen Tanganyika 1949, attorney-gen Trinidad and Tobago 1953, chief justice Br Honduras (later Belize) 1957-72, judge of the Cts of Appeal of Bermuda, the Bahamas and the Turks and Caicos Islands 1974-75; judge of the ct of Appeal of Belize 1974-81; chm of integrity cmmn of Nat Assembly of Belize 1981-87; memb of Belize Advsy Cncl 1985; kt 1961; *Recreations* cricket, tennis, gardening; *Clubs* Barbados Yacht, Pickwick CC Barbados; *Style*— Sir Clifford Inniss; 11/13 Oriole Ave, Belmopan, Belize

INNOCENT, Harold Sidney; s of Harry William Harrison (d 1932), and late Jennie Henry; *b* 18 April 1933; *Educ* Broad St Secondary Modern Coventry, Churchfield HS Coventry; *Career* actor; Nat Serv RAF; appeared with NT, RSC, Old Vic Company; West End: The School for Scandal, The Importance of Being Earnest, Pericles, Dear Antoine, The Magistrate, Donkey's Years; The Grace of Mary Travers at Royal Court, Rocket to the Moon and Ascent of Mount Fiji at Hampstead Theatre Club; Sir Despard in Ruddigore for New Sadler's Wells Opera Co; Films incl: Casanova, The Tall Guy, Buster, Henry V, Little Dorritt, The Big Steal, The Yellow Dog, Without a Clue; TV incl: An Englishman Abroad, Porterhouse Blue, Paradise Postponed, Tale of Two Cities; American TV incl: Have Gun - Will Travel, Gun Smoke, Ben Casey, Alfred Hitchcock Presents, The New Breed, Sea Hunt; *Recreations* reading, travel, music (particulary opera), letter writing; *Style*— Harold Innocent, Esq; 367 King's Rd, London SW6 4RJ; c/o Susan Angel, Susan Angel Associates Ltd, 12 D'Arblay St, London W1V 3FP (☎ 01 439 3086)

INSALL, Donald W; OBE (1981); s of William R Insall (d 1966), of Bristol, and Phyllis Irene, *née* Hill (d 1987); *b* 7 Feb 1926; *Educ* Bristol GS, Bristol Univ (RWA), RASA; *m* 13 June 1964, Libby, da of Malcolm H Moss, of Nanpantan, Loughborough, Leics; 2 s (Robert 1965, Christopher 1968), 1 da (Hilary 1972); *Career* WWII regnl HQ Staff Coldstream Gds; currently dir (princ 1958) Donald W Insall & Assocs Ltd (specialists in architectural conservation, conservation conslts City of Chester 1970-87); awards incl: The Queen's Silver Jubilee Medal 1977, Europa Nostra Medal, Euro Architectural Heritage Awards; visiting lectr RCA 1964-69, adjunct prof Univ of Syracuse 1971-81, visiting prof Coll of Europe, Catholic Univ of Leuves Belgium 1980-; conslt architect Worshipful Co of Goldsmiths; Acade,osoam (and memb selection/hanging ctee) Royal West of England Acad, Fell Soc of Antiquaries of London, memb UK cncl Int Cncl of Monuments and Sites, memb cncl RSA 1976-78 (FRSA 1948); memb: Econ Res Cncl, RA (Reynolds Club), Historic Bldgs Cncl for England 1971-83, Ancient Monuments Bd for England 1980-83, cmmr The Historic Bldgs and Monuments Cmmn for England 1984-; memb advsy ctee Getty Grants Programme 1988-; life memb: SPAB (and cncl memb), Georgian Gp, Victorian Soc, Royal Photographic Soc, Nat Tst, Kew Soc; hon memb Bath Preservation Tst, hon sec The Conf on Trg in Architectural Conservation; FRIBA 1968, FRTPI 1973, RWA 1985; *Books* The Case of Old Buildings Today (1973), Chester: A Study in Conservation (1968), Conservation in Action (1982), Historic Buildings: Action to Maintain the Expertise for their Care & Repair (1974), contrib Encyclopaedia Britannica film: Buildings - Who Cares? (ITV); *Recreations* visiting, photographing, enjoying places, appreciating craftsmanship; *Clubs* Athenaeum; *Style*— Donald Insall, Esq, OBE; 73 Kew Green, Richmond, Surrey; Donald W Insall & Associates Ltd, 19 West Eaton Place, London SW1 8LT (☎ 01 245 9888, fax 01 235 4370)

INSCH, Dr Gordon McConochie; s of James Gordon Insch (d 1977), and Alice Helen Goulding McConochie (d 1963); *b* 18 June 1927; *Educ* Morrison's Acad Crieff, St Andrew's Univ, Glasgow Univ (BSc, PhD); *m* 1954, Audrey Keith, da of George Keith Drew (d 1957); 1 s (Keith), 1 da (Lindsay); *Career* dir: Br Nuclear Design & Construction Ltd 1969-75, Atomic Power Constructions Ltd 1971-; mktg mangr Nat Nuclear Corpn Ltd 1987-; CEng, FIMechE, FInstP; *Recreations* golf; *Clubs* Centro Español de Londres; *Style*— Dr Gordon Insch; National Nuclear Corpn Ltd, Risley, Warrington, Cheshire WA3 6BZ (☎ 0925 51291 telex 627727); Woodlands 50 Leigh Rd, Prestbury, Macclesfield, Cheshire SK10 4HX (☎ 0625 829505)

INSKIP, Hon Mrs (Clare Elizabeth Anne); *née* Buxton; da of 2 Baron Noel-Buxton (d 1980); *b* 1954; *m* 1977, Owen Hampden Inskip; *Style*— Hon Mrs Owen Inskip

INSKIP, Henry Thurston; JP; s of Geoffrey May Inskip, JP (d 1959), and Lily Ethel, *née* Thurston (d 1979); *b* 2 April 1934; *Educ* Bedford Sch; *m* 9 May 1959, Margaret Vera, da of William James Topping, of Saffron Walden, Essex; 1 s (Charles b 1962), 2 da (Elizabeth b 1963, Amanda b 1963); *Career* chartered surveyor; sr ptnr E H C Inskip & Son architects and surveyors (fnded by gf in 1900); FRICS; *Recreations* history, photography, genealogy; *Style*— Henry Inskip, Esq, JP; 8 Rothsay Gardens, Bedford MK40 3QB (☎ 0234 266784); E H C Inskip and Son, 47 Goldington Rd, Bedford MK40 3LG (☎ 0234 261266)

INSKIP, His Hon Judge John Hampden Inskip; QC (1966); s of Sir John Hampden Inskip, KBE, sometime Lord Mayor of Bristol (yr bro of 1 Viscount Caldecote), by his w Hon Janet, *née* Maclay, 2 da of 1 Baron Maclay; *b* 1 Feb 1924; *Educ* Clifton, King's Coll Cambridge; *m* 1947, Ann Howell, yr da of late Lt-Col Owen Stanley Davies, DSO, MC, TD, RE, by his w, subsequently Lady Gueterbock; 1 s (Owen b 1953), 1 da (Diana b 1950); *Career* barr Inner Temple 1949, dep chm Hants QS 1967-71, rec 1970-82, memb Criminal Law Revision Ctee 1973-82, pres Transport Tbnl 1982-, Circuit judge (Western) 1982-; *Style*— His Hon Judge Inskip, QC; Clerks, Bramshott, Liphook, Hants

INSKIP, Hon Piers James Hampden; s and h of 2 Viscount Caldecote; *b* 20 May 1947; *Educ* Eton, Magdalene Coll, Cambridge; *m* 1, 1970, (m dis 1981), Susan Bridget, da of late W P Mellen, of Hill Farm, Gt Sampford, Essex; m 2, 1984, Kristine Elizabeth, da of Harvey Holbrooke-Jackson, of 12 Abbots Close, Ramsey, Cambs; 1 s (Thomas James b 22 March 1985); *Career* Investmt Research, Chase Manhattan Equities; *Recreations* golf, tennis; *Style*— The Hon Piers Inskip

INSOLE, Douglas John; CBE (1979); s of John Herbert Insole (d 1970), and Margaret Rose Insole, *née* Moore; *b* 18 April 1926; *Educ* Sir George Monoux GS, St Catharine's Coll Cambridge (MA); *m* 1948, Barbara Hazel (decd); 3 da (Susan b 1950 (decd), Anne b 1953, Gwenda b 1958); *Career* capt: Cambridge Univ CC 1949, Essex CCC 1950-60, England (9 appearances), vice capt S Africa tour 1956; chm England selectors 1964-68, mangr England tour to Australia 1978-79 and 1982-83, chm Essex CCC, TCCB, tstee MCC; memb FA cncl; JP Chingford Bench 1962-74; Town & City Properties 1970-75, Fosroc Int 1975-85, Trollope & Colls Hldgs 1975-; *Recreations* cricket, soccer, jazz; *Clubs* MCC, Essex CCC, East India & Sports; *Style*— Douglas Insole, Esq, CBE; 8 Hadleigh Ct, Crescent Rd, Chingford, London E4 6AX (☎ 01 529 6546); 10 East Rd, London N1 6AJ (☎ 01 490 1939)

INSTANCE, David John; s of Horace Arthur Instance, and Ellen Rosina, *née* Perkins; *b* 15 Dec 1938; *Educ* Woolwich Poly (HNC Engineering); LSPGA (Dip Printing Mgmnt); *m* 19 Oct 1963, Lydia Fiamma, da of Carlo Lago (d 1984); 2 s (Simon David, Andrew Edward); *Career* Nat Serv Lt RE, served Malaya; chm and md Instance Gp of Cos; holder of many patents covering engrg/printing application; dir of num subsidiary cos incl: Ditchling Press Ltd, Inprint Systems Italy, Inprint Systems France, Inprint Systems USA, Cybertest USA; *Recreations* reading, opera, skiing, walking; *Style*— David Instance, Esq; Guinea Hall, Sellindge, nr Ashford-Kent TN25 6EG (☎ 030 381 3115); David J Instance Ltd, T/A Inprint Systems, Maidstone Road, Paddock Wood, Tonbridge, Kent TN12 6DF

INSTONE, Ralph Bernard Samuel; s of Capt Alfred Instone, JP (d 1957), and Phyllis Hilda, *née* Goldberg (d 1971); *b* 27 July 1918; *Educ* Westminster, Christ Church Oxford (classical scholar); *m* 11 March 1941 (m dis 1973), Sybil Esther, da of Jack Palca (d 1920); 3 s (Daniel b 1947, Stephen b 1954, Simon b 1957), 1 da (Sara b 1946, d 1969); *Career* Army 1939-46, Inf 1939-41, GCHQ 1941-44, ret Capt; educn offr Notts & Derby 1945-46; called to bar Inner Temple 1945, in practice Lincoln's Inn 1946-, numerous articles on co law in legal & accountancy jls, *Recreations* lawn tennis, bridge; *Clubs* Roehampton; *Style*— Ralph B S Instone, Esq; 18 Fairacres, Roehampton Lane, London SW15 5LX; 7 New Sq, Lincoln's Inn, London WC2A 3QS

INVERARITY, James Alexander (Sandy); s of William Inverarity (d 1978), and Alexina, *née* Davidson (d 1978); *b* 17 Sept 1935; *Educ* Loretto; *m* 8 March 1960, Jean Stewart, da of James Rae Gellatly (d 1979); 1 s (Graeme b 1964), 2 da (Catherine b 1960, Alison b 1962); *Career* farmer, CA and co dir; pres NFU of Scotland 1970-71; memb: Eggs Authy 1971-74, governing body E of Scotland Coll of Agric 1974-, Farm Animal Welfare Cncl 1978-88, Panel of Agric Arbiters 1983-, governing body Scottish Crop Res Inst 1984-, Dairy Produce Quota Tbnl for Scotland 1984-85; dir: Scottish

Agric Securities Corpn plc 1983- (chm 1987-), Utd Oilseeds Prodrs Ltd 1985- (chm 1987-); *Recreations* shooting, curling; *Clubs* Farmers, Royal Scottish Automobile; *Style*— Sandy Inverarity, Esq; Cransley Liff, by Dundee (☎ 0382 580327)

INVERFORTH, 4 Baron (UK 1919); Andrew Peter Weir; only s of 3 Baron Inverforth (d 1982), and Jill Elizabeth Inverforth, *née* Thornycroft, *qv*; *b* 16 Nov 1966; *Educ* Marlborough; *Heir* unc, Hon John Vincent Weir; *Style*— The Rt Hon the Lord Inverforth; 27 Hyde Park St, London W2 2JS (☎ 01 262 5721);

INVERFORTH, Iris, Baroness; Iris Beryl; da of late Charles Vincent, 4 Bn The Buffs; *m* 26 June 1929, 2 Baron Inverforth (d 1975); 2 s (late 3 Baron, Hon (John) Vincent Weir, *qv*); *Style*— The Rt Hon Iris, Lady Inverforth; 24 Clarence Terrace, Regents Park, London NW1 4RD

INVERFORTH, Baroness; Jill Elizabeth; o da of John Ward Thornycroft, CBE (d 1989), of Bembridge, IOW; *m* 26 Jan 1966, 3 Baron Inverforth (d 1982); 1 s (4 Baron *qv*), 1 da (Hon Clarinda Weir b 22 May 1968); *Style*— The Rt Hon Lady Inverforth; 27 Hyde Park St, London W2 2JS (☎ 01 262 5721)

INVERURIE, Master of; Hon James William Falconer Keith; s and h of Lord Inverurie; *b* 15 April 1976; *Style*— The Master of Inverurie

INVERURIE, Lord; Michael Canning William John Keith; Master of Kintore; assumed surname of Keith in lieu of Baird; s and h of 12 Earl of Kintore; *b* 22 Feb 1939; *Educ* Eton, RMA Sandhurst; *m* 1972, Mary Plum, da of late Sqdn Ldr E G Plum, of Rumson, NJ; 1 s, 1 da; *Heir* s, Master of Inverurie; *Career* former Lt Coldstream Gds; *Style*— Lord Inverurie; The Stables, Keith Hall, Inverurie, Aberdeen (☎ 0467 20495)

IPSWICH, Archdeacon of; *see*: Gibson, The Ven Terence Allen

IPSWICH, Viscount; Henry Oliver Charles FitzRoy; s and h of Earl of Euston; *b* 6 April 1978; *Style*— Viscount Ipswich

IRBY, Charles Leonard Anthony; s of The Hon Anthony P Irby (d 1986), of Osborne House, South Bolt on Gardens, London, SW5, and Mary, *née* Apponyi (d 1952); *b* 5 June 1945; *Educ* Eton; *m* 23 Sept 1971, Sarah Jane, da of Col David G Sutherland, MC, of 51 Victoria Road, London, W8; 1 s (Nicholas Charles Anthony b 10 July 1975), 1 da (Caroline Sarah b 21 May 1977); *Career* dir Baring Brothers & Co Ltd 1984-; FCA; *Recreations* travel, photography, skiing; *Clubs* City; *Style*— Charles Irby, Esq; 125 Blenheim Cres, London, W11 2EQ (☎ 01 221 2979); The Old Vicarage, Chieveley, Newbury, Berks, RG16 8UX (☎ 0635 748 117); Baring Bros & Co Ltd, 8 Bishopsgate, London, EC2N 4AE (☎ 01 283 8833, fax 01 283 2224)

IRBY, (George Anthony) Peter; s of Hon Anthony Peter Irby (d 1986), and Mary, *née* Apponyi (d 1952); *b* 3 June 1942; *Educ* Eton; *m* 10 Oct 1981, Ginger Kay, da of Frank E Wallace (d 1977), of Texas, USA; 2 s (Edward b 1986, Richard Peter Anthony Wallace b 1988), 2 da (Mary (decd), Katharine b 1984); *Career* Maj Royal Green Jackets 1961-79; advertising mangr (Europe & ME) New York Times 1981-; *Recreations* golf; *Style*— Peter Irby, Esq; Hill House, 64 Honor Oak Road, London SE23 3RZ; The New York Times, 76 Shoe Lane, London EC4A 3JB (☎ 01 353 2174/ 3472, fax 01 583 1458, telex 263317 NYKTMS G)

IREDALE, (John) Martin; s of John Leslie Iredale (d 1988), of 44 Whitehouse Rd, Woodcote, Reading, and Hilda, *née* Palfry; *b* 10 June 1939; *Educ* Abingdon Sch; *m* 14 Sept 1963, (Margaret) Anne, da of Reginald Walter Jewell (d 1968), of 15 Winser Drive, Reading; 3 s (Edward b 1 May 1965, Mathew b 3 Oct 1966, William b 18 May 1976), 1 da (Hannah b 30 March 1973); *Career* CA and licensed insolvency practitioner; ptnr: Cork Gully 1971-, Coopers & Lybrand 1983-; sec Royal Shakespeare Theatre Tst 1970-, govr Royal Shakespeare Theatre 1981-, memb Hodgson Ctee On Profits of Crime and Their Recovery 1981-82, also Old Abingdonian Club 1982-84, chm Cornhill Club 1985-86; Freeman City of London 1973, Liveryman Worshipful Co Carmen 1978, FCA 1963, FIPA 1985; *Books* Receivership Manual (with C J Hughes, 1987); *Recreations* waiting on my family; *Clubs* Leander, Cornhill, Reading Abbey Rotary; *Style*— Martin Iredale, Esq; Holybrook Farm House, Burghfield Bridge, Reading RG3 3RA (☎ 0734 575 108); Cork Gully, Shelley House, 3 Noble St, London EC2V 7DQ (☎ 01 606 7700, fax 01 606 9887, car tel 0860 522 370, telex 884730 CORKGY G)

IREDALE, Dr Roger Oliver; s of Fred Iredale (d 1978), of Sussex, and Elsie Florence, *née* Hills; *b* 13 August 1934; *Educ* Harrow Co GS, Univ of Reading (BA, MA, PhD), Peterhouse Cambridge ; *m* 1968, Mavis, da of Charles Frederick Bowtell, of York; 1 s (Simon Crispian b 1974), 1 da (Rachel Samia b 1971); *Career* teacher Hele's Sch Exeter 1959-61, lectr (later sr lectr) Bishop Otter Coll Chichester 1962-70, Br Cncl offr and maitre de conferences Univ of Algiers 1970-72; lectr Chichester Coll of Further Educn 1972-73; Br Cncl Offr Madras 1973-75; lectr in educn Univ of Leeds 1975-79; chief educn advsr overseas Devpt admin FCO 1983- (educn adsr 1979-83) memb Cwlth Scholarship Cmmn 1984-, cmmr Sino-Br Friendship Scholarship Scheme 1986-, govr: SOAS 1983-, Queen Elizabeth House Oxford 1986-87, The Cwlth of Learning; poems for BBC Radio 3 and in anthologies and jls; *Publications* Turning Bronzes (poems, 1974), Out Towards the Dark (poems, 1978); articles in Comparative Education and other jls; *Recreations* sailing, poetry, writing, restoring the discarded; *Style*— Dr Roger Iredale; Overseas Development Administration, Eland House, Stag Place, London SW1E 5DH (☎ 01 273 0125)

IRELAND, Adrian William Velleman; *b* 1 Mar 1945; *Educ* Stowe; *m* 19 July 1975, (Victoria) Jane, da of Maj Myles Harry Cooper (d 1986), of Bideford, Devon; 2 s (Rupert b 1977, Frederic b 1979); *Career* with Akroyd and Smithers stock jobbers until 1986, dir S G Warbury Securities 1986-; *Recreations* travel, cricket, food; *Clubs* City of London, Boodles, MCC; *Style*— Adrian Ireland, Esq; 7 Dalebury Rd, London SW17; 1 Finsbury Ave, London EC2 (☎ 01 606 1066)

IRELAND, Norman Charles; s of Charles Ireland (d 1980), and Winifred Alice Ireland (d 1962); *b* 28 May 1927; *Educ* UK, USA, India; *m* 18 Aug 1953, Gillian Margaret (Gill), da of William James Harrison (d 1976); 1 s (David Alistair b 30 April 1958), 1 da (Jennifer Fiona b 11 Nov 1955); *Career* RAF 1945-48; Avon Rubber 1954-65, chief accountant Utd Glass 1965-67, fin dir BTR 1967-87 (ret as exec 1987); chm: London & Met plc 1986-, Bowater Industs plc 1987-, Bricom Gp 1988-, The Housing Fin Corpn 1988-; non exec dir 1987-: BTR plc, Meggitt Hldgs plc, Etam plc, Savage Gp plc, Scottish Heritable Tst plc, WA Hldgs plc; MICAS, memb Inst of Cost and Mgmnt Accountants; *Recreations* gardening, watching and listening to music, ballet, opera; *Style*— Norman Ireland, Esq

IRELAND, Sheriff Ronald David; QC (1964); s of William Alexander Ireland (d 1969), and Agnes Victoria Brown (d 1958); *b* 13 Mar 1925; *Educ* Watson's Coll Edinburgh, Balliol Coll Oxford (MA), Univ of Edinburgh (LLB); *Career* advocate of the Scottish Bar 1952, prof of Scots law Univ of Aberdeen 1958-71, dean of the Faculty of Law 1964-67; Sheriff of Lothian and Borders 1972-88, dir Scottish Cts Admin 1975-78, Sheriff Princ of Grampian Highland and Islands 1988-; *Clubs* New (Edinburgh), Royal Northern and Univ (Aberdeen), Highland (Inverness); *Style*— Sheriff Ronald Ireland, QC; 6a Greenhill Gardens, Edinburgh; The Castle, Inverness

IRELAND, Hon Mrs Sheila Marian; *née* Poole; da of 1 Baron Poole, CBE, TD, PC; *b* 1940; *m* 1, 1966 (m dis), Cob Stenham, *qv*; m 2, 1980, George Ian Kenneth Ireland; *Style*— The Hon Mrs Ireland; 9 Albert Place, London W8

IREMONGER, (William) John; s of Rev William George Iremonger, (d 1964), and Ruth Ida, *née* Gascoigne (d 1964); *b* 10 April 1912; *Educ* Hurstpierpoint, Keble Coll Oxford, Grenoble Univ France; *m* 8 Nov 1947, Christine Margaret, da of Lewis Gottwaltz (d 1928), of The Nook, Southern Down, S Wales; 2 s (Jonathan b 19 March 1953, Robert b 16 July 1962), 4 da (Susan b 24 July 1949, d 1950, Penelope b 15 Nov 1950, Joanna b 20 July 1955, Nicola b 1 April 1958); *Career* WWII Flying Offr RAF 1940-46; started own business (hotel and property) 1947, underwriting memb Lloyds 1974-, vice chm Dorset CC (memb 1968-); *Recreations* walking, music, photography; *Clubs* Lansdowne; *Style*— John Iremonger, Esq; The Choughs, 95 Golf Links Rd, Ferndown, Dorset BSZZ 8BU (☎ 0202 874 325); Breton, Loubes Bernac, 47120 Duras, France; 55 Kensington Court, London W8 (☎ 01 937 8922)

IREMONGER, Thomas Lascelles; s of Lt-Col H E W Iremonger, DSO, RMA (d 1937); *b* 14 Mar 1916; *Educ* Oriel Coll Oxford; *m* 1937, Lucille d'Oyen, FRSL (d 1989), da of Basil Oscar Parks, JP (d 1947); 1 da; *Career* Lt RNVR WWII; district offr Colonial Admin Serv (W Pacific) 1939-46; underwriting memb of Lloyd's; MP (C) Ilford North 1954-74; editor of Overseas; author of works on penal system and economics; *Recreations* small boat sailing (sailed for Oxford v Cambridge 1938); *Style*— Thomas Iremonger, Esq; 34 Cheyne Row, Chelsea, London SW3; The Giant's House, Newbourn, nr Woodbridge, Suffolk; La Voûte, Montignac-le-Coq, 16390 St Séverin, France

IRESON, Prof (John) Clifford; s of John Leonard Ireson (d 1962), of Kettering, Northamptonshire, and Doris Helena, *née* Busby (d 1987); *b* 29 Jan 1922; *Educ* Kettering GS, Univ Coll Nottingham, Sorbonne, London (BA, MA), Sorbonne (Docteur ès Lettres); *m* 2, 10 Dec 1949, Barbara Amy, da of Thomas Sudbury Francis (d 1971), of Brighton, Sussex; 2 s (Richard b 1952, Nicholas b 1958), 1 da (Jane b 1950); *Career* serv WWII RAF 1942-45; asst lectr (later lectr and reader) Univ of Leeds 1950-64, prof of french Univ of Sheffield 1964-69, dean faculty of arts Univ of Hull 1978-80, prof of modern french literature Univ of Hull 1969-82 (prof emeritus 1982-); chm Assoc of Univ Profs of French 1977-78; pres Nat Cncl for Modern Languages 1972-75 and 1977-80; Chevalier de l'Ordre National du Mérite (France) 1982; *Books* L'Oeuvre poétique de Gustave Kahn (1962), Threnody for four Voices (1961), Lamartine: A Revaluation (1969), Imagination in French Romantic Poetry (1970), The Relevance of the Romantics (1980); *Recreations* creative gardening, restoration of old houses; *Style*— Prof Clifford Ireson; Les Hautes Rives, 8 rue St Georges, Rochecorbon, 37210 Vouvray, France (☎ 47 52 56 01)

IRISH, John George Augustus; s of Albert Edwin Irish, of Hinton St George, Somerset (d 1986), and Rosa Anna Elizabeth, *née* Norris (d 1961); *b* 1 August 1931; *Educ* Crewkerne Sch, LSE (BSc); *m* 1, 1953 (m dis 1967) Joan, *née* Hall; 1 s (Timothy b 1964), 1 da (Nicola b 1962); m 2, 1968, Isabel Josephine, o da of Bernhard Berenzweig, of Harrow on the Hill, Middx; 4 s (Jonathan b 1970, Nicholas b 1972, Hugo b 1979, Charles b 1981); *Career* cmmnd Nat Serv 1952-54; exec Marks and Spencer 1954-65, retail dir David Greig 1965-70; chm: Spar UK Ltd 1983- (md 1981-), Eight Till Late Ltd 1981-; vice chm Spar Guild of Grocers 1984-; chief exec: Spar Food Distributors, Landmark Cash and Carry Ltd, Spar Landmark Services 1985-; dir IGT (Amsterdam based trading co of Int Spar) 1983-; dep chm Retail Consortium, memb NEDC Distributive Trades, chm voluntary gp mgmnt ctee Inst of Grocery Distribution, memb cncl and fund raising ctee Nat Grocers' Benevolent Fund 1983-; Supermarketing "Man of the Year" 1986, Independent Grocer Gold Award 1987; govr Orley Farm Sch Middx; FIGD 1985; *Recreations* history, conservation, education; *Clubs* IOD; *Style*— John Irish, Esq; Fourbuoys House Georgian Way, Harrow on the Hill, Middx HA1 3LF (☎ 01 864 6953); Spar (UK) Ltd, 32-40 Headstone Drive, Harrow, Middx HA3 5QT (☎ 01 863 5511, telex 923215 SPARHA)

IRISH, Sir Ronald Arthur; OBE (1963); s of Arthur Irish (d 1968); *b* 26 Mar 1913; *Educ* Fort St HS; *m* 1960, Noella Jean Austin, da of Leslie Stuart Fraser; 3 s; *Career* former sr ptnr Irish Young and Outhwaite CA's, pres Inst of CAs Aust 1956-58, chm Manufacturing Industs Advsy Cncl 1966-72, pres Tenth Int Congress of Accountants 1972, former chm Rothmans of Pall Mall (Australia) Ltd; life memb: Australian Soc of Accountants 1972, Inst of CAs in Australia 1974; hon fell Univ of Sydney 1986; FCA; kt 1970; *Books* Auditing; *Clubs* Union and Australian (Sydney); *Style*— Sir Ronald Irish, OBE; 2803/85 Spring St, Bondi Junction, NSW 2022, Australia

IRONS, Jeremy John; s of Paul Dugan Irons (d 1983), and Barbara Anne Brereton Brymer, *née* Sharpe; *b* 19 Sept 1948; *Educ* Sherborne, Bristol Old Vic Theatre Sch; *m* 23 March 1978, Sinead Mary, da of Cyril James Cusack, actor; 2 s (Samuel b 16 Sept 1978, Maximilian b 17 Oct 1985); *Career* actor; stage appearances incl: Godspell 1971, Wild Oats RSC 1975, Simon Gray's Rear Column (Clarence Derwent Award) 1976, TV Brideshead Revisited (TV Times Best Actor Award) 1982; Films: French Lieutenant's Woman (Variety Club Best Actor Award), Moonlighting 1982, The Captains Doll (BBC TV film) 1982, The Wild Duck (Australian film of Ibsen play) 1983, Betrayal 1983, Swann in Love 1983, The Mission 1985, Deadringers (1988), Chorus of Disapproval (1988), Danny Champion of the World (1988); Broadway: The Real Thing 1984 (Tony Award Best Actor, Drama League Distinguished Performance Award); RSC 1986-87 Winters Tale, The Rover, Richard II; Dead Ringers (Best Actor, New York Critics Award) 1988; *Recreations* sailing, riding, skiing, flying; *Style*— Jeremy Irons, Esq; c/o Hutton Mangement, 200 Fulham Rd, London SW10

IRONSIDE, Hon Charles Edmund Grenville; s and h of 2 Baron Ironside; *b* 1 July 1956; *m* 17 Aug 1985, Hon Elizabeth Mary Law, eldest da of 2 Baron Coleraine; 1 da (Emily Charlotte b 23 Oct 1988); *Style*— The Hon Charles Ironside; 25 Patience Rd, London SW11

IRONSIDE, 2 Baron (UK 1941); Edmund Oslac Ironside; s of Field Marshal 1 Baron Ironside, GCB, CMG, DSO (d 1959); *b* 21 Sept 1924; *Educ* Tonbridge Sch; hon CGIA 1986; *m* 1950, Audrey Marigold, da of late Col the Hon Thomas George Breadalbane Morgan-Grenville, DSO, OBE, MC (3 s of Lady Kinloss in her own right); 1 s, 1 da; *Heir* s, Hon Charles Ironside; *Career* Lt RN 1943-52; Marconi Co 1952-59, English Electro Leo Computers 1959-64, Cryosystems Ltd 1964-68, Int Research and Devpt Co Ltd 1968-84, NEI plc 1984-; memb: organising ctee British Library 1972-74, select ctee European Communities 1974-; chm Science Reference Library Advsy Ctee 1975-85; pres: Electric Vehicle Assoc of Great Britain 1975-83, European Electric Road Vehicle Assoc 1980-82 (vice-pres 1978-80), Sea Cadet Corps Chelmsford 1959-88; vice-pres: Inst of Patentees and Inventors 1976-, Parly and Scientific Ctee 1977-80 and 1983-86 (dep chm 1974-77); tres All Pty Energy Studies Gp 1979-; privy cncl memb of court City Univ 1975- (memb cncl 1986-88); memb court Essex Univ 1982- (memb cncl 1984-87); Master Worshipful Co of Skinners 1981-82; *Books* Highroad to Command (1972); *Clubs* Royal Ocean Racing; *Style—* The Rt Hon the Lord Ironside; Priory House, Old House Lane, Colchester Essex CO4 5RB

IRONSIDE, Hon Mrs (Elizabeth Mary); *née* Law; da (by 1 m) of 2 Baron Coleraine; *b* 4 Feb 1961; *m* 17 Aug 1985, Hon Charles Edmund Grenville Ironside, only s of 2 Baron Ironside; 1 da (Emily Charlotte b 23 Oct 1988); *Style—* The Hon Mrs Ironside; 25 Patience Road, London SW11

IRONSIDE, Mariot, Baroness; Mariot Ysabel; da of Lt Charles Cheyne, ISC (d 1891); *b* 3 June 1888; *m* 1915, 1 Baron Ironside, GCB, CMG, DSO (d 1959); 1 s (2 Baron), 1 da (Hon Mrs Hendry); *Style—* The Rt Hon Mariot, Lady Ironside; Hampton Court Palace, East Molesey, Surrey (☎ 01 977 2069)

IRONSIDE, Thomas David; WS; s of William Bickerstaff Ironside, of Scotland, and Iona Margaret McKay; *b* 2 June 1955; *Educ* Hutchesons' Boys' GS Glasgow, Edinburgh Univ (LLB); *m* 10 Sept 1983, Anne, da of William Kenny; *Career* slr; Notary Public 1979; *Recreations* sailing; *Style—* David Ironside, Esq, WS; The Alders, Balnearn, Lochtayside, Perthshire; Struan House, The Square, Aberfeldy PH15 2DD (☎ 0887 20820)

IRVINE, Rt Hon Sir Bryant Godman; PC (1982); s of William Henry Irvine, and Ada Mary, *née* Bryant, of Toronto; *b* 25 July 1909; *Educ* Upper Canada Coll Toronto, St Paul's, Magdalen Coll Oxford (MA); *m* 1945, Valborg Cecilie, da of late Peter Frederick Carslund, of Fyn, Denmark; 2 da; *Career* serv WWII RNVR, Lt-Cdr (at sea and on staff C-in-C Western Approaches and cdr US Naval Forces Europe); barr 1932; farmer, memb exec ctee NFU (E Sussex) 1947-84 (branch chm 1956-58); chm: SE Agric Land Tbnl 1954-56, YCs' Union 1946-47; Parly candidate (C) Wood Green and Lower Tottenham 1951, MP (C) Rye 1955-83; PPS to: min Educn and parly sec Miny Educn 1957-59, fin sec Treasy 1959-60; chm: Cons Horticulture Sub-Ctee 1960-62, All-Party Tourist and Resort Ctee 1964-66; vice-chm Cons Ctee on Agric 1964-70, memb select ctee Agric 1967-69, jt sec 1922 Ctee 1965-68 (hon tres 1974-76), jt sec and vice-chm Cons Cwlth Affairs Ctee 1957-66, memb exec ctee Cwlth Parly Assoc UK branch 1964-76 and 1982-83 (memb gen cncl and hon tres 1970-73), chm British-Canadian Parly Gp 1964-83, vice-chm Cons Foreign and Cwlth Affairs Ctee 1973-76 (jt sec 1967-73), memb Speaker's Panel Chairmen 1965-76, dep chm Ways and Means Ctee House of Commons and dep speaker 1976-82, represented Mr Speaker at the Millenium of Tynwald IOM 1979, Cwlth Speakers Conference Ottawa 1981, 150 Anniversary of Parly Govt Cayman Islands 1982, ldr Parly Delgn to UNO 1982; pres Southern Counties Agric Trading Soc 1983-86; CInstCE 1938-74; Kt 1986; *Clubs* Carlton, Pratt's, Naval; *Style—* The Rt Hon Sir Bryant Godman Irvine; Flat 91, 24 John Islip St, London SW1 (☎ 01 834 9221); Great Ote Hall, Burgess Hill, W Sussex (☎ 044 46 2179)

IRVINE, Dr Donald Hamilton; CBE (1987, OBE 1979); s of Dr Andrew Bell Hamilton Irvine, and Dorothy Mary, *née* Buckley; *b* 2 June 1935; *Educ* King Edward VI's GS Morpeth, Med Sch Univ of Newcastle-upon-Tyne (MB BS, MD); *m* 1, 16 July 1960 (m dis 1985), Margaret Mary, da of late Francis McGuckin of Ponteland, Northumberland; 2 s (Alastair b 1962, Angus b 1968), 1 da (Amanda b 1966); m 2, 28 June 1986, Sally, da of Stanley Arthur Day, of Bellingham, NSW; *Career* princ GP Lintonville Med Gp Northumberland 1960-, regnl advsr GP Regnl Postgrad Inst for Med and Dentistry Univ of Newcastle upon Tyne 1973-; memb Gen Med Cncl 1979- (chm of ctee of standards and med ethics); RCGP: memb cncl 1968-, hon sec 1972-78, chm of cncl 1982-85 ; chm Jt Ctee on Postgrad Trg for GP 1988- (memb 1976); memb UK Central Cncl for Nursing Midwifery and Health Visiting 1983-; chm: bd govrs MSD Fndn 1983-, project mgmnt ctee of the Northern Regnl Study of Standards and Performance in GP 1979-; MRCGP 1965, FRCGP 1972; fell BMA: RSM; *Books* The Future General Practioner - Learning and Teaching (jtly 1972); *Recreations* gardening, bird watching, going to the theatre; *Style—* Dr Donald Irvine, Esq, CBE; Mole End, Fairmoor, Morpeth, Northumberland (☎ 0670 515746); 11 Cedarland Ct, Roland Gardens, London SW7 3RW (☎ 01 373 5234); Lintonville Med Gp, Lintonville, Old Lane, Ashington, Northumberland (☎ 0670 812772, fax 0670 510046)

IRVINE, His Honour Judge James Eccles Malise; yr s of Brig-Gen Alfred Ernest Irvine, CB, CMG, DSO (d 1962), of Wotton-under-Edge, Glos, and Katharine Helen (d 1984), elder da of Lt-Gen Hamilton Maximilian Christian Williams Graham, CMG (d 1931); *b* 10 July 1925; *Educ* Stowe, Merton Coll Oxford (MA); *m* 24 July 1954, Anne, eld da of Col Geoffrey Egerton-Warburton, DSO, TD, JP, DL (d 1961); ggs of Rev Rowland Egerton-Warburton, bro of 8 and 9 Bts Grey-Egerton), of Grafton Hall, Malpas, Cheshire, and Hon Georgiana Mary Dormer, MBE (d 1955), eld da of 14 Baron Dormer; 1 s (David b 1963), 1 da (Susan b 1961); *Career* WWII served Grenadier Gds 1943-46 (Hon Capt 1946); barr Inner Temple 1949, prosecuting counsel for inland revenue on Oxford circuit 1965-71, dep chm Glos QS 1967-71, circuit judge 1972-; Lay Judge of Ct of Arches for Province of Canterbury and of Chancery Ct of York for Province of York 1981-; *Books* Parties and Pleasures: the Diaries of Helen Graham 1823-26 (1954); *Style—* His Honour Judge Irvine; c/o Oxford Combined Crown and County Court Centre, St Aldates, Oxford OX1 1TL

IRVINE, John Ferguson; CB (1983); s of Joseph Ferguson Irvine (d 1980), of Scotland, and Helen Dick Irvine, *née* Gardner (d 1985); *b* 13 Nov 1920; *Educ* Ardrossan Acad, Glasgow Univ (MA); *m* 1, 1945, Doris, da of Thomas Partidge (d 1952), of Birmingham; 2 s (Graham b 1966, Richard b 1970), 1 da (Gwyneth b 1949); m 2, 1980, Christine Margot, da of Thomas Tudor, of Staffs; 2 s (Thomas b 1982, William b 1983), and 1 step s (John b 1977); *Career* Flt Lt flying boat capt Atlantic, North Sea, Indian Ocean; administrative civil servant: Scottish Office 1946, N Ireland civil servant 1948, asst sec 1959, under sec 1971, permanent sec 1976, ret 1983 as permanent sec Dept of Environment for N Ireland; seconded chief exec Ulster Transport Authy and N Ireland Transport Hldg Co 1976-78; chief exec Indust Therapy Organisation (Ulster) Ltd 1983-; *Recreations* distance running, soccer, Mallorca; *Style—* John Irvine, Esq, CB; c/o Allied Irish Bank, Donegall Square East, Belfast; Industrial Therapy Organisation, Downpatrick, Co Down BT30 (☎ (0396) 2647)

IRVINE, Michael Fraser; MP (C) Ipswich 1987-; s of Rt Hon Sir Arthur James Irvine, QC, MP (d 1978) of London, and Eleanor, *née* Morris; *b* 21 Oct 1939; *Educ* Rugby, Oriel Coll Oxford (BA); *Career* barr 1964-; Parly candidate (C) Bishop Auckland 1979; *Recreations* hill-walking in Scotland; *Style—* Michael Irvine, Esq, MP; 1 Crown Office Row, Temple, London EC4Y 7HH (☎ 01 583 9292, telex 8953152, fax 01 353 9292)

IRVINE, Norman Forrest; QC (1973); s of William Allan Irvine (d 1944), and Dorcas Forrest (d 1975); *b* 29 Sept 1922; *Educ* HS of Glasgow, Glasgow Univ (BL); *m* 1964, Mary Lilian Patricia, da of Ernest Victor Constable (d 1976); 1 s (James b 1965); *Career* Lt RCS 1942-45 served Middle E and India; slr Scotland 1943, Staff Capt HM Claims Cmmn 1945-46, barr Grays Inn 1955, rec of the Crown Court 1974-86; *Recreations* writing novels; *Style—* Norman Irvine, Esq, QC; Park House, Upland Park Road, Oxford (☎ 0865 513570)

IRVINE OF LAIRG, Baron (Life Peer UK 1987) Alexander Andrew Mackay Irvine; QC (1978); s of Alexander Irvine and his w Margaret Christina, da of late Alexander Macmillan; *b* 23 June 1940; *Educ* Inverness Royal Acad, Hutchesons' Boys' GS Glasgow, Glasgow Univ (MA, LLB), Christ's Coll Cambridge (BA, LLB); *m* 1974, Alison Mary, yst da of Dr James Shaw McNair, MD; 2 s (Hon David b 1974, Hon Alastair b 1976); *Career* barr Inner Temple 1967, bencher 1985, rec 1985-88; lectr LSE 1965-69; *Recreations* collecting paintings, reading, theatre, cinema; *Clubs* Garrick; *Style—* Baron Alexander Irvine of Lairg, QC; 11 King's Bench Walk, Temple, London EC4Y 7EQ (☎ 01 583 0610, fax 01 583 9123 3690, telex 884620 BARLEX)

IRVINE ROBERTSON, Alexander; TD (1945), DL (1961 Stirlingshire); s of Duncan Irvine Robertson (d 1953), of Stirling, and Winifred Penelope Drummond (d 1984); *b* 12 Nov 1912; *Educ* Fettes, Edinburgh Univ (MA, LLB); *m* 1939, Jean Margaret, da of late Rev Alexander Garden Fraser, CBE; 3 s (Alistair, James, John), 1 da (Penelope); *Career* 2 Lt TA 1931, WWII served BEF, Lt-Col 1950; Bt-Col 1953, slr Mathie Macluckie & Lupton 1937-, cncllr Royal Burgh of Stirling 1946-50, chm Stirlingshire T & AF Assoc 1965-68, dir of various cos; *Recreations* golf; *Style—* Alexander Irvine Robertson, Esq, TD, DL; 6 Abercromby Place, Stirling (☎ 0786 74526)

IRVING, Barrie Leslie; s of Herbert Leslie Irving, of Jersey, CI, and Joan Fletcher, *née* Robinson (d 1977); *b* 6 Oct 1942; *Educ* Stowe, Pembroke Coll Cambridge (BA), Graduate Sch of Univ of California at Berkeley (MA); *m* 1, 11 July 1964 (m dis 1982), (Pamela) Jane, da of Capt Ronald Leese (ka 1943); 2 s (Dominic Paul b 25 May 1972, Benjamin Alec James b 16 March 1985), 1 da (Samantha Jane b 15 May 1968); *Career* psychologist and criminologist; res staff Inst of Human Devpt Univ at California Berkeley 1965-66, professional staff (later memb mgmnt ctee) Tavistock Inst of Human Relations London 1966-79, dir The Police Fndn 1980-; special assignments incl: conslt to the official slr for Sir Henry Fisher's Inquiry into the Murder of Maxwell Confait 1977, res conslt to the Royal Cmmn on Criminal Procedure 1979; memb and cnsllr Nat Step Families Assoc; *Books* The Psychological Dynamics of Smoking (1968), Tied Cottages in British Agriculture (1975), Police Interrogation (1980), Regulating Custodial Interviews (1988), Changes of Pace (1989); *Recreations* tennis, golf, fencing, music (piano playing); *Clubs* Naval and Military; *Style—* Barrie Irving, Esq; The Police Foundation, 314-316 Vauxhall Bridge Rd, London SW1Y 1AA (☎ 01 828 1438/9)

IRVING, Dr (John) Bruce; s of Edward James Bruges Irving (d 1976), of Balgownie, Kirkintilloch, and Marjorie Olive, *née* Dumbleton; *b* 19 June 1942; *Educ* Lenzie Acad, Univ of Glasgow (BSc, PhD), Univ of Stirling (MSc); *m* 14 June 1969, Margaret Anna, da of James Elgin McWilliam (d 1976), of Uphall, W Lothian; 2 s (Christopher b 1971, Peter b 1973), 1 da (Anna b 1978); *Career* researcher Nat Engrg Lab E Kilbride 1969-78, info systems mangr (former project co-ordinator) Chloride Tech Ltd Manchester 1978-85, dir info technol Dumfries and Galloway Regnl Cncl 1986-; Laird of Bonshaw; former pres: Ayrshire Philatelic Soc, Dumfries Philatelic Soc; FBIM 1988; *Recreations* outdoor pursuits, family history, philately; *Style—* Dr Bruce Irving; Bonshaw Tower, Kirltebridge, Lockerbie, Dumfriesshire DG11 3LY (☎ 046 15 256)

IRVING, Charles Graham; MP (C) Cheltenham Oct 1974-; s of Charles Graham Irving, of Cheltenham, and Ethel Maude, *née* Collett (d 1957); *b* 6 May 1923; *Educ* Cheltenham GS, Lucton Sch Herefordshire; *Career* chm: Irving Hotels Ltd Cheltenham and London 1964-75, Western Travel Co 1986-; conslt public affairs Dowty Gp plc 1986- (dir public relations 1964-86); chm: House of Commons Catering Ctee 1979-, All Pty Gp Mental Health; tres All Pty Gp Penal Affairs; memb: Cheltenham Borough Cncl 1948- (chm fin and policy 1959-84 and 1987-), Gloucestershire CC 1948-81 (chm social servs 1975-81, hon alderman 1981); Mayor of Cheltenham 1958-60 and 1971-72; chm: Stonham Housing Assoc Ltd 1974-, SW Midlands Soc; vice chm NACRO 1975-, fndr memb Nat Victims' Support Schemes 1973-, fndr pres Cheltenham and Dist Housing Assoc, pres Cheltenham and N Cotswolds Eye Therapy Tst; Freeman Borough of Cheltenham 1976; *Books* After-care in the Community, Case of the Meter Victims, House of Commons Cookery Book; *Recreations* antiques, social work; *Clubs* St Stephen's Constitutional, St James's; *Style—* Charles Irving, Esq, MP; The Grange Malvern Rd, Cheltenham, Glos (☎ 0242 523083); Constituency Office: Douglas House, Vittoria Walk, Cheltenham (☎ 0242 522958); House of Commons, London SW1A OAA (☎ 01 219 4095)

IRVING, Rear Adm Sir Edmund George; KBE (1966, OBE 1944), CB (1962); s of George Clerk Irving (d 1956), Ethel Mary Frances, *née* Poole (d 1964) of British N Borneo; *b* 5 April 1910; *Educ* St Anthony's Eastbourne, RNC Dartmouth; *m* 1, 1936, Margaret Scudamore (d 1974), da of Richard Edwards, MBE; 1 s, 1 da; m 2, 1979, Esther Rebecca Ellison; *Career* joined RN 1924, served WWII, Capt 1951, Rear Adm 1960, ADC to HM The Queen 1960, Hydrographer of the Navy 1960-66, ret; memb NERC 1967-74; pres: RIN 1967-69, RGS 1970-72; tstee Nat Maritime Museum 1972-81; acting conservator of the River Mersey 1975-85; FRGS, FRICS, FRIN, FRSA; *Recreations* horticulture; *Clubs* Army and Navy; *Style—* Rear-Adm Sir Edmund Irving, KBE, CB; Camer Green, Meopham, Kent DA13 0XR (☎ 0474 813 253)

IRVING, James Wyllie; TD; s of John Irving, MBE (d 1931), and Jessie Howatson Mitchell Wyllie (d 1925); *b* 21 April 1914; *Educ* Fettes, Glasgow Univ; *m* 31 March 1937, Henrietta Mary, da of Henry Purcell (d 1940), of Co Dublin; 2 da (Christine b 1946, Pamela b 1948); *Career* Maj Cheshire Regt 1939-45; KOSB (TA) 1948-59; controller SW Scotland Civil Defence Gp 1960-68; slr; ptnr Primrose and Gordon Dumfries 1937-; memb bd mgmnt Dumfries and Galloway Hosps 1965-71 (chm 1968-71); chm: bd of mgmnt Dumfries and Galloway and Crichton Royal Hosps 1972-74,

Dumfries and Galloway Health Bd 1973-80; sec: County of Dumfries Valuation Appeal Ctee 1956-72, SW Scotland Local Employment Ctee 1960-74, Local Bd of Dirs Scottish Union & Nat Insurance Co 1973-85; dir Dumfries Trading Estate Ltd 1961-; SSC, Hon Sheriff South Strathclyde Dumfries and Galloway 1963-, Notary Public; *Recreations* reading, gardening; *Style*— James Irving, Esq, TD; Kirkbrae (The Old Manse), Lochrutton, Nr Dumfries DG2 8NH (☎ 038 773 301); 92 Irish St, Dumfries (☎ Dumfries 67316)

IRVING OF DARTFORD, Baron (Life Peer UK 1979); Sydney Irving; PC (1969), DL (Kent 1976); s of Sydney Irving, of Newcastle upon Tyne; *b* 1 July 1918; *Educ* Pendower Sch Newcastle upon Tyne, LSE; *m* 1942, Mildred, da of Charlton Weedy, of Morpeth; 1 s, 1 da (and 1 s decd); *Career* sits as Labour Peer in House of Lords; chm S Regional Council of Labour Party 1965-67, memb Dartford Borough Cncl 1952-, memb NW Kent Divnl Exec Kent Education Ctee 1952-74; MP (Lab and Co-op) Dartford 1955-70 and Feb 1974-79, opposition whip (S and S Western) 1959-64, treasurer of the Household and dep chief govt whip 1964-66, chm of Ways and Means and dep speaker 1968-70, formerly chm of Select Ctees; *Style*— Rt Hon Lord Irving of Dartford, PC, DL; 10 Tynedale Close, Dartford, Kent (☎ (32) 25105)

IRWIN, Basil William Seymour; MC (1945), TD (1946), DL (Greater London 1967); s of Major William James Irwin (d 1960); *b* 27 May 1919; *Educ* Tonbridge; *m* 1949, Eleanor Ruth, da of Edwin Burgess; *Career* Brevet Col, served Europe and Middle East; TAVR, ADC to HM The Queen 1968-73; former merchant banker, vice chm Ionian Bank Ltd until 1978; stockbroker with Pinchin Denny & Co; chm Archimedes Investment Trust plc; dir Grahams Rintoul Investment Tst plc; *Clubs* Special Forces; *Style*— Basil Irwin, Esq, MC, TD, DL; The Thatch, Stansted, Essex (☎ 0279 812207)

IRWIN, Maj-Gen Brian St George; CB (1975); s of Lt-Col Alfred Percy Bulteel Irwin, DSO (d 1976), of Maumfin, Moyard, Co Galway, and Eileen, *née* Holberton (d 1974); *b* 16 Sept 1917; *Educ* Rugby, RMA Woolwich, Trinity Hall Cambridge (MA); *m* 23 Dec 1939, Audrey Lilla, da of Lt-Col Hugh Barkley Steen, IMS (d 1951), of Dunboe, Shepperton-on-Thames, Middx; 2 s (Michael St George b 1940, (Brian) Christopher b 1946); *Career* cmmnd 2 Lt RE 1937; WWII served: Western Desert 1941-43 (despatches), Sicily and Italy 1943-44 (despatches), Greece 1944-45; Cyprus 1956-59 (despatches) and 1961-63, dir of mil survey MOD 1965-69, Maj-Gen 1969-74, dir gen Ordnance Survey 1969-77, ret Army 1974; under sec Civil Serv 1974-77; Col Cdr RE 1977-82; FRICS 1949- (cncl memb 1969-70 and 1972-76), FRGS 1960- (memb of cncl 1966-70, vice pres 1974-77); *Recreations* golf, genealogy; *Clubs* Army and Navy; *Style*— Maj-Gen Brian Irwin, CB; 16 Northerwood House, Swan Green, Lyndhurst, Hampshire SO43 7DT (☎ 042 128 3499)

IRWIN, (Frederick George) Ernest; s of George Irwin, and Margaret Irwin; *b* 19 Nov 1933; *Educ* Trinity Coll Dublin (BA, BAI), Iowa State Univ (MSc); *m* 11 Sept 1964, Juliet Faith, da of Antony Alexander Fitzgerald Tatlow; 1 s (George b 14 April 1972), 2 da (Katharine b 19 March 1969, Aisling b 31 May 1966); *Career* area engr DuPont Construction 1958-61; Ove Arup and Ptnrs: design engr London 1961-64, chief engr Ghana 1964-68, regnl assoc 1968-75, dir 1975- (head of Birmingham office responsible for: engrg design of Int Convention Centre Birmingham, Nat Exhibition Centre extension, land reclamation projects); chm: ICE res sub-ctee 1985-, ICE report construction res and devpt (published 1987); memb: ICE cncl 1985-87, ctee Birmingham Good Design Initiative; tstee Lench's Tst; FICE, FIStructE; *Recreations* golf, sailing, drawing; *Clubs* Edgbaston Golf, Barnt Green Sailing; *Style*— Ernest Irwin, Esq; 46 Selly Wick Rd, Selly Park, Birmingham B29 7JA; Ove Arup & Ptnrs, 3 Duchess Place, Edgbaston, Birmingham, B16 8NH (☎ 021 454 6261, fax 021 454 8853, telex 339468)

IRWIN, Felicity Ann; *née* Green; JP (Poole 1985); da of Lt-Col Arthur Thomas Begg Green, ED (d 1982), and Doris, Lady Pechell, *qv*; *b* 7 June 1947; *Educ* Queen Margaret Coll Wellington New Zealand; *m* 12 March 1969, (Alastair) Giles Irwin, s of Dr Desmond Irwin, of Clarendon House, Woodford Green, Essex; 3 da (Charlotte Ann b 26 Aug 1970, Candida Jane b 21 Dec 1973, Claudia b 14 Dec 1976); *Career* regnl exec Television South 1987-; hon sec Wessex branch IOD; chm: Relate Bournemouth, Dorset Family Conciliation Service, Poole and East Dorset Branch NSPCC; MInstD 1977, MIPR 1988; *Recreations* royal tennis, lawn tennis, water skiing; *Style*— Mrs Giles Irwin, JP; Stanbridge House, Stanbridge, Wimborne, Dorset BH21 4JD (☎ 0258 840129); TVS, Poole Art Centre, Poole, Dorset (☎ 0202 684375, fax 0202 682263)

IRWIN, Ian Sutherland; CBE (1982); s of Andrew Campbell Irwin (d 1967), of Glasgow, and Elizabeth Ritchie, *née* Arnott; *b* 20 Feb 1933; *Educ* Whitehill Sr Secdy Sch Glasgow, Glasgow Univ (BL); *m* 2 May 1959, (Margaret Miller) Maureen, da of John Scoullar Irvine, of Edinburgh; 2 s (Graeme Andrew b 1961, Derek John b 1965); *Career* Nat Serv Sgt RAPC attached to 1 Bn Seaforth Highlanders 1957-59; Hon Col 154 Regt RCT (V) 1986-; accountant Kirkcaldy Linoleum Mkt 1959-60, commercial mangr Scottish Omnibuses Ltd 1960-64, gp sec Scottish Tport Gp 1969-75 (gp accountant 1965-68), chm and chief exec Nat Bus Gp 1987- (dir and md 1975-86), non-exec dir Scottish Mortgage & Tst 1986-; dir Scottish Business in the Community, cncl memb CBI and CBI Scotland, hon vice-pres Int Union Public Tport, pres Bus and Coach Cncl 1979-80, vice-pres Inst of Tport 1984-87; CIPFA, FCIT, CBIM, FInstD; *Recreations* golf, gardening, reading; *Clubs* Caledonian, MCC; *Style*— Ian Irwin, Esq, CBE; Kilrymont, 6A Esher Belmont Rd, Edinburgh EH12 6EX (☎ 031 337 7098); Scottish Tport Gp, 114/116 George St, Edinburgh EH2 4LX (☎ 031 226 7491)

IRWIN, Sir James Campbell; OBE (1945), ED (1947); s of Francis James Irwin (d 1948), and Annabella Margaret Campbell, *née* Mann (d 1945); *b* 23 June 1906; *Educ* Queen's Sch, St Peter's Collegiate Sch, St Mark's Coll Adelaide Univ, (hon fell 1973), Staff Coll Haifa (psc); *m* 1933, Kathleen Agnes, da of Gilbert William Orr (d 1960); 1 s, 1 da; *Career* Lt-Col Royal Aust Artillery 2/AIF active service abroad: Middle East, New Guinea, Morotai, Philippine Islands; architect; Lord Mayor of Adelaide 1963-66, memb Adelaide City Cncl 1935-72; pres and chm Adelaide Festival of Arts 1963-73, memb Nat Capital Planning Ctee Canberra 1964-70, pres Home for Incurables 1966-81, chm Co-op Fndn 1981-87; pres Toc H (SA) 1952-55 and 1985-87, life fell RAIA (pres 1962-63); FRIBA (life fell); kt 1971; *see Debrett's Handbook of Australia and New Zealand for further details*; *Clubs* The Adelaide, Naval Military and Air Force (S Australia); *Style*— Sir James Irwin, OBE, ED; 124 Brougham Place, N Adelaide, S Australia 5006 (☎ 267 2839)

IRWIN, Lord; James Charles Wood; s and h of 3 Earl of Halifax; *b* 24 August 1977; *Style*— Lord Irwin; Garrowby, York YO4 1QD

IRWIN, Dr Michael Henry Knox; s of William Knox Irwin, FRCS, MD (d 1973), of Watford Heath, Herts, and Edith Isabel Mary, *née* Collins; descendant of John Knox; *b* 5 June 1931; *Educ* Merchant Taylors' Sch, St Bart's Hosp London (MB, BS), Columbia Univ NY (MPH); *m* 1, 1958 (m dis 1982), Elizabeth Miriam, *née* Naumann; 3 da (Christina, Pamela, Diana); m 2, 1983, Frederica Todd, da of Frederick Gordon Harlow, of Savannah, Ga, USA; *Career* physician; joined UN 1957, UN medical dir 1969-73, dir of personnel UN Devpt Programme 1973-76, UNICEF rep in Bangladesh 1977-80, sr advsr UNICEF 1980-82, medical dir UN, UNDP and UNICEF 1982-; conslt American Assoc of Blood Banks 1984-; Offr Cross Int Fedn of Blood Donor Organisations 1984; *Books* Overweight: a Problem for Millions (1964), What Do We Know About Allergies? (1972), Nuclear Energy: Good or Bad? (1984), The Cocaine Epidemic (1985); *Recreations* travelling, bicycling, writing; *Clubs* Royal Soc of Medicine (London); *Style*— Dr Michael Irwin; One West 89th St, New York, NY 10024, USA (☎ 212 595 7714); United Nations, New York, NY 10017, USA (☎ 212 754 7082)

IRWIN, Hon Mrs; Hon Mikaela; *née* Rawlinson; da of Baron Rawlinson of Ewell, PC, QC, by his 1 w, Haidee; *b* 1941; *m* 1964, Jonathan Irwin Goffs, s of John Irwin, of Chiswick; 4 s; *Style*— The Hon Mrs Irwin; Sandymount House, Digby Bridge, Sallins, Co Kildare, Ireland

ISAAC, David Ward; s of Augustus William Isaac, of Westmead, Willoughby, Boston, Lincs, and Jessica Doreen, *née* Beaulah; *b* 23 June 1933; *Educ* Bootham Sch York; *m* 14 Sept 1957, Eileen Mary, da of Reginald Lennard Victor Hayman (d 1972); 2 s (Martin b 1961, Stephen b 1972), 2 da (Jennifer b 1959, Heather b 1965); *Career* Nat Serv RMP 1950-52; md: GN Beulah Ltd 1961, Thomas Linnell (Boston) Ltd 1972 (main bd dir Northampton 1976); Appleby & Sons Ltd Bristol 1983, Appleby Westward Ltd 1984 (and for gp 1988); regnl dir Amalgamated Foods Ltd 1980, regnl chm Nat Guild of Spar Grocers; *Recreations* tennis, swimming, walking; *Clubs* Tavistock and Whitchurch Tennis, Tavistock GC; *Style*— David Isaac, Esq ; Appleby Westwald GP plc, PO Box 3, Callington Rd, Saltash, Cornwall PL12 6LT, (☎ 0752 843171, telex 45106)

ISAACS *see also*: Rufus Isaacs

ISAACS, Dame Albertha Madeline; DBE (1974); da of late Robert Hanna, and Lilla, *née* Minns; *b* 18 April 1900; *Educ* Cosmopolitan HS and Victoria HS Nassau; *m* ; 3 s, 1 da; *Career* memb Progressive Liberal Party, senator 1968-72, memb of PLP's Nat Gen Cncl and of Cncl of Women; *Style*— Dame Albertha Isaacs, DBE; c/o Progressive Liberal Party, Head Office, Nassau, Bahamas

ISAACS, Dr Anthony Donald; s of David Isaacs, of London, and Rosa, *née* Hockman ; *b* 18 Jan 1931; *Educ* London Univ and Charing Cross Hosp London Univ (MB BS, DPM); *m* 15 Dec 1963, Elissa, da of Isaac Cedar (d 1977), 1 s (Timothy b 13 Sept 1967), 1 da (Catherine b 28 Oct 1964); *Career* Nat Serv RAMC Lt to Capt 1955-57; conslt psychiatrist Bethlem Royal and Maudsley Hosp 1963-, sub-dean Inst of Psychiatry London Univ 1982-; vice chm grants ctee King Edward's Hosp Fund for London; Freeman City of London 1962; FRCP, FRCPsych, FRSM; *Books* Studies in Geriactric Psychiatry (1978), Psychiatric Examination in Clinical Practise (1981); *Style*— Dr Anthony Isaacs; The Maudsley Hospital, Denmark Hill, London SE5 (☎ 01 703 6333 ext 2369)

ISAACS, Anthony Hyman; s of Eric Hyman Isaacs (d 1985), and Marjorie Josephine, *née* Solomon (d 1983); *b* 9 August 1934; *Educ* Cheltenham Coll, Pembroke Coll Cambridge (BA); *m* 31 March 1964, Jennifer Irene, da of Sir James Cameron, CBE, TD, *qv*; 3 s (Roderick b 1968, Matthew b 1972, Oliver b 1976), 2 da (Jessica b 1966, Diana b 1970); *Career* RN 1952-54, Sub-Lieut RNVSR; Stephenson Harwood (formerly Stephenson Harwood & Tatham): articled to Sir Anthony Lousada 1957-60 (ptnr 1964, sr ptnr 1987); co-opted memb Co Law Ctee of the Law Soc; memb: Slr's Disciplinary Tbnl 1988, cncl Peper Harow Fndn, advsy ctee The Rehearsal Orchestra, Law Soc; *Recreations* music, gardening, theatre; *Clubs* Garrick, City Law; *Style*— Anthony Isaacs, Esq; Jordans, Eashing, nr Godalming, Surrey, GU7 2QA; One St Paul's Churchyard, London, EC4M 8SH (☎ 01 329 4422, fax 01 606 0822, telex 886789 SHSPC G)

ISAACS, Prof Bernard; s of Louis Isaacs (d 1970), of Glasgow, and Rosine Naomi, *née* Lion (d 1958); *b* 20 July 1924; *Educ* Kilmarnock Acad, Glasgow Univ (MB ChB, MD); *m* 27 Aug 1957, Dorothy Beulah, da of Abe Berman (d 1958), of Glasgow; 3 s (Lionel b 1959, Michael b 1962, Alick b 1968), 1 da (Aubrey b 1962); *Career* Capt (formerly Lt) RAMC 1948-50; conslt physician in geriatric med: Forest Hall Hosp Glasgow 1961-64, Glasgow Royal Infirmary 1964-74; Charles Hayward prof of geriatric med Univ of Birmingham 1975-89; memb: S Birmingham Health Authy 1981-85, Br Geriatric Soc 1957-89; FRCP (Glasgow 1961, Edinburgh 1974, London 1986); *Books* Survival of the Unfittest (1971), Giants of Geriatrics (1989); *Style*— Prof Bernard Isaacs; 33 Greville Drive, Birmingham B15 2UU (☎ 021 440 3418); Hayward Building, Selly Oak Hospital, Birmingham B29 6JL (☎ 021 472 5313)

ISAACS, Geoffrey Lewis; s of Laurence Isaacs (d 1955), of 8 Pembroke Rd, Moor Park, Northwood, Middx, and Gladys Rachel, *née* Jacobs, (d 1982); *b* 29 Sept 1935; *Educ* Merchant Taylors', Coll of Law; *m* 23 Sept 1960, (Barbara) Jane, da of Charles Stanley Catlow, of 66 Church Rd, Weston Favell, Northampton; 2 s (Mark b 1961, Tom b 1968), 1 da (Caroline b 1964); *Career* admitted slr 1958, ptnr Tarlo Lyons 1960; dir: Kerax Ltd, Whittendell Electrical Mfrg Co (Watford) Ltd, Soil Structures Int Ltd, OH1 UK Ltd, Servequip Ltd, Broadoak Flexible Packaging Ltd, Ralvin Pacific Properties Inc California; Freeman City of London 1979, memb Worshipful Co Painters - Stainers 1979; memb Law Soc 1958; *Recreations* golf, travel, theatre, walking; *Clubs* City Livery, Moor Park GC, Old Merchant Taylors; *Style*— Geoffrey Isaacs, Esq; Benthills, 1 Kings Farm Rd, Chorleywood, Herts WD3 5HF (☎ 09278 3340); High Holborn House, 52/54 High Holborn, London WC1V 6RU (☎ 01 405 2000, fax 01 405 3976, telex 267572)

ISAAMAN, Gerald Michael; s of Asher Isaaman (d 1975), and Lily Finklestein; *b* 22 Dec 1933; *Educ* Dame Alice Owens GS; *m* 1962, Delphine, da of Arnold Bertram Walker, of Whitby, Yorks; 1 s (Daniel); *Career* journalist: N London Observer Series 1950, Hampstead and Highgate Express 1955 (ed 1968-); chm: mngmnt bd Camden Arts Tst 1970-82, exhibitions ctee Camden Arts Centre 1971-82, Russell Housing Soc 1976-82; memb Camden Festival Tst 1982-, bd memb Assoc of Br Eds 1985-, fndr tstee Arkwright Arts Tst 1971; chm tstees King's Cross Disaster Fund 1987-; *Recreations* listening to jazz, collecting postcards, pontificating; *Style*— Gerald Isaaman,

Esq; 9 Lyndhurst Road, Hampstead, London NW3 5PX (☎ 01 794 3950); Hampstead and Highgate Express, Marlborough House, 179/189 Finchley Rd, London NW3 6LB (☎ 01 794 5691)

ISDELL-CARPENTER, Peter; s of Richard Isdell-Carpenter, OBE (d 1986), and Rosemary, *née* Ashworth; *b* 18 Nov 1940; *Educ* Marlborough, St John's Coll Oxford (BA); *m* 28 Sept 1966, Antoinette, da of Louis Cass (d 1952); 1 s (Simon b 1968), 2 da (Katherine b 1968, Nicola b 1970); *Career* Birds Eye Foods Ltd 1964-69, Greys Advertising 1969-70, dir Young and Rubicam Advertising Ltd 1970-78, md Sea Tack Ltd 1978-81, dir of mktg Young and Rubicam (Europe) Ltd 1981-; *Recreations* sailing, skiing, music; *Style—* Peter Isdell-Carpenter, Esq; The Manor House, Newton Valence, nr Alton, Hants (☎ 042058 295); Young and Rubicam Europe Ltd, Greater London House, Hampstead Rd, London NW1 (☎ 01 387 9366, car tel 0836 253 800)

ISHAM, Sir Ian Vere Gyles; 13 Bt (E 1627), of Lamport, Northamptonshire; s of Lt-Col Vere Arthur Richard Isham, MC (d 1968), and suc to kinsman Sir Gyles Isham, 12 Bt (d 1976); *b* 17 July 1923; *Educ* Eton, Worcester Coll Oxford; *Heir* bro, Norman Isham (*qv*); *Career* marketing analyst and cartographer; *Clubs* Overseas; *Style—* Sir Ian Isham, Bt; 40 Turnpike Link, Croydon, Surrey (☎ 01 686 1256)

ISHAM, Norman Murray Crawford; OBE; s of late Lt-Col Vere Arthur Richard Isham, MC; hp of bro, Sir Ian Isham, 13 Bt; *b* 28 Jan 1930; *Educ* Stowe, Univ of Cape Town; *m* 1956, Joan, da of late Leonard James Genet, of Umtali, Zimbabwe; 2 s, 1 da; *Career* architect; civil serv; *Style—* Norman Isham, Esq, OBE; 5 Langton Way, Park Hill, Croydon, Surrey CRO 5JJ

ISHERWOOD, (Samuel) Geoffrey; s of Samuel Rawlinson Isherwood (d 1973), of Blackburn, and Hilda, *née* Chadwick; *b* 28 Sept 1947; *Educ* Clitheroe GS; *m* 9 Sept 1972, Christine, da of Albert Ward (d 1963), of Blackburn; 3 da (Joanne b 1973, Claire b 1976, Pamela b 1980); *Career* slr, ptnr Forbes & Ptnrs; *Recreations* golf, Rotary, motor sport; *Clubs* Wilpshire Golf, Clitheroe Rotary, Lancs Automobile; *Style—* Geoffrey Isherwood, Esq; Carter House, 28 Castle St Clitheroe, Lancashire (☎ 0200 27228, fax 0200 28777)

ISLES, Maj-Gen Donald Edward; CB (1978), OBE (1968); s of Harold Isles (d 1956), and Kathleen, *née* Trenam (d 1979); *b* 19 July 1924; *Educ* Roundhay Sch Leeds, Leeds Univ, RMCS, Jt Serv Staff Coll; *m* 1948, Sheila Mary, *née* Thorpe; 3 s, 1 da; *Career* cmmnd Duke of Wellington's Regt 1943; CO 1 DWR 1965-67, Col GS Royal Armaments Res and Devpt Estab 1971-72, dir of Munitions Br Def Staff Washington 1972-75, dir-gen of Weapons MOD 1975-78, Col DWR 1975-82, ret; dir and dep mangr Br Mfr & Res Co Ltd Grantham 1979-; *Recreations* squash, tennis, shooting; *Clubs* Army and Navy; *Style—* Maj-Gen Donald Isles, CB, OBE; c/o Lloyds Bank plc, 6 Pall Mall, London SW1Y 5NH (☎ office: 0476 65577, telex 37635)

ISMAY, Walter Nicholas; s of John Ismay (d 1962), of Maryport, Cumbria, and Grace, *née* Beasant (d 1980); *b* 20 June 1921; *Educ* Taunton's Sch Southampton, King's Coll London (BSc), Carnegie Inst of Technol Pittsburgh USA; *Career* WW11 1943-46, Capt (final rank), gen list rocket devpt UK, served Combined Intelligence Ops and Special Projectile Ops Gp Germany; tech dir metals div ICI 1957-58, engr dir Yorks Imp Metals Ltd 1958-67, dep chm Yorks Imp Plastics Ltd 1961-67, dep chm and md Milton Keynes Devpt Corpn 1967-71, asst to md McKechnie Bros Ltd (parent co) and md Worcester Parsons Ltd 1972-82; FIMechE 1949- (former cncl memb); *Recreations* sailing; *Clubs* Royal Lymington Yacht; *Style—* Walter Ismay, Esq; Pitlundie, Monument Lane, Walhampton, Lymington, Hants SO41 5SE (☎ 0590 673032)

ISRAEL, Rev Dr Martin Spencer; s of Elie Benjamin Israel (d 1980), of Johannesburg, SA, and Minnie, *née* Israel (d 1957); *b* 30 April 1927; *Educ* Parktown Boys HS Johannesburg SA, Univ of the Witwatersrand SA (MB, ChB); *Career* registrar in pathology Royal Hosp Wolverhampton 1953-55; RAMC 1955-57, Capt; RCS: res fell in pathology 1957-60, lectr in microbiology 1961-66, sr lectr in pathology 1967-81, hon lectr 1982; curate St Michael Cornhill London 1974-76, asst priest Holy Trinity with All Saints S Kensington 1977-82 (p-in-c 1983); pres Guild of Health and Churches' Fellowship for Psychical and Spiritual Studies; MRCP 1952, FRCPath 1975; *Books* General Pathology (with J B Walter 1963), Summons to Life (1974), Precarious Living (1976), Smouldering Fire (1978), The Pain that Heals (1981), Living Alone (1982), The Spirit of Counsel (1983), Healing as Sacrament (1984), The Discipline of Love (1985), Coming in Glory (1986), Gethsemane (1987), The Pearl of Great Price (1988), The Dark Face of Reality (1989), The Quest for Wholeness (1989); *Style—* The Rev Dr Martin Israel; Flat 2, 26 Tregunter Rd, London SW10 9LH

IVANOVIĆ, Vane (Ivan) Stevan; s of Dr Ivan R Ivanović (d 1949), of Zagreb, and Milica, *née* Popović (d 1969); *b* 9 June 1913; *Educ* Westminster, Peterhouse Cambridge (BA, MA); *m* 1939, June Veronica, da of Rev John L Fisher, Canon of Colchester (d 1970); 2 s (Ivan Božidar, Andrija), 1 da (Milica); *Career* serv WWII, Middle E & Italy, Maj; chm: Yugoslav Shipping Ctee 1941 (memb 1941-45), Assoc of Free Yugoslavs 1949-69, Ivanovic & Co 1949-67; consul-gen Monaco in London 1967-; Offr Order of Grimaldi (Monaco) 1975; *Recreations* diving and spear fishing, track and field athletics, jogging, sailing (motor yacht 'Taro'); *Clubs* White's, MCC, Brooks's; *Style—* Vane Ivanovic, Esq, Consul-General of Monaco; 1 Ruelle Ste Barbe, Monaco (☎ 300996); 4 Audley Sq, London W1 (☎ 01 629 0734)

IVE, John Patrick Francis; s of Frank George Ive (d 1973); *b* 20 April 1933; *Educ* Downside; *m* 1956, Elizabeth Anne, *née* Holmes; 2 children; *Career* chm: Hartley Cooper & Co Ltd 1975-79, Hartley Cooper Hldgs Ltd 1977-79; md Market Security Minet Hldgs plc; dir Brownstone Reinsurance Co Ltd (Isle of Man); *Recreations* golf, bird watching, stamp collecting; *Clubs* Annabel's, Knickerbocker (New York), MCC; *Style—* John Ive, Esq; Fidler's Hall, Shackleford, Godalming, Surrey (☎ 0483 810737)

IVEAGH, 3 Earl of (UK 1919); Sir Arthur Francis Benjamin Guinness; 3 Bt (UK 1885); also Baron Iveagh (UK 1891), Viscount Iveagh (UK 1905), Viscount Elveden (UK 1919); s of Maj Arthur Onslow Edward Guinness, Viscount Elveden (ka 1945 - 2 s of 2 Earl), and Lady Elizabeth Hare, da of 4 Earl of Listowel (d 1931); suc gf, 2 Earl of Iveagh, KG, CB, CMG 1967; 1 cous of Rt Hon Paul Channon, MP; *b* 20 May 1937; *Educ* Eton, Trinity Coll Cambridge, Univ of Grenoble; *m* 1963 (m dis 1984), Miranda Daphne Jane, da of Maj Charles Michael Smiley, of Castle Fraser, Aberdeenshire; 2 s (Viscount Elveden, Hon Rory Michael Benjamin b 12 Dec 1974), 2 da; *Heir* s, Viscount Elveden; *Career* memb Irish Senate 1973-77; chm Guinness Group; *Clubs* White's, Royal Yacht Sqdn, Kildare St and Univ (Dublin); *Style—* The Rt Hon the Earl of Iveagh; Guinness Ireland Ltd, St James's Gate Brewery, Dublin 8 (☎ 0001 753645)

IVENS, Michael William; CBE (1983), Ord Nob Del Cihgolo M 1 state (Ccu d: Gtazia Magistrate 1987); s of Harry Guest Ivens, and Nina Ailion; *b* 15 Mar 1924; *Educ* Quinton Sch London; *m* 1, 3 March 1951, Rosalie Joy, da of Bertrand Turnbull (d 1943); 3 s, 1 da; m 2, 17 July 1971 Katherine Patricia, da of John Kellock Laurence; 2 s; *Career* mangr communications dept ESSO 1955-68, jt ed Twentieth Century 1967-72, dir Standard Telephone 1970-71; dir: Fndn for Business Responsibilities 1968-, Aims of Indust 1971-; jt fndr & vice-pres Freedom Assoc 1973-, jt fndr & tstee Research Fndn for Study of Terrorism 1986-; *Books* The Practice of Industrial Communication (1963), Case Studies in Management (1964), The Case for Capitalism (1967), Industry and Valves (1970), Prophets of Freedom & Enterprise (1975); Backman Book of Freedom Quotes (jt ed, 1978); *poetry* Another Sky (1963), Last Waltz (1964), Private and Public (1968), Born Early (1975), No Woman is an Island (1983); *Recreations* writing, reading, campaigning; *Clubs* Carlton; *Style—* Michael Ivens, Esq, CBE; Aims of Industry, 40 Doughty St, London WC1 (☎ 01 405 5195)

IVENS-FERRAZ, Lady Almary (Bridget); *née* Coke; da of 6 Earl of Leicester; *b* 1938; *m* 1963, Peter Ivens-Ferraz; 4 da; *Style—* Lady Almary Ivens-Ferraz; 19 Lady Smith St, Dan Pienaat, Bloemfontein, Orange Free State, S Africa; 33 Sixth Ave, Parktown N, Johannesburg, S Africa

IVES, Prof Kenneth James; s of Walter Leslie Ives (d 1966), of NW London, and Grace Amelia Ives, *née* Curson (d 1983); *b* 29 Nov 1926; *Educ* William Ellis GS London, Univ Coll London (BSc, PhD, DSc); *m* 29 March 1952, Brenda Grace, da of Rev Frederick Walter Tilley (d 1987), of Leatherhead, Surrey; 1 s (Matthew b 1962), 1 da (Cherrill (Mrs Theobald) b 1953); *Career* asst engr Metropolitan Water Bd London 1948-55, prof lectr and reader Univ Coll London 1955-84, res fell Harvard Univ USA 1958-59, visiting assoc prof Univ of N Carolina USA 1964, visiting prof Delft Univ NL 1977, Chadwick prof Univ Coll London 1984-; expert advsr on environmental health WHO 1966-, hon exec ed Int Assoc on Water Pollution Res and Control 1984-; FICE 1952, MASCE 1959, FEng 1986; *Books* The Scientific Basis of Filtration (1975), The Scientific Basis of Flocculation (1978), The Scientific Basis of Flotation (1984), and 100 articles in jls; *Recreations* squash, ballroom dancing; *Style—* Prof Kenneth Ives; Department of Civil and Municipal Engineering, Univ Coll London, Gower St, London WC1E 6BT (☎ 01 380 7224, fax 01 387 8057, telex 296273 UCLENG G)

IVES, William Leonard; OBE (1959); s of Alfred Leonard Ives (d 1962), and Ada Smith (d 1968); *b* 20 April 1906; *Educ* Alleynes GS, King's Coll London (LLB); *m* 1935, Margaret Joyce, da of James Antony (d 1980); *Career* Wing Cdr RAF 1940-45 (despatches), sr offr ic Danube Allied cmd for Austria 1944-45; barr (Middle Temple) 1930; dep parly offr Metropolitan Water Bd 1930-34; dep chm Br Waterways 1955-62, chm nat jt cncl for Inland Waterways Indust 1955-62; memb: cncl Water Companies Assoc 1965-, chartered Inst of Tport 1978-; *Recreations* bridge, foreign travel, RAF; *Style—* William Ives, Esq, OBE; North Down, Upper Stoneborough Lane, Budleigh, Salterton (☎ 039 54 2077)); Tendring Hundred Water Works Company, Manningtree, Essex (☎ 0206 392155, fax 0206 395541)

IVISON, David Malcolm; s of John Ivison (d 1979), of Lichfield and Ruth Ellen *née* Summerfield; *b* 22 Mar 1936; *Educ* King Edward VI Sch Lichfield; *m* 4 Apr 1961, Lieselotte, da of Johannes Verse of Germany; 1 s (Marcel b 1963), 1 da (Nicola b 1965); *Career* RMA Sandhurst 1954-55, RASC 1955-58, Gurkha Tport Regt 1958-80 serv Malaya and Borneo, Army Staff Coll Camberley 1967-68, Lt Col NATO HQ Belgium 1980-83; distribution mangr Tate and Lyle 1984-85, chief exec Inst of Road Tport Engrs 1985-88; MBIM 1969, FCIT 1976, MILDM 1979, MIRTE 1986; *Recreations* swimming, languages, reading; *Style—* David Ivison, Esq; 1 Dundaff Close, Camberley, Surrey, GU15 1AF, (☎ 0276 27778)

IVON JONES, Geoffrey Hugh; DFC (1944); s of Harold Ivon Jones (d 1950), and Gladys Muriel, *née* Fitzgerald (d 1941); *b* 24 May 1916; *Educ* Dauntseys, King Edward VII Sheffield; *m* 16 March 1944, Irina Maya, da of Maj W H Elkins, OBE (d 1968); 1 s (Brian b 1944), 1 da (Tatiana b 1947); *Career* joined 28 Essex Bn TA 1937, embodied 1939, cmmnd RA 1941; serv WWII: Capt 652 Air OP Sqdn 1941-46; md IPPC (Southern) Ltd; ret; *Recreations* falconry, punt gunning, shooting, salmon and trout fishing, stalking, restoring antique furniture; *Clubs* Br Falconers; *Style—* Geoffrey H Ivon Jones, Esq, DFC; 35 East Stratton, nr Winchester, Hampshire SO21 3DU (☎ 0962 89373)

IVORY, (James) Angus; s of Basil Gerritsen Ivory (d 1973), of Jamaica, and Joan Mary, *née* White; *b* 31 July 1931; *Educ* Eton, Guelph Univ Agric Dep Trinity Coll, Toronto Univ Canada (BA); *m* 26 Oct 1956, Nancy Ann, da of William Park, of Toronto, Canada; 2 s (Gavin b 1957, Colin b 1959), 1 da (Gillian b 1964); *Career* md Brown Brothers Harriman Ltd, previously Clark Dodge & Co Inc 1960-74; chm Wall Street Int Corpn 1967-70; memb: Cncl US Investmt Community 1967-70, UK Assoc of New York Stock Exchange, Firms 1980-82, Cncl Securities Indust 1980-82; *Recreations* hunting, farming; *Clubs* Lansdowne; *Style—* Angus Ivory, Esq; Greenway Farm, Tockenham, Swindon SN4 7PP (☎ 079385 2367); 11 Warwick Square, London SW1 (☎ 01 834 5968); Brown Bros Harriman Ltd, Garden Hse, 18 Finsbury Circus, London EC2M 7BP

IVORY, Brian Gammell; s of Eric James Ivory (*qv*); *b* 10 April 1949; *Educ* Eton, Magdalene Coll Cambridge (MA); *m* 21 Feb 1981, Oona Mairi Macphie, da of Archibald Ian Bell-MacDonald (d 1987); 1 s (Euan b 1986); *Career* CA; dir The Highland Distilleries Co plc 1978 (and principal subsidiary) Matthew Gloag & Son Ltd 1987-; Scottish Arts Cncl - cncl memb 1983; chm Combined Arts Cttee and memb of Policy & Resources Cttee 1984; *Recreations* the arts, farming, hill-walking, travel; *Clubs* New (Edinburgh); *Style—* Brian Ivory; Brewlands, Glenisla, by Glairgowrie, Perthshire PH11 8PL; 12 Anne St, Edinburgh EH4 1PJ; The Highland Distilleries Company plc, 106 West Nile St, Glasgow G1 2QY (☎ 041 322 7511, fax 041 332 6697)

IVORY, James Francis; s of Capt Edward Patrick Ivory, US Army (d 1967), of Dinuba California, and Hallie Millicent, *née* De Loney (d 1963); *b* 7 June 1928; *Educ* Univ of Oregon (BA), Univ of Southern California (MA); *Career* founder Merchant Ivory Produs (with Ismail Merchant and Ruth Prawer Jhabvala) 1963; films incl: Shakespeare Wallah (1965), Savages (1972), Autobiography of a Princess (1975), Roseland (1977), Hullabaloo Over Georgie and Bonnie's Pictures (1978), The Europeans (1979), Quartet (1981), Heat and Dust (1983), The Bostonians (1984), A Room with a View (1986, nominated best dir Acad Awards 1987), Maurice (1987, Silver Lion Venice Film Festival), Slaves of New York (1989); Guggenheim fell 1975; memb: Dirs Guild of America, Writers Guild of America; *Recreations* looking at pictures; *Style*— James Ivory, Esq; Patroon St, Claverack, New York 12513, USA (☎ 518 851 7808); Merchant Ivory Productions, 46 Lexington St, London W1 (☎ 01 437 1200/01 439 4335)

IZAT, (Alexander) John Rennie; s of Sir James Rennie Izat (d 1962), of Balliesk, and Lady (Eva Mary Steen) Izat, *née* Cairns (d 1984); *b* 14 July 1932; *Educ* Trinity Coll Glenalmond, Oriel Coll Oxford (MA); *m* 12 April 1958, Frederica Ann, da of Colin Champness McNiel, of Hants; 1 s (Alexander b 1959), 2 da (Davina b 1958, Rosann b 1963); *Career* stockbroker; ptnr Williams de Broe & Co London 1955-75; John Izat & Ptnrs: Balliliesk and Naemoor 1961-87, High Cocklaw 1987-; dir: United Auctions (Scotland) Ltd, Holiday Cottages (Scotland) Ltd, Cromlix Estates, C Champness & Co, Shires Investmt plc, Wiston Invesmt Co; chm: U A Properties Ltd, U A Forestry Ltd; farmer; past pres Fife-Kinross NFU & Kinross Agric Assoc, dir Royal Highland Agric Assoc 1985-; chm: Scottish Woods and Forest Awards Sch Shield Competition; memb cncl Trinity Coll Glenalmond; JP; *Recreations* shooting, suffolk sheep; *Style*— John Izat, Esq, JP; High Cocklaw, Berwick-upon-Tweed TD15 1UZ (☎ 0289 86591)

IZATT, Gordon Wilson; s of Alexander Izatt (d 1960), and Elizabeth Smith, *née* Brown; *b* 21 April 1921; *Educ* Glasgow HS, Glasgow Univ (BL); *m* 1, 1945, Kathleen Edith, *née* James (d 1975); 3 da (Lesley b 1946, Elizabeth b 1948, Fiona b 1951); m 2, 1980, Mary Drummond Sempill, da of James Watson Thomson Geddie (d 1973); *Career* WWII Sub Lt RN (Fleet Air Arm) 1941-46, served Home, Eastern and Med Fleets inc Salerno landings; slr, snr ptnr Condie Mackenzie & Co WS Perth ret 1987; pres Soc of Procurators & Slrs in the city and co of Perth 1983-85; tstee numerous family tsts and co dir; memb of Lloyds; *Recreations* golf; *Clubs* Royal Perth Golf Soc, Co and City, Royal and Ancient Golf, Hon Co of Edinburgh Golfers; *Style*— Gordon W Izatt, Esq; Chapel Green House, Earlsferry, Leven, Fife KY9 1AD (☎ 0333 330422)

J

JACK, Hon Sir Alieu Sulayman; *b* 14 July 1922; *Educ* St Augustine's Sch; *m* 1936, Yai Marie Cham; 4 s, 4 da (and 1 da decd); *Career* md Gambia Nat Trading Co 1948-72, min for Works and Communications The Gambia 1972-77, speaker of the House of Representatives Gambia 1977- (also 1962-72); Grand Cdr and Chancellor National Order of The Gambia 1972; kt 1970; *Style—* Hon Sir Alieu Jack; PO Box 376, Banjul, The Gambia (☎ 930 2204; House of Representatives, The Republic of The Gambia (☎ 241)

JACK, Gordon Daniel; s of Dr James Dalrymph Jack, MC (d 1943), of Durham, and Bessie, *née* Cross (d 1939); *b* 21 June 1918; *Educ* Durham Sch, Edinburgh Univ (MB ChB); *m* 27 Sept 1947, Eileen Lydia, da of Alwyn Howarth Thwaite (d 1954), of Coxhoe, Co Durham; 1 s (Antony b 1952), 1 da (Allison b 1949); *Career* MO (surgn) RAF mobile field hosp Bengal Burma Cmd 1944-46; trainee dept of Surgery Edinburgh 1947-52, cardiothoracic surgn Wythenshaw Hosp 1952-77; FRCS Edinburgh; *Recreations* golf, gardening, bird watching; *Clubs* Royal St Davids GC;; *Style—* Gordon Jack, Esq; Llechwedd Du Bach, Harlech, Gwynedd LL46 2UU (☎ Harlech 780 427)

JACK, (John) Michael; MP (C) Flyde 1987-; s of Ralph Niven, of York, and Florence Edith, *née* Reed; mothers family Hewish of Devon said to have arrived with William the Conqueror; *b* 17 Sept 1946; *Educ* Bradford GS, Bradford Tech Coll, Leicester Univ (BA Econ, MPhil); *m* 1976, Alison Jane, da of Cncllr Brian Rhodes Musgrave; 2 s (Edmund b 1979, Oliver b 1981); *Career* sale dir L O Jeffs Ltd 1980-87, previously with Marks & Spencer and Procter & Gamble; *Recreations* motor sport, Boule player; *Style—* Michael Jack, Esq, MP; House of Commons, Westminster, London SW1A 0AA

JACK, Raymond Evan; QC (1982); s of Evan Stuart Maclean Jack, and Charlotte, *née* Fry; *b* 13 Nov 1942; *Educ* Rugby, Trinity Coll Cambridge (MA); *m* 1 Oct 1976, Elizabeth Alison (Liza), da of Canon James Seymour Denys Mansel, KCVO; 1 s (Alexander b 1986), 1 da (Katherine b 1979, Lucy b 1981); *Career* called to the Bar Inner Temple 1976, SE Circuit;; *Style—* Raymond Jack, Esq, QC; 1 Hare Court, Temple, London EC4Y 7BE (☎ 01 353 3171, 01 583 9127, telex 8814348)

JACK, Prof Robert Barr; s of Robert Hendry Jack (d 1966), of Ayrshire, and Christina Alexandra, *née* Barr (d 1961); *b* 18 Mar 1928; *Educ* Kilsyth Acad, Glasgow HS, Glasgow Univ (MA, LLB); *m* 1958, Anna Thorburn, da of George Harris Thomson, of Glasgow; 2 s (Robert Thomson Barr b 1961, David George b 1963); *Career* slr; sr ptnr McGrigor Donald Glasgow and Edinburgh; prof of mercantile law Glasgow; memb: co law ctee Law Soc of Scotland 1971- (convener 1978-85), Scottish Law Cmmn 1974-77, DOT advsr panel co law 1980-82, Cncl for the Securities Industry 1983-85; lay memb Cncl of the Stock Exchange 1984-86, independent Bd of the Securities Assoc Ltd 1986-, Scottish observer on DOT Insolvency Law Review Ctee 1977-82; chm: Brownlee plc 1984-86, Joseph Dunn (Bottlers) Ltd 1983-, Review Ctee on Banking Servs Law 1987-; dir: Bank of Scotland 1985-, Scottish Met Property plc 1980-, Scottish Mutual Assurance Soc 1987-, Clyde FC Ltd 1980-; chm Scottish Nat Cncl of YMCAs 1966-73 (pres 1983-), govr Hutchesons' Educnl Tst Glasgow 1978-87 (chm 1980-87), chm The Turnberry Tst; *Publications* Various Aspects of Company Law, The Statutory Regulation and Self-Regulation of the City; *Recreations* golf, football, the Isle of Arran; *Clubs* Caledonian, Western (Glasgow), Pollok Golf, Shiskine Golf and Tennis (Isle of Arran); *Style—* Prof Robert Jack; 39 Mansewood Road, Glasgow G43 1TN (☎ (041) 632 1659); McGrigor Donald, Pacific House, 70 Wellington Street, Glasgow G2 6SB (telex 778744 MCGDGLWG)

JACK, Roland Maclean; s of Evan Stuart Maclean Jack, and Charlotte Ellen, *née* Fry; *b* 22 July 1948; *Educ* Oundle; *m* 24 June 1978, Hon Fiona Georgina, da of Lord Ironside; 1 s (Oliver Edmund Maclean b 7 Nov 1983), 1 da (Anthea Audrey Charlotte b 30 March 1985); *Career* dir: Turner Porter Assocs 1984-85, McCann Consultancy 1986-88; managing ptnr Dark Horse Design 1988-; *Recreations* running, photography; *Style—* Roland Jack, Esq; The Old Vicarage, Lyford, nr Wantage, Oxfordshire OX12 0EF; The Old Vicarage Studio, Lyford, nr Wantage, Oxfordshire OX12 0EF (☎ 023587 8036, fax 023587 8084)

JACK, Dr William Logan; JP (Hertfordshire); s of Dr Robert Lockhart Jack, DSC (d 1964), of 52 Clowes St, Melbourne, Aust, and Frances Augusta, *née* Marr (d 1963); *b* 25 Dec 1907; *Educ* St Peter's Coll Adelaide, Univ of Adelaide (MB BS); *m* 15 May 1940, Dorothy Margaret, da of Lt-Col G W Dryland, of Pitfour, Kington, Hereford; 3 s (Robert Logan b 1941, William Logan b 1946, Ian Logan b 1948), 2 da (Felicity Logan (Mrs Hutchings) b 1943, Veronica Logan (Mrs Allen) b 1948); *Career* surgn Kington Hosp 1933-78; chm KUDC 1947-52 (memb 1945), govr Lady Hawkins Sch Kington 1952-, chm Kington Horse Show 1951-72, fndr memb (currently pres) Llangaorse SC 1952-, vice-pres (formerly chm) N Hereford Cons Assoc, vice chm Hereford & Worcs branch Magistrates Assoc 1972-77; *Style—* Dr William Jack, JP; Huntington Court, Huntington Kingdon, Hereford (☎ 0544 230330)

JACKLIN, Robert Arthur; s of Frederick Arthur Jacklin (d 1978), of Colchester, Essex, and Edith Emily, *née* Howard (d 1982); *b* 10 April 1934; *Educ* Culford Sch Bury St Edmonds, Emmanuel Coll, Cambridge (MA); *m* 20 April 1967, Penelope Grace, da of Charles Arthur Godwin Lywood, (d 1970); 1 s (Michael b 1969), 2 da (Annabel b 1970, Rosamond b 1975); *Career* Nat Serv 2 Lt RA 1953-55, Capt Essex Yeo (TA) 1955-65; slr 1962; sr ptnr Sparling Benham & Brough 1984 (ptnr 1969-); former pres: dist sports cncl Rotary Club, vice chm Age Concern Colchester, hon sec Abbeyfield Colchester Soc; memb Law Soc 1962; *Recreations* sailing, music, fell walking; *Clubs* Colchester Garrison Officers, Royal Harwich YC; *Style—* Robert Jacklin, Esq; 3 West Stockwell St, Colchester, Essex, CO1 1HQ, (☎ 0206 577767, fax 0206 564551)

JACKMAN, Bernard George Lovell; s of Leonard Jackman (d 1962); *b* 29 Oct 1914; *Educ* Bablake Sch Coventry, London Univ; *m* 1940, Joyce Alfreda, *née* Litchfield; 1 s, 1 da; *Career* dir and gen mangr Lockheed Hydraulic Brake Co Ltd 1956-64, md Rover Co Ltd and Rover-Triumph (BL) 1972-75, industrial conslt Bernard Jackman Ltd 1975-84, chm Stonefield Vehicles Ltd 1977-80; dir: Export Packing Service Ltd Banbury, Manor Armour Ltd Bridgwater 1977-84; Freeman City of London, Liveryman Worshipful Co of Clockmakers (Master 1984); CEng; *Recreations* shooting, fishing, veteran cars; *Clubs* Flyfishers', Veteran Car; *Style—* Bernard Jackman, Esq; Stour View, Halford, nr Shipston on Stour, Warwicks

JACKMAN, Air Marshal Sir (Harold) Douglas; KBE (1959, CBE 1943), CB (1946); s of A J Jackman (d 1938); *b* 26 Oct 1902; *Educ* HMS Worcester; *m* 1931, Marjorie Leonore, da of A Hyland (d 1960); *Career* joined RAF 1926, served WWII (despatches 5), Gp Capt 1941, idc 1948, Air Vice-Marshal 1953, AOC 40 Gp RAF 1953-55, dir-gen of equipment Air Miny 1955-58, Air Marshal 1958, AOC-in-C Maintenance Cmd 1958-61, ret 1961; co-ordinator Anglo-American relations Air Miny 1961-64; Order of George with Swords Greece 1946, AFC Greece 1946; *Recreations* golf, woodworking; *Clubs* Durban Country, Overseas; *Style—* Air Marshal Sir Douglas Jackman, KBE, CB; 7 Poynton Place, Durban 4001, South Africa (☎ 294151)

JACKMAN, Frederick Charles; s of Stanley Charles Jackman (d 1978), of Brentwood, Essex, and Lilian May, *née* Brassett; *b* 29 Feb 1944; *Educ* Warren Sch Dagenham, Barking Coll of Technol, Borough Poly (HNC); *m* 14 June 1969, Zarene, da of Karim Gulam Husain (d 1973), of London; *Career* Stinton Jones & Ptnrs 1960-64, Costain Construction 1964-66, TP Bennett & Son 1966-69, Arvp Assocs 1969-73, Upton Assoc Bldg Servs consulting engrs 1973- 9resident Dubai 1976, sr ptnr 1979-); MConsE, FCIBSE, FIHospE; *Recreations* travel, walking, fishing; *Clubs* Phyllis Court (Henley); *Style—* Frederick Jackman, Esq; New House, Holyport Rd, Maidenhead, Berks (☎ 0628 34102); Upton Associates, Pilot House, West Wycombe Rd, High Wycombe, Bucks HP12 3AB (☎ 0494 450 931, telex 83684)

JACKSON, Andrew Graham; s of Thomas Armitage Geoffrey Jackson (d 1985), and Hilda Marion Jackson; *b* 5 May 1937; *Educ* Denstone Coll, Jesus Coll Cambridge (MA); *m* 1964, Christine Margaret, da of Charles Edward Chapman, of Oundle; 1 s (Matthew b 1971), 2 da (Sarah b 1967, Claire b 1969); *Career* Lt Nat Serv Served Suez 1956; Stewarts & Lloyds Corby 1960-67, joined Denco Hldgs Ltd 1967 (sales mangr 1967-69, sales dir 1969-72, dep md 1972-77, gp md 1977-85), dir AMEC Projects Ltd 1985-86, md Keg Services Ltd 1986-; Lloyds underwriter; pres Hereford Dist Scouts Assoc; Liveryman: Worshipful Co of Carmen, Worshipful Co of Engrs; CEng, MBIM, FIMechE; *Recreations* squash, water skiing, scuba diving; *Clubs* RAC; *Style—* Andrew Jackson, Esq; The Orchard, Lyde, Hereford (☎ 0432 272 830); Keg Services Ltd, Twyford Rd, Hereford HR2 6JR (☎ 0432 353 300, fax 0432 268 141)

JACKSON, Andrew Joseph; s of Joseph William Jackson, and Dorothy Mary, *née* Swingler; *b* 3 June 1955; *Educ* Queens Coll Taunton (LLB); *m* 22 May 1982, Morag Elizabeth Anne, da of William John Lewis, of Bournemouth; 2 s (Marc Andrew b 1985, James William b 1987); *Career* slr, ptnr Messrs Turners Slrs, dir A & M Properties Dorset Ltd; *Style—* Andrew Jackson, Esq; Morn Gate Park, Dorchester, Dorset; Turners, 1 Poole Road, Bournemnouth, Dorset DT2 9DS (☎ 0202 291291)

JACKSON, Andrew Michael; s of Anthony Hargreaves Jackson, of Boughton, Northampton, and Evelyn Mary, *née* Anson (d 1987); *b* 27 Feb 1940; *Educ* Sedbergh; *m* 1 April 1967, Jillian Felicity, da of Denys Gordon Parfitt, of Shalford, Guildford, Surrey; 1 s (David Richard Anthony b 5 March 1968); *Career* admitted slr 1965, ptnr Hutson Poole 1984, Notary Public 1986; memb Guildford Rotary Club, cncl memb Guildford and Dist C of C, sec Surrey Business Enterprise Agency; memb Law Soc 1965, Notaries Soc 1986; *Recreations* inland cruising, carriage driving; *Clubs* The County (Guildford); *Style—* Andrew Jackson, Esq; Tangley Field, Wonersh, Guildford, Surrey GU5 0PY (☎ 0483 65719); Hutson Poole Solicitors, 17 & 18 Quarry St, Guildford, Surrey GU1 3XA (☎ 0483 65244, fax 0483 575 961)

JACKSON, Ashley Norman; s of Norman Valentine Jackson (POW Malaya, executed 1944/45), and Dulcie Olga, *née* Scott (Mrs Haigh); *b* 22 Oct 1940; *Educ* St Joseph's Singapore, Holyrood Barnsley S Yorks, Barnsley Coll of Art; *m* 22 Dec 1962, (Patricia) Anne, da of Donald Hutchinson, of Barnsley, S Yorks; 2 da (Heather b 11 Nov 1968, Claudia b 15 Sept 1970); *Career* artist; exhibited: RI, RBA, RWS, Britain in Watercolour, UA; one man shows: Upper Grosvenor Gallery, Mall Gallery, Christina Foyle Gallery, Spanish Inst of Culture, London, New York, Chicago, San Francisco, Washington, Dallas; works in the collections of: MOD, RN, NCB, British Gas, NUM; own tv series on BBC 1, Channel 4 and PBS in America; memb bd of govrs Barnsley Coll of Art, chm Yorks Watercolour Soc, bd memb and appeals chm Prince's Youth Business Tst W Yorks, chm: FRSA 1964; *Books* My Own Flesh and Blood (1981), The Artist's Notebook (1985), Ashley Jackson's World of Art 1 and 2 (1988); *Style—* Ashley Jackson, Esq; The Studio, 13-15 Huddersfield Rd, Holmfirth, Huddersfield (☎ 0484 686460)

JACKSON, Barry Trevor; s of late Arthur Stanley Jackson, of Chingford, and Violet May, *née* Fry; *b* 7 July 1936; *Educ* Sir George Monoux GS, King's Coll London, Westminster Med Sch; *m* 1962, Sheila May, da of late Bert Wood, of Bollington Cheshire; 2 s (Simon, James), 1 da (Sarah); *Career* surgn to HM's Household 1983-; conslt surgn: St Thomas' Hosp 1972-, King Edward VII Hosp for Offrs 1983-; sec Assoc Surgn of GB and Iceland 1986-; memb: Ct of Examiners RCS England 1983-, Cncl RSM; MS, FRCS; *Recreations* book collecting, reading, opera, the arts generally; *Clubs* Athenaeum; *Style—* Barry Jackson, Esq; Mapledene, 7 St Matthew's Ave,

Surbiton, Surrey KT6 6JJ; St Thomas' Hosp, London SE1 7EH; 53 Harley Street, London W11DD

JACKSON, Betty (Mrs David Cohen); MBE (1987); da orf Arthur Jackson (d 1977), of Lancs, and Phyllis Gertrude, *née* Rains (d 1983); *b* 24 June 1949; *Educ* Bacup and Rawtenstall GS Lancs, Birmingham Coll Art and Design; *m* 14 Jan 1986, David Cohen, s of Mansour Cohen (d 1977), of Marseille, France; 1 s (Oliver Mansour b 1987), 1 da (Pacale Phyllis b 1986); *Career* chief designer Quorum 1973, fndr Betty Jackson Ltd 1981; fell Birmingham Univ 1988, Br Designer of the Year 1985; RDI 1988; *Clubs* Moscow, Grouchos; *Style—* Miss Betty Jackson; 33 Tottenham St, London W1P 9PE (☎ 01 631 1010, fax 01 323 0609, car tel 0860 371 601, telex 25663 Betty J G)

JACKSON, Very Rev Brandon Donald; s of Herbert Jackson (d 1977), and Millicent, *née* Haddock (d 1980); *b* 11 August 1934; *Educ* Stockport Sch, Liverpool and Oxford Univs (LLB); *m* 1958, Mary Lindsay, da of John Philip; 2 s (Timothy Philip b 1959, Robert Brandon b 1961), 1 da (Sarah Lindsay b 1964); *Career* curate: Chist Church New Malden Surrey 1958-61, St George Leeds 1961-65; vicar St Peters Shipley 1965-77, provast Bradford Cath 1977-89, Dean of Lincoln 1989-; memb: Gen Synod of the C of E 1970-77 and 1980-87, Gen Synod Marriages Cmmn 1974-78; church cmmr 1971-73; memb: Cncl of Wycliffe Hall Oxford 1971-85, St John's Coll Nottingham 1986; govr Harrogate Coll 1974-84, and Bradford GS 1977, scriptwriter consIt Stars on Sunday, Emmerdale Farm; provost; *Recreations* sport, cricket, squash, fell-walking, fishing, reading; *Style—* The Very Rev the Dean of Lincoln; The Deanery, Lincoln, LN2 1PX

JACKSON, Calvin Leigh Raphael; s of Air Cdre John Arthur George Jackson CBE, DFC, AFC, of Somerset House, Wimbledon Common, London and Yolanda de Felicé Jackson; *b* 13 August 1952; *Educ* Douai Sch, Kings Coll, Univ of London (LLB, LLM) Corpus Chrish Coll Cambridge (MPhil); *Career* called to the Bar Lincolns Inn 1975, practice at bar 1981-83, govt legal serv 1983-85, sr compensation consIt William M Mercer Fraser Ltd 1985-87, sr tax mangr Deloitte Haskins & Sells 1987-; memb Hon Soc of Lincolns Inn;; *Clubs* Utd Oxford and Cambridge; *Style—* Calvin Jackson, Esq; c/o Deloitte Haskins & Sells, Business and Executive Tax Group, PO Box 198, Hillgate House, 26 Old Bailey, London EC4M 7PL (☎ 01 248 3913), fax (01 236 2367), telex 8955899 DHSHHG

JACKSON, Charles Vivian; s of Louis Charles Jackson, MC, of E Sussex, and Sylvia, *née* Kerr; *b* 2 July 1953; *Educ* Marlborough, Magdalen Coll Oxford (MA), Stanford (MBA); *m* 12 Feb 1982, Frances Miriam, da of Frederick Schwartzstein (d 1982), of NJ; 1 s (David b 1985), 1 da (Rebecca b 1983); *Career* dir: Warburg Investmt Mgmnt 1985-, Mercury Bond 1985-, Munich London 1986-; md Mercury Asset Mgmnt Hldgs 1987- (dir 1986-87); *Clubs* Travellers'; *Style—* Charles Jackson, Esq; 33 King William St, London EC4R 9AS (☎ 01 280 2800)

JACKSON, Christopher Murray; MEP (C) Kent East 1979-; s of Rev Howard Murray Jackson (d 1955), and Doris Bessie Jackson; *b* 24 May 1935; *Educ* Kingswood Sch Bath, Magdalen Coll Oxford (MA), Frankfurt Univ, LSE; *m* 1971, Carlie Elizabeth, da of Bernard Sidney Keeling; 1 s, 1 da; *Career* d Nat Serv cmmd pilot RAF; former dir of corporate devpt Spillers Ltd, Cons pty spokesman on co-operation with developing countries 1981-1986, Cons party spokesman on agric 1987; *Style—* Christopher Jackson Esq, MEP; Sevenoaks, Private Office. 8, Wellmeade Drive, Kent TN13 1QA (☎ 0732 456688)

JACKSON, Daphne Diana; da of Maj Thomas Casey MC, (d 1958), of Nairobi, Kenya, and Agnes Nora, *née* Gradden; *b* 8 Oct 1933; *Educ* Folkestone GS; *m* 18 July 1953, John Hudleston Jackson, s of Henry John Huddlestone Jackson, (d 1945), of Newcastle, Staffs; *Career* personnel and central servs off borough engr and surveyor's dept London Borough of Hounslow 1968-86, asst personnel offr city engrs dept City of Birmingham 1986-; chairperson Gen Advsy Ctee IBA 1985- (memb 1980-), memb nat employment ctee, Nat Assoc for the Care and Rehabilitation of Offenders 1984-86, memb WI and Soroptimist Int; Freeman City of London 1980, memb Worshipful Co of Chartered Secs and Admins 1980; ACIS; *Recreations* bereavement cnsllr, reading, embroidery, learning about antiques; *Style—* Mrs John Jackson; 3 Manor Ct, Cleeve Prior, Evesham, Worcs WR11 5LQ (☎ 0789 772817); Personnel Div, City Engineer's Department, 1 Lancaster Circus, Queensway, Birmingham (☎ 021 300 7842)

JACKSON, Prof Daphne Frances; OBE 1987; da of Albert Henry Jackson (d 1951), of Peterborough, Cambs, and Frances Ethel, *née* Elliot (d 1985); *b* 23 Sept 1936; *Educ* Peterborough GS for Girls, Imperial Coll of Sci and Technol London (BSc, ARCS), Battersea Coll of Technol London (PhD), Univ of London (DSc); *Career* lectr Battersea Coll of Tech 1960-66, prof of physics and head dept of physics Univ of Surrey 1971- (reader 1967-71), dean faculty of sci Univ of Surrey 1984-88; visiting prof: Univ of Maryland 1970, Université de Louvain Belgium 1972, Univ of Lund Sweden 1980-82; visiting physicist Inst Cancer Res 1979-80; dir: Surrey Med Imaging Systems Ltd 1986-, Surrey Univ Press 1984-; memb: BBC Sci Cnslt Gp, USC physical sci sub-ctee, advsy cncl R & D for Fuel and Power, cncl IEE, W Surrey and NE Hants DHA (vice chm 1983-84), CSTI Health Care Advsy Ctee; hon sec Women's Engrg Soc (pres 1983-85), tstee Verena Holmes Lectur Fd, hon pres Hereward (Peterborough) SATRO, memb cncl Surrey SATRO; Freeman City of London, Liveryman Worshipful Co of Engrs; Hon DUniv Open Univ 1987 Hon DSc Exeter Univ 1988; FInstP 1966, FIEE 1984; *Books* Imaging With Ionising Radiations (jtly 1982), Nuclear Sizes and Structure (jtly, 1977), Nuclear Reactions (1970), Concepts of Atomic Physics (1971); *Recreations* writing, helping women and girls in science and engineering;; *Clubs* Nat Liberal; *Style—* Prof Daphne Jackson, OBE; 5 St Omer Rd, Guildford, Surrey GU1 2DA (☎ 0483 573 996); Dept of Physics, Guildford, Surrey GU2 5XH (☎ 0483 509166, fax 0483 300 803, telex 859331)

JACKSON, Prof David Cooper; s of Rev James Jackson (d 1983), and Mary Emma Jackson; *b* 3 Dec 1931; *Educ* Ashville Coll Harrogate, Brasenose Coll Oxford (BCL, MA); *m* 1967, Roma Lilian, da of late William Pendergast; *Career* barr Inner Temple; pt/t prof of law Univ of Southampton (prof of law 1971-84, dean 1972-75, and 1978-81, dep vice chllr 1983-84); consIt: Inst of Maritime Law Southampton (dir 1983-84; 1987), Shipping Legislation UNCTAD 1979-80 and 1983-84; vice pres Immigration Appeal Tbnl; visiting prof: QMC London 1969, Arizona State Univ 1976; Sir John Latham prof of law Monash Univ Aust 1966-70; *Books* Principles of Property Law (1967), The Conflicts Process (1975), The Enforcement of Maritime Claims (1985), World Shipping Laws (gen ed, 1979), Civil Jurisdiction and Judgment: Maritime Claim (1987); *Recreations* travel; *Style—* Prof David Jackson; office: 231 Strand, London (☎ 01 353 8060)

JACKSON, Sir (John) Edward; KCMG (1984, CMG 1977); *b* 21 August 1925; *Educ* Ardingly, Corpus Christi Coll Cambridge; *m* 1952, Eve Stainton, *née* Harris; 2 s, 1 da; *Career* Sub Lt 1943-46 RNVR; Dip Serv; Br Embassy Paris 1949-52, Br Embassy Bonn 1956-59, NATO Def Coll 1969, cnsllr and political advsr Br Mil Govt Berlin 1969-73, head def dept FCO 1973-75, head UK Delgn on Mutual and Balanced Reduction of Forces in Central Europe (ambassadpr) 1980-82, ambassador to Brussels 1982-85 (Havana 1975-79); chm Brecon Beacons Natural Waters - Spadel (UK) Ltd 1985-; dir: Herbert Mueller Ltd, Sheppee Holdings Ltd, MEI Engrg plc 1987-, Armistice Festival 1985-; tstee Imperial War Museum 1985-, chm Anglo-Belgian Soc, dep chm Belgo-Luxembourg C of C; *Recreations* tennis, golf, the arts.; *Clubs* Travellers, Anglo-Belgian, Hurlingham; *Style—* Sir Edward Jackson, KCMG

JACKSON, Enid, Lady; Enid; da of Stanley Hugh Groome (d 1965), of Kingston-upon-Thames; *m* 1, 1937 (m dis 1950), as his 2 w, (Alfred) Chester Beatty (d 1983); m 2, 1953, Sir John Montrésor Jackson, 6 Bt (d 1980); *Style—* Enid, Lady Jackson; Rose Cottage, Charing, Kent TN27 0EN

JACKSON, Gordon Cameron; OBE (1979); s of Thomas Jackson (d 1946), of Glasgow, and Margaret McGregor, *née* Fletcher (d 1972); *b* 19 Dec 1923; *Educ* Hillhead HS Glasgow; *m* 2 June 1951, Rona Arbuthnot, da of James Anderson (d 1961), of Edinburgh; 2 s (Graham b 1959, Roderick b 1961); *Career* actor; films: Four men went to France (1941), Whisky Galore (1948), Tunes of Glory (1960), Great Escape (1962), The Whistle Blower (1987), The Shooting Party (1985); theatre: Moby Dick (1955), Macbeth (1966), Wise Child (1967), Hamlet (1969), Hedda Gabler (1970), Noah and Twelfth Night (1976), A Town Like Alice (1981), Cards on the Table and Mass Appeal (1983), The Kingfisher (1987); TV: Upstairs Downstairs (1970-1975), The Professionals (1977-1981), My Brother Tom (1986), Noble House (1987), Look to the Lady, Winslow Boy; Clarence Derwent Award 1969, Royal TV Soc Award 1975, USA Emmy Award 1976, Australian Logie Award 1982; *Recreations* music (especially Mozart), gardening; *Clubs* Garrick; *Style—* Gordon Jackson, Esq, OBE; ICM Ltd, 388 Oxford Street, London W1N 9HE (☎ 01 629 8080, telex 885974)

JACKSON, Graeme; s of Lewis Reginald Jackson, and Winifred Ivy Jackson; *b* 13 Mar 1943; *Educ* Brighton Coll; *m* 1, 22 Nov 1963, Elizabeth (decd); 1 s (Richard Andrew St John b 22 April 1964); m 2, 10 Aug 1972 (m dis 1980), Janet, da of Robert Tyndall; *Career* jr surveyor Ibbet Moseley Card 1959-61, surveyor Donaldson & Co 1961-64, dir Central of Dist Properties plc 1966-71 (surveyor 1964-66), chm London and Manchester Securities plc 1971-83, chm and chief exec Warringtons plc 1986-; *Recreations* ocean racing, real tennis, opera; *Clubs* RORC, Island SC, Queens (Royal Berkshire); *Style—* Graeme Jackson, Esq; 56 Grosvenor Hill, London W1X 2JE (☎ 01 499 2997); Burnside Cottage, Isle-of-Harris, Western Isles, Scotland; 12 Commandore Club, Punta Gorda, Florida, USA; 74 Grosvenor St, London W1X 9DD (☎ 01 491 2768, fax 01 499 0589, car 0860 344539)

JACKSON, Ina, Lady; Ina; da of James Leonard Joyce, FRCS, of Reading; *m* 1966, as his 2 w, Sir William Jackson, 7 Bt (d 1985); *Style—* Ina, Lady Jackson; 8 West View, Brampton, Cumbria CA8 1QC

JACKSON, John Fabian Brindley; CBE (1976); s of John Millington Jackson (d 1918), and Elise, *née* Wood (d 1975); *b* 8 May 1912; *Educ* Giggleswick sch, Manchester Univ (BSc); *m* 1940, Winifred Elaine, da of Raymond Swift (d 1977), 2 s (Roger, Simon), 2 da (Ann, Katherine); *Career* dir of research Br Steel Castings Research Assoc 1949-54, dir APV Hldgs Ltd 1961-77; chm: PI Castings Gp Ltd 1971-82, Crawley Indust Gp 1973-76; consIt to Dept of Indust 1977-80 , dep chm Defence Mfrs Assoc 1979-81; *Recreations* fly fishing, philately, genealogy; *Clubs* RAC;; *Style—* John Jackson, Esq, CBE; Out Rake, Coniston, Cumbria (☎ (0966) 41363); La Rambla del Mar, Los Realejos, Bajo, Tenerife

JACKSON, (Henry) John; s of James William Jackson, and Annie Margaret, *née* Best; *b* 10 Sept 1937; *Educ* Hackney Downs GS, Pitman's Coll; *m* 17 Aug 1972, Jill Yvonne, da of Albert Horace Ireson, OBE, of Seaford E Sussex; *Career* served: 67 Trg Regt RAC 1955, 1 King's Dragoon Gds 1956-58, 28 Cwlth Inf Bde, 17 Gurkha Div Malaya; telephone typist Press Assoc Sport 1952-54, sub ed The Scotsman 1954-55, racing reporter and sub ed Press Assoc Sport 1958-62, racing sub ed Daily Telegraph Sport 1962-66, reporter Ilford Pictorial 1966-67, educn and parly corr London Evening News 1967-75, parly rep Press Assoc 1975-76, freelance 1976-79, reporter Saudi Press Agency 1979-80, ed Municipal Journal 1980 (dir 1986-); pres London Govt PR Assoc; memb: Cromwell Assoc, Br Horse Soc, Br Field Sports Soc, Assoc of Civil Defence and Emergency Planning Offrs, Soc Industl Emergency Servs Offrs, Redbridge LBC 1968-74; Parly candidate (c) Erith Crayford 1970 and Hornchurch 1974, chm Ilford North Cons Assoc 1972-74; Freeman City of London, memb Worshipful Co of Loriners; MICD 1987; *Recreations* horseriding, cricket, English Civil War history; *Clubs* MCC, Carlton, City Livery; *Style—* John Jackson, Esq; Wingfield Farm, Wing, Leighton Buzzard LU7 0LD (☎ 0296 688 972); Municipal Journal, 178-202 Great Portland Street, London W1N 6NH (☎ 01 637 2400, fax 01 631 4338, telex 262568)

JACKSON, John Maxwell (Max); s of Herbert Wilfred Jackson (d 1965), and Dorothy, *née* Jefferson (d 1941); *b* 24 May 1915; *Educ* Hymers Coll Hull; *m* 10 Aug 1943, Caroline Jane Bainbridge, da of David Adams (d 1983), of Newcastle Emlyn, Dyfed, S Wales; 1 s (Geoffrey Philip b 1945); *Career* WWII Lt RNVR Special Branch on staff of DMWD 1942-45, CEAD Fort Halstead Kent 1942, CSPDE Aberport S Wales 1943-45; Metal Box Co Ltd (now MB Gp) 1932-68: craft apprentice trg as engr 1932 (war serv 1941-46), mangr product design dept 1946, tech mangr Plastics Div 1953 (gen mangr 1961, resigned 1968); md Standard Containers Ltd and Chromax Ltd 1969 (Chromax sold to Metal Box 1974); chm and md Cleamax Ltd 1975, chm and md Hinterland Ltd 1983; inventor with 41 patented designs incl: parachute landing system with retarding rockets 1941 (the original patent 581726 covering the system now used by Russians for landing space craft and heavy armaments), remot control toy car 1946 (first known remote control car to be mass produced), machine for producing first liquid detergent bottles 1960, multi-colour printing machine for cans 1969 (an invention which turned £1000 into £3 000 000), toy water rocket 1983 (used in conjunction with Max Jackson Accelerometer to demonstrate Newton's laws of motion, on permanent display at Sci Museum Kensington); Freeman: City of London 1962, Worshipful Co of Horners; *Recreations* handicrafts; *Style—* Max Jackson, Esq; Chalgrove, Penybanc, Llechryd, Cardigan, Dyfed SA43 2NR; Cleamax Ltd, Mill Green Works, Hatfield, Herts AL9 5NZ (☎ 07072 71725)

JACKSON, Judith Margaret (Mrs John Horam); da of Ernest Jackson, MBE (d 1970), and Lucy Margaret Jackson; *b* 1 May 1936; *Educ* Dartington Hall Sch, Univ of

London (BA, LGSM), Univ of Paris (Dip Civ Fr); *m* 6 June 1963 (m dis 1976), Peter Jopp, s of George Jopp (d 1969); 2 s (Fraser b 1965, Lincoln b 1968); m 2, John Rhodes Horam; *Career* TV presenter Associated rediffusion 1961-65 and BBC 1965-80; motoring ed: The Sunday Times 1970-84, The Guardian 1987-; dir: UK 2000 1987-, Dartington Int Summer Sch 1984-; ctee memb WOMAC (Women on the Move Against Cancer); *Books* Man and the Automobile (1979); *Recreations* music, cookery; *Style—* Miss Judith Jackson; 6 Bovingdon Rd, London SW6 2AP (☎ 01 736 8521)

JACKSON, Keith Arnold; s of late John Keith Jackson and hp of kinsman, Sir Robert Jackson, Bt; *b* 1921; *m* Pauline Mona, da of B P Climo, of Wellington, NZ; 4 s, 1 da; *Style—* Keith Jackson, Esq; Coast Rd, Wainuiomata, New Zealand

JACKSON, Keith William; s of William Henry Jackson (d 1979), of Liverpool, and Elsie May, *née* Cockburn; *b* 21 Nov 1942; *Educ* Liverpool Coll, Liverpool Univ (LLB); *m* 21 June 1969, (m dis 1979), Janet Mary, da of George Cecil Lees, of Wirral; 2 da (Sarah Ann b 1974, Louise Claire (twin) b 1974); *Career* slr; ptnr Philip Jones Hillyer & Jackson of Chester and Bebington; hockey: English Univs, Lancs (capt 1975-76), of England and England B, pres Lancs Hockey Assoc 1986-88; cricket: rep Liverpool competition winners Steiner Cup 1975, capt Neston CC 1974-75; *Recreations* golf, cricket, squash, gardening; *Clubs* Eaton Park GC, Neston CC, Northern Hockey; *Style—* Keith Jackson, Esq; Parry's Well, The Rake, Burton, South Wirral, Cheshire (☎ 051 336 2735); 26/28 Mercia Square, Chester (☎ 0244 45551, fax 0244 42824)

JACKSON, Kenneth (Ken); s of Joseph Henry Jackson (d 1965), of Dewsbury, and Ada, *née* Smith (d 1981); *b* 23 Sept 1939; *Educ* Dewsbury Wheelwright GS, Batley Tech and Art Coll, Harvard Business Sch; *m* 25 Aug 1962, Elisabeth Joyce, da of David William Wilks (d 1975), of Dewsbury; 1 s ((Stephen) David b 8 Feb 1970); *Career* md Spencer & Halstead Ltd 1971 (personnel dir 1968-), vice pres Bonded Abrasives Europe Carborundum & Co USA 1978, vice pres sales and mktg abrasives carborundum div Sohio 1981, gp md Carborundum Abrasives plc (now Carbo plc 1984), non exec chm Autogem (Hldgs) Ltd 1986; *Recreations* travel, gardening; *Style—* Ken Jackson, Esq; Savile Ings Farm, Holywell Green, Halifax, W Yorks HX4 9BS (☎ 0422 72608); Carbo plc, Lakeside, PO Box 55, Trafford Pk, Manchester M17 1HP (☎ 061 872 2381, fax 061 872 1471, telex 667344 CARBOM G)

JACKSON, The Very Rev Lawrence; s of Walter Jackson (d 1947), and Edith, *née* Gray (d 1955); *b* 22 Mar 1926; *Educ* Alderman Newton's Sch Leicester, King's Coll London (AKC);; *m* 1955, Faith Anne, da of Philip Henry Seymour, of Suffolk; 4 da (Charlotte b 1955, Deborah b 1957, Rachel b 1961, Lucy b 1966); *Career* asst curate St Margaret's Leicester 1951-54; vicar: Wymeswold 1955-59, St James The Greater Leicester 1959-65, Coventry 1965-73; canon Coventry Cathedral 1967-73, provost of Blackburn 1973-; memb of the Gen Synod of the C of E 1974-, church cmmr 1981-, sr chaplain ACF Leics, Rutland and Warwickshire 1955-70; Liveryman Worshipful Co of Fruiterers; *Recreations* music, architecture, theatre, countryside, after-dinner speaking; *Clubs* Carlton, East India, Eccentric, Lord's Taverners, Forty, Lighthouse; *Style—* The Very Reverend Jackson; The Provost's House, Preston New Rd, Blackburn BB2 6PS (☎ (0254) 52502); Provost's Office, Cathedral Close, Blackburn BB1 5AA (☎ 0254 51814)

JACKSON, Hon Sir Lawrence Walter; KCMG (1970); s of Lawrence Stanley Jackson; *b* 27 Sept 1913; *Educ* Fort St Sch, Sydney Univ; *m* 1937, Mary, da of T H Donaldson; 1 s, 2 da; *Career* chief justice Supreme Ct WA 1969-77 (judge 1949), chllr WA Univ 1968-81; kt 1964; *Style—* The Hon Sir Lawrence Jackson, KCMG; 57 Lisle St, Mt Claremont, W Australia 6010

JACKSON, (Deirdre Ruth) Lucy; *née* Clokie; da of Hugh James Clokie (d 1958), and Patricia Ruth Wales, *née* Bond (d 1956); *b* 13 April 1930; *Educ* privately, London Univ (BA, Medau Dip); *m* 1, 14 May 1956, Dr Hellmuth Heitz, s of Dr Julius Heitz (d 1923); 2 s (John Julian b 1962 James Alexander (twin) b 1962), 1 da (Lanya b 1960); m 2, 12 Sept 1970, Ian MacGilchrist Jackson, s of Dr Ernest Jackson (d 1929); *Career* internationally reknowned teacher of Medau Method (fitness training prog achieved through natural rhythmic body-movement), author of books on Medau Method; *Style—* Mrs Ian Jackson; 23 Springfield Rd, London NW8 0QJ (☎ 01 624 3580)

JACKSON, Marilyn; da of Alfred Thomas Wilson (d 1988), of 26 Appletree Gdns, Walkerville, Newcastle Upon Tyne, and Mary Wilhelmina, *née* Liddie; *b* 27 Jan 1945; *Educ* Stephenson Meml HS Wallsend, Coll of Further Educn Whitley Bay; *m* 15 Oct 1966, David Henry Jackson, s of Henry Jackson (d 1983); 2 da (Peta b 1969, Trudi b 1973); *Career* fashion model 1966-79, TV hostess Opportunity Knocks 1967-68, admin Jeanette McNamee Model Agency 1977-78, personnel offr Co-op Laundry Soc Wallsend 1978-80, asst to indust dir T Rossling & Co 1980-87, co sec Regnl Engrs Distributors Gp Ltd 1982-, memb Bd G & AE Slingsby Ltd Hull 1988- (admin mangr 1987); sec Battle Hill Townswomen Guild 1975-78 (chm 1972-75); *Recreations* housework!; *Style—* Mrs Marilyn Jackson; 82 Montagu Ave, Gosforth, Newcastle Upon Tyne NE3 45B (☎ 091 285 3752); G & A E Slingsby Ltd, Leads Rd, Hull HU8 0DD (☎ 0482 838 880, fax 0482 878 827)

JACKSON, Michael Edward Wilson; s of Sqdn Ldr Edward Grosvenor Jackson, of The Field House, E Rigton, Yorks, and Yvonne Brenda Jackson, OBE, *née* Wilson; *b* 16 Mar 1950; *Educ* The Leys Sch, Cambridge Univ (LLB); *m* 19 April 1980 (m dis), Prudence Elizabeth Robinson, da of Michael John Boardman, of White Howe, Norfolk; *Career* dir The Guidehouse Gp plc 1983-; FCA 1986; *Recreations* tennis; *Clubs* The Vanderbilt Tennis, RAC, Annabel's; *Style—* Michael Jackson, Esq; 80 Deodar Rd, Putney, London SW15 (☎ 01 874 4564); Vestry House, Greyfriars Passage, Newgate St, London EC1R 7BA (☎ 01 606 6321)

JACKSON, (Richard) Michael; CVO (1983); s of Richard William Jackson (d 1979), of Bexhill, and Charlotte, *née* Wrightson; *b* 12 July 1940; *Educ* Darlington GS, Paisley GS, Glasgow Univ (MA); *m* 27 Dec 1961, Mary Elizabeth (Mollie), da of Dr Andrew Symington Kitchin (d 1978), of Skelmorlie, Ayrshire; 1 s (Andrew b 1968), 1 da (Dorothy b 1963); *Career* SO 1961-72, transferred to Dip Serv 1975, The Hague 1972-75, Euro Integration Dept FCO 1975-76, Panama City 1976-79, Arms Control and Disarmament Dept FCO 1979-81, Buenos Aires 1981-82, Falkland Islands Dept FCO 1982, Stockholm 1982-87, Seoul 1987-; Cdr of Order of Northern Star Sweden 1983; *Recreations* bird-watching, real ale; *Style—* Michael Jackson, Esq, CVO; FCO (Seoul), King Charles Street, London SW1 2AH

JACKSON, Michael Rodney; s of John William Jackson, of North Humberside, and Nora, *née* Phipps (d 1984); *b* 16 April 1935; *Educ* Queen Elizabeth GS Wakefield, Queens' Coll Cambridge (MA, LLM); *m* 1968, Anne Margaret, da of Prof Eric William Hawkins, CBE, of North Humberside; 2 s (Nicholas b 1969, Richard b 1972); *Career* slr 1962; rec of the Crown Ct 1985-, Notary Public 1967; *Recreations* fell walking; *Clubs* Royal Cwlth Soc; *Style—* Michael Jackson, Esq; 11 The Paddock, Swanland, North Ferriby, North Humberside HU14 3QW (☎ 0482 633278); PO Box 47, Victoria Chambers, Bowlalley Lane, Hull HU1 1XY (☎ 0482 25242, telex 592419, fax 0482 212974)

JACKSON, Sir Michael Roland; 5 Bt (UK 1902), of Stansted House, Stansted, Essex; s of Sir (Walter David) Russell Jackson, 4 Bt (d 1956), and Kathleen, *née* Hunter (d 1975); *b* 20 April 1919; *Educ* Stowe, Clare Coll Cambridge (MA); *m* 1, 1942 (m dis 1969), (Hilda) Margaret, da of Cecil George Herbert Richardson, CBE (d 1976); 1 s, 1 da; m 2, 1969, Hazel Mary, da of Ernest Harold Edwards (d 1981); *Heir* s, Thomas Jackson; *Career* WWII, Flt Lt RAFVR; engr ret 1979; CEng, MIEE, FIQA;; *Style—* Sir Michael Jackson, Bt; Dragon Cottage, Dragon's Green, Horsham, W Sussex

JACKSON, Sir Nicholas Fane St George; 3 Bt (UK 1913), of Eagle House, Wimbledon, Surrey; s of Sir Hugh Nicholas Jackson, 2 Bt (d 1979), and Violet, Lady Jackson, *qv*; the 1 baronet, Sir T G Jackson, Bt, was the architect responsible for many buildings in Oxford incl Examination Schools Brasenose, Hertford and Trinity Coll Oxford; *b* 4 Sept 1934; *Educ* Radley Coll, Wadham Coll Oxford, Royal Acad of Music; *m* 1, 1961 (m dis 1968), Jennifer Ann, da of F A Squire, of 8 Marylebone St, Wondon W1; m 2 1972, Nadia Francoise Genevieve, da of Georges Michard, of St Etienne, France; 1 s; *Heir* s, Thomas Graham St George Jackson b 5 Oct 1980; *Career* organist, harpsichordist and composer; organist: St Anne's Soho 1963-68, St James's Piccadilly 1971-74, St Lawrence Jewry 1974-77; organist and master of the choristers St David's Cathedral 1977-84, musical dir and fndr St David's Cathedral Bach Festival 1979; concert tours: USA, France, Germany, Spain, Japan, Belgium; dir Festival Bach at Sante Creos Spain 1987; dir Concertante of London 1987-; jr Warden Worshipful Co of Drapers 1985-86; LRAM, ARCM; *Books* compositions published by Boosey & Hawkes, Cardiff Univ Press, Anglo American Publishers; *Recreations* travel, writing; *Style—* Sir Nicholas Jackson, Bt

JACKSON, Dr Oliphant Fairburn; s of Edward Ellis Jackson (d 1928), of Matlock, Derbys, and Elisabeth Duff, *née* Mitchell (d 1964, *see* Jackson of Fairburn, Burke's Landed Gentry 1952 edn); *b* 19 May 1923; *Educ* Dulwich, Royal Dick Sch of Vet Studies Edinburgh, Univ of London Royal Free Hosp Sch of Med (PhD); *m* 29 March 1949, Elizabeth Katharine Marion, da of Col Sir Lionel Hall, Bt, MC (12 Bt Hall of Dunglass, d 1975), of Scorton, Yorks; 2 s (James Ellis b 1959, Anthony Oliphant b 1961), 1 da (Rosemary Frances b 1955); *Career* RNVR, Lt 1941-46: destroyers, N Atlantic, Med, Normandy Landings; veterinary surgn private practice Darlington 1951-56 and Ndola N Rhodesia 1956-66) curator the comparative biology unit Royal Free Hosp 1966-80, specialist reptile clinician 1980-86; ret 1986; chm The Br Chelonia Gp; MRCVS; *Books* Diseases of the Reptilia, BSAVA Exotic Pets Manual; *Recreations* cricket, Scottish country dancing, breeding Texel sheep; *Style—* Dr Oliphant Jackson; Little Stagenhoe, Horningtoft, Dereham, Norfolk NR20 5ED

JACKSON, Hon Mrs (Pamela); *née* Freeman-Mitford; 2 da of 2 Baron Redesdale, JP (d 1958), and Sydney, *née* Bowles (d 1963), and sis of Nancy, Jessica, and Unity Mitford, Hon Lady Mosley, and (Debo) Duchess of Devonshire; *b* 25 Nov 1907; *m* 1936 (m dis 1951), Wing Cdr Prof Derek Ainslie Jackson, OBE, DFC, AFC, RAFVR, s of Sir Charles Jackson; *Style—* The Hon Mrs Jackson; Woodfield House, Caudle Green, Cheltenham, Glos (☎ 028 582 300)

JACKSON, (Kevin) Paul; s of T Leslie Jackson, of 22 Welsby Ct, Eaton Rise, London W5, and Jo, *née* Spoonley; *b* 2 Oct 1947; *Educ* Gunnersbury GS, Exeter Univ (BA); *m* 21 Aug 1981, Judith Elizabeth, da of John Charles Cain, DSO, of The Old Bakery, Cowden, Kent; 2 da (Amie b 1981, Katie b 1984); *Career* stage mgmnt: Marlowe Theatre Canterbury 1970, Thorndike Theatre Leatherhead 1971; prodn work BBC TV: Two Ronnies, 3 of a Kind, Carrott's Lib, The Young Ones, Happy Families 1971-82; freelance prodr and dir Canon and Ball, Girls on Top 1982-84; prodr and chm Paul Jackson Prodns: Red Dwarf, Don't Miss Wax, Saturday Live 1984-86; md NGTV 1987, Guardian columnist 1988, chm Comic Relief 1987-, cncl memb Charity Projects 1988-, memb IPPA Cncl 1987-88; BAFTA 1983 and 1984; *Recreations* theatre, rugby, travel, food and wine, friends and family; *Style—* Paul Jackson, Esq; 24 Denmark St, London WC2H 8NJ (☎ 01 379 5953, fax 379 0831, telex 21760 RANGO G)

JACKSON, Paul Mervyn; s of Brian Mervyn Jackson (d 1979), and Margaret Irene, *née* Scythes; *b* 12 July 1947; *Educ* Cranleigh; *m* 15 June 1974, Nina Ann, da of Robert Ferdinand Delliére; 2 da (Portia b 12 June 1977, Olivia b 19 April 1979); *Career* surveyor; fndr Victory Land Ltd 1983; Freeman City of London 1972, Liveryman Worshipful Co of Merchant Taylors 1978; FRICS 1970;; *Recreations* golf, tennis, formula 1 motor racing; *Style—* Paul Jackson, Esq; The Old Farm, 6 Fife Rd, London SW14 7EP; Victory Land Ltd, 46/47 Pall Mall, London SW1Y 5JG (☎ 01 408 1067, fax 01 493 8633, car tel 0836 292 562)

JACKSON, Peter Grayling; *Career* publisher and md of News Int Hachette Ltd (publishers of Elle Magazine in Britain and SKY Magazine throughout Europe) previously ed of Sunday Times Magazine, and SUNDAY (News of the World's magazine); twice winner of Editor of the Year award (presented by Br Soc of Magazine Editors) for work on: TV Times 1974, and SUNDAY 1981; *Clubs* RAC, Steering Wheel; *Style—* Peter Jackson, Esq; c/o News International Hachette Ltd, 4-12 Lower Regent Street, London SW1 (☎ 01 930 9050)

JACKSON, Peter Guy; s of Edwin Arthur Jackson (d 1953), of 13 North St, Ashford, Kent, and Grace Marion, *née* Rudd (d 1942); *b* 5 Nov 1921; *Educ* Ashford GS, Herne Bay Coll; *m* 1, 26 April 1943, Joan Dorothy (d 1951), da of Wilfred Abraham Caton (d 1980), of Essex; 2 s (Richard Peter Caton b 1945, d 1947, James Edwin Caton b 1947), 1 da (Anne b 1949); m 2, 17 May 1952 (m dis 1984), Barbara Eveline Caton; 2 da (Jane b 1955, Gillian b 1958); m 3, 2 Feb 1985, Janice Wager; *Career* Cadet Br India Steam Navigation Co 1939-42; RNR: Sub Lt 1943-45, Lt 1945-63, Lt-Cdr 1963-66; E C Harris & Ptnrs chartered quantity surveyors: joined 1952, ptnr 1962, conslt 1978-; Studying for Lay Miny Anglican Church; Freeman City of London, Liveryman Worshipful Co of Needlemakers; ARICS 1949, FRICS 1962; *Recreations* gardening, DIY, model making; *Style—* Peter Jackson, Esq; Richmond Cottage, Fambridge Rd, Althorne, Chelmsford, Essex CM3 6BZ (☎ 0621 741 022); c/o E C Harris Partners, The Old Rectory, Church Rd, Bowers Gifford, Basildon, Essex (☎ 0268 559 666, fax 0268 858 153)

JACKSON, Peter John Edward; s of David Charles Jackson (d 1977), of Kent, and Sarah Ann, *née* Manester; *b* 14 May 1944; *Educ* Brockley County GS, Sprachen und

Dolmetscher Inst Hamburg, Univ of London (LLB), Tübingen Univ W Germany (DJur); *m* 23 Sept 1967, Ursula Henny, da of Paul Schubert (d 1945), and Henny Schubert (d 1980) of Hamburg; 2 da (Philippa b 1972, Pia b 1984); *Career* barr Middle Temple, and N Ireland, dep circuit judge 1979-81, asst rec 1982-83, rec of Crown Ct 1983-; ptnr Campbell & Jackson Int Arbitral & Legal Conslts; *Recreations* horse riding, German language, German law; *Style*— Dr Peter Jackson; Pump Court Temple, London EC4Y 7AH (☎ 01 583 9389 and 353 5597, fax 583 5122); 16 Place Roupe 1000, Brussels (☎ 01 510 3211, fax 01 512 6586, telex 22806 FIDUCI(Belge))

JACKSON, Air Vice-Marshal Sir Ralph Coburn; KBE (1973), CB (1963); s of Ralph Jackson (d 1937), and Phillis Cooper, *née* Dodds (d 1964); *b* 22 June 1914; *Educ* Oakmount Westmorland, Guy's Hosp; *m* 1939, Joan Lucy, da of Lewellin de Sidnia Crowley (d 1952); 2 s, 2 da; *Career* joined RAF 1938, WWII served: France, Russia, W Africa (despatches twice) conslt in med RAF Hosps 1946-66: Aden, Halton, Wegberg Gp Capt 1957, MacArthur lectr Edinburgh Univ 1959, Air Cdre 1961, conslt advsr in med RAF 1966-74, advsr in med CAA 1966-75, Air Vice-Marshal 1969, QHP 1969-75, sr conslt RAF 1971-75, chm Def Med Servs Post Grad Cncl 1973-75, med referee to various life insurance cos 1976-88; Hon: civil conslt in med to RAF 1975-, hon med conslt RAF Benevolent Fund 1975-, dir and med advsr French Hosp Rochester 1986-; Lady Cade Medal RCS 1960; Freeman city of London Liveryman Worshipful Soc of Apothecaries; FRCP (London and Edinburgh), MRCS; *Recreations* bird and wildlife watching, genealogy; *Clubs* RAF; *Style*— Air Vice-Marshal Sir Ralph Jackson, KBE, CB; Piper's Hill, Marwell, Westerham, Kent TN16 1SB (☎ Westerham 0959 64436)

JACKSON, Richard Anthony; s of Harold Reginald Jackson (d 1948), of Harrogate, Yorks, and Irene Dallas, *née* Nelson (d 1968); *b* 31 Mar 1932; *Educ* Cheltenham Coll; *Career* Nat Serv RE 1950-52; salesman Henry A Lane & Co Ltd 1953-56, merchandising asst Walt Disney Prodns Ltd 1956-59, dir Richard Jackson Personal Mgmnt Ltd (actors representation), produced plays in London West End and on Fringe; incl: Madame de Sade (Kings Head 1975), Charles Trenet in concert (Royal Albert Hall 1975),The Bitter Tears of Petra Von Kant (New End 1976), An Evening with Quentin Crisp (Duke of Yorks and Ambassadors 1978), The Singular Life of Albert Nobbs, Alterations, Tribute to Lili Lamont (New End 1978), Flashpoint (New End and Mayfair 1978), A Day in Hollywood, A Night in The Ukraine (New End and Mayfair 1979 - Winner of Evening Standard Award for Best Musical and Plays and Players Award for Best Comedy), The Square, La Musica, Portrait of Dora (New End 1979) Appearances (Mayfair 1980), A Galway Girl (Lyric Studio 1980), Bar and Ger (Lyric Studio 1981), Latin (Lyric Studio 1983), The Human Voice (with Susannah York, performed world-wide since 1984) Swimming Pools at War (Offstage 1985), Matthew, Mark, Luke and Charlie (Latchmere 1986), I Ought to be in Pictures (offstage 1986), Pier Pasolini (offstage 1987), Creditors, Latin (New End 1989); memb BAFTA; *Recreations* table tennis, crosswords; *Clubs* Green Room; *Style*— Richard Jackson, Esq; 48 William Mews, London SW1X 9HQ (☎ 01 235 3759); 59 Knightsbridge, London SW1X 7RA (☎ 01 235 3671)

JACKSON, Maj Richard Francis Laidlay; TD (1945); s of Francis Crichton Jackson (d 1947), and Frances Isobel, *née* Laidlay (d 1963); *b* 19 July 1917; *Educ* Tonbridge, Wye Coll London; *m* 30 Dec 1944, Anne Kythe Mackenzie, da of Walter Lee (d 1940), of India; 3 da (Jacqueline (Mrs Scott) b 23 April 1947, Penelope (Mrs Shaw) b 5 Oct 1949, Frances (Mrs Geoghegan) b 29 Nov 1951); *Career* cmmnd RA (TA) 1939, AA Cmd 1939-42, served Ceylon 1942-43, Burma 1943-44 (DAQMG); ptnr Wood Hanbury Rhodes & Jackson 1945-66, chm Morris Hanbury Jackson 1980 (ptnr and dir 1966-81); memb: Pony Club 1965-68, Cons Assoc 1965-70; *Recreations* croquet, gardening; *Style*— Maj Richard Jackson, TD; Shipley Hall, Brooks Gn, Horsham, W Sussex (☎ 0403 741 409)

JACKSON, Richard Peter; s of Richard Charles Jackson (d 1982), of Newlands, Fowlmere, Cambs, and Allison Mary Clare, *née* Hicks; *b* 21 Mar 1944; *Educ* Bishop's Stortford Coll Herts, City Univ London (BSc); *m* 1, 30 April 1966 (m dis 1986), Rosemary Phyllis Choat Stickels, da of Samuel Harry Choat Jenkins, of Rougham Hill, Bury St Edmunds, Suffolk; 2 s (Piers b 1970, Giles b 1972); m 2, 24 July 1987, Annabel Gemma Jane (formerly Mrs Gunn), da of Maj Rodney Charles Hitchcock (d 1969), of Branch Hill, Hampstead, London; *Career* indentured engr George Wimpey & Co London 1963-69, structural engr Firth Cleveland Jamaica 1969-71, sec engr Bullen & Ptnrs Croydon 1971-73, assoc John Powlesland & Assoc Colchester 1973-76, sr ptnr Richard Jackson Partnership Hadleigh Ipswich Suffolk and London Docklands 1976-, ctee memb E Anglian Branch Faculty of Bldg (former chm), ctee memb E Anglian branch Lighthouse Club; CEng 1969, FIStructE 1983, MICE 1971, MConsE 1983; *Recreations* tennis, skiing; *Clubs* Placemakers, Cavaliers Colchester, Lighthouse; *Style*— Richard Jackson, Esq; Hill Barn, Hitcham, Ipswich, Suffolk (☎ 0449 741 399); Richard Jackson Ptnrship, Consulting Civil & Structural Engineers, 26 High St, Hadleigh, Ipswich, Suffolk IP7 5AP (☎ 0473 823 939, fax 0473 823 226, car tel 0836 512 870)

JACKSON, Sir Robert; 7 Bt (UK 1815), of Arlsey, Bedfordshire; s of Maj Francis Gorham Jackson (d 1942, 2 s of 4 Bt); suc kinsman, Sir John Montrésor Jackson, 6 Bt 1980; *b* 16 Mar 1910; *Educ* St George's Coll; *m* 1943, Maria E Casamayou, of Montevideo, Uruguay; 2 da; *Heir* kinsman, Keith Jackson; *Clubs* English (Montevideo); *Style*— Sir Robert Jackson, Bt; Santiago de Chile 1243, Montevideo, Uruguay (☎ 905487)

JACKSON, Cdr Sir Robert Gillman Allen; KCVO (1962), CMG (1944), OBE (1941); s of Archibald Jackson, of Melbourne (d 1928), by his w, Kathleen Crooke (d 1943); the Jackson family arrived in Australia in 1862; *b* 8 Nov 1911; *Educ* Mentone GS Victoria; *m* 1950, (Barbara) Baroness Jackson of Lodsworth, DBE (d 1981), da of Walter Ward, of Felixstowe, Suffolk; 1 s (Robert); *Career* RAN 1929, transferred to RN 1937, seconded to Br Army as CSO to Cdr-in-Chief Malta 1939, dir-gen ME Supply Centre 1941-44, princ advsr Br War Cabinet Min in ME, special duties with C-in-C Greece 1944; sr dep dir-gen UNRRA 1945-47, HM Treasy 1949, loaned to Aust Govt 1959-62 (established Miny of Nat Devpt), advsr Govt of India on devpt plans 1953-67, advsr pres of Ghana and chm Ghana Devpt Cmmn 1957-60, special conslt to admin of UN Devpt Programme at HQ and in 50 countries in Asia, Africa and the ME 1962-71, advsr pres Liberia 1962-80, UN Cmmr i/c Study of the Capacity of the UN Devpt System 1968-70, consulting dir McKinsey & Co Inc 1970-79; UN under-sec gen i/c: assistance to Bangladesh 1972-74, assistance to Zambia 1973-78; co-ordinator of UN assistance to: Indo-China 1975-78, Rep Cape Verde 1975-78; special advsr admin of UN Devpt Programme 1978-79, under-sec-gen and sr advsr UN 1984-, sr conslt Volta River Authy 1962-; advsr various industl gps and fin insts; memb jury Institut de la Vie; kt 1955; *Recreations* reading, breeding white tigers, deep sea fishing; *Clubs* Brooks's, Melbourne, Victoria; *Style*— Cdr Sir Robert Jackson, KCVO, CMG, OBE; United Nations, New York City 10017, USA (☎ (212) 754 5004); Hotel Richemond, Geneva, Switzerland (☎ (21) 31 14 00)

JACKSON, Robert Victor; MP (C) Wantage 1983-; *b* 24 Sept 1946; *Educ* Falcon Coll S Rhodesia, St Edmund Hall Oxford, All Souls Coll Oxford; *m* 1975, Caroline Frances, DPhil, MEP (C) Wilts 1984-, da of G H Harvey; 1 s decd; *Career* former ed The Round Table and International Affairs (Chatham House); memb Oxford City Cncl 1969-71, political advsr to Employment sec 1973-74, contested (C) Manchester Central Oct 1974, memb Cabinet of Sir Christopher Soames (now Lord Soames, *qv*) EEC Cmmn 1974-76, chef de cabinet to Pres EEC Econ and Social Ctee Brussels 1976-78, special advsr to Lord Soames as Govr Rhodesia 1979-80, rapporteur European Parl Budget Ctee 1982-; parl under sec of state, Dept of Educn and Science, with responsibility for Higher Educn and Sci 1987-; author of several books; *Style*— Robert Jackson, Esq, MP; New House, Southmoor, Oxfordshire (☎ 0865 821243); 74 Carlisle Place, London SW1 (☎ 01 828 6113)

JACKSON, Dr (William) Roland Cedric; s and h of Sir Thomas Jackson, 8 Bt, *qv*; *b* 9 Jan 1954; *Educ* Wycliffe Coll, St Peter's Coll Oxford (MA), Exeter Coll Oxford (DPhil); *m* 1977, Nicola Mary, yr da of Prof Peter Davis, of St Mawes, Cornwall; 2 s (Adam William Roland b 1982, James Anthony Foljambe b 1984); *Style*— Dr Roland Jackson; 44 Kingsmead, Nailsea, Bristol, Avon (☎ 0272 856481)

JACKSON, Rupert Matthew; QC (1987); s of George Henry Jackson (d 1981), and Nancy Barbara, *née* May; *b* 7 Mar 1948; *Educ* Christ's Hosp, Jesus Coll Cambridge (MA, LLB); *m* 20 Sept 1975, Claire Corinne, da of Harry Potter (d 1979); 3 da (Corinne b 1981, Chloe b 1983, Tamsin b 1985); *Career* called to bar Middle Temple 1972, practising SE circuit; FRSA; *Books* Professional Negligence (jtly second edn 1987); *Style*— Rupert Jackson, Esq, QC; The Old House, The Street, West Horsley, Surrey (☎ 048 652 780); 2 Crown Office Row, Temple, London EC4Y 7HJ (☎ 01 583 8155, fax 01 583 1205)

JACKSON, Hon Mrs Edward (Susannah Albinia); *née* Chaytor; yst da of late (Alfred) Drewett Chaytor, of Spennithorne Hall, Leyburn, Yorks; *b* 13 Nov 1939; *m* 1971, as his 2 w, Capt Hon Edward Lawies Jackson, RHG (d 1982), o son of 3 Baron Allerton, *qv*; 2 da (Olivia Susannah b 1975, Katharine Elizabeth b 1978); *Career* photographer; *Style*— Hon Mrs Edward Jackson; The Old Rectory, Cottisford, Brackley, Northants NN13 5SW

JACKSON, Thomas St Felix; s and h of Sir Michael Roland Jackson, 5 Bt; *b* 27 Sept 1946; *Educ* Stowe, Southampton Univ (BA); *m* 1980, Georgina Victoria, da of George Harold Malcolm Scatliff, of Springlands Farm, Wineham, Sussex; 2 da (Lucy Harriet b 1982, Charlotte Dare b 1986); *Career* md Billington Jackson Advertising Ltd; *Recreations* golf, cricket, photography, reading; *Clubs* Royal Wimbledon Golf, Naval and Military, MCC; *Style*— Thomas Jackson, Esq; 30 Westover Road, London SW18 (☎ 01 874 3550); Billington Jackson Advertising Ltd, 219 King's Road, London SW3 5EJ (☎ 01 351 0006)

JACKSON, Sir (William) Thomas; 8 Bt (UK 1869), of The Manor House, Birkenhead; s of Sir William Jackson, 7 Bt (d 1985), and his 1 w, Lady Ankaret Cecilia Caroline Howard (d 1945), da of 10 Earl of Carlisle; *b* 12 Oct 1927; *Educ* Mill Hill, RAC Cirencester; *m* 1951, Gilian Malise, eld da of John Stobart, MBE, of Farlam Ghyll, Brampton, Cumbria; 3 s (Roland b 1954, Piers Anthony b 1955, Jolyon Thomas b 1957); *Heir* s, (William) Roland Cedric, *qv*; *Style*— Sir Thomas Jackson, Bt; Routen, Ennerdale, Cleator, Cumbria CA23 3AU

JACKSON, Violet, Lady; Violet Marguerite Loftus; yr da of Loftus St George (d 1952) and Marguerite Isabel Clifford, *neé* Borrer (d 1956); *b* 11 Mar 1904; *m* 15 July 1931, Sir Hugh Nicholas Jackson, 2 Bt (d 1979); 1 s (Nicholas, 3 Bt, *qv*), 1 da (Louise, Mrs M Taraniuk); *Style*— Violet, Lady Jackson; 38 Oakley St, London SW3 5HA

JACKSON, Gen Sir William Godfrey Fothergill; GBE (1975), OBE (1958), KCB (1971, MC & bar 1940, 1943); s of Col Albert Jackson (d 1956), and Eleanor Mary Fothergill (d 1978), of Ravenstonedale, Cumbria; *b* 28 August 1917; *Educ* Shrewsbury, RMA Woolwich, King's Coll Cambridge (MA); *m* 1946, Joan Mary, da of Capt C P Buesden, of Bournemouth; 1 s, 1 da; *Career* cmmnd RE 1937, served WW II Norway, N Africa, Sicily, Italy, Far East; dep dir Staff Duties War Office 1962-64, IDC 1965, dir CDS's Unison Planning Staff 1966-68, asst CGS Op Requirements MOD 1968-70, GOC-in-C Northern Cmd 1970-72, QMG 1973-76, mil historian Cabinet Office 1977-88, govr & C-in-C Gibraltar 1978-82; ADC Gen to HM The Queen 1974-76; Col Cmmdt: RE 1971-81, Gurkha Engrs 1971-76, RAOC 1973-78, Hon Col Engr & Rlwy Staff Corps RE TAVR 1977-; KStJ 1978; *Books* Attack in the West (1953), Seven Roads to Moscow (1957), Battle for Italy (1967), Battle for Rome (1969), Alexander of Tunis (1971), The North African Campaigns (1975), Overlord: Normandy 1944 (1978), Vol VI British Official History of the Mediterranean and Middle East Campaigns (Pt 1 1984, Pt 2 1987 Pt 3 1988), Withdrawal from Empire (1986) Rock of the Gilvaltians (1987), Alternative Third World War (1987); *Clubs* Army & Navy; *Style*— Gen Sir William Jackson, GBE, KCB, MC; Royal Bank of Scotland, Holt Branch, Whitehall, London SW1; West Stowell Place, Oare, Marlborough, Wilts

JACKSON, William Unsworth; CBE (1985); s of William Jackson (d 1959), and Margaret Esplen, *née* Sunderland (d 1984); *b* 9 Feb 1926; *Educ* Alsop HS Liverpool; *m* 1952, Valerie Annette, da of Robert Henry Llewellyn (d 1966); 1 s (Philip b 1957), 1 da (Deborah b 1954); *Career* slr; chief exec Kent CC 1973-86, pres Soc of Local Authy Chief Execs 1985-86, dir Kent Econ Devpt Bd 1982-86, tstee Charity Aid Fndn 1986-; *Recreations* gardening; *Clubs* Royal Overseas; *Style*— William Jackson, Esq, CBE; 34 Yardley Park Rd, Tonbridge TA9 1NF (☎ 0732 351078)

JACKSON OF BURNLEY, Baroness; Mary Elizabeth; da of Dr Robert Oliphant Boswall (d 1977); *m* 1938, Baron Jackson of Burnley (Life Peer, d 1970); 2 da (Hon Mrs Freeston, Hon Mrs Moffatt); *Style*— The Rt Hon the Lady Jackson of Burnley; Flat 6, Ritchie Court, 380 Banbury Road, Oxford.

JACKSON-STOPS, Timothy William; s of Anthony Ashworth Briggs (d 1987, who assumed by deed poll the surnmane of Jackson-Stops 1949), and Jean Jackson, *née* Jackson-Stops; *b* 20 August 1942; *Educ* Eton; *m* 27 June 1987, Jenny; *Career* chm Jackson-Stops & Staff; FRICS (1975); *Recreations* skiing, shooting, fishing, sailing; *Clubs* Buck's; *Style*— Timothy Jackson-Stops, Esq; Wood Burcote, Towcester, Northants NN12 7JP (☎ 0327 50443); 14 Curzon Street, London W1Y 7FH (☎ 01

499 6291, fax 01 495 2936)

JACOB, Lt-Gen Sir (Edward) Ian Claud; GBE (1960), KBE (1946, CB 1944, CBE 1942); s of Field Marshal Sir Claud Jacob, GCB, GCSI, KCMG (d 1948); *b* 27 Sept 1899; *Educ* Wellington, RMA Woolwich, King's Coll Cambridge (BA); *m* 1924, Cecil Bisset, da of Maj-Gen Sir Francis Treherne (d 1955); 2 s (*see* Jacob, Cdr John C); *Career* 2 Lt RE 1918, Bde Maj Canal Bde Egypt 1936-38, Maj 1938, mil asst sec Ctee of Imperial Def 1938-39, served WW II, mil asst sec War Cabinet 1939-46, Col 1942, Brig 1943, Temp Maj-Gen 1945, ret with hon rank of Maj-Gen 1946; recalled to be Chief Staff Offr to Min Def with temp rank of Lt-Gen 1952; controller Euro service BBC 1946-48, dir external service BBC 1948-51, dir-gen BBC 1952-60; dir: Fisons 1960-70, EMI Ltd 1960-73; chm: Covent Garden Market Authy 1961-66, Blyth Breeding Co 1968-85, Matthews Hldgs 1970-76; tstee Imperial War Museum 1970-76; cllr E Suffolk 1960-70, JP Suffolk 1961-69, alderman 1970-74, cllr Suffolk 1974-77; DL Suffolk 1964-85; *Recreations* golf; *Clubs* Army & Navy (chm 1959-67); *Style*— Lt-Gen Sir Ian Jacob, KBE, CB, CBE; The Red House, Woodbridge, Suffolk IP12 4AD (☎ 039 43 2001)

JACOB, Sir Jack (Issac Hai); QC (1976); s of Jacob Isaiah Jacob (d 1936), of Shanghai, China; *b* 5 June 1908,Shanghai; *Educ* Shanghai Public Sch for Boys, LSE, UCL (LLB); *m* 1940, Rose Mary Jenkins, da of John William Samwell (d 1918); 2 s; *Career* WWII RAOC, Staff Capt WO 1943-45; called to the Bar Gray's Inn 1930, master Supreme Ct (Queen's Bench) 1957-75, memb Senate of Inns of Court and the Bar 1975-78, sr master Supreme Court Queen's Bench Div 1975-80, Queen's Remembrancer 1975-80, hon bencher Gray's Inn 1978; hon lectr in Law UCL 1959-74 (fell 1966), visiting prof English Law 1974-87; visiting prof: Sydney Univ NSW 1971, Osgoode Hall Law Sch, York U Toronto 1971; dir Inst of Advanced Legal Studies London Univ 1986-88; memb Lord Chllr's Dept Ctees on: (Pearson) Funds in Ct 1958-59, Revision of Rules of Supreme Ct 1960-65, (Payne) Enforcement of Judgement Debts 1965-69, (Winn) Personal Injuries Litigation 1966-68, (Kerr) Foreign Judgements 1976-80; advsy ed Court Forms 1962-, ed Annual Practice 1961-66; gen ed: Supreme Court Practice 1967-, Civil Justice Quarterly 1982-; pres Assoc of Law Teachers; vice pres: Selden Soc (cncl memb), Inst of Legal Execs, Industrial Law Soc; memb Gen Ctee, Bar Assoc for Commerce Finance and Industry; memb: Ct of Govrs Poly of Centl London 1970-88, Broderers' Co 1977; Freeman City of London 1976; hon memb: Cncl of Justice 1987, Soc of Public Teachers of Law; hon fell Central London Poly 1988, Hon LLD: Birmingham 1978, London 1981; Dr Juris hc (Würzburg, Bavaria) 1982; kt 1979; *Style*— Sir Jack Jacob, QC; 16 The Park, Golders Green, London NW11 7SU (☎ 01 458 3832)

JACOB, Cdr John Claud; DL Suffolk 1988; s of Lt-Gen Sir Ian Jacob, GBE, CB, DL, *qv*; *b* 9 June 1925; *Educ* Sherborne Sch; *m* 1948, Rosemary Elizabeth, da of Leonard Shuter (d 1960); 2 s; *Career* entered RN 1943, served WW II, Home and East Indies Stations, served Suez 1956, Cdr 1957, ret 1962; farmer; chm Radio Orwell 1971-, joined with Saxon Radio (founded 1981) as wholly owned subsid of Suffolk Gp Radio, chm 1981-87; tres Aldeburgh Fndn 1980-; chm Organic Farmers and Growers Ltd 1975-86; *Clubs* Farmers'; *Style*— Cdr John Jacob, RN; c/o Radio Orwell, Electric House, Lloyds Ave, Ipswich, Suffolk (☎ 0473 216971); 74 Lee Rd, Aldeburgh, Suffolk IP5 5EY (☎ 072 885 2491)

JACOB, Robin Robert Raphel Hayim; QC (1981); s of Sir Jaek I H Jacob, of London, and Rose Mary, *née* Samwell; *b* 26 April 1941; *Educ* Mountgrace Comprehensive Sch, St Paul's Sch, Trinity Coll Cambridge, (MA), LSE (LLB); *m* 1967, Wendy, da of Leslie Huw Thomas Jones; 3 s (Sam b 1970, Matthew b 1972, Oliver b 1975); *Career* barr 1965, jr counsel to Treasy in patent matters 1976-81; *Style*— Robin Jacob Esq, QC; Francis Taylor Building, Temple, London EC4

JACOB, Rev Canon Dr William Mungo; s of John William Carey Jacob (d 1982), of Ringstead, Hunstanton, Norfolk, and Mary Marsters, *née* Dewar (d 1959); *b* 15 Nov 1944; *Educ* King Edward VII Sch Kings Lynn, Hull Univ (LLB), Linacre Coll Oxford (BA, MA), Edinburgh Univ (Dip in Pastoral Studies), Exeter Univ (PhD); *Career* asst curate Wymondham Norfolk 1970-73, asst chaplain Exeter Univ 1973-75, dir of pastoral studies Salisbury and Wells Theol Coll 1975-80 (vice princ 1977-80), sec ctee for theol educn advsy cncl for Church's Miny 1980-86, warden Lincoln Theol Coll and prebendary of Gretton in Lincoln Cathedral 1986-; *Style*— The Rev Canon Dr William Jacob; The Warden's House, Drury Lane, Lincoln LN1 3BP (☎ 0522 258 79); Lincoln Theological Coll, Lincoln LN1 3BP (☎ 0522 5388 85)

JACOBS, Prof Arthur David; s of Alexander Susman Jacobs (d 1972), and Estelle, *née* Isaacs (d 1981); *b* 14 June 1922; *Educ* Manchester GS, Oxford Univ (MA); *m* 4 Nov 1953, Betty Upton Hughes; 2 s (Julian b 1957, Michael b 1960); *Career* served WWII 1942-46; music critic Daily Express 1947-52, freelance writer on music 1953-, prof RAM 1964-79, head music dept Huddersfield Poly 1979-84, fndr ed British Music Yearbook 1972, memb bd eds Opera magazine 1962-; *Books* incl: Music Loner's Anthology (1948), Gilbert and Sullivan (1951), Choral Music (1963), Libretto of Opera One Man Show by Nicholas Maw (1964), Pan Book of Opera (with Stanley Sadie, expanded edn 1984), A Short History of Western Music (1972), The New Penguin Dictionary of Music (new edn 1978), Arthur Sullivan: a Victorian musician (1984), Pan Book of Orchestral Music (1988), The Penguin Dictionary of Musical Performers (1989), many opera translations incl Berg's Lulu; *Style*— Prof Arthur Jacobs; 10 Oldbury Close, Sevenoaks, Kent TN15 9DJ (☎ 0732 884006)

JACOBS, David Lewis; DL (Greater London 1983); s of late David Jacobs and late Jeanette Victoria, *née* Goldsmid; *b* 19 May 1926; *Educ* Belmont Coll, Strand Sch; *m* 1, 15 Sept 1949 (m dis 1972), Patricia Bradlaw; m 2, 1975 Caroline Munro (d 1975); m 3, 1979, Mrs Lindsay Stuart Hutcheson; 1 s (Jeremy decd), 3 da (Carol, Joanna, Emma), 1 step s (Guy); *Career* RN 1944-47; radio/tv broadcaster; first broadcast Navy Mixture 1944; announcer: Forces Broadcasting 1944-45 (chief), Radio SEAC Ceylon 1945-47 (asst station dir 1947); freelance, BBC & radio Luxembourg top disc-jockey 1947-53; radio credits incl: Housewive's Choice, Journey into Space, BBC Jazz Club, Pick of the Pops, Any Questions, Any Answers, Melodies for You, David Jacobs show; TV credits incl: 6 Royal Command Performances, Juke Box Jury, Top of the Pops, Little Women, What's my Line, Miss World, Eurovision Song Contest, Come Dancing, Questions and many others; Man in the Moon UK Ltd 1986-, chm Think British Campaign 1985 (dep chm 1983-85); pres: National Children's Orchestra, Royal Br Legion (Kingston); vice-pres: Stars Organisation for Spastics (past chm), Wimbledon Girls Choir; awards: RSPCA Richard Martin Award, Variety Club, BBC TV Personality 1960, BBC Radio Personality 1975, Sony Gold Award Outstanding Radio Contribs 1985, Sony Hall of Fame 1988; *Books* Jacobs Ladder (1963), Caroline (1978), Any Questions? (with Michael Bowen, 1981); *Recreations* talking and listening, hotels; *Clubs* Garrick, St James's, Helford River Sailing; *Style*— David Jacobs, Esq, DL; 203 Pavilion Rd, London SW1X 0BJ (☎ 01 245 0007)

JACOBS, Donald; s of Harry Jacobs (d 1980), of London, and Hetty, *née* Lands; *b* 21 April 1931; *Educ* Grocers Co Sch; *m* 8 Oct 1958, Jeanette, da of Bert Conway (d 1967), of Croydon; 2 s (Jonathan b 1962, Simon b 1965); *Career* chartered accountant; dir: Walker Bros Civil Engrg Ltd, Disjay Ltd, Metropolis Finance Ltd 1987; *Recreations* tennis, music, theatre, travel; *Style*— Donald Jacobs, Esq; 20 Cheyne Walk, London NW4 3QJ (☎ 01 202 5708); 47 St Johns Wood, High Street, London NW8 7NJ

JACOBS, Godfrey Frederick; s of Frederick George Jacobs (d 1963), of Woodford, Essex, and Louise Lily, *née* Phipps; *Educ* South West Essex Tech Coll, Wansfell Coll Essex; *m* Hazell Thirza, *née* Robertson; 2 da (Lorne Alison b 10 June 1958, Clare Morag b 13 April 1960); *Career* Nat Serv Tport Cmd RAF 1949-51; dir (overseas) English Property Corpn 1968-75, gen property mangr MTRC Hong Kong 1976-79; 1979-86: exec dir US Assets Ltd, dir and pres AMP Property Services, Ing of San Francisco, chm Copthorn Hldgs Ltd (Toronto); chm Suncrest Devpts plc 1986-; memb: World Wildlife Fund of Canada, Community Assoc for Riding for Disabled (Canada), Zoo Canadians for Wildlife, Utd Wards Club of London; Freeman City of London 1964, Liveryman Worshipful Co of Painter Stainers 1964, Former Master Hon Co of Freemen of the City of London in N America; FSVA 1963, ABIM 1966, FCIArb 1977, FIOD 1961; *Recreations* charity work; *Clubs* Naval, City Livery; *Style*— Godfrey Jacobs, Esq

JACOBS, John Robert Maurice; s of Robert Jacobs (d 1934), and Vivian Jacobs (d 1978); *b* 14 Mar 1925; *Educ* Maltby GS; *m* 25 Jan 1949, Rita, da of Joseph Wragg (d 1957), of Woodsetts, Worksop, Notts; 1 s (Johnathan b 1960), 1 da (Joanna b 1957); *Career* Sgt Fl Engr 1944; Br Int professional golfer 1954-58 player Ryder cup 1955 (non playing Capt 1979, 1981); dir Euro Tour 1971-76; *Books* Golf (1979), Play Better Golf (1969), Practical Golf (1973), Golf Doctor (1979), Practical Golf, Jacobs Impact on Golf; *Recreations* fishing, shooting, golf; *Clubs* Brockenhurst, Bramshaw, Sandy Lodge, Wakenona (USA); *Style*— John Jacobs, Esq; Stable Cottage, Chapel Lane, Lyndhurst, Hamps (☎ 042 128 2743)

JACOBS, Hon Sir Kenneth Sydney; KBE (1976); s of Albert Sydney Jacobs; *b* 5 Oct 1917; *Educ* Knox GS NSW, Sydney Univ Aust (BA, LLB); *m* 1952, Eleanor Mary Neal; 1 da; *Career* barr NSW 1947, QC 1958, Supreme Court of NSW Australia: judge 1960, judge of appeal 1966, pres Court of Appeal 1972, justice of High Ct of Aust 1974-79; *Style*— The Hon Sir Kenneth Jacobs, KBE; Crooks Lane Corner, Axford, Marlborough, Wilts SN8 2HA

JACOBS, Prof Louis; s of Harry Jacobs (d 1968), of Manchester, and Lena, *née* Myerstone (d 1956); *b* 17 July 1920; *Educ* Manchester Central HS, UCL (BA, PhD); *m* 28 March 1944, Sophie, da of Israel Lisagorska (d 1945), of London; 2 s (Ivor b 1945, David b 1952), 1 da (Naomi b 1947); *Career* rabbi: Central Synagogue Manchester 1948-1954, New West End Synagogue London 1954-60; tutor Jews' Coll London 1959-62, dir Soc Study of Jewish Theology 1962-64, rabbi New London Synagogue 1964- visiting prof: Havrard Divinity Sch 1985-86, Lancaster Univ 1988-; Hon fell: UCL 1988, Leo Baeck Coll London 1988; former pres London Soc for Study of Religion, pres Assoc for Jewish Studies; hon Citizen: Texas 1961, New Orleans 1963; Hon DHL: Spertus Coll 1987, Hebrew Union Cincinnati USA 1989, Jewish Theological Seminary New York 1989; *Books* We Have Reason To Believe (1957), Studies in Talmudic Logic (1961), Principles of the Jewish Faith (1964), A Jewish Theology (1973), Hasidic Prayer (1977), Jewish Mystical Testimonies (1977), The Talmudic Argument (1985-); *Recreations* hillwalking, theatre, cinema; *Style*— Rabbi Louis Jacobs; 27 Clifton Hill, St John's Wood, London NW8 OQE (☎ 01 624 1299); The New London Synagogue, 33 Abbey Rd, London NW8 (☎ 01 328 1026/7)

JACOBS, Michael Edward Hyman; s of Harry Ronald Jacobs (d 1966), of London, and Edmonde, *née* London; *b* 21 May 1948; *Educ* St Paul's Sch, Birmingham Univ (LLB); *m* 5 March 1973, Ruth Jacobs; 2 s; *Career* admitted slr 1972, ptnr Nicholson Graham and Jones 1976-; author of articles on corporate and personal taxation, contrib to Taxation and Tolley's Tax Planning 1989; Freeman City of London 1983, Liveryman Worshipful Co of Solicitors' 1987; memb Law Soc; FBIM 1983; *Style*— Michael Jacobs, Esq; Nicholson Graham & Jones, 19-21 Moorgate, London EC2R 6AU (☎ 01 628 9151, fax 01 638 3102, telex 8811848)

JACOBS, Peter; s of Bertram Jacobs (d 1982), and Phyllis Jacobs (d 1982); *b* 26 Sept 1938; *Educ* Merchant Taylors, Queen's Coll Cambridge (MA); *m* 21 Dec 1974, Susan Frances, da of Eric Simeon Boyes; 2 da (Sarah b 1977, Helen b 1978); *Career* 2 Lt 1958-59, Royal Hampshire Regt 1957-59; mktg res; fencing: Br Epee Champion (1962, 1964, 1970), Br Olympic Teams (1964, 1968), Cwlth Team (1962, 1966, 1970), mangr Br Olympic Team (1972, 1976), World Univ Epee Champion 1963; vice-pres Amateur Fencing Assoc, memb Exec Ctee Int Fencing Fedn 1985-88 (memb Statutes Ctee 1977-); Liveryman Worshipful Co of Weavers 1971; *Style*— Peter Jacobs, Esq

JACOBS, Sqdn-Ldr Vivian Kenneth; s of Frederick Charles Jacobs (d 1959), of Auckland, NZ, and Jane Ellen, *née* Ransley (d 1954); *b* 18 Sept 1918; *Educ* Mount Albert GS Auckland, Auckland Teachers Trg Coll (Teachers' C Primary Sch Cert), Auckland Univ Coll (Teachers' C Primary Sch Cert) , Royal Scottish Acad of Music Glasgow (Music in Educn); *m* 19 April 1945 (m dis 1963), 1 s (Martin Julian b 1951), 1 da (Louisa Fan b 1956); *Career* RNZAF 1940, cmmnd 1941, 136 Fighter Sqdn 1941, Sqdn-Ldr OC Wingate Clandestine Airfield, RAF Broadway N Burma 1944; Personal Staff Offr to Air Marshal Sir Victor Goddard AOA SE Asia Air Force; cmmnd RAF 1947; graduate RAF Staff Coll Bracknell 1949; Air Miny 1950-52 OC 45 Sqdn FEAF, Singapore, Butterworth, Malaya 1953-56; Cadet Staff Liason 61 Gp 1956-57; outside sales rep Russell & Somers Travel Agents Auckland 1958-61, mangr own travel agency Auckland 1962-66, sales mangr South Pacific US Travel Serv (US Govt Dept of Commerce) Sydney, Aust 1967-69, South Pacific sales dir Kneisel Travel Portland, Oregon 1970-74, own agency 1975-82; chorus master for NZ Opera Co 1959-60, choir master NSW Police Choir Sydney 1968, estab Jubilee Theatre Arts Soc Norwich 1985, developed project to creat a music theatre acad for full trg in music theatre for youngsters 18-25 years to be a registered charity, produced series of Gilbert & Sullivan operettas for 10-17 year olds 1985-88 in Norwich; nominee Unsung Hero of 1987 Award Norwich; *Recreations* music theatre and working with young people in musical prodns; *Clubs* RAF; *Style*— Sqdn-Ldr Vivian Jacobs; 31 Cuckoofield Lane,

Mulbarton, Norfolk NR14 8AY; General Director, Jubilee Theatre Arts Soc, P.O.Box 156, Norwich NR3 1QQ (☎ 0508 70072)

JACOBS, Sir Wilfred Ebenezer; GCMG (1982), KCVO (1977, OBE 1959, QC 1959); s of William Henry Jacobs and Henrietta Du Bois; *b* 19 Oct 1919; *Educ* Grenada Boys' Secdy Sch; *m* 1947, Carmen Sylva, da of Walter, and Flora Knight; 1 s, 2 da; *Career* barr 1946, registrar and additional magistrate St Vincent 1946, magistrate Dominica 1947, St Kitts 1949, attorney-gen Leeward Islands 1957-59, Antigua 1960; memb Legislative Cncl St Vincent, Dominica, St Kitts, Antigua 1947-60; slr-gen and actg attorney-gen Barbados 1961-63, plc; and MLC 1962-63, DPP 1964, judge Supreme Court Judicature 1967, govr Antigua 1967-81; KStJ; kt 1967; *Style—* Sir Wilfred Jacobs, GCMG, KCVO, OBE, QC; Governor's Residence, Antigua, West Indies

JACOBSON, Hon Colin; s of Baron Jacobson (Life Peer, d 1988); *b* 1941; *m* 1972, Josephine, da of John William Gates; *Style—* The Hon Colin Jacobson; 48 Parkway, NW1

JACOBSON, Ivor Julian; s of Harry Jacobson (d 1980), and Rae, *née* Tatz (d 1950); *b* 6 May 1940; *Educ* King Edward VII Sch Johannesburg, Univ of Witwatersrand S Africa (BComm); *m* 23 Dec 1963, Joan Yocheved, da of Isiah Adelson (d 1984); 1 s (Russell b 1965), 2 da (Lauren b 1968, Amanda b 1970); *Career* articled clerk Levitt Kirson Gross & Co 1963-65, trainee mangr and dir Brown Bros Shipping Co (Pty) Ltd 1966-67, fndr and md Int Shipping Co (Pty) Ltd 1968-87, chief exec Trade and Indust Gp (with subsids in many countries inc: S Africa, UK, USA, Singapore, Aust, Belgium, the Netherlands) 1973-; *Recreations* squash, horse riding; *Clubs* The Transvaal Automobile; *Style—* Ivor Jacobson, Esq; 200 North St, Harrison, New York 10528, USA (☎ 914 667 7299); 16 East 34 St, New York 10016 (☎ New York 212 6862420, telex 220710, fax 212 213 1347)

JACOBSON, Julian; s of Herbert Lawrence Jacobson, of San Jose, Costa Rica, and Fiora, *née* Ravasini; *b* 13 April 1953; *Educ* Coll Mellerio Rosmini Domodossola Italy, Univ De Geneve Switzerland; *Career* Du Pont de Nemours Int Sa Geneva Switzerland 1974-76, Kidder Peabody (Suisse) SA, Geneva Switzerland 1976-79, md (joined 1980) Kidder Peabody Int Ltd 1985-, dir Pasfin Servizi Finanziari SPA Milan Italy 1988-; *Recreations* tennis, skiing, basketball; *Style—* Julian Jacobson, Esq; 7 Lincoln Ho, Basil St, London SW3 1AN (☎ 01 589 2237); Kidder Peabody Int Ltd, 107 Cheapside, London EC2V 6DD (☎ 01 480 8115, fax 01 726 2796, car tel 0836 203 333, telex 884694)

JACOBSON, Hon Pamela; da of Baron Jacobson (Life Peer, d 1988); *b* 1944; *Style—* The Hon Pamela Jacobson; Witteys Lane, Thorncombe, nr Chard, Som

JACOBSON, Hon Philip; s of Baron Jacobson (Life Peer, d 1988); *b* 1938; *m* 1967, Ann, da of late Gilbert Mathison; *Style—* The Hon Philip Jacobson; 29 Carmalt Gdns, London SW15

JACOBSON, Baroness; Phyllis June; da of late Frank S Buck; *m* 1938, Baron Jacobson, MC (Life Peer, d 1988); 2 s, 1 da; 6 Avenue Road, St Albans, Herts

JACOBY, Hans Gert; *b* 7 July 1926; *Educ* Taplow GS, Westminster Tech Coll, Imperial Coll London, City and Guilds (BSC Eng); *m* 1955, Patricia Rose; 1 s; *Career* chm Br Mantle Mfrs Assoc 1973-77 (memb exec bd), fndr memb and current chm (1977-) Clothing Export Cncl, md Jacoby & Bratt and Assoc Cos, chm Export Advsy Gp for Clothing (Economic devpt ctee of Clothing Indust); *Style—* Hans Jacoby Esq; 7 Kingwood Pk, Hendon av, Finchley, N3 (☎ 01 346 3763)

JACOMB, Sir Martin Wakefield; s of Hilary and Félise Jacomb; *b* 11 Nov 1929; *Educ* Eton, Worcester Coll Oxford (MA); *m* 1960, Evelyn Helen, da of Richard Frank Heathcoat-Amory (d 1957; gs of Sir John Heathcoat-Amory, 1 Bt), and Hon Margaret Irene Gaenor Scott-Ellis, da of 8 Baron Howard de Walden (d 1946); 2 s, 1 da; *Career* barr Inner Temple 1955-68; dep chm Barclays Bank plc 1985, chm Barclays de Zoete Wedd 1986; dir: Bank of England 1986-, Christian Salvesen plc 1974-87, Commercial Union Assur Co plc 1984- (dep chm 1987), Br Gas plc 1981-87, Royal Opera House Covent Garden Ltd, The Daily Telegraph plc 1986-, Rio Tinto Zinc Corpn plc 1987-; external memb fin ctee Oxford Univ Press 1971-; tstee Nat Heritage Meml Fund 1982-; *Style—* Sir Martin Jacomb; Barclays Bank plc, 54 Lombard St, London EC3P 3AH (01 626 1567); Barclays de Zoete Wedd, PO Box 188, Ebbgate House, 2 Swan Lane, London EC4R 3TS (01 623 2323)

JACOMB-HOOD, Edward Wykeham; s of Canon Francis Edward Shaw Jacomb-Hood (d 1960), of Chichester, and Margaret Irene, *née* Chilver (d 1963); *b* 18 Mar 1920; *Educ* Lancing, King's Coll London (Bsc); *m* 25 June 1955, Honor Margaret, da of Sidney Edward Jones (d 1942), of London; 1 s (Anthony Wykeham b 1959), 2 da (Anna Margaret b 1956, Julia Honor b 1957); *Career* WWII Capt Royal Bombay Sappers and Miners RE; ptnr Livesey and Henderson Consulting Engrs 1959-66, conslt Dobbie and Ptnrs 1967-; memb: Synod diocese of Chichester, mid-Sussex NADFAS; Liveryman City of London 1984 (Freedom 1986); memb Assoc of Consulting Engrs 1966; FICE 1963; *Recreations* gardening, photography, walking, skiing, bridge; *Clubs* Athenaeum; *Style—* Edward Jacomb-Hood, Esq; Backwoods, Lindfield, Haywards Heath, Sussex RH16 2EN (☎ 04447 3310); Dobbie and Partners, 17 Lansdowne Rd, Croydon CR9 3UN (☎ 01 686 8212, fax 01 681 2499, telex 917 220)

JACQUES, Hon Ann; da of Baron Jacques (Life Peer); *b* 1941; *Style—* The Hon Ann Jacques

JACQUES, Hon Cecil Philip; s of Baron Jacques (Life Peer); *b* 20 Sept 1930; *Educ* Univ Coll London (BSc), Univ of London; *m* 1, 1960 (m dis 1977), Rita Ann Florence Hurford; 2 s; m 2, 1983, Mrs Carrine Royston, *née* Johnson; 2 s (John, Neil); *Career* sr staff eng Lockhead Missiles and Space Co Inc Sunnyvale California 1960-; *Clubs* Br American of Northern California Inc; *Style—* The Hon Cecil Jacques; 873 Somerset Drive, Sunnyvale, CA 94087; work (☎ 408 742 1669, 408 742 1932, 408 742 1933)

JACQUES, Baron (Life Peer UK 1968); John Henry Jacques; JP (Portsmouth); s of Thomas Dobson Jacques (d 1941), and Annie Bircham (d 1972); *b* 11 Jan 1905; *Educ* Victoria Univ Manchester (BCom), Co-op Coll Manchester; *m* 1929, Constance (d 1987), da of Harry White (d 1950), of Birmingham; 2 s, 1 da; *Career* sits as Labour Peer in Lords; chief exec Portsea Island Co-op Soc Ltd Portsmouth 1945-65, pres Co-op Congress 1961, chm Co-op Union 1964-70, pres Retail Trades Educn Cncl 1971-75, a lord in waiting (Govt whip) 1974-77 and 1979, a dep chm of Ctees 1977-85; *Clubs* Co-operative (Portsmouth); *Style—* The Rt Hon the Lord Jacques, JP; 23 Hilltop Crescent, Cosham, Portsmouth, Hants PO6 1BB (☎ 0705 375511)

JACQUES, Hon Paul; yr s of Baron Jacques (Life Peer); *b* 8 Jan 1932; *Educ* Edinburgh Univ (MB, ChB); *m* 20 Sept 1958, Nina Mollie, da of James MacKenzie, of Leigh-on-Sea, Essex; 1 s, 3 da; *Style—* The Hon Paul Jacques; Pinestead, 16 Twentylands Drive, East Leake, Loughborough, Leics

JACQUES, Peter Roy Albert; s of George Henry Jacques (d 1984), and Ivy Mary, *née* Farr (1988); *b* 12 August 1939; *Educ* Archbishop Temple's Sch, Newcastle-on-Tyne Poly (BSc), Leics Univ; *m* 21 Aug 1965, Jacqueline Anne, da of Robert George Sears, of Worthing; 1 s (Jonathan Peter), 1 da (Tamsin Eleanor); *Career* bldg labourer 1955-58, mkt porter 1958-62, teacher 1966-67, asst TUC Socl Insur and Industl Welfare Dept 1968-72 (ctee sec 1972-); memb: Nat Insur Advsy Ctee 1972-78, Health Educn Cncl 1974-87, Royal Cmmn on NHS 1976-79, NHS London Advsy Ctee 1979-82, Industl Injuries Cncl 1972-, Health & Safety Cmmn 1974-, EC Ctee on Health & Safety 1976-, sec Health Servs Ctee 1979-, Socl Securtiy Advsy Ctee 1980-, Civil Justice Review Advsy Ctee 1985-1988; *Recreations* yoga, gardening, walking, golf, reading; *Style—* Peter Jacques, Esq; TUC, Congress Ho, Gt Russell St, London WC1B 3LS (☎ 01 636 4030)

JACQUIER, Claire; da of Léon Jacquier (d 1931), and Elsa Gladys Jacquier, *née* Donner (d 1978); *Educ* Downham; *Career* painting and writing; *Style—* Miss Claire Jacquier

JAFFAR, Fouad Khaled; s of Khalid Mohammed Jaffar, ambassador Touk 1963-65, head of Diplomatic and Political Dept, and Miriam Abdullah Al-Askar; *b* 24 Nov 1945; *Educ* Wittleberry Sch, Concord Coll Tunbridgewells, Leeds Univ (BA Econ/Politics); *m* 11 Aug 1971, Elizabeth Jane, da of Herbert Vaughan Burke (d 1981); 1 s (Khaled b 1978), 1 da (Sara b 1975); *Career* UK dirships: Kuwait Invest Off (dep chm and gen mangr), Autobar Gp Ltd (dep chm 1982)-, Autobar Industs Ltd (chm 1983), Hays Gp Ltd (chm 1983-87), Hays Hldgs Ltd (vice-chm 1980-87), St Martins Hldgs Ltd (chm 1974-), St Martins (Indust) Ltd (dir 1980-), St Martins Property Corp Ltd and St Martins Property Invest Ltd (vice chm 1974- and 1975-), Timeregal Ltd (chm 1980-); Germany dirships: Zach AG and Westend Industl GmbH (md 1984-); Dutch dirships: Autobar Gp BV (md 1981-), Univend BV (memb suprvisory Bd); Spanish dirships: Industs del Papel y de la Celulosa Sa (pres 1984-), Prima Inmobilaira Sa and Torras Hostench Sa (vice-pres 1987-), Cros Sa (dir 1987-); Singapore dirships: Overseas Union Bank Centre (dir 1984-), Sassoon Hldgs Pte Ltd (vice-chm 1986-); Malaysia: dir United Plantations Berhad 1982-; Hong Kong dirships: Dao Heng Bank and Duo Heng Hldgs (dep-chm 1984-); *Recreations* walking, cycling, swimming; *Style—* Fouad Jaffar, Esq; Kuwait Investment Office, St Vedast House, 150 Cheapside, London EC2

JAFFE, Prof (Andrew) Michael; CBE; s of Arthur Daniel Jaffé, OBE, of 59 Putney Hill, London SW15, and Marie Marguerite, *née* Strauss; *b* 3 June 1923; *Educ* Eton (King's Scholar), King's Coll Cambridge (foundation scholar, MA, DLitt), Courtauld Inst of Art, Harvard, NY Inst of Fine Arts; *m* Patricia Ann Milne Henderson, da of Alexander Roy; 2 s (Daniel, Benjamin), 2 da (Deborah, Dorothea); *Career* served RNVR, Lt Cdr retd; dir Fitzwilliam Museum Cambridge 1973-, prof history of western art 1973-, fell King's Coll Cambridge 1952, fell Cwlth Fund Harvard and NY Univ 1951-53, asst lectr in fine arts Cambridge 1956 (lectr 1961), prof renaissance art Washington Univ 1960-61, visiting prof Harvard 1961 (1968-69), reader in hist of western art Cambridge 1968, head dept of hist of art Cambridge 1969-73, organiser Jordaens Exhibn Ottawa 1968-69; memb Cambridge Festival Bd, bd memb Eastern Arts Assoc; Nat Tst: regnl ctee (Wessex), art panel; govr Br Inst of Florence (representing vice-chllrs and princs); FRSA 1969; *Books* Van Dyck's Antwerp Sketchbook (1966), Rubens (1967), Jordaens (1968), Rubens and Italy (1977), author of articles and reviews (art historical) in Euro and N American jls, etc; *Recreations* viticulture; *Clubs* Brooks's, Beefsteak, Turf; *Style—* Prof Michael Jaffe, CBE; Grove Lodge, Trumpington St, Cambridge

JAFFRAY, Anne, Lady; Anne; only da of Capt John Otho Paget, MC (d 1934), of Thorpe Satchville Hall, Leics; *Educ* Langford Grove, Schs: France, Germany; *m* 1, 1942 (m dis 1950), Sir John Godfrey Worsley-Taylor, 3 Bt (d 1952); 1 da (Annette Pamela, *qv*); m 2, 1950, Col Sir William Edmund Jaffray, 4 Bt, TD, JP, DL (d 1953); 1 s (William Otho, 5 Bt, *qv*); *Career* memb Hants CC 1964-79; *Recreations* tennis, fishing, field-sports; *Style—* Anne, Lady Jaffray; Haydown House, Weston Patrick, Basingstoke, Hants

JAFFRAY, Nicholas Gordon Alexander; s and h of Sir William Jaffray, 5 Bt, *qv*; *b* 1 Nov 1951; *Style—* Nicholas Jaffray Esq

JAFFRAY, Sir William Otho; 5 Bt (UK 1892), of Skilts, Studley, Warwickshire; s of Lt Col Sir William Edmund Jaffray, 4 Bt, TD, JP, DL (d 1953); *b* 1 Nov 1951; *Educ* Eton; *m* 9 May 1981, Cynthia Ross Corrington, da of William M Geering, of Montreal, Quebec, Canada; 2 s (Nicholas b 1982, Jack Henry William b 3 Aug 1987), 1 da (Alexandra Marina Ross b 1984); *Heir* s, Nicholas Gordon Alexander b 18 Oct 1982, *qv*; *Career* property conslt; *Style—* Sir William Jaffray, Bt; The Manor House, Priors Dean, Petersfield, Hants (☎ 073 084 483)

JAGGARD, Anthony John Thorrold; JP (1976); s of Rev Arthur William Percival Jaggard (d 1967), of Guilsborough Vicarage, Northamptonshire, and Isabel Louise May, *née* Capell (d 1972); *b* 5 June 1936; *Educ* Bedford Sch, Liverpool Sch of Architecture Univ of Liverpool; *m* 29 April 1961, (Elizabeth) Jane, da of Col Sir Joseph William Weld, OBE, TD (former Ld-Lt Dorset 1964-84), of Lulworth Manor, Dorset; 2 s (Oliver b and d 3 April 1970, Simon (twin) b 3 April 1970), 3 da (Victoria b 14 Jan 1962, Charlotte b 27 Jan 1964, Sarah b 5 March 1968); *Career* Cheshire (Earl of Chester's) Yeomanry 1958-67 (Capt 1964, Adj 1967), RARO 1967-86; ptnr John Stark and Ptnrs architects 1965-; projects incl consultation on: Callaly Castle Northumberland, Hoddam Castle Dumfries, Ince Castle Cornwall, Lulworth Castle Dorset, Wardour Castle Wiltshire; designed or remodelled new houses at Gaston Grange Bentworth Hants, Longford House Sydling St Nicholas Dorset, Lulworth Castle House Dorset, Oakfield Park Mortimer Berks, contributor Archaeological Journal; memb exec cncl S Dorset Cons Assoc 1965-81; cncl memb: Dorset Nat Hist and Archaeological Soc 1969-, Dorset Cncl of St John 1978-81; dir Dorset Bldgs Preservation Tst 1984-, cncl memb Royal Archaeological Inst 1987; Liveryman Worshipful Co of Painter Stainers 1975; FRSA 1986; *Recreations* old buildings, gardening, shooting; *Clubs* Cavalry and Guards; *Style—* Anthony Jaggard, Esq, JP; Winfrith Court, Winfrith Newburgh, Dorset DT2 8JR (☎ 0305 852 800)); John Stark and Partners, 13 and 14 Princes St, Dorchester DT1 1TW (☎ 0305 262636, fax 0305 260960)

JAGGARD, Joan; da of Joseph Wright (d 1942), and Ethel Anne, *née* Payne; *b* 15 Jan 1924; *Educ* Hesketh Fletcher Sch For Girls, Wigan Tech Mining Coll, Manchester Tech, Nottingham Univ; *m* 15 Jan 1956, Donald William Jaggard (d 1977), s of Arthur

Jaggard (d 1935); *Career* WWII served ATS 1942-47; employed in textile indust 1947-53 (sales rep 1953-57), sales promotion exec in packaging indust 1957-63; fndr DW Jaggard and Assocs Ltd 1963 (selling commercial vehicle trailer equipment; invented and took copyright on Tiltman Services - a national repair service for Tilt Trailer and curtain sided vehicles - 1987); campaigner for improved safety critical factors and safety standards for vehicle components; supporter of Direction of Youth in Employment; *Recreations* gardening, music, reading, travel; *Style—* Mrs Joan Jagggard; Jaggards Tiltman Ltd, 40 High St, Edwinstowe Mansfield (☎ 823033, fax 0623 824602)

JAGGER, Cedric Sargeant; s of Charles Sargeant Jagger, MC, ARA (d 1934), of London, and Violet Constance *née* Smith (d 1964); *b* 14 June 1920; *Educ* Westminster; *m* 1, 22 March 1952 (m dis 1972), Jane Angela, da of James Hynds (d 1975); 1 s (Christopher b 18 May 1958), 1 da (Linsday b 19 Sept 1954); m 2, 5 April 1972, Christine, da of James Fergus Brown of Sevenoaks, Kent; *Career* WWII RA 1940-46, served 8 Army ME 1942-, then N Africa, Sicily and Italy, WOII at end of war; permanent staff ICI 1938-72, p/t memb and chm of selection bds CS Cmmn 1973-86, p/t asst curator and keeper of the Clockmakers Co Collection Guildhall London 1974-88; horological historian and author 1968-; memb The Stable Theatre Tst, life memb Hastings and St Leonards Museum Assoc, Friend of Rye Harbour Nature Reserve; JP Hampshire 1975; Liveryman Worshipful Co of Clockmakers 1980 (Freeman 1975); memb Soc of Authors (1987); *Books* Clocks (1973), The World's Great Clocks and Watches (1977), Royal Clocks - The British Monarchy and its Timekeepers 1300-1900 (1983), The Artistry of the English Watch (1988); *Recreations* principally work - also photography and music; *Clubs* The Arts; *Style—* Cedric Jagger, Esq

JAGGS, Michael Richard Moore; s of Rev Arthur Ernest Jaggs (d 1975), of Tilford Vicarage, Tilford, Surrey, and Mary Enid, *née* Moore; *b* 7 Nov 1937; *Educ* Wells Cathedral Sch, Pierrepont Sch, City Univ (FBDO, PhD); *m* 1, 15 Sept 1962 (m dis), Gillian, da of (Francis) Allen Ayre, MBE (d 1969); 2 s (Richard, Alexander), 2 da (Sarah, Sophie); m 2, 30 Aug 1980, Janet Elizabeth, *née* Talbot; *Career* qualified dispensing optician 1956, in private practice 1961-, practice merged with Dollond & Aitchison 1988, hosp appt Odstock Hosp Salisbury; in control of Crofting Ltd (investmt co); chm bd of govrs Pierrepont Sch Surrey; Freeman City of London, Liveryman Worshipful Co of Spectacle Makers; fell: Assoc of Br Contact Orgn, Royal Soc of Health, Br Contact Lens Assoc; *Books* Scleral lenses - a clinical guide (1980); *Recreations* skiing, sailing, swimming; *Style—* Michael Jaggs, Esq; Turnpike Field, Hartley Wintney, Hampshire RG27 8HY (☎ 025126 2658); 7 Wigmore St, London W1 (☎ 01 935 4280)

JAKES, Clifford Duncan; s of Ernest Thomas James (d 1963), of Leigh on Sea, Essex; *b* 29 Dec 1942; *Educ* Westcliff HS Southend-on-Sea, Aston Univ; *Career* articled Wilkins Kennedy & Co London 1960-65, mgmnt trainee Tube Investmts Ltd 1966-67, fin dir Raleigh Cycles (Malaysia) 1968-71, fin controller (overseas div) Raleigh Industries Ltd Nottingham 1971-73, fin dir and md Warren Plantation Hldgs London 1974-81, mgmnt conslt 1982, gp md Link House Pubns 1983-; FCA; *Recreations* theatre, sport, preservation of wild life; *Clubs* City, Selangor (Malaysia), Bengal (Calcutta); *Style—* Clifford Jakes, Esq; 10 Harley St, Leigh on Sea, Essex (☎ 0702 75758); Link House Publications plc, Robert Rogers House, New Orchard, Poole, Dorset (☎ 0202 671171)

JAKEWAY, Sir (Francis) Derek; KCMG (1963), CMG (1956, OBE 1948); s of Francis Edward Jakeway; *b* 6 June 1915; *Educ* Hele's Sch Exeter, Exeter Coll Oxford (MA); *m* 1941, Phyllis Lindsay Watson; 3 s; *Career* entered Colonial Service (Nigeria) 1937, sec to Seychelles Govt 1946-49, chief sec: Br Guiana 1955-59, Sarawak 1959-63, govr and C-in-C Fiji 1964-68, ret; chm Devon Area Health Authy 1974-82; KStJ 1964; *Style—* Sir Derek Jakeway, KCMG, CMG, OBE; 78 Douglas Ave, Exmouth, Devon (☎ 039 582 271342)

JAKOBOVITS, Baron (Life Peer UK 1988) Immanuel; s of Rabbi Dr Julius Jakobovits; *b* 8 Feb 1921,Konigsberg, Germany; *Educ* London Univ, Jews' Coll London, Yeshivah Etz Chaim London; *m* 1949, Amélie, da of Rabbi Dr Elie Munk; 2 s (Dr Hon Julian b 1950, Rabbi Hon Samuel b 1951), 4 da (Esther (Hon Mrs Pearlman) b 1953, Jeanette (Hon Mrs Turner) b 1956, Aviva (Hon Mrs Adler) b 1958, Elisheva (Hon Mrs Homburger) b 1966); *Career* minister of three London synagogues 1941-49; Chief Rabbi of Ireland 1949-58; Rabbi Fifth Ave Synagogue (New York) 1958-67; Chief Rabbi of The United Hebrew Congregations of the Br Cwlth of Nats 1967-; kt 1981; *Books* Jewish Medical Ethics (1959), Jewish Law Faces Modern Problems (1965), Journal of a Rabbi (1966), The Timely and the Timeless (1977), If Only My People...Zionism in My Life (1984); co-author of The Jewish Hospital Compendium (1963), etc; *Style—* The Rt Hon Lord Jakobovits; Adler House, Tavistock Sq, London WC1 (☎ 01 387 1066)

JAMAL, Mahmood; s of Maulana Jamal Mian, of Firangi Mahal, and Kaniz Fatima Asar; *Educ* St Joseph's Sch Dacca, SOAS, London Univ (BA); *Career* poet, prodr and dir; poems broadcast on Radio 3 and published in various magazines including London Magazine; prodr of TV films, Majdhar Channel 4 1984; dir: Sanctuary Challenge Channel 4 1986, Environment of Dignity Channel 4 1986; co-fndr Retake Film and Video Collective (winner BFI Independent Film and TV Award 1988), co-ed Black Phoenix Magazine 1979-, lit advsr and vice chm steering ctee Roundhouse Arts Centre 1984, winner Minority Rights Gp Award for poetry and translation 1985, lit advsr to Gtr London Arts 1986-, advsr and memb editorial bd Third Text Quarterly 1987-, participant in poetry in festivals all over the country including the Arts Cncl Festival Southbank; memb Assoc of Admin Accountants; *Books* Coins for chgaron (1976), Silence Inside A Guns Mouth (1984); ed and translator Penguin Book of Modern Urdu Poetry (1986); *Recreations* tennis, squash, cricket; *Clubs* South Hampstead Lawn Tennis; *Style—* Mahmood Jamal, Esq; 69 Dartmouth Rd, London NW2 4EP (☎ 01 452 8170); 19 Liddell Rd, London NW6 (☎ 01 328 4676)

JAMES, Alan Murray; s of Harold Birkett James (d 1961), of Sutton, Surrey, and Nellie Beatrice, *née* Covington (d 1981); *b* 24 Feb 1925; *Educ* Sutton Valence Sch, Univ of Birmingham (RE Army Course), Clare Coll Cambridge (MA); *m* 7 June 1952, Janette Mary, da of Harold Pridmore Lack (d 1974); 3 da (Linda b 1954, Susan b 1956, Mandy b 1961); *Career* WWII RE 1943-47, cmmnd 1945, KGVD Bengal Sappers and Miners 1945-47, Capt 1947, serv Indonesia and Malaysia; md and chm Tate and Lyle Tech Servs 1961-75, md Tate and Lyle Enterprises 1969-75, chm Sugar Knowledge Int 1981-, dir Sugar Indust Technologists Inc 1965-78, pres Sugar Processing Res 1972-74; Cambridge Univ Rugby Blue 1948 and 1949; Lloyds underwriting memb 1982-; Freeman City of London 1948, Worshipful Co of Loriners; *Recreations* tennis, squash, travel; *Clubs* RAC, Bromley CC, Middleton, Richmond FC, Cambridge RUFC; *Style—* Alan James, Esq; 12 Shornefield Close, Bickley, Kent BR1 2HX (☎ 01 467 4579, telex 934968); 16 Crossbush Rd, Felpham, W Sussex PO22 7LS

JAMES, Hon Anthony Christopher Walter Paul; 2 s of 5 Baron Northbourne; *b* 14 Jan 1963; *Style—* The Hon Anthony James; 11 Eaton Place, London SW1

JAMES, Charles Edwin Frederic; s of Frederic Crockett Gwilym James (d 1970), formerly tres of the Great Universal Stores Ltd, and Marjorie Peggy, *née* Peace (d 1976); *b* 17 April 1943; *Educ* Trent Coll Derbyshire, Selwyn Coll Cambridge (MA); *m* 1968, Diana Mary Francis, da of James Francis Thornton (d 1977), formerly chm and md William Thornton & Sons Ltd; 2 s (Daniel b 1971, Philip b 1973); *Career* barr 1965, barr-at-law practising Northern Circuit, rec of the Crown Ct 1982-; *Recreations* family pursuits; *Clubs* Cambridge Univ Cricket, Royal Liverpool Golf, Royal Mersey Yacht; *Style—* Charles James, Esq; Broomlands, 38 Vyner Road South, Birkenhead, Merseyside L43 7PR (☎ 051 652 1951); Refuge Assurance House, Derby Square, Liverpool L2 1TS (☎ 051 709 4222)

JAMES, Hon Charles Walter Henry; eldest s & h of 5 Baron Northbourne, qv; *b* 14 June 1960; *Educ* Eton, Magdalen Coll Oxford; *m* 3 Oct 1987, Catherine Lucy, o da of W Ralph Burrows, of Prescot, Lancs; *Career* dir: Rede Investmts Ltd, Redesdale Investmts Ltd, Betteshanger Farms Ltd; *Recreations* art collector; *Clubs* Annabels; *Style—* The Hon Charles James; Stoneheap Farm, Studdal, Deal, Kent (☎ (0304) 361130); Betteshanger Farms Ltd, Home Farm, Betteshanger, Deal, Kent (☎ 0304 611281, telex 965837)

JAMES, Christopher John; s of John Thomas Walters James, MC (d 1978), of Monmouth, and Cicely Hilda, *née* Puton (formerly Motteram) (d 1970); *b* 20 Mar 1932; *Educ* Clifton, Magdalene Coll Cambridge (MA); *m* 20 Sept 1958, Elizabeth Marion Cicely, da of Thomas Finlayson Thomson (d 1977), of Winchester; 1 s (Timothy b 10 Dec 1959), 1 da (Caroline b 10 Oct 1962); *Career* Nat Serv cmmn RA 1951-52, TA 1952-60; admitted slr 1958, dep sr ptnr Martineau Johnson 1987- (formerly ptnr Johnson & Co 1960-87); Birmingham Midshires Building Soc (formerly Birmingham & Bridgwater Bldg Soc, previously Birmingham Bldg Soc): dir 1980-, dep chm 1988-; pres Birmingham Law Soc 1983-84, chm body govr Edgbaston HS for Girls 1987-; gen cmmr for income tax N E Warwicks 1974-82; memb Law Soc 1958; *Clubs* Little Aston GC; *Style—* Christopher James, Esq; Martineau Johnson, St Philips House, St Philips Place, Birmingham B3 2PP (☎ 021 200 3300, fax 021 200 3330, telex 339793)

JAMES, His Honour Judge Christopher Philip; s of Herbert Edgar James, CBE (d 1977); *b* 27 May 1934; *Educ* Felsted, Magdalene Coll Cambridge; *Career* barr Gray's Inn 1959, rec Crown Ct 1979, circuit judge 1980-; *Clubs* United Oxford and Cambridge Univ; *Style—* His Honour Judge James

JAMES, Hon (Veronica) Clare; da of Baron Saint Brides, GCMG, CVO, MBE (Life Peer), *qv*, and his 1 w Elizabeth Margaret, *née* Piesse (d 1966); *b* 14 Sept 1950; *Educ* Wycombe Abbey, London Univ (BSc Econ), RSA Dip in Teaching English as a Foreign Language; *m* 10 Jan 1970 (m dis 1978), Dr Patrick Duncan, s of Patrick Baker Duncan (d 1967); 1 s (Patrick b 1973); *Career* teacher of English as a Foreign Language London 1977-80 (Int Business Colls Ltd) and Stockholm 1980-; freelance translator from Swedish to English 1982-; authorised by Swedish Bd of Trade as Public Translator from Swedish into English 1987; employee of own company The Word Shop (Sprakverksta'n AB) 1986-; conslt on English language work; *Recreations* reading, travel; *Style—* The Hon Clare James; Köpenhamnsgatan 24, 2 tr, S-164 42 Kista, Sweden (☎ 010 46 8 750 8846)

JAMES, Rt Rev Colin Clement Walter; *see*: Wakefield, Bishop of

JAMES, Sir Cynlais (Kenneth) Morgan; KCMG (1985, CMG 1976); s of Thomas and Lydia James; *b* 29 April 1926; *Educ* Trinity Coll Cambridge; *m* 1953, Mary, da of Richard Désriré Girouard by his w Lady Blanche Maud de la Poer Beresford (da of 6 Marquess of Waterford, KP, and Lady Beatrix Fitzmaurice, da of 5 Marquess of Lansdowne), also sis of the architectural historian Mark Girouard, *qv*; 2 da; *Career* served RAF 1944-47; FO (now FCO) 1951: former sec Moscow, head W Euro Dept FCO and min Paris; ambass Poland 1981-83, under-sec of state FCO 1983, ambass Mexico 1983-86; dir-gen Canning House 1987-; Order of the Aztec Eagle (First Class); Doctor Honoris Causa of the Mexican Acad of Int Law; *Clubs* Brooks's, Pratt's, Travellers' (Paris), Beefsteak; *Style—* Sir Cynlais (Kenneth) James, KCMG; Canning House, 2 Belgrave Square, London SW1

JAMES, Prof David Edward; s of Charles Edward James (d 1982), of Eastleigh, Hants, and Dorothy Hilda, *née* Reeves (d 1984); *b* 31 July 1937; *Educ* Peter Symonds Sch Winchester, Univ of Reading (BSc), Univ of Oxford (Dip Ed), Univ of London (Dip Further Ed), Univ of Durham (MEd); *m* 30 March 1963, Penelope Jane, da of Lt Cdr Edward J Murray, of Bradford-on-Avon, Wilts; 2 s (Philip b 1966, Christopher b 1969), 1 da (Lucy b 1964); *Career* lectr in zoology and psychology City of Bath Tech Coll 1961-63, lectr in sci and psychology St Mary's Coll of Educn Newcastle-on-Tyne 1963-64; Univ of Surrey: lectr in educnl psychology 1964-68, res lectr in educn 1968-69, dir of adult educn 1969-80, prof of adult educn 1980-81, prof and head of dept of educnl studies 1981-; chm: Br Assoc for Educnl Gerontology, Preretirement Assoc of GB and NI; memb: bd of educn Royal Coll of Nursing, educn ctee Royal Coll of Midwives, governing body Centre for Int Briefing, Moor Park Tst for Christian Adult Educn, Weald Community Sch, Croydon Coll, Gen Nursing Cncl 1972-80, UK Central Cncl for Nursing Midwifery and Health Visiting 1980-83, English Nat Bd for Nursing Midwifery and Health Visiting 1983-88; AFBPsS 1966, CIBiol, MIBiol 1963, FRSH 1974, FRSA 1974; *Books* A Students guide to Efficient Study (1966), Introduction to Psychology (1968); *Recreations* farming; *Style—* Prof David James; Dept of Educational Studies, University of Surrey, Guildford GU2 5XH (☎ 0483 571281 ext 3122, fax 300803, telex 859331)

JAMES, Dr David Geraint; s of David James (d 1968), of Treherbert, Wales, and Sarah, *née* Davies (d 1978); *b* 2 Jan 1922; *Educ* Pontypridd Co Sch, Jesus Coll Cambridge (MA, MD), Middx Hosp Univ of London (MRCS, LRCP, MRCP), Columbia Univ NY; *m* 18 Dec 1951, Prof Dame Sheila Patricia Violet Sherlock, DBE; 2 da eamanda b 15 Sept 1958, Auriole b 7 Dec 1963); *Career* Surgn-Lt RNVR 1946-48; serv: HMS Halcyon, HMS Theseus; conslt physician RN 1972-85; dean of studies Royal Northern Hosp London 1968-88 (conslt physician 1959-), prof med Univ of London and Miami; pres: Harvey Soc London 1963, Osler Club London, Med Soc London 1980; fndr London Med Ophthalmology Soc 1964, organising soc World Congress History of Med 1972, conslt ophthalmic physician St Thomas Hosp London;

cncl memb: RCP 1983, Huntarian Soc 1984; pres London Glamorganshire Soc 1971-75, fndr pres World Assoc of Sarcoidosis 1987, ed Int Jl Sarcoidosis, vice pres Post Grad Med Fedn; hon corr Thoracic Soc of: France, Italy, Portugal, French Nat Acad of Med; white robed memb Bardic Circle of Wales 1984; Freeman: Worshipful Co of Apothecaries 1960-, City of London; Hon LLD Univ of Wales 1982; FRCP 1964; *Books* Textbook of Infectins (1957), Colour Atlas of Respiratory Diseases (1981), Sarcoidosis (1985), W B Saunders; *Recreations* tennis, rugby, international Welshness; *Clubs* Athenaeum; *Style*— Dr Geraint James; 41 York Terrace East, Regent's Park, London NW1 4PT (☎ 01 486 4560); 149 Harley St, London W1N 1HG (☎ 01 935 4444)

JAMES, Hon Mrs (Deborah Katherine Louise); *née* Suenson-Taylor; 2 da of 2 Baron Grantchester, QC; *b* 9 April 1957; *m* 1977, Michael James; *Style*— The Hon Mrs James; Windsor, Church Rd, West Wittering, W Sussex

JAMES, Derek Claude; s of Cecil Claude James (d 1987), and Violet, *née* Rudge (d 1974); *b* 9 Mar 1929; *Educ* King Edwards GS Birmingham, Open Univ (BA); *m* 16 Oct 1954, Evelyn, *née* Thomas; 1 s (Stephen b 1955), 1 da (Kathryn (Mrs Dawson) b 1956); *Career* RA 1947-49; local govt 1946-69: Birmingham, Coventry, Bradford; Leeds City Cncl: princ offr 1969-73, dep dir of social servs 1973-78, dir of social servs 1978-; pres Nat Assoc of Nursery and Family Care 1988-; memb: St Annes Shelter & Housing Action Ltd Leeds 1976-, Yorks RHA 1976-82, Nat Advsy Cncl for Employment of Disabled People 1985-89; memb Assoc of Dirs of Social Servs; *Recreations* gardening, watching sport; *Style*— Derek James, Esq; Hill House, Woodhall Hills, Calverley, Pudsey, West Yorkshire LS28 5QY (☎ 0532 578 044); Dept of Social Service, Sweet St, Leeds 11 (☎ 0532 463 400)

JAMES, Air Vice Marshal Edgar; CBE (1966), DFC (1945, AFC X1948 and bar 1959); s of Richard George James (d 1967), and Gertrude, *née* Barnes (d 1942); *b* 19 Oct 1915; *Educ* Neath GS; *m* 1941, Josephine, da of John Steel (d 1980), of Harrogate; 2 s (Stephen b 1945, David b 1949); *Career* RAF 1939-, cmmnd 1940, 305 and 107 Sqdns NW Europe (King's Commendation for Meritorious Service in the Air 1943 and 1944), CO 68 Sqdn 1954-55 Germany (Queens commendation 1956), chief instr and asst cmdt Centl Flying Sch 1959-61, dir operational regts MoD 1962-65, cdr Br Forces Zambia 1966, Air Vice Marshal 1967, dep controller Miny of Technol 1967-69, ret 1969; aviation conslt 1970-86; FRAeS 1971; *Recreations* sailing, golf; *Clubs* RAF, Royal Western Y C; *Style*— Air Vice Marshal James; Low Mead, Traine Paddock, Modbury, Devon PL21 0RN (☎ 0458 830 492)

JAMES, Edward Frank Willis; s of William Dodge James, CVO, JP, DL, and Evelyn, CBE (da of Sir Charles Forbes of Newe, 4 Bt, DL, by Helen, 2 da of Sir Thomas Moncreiffe of Moncreiffe, 7 Bt); Edward is hence 2 cous once removed of Sir Iain Moncreiffe of that Ilk, 11 Bt, and 3 cous of 24 Earl of Erroll); *b* 16 August 1907, (HM King Edward VII stood sponsor); *Educ* Eton, Ch Ch Oxford; *m* 1931 (m dis 1934), Tillie (Ottilie Ethel) Losch, the actress and da of Eugene Losch, of Vienna; *Career* lord of the manors of West Dean and Binderton, patron of the living of West Dean; late hon attaché Rome; novelist, collector of paintings, particularly surrealist ones; *Style*— Edward James, Esq; 3 Culross St, London W1

JAMES, Edwin Kenneth George; s of Edwin Percy (d 1956), and Jessie Marion, *née* Clarke; *b* 27 Dec 1916; *Educ* Latymer Upper Sch, Univ of London (BSc); *m* 1941, Dorothy Margaret, da of Arthur Pratt (d 1961), of London; 1 da (Carolyn Margaret b 1943); *Career* WO 1938, Chem Def Expl Stn 1942, Austral Field Sxpl Stn 1944-46, Operational Res Gp US Army MD USA 1950-54, dir Biol and Chemical Def MOD 1961; HM Treasy 1967, chief scientific offr Civil Serv Dept 1970; chief exec PAG Ltd 1977-87, chm Photon plc and Pagsolar Technol Ltd 1986-; silver medal of Operational Res Soc 1979; FRCS, FOR; *Clubs* Athenaeum; *Style*— Kenneth James, Esq; 5 Waterseet Rd, Harnham, Salisbury, Wilts (☎ 0722 334099)

JAMES, Rev Canon Eric Arthur; s of John Morgan James and Alice Amelia James; *b* 14 April 1925; *Educ* Dagenham County HS, King's Coll London (MA, BD, FKC); *Career* asst curate St Stephen with St John Westminster 1951-55, chaplain Trinity Coll Cambridge 1955-59, select preacher to Univ of Cambridge 1959-60, vicar St George Camberwell and warden Trinity Coll Mission 1959-64, dir Parish and People 1964-69, canon residentiary and precentor Southwark Cathedral 1966-73, proctor in convocation 1964-72, canon residentiary and missioner Diocese of St Albans 1973-83, hon canon 1983-, preacher to Gray's Inn 1978-; commissary to: Bishop of Kimberley 1965-67, Archbishop of Melanesia 1969-; examining chaplain to: Bishop of St Albans 1973-83, Bishop of Truro 1983-; dir Christian Action 1979-, chaplain to HM The Queen 1984-; *Books* The Double Cure (1957, second edn 1980), Odd Man Out (1962), Spirituality for Today (ed 1968), Stewards of the Mysteries of God (ed 1979), A Life of Bishop John A T Robinson, Scholar, Pastor, Prophet (1987), Where Three Ways Meet (ed 1987), God's Truth (ed 1988); *Recreations* music; *Clubs* Reform, Royal Cwlth Soc; *Style*— The Rev Canon Eric James; 11 Denny Crescent, Kennington, London SE11 4UY; Christian Action, St Peter's House, 308 Kennington Lane, London SE11 5HY (☎ 01 735 2372)

JAMES, Dr (David William) Francis; s of Thomas Martin James (d 1962), of Harefield, Middx, and Margaret Anne, *née* Francis (d 1984); *b* 29 Mar 1929; *Educ* Cyfarthfa GS, Univ of Wales (BSc), Univ of London (PhD); *m* 4 April 1953, Elaine Maureen, da of Thomas Hewett (d 1955); 2 da (Rosalind b 1955, Heather b 1958); *Career* Flying Offr RAF 1954-56 (educn offr); res offr ICI Ltd 1956-60, lectr and sr lectr Univ of Wales Bangor 1960-71, dep princ Glamorgan Poly 1971-72, dir Poly of Wales 1972-78, dir and chief exec Br Ceramic Res Ltd; chm Leek and Dist Camera Club; memb: Methodist Church, cncl Nat Academic Awards (CNAA) 1975-82; chm Ctee for Res Degrees (CNAA) 1980-86 (memb 1976-82); memb: SERC Polys Ctee 1975-78, trg ctee Wales Cncl for Disabled 1974-78; hon fell Poly of Wales 1986; FRSA 1976, FICeram 1985; *Recreations* photography, DIY; *Clubs* Royal Cwlth Fedn; *Style*— Dr Francis James; Fairways, Birchall, Leek, Staffs (☎ 0538 373311); British Ceramic Res Ltd (Ceram Research), Queen's Road, Penkhull, Stoke-on-Trent, Staffs (☎ 45431, fax 0782 412331, telex 36228 BCRA G)

JAMES, Gerald Reaveley; s of Capt William Gilbert Ferdinand James (d 1965), of Deer Orchard House, Cumberland, and Annie, *née* Rydiard (d 1985); *b* 7 Sept 1937; *Educ* Sedbergh; *m* 5 Dec 1964, Gisela, da of Erich Christian Hess (ka 1943); 3 s (Christian Gilbert Furnival b 22 July 1967, Andrew Francis Reaveley b 17 Oct 1968, Alexander Gerald Reaveley b 11 Feb 1981); *Career* RA 1955, 16 Ind Para Bde 1956-58; Peat Marwick Mitchell 1958-64, Hill Samuel & Co Ltd 1964-68, Baring Bros & Co Ltd 1968-72, dir Henry Ansbacher & Co Ltd 1972-76, conslt Singer & Friedlander 1976-78; dir: Belhaven Brewery & Co Ltd 1978-82, Norton Telecoms Gp plc 1978-82, VW Thermax plc 1982-83; chm: Astra Hldgs plc 1981-, Astra Hldgs Corp (USA) 1986-, Astra (Canada) 1986-, Kilgore Corpn USA 1987-, Br Mfr & Res Co Ltd 1988-; Freeman City of London 1989, Liveryman Worshipful Co of Gunmakers 1989 (Freeman 1988); FCA 1964, FIOD 1984, MBIM 1980; *Recreations* shooting, fishing, cricket, rugby, tennis; *Clubs* Naval & Mil, Roehampton; *Style*— Gerald James, Esq; 2 Laurel Road, Barnes, London SW13 0EE (☎ 01 876 1436); Deer Orchard House, Cockermouth, Cumbria; 6 St James's Place, London SW1 (☎ 01 495 3787, fax 01 495 0493, telex 295279)

JAMES, Geraldine; da of Gerald Thomas (d 27 May 1987), of Cornwall, and Annabella, *née* Doogan (d 6 May 1987); *b* 25 Oct 1955; *Educ* Downe House Sch Newbury, Drama Centre London; *m* 28 June 1986, Joseph Sebastian Blatchley, s of John Blatchley; 1 da (Eleanor b 20 June 1985); *Career* actress; worked in repertory theatre at Chester, Exeter and Coventry 1972-75 roles incl Miss Julie, Desdemona, Raina, Annie Sullivan; fringe theatre in London incl: Almost Free 1976, Little Theatre 1976, Bush 1983, Man in the Moon 1986; other work incl: The White Devil Oxford Playhouse 1981, When I was a Girl I Used to Scream and Shout Whitehall Theatre 1987, Cymbeline NT 1988, Portia in The Merchant of Venice Peter Hall Co 1989; TV incl: Dummy 1977 (BAFTA Best Actress nomination), Love Among The Artists 1978, The History Man 1980, Jewel In The Crown (BAFTA Best Actress nomination), Blott on the Landscape 1984, Echoes 1987; films incl: Sweet William 1978, Night Cruiser 1978, Gandhi 1981, Wolves of Willoughby Chase 1988, The Tall Guy 1988; *Recreations* music; *Style*— Miss Geraldine James; Julian Belfrage Assoc, 68 St James Street, SW1 (☎ 01 491 4400)

JAMES, Glen William; s of Clifford Vizetelly James, of Long Ashton, Bristol, and Kathleen Mary Flora, *née* Doull; *b* 22 August 1952; *Educ* King's Coll Sch Wimbledon, New Coll Oxford (MA); *m* 15 Aug 1987, Amanda Claire, da of Philip Dorrell, of Worcester; *Career* admitted slr 1976, ptnr Slaughter and May 1983-; Freeman City of London Slrs Co; memb Law Soc; *Recreations* music, reading, various sports; *Clubs* RAC; *Style*— Glen James, Esq; Slaughter and May, 35 Basinghall St, London EC2V 5DB (☎ 01 600 1200, fax 01 600 0289, telex 883486/888926)

JAMES, Helen; *née* Shaw; da of Peter Shaw, and Joan Mary, *née* Turner; *b* 29 Mar 1951; *Educ* Cheadle Hulme Sch, Girton Coll Cambridge (MA); *m* 30 August 1976, Allan James, s of Thomas Raymond James; 1 s (Peter Thomas b 26 March 1979), 2 da (Clare Elizabeth b 21 Oct 1980, Sarah Linda b 29 Sept 1985); *Career* actuary; trainee Equity and Law 1972-74, ptnr Clay & Ptnrs 1977- (joined 1975); *Style*— Mrs Helen James; 15 Church Ave, Ruislip, Middx HA4 7HX (☎ 0895 631 758); Clay & Partners 61 Brook St, London W1 (☎ 01 408 1600)

JAMES, Henry Leonard; CB (1979); s of Leonard Mark James (d 1967), of Birmingham, and Alice Esther, *née* Jones (d 1971); *b* 12 Dec 1919; *Educ* King Edward VI Sch Birmingham; *m* 26 Mar 1949, Sylvia Mary, da of Rupert John George Bickell (d 1952), of Bournemouth; *Career* ed The Window Miny Nat Insur 1947-51, press offr Miny Pension and Nat Insur 1951-55, head (films, radio, tv) Admlty 1955-61, dep chief info offr Miny of Educn 1961-64, dep press sec to PM 1964-69 (press sec 1970-71 and 1979), chief info offr Miny of Housing 1969-70, dir of info DOE 1971-74, dir gen COI 1974-78, PRO Vickers Ltd 1978, dir gen Nat Assoc of Pension Funds 1980-86; assoc dir Godwins Ltd 1987-; memb: BOTB 1980-84, cncl RSPCA 1980-83; FIPR (pres 1979), FCAM (vice pres 1984-), FRSA; *Recreations* literary and visual arts; *Style*— Henry James, Esq, CB; 53 Beaufort Rd, London W5 3EB (☎ 01 997 3021); Godwins Ltd, Briarcliff House, Kingsmead, Farnborough, Hampshire GU14 (☎ 0252 544 484, fax 0252 522 206, telex 858241)

JAMES, Prof Ioan Mackenzie; s of Reginald Douglas James (d 1966), of Norwood, Broad Oak, Heathfield, Sussex, and Jessie Agnes, *née* Surridge (d 1982); *b* 23 May 1928; *Educ* St Pauls London, Queen's Coll Oxford; *m* 1 Jul 1961, Rosemary Gordon, da of William George Stewart (d 1953); *Career* Cwlth fund fell: Princeton, Berkeley, Inst for Advanced Study 1954-55; Tapp res fell Gonville and Caius Coll Cambridge 1956, reader in pure mathematics Oxford 1957-69, sr res fell St John's Coll Oxford 1959-69, Savilian prof of geometry Oxford 1970-; pres London Mathematical Soc 1985-86 (tres 1969-79), govr St Paul's Sch and St Paul's Girls Sch 1970; hon fell St John's Coll Oxford 1987, professorial fell New Coll Oxford 1987, FRS 1968; *Books* The Topology of Stiefel Manifolds (1976), General Topology and Homotopy Theory (1984), Topological and Uniform Spaces (1987), Fibrewise Topology (1988); *Style*— Prof Ioan James; Mathematical Institute, 24-29 St Giles, Oxford OX1 3LB (☎ 0865 273 541)

JAMES, Hon Mrs (Jaquetta Mary Theresa); da of 11 Baron Digby, KG, DSO, MC, TD (d 1964); *b* 28 Oct 1928; *Educ* Sherborne Sch for Girls; *m* 1950, David Pelham Guthrie-James, MBE, DSC (d 1986), s of Wing-Cdr Sir Archibald James, KBE, MC (d 1979); 4 s, 2 da; *Career* memb: Mid-Sussex Hosp Mgmnt Ctee 1960-68, Dorset Area Health Authority 1974-81; chm Hamilton Lodge Sch for Deaf Children Brighton 1962-80; *Recreations* gardening; *Style*— The Hon Mrs James; Torosay Castle, Craignure, Isle of Mull, Argyll PA65 6AY (☎ 068 02 421)

JAMES, Jeremy Edward; s of Herbert Edward James, of Beckenham, Kent, and Edith Marjorie, *née* Day; *b* 6 June 1941; *Educ* Dulwich; *m* 1 (m dis 1978), Suzanne; 1 s (Richard David b 1964), 1 da (Tanya b 1968); m 2, 7 June 1980, Jacqueline, da of Thomas Walter Latter (d 1975); 1 da (Alison b 1982); *Career* controller Air Hldgs 1964-69; dir: Williams Hudson 1970-79, Sungate Resources 1980-83, Stockton Hldgs 1984-, Inoco plc 1986-; FCA 1965; *Recreations* golf, sailing; *Clubs* Langley Park Golf ; *Style*— Jeremy James, Esq; Gaiters, Bishops Walk, Croydon, Surrey CR0 5BA (☎ 01 654 4213); Stockton Holdings (UK) Ltd, 47 Duke Street, St James's, London SW1Y 6QX (☎ 01 930 6096, fax 01 930 9613, telex 295899, car tel 0836 280176

JAMES, John Denis; s of Kenneth Alfred James, of Alvechurch, Worcestershire, and Pauline Audry, *née* Haymen; *b* 30 August 1950; *Educ* Bridley Moor GS Redditch; *m* 3 Sept 1975, Barbara Elizabeth, da of John Thorpe, of Birmingham; 1 s (Christopher John b 1975), 1 da (Emma Louise b 1978); *Career* trainee photographer Redditch Indicator 1965, sr photographer Birmingham Post and Mail 1972, Midland Photographer of the Year 1981 and 1987, Midland News Photographer of the Year 1987, Nat Br Press Award Photographer of 1987, Kodak News Photographer of 1987; memb Inst of Journalists; *Recreations* off road buggy racing; *Style*— John James, Esq; 2 Boultons Lane, Crabbs Cross, Redditch, Worcs B97 5NY (☎ 0527 44797); Birmingham Post and Mail, Colmore Circus, Birmingham (☎ 021 236 3366)

JAMES, Jonathan Elwyn Rayner; QC 1988; s of Basil James, of Brockham, Surrey, and Moira Houlding, *née* Rayner; *b* 26 July 1950; *Educ* King's Coll Sch Wimbledon,

Christ's Coll Cambridge (MA, LLM), Brussels Univ Licencié Spécial en Droit Européen; *m* 3 Jan 1981, Anne, da of Henry McRae (d 1984); 1 s (Daniel Charles Rayner b 23 Dec 1981); *Career* called to the Bar Lincoln's Inn 1971; *Books* EEC Anti Trust Law (jt ed 1975), Copinger and Skone James on Copyright (jt ed 1980); *Recreations* DIY, squash, opera, travel; *Style—* Jonathan James, Esq, QC; 5 New Sq, Lincoln's Inn, London WC2A 3RJ (☎ 01 404 0404)

JAMES, (David) Keith Marlais; s of James Lewis James, of 9 The Mount, Dinas Powis, S Glamorgan, and Margaret Evelyn; *b* 6 August 1944; *Educ* Cardiff HS, West Monmouth Sch, Queens' Coll Cambridge (BA, MA); *m* 4 Aug 1973, Kathleen Linda, da of Wilfred Lawson Marrs, OBE (d 1981), of Cyncoed, Cardiff; 1 s (Thomas b 1983), 2 da (Alys b 1978, Elizabeth b 1980); *Career* slr; ptnr Phillilps and Buck 1969-; dir: various cos in Hamard Gp 1977-86, Bank of Wales plc 1988-; chm: Welsh Exec of Un Assoc 1977-80, Welsh Centre for Int Affrs 1979-84; memb: UK mgmnt ctee Freedom from Hunger Campaign 1978-87, Welsh mgmnt ctee of Inst of Dirs 1985-, Ct of UWIST 1985-88, Cncl of UWIST 1985-88, Advsy Panel of Cardiff Business Sch 1986-, Cncl Univ of Wales Coll of Cardiff 1988; vice pres Cardiff Business Club 1987-, hon sec Inst of Welsh Affrs 1987-; memb: Law Soc, IOD; *Recreations* golf, skiing; *Clubs* Cardiff and County, Royal Porthcawl Golf; *Style—* Keith James, Esq; Trehedyn Cottage, Peterston-Super-Ely, S Glamorgan; 14 Caerfai Road, St Davids, Dyfed; Phillips and Buck, Fitzalan House, Fitzalan Court, Cardiff (☎ 0222 471147, fax 0222 463447, telex 497625 (Filbuk G) DX 33016)

JAMES, Keith Royston; s of William Ewart Gladstone James, of Birmingham, and Lilian Elizabeth James (d 1966); *b* 22 August 1930; *Educ* King Edward VI Camp Hill Sch Birmingham, Univ of Birmingham; *m* 6 May 1961, Venice Imogen, da of Maj Henry St John Murray Findlay (d 1954); 1 s (William b 1964), 3 da (Rohaise b 1966, Selina b 1968, April b 1971); *Career* admitted slr 1954, sr ptnr Needham & James; dir: Technol & Law 1980, A E Westwood Ltd 1969, Turley Sheet Metal Prods 1969; chm Soc for Computers & Law 1988; *Books* A Guide to the Electronic Office for Practising Solicitors; articles on the application of technology to the law; *Recreations* shooting, walking, tennis; *Clubs* Athenaeum (Birmingham); *Style—* Keith James, Esq; Norton Curlieu, nr Warwick CV35 8JR (☎ 092 684 2372); Needham & James, Windsor House, Temple Row, Birmingham B2 5LF (☎ 021 200 1188, fax 021 236 9228, telex 338460 NEEJAM G, car tel 0860 513882)

JAMES, Martin Jonathan; s of Kenneth Charles James, of Christchurch, NZ, and Beatrice Rose, *née* Dickson; *b* 22 Sept 1961; *Educ* NZ Sch of Dance; *m* 8 Feb 1985, Adrienne Jane Terehunga, da of Fl Lt James Matheson, DFC, of Christchurch, NZ ; *Career* Royal NZ Ballet 1981, awarded Queen Elizabeth II Arts Cncl Grant for study in America 1982, promoted princ dancer, first one man graphic arts exhibition Molesworth Gallery NZ 1984, gained int recognition fourth World Ballet competition Japan 1984, London Festival Ballet 1985- (princ dancer 1987-); roles incl: Albrecht and Hilarion in Giselle, Franz in Coppelia, Prince in The Nutcracker, Toreodor in Petit's Carmen, Paris in Ashton's Romeo and Juliet; Paris Summer season 1987 incl: Kevin Haigen's Meditation (with Natalia Makarova), Spectre de la Rose, Le Corsaire, Makarova's Swan Lake, title role in Cranko's Onegin; Oedipus in Sphinx (Glen Tetley), title role Apollo (Balanchine), Symphony in C (Balanchine), Napoli (Bournonville), Lano (Christopher Bruce), Bull in Cruel Garden (Christopher Bruce); guest appearances Hong Kong, Paris, Le Creusot; memb Educn Dept London Festival Ballet, yearly engagements Ilkley Seminar Summer Sch; ARAD 1979, Solo Seal 1980; *Recreations* tennis, painting, rugby, swimming, therapeutic massage; *Clubs* Elmwood Tennis, Burnside Rugby; *Style—* Martin James, Esq; New Zealand (☎ 581 1245); London Festival Ballet, 39 Jay Mews, London SW7 2ES

JAMES, Michael; s of Aubrey Charles James (d 1986), of Chilcompton, Somerset, and Ada Emily, *née* Milsom (d 1938); *b* 19 Feb 1925; *Educ* Wells Cathedral Sch, RWA Sch of Architecture; *m* 4 April 1953, Margaret Rose (d 1984), da of George Brazier; 1 adopted da (Sarah Nicola b 12 May 1959); *Career* WW11 1943-1946, Lt 18 Cavalry Indian Army 1945-46, Capt SSO Razmak NW Frontier 1946; architect and town planner in private practices 1952-, chm Elsworth Sykes Ptnrs Ltd 1985-; magistrate Highgate Ct 1967-84; FRIBA 1950, MRTPI 1954, ACIArb 1980; *Recreations* golf; *Clubs* Reform; *Style—* Michael James, Esq ; The Coach House, 49a Maresfield Gardens, London NW3 5TE (☎ 01 435 5501); Elsworth Sykes Partnership, 287 Regent St, London W1R 8BX (☎ 01 409 2662)

JAMES, Michael Leonard; s of Leonard James, of Portreath, Cornwall.; *b* 7 Feb 1941; *Educ* Latymer Upper Sch, Christ's Coll Cambridge (MA); *m* 1975, Jill Elizabeth, da of George Tarján, OBE, of Budapest; 2 da (Ruth b 1978, Susanna b 1980); *Career* entered Br govt serv 1963, private sec to Rt Hon Jennie Lee MP Min for the Arts 1966-68, DES 1968-71; planning unit of Rt Hon Margaret Thatcher MP sec of state for educn & sci 1971-73, asst sec 1973, DCSO 1974, advsr to OECD Paris and UK govr Int Inst for Mgmnt of Technol (IIMT) Milan 1973-75, specialist duties 1975-78, dir Int Atomic Energy Agency Vienna 1978-83, advsr on Int Rels, Cmmn of the Euro Communities Brussels 1983-, chm The Hartland Press Ltd 1985-; govr: E Devon Coll of Further Educn Tiverton 1985-, Colyton GS 1985-, Sidmonth Community Coll 1988; chm bd of mgmnt Axe Vale Further Educn Unit Seaton 1987-(memb 1985-); memb: Exeter Social Security Appeal Tbnl 1986-, Exeter and Taunton VAT Appeal Tbnl 1987-; hon fell Univ of Exeter; FRSA; *Books* Internationalization to Prevent the Spread of Nuclear Weapons (1980), articles on int relations and nuclear energy, four novels under a pseudonym (SW Arts Literary Award 1984); *Clubs* Athenaeum, United Oxford & Cambridge Univ, Int PEN, Devon and Exeter Institution; *Style—* Michael James, Esq; Cotte Barton, Branscombe, Devon

JAMES, Dame Naomi Christine; DBE (1979); da of Charles Robert Power; *b* 2 Mar 1949; *Educ* Rotorua Girls' HS NZ; *m* 1976, Robert James (d 1983); 1 da (b 1983); *Career* former language teacher and hairdresser; yachtswoman: winner Binatone Round Britain and Ireland Race in trimaran Colt Cars GB 1982, NZ Yachtsman of the Year 1978, recipient Royal Yacht Sqdn Chichester Trophy 1978, winner Ladies' Prize Observer Transatlantic Race 1980 (women's record for solo crossing), circumnavigated world as first woman solo via Cape Horn Sept 1977-June 1978; tstee Nat Maritime Museum; writer and presenter BBC documentary Polynesian Triangle (Great Journeys Series) 1989; *Books* Women Alone (1978), At One With the Sea (1979), At Sea on Land (1981), Courage at Sea (1987); *Recreations* tennis, golf, skiing; *Clubs* Royal Dart Yacht, Royal Western Yacht; *Style—* Dame Naomi James, DBE

JAMES, Noel David Glaves; OBE (1964), MC (1945), TD (1946); s of Rev David Taliesin Robert James (d 1935), and Gertrude Ethel Ellen, *née* Glaves (d 1963); *b* 16 Sept 1911; *Educ* Haileybury, RAC Cirencester; *m* 29 Dec 1949, (Laura) Cecilia (d 1970), da of Sir Richard Winn Livingstone (d 1960); 3 s (Timothy b 1952, Jeremy b 1961, Alastair b 1954, d 1960); *Career* cmmnd 2 Lt RA TA 1933; WWII 1939-46 served: France (Dunkirk), Belgium, Persia, Iraq, Palestine, Syria, Italy (despatches); land agent 1933-39, bursar Corpus Christi Coll Oxford 1946-51, land agent Oxford Univ and estates bursar Brasenose Coll Oxford 1951-61, agent for Lord Clinton and The Clinton Devon Estates 1961-76; fell Corpus Christi Coll and Brasenose Coll; pres: Royal Forestry Soc 1962-64, Chartered Land Agents Soc 1957-58; FRICS 1950; *Books* Working Plans for Estate Woodlands (1948), Notes on Estate Forestry (1949), An Experiment in Forestry (1951), The Foresters Companion (fourth edn 1989), The Trees of Bicton (1969), The Arboriculturalist's Companion (1972), A Book of Trees Anthology (1973), Before The Echoes Die Away (1980), A History of English Forestry (1981), A Forestry Centenary (1982), Gunners at Larkhill (1983), Plain Soldiering (1987); *Recreations* forestry, shooting, country life; *Clubs* Army and Navy; *Style—* N D G James, Esq, OBE, MC, TD; Blakemore House, Kersbrook, Budleigh Salterton, Devon EX9 7AB (☎ 03954 3886)

JAMES, Professor the Hon Oliver Francis Wintour; s of Baron James of Rusholme (Life Peer), of Leyburn N Yorks, and Cordelia Wintour, Lady James, of Rusholme; *b* 23 Sept 1943; *Educ* Winchester, Balliol Coll Oxford (MA, BM, BCh); *m* 1965, Rosanna, da of Maj Gordon Bentley Foster (d 1963), of Sleightholme Dale, Fadmoor, York; 1 s (Patrick b 1967), 1 da (Helen b 1970); *Career* landowner (170 acres); prof of med Univ of Newcastle upon Tyne, tstee Sir James Knott Tst; FRCP; *Recreations* golf, tennis, wine; *Style—* Prof Oliver James; Sleightholmedale, Lodge, West Kirbymoorside, York; Freeman Hospital, Newcastle upon Tyne NE7 7DN

JAMES, Hon Ophelia Mary Katherine Christine Aliki; only da of 5th Baron Northbourne; *b* 23 August 1969; *Style—* The Hon Ophelia James; 11 Eaton Place, London SW1

JAMES, (William) Paul; s of Sir Frederick Seton James, KCMG, KBE (d 1934), and Lady Doris Francis Vamee (d 1956); *b* 22 August 1921; *Educ* Hailerbury, PCL (Dip Arch); *m* 4 Jan 1947, (Florence) Peggy, da of Josephy Harvey; 1 s (Julian Paul b 1958), 3 da (Jennifer b 1948, Fenella b 1952, Caroline b 1954); *Career* WWII RAF 1940-45; architect on staff of Lord Holford 1950-60, princ in private practice 1960-67, seconded planning conslt DHSS 1967-68, fndr ptnr and chm Hosp Design Partnership (London, Leeds and Birmingham) 1968-79, int conslt in hosp planning 1979-; author of numerous articles in professional jls 1970-85; chm Royal Turnbridge Wells Civic Soc; ARIBA 1950, FRIBA 1970; *Books* Hospitals - Designs and Development (1986); *Recreations* lawn tennis, walking, reading, travel, writing; *Clubs* Sloane; *Style—* Paul James, Esq; Lawnside, 3 Hungershall Park, Tunbridge Wells, Kent (☎ 0892 25726)

JAMES, Dr Peter Charles; *b* 15 Jan 1943; *Educ* Magdalen Coll Oxford (MA), UCL (PhD), Univ of London (BSc); *m* 12 June 1971, Vivien Elizabeth, *née* Bell; 1 s (Christian Stuart b 1974), 2 da (Charlotte Magdalen b 1976, Catherine Eleanor b 1982); *Career* OECD Paris 1968-73, N Carolina Nat Bank 1973-, md Carolina Bank Ltd 1978-87, gp chief exec Panmure Gordon Bankers Ltd 1987-; *Recreations* music, reading, sports; *Clubs* Hurlingham; *Style—* Dr Peter James; 15 Hobury St, London SW10; Robins, Upper Wardley, Milland, Liphook, Hants; Panmure Gordon Bankers Ltd, 14 Moorfields, Highwalk, London EC2

JAMES, Peter John; s of John Burnett James, and Cornelia, *née* Kates; *b* 22 August 1948; *Educ* Charterhouse, Ravensbourne Coll of Art & Design; *m* 21 April 1979, Georgina Valerie James, da of T D Wilkin, of Hove, Sussex; *Career* dir: Quadrant Films Toronto 1972-75, Yellowbill Ltd 1977, Cornelia James Ltd, currently md Cornelia James Contracts Ltd and md Cornelia James Neckwear Ltd; film prodr: Spanish Fly 1976, Biggles 1985 (assoc prodr); Freeman City of London 1980, Worshipful Co of Glovers; Royal Warrant Holder Queens Warrent for Glove Mfrs; memb Soc of Authors, Soc for Psychical Res; *Books* Dead Letter Drop (1981), Atom Bomb Angel (1982), Billionaire (1983), Possession (1988), Dreamer (1989); *Recreations* golf, tennis, skiing, vintage sports cars, wine, food; *Clubs* Tramps, Jaguar Owners; *Style—* Peter James, Esq; Cornelia James Ltd, 123 Havelock Rd, Brighton BN1 6GS (☎ 0273 508 866, fax 0273 541 656, car tel 0836 213 569, telex 877057)

JAMES, Prof Peter Maunde Coram; VRD (1964); s of Capt Vincent Coram James (d 1972), of London, and Mildred Ivy, *née* Gooch (d 1982); *b* 2 April 1922; *Educ* Westminster, Univ of London (LDS, RCS, MDS), Univ of St Andrews (DPD); *m* 27 Nov 1945, Denise Mary, da of John Waring Bond (d 1948), of Gravesend; 4 s (Nicholas, John, Martin, Richard); *Career* Surgn Lt RNVR 1945-48, demobbed 1948, continued in RNVR (later RNR) until ret Surgn Lt Cdr 1963; registrar res asst and hon lectr Inst of Dental Surgery Univ of London 1949-55; Royal Dental Hosp: sr lectr dept of children's dentistry 1955, asst dean 1958-66, hon conslt dental surgn 1961, dir dept of childrens dentistry 1962; reader in preventive dentistry Univ of London 1965; Univ of Birmingham: John Humphreys prof of dental health and head of dept of dental health 1966-87, dir dental sch 1978-82, postgrad advsr in dentistry 1983-86; emeritus prof 1987-; conslt advsr in community dentistry DHSS 1977-82, West Midlands regnl advsr Faculty of Dental Surgery RCS 1976-82, chm specialist advsy ctee in Community Dental Health and memb Jt Ctee for Higher Trg in Dentistry (RCS) 1981-86; ed Community Dental Health; pres Br Dental Assoc Central Counties branch 1981-82; memb: Birmingham Area Health Authy 1979-82, Birmingham Central DHA 1982-85; Br Soc for the Study of Community Dentistry, fndr pres and hon life memb RSM, hon life memb Br Dental Assoc, former pres and hon life memb Br Paedodontic Soc; *Recreations* walking, reading, music, messing about in boats; *Style—* Prof Peter James, VRD; The Pump House, Bishopton Spa, Stratford-upon-Avon, Warwickshire CV37 9QY (☎ 0789 204 330)

JAMES, Prof Philip Seaforth; s of Dr Philip William James, MC (d 1934), of Croydon, Surrey, and Muriel Lindley, *née* Rankin (d 1971); *b* 28 May 1914; *Educ* Charterhouse, Trinity Coll Oxford (MA), Yale Law Sch; *m* 4 Jan 1954, Wybetty, da of Claus Pieter Gerth (d 1968), of Enschede, Holland; 2 s (Nicholas b 1955, Edward b 1958); *Career* WWII RA 1940-45 Burma, Maj (despatches); barr Inner Temple 1939, fell and tutor Exeter Coll Oxford 1946-49, Bar practice 1949-52, prof of law and head of dept Univ of Leeds 1952-75, prof and chm of law faculty Univ of Buckingham 1975-81; visiting prof: Yale Univ and Univ of Louisville USA 1960-61, Univ of S Carolina 1972-73, NY Law Sch 1981-83; pres Soc of Public Teachers of Law 1971; chm Yorks Rent Assessment Ctee 1966-75, govr Swinton Con Coll 1970-81, assessor to Co Ct on race relations 1972-; Freedom of Madison Indiana 1961; hon memb Mark Twain Soc 1979; Hon LLD Univ of Buckingham 1987; *Books* Introduction to English Law (1950),

General Principles of the Law of Torts (1958); *Recreations* gardening; *Clubs* Nat Lib; *Style—* Prof Philip James; Chestnut View, Whitfield, nr Brackley, N Hants NN13 5TQ (☎ 02805 246); Walk Mill Cottage, Duddon Bridge, Broughton-in-Furness, Cumbria LA20 6EU (☎ 06576 788)

JAMES, Prof (William) Philip Trehearne; s of Jenkin William James (d 1944), and Lilian Mary James, *nér Shaw*; *b* 27 June 1938; *Educ* Ackworth Sch Pontefract Yorks, UCL (BSc), UCH (MB, BSc, MD); *m* 1961, Jean Hamilton, da of James Lingford Moorhouse (d 1977); 1 s (Mark), 1 da (Claire); *Career* asst dir MRC Dunn Nutrition Unit Cambridge 1974-82, dir Rowett Res Inst Aberdeen 1982-, hon res prof Aberdeen Univ; memb ctees: MAFF Applied Food and Nutrition Res, Novel Food Prods, Dirs of Food Res, DHSS Toxicity, Nat Nutritional Surveillance; formerly chm Working Pty on Nat Advsy Ctee of Nutrition Educn, vice-chmn FAO/WHO/UNU Expert Consultation on Energy and Protein Requirement of Man 1981-85; chm: FAO Expert Consultation on Nat Energy Needs 1987, UK Nat Food Alliance 1987-, Coronary Prevention Group 1988-; memb Nutrition Advsy Ctee WHO Euro Regn 1985-, consultation on Nutrition and Health WHO 1989; meml lectures: Cuthbertson 1979, Ames 1985, Middleton 1986, Davidson 1987, Minshull 1989, Mehta Oration India 1985, Peter Beckett Dublin 1983; *Books* on European Food Policy 1989, Manual for Calculating Energy Requirements 1989; papers on nutrient absorption, energy and protein metabolism, health policy and food labelling; *Recreations* talking, writing government reports, eating; *Clubs* Athenaeum (London); *Style—* Prof Philip James; Wardenhill, Bucksburn, Aberdeen, Scotland AB2 9SA (☎ 0224 712623); The Rowett Research Institute, Greenburn Rd, Bucksburn, Aberdeen, Scotland AB2 9SB (☎ 0224 712751, fax 0224 715349, telex 739988)

JAMES, Richard Austin; CB, MC (1945); s of Thomas Maurice James (d 1962), of Kent, and Hilda Joan, *née* Castle (d 1987); *b* 26 May 1920; *Educ* Clifton, Emmanuel Coll Cambridge; *m* 1948, Joan Betty, da of Albert Malcolm Boorer (d 1932); 2 s (Thomas, Andrew), 1 da (Sally); *Career* RE 1939-41, Queen's Own Royal West Kent Regt 1941-46 served in Middle East and Europe (despatches); Home Off 1948, private sec to Chllr of the Duchy of Lancaster (Lord Hill and the late Mr Iain Macleod) 1960 (asst sec 1961), dep receiver Met Police Dist 1970-73, asst under-sec of state Home Off 1974-76, receiver Met Police Dist 1977-80, dep under-sec of state 1980, memb cncl of Mgmnt of Distressed Gentlefolk Aid Assoc 1982- (gen sec 1981-82), memb ctee of mgmnt Sussex Housing Assoc for the Aged 1985-; Freeman City of London; *Recreations* cricket, garden construction; *Clubs* Athenaeum, MCC; *Style—* Richard James, Esq, CB, MC; Cedarwood, Redbrook Lane, Buxted, E Sussex TN22 4QH

JAMES, Hon Roderick Morrice; s (by 1 m) of Baron Saint Brides (Life Peer); *b* 1956; *m* 24 Oct 1981, Harriet S, yst da of Lt-Cdr John Benians, of Waterfield, Headley, Hants; 2 s (Caspian b 1985, Pasco b 1987); *Style—* The Hon Roderick James; c/o Rt Hon Lord Saint Brides, GCME, CVO, MBE, PC, Cap St-Pierre, 83990, Saint-Tropez, France

JAMES, Hon Sebastian Richard Edward Cuthbert; 3 and yst s of 5th Baron Northbourne; *b* 11 Mar 1966; *Educ* Eton, Magdalen College Oxford; *Career* Assoc Cnslt Bain UK Ltd; *Recreations* skiing, sailing, travel; *Clubs* The Lily, Ronnie Scotts; *Style—* The Hon Sebastian James

JAMES, Lady Serena Mary Barbara; *née* Lumley; JP (Richmond); da of late 10 Earl of Scarbrough, KG, GBE, KCB, TD; *b* 1901; *m* 1923, as his 2 w (he m 1 Lady Evelyn Wellesley, da of 4 Duke of Wellington; 1 s), Hon Robert James, s of late 2 Baron Northbourne; 2 da (*see Baron Westbury*); *Career* DStJ; *Style—* Lady Serena James, JP; St Nicholas, Richmond, Yorks

JAMES, Stephen Lawrence; s of Walter Amyas James (d 1970), of Clifton, Bristol, and Cecile Juliet, *née* Hillman (d 1970); *b* 19 Oct 1930; *Educ* Clifton, St Catharine's Coll Cambridge (BA); *m* 1955 (m dis 1986), Patricia Eleanor Favell, da of Reginald Cave (d 1968), of Bristol; 2 s (Oliver, Benedict), 2 da (Gabrielle, Miranda); *Career* admitted slr 1959, sr ptnr Simmons & Simmons 1980; dir: Horace Clarkson plc, Sofipac (London) Ltd, memb Worshipful Co of Glaziers 1964; memb Law Soc 1959; *Recreations* yachting (yacht, 'Jacobite'), gardening; *Clubs* Royal Yacht Sqdn, Royal Thames Yacht, Royal Lymington Yacht, Royal Ocean Racing; *Style—* Stephen James, Esq; Widden, Shirley Holms, Lymington, Hants SO41 8NL (☎ 0590 682226); 20 Queen's Gate Gardens, London SW7 5LZ (☎ 01 581 4953); Simmons and Simmons, 14 Dominion Street, London EC2M 2RJ (☎ 01 628 2020, fax 01 588 4129, telex 888562 SIMMON G); car ☎ 0836 2238 03

JAMES, Terence (Terry); s of Robert Joseph James (d 1986), of Long Stratton, Norfolk, and Nellie Wallis James, *née* Beare; *b* 6 June 1935; *Educ* Paston Sch, Magdalene Coll Cambridge (MA); *m* 12 Aug 1958, Julie Estelle, da of Charles Anderson Robson (d 1953), of Shelford, Cambs; 1 s (Michael b 1962), 1 da (Linda b 1961); *Career* Nat Serv RAF 1953-55; dir Fisons plc 1976-80; chm: FBC Ltd 1980-86, Chlor-Chem 1982-, Schering Hldgs Ltd 1986-; non exec dir Berol Europa 1988-; memb CBI Regnl Cncl; FID 1984; *Recreations* golf, contemplative indolence; *Clubs* John O'Gaunt GC; *Style—* Terry James, Esq; Schering Holdings Ltd, Mount Pleasant House, Huntingdon Road, Cambridge CB3 0DA (☎ 0223 323222, fax 0223 66853, telex 81654)

JAMES, Thomas Freedom; s of William Ewart James (d 1948), the first engineer and surveyor to Welwyn Garden City; *b* 4 April 1919; *Educ* Hitchin GS, Herne Bay Coll; *m* 1948, June Elizabeth, da of William Harriman Moss (d 1961), of Blue Hill Farm, Wattons; 3 s (William, Alan, Charles) , 1 da (Anne); *Career* WWII: chief offr troopship Eastern Prince of the Furness Prince Line; joined NZ Shipping Co 1936, bldg and civil engr; chm The William Moss Gp Ltd 1977-83; FIOB, FFB; *Recreations* gardening, bee-keeping, DIY; *Style—* Thomas James, Esq; Broadgates, Potkiln Lane, Jordans, Beaconsfield, Bucks (☎ 02407 4277)

JAMES, Thomas Garnet Henry (Harry); CBE (1984); s of Thomas Garnet James (d 1956), and Edith, *née* Griffiths (d 1958); *b* 8 May 1923; *Educ* Neath GS, Exeter Coll Oxford, (BA, MA); *m* 15 Aug 1956, Diana Margaret, da of Harold Lancelot Vavasseur Durell (d 1929); 1 s (Stephen Garnet Vavasseur b 1958); *Career* WWII cmmnd RA serv NW Europe 1942-45; keeper Egyptian & Assyrian antiquities Br Museum 1974-88 (prev dep keeper and asst keeper, joined 1951); Laycock student Worcester Coll Oxford 1954-60, Wilbor fell The Brooklyn Museum NY 1964, visiting prof Coll de France Paris 1983; hon chm bd of govrs Inst of Egyptian Art & Archaeology Memphis State Univ 1985-; chm: Egypt Exploration Soc 1983-, advsy ctee Freud Museum 1986-; FBA 1976; *Books* The Mastaba of Khentika (1953), Hieroglyphic texts in the Br Museum (I 1961, IX 1970), The Hekanakhte Papers (1962), Corpus of Hieroglyphic Inscriptions in the Brooklyn Museum (I 1974), Pharaoh's People (1984), Ancient Eqypt (1988); *Recreations* music, cooking; *Clubs* United Oxford and Cambridge; *Style—* T G H James, Esq, CBE; 14 Turner Close, London NW11 6TW (☎ 01 455 9221)

JAMES, Prof Vivian Hector Thomas; s of William Percy James (d 1970), of London, and Alice May James (d 1936); *b* 29 Dec 1924; *Educ* Latymer's Upper Sch, Univ of London (BSc, PhD, DSc); *m* 20 April 1958, Betty Irene, da of Frederick Pike (d 1941), of London; *Career* joined RAF 1942, serv as cmmnd pilot in UK and M East, released Fl Lt 1946; sci staff Nat Inst for Med Res 1952-56, reader in chemical pathology St Marys Hosp Med Sch 1962-67 (lectr 1956-62), prof of chemical endocrinology Univ of London 1967-73, prof and head of dept of chemical pathology St Marys Hosp Med Sch Univ of London 1973-, chm div of pathology St Marys Hosp 1981; memb Herts AHA 1967-72, sec clinical endocrinology ctee MRC 1976-82, chm human pituitary collection MRC, pres section of endocrinology RSM 1976-78, gen sec Soc for Endocrinology 1979-83 (tres 1983-), dep sec gen Int Soc of Endocrinology 1986-, sec gen Euro Fedn of Endocrine Socs 1987-, ed Clinical Endocrinology 1972-74; Freedom of Haverfordwest; FRCPath, Fiorino D'Oro City of Florence 1977; *Books* Hormones in Blood (1983), The Adrenal Gland (1979); *Recreations* languages; *Clubs* RSM; *Style—* Prof Vivian James; Dept of Chemical Pathology, St Mary's Hospital Medical School, London W1 1PG (☎ 01 723 1252)

JAMES, Prof Walter; CBE (1977); s of George Herbert James, and Mary Kathleen, *née* Crutch; *b* 8 Dec 1924; *Educ* Royal GS Worcester, St Luke's Coll Exeter, Univ of Nottingham (BA); *m* 21 Aug 1948, Joyce Dorothy, da of Frederick George Allan Woollaston (d 1975); 2 s (Alan b 1962, Andrew b 1965); *Career* lectr adult educn Univ of Nottingham 1948-69, prof educnl studies Open Univ 1969-84 (dean and dir 1969-77); UK rep Cncl of Europe working parties on: Devpt of Adult Educn 1973-81, Adult Educn for Community Devpt 1982-87, Adult Educn for Change 1988- (project dir 1982-87); chm: Nat Cncl for Voluntary Youth Servs 1970-76, Review of Trg p/t Youth and Community Workers 1975-77, Religious Advsy Bd, Scout Assoc 1977-82, In Serv Trg and Educn Panel for Youth and Community Work 1978-82, Cncl for Educn and Trg in Youth and Community Work 1982-85; tstee: Trident Educnl Tst 1972-86, Young Volunteer Force Fndn 1972-77, Community Projects Fndn 1977-; pres Inst of Playleadership 1972-74, Fair Play for Children 1979-82; *Books* The standard of Living (with F J Bayliss, 1964), Virginia Woolf Selections from her Essays (ed 1966); contrib: Encylopaedia of Education (1968), Teaching Techniques in Adult Education (1971), Mass Media and Adult Education (1971); The Development of Adult Education (with H Janne and P Dominice, 1980), The 14 Pilot Experiments Vols 1-3 (1984), Handbook on Co-operative Monitoring (1986); *Recreations* living; *Style—* Prof Walter James, CBE; 18 Dartmouth Ct, Dartmouth Grove, London SE10 8AS (☎ 01 692 4114)

JAMES, (Arthur) Walter; s of William John James, OBE (d 1921), of Southampton, and Ethel Lucy, *née* Wooster (d 1975); *b* 30 June 1912; *Educ* Uckfield GS, Keble Coll Oxford (MA), Br Sch At Rome; *m* 1, 1939 (m dis 1956), Elisabeth, da of late Richard Rylands Howroyd, of Little Hampton Chester; 1 da (Jennifer); m 2, (Anne) Jocelyn, da of C A Leavy Burton (d 1959); 1 da (Sophie b 1971), 1 adopted s (Matthew 1962), 2 adopted da (Emma b 1959, Henrietta b 1960); *Career* ldr writer Manchester Guardian 1937-46, ed Times Educational Supplement 1952-69 (dep ed 1947-51), ed Technology 1957-60, special advsr Education Times Newspapers 1969-71, reader in journalism Univ of Canterbury 1971-74, princ St Catharine's, Windsor 1974-82; contested (Lib) Bury, Lancs 1945; memb: gen advsy cncl BBC 1956-64, cncl Industl Design 1961-66, Br American Assocs 1964-82, cncl RSA 1964; govr Central Sch Art and Design 1961-66; *Books* ed: Temples and Faiths (1958), The Christian In Politics (1962), The Teacher And His World (1962), A Middle-Class Parent's Guide To Education (1964), Amy Buller and the Founding of St Catharine's Cumberland Lodge (1978); *Recreations* gardening; *Clubs* Nat Lib; *Style—* Walter James, Esq; 1 Cumberland Mews, Windsor Great Park, Berks SL4 2HP (☎ 0784 313 77)

JAMES, William Stirling; s of Wing Cdr Sir Archibald William Henry James, KBE, MC, and Eugenia, *née* Morris; *b* 20 Nov 1941; *Educ* St Georges Coll Rhodesia, Stonyhurst, Magdalene Coll Cambridge (MA); *Career* Morgan Grenfell & Co Ltd 1964-65, Touche Ross & Co London 1965-68 (NY 1968-69), Hill Samuel & Co Ltd 1969-(dir 1980-); farmer; external memb Lloyds; ACA 1968, FCA 1978; *Recreations* shooting, bridge; *Clubs* Boodles, Pratts, Annabels; *Style—* William James, Esq; 12 Godfrey St, London SW3 3TA (☎ 01 352 4097); Champions Farm, Pulborough, Sussex RH20 3EF; 100 Wood St, London EC2P 2AJ (☎ 01 628 8011)

JAMES OF RUSHOLME, Baron (Life Peer UK 1959); Eric John Francis James; s of late Francis William James, of Parkstone, Dorset; *b* 13 April 1909; *Educ* Taunton's Sch Southampton, Queen's Coll Oxford; *m* 1939, Cordelia Mary, sis of the former ed of the *Evening Standard* Charles Wintour and da of Maj-Gen FitzGerald Wintour, CB, CBE, and his w Alice (who was sis of Sir Augustus Foster, 4 & last Bt); 1 s; *Career* high master Manchester GS 1945-62, vice-chllr Univ of York 1962-72; chm: Headmasters' Conference 1953-54, Communications Research Ctee in Building Indust 1963, Inquiry into Teacher Trg 1971, Personal Social Servs Council 1973-76, Royal Fine Art Cmmn 1976-79; Hon LLD McGill York (Toronto), Hon DLitt New Brunswick, DUniv York, Hon FRIBA 1979, Hon Fell Queen's Coll Oxford; kt 1956; *Books* Science and Education, An Essay on the Content of Education, Education Second Leadership,; *Style—* The Rt Hon the Lord James of Rusholme; Penhill Cottage, West Witton, Leyburn, N Yorks

JAMES-DUFF, David Robin Millais; s of Capt Christopher Alexander James, RN (d 1969), and Cynthia Swire (d 1970); *b* 29 May 1945; *Educ* Trinity Coll Glenalmond, RAC Cirencester; *m* 1, 14 March 1970 (m dis 1982), Monica Jean, da of Thomas G Browne; 1 s (Rory b 1978), 3 da (Fiona b 1971, Tania b 1973, Nicola b 1980); m 2, 20 Feb 1988, Jayne Elizabeth, da of James Bryce, of Couper Angus; *Career* vice chm Br Field Sports Soc in Scotland, coordinator for Operation Raleigh Grampian Regn; memb Royal Co of Archers (Queen's Bodyguard for Scotland); *Recreations* golf, cricket, tennis, field sports; *Clubs* Royal and Ancient, St Andrews, MCC; *Style—* David James-Duff, Esq; Hatton Castle, Turriff, Aberdeenshire (☎ 0888 62279); Estate Office, Hatton Estates, Turriff (☎ 0888 63624)

JAMESON, Andrew David; s of Stanley Jameson, of Liverpool, and Diane Selina, *née* Cook; *b* 19 Feb 1965; *Educ* Chesterfield HS Crosby, Kelly Coll Tavistock, Arizona State Univ (BSc, BA); *Career* investmt banking Banque Indosuez London 1989; swimmer; Cwlth Games 1986 Gold Medallist 100m Butterfly (Cwlth record holder), World Champs 1986 Bronze Medallist 100m Butterfly; Euro Champs 1987 Gold Medallist 100m Butterfly, World Univ Games 1987 (Capt Br team) Gold Medallist

100m Freestyle and 100m Butterfly; Australian and American Open 1988 Champion 100m Butterfly, Olympic Games 1988 Bronze Medallist 100m Butterfly; Br Swimmer of the Year 1985; *Style—* Andrew Jameson, Esq; 114 Chesterfield Rd, Great Crosby, Liverpool L23 9TT (☎ 051 924 2698); Banque Indosuez, 52-62 Bishopsgate, London EC2N 4AR (☎ 01 638 3600, fax 01 628 4724, telex 892967 INDOSU G)

JAMESON, Derek; s of Mrs E Barrett; *b* 29 Nov 1929; *Educ* elementary schs East London; *m* 1, 1948, Jacqueline Sinclair (decd); 1 s, 1 da; m 2, 1971 (m dis 1977), Pauline Tomlin; 2 s; m 3, 1988, Ellen Petrie; *Career* Reuters 1944-60; ed: London American 1960-61, Daily Express 1961-63, Sunday Mirror 1963-75; Northern ed Daily Mirror 1975-76, managing ed Daily Mirror 1976-77; ed: Daily Express 1977-78, Daily Star 1978-80, News of the World 1981-83; TV and Radio commentator; *Style—* Derek Jameson, Esq; BBC Radio 2, Broadcasting House, London W1A 1AA (☎ 01 927 4652)

JAMESON, Julian Richard Musgrave; yr s of Thomas Ormsby Jameson (d 1965), and Joan Moira Maud (d 1953), da of Sir Richard John Musgrave, 5th Bt, DL, JP; *b* 6 June 1928; *Educ* St Colomba's; *m* Anne Dwyer; 1 s, 1 da; *Career* memb Stock Exchange 1962, shareholder and ptnr Goodbody Dudgeon (Stockbrokers); *Style—* Julian Jameson, Esq; Garretstown, Dunshaughlin, Co Meath, Eire; Dudgeon, 25 Suffolk St, Dublin 2 (☎ (0001) 777314; telex 25299)

JAMESON, Hon Mrs (Margaret Miranda); *née* Lampson; da of 1 Baron Killearn, GCMG, CB, MCO, PC (d 1964); *b* 1923; *m* 1946, Geoffrey John Eustace Jameson; 1 s; *Style—* The Hon Mrs Jameson; 64 Limerston St, London SW10

JAMESON, Air Cdre Patrick Geraint (Jamie); CB (1959), DSO (1943), DFC (1940, and bar 1941); s of Robert Delvin Jameson (d 1952), of Delvin Lodge, and Katherine Lenora Jameson, *née* Dick (d 1965); *b* 10 Nov 1912; *Educ* Hutt Central, Hutt Valley HS; *m* 1941, Hilda Nellie Haiselden, da of Bertie Fitzherbert Webster, of NZ; 1 s (John), 1 da (Suzanne); *Career* joined RAF 1936, No 8 FTS Montrose 1936, posted to No 46 Fighter Sqdn Norwegian Campaign 1940, cmd 266 Spitfire Sqdn (Battle of Britain), 12 Gp Wing Leader based at Wittering 1941-42, (Dieppe Operation) Wing Leader North Weald leading Norwegian Spitfire Wing 1942, HQ No 11 Gp 1943, planning fighter ops 1944, Cdr 122 Mustang Wing in Normandy Beach-head, Belgium, Holland, Germany, Denmark, Staff Coll 1946, Air Miny Fighter Operational Trg, 1949 OC Day Fighter Leaders Sch & Gp Capt Ops Central Fighter Estab, OC RAF Station Wunstorf Germany 1952, SASO HQ No 11 Gp 1954, Air Cdre 1956, apptd SASO of 2nd TAF RAF Germany, Task Force Cdr Operation Grapple (Christmas Island) 1959; ret 1960; mentioned in despatches 5 times; Norwegian War Cross with Swords, Cdr Order of Orange-Nassau, American Silver Star; *Recreations* fishing, shooting, golf; *Clubs* RAF, Hutt, Hutt Golf; *Style—* Air Cdre Jamie Jameson, CB, DSO, DFC; 70 Wai-iti Crescent, Lower Hutt, New Zealand (☎ Wellington 697693)

JAMESON, (Arthur) Roy; s of Arthur Jameson (d 1945), and Jessie, *née* Wright (d 1947); *b* 27 Dec 1930; *Educ* Hutton GS, Univ of London (LLB, LM TPI); *m* 5 Aug 1961, Pauline, da of John Charles Crook (d 1966); 1 s (Andrew Roy b 1965), 2 da (Caroline Judith b 1963, Alison Claire b 1968); *Career* slr and notary public; clerk Fulwood UDC 1968-74; hon sec Preston Incorporated Law Soc 1976-80 (pres 1986-87), vice-pres Assoc of North Western Law Socs, local rep Slrs' Benevolent Assoc, memb cncl Provincial Notaries' Soc 1987-; clerk to Bd of Mgmnt of Royal Cross Sch for the Deaf, Preston 1969-, clerk to Withnell Parish Cncl 1974-77, govr Hutton GS; *Recreations* fencing, amateur dramatics; *Style—* Arthur Jameson, Esq; 11 Regent Drive, Fulwood, Preston, Lancashire PR2 3JA (☎ 0772 719312); 8 Lone St, Preston, Lancashire PR1 2LD (☎ 0772 555616)

JAMIESON, Alister Charles; s of Major Gerald Alister Jamieson (d 1916), and Ruth Margaret Davy, *née* Cobbold (d 1972); *b* 7 Sept 1913; *Educ* Dragon Sch Oxford, Marlborough, Trinity Hall Cambridge (MA); *m* 21 Nov 1940, Joan May, da of John C Stronach, CMG (d 1967); 2 s (Michael b 1942, David b 1945); *Career* mil serv E Africa and Br Mil Admin Eritrea, Lt-Col; sr dist offr Colonial Admin; *Style—* Alister Jamieson, Esq; 8 Gatchell Green, Trull, Taunton, Somerset (☎ 0823 279943)

JAMIESON, Andrew Thomas; s of Alexander Jamieson (d 1960), and Catherine Elizabeth, *née* MacDonald (d 1977); *b* 16 Feb 1928; *Educ* George Heriots Sch Edinburgh, Univ of Edinburgh (BSc); *m* 18 March 1953, Evelyn Hall, da of James Andrew Hiddleston (d 1983); 1 s (Alexander James Andrew b 1958), 1 da (Elizabeth Helen Hall b 1956); *Career* Nat Serv 1950-52; dir Panmure Gordon Ltd 1987- (ptnr 1964-86, fin dir 1986-); chm Hemel Hempstead Cons Assoc 1972-74; Freeman City of London, Liveryman Worshipful Co of Actuaries; FFA 1951, AIA, FSS 1956; *Books* Investment Management (with J G Day, 1974); *Recreations* hill walking, cattle rearing; *Clubs* Caledonian, Actuaries; *Style—* Andrew Jamieson, Esq; Rookwoods, Sible Hedingham, Essex; Aile de Chateau de Commandre, St Siffret, France; 14 Moorfields Highwalk, London EC2

JAMIESON, Maj David Auldjo; VC (1944); s of Sir Archibald Jamieson, KBE, MC; *b* 1 Oct 1920; *Educ* Eton; *m* 1, 1948, Nancy (d 1963), da of Robert Elwes, JP; 1 s, 2 da; m 2, 1969, Joanna, da of Edward Woodall; *Career* 2 Lt Royal Norfolk Regt 1939, Capt 1940; dir: Australian Agric Co 1949-78 (govr 1952-76), Australian Mutual Provident Soc (UK) 1963- (dep chm 1973-), Nat Westminster Bank plc 1983-87; Lt HM Body Guard of Hon Corps of Gentlemen at Arms 1986- (memb 1968-); High Sheriff Norfolk 1980; *Style—* Major David Jamieson, VC; The Drove House, Thornham, Hunstanton, Norfolk (☎ 048 526 206)

JAMIESON, Wing Cdr Harold Clive (Jamie); OBE (1967, MBE 1966); s of Harold Jamieson (d 1968), of 33 Cornwall Ave, Welling, Kent, and Hannah Marie, *née* Mathias (d 1981);; *b* 31 Mar 1930; *Educ* Godalming Co GS, Guildford Tech Coll, London Univ (HNC), SW London Coll (HND); *m* 24 March 1951, Gwendoline May, da of Edward Hunt (d 1957), of 15 Teignmouth Rd, Welling, Kent; 1 s (Martin b 1957), 4 da (Nicola b 1954, Lynne b 1957, Edwina b 1960, Tracy b 1960); *Career* Electronic Offrs' Course RAF Henlow 1952, OC Elec Trg RAF Halton 1952-57, Univ Grad Elec Course 1957 (Fl Lt), Flying Course 1958, OC Ground Elecs RAF Wyton 1959-62, OC Special signals Unit Berlin, Sqdn Ldr 1962-67, OC Special HQSC RAF Medmenham, Wing Cdr EN HQ 90 Gp RAF Medmenham 1969-72; commendations 1963 and 1965; divnl mangr Perkin- Elmer (UK) Ltd 1972-76, prod dir Richard Garrett Engrg Ltd 1976-79 (md 1979-80), dir AFA Minerva (EMI) Ltd 1980-82, md Oceanics SPL Ltd 1982-; tres CMS Farnham & Aldershot Deanery Assoc; CEng MRAES 1964, EEng MIERE 1965; *Recreations* antiques, church, travel; *Style—* Wing Cdr H C Jamieson, OBE; Jayview, Shortheath Rd, Farnham, Surrey (☎ 0252 723965); Oceanics Spl Ltd, Invincible Rd, Farnborough, Hants GU14 7SY(☎ 0252 514941 Ext. 201, fax 0252 510777, tlelx 858862)

JAMIESON, James McAulay; s of Crawford John Baird Jamieson (d 1978), of Blackheath, London, and Elizabeth, *née* McAulay; *b* 5 June 1939; *Educ* St Dunstans Coll; *m* 12 Dec 1964, (Frances) Vivian, da of Col Francis Alan Forman (d 1980) of Eltham; 2 s (Alan b 3 Feb 1970, William b 3 Oct 1932); *Career* Everett Morgan and Grundy 1958-64, qualified CA 1964; Price Waterhouse: Jamaica 1964-68, NY 1968-72, London 1972-; FCA 1964; *Recreations* golf; *Clubs* Royal St Georges GC, Royal Blackheath GC, Littlestone GC; *Style—* James Jamieson, Esq; 23 Morden Rd, Blackheath, London SE3 OAD (☎ 01 852 0050); 16 Aynsley Court, Strand St, Sandwich, Kent (☎ 0304 615093); Price Waterhouse, Southward Towers, 32 London Bridge St, London SE1 9SY (☎ 01 407 8989, fax 01 407 0545)

JAMIESON, Maj Lenox Harvey; s of Lt-Col Harvey Morro Harvey-Jamieson, OBE, TD, DL, WS, *qv* late of Moray Place, Edinburgh, and Maude Frances Wilmot Ridout; ggf: James Wilcocks Carrall created honorary Mandarin and order of Double Dragon 1900 (1849-1902), ggf: Maj Gen Sir Robert Murdoch-Smith, KCMG (1835-1900) late RE excavated sites of antiquity in Mediterranean and Persia 1854-85: many artefacts now in Br Museum, gggf: John Hayter, painter in ordinary to Queen Victoria (1800-85), gguncle: Sir George Hayter (1792-1871): painter; *b* 23 Feb 1937; *Educ* Edinburgh Acad, Univ of Edinburgh; *m* 8 May 1981, Audrey Mackay, da of David Mackay Paterson (d 1981), late of Woodcliff, Kilmacolm, Renfrewshire; *Career* cmmnd RE 1959, served in Far East, Middle East, UK, attached RN HMS Fearless 1965-67, sr personnel offr Scotland 1982-; memb Queen's Body Guard for Scotland (Royal Co of Archers) 1971-; *Recreations* archery, gardening, model engineering, vintage motor cars; *Clubs* Army and Navy, 20 Ghost; *Style—* Maj Lenox Jamieson; c/o Army and Navy Club, Pall Mall, London

JAMIESON, Lady Mariegold (Magdalene); *née* Fitzalan Howard; da of 3 Baron Howard of Glossop, MBE (d 1972), and Baroness Beaumont, OBE (d 1971); sis of 17 Duke of Norfolk, KG, CB, CBE, MC, DL; *b* 1919; *Educ* private; *m* 1957, Gerald James Auldjo Jamieson, s of Sir Archibald Auldjo Jamieson, KBE, MC; 2 s; *Style—* Lady Mariegold Jamieson; 17 Elvaston Place, London SW7; Yarrow House, Elmham, Dereham, Norfolk

JANAS, Ludovic Joseph; s of Wojciech Janas (d 1938), and Apolonia, *née* Tengowska (d 1945); *b* 31 August 1926; *Educ* Univ Coll Cork (BA), Birkbeck Coll Univ of London; *Career* computer conslt; statistician N Br and Mercantile Insur Co Ltd 1952-60; chief programmer: Commercial Union Assur Co Ltd 1960-64, Wiggins Teape Ltd 1964-72 (asst dep mangr 1966-70, gp systems mangr 1970-72); dir computing and mgmnt servs King's Coll Hosp London 1972-73, dep mangr Phoenix Assur plc Bristol 1973-85 (mgmnt servs mangr Phoenix Assur 1985-86), computer mangr Sun Alliance Gp 1985-86, PA to chm IBM Computer Users Assoc 1986-87; served on computer res ctee of: Br Insur Assoc, Data Protection Ctees, CBI; fell: Br Computer Soc, Royal Statistical Soc; memb Royal Inst of Philosophy; *Recreations* badminton, mountaineering; *Style—* Ludovic Janas, Esq; Wint Hill House, Wint Hill, Banwell, Avon BS24 6NN

JANCAR, Dr Joze; s of Josip Jancar (d 1971), of Zalna, and Marija, *née* Tomlje; *b* 23 May 1920; *Educ* Real Gymnasium Ljubljana, Ljubljana Univ, Gray Univ, Galway Univ, Dublin Univ (MB, BCh, BAO, DPM); *m* 18 Oct 1945, Marija, da of Anton Hribar (1968), of Ponova Vas; 2 s (Joseph b 1953, Martin b 1956), 1 da (Sonja b 1950); *Career* asst MO Ballinasloe 1952, registrar Mercer's Hosp Dublin 1954; Stoke Park Hosp Bristol: jr hosp MO 1956-59, sr hosp MO 1959-61, conslt psychiatrist 1961-85, hon conslt psychiatrist 1985; clinical lectr in mental health Univ of Bristol 1961-85;Blake Marsh lectr awarded Burden res gold medal and prize 1971, 1974; distinguished achievement award for scientific literature IASSMO New Delhi 1985, vice pres RCPsych 1981-83, pres Bristol Medico-Chirurgical Soc 1985-86, memb Bristol Medico-Historical Soc; med memb Mental Health Review Tbnl, med memb Mental Health Act Cmmn 1983-87, cncl memb Burden Inst Bristol; hon offr Cncl Int Assoc for the Sci Study of Mental Deficiency 1988; Freeman City of London 1980, Liveryman Worshipful Co of Apothecaries 1980; memb BMA 1952, FRSM 1969, FRCPsych 1971 (hon 1988); *Books* Stoke Park Studies - Mental Subnormality (1961), Clinical Pathology in Mental Retardation (jtly 1968),; *Recreations* history, travel, languages; *Clubs* Savages (Bristol); *Style—* Dr Joze Jancar; Emona, Beaufort Place, Frenchay, Bristol BS16 1PE (☎ 0272 567 891); Stoke Park Hospital, Stapleton, Bristol BS16 1QU (☎ 0272 655261)

JANES, (John) Douglas Webster; CB (1975); s of John Arnold Janes (d 1949), and Maud Mackinnon, *née* Webster (d 1938); *b* 17 August 1918; *Educ* Trinity Acad Edinburgh, Southgate Co Sch Middx, City and Guilds Coll London Univ (BScEng, DIC); *m* 1943, Margaret Isabel, *née* Smith (d 1978); 1 s, 2 da; m 2, 1986, Joan Walker; *Career* princ fin offr Miny of Housing and Local Govt DOE 1968-73 (dep sec 1973), chief exec Maplin Devpt Authy 1973-74, dep sec NI Off 1974-79; various mgmnt orgn reviews 1979-81, memb Home Grown Timber Advsy Ctee 1979-81 (chm 1981-); sec Bach Choir 1981-89; ACGI; *Recreations* singing in choirs, using my hands; *Style—* Douglas Janes Esq, CB

JANION, Rear-Adm Sir Hugh Penderel; KCVO (1981); s of Capt Ralph Penderel Janion RN (d 1963), and Winifred Derwent, *née* Craig (d 1983); *b* 28 Sept 1923; *Educ* RNC Dartmouth; *m* 1956, Elizabeth Monica, da of Col Cecil Leonard Ferard (d 1970); 1 s, 1 da; *Career* joined RN 1937, served WWII Russian convoys, invasions of Sicily and Italy, served Korean War Inchon landing, Cdr 1958, cmd HMS Jewel, exec offr HMS Ark Royal, Capt 1966, cmd HMS Aurora, cmd HMS Bristol, Rear Adm 1975, ADC to HM The Queen 1975, Flag Offr Royal Yachts 1975-81; extra equerry to HM The Queen 1975-; younger brother Trinity House 1976-; *Recreations* golf, sailing, gardening; *Clubs* Naval & Military, Royal Yacht Sqdn, Royal Naval & Royal Albert, Imperial Poona Yacht, Sherborne Golf; *Style—* Rear Adm Sir Hugh Janion, KCVO; King's Hayes, Batcombe, Shepton Mallet, Somerset BA4 6HF (☎ 074 985 300)

JANMAN, (Timothy Simon) Tim; MP (C) Thurrock 1987-; s of J Janman, of Banbury, and Irene, *née* Frith; *b* 9 Sept 1956; *Educ* Sir William Borlase GS, Univ of Nottingham (BSc); *Career* Ford Motor Co 1979-83 (industl rels), IBM UK Ltd 1983-87 (sales), sec Cons Backbench Employment Ctee 1987-88; vice chm 1988-); vice pres: Jordan is Palestine Ctee, Selsdon Gp; *Recreations* theatre, restaurants, reading; *Style—* Tim Janman, MP; House of Commons, London SW1A 0AA (☎ 01 219 4001)

JANNER, Baroness; Elsie Sybil; CBE (1968), JP (Inner London 1936); da of Joseph Cohen; *Educ* Centl Newcastle HS, S Hampstead HS, Switzerland; *m* 1927, Baron Janner (Life Peer, d 1982); 1 s (Greville *qv*), 1 da (Lady Morris of Kenwood); *Career* contested (Lab) Mile End LCC 1947, pres Brady Clubs and Settlement; former chm: Juvenile Cts Panel, Stonham Housing Assoc Advsy Bd 1975-83, Thames Bench

Magistrates 1975; pres: Stonham Housing Assoc, Brady Clubs and Settlement Whitechapel; vice pres (former hon tres) Magistrates Assoc, vice chm Mitchell City of London Charity and Educnl Fndn, 1986-; chm Stonham Meml Tst; tstee Barnett Janner Charitable Tst, exec Inst of Advanced Motorists 1974-88 (dep chm 1981-85); hon vice-pres Fedn of Women Zionists, pres Brady-Maccabi Youth and Community Centre Edgware, vice pres Assoc Jewish Youth; Freeman City of London; *Books* Barnett Janner - A Personal Portrait (1984); *Style*— The Rt Hon the Lady Janner, CBE, JP; 45 Morpeth Mansions, Morpeth Terrace, London SW1P 1ET (☎ 01 828 8700)

JANNER, Hon Greville Ewan; QC (1971), MP (Lab) Leicester West 1974-; s of Baron Janner (Life Peer, d 1982) and Baroness Janner, *qv*; *b* 11 July 1928; *Educ* Bishop's Coll Sch Canada, St Paul's Sch, Trinity Hall Cambridge, Harvard Law Sch USA; *m* 1955, Myra Louise, *née* Sheink; 1 s, 2 da; *Career* barr 1955, author, journalist, broadcaster; contested (Lab) Wimbledon 1955, MP (Lab) Leicester North West 1970-74, memb select ctee on Employment, chm All-Pty Safety Gp, vice chm All-Pty Parly Ctee for Release of Soviet Jewry; pres Retired Exec's Action Clearing House (REACH) 1980-; vice pres World Jewish Congress 1981-86; former dir Jewish Chronicle Newspaper Ltd, dir Ladbroke plc 1986-; pres Bd of Deputies British Jews 1979-85, first pres Cwlth Jewish Cncl 1982-; FIPM 1976; *Recreations* Magic Circle; *Style*— The Hon Greville Janner, QC, MP; House of Commons, London SW1 0AA (☎ 01 219 4469)

JANNEY, Rodney Turnbull; s of Robert Turnbull Janney (d 1968), of Sutton Coldfield, and Edna Ruth, *née* Goodwin (d 1974); *b* 18 Mar 1940; *Educ* Trinity Coll of Music (LTCL); *m* 29 July 1968, Jennifer Maureen, da of Thomas Charles Roderick (d 1952); *Career* oboe and cor anglais reedmaker 1971-; *Recreations* hill walking, listening to music, drawing; *Style*— Rodney T Janney, Esq; Bearnock Lodge, Glenurquhart, Inverness-shire

JANSEN, Cletus Patrick; *Career* md: GEC Projects and Automation Gp (all subsidiary cos of GEC plc), GEC Electrical Projects Ltd (gained Queen's Award for Export in 1982 and 1983), GEC Industl Controls Ltd, GEC Mechanical Handling Ltd, GEC Robot Systems Ltd, GEC Automation Projects Inc (USA), GEC Machines Ltd, GEC Small Machines and GEC Marine & Industl Gears Ltd; *Style*— Cletus Jansen, Esq; GEC Electrical Projects Ltd, Boughton Rd, Rugby, Warwicks CV21 1BU (☎ 0788 2144)

JANSZ, Dr Clifford Cyril Arthur; s of Sir Herbert Eric Jansz, CMG (d 1976), of Fortis House, Hammers Lane, Mill Hill, London, and Beatrix, *née* Van Langenberg (d 1954); *b* 13 Jan 1924; *Educ* St Peters Coll Colombo Sri Lanka, Univ of Ceylon (MB BS), Great Ormond Street Hosp for Sick Children (DCH), Inst of Public Health Gt Portland Place London (DPH), Birkbeck Coll London; *m* 19 April 1949, Margaret (Peggy) Louise, da of Stanley Studholm Wallbeoff (d 1957), of The Park, Lady McCallums Drive, Kandy, Sri Lanka; 1 s (Richard), 4 da (Ann, Sabrina, Litza, Natania); *Career* MO Govt Health Serv Sri Lanka 1949-54, asst MO Essex CC 1959-63, sr asst MO Middx 1963-64, sr MO London Borough Brent 1964-66, princ MO London Borough Greenwich 1966-69, chief health servs offr London Borough Hammersmith 1969-72, dir health servs London Borough Harrow 1973-74, dist community physician and MO of Environmental Health 1974-89, ret 1989; tstee CJ Ward Tst Harrow 1973-89; memb BMA 1955, FFCM 1982 (memb 1973); *Recreations* tennis, photography, model railways; *Style*— Dr Clifford Jansz; Fortis House, Hammers Lane, Mill Hill, London NW7 4DJ (☎ 01 959 1565); Northwick Park Hospital, Watford Rd, Harrow HA1 3UJ (☎ 01 864 5311 ext 2786/01 864 2668)

JANVRIN, Vice Adm Sir (Hugh) Richard Benest; KCB (1969, CB 1965), DSC (1940); s of Rev Canon Claud William Janvrin (d 1965), of Fairford, Glos, and Irene Monica, *née* Turner (d 1981); *b* 9 May 1915; *Educ* RNC Dartmouth; *m* 1938, Nancy, da of late F B Fielding, of Gloucester; 2 s; *Career* joined RN 1929, Lt 1937, served WWII, Capt 1954, dir Tactics and Weapons Policy Admty 1962-63, Rear Adm 1964, Flag Offr Aircraft Carriers 1964-66, Dep Chief of Naval Staff 1966-68, Vice Adm 1967, Flag Offr Naval Air Cmd 1968-70, ret 1971; *Style*— Vice Adm Sir Richard Janvrin, KCB, DSC; Allen's Close, Chalford Hill, Stroud, Glos GL6 8QJ (☎ 0453 882336)

JAQUES, John Michael; MBE (1988); s of William Edward Jaques, of La Providence, Rochester, Kent, and Gertrude, *née* Scott (d 1980); *b* 29 Sept 1930; *Educ* Cambridge HS; *m* 27 Jan 1962, Caroline, da of Philip Reddie Knapman, of Stanton Drew, Avon; 2 s (Rupert b 1962, Matthew b 1964); *Career* architect; sr ptnr Jaques Muir & Ptnrs chartered architects; practice cmmns incl: housing schemes, banks, religious bldgs, sports centres, museums, theatres, laboratories and med bldgs, telecommunication centres, planning studies; architect for major restoration work to Church of the Holy Sepulchre Jerusalem; cncl memb The Anglo Jordanian Soc 1980-86; ctee memb Friends of St John Ophthalmic Hosp Jerusalem 1982-86; OStJ 1985, Order of El Istiqlal (Jordan) 1977; RIBA, FRSA; *Recreations* shooting, hunting, fishing, painting, glass engraving, visiting ancient antiquities; *Clubs* Arts; *Style*— John M Jacques, Esq, MBE; 8 Vine Yard, Sanctuary St, London SE1 1QL (☎ 01 357 7428, fax 01 357 7650)

JARDINE, Sir Andrew Colin Douglas; 5 Bt (UK 1916), of Godalming, Surrey; er s of Brig Sir Ian Liddel Jardine, 4 Bt, OBE, MC (d 1982), and Priscilla, Lady Jardine, *qv*; *b* 30 Nov 1955; *Educ* Charterhouse; *Heir* bro, Michael Ian Christopher Jardine; *Career* served Royal Green Jackets 1975-78; C T Bowring & Co 1979-81, Henderson Admin Gp plc 1981-; *Style*— Sir Andrew Jardine, Bt

JARDINE, Sheriff James Christopher Macnaughton; s of James Jardine (d 1952), of Glasgow, and Jean Paterson Stuart (d 1966); *b* 18 Jan 1930; *Educ* Glasgow Acad, Gresham House Sch, Ayrshire Univ of Glasgow (BL); *m* 1955, Vena Gordon, da of Daniel Gordon Kight (d 1973), of Renfrewshire; 1 da (Susan); *Career* slr princ Nelson & Mackay 1955-56, ptnr McClure Naismith Brodie & Co Slrs Glasgow 1956-69; Sheriff of: Stirling Dunbarton & Clackmannan (later N Strathclyde) at Dumbarton 1969-79, Glasgow and Strathkelvin 1979-; *Recreations* boating, music, theatre, ballet, opera; *Style*— Sheriff James Jardine; Sheriff's Chambers, Sheriff Court of Glasgow and Strathkelvin, 1 Carlton Place, Glasgow G5 9DA

JARDINE, Michael Ian Christopher; s of late Brig Sir Ian Liddel Jardine, 4 Bt, OBE, MC (d 1982), and Priscilla, Lady Jardine, *qv*; hp of bro, Sir Andrew Jardine, 5 Bt, *qv*; *b* 1958; *m* (Maria) Milky; 1 s; *Style*— Michael Jardine, Esq; 36B Argyle Rd, Ealing, London W13 8AA

JARDINE OF APPLEGIRTH, Sir Alexander Maule; 12 Bt (NS 1672), of Applegirth, Dumfriesshire; 23 Chief of Clan Jardine; s of Col Sir William Edward Jardine of Applegirth, 11 Bt, OBE, TD, JP, DL (d 1986), and Ann Graham Maitland; *b* 24 August 1947; *Educ* Gordonstoun; *m* 9 Oct 1982, Mary Beatrice, posthumous only child of Hon John Cross (yst s of 2 Viscount Cross), by Sybil Anne, *née* Murray, who m subsequently Lt-Cdr James Parker-Jervis, RN (ggs of Hon Edward Parker-Jervis, 2 s of 2 Viscount St Vincent); 1 s (William Murray b 1984), 2 da (Kirsty Sybil b 1986, Jean Maule b 1988); *Heir* s, William Murray; *Career* farmer; memb Queen's Body Guard for Scotland (Royal Co of Archers); *Recreations* shooting, fishing, curling; *Style*— Sir Alexander Jardine of Applegirth, Bt; Ash House, Thwaites, Millom, Cumbria LA18 5HY (☎ 06576 331)

JARMAN, David Alexander Elijah; JP (Surrey 1983); s of Lt-Cdr Alexander William Jarman, RNVR (d 1985), and Ivy L Jarman; *b* 16 Jan 1936; *Educ* Tiffin Sch Kingston-on-Thames; *m* 22 Dec 1962, Brenda Mary, da of Dr Douglas Arthur Blount (d 1966), of Dunstable, Beds; *Career* mangr Road Tport Indust until 1969, barr Inner Temple 1969, practiced SE circuit 1969-81, legal advsr Br Aerospace plc 1981; memb : Magistrates Assoc, Bar Assoc for Commerce Fin and Indust ; *Recreations* yachting, gardening, genealogy and local history; *Clubs* Nat Lib, Middle Thames YC; *Style*— David Jarman, Esq, JP; c/o British Aerospace plc, 11 Strand, London WC2N 5JT (☎ 01 930 1020)

JARMAN, Michael Charles; JP (1978); s of Charles Bertram Jarman; *b* 12 June 1936; *Educ* Rossall; *m* 1965, Helen Barbara, da of Cecil Charles Robinson; 1 s, 3 da; *Career* md Avenue Farms Ltd 1964-, Miden Properties Ltd 1964-; govr Agric Soc; MInst M 1981 (gen cmmr 1984), memb Mktg Soc 1979, FID, FCA; *Recreations* salmon fishing, equestrian sports, farming; *Clubs* Farmers'; *Style*— Michael Jarman, Esq, JP; Castle Fields, Buckingham (☎ 0280 812127);

JARMAN, Nicolas Francis Barnaby; QC (1985); s of Archibald Seymour Jarman (d 1982), of Brighton, and Helen Marie Klenk; *b* 19 June 1938; *Educ* Harrow, Ch Ch Oxford (MA); *m* 1973 (m dis 1977), Jennifer Michelle, da of Michael Lawrence Lawrence-Smith (d 1988), of Suffolk; 1 da (Jemima b 1975); *Career* JVO Mons Offr Trg Sch 1957, cmmnd RA 1957, served Cyprus; barr Inner Temple 1965-, practicing Midlands & Oxford circuit, rec of Crown Ct 1982-; *Recreations* flyfishing, France; *Style*— Nicolas Jarman, Esq, QC; 13 Blithfield St, London W8 6RH (☎ 01 937 0982); 4 King's Bench Walk, Temple, London EC4 (☎ 01 353 3581)

JARMAN, Roger Whitney; s of Reginald Cecil Jarman, and Marjorie Dix, *née* Whitney (d 1970); *b* 16 Feb 1935; *Educ* Cathays HS Cardiff, Univ of Birmingham (BSocSc); *m* 1959, Patricia Dorothy, da of Trevor Henry Odwell (d 1977); 1 s (Christopher b 1960); *Career* instr in lab studies Vauxhall Motors 1960-62, recruitment offr Vauxhall Motors 1962-64, asst sec appt bd Bristol Univ 1964-68, princ Civil Serv Cmmn 1968-72, princ Welsh Off Euro Div 1972-74, asst sec Devolution Div 1974-78, asst sec perm sec div 1978-80, under-sec Land Use Planning Gp 1980-83, under sec Tport Highways and Planning Gp Welsh Off 1983-88, under sec Housing Health and Social Servs Policy Gp; *Recreations* reading, cooking, walking; *Clubs* Civil Serv; *Style*— Roger Jarman, Esq; Welsh Office Cathays Park, Cardiff (☎ 0222 825257)

JARMAN-PRICE, Russell; s of Robert Eustace Price, JP, and Redena Mary, *née* Stockdale; *b* 18 May 1954; *Educ* Priory GS Shrewsbury, Univ of Loughborough (BSc); *m* 1 Sept 1988, Amanda Jayn Jarman, da of Maj Roy Longden Rozler; *Career* account exec Benton of Bowles (London) 1976-78, account mangr T13WA (London) 1976-80, account dir Gold Greenlees Trott 1980-81, bd account dir Hedger Mitchel Stark 1981-84; md Still Price Court Twivy De Sourza Ltd 1985-;IPA; *Recreations* riding, painting, driving, walking, cinema; *Clubs* Burkes; *Style*— Russell Jarman-Price, Esq; 30 New Oxford St, London WC1A 1NP (☎ 01 636 3377, fax 01 631 4322, car tel 0836 228 970, 0860 305 093)

JARRATT, Sir Alexander Anthony (Alex); CB (1968); s of Alexander Jarratt (d 1943), and Mary Jarratt (d 1970); *b* 19 Jan 1924; *Educ* Royal Liberty GS Essex, Univ of Birmingham (BCom); *m* 1946, Mary Philomena, da of Louis Keogh (d 1932); 1 s, 2 da; *Career* Petty Offr Fleet Air Arm, served Far East; civil servant: Miny of Power 1949-64, seconded Treasy 1953-54, Cabinet Off 1964-65, sec Prices and Incomes Bd 1964-68, dep under-sec Dept of Employment and Productivity 1968-70, dep sec Miny of Agric 1970; chief exec IPC and IPC Newspapers 1970-73, chm and chief exec Reed Int 1974-85 (dir 1970-), dep chm Midland Bank 1980-, dep chm Prudential Corpn 1987-, dir ICI 1975, Thyssen-Bornemisza Gp 1972-, chm Smiths Industs plc 1985-; pres Advertising Assoc 1979-83, former memb NEDC; former chm CBI Econ Policy Ctee and Employment Policy Ctee, former memb President's Ctee CBI; chm Industl Soc 1975-79 (currently memb); chm Henley Admin Staff Coll; govr Ashridge Mgmnt Coll, chllr Univ of Birmingham (Hon LLD) 1983-; Hon DSc Cranfield, DUniv Brunel; FRSA; kt 1979; *Recreations* the countryside, reading; *Clubs* Savile; *Style*— Sir Alex Jarratt, CB; Smiths Industries plc, 765 Finchley Rd, Childs Hill, London NW11 8DS (☎ 01 458 3232, telex 928761)

JARRETT, Dr (Boaz) Antony; s of Frank Jarrett (d 1963), of Cox Corner, Ockley, Surrey, and Ethel Mary, *née* Budden; *b* 24 July 1923; *Educ* Windsor Co Boy's Sch, Imperial Coll London (BSc, PhD, DIC, ACGI); *m* 2 Oct 1948, Patricia Eveline, da of Arthur White (d 1976), of Forest Row, Sussex; 2 da (Lianne b 6 Sept 1951, Naomi b 11 Sept 1955); *Career* Sub-Lt (A) RNVR air engr 1943-46; res contract Imp Coll 1946-48, gen factory mangr Lucas Cav Ltd 1949-63, md Eaton-Env Ltd 1963-66, tech dir Lucas Cav Ltd 1966-81, gp dir prod techol Lucas Industs plc 1981-86; pres Old Centralians (Engrs' Alumnus Assoc of Imp Coll) 1986-87, memb tech ctee RAC, former govr Claremont Fan Ct Sch Esher (chm CDT ctee); Freeman City of London 1984, Liveryman Worshipful Co of Engrs 1984; FIMechE 1965, MSAE 1978, FCGI 1981, FEng 1983, FRSA 1984; *Clubs* RAC; *Style*— Dr Antony Jarrett; c/o Royal Automobile Club, 85 Pall Mall, London SW1Y 5HS

JARRETT, Sir Clifford George; KBE 1956 (CBE 1945), CB (1949); s of George Jarrett; *b* 1909; *Educ* Dover Co Sch, Sidney Sussex Coll Cambridge; *m* 1, 1933, Hilda Goodchild (d 1975); 1 s, 2 da; m 2, 1978, Mary, da of C Beacock; *Career* Home Off 1932, Admty 1934, dep sec Admty 1950-61, perm sec 1961-64; perm under-sec Miny of Pensions and National Insur (later DHSS) 1964-70; tstee Nat Maritime Museum 1969-81, chm: Dover Harbour Bd 1971-80, Tobacco Res Cncl 1971-78; memb Civil Serv Security Appeals Panel to 1982; *Style*— Sir Clifford Jarrett, KBE, CB; 1 The Coach House, Derry Hill, Menston, Ilkley, W Yorks

JARROW, Bishop of 1980-; Rt Rev Michael Thomas Ball; s of Thomas James Ball (d 1966), of Eastbourne, and Kathleen Obena Bradley, *née* Morris (d 1980); *b* 14 Feb 1932; *Educ* Lancing, Queens' Coll Cambridge (BA, MA); *Career* schoolmaster 1955-75; chaplain for higher educn in Brighton Area 1975-80, curate Whiteshill Stroud 1971-75, parish priest Stanmer and Falmer 1975-80; prior of Stroud Glos 1963-75, co fndr Community of the Glorious Ascension 1960; involved in: governing body various ind schools, drug rehabilitation unit, school for violent or difficult children; pres local hospice; fell Woodward Corpn, provost N Div Woodward Schs 1985-86; *Recreations* sport, music, housework; *Style*— The Rt Rev the Bishop of Jarrow; Melkridge House, Gilesgate, Durham DH1 1JB (☎ 091 3843797)

JÄRVI, Neeme; s of August Järvi (d 1960), and Elss Järvi (d 1984); musical family, bro Vallo Järvi conductor, theatre 'Estonia' Tallinn Estonia; *b* 7 June 1937; *Educ* Tallinn Music Sch Leningrad, Conservatory of Music Rimski-Korsakov (post grad); *m* 1961, Lillia Järvi; 2 s (Paavo, Kristjan), 1 da (Maarika); *Career* music dir Estonian Radio Symphony Orchestra, theatre opera and ballet Estonia 1960-73, Estonian State Symphony Orchestra 1973-80, concerts and tours with Leningrad and Moscow Orchestras, emigration to USA 1980; music dir Gothenburg Symphony Orchestra Sweden 1980-, musical dir and chief conductor The Scottish Nat Orchestra 1984-, concerts and opera performance: Met New York, Philadelphia, Boston, Chicago, San Francisco, Los Angeles, German Orchestra, London Orchestra (Philharmonic LPO, LSO), Canada, Mexico, Brazil; recordings with EMI, Philips, DG, BIS, Chandos; *Style*— Neeme Järvi Esq; 130 West 67 Street, apt 21 H, New York, NY 10023, USA; 3 La Belle Place, Glasgow G3 7LH (☎ (041) 332 7244, telex 777751)

JARVIS, David; s of Harold Jarvis (d 1945), and Phyllis Emma, *née* Hart; *b* 9 Mar 1941; *Educ* Gillingham GS, Maidstone Coll of Tech; *m* 9 Feb 1963, Willamina Bell, da of William Herbert Colby; 1 s (Julian David b 1966), 2 da (Andrea Claire b 1968, Nicola Emma b 1976); *Career* Anderson Clayton: controller and tres Milne and Cosa 1963-68, fin admin Peru 1968-70, gen mangr Consumer Prods Div Mexico 1970-78; gen mangr Int Business Devpt The Pillsbury Co USA 1978-81, vice-chm and chief fin offr Norwest Corpn USA 1981-86, md Saloman Bros USA UK 1986-; voyageur Outward Bound Sch Minnesota, ex tstee Fin Accounting Standards Bd USA; ACMA 1960; *Recreations* tennis, golf; *Clubs* Canning, Riverside; *Style*— David Jarvis, Esq; 64 Cadogan Sq, London SW1 (☎ 01 584 2007); The Small House, Great Rissington, Glos(☎ 0451 21727); Salomon Bros Int, Victoria Plaza, 111 Buckingham Palace Rd, London SW1W OSB (☎ 01 721 3974, fax 01 736 5773, telex 886441)

JARVIS, David William; s of George Harry Jarvis, and Doris Annie, *née* Mabbitt; *b* 25 April 1947; *Educ* City of London Sch, Univ of Exeter (BA); *m* 1972, Elizabeth Ann Rowena, da of Fergus Ferguson (d 1969); 1 s (John David George b 1982), 2 da (Rowena Gilliam b 1978, Katherine Elizabeth b 1980); *Career* dir of fin Harvey of Bristol Ltd; dir: John Harvey & Sons Ltd, John Harvey & Sons (Espana) Ltd, Jhesa, Fernando A De Terry Sa, A Delor & Cie Sa, Commercial Agencie (Spain), Commercial Agencies (Tenerife), John Harvey & Sons (Portugal) Ltd, Palomino & Vergara SA; FCCA; *Recreations* sports, walking, reading, current affairs; *Style*— David Jarvis, Esq; Harveys of Bristol, Harvey House, Whitechurch Lane, Whitchurch, Bristol (☎ 0272 836161)

JARVIS, John Manners; s of Donald Edward Manners Jarvis, TD, of Rockbourne, Hants, and Theodora Brixie, *née* Bryant; *b* 20 Nov 1947; *Educ* Kings Coll Sch Wimbledon, Emmanuel Coll Cambridge (MA); *m* 5 May 1972, Janet Rona, da of Eric Cresswell Kitson, OBE (d 1975), of Mersham,Kent; 2 s (Christopher b 1974, Fergus b 1976); *Career* barr 1970, practice at commercial Bar, asst rec; govr Kings Coll Sch Wimbledon; *Recreations* tennis, sailing, skiing, cycling, music; *Clubs* Hurlingham; *Style*— John Jarvis, Esq; 3 Gray's Inn Place, Gray's Inn, London WC1R 5EA (☎ 01 831 8441, fax 01 831 8479)

JARVIS, Patrick William; CB 1984; s of Arthur Frederick Jarvis (d 1950), and Marjorie Winifred, *née* Adams; *b* 27 August 1926; *Educ* Co GS Gillingham, Royal Dockyard Sch, RN Engrg Coll Devonport, RNC Greenwich (BSc); *m* 21 July 1951, Amy Jarvis, da of Albert Ryley (d 1983), 2 s (Anthony, Robin); *Career* joined MOD 1951: various appts 1951-74, dir ship prodn 1979-81, dir ship design and engrg 1981-83, dep controller of the Navy (warships) 1983-86, ret 1986; FIEE 1949, FiMarE 1983, FRINA 1983, RCNC; *Style*— Patrick Jarvis, Esq, CB

JASPER, Robin Leslie Darlow; CMG (1963); s of T D Jasper, of Beckenham; *b* 22 Feb 1914; *Educ* Dulwich, Clare Coll Cambridge; *m* 1, 1940 (m dis), Jean, da of late Brig-Gen J K Cochrane, CMG; m 2, 1966, Diana Speed, *née* West; 2 step da; *Career* Wing Cdr RAFVR 1940-45; princ India Off (later Cwlth Rels Off) 1945, concerned with resettlement of the Sec of State's services in India 1947-48, Br dep high cmmnr Lahore Pakistan 1949-52, advsr London Conferences on Central African Fedn and visited Central Africa in this connection 1952-53, cnsllr HM Embassy Lisbon 1953-55, visited Portguese Africa 1954, Cwlth Rels Off 1955-60 (head of Info Policy Dept 1958-60); attached to UK delgn to the UN 1955 and 1956, Br dep high cmmnr Ibadan Nigeria 1960-64, cnsllr Cwlth Off 1965-67, consul-gen Naples 1967-71, ret 1972; *Recreations* tennis, rugby fifes, wind music, 17th century church sculpture, claret; *Clubs* MCC, Jesters; *Style*— Robin Jasper, Esq, CMG; c/o Royal Bank of Scotland, Drummonds Branch, 49 Charing Cross, London SW1

JAUNCEY, Hon Arabella Bridget Rachel; da of Baron Jauncey of Tullichettle (Life Peer) and his 1 w, Jean, *née* Cunninghame Graham; *b* 14 April 1965,; *Style*— The Hon Arabella Jauncey; c/o The Rt Hon Lord Jauncey of Tullichettle, Tullichettle, Comrie, Perthshire

JAUNCEY, Hon James Malise Dundas; er s of Baron Jauncey of Tullichettle (Life Peer) and his 1 w Jean, *née* Cunninghame Graham (now Lady Polwarth); *b* 29 Sept 1949; *Educ* Radley, Univ of Aberdeen (LLB); *m* 1, 26 April 1980 (m dis 1986), Caroline Elizabeth, da of Charles Ede, of The Garden House, Hollington, Newbury, Berks; 2 da (Sophie b 1980, Eleanor b 1983); m 2, 10 Sept 1988, Sarah Jacqueline, da of Peter David Ludovic Lindsay (d 1971), of Meribel Les Allues, Savoie, France; *Career* City of Westminster Arts Cncl Travelogue Award 1975 and 1976; fndr ed and publisher Radio Month 1979-82; organiser: The Local Radio Awards 1979-81, Edinburgh Int Radio Festival 1982; fndr ed and publisher Cable and Satellite News and Cable and Satellite Europe 1982-84; *Books* Pan Book of Horror Stories (1971), Gaslight Tales of Terror (1975); *Recreations* skiing, music; *Style*— The Hon James Jauncey; 16 Ormeley Rd, London SW12 9QE (☎ 01 673 4980)

JAUNCEY, Hon Simon Helias; yr s of Baron Jauncey of Tullichettle (Life Peer) and his 1 w, Jean, *née* Cunninghame Graham (now Lady Polwarth); *b* 8 Oct 1953,; *Educ* Radley; *m* 1979, Aurora, da of Juan de Jesus Castaneda, of Apartado Aereo 33394, Bogota, Colombia; 2 s (Jeremy Cunninghame b 1984, Thomas Charles b 1987); *Style*— The Hon Simon Jauncey; 128 Cavendish Drive, London E11

JAUNCEY OF TULLICHETTLE, Baron (Life Peer UK 1988); Charles Eliot Jauncey; o c of Capt John Henry Jauncey, DSO, RN (d 1958); *b* 8 May 1925; *Educ* Radley, Christ Church Oxford (MA), Univ of Glasgow (LLB); *m* 1, 1948 (m dis 1969), Jean, da of Adm Sir Angus Cunninghame Graham; 2 s, 1 da; m 2, 1973 (m dis 1977), Elizabeth, widow of Maj John Ballingal, MC; m 3, 1977, (Sarah) Camilla, da of late Lt-Col Charles Cathcart, DSO (ggs of 2 Earl Cathcart); 1 da (Hon Cressida Jane b 1981); *Career* served WWII Sub-Lt RNVR; advocate 1949; Kintyre Pursuivant of Arms 1955-71; sheriff principal Fife and Kinross 1971-74; judge Cts of Appeal Jersey and Guernsey 1972-79; senator Coll of Justice Scotland 1979-88; Lord of Appeal in Ordinary 1988-; Hon Master of Bench of Middle Temple 1988; memb Royal Co Archers (Queen's Bodyguard for Scotland); *Recreations* shooting, fishing, genealogy, bicycling; *Clubs* Royal (Perth); *Style*— The Rt Hon Lord Jauncey of Tullichettle; Tullichettle, Comrie, Perthshire (☎ 0764 70349); 1 Plowden Buildings, Temple, London EC4 (☎ 01 583 4246)

JAWARA, Hon Sir Dawda Kairaba; GCMG, GMRG; *b* 16 May 1924; *Educ* Muslim Primary Sch, Methodist GS, Achimota Coll (Vet Sch), Univ of Glasgow; *Career* princ veterinary offr for The Gambia govt 1957-60 (vet offr 1954-57); ldr People's Progressive Party The Gambia 1960, min of Educn 1960-61, premier 1962-63, PM 1963-70, pres The Republic of Gambia 1970-; Grand Cross Order of Lebanon 1966, Nat Order of Republic of Senegal 1967, Order of Propitious Clouds of China (Taiwan) 1968, Nat Order of Republic of Guinea 1973, Grand Offr Order of Islamic Republic of Mauritania 1967; Grand Cordon of most Venerable Order of Knighthood Pioneers of Republic of Liberia 1968, Grand Commander Nat Order of Federal Republic of Nigeria 1970, Grand Master Order of the Republic of The Gambia 1972, Hon GCMG 1974; Commander of Golden Ark (Netherlands) 1979; Peutinger Gold Medal Peutinger-Collegium Munich 1979, Agricola Medal 1980; DSc (Ife Univ), DSc (Colorado State Univ); kt 1966; *Books* Sir Dawda Speaks (1971), Sunrise in the Sahel (forthcoming); *Recreations* golf, gardening; *Style*— Hon Sir Dawda Jawara, GCMG; State House, Banjul, The Gambia

JAY, Sir Antony Rupert; s of Ernest Jay (d 1957), of London, and Catherine Mary, *née* Hay (d 1981); *b* 20 April 1930; *Educ* St Paul's, Magdalene Coll Cambridge (BA, MA); *m* 15 June 1957, Rosemary Jill, da of Leslie Watkins, of Stratford upon Avon; 2 s (Michael b 1959, David b 1972), 2 da (Ros b 1961, Kate b 1964); *Career* Nat Serv Royal Signals 1952-54 (2 Lt 1953), Lt TA 1954; BBC 1955-64: ed Tonight 1962-64, head Talks Features 1963-64; ed A Prime Minister on Prime Ministers 1977; writer: Royal Family (1969), Yes Minister (3 series with Jonathan Lynn, 1980-82), Yes Prime Minister (2 series 1985 and 1987); BAFTA Writers Award 1988; memb Anna Ctee on Future of Broadcasting 1974-77; Hon MA Sheffield 1987, Hon DBA Int Mgmnt Centre Buckingham 1988; *Books* Management and Machiavelli (1967), To England with Love (with David Frost, 1967), Effective Presentation (1970), Corporation Man (1972), The Complete Yes Minister (with Jonathan Lynn, 1984), Yes Prime Minister (1986, vol II 1987); *Style*— Sir Antony Jay; Video Arts Ltd, Dumbarton House, 68 Oxford St, London W1N 9LA (☎ 01 637 7288)

JAY, Prof Barrie Samuel; s of Maurice Bernard Jay (d 1959), of London, and Julia, *née* Sterling (d 1965); *b* 7 May 1929; *Educ* Perse Sch Cambridge, Gonville and Caius Coll Cambridge (MB, BChir, MA, MD); *m* 19 Jan 1954, Marcelle Ruby, da of Alan Byre (d 1968), of Paris; 2 s (Robert b 1959, Stephen b 1961); *Career* conslt ophthalmic surgn London Hosp 1965-79, conslt surgn Moorfields Eye Hosp 1969-, dean Inst of Ophthalmology London 1980-85, conslt advsr in ophthalmology DHSS 1982-88, prof of clinical ophthalmology Univ of London 1985-; pres Faculty of Ophthalmologists 1986-88, vice pres Coll of Ophthalmologists 1988-; Liveryman: Worshipful Co of Apothecaries (memb ct 1985-), Worshipful Co of Barbers; FRCS 1962, FRPSL 1986; *Books* System of Ophthalmology vol XI (jtly 1969), Postal History of Great Britain and Ireland (jtly 1981), British County Catalogue of Postal History, vols 1-4 (jtly 1978-88); *Recreations* postal history, gardening; *Style*— Prof Barrie Jay; 10 Beltane Drive, London SW19 5JR (01 947 1771)

JAY, Baron (Life Peer UK 1987), of Battersea in Greater London; Douglas Patrick Thomas Jay; PC (1951); s of Edward Aubrey Hastings Jay (d 1950); *b* 23 Mar 1907; *Educ* Winchester, New Coll Oxford; *m* 1, 1933 (m dis 1972), Margaret Christian, eld da of late J C Maxwell Garnett, CBE; 2 s (Hon Peter, Hon Martin), 2 da (Hon Mrs Pennant-Rea, Hon Mrs Boyd); m 2, 1972, Mary Lavinia, da of Maj Hugh Lewis Thomas, of 12 Woodlands Park, Merrow, Guildford; *Career* on staff of The Times 1929-33 and The Economist 1933-37, city ed Daily Herald 1937-40; MP (Lab): Battersea N 1946-74, Wandsworth Battersea N 1974-83; asst sec Miny of Supply 1940-43, princ asst sec BOT 1943-45; PA on econ affrs to PM 1945-46, fin sec Treasy 1950-51, econ sec Treasy 1947-50, pres BOT 1964-67; chm: Common Mkt Safeguards Campaign 1970-77, London Motorway Action Gp 1968-80; dir: Courtaulds 1967-70, Trade Union Unit Tst 1967-80; fell All Souls Coll Oxford 1968- (and 1930-37); *Books* The Socialist Case (1937), Socialism in the New Society (1962), After the Common Market (1968), Change and Fortune (1980), Sterling, A Plea for Moderation (1985); *Style*— The Rt Hon Lord Jay; Causeway Cottage, Minster Lovell, Oxford OX8 5RN (☎ 0993 775 235)

JAY, Hon Mrs (Jane Malca); *née* Mishcon; da of Baron Mishcon (Life Baron); *b* 1950; *m* 1971 (m dis), Anthony Jay; 1 s (Adam), 1 da (Lucy); *Style*— Hon Mrs Jay

JAY, John Philip Bromberg; s of Alec Jay and (Helena) June Jay; *b* 1 April 1957; *Educ* UCS, Magdalen Coll Oxford (BA); *m* 15 Aug 1987, Susy, da of Donald Streeter; *Career* reporter Western Mail 1979-81; city reporter: Thomson Regnl Newspapers 1981-83, Sunday Telegraph 1984-86; city ed Sunday Times 1986 (dep business ed 1988); *Recreations* walking, cinema, theatre; *Style*— John Jay, Esq; The Sunday Times, 1 Pennington St, London E1 (☎ 01 782 5766, fax 01 782 5658)

JAY, Hon Mrs (Margaret Ann); *née* Callaghan; er da of Baron Callaghan of Cardiff, KG, PC (Life Peer), *qv*; *b* 1939,R[; *m* 1961 (m dis 1986), Hon Peter Jay, *qv*; 1 s, 2 da; *Style*— The Hon Mrs Jay; 111 Ledbury Road, Notting Hill Gate, London W11 2AQ

JAY, Hon Martin; yr s of Baron Jay, PC (Life Peer), *qv*; *Educ* Winchester, New Coll Oxford (BA); *m* 1969, Sandra, *née* Williams; 1 s (Adam b 1976), 2 da (Claudia b 1971, Tabitha b 1972); *Career* industrialist; *Style*— The Hon Martin Jay; Bishop's Court, Bishop's Sutton, Alresford, Hants

JAY, Hon Peter; er s of Baron Jay, PC (Life Peer), *qv*; *b* 7 Feb 1937; *Educ* Winchester, Christ Church Oxford, (MA); *m* 1, 1961 (m dis 1986), Hon Margaret Ann, er da of Baron Callaghan of Cardiff, KG, PC (Life Peer), *qv*; 1 s, 2 da; m 2, Emma, da of P K Thornton; 1 s; *Career* Midshipman and Sub Lt RNVR 1956-57; former pres Oxford Union; economics ed The Times 1967-77, assoc ed Times Business News 1969-77, presenter Weekend World ITV 1972-77; ambass to USA 1977-79, conslt

Economist Gp 1979-81; dir Econ Intelligence Unit 1979-83; chm Nat Cncl for Voluntary Orgns 1981-; chm and chief exec TV AM 1980-83 (presenter 1983-), presenter A Week in Politics 1985-, ed Banking World 1983-; private sec to Jt Perm sec 1964, princ 1964-67, HM Treasy Economics ed The Times 1967-77; dir: New Nat Theatre Washington DC 1979-81, Landen Press Ltd 1983-; visiting scholar Brookings Inst 1979-80, Wincott Meml lectr 1975, Copland Meml lectr 1980; COS to Robert Maxwell (publisher of Mirror Gp Newspapers, chm BPCC plc and Pergamon Hldgs) 1986-; chm: NACRO 1976-77, United Way (UK) Ltd 1982-83 and various United Way subsidiaries; memb cncl Cinema and TV Benevolent Fund 1982-83, govr Ditchley Fndn 1982-; holds various broadcasting honours and TV awards; *Recreations* sailing (yacht 'Norvantes'); *Clubs* Garrick; *Style—* The Hon Mr Jay; 39 Castlebar Rd, London W5 2DJ (☎ 01 998 3570)

JAY, Peter Alfred; s of Edgar Jay (d 1949), of Lancing Sussex, and Edith, *née* Marks (d 1974); *b* 24 June 1930; *Educ* Cheltenham, Oriel Coll Oxford (BA); *m* 18 Oct 1966, Jane Ohna Campbell *née* Miller, da of Maj Gordon Logan Millar (d 1959), of Troon, Ayrshire; *Career* Nat Serv Sub Lt RNVR, trained Russian interpreter, later Lt seaman branch RNVR; fndr Peter Jay and Ptnrs electrical conslts 1956 (later conslt engrs and bldg servs 1966), advsr to Nat Tst on electrical installation, advsr on electrical installations and lighting to Central Cncl for the Care of Churches; chm Paddington Waterways and Maida Vale Soc; vice pres Illuminating Engr Soc 1974- 77; MInstP 1972, FIOA 1976, FCIBSE 1978, FRSA 1989; *Books* Electrical Installation (with J Hersley, 1962), author various papers and articles on lighting; *Recreations* music; *Style—* Peter Jay, Esq; 1 Penfold Place, London NW1 6RJ (☎ 01 262 3147, fax 01 723 1559)

JAYES, Anthony Peter; s of Grayson Jayes (d 1982), of Walsall, and Doris Ada, *née* Green (d 1985); *b* 11 May 1939; *Educ* Elmore Green HS, Bloxwich Walsall, Univ of London (LLB); *m* 4 June 1966, Mary Patricia, da of Thomas Donaghy, of Aldridge, West Midlands; 1 s (Stephen Charles b 12 Feb 1968), 1 da (Ursula Frances b 2 Jan 1972); *Career* articled clerk Ridsale Cozens & Purslow CAs Walsall 1956-62, Peat Marwick Mitchell & Co 1962-64, Cooper Bros 1962-64, princ lectr in taxation Sandwell Coll 1964-; practising CA (later ptnr Jayes Scriven & Co Rugeley Staffs) 1964-84; hon auditor: Beaudesert Tst 1965-75, Rugeley CAB 1984-87; tres local branch Cons and Unionist Party 1974-88; hon auditor Colwich and Little Haywood Village Hall 1982-; qualified MCC coach 1983; FCA 1962, ATII 1965; *Recreations* village CC; *Clubs* Uttoxeter GC; *Style—* Anthony Jayes, Esq; Pennycroft, The Orchard, Coley Lane, Little Haywood, Stafford ST18 0UJ (☎ 0889 882 641); Jayes Scriven & Co, Chartered Accountants, Crossley Stone, Rugeley, Staffs (☎ 08894 77743)

JAYES, Percy Harris; s of Thomas Harris Jayes (d 1954), of Bickley, Kent, and Jessie May, *née* Sanders (d 1955); *b* 26 June 1915; *Educ* Merchant Taylors', St Bart's Hosp Med Coll (MB BS); *m* 1, 1945, Kathleen Mary, da of William Harrington (d 1960), of Finaha Castletownbere, Co Cork; 2 s (Brian b 1946, Michael b 1951), 1 da (Catherine b 1954); m 2, 26 Aug 1964, Aileen Mary, da of George McLaughlin, of East Grinstead, 1 s (Simon b 1965), 1 da (Susannah b 1966); *Career* conslt RAF 1960-85; Queen Victoria Hosp East Grinstead 1948-73, St Bartholemew's Hosp 1950-73, King Edward VII Hosp for Offrs 1960-85; *Recreations* gardening; *Style—* Percy H Jayes, Esq; Barton St Mary, East Grinstead, W Sussex RH19 3UB

JEANNERET, Hon Mrs; (Marian Elizabeth); da of Baron Hobson (Life Peer d 1966); *b* 1942; *Educ* Newnham Cambridge (MA, PhD); *m* 1968, Michel Jeanneret; *Style—* The Hon Mrs Jeanneret; 18 South Vale, London SE19 (☎ 01 771 5094)

JEANS, Michael Henry Vickery; s of Henry Tendron Wilson Jeans, of Bullaven, 24 Woodside Ave, Walton-on-Thames, Surrey, and Joan Kathleen, *née* Vickery; *b* 14 Mar 1943; *Educ* St Edward's Sch Oxford, Univ of Bristol (BA); *m* 1, 27 June 1970 (m dis 1981), Iris Carla, da of Franco Dell'Acqua, of Milan, Italy; m 2, 12 Jan 1987, Paula Wendy, da of David Arthur Spraggs, of Thorpe Bay, Essex; 1 s (James b 25 Aug 1987), 1 da (Rebecca (twin) b 25 Aug 1987); *Career* CA; trainee accountant Peat Marwick McLintock (formerly Peat Marwick Mitchell) 1964-67, asst accountant Blue Circle Gp 1967-70, ptnr Peat Marwick McLintock 1981- (conslt 1970-); vice pres Inst of Mgmnt Conslts 1987-; govr Haberdashers' Aske's Sch Elstree, memb St Matthews Bayswater PCC; Freeman City of London 1965, Liveryman Worshipful Co of Haberdashers 1965 (Memb of Ct 1985); FIMC 1970, FCMA 1971, FCA 1972, MMS 1984; *Recreations* tennis, opera, theatre, Italy; *Clubs* Kingston Rowing, Mensa, Soc of London Ragamuffins; *Style—* Michael Jeans, Esq; 15 Queen's Mews, Bayswater, London W2 4BZ (☎ 01 727 5629); Peat Marwick McLintock, 1 Puddle Dock, Blackfriars, London EC4V 3PD (☎ 01 236 8000, fax 01 248 6552, telex 8811541 pmmlon g)

JEAPES, Maj Gen Anthony Showan (Tony); CB (1987), OBE (1977), MC (1959); s of Stanley Arthur Bernard (d 1971), and Dorothy Irene, *née* Showan (d 1979); *b* 6 Mar 1935; *Educ* Raynes Park GS, RMA Sandhurst, Staff Coll Camberley, NDC Latimer; *m* 1959, Jennifer Clare, da of Lt Col Oliver Geoffrey Woodhouse White, DSO, OBE (d 1975), of Coombe Bissett; 1 s (Benjamin Patrick b 1965), 1 da (Antonia Clare b 1968); *Career* enlisted 1953, cmmnd Dorset Regt 1955, joined 22 Special Air Serv Regt Malaya 1958, serv Oman and Trucial States, India, Kenya, USA (with US Special Forces) and in Malaysia, directing staff Army Staff Coll 1972-74, CO 22 SAS Regt 1974-77, Br Mil Advsy Team Bangladesh 1977-79, dep cmdt Sch of Inf 1979-81, cmd 5 Airborne Bde 1982-85, cmd Land Forces NI 1985-87, gen OC SW Dist 1987; *Books* SAS: Operation Oman (with William Kimber, 1981); *Recreations* offshore sailing, deer conservation, shooting; *Style—* Maj Gen Anthony Jeapes

JEBB, Dom (Anthony) Philip; s of Reginald Douglas Jebb, MC (d 1977), of King's Land, Shipley, Horsham, Sussex, and Eleanor Philippa (d 1979), da of Hilaire Belloc; *b* 14 August 1932; *Educ* Downside, Christ's Coll Cambridge (MA); *Career* clothed as a monk of Downside 1950, ordained priest 1956, curate Midsomer Norton 1960-62, headmaster Downside 1980- (teacher 1960-, housemaster 1962-75, dep headmaster 1975-80); chm SW Div HMC 1988, archivist and annalist English Benedictine Congregation 1972-, memb EBC Theol Cmmn 1969-82 (chm 1979-82), del to Gen Chapter EBC 1980-; memb cncl: Somerset Records Soc 1975-, Bath Univ 1983-87; memb: Ctee Area 7 Secdy Heads Assoc 1984-87, Somerset Archaeological Soc 1975- (tstee 1989), HMC, SHA; vice pres SW Amateur Fencing Assoc; principal speaker AGM of WI in The Albert Hall 1988; Chaplain of Magistral Obedience Br Assoc SMOM 1978; *Books* Missale de Lesnes (ed 1964), Religious Education (ed 1968), By Death Parted (ed 1986), Widowed (1973), Consider Your Call (contrib 1978), A Touch of God (contrib 1982); *Recreations* fencing, archaeology, cosmology, canoeing; *Clubs* East India, Stratton-on-the-Fosse Cricket (pres); *Style—* Dom Philip Jebb, Esq; Downside Abbey, Stratton-on-the-Fosse, Bath BA3 4RJ (☎ 0761 232 206)

JEBB, Lionel Richard; s of Richard Lewthwaite Jebb (d 1961), of The Lyth, Ellesmere, and Marjorie Joy, *née* Jacobs; *b* 21 Dec 1934; *Educ* Shrewsbury, Merton Coll Oxford (MA); *m* 28 May 1960, Corinna Margaret, da of Charles Peter Elmhirst Hawkesworth, of Aldborough House, Boroughbridge, N Yorks; 2 s (Richard b 1961, Andrew b 1966), 1 da (Sophie b 1963); *Career* farmer and landowner; memb: Shropshire CC 1970-81 (chm resources sub-ctee 1978-81), cncl CLA 1975-; chm Shropshire: branch CLA 1985-88, ctee of COSIRA 1982-, Rural Devpt Forum 1985-, Wildlife Fund 1981-88; lay chm Ellesmere Deanery Synod 1970-74 and 1980-85; vice chm: Walford Coll of Agric 1981-88, Adcote Sch Shrewsbury 1970-; memb: Rural Voice 1981-88, Rural Employment Gp, NEDC Agric Sector Gp 1987-89; *Recreations* shooting; *Clubs* Royal Overseas League; *Style—* L R Jebb, Esq; The Lyth, Ellesmere, Shropshire SY12 0HR

JEBB, Hon Miles Alvery Gladwyn; s and h of 1 Baron Gladwyn, GCMG, GCVO, CB, qv; *b* 3 Mar 1930; *Educ* Eton, Magdalen Coll Oxford (MA); *Career* 2 Lt Welsh Gds, Pilot Offr RAFVR; sr mgmnt with British Airways to 1983; *Books* The Thames Valley Heritage Walk (1980), A Guide to the South Downs Way (1984), Walkers (1986), A Guide to the Thames Path (1988); *Recreations* long distance walking; *Clubs* Brooks's, Beefsteak; *Style—* The Hon Miles Jebb; E1 Albany, Piccadilly, London W1

JEEVES, Prof Malcolm Alexander; s of Alexander Frederic Thomas Jeeves (d 1977), and Helena May, *née* Hammond (d 1975); *b* 16 Nov 1926; *Educ* Stamford Sch, St John's Coll Cambridge (BA, MA, PhD), Harvard; *m* 7 April 1955, Ruth Elisabeth, da of Oscar Cecil Hartridge (d 1983); 2 da (Sarah b 1958, Joanna b 1961); *Career* Army 1945-48, cmmnd Royal Lincs Regt, served 1 Bn Sherwood Foresters BAOR; lectr dept of psychology Univ of Leeds 1956-59, fndn prof and head of dept of psychology Univ of Adelaide S Aust 1959-69 (dean Faculty of Arts 1963-64), fndn prof of psychology Univ of St Andrews 1969- (vice princ 1981-85); pres: Int Neuropsychological Symposium 1985-, psychology section Br Assoc for the Advancement of Sci 1988-89; memb: cncl Sci and Engrg Res Cncl 1985-89, neuroscience and mental health bd MRC 1985-89, cncl Royal Soc Edinburgh 1986-89; Hon Sheriff East Lothian and Tayside; FRSE 1980, FBPsS, memb Experimental Psychology Soc; *Books* Thinking in Structures (with Z P Dienes, 1965), The Effects of Structural Relations upon Transfer (with Z P Dienes, 1968), The Scientific Enterprise and Christian Faith (1969), Experimental Psychology: an introduction For Biologists (1974), Psychology and Christianity: the view both ways (1976), Analysis of Structural Learning (with G B Greer 1983), Free to be Different (with R J Berry and D Atkinson 1984), Behavioural Sciences: a Christian perspective (1984), Psychology - through the eyes of faith (with D G Myers 1987); *Recreations* fly fishing, music, walking; *Style—* Prof Malcolm Jeeves; 7 Hepburn Gdns, St Andrews, Fife, Scotland (☎ 0334 73545); Department of Psychology, University of St Andrews, St Andrews, Fife, Scotland KY16 9JU (☎ 0334 76161 ext 7173, fax 0334 75851)

JEEWOOLALL, Sir Ramesh; s of Shivprasad Jeewoolall; *b* 20 Dec 1940; *Educ* Mauritius Inns of Court Law Sch; *m* 1971, Usweenee Reetoo; 2 s; *Career* barr Middle Temple 1968, magistrate 1971-72; chm Mauritius Tea Devpt Authy 1972-76; memb Mauritius Parl 1976-, speaker House of Assembly 1979-; kt 1979; *Style—* Sir Ramesh Jeewoolall; Q1, Farquhar Ave, Quatre Bornes, Mauritius (☎ 4 5918)

JEFFARES, Prof Alexander Norman (Derry); s of Cecil Norman Jeffares (d 1950), and Agnes, *née* Fraser (d 1970); *b* 11 August 1920; *Educ* Dublin HS, Trinity Coll Dublin (BA, MA, PhD), Oriel Coll Oxford (MA, DPhil); *m* 1, 29 July 1947, Jeanne Agnes, da of Emil Calembert (d 1932), of Brussels; 1 da (Felicity Anne b 1 Jan 1949); *Career* lectr in classics Trinity Coll Dublin 1943-44, lectr in Eng Groningen Univ 1946-48, lectr Edinburgh Univ 1949-51, Jury prof of Eng Univ of Adelaide S Aust 1951-56, prof of Eng lit Univ of Leeds 1957-74, prof of Eng studies Univ of Stirling 1974-86; md Acad Advsy Servs Ltd 1970-, dir Colin Smthe Ltd 1978-; vice-pres Film & TV Cncl S Aust 1951-56; vice chm: Muckhart Community Cncl 1976-86, Scottish Arts Cncl 1978-84; pres PEN Scotland 1986-89, chm Book Tst Scotland 1985-88, vice-pres The Roy Soc of Scotland 1988-; memb ACGB 1980-84, life fell Assoc for Cwlth Lit and Language studies (chm 1966-68), hon life pres Int Assoc for the Study of Anglo-Irish Literature 1973-; FAHA (1970), FRSL (1965), FRSE (1981), FRSA (1963), AM (1988); *Books* W B Yeats: Man and Poet (1949, 1966), A Commentary on the Collected Poems of Yeats (1968), The Circus Animals (1970), A Commentary on the Collected Plays of Yeats (with A S Knowland, 1975), Restoration Drana (4 vols, 1974), A History of Anglo-Irish Literature (1982), Poems of Yeats: A New Selection (1984, 1987), Brought Up in Dublin (poems, 1987), Brought Up to Leave (poems 1987), W B Yeats, A New Biography (1989); *Recreations* drawing, motoring, restoring old houses; *Clubs* Athenaeum, Royal Cwlth Soc; *Style—* Prof Derry Jeffares; Craighead Cottage, Fifeness, Crail, Fife (☎ 0333 50898)

JEFFCOATE, Sir (Thomas) Norman Arthur; s of Arthur Jeffcoate (d 1914), of Nuneaton; *b* 25 Mar 1907; *Educ* King Edward VI Sch Nuneaton, Univ of Liverpool (MB, ChB, MD); *m* 1937, Josephine Lindsay (d 1981); 4 s; *Career* consultant obstetrician and gynaecologist Royal Liverpool United Hosp 1932-72; prof of obstetrics and gynaecology Liverpool Univ 1945-72, emeritus 1972-; pres Royal Coll of Obstetricians and Gynaecologists 1969-72; kt 1970; *Books* Principles of Gynaecology 1957 (fifth edn 1987, renamed Jeffcoate's Principles of Gynaecology"; *Style—* Sir Norman Jeffcoate; 6 Riversdale Rd, Liverpool, Merseyside LI9 3QW (☎ 051 427 1448)

JEFFERIES, Col Patrick Hugh Mostyn; s of Norman Jefferies (d 1952), and Anne Isobel, *née* Lucas (d 1974); *b* 22 Sept 1919; *Educ* Bromsgrove, RMC Sandhurst; *m* 6 Oct 1945, (Adelaide) Elizabeth (d 1970), da of Daniel Edward Buckney (d 1964), of Seaford, Sussex; 2 s (Hugh b 1948, Paul b 1953), 1 da (Clare b 1951); *Career* WWII cmmnd Worcs Regt 1939, India 1939-44, BAOR 1945-50, Staff Coll Camberley 1951, GHQ M East 1952-55, MOD 1956-59, Cdr 4 Bn Queen's Own Nigeria Regt 1960-62, HQ Allied Mobile Force NATO 1963-66, mil attaché Tehran and Kabul 1967-70, HQ Northern Army Gp NATO 1970-73; *Recreations* growing vines and making wine; *Clubs* Army and Navy; *Style—* Col Patrick Jefferies; Puck's Hill, Lulsley, Knighwick, Worcestershire WR6 5QW (☎ 0886 21665)

JEFFERIES, Patrick Vernon; s of Lt Col Frederick William, of 35 Kings Rd, Barnet, Herts, and Barbara Millicent, *née* Short; *b* 12 June 1935; *Educ* Haileybury, Law Socs Sch of Law; *m* 26 May 1962, Angela Margaret, da of Capt George Francis Hounslow Blunt, of The Priory, Abbotskerswell, Newton Abbot, Devon; 2 da (Margo b 1966,

Anna b 1969); *Career* Nat Serv 2Lt RA 1958-60; admitted slr 1958, sr ptnr Merton Jones Lewsey & Jefferies 1979-; memb Law Soc, veteran memb HAC 1965; Freeman City of London 1966, Liveryman Worshipful Co of Merchant Taylors 1976; *Recreations* sailing, DIY; *Clubs* HAC Mess, Bosham Sailing; *Style—* Patrick Jefferies, Esq; Shamrock Cottage, Bosham Lane, Bosham, Chichester, W Sussex PO18 8AL; 13 Finchley Lodge, Gainsborough Rd, London N12 8AL; 753 High Rd, London N12 8LG (☎ 01 446 4301, fax 01 446 5117, telex 23538 MJLJG)

JEFFERIES, Roger David; s of George Edward Jefferies, of Tetbury, Glos, and Freda Rose, *née* Marshall; *b* 13 Oct 1939; *Educ* Whitgift Sch Croydon, Balliol Coll Oxford (BA, BCL); *m* 1, 1962 (m dis 1974), Jennifer Anne, da of Leslie Ernest Southgate (d 1984), of Rowhedge, Essex; 1 s (William b 1965), 2 da (Sophie b 1967, Polly b 1970); m 2, 1974 (m dis 1984), Margaret Sealy, *née* Pointer; m 3, 1984, Pamela Mary Elsey, da of Benjamin Arnet Holden, of Harpenden, Herts; 1 s (Harry b 1986); *Career* articled clerk to Sir Charles Barratt town clerk Coventry 1961-64, admitted slr 1965, asst slr Coventry City Cncl 1965-68, asst town clerk Southend Co Borough Cncl 1968-70, dir of ops London Borough of Hammersmith 1970-75, chief exec London Borough of Houslow 1975-; clerk: Mortlake Crematorium Bd 1973-, W London Waste Authy 1986-; under-sec (on secondment) DOE 1983-85; sec Hounslow Arts Tst 1975-; memb: Cncl RIPA 1982-88, Bd of Pub Fin Fndn, regnl advsy ctee Arts Cncl 1984-88; jr vice pres Soc of Local Authy Chief Execs; memb Law Soc 1975; *Books* Tackling the Town Hall (1982); *Recreations* theatre, cooking, growing vegetables; *Style—* Roger Jefferies, Esq; Civic Centre, Lampton Rd, Hounslow, Middx (☎ 01 570 7728, fax 01 572 4819)

JEFFERIES, Stephen; s of George Frederick Jefferies, of Birmingham, and Kitty Barbara, *née* Salisbury; *b* 24 June 1951; *Educ* Royal Ballet Sch (Upper); *m* 1972, Rashna, da of Homi B Minocher Homji; 1 s (Christopher b 1985), 1 da (Lara b 1982); *Career* all major roles with the Royal Ballet & Nat Ballet of Canada, 18 roles created; ARAD; *Recreations* golf; *Style—* Stephen Jefferies, Esq; Royal Opera House, Covent Garden, London WC2 (☎ 01 240 1200)

JEFFERS, Prof John Norman Richard; s of Lt-Col J H Jeffers, OBE (d 1980), of Woodhall Spa, Lincs, and Emily Matilda Alice, *née* Robinson (d 1974); *b* 10 Sept 1926; *Educ* Portsmouth GS, Benmure Forestry Sch Dunoon; *m* 25 July 1951, Edna May, da of Earnest Reginald Parratt (d 1973), of Farnham, Surrey; 1 da (Ysanne b 11 July 1963); *Career* Forestry Cmmn: res forester 1944-53, princ statistician 1953-68: dir Mertewood Res Station Nature Conservancy 1968-73, dep dir Inst of Terrestrial Ecology (NERC) 1973-75 (dir 1976-86), visiting prof dept of statistics Univ of Newcastle 1986-, visiting prof Maths Inst Univ of Kent 1988-, hon prof cmmn for integrated survey of nat resources Academia Sinica Peoples Republic of China; memb Grange and Dist Concert Club, memb PCC; DSc (honouris causa) Univ of Lancaster; FIS, FRSS, FIBiol, FCHIFOR, memb Biometric Soc; *Books* Experimental Design and Analysis in Forestry (1953), An Introduction to Systems Analysis: with ecological examples (1978); *Recreations* military, history; *Clubs* Athenaeum; *Style—* Prof John Jeffers; Ellerhow, Lindale, Grange-over-Sands, Cumbria LA11 6NA (☎ 05395 33731)

JEFFERS, Raymond Jackson; s of George Dennis Jeffers, of Albany, Ipswich, Suffolk, and Jeanine, *née* Jacquier; *b* 5 August 1954; *Educ* Stanwell Sch Penarth, Aberystwyth Univ Coll of Wales (LLB), Wadham Coll Oxford (BCL); *m* 4 Sept 1982, Carol Elizabeth, da of John Bernard Awty, of Freshwater, IOW; *Career* admitted slr 1980, ptnr corporate dept Linklaters & Paines 1986-; memb Employment Law Sub-ctee City of London Slrs Co 1987 (memb Commercial Law Sub-Ctee 1986); memb Law Soc 1980; *Recreations* ornithology, badminton, golf, tennis; *Style—* Raymond Jeffers, Esq; Barrington House, 59-67 Gresham St, London EC2V 7JA (☎ 01 606 7080, fax 01 606 5113, telex 884349/888167)

JEFFERSON, (John) Bryan; CBE (1983); s of John Jefferson (d 1940), of Sheffield, Yorks, and Marjorie, *née* Oxley; *b* 26 April 1928; *Educ* Lady Manners Sch Bakewell Derbyshire, Univ of Sheffield (Dip Arch); *m* 26 July 1954 (m dis 1965), Alison Mary, da of Basil Gray (d 1960); 3 s (Timothy b 1955, David b 1958, Peter b 1960); *Career* Nat Serv RAF 1948-50; asst Morrison and Ptnrs Derby 1956-57, estab practice Sheffield 1957, Jefferson Sheard and Ptnrs (London, Sheffield, Peterborough) 1960-; DOE 1984-: dir gen of design servs Property Servs Agency, chief architectural advsr to Sec of State for Enviroment; pres Sheffield Soc of Architects 1973-74, chm RIBA Yorks Region 1974-75, pres Concrete Soc 1977-78, pres RIBA 1979-81; Freeman City of London 1982; hon fell RAIC 1981, Hon Doc Civil Engrg Univ of Bradford 1987; RIBA 1954, RSA 1983; *Recreations* sailing, music, skiing; *Clubs* Royal Western YC; *Style—* Bryan Jefferson, Esq, CBE; 6 St Andrews Mansions, Dorset St, London W1H 3FD (☎ 01 486 6219); Dept of Enviroment, 2 Marsham St, London SW1P (☎ 01 276 3625)

JEFFERSON, Lady Caragh Seymour; *née* Le Poer Trench; da of late 6 Earl of Clancarty; *b* 1933; *m* 1, 1953 (m dis 1961), Lt-Cdr John Anthony Lake, RN; 1 s, 2 da; m 2, 1961, Capt Arthur Jay Oken, USAF; m 3, 1966, Capt Donald Van Horn Lee, USAF; m 4; m 5, Mr Jefferson; *Style—* Lady Caragh Jefferson

JEFFERSON, David John; s of Edward Hennings Jefferson (d 1959), of Maidenhead, Berks, and Margaret Agatha, *née* Young (d 1977); *b* 14 June 1932; *Educ* Windsor GS; *m* 6 Jan 1962, Barbara Anne, da of Richard Bevington Cooper, of Arnside, Cumbria, 1 s (Peter b 1968), 2 da (Sarah b 1963, Lucy b 1970); *Career* 2Lt Intelligence Corps 1957-58; sr ptnr Maxwell Batlev Slrs 1985- (ptnr 1963-); memb cncl Law Soc 1968-, chm Incorporated Cncl of Law Reporting for England and Wales 1987-; memb: Datchet Parish Cncl 1965-83 (chm 1971-73), Eton RDC 1967-74, Royal Borough of Windsor and Maidenhead Cncl 1974-83; chm Church Adoption Soc 1977-88; Freeman City of London 1969, Liveryman Worshipful Co of Slrs 1969; memb: Law Soc 1957; *Recreations* conversation, music, ballet, opera, theatre, swimming, skiing, collecting (books, drawings and water colours); *Clubs* Special Forces, Royal Thames YC, City of London, Leander; *Style—* David Jefferson, Esq; The Vyne, Deep Field, Datchet, Berks SL3 9JS (☎ 0753 43087); Maxwell Batley, 27 Chancery Lane, London WC2A 1PA (☎ 01 405 7888, fax 01 242 7133, telex 287170)

JEFFERSON, Sir George Rowland; CBE (1969); s of Harold Jefferson and Eva Elizabeth Ellen; *b* 26 Mar 1921; *Educ* Dartford GS; *m* 1943, Irene, da of Frederick Watson-Browne; 3 s; *Career* REME; dir: Br Aerospace (former chm and md Dynamics Gp), Br Scandinavian Aviation, Hawker Siddeley Dynamics; memb NEB 1979-80; dep chm Post Office 1980, dir Babcock Int 1980-87, chm BT 1981-87, non-exec dir Lloyds Bank plc 1986-, chm Natthew Hall plc 1987-88; memb: NEDC 1981-84, NICG 1980-84; Freeman City of London; Hon DSc Bristol 1984, Hon DUniv of Essex 1985; FEng, Hon FIMechE, FIEE, FRAeS, FRSA, CBIM, FCGI; kt 1981; *Style—* Sir George Jefferson, CBE; 14 South Audley St, London W1Y 5DP

JEFFERY, Brian Maurice; s of Maurice Frank Jeffery (d 1968); *b* 24 June 1941; *Educ* Northampton GS, Univ of Birmingham; *m* 1963, Susan, *née* Fearn; 1 s, 1 da; *Career* chm and md Swift and Co Ltd 1978-81, chief exec Alfred Marks Gp 1981-; *Recreations* sport, music; *Clubs* RAC, Durrant's; *Style—* Brian Jeffery, Esq; The Tumbles, Hersham, Bude, Cornwall (☎ 028 882 251); Alfred Marks Bureau Ltd, ADIA House, 84/86 Regent St, London W1R 5PA (☎ 01 437 7855, telex 298240)

JEFFERY, David John; s of Stanley John Friend Jeffery (d 1972), and Sylvia May, *née* Mashford; *b* 18 Feb 1936; *Educ* Sutton HS Plymouth, RNC Greenwich, Croydon Coll of Technol, RCDS; *m* 28 March 1959, Margaret, da of George Yates (d 1983); 1 s (Christopher b 6 Aug 1968), 2 da (Karen b 6 Sept 1962, Susan b 27 July 1964); *Career* Nat Serv RAOC 1954-56; Admty Dir Stores Dept 1956-66 (Devonport, Risley, Singapore, London) MOD 1968-70, princ Treasy Centre for Admin Studies 1970-72, mgmnt sci trg advsr Malaysian Govt Kuala Lumpur 1972-74, princ Civil Serv Dept 1974-76, sr princ MOD 1976-80, asst sec and princ Supply and Tport Offr (Naval) Devonport 1980-83, dep dir Supplies and Tport 1984, dir Armaments and Mgmnt Servs, RN Supply and Tport Serv 1984-86, chief exec river and bd memb Port of London Authy 1986-, chm: Port Publishing 1986-, PLACON Ltd 1987-; tstee dir Pilots Nat Pension Fund 1988-, dir Br Ports Fedn Ltd 1988-, chm Estuary Servs Ltd 1988-; memb: mgmnt ctee Br Ports Assoc 1986-88, Ind Assoc of Ports and Harbours 1986-; memb: Worshipful Co of Watermen and Lightermen of River Thames 1987-; Freeman City of London 1987; *Style—* David Jeffery, Esq; The Old Coach House, Nunney, Frome, Somerset BA11 4LZ; Flat 4, 91 Lansdowne Way, London SW8; Port of London Authority, Europe House, World Trade Centre, London E1 9AA (☎ 01 481 8484, fax 01 481 0313, telex 941 3062 PLALON G)

JEFFERY, Duncan Charles; s of Henry C Jeffery, of Gt Yarmouth, and Ada E Jeffrey; *b* 15 Dec 1952; *Educ* Gt Yarmouth GS; *m* 11 Aug 1979, Mary Elizabeth, da of William John Hayden, TD; *Career* Euro corr Press Assoc 1976, asst ed Eastern Daily Press 1984, ed Southern Evening Echo 1986; memb Guild of British Newspaper Eds; *Recreations* golf, sailing, cookery, antiquarian books; *Clubs* Farmers; *Style—* Duncan Jeffery, Esq; 45 Above Bar, Southampton, Hants (☎ 0703 634134, fax 0703 630428)

JEFFERY, Edgar Charles; s of Edred Fleetwood Jeffery (d 1953), of The Parade, Epsom, and Grace, *née* Friston (d 1977); *b* 6 August 1922; *Educ* Tiffin Sch Kingston-upon-Thames, Architectural Assoc; *m* 18 May 1963, Barbara Joyce, da of Maj Frank Herbert Briggs (d 1981), of Silvretta, Torquay; 1 da (Fiona Jane b 1964), 1 s (David William b 1966); *Career* architect, chartered surveyor, county architect Northumberland 1973-85; chm Timber Res and Devpt Assoc N Region 1988-89; maj works: Queens Hall Arts Centre Hexham 1983, County Hall Morpeth 1983, Duchess High Sch Alnwick 1980; ARIBA, ARICS, FRSA; *Recreations* water colours, water sports, walking, working; *Style—* Edgar Jeffery, Esq; Lea House, Fladbury, Worcs WR10 2QW

JEFFERY, Keith Howard; s of James Walter Jeffery (d 1959), of Northwood, Middx, and Ruth, *née* Auld (d 1977); *b* 10 April 1926; *Educ* Merchant Taylors', Pembroke Coll Oxford (MA); *Career* Lt RHA 1946 served: Italy, Austria, Middle East (despatches Palestine 1948); admin Civil Serv 1950, Air Miny 1950-61, Cabinet Off 1961-63, sec Robbins' Ctee on Higher Educn 1963-64, Off of the Min for the Arts 1964-70, Arts Cncl of GB 1970-82; London Rep of the FVS Fndn of Hamburg 1970-; FRSA 1978; *Recreations* music, theatre; *Clubs* Garrick; *Style—* Keith Jeffery, Esq; North Grange, Langley Park, Buckinghamshire

JEFFERY, Ralph Arnold; s of Henry John Jeffery (d 1957), of London, and Lucy Ethel, *née* Hartell (d 1975); *b* 23 April 1920; *Educ* Plaistow GS, Goldsmiths Coll London (NDD, ATD); *m* 26 Dec 1970, Jean Elizabeth, da of Leonard Ash, of Rogate, W Sussex; 2 s (Nicholas Simon, Alexander Ralph); *Career* RAF 1942-47, cmmnd 1943, Fl Lt 1944, seconded Air Miny 1945; teacher and lectr St Dunstan's Coll Woolwich Sch of Art 1947-63, inspr 1963, staff inspr 1979, ret 1982; DES assessor: Design Cncl, Crafts Cncl, Schs Cncl; memb Gulbenkian Ctee for the Arts in Schs, chm Schs Cncl A Level Conference 1979, co-fndr Open Coll of the Art, govr West Surrey Coll of Art; author report to Royal Soc of Arts on Young Designers in Indust; artist, exhibited Royal Acad and London Gp; FRSA 1981, hon fell NSAED 1985; *Recreations* painting, music, gardening; *Style—* Ralph Jeffery, Esq; Broad Oak, Fyning Lane, Rogate, Petersfield, Hants (☎ 073 080 615)

JEFFERY, Very Rev; Robert Martin Colquhoun; s of Norman Clare Jeffery (d 1972), and Gwenedd Isabel, *née* Field; *b* 30 April 1935; *Educ* St Paul's Sch, King's Coll London (BD, AKC); *m* 4 May 1948, Ruth Margaret, da of Everard Tinling (d 1978), of Surrey; 3 s (Graham b 1969, Hilary b 1971, Charles b 1975), 1 da (Phillipa b 1975); *Career* asst curate: St Aidan Grangetown 1959-61, St Mary Barnes 1961-63; asst sec Missionary and Ecumenical of Church Assembly 1964-68, sec Dept of Mission and Unity Br Cncl of Churches 1968-71, vicar St Andrew Headington 1971-78, rural dean Cowley 1972-78, Lichfield diocesan missioner 1978-80, memb Gen Synod of C of E 1982, archdeacon of Salop 1980-87, dean of Worcester 1987-; *Books* Christian Unity and the Anglican Community (with D M Paton, 1965 and 1968), Unity in Nigeria (1964), Areas of Ecumenical Experiment (1968), Ecumenical Experiments: A Handbook (1971), Case Studies in Unity (1972); *Recreations* local history, cooking; *Style—* The Very Rev the Dean of Worcester; 10 College Green, Worcester (☎ 0905 27821)

JEFFREY, John Christopher; s of Cyril Henry Jeffrey (d 1985), and Mary Elizabeth, *née* Jones; *b* 21 July 1942; *Educ* Clifton Coll Bristol; *m* 27 Sept 1974, Diana Lisa, da of Cecil Raymond (d 1988), of Messiter-Tooze; 2 s (Justin b 1971, Nicholas b 1975); *Career* CA 1977; Deloitte Haskins & Sells: ptnr Zambia 1970-75, ptnr i/c Kitwe Zambia 1975-78, managing ptnr Lusaka Zambia 1978-84, ptnr i/c Leeds Bradford 1984-85, managing ptnr N Region Manchester Liverpool Newcastle Leeds; FCA 1965; *Recreations* golf, skiing; *Clubs* St James, Manchester-Prestbury Golf; *Style—* John C Jeffrey, Esq; Greenbank, Chelford Road, Prestbury, Cheshire SK10 4PT (☎ 0625 828 979); Deloitte Haskins & Sells, Bank House, Charlotte Street, Manchester M1 4BX (☎ 061 236 9565, fax 061 228 3920, car tel 0860 612 082, telex 666383)

JEFFREY, Capt John Robert (Ian); OBE (1965); s of James Jeffrey (d 1964), of Glenpatrick, Renfrewshire, and Mina Sadler, *née* Ferguson (d 1949); *b* 1 Dec 1922; *Educ* Johnstone HS Renfrewshire; *m* 25 Sept 1948, Elizabeth Comfort, da of Roger Newton Goode (d 1926), of Des Moines, Iowa, USA; 1 s (J Stuart b 1951), 2 da (Sandra (Mrs Cleaver) b 1949, Wendy (Mrs Tobi) b 1955); *Career* WW11: RAFVR

1941, serv No 53 and No 86 Sqdns Coastal Cmd 1942-45 (despatches); seconded to BOAC 1945, Capt 1947; Cdr flying: Liberator, Constellation 049, Stratocruiser, DC Seven Seass, Boeing 707, Boeing 747; Boac Trg Capt, instrument rating examiner 1959, Master Air Pilot, Sr Capt first class 1959, ret 1977; dir ECG Consits Ltd 1966-; memb exec ctee BALPA 1960-66 (fin chm 1960-62, chm centl bd 1962-66); memb: Nat Jt Cncl for Civil Air Tport 1962-66, Air League Cncl 1967-79; assessor Fay Inquiry into Munich air crash 1968-69; chm Frimley and Camberley UDC 1963-65 (memb 1959-65), Party candidate (Cons) Coventry SW 1974 (twice), JP 1966-86; Freeman City of London 1957, Liveryman Guild of Air Pilots and Navigators 1965; FCIT 1970, MRAEs 1966; *Clubs* RAF; *Style*— Capt Ian Jeffrey, OBE; 21 Billing Rd, London SW10 9VL (☎ 01 352 0760); 2 Canary Wharf, London E14 9SJ (☎ 01 942 2488, car phone 0836 205 401, telex 22891)

JEFFREY, Nicholas; s of Manfred Jeffrey, MD, DPM, of Essex, and Doris MacKay *née* Spouge; *b* 6 June 1942; *Educ* Ecclesfield GS, Univ of Sheffield (LLB); *m* 1965, Dianne Michelle, da of Cyril Cantor (d 1985); 2 s (Alexander b 1966, David b 1969), 2 da (Danya b 1968, Miranda b 1971); *Career* dir of Cantors plc and all subsidiary companies 1967- (chief exec 1980-); *Recreations* shooting, sailing; *Style*— Nicholas Jeffrey, Esq; Riley Croft, Eyam, Derbyshire; Cantors plc, 164-170 Queens Rd, Sheffield S2 4DY (☎ 0742 766461, telex 547037, fax 0742 769070)

JEFFREY, Hon Mrs; (Oonagh Elizabeth); *née* Gibson; da of 3 Baron Ashbourne; *b* 1935; *m* 1963, John William Jeffrey; 1 s, 1 da; *Style*— The Hon Mrs Jeffrey; Alding, Grayswood Rd, Haslemere, Surrey

JEFFREY, Walter Johnstone; s of George Jeffrey (d 1974), and Agnes McCallum Strain; *b* 20 June 1939; *Educ* The GS Carlise Cumbria, Univ of Durham (BA); *Career* gen sec Writers' Guild of GB; *Style*— Walter Jeffrey, Esq; 37 South Hill Park, London NW3 2ST; Writers Guild of GB, 430 Edgware Rd, London W2 1EH

JEFFREY-COOK, John; *b* 5 Jan 1936; *Educ* Whitgift Middle Sch Croydon; *m* 12 May 1962, Gillian Audrey, da of Ronald Albert Kettle (d 1982), of Croydon; 2 s (Richard Daniel b 1964, Malcolm John b 1970, d 1981), 1 da (Fiona Elizabeth b 1966); *Career* managing ed of taxation books Butterworth Law Publishers 1966-77, dir of pubns Deloitte Haskins & Sells 1977-85, ptnr Moores & Rowland 1985-; memb: ctee London & Dist Soc of CAs 1966-77, cncl Inst of Taxation 1977- (tres 1981-88); Freeman City of London 1980, memb Worshipful Co of CAs 1980; FCA 1958, FCIS 1959, FTII 1964; *Books* Simon's Taxes (ed 1970), Simon's Taxes Intelligence and Cases (1973), Butterworths Orange Tax Handbook (1976), de Voil's Value Added Tax (1973), Foster's Capital Taxes Encyclopaedia (1976), Moores Rowland Yellow and Orange Tax Guides (ed 1987-); *Recreations* genealogy, cinema; *Style*— John Jeffrey-Cook, Esq; 32 Campion Close, Croydon, Surrey CRO 5SN, (☎ 01 688 3887), Moores & Rowland, Clifford's Inn, London EC4A 1AS, (☎ 01 831 2345, fax 01 831 6123, telex 886 504 MARCA)

JEFFREYS, Annie-Lou, Lady Jeffreys; (Anne Louise) Annie-Lou; da of His Hon Judge Sir (William) Shirley Worthington-Evans, 2 Bt (d 1971, when Btcy became extinct); *b* 1934; *m* 1967 (m dis 1981), 2 Baron Jeffreys, *qv*; 1 da (Sophie Lousie); *Style*— Annie-Lou, Lady Jeffreys; The Cottage, Willesley, Tetbury, Glos

JEFFREYS, 3 Baron; Christopher Henry Mark Jeffreys; s of 2 Baron Jeffreys (d 1986), and Mrs Alexander Clarke, of Foxhill House, Hawling, Glos; *b* 22 May 1957; *m* 22 Aug 1985, Anne Elisabeth, da of Antoine Denarie, and Mrs Derek Johnson, of Boden Hall, Scholar Green, Cheshire; 1 da (Hon Alice Mary b 1986); *Heir* bro Alexander Charles Darell Jeffreys; *Career* futures broker; *Recreations* country sports, skiing; *Clubs* Whites, Annabels; *Style*— Rt Hon Lord Jeffreys; Bottom Farm, Eaton, Grantham, Lincolnshire NG32 1ET

JEFFREYS, Hon George Christian Darell; raised to the rank of a Baron's son 1961; s of Capt Christopher John Darell Jeffreys, MVO (ka 1940, only s of 1 Baron Jeffreys), and Lady Rosemary Beatrice, *née* Agar (d 1984), da of 4 Earl of Normanton; *b* 2 Dec 1939; *Educ* Eton, RMA Sandhurst; *m* 3 April 1967, (Karen) Elizabeth Mary, da of Col Hugo Meynell, MC, JP, DL (d 1960), of Hollybush Park, Newborough, Burton-on-Trent; 1 s (Christopher b 1988), 2 da (Zara Serena b 1972, Susannah Elizabeth b 1975); *Career* Capt Gren Gds 1964, ret 1966; with C T Bowring & Co Ltd 1966-68, joined Seccombe Marshall & Campion plc 1968 (co sec 1974, dir 1976, md 1978-87); with RIM Fund Mgmnt Ltd 1987-88; *Recreations* hunting, shooting, golf, cricket; *Clubs* Boodle's; *Style*— The Hon George Jeffreys; The Green Farm, Tidmington, Shipston-on-Stour, Warwicks CV36 5LR (☎ 0608 61423)

JEFFREYS, Graham Phillip; s of Kenneth Leopold Jeffreys, of Esher, Surrey, and Phyllis Hilda Eileen, *née* Welch; *b* 17 July 1953; *Educ* St John's Leatherhead; *m* 31 March 1979, Jill Elaine, da of Robert Henry Verrills, of 71 Wordsworth Drive, Cheam, Surrey; 2 da (Louise b 1980, Rachel b 1985), 1 s (Samuel b 1983); *Career* CA 1975-; princ: Jeffrey's & Co 1979-, Acorn Jeffreys Ltd 1982-, Guildford Business Centre Ltd; tres Rushmoor Hart Leonard Chesire Fndn Family Support Serv; *Recreations* swimming, gardening; *Style*— Graham Jeffreys, Esq; Upcott Farm, Wellington, Somerset; Roselea, 15 Down Rd, Guildford, Surrey (☎ 0482 26808, fax 0483 65056, car tel 0860 376484)

JEFFREYS, Martyn Edward; s of William Herbert Jeffreys (d 1961), of Ealing, and Nora Emilie, *née* Crane; *b* 20 Jan 1938; *Educ* St Clement Danes, Bristol Univ (BSc); *m* 29 Oct 1961, Carol, da of Marcel Faustin Boclet (d 1964), of Twickenham; 2 s (Andrew b 1962, Adam b 1968), 1 da (Katy b 1965); *Career* operational res scientist Br Petroleum 1961-63, sr mathematician and mangr mathematical programming div SD-Scicon (formerly CEIR Ltd) 1964-67, chief mgmnt sciences conslt and head professional servs SIA Ltd 1968-70, sr ptnr Wootton Jeffreys & Ptnrs 1971-84, exec chm Wootton Jeffreys Systems Ltd 1985-86, chm Jeffreys Systems plc 1987-; FBCS 1973; *Style*— Martyn Jeffreys, Esq; 196 Epsom Road, Merrow, Guildford, Surrey GU1 2RR (☎ 0483 39598); Jeffreys House, 21 Normandy Street, Alton, Hampshire GU34 1DD (☎ 0420 541541, fax 0420 541640, car tel 0836 283850)

JEFFREYS, Dr Roy Arthur; s of Arthur Thomas George Jeffreys (d 1981), and Elsie Clara, *née* Pegler (d 1976); *b* 7 April 1926; *Educ* Kilburn GS, King's Coll London (BSc, AKC, MSc, PhD); *m* 1 Dec 1951, Joyce Margaret Dorothy, da of Stanley Holloway, DCM, MM (d 1963); 3 s (Paul Robert b 1956, Charles Francis b 1960, Timothy b 1964); *Career* co dir Research Div Kodak Ltd 1981-(dir of res 1978-88), ret 1988; conslt R & D mgmnt 1989-; chm Personnel Policy Ctee Royal Soc of Chem, sr fell Brunel Mgmnt Prog, industl assoc Royal Holloway Coll, vice chm Special Health Authy; FBIM, FInstD, FRSocChem, CChem, Hon FRPS; *Recreations* marathon running; *Style*— Dr Roy Jeffreys; 2 Hillview Rd, Hatch End, Pinner, Middx (☎ 01 428 4173); Research Division, Kodak Ltd, Headstone Drive, Harrow, Middx, HA1 4TY (☎ 01 428 4380); Brunel Management Programme, B1055, Brunel University Uxbridge, Middx UB8 3PH

JEFFRIES, Lionel Charles; s of Bernard Jackson, and Elsie Jackson; *b* 19 June 1926; *Educ* Queen Elizabeths GS Wimborne Dorset, RADA (Dip, Kendal Award 1947); *m* 30 June 1951, Eileen, da of William Walsh (d 1963); 2 da (Elizabeth, Martha), 1 s (Timothy); *Career* War Serv 1939-45, Capt Oxford and Bucks LI Burma, RWAFF (Burma Star); actor (stage and film) 1949-, film prodr, dir, screen writer; appeared in: 7 West End plays, over 100 feature films, Broadway (Pygmalion 1987); wrote and dir: The Railway Children 1972, The Amazing Mr Blunden, The Water Babies 1979; TV films: Danny, Chorus of Disapproval 1988, Ending Up 1989; *Recreations* oil painting, swimming; *Clubs* St James; *Style*— Lionel Jeffries, Esq; John Redway & Assocs Ltd, 16 Berners St, London W1P 3DD (☎ 01 637 1612)

JEFFRIES, Michael Makepeace Eugene; s of William Eugene Jeffries (d 1975), of Port of Spain, Trinidad, and Margaret, *née* Makepeace; *b* 17 Sept 1944; *Educ* Queens Royal Coll Port of Spain Trinidad, Poly of North London (Dip Arch); *m* 10 Sept 1966, Pamela Mary, da of Sir Gordon Booth, KCMG, CVO, of Walton-on-the-Hill, Surrey; 2 s (Andrew b 1969, Simon b 1973), 2 da (Kathryn b 1971, Victoria b 1975); *Career* John Laing and Sons Ltd 1963-67, Deeks Bousell Ptnrship 1968-73, Bradshaw Gass and Hope 1973-75; Atkins Sheppard Fidler and Assocs (WS Atkins Gp) 1975-: dir 1978, chm and md 1979; dir WS Atkins Conslts 1979; chm Banstead Round Table 1980, cncl memb London C of C; RIBA 1973, FRSA 1987; *Recreations* golf, sailing, skiing, water colours, antiquarian horology; *Style*— Michael Jeffries, Esq; Sixways, Court Rd, Banstead, Surrey SM7 2NQ (☎ 0737 359 518); Woodcote Grove, Ashley Rd, Epsom, Surrey KT18 5BW (☎ 03727 23 555, fax 03727 43 006, car tel 0860 366 251, telex 266701 ATKINS G)

JEFFS, Julian; QC (1975); s of Alfred Wright Jeffs (d 1974); *b* 5 April 1931; *Educ* Mostyn House Sch, Wrekin Coll, Downing Coll Cambridge; *m* 1966, Deborah, *née* Bevan; 3 s; *Career* barr, rec 1975, bencher Gray's Inn 1981, chm Patent Bar Assoc 1981-; memb ctee of mgmnt Int Wine and Food Soc 1965-67 and 1971-82, vice pres Circle of Wine Writers (chm 1970-72); gen ed Faber's Wine Series; *Books* Sherry (1961, third edn 1982), Clerk & Lindsell on Torts (ed fifteenth edn 1982), The Wines of Europe (1971), Little Dictionary of Drink (1973), Encyclopedia of United Kingdom and European Patent Law (jtly 1977); *Recreations* wine, walking, old cars, Iberian things; *Clubs* Beefsteak, Garrick, Reform, Saintsbury; *Style*— Julian Jeffs, Esq, QC; Francis Taylor Bldg, Temple, London EC4 (☎ 01 353 5657); Church Farm House, East Ilsley, Newbury, Berks (☎ 063 528 216)

JEGER, Baroness (Life Peer UK 1979); Lena May Jeger; da of Charles Chivers (d 1971), of Yorkley, Glos and Eugenie Alice James (d 1969); *b* 19 Nov 1915; *Educ* Southgate Co Sch Middx, Birkbeck Coll London Univ (BA); *m* 1948, Dr Santo Wayburn Jeger, MP (d 1953); *Career* sits as Labour peer in House of Lords; on London staff Manchester Guardian 1951-54 and 1961-; MP (L): LCC 1951-54, Holborn and St Pancras South Nov 1953-1959 and 1964-74, Camden Holborn and St Pancras South 1974-79; memb Nat Exec Ctee Labour Party 1968-80 (vice chm 1978-79, chm 1979-80); UK rep Staus of Women Cmmn UN 1967, memb Consultative Assembly of Cncl of Europe and Western European Union, memb Chm's Panel House of Commons 1971-79; oppn spokesman (Lords) Social Security 1983-; *Style*— The Rt Hon the Lady Jeger; 9 Cumberland Terrace, Regent's Park, London NW1

JEHANGIR, Sir Hirji Cowasji; 3 Bt (UK 1908), of Bombay; s of Sir Cowasji Jehangir, 2 Bt, GBE, KCIE, OBE (d 1962); *b* 1 Nov 1915; *Educ* St Xavier's Sch Bombay, Magdalene Coll Cambridge; *m* 10 Aug 1952, Jinoo, er da of Kakushroo H Cama; 2 s (Jehangir, Adi b 1956); *Heir* s, Jehangir Hirji Jehangir, b 23 Nov 1953, m 21 March 1988, Jasmine, da of Beji Billimoria; *Career* chm Jehangir Art Gallery Bombay, merchant and landlord; chm: Jehangir Charity Tst, Pavsi Public Sch Soc; *Clubs* Willingdon (Bombay), Brooks's; *Style*— Sir Hirji Jehangir, Bt; Readymoney House, 49 Nepean Sea Rd, Bombay 36, India; 24 Kensington Court Gdns, Kensington Court Place, London W8

JEJEEBHOY, Sir Jamsetjee; 7 Bt (UK 1857), of Bombay; s of Rustamjee J C Jamsetjee (d 1947), n of 4 Bt; suc kinsman Sir Jamsetjee Jejeebhoy 1968, when he assumed the name of Jamsetjee Jejeebhoy in lieu of Maneckjee Jamsetjee Jejeebhoy; *b* 19 April 1913; *Educ* Univ of Bombay (BA); *m* 1943, Shirin Jehangir H Cama; 1 s (Rustomjee b 16 Nov 1957), 1 da (Ayesha); *Heir* s, Rustomjee Jejeebhoy; *Career* chm: Sir Jamsetjee Jejeebhoy Charity Funds, Sir J J Parsee Benevolent Instn, Seth Rustomjee Jamsetjee Jejeebhoy Gujrat Sch Fund, M F Cama Athornan Instn & M M Cama Educn Fund, Bombay Panjrapole, HB Wadia Alash-Behram Funds, Iran League, K R Cama Oriental Inst; tstee: A H Wadia Charity Tst, Byramujee Jeejeebhoy Parsi Charitable Instn, Zorastrian Bldg Fund, Cowasji Behramji Divecha Charity Tst, Parsee Surat Charity Fund, Framjee Cowasjee Inst; memb exec ctee Bomanjee Dinshaw Petit Parsee Gen Hosp, created special exec magistrate 1977; *Clubs* Willingdon Sports, WIAA, Royal Western India Turf, Poona; *Style*— Sir Jamsetjee Jejeebhoy, Bt; Beaulieu, 95 Worli Seaface, Bombay 400 025, India (☎ 4930955); Maneckjee Wadia Bldg, 127 Mahatma Gandhi Rd, Fort, Bombay 400 001, India (☎ 273843)

JEJEEBHOY, Rustomjee; s and h of Sir Jamsetjee Jejeebhoy, 7 Bt, of Bombay, and Shirin Jamsetjee Jejeebhoy; *b* 16 Nov 1957; *Educ* Bombay Univ (BCom, LLM); *m* 1984, Delara Jal Bhaisa, da of Jal Nariman Bhaisa, of Bombay; 1s (Jehangir b 20 Jan 1986); *Career* tstee: Sir Jamsetjee Jejeebhoy Parsee Benevolent Instn, Sir Jamsetjee Jejeebhoy Charity Fund, M F Cama Athornan Instn & M M Cama Educn Fund; service legal offr, TATA Exports Ltd Bombay 1983; dir: Beaulieu Inv Pvt Ltd 1975, Dawn Threads Pvt Ltd 1984, Palmera Inv Pvt Ltd 1984; *Recreations* sports, music, reading; *Clubs* Willingdon Sports, Royal Western India Turf; *Style*— Rustomjee Jejeebhoy, Esq; Beaulieu 95 Worli Seaface, Bombay 400 025 (☎ 4938517); Block A, Shivsagar Estates, Dr Annie Besant Rd, Worli, Bombay 400018 (☎ 494 8573)

JELF, Maj-Gen Richard William; CBE (1947, OBE 1944); s of Sir Ernest Arthur Jelf (d 1950, King's Remembrancer and Master of the Supreme Ct), of Pinner, Middx, and Rose Frances, *née* Reeves (d 1923); *b* 16 June 1904; *Educ* Cheltenham, RMA Woolwich; *m* 23 July 1928, Nowell, da of Maj Nowell Sampson-Way (d 1948), of Manor House, Henbury, Bristol; 3 s (Timothy b 1929, Nicholas b 1932, Jeremy b 1943), 1 da (Jan b 1943); *Career* cmmnd RA 1924, Staff Coll Quetta 1936-37, memb directing staff Staff Coll Camberley 1942, GSO1 49 Div 1942-44, CO Northumberland Hussars 1944-45, Col GS 8 Corps 1945, cdr Cologne Dist CCG 1946, dep dir staff duties WO 1946-47, IDC 1948, cdr RA 1 Div 1948-49, dep dir RA WO 1949, dep chief organization and trg SHAPE 1950-52, COS Eastern Cmd 1955-57, cmdt Police Coll 1957-63, regnl dir Civil Def 1963-68; ADC to HM The Queen 1952; hon sec RNLI Lyme Regis 1972-84; *Style*— Maj-Gen Richard Jelf, CBE; Library Cottage, Marine Parade, Lyme Regis, Dorset (☎ 02974 3284)

JELLEY, Lt-Col Marcus; OBE (1944), TD, DL (1950); s of Harry George Jelley (d 1937); *b* 18 Oct 1908; *Educ* Berkhamsted Sch; *m* 1945, Elizabeth Gwendolen, *née* Noll; 2 s, 2 da; *Career* Lt-Col RA,served NW Europe; former co dir; JP Northants 1946-76; *Style*— Lt-Col Marcus Jelley, OBE, TD, DL; Southlands, 5 The Avenue, Dallington, Northampton (☎ 0604 51704)

JELLICOE, (Patricia) Ann; OBE (1984); da of Maj John Andrea Jellicoe (d 1975), and Frances Jackson Henderson; *b* 15 July 1927; *Educ* Polam Hall Sch Darlington, Queen Margaret's Sch Castle Howard York, Central Sch of Speech & Drama; *m* 1962, David Roger Mayne; 1 s (Tom b 1969), 1 da (Katkin b 1966); *Career* theatre director, playwright and actress; fndr Cockpit Theatre Co to experiment with Open Stage 1952-54, taught acting and directed plays Central Sch of Speech and Drama 1954-56, literary mangr Royal Court Theatre 1972-74, set up first community play in Lyme Regis 1978, fndr Colway Theatre Tst (also dir) to produce and develop community plays; princ plays incl: The Confederacy 1952, The Frogs 1952, The Sport of My Mad Mother 1958, The Nigger Hunt 1958, The Knack 1962, Shelley 1965, A Worthy Guest 1974, Flora & The Bandits 1975, The Bargain 1979, The Tide 1980, The Poor Man's Friend 1981, The Garden 1982, The Western Women 1984, Entertaining Strangers 1985, Money and Land 1988; Elsie Fogarty Prize 1947, 3rd prize Observer Playwriting Competition 1956; pres Colway Theatre Tst; *Books* Some Unconscious Influences in the Theatre (1967), The Shell Guide to Devon (with Roger Mayne, 1975) Community Plays How to Put Them on (1987); *Recreations* reading theatrical biography; *Style*— Ms Ann Jellicoe, OBE; Colway Manor, Lyme Regis, Dorset DT7 3HD

JELLICOE, Sir Geoffrey Alan; CBE (1961); s of George Edward Jellicoe; *b* 8 Oct 1900; *Educ* Cheltenham, Architectural Assoc; *m* 1936, Ursula, da of Sir Bernard Pares, KBE, DCL; *Career* former sr ptnr Jellicoe & Coleridge Architects; former pres Inst Landscape Architects, hon pres Int Fedn Landscape Architects; former memb Royal Fine Art Cmmn, former tstee Tate Gallery; FRIBA, PPILA, FRTPI; kt 1979; *Style*— Sir Geoffrey Jellicoe, CBE; 14 Highpoint, North Hill, Highgate, London N6 4BA (☎ 01 348 0123)

JELLICOE, 2 Earl (UK 1925); George Patrick John Rushworth Jellicoe; KBE (1986), DSO (1942), MC (1944), PC (1963); also Viscount Jellicoe (UK 1917), and Viscount Brocas (UK 1925); s of Adm of the Fleet 1 Earl Jellicoe, GCB, OM, GCVO (d 1935); *b* 4 April 1918; *Educ* Winchester, Trinity Coll Cambridge; *m* 1, 23 March 1944 (m dis 1966), Patricia Christine, o da of Jeremiah O'Kane, of Vancouver, Canada; 2 s (Viscount Brocas, Hon Nicholas Charles b 1953), 2 da (Lady Alexandra Patricia Gwendoline b 1944, Lady Zara Lison Josephine b 1948); m, 2, 1966, Philippa Ann, da of late Philip Dunne, of Gatley Park, Leominster; 1 s (Hon John Philip b 1966), 2 da (Lady Emma Rose b 1967, Lady Daisy b 1970); *Heir* s, Viscount Brocas; *Career* page of honour to HM King George V1; WWII: ME Lt-Col Coldstream Gds, 1 SAS Regt, Special Boat Serv Regt, (wounded, despatches thrice, Legion of Honour, French Croix de Guerre, Greek War Cross); ld-in-waiting to HM Feb-June 1961; parly under-sec Miny of Housing and Local Govt 1961-62, min of state HO 1962-63, first Lord of the Admty 1963-64; Lord Privy Seal, Min in charge Civil Service, Leader of House of Lords 1970-73; chm: MRC 1982-, E Euro Trade Cncl 1986-, Davy Corp 1985-, Booker Tate 1988-; chllr Southampton Univ; dir: Tate & Lyle plc (chm 1978-83), Sotheby's Hldgs 1973-, S G Warburg & Co 1973-88, Morgan Crucible 1974-88, Smiths Industs 1973-86; pres London C of C 1979-88; chm: Brit Overseas Trade Bd 1983-86, Parly & Scientific Ctee 1980-83, Prevention of Terrorism Act Review 1982-83, East Euro Trade Cncl 1986-, Cncl of King's Coll London 1974-83; *Recreations* travel, skiing; *Clubs* Brooks's, Special Forces; *Style*— The Rt Hon the Earl Jellicoe, KBE, DSO, MC, PC; Tidcombe Manor, Tidcombe, nr Marlborough, Wilts (☎ 026 489 225); 97 Onslow Sq, London SW7 (☎ 01 584 1551)

JELLICOE, Hon Nicholas Charles Joseph John; s of 2 Earl Jellicoe, DSO, MC, PC; hp of bro, Viscount Brocas; *b* 23 Mar 1953; *Educ* Eton, Univ of York; *m* 29 Dec 1982, Patricia Ruiz de Castilla, da of late Count Arturo Ruiz de Castilla, of Madrid, Spain, and Lima, Peru; 1 da (Zoë Anaya b 15 June 1988); *Style*— The Hon Nicholas Jellicoe; 14A Willow Bridge Rd, London N1 2LA (☎ 01 359 7266)

JENKIN, The Hon Bernard Christison; yr son of Baron Jenkin of Roding, *qv*; *Educ* Highgate, William Ellis Sch, CCC Camb; *m* 24 Sept 1988, Anne Caroline, da of late Hon Charles Strutt and sis of 6 Baron Rayleigh, *qv*; *Style*— The Hon Bernard Jenkin; 32 Fairfield Road, London E3 2QB

JENKIN, Rev the Hon Charles Alexander Graham; er s of Baron Jenkin of Roding, *qv*; *Educ* Highgate, UCL, Westcott House Cambridge; *m* 1984, Susan, da of Roy Collins; 1 da (Alexandra Emily b 21 Feb 1989); *Career* ordained 1984; *Style*— The Rev the Hon Charles Jenkin; St Anne's House, St Anne's Rd, Canvey Island, Essex SS8 7LS

JENKIN, Rear-Adm (David) Conrad; CB (1983); s of C Jenkin; yr bro of The Rt Hon Lord Jenkin of Reading *qv*; *b* 25 Oct 1928, ; *Educ* RNC Dartmouth; *m* 1958, Jennifer Margaret Nowell; 3 s, 1 da; *Career* RN 1942, Flag Offr First Flotilla 1981-82, Cmdt Jt Serv Def Coll 1982-84; *Style*— Rear-Adm Conrad Jenkin, CB; Knapsyard House, West Meon, Hants GU32 1LF (☎ 073 086 227)

JENKIN, The Hon Flora Margaret; yr da of Lord Jenkin of Roding, *qv*; *Educ* St John's Coll Durham; *Style*— The Hon Flora Jenkin

JENKIN, Ian Evers Tregarthen; OBE (1984); s of late Henry Archibald Tregarthen Jenkin, OBE, of The Firs, Norton, Worcs, and Dagmar, *née* Leggott (d 1969); *b* 18 June 1920; *Educ* Stowe, Slade Sch of Fine Art, Camberwell Sch of Art and Crafts, Trinity Coll Cambridge MA; *Career* mil serv Capt RA 1940-46; dir and co-fndr (with Lord Young of Dartington) Open Coll of The Arts 1986-, curator Royal Acad Schs 1985-86, pncpl Camberwell Sch of Art and Crafts 1975-85, ret; sec and tutor Slade Sch of Fine Art, UCL 1949-75; memb: art panel Arts Cncl 1979-82 (also vice-chm), Crafts Cncl 1981-84, Educn Ctee 1981-84 (also chm), nat advsy body for Public Sector Higher Educn Art and Design Working Gp 1982-85, Nat Conservation Advsy Ctee 1984-86; chm: Painting Faculty 1977-86, Combined Fine Arts Faculty 1986-; (cncl memb 1981-), Gulbenkian Fndn Craft Initiative Working Pty 1985-; govr: Hounslow Borough Coll 1976-81, W Surrey Coll of Art and Design 1975-, Wimbledon Sch of Art 1985-, Loughborough Coll of Art 1985-, Norfolk Coll of Art & Design 1988-; memb exec ctee Arts Servs Grants Ltd 1977 (vice-chm 1983-); fndr and tstee Camberwell Residential Academic and Fellowship Tst, pres Dulwich Decorative and Fine Arts Soc 1984-; tstee: Sir Stanley Spencer Meml Tst 1982-, Birgit Skiöld Meml Tst 1988-; memb advsy ctee Paintings in Hospitals 1982-; dir of the Guild of St George 1986- (companion 1984-); *Publications* Disaster Planning and Prepardness, A Survey of Practices and Procedures, Br Library R & D Report (1986), An Outline Disaster Control Plan, Br Library Information Guide (1987), William Johnson, His Contribution to Art Educn (1981);; *Recreations* painting, gardening, farming; *Clubs* Athenaeum, Bucks, Arts; *Style*— Ian Jenkin, Esq, OBE; Grove Farm, Fifield, Maidenhead, Berks SL6 2PF (☎ 0628 24486); The Open Coll of The Arts, 18 Victoria Park Sq, London E2 9PF (☎ 01 980 6263)

JENKIN, The Hon Nicola Mary; er da of Baron Jenkin of Roding, *qv*; *Educ* N London Collegiate Sch, Royal Coll of Music, Hochschule für Musik Vienna; *Style*— The Hon Nicola Jenkin; 217 Bravington Road, London W9 3AR

JENKIN OF RODING, Baron (Life Peer UK 1987); (Charles) Patrick Fleeming Jenkin; PC (1973); s of Charles O F Jenkin (d 1939), of Gerrards Cross, Bucks; er bro of Rear Adm David Conrad Jenkin, *qv*; *b* 7 Sept 1926; *Educ* Clifton, Jesus Coll Cambridge; *m* 1952, Alison Monica, da of Capt P S Graham, RN; 2 s, 2 da; *Career* Queen's Own Cameron Highlanders 1945-48; barr Middle Temple 1952-57, Distillers Co Ltd 1957-70; memb Hornsey Borough Cncl 1960-63; govr Westfield Coll London Univ 1964-70; MP (C) Wanstead and Woodford 1964-87; jt vice-chm Cons Parly Trade and Power Ctee 1966, oppn front bench spokesman on Treasy, Trade and Econ Affrs 1965-70, fin sec to Treasy 1970-72, chief sec to Treasy 1972-74, min for Energy Jan-March 1974, shadow spokesman on energy and memb Shadow Cabinet 1974-76; shadow spokesman on: Social Servs 1976-79 (sec of state 1979-81), Indust 1981-83, DOE 1983-85; chm: Friends' Provident Life Off; chm: Crystalete Hldgs plc, Lamco Paper Sales Ltd; dir Nat Econ Res Assocs Inc (UK off); advsr Arthur Andersen & Co; chm: UK-Japan 2000 Gp, Taverner Concerts Tst; vice-pres: Nat Assoc of Local Cncls, Greater London Area Conservatives, Cncl Guide Dogs for the Blind Assoc; pres Friends of Wanstead Hosp; *Recreations* gardening, music, bricklaying, sailing; *Clubs* West Essex Conservative; *Style*— The Rt Hon Lord Jenkin of Roding, PC; Home Farm, Matching Rd, Hatfield Heath, Bishop's Stortford, Herts CM22 7AS; 703 Howard House, Dolphin Sq, London SW1 3LX

JENKINS, Prof Aubrey Dennis; s of Arthur William Jenkins (d 1982), and Mabel Emily, *née* Street (d 1970); *b* 6 Sept 1927; *Educ* Dartford GS, Sir John Cass Tech Inst, Kings Coll London (BSc, PhD, DSc); *m* 29 Dec 1987, Jitka, da of Josef Horsky (d 1975); *Career* res chemist Courtaulds Fundamental Res Laboratory 1950-60, res mangr Gillette Fundamental Res Laboratory 1960-64, prof polymer sci Univ of Sussex 1964-; sec Macromolecular Div Int Union of Pure and Applied Chemistry, memb Brighton Health Authy; FRSC 1945; *Books* Kinetics of Vinyl Polymerization (1958), Reactivity Mechanism and Structure in Polymer Chemistry (1974), Polymer Science (1972); *Recreations* music, travel; *Clubs* Great Britain, East Europe Centre; *Style*— Prof Aubrey Jenkins; Shoe Box Cottage, 115 Keymer Road, Hassocks, W Sussex BN6 8QL (☎ 07918 5410); School of Chemistry and Molecular Sciences, Univ of Sussex, Brighton, Sussex BN1 9QJ (☎ 0273 678321)

JENKINS, Brian Garton; s of Owen Garton Jenkins (d 1963), and Doris Enid, *née* Webber (d 1986); *b* 3 Dec 1935; *Educ* Tonbridge, Trinity Coll Oxford (MA); *m* 2 Jun 1967, (Elizabeth) Ann, da of John Philip Manning Prentice (d 1981), of Suffolk; 1 s (Charles b 1973), 1 da (Julia b 1971); *Career* 2 Lt RA 1955-57 served Gibraltar; CA; head audit Coopers & Lybrand 1988-(ptnr 1969-, joined 1960); pres ICAEW 1985-86; govr Royal Shakespeare Theatre 1981-; Alderman City of London 1980- (Sheriff 1987-88); Liveryman: Worshipful Co of CAs 1980- (Jr Warden 1988), Worshipful Co of Merchant Taylors Co 1984-; ACA 1963, FCA 1974, FRSA 1980; *Books* An Audit Approach to Computers (jtly 1978,1986) ; *Recreations* garden construction, old books, large jigsaw puzzles, ephemera; *Clubs* Brooks's, City of London, City Livery; *Style*— Brian Jenkins, Esq; Plumtree Court, London EC4A 4HT (☎ 01 583 5000, fax 01 822 4652)

JENKINS, Brian Stuart; s of Harold Griffith Jenkins (d 1970), of Christleton, Chester, and Ida Lily, *née* Stuart (d 1986); *b* 26 May 1934; *Educ* Shrewsbury; *m* 5 Sept 1959, Teresa Sheelagh, da of Stephen George Ronan (d 1980), of Wigfair Isaph, St Asaph, N Wales; 2 s (Nicolaus Stuart b 13 March 1961, Simon Spencer b 26 March 1962), 1 da (Vanessa Stephanie b 7 July 1965); *Career* RN 1952-54, Midshipman 1953 (served HMS Surprise, fleet despatch vessel Med Fleet), Mersey Div RNR, ret Lt 1960; CA; sr ptnr Haswell Bros 1970-; chm Wrexham and East Denbighshire Water Co 1987- (dir 1969-), memb Wales Regnl Bd TSB Gp plc; FCA 1966; *Recreations* sailing, field sports; *Clubs* Royal Yacht Sqdn; *Style*— Brian Jenkins, Esq; 1 Union St, Chester (☎ 0244 320 532)

JENKINS, Hon Charles Arthur Simon; s of Baron Jenkins of Hillhead (Life Peer), *qv*; *b* 25 Mar 1949; *Educ* Winchester, Holland Park Sch, New Coll Oxford; *m* 11 Sept 1971, Ivana Alexandra, da of Ing Ivo Vladimir Sertic (d 1986), of Zagreb, Yugoslavia; 2 da (Alexandra Dorothea b 14 March 1986, Helena Harriet b 13 May 1988); *Career* Euro ed Economist Intelligence Unit 1975-, ed Euro Trends: (quarterly magazine on Euro affrs); memb Clapham Soc planning and transport ctee; *Style*— The Hon Charles Jenkins; Economist Intelligence Unit, 40 Duke Street, London W1A 1DW (☎ 01 493 6711)

JENKINS, Clive Ferguson; s of Merlyn Jenkins (d 1975), and Annie Elizabeth, *née* Davies (d 1970); *b* 19 Oct 1936; *Educ* Dynevor Secdy Sch Swansea, Welsh Sch of Architecture Cardiff (Dip Arch); *m* 11 Aug 1962, Pauline Helen, da of William George Sutton (d 1974), of Swansea; 1 s (Craig Warren b 1969), 1 da (Kimberley Sian b 1967); *Career* chartered architect private practice, dir PM Devpts Ltd 1987; fndr sec Welsh Water Ski Ctee 1963, Welsh Water Ski Jumping Champion 1970 (overall runner up 1970); FRIBA ; *Recreations* snow skiing, scuba diving; *Clubs* British Water Ski Fed; *Style*— Clive F Jenkins, Esq; 8 Northway, Bishopston, Gower, W Glam (☎ 044 128 2210); 42 Newton Road, Oystermouth, Swansea (☎ 07920 361830)

JENKINS, Prof David; s of Alfred Thomas Jenkins (d 1960), and Doris Cecelia, *née* Hutchings; *b* 1 Mar 1926; *Educ* Marlborough, RVC (MRCVS), Univ of Cambridge (MA), Univ of Oxford (PhD, BSc); *m* 8 April 1961, Margaret, da of James Wellwood Johnson (d 1958); 1 s (Gavin b 1969), 1 da (Fenella b 1967); *Career* vertebrate ecologist Nature Conservancy 1956-72; asst dir (res) Scotland Inst of Terrestrial Ecology 1966-72, head Banchory Res Station 1972-86; hon prof Aberdeen 1986-; chm Scientific Advsy Ctee World Pheasant Assoc 1976-; FRSE; *Books* Population Control in Protected Partridges (1961), Social Behaviour in the Partridge (1963), Population Studies on Red Grouse in N E Scotland (with A Watson and G R Miller, 1963), Population Fluctuations in the Red Grouse (with A Watson and G R Miller, 1967), Structure and Regulation of a Shelduck Population (with M G Murray and P Hall, 1975), Ecology of Otters in Scotland and Otter Breeding and Dispersion in mid-Deeside, Aberdeenshire in 1974-79 (1980); *Recreations* natural history, gardening; *Style*— Prof David Jenkins; Whitewalls, Aboyne, Aberdeenshire AB3 5JB

JENKINS, Dr David Anthony Lawson; s of Phillip Ronald Jenkins (d 1969), of Leigh on Sea, Essex, and Olive Lilian, *née* Lear (d 1938); *b* 5 Dec 1938; *Educ* Dauntseys Sch Wilts, Clare Coll Cambridge (BA, DPhil); *m* 13 Feb 1963, Evanthia, da of Spirithonos Nicolopoulou, of Patras; 2 s (Charles David b 19 June 1969, Anthony Phillip b 8 Aug 1970); *Career* Br Petroleum 1961-: chief geologist BP exploration 1979-82, sr vice pres exploration and prodn BP Canada 1983-84, gen mangr BP exploration 1985-88, Br Petroleum Devpt and chief tech exec BP exploration 1988-; fell Geological Soc, AAPG; *Recreations* tennis, theatre, gardening; *Style*— Dr David Jenkins; Ardennes, East Rd, St George's Hill, Weybridge; Britannic Ho, Moor Lane, London EC2Y 9BU (☎ 01 920 7765, fax 01 920 4192, telex 888811)

JENKINS, Edward Victor; s of Ernest Victor Jenkins (d 1977), of Hedd Wyn, Chandag Rd, Keynsham, Bristol, and Winifred Agnes, *née* Capron (d 1983); *b* 17 August 1932; *Educ* Frays Coll Uxbridge, Ealing GS, Northampton Engrg Coll (BSc), Imperial Coll London (DIC); *m* 5 Sept 1959, Elisabeth, da of Hubert Deacon Harrison, OBE, MC (d 1987), of Victoria, Vancouver, British Columbia, Canada; 1 s (Christopher b 1965), 1 da (Victoria b 1968); *Career* Nat Serv RE 1956-58; engrg pupil 1951-53, Holland and Hannen & Cubitts Ltd 1958-66; G Maunsell & Ptnrs: section and resident engr 1966-72, sr engr 1972-73, assoc 1973-75, project ptnr seconded to Maunsell Consults Asia, Hong Kong 1978-81; md G Maunsell & Ptnrs 1987-, dir Maunsell Int; FICE, MConsE; *Recreations* sailing, rugby football, choral singing; *Clubs* Army & Navy, Royal Hong Kong Yacht; *Style*— Edward Jenkins, Esq; Yeoman House, 63 Croydon Rd, London SE20 7TP (☎ 01 778 6060, fax 01 659 5568, telex 946 171)

JENKINS, Dr Elizabeth; da of George Woodward Turner (d 1962), of Anglesey, and Elsie Aggie, *née* Fox; *b* 15 Feb 1922; *Educ* Withington Girls Sch Manchester, Victoria Univ of Manchester (MB ChB); *m* 25 Mar 1944, Sqdn Ldr Richard John Jenkins, s of the late Rev John Jenkins; 1 s (Simon b 1947), 2 da (Anne Elizabeth Rees-Jenkins b 1949, Diana Margaret (Mrs Gray-Buchanan) b 1952); *Career* MO Govt of Aden 1954-56; assoc specialist in psychiatry St John's Hosp Lincoln 1964- (prev med asst and clinical asst); memb Lincoln City Cncl 1976-77 (chm soc serv 1983-); dir Family Policy Studies Centre 1988-, dep chm Lincoln Cons Assoc 1983-86; O St J 1972; *Recreations* local community, gardening; *Style*— Dr Elizabeth Jenkins

JENKINS, Very Rev Frank Graham; s of Edward Jenkins (d 1961), of Glamorgan, and Miriam Martha Jenkins, *née* Morse (d 1978); *b* 24 Feb 1923; *Educ* Cyfarthfa Castle Sch Merthyr Tydfil, Port Talbot Secdy GS, St Davids Coll Lampeter (BA), Jesus Coll Oxford (BA, MA), St Michael's Coll Llandaff; *m* 1 Aug 1950, Ena Doraine, da of Eardley Morgan Parry (d 1970), of Port Talbot; 2 s (Timothy b 1955, Peter b 1958), 1 da (Caroline b 1951); *Career* cmmnd Welch Regt 1944-46 (Capt), CF (TA) 1956-61; curate of Llangeinor 1950-53, minor canon Llandaff Cathedral 1953-60, vicar of Abertillery 1960-64, vicar of Risca 1964-75, vicar of Caerleon 1975-76, dean of Monmouth 1976-; *Style*— The Very Rev the Dean of Monmouth; The Deanery, Stow Hill, Newport, Gwent NP9 4ED (☎ 0633 63338)

JENKINS, Prof George Charles; s of John Robinson Jenkins (d 1969), of Stoneygate, Leics, and Mabel Rebecca,*née* Smith (d 1985); *b* 2 August 1927; *Educ* Wyggeston Leics, St Bartholomew's Hosp Med Coll, Univ of London (MB BS, PhD); *m* 28 April 1956, Elizabeth Claire, da of Cecil Joseph Welch (d 1963), of Carlton Rd, Ealing; 1 s (Mark Andrew b 15 Nov 1957), 2 da (Nicola Claire b 11 April 1961, Camilla Anne b 3 Jan 1963); *Career* Sqdn Ldr RAF (Med branch) 1952-54, civilian conslt haematologist RN 1978; conslt haematologist: N Middx Hosp 1963-65, London Hosp 1965-; reader in haematology Univ of London 1971-74, prof of haematology Univ Of London at London Hosp Med Coll 1974-; vice pres RCPath 1982-84, pres Br Soc for Haematology 1988-, chm exec cncl Br Acad Forensic Sci; patron Home Farm Tst; Freeman City of London 1961, memb Worshipful Co Spectacle Makers 1961; FRCPath 1975; *Books* Advanced Haematology (jt ed and author); *Recreations* fishing, music, theatre going; *Style*— Prof George Jenkins; 19 Bush Hill, London N21 2DB (☎ 01 360 1484); London Hosp Med Coll, Whitechapel, London E1 2AD (☎ 01 377 7178)

JENKINS, Graeme James Ewers; s of Kenneth Arthur Jenkins, of London, and Marjorie Joyce, *née* Ewers; *b* 31 Dec 1958; *Educ* Dulwich, Gonville and Caius Coll Cambridge (MA), RCM London (ARCH); *m* 19 July 1986, Joanna, da of Christopher Charles Cyprian Bridge, ERD of E Sussex; *Career* music dir Glyndebourne Touring Opera 1985-; conducted Glyndebourne Festival Opera, English Nat Opera, Scottish Opera, Kent Opera, Geneva Opera, Amsterdam Opera, princ British orchestras; *Recreations* reading, cooking; *Clubs* Savile; *Style*— Graeme Jenkins, Esq; Pond Cottage, Friston, Nr Eastbourne, E Sussex BN20 0AG (☎ 0323 423400)

JENKINS, Prof Harold; s of Henry Jenkins (d 1932), of Shenley Church End, Bucks, and Mildred, *née* Carter (d 1959); *b* 19 July 1909; *Educ* UCL (BA, MA), Witwatersrand (DLitt); *m* 23 Jan 1939, Gladys Grace (d 1984), da of Albert George Victor Puddifoot (d 1960), of London; *Career* William Noble fell of Liverpool 1935-36; Univ of Witwatersrand SA: jr lectr in English 1936-38, lectr 1938-44, sr lectr 1945; reader in English UCL 1946-54 (lectr 1945-46), prof of English Westfield Coll London 1954-67, visiting prof Duke Univ USA 1957-58, regius prof of rhetoric and English literature Univ of Edinburgh 1967-71 (prof emeritus 1971-), visiting prof Univ of Oslo 1974; gen ed The Arden Shakespeare 1958-82; memb editorial bd: Shakespeare Survey 1964-72, Studies in English Literature 1961-78; contrib: Modern Language Review, Review of English Studies, The Library, Studies in Bibliography, Shakespeare Survey; cncl memb Malone Soc 1955-89; winner Shakespeare Prize Stiftung FVS Hamburg 1986; Hon DLitt Iona Coll New Rochelle NY USA 1983; memb: Int Shakespeare Assoc, Int Assoc of Univ Profs of English; *Books* The Life and Work of Henry Chettle (1934), Edward Benlowes (1952), The Structural Problem in Shakespeare's Henry IV (1956), The Catastrophe in Shakespearean Tragedy (1969), Hamlet (ed 1982); *Clubs* Athenaeum; *Style*— Prof Harold Jenkins; 22 North Crescent, Finchley, London N3 3LL

JENKINS, Hugh Royston; s of Hubert Graham (d 1977), of Llanelli, S Wales, and Violet, *née* Aston; *b* 9 Nov 1933; *Educ* Llanelli GS; *m* (m dis); *Career* LCC 1956-63, md CIN Properties Ltd 1969-73 (asst property controller 1963-69), dir gen NCB Pension Funds 1973-85, chief exec Heron Fin Corpn LA 1985-86, gp investmt dir Allied Dunbar Assur plc 1986-, chm and chief exec Allied Dunbar Asset Mgmnt plc 1986-, chm Dunbar Bank plc 1986-; formerly: lay memb Int Stock Exchange, memb City Capital Markets Ctee, vice chm Nat Assoc of Pension Funds and chm of the Investmt Ctee, non-dir Stock Conversion plc, non-exec dir London and Manchester Assur plc; currently non exec dir: Heron Int NV, Unilever Pensions Ltd, IBM Pension Tst Co Ltd, Property Advsy Ctee DOE; FRICS, FPMI, memb Anglo-American Real Estate Inst; *Recreations* theatre; *Clubs* Garrick; *Style*— Hugh Jenkins, Esq; 3 Christchurch Terrace, Chelsea SW3; Sackville House, 9-15 Sackville St, London W1 (☎ 01 434 3211, fax 01 494 3067, car 0850 359088)

JENKINS, Cdr Humphrey Leoline; OBE (1954), DSC (1945, bar 1945); s of Rev Thomas Leonard Jenkins (d 1943), and Caroline Mabel, *née* Turton (d 1956); *b* 11 June 1903; *Educ* Twyford Sch, Winchester, RN Colls Osborne, Dartmouth; *m* 25 Jan 1941, Margaret Campbell, da of Canon Edward Francis Campbell-Ward (d 1940), of Somerset; 1 s (Richard); *Career* Midshipman HMS Valiant Atlantic 1921-23, cmmnd Sub-Lt 1924, Lt HMS Iroquois China 1925-28, Marlborough Atlantic 1928, Argus Atlantic 1929, Rosemary Fishery protection 1929-30, Bideford E Indies, Enterprise; Lt Cdr HMS Kempenfelt Home Fleet 1934-37, Newcastle 1937-39, Cdr HMS Revenge Atlantic & E Indies 1939-42 (Larne, Welfare, Fly), SO 5 MS Flotilla Med 1944-46, Rooke KHM & Cap Dockyard Gibraltar 1949-51, HMNZS Philomel Supt HMNZN Dockyard Auckland NZ (despatches 1943 & 45); Croix de Guerre 1945; *Recreations* survival; *Clubs* Anglo Belgian; *Style*— Cdr Humphrey L Jenkins; Rose Cottage, Culver Gdns, Malmesbury, Wilts SN16 9BY (☎ 0666 823177)

JENKINS, Dr Ivor; CBE (1970); s of Thomas Jenkins (d 1955), of Gwynfryn, Kingsbridge, Gorseinon, Swansea, and Mary Emily Ellen, *née* Evans (d 1959); *b* 25 July 1913; *Educ* Gowerton GS, Univ Coll Swansea (BSc, MSc, DSc); *m* 19 April 1941, Caroline Wijnanda, da of William John James (d 1961), of 47 Roxeth Hill, Harrow, Middlesex; 2 s (Brian James b 4 April 1944, Peter Anthony b 15 Feb 1947); *Career* chief metallurgist GEC Hirst Res Centre 1952-61; dir for res: Manganese Bronze Hldgs Ltd 1961-69, Delta Metal Co Ltd 1969-78; pres: Inst of Metallurgists 1956-66, Inst of Metals 1968-69; Williams Prize Iron and Steel Inst 1946, Platinum Medal The Metals Soc 1978; fell: American Soc of Metals 1974, UC Swansea 1986; pres Onehouse Harleston and Shelland (Suffolk) Community Cncl 1974-80; FEng 1979, FIM 1948 (pres 1965-66); *Books* Controlled Atmospheres for the Heat Treatment of Metals (1946); *Recreations* walking, swimming; *Clubs* Athenaeum, Anglo-Belgian; *Style*— Dr Ivor Jenkins, CBE; 31 Trotyn Croft, Aldwick Felds, Aldwick, Bognor Regis, W Sussex PO21 3TX (☎ 0243 828749)

JENKINS, John George; CBE; s of George John Jenkins, and Alice Maud, *née* Prickett; *b* 26 August 1919; *Educ* Winchester, Univ of Edinburgh; *m* 1948, Chloe Evelyn, da of John Kenward; 1 s (Martin), 3 da (Alison, Penelope, Jocelyn); *Career* farmer landowner (694 acres); dir Agric Mortgage Corpn 1969-, chm Utd Oilseeds Ltd 1983-87; pres NFU of Scotland 1960-61; *Recreations* tennis, bridge; *Clubs* Farmers; *Style*— John Jenkins, Esq, CBE

JENKINS, Hon Mrs (Judith Catharine Dean); da of Baron Soper (Life Peer); *b* 1942; *m* 1970, Alan Jenkins; *Style*— The Hon Mrs Jenkins

JENKINS, Maurice; s of David Jenkins (d 1978), and Josephine Lily Jenkins; *b* 9 July 1925; *Educ* Acklam Sch Middlesborough, Univ of Manchester, Univ of London; *m* 1951, Dorothy, *née* Tait; 1 s, 2 da; *Career* admin offr HM Overseas Civil Serv Nigeria 1951-62; chm Rugby Portland Cement Co plc 1984- (dep chm 1976-84, md 1968-84), chm and dir of assoc cos Cockburn Cement Ltd W Aust 1974-; memb London Bd Norwich Union Insur Gp 1974-80, dir AP Bank Ltd 1981-; vice pres Nat Cncl of Bldg Material Prodrs 1976-; memb Nat Econ Devpt Ctee for Civil Engrg 1972-82; cncl memb CBI 1984-; *Recreations* business, family; *Style*— Maurice Jenkins, Esq; 5 Bilton Rd, Rugby, Warwicks (☎ 0788 65547); Rugby Portland Cement Co plc, Crown House, Rugby CV21 2DT (☎ 0788 2111, telex 31523)

JENKINS, HE Michael Romilly Heald; CMG (1984); s of Romilly James Heald Jenkins (d 1969), and Celine Juliette Haeglar; *b* 9 Jan 1936; *Educ* King's Coll Cambridge (BA); *m* 1968, Maxine Louise, da of Dudley Hodson (d 1982); 1 s (Nicholas 1975), 1 da (Catherine b 1971); *Career* HM Dip Serv 1959-; Paris, Moscow, Bonn; dep sec-gen of Euro Cmmn 1981-83, asst under-sec of state FCO 1983-85, min HM Embassy Washington 1985-87; Br ambass The Hague 1988-; *Books* Arakcheev, Grand Vizir of the Russian Empire (1969), contributions to History Today; *Clubs* MCC; *Style*— HE Michael Jenkins, CMG; c/o Foreign & Commonwealth Office, London SW1

JENKINS, Nicholas Stephen; s of Walter Walker Jenkins (d 1982), of Tanglewood, Pyrford, Surrey, and Teresa Davis, *née* Callens ; *b* 8 Feb 1954; *Educ* Salesian Coll Chertsey, Harlow Coll; *m* 25 Oct 1974, Marion Joanne, da of Henry Alex Findlay (d 1966), of Charham, Kent; 2 s (Joel, Jordan); *Career* PR conslt; formed Jenkins of Rochester Agency 1975-; nat fund raiser Concern Universal Charity; MIPR; *Recreations* tennis, helicopters; *Clubs* Castle (Rochester), Roffen, St James ; *Style*— Nicholas Jenkins, Esq; Castle Chambers, Castle Hill, Rochester, Kent; Berkeley House, 186 High St, Rochester, Kent ME1 1EY (☎ 0634 408 325, fax 0634 830 930, car tel 0860 414285, telex 94015848 JORG G)

JENKINS, Sir Owain Trevor; s of Sir John Lewis Jenkins, KCSI (d 1912); bro of Rt Hon Lord Jenkins (d 1967), and of Sir Evan Meredith Jenkins, GCIE, KCSI (d 1985); *b* 20 Feb 1907; *Educ* Charterhouse, Balliol Coll Oxford; *m* 1940, Sybil Léonie, da of Maj-Gen Lionel Herbert, CB, CVO (d 1929); *Career* served WWII 45 Cavalry IA, Maj; joined Balmer Lawrie & Co)Calcutta) 1929, (md 1948-59); pres: Bengal C of C and Indust 1956-57, Assoc Assoc C of Cs of India 1956-57, UK Citizens Assoc 1957-58; dir: Calcutta Electric Supply Corpn, MacLeod Russel & Co Ltd, and other cos 1960-82; kt 1958; *Books* The Dark Horse (with Rumer Godden, 1981), Merchant Prince, Memoirs (1987); *Clubs* Oriental; *Style*— Sir Owain Jenkins; Boles House, East St, Petworth, W Sussex GU28 0AB (☎ 0798 42531)

JENKINS, Peter George James; s of Kenneth E Jenkins, of Norfolk, and Joan, *née* Croger (d 1981); *b* 11 May 1934; *Educ* Culford Sch, Trinity Hall Cambridge (BA, MA), Oxford Univ (MA), Univ of Wisconsin USA; *m* 1, 1960, Charlotte (d 1970), da of John Strachey; 1 da (Amy b 20 Oct 1963); m 2, 28 Dec 1970, Mary Louisa (Polly), da of Philip Toynbee; 1 s (Nathaniel b 10 Jan 1985), 2 da (Milly b 5 Dec 1971, Flora b 17 Dec 1976); *Career* journalist; Fin Times 1958-60; The Guardian 1960-85: labour corr 1963-70, Washington corr 1972-74, political commentator and policy ed 1974-85; theatre critic The Spectator 1978-81, political columnist The Sunday Times 1985-87, assoc ed The Independent 1987-; first stage play Illuminations (1980), TV series

Struggle (1983); Granada TV Journalist of the Year 1978; *Books* The Battle of Downing Street (1970), 1987 Mrs Thatcher's Revolution - The Ending of the Sociatlist Era (1987); *Clubs* Garrick; *Style—* Peter Jenkins, Esq; 1 Crescent Grove, London SW4 7AF (☎ 01 622 6492); The Independent, 40 City Rd, London EC1Y 2DB (☎ 01 253 1222)

JENKINS, Peter Sefton; s of John Harry Sefton Jenkins (d 1978), of Croft Lodge, Bramley, Northants, and Helen Summers, *née* Staveley; *b* 9 Feb 1948; *Educ* King's Sch Canterbury, St Edmund Hall Oxford (MA); *m* 8 June 1972, Jacqueline, da of John Mills (d 1976); 2 s (Benjamin b 13 June 1975, Christopher b 7 April 1979); *Career* HM Customs and Excise 1969-86: private sec to chm 1972-74, Cabinet Off 1974-77, involved in EC negotiations on customs duty harmonisatoins 1977-79, private sec to Chllr of Exchequer 1979, asst sec VAT Admin 1983-86; ptnr VAT and customs gp Ernst & Whinney 1986-; memb VAT Practioners Gp 1988; *Recreations* squash, music (violin, singing), opera, walking; *Clubs* Reform; *Style—* Peter Jenkins, Esq; 63 Guibal Road, London, SE12 (☎ 01 857 1548), Ernst Whinney, Becket House, 1 Lambeth Palace Road, London, SE1 7EU (☎ 01 928 2000, fax 01 928 1345)

JENKINS, (William Martyn) Peter; s of Cyfaude Glyndwr Jenkins, of Swansea, and Helen Phillips, *née* Frew; *b* 4 Feb 1954; *Educ* Bishop Gore GS Swansea, King's Coll Cambridge (MA), London Business Sch (MBA); *m* 18 Dec 1976, Deborah Jenkins, da of Maj Ronald Jarman, of Whitstable; 2 s (Matthew b 5 June 1985, Eliot b 18 Aug 1988); *Career* princ Booz Allen and Hamilton 1981-86, md Spicer and Oppenheim Conslts 1986-; *Style—* Peter Jenkins, Esq; 7 Papillons Walk, Blackheath Park, London SE3 9SF (☎ 01 852 6561); Friary Court, 65 Crutched Friars, London EC3N 2NP (☎ 01 480 7766, fax 01 480 6958, car tel 0860 633571, telex 884257)

JENKINS, (Arthur) Robert; CBE 1972; s of Edgar Jackson Jenkins and Ethel Mary, *née* Bescoby; *b* 20 June 1908; *Educ* Rotherham GS, Univ Sheffield; *m* 28 Oct 1933, Margaret Fitton, da of Bernard Jones; 1 s (Robert Iain Bescoby, b 1943) 3 da (Angela Margaret b 1935, Bridget Elaine b 1938, Caromy b 1942); *Career* dir (later chm) Robert Jenkins & Co Ltd Gp (Robert Jenkins Hldgs Ltd) 1933-75; memb nat exec NSPCC (chm Rotherham branch), pres Rotherham CofC, former magistrate and chm Rotherham Borough Bench; chm Br Welding Res Assoc, pres Inst of Welding (after amalgamation pres Weld Inst); FIMechE, Hon FWeldI; *Style—* Robert Jenkins, Esq, CBE; (☎ 0439 70931)

JENKINS, Simon David; s of Dr Daniel Jenkins and Nell Jenkins; *b* 10 June 1943; *Educ* Mill Hill, St John's Coll Oxford (BA); *m* 1978, Gayle Hunnicutt, the actress; 1 s (Edward Lloyd b 24 Feb 1982), 1 step s (Nolan); *Career* with *Country Life* 1965, news ed TES 1966-68; ed: *Crossbow* 1968-70, *Evening Standard* 1976-78 (previously dep ed and columnist 1969-74), 'Insight' on *Sunday Times* 1974-75; political ed *The Economist* 1979-86; Columnist, Sunday Times 1986-; memb: British Railways Bd 1979-, London Regnl Tport Bd 1983-86, Historic Building and Monument Commission 1985-, and South Bank Bd 1985-; dir Municipal Journal Ltd; author, books include: *Newspapers: the power and the money* (1979), *The Companion Guide to Outer London* (1981), *Images of Hampstead* (jointly, 1983); *Style—* Simon Jenkins, Esq; 174 Regent's Park Rd, NW1 (☎ 01 722 4022)

JENKINS, Trevor Westover; CPM (1953), QPM (1955); s of Cecil Sydney Westover Jenkins (d 1952), of Blackheath, and Helen Maud, *née* Williams (d 1953); *b* 24 Dec 1914; *Educ* St Peters Sch York; *m* 25 Aug 1945, Joan Mary, da of John Patrick (d 1953), of Nairobi; 2 s (Michael b 1946, Philip Moore b 1953); *Career* Colonial Police Serv 1935-60 (despatches 1957), attached South African Forces, Kenya 1940-43, asst cmmr and dir Intelligence and Security Kenya 1952-56; Gold Coast Police 1946-51, dep cmmr Nigeria Police 1956-60 (ret); MOD 1960-78, Def Security Offr HQ's BFNE Cyprus 1970-74 (ret); *Recreations* golf; *Clubs* Naval and Military (London), Aldeburgh Golf (Suffolk);; *Style—* Trevor W Jenkins, Esq, CPM, QPM; 3 Mariners Ct, Aldeburgh, Suffolk (☎ 072 885 3456)

JENKINS, Vivian Evan; MBE (1945); s of Arthur Evan Jenkins (d 1967), of 141 Pencisely Rd, Llandaff, Cardiff, and Blodwen, *née* Evans (d 1948); *b* 12 Sept 1918; *Educ* Univ Of Wales GS (BA); *m* 19 Dec 1946, Megan Myfanwy, da of Aneurin Evans (d 1923), of Pontypridd, Glamorgan; 1 s (John David b 7 Dec 1947), 1 da (Mair Elizabeth (Mrs Brewer) b 8 June 1955); *Career* RCS 1940, cmmnd 1943, Lt parachutist 1 and 6 Airbourne Divs 1942-46, serv France, Belgium, Germany, India and Palestine; child care offr and asst childrens offr Glamorgan CC 1949-52, inspr SW regn Home Office Childrens Dept, Inspectorate 1952, Leeds regn Home Off Inspectorate 1957, dir social servs Cardiff City Cncl 1971, memb (later chm) selection bds Civil Serv Commn (exec offr appts) 1977-81,; *Recreations* golf, rugby, cricket; *Clubs* Radyr GC, Probus (Cardiff West); *Style—* Vivian Jenkins, Esq, MBE; 24 Windsor Rd, Radyr, Cardiff CF4 8BQ (☎ 0222 842 485)

JENKINS OF HILLHEAD, Baron (Life Peerage UK 1987), of Pontypool in the Co of Gwent Roy Harris Jenkins; PC (1964); o s of Arthur Jenkins (d 1946; MP (Lab) Pontypool 1935-46, Parly Sec Miny Town and Country Planning then Educn 1945 and PPS to Rt Hon Clement Attlee (later 1 Earl Attlee) 1940-45), and Hattie Jenkins; *b* 11 Nov 1920; *Educ* Abersychan GS, Balliol Oxford (hon fellow 1969); *m* 1945, Dame (Mary) Jennifer, DBE (chm Nat Tst 1986-; former chm: Historic Bldg Cncl for England 1975-85, Consumers' Assoc; tstee The Wallace Collection), da of Sir Parker Morris (d 1972; expert on housing after whom Parker Morris standards are named); 2 s, 1 da; *Career* RA 1942-43, special intelligence 1943-46 (Capt), ICFC 1946-48, contested (Lab) Solihull 1945; MP (Lab): Southwark Central 1948-50, Birmingham Stechford 1950-76; former chm and memb exec Fabian Soc; PPS to Cwlth Relations Sec 1949-50, memb UK Delegn to Cncl of Europe 1955-57; memb ctee of mgmnt Soc of Authors; dir John Lewis Ptnrship 1962-64; Min Aviation 1964-65, home sec 1965-67, chllr of the Exchequer 1967-70, dep ldr Lab Party 1970-72; awarded Charlemagne and Robert Schuman prizes for services to Euro unity 1972; former govr Br Film Inst; vice-pres Inst Fiscal Studies 1970-; home sec 1974-76; pres Br in Europe (EEC membership referendum) 1975; dep chm Common Market Campaign; pres Lab Ctee for Europe; chm Lab Euro Ctee; pres UK Cncl Euro Movement, pres Univ of Wales Inst of Sci and Technol 1975-81; tstee Pilgrims Tst 1973-; pres European Cmmn 1977-81; dir Morgan Grenfell Hldgs 1981-82; - founder memb: Cncl for Social Democracy Jan 1981, SDP March 1981; contested (SDP) Warrington 1981; MP (SDP) Glasgow Hillhead (by-election) 1982-87; elected first SDP ldr 1982, resigned 1983, having led Alliance with Rt Hon David Steel into June 1983 Election; chllr of Oxford Univ 1987-; *Publications include* Mr Attlee: An Interim Biography, Pursuit of Progress, Mr Balfour's Poodle, Sir Charles Dilke, Asquith, Afternoon on the Potomac, What Matters Now, Nine Men of Power, Partnership of Principle, Truman, Baldwin, Gallery of Twentieth Century Portraits European Diary 1977-81; *Clubs* Brooks's, Athenaeum, Reform, Pratt's, Utd Oxford and Cambridge Univ; *Style—* The Rt Hon Lord Jenkins of Hillhead, PC; St Amand's House, East Hendred, Oxon; 2 Kensington Park Gdns, London W11 (☎ 01 727 5262); House of Lords, London SW1

JENKINS OF PUTNEY, Baron (UK 1981); Hugh Gater Jenkins; s of Joseph Walter Jenkins (d 1955), and late Florence, *née* Gater; *b* 27 July 1908; *Educ* Enfield GS; *m* 1936, Marie Ethel, da of Sqdn-Ldr Ernest Christopher Crosbie, RAF; *Career* sits as Labour Peer in House of Lords; served WW II, Fl-Lt RAF, UK, Burma, Pacific; employee of Prudential Assurance Co 1930-40; head English Programmes Rangoon Radio 1945; research offr National Union of Bank Employees (editor The Bank Officer) 1946-50; asst gen-sec Actors Equity 1950-64; MP (Lab) Wandsworth (Putney) 1964-79, min Arts 1974-76; memb National Theatre Bd 1976-; dir: Theatres Trust 1977-86, pres Soc for Cultural Revalution in the USSR; vice pres: Theatres Advsy Cncl 1980-; pres Battersea Arts Centre 1985-; vice pres CND 1981- (chm 1979-81, Aldermaston Marcher); *Books* The Culture Gap (1979), Rank and File (1980); *Recreations* reading, writing (radio plays), listening, talking, looking, avoiding retirement; *Style—* The Rt Hon the Lord Jenkins of Putney; House of Lords, London SW1 (☎ 01 219 6706, 01 836 8591)

JENKINS-MCKENZIE, Dulcibel Edna; da of Brig Ralph Alexander Broderick (d 1971), and Dulcie Broderick, *née* Lunt (d 1982); *b* 1 August 1918; *Educ* Badminton Sch Bristol, Birmingham Univ (BA), Birkbeck Coll, Maria Grey Coll, Coll of Law; *m* 1, 1944, John Rickatson Jenkins, s of Harold Carnegie Jenkins (d 1945); 2 s (Brian Harold Broderick b 1945, David Christopher Broderick b 1947); m 2, 1973, William McKenzie, s of Daniel McKenzie; *Career* teacher and lawyer, HM Inspr of Factories 1941-44, lectr West London Coll 1964-68, practising barr 1967-69, sr legal asst Dept of Trade 1969-82; chm Rent Assessment Ctee 1982-; Art Exhibition Burgh House London (1984), Befriender Charing Cross Hosp , memb Itchenor PPC; Freeman City of London; *Books* Chronicles of John R Jenkins, Steps to the Bar; *Recreations* travelling, painting, languages, swimming; *Clubs* Itchenor SC, Hurlingham; *Style—* Mrs Dulcibel E Jenkins-McKenzie; 89 Cornwall Gdns, London SW7 4AX (☎ 01 584 7674); Greengates, Itchenor, Chichester (☎ 0243 512 411); Rent Assessment Panel, Berners Street, London W1

JENKINSON, Austen David Poles; s of David Barnes Jenkinson (d 1961), and May, *née* Cooper (d 1962); *b* 20 Mar 1914; *Educ* Wellingborough Sch, Sheffield Univ (ARIBA); *m* 16 March 1940, Stacey, da of Leonard Augustus Stacey (d 1932); 1 s (Vivian Paul b 1946), 1 da (Susan Amanda b 1949); *Career* WWII 1940-45, (despatches twice), Staff Capt at Gen Alexander's HQ Caserta, Italy with pres service in Egypt, Palestine, Western Desert, and Sicily; chartered architect, sr ptnr Jenkinson, Palmer and Associate; memb cncl Sheffield Sch of Architects 1963-80; RIBA; *Recreations* architectural research and photography; *Clubs* Rotherham; *Style—* Austen D P Jenkinson, Esq; 3 Holling Moor Lane, Wickersley, Rotherham S66 0AL (☎ 0709 543554); Mountenoy Rd, Rotherham S60 2AL (☎ 0709 365678)

JENKINSON, Dermot Julian; s of Julian Charles Lewis Jenkinson, and Diana Catherine Baird; *b* 2 Dec 1954; *Educ* Eton, Eurocentre (Lausanne and Cologne); *m* 2 May 1979, Miranda Jane, da of John Maxwell Menzies; 1 s (Oliver John Banks), 1 da (Emily Lavinia); *Career* dir: John Menzies plc 1985, Frank Smythson Inc 1985, Telegroup (Holdings) Ltd 1983; chm Early Learning Centres Inc 1986; *Clubs* Turf, New; *Style—* Dermot J Jenkinson, Esq; Philpstoun House, Linlithgow, West Lothian, Philpstoun (☎ 050 683 4287); 108 Princes Street, Edinburgh (☎ 031 225 8555)

JENKINSON, Lady; Frances; da of Harry Stremmel, of New York, USA; *m* 9 Oct 1943, Sir Anthony Banks Jenkinson, 13 Bt (d 1989); 1 s (Sir John Banks, 14 Bt, *qv*), 2 da (Jennifer Ann b 26 Nov 1947, Emily Frances Joan b 2 Sept 1953); *Style—* Lady Jenkinson; 491 South Church Street, Georgetown, Grand Cayman, West Indies

JENKINSON, Frances Caroline; da of Capt Robert Charles Horace Jenkinson (d 1970), and Gwyneth Margaret Llewellyn, *née* Mathews (d 1987); *b* 30 April 1942; *Educ* Fritham House Hants; *Career* social sec to Belgian Ambass in London; *Recreations* walking (with dog), ballet, gardening; *Style—* Miss Frances Jenkinson; 34 De Morgan Rd, London SW6 (☎ 01 731 0726); Belgian Embassy, 103 Eaton Sq, London SW1, (☎ 01 235 5422)

JENKINSON, Sir John Banks; 14 Bt (E 1661), of Hawkesbury, Co Gloucester; o s of Sir Anthony Banks Jenkinson, 13 Bt (d 1989); *b* 16 Feb 1945; *Educ* Eton, Univ of Miami USA; *Heir* kinsman, Julian Charles Lewis Jenkinson b 1926; *Style—* Sir John Jenkinson, Bt; 15920 South West 238th St, Homestead, Florida 33031, USA; Hawkesbury, Chippenham, Wilts

JENKINSON, Valerie Robertson; da of late William Mar Erskine, and Flora Ernestine, *née* Robertson; *b* 16 Mar 1934; *Educ* St Paul's Girls Sch Hammersmith; *m* 1 March 1962, Eric Reginald Jenkinson, s of Percy Jenkinson; *Career* SRN 1960; Various posts (trg St Bartholomews Hosp Rochester 1957-60) Medway Health Authy 1960-79, registerd clinical nurse tutor 1973, commissioning nurse New Maidstone Dist Gen Hosp Maidstone Health Authy 1973-83, dir nursing servs Canterbury gen unit Canterbury and Thanet Health Authy 1983-; *Recreations* cooking, gardening, music; *Style—* Mrs Eric Jenkinson; Invermar, 26 Richdore Rd, Waltham, nr Canterbury, Kent CT4 5SJ (☎ 0227 70 477), Kent and Canterbury Hosp, Canterbury, Kent CT1 3NG (☎ 0227 766 877, ext 4300)

JENKS, (Maurice Arthur) Brian; s and h of Sir Richard Atherley Jenks, 2 Bt; *b* 28 Oct 1933; *Educ* Charterhouse; *m* 1962, Susan L, da of Leslie Allen, of Glenside, Star Lane, Hooley, Surrey; 1 da; *Career* chartered accountant; *Recreations* wine, racing; *Style—* Brian Jenks Esq

JENKYNS, Richard Henry Austen; s of Henry Leigh Jenkyns (whose mother Winifred was gda of the Rev James Austen-Leigh, himself n of Jane Austen), of Aldeburgh; *b* 18 Mar 1949; *Educ* Eton, Balliol Coll Oxford; *Career* writer and classicist; fell All Souls Oxford 1972-81, lectr in classics Bristol Univ 1978-81, fell Lady Margaret Hall Oxford 1981-; *Books* The Victorians and Ancient Greece (1980, winner of Arts Cncl Nat Book Award 1981 and Yorkshire Post Book Award 1981), Three Classical Poets (1982); *Recreations* playing the piano, looking at buildings; *Style—* Richard Jenkyns Esq; Lady Margaret Hall, Oxford (☎ 0865 274300)

JENNER, Michael Eugene; s of Eugene Jenner (d 1945), and Beatrice Jenner (d 1976); *b* 7 Jan 1936; *Educ* St George's Coll Surrey; *m* 9 June 1962, Jane Elizabeth, da of Harold Goodhew Turner, CMG (d 1978); 1 s (Mark Eugene b 1963), 2 da (Clare Elizabeth b 1967, Lucy Jane b 1972); *Career* CT Bowring 1952-: asst dir 1967, dir

Marine Div 1969, dep chief exec 1971, chief exec 1974; jt dep chm CT Bowring (Insurance Hldgs) Ltd 1976, ch exec CT Bowring Insurance 1979, dir parent bd CT Bowring & Co 1979; dir: Bowring Tyson, CTB Offshore Oil UK, Terra Nova Insurance Brokers; fndr & chm: Jenner Fenton Slade Ltd 1980, JFS Reinsurance Brokers 1981; chm LIBC 1987; ACII; *Recreations* golf, racehorse owner; *Clubs* Piltdown Golf, Royal St George's Golf, Royal Cinque Port Golf, Annabels; *Style*— Michael Jenner; Moons Farm, Barcombe Rd, Piltdown, nr Uckfield, E Sussex (☎ 082 2037); 42 Cadogan Lane, SW1 (☎ 235 5832); Jenner Fenton Slade Ltd, Knollys House, 47 Mark Lane, London EC3R 7QH (☎ 01 929 4500)

JENNER, Victor John; JP (Hants 1975); s of Leonard Jenner (d 1954), and Daisy Beatrice, *née* Dormer (d 1939); *b* 20 Mar 1926; *Educ* Portsmouth Northern GS; *m* 15 May 1945, Ann Lilian May, da of Frank Godfrey Welch (d 1955), of Portsmouth; 1 s (John Colin b 1946), 1 da (Linda Ann b 1947); *Career* Oxford and Bucks LI 1945, 2 Bn Hants Regt 1945, 8 Bn Suffolk Regt 1946-47; Wadham Bros Ltd 1947-50, Harris & Parkin Ltd 1950-52; md Harbottle-Leeson Ltd 1952-, chm EMMA Ltd (consortium of 26 cos) 1976-; Portsmouth: dep chm Juvenile Panel 1982-; chm: Licensing Ctee 1978-, Hants Standing Conf of Licensing 1982-, Licensing Justices Ports 1976-; memb: Electricity Consultative Cncl (Southern Area) 1972-, Manpower Servs Bd (Southern Area) 1980-84, Portsmouth Cathedral Business Mens Ctee 1955-; chm: Freight Tport Assoc (Portsmouth area) 1962-65, Hants & Dorset Branch Electrical & Electronic Industs Benevolent Assoc 1972-77 (pres 1977-), Portsmouth Poly Govrs 1985-, Fin & Gen Purposes Ctee 1985-; pres: Portsmouth Incorp C of C 1972-, UK Commercial Traveller Assoc (Portsmouth and Southsea) 1965-; memb Portsmouth & SE Hants Health Authy 1984-; chm of tstees St Petroc Community 1972-; Freeman City of London 1973, Liveryman Worshipful Co of Carmen 1973; FBIM 1980, FIOD 1967, MITA 1985; *Recreations* gardening; *Clubs* "1664"; *Style*— Victor J Jenner, Esq, JP; Vannic, Well Hill, Hambledon Rd, Denmead, Hants PO7 6HB (☎ 0705 255919); Harbottle-Leeson Ltd, Asquith House, 22 Middle St, Portsmouth, Hants PO5 4BJ (☎ 0705 820535, fax 0705 295655, car 0836 617623)

JENNER-FUST, Major Richard; s of Lt Richard Jenner-Fust, OBE (ka 1942), and Thea Wilmer (d 1981); *b* 24 July 1942; *Educ* Eton, Royal Mil Acad Sandhurst, RAC Cirencester; *m* 20 May 1972, Jane Daphne, da of Col Douglas Ian MacArthur Finlayson; 1 s (Thomas b 1978), 2 da (Alexandra b 1974, Jemima b 1981); *Career* joined Scots Gds 1962, Capt 1966, Maj 1971, served in Malaya & Borneo; landowner; *Recreations* skiing, fishing, music; *Style*— Maj Richard Jenner-Fust; Hill Court, Hill, Berkeley, Gloucs

JENNINGS, Sir Albert Victor; s of John Thomas Jennings; *b* 12 Oct 1896; *Educ* Eastern Rd Sch Melbourne; *m* 1922, Ethel Sarah, d of George Herbert Johnson; 2s; *Career* founder and chm A V Jennings Industries (Australia) Ltd 1932, ret 1972; manufacturing Industries Advsy Cncl to Cwlth Govt 1962-72; FAIB, FAIM, FIOB (UK); kt 1969; *Clubs* Melbourne, Commonwealth, Savage; *Style*— Sir Albert Jennings; Ranelagh House, Rosserdale Cres, Mt Eliza, Vic 3930, Australia

JENNINGS, Hon Mrs; (Catherine Frances); *née* Donaldson; yr da of Baron Donaldson of Kingsbridge (Life Peer), *qv*; *b* 18 Nov 1945; *m* 1973, G Mark Jennings; children; *Style*— The Hon Mrs Jennings; 57 Winsham Grove, London SW11 6NB

JENNINGS, Charles James; s of Douglas Vivian Jennings, MC, Witley Manor, Witley, Surrey, and Virginia, *née* Turle; *b* 27 Oct 1951; *Educ* Harrow, Durham Univ (BA); *m* 8 May 1976, Julia Frances, da of Philip Whiffen, of Mole End, Oxshott, Cobham, Essex; 1 s (Simon Charles b 1980), 1 da (Anna Francis b 1978); *Career* Freshfields 1980-82, ptnr Wilde Sapte 1986-; memb Law Soc, City of London Solicitors Co; *Recreations* tennis, gardening; *Clubs* City of London; *Style*— Charles Jennings, Esq; Kingsdown Farm, Burwash Common, Etchingham, Sussex; Queensbridge House, 60 Upper Thames St, London EC4 (☎ 01 236 3050)

JENNINGS, Hon Mrs (Deanna Christine); *née* Layton; o da of 2 Baron Layton (d 1989); *b* 19 Oct 1938; *Educ* St Paul's Girls' Sch, St Bartholomew's Hosp Med Sch London (MB, BS); *m* 1964, Melvin Calverley Jennings, s of Dr Calverley Middlemiss Jennings, MB, FRCS; 3 s; *Career* medical practitioner, principal in general practice Reigate; MRCS, LRCP, MBBS; *Style*— The Hon Mrs Jennings; Barn Ridge, 18 High Trees Rd, Reigate, Surrey RH2 7EJ (☎ 0737 40847)

JENNINGS, (Roland) Godfrey; s of Sir Roland Jennings (d 1969), and Lady Hannah Holmes, *née* Peacock; *b* 25 April 1925; *Educ* Harrow Sch, Cambridge Univ (MA); *m* 8 May 1954, Gillian Fay, da of Dr Montague Alan Watson (d 1982); 1 s (Adam b 1965), 2 da (Amanda b 1955, Annabel b 1957); *Career* Sub Lieut RNVR 1943-46; qual chartered accountant 1952; chm Sunderland and S Shields Water Co 1987- (dir 1978-), dir N of England Bldg Soc 1986-; FCA, IOD; *Recreations* golf, shooting, fishing; *Style*— Godfrey Jennings, Esq; Seacot, Links Road, Bamburgh, Northumberland; 19 Borough Road, Sunderland, Tyne & Wear SR1 1LA (☎ 091 5650 5651, fax 091 514 2083)

JENNINGS, James; JP (Cunningham 1969); s of Mark Jennings (d 1977), and Janet, *née* McGrath (d 1977); *b* 18 Feb 1925; *Educ* St Palladius Sch Dalry, St Michael's Coll Irvine; *m* 1, 1943, Margaret Cook, *née* Barclay; 3 s (Daniel Mark, David Mark, James), 2 da (Janette Matilda, Marie Elizabeth); m 2, 18 Oct 1974, Margaret Mary (Greta), *née* Hughes, JP; 2 da (Frances, Jaqueline); *Career* RAF 1942-46; involved Steel Ind 1946-79; memb: Ayr CC 1958, Strathclyde Regnl Cncl 1974 (vice-convener 1982-86), Police Cncl GB, Police Cncl UK 1978-79, LACSAB 1986-88; chm: Ayr CC Police and Law Ctee 1964-70, Ayrshire Jt Police Ctee 1970-75, Cunninghame Justices Ctee 1975-, N Ayrshire Crime Prevention Panel 1970-82, Police and Fire Ctee, Strathclyde Regnl Cncl 1978-82; vice-chm, chm Police Negotiating Bd (official side) 1984-88 (memb 1988-); Parly Candidate (Lab) Perth and E Perthshire 1966; jt patron Mayfest Ltd; vice-pres St Andrew's Ambulance Assoc; hon-pres: Scottish Retirement Cncl, Princess Louise Scottish Hosp (Erskine Hosp); hon vice-pres: SNO Chorus, Royal Br Legion Scotland (Dalry and Dist branch); patron Assoc Youth Clubs Strathclyde; dir European Summer Special Olympic Games 1990 (Strathclyde) Ltd 1988-; *Recreations* local community involvement; *Clubs* Royal Scottish Automobile (Glasgow), Garnock Lab (chm), St Andrew's Sporting (chm and hon life patron); *Style*— James Jennings, Esq, JP; 4 Place View, Kilbirnie, Ayrshire KA25 6BG (☎ 0505 3339); Strathclyde Regnl Cncl, India St, Glasgow G2 4PF (☎ 041 227 3395, fax 041 227 2870, car telephone 0836 634 839, telex 77428)

JENNINGS, John Southwood; CBE (1985); s of George Southwood Jennings (d 1978), of Crowle, Worcs, and Irene Beatrice, *née* Bartlett; *b* 30 Mar 1937; *Educ* Oldbury GS, Birmingham Univ (BSc), Edinburgh Univ (PhD), London Business Sch (Sloan fell); *m* 1961, Gloria Ann, MB, CHB, LRCP, MRCS, da of Edward Albert Griffiths (d 1985), of Hope Cove, Devon; 1 s (Iain), 1 da (Susan); *Career* geologist; chief geologist Shell UK Exploration and Prodn Ltd London 1968-70, exploration mangr Petroleum Devpt Oman Ltd 1971-75 (prodn mangr 1975-76) gen mangr and chief rep Shell Gp of Cos in Turkey 1976-79, md exploration and prodn Shell UK Ltd London 1979-84, exploration and prodn co-ordinator Shell Int Petroleum Maatschappij BV The Hague 1984-, md Royal Dutch-Shell Gp 1987-; FGS; *Recreations* flyfishing, shooting, photography, travel; *Clubs* Flyfishers', Brooks's; *Style*— John Jennings, Esq, CBE; Chequers Farm, Crowle, Worcester (☎ 090 560 634); Nassaulaan 7, 2514 JS The Hague, The Netherlands (☎ 070 65 18 97); office: Carel van Bylandtlaan 30, The Hague, The Netherlands (☎ 070 773 766, telex 36000)

JENNINGS, Marie Patricia; s of Harold Robert Jennings, and Phyllis Hortense; *b* 25 Dec 1930; *Educ* Presentation Convent Coll Sprinagar Kashmuir; *m* 1, (m dis), Michael Keegan; 1 s (Michael Geoffrey b 18 July 1962); m 2, 3 Jan 1976, (Harry) Brian, s of Harry Locke; *Career* md The Roy Bernard Co Ltd 1960-65; special advsr: Stanley Tools 1961-, The Unit Tst Assoc 1976-, The Midland Bank Gp 1978-; dir The PR Consits Assoc 1979-84 (consit); dir Cadogan Mgmt Ltd 1984-; cncl memb: Fin Int Mangrs and Brokers Regnl Assoc 1986-, Insur Ombudsman Bureau 1988-; memb exec ctee Wider Share Ownership Cncl 1987-; hon tres Nat Assoc Womens Clubs (memb Fin and Gen Purposes Ctee) 1977-87; Woman of the Year 1969; memb: Inst of PR, NUJ; *Books* The Money Guide (1983), Getting the Message Across (1988), Women and Money (1988), Money Go Round (LWT 1977), Moneys Spinner (C4 1985); *Recreations* reading, writing; *Clubs* IOD; *Style*— Ms Marie Jennings; 37 Cadogan St, Sloane Sq, London SW3 2PR; The Old Toll House, Stancombe, Stroud, Glos (☎ 01 589 9778); Cadogan Management Ltd, 53 Haymarket, London SW1; The Court House, Bisley, Stroud, Glos GL6 7AA (☎ 01 930 4241/0452 770003, fax 01 930 6993/0452 770058)

JENNINGS, Paul Francis; s of William Benedict Jennings (d 1953), of Coventry, and Mary Gertrude (d 1960); *b* 20 August 1918; *Educ* King Henry VIII Coventry, Douai Sch; *m* 9 Feb 1952, Celia, da of Eric Blom, CBE (d 1959), of London; 3 s (Matthew b 8 July 1954, Quentin b 13 Dec 1962, Hilary b 28 April 1959), 3 da (Susanna (Mrs Gibbons) b 17 Dec 1952, Theodora (Mrs Boyd) b 28 Nov 1956, Christiana b 3 June 1965); *Career* Lt RCS, served India; script writer COI 1946, copywriter Colman Prentis and Varley 1947; columnist: Observer's humour column Oddly Enough 1949-66, Times, Telegraph, Punch, etc; documentaries: The Hopping Basket (1965), The Great Jelly of London (1967), The Train to Yesterday (1974), The Book of Nonsense (1977), A Feast of Days (ed, 1982); TV career includes: Down You Go in the 1950's, fndr memb of Face the Music; FRSL, FRSA; *Books* Oddly Enough (1950), Even Oddlier (1952), Oddly Bodlikins (1953), Next to Oddliness (1955), Model Oddliness (1956), Gladly Oddly (1958), Idly Odly (1959), I Said Oddly, Diddle I? (1961), Oodles of Oddlies (1963), Jenguin Pennings (1963), Oddly Ad Lib (1965), I was Joking of Course (1968), The Living Village (1968), It's an Odd Thing But (1971), Britain as she is Visit (1976), I Must Have Imagined It (1977), And Now for Something Exactly the Same (novel, 1977), Paul Jennings Companion to Britain (1982), Golden Oddlies (1983), East Anglia (1986); *Recreations* singing (London philharmonic Choir); *Style*— Paul Jennings, Esq

JENNINGS, Percival Henry; CBE (1953); s of Canon Henry Richard Jennings (d 1951), and Susan, *née* Milton (d 1952); *b* 8 Dec 1903; *Educ* Christ's Hosp; *m* 23 June 1934, Margaret Katharine Musgrave, da of late Brig Gen Hugh Stuart Rogers, CMG, DSO (d 1951), 3 da (Penelope b 1938, Margaret b 1940, Josephine b 1947); *Career* overseas audit service: asst auditor Northern Rhodesia 1927-31, asst auditor Mauritius 1931-35, auditor Br Honduras 1935-38, dep dir Gold Coast 1938-45, dep dir Nigeria 1945-48; dir of audit Hong Hong 1948 (dep dir gen 1955-60), dir gen overseas audit serv 1960-63; pres Penzance MorRad Library; *Recreations* golf, gardening; *Clubs* Royal Cwlth Soc, Royal Overseas League, West Cornwall GC; *Style*— Percival Jennings, Esq, CBE; Littlewood, Lelant, St Ives, Cornwall (☎ 0736 753407)

JENNINGS, Sir Raymond Winter; QC (1945); s of Sir Arthur Oldham Jennings, MBE (d 1934); *b* 12 Dec 1897; *Educ* Rugby, RMC Sandhurst, Oriel Coll Oxford (MA, BCL); *m* 1930, Sheila Helen Grant (d 1972); 1 s, 1 da; *Career* served WWI Lt Royal Fusiliers; barrister Inner Temple 1922, bencher Lincoln's Inn 1951, master of the Ct of Protection 1956-70; kt 1968; *Recreations* fishing; *Clubs* Athenaeum; *Style*— Sir Raymond Jennings, QC; 14c The Upper Drive, Hove, East Sussex BN3 6GN (☎ 0273 773361)

JENNINGS, Prof Sir Robert Yewdall; QC (1969); s of Arthur Jennings, of Idle, Yorks; *b* 19 Oct 1913; *Educ* Belle Vue G S Bradford, Downing Cambridge (LLB, hon fell 1982), Harvard; *m* 1955, Christine Dorothy, da of late H Bernard Bennett, of Lydd, Kent; 1 s, 2 da; *Career* served WWII Intelligence Corps (Major); asst lectr law LSE 1938-39, fell Jesus Coll Cambridge 1939- (sr tutor 1949-55, then pres, hon fell 1982), barr Lincoln's Inn 1943 (hon bencher 1970), reader in int law Cncl of Legal Educn 1959-70, Whewell prof int law Cambridge 1955-81, vice pres Inst of Int Law 1979-81, pres 1981-83, hon memb 1985; judge Int Ct of Justice The Hague 1982-; jt ed: International and Comparative Law Quarterly 1955-61, British Year Book of International Law 1960- Hon LLD Hull Univ 1987, Hon Dr Juris Univ of Saarland 1988; kt 1981; *Clubs* Utd Oxford and Cambridge Univ, Haagsche Plaats Royaal (The Hague); *Style*— Prof Sir Robert Jennings, QC; Jesus College, Cambridge (☎ 0223 68611); Peace Palace, 2517 KJ The Hague, Neths

JENNISON, John Ronald; JP (Borough of Macclesfield, 1967-); s of John Jennison (d 1942), of Manchester, and Lilian Ena, *née* Mould (d 1964); family fnded Belle Vue Zoological Gdns Manchester in 1834; *b* 2 April 1921; *Educ* Beech Hall Prep Sch Macclesfield, Worksop Coll Notts; *m* 18 Sept 1951, Jean Lisle, da of Harold Harrison (d 1948), of Macclesfield; 1 s (John Henry Nicholas b 1956), 3 da (Caroline Louise b 1959, Jean Rosalind b 1963, Penelope Jeanette Lisle b 1965); *Career* Service in N Africa and Italy RASC 1939-44; chm James Kershaws Silk Mill (Macclesfield) Ltd 1964-74; Mayor of Maclesfield Borough 1966-67; *Style*— John R Jennison, Esq, JP; Grey Stead, 144 Prestbury Road, Macclesfield, Cheshire SK10 3BR (☎ 0625 22795)

JENRICK, William John; s of Sidney Thomas Jenrick, of Dukinfield, Cheshire, and Ivy Jenrick, *née* Barret; *b* 23 Nov 1940; *Educ* Ducie H S; *m* 1975, Jennifer Ann, da of Eric Alexander Robertson (d 1979); 1 s (Robert b 1982), 1 da (Jane b 1979); *Career* md: Cannon (Holdings) Ltd, Cannon Industries Ltd; chm Charlton & Jenrick Ltd; pres Round Table 1981 (chm 1980); capt Shropshire Minor Cnty Chess Team 1982-83; chm chief exec Ctee Soc of British Gas Industry 1985; ACMA; *Recreations* chess; *Style*—

William Jenrick Esq; Lark Rise, Haughton Lane, Shifnal, Shropshire (☎ 0952 461311; office 0902 43161)

JENSEN, Michael Harold; s of Eric Axel Jensen (d 1964); *b* 24 Oct 1942; *Educ* St Lawrence Coll; *m* 1969, Linda, da of Ernest Edwards; 2 da; *Career* md: Eden Ct Property Co Ltd 1968-, HL Thomson Ltd 1976-, HL Thomson (E Anglia) Ltd 1977-, Hogg Robinson Gardner Mountain Int Ltd 1977-; exec dir Willis Faber & Dumas Ltd (insurance brokers) 1981-87, chm Jensen Dickens Ltd (insur brokers); memb Worshipful Co of Carmen 1978, Freeman City of London 1978; memb Lloyd's 1980; *Recreations* shooting, sailing (yacht, MY Cheoy Lin); *Clubs* Lloyd's Yacht, Haven Ports Yacht, Deben Yacht.; *Style—* Michael Jensen, Esq; Oaken, Falconers Park, Sawbridgeworth, Herts; Moorings, Navere Meadows, Woodbridge, Suffolk; Jensen Dickens Ltd, Lloyd's Ave Hse, 6 Lloyd's Ave, London EC3N 3AX (☎ 01 480 6474)

JENSEN, Thomas George; s of Thomas Swensen Jensen (d 1963), and Ruth Ordell,*née* Ford; *b* 20 Jan 1948; *Educ* Nederland Opliedings Instituut Voor Het Buitenland (BA),; *m* 1 March 1971, Miki Hotta, da of Kuniyoshi Hotta, of Japan; 1 da (Katura Renia b 1972); *Career* vice pres Seattle First Nat Bank 1973-83, asst gen mangr Saudi Investmt Bank 1983-86, dir IBJ Int Ltd 1986-; *Recreations* tennis; *Style—* Thomas Jensen, Esq; 5 Brasenose House, 35 Kensington High St, London W8 5BA (☎ 01 937 2516); IBJ International, Bucklersbury House, 3 Queen Victoria St, London EC4N 8HR (☎ 01 236 1090)

JEPHCOTT, Sir (John) Anthony; 2 Bt (UK 1962), of East Portlemouth, Co Devon; s of Sir Harry Jephcott, 1 Bt (d 1978), and Doris, da of Henry Gregory; *b* 21 May 1924; *Educ* Aldenham, St John's Coll Oxford, LSE; *m* 1, 1949 (m dis 1978), Sylvia Mary, da of Thorsten F Relling, of Wellington, NZ; 2 da; m 2, 1978, Josephine Agnes, da of Philip Sheridan, of Perth, WA; *Heir* bro, Neil Jephcott; *Career* 1939-45 war with REME, later RAEC, formerly manufacturer of anaesthesia equipment, md: Penlon Ltd 1952-73, Pen Medic Ltd NZ 1973-78; *Style—* Sir Anthony Jephcott, Bt; 21 Brilliant St, St Heliers, Auckland 5, New Zealand

JEPHCOTT, Neil Welbourn; s of Sir Harry Jephcott, 1 Bt (d 1978), and hp of bro, Sir Anthony Jephcott, 2 Bt; *b* 3 June 1929; *Educ* Aldenham, Emmanuel Coll Cambridge (MA); *m* 1, 1951, Mary Denise (d 1977), da of Arthur Muddiman, of Abbots Mead, W Clandon, Surrey; m 2, 1978, Mary Florence, da of James John Daly (d 1950); *Career* professional engineer; *Recreations* sailing; *Clubs* Royal Ocean Racing; *Style—* Neil Jephcott, Esq; Thalassa, East Portlemouth, Salcombe, S Devon

JEREMIAH, Melvyn Gwynne; s of Bryn Jeremiah (d 1967), of Gwent, and Fanny Evelyn Mary, *née* Rogers (d 1987); *b* 10 Mar 1939; *Educ* Abertillery County Sch; *m* 1960 (m dis 1970), Clare, da of William Bailey, of Devon; *Career* appt HO 1958, Customs and Excise 1963, Cabinet Off 1975, Treas 1976, Welsh Off 1979, dir Ashley Gdns Freeholds Ltd 1986-; chief exec Disablement Servs Authy 1987-; sec Assoc of First Div Civil Servants 1967-70; *Recreations* work, people; *Clubs* Reform; *Style—* Melvyn Jeremiah, Esq; 110 Ashley Gdns, Thirleby Rd, London SW1P 1HJ (☎ 01 828 1588); Bwthyn Llon, St Harmon Road, Rhayader, Powys LD6 5LS (☎ 0597 810286); 14 Russell Sq, London WC1B 4EP (☎ 01 636 6811, fax 01 631 4581)

JERMAN, (Herbert) Noel; CBE (1967); s of John Maurice Jerman (d 1960), of Kerry, Powys; *b* 11 Dec 1909; *Educ* Newtown County Boys' Sch, Univ Coll Wales Aberystwyth (MA, DipEd); *m* 1939, Blodwen Elizabeth (d 1987), da of George Jenkins (d 1940), of Aberystwyth; *Career* WW II, Sqdn Ldr RAFVR; keeper maps prints and drawings Nat Library of Wales 1935-41; princ: Miny Town and Country Planning 1946-51, Welsh Office Miny Housing and Local Govt 1951-57; asst sec Welsh Off 1957-70, chief offr for Wales Cncl for Small Industs in Rural Areas 1970-77, small business conslt Welsh Dvpt Agency 1977-80; chm: Cambrian Archaeological Assoc 1963-69 (pres 1980-81), Offa's Dyke Assoc 1970-79 (pres 1979-80), Standing Conf of Rural Community Cncls in Wales 1971-78, Powys Rural Cncl 1974-77, Rent Scrutiny Bd for Mid-Wales 1972-74, Clwyd/Powys Archaeological Tst 1974-84, art and archaeology ctee Bd of Celtic Studies 1979-85, St John Cncl for Montgomeryshire 1981-, Powysland Club 1981-85 (vice pres 1985-), Mid-Wales Branch CS Retirement Fellowship 1983-; memb: ct Univ of Wales 1965-, ct and cncl Univ Coll Wales Aberystwyth 1972-77, ct and cncl Nat Library Wales 1973-, Rent Assessment Panel for Wales 1972-82, Welsh Place Names Advsy Ctee 1974-83, Mental Health Review Tbnl for Wales 1976-82, Welsh Folk Museum Governing Ctee 1976-, Royal Welsh Agric Soc 1978-; High Sheriff Powys 1983-84; OStJ (1984); FSA; Legion of Merit (US), OStJ (1984); *Books* Guide to Church and Village of Kerry (1976); *Recreations* gardening; *Clubs* Civil Service; *Style—* Noel Jerman Esq, CBE; Dolforgan Gardens, Kerry, Newtown, Powys SY16 4DN (☎ 0686 88 204)

JERRAM, Col Edward Jenner; MC (1940); s of Herbert William Jerram (d 1922), and Isabella Gertrude; *b* 5 Jan 1903; *Educ* Sherborne Sch, RMA Sandhurst; *m* 12 July 1952, Barbara Effie, da of late Lt Col Edward Armstrong, CMG, DSO, of Port Madoc; 1 s (Christopher Edward Jenner b 1953); *Career* regular army 1923-45, Bn Cdr N Ireland, Normandy, Palestine, Egypt, A/Brig cmd 7 Int Bde M East 1946, Sub Dist Cdr E Palestine 1947-48, ret Col 1954; *Recreations* fishing; *Clubs* Army & Navy; *Style—* Col Edward J Jerran, MC; Poplars Farm House, Evenlode, Moreton-in-Marsh, Gloucs

JERRAM, Maj-Gen Richard Martyn; CB (1984), MBE (1960); s of Brig R M Jerram, DSO, MC (d 1974), and Monica, *née* Gillies (d 1975); *b* 14 August 1928; *Educ* Marlborough, RMA Sandhurst; *m* Feb 1987, Susan, *née Roberts*, widow of Mr John Naylor; *Career* cmmnd RTR 1948, Instr Staff Coll Camberley 1964-67, CO 3 RTR 1969-71, Brig 1976, Maj-Gen 1981, dir RAC MOD 1981-84, Col Cmdt RTR 1982-88; *Clubs* Army & Navy; *Style—* Maj-Gen Richard Jerram, CB, MBE; Trehane, Trevanson, Wadebridge, Cornwall PL27 7HB (020 881 2523)

JERVIS, Hon Edward Robert James; s and h of 7 Viscount St Vincent; *b* 12 May 1951; *Educ* Radley; *m* 1977, Victoria Margaret, da of Wilton Joseph Oldham, of Jersey; 1 da (Emma Margaret Anne b 1980); *Career* co dir; *Recreations* skiing, water sports, chess, backgammon; *Style—* The Hon Edward Jervis; Colinas Verdes 26, Bensafrim, Lagos 8600, Algarve, Portugal

JERVIS, Roger David; s of David William Jervis, of Northampton, and Ada Ellen, *née* Barker; *b* 1 May 1942; *Educ* Northampton GS; *m* 11 March 1967, Carole Margaret, da of George Coles Ashton, of Northampton; 1 s (Guy b 1972), 1 da (Katie b 1969); *Career* articled Dutton and Co Northampton 1959-65, co sec and dep to gp accountant Wilson plc property co's 1965-69, fndr Jervis and Ptnrs 1970-; Kingsthorpe GC Northampton: hon tres 1974-82, capt 1982, tstee 1974-88; hon tres Northants Golf Union 1982-; govr: Northampton Sch for boys, Abington Vale Middle Sch; FCA 1965; *Recreations* golf, horse racing; *Clubs* Northampton County, Kingstorpe GC; *Style—* Roger Jervis, Esq; 38 Thorburn Rd, Northampton (☎ 0604 408 277); 20/22 Harborough Rd, Northampton (☎ 0604 714 600, fax 0604 719 304)

JERVIS, Hon Ronald Nigel John; s of 7 Viscount St Vincent; *b* 1954; *Educ* Eton, Durham Univ; *m* 1983, Gillian Lois, *née* Sharp; 1 s (David Stephen), 1 da (Sarah Francis); *Career* software engineer; *Recreations* books, music, gardening, foreign travel; *Style—* The Hon John Jervis

JERVOIS, David Reginald Warren; s of Reginald Charles Warren Jervois (d 1978), and Hettie Florence, *née* Clark; *b* 4 Dec 1928; *Educ* Marlborough Coll, Peterhouse Cambridge (BA); *m* 20 Sept 1958, Pamela Joan, da of Stanley James Hill (d 1979); 1 da (Jane Elizabeth b 1969); *Career* admitted slr 1957, notary public 1957; ptnr Woollcombe Watt & Co 1963-; clerk to Cmmrs of Income Tax Newton Abbot Teignbridge Div 1973-, chm Torquay Supp Benefit Appeal Tribunal 1982-, fndr memb Bovey Tracey Rotary Club (pres 1981); hon sec: S Devon CC, Torbay Hockey Club 1969-, Devon Co Hockey Assn 1987-; *Recreations* cricket, hockey, golf, model railways, philately; *Clubs* S Devon Cricket, MCC, Dragoons Cricket, Torbay Hockey, Stover Golf; *Style—* David R W Jervois, Esq; Lower Close, Chapple Road, Bovey Tracey, Devon TQ13 9JX (☎ 0626 833292); Church House, Queen Street, Newton Abbot, Devon (☎ 0626 52601)

JERVOISE, John Loveys; s of Capt John Loveys, MC (d 1974), of Chudleigh, Devon, and Barbara Tristram Ellis, o da of Arthur Tristram Ellis Jervoise (d 1942); descended maternally from Sir Thomas Jervoise, MP (d 1654), who acquired Herriard through his marriage to Lucy, eldest da of Sir Richard Powlet (*see* Burke's Landed Gentry, 18 edn, vol I, 1965); *b* 16 July 1935; *Educ* Hardye's Sch Dorchester, MacDonald Coll McGill Univ (Dip Agric), Seale-Hayne Agric Coll (Dip Farm Mgmnt); *m* 12 Aug 1961, Jane Elizabeth, eldest da of James Henry Lawrence Newnham (d 1975), of Stokelake, Chudleigh, Devon; 2 s (John Tristram b 3 May 1962, Anthony Richard b 2 Aug 1964), 2 da (Sarah Jane b 18 Nov 1965, Anne Elizabeth b (twin) 18 Nov 1965); *Career* nat serv: Lt Devonshire Regt 1953-56, Capt 4/5 Bn Royal Hampshire Regt, TA 1960-68; farmer and landowner; Basingstoke Rural DC 1964-74; chm Planning Ctee 1970-74 Basingstoke and Deane Borough Cncl 1974-78, chm Planning Ctee 1977-78; dir Mid Southern Water Co 1974-, chm Hampshire Branch Country Landowners Assoc 1986-88, pres Black Welsh Mountain Sheep Breeders Assoc 1980-82; MInstPet; *Recreations* hunting, shooting, walking; *Clubs* Naval and Military, RAC, The Devon and Exeter Inst (Exeter); *Style—* John Loveys Jervoise, Esq; Herriard Park, Basingstoke, Hampshire RG25 2PL (☎ 0256 83252); Estate Office, Herriard Park, Basingstoke, Hants (☎ 0256 83275)

JESSEL, Hon Mrs Amelia Grace; *née* FitzRoy; da of 2 Viscount Daventry (d 1986); *b* 26 Mar 1930; *Educ* East Haddon Hall Sch 1946; *m* 1950 (m dis 1978), as his 1 wife, Capt David Charles George Jessel (d 1985), Coldstream Gds (s of late Sir Richard Hugh Jessel); 1 s, 1 da; *Career* gun dog trainer, field trial and internat show judge; memb Council for Guide Dogs for the Blind Assoc, Pres: South and west Counties Field trial Soc, Meon Valley Working Spaniel Club; *Recreations* stalking, fishing, sailing; *Style—* The Hon Mrs Jessel; Bridge Cottage, Stoke Charity, Winchester, Hants (☎ 0962 760259)

JESSEL, Betty, Lady; (Joan) Betty; *née* Ewart; da of late Dr David Ewart, OBE, MD, FRCS, of Chichester; *m* 1, 1933 (m dis 1946), 2 Baron Russell of Liverpool. CBE, MC (d 1981) 1 da;m 2, 1948, as his 2 wife, Sir George Jessel, MC, 2 Bt (d 1977); *Recreations* gardening; *Clubs* Army and Navy; *Style—* Betty, Lady Jessel; Ladham House, Goudhurst, Kent TN17 1DB (☎ 0580 211203)

JESSEL, Sir Charles John; 3 Bt (UK 1883), of Ladham House, Goudhurst, Kent; s of Sir George Jessel, MC, 2 Bt (d 1977); *b* 29 Dec 1924; *Educ* Eton, Balliol Coll Oxford; *m* 1, 1956, Shirley Cornelia (d 1977), da of John Waters, of Northampton; 2 s, 1 da; m 2, 1979 (m dis 1983), Gwendolyn Mary, da of late Laurance Devereux, OBE, and widow of Charles Langer; *Heir* s, George Jessel; *Career* Lt 15/19 Hussars (despatches) WWII; Northampton Inst of Agriculture 1951-52, farmer 1953-85, in partnership with son 1985-; chm Ashford NFU 1963-64, chm Canterbury Farmers Clubs 1972-, pres Kent branch Men of the Trees 1979-83, pres Br Soc of Dowsers 1987; JP Kent 1960-78; *Recreations* gardening, planting trees; *Clubs* Cavalry and Guards; *Style—* Sir Charles Jessel, Bt; South Hill Farm, Hastingleigh, nr Ashford, Kent (☎ 023 375 325)

JESSEL, David Charles George; s of Sir Richard Hugh Jessel (d 1979, bro of Sir George Jessel, 2 Bt); *b* 20 June 1924; *Educ* Eton; *m* 1, 1950 (m dis 1978), Amelia Grace FitzRoy, da of Viscount Daventry *qv*; 1 s, 1 da; m 2; 1980, Matilda McCormick; *Career* served Coldstream Gds 1942-48, ret as Capt; joined Jessel Toynbee & Co Ltd 1948, (chm and md 1963-77); chm Bernard Sunley Investment Trust 1977-80; dep chm Eagle Star Hldgs 1980-; chm & dep chm London Discount Market Assoc 1967-71; chm Intervention Bd for Agric Produce 1980-; dir BAT Industries 1984-, Great Portland Estates 1961-77, UDS 1982-3; FIB; *Recreations* fishing, shooting, sailing; *Clubs* Cavalry and Guards; *Style—* David Jessel Esq; 22 Cambridge Rd, London SW11 4RR (☎ 01 228 8445)

JESSEL, 2 Baron (UK 1924); Sir Edward Herbert Jessel; 2 Bt (UK 1917), CBE (1963); s of 1 Baron Jessel, CB, CMG (d 1950), and Maud (d 1965), 5 da of late Rt Hon Sir Julian Goldsmid, 3 Bt, MP ; *b* 25 Mar 1904; *Educ* Eton, Ch Ch Oxford (MA); *m* 1, 1935 (m dis 1960), Lady Helen Maglona Vane-Tempest-Stewart, 3 da of 7 Marquess of Londonderry, KG, MVO, TD, PC (d 1949); 1 da (1 s and 1 da decd); m 2, 1960, Jessica, da of late William de Wet; *Heir* none; *Career* barr Inner Temple 1926; formerly with: Textile Machinery Makers Ltd, Truscon Ltd, Westminster Trust; chm Assoc of Independent Unionist Peers 1959-64, a dep speaker House of Lords 1963-77, chm Associated Leisure Ltd until 1984; *Clubs* Garrick, White's; *Style—* The Rt Hon the Lord Jessel, CBE; 4 Sloane Terrace Mansions, London SW1 (☎ 01 730 7843)

JESSEL, George Elphinstone; s and h of Sir Charles Jessel, 3 Bt, and Shirley Cornelia Jessel, *née* Waters (d 1977), of South Hill Farm, Hastingleigh, Ashford, Kent; *b* 15 Dec 1957; *Educ* Milton Abbey, RAC Cirencester; *m* 10 Dec 1988, Rose Amila Coutts-Smith; *Career* cmmd Lt 15/19 Royal Hus, Germany, Canada and Cyprus 1978-82; farmer, ptnr with father 1985-; *Recreations* skiing, travelling; *Clubs* Cavalry & Guards, London Farmers; *Style—* George Jessel, Esq; Stoakes Cottage, Hastingleigh, Ashford, Kent TN25 5HG (☎ 023 375 216); South Hill Farm, Hastingleigh, Ashford, Kent TN25 5HL (☎ 023 375 325)

JESSEL, Oliver Richard; er s of Cdr Richard Frederick Jessel, DSO, OBE, DSC, RN (d 1988), of Marden, Kent; er bro of Toby Jessel, MP; *b* 24 August 1929; *Educ* Rugby; *m* 1950, Gloria Rosalie Teresa, *née* Holden; 1 s, 5 da; *Career* chm Jessel Trust 1971-; chm Charles Clifford Industries (non-ferrous metals gp) 1978-81; former chm London, Australian & Gen Exploration Co; fndr New Issue Unit Tst, Castle Communications plc; formed numerous mergers;; *Clubs* Garrick; *Style*— Oliver Jessel Esq; Merrington Place, Rolvenden, Cranbrook, Kent TN17 4PJ (☎ 0580 241428)

JESSEL, Toby Francis Henry; MP (Cons Twickenham 1970-); yr s of Cdr Richard Jessel, DSO, OBE, DSC, RN (d 1988), and Winifred May (d 1977), da of Major Walter Levy D.S.O and Hon Mrs Levy (later Hon Mrs Ionides) da of 1 Viscount Bearsted; *b* 11 July 1934; *Educ* RNC Dartmouth, Balliol Oxford; *m* 1, 1967 (m dis), Phillppa Brigid, *née* Jephcott; 1 da (decd); m 2, 1980, Eira Heath; *Career* Sub Lt RNVR 1954; parly Candidate (Cons) Peckham 1964, Hull N 1966; chm Cons Arts and Heritage Ctee; memb Cncl Europe 1976-; GLC memb Richmond 1967-73; Liveryman Worshipful Co of Musicians; Chevalier de l'Ordre de la Couronne Belgium; *Recreations* piano, gardening, skiing, swimming; *Clubs* Garrick, Hurlingham; *Style*— Toby Jessel Esq, MP; Old Court House, Hampton Court, E Molesey, Surrey KT8 9BW

JESSUP, Graham Marcus; s of Basil Graham Jessup (Maj ret), of Ash Platt, Kent (d 1979), and Jessie Laura Jessup, *née* Chappell (d 1979); *b* 14 Feb 1947; *Educ* Sevenoaks Sch, Bristol Univ (BSc); *m* 17 Aug 1967, Susan Janet Melland, da of Peter William Gilpin, (Gp Capt ret), of Culvers Close, Oxon; 2 s (Simon b 1972, Richard b 1974); *Career* client servs dir Newton & Godin Ltd; dir: Newton & Godin Ltd 1982-, Promotional Campaigns Ltd 1982-, Dowton Advertising Ltd 1980-82; *Recreations* golf, sailing; *Clubs* Knole Park Golf; *Style*— Graham M Jessup, Esq; Parksland Cottage, 7 Weald Rd, Sevenoaks, Kent; Newton & Godin Ltd, Union House, The Pantiles, Tunbridge Wells, Kent (☎ 0892 510520, car ☎ 0860 325 374)

JEUNE, Senator Reginald Robert; OBE (1979); s of Reginald Valpy Jeune (d 1974), and Jessie Maud, *née* Robinson (d 1945); *b* 22 Oct 1920; *Educ* De La Salle Coll Jersey; *m* 1946, Monica Lillian, da of Hedley Charles Valpy, of Jersey; 2 s (Richard Francis Valpy b 1949, Nicholas Charles b 1954), 1 da (Susan Elizabeth b 1958); *Career* slr of the Royal Court of Jersey 1945-; ret sr ptnr Mourant du Feu & Jeune now conslt with that firm; Senator of States of Jersey (pres fin & econs ctee), chm: Cwlth Parly Assoc, Exec Jersey Branch, TSB Channel Islands Ltd; memb TSB Gp plc Bd; chm Jersey Electricity Co Ltd; consul for the Netherlands (Jersey); OStJ, Chevalier of the Order of Orange Nassau, Offr of the Ordre de Merite Nationale; *Recreations* golf; *Clubs* Carlton (UK), RAC, MCC, Victoria (Jersey), United, Royal Jersey Golf, La Moye Golf; *Style*— Senator Reginald R Jeune, OBE; Messrs Mourant du Feu & Jeune, 18 Grenville St, St Helier, Jersey, CI (☎ 0534 74343, fax 0534 79064, telex 4192064)

JEWELL, David John; s of Wing Cdr John Jewell, OBE (d 1985), of Porthleven, Cornwall, and Rachel, *née* Miners (d 1962); *b* 24 Mar 1934; *Educ* Blundell's, St John's Coll Oxford (MA, MSc); *m* 23 Aug 1958, Katharine Frida, da of Prof Hans Sigmund Heller (d 1974), of Bristol; 1 s (John Edward), 3 da (Rachel Susannah, Sarah Josephine, Tamsin Mary Katharine); *Career* Nat Serv pilot offr RAF 1952-54; head of science dept Eastbourne Coll 1958-62, Winchester Coll 1962-67, dep head Lawrence Weston Sch Bristol 1967-70, head master Bristol Cathedral Sch 1970-79, head master Repton 1979-87, Master Haileybury and Imp Serv Coll 1987-; nat rep and chm HMC sub ctees, chm elect HMC ; FRSA 1981; *Recreations* music, cricket, Cornwall; *Clubs* East India, MCC, Bristol Savages; *Style*— David Jewell, Esq; The Master's Lodge, Haileybury, Hertford SG13 7NU (☎ 0992 462 352)

JEWERS, William George; CBE (1982, OBE 1976); s of William Jewers (d 1925), and Hilda, *née* Ellison (d 1964); *b* 18 Oct 1921; *Educ* Liverpool Inst HS; *m* 1955, Helena Florence, da of Frederick Sleight Rimmer (d 1959); 1 s (Keith b 1958), 1 da (Patricia b 1955); *Career* F/O RAFVR 1941-46, 265 Sqdn Indian Ocean 1943-44, Burma 194 Sqdn 1945; joined Liverpool Gas Co 1938, dir fin West Midlands Gas Bd 1968-69, dir fin Gas Cncl 1969-73, md finance Br Gas Corpn 1976- 86 (dir fin 1973-76), md fin Br Gas plc 1986-87;; *Recreations* music, reading; *Style*— William Jewers, Esq, CBE; 17 South Park View, Gerrards Close, Bucks SL9 8HN (☎ 0753 886169)

JEWISS, John E; s of John W Jewiss (d 1978), and Marjorie Jewiss Bailey; *b* 4 April 1944; *Educ* Selhurst Grammar Sch; *m* 1966, Sandra, da of Gerald A J Peacock, 2 da (Paula b 1968, Kerry b 1970); *Career* chm Hartley Cooper Gp Hldgs 1982-83; Dir: C E Heath Gp 1973-77, Hartley Cooper Gp 1977-81; md Gibbs Hartley Cooper 1983-85; independent mgmnt conslt 1985-; *Recreations* cricket, badminton, music, drama, art; *Clubs* Les Ambassadeurs, Wellington; *Style*— John Jewiss, Esq; Hoddydodd Hall, Spains Hall Rd, Willingale, Essex CM5 0QD; Hoddydodd Hall, Willingale, Essex

JEWITT, Anthony John; s of John Jewitt and Ellen, *née* Tatlock; *b* 7 Oct 1935; *Educ* Chingford GS, Harvard Business Sch; *m* 26 July 1958, Janet Julia, *née* Smith; 3 da (Marie Julia Anne b 28 June 1960, Jennie Anne Louise b 15 July 1962, Catherine Jane b 8 April 1965); *Career* served in army 1958-60, Capt; gp chm ICC Info Gp Ltd; dir: SI Management Ltd, Mar-Com Systems Ltd; BIM, MInstM, MICSA ; *Recreations* skiing, tennis, horse racing; *Clubs* St James's; *Style*— Anthony Jewitt, Esq; Majenca, Pelling Hill, Old Windsor, Berks SL4 2LL (☎ 0753 865289); ICC Information Group Ltd, Field House, 72 Oldfield Rd, Hampton, Middx TW12 2HQ (☎ 01 783 1122, fax 01 783 0049, telex 296090)

JEWITT, Cdr Dermod James Boris (Toby); DSC; s of Capt Reuben James Charles Jewitt (d 1958), and Enid Alice, *née* Bagot; *b* 13 Oct 1908; *Educ* RNC; *m* 1, March 1941 (m dis 1951), Pamela Mary Scrutton; 2 da (Sarah Mary (Mrs Best) b 1943, Penelope Anne (Mrs Allanson-Bailey) b 1946); m 2, 19 Sept 1960, Emma Jane,da of Reginald Martin Vick, OBE; 1 s (Charles James Bagot b 1965); *Career* RNC Dartmouth 1922-25, HMS: Valiant 1926-28, Seraph 1930-32, Amazon 1932-33, Keith 1933-34, Sussex 1934-35, Wolsey 1935-36, Ivanhoe 1936-39; Cdr HMS: Northern Spray 1939-40, Vimy 1940-41, Winchester 1941-42, Meteor 1942-44, Hasdrubal 1945, President 1945-47 Nereide 1947-49, Jt Serv Staff Coll 1949-50, invalided 1950 (despatches twice); Scruttons Ltd: master stevedores 1950, indust dir, chm London Ocean Trade Employers 1971-72; *Recreations* walking, golf, fishing; *Style*— Cdr Toby Jewitt, DSC; Pelham Lodge, Pelham Lane, Crediton, Devon EX17 1ED (☎ 036 32 3827)

JEWITT, John James; OBE (1979), JP (1966); s of John James Jewitt, MBE (d 1984), of Sheffield, and Edna May, *née* Hobson; *b* 28 Feb 1924; *Educ* Firth Park GS; *m* 1, 27 Aug 1948, Dorothy Allice (d 1974), da of Lawrence Dungworth (d 1965), of Derby; 1 s (Christopher b 1951), 1 da (Alison b 1958 d 1974) m 2, 20 March 1976, Meinir Constance, da of Sydney Thomas Bailey (d 1987), of Sheffield; 1 s (Marc b 1978), 1 da (Claire b 1976); *Career* dir J C H Castings 1974-83, Radio Hallam 1974-; chm Thos C Hurdley 1978-86, md Footprint Tools Ltd 1970- (chm 1984); pres Sheffield Junior Chamber of Commerce 1959-60; chm: selection ctee Sheffield Outward Bound Tst 1965-72, cncl of S Yorkshire and Hallamshire Boys Clubs 1976-, mgmnt ctee and Chm Hillsborough Boys Club Sheffield 1969-, Sheffield Light Trades Employers Assoc 1974-77; pres Cncl of Hand Tools for Europe (14 countries) 1988- (pres 1988-90), pres Fedn of Br Hand Tools Manufacturers 1985-87; memb: Nat Cncl of Assoc of Boys Clubs 1964-, Local Affairs Ctee Chamber of Commerce 1978-; Freeman Worshipful Co of Cutlers in Hallamshire; *Recreations* sailing, wind surfing, squash, skiing; *Clubs* Sheffield, Lansdowne,; *Style*— John Jewitt, Esq, OBE, JP; The Homestead, Pinfold Hill, Curbar, via Sheffield S30 1YL (☎ 0433 31500); Footprint Tools Ltd, PO Box 19, Hollis Croft, Sheffield S1 3HY (☎ 0742 753200)

JEWITT, Ronald William; s of Cyril George Jewitt (d 1982), of Newport, Gwent, and Hilda Laura Jewitt (d 1972); *b* 25 Jan 1942; *Educ* Newport HS, Newport and Mon Tech Coll, Brunel Coll of Advanced Tech; *m* 30 March 1963, June Rose, da of Reginald Barley (d 1982), of Newport, Gwent; 2 s (Peter Ronald b 1964, David Charles b 1965), 1 da (Penelope Anne b 1967); *Career* asst chemist Monsanto Chemicals Ltd 1958-62, dep analyst Expandite Ltd 1962-64, res and devpt chemist Burt Boulton and Haywood Ltd 1964-66, analytical chemist London Tport 1966; pres: Caversham and Mapledurham Royal Br Legion, Reading Mid-Week Assoc Cricket League, Royal Berks Sports and Social Club; chm Caversham Cons Assoc; memb: Reading Borough Cncl 1973- (housing chm 1979-84, Mayor 1984-85, dep Mayor 1985-86), Berks CC 1977- (ldr 1986-); *Recreations* walking, swimming; *Style*— Ronald Jewitt, Esq; 98 Chiltern Road, Caversham, Reading, Berkshire RG4 OJD (☎ 0734 481147); 55 Lot's Road, London SW10 (☎ 01 352 3727, ext 37)

JEWKES, Gordon Wesley; CMG (1980); s of Jesse Jewkes (d 1943), and Anne Plumb (d 1983); *b* 18 Nov 1931; *Educ* Barrow in Furness GS; *m* 1954, Joyce, da of John Lyons (d 1975); 2 s (Nigel, Stephen); *Career* Home Civil Serv 1948-68; Nat Serv and Army Emergency Reserve (AER), Capt RAOC 1968; first sec Cwlth later Foreign & Cwlth Off, consul (commercial) Chicago 1969-72, dep high cmmnr Port of Spain 1972-75, head of Finance Dept Foreign and Cwlth Off, finance offr Diplomatic Serv 1975-79; consul-gen: Cleveland 1979-82, Chicago 1982-85, New York; govr Falkland Islands and high cmmnr Br Antarctic Territory 1985-88; dir-gen Trade and Investmts 1989-; *Recreations* music, walking, travel; *Clubs* Travellers'; *Style*— Gordon Jewkes, Esq, CMG; c/o Foreign & Commonwealth Office, King Charles St, London SW1A 2AH

JEWSON, Richard Wilson; s of Charles Boardman Jewson (d 1981), of Norfolk, and Joyce Marjorie, *née* Laws; *b* 5 August 1944; *Educ* Rugby, Pembroke Coll Cambridge (MA); *m* 1965, Sarah Rosemary, da of Henry Nevill Spencer, of Kenilworth; 1 s (William b 1968), 3 da (Henrietta b 1966, Charlotte b 1970, Camilla b 1976); *Career* md Jewson Ltd 1974-86, dir Eastern Counties Newspaper Gp Ltd 1982, md Meyer Int plc 1986; memb of Cncl of Univ of E Anglia 1980-; CBIM; *Recreations* gardening, tennis; *Clubs* Boodle's, Royal W Norfolk GC, RSA; *Style*— Richard Jewson, Esq; Dades Farm, Barnham Broom, Norfolk NR9 4BT (☎ 060 545237); Villiers House, The Strand, London (☎ 01 839 7766)

JEYNES, Edward Raymond; s of Albert Edward Jeynes (d 1977), and Florence Kate Jeynes, *née* White; *b* 23 June 1922; *Educ* Central GS; *m* Jacqueline Mary, da of Ralph Parsons, of Scotland; 1 s (Matthew Simon b 1988), 3 da (Susan Carole b 1958, Deborah Ruth b 1966, Catherine Tamsin b 1986); *Career* CA; sr ptnr West Midlands Price Waterhouse 1982; chm: Wheway plc, Eliza Tinsley Gp plc; dep chm Healey Mouldings Ltd; dir: Joseph Webb plc, Archibald Kenrick & Sons Ltd, Noel Penny Turbines Ltd, Heart of England Bldg Soc; *Style*— Edward Jaynes; The Woodlands, Dunley, nr Stourport-on-Severn, Worcs DY13 0TZ (☎ 029 93 2001)

JHABVALA, Ruth Prawer; da of Marcus Prawer (d 1948), and Eleaonora, *née* Cohn (d 1983); *b* 7 May 1927; *Educ* Hendon Co Sch London, London Univ (MA); *m* 16 June 1951, Cyrus Jhabvala, s of Shiavakshah Jhabvala (d 1973); 3 da (Renana b 1952, Ava b 1955, Firoza b 1957); *Career* authoress: films: Shakespeare wallah 1964, Autobiography of a Princess 1975, The Bostonians 1985, Room With A View 1986; Hon DLitt London; FRSL; *Books* To Whom She Will (1955), The Nature of Passion (1956), The Householder (1960), Heat and Dust (1975), Out of India (1986), Three Continents (1987); *Style*— Mrs Ruth Jhabvala; 400 East 52nd St, New York, NY 10022, USA; c/o John Murray, 50 Albemarle St, London W1

JOACHIM, Dr Margaret Jane; *née* Carpenter; da of Reginald Carpenter, DSO, of Pensilva, Cornwall, and Joyce Margaret, *née* Howard (d 1977); *b* 25 June 1949; *Educ* Brighton & Hove HS, St Hugh's Coll Oxford (MA), W Midlands Coll of Educ, Univ of Birmingham (PhD); *m* 2 July 1970, Paul Joseph Joachim s of Joseph Joachim, of Marlborough, Wilts; *Career* Vol Serv WRNR serv HMS Sussex 1965-67, offr cadet OTC Oxford Univ 1967-70; teacher Stourbridge Girls HS 1971-73 (pt/t 1973-76), pt/t lectr Univ extramural and WEA 1972-77, post-doctoral res fell geol Univ of Birmingham 1976-79; programmer BOC Datasolve 1979-80, programmer and conslt IP Sharp Assocs 1980-84, futures database mangr Rudolf Wolff & Co Ltd 1984-87, sales exec (UK Insur Servs) EDS Ltd 1988-; fndr: Oxford Univ Gilbert & Sullivan Soc, The Steam Apprentice club, chm working gp (Int) to establish womens lobby in Brussels, friend Ironbridge Gorge Museum; Parly candidate (Lib): W Glos 1979, (Alliance) Finchley 1983, Epsom and Ewell 1987; chm Fawcett Soc 1984-87, pres elect Womans Lib Fedn 1988, memb exec ctee 300 Gp 1988-, jt co-ordinator WIPL 1987-88; FRES 1977, AMI Geol 1978; *Recreations* reading, sailing, walking, singing, visiting traction engine rallies, making jam; *Clubs* Reform; *Style*— Dr Margaret Joachim; 8 Newburgh Rd, London W3 6DG (☎ 01 993 0936), EDS Ltd, Devonshire House, Mayfair Place, London W1X 5FH (☎ 01 499 9588, fax 01 499 8526, telex 295449 EDSW)

JOB, Rev Canon (Evan) Roger Gould; s of Thomas Brian Job (d 1985), of Ipswich, and Elsie Maud Gould (d 1987); *b* 15 May 1936; *Educ* The Kings Sch Canterbury, Magdalen Coll Oxford (BA, MA), Cuddesdon Theol Coll; *m* 4 July 1964, Rose Constance Mary, da of Lt Col Stanley Gordon, MC, TD (d 1982), of Hooton, Wirral; 2 s (Jonathan b 1967, Christopher b 1971); *Career* Nat Serv RN 1955-57; ordained: deacon 1962, priest 1963 in Liverpool Cathedral; asst curate Liverpool Parish Church 1962-65, vicar St John New Springs Wigan 1965-70, minor canon and precentor Manchester Cathedral 1970-74, precentor and sacrist Westminster Abbey 1974-79, canon residentiary precentor and sacrist Winchester Cathedral 1979-; Winchester area chm Royal Sch of Church Music 1984-, local pres Save the Children Fund 1981-, chm Winchester and Dist Christian Cncl 1986-87; *Recreations* gardening, piano; *Style*— The Rev Canon Roger Job; 8 The Close, Winchester SO23 9LS (☎ 0962 53137)

JOBERNS, Geoffrey Lewis; s of William Lewis Joberns; *b* 6 Nov 1929; *Educ* Solihull

Public Sch; *m* 1955, Barbara Anne, *née* Hemming; 1 s (Stephen Lewis b 1969), 2 da (Karen Elizabeth Gaymond, b. 1957 Louise Anne b 1960); *Career* solicitor 1956; memb Lloyds Underwriters 1979; chm: Packwood Properties Ltd, Packwood Developments Ltd, Packwood Construction Ltd, Packwood Investments Ltd. Thornlake Ltd, Cotswold; *Recreations* golf; *Clubs* Shirley Golf, Midlands Sporting, Bentley Drivers, Avenue Bowling; *Style*— Geoffrey Joberns Esq; Packwood Towers, Windmill Lane, Packwood, Solihull, West Midlands (☎ 056 45 2267)

JOBSON, Lady Lavinia (Anne); *née* Brabazon; da of 14 Earl of Meath; *b* 1945; *m* 1969, John Ernest Baron Jobson; 1 s, 3 da; *Style*— Lady Lavinia Jobson; Barnacullia, Kilmacanoge, Co Wicklow, Eire

JOBSON, Timothy Akers; s of Maj Edward Oliver Akers Jobson (d 1965), of London W8, and Joan, *née* Webb, of Stourbridge; *b* 16 July 1944; *Educ* Bromsgrove Sch, Keble Coll Oxford (MA); *m* 1, 27 July 1970 (m dis 1980), (Gloria) Lee, da of Reginald Bazeley; 1 s (Simon b 1973), 1 da (Annie b 1974); m 2, 7 April 1982, Susan Freda Jeavons, da of Cyril Edward Marshall; *Career* admitted slr 1968; ptnr: Lyon Clark & Co W Bromwich 1970-84, Keely Smith & Jobson Lichfield 1985-; dep chm W Bromwich & Dist YMCA 1979- (dir trg orgn YTS 1987-); memb Law Soc 1968; *Recreations* sailing, swimming; *Clubs* Barnt Green SC (hon sec 1981-86); *Style*— Tim Jobson, Esq; 6 Redhouse Rd, Tettenhall, Wolverhampton WV6 8ST; Keely Smith & Jobson, 16 Bore Street, Lichfield Staffs WS13 6LL (☎ 0543 414 222, fax 0543 258 469)

JOCELYN, Doctor Henry David; s of John Daniel Jocelyn (d 1956), and Phyllis Irene *née* Burton (d 1977); *b* 22 August 1933; *Educ* Canterbury Boys' HS NSW, Univ of Sydney (BA), St John's Coll Univ of Cambridge (MA PhD); *m* 22 Oct 1958, Margaret Jill , da of Bert James Morton (d 1984); 2s (Luke b 1962, Edmund b 1968); *Career* memb academic staff Univ of Sydney 1960-73; Hulme prof Latin Univ of Manchester 1973-; *Style*— Dr Henry D Jocelyn; 4 Clayton Avenue, Manchester, M20 0BN (☎ 061 434 1526); Department of Greek and Latin, University of Manchester, M13 9PL (☎ 061 275 3022)

JOCELYN, Hon James Michael; s of 9 Earl of Roden; *b* 12 April 1943; *Educ* Stowe, Trinity Coll Dublin; *Style*— The Hon James Jocelyn; Glynsk, Connemara, nr Cashel, Co Galway, Eire

JOCELYN, Robert John; does not use courtesy title of Viscount; s and h of 9 Earl of Roden; *b* 25 August 1938; *Educ* Stowe; *m* 1, 1970 (m dis 1982), Sara Cecilia, da of Brig Andrew Dunlop, of Que Que, Zimbabwe; 1 da (Cecilia Rose b 1976); m 2, 1986, Ann Margareta Maria, da of Dr Gunnar Henning, of Goteborg, Sweden; *Heir* bro, Hon Thomas Jocelyn; *Career* insurance broker; *Style*— Mr Robert Jocelyn; 4 The Boltons, London SW10 9TB

JOCELYN, Hon Thomas Alan; 2 s of 9 Earl of Roden; hp of bro, Viscount Jocelyn; *b* 4 Oct 1941; *Educ* Stowe, RNC Dartmouth; *m* 1966 (m dis 1983), Fiona, da of Capt Rudland Dallas Cairns, DSC, RN, of Co Wexford; 2 da, 1 s; *Career* Lt-Cdr RN (ret 1979); *Style*— Lieutenant Commander The Hon Thomas Jocelyn, RN

JODRELL, Michael Francis Mostyn Owen; s of Col Herbert Lewis Mostyn-Owen (d 1972), and Susan Dorothy, *née* Jodrell-Ransden (d 1965); *b* 9 Dec 1935; *Educ* Eton; *m* 25 April 1964, Veronica Mary, da of Lt-Col Oskar Leslie Boord, MC (d 1967); 2 s (Henry b 28 April 1967, William b 8 Oct 1969); *Career* Lt Grenadier Gds; ptnr Rowe & Pitman 1972-86, vice-chm Mercury Rowan Mullens 1966-; Liveryman Worshipful Co of Fishmongers; *Recreations* photography, gardening, shooting; *Clubs* Pratts; *Style*— Michael M B Jodrell, Esq; Leigh Court, Shaftesbury, Dorset (☎ 074 788 261); 33 King William St, London EC4 (☎ 01 280 2900)

JOEL, Hon Sir Asher Alexander; KBE (1974, OBE 1956), AO (1986); s of Harry Joel and Phoebe Joel; *b* 4 May 1912; *Educ* Enmore Pub Sch, Cleveland St HS Sydney; *m* 1, 1937 (m dis 1948); 2 s; m 2, 1949, Sybil, da of Frederick Mitchell Jacobs; 1 s, 1 da; *Career* MLC (Country Party) NSW 1957-78, dir Royal North Shore Hosp 1959-81, chm Asher Joel Media Gp, chm Mt Isa Television Pty Ltd; Public Relations Inst Man of Achievement Award 1970; Order of Sikatuna (Philippines) 1975, Knight Cdr Order of Rizal (Philippines) 1978; kt 1971; *see Debrett's Handbook of Australia and New Zealand for further details*; *Books* Australian Protocol and Procedures; *Style*— The Hon Sir Asher Joel, KBE, AO; 120 Clarence St, Sydney, NSW 2000, Australia

JOELSON, Stephen Laurance Robert; s of Maurice Joelson, of London, and Maureen Michelle, *née* Wien; *b* 28 Feb 1956; *Educ* Latymer Upper Sch, Reading Univ (LLB), Inns of Court Sch of Law; *Career* barr Gray's Inn 1980; *Recreations* skiing, football; *Clubs* Holmes Place, The Bank;; *Style*— Stephen Joelson, Esq; 3 New Square, Lincoln's Inn, London, WC2A 3RS (☎ 01 242 2523, fax 01 831 6968)

JOFFE, Joel Goodman; s of Abraham Michael Joffe (d 1984), of Johannesburg, and Dena, *née* Idelson (d 1984); *b* 12 May 1932; *Educ* Univ of Witwatersrand Johannesburg (B Com, LLB); *m* 1 Nov 1962, Vanetta, da of François Pretorius (d 1975), of Port Elizabeth, S Africa; 3 da (Deborah b 11 June 1963, Lisa b 13 Aug 1964, Abigail b 4 Sept 1969); *Career* lawyer SA 1954-65; admin dir Abbey Life Assur plc 1966-70; dep chm (formerly dir and md) Allied Dunbar Assur plc 1971-; chm: Swindon Cncl of Voluntary Servs 1973-80, Oxfam 1980-88 (tstee, hon sec and chm of its exec ctee);; *Recreations* tennis, squash, cycling; *Style*— Joel Joffe, Esq

JOHANSEN, Hon Mrs (Jane); *née* Blyton; eldest da of Baron Blyton, Life Peer (d 1987); *b* 1920; *m* 1943, John Johansen (d 1955); children; *Style*— The Hon Mrs Johansen; 139 Brockley Ave, S Shields, Tyne and Wear

JOHANSEN-BERG, Rev John; s of John Alfred Johansen-Berg, of Middlesbrough, Cleveland, and Caroline, *née* Gettings; *b* 4 Nov 1935; *Educ* Acklam Hall GS, Leeds Univ (BA, BD), Cambridge Univ (MA); *m* 17 July 1971, Joan Scott, da of James Parnham, of Leeds, Yorks; 2 s (Mark b 1973, James (Jake) b 1977), 1 da (Heidi b 1974); *Career* tutor Westminster Coll Cambridge 1961-62, ordained 1962, minister St Nimian's Presbyterian Church Luton Beds 1962-70, fndr minister St Katherine of Genoa Church Dunstable, Beds 1966-70, frontier mission work in Everton Liverpool resulting in the building of the Rock Church Centre 1970-77, minister St Andrew's United Reformed Church Ealing 1977-86, fndr Community for Reconciliation 1984 (pastoral leader Birmingham 1986-); moderator: United Reformed Church 1980-81, Free Church Federal Cncl 1987-88; memb Br Cncl of Churches Assemby (SA Advsy Ctee, Namibia Advsy Gp), fndr sponsor Christian Concern for SA (former vice chm); memb and former chm: Christian Fellowship Tst, Namibia Christian Exchange; chm: Clergy Against Nuclear Arms, Church and Soc Dept of URC 1972-79, BCC Working Party which produced Non-Violent Action: A Christian Apprisal (SCM 1973), Violence, Non-Violence and Social Change (BCC 1977), URC Gp which produced Good News the Poor: New Enterprise in Mission (URC 1982); jt ed The Journal of the Presbyterian Historical Soc 1964-70; *Books* Arian or Arminian? Presbyterian Continuity in the Eighteenth Century (1969); *Recreations* walking, mountain climbing/walking, badminton, tennis, golf; *Style*— The Rev John Johansen-Berg; Barnes Close, Chadwich Manor, nr Bromsgrove, Worcs B61 ORA (☎ 0562 710231); Community for Reconciliation, Barnes Close, Chadwich Manor, nr Bromsgrove, Worcs B61 ORA

JOHN, (Richard) Alun; s of Thomas Guy John (d 1969), and Edith, *née* John (d 1979); *b* 7 April 1948; *Educ* Whitchurch GS; *m* 14 June 1980, (Elizabeth) Sara, da of Denis W Kent, of Beaconsfield, Bucks; 1 s (Guy b 7 Oct 1985); *Career* photographer South Wales Echo and Western Mail 1966, photographer The Press Assoc 1977, ed The Associated Press; dep picture ed: Evening Standard 1981, Mail on Sunday 1982; picture ed: The Independant 1986, The European 1988-; external examiner Trent Poly Nottingham, selector RPS Exhibitions 1988-89, conslt picture ed Thomson Rndn; Gerald Barry Award in What the Papers Say Award 1987;; *Books* Newspaper Photography (1988); *Recreations* travel, writing, shooting; *Style*— Alun John, Esq; Randall Mead, Binfield Berks RG12 5EL; Mirror Newspapers, Holborn Circus, London (☎ 01 353 0246)

JOHN, Arthur Walwyn; CBE (1967, OBE 1945); s of Oliver Walwyn John (d 1953), of Cardiff, and Elsie Maud, *née* Davies; *b* 1 Dec 1912; *Educ* Marlborough; *m* 1, 24 Sept 1949, Elizabeth Rosabelle (d 1979), yr da of Ernest David Williams, of Radyr, Cardiff; 1 s (Oliver b 1961), 2 da (Ann b 1952, Sarah b 1953); m 2, 30 May 1986, Bonita Lynne, da of Sebastian Maritano; *Career* joined army 1939, cmmnd 1940, War Office 1941, DAQMG First Army 1942, HQ Allied Armies in Italy 1942, AQMG Allied Forces HQ 1944 (despatches 1943 and 1945); asst to commercial mangr (collieries) Powell Duffryn Associated Collieries Ltd 1936; chief accountant John Lewis & Co Ltd 1945; dep dir-gen of finance NCB 1946, dir-gen 1955, bd memb 1961-68, chm coal products divn 1962-68; dir: Unigate Ltd 1969-75, Property Holding and Investment Tst Ltd 1976-87 (chm 1982-84), Reed Stenhouse Cos Ltd Canada 1977-84, J H Sankey & Son Ltd 1965-86, Schroder Property Fund 1971-88, Teamdale Distribution Ltd 1982- (chm 1982-), Chartered Accountants Tstees Ltd 1982-87, Wincanton Contracts Finance Ltd 1983-85, Chase Property Holdings plc 1986-87 (chm 1986-87); memb Price Cmmn 1976-77; memb court: Univ of Wales Aberystwyth, City Univ; Freeman of City of London, memb court of Worshipful Co of Chartered Accountants 1977- (Master 1981-82); FCA; *Recreations* gardening, golf, walking; *Clubs* Army and Navy; *Style*— Arthur John, Esq, CBE; Limber, Top Park, Gerrards Cross, Bucks SL9 7PW (☎ 0753 884811)

JOHN, Huw Stradling; s of Alfred Stradling John, JP (d 1982), of Pontypridd, and Glwady Clarrisa, *née* Rees; *b* 21 August 1941; *Educ* Wycliffe Coll, Univ Coll Cardiff; *m* 25 Sept 1971, Margaret Joan, da of Henry Goode; 2 s (Edward b 1976, Oliver b 1983), 1 da (Victoria b 1973) ; *Career* chartered accountant, ptnr Alfred S John 1968-80; FICA 1967; *Recreations* golf, swimming, walking; *Clubs* Cardiff Golf; *Style*— H S John, Esq; Cardiff, (☎ 761 728)

JOHN, Hon Mrs (Jane Lesley); *née* Nicol; da of Alexander Douglas Ian Nicol, by his w, Baroness Nicol (Life Peeress); *m* 1984, Edward John, only s of J E John, of Margam, Port Talbot, W Glam; *Style*— Hon Mrs John

JOHN, Hon Mrs; Hon (Mary) Joan Fenella Hope; *née* Hope-Morley; da of 2 Baron Hollenden, JP (d 1977); *b* 1915; *m* 1, 1941 (m dis 1965), David Babington Smith, s of late Sir Henry Babington Smith, GBE, CH, KCB, CSI; 1 da; m 2, 1966, Geoffrey John; *Style*— The Hon Mrs John; Lime House, Kintbury, Newbury, Berks

JOHN, Maldwyn Noel; s of Thomas Daniel John (d 1944), of Pontypridd, Glamorgan, and Beatrice May, *née* Clare (d 1971); *b* 25 Dec 1929; *Educ* Pontypridd GS, Univ Coll Cardiff (BSc); *m* 27 June 1953, Margaret, *née* Cannell; 2 s (Steven Thomas b 1959, Paul David b 1962); *Career* Met Vickers Electrical Co Manchester 1950-59, Atomic Energy Estab UKAEA Winfrith 1959-63, chief engr and divnl mangr AEI/GEC Manchester 1963-69; Kennedy & Donkin Consulting Engrs: chief electrical engr 1969-72, ptnr 1972-87, chm 1987-; pres Inst of Electrical Engrs 1983-84, memb ct UWIST 1984-88, memb Overseas Projects Bd 1987-, bd dir Nat Inspection Cncl for Electrical Installation Contractors (NICEIC) 1988-; govr Broadwater County Secdy Sch Godalming Surrey; Freeman: City of London 1987, Worshipful Co of Engrs 1987; CEng 1966, FIEE 1969, MConsE 1973, FEng 1979, FIEEE 1985; *Books* Practical Diakoptics for Electrical Networks (co author 1969), Power Circuit Breakers Theory & Design (co author, first edn 1975, second edn 1982); *Recreations* golf; *Clubs* Bramley GC (Surrey); *Style*— M N John, Esq; Kennedy & Donkin Gp Ltd, Westbrook Mills, Godalming, Surrey GU7 2AZ (☎ 048 68 25900, fax 04868 25136, telex 859373 KDHO G)

JOHN, Richard; CBE (1969), JP (Glam 1969); s of Edward John (d 1947), and Catherine John (d 1928); *b* 5 June 1904; *Educ* Barry Sec Sch, Cardiff Tech Coll, Univ Coll Cardiff; *m* 1932, Bessie Louise, da of Walter John Dunn (d 1981); 1 s (David Roydon); *Career* slr 1938, special conslt Glan Constab 1938-52, county prosecuting sir Glam Constab 1938-52, county slr 1943-69, hon sec Lord Chllr's Advsy Ctee Glam 1953-69, clerk of the peace and county clerk Glam 1953-69, clerk South Wales Police Authy, 1969, chm Cncl and Fin Ctee The Univ of Wales Coll of Medicine 1956-88, fndr memb mgmnt ctee Tenovus Cancer (chm of trustees) 1966-88; memb ct of govrs Univ of Wales and Univ of Cardiff 1953-88, Erroll Cmmn reviewing liquor licensing laws of England & Wales 1971-72, memb bd Civic Trust for Wales, sr tstee Cardiff YMCA; OStJ 1965; OM (W Germany) 1963; Hon LLD Wales 1974; *Recreations* gardening, shooting, fishing; *Clubs* Cardiff & County; *Style*— Richard John Esq, CBE, JP; 22 Fairwater Rd, Llandaff, Cardiff CF5 2LD (☎ 0222 562891)

JOHN, Sir Rupert Godfrey; s of Donelley Westmore John (d 1951); *b* 19 May 1916; *Educ* St Vincent G S, London Univ (BA, DipEd), New York Univ; *m* 1937, Hepsy, da of Samuel Norris; 3 s, 1 da (and 1 s decd); *Career* barrister Gray's Inn; first asst master St Kitts/Nevis G S 1943, asst master St Vincent GS 1944-52, private law practice St Vincent 1952-58, magistrate Grenada WI 1958-60, acting attorney-gen Grenada 1960-62; human rights offr UN 1962-70, memb int team of observers Nigeria 1969-70, sr human rights offr 1970, govr St Vincent 1970-76; memb: Barclays Bank Int Ltd Policy Advsy Ctee (St Vincent) 1977-85, West India Ctee; special fellow to UN Inst of Trg and Res 1978-85, founded Assoc of Sr Citizens of St Vincent and The Grenadines; pres Caricare, Caribbean Inst for observance and protection human rights and democratic and humanitarian principles 1987-88; Caricare Human Rights Awards 1988; pres Caricare, Caribbean for observance and protection of human rights and democratic and humanitarian principle 1987; KStJ 1971; kt 1971;; *Recreations* reading, walking, swimming; *Clubs* Royal Commonwealth Soc; *Style*— Sir Rupert John; PO Box 677, Cane Garden, St Vincent, West Indies (☎ 809 4561500)

JOHN-MACKIE, Baron (Life Peer UK 1981); John Mackie; s of Maitland Mackie, OBE, farmer, and Mary, *née* Yull; er bro of Baron Mackie of Benshie and Sir Maitland Mackie, Lord-Lieut of Aberdeenshire; *b* 24 Nov 1909; *Educ* Aberdeen GS, N of Scotland Coll of Agric; *m* 1934, Jeannie Inglis, da of Robert Milne; 3 s, 2 da; *Career* sits as Labour Peer in Lords; farmer in Essex; MP (Lab) Enfield E 1959-74, jt parly sec Miny of Agric 1964-70; chm Forestry Commission 1976-79; oppn agriculture spokesman; *Style*— The Rt Hon the Lord John-Mackie; Harold's Park, Nazeing, Waltham Abbey, Essex (☎ 099 289 2202)

JOHNS, Brooke Elliot Mackelcan; s of Jack Elliot Mackelcan Johns (d 1969) and Janet Johns, *née* Price; *b* 20 Sept 1939; *Educ* Marlborough Coll; *m* 1965, Angela Christine (d 1986), da of Sir William Albert Fairbairn 5 Bt (d 1972); 2 s (Jeremy b 1967, Anthony b 1971); *Career* chartered accountant; *Recreations* skiing, sailing, travel, gardening; *Style*— Brooke Johns Esq; Marshcroft, Lime St, Eldersfield, Glos GL19 4NX (☎ 045 284 433)

JOHNS, David John; *b* 29 April 1931; *Educ* St Brendans Coll Bristol, Univ of Bristol (BSc, MSc), Loughborough Univ of Technol (PhD, DSc); *m* 27 March 1954, Sheila Jean, *née* Read; 1 da (Susan Mary Ann (Mrs Butler)); *Career* student apprentice (later tech offr section ldr) Br Aeroplane Co Ltd 1949-57, sr tech offr Sir W G Armstrong Whitworth A/C Ltd 1957-58, lectr Cranfield Inst of Technol 1958-63; Loughborough Univ of Technol 1964-83: reader, prof, head of dept of tport technol, dean of sch of engrg, sr pro vice-chllr; dir City Poly Hong Kong 1983-89; vice-chllr and princ Univ of Bradford 1989-; memb: (later chm) Aeronautical Res Cncl Dynamics Ctee 1970-80, (later vice pres and pres elect) cncl Inst of Acoustics 1979-83, (later chm) Environmental Pollution Advsy Ctee (Hong Kong) 1984-88, Vocational Trg Cncl (Hong Kong) 1984-89, Hong Kong Productivity Cncl 1984-89, cncl Hong Kong Inst of Engrs 1984-89; CEng 1968, FRAeS 1969, FIOA 1977, FCIT 1977, FHKIE 1984, FAeSI 1986; *Books* Thermal Stress Analyses (1965); *Recreations* walking, bridge, music; *Clubs* Hong Kong, Royal Hong Kong Jockey; *Style*— Prof David Johns; Vice Chancellor's Office, Univ of Bradford, West Yorks BD7 1DP (☎ 0274 733 466, fax 0274 305 340)

JOHNS, Helen Mary; da of Maurice Charles Johns, of Bradford-on-Avon, Wilts, and Sophie, *née* Rees; *b* 10 Sept 1948; *Educ* City of Bath Girls GS, Univ of Kent at Canterbury (BA); *Career* md Book Incentives Ltd; memb: Inst of Sales Promotion, Br Promotional Merchandise Assoc, Network; winner of Docklands Devpt Corpn Enterprise Award 1987; *Recreations* theatre, cinema, food and wine, music; *Clubs* St Katharine Yacht, Docklands Business; *Style*— Ms Helen Johns; 54 Manor Lane, London SE13 5QP (☎ 01 318 3085); Book Incentives Ltd, 519 Butlers Wharf Business Centre, 45 Curlew St, London SE1 2ND (☎ 01 378 6637)

JOHNS, Michael Stephen Mackelcan; s of Jack Elliot Mackelcan Johns (d 1968), Starveacres, Radlett, Herts, and Janet, *née* Price; *b* 18 Oct 1943; *Educ* Marlborough; *m* 1, 20 Sept 1968 (m dis 1975), Joanna Turner, *née* Gilligan; 2 s (Alexander b 16 Sept 1971, Toby b 1 Sept 1973); m 2, 10 March 1979, Gillian, da of Geoffrey Duckett White, of Perth, Western Aust; 1 da (Sophie b 2 Feb 1984); *Career* slr; ptnr Nicholson Graham & Jones 1973- (managing ptnr 1987-), non exec dir Normans Gp plc 1979-; memb: Law Soc, IOD; *Recreations* golf, cricket, gardening; *Clubs* MCC, St Georges Hill GC; *Style*— Michael Johns, Esq; 22 Bowerdean Street, London SW6 3TW (☎ 01 731 7607); 19-21 Moorgate, London EC2R 6AU (☎ 01 628 9151, fax 01 638 3102 telex 8811848)

JOHNS, Patricia Holly (Pat); da of W A H Harris, and V F Harris, *née* Chinnery; *b* 13 Nov 1933; *Educ* Blackheath HS, Girton Coll Cambridge (BA, MA), Hughes Hall Cambridge (Cert Ed); *m* 2 Aug 1958, Michael C.B Johns (d 1965), s of Alfred S Bedford Johns, of Exeter; 1 s (Paul b 1961), 1 da (Sarah b 1964); *Career* mathematics teacher: Cheltenham Ladies Coll 1957-58, Macclesfield HS 1958-60; St Albans HS: mathematics teacher 1966-70, head of mathematics and dir of studies 1970-75; sr mistress Gordonstoun Sch 1975-80, headmistress St Mary's Sch Wantage 1980-; lay reader 1979-; SHA, GSA; *Recreations* singing, corgis, travel; *Style*— Mrs Pat Johns; 3 Post Office Lane, Wantage, Oxon; St Mary's School, Wantage, Oxon (☎ 021 57 3571)

JOHNS, Peter Andrew; s of Lt John Francis, DSC, RNVR, of Porthcawl, and Megan, *née* Isaac; *b* 31 Dec 1947; *Educ* Bridgend GS, UCL (BSc); *m* 12 Aug 1985, Rosanne Helen Josephine, da of Capt William John Howard Slayter, RA, of Oxted, Surrey; 1 s (Jack b 1987); *Career* non-exec dir: Merchant Bank of Central Africa 1985-; dir NM Rothschild & Sons Ltd 1987-; ACIB 1975; *Recreations* golf, tennis, books; *Clubs* RAC; *Style*— Peter Johns, Esq; 56 Canonbury Park South, London N1 2JG (☎ 01 354 3570); New Ct, St Swithins Lane, London EC4P 4DU (☎ 01 280 5000, fax 01 280 5400, telex 888031)

JOHNS, Air Vice Marshall Richard Edward; CBE (1985 OBE 1978), LVO (1972);; s of Lt-Col Herbert Edward Johns, RM (d 1977), of Emsworth, Hants, and Marjory Harley, *née* Everett; *b* 28 July 1939; *Educ* Portsmouth GS, RAF Coll Cranwell; *m* 23 Oct 1965, Elizabeth Naomi Anne, da of Air Cdre Frederick John Manning (d 1988), of Eynsham, Oxford; 1 s (Douglas b 1972), 2 da (Victoria b 1970, Harriet b 1974); *Career* RAF, No 64 (F) Sqdn 1960-63, No 1417 (FR) Flt Aden 1965-67, flying instr duties 1968-71 (including tuition of HRH The Prince of Wales 1970-71), Staff Coll 1972, PSO/CINC NEAF 1973, No 3 (F) Sqdn as CO 1975-77, MOD Air Staff 1978-81, Stn Cdr and Harrier Force Cdr RAF Gutersloh 1982-84, RCDS 1985, SASO HQ RAF Germany 1986-88; SASO, HQ Strike Cmd 1989-; *Recreations* military history, rugby, cricket; *Clubs* RAF; *Style*— Air Vice-Marshal Richard Johns, CBE, OBE, LVO; c/o Lloyds Bank (R3), 6 Pall Mall, London SW1

JOHNSON; *see*: Campbell-Johnson

JOHNSON, Dr Adrian Mackey; CBE (1968); s of Dr A M Johnson (d 1922), of Sydney, and Mary Jane Flood (d 1970); *b* 19 Jan 1916; *Educ* St Ignatius' Coll Riverview, Sydney Univ; *m* 1942, Margaret Flood, da of Valentine Flood Nagle, of Albury, solicitor (d 1948); 2 s, 3 da (1 s decd); *Career* Capt AAMC in 25 Fd Regt; AIF 1940-42; consultant Hon Gp Capt 1944; dermatologist, univ lecturer in dermatology Sydney Univ 1966-76, hon physician and head dept of dermatology Royal Prince Alfred Hospital 1954-81; hon conslt RPAH 1981-; conslt dermatologist RAAF; chm Christian Childrens Fund of Australia; *Recreations* racing, bowls; *Clubs* University, Royal Sydney Golf, Univ & Sch (S&C); *Style*— Dr Adrian Johnson, Esq, CBE; 1B/5 Thornton St, Darling Point, NSW 2027; 149 Macaumrie St, Sydney 272991

JOHNSON, Alan Michael Borthwick; s of Dennis Daniel Borthwick Johnson, OBE (d 1976), of Calderstones, Liverpool, and Nora, *née* MacLeod; *b* 7 June 1944; *Educ* Liverpool Coll 1951-63, CCC Oxford (MA); *Career* called to the Bar Middle Temple (Wandsworth Scholar) 1971; Gray's Inn ad eundem 1973-; memb Criminal Bar Assoc; *Clubs* Oxford Society; *Style*— Alan Johnson, Esq; 1 Farm Place, London W8 7SX; 14 Gray's Inn Square, Gray's Inn, London WC1R 5JP (☎ 01 242 0858, fax 01 242 5434)

JOHNSON, Hon Mrs (Anne); *née* Robbins; da of Baron Robbins, CH, CB (Life Peer, d 1984), and Baroness Robbins, *qv*; *b* 16 Oct 1925; *Educ* UCL; *m* 1958, Christopher Johnson, *qv*; 1 s, 3 da; *Style*— The Hon Mrs Johnson; 39 Wood Lane, London N6 (☎ 01 340 4970)

JOHNSON, Prof Barry Edward; s of Edward Johnson (d 1964), of Burgess Hill, Sussex, and Evelyn May, *née* Bailey (d 1980); *b* 1 August 1937; *Educ* Epsom Co GS, Hobart State HS, Univ of Tasmania (BSc), Univ of Cambridge (PhD); *m* 1 Nov 1961 (m dis 1979), Jennifer Pat, da of Arthur Stuart Munday (d 1968), of Hitchin, Herts; 2 s (Martin b 1963, Adrian b 1966), 1 da (Susan b 1964); *Career* instr Univ of California Berkeley 1961-62, lectr Univ of Exeter 1963-65; Univ of Newcastle-upon-Tyne: lectr 1965-68, reader 1968-69, prof pure mathematics 1969-, dean faculty of sci 1986-89; visiting prof Univ of Yale New Haven USA 1970-71 (visiting lectr 1962-63); pres London Mathematical Soc 1980-82 (cncl memb 1975-78); govr Royal GS Newcastle 1987-; FRS 1978; *Books* Cohomology in Banach Algebras (1970); *Recreations* reading, travel; *Style*— Prof Barry Johnson; 12 Roseworth Crescent, Gosforth, Newcastle upon Tyne NE3 1NR (☎ 091 284 5363); Dept of Mathematics and Statistics, The Univ, Newcastle upon Tyne NE1 7RU (☎ 091 232 8511, fax 091 261 1182)

JOHNSON, Christopher Louis McIntosh; s of Donald McIntosh Johnson, MP for Carlisle 1955-64 (d 1978); *b* 12 June 1931; *Educ* Winchester, Magdalen Coll Oxford; *m* 1958, Hon Anne, *qv*; 1 s, 3 da; *Career* Capt RAEC; dir Financial Times 1972-76 (foreign ed 1965-67, managing ed 1967-70, dir business enterprises div 1971-72); econ advsr Lloyds Bank 1976-, visiting prof (in econs) Surrey Univ 1986-; *Books* Anatomy of UK Finance, North Sea Energy Wealth, Measuring the Economy; *Recreations* sailboarding, music; *Clubs* Overseas Bankers; *Style*— Christopher Johnson Esq; 39 Wood Lane, London N6 (☎ 01 340 4970)

JOHNSON, Colin Trevor; s of Richard Johnson (d 1986), of Eccles, Manchester, and Annie Evelyn, *née* Breakell; *b* 11 April 1942; *Educ* Worsley Techn Coll, Salford Sch of Art, Manchester Coll of Art; *Career* artist; one-man exhibitions incl: Monks Hall Museum and Art Gallery Eccles 1961 (1963, 1969, 1972, 1978), N W Arts Centre Manchester 1974, Victoria Gallery Harrogate 1975 and 1977, Granada TV 1968 (1969, 1973, 1976), RNCM 1974 (1978, 1987), Theatre Royal York 1976, Derby City Art Gallery 1980, Salt House Gallery St Ives Cornwall 1981 and 1984, Libertys London 1983, Barbican 1984, Harrogate Gallery 1986, Brewhouse Art Centre Tauton 1987, Buxton Art Gallery 1988; Bridgewater Arts Gallery 1989, Swinton Art Gallery 1969, 1972 and 1989, mixed exhibitions incl: Park Sq Gallery Leeds 1972-74, Manchester Acad and Manchester City Art Gallery 1976 (1982-89), Royal Acad Business Galleries 1983-85; public collections incl: BBC TV, Derby City Art Gallery, Lancs Libraries, Manchester Univ, Salford Univ, City of London, City of Manchester; artist-in-residence: Manchester Festival 1980, City of London Festival 1984, Wigan Int Jazz Festival 1986 and 1987, Int Nuclear Physics Conf 1986; cmmns: Granada TV 1968, BBC N W 1975, Royal Exchange Theatre Manchester 1978; dir: Swinton & Pendlebury Festival 1973, Bolton Festival 1979; memb ctee Friends of St Ives Cornwall, assoc memb Penwith Soc of Arts, hon friend Manchester Camerata Orchestra; memb Manchester Acad of Fine Arts; *Recreations* travelling, collecting books, tiles, jugs; *Style*— Colin Johnson, Esq; 27 Bedford Rd, St Ives, Cornwall TR26 1SP (☎ 0736 794 622)

JOHNSON, Colpoys Guy (Matt); s and h of Sir Peter Johnson, 7 Bt; *b* 13 Nov 1965; *Educ* Winchester, Kings Coll London (BA); *Career* banker Midland Montagu; FRGS; *Recreations* yachting, fly fishing; *Clubs* Royal Ocean Racing, RLYC;; *Style*— Colpoys Johnson, Esq; Dene End, Buckland Dene, Lymington, Hants SO41 9DT (☎ 0590 75921); No 1 Harbut Rd, London, SW11 2RA, (☎ 01 223 0352)

JOHNSON, David Gordon; s of Sidney Burnup Johnson, of Newcastle upon Tyne, and Pearl, *née* Jenkinson; *b* 13 Dec 1951; *Educ* Dame Allan's Boys' Sch, Newcastle Upon Tyne, Univ of Manchester (BSc); *m* 1, Lesley Annis Johnson (m dis 1986); 2 s (James Scott b 1981, Mark David b 1983); m 2, 17 May 1988, Judith Ann, da of Gerald Arthur Vernon Leaf, of Leeds; *Career* ptnr Duncan C Fraser and Co 1977, dir William M Mercer Fraser Ltd 1986; cncl memb Soc of Pension Conslts, memb pilot ctee AOPA (UK); Freeman: City of London 1989, Worshipful Co of Actuaries 1989; FIA 1976; *Recreations* private aviation, motor racing; *Clubs* Reform; *Style*— David G Johnson, Esq; 2 Aldenham Grove, Radlett, Herts; 8 Collingwood Crescent, Ponteland, Newcastle upon Tyne; William M Mercer Fraser Ltd, Telford Hse, 14 Tothill St, London (☎ 01 222 9121, fax 01 222 6140)

JOHNSON, David John Crump; s of Stanley Charles Johnson (d 1983), of Little Knoll, Dunsley Kinver, Stourbridge, West Midlands, and Mary, *née* Blumsom; *b* 10 Mar 1938; *Educ* King Edward V GS Stourbridge, Univ of Bristol; *m* 25 Aug 1962, Valerie Margaret, JP, da of Arthur Henry Heathlock Englefield, of 9 Walker Ave, Wollescote, Stourbridge; 3 da (Katherine Jane b 1966, Victoria Louise b 1968, Kirsty Valerie b 1972); *Career* CA 1962; articled clerk Agar Bates Neal & Co (now Deloitte Haskins & Sells) Birmingham 1958-62, Stanley C Johnson & Son Stourbridge 1962-; former pres: Wollaston Lawn Tennis Club 1977-85, Stourbridge Rotary Club 1978-79; FCA, memb Inst Taxation; *Recreations* lawn tennis, walking, literature; *Style*— David Johnson, Esq; Yew Tree House, Shenstone, Kidderminster, Worcs DY10 4BY (☎ 056 283 464; 22 Worcester St, Stourbridge, West Midlands DY8 1BH (☎ 0384 395380 or 372008, fax 0384 440468)

JOHNSON, Hon Mrs (Diana Gillian Amanda); *née* Pritchard; da of Baron Pritchard (Life Peer); *b* 1948; *Educ* Georgetown Univ, USA (BA) 1974; *m* 1, 1969 (m dis 1977), David Huntington Williams; 2 s; m 2, 1984, Harry Johnson, s of Henry Leslie Johnson, of Offchurch Bury, Warwicks; 2 d; *Career* writer, equestrian mangr, farmer; *Clubs* Lyford Cay (Bahamas), Pytchley Hunt, Warwicks Hunt; *Style*— The Hon Mrs Johnson; Red House Farm, Campion Hills, Royal Leamington Spa, Warwicks

JOHNSON, Donal Keith; s of Edmund Donald Johnson (d 1971), and Jean Marion, *née* Chapter (d 1970); *b* 11 June 1928; *Educ* Magdalen Coll Sch Oxford; *m* 8 Aug 1955, Hilary Anita, da of Capt Frank Smith (d 1938), of Stanhope Farm, Stanwell, Middx; 1 s (Neil b 1960), 1 da (Sarah b 1958); *Career* CA, sr ptnr Bryden Johnson and Co 1970- (ptnr 1958); FCA 1953; Liveryman Worshipful Co of Needlemakers 1969, Freeman City of London 1968; FCA 1953; *Recreations* golf; *Clubs* RAC; *Style*— Donal Johnson,

Esq; The Downe House, Ricketts Hill, Tatsfield, Westerham, Kent (tel: 0959 77318); Bryden Johnson and Co, Kings Parade, Lower Coombe Street, Croydon CRO 1AA (☎ 01 686 0255, fax 01 688 5620, telex 928110 BJCO G)

JOHNSON, Hon Elizabeth Ann Cynlais; da of Baron Evans of Claughton (Life Peer); *b* 1957; *Educ* BEd; *m* 18 March 1989, Ian Frederick Johnson; *Style*— Hon Elizabeth Johnson;

JOHNSON, Hon Mrs (Frances Ann); *née* Guest; da of 2 Viscount Wimborne, OBE, JP, DL; *b* 18 Nov 1942; *m* 1971, Ernest Johnson; *Style*— The Hon Mrs Johnson; 420 E 86th St, NYC, New York, USA

JOHNSON, Frank Robert; s of Ernest Johnson, and Doreen, *née* Skinner; *b* 20 Jan 1943; *Educ* Chartesey Secdy Sch Shoreditch, Shoreditch Secdy Sch; *Career* reporter: Walthamstow Post 1960-61, Walthamslow Guardian 1961-65, North Western Evening Mail 1965-66, Nottingham Evening Post and Guardian Journal 1966; asst Lobby corr Liverpool Daily Post 1966-68, lobby corr Liverpool Echo 1968-69, political staff Sun 1969-72, parly sketch writer and ldr writer Daily Telegraph 1972-79, columnist Now! Magazine 1979-81; The Times: parly sketch writer 1981-83, Paris diarist 1984, Bonn corr 1985-86, parly sketch writer 1986-87; assoc ed 1987; prin assoc ed Sunday Telegraph 1988; awards: Parly Sketch Writer of the Year 1977, Granada What the Papers Say 1977, Colunuist of the Year 1981, British Press 1981; *Recreations* opera, ballet; *Clubs* Beefsteak, Garrick; *Style*— Frank Johnson, Esq; 24a St Petersburgh Place, London W2 4LB; Sunday Telegraph, Peterborough Court at South Quay, 181 Marsh Wall, London E14 9SR (☎ 01 538 5000, fax, 01 538 1330, telex 22874 TELLDNG)

JOHNSON, Frederick Duncan John; OBE (1986); s of Frederick Johnson, BEM (d 1964), of Oak Hurst, Waterworks Road, Otterbourne, Hants, and Agnes Paton, *née* MacAlpine (d 1964); *b* 24 Sept 1932; *Educ* Peter Symonds' Sch Winchester, Univ of Southampton (BSc); *m* 11 Aug 1956, Ann Margaret, da of Bernard Bradley Bond Smyth (d 1986) of Duneside, Church Lane, Sutton on Sea, Lincs; 1 s (Stirling Duncan Arthur b 4 Jan 1958), 1 da (Sally Ann b 21 Aug 1962); *Career* motorway engr Surrey CC 1965-68, supt engr SE Rd Construction Unit Dept of Tport 1968-70, Co Surveyor Somerset CC 1975-(dep 1970-75); past sec Co Surveyors' Soc (centenary pres 1985-86); memb Street Works Advsy Ctee of Dept of Tport, FICE 1985, FIHT 1982, FBIM 1970, CEng; *Recreations* golf, sports, landscape gardening; *Clubs* RAC; *Style*— Frederick D J Johnson, Esq, OBE; County Hall, Taunton, Somerset (☎ 0823 55600)

JOHNSON, Harold Graham; s of Harold Johnson (d 1979) of Chatteris, Cambs, and Irene Hetherington, *née* Clowes (d 1988); *b* 11 Dec 1933; *Educ* March GS, Queen Mary Coll Univ of London (BSc), Imperial Coll Univ of London (DIC); *m* 5 Nov 1966, Jennifer Mary, da of Leonard Victor Harold Hazelton (d 1959), of St Albans, Herts; 2 s (Adrian b 1970, Philip b 1972); *Career* Nat Serv, Lt RE 1956-58; asst engr: Minsty of Works, Aldermaston 1954-56, asst engr Sir William Halcrow and Ptnrs 1958-61; engr Balfour Beatty (Tanzania and Nigeria) 1961-63, exec engr Uganda govt 1964-66, Sir William Halcrow and Ptnrs 1966-88 (assoc 1977, dir 1982), ptnr Halcrow Int Partnership 1983, ptnr The Halcrow Partnership 1988-; past memb : PCC (Holy Trinity Brompton, St Mary Beaconsfield, St Helen Abingdon), Abingdon Deanery Synod; former sec UNA Beaconsfield; cuidadano honorario San Pedro Sula Honduras 1975; CEng, FICE, FIWEM, CDipAF, FRSA; *Recreations* sailing, walking, gardening; *Style*— H Graham Johnson, Esq; Caledon, 23 Picklers Hill, Abingdon, Oxon OX14 2BB, (☎ 0235 20907); Burderop Park, Swindon, Wilts SN4 OQD, (☎ 0793 812479), fax 0793 812089, telex 44844 Halwil G

JOHNSON, Henry (Stuart); s of Hubert Johnson (d 1960), and Eva, *née* Webster; *b* 9 Nov 1945; *Educ* Abbotsholme Sch; *m* 9 Oct 1971, Bridget Jane, da of Sqn Ldr Dennis A Barry, of Sheffield; 1 s (Matthew b 1974), 1 da (Charlotte b 1976); *Career* md King, Taudevin & Gregson (Hldgs) Ltd; dir: Vaba Industries Ltd, Virtrifix Int Ltd, GTI (Hldgs) Ltd; commercial dir Mills Brothers (Sheffield) Ltd 1966-72, mktg dir Coldflow Ltd 1972-75; cncl memb CBI, memb Sheffield Univ Cncl, Tres Sheffield Univ; *Recreations* power boating, water skiing; *Style*— Stuart Johnson, Esq; 6 Slayleigh Lane, Sheffield S10 3RF (☎ 0742 754428); 39 Scotland St, Sheffield S3 7BT (☎ 0742 727107, telex 547359, fax 0742 754428)

JOHNSON, Hugh Eric Allan; s of Maj Guy Francis Johnson, CBE (d 1949), of London, and Grace Enid Marian, *née* Kittel; *b* 10 Mar 1939; *Educ* Rugby, King's Coll Cambridge (BA, MA); *m* 13 March 1965, Judith Eve, da of Col Antony Gibbons Grinling, MBE, MC(d 1982), of Dyrham, Glos; 1 s (Redmond b 1970), 2 da (Lucy b 1967, Kitty-Alice b 1973); *Career* staff writer Vogue and House & Gdn 1960-63, ed Wine & Food (sec Wine & Food Soc 1963-65), travel ed Sunday Times 1967 (wine correspondent 1962-67), ed Queen 1968-70, pres Sunday Times Wine Club 1973-, ed dir The Garden 1975-, gdn correspondent New York Times 1985-86; chm: Winestar Prodns Ltd, The Movie Business, The Hugh Johnson Collection Ltd; Wine conslt: Jardines Wine and Br Airways; films: How to Handle A Wine (video 1984), Wine - A Users Guide, Vintage - A History of Wine (with WGBH Boston and Channel 4 1989); churchwarden St James Gt Saling 1974-; *Books* Wine (1966 revised 1974), The World Atlas of Wine (1971 revised 1987, 1985), The International Book of Trees (1973 revised 1984), The California Wine book (with Bob Thompson 1976), Hugh Johnson's Pocket Wine Book (annually 1977-), The Principles of Gardening (1979 revised 1984), Understanding Wine (1980), Hugh Johnson's Wine Companion (1983 revised 1987), The Atlas of German Wines (1986), The Hugh Johnson Cellar Book (1986), The Wine Atlas of France (with Hubrecht Duijker 1987), The Story of Wine (1989); many articles on gastronomy, gardening, travel;; *Recreations* gardening, travel, pictures; *Clubs* Garrick; *Style*— Hugh Johnson; 73 St James's St, London SW1

JOHNSON, Hugh Stringer; s of Richard Stringer Johnson, CBE, TD (d 1981), of Medbourne Manor, Market Harborough, Leics, and Isabel Alice, *née* Hezlett; *b* 24 May 1939; *Educ* Sherborne, Gonville and Caius Coll Cambridge (MA, LLB); *m* 4 March 1967, Marie-Odile, da of Comte Antoine Tillette De Clermont-Tonnerre, of 5 Rue De Mouchy, Versailles; 2 s (Antony b 1967, Charles b 1971), 1 da (Marie-Caroline b 1969); *Career* admitted slr 1966, ptnr Biddle & Co London 1966-; Freeman City of London 1970, Liveryman Worshipful Co of Ironmongers 1970; *Style*— Hugh Johnson, Esq; 5 Lichfield Rd, Kew, Richmond, Surrey TW9 3JR (☎ 01 948 4518); 1 Allee Adrienne, Bois De La Chaize, Noimoutier-En-L'Ile, France; 1 Gresham St, London EC2 (☎ 01 606 9301)

JOHNSON, Air Vice Marshal James Edgar; CB (1965), CBE (1960, DSO and two Bars 1943, 1944, DFC 1941, and Bar 1943); s of Alfred Edward Johnson (d 1953), and Beatrice May Rossell (d 1978); *b* 9 Mar 1915; *Educ* Loughborough GS, Nottingham Univ; *m* 14 Nov 1942 (m dis), Pauline Ingate; 2 s (Michael James Barrie b 1944, Christopher b 1945); *Career* Air Offr cmd Middle East 1963-60 (ret 1966); DL Leicestershire; dir: Aircraft Equipment (Int) Ltd, Westminster Scaffolding Ltd; Legion of Merit (USA), DFC (USA), Air Medal (USA), Legion d'Honneur (France), Order of Leopold (Belgium), Croix de Guerre (Belgium); *Recreations* fishing & writing; *Clubs* RAF; *Style*— Air Vice Marshal James Johnson, CB, CBE, DSO, DFC; The Stables, Hargate Hall, Buxton, Derbyshire (☎ 0298 871522); Astra House, Moss Lane, Bramhall, Stockport, Cheshire (☎ 061 440 9696)

JOHNSON, Sir John Rodney; KCMG (1988, CMG 1980); s of Edwin Done Johnson, OBE (d 1967), of Kendal, Cumbria, and Florence Mary, *née* Clough (d 1980); *b* 6 Sept 1930; *Educ* Manchester GS, Oxford Univ (BA 1954, MA 1955); *m* 11 Sept 1956, Jean Mary, da of Ernest Lewis (d 1949), of Manor Farm, Eyton; 3 s (Nicholas b 1957, Charles b 1962, Edward b 1967), 1 da (Julia b 1959); *Career* 2 Lt RA (nat serv) 1949-51; HM Overseas Civil Service 1955-64, dist offr later dist cmmr Kenya; HM Diplomatic Service 1966-, 1 Sec FCO 1966-69, Head of Chancery, British Embassy, Algiers 1969-72, Dep High Cmmr Barbados 1972-74, Political Counsellor British High Cmmn Nigeria 1975-78, Amb to Chad and Head of W African Dept FCO (concurrently) 1978-80, British High Cmmr to Zambia 1980-84, Asst Under Sec of State (Africa) 1984-86; British High Cmmr to Kenya 1986-; memb ctee of Vice-Chancellors and Principals of UK Univs 1964-65 (sr administrative asst); memb Cncl Royal African Soc; *Recreations* climbing, travel in remote places, tennis; *Clubs* Travellers', Muthaiga Country, Mombasa, Climbers'; British High Commission, Box 30465, Nairobi, Kenya (☎ 010254 2 335944)

JOHNSON, Kenneth Walford; s of Edward Stanley Johnson (d 1974), and Esma Vera May Johnson (d 1982); *b* 21 Nov 1921; *Educ* Merchant Taylors' London Univ (LLB); *m* 15 Oct 1952, Nerys Gwendolen (d 1985), da of Dr Richard Tudor Edwards (d 1971), of Stanmore; 2 da (Janet b 1955, Katharine b 1958); *Career* WW II RAF (Flying Offr) 1941-46; taxation specialist; dir cos in Robert Luff Gp 1968-, Moor Park (1958) Ltd 1981-; CA; *Recreations* golf, bridge, listening to music; *Clubs* Moor Park Golf, Sandy Lodge Golf; *Style*— Kenneth Johnson, Esq; 97 Wolsey Road, Moor Park, Northwood, Middx HA6 2ER (☎ 09274 24367)

JOHNSON, Michael Francis George; s of Dr Walter James Johnson (d 1979), of Great Witley, Worcester, and Phyllis Lucy, *née* Hayward (d 1979); *b* 26 Mar 1942; *Educ* Shrewsbury Sch, Insead, Fontainebleau (MBA); *m* 1, 10 April 1971 (m dis 1983), Jose Marie Lucie Simone, da of Dr Alfred Viau (d 1968), of Port Au Prince, Haiti; 2 s (Benjamin b 1974, Jeremy b 1982), 1 da (Alix b 1976); m2, 1 Feb 1984, Jane Elizabeth da of John Merrick, of Stedham, Midhurst, W Sussex; 1 s (Oliver b 1985); *Career* CA 1966, md Synkin SA Brussels 1973-78; dir: ERA Gp plc 1981-87, Surfachem Gp plc 1987-; fin dir Broad Street Gp plc 1986-88; CHM: chm: Chiltern Engrg Ltd 1986-, W Notting Ltd 1988, Dudes Clothing Ltd 1988; vice chm Octavia Hill & Rowe Housing Assoc; *Recreations* tennis, cross country running; *Style*— Michael Johnson, Esq; Bassett House, Claverton, Bath; 9 Needham Road, London W11 (☎ 01 229 5423); 44 hanover St, Liverpool L1 4AA (☎ 051 708 7323, fax 051 708 5381, car telephone 0860 338 187)

JOHNSON, Michael Ross; s of Myron Johnson (d 1972), of Delphi, Indiana, USA, and Eileen Rahilly Johnson (d 1975); *b* 23 Nov 1938; *Educ* San Jose State Coll (BA), Columbia Univ NY; *m* 28 May 1966, Jacqueline, da of Joseph Zimbardo; 3 da (Stephanie, Raphaëlle, Delphine); *Career* editorial staff Hayward Daily Review 1960-61; The Associated Press: Corr Charleston W Virginia 1962-63, ed NY 1964-66, Corr Moscow 1967-71; bureau chief McGraw-Hill World News Paris 1971-76 (dir 1976-82), ed in chief Int Mgmnt 1982-; memb: American Soc of Magazine Ed, Paris America Club, Overseas Press Club; *Recreations* piano, weight lifting, juggling flaming torches; *Clubs* Wig and Pen; *Style*— Michael Johnson, Esq; Int Mgmt, 34 Dover St, London W1X 4BR

JOHNSON, Michael Sloan; s of Maj Harold Bell Johnson, TD, TA (Res) (d 1975), and Jean Louise *née* Sloan; *b* 3 June 1947; *Educ* Upper Canada Coll Toronto, St Andrews Scots Sch Buenos Aires Argentina, Trinity Coll Cambridge (BA, LLB, MA, LLM); *m* 27 July 1972, Judith Mary, da of Arthur Lawton, of Crewe, Cheshire; 1 s (Matthew Richard b 7 Sept 1979), 1 da (Rosalind Mary b 5 Nov 1980); *Career* barr Lincoln's Inn 1971, memb Northern circuit 1972-, Chancery practitioner Manchester 1972-; Churchwarden St Mary's Parish Church Hawkshaw Bury Lancs 1986-; pres Cambridge Univ Law Soc 1969, memb Ecclesiastical Law Soc 1988-; *Recreations* music, modern languages, wine; *Clubs* Portico Library Manchester; *Style*— Michael Johnson, Esq; 7 Troutbeck Close, Hawkshaw, Bury, Lancs BL8 4LJ (☎ 020 488 4088); Crown Sq Chambers, 1 Deans Ct, Crown Sq, Manchester M3 3HA (☎ 061 833 9801, fax 061 835 2483, Document Exchange 14326 Manchester)

JOHNSON, Lt Col Neil Anthony; TD (1986); s of Anthony Johnson, of Glamorganshire, and Dilys Mabel Vera, *née* Smith; *b* 13 April 1949; *Educ* Canton Sch Cardiff, RMA Sandhurst; *m* 1971, Judith Gail, da of Dr Ian Ferguson (d 1978), of Cardiff; 3 da (Sarah b 1973, Amanda b 1975, Victoria b 1977); *Career* Comd Offr 1987-88 4 Bn The Royal Green Jackets (on secondment from Jaguar Cars Ltd 1982-87); dir Jaguar Cars Ltd 1977-82, exec dir Br Leyland Ltd; Freeman City of London, Liveryman Worshipful Co of Coach Makers and Coachharness Makers; FIMI, MInstM, MBIM; *Recreations* shooting, reading, riding, farming; *Clubs* Army and Navy, RA, Royal Green Jackets; *Style*— Lt-Col Neil Johnson, TD; Hillhampton Farm, Great Witley, Worcester (☎ 029 921 896604); 56 Davies St, Mayfair (☎ 01 629 3674)

JOHNSON, Nevil; s of Geoffrey Enoch Johnson (d 1962), of Darlington, and Doris, *née* Thompson, MBE; *b* 6 Feb 1929; *Educ* Queen Elizabeth GS Darlington, Univ Coll Oxford (BA, MA); *m* 29 June 1957, Ulla, da of Dr Peter van Aubel, Distinguished Serv Cross of Fed Repub of Germany (d 1964), of Dusseldorf; 2 s (Peter b 4 June 1961, Christopher b 3 Oct 1964); *Career* Nat Serv Army REME 1947-49; admin class Home Civil Serv 1952-62 (princ minys: supply, housing, local govt); lectr politics Univ of Nottingham 1962-66, sr lectr politics Univ of Warwick 1966-69; reader comparative study of insts and professorial fell Nuffield Coll Univ of Oxford 1969-, hon ed pub admin journal of Royal Inst Pub Admin 1967-81, memb Econ and Social Res Cncl 1981-87, pt/t memb Civil Serv Cmmn 1982-85; chm: bd Faculty of Social Studies Univ of Oxford 1976-78, Study of Parl Gp 1984-87; town cncllr Abingdon 1976-78; memb Political Studies Assoc; *Books* Parliament & Administration: the Estimates Committee 1945-65 (1966), Government in the Federal Republic of Germany (1973 and 1983), In Search of the Constitution (1977 and 1980), The Limits of Political Science (1989); *Recreations* jogging, swimming; *Clubs* Oxford and Cambridge; *Style*— Nevil Johnson,

Esq; 2 Race Farm Cottages, Race Farm Lane, Kingston Bagpuize, Oxon (☎ 0865 820777); Nuffield Coll, Oxford

JOHNSON, Hon (Patricia Mary); *née* French; da of late 6 Baron De Freyne; *b* 1917; *m* 1941, Reginald Johnson (d 1958); 1 s, 1 da; *Style*— The Hon Mrs Johnson; 4, Linley Court, Rouse Gardens, SE21

JOHNSON, Paula Joan; da of Maj Grosvenor Marson Johnson (d 1981), and Diana Margery Joan, *née* Webb; *b* 12 Sept 1953; *Educ* Atherley C of E Church Sch Southampton, Univ of Exeter (BA); *m* 20 April 1985, Lance Hamilton, s of John Harold Poynter, of Castillon Du Gard, Remoulins, Gard, France; *Career* asst literary ed Now! Magazine 1979-81, asst literary ed Mail on Sunday 1982-83, literary ed Mail on Sunday 1983-; *Recreations* singing, travel; *Clubs* Royal London Yacht, Lansdowne; *Style*— Miss Paula Johnson; Donnington, nr Newbury, Berks; Billing Place, London; Northcliffe Ho, Tudor St, London EC4Y 0JA (☎ 01 353 6000, fax 01 353 1866)

JOHNSON, Peter Alec Barwell; s of Oscar Ernest Johnson (d 1968), of Rippington Manor, Great Gransden, Cambridgeshire, and Marjorie, *née* Barwell; *b* 26 July 1936; *Educ* Uppingham; *m* 3 July 1965, Gay Marilyn, da of Douglas Bennington Lindsay, of 27 Ave de Bude, Geneva, Switzerland; 2 da (Juliet b 1966, Annabel b 1970); *Career* tstee and fndr: The Br Sporting Art Tst Ctee of the World of Watercolours and Drawing Fair, East Anglian Ctee of the Historic Houses Assoc; chm and md Oscar & Peter Johnson Ltd, vice-chm Cromwell Museum, patron of the Art Project for Addenbrooke's Hosp; cncl memb: Br Antique Dealers Assoc 1970-80, Kensington & Chelsea C of C Ctee of West London Family Serv Unit; guide Chelsea Physic Garden; chm: Cleaner Royal Borough, Hans Town Ward Cons 1969-72; br delegate Conseil Internationale de la Chasse; *Books* The Nasmyth Family (with E Money 1977); *Recreations* gardening, riding, reading; *Clubs* Bucks, Hurlingham; *Style*— Peter Johnson, Esq; 1 The Little Boltons, London SW10 (☎ 01 373 7038); Rippington Manor, Great Gransden, Cambridge; Oscar & Peter Johnson Ltd, Lowndes Lodge Gallery, 27 Lowndes St, London SW1X 9HY (☎ 01 235 6464, fax 01 823 1057, car 0860 335980)

JOHNSON, Peter Charles; s of William Arthur Johnson, of 55 Norrice Lea, London N2 and Suzanne Renee, *née* Roubitschek; *b* 12 Nov 1950; *Educ* Merchant Taylors Sch Crosby, Pembroke Coll, Cambridge (MA); *m* 27 July 1974, Judith Anne, da of Vincent Larvan of Oxford Court, Trafalgar Road, Southport; 2 s (Matthew b 1980, Elliot b 1982), 2 da (twins Charlotte, Sophie b 1987); *Career* appt Herbert Smith and Co 1973-75, slr 1975, sr ptnr Alexander Johnson; Freeman City of London, Liveryman Worshipful Co of Distillers 1978-; memb Law Soc; *Recreations* sailing; *Clubs* Wig and Pen; *Style*— Peter Johnson, Esq; 12 Wallace Road, London N1 (☎ 01 987 5611); Scott House, Admirals Way, South Quay, Isle of Dogs, London E14 (☎ 01 538 5621, fax 01 538 2442)

JOHNSON, Sir Peter Colpoys Paley; 7 Bt (GB 1755), of New York, North America; s of Lt-Col Sir John Johnson, 6 Bt, MBE (d 1975); *b* 26 Mar 1930; *Educ* Wellington Coll, RMC of Science Shrivenham; *m* 1, 1956, (m dis 1972), Clare, da of Dr Nigel Bruce; 1 s, 2 da; m 2, 1973, Caroline Elisabeth, da of Wing Cdr Sir John Hodsoll, CB (d 1971); 1 s; *Heir* s, Colpoys Guy Johnson; *Career* RA 1949-61 (Capt); publisher; dir Nautical Publishing Co Ltd 1971-81, publisher nautical books Macmillan London Ltd 1981-86, author and consultant editor 1986-; *Books* Ocean Racing and Offshore Yachts (1970 and 1972), Boating Britain (1973), Guinness Book of Yachting Facts and Feats (1975), Guinness Guide to Sailing (1981), This is Fast Cruising (1986), Encyclopedia of Yachting (1989), and 3 reference works; *Recreations* sailing, DIY; *Clubs* Royal Yacht Squadron, Royal Ocean Racing, Royal Lymington Yacht; *Style*— Sir Peter Johnson, Bt; Dene End, Buckland Dene, Lymington, Hampshire SO41 9DT (☎ 0590 75921, fax 0590 72885)

JOHNSON, Brig Peter Dunbar; s of Dr P Dunbar Johnson (d 1984), of Tapshaw, Male Hill, St Leonards-on-Sea, Sussex, and Barbara Leigh, *née* Hutton; *b* 15 April 1931; *Educ* Sherborne, RMA Sandhurst, Staff Coll (psc), Jt Servs Staff Coll (jssc), Royal Coll of Defence (rcds);; *m* 1961, Marthe Marie Eugenie, da of Marquis Yvés de Simon de Palmas (d 1975), of LàRaterie, Corbery, Loches, France; 3 s Mark, Stephen, Paul); *Career* cmmnd Royal Sussex Regt 1951, CO 5 Queens 1971-73; dep dir Manning 1981-84; gen sec Off Assoc 1984-; ADC to HM The Queen 1983-; *Recreations* golf, ski-ing, gardening; *Clubs* Army & Navy, Royal St George's (Sandwich); *Style*— Brig P D Johnson; Homestall, Doddington, Kent ME9 0HF (☎ 079 586 212); Offs Assocn, 48 Pall Mall, London SW1

JOHNSON, Peter Lincoln; s of Lincoln Ernest Johnson (d 1949), of Birstall, Leics, and Lilian Gertrude, *née* Pearce; *b* 12 June 1943; *Educ* Loughborough GS; *m* 1 June 1982, Lynne Marie, da of Harry Westwell of Lanzarote, Canary Islands; *Career* creative direction on advertising campaigns: Jensen Motor Cars 1964, Schweppes 1966-68, Jaeger 1968-70, Bally Shoes 1968-70, Barratt Developments 1971-83, Dixons 1984-86, NE Electricity 1984-87, English Estates 1988-, Cameron Hall Devpt 1988-; *Recreations* music, walking, cookery; *Clubs* The Sloane Club; *Style*— Peter Johnson, Esq; The Mill, Black Hall Mill, Steel, Hexham, Northumberland NE47 OLF (☎ 043473 432); Redheads Advertising Ltd, 23 Quayside, Newcastle upon Tyne NE1 3NX (☎ 091 232 1272)

JOHNSON, Rex Sutherland; s of Adam Sutherland Johnson (d 1950), and Grace Elizabeth, *née* Bedwell (d 1988); *b* 24 August 1928; *Educ* Royal HS Edinburgh, George Heriots Sch Edinburgh (Dip Arch); *m* 24 Aug 1957, Betty Elsie, da of Herbert Charles Manning (d 1974), of Witham, Essex; 2 s (Mark Sutherland b 1958, Michael Charles b 1960); *Career* RN 1947-48; sr architect TP Bennett & Son London 1946-61, jr ptnr Oliver Law & Ptnrs London 1961-63, ptnr Ronald Ward & Ptnrs London 1963-, dir Ronald Ward International Ltd 1980-; cncl memb London C of C and Indust 1976-, former chm Platt Cons Soc Kent 1976-79, sr vice pres United Ward Club of the City of London 1988, former pres and rotarian Westminster and Pimlico Rotary Club; Freeman of the City of London 1969, jr Warden Guild of Freeman City of London 1988, Liveryman Worshipful Co of Carmen, Liveryman Worshipful Co of Woolmen (ct memb); FRIBA 1968, FCIArb 1971; *Recreations* golf, photography, architecture, travel; *Clubs* City Livery, Caledonian; *Style*— Rex Johnson, Esq; 'Whitepines', Longmill Lane, Crouch, Nr Sevenoaks, Kent TN15 8QB; Ronald Ward & Partners, 29 Chesham Place, Belgrave Square, London SW1X 8HD (☎ 01 235 3361)

JOHNSON, Richard Keith; s of Keith Holcombe Johnson (d 1972), of Essex, and Frances Louisa Olive, *née* Tweed (d 1962); *b* 30 July 1927; *Educ* Parkfield Sch, Felsted, RADA; *m* 1, 9 Feb 1957 (m dis 1964), Sheila, da of Herbert Sweet (d 1988), of London; 1 s (Jervis b 1959), 1 da (Sorel b 1961); m 2, 15 March 1965 (m dis 1966), (Marilyn Pauline) Kim Novak of USA; m 3, 2 July 1982, Marie Louise, *née* Norlund, of London; 1 s (Nicholas b 1979), 1 da (Jennifer b 1984); *Career* served RN (supply asst HM Yacht Victoria and Albert 1945-48; actor and producer; first stage appearance Hamlet Opera House Manchester 1944; major roles incl: Marius Tertius in The First Victoria 1950, Pierre in The Madwoman of Chaillot 1951, Demetrius in A Midsummers Night's Dream 1951, George Phillips in After my Fashion 1952, Beauchamp Earl of Warwick in The Lark 1955, Laertes in Hamlet 1955, Jack Absolute in The Rivals 1956, Lord Plynlimmon in Plaintiff in a Pretty Hat 1956; RSC 1957-62 roles incl: Orlando in As You Like It, Mark Anthony in Julius Caesar, Leonatus in Cymbeline, Ferdinand in The Tempest, Romeo in Romeo and Juliet, Sir Andrew Agvecheek in Twelfth Night, title role in Pericles, Don Juan in Much Ado About Nothing; National Theatre 1975-78 roles incl: Charles in Blithe Spirit, Pinchwife in the Country Wife, Pilate in The Passion, title-role in The Guardsman; UK tour Death Trap 1982, first film appearance in Captain Horatio Hornblower 1950; films incl: Never So Few 1959, The Haunting 1963, The Pumpkin Eater 1964, Operation Crossbow 1965, Khartoum 1966, Deadlier than the Male 1966, Hennessy 1975; first TV appearance 1949; leading roles in TV prodns incl: Rembrandt, Anthony and Cleopatra, Claudius in Hamlet, The Member for Chelsea, Cymberline; recent TV films incl A Man for All Seasons and Voice of the Heart 1988; prodr of films incl: The Biko Inquest, Serjeant Musgrave's Dance, The Playboy of the Western World, Old Times, Turtle Diary, Castaway, The Lonely Passion of Judith Hearne; fndr chm and it chief exec Utd Br Astists 1982- memb cncl BAFTA 1976-78;; *Books* Hennessy (original story for film 1974); *Recreations* gardening, music, travel; *Style*— Richard Johnson, Esq; 2 Stokenchurch St, London SW6 3TR (☎ 736 5920)

JOHNSON, Hon Mr Justice Robert Lionel; s of Edward Harold Johnson (d 1986), and Ellen Lydiate Johnson, of Surrey; *b* 9 Feb 1933; *Educ* Watford GS, LSE (LLB); *m* 1957, Linda Mary, da of Charles William Bennie (d 1975), of Durham; 1 s (Robert b 1968), 2 da (Melanie b 1961, Edwina b 1962); *Career* barr Grays Inn 1957, rec Crown Ct 1977, QC 1978, memb Bar Cncl 1980-88 (vice-chm 1987, chm 1988), High Ct Judge (Family Div) 1989-; memb nat exec ctee and tstee Cystic Fibrosis Res Tst 1964-, hon sec Int Cystic Fibrosis (Mucoviscidosis) Assoc 1984-89; *Recreations* gardening, charitable work; *Style*— Hon Mr Justice Robert Johnson; Royal Cts of Justice, Strand, London WC2A 2LL

JOHNSON, Sir Robin Eliot; 7 Bt (UK 1818), of Bath; s of Maj Percy Eliot Johnson (d 1962), and kinsman, Sir Victor Johnson, 6 Bt (d 1986); *b* 1929; *Educ* St John's Coll Johannesburg; *m* 1954, Barbara Alfreda, da of late Alfred T Brown, of Germiston, Transvaal; 1 s, 2 da; *Style*— Sir Robin Johnson, Bt

JOHNSON, Sir Ronald Ernest Charles; CB (1961), JP (Edinburgh 1972); s of Ernest Johnson (d 1965); *b* 3 May 1913; *Educ* Portsmouth GS, St John's Coll Cambridge (MA); *m* 1938, Elizabeth Gladys Nuttall; 2 s (and 1 s decd); *Career* served WW II: Sub Lt (special) RNVR, Eastern Theatre; entered Scottish Off 1935; sec: Scottish Home and Health Dept 1963-72 (under-sec 1956-62), Cmmns for Scotland 1972-78; memb: Scottish Records Advsy Cncl 1975-81, Ctee on Admin of Sheriffdoms 1981-82; chm Fire Serv Res and Trg Tst 1976-89; pres: Edinburgh Bach Soc 1973-86; kt 1970; *Recreations* church organ; *Style*— Sir Ronald Johnson, CB, JP; 14 Eglinton Crescent, Edinburgh, Scotland EH12 5DD (☎ 031 337 7733)

JOHNSON, Stanley Patrick; s of Wilfred Johnson, and Irene Johnson; *b* 18 August 1940; *Educ* Sherborne, Exeter Coll Oxford (MA); *m* 1, 1963 (m dis 1979) Charlotte Offlow Fawcett; 3 s (Alexander, Leo, Joseph), 1 da (Rachel); m 2, 1981, Mrs Jennifer Kidd; 1 s (Maximilian), 1 da (Julia); *Career* on staff of Int Planned Parenthood Fedn London 1971-73; consultant to UN Fund of Population Activities 1971-73; head of Prevention of Pollution and Nuisances Div EEC 1973-77; advsr to head of Environment and Consumer Protection Service EEC 1977-79; MEP (EDE) Jow and E Hants 1979-84; Environmental Advsr to EEC Cmmn Brussels; Newdigate Prize for poetry, 1962; Greenpeace Prize 1984; RSPCA Richard Martin Award 1982; *Books* Life Without Birth (1970), The Green Revolution (1972) The Population Problem (1973), The Politics of the Environment (1973), Antarctica - Last Great Wilderness (1984), World Population and the United Nations (1988); *Novels* Gold Drain (1967), Panther Jones for President (1968), God Bless America (1974), The Doomsday Deposit (1980), The Marburg Virus (1982), Tunnel (1984), The Commissioner (1987), Dragon (1989); *Recreations* writing, travel; *Clubs* Savile; *Style*— Stanley Johnson, Esq,; West Nethercote, Winsford, Minehead, Somerset

JOHNSON, Timothy Charles; s of John Arthur Johnson, of Wakefield, and Louis Jessie, *née* Hewitt; *b* 10 Nov 1945; *Educ* Fakenham GS; *m* 25 March 1972, Elizabeth Mary, da of Ben Blake (d 1977); 1 s (William Timothy b 12 March 1978); *Career* architect: own practice 1971-88; property developer: dir Mand Developments Ltd, sole proprietor Jexin Properties, ptnr Kenwood Developments; past chm Holt Round Table; *Recreations* game shooting, squash, swimming, weight training, skiing, wine; *Clubs* Holt 41, Aylsham Squash; *Style*— Timothy C Johnson, Esq; Branksome House, 166 St Clements Hill, Norwich, Norfolk NR3 4DG (☎ 0603 415068); Apartment 120, Les Cardibes Avenue, Chevalier D'Alphonse, Le Cap d'agde, France; 35 Whiffler Rd, Norwich NR3 2AW (☎ 0603 415068, 485376, fax 0603 787496, car tel 0860 200994)

JOHNSON, Victor Horace (Johnnie); s of late Herbert Johnson; *b* 14 May 1920; *Educ* Handsworth GS, Birmingham Sch of Architecture; *m* 1972, Gillian Margaret, *née* Longmore; 2 s, 1 da, 2 step s, 1 step da; *Career* chartered builder; md Herbert Johnson Ltd 1946-61; chm: Page-Johnson Builders Ltd 1961-72, West European Building Corp Ltd 1969-78; dir Bovis Ltd 1972-74; chm Page Johnson Homes Ltd 1972-; fndr: The Johnnie Johnson Tst 1961-, The Johnnie Johnson Adventure Tst/ Youth Afloat 1972-; *Recreations* flying, sailing, (yacht 'British Maid'), forestry, farming; *Clubs* RAF, Lloyd's Yacht, Royal Dart Yacht, Royal Perth Yacht (W Australia); *Style*— Victor Johnson, Esq; Elmdon House, Elmdon Park, Solihull, West Midlands (☎ 021 743 5340); Farthings, Beacon Rd, Kingswear, Dartmouth, Devon (☎ 080 425 577); 5 Vervain Way, Riverton, Perth, WA 6155 (☎ 457 4789)

JOHNSON, Capt William Jefferson; OBE (1965), MVO (1962); s of Lancelot Johnson (d 1953), of Workington, Cumbria, and Janet, (*née* Muir (d 1959); *b* 13 August 1909; *Educ* Workington GS; *m* 1, 29 Dec 1938 (m dis 1950), Marjorie Claire, *née* Wigglesworth; 2 s (Graeme b 1941, Neil b 1945); m 2, 21 Sept 1950, Wendy Mhairi, da of John McNicol (d 1954); 1 da (Jean b 1953); *Career* pilot III (F) Sqdn 1931-35, flying instr No 4 FTS 1936-38, transfer to reserve 1939, recalled with VR cmmn as flying instr Desford and Kingstown Carlisle 1940, test pilot RAF Silloth, released to civil aviation 1942; assoc Airways Jt Ctee Liverpool 1942; Scottish Airways: Capt and flight mangr 1946-53, mangr flight ops trg 1953-74 chm IATA Flight Crew trg ctee 1967-74,cmd Royal flight to S America 1962; master Air Pilot Certificate 1953; memb: Rotary 1966-87, London Diocesan Synod 1976-80, Malcolm Sargent Festival choir, Woking Choral Soc; sec Samaritans Weybridge branch 1977-81, steward and guide Guildford Cathedral 1986-; Freeman City of London, Liveryman Worshipful Co Air Pilots and Air Navigators 1957; FCIT 1964; *Recreations* mountaineering, music, choral singing; *Clubs* Royal Air Force; *Style*— Capt William Johnson, OBE, MVO; Rivey Lodge, 94 Old Woking Rd, West Byfleet, Surrey KT 14 6HU (☎ 09323 43 164)

JOHNSON SMITH, Sir Geoffrey; DL, MP (Cons Wealden 1983-); s of J Johnson Smith; *b* 16 April 1924; *Educ* Charterhouse, Lincoln Coll Oxford; *m* Jeanne Pomeroy; 2 s, 1 da; *Career* WWII Capt RA 1942-47 (UK, Belgium, India); BBC TV 1953-54 and 1955-59; memb LCC 1955-58; MP (Cons): Holborn and St Pancras South 1959-64, East Grinstead 1965-1983; PPS BOT and Miny Pensions 1960-63, opposition whip 1965, a vice-chm Cons Party 1965-71, parly under-sec of state for Def 1971-72, parly sec CSD 1972-74; former memb IBA gen advsy cncl; memb: exec 1922 Ctee 1979-, (vice chm 1988); military ctee N Atlantic Assembly 1981- (chm 1985, ldr of Br delgn to NAA 1987-), bd LWT (Hldgs) 1982-; govr British Film Inst 1981-87; vice chm Cons Defence Ctee, (chm 1988); chm Thames Salmon Tst 1987; kt 1982; *Recreations* fishing, tennis; *Clubs* Travellers'; *Style*— Sir Geoffrey Johnson Smith, DL, MP; House of Commons, London SW1 (☎ 01 219 4158)

JOHNSON-FERGUSON, Ian Edward; s and h of Sir Neil Johnson-Ferguson, 3 Bt, TD, JP, DL, *qv*; *b* 1 Feb 1932; *Educ* Ampleforth, Trinity Coll Cambridge (BA), Imperial Coll London (DIC); *m* 9 April 1964, Rosemary Teresa, yr da of Cecil John Whitehead, of The Old House, Crockham Hill, Edenbridge, Kent; 3 s (Mark Edward, b 14 Aug 1965, Paul Duncan b 20 Aug 1966, Simon Joseph b 23 July 1967); *Style*— Ian Johnson-Ferguson, Esq

JOHNSON-FERGUSON, Lt-Col Sir Neil Edward; 3 Bt (UK 1906), of Springkell, Co Dumfries, Kenyon, Newchurch-in- Culcheth, Co Palatine of Lancaster, and Wiston, Co Lanark; TD, JP (Dumfriesshire 1954), DL (Dumfriesshire 1957); s of Col Sir Edward Alexander James Johnson-Ferguson, 2 Bt, TD, JP, DL (d 1953), and Hon Elsie Dorothea, *née* McLaren (d 1972), da of 1 Baron Aberconway; *b* 2 May 1905; *Educ* Winchester, Trin Coll Camb (BA); *m* 20 Jan 1931, Sheila Marion (d 1985), er da of Col Herbert Swynfen Jervis, MC (d 1965), of Tilford, Surrey; 4 s (Ian Edward *qv*, Christopher Charles b 14 April 1933, Michael Herbert JP b 27 Sept 1934, Nicholas Swynfen b 28 Dec 1938); *Heir* s, Ian Edward Johnson-Ferguson, *qv*; *Career* RAE Farnborough 1928-39, UKAE Seascale 1949-56, Maj Lanarkshire Yeo, Lt Col RCS (TA); memb Dumfries CC, vice-lt Co of Dumfries 1956-80; Legion of Merit (USA); *Recreations* shooting, forestry, photography; *Style*— Sir Neil Johnson-Ferguson; Springkell, Lockerbie, Dumfrieshire (☎ 046 16 230)

JOHNSON-GILBERT, Christopher Ian; s of Thomas Ian Johnson-Gilbert, of St Johns Wood, London, and Gillian June, *née* Pool; *b* 28 Jan 1955; *Educ* Rugby, Worcester Coll Oxford (BA); *m* 25 July 1981, Emma Davina Mary, *née* Woodhouse, da of Hon C M Woodhouse, DSO, OBE; 2 da (Cordelia b 14 June 1983, Jemima b 24 July 1985); *Career* admitted slr 1980, ptnr Linklaters & Paines 1986-; memb City of London Slrs Co; *Clubs* MCC, RAC, Vincents, Grannies CC; *Style*— Christopher Johnson-Gilbert, Esq; House A-5, Wah Kwong Cliff, 200 Victoria Rd, Hong Kong (☎ 5 8551 744); Linklaters & Paines, 14th Floor Alexandra House, Chater Rd, Central, Hong Kong (☎ 5 8424888, fax 5 8108133)

JOHNSON-GILBERT, Ronald (Stuart); OBE (1976); s of Sir Ian Johnson-Gilbert, CBE (d 1974), and Lady Rosalind Sybil Johnson-Gilbert, *née* Bell-Hughes (d 1977); *b* 14 July 1925; *Educ* Edinburgh Acad; Rugby; Brasenose Coll, Oxford (MA); *m* 10 March 1951, Ann Weir, da of Surgn Cmmdr Thomas Drumond (d 1953); 3 da (Ann Clare b 1953, Emma b 1954, Lydia b 1957); *Career* trainee John Lewis Partnership 1950-51; sec RCS 1962-88 (asst sec 1951-61); sec: Faculty of Dental of Surgery 1958-87, Faculty of Anaesthetists 1958-83, Int Fedn Surgical Colls 1967-74; hon sec Med Cmmn on Accident Prevention 1984-88; awarded: John Tomes Medal 1980, Mc Neill Love Medal 1981, RACS Medal 1985; Bradlaw Orator 1988; Hon FFARCS 1983, Hon FDSRCS 1987, Hon FRCS 1987, FRSM 1985; *Recreations* writing, art, music, golf; *Clubs* Confreres; *Style*— Ronald Johnson-Gilbert, Esq, OBE; Home Farm, Lower Road, Castle Rising, King's Lynn, Norfolk

JOHNSON-GILBERT, Ronald Stuart; OBE (1977); s of Sir Ian Anderson Johnson-Gilbert, CBE, DL, JP (d 1974), of Edinburgh, and Rosalind Sybil, *née* Bell-Hughes (d 1977); *b* 14 July 1925; *Educ* Edinburgh Acad, Rugby, Brasenose Coll Oxford (MA); *m* 10 March 1951, Ann Weir, da of Capt Thomas Weir Drummond, RNVR, TD (d 1953), of Greenock; 3 da (Clare Chevalier, Emma, Lydia Smith); *Career* Intelligence Corps 1943-46; sec Royal Coll of Surgeons of England 1951-88 (formerly asst sec), sec Int Fedn of Surgical Colls 1962-72, hon sec and then hon tres Med Cmmn on Accident Prevention 1980-; Hon FFARCS 1983, Hon FRCS 1987, Hon FDSRCS 1987, Hon FRCSI 1989; *Recreations* literature, golf, music; *Style*— Ronald Johnson-Gilbert, Esq, OBE; Home Farm, Castle Rising, Kings Lynn, Norfolk (☎ 055 387 720)

JOHNSON-GILBERT, Thomas Ian; s of Sir Ian Johnson-Gilbert, CBE (d 1974), and Rosalind Sybil, *née* Bell-Hughes (d 1976); *b* 2 June 1923; *Educ* Edinburgh Acad, Rugby Sch, Trinity Coll Oxford (MA); *m* 25 Nov 1950, Gillian June, da of Gordon Desmond Pool (d 1942), of London; 1 s (Christopher b 1955), 1 da (Catherine b 1952); *Career* Flt Lt VR 1943-46; admitted slr 1950, snr ptnr Coward Chance 1980-87 (ptnr since 1954), jt sen ptnr Clifford Chance 1987-89; memb: Law Soc (cncl 1970-88), City of London slrs Co, Int Bar Assoc; *Recreations* reading, arts, travel, spectator sport; *Clubs* Athenaeum; City of London, MCC; *Style*— Thomas Johnson-Gilbert, Esq; Clifford Chance, Royex House, Aldermanbury Square, London EC2 (☎ 01 600 0808, fax 01 726 8561, telex 895 9991)

JOHNSON-HILL, Nigel; s of Kenelm Clifton Johnson-Hill, JP (d 1977), and Joyce Wynne, *née* Booth; *b* 8 Dec 1946; *Educ* Rugby; *m* 23 Oct 1971, Catherine, da of Edward Sainsbury TD; 1 s (Sam b 1978), 2 da (Chloe b 1976, Anna b 1981); *Career* bank offr Hong Kong & Shanghai Banking Corp 1965-73, stockbroker WI Carr (Overseas) 1973-78, md Hoare Govett 1978-87; stockbroker and chief exec Hoenig & Co Ltd 1988-; memb Stock Exchange 1979, The Securities Assoc 1988; *Recreations* wine, skiing, tennis; *Clubs* Oriental, Hong Kong; *Style*— Nigel Johnson-Hill, Esq; Park Farm, Milland, Liphook, Hampshire, GU30 7JT; C/o Hoenig & Co Ltd, 5 London Wall Bldgs, Finsbury Circus, London EC2M 5NT (☎ 01 588 6622, fax 588 6497)

JOHNSON-LAIRD, Dr Philip Nicholas; s of Frederick Ryberg Johnson-Laird (d 1962), of London, and Dorothy *née* Blackett (d 1947); *b* 10 Oct 1936; *Educ* Culford Sch, Univ Coll, London (BA, PhD); *m* 1 Aug 1959, Maureen Mary Bridget, da of John Henry Sullivan (d 1948); 1 s (Benjamin b 1966), 1 da (Dorothy b 1971); *Career* asst lectr, Psychology, Univ Coll, London, 1966-67 (lectr 1967-73), visiting memb, The Inst for Advanced Study, Princeton, New Jersey 1971-72, reader in experimental pysch Univ of Sussex, 1973-78 (prof 1978-82), visiting fell, cognitive sci prog Stanford Univ Spring 1980; visiting prof: pysch Stanford Univ Spring 1985, pysch Princeton Univ, Spring 1986 and 1987; asst dir MRC Applied Pysch Unit Cambridge 1988-; fell Darwin Coll Cambridge; memb Experimental Pysch Soc, Br Pysch Soc; Doctorate Göteborg Sweden 1983, FBA 1986; *Books* Pyschology of Reasoning (jtly P C Watson 1972), Language and Perception (jtly G A Miller 1976), Mental Models (1983), The Computer and the Mind (1988); *Style*— Dr Philip Johnson-Laird; MRC Applied Psychology Unit, 15 Chaucer Road, Cambridge (☎ 0223 355 294)

JOHNSON-MARSHALL, Lady; Joan Mary; *née* Brighouse; *b* 29 August 1914; *m* 1937, Sir Stirrat Johnson-Marshall, CBE (d 1981), sometime chief architect to Miny of Educn; 2 s (and 1 s decd), 1 da; *Recreations* beekeeping, gardening, spinning; *Style*— Lady Johnson-Marshall; Curtis Mill, Lower Kilcott, Hillsley, Wotton-under-Edge, Glos (☎ 045 423 697)

JOHNSON-MARSHALL, Percy Edwin Alan; CMG (1975); s of Felix William Norman Johnson-Marshall (d 1957), and Kate Jane, *née* Little (d 1975); *b* 20 Jan 1915; *Educ* Queen Elizabeth Sch Kirkby Lonsdale Liverpool, Edinburgh Univ (MA); *m* 1944, April Phyllis Trix, da of Harold Bridger, of Argentina; 3 s (William, Stirling, Nicholas), 4 da (Mary, Katherine, Caroline, Ursula); *Career* RE in India and Burma 1942-46, Major; asst regnl planning offr LCC i/c of London's reconstruction areas including: Stepney, Poplar (Lansbury), South Bank, City (including Barbican); sr lectr, reader and prof Edinburgh Univ 1964-85, planning conslt 1960-; RTPI, DistTP; *Books* Rebuilding Cities (1966); *Recreations* reading, writing, photography, travelling, hill walking; *Clubs* Edinburgh Univ Staff; *Style*— Prof Percy Johnson-Marshall, CMG; Bella Vista, Duddingston Village, Edinburgh (☎ 031 661 2019); Percy Johnson Marshall Ptnrs, 64 The Causeway, Duddington, Edinburgh

JOHNSTON, Alan Charles MacPherson; QC (1980); s of Hon Lord Dunpark, *qv*, and Katherine Margaret, *née* Mitchell (d 1982); *b* 13 Jan 1942; *Educ* Loretto Sch, Jesus Coll Cambridge (BA), Univ of Edinburgh (LLB); *m* 30 July 1966, Anthea Jean, da of John Blackburn (d 1985); 3 s (Alexander b 1969, Charles b 1971, Nicholas b 1974); *Career* advocate 1967, memb standing jr cncl Scottish Home & Health Dept 1972-78, tres Faculty Advocates 1978- (advocate depute 1979-82); chm: Industl Tbnl 1982-88, Med Appeal Tbnl 1984-; *Recreations* fishing, golf, shooting; *Clubs* New (Edinburgh), Univ Pitt Cambridge; *Style*— Alan Johnston, Esq, QC; 3 Circus Gdns, Edinburgh EH3 6TN (☎ 031 225 1862); Parkend, Stichill, Roxburghshire; Advocate Library, Parl House, Edinburgh (☎ 031 226 5071)

JOHNSTON, The Hon Lord Alastair McPherson; TD (1948), QC (1958); s of The Rev Alexander McPherson Johnston (d 1957), and Eleanora Guthrie Wyllie (d 1966); *b* 15 Dec 1915; *Educ* Merchiston Castle Sch, Cambridge Univ (BA), Univ of Edinburgh (LLB); *m* 1, 10 Dec 1939, Katharine Margaret, da of Charles Mitchell, of Chislehurst (d 1957); 3 s (Alan Charles Macpherson b 1942, Alasdair Bryan Mitchell b 1948, Colin Lindsay Wyllie b 1952); m 2, 29 Sept 1984, Kathleen Elizabeth, da of Cochrane Welsh (d 1954), of Eire; *Career* Maj TA UK 1939, served ME (Haifa psc) 1942-45 (despatches); memb Faculty of Advocates Scotland 1946, standing junior counsel various Govt Depts 1948-58, Sheriff Princ Dumfries and Galloway 1966-68; memb Scottish Law Commission 1968-71, Senator Coll of Justice Scotland and Lord of Session with the honorary title of Lord Dunpark 1971-; chm: Edinburgh Legal Dispensary 1961-, Royal Artillery Assoc (Scotland) 1962-80, Cockburn Assoc (Edinburgh Civic Tst 1968-72), St George's Sch for Girls Edinburgh 1973-89; hon pres Edinburgh Marriage Guidance Cncl 1975-86, pres Scottish Univs Law Inst 1977-; *Publications* jt ed: 3 ed Walton on Husband and Wife, 7 ed Gloag & Henderson's Introduction to the Law of Scotland; *Recreations* walking, golf; *Clubs* New (Edinburgh), The Honourable Company of Edinburgh Golfers; *Style*— The Hon Lord Dunpark, TD, QC; 17 Heriot Row, Edinburgh EH3 6HP (☎ 031 556 1896); Parliament House, Edinburgh

JOHNSTON, Sir Alexander; GCB (1962, CB 1946), KBE (1953); s of Alexander Simpson Johnston (d 1960); *b* 27 August 1905; *Educ* George Heriot's Sch Edinburgh, Edinburgh Univ; *m* 1947, Betty Joan, CBE, *qv*; 1 s, 1 da; *Career* civil servant: Treasy, MO, cabinet Off; chm Bd of Inland Revenue 1958-68; dep chm: Monopolies Cmmn 1969-76, Take-Over Panel 1970-83, Cncl for the Securities Indust 1978-83; Hon DSc London Univ 1977; Hon LLD Leicester Univ 1986;; *Recreations* gardening; *Clubs* Reform; *Style*— Sir Alexander Johnston, GCB, KBE; 18 Mallord St, London SW3 6DU (☎ 01 352 6840)

JOHNSTON, Arthur Robert Court; s of William Court Johnston, MC (d 1946), of Carlisle, and Mabel Caroline, *née* Tucker; *b* 22 July 1924; *Educ* St Bees, Liverpool Univ Sch of Architecture (BArch); *m* 13 June 1953, (Sylvia) Fay, da of George Lionel Spencer Lightfoot, OBE (d 1972), of Carlisle; 2 s (Richard b 1955, Adrian b 1961), 1 da (Sarah b 1963); *Career* architect; served Queen's Royal and Border Regts 1943-46; dir Johnston & Wright 1950-; fndr chm Cumbrian Best Kept Village Competition 1957-; FRIBA 1958; *Recreations* arts, sport, travel; *Clubs* Border and County (Carlisle); *Style*— Arthur Johnston, Esq; Hill Crest, Beaumont, Carlisle, Cumbria CA5 6EF (☎ 022 876 277); 15 Castle Street, Carlisle, Cumbria, CA3 8TD (☎ 0228 25161, fax 0228 515 559)

JOHNSTON, Barrie Colin; s of Alfred John Johnston, OBE (d 1964); *b* 7 August 1925; *Educ* Epsom Coll; *m* 1952, Cynthia Anne, *née* Clark; 1 s (Alastair John), 1 da (Nicola Mary); *Career* Lt RM Far East; merchant banker (ret); dir: Charterhouse Japhet Ltd 1973-84, T H White Ltd 1981-87, Mountleigh Gp Ltd plc 1983-, Mornington Bldg Soc 1988-; memb: mgmnt ctee The Pension Fund Property Unit Tst 1966-, mgmnt ctee Charities Property Unit Tst 1967-88, cncl Dr Barnardos 1980-, memb cncl King Georges Fund for Sailors 1982-, (hon tres 1985-); fin advsr Charities Aid Fndn 1976-; memb fin ctee Spastics Soc 1984-88; FPMI, ASIA; *Recreations* sport, travel; *Style*— Barrie Johnston, Esq; Yew Cottage, 8 The Green, Ewell, Surrey (☎ 01 393 2920)

JOHNSTON, Lady; Betty Joan; CBE 1989;; da of Edward Harris; *Educ* Cheltenham Ladies' Coll, St Hugh's Coll Oxford; *m* 1947, Sir Alexander Johnston, GCB, KBE, *qv*; 1 s, 1 da; *Career* barr Gray's Inn 1940; JP Inner London 1966; dep parly counsel Law Cmmn 1975-83, standing counsel General Synod 1983-88; chm: Girls' Public Day Schs Tst 1975-, Francis Holland (C of E) Schs Tst 1978-, Governing Bodies Girls' Public Schs 1979-, Independent Schs Jt Cncl 1983-86, memb cncl Queen's Coll London;

Style— Lady Johnston, JP; 18 Mallord St, London SW3 6DU (☎ 01 352 6840)

JOHNSTON, Brian Alexander; OBE, MC; s of Lt-Col C E Johnston, DSO, MC (d 1922), and Pleasance, *née* Alt (d 1957); *b* 24 June 1912; *Educ* Eton, New Coll Oxford (BA); *m* 22 April 1948, Pauline, da of Col William Tozer, CBE, TD (d 1971); 3 s ((Charles) Barry b 22 April 1949, (William) Andrew b 27 March 1954, (Philip) Ian b 2 May 1957), 2 da (Clare Eileen b 14 Sept 1951, Joanna Jane b 28 Nov 1965); *Career* WWII: 2 Bn Gren Gds 1940-45 (demob as Maj), served Normandy Campaign, capture of Brussels and Nijmegen Bridge, crossing the Rhine; broadcaster and commentator BBC: memb of staff 1946-72, cricket commentator TV 1946-70, cricket commentator on radio Test Match Specials 1970-, BBC cricket corr 1963-72; freelance: In Town tonight, Down Your Way, ceremonial and royal occasions; *Books* Lets Go Somewhere (1952), Armchair Cricket (1957), Stumped for a Tale (1965), The Wit of Cricket (1968), All About Cricket (1972), Its Been A Lot of Fun (1974), Its a Funny Game (1978), Rain Stops Play (1979), Chatterboxes (1983), Brian Johnston's Guide to Cricket (1986), Now Here's a Funny Thing (1984), Its Been a Piece of Cake (1989); *Recreations* cricket, golf, theatre; *Clubs* MCC; *Style*— Brian Johnston, Esq, OBE, MC; 43 Boundary Rd, St John's Wood, London NW8 OJE (☎ 01 286 2991)

JOHNSTON, David Lawrence; s of Herbert David Johnston (d 1983), and Hilda Eleanor, *née* Wood, of Chichester, Sussex; *b* 12 April 1936; *Educ* Lancastrian Sch Chichester, King's Coll Durham Univ (BSc); *m* 7 July 1959, Beatrice Ann, da of John Turnbull Witten (d 1973); 3 da (Fiona b 1960, Pauline b 1961, Kate b 1970); *Career* Lt RN 1959-62, electrical offr HMS Eastbourne 1960-62; MOD 1962-87: overseeing Wallsend 1962-63, design Bath 1963-66, prodn and project mgmnt Devonport Dockyard 1966-73, Dockyard dept policy Bath 1973-76, design Bath 1976-79, prodn and planning Portsmouth Dockyard 1979-81, asst under sec of state and dir Devonport Dockyard Ltd 1984-87, chm DDL 1985-87 (Mgmnt buy out Co), dep chm DML 1987; mgmnt conslt 1988; dir gen Nat Instruction Cncl for Electric Installation Contracting (NICEIC) 1989-; vice pres Plymouth and Dist Br Inst of Mgmnt; pres Plymouth Civil Serv Sports Assoc 1984-88, govr Plymouth CFE 1984-88; FIEE 1980, FBIM 1982, RCNC; *Recreations* walking, gardening, modernizing houses; *Clubs* Army and Navy; *Style*— David Johnston, Esq; The Old Orchard, Harrowbeer Lane, Yelverton, Devon PL20 6DZ; 40 Sawsbury Square, Kennington, London (☎ 0822 854 310); Vintage House, 36/37 Albert Embankment, London SE1 7UJ (☎ 01 582 7746, fax 01 820 0831)

JOHNSTON, (John) Douglas Hartley; s of Dr John Johnston (d 1982) and Rhoda Margaret *née* Hartley; *b* 19 Mar 1935; *Educ* Manchester GS, Cambridge Univ (MA, LLB, PhD), Harvard Law Sch (LLM); *Career* barr Lincoln's Inn 1963; princ asst and slr Inland Revenue 1986- (legal asst 1968, sr legal asst 1971, asst slr 1976); Sidesman, Great St Marys Ch Cambridge; *Recreations* walking, gardening, listening to music; *Style*— Douglas Johnston, Esq; Solicitor's Office, Inland Revenue, Somerset House, London, WC2, (☎ 01 438 6228, fax 01 438 6246)

JOHNSTON, Edward Ingram; s of Samuel William Johnston (d 1954); *b* 27 May 1930; *Educ* Portora Royal Sch; *Career* dir: UDT Bank Ltd, Securicor (Ulster) Ltd, TSB of Northern Ireland plc, Citron Estates (Belfast) Ltd; chm United Dominions Tst (car plant) Ltd; FCA; *Recreations* reading, music, sport; *Style*— Edward Johnston, Esq; 89 Whiterock Rd, Killinchy, Co Down, NI

JOHNSTON, Hon Lady; Hon Elizabeth Rosemary; JP (Berks); da of 2 Baron Hardinge of Penshurst, GCB, GCVO, MC, PC (d 1960) and Helen, Lady Hardinge of Penshurst (d 1979); *b* 3 April 1927; *m* 1949, Lt-Col Sir John F D Johnston, GCVO, MC, *qv*; 1 s, 1 da; *Career* formerly WRNS professional photographer; *Style*— The Hon Lady Johnston, JP; Stone Hill, Newport, Dyfed

JOHNSTON, Frederick Patrick Mair; s of Frederick Mair Johnston (d 1973), of Falkirk, and Muriel Kathleen Johnston, *née* Macbeth; The Johnston family have had a continuous controlling interest in Johnston Press plc and its predecessor since 1767; *b* 15 Sept 1935; *Educ* Lancing Coll Sussex, New Coll Oxford (MA); *m* 1961, Elizabeth Ann, da of Robert Thomas Jones, of Montgomery, Wales; 2 s (Michael b 1962, Robert b 1964); *Career* cmmnd Royal Scots Fusiliers, served East Africa 4th Uganda Bn KAR 1955-56; chm: Johnston Newspaper Gp 1973-, Dunn & Wilson Gp 1976-; dir: Johnston Press plc (F Johnston & Co Ltd until 1988) 1962-; memb Press Cncl 1974-88; pres: Young Newspapermen's Assoc 1968-69, Forth Valley Chamber of Comm 1972-73, Scottish Newspaper Proprietors' Assoc 1976-78; chm Central Scot Manpower Ctee 1976-83; tres Soc of Master Printers of Scotland 1981-86, Cwlth Press Union 1987-, sr vice pres Newspaper Soc 1988-; *Recreations* reading, travelling; *Clubs* New Club, Edinburgh/Royal Cwlth Soc London; *Style*— Frederick P M Johnston, Esq; 1 Grange Terrace, Edinburgh EH9 2LD (☎ 031 667 9201); 53 Manor Place, Edinburgh EH3 7EG (☎ 031 225 3361)

JOHNSTON, Geoffrey Edward Forshaw; s of late Ronald Douglas Graham Johnston, of Hallhouse, Fenwick Ayrshire, Scotland, and Nancy Forshaw, *née* Price; *b* 20 June 1940; *Educ* Loretto Sch, Musselburgh, Univ of St Andrews (LLB); *m* 21 Dec 1964, Elizabeth Anne, da of Maj William Lockhart; 2 da (Susannah b 1968, Victoria b 1969); *Career* articled accountant 1962-65; CA: Touche Ross and Co, Arbuckle Smith Hldgs Ltd 1965- (mgmnt trainee 1965-67, dir subsidiary bd 1972, led mgmnt buyout of gp 1984, gp md 1984-); nat vice chm Inst of Freight Forwarders 1988- (Scot chm 1984-86), dir and govr Lomond Sch Ltd; memb: Scot Valuation Advsy Cncl 1982-, Merchant House of Glasgow; FILDM, FIFF, MBIM, IOD; *Recreations* sailing, skiing, hillwalking, golf; *Clubs* Royal Northern & Clyde YC, RHU, Dunbartonshire; *Style*— Geoffrey Johnston, Esq; Arbuckle Smith and Co Ltd, 91 Mitchell St, Glasgow G1 3LS

JOHNSTON, Gilbert; s of David Kidd Johnston of Dundee (d 1953), and Agnes Penman, *née* Neish (d 1957); *b* 11 Mar 1932; *Educ* Harris Acad Dundee; *m* 24 Apr 1957, Aileen Brown, da of John Brown of Dundee (d 1955); 2 s (Scott b 1959, Derek b 1962); *Career* nat serv: 2 Lt Army 1956-58; qual CA 1956; worked ICI and Rolls Royce; gp chief exec J C Bamford Excavators Ltd 1977- (dealer dept mangr 1964, gp planning dir 1972); memb Midland Indust Cncl; CBIM; *Recreations* swimming, golf, gardening, music, reading; *Style*— Gilbert Johnston, Esq; J C Bamford Excavators Ltd, Rocester, Uttoxeter, Staffs ST14 5JP (☎ 0889 590312, fax 0889 590769, telex 36 372)

JOHNSTON, Sheriff (Alexander) Graham; WS (1971); s of Hon Lord Kincraig, *qv*, of Westwood, Kings Rd, Longniddry, and Margaret Joan, *née* Graham; *b* 16 July 1944; *Educ* Edinburgh Acad, Strathallan Sch, Edinburgh Univ (LLB), Univ Coll Oxford (BA); *m* 1 (m dis 1982), Susan Gay Horne; 2 s (Robin Graham Jolyan b 30 Nov 1973, Paul Mark b 20 Oct 1975); m 2, 6 Feb 1982, Angela Astrid Synnove Anderson, da of Maier Olsen, of Cupar, Fife; *Career* ptnr Hagart & Burn-Murdoch WS 1972-82; Sheriff: Grampian Highlands & Islands Aberdeen 1982-85, Glasgow & Strathkelvin at Glasgow 1985-; ed Scottish Civil Law Reports 1987-; hon fell Inst of Professional Investigators 1979; *Recreations* golf, bridge, puzzles; *Clubs* Elie Golf House, Vincents (Oxford), Oxford & Cambridge Golfing Soc; *Style*— Sheriff Graham Johnston, WS; 3 North Dean Park Ave, Bothwell, Lanarkshire (☎ 0698 852 177); Prospect Cottage, Elie, Fife; Sheriff Court, 1 Carlton Place, Glasgow (☎ 041 429 8888)

JOHNSTON, Lady Helen Torrey; *née* Du Bois; da of Benjamin Franklin Du Bois; *m* 1941, Sir Thomas Alexander Johnston, 13 Bt (d 1984); 1 s (Sir Thomas Alexander, 14 Bt), 2 da (Helen Du Bois b 1944: m 1969, Phillip Thomas Sargent; Leslie Sheldon b 1951: m 1972, David Charles Krempa); *Style*— Lady Johnston; 350 W Delwood Drive, Mobile, Alabama 36606, USA

JOHNSTON, Dr Ian Alistair; s of Donald Dalrymple Johnston (d 1985), and Muriel Joyce Johnston; *b* 2 May 1944; *Educ* Royal GS High Wycombe, Birmingham Univ (BSc, PhD); *m* 1973, Mary Bridget, and Francis Patrick Lube (d 1985); 1 s (Donald b 1979), 1 da (Claire b 1981); *Career* asst princ Dept of Employment 1969, princ 1973, asst sec 1978, under sec 1984; private sec Sir Denis Barnes 1972-74; first sec Br Embassy Brussels 1975-78; advsy conciliation Service 1978-84; dir Planning and Resources Manpower Services Cmmn 1984-85; chief exec Manpower Services Cmmn (VET GP) 1985-87, dep dir-gen Manpower Services Cmmn (now Trg Agency) 1987-; *Recreations* bird watching, skiing, tennis; *Style*— Dr Ian Johnston; Dent Employment Training Agency, Moorfoot, Sheffield 1 (☎ 0742 704108)

JOHNSTON, Ian Andrew Hill; s of John Hill Johnston (d 1962), of Bearsden, Glasgow, and Ethel, *née* Andrew (d 1987); *b* 9 July 1926; *Educ* Jordan Hill Coll Sch, Glasgow Univ (BSc); *m* 4 Feb 1956, Gwenyth Claire, da of John Lloyd (d 1981), of Glasgow; 1 s (Ian Lloyd b 2 April 1959), 1 da (Sally Eve b 2 Oct 1957); *Career* dir: Trusthouse Forte plc, Gen Accident Life; co cncllr N Yorks 1970-77; *Recreations* skiing, shooting; *Clubs* Caledonian London; *Style*— Ian Johnston, Esq; THF plc, 166 High Holborn, London WC1V 6TT (☎ 01 836 7744)

JOHNSTON, Cdr Ian Edgar; OBE (1981); s of Maj Alan Robert Charles Johnston (d 1970), of Emsworth, Hants, and Evelyn Beatrice, *née* Edgar (d 1961); *b* 17 May 1929; *Educ* RNC Dartmouth, RNC Greenwich; *m* 6 Aug 1955, Marcia Elaine, da of Douglas Sioda Macnamara Faulkner (d 1970), of Melbourne, Australia; 2 da (Sara b 1956, Marguerite b 1960); *Career* Entered RNC Dartmouth 1943, served MTBs , destroyers, cruisers, aircraft carriers 1944-67, Naval Staff Washington DC 1968-70, jt servs Staff Coll Latimer 1970, Directorate of Naval Operational requirements - data processing 1971-73, 2i/c RNAS Yeovilton 1973-75, Queen's Harbourmaster and Cdr Dockyard Gibraltar 1975-78, CO HMS President and Naval Liaison Offr London 1978-82; Br Diabetic Assoc 1982, lectr London Mgmnt centre 1983-; cross country commentator Br Horse Soc; hon Sheriff Monterey Cal (1969); Freeman City of London 1980; FBIM (1982), ICFM (1986); *Recreations* field sports, horse trials; *Clubs* Anchorites; *Style*— Cdr I E Johnston, OBE, RN; Holbrook, Yetminster, Sherborne, Dorset DT9 6HQ; 27 St Mary-le-Park Court, Albert Bridge Rd, London SW11 (☎ 01 223 3793); British Diabetic Association, 10 Queen Anne St, London W1M OBD (☎ 01 323 1531, fax 01 637 3644)

JOHNSTON, Sir John Baines; GCMG (1978, KCMG 1966, CMG 1962), KCVO (1972); s of Rev Andrew Smith Johnston (d 1966); *b* 13 May 1918; *Educ* Banbury GS, Queen's Coll Oxford (MA); *m* 1969, Elizabeth Mary, da of John Foster Crace (d 1960); 1 s (John b 1970); *Career* served WW II Maj Gordon Highlanders; Colonial Off 1947-57; dep high cmmr S Africa 1959-61; Br high cmmr: Sierra Leone 1961-63, Rhodesia 1963-65, Malaysia 1971-74, Canada 1974-78, ret; chm the ARELS Examination Tst; govr BBC 1978-85, memb Disasters Emergency Ctee; *Style*— Sir John Johnston, GCMG, KCVO; 5 Victoria Rd, Oxford OX2 7QF (☎ 0865 56927)

JOHNSTON, Lt-Col Sir John Frederick Dame; GCVO (1987, KCVO 1981, CVO 1977, MVO 1971), MC (1945); s of Frederick Horace Johnston (d 1935), and Winifred Emily, *née*, Dame (d 1983); *b* 24 August 1922; *Educ* Ampleforth; *m* 4 Nov 1949, Hon Elizabeth Rosemary, *qv*, da of 2 Baron Hardinge of Penshurst, GCB, GCVO, MC, PC (d 1960); 1 s (Christopher Michael b 1951), 1 da (Joanna Elizabeth b 1953); *Career* Grenadier Gds 1941-64 (cmd 1 Bn 1962-64); comptroller Lord Chamberlain's Office 1981-87 (asst comptroller 1964-81); Freeman City of London 1985; recipient of 32 foreign orders and decorations; *Recreations* gundogs, golf; *Clubs* Boodle's, Pratt's, Swinley Forest Golf; *Style*— Lt-Col Sir John Johnston, GCVO, MC; Stone Hill, Newport, Dyfed (☎ 0239 820978); Studio Cottage, The Great Park, Windsor, Berks SL4 2HP (☎ 0784 31627)

JOHNSTON, Capt John Richard Cox (Johnnie); CBE (1976); s of John Samuel Cox Johnston (d 1929), of Elm Bank, Worplesdon, nr Guilford, Surrey, and Florence, *née* Knight (d 1957); *b* 29 August 1923; *Educ* RNC Dartmouth; *m* 22 Jan 1949, Audrey Margaret, da of Gordon Johnston Humbert (d 1974), of Budleigh Salterton, Devon; 1 s (Colin b 5 March 1954), 1 da (Vivien b 31 Jan 1950); *Career* Midshipman Durban, Dorsetshire and King George V 1941-42, Sub-Lt 59 LCA Flotilla 1942-44, Lt flying trg 1944-49, qual as Air Weapons Offr 1949, Gp Air Weapons Offr Theseus and Glory Off Korea 1950-51, Lt Cdr Indefatigable 1951-53, Warrior (for H Bomb tests) 1956-57, Directorate of Air Warfare 1957-59, Cdr Ulster 1960-61, JSSC 1962, DSD RN Staff Coll 1963-64, Fleet Ops Offr to CinC HF 1964-66; Capt: Tartar 1967-68, MOD 1969-72, Osprey 1972-74, Bulwark 1974-76; chief exec Nat Smallbore Rifle Assoc 1977-80; vice chm S Dorset Cons Assoc; FRAeS, FBIM; *Recreations* fishing, shooting, gundog training; *Style*— Capt Johnnie Johnston, CBE, RN; Old Barn Cottage, Affpuddle, Dorchester, Dorset DT2 7HH (☎ 0305 848268)

JOHNSTON, Leslie; s of John Bruce Johnston (d 1935), of Hillside, Belfast, and Emma Belinda, *née* Atkinson (d 1933); *b* 15 Feb 1909; *Educ* Royal Belfast Academical Inst, Queen's Univ Belfast (BCommSc), Open Univ (BA); *m* 10 June 1938, Dorothy Jane, da of Capt Thomas Matthews Wright (d 1939); 2 da (Janet Bruce b 1939, Vivien Louise b 1943); *Career* md Ulster Bank Tst Co 1970-; cncllr Heath Ward S Kesteven DC 1977-87; OStJ; *Recreations* bridge, walking, gardening; *Clubs* Grantham Cons, Sleaford Golf, St John House; *Style*— Leslie Johnston, Esq; Laburnum Cottage, Frieston, Caythorpe, Grantham, Lincs NG32 3BY (☎ 0400 72563)

JOHNSTON, Lt-Gen Sir Maurice Robert; KCB (1981), OBE (1971); s of Brig Allen Leigh Johnston, OBE; *b* 27 Oct 1929; *Educ* Wellington, RMA Sandhurst; *m* 1960, Belinda Sladen; 1 s, 1 da; *Career* cmmnd RA 1949, transferred Queen's Bays 1954, Mil Asst to CGS 1968-71, CO 1 Queen's Dragoon Gds 1971-73, Cdr 20 Armd Bde 1973-75, Brig Gen Staff HQ UK Land Forces 1977-78, Sr Directing Staff RCDS 1979-

80, Asst CGS 1980, Dep Chief Def Staff 1981-83; ret 1984; co dir; *Style*— Lt-Gen Sir Maurice Johnston, KCB, OBE; Ivy House, Worton, Devizes, Wilts (☎ 0380 3727)

JOHNSTON, Richard Graves; JP (1962), DL (1963); s of George Paul Graves Johnston, JP (d 1955); *b* 4 July 1914; *Educ* Canford Sch Dorset, Trinity Coll Dublin; *m* 1945, Lydia Constance, da of Lt-Col Michael John Furnell; 3 children; *Career* landowner, company director, High Sheriff Co Armagh 1959; *Recreations* hunting, water skiing; *Clubs* Kildare St (Dublin); *Style*— Richard Johnston Esq, JP, DL; Kilmore House, Kilmore Armagh (Co), N Ireland (☎ 0762 871234)

JOHNSTON, Robert William Fairfield; CMG (1960), CBE (1954), MC (1917), TD (1936) and 3 bars (1947); s of Capt Robert Johnston, The Royal Scots (d 1949); *b* 1 May 1895; *m* 1922, Agnes Scott, *née* Justice (d 1980); 1 s; *Career* Civil Service 1910, served Royal Scots 1910-21, Gordon Highlanders 1922-47 (secondment RA 1943-44), Lt-Col 1940; TA 1910-47; asst sec MOD, cllr Foreign Office, memb UK Delgns to NATO and OEEC 1953-61, ret 1962; *Style*— Robert Johnston, Esq, CMG, CBE, MC, TD; 8 Broad Ave, Queen's Park, Bournemouth, Dorset BH8 9HG (☎ (0202) 37438)

JOHNSTON, Sir (David) Russell; MP (SLD) Inverness, Nairn and Lochaber 1983-, (Inverness 1964-83) (Lib 1964-88, SLD 1988);; s of David Knox Johnston (d 1972); *b* 1932; *Educ* Portree HS Isle of Skye, Edinburgh Univ; *m* 1967, Joan Graham, da of Donald Menzies; 3 s; *Career* Nat Serv, cmmnd Intelligence Corps (2 i/c Berlin); winner of debating trophies: *The Scotsman* 1956 and 1957, *The Observer* mace 1961; memb Royal Cmmn on Scottish local govt 1966; chm Scottish Lib Pty 1970-, ldr 1974-86 (pres 1988-), former def spokesman; first UK Lib memb of Euro Parl 1973-75 and 1976-79 (vice pres Political Ctee 1976-79), stood at first Euro direct election 1979; Lib spokesman on foreign and cwlth 1970-75, 1979-75, and Scotland 1970-73, 1975-83, 1985-87, Alliance spokesman on Scotland and European community affrs 1987, dep ldr SLD; spokesman: foreign and cwlth affrs, Euro community affrs; kt 1985; *Publications* Highland Development; To be a Liberal, Scottish Liberal Party Conference Speeches 1971-78, 1979-86; *Clubs* Scottish Liberal; *Style*— Sir Russell Johnston, MP; House of Commons, London SW1A 0AA

JOHNSTON, Thomas; OBE (1982); s of John Watson Johnston (d 1970), of Skelmorlie; *b* 27 June 1927; *Educ* Royal Tech Coll, Glasgow Univ (BSc); *m* 24 Dec 1949, Gwendoline Jean, *née* Bird; 1 s, 3 da; *Career* md Barr & Stroud Ltd 1977-, chm Pilkington Electro-Optical Materials Ltd 1986 dir: Pilkington Electro-Optical Div 1979, W Bd Bank of Scotland 1984-, Scottish Amicable Life Assur Soc 1987-; memb: Scottish Industl Devpt Advsy Bd, Scottish Engrg Employers Assoc, Ct of Strathclyde Univ; FIProdE, FRSA; *Recreations* high hills, grand opera, cottage garden; *Clubs* Western; *Style*— Thomas Johnston, Esq, OBE; 43 Strathblane Rd, Milngavie, Glasgow G62 8HA; Barr & Stroud Ltd, Anniesland, Glasgow G13 1HZ (☎ 041 954 9601, fax 041 954 2380)

JOHNSTON, Sir Thomas Alexander; 14 Bt (NS 1626); only s of Sir Thomas Alexander Johnston, 13 Bt (d 1984); *b* 1 Feb 1956; *Heir* none; *Style*— Sir Thomas A Johnston, Bt; 350 West Delwood Drive, Mobile, Alabama 36606, USA

JOHNSTON, Dr Thomas Lothian (Tom); DL (City of Edinburgh 1987); s of Thompson Braidford Johnston (d 1981), and Janet Bell, *née* Lothian (d 1969); *b* 9 Mar 1927; *Educ* Hawick HS, Edinburgh Univ (MA 1951, PhD 1955), Stockholm Univ; *m* 20 July 1956, Joan Winifred, da of Ernest Chalmers Fahmy, FRCSE, FRCPE, FRCOG (d 1983), of Edinburgh; 2 s (David b 1961, Andrew b 1963), 3 da (Caroline b 1959, Christine b 1967, Katharine b 1967); *Career* Sub Lt RNVR 1944-47; lectr in political economy Edinburgh Univ 1953-65; prof of economics Heriot-Watt Univ 1966-76, chm Manpower Services Ctee for Scotland and economic conslt to Sec of State for Scotland 1977-, princ and vice-chllr Heriot-Watt Univ 1981-88 (now princ emeritus); arbitrator and memb: Scottish Milk Mktg Bd 1967-72, Scottish Telecommunications Bd 1977-81; visiting academic: Univ of Illinois 1962-63, Queens Univ Canada 1965, Int Inst of Labour Studies Geneva 1973, Western Australia Inst of Technol 1979; chm MSC Scotland 1977-80; head of Inquiry into Water Strike 1983; Hon Dr Univ of Edinburgh 1986; foreign memb Royal Swedish Acad of Engrg Sciences; FRSE 1979, CBIM 1983, FRSA 1983, FIPM 1985; Cdr Royal Swedish Order of the Polar Star 1985; *Recreations* walking, gardening; *Style*— Prof Tom Johnston; 14 Mansionhouse Rd, Edinburgh EH9 1TZ (☎ 031 667 1439)

JOHNSTON, William Bryce; s of William Bryce Johnston, ISO (d 1963), of Edinburgh, and Isabel Winifred Chester, *née* Highley (d 1953); *b* 16 Sept 1921; *Educ* George Watson's Coll Edinburgh, Edinburgh Univ (MA, BD); *m* 9 Oct 1947, Ruth Margaret, da of Rev James Arthur Cowley (d 1960), of Edinburgh; 1 s (Iain Arthur Bryce b 19 Dec 1950 (Ft Lt RAF)), 2 da (Fiona Margaret b 6 Nov 1952, Rosemary Swan (Mrs McCulloch) b 18 Feb 1958); *Career* Chaplain to the Forces 1945-49; minister: St Andrew's Church Bo'ness 1949-55, St George's Church Greenock 1955-64, Colinton Parish Church 1964-; Chaplain HM Prison Greenock 1959-64; convenor Gen Assembly Ctees: Church and Nation 1972-76, Inter-Church Relations 1979-81; moderator of the Gen Assembly 1980-81, Chaplain-in-Ordinary to HM The Queen in Scotland 1981-; chm Judicial Commn 1986-, visiting lectr in Social Ethics Heriot-Watt Univ 1966-87, tstee Scottish Nat War Memorial 1981-, memb Bdcasting Cncl for Scotland 1983-87; Hon DD Aberdeen Univ 1980, Hon DLitt Heriot-Watt Univ 1989; *Books* translation: Karl Barth, Dogmatics (1960), John Calvin: Epistle To The Hebrews (1963); Ethics and Defence (ed 1987); *Recreations* organ-playing, bowls; *Clubs* New (Edinburgh); *Style*— The Very Rev William Johnston; The Manse of Colinton, Edinburgh EH13 0JR (☎ 031 441 2315)

JOHNSTON, William James; s of Thomas Hamilton Johnston (d 1951), of Enniskillen, Co Fermanagh, and Mary Kathleen, *née* Bracken (d 1977); *b* 3 April 1919; *Educ* Portora Royal Sch Enniskillen Co Fermanagh; *m* 6 Dec 1943, Joan Elizabeth Nancye, da of Rev William John Young (d 1927), of Newtownbutler, Co Fermanagh; 2 da (Dr Heather Johnston b 1945, Mrs Janet Moore b 1948); *Career* qualified CA 1942; dep sec Antrim CC 1944-68, dep Town Clerk Belfast Corpn 1968-73, town clerk and chief exec Belfast City Cncl 1973-79, sec Assoc of Local Authorities NI 1979-82; memb NI advsy bd, Abbey National Building Soc 1982-; BBC NI advsy cncl 1965-69, Bd of Arts Cncl of NI 1974-80, Local Govt Staff Cmmn 1974-84, NI Tourist Bd 1980-85, NI Australian Bicentennial Ctee; chm Public Serv Trg Cncl 1974-83; FCA; *Recreations* golf, live theatre, travel; *Clubs* Royal Portrush GC, Cushendall GC, Malone GC; *Style*— William Johnston, Esq; 47 Layde Rd, Cushendall, Ballymena, Co Antrim BT44 0NQ; Flat 4, 29 Windsor Ave, Belfast BT9 6EJ (☎ 02667 71 211, 0232 660 793)

JOHNSTON OF ROCKPORT, Baron (Life Peer UK 1987), of Caversham, Co Berks; Sir Charles Collier Johnston; TD; s of Capt Charles Moore Johnston (ka Battle of Somme 1916), and Muriel Florence Edmeston, *née* Mellon (d 1963); *b* 4 Mar 1915; *Educ* Rockport Preparatory Sch, Craigavad Co Down, Tonbridge Sch; *m* 1, 15 June 1939 (m dis 1979), Audrey Boyes, da of late Edgar Monk; 2 s (Hon Michael Charles b 20 Oct 1942, Hon Timothy Courtenay b 29 May 1945); m 2, 1 Sept 1981, Mrs Yvonne Shearman, da of late Reginald Marley; *Career* chm Standex International Ltd 1951-77 (formerly Roehlen-Martin Ltd, md 1948-76), engravers and engrs Ashton Rd, Bredbury, Cheshire; chm: Thames and Kennet Marina Ltd 1982-, James Burn International 1986- (dir 1983), Standex Hldgs Ltd 1986-, Macclesfield Constituency Cons Assoc 1961-65; hon tres NW Cons, memb Cons Bd of Finance 1965-71, chm NW Area Cons 1971-76, memb exec ctee Nat Union of Cons and Unionist Assocs 1965-88 (chm 1976-81), pres Nat Union of Cons and Unionist Assocs 1986-87, Nat chm Cons Friends of Israel 1983-86, memb Boyd Cmmn as official observers of elections held in Zimbabwe/Rhodesia April 1980; *Recreations* spectator sports, travelling, gardening; *Clubs* Royal Corinthian Yacht (Cowes); *Style*— The Lord Charles Johnston of Rockport, TD; House of Lords, London SW!

JOHNSTON-JONES, David Ranald; s of Lt Col Kenneth Charles Johnston-Jones, MBE, MC (d 1970), and Stella Margaret, *née* Sharvill (d 1988); *b* 14 Oct 1926; *Educ* Bedford Sch, New Coll Oxford (MA); *m* 24 April 1954, Millicent Elspeth, da of Reginald Douglas Gibbs (d 1987); 1 s (Nicholas b 1963), 3 da (Virginia b 1956, Vivienne b 1957, Valerie b 1960); *Career* Capt RM and Intelligence Corps 1945-48; active service in Palestine; civil assist WO 1951-58, serv in London, Egypt, Cyprus; sch master 1958-86; rector of Morrisons Acad (Crieff) 1974-78; headmaster of Merchant Taylors Sch (Crosby) 1979-86; *Books* The Deathless Train, The Life and Work of R S Surtees (1974), The Cambridge Guide to Literature in English (contrib 1988); *Recreations* writing, lecturing, C19 literature; *Style*— David R Johnston-Jones, Esq; 12 Ferry Path, Cambridge CB4 1HB (☎ 0223 358916)

JOHNSTONE, Adam; s of Maj Richard Johnstone, (d 1919), of Fulford Hall, Wythall, Worcs, and Florence Catherine May, *née* Harris (d 1957); *b* 28 August 1912; *Educ* Greshams Sch Holt Norfolk; *m* 1, 24 March 1946, Ella Mary (d 1971), da of Maj Godfrey Edmonds, of Kingsbridge, Devon; 2 da (Laurelie b 4 March 1947, Janet b 22 Sept 1949); m 2, 3 June 1972, Monica Katharine Mary, da of Wilfred Hodsoll; *Career* RASC 1939-47: Maj 1942 (POW Japan 1942-45); Kleinwort Son & Co and subsidiaries 1947-54: jt md Fendrake Ltd, pres Drake America Corp USA, chm Mark Cross USA; chm Sales Audits Ltd 1954-64, visiting prof of mktg Inst European d'Administration des Affaires Fontainbleau France 1958-64, chief exec Motherwell Bridge Contracting & Trading Co Ltd 1964-67, dep chm Gallaway Mechanical Services 1973-79, chm J Broadwood & Sons Ltd 1974-83; pres of appeal RAM, chm Broadwood Charitable Tst, pres PMA, memb Cons Assoc; MInstM 1948, charter memb American Inst Mgmnt 1949; *Recreations* gardening, travel, photography, wine; *Clubs* Naval and Military, Wig and Pen; *Style*— Adam Johnstone, Esq; Temple Wood, Capel, Surrey

JOHNSTONE, Air Vice-Marshal Alexander Vallance Riddell; CB (1966), DFC (1940), AE, DL (Glasgow); s of Alexander Lang Johnstone (d 1950) and Daisy, *née* Riddell; *b* 2 June 1916; *Educ* Kelvinside Acad; *m* 1940, Margaret, da of James T Croll, of Glasgow; 1 s, 2 da; *Career* RAF 1935-68: fndr and first CAS Royal Malayan Air Force 1957-58, dir of personnel Air Miny 1962-64, Cdr Air Forces Borneo 1964-65, Air Offr Scotland 1965-68, Cdr Air N Atlantic 1965-68; vice chm cncl TA&VRA 1969-79, chm Climax Cleaning Co Ltd 1980-; *Recreations* golf; *Clubs* RAF; *Style*— Air Vice-Marshal Alexander Johnstone, CB, DFC, AE, DL; 36 Castle Brooks, Framlingham, Woodbridge, Suffolk IP13 (☎ 0728 723770)

JOHNSTONE, David William Robert; s of William Johnstone (d 1948), and Elizabeth Hankin Johnstone, *née* Hedley; *b* 20 Nov 1936; *Educ* St Bees Sch, Clare Coll Cambridge (MA); *m* 1962, Penelope Susan, da of Dr David Robert Sloan, of Blagdon, Bristol; 3 da (Penelope Harriet b 1964, Jessica Lucy b 1966, Bryony Aileen b 1969); *Career* Lt Royal Northumberland Fusliers; CA; articled clerk Whinney Smith & Whinney London 1960-63 (staff 1963-65); joined Grace Darbyshire & Todd (later Grace Ryland) 1965, ptnr 1967 (merged with Thomson McLintock & Co 1969); fndr Dartington & Co Ltd 1979, chief exec of Dartington & Co Gp plc; dir: TSW TV South West plc 1980-, The Burns-Anderson Gp plc 1987-, Spafax Hldgs plc 1969-, J T Gp Ltd 1979-; FCA; *Recreations* gardening, walking, theatre, music; *Style*— David Johnstone, Esq; Lake House, Grib Lane, Blagdon, Bristol BS18 6SA (☎ 0761 62533); Dartington & Company, Bush House, 72 Prince Street, Bristol BS1 4QD (☎ 0272 213206)

JOHNSTONE, Hon Francis Patrick Harcourt (Vanden-Bempde-); s and h of 5 Baron Derwent, LVO, *qv*; *b* 23 Sept 1965; *Educ* Eton, Edinburgh Univ; *Style*— The Hon Francis Vanden-Bempde-Johnstone; Hackness Hall, Scarborough, N Yorks

JOHNSTONE, Sir Frederic Allan George; 10 Bt (NS 1700), of Westerhall, Dumfriesshire; s of Sir George Frederic Thomas Tankerville Johnstone, 9 Bt (d 1952); *b* 23 Feb 1906; *Educ* Imperial Service Coll; *m* 1, 1933 (m dis 1941), Gladys Hands; m 2, 1946, Doris, da of late W L Shortridge, of Blackheath, SE; 2 s; *Heir* s, George Johnstone; *Style*— Sir Frederic Johnstone, Bt; Urry's Cottage, Freshwater, Isle of Wight

JOHNSTONE, (John) Raymond; o s of Capt Henry James Johnstone, RN, of The Myretoun, Menstrie, Clackmannanshire (d 1947, fourth in descent from John Johnstone, who commanded the artillery at the Battle of Plassey, to which victory he substantially contributed, and who was s of Sir James Johnstone, 3 Bt), and Margaret Alison McIntyre (d 1984); *b* 27 Oct 1929; *Educ* Eton, Trinity Coll Cambridge (BA pure mathematics); *m* 1979, Susan Sara, da of Christopher Gerald Gore (d 1955), widow of Peter Quixano Henriques (d 1974), and of Basil Ziani de Ferranti; 5 step s , 2 step da; *Career* chm Murray Johnstone Ltd 1984- (md 1968-88); chm Dominion Insurance 1978, chm (1983-85) and dir Scottish Amicable Life Assurance Soc 1971, chm Murray Technology Ltd; dir: Scottish Fin Enterprise, Alva Estates, Hope Street Fund SA, Pacific Fund SA, Glasgow Cultural Enterprise; Fund SA, Kemper-Murray Johnstone International Inc, Yamaichi-Murray Johnstone Ltd, Landel Insurance Hldgs; also dir various Murray Johnstone subsids; hon pres Scottish Opera (chm 1983-86); memb Scottish Ctee, Scottish Econ Cncl, Nature Conservancy Cncl; *Recreations* fishing, music & farming; *Clubs* Western (Glasgow); *Style*— Raymond Johnstone, Esq; Murray Johnstone Ltd, 7 West Nile St, Glasgow G1 2PX (☎ (041) 226 3131) Wards, Gartocharn, Dunbartonshire G83 8SB (☎ 038 983 321, telex: 778627, fax: 041 248 5420)

JOHNSTONE, (George) Richard Douglas; s and h of Sir Frederic Johnstone, 10 Bt; *b* 21 August 1948; *Educ* Magdalen Coll Oxford; *m* 1976, Gwyneth, da of Arthur

Bailey; 1 s (Frederic b 1981); *Career* dir D E Barnard Systems Ltd, mgmnt consits; *Style*— Edward Johnstone Esq

JOHNSTONE, Prof Robert Edgeworth; s of Col Sir Walter Edgeworth-Johnstone, KBE, CB (d 1936), and Helen Gunning Edgeworth-Johnstone, *née* Waters (d 1953); *b* 4 Feb 1900; *Educ* Wellington Coll, RMA, Manchester Univ (BSc Tech), London Univ (MSc, DSc); *m* Jessie Marjory (d 1981), da of R T Creig (d 1903); 2 s (Richard b 1938, Walter b 1944), 1 da (Rosemary b 1940); *Career* chemical engr; various appts Britain, Kenya & Trinidad; British Security Co-ordination 1942-46; asst dir Ordnance Factories 1951; prof of chemical engrg Univ of Nottingham 1960-67; Liveryman of the Salters' Co; FRIC; FIChemE; FIMechE; *Books* Pilot Plants & Model Experiments in Chemical Engineering (1956 with M W Thring), The Lost World: Does it Exist? (1978 as Robert Johnstone), Samuel Butler on the Resurrection (1980 Ed), Over 40 scientific papers; *Recreations* music, pistol shooting, philosophy; *Clubs* Athenaeum; *Style*— Prof Robert E Johnstone; c/o Barclays Bank plc, 139 North Street, Brighton BN1 1RU

JOICEY, Hon Andrew Hugh; yr s of 4 Baron Joicey, *qv*; *b* 24 Dec 1955; *Educ* Eton, Christchurch Oxford; *Career* Farmer; *Style*— The Hon Andrew Joicey

JOICEY, Hon James Michael; s and h of 4 Baron Joicey; *b* 28 June 1953; *Educ* Eton, Ch Ch Oxford; *m* 16 June 1984, Harriet, da of Rev William Thompson, of Oxnam Manse, Jedburgh, Roxburghshire; 1 da (b 25 June 1988); *Style*— The Hon James Joicey; Hall Cottage, Woodcott, Whitchurch, Hampshire RG28 7PY

JOICEY, 4 Baron (UK 1906); Sir Michael Edward Joicey; 4 Bt (UK 1893); s of 3 Baron Joicey (d 1966), and Lady Joan Lambton, da of 4 Earl of Durham; through his mother Lord Joicey is 1 cous to Lord Home of the Hirsel and (6) Duke of Sutherland; *b* 28 Feb 1925; *Educ* Eton, Ch Ch Oxford; *m* 1952, Elisabeth, da of Lt-Col Hon Ian Melville, TD, yst s of 11 Earl of Leven and Melville; 2 s, 1 da; *Heir* s, Hon James Joicey; *Career* served WW II Capt Coldstream Gds; MFH The N Northumberland 1954-74; DL Northumberland 1985; *Recreations* shooting, stalking, fishing; *Clubs* Kennel, Lansdowne, N Counties (Newcastle); *Style*— The Rt Hon the Lord Joicey; Loch Choire Lodge, Kinbrace, Sutherland (☎ 043 13 222); Etal Manor, Berwick-on-Tweed (☎ 089082 205)

JOICEY-CECIL, James David Edward; s of late Edward Wilfrid George Joicey-Cecil; *b* 24 Sept 1946; *Educ* Eton; *m* 1975, Jane Susanna Brydon, da of late Capt P W B Adeley; 2 da; (Katherine Mary b 1978, Susanna Maud b 1981); *Career* memb Stock Exchange 1978-, ptnr James Capel & Co 1978-; FCA; *Clubs* Annabel's, City; *Style*— James Joicey-Cecil, Esq; 49 Clapham Common South Side, London SW4 (☎ 01 622 0576)

JOINER, Dr Charles Louis; s of Maj C A Joiner (d 1952), of Whyteleafe, Surrey, and Kathleen, *née* O'Malley (d 1978); *b* 21 Jan 1923; *Educ* Tonbridge Sch, Guys Hosp Med Sch (MB,BS,MD); *m* 9 Dec 1947, Helen Mary, da of Basil Reginald Lovell, MBE (d 1984) of Littleton, Hants; 1 s (David b 1961), 1 da (Sarah b 1958); *Career* RAMC 1946-48; physician to Guys Hosp Bromley, Gp of Hosps 1959-88, hon physician to the Army 1974-88, chief conslt physician Sun Alliance Insur Co; FRCP, FRSM; *Books* Short Text Book of Medicine (1969); *Recreations* shooting, English lit and history, antique porcelain; *Clubs* Athenaeum; *Style*— Dr Charles Joiner, MD; Ashton, Mead Road, Chislehurst, Kent (☎ 01 467 4060), Suite 302, Emblem House, 27 Tooley Street, London SE1 (☎ 01 407 0292)

JOLL, Hon Mrs (Katharine Mary); *née* Howard; 2 da (by 1 m) of 4 Baron Strathcona and Mount Royal; *b* 1956; *m* 1, 1975, Gavin Michael Strachan, of Edinburgh; m 2, 1982 (having resumed her maiden name), William Evelyn Hinton Joll, s of Evelyn Joll, of, S Kensington; 1 s (Harry b 1983), 2 da (Flora b 1985, Hannah b 1988); *Style*— The Hon Mrs Joll; 17 Durand Gdns, London SW9 0PS

JOLLES, Dr Alicia; da of Dr B A Jolles (d 1985), of Northampton, and Miriam, *née* Blake; *b* 24 Dec 1947; *Educ* Northampton HS, Univ of London Westfield Coll, (BA, PhD); *m* 10 June 1981, Martin Geoffrey Greenham, s of Geoffrey Basil Herbert (d 1974); 1 s (Edward b 21 Jan 1987), 2 da (Susannah b 20 Oct 1982, Katharine b 8 Aug 1985); *Career* Coward Chance: slr 1977, ptnr 1981 (known as Clifford Chance 1987-); Freeman City of London, memb: Law Soc, City of London Slrs Co; *Recreations* family, sailing, gardening; *Style*— Dr Alicia Jolles; 23 Alwyne Rd, London N1 2HN (☎ 01 226 8159); The Gables, East Bergholt, Suffolk; Clifford Chance, 19 New Bridge St, London EC4V 6BY (☎ 01 353 0211, fax 01 489 0046, telex 887847)

JOLLES, Bernard Nathan; s of Dr Benjamin Jolles (d 1985), of Northampton, and Miriam, *née* Blake; *b* 23 August 1949; *Educ* Bedford Sch, St John's Coll Cambridge (MA), Balliol Coll Oxford (MSc), London Business Sch (MSc); *m* 1 Dec 1986, Pamela, da of Horace Knight (d 1973), of Hastings; *Career* merchant banker; dir: Samuel Montagu & Co Ltd 1982-87; Henry Ansbacher & Co Ltd 1988-; *Recreations* flying, golf, skiing, tennis; *Style*— Bernard N Jolles, Esq; 110 Regent's Park Rd, London NW1 8UG (☎ 01 722 5522)

JOLLIFFE, Sir Anthony Stuart; GBE (1982), JP (City of London); s of Robert Jolliffe; *b* 12 August 1938; *Educ* Porchester Sch Bournemouth; *m* 1962, Anne Elizabeth Phillips; 1 s, 2 da; *Career* lord mayor London 1982-83 (Sheriff 1980-81, alderman Candlewick Ward 1975-, hon tres Sheriff's & Recorder's Fund, pres Candlewick Ward Club); memb: Governing Body Utd Wards Club, Guild of Freemen, Court Painter Stainers' Co, Court Chartered Accountants in England & Wales, Wheelwrights' Co, Cncl Operation Drake Fellowship, Heritage of London Tst Special Ctee, Variety Club of GB; tstee Police Fndn; vice chm St John Ambulance Assoc City of London Branch, OStJ 1981; vice pres European League for Economic Cooperation, hon tres Britain in Europe Residual Fund; chartered accountant 1964- and sr ptnr Jolliffe Cork & Co, also int chm Jolliffe Cork Ingram; dir: E Fogarty & Co, SAS Catering, Nikko Trading UK, Capital for Industry, Erskine House Investments, Marlborough Property Hldgs (Devpts) & subsids, Albany Commercial & Industl Devpts, Gantry Railing, Specialweld; FCA, FRSA, ATII; *Recreations* classic cars, theatre, sailing (yacht 'Kleen Sweeps'); *Clubs* City Livery, Royal London Yacht, Thames Motor Yacht; *Style*— Sir Anthony Jolliffe, GBE, JP; c/o Thornton Baker & Co, Fairfax House, Fulwood Place, London WC1; Oakwood, 2 Park Close, Batchworth Heath, Rickmansworth, Herts (☎ Northwood 29877); c/o Jolliffe Cork & Co, Elvian House, 18/20 St Andrew St, London EC4A 3AE

JOLLIFFE, John Anthony; s of Donald Norman Jolliffe (d 1967), of Dover, Kent and Edith Constance Mary, *née* Lovegrove; *b* 1 August 1937; *Educ* Dover Coll; *m* 1, 5 June 1965 (m dis 1983), Jacqueline Mary, *née* Smith, 1 s (Jeffrey b 1968), 1 da (Jenny b 1966); m2, 3 Aug 1984 (m dis 1986), Irmgard Elizabeth, *née* Melville; 1 s (Andrew b 1985); *Career* Nat Serv RAF 1955-57, ptnr R Watson & Sons 1967- (joined 1957); examiner in pension funds Inst of Actuaries 1970-75 (tutor 1965-70), tres Assoc Consulting Actuaries 1980-84, dir London Aerial Tours Ltd 1983-; chm: ACA local govt Superannuation Ctee 1975-, NAPF Int Ctee 1986-88, European Fedn of Retirement Provison 1988-; cncl memb Nat Assoc of pension Funds 1983-; memb UK Steering Ctee for Local Govt superannuation 1975-; Freedman City of London, Liveryman Co of Actuaries; FIA 1964, FPMI 1977, ASA (USA) 1971; *Recreations* flying, tennis, travel; *Clubs* Reform, Birmingham; *Style*— John Jolliffe, Esq; Sunhurst Clay Lane, South Nutfield, Redhill, Surrey, RH1 4EG (☎ 0737 762441); Watson House, London Road, Reigate, Surrey RH2 9PQ (☎ 0737 241144, fax 0737 241496, telex 946070)

JOLLIFFE, Hon John Hedworth; s of 4 Baron Hylton (d 1967), and Perdita, da of Raymond Asquith, es of 1 Earl of Oxford and Asquith; *b* 1935; *Educ* Eton, Ch Ch Oxford (BA); *m* 1965, Hon Victoria Catherine Elizabeth, *née* Eden, da of 7 Baron Henley (d 1977); *Career* dir Bain Dawes (insurance brokers); Kt SMO Malta; *Books* Raymond Asquith, Life & Letters; *Clubs* Brooks's, Beefsteak, Pratt's, Polish Hearts; *Style*— The Hon John Jolliffe; Church House, Chesterblade, Shepton Mallet, Somerset BA4 4QX, (☎ 0749 88413)

JOLLIFFE, Robert St John; s of Robert Jolliffe, of Firs Lodge, Troutstream Way, Loudwater, Rickmansworth, Herts, and Vi Dorothea, *née* Crumbleholme; *b* 26 June 1943; *Educ* Watford GS; *m* 12 July 1968, Sarah Anne, da of Maj W N Spraggs (d 1988), of 16 Gatehill Rd, Northwood, Middx; 2 s (James b 1973, Charles b 1976); *Career* CA; ptnr: Fryer Whitehill resigned 1975, Jolliffe Cork & Co 1975-82, Grant Thornton resigned 1988; fin dir: Automagic Hldgs plc 1988-, Country Classic Cars 1988-; non-exec dir CP Carpets (Kidderminster) Ltd 1988; pres Bishopsgate Ward Club 1988-89, Freeman City of London 1969, Liveryman Worshipful Co of Painter-Stainers 1969; FCA 1979; *Recreations* golf, music, sailing; *Clubs* Moor Park GC, Edgbaston Priory Birmingham, Royal Soc of St George, IOD, City Livery; *Style*— Robert Jolliffe, Esq; Cobblers, Rooks Hill, Loudwater, Rickmansworth, Herts WD3 4HZ (☎ 0923 771 834); Automagic House, Coldharbour Lane, Harpenden, Herts (☎ 0582 460 960, fax 05827 64547, car tel 0860 318 662)

JOLLIFFE, Hon William Henry Martin; s and h of 5 Baron Hylton; *b* 1 April 1967; *Style*— The Hon William Jolliffe

JOLLY, Lt Cdr Edward John; s of Thomas Alfred Jolly, of Stubbington, and Kate Aline Mary, *née* Attle; *b* 11 Mar 1941; *Educ* Glendale GS London, Loughborough Univ (MSc); *m* 1, 18 Sept 1965, Sally Russ; 1 s (Leslie James b 1966); m 2, 3 May 1986, Patricia Elizabeth Jolly; *Career* entered Mil Serv 1957, trained in med laboratory sci, cmmnd 1970, RNC Greenwich (trained in radiological protection for appts in nuclear submarine support), Inst of Naval Medicine Alverstoke (submarine environmental res), RN Staff Coll 1981, MOD 1981-85, ret; safety and security mangr The Stock Exchange 1985-; *Recreations* walking, badminton; *Style*— Lt Cdr Edward Jolly; 164 Teg Down Meads, Winchester, Hants (☎ 0962 65583); The Stock Exchange, London EC2N 1HP (☎ 01 588 2355)

JOLLY, Air Cdre Robert Malcolm; CBE (1969); s of Robert Imrie Jolly (d 1940), and Ethel Thompson Jolly, *née* Elliott (d 1967); *b* 4 August 1920; *Educ* Skerry's Coll Newcastle; *m* 1946, Josette Jacqueline, da of Gabrielle Baindeky (d 1934); *Career* served in RAF 1940-75; Malta 1941-1945, Egypt 1945, Iraq 1945-1946, Malta 1946-1949, dir Personnel Services RAF 1970-75, Air Cdre, ret; md Leonard Griffiths and Assocs 1975-77, vice-pres MWS Consultants Inc 1978-80, computer advsr to Cyprus Govt 1981; gen mangr & dir of Diebold Res Program 1984-85; *Recreations* boating, gardening, DIY; *Clubs* RAF; *Style*— Air Cdre Robert Jolly, CBE

JOLOWICZ, Prof John Anthony (Tony); s of Prof Herbert Felix Jolowicz (d 1954), of London and Oxford, and Ruby Victoria, *née* Wagner (d 1963); *b* 11 April 1926; *Educ* Oundle, Trinity Coll Cambridge (MA); *m* 8 Aug 1957, Poppy, da of Norman Stanley; 1 s (Nathaniel Herbert b 20 July 1963), 2 da (Kate (Mrs Little) b 4 May 1959, Sophie b 26 June 1961); *Career* Lt RASC 1944-48; called to the Bar 1952, master of the bench Grays Inn 1978; Univ of Cambridge: asst lectr 1955, lectr 1959, reader 1972, prof of comparative law 1976-, chm faculty of law 1984-86, (fell Trinity Coll 1952-); prof associè Univ de Paris II 1976-, Lionel Cohen lectr Univ of Jerusalem 1983; pres SPTL 1986-87, ed of various law jls and author of various legal works; Hon Dr Universidad Nacional Autónoma de México 1985; *Recreations* reading, music, travel; *Clubs* Leander, RAC; *Style*— Prof J A Jolowicz; West Green House, Barrington, Cambridge CB2 5SA (☎ 0223 870 495); La Truffière, 47120 St Jean-de-Duras, France; Trinity College, Cambridge CB2 1TQ (☎ 0223 338 400, 0223 338 461, fax 0223 338 564)

JOLY, Hon Mrs Diana Olive; *née* Newall; da of 1 Baron Newall, GCB, OM, GCMG, CBE, AM (d 1963); *b* 1927; *m* 1956 (m dis 1967), John Leonard Joly; 1 da (Harriet Diana b 1960); *Style*— The Hon Mrs Diana Joly; Tower House, 8 Reybridge, Lacock, Chippenham, Wilts

JOLY, John Leonard; OBE (1973); s of Kenneth Henry Joly, OBE (d 1957), and Ethel Gertrude, *née* Bickmore (d 1987); *b* 12 Nov 1924; *Educ* Haileybury, Oriel Coll Oxford (MA); *m* 1, 16 Sept 1956, Diana Olive, da of Marshal of the RAF Lord Newall, GCB, OM, GCMG, CBE, AM (d 1964); 2 da (Susan Rosemary b 1957 (d 1974), Harriet Diana b 1960); m 2, 22 Dec 1967, Yvonne Irene, da of John Sothorn Lawrence, of Minehead Somerset; 1 s (Dominic John b 1967); *Career* Pilot Fleet Air Arm, Lt (A) RNVR 1943-47, 1 Carrier Sqdn Pacific Fleet; chm: Henry Heald & Co SAL Beirut 1964-, Heald Trading & Co SAL 1964-; author; *Books* Coral Circus (1951), The Destined Hour (1960, A Wreck of Paradise (1975); *Recreations* golf, tennis; *Clubs* Oriental, St George's, Golf of Lebanon; *Style*— John L Joly, OBE; Domaine des Fleurs, Chimin des Aspres, 06130 Grasse, France (☎ 93706366); Lebanon (☎ 893184, telex 42364 LEBANON)

JOLY DE LOTBINIERE, Lt-Col Sir Edmond; s of Brig-Gen Henri Gustave Joly de Lotbinière, DSO, JP (descended from Michel, Marquis de Lotbinière, sole French subject of Canadian birth to be created a Marquis, thus honoured by Louis XVI in 1784) and Mildred, da of Charles Seymour Grenfell (first cous of Field Marshal 1 Baron Grenfell, GCB, GCMG, PC); *b* 17 Mar 1903; *Educ* Eton, RMA Woolwich; *m* 1, 1928 (m dis 1937), Hon Elizabeth Jolliffe (da of 3 Baron Hylton); 2 s (Thomas and Michael, *qqv*); m 2, 1937, Helen (d 1953), da of Dr Hartley Ferrar, of NZ; m 3, 1954, as her 2 husb, Evelyn Adelaide (b 1904, d 1985, er da of Nigel Dawnay, s of Hon William Dawnay, JP, DL, 6 s of 7 Viscount Downe), widow of Lt-Col James Innes, DSO (*see* Hall, Sir John Bernard, 3 Bt); *Career* cmmnd RE 1923, ret 1928; RARO 1928-45, served Abyssinia, E Africa (despatches), Lt-Col 1943; pres Bury St Edmunds Conservative Assoc 1972-79 (chm 1953-72), chm and md building material companies;

chm Eastern Provincial Area Cons Assoc 1961-65 (pres 1969-72); kt 1964; *Clubs* Naval and Military; *Style*— Lt-Col Sir Edmond Joly de Lotbinière; Horringer Manor, Bury St Edmunds, Suffolk (☎ 028 488 208); Lignacite (Brandon) Ltd, Victoria Works, Brandon, Suffolk (☎ 0842 810 678)

JOLY DE LOTBINIERE, Michael Edmond; 2 s of Lt-Col Sir Edmond Joly de Lotbinière, *qv*, by his 1 w, Hon Elizabeth Joliffe (da of 3 Baron Hylton); *b* 3 Feb 1932; *Educ* Eton, Downing Cambridge; *m* 1956, Angela, yr da of Col Eugene St John Birnie, of Belgravia, by Lady Kathleen Courtenay, 3 da of 16 Earl of Devon; 2 s, 1 da; *Career* former tobacco farmer (Rhodesia); dir building materials-manufacturing cos; *Style*— Michael Joly de Lotbinière, Esq; Rougham House, Bury St Edmunds, Suffolk

JOLY DE LOTBINIERE, Thomas Henry; s of Lt-Col Sir Edmond Joly de Lotbinière, *qv*, by his 1 w, Hon Elizabeth Jolliffe (da of 3 Baron Hylton); *b* 18 July 1929; *Educ* Eton, Trinity Coll Cambridge (BA); *m* 15 Sept 1953, Prudence Mary, da of Thomas Richard Bevan (d 1970), of Hadlow Down; 1 s (Nicholas b 1955), 2 da (Lucy b 1957, Henrietta b 1960); *Career* memb Stock Exchange 1959; sr ptnr Grenfell & Colegrave (stockbrokers) 1978-86; chm CIBC Securities Europe Ltd 1986-; vice- pres Canadian Imperial Bank of Commerce 1986- ; *Recreations* gardening, shooting; *Clubs* City of London; *Style*— Thomas Joly de Lotbinière, Esq; Cottons Centre, Cottons Lane, London SE1 2QL (☎ 01 234 6000, fax 01 407 4127, telex 28902)

JONAS, Christopher William; s of Philip Griffith Jonas, MC (d 1982), of Oxted, Surrey, and Kathleen Marjory, *née* Ellis; *b* 19 August 1941; *Educ* Charterhouse, Coll of Estate Mgmnt, London Business Sch; *m* 30 Nov 1968, (Jennifer Susan) Penny, da of Bernard Leslie Barker (d 1976), of Fulbeck, Grantham; 3 s ((Leslie) Peter b 16 April 1970, Toby Philip b 10 Nov 1971, Max Christopher b 2 Feb 1977), 1 da (Freya Josephine Wendy b 4 Feb 1981); *Career* TA Inns of Ct Regt 1959-66; Jones Lang Wootton 1959-67; Drivers Jonas: ptnr 1967-82, manging ptnr 1982-87, sr ptnr 1987-; memb Gen Cncl RICS, property advsr Staffs CC 1982-; bd memb: Port of London Authy 1985-, The Securities Assoc 1988-; chm Econs Res Assoc (USA), memb: Urban Land Inst USA, American Soc of Real Estate Cnsllrs; tstee Property Centre City Univ; Liveryman: Worshipful Co of Clothworkers 1962, Worshipful Co of Chartered Surveyors 1978; FRICS 1975, FRSA, FIOD; *Recreations* Wagner, other music, skiing, tennis; *Clubs* Naval and Military, Toronto (Toronto); *Style*— Christopher William Jonas, Esq; Drivers Jonas, 16 Suffolk St, London SW1Y 4HQ (☎ 01 930 9731, fax 01 930 3690, telex 917080)

JONAS, George Siegfried; s of George Jonas (d 1942), and Frieda, *née* Glaser (d 1942); *b* 2 Jan 1928; *Educ* Barnton Brunner Sr Sch, LSE (LLB); *m* 23 Dec 1951, Frieda, da of the late Marcus Reinert; 1 s (Steven Michael b 1956), 1 da (Helen Ann b 1959); *Career* slr; snr ptnr George Jonas & Co; cncl memb Birmingham Law Soc 1965- (pres 1979-80, vice pres 1978-79, hon Life memb 1985-) and chm litigation and legal and ctee 1972-79; chm No 6 Regnl Devpt Slr Ctee 1984-87; chm Cncl of Mgmnt City of Birmingham Symphony Orch 1974- (dep chm 1971-74, memb 1966-); memb Birmingham City Cncl 1959-65 and 1966-69, chm Public Library Ctee 1962-65; Lab pty candidate Hall Green 1966; fndr tstee Cannon Hill Tst, chm The Margery Fry Memorial Tst 1970-85, former chm W Midlands Campaign for Abolition of Capital Punishment; awarded Gold Medal of the Birmingham Civic Soc (1986); *Recreations* music, cricket, modern transport; *Clubs* The Birmingham; *Style*— George S Jonas, Esq; 15 Burke Avenue, Birmingham B13 9XB (☎ (021) 777 3773); 5 Waterloo St, Birmingham B2 5PG (☎ (021) 0660, telex 334 786 GJONASG)

JONAS, Peter; s of Walter Adolf Jonas (d 1965), of Hamburg and London, and Hilda May, *née* Ziadie; *b* 14 Oct 1946; *Educ* Worth Sch, Univ of Sussex (BA), Royal Northern Coll of Music (LRAM), Royal Coll of Music (CAMS), Eastman Sch of Music, Univ of Rochester USA; *Career* Chicago Symphony Orch: asst to music dir 1974-76, artistic admin 1976-85; dir of artistic admin Orchestral Assoc of Chicago 1977-85 (Chicago Symphony Orch, Civil Orch of Chicago, Chicago Symphony Chorus, Allied Arts Assoc, Orchestra Hall), md ENO 1985-; memb: bd of mgmnt Nat Opera Studio 1985-, cncl RCM 1988-; *Recreations* music, theatre, architectural models, Eastern Europe; *Clubs* Athenaeum; *Style*— Peter Jonas, Esq; 18 Lonsdale Place, Barnsbury Street, London N1 1EL (☎ 01 609 9427); English National Opera, London Coliseum, St Martins Lane, London WC2N 4ES (☎ 01 836 0111)

JONDORF, Dr W(erner) Robert; s of Wilhelm Jondorf (d 1957), and Irmgard Jondorf (d 1937); *b* 2 Dec 1928; *Educ* King Henry VIII GS, Abergavenny Univ Coll Cardiff (BSc), St Mary's Hosp Med Sch London (PhD); *m* 25 July 1963, Gillian, da of Royal Digby Moore (d 1975), of Oakington, Cambs; 4 da (Harriet b 1964, Sarah b 1965, Miranda (twin) b 1965, Alice b 1969); *Career* visiting scientist: dept of chemical pharmacology Nat Heart Inst, Nat Insts of Health Bethesda Md USA 1957-60; special lectr Chester Beatty Res Inst London 1961-, special res fell dept of biochemistry Univ of Glasgow 1962-63; guest worker: Nat Cancer Inst, Nat Insts of Health Bethesda (Md 1964-65); assoc res prof dept of pharmacology The George Washington Univ Med Center Washington DC USA 1968-71 (asst res prof 1963-68), Leverhulme res fell dept of pharmacology Univ of Glasgow 1971-73, res fell dept of biochemistry Univ of Cambridge 1973-74, res scientist RSS Labs Newmarket Suffolk 1974-79; Swiss Nat Fund supported guest faculty, Inst of Pharmacology Univ of Berne Switzerland 1979-81, memb scientist endocrinology section Bourn Hall Clinic Bourn Cambridge 1982-85, guest faculty memb Inst of Pharmacology Univ of Berne Switzerland 1986-, visiting Res Fell Mayo Clinic Rochester MN 55905 USA 1988; numerous scientific publications: Mechanism of Action of Drugs, Evolution, Species, Age and Hormone Dependence on Response to Drugs and Toxic Agents; *Books* Signals to Noise (1963), Messages from Planet Earth (1978), Through the Gates of Time (1987); *Recreations* chess, motorcylcing, civic affairs, study of Central and S American civilisations, poetry; *Style*— Dr W Robert Jondorf; 3 Gough Way, Cambridge CB3 9LN

JONES, Alan Martin; s of John Edward Jones (d 1977), and Ina Majorie Jones, *née* Hartshorne (d 1987); *b* 27 Sept 1941; *Educ* Brewood GS; *m* 5 Sept 1964, Valerie, da of Edward Mitchell, of Wolverhampton; 1 s (Sean b 1966); *Career* financial dir; D F Bevan (Holdings) plc 1974-86, Wheway Distribution Ltd 1986-87; md Wheway Secretarial Services Ltd 1987-; FCCA; ACMA; *Style*— Alan M Jones, Esq; 5 Firsway, Wightwick, Wolverhampton, WV6 8BJ (☎ 0902 762051); Trinity Court, Newton Road, Great Barr, Birmingham B43 6RP (☎ 021 357 9474); car telephone (0860) 523820

JONES, Alan Wingate; s of Gilbert Victor Jones (d 1971), of Kingswood, Surrey, and Isobel Nairn Wilson; *b* 15 Oct 1939; *Educ* Sutton Valence Sch, Kings Coll Cambridge (MA); *m* 4 July 1974, Judith Ann, da of George William Curtis (d 1952); 1 s (Mark b 1975), 1 da (Sophie b 1980); *Career* md Plessey Electronic Systems, dir Plessey Co plc; *Recreations* skiing, opera; *Clubs* RAC; *Style*— Alan W Jones, Esq; Green Croft, Green Lane, Churt, Farnham, Surrey (☎ 0428 713189); Plessey Company, Addlestone, Surrey (telex 936082); car tel 0860 379 019

JONES, Allen; s of William Jones, and Madeline, *née* Aveson; *b* 1 Sept 1937; *Educ* Ealing GS for Boys, Hornsey Sch of Art, RCA; *m* 1964 (m dis 1978), Janet, *née* Bowen; 2 da (Thea b 1967, Sarah (twin) b 1967); *Career* teacher of lithography Croydon Coll of Art 1961-63, teacher of painting Chelsea Sch of Art 1966-68; painter; first int exhibition Paris Biennale 1961; one man exhibitions incl: Arthur Tooth & Sons (London), Richard Feigen Gallery (NYC, Chicago and Los Angeles), Marlborough Fine Art (London), Seibu (Tokyo), Waddington Galleries (London), James Corcoran Gallery (Los Angeles), Galerie Patrice Trigano (Paris); ICA graphic retrospective 1978, retrospective of painting Walker Art Gallery (Liverpool) 1979; cmmns incl: Liverpool Int Garden Festival 1984, sculpture for Cottons Atrium London Bridge City 1987; designer of sets for TV and stage in UK and Germany (incl sets and costumes for Rambert Dance Co 1989); RA; *Books* Allen Jones Figures (1969), Allen Jones Projects (1971), Waitress (1972), Sheer Magic (1979); *Recreations* gardening; *Clubs* Zanzibar, Garrick; *Style*— Allen Jones, Esq; c/o Waddington Galleries, 11 Cork St, London W1X 1PD (☎ 01 437 8611, fax 01 734 4146)

JONES, Dr Alun Denry Wynn; s of Thomas D Jones (d 1982) of Penygroes Dyfed and Ray, *née* Morgan; *b* 13 Nov 1939; *Educ* Amman Valley GS Ammanford, Christ Church Oxford (MA, D Phil); *m* 22 Aug 1964, Ann, da of Brinley Edwards (d 1955), of Bettws, Dyfed; 2 da (Helen b 1966, Ingrid b 1969); *Career* sr student Cmmn for the Exhibition of 1851 1964-66, sr res fell UKAEA 1966-67, Lockheed Missiles and Space Co California 1967-70, tutor Open Univ 1971-82, dep ed Nature, Macmillan Jnls 1972- (joined 1971), Br Steel Corpn 1974-77, Br Steel Overseas Servs 1977-81, asst dir Tech Change Centre 1982-85, dir and sec Wolfson Fndn 1987- (dep dir 1986-87); Br Assoc for Advancement of Sci: sec of working pty on social concern and biological advances 1972-74, memb section X ctee 1981-; Br Library: memb advsy cncl 1983-85, document supply centre advsy ctee 1986-; memb cncl Nat Library of Wales 1987- (govr 1986-); FInstP 1973, CPhys 1987, CDipAF 1977; *Books* Our Future Inheritance: Choice or Chance (jtly 1974); *Recreations* Welsh culture, gardening, theatre; *Style*— Dr Alun Jones; 4 Wheatsheaf Close, Woking, Surrey GU21 4BP; 251/256 Tottenham Court Rd, London W1A 1BZ (☎ 01 580 6441)

JONES, Andrew Bryden; s of David Jones, 1 Sheriffmuirlands Rd, Causewayhead, Stirling, Scotland, and Ellen Milne, *née* Rennie (d 1983); *b* 31 Mar 1948; *Educ* HS of Stirling; *m* 9 Feb 1974, Rosemary Ann, da of Norman Thomas Clarke, of 7 Ardmore Lane, Buckhurst Hill, Essex; 2 s (Alasdair David b 1975, Douglas Ian b 1976); *Career* apprentice CA Dickson Middleton & Co Stirling 1965-70, qualified 1970, sr accountant in tax Arthur Andersen Glasgow 1970-71, mangr in tax Edward Moore & Co London 1971-74, supervisor to mangr Whinney Murray & Co London 1974-79; Ernst & Whinney: ptnr 1979, ptnr i/c of tax London 1984, nat tax ptnr 1988, co-ordinating ptnr of firm's exec 1988; MICAS 1970; *Recreations* watching sons play sport, golf, reading; *Style*— Andrew B Jones, Esq; 6 Oaklands Dr, Bishops Stortford, Herts CM23 2BZ (☎ 0279 506152); Ernst & Whinney, Becket House, 1 Lambeth Palace Rd, London SE1 7EU (☎ 01 928 2000, fax 01 928 1345)

JONES, Anne; da of Sydney Joseph Pickard (d 1987), and Hilda Everitt, *née* Bird; *b* 8 April 1935; *Educ* Harrow Weald Co Sch, Westfield Coll London (BA), King's Coll London (PGCE); *m* 9 Aug 1958 (m dis 1988), Cyril Gareth Jones, s of Lyell Jones (d 1936); 1 s (Christopher b 24 July 1962), 2 da (Catherine Rachel b 8 Aug 1963, Rebecca Madryn b 15 March 1966); *Career* asst mistress: Malvern Girls Coll 1957-58, Godolphin and Latymer Sch 1958-62, Dulwich Coll 1964; sch cnsllr Mayfield London 1965-71, dep head Thomas Calton Sch London 1971-74; head: Vauxhall Manor Sch 1974-81, Cranford Community Coll 1981-87, dir of educn programmes Training Agency Employment Dept 1987-; former chm Area Manpower Bd London SW; cncl memb CRAC; FRSA (cncl memb), hon memb City and Guilds Inst; *Books* Counselling Adolescents: School and after (1986), Leadership for Tomorrows Schools (1987); *Recreations* walking, dining, swimming, boating; *Style*— Mrs Anne Jones; The Training Agency, Moorfoot, Sheffield S1 4PQ (☎ 0742 70 4221)

JONES, Rt Hon Aubrey; PC (1955); s of Evan and Margaret Aubrey Jones; *b* 20 Nov 1911; *Educ* Cyfartha Castle Secdy Sch Merthyr Tydfil, LSE; *m* 1948, Joan, da of G Godfrey-Isaacs; 2 s; *Career* editorial staff The Times 1937-39 and 1947-48; contested SE Essex 1945 and Heywood and Radcliffe 1946; MP (Unionist) Birmingham Hall Green 1950-65, PPS to min of State Econ Affrs 1952 and to min of Materials 1953; min of Fuel and Power 1955-57, min of Supply 1957-59; chm Prices and Incomes Bd 1965-70; pres Oxford Energy Policy Club 1976-88, sr research assoc St Antony's Coll Oxford 1979-82, fellow commoner Churchill Coll Cambridge 1972, 1982-86; dir: Black & Decker 1977-83, Thomas Tilling 1970-82 and formerly dir GKN and Courtaulds; chm: Cornhill Insurance 1971-74 (dir 1971) and formerly Staveley and Laporte Industs; visiting fell Science Policy Res Unit (Sussex Univ) 1986; hon fellow LSE 1959 (memb Court of Govrs 1964), Hon DSc Bath; *Style*— The Rt Hon Aubrey Jones; Arnen, Limmer Lane, Felpham, Bognor Regis, W Sussex (☎ 024 369 2722)

JONES, (Stephen) Barry; MP (Lab) Alyn and Deeside 1983-; s of Stephen Jones by his w Grace; *b* 1937; *m* Janet Davies; 1 s; *Career* MP (Lab) Flint E 1970-1983, parly under-sec Wales 1974-79, oppn front bench spokesman: Employment 1981-Nov 1983, Wales and memb shadow cabinet Nov 1983-87; *Clubs* Connah's Quay Labour; *Style*— Barry Jones, Esq, MP; 30 Paper Mill Lane, Oakenholt, Flint, Clwyd (☎ (035 26) 3430)

JONES, Maj-Gen Basil Douglas; CB (1960), CBE (1950); s of Rev Benjamin Jones (d 1940), and Emma Wonnacott (d 1945); *b* 14 May 1903; *Educ* Plymouth Coll, RMC Sandhurst; *m* 1932, Katherine Holberton (d 1986), da of Col Hubert William Man, CBE, DSO (d 1956); 1 s (Michael), 2 da (Alison, Penelope); *Career* 2nd Lt Welch Regt 1924; transferred to RAOC 1935, Maj 1939, served with Australian Military Forces in Australia & New Guinea 1941-43, Temp Brig 1947, Maj Gen 1958, ADC to HM The Queen 1956-58, Inspr RAOC 1958-60, ret Col Cmdt RAOC 1963-67; *Recreations* golf, croquet, gardening; *Style*— General Basil D Jones, CB, CBE; Churchfield, All Saints Lane, Sutton Courtenay, Abingdon, Oxon (☎ 0235 848261)

JONES, Benjamin George; CBE (1979); s of Thomas Jones, and Rachel, *née* Thomas; *b* 18 Nov 1914; *Educ* Aberaeron Sch, Univ Coll of Wales (LLB); *m* 6 April 1946, Menna Wynn, da of Rev Evelyn Wynn Jones, of Holyhead; 1 s (Richard Wynn b 27 Aug 1948), 1 da (Rhiannon Eland b 24 Sept 1952); *Career* RAF 1940-46; slr, ptnr: Cecil Williams 1946-60, Linklaters & Paines 1963-78; chm: London Welsh Assoc 1954,

Cncl for Welsh Language 1973-78; pres Hon Soc of Cymmrodorion 1982- (dep sec 1960-63, sec 1963-73), contested (L) Merioneth 1959, memb Gen Advsy Cncl BBC 1970-78, vice-pres and memb cte Univ Coll of Wales 1975-86 cncl memb Nat Library of Wales, former dep chm Agric Land Tribunal SE Area; Hon LLD Wales 1983; *Recreations* walking, music, visiting art galleries; *Clubs* Reform; *Style—* Benjamin Jones, Esq, CBE

JONES, Brenda; da of Edward Jones (d 1950), and Margaret Jones, *née* Thomas (d 1981); *b* 20 Oct 1938; *Educ* Blackburne House Liverpool, Univ Coll of N Wales Bangor,; *m* 1973, Roger Houghton, s of Geoffrey Houghton; 1 s (Geoffrey b 1966), 2 da (Jane b 1968, Daisy b 1975); *Career* Kenya corr The Guardian, dep prodn ed Sunday Times Business News, dep ed Cosmopolitan, woman's ed Sunday Times Magazine; *Books* Cosmopolitan's Guide to Getting Ahead (1981); *Style—* Ms Brenda Jones; Sunday Times Magazine (☎ 01 833 7188)

JONES, Brian Robert; s of Charles Robert (d 1973), and Ellen Elsie Walker; *b* 7 Jan 1946; *Educ* Wallington GS; *m* 1968, Sandra Thirlwall, da of William Davies (d 1953); 1 da (Elaine b 1969); *Career* fell of the Institute of Actuaries (FIA); gen mangr and actuary Royal London Mutual Insurance Soc Ltd 1987- (dir 1985-); chm Royal London Unit Tst Mangrs Ltd 1987- (dir 1981-); *Recreations* gardening, reading, enjoyment of the countryside; *Style—* Brian Jones, Esq; "Tarkwa", Daisy Green, Groton, Boxford, nr Colchester, Essex CO6 5EN (☎ (0787) 210814); Royal London House, Middleborough, Colchester, Essex CO1 1RA (☎ (0206) 761761, fax (0206) 578449, telex 987723)

JONES, (Martin) Bruce; s of Edward Stanley Johes (d 1955), and Elvia Hinton, *née* Bloomer; *b* 28 August 1940; *Educ* Cheltenham, Oriel Coll Oxford (BA); *m* 1 Jan 1971, Gillian Ruth, da of Harold Earley Moxon (d 1974); 1 s (Crispin b 1974), 2 da (Abigail b 1972, Isabelle b 1980); *Career* market res exec Market Investigations Ltd 1962-70, investmt analyst Strauss Turnbull & Co 1970-77, sr investmt analyst WI CARR/CARR SEBAG 1977-82; dir investmt res Kitcat & Aitken 1982-; AMSIA; *Recreations* antiques; *Style—* Bruce Jones, Esq; Whitworth La, Loughton, Milton Keynes, Beds MK5 8EB (☎ 0908 670 393); Kitcat & Aitken, 71 Queen Victoria St, London EC4V 4DE (☎ 01 489 1966, fax 01 329 6150, telex 888297)

JONES, Bryan Sydney Powell; s of Leonard Stanley Jones (d 1946), and Ethel, *née* Angle (d 1981); *b* 20 Feb 1932; *Educ* Watford Boys GS, Jesus Coll Cambridge (MA, LLM); *m* 18 Aug 1962, Jennifer Marion, da of Claude Gilbert Betts (d 1984); 1 s (Christopher b 1968), 2 da (Catherine b 1964, Alison b 1966); *Career* Nat Serv pilot officer RAF 1950-51, Flt Lt Royal Aux AF 1960; admitted slr 1957, ptnr JW Ward & Son 1963-; memb Bath CC 1963-72, chm govrs Bath Coll Higher Educn 1967-74, pres Bath Law Soc 1977-79, vice chm Avon CC 1988-(memb 1985-); charter memb Bath Lions Club 1963-; memb Law Soc; *Recreations* walking; *Style—* Bryan Jones, Esq; 92 High St, Marshfield SN14 8LS (☎ 0225 891 053); 52 Broad St, Bristol BS1 2EP (☎ 0272 292 811, fax 0272 290 6863)

JONES, Charles Lloyd; CMG (1978); s of Sir Charles Lloyd Jones (d 1958), of NSW, and Hannah Beynon Lloyd Jones, OBE (d 1982); *b* 4 Dec 1932; *Educ* Cranbrook Sch Sydney NSW, Univ of Sydney NSW; *Career* chm David Jones Ltd Sydney 1963- 80 (alternate dir 1956, full dir 1957-80), pres Cr Retail Traders' Assoc NSW 1976-78; hon consul-gen Finland 1972-, vice-pres Finnish Aust Chamber of Commerce 1973-; tstee: William Dobell Art Fndn 1971-; Art Gallery of NSW 1972- (pres bd of tstees 1980-83), pres Aust Cr Retailers Assoc 1980-83 (vice pres 1976-80), memb bd Sydney Hosp, vice-pres French C of C Sydney; Cdr Order of Offr OM Italy, Lion of Finland 1982; *Clubs* Royal Sydney GC; *Style—* Charles Jones Esq, CMG; 294 Old South Head Rd, Watsons Bay 2030 NSW; Summerlees Farm, Yarramalong Rd, Yarramalong, 2259 NSW

JONES, Christopher Kenneth; s of William Henry Jones (d 1942), and Dorothy Irene, *née* Tonge; *b* 22 Mar 1939; *Educ* Sir Roger Manwood's GS Sandwich, Univ of Southampton's Sch of Navigation; *m* 29 June 1963, (Moira) Jane, da of Gp Capt David Fowler McIntyre, DFC (d 1957), of Lochgreen House Troon Ayrshire; 2 s (Mark b 1964, Neil b 1965), 1 da (Amanda b 1967); *Career* third offr Union-Castle Mail SS Co Ltd 1959-62, merchandise dir Peter Robinson/Top Shop Ltd 1964-72, dep md Richard Shops Ltd 1972-76, md Bally London Shoe Co Ltd 1976-80, chief exec Lillywhites Ltd 1980-84, md retail activities Seaco Inc 1984-86; dir The Valentine Publishing Gp plc 1989; Freeman City of London; FRSA 1974; *Recreations* skiing, golf; *Style—* Christopher Jones, Esq; 12 Hamilton Drive, Sunningdale, Berkshire SL5 9PP (☎ 0990 21837); 31 Curzon St, London W1Y 7AE (☎ 01 499 0154, 01 491 9230, fax 0990 23371, telex 23727 SAXET G)

JONES, Christopher Michael Stuart; s of Flt Lt Richard Leoline Jones, RAFVR, of Whitney, Oxon, and Elizabeth Margaret, *née* Cook; *b* 1 Jan 1944; *m* 1 Sept 1966, Jennifer Amy, da of Leonardus Franciscus Aarts, of Wolverhampton, Midlands; 1 s (Richard b 3 June 1970), 1 da (Victoria b 16 Oct 1973); *Career* Sales mangr RH Macy New York USA 1964; James Beattie: buyer Wolverhampton 1965, gen mangr Birkenhead 1972; James Beattie Solihull: gen mangr 1974, gp merchandise controller 1977, merchandise dir 1979, jt md 1984; memb steering ctee Wolverhampton Ptnrs in Progress; *Recreations* gardening, DIY, collecting antique clocks; *Clubs* Rotary and 41 (Tettenhall); *Style—* Christopher Jones, Esq; Woodbury, Wergs Rd, Tettenhall, Wolverhampton WV6 8TD (☎ 0902 759 200); James Beattie plc, Victoria St, Wolverhampton WV1 (☎ 0902 22 311, fax 0902 28 144)

JONES, (Robert Miles) Christopher; s of Rev Richard Ebenezer Jones (d 1937), of Whittington Rectory, Nr Cheltenham, Glos, and Mary Helen, *née* Jenkins (d 1967); *b* 9 July 1922; *Educ* Haileybury, Royal Agric Coll; *m* 6 June 1952, Sandra Mary 9d 1986), da of Lt-Col William Franklin Beavan, OBE, DL (d 1985), of Halkyn Castle, Flint; 2 s (Richard b 1953, David b 1956), 1 da (Susan b 1954); *Career* RAF 1940-46, cmmnd 1941, serv ME 1941-44, Europe 1944-46; land agent to Duke of Westminster 1950-84, Tstees of Grosvenor Estate 1950-84; FLAS, FAI, FRICS; *Recreations* shooting and fishing; *Style—* R M C Jones, Esq; Langstone Court, Llangarron, Ross-on-Wye, Herefordshire, HR9 6NR, (☎ 098 984 254)

JONES, (John) Clement; CBE (1972); only s of Clement Daniel Jones (d 1916), of Haverfordwest; *b* 22 June 1915; *Educ* Ardwyn, Aberystwyth, (BA Open Univ 1983); *m* 1938, Marjorie, da of George Gibson, of Llandrindod Wells; 3 s; *Career* journalist and broadcaster; editor and dir Express and Star Wolverhampton 1960-75; Cwlth and UNESCO media conslt 1975-, exec dir Beacon Radio (programming) 1974-8, pres Guild Br Newspaper Editors, govr British Inst of Human Rights 1971-85; FRSA ; *Recreations* gardening, beekeeping, writing, broadcasting; *Clubs* Athenaeum; *Style—* J Clement Jones, Esq, CBE; 7 South View Drive, Walton on the Naze, Essex CO14 8EP

JONES, Clive Lawson; s of John Lawson Jones (d 1986), and Gladys Irene, *née* Danies; *b* 16 Mar 1937; *Educ* Cranleigh Sch, Univ of Wales (BSc); *m* 4 April 1961, Susan Brenda, da of late Walter Angus McLeod; 1 s (Robin b 26 Dec 1964), 1 da (Tracy b 28 Dec 1966); *Career* with: BP 1957-61, Texaco Trinidad 1961-68; princ DTI 1968-73, asst sec Dept of Energy 1973-77, energy cnsllr Br Embassy Washington DC 1977-81, undersec Dept of Energy 1981-82, dir energy policy EC 1982-86, dep dir gen for energy EC Cmmn 1987-; *Style—* Clive Jones, Esq; 37 Rue Maredye, 1150 Brussels, Belgium; 5 Burlington Gardens, London W4; CEE DGXVII 200 Rue De La Loi, 1049 Brussels, Belgium (☎ 010 32 2 235 7096)

JONES, David Alan Freeborn; s of Daniel Edward (d 1966), of King's Norton, Birmingham, and Winnifred Kate, *née* Freeborn; *b* 28 Mar 1943; *Educ* King's Norton GS Nottingham Univ (LLB Hons); *m* 15 Feb 1969, Mavis, da of John Douglas (d 1961), of Northumbria; 1 s (Nicholas 1971), 2 da (Rachel b 1973, Hannah b 1980); *Career* called to the Bar Gray's Inn 1967, in practice Birmingham 1969-, head of chambers 1985, organiser deliverer and publisher Annual Lecture to the Birmingham Bar and Midland and Oxford Circuit on Criminal Law, law lectr Birmingham Coll of Commerce 1965-68; Criminal Bar Assoc; *Recreations* cricket, golf, ornithology, gardening, tennis; *Clubs* Alvechurch CC, Fulford Heath & Aberdovey GCs, RSPB; *Style—* David Jones, Esq; 12 Cherry Hill Ave, Barnt Gn, Birmingham B45 8LA (☎ 021 445 1935); 3 Fountain Ct, Steelhouse Lane, Birmingham B4 6DR (☎ 021 236 5854, fax 021 236 7008)

JONES, Rev David Ian Stewart; s of Rev John Milton Granville Jones (d 1986), and Evelyn Moyes Stewart, *née* Chedburn (d 1965); *b* 3 May 1934; *Educ* St John's Sch Leatherhead, Selwyn Coll Cambridge (MA); *m* 19 Aug 1967, Susan Rosemary, da of Eric Arthur Hardy-Smith (d 1958); 1 s (Benedict b 12 Sept 1970), 1 da (Katherine (twin) b 1970); *Career* RCS 1952-54; ordained priest Manchester Cathedral 1960, curate Oldham Parish Church 1959-62, vicar All Saints, Elton, Bury, Lancs 1962-66, asst conduct & chaplain Eton 1966-70 (conduct & sr chaplain 1970-74), headmaster Bryanston 1974-82, rector Bristol City Parish 1982-85; dir Lambeth Charities 1985-; *Recreations* reading, walking, music; *Clubs* East India, Devonshire, Sports and Public Schools; *Style—* The Rev David Jones; 127 Kennington Road, London SE11 6SF (☎ 01 735 2531, office 01 735 1925)

JONES, (John) David; s of John Trevor Jones, of The Orchard, 5 Allerton Beeches, Liverpool, and Mair Eluned Jones; *b* 11 Oct 1955; *Educ* Liverpool Coll, Oxford Univ (MA), London Univ (PhD); *Career* insur analyst L Messel & Co 1981-83, asst dir and head of French res E B Savory Milln & Co 1983-86, assoc dir and head of French res Warburg Securities 1986-; registered rep Stock Exchange 1987, memb Société Francaise des Analystes Financiers 1988; *Recreations* classical music, theatre, cinema, reading; *Clubs* United Oxford & Cambridge University, Oxford Soc, Bow Gp; *Style—* David Jones, Esq; 147 Boulevard St Michel, 75005, Paris (☎ 010 331 4633 8480); 17 Hale House, Bessborough Gardens, 7 Drummond Gate, London SW1 V2HS; Warburg Securites, c/o Bacot-Allain, 13 Rule Lafayette, 75009, Paris (☎ 010 331 4016 3306)

JONES, David Morris; s of Capt Morris Jones, MN (ka 1941) of Beaumaris, Anglesey, and Menna Lloyd, *née* Evans; *b* 24 Mar 1940; *Educ* Beaumaris GS, Univ Coll Bangor (BA, Dip Ed); *m* 3 Dec 1971, Patricia; 2 da (Sian b 24 Nov 1976, Eira b 17 Feb 1980); *Career* journalist Liverpool Daily Post and Echo Ltd 1962-63; BBC Wales: news asst 1963-64, sr news asst 1964-67, chief news asst 1967-71, TV news prodr 1971-82, managing ed news and current affairs 1982- 85, ed Wales news and current affairs 1985-; memb: Radio TV News Dirs Assoc (USA), Royal TV Soc; *Recreations* sailing; *Style—* David Jones, Esq; BBC, Broadcasting House, Llandaff, Cardiff, S Glam (☎ 0222 564 888, fax 0222 555 960)

JONES, Hon Mrs (Deborah Katherine Louise); *née* Suenson-Taylor; 2 da of 2 Baron Grantchester, CBE, QC; *b* 9 April 1957; *Educ* Cheltenham Ladies' Coll; *m* 1977, Michael Paul Jones; 1 s (Christopher Michael b 1987); *Style—* The Hon Mrs Jones; Windsor, Church Road, W Wittering, W Sussex

JONES, Della Louise Gething; da of Cyril Vincent Jones (d 1982), and Eileen Gething Jones; *Educ* Neath Girls GS, Royal Coll of Music (LRAM, ARCM, GRSM); *m* 2 April 1988, Paul Anthony Hooper Vigars, s of Norman Vigars; *Career* mezzo-soprano; soloist ENO 1977-82 incl: title role in Carmen, Dorabella in Cosi Fan Tutti, roles in many Rossini operas; sung with all maj Br opera cos and at opera houses and concert halls throughout Europe, USA and USSR incl: Dido in Les Troyens WNO 1987, Ramiro in Finta Giardinera and Cecilio in Lucio Silla Mostly Mozart Festival NY, Sorceress in Dido and Aeneas Buckingham Palace 1988 (tercentenary celebration of William and Mary); Laurence Olivier Award nomination for Rosina in The Barber of Seville ENO 1988; extensive recordings, frequent radio and tv broadcasts; *Recreations* collecting elephants, visiting Venice for Bellini, writing cadenzas, animal welfare; *Style—* Miss Della Jones; Music International, 13 Ardilaun Rd, Highbury, London N5 2QR (☎ 01 359 5183)

JONES, Dennis; s of Dennis, and Emily, *née* Buckley; *b* 17 Feb 1950; *Educ* Urmston GS; *m* 25 Aug 1984, Joan, da of Norman Bernard Cronshaw (d 1983); 3 s (Gary b 1958, Mark b 1960, Simon b 1967), 1 da (Johanna b 1968); *Career* dir: Hazlewood Foods plc 1975-, Irishwire Products plc 1986-; FCA; *Recreations* golf; *Clubs* Club de Golfe Las Brisas; *Style—* Dennis Jones, Esq; Hazlewood Foods plc, Rowditch, Derby DE1 1NB (☎ (0332) 295295)

JONES, Donald Keith; s of David Burne Jones (d 1965), of Handsworth Birmingham, and Peggy, *née* Lane (d 1930); *b* 29 Mar 1930; *Educ* Handsworth Coll Birmingham; *m* 20 March 1956, Barbara, da of Sidney Hinchcliffe, of Wakefield, Yorks; 1 da (Amanda Louise b 28 Aug 1958); *Career* Pilot Offr RAF: Flying Trg 1951, 20 sqdn 1953; ESSO UK plc, div dir: industrial/consumer 1970, planning and economics 1973, dir int and specialties 1975-85; dir Br Road Fedn 1983-88; chm Mid Surrey Health Authy 1986-; *Recreations* golf, walking, music and dining out; *Clubs* Betchworth Park GC; *Style—* Donald Jones, Esq; Latchetts, Park Lane, Reigate, Surrey RH2 8JX (☎ 07372 46 016); West Park Hospital, Horton Lane, Epsom, Surrey KT19 8PB (☎ 03727 27 811)

JONES, Donald Pryse; s of Evan Lewis Jones (d 1960), of Wye Lodge, Rhayader, Powys, and Florence Agnes Norah Jones (d 1988); *b* 16 April 1922; *Educ* Builth Wells Primary and Secdy Schs; *Career* served as Sgt Europe and N Africa 1941-46; slr; dir: Wyeside Arts Centre Ltd for 11 yrs, Builth Wells Golf and Gen Devpt Co Ltd for 22 yrs promoter and chm Wyeside Arts Centre Builth Wells; *Recreations* theatre, arts; *Style—* Donald Jones, Esq; Manchester House, High St, Builth Wells, Powys

JONES, Prof Douglas Samuel; MBE (1945); s of Jesse Dewis Jones (d 1932) and Bessie *née* Streather; *b* 10 Jan 1922; *Educ* Wolverhampton GS, Corpus Christi Coll Oxford (MA 1947, Hon fell 1980), Univ of Manchester (DSc); *m* 23 Sept 1950, Ivy da of Henry Styles (d 1932); 1 s (Philip b 1960), 1 da (Helen b 1958); *Career* WWII Flt Lt RAFVR 1941-45; fell Cwlth Fund MIT 1947-48; Univ of Manchester (asst lectr, lectr, sr lectr) 1948-57, res prof NY Univ 1955, prof Mathematics Univ of Keele 1957-64, visiting prof Courant Inst 1962-63, Ivory Prof of Mathematics Univ of Dundee 1964-; memb: Mathematical Sci Sub ctee 1971-86 (chm 1976-86), cncl Royal Sec 1973-74, UGC 1976-86, Computer Bd 1977-82, visiting ctee OU 1982-87, cncl Inst of Mathematics and its Applications 1982 (pres 1988-); Keith Prize Royal Soc of Edinburgh 1974, van der Pol gold medal of Int Union of Radio Sci 1981, Naylor Prize of London Mathematical Soc 1987; hon DSc Univ of Strathclyde 1975; FIMA 1964, FRSE 1967, FRS 1968; *Books* Electrical and Mechanical Oscillations (1961), Theory of Electromagnetism (1964), Generalised Functions (1966), Introductory Analysis Vol 1 (1969, Vol 2 1970), Methods in Electromagnetic Wave Propagation (1979, reissued as 2 volumes in 1987), Elementary Information Theory (1979), The Theory of Generalised Functions (1982), Differential Equations and Mathematical Biology (1983), Acoustic and Electromagnetic Waves (1986), Assembly programming and the 8086 Microprocessor (1988); *Clubs* Oxford and Cambridge; *Style*— Prof Douglas Jones, MBE; Department of Mathematics and Computer Science, The University, Dundee, DD1 4HN (☎ (0382) 23181)

JONES, (Ernest) Edward (Ted); s of William Edward (Ted) Jones (d 1976), of 25 Rose Cres, Scawthorne, Doncaster, and Eileen, *née* Gasser (d 1986); *b* 15 Oct 1931; *Educ* Sheffield De La Salle Coll, Hopwood Hall Coll of Educn, Manchester Univ, Sheffield Poly (Cert Ed, DipSc, DEM); *m* 27 Dec 1955, Mary Ellen, da of (Joseph) Rennison Armstrong (d 1955); 1 s (Peter Edward b 22 Nov 1956), 1 da (Elizabeth Mary b 1 Feb 1958); *Career* Nat Serv, RAF (lectr in RADAR systems); sch master 1953-; memb Doncaster Met BC 1980-(vice chm Educn ctee 1983-, chm Further Educn Ctee 1983-); chm: Doncaster Community Health Cncl 1981-, Trent Regn Assoc of Health Cncls 1988-, Assoc Yorks and Humberside Educn Authy 1988, S Yorks Int Archaeological Ctee 1987-; memb: exec Yorks Art Assoc 1983, Yorks and Humberside Museums Cncl 1983-, Cncl Nat Museums Assoc, Ct of Hull Univ 1983-, Sheffield Univ Cncl 1983-; memb of former Doncaster Co Borough Cncl 1962-74, S Yorks CC 1973-77; memb of cncl Bradford Univ 1986-; chm S Yorks CC 1975-76 (dep chm 1973-75); FRSA 1983, MRSH 1974; *Recreations* music, fine arts, gen interest in sport, fell-walking, caravanning; *Style*— Ted Jones, Esq; 11 Norborough Rd, Doncaster, S Yorks (☎ 0302 66122); Mansion House, Doncaster

JONES, Edward Appleby; s of Wilfred Jones (d 1977); *b* 21 April 1926; *Educ* Bede Collegiate Boys Sch Sunderland; *m* 1949, Jessie Isabell, *née* Green; 1 s (Antony David); *Career* Sgt (Air Gunner) RAF; cost accountant Garricks (Caterers) Ltd 1951-63, regional accountant Cooperative Wholesale Soc 1963-69, fin dir and co sec: RB Bolton (Mining Engrg) Ltd 1969-85, RB Bolton (Hydraulics) Ltd 1969-85, RB Bolton (Engrs) Ltd 1969-85, General Mining & Engrg Services Ltd 1977-85; *Recreations* gardening, travel, reading; *Style*— Edward Jones Esq; Hartside, 177 Newcastle Rd, Sunderland (☎ 488129)

JONES, Rt Hon Lord Justice; Rt Hon Sir Edward Warburton Jones; PC (1979), PC (N Ireland 1965); s of Hume Riversdale Jones, LLD, Resident Magistrate, and Elizabeth Anne Phibbs; yr bro of Gen Sir Charles Jones, GCB, CBE, MC, *qv*; *b* 3 July 1912; *Educ* Portora Royal Sch Enniskillen N Ireland, Trinity Coll Dublin (LLB); *m* 1, 1941, Margaret Anne Crosland (d 1953), da of William Smellie (d 1955); 3 s (Graham, Peter, Hume); m 2, 1953, Ruth Buchan Smellie (sis of his l w); 1 s (Charles); *Career* served WW II Royal Irish Fusiliers, Hon Lt-Col 1946; MP (U) Londonderry 1951-68 (NI Parl); barrister NI 1936 and Middle Temple 1964, QC (NI) 1948, jr crown counsel Belfast 1945-55, attorney-gen NI 1964-68, High Court Judge NI 1968-73, Lord Justice of Appeal NI 1973-84, Hon Master of Bench Middle Temple 1982-; vice pres College Historical Soc Trinity Coll Dublin; kt 1973; *Books* Jones L J His Life and Times an autobiography; *Recreations* golf, sailing; *Clubs* Army & Navy, Royal Portrush Golf, Ulster Reform; *Style*— The Rt Hon Lord Justice Jones; Craig-y-Mor, Trearddur Bay, Anglesey (☎ 860406); The Lodge, Spa, Ballynahinch, Co Down, N Ireland (☎ 562240)

JONES, Sir (Charles) Edward Webb; KCB (1989), CBE (1985); s of Gen Sir Charles Jones, GCB, CBE, MC (d 1988), of Amesbury Abbey, Amesbury, Wilts, and Ouida Margaret Jones; *b* 25 Sept 1936; *Educ* Portora Royal Sch Enniskillen NI; *m* 20 Feb 1965, Suzanne Vere, da of G R P Leschallas, of Little Canon, Wateringbury, Kent; 2 s (Hume b 1967, Benjamin b 1978), 1 da (Jemma b 1971); *Career* cmmnd Oxford and Bucks LI 1956, Green Jackets 1958, Royal Green Jackets 1967, Maj DAA and QMG HQ 7 Armd Bde 1968, Lt-Col dir staff Staff Coll 1973, CO 1 Bn Royal Green Jackets 1974, Col MO4 MOD 1976, RCDS 1980, Brig Cdr 6 Armd Bde 1981, Cdr Br Military Advsy and Trg Team Zimbabwe 1983, Maj-Gen Dir Gen TA and Orgn 1985, Cdr 3 Armd Div 1987, Lt-Gen QMG 1988; *Recreations* fishing, golf; *Clubs* Army and Navy; *Style*— Sir Edward Jones, KCB, CBE

JONES, Sir (William) Elwyn Edwards; s of Rev Robert William Jones; *b* 1904; *Educ* Bootle Secondary Sch, Univ of Wales (BA, LLB); *m* 1936, Dydd, da of Rev Tegla Davies; 1 s, 2 da; *Career* solicitor 1927; town clerk Bangor 1939-69; MP (Lab) Conway Div Caernarvonshire 1950-51; Cncl and Court of Govrs and Tres Univ Coll of N Wales, Court of Govrs Univ of Wales; kt 1978; *Style*— Sir Elwyn Jones; 23 Glyngarth Court, Glyngarth, Menai Bridge, Gwynedd, N Wales (☎ 0248 713 422)

JONES, Emlyn Bartley; MBE (1975); s of Ernest Jones, MM (d 1955), of Buckley Clywd, and Sarah Jones (d 1982); *b* 9 Dec 1920; *Educ* Alun GS Mold Clwyd, Normal Coll Bangor N Wales (Teachers Cert), Loughborough Coll (Dip Physical Ed); *m* 27 March 1944, (Constance) Inez, da of Richard William Jones, of Mold, Clwyd; 1 da (Madeleine Bartley (Mrs Ward) b 11 Oct 1946); *Career* Fl Lt Radar Branch 1941-46, cmmnd 1943, PO demobbed 1946; teacher history and physical educn Flint Modern Secdy Sch Clwyd 1946, tech rep CCPR N Wales 1947-51, tech advsr CCPR London HQ 1951- 62, tv sports commentator ITV 1955-, dir Crystal Palace Nat Sports Centre 1962-78, dir gen The Sports Co 1978-83, self empld conslt sport and leisure 1983-; pres Br Assoc Nat Sports Admins, chm Physical activities ctee Nat Assoc Boy's Clubs, individual memb CCPR, govr Dulwich Coll, fndr co memb London Sports Med Inst; FBIM 1984; *Books* Learning Lawn Tennis (1960), Sport in Space (1985); *Recreations* golf, skiing, watching sport, reading, walking; *Clubs* Royal Air Force; *Style*— Emlyn Jones, Esq, MBE; Chwarae Teg, 1 B Allison Grove, Dulwich, London SE21 7ER (☎ 01 693 7528)

JONES, Prof Emrys; s of Samuel Garfield Jones (d 1969), and Annie, *née* Williams (d 1983); *b* 17 August 1920; *Educ* Aberdare Boy's GS, Univ Coll of Wales Aberystwyth (BSc, MSc, PhD); *m* 7 Aug 1948, Iona Vivien, da of Richard Hywel Hughes (d 1972); 2 da (Catrin b 1955, Rhianon b 1958, d 1980); *Career* asst lectr geography Univ Coll London 1947-50, lectr and sr lectr Queen's Univ Belfast 1950-58, reader and prof LSE 1959-84, emeritus 1984; Royal Geographical Soc: fell 1947, cncl memb 1972-78, vice pres 1978-83, chm Regnl Studies 1968-70; chm Hon Soc of Cymmrodorion 1983- (cncl memb 1978-), memb Govt Ctee of Enquiry into Allotment 1969; conslt in planning and urbanisation; hon DSc Queen's Univ Belfast 1978, Royal Geographical Soc Victoria Medal 1977; fell: Univ of Wales 1946-47, Rockefeller Fndn NY; *Books* Social Geography of Belfast (1960), Introduction to Human Geography (1964), Towns & Cities (1965), Atlas of London (1970), Cities (with E Van Zandt 1974), Introduction to Social Geography (with J Eyles, 1977); *Recreations* books, music; *Clubs* Athenaeum; *Style*— Prof Emrys Jones; 2 Pine Close, North Rd, Berkhamsted, Herts HP4 3BZ (☎ 0442 875 422)

JONES, Sir (William) Emrys; s of late William Jones; *b* 6 July 1915; *Educ* Llandovery GS, Univ Coll of Wales; *m* 1, 1938 (m dis 1966), Megan Ann Morgan; 3 s; m 2, 1967, Gwyneth George; *Career* MAFF: chief agric advsr 1967-71, dir-gen agricultural devpt and advsy serv 1971-73; princ Agricultural Coll Cirencester 1973-78, emeritus 1978-85; dir Lloyds Bank (N and E Midlands Region) 1978-, chm Velcourt Mgmnt Servs 1983-84; kt 1971; *Clubs* Farmers'; *Style*— Sir Emrys Jones; The Draey, 18 St Mary's Park, Louth, Lincs

JONES, Sir Ewart Ray Herbert; s of William Jones (d 1924); *b* 16 Mar 1911; *Educ* Grove Park Sch Wrexham, Univ Coll of N Wales Bangor, Manchester Univ (MA, DSc, PhD); *m* 1937, Frances Mary Copp; 1 s, 2 da; *Career* Sir Samuel Hall prof of chemistry Manchester Univ 1947-55, Waynflete prof of chemistry Oxford Univ 1955-78, emeritus 1978-; hon fellow Magdalen Coll Oxford (fellow 1955-78); chm Anchor and Guardian Housing Assoc 1979-84; FRS; kt 1963; *Style*— Sir Ewart Jones; 6 Sandy Lane, Yarnton, Oxford OX5 1PB (☎ 086 75 2581)

JONES, Sir Francis Avery; CBE (1966); s of Francis Samuel Jones; *b* 31 May 1910; *Educ* Sir Leman Sch Beccles, London Univ; *m* 1, 1934, Dorothy Bessie (d 1983), da of Henry Pfirter; 1 s; m 2, 1983, K Joan Edmunds; *Career* physician Gastroenterological Dept Central Middx Hosp 1940-74, consulting physician 1974; consultant St Mark's Hosp 1948-78, consulting gastroenterologist 1978; consultant RN 1950-78, consulting gastroenterologist 1978; hon consulting physician St Bartholomew's Hosp 1978; kt 1970; *Style*— Sir Francis Jones, CBE; Mill House, Nutbourne, Pulborough, W Sussex

JONES, (Cyril) Gareth; s of Lyell Jones (d 1937), and Ceridwen, *née* Jenkins; *b* 28 May 1933; *Educ* Nantyglo GS, Christ's Coll Cambridge (MA), Birkbeck Coll London (PhD); *m* 1, 9 Aug 1958 (m dis 1988), Anne, da of Sidney Pickard (d 1987), of Bampton, Oxfordshire; 1 s (Christopher b 24 July 1962), 2 da (Katy b 8 Aug 1963, Becky b 15 March 1966); m 2, 14 Jan 1989, Helen Patricia Rahming; *Career* RAF 1954-56, Pilot Offr 1954, Flying Offr 1955; asst master: Stationers' Company's Sch 1957-59, Dulwich Coll 1959-63; ESSO Petroleum Co 1963-69: asst econ advsr mktg, mangr nat trade sales div, stategic planning advsr; Booz Allen and Hamilton Int Mgmnt conslts 1969-73 (vice pres 1973, managing ptnr UK 1974), dir Booz Allen & Hamilton Inc 1981-84, managing ptnr Ernst & Whinney mgmnt conslts 1985-; memb exec ctee Arthritis and Rheumatism Res cncl 1973-86, bd memb Welsh Water Authy 1981-85; co-opted memb ILEA 1969-72; govr: Thames Poly, Philippa Fawcett Coll, Walbrook Coll; Hon FIAM 1987; Soc of Business Economists, Strategic Planning Soc; *Books* Strategy for Schools (jtly 1964), Persepctives in Manpower Planning (jtly 1967); *Recreations* travel, walking, opera; *Clubs* Reform; *Style*— Dr Gareth Jones; 62 Thurlow Park Rd, London, SE21 (☎ 01 670 6310); Tregraig House, Bwlch, Powys (☎ 0874 730 650); Becket House, 1 Lambeth Palace Rd, London SE1 (☎ 01 928 2000, fax 01 928 1345)

JONES, Prof Gareth Hywel; QC (1986); s of Benjamin Thomas Jones (d 1967), and Mabel Jane Jones (d 1977); *b* 10 Nov 1930; *Educ* Porth Co GS, VCL (LLB), St Catherines Coll Cambridge (MA, LLD), Harvard Univ (LLM); *m* 21 March 1959, Vivienne Joy, da of Colin Edward Packridge (d 1983); 2 s (Christopher b 1960, Steven b 1961), 1 da (Alisa b 1965); *Career* Vice Master Trinity Coll Cambridge 1986- (fell 1961-, Downing prof of the Law of England 1975-); fell UCL 1988; FBA 1982; *Clubs* Beafsteak; *Style*— Prof Gareth Jones; Trinity Coll, Cambridge CB2 1TQ (☎ 0223 338 473)

JONES, Geoffrey Arthur Hesketh; MBE (1944); s of Arthur Dansey Jones, OBE, MVO (d 1936), of Guildford, and Edith Agnes, *née* Nash (d 1968); *b* 13 July 1913; *Educ* Lancing, Hertford Coll Oxford (BA); *m* 6 Oct 1981, Diana Elizabeth, da of Charles Reid; *Career* WWII Royal Signals 1939-45; 2 Lt 50 Divnl Signals 1940, Capt Adj 50 Divnl Eygpt 1942 (despatches), Maj GS02 to chief signal offr 13 Corps Sicily and Italy 1943 (despatches), GS02 Signals WO 1945; chm Stephenson Clarke Ltd 1965 (sec 1950, md 1960), dep chm Powell Duffryn Ltd 1975 (dir 1962); chm: Shoreham Port Authy 1961-83, Southampton Isle of Wight and South of England Royal Mail Steam Packet Co Ltd 1974-87; *Recreations* golf, gardening, painting; *Clubs* Army and Navy; *Style*— Geoffrey Jones, Esq, MBE; Tilford Cottage, Guildford, Surrey

JONES, Air Marshal Sir George; KBE (1953, CBE 1942), CB (1943), DFC (1918); s of Henry Jones (d 1897), and Jane Jones (d 1933); *b* 18 Oct 1896; *Educ* Rushworth Sch; *m* 1920, Muriel Agnes, da of Mrs F Stone (d 1936); 1 s; *Career* served WW I Gallipoli, France, Germany (despatches), joined RAAF 1920, served S W Pacific and Australia, dir Personnel Services 1936-39, dir of Training RAAF 1939-42, Chief of Air Staff RAAF 1942-52, Air Marshal 1946; dir Ansett Transport Industries 1954-78, ret; *Clubs* Naval and Military (Melbourne); *Style*— Air Marshal Sir George Jones, KBE, CB DFC; Flat 10, 104 Cromer Rd, Beaumaris, Vic 3193, Australia (☎ (583) 4230)

JONES, George Briscoe; CBE (1988); s of Arthur Briscoe Jones (d 1975), and Mary Alexandra, *née* Taylor (d 1982); *b* 1 June 1929; *Educ* Caldy Grange GS, Wallasey GS; *m* 26 March 1955, Audrey Patricia, da of Thomas Arthur Kendrick (d 1976); 2 da (Christine Jennifer (Mrs Rayner) b 22 May 1958, Deborah Ann (Mrs Campbell) b 4 July 1961); *Career* Army 1947-49; clerk to commercial mangr and co sec BEC Ltd 1949-67, planning mangr agric div Unilever 1967-71, dir BOCM Silcock 1974-82 (corporate planning mangr 1971-74), chm Unitrition Int Ltd 1976-82; dir: Cooperative Devpt Agency 1982, Job Ownership Ltd 1984-, Partnership in Business Ltd 1988-; chm Pavillon Theatre Gp Basingstoke; *Recreations* reading, drama, painting, sculpture, metalwork, chess, bridge; *Clubs* Farmers; *Style—* George Jones, Esq, CBE; 3 Beverley Close, Basingstoke, Hants (☎ 0256 282 39); 21 Panton St, London SW1 (☎ 01 839 2985, fax 01 839 1215)

JONES, Prof George William; s of George William Jones (d 1973), of Wolverhampton, and Grace Annie, *née* Cowmeadow (d 1982); *b* 4 Feb 1938; *Educ* Wolverhampton GS, Jesus Coll Oxford (BA, MA), Nuffield Coll Oxford (DPhil); *m* 14 Sept 1963, Diana Mary, da of Henry Charles Bedwell (d 1982), of Kidlington; 1 s (Maxwell b 1969), 1 da (Rebecca b 1966); *Career* lectr Univ of Leeds 1965-66 (asst lectr 1963-65); LSE & Political Sci: lectr 1966-71, sr lectr 1971-74, reader 1974-76, prof of govt 1976-; memb Layfield Ctee on local govt fin 1974-76, vice-chm Political Sci and Int Rels Ctee of Social Sci Res Cncl 1978-81 (memb 1977-81); FRHists 1980, RIPA 1963 (memb cncl 1985-);; *Books* Borough Politics (1969), Herbert Morrison (co-author 1973), Political Leadership in Local Authorities (co-ed 1978), New Approaches to the Study of Central-Local Government Relationships (ed 1980), The Case for Local Government (co-author 1985), Between Centre and Locality (co-ed 1985); *Recreations* cinema, eating, reading, dancing; *Clubs* National Film; *Style—* Prof George Jones; Dept of Govt, London School of Economics and Political Science, Houghton St, London WC2A 2AE (☎ 01 405 7686, fax 01 242 0392, telex 24655 BLPES G)

JONES, Geraint Martyn; s of Robert Kenneth Jones, of Luton, and Frances Elizabeth, *née* Mayo; *b* 15 July 1948; *Educ* St Albans Sch, Christs Coll Cambridge (MA, LLM), Inns of Court Sch of Law; *m* 29 Jul 1978, Caroline Mary Jones, da of Lt Peter Edwin Cecil Eyres, RNVR (d 1975); 1 s (Robert b 1980), 1 da (Louisa b 1982); *Career* called to the Bar Grays Inn 1972, practised London 1972-74; practised S E circuit mainly in Cambridge 1974-; principally commercial, property and employment law; chm Rent Assesment ctees 1985-; chm Madingley Sch Tst 1988-; memb: RYA, RNLI, OGA; *Recreations* sailing, golf, jazz, carpentry, reading; *Clubs* Cambs Co Farmers, Cambs Rugby, Toft Red Lion Rowing, Royal Norfolk and Suffolk YC; *Style—* Geraint Jones, Esq; Fenners Chambers, 5 Gresham Rd, Cambridge CB1 2EP (☎ 0223 68761, fax 0223 313007); Lamb Building, Temple, London EC4

JONES, Geraint Stanley; s of Rev David Stanley Jones (d 1974); *b* 26 April 1936; *Educ* Pontypridd G S, Univ Coll N Wales Bangor (BA, DipEd); *m* 1961, Rhiannon, da of Emrys Williams (d 1971); 2 da (Sioned b 1965, Siwan b 1966); *Career* served RAEC, Sgt; BBC studio mangr 1960-62, TV producer 1965-73, asst head Programmes 1973-74, head Programmes Wales 1974-81, controller BBC Wales 1981-; *Recreations* music, painting; *Clubs* Cardiff & County; *Style—* Geraint Jones Esq; 12 Lady Mary Road, Roath Park, Cardiff, S Glam (☎ 0222 751038)

JONES, Dr Gerald; s of John Jones, and Gladys *née* Roberts; *b* 25 Jan 1939; *Educ* Swansea GS, Merton Coll Oxford, London Hosp Med Coll (BA, BM, BCh, FRCP, PhD); *m* 1 Aug 1964, (m dis 1988), Anne da of Walter Heatley Morris (d 1977) 1 s (Jonathan Robert b 1976), 2 da (Paula Caroline b 1969, Katharine Helen b 1970); *Career* Hosp appts 1965-69, med res 1969-74, private indust 1974-75, sr princ med offr Medicines Div Dept of Health; *Recreations* music, reading; *Style—* Gerald Jones, Esq; Medicines Division, Market Towers, 1 Nine Elms Lane, Vauxhall, London, SW8 5NQ (☎ 01 720 2188 ext 3134)

JONES, (Robert) Gerallt Hamlet; s of Rev Richard Emrys Jones (d 1969), of Ynys Môn, and Elizabeth Ellen (d 1988); *b* 11 Sept 1934; *Educ* Denstone Coll, VCNW (BA, MA, Dip Ed); *m* 15 Sept 1962. Susan Lloyd, da of Richard Heber Lloyd Griffith (d 1975), of Borth-Y-Gest; 2 s (Rhys Gerallt b 1969, Dafydd Gerallt b 1972), 1 da (Ceri Rhiannon b 1964); *Career* lectr educn VCW 1960-65, princ Mandeville Teachers Coll Jamaica 1965 -67, Warden and headmaster Llandovery Coll 1967-76, sr tutor extra-mural dept VCW 1979-88, Warden Gregynog Hall VCW 1988-; author of TV documentaries and series incl Joni Jones; winner: prose medal Nat Eisteddfod 1977 and 1979, Hugh McDiarmid Trophy 1987; ed Taliesin 1986-; memb Broadcasting Cncl Wales 1967-72, chm Welsh Acad 1982-87, dir Aberystwyth Devpt Studies Course 1986-, memb Welsh Arts Cncl 1987-; memb Yr Academi Cymreig (the Welsh Acad) 1964; *Books* author of 35 vols in Welsh lang incl: ymysg y Drain (1959), cwlwm (1962), Y Foel Fawr (1962), Poetry of Wales 1930-70 (1972), Jamaican Landscape (1969), Jamaican Interlude (1972), Triptych (1977), Cafflogion (1979), Tair Drama (1988), Seicoleg Cardota (1989), Cerddi 1959-89 (1989); *Recreations* cricket, hill-walking; *Style—* Gerallt Jones, Esq; Leri, Dolybont, Borth, Dyfed (☎ 0970 871 525); Gregynog Hall, University of Wales, Newtown, Powys (☎ 0686 87 224)

JONES, Gerard; PC (1952); s of Timothy Jones (d 1959), of Bandon, Co Cork; *b* 15 June 1919; *Educ* Rockwell Coll, Presentation Coll Cork; *m* 1956, Breda, da of Partick Brooder, of Dublin; 4 children; *Career* dir: Irish Shipping Ltd ret 1970, Securicor ret 1978, Dublin Shipping ret, Palgrave Murphy Ltd ret; dir Jones Gp Ltd 1973-; hon Belgian consul 1968; *Recreations* sailing, gardening; *Clubs* United Services (Dublin), Royal Cork Yacht, Royal Yacht (Majorca), Real Club Nautico Palma; *Style—* Rt Hon Gerard Jones; 3 Roebuck House, Stag Place, London (☎ 01 828 0537); 7 Alamar, Nerja, Spain

JONES, (Thomas) Glanville; s of Evan James Jones (d 1981), of London, and Maggie Jones, *née* Evans (d 1972); *Educ* Clement Danes GS, London Univ Coll London (LLB Hons), Inns of Ct Sch of Law; *m* 29 Aug 1964, Valma Shirley, da of Ivor Jones, of Swansea; 3 s (Aled Prydderch b 1966, Dyfan Rhodri b 1968, Geraint Islwyn b 1971); *Career* barr; called to the Bar 1956, rec of Crown Ct; chm The Guild for the Promotion of Welsh Music 1970-; *Recreations* music, rugby, reading; *Clubs* Ffynone (Swansea); *Style—* T Glanville Jones, Esq; "Gelligron", 12 Eastcliff, Southgate, West Glam SA3 2AS (☎ 044 128 3118); Angel Chambers, 94 Walter Rd, Swansea SA1 5QA (☎ 0792 464623)

JONES, Sir Glyn Smallwood; GCMG (1964, KCMG 1960, CMG 1957), MBE (1944); s of Gwilym Ioan Jones (d 1942); *b* 9 Jan 1908; *Educ* King's Sch Chester, St Catherine's Oxford (MA, hon fell); *m* 1942, Nancy Madoc Featherstone; 1 da (and 1 s decd); *Career* entered Colonial Service (N Rhodesia) 1931, min for Native Affairs and chief cmmr N Rhodesia 1959, chief sec Nyasaland 1960-61, govr Nyasaland 1961-64, govr-gen and C in C Malawi 1964-66; advsr on govt admin to PM of Lesotho 1969-71; British Govt observer Zimbabwe elections 1980; dep chm Lord Pearce Cmmn for test of Rhodesian Opinion 1971-72; KStJ; *Recreations* fishing, golf; *Clubs* MCC, Athenaeum, Royal Commonwealth Soc; *Style—* Sir Glyn Jones, GCMG, MBE; Little Brandfold Cottage, Goudhurst, Kent TN17 1JJ (☎ 0580 211386)

JONES, Gordon Pearce; s of Alun Pearce Jones (d 1979), of Swansea, and Miriam Jones; *b* 17 Feb 1927; *Educ* Swansea GS, Univ of Wales (BSc); *m* 15 Dec 1951, Gloria Stuart, da of Stuart Carr Melville, of Edinburgh; 2 s (Huw b 3 Feb 1960, (twin) Hywel), 1 da (Elspeth b 14 July 1957); *Career* Lt RN 1947-51; scientist Br Iron and Steel Res Assoc 1951-56 raw material planning Iron and Steel Ind 1956-64, UK Sales Mangr Esso Petroleum Co Ltd 1961-64, mktg sales dir English Steel Corpn 1964- 68, dir gen mangr Murex 1968-70, md Rotherham Tinsley Steels 1970 md Firth Vickers 1974-79, dir TW Ward plc 1979-82; chm: Yorkshire Water 1983-, Water Authys Assoc; memb pres ctee CBI; *Recreations* reading, music, opera, railway history, travel; *Clubs* Naval and Military; *Style—* Gordon Jones, Esq; (☎ 0709 364 588); Yorkshire Water, Albion St, Leeds (☎ 0532 448 201, fax 0532 443 071)

JONES, Graham Edward; s of Edward Thomas Jones (d 1980), and Dora Rachel, *née* Hughes; *b* 22 Sept 1944; *Educ* Birkenhead Sch, Fitzwilliam Coll Cambridge (MA); *m* 29 Oct 1976, Vanessa Mary Heloïse; *Career* asst master Charterhouse 1961 (later head of econs and politics and housemaster), seconded to BP 1981, awarder in economics Oxford and Cambridge Exam Bd 1979-, reviser in econs JMB 1981-, headmaster Repton 1987-; FRSA; *Recreations* painting, walking, music, cooking, the classics; *Style—* Graham Jones, Esq; The Hall, Repton, Derby DE6 6FH (☎ 0283 702375)

JONES, His Hon Judge Graham Julian; s of David John Jones, CBE (d 1974), Town Clerk of Borough of Rhondda, and Edna Lillie Jones, *née* Marshall; *b* 17 July 1936; *Educ* Porth Co GS, Cambridge Univ (MA, LLM); *m* 30 Aug 1961, Dorothy, da of James Smith Tickle (d 1980), of Abergavenny; 2 s (Nicholas David Julian b 1963, Timothy James Julian b 1968), 1 da (Sarah Elizabeth b 1965); *Career* ptnr Morgan Bruce & Nicholas (slrs Cardiff) 1961-85; dep circuit judge 1975-78, recorder 1978-85, circuit judge Wales & Chester circuit 1985-; pres Assoc Law Soc of Wales 1982-84; memb Lord Chllr Legal Aid advsy ctee 1980-85; *Recreations* golf, boats; *Clubs* Cardiff and County, Radyr Golf (Cardiff); *Style—* His Hon Judge Graham Jones; Plowden, 17 Windsor Rd, Radyr, Cardiff (☎ 0222 842669)

JONES, Gwilym Haydn; MP (C) Cardiff North 1983-; s of Evan Haydn Jones and Mary Elizabeth Gwenhwyfar, *née* Moseley; *b* 1947; *Educ* London and S Wales; *m* 1974, Linda Margaret, da of David Mathew John (d 1980), of Cardiff; 1 s (Grant), 1 d (Fay); *Career* insurance broker, dir Bowring Wales Ltd; memb Cardiff City Cncl 1969-72 and 1973-83, parly election agent SE Cardiff Feb and Oct 1974, memb The Select Ctee on Welsh Affairs 1983-; sec Welsh Cons Backbenchers 1984-, sec All Party Parliamentary Group for the Fund for the Replacement of Animals in Medical Experiments; *Recreations* golf, model railways; *Clubs* County Conservative, Cardiff & County, Rhiwbina Rugby, United Services Mess; *Style—* Gwilym Jones Esq, MP; House of Commons, London SW1 (☎ 01 219 3000)

JONES, Sir Harry Ernest; CBE (1955); s of Harry Charles Ofield Jones (d 1947); *b* 1 August 1911; *Educ* Stamford Sch, St John's Coll Cambridge (BA); *m* 1935, Phyllis Eva, da of Alfred Dixon (d 1963); *Career* entered N Ireland Civil Service 1934, perm sec Miny of Commerce 1955, agent in Great Britain for N Ireland 1970-76; *Recreations* fly-fishing; *Clubs* Stowe Fly-Fishing, Willowbrook Fly-Fishers; *Style—* Sir Harry Jones, CBE; Homelea, Nassington, Peterborough (☎ 0780 782675)

JONES, (John) Hugh; s of late Thomas Hugh Jones and Mary Jones; *b* 6 August 1916; *Educ* Gowerton GS; *m* 1, 1948, Ilby, *née* Rowland (decd); 1 s, 2 da; *m* 2, 1967, Joan, *née* Freeston; *Career* Lloyds Bank Ltd 1934-77 (chief registrar 1964), dir and chief exec Joint Credit Card Ltd 1974, dir London Shop plc and subsids 1977- (chm 1980-86, vice-chm 1986), vice pres Baptist Housing Assoc Ltd 1974-88; FCIB 1952; *Recreations* music, literature, country activities (local village affairs), gardening, rugby, charitable work; *Style—* Hugh Jones, Esq; Culverden, The Thatchway, Angmering, West Sussex BN16 4HJ (☎ 0903 772 006); London Shop plc, Beaumont House, 179-187 Arthur Rd, London SW19 8AF (☎ 01 947 2204, telex 928242, fax 01 947 7876)

JONES, Ven (Thomas) Hughie; s of Edward Teifi Jones (Battery Sgt RA, d 1973), of Cardiff, and Ellen, *née* Jones (d 1978); *b* 15 August 1927; *Educ* William Hume's Sch Manchester, Univ of Wales (Cardiff, BA), Univ of London (BD), Univ of Leicester (MA); *m* 26 Dec 1949, Beryl Joan, da of late Robert William Henderson (Corpl RAMC), of Chepstow; 2 da (Susan b 1951, Christine b 1954); *Career* volunteered Fleet air Arm 1944, deferred, never served; warden Bible Trg Inst Glasgow 1949-57, minister John St Baptist Church Glasgow 1951-54, teacher and lectr Leicester & Leicestershire Educn Authies 1955-75, princ Hind Leys Coll Shepshed Leics 1976-81, rector The Langtons Leics 1981-86, adult educn offr Diocese of Leicester 1981-84, archdeacon of Loughborough 1986-; memb: Welsh Soc, Crime Prevention Panel, Local Educn Authy; FBIM 1974, FRAS 1977; *Recreations* gardening, bee keeping, entomology, genealogy, literature, Welsh affairs; *Clubs* Carlton, Leicestershire, Leics Co Cricket; *Style—* The Ven the Archdeacon of Loughborough; The Archdeaconry, Church Rd, Glenfield, Leicester LE3 8DP (☎ 0533 311 632); Church House, 3-5 St Martins East, Leicester LE1 5FX (☎ 0533 27445)

JONES, Hywel Francis; s of Brymor Jones (d 1957), of Morriston, Swansea, and Maggie Beatrice, *née* Francis (d 1987); *b* 28 Dec 1928; *Educ* Swansea GS, St John's Coll Cambridge (BA, MA); *m* 10 March 1959, Marian Rosser, da of Sidney Craven (d 1951), of Morriston, Swansea; 1 da (Sharon); *Career* Nat Serv RAPC 1953-55; dep co tres Breconshire CC 1956-59, asst co tres Carmarthenshire CC 1959-66, borough tres Port Talbot Borough Cncl 1966-75, memb cmmn Local Admin in Wales 1975-(sec 1975-85), local ombudsman 1985-; memb Public Works Loan Bd 1971-75, fin advsr AMC 1972-74; tres Royal Nat Eisteddfod of Wales 1975-, memb Gorsedd of Bards 1977; CIPFA 1953; *Recreations* music, reading, gardening; *Style—* Hywel F Jones, Esq; Godre'r Rhiw, 1 Lon Heulog, Baglan, Port Talbot SA12 8SY (☎ 0639 813 822); Derwen House, Court Rd, Bridgend CF31 1BN (☎ 0656 61 325)

JONES, Hywel Glyn; s of Thomas Glyndwr Jones (d 1984), and Anne, *née* Williams (d 1978); *b* 1 July 1948; *Educ* Whitchurch GS Cardiff, Trinity Coll Cambridge (MA); *m* 1 Aug 1970, Julia Claire, da of Lionel Davies; *Career* univ lectr in econ Univ of Warwick 1971-73, univ lectr in Econ of the Firm Oxford Univ 1973-77 (fell Linacre Coll, coll lectr Worcester Coll 1973-77), dir and chief exec the Henley Centre 1981-85 (dir of int forecasting 1977-81); chm: Hywel Jones & Assocs 1985-, Fixpoint Ltd 1988-; *Books* Second Abstract of British Historical Statistics (with BR Mitchell 1970), An Introduction to Modern Theories of Economic Growth (1974), Full Circle into the Future?, Britain into the 21st Century (1984); *Recreations* conversation, walking, military history; *Style—* Hywel Jones, Esq; 59 Yarnells Hill, Oxford OX2 9BE (☎ 0865 240 916); Fixpoint Ltd, Euston House, 81-103 Euston St, London NW1 2ET (☎ 01 387 0019, fax 01 872 0095)

JONES, (Charles) Ian (McMillan); s of Wilfred Charles Jones (Lt Devonshire Regt, d

1986), of Wroxham, Norfolk, and Bessie, *née* McMillan; *b* 11 Oct 1934; *Educ* Bishop's Stortford Coll, St John's Coll Cambridge (BA, PGCE); *m* 9 Aug 1962, Jennifer Marie, da of Alec Potter (d 1980), of Hertford; 2 s (William b 18 Jan 1964, Robert b 28 Jan 1970); *Career* Nat Serv 1953-55, cmmnd RA, Subalt 45 Field Regt in BAOR, Regtl Motor Tport Offr, TA 1955-57, Lt Herts Yeomanry; hd geography dept Bishop's Stortford Coll 1960-70 (asst to headmaster 1967-70), vice princ King Williams Coll IOM 1971-75, headmaster Bedford Sch 1975-86, dir of Studies Britannia RNC Dartmouth 1986-88, project dir The Centre for Br Teachers Negara Brunei Darussalam 1988-, educnl advsr Kolej Tuanku Ja'afar Malaysia 1988-; played for: England Hockey XI 1959-64, GB Hockey XI 1959-64; competed in Rome and Tokyo Olympics, mangr/coach England Hockey XI 1967-69; English Schoolboy Hockey Assoc: chm 1976-86, pres 1980-88; mangr England Schoolboy Hockey XI 1967-77; memb: Ctee of Headmasters Conf 1981-83, IOM Sports Cncl 1972-75; chm ISIS Centl 1981-83; FBIM 1981, FRSA 1981; *Recreations* hockey, cricket, squash, golf; *Clubs* MCC, Hawks, Pantai Mentiri Golf (Brunei); *Style*— Ian Jones, Esq; Riverain, Staitheway Rd, Wroxham, Norwich, Norfolk NR12 8TH (☎ 0603 782 307); Centre for British Teachers, Quality Ho, Quality Ct, Chancery Lane, London WC2A 1HP (☎ 01 242 2982/5, fax 01 242 0474)

JONES, Ian Quayle; WS; s of Arnold Bates Jones (d 1977), of Poynton, Cheshire, and Lilian Quayle Jones; *b* 14 July 1941; *Educ* Strathallan Sch, Edinburgh Univ (MA, LLB); *m* 24 Feb 1968, Christine Ann, da of Kenneth Macrae, WS (d 1984), of Edinburgh; 2 s (Simon Quayle b 1977, Richard Ian b 1980), 1 da (Stephanie Margaret b 1974); *Career* ptnr Cowan and Stewart WS 1968-72, fund mangr Ivory & Syme 1972-74; mangr, asst dir, dir British Linen Bank Ltd 1974-83; jt md Quayle Munro 1983-; govr Strathallan Sch; *Recreations* golf, skiing, fishing; *Clubs* Hon Co of Edinburgh Golfers; *Style*— Ian Jones, Esq; The Stone House, 1 Pentland Road, Edinburgh (☎ 031 441 3034); 42 Charlotte Square, Edinburgh EH2 4HQ (☎ 031 226 4421, fax 031 225 3391)

JONES, Iddon Lloyd; JP (1979); s of Morris Jones (d 1963), of Harlech, and Dorothy Lloyd, *née* Roberts (d 1986); *b* 1 Nov 1933; *Educ* Barmouth GS, UCW Swansea (BSc); *m* 7 Sept 1968, Ann, da of Harry Trefor Jones, of Criccieth; 1 s (Huw Lloyd b 22 May 1972), 1 da (Nai Lloyd b 29 Sept 1970); *Career* Nat Serv 1955-57: cmmnd flying offr RAF (airfield construction branch); James Williamson & Ptnrs cnslt engrs 1957- (currently ptrn NW off); work incl: Ffestiniog Pumped Storage Project, Wylfa nuclear power station, Dinorvig pumped storage scheme, N Sea oil related work offshire Shetlands; md Merz Rendel Williamson Ltd; dir Williamson Tech Servs; former capt Penmaenmawr Golf Club; C Eng, FICE, FIHT, M ConsE; *Recreations* golf; *Clubs* RSAC, Penmaenmawr Golf; *Style*— Iddon Jones, Esq, JP; Treflys, Colwyn Old Road, Penmaenmawr, Gwynedd LL84 6RD (☎ 0492 623 622); 11 Wynnstay Road, Colwyn Bay, Clwyd LL29 8NB (☎ 0492 531 833)

JONES, Rev Canon Idwal; s of late Henry Arthur Jones, and late Margaret Ann, *née* Williams; *b* 19 July 1913; *Educ* Univ of Wales (BA), St Michaels Coll Llandaff; *m* 14 June 1945, Jean Margaret, da of Herbert John Shuttleworth; 2 s (Timothy Arthur b 20 April 1951, David Christopher b 26 Feb 1954); *Career* RAChD 1944-50, Normandy Campaign Assault Unit; vicar: Cuddington Surrey 1950-63, Royal Leamington Spa 1963-80; hon canon Coventry Cath 1972; nat vice chm C of E Men's Soc, pres Leamington and Warwick Branch Arthiritic and Rheumatic Cncl, vice pres Leamington and Warwick United Nations Assoc; hon Chaplain to the Forces, asst Chaplain OStJ; *Books* Warwickshire Village Histories: Birdingbury (1983), Grandborough (1986); *Recreations* local history, walking, country preservation; *Style*— The Rev Canon Idwal Jones; Leam Cottage, Birdingbury, nr Rugby CV23 8EL (☎ 0926 632896)

JONES, Ieuan Wyn; MP (Plaid Cymru) Ynys Mon 1987; s of Rev John Jones (d 1977), of Gwynedd, and Mair Elizabeth Jones, *née* Pritchard; *b* 22 May 1949; *Educ* Pontardawe GS Ysgol-Y-Berwyn, Y Bala & Liverpool Poly (LLB); *m* 1974, Eirian Llwyd, da of John Nefydd Jones, of Clwyd; 2 s (Gerallt b 1975, Owain b 1978), 1 da (Gwenllian b 1977); *Career* slr 1973, ptnr William Jones & Talog Davies Ruthin Clwyd 1974 (ptnr branch in Llangefni 1985-); *Recreations* sport, local history; *Style*— Ieuan Jones, Esq; Ty Newydd Rhosmeirch, Llangefni (☎ 0248 72261, 0248 723599): House of Commons (☎ 219 5021)

JONES, Jack Anthony; s of Jack Jones (d 1973), and Patricia, *née* Hacket; *b* 12 Oct 1957; *Educ* Chatham House GS Ramsgate, Nottingham Univ (BSc), Imp Coll of Sci & Technol (MSc); *m* 30 May 1981, Bridget Jane, da of Peter Linington, of Somali Farm, Birchington, Kent; 1 s (Christopher Peter b 24 Sept 1987); *Career* minging engr: Gold Fields of SA 1979-80, Shell (SA) 1980-82, Shell (Botswana) 1982-83; investmt analyst Phillips & Drew 1984-; MIMM 1985, CEng 1986; *Style*— Jack Jones, Esq; Ashleigh, 11A Johns Rd, Meopham, Kent DA13 0LD (☎ 0474 814 720); Phillips & Drew, 120 Moorgate, London EC2H 6XD (☎ 01 628 4444)

JONES, Jack James Larkin; CH (1978), MBE (1950); s of George Jones (docker, d 1963), of Liverpool, and Ann Devoy (d 1963); *b* 29 July 1913; *Educ* Elementary Sch Liverpool, Toxteth Tech Sch Liverpool; *m* 1938, Evelyn Mary, da of Joseph Taylor, RSM (d 1954), of Knutsford; 2 s (Jack, Michael); *Career* served Spanish Civil War, (wounded Ebro Battle 1938); first employed in engrg and docks industs, gen sec Tport & Gen Workers Union 1969-78, dep chm Nat Ports Cncl 1967-79, chm Int Ctee Nationalised Industs & Tport Ctees of TUC, memb ACAS Bd 1974-78, vice pres Int Tport Workers Fedn 1972-; pres EFTA Trade Union Cncl; FCIT; *Books* The Incompatibles (1967), A to Z of Trades Unionism and Industrial Relations (with Max Morris, 1982), 'Union Man' (autobiography 1986); *Recreations* walking; *Clubs* Tom Mann Trades (Coventry); *Style*— Jack Jones, Esq, CH, MBE; 74 Ruskin Park House, Champion Hill, London SE5 8TH; (☎ 01 274 7067)

JONES, James; s of James Bertram Jones (d 1969); *b* 1 Mar 1925; *Educ* Kelvinside, Royal Tech Coll, West of Scotland Commercial Coll; *m* 1953, Janet Young Mitchell, *née* Lockhart; 1 s (Stephen b 1960), 1 da (Carol b 1961); *Career* mgmnt conslt; md: David Scott & Co Ltd 1960-68, L Sterne & Co Ltd 1968-71, J Jones (Glasgow) Ltd 1971-, Blairs Ltd 1974-; *Recreations* golf; *Clubs* Reform, Naval and Military, Royal Aero, Caledonian; *Style*— James Jones Esq; 97 Kelvin Ct, Glasgow G12 0AH (☎ 041 221 1715)

JONES, Hon James Glynmore; o s of Baron Maelor (Life Peer); *Style*— The Hon James Jones

JONES, Janet Eveline; JP (1979); da of Edward Leslie Coppack, JP (d 1981), of 'Colherne', Bryn Arnold Connah's Quay, Clwyd, and Agnes Jamieson, *née* McRae; *b* 27 June 1930; *Educ* Hawarden GS, The Froebel Educ Inst (dip); *m* 21 Aug 1954, Thomas Mathias Jones, s of David Elwyn Jones (d 1971), of Bryn Arnold, Connah's Quay, Clwyd; 2 s (Christopher Thomas b 1960 David Edward b 4 Jan 1962), 1 da (Helen Lesley (Mrs Byrne) b 9 Jan 1958); *Career* hd teacher Astmoor Infants Sch 1971-81, pres NAHT Halton South 1975- 76, nat chm Br Assoc for Early Childhood Educn 1986-89 (chm Cheshire branch 1979-80), disability retirement 1981; pres Runcorn and Dist Soroptimists 1985, sch govr, fndr memb Cheshire Woman of the Year Steering Ctee; co chm Womans Nat Cmmn 1987-89, patron Prix de Femmes d' Europe; writer of various reports and submissons to select ctees on educ and writer of reports for Womans Nat Ctee; *Recreations* reading, swimming, photography; *Clubs* The Soroptimist; *Style*— Mrs Janet Jones, JP; 8 Kenilworth Ave, Runcorn, Cheshire WA7 4XQ (☎ 0928 574 223); Woman's National Commission, Cabinet Office, Government Offices, Great George St, London SW1P 3AQ (☎ 01 233 4208); BAECE, 111 City House, 463 Bethnal Green Rd, London E2 9QH (☎ 01 739 7594)

JONES, Jeffrey Richard; CBE (1979); s of Rev Thomas Jones (d 1962), and Winifred Jones, *née* Williams; *b* 18 Nov 1921; *Educ* Grove Park Wrexham, Denstone Coll Staffs, Keble Coll Oxford (MA); *m* 1955, Ann Rosaleen, da of Michael Carberry (d 1963), of Derbys; 1 s (Thomas), 1 da (Philippa); *Career* Fl Lt (Pilot) RAFVR 1941-46; art master Mountgrove Comprehensive Sch Middx 1953-54, called to the bar Middle Temple 1954; chief justice: Kano State Nigeria 1975-80, Rep of Kiribati 1980-85; pres Ct of Appeal Kiribati 1981-85, memb Court of Appeal Vanuatu Islands 1983 and Solomon Islands 1984; *Recreations* duck shooting, sea fishing, golf, art; *Style*— Hon Jeffrey Jones, Esq, CBE; Bradley Cottage, Bradley Lane, Holt, Wilts (☎ 0225 782004)

JONES, Hon Mrs (Jennifer Margaret); da of Baron Pilkington (Life Peer, d 1983) by 1 w, Rosamond Margaret Rowan (d 1953); *b* 1933; *m* 1958, Dennis Jones; children; *Style*— The Hon Mrs Jones; Swallow Cottage, Burbage, Leics

JONES, Group Captain Jeremy Frederick Billings; s of Air Cdre Philip Jones, CBE (d 1978), and Nowelle, *née* Billings (d 1985); *b* 16 August 1931; *Educ* Radley, RAF Coll Cranwell; *m* 30 Aug 1956, Imogene Eve Patricia Knox, da of Lt-Col Geoffrey Hayes, DSO (d 1976); *Career* RAF, cmmnd 1952, Pilot 2 Sqdn 1952-54, Flt Cdr 94 Sqdn 1955-56, trials Fighter Weapons Sch 1956-57, Central Fighter Estab 1958, Guided Weapons Trials Sqdn 1959-61, Air Miny (ops staff) 1961-62, RAF Staff Coll Bracknell 1963-64, USAF exchange duties Florida 1964-67, Wing Cdr (trng) HQ Fighter Cmd 1967-68, cmd 11 Sqdn 1969-71 Nat defence Coll 1971-72, dir staff Nat Defence Coll 1972-74, personnel Air 1 MOD 1974-76, chief fighter branch HQ AA FCE 1976-80, Dep Capt The Queen's Flight 1981-89, ADC to HM The Queen 1981-89; memb Nat Tst, CGA; chm Anatolian Shepherd Dog Club 1982-84, Supporter PDSA and NCDL; *Recreations* animals, travelling, walking, country pursuits; *Clubs* RAF; *Style*— Gp Capt Jeremy Jones; Orchard House, Orchard Lane, Helford, Cornwall (☎ 032 623 368); The Queen's Flight, RAF Benson, Oxfordshire OX9 6EE (☎ 0491 35055, fax 0491 37766, telex 547271)

JONES, Hon Mrs Joanna Catherine; *née* Grant; da of Maj Sir Arthur Lindsay Grant, 11 Bt (ka 1944), and Baroness Tweedsmuir of Belhelvie (Life Peeress, d 1978); *b* 1935; *m* 1954 (m dis 1966), Dominick Jones, s of Sir (George) Roderick Jones, KBE; 1 s; *Style*— The Hon Mrs Joanna Jones; c/o Romily Jones, 162 Elborough Street, London SW18 5DL

JONES, John Elfed; CBE (1987); s of Urien Maelgwyn Jones (d 1978); *b* 19 Mar 1933; *Educ* Blaenau Ffestiniog GS, Denbighshire Tech Coll, Heriot-Watt Coll; *m* 1957, Mary Sheila, da of David Thomas Rosser; 2 da (Bethan, Delyth); *Career* Flying Offr RAF; chartered electrical engr CEGB 1949-1969, dep md Anglesey Aluminium Metal Ltd 1969-79, under-sec (indust) Welsh Off 1979-82, chm Welsh Water Authy 1982-; chm Bwrrdd Yr Iaith Gymraeg (Welsh Language Bd) 1988-; CEng, FIEE, FRSA; *Recreations* fishing (salmon and trout), attending Eisteddfodau; *Style*— John Elfed Jones Esq, CBE; Ty Mawr, Coety, Penybontarogwr, Morgannwg Ganol CF35 6BN (☎ 0656x 653039); Welsh Water Authority, Cambrian Way, Brecon, Powys LD3 7HP (☎ 0874 3181)

JONES, (Henry) John Franklin; s of late Lt-Col James Walker Jones, DSO, and Doris Marjorie, *née* Franklin; *b* 6 May 1924; *Educ* Blundell's, Merton Coll Oxford; *m* 10 Dec 1949, Jean Verity, da of Samuel Robinson, CMG (d 1973), of London; 1 s; *Career* WWII serv Ordinary Seaman RN 1943, Intelligence Staff Eastern Fleet 1944; Univ of Oxford: fell and tutor jurisprudence 1949-56, Univ sr lectr 1956-62, fell and tutor English Lit 1962-79, prof of poetry 1979-84; Dill Meml lectr Queen's Univ Belfast 1983; football corr The Observer 1956-59; tv appearances incl The Modern World 1988; publications incl: The Egotistical Sublime (1954, fifth edn 1978), The British Imagination (contrib 1961), on Aristotle and Greek Tragedy (1965, fifth edn 1980), Dickens and the Twentieth Century (contrib 1962), John Keats' Dream of Truth (1969, second edn 1980), The Morality of Art (1969), The Same God (1971), Dostoevskey (1983, second edn 1985); *Style*— John Jones, Esq; Holywell Cottage, Oxford (☎ 0865 247 702); Yelands, Brisworthy, Shaugh Prior, Plympton, Devon (☎ 075 539 310)

JONES, Sir John Lewis; KCB (1983), CMG (1972); *b* 17 Feb 1923; *Educ* Christ's Coll Camb (MA); *m* 1948, Daphne Nora (*née* Redman); *Career* RA 1942-46, Sudan Govt 1947-55, MOD 1955-85; *Clubs* United Oxford and Cambridge; *Style*— Sir John Jones, KCB, CMG

JONES, Sir Keith Stephen; s of S W Jones; *b* 7 July 1911; *Educ* Newington Coll Sydney Univ; *m* 1936, Kathleen, da of A E Abbott; 3 s; *Career* memb Newington Coll Cncl 1951-70, CMO NSW State Emergency Servs 1968-74, memb NSW Med Bd 1971-81, pres Aust Med Assoc 1973-76; chm: Australasian Med Publishing Co 1976-82, Nat Specialist Qualifications Advsy Ctee 1979-82, Blue Cross Assoc of Aust 1983-85, pres MBF of Aust 1983-86; emeritus consultant surgn Manly Dist Hosp 1982-; Gold Medal Aust Med Assoc 1976; FRCS, FRACS. FRACGP, FACEM; kt 1980; *Style*— Sir Keith Jones; 123 Bayview Village, Cabbage Tree Rd, Bayview, NSW 2104 Australia (☎ 02 997 2876)

JONES, Sir (John) Kenneth (Trevor); CBE (1956), QC (1976); s of John Jones; *b* 11 July 1910; *Educ* King Henry VIII GS Abergavenny, Univ Coll of Wales, St John's Coll Cambridge; *m* 1940, Menna Jones; 2 s; *Career* served WW II RA; barrister Lincoln's Inn 1937; entered Home Office 1945, Legal Advsr Home Office 1956-77; memb Standing Ctee on Criminal Law Reform 1959-80; kt 1965; *Clubs* Athenaeum; *Style*— Sir Kenneth Jones, CBE, QC; 7 Chilton Court, Walton on Thames, Surrey KT12 1NG (☎ (0932) 226890)

JONES, Hon Mr Justice; Hon Sir Kenneth George Illtyd; s of Richard Arthur Jones; *b* 26 May 1921; *Educ* Brigg GS, Univ Coll Oxford (MA); *m* 1, 1947, Dulcie

Thursfield (d 1977); 1 s, 2 da; m 2, 1978, June Patricia, da of Leslie Arthur Doxey (banker 1969, Treasurer 1987); *Career* served WW II RA; barrister Gray's Inn 1946, QC 1962, recorder: Shrewsbury 1964-66, Wolverhampton 1966-71; bencher 1969, recorder of the Crown Court 1972, Circuit Judge 1972, Judge of the High Court of Justice (Queen's Bench Div) 1974-88; kt 1974; *Style*— The Hon Mr Justice Jones; Royal Courts of Justice, Strand, London WC2A 2LL

JONES, Laurance Aubrey; s of Aubrey Joseph Goldsmid Jones, of The Chestnuts, Godmanchester, Huntingdon, and Frances Laura, *née* Ward; *b* 7 April 1936; *Educ* King's Sch Rochester; *m* 8 July 1961, Joan, da of Douglas Stanley Sargeant, of 6 Jeffery Close, Staplehurst, Kent; *Career* Nat Serv RAF 1954-56; Royal Insur Gp 1953-54 and 1956-57, Nat Employers Mutual Gen Insur Assoc Ltd 1957-58, co sec Marchant & Tubb Ltd 1959-67, jt sec Tollemache & Cobbold Gp Cambridge 1967-70, dep sec Int Timber Corpn Ltd 1970-77; gp sec Land Securities plc 1977-; cncl memb Chartered Secs East Anglian Branch; Freeman Maidstone 1957, City of London 1981; Liveryman Worshipful Co of Chartered Secs and Administrators 1981; FCIS (assoc 1968, fell 1972); *Recreations* tennis, skiing, golf, travel, bridge; *Clubs* Chesterford Country, Union Jack; *Style*— Laurance Jones, Esq ; Florus House, Widdington, Saffron Walden, Essex CB11 3SB; 99 Le Panoramic, Thollon Les Memises, 74500 Evian Les Bains, France (☎ 01 353 4222, fax 01 353 7871, telex 934019)

JONES, Air Marshal Sir Laurence Alfred; KCB (1984), AFC (1971); s of Benjamin Howel and Irene Dorothy Jones; *b* 18 Jan 1933; *m* 1956, Brenda Ann Jones; 2 da; *Career* RAF Coll Cranwell 1951-53, served M East and Germany; rcds, jssc, psc; SASO Strike Command 1982-84, ACAS (operations) 1984, ACDS (programmes) 1985-86, ACAS 1986-87; Air Member for Personnel 1987-; *Style*— Air Marshal Sir Laurence Jones, KCB, AFC; c/o Ministry of Defence, Main Building, Whitehall, London SW1A 2HB

JONES, Martin Peter; s of George Pageant Jones (d 1984), and Kathleen Marie, *née* Wood (d 1966); *b* 13 Mar 1946; *Educ* Shrewsbury Sch, Coll of Law Guildford; *m* 14 April 1973, Judith Wilkinson, da of Eric Bowyer (d 1978); 2 da (Alexandra b 1975, Abigail b 1977); *Career* slr; *Recreations* restoring and using vintage & post vintage cars; *Style*— Martin P Jones, Esq; Green Cottage, The Green, Higher Kinnerton, nr Chester, Clwyd (☎ 0244 660283); Martin P Jones & Co, 62 North-gate Street, Chester CH1 2H7 (☎ 0244 313577, fax 0244 318928)

JONES, Martyn David; MP (L) Clwyd South West 1987-; s of Vernon Pritchard Jones, of Wrexham, and Violet Gwendoline Jones, *née* Griffiths; *b* 1 Mar 1957; *Educ* Grove Park GS Wrexham, Trent Poly (MIBiol); *m* 1974, Rhona, da of Roger Bellis, of Wrexham; 1 s (Nicholas b 1984), 1 da (Linzi b 1974); *Career* county cnsllr 1981-; *Recreations* backpacking, target shooting, sailing; *Clubs* Wrexham Lager Sports & Soc, Wrexham British Rail; *Style*— Martyn Jones, MP; 5 Maesyr Haf, Smithy Lane, Wrexham (☎ Wrexham 263236); House of Commons London SW1A 0AA (☎ 01 219 3417)

JONES, Maude Elizabeth; CBE (1973); 2 da of Edward William Jones (d 1953), of Dolben, Ruthin, N Wales; *b* 14 Jan 1921; *Educ* Brynhyfryd Sch for Girls Ruthin; *Career* joined foreign relations dept Joint War Orgn BRCS and Order of St John 1940, dir Jr Red Cross 1960 (dep dir 1949), dep dir-gen for branch affairs BRCS 1966, memb joint ctee Order of St John and BRCS 1966-77, dep dir-gen British Red Cross Soc 1970-77; memb: National Cncl of Social Services 1966-77, FANY 1966-77; govr St David's Sch Ashford Middx; SSStJ 1959; *Recreations* music, gardening, reading; *Clubs* New Cavendish; *Style*— Miss Maude Jones, CBE; Dolben, Ruthin, N Wales (☎ 082 42 2443)

JONES, (Christopher) Maurice; DL (Hants 1984); s of Sydney Edward Jones (d 1942), of Evelyn Gardens, London SW7, and Margaret Jesse, *née* Collis-Sandes (d 1956); *b* 17 May 1919; *Educ* Rugby, Trinity Coll Cambridge (MA); *m* 3 May 1947, Isobel Gwyn, da of William Reginald Bown; 1 s (Nicholas b 1952), 2 da (Susannah (Mrs Lyle) b 1948, Caroline b 1950); *Career* WWII cmmnd RA POW Singapore (worked on Siam-Burma railway) 1939-45; md John Lewis Partnership 4,000 Acre Estate Hants 1946-81; memb Hants CC 1965-(chm 1984-86); chm: Glebe ctee Winchester Diocese 1974, Test and Itchen Fishing Assoc 1972-81; pres Romsey Show 1981; *Recreations* NH racing, country pursuits, visiting old churches; *Style*— Maurice Jones, Esq, DL; One, The Grange, Longstock, Stockbride, Hants

JONES, Medwyn; s of Capt Ieuan Glyn Du Platt Jones (ret), of Llandbedr Duffryn, Clwyd, N Wales, and Margaret, *née* Owen; *b* 13 Sept 1955; *Educ* Scorton Sch, Chester GS, Sheffield Univ (LLB), The Coll of Law; *Career* slr Theodore Goddard 1980-81 (articled clerk 1978-80), ptnr Walker Martineau 1983- (slr 1981-83); memb Australian Business in Europe; memb City of London Solicitor's Company 1988; memb Law Society 1980; *Recreations* skiing, squash, sailing, weight-training; *Style*— Medwyn Jones, Esq; Walker Martineau, 64 Queen St, London EC4R IAD (☎ 01 236 4232, fax 01 236 2525)

JONES, Michael Lynn Norman; s of Lynn Daniel Jones, of, Rhiwbina, Cardiff, and Mary Hannah, *née* Edwards; *b* 14 Jan 1943; *Educ* Neath Boys GS, Jesus Coll Oxford (BA, MA), Coll of Law; *m* 16 April 1974, Ethni, da of Gwynfryn Morgan Daniel (d 1960), of Llys-y-Coed, West Orchard Cres, Llandaff, Cardiff; 1 s (Garmon b 1975), 3 da (Mererid b 1976, Gwenfair b 1979, Rhiannon b 1982); *Career* slr; ptnr C Hugh James & Ptnrs Cardiff 1966, sr ptnr Hugh James Jones & Jenkins Cardiff 1970-; memb: Wales and Chester Circuit Advsy Ctee 1971-77, Curriculum Cncl Wales 1988-; asst sec Cardiff and Dist Law soc 1969-; govr: Coed-y-G of Welsh Primary Sch 1985-, Glantaf Welsh HS 1988; elder Salem Presbyterian Church of Wales Canton Cardiff 1988; memb: Law Soc 1966, CIArb 1987; *Recreations* gardening, walking; *Clubs* Cardiff & County, Oxford Union; *Style*— Michael Jones, Esq; Allt-y-Wennol, Peterston-super-Ely, Cardiff (☎ 0446 760 383); Hugh James, Jones & Jenkins, Arlbee Ho, Greyfriars Rd, Cardiff (☎ 0222 224 871, fax 0222 388 222)

JONES, (Philip) Michael Thyer; s of Philip Emlyn Thyer Jones, DFC (d 1974), of Gorseinon, S Wales, and Elizabeth Vivien Thyer, *née* Fannon; *b* 21 April 1914; *Educ* Roan Sch Blackheath; *m* 21 May 1965, Barbara Mary, da of George Johnstone, of Thornhill, Dumfriesshire, Scot; 3 da (Fiona b 1981, Katey b 1974, Alison b 1970); *Career* Int Stock Exchange 1959-63; Capel-Cure Myers: various posts 1959-63, head investmts 1969-70, ptnr fin and admin 1970-85; tech servs dir Capel-Cure Myers Capital Mgmnt; MInstAM 1970; *Recreations* flying, rock climbing, deep sea fishing, skiing, shooting; *Style*— Michael Jones, Esq; 65 Holborn Viaduct, London EC1A 2EU (☎ 01 236 5080, fax 01 329 4271, telex 9419251)

JONES, Nicholas (John); s of John Sterry Jones, and Ann Margaret, *née* Dunand; *b* 18 July 1958; *Educ* Malvern Coll, Royal Scottish Acad of Music, Int Cello Centre (ARCM); *m* 17 Dec 1983, Isobelle Lillian, da of John McGuinness, of Strabane, N Ireland; *Career* concert cellist and musical dir; given concerts at major festivals and regular Purcell Room recitals; founded Johannes Piano Trio with Michael Bochmann and Iwan Llewelyn Jones; principal cello English String Orchestra; *Recreations* walking, reading, looking at art, theatre, opera, conversation, humour; *Style*— Nicholas Jones, Esq; Tanybryn, Rhydypennan, Bow Street, Dyfed SY24 5AD (☎ 0970 820 300); Arts Centre, Penglais, Aberystwyth, Dyfed SY23 3DE (☎ 0970 4277)

JONES, Nicholas Graham; s of Albert William Jones, and Gwendolen Mary Muriel Taylor-Jones, *née* Phillips; *b* 13 August 1948; *Educ* Latymer Upper, St Catherine's Coll Oxford (MA); *m* 25 Sept 1976, Shelagh Ann, da of Robert Maitland Farror; 1 s (Benjamin Nicholas Farror b 1986); *Career* film ed and prodr BBC 1969, barr 1975 Inner Temple; *Recreations* sailing, walking, music; *Clubs* Royal Ocean Racing, Bar Yacht, Frensham Pond Sailing; *Style*— Nicholas Jones, Esq; 4 Brick Court, Temple, London EC4Y 9AD (☎ 01 583 8455, fax 01 353 1699)

JONES, Nicholas Michael Houssemayne; s of Henry J E Jones of Kitsbury Orchard, nr Moreton-in-Marsh, Glos, and Patricia Rose, *née* Holland; *b* 27 Oct 1946; *Educ* Winchester Coll, London Business Sch (MSc); *m* 25 March 1971, Veronica Anne, da of Brig The Hon R G Hamilton- Russell, DSO, LVO, qv; 1 s (Oliver Mark b 5 April 1977), 1 da (Rowena Rose b 5 Sept 1975); *Career* with Peat Marwick Mitchell 1965-73, dir J Henry Schroder Wagg & Co 1975-87; md Lazard Brothers & Co 1987-; FCA 1969; *Recreations* racing, tennis, stalking, bridge, painting; *Style*— Nicholas Jones, Esq; Rectory Farmhouse, Church Enstone, Oxfordshire OX7 4NN; 12 Paulton's St, London SW3 5DR; Lazard Brothers & Co, Limited, 21 Moorfields, London EC2P 2HT (☎ 01 588 2721)

JONES, Ven Noel Debroy; CB (1986); s of Brinley Jones, of Gwent, and Gwendoline Alice, *née* White (d 1988); *b* 25 Dec 1932; *Educ* West Monmouth Sch for Boys, St Davids Coll (BA), Wells Theol Coll; *m* 1969, Joyce Barbara Leelavathy, da of Arumugam Arulanandam (d 1979), of Singapore; 1 s (Benjamin b 1972), 1 da (Vanessa b 1970); *Career* clerk in Holy Orders 1955, Parishes Diocese of Monmouth; vicar of Kano N Nigeria 1960, Chaplain Royal Navy 1962, Chaplain of the Fleet 1984-, Queens Hon Chaplain 1983; GSM; *Recreations* formerly rugby, squash, music, family; *Clubs* Sion Coll; *Style*— The Ven Noel Jones, Chaplain of the Fleet; 111 Belgrave Road, SW1 (☎ 834 1097); 1 Eastway Terrace, RN Eastway, Southsea (☎ 0705 737468); Ministry of Defence, Lacon House, Theobalds Road WC1X 8RY (☎ 01 430 6847)

JONES, (Cyril) Norman; s of Norman Jones (d 1963), of Cheshire, and late Rosa Beatrice, *née* Best; *b* 26 Oct 1916; *Educ* Prizes Birkenhead Sch, Univ of Liverpool (LLB, LLM); *m* 20 June 1942, Megan Margaret, da of Thomas Henry Roberts (d 1952), of Cheshire; 2 da (Diana Margaret b 1954, Amanda Lois b 1956), 1 adopted s (Philip Norman b 1951); *Career* Fl-Lt RAF 1940-, Actg Sqdn Ldr 1946, Adj to RAAF; church warden Shearsby Parish Church, pres Leicester Family Service Unit, int cnsllr and dist govr Lions Club; rural dist cncllr Lutterworth, chm Leicester Cons Cwlth Soc, sec and pres Leicester Round Table 500, sec Leicester Boy Scouts Assoc, life govr Cancer Res; *Recreations* classical music, literature; *Clubs* Bath and County, Bath, Leicestershire Cons; *Style*— Norman Jones, Esq; Greensleeves, Market Place, Box, Wilts SN9 NZ (☎ 0225 743758)

JONES, Dr Norman Fielding; s of William John Jones (d 1968), of Aberbeeg, Gwent, and Winifred, *née* Evans (d 1974); *b* 3 May 1931; *Educ* Christ Coll Brecon, King's Coll Cambridge (MA, MD), St Thomas's Hosp Med Sch (B Chir), Univ of N Carolina; *m* 15 March 1958, Ann Pye, da of Dr Charles Cecil Howard Chavasse (d 1971), of Alcester, Warwicks; 3 s (Christopher b 1960, Richard b 1963, Michael b 1967); *Career* Nat Serv 1949-50; conslt physician St Thomas's Hosp London 1967-, physician King Edward VII's Hosp for Offrs 1977-, chm dist mgmnt team and staff ctee St Thomas's Hosp 1977-78, conslt physician Met Police 1980-, hon conslt physician Army 1980-, chm RCP ctee on Renal Disease 1980-, chief med offr Equitable Life Assur Soc 1985-, hon conslt physician Royal Hosp Chelsea 1987-, sr censor and vice pres RCP 1989-; FRCP 1970, memb Nat, European and Internat Socs of Nephrology; *Books* Recent Advances in Renal Disease (ed 1975), Renal Disease (ed with Sir Douglas Black, 1979), Recent Advances in Renal Medicine (ed with D K Peters, 1982); *Recreations* iconology, modern English literature; *Clubs* United Hospitals; *Style*— Dr Norman Jones; 1 Annesley Rd, London SE3 0JX (☎ 01 856 0583); St Thomas's Hosp, London SE1 7EH (☎ 01 928 9292)

JONES, Norman Henry; QC (1985); s of Warrant Offr Henry Robert Jones, DFM, and Charlotte Isabel Scott, *née* Davis; *b* 12 Dec 1941; *Educ* Bideford GS, North Devon Tech Coll, Univ of Leeds (LLB, LLM); *m* 28 March 1970, Trudy Helen, da of Frederick George Chamberlain (d 1974), of Werrington, Peterborough; 2 s (Gareth b 22 Dec 1977, Nicholas b 14 April 1981), 1 da (Helena b 6 April 1983); *Career* barr Middle Temple 1968, Recorder 1987; *Recreations* boats; *Style*— Norman Jones, Esq, QC; Danehurst, Greenfield Lane, Guiseley, Leeds LS20 9HF (☎ 0943 781 92); Park Court Chambers, 40 Park Cross St, Leeds LS1 2QH (☎ 0532 433 277, fax 0532 421 285, telex 666135 LEEDS)

JONES, Norman Herbert; MBE; s of Edward Samuel Jones, and Elizabeth Caroline, *née* Meyer; *b* 17 July 1905; *Educ* Marlborough; *m* (m dis), Margaret Elizabeth Noel (Miggs), 2 da of Donald Clarke; 4 s; m 2, Ann Tovey; 1 s, 2 da; *Career* 601 Sqdn Aux Air Force 1930-37, RNVR 1938-45, served in destroyers and minesweepers; dir: Samuel Jones & Co, Wiggins Teape & Co Ltd; chm Rollason Aircraft and Engines, memb Esher UDC; pres Tiger club; *Recreations* sailing, flying; *Clubs* London Aero, Tiger; *Style*— Norman Jones, Esq; 4 Darley Gate, Meads, Eastbourne; Castlewater, Rye, E Sussex

JONES, Capt Norman Leslie; TD (1986); s of Dudley Frederick Saville Jones (d 1967), of Birkenhead, Wirral, and Margaret, *née* Thompson; *b* 15 Jan 1948; *Educ* St Hugh's RC Secondary Sch Birkenhead, Liverpool Coll of Commerce, Chester Coll of Law; *m* 8 Sept 1973, Maria Teresa, da of John Cubells (d 1988), of Higher Bebington, Wirral; 1 s (Daniel b 1985), 2 da (Rebeca b 1978 (d 1979), Stephanie b 1983); *Career* TA 1968-, 208 (Merseyside) Gen Hosp RAMC (V) Liverpool, cmmd Unit Raymaster 208 (Merseyside) Gen Hosp RAMC (V) 1978, Capt 1980; slr of the Supreme Ct 1976; legal advsr Radio Merseyside Helpline, vice chm Prenton Prep Sch Parents' Assoc 1988; fell Inst Legal Execs 1973, memb Law Soc 1976; *Recreations* writing, gardening, furniture restoration; *Style*— Capt Norman Jones, TD; 9 Reservoir Rd North, Prenton, Birkenhead, Wirral (☎ 051 608 4723); 11 & 61 Hamilton Sq, Birkenhead, Wirral (☎ 051 647 4051, fax 051 666 1632)

JONES, Norman William; CBE (1984), TD (1962); s of James William Jones (d 1957), and Mabel, *née* Pyewell (d 1972); *b* 5 Nov 1923; *Educ* Gravesend Sch; *m* 1950, Evelyn June, da of Gilbert Hall (d 1977); 2 s; *Career* served HM Forces 1942-47, Major Airborne Forces Europe and Burma; Lloyds Bank plc: dir 1976-, group chief exec 1978-83, dep chm 1984-; chm Australia & New Zealand Trade Advsy Ctee (BOTB) 1985-88; FIB; *Recreations* sailing, photography; *Clubs* Overseas Bankers'; *Style—* Norman Jones, Esq, CBE, TD; Rowans, 21 College Ave, Grays, Essex RM17 5UN (☎ 0375 73101); Lloyds Bank plc, 71 Lombard St, London EC3P 3BS (☎ 01 626 1500)

JONES, Penry; s of Joseph William Jones (d 1973), of Cheshire, and Edith Emily, *née* Edward (d 1972); *b* 18 August 1922; *Educ* Rock Ferry HS Cheshire, Liverpool Univ; *m* 1948, Beryl Joan, da of Rev James Fielden Priestley (d 1950), of Lancs; 2 da (Felicity, Siân); *Career* gen sec YMCA Altrincham 1942-44; sec Student Christian Movement for Oxford and Univs of SW England 1945-47; represented Churches on Youth Delgn to Soviet Union 1945-46; Parly candidate (Lab) Berwick and E Lothian 1955 and 1959; chm World Cncl of Churches' Dept of Communication 1968-75; indust sec Iona Community (Scot) 1948-57; prodr religious progs ABC TV 1958-64, religious progs offr ITA 1964-67, head of religious broadcasting BBC 1967-72, chief asst (Television) IBA 1972-82; fndr memb tv selection ctee Nat Film Archive (BFI) 1960; *Recreations* hill walking, watching Rugby football, films; *Clubs* Reform; *Style—* Penry Jones, Esq; Erraid House, Isle of Iona, Argyll PA76 6SJ (☎ Iona 448)

JONES, Brig Percival de Courcy; OBE (1953); s of Percy de Courcy Jones (d 1922); *b* 9 Oct 1913; *Educ* Oundle Sch, Sandhurst; *m* 1, 1947 (m dis 1951), Anne, *née* Hollins; 1 s; m 2, 1962, Elaine Mary, da of Harry Charles Connatty, of Co Cork, and widow of Onslow Garnett; 1 step da (*see* Hilary Rose Burt); *Career* Army 1933-62, retired: cmmnd KSLI 1933, WWII (France, Burma) cmd 1 Northamptons 1945, Lt-Col 1952, cmd KSLI 1953-55, Col Q War Office 1955-58, Brig 1961; chief sec Royal Life Saving Soc 1965-75 (dir 1969-75), Silver Medal Federacion Int de Sauvetage 1976, cllr Aylesbury Vale DC 1976-79; *Recreations* skiing, gardening; *Clubs* Light Infantry; *Style—* Brig P de C Jones, OBE; 6 Port Hill Gdns, Shrewsbury, Salop (☎ 0743 247 904)

JONES, Peter Boam; s of Cecil Walley Jones, of Cheshire, and Dorothy, *née* Boam; *b* 11 June 1930; *Educ* Nantwich and Acton GS; *m* 1960, Patricia Ann, da of Tom Dewhurst, JP, of Worcestershire; 1 s (Anthony b 1963), 1 da (Victoria b 1967); *Career* Nat Serv 1953-55, cmmnd Lt RAOC 1954; ptnr Touche Ross & Co Birmingham 1965-82, dep chm Maxim Investmt Gp, chm Time Craft Designs Ltd; dir: Saracens Cycles Ltd, Aquarian Hldgs Gp; pres: Birmingham and W Midland Soc of Chartered Accountants 1980-81, Birmingham CA Students Soc 1979-80; Freeman City of London, Liveryman Worshipful Co of Chartered Accountants; FCA; *Recreations* gardening, tennis, travelling; *Clubs* Birmingham; *Style—* Peter Jones, Esq; The Heath, Longdon Heath, Upton upon Severn, Worcestershire (☎ 06846 4495)

JONES, Peter Eldon; s of Wilfrid Eldon Jones (d 1985), of Kingston upon Thames, and Jessie Meikle, *née* Buchanan (d 1970); *b* 11 Oct 1927; *Educ* privately, Surbiton GS, Kingston poly, UCL (DipTP); *m* 1, 1954 (m dis 1984), Gisela Marie, da of Maj Landforstmeister Karl Heinrich von Arnswaldt (d 1985) of Celle, W Germany; 2 s (Christopher b 1955, Andrew b 1958), 1 da (Hella b 1962); m 2, 1985, Claudia Ann Mary Milner-Brown, da of John Alan Laurence of Chatham Hall, Gt Waltham, Essex; *Career* sr asst architect Powell and Moya 1950-54, joined LCC Arch Dept 1954, dep sch arch LCC 1960-65, town devpt architectural planner GLC 1965-71, tech policy architect GLC 1971-74, educ architect ILEA 1974-82, acting dir of architecture 1980-82, dir architecture and superintending architecture Met Bldgs GLC/ILEA 1982-86; dir Watkins Gray Peter Jones Ltd 1986-; conslt: Watkins Gray Int, DES; pt/t tutor Kingston Poly, chm Abbeyfield, Pirbright Bldg ctee; pres Soc Chief Architects of Local Authies 1983-84; Freeman: City of London 1968, Worshipful Co of Chartered Architects 1988; vice pres RIBA 1985-86, FRIBA, FRTPI, FRSA, FCSD; *Books* Good House Design (1956); *Recreations* photography, travel, bridge, golf; *Clubs* Woking Golf; *Style—* Peter Jones, Esq; Watkins Gray Peter Jones Ltd, Alexander House, 1a Spur Rd, Orpington Kent (☎ 0689 36141, fax 0689 35152)

JONES, Peter George Edward Fitzgerald; CB (1986); s of Dr John Christopher Jones (d 1960), of Sussex, and Emily Isabel Howell (d 1954); *b* 7 June 1925; *Educ* Fairfield Sch Birmingham, Dulwich Coll London, Croydon Tech, Battersea Poly, (BSc (London), Physics 1st Hons); *m* 1, 8 July 1950, Gwendoline Iris (d 1964), da of George Edwin Humphreys (d 1952), of London; 2 s (Graham b 1951, Laurence b 1956 (decd)); m 2, 17 June 1967, Jacqueline Angela, da of Clifford Meyer Gilbert, of Newbury; 2 s (Christopher b 1968, Jason b 1971), 1 da (Tracey b 1969); *Career* RAF 1943-47, pilot F/O, UK, India, Malaya, China; GEC Research Labs Wembley 1951-54 (sr scientist); UKAEA 1954-73 & MOD 1973-87; dir Atomic Weapons Research Establishment, dep under sec 1982-87; sr scientific offr 1954-58, principal 1958-63, supt electronics research 1964-66, sr supt warhead electronics 1966-68, snr supt special systems 1968-74, chief of warhead devpt 1974-76, dep dir 1976-80, princ dep dir 1980-82, dir 1982-87 (ret 1987); thermonuclear tests Christmas Island 1957-58, participation with USA under mutual defence agreement 1958-87 with underground tests 1974-87, devpt of chevaline and trident 1968-87; FInstP; *Recreations* motoring, flying; *Style—* Peter Jones, Esq; Rhyd-y-Felin, Upper Llanover, Abergavenny, Gwent NP7 9DD

JONES, Peter Henry Francis; s of Eric Roberts Jones, MBE, of Swansea, and Betty Irene, *née* Longhurst (d 1981); *b* 25 Feb 1952; *Educ* Bishop Gore GS Swansea, Newport HS Gwent, Balliol Coll Oxford (MA); *m* 3 June 1978, Anne Elizabeth, da of David Jones, DFC, of Cheadle; 2 da (Clare b 14 May 1980, Eleanor b 14 July 1982); *Career* admitted slr 1977, ptnr Darlington & Parkinson 1979- 87; ptnr John Howell & Co Sheffield 1987-; memb Law Soc's Family Law Ctee; chm Legal Servs Conference 1986-, memb Lord Chllr's Advsy Ctee on Legal Aid 1983-; *Recreations* cricket, tennis, rugby, reading; *Style—* Peter Jones, Esq; 11 Endcliffe Grove Ave, Sheffield S10 3EJ (☎ 0742 660 303); 427/431 London Rd, Sheffield S2 (☎ 0742 501 000)

JONES, Philip Mark; CBE (1986, OBE 1977); s of John Jones (d 1957), and Mabel, *née* Copestake (d 1980); *b* 12 Mar 1928; *Educ* RCM (ARCM); *m* 1 Aug 1956, Ursula, da of Walter Strebi (d 1981); *Career* princ trumpet with all maj orchestras London 1949-72, fndr and dir Philip Jones Brass Ensemble 1951-86; dir wind & Percussion dept: Royal Northern Coll of Music Manchester 1975-77, Guildhall Sch Music and Drama City of London 1983-88; ed Just Brass Series Chester Music London 1975-; princ Trinity Coll of Music London 1988-; created over fifty gramaphone records with Philip Brass Ensemble; memb Arts Cncl GB 1984-88; memb Worshipful Co of Musicians 1987-, Freeman City of London 1988; Hon FTCL 1988; Royal Soc Musicians 1951-; FRNCM 1977, FRCM 1983, FRSA 1983, FGSM 1984; *Recreations* mountain walking, skiing; *Style—* Philip Jones, Esq, CBE; 14 Hamilton Terrace, London NW8 9UG (01 286 9155)

JONES, Sir (Thomas) Philip; CB (1978); *b* 13 July 1931; *Educ* Cowbridge GS, Jesus Coll Oxford (BA); *m* 1955, Mary; *Career* asst princ Miny of Supply 1955, princ Miny of Aviation 1959, on loan to HM Treasury 1964-66, pps to min of Aviation 1966-67, asst sec Miny of Technol subsequently Miny of Aviation Supply 1967-71; under sec: DTI 1971, Dept of Energy 1974; dep sec Dept of Energy 1976-83; memb British Nat Oil Corpn 1980-82, chm Electricity Cncl 1983-; kt 1986; *Style—* Sir Philip Jones, CB; Electricity Council, 30 Millbank, London SW1P 4RD (☎ 01 834 2333)

JONES, (William) Quentin; s of William Stephen Jones (d 1981), and Joan Constance, *née* Reach; *b* 18 Nov 1946; *Educ* Bradfield, Coll of Estate Mgmnt London; *m* 1, 4 Oct 1970 (m dis 1982), Jane Elizabeth; 4 s (Richard b 1973, Gregory Chamberlain b 1973, Russell Chamberlain b 1975, Edward b 1976); m 2, 5 April 1984, Diana Mary, da of Maj Albert Henry Hilton; *Career* chm JM Jones & Sons (Hldgs) Ltd 1981 (dir 1970); Freeman City of London, Liveryman Worshipful Co of Masons; FRICS 1969; *Recreations* tennis, swimming; *Style—* Quentin Jones, Esq; Greenacres, Lambridge Wood Rd, Henley on Thames, Oxon RG9 3BP (☎ 0491 573 200); JMJ House, Norden Rd, Maidenhead, Berks SL6 4BW (☎ 0628 771 144, fax 0628 771 633, car tel 0836 220 506)

JONES, Ralph Godfrey; s of William Ewart Jones (d 1971), of Ammanford, Wales, and Emily Frances (d 1969); *b* 6 April 1926; *Educ* Amman Valley GS, Swansea Univ (BSc); *m* 27 Sept 1947, Dorothy Lilian, da of Leonard Heath (d 1955), of Syston, Leics; 3 s (Vincent b 7 June 1948, David b 22 March 1953, Godfrey (twin) b 1953); *Career* fndr Preci-Spark Ltd (sub contractor to the aero-space indust) 1960; Freeman City of London 1974, Liveryman Worshipful Co of Fanmakers 1974; *Recreations* equestrian activities; *Style—* Ralph Jones, Esq; Sandhills Cottage Farm, Newtown, Linford, Leics (☎ 0530 242 275) Preci-Spark Ltd, Syston, Leics (☎ 0533 607 911, fax 0533 609 461, telex 342125 PRECI G)

JONES, (Raymond) Ray (John); s of Hubert Clarence Eric Jones, of Staffs, and Florence Evelyn Jones, *née* Bettles; *b* 31 Dec 1934; *Educ* Queen Elizabeth GS Staffs; *m* 1958, Margaret Heather (d 1988), da of George Clamp (d 1976), of Staffs; 2 da (Helen Susan b 1964, Claire Elizabeth b 1967); *Career* jt md The Tamworth Herald Co Ltd, Newspaper Publishers & Printers 1985; dir: Echo Press (1983) Ltd 1983-, Lichfield Mercury Ltd 1986-; *Recreations* music, gardening; *Clubs* Rotary (Tamworth Anker, founder press); *Style—* Ray Jones, Esq; 9 Moor Lane, Bolehall, Tamworth, Staffs (☎ 0827 54800); 10 Aldergate, Tamworth, Staffs (☎ 0827 60741)

JONES, Rhidian Huw Brynmor; s of Rev Preb Ivor Brynmor Jones, RD (d 1982), of Sutton Coldfield, Warwickshire, and Elizabeth Mary, *née* Morris; *b* 13 July 1943; *Educ* Queen Mary's GS Walsall, Keble Coll Oxford (MA); *m* 8 Aug 1970, Monica Marianne, da of Bror Eric Sjunne Sjöholm (d 1957), of Halmstad, Sweden; 1 s (Gavin b 1982), 1 da (Anna b 1978); *Career* trainee sec asst Selection Tst Ltd 1966-68, legal asst Total Oil GB Ltd 1968-69, co sec J E Lesser (Hldgs) Ltd 1969, asst sec Granada Gp Ltd 1970-76, articled clerk and asst slr Herbert Smith and Co 1976-80, sr asst slr Kenneth Brown Baker Baker 1980-81, ptnr Turner Kenneth Brown 1981-; vice-pres Ealing RUFC; cncl memb Anglo Swedish Soc; Freeman City of London Slrs' Co 1979; FCIS 1976, memb Law Soc 1978, FBIM 1987, MInstD 1987; *Recreations* rugby, Scandinavian studies; *Clubs* Wig and Pen; *Style—* Rhidian Jones, Esq; Roseleigh, 80 Elers Road, Ealing, London W13 9QD (☎ 01 579 9785); Turner Kenneth Brown, Slrs, 100 Fetter Lane, London EC4A 1DD (☎ 01 242 6006, fax 01 242 3003, telex 297696 TKBLAW G)

JONES, Robert Alan; s of William Arthur Jones (d 1967), of London, and Nellie Catherine, *née* Swinnerton (d 1980); *Educ* Eltham Coll; *m* 20 March 1954, Brenda, da of Gerald Charles Candish Dixon (d 1986); 1 s (Haydn b 1966), 2 da (Persephone b 1964, Anneliese b 1968); *Career* Nat Serv 1948-50, cmmnd 2 Lt (served in Libya); md Crown House Eng Ltd (formerly FH Wheeler Ltd) 1967, chm CHE Ltd 1974-79, dir Balfour Kilpatrick 1979 (md 1989); Liveryman Worshipful Co of Glaziers and Painters of Glass 1970; C Eng, FIEE, FCIBSE, CBIM; *Recreations* golf, literature, gardening; *Clubs* Betchworth Park Golf, RAC; *Style—* Robert Jones, Esq

JONES, Robert Brannock; MP (C) West Hertfordshire 1983-; s of Ray Elwin and Iris Pamela Jones; *b* 26 Sept 1950; *Educ* Merchant Taylors', St Andrews Univ (MA); *Career* memb: St Andrews Burgh Cncl 1972-75, Fife CC 1973-75, Chiltern Dist Cncl 1979-83; contested (C): Kirkcaldy Oct 1974, Teesside Stockton 1979; *Style—* Robert Jones Esq, MP; House of Commons, London SW1

JONES, Robert Henry; TD (1967); s of George Samuel Jones (d 1986), and Gertie Gladys Nash; *b* 10 April 1933; *Educ* Rendcomb Coll Cirencester (Open Scholarship), Bristol Business Sch, London Business Sch; *m* 18 July 1973, Valerie Ann, da of Edmund Norman Underwood (d 1982); 1 s (Paul Harris b 1963), 1 da (Caroline b 1975); *Career* Nat Serv Offr in Devonshire Regt Active Service (Mau Mau Campaign) Kenya 1953-54, TA Service (Glosters) 1954-67, final rank Major; independent professional chm, non-exec dir and adviser; md Lonsdale Printing and Packaging 1969-76; chm: Howard Jones Gp Ltd 1980-88, CWF Contractors 1980-85, Dataforms Ltd 1981-84 Blatchford Ltd (1987-), West of England Branch IOD 1984-; Southgate 1 XI Hockey 1960-61, West Gloucester 1961-69, represent TA 1957-58; *Recreations* tennis, shooting, music, sailing, hockey, skiing; *Clubs* Clifton, Institute of Directors, Bristol Commercial; *Style—* Robert H Jones, Esq, TD; 26 Duchess Rd, Clifton, Bristol BS8 2LA, (☎ 0272 737801)

JONES, (Owen Griffith) Ronald; s of William Tascar Jones, of Brynaman, Dyfed, and Bronwen Eirlys, *née* Jenkins; *b* 11 Dec 1948; *Educ* Amman Valley GS, Univ Coll Cardiff (BSc); *m* 10 July 1970, (Elizabeth) Cheryl; 1 da (Nia Mair b 1 Feb 1983); *Career* ptnr Arthur Andersen & Co 1983; tstee The Community Tst, dir Theatr Dalier Sylw, memb Welsh Language Bd, cncl memb Inst of Welsh Affrs; FICA 1974; *Style—* Ron Jones, Esq; 43A Hollybush Rd, Cardiff (☎ 0222 762 351); Arthur Andersen & Co, 21 Park Place, Cardiff (☎ 0222 371 353)

JONES, Roy Vincent; OBE (1966); s of Reginald Edward Jones (d 1968); *b* 6 July 1926; *Educ* Wolverhampton GS, Oxford Univ (MA); *m* 1948, Phillipa, da of Walter Whillock (d 1973); 2 children; *Career* md Guinness Peat Int; dir: Guinness Peat Securities, Guinness Peat Financial Services 1983-, Guinness Peat Trading, Guinness Peat (Overseas), North Delta Line; dir (Nigeria): Northern Expellers Ltd, Nigeria Bulk

Oil Co, Funtua Cottonseed Crushing Co, Lewis and Peat (Nigeria Rubber Industries); *Recreations* golf, fishing, coastal cruising; *Style—* Roy Jones Esq, OBE; Goetre Hill, Meifod, Powys (☎ (093 884) 378); Flat 15, Ivory House, St Katharine By The Tower, London E1 (☎ 01 481 9793); Guinness Peat International Ltd, PO Box 442, 32 St Mary At Hill, London EC3P 3AJ (☎ 01 623 9333; telex 885849)

JONES, Dr Schuyler; s of Schuyler Jones, of Wichita, Kansas, USA, and Ignace, *née* Mead; *b* 7 Feb 1930; *Educ* Wichita HS, Univ of Edinburgh (MA), Univ of Oxford (MA, DPhil); *m* 20 Dec 1955, Lis Margit Sondergaard, da of Malling Rasmussen, of Karlby, Denmark; 1 s (Peter Rasmussen b 2 Aug 1956), 1 da (Hannah Lis b 3 Oct 1962) ; *Career* Oxford Univ: lectr in Ethnology 1970-71, curator Pitt Rivers Museum 1985-, (asst curator 1971-85) hd Dept of Ethnology and Prehistory 1985-; anthropological expeditions: N Africa, The Sahara, W Africa 1951, French Equatorial Africa, Belgian Congo, E Africa 1952, S Africa, The Zambezi and Congo Rivers 1953, French W Africa, The Sahara 1954, Eastern Med 1956, Greek Is 1957, Turkey, Iran, Afghanistan, Pakistan, India, Nepal 1958, Pakistan, Kashmir, Afghanistan 1959, Nuristan 1960-70, Central China, Gobi Desert, Chinese Turkestan 1984, E Africa 1985, Central China, Tibet, Gobi Desert 1986, S China, Chinese Turkestan, Hunza, Gilgit 1988; Cncl memb RAI 1986-; *Books* Sous le Soleil Africain (1955), Under the African Sun (1956), Annotated Bibliography of Nuristan (Kafiristan) & the Kalash Kafirs of Chitral (1966), The Political Organization of the Kam Kafirs (1967), Men of Influence in Nuristan (1974), Nuristan (with Lennart Edelberg 1979), Hunting & Trading on the Great Plains 1859-1875, by James R Mead (ed 1986) ; *Style—* Dr Schuyler Jones; Pitt Rivers Museum, Oxford Univ, South Parks Rd, Oxford OX1 3PP (☎ 0865 270 924)

JONES, Sir Simon Warley Frederick Benton; 4 Bt (UK 1919), of Treeton, West Riding of Yorks, JP (Lincs 1971); s of Lt-Col Sir Peter Fawcett Benton Jones, 3 Bt, OBE (d 1972), and Nancy, *née* Pickering; *b* 11 Sept 1941; *Educ* Eton, Trinity Coll Cambridge; *m* 14 April 1966, Margaret Fiona, eldest da of David Rutherford Dickson, of Bentley Manor, nr Ipswich; 3 s, 2 da; *Heir* s, James Peter Martin Benton Jones b 1 Jan 1973; *Career* farmer, High Sheriff Lincs 1977-78; *Recreations* shooting, fishing; *Style—* Sir Simon Benton Jones Bt, JP; Irnham Hall, Grantham, Lincs (☎ 047 684 212); Sopley, Christchurch, Dorset

JONES, (John) Stanley; s of George White Jones (d 1958), of Wigan, Lancs, and Elizabeth Jones; *b* 10 June 1933; *Educ* Wigan GS, Wigan Art Sch (NDD), Slade Sch of Art UCL (Slade Dip in Fine Art), Ecole des Beaux Arts Paris; *m* 18 March 1961, Jennifer Francis, da of Lawrence Frederick Stone; 1 s (Matthew b 4 June 1965), 1 da (Liza b 17 Dec 1962); *Career* lectr in lithography Slade Sch of Fine Art UCL 1958, co fndr Curwen Studio London 1958, dir Curwen Prints Ltd 1962-; pres Printmakers Cncl, memb Royal Soc of Painter Etchers; *Books* Lithography for Artists (1963); *Recreations* walking, appreciation of music; *Style—* Stanley Jones, Esq; Curwen Prints Ltd, 114 Tottenham Court Road, Minford Place, London W1P 9HL (☎ 01 387 2618)

JONES, Stewart Elgan; s of Gwilym John Jones (d 1987), of Flecknoe, Warwickshire, and Elizabeth, *née* Davies; *b* 20 Jan 1945; *Educ* Cheltenham, The Queen's Coll Oxford (MA); *m* 21 July 1979, Jennifer Anne, da of Maj James Ian Leonard Syddall (d 1963), of Riseley, Berks; 2 da (Eleanor b 2 July 1980, Clementine b 19 Nov 1981); *Career* barr Grays Inn 1972, memb of Western Circuit, asst recorder Crown Ct 1985; *Recreations* home, hearth, the great outdoors; *Clubs* MCC; *Style—* Stewart E Jones, Esq; 3 Paper Buildings, Temple, London, EC4Y 7EU (☎ 01 583 8055, fax 01 353 6271)

JONES, Dr Sydney; CBE (1971); s of John Daniel Jones (d 1942), of 3 Brynglas, Penydarren, Merthyr Tydfil, Glam, and Margaret Anne, *née* Evans (d 1958); *b* 18 June 1911; *Educ* Cyfarthfa GS Merthyr, Cardiff Tech Coll, Univ of Cardiff (BSc), Univ of Birmingham (PhD), City Univ (DSc); *m* 23 July 1938, (Winifred) Mary, da of Joseph Boulton (d 1942), of Evesham, Worcs; 2 s (David Michael, Peter Howard), 1 da (Marilyn Gwenda); *Career* early career to 1956: engr GEC, lectr Birmingham and res TRE Malvern; head Armament Dept 1957-59, applications dir CEGB 1959-61, tech dir RB Pullin 1961-62, memb of bd BRB (formerly dir of res) 1962-75; MacRobert Award 1975; chm: BR Hovercraft Ltd, SIRA 1962-75; fndr Conformable Wheel Co Ltd 1975-; former govr Malvern Girls Coll; Freeman Worshipful Co of Scientific Instrument Makers 1976; City Univ (DSc) 1977; Design Cncl/Toshiba Award 1989; FEng; *Style—* Dr Sydney Jones, CBE; Cornerstones, Back Lane, Malvern, Worcs WR14 2 HJ (☎ 0684 572 566)

JONES, Terence Graham Parry (Terry); s of late Alick George Parry Jones, and Dilys Louise, *née* Newnes (d 1971); *b* 1 Feb 1942; *Educ* Royal GS Guildford, St Edmund Hall Oxford; *m* 20 June 1970, Alison, da of James Veitch Telfer; 1 s (William George Parry b 1976), 1 da (Sarah Louise Parry b 1974); *Career* writer and performer Monty Python's Flying Circus (BBC TV) 1969-75; film dir: Monty Python and the Holy Grail 1974, Monty Python's Life of Brian 1978, Monty Python's Meaning of Life 1981, Personal Services 1986, Erik the Viking 1989; *Books* Chaucer's Knight (1980), Fairy Tales (1981), The Saga of Erik the Viking (1983), Nicobobinus (1986), The Curse of the Vampire's Socks (1988), Attacks of Opinion (1988); *Style—* Terry Jones, Esq; 68A Delancey St, London NW1 (☎ 01 284 0242)

JONES, Timothy Arthur; s of Canon Idwal Jones, of Leam Cottage, Birdingbury, Warwicks, and Jean Margaret, *née* Shuttleworth; *b* 20 April 1951; *Educ* Christ's Hosp Horsham, Jesus Coll Cambridge, LSE, Coll of Law Chancery Lane; *m* 21 July 1979 (m dis 1988); 1 da (Harriet b 1980); *Career* barr Inner Temple 1975, practising Midland and Oxford circuit; parly candidate (Lib): Warwick and Leamington 1974, Mid Staffordshire 1983 and 1987; memb standing ctee Cambridge Union 1971, vice-chm League of Friends Rugeley Hosp 1985-; memb Admin Law Bar Assoc; *Recreations* theatre, walking, ornithology; *Style—* Timothy Jones, Esq; 25 Kingsley Wood Rd, nr Rugeley, Staffs WS15 2UF; St Ive's Chambers, 9 Fountain Ct, Steelhouse Lane, Birmingham B4 6DR (☎ 021 236 0863/0929/8952)

JONES, Trevor Courtney; s of William Jones (d 1979), of Hereford, and Edith Frances, *née* Webb (d 1963); *b* 14 August 1929; *Educ* Newport HS, Cardiff Univ (MM); *m* 24 Oct 1975, Rosemary Morley, da of Henry Vaughan Lowndes (d 1951), of Cheshire; 1 s (Simon Geoffrey b 30 Oct 1977); *Career* Master Mariner Union Castle Mail Steamship Co 1952-60, theatre mangr Royal Opera House 1971- (asst theatre mangr 1960-71); memb Covent Garden Forum; memb Hon Co of Master Mariners 1970; *Recreations* sailing, music, opera, ballet, theatre, reading; *Style—* Trevor Jones, Esq; 132 Tachbrook St, London SW1 (☎ 01 834 5273); The White Lodge, The Warren, Caversham, Berks; 42 Rue Des Lingots, Honfleur, Calvados, France 14600; Royal Opera House, Covent Garden, London WC2E 9DD (☎ 01 240 1200, fax 01 836 1762, telex 27988 COVGAR G)

JONES, Sir (Owen) Trevor; s of Owen and Ada Jones, of Dyserth; *b* 1927; *Career* memb Liverpool City Cncl 1968, Liverpool District Cncl 1973-, ldr Liverpool City Cncl; memb Merseyside Devpt Corpn 1981-; pres Liberal Party 1972-73, contested (Lib) Liverpool Toxteth 1974; kt 1981; *Style—* Sir Trevor Jones; Town Hall, Liverpool L2 3SW

JONES, (Gwilym) Wyn; CBE (1977); s of Rev John Jones, MA, BD (d 1943), and Elizabeth, *née* Roberts (d 1929); *b* 12 July 1926; *Educ* Llanrwst GS, UCNW (BA), Univ of London; *m* 2 June 1951, Ruth, da of the late John Henry Thomas; 1 s (Gareth Wyn b 28 Sept 1964), 1 da (Nerys Wyn b 25 Feb 1956); *Career* WWII served RN 1944-47; colonial admin Gilbert & Ellice Is, Tarawa, Phoenix Is & Ocean Is 1950-61 sec to Chief Min Cncl of Mins Solomon Is 1961-77 (asst sec 1961, sr asst sec 1967, dep chief sec 1974), govr Montserrat 1977-80; admin Cwmni Theatr Cymru (Welsh Nat Theatre) 1982-85; memb Gwynedd Health Authy 1982-; *Recreations* walking alone; *Style—* Wyn Jones, Esq, CBE; Y Frondeg, 13 Warren Drive, Deganwy, Gwynedd LL31 9ST (☎ 0492 833 77)

JONES, (Ieuan) Wyn; s of Tom Jones (d 1978), of Haverfordwest, and Dilys Vaughan Jones, *née* Williams (d 1959); *b* 8 Dec 1928; *Educ* Ellesmere Coll, Univ of London, Univ of Liverpool, BA (Arch) Lond., Dip, CD (Livpl); *m* 11 July 1959, Elfrida Mary, da of Michael Ionides (d 1978), of Surrey; 1 s (Gareth b 1962), 1 da (Emma b 1960); *Career* architect: dep architect MOD Iraq 1956-59, ptnr Hirst & Jones, Moore Simpson & Ptnrs 1959-68; ptnr Wyn Jones, Paul Andrews & Associates 1968 - cmmns inc numerous domestic & commercial buildings in West Wales, PCC Admin Building Texaco Refinery; also numerous restorations, St Mary Haverfordwest; Picton Castle & Pembroke Castle; 3 Civic Tst Awards (1968, 1970, 1982) and Welsh Office Housing Medal (1968); architect to St Davids Diocesan Bd of Finance, FRIBA (1969); JP (1972); *Recreations* hunting, gardening, sketching, historical buildings; *Style—* Wyn Jones, Esq, JP; Blaencilgoed House, Ludchurch, Narberth, Dyfed (☎ 083 483 605); 22 High Street, Haverfordwest, Dyfed, (☎ 0437 5156)

JONES, Wynn Rees; s of Iorwerth Jones of Machynlleth, Powys, and Catherine Jane *née* Rees; *b* 18 Feb 1941; *Educ* Machynlleth GS; *m* 28 April 1962, Eira, da of Trevor Jones (d 1962); 2 da (Karen Wynn b 18 Sept 1963, Nia Wynn b 16 Nov 1967); *Career* Barclay's Bank: mangr Port Talbot 1978-81, gen mangr asst Lombard St 1982-83, local dir S Wales Regnl Office 1984-87, retail dir Shrewsbury Regnl Office 1988-; memb Cncl Nat Museum of Wales; ACIB; *Recreations* antiques, motoring, all sport; *Style—* Wynn Jones, Esq; South Lodge, Norton, Shifnall, Shropshire TF11 9EE; Barclays Bank Plc, Regional Office, St Marys Place, Shrewsbury, SY1 1DU (☎ 0743 232901, fax 0743 231630)

JONES-PARRY, Sir Ernest; s of John Parry (d 1958); *b* 16 July 1908; *Educ* St Asaph, Univ of Wales (MA), London Univ (PhD); *m* 1938, (Marjorie Elizabeth) Mary, da of Hugh Garfield Powell (d 1926); 2 s (Rupert, Tristram); *Career* lectr in History Univ Coll of Wales 1935-40; Miny of Food 1941, Miny of Agric Fisheries and Food 1954 (under-sec 1957-64); exec dir: Int Sugar Cncl 1965-67, Int Sugar Orgn 1968-78; kt 1978; *Publications* The Spanish Marriages 1841-46 (1936), The Correspondence of Lord Aberdeen and Princess Lieven 1832-1854 (2 vols Royal Historical Soc 1938-39); *Recreations* reading, watching cricket; *Clubs* Athenaeum; *Style—* Sir Ernest Jones-Parry; Flat 3, 34 Sussex Sq, Brighton, Sussex BN2 5AD (☎ 0273 688894)

JONES-WILLIAMS, Dafydd Wyn; OBE (1970), MC (1942), TD (1954), DL (1958); John Jones-Williams (d 1936), of Dolgellau, and Lowry Jones-Williams (d 1971); *b* 13 July 1916; *Educ* Dolgellau GS, UCW Aberystwyth (LLB); *m* 1945, Rosemary Sally, eldest da of late A E Councell, of Blaenau Hall, Rhydymain; 2 da, both adopted (Susan, Sarah); *Career* formerly cmd 446 (Royal Welch) AB LAA Regt RA (TA); servd with HAC and X Royal Huss (W Desert); slr, clerk of the peace and clerk of Merioneth CC 1954-70, Circuit Admin for Wales & Chester Circuit 1970-75, Local Govt Ombudsman for Wales 1975-80; memb of Hughes Parry Ctee on Legal Status of Welsh Language 1963-65; former memb: Nature Conservancy and chm Ctee for Wales, Prince of Wales Ctee and Exec Ctee; memb of Cncl on Tribunals 1978-86; chm Merioneth and Montgomerys T & AFA; *Recreations* reading, golf, motoring, snooker; *Clubs* Army & Navy, Royal St David's and Dolgellau Golf; *Style—* Dafydd Jones-Williams, Esq, OBE, MC, TD, DL; Bryncoedifor, Rhydymain, Dolgellau (☎ 034141 635)

JOPLING, Rt Hon (Thomas) Michael; PC (1979), MP (C) Westmorland and Lonsdale 1983-; s of late Mark Bellerby Jopling; *b* 10 Dec 1930; *Educ* Cheltenham, King's Coll Newcastle; *m* 1958, Gail, da of late Ernest Dickinson; 2 s; *Career* farmer, contested (C) Wakefield 1959, memb Nat Cncl NFU 1962-64, memb UK exec Cwlth Parly Assoc 1974-79 and 1987-(vice chm 1977-79, memb int exec 1988-), MP (C) Westmorland 1964-1983, PPS to Min Agric 1970-71, asst govt whip 1971-73, lord cmmr Treasury 1973-74, oppn whip 1974, oppn spokesman Agric 1974-79, shadow min Agric 1975-76, parly sec to Treasury and govt chief whip 1979-1983; Miny Agric, Fishery and Food 1983-87; pres EEC Cncls of Agric, Fishery Ministers Jul-Dec 1986; hon sec Br and American Parly Gp 1987-, memb Foreign Affairs select Ctee 1987; *Style—* The Rt Hon Michael Jopling, MP; Ainderby Hall, Thirsk, N Yorks (☎ 0845 567 224); Clyder Howe Cottage, Windermere, Cumbria (☎ 096 62 2590)

JORDAN, Andrew; s of Andrew Jordan, of Belfast, and Bessie Jordan (d 1977); *b* 12 Mar 1950; *Educ* Queen's Univ Belfast (BSc), Univ of Cambridge (Dip Mathematical Statistics), Cranfield Sch Mgmnt (MBA); *Career* statistician Unilever Res Ltd 1974-77 (statistician overseas devpt admin 1977-79, investmt controller 3i 1980-84); dir Coopers & Lybrand 1985-; *Recreations* squash, diving, skiing; *Style—* Andrew Jordan, Esq; 8A Belvedere Drive, Wimbledon, London SW19 7BY (☎ 01 947 0183); Coopers & Lybrand, Plumtree Ct, London EC4A 4HT (☎ 01 822 4695, fax 01 822 4681)

JORDAN, Dr Carole; da of Reginald Sidney Jordan, and Ethel May, *née* Waller; *b* 19 July 1941; *Educ* Harrow Co GS for Girls, UCL (BSc, PhD); *Career* res assoc Jt Inst for Laboratory Astrophysics Univ of Colorado USA 1966, post doctoral appt UKAEA Culham Lab 1966-69; SRC's Astrophysics Res Unit Culham Laboratory: post doctoral res asst 1969-71, sr scientific offr 1971-73, princ scientific offr 1973-76; univ lectr Dept Theoretical Physics Oxford Univ, fell and tutor in physics Somerville Coll Oxford 1976-; sec RAS 1981-, memb SERC 1985-; FInstP 1973, FRAS 1966, memb IAU 1967; *Recreations* gardening; *Style—* Dr Carole Jordan; Dept of Theoretical Physics, Univ of Oxford, 1 Keble Rd, Oxford OX1 3NP (☎ 0865 273 980, fax 0965 273 418, telex 83245 NUCLOX)

JORDAN, Francis Leo (Frank); QPM (1982); s of Leo Thomas Jordan (d 1967), of

Stone, Staffs, and Mary Moloney (d 1982); *b* 15 June 1930; *Educ* St Joseph's Coll; *m* 1951, Ruth, da of James Ashmore (d 1970), of Cheshire; 1 s (Francis b 1958), 2 da (Karen b 1957, Diane b 1962); *Career* joined Staffs Police 1950 attaining rank of Chief Superintendent, seconded to Cyprus Police during EOKA emergency 1956-58, staff offr to HO Police Inspectorate 1975, asst chief constable W Midlands 1976, dep chief constable of Kent 1979, Chief Constable of Kent 1982-; chm Kent Children's House Soc 1979-81 (hon patron), memb Kent County Ctee of Soldiers, Sailors and Airmens Families Assoc, vice-pres Assoc of Kent Cricket Clubs; CBIM; *Recreations* shooting, walking, old buildings, travel; *Clubs* Royal Overseas League; *Style—* Frank Jordan, Esq, QPM; The Residence, Police Headquarters, Sutton Road, Maidstone ME15 9DD; Police Headquarters, Sutton Road, Maidstone, Kent ME15 9BZ (☎ 0622 690690, telex 96132)

JORDAN, Gayton (Gay); da of Stafford Walter Beckett (d 1985), of Shaldon, South Devon, and Catharine Barbara, *née* Marshall (d 1982); *b* 26 Feb 1951; *Educ* Convent of Notre Dame Teignmouth Devon, UCL (LLB, LLM); *m* 19 April 1976, David Jordan, s of William Henry Jordan; *Career* asst sec The Chartered Assoc of Certified Accountants (former asst professional educn sec) 1978-86, dir Inst of Trading standards admin 1987-; Fell RSPB (memb Enfield local gp); *Recreations* reading, hill walking, travel/camping in Africa, bird/animal watching; *Style—* Mrs Gay Jordan; Flat 2, 6 Warwick Rd, New Southgate, London N11 2TU (☎ 01 368 8122); Units 4 and 5, Hadleigh Business Centre, 351 London Rd, Hadleigh Essex SS7 2BT (☎ 0702 559 922, fax 0702 559 902)

JORDAN, Gerard Michael; s of Arthur Thomas Jordan (d 1971), of Upton, Wirral, Cheshire, and Ruby Eveline, *née* Charlton (d 1979); *b* 25 Sept 1929; *Educ* Grange Sch Birkenhead, Univ of Liverpool (BEng); *m* 26 March 1955, Vera Maud, da of George Peers (d 1967), of Bidston, Cheshire; 1 s (Paul Cahrlton b 1966), 1 da (Nichola Lesley b 1961); *Career* engr offr Mercantile Marine, gp engr Proctor & Gamble UK 1955-59; UKAEA: princ professional and tech offr 1959-72, asst dir 1972-75, dep dir 1975-84, dir of engrg 1984-87, dir of Dounreay Estab 1987-; cnslt (ex officio) Highlands Regnl Cncl and Highland and Islands Devpt Bd, indust rep to CBI Highlands region cncl memb Thurso Tech Coll; MIMechE; *Recreations* golf, sailing, DIY; *Style—* Gerard Jordan, Esq; The Cottage, Reay, Caithness, Scotland KW14 7RE (☎ 0847 81202); Dounreay Nuclear Power Development Establishment, Thurso, Caithness, Scotland KW14 7TZ (☎ 0847 62121)

JORDAN, John Oliver Philip ; s of Arther Oliver Jordan (d 1976), of Southampton, and Daisy Gertrude, *née* Jerrim (d 1980); *b* 4 Feb 1936; *Educ* Barton Peverel GS; *m* 30 April 1960, Ann Lochhead, da of Maj Donald Robert Daniels (d 1988), of Southampton; 2 s (Peter John 1961, Andrew b 1966), 2 da (Elizabeth b 1963, Alison b 1968); *Career* Nat Serv cmmnd RAPC, 6 years Army Emergerncy Reserve RAPC (Capt/pay-master); CA 1957; currently sr ptnr Jordan Brookes & Co; FCA 1966, ATII; *Style—* John Jordan, Esq; Parmenter Ho, Tower Rd, Winchester SO23 8TD (☎ 0962 52 263, fax 0962 841 197)

JORDAN, Michael Anthony; s of Charles Thomas Jordan (d 1956), of The Ferns, Duffield, Derbys, and Florence Emily, *née* Golder (d 1977); *b* 20 August 1931; *Educ* Haileybury; *m* 9 Dec 1956, Brenda Elizabeth, *née* Gee; 1 s (Mark b 1959), 1 da (Fiona b 1961); *Career* joined RH March Son & Co 1958 (ptnr 1959-68; ptnr: Saker & Langdon Davis 1968, WH Cork Gully & Co 1968-80, and Lybrand 1980-; sr ptnr Cork Gully 1983-; govr Royal Shakespeare Theatre 1979; High Ct of Justice Isle of Man (jt insprinto affairs of The Savings and Investmt Bank Ltd 1979); FCA; *Recreations* opera, diy; *Style—* Michael Jordan, Esq; Ballinger farm, Ballinger nr Missenden, Bucks HP16 9LQ (☎ 02406 3298); Shelley House, 3 Noblĕ St, London EC2V 7DQ (☎ 01 606 7700 fax 01 606 9887, telex 884 730 Corkgy G)

JORDAN, Air Marshal Sir Richard Bowen; KCB (1956, CB 1947), DFC (1941); s of Alfred Ormand Jordan (d 1942); *b* 7 Feb 1902; *Educ* Marlborough, RAF Coll Cranwell; *m* 1932, Freda Monica Minton Haines (d 1985), da of Mrs Miles Bruton (d 1950); 1 da; *Career* joined RAF 1921, served WWII, Gp Capt 1941, Air Cdre 1947, Air Vice-Marshal 1951, Air Marshal 1956, dir-gen orgn Air Miny 1953-55, AOC-in-C Maintenance Cmd 1956-58, ret 1958; Polonia Restituta 1942, Orange Nassau 1948; *Recreations* shooting, gardening; *Style—* Air Marshal Sir Richard Jordan, KCB, DFC; 4 Stonegate Court, Stonegate, Wadhurst, East Sussex TN5 7EQ

JORDAN, Terence; s of late Thomas William Jordan, and Elsie Elizabeth, *née* Davies; *b* 29 July 1936; *Educ* Hazeltine Sch Lower Sydenham; *m* 1, 17 March 1955 (m dis), Margaret Route; 1 s (Barry John b 1957), 1 da (Karen b 1960); m 2, 7 Sept 1964 (m dis), Valerie Ann Eustace; 1 s (Neil b 1966); m 3, 10 March 1986, Herchel Maclear-Williams (*née* Maclear-Morris); 1 step da (Charlotte Rachael Maclear b 1975); *Career* md Terrys Jewellers Ltd 1979-, dir Ratners Jewellers plc 1984-, md Ernest Jones Ltd 1988-, md Zales Jewellers 1988-; *Recreations* golf, travel, philately; *Clubs* Flackwell Heath Golf; *Style—* Terence Jordan, Esq; Ratners HQ, 25 Great Portland Street, London W1

JORDAN, William Brian; s of Walter Jordan (d 1974), and Alice Jordan *née* Heath; *b* 28 Jan 1936; *Educ* Dudley Rd Jr Sch, Barford Rd Secdy Mod Birmingham; *m* 8 Nov 1958, Jean Ann, da of Ernest Livesey; 3 da (Pamela, Lisa, Dawn); *Career* pres AEU 1986; memb: TUC gen and major ctees, NEDC, engrg indust trg bd; advsy (ACAS); pres Euro metalworkers (EEC), Br section Int Metalworkers Fedn; govr: LSE Manchester Business Sch; memb BBC Bd of Govrs 1988; *Recreations* reading, most sports; *Clubs* E57 Working man's club Birmingham, Austin Sports & Social Club; *Style—* William Jordan, Esq; 110 Pechkam Rd, London, SE15 5EL (☎ 01 703 4231, fax 01 701 7862)

JOSCELYNE, Richard Patrick; s of Dr Patrick Joscelyne (d 1963), of Westbury-on-Trym Bristol, and Rosalind Effie Joscelyne, later Adams, *née* Whitcombe; *b* 19 June 1934; *Educ* Bryanston, Queens Coll Cambridge (MA); *m* 1, 5 Feb 1961 (m dis 1988), Vera Lucia Melo, da of Dr Joaquim Ovidio Melo (d 1983), of Brazil; 1 s (Richard b 1964), 1 da (Patricia b 1963); m 2, 1988, Rita Irangani, da of Eric Dias (d 1961) of Colombo, Sri Lanka; *Career* Br Cncl: Montevideo 1962-67, Moscow 1967-69, Madrid 1969-73, dir N and Latin America dept 1973-77, rep Sri Lanka 1977-80, controller Asia and America div 1980-82, controller fin 1982-87, Spain 1987-; Encomienda De La Orden De Merito Civil (Spain 1988); *Style—* Richard Joscelyne, Esq; c/o British Council, 10 Spring Gardens, London SW1A 2BN (☎ 01 930 8466)

JOSE, (Thomas) Leonard; JP; s of William José (d 1967), of Penzance, and Jessie, *née* Brown Wark (d 1974); *b* 11 May 1926; *Educ* Schs in Cornwall, Scotland and England; *m* 29 March 1952, Gwendoline Joyce, da of Archibald Butler (d 1945), of Hounslow; 1 s (Alan S M), 2 da (Karen, Miranda); *Career* London Scottish (Gordon Highlanders) TA 1948-52: Lance-Corpl 1949, Corpl 1950, Sgt 1951; Kenya Police Reserve Inspr pt/t 1953-55; Lloyds 1944-87 (memb 1977); HP Motor Policies 1944-48, Hogg Robinson & Capel Cure 1948-49, Arbon Langrish & Co Ltd 1949-55, Ernest A Notcult & Co Ltd 1955-87 (later Eastern Produce Hldgs, Clarkson Puckle, now Bain Clarkson); Magistrate Bromley Bench 1979, PR exec Bromley Borough C of C; govr: Valley Primary Sch Shortlands, Princess Plain Primary Bromley; sidesman and chm rooms ctee Bromley Parish Church; life memb: Nat Tst for Scotland, Cornwall Naturalists Tst; Freeman City of London 1959; memb: Guild of Freeman, Liveryman Worshipful Co of Carmen 1982; memb Chartered Insurance Inst, registered Insur Broker; *Books* Road Transport Safety and Security Handbook (contrib, 1982); *Recreations* cooking, golf, reading, walking; *Clubs* Bromley Conservatives, City Livery; *Style—* Leonard José, Esq, JP; 14 The Glen, Shortlands, Bromley, Kent BR2 0JB (☎ 01 464 3548)

JOSEPH, Bernard Michael; s of Harry Toby, of London, and Esther *née* Markson; *b* 27 Sept 1948; *Educ* Bede GS for Boys; *m* 12 Oct 1980, Ruth Lesley-Ann, da of Jo Trent of London; 1 s (Darren Paul b 2 Sept 1985), 1 da (Danielle Natasha b 20 May 1983); *Career* CA, trainee Jennings Johnson 1971-75, Peat Marwick & Mitchell 1975-77, Nash Broad & Co 1977-79 (sole practitioner 1979-88), ptnr Johnsons 1988-; tres Voluntary Action Westminster; memb Worshipful Co of CAs, Freeman City of London; memb Nat Fedn Self Employed; *Clubs* Round Table; *Style—* FICA 1975 , MInstD, Bernard Joseph, Esq; 3 Hillersdon Ave, Edgware, Middx, HA8 7SG (☎ 01 958 5746), City Chambers, 285 City Rd, London EC1V 1LA (☎ 01 250 3134, fax 01 253 0289)

JOSEPH, Ernest Alex; s of Felix Joseph (d 1941); *b* 3 Jan 1923; *Educ* Townley Castle Sch London, Philanthropin Frankfurt; *m* 1950, Sylvia Ray, *née* Findon; 1 s, 1 da; *Career* dir Lanca plc; ret; *Recreations* music, swimming, gardening; *Clubs* Marco Polo (Hong Kong); *Style—* Ernest Joseph, Esq; 10 Monkville Ave, London NW11 (☎ 01 455 7682)

JOSEPH, Jack Michael; s of Joseph Joseph (d 1918), of London, and Catherine Joseph (d 1932); *b* 3 April 1910; *Educ* Essex Co HS, Westham Tech Coll; *m* 2 Sept 1934, Bertha, da of Moss Harris (d 1936); *Career* RAF LAC fitter 1942-43, Flying Offr ops navigator 1943-45, Flying Offr educnl and vocational trg offr 1945-46; jr clerk Sedgwick Collins Ltd 1926-27, branch mangr Barclays Bank Ltd Bow 1954-70 (served in various branches 1927-54), estate mgmnt C Henry Bond & Co 1971-73, dir Rowanband Ltd; chm: Frizcount Ltd, Honourgold Ltd, Griceglen Ltd, Vetchtree Ltd, Bryanston Sq Res Assoc Ltd; chm Bryanston Square Tst, govr Coopers Co & Coborn Educnl Fndn 1968-88; former pres Rotary Club of Bow 1970, memb Rotary Club of Bethnal Green; former hon tres: Br Czechoslovak friendship League, Br Hosp in Vietnam; former nat exec memb Banking Insur & Fin Union; hon tres: local branch Br Red Cross 1961-70, local branch Air Trg Corps 1969-70; chm local Nat Savings Ctee 1954-70, former tbnl memb Miny of Lab 1960-69; Freeman City of London 1962, Liveryman Worshipful Co of Coopers 1967; *Recreations* walking, watching cricket and football, campaigning for social justice; *Clubs* RAC, Cricketers of London; *Style—* Jack Joseph, Esq; 8 Bryanston Sq, London W1H 7FF (☎ 01 262 0353)

JOSEPH, Baron (Life Peer UK 1987), of Portsoken, in the City of London; Sir Keith Sinjohn Joseph; 2 Bt (UK 1943), CH (1986), PC (1962); o s of Sir Samuel George Joseph, 1 Bt (d 1944), and Edna Cicely, *née* Phillips (d 1981); *b* 17 Jan 1918; *Educ* Harrow, Magdalen Oxford; *m* 6 July 1951 (m dis 1985), Hellen Louise, yr da of Sigmar Guggenheimer, of NY; 1 s (James), 3 da (Emma Catherine Sarah b 1956, Julia Rachel b 1959, Anna Jane Rebecca b 1964); *Heir* (to baronetcy) s, Hon James Samuel Joseph b 27 Jan 1955; *Career* serv WWII in Italy as Capt RA (wounded, despatches); barr Middle Temple 1946, common cnclman of City of London for Ward of Portsoken 1946, alderman 1946-49; contested (C) Baron's Ct 1955; MP (C) Leeds NE 1956-87; pps to Parly Under-Sec of State CRO 1957-59, parly under-sec Miny Housing and Local Govt 1959-61, min of state BOT 1961-62, min Housing and Local Govt and min for Welsh Affrs 1962-64; sec of state for: Social Services DHSS 1970-74, Industry 1979-81, Educn 1981-86; co-fndr and first chm Fndn for Mgmnt Educn 1959; fndr and first chm Mulberry Housing Tst 1965-69; fndr and chm Mgmnt Ctee Centre for Policy Studies Ltd 1974-79; chm Cons Pty Advsy Ctee on Policy; Liveryman Worshipful Co of Vintners'; Fell of All Souls' Coll Oxford; *Style—* The Rt Hon Lord Joseph, CH, PC; 63 Limerston Street, Chelsea, London SW10 0BL

JOSEPH, Sir (Herbert) Leslie; DL (Mid Glam 1982); s of late David Ernest Joseph, and Florence Joseph; *b* 4 Jan 1908; *Educ* King's Sch Canterbury (govr 1968-); *m* 1934, Emily Irene, da of late Dr Patrick Murphy, of Aberdare; 2 da (dec); *Career* serv WWII RE, Major, Abyssinia, Sudan, Egypt; vice chm THF 1970-80; former pres Assoc Amusement Parks Proprietors, former chm Nat Amusements Cncl, Amusement Caterers' Assoc and Housing Production Bd for Wales; High Sheriff Mid-Glam 1975-76; kt 1952; *Style—* Sir Leslie Joseph, DL; Coedargraig, Newton, Porthcawl, Mid-Glamorgan (☎ (065 671) 2610)

JOSEPH, Neville Anthony; s of Jack Joseph (d 1985), of Stanmore, Middx, and Lily Joseph, *née* Libo; *b* 27 Feb 1937; *Educ* Ilfracombe GS, Bancrofts Sch; *m* 10 Oct 1962, Elna; 1 s (Philip Michael b 1964), 2 da (Viola Elna b 1966, Alexandra Louise b 1968); *Career* chartered accountant 1959-; md private bankers; FCA; FCIS; FTII; *Recreations* computers; *Style—* Neville A Joseph, Esq; Marlowe House, Hale Road, Wendover, Bucks HP22 6NE (☎ (0296) 62 3167)

JOSLIN, Chief Constable Peter David; QPM (1983); s of Frederick William Joslin, of Essex, and Emma, *née* Smith (d 1979); *b* 26 Oct 1933; *Educ* King Edward VI GS Chelmsford, Essex Univ (BA); *m* 26 Oct 1933, Kathleen Josephine, da of Patrick Monaghan, of Eire; 2 s (Russell b 1961, Stephen b 1964), 1 da (Angela b 1972); *Career* police offr, presently chief constable Warks Constabulary, formerly dep chief constable Warks Constabulary 1977, asst chief constable (ops) Leics Constabulary 1976, chief supt Leics Constabulary 1974, police constable to supt Essex Police 1954-74; *Recreations* cricket, football, golf, swimming, gardening, house renovation, after dinner speaking, good wines; *Clubs* RAC; *Style—* Chief Constable Peter Joslin, QPM; Warwickshire Constabulary, PO Box 4, Leek Wootton, Warwick CV35 7QB (☎ 0926 411 111, telex 31548)

JOSLING, Frederick John; s of John Frederick Josling (d 1975), and Emily Esther, *née* Baker (d 1987); *b* 22 Sept 1930; *Educ* St Albans Sch; *m* 1 April 1961, Elisabeth Mary, da of Thomas Reginald Harrison (d 1970); 2 s (Nicholas b 1966, William b 1970), 1 da (Emma b 1963); *Career* dir Lopex plc 1980-83, dep chm Kirkwoods 1981-86, md Interlink 1973-80 (chm 1981); chm: ASL Central 1986-88, ASL Alliance 1987-;

FIPA, FCAM; *Recreations* cricket, gardening; *Clubs* MCC, Lord's Taverners (chm 1976-78), Reform; *Style—* F J Josling, Esq; Badger's Holt, Caddington, nr Luton, Beds LU1 4AD (☎ 0582 23797); ASL Alliance Ltd, 30 Gray's Inn Rd, London WC1X 8HR (☎ 01 242 4444, fax 01 404 4165)

JOSSE, DR (Silvain) Edouard; OBE (1983); s of Albert Josse, of London, and Charlotte, *née* Karolicki; *b* 8 May 1933; *Educ* Highgate Sch, Middx Hosp Med Sch, Univ of London (MB, BS, DMJ); *m* 15 May 1960 (m dis 1983), Lea, da of Alter Majer Ber (d 1977); 2 s (David b 22 July 1961, Jeremy b 14 July 1968), 1 da (Ann b 19 Sept 1964); *Career* gen med practitioner 1962, sr forensic med examiner Metropolitian Police 1964, regnl advsr in gen practice NE Thames Region Br Postgrad Med Fedn Univ of London 1976; GP memb NE Thames RGA, memb Standing Ctee on Postgrad Med Educn, sec gen UEMO 1982-86; memb Enfield & Haringey Family Practitioners Ctee, chm Enfield & Haringey Local Med Ctee; MRCS, LRCP, FRCGP (1977), FZS, APSGB, MLS, BAFS; memb: BMA (1956), RSM (1978); *Recreations* skiing, gardening, history, good wine tasting; *Clubs* MCC, Middx CC; *Style—* Dr Edouard Josse, OBE; 24 Broad Walk, Winchmore Hill, London N21 3DB (☎ 01 886 8886); British Postgraduate Med Fedn, West Wing, Nurses Home, N Middx Hosp, Sterling Way, Edmonton, London N18 1QX (☎ 01 803 5313, fax 01 884 2773, car 0836 243330)

JOST, Dr H Peter; CBE (1969); s of Leo Jost (d 1941); *b* 25 Jan 1921; *Educ* Liverpool Tech Coll, Manchester Coll of Technol; *m* 1948, Margaret Josephine, da of Michael Kadesh (d 1952); 2 da; *Career* chm: K S Paul Gp, Assoc Technol Gp; co dir; lord president's nominee on Ct of Salford Univ 1970-87, first pres Int Tribology Cncl 1973-, chm Manchester Technol Assoc in London 1976-, pres Manchester Technol Assoc 1984-85; memb Parly and Scientific Ctee 1976- and Steering Ctee 1983-; pres Inst Prodn Engrs 1977-78, memb Cncl Engrg Instns 1977-84 (chm Home Affairs Ctee 1980-84); vice pres Inst Mech Engrs 1987; hon industl prof Liverpool Poly; and hon Prof Univ of Wales, Liveryman of Worshipful Co of Engrs, and Freeman of City of London, chm: K S Paul Gp, Assoc Technol Gp; co dir; Hon DSc Salford 1970, Hon DTech Cncl for Nat Academic Awards 1987, Hon DrSc Slovak Univ 1987; Hon DEng Leeds Univ 1989, State Legistative Commendation of State of California (USA) 1978; Gold Insignia of Order of Merit of Polish People's Republic 1986; *Recreations* music, gardening; *Clubs* Athenaeum; *Style—* Dr H Peter Jost, CBE; Hill House, Wills Grove, Mill Hill, London NW7 1QL (☎ 01 959 3355); K S Paul Products Ltd, Nobel Rd, Eley Estate, London N18 3DB (☎ 01 807 4567)

JOST, Hon Mrs (Marylyn Jane); *née* Macdonald; da of Rt Hon Lord MacDonald of Gwaenysgor 2 Baron McDonald of Gwaenysgor and Leslie Margaret; *b* 10 Oct 1951; *m* 1977, Peter Ronald, s of Ronald Jost of 5 Manor Grove, Fifield, Maidenhead, Berks; 2 s (Edward b 1980, Thomas b 1983) 1 s (decd); *Style—* The Hon Mrs Peter Jost

JOUGHIN, Michael; CBE (1971), JP (County of Moray); s of John Clague Joughin (d 1960), and May, *née* Hocken (d 1957); *b* 26 April 1926; *Educ* Kelly Coll Tavistock Devon; *m* 1, 1948, Lesley; 1 s (James), 1 da (Gail); m 2, 1981, Anne; *Career* Lt RM 1944-52, seconded 1946-49 Fleet Air Arm, ditched off Malta 1949, invalided 1952, Capt 11th Bn (TA) Seaforth Highlanders 1952-53; chm: N of Scotland Hydro-Electric Bd 1983-, N of Scotland Milk Mktg Bd Inverness 1974-83, Grassland and Forage Ctee JCC, Scottish Agric Dvpt Cncl 1971-80, Govrs of N of Scotland Coll of Agric Aberdeen 1969-72, Govrs of Blairmore Preparatory Sch Nr Huntly 1966-72, NEDC's Working Party on Livestock, N of Scotland Grassland Soc 1970-71, Elgin Mkt Green Auction Co 1969-70; pres Nat Farmers Union of Scot 1964-66; govr: Animal Diseases Research Assoc Edinburgh 1969-74, Scottish Plant Breeding Station Pentlandfield 1969-74, Rowett Research Inst Aberdeen 1968-74; memb: Awards Ctee the Massey-Ferguson Nat Award for Services to UK Agric, Scottish Constitutional Ctee, (Douglas-Home Ctee) 1969-70, Intervention Bd for Agric Produce London 1972-76, Nat Econ Devpt Cncl for Agric 1967-70, Agric Mktg Devpt Exec Ctee London 1965-68, Br Farm Produce Cncl London 1965-66, Br Farm Produce Cncl London 1965-66, Selection Ctee Nuffield Farming Scholarships; fndr presenter Farming Programme Country Focus Grampian TV 1961-64 and 1967-69; farmer 700 acres; FRAS, CBIM; DL County of Moray 1974-80; *Recreations* sailing; *Clubs* New (Edinburgh), RNSA, RMSC, Goldfish; *Style—* Michael Joughin Esq, CBE, JP; Elderslie, Findhorn, Moray (☎ 0309 30277); North of Scotland Hydro-Electric Bd, Rothesay Terrace, Edinburgh (☎ 031 225 1361)

JOURDAIN, James William; s of Henry James Jourdain (d 1966); *b* 28 Feb 1928; *Educ* Radley Coll; *m* 1953, Molly Elizabeth, da of Paul Gustavus Arthur Anthony OBE; 2 s (Richard, Michael), 2 da (Diana, Nicola); *Career* served RNVR 1946-48; md Blyth Greene Jourdain & Co Ltd 1969-; dir: Ireland Blyth & Co Ltd (Mauritius) 1972-, Bank of Mauritius 1967-69; chm Blyth Bros & Co Ltd Mauritius 1964-69, md Swire Blyth & Co Ltd London 1980-; *Recreations* sport, music, travel; *Clubs* City of London, MCC; *Style—* James Jourdain Esq; Tazar, Whiteman's Green, Cuckfield, Sussex (☎ (0444) 454723)

JOURDAN, Martin Hubert Thomas; s of Charles Henry Hans Jourdan; *b* 22 Nov 1940; *Educ* Mill Hill Sch, Harvard Business Sch; *m* 1963, Enid Valerie; 3 children; *Career* chairmaker; chm: Parker Knoll plc 1976- (furniture and textiles), Southern Regn CBI 1977-; chm: Southern Region CBI 1981-83, Lambert Howarth Gp plc 1985-; *Recreations* walking, shooting, fishing; *Clubs* Old Millhillians; *Style—* Martin Jourdan Esq; The Courtyard, Frogmoor, High Wycombe, Bucks (☎ (0494) 21144)

JOWELL, Prof Jeffrey Liones; s of Jack Jowell, of Cape Town, SA, and Emily, *née* Katzaenellenbogen; *b* 4 Nov 1938; *Educ* Univ of Cape Town (BA, LLB), Hertford Coll Oxford (BA, MA), Harvard Law Sch (LLM, SJD); *m* 8 Dec 1963, Frances Barbara, da of Dr Moses Suzman, of Johannesburg; 1 s (Daniel b 11 June 1969), 1 da (Joanna b 2 Sept 1967); *Career* barr Middle Temple 1965; res asst Harvard Law Sch 1966-68, fell jt centre urban studies Harvard and MIT 1967-68, assoc prof law and admin studies York Univ Toronto 1968-71; LSE: Leverhulme fell urban legal studies 1972-74, lectr law 1974-75; Social Sci Res Cncl: chm social sci and law ctee 1981-84, vice-chm govt and law ctee 1982-84; chm ctee of heads Univ Law Schs 1984-86, memb Nuffield Ctee Town and Country Planning 1983-86, Lionel Cohen lectr Hebrew Univ of Jerusalem 1983; Faculty of Law UCL: prof public law 1975-, dean 1979-, head dept 1982-; Hon DJur Athens 1987, Hon LLD Ritsumeikan 1988; *Books* Law and Bureaucracy (1975), Lord Denning: The Judge And The Law (jt ed 1984), The Changing Constitution (jt ed 1985); *Recreations* tennis, exploring Exmoor; *Clubs* Garrick; *Style—* Prof Jeffrey Jowell; 7 Hampstead Hill Gardens, London NW3 2PH (☎ 01 794 6645); Hantons, Exford, Somerset TA24 7LY; UCL, Gower St, London WC1 (☎ 01 380 7014)

JOWETT, (Edward) Ian; s of Eddie Jowett (d 1966), of 145 Moore Ave, Bradford 7, W Yorks, and Maud Alberta, *née* Holmes (d 1974); *b* 23 July 1928; *Educ* Bradford GS, Queen's Coll Oxford (MA,BCL); *m* 20 Oct 1962, Eileen Elizabeth, da of Stanley James Adamson (d 1969), of 94 Ashingdon Road, Rochford, Essex; 2 da (Susan b 1964, Carolyn b 1967); *Career* nat serv in Army, served: Palestine, Egypt, Libya 1947-49; called to the Bar (Middle Temple) 1952; asst to co sec Richard Thomas and Baldwins Ltd 1955-62, legal mangr Total Oil (GB) Ltd 1962-74, dir legal affairs Ford Motor Credit Co Ltd 1974-78, dir legal affairs Euro Credit Operations Ford of Europe Inc 1978-; fndr memb Bar Assoc of Commerce, Fin and Indust; elder Utd Reform Ch; Bar Cncl 1955; *Books* author articles in learned jnls and law review article in Title Retention Clauses (1980); *Recreations* cricket, ornithology, travelling; *Clubs* RCS; *Style—* Ian Jowett, Esq; 10 Arundel Gardens, Westcliff-on-Sea, Essex SSO OBJ (☎ (0702) 344 182); 1 Hubert Road, Brentwood, Essex CM14 4QL (☎ (0277) 224 400, fax (0277) 231 649, telex 995184 FMCCBWG

JOWITT, Harold John Duncan Mackintosh; s of Rev John Duncan Jowitt (d 1944), and Mary Margaret Stanton (d 1960); *b* 23 August 1911; *Educ* Glasgow Acad, Marlborough Coll, Univ of Nottingham (BA); *m* 1 April 1939, Kathleen Joyce, da of Thomas Clark (ka 1915); 1 s (Peter b 1942), 2 da (Christina b 1945, Caroline b 1952); *Career* WWII Sqdn Ldr RAF, intelligence duties, bomber cmd (despatches) 1940-46; in motor indust 1929-32, various appts in technical and adult educn, asst dir of educn Somerset CC 1951-54, chm and chief exec Dobson Park Industs plc 1970-76 (dep chm 1961-70, dir 1956-61, mgmnt offr 1954-56), memb Midlands Postal Bd 1974-78, hon sec N Midlands Cncl YHA 1936-39, memb FO sponsored exchanges between officials of Somerset and Lower Saxony 1950, (51, 52), hon dep tres UN Assoc (England and Wales) 1966-70, memb UK nat ctee for UNICEF 1967-70, pres Mapperley Hosp League of Friends 1973-80, chm Southwell Minster Appeal 1976-78, chm: Southwell Cathedral Preservation Tst 1978-, Nottingham Fights Strokes Assoc 1985-; FRSA 1972;; *Recreations* travel, gardening; *Style—* Harold Jowitt, Esq; Burgage Paddock, Southwell, Notts NG25 0ER (☎ 0636 812261)

JOWITT, Juliet Diana Margaret; *née* Brackenbury; JP (N Yorks 1973); da of Lt-Col Robert Henry Langton Brackenbury, OBE (d 1978) and Eleanor Trewlove, *née* Springman (d 1971); *b* 24 August 1940; *Educ* Hatherop Castle; Switzerland and Spain; *m* 1963, (Frederick) Thomas Benson Jowitt; 1 s, 1 da; *Career* assoc shopping ed House & Garden and Vogue 1966-69; proprietor Wood House Design (Interior Design) 1971-, memb Interior Decorators' and Designers' Assoc (IDDA) (memb: combined Juvenile Panel (Thirsk) 1976 combined Domestic Panel 1987); memb: IBA 1981-86, Domestic Coal Consumers' Cncl 1985, Potato Mktg Bd 1986-; dir Yorkshire TV Ltd 1987; *Style—* Mrs Thomas Jowitt, JP; 11 St George's Sq, London SW1V 2HX; Thorpe Lodge, Littlethorpe, Ripon, N Yorks HG4 3LU

JOWITT, Peter John Russell; s of Harold John Duncan Mackintosh Jowitt, of Burgage Paddock, Southwell, Notts, and Kathleen Joyce, *née* Clark; *b* 30 July 1942; *Educ* Bryanston, Univ of Nottingham (Bed); *Career* asst master Cheltenham Coll 1979-82, dep headmaster Cokethorpe Sch 1982-84, head of modern languages Claires Ct Sch 1985-89, dir Monksoft Ltd 1988-; memb Ctee Nat Sch's Regatta 1973-, selector GB Jr Rowing Team 1974-76, chm jr rowing ctee and memb exec ctee Amateur Rowing Assoc 1978-79, memb jr cmmn FISA 1979-84 (holder umpire's license 1971-), chef de mission Moscow 1979, chm Kitchin Soc 1989- (sec 1986-89); memb Physical Educn Assoc; *Recreations* ocean racing, rowing administration, computer assisted language learning; *Clubs* Lloyd's YC, Leander; *Style—* Peter Jowitt, Esq; Burgage Mews, Southwell, Notts NG25 0ER (☎ 0636 813545, fax 0636 815442, car 0836 507861)

JOY, Peter; OBE (1969); s of Neville Holt Joy (d 1935), of Marelands, Bently nr Farnham, Surrey, and Marguerite Duff *née* Beith; *b* 16 Jan 1926; *Educ* Down House Sch, Pembridge, Herefs; New Coll Oxford; *m* 2 May 1953, Rosemary Joan, da of Maj Harry Hamilton Hebden (d 1939), of Eday Royal Fusilers, and Eday, Orkney; 2 s (Nicholas b 1954, Rupert b 1963), 2 da (Caroline b 1955, Henrietta b 1960); *Career* RAF 1944-47, leading aircraftsman; joined FO 1952; first sec: Ankara 1959-61, New Delhi 1961-64, Beirut 1968-73; cnsllr and later dep High Cmmr, Kuala Lumpur 1979-80, ret FCO 1986; cnclr FCO; *Recreations* reading, shooting, fishing; *Clubs* Ex-Travellers; *Style—* Peter Joy, Esq; The Old Rectory, Stoke Bliss, Tenbury Wells, Worcestershire; Carrick House, Eday, Orkney

JOY, Thomas Alfred; LVO (1979); s of Alfred George Joy (d 1962), and Ann Carpenter (d 1955); *b* 30 Dec 1904; *Educ* Bedford House Sch Oxford; *m* 1932, Edith Lizzie, da of Richard Ellis (d 1906); *Career* asst Bodleian Library Oxford 1919, buyer and cataloguer J Thornton & Son Univ Booksellers Oxford 1925-35 (indentured apprentice 1919-25), mangr circulating library and book dept Harrods 1935-45, Army & Navy Stores: mangr book dept and fndr library 1945-56, merchandise mangr 1956, dep md 1956-65; employers rep Bookselling and Stationery Trade Wages Cncl 1946-79, leader employers' side 1957; memb: Nat Chamber of Trade 1946-51, Wholesale Trades Advsy Ctee 1946-51, Book Trade Ctee 1948, Arts Cncl working pty on obscene pubns 1968-69, sub-ctee on Pub Lending Rights 1970; pres: Hatchards 1985- (and 1965-85, began Hatchards Authors of the Year parties 1966, Booksellers Assoc of GB and Ireland 1957-58 (hon life memb 1983), Book Trade Benvt Soc 1974-; inaugurated Nat Book Sale (1st chm of ctee 1954-65), hon life memb: Soc of Bookmen, Booksellers Assoc of GB and I 1983; FRSA; Jubilee Medal 1977; *Books* The Right Way to Run a Library Business (1949), Bookselling (1953), The Truth about Bookselling (1964), Mostly Joy (autobiography 1971), The Bookselling Business (1974); *Recreations* motoring, gardening, salmon fishing; *Style—* Thomas Joy Esq, LVO; 13 Cole Park Gardens, Twickenham, Middlesex TW1 1JB; Hatchards, 187 Piccadilly, London W1V 9DA (☎ 01 439 9921, telex 953970)

JOYCE, Michael Herbert; JP (1981); s of Tom Joyce, and Mary Jackson; *b* 5 April 1933; *Educ* King Edward XII Sch Lytham St Annes Lancs, St Bees Sch Cumbria; *m* 8 Sept 1956, Sheila, da of Hubert Taylor; 2 s (Nicholas Tom b 14 Oct 1959, Andrew Michael b 15 Oct 1960); *Career* 5 RTR 1958-60;ptnr McKeith Dickinson & Ptnrs 1970-83, md Omn's Devpts 1983-, JP 1981; *Recreations* golf; *Clubs* St Annes Old Link S, Aloha (Marbella); *Style—* Michael Joyce, Esq; 6 Lindsay Court, New Road, St Anes-On-Sea (☎ 0253 465 96); 4 South King St, Blackpool (☎ 0253 20 016)

JOYCE, William Jesson (Bill); CBE (1968); s of Geoffrey Joyce (d 1937), of Blackfordby, Burton-on-Trent, and Dorothy Lilian, *née* Jesson (d 1983);; *b* 5 Dec 1917; *Educ* Ashby-de-la-Zouch GS; *m* 28 April 1946, Isabel Mary, (d 1985), da of late James Keir Simpson, of Christchurch, NZ; 2 da (Marianne b 26 April 1952, Margaret b 11

June 1956); *Career* WWII Guardsman then Coldstream Gds, Royal Leics Regt, serv N Africa and Italy, (despatches); staff FW Woolworth & Co Ltd at Taunton Exeter Bristol and Plymouth 1936-39; Elder Dempster Lines Ltd: joined 1946, Ghana mangr 1962-65, Nigeria mangr 1965-66; dir and West Coast mangr: Elder Dempster Agencies Ltd, Sierra Leone Shipping Agencies, Liner Agencies (Ghana) Ltd, Elder Dempster Agencies (Nigeria) Lt, West Africa Properties (Nigeria) Ltd, Elder Dempster Agencies (Gambia) Ltd 1966-72, ret 1973; *Style*— Bill Joyce, Esq, CBE; 3 Upton Close, Upton, Wirral, Merseyside L49 6NA (☎ 051 677 3827)

JOYNSON, Lt Col (Henry) Calvert (Weaver Glazebrook); s of Col NHW Joynson (d 1984), and Cecile Joynsons, *née* Stanley Clarke; *b* 6 Oct 1934; *Educ* Harrow, RMAS; *m* 20 March 1958, Diane Helen, da of Col Hugh Dalton Turrall, of Dolton, Devon; 2 s (Charles b 1959, Andrew b 1981), 1 da (Tiffany b 1967); *Career* mil serv, cmmnd 1955, Maj 14/20 Kings Hussars 1966, Lt Col 1980, ret 1983; chm NFSE (Devon) Ltd 1987, MBIM; *Recreations* golf, bibliophily; *Style*— Lt Col H C Joynson, Esq; Calverlei House, Chawleigh, Chulmleigh, Devon (☎ (0769) 80146); CPA Ltd, 350 Kings St, London W6 (car (☎ (0836) 592291)

JOYNSON, (George) Colin (Whittell); s of George Whittell Joynson (d 1965), and Joan Lily, *née* Heyworth (d 1951); *b* 9 April 1929; *Educ* Stowe; *m* 3 April 1954, Jean Emilia Hilda, da of Ralph Wicksteed (d 1962); 1 s (Richard b 1959), 1 da (Nicola b 1955); *Career* aircraftsman RAF; former commodity broker and memb of leading UK Exchanges; dir Richard Joynson Ltd 1965-; chm: London Wool 1965, Coffee Terminal Mkt of London 1970; business broker 1971-; Business Search Unit 1979- memb of Olympic Bobsleigh Team 1948; *Clubs* Gresham, St Moritz Tobogganing; *Style*— Colin Joynson, Esq; Douglas House, Queensberry Road, Kettering, Northamptonshire NN15 7HL (☎ 0536 85115)

JOYNSON, Kenneth Mercer; s of Edgar Hilton Joynson (d 1974), and Nellie, *née* Clausey (d 1943); *b* 8 Oct 1926; *Educ* Lymn GS Cheshire, Wolverhampton Tech Teachers Coll (Cert Ed); *m* 22 Sept 1951, Ruth Madeleine, da of Cyril Bentley Jackson (d 1931); 1 s (Richard b 25 Jan 1956); *Career* CA; asst accountant Bell & Nicholson Ltd Birmingham 1951-57, accountant Newey Eyre Ltd Birmingham 1957-59, sr audit mangr Impey Cudworth Co Birmingham 1959-62, princ Joynson & Co Sutton Colfield 1963-66, sr lectr and head accounting studies, Peterborough Regnl Coll 1967-80, lectr examiner Chartered Building Socs Inst 1972-86, princ Joynson & Co Peterborough 1981-; disabled through Polio 1931, vice chm (later chm) polio Fellowship Birmingham 1953-65, chm Age Concern Deepings and Dist Lincolnshire 1972-; various offices 1958- 67: W Midland Lib Pty, Rutland and Stamford Lib Assoc, Stamford and Spalding Lib Assoc; now memb SLD, parish cncllr Deeping St James Parish Cncl 1979-83, cncllr South Kesteven Dist Cncl 1983-89; ACA 1951, FCA 1961; *Recreations* marathon running, association football; *Clubs* Peterborough Athletics, Stamford Town FC; *Style*— Kenneth Joynson, Esq; 39 Manor Way, Deeping St James, Peterborough PE6 8PS (☎ 0778 343 506); Cushing Fairbairn Wardle & Co, 73 Park Rd, Peterborough PE1 2JN (☎ 0733 313 600)

JOYNSON, Peter Assheton; JP (1976); s of Maj Will Joynson (d 1970), of Perths, and Mary Hamilton Clegg (d 1971); *b* 9 May 1928; *Educ* Eton, RAC Cirencester; *m* 14 May 1955, Catherine Hilda Douglas, da of Col A V C Douglas, of Mains (d 1977); 1 s (Michael William b 1959), 1 da (Theresa Cicely b 1961); *Career* land agent, ptnr fndr Managed Estates, Stirling; memb Justice Prison Ctee 1980, chm Belhaven Hill Sch Governors 1977-88, memb Queen's Bodyguard of Scotland (Royal Co of Archers) 1965-; MRAC, FRIC; *Recreations* shooting, fishing, hill walking; *Clubs* New (Edinburgh), Flyfishers; *Style*— Peter A Joynson, Esq, JP; Laraich, Aberfoyle, By Stirling (☎ 08772 232); Managed Estates, 18 Maxwell Place, Stirling FK8 1JU (☎ 0786 62519)

JUCKES, Col William Geoffrey; MBE (1956), TD, DL (1969); s of Geoffrey Juckes (d 1946), of Hull, and Alice Olivia, *née* Murdo (d 1972); family farmers in Shrops for 13 known generations; *b* 28 Sept 1909; *Educ* Boteler GS Warrington; *m* 27 May 1937, Kathleen Mary, da of Ernest Foster (d 1923), of Bath; 1 s (Geoffrey b 1950), 2 da (Pauline b 19 Feb 1938, Gillian Anita b 21 Aug 1942); *Career* Hants Regt TA wounded N Africa 1943; Westminster Bank Hull 1926, mangr Andover 1953, mangr Newbury 1966; ret 1970; Co Cmdt ACF 1960-70; *Recreations* cricket, rugby; *Clubs* Naval & Military, MCC; *Style*— Col William G Juckes, MBE, TD, DL; Hatchway Cottage, Vernham Dean, Andover, Hampshire (☎ 026487 205)

JUDAH, Nigel Leopold; s of Edward Joseph Judah (d 1966), and Sylvia Sarah, *née* Frank (d 1970); *b* 6 Dec 1930; *Educ* Charterhouse, Lausanne Univ; *m* 1970, Phoebe; 1 s (Samuel b 1978), 2 da (Henrietta b 1972, Hannah b 1975); *Career* CA; finance dir and sec Reuters Hldgs plc 1981 (joined 1955, sec and chief accountant 1960, sec and asst gen mangr 1967); dir: Reuters Hldgs plc, Reuters Ltd, Visnews Ltd; Order of Merit (Italy); FCA; *Recreations* opera, wine, collecting pictures, tennis; *Clubs* Brooks's; *Style*— Nigel Judah, Esq; 49 Addison Ave, London W11 4QU (☎ 01 603 7628); Reuters Ltd, 85 Fleet St, London EC4P 4AJ (☎ 01 250 1122)

JUDD, Allan Frederick; s of Frederick James Judd (d 1950), of Surbiton, Surrey, and Ruth Emma, *née* Mansell (d 1967); *b* 17 August 1911; *Educ* Kingston GS, Wimbledon Tech Coll, Law Soc Sch of Law; *m* 1, Dorothy Frances Judd (d 1968); 1 s (Richard Allan Follett Judd b 1942), m 2, Violet Muriel Bell, da of Joseph George Follett, of Hove, Sussex; 1 step s (David John Bell b 1942); *Career* joined RA 1940, cmmnd 1941; served: 2 Army Fr and Ger, Belson liberation and rehabilitation of camp inmates, mil govt Miden, judge intermediate; admitted slr 1934, ptnr Simmonds church Smiles 1946-89; clerk General cmmn of Taxes: West Brixton Div 1949-86, First East Brixton Div 1971-86; sec Lord Chllr Advsy Ctee 1960-89, hon legal advsr office Assoc (Br Legion); memb Met Water Bd 1956-59; pres: Rotary Club Wandsworth 1975-76, Holborn Law Soc (fnds memb) 1963-64; memb Holborn Borough Cncl 1950-64 (Mayor 1959-60 and 1963-64), JP, Alderman 1961; memb Utd Ward Club City of London; Freeman City of London, memb Worshipful Co of Fruiterers; MIOD; *Clubs* Carlton, Kingston Rowing, Luxembourg Soc; *Style*— Mr Judd, Esq; 13 Bedford Row, London WC2

JUDD, (Eric) Campbell; DBE (1974), LVO (1984, MVO 1956); Frederick William Judd (d 1951), and Marjorie Katherine, *née* Bell (d 1956); *b* 10 August 1918; *Educ* Wellington, St Thomas Collegiate, Univ of Toronto; *m* 8 Nov 1947, Janet Creswell, da of George Frederic Fish (d 1940), of Nottingham; 2 s (Richard b 1951, Anthony b 1956), 1 da (Susan b 1949); *Career* air crew observer RCAF & RAF (attached), N Atlantic Ferry cmd; Bomber cmd: Malta, Far East, W Indies 1939-45; ret sqdn ldr RCAF Res 1945; Unilever Ltd 1946, Utd Africa Co Ltd Nigeria 1946-60 (dir 1953-60, chm 1957-60), dir UAC Ltd London 1960-77 (md 1968-77, dep chm & joint md 1969-77); memb House of Assembly W Nigeria 1955-56; chm: BNEC Africa 1969-72, advsy gp BOTB 1972-74, W Africa Ctee London 1976-85 (vice chm 1963-76); memb cncl & exec ctee Royal Africa Soc 1975-83 (vice pres 1983-86); life memb: Bomber Cmd Museum Hendon, Burma Bomber Assoc Canada, RAF Assoc UK, Royal Br Legion; *Recreations* golf, theatre, cricket, reading, music; *Clubs* MCC, Pathfinder, Mid-Herts golf; *Style*— Campbell Judd, Esq, CBE, LVO; 23 Townsend Lane, Harpenden, Herts AL5 2PY (☎ 05827 2617); 8 Albany Ct, Petty France, London SW1 (☎ 01 799 2162)

JUDD, Clifford Harold Alfred; CB (1987); s of Alfred Ernest Judd (d 1966), and Florence Louisa, *née* Peacock; *b* 27 June 1927; *Educ* Christs Hosp, Keble Coll Oxford; *m* 9 Aug 1951, (Elizabeth) Margaret, da of late Albert William Holmes; 2 da (Caroline b 1969, Rosemary b 1970); *Career* Nat Serv 2 Lt RA 1947-48 (invalided out); HM Treasy: exec offr 1948, through ranks princ 1964, sr princ 1969, asst sec 1973, under sec (Treasy offr of Accounts) 1981-87; memb Royal Patriotic Fund Corpn 1987-; *Recreations* cricket, golf, DIY; *Clubs* Sevenoaks Vine CC, Knole Park GC; *Style*— Clifford Judd, Esq, CB; 4 Colets Orchard, Otford, Sevenoaks, Kent TN14 5RA (☎ 09592 2398)

JUDD, Frank Ashcroft; s of Charles W Judd, CBE (d 1974), of Surrey, and Helen Osborn Judd, JP, *née* Ashcroft (d 1982); *b* 28 Mar 1935; *Educ* City of London Sch, LSE (BSc); *m* 1961, Christine Elizabeth Louise, da of Frederick Ward Willington (d 1966), of Kent; 2 da (Elizabeth, b 1967, Philippa b 1969); *Career* F/O RAF 1957-59; gen sec of Int Voluntary Service 1960-66; MP 1966-79; PPS to: Min of Housing and Local Govt 1967-70, Leader of Opposition 1970-72; jr opposition defence spokesman 1972-74, Parly Under Sec of State for Defence for the RN 1974-76, Min for Overseas Devpt 1976-77, Min of State FCO 1977-79, assoc dir Int Defence & Aid Fund for Southern Africa 1979-80, dir Voluntary Service Overseas 1980-85, dir Oxfam 1985-; for LSE; memb Cncl of Overseas Devpt Inst; chm Int Cncl of Voluntary Agencies; Hon DLitt; Hon fell Portsmouth Poly; govr LSE; memb Cncl of Overseas Devpt Inst; chm Int Cncl of Voluntary Agencies; FRSA; *Books* (Jt author) Radical Future (1967), Fabian International Essays (1970), Purpose in Socialism (1973); *Recreations* hill walking, family holidays; *Clubs* Royal Cwlth Soc; *Style*— Frank Judd, Esq; Belmont, 21 Mill Lane, Old Marston, Oxford OX3 0PY (☎ 0865 721 447); Oxfam, 274 Banbury Rd, Oxford OX2 7DZ (☎ 0865 56777)

JUDD, Bt-Col George Richard; TD, DL (Essex 1948); s of Edward Thomas Judd, JP (d 1963); *b* 26 April 1914; *Educ* Gresham's Sch Norfolk; *m* 1956, Mary Stuart, *née* Paton; 3 s; *Career* Lt-Col 1943 304 Field Regt RA (TA), Essex Yeo 1947-51, Bt-Col 1951, Hon-Col 1965-69; chartered surveyor, ptnr Strutt & Parker; High Sheriff Essex 1974; FRICS; *Clubs* Boodle's, City of London; *Style*— Col George Judd, TD, DL; Bouttells House, Kersey, Ipswich, Suffolk IP7 6DY (☎ 0473 828 044)

JUDD, Lionel Henry; s of John Basil Thomas Judd (d 1983), and Cynthia Margaret Georgina, *née* White-Smith; *b* 24 Oct 1945; *Educ* Leys, and Downing Coll, Camb (MA); *m* 19 Sept 1970, Janet Elizabeth, da of Arthur Boyton Fraser (d 1966), of The Limes, Stansted, Essex; 1 s (Edward b 1972), 1 da (Alexandra b 1975); *Career* slr 1972; ptnr Darley Cumberland 1975-; *Recreations* rowing, country pursuits, travel; *Clubs* Leander; *Style*— Lionel Judd, Esq; Little Coombe, Wendover, Bucks HP22 6EQ; 36 John St, London WC1N 3BH (☎ 01 242 0422, fax 01 831 9081)

JUDD, Vincent Sydney; s of Sydney Arthur Judd, of 9 Manor Rd, Wheathampstead, Herts, and Hilda Lillian Judd; *b* 15 April 1944; *Educ* St Albans Sch; *m* 16 Sept 1968, Betty, da of James Humphrey, of 60 Larke Way, Leagrave, Beds; 4 da (Christine b 1971, Eve b 1972, d 1973, Sally b 1976, Fiona b 1978); *Career* qualified CA 1966, insolvency practitioner; memb ICEAW; *Recreations* transport, photography, gardening; *Style*— Vincent Judd, Esq; 7 High St, Harpenden, Herts (☎ 05827 62 649, 05827 68 936, fax 0582 460 674)

JUDD, Lady Zinnia Rosemary; *née* Denison; da of 4 Earl of Londesborough (d 1937); *b* 1937,(posthumously); *m* 1, 1957 (m dis 1961), Peter Comins; 1 s (Timothy b 1958, changed name to Pollock after 1968); m 2, 1961 (m dis 1964), John David Leslie Melville (only s of Hon David Leslie Melville, MBE, 3 s of 11 Earl of Leven and Melville); m 3, 1964 (m dis 1967), Maj Hugh Cantlie, Scots Gds; 1 s (Charles); m 4, 1968 (as his 3 w), Ralph John Hamilton Pollock, publisher (d 1980, gggs of Rt Hon Sir Frederick Pollock, 1 Bt); m 5, 1982, James (Jamie) H Judd; *Style*— Lady Zinnia Judd; Stewkley Grange, Leighton Buzzard, Beds

JUDGE, David Leslie; s of Harry Judge, MC, of Islington, London,and Joan Beryl, *née* Tomey (d 1978); *b* 23 May 1942; *Educ* Malvern Coll, Merton Coll, Oxford (MA); *m* 19 Sept 1964, Angela Monica da of Col Edward Douglas Lawson Whatley, OBE, TD, DL, (d 1981), of Malvern, Worcs; 1 s (Edward b 1971), 1 da (Joanna b 1969); *Career* slr 1969, sec Abbeyfield (Malvern) Soc Ltd, hon slr and ctee memb Malvern CAB, church warden St Johns, Clerk to Malvern Hills Conservators 1979-; memb Law Soc 1967-; *Recreations* field sports, fishing, shooting, stalking; *Style*— David Judge, Esq; Shuttifield Cottage, Birchwood, Storridge, Malvern, Worcs WR13 5HA (☎ 08864 243); Priors Croft, Grange Rd, Malvern, Worcs (☎ 0684 892298)

JUKES, John Andrew; CB (1968); s of Capt (Andrew) Munro Jukes (d 1918), and Gertrude Elizabeth, *née* King (d 1957); *b* 19 May 1917; *Educ* Shrewsbury, St John's Coll Cambridge (MA), LSE (BSc); *m* 19 June 1943, Muriel, da of Frederick James Child; 2 s (Andrew b 1946, David b 1952), 2 da (Margaret (Mrs Condick) b 1944, Rosemary (Dr Fowler) b 1950); *Career* hon cmmn RAF 1940; econ advsr: econ section Cabinet Off/Treasy 1948-54, UK Atomic Energy Authy 1954-64; dep dir gen and dep sec dept econ affrs 1964-69, dep sec Miny of Tport 1969-71; dep sec DOE: econs and resources 1970-72, enviromental protection 1972-74; dir gen highways Dept of Tport 1974-77, exec bd memb CEGB 1977-80; memb: SDP 1981-87, SLD 1988-; London Borough of Sutton: rep on Cncl for Socl Democracy 1982-86, cncllr 1986-, chm fin sub ctee and resources sub ctee; memb Merton and Sutton Dist Health Authy 1986-; *Recreations* gardening; *Style*— John Jukes, Esq, CB; 38 Albion Rd, Sutton, Surrey SM2 5TF (☎ 01 642 5018)

JUKES, Paul Francis; s of Frederick Jukes (d 1987), of London, and Mary, *née* Galloway (d 1980); *b* 23 August 1952; *Educ* St Ignatius Coll North London, Middlesex Poly; *m* 6 April 1974, Geraldine, da of James Fahey, of London; 4 s (Adam b 1975, Christopher b 1978, Jeremy b 1981, Daniel b 1984); *Career* Cooper Lancaster CAs 1971-76, The Br CECA Co Ltd 1976- (appointed md 1982), Cobham Catholic Boys FC, sch govr St Paul's RC First Sch, memb Parish Pastoral Cncl Sacred Heart Cobham; FCA 1981, FInstD, FBIM; *Recreations* running, particularly road running; *Clubs* RAC; *Style*— Paul Jukes, Esq; The British CECA Co Ltd, Rowan Ct, 56 High

St, Wimbledon Village, London SW19 5EE (☎ 01 946 7774, fax 01 947 3873, telex 928041)

JULIAN, Prof Desmond Gareth; s of Dr Frederick Bennett Julian, MC (d 1958), and Jane Frances, *née* Galbraith (d 1956); *b* 24 April 1926; *Educ* Leighton Park Sch, St John's Coll Cambridge (MA,MD), Middx Hosp London; *m* 1, 8 July 1956, Mary Ruth (d 1964), da of John Jessup (d 1968); 1 s (Paul Richard b 1962), 1 da (Claire Frances b 1960); m 2, 10 Dec 1988, Claire, da of Frederick Bolam Marley; *Career* RNVR 1949-51; conslt cardiologist Sydney Hosp Aust 1961-64, conslt cardiologist Royal Infirmary Edinburgh 1964-74, prof of cardiology Newcastle-upon-Tyne Univ 1975-86, conslt med dir Br Heart Fndn 1986-; hon MD Gothenburg 1986; FRCP London, Edinburgh, Aust; *Books* Cardiology (1970; 5 edn 1988); *Recreations* skiing, walking; *Clubs* Athenaeum; *Style*— Prof Desmond Julian; Flat 1, 36 Frognal, London NW3 6AG (☎ 01 794 9314); Old Darras Hall, Edge Hill, Ponteland, Newcastle-upon-Tyne NE20 9RR; British Heart Foundation, 102 Gloucester Place, London W1H 4DN (☎ 01 935 0185)

JULIEN, Michael Frederick; *b* 22 Mar 1938; *Educ* St Edward's Sch Oxford; *m* ; 3 children; *Career* gp fin dir BICC Ltd 1976-1983; gp finance dir Midland Bank 1983-86; md Finance and Admin Guinness plc 1987-; memb 100 Gp of Chartered Accountants; liveryman Worshipful Company of Barber-Surgeons; vice-pres Br Digestive Fndn; FCA, FCT; *Clubs* City Livery Club; *Style*— Michael F Julien, Esq; Bendochy, Ellesmere Rd, Weybridge, Surrey KT13 OHQ (☎ (0932) 844999); Guinness plc, 39, Portman Square, London W1H 9HB (☎ 01 486 0288)

JUNGELS, Dr Pierre; s of Henri Jungels, former pres of Labaz; *b* 18 Feb 1944; *Educ* Univ of Liege (Ing Civ), California Inst of Technol (PhD); *m* 2 1988 Caroline, da of Dr Srg Benc of Worster; 2 children; *Career* gen mangr and chief exec Petrangol (Angola) 1977-80; md and chief exec Petrofina (UK) 1981-, chm/dir various Petrofina subsidiaries in UK, Belgium and France, elected to main bd of Petrofina SA Brussels; pres The Inst of Petroleum 1986-88; *Recreations* tennis, skiing; *Clubs* Anglo-Belgian; *Style*— Dr Pierre Jungels; Oak Farm, Jesses Lane, Peaslake, Surrey GU5 9RT (☎ 048 641 2142) Petrofina (UK) Ltd, Petrofina House, Ashley Ave, Epsom KT18 5AD (☎ 037 27 26226)

JUNGIUS, Vice-Adm Sir James George; KBE (1977), DL (Cornwall 1982); s of Maj E Jungius, MC; *b* 15 Nov 1923; *Educ* RNC Dartmouth; *m* 1949, Rosemary Frances Turquand Matthey; 3 s; *Career* RN: served WWII Atlantic and Med, Commando Ops Adriatic, asst naval attaché Washington, asst chief Naval Staff Operational Requirements 1972-74, Rear Adm 1972, Vice-Adm 1974, Dep Supreme Allied Cdr Atlantic 1975-77, Supreme Allied Cdr's Atlantic rep Europe 1978-80, ret; navigation specialist; fell Wood Corpn (Wester div); OStJ (chm cncl for Cornwall); CBIM; *Recreations* sailing, fishing; *Clubs* Pilgrims, RN club of 1765 and 1785, overseas league; *Style*— Vice Adm Sir James Jungius, KBE, DL; c/o National Westminster Bank, 26 Molesworth St, Wadebridge, Cornwall PL27 7DL

JUNOR, Sir John; s of Alexander Junor, of Black Isle; *b* 15 Jan 1919,Glasgow,; *Educ* Glasgow Univ (MA); *m* 1942, Pamela Welsh; 1 s, 1 da; *Career* serv WWII RNVR; contested (Lib): Kincardine and W Aberdeen 1945, Edinburgh E 1948, Dundee W 1951; journalist; ed Sunday Express 1954-86 (chm 1968-86); dir: Express Newspapers (formerly Beaverbrook Newspapers) 1960/86, Fleet Hldgs 1982-85; kt 1980; *Books* The Best of JJ (1981); *Recreations* golf; *Clubs* Royal and Ancient; Walton Heath; *Style*— Sir John Junor; c/o Utd Newspapers, Tudor St, London EC4Y OHR

JUPP, Clifford Norman; CMG (1966); s of Albert Leonard Jupp (d 1959), and Marguerite Isabelle Day Winter (d 1962); *b* 24 Sept 1919; *Educ* Perse Sch Cambridge, Trinity Hall Cambridge (MA); *m* 1945, Babbs, da of Arthur Babbs (d 1964); 1 s (Peter), 2 da (Jane, Carol); *Career* WWII 1940-46, Capt Commandos 1946-70; Foreign and Diplomatic Service: FO 1941-43, Beirut 1947-49, NY 1949-51, FO 1951-53, Cairo 1953-56, Kabul 1956-58, FO 1958-61, Brussels 1961-63, Belgrade 1963-66; BOT 1966-70; Burton Gp 1970-72; dir Br Textile Confederation 1973-76, ret; *Style*— Clifford Jupp Esq, CMG; Tigh Nan Cruitean, Kildalton, Isle of Islay PA42 7EF; Argyll, Scotland

JUPP, Hon Mr Justice; Hon Sir Kenneth Graham Jupp; MC (1943); s of Albert Leonard Jupp, shipbroker; *b* 2 June 1917; *Educ* Perse Sch Cambridge, Univ Coll Oxford (MA); *m* 1947, Kathleen Elizabeth, da of Richard Owen Richards, farmer, of Morton Hall, Morton, Salop; 2 s, 2 da; *Career* Major, served WWII, Europe and N Africa 1939-43, on WO Selection Bd 1943-46; barr Lincoln's Inn 1945, dep chm Cambs and Isle of Ely QS 1965-71, recorder Crown Ct 1972-75, QC 1966, High Ct Judge (Queen's Bench) 1975-, Presiding Judge NE Circuit 1977-81; chm Ind Schs Tbnl 1964-67, chm Public Enquiry into Fire at Fairfield Home Nottingham 1975; kt 1975; *Recreations* music, reading,; *Clubs* Garrick; *Style*— The Hon Mr Justice Jupp, MC; Royal Courts of Justice, Strand, London WC2

JURKIEWICZ, Hon Mrs (Enid Aughard); *née* Jones; da of Baron Maelor (Life Peer); *m* , E Jurkiewicz; *Style*— The Hon Mrs Jurkiewicz; 16 Snowdon Drive, Wrexham, Denbighshire

JURY, Capt Peter Charles Cotton; s of Col Edward Cotton Jury, CMG, MC (d 1966); *b* 30 August 1919; *Educ* Rugby, King's Coll Cambridge; *m* 1953 (m dis), (Ursula Joan) Sally, da of Maj Gen Sir William Abraham, CBE (d 1980); 2 da (Sophie, Polly); *Career* Capt 13/18 Royal Hussars: BEF 1939-40, BLA 1944-45; md Shelbourne Hotel Ltd Dublin 1947-60, Tst Houses Ireland Ltd 1960-72, dir Tst House Hotels 1967-71, chm Trusthouse Forte Ireland Ltd 1972-80, pres Int Hotel Assoc 1977-78, dir Minibar (UK) Ltd 1986-; *Clubs* Sloane; *Style*— Capt Peter Jury; The Old Vicarage, Beadlam, Nawton, York YO6 5ST (☎ 0439 71220)

JUSTHAM, David Gwyn; s of John Farquhar Richard Justham (d 1948); Margaret Anne, *née* John (d 1969); *b* 23 Dec 1923; *Educ* Bristol GS; *m* 31 March 1950, Isobel Thelma, da of George Gordon Thomson, MC (d 1968); 1 s (Jamie b 1951), 1 da (Julia b 1954); *Career* Flt Lt (pilot) RAF 1941-46; slr 1949; various appts with ICI plc 1955-65 and IMI plc 1965-85; dir IMI plc 1968-85, Nat Exhibition Centre Ltd 1979- (chm 1982-), H Samuel plc 1981-84, Central Ind TV plc 1981- (chm 1986-); chm Birmingham Hippodrome Theatre Tst Ltd 1979-, memb cncl of mgmnt CBSO 1984-88, pres Birmingham Chamber of Industry and Commerce 1974-75, gen cmmr of Income Tax 1972-77; High Sheriff W Midlands 1981-82; hon life memb ct of govrs 1986 (memb 1976-), Univ of Birmingham: dep pro vice chllr 1987-; *Recreations* opera, theatre; *Clubs* Army & Navy; *Style*— David Justham, Esq; 9 Birch Hollow, Edgbaston, Birmingham B15 2QE (☎ 021 454 0688)

JUSTICE, Nicholas Alexander; *b* 17 August 1945; *Educ* Christ's Coll, Ch Ch NZ, Univ of Canterbury NZ (BE, ME); *m* 28 Dec 1968, Patricia; 1 s (Andrew b 1981), 2 da (Emma b 1976, Anetta b 1982); *Career* chief engr Hawker Siddeley Dynamics Engrg Ltd 1981; md Strategic Systems Technol Ltd 1983-; memb Inst of Measurement & Control; *Style*— Nicholas A Justice, Esq; 14 Landons Close, London E14 9QQ (☎ 01 538 8228, fax 01 515 3887)

K

KABERRY, Hon Andrew Murdoch Scott; 2 s of Baron Kaberry of Adel (Life Peer); *b* 22 Sept 1946; *Educ* Repton, East Anglia Univ (BA); *Career* FCA 1972, chartered accountant; *Style*— The Hon Andrew Kaberry; Thorp Arch Hall, Boston Spa, W Yorks

KABERRY, Hon Christopher Donald; s and h (to baronetcy only) of Baron Kaberry of Adel (Life Peer UK 1983); *b* 14 Mar 1943; *m* 25 March 1967, Gaenor Elizabeth Vowe, yr da of Cecil Vowe Peake, MBE, of Redbourn, St Albans, Herts; 2 s (James b 1970, Angus b 1972), 1 da (Claire b 1974); *Style*— The Hon Christopher Kaberry; The Croft, Rookery Lane, Wymondham, Melton Mowbray, Leics LE14 2AU (☎ 057 284 663)

KABERRY, Hon Simon Edward John; 3 and yst s of Baron Kaberry of Adel (Life Peer); *b* 14 Dec 1948; *Educ* Repton; *Career* solicitor 1974; *Style*— The Hon Simon Kaberry; Adel Willows, Otley Rd, Leeds 16

KABERRY OF ADEL, Baron (Life Peer UK 1983); Sir Donald Kaberry; 1 Bt (UK 1960), of Adel cum Eccup, City of Leeds; TD (1947), DL (W Yorks 1976); s of Abraham Kaberry (d 1954), of Leeds, and Lily, *née* MacKenzie; *b* 18 August 1907; *Educ* Leeds GS, Leeds Univ; *m* 3 Sept 1940, Lily Margaret, da of late Edmund Scott, of Morley, W Yorks; 3 s; *Heir* to baronetcy only, s, Christopher Donald Kaberry, *qv*; *Career* sits as Conservative Peer in House of Lords; served WW II, RA, Dunkirk and NW Europe (despatches 2), Actg Col; solicitor 1930; memb Leeds City Cncl 1930-39 and 1946-50; MP (C) Leeds NW 1950-83; asst govt whip 1952-55, parly sec BOT 1955; memb: Select Ctee Nationalised Industries 1961-83, Speaker's Panel of Chairmen 1974-83; chm Select Ctee Industry and Trade 1979-83; vice chm Cons Pty 1955-61, chm Assoc of Cons Clubs 1961-, pres York Area Cncl of Cons Pty 1966- (chm 1951-55, dep pres 1956-65); former chm: Yorkshire Chemicals Ltd, W H Baxter Ltd, E Walker & Co Ltd; pres Leeds Branch Dunkirk Veterans Assoc; chm Leeds Teaching Hosps 1961-75 (chm Special Tstees 1975-86); *Clubs* Carlton, St Stephen's, Constitutional, Leeds; *Style*— The Rt Hon the Lord Kaberry of Adel TD, DL; 1 Otley Rd, Harrogate, N Yorkshire HG2 0DJ

KADOORIE, Baron (Life Peer UK 1981), of Kowloon in Hong Kong and of the City of Westminster; Sir Lawrence; CBE (1970), JP (1936); s of Sir Elly Kadoorie, KBE (d 1944); *b* 2 June 1899; *Educ* Cathedral Sch Shanghai, St Vincent's Eastbourne, Clifton; *m* 1938, Muriel, *née* Gubbay; 1 s, 1 da; *Career* joint proprietor Sir Elly Kadoorie & Sons; chm: Sir Elly Kadoorie Successors Ltd, China Light and Power, Schroders Asia Ltd, Nanyang Cotton Mill Ltd; dir: Sir Elly Kadoorie & Sons Ltd, and vaious other companies; kt 1974; *Recreations* sports cars, photography, Chinese works of art; *Clubs* Hong Kong, Jewish Recreation; *Style*— The Rt Hon the Lord Kadoorie, CBE, JP; 24 Kadoorie Ave, Kowloon, Hong Kong (☎ 7116129)

KADOORIE, Hon Michael David; s of Baron Kadoorie (Life Peer); *b* 1941; *m* Betty, da of J E Tamayo, of Florida, USA; 2 da (Natalie b 1986, Bettina b 1987); *Style*— The Hon Michael Kadoorie; No 68 Deep Water Bay Road, Hong Kong

KADRI, Sibghatullah; s of Alhaj Maulana Firasatullah Kadri, of 33 Wavertree Road, London SW2, and Begum Tanwir Fatima, *née* Hamidi (d 1986); *b* 23 April 1937; *Educ* Christian HS Budown UP India, SM Sci Coll Karachi Pakistan, Karachi Univ Pakistan, Inns of Court School of Law London; *m* 4 Oct 1963, Carita Elisabeth da of Stig Ole Sigvward Idman (d 1973), of Helsinki; 1 s (Sadakat b 1964), 1 da (Maria Fatima b 1965); *Career* BBC External Serv 1965-68, prodr and presenter BBC Home Serv, visiting lectr in Urdu Holborn Coll 1966-68, called to the Bar Inner Temple 1969, head of chambers 1973-; Pakistan Students Fedn in Br: gen sec 1961-62, vice pres 1962-63; pres Inner Temple Students Assoc 1968-69; standing Conference of Pakistani Organisation: gen sec 1975-78, pres 1978-84; convenor Asian Action Ctee 1976, vice chm Jt Ctee Against Racism, chm Soc of Black Lawyers 1981-83, sec Br Lawyers Ctee for Human Rights and Justice in Pakistan 1984-, chm Asian Lawyers Conference, memb Bar Cncls Race Relations ctee 1989 (1982-85,1988); *Style*— Sibghatullah Kadri, Esq; 100 Girdwood Rd, London SW18 5QT (☎ 01 789 1941); 11 Kings Bench Walk, Temple, London EC4Y 7EQ (☎ 01 353 4931/2, 01 583 0695/8, fax 01 353 1726)

KAGAN, Hon Anne Eugenia; da of Baron Kagan (Life Peer); *b* 1965; *Style*— The Hon Anne Kagan

KAGAN, Hon Daniel; s of Baron Kagan (Life Peer); *b* 1953; *Style*— The Hon Daniel Kagan

KAGAN, Baron (Life Peer UK 1976); Joseph Kagan; s of Benjamin Kagan (d 1988, aged 109); *b* 6 June 1915; *Educ* High Sch Kaunas Lithuania, Leeds Univ; *m* 1943, Margaret Stromas; 2 s, 1 da; *Career* dir Kagan Textiles, chm Gannex Gp of Cos (founded 1951); kt 1970 (annulled 1981); *Style*— The Rt Hon the Lord Kagan; 15 Fixby Rd, Huddersfield, Yorks (☎ 0484 25202); Barkisland Hall, Barkisland, Halifax, W Yorks (☎ Elland 0422 74121)

KAGAN, Hon Michael George; s of Baron Kagan (Life Peer); *b* 1950; *Style*— The Hon Michael Kagan

KAHN, Baron (Life Peer UK 1965); Richard Ferdinand Kahn; CBE (1946); s of late Augustus Kahn, of London; *b* 10 August 1905; *Educ* St Paul's, King's Coll Cambridge; *Career* temp civil servant in various govt depts 1939-46, prof of econs Cambridge Univ 1951-72, fell King's Coll Cambridge; FBA 1960; *Books* Selected Essays on Employment and Growth (1973), The Making of Keynes' General Theory (1984); *Clubs* United Oxford and Cambridge; *Style*— The Rt Hon the Lord Kahn, CBE; King's College, Cambridge CB2 1ST (☎ 0223 350411/353311)

KALDOR, Hon Mary Henrietta; da of Baron Kaldor (Life Peer, d 1986); *b* 1946; *Books* The Baroque Arsenal (1982); *Style*— The Hon Mary Kaldor; c/o André Deutsch Ltd, 105 Great Russell St, WC1 (☎ 01 580 2746)

KALISHER, Michael David Lionel; QC (1984); s of Samuel Kalisher (d 1966), and Rose, *née* Chester (d 1970); *b* 24 Feb 1941; *Educ* Hove Co GS, Bristol Univ (LLB); *m* 1967, Helen, da of Albert Edward McCandless, of N Ireland; 1 s (Jason b 1972), 2 da (Justine b 1969, Natasha b 1973); *Career* slr 1965-69, barr 1970, rec Crown Ct 1985; *Recreations* squash, tennis, reading; *Clubs* Roehampton; *Style*— Michael Kalisher, Esq, QC; 1 Hare Court, Temple, London EC4 (☎ 01 353 5324, fax 01 353 0667)

KALMS, (Harold) Stanley; s of Charles Kalms (d 1978), and Cissie, *née* Schlagman; *b* 21 Nov 1931; *Educ* Christ's Coll Finchley; *m* 28 Feb 1954, Pamela Audrey, da of Morris Jimack (d 1968), of London; 3 s (Richard b 10 March 1955, Stephen b 3 Dec 1956, Paul b 6 March 1963); *Career* chm Dixons Gp plc; non exec dir British Gas plc 1987-; chm: Jews' Coll, Jewish Educnl Devpt Tst; Hon City and Guilds Insignia Award in Technology (Hon CGIA) 1988; *Recreations* communal educnl activities, sailing; *Style*— Stanley Kalms, Esq; Dixons Gp plc, 29 Farm St, London W1X 7RD (☎ 01 499 3494, fax 01 629 1410, telex 923427)

KAMIL, Geoffrey Harvey; s of Peter Kamil of Princess Court, Harrogate Road, Leeds and Sadie, *née* Morris; *b* 17 August 1942; *Educ* Leeds GS, Leeds Univ (LLB); *m* 17 March 1968, Andrea Pauline, da of Gerald Ellis, of The Fairways, The Fairway, Leeds; 2 da (Sharon b 1969, Debra b 1971); *Career* slr of Supreme Ct of Judicators 1968-, ptnr J Levi Leeds 1974-87, stipendiary magistrate W Midlands (dep stipendiary magistrate 1985), asst rec of Crown Ct 1986-; memb: ctee of Leeds Law Soc 1982-87, Leeds Cts ctee 1983-87, Leeds Duty Slr Ctee 1985-87; sec Stonham's Kirkstall Lodge Leeds 1974-87; *Recreations* golf, sailing, swimming, collectors cars; *Clubs* Shirley Park GC, Moor Allerton GC; *Style*— Geoffrey Kamil, Esq

KAN, Sir Yuet-Keung; GBE (1979, CBE 1967, OBE 1959), JP; s of Kan Tong Po, JP; *b* 26 July 1913; *Educ* Hong Kong Univ, London Univ (BA); *m* 1940, Ida; 2 s, 1 da; *Career* solicitor; chm Hong Kong Trade Devpt Cncl 1979-83; pro-chllr Chinese Univ of Hong Kong; Hon LLD Hong Kong Univ, Chinese Univ; kt 1972; *Style*— Sir Yuet-Keung Kan, GBE, JP; Swire House, 11 Floor, Chater Rd, Hong Kong (☎ Hong Kong 238181)

KANE, Wing Cdr (Morris) Michael; MBE (1939); s of Edward Michael Kane (d 1937), of Dublin and London, and Gertrude Mary, *née* Pentony (d 1972); *b* 26 Feb 1913; *Educ* private; *m* 9 Oct 1940, Oonagh Isabelle, da of Capt Walter Benjamin Palmer, OBE, RNR (d 1926); 1 s (Timothy b 1952), 2 da (Susanna b 1942, Penelope b 1946); *Career* cmmnd Pilot Offr RAF 1934, 18 Sqdn Heyford 1935, sqdn Abingdon 1935, 39 Sqdn Risalpur NWFP India 1936, Central Flying Sch 1939, Flt Cdr No 2 Flying Trg Sch 1939, promoted Sqdn Ldr and posted Flt Cdr 10 Sqdn 1941 (POW Germany 1941-45, despatches for distinguished serv) Wing Cdr Air Staff Air Miny 1945, memb Jt Intelligence Staff and Chief Intelligence Offr FEAF 1948, RAF Staff Coll 1950; Wing Cdr: (Orgn) HQ Tport Cmnd 1951 (Flying) RAF Abingdon; posted special duties 1952, cmmnd RAF Andover 1955, for personnel memb Staff of Air Miny 1959, ret 1960; int staff NATO 1960-62, chm John F Rich Co Ltd 1967- (designate md 1962-63, md); co cmmr St John Ambulance Oxfordshire 1964-74; memb: St John Cncl Oxfordshire, British Schools and Univs Fndn 1962; tstee Albertus Magnus Tst 1980; FInstD 1964, FBIM 1985, MICFM 1985; Knight of Malta 1963, Cross Pro Merito Melitensi 1970, Officer Pro Merito Melitensi 1986; *Recreations* drawing, reading, listening to music, watching cricket, rugby; *Clubs* RAF, Directors; *Style*— Wing Cdr Michael Kane, MBE; Brimpton House, Milton Common, Oxford OX9 2JN (☎ 0844 729229)

KANTOROWICZ TORO, Donald; s of Rodolph Kantorowicz, and Blanca Livia, *née* Toro; *b* 4 August 1943; *Educ* Jesuit Sch Cali Colombia, Salem Sch Germany, St Joseph Sch Boston USA, German Sch Cali Colombia, Hochschule für Welthandel Vienna (MBA), LSE, Faculté de Droit et Sciences Economiques Paris (DEconSc); *m* 12 Sept 1973 (m dis 1986), Chantal, *née* Lancrenou; 2 da (Melanie b 1976, Johana b 1978); *Career* Banque de L'Union Européenne Paris 1969-71, asst mangr Bank of Amercia Paris 1972-77, asst vice pres Bank of America Madrid 1977-78, vice pres and mangr Bank of America Barcelona 1979-80, md and chief exec Consolidado UK Ltd 1980-; memb French Fin Assoc Paris; *Recreations* skiing, sailing, classical music, history; *Clubs* Overseas Bankers, Jockey (Bogora), Interalie Paris, Marks; *Style*— Donald Kantorowicz Toro, Esq; 11 South Terrace, London SW7 (☎ 01 584 8185); Consolidado UK Ltd, The Old Deanery, Dean's Court, London EC4V 5AA (☎ 01 236 2095, fax 01 489 0409, telex 291109)

KAPP, Carlo David; s of Robert Scope Kapp (d 1975), of Hayling Island, Hampshire, and Paolo Luisa, *née* Putoto; *b* 31 July 1947; *Educ* Ladybarn Sch Manchester; *m* 1, 28 March 1970 (m dis 1978), Jean Gillian, da of Aubrey Charles Overington (d 1980), of Richmond, Surrey; 1 da (Kelli Ann b 4 July 1977); m 2, 30 Oct 1979, Basia Evelyn, da of Dr Abraham Seinwel Bardach (d 1988), of London; 1 s (Daniel Joseph b 5 Oct 1980), 1 da (Pippa Luisa b 25 Feb 1983); *Career* jt display mangr Marshal & Snelgrove Manchester 1966-67, des dir Kempthorns Richmond 1967-68, interior display mangr Debenham & Forebody 1968-70, display mangr Swears & Wells Gp, overseas sabbatical 1971-74, creative servs mangr Estee Luder Gp (UK) 1974-81; chm and md: Dawson Kapp Overseas 1981-88, DKO Gp plc 1988-; govr RNLI; memb: Addison Gardens Garden Ctee, Greenpeace; *Recreations* shooting, golf, skiing, marathon running, sailing; *Clubs* RAC, Les Ambassadors, Wimbledon Park GC; *Style*— Carlo Kapp, Esq; Kiln House, 1 New King's Rd, London SW6 (☎ 01 727 6533, fax 01 727 6538)

KARA, Peter Bhupatsingh; s of Bhimsingh Kara (d 1968), of S Africa; *b* 5 July 1944; *Educ* Damelin Coll S Africa; *m* 1969, Gita, da of Gulabsingh Parmar, of India; 1 s, 1

da; *Career* fin dir Arthur Woollacott Holdings Ltd; dir: Wrappings & Packings (Engineering) Ltd, R Peters (London) Ltd, Eulatimex Ltd, Gwelo Mfrg Co Ltd, Charles Pretzlik & Son Ltd, Levril Gp plc, Interactive Educational Services Ltd, Lowfield Securities Ltd (md); memb Assoc of Certified Accountants; *Recreations* windsurfing, squash, yoga; *Style*— Peter Kara Esq; 11 Fitzroy Sq, London W1 (☎ 01 388 9591); 73 Windmill Hill Drive, Bletchley, Bucks

KARK, Austen Steven; CBE (1987); s of Maj Norman Kark, and Ethel, *née* Goldberg (d 1980); *b* 20 Oct 1926; *Educ* Upper Canada Coll Toronto, Nautical Coll Pangbourne, RNC, Magdalen Coll Oxford (MA); *m* 1, 1949 (m dis 1954), Margaret Solomon, da of S Schmahmann, of S Africa; 2 da (Catherine b 1950, Teresa b 1953); m 2, 1954, Nina Mary (novelist Nina Bawden *qv), da of Cdr Charles Mabey (d 1976), of Herne Bay; 1 da (Perdita b 1957), 2 step s (Nicholas Bawden (d 1983), Robert Bawden)*; *Career* Midshipman RIN 1944-46, E Indies Flt, HMS Nelson, HMS London; dir first prodn Sartres 'The Flies' Oxford 1948; BBC: joined 1954, head S Euro Serv 1964, E Euro and Russian Serv 1972; ed World Serv 1973, controller English Services 1974, advsr the late Lord Soames on election broadcasting Rhodesia, chm Harare Govt Report on Radio and TV Zimbabwe, md external broadcasting 1984-86 (dep md 1981-84) ret 1986; chm: UK Alumni Salzburg seminar in American Studies 1979-85, CPC Guide books 1987; dir Canadian Prodns Ltd 1988; *Recreations* real tennis, travelling, mosaics; *Clubs* Oriental, MCC, Royal Tennis Ct; *Style*— Austen Kark, Esq, CBE; 22 Noel Road, London N1 8HA

KARN, Roger; s of Frederick Peter Karn (d 1988), of West Byfleet, Surrey, and Beryl, *née* Seaman; *b* 8 Sept 1953; *Educ* King's Coll Taunton, Trinity Coll Cambridge (MA); *Career* slr; contested New Forest (Lib SDP Alliance) 1987; *Recreations* bridge, motoring; *Clubs* National Liberal; *Style*— Roger Karn, Esq; 2nd Floor Flat, 38 Great Pulteney St, Bath, Avon BA2 4BZ (☎ 0225 444878); Sylvester & Mackett, Castle House, Castle St, Trowbridge, Wilts BA14 8AX (☎ 0225 755621, fax 0225 769055, telex 444258)

KARN, Prof Valerie Ann; da of Arthur Frederick Thomas Karn (d 1968), and Winnifred Alice Whisson; *b* 17 May 1939; *Educ* Newquay Co GS, Lady Margaret Hall Oxford (BA), Univ of the Punjab Lahore Pakistan, Grad Sch of Design Harvard Univ; 1 da (Jacqui b 1974); *Career* res fell inst of social and econ res York Univ 1964-66, sr lectr centre for urban and regnl studies Birmingham Univ (formerly res assoc, lectr) 1966-84, res fell Urban Inst and advsr to the Dept of Housing and Urban Development Washington DC USA 1979-80, prof of environmental health and housing Salford Univ and dir Salford Centre for Housing Studies 1984-; memb: NW regnl ctee Anchor Housing Assoc 1986-88, Ctee of Inquiry into Glasgows Housing 1986-88; chm supervisory gp of the feasibility study for Hulme Estate Manchester 1986-88, memb academic bd Salford Coll of Technol 1987-(formerly chm special projects ctee Copec Housing Tst Birmingham); res offr to the Central Housing Advsy Ctee 1967-69 (memb sub ctee housing mgmnt The Cullingworth Ctee 1967-69), memb housing servs advsy gp DOE 1976-79, memb Duke of Edinburgh's Inquiry into Br Housing 1984-85, special cmmr Cmmn for Rural Equality (on an inquiry into Liverpool City Cncl'c housing allocations) chm research steering gp Nat Fedn Housing Assocs 1988-(memb 1984-), external advsr Inst of Housings professional qualification, chm editorial bd Roof (Shelter's housing jl 1986); memb Assoc of the Inst of Housing; *Books* various articles and books incl: Retiring to the Seaside (1977), The Consumers Experience of Housing (ed with C Ungerson, 1980), Home Ownership in the Inner City (with P Williams and J Kemeny, 1985), Race, Class and Public Housing (with J Henderson, 1986); *Recreations* gardening; *Style*— Prof Valerie Karn; 71 Barton Rd, Worsley M28 4PF (☎ 061 794 7791); Environmental Health and Housing, Telford Building, Univ of Salford, Salford M5 (☎ 061 736 5843, ext 7308)

KARNEY, Andrew Lumsdaine; s of Rev Gilbert Henry Peter Karney, and Celia Finch Wigham, *née* Richardson; gf Rt Rev Arthur B L Karney, First Bishop of Johannesburg; *b* 24 May 1942; *Educ* Rugby, Trinity Coll Cambridge; *m* 1969, Beryl Fleur, da of late Louis Goldwyn, of Australia; 1 s (Peter John b 1972); *Career* staff memb UN Relief and Works Agency Beirut and Gaza Strip 1963-64; devpt engr for Standard Telephones and Cables London and Paris 1965-68; sr scientist Gen Electric Co Hirst Res Centre 1968-71, planning engr communications Br Gas Corpn 1972-73, conslt Logica plc 1973-, md Logica Communications and Electronic Systems Ltd 1984-; dir: Cable London plc 1984-86, Logica General Systems Spa Italy 1984-, Logica Technol Servs Ltd Hong Kong 1986-, Logica plc 1986-, Logica Data Architects Inc USA 1988; *Recreations* travel, photography; *Style*— Andrew Karney, Esq; 16 Kemplay Rd, London NW3 1SY; Logica, 64 Newman St, London W1A 4SE (☎ 01 637 9111, telex 27200)

KARTEN, Ian Herman; s of Israel Karten (d 1945), and Helen, *née* Baron (d 1976); *b* 14 Dec 1920; *Educ* private, London Univ (BSc); *m* 9 December 1968, Mildred Elizabeth Hart, da of Selim Laurence Hart (d 1973); *Career* RAF: cmmnd (technical branch) Pilot Offr 1942; serv HQ Bomber Cmd, Air Disarmament Denmark, (despatches 1946), demobilised Flt Lt 1946; Multitone Electronics plc (formerly Multitone Electric Co Ltd): joined 1947, mfrg mangr, export mangr, gen mangr, md 1961, chm and chief exec offr 1978-; *Recreations* reading, music; *Style*— Ian Karten, Esq; The Mill House, Newark, Ripley, Surrey GU23 6DP (☎ 0483 225 020); Multitone Electronics plc, 12 Underwood St, London N1 7JT (☎ 01 253 7611, fax 01 253 8409, telex 266518)

KASER, Michael Charles; s of Charles Joseph Kaser (d 1983), of St Albans, Herts, and Mabel Lucina, *née* Blunden (d 1976); *b* 2 May 1926; *Educ* Gunnersbury Catholic GS, Wimbledon Coll, Kings Coll Cambridge (BA, MA), Oxford Univ (MA); *m* 13 May 1954, Elizabeth Ann Mary, da of Cyril Gascoigne Piggford (d 1956), of Springs, SA; 4 s (Gregory b 1955, Matthew b 1956, Benet b 1959, Thomas b 1962), 1 da (Lucy b 1968); *Career* economist; chief sci advsr dept Miny of Works 1946-47, economic intelligence dept FO 1947-51, second sec HM Embassy Moscow 1949, economic affrs offr UN Economic Cmmn for Europe Geneva 1951-63, visiting prof Graduate Inst of Int Studies Univ of Geneva 1959-63; Univ of Oxford: Leverhulme res fell St Antony's Coll 1960-62, faculty fell St Antony's Coll 1963-72, faculty lectr in Soviet economics 1963-72, govr Plater Coll 1968-, professorial fell St Antony's Coll 1972-, reader in economics 1972-, assoc fell Templeton Coll 1983-, dir Inst of Russian Soviet and East Euro Studies 1988-, chm advsy cncl for Adult Educn Oxford 1972-78, Latin preacher Univ Church of St Mary the Virgin 1982; visiting fell Henley Mgmnt Coll 1986-; sec Cwlth Assoc of Geneva 1956-63; memb: cncl Royal Economic Soc 1976-86 and 1987-, Royal Inst of Int Affrs 1979-85 and 1986-, exec ctee Int Economic Assoc 1974-83 and 1986- (gen ed 1986-), Int Social Sciences Cncl (UNESCO) 1980-, advsy bd Inst for East West Security Studies NY 1989-; chm: Coordinating Cncl of Area Studies Assocs 1986-88, Wilton Park Acad Cncl (FCO) 1986-; pres Br Assoc for Soviet Slavic and East Euro Studies 1988- (previously first chm and then ctee memb Nat Assoc for Soviet and East Euro Studies 1964-); sec Br Acad Ctee for S E Euro Studies 1988-; *Books* Comecon: Integration Problems of the Planned Economies (1965 and 1967), Soviet Economics (1970), Health Care in the Soviet Union and Eastern Europe (1976); jtly: Planning in Eastern Europe (1970), The New Economic Systems of Eastern Europe (1975), The Soviet Union since the Fall of Skrushchev (1975), Soviet Policy for the 1980's (1982); gen ed: The Cambridge Encyclopedia of Russia and the Soviet Union (1982), The Economic History of Eastern Europe 1919-75 (3 vols 1985-86); *Recreations* walking; *Clubs* Reform; *Style*— Michael Kaser, Esq; 7 Chadlington Rd, Oxford OX2 6SY (☎ 0865 515 581); St Antony's Coll, Oxford OX2 6JF (☎ 0865 596 51, fax 0865 270 708)

KASKET, Esther; *née* Laredo; da of Joseph Solomon Laredo (d 1972), and Allegra, *née* Maratchi; both families mentioned in histories of Moroccan, Gibraltarian, Spanish and Mancinian Jewry; the Laredos (Christians and Jews) granted coat of arms in 1254 by Don Alfonso VIII; *b* 16 Mar 1930; *Educ* Mrs Pratt's Private Eng Sch Mazagan Morocco, Lycée de jeunes filles Casablanca, Manchester HS for Girls, Newnham Coll Cambridge (BA, MA); *m* 20 April 1958, Harold Kasket, s of Maurice Kasket (d 1969); 1 s (Alan Joseph b 1963), 1 da (Anna Caroline b 1962); *Career* exec with Mullens & Co, govt brokers 1951-59, pt/t teaching 1959-68, returned to stockbroking James Capel & Co 1968-76; joined Laurence Prust & Co (then a ptnr) 1976, ptnr Laurence Prust & Co Ltd 1985-86, memb exec bd Laurence Prust Broking Securities Ltd 1987- (dir 1986-); ctee memb Woman of the Year Assoc; exhibited paintings and drawings at Hampstead Arts Club and Stock Exchange Art Soc; *Recreations* painting, horse-riding, gardening, theatre, music; *Clubs* Parrot; *Style*— Mrs Esther Kasket; 7 Lymington Rd, London NW6 1HX (☎ 01 794 5251); 27 Finsbury Sq, London EC2A 1LP (☎ 01 628 1111, telex 924081, fax 01 638 7660)

KASSEM, Tarek Jamal Hamid; s of Jamal Hamid Kassem, and Nadida Saeed, *née* Fahoum; *b* 28 August 1946; *Educ* City of London Poly; *m* 1, Salma Rayes (m dis 1984); 1 s (Khaled Tarek b 1975); m 2, 28 June 1985, Susan Wendy Mary, JP, da of Harold James Boylet, of Guildford, Surrey; *Career* trainee: Arabian American Oil Co Dahran Saudi Arabia, Electro-Components Hldgs Ltd 1969-70; asst sec George Wills & Co Hldgs Ltd 1970-73, Vickers de Costa London 1973-74, Arab Bank Investmt co Ltd 1974-87, Quanta Gp Hldgs Ltd 1987-; memb Arab Bankers Assoc London; dir: non exec Malvern Property Co plc 1986, exec R & G Fin Consultants Ltd 1988, non-exec Walker Crisps Weddle Beck plc 1989; FIMBRA; *Recreations* tennis, photography, reading; *Style*— Tarek Kassem, Esq; Empire House, 8-14 St Martin's-le-Grand, London EC1A 4AD (☎ 01 606 7491, fax 01 606 9827, telex 886318 Quanta G)

KATZ, Sir Bernard; s of Max Katz (d 1971); *b* 26 Mar 1911; *Educ* Leipzig Univ (MD), London Univ (PhD, DSc); *m* 1945, Marguerite Penly; 2 s; *Career* serv WWII Flt Lt RAAF; prof and head of biophysics dept UCL 1952-78, emeritus prof 1978-; Nobel Prize (jtly) for Physiology and Medicine 1970; FRS 1952; kt 1969; *Style*— Sir Bernard Katz; University College, London WC1E 6BT (☎ 01 387 7050)

KAUFMAN, Rt Hon Gerald Bernard; PC (1978), MP (Lab) Manchester Gorton 1983-; s of Louis Kaufman and Jane Kaufman; *b* 21 June 1930; *Educ* Leeds GS, Queen's Coll Oxford; *Career* political staff Daily Mirror 1955-64, political corr New Statesman 1964-65, Lab parly press liaison offr 1965-70; MP (Lab) Manchester Ardwick 1970-83, parly under-sec Environment 1974-75, min of state Dept of Indust 1975-79; oppn front bench spokesman and memb shadow cabinet: Environment 1980-83, Home Affrs 1983-87, Foreign and Cwlth Affairs 1987-; *Style*— The Rt Hon Gerald Kaufman, MP; 87 Charlbert Ct, Eamont St, London NW8 (☎ 01 722 6264)

KAVANAGH, Patrick Joseph; s of H E (Ted) Kavanagh (d 1958), and Agnes O'Keefe (d 1985); *b* 6 Jan 1931; *Educ* Douai Sch, Lycée Jaccard, Merton Coll Oxford (MA); *m* 1, 1956 Sally Phillips (d 1958), da of Hon Mrs R N Phillips (Rosamond Lohmann), and Lord Milford; m 2, 1964, Catherine, da of Sir John Ward, KCMG, of St Margaret's Bay, Kent; 2 s (Cornelius b 1966, Bruno b 1969); *Career* actor 1959-70; writer, columnist The Spectator 1983-; *Poems* One and One (1960), On the Way to the Depot (1977), About Time (1970), Edward Thomas in Heaven (1974), Life Before Death (1979), Selected Poems (1982), Presences (1987); *novels*: A Song and Dance (1968, Guardian Fiction Prize), A Happy Man (1972), People and Weather (1979), Only by Mistake (1986), The Perfect Stranger (autobiography, Richard Hillary Prize 1966); *for children*: Scarf Jack (1978), Rebel for Good (1980); *edited*: Collected Poems of Ivor Gurney (1982), Oxford Book of Short Poems (with James Michie), People and Places (1988); *Style*— P J Kavanagh, Esq; c/o A D Peters, 10 Buckingham St, London WC1

KAY, Sir Andrew Watt; s of David Watt Kay; *b* 14 August 1916; *Educ* Ayr Acad, Glasgow Univ (MD, CHM, DSc); *m* 1943, Janetta Main Roxburgh; 2 s, 2 da; *Career* served WWII Maj RAMC; prof of surgery Sheffield Univ 1958-64, Regius prof of surgery Glasgow Univ 1964-81; pt/t chief sci Scottish Home and Health Dept 1973-81; chm Scottish Hosp Endowments Res Tst 1982-89 FRCS, FRSE; kt 1973; *Books* Textbook of Surgical Physiology; *Recreations* gardening; *Style*— Sir Andrew Kay; 14 North Campbell Ave, Milngavie, Glasgow G62 7AA (☎ 041 956 3378)

KAY, Brian Muir; s of Dr Herbert Kay, of Nunthorpe, Middlesborough, and Jean, *née* Kerr; *b* 15 Sept 1957; *Educ* St Peter's Sch York, Bristol Univ (BA); *Career* journalist; Yorkshire Evening Post 1980, Yorkshire Post 1986, Argos Consumer Journalist of the Year 1987, Campaigning Journalist of the Year British Press Awards 1988; *Recreations* travel, skiing, champagne, slow cars; *Style*— Brian Kay, Esq; Headingley, Leeds (☎ 05362 758 849); Yorkshire Post, Wellington St, Leeds LS1 1RF (☎ 0532 432 701 ext 347)

KAY, Brian Wilfrid; s of Wilfrid Ernest Kay (d 1953), of Chester, and Jessie Ashby Howe (d 1947); *b* 30 July 1921; *Educ* Kings Sch Chester, Univ Coll Oxford (MA); *m* 5 April 1947, Dorothea Sheppard, da of Rev Eric John Lawson; 2 da (Sarah b 1948, Elizabeth b 1951); *Career* asst master in classics Birkenhead Sch 1947-59, head of classics Liverpool Collegiate Sch 1959-64, HM inspr of Schs 1964-81 (staff inspr 1971-77, chief inspr 1977-81), sr res fell Culham Coll Inst 1982-; church warden, lay chm PCC; *Recreations* music, gardening, architectural history; *Style*— Brian Kay, Esq; Pond Cottage, Botolph, Claydon, Buckingham MK18 2NG (☎ 029 671 3477)

KAY, John William; QC (1984); s of Christopher Herbert Kay (d 1970), of Blundellsands, nr Liverpool, and Ida Muriel, *née* Harper; *b* 13 Sept 1943; *Educ* Denstone Coll, Christ's Coll Cambridge (MA); *m* 1966, Jeffa, da of Maj Graham

Bourke Connell, MBE (d 1968); 1 s (Benedict b 1975), 2 da (Amanda b 1969, Tiffany b 1971); *Career* barr Gray's Inn 1968; tutor in Law Liverpool Univ 1968-69, in practice Northern Circuit 1968-, rec of the Crown Ct 1982-; *Recreations* gardening, genealogy, horse racing; *Clubs* Athenaeum (Liverpool); *Style—* John Kay, Esq, QC; Markhams, 17 Far Moss Rd, Blundellsands, Liverpool L23 8TG (☎ 051 924 5804); 1 Exchange Flags, Liverpool L2 3XN (☎ 051 236 7747); 1 Temple Gardens, London NW11

KAY, Jolyon Christopher; s of Colin Mardall Kay (d 1950), and Gertrude Fanny Kay (d 1983); *b* 19 Sept 1930; *Educ* Charterhouse, St John's Coll Cambridge (BSc); *m* 19 May 1956, Shirley Mary, *qv*, da of Thomas John Clarke (d 1983); 2 s (Tim b 1957, Toby b 1969), 2 da (Gigi b 1959, Katherine b 1965); *Career* design engr Albright and Wilson 1954-58, sr scientific offr AERE and UKAEA 1958-61, Battelle Inst Geneva 1961-64, For and Cwlth Off 1964-, HM consul gen Dubai UAE 1985; *Recreations* skiing, croquet, acting; *Style—* Jolyon Kay, Esq; Little Triton, Blewbury, Didcot, Oxon OX11 9PE (☎ 0235 850 010); British Embassy, PO Box 65, Dubai, UAE (☎ 9714 521 070, fax 971 525 750, car telephone 971 50 38283, telex 45426 PROD EM)

KAY, Maurice Ralph; QC; s of Ralph Kay (d 1981), of Knutsford and Hylda Jones; *b* 6 Dec 1942; *Educ* William Holmes GS Manchester, Sheffield Univ (LLB, PhD); *m* 24 July 1968, Margaret Angela, da of Joseph Bernard Alcock, of Formby (d 1985); 4 s (Jonathan b 1969, Dominic b 1971, Oliver 1975, Tristan b 1982); *Career* lectr: Univ of Hull 1967-72, Univ of Manchester 1972-73; prof of law, Univ of Keele 1973-83; barr 1975-, memb Grays Inn Wales and Chester Circuit, asst recorder 1987-; *Books* ed and contrib legal text books,; *Recreations* music, theatre, sport; *Clubs* Reform; *Style—* Maurice Kay, Esq, QC; 3 Paper Buildings, Temple, London, EC4Y 7EU, (☎ 01 583 8055/ 0244 323070, fax 01 353 6271/0244 42930/0270 626736)

KAY, Nigel Jeffrey Randle; s of James Arthur Randle Kay (d 1982), of Newton Hall, Clitheroe, Lancs, and Giffard Jeffrey, *née* Wilding; *b* 9 Sept 1939; *Educ* Stowe, Manchester Univ (BSc); *m* 2 Sept 1967, Margaret Rose, da of Ian Bowman Thorburn (d 1972), of Blackpool; 3 da (Amanda b 1970, Leysa b 1971, Timara b 1974); *Career* chm Colson & Kay Ltd 1972, dir Cransley Sch Ltd 1984; *Recreations* sailing, skiing, shooting; *Clubs* Royal Thames Yacht; *Style—* Nigel Kay, Esq; Farmwood House, Chelford, Cheshire (☎ 0625 861560); 12 Swan St, Wilmslow, Cheshire (☎ 0625 533878, fax 0625 524392)

KAY, Shirley; da of Thomas John (d 1983), of Hackleton House, Northants, and Jessie Clarke, *née* McColl (d 1963); *b* 13 May 1933; *Educ* Northampton HS, Girton Coll Cambridge (BA); *m* 19 May 1956, Jolyon Christopher Kay, *qv*, s of Colin Mardall Kay (d 1950), of West Thurrock, Essex; 2 s (Tim b 1957, Toby b 1969), 2 da (Gigi b 1959, Katharine b 1964); *Career* writer and TV presenter; *Books* The Arab World (1967), Morocco (1980), Emirates Archaeological Heritage (1986); *Recreations* skiing, camping, gardening; *Style—* Mrs Shirley Kay; Little Triton, Blewbury, Didcot, Oxon OX11 9PE (☎ 0235 850 010); Dubai TV, Dubai UAE

KAY-SHUTTLEWORTH, Hon David Charles; s of 5 Baron Shuttleworth; *b* 29 August 1978; *Style—* The Hon David Kay-Shuttleworth

KAY-SHUTTLEWORTH, Hon Edward Roger Noël; 3 and yst s of late 4 Baron Shuttleworth; *b* 28 June 1962; *Style—* The Hon Edward Kay-Shuttleworth

KAY-SHUTTLEWORTH, Hon Robert James; 2 s of late 4 Baron Shuttleworth, MC; *b* 27 May 1954; *Educ* Eton; *Career* late Lt Coldstream Gds Res; *Style—* The Hon Robert Kay-Shuttleworth

KAY-SHUTTLEWORTH, Hon Thomas Edward; s and h of 5 Baron Shuttleworth; *b* 29 Sept 1976; *Style—* The Hon Thomas Kay-Shuttleworth

KAY-SHUTTLEWORTH, Hon William James; s of 5 Baron Shuttleworth; *b* 29 Nov 1979; *Style—* The Hon William Kay-Shuttleworth

KAYE; *see*: Lister-Kaye

KAYE, Alan; s of Wallace Kaye (d 1978), of Horwich, and Nellie Elizabeth, *née* Cookson; *b* 24 June 1936; *Educ* Rivington and Blackrod GS; *m* 21 June 1958, Betty, da of Ernest Rainford (d 1970), of Adlington, Lancs; 1 s (Andrew b 1960), 1 da (Janet b 1961); *Career* dep gen mangr (Filter Div) Automotive Products plc 1969-70, Dobson Park Industs plc: fin dir (Mining Equipment Div 1970-74, chief exec 1974-80), dep chief exec 1984, chief exec 1985; *Recreations* gardening, music, reading, walking; *Style—* Alan Kaye, Esq; Mill Hill Farm, Mill Lane, Goosnargh, Preston, Lancs PR3 2JX (☎ 0722 865014); Dobson Park Industries plc, Dobson Park House, Manchester Rd, Ince, Wigan, Lancs WN2 2DX (☎ 0942 31421, telex 67355, fax 0942 47058)

KAYE, Sir David Alexander Gordon; 4 Bt (UK 1923), of Huddersfield, Co York; s of Sir (Henry) Gordon Kaye, 2 Bt (d 1956); suc bro, Sir Stephen Kaye, 3 Bt, 1983; *b* 26 July 1919; *Educ* Stowe, Cambridge Univ (BA); *m* 1, 10 Oct 1942 (m dis 1950), Elizabeth Rosemary, only da of Capt Malcolm Hurtley, of Baynards Manor, Horsham, Sussex; m 2, 15 June 1955, Adelle Frances, da of Denis Lionel Thomas, of Brisbane, Qld; 2 s, 4 da; *Heir* s, Paul Henry Gordon Kaye; *Career* MRCS Eng, LRCP London; *Style—* Sir David Kaye, Bt; Yerinandah, Moggill Rd, The Gap, Brisbane, Queensland, Australia

KAYE, David Raymond; s of Michael Kaye (d 1981), and Elizabeth, *née* Wasserman; *b* 29 Mar 1932; *Educ* Nottingham HS, St Pauls, Cambridge Univ (MA), Univ of Michigan USA, Oxford Univ (Dip Stats); *m* 15 Oct 1966, Sara Frances, da of Edwyn Lyte (d 1979); 2 s (James b 1970, George b 1972), 1 da (Sophie b 1967); *Career* 2/Lt RA 1952; Shell Int Petroleum 1958-62, Andersen Consulting (Arthur Anderson & Co) 1962- (ptnr 1967); tstee Charities Effectiveness Review Tst; FSS, FOR, FIMC; *Recreations* walking, sculpture; *Clubs* Athenaeum, Reform; *Style—* David Kaye, Esq; 37 Wood Lane, London N6 5UD (☎ 01 340 1624); Anderson Consulting, 2 Arundel St, London WC2R 3LT (☎ 01 438 3606, fax 01 831 1133)

KAYE, Col Douglas Robert Beaumont; DSO (1942), bar (1945); s of Robert Walter Kaye, JP (d 1957), of Great Glen Manor, Leics, and Marian, *née* Robinson (d 1946); *b* 18 Nov 1909; *Educ* Harrow Sch; *m* 16 Nov 1946, (Florence) Audrey Emma, da of Henry Archibald Bellville (d 1930), of Tedstone Ct, Bromyard, Hereford; 1 s (John b 1951), 1 da (Sarah (Mrs Gilbert) b 1947); *Career* 2 Lt Leics Yeo 1928, 10 Royal Hussars 1931, DAPM Jerusalem, 1939-41, APM Cairo HQ 30 Corps 1941-43, Lt-Col cmdg 10 Royal Hussars N Africa, Italy 1943-46, wounded (despatches twice) psc 1946, Bde Maj 30 Lowland Ind Armd Bde TA 1947-49, Lt-Col cmdg 16/5 Queens Royal Lancers 1949-51, AA & QMG 56 London Armd Div TA 1952-54, Col, Cmdt & chief instructor Gunnery Sch RAC Centre 1954-56; hon sec: Newmarket & Thurlow Hunt 1959-70 (MFH 1957-59), Puckeridge & Thurlow 1970-88; JP Cambs 1961, DL 1963, High Sheriff Cambs & Isle of Ely 1971, chm Newmarket DC 1972-74 (dcncllr 1958-74), memb E Cambs DC 1974-83; Lord of the Manor of Brinkley; *Recreations* hunting, shooting; *Clubs* Cavalry; *Style—* Col Douglas Kaye, DSO; Brinkley Hall, Newmarket, Suffolk (☎ 0638 76202)

KAYE, Sir Emmanuel; CBE (1967); *b* 29 Nov 1914; *Educ* Richmond Hill Sch, Twickenham Tech; *m* 1946, Elizabeth Cutler; 1 s, 2 da; *Career* fndr chm The Kaye Organisation 1966-; chm: Lansing Bagnall, Lansing Bagnall Int (Switzerland), Lansing Leasing, Elvetham Hall Ltd, Lansing GmbH (W Germany), Pool & Sons, Hawkington Ltd, Hadley Contract Hire 1973-78, Henley Forklift Gp 1976-79, Bonser Engrg 1978-81, Lina-Loda Ltd, Kaye Office Supplies, Kaye Steel Stockholders; memb CBI Cncl and Econ & Fin Policy Ctee 1985-; chm Thrombosis Res Tst; FBIM, FRSA; kt 1974; *Clubs* Brooks's; *Style—* Sir Emmanuel Kaye, CBE; Hartley Place, Hartley Wintney, Hants RG27 8HT; 25 St James's Place, SW1A 1NH

KAYE, Dr Georges Sabry; s of Dr Georges Kaye, of Beirut, The Lebanon, and Claire, *née* De las Case; *b* 21 May 1949; *Educ* Villa St Jean, Fribourg, Ratcliffe Coll Leicester, King's Coll London (BSc), Westminster Hosp Med Sch (MB, BS); *m* 18 Dec 1982, Georgina Margaret, da of Simon Harold John Arthur Knott, of Hammersmith, London; 1 s (Charles Edwin Georges b 20 June 1985), 2 da (Alice Georgina Claire b 1 Jan 1987, Olivia Sarah Louise b 25 Oct 1988); *Career* physician-in-charge occupational health dept Cromwell Hosp 1986-; co physician to: GEC, Salomon Bros Int, Air France; memb BMA 1974; *Books* La Soif (The Thirst) (1976); *Recreations* french literature, lute playing; *Clubs* The Reform; *Style—* Dr Georges Kaye; 4 Lord North St, London SW1; 2nd Braco Castle, Perthshire; Cromwell Hospital, Cromwell Road, London SW5 (☎ 01 370 4233)

KAYE, Jeremy Robin; s of Kenneth Brown Kaye (d 1985), of Doncaster, and Hannah Eleanor Christabel, *née* Scott; *b* 25 Sept 1937; *Educ* Eastbourne Coll, Worcester Coll Oxford (BA, MA); *Career* Nat Serv Bombardier RA 1956-58; barr Inner Temple 1962, asst sec Limmer and Trinidad Lake Asphalt Co Ltd 1962-67, chief legal offr and asst sec Limmer Hldgs Ltd 1967-72, dir Arbuthnot Latham Bank Ltd (sec 1973-); sec: Arbuthnot Latham Hldgs Ltd 1975-81, Dow Scandia Hldgs Ltd 1982-86, Secure Tst Gp plc 1987-; lay chm East Grinstead Deanery 1977-87 (sec 1967-77), memb Chichester Diocesan Synod 1970-73 and 1988-; FCIS; *Recreations* gardening, cricket, golf; *Clubs* MCC, Holtye GC; *Style—* Jeremy Kaye, Esq; 64 Blount Ave, East Grinstead, West Sussex RH19 1JW (☎ 0342 321 294); 131 Finsbury Pavement, Moorgate, London EC2A 1AY (☎ 01 280 8514, fax 01 638 1545, telex 885970)

KAYE, Col Michael Arthur Chadwick Porter; TD (1948), DL (W Yorks 1974-); s of Col Harold Swift Kaye, DSO, MC (d 1953), of St Johns Lodge, Wakefield, Yorks, and Dora Margaret, *née* Porter (d 1968) ; *b* 11 Jan 1916; *Educ* Harrow, Pembroke Coll Cambridge (MA); *m* 21 June 1941, Betty (d 1973), da of Maj Gen EA Sutton, CB, CBE, MC (d 1964), of Highcliffe, Hants; 2 s (Colin b 20 July 1943, Patrick b 3 Feb 1945), 1 da (Anne b 23 March 1942); *Career* 4 KOYLI: 2 Lt 1935-47, Lt - Col 1947-51, Col 1951-55, Hon Col 1955- 66, Cmdt West Riding ACF 1955-59; ADC to HM The Queen 1969-71; chm Marshall Kaye & Marshall Ltd 1953-68; memb exec ctee ACF Assoc 1956- 88, chm Yorks TA and VR Assoc 1968-73, Yorks regnl organiser Br Heart Fndn 1968-82, memb bd of visitors New Hall Detention Centre 1970-86, cmmmr of taxes Wakefield Dist 1977-, DL W Riding and City of York 1960-74; *Recreations* cricket, travel ; *Clubs* Yorks, MCC, I Zingari; *Style—* Col Michael Kaye, TD, DL; 224, Mount Vale, York YO2 2DL (☎ 0904 36760)

KAYE, Michael Kaye; s of Harry Kay (d 1973), and Annie, *née* Steinberg (d 1943); *b* 27 Feb 1925; *Educ* West Ham Secdy Sch; *m* 1, 28 March 1950 (m dis 1959), Muriel, da of Barnet Greenberg (d 1973), of London; 1 da (Ann b 9 July 1952); m 2, 6 Sept 1962, Fay, da of Morris Bercovitch (d 1950), of London; *Career* REME 1943-45, Intelligence Corps 1945-47; journalist and PR 1947- 53, mktg and PR tobacco indust 1953-61, PR mangr Rothmans Ltd 1961-74, PR dir Carreras Rothmans Gp 1974-76, dir Peter Stuyvesant Fndn 1963-76, gen admin Rupert Fndn 1972-76, md LSO 1976-80, arts dir GLC 1980-83; gen admin: South Bank Concert Halls 1980-83, Young Concert Artists Tst 1983-; festival dir City of London Festival 1984-; Whitechapel Art Gallery 1964-75: tstee, fin chm, memb gen purposes ctee; tstee Youth & Music 1970-78; FRSA 1986; *Recreations* music, photography; *Style—* Michael Kaye, Esq; 3 Coppice Way, London E18 2DU (☎ 01 989 1281); City Arts Trust, 230 Bishopsgate, London EC2 (☎ 01 377 0540, fax 01 377 1972)

KAYE, Capt Paul Henry Gordon; s (by 2 m) and h of Sir David Alexander Gordon Kaye, 4 Bt, *qv* ; *b* 19 Feb 1958; *m* 1984, Sally Ann Louise; *Career* cmmnd RAE 1982, Capt; memb Young National Party; *Recreations* rugby union, scuba diving; *Style—* Capt Paul Kaye; 73 Moggill Rd, The Gap, Qld, Australia 4061

KAYE, Simon; s of Isaac Kaye (d 1964), of 20 Rutland Park Gardens, London, and Dora, *née* Liborvitch (d 1964); *b* 22 July 1935; *Educ* Wycombe Sch; *m* 8 Sept 1957, Sylvia Adrienne, da of Michael Kagan (d 1982); 2 s (Jeremy b 22 Oct 1959, Trevor b 6 May 1966), 1 da (Elaine b 24 Sept 1962); *Career* entered film indust 1953, sound mixer 1962, dir Siren Sound 1967-, recorded over sixty Br and American films; 9 Br Acad Nominations: Charge of the Light Brigade, Lion in Winter, Oh! What a Lovely War, Sunday, Bloody Sunday, A Bridge too Far, Reds, Ghandi, Indiana Jones and the Temple of Doom, Cry Freedom; 3 Oscar Nominations: Reds, Ghandi, Platoon; 3 BAFTA Awards: Oh! What a Lovely War, A Bridge too Far, Cry Freedom; 1 Oscar for Platoon; *Style—* Simon Kaye, Esq; 39 Bellfield Ave, Harrow Weald, Middx HA3 6ST (☎ 01 428 4823); Siren Sound, 97/99 Dean St, London W1V 5RA (☎ 01 437 3114)

KAYE, William; s of Henry Kaye (d 1958), of Wakefield, and Alice Kaye (d 1964) ; *b* 26 Feb 1914; *Educ* Thornes House Sch; *m* 21 June 1937, (Emma) May (d 1947), da of Rowland Harrison, of Wakefield; m 2, June 1949, (Elizabeth) Branwen (d 1982), da of Rev Thomas Elwy-Williams, of Trefriw, N Wales; *Career* served in RAF 1942-44; civil servant, ret 1970; memb Governing Cncl Fedn of Environment Socs 1968-70; patron Nat Domesday Celebrations 1986; memb Manorial Soc of GB; Lord of the Manor of Hulland Derbyshire; *Recreations* music, gardening, golf, studies in medieval history; *Clubs* Civil Service, Betws-y-Coed Golf; *Style—* William Kaye, Esq; Minffordd, Capel Garmon, Llanrwst, Gwynedd (☎ 0492 069 02 483)

KAYLL, Wing-Cdr Joseph Robert; DSO, OBE (1941), DFC (1940) JP (Sunderland), DL (Tyne & Wear); s of Maj Joseph Pelham Kayll, MBE (d 1971); *b* 12 April 1914; *Educ* Stowe; *m* 1940, Annette Lindsey, *née* Nisbet; 2 s; *Career* Wing-Cdr RAF; timber importer; *Recreations* sailing, shooting; *Clubs* Royal Ocean Racing, RNYC, SYC, WBA; *Style—* Wing-Cdr Joseph Kayll, DSO, OBE, DFC, JP, DL; Hillside House, Hillside, Sunderland (☎ 0915 283282); Joseph Thompson & Co Ltd, Hendon Lodge Sawmills, Sunderland (☎ 091 51 44663)

KAZANTZIS, (Lady) Judith Elizabeth; *née* Pakenham; does not use style of Lady; da of 7 Earl of Longford, KG, PC; *b* 1940; *Educ* Somerville Coll Oxford; *m* 1963, Alexander John Kazantzis, s of Constantine Kazantzis (d 1981); 1 s, 1 da; *Career* writer and poet; *Style—* Mrs Alexander Kazantzis; 32 Ladbroke Grove, London W11; The Foreman's, nr Glynde, Sussex

KEABLE-ELLIOTT, Dr (Robert) Anthony; OBE; s of Robert Keable (d 1927), and Jolie, *née* Buck (d 1924); *b* 14 Nov 1924; *Educ* Sherborne, Guys Hosp London (MB, BS); *m* 9 May 1953, Gilian Mary, da of Brig Colin Ross Marshall Hutchinson, DSO, MC (d 1943); 4 s (David b 1954, Ian b 1956, Trevor b 1958, Simon b 1960); *Career* GP 1948-88; BMA: memb 1949-, cncl memb 1964-, chm gen med servs ctee 1964-68, tres 1981-86; memb Fin Corpn of Gen Practice 1974-79, dir BMA Servs Ltd, chm jl ctee BMA 1988-; fndr memb Chiltern Med Soc 1956 (pres 1964); chm Ibstone PC; Freeman: City of London 1986, Soc of Apothecaries of London 1986; FRCGP 1964, Fell BMA 1987; *Recreations* golf, sailing, gardening; *Style—* Dr Tony Keable-Elliott, OBE; Peels, Ibstone, High Wycombe, Bucks

KEAL, Anthony Charles (Tony); s of Maj Kitchener Keal, of Thornton Dale, Yorkshire, and Joan Marjorie, *née* Ayling; *b* 12 July 1951; *Educ* Stowe, New Coll Oxford Univ (BA); *m* 24 Nov 1979, (Janet) Michael, da of John Charles King, of Javea, Spain; 3 s (Julian Charles b 1982, Jonathan David b 1986, Christopher b 1987); *Career* slr Allen & Overy 1976, slr and co sec Libra Bank plc 1976-78, ptnr Allen & Overy 1982- (slr 1978-82); memb: Law Soc, Worshipful Co of Slrs; *Recreations* sailing, travel, family; *Clubs* Thames Sailing, Twickenham YC; *Style—* Tony Keal, Esq; 9 Cheapside, London EC2V 6AD (☎ 01 248 9898, fax 01 236 2192, telex 8812801/2)

KEANE, Sheriff Francis Joseph; s of Thomas Keane (d 1967), of W Lothian, and Helen Flynn; *b* 5 Jan 1936; *Educ* Blairs Coll Aberdeen, Gregorian Univ Rome (PHL), Edinburgh Univ (LLB); *m* 19 April 1960, Lucia Corio, da of John Morrison (d 1983), of Glasgow; 2 s (Paul b 1963, Mark b 1965), 1 da (Lucy b 1961); *Career* slr; ptnr McCluskey Keane & Co Edinburgh 1959; depute procurator fiscal: Perth 1961, Edinburgh 1963; sr depute procurator fiscal Edinburgh 1971, sr legal asst Crown Off Edinburgh 1972, procurator fiscal Airdrie 1976, regnl procurator fiscal South Strathclyde Dumfries and Galloway 1980; pres Procurators Fiscal Soc 1982-84; Sheriff Glasgow and Strathkelvin 1984; *Recreations* music, tennis, painting; *Style—* Sheriff Francis Keane; 24 Marlborough Ave, Glasgow G11 7BW (☎ 041 339 7180); Sheriffs Chambers, Sheriff Court of Glasgow and Strathkelvin, PO Box 23, 1 Carlton Pl, Glasgow G5 9DA (☎ 041 429 8888)

KEANE, John Charles; s and h of Sir Richard Keane, 6 Bt; *b* 16 Sept 1941; *Educ* Eton, Ch Ch Oxford; *Style—* John Keane Esq; c/o Cappoquin House, Cappoquin, Co Waterford, Ireland

KEANE, Philip Vincent; s of Bernard Vincent Keane (d 1983), of London, and Brenda Ellen Margaret, *née* Ford; *b* 11 August 1940; *Educ* Wimbledon Coll GS, LSE (BSc); *m* 18 Sept 1965 (Kathleen) Winifred, da of William Aloysius Thomson (d 1987), of London; 2 da (Angelina Teresa b 14 Sept 1968, Noelle Francesca b 16 Dec 1969) ; *Career* tstee dept Lloyds Bank 1964-66, sr investmt analyst Esso Pension Tst 1967-71, head of investmt res Mercantile & Gen Reinsurance 1971-75, equity fund mangr Prudential Pensions 1976-77, investmt mangr Rea Bros Ltd 1977-81; dir: Wardley Investmt Mgmnt Ltd 1981-82, HK Unit Tst Mangrs Ltd, Rea Bros (Investmt Mgmnt) Ltd 1982-; AMSIA; *Recreations* travel, photography, skiing, lit; *Style—* Philip Keane, Esq; 70 Pine Grove, off Lake Rd, Wimbledon, London SW19 7HE; Rea Bros plc Alderman's House, Alderman's Walk, London EC2 (☎ 01 623 1155 ext 246)

KEANE, Sir Richard Michael; 6 Bt (UK 1801), of Cappoquin, co Waterford; s of Lt-Col Sir John Keane 5, Bt, DSO (d 1956), and Lady Eleanor Hicks-Beach (d 1960), da of 1 Earl St Aldwyn; *b* 29 Jan 1909; *Educ* Sherborne, Ch Ch Oxford; *m* 1939, Olivia Dorothy, da of Oliver Hawkshaw, TD; 2 s, 1 da; *Heir* s John Charles Keane; *Career* served with Co of London Yeo and 10 Royal Hussars 1939-44, liaison officer (Maj) with HQ Vojvodina Yugoslav partisans 1944, attached British Military Mission Belgrade 1944-45; diplomatic correspondent: Reuters 1935-37, Sunday Times (also asst to editor) 1937-39; publicity consultant to ICI Ltd 1950-62; farmer; *Recreations* fishing, farming; *Style—* Sir Richard Keane, Bt; Cappoquin House, Cappoquin, Co Waterford, Ireland (☎ 058 54004)

KEAR, Graham Francis; s of Richard Walter Kear (d 1976), and Eva, *née* Davies (d 1967); *b* 9 Oct 1928; *Educ* St Julien's HS Newport, Balliol Coll Oxford (BA); *m* 9 Oct 1978, Joyce Eileen, da of Frank Bartram Parks (d 1973); *Career* Nat Serv RAF 1947-49; Civil Serv: Miny of Supply 1951-52 and 1954-57, UK Delg to Euro Coal and Steel Community 1953-54, Miny of Aviation 1957-59 and 1960-63, NATO Maintance and Supply Agency 1959-60, MOD 1963-65, Cabinet Off 1968-71, Miny of Aviation DTI 1971-72, under sec Dept of Energy 1974-80; assoc fell Harvard Univ 1972-73; asst sec Abbeyfield Richmond Soc 1984-, tres Parochial Church Cncl 1985- (memb 1983-); *Recreations* reading; *Style—* Graham Kear, Esq; 28 Eastbourne Rd, Brentford, Middx (☎ 01 560 4746); Abbeyfield, 4 Ennerdale Rd, Kew, Richmond, Surrey (☎ 01 948 3977)

KEARLEY, Chester Dagley Hugh; s of late Hon Mark Hudson Kearley (s of 1 Viscount Devonport); kinsman and hp of 3 Viscount Devonport; *b* 29 April 1932; *m* 1974, Josefa Mesquida; *Style—* Chester Kearley, Esq; S Patos, 466 Denia, Alicante, Spain

KEARLEY, Hon Marilyn Whitson; da of late 2 Viscount Devonport

KEARNEY, Hon Sir William John Francis; CBE (1976); s of W J K Kearney; *b* 8 Jan 1935; *Educ* Wolstanton CGS, Sydney GS, Sydney Univ, Univ Coll London; *m* 1959, Jessie, da of L Yung; 3 da; *Career* dormant cmmn as admin of Papua New Guinea 1973, high cmmr of PNG 1973-75, judge Supreme Ct PNG 1976-82, dep chief justice 1980-82, judge Supreme Ct Northern Territory 1982-, Aboriginal Land cmmr 1982-; kt 1982; *Style—* The Hon Sir William Kearney, CBE; Judges' Chambers, Supreme Court, Darwin, NT 5790, Australia

KEARNS, Lady; Betty; *née* Broadbent; da of Newton Broadbent, of Burnley; *m* 1946, Sir Frederick Matthias Kearns, KCB, MC (d 1983); 1 da; *Style—* Lady Kearns; 26 Brookway, Blackheath, London SE3 (☎ 01 852 0747)

KEARSLEY, Eric Saxon; s of William Kearsley (d 1940), of Prenton, Birkenhead, Ches, and Catherine, *née* Mason (d 1953); *b* 24 Oct 1915; *Educ* Birkenhead Sch; *m* 9 Aug 1941, (Margaret) Joan, da of William Sinton (d 1950), of Heswall, Wirral, Ches; 1 s (David b 1947), 1 da (Susan (Mrs Gwaspari) b 1949); *Career* WWII serv: cmmnd 2 Lt TA 1939, Lt France 1940, Capt 1941, Maj N Africa and Italy 1943 (POW Germany 1943-45), demobbed 1946; Dep Cmdt Derbys Army Cadet Force 1953-55; admitted slr 1938, export mangr Staveley Coal & Iron Co Ltd 1946-51, sales mangr Staveley Iron & Chemical Co Ltd 1951-60, asst gen sales mangr Stanton & Staveley Co 1960-68, mangr staff devpt Stanton & Staveley 1968-73, ret 1973; memb Law Soc 1939; Distinguished Service Cross America 1946; *Style—* Eric Kearsley, Esq, DSO

KEAST, Roger John; s of Horace Keast, of Gwellyets, Truro, Cornwall, and Margaret, *née* Legard; *b* 4 Dec 1942; *Educ* Truro Sch, Exeter Univ (LLB); *m* 1, 25 March 1970 (m dis 1975), Anne Elizabeth, da of Norman Samuel Cross, of Lanteague, Goonhavern, Truro, Cornwall; m 2, 9 July 1976, (Elizabeth) Ann, da of Albert John Folland (d 1982), of W Forde, Stockleigh, Pomeroy, Devon; 1 s (Paul Edward John b 15 Nov 1977), 2 step da (Sarah Annette Radford b 14 July 1966, Carole Suzanne Radford b 20 Nov 1967); *Career* Stephens and Scown St Austell Exeter 1963-: articled clerk 1963-66, slr 1966-70, ptnr 1970-, dep sr ptnr 1986-; memb Exeter City Cncl 1968-81, Mayor City of Exeter 1977-78; hon slr Devon Young Farmers Club 1968-, memb cncl Exeter Univ 1979-, hon slr Som and Dorset Railway Tst 1982-, fndr memb Exeter Castle Rotary Club 1985-; hon alderman; Hon MA Exeter Univ 1978; memb Law Soc 1966; *Style—* Roger Keast, Esq; Arroya House, Mount Rise, Kenn, Nr Exeter, Devonshire (☎ 0392 832889); 27/28 Southernhay East, Exeter, (☎ 0392 210700, fax 0392 74010)

KEAT, Alan Michael; s of Ernest Frank Keat, of Liphook, Surrey, and Joyce Evelyn, *née* Curtis; *b* 12 May 1942; *Educ* Charterhouse, Merton Coll Oxford (MA); *m* 9 July 1966, Lorna Marion, da of Horace Henry Wilson, of Chesterfield, Derbys; 3 da (Anna b 19 Oct 1968, Jane b 18 Sept 1972, Rebecca b 22 June 1975); *Career* slr 1966, ptnr Travers Smith Braithwaite 1970-, non-exec dir Beazer plc 1986-; *Style—* Alan Keat, Esq; 6 Snow Hill, London EC1A 2AL (☎ 01 248 9133, fax 01 236 3728, telex 887117)

KEATING, Frank; s of Bryan Keating, of Cheltenham, Glos, and Monica, *née* Marsh; *b* 4 Oct 1937; *Educ* Belmont Abbey, Douai; *m* 1987, Jane A Sinclair; *Career* prodr Independent Television 1963-64; columnist: The Guardian 1975-, Punch 1982-; TV series incl: Maestro (BBC 1), Italy, My Italy (ITV); Sportswriter of Year 1978, 1980; Magazine Writer of Year 1987; *Books* Bowled Over, Another Bloody Day in Paradise, High, Wide and Handsome, Gents and Players; *Recreations* Channel 4, Radio 4, gardening; *Clubs* Chelsea Arts; *Style—* Frank Keating, Esq; Church House, Marden, Hereford; The Guardian, London (☎ 01 278 2332)

KEATING, Henry Reymond Fitzwalter (Harry); s of John Hervey Keating (d 1950), and Muriel Margharita, *née* Clews (d 1986); *Educ* Merchant Taylors Sch, Trinity Coll Dublin (BA); *m* 3 Oct 1953, Sheila Mary, da of William Ford Mitchell, ISO (d 1968); 3 s (Simon b 1955, Piers b 1960, Hugo b 1964), 1 da (Bryony 1957); *Career* Army 1945-48; journalist 1952-63; chm: Crime Writers Assoc 1970-71, Soc of Authors 1982-84; *Books* Death and the Visiting Firemen (1959), The Perfect Murder (1964), The Murder of the Maharajah (1980), The Lucky Alphonse (1982), Under A Monsoon Cloud (1986), Dead on Time (1988); *Style—* H R F Keating, Esq; 35 Northumberland Place, London W2 5AS (☎ 01 229 1100)

KEATING, John David; s of Peter Steven Keating (d 1944, war casualty), of York, and Muriel Emily Alice Lamport; *b* 18 June 1943; *Educ* Dorset Inst and Highbury Coll (Portsmouth); *m* 28 Aug 1970, Linda Margaret, da of Sidney Reginald Hall, of Blackheath, London SE12; 1 s (Matthew b 1971), 1 da (Sarah b 1973); *Career* sea-going purser with Peninsular & Oriental SNCO 1960-70, reserve serv with RN (Lt) 2 Submarine Div 1970-71; asst to md (CWS) 1972-74, UK divnl accountant Borden Chemical Corpn 1975-81, fndr dir and proprietor WRA Ltd 1982-; dir: WRA Hldgs Ltd 1984-, WRA (Offshore) Ltd (Sub-Sea Devpt) 1985-; md Wessex Resins & Adhesives Ltd; elected memb for Ringwood South Ward of New Forest Dist Cncl 1987-; FCCA 1977, MHCIMA, ACCA; *Recreations* sailing, skiing; *Clubs* Naval, Royal Naval Sailing Assoc; *Style—* John Keating, Esq; Greenways, Hightown Hill, Ringwood, Hampshire (☎ 0425 475 446); Wessex Resins & Adhesives Ltd, Wessex House, 189-193 Spring Rd, Southampton (☎ 0703 444 744, telex 47388, fax 0703 431 792)

KEATINGE, Sir Edgar Mayne; CBE (1954); s of Gerald Francis Keatinge, CIE (d 1965); *b* 3 Feb 1905; *Educ* Rugby, South Africa; *m* 1930, Katharine Lucile, da of Reginald John Burrell (d 1948); 1 s, 1 da; *Career* joined Suffolk Yeo 1937, Cmdt School of Artillery W Africa 1942-43, Lt-Col RA; MP (C) West Suffolk Bury St Edmunds Div 1944-45; memb Panel Land Tbnl SW Area 1948-74, chm Wessex Area Nat Union of Cons Assocs 1951-54, govr Sherborne Sch 1951-74; memb cncl Royal African Soc 1970-80; kt 1960; *Clubs* Carlton, Boodle's; *Style—* Sir Edgar Keatinge, CBE; Teffont, Salisbury, Wilts SP3 5RG (☎ 072 276 224)

KEATINGE, Prof William Richard; s of Sir Edgar Keatinge, of Teffont Evias, Salisbury, Wilts, and Katherine Lucille; *b* 18 May 1931; *Educ* Upper Canada Coll, Rugby, Cambridge Univ (MA, MB BChir, PhD); *m* 15 Oct 1955, Margaret Ellen Annette, da of David Hegarty (d 1973), of Porstmouth; 1 s (Richard), 2 da (Claire, Mary); *Career* RNVR seconded for res at Cambridge Univ 1956-58; dir of studies in medicine and jr res fell Pembroke Coll Cambridge 1958-60, fell Cardiovascular Res Inst San Francisco 1960-61, MRC post and fell Pembroke Coll Oxford 1961-68, head of physiology dept London Hosp Med Coll 1981- (reader 1968-71, prof 1971-); memb: Physiological Soc 1959, RSM; MRCP 1984; *Books* Survival In Cold Water, Local Mechanisms Controlling Blood Vessels; *Recreations* archaeology, sailing; *Style—* Prof William Keatinge; Dept of Physiology, The London Hospital Medical College, Turner St, London E1 2AD (☎ 01 377 7623)

KEATLEY, (Robert) Bryan; TD (1961); s of James Walter Stanley Keatley (d 1978), of Royston, and Helen Rankin Thompson; *b* 21 Mar 1930; *Educ* Aldenham, St Catharines Coll Cambridge (MA); *m* 14 Sept 1957, Diana, da of Frank Harvey, of Bishops Stortford; 2 s (Robert b 1967, Richard (twin) b 1967), 2 da (Georgina b 1960, Regina b 1962); *Career* chartered surveyor and land agent; ptnr Humberts London 1962- (sr ptnr 1980-85); regular army 1949-50, TA Cambs Regt (16 Airborne Div), Maj & OC Herts Regt; Nat Tst fin ctee 1983, estates panel 1983, Enterprise Bd 1984; dir Landplan Ltd 1974, chm Formfield (BES) 1984, dir Rural Assets 1987; Freeman of City of London 1978, Liveryman Worshipful Co of Farmers, cmmr of taxes 1960, chm Herts (Hadhams branch) Royal Br Legion 1984; FRICS, FRSA; *Recreations* shooting, conservation, gardens, browsing; *Clubs* Boodle's, Farmers'; *Style—* Bryan Keatley, Esq, TD; Hadham Park, nr Bishops Stortford, Herts CM23 1JH (☎ 0279 52040); Humberts, 25 Grosvenor Street, London (☎ 01 629 6700, telex 27444, fax 01 493 4346)

KEATLEY, John Rankin Macdonald; s of James Walter Stanley Keatley (d 1978), of Royston, and Helen Rankin Thompson; *b* 20 August 1933; *Educ* Aldenham, RAC Circencester; *m* 1964, Carolyn Margaret, da of Rodney Telford Morell, of Melbourne,

Australia; 1 s (James b 1965), 1 da (Arabella b 1967); *Career* 2 Lt Duke of Wellington's Regt Korea 1952-53, Capt Herefordshire Regt TA; Parly candidate (C) Hemsworth 1964; chm Applied Botanics plc 1984-, leader Cambridge CC 1967-69, tstee Cambridge Museum of Technol 1970-; dir REA Holdings plc; pres SW Cambridgeshire Cons Assoc; memb ctee Contemporary Art Soc 1989; *Clubs* Lansdowne; *Style*— J R M Keatley, Esq; Melbourn Lodge, Royston, Herts SG8 6AL (☎ 0763 60680)

KEATLEY, William Halliday; TD (1970); s of James Walter Stanley Keatley (d 1978), of Royston, and Helen Rankin, *née* Thompson; *b* 22 Sept 1935; *Educ* Aldenham, St Catharine's Coll Cambridge (MA); *m* 3 Sept 1965, (Elizabeth) Jane, da of Capt Thomas Abdy Combe (d 1984); 2 da; *Career* 2 Field Batty Gold Coast RWAFF 1954-56, Cambs Regt and Suffolk and Cambs Regt 1956-72; John Prust & Co 1959-71 (ptnr 1965), Laurence Prust & Co 1971-85 (dep sr ptnr 1983), sr ptnr Laurence Keen & Co 1986-, non-exec dir Pershing & Co Ltd; memb Int Stock Exchange; *Style*— W H Keatley, Esq, TD; Heddon Hall, Parracombe, N Devon EX31 4QL (☎ 059 83 409); Laurence Keen & Co, 49-51 Bow Lane, Cheapside, London EC4M 9LX (☎ 01 489 9493)

KEATS, Helen; da of Fred Grant, of Harrow, Middx, and Margaret, *née* Braunsberg (d 1982); *b* 29 June 1947; *Educ* Peterbourgh St Margaret's HS, Wimbledon Sch of Art (BA); *m* 10 Sept 1967, Louis Maurice Keats, s of Sam Keats; 2 da (Tara b 1968, Sara b 1972); *Career* painter, lithographer, etcher & photographer; exhibitions incl: Ben Uri London and major venues abroad; memb: cncl Ben Uri Art Soc, ctee Print Makers Cncl; FPMC 1985; *Recreations* walking, swimming, music; *Style*— Mrs Helen Keats; 21 Lonsdale Rd, London SW13 9JP (☎ 01 741 0377)

KEATS, Louis Maurice; s of Samuel Keats, of Middx and Brussels, and Betty, *née* Young; *b* 23 Feb 1944; *Educ* Preston Manor GS; *m* 10 Sept 1967, Helen, da of Fred Grant, of Middx; 2 da (Tara b 1968, Sara b 1972); *Career* sr ptnr Keats Poulter (CAs) 1972, chm Data Servs Gp 1987 (dir 1984), dir Nat Youth Jazz Orchestra 1984, chm Ben Uri Art Soc 1988; FCA 1969, FCCA 1982, FBIM 1981; *Recreations* art, music, classic motor cars; *Style*— Louis M Keats, Esq; 21 Lonsdale Road, London SW13 9JP; 33 Cork Street, London W1X 1HB (☎ 01 439 1986, fax 01 734 3106)

KEAY, Hon Mrs (Julia Margaret); *née* Atkins; 2 da of Baron Colnbrook (Life Peer), *qv*; *b* 16 Sept 1946; *m* 1, 5 March 1966 (m dis 1972), David Charles Roderick, er s of Rev Charles Roderick; m 2, 1972, John Stanley Melville Keay; 2 s, 2 da; *Style*— The Hon Mrs Keay; Succoth, Dalmally, Argyll

KEBLE-WHITE, (Arthur) James; s of Capt Geoffrey Meredith Keble Keble-White, RN (d 1961), of Hants and Violet Gertrude Alice, *née* Preston (d 1963); *b* 29 May 1930; *Educ* Winchester, Trinity Coll Oxford (MA); *m* 7 May 1955, Penelope Mary, da of John Newsam McClean (d 1986), of Cirencester, Glos; 3 da (Caroline b 1957, Julia b 1959, Diana b 1964); *Career* chartered engr; dir Ove Arup & Ptnrs, md Carrier Engrg Co Ltd (resigned 1974); FIMechE, FCIBSE; *Style*— James Keble-White, Esq; Bordocks, Wisborough Green, Billingshurst, Sussex RH14 0HA (☎ 0403 700276); Ove Arup & Ptnrs, 13 Fitzroy St, London W1P 6BQ (☎ 01 636 1531)

KEE, Robert; s of Robert Kee (d 1958), and Dorothy Frances, *née* Monkman (d 1964); *b* 5 Oct 1919; *Educ* Rottingdean Sch Sussex, Stowe, Magdalen Coll Oxford (MA); *m* 1, 1948, Janetta, da of G H J Woolley; 1 da (Georgiana); m 2, 1960, Cynthia Charlotte, da of Edward Judah; 2 s (Alexander, Benjamin (decd)), 1 da (Sarah); *Career* author and broadcaster, TV interviewer, presenter, documentary maker (BBC and ITV) 1958-, Richard Dimbleby Award 1976, Jacobs Award (Dublin) for BBC Ireland (1981); memb: ACTT, Equity; *Publications* A Crowd is not Company (1948), The Impossible Shore (1949), A Sign of the Times (1956), Broadstrop in Season (1959), Refugee World (1961), The Green Flag (1972), Ireland: A History (1981), 1939 (1984), 1945 (1985), Trial and Error (1986); *Style*— Robert Kee, Esq; c/o Lloyds Bank Ltd, 112-114 Kensington High St, London W8 4SN; c/o Anthony Sheil Associates, 43 Doughty St, London WC1N 2LF (☎ 01 405 9351)

KEE, His Hon Judge William; s of Robert Kee (d 1958), and Dorothy Frances, *née* Monkman (d 1964); *b* 15 Oct 1921; *Educ* Stowe; *m* 1953, Helga Wessel, da of Erling Christian Haneborg Eckhoff (d 1980); 1 s (Peter William b 1960), 3 da (Christine Frances b 1954, Susanna Helga b 1957, Karen Mary b 1964); *Career* Army 1941-46, Orkneys and India, attached 9 Gurkha Rifles, staff capt; barr Inner Temple 1948, jt chm Ind Sch Tbnl 1971-72; princ judge for County Cts in Kent 1985-, circuit judge 1972-; *Books* Divorce Case Book (1950), contributor Encyclopaedia of Court Forms and Halsbury's Laws of England; *Recreations* walking, listening to music; *Style*— His Hon Judge Kee; Oak Hill Cottage, 8 Oak Hill Road, Sevenoaks, Kent TN13 1NP (☎ Sevenoaks 452737)

KEEBLE, Sir (Herbert Ben) Curtis; GCMG (1982, KCMG 1978, CMG 1970); s of Herbert Keeble; *b* 18 Sept 1922; *Educ* Clacton County HS, London Univ; *m* 1947, Margaret Fraser; 3 da; *Career* served WWII; Dip Serv: served Berlin, Washington, Jakarta; former cnsllr and head Euro Econ Orgns Dept FCO; commercial cnsllr Berne 1965-68, min Canberra 1968-71, asst under-sec of state FCO 1971-73, ambass German Democratic Republic 1974-76, dep under-sec FCO (chief clerk) 1976-78, ambass to USSR 1978-82, ret; int affairs conlt; govr BBC, memb cncl Royal Inst of Int Affairs, Sch of Slavonic and East European Studies; chm GB/USSR Assoc; *Books* The Soviet State (1984); *Recreations* sailing; *Style*— Sir Curtis Keeble, GCMG; Dormers, St Leonards Rd, Thames Ditton, Surrey (☎ 01 398 7778)

KEEBLE, Donovan Horace Leslie; MC (1945), TD (1975); s of Horace Keeble (d 1967), and Dorothy Lesley, *née* de Caux (d 1938); *b* 11 Jan 1912; *Educ* Thornton Heath Sch, King's Coll London (BSc), Battersea Poly; *m* 12 June 1937, Joan Florence, da of Edwin John Tessier (d 1960); 2 da (Domini b 20 Feb 1939, d 1987, Hulda b 19 July 1943); *Career* cmmnd 2 Lt RE TA 1938, Lt 226 Field Co 48 S Midland Div 1939, Capt 1940, Maj 53 SW Div 1941, SO2 (RE) with CE 21 Army Gp, released from embodied serv 1946, ret hon Maj 1975; engr Croydon London CC and Reading 1932-39; asst md 1946-51: Cheecol Processes Ltd, Permacem Paint Co Ltd; chief engr Nat Bldg and Housing Bd S Rhodesia 1951-53, fndr ptnr Maggs and Keeble Consulting Engrs S Rhodesia 1953-62; fndr dir: and chm BMMK and Ptnrs consulting engrs 1962-81, Southern Testing Laboratories Geotechnical Conslts 1962-; fndr and first chm Assoc of Consulting Engrs S Rhodesia, former chm Borrowdale Road Cncl S Rhodesia, former pres E Grinstead Rotary Club; chm Borrowdale constituency under PM S Rhodesia 1961; FICE 1938, FIHT 1947, MConsE; *Recreations* pottery and ceramics, swimming, walking, travelling; *Clubs* RAC; *Style*— Donovan Keeble, Esq, MC, TD; Regency Cottage, Fairwarp, E Sussex TN22 3BE (☎ 08257 2940); Fermoyle Ballinskelligs, Co Kerry, Rep of Ireland; P O Box 1834, Harare, Zimbabwe; Keeble House, Stuart Way, E Grinstead, W Sussex RH19 4QA (☎ 0342 313 156, fax 0342 410 321, telex 95637 TELSER)

KEEBLE, Maj Robert; DSO (1940), MC (1945), (TD 1946); s of Edwin Percy Keeble (d 1942), of Summer Lodge, Kenilworth, and Alice Elizabeth, *née* Langford (d 1966); *b* 20 Feb 1911; *Educ* King Henry VIII Sch Coventry, Staff Coll Camberley; *Career* territorial cmmn RE 1933, Capt 1936, Maj 1940, served in Middle East under Dir Mill Ops and Plans War Off, N Ireland 1942-43, Offr i/c 582 Army Field Co RE Normandy 'D' Day France, Germany 1944, twice wounded (despatches 1941, 1946), demobbed 1946; engr apprentice Alfred Herberts Coventry; Portland Cement Co: joined 1931, works mangr Harbury Warwicks 1946-52, appt i/c prodn UK 1952, appt i/c prodn of all overseas cos 1965, memb main bd of dir 1970, dir Aberthaw & Bristol Channel 1970; ret 1974; govr Hull Univ 1960, hon er bro Trinity House Hull 1965; Freeman City of London 1938, Liveryman Worshipful Co of Fanmakers; *Recreations* fishing, sailing; *Clubs* Army and Navy; *Style*— Maj Robert Keeble, DSO, MC, TD; 15 Fernhill Close, Kenilworth, Warwicks (☎ 0926 556 68)

KEEGAN, Sheila Mary; da of James Keegan, of London (d 1986), and Elizabeth, *née* Tinnenny; *b* 25 July 1952; *Educ* Portsmouth Poly (BA), LSE (MSc); *m* 4 Sept 1982, James Michael Ryan; 1 da (Carolyn b 1985); *Career* assoc dir Cooper Res & Mktg 1975-79; dir: Business Decisions Ltd 1979-83, Cambell Keegan Ltd 1983-; MRS 1975- (full memb 1983); *Style*— Ms Sheila Keegan; Campbell Keegan Ltd, Plaza 535, Kings Rd, London (☎ 01 823 3777)

KEELING, Christopher Anthony Gedge; s of Sir Edward Keeling, MC, MP, DL (d 1954), of 20 Wilton Street, London SW1, and Martha Ann, *née* Darling; *b* 15 June 1930; *Educ* Eton, RMA Sandhurst; *m* 1, 20 Sept 1955 (m dis 1972), Veronica, da of Alec Waugh, the writer (d 1980), of Edrington, Silchester, Berks; 2 s (Simon Alexander Edward, d 1982, Julian James), 1 da (Nicola Sara); m 2, 1974, Rachael Macdonald; *Career* Capt Grenadier Gds 1948-56; chm Fenchurch Underwriting Agencies Ltd, dir Fenchurch Insurance Holdings Ltd; dir: Jago Venton Underwriting Agencies Ltd, Castle Underwriting Agencies Ltd, Burton Rowe & Viner Ltd; chm Venton Underwriting Agency Ltd; Freeman City of London, Liveryman Worshipful Co of Fishmongers 1955;; *Recreations* shooting, reading, watching cricket ; *Clubs* White's, MCC, Beefsteak; *Style*— Christopher Keeling, Esq; Leyden House, Thames Bank, London SW14 7QR (☎ 01 876 7375); Boundar House, 7 Jewry Street, London EC3N 2EX (☎ 01 488 2388; fax, 01 481 9467; telex, 884442 LOQOTE G)

KEELING, Surgn Rear Adm John; CBE (1978); *b* 28 Oct 1921; *Educ* Queen Elizabeth's Sch Hartlebury, Birmingham Univ; *m* 1948, Olwen Anne; 2 s (1 decd); *Career* RN 1946, Fleet Air Arm until 1975; dir environmental med 1975-77, dep med dir-gen (Naval) 1977-80, dir of med policy and plans MOD 1980-83, chm NATO Jt Civil Mil Med Gp 1981-83; QHP 1977-83; MFOM; *Recreations* caravanning, microcomputers; *Clubs* Army and Navy; *Style*— Surgn Rear Adm John Keeling, CBE; Merlin Cottage, Brockhampton, Hereford HR1 4TQ (☎ 098986 649)

KEELING, John Arthur Bernard; DFC (1943); s of Sir John Henry Keeling (d 1978); *b* 31 Oct 1922; *Educ* Eton, Christ Church Oxford (MA); *m* 1961, Mary Jocelyn, da of Eric Heseltine Wenham (d 1959); 2 s; *Career* served RAF 1941-45, Fl-Lt, NW Europe, Malta and Italy; CA 1949; chm: London & Yorks Tst Hldgs Ltd 1965-88 (dir 1952-88), W Riding Worsted & Woollen Mills Ltd 1968-75 (dir 1959-75), Close Bros Gp plc 1975-87 (dir 1959-87); dir: Bowater Industs plc 1968-88, RIT and Northern plc 1968-85; advsr Br Airways Pension Fund 1959-85, chm St Michael's Hospice Hastings 1988-; farmer 1967-; *Recreations* travel, gardening; *Clubs* White's; *Style*— John Keeling Esq, DFC; 48 Melton Ct, Old Brompton Rd, London SW7 3JH (☎ 01 584 0333); Hurst Hse, Sedlescombe, Sussex (☎ 042 487 340)

KEELING, Robert William Maynard; s of Dr George Sydney Keeling (d 1957), of Attleborough, Norfolk, and Florence Amy Maynard (d 1951); *b* 16 Dec 1917; *Educ* Uppingham, Corpus Christi Coll Cambridge; *m* 1942, Kathleen Busill, da of Herbert Busill-Jones, JP (d 1955), of Staffs; 1 s (Jonathan b 1952), 2 da (Anne b 1945, Karen b 1948); *Career* Army 1939-46, Maj RASC, served Western Desert, Libya, Palestine, Trans-Jordan, Egypt, Greece, Berlin (despatches 1944); GSO 2, control cmmn for Germany 1945; FO (German Economic Dept) 1946-47, slr 1950, rec Crown Ct 1980-; Kt Cdr Order of Civil Merit of Spain 1967; *Recreations* travel, painting; *Style*— Robert Keeling, Esq; Vale Bank, Chadlington, Oxford; 44 The Boilerhouse, Shad Thames, London SE1

KEEN, Charles William Lyle; s of Harold Hugh Keen (d 1974), and Catherine Eleanor Lyle, *née* Cummins; *b* 4 July 1936; *Educ* Winchester, New Coll Oxford (MA); *m* 21 July 1962, Lady (Priscilla) Mary Rose, *qv*, da of 6 Earl Howe, CBE (d 1984); 1 s (William b 1970), 3 da (Laura b 1963, Eleanor b 1965, Alice b 1966); *Career* Lt The Royal Dragoons; local dir Barclays Bank: Reading 1967-71 (sr local dir 1974-81); Nottingham 1971-74; dir: Barclays Unicorn Gp Ltd 1978-81, Barclays Merchant Bank 1981-87, Barclays de Zoete Wedd Hldgs Ltd 1986-87; regnl dir Barclays Bank 1987-; AIB 1964; *Books* The Mondragon Experience (1977); *Recreations* rural sports and pastimes; *Style*— Charles Keen, Esq; St Mary's Farm House, Beenham, Reading, Berks (☎ 0734 713705); 2 Circus Place, London Wall, London EC2

KEEN, Frank William Ernest; s of Frederick Henry Ernest Keen (k/a 1945) and Elsie Dora, *née* Muckett (d 1977); *b* 28 Jan 1929; *Educ* Prices GS Fareham Hants; *m* 4 March 1950, Doreen May, da of George Charles Salmon (d 1980); 2 da (Sandra Anne (Mrs Meggs) b 1952, Rossalyn (Mrs Watchorn) b 1955); *Career* Nat Serv RE 1947-49; local govt offr (engr and surveyor 1944-60), princ own firm of surveyors 1960-83; former memb Bognor Regis Round Table and Rotary Club; memb: W Sussex CC 1968- (chm Highways ctee), Sussex Police Authy 1977- (chm 1985-88); Freeman City of London, Liveryman Worshipful Co of Painter Stainers; FRICS, FSVA, MICE, FIHT; *Recreations* golf; *Style*— Frank Keen, Esq; 4 St Richard's Drive, Bognor Regis, West Sussex PO21 3BH (☎ 0243 263 350)

KEEN, Lady (Priscilla) Mary Rose; *née* Curzon; da of 6 Earl Howe, CBE; *b* 12 Feb 1940; *Educ* Lawnside Worcs, Oxford; *m* 1962, Charles William Lyle Keen, *qv*; 1 s, 3 da; *Books* The Garden Border Book; *Recreations* gardening; *Style*— Lady Mary Rose Keen; St Mary's Farm, Beenham, Reading, Berks (☎ 0734 713705)

KEEN, Robert Victor; s of Hedley Victor Keen (d 1978), and Elsie Frances, *née* Bush (d 1976); *b* 1 Jan 1934; *Educ* Simon Langton Sch, Canterbury; *m* 1, (m dis 1966), Christine, *née* Brind; 1 s (Justin Robert b 19 July 1958), 1 da (Naomi Theresa b 30 May 1961); m 2, 30 Nov 1966, Pamela Rosina, da of Ralph Knight; 1 s (James Thomas b 6 April 1971); *Career* Nat Serv, cmmnd The Buffs 1954-56; PT mangr (plastics/ chemicals) Distillers Co 1956-64, account gp dir J Walter Thompson 1964-68, md

Interpublic PR 1968-74, dir (int corp affairs) Ranx Xerox 1974-80, chm Charles Barker Traverse-Healy 1980-; JP 1984-88; MIPR; *Recreations* sailing; *Clubs* Royal Lymington YC; *Style—* Robert Keen, Esq; Rivendell, Ridgeway Lane, Lymington, Hants; 44 Andrewes House, Barbican, London EC2 (☎ 0590 73030); 30 Farringdon St, London EC4A 4EA (☎ 01 634 1000, fax 236 0170, telex 883588/887928)

KEEN, Dr Timothy Frank; s of Frank Keen, MBE (d 1986), of Keensacre, Burnham Beeches, Bucks, and Lillian, *née* Hooley (d 1976); *b* 9 Nov 1953; *Educ* St Paul's, Nottingham Univ (BSc, PhD); *m* 6 Aug 1983, Victoria Ann, da of Jeffrey James Brandon, of Keyworth, Notts; 1 s (Henry b 20 Feb 1986), 1 da (Lucinda b 15 June 1987); *Career* md Keen Computers Ltd 1978-84, gen mangr Intelligence Res Ltd 1985, chm and chief exec Keen Ltd 1985-; chm and cncl memb Computer Retailters Assoc 1978-83, cncl memb Parly Info Ctee 1983-86, dir Nottingham Info Technol Ctee 1983-84; pres Britwell Carnival Charity; FBIM 1981, FIOD 1981, MBCS 1982; *Recreations* fly fishing, shooting, breeding highland cattle; *Clubs* RAC; *Style—* Dr Timothy Keen; Keensacre, Burnham Beeches, Bucks SL2 3TA (☎ 028 14 4404); Keen Ltd, PO Box 551, Slough SL2 3TT (☎ 02914 6501, fax 02814 2417, car tel 0836 718 432)

KEENE, Bryan Richard; s of Edward Stanley William Keene (d 1963), of Weybridge, and Sybil White, *née* Holmes; *b* 14 Sept 1937; *Educ* St James' Boys Sch Weybridge; *Career* Securities Agency Ltd/Drayton Corpn Ltd 1963-74, asst dir Samuel Montagu & Co Ltd 1974-84, dir and co sec MIM Ltd 1984-; dir: MIM Devpt Capital Ltd 1984-, Elliot Assocs Ltd 1984-, Anglo-Scottish Securities Ltd 1986-, Staple Investmt Tst Ltd 1986-; co sec: MIM Britannia Ltd 1986-, MIM Britannia Unit Tst Mangrs Ltd 1986-; sec Parochial Church Cncl of Weybridge; FCIS 1968, ATII 1977; *Style—* Bryan Keene, Esq; Woodside, Winterbourne Grove, Weybridge, Surrey (☎ 0932 841708); 11 Devonshire Sq, London EC2M 4YR (☎ 01 626 3434)

KEENE, Gareth John; s of Victor Horace Keene, of Kent, and Muriel Olive, *née* Whitehead; *b* 31 Mar 1944; *Educ* Tonbridge, St John's Coll Cambridge (MA, LLM); *m* 1, 1969 (m dis 1983), Georgina, da of David Walter Patrick Thomas, of Cambs; 3 s (Timothy b 1973, David b 1975, Jonathan b 1979); m 2, 1983, Charlotte Louise, da of Peter Frank Lester (d 1985), of Devon; *Career* barr Grays Inn 1966; int legal consit; dir TSW TV SW Hldgs plc 1980-; tstee Int Musicians Seminar; sec Euro Community Chamber Orchestra Tst; chm Beaford Arts Centre; *Books* Sacred and Secular (with Adam Fox, 1975); *Recreations* music; *Clubs* Royal Soc of Medicine; *Style—* Gareth Keene, Esq; Buttermead, Manaton, Newton Abbot, Devon TQ13 9XG (☎ 064722 208, fax 064722 410)

KEENLYSIDE, Brig Richard Headlam (Dick); CBE (1957), DSO (1946); s of Capt Guy Francis Headlam Keenlyside (ka France 1914), and late Rose Margaret, *née* Knyvett; *b* 13 May 1909; *Educ* Charterhouse, RMA Woolwich; *m* 1, 1937, Aileen Evelyn D'Auvergne (d 1960), da of Capt Nigel Hogg (ka 1916); 2 da (Susan (Mrs Vale) b 1939), Jane (Mrs Jacob) b 1940); m 2, 28 April 1962, Ann Christian, wid of Maj-Gen F N Mitchell, da of Maj Nigel Livingstone-Learmonth (ka 1915); 3 step da (Mona Mitchell, CVO, Josephine (Mrs Robinson), Marion (Mrs Weston)); *Career* cmmnd 2 Lt 1929, served England 1929-34, India (now Pakistan) 1935-39, (Capt) France 1939, (Maj) France, Belgium, Dunkirk, England 1940; Egypt, Sudan, Eritrea, Palestine 1940-42; Tripoli, Algeria, Normandy, Belgium, Holland, Germany (Lt Col) 1943-45; Regtl Cdr and WO England 1945-50, SO Germany 1950-53, Regtl Cdr England 1953-54, SO Singapore 1954-57, Cdr RA 56 (London) Div 1958-61, ret 1961; dir CLA Game Fair 1963-74; *Recreations* shooting, golf, playing the piano; *Clubs* Army & Navy; *Style—* Brig R H Keenlyside, CBE, DSO; Valley Farm, Blackford, Yeovil, Somerset BA22 7EF (☎ 0963 40304)

KEEP, Hugh Charles John Martin; s of John Frederick Charles Keep; *b* 21 Nov 1945; *Educ* Bradfield; *m* 1970, Rosemary Isabel, da of James Stuart Smith; 3 s; *Career* dir: Keep Brothers Ltd 1973-88, Elders Finance Ltd 1987-; Elders Keep Ltd 1988-; *Recreations* flyfishing, gardening, reading, bee-keeping, tennis; *Style—* Hugh Keep, Esq; The Old Rectory, Lockhill, Upper Sapey, Worcester WR6 6XR

KEEPING, Bryan Edward; s of Douglas William Joseph Keeping (d 1967), of Poole, and Ena Anne, *née* Coombes; *b* 23 Mar 1936; *Educ* Poole GS, Balliol Coll Oxford (MA); *m* 19 Oct 1963, Christine Margaret, da of Arthur Ivor Brown (d 1973), of Newport, Gwent; 1 s (David b 1965) 1 da (Jennifer b 1968); *Career* Nat Serv RAF 1955-57; sr ptnr Trevanions slrs 1988- (ptnr 1965-); memb Poole Rotary Club; *Recreations* golf, boating; *Clubs* Parkstone GC, RMYC; *Style—* Bryan Keeping, Esq; 20 Greenwood Ave, Poole, Dorset, BH1 48QD (☎ 0202 709 608); Trevanions, 15 Church Road, Parkstone, Poole, Dorset BH1 48UF (☎ 0202 715 815, fax 0202 715 511)

KEER, Colin John Gordon; s of Maj Martin Cordy Keer, MC, of Violet Cottage, Blockley, Gloucs, and Leila Lorna *née* Troup; *b* 19 April 1950; *Educ* Radley, Magdalene Coll Cambridge, (MA); *Career* asst mangr Price Waterhouse 1976- (1972-76), dir Samuel Montagu & Co Ltd 1984- (1976-86), md Bankers Tst Co 1986-;; *Recreations* tennis, gardening; *Style—* Colin Keer, Esq; Bankers Trust Co, Dashwood House, 60 Old Broad St, London, EC2P 2EE (☎ 01 726 4141, fax 01 382 2256)

KEETON, Prof George Williams; s of John William Keeton (d 1958), of Sheffield, and Mary Emma, *née* Williams (d 1948); *b* 22 May 1902; *Educ* City Central Sch Sheffield, Gonville and Caius Coll Cambridge (BA, LLB, MA, LLM, LLD); *m* 1, 25 February 1924 (m dis 1947), Gladys Edith, da of Thomas Calthorpe (d 1955), of Sheffield; 2 s ((Cecil) Peter Calthorpe b 12 Jan 1928, Michael George Williams b 14 March 1929); m 2, 18 Dec 1947, (Kathleen) Marian, da of Charles Archibald Willard (d 1970), of Leighton Buzzard, Beds; *Career* called to the Bar Gray's Inn 1928, reader in law and politics Hong Kong Univ 1924-27, sr lectr in law Manchester Univ 1928-31; UCL: reader in English law 1931-37, prof of English law and head law dept 1937-69, vice-prof 1966-69; asst prof Brunel Univ 1969-76, distinguished visiting prof Univ of Miami 1970-74, emeritus prof 1976-; pres: Soc of Pub Teachers of Law 1961-62, London Inst of World Affrs 1948-88; FBA 1964; *Books* The Development of Extraterritoriality in China (1928), The Law of Trusts (1934, 11 edn 1983), Equity (with LA Sheridan, 3 edn 1987), Lord Chancellor Jeffreys (1964), The Norman Conquest and the Common Law (1966), The Comparative Law of Trusts (1976), Harvey Hasty (1978); *Style—* Prof George Keeton; Picts Close, Picts Lane, Princes Risborough, Bucks HP1M 9DX

KEEVIL, (Ambrose) Clement (Arthur); s of Col Sir Ambrose Keevil, KBE, MC, DL (d 1973); *b* 21 Sept 1919; *Educ* Tonbridge, Queen's Coll Oxford (BA); *m* 1945, Olwen Marjorie Enid, da of John Gibbins; 2 s (Philip m Augusta McGrail, Julian m Mary Harrison), 1 da (Harriet); *Career* served Middx Regt, RA (Adj), GSO 2 (AIR) AFHQ Italy (despatches); a fndr dir Fitch Lovell plc (dep chm until ret 1983), fndr memb and chm Fish Farming Branch NFU; Master Worshipful Co of Poulterers 1966-67, Freeman City of London; FRSA; *Recreations* painting; *Clubs* Army and Navy, MCC; *Style—* Clement Keevil, Esq; Buckwell Place, Herstmonceux, East Sussex BN27 4JT (☎ 0323 832157)

KEEVIL, Philip Samuel; s of Arnold Herbert Keevil (d 1965), of Lewes, Sussex, and Gladys Cecilia, *née* Haydon (d 1982); *b* 24 Sept 1937; *Educ* Brockenhurst County HS; *m* 27 Feb 1960, Joan Kathleen, da of Wallace Henry Brown, of S Wigton, Leicester; 1 s (Andrew b 1960), 1 da (Vicky b 1963); *Career* architect in private practice; md: Applied Cad Servs Ltd, Computer Graphics 1984-; fndr chm Actocad User Gp UK; former pres Nene Rotary Club; *Recreations* squash, music; *Clubs* Northampton and County; *Style—* Philip Keevil, Esq; The Bungalow, 1 Sandringham Rd, Northampton; Applied Cad Services Ltd, Ashton House, Kent Rd, Northampton NN5 6XB (☎ 0604 587921)

KEEYS, Geoffrey Foster; s of Richard Kipling Foster Keeys, and Joan, *née* Anderson; *b* 29 Oct 1944; *Educ* Abingdon Sch, Univ of Manchester (LLB); *m* 4 April 1970, Christine Mary (Donna), da of Henry Albert Lavers, of Newbury; 1 s (Henry Foster b 16 April 1976), 1 da (Georgia Ellen b 22 May 1974); *Career* graduate trainee Mobil Oil 1966-68, various personnel positions to dir personnel and ind relations (Europ and World export) Massey Ferguson 1968-82, dir gp personnel Chubb & Son plc 1982-84, gen mangr personnel and admin servs Prudential Corpn plc 1984-; memb advsy bds: Personnel Mgmnt (Magazine Inst Personnel Mgmnt), centre strategic mgmnt and change Univ of Warwick; non exec dir Employee Rels Ltd; memb nat ctee Nat Assoc Boys Clubs; MIPM; *Recreations* golf, cricket; *Clubs* RAC; *Style—* Geoffrey Keeys, Esq; Prudential Corpn, 142 Holborn Bars, London EC1N 2NH (☎ 01 936 0241)

KEFFER, John W; s of James Morgan Keffer (d 1935), and Dove, *née* Douglas (d 1934); *b* 5 June 1923; *Educ* Texas Technol Univ (BA), The Univ of Texas (JD), Johns Hopkins Univ (MA); *m* 25 Aug 1954, Natalia, da of Baron Giulio Blanc (d 1978), of Le Chateau, Tolochenaz, Switzerland; 2 s (Charles b 1955, d 1959, John b 1957); *Career* ensign USNR 1943, served Europe 1944-45: Normandy Invasion 1944, Invasion Southern France 1944, Lt (JG); served Pacific 1945-46: Okinawa, Philippines, Occupation of Japan; lawyer 1950-53: Schuster & Davenport NY, Travieso Paul Caracas Venezuela; gen counsel: Esso Standard Oil Havana Cuba 1954-60, Coral Gables Florida 1960-63, Creole Petroleum Corpn Caracas Venezuela 1964-73, Esso Europe London 1973-85, Counsel Fulbright & Jaworski London 1986-; chm tstees American Museum in Britain 1982- (tstee 1979-), memb advsy bd Royal Acad 1987-; memb: Int Bar Assoc, American Bar Assoc, Texas Bar; *Recreations* photography, collecting paintings, drawings, watercolours, antiques; *Clubs* Garrick, Brooks's, Univ (NY), Circolo Della Caccia (Rome); *Style—* John Keffer, Esq; Fulbright & Jaworski, 2 St James's Place, London SW1A 1NP (☎ 01 629 1207, fax 01 493 8259, telex 28310)

KEIGHTLEY, Maj-Gen Richard Charles; CB (1987); s of Gen Sir Charles F Keightley, GCB, GBE, DSO (d 1974), and Joan Lydia, da of Brig-Gen G N T Smyth-Osbourne, CB, CMG, DSO (d 1942); *b* 2 July 1933; *Educ* Marlborough, RMA Sandhurst; *m* 21 Oct 1958, Caroline Rosemary, da of Col Sir Thomas Butler, 12 Bt, DSO, OBE, MVO, *qv*; 3 da (Charlotte (Mrs Jenkinson) b 21 March 1961, Arabella b 31 July 1962, Victoria b 3 Dec 1965); *Career* cmmnd 5 Royal Inniskilling Dragoon Gds 1953; served Suez Canal Zone, Far East, Libya, N I, Germany, Cdr 1972-75; Cdr: Task Force E 1978-79, Western Dist 1982-83, Cmdt RMA Sandhurst 1983-87, Col 5 Royal Inniskilling Dragoon Gds 1986-; chm: Combined Servs Polo Assoc 1982-87, W Dorset Health Authy 1988-; *Recreations* equitation, field sports, cricket, farming; *Clubs* Cavalry and Guards'; *Style—* Maj-Gen Richard Keightley, CB; Kennels Cottage, Tarrant Gunville, Blandford, Dorset DT11 8JQ (☎ 025889 418); Somerleigh Gate, Dorset County Hospital, Dorchester, Dorset (☎ 0305 63123)

KEIL, Charles George; *b* 7 Mar 1933; *Educ* St Bartholomew's GS Newbury, Queen Mary Coll Univ of London; *m* 23 April 1960, Janette Catherine; 2 s (Duncan b 1963, Ewan b 1964), 1 da (Fiona b 1962); *Career* RAF (fighter pilot) Flt Lt, served Canada, Germany, France, Cyprus 1951-55; ed of monthly aviation journal "Aircraft Engineering" 1959-65, dir John Fowler & Ptnrs Ltd (PR conslts) 1971-73, md Harrison Cowley PR Ltd 1974-; dir: Harrison Cowley Advertising (Midlands) Ltd 1975-, Harrison Cowley Photographic Ltd 1978-; chm: Harrison Cowley PR Ltd 1988-, Hall Harrison PR Gp (Birmingham, Bristol, Edinburgh, Maidenhead, Manchester and Southampton) 1988-; *Recreations* reading, dog walking, painting, activity holidays; *Style—* Charles Keil, Esq; Illyria, 536 Streetsbsrook Rd, West Midlands B91 1RD (☎ 021 705 0773); Harrison Cowley Public Relations Ltd, 154 Great Charles St, Birmingham B3 3HU (☎ 021 236 7532)

KEIR, James Dewar; QC; s of Lt-Col David Robert Keir, DSO (d 1947), of Edinburgh, and Elizabeth Lunan, *née* Ross (d 1975); *b* 30 Nov 1921; *Educ* Edinburgh Acad, Ch Ch Oxford (MA); *m* 7 July 1948, Jean Mary, da of Rev Edward Percival Orr (d 1970), of Diss, Norfolk; 2 s (Robert b 17 Sept 1954, Simon b 29 March 1957), 2 da (Alison b 22 Aug 1950, Caroline b 11 Feb 1952); *Career* Capt Balck Watch (RHR) served: ME Italy, Austria; called to the Bar Inner Temple 1949, legal advsr Utd Africa Co Ltd 1954, head of legal servs Unilever Ltd 1973, jt sec Unilever NV and Unilever plc 1976-84; dir Open Univ Educn Enterprises Ltd 1983-; chm City and East London Family Practitioner Ctee 1985-, pres East Grinstead RFC 1969-88; chm: East Grinstead Decorative and Fine Arts Soc 1987-, Pharmacists Review Panel 1986-, Monopolies and Mergers Cmmn 1987-; *Recreations* watching rugby, opera, reading; *Clubs* Caledonian; *Style—* James Keir, Esq, QC; The Crossways, 1 High St, Dormansland, Lingfield, Surrey RH7 6PU (☎ 0342 834621)

KEIR, Lady (Elizabeth) Sophia Rhiannon; *née* Paget; da of 7 Marquess of Anglesey, DL; *b* 14 May 1954; *m* 1983, Robert Keir, s of James Dewar Keir, QC, *qv*; *Style—* Lady Sophia Keir

KEIR WATSON, Robin; s of Robert Keir Watson (d 1929); *b* 12 Sept 1915; *Educ* Hillhead HS Glasgow, Glasgow Univ; *m* 1950, Veronica Josephine Yolande (d 1979); *Career* chartered engr and accountant; chm Associated Engineering Ltd 1970-80; Freeman City of London, Liveryman Worshipful Co of Shipwrights 1972; recipient of Cncl of Inst of Petroleum Award in recognition of servs to the Inst 1983; *Recreations* educnl res in energy subjects, walking, voluntary work of educnl nature; *Clubs* Caledonian, Western (Glasgow); *Style—* Robin Keir Watson, Esq; 18 Kelvin Court, Glasgow G12 OAB (☎ 041 334 8763)

KEITH, Hon Alastair James; s of Baron Keith of Castleacre (Life Peer); *b* 1947; *Educ* Eton, Harvard Univ (BA, MBA); *m* 1983, Jayne Will, yr da of late Walter C

Teagle, Jr; 1 s (Alexander b 1984), 1 da (Serena b 1986); *Career* banker; *Style*— The Hon Alastair Keith; 150 East 73, New York City, New York, USA

KEITH, Hon Alexander Lindsay; s of Baron Keith of Kinkel (Life Peer); *b* 1967,(twin); *Style*— The Hon Alexander Keith

KEITH, Lady Ariel Olivia Winifred; *née* Baird; CVO; 2 da of 1 Viscount Stonehaven, PC, GCMG, DSO (d 1941), and Countess of Kintore (d 1974); *b* 16 August 1916; *m* 25 April 1946 (m dis 1958), Sir Kenneth Alexander Keith (now Lord Keith of Castleacre); 1 s, 1 da; *Career* lady-in-waiting to HRH Princess Alice, Countess of Athlone 1940; *Style*— Lady Ariel Keith, CVO; Flat B, 9 Cadogan Sq, London SW1X 0HT (☎ 01 235 5343)

KEITH, Hon Deborah Jane; da of Baron Keith of Kinkel (Life Peer); *b* 1957; *Style*— The Hon Deborah Keith

KEITH, Hon Hugo George; s of Baron Keith of Kinkel (Life Peer); *b* 1967; *Style*— The Hon Hugo Keith

KEITH, Ian Douglas; s of Leonard Douglas Keith, and Bertha Musker, *née* Strathan; *b* 13 Oct 1929; *Educ* Strathallan Forgandenny Perth; *m* 5 Sept 1959, Rosemary Enriqueta, da of Col William Herbert Treays (d 1960), of Treetops, Orpington, Kent; 3 da (Sophie Henrietta b 1963, Sarah Louise b 1965, Fiona Mary b 1967); *Career* Nat Serv RASC 1954-56, Actg Capt Plymouth Tport Off for Devon and Cornwall during Nat Tport Strike, asst Adj SW HQ Taunton; slr 1960, ptnr Whitley Hughes & Luscombe 1963 (amalgamated with Donne Mileham & Haddock 1986); Notary Public 1963; chm govrs Handcross Prep Sch 1976-87, sole clerk to NHSS Tbnl for Eng and Wales; memb Law Soc; *Recreations* sailing, tennis, gardening; *Clubs* Bosham Sailing Club; *Style*— Ian Keith, Esq; 25 Queens Sq, Crawley, West Sussex, RH10 1EU (☎ 0293 545971, fax 0293 543760)

KEITH, Hon Iona Delia Mary Gaddis; da of Lord Inverurie, *qv*; *b* 1978; *Style*— The Hon Iona Keith

KEITH, Hon James Alan; s of Baron Keith of Kinkel (Life Peer); *b* 1959; *m* 21 Nov 1987, Eleanor, yr da of Col M F F Woodhead; *Style*— The Hon James Keith

KEITH, Penelope Anne Constance; da of Frederick Hatfield, and Constance Mary Keith; *m* 1978, Rodney Timson; *Career* actress; *plays in London include* The Norman Conquests (1974), Donkey's Years (1976), Hay Fever (1983); *TV series include* The Good Life (1974-77), To The Manor Born (1979-81), Sweet Sixteen (1983); *Style*— Miss Penelope Keith; c/o Howes & Prior, 66 Berkeley House, Hay Hill, London W1

KEITH, Capt (James) Robin Glyn; s of Col Norman Alistair Keith (d 1983), and Monica Margaret, *née* Price, (d 1988); *b* 13 Mar 1944; *Educ* Tonbridge; *m* 8 Jan 1979, Wendy Gay, da of Wing Cdr Harvey Heyworth (d 1957); 1 s (James b 1979); *Career* cmmnd 14/20 Kings Hussars 1962-68, attached Army Wings Course Middle Wallop (later to Army SAir Corps) 1964-68; commercial helicopter pilot Bristow Helicopters Ltd overseas: American Basin, Ghara, Dahorney, Indonesia, Malaysia, Singapore, West Aust 1968-74; md and fndr McAlpine Helicopters 1974-87 (fndr McAlpine Helicopters Servs NZ 1984), fndr European Helicopters Ltd 1988-; memb British Assoc fo Shooting and Conservation; Upper Freeman of Guild of Air Pilots and Navigators 1984; memb Royal Aeronautical Soc 1988; *Recreations* shooting, deer stalking, fishing; *Clubs* Cavalry and Guards; *Style*— Capt Robin Keith; Kingfisher's Cottage, Nelson Close, Stockbridge, Hants (☎ 0264 810 300); (☎ 0264 810 300, fax 0264 810 260, car tel 0836 275 143)

KEITH, Hon Thomas Hamilton; s of Baron Keith of Kinkel (Life Peer); *b* 1961; *Educ* Magdalen Coll Oxford; *Career* barr; *Style*— The Hon Thomas Keith

KEITH OF CASTLEACRE, Baron (Life Peer UK 1980); Kenneth Alexander Keith; s of Edward Charles Keith (d 1972), naturalist and writer, of Swanton Morley House, Dereham, Norfolk; *b* 30 August 1916; *Educ* Rugby; *m* 1, 25 April 1946 (m dis 1958), Lady Ariel Olivia Winifred Baird, 2 da of 1 Viscount Stonehaven, GCMG, DSO, PC, and (Ethel) Sydney, Countess of Kintore; 1 s, 1 da; m 2, 1962 (m dis 1972), Mrs Nancy (Slim) Hayward (formerly w of (1) Howard Hawks, the film dir, and (2) Leland Hayward, theatre and film agent); m 3, 1973, Marie-Luz, da of Capt Robert Peel Dennistoun-Webster, RN, and formerly wife of (1) Adrian Donald Henderson and (2) James Robert Hanbury; *Career* 2 Lt Welsh Gds 1939, Lt-Col 1945, served in N Africa, Italy, France and Germany (despatches, Croix de Guerre with Silver Star), asst to dir-gen Political Intelligence Dept FO 1945-46, merchant banker and industrialist; vice-chm BEA 1964-71, chm Hill Samuel Gp Ltd 1970-80, dir British Airways 1971-72, chm and chief exec Rolls-Royce Ltd 1972-80, Beecham Gp Ltd (dir 1949-87, vice-chm 1956-65 and 1974-87, chm Beecham Group 1985-86); dir: Eagle Star Insur Co 1955-75, Nat Provincial Bank 1967-69, Standard Telephones and Cables Ltd, (chm 1985); chm Arlington Securities 1982-; kt 1969; *Recreations* farming, shooting, golf; *Clubs* White's, Pratt's, Links (NY); *Style*— The Rt Hon the Lord Keith of Castleacre; 9 Eaton Sq, London SW1W 9DB (☎ 01 730 4000); The Wicken House, Castle Acre, Norfolk (Castle Acre 225)

KEITH OF KINKEL, Baron (Life Peer UK 1976); Hon Henry Shanks Keith; PC (1976); s of Baron Keith of Avonholm (Life Peer, d 1964); *b* 7 Feb 1922; *Educ* Edinburgh Acad, Magdalen Oxford (Hon Fell 1977), Edinburgh Univ; *m* 1955, Alison Hope Alan, da of Alan Brown; 4 s (incl twins); 1 da; *Career* Scots Gds 1941-45 (despatches), advocate Scottish Bar 1950, barr Gray's Inn 1951, QC (Scot) 1962, Sheriff of Roxburgh, Berwick and Selkirk 1970-71, dep chm Parly Boundary Cmmn for Scotland 1976, senator of College of Justice in Scotland with judicial title of Lord Keith 1971-77, Lord of Appeal in Ordinary 1977-, chm ctee on powers of the Revenue Depts 1980-83; hon fell Magdalen Coll Oxford 1977; *Clubs* Flyfishers'; *Style*— Rt Hon the Lord Keith of Kinkel, PC; Woodend, Strathtummel, by Pitlochry, Perthshire (☎ Tummel Bridge 255)

KEITH-LUCAS, Prof Bryan; CBE (1983); s of Dr Keith Lucas (ka 1916), and Alys, *née* Hubbard (d 1955); *b* 1 August 1912; *Educ* Gresham's Sch Holt, Pembroke Coll Cambridge (MA), Univ of Kent at Canterbury (DLitt); *m* 24 Oct 1946, Mary Ross, MBE (Sheriff of Canterbury 1971), da of Dr J Hardwicke (d 1940), of Woolpit, Suffolk; 1 s (Peter b 1950), 2 da (Jane (Mrs Bird) b 1948, Polly (Mrs Dangerfield) b 1950); *Career* enlisted Buffs 1939; Sherwood Foresters: cmmnd 1940, Adj 2/5 Bn 1941, serv N Africa and Italy 1942-44, (despatches 1943), Maj DAAG Cyprus 1945-46; slr 1937; asst slr: Royal Borough of Kensington 1937-46, Nottingham 1946-48; sr lectr Oxford Univ 1948-65, fell Nuffield Coll 1950-56 (bursar 1957-65), prof of govt Univ of Kent at Canterbury 1965-77; city cncllr Oxford 1950-65, parish cncllr Cumnor 1950-56; pres Kent: Assoc of Parish Cncls 1976-81, Fedn of Amenity Socs 1976-81; chm Canterbury Soc 1972-75; pres: the Kent Soc 1985-88, The Stour Valley Soc 1982-; chm Nat Assoc of Parish Cncls 1964-70; chm Cmmn on Elections: Sierra Leone 1954, Mauritius 1955-60; memb: Roberts Ctee on Public Libraries 1957-59, Mallaby Ctee on Staffing in Local Govt 1964-67, Royal Cmmn on Elections in Fiji 1975, Local Govt Cmmn for Eng 1965-66; hon fell Inst of Local Govt Studies Birmingham Univ 1973; *Publications*: The English Local Government Franchise (1952), English Local Government in the 19th and 20th Centuries (1977), History of Local Government in the 20th Century (with P G Richards, 1978), The Unreformed Local Government System (1979), Parish Affairs (the Government of Kent under George III) (1986); *Recreations* walking; *Clubs* Nat Lib; *Style*— Prof Bryan Keith-Lucas, CBE; 7 Church St, WYE, Ashford, Kent TN25 5BN (☎ 0233 812 621)

KEITH-MURRAY, Maj Peter; s of late David Keith-Murray, and hp of kinsman, Sir Patrick Murray of Ochtertyre, 12 Bt; *b* 12 June 1935; *m* 1960, Judith Anne, da of late William Andrew Tinsley; 1 s, 1 da; *Style*— Maj P Keith-Murray

KELBIE, Sheriff David; s of Robert Kelbie, of Plymouth, and Monica Eileen Pearn; *b* 28 Feb 1945; *Educ* Inverurie Acad, Aberdeen Univ (LLB); *m* 1966, Helen Mary, da of William Ross Smith, of Aberdeen; 1 s (Alasdair David b 1975), 1 da (Catriona Helen b 1972); *Career* passed advocate 1968; Sheriff: North Strathclyde at Dumbarton 1979-86, Grampian, Highland and Islands, Aberdeen, Stonehaven 1986-; *Recreations* sailing, hill walking; *Style*— Sheriff David Kelbie; 38 Earlspark Drive, Bieldside, Aberdeen (☎ 0224 868237); Aberdeen Sheriff Ct (☎ 0224 572780)

KELBURN, Viscount of; David Michael Douglas Boyle; s and h of 10 Earl of Glasgow; *b* 15 Oct 1978; *Style*— Viscount of Kelburn

KELLAND, John William; LVO (1977), QPM (1975); s of William John Kelland (d 1976), of Devon, and Violet Ethel, *née* Olsen (d 1983); *b* 18 August 1929; *Educ* Sutton HS, Oxford Sch, Plymouth Poly; *m* 1, 14 May 1963, Brenda Nancy (d 1985), da of Edward Foulsham (d 1948), of London; 2 s (Michael John b 1950, Andrew b 1953): m 2, 17 May 1986, Frances Elizabeth, da of Thomas Byrne (d 1953), of Ireland; 1 step da (Jean Margaret McDonald b 1963); *Career* Nat Serv RAF Pilot Offr 1947-49; inspr Plymouth City Police 1950-67, supt Devon and Cornwall Constabulary 1968-72 Sr Cmd Course Police Staff Coll 1972, asst chief constable Cumbria Constabulary 1972-74, cmmr Royal Fiji Police 1975-78, dir sr cmd trg Police Staff Coll UK 1978-80, ret; fndr Mgmnt Consultancy 1981; 1981-85: chm Civil Serv Selection Bds, sr conslt Royal Isnt of Public Admin, sr lectr Business Studies Cornwall Coll of Higher Educn, facilitator Interpersonal Skills Seminar; overseas police advsr and inspr gen of Dependent Territories Police FCO 1985-; FBIM 1972; *Recreations* sport, wild life, travel, choral singing; *Clubs* Royal Overseas, Civil Serv; *Style*— John Kelland, Esq, LVO, QPM; Foreign and Commonwealth Office, Room 89C, Old Admiralty Building, Whitehall (☎ 01 210 6330)

KELLAR, David Crawford; s of Prof Robert James Kellar (d 1980), of Edinburgh, and Gertrude Crawford, *née* Aitken (d 1980); *b* 30 Mar 1932; *Educ* Rugby, Edinburgh Univ (MA, LLB); *m* 25 June 1960, Agnes Gilchrist, da of Leslie James Hastie, of Dumfries; 1 s (Ewen b 1962), 1 da (Gail b 1966); *Career* slr, Notary Public estate agent; sec Faculty of Procurators of Dumfriesshire 1968-88, pres Scottish Law Agents Soc 1984-86; *Recreations* photography, cookery, jazz piano; *Clubs* New (Edinburgh); *Style*— David Kellar, Esq; Woodlea, Shawhead, Dumfries (☎ 0387 73 324); 5 Sheffield Terr, London W8; 135 Irish St, Dumfries DG1 2NT (☎ 0387 55351, fax, 0387 57306)

KELLAS, Arthur Roy Handasyde; CMG (1963); s of Henry Kellas (d 1923), of Aberdeen, and Mary, *née* Brown (d 1956); *b* 6 May 1915; *Educ* Aberdeen GS, Univ of Aberdeen (MA), Balliol Coll Oxford (BA), Ecole des Sciences Politiques Paris; *m* 27 Aug 1952, (Katharine) Bridget, da of Sir John Le Rougetel, KCMG, MC (d 1975), of Alton, Hants; 2 s (Ian b 1955, Roger b 1958), 1 da (Miranda b 1953); *Career* WWII 2 Lt 7 Bn Border Regt 1939-40 (10 Ind Company 1940), Lt 1 Bn Parachute Regt 1941-43, Capt SOE 1943-44; Dip Serv; third sec 1939, third sec Tehran Embassy 1944-47; first sec: Helsinki Legation 1949-51, Cairo Embassy 1951-52, Baghdad Embassy 1954-58; cnsllr: Tehran Embassy 1958-62, Tel Aviv Embassy 1964-65; ambass: Kathmandu 1966-70, Aden 1970-72; high cmmr Tanzania 1973-75; FRGS 1960; Pahlavi Order (Lion and Sun) Iran 1960; *Clubs* Utd Oxford and Cambridge Univ; *Style*— Arthur Kellas, Esq, CMG; Inverockle, Achateny, Acharacle, Argyll, Scotland (☎ 097 23265); 59 Cockburn St, Edinburgh (☎ 031 2262398)

KELLAWAY, Richard James; s of Francis Percival Hamley Kellaway (d 1979), of Reading, and Mildred Alice, *née* Neal; *b* 30 May 1945; *Educ* Presentation Coll Reading, Pembroke Coll Cambridge (MA); *m* 18 Oct 1970, Marie-Louise Anne, da of Vincent Michael Franklin (d 1955), of Beckenham; 2 s (Nicholas Franklin b 7 March 1975, Christopher Michael b 4 Aug 1984), 1 da (Antonia Helen b 4 Oct 1972); *Career* commercial mangr Paktank Storage Co Ltd 1968-73, dir Tankfreight Ltd Co 1973-77; md: Felixstowe Tank Devpt Ltd 1975-77, Unitank Storage (div of Tate & Lyle plc) 1979-(joined 1977); chm Tees Storage Co Ltd; dir: Unitank Terminal Serv (USA), Fima-Unitank (Malaysia), Wymondham Oil Storage Co Ltd, Unitank Pencol Ltd; cncllr London Borough of Bromley 1971-74, Parly candidate (C) Bristol South 1974; FInstPet; *Recreations* music, golf; *Clubs* Carlton, Wig and Pen, Winter Hill GC; *Style*— Richard Kellaway, Esq; Somerley, Startins Lane, Cookham Dean, Berks SL6 9TS (☎ 06284 2605); Unitank Storage Co, Nicholson House, High St, Maidenhead, Berks SL6 1LQ (☎ 0628 771 242, fax 0628 771 678, telex 847862)

KELLEHER, Brig Dame Joan Evelyn; DBE (1965); da of Kenneth George Henderson; *b* 24 Dec 1915; *Educ* privately; *m* 1970, Brig M F H Kelleher, OBE, MC, late RAMC; *Career* joined ATS 1941, cmmnd 1941, WRAC 1949, dir Women's Royal Army Corps 1964-67; hon ADC to HM The Queen 1964-67; *Recreations* golf, gardening; *Style*— Brig Dame Joan Kelleher, DBE; c/o Midland Bank, 123 Chancery Lane, London WC2A 1QH

KELLER, Hon Mrs (Susan Henriette); da of Baron Schon (Life Peer); *b* 23 Oct 1941; *Educ* Badminton Sch Bristol, Ecole Hoteliere Switzerland; *m* 1964, Richard Henry Keller, s of Arthur Keller; 2 s (Philip Henry b 1965, Nicholas Frank b 1970), 1 da (Annabel Jane b 1967); *Career* aerobics teacher; *Recreations* aerobics, tennis, antiques; *Clubs* Annabel's; *Style*— The Hon Mrs Keller; Hillmorton, Wills Grove, Mill Hill Village, London NW7 (☎ 01 959 4442)

KELLETT, Anthony; s of Albert Kellett (d 1980), and Lilian, *née* Holroyd; *b* 24 Sept 1937; *Educ* Batley GS, Leeds Sch of Architecture (Dip Arch); *m* 4 Sept 1964 (m dis 1984); 2 s (Anthony John b 1967, Martin James b 1970); *Career* CA; ptnr: Davidson Marsh & Co 1971-79, Kellett & Robinson 1980-; pres IOM Soc of Architects and Surveyors; FFAS, ACIArb, RIBA; *Recreations* painting; *Clubs* Ellan Vannin, Rotary of Rushen and Western Mann; *Style*— Anthony Kellett, Esq; 32 Birch Hill Ave, Onchan,

Douglas, IOM (☎ 0624 72255); Sydney Mount, Bucks Rd, Douglas, IOM (☎ 0624 28141)

KELLETT, Audrey, Lady Kellett; Audrey Margaret; *née* Phillips; *m* 1938, Sir Stanley Everard Kellett, 6 Bt (d 1983); 1 s (Sir Stanley, 7 Bt, *qv*), 1 da; *Style—* Audrey, Lady Kellett; 33 Caroma Avenue, Kyeemagh, NSW 2216, Australia

KELLETT, Sir Brian Smith; s of Harold Lamb Kellett (d 1935) and Amy Elizabeth, *née* Smith (d 1984); *b* 8 May 1922; *Educ* Manchester GS, Trinity Coll Cambridge; *m* 1947, Janet Lesly Street; 3 da; *Career* civil servant with Admty, Miny of Tport 1942-48, Sir Robert Watson-Watt & Partners 1948-49, Pilkington Bros 1949-55; former chm Br Aluminium Co; chm: Tube Investments (TI Gp) 1976-84 (md 1968-82), Port of London Authy 1985-; dir: Unigate 1974-, Nat Westminster Bank 1981-, Lombard North Central 1985-, Investmt Mgmnt Regulatory Orgn 1987-; govr: Imperial Coll 1979-, London Business Sch 1976-84; kt 1979; *Style—* Sir Brian Kellett; The Old Malt House, Deddington, Oxford OX5 4TG

KELLETT, Ida, Lady; Ida Mary Grace Weaver; *m* 7 May 1952, Sir Henry de Castres Kellett, 5 Bt (d 1966); *Style—* Ida, Lady Kellett

KELLETT, Peter; s of Milton Hampden Kellett (d 1966), and Margaret Mary, *née* Hart; *b* 29 August 1927; *Educ* Cotton Coll N Staffs, St Andrews Univ (BSc); *m* 5 Sept 1949, Jean Mcintosh, da of Robert Fulcar Browning (d 1936); 2 s (Michael b 1954, David b 1965), 2 da Jane b 1950, Sarah b 1962); *Career* head of computing and res (later gen mangr) Elliott Automation Computers Ltd 1967, fndr Lamerholm Ltd 1975; currently chm and md: Lamerholm Fleming Ltd, Lamerholm Ltd, Fleming Instruments Ltd; FIEE, CEng; *Recreations* hill walking, woodworking, eighteenth and nineteenth century literature; *Style—* Peter Kellett, Esq; Fife House, Graveley, Herts (☎ 0438 352175); Lamerholm Fleming Ltd, Caxton Way, Stevenage, Herts SG1 2DE (☎ 0438 728844, fax 0438 742326, telex 82385)

KELLETT, Sir Stanley Charles; 7 Bt (UK 1801), of Lota, Cork; s of Sir Stanley Everard Kellett, 6 Bt (d 1983), and Audrey Margaret, *née* Phillips; *b* 5 Mar 1940; *m* 1, 1962 (m dis 1968), Lorraine May, da of F Winspear; m 2, 1968, Margaret Ann, da of James W Bofinger; m 3, 1982, Catherine Lorna, da of W J C Or; 1 da (Leah Catherine Elizabeth, b 1983); *Style—* Sir Stanley Kellett, Bt; 58 Glad Gunson Drive, Eleebana, NSW Australia

KELLETT-BOWMAN, Edward Thomas; JP (Middx 1966); s of Reginald Edward Bowman (d 1934), and Mabel Bowman; *b* 25 Feb 1931; *Educ* Reed's Sch, Slough Coll of Technology (DMS), Cranfield Inst of Technology (MBA); *m* 1, 1960, Margaret Blakemore (d 1970); 3 s, 1 da; m 2, 1971, (Mary) Elaine Kellett (Dame Elaine Kellett-Bowman, MP, *qv*); *Career* MEP (EDG): Lancs E 1979-84; Hants Central 1988-; FBIM; *Recreations* shooting, tennis, swimming; *Style—* Edward Kellett-Bowman, Esq, JP; 28 Fairholme Rd, London W14 9JX

KELLETT-BOWMAN, Dame (Mary) Elaine; *née* Kay; DBE (1989), MP (C) Lancaster 1970-; da of late Walter Kay; *b* 8 July 1924; *Educ* Queen Mary's Sch Lytham, The Mount Sch York, St Anne's Coll Oxford; *m* 1, 1945, Charles Norman Kellett (d 1959); 3 s, 1 da; m 2, 1971, Edward Thomas Kellett-Bowman, MEP, JP, *qv*; 3 step s, 1 step da; *Career* farmer; welfare worker London and Liverpool; barr Middle Temple 1964; contested (C): Nelson and Colne 1955, S W Norfolk 1959 and 1959 by-election, Buckingham 1964 and 1966; memb Press Cncl 1964-68; alderman Camden Boro 1968-74, chm Welfare Ctee 1969; MEP (EDG) Cumbria 1979-84; *Clubs* English Speaking Union; *Style—* Dame Elaine Kellett-Bowman, DBE, MP; Slyne Grange, Slyne, nr Lancaster LA2 6AU

KELLEY, Malcolm Percy; s of Percy William Alfred Kelley (d 1978), and Gladys Beatrice Kelley (d 1986); *b* 21 July 1931; *Educ* Thames Valley GS; *m* 24 Aug 1957, Pamela, da of John Edward Conway (d 1968); *Career* sales dir: Penguin Books Ltd 1970-72, Ladybird Books Ltd 1972-73; md Ladybird Books Ltd 1973-; dir Longman Group 1981-; *Recreations* rugby football, reading, cooking, jogging; *Clubs* Rosslyn Park and Leicester RFC; *Style—* Malcolm Kelley, Esq; 50 Outwoods Rd, Loughborough, Leics LE11 3LY; Ladybird Books Ltd, Beeches Road, Loughborough, Leics (telex 341347, fax 234672)

KELLOCK, His Hon Judge Thomas Oscar; QC (1965); s of Thomas Herbert Kellock, (d 1922), and Margaret Brooke (d 1972); *b* 4 July 1923; *Educ* Rugby, Clare Coll Cambridge (BA); *m* 18 March 1967, Jane Ursula, da of Arthur George Symonds (d 1944), of Dorset; *Career* RNVR (special branch) 1944-46; barr Inner Temple 1949, bencher 1973; dir Legal Div Cwlth Secretariat 1969-72, circuit judge 1976-; *Recreations* travelling; *Clubs* Reform; *Style—* His Hon Judge T O Kellock, QC; 8 Huntingdon Drive, The Park, Nottingham NG7 1BW (☎ 0602 418304); 8 Kings Bench Walk, Inner Temple, London EC4Y 7DU

KELLY, Bernard Noel; s of Sir David Kelly, GCMG, MC (d 1959), of Tara House, Co Wexford, and Comtesse de Vaux; *b* 23 April 1930; *Educ* Downside; *m* 11 July 1952, Lady Mirabel Magdalene Fitzalan Howard, sister of 17 Duke of Norfolk *qv*; 7 s, 1 da; *Career* Capt 8 Queen's Royal Irish Hussars incl reserves 1948-60; slr 1956; ptnr Simmons and Simmons 1958-62; banker; dir S G Warburg & Co 1963-76, Barnes Gp Inc (USA) 1975-, Investmt AB Ostermalm (Sweden) 1976-, Lazard Bros and Co Ltd 1980- (vice-chm and md 1981-85); chm: First Equity Servs Ltd 1987-, Lazard Bros & Co (Guernsey) Ltd 1987-, Lazard Bros & Co (Jersey) Ltd 1987-; *Clubs* Athenaeum, Brooks's, Kildare & University (Dublin); *Style—* Bernard Kelly, Esq; 21 Moorfieelds, London EC2 (☎ 01 588 2721)

KELLY, Air Vice-Marshal (Herbert) Brian; CB (1983), LVO (1960); s of Surg Capt James Cecil Kelly, DSC (d 1961), of Clonmore, Charing, Kent, and Meta Matheson, *née* Fraser (d 1971); *b* 12 August 1921; *Educ* Epsom Coll, St Thomas's Hosp London Univ (MB, BS 1943, MRCP (Lond) 1945, MD 1948, FRCP 1968); *Career* registered med practitioner; med offr RNVR 1945-48; conslt in med RAF Hosps: Aden, Ely, Nocton Hall, Singapore, Cyprus, Germany; med branch RAF 1953-83, sr conslt to RAF 1979-83 (formerly conslt advsr in med), ret; conslt medical advsr to PPP Medical Centre, conslt advsr to CAA; QHS 1978-83; Liveryman Worshipful Soc of Apothecaries, Freeman City of London; DCH 1966, QHS 1978-83, MFOM 1982, FRSM 1948, Fell Med Soc of London 1959; *Recreations* choral singing, DIY; *Clubs* RAF; *Style—* Air Vice-Marshal Brian Kelly, CB, LVO; 32 Chiswick Quay, Hartington Rd, London W4 3UR (☎ 01 995 5042)

KELLY, Brian Owen; s of George Alfred Kelly (d 1984), and Delia, *née* Cafferkey (d 1984); *b* 9 Jan 1943; *Educ* Presentation Coll Reading, Farnborough Coll of Technol; *m* 17 Oct 1970, (Ann) Christie, da of Fred Payne (d 1985); *Career* scientific asst Servs Experimental Res Laboratory 1959-64, experimental offr Admty Compass Observatory 1964-70, sr engr Bendix Aerospace Michigan USA 1970-73, vice pres Utd Detector Technol LA 1973-78, md Centronic Optical Systems Ltd, Croydon 1985- (gen mangr 1978-85); memb cncl Defense Manufacturers Assoc; govr: Rowdown HS Croydon, Addington HS Croydon; MIERE 1975, M Inst P 1979, FBIM 1980, C Phys; *Recreations* golf, bridge, chess; *Style—* Brian Kelly, Esq; Green Roops, Dower House Crescent, Tunbridge Wells, Kent TN4 0TT; Centronic House, King Henry's Drive, Croydon CR9 0BG (☎ 0689 42 121, fax 0489 43 053, telex 876 474 CENTRO G)

KELLY, Charles Henry; CBE (1986), QPM (1978, DL (Staffs 1979)); s of Charles Henry Kelly (d 1984), and Phoebe Jane Kelly (d 1948); *b* 15 July 1930; *Educ* Douglas HS for Boys IOM, London Univ (LLB); *m* 1952, Doris; 1 s (Kevin), 1 da (Lynne); *Career* asst chief constable Essex 1972-76, dep chief constable Staffordshire 1976-77, chief constable Staffordshire 1977-; CStJ 1983; *Recreations* music, cricket, reading; *Clubs* Special Forces; *Style—* Charles Kelly, Esq, CBE, QPM, DL; Baswich House, Cannock Rd, Stafford ST17 0QG (☎ 0785 57717)

KELLY, Christopher Aliaga; s of Ambrose Aliaga Kelly (d 1953); *b* 28 Sept 1920; *Educ* St Mary's Coll Dublin; *m* 1948, Cynthia Averill, da of Lt-Col the Hon Thomas George Breadalbane Morgan-Grenville DSO, OBE (d 1965); 1 s, 1 da; *Career* jt md: Cookson Group; dir: Allied Irish Banks Ltd; chm: Goodlass Wall Ltd, Alexander Fergusson Ltd, dir: Fry's Diecastings, Goodlass Nerolac Paints India, Valentine Varnish & Lacquer; past pres Confedn of Irish Industry; *Clubs* Stephens Green (Dublin); *Style—* Christopher Kelly, Esq; 10 Rawlings St, London SW3 (☎ 01 584 1155)

KELLY, David; s of Bernard Myrddin Kelly (d 1977), and Mabel Elizabeth, *née* Beard; *b* 29 Oct 1936; *Educ* Stonyhurst Coll, Lincoln Coll Oxford (MA); *Career* Queen's Own Lancs Regt 1955-57 (served Roy W Africa Frontier Force 1957); TA E Lancs Regt; barr 1962, ICI 1962-67, Amalgamated Metal Corpn and Metal Corpn 1967-72, Woodan-Duckham Gp 1972-74, B Elliott plc 1974-84, The Octluy Gp (Hldgs) 1985-; *Recreations* tennis, golf, skiing; *Clubs* Utd Oxford & Cambridge; *Style—* David Kelly, Esq; 19 Kingslawn Close, Howards Lane, Putney, London SW15 6QJ (☎ 01 789 3344); Brettenham House, Lancaster Place, London WC2E 7EZ (☎ 01 836 2466, fax 01 836 5938)

KELLY, (Richard) Denis Lucien; MC (1944); s of Capt Richard Cecil Kelly, OBE (d 1959), and Joan Maisie, *née* Collings (d 1947); *b* 31 Jan 1916; *Educ* Marlborough, Balliol Coll Oxford (BA); *m* 1, 2 Oct 1945 (m dis 1954), Anne Marie Stuart, da of James Stuart Anderson (d 1940), of Hinton House, Christchurch; 1 da (Victoria Marie Teresa b 5 Dec 1951); m 2, 1958, Marjorie Ashley Cooper (d 1960); *Career* 2 Lt Surrey & Sussex Yeo TA 1938, Capt Indian Mountain Artillery 1942, Maj 1944, served NW Frontier and two Burma Campaigns, cmd 25 Indian Mountain Artillery Batt during final campaign; barr Middle Temple 1942, dep chm of QS, rec of the Crown Ct 1972-80, emeritius bencher of the Middle Temple 1976 (emeritus 1987), lit asst Sir Winston Churchill 1947-57; *Books* The Second World War (1959), The Ironside Diaries 1937-40 (with Col R MacLeod, DSO, MC, 1962); *Clubs* Garrick; *Style—* Denis Kelly, Esq, MC; 3 Temple Gardens, Temple, London EC4Y 9AU (☎ 01 353 4949); Lamb Building, Temple, London EC4Y 7AS (☎ 01 353 6701)

KELLY, Dominic Noel David Miles Charles; s of Bernard Noel Kelly, *qv*, and Lady Mirabel Magdalene Fitzalan Howard, sis of 17 Duke of Norfolk; *b* 24 June 1953; *Educ* Worth Abbey; *m* 3 Oct 1982, Miranda Rita, da of Lance Macklin; 3 da (Sabine b 21 April 1983, Alice b 9 March 1985, Celina b 24 Oct 1987); *Career* cmmnd Queen's Royal Irish Hussars 1971, resigned 1977 ; *Recreations* tennis; *Clubs* Pratt's, Hurlingham; *Style—* Dominic Kelly, Esq; 17/19 Shellwood Road, London SW11 5BJ (☎ 01 228 1109); 50 Sullivan Road, London SW6 3DX (☎ 01 731 1303, fax 01 731 5644, car tel 0836 638893 or 212874)

KELLY, (Robert Henry) Graham; s of Thomas John Kelly (d 1960), and Emmie, *née* Greenlees (d 1982); *b* 23 Dec 1945; *Educ* Baines GS Lancs; *m* 18 July 1970, Elizabeth Anne, *née* Wilkinson; 1 s (Stephen b 1974), 1 da (Alison b 1972); *Career* Barclays Bank 1964-68, sec the Football League 1979-88, chief exec The FA 1989-; FCIS 1973; *Style—* Graham Kelly, Esq; 16 Lancaster Gate, London W2 3LW (☎ 01 262 4542)

KELLY, John Anthony Brian; RD (1974); s of Lt Cdr Brian James Parmenter Kelly, DSC, of Bangor Co Down, N Ireland, and Ethne Mary, *née* Ryan (d 1977); *b* 21 August 1941; *Educ* Bangor GS N Ireland, Fort Augustus Abbey Sch Scotland, Queen's Univ Belfast (LLB); *m* 28 March 1973, Denise Anne, da of Richard James Circuit, of St Albans; 2 s (Christopher b 1977, Nicholas b 1982), 2 da (Katrina b 1973, Joanna b 1975); *Career* Lt Cdr RNR 1959-84; Price Waterhouse and Co 1963-68 (qualified 1967), exec Old Broad St Securities 1968-70, exec and assoc Laurie Milbank and Co 1970-78, dir Brown Shipley and Co Ltd 1982- (mangr 1978), non exec dir Consult plc 1986, non exec dir TAG Hldgs Ltd 1988; memb PCC St Teresa's Church Beaconsfield 1983-, memb Cncl of Co operation Ireland; Liveryman Worshipful Co of Founders; FICA; *Recreations* walking, reading, poetry, tennis; *Clubs* The Naval, Royal Ulster Yacht; *Style—* John Kelly, Esq, RD; Cherrytrees, Penn Rd, Beaconsfield, Bucks HP9 2LW; c/o Brown Shipley & Co Ltd, Founders Court, Lothburg, London EC2R 7HE (☎ 01 606 9833, fax 01 796 4875)

KELLY, Rt Hon Sir John William (Basil); PC (1984); s of Thomas William Kelly (d 1955), of NI, and Emily Frances, *née* Donaldson (d 1966); *b* 10 May 1920; *Educ* Methodist Coll Belfast, Trinity Coll Dublin (BA, LLB) ; *m* 1957, Pamela, da of Thomas Colmer Colthurst (d 1960), of Aldershot; *Career* barr NI 1944-; barr Middle Temple 1970, MP NI 1964-72, attorney gen NI 1968-72, judge of High Ct NI 1973-85, Lord Justice of Appeal Supreme Ct of Judicature NI 1984-; kt 1984; *Recreations* golf, travel, music; *Style—* Rt Hon Sir Basil Kelly, PC; Royal Courts of Justice, Belfast BT1 3JF

KELLY, Laurence Charles Kevin; s of Sir David Kelly, GCMG, MC (d 1959); *b* 11 April 1933; *Educ* Downside, New Coll Oxford (MA); *m* 1963, Linda, da of Maj R G McNair Scott, and Hon Mrs Scott, of Huish House, Old Basing, Hants; 1 s, 2 da; *Career* Lt Life Gds 1949-52; served Foreign Off 1955-56, Guest Keen and Nettlefolds 1956-72, dir GKN Int Trading 1972, dir Helical Bar 1972- (chm 1984-), chm Queenborough Steel Co 1980-; vice-chm British Steel Consumers' Cncl 1974- (resigned 1985); memb: bd N Ireland Devpt Agency 1972-78, Monopolies and Mergers Cmmn 1982-; Dir: KAE Ltd 1985-, Morganite Int Ltd 1984-; sr assoc memb St Antony's Coll Oxford 1985; FRGS; *Books* Lermontov: Tragedy in the Caucasus (1978), St Petersburg (1981), Moscow (1983); *Recreations* tennis, swimming, shooting; *Clubs* Brooks's, Turf, Beefsteak, University (Dublin); *Style—* Laurence Kelly, Esq; 44 Ladbroke Grove, London W11 (☎ 01 727 4663)

KELLY, Lady; (Renée) Marie-Noële Ghislaine; *née* de Jourda de Vaux; da of

Comte de Jourda de Vaux, and Baronne Snoy; *b* 25 Dec 1901; *Educ* abroad; *m* 1929, as his 2 w, Sir David Kelly, GCMG, MC (d 1959; a Knight of Malta and ambassador successively to Berne, Argentina, Turkey (USSR); 2 s; *Career* writer: numerous articles in: Times, Connoisseur, Country Life; Friend of St John and St Elizabeth's Hosp; govr St Clare's Coll Oxford; vice-pres: Anglo-Turkish Assoc, Anglo-Belgian Cncl; Dame of Hon and Devotion SMO Malta; *Books* Turkish Delights (1951), Mirror to Russia (1952), Picture Book of Russia (1952), This Delicious Land Portugal, Dawn to Dusk (1956); *Recreations* swimming, walking; *Style*— Lady Kelly; 27 Carlyle Sq, London SW3 (☎ 01 352 9186)

KELLY, Matthias John; s of Ambrose Kelly, of Dungannon, Co Tyrone, N Ireland, and Anne, *née* McKiernan (d 1973); *b* 21 April 1954; *Educ* St Patrick's Secdy and St Patrick's Acad Dungannon Co Tyrone, Trinity Coll Dublin (BA, LLB), Cncl Legal Educn London; *m* 5 May 1979, Helen Ann, da of Peter Joseph Holmes (d 1974), of Longford, Ireland; 1 s (Peter b 1986), 1 da (Anne b 1987); *Career* called to the Bar: Gray's Inn 1979, N Ireland 1983, Republic of Ireland 1983; admitted attorney: New York 1986, USA Federal Bar 1987; hon life memb Br Soc of Criminology 1986; FLBA 1981, CLBA 1987, memb Soc of Labour Lawyers 1979; *Recreations* squash, walking, cylcing, reading; *Style*— Matthias Kelly, Esq; 33 Langbourne Ave, Highgate, London N6 6PS (☎ 01 348 0208); 14 Gray's Inn Sq, Gray's Inn, London WC1R 5JB (☎ 01 242 0858, fax 01 242 5434)

KELLY, Dr Michael; CBE (1983), JP ((Glasgow 1973), DL (1983)); s of David Kelly (d 1972); *b* 1 Nov 1940; *Educ* Univ of Strathclyde (BSc, PhD); *m* 1965, Zita, da of Hugh Harkins; 3 children; *Career* economics lectr Strathclyde Univ 1967-84; Lord Provost of Glasgow (and *ex officio* Lord-Lieut) 1980-, Lord Rector Univ of Glasgow 1984-87, chm Royal Scottish Soc for Prevention of Cruelty to Children 1987-; pres Inst of Mktg (Strathclyde Branch) 1986- (fell 1989), memb Scottish ABSA 1986-; hon LLB Glasgow Univ 1983; OStJ 1984; *Recreations* football, photography, philately, phillumeny (ie collecting match books & boxes); *Style*— Dr Michael Kelly, CBE, JP; 50 Aytoun Rd, Glasgow G41;

KELLY, Philip John; s of William Kelly (d 1979), of Crosby, Merseyside, and Mary Winifred, *née* Ellison; *b* 18 Sept 1946; *Educ* St Mary's Coll Crosby, Leeds Univ (BA); *m* 12 Nov 1988, Dorothy Margaret Jones; 2 s (Matthew b 1980, Robert b 1986); *Career* freelance jounalist and PR conslt 1970-87; co-fndr: Leveller 1976, State Research 1977; ed Tribune 1987-; chm London Freelance Branch NUJ 1983; cncllr (Lab) London Borough of Islington 1984-86; *Recreations* railways, model railways; *Clubs* Red Rose; *Style*— Philip Kelly, Esq; 58 Windsor Rd, London N7 6JL; Tribune, 308 Grays Inn Rd, London WC1X 8DY (☎ 01 278 0911)

KELLY, Rosaline; da of Laurence Kelly (d 1951), of Drogheda, and Ellen, *née* Fogarty (d 1967); *b* 27 Nov 1922; *Educ* St Louis Convent Carrickmacross Co Monaghan, Nat Univ of Ireland; *Career* publishing conslt; visiting lectr in journalism London Coll of Printing 1981-85; pres (only woman so far) Nat Union of Journalists 1975-77 (memb of Honour 1979); memb Press Cncl 1977-80 (only woman ever to represent Press on cncl); *Style*— Ms Rosaline Kelly; c/o Robert Fleming, Bankers, Hexagon House, 28 Western Rd, Romford RM1 3LB

KELSEY, Alan Howard Mitchell; s of Emanuel Kelsey (d 1985), of London, and Dorothy Mitchell, *née* Smith; *b* 10 April 1949; *Educ* Kings Coll Sch Wimbledon, Oriel Coll Oxford (BA, MA); *m* 12 March 1977, Sarah D'Oyly, da of Robin Carlyle Sayer, of Little Walsingham, Norfolk; 2 s (Guy b 21 Feb 1980, William b 29 July 1980), 1 da (Keziah b 19 Jan 1978); *Career* Kitcat & Aitken: t'port investmt analyst 1975-, head of res 1987-; dir RBC Dominion Securities Int 1988-; chm local cons Assoc 1985-88; memb cncl of The Society of Investmt Analysts 1986-88; memb Int Stock Exchange; *Recreations* rowing; *Clubs* Brooks's; *Style*— Alan Kelsey, Esq; The Priory, Little Waldingfield, Suffolk C010 0SW; Flat 90, Marlborough, Walton St, London SW3 (☎ 01 584 4238); Kitcat & Aitken, 6th Floor, RBC Centre, 71 Queen Victoria St, London EC4V 4DE (☎ 01 489 1966, fax 01 329 6150, telex 888297)

KELSEY, Maj-Gen John; CBE (1968); s of Benjamin Richard Kelsey and Daisy, *née* Powell; *b* 1 Nov 1920; *Educ* Royal Masonic Sch, Emmanuel Coll Cantab, Royal Mill Coll of Sci (BSc), UCL (BSc); *m* 1, 1944, Phyllis Margaret, da of Henry Smith, of Chingford; 1 s, 1 da; *Career* RE 1940 N Africa and Europe, mil survey units in UK, North Africa, West Indies and Germany; snr instr Geodsy Sch of military survey 1951-53; affr Ordnance Survey 1954-59; dir of Field Survey Ordnance Survey 1969-72, dir mil survey MOD 1972-77, sec Western Euro Sub Cmmn of Int Cmmn for Artificial Satellites 1967-71 (pres 1971-75); chm: Working Party Satellite Geodsy 1975-86, Survey and Mapping Conference Steering Gp 1981-87; non exec dir Wild Heerburg UK Ltd, cnslt to Wild Heerburg Ltd and Ernst Leitz Wetzlar GmbH, RGS, Royal Inst of chartered surveyors; *Style*— Maj-Gen John Kelsey, CBE

KELSEY, Julian George; CB (1982); s of William Kelsey (d 1953), of Marylebone, and Charlotte Ann, *née* Paull (d 1963); *b* 28 August 1922; *Educ* Brockenhurst GS; *m* 1944, Joan, da of Fred Singerton (d 1959), of Midsomer Norton; 1 da (Anne); *Career* served WW II RAC Capt, SOE (Europe) Force 136 and No 11 Searcher Party Team SE Asia; entered Civil Service 1939, joined Miny of Agric, Fisheries and Food 1951, dir of Establishments 1971-76, Fisheries sec 1976-80, dep sec 1980-82; conslt Glengrove Gp 1983-; *Clubs* Special Forces; *Style*— Julian Kelsey, Esq, CB; Shaston House, St James, Shaftesbury, Dorset SP7 8HL (☎ 0747 51147)

KELSEY, Michael Edward; TD (1969), ADC (1987); s of W Cdr George Thomas Kelsey OBE, RAFVR (d 1980); *b* 16 April 1935; *Educ* Berkhamsted Sch, King's Coll London (BSc); *m* 1961, Anthea Mabel, da of Dr Arthur Sproul McFarlane (d 1978); 2 s, 1 da; *Career* Col TA; chartered eng dir and chief exec Engineering Employers Wester Assoc, chm and chief exec: Crouse Hinds (UK) Ltd, Arrow-Hart (Europe) Ltd, Cablok Co Ltd 1979-86; md Sealed Motor Construction Co 1976-79; *Recreations* skiing, sailing, gardening; *Clubs* Royal Dart Yacht, Royal Western Yacht Club of England; *Style*— Michael Kelsey, Esq, TD, ADC; The Little Field, Green Lane, Tavistock, Devon

KELTON, Michael John St Goar; s of Gerald St Goar Kelton (d 1972), and Beatrice Millicent, da of J B Body, md S Pearson & Co (responsible for many engrg devpts in Mexico *ca* 1900, inc draining of Valley of Mixico, construction of Vera Cruz habour and founding Mexican Eagle Oil Co); *b* 25 Mar 1933; *Educ* Stowe, Queens' Coll Camb (MA); *m* 19 June 1958, Joanna Elzabeth, da of Sir (William) John Peel, MP (*C*) Leicester SE 1957-74; 3 s (Jeremy b 1960, Capt R Scots Drag Gds, Andrew b 1961, Simon b 1966); *Career* Capt 3 Carabiniers (now R Scots Drag Gds); merchant banker: Lazard Bros 7 Co Ltd 1957-, dir Lazard Securities until 1971; stockbroker: late Scott, Goff and Handcock, and Raphael Zorn 1976-; *Recreations* shooting, fishing, golf; *Clubs* Cavalry and Guards, Flyfishers', Hawkley Common Golf; *Style*— Michael Kelton, Esq; Pipers Well, Churt, Farnham, Surrey GU10 2NT (☎ 042 871 3194); Raphael Zorn, 10 Throgmorton Ave, London EC2 (☎ 01 628 4000)

KEMBALL, Christopher Ross Maguire; MBE (Mil 1973); s of John Patrick Gerard Kemball, of Vila Praia De Ancora, Portugal, and Rachel Lucy, *née* Vernon; *b* 29 Dec 1946; *Educ* Ampleforth, Pembroke Coll Cambridge (BA Hons Law); *m* 3 Feb 1979, Frances Maria, da of Richard Peter Angelo Monico, Flight Lt RAF (d 1945); 1 s (Charles b 1983); *Career* Regular Army Capt (acting Maj) Royal Green Jackets 1968-75; Sultan's Armed Forces, Maj Northern Frontier Regt 1972-73; dir Kleinwort Benson Ltd 1975-86, vice-chm Kleinwort Benson Hldgs Inc 1984-86; md Dillon, Read & Co Inc 1986-, exec md and co-head Dillon, Read Ltd 1987-; *Recreations* opera, swimming, skiing, shooting; *Clubs* Royal Automobile; *Style*— Christopher Kemball, Esq, MBE; Dillon Read Ltd, Devonshire House, Mayfair Place, London W1X 5FH (☎ 01 493 1239)

KEMBALL, Air Vice-Marshal (Richard) John; CBE (1981); s of Richard Charles Kemball (d 1983), of Colchester, and Margaret James, *née* Robson (d 1987); *b* 31 Jan 1939; *Educ* Uppingham; *m* 1962, Valerie Geraldine, da of Maj Albert John Webster, RA, of Sussex; 2 d (Katherine b 1964, Samantha b 1966); *Career* cmmnd RAF 1957, served France, Middle E, USA; cmd No 54 Sqdn, RAF Laarbruch; Cmdt RAF Central Flying School 1983-85; Cdr Br Forces Falkland Islands 1985-86; ACDS (Intelligence) 1987; *Recreations* field sports, cricket, tennis, skiing; *Clubs* RAF; *Style*— Air Vice-Marshal John Kemball, CBE; c/o Midland Bank, 46 Market Hill, Sudbury, Suffolk CO10 6ES

KEMBALL-COOK, Lt-Col Brian Hartley; s of Sir Basil Alfred Kemball-Cook, KCMG, CB (d 1949), and Nancy Annie, *née* Pavitt (d 1959); *b* 12 Dec 1912; *Educ* Shrewsbury Sch, Balliol Coll Oxford (BA, MA); *m* 2 Aug 1947, (Gladys) Marian, da of Robert Charles Reginald Richards, OBE (d 1979); 3 s (David b 1952, Oliver b 1955, Geoffrey b 1955), 1 da (Jessica b 1948); *Career* Intelligence Corps 1940-46; UK Port Security Control 1941-44, Supreme HQ, Allied Expdn Force 1944-45, G2 30 Corpc Germany 1945-46, Regnl intelligence offr and political advsr to Regnl Cmmr Hanover 1946 (despatches 1945); princ Miny of Tport 1946-47, sr classics master Repton 1947-56 (sixth form classics master 1936-40); headmaster: Queen Elizabeth's GS Blackburn 1956-65, Bedford Modern Sch 1965-77; chm Beds Music Festival 1966-77, tutor Workers' Educnl Assoc 1972-77, lectr Womens' Insts 1983-; memb HMC 1956; *Books* ed Shakespeare's Coriolanus (1955), contributed to Education: Threatened Standards 1972, translated into English Hexameters Homer's Odyssey; *Recreations* Mountaineering, Music; *Clubs* Climbers Club; *Style*— Lt-Col Brian Kemball-Cook; 23 Grosvenor Rd, East Grinstead, West Sussex RH19 1HS (☎ 0342 323360)

KEMBER, Anthony Joseph; s of Thomas Kingsley Kember (d 1968), and May Lena, *née* Pryor (d 1972); *b* 1 Nov 1931; *Educ* St Edmund Hall Oxford (MA); *m* 3 Aug 1957, Drusilla Mary, da of Geoffrey Lionel Boyce, of Broad Oak, Cambridge Park, Twickenham, Middx; 1 s (Julian James Kingsley b 18 May 1960), 2 da (Selina May b 28 April 1962, Perdita Jane b 15 Jan 1965); *Career* dep house govr and sec to bd of govrs Westminster Hosp 1961-69, gp sec Hillingdon Gp Hosp Mgmnt Ctee 1969-73, area admin Kensington and Chelsea and Westminster AHA (teaching) 1973-78, currently gen mangr SW Thames RHA; chm Regnl Gen Mangrs 1987; tstee Disabled Living Fndn 1981-; AHSM 1963; *Recreations* royal tennis, lawn tennis, painting, golf; *Clubs* Exiles, Royal Tennis Court Hampton Court Palace; *Style*— Anthony Kember, Esq; 16 Orchard Rise, Richmond Upon Thames, Surrey TW10 5BX (☎ 01 876 5192); SW Thames RHA, 40 Eastbourne Terr, London W2 3QR (☎ 01 262 8011, 01 262 6481)

KEMBERY, John Philip; s of Alec George Kembery, of Keynsham, Somerset; *b* 6 Oct 1939; *Educ* Queen Elizabeth's Hosp Bristol, Univ of Surrey; *m* 1964, Marjorie Carolyn, da of Gilbert James Bowler, of Bridge End House, Much Cowarne, Herefs; 2 s; *Career* ed: Alcan Extrusions 1975-80, Alcan Metal Centres 1980-81; chm: McKechnie Metals (non ferrous metal mfrs) (md 1981-87), PSM Int; dir McKechnie plc 1986-; pres Br Non Ferrous Metals Fedn 1988-; fell Inst of Metals; FID; *Recreations* golf, shooting, good food; *Style*— John Kembery, Esq; 37 Broad Oaks, Solihull, W Midlands (☎ 021 705 3214); McKechnie plc, Leighswood Rd, Aldridge, Walsall, W Midlands WS9 8DS (☎ 0922 743887)

KEMBLE, Cdr (Theodore Patrick) Kenneth; s of Arthur Kenneth Kemble (d 1945), of Runwellhall, Essex, and Celia Arden, *née* Slocock (d 1974); *b* 18 May 1907; *Educ* Lambrook Bracknell, Radley; *m* 1, 1932 (m dis), Dorothy Sadie Nelson (d 1987); 1 da (Shirley Derris Mary b 1934); m 2, 1952, Peggy Fairbairn (d 1972), wid of Hon J V Fairbairn; m 3, 1979, Hélène Charlotte Hill, da of late Grant Richards, wid of Charles Hill, of Bristol (d 1976); *Career* Midshipman 1927, Lt HKNVF 1933 (1 Lt HMS Cornflower), Lt RNVR 1939, Lt Cdr 1941, Cdr 1941, Cdr 1944, ret 1947; slr 1932, special constable Metropolitan Mounted Police; legal advsr: Int Aeradio Ltd 1947-68, Sale Tilney Gp 1952-72; chm Spencer Turner & Boldero Ltd 1960-70, dir various firms; candidate (Cons) North Paddington 1950; *Recreations* racing as owner and permit holder; *Clubs* Whites, Naval; *Style*— Cdr Kenneth Kemble; Clover House, Winson, nr Cirencester, Gloucestershire

KEMMIS, Hon Mrs (Bridget Mary Dean); 2 da of Baron Soper (Life Peer); *b* 17 Dec 1933; *m* 15 Sept 1956, Owen Henry Kemmis, MA, o s of late Hubert Beresford Kemmis; 1 s; *Style*— The Hon Mrs Kemmis

KEMP, Alan Scott; s of Alexander Scott Kemp (d 1968), of Edinburgh, and Christina Margaret, *née* Stocks (d 1965); *b* 2 April 1944; *Educ* George Heriots Sch Edinburgh; *m* 9 Dec 1967, June, da of John Christie (d 1986), of Edinburgh; 2 s (Grame , Martin); *Career* dep mangr The Edinburgh Investmt Trust plc 1974-84, investmt dir Dunedin Fund Mangrs Ltd 1985-; memb Murrayfield/Cramond Rotary Club, dir Edinburgh Sports Club Ltd, MICAS; *Recreations* golf, squash; *Style*— Alan Kemp, Esq; 65 Whitehouse Rd, Edinburgh EH4 6PE (☎ 031 312 7182); Dunedin Fund Mangers Ltd, Dunedin Ho, 25 Ravelston Tce, Edinburgh EH4 3EX (☎ 031 315 2500, fax 031 315 2222, telex 72229)

KEMP, Arnold; s of Robert Kemp (d 1968), of Edinburgh, and Meta Elizabeth, *née* Straestan; *b* 15 Feb 1939; *Educ* Edinburgh Acad, Edinburgh Univ (MA); *Career* sub ed: The Scotsman 1959-62, The Guardian 1962-65; The Scotsman: prodn ed 1965-70, London ed 1970-72, dep ed 1972-81; ed Glasgow Herald 1981-; *Clubs* Caledonian, Glasgow Arts; *Style*— Arnold Kemp, Esq; Glasgow Herald, 195 Albion St, Glasgow G1 1QP (☎ 011 552 6255, fax 041 552 2288

KEMP, Athole (Stephen) Horsford; LVO (1983), OBE (1958, MBE 1950); s of Sir Joseph Horsford Kemp, CBE (d 1950), and Mary, *née* Stuart (d 1954); *b* 21 Oct 1917; *Educ* Westminister, Ch Ch Oxford (MA); *m* 3 Aug 1940, (Marjorie) Alison, da of Geoffrey Rowley Bostock (d 1961); 2 s (Richard b 27 Oct 1948, Charles b 29 Aug 1952), 1 da (Katherine b 27 Nov 1950); *Career* cmdr RA 1939-46; Malayan CS: appointed on secondment from RA 1940 (recalled to RA 1941, POW Singapore and Thailand Burma Railway 1942-45), reverted to Malayan CS 1946, sec to govt Fedn of Malaya 1955-57, dep perm sec PM's Dept Malayasia 1957-61; Royal Cwlth Soc: dep sec gen 1964-67, sec gen 1967-83 (ret), hon sec library trust 1984-, hon chief examiner cwlth essay comp; memb rights of way ctee CPRE Oxon; Oxford Fieldpaths Soc: Memb exec ctee 1983, vice chm 1985; Open Spaces Soc: local correspondent W Oxon 1983, clerk Langford PCC; Freeman City of Winnipeg Manitoba Canada 1969; JMN (Johan Mangku Negara) Malaysia 1958; *Recreations* gardening, rights of way, wine; *Clubs* Royal Cwlth Soc; *Style—* Stephen Kemp, Esq, LVO, OBE; Lockey House, Langford, Lechlade, Glouc GL7 3LF (☎ 036 786 239); Commonwealth House, 18 Northumberland Ave, London WC2N 5BJ (☎ 01 930 6733)

KEMP, Brian William; s of William Kemp (d 1984), of Solihull, and Muriel Beatrice, *née* Taylor; *b* 29 Jan 1939; *Educ* Moseley GS Birmingham; *m* 1, 15 Feb 1964 (m dis 1988), Mary Christine, da of Harry Hughes, of Birmingham; 2 s (Andrew b 1970, Jonathan b 1973), 1 da (Alison b 1967); m 2, 20 May 1988, Sheila Margaret, da of Walter Patrick of Birmingham; *Career* sr ptnr Allenbrooke Kingsley Mills (formerly R Kingsley Mills and Co) 1986- (ptnr 1970-); FCA 1962, ATII 1965; *Recreations* yachting; *Clubs* Salcombe YC; *Style—* Brian Kemp, Esq; Allenbrooke Kingsley Mills, 614 Stratford Rd, Birmingham B11 4BE (☎ 021 777 6762, fax 021 777 2319)

KEMP, Charles James Bowring; s of Capt Michael John Barnett Kemp, ERD (d 1982), of Winchcombe, Glos, and Brigid Ann Vernon-Smith, *née* Bowring; *b* 27 April 1951; *Educ* Shrewsbury Sch, University Coll Univ of London (LLB); *m* 21 Dec 1974, Fenella Anne, da of Harry Herring, of Cropwell Butler, Nottingham; 1 s (Marcus b 28 Feb 1979), 1 da (Sophie b 11 Feb 1977); *Career* called to the Bar Gray's Inn 1973, asst rec 1987; parish cllr Chailey PC; *Recreations* tennis, swimming, golf, country pursuits; *Style—* Charles Kemp, Esq; Keepers, Cinder Hill, Chailey, nr Lewes, East Sussex BN8 4HP (☎ 082 572 3168); 1 King's Bench Walk, Temple, London EC4Y 7DB (☎ 01 583 6266, fax 01 583 2068)

KEMP, David Stephen; s of Stephen Nicholas Kemp (d 1967), of Bromley, Kent, and Mary Grace, *née* Gibbs (d 1976); *b* 14 Dec 1928; *Educ* Tonbridge, Brasenose Coll Oxford (MA); *m* 16 April 1966, Marion Elizabeth, da of late Dr Maurice Sibley Blower, of Rake, Hants; 3 s (Anthony David b 1967, William James Stephen b 1971, Peter John b 1973); *Career* 2 Lt Duke of Wellingtons Regt 1948; articled clerk E F Turner & Sons 1952, admitted slr 1955; Tonbridge Sch: asst master 1956, housemaster 1969, second master 1971; played hockey for Kent; pres Tonbridge Cricket and Hockey Club, lay memb Tunbridge Wells Health Authy, chm of govrs Marlborough House Sch; Liveryman Worshipful Co of Skinners 1954; *Recreations* cricket, golf, reading; *Clubs* Vincents, MCC, Bude & N Cornwall GC; *Style—* David Kemp, Esq; Summerlands, Portman Park, Tonbridge, Kent TN9 1LW (☎ 0732 350 023); Tonbridge Sch, Tonbridge, Kent (☎ 0732 365 555)

KEMP, Rt Rev Eric Waldram; *see*: Chichester, Bishop of

KEMP, Harry Vincent; s of Alfred Vincent Kemp (d 1959), of Pinner, Middx, and Lucy Edith, *née* Tomkins (d 1946); *b* 11 Dec 1911; *Educ* Stowe, Clare Coll Cambridge (BA, MA), London Univ Inst of Educn (Teaching Dip); *m* 1, 9 July 1941 (m dis 1952), (Lilian) Alix (d 1966), da of Herr Eiermann, of Nuremburg; 1 s (Hugh McDowell b 31 July 1953); m 2, 5 Oct 1957 (m dis 1976), Eunice Ellen, *née* Frost; *Career* WWII RA 1940-41, cmmnd RAOC 1941, released Capt EME 1946; teacher 1935-71, ret 1971; poet; *Books* poetry: Epilogue III (contrib, ed with Laura Riding and Robert Grave 1937), The Left Heresy (with Laura Riding and Robert Graves 1939), Poems as of Now (1969), Poems as of Then (1972), Poems in Variety (1977), Ten Messengers (with Witold Kawalec, 1977), Verses for Heidi (with Harry Gordon, 1978), Collected Poems (1985); *Recreations* cricket, travel, mathematical logic; *Clubs* MCC, Cryptics, Stowe Templars; *Style—* Harry Kemp, Esq; 6 Western Villas, Western Rd, Crediton, Devon EX17 3NA (☎ 03632 3502)

KEMP, Hubert Bond Stafford (Hugh); s of John Stafford Kemp (d 1966), of Cardiff, and Cecilla Isabel, *née* Bond (d 1964); *b* 25 Mar 1925; *Educ* Cardiff HS, Univ of South Wales, St Thomas' Hosp and Univ of London (MB BS, MS); *m* 22 June 1967, Moyra Ann-Margaret, s of William Arthur Odgers (d 1951), of Johannesburg; 3 da (Sian b 16 Jan 1961, Sarah b 10 Oct 1962, Louise b 4 June 1975); *Career* hon conslt Royal Nat Orthopaedic Hosp London and Stanmore 1965-74, sr lectr of Orthopaedics 1965-74 (hon sr lectr 1974-), Hunterian prof RCS 1969; visiting prof VII Congress of Soc Latino America de Orthopedia y Traumatologica 1971; chm London Bone Tumour Unit 1985; memb MRC working parties: Tuberculosis of the Spine 1974-, Osteosarcoa 1985; MRCS 1947, LRCP 1947, FRCSE 1960, FRCS 1970; *Books* Orthopaedic Diagnosis (jtly 1984), A Postgraduate Textbook of Clinical Orthopaedics (contrib 1983), Bailliere's Clinical Oncology (contrib 1987); *Recreations* fishing, painting; *Style—* Hugh Kemp, Esq; 55 Loom Lane, Radlett, Herts WD7 8NX (☎ 0923 854 265); 107 Harley St, London W1N 1DG (☎ 01 935 2776)

KEMP, Prof Martin John; s of Ferderick Maurice Kemp, of Watton, Norfolk, and Violet Anne, *née* Tull; *b* 5 Mar 1942; *Educ* Windsor GS, Downing Coll Cambridge (BA, MA), Courtauld Inst of Art London Univ; *m* 27 Aug 1966, Jill, da of Dennis William Lightfoot, of Bisham, Marlow, Bucks; 1 s (Jonathan b 1976), 1 da (Joanna b 1972); *Career* lectr history of western art Dalhousie Univ Nova Scotia Canada 1965-65, lectr fine arts Univ of Glasgow 1966-81, prof fine arts Univ of St Andrews 1981-, memb Inst for Advanced Study Princeton 1984-85, Slade prof Univ of Cambridge 1987-88, Benjamin Sonenberg visiting prof Inst of Fine Arts NY Univ; dir St Andrews Festival plc, hockey coach St Andrews Univ and Madras Coll (ladies), selector Scottish Univs Mens Hockey Team; tstee Nat Galleries of Scotland 1982-87, Victoria and Albert Museum 1986-; hon prof of history Royal Scottish Acad 1985-; FRSA 1983, HRSA 1985, HRIAS 1988; *Recreations* sport especially hockey; *Style—* Prof Martin Kemp; Orillia, 45 Pittenweem Rd, Anstruther, Fife, Scotland; Dept of Fine Art, Univ of St Andrews, St Andrews, Fife

KEMP, Michael Alfred Lawrence; s of Alfred Lawrence Kemp (d 1968), and Margaret, *née* Smith; *b* 19 Mar 1941; *Educ* Greenwich Central Sch; *m* 1, 1965, Janet Anne, da of Charles Blogg, OBE; 1 s (Lawrence Michael b 1968); m 2, Patricia Deborah, da of Jack Kitching (d 1986); 1 s (Paul Lawrence Michael b 1971), 1 da (Lindsay b 1974); *Career* dir: G & L Ralli Investmt & Tstee Co Ltd 1973- (md 1977), G & L Ralli Finance Co Ltd 1972- (md 1977-); md Ralli Investmt Co Ltd 1979-; dir: Ralli Bondite Ltd 1981-, Frowds Ltd 1983-; Assoc Soc of Investmt Analysts; *Recreations* gardening, rugby union supporter, horseracing; *Clubs* City of London; *Style—* Michael A L Kemp, Esq; 5 Westott Close, Bickley, Kent BR1 2TU (☎ 01 468 7347)

KEMP, Peter Mant MacIntyre; DSO (1945); s of Sir Norman Wright Kemp (d 1937), and Olivia Maria, *née* Martin (d 1946); *b* 19 August 1915; *Educ* Wellington, Trinity Coll Cambridge (MA); *m* 20 Nov 1946 (m dis 1958), Cynthia Margaret, da of Col Vivian Henry CB (d 1930); *Career* cmmnd 1940, Capt 1940, Maj 1943, Lt-Col 1946; author; life assur underwriter Imperial Life of Canada; *Books* Mine Were of Trouble (1957), No Colours or Crest (1958), Aims for Oblivion (1961), Br Glin Vietnam (jtly 1969); *Recreations* tavern talk and travel; *Clubs* White's, Pratt's, Special Forces, Chelsea Arts; *Style—* Peter Kemp, Esq, DSO; 24 Radnor Walk, London SW3 4BN (☎ 01 352 9356)

KEMP, Robert Thayer; s of Robert Kemp (d 1968), and Ada, *née* Thayer; *b* 18 June 1928; *Educ* Bromley GS, London Univ (BA); *m* 1951, Gwendolyn Mabel, da of Rev Charles Stanley Minty (d 1930); *Career* dir Int Gp Export Credits Guarantee Dept 1985-88 (formerly under sec 1975-85, asst 1970-75); *Recreations* gardening, theatre, music; *Clubs* Overseas Bankers; *Style—* Robert Kemp, Esq; ECGD, PO Box 272, Export House, 50 Ludgate Hill, London EC4M 7AY (☎ 01 382 7649)

KEMP, Roy; s of Robert Godfrey Kemp (d 1926); *b* 15 May 1911; *Educ* Uppingham; *m* 1935, Elisabeth Marie Lynn, *née* Aspinall; 2 s, 1 da; *Career* divnl offr Nat Fire Serv (GB and N Ireland), dep chm Leicester Bldg Soc 1955-81, chm Allen Bastick & Billson Ltd 1946-, chm Belgrave & Wigston Ltd 1959-, pres Leicester & Dist Hosiery Mfrs Assoc Ltd 1971-72; *Recreations* rugby football refereeing, squash racquets; *Clubs* Leicestershire, Leicestershire Golf, Stoneygate FC; *Style—* Roy Kemp, Esq; Remlak, 28 The Oval, Oadby, Leicester LE2 5JB (☎ 0533 712 081)

KEMP, Hon St John Durival; s and h of 1 Viscount Rochdale, OBE, TD, DL; *b* 15 Jan 1938; *Educ* Eton; *m* 1, 1960 (m dis 1974), Serena Clark-Hall; 2 s, 2 da; m 2, 1976, Elizabeth Anderton; *Style—* The Hon St John Kemp; Rosetrees, Portinscale, Keswick, Cumbria CA12 5TZ

KEMP, Dr Thomas Arthur; s of Fred Kemp (d 1922), and Edith, *née* Peters (d 1973); *b* 12 August 1915; *Educ* Denstone Coll, St Catherines Coll, Cambridge (MA), St Mary's Hosp Med Sch London (MD); *m* 28 Nov 1942, Ruth May, da of Wing-Cdr George Henry Keat (d 1986), of Northwood, Mddx; 1 s (Thomas b 1943), 1 da (Catherine b 1948); *Career* RAMC 1943-47, served Middle East 1944-47, Maj med specialist 1945, Lt-Col offr i/c med dir 1946; conslt physician: St Mary;s Hosp 1947-75, Paddington Gen Hosp 1950-75, Army 1972-75; examiner Univ of Lond on and Glasgow, hon dec RSM 1961-67, pres Br Student Health Assoc 1062-63; govr: Denstone Coll 1953-85, St Martin's Sch Northwood 1960-88 (chm 1984-88); played RF for England 1937, 1939, 1948 (capt), England selector 1954-61, pres RFU 1971-72; fell Middland dir Woodward Schs 1962-85, (with Travelling Fellowship 1967; FRSM, FRCP; *Clubs* Hawks (Cambridge); *Style—* Dr Thomas Kemp; 2 Woodside Rd, Northwood, Middx HAG 3QE

KEMP, Timothy; s of Capt Maurice Kemp, TD, of Walton-on-the-Hill, Surrey, and Gwendoline, *née* Atkinson (d 1979); *b* 16 April 1948; *Educ* Cranleigh; *m* 12 Jan 1974, Susan Elouise, da of Graham Cox (d 1982), of Chipstead, Surrey; 1 s (Robert 20 March 1980), 1 da (Katie 27 March 1978); *Career* Hon Artillery Co TA 1967-74; insur broker; elected memb of Lloyd's 1979, Gibbs Hartley Cooper Ltd 1971-(dir 1985); ACII 1971; *Recreations* golf, gardening; *Clubs* HAC, Lloyd's GC, Royal Ashdown Forest GC; *Style—* Timothy Kemp, Esq; Rush Green, Forest Row, E Sussex; Gibbs Hartley Cooper Ltd, Bishops Court, 27/33 Artillery La, London E1 7LP (☎ 01 247 5433)

KEMP-GEE, Hon Mrs (Lucy); *née* Lyttelton; 3 da of 10 Viscount Cobham (d 1977); *b* 1954; *m* 1980, Mark Norman Kemp-Gee, *qv*; 3 s; *Style—* The Hon Mrs Kemp-Gee; Beech Tree Cottage, Preston Candover, Basingstoke, Hants RG25 2EJ

KEMP-GEE, Mark Norman; yr s of Bernard Kemp-Gee, of London W8; *m* 26 July 1980, Hon Lucy, *qv*; 3 s; *Career* memb Stock Exchange 1970; sr ptnr Greig, Middleton & Co (stockbrokers); *Style—* Mark Kemp-Gee Esq; 10 Orlando Rd, Clapham Old Town, London SW4 0LF (☎ 01 720 2969); Greig, Middleton & Co, 78 Old Broad St, London EC2M 1JE (☎ 01 920 0481; telex 887296)

KEMP-WELCH, John; s of Peter Wellesbourne Kemp-Welch, OBE (d 1964), and Peggy Penelope, *née* Hunter; sr rep of the family descended from Martin Kemp-Welch (1772-1837), who assumed, by Royal Licence, 1795, the additional name of Welch, in compliance with the testamentary injunctions of his maternal unc, George Welch, banker and fndr of the banking house of Welch Rogers Olding and Rogers; *b* 31 Mar 1936; *Educ* Winchester; *m* 1964, Diana Elisabeth, da of Dr A W D Leishman, FRCP (d 1978); 1 s, 3 da; *Career* memb Stock Exchange 1959, jt sr ptnr Cazenove & Co (stockbrokers); dir: Lowland Investmt Co plc, Updown Investmt Co plc; govr Ditchley Fndn; memb: Courtauld Inst of Art Tst, tstee Kings Medical Res Tst. dir: Garrows Farm Ltd 1964, Savoy Hotel plc 1985-; govr North Foreland Lodge Sch; CBIM; *Recreations* shooting, farming, the hills of Perthshire; *Clubs* White's, City of London, MCC; *Style—* John Kemp-Welch, Esq; Little Hallingbury Place, Bishop's Stortford, Herts; Garrows, Amulree, Dunkeld, Perthshire; Cazenove & Co, 12 Tokenhouse Yard, London EC2R 7AN (☎ 01 588 2828; telex 886758)

KEMPE, John William Rolfe; CVO (1979); s of William Alfred Kempe (d 1922), of Nairobi, and Kunigunda, *née* Neville-Rolfe (d 1959); *b* 29 Oct 1917; *Educ* Stowe, Clare Coll Cambridge (MA); *m* Barbara Nan Stephen, da of Dr Charles Reginald Ralston Huxable, MC (d 1950), of Sydney; 2 s (Nicholas b 5 May 1959, Clive b 26 May 1961), 1 da (Penelope b 21 April 1964); *Career* WW11 serv RAF: flying Spitfires (602 Sqdn), Beaufighters, Mosquitoes (Night Fighers) N Africa and Med, Wing Cdr 153 and 255 Night Fighter Sqdns 1943-44; BOT 1945-46, sec John Brown & Thos Firth (Overseas) Ltd 1946-47, head maths dept Gordonstoun 1948-51, princ Hyderabad Public Sch Deccan India; headmaster: Corby GS 1955-67, Gordonstoun 1967-78; ret 1979; mountaineering in Alps, India and Peru; memb: Everest Fndn ctee 1956-62, Brathay Exploration ctee 1969-70; vice-chm Euro Atlantic Movement Team 1980-, chm Round Square Int Serv 1980-88, govr Stamford Sch 1979-89; tstee Kurt Hahn Tst, Thornton Smith Tst, Plevins Charity; *Clubs* Alpine, English Speaking Union; *Style—* John Kempe, Esq; Maple Tree Cottage, 24 Old Leicester Rd, Wansford PE8 6JR

KEMSLEY, Col Sir Alfred Newcombe; KBE (1980), CMG (1973, CBE 1960, MSM,

ED); s of late Alfred Kemsley; *b* 29 Mar 1896; *Educ* Adelaide Business Training Acad; *m* 1, 1921, Glydus Logg (decd); m 2, 1925, Jean Oldfield (decd); m 3, 1972, Anne Copsey; *Career* company dir, involved in town planning, broadcasting; business conslt; chm Blamey Memorial Ctee 1978, memb gen Sir Edmund Herring Memorial Ctee 1982; kt 1978; *Style*— Col Sir Alfred Kemsley, KBE, CMG, CBE, MSM, ED; 41 Bay St, Brighton, Vic 3186, Australia

KEMSLEY, Viscountess; Lady Hélène Candida; *née* Hay; da of 11 Marquess of Tweeddale (d 1967); *b* 1913; *m* 1933, 2 Viscount Kemsley; 4 da; *Career* DStJ; *Style*— The Rt Hon the Viscountess Kemsley; Field House, Thorpe Lubenham, Market Harborough, Leics

KEMSLEY, Viscount (UK 1945); Sir (Geoffrey) Lionel Berry; 2 Bt (UK 1928), DL (Leics 1972); Baron Kemsley (UK 1936); s of 1 Viscount Kemsley, GBE (d 1968); *b* 29 June 1909; *Educ* Marlborough, Magdalen Coll Oxford; *m* 1933, Lady Hélène Hay, *qv*; 4 da; *Heir* nephew, Richard Gomer Berry, b 1951, s of late Hon Denis Gomer Berry, TD; *Career* served WW II as Capt Gren Gds (invalided out 1942); dep chm Kemsley Newspapers Ltd 1938-59, MP (C) Buckingham 1943-45; Master of Spectacle Makers' Co 1949-51 and 1959-61; CC Northants 1964-70, High Sheriff Leics 1967, chm St Andrew's Hosp Northampton 1973-84, pres Assoc of Independent Hosps 1976-83, memb Chapter Gen of OStJ; FRSA; KStJ; *Clubs* Turf, Pratt's, Royal Overseas; *Style*— The Rt Hon the Viscount Kemsley, DL; Field House, Thorpe Lubenham, Market Harborough, Leics (☎ 0858 62816)

KENCH, Eric Arthur; s of Joseph Peter Kench, of Oxfordshire, and Ethel Catherine, *née* Younger; *b* 30 Sept 1952; *Educ* Henley GS; *m* 20 July 1974, Kathleen Jennifer, da of Philip Hague (d 1980); 1 s (David b 1979), 2 da (Caroline b 1981, Sarah b 1982); *Career* CA; formed E A Kench & Co 1982, past chm Thames Valley Young CA Gp, Thames Valley rep ICA (E&W) Smaller Practitioners Ctee 1984-, memb ICA Changing Environment Gp 1984-87, pres Thames Valley Soc of CAs 1987-88; FCA; *Recreations* squash, flying (private pilot), working; *Style*— Eric Kench, Esq; 5 All Hallows Rd, Caversham, Reading RG4 0LP (☎ 0734 475624); E A Kench & Co, 8 Station Rd, Henley-on-Thames RG9 1AY (☎ 0491 578207)

KENDAL, Felicity Anne; da of Geoffrey Kendal, of Swan Ct, Chelsea, London, and Laura, *née* Liddell; *Educ* convents in India; *m* 1, 1969 (m dis 1976), Drewe Henley; 1 s (Charles b 23 Jan 1973); m 2, Michael Edward Rudman, s of Duke Rudman, of Dallas, Texas; 1 s (Jacob Henry b 1 Oct 1987); *Career* grew up touring and acting with parents theatre co in India and Far East, London debut in Minor Murder (Savoy) 1967; plays: Henry V and The Promise (Leicester) 1968, Back to Methuselah (Nat Theatre) 1969, A Midsummer Nights Dream and Much Ado About Nothing (Regents Park) 1970, Kean (Oxford) 1970 and (London) 1971, Romeo and Juliet, 'Tis Pity She's a Whore and The Three Arrows 1972, The Norman Conquests (Globe) 1974, Once Upon a Time (Bristol) 1976, Arms and the Man (Greenwich) 1978, Clouds (Duke of York's) 1978, Amadeus (NT) 1979, Othello (NT) 1980, On the Razzle (NT) 1981, The Second Mrs Tanqueray (NT) 1981, The Real Thing (Strand) 1982, Jumpers (Aldwych) 1985, Made in Bangkok (Adlwych) 1986; TV: The Good Life 1975-77, Twelfth Night 1979, Solo 1980 and 1982, The Mistress 1985; films: Shakespeare Wallah 1965, Valentino 1976; awards: Variety Club Most Promising Newcomer 1974, Best Actress 1979, Clarence Derwent Award 1980, Variety Club Woman of the Year Best Actress Award 1984; *Recreations* golf; *Clubs* RAC, Royal Mid Surrey GC, Dyrem Pk GC; *Style*— Miss Felicity Kendal; Chatto & Linnit, Prince of Wales Theatre, Coventry St, London W1 (☎ 01 930 6677, fax 01 930 0091)

KENDALL, Rev Frank; s of Norman Kendall (d 1976), of Ripon, Yorkshire, and Violet, *née* Bloor; *b* 15 Dec 1940; *Educ* Bradford GS, Corpus Christi Coll Cambridge (MA), London Univ (Dip in Religious Studies); *m* 20 Feb 1965, Brenda, da of Walter Isaac Pickin (d 1982), of Royston; 1 s (Andrew b 1970), 1 da (Angela b 1969); *Career* Civil Serv; asst princ then princ Miny of Public Building and Works 1962-70, princ Dept of Economic Affairs 1967-68, princ and asst sec DOE 1970-84, under sec and NW regnl dir Depts of the Environment and Tport 1984-; ordained: deacon 1974, priest 1975; hon curate: Lingfield 1974-75 and 1978-82, Limpsfield 1982-84 (Diocese of Southwark), Sketty 1975-78 (Diocese of Swansea and Brecon); licensed preacher Diocese of Manchester 1984-; *Recreations* painting, DIY; *Style*— The Rev Frank Kendall; 9 Abberton Rd, Withington, Manchester M20 8HX (☎ 061 434 5657); Depts of the Environment and Tport, Sunley Tower, Piccadilly Plaza, Manchester M1 4BE (☎ 061 832 9111, fax 061 838 5790, telex 668767)

KENDALL, George Langton; JP (1966 Bucks); s of Gordon Kendall (d 1972), of Leics, and Elsie Winifred, *née* Breeze; coat of arms 1448 confirmed under seal by Clarenceux King of Arms; John Kendall, sec to Richard III, killed at Bosworth Leics; *b* 19 June 1927; *Educ* Haileybury; *m* 13 June 1959, Elizabeth Jane, da of William George Eric Shand, of NZ; 1 s (Angus b 1960), 1 da (Mary-Anne b 1962); *Career* Sub Lt RNVR, served Far East; chartered surveyor; chm and sr ptnr Raffety Buckland 1980-87, dir Raffety Buckland & Co Ltd 1987, chm Wickham Rye & Co 1979-; memb: Cncl RICS 1956-59, Wycombe Borough Cncl 1966-69, Bow Gp 1955-65; memb and chm personnel ctee Bucks CC 1970-77; memb: Bucks Business Gp (set up under Local Govt Act 1984) 1985-88, cncl Univ of Buckingham 1986-; gen cmmr of taxes 1983-; High Sheriff Bucks 1986-87; life memb Primrose League; Liveryman Worshipful Co of Chartered Surveyors; FIOD; *Recreations* golf, shooting, sailing, crew memb Taiseer IV (first winner Britannia Cup Cowes 1951); *Clubs* Naval, MCC, Leander; *Style*— George Kendall, Esq, JP; 30 High St, High Wycombe, Bucks (☎ 0494 21234, fax 0494 36362)

KENDALL, John Melville; s of Capt Charles Edward Kendall (d 1978), of Great Nineveh, Benenden, Kent, and Cara Honoria, *née* Pelly; *b* 1 Sept 1931; *Educ* Ampleforth; *m* 23 Feb 1971, Anthea Diana, da of Col T D Partridge; 1 s (Mark b 12 Jan 1972), 1 da (Sophia b 4 July 1973); *Career* Lt RN 1952-56; chm Charks Kendall Gp of Cos 1978-; Order of Sultan Qaboos Sultanate of Oman; *Recreations* sailing, skiing, hunting; *Clubs* Brooks's; *Style*— John Kendall, Esq; Coombe Priory, Shaftesbury, Dorset; 7 Albert Ct, Prince Consort Rd, London SW7 2BJ (☎ 01 589 1256, fax 01 581 5761, telex 919060)

KENDALL, Lady; Kathleen Ruth (Whitfield); da of Roland Abel Phillipson (d 1925), of Bournemouth; *b* 20 Nov 1904; *Educ* Bournemouth Collegiate Sch; Les Allières Lausanne, Switzerland; *m* 1947, as his 2 w, Sir Maurice George Kendall (d 1983), s of John Roughton, of Derby, prof of statistics London Univ 1949-61, dir World Fertility Survey 1972-80, chm Scientific Control Systems; *Recreations* languages, reading, skiing; *Style*— Lady Kendall; c/o Barclays Bank, 117 Dulwich Village, Dulwich, London SE21 7BD

KENDELL, Prof Robert Evan; s of Robert Owen Kendell (d 1954), and Joan, *née* Evans (d 1986); *b* 28 Mar 1935; *Educ* Mill Hill Sch, Peterhouse Cambridgs (BA, MA, MB BChir, MD), King's Coll Hosp Med Sch London); *m* 2 Dec 1961, Dr Ann Whitfield, da of Dr Gerald Whitfield (d 1972), of Lindfield, Sussex; 2 s (Patrick b 1968, Harry b 1970), 2 da (Katherine b 1965, Judith b 1966); *Career* registrar later sr registrar The Maudsley Hosp London 1962-66, res worker Inst of Psychiatry London 1966-70, visiting prof Univ of Vermont Coll of Med USA 1969-70, reader in psychiatry Inst of Psychiatry London 1970-74, prof of psychiatry Univ of Edinburgh 1974- (dean faculty of med 1986-), Gaskell Gold Medal RCPsych 1967, Paul Hoch Medal American Psychopathological Assoc 1988; WHO: chm expert ctee on alcohol consumption 1979, memb expert advsy panel on mental health 1979-; memb MRC 1984-88; FRCP 1974, FRCPE 1977, FRCPsych 1979; *Books* The Classification of Depressive Illnesses (1968), The Role of Diagnosis in Psychiatry (1975), Companion to Psychiatric Studies (ed, second edn 1988); *Recreations* overeating, walking up hills; *Clubs* Climbers; *Style*— Prof R E Kendall; 3 West Castle Rd, Edinburgh EH10 5AT (☎ 031 229 4966); University Dept of Psychiatry, Royal Edinburgh Hospital, Edinburgh EH10 5HF (☎ 031 447 2011)

KENDRA, Rev Kenneth Ernest; OBE (1966) ; s of Ernest Kendra (d 1938), of Newton Upon Derwent, Yorks, and Emily, *née* Lister; *b* 27 Oct 1913; *Educ* Wilberforce Sch York, Univ of Leeds (BA, MA), Scholae Cancellarii Lincoln; *m* 14 July 1951, Kathleen, da of Alderman Charles W Whatley, OBE (d 1960), of Burderop, Chiseldon, Marlborough, Wilts; 2 da (Emily Jane, Judith Anne Morse); *Career* chaplain: to the forces 1945, 6 Airborne Div 1946; sr Chaplain 3 Inf Div 1953, chaplain RMA Sandhurst 1954, sr chaplain 5 Inf Bde 1958, dep asst to chaplain Gen BAOR 1963, sr chaplain supreme HQ Far East 1968, ret 1971; ordained: deacon 1942, priest 1943; curate Pocklington Yorks 1943-45, vicar Lee on the Solent Hants 1971-80; chm Mere and District Historical Soc ; *Style*— The Rev Kenneth Kendra, OBE; Highfields, Castle Hill Lane, Mere, Wilts BA12 6JB, (☎ 0747 860823)

KENDREW, Sir John Cowdery; CBE (1963); s of Wilfrid Kendrew; *b* 24 Mar 1917; *Educ* Clifton, Trinity Coll Cambridge (ScD, PhD); *Career* served WWII Miny of Aircraft Prod, Hon Wing Cdr RAF ME and SE Asia; dep chm MRC Laboratory of Molecular Biology Cambridge 1946-74, dir gen Euro Molecular Biology Laboratory 1975-82, jt winner Nobel Prize Chemistry 1962, Royal Soc Royal Medal 1965; memb cncl UN Univ 1980-86 (chm governing cncl 1983-85); pres: St John's Coll Oxford 1981-87, Br Assoc for the Advancement of Sci 1974, Int Cncl of Scientific Unions 1983; Hon fell Peterhouse and Trinity Coll Cambridge; Hon DSc: Reading, Keele, Exeter, Buckingham, Madrid; Hon DUniv Stirling, Hon Prof Univ of Heidelberg 1982; FRS; kt 1974; *Clubs* Athenaeum; *Style*— Sir John Kendrew, CBE; The Guildhall, 4 Church Lane, Linton, Cambridge (☎ 0223 891 545)

KENDREW, Richard Adrian; s of George Richard Hamilton Kendrew, of Harrogate, N Yorks, and Eileen Tipple, *née* Wood, of Ilkley, W Yorks; *b* 28 Sept 1944; *Educ* Malvern; *m* 1, 1970 (m dis), Frances Elizabeth; 1 s (Adrian b 1973); m 2, 1983, Elizabeth Anne, da of Ronald Merrick; *Career* slr in private practice, memb cncl Law Soc 1984-; *Recreations* foreign travel; *Clubs* Carlton; *Style*— Richard Kendrew, Esq

KENDRICK, Clinton Jansen; *b* 2 August 1943; *Educ* Phillips Acad, Yale Univ (BA Eng Lit), New York Univ Graduate Sch; *m* 11 Oct 1970, Mary Claudell Jallande; 1 s (Nicholas b 1974), 1 da (Charlotte Fortier b 1977); *Career* pres Alliance Capital Mgmnt Corp New York, chm Alliance Capital Mgmnt Int Inc London; *Style*— Clinton Kendrick, Esq; 1345 Avenue of the Americas, New York 10105 (☎ 212 969 1030); 43 Upper Grosvenor Street, London W1X 9PG

KENILOREA, Rt Hon Sir Peter; KBE, PC (1979); *b* 23 May 1943; *Educ* Univ and Teachers' Coll NZ; *m* 1971, Margaret Kwanairara; 2 s, 2 da; *Career* PM Solomon Islands 1978-81, chief min 1976-78; MLA Solomon Islands 1976-; *Style*— The Rt Hon Sir Peter Kenilorea, KBE, PC; Legislative Assembly, Honiara, Guadalcanal, Solomon Islands

KENILWORTH, Jacqueline, Baroness; Jacqueline Paulette; *née* Gelpi; da of late Robert Gelpi, of Lyon, France; *m* 28 Aug 1948, 3 Baron Kenilworth (d 1981); 1 s (4 Baron), 1 da (Hon Mrs McCarraher); *Style*— The Rt Hon Jacqueline, Baroness Kenilworth; 2 Lexham Walk, London W8 (☎ 01 370 6805)

KENILWORTH, 4 Baron (UK 1937); (John) Randle Siddeley; only s of 3 Baron Kenilworth (d 1981); *b* 16 June 1954; *Educ* Northease Manor, London Coll of Furniture; *m* 1983, Kim, only da of Danie Serfontein, of Newcastle upon Tyne; *Style*— The Rt Hon the Lord Kenilworth; 52 Hartismere Rd, London SW6

KENNAIR, William Brignall; s of Joseph Terry Kennair, of Newcastle upon Tyne, and Nancy, *née* Neasham; *b* 6 June 1956; *Educ* Royal GS Newcastle upon Tyne, UCL (LLB); *m* 2 Aug 1980, Karen Elizabeth, da of Keith John Williams, of Cardiff; *Career* ptnr John Venn & Sons London 1986- (articled clerk 1978-83, assoc 1983-86), Notary Public; (John Venn & Sons notaries and translators); Freeman City of London 1983-, Liveryman Worshipful Co of Scriveners 1983-; memb Assoc Int De Jeunes Avocats 1985-; *Recreations* cuisine, wine, travel; *Style*— William Kennair, Esq; John Venn & Sons, Imperial House, 15-19 Kingsway, London WC2B 6UU (☎ 01 836 9522, fax 01 836 3182, telex 262582 VENLEX G)

KENNARD, Maj David Arthur; MC (1942) and bar (1945); s of Maj Arthur Molloy Kennard (d 1918), and Evelyn Mary, *née* Kennedy (d 1955); *b* 4 Jan 1916; *Educ* Charterhouse, RMC Sandhurst; *m* 17 April 1952, Prudence Elizabeth Struan, da of Maj Grange Inglis Kirkcaldy (d 1979), of Aberdeen; 2 s (Rodney b 1953, Andrew b 1956), 1 da (Susan b 1959); *Recreations* shooting, antique clocks; *Clubs* Cavalry and Guards', English Speaking Union; *Style*— Maj David Kennard, MC; Cool, Auchterarder, Perthshire PH3 1DR (☎ 0764 62655)

KENNARD, Sir George Arnold Ford; 3 Bt (UK 1891), of Fernhill, co Southampton; s of late Sir Coleridge Kennard, 1 Bt; suc bro, Sir Laurence Ury Charles Kennard, 2 Bt 1967; *b* 27 April 1915; *Educ* Eton; *m* 1, 1940 (m dis 1958), Cecilia Violet Cokayne, da of Maj Cecil John Cokayne Maunsell, JP; 1 da; m 2, 1958 (m dis 1974), Mrs Molly Jesse Rudd Miskin, da of late Hugh Wyllie, of Fishbourne, Sussex; m 3, 1985, Nicola, da of Capt Peter Gawan Carew (d 1966) and formerly w of Charles Louis Breitmeyer; *Heir* none; *Career* 1939-45 War (despatches twice, prisoner), Lt-Col (cmdg) late 4 Queen's Own Hussars; Midland rep for Cement Marketing Co; *Clubs* Cavalry and Guards; *Style*— Sir George Kennard, Bt; Cogwell, Tiverton, Devon (☎ Tiverton 2154)

KENNARD, Michael Frederick; s of Julius Kennard (d 1986), and Phyllis, *née*

Swyers; *b* 2 Feb 1927; *Educ* Univ Coll Sch London, Northampton Eng Coll, Univ of London (BSc); *m* Sept 1955, Ruth, 2 da (Elaine b 1958, Emma b 1964); *Career* civil engr, Sir William Halcrow and Ptnrs 1948-52, Cubitts Ltd 1953-54, Sandeman Kennard and Ptnrs 1954-70 (ptnr 1955-70), sr ptnr Rofe Kennard and Lapworth 1985- (ptnr 1970-85), conslting engr specialising dams, geotech engng and water engng; appt by Min of Agric to Drainage Ctee Thames Water Authy 1986-, chm Br Section of Int Cmmn of Large Dams 1977-80; FIWEM, FICE 1952; *Books* tech papers on dams and water engng; *Style*— Michael Kennard, Esq; 25 Talbot Crescent, London NW4 4HS; Rofe Kennard and Lapworth; 2/4 Sutton Court Road, Sutton, Surrey SM1 4SS (☎ 01 643 8201, fax 01 642 8469, telex 946688)

KENNARD, Nigel Robert; s of Herbert Edward Kennard (d 1971), of Guernsey, and Esther Mary, *née* Plummer; *b* 23 July 1944; *Educ* Lancing; *m* 15 March 1969, Anne Jane, da of Kenneth Embden Archer, of Sussex; 2 s (Edward b 1973, James b 1976); *Career* chartered accountant in own practice 1978; dir Kesgrave Hall Sch Ltd 1984, fin chm English Guernsey Cattle Soc (bred champion Guernsey cow RASE 1987); FCA; *Recreations* cattle breeding, hockey; *Style*— Nigel R Kennard, Esq; Instead Manor, Weybread, Diss, Norfolk IP21 5UH (☎ 0379 852350)

KENNARD, Prof Olga; OBE (1988); da of Joir Weisz, and Catherina, *née* Sternberg (d 1988); *b* 23 Mar 1924; *Educ* Prince Henry VIII GS, Cambridge Univ (ScD); *m* m 1948 (m dis 1961), Dr David William Kennard; 2 da (Susanna Clare b 1955, Julia Sarah b 1958); *Career* res asst Cavendish Lab Cambridge 1944-48; MRC: vision Res Unit 1948-51, Nat Inst for Med Res 1951-61, external staff Univ Chem Lab Cambridge 1961-, special appt 1971-; scientific dir Cambridge Crystallographic Data Centre 1965-, visiting prof London Univ 1988-; memb numerous ctees of scientific socs, author scientific papers and books on scientific data; FRS 1987; *Recreations* swimming, cooking, reading; *Style*— Prof Olga Kennard, OBE; Crystallographic Data Centre, Univ Chemical Lab, Lensfield Rd, Cambridge CB2 1EW (☎ 0223 336408, fax 0223 336362)

KENNAWAY, Prof Alexander; s of Dr Noah Barou (d 1955), and Mrs Sophie Barou (d 1956); *b* 14 August 1923; *Educ* St Paul's, Pembroke Coll Cambridge (MA); *m* 1, 1947 (m dis 1970), Xenia Rebel; 2 s (Igor b 1947, Edward b 1956), 1 da (Nadia b 1950); m 2, 1973, Jean Simpson, da of Stanley Church (d 1982); *Career* WWII Lt-Cdr served: Med, East Indies, Pacific; consulting engr 1966-; dir: BTR Industs 1960-66, Lankro Chemicals 1970-77, Thomas Jourdan Gp 1976-82; chm Terrafix Ltd 1983-; visiting prof of chemical (now mechanical) engrg Imperial Coll 1976-; memb bd Civil Aviation Authy 1979-82, sometime memb standing advsy ctee on artificial limbs DHSS; *Books* contrib: Plastics in Surgery (1956), Polythene, Its Technology and Uses (1958), sole author: Engineers in Industry, A Management Guide Self Improvement (1981), chapters in The British Malaise (1982); *Recreations* sailing, chess, music, self-education, thinking; *Clubs* Royal Naval Sailing Assoc; *Style*— Prof Alexander Kennaway; 12 Fairholme Cres, Ashtead, Surrey KT21 2HN (☎ 0372 277 678); Imperial College of Science and Technology, Exhibition Rd, London SW7

KENNAWAY, John-Michael; s and h of Sir John Kennaway, 5 Bt and Christina Veronica, *née* Urszenyi; *b* 17 Feb 1962; *Educ* King Edward's Sch Bath, Hampshire Coll of Agriculture; *m* 22 Oct 1988, Lucy Frances, yr da of Dr Jeremy Houlton Bradshaw- Smith, of Ottery St Mary, Devon; *Career* ornamental fish farmer, landowner (1200 acres); *Recreations* shooting, scuba diving; *Style*— John-Michael Kennaway, Esq; Escot, Ottery St Mary, Devon EX11 1LU (☎ 0404 822 429); Parklands Farm, Escot, Ottery St Mary, Devon (☎ 0404 822 188)

KENNAWAY, Mary, Lady; Mary Félicité; da of Rev Stewart Gordon Ponsonby (d 1950); *b* 11 Sept 1898; *m* 1931, Sir John Kennaway, 4 Bt (d 1956); 1 s, 2 da; *Style*— Mary, Lady Kennaway; Gittisham Hill House, Honiton, Devon

KENNEDY, Charles Peter; MP (SDP) Ross, Cromarty and Skye; 1983-88, SLD 1988-; s of Ian Kennedy and Mary MacVarish, *née* MacEachen, of Fort William; *b* 25 Nov 1959; *Educ* Lochaber HS Fort William, Glasgow Univ (MA), Indiana Univ USA (Fulbright Scholarship); *Career* journalist BBC Highland Inverness 1982; graduate student/lecturer (speech communications and British politics) Indiana Univ USA 1982-83; chm SDP Cncl for Scotland 1983; *Recreations* music, reading, writing; *Clubs* National Liberal; *Style*— Charles Kennedy Esq, MP; House of Commons, London SW1

KENNEDY, Sir Clyde David Allen; s of late D H Kennedy; *b* 20 Nov 1912; *Educ* Mount Albert GS, Auckland Univ; *m* 1937, Sarah Stacpoole; 2 s, 1 da; *Career* company dir Aust Casing Co Pty Ltd 1939-82, chm Sydney Turf Club 1972-77 and 1980-83 (dir 1964-83, vice-chm 1967-72); memb Totalizator Agency Bd of NSW 1965-82, chm Spinal Research Foundation; kt 1973; *Style*— Sir Clyde Kennedy, Esq; 13A/23 Thornton St, Darling Point, NSW 2027, Australia

KENNEDY, Lord David Thomas; s of 7 Marquess of Ailsa, OBE, DL; *b* 3 July 1958; *Educ* Strathallan Sch, Berks Coll of Ag; *Career* farmer; *Recreations* shooting, fishing, vintage car restoration, travel; *Clubs* New (Edinburgh); *Style*— Lord David Kennedy; Morriston Farm, Maidens, Maybole, Ayrshire

KENNEDY, Ambassador Eamon; s of Luke William Kennedy (d 1980), of Dublin, and Ellen Stafford (d 1955); maternal gf, Matthew Stafford, memb of Irish Senate (late 30's); both gfs participated in 1916 Rising in Dublin; *b* 13 Dec 1921; *Educ* UC Dublin (MA, B Comm), Nat Univ of Ireland (Ph D); *m* 1960, Barbara Jane, da of William Black (d 1980), pres of Chock Full Coffee Corpn, of NY; 1 s (Mark b 1970) 1 da (Helen b 1967); *Career* entered Dept Foreign Affrs 1943; consul NY 1947; second Sec Ottawa 1947; first sec: Washington 1949, Paris 1950, (and acting chief of protocol) Dept FA 1954; cncllr Perm Mission UN NY 1956; ambass: Fedn Rep Nigeria 1961, Fedn Rep Germany 1964, France 1970; perm rep to UN 1974; ambass: Britain 1978, Italy, Turkey and Libya 1983-; Grand Cross of Merit of France 1974, Grand Cross of Merit of Federal Republic of Germany 1970; *Recreations* golf, theatre, music; *Clubs* Acquasanta (Rome), Old Collegians Rowing (Dublin); *Style*— His Excellency Mr Eamon Kennedy; Via Valle delle Camene 3, 00184 Roma, Italy (☎ 778035); Embassy of Ireland, Largo del Nazareno 3, 00187 Roma, Italy

KENNEDY, Francis; CBE (1977, MBE 1958); s of James Kennedy; *b* 9 May 1926; *Educ* Manchester and London Univs; *m* 1957, Anne O'Malley; 2 s, 2 da; *Career* Colonial Service Nigeria 1953-63, Foreign Service 1964 (served Kuching, Dar-es-Salaam, Istanbul, Atlanta, Lagos); ambass to Angola and ambass non-resident to São Tomé and Principe 1981-83, HM consul-gen at New York and dir-gen British Trade Devpt USA 1983-; *Clubs* Brooks's; *Style*— Francis Kennedy Esq, CBE; British Consulate-General, 845 Third Avenue, New York, NY 10022, USA; c/o Foreign and Commonwealth Office, King Charles St, London SW1

KENNEDY, Geoffrey Farrer; s of Sir John MacFarlane Kennedy, OBE (d 1954), of Shalford, Surrey, and Lady Dorothy Farrer Kennedy (d 1974); *b* 30 Oct 1908; *Educ* Oundle, Trinity Coll Cambridge (BA, MA); *m* 1, 1938 (m dis 1948), Daska, *née* Ivanovic; 1 s (John Alexander b 1942), 3 da (Tessa Georgina b 1939, Marina Milica b 1939, Caroline Bella b 1944); m 2, 6 June 1950, Daphne, da of Graham Sinclair Summersell (d 1951), of Oxshott; 2 s (Christopher Michael Graham b 1954, Anthony Geoffrey Richard b 1957); *Career* student apprentice Bth Rugby 1930-32, sr ptnr Kennedy & Donkin 1964-75 (asst engr 1932-34, ptnr 1934-64), sr conslt Kennedy & Donkin Gp and Kennedy & Donkin Int Consulting Engrs 1975-; chm: Br Conslts Bureau 1969-72, Assoc of Consulting Engrs 1972-73; Hon FIEE, FInstCE, Hon MConsE, FIMechE, memb ASME, FCIT; Order of Merit First Class Egypt 1959; *Books* A History of Kennedy & Donkin 1889-1989 (1989); *Recreations* yachting, walking; *Clubs* Royal Yacht Squadron, Royal Thames YC; *Style*— Geoffrey Kennedy, Esq; Lowsley House, Liphook, Hants (☎ 0428 723120); Kennedy & Donkin Gp, Westbrook Mills, Godalming, Surrey (☎ 04898 25900)

KENNEDY, Graham Norbert; *b* 21 Oct 1936; *Career* sr exec James Capel & Co; memb: Stock Exchange 1974, Cncl of Stock Exchange; jt chm Cncl's Quotations Ctee; *Recreations* golf, shooting, music; *Clubs* Boodles, City of London; *Style*— Graham Kennedy, Esq; Hatchetts, Church Lane, Worting, Basingstoke, Hants (☎ 0256 21764); James Capel & Co, James Capel House, 6 Bevis Marks, London EC34 7JQ (☎ 01 929 2101, telex 888866)

KENNEDY, Iain Manning; s of William Stanley Kennedy (d 1983), and Pamela Ellen, *née* Manning; *b* 15 Sept 1942; *Educ* Glenalmond, Pembroke Coll Cambridge (MA); *m* 18 Aug 1971, Ingrid Annette, da of Andersson Holgar Adolf Herr (d 1986); 2 da (Lucy Gunilla b 1974, Anna Ingrid b 1976); *Career* dir Church & Co plc 1974-; *Recreations* golf, philately; *Style*— Iain Kennedy, Esq; 3 Townsend Close, Hanging Houghton, Northampton NN6 9HP (☎ 0604 880755); office (☎ 0604 51251)

KENNEDY, Ian Philip; s of Major Algernon Thomas Kennedy, TD, of Norwood Lodge, York Rd, Weybridge, Surrey, and Marie Dolores, *née* Dorté (d 1984); *b* 22 July 1932; *Educ* Downside, Guildford Tech Coll (BSc); *m* 17 Sept 1960, Sheila Veronica, da of Arnold Albert Crook (d 1961); 1 s (Andrew b 10 Dec 1964), 1 da (Carole b 26 July 1961); *Career* Nat Serv cmmnd 2 Lt RAOC 1951-53, TA 1953-55 (Lt 1954); Wiggins Teape Gp Ltd 1953-89: sales and mktg dir industl papers 1964-70, gen mangr Stoneywood Paper Mill Aberdeen 1970-78, divnl gen mangr printings writings and carbonless papers 1979-81, divnl gen mangr printing and writing papers photographic and drawing office papers 1981-84, chief exec fine papers (also gp bd dir) 1984-89; chm bd of tstees Wiggins Teape Pension Fund 1987; former pres Eupagraph, former chm NE Scotland Productivity Assoc; Br Paper and Board Indust Fedn: former chm commercial ctee, former memb industl rels ctee Freeman: City of London 1954, Worshipful Co of Grocers 1954; MInstM 1970; *Recreations* gardening, reading, photography, music; *Style*— Ian Kennedy, Esq; Tudor House, Cricket Hill Lane, Yateley, Surrey; The Wiggins Teape Gp Ltd, Gateway House, Basing View, Basingstoke, Hants (☎ 0256 842 020)

KENNEDY, James; OBE (1976), DL (1963); s of Alexander Milroy Kennedy (d 1951), of Edinburgh, and Mary Augusta Raeburn Inches (d 1944); *b* 2 August 1907; *Educ* Glenalmond Coll, Jesus Coll Cambridge (BA); *m* 1941, Horatia Bedford, da of Thomas Bedford Franklin, FRSE (d 1960), of Edinburgh; *Career* RAF 1940-45, UK and Egypt, sqdn ldr 1945; chm Jenners Ltd Edinburgh 1951-82 (jt md 1946-73, pres 1987); dir: Edinburgh Chamber of Commerce 1954-57, Scottish Provident Inst 1959-81; master co of Merchants City of Edinburgh 1957-59; memb Bd of Mgmnt Edinburgh Savings Bank 1946-75 (chm 1969-75); chm: Tstee Savings Bank of South Scotland 1975-79; DL to City and County of the City of Edinburgh 1963-84, memb Queens Body Guard for Scotland (The Royal Co of Archers) 1936; *Recreations* deer stalking, salmon fishing, golf, gardening; *Clubs* New (Edinburgh), Muirfield, Gullane; *Style*— James Kennedy, Esq, OBE, DL; 19 Clarendon Cres, Edinburgh EH4 1PU (☎ 031 332 3400)

KENNEDY, Joanna Alicia Gore; *née* Miss Ormsby; da of Capt Gerald Anthony Gore Ormsby, DSC, DSO, RN (ret), of Stoke Row, Oxfordshire, and Nancy Mary (Susan), *née* Williams (d 1974); *b* 22 July 1950; *Educ* Queen Anne's Sch Caversham, Lady Margaret Hall Oxford (MA); *m* 21 July 1973, Richard Paul Kennedy; 2 s (Peter b 1985, David b 1988); *Career* sr engr Ove Arup & Ptnrs 1979- (design engr 1972, asst resident engr (Runnymede Bridge) 1977), project admin Arup Assocs 1987; memb: Engrg Cncl 1984-86, and 1987-, Cncl Inst of Civil Engrs 1984-87, Advsy Cncl RNEC Manadon 1988-; govr Downe House Sch; FRSA 1986, CEng, MICE, ACIArb; *Style*— Mrs Joanna Kennedy; Ove Arup & Partners, 13 Fitzroy St, London W1P 6BQ (☎ 01 636 1531, fax 01 580 3924)

KENNEDY, Rt Rev Monsignor John; s of James Kennedy (d 1961), and Alice, *née* Bentham (d 1978); *b* 31 Dec 1930; *Educ* St Joseph's Coll Upholland, English Coll Rome (PhL, STL), Campion Hall Oxford (M Phil); *Career* curate: St John's Wigan 1956-64, St Austin's St Helens 1964-66, St Edmund's Waterloo Liverpool 1966-68; lectr Christ's Coll Liverpool 1968-83 (head Theology Dept 1975-), rector English Coll Rome 1984-; *Books* Priest & People (contrib 1968); *Recreations* golf, cricket; *Clubs* Shaw Hill Golf and Country; *Style*— The Rt Rev Monsignor Kennedy; 45 Via Monserrato, Roma 00186, Italy (☎ 686 4185)

KENNEDY, Ludovic Henry Coverley; s of Capt Edward Kennedy, RN (ka 1939; ggs of Hon Robert Kennedy, bro of 1 Marquess of Ailsa and 3 s of 11 Earl of Cassillis), and Rosalind, da of Sir Ludovic Grant, 11 Bt of Dalvey; *b* 3 Nov 1919; *Educ* Eton, Ch Ch Oxford; *m* 1950, Moira Shearer (formerly ballerina with Sadler's Wells Ballet, actress (including The Red Shoes), and lecturer), da of Harold King; 1 s, 3 da; *Career* Lt RNVR; contested (Lib) Rochdale 1958 and 1959; writer and broadcaster; West German Cross of Merit 1st class; *Books* 10 Rillington Place, Pursuit, The Airman and the Carpenter, On the Way to the Club (autobiography); *Clubs* Brooks's, Army and Navy, Beefsteak, MCC; *Style*— Ludovic Kennedy, Esq; c/o Rogers, Coleridge & White, 22 Powis Mews, London W11 1JN

KENNEDY, Sir Michael Edward; 8 Bt (UK 1836), of Johnstown Kennedy, Co Dublin; s Lt-Col Sir (George) Ronald Derrick Kennedy, 7 Bt, OBE (d 1988); *b* 12 April 1956; *Educ* Rotherfield Hall Sussex; *m* 1984, Helen Christine Jennifer, da of Patrick Lancelot Rae, of Nine Acres, Halstead, Kent; 2 da (Constance b 1984, Josephine b 1986); *Heir* uncle, Mark Gordon Kennedy b 3 Feb 1932; *Style*— Michael Kennedy, Esq; Johnstown Kennedy, Rathcoole, Co Dublin; c/o Noelle, Lady Kennedy, Harraton Square Church Lane, Exning, Suffolk

KENNEDY, Neil Richard; s of Walter Kennedy (d 1988), and Vera Nancy Kennedy; *b* 6 Mar 1946; *Educ* Uppingham; *m* 1, Georgina Theresa, *née* Tolhurst (d 1979); 2 s

(Angus b 19 Jan 1973, James b 7 Sept 1978), 2 da (Caroline b 28 Oct 1971, Elizabeth b 8 Oct 1976); m 2, 28 Nov 1980, Johanna, da of Gert Woudstra, of Holland; *Career* Colman Prentis & Valley Ltd 1963-65, dep md Childs-Greene Assocs Ltd 1965-76, md Brunnings plc 1976-78, vice chm BSB Dorland Ltd 1978-; tstee Burnham YC (former cdre); *Books* Retail Handbook (1988); *Recreations* skiing, sailing, shooting; *Clubs* Royal Burnham YC, Royal Thames YC; *Style*— Neil Kennedy, Esq

KENNEDY, Nigel Paul; s of John Kennedy, and Scylla, *née* Stoner; *b* 28 Dec 1956; *Educ* Yehudi Menuhin Sch, Juillard Sch of Performing Arts; *Career* solo violinist; debut at Festival hall with Philharmonia Orch 1977, Berlin debut with Berlin Philharmonia 1980, Henry Wood Promenade debut 1981, New York debut with BBC Symphony Orch 1987, tour of Hong Kong and Aust with Hallé Orch 1981, recordings incl: Tchaikovsky, Sibelius, Vivaldi, Elgar Violin Concerto (record of the Year 1985, Gold Disc), Bruch Mendellsohn, Walton Violin and Viola, and Let Loose; *Recreations* golf, driving, football, cricket, boxing; *Style*— Nigel Kennedy, Esq; c/o Helen Turner, Terry Harrison Artists Management, 9a Penzance Place, London W11 4PE (☎ 01 221 7741/ 2, fax 01 221 2610, telex 25872 TERRYH G)

KENNEDY, Noelle, Lady; Noelle Mona; *née* Green; da of Charles Henry Green, of Hunworth, Melton Constable, Norfolk; *m* 1949, Lt-Col Sir (George) Ronald Derrick Kennedy, 7 Bt, OBE, RA (d 1988); 1 s (Sir Michael, 8 Bt, *qv*), 1 da (Carolyn Phyllis (Mrs Jan Blaauw) b 1950); Harraton Square, Church Lane, Exning, Suffolk

KENNEDY, Hon Mr Justice; Hon Sir Paul Joseph Morrow Kennedy; QC (1973); s of Dr Joseph Morrow Kennedy, of Sheffield, and Bridget Teresa Kennedy; *b* 12 June 1935; *Educ* Ampleforth, Gonville and Caius Coll Cambridge; *m* 1965, Hon Virginia, *qv*, da of Baron Devlin; 2 s, 2 da; *Career* barr Gray's Inn 1960, rec 1972, bencher 1982, High Court Judge 1983-, presiding judge NE circuit 1985-; kt; *Style*— The Hon Sir Justice Kennedy, QC; Royal Courts of Justice, Strand, London WC2A 2LL

KENNEDY, Tessa Georgina (Mrs Elliott Kastner); da of Geoffrey Farrer Kennedy, of Lowsley House, Liphook, Hants, and Daska McLean, *née* Ivanovic; *b* 6 Dec 1938; *Educ* Oak Hall Haslemere Surrey, Ecole de Beaux Arts Paris; *m* 1, 27 Jan 1958 (m dis 1969), Dominick Evelyn Bede Elwes, s of Simon Elwes (d 1975); 3 s (Cassian b 1959, Damian b 1960, Cary b 1962); m 2, 26 June 1971, Elliott Kastner; 1 s (Dillon b 1970), 1 da (Milica b 1972); *Career* interior designer, clients incl: John Barry, Sam Spiegel, Richard Burton, Stanley Kubrick, Viscount Hambledon, De Beers, BUPA Hosps, HM King of Jordan, Michael Winner, Candice Bergen, Rudolf Nureyev, George Harrison, currently Claridges; memb ISID; *Recreations* tennis, movies, watching american football; *Style*— Miss Tessa Kennedy; 2 Hyde Pk Gdns, London W2 2LT (☎ 01 723 4686); 1 East 62nd St, New York, NY 10021; Studio 5, 91/97 Freston Rd, London W11 4BD (☎ 01 221 4546, fax 01 229 2899, car 0836 201 980)

KENNEDY, Air Chief Marshal Sir Thomas Lawrie; GCB (KCB 1980, CB 1978), AFC (1953) and Bar (1960); s of James Domoné Kennedy and Margaret Henderson, *née* Lawrie; *b* 19 May 1928; *Educ* Hawick HS, RAF Coll Cranwell; *m* 1959, Margaret Ann Parker; 1 s, 2 da; *Career* Cmmnd RAF 1949; Dep C-in-C RAF Strike Cmd 1979-81, C-in-C RAF Germany and Cdr Second Allied Tactical Air Force 1981-83, Air Memb for Personnel, Air Force Bd 1983-; Air ADC to HM 1983-; *Style*— Air Chief Marshal Sir Thomas Kennedy, GCB, AFC, ADC; c/o MOD, Whitehall, London SW1

KENNEDY, Hon Lady; Hon Virginia; da (twin) of Baron Devlin (Life Peer); *b* 1940; *m* 1965, The Hon Mr Justice (Paul) Kennedy, *qv*; 2 s, 2 da; memb of Press Cncl 1987-; *Style*— The Hon Lady Kennedy; c/o The Hon Mr Justice Kennedy, Royal Courts of Justice, Strand, London WC2A 2LL

KENNEDY, William Michael Clifford; s of Dr Clifford Donald Kennedy, FRCS, FRCSE, and Isobel Sinclair Kennedy (d 1984); *b* 29 Oct 1935; *Educ* Rugby, Merton Coll Oxford (BA, PPE); *m* 1962, Judith Victoria, da of Kenneth Fulton Gibb, of Fife; 1 s (Niall b 1964), 1 da (Tessa b 1965); *Career* CA; dir: Martin Currie Inc 1978-, Martin Currie Investment Mgmnt Ltd 1978-, The Scottish Life Assurance Co 1976-, The Scottish Eastern Investmt Tst plc 1982-, Venture Associates SA 1978-, Martin Currie Pacific Tst 1985-; fin advsr Royal Scottish Acad; *Recreations* shooting, fishing, golf, gardening, music; *Clubs* New (Edinburgh); Hon Co of Edinburgh Golfers; *Style*— Michael Kennedy, Esq; Oak Lodge, Inverest, Midlothain EH21 7TE (☎ 031 665 8822); 29 Charlotte Square, Edinburgh EH2 4HA (☎ 031 225 3811, telex 72505)

KENNERLEY, Prof (James) Anthony Machell (Tony); s of William James Kennerley, of Bankhall Lane, Hale, Cheshire, and Vida May, *née* Machell (d 1984); *b* 24 Oct 1933; *Educ* Altrincham GS, Rhyl GS, Univ of Manchester (BSc), Imp Coll London (MSc); *m* 12 Jan 1978, Dorothy Mary, da of George Paterson Simpson; 1 s (David James b 20 Nov 1978), 1 da (Elizabeth Lindsay (twin) b 20 November 1978); *Career* PO RAFVR 1952-57, Flying Offr RCAF 1959-62; aerodynamicist: AV Roe & Co Manchester 1955-58, Pratt & Whitney USA 1958-59; asst prof of mathematics Univ of new Brunswick Canada 1962-67, dir of studies Manchester Business Sch 1967-69, assoc prof of business admin Columbia Univ Business Sch NY 1969-70, sr lectr mktg and quantitative methods London Business Sch 1970-73, dir Strathclyde Univ Business Sch 1973-83 (prof 1973-83); dir S Scotland Electricity Bd 1976-83; chm: arbitration panel Scottish Milk Mktg Bd 1981-83, W Surrey and NE Hants Health Authy 1986-; arbitrator ACAS 1976-; memb Bridgegate Tst Glasgow 1981-84; AFMIA, MIMechE, AFRACS, FBIM; *Books* Guide To Business Schools (1985); *Recreations* flying, travelling; *Clubs* Reform; *Style*— Prof Tony Kennerley; 5 Old Rectory Gdns, Busbridge, Godalming, Surrey GU7 1XB (☎ 04868 28108); West Surrey and North East Hampshire Health Authority, Abbey House, 282 Farnborough Rd, Farnborough, Hants GU14 7NE (☎ 0252 548 881)

KENNERLEY, Peter Dilworth; s of John Dilworth Kennerley, and Margery, *née* Dugard (d 1977); *b* 9 June 1956; *Educ* Collyers Sch, Sidney Sussex Coll Cambridge (MA); *Career* TA Maj Royal Yeo 1986; Simmons & Simmons: joined 1979, admitted slr 1981, ptnr 1986; sec Panel on Takeovers and Mergers 1986-88; memb Law Soc; *Clubs* Cavalry and Guards; *Style*— Peter Kennerley, Esq; 13 Gauden Rd, London SW4 6LR (☎ 01 720 5160); Simmons & Simmons, 14 Dominion St, London EC2M 2RJ (☎ 01 628 2020, fax 01 588 4129, telex 888562)

KENNET, 2 Baron (UK 1935); Wayland Hilton Young; s of 1 Baron Kennet, GBE, DSO, DSC, PC (d 1960), and Kathleen, da of Rev Canon Lloyd Stewart Bruce (3 s of Sir James Bruce, 2 Bt) and widow of Capt Robert Falcon Scott, CVO, RN, the Antarctic explorer; Lady Kennet was a sculptor whose works include the statue of her first husband in Waterloo Place; *b* 2 August 1923; *Educ* Stowe, Trinity Coll Cambridge (MA), Perugia, Harvard; *m* 24 Jan 1948, Elizabeth Ann, da of Capt Bryan Fullerton Adams, DSO, RN; 1 s, 5 da; *Heir* s, Hon Thoby Young; *Career* sits as SDP peer in House of Lords; RN 1942-45, FO 1946-47 and 1949-51, del Parly Assemblies WEU and Cncl of Europe 1962-65, parly sec Miny of Housing and Local Govt 1966-70, Labour oppn spokesman Foreign Affrs and Science Policy 1971-74; chm: Advsy Ctee on Oil Pollution of the Sea 1970-74, CPRE 1971-72, Int Parly Conferences on the Environment 1972-78; MEP 1978-79, SDP Whip in House of Lords 1981-83, SDP spokesman on Defence and Foreign Affrs 1981-; Hon FRIBA; author and journalist; *Recreations* sailing, walking; *Style*— The Rt Hon the Lord Kennet; House of Lords, London SW1

KENNETT-BROWN, David; JP (Willesden 1975-); s of Thomas Kennett Brown (d 1979), and Vanda, *née* Low; *b* 29 Jan 1938; *Educ* Durston House Ealing, Monkton Combe Sch Bath, Lincoln Coll Oxford (MA), London Univ (Dip Crim); *m* 1966, Wendy Margaret, da of Frederick Gordon Evans (d 1984); 1 s (Neil b 1969), 2 da (Kathryn b 1967, Alison b 1971); *Career* churchwarden St John's Church W Ealing 1973-86, dep chm Juvenile & Domestic Cts Panel 1979-82, chm London Rent Assessment Panel 1979-82, pres Central & South Middx Law Soc 1982-, chm Inner London Juvenile Cts 1983-, Metropolitan stipendiary magistrate 1983-, asst Crown Ct recorder 1984-; FCIArt; *Recreations* walking, gardening, family life; *Style*— David Kennett-Brown, Esq, JP; 34 The Mall, Ealing, London W5; Inner London Magistrates Ct Service, Bush House, NW Wing, Aldwych, Strand, London WC2

KENNON, Vice Adm James Edward Campbell; KCB (1982), CBE (1974, OBE 1962); s of Robert Kennon, MC, FRCS, and Florence Ethel,*née* Warton; *b* 26 Nov 1925; *Educ* Stowe; *m* 1950, Anne, da of Capt Sir Stuart Paton, KCVO, CBE, RN (ret); 2 s, 1 da; *Career* joined RN 1943, Sec to C-in-C Fleet 1968-70, Sec to First Sea Lord 1971-74, Asst Chief of Naval Staff Policy 1978-79, Chief of Naval Supply and Secretariat Offr 1979-81, Port Admiral Rosyth 1980-81, Vice-Adm 1981, Chief of Fleet Support 1981-83; *Recreations* gardening, walking; *Clubs* Army and Navy; *Style*— Vice Adm Sir James Kennon, KCB, CBE; c/o National Westminster Bank, 26 Haymarket, London SW1

KENNY, Dr Anthony John Patrick; s of John Kenny, and Margaret, *née* Jones; *b* 16 Mar 1931; *Educ* St Joseph's Coll Upholland, Gregorian Univ Rome, St Benet's Hall Oxford (DPhil); *m* 2 April 1966, Nancy Caroline, da of Henry T Gayley Jr, of Ithaca, NY, USA; 2 s (Robert b 1968, Charles b 1970); *Career* master Balliol Coll Oxford 1978-89, warden and sec Rhodes Tst Oxford 1989-; vice pres Br Acad 1986-88; Hon DLitt Bristol 1982, Hon DHumLitt Denison Ohio 1986, Hon DCL Oxon 1987, Hon Liverpool 1988; *Books* Descartes (1968), Wittgenstein (1973), Will, Freedom and Power (1975), Freewill and Responsibility (1978), The God of the Philisophers (1979), A Path from Rome (1986), The Road to Hillsborough (1986), The Heritage of Wisdom (1987), Reason and Religion (1987); *Clubs* United Oxford and Cambridge, Athenaeum; *Style*— Dr Anthony Kenny; Balliol College, Oxford

KENNY, His Honour Judge Anthony Marriott; s of Noel Edgar Edward Marriott Kenny, OBE (d 1972), of Zimbabwe and Zambia, and Cynthia Margaret Seton, *née* Melville; *b* 24 May 1939; *Educ* St Andrew's Coll, Christ's Coll Cambridge (MA); *m* 1969, Monica, da of Hector Bennet Grant Mackenzie, of S Africa; 3 s (Julian Hector Marriott b 1972, Christian Edward Mackenzie b 1977, Nicholas William Mackenzie b 1983); *Career* barr Grays Inn 1963, recorder of the Crown Ct 1980-, circuit judge 1987, practice SE circuit; *Recreations* travelling, skiing, music, reading, tennis; *Style*— His Honour Judge Kenny; Melbury Place, Wentworth, Surrey GU25 4LB

KENNY, Gen Brian Leslie Graham; CBE (1979), KBE (1985); s of Brig James Wolfenden Kenny, CBE (d 1978); *b* 18 June 1934; *Educ* Canford; *m* 1958, Diana Catherine Jane, da of Brig Felton Arthur Hamilton Mathew, OBE, MC (d 1977); 2 s; *Career* CO Queen's Royal Irish Hussars 1974-76, Col GS HQ 4 Armd Div 1976-78, Brig 1978, cmd 12 Armd Bde 1978-80, Maj-Gen 1982, GOC 1 Armd Div 1982-83, dir Army Staff Duties MOD 1983-85, Col Cmdt Royal Army Veterinary Corps 1983-, Col QRIH 1985, cmd (BR) Corps 1985-87, C-in-C BAOR/Comd NORTHAG 1987, gen 1987; govr Canford Sch; *Recreations* cricket, tennis, skiing; *Clubs* MCC, IZ, Free Foresters, Cavalry and Guards'; *Style*— Gen Sir Brian Kenny, KCB, CBE; c/o Lloyds Bank plc, 19 Obelisk Way, Camberley, Surrey GU15 3SE

KENNY, Michael James; s of James Kenny, of Blackburn, Lancashire, and Ellen, *née* Gordon; *b* 10 June 1941; *Educ* St Francis Xavier's Coll Liverpool, Liverpool Coll of Art, Slade Sch of Fine Art; *m* 1, July 1962 (m dis), Gillian Wainwright; m 2 (m dis), June 1968, Rosemary Flood; m 3, 20 Dec 1978, Angela Helen, da of Maj Anthony Smith of Dorset; 1 s, 2 da; *Career* visiting lectr Slade Sch of Fine Art 1970-82, dir of fine art studies Goldsmith's Coll London 1983-88; worked at: Tate Gallery, V & A Museum, British Museum; numerous one-man exhibitions in: Paris, Milan, Tokyo, Frankfurt, etc; memb: Cathedrals Advsy Ctee, bd of govrs The London Inst; ARA 1976, RA 1986; *Recreations* ornithology; *Clubs* Chelsea Arts; *Style*— Michael Kenny, Esq; 71 Stepney Green, London E1 3LE (☎ 01 790 3409); Annely Juda Fina Art, 11 Tottenham Mews, London W1P 9PJ (☎ 01 637 5517/8/9)

KENNY, Sir Patrick John; s of Patrick John Kenny (d 1958), and Agnes Margaret Kenny (d 1953); *b* 12 Jan 1914; *Educ* Marcellin Coll, Sydney Univ (MB, BS, MS); *m* 1942, Beatrice Ella, da of Cecil James Hammond (d 1963); 2 s; *Career* Maj, served UK, Mid E, SWPA; conslt emeritus surgn St Vincent's Hosp and Lewisham Hosp Sydney (surgn 1946-79); pres Royal Australasian Coll of Surgns 1969-71; FRCS, FRACS, Hon FRCPS (Glasgow); kt 1976; *Style*— Sir Patrick Kenny; 13 David St, Mosman, Sydney, NSW 2088, Australia (☎ 960 2820)

KENNY, Prof Phillip Herbert; s of Robert Kenney, of King's Lynn, and Moira, *née* Davies; *b* 9 August 1948; *Educ* Bristol Univ (LLB), Cambridge Univ (Dip Crim), Univ of Columbia (LLM); *m* 7 Aug 1970, Ann Mary, da of Harold Langley (d 1970), of Winchester; 1 s (Stephen b 1982), 3 da (Julia b 1975, Angharad b 1977, Helen b 1979); *Career* slr; head of Law Dept Newcastle Poly 1980-, former Univ and Poly lectr; *Recreations* pigeon racing, walking, sailing; *Clubs* North of England Homing Union; *Style*— Prof Phillip Kenny; 105 Kenton Rd, Gosforth NE3 4NL; Newcastle upon Tyne Polytechnic, Newcastle upon Tyne

KENNY, Thomas; s of John Kenny (d 1944), and Lucy, *née* O'Dea (d 1960); *b* 3 June 1919; *Educ* Univ Sch Dublin, Nat Univ of Ireland; *m* 1944, Blanche, da of Frank Aubrey Blanche, of Surrey; 1 s, 1 da; *Career* chm: GEI Int plc, Sheffield Forgemasters plc, CDB Investmts Ltd, Industrial Funding Tst Ltd, Campden Hill Gate Ltd; FCA; *Recreations* fly fishing, racing; *Clubs* Arts, City of London, Flyfishers'; *Style*— Thomas Kenny, Esq; Brettenham House, Lancaster Place, London WC2E 7EN (☎ 01 379 7555); 10 Campden Hill Gate, Duchess of Bedford's Walk, London W8

KENRICK, Martin John; s of William Edmund Kenrick (d 1981), of Birmingham, and

Elizabeth Dorothy Magdalen, *née* Loveday; family non-conformists who settled with others in Midlands, family firm run by sixth generation; *b* 5 Feb 1940; *Educ* Newlands Sch, Rugby Sch, Trinity Coll Dublin (MA, BComm), Cranfield Inst of Tech (MSc); *m* 21 Feb 1970, Christine Mary, da of Charles Ronald Wingham (d 1972), of St Albans, Herts; 1 s (Hilgrove b 1977), 2 da (Tanya b 1972, Helen b 1973); *Career* guardian Birmingham Assay Office 1971-; Cmmr of Taxes 1972; md Archibald Kenrick & Sons Ltd 1973-78 (chm 1978-), dir Birmingham R & D Ltd 1985-(chm 1985-87), hon life memb ct of govrs Birmingham Univ 1978 (memb cncl 1981-, memb fin and gen purpose ctee 1987-); Birmingham Chamber of Indust and Commerce: cncl memb 1981-, memb gen purposes ctee 1982-, chm educn ctee 1985-, working pty for Indust Year 1985-86; memb mgmnt ctee W Midlands Regnl Mgmnt Centre 1978-82; dir: Black Country Museum Tst 1987-, Birmingham Chamber Trg Ltd 1986-87; chm: policy gp Birmingham Local Employers Network 1987-, W Midlands Region Industry Matters 1987-; *Recreations* ornithology, skiing, tennis, squash, hockey, gardening; *Style—* Martin J Kenrick, Esq; The Mount, 37 Richmond Hill Rd, Edgbaston, Birmingham B15 3RR (☎ 021 454 4720); Archibald Kenrick & Sons Ltd, PO Box 9 West Bromwich, West Midlands B70 6DB (☎ 021 553 2741, fax 021 500 6332, telex 336470 KENRIC G)

KENROY, James Royston; s of Ronald Victor Kenroy, of Hampshire, and Marjorie Barbara, *née* Hughes (d 1987); *b* 10 Jan 1932; *Educ* Tonbridge; *m* 25 June 1966, (Margaret) Deirdre, da of Rev (Gordon) Ronald Paterson, MBE; 2 da (Vanessa b 17 Aug 1967, Rebecca b 15 Oct 1968); *Career* admitted slr 1956, sr ptnr Glanvilles 1983-; pres Hants Inc Law Soc 1985-86, fndr chm Portsmouth and S E Hants Conveyancing Protocol 1986-, int rel offr RTBI 1968-70, ed World Cncl of Young Mens' Serv Clubs 1970-72; dep coroner City of Portsmouth 1984-, pt/t chm Soc Sec Appeal Tbnls 1987-; memb Coroners Soc; *Recreations* family life; *Clubs* RN and Royal Albert YC; *Style—* James Kenroy, Esq; 16 Landport Terr, Portsmouth (☎ 0705 827231, fax 0705 753611, telex 86538)

KENSINGTON, 8 Baron (I 1776 and UK 1886); Hugh Ivor Edwardes; s of Capt Hon Owen Edwardes (d 1937, 2 s of 6 Baron Kensington, CMG, DSO, TD, JP, DL); suc unc, 7 Baron, 1981; *b* 24 Nov 1933; *Educ* Eton; *m* 1961, Juliet Elizabeth Massy, da of Capt Alexander Massy Anderson (d 1943); 2 s (Hon Owen b 21 July 1964, Hon Rupert b 25 Jan 1967), 1 da (Hon Amanda, *qv*); *Heir* s, Hon William Owen Alexander Edwardes; *Career* farmer and thoroughbred breeder; *Recreations* horse breeding, shooting; *Clubs* Boodle's, Durban; *Style—* The Rt Hon the Lord Kensington; Friar Tuck, PO Box 549, Mooi River, 3300 Natal, S Africa (☎ 033322 36323)

KENSWOOD, Catherine, Baroness; Catherine (Chilver-Stainer); da of Frank Luxton; *b* 10 Nov 1895; *m* 1962, as his 2 wife, 1 Baron Kenswood (d 1963); *Style—* Catherine, Lady Kenswood; c/o Barclays Bank, 25 Soho Square, London

KENSWOOD, 2 Baron (UK 1951); John Michael Howard Whitfield; s of 1 Baron Kenswood (d 1963); *b* 6 April 1930; *Educ* Trinity Sch Ontario, Harrow, Grenoble Univ, Emmanuel Coll Cambridge; *m* 1951, Deirdre Anna Louise, da of Colin Malcolm Methven, of Errol, Perthshire; 4 s (Hon Michael b 1955, Hon Anthony b 1957, Hon Steven b 1958, Hon Benjamin b 1961), 1 da (Hon Anna Louisa b 1964); *Heir* s, Hon Michael Whitfield; *Style—* The Rt Hon the Lord Kenswood; Domaine de la Foret, 31340 Villemur sur Tarn, France

KENT, Geoffrey Charles; s of Percival Whitehead Kent, and Madge Kent; *b* 2 Feb 1922; *Educ* Blackpool GS; *m* 1955, Brenda Georgine; *Career* WWII, Coastal Cmd RAF; joined Imperial Gp 1958: jt md John Player 1969 (chm and md 1975-78), memb Imperial Gp Bd 1975-86; chm and chief exec: Courage Ltd 1978-81, Imperial Group plc 1981-86; chm Mansfield Brewery plc 1989-; dir: Lloyds Bank plc 1981-, Lloyds Bank Int 1983-85, Lloyds Merchant Bank Hldgs 1985-87; memb Lloyds of London 1985-; dep chm: Cora plc 1986-, John Howitt Group Ltd 1986-; FIM, CBIM; *Recreations* flying (full instrument rating), skiing; *Clubs* RAF; *Style—* Geoffrey Kent, Esq; Hill House, Gonalston, Notts NG14 7JA (☎ 0602 663303)

KENT, Sir Harold Simcox; GCB (1963, KCB 1954, CB 1946), QC (1973); s of Percy Horace Braund Kent, OBE, MC (d 1963), of Clavering, Cooden, Sussex, and Anna Mary, *née* Simcox; *b* 11 Nov 1903; *Educ* Rugby, Merton Coll Oxford; *m* 14 April 1930, Zillah (d 1987), da of Henry Rees Lloyd; 1 s, 1 da (decd); *Career* barr Inner Temple 1928; Parliamentary Cncl 1940-53; HM Procurator-Gen and Treasy Slr 1953-63; slr: Bank Rate Tribunal 1957, Vassall Tribunal 1962; Standing Cnsl to Church Assembly and Gen Synod 1964-72; memb Security Cmmn 1967-72; vicar-gen Province of Canterbury 1970-76; dean of Arches Ct of Canterbury and auditor of Chancery Ct of York 1972-76; commissary to Dean and Chapter of St Paul's Cathedral 1976-; *Books* In on the Act (1979); *Clubs* United Oxford and Cambridge Univ; *Style—* Sir Harold Kent, GCB, QC; Alderley, Calf Lane, Chipping Campden, Glos (☎ 0386 840421)

KENT, John Philip Cozens; s of John Cozens Kent, DCM, and Lucy Ella, *née* Binns (d 1984); *b* 28 Sept 1928; *Educ* Minchenden Co GS, UCL (BA, PhD); *m* 21 Oct 1961, Patricia Eleanor, da of Lionel Maldwyn Bunford (d 1961); 1 s (Philip b 1962), 1 da (Hilary b 1965); *Career* Nat Serv 1951-53, 2 Lt RASC 1952; Br Museum Dept of Coins and Medals: asst keeper 1953-74, dep keeper 1974-83-, keeper 1983-; pres: Br Assoc of Numismatic Socs 1974-78, Royal Numismatic Soc 1984-89, London and Middx Archaelogical Soc 1985-88, Barnet and Dist Local Hist Soc 1980-; FRNS 1948, FSA 1961, FBA 1986, FMA 1988; memb Institute de Sintra 1986; *Books* Late Roman Bronze Coinage (jtly 1960), Wealth of the Roman World (with K S Painter, 1977), Roman Coins (1978), 2000 Years of British Coins and Medals (1978), Roman Imperial Coinage Vol VIII, The Family of Constantine I 337-364 (1981), A Selection of Byzantine Coins in the Barber Institute of Fine Arts (1985), British Museum Catalogue of Celtic Coins Vol I (with M R Mays, 1987), Catalogue of Silver Coins of the East Celts and other Balkan Peoples (with M R Mays, 1987); *Recreations* local history and archaeology, mediaeval music, railway history; *Style—* Dr John Kent; 16 Newmans Way, Hadley Wood, Barnet, Herts EN4 OLR; Dept of Coins and Medals, British Museum, London WC1B 3DG (☎ 01 323 8170)

KENT, John Sutcliffe; s of John Kent (d 1970), of Essex, and Elsie Kent, *née* Sutcliffe; *b* 27 Jan 1930; *Educ* Pangbourne Nautical Coll Berks; *m* 3 June 1958, Jean Margaret, da of James Lennox (d 1982), of Essex; 2 da (Elizabeth Ann b 1960, Hilary Alison b 1964); *Career* Lt RNVR 1951-53; dir: Guild of Architectural Ironmongers, Kent Blaxill & Co Ltd; *Recreations* golf, bowling; *Clubs* Colchester Garrison Officers, Colchester Gc; *Style—* John Kent, Esq; Hill House, Gravel Hill, Nayland, Colchester CO6 4JB; Kent Blaxill & Co Ltd, PO Box 17, Colchester CO2 9SY

KENT, Dr Paul Welberry; JP (1972); s of Thomas William Kent (d 1975), of Doncaster, and Marion, *née* Cox (d 1954); *b* 19 April 1923; *Educ* Doncaster GS, Birmingham Univ (BSc 1944, PhD 1947), Jesus Coll Oxford (MA 1951, DPhil 1953, DSc 1966); *m* 23 Aug 1952, Rosemary Elizabeth Boutflower, da of Maj Charles Herbert Boutflower Shepherd, MC, TD (d 1980), of Oxford; 3 s (Anthony b 1955, Richard b 1961, Peter b 1964), 1 da (Deborah b 1957); *Career* asst lectr, subsequently ICI Fell, Birmingham Univ 1946-50; visiting fell Princeton Univ NJ 1948-49; demonstrator in biochemistry Oxford Univ 1950-72; student, tutor and Dr Lees Reader Christ Church Oxford 1955-72 (emeritus student 1972-); master Van Mildert Coll Durham Univ 1972-82, research dir Durham Univ 1972-82; biochemical conslt, visiting prof Windsor Univ Ontario 1971 and 1980; memb: Oxford City Cncl 1964-72, Ctee Biochemical Soc 1963-67, Chemical Cncl 1965-70, Advsy Ctee Cystic Fibrosis Res Cncl 1977-82; govr: Oxford Coll of Technol, subsequently Oxford Poly 1964-72 and 1983 (vice-chm 1966-69, chm 1969-70), St Chad's Coll Durham 1976-, Pusey House Oxford 1983-; memb Oxford Poly Higher Educn Corpn 1988- (dep chm); hon fell Canterbury Coll Ontario 1974, Hon DLitt Drury Coll USA 1973, Verdienstkreuz (Bundes Republik) 1970; author of articles in scientific journals and jt author of scientific monographs; FRSC 1950; *Books* Biochemistry of the Amino Sugars (with M W Whitehouse 1955), International Aspects of the Provision of Medical Care (1976); *Recreations* travel, flute and organ music; *Clubs* Athenaeum; *Style—* Dr Paul Kent; Bricoe Gate, Baldersdale, Barnard Castle, Co Durham DL12 9UL; 18 Arnolds Way, Cumnor Hill, Oxford OX2 9JB (☎ 0865 862087)

KENT, Roderick David; s of Dr Basil Stanley Kent, of Wheat House, Wheathold, Ransdell, Hants, and Vivien Margaret, *née* Baker; *b* 14 August 1947; *Educ* King's Sch Canterbury, CCC Oxford (MA 1970); *m* 12 Aug 1972, Belinda Jane, da of W H Mitchell (d 1983), of Francheville, Grouville, Jersey; 3 da (Sophie b 1974, Nicola b 1976, Tiffany b 1978); *Career* with J Henry Schroder Wagg & Co Ltd 1969-71, Banque Blyth (Paris) 1971, Institut Européen d'Administration des Affaires (INSEAD) 1971-72, Triumph Investment Tst 1972-74; Close Bros 1974- (md 1975-); chm bd of govrs Inhurst House Sch; Liveryman of Worshipful Co of Pewterers; MBA 1972; *Recreations* sport; *Style—* Roderick Kent Esq; Close Brothers Ltd, 36 Great St Helens, London EC3A 6AP (☎ 01 283 2241, fax 01 623 9699, telex 8814274); Wolverton Cottage, Wolverton, nr Basingstoke, Hants RG26 5SX (☎ 0635 298 276)

KENT, Brig Sidney Harcourt; OBE (1944); s of Maj Geoffrey Harcourt Kent (d 1979), of Hindhead, and Muriel Hutton, *née* Potts (d 1981); *b* 22 April 1915; *Educ* Wellington Coll, RMC Sandhurst; *m* 5 March 1945, Nina Ruth, da of Gen Sir Geoffry Arthur Percival Scoones, KCB, KBE, CSI, DSO, MC (d 1975), of Ashdon, Essex; 1 s (Simon b 1948), 1 da (Susan b 1946); *Career* 2 Lieut KOYLI, Lieut-Col 1944, Brig 1944; GSO1 8 Army 1944, BGS Allied Land Forces SE Asia 1944; cmd 128 Inf Bde (TA) 1960-63; man and sec Turf Bd 1965, gen man and chief exec Jockey Club 1969, advsr Royal Horse Soc Teheran 1978, tech advsr Nicosia Race Club 1979, conslt steward Jamaica Racing Cmmn 1984-86; dir racing Macao Jockey Club 1989; *Recreations* farming, travel, vintage cars; *Style—* Brig Sidney H Kent, OBE; The Old Vicarage, Kingsey, Aylesbury, Bucks (☎ 0844 291 411); Maroni Village, Larnaca, Cyprus (☎ 0433 2614)

KENT, Trevor Lincoln; s of Ernest George Kent (d 1987), of Gerrards Cross, Bucks, and Evelyn Gertrude Mary, *née* Fuller; *b* 28 Mar 1947; *Educ* Denstone Coll, London Coll of Commerce; *m* 7 July 1979, Angela Christine, da of Gp Capt John Thornhill Shaw, DSO, DFC, AFC (d 1975), of Worplesdon, Surrey; 4 s (Toby d 1980, Lincoln b 1982, Warwick b 1983, Leicester b 1987); *Career* served with various estate agents, sr ptnr Trevor Kent & Co 1971-; dist cncllr South Bucks DC 1978-82; pres Nat Assoc of Estate Agents May 1989-, memb Jt Professional Working Pty on Conveyancing Reform, licenced asst CoE, govr Park Crescent Sch for Disabled Children; fell Nat Assoc of Estate Agents; *Recreations* playing cricket, watching the garden grow, separating the boys, not dieting; *Style—* Trevor Kent, Esq; The Nat Assoc of Estate Agents, 21 Jury St, Warwick CV34 4EH (☎ 0926 496800, fax 0926 400 953)

KENTISH, Lt Cdr William; VRD (1968, and clasp 1974); s of Capt William Kentish (d 1954), of 41 Amesbury Rd, Moseley, Birmingham, and Florence Gladys Louise Kentish (d 1963); *b* 14 Sept 1918; *Educ* King Edwards Sch Birmingham, Cambridge Univ (MA, LLM); *m* 1, 1952 (m dis 1954), Daphne, *née* Cunynghame; m2, 1957 (m dis 1967), Sylvia Mary, *née* Abbotts; 2 s (William David b 10 Jan 1958, Miles Adrian b 20 April 1959); *Career* Sub Lt RNVR trg HMS King Alfred 1939, served with Naval ASDIC trawlers in Bristol Channel 1939-40, HMS Arethusa 1940-42, drafted to HMS Carnarvon Castle 1942, Lt 1942, served in HMS Rockrose and as Gunnery Offr HMS Artic Explorer in convoys from Cape Town to Durban and back 1943, Co HM Fairmile Motor Launch 857 1944-45, active serv in Burma 1945, demob 1946; re-joined RNVR 1950, Navigating Pilotage Certificate 1955 served in HMS Truelove and HMS Sheffield, Lt Cdr 1956, trained as Naval Control of Shipping Offr 1960-74; admitted slr 1948; ptnr: James Kentish & Atkins, Kentish & Co, Cottrell & Co, Cottrell Son & Wm Kentish, Cottrell Kentish & Bache, Haynes Duffell Kentish & Co; Notary Public 1965; cncl memb Birmingham Law Soc 1980-84, hon sec Cons Political Gp; memb Law Soc; *Recreations* golf, swimming; *Clubs* MCC, Birmingham, Edgbaston GC; *Style—* Lt Cdr William Kentish, VRD; 88 Salisbury Rd, Moseley, Birmingham B13 8JY (☎ 021 449 3933); Essex House, 27 Temple St, Birmingham B2 5RQ (☎ 021 643 1235, fax 021 643 1314)

KENTRIDGE, Sydney; QC (1984); s of Morris Kentridge (d 1964), of Johannesburg, and May, *née* Shafner (d 1971); *b* 5 Nov 1922; *Educ* King Edward VII Sch Johannesburg, Univ of Witwatersrand (BA), Oxford Univ (MA); *m* 15 Jan 1952, Felicia, da of Max Geffen, of Johannesburg (d 1977); 2 s (William, Matthew), 2 da (Catherine, Elizabeth); *Career* WWII Lt SA Forces served E Africa, Sicily, Italy; memb: Johannesburg Bar 1949-, sr counsel SA 1965; called to Bar Lincoln's Inn 1977 ; bencher Lincoln's Inn, hon fell Exeter Coll Oxford, Roberts lectr Univ of Pennsylvania 1979, Granville Clark Prize (VSA) 1978; judge of the Cts of Appeal of Jersey, Guernsey and Republic of Botswana; Hon LLD: Leicester 1985, Cape Town 1987, Seaton Hall, New Jersey 1978; *Recreations* opera-going; *Clubs* Athenaeum; *Style—* Sydney Kentridge, Esq, QC; 1 Brick Court, Temple, London EC4 (☎ 01 583 0777, fax 01 583 9401)

KENWARD, Elizabeth; MBE (1986); da of Brian Charles Durant Kemp-Welch (d 1950), of Kineton, Warwicks, and Verena, *née* Venour (d 1968); *b* 14 July 1906; *Educ* privately and Les Tourelles Brussels; *m* 22 June 1932 (m dis 1942), Capt Peter Trayton Kenward, late 14/20 Hus (decd), s of late Edward Kenward, of Mill Farm House, Tenterden, Kent; 1 s (Jim Trayton b 1933); *Career* social ed; Jennifer of

Jennifer's Diary (Tatler 1944-59, Queen Magazine 1959-70, Harpers & Queen 1970-); Off Sister of St John 1986; *Recreations* flat racing, theatre, flying (quickest trip Caracus and back for a dinner party by Air France Concorde); *Clubs* Annabels; *Style*— Mrs Elizabeth Kenward, MBE; Harpers & Queen, 72 Broadwick St, London W1V 2BC

KENWORTHY, Hon Basil Frederick de la Pole; TD (1958); 3 s of 10 Baron Strabolgi (d 1952), and his 1 w, Doris (d 1988), da of Sir Frederick Whitley Whitley-Thomson, JP, MP; *b* 24 Mar 1920; *Educ* Oundle, Lincoln Coll Oxford (BA, MA); *m* 18 March 1948 (m dis 1965), Chloë, 2 da of Henry Gerard Walter Sandeman and Hon Phyllis Legh, da of 2 Baron Newton, PC; 3 da (Mrs William Healey b 1949, Mrs John Vincent b 1950, Mrs Sebastian Kent b 1958); *Career* Capt RA (TA Reserve), served Norway, India, Palestine, Western Desert, Greece, Crete and Germany; FInstPet, MInstT; *Recreations* shooting, music; *Clubs* Hurlingham, Anglo-Turkish Assoc, Turco-British Assoc, Istanbul, Lincoln Soc, Oxford Union Soc; *Style*— The Hon Basil Kenworthy, TD; c/o Nat Westminster Bank, Onslow Gdns, London SW7

KENWORTHY, Frederick John; s of Rev Fred Kenworthy, MA, BD (d 1974), Ethel Kenworthy, *née* Radcliffe; *b* 6 Dec 1943; *Educ* William Hulme's GS Manchester, Univ of Manchester (BA); *m* 1968, Diana, da of Reginald Flintham (d 1948); 1 da (Hannah Frances b 1983); *Career* asst princ MOD (Navy) 1966; Treasy centre for Admin Studies 1968-69; Br Steel Corpn Sheffield 1969; princ MOD 1972; Royal Cmmn on the Press Secretariat 1974; asst sec, dir Weapons Resources and Progs (Naval) MOD 1979-83; head of Resources and Progs Authy; RN Size and Shape Policy MOD 1983-86; *Recreations* music, sport, photography; *Clubs* Lonsdown, Tennis, Squash, Racquets (Bath); *Style*— Frederick Kenworthy, Esq

KENWORTHY, Joan Margaret; da of Albert Kenworthy (d 1984), and Amy, *née* Cobbold (d 1965); *b* 10 Dec 1933; *Educ* GS for Girls Barrow-in-Furness, St Hilda's Coll Oxford (BLitt, MA); *Career* temp tutorships: St Hugh's Coll Oxford 1958-59, Bedford Coll London 1959-60; asst lectr Univ of Liverpool 1960-63 (lectr 1963-73, sr lectr 1973-77) Warden Salisbury Hall 1966-77, Morton House 1974-77; pncpl St Mary's Coll Univ of Durham 1977-; FRGS, FRMetS; memb: Inst of Br Geographers, Geography Assoc, Br Ecol Soc, African Studies Assoc; *Books* contrib to several books on climatology and Africa; *Clubs* Royal Cwlth Soc; *Style*— Miss Joan M Kenworthy; 1 Elvet Garth, South Rd, Durham DH1 3TP (☎ 091 384 3865); St Mary's Coll, University of Durham, Durham DH1 3LR (☎ 091 374 2700)

KENWORTHY, Rev the Hon Jonathan Malcolm Atholl; s of late 10 Baron Strabolgi by 1 w, Doris, da of Sir Frederick Whitley Whitley-Thomson, JP, MP; hp of bro, 11 Baron, *qv*; *b* 16 Sept 1916; *Educ* Oundle, Pembroke Coll and Ridley Hall Cambridge (MA); *m* 1, 1943, Joan Marion (d 1963), da of late Claude Gilbert Gaster, of Tunbridge Wells; 2 da (Mrs D Brown b 1944, Mrs G Collins b 1946); m 2, 1963, Victoria Hewitt; 2 s (Andrew b 1967, James b 1971), 1 da (Penelope b 1964); *Career* served WW II, CF NW Europe 1944, NE India 1945-47; rector St Clement's Oxford 1947-54, vicar Hoddesdon 1954-63, vicar All Saints' Burton-on-Trent 1963-65, chaplain St John's Bangalore 1965-66, vicar Christ Church Penge 1966-75, rector Yelvertoft and Lilbourne 1975-82; *Style*— The Rev the Hon Malcolm Kenworthy; 37 North Rd, Combe Down, Bath (☎ 0225 835447)

KENWORTHY-BROWNE, Dr (James) Michael; s of Bernard Evelyn Kenworthy-Browne (d 1979), of Herts; bro Peter Kenworthy-Brown, *qv*; *b* 22 Mar 1936; *Educ* Ampleforth, Oriel Oxford (MA, BM, BCh, MRCP (UK), FRCGP); *m* 1, 1962, Anne (d 1983), da of Vernon Mayer (d 1982); 1 s (Nicholas b 1971), 3 da (Joanna b 1966, Frances b 1966, Michelle b 1966); *Career* nat serv 2 Lt Cyprus 1956-57; med practitioner Oxford City and Univ, past gen med and cardiac registrar Radcliffe Infirmary 1967-79, past course organizer Gen Practice Training Oxford City and County 1975-83; *Recreations* travel, wine appreciation; *Clubs* RAC, Pall Mall, Vincents; *Style*— Dr Michael Kenworthy-Browne, Esq; Heron Hill, Harberton Mead, Oxford OX3 0DB (☎ 0865 66568); The Jericho Health Centre, Walton Street, Oxford OX2 6NW (☎ 0865 52971)

KENWORTHY-BROWNE, (Bernard) Peter Francis; s of Bernard Evelyn Kenworthy-Browne (d 1979), formerly of Wellbury, nr Hitchin, Herts, and Margaret Sibylla (d 1985), o da of Sir George Hadcock, KBE, FRS; bro Dr Michael Kenworthy-Browne, *qv*; *b* 11 May 1930; *Educ* Ampleforth, Oriel Coll Oxford (MA); *m* 3 Oct 1975 (m dis 1982), Jane Elizabeth, da of late Denis Malcolm Mackie; *Career* Nat Serv, 2 Lt Irish Guards 1949-50, Lt (Reserve) 1953; barr Lincoln's Inn 1955, Oxford and Midland and Oxford Circuits 1957-82, rec of the Crown Ct 1981-82, registrar of the Family Division of High Ct of Justice 1982-; *Recreations* music, photography, gardening, sports; *Style*— Peter Kenworthy-Browne, Esq; 30 Dewhurst Rd, London W14 0ES (☎ 01 602 9580); Principal Registry, Family Div, Somerset House, Strand, WC2R 1LP

KENYON, Sir George Henry; JP (Cheshire 1959), DL (Chester 1969), DL (Manchester 1983);; s of George Henry Kenyon; *b* 10 July 1912; *Educ* Radley, Manchester Univ (LLD); *m* 1938, Christine Dorey, *née* Brentnall; 2 s, 1 da; *Career* chm: William Kenyon & Sons Ltd 1961-82 (dir 1942-), Williams and Glyn's Bank Ltd 1978-83 (dir 1972-83), S Tameside Bench 1974-82, cncl Manchester Univ 1972-80; dir: Manchester Ship Canal 1972-, Royal Bank of Scotland 1979-83; kt 1976; *Style*— Sir George Kenyon, JP, DL; Limefield House, Hyde, Cheshire (☎ 061 368 2012)

KENYON, Col John Frederick; OBE (1970), MC (1944); s of Lt-Col Herbert Edward Kenyon, DSO (d 1958), of Pradoe, Oswestry, Shropshire, and Gwendoline Ethel Graham, *née* Ommanney (d 1958); *b* 30 Dec 1921; *Educ* Marlborough, Staff Coll Camberley, Jt Servs Staff Coll Latimer; *m* 1, 8 Aug 1947 (m dis 1960), Jean Molyneux, da of Howard Godfrey, MC (d 1964), of Wilts; 2 s (John b 24 Oct 1948, Richard b 3 Dec 1951); m 2, 5 Aug 1960 (m dis 1981), Margaret Bowker Remington; m 3, 20 July 1982, Janet Mary, da of Fisher Maddicott, of Devon; *Career* cmmnd RA India 1942, Burma 1943-46, NWFP India 1946-47, Instr in Gunnery 1948-50, Staff Coll Camberley 1951, Suez Canal 1952-54, Jt Servs Staff Coll 1959, Cdr Chestnut Troop RHA 1960-61, Mil Asst to C-in-C Far East Land Forces 1962-64, GSO operations, Intelligence & Security HQ 1 Br Corps 1966-69, Def Naval & Mil Attaché Brussels 1971-73; Pres Freemen of England, chm Shrewsbury Abbey Restoration Project govr Derwen Trg Coll for the Handicapped patron Br Torch Delegation; co cncllr Shropshire Co Cncl 1977-85; Freeman City of London 1983, Grand Master Freeman of Shrewsbury 1973; *Recreations* conservation on estates, fighting bureaucracy, shooting, tennis; *Clubs* Farmers; *Style*— Col John Kenyon, OBE, MC; Pradoe, Oswestry, Shropshire SY11 4ER (☎ 0691 88218)

KENYON, 5 Baron (GB 1788); Sir Lloyd Tyrell-Kenyon; 5 Bt (GB 1784), CBE (1972), DL (Flint 1948); s of 4 Baron Kenyon (d 1927); *b* 13 Sept 1917; *Educ* Eton, Magdalene Coll Cambridge; *m* 1946, Leila Mary, da of Cdr John Wyndham Cookson, RN (ret), by the Cdr's w Mary (da of Sir Alan Colquhoun, 6 Bt, KCB, JP, DL, and Aunt of Countess of Arran); Leila was wid of Hugh William Jardine Ethelston Peel; 3 s (Hon Lloyd b 1947, Hon Richard b 1948, Hon Thomas b 1954), 1 da (Hon Katharine b 1959); *Heir* s, Hon Lloyd Tyrell-Kenyon; *Career* 2 Lt Shrops Yeo 1937, Lt RA (TA), ret 1943 with hon rank of Capt; dir Lloyds Bank Ltd 1962-85 (chm NW bd 1962-88); pres Univ Coll of N Wales Bangor 1947-82; chm Nat Portrait Gallery 1966-88 (tstee 1953-88); memb: Royal Cmmn on Historical MSS 1966-, bd Ancient Monuments for Wales 1979-87, CCllr Flint 1946 (chm 1954-55); Hon LLD Wales 1958; *Clubs* Brooks's, Cavalry & Guards, Beefsteak; *Style*— The Rt Hon the Lord Kenyon, CBE, DL; Cumbers House, Gredington, Whitchurch, Salop SY13 3DH (☎ 094 874 330)

KEOGH, Colin Denis; s of John Denis Keogh, of SA, and Hillary Joan, *née* Campbell; *b* 27 July 1953; *Educ* St John's Coll SA, Eton, Univ Coll Oxford (MA), INSEAD (MBA); *m* 26 Aug 1978, Joanna Mary Martyn, da of John Frederick Leapman; 2 s Thomas b 27 March 1982, William b 6 May 1986), 1 da (Kate b 6 Nov 1984); *Career* Arthur Andersen & Co 1978-82, INSEAD 1982-83, Saudi Int Bank 1983-85, dir Close Bros Ltd 1985-; memb Inst Taxation; *Recreations* sport, theatre; *Style*— Colin Keogh, Esq; 66 Manville Rd, London SW17 8JL (☎ 01 672 1340); Close Brothers Ltd, 36 Great St Helen's, London EC3A 6AP (☎ 01 283 2241, fax 01 623 9699)

KEOHANE, Desmond John; s of William Patrick Keohane (d 1971), and Mabel Margaret, *née* Coleman; *b* 5 July 1928; *Educ* Borden GS Sittingbourne Kent, Univ of Birmingham (BA), Univ of London (PGCE); *m* 13 Aug 1960, Mary, da of Patrick Kelliher of Northampton; 2 s (Jeremy b 1961, John b 1968), 2 da (Ann b 1963, Clare b 1964); *Career* Nat Serv Flying Offr educn branch RAF; sch teacher and coll lectr, vice princ Havering Tech Coll 1969-71 (hd Dept of Soc and Academic Studies 1964-69); princ: Northampton Coll of Further Educn 1971-76, Oxford Coll of Further Educn 1976-; govr: Thomas Beckett Sch Northampton 1973- (chm 1983-), St Mary's Sch Northampton 1972-, Oxford Sch 1982-86, Oxford Poly 1983-87, Oxford Area Arts Cncl 1980-85; memb: bd Berks and Oxon Area Manpower 1985-89, cncl Secdy Examinations 1983-86, southern regnl cncl for Further Educn 1977-, Special Employment Measures Advsy Gp (MSC) 1986-89; FBIM 1981; *Recreations* watching cricket, walking, reading; *Style*— Desmond Keohane, Esq; 14 Abington Park Cres, Northampton, NN3 3AD (☎ 0604 38829), Oxford College of Further Education, Oxpens Rd, Oxford, OX1 1SA (☎ 0865 245871, fax 0865 248871)

KEOHANE, Dr Kevin William; CBE (1976); s of William Patrick Keohane (d 1971), and Mabel Margaret, *née* Coleman; *b* 28 Feb 1923; *Educ* Borden GS, Univ of Bristol (BSc, PhD); *m* 26 Feb 1949, Mary Margaret Patricia, da of Charles Ashford (d 1938); 1 s (Stephen b 1964), 3 da (Elizabeth b 1952, Katharine b 1953, Hilary b 1957); *Career* served WWII RAF 1943-46 (Far E); prof of sci educn Univ of London 1968-76 (prof of physics 1964-68), rector Roehampton Inst of Higher Educn 1976-88; chm: Taylor & Francis Inc (dir and exec vice chm 1974-), Nuffield Chelsea Curriculum Tst 1976- (dir Nuffield Fndn Sci Teaching Projects 1966-76), Royal Soc Leverhulme prof to Brazil 1971, vice chm int advsy panel Chinese Prov Univs Project 1985-; memb: Richmond Twickenham and Roehampton Health Authy 1987-, Merton Local Educn Authy 1988, cncl of Univ of Surrey 1988-; KSG 1983; *Recreations* rugby (spectator), bee-keeping; *Clubs* Roslyn Park RFC, Athenaeum; *Style*— Dr Kevin Keohane, CBE; 3 Thetford Road, New Malden KT3 5DN (☎ 01 942 6861)

KEOWN-BOYD, Henry Gerald; s of Sir Alexander Keown-Boyd, KBE, CMG (d 1954), and Joan Mary, *née* Partridge (d 1975); *b* 15 Oct 1932; *Educ* Eton; *m* 1963, Jeannette Marie, da of Christo Stamatopoulo (d 1965), of Egypt; 1 da (Joanna b 1969); *Career* served 11 Hussars Germany and Malaya 1951-54 (Lt); business 1955-80; *Books* A Good Dusting (1986); *Recreations* reading, writing, walking, fishing; *Clubs* Royal Overseas League; *Style*— Henry Keown-Boyd, Esq; Old Rectory, Thornbury, nr Bromyard, Herefordshire

KEPPEL, Hon Mrs Arnold; Mildred; da of William Stanley Rodber (d 1968), of Richmond Yorks, and Elizabeth, *née* Earl (d 1947); *b* 21 Sept 1914; *Educ* HS for Girls Richmond; *m* 1, Flying Offr Allan Carter, RAF (decd); 1 s (Michael); m 2, 1952, as his 3 w, Hon Arnold Keppel (d 1964), 2 s of 8 Earl of Albemarle, GCVO, CB, JP (d 1943), and Lady Gertrude, only child of 1 and last Earl Egerton of Tatton; *Recreations* painting; *Style*— The Hon Mrs Arnold Keppel; 1a Swan Ct, Southsea Rd, Datchet, Berks (☎ 0753 43928)

KER-LINDSAY, Hon Mrs (Anne Bradbury); da of 2 Baron Bradbury; *b* 19 Sept 1947; *m* 1970, Alastair James Ker-Lindsay; 4 s (James b 4 May 1972, Mark b 21 June 1973, John Alexander b 10 Aug 1977, Adam Ronald b 28 Feb 1979), 1 da (Laura Anne b 27 April 1975); *Style*— The Hon Mrs Ker-Lindsay; Manor House, 26 St John's Wood Park, London NW8 6QP

KERBY, John Vyvyan; s of Dr Theo Rosser Fred Kerby (d 1947), and Constance Mary, *née* Newell (d 1954); *b* 14 Dec 1942; *Educ* Eton, Christ Church Oxford (MA); *m* 23 June 1978, Shirley Elizabeth, da of Sydney John Pope (d 1970); 1 step s, 1 step da; *Career* temp asst princ Colonial Off 1965-67, asst princ Miny of Overseas Devpt 1967-70, private sec to Parly Under Sec FCO 1970-71, princ ODA 1971-74 and 1975-77, asst sec ODA 1977-83; head Br Devpt Div in Southern Africa 1983-86), under sec and prince estabs offr ODA 1986-(Civil Serv Selection Bd 1974-75; *Recreations* gardening, entomology, cricket; *Style*— John Kerby, Esq; Overseas Development Administration, Eland House, Stag Place, London, SW1 (☎ 01 273 0380)

KERNICK, Robert (Robin) Charles; s of John Wilson Kernick, OBE (d 1974), and Myrth Gwendoline, *née* Whittall (d 1989); *b* 11 May 1927; *Educ* Blundells, Sidney Sussex Coll Cambridge (MA); *m* 1, 1951, Gillian, da of late Brig John Burne; 1 s (Mark Robert John b 1957), 1 da (Georgina Mary b 1954); m 2, Elizabeth, da of Surgn Rear Adm Sir Henry White, KCVO, CBE (d 1976); *Career* Capt Queen's (late King's) Dragoon Gds: Palestine, N Africa; dir Grand Metropolitan Ltd 1972-75, md IDV Ltd 1972-75, chm Corney and Barrow Ltd 1981-88; clerk of The Royal Cellars 1978-; *Recreations* golf, shooting, skiing; *Clubs* Cavalry & Guards, MCC, Huntercombe GC, Swinley Forest GC; *Style*— Robin Kernick, Esq; 12 Helmet Row, London EC1 (☎ 01 251 4051, fax 01 608 1373)

KERR; *see*: Blair-Kerr

KERR, Dr Archibald Brown; OBE (1945), CBE (1968), TD; s of Robert Kerr (d 1948), of Glasgow, and Janet Harvey, *née* Brown (d 1950); *b* 17 Feb 1907; *Educ* Glasgow HS, Univ of Glasgow (BSc, MB, ChB); *m* 16 Feb 1940, Jean Margaret, da of John Cowan, MBE (d 1972), of Calcutta, and Irvine, Ayrshire; 1 da (Winifred); *Career*

Univ OTC 1923-38 (cmmnd 1927), TA RAMC 156 (Lowland) Field Ambulance (embodied serv 1939-45), No 23 (Scottish) Gen Hosp 1940, Lt-Col OC Surgical Divn; served: Palestine, France, Germany (Col cmdg); demob 1945; asst to prof of pathology Univ of Glasgow 1931-33, surgn to outpatients Western Infirmary Glasgow 1932-39, surgn Royal Alexandra Infirmary Paisley 1946-54, asst surgn Western Infirmary Glasgow 1946-54, lectr in clinical surgery Univ of Glasgow 1946-72, surgn i/c wards Western Infirmary Glasgow 1954-72 (hon surgn 1972-present); pres Royal Medico Chirurgical Soc of Glasgow 1951-52, pres RCPS (Glasgow) 1964-66; LLD Univ of Glasgow 1973; FRFPS (Glasgow) 1933, FRCS Ed 1934, FRCS Glas 1962; *Books* The Western Infirmary 1874-1974, A Century of Service to Glasgow (1974); *Recreations* golf, gardening; *Clubs* Royal Scottish Automobile, Glasgow Univ Coll; *Style—* Dr Archibald Kerr, CBE, OBE, TD; 10 Iain Rd, Bearsden, Glasgow G61 4LX (☎ 041 942 0424)

KERR, Colin Alan Lincoln; s of William Kerr (d 1967), of London, and Emily Jessica Kerr (d 1984); *b* 15 June 1929; *Educ* Bristol GS, Regent St Poly, Coll of Estate Mgmnt; *m* 17 Oct 1958, Francoise Marie Jeanne Marcelle, da of George Gavin (d 1986), of Paris; 2 s (Anthony Marc George Lincoln b 6 April 1971, Stephane Pierre Lincoln b 11 Nov 1961), 1 da (Delphine Marie Ingrid b 28 May 1974); *Career* cmmnd RA 1952-54; Edward Erdman: joined 1949-51, rejoined 1954, jt sr ptnr 1976, sr ptnr 1986; chm commercial prop ctee RICS 1983-86, dir fin devpt bd NSPCC 1983-; Freeman City of London, Liveryman Worshipful Co of Chartered Surveyors 1979; AAI 1951, FRICS 1962; *Recreations* sailing, golf, skiing; *Clubs* Oriental, Royal Lymington YC, Little Ship, Highgate GC; *Style—* Colin Kerr, Esq ; Blue Orchard, Courtenay Ave, Highgate, London N6 4LP; Hammeux Des Piste, Megeve, France; 6 Grosvenor St, London W1 (☎ 01 629 8191, fax 01 409 2757, telex 28169)

KERR, Dr David Leigh; s of Myer Woolf Kerr (d 1968), and Paula, *née* Horowitz (d 1963); *b* 25 Mar 1923; *Educ* Whitgift Sch, Middlesex Hosp Med Sch, London Univ (MB, BS); *m* 1, 14 Sept 1944 (m dis 1969), (Margaret) Aileen, da of Clifford Saddington (d 1933); 2 s (Nicholas, Maxwell), 1 da (Sara); m 2, 3 April 1970, Margaret Palmer, da of John Dunlop; 1 s (Paul), 2 da (Ruth, Emma); *Career* GP 1946-82, chief exec Industl Orthopaedic Soc 1982-87; London ccnclr 1958-65, cnclr London Borough of Wandsworth 1962-65; MP Wandsworth Central (now Wandsworth Tooting) 1964-70, pps to Mrs Judith Hart 1967-68; chm Bishops Hatfield Girls' Sch Campaign Ctee; govr: London Sch of Hygiene and Tropical Med 1960-62, Br Film Inst 1965-72, Chllr's Sch Brookmans York, Brookmans Park Primary Sch; vice pres and tstee Health Visitors' Assoc; MRCGP 1952, FRSM; *Recreations* cinema, theatre, music, reading other peoples' biographies; *Clubs* RSM; *Style—* Dr David Kerr; 19 Calder Ave, Brookmans Park, Hatfield AL9 7AH (☎ 0707 53954)

KERR, Jill; da of Eric David Kerr, MC, of Barn Cottage, Cryers Hill Lane, Widmer End, High Wycombe, Bucks, and Betty, *née* Knight; *b* 2 July 1949; *Educ* Univ of York (BA, MA); *Career* dept MSS and early printed books Trinity Coll Dublin 1971-72, photo-archives Courtauld Inst Univ of London 1973-75, Dean and Chapter Canterbury Cathedral (estab system for recording the restoration of the stained glass) 1975, Radcliffe Tst Scheme for the Crafts 1974-75, sec Corpus Vitrearum Medii Aevi GB (Br Acad) 1975-84, inspr Historic Bldgs and Monuments Cmmn for England (English Heritage) 1984-88, head Western region historic bldgs div English Heritage 1988-; memb: Br Soc of Master Glass Painters 1969- (cncl memb and hon jt ed of the soc's jl 1983-86), Br Archaeological Assoc 1972- (cncl memb 1981-85), Assoc for Studies in the Conservation of Historic Bldgs 1984- (visits sec 1988-), stained glass advsy ctee Cncl for the Care of Churches of the C of E 1984-; hon sec to the tstees Ely Stained Glass Museum 1978-84; various contribs to specialist literature; Freeman City of London 1984, Liveryman Worshipful Co of Glaziers Painters and Stainers of Glass; *Recreations* talking, travelling; *Style—* Miss Jill Kerr; Historic Buildings and Monuments Commission for England, Fortress House, 23 Savile Row, London W1X 2HE (☎ 01 734 6010, fax 01 434 1799, telex 892091 HBM CFHG)

KERR, Lord John Andrew Christopher; s of late Capt Andrew William Kerr, RN (gs of 7 Marquess of Lothian) and bro of 12 Marquess of Lothian; raised to the rank of a Marquess's son 1941; *b* 1927; *Educ* Ampleforth, Christ Church Oxford; *m* 1949, Isabel Marion, da of Sir Hugh Gurney, KCMG, MVO, and Mariota, da of Rt Hon Sir Lancelot Carnegie, GCVO, KCMG (d 1933); 3 s (William b 1950, David b 1952, Andrew b 1955), 2 da (Marion b 1960, Catherine b 1965); *Career* late Capt Scots Guards; chm Bloomsbury Book Auctions 1983- (formerly mangr book dept of Sotheby's); *Style—* Lord John Kerr; Holly Bank, Wootton, Woodstock, Oxford

KERR, Rt Hon Sir John Robert; AK (1976, AC 1975), GCMG (1976, KCMG 1974, CMG 1966), GCVO (1977), PC (1977); s of Harry Kerr (d 1962), and Laura May, *née* Cardwell (d 1972), of Sydney; *b* 24 Sept 1914; *Educ* Fort St Boys' HS Sydney, Sydney Univ (LLB); *m* 1, 1938, Alison (d 1974), da of Frederick Worstead, of Sydney; 1 s, 2 da; m 2, 1975, Mrs Anne Dorothy Robson, DStJ, da of late John Taggart; *Career* 2 AIF 1942-46 (Col); barr 1938-66; first princ Aust Sch of Pacific Admin 1946-48, organising sec S Pacific Cmmn 1946-47, QC 1953; pres: NSW Bar Assoc 1964, Law Cncl of Australia 1964-66, Law Assoc for Asia and Western Pacific 1966-70; presided at Third Cwlth and Empire Law Conf Sydney 1965, hon life memb Law Soc of England and Wales 1965-, hon memb American Bar Assoc 1967-; Federal Judge 1966-72, Chief Justice of NSW 1972-74, lieut-govr NSW 1973-74, govr-gen Australia 1974-77; KStJ 1974 *see Debretts Handbook of Australia and New Zealand*; *Clubs* Union (Sydney); *Style—* The Rt Hon Sir John Kerr, AK, GCMG, GCVO QC; Suite 2404, 56 Pitt St, Sydney, NSW, Australia 2000

KERR, Rt Hon Lord Justice; Rt Hon Sir Michael Robert Emanuel; PC (1981); s of Alfred Kerr; *b* 1 Mar 1921; *Educ* Aldenham, Clare Cambridge; *m* 1, 1952 (m dis 1982), Julia (actress, played Mrs Dale's da-in-law in Mrs Dale's Diary on BBC radio), da of Joseph Braddock; 2 s, 1 da; m 2, 1983, Diana Sneezum, yr da of H Neville Sneezum, of Gothic House, E Bergholt, Suffolk; 1 d; *Career* served WW II Fl-Lt RAF; barr 1948, QC 1961, dep chm Hants QS 1961-71, Lord Justice of Appeal 1981-, High Ct Judge (Queen's Bench) 1972-81, chm Law Commission 1978-81, Lord Justice of Appeal 1981-, first chm Supreme Ct Procedure Cncl 1982-; pres Chartered Inst of Arbitrators 1983-; pres Br German Tourists Assoc 1985-; memb cncl mgmnt Br Inst Int and Comparative Law 1973-, chm Lord-Chllr's Inter Deptl Ctee on EEC Judgements Convention 1974-, vice pres Br Maritime Law Assoc 1977-, memb Inst Advanced Legal Studies 1979-85; chm ctee mgmnt Centre Commercial Law Studies QMC 1980-; kt 1972; *Style—* The Rt Hon the Lord Justice Kerr, PC; Royal Courts of Justice, Strand, London WC2A 2LL

KERR, Lord Ralph William Francis Joseph; s of 12 Marquess of Lothian, KCVO; *b* 7 Nov 1957; *Educ* Ampleforth; *m* 1, 1980 (m dis 1987), Lady Virginia Mary Elizabeth, *qv*, da of 11 Duke of Grafton, KG; m 2, 5 March 1988, Marie-Claire, yr da of Donald Black, MC, of Edenwood, Cupar, Fife; 1 s (John Walter Donald Peter b 8 Aug 1988); *Career* political res, pianist, currently estate mangr and songwriter; *Recreations* playing the piano; *Style—* Lord Ralph Kerr; 20 Upper Cheyne Row, London SW3 (☎ 01 352 7017); Melbourne Hall, Melbourne, Derby (☎ 033 16 2263)

KERR, The Rt Rev Robert (Ray); *see*: Bradford, The Bishop of

KERR, Thomas Henry; CB (1983); s of Albert Edward Kerr, of Westborough, Newark (d 1963); *b* 18 June 1924; *Educ* Magnus GS Newark, Univ Coll Durham Univ (BSc); *m* 1946, Myrnie Evelyn Martin, da of Edward Hughes, of Newark, Notts (d 1965); *Career* Fl Lt, served Europe and Africa, pilot RAFVR 1942-53, Aero Flight RAE 1949-55, Head Supersonic Fl Gp 1955-59, Sci Advsr to C-in-C Bomber Cmd High Wycombe 1960-64, Head Assessment Div Weapons Dept RAE 1964-66, dep dir and dir of Def Operational Analysis Estab 1966-70, Head Weapons Res Gp, Weapons Dept RAE 1970-74, dir: Nat Gas Turbine Estab 1974-80, Royal Aircraft Estab 1980-84; R & D dir Royal Ordnance plc 1984-85, Tech dir Hunting Engrg 1986; *Recreations* bridge, water, ski-ing, tennis, badminton; *Style—* Thomas Kerr, Esq, CB; Bundu, 13 Kingsley Ave, Camberley, Surrey GU15 2NA (☎ 0276 25961); Hunting Engineering, Ampthill, Bedford (☎ 0525 403431

KERR, Lady Virginia Mary Elizabeth; *née* FitzRoy; da of 11 Duke of Grafton, KG; *b* 1954; *m* 1980 (m dis 1987), Lord Ralph Kerr, *qv*; *Style—* Lady Virginia Kerr; 20 Upper Cheyne Row, London SW3 (☎ 01 352 7017); Melbourne Hall, Melbourne, Derby (☎ Melbourne 2263)

KERRISON, Roger Edmund Fulke; yr s of Roger Fulke Kerrison, JP (d 1976), of Burgh Hall, Aylsham, Norfolk, and Cecil Scott, *née* Craft (d 1983); descended from Matthias Kerrison, of Seething, Norfolk, b 1650 (*see* Burke's Landed Gentry, 18 edn, vol II, 1969); *b* 21 Jan 1920; *Educ* Eton, Trinity Coll Camb; *m* 21 Sept 1942, (Edith) Anne Edmonstone, o da of Maj Lewis Aloysius Macdonald Hastings, MC, late RFA (d 1966); 1 s (Philip Roger Stephen b 18 Feb 1950, d 1978), 2 da (Caroline) Felicity (Mrs Sandford Cox) b 19 Sept 1943, Theresa Mary (Mrs Marlborough Pryor) b 2 April 1948); *Career* served WW II as Lt Cdr RNVR (FAA) 1940-45; md A R Taylor & Co Ltd 1951-76; dir Olympia Ltd; Lloyd's Underwriting Name 1965-; farmer; Freeman of City of Norwich; *Recreations* fishing, shooting; Sloley Lodge, nr Norwich, Norfolk (☎ 069 269 253)

KERRUISH, Sir (Henry) Charles; OBE (1964); *b* 23 July 1917; *Educ* Ramsey GS; *m* 1, 1944, Margaret Gell; 1 s, 3 da; m 2, 1975, Kay Warriner; *Career* farmer; speaker House of Keys 1962- (memb 1946-); regnl cnclr Br Isles & Med Cwlth Parly Assoc 1975-77, memb Ct Liverpool Univ 1974-; vice pres Cwlth Parly Assoc 1983, pres 1984-; kt 1979; *Style—* Sir Charles Kerruish, OBE; Ballafayle, Maughold, IOM (☎ 0624 812293)

KERRY, Alan James; s of James Leslie Kerry (d 1951), of Cardiff, and Constance Mary, *née* Langley (d 1976); *b* 4 Mar 1921; *Educ* Leeds GS, Leeds Univ (LLB); *m* 7 July 1951, Margaret Gwenllian Trevor, da of George Trevor Jones Morris (d 1970), of Glamorgan; 1 s (James b 1954), 1 da (Alison b 1959); *Career* Actg Lt Cdr RNVR Western Approaches; slr, sr ptnr Ford & Warren (Leeds); dir Provincial Building Soc 1962-88, chm Nat & Provincial Building Soc 1983-88; pres Leeds Law Soc 1982-83; *Recreations* fishing, gardening; *Clubs* Leeds; *Style—* Alan J Kerry, Esq; 26A Rutland Drive, Harrogate HG1 2NS (☎ 0423 65154); 5 Park Square, Leeds LS1 2AX (☎ 0532 436601, telex 556371, fax 0532 420905)

KERRY, Francis Robert; s of Francis Kerry (d 1935); *b* 24 Oct 1914; *Educ* Burton-on-Trent GS; *m* 1965, Zena Pamela, da of Ewart Illsley (d 1972); 6 children; *Career* pres Fine Art Developments plc and assoc co's: dir Mayflower Finance (Burton) Ltd; *Recreations* yachting; *Style—* Francis Kerry, Esq; Drakelow House, Burton-on-Trent, Staffs (☎ 0283 68106); Casa Drakelow, 60 Urbanizaciones, Playa Fotges, Muro, Mallorca

KERRY, 23 Knight of (first recorded use of title 1468; The Green Knight); Maj Sir George Peter Maurice FitzGerald; 5 Bt (UK 1880), of Valentia, Co Kerry, MC (1944); the title Knight of Kerry was conferred upon his son Maurice by John Fitz Thomas FitzGerald, Earl of Decies and Desmond, by virtue of his royal seigniory as a Count Palatine and his descendants have ever since been so styled in Acts of Parliament, patents under the Great Seal and other documents; the first baronet was 19 Knight of Kerry; 2, but only surviving, s of Capt 22 Knight of Kerry (Sir Arthur Henry Brinsley FitzGerald, 4 Bt, d 1967), and Mary, *née* Forester; *b* 27 Feb 1917; *Educ* Harrow, RMC Sandhurst; *m* 1939, Angela Dora, da of late Capt James Rankin Mitchell; 1 s, 1 da (Rosanna, m Count Richard Gurowski); *Heir* s, Adrian James Andrew Denis FitzGerald; *Career* 2 Lt Irish Gds cmmnd 1937, served Palestine 1938 (despatches), and Norway, N Africa, Italy 1939-45, Maj 1943, ret 1948; *Style—* Major the Knight of Kerry, Bt, MC; Colin's Farm House, 55 High Street, Durrington, Salisbury, Wilts SP4 8AQ (☎ 0980 52242)

KERRY, Sir Michael James; KCB (1982, CB 1976), QC (1984); s of Russell Kerry (d 1948), and Marjorie, *née* Kensington (d 1967); *b* 5 July 1923; *Educ* Rugby, St John's Coll Oxford (MA); *m* 1952, Sidney Rosetta Elizabeth, *née* Foster; 1 s, (Patrick b 1965), 2 da (Lucy, Frances); *Career* barr Lincoln's Inn 1949, joined BOT as legal asst 1951, slr DTI 1973-80 (princ asst slr 1972), HM procurator gen and treasy slr 1980-84, bencher Lincolns Inn 1984, dep chm Lautro Ltd 1987; Hon fell St Johns Coll Oxford 1986; *Recreations* Golf; *Style—* Sir Michael Kerry, KCB, QC; S Bedales, Lewes Rd, Haywards Heath, W Sussex (☎ 044 486 303)

KERSEN, Mark; s of Harry Kersen (d 1967), and Ann Kersen (d 1985); *b* 23 Oct 1935; *Educ* Strodes GS Egham Surrey; *m* 8 Sept 1962, Ann Jeanette; 1 s (Timothy b 1969); *Career* Nat Serv 1958-59; copy boy Manchester Guardian 1952; journalist: Windsor, Slough and Eton Express 1952-56; Slough Express, Express & Star Wolverhampton 1959- (feature writer, dep News ed); ed Shropshire Star 1970-72, Express & Star 1972 (dir 1973, gen mangr 1978, md 1981); dir Midland News Assoc, memb Newspaper Panel, memb Monopolies Cmmn; pres W Midlands Newspaper Soc 1985; *Style—* Mark Kersen, Esq; Express & Star Ltd, 50-51 Queen St, Wolverhampton WV1 3BU (☎ 0902 313 131, fax 0902 21 467, car tel 0860 542 274, telex 335490)

KERSHAW, Sir (John) Anthony; MC (1943), MP (C) Stroud 1955-87; s of Judge John Felix Kershaw (d 1927); *b* 14 Dec 1915; *Educ* Eton, Balliol Coll Oxford (BA); *m* 1939, Barbara, da of Harry Mitton Crookenden (d 1953); 2 s, 2 da; *Career* WWII: 16/5

Lancers, Reserve Forces 1946-56, CO Royal Gloucs Hussars 1953-56, (C) psc; barr 1939; City of Westminster cnllr 1946-49, cnllr LCC 1948-51, MP Stroud 1955-87, parly sec Miny of Public Building and Works 1970, parly under-sec of state FCO 1970-73, parly under-sec of State for Def (RAF) 1973-74, chm House of Commons select ctee on foreign affrs 1979-87, vice chm British Cncl 1975-87, kt 1981; *Recreations* field sports; *Clubs* White's; *Style*— Sir Anthony Kershaw, MC; West Barn, Didmarton, Badminton, Glos GL9 1DT (☎ 045 423 630)

KERSHAW, Cissie, Baroness; Cissie Burness; da of Charles E Smyth, of Friern Barnet; *m* 1933, 2 Baron Kershaw (d 1961); *Style*— The Rt Hon Cissie, Lady Kershaw; 29 St Ann's Rd, Newquay, Cornwall

KERSHAW, David Robert; s of Noel Ernest Kershaw, TD, and Dorothy Anne, *née* Cheyne, b 1953; *Educ* Urmston GS, Trinity Coll Cambridge (MA); *m* 1978, Christine Anne, da of late John Spear Sexton; 3 s (Oliver James b 1979, Toby Thomas b 1984, Charles Henry Alexander b 1986); *Career* slr 1978; specialist in corporate fin, mergers and acquisitions and banking, asst slr Slaughter & May 1978-82; ptnr Ashurst Morris Crisp 1986- (slr 1982, assoc 1984-86); *Recreations* classical guitar, windsurfing, tennis, literature; *Style*— David Kershaw, Esq; Ashurst Morris Crisp, Broadgate House, 7 Eldon Street, London EC2M 7HD (☎ 01 247 7666, fax 01 377 5659)

KERSHAW, Hon Donald Arthur; JP (Richmond Upon Thames); s of 1 Baron Kershaw, OBE (d 1961); *b* 1915; *m* 1942, Barbara Edith, da of Lt-Col Cecil Graham Ford (d 1968), of Richmond, Surrey; 2 s (Ian, Mark); *Career* slr 1939; RAF 1940-45; *Style*— The Hon Donald Kershaw, JP; 32 Hans Rd, London SW3 (☎ 01 581 2627)

KERSHAW, His Hon Judge Henry Aidan; s of Rev Henry Kershaw (d 1970), and Hilda Shaw, *née* Brooker-Carey; *b* 11 May 1927; *Educ* St John's Leatherhead, Brasenose Coll Oxford (BA); *m* 31 March 1960, Daphne Patricia, wid of Dr C R Cowan, da of George Egerton Howlett (d 1960); 2 s (Michael b 1961, Nicholas b 1963), 2 step s (Charles b 1951, Richard b 1956); *Career* RN 1946-48; barr Inner Temple 1953, practised Northern Circuit 1953-76; assr rec Oldham Quarter Sessions 1970-71, rec Crown Ct 1972-76, circuit Judge 1976; cncllr Bolton County Borough Cncl 1954-57; dep chm Agric Land Tbnl 1972-76, chm (later vice pres) Lancs Sch Golf Assoc 1981, vice pres Eng Sch Golf Assoc, exec memb Lancs Union of Golf Clubs 1985-89; *Recreations* golf, skiing, oil painting, music; *Clubs* Royal and Ancient GC, St Andrews, Bolton GC (capt 1983-84), West Hill GC, Ski Club of Great Britain; *Style*— His Hon Judge Kershaw; Broadhaven, 54 St Andrew's Rd, Lostock, Bolton (☎ 0204 47 188)

KERSHAW, Joseph Anthony; s of Joseph Henry Kershaw, of Preston; *b* 26 Nov 1935; *Educ* Ushaw Coll Durham, Preston Catholic Coll SJ; *m* 1959, Ann, da of John Whittle (d 1964), of Preston; 3 s, 2 da; *Career* short serv cmmn RAOC, Lt; Unilever Ltd 1958-67, gp mktg mangr Co-Op Wholesale Soc (CWS) 1967-69; md: Underline Ltd 1969-71, merchant div Reed Int Ltd 1971-73; head of mktg (non-foods) CWS 1973-75; first dir Nat Consumer Cncl 1975; independent mgmnt conslt 1975-; assoc dir Foote Cone & Belding Ltd 1979-84; dir: John Stork & Ptnrs Ltd 1980-84, Allia (UK) Ltd 1984; chm: Antonian Investmt Ltd 1985-87, Organised Business Data Ltd 1987-89; memb IOD; *Recreations* fishing, shooting, cooking, CPRE, balloon pilot; *Style*— Joseph Kershaw, Esq; Westmead, Meins Rd, Blackburn, Lancs BB2 6QF (☎ 0254 55915)

KERSHAW, Katharine, Baroness; Katharine Dorothea; da of Charles H Staines, of Clapham; *m* 1935, 3 Baron Kershaw (d 1962); 1 s (4 Baron), 1 da (Mrs David Pickett b 1943); *Style*— The Rt Hon Katharine, Lady Kershaw; 2 Coombe Court, 84b Worcester Rd, Sutton, Surrey SM2 6QH

KERSHAW, (Philip) Michael; QC (1980); s of His Hon Philip Kershaw (d 1986), and Michaela Kershaw, *née* Raffael; *b* 23 April 1941; *Educ* Ampleforth, St John's Coll Oxford; *m* 30 Dec 1980, Anne; 1 s (Francis Edward b 23 Aug 1984); *Career* called to the Bar Grays Inn 1963, rec 1980; *Style*— Michael Kershaw, Esq, QC; 5 Essex Court, Temple, London EC4Y 9AH (☎ 01 353 4363, fax 01 583 1491)

KERSHAW, Hon Peter John; s of 1 Baron Kershaw, OBE (d 1961); *b* 19 July 1924; *Educ* Queen Elizabeth's GS Barnet, King's Coll London (BSc); *m* 1948, Brenda Margaret, da of James Austin Smith (d 1966), of Brighton; 1 s (Michael b 1951); *Career* Sub Lt RNVR 1945-46; chartered civil engr; dir and chief engr of Sir Robert McAlpine & Sons Ltd 1977-, ret 1987; FEng, FICE; *Style*— The Hon Peter Kershaw; 22 Orchard Rise, Richmond, Surrey TW10 5BX (☎ 01 876 2660)

KERSHAW, (John) Stephen; s of Raymond Newton Kershaw, CMG, MC (d 1981), and Hilda Mary, Kershaw (d 1989); *b* 21 Dec 1931; *Educ* Cheltenham, New Coll Oxford; *Career* investmt mgmnt, incl in developing countries of Br Cwlth; former dir: Bandanga Tea Plantations Ltd, Henckell du Buisson & Co Ltd, Plantation Tst Co plc; fndr memb Stock Exchange Sailing Assoc 1961; memb: Bow Gp 1961-76 (memb corp taxation res gp 1967-69, memb overseas devpt res gp 1974-76), Cons Cwlth and Overseas Cncl 1972-76; *Publications*: Referendum (jtly 1975), author of various articles in investmt journals and newspapers; *Recreations* travel, economic conumdrums, old cars; *Clubs* Oriental; *Style*— Stephen Kershaw, Esq; 139 Pavilion Rd, London SW1X 0BL; Puerto Sotogrande, Spain

KERTESZ, Lady Gillian Moyra Katherine; *née* Cecil; da of 6 Marquess of Exeter, KCMG (d 1981), and his 1 w, Lady Mary, *née* Montagu Douglas Scott (d 1984), da of 7 Duke of Buccleuch; *b* 8 Mar 1935; *m* 1, 23 Nov 1954 (m dis 1979), Sir Giles Henry Charles Floyd, 7 Bt; 2 s (David, Henry); m 2, 24 April 1979, George Michael Kertesz, s of Zoltan Kertesz (d 1975), of Budapest and Nagyvard; *Career* Coronation Medal (1953); *Style*— Lady Gillian Kertesz; 57 Peel St, London W8 7PA (☎ 01 727 5898); Holly House, Northchapel, nr Petworth, W Sussex (☎ 042 878 580)

KESSLER, David Francis; s of Leopold Kessler, MIMM (d 1944), and Annette Grace, *née* Loeb (d 1936); Leopold Kessler led the El Arish Expedition in 1903 to survey the possibility of Jewish settlement in N Sinai; *b* 6 June 1906; *Educ* Leighton Park Sch, Clare Coll, Cambridge Univ (BA); *m* 20 Dec 1938, Mary Matilda, da of Charles Bray (d 1959), of Upper Basildon, Berks; 1 s (Charles b 1952), 3 da (Josephine b 1941, Elizabeth b 1947, Nikola b 1948); *Career* Major RA, seconded Iraq Levies 1942-44, Political Warfare Exec 1944-45, Br Econ Mission to Greece 1946; publisher; chm Jewish Chronicle Ltd 1958-87 (md 1936-73), fndr and former chm Vallentine Mitchell and Co Ltd publishers, former chm Wiener Library and Inst of Contemporary Hist; former pres Buckingham Liberal Assoc, hon pres CBF World Jewish Relief 1986; tstee: Open Univ Fndn 1984-, cncl Minority Rights Gp; Freeman Stationers and Newspaper Makers Co; *Books* The Falashas the Forgotten Jews of Ethiopia (1982); *Recreations* gardening, archaeology, travel; *Clubs* Athenaeum; *Style*— David F Kessler, Esq; 25 Furnival St, London EC4A 1JT (☎ 01 405 9252)

KESWICK, Hon Mrs (Annabel Térèse); *née* Fraser; yr da of 15 Lord Lovat; *b* 15 Oct 1942; *m* 1, 1964 (m dis 1978), 14 Lord Reay; 2 s, 1 da;m2, 1985, Henry Neville Lindley Keswick, eld s of Sir William Keswick, of Glenkiln, Shawhead, Dumfries; *Style*— Hon Mrs Keswick; 10 Egerton Pl, London SW3 2EF

KESWICK, (John) Chippendale Lindley; s of Sir William Keswick *qv*, of Theydon Bois, Essex; *b* 2 Feb 1940; *Educ* Eton, Univ of Aix Marseilles; *m* 1966, Sarah *qv*, da of The Earl of Dalhousie, of Angus Scotland; 3 s (David b 1967, Tobias b 1968, Adam b 1973); *Career* dir: Persimmon plc 1984, Hunters & Frankau Gp Ltd 1986-, Hambros plc (jt dep chm 1986-), Charter Consolidated plc 1988-; chm Hambros Bank Ltd; cncl memb Cancer Res Campaign 1978-; hon tres Children's Co Holidays Fund; memb Royal Bodyguard of Archers; *Recreations* bridge, field sports; *Clubs* Whites, Portland (chm); *Style*— Chippendale Keswick, Esq; c/o Hambros Bank Ltd, 41 Tower Hill, London EC3N 4HA (☎ 01 480 5000, telex 883851, fax 01 702 4424)

KESWICK, Lady; (Celia) Clare Mary Alice; da of Gervase Elwes by his w Lady Winifrede, *née* Feilding, 4 da of 8 Earl of Denbigh; *b* 13 Jan 1905; *m* 1940, Sir John Keswick, KCMG (d 1982), sometime chm and dir Jardine Matheson & Co; 1 da; *Style*— Lady Keswick; Portrack House, Holywood, Dumfries (☎ Newbridge 276); 5 Chester Place, NW1

KESWICK, Henry Neville Lindley; s of Sir William Johnston Keswick, *qv*; *b* 29 Sept 1938; *Educ* Eton, Trinity Coll Cambridge (BA); *m* 1985, Annabel Térèse (Tessa), da of 15 Baron Lovat, *qv*; *Career* nat serv cmmn Scots Guards 1956-58; dir Jardine Matheson & Co Ltd 1967 (chm 1972-75); dir: Sun Alliance & London Insurance 1975-, Robert Fleming Hldgs; chm Matheson & Co Ltd 1975-; *Recreations* country pursuits; *Clubs* White's, Turf, Third Guards; *Style*— Henry Keswick, Esq; Matheson & Co Ltd, 3 Lombard Street, London EC3V 9AQ (☎ 5284000, fax 6235024)

KESWICK, Lady Sarah; *née* Ramsay; da of 16 Earl of Dalhousie, KT, GCVO, GBE, MC; *b* 1945; *m* 1966, Chippendale Keswick, *qv*; 3 children; *Style*— Lady Sarah Keswick; 1a Ilchester Place, London W14 (☎ 01 603 2873); Auchendolly House, Old Bridge of Urr, Castle Douglas, Kirkcudbrightshire (☎ 055 665 265)

KESWICK, Simon; s of Sir William Keswick, *qv*; the firm of Jardine Matheson was founded in 1832 by William Jardine and James Matheson; the Keswicks of Dumfries married into the Jardine family in the mid-nineteenth century; *Educ* Eton, Trinity Coll Cambridge; *Career* chm Jardine Matheson 1983-; *Style*— Simon Keswick Esq; Jardine Matheson & Co, 3 Lombard St, London EC3

KESWICK, Sir William Johnston; s of Maj Henry Keswick (d 1926), of Cowhill Tower, Dumfries, and Winifrede Johnston; *b* 6 Dec 1903; *Educ* Winchester, Trinity Coll Cambridge; *m* 1937, Mary, da Rt Hon Sir Francis Lindley, GCMG (d 1950); 3 s (Henry *qv*, (John) Chippendale *qv*, Simon *qv*), 1 da; *Career* Brig 21 Army Gp (Europe and Egypt); dir: Matheson & Co Ltd 1943-75 (chm 1949-66), Hudson's Bay Co 1943-72, Bank of England 1955-73, BP Co Ltd 1950-73, Jardine Matheson & Co Ltd (Hong Kong & Far East); memb: Royal Co of Archers (Queen's Bodyguard for Scotland), National Gallery; kt 1972; *Recreations* gardening; *Clubs* White's; *Style*— Sir William Keswick; Theydon Priory, Theydon Bois, Essex (☎ 037 881 2256); Glenkiln, Shawhead, Dumfries, Scotland

KETT WHITE, Cllr John Roderick; s of Sqdn-Ldr Cyril Thomas (Jack) White MBE (d 1953), of Exeter and Singapore, and Frances Ada Lean (d 1979), later Mrs Johnny Johnson; *b* 2 Jan 1938; *Educ* private, public and state GS, Kitchener Scholar Guys Hosp Med and Dental Sch Univ of London; *m* 16 May 1964, Elizabeth Anne, da of Frederick Sidney Kett (d 1981), of Axminster, Devon; 2 s (Charles Rupert b 1966, Thomas Anthony b 1967), 1 da (Anna Sophia b 1965); *Career* landowner; dental surgn (RCS) Wilton Place SW1 1962, sr house offr Bristol Dental Hosp 1969; gen practise Devon, Somerset, Avon 1964-87; dist cncllr Wansdyke 1981-,ldr and chm Policy and Resource Ctee Wansdyke Cncl 1979-82; memb Bristol Health Authy, chm Bathovon Div N Somerset Cons Assoc; various papers inc: Mgmnt of change of Local Govt, A New Way of Treating the Patient, Wansdyke Experience, Origin of a New Experience; *Recreations* the arts, the countryside; *Clubs* Bath Clinical Soc; *Style*— Cncllr John Kett-White, Esq; Iford Park, Hinton Charterhouse, Nr Bath (☎ 022 122 3228); Wansdyke Cncl, 'The Hollies', Midsomer Morton, Bath (☎ 0761 417785)

KETTELEY, John Henry Beevor; s of John Joseph Beevor Ketteley (d 1975), and Violet, *née* Robinson; *b* 9 August 1939; *Educ* Brentwood Sch Essex, Hackley Sch Tarrytown NY USA; *m* 15 April 1967, Susan Elizabeth, da of Robert Charles Jay Gordon, of Great Wakering, Essex; 2 s (Stephen b 13 Nov 1973, Thomas b 20 Aug 1985), 2 da (Sara b 11 July 1969, Alexandra b 15 Nov 1970); *Career* exec dir S G Warburg & Co Ltd 1972-81, non exec dir (dep chm) BTP plc 1978-, md Rea Bros plc 1981-83, exec dir Barclays De Zoete Wedd Ltd 1983-87; non exec dir: Fairholt plc 1987-89, Boosey & Hawkes plc 1987-; Freeman City of London 1978, Liveryman Worshipful Co of CAs 1978; FCA 1970; *Recreations* sailing, golf, tennis, squash; *Clubs* Royal Burnham YC, Royal Corinthian YC; *Style*— John Ketteley, Esq; Keeway, Ferry Rd, Creeksea, Burnham on Crouch, Essex CMO 8PL (☎ 0621 783748, fax 0621 784966, car 0836 281485); Clos Beausoleil, Quartier Garigouille, 30670 Aigues Vives, France

KETTLE, Capt Alan Stafford Howard; CB (1984); s of Arthur Stafford Kettle, and Marjorie Constance, *née* Clough; *b* 6 August 1925; *Educ* Rugby; *m* 1952, Patricia Rosemary, *née* Gander; 2 s; *Career* joined RN 1943, Cdr 1959, Capt 1968, ADC 1977; entered Civil Service as asst under-sec 1977, gen mangr HM Dockyard Chatham 1977-84; *Style*— Capt Alan Kettle, CB, RN; 3 Leather Tor Close, Grangelands, Yelverton PL20 6EQ

KETTLEWELL, Cmdt Dame Marion Mildred; DBE (1970, CBE 1964); da of George Wildman Kettlewell, and Mildred Frances, *née* Atkinson; *b* 20 Feb 1914; *Educ* Godolphin Sch Salisbury, St Christopher's Coll Blackheath; *Career* worked for Fellowship of Maple Leaf Alta Canada 1935-38, worked for Local Cncl 1939-41; joined WRNS 1941, cmnd as Third Offr 1942, Supt WRNS on staff of Flag Offr Air 1961-64, Supt Trg and Drafting 1964-67, dir WRNS 1967-70, gen sec GFS 1971-78, pres Assoc of Wrens 1981-; *Recreations* needlework, walking, ornithology; *Style*— Cmdt Dame Marion Kettlewell, DBE; Flat 2, 9 John Islip St, London, SW1P 4PU

KETTLEWELL, Capt Nigel Ion Charles; s of Cdr Charles Robert Kettlewell (d 1963); *b* 19 Mar 1934; *Educ* Allhallows Sch, RNC Dartmouth; *m* 1964, Lady Serena Jane, *qv*, *née* Dundas, da of 3 Marquess of Zetland; 1 s (Robert b 1965), 2 da (Melissa b 1968, Charlotte b 1970); *Career* qualified in Signals 1960, Staff Coll 1965, served HM Yacht Britannia 1957-58 and 1963-64, in command HM ships Rhyl 1974-75, Brighton 1975-76, MOD 1976-86, Capt RN 1979, chief naval signal offr 1983-86; ADC to HM The Queen 1986-88, Cdre Cmdg HMS Drake 1986-88; ret 1988 companion IERE 1986; yr bro fo Trinity House 1978; *Recreations* gardening, industrial archaeology; *Clubs* Naval and Military; *Style*— Capt Nigel Kettlewell, RN; The Old Rectory, Newton Toney, Salisbury, Wilts (☎ 098 064 311)

KETTLEWELL, Lady Serena Jane; *née* Dundas; da of 3 Marquess of Zetland, ED, DL; *b* 10 Sept 1940; *m* 1964, Capt Nigel Ion Charles Kettlewell, RN, *qv*; 1 s, 2 da; *Style*— Lady Serena Kettlewell; The Old Rectory, Newton Toney, Salisbury, Wilts (☎ 098 064 311)

KEVILL-DAVIES, Christopher Evelyn; CBE (1973), JP (1954-82), DL (1974-82 Norfolk); s of William A S H Kevill-Davies, JP (ka 1915), of Croft Castle, Hereford, and Dorothy Mortlock, *née* Lacon (d 1985); *b* 12 July 1913; *Educ* Radley; *m* 23 June 1938, Virginia Louisa, da of Adm Ronald Arthur Hopwood, CB (d 1949), of 7 Sloane Gardens, London SW1; 1 s (Rev Christopher Charles b 1944), 1 da (Anne Margaret (Mrs Bartholomew) b 1939); *Career* served WWII Suffolk Yeo 1939-43 and Gren Gds 1943-45 in (France, Belgium and Germany) Capt memb Gt Yarmouth Borough Cncl 1946-53; chm Norfolk Mental Deficiency HMC 1950-69; vice chm: E Anglican Regnl Health Authy 1974-82; chm E Lacon & Co, Brewers, Gt Yarmouth 1963-75 (dir 1936, vice chm 1946); memb gen Cncl King Edward Hosp Fund for London 1972; High Sheriff of Norfolk 1965; Liveryman Worshipful Co of Fishmongers 1967; *Clubs* Cavalry and Guards', RAC, Norfolk; *Style*— Christopher Kevill-Davies, CBE, JP, DL; 11 Hale House, 34 de Vere Gardens, London W8 5AQ (☎ 01 937 5066)

KEVILLE, Sir (William) Errington; CBE (1947); s of William Edwin Keville (d 1941); *b* 3 Jan 1901; *Educ* Merchant Taylors' Sch; *m* 1928, Ailsa Sherwood McMillan; 3 s, 2 da; *Career* memb Cncl Chamber of Shipping 1940- (vice pres 1960, pres 1961); memb: bd Port of London Authority 1943-59, ctee Lloyds Register of Shipping 1957-68; dir: Shaw Savill & Albion Co Ltd 1941-68 (former dep chm), Furness Withy & Co Ltd 1950-68 (chm 1962-68); chm: Gen Cncl of Br Shipping 1961, Int Chamber of Shipping 1963-68, Ctee of European Shipowners 1963-65, Ctee of European Nat Shipowners' Assocs 1963-65; dir Nat Bank of NZ 1946-75; kt 1962; *Recreations* walking, gardening; *Style*— Sir Errington Keville, CBE; Stroud Close, Grayswood, Haslemere, Surrey GU27 2DJ (☎ 0428 3653)

KEY, Brian Michael; MEP (Lab) S Yorks 1979-; s of Leslie Granville Key, and Nora Alice, *née* Haylett; *b* 1947,Sept; *Educ* Darfield Primary Sch, Wath upon Dearne GS, Liverpool Univ (BA Hons); *Career* Offr W Riding County Cncl 1970-73, Sr admin offr S Yorks County Cncl 1973-79; MEP 1979; *Style*— Brian Key Esq, MEP; 25 Cliff Road, Darfield, Barnsley, Yorks; office: 36 Nelson St, Rotherham S65 1EX (☎ 0709 75944)

KEY, Geoffrey George Bamford; s of George Key (Sgt RA, d 1967), of Manchester, and Marion, *née* Bamford; *b* 13 May 1941; *Educ* High Sch of Art Manchester, Regnl Coll of Art Manchester (Nat Dip of Design, Dip of Associateship of Manchester, Postgrad in Sculpture); *Career* major exhibitions: Salford Art Gallery 1966, Manchester Univ 1969, Erica Bourne Gallery London 1974, Salon d'Automne Clermont Ferrand France 1974, Nancy France 1974, Gallery Tendenz Germany 1977, Lausanne Switzerland 1980, Madison Avenue NY 1980, Solomon Gallery Dublin 1983, Solomon Gallery London 1985; work incl in the collections of: Salford Art Gallery, Manchester City Art Gallery, Bolton Art Gallery, NW Arts Assoc, Manchester Univ, Wigan Corpn, Granada TV; council memb: Friends of Salford Art Gallery, Manchester Acad of Fine Art (memb 1970); *Books* G Key A Book of Drawings and Interview (1975), Daydreams (1981); *Recreations* collecting 16th & 17th century works of art; *Style*— Geoffrey Key, Esq; 59 Acresfield Rd, Pendleton, Salford 6, Lancashire (☎ 061 736 6014)

KEY, (Simon) Robert; MP (C) Salisbury 1983-; s of The Rt Rev John Maurice Key (d 1984), and Agnes Joan (Dence); Rt Rev John Key (d 1984) was Bishop of Sherborne (1946-60) and Bishop of Truro (1960-73); *b* 22 April 1945; *Educ* Salisbury Cathedral Sch, Sherborne, Clare Coll Cambridge (MA); *m* 1968, Susan Prisilla Bright, da of Very Revd Thomas Thurstan Irvine, former Dean of St Andrews; 2 s (James (decd), Adam b 1974), 2 da (Sophy b 1977, Helen b 1979); *Career* MP for Salisbury (C) 1983-; memb of Commons Select Ctee on Educn Sci and the Arts 1983-86; chm Cncl for Educn in the Cwlth 1984-87; memb UK Nat Cmmn for UNESCO 1985-86; pps to:Rt Hon Edward Heath MP 1984-85, Min of State for Energy 1985-87, Chris Patten MP, Min for Overseas Devpt 1987-; *Clubs* Athenaeum; *Style*— Robert Key, Esq, MP; 12 Brown St, Salisbury, Wilts (☎ 0722 333141); House of Commons, London SW1

KEYDEN, James Aitken; s of John Keyden (d 1969); *b* 15 May 1909; *Educ* Glasgow HS; *m* 1940, Doris Margaret, nee Crawford; 2 s (and 1 decd), 3 da (and 1 decd); *Career* CA, dir Scottish Utd Investors Ltd 1961-80, chm Rowan & Boden Ltd 1968-71, dir: Pressed Steel Co Ltd 1953-63, Scottish Gas Bd 1964-73, Brown Shipley & Co Ltd 1979-84, Volvo Trucks (GB) Ltd 1966-84, George Blair plc; *Recreations* golf, fishing; *Clubs* Royal Scottish Automobile; *Style*— James Keyden, Esq; Craigie Burn, Glencairn Rd, Kilmacolm, Renfrewshire (☎ 050 587 2478)

KEYES, Hon Adrian Christopher Noel; s of 2 Baron Keyes *qv*; *b* 1962; *Educ* Lancing; *Style*— The Hon Adrian Keyes

KEYES, Hon Charles William Packe; s and h of 2 Baron Keyes *qv*; *b* 8 Dec 1951; *m* 1978, Sadiye Yasmin, da of Mahir Coskun, of Istanbul; *Style*— The Hon Charles Keyes

KEYES, Hon Elizabeth Mary; da of Adm of the Fleet 1 Baron Keyes, GCB, KCVO, CMG, DSO (d 1945) and Eva Mary Salvin (d 1973), da of Edward Salvin Bowlby, DL, of Gilston Park, Herts an Knoydart, Inverness (whose er s was awarded a posthumous VC for leading Commando raid on Gen Rommel's HQ at Sidi Rafa, Libya 1941); *b* 10 May 1915; *Educ* Westonbirt; *Career* WW II 1939-45 with VAD (RN); smallholder (ret), former breeder of Anglo-Arabs (Working Hunter of the Year 1960), beef cattle and geese; *Books* Geoffrey Keyes, VC of the Rommel Raid (1966); *Recreations* conservation; *Clubs* Nat Farmers' Union, VAD (RN) Assoc; *Style*— The Hon Elizabeth Keyes; Wood Lane Cottage, Tingewick, Buckingham MK18 4QS (☎ 02804 303)

KEYES, Hon (Leopold Roger) John; s of 2 Baron Keyes *qv*; *b* 1956; *Style*— The Hon John Keyes

KEYES, 2 Baron (UK 1943); Sir Roger George Bowlby Keyes; 2 Bt (UK 1919); s of Adm of the Fleet 1 Baron Keyes, GCB, KCVO, CMG, DSO, DCL (d 1945), and Eva Mary Salvin, *née* Bowlby (d 1973); *b* 14 Mar 1919; *Educ* King's Mead Sch Seaford, RNC Dartmouth; *m* 6 Dec 1947, Grizelda Mary, da of late Lt-Col William Packe, DSO; 3 s (Hon Charles *qv*, Hon John *qv*, Hon Adrian b 1962), 2 da (Hon Mrs Martyn Crompton b 1950, Hon Mrs Thoby Young b 1958); *Heir* s, Hon Charles Keyes; *Career* WWII serv RN N Sea and Med 1939-45, ret 1949; co dir, conslt; author; *Books* Outrageous Fortune (1984),Un Règne Brisé (1985), Echec au Roi (1986), Een Beproeft Koning (1986), Complot Tegen de Koning (1988); *Clubs* Institute of Directors; *Style*— The Rt Hon the Lord Keyes; Elmscroft, Charlton Lane, West Farleigh, nr Maidstone, Kent ME15 0NY (☎ 0622 812477)

KEYNES, Hon Mrs (Anne Pinsent); *née* Adrian; da of 1 Baron Adrian, OM (d 1977), and Hester, *née* Pinsent, DBE, BEM (d 1966); *b* 27 May 1924; *Educ* Downe House, Somerville Coll Oxford (MA); *m* 1945, Richard, FRS, s of Sir Geoffrey Keynes (d 1982), and Margaret (da of Sir George Darwin, KCB, FRS, of Newnham Grange, Cambridge); 3 s (Randal b 1948, Roger b 1951, Simon b 1952), and 1 s decd; *Style*— The Hon Mrs Keynes; 4 Herschel Rd, Cambridge (☎ 0223 353107); Primrose Farm, Wiveton, nr Holt, Norfolk (☎ 0263 740317)

KEYS, David Chaloner; s of John Henry Keys (d 1982), of Sussex, and Jean Winifred, *née* Glover (d 1970); *b* 12 Feb 1934; *Educ* Merchant Taylors Sch, St John's Coll Oxford (MA); *m* 2 June 1959, Pamela Helen, da of Philip Henry Megson (d 1984), of Cheshire; 3 da (Charlotte b 1962, Harriet b 1965, Rebecca b 1973); *Career* flying offr RAF 1953-55, private sec to dep govr Bank of Eng 1963 (joined 1958), seconded to UK Treasy Delgn Washington 1964-66; seconded as md Bank of Mauritius 1968-70; Morgan Grenfell 1971- (dir MG Gp 1987-88, M G & Co Ltd 1973-88); chm E Surrey Health Authy 1988-; dir: Norwich Union Insurance Group 1988-, A De Gruchy & Co Ltd 1982- (chm 1988-); non exec dir: HFC Tst and Savings Ltd 1982-; *Recreations* reading, travelling, ornithology; *Style*— David Keys, Esq; Tower Hill House, Tower Hill, Dorking, Surrey RH4 2AP (☎ 0306 885625); 23 Great Winchester St, London EC2P 2AX (☎ 01 588 4545)

KEYS, Sir (Alexander George) William; AC (1988), OBE (1970), MC (1951); s of John Alexander Binnie Keys and Irene Daisy Keys; *b* 2 Dec 1923; *Educ* Hurlstone Ag HS; *m* 1950, Dulcie Beryl, *née* Stinton; *Career* Capt, served New Guinea, Borneo and Korea; Nat sec RSL of Aust 1961-78, Nat pres 1978-88, Nat pres Korea and S E Asia Forces Assoc of Aust (life memb 1965), pres Int Fedn of Korean War Veterans' Assoc tstee Aust War Memorial, dep chm Canberra Permanent Building Soc; MC 1951, OBE 1970, Order of Korean Nat Security Merit 1981; kt 1980; *Style*— Sir William Keys, AC, OBE, MC; Glenlee, PO Box 455, Queanbeyan, NSW 2620, Australia (☎ 97 5440)

KEYS, William Herbert; s of George William Keys, of London (d 1951), and Jessie Florence, *née* Powell (d 1965); *b* 1 Jan 1923; *Educ* S London GS; *m* 28 May 1949, Enid, da of William Gledhill, of New Zealand (d 1954); 2 s (Keith b 1950, Ian b 1952); *Career* WO 2 6 City of London Rifles, RE, RA, Served NW Europe 1939-496; gen sec SOGAT 1974-85 (nat organiser 1953-61, sec London 1961-71, gen pres 1971-74); chm: TUC Printing Ctee 1974-85, TUC Employment Policy Organisation Ctee 1976-85, Trade Union Co-ordinating Ctee 1984-87, TUC/Labour Pty Liaison Ctee 1981-85; jt chm Pulp and Paper Div Int Chemical 1976-85; memb various TUC Ctee: Equal Right 1974-85, Race Relations 1974-85, Media 1977-85, Economic 1981-85, Gen Purposes 1982-85; memb: Central Arbitration Ctee 1977-, Manpower Services Cmmn 1979-85, Cmmn of Racial Equality 1977-81, European Social Fund 1979-86, ACAS 1976-; *Recreations* music; *Style*— William Keys, Esq

KHANGURA, Jagpal Singh; s of Joginder Singh Khangura (d 1978), of Latala, Punjab, India, and Harnam Kaur Khangura (d 1942); *b* 12 May 1937; *Educ* Punjab Univ (BA); *m* 17 Sept 1960, Gurdial Kaur Khangura; 2 s (Jasbir Singh b 1963, Satbir Singh b 1967); *Career* sub-postmaster 1963-81, hotelier 1981-86, chief exec Premier Hotel Gp 1986-; vice chm Hounslow Community Relations Cncl 1982-87, gen sec Indian Workers Assoc 1987-; cncllr London Borough of Hounslow 1986-; *Recreations* gardening; *Style*— Jagpal Khangura, Esq; 85 Byron Ave, Cranford, Middx (☎ 01 897 8508); Premier Hotels, West End Rd, Ruislip, Middx (☎ 0895 621000, fax 0895 621635, telex 892514)

KHASRU, (Mohammed) Ameer; s of Abdur Rahman Khasru, of Bangladesh, and Saleha Khasru; *b* 28 Jan 1942; *Educ* Collegiate Sch Chittagong, Univ of Dhaka (BCom); *m* 4 March 1965, Chantal Berthe, da of Andre Faucher (d 1979), of France; 1 s (Stephane Reza b 1966), 1 da (Ambreen Joy b 1970); *Career* snr ptnr Khasru & Co London; chief accountant: Burmah Eastern Ltd, Chittagong Bangladesh 1968-71; snr lectr Business Studies SW London Coll 1971-74, trng mangr 1974-78; FCA; *Recreations* swimming, tennis, theatre, reading, good food; *Clubs* Asian City (tres); *Style*— Ameer Khasru, Esq; 236 Linen Hall, 162 Regent Street, London W1R 5TB (☎ 01 437 5401)

KIBBEY, (Sidney) Basil; s of Percy Edwin Kibbey (d 1939), of Mickleover, and Winifred, *née* Garratt (d 1968); *b* 3 Dec 1916; *Educ* Derby Sch, Admin Staff Coll Henley; *m* 3 June 1939, (Violet Gertrude) Jane, da of John George Eyre (d 1956), of Lincs; 1 s (Paul b 1943), 1 da (Anna (twin) b 1943); *Career* princ Miny of Nat Insur 1951, sec Nat Insur Advsy Ctee 1960-62, asst sec Miny of Pensions & Nat Insur 1962; under-sec DHSS 1971-76, visiting lectr Civil Serv Coll 1976-; *Recreations* photography, gardening; *Clubs* English-Speaking Union; *Style*— Basil Kibbey, Esq; 29 Beaulieu Close, Datchet, Berks SL3 9DD (☎ 0753 49 101)

KIDD, John Edward Aitken; s of Maj Edward Daltrey Kidd (d 1979), and Hon Janet Gladys, *née* Aitken (d 1988), da of 1 Baron Beaverbrook; *b* 12 Dec 1944; *Educ* Harrow; *m* 2 April 1973, Wendy Madeleine, da of Sir John Rowland Hodge MBE; 1 s (Jack Edward b 1973), 2 da (Jemma Madeleine b 1974, Jodie Elizabeth b 1978); *Career* Jr Euro Individual Showjumping Champion 1962; represented GB in Europe, USA and Africa 1964-72; represented England 11 v The Commonwealth (Polo) on Int Day at Windsor 1972; dir: London United Investmts plc 1977-81, Aitken Home plc 1982-86; chm Columbia Laboratories Inc USA 1987-; dir: Careplus Inc USA 1987-, All England Jumping Course Hickstead 1989-; *Books* Reins In Our Hands, 1966, Take Off, 1974, Biographies On Showjumping Career; *Recreations* polo; *Clubs* Buck's; *Style*— John Kidd, Esq; Hilliers, Petworth, West Sussex; Holders House, St James, Barbados; Suite 1809, 745 Fifth Ave, New York City, NY, USA

KIDD, Sir Robert Hill; KBE (1979), CB (1975); s of Andrew Kidd (d 1947), and Florence, *née* Hill (d 1963); *b* 3 Feb 1918; *Educ* Royal Belfast Academical Inst, Dublin Univ (BA, BLitt); *m* 1942, Harriet Moore, da of Rev E H Williamson, BLitt, PhD, of Ballina and Tralee, Eire; (3 s, 2 da); *Career* actg Maj SEAC, cmmnd 1942, Royal Ulster Rifles, later attached to Intelligence Corps; NI Civil Serv 1947-79 (head of NICS 1976-79); dir Allied Irish Banks Ltd; chm Belfast Car Ferries Ltd, NI chm of Cooperaton North 1982-86; pro chancellor and chm cncl New Univ of Ulster 1980-84; tstee: Scot Irish Tst, Ulster Historical Fndn 1980-; Hon DLitt Univ of Ulster 1985; *Recreations* gardening, photography; *Clubs* Civil Serv; *Style*— Sir Robert Kidd, KBE, CB; 24 Massey Court, Belfast, BT4 3GJ (☎ 768694)

KIDDY, Dennis; s of Thomas William Kiddy (d 1987), and Violet, *née* Snead; *b* 6 Dec 1951; *Educ* Blackpool GS, Worcester Coll Oxford (MA); *Career* musician, organ scholar Worcester Coll Oxford Univ 1970-73, dir of music: Beaudesert Park 1974-75, Repton Prep Sch 1975-83, Wymondham Coll 1983-84; devpt offr St Edmund's Sch Canterbury 1984-; hon sr memb Darwin Coll Univ of Kent 1986, dir of music Lambeth Conf 1988; *Recreations* cooking; *Style*— Dennis Kiddy, Esq; St Edmund's Sch, Canterbury, Kent CT2 8HU (☎ 0227 454 575)

KIDNER, David Hudson; OBE (1985); s of Clifford Hudson Kidner (d 1970), and Elspeth Mary, *née* Creeke (d 1973); *b* 13 Mar 1931; *Educ* Burnley GS; *m* 1954, (Elizabeth) Alison, da of Austin Marshall (d 1969), of Mawgan Porth Cornwall; 3 s (Paul, Alan, Brian); *Career* asst clerk Burnley Borough Magistrates Ct 1947, princ clerk Wallington Magistrates' Ct 1953; slr 1964; clerk to the Justices for Five Petty Sessional Divs Isle of Ely Cambs 1966, clerk to the Justices Coventry 1973, hon sec Justices' Clerks Soc 1976-81, pres Justices' Clerks' Soc 1983-84; chm Coventry Diocesan Bd for Social Responsibility 1980-; *Recreations* walking, rugby (spectator); *Style*— David Kidner Esq, OBE; St Mary's Hall, Coventry CV1 5RH (☎ (0203) 25555 ext 2114)

KIDSON, Capt Ian Harold; s of Capt Harold Brookes Kidson (d 1969), of 7 Clifton Rd, Tettenhall, Wolverhampton, and Dorothea, *née* Johnston (d 1975); *b* 8 Feb 1920; *Educ* Malvern; *m* 1 Sept 1954, Anne Augusta, da of Leonard Dudley Braithwaite (d 1970), of Fosse House, Stourbridge Rd, Wombourn, Wolverhampton; 3 s (Jonathan b 1956, Bruce b 1958, Paul b 1962), 3 da (Elena b 1955, Suzanne b 1964, Annabel b 1974); *Career* cmmnd 2 Lt 2/6 S Staffs Regt (TA) 1939, Capt (co cdr) 6 Bn KOYLI 1942, 4/6 Bn KAR Serv overseas (E Africa, Ceylon, India, Burma) 1943-46; articled clerk to CA 1937-39 and 1946-48, sales rep agric engrs 1948-50, co sec and dir Multiple Retail Grocers 1950-61 (md 1961-62), JW Braithwaite & Son Ltd (bookbinders) 1962-: co sec 1965-70, chm and md 1970-; chm Church Eaton Branch Stafford Cons Assoc 1971-87, church warden Church Eaton Stafford 1983-86, pres Glebelands Sports Assoc 1983-; memb bd govrs PNEU Sch 1958-78, chm 1975-78, bd visitors HM Prison Featherstone Staffs 1979-88; memb Br Printing Industs Fedn (pres Midland Region 1974); *Recreations* tennis, shooting, gardening; *Style*— Capt Ian Kidson; Little Onn Hall, Church Eaton, Stafford ST20 OAU (☎ 0785 840 154); J W Braithwaite & Son Ltd, PO Box 20, Pountney St, Wolverhampton, W Mids WV2 4HY (☎ 0902 52209, fax 0902 352918)

KIDSTON, Hon Mrs (Patricia Anne); *née* Manners; da of 4 Baron Manners, MC (d 1972); *b* 1927; *m* 1946, John Bonham Kidston (d 1968), gs Sir George Bonham, 2 Bt; 2 s (Francis b 1947, Jonathan b 1951), 1 da (Virginia b 1953); *Style*— The Hon Mrs Kidston; Breach Farm, Dummer, Basingstoke

KIDSTON-MONTGOMERIE OF SOUTHANNAN, Col George Jardine; DSO (1942), MC (1941), DL (Wilts 1960); s of Richard Logan Kidston (d 1920), of Beecham Court, Newbury, and Sophia Egidia Gwendolin Montgomerie; recognised by Lord Lyon King of Arms upon his succession to feudal barony of Wouthannan, Ayrshire through his maternal grandmother Lady Sophia Montgomerie, co-heiress to her father 14 Earl of Eglinton and Winton; *b* 8 Mar 1907; *Educ* Eton, RMC Sandhurst; *m* 26 July 1932, Lydia Cecelia, da of Maj P Mason, DSO (ka 1915); 1 s (Robert Alexander b 1936), 1 da (Philippa Sophia b 1934); *Career* joined 12 Royal Lancers 1926, cmd 12 RL 1942-43, cmd 4 Hussars 1947-49; Col Queens Royal Irish Hussars 1965-69; memb Royal Co of Archers (Queen's Body Guard for Scotland); one of HM's Hon Corps of Gentlemen-at-Arms; *Recreations* hunting, shooting, fishing; *Clubs* White's, Cavalry and Guards'; *Style*— Col George Kidston-Montgomerie of Southannan, DSO, MC, DL; Longbottom, Biddesden, Andover, Hants; Fairlie Craig, Fairlie, Ayrshire (☎ Chute Standen 226)

KIELY, Dr David George; s of George Thomas Kiely (d 1964), of Ballynahinch, Co Down, and Susan Wolfenden (d 1972); *b* 23 July 1925; *Educ* Down HS Downpatrick, Queen's Univ Belfast (BSc, MSc), Sorbonne (DSc), Royal Naval Staff Coll; *m* 17 Aug 1956, Dr Ann Wilhelmina, da of John William Kilpatrick (d 1961), of Kilwarlin House, St James's, Hillsborough, Co Down; 1 s (Patrick b 1964), 1 da (Fiona b 1961); *Career* Civil Serv MOD, appts RNS Serv 1944-incl: hd of Electronic Warfare Div ASWE 1965-68, hd of Communications and Sensor Dept ASWE 1968-72, Under Sec 1972, Dir Gen Telecommunications PE MOD 1972-74, Dir Gen Stategic Electonic Systems PE MOD 1974-76, Dir Gen Electroics Res 1976-78, Dir Naval Surface Weapons ASWE 1978-83, The Chief Naval Weapon Systems Engr 1983-84; chm R & D Policy Ctee of the General Lighthouse Authys of the UK and Eire 1974-; gp Chief Exec Chemring plc 1984-85, conslt engr 1985-; govr Portsmouth Coll of Technol 1965-69, chm Chichester Cathedral cncl 1985- (memb 1982-); CEng, FIEE, CPhys, FInstP; *Books* Dielectric Aerials (1953), Marine Navigational Aids for Coastal Waters of the British Isles (1987), Naval Electronic Warfare (1988) Naval Surface Weapons (1988); *Recreations* fly fishing, gardening, aviculture; *Clubs* Naval and Military; *Style*— Dr David Kiely; Cranleigh, 107 Havant Road, Emsworth, Hampshire PO10 7LF (☎ 0243 372250)

KIENDL, Hon Mrs (Judith Caroline); *née* Ross; yr da of Baron Ross of Newport (Life Peer), *qv*; *b* 1 Nov 1952; *m* Theodore Kiendl; 65 Tyrwhitt Road, Brockley, London SE14

KIER, Michael Hector; s of Mogens Kier, and Birthe, *née* Andreasen; *b* 22 Oct 1946; *Educ* Repton, King's Coll London; *m* 15 May 1971, Jane Elizabeth, da of J R Childs; *Career* insur broker C E Heath plc 1968-77 (dir 1986-), jt md: Fielding Juggins Money & Stewart 1981-86, Heath Fielding Insur Broking Ltd 1986-, chm C E Heath Latin America Ltd 1986-; *Style*— Michael Kier, Esq; C E Heath plc, 150 Minories, London EC3N 1NR (☎ 01 488 2488, fax 01 480 7464, telex 8813001)

KIKANO, Khalil Naoum; *b* 20 August 1938; *m* 22 Nov 1959, Hanne, 1 s (Naoum b 1960), 2 da (Margo b 1964, Lara b 1969); *Career* Banque Sabbag SAL Beirut 1956-63, mangr of audit Whinney Murray & Co 1964-68; The Royal Bank of Canada: mangr (Middle E) SAL Beirut 1969-77, regnl offr of (Middle E and Africa) Montreal 1977, gen mangr (Middle E and Africa) London 1982, vice-pres of (Middle E and Africa) 1983, vice-pres of lending 1988; memb Centre of Arbitration and Concilliation Union of Arab Banks; *Clubs* RAC; *Style*— Khalil Kikano, Esq; 6 Cornwall Mansions, 33 Kensington Ct, London W8 5BG (☎ 01 937 9346); The Royal Bank of Canada, 71 Queen Victoria St, London EC4V 4DE (☎ 01 489 1188, fax 01 329 6065, telex 929111)

KILBRACKEN, 3 Baron (UK 1909); John Raymond Godley; DSC (1945); s of 2 Baron Kilbracken, CB, KC (d 1950), and his 1 w, Elizabeth, *née* Hamilton; bro of Prof Hon Wynne Godley, the economist, and gs of 1 Baron who was Gladstone's private sec and a perm under-sec for India; *b* 17 Oct 1920; *Educ* Eton, Balliol Coll Oxford, (MA); *m* 1943 (m dis 1949), Penelope, da of Rear Adm Sir Cecil Reyne, KBE (d 1958); 1 s (Hon Christopher b 1945; and 1 s decd Simon); m 2, 1981, Susan, da of late Norman Heazlewood; 1 s (Hon Seán b 1981); *Heir* s, Hon Christopher Godley; *Career* sits as Lab peer in House of Lords; serv WWII RNVR Fleet Air Arm, Lt Cdr; journalist and author; winner of Times Educnl Supplement Information Book Award 1982 for books for children aged 10-16; *Books* Tell Me The Next One (1950), The Master Forger (1951), Living Like A Lord (1954), A Peer Behind The Curtain (1959), Shamrocks and Unicorns (1962), Van Meegeren (1967), Bring Back My Stringbag (1979), The Easy Way to Bird Recognition (1982), The Easy Way to Tree Recognition (1983), The Easy Way to Wild Flower Recognition (1984); *Recreations* bird watching; *Style*— The Rt Hon Lord Kilbracken, DSC; Killegar, Cavan, Rep of Ireland (☎ Cavan 34309)

KILBRANDON, Baron (Life Peer UK 1971); Charles James Dalrymple Shaw; PC (1971); s of James Edward Shaw, DL (d 1954), of High Greenan, Ayr; *b* 15 August 1906; *Educ* Charterhouse, Balliol Coll Oxford (BA), Edinburgh Univ (LLB); *m* 1937, Ruth Caroline, da of Frank Morrison Seafield Grant, of Knockie, Inverness; 2 s (Hon Patrick b 1938, Hon Michael b 1944), 3 da (Hon Mrs Christopher Orme-Smith b 1940, Hon Mrs Thomas Shephard, Hon Elizabeth b 1948); *Career* advocate Scotland 1932, KC 1949, sheriff of Ayr and Bute 1954-57, of Perth and Angus 1957-58, dean of Faculty of Advocates 1957-59, a Lord of Session with title of Lord Kilbrandon 1959-71, a Lord of Appeal in Ordinary 1971-76, chm Scottish Law Cmmn 1965-71; hon fell Balliol Coll, visitor 1974-86; hon bencher Gray's Inn 1971; Hon DSc Edinburgh, Hon LLD Aberdeen; *Clubs* New, Royal Highland YC (Oban); *Style*— The Rt Hon The Lord Kilbrandon, PC; Kilbrandon House, Balvicar, by Oban, Argyll PA34 4RA (☎ Balvicar 239)

KILBY, Michael Leopold; MEP; s of Guy Kilby (d 1972) and Grace; *b* 3 Sept 1924; *Educ* Coll of Technol; *m* 21 March 1952, Mary, da of Eric Sanders (d 1981); 3 s (Guy, Marcus, Robert); *Career* former exec of General Motors Corpn: (head of Euro planning, govt and trade relations 1972-79, Euro Sales mktg and serv mangr, plant mangr 1966-71); author, novels incl Man at the Sharp End and Mammon Inc; *Recreations* cricket; *Clubs* Beds CC, Dunstable Town CC, Luton CC; *Style*— Michael Kilby Esq, MEP; Grange Barn, Haversham Village, Milton Keynes, Bucks MK19 7DX (☎ 0908 313 613; Nat-West, High Street, Stony Stratford, Bucks

KILDARE, Marquess of; Maurice FitzGerald; s and h of 8 Duke of Leinster by his 2 w, Anne, *née* Smith; *b* 7 April 1948; *Educ* Millfield; *m* 1972, Fiona Mary Francesca, da of late Harry Hollick, of Sutton Courtenay, Abingdon; 1 s, 2 da (Lady Francesca b 6 July 1976, Lady Pollyanna b 9 May 1982); *Heir* s, Earl of Offaly b 12 Jan 1974; *Career* landscape gardener and designer Maxwell Communications Corpn plc, Headington, Oxon; pres Oxfordshire Dyslexia Assoc 1978-, patron Sequal; *Recreations* shooting, fishing, riding, squash, sailing; *Style*— Marquess of Kildare; Courtyard House, Oakley Park, Frilford Heath, Oxon OX13 6QW

KILFEDDER, James Alexander; MP (Ulster Popular Unionist Pty 1980-, Down N 1970-); s of Robert Kilfedder (d 1964), of Eastonville, Millisle, Co Down; *b* 16 July 1928; *Educ* Portora Royal Sch Enniskillen, Dublin Univ; *Career* Irish barr 1952, Gray's Inn 1958, MP (UU) Belfast W 1964-66, Official Unionist memb: NI Assembly 1973-74, NI Convention 1975-76, second NI Assembly 1982-86, resigned from Official Unionist Pty 1979 to stand as UU, fndr memb and ldr Ulster Popular Unionist Pty 1980-, speaker NI Assembly 1982-86; *Style*— James Kilfedder, Esq, MP; 96 Seacliff Rd, Bangor, Co Down BT20 5EZ, Northern Ireland

KILGOUR, Dr John Lowell; CB (1987); s of Ormonde John Lowell Kilgour (d 1946), of Aberdeen, Scotland, and Catherine, *née* MacInnes (d 1925); *b* 26 July 1924; *Educ* St Christophers Hove Sussex, Aberdeen GS, Aberdeen Univ (MB, ChB); *m* 24 Oct 1955, Daphne, da of Walter Tully (d 1958), of Otterburn, Northumberland; 2 s (Alastair Hugh Lowell, Simon Walter Lowell); *Career* Lt RAMC 1947-48, Capt RAMC 1948-50, Maj: 26 Field Ambulance Korea 1950-52, Depot and Trg Estab RAMC 1953-54; Lt Col CO 23 Parachute Field Ambulance 1954-57 (served Suez, Cyprus), registrar Queen Alexandra Mil Hosp 1957-59, Gen Staff Coll Camberley 1959-60, DADG WO 1960-61, ADMS GHQ FARELF (Singapore, Brunei) 1961-64, Jt Servs Staff Coll 1964-65, Cmdt RAMC Field Trg Sch 1965-67; joined Med Civil Serv 1968, med offr in med manpower postgrad med educn implementation of Todd Report, sr med offr 1970-71, princ med offr head of Int Health Div DHSS 1971-73, chief med advsr and undersec Miny of Overseas Devpt 1973-78, seconded dir of coordination (D2) WHO Geneva until 1983, dir and under sec Prison Med Serv Home Off 1983-; ldr of UK delegations to WHO and Cncl of Euro Public Health Ctees 1971-78; chm: Ctee for Surveillance of Communicable Diseases 1976, EPHC 1976; govr London Sch of Tropical Med and Hygiene 1986- (visiting lectr 1973-); memb: UN Advsy Ctee on Coordination 1978-83, exec ctee Royal Cwlth Soc of the Blind, cncl Liverpool Sch of Tropical Med 1973-87; Cons Speaking Prize (London and SE) 1967; MRCGP 1961, FFCM 1974; *Books* Medical Migration (1971), Global Impact of Aids (1988), plus numerous contriutions to medical and general publications; *Clubs* Athenaeum, Hurlingham, Royal Windsor Racing; *Style*— Dr Kilgour, CB; Stoke House, 22 Amersham Road, Chesham Bois, Bucks HP6 5PE (☎ 0494 726 100); Cleland House, Page Street, London SW1P 4LN (☎ 01 211 8091)

KILKENNY, Bernard Crook; s of William Kilkenny (d 1985), of Branksome Park, Poole, Dorset, and Lilian, *née* Crook; *b* 6 Sept 1928; *Educ* Beaumont Coll, New Coll Oxford (BA, BSc, DPhil, MA); *m* 1 Feb 1958 (m diss 1985), Patricia Ann, da of Thomas William Howard, of Northwood, Middlesex; 2 s (Charles b 1965, Neville b 1966), 2 da (Elizabeth b 1959, Caroline b 1961); *Career* Royal Horse Artillery 1952-54; HAC 1954-62; dir: Allied Breweries 1969-78 (jt md (UK) Ltd 1973-8, dep chm (UK) Ltd, chm (UK) Ltd & subsid Cos 1975-8; dir: Scottish & Newcastle Breweries plc; chm: Thistle Hotels, William Younger & Co, Home Brewery, Waverley Vintners Ltd; *Recreations* golf, sailing, skiing, shooting, bridge; *Clubs* Royal Thames YC, Moor Park GC, Hon Co of Edinburgh Golfers; *Style*— Bernard Kilkenny, Esq; 45 Heriot Row, Edinburgh EH3 6EX (☎ 031 225 7729); 17 Eaton Mansions, Cliveden Place, London; Scottish & Newcastle Breweries plc, 111 Holyrood Rd, Edinburgh (☎ 031 556 2591, telex: 72356)

KILLANIN, 3 Baron (UK 1900); Sir Michael Morris; 3 Bt (UK 1885); MBE (1945), TD (1945); s of Lt-Col Hon George Morris, Irish Gds (ka 1914, yr bro of 2 Baron) by his w Dora Wesley Hall; gs of 1 Baron, formerly Lord Chief Justice of Ireland and later Lord of Appeal in Ordinary; suc unc 1927; *b* 30 July 1914; *Educ* Eton,

Sorbonne, Magdalene Coll Cambridge (MA); *m* 1945, Sheila Mary, MBE, da of late Rev Canon Douglas Dunlop, of Co Galway; 3 s, 1 da; *Heir* s, Hon George Morris; *Career* serv WWII KRRC: Bde Maj 30 Armd Bde, (Normandy Landing); journalist on Daily Express, then Daily Mail (reported on Chinese/Japanese War 1937-38); formerly dir: Irish Shell Ltd, Beamish & Crawford Ltd, Ulster Bank Ltd, Syntex (Ireland) Lte; formerly chm: Northern Telecom (Ireland) Ltd, Gallaher (Dublin) Ltd, Chubb Ireland Ltd, Hibernian Life Assoc Ltd, Ulster Investmt Bank Ltd, Lombard & Ulster Banking Ireland Ltd; memb Lloyd's; pres Olympic Cncl of Ireland 1950-73; Int Olympic Ctee: memb 1952, memb exec bd 1967, vice pres 1968, pres 1972-80, hon life pres 1980-; memb (nominated by Irish Govt): Cultural Relations Ctee 1947-72, Nat Monuments Advsy Cncl 1947-80, Irish Red Cross Soc 1947-72, Irish Sailors and Soldiers Land Tst 1955-; chm: Irish Govt Nat Heritage Cncl 1988-, Irish Govt Cmmn on Thoroughbred Breeding and Racing 1982-; steward of Turf Club 1973-75 and 1981-83; memb: Irish Nat Hunt Steeplechase Ctee, Royal Irish Academy 1952, French Acad of Sports 1974; hon life memb Royal Dublin Soc 1981; Hon LLD Nat U of Ireland 1975, Hon DLitt New U of Ulster 1977; decorations include: Kt of Honour and Devotion SMOM 1943, Medal Miroslav Tyrs (Czech) 1970, Cdr Grand Cross (FDR) 1972, Star of Sacred Treasure (2 cl, Japan) 1972, Grand Offr Order of Merit (Italy) 1973, Grand Cross Order of Civil Merit (Spain) 1976, Grand Offr Order of Republic (Tunis) 1976, Grand Offr Order of Phoenix (Greece) 1976, Order of Madara Rider (Bulgaria), Cdr Legion of Honour (Fr) 1980, Olympic Order of Merit (gold) 1980; *Books* Sir Godfrey Kneller, The Shell Guide to Ireland (with Prof Michael Duignan, 1962), The Olympic Games (with John Rodda, 1975/1983), Olympic Games - Moscow - Lake Placid (1979/1983), My Olympic Years (autobiography, 1983), My Ireland (1987); *films* (with John Ford) The Quiet Man (1952), The Rising of the Moon, The Playboy of the Western World, Gideon's Day; *Clubs* Garrick, Beefsteak, County (Galway), Stephen's Green (Dublin); *Style*— The Rt Hon the Lord Killanin, MBE, TD; St Annins, Spiddal, Co Galway; 9 Lower Mount Pleasant Ave, Dublin 6

KILLEARN, 2 Baron (UK 1943); Sir Graham Curtis Lampson; 4 Bt (UK 1866); s of 1 Baron Killearn, GCMG, CB, MVO, PC (d 1964), sometime envoy to China and Egypt (s of Norman George Lampson who was yst s of Sir Curtis Miranda Lampson, 1 Bt, dep chm of Atlantic Telegraph Co which laid the first Atlantic telegraph cable 1865), by his 1 w, Rachel Mary Hele (d 1930), da of William Wilton Phipps and Dame Jessie, DBE, JP, da of William Butler Duncan, of 1 Fifth Ave, New York; suc 1 cous once removed, Sir Curtis George Lampson, 3 Bt, 1971; *b* 28 Oct 1919; *Educ* Eton, Magdalen Coll Oxford (MA); *m* 15 May 1946, Nadine Marie Cathryn, o da of Vice Adm Cecil Horace Pilcher, DSO; 2 da (Hon Mrs Meynell, Hon Lady Bonsor *qqv*); *Heir* half-bro, Hon Victor Lampson, *qv*; *Career* formerly Maj Scots Gds, served ME, Italy; Bronze Star (USA); *Style*— The Rt Hon the Lord Killearn; 58 Melton Court, Old Brompton Road, London SW7 3JJ (☎ 01 584 7700)

KILLEARN, Dowager Baroness; Jacqueline Aldine Leslie; da of Marchese Senator Sir Aldo Castellani, KCMG, FRCP, FACP; *m* 1934, as his 2 w, 1 Baron Killearn, GCMG, CB, MVO, PC (d 1964); *Style*— The Rt Hon the Dowager Lady Killearn; 23 Harley St W1; Haremere Hall, Etchingham, E Sussex

KILLEN, Hon Sir (Denis) James; KCMG (1982); s of James Walker Killen (decd), and Mabel E Sheridan; *b* 23 Nov 1925; *Educ* Brisbane GS, Qld Tech Coll, Qld Univ (LLB); *m* 1949, Joyce Claire, da of Col E Buley; 2 da (and 1 decd); *Career* barr 1965, MHR (Lib) Moreton Qld 1955-, min for Navy 1969-71, min for Defence 1976-82, vice pres of the Executive Cncl and ldr of the House of Representatives 1982-; *see Debrett's Handbook of Australia and New Zealand for further details*; *Style*— The Hon Sir James Killen, KCMG; 22 Cook St, Yeronga, Qld 4104, Australia

KILLICK, Sir John Edward; GCMG (1979, KCMG 1971, CMG 1966); s of Edward William James Killick (d 1972); *b* 18 Nov 1919; *Educ* Latymer Upper Sch, UCL (fell), Bonn Univ; *m* 1949, Lynette du Preez, da of William Oxenham Leach (d 1984); m 2, 1985, Irene Monica Harries, OBE, da of Malcolm Henry Easton; *Career* WWII Capt (Army) W Africa and W Europe; Dip Serv 1946-; asst under-sec of state 1968-71, ambass USSR 1971-73, dep under-sec of state 1973-75, ambass and permanent UK rep to NATO 1975-79, ret; dir Dunlop SA 1980-85; pres Br Atlantic Ctee; *Recreations* golf; *Clubs* Brooks's, East India Devonshire, Sports and Public Schs; *Style*— Sir John Killick, GCMG; Challoner's Cottage, 2 Birchwood Ave, Southborough, Kent TN4 0UE

KILLINGBECK, Bernard Richard; s of Robert William Killingbeck, of Norfolk, and Gertrude Edith (d 1981); *b* 20 August 1950; *Educ* St Joseph's Coll, Ipswich; *m* 21 July 1979, Catherine Margaret, da of George Gibson Cargill (d 1969), of Norfolk; *Career* dir of private food, soft drinks and cosmetic co; *Recreations* golf; *Style*— Bernard R Killingbeck, Esq; Abbey Farm, Guestwick, Norfolk NOR 20QW (☎ 036 284242)

KILMAINE, 7 Baron (I 1789); Sir John David Henry Browne; 13 Bt (NS 1636); s of 6 Baron Kilmaine, CBE (d 1978); *b* 2 April 1948; *Educ* Eton; *m* 1982, Linda, yr da of Dennis Robinson; 1 s, 1 da (Alice b 1985); *Heir* s, Hon John Francis Sandford Browne b 4 April 1983; *Career* dir: Fusion (Bickenhill) Ltd 1969-, Whale Tankers Ltd 1974-; *Style*— The Rt Hon the Lord Kilmaine

KILMARNOCK, 7 Baron (UK 1831); Alastair Ivor Gilbert Boyd; s of 6 Baron Kilmarnock, MBE, TD (d 1975), and of Hon Rosemary Guest (d 1971), da of 1 Viscount Wimborne. Lord Kilmarnock's f (6 Baron) changed his family name from Hay to Boyd 1941, having succeeded his bro, the 22 Earl of Erroll (in the UK Barony only) the same year; in descends from the 18 Earl of Erroll cr 1 Baron Kilmarnock who m (1820) Elizabeth FitzClarence, a natural da of William IV by the actress Mrs Jordan; *b* 11 May 1927; *Educ* Bradfield, King's Cambridge; *m* 1, 1954 (m dis 1969, she d 1975) Diana Mary, da of D Grant Gibson; m 2, 1977, Hilary Ann, da of Leonard Sidney Bardwell; *Heir* bro, Hon Robin Jordan Boyd; *Career* joined SDP 1981; vice-pres Inst Sales & Mktg Mgmnt 1981-; Late Lt Irish Gds, serv Palestine 1947-48; chief of Clan Boyd, page to Lord High Constable of Scotland at Coronation of HM King George VI; Sabbatical Year (1958), The Road from Ronda (1969), The Companion Guide to Madrid and Central Spain (1974); *Clubs* Pratt's; *Style*— The Rt Hon the Lord Kilmarnock; 1 Bridge St, Thornborough, Bucks MK18 2DN; Apartado 12, Ronda, Malaga, Spain

KILMISTER, (Claude Alaric) Anthony; s of Dr Claude Emile Kilmister (d 1951), of Swansea, S Wales, and Margaret E Mogford *née* Gee; *b* 22 July 1931; *Educ* Shrewsbury; *m* 24 May 1958, Sheila, da of Lawrence Harwood (d 1984), of Hyde, Cheshire; *Career* Nat Serv 1950-52, cmmnd Army; NCB 1952-55, and with (C) Pty Orgn 1954-60, gen sec Cinema and TV Benevolent Fund (1972) 1962-72 (asst sec 1960-61), fndr memb and dept chm of Prayer Book Soc (and its forerunner BCP Action Gp) 1972-, exec dir Parkinsons Disease Soc 1972-; founding ctee memb Action for Neurological Diseases 1987-; *Books* The Good Church Guide (1982), When Will Ye be Wise? (1983), My Favourite Betjeman (1985); *Recreations* writing, walking; *Clubs* Athenaeum; *Style*— Anthony Kilmister, Esq; 36 The Drive, Northwood, Middx HA6 1HP (☎ 092 74 24278); 36 The Portland Place, London W1N 3DG (☎ 01 255 2432)

KILPATRICK, Dr Ann Wilhelmina; da of John William Kilpatrick (d 1961), of Kilwarlin Ho, St James's, Hillsborough, Co Down, N I, and Anna Maria, *née* Brereton (d 1973); *b* 14 May 1924; *Educ* The Methodist Coll Belfast, Queen's Univ Belfast (MB, BCh, BAO, DPH), London Univ (DCH); *m* 17 Aug 1956, Dr David George Kiely, s of George Thomas Kiely (d 1964), of Ballynahinch, Co Down, N Ireland; 1 s (Patrick b 1964), 1 da (Fiona b 1961); *Career* med paediatric registrar Alder Hey Childrens Hosp Liverpool 1951; asst med offr of health: Walsall 1952, Downpatrick 1954, Portsmouth 1956 (sen clinical med offr 1978); chm of govrs East Shore Special Sch Portsmouth, govr Cliffdale First and Middle Special Schs Portsmouth; current specialist in assessing devpt of young children (from birth to five years) by interactive testing; BMA 1948, MFCM 1974, associate memb BPA 1982; *Recreations* fly fishing, gardening, foreign travel; *Style*— Dr Ann Kilpatrick; Cranleigh, 107 Havant Rd, Emsworth, Hants PO10 7LF (☎ 0243 372 250); The School Clinic, Battenburg Ave, Portsmouth, Hants (☎ 0705 664 235, 0705 611 398)

KILPATRICK, Sir Robert; CBE (1979); s of Robert Kilpatrick (d 1974), of 4 Plantation Row, Coaltown of Wemyss, Fife, and Catherine Sharp, *née* Glover (d 1944); *b* 29 July 1926; *Educ* Buckhaven HS, Edinburgh Univ (MB ChB, MD); *m* 28 Oct 1950, Elizabeth Gibson Page, da of Alexander Sharp Forbes, of The Barn, 12 Mill Lane, Smeeton Westerby, Leics; 2 s (Neil b 25 March 1956, John b 28 May 1959), 1 da (Katherine b 9 Aug 1951); *Career* Univ of Sheffield: lectr 1955-56, prof of clinical pharmacology and therapeutics 1966-75, dean of faculty of med 1970-73; Univ of Leicester: dean faculty of med 1975-, prof and head of dept of clinical pharmacology and therapeutics 1975-83, prof of med 1984-; designate pres Gen Med Cncl Feb 1989-; Hon Doc Univ of Edinburgh 1987; FRCP Edinburgh 1953, FRCP 1966, memb Physiological Soc 1960; Kt 1986; *Recreations* golf, gardening; *Clubs* Royal and Ancient; *Style*— Sir Robert Kilpatrick, CBE; The Barn, 12 Mill Lane, Smeeton Westerby, Leics LE8 0QL (☎ 0533 79 2202); General Med Cncl, 44 Hallam St, London W1N 6AE (☎ 01 580 7642, fax 01 436 1383)

KILPATRICK, prof (George) Stewart; O B E (1986); s of Hugh Kilpatrick (d 1951), of Edinburgh, and Annie Merricks, *née* Johnstone Stewart (d 1972); *b* 26 June 1925; *Educ* George Watson's Coll Edinburgh, Edinburgh Univ Med Sch (MB ChB, MD); *m* 11 May 1954, Joan, da of Martin Askew (d 1970), of Cornwall; *Career* Nat Serv Maj RAMC 1949-51; Univ of Wales Coll Med 1970-: dean of clinical studies 1970-87, vice-provost 1987-, prof and head of dept of tuberculosis and chest diseases; conslt physician S Glam Health Authy; chm: Assoc of Med Deans of Europe, cncl for the Assoc of the Study of Med Educn, scientific ctees of Int Union Against Tuberculosis and Lung Disease; MRCPE 1952, FRCPE 1966, FRCP 1972; memb: Assoc of Physicians of GB and Ireland, Br Thoracic Soc, Soc of Physicians in Wales; *Recreations* foreign travel, photography, reading; *Style*— Prof Stewart Kilpatrick, OBE

KILROY, Patrick Canice; s of Thomas Kilroy (d 1976), and Mary, *née* Devine (d 1977); *b* 12 Oct 1929; *Educ* St Kieran's Coll Kilkenny, Univ Coll Dublin; *m* 1958, Dorothy, da of Michael Donnelly, of Dublin (d 1958); 2 s (Mark, Stephen), 3 da (Aisling, Helen, Cliona); *Career* slr; chm Gowan Gp Ltd; dir: The Nat Theatre Soc Ltd, Waterford Glass Gp plc, Irish Distillers Gp plc, Banque Nationale de Paris (Ireland) Ltd, Silvermines plc, Irish Life Assur Co plc; chm: Church & Gen Insur Co plc, Union Camp (Ireland) Ltd; Chev de l'Ordre Nat du Mérite; *Recreations* golf, tennis; *Clubs* Miltown Golf, Fitzwilliam Lawn Tennis; *Style*— Patrick Kilroy, Esq; Anerley, 45 Cowper Rd, Dublin 6 (☎ 975283); office: 69 Lower Leeson St, Dublin 2 (☎ 766166, fax 767823)

KILROY-SILK, Robert; MP (Lab) Knowsley North 1983-86; s of William Silk (d 1943); *b* 19 May 1942; *Educ* Secdy Modern Sch, Sparkhill Commercial Sch, Saltley GS, LSE; *m* 1963, Jan, da of William Beech; 1 s, 1 da; *Career* lectr Liverpool Univ 1966-74, govr Nat Heart and Chest Hosp 1974-77; MP (Lab) Ormskirk Feb 1974-1983, PPS to Min of Arts 1975-76, memb select ctee on Race Relations and on Wealth Tax 1974-75, vice chm PLP Home Affrs Gp 1976-79, chm PLP Civil Liberties Gp 1979-84, chm Parly Penal Affrs Gp 1979-86, memb select ctee Home Affrs 1979-84, chm PLP Home Affrs Gp 1983-84, frontbench spokesman Home Affrs 1984-86; TV presenter Kilroy 1986-; columnist Times 1987-; *Publications* Socialism since Marx (1973), The Ceremony of Innocence (novel 1984), Hard Labour: The Political Diary of Robert Kilroy-Silk (1986); *Recreations* gardening; *Style*— Robert Kilroy-Silk, Esq; Kilroy, BBC TV, Lime Grove, London (☎ 01 576 7821)

KIM, Sang Man; Hon KBE (1981); *b* 9 Dec 1909; *Educ* Korea, LSE (Hon Fell 1981), Univ of Japan; *Career* dir Dong-A Ibow (daily newspaper) 1949, pres 1971-77, hon chm 1981; exec dir & publisher Kyong Bang (publishing co) Ltd 1961, audior 1966; chm Press Assoc of Asia 1976; fndr pres Korea-Britain Soc 1965 hon pres 1979-); awarded Hon KBE for promoting UK-Korean cultural contacts; *Style*— Dr Kim Sang Man, KBE; 5 Kahoe-Dung Chon Gno-Gu, Seoul, Republic of Korea

KIMBALL, Baron (Life Peer UK 1985); Marcus Richard Kimball; DL (Leics 1984); s of late Maj Lawrence Kimball, JP, DL, sometime MP Loughborough, by his 1 w, Kathleen Joan, only surviving da of Richard Ratcliff, of Stanford Hall, Loughborough, by his w Christine (3 da of Vaughan Hanning Vaughan-Lee, JP, DL, sometime MP W Somerset); *b* 18 Oct 1928; *Educ* Eton, Trinity Coll Cambridge; *m* 1956, June Mary Fenwick, only da of Montagu John Fenwick (whose mother Millicent was da of Rt Hon Lord Robert Montagu, 2 s of 6 Duke of Manchester), of Great Stukeley Hall, Huntingdon; 2 da (Hon Mrs Gibbs, Hon Mrs Straker *qqv*); *Career* Lt Leics Yeo (TA) 1947, Capt 1952, Maj 1955; MP for Gainsborough Div of Lincs (C) 1956-83, CC Rutland 1955-, PC rep Council of RCVS 1969-82 (Hon ARCVS 1982); external memb Cncl Lloyds 1982-86 (re-elected 1987); dir: Royal Tst Bank 1970-, Royal Tst Asset Mgmnt 1987-; Maybox Gp plc 1984-; chm Br Field Sports Soc 1966-82; kt 1981; *Recreations* fox hunting, past jt master of FitzWilliam and Cottesmore; *Clubs* White's, Pratt's; *Style*— Rt Hon Lord Kimball, DL; Great Easton Manor, Market Harborough, Leics LE16 8TB (☎ 0536 770333); Altnaharra, Lairg, Sutherland IV27 4AE (☎ 054 981 224)

KIMBER, Sir Charles Dixon; 3 Bt (UK 1904); s of Sir Henry Dixon Kimber, 2 Bt (d 1950); *b* 7 Jan 1912; *Educ* Eton, Balliol Coll Oxford; *m* 1, 1933 (m dis 1950), Ursula, da of late Ernest Roy Bird, MP; 3 s; m 2, 1950 (m dis 1965), Margaret, da of Francis John Bonham; 1 da; *Heir* s, Timothy Kimber *qv*; *Style*— Sir Charles Kimber, Bt; No 2

Duxford, Hinton Waldrist, nr Faringdon, Oxon (☎ Longworth 820004)

KIMBER, Timothy Roy Henry; s and h of Sir Charles Dixon Kimber, 3 Bt; *b* 3 June 1936; *Educ* Eton; *m* 1, 1960 (m dis 1974), Antonia Kathleen Brenda, da of Sir Francis John Watkin Williams, 8 Bt, QC; 2 s; m 2, 1979, Susan Hare, da of late J K Brooks, of Newton Hall, Lancs, and widow of Richard Coulthurst North; *Career* banker; dir Lazard Bros & Co Ltd; *Clubs* Boodle's; *Style*— Timothy Kimber, Esq; Newton Hall, via Carnforth, Lancashire (☎ 0468 71232, work 05242 72146); 7 Chelsea Lodge, 58 Tite St, London SW3 (☎ 01 351 1656)

KIMBER-SMITH, Geoffrey; s of Alan Harold Kimber-Smith, of Wilts, and Dorothy Coulthard Wood; *b* 15 April 1950; *Educ* Glasgow Acad, Royal GS High Wycombe, Derby Poly; *m* 2 s (Mathew b 1974, Thomas 1984); *Career* accountant, Lion Oil Tool Ltd 1985-, AGK Motors (Wokingham) Ltd 1986-; D Cooper (Engr) Ltd 1976, DP Media Servs 1983-85, Gramak (Engr) 1984-; *Recreations* motor racing; *Style*— Geoffrey Kimber-Smith, Esq; 26 Mill Close, Wokingham, Berks; Admiralty Road, Gr Yarmouth, Norfolk (☎ 0493 856414, telex 975210)

KIMBERLEY, 4 Earl of (UK 1866); Sir John Wodehouse; 11 Bt (E 1611); also Baron Wodehouse (GB 1797); s of 3 Earl of Kimberley, CBE, MC (d 1941) and Frances Margaret Irby, niece of Lord Boston; *b* 12 May 1924; *Educ* Eton, Magdalene Coll Cambridge; *m* 1, 1945 (m dis 1948), Diana Evelyn, da of late Lt-Col the Hon Sir Piers Walter Legh, GCVO, KCB, CMG, CIE, OBE (yr s of 2 Baron Newton); m 2, 1949 (m dis 1952), Carmel June (Dunnett), da of late Michael Maguire, of Melbourne, Aust; 1 s; m 3, 1953 (m dis 1960), Mrs Cynthia Abdy Westendarp, da of E Abdy Collins, FRCS, MRCP, of The Chantrey, Saxmundham, Suffolk; 2 s; m 4, 1961 (m dis 1965), Margaret, da of Alby Simons; 1 s; m 5, 1970 (m dis 1982), Gillian, da of Col Norman Ireland-Smith, and formerly w of John Raw; m 6, 1982, Jane, da of Lt-Col Christopher d'A P Consett, DSO, MC, of Osgodby Hall, Thirsk, N Yorks; *Heir* Lord Wodehouse b 1951; *Career* served as Lt Gren Gds in Armoured Div 1943-45; former Lib spokesman on aviation and aerospace, defence, voluntary community services; left Lib Pty May 1979, has since sat as Cons Peer in House of Lords; delegate to N Atlantic Assembly 1981-; memb: House of Lords All Pty Defence Study Gp (Hon Sec 1978-), Air League Cncl 1981, Assoc Cons Peers, Br Maritime League Cncl, Royal Utd Services Inst, Int Inst for Strategic Studies, Br Atlantic Ctee; ARAeS; vice-pres World Cncl on Alcoholism, chm National Cncl on Alcoholism 1982-85, dir Airship Industs (UK) Ltd, R J Levitt Gp of Cos Ltd; *Recreations* fishing, shooting, racing, gardening, bridge; *Clubs* Whites's, MCC, House of Lords' Yacht, House of Lords' Fly Fishing, Falmouth Shark Angling (pres); *Style*— The Rt Hon the Earl of Kimberley; Hailstone House, Cricklade, Wilts SN6 6JP (☎ 0793 750344)

KIMMINS, Malcolm Brian Johnston; s of Lt-Gen Sir Brian Kimmins, KBE, CB, DL (d 1979); *b* 12 Feb 1937; *Educ* Harrow, Grenoble Univ; *m* 1968, Jane, da of Thomas Douglas Pilkington; (1 s, 2 da); *Career* chief exec, Corney & Barrow Ltd; *Recreations* horse racing, golf, shooting; *Clubs* White's, Jockey; *Style*— Malcolm Kimmins Esq; Corney & Barrow Ltd, 12 Helmet Row, London EC1V 3NN (☎ 01 251 4051)

KIMPTON, Hon Mrs (Rachel Elizabeth); da of 1 Baron Hazlerigg (d 1949); *b* 1904; *m* 1928, Col Anthony Charles Ward Kimpton, Herts Yeo; 1 s, 2 da; *Style*— The Hon Mrs Kimpton; Pythouse, Tisbury, Wilts

KINAHAN, Maj-Gen Oliver John; CB (1981); s of James Kinahan; *b* 17 Nov 1923; *Educ* Queen's Univ Belfast; *m* 1950, Margery Fisher; 1 s, 2 da; *Career* RIF 1942, Nigeria Regt RWAFF 1943-46, Instr Sch of Signals and Sch of Inf 1947-51, RAPC 1951; Cmdt RAPC Trg Centre 1974-75, Ch Paymaster HQ UKLF 1975-76, Dep Paymaster-in-Chief Army 1977-78, Paymaster-in-Chief and Inspr of Army Pay Servs 1979-83, ret; *Style*— Maj-Gen Oliver Kinahan, CB; c/o Williams and Glyn's Bank, Kirkland Hosue, Whitehall, London SW1

KINAHAN, Sir (Robert George Caldwell) Robin; ERD (1946), JP (1950); s of Henry Kinahan (d 1958); *b* 24 Sept 1916; *Educ* Stowe; *m* 1950, Coralie Isabel, da of Capt Charles de Burgh, RN (d 1968); 2 s, 3 da; *Career* Capt RA 1939-45, served France and Far East; cllr and alderman Belfast Corpn 1949-64; High Sheriff: Belfast (1955), Co Antrim (1969); MP (NI) Clifton 1958-59, Lord Mayor of Belfast 1959-61; dir: Gallaher Ltd 1967-81, Nat West Bank 1973-83, Eagle Star Insur Co (local) to 1981, STC (NI) Ltd, Abbey Life (Ireland) Ltd 1981-87; chm: Bass Ireland Ltd 1958-78, Inglis & Co Ltd 1962-82, E T Green Ltd 1964-82, Ulster Bank Ltd 1970-82 (dep chm 1964-70), Abbeyfield Belfast Soc 1983-, Cheshire House (NI) 1983-87; Lord-Lt Co, Borough of Belfast 1985- (DL 1962); kt 1961; *Recreations* gardening, farming; *Style*— Sir Robin Kinahan, ERD, JP, DL, HM Lord-Lieut for Co Borough of Belfast; Castle Upton, Templepatrick, Co Antrim, N Ireland (☎ 08494 32466)

KINCADE, Dr James; CBE (1988); s of George Kincade (d 1965), and Rebecca Jane, *née* Lyons (d 1983); *b* 4 Jan 1925; *Educ* Foyle Coll Londonderry, Trinity Coll Dublin (MA), Oriel Coll Oxford (BLitt, MA), Edinburgh Univ (PhD); *m* 26 Aug 1952, (Elizabeth) Fay, da of James Anderson Piggot, OBE, JP, DL (d 1961); 1 s (James Anderson b 26 Aug 1953), 1 da (Ruth b 20 Feb 1956); *Career* RAF 1943-47 (cmmnd 1944); teacher Merchiston Castle Sch 1952-61 (hd of english 1955-61), visiting prof of philosophy Indiana Univ 1959; headmaster: Dungannon Royal Sch 1961-74, Methodist Coll Belfast 1974-88; Queen's Univ Belfast: memb senate, chm Career Advsy Ctee, memb Standing Ctee; cncl memb Cncl of Catholic Maintained Schs; memb educn ctee UTV 1979-85, nat govr for NI BBC 1985-; SHA 1961-88, HMC 1974-88; *Recreations* gardening, walking; *Style*— Dr James Kincade, CBE; 23 Adelaide Park, Belfast, NI BT9 6FX (☎ 0232 664 349)

KINCHIN SMITH, Michael; OBE (1987); s of Francis John Kinchin Smith (d 1958), of 34 Emperor's Gate, London SW7 and Dione Jean Elizabeth May (d 1963), da of Sir Francis Henry May, GCMG, sometime Govr of Hong Kong; *b* 8 May 1921; *Educ* Westminster, Christ Church Oxford (MA); *m* 20 Sept 1947, Rachel Frances, da of Rt Hon Sir Henry Urmston Willink, 1 Bt, MC, QC, (d 1973, Master of Magdalene Coll Cambridge); 4 s (Christopher b 1950, John b 1952, David b 1954, Robert b 1960), 2 da (Lavinia b 1948, Juliet b 1957); *Career* war serv with Coldstream Gds: Italian Campaign, Capt (despatches); commercial and admin trainee ICI Ltd 1947-50; BBC 1950-78: various admin posts controller, staff admin 1967-76; lay asst to Archbishop of Canterbury 1979-84; appts sec to Archbishops of Canterbury and York and sec to Crown Appts Cmmn 1984-87; chm exec cncl RIPA 1975-77; vice chm IPM 1978-80; memb Gen Synod C of E 1975-78; CIPM; *Recreations* walking, local history, genealogy; *Clubs* Utd Oxford and Cambridge; *Style*— Michael Kinchin Smith Esq, OBE; The Old Bakery, Epwell, Banbury, Oxon OX15 6LA (☎ 029 578773)

KINCRAIG, Hon Lord; Robert Smith Johnston; s of William Turner Johnston, iron merchant, of Glasgow; *b* 10 Oct 1918; *Educ* Strathallan, St John's Coll Cambridge, Glasgow Univ; *m* 1943, Margaret Joan, da of Col A Graham, of Glasgow; 1 s, 1 da; *Career* advocate 1942; QC 1955; sheriff Roxburgh & Berwick 1964-70; senator Coll of Justice and Lord of Session 1972-87, with title of Lord Kincraig; dean Faculty of Advocates 1970-72; *Recreations* golf, gardening, curling; *Clubs* Hon Co Edinburgh Golfers; *Style*— The Hon Lord Kincraig; Westwood, Longniddry, E Lothian (☎ 0875 52849)

KINDER, John Russell; s of Herbert Kinder, of Leicester, and Kathleen Margaret, *née* Sarson; *b* 10 Nov 1937; *Educ* Wyggeston GS Leicester, Corpus Christi Coll Oxford (MA in PPE); *m* 1964, Diana Christine, da of Frederick Gordan Evans (d 1984); 4 s (Mark Russell b 1966, Andrew John b 1967, Stephen James b 1970, Jonathan Charles b 1974); *Career* RAF 1956-58; dir: William Brandts Sons & Co Ltd 1975-77; jt md Warwick Engineering Investmts Ltd 1978-80; md CH Industrials plc 1980-; dir: Aston Martin Lagonda 1980-83, Aston Martin Tickford 1981-; FICA; *Recreations* tennis, sailing, christian youth work; *Style*— John Kinder, Esq; 23 Woodville Gardens, Ealing, London W5 2LL (☎ 997 1207); CH Industrials, 33 Cavendish Square, London W1 (☎ 491 7860)

KINDERSLEY, Hon Anna Lucy; da of 3 Baron Kindersley; *b* 1965; *Style*— The Hon Anna Kindersley

KINDERSLEY, Christian Philip; s of Hon Philip Leyland Kindersley, of The Coach House, Northwick Park, Blockley, Gloucs, and Valerie Violet Gwendolen, *née* French; *b* 19 Mar 1950; *Educ* Eton; *m* 5 May 1973, Hilary Luise, da of David Radcliffe Guard (d 1979); 1 s (Alexander), 2 da (Vanessa, Davina); *Career* ptnr Cazenove & Co 1982- (joined 1970); Freeman City of London 1983, Liveryman Worshipful Co of Fishmongers 1983; *Recreations* shooting, tennis, reading; *Clubs* White's, City of London; *Style*— Christian Kindersley, Esq; 27 Eglantine Rd, London SW18 2DE (☎ 01 870 1091); 12 Tokenhouse Yard, London EC2R 7AN (☎ 01 588 2828, fax 01 606 9205, car tel 0860 353 612, telex 886758)

KINDERSLEY, David Guy Barnabas; MBE (1979); s of Guy Kindersley, OBE, JP, variously barr, stockbroker, MP, publisher and brewer (bro of 1 Baron Kindersley, GBE), by his w Kathleen, da of Sir Edmund Elton, 8 Bt; *b* 11 June 1915; *Educ* Marlborough; *m* 1957, Barbara, *née* Spells, wid of Martin Petrie; 2 s, 1 da; *Career* stone carver and alphabet designer, former pupil of the sculptor Eric Gill; late advsr to MOT for street name signs and Shell Film Unit for titles conslt Letraset 1964-; chm Wynkyn de Worde Soc 1976; *Clubs* Arts; *Style*— David Kindersley Esq, MBE; 152 Victoria Rd, Cambridge CB4 3DZ (☎ 0223 62170)

KINDERSLEY, Hon Dickon Michael; s of 3 Baron Kindersley; *b* 1962; *Style*— The Hon Dickon Kindersley

KINDERSLEY, Gay; s of Hon Philip Kindersley (4 s of 1 Baron Kindersley, GBE) by his 1 w, Oonagh, yst da of Hon Arthur Guinness (2 s of 1 Earl of Iveagh), who m 2, 4 Baron Oranmore and Browne and 3, Miguel Ferreras; *b* 2 June 1930; *Educ* Eton; *m* 1, 1956 (m dis 1976), Margaret, da of Hugh Wakefield, of Mount St, Mayfair; 2 s, 2 da; m 2, 1976, Philippa Harper; 2 s; *Career* gentleman rider (amateur jockey) and trainer; *Clubs* Turf; *Style*— Gay Kindersley, Esq; Parsonage Farm and Stables, East Garston, Newbury, Berks (☎ Great Shefford (048 839) 301/279)

KINDERSLEY, Hon Hugh Francis; s of 3 Baron Kindersley; *b* 1956; *Educ* Eton; *m* 27 June 1987, (Evelyn) Rosamund, eld da of Gwent Forestier-Walker, of Whitelead, Bucks; 1 da (Rosanna b 1987); *Style*— The Hon Hugh Kindersley; 6 Kay Rd, London SW9 9DE

KINDERSLEY, Hon Philip Leyland; s of 1 Baron Kindersley, GBE (d 1954); *b* 11 Mar 1907; *Educ* Eton, Christ Church Oxford; *m* 1, 1929 (m dis 1936), Oonagh, da of Hon (Arthur) Ernest Guinness (d 1949, 2 s of late 1 Earl of Iveagh); 1 s, 1 da (decd); m 2, 1936, Valerie Violet (formerly w of late 4 Baron Brougham), da of Hon Gerald French, DSO (2 s of late 1 Earl of Ypres, KP, GCB, OM, GCVO, KCMG, PC) 1 s, 2 da; *Career* serv WWII in N Africa (wounded, POW); Capt Coldstream Gds; stockbroker, ret 1977; chm Lingfield Racecourse, ret 1982; *Recreations* hunting; *Clubs* White's; *Style*— The Hon Philip Kindersley; High Paddocks, Lye Green, Crowborough, Sussex (☎ Crowborough 3127)

KINDERSLEY, Lt-Col (Claude) Richard (Henry); DSO (1944), MC (1943); s of Lt Col Archibald Ogilvie Littleton Kindersley, CMG, DL (d 1955), and Edith Mary Kindersley, *née* Craven (d 1936); *b* 11 Dec 1911; *Educ* Wellington, Trinity Coll Cambridge (MA); *m* 5 Oct 1933, Vivien Mary, da of Sqdn Ldr Charles John Wharton Darwin, DSO (d 1941); 3 da (Gloria b 1940, Avril b 1944, Susan b 1948); *Career* cmmnd HLL 1933, served 2 Bn HLI (NW Frontier, Palestine, Middle E 1936-43); 1 Bn HLI (France and Germany) 1944-45, Cdr 1 Bn HLI 1945, Inf Boys Bn 1953-54, ret 1955; DL 1962-74, Hants 1974, IOW High Sheriff 1974; Vice-Ld Lt 1979-86; pres IOW branch CLA, dir The Trade Counter Ltd; *Recreations* sailing; *Clubs* Royal Yacht Sqdns, Royal Solent YC; *Style*— Lt-Col Richard Kindersley; Hamstead Grange, Yarmouth, Isle of Wight (☎ 0983 760230)

KINDERSLEY, 3 Baron (UK 1941); Robert Hugh Molesworth Kindersley; 3 Baron (UK 1941), DL (Kent 1986); s of 2 Baron Kindersley, CBE, MC (d 1976); *b* 18 August 1929; *Educ* Eton, Trinity Coll Oxford, Harvard Business Sch; *m* 4 Sept 1954, Venice Marigold (Rosie), da of late Lord (Arthur) Francis Henry Hill (yr s of 6 Marquess of Downshire); 3 s, 1 da; *Heir* s, Hon Rupert Kindersley; *Career* Lt Scots Gds, Malaya 1948-49, dir: Lazard Bros & Co Ltd 1960-, London Assur 1957-, Sun Alliance & London Insur Gp 1965-, Witan Investmt Co Ltd 1958-85, Swedish Match Co 1973-85, Maersk Co Ltd 1986-, Br Match Corpn Ltd 1969-73, Marconi Co Ltd 1963-68, English Electric Co Ltd 1966-68, GEC Ltd 1968-70, Steel Co of Wales 1959-67; chm Cwlth Devpt Corpn 1980-; dep chm ECGD Advsy Cncl 1975-80; chm Br Bankers Assoc 1976-78, fin advsr to Export Gp for the Constructional Industs 1961-85; pres Anglo-Taiwan Trade Ctee 1976-86; memb: Inst Int d'Etudes Bancaires 1971-85, Ct Worshipful Co of Fishmongers 1973-; *Recreations* all sports, farming, gardening; *Clubs* All England Lawn Tennis and Croquet (memb ctee), All England Club Wimbledon (memb ctee), Queen's, MCC, Pratt's; *Style*— The Rt Hon the Lord Kindersley; West Green Farm, Shipbourne, Kent TN11 9PU (☎ 0732 810293); 25 Grafton Square, London SW4 0DB (☎ 01 622 1198); 21 Moorfields, London EC2P 2HT (☎ 01 588 2721)

KINDERSLEY, Hon Rupert John Molesworth; s and h of 3 Baron Kindersley; *b* 11 Mar 1955; *Educ* Eton; *m* 1975, Sarah Anne, da of late John D Warde; 1 s (Frederick b 1987), 1 da (Rebecca b 1985); *Style*— The Hon Rupert Kindersley; 22 Sugden Road, London SW11 5EF

KINDERSLEY, Hon Mrs Philip; Violet Valerie; *née* French; da of Lt-Col Hon Gerald French, DSO (2 s of 1 Earl of Ypres and an author); *b* 1909; *m* 1, 1931 (m dis 1934), 4 Baron Brougham and Vaux (d 1967); 1 s decd ; m 2, 1936, as his 2 w, Hon Philip Kindersley, 4 s of 1 Baron Kindersley, GBE; 1 s, 2 da (Mrs Robert Philipson-Stow and Hon Mrs Peregrine Fairfax); *Style—* The Hon Mrs Kindersley; High Paddocks, Lye Green, Crowborough, Sussex (☎ 3127)

KING, Sir Albert; OBE (1958), JP; s of George King (d 1915); *b* 20 August 1905; *Educ* Primrose Hill Leeds; *m* 1928, Pauline Riley; 1 da; *Career* full-time offr AUEW 1942-70, Leeds div sec 1942-52, div organiser 1952-70, TUC regnl sec 1958-70, ret; ldr Labour Gp Leeds Met DC 1975-78; kt 1975; *Recreations* walking, reading; *Clubs* Beeston WMC; *Style—* Sir Albert King, OBE, JP; 25 Brookhill Ave, Leeds LS17 8QA (☎ 0532 684684)

KING, Alison; OBE (1978); da of Frank Ernest King (d 1963), and Maude, *née* Matthews (d 1960); *b* 20 August 1913; *Educ* Kings House Sch, Tollingham HS; *Career* Flt-Capt (Ops) ATA 1940-45; chm Br Womens Pilots Assoc 1956-64, gen sec Nat Fedn Womens Inst 1959-69; dir: Womens Jr Air Corps 1952-58, WRVS Off Premises Ltd 1969-78; co-ordinator properties WRVS 1974-78 (memb Housing Assoc Ctee 1973-83); *Books* Golden Wings (1956); *Clubs* Univ Womens; *Style—* Miss Alison King, OBE; Delaware, Cirencester St, London W2 5SR (☎ 01 778 4087); 87 Kenilworth Court, Lower Richmond Road, Putney, London SW15 1HA

KING, Prof Anthony Stephen; s of Harold Stark King (d 1949), and Marjorie Mary, *née* James (d 1982); *b* 17 Nov 1934; *Educ* Queen's Univ Kingston, Ontario Canada (BA), Oxford Univ (BA, DPhil); *m* 1, 1965, Vera Karte (d 1972); m 2, Janet Frances Mary, da of Adm of the Fleet Sir Michael Pollock, KGCB, DSO, *qv*, of The Ivy House, Churchstoke, Montgomery, Powys; *Career* fell Magdalen Coll Oxford 1961-65; Univ of Essex 1966-: sr lectr in govt 1966-67, reader 1967-69, prof 1969-, academic pro-vice-chllr 1986-89; fell center for advanced study in the behavioural scis Stanford California 1977-78, visiting prof of public int affrs Princeton Univ 1984; *Books* Westminster and Beyond (with Anne Slaman, 1973), British Members of Parliament (1974), Why is Britain Becoming Harder to Govern? (ed 1976), The New American Political System (ed 1978), Britain Says Yes: The 1975 Referendum on the Common Market (1977), The British Prime Minister (ed, second edn 1985); *Recreations* music, holidays, walking; *Clubs* Royal Cwlth Soc; *Style—* Prof Anthony King; Dept of Govt, University of Essex, Wivenhoe Park, Colchester, Essex CO4 3SQ (☎ 0206 873393)

KING, Barbara Sarah; da of John Henry Otty (d 1978), of Yorks, and Florence Harriet, *née* Robinson (d 1985); *b* 14 June 1946; *Educ* Secdy Modern Otley, private; *m* 21 July 1962, James King; 1 s (James Martin b 1964, d 1964), 1 da (Sarah Jane b 1972); *Career* md Slimming Magazine Clubs Ltd 1988- (exec dir 1985-), dir Argus Consumer Magazine Div 1988; contrib to health and diet pubns; MIOD, MInstM; *Recreations* reading, writing, wine making; *Style—* Mrs Barbara King

KING, Brian Maurice; s of Maurice James King, and late Grace Mary, *née* Escott; *b* 8 August 1933; *Educ* Westcliff HS, Southend Sch of Architecture; *m* 23 Aug 1958, Joan, da of Arthur Rouse; 2 s (Andrew James b 1961, Daniel John b 1963); *Career* architect and landscape architect; formed own practice 1982; chm Wells Housing Assoc; served in Friends Ambulance Unit Int Serv 1956-58; ARIBA; *Recreations* dinghy sailing, painting, drawing, walking; *Clubs* Wilsonian; *Style—* Brian King, Esq; 67 Kingswood Rd, Bromley, Kent BR2 0NL (☎ 01 460 7658); 34 Hill Rise, Richmond, Surrey TW10 6UA (☎ 01 948 8191/2)

KING, Col Bryan Arthur George; TD (1972); s of George Henry King (d 1965), of Wallasey, and Ethel, *née* Hughes; *b* 29 April 1930; *Educ* Birkenhead Sch; *m* 21 May 1960, Elizabeth, da of late Jack Oddy, of Chester; 2 da (Jane b 1962, Julia b 1967); *Career* TA 1959-69, 4 Bn Cheshire Regt, Mercian Vols and Cheshire ACF, Col 1978, memb Regtl Cncl Cheshire Regt, mil memb NW Eng TAVR; ptnr Wayman Hales Slrs Chester, hon slr Cheshire Regt; memb cncl Law Soc; govr The Queen's Sch Chester, pres Deeside Ramblers Hockey Club; *Recreations* travel, gardening; *Clubs* Army and Navy, Chester City; *Style—* Col Bryan King, TD; Taluca, Church La, Upton By Chester, Cheshire (☎ 0244 381 436); 12 White Friars, Chester (☎ 0244 321 122, fax 0244 43642)

KING, Hon Mrs (Elizabeth Patricia); *née* White; da of 4th Baron Annaly, MC, and Lady Lavinia Spencer, da of 6th Earl Spencer, KG, GCVO, VD, PC; is 1 cous once removed of HRH Princess of Wales; *b* 5 Nov 1923; *m* 1945, Lt Cdr Osborne King, DSC, DL, RNVR, *qv*; 1 s (James b 1952, m 1981 Sally, da of Alan Walker-Gray), 2 da (Elizabeth Lavinia Sara b 1946, m 1969 David Hugh Montgomery; Patricia Rose, b 1947, m 1970, Antony Douglas North); *Style—* The Hon Mrs King; Rademon, Crossgar, Co Down, N Ireland (☎ 0396 830214)

KING, Evelyn Mansfield; s of Harry Percy King, and Winifred Elizabeth, *née* Paulet; *b* 30 May 1907; *Educ* Cheltenham, King's Coll Cambridge (MA); *m* 6 April 1935, Hermione Edith, da of Arthur Felton Crutchley DSO RN; 1 s (John Mansfield Paulet), 2 da (Diana (Mrs Gabb), Jenifer (Lady Jenifer Patricia Cooke); *Career* joined Army 1940, Lt-Col; corr Sunday Times 1928-30, asst master Bedford Sch 1930, headmaster and warden Clayesmore Sch 1935-50, MP (Lab) Penryn and Falmouth div of Cornwall 1945-50, Parly sec min of Town and Country Planning 1947-50, resigned Lab Pty 1951 and joined Cons Pty contested Southampton (Itchen) 1959; MP (C) S Dorset 1964-79; memb pty delegations: Bermuda and Washington 1946, Tokyo 1947, Cairo and ME 1967, Jordon and Persian Gulf 1968, Kenya and Sechelles 1969, Malta 1970 (1dr); memb select ctee on Overseas Aid 1971, chm Food Ctee 1971; *Books* Printer to the House, Biography of Luke Honsard (with J C Trewin, 1962); *Clubs* Carlton; *Style—* Evelyn King, Esq; Embley Manor, Romsey, Hampshire; 11 Barton St, London SW1 (☎ 0794 512 342)

KING, Francis Henry; CBE (1985); s of Eustace Arthur Cecil King (d 1937), and Faith Mina, *née* Read; *b* 4 Mar 1923; *Educ* Shrewsbury, Balliol Coll Oxford (MA); *Career* Br Cncl Offr 1950-63; lectr Florence Italy 1950-51, lectr Salonica and Athens Greece 1951-57, asst rep Finland 1957-58, reg dir Kyoto Japan 1958-63; drama critic Sunday Telegraph 1976-88; Internat pres PEN 1986-89; FRSL 1958-; *Books* The Dividing Stream (Somerset Maughan Award, 1951), The Man on the Rock (1957), The Custom House (1961), The Needle (1975), Act of Darkness (1983), Voices in an Empty Room (1984), The Woman Who Was God (1988); *Recreations* mountaineering and pot-holing; *Style—* Francis King, Esq, CBE; 19 Gordon Pl, London W8 4JE (☎ 01 937 5715)

KING, Gen Sir Frank Douglas; GCB (1976, KCB 1972, CB 1971), MBE (1953); s of Arthur King; *b* 9 Mar 1919; *Educ* Wallingford G S; *m* 1946, Joy Emily; 1 s, 2 da; *Career* joined Army 1939, serv WWII, cmd Parachute Bn Gp Cyprus 1960-62, cmd Inf Bde Gp Germany 1962-64, Brig 1965, Maj-Gen 1966, dir Land/Air Warfare MOD (Army) 1966-68, Cmdt RMCS 1969-71, GOC-in-C Strategic Cmd 1971, dep C-in-C UKLF 1972-73, GOC NI 1973-75, Gen 1976, Cdr Northern Army Gp and C-in-C BAOR 1976-78, ADC Gen to HM The Queen 1977-78, ret; chm: John Taylor Tst 1978-88, Assets Protection Int Ltd 1981-86; mil advsr Short Bros Ltd Belfast 1979-84; dir Control Risks Ltd 1979-86, Kilton Properties, Springthorpe Property Co, PLAZA Fish Ltd; dir Airborne Forces Charitable Devpt Tst 1988, tstee Airborne Forces Security Tst 1981-, memb cncl Air League 1982-; *Clubs* Ashridge Golf, Berks Golf, Army & Navy; *Style—* Gen Sir Frank King, GCB, MBE; c/o William and Glyn's Bank, Columbia House, 69 Aldwych, London WC2

KING, Henry Edward St Leger; s of Robert James King and Dorothy Louisa Marie *née* Wickert; *b* 11 Oct 1936; *Educ* Whitgift Mid Sch, Fitzwilliam Coll Cambridge (MA, LLB); *m* 10 April 1964, Kathleen Bridget, da of William Wilcock (d 1971); 1 s (Simon b 1969, d 1984), 1 da (Alexandra b 1966); *Career* Nat Serv 2 Lt 1959-61; slr; ptnr Denton Hall Burgin & Warrens 1967-; dir: Belhaven plc, Rentokil Gp plc, Gulf & Wester Gp Ltd, Capital Equipment Leasing Ltd, GKN Chep Ltd, Brambles UK Ltd, Brambles Europe Ltd, Cleanway Hldgs Ltd, DMR UK Ltd; *Recreations* travel, theatre, music; *Style—* Henry King, Esq; Denning House, 5 Chancery Lane, London WC2A 1LF (☎ 01 242 1212)

KING, Ian Charles; s of Thomas Charles King (d 1959), of Finchley, London N3, and Winifred Alice, *née* Carter (d 1904); *b* 8 Feb 1904; *Educ* Univ Coll Sch London, Bartlett Sch of Achitecture Univ of London (Dip Arch); *m* 1, (m dis 1977); 2 s (Julian Charles Lintern b 13 April 1965, Oliver Roland b 21 March 1969), 2 da (Sharon Louise b 29 Sept 1971); m 2, 15 Feb 1980, Nathalie Jane, da of Benode Singh (d 1987); *Career* architect in private practice since 1964, now chm Ian C King Ltd Chartered Architect; govr Univ Coll Sch Hampstead London, hon tres Architects Benevolent Soc; Freeman City of London 1981, Liveryman Worshipful Co of Glassellers 1982, Liveryman Worshipful Co of Chartered Architects 1988; MRIBA 1960; *Recreations* lawn tennis, theatre, veteran cars, metal toy collector; *Clubs* All England Lawn Tennis, The Hurlingham; *Style—* Ian King, Esq; 214 Ashley Grds, Emery Hill St, London SW1 PIPA (☎ 01 828 4400); 77/83 Upper Richmond Rd, London SW15 2DT (☎ 01 785 3408, fax 01 780 1949)

KING, Jack Naisbitt; s of John George King (d 1944), and Grace, *née* Naisbitt; *b* 19 Sept 1928; *Educ* Bedford Modern Sch, Emmanuel Coll Cambridge (BA, MA), Adelaide Univ (MA); *m* 4 s, 3 da; *Career* bursar and sec of tstees Wolfson Coll 1968-79, dir Wolfson Coll course and programme 1979-, (vice-pres 1984-88); tstee Royal Opera House Tst (and Endowment Fund) 1985-; memb: Cambridge Police Authy 1980-, Int Steering Gp for res into policing and social order in Europe and US; chm Fairleigh Dickinson Fndn New Jersey 1981-; tstee Cluff Fndn, Gosnold UK Tst; Freeman City of London; memb: Worshipful Co of Blacksmiths, Co of Waterman & Lightermen of River Thames; Yates Medallion 1980, Hon DHL William Jewell Coll Missouri; FRSA; *Clubs* Leander, RAF, City Livery; *Style—* Jack King, Esq; Wolfson Coll, Cambridge, Cambs CB3 9BB (☎ 0223 335 900)

KING, James Archibald; s of John Howard King, (d 1973), of Ballater, and Margaret Whyte Smail, *née* Bannatyne; *b* 25 May 1951; *Educ* Melville Coll Edinburgh, Strathclyde Univ (BA); *m* 1, 8 Oct 1977 (m dis 1982), Amanda Jane, da of Alan Lea Ferrand, of Woodside, Minshull Vernon, Cheshire; m 2, 29 Jan 1983, Katharine Stein, da of Henry Stein McCall of High Auchengere, Rhu, Dunbartonshire; *Career* account exec Grey Advtg 1972-74, account dir: French Gold Abbott 1974-79, Abbott Mead Vickers 1979-81; dir Ogilvy & Mather (Scotland) 1981-87, client servs dir Hall Advtg 1987-89; dir Lethendy Estates 1989-; MIPA (1982); *Recreations* sailing, shooting, skiing, photography; *Clubs* RORC (memb ctee 1980-81), Royal Northern & Clyde YC (memb Ctee 1981- 83), Annabels; *Style—* James King, Esq; 7 Royal Circus, Edinburgh EH3 6TL (☎ 031 225 2882); Lethendy Estates Ltd, Tower of Lethendy, Meikleour, Perthshire PH2 6EQ (☎ 025 084 344)

KING, Sir James Granville Le Neve; 3 Bt (UK 1888), of Campsie, Stirlingshire, TD (1944); s of Sir John Westall King, 2 Bt (d 1940); *b* 17 Sept 1898; *Educ* Eton, King's Coll Cambridge; *m* 1928, Penelope Charlotte, only da of Capt Edmund Moore Cooper Cooper-Key, CB, MVO, RN (ret); 1 s, 2 da; *Heir* s John Christopher King; *Career* Maj 99 Field Brig RA (TA); jt master S Berks Foxhounds 1935-39; *Style—* Sir James King Bt, TD; Church Farm House, Chilbolton, Stockbridge, Hants (☎ 026 474 273)

KING, John Christopher; s and h of Sir James King, 3 Bt, TD, *qv*; *b* 31 Mar 1933; *Educ* Eton; *m* 1, 3 Oct 1958 (m dis 1972), Patricia Monica, o da of late Lt-Col Kingsley Osbern Nugent Foster, DSO, OBE; 1 s, 1 da; m 2, 1984, Mrs (Aline) Jane Holley, er da of Col Douglas Alexander Brett, GC, OBE, MC; *Career* Sub Lt RNVR, 1 Lt Berkshire Yeo TA; memb Stock Exchange 1958-73; *Recreations* sailing, shooting; *Clubs* Brooks's; *Style—* John King, Esq; Church Farm House, Chilbolton, Stockbridge, Hants

KING, John Edward; s of late Capt Albert Edward King, and Margaret King; *b* 30 May 1922; *Educ* Penarth Co Sch, SOAS London; *m* 1, 1948 (m dis), Pamela, *née* White; 1 da; m 2, 1956, Mary Margaret, *née* Beaton; *Career* WWII 1941-47: Rifle Bde, RWF, Nigeria Dept; served Chindit campaign Burma (despatches); Overseas Civil Serv: cadet Colonial Admin Serv N Nigeria 1947, permanent sec Fed Govt of Nigeria 1960, ret 1963; CRO 1963, navy dept MOD 1966-69, private sec to Sec of State for Wales 1969-71, asst sec Welsh Off 1971-77, princ estab offr and under sec Welsh Off 1977-82, conslt Dept of Educn and dir china studies centre Univ Coll Cardiff 1984-87; civil serv memb Civil Serv Cmmn final selection bd 1977-82 (external memb 1982-86); *Recreations* books, swimming, tennis, watercolour painting; *Clubs* Civil Service, Llandaff Inst, Llandaff Lawn Tennis; *Style—* John King, Esq; Fairfields, Fairwater Road, Llandaff, Cardiff CF5 3LF (☎ 0222 562825)

KING, (Kenneth George) Jonathan; s of Ailsa King; *b* 6 Dec 1945; *Educ* Trinity Coll Cambridge; *Career* entertainer; entered tv ind 1964, recording artist Everyone's Gone To The Moon 1965; tv: presenter and creator Entertainment USA and No Limits (BBC 2); *Style—* Jonathan King, Esq; 1 Wyndham Yard, Wyndham Place, London W1H 1AR (☎ 01 402 7433, fax 01 402 2866, telex 298976)

KING, Hon Mrs (Madeleine Coleman); da of Baron Cohen of Brighton (Life Peer, d 1966); *b* 11 July 1946; *Educ* Univ of London (BA); *m* 1978, Ross King, s of Kenneth King (d 1958); 1 s, 1 da; *Career* barr Inner Temple 1971, barr and slr in Alberta Canada 1983; *Style—* The Hon Mrs King; 3222, 3rd St SW, Calgary, Alberta T2S 1V3, Canada (☎ 403 243 4899)

KING, Prof Mervyn Allister; s of Eric Frank King, and Kathleen Alice, *née* Passingham; *b* 30 Mar 1948; *Educ* Wolverhampton GS, King's Coll Cambridge (BA, MA); *Career* jr res offr Dept of Applied Econs (memb Cambridge Growth Project) 1969-73, Kennedy Scholarship Harvard Univ 1971-72; Cambridge Univ: fell and dir studies St John's Coll 1972-77, res offr dept of applied econs 1972-76, lectr faculty of econs 1976-77, visiting prof of econs Harvard Univ 1982, Esmee Fairbairn prof of investmt Univ of Birmingham 1977-84, visiting prof of econs MIT 1983-84, prof of econs LSE 1984-; memb: Meade Ctee on Taxation (sec) 1975-78, prog ctee Econometric Soc Congress 1974, 1979, 1985, econs ctee ESRC 1980-82, res ctee ENSAE Paris 1985, exec ctee IFS 1985, Econ Policy Panel 1985-86, CLARE Gp 1976-85, ed bd Jl of Industl Economics 1977-83, cncl and exec ctee Royal Econ Soc 1981-86; co dir ESRC Res Prog on Taxation Incentives and Distribution of Income LSE 1979-; res: assoc NBER 1978-, fell Centre for Econ Policy Res 1984-; co dir (with C Goodhart) fin mkts gp LSE 1987-; asst ed Econ Jl 1974-75 assoc ed Jl of Public Econs 1982-, managing ed Review of Econ Studies 1978-83, memb ed bd American Econ Review 1985-, chm Soc of Econ Analysis; Walras-Bowley lectr Econ Soc, Review of Econs lectr Cambridge, assoc memb inst of fiscal and monetary policy Miny of Fin Japan; conslt: NZ treasy 1979, OECD 1982, Royal Cmmn on Distribution of Income and Wealth; res fell INSEE Paris 1977, hon res fell UCL; Helsinki Univ Medal 1982; *Books* Public Policy and the Corporation (1977), The British Tax System (with J A Kay 1978, 4 edn 1986), Indexing for Inflation (ed with T Liesner 1975), The Taxation of Income from Capital: A Comparitive Study of the US, UK, Sweden and West Germany (with D Fullerton et al 1984), numerous articles; *Style*— Prof Mervyn King; Lionel Robbins Building, London School of Economics, Houghton St, London WC 2AE (☎ 01 405 7686)

KING, Michael William; s of Alfred William King (d 1983), and Jessie, *née* Carter; *b* 31 August 1934; *Educ* Univ of London (BA); *m* 5 March 1960, Teresa, da of Ben Benjamin (d 1965); 1 s (Russell William b 1963), 1 da (Sarah Elizabeth b 1961); *Career* Nat Serv Royal West Kent Regt 1956-57; mgmnt tnee then leading buyer Ford Motor Co 1958-64, AEI Hotpoint 1964-68: purchasing mangr 1964, prodn mangr 1965, central ops mangr 1966; Lake and Elliot 1968-72: main bd dir and div chief 1968, gp devpt dir 1971; gp chief exec Heatrae Sadia Internat 1972-84, business conslt 1984-, various directorships and consultancies incl chief exec East Anglian Regnl Health Authy (three year project); Freeman City of London, Liveryman Worshipful Co of Coopers; MBIM, MIOD; *Recreations* tennis, skiing, music, antiques; *Style*— Michael King, Esq; Moat Cottage, Pleshey, Essex CM3 1HG (☎ 0245 37 202, fax 0245 37 242)

KING, Nicholas Geoffrey; s of Geoffrey Thomas King, of Cross Cottage, Barford St Martin, Salisbury, Wiltshire, and Rita Mary, *née* Bull; *b* 21 July 1951; *Educ* Canford Sch Dorset; *m* 1, 12 Oct 1974 (m dis 1983), Lillian Amanda Rosemary da of John Langrigg Kirconel; 2 da (Julia b 1978, Abigail b 1982); m 2, Jane Carol, da of Gywnvor Nicholas; *Career* AC 1970-76; Charles Church Devpts Ltd: chief accountant 1976-78, gp fin dir 1978-87, gp md 1987-; fund raiser and supporter Cons Pty; FCA 1974, memb Lloyds 1985-; *Recreations* shooting, farming; *Style*— Nicholas King, Esq; Hughenden Chase, Denner Hill, Gt Missenden, Buckinghamshire (☎ 024024 2384); Charles Church Developments plc, Charles Church House, Knoll Rd, Camberley, Surrey (☎ 0276 62299, fax 0276 62712)

KING, Vice Adm Sir Norman Ross Dutton; s of Sir Norman King, KCMG (d 1963), and Lady Mona King, *née* Dutton (d 1982); family name which was adopted from town of Dutton in Cheshire can be traced back to Sir Thomas Dutton of Dutton, Sheriff of Cheshire in 1226; *b* 19 Mar 1933; *Educ* Fonthill Sch, RNC Dartmouth; *m* 1967, Patricia Rosemary, da of Dr Lionel Brian Furber (d 1981); 2 da (Annabelle b 1970, Melissa b 1978); *Career* CO HMS Leopard 1967-68; XO HMS Intrepid 1972-73; NA to Second Sea Lord 1975-77; RCDS 1978; Co HMS Newcastle 1979-80; Dir of Naval Offr Appts (Seamen Offrs) 1983-84, Cmdr Br Navy Staff Washington, Br Naval Attaché Washington, UKNLR to SACLANT 1985-86; Naval Sec 1987, chief of Staff to Cdr Allied Naval Forces S Europe 1988-; *Recreations* tennis, music, chess; *Clubs* Royal Navy of 1765 and 1785; *Style*— Vice Adm Sir Norman King, KBE; c/o Lloyds Bank, Faversham, Kent

KING, Lt-Cdr (James) Osborne; DSC (1945), DL (Co Down); s of James King (d 1943); *b* 8 Oct 1914; *Educ* Campbell Coll; *m* 1945, Hon Elizabeth (*see* Hon Mrs (E P) King); *Career* Lt Cdr RNVR, serv WWII; estate agent, dir Bowring (Members Agency) Ltd, dir/sec Rademon Dvpts Ltd, chm Stubber Securities Ltd, dir Gwydir Valley Agric Investmts Pty Ltd (Australia); chm: Montgomery Hldgs, O'Sullivan Properties Ltd; Vice-Lord Lt Co Down; *Recreations* shooting; *Clubs* Kildare St (Dublin); *Style*— Lt Cdr Osborne King, DSC, DL; Rademon, Crossgar, Co Down, N Ireland (☎ 0396 830214)

KING, Patrick Thomas Colum; s of Patrick William King (d 1978), Pro Ecclesia Et Pontifice, and Agnes Norah, *née* Lynch, MBE; *b* 27 May 1938; *Educ* St George's Coll Weybridge, LSE, London Univ (LLB, LLM); *Career* admitted slr 1962, ptnr Herbert Smith 1968- (asst slr 1962-65, assoc 1965-68); capt: Blackheath FC 1964-66, Hampshire RFU 1965-67, Barbarian 1965, Munster Interprovincial 1966, Ireland Trials 1966; pres Hants RFU 1983-86 (tres 1971-82), hon vice pres London Div RFU 1988 (sec 1979-86) memb: Scriveners Co, City of London Slrs Co; La Medaille de la Ville de Paris 1980; *Recreations* rugby union football, horse racing, historical res, opera; *Clubs* Reform, Barbarians RFC, MCC, City of London Catenians; *Style*— Patrick King, Esq; 14 Regents Court, St George's Avenue, Weybridge KT13 0DQ (☎ 0932 847013); Watling House, 35 Cannon Street, London EC4M 5SD (☎ 01 489 8000, fax 01 236 5733)

KING, Air Vice-Marshal Peter Francis; CB (1987), OBE (1964); s of William George King, MBE (d 1968), of Huntingdon, and Florence Margaret, *née* Sell (d 1955); *b* 17 Sept 1922; *Educ* Framlingham Coll, King's Coll London, Charing Cross Hosp London, Univ of Edinburgh (FRCSE, DLO, MRCS, LRCP, MFOM); *m* 1945, Doreen Maxwell, da of Jorgen Hansen-Aarõe (d 1960), of Northwood; 1 s (Peter), 1 da (Suzanne); *Career* cmmnd RAF 1945, serving offr and conslt in otolaryngology, specialist in otorhinolaryngology, employed in Cosford, Ely, Fayid, Halton and CME, conslt in otorhinolaryngology 1955, Hunterian prof RCS 1964, conslt advsr in otorhinolaryngology 1966-83, Air Cdre 1976, reader aviation med Inst of Aviation Med 1977-79, Whittingham prof in aviation med IAM and RCP 1979-83, Air Vice-Marshal 1983-, dean RAF Med 1983-85, sr conslt RAF 1985-, conslt: Herts HA 1963-, CAA 1973-, King Edward VII Hosp Midhurst, 1987; hon surgn to HM The Queen 1979-87; examiner for dip in Aviation Med RCP 1980-; pres Section of Otology RSM 1977-78; chm Br Soc of Audiology 1979-81; vice-chm RNID 1980-; memb cncl Br Assoc of Otolaryngologists 1960-; editorial bd Br Journal of Audiology 1980-; Cmdr Order of St John (1987); *Recreations* sculpture, looking at prints; *Clubs* RAF; *Style*— Air Vice-Marshal Peter King, CB, OBE; Squirrel's Nook, Oak Glade, Northwood, Middlesex HA6 2TY (☎ Northwood 23961)

KING, Hon Philip James Stephen; s of Baron King of Wartnaby (Life Peer); twin with Rupert *qv*; *b* 1950; *Educ* Harrow; *Style*— The Hon Philip King; 77 Stanhope Mews East, London SW7

KING, Sir Richard Brian Meredith; KCB (1975, CB 1970), MC (1944); s of Bernard King (d 1968), of Claygate, Surrey, and Dorothy, *née* Scrivener (d 1974); *b* 2 August 1920; *Educ* Kings Coll Sch Wimbledon; *m* 24 Dec 1944, (Blanche) Phyllis, da of Edward Owen Roberts (d 1975), of Shalbourne, Wilts; 3 da (Hilary b 1949, Julian b 1956, Pauline b 1946); *Career* cmmnd N Irish Horse 1941 (1941-46), Capt 1944, Maj 1945, serv N Africa and Italy; Civil Serv: Air Miny 1939-41, Miny of Works 1946, seconded to HM Treasy 1933-55, PPS to Min of Works 1956-57, seconded to Cabinet Secretariat 1958-61, sec gen of independence constitutional conferences for Malta 1959 (Kenya 1960, W Indies Fedn 1960, Fedn for Rhodesa N Rhodesia and Nyasaland 1961), asst sec dept of tech cooperation 1961, perm sec Miny of Overseas Devpt 1973 (under sec 1964, dep sec 1968), exec sec World Bank/IMF jt devpt ctee 1976-80, sr advsr to S G Warburg & Co Ltd 1980-85, devpt fin conslt 1985-; *Books* Planning the British Aid Programme (1971), Criteria for Europe's Development Policy to the Third World (1974); *Recreations* music, lawn tennis, gardening; *Clubs* All-England Lawn Tennis; *Style*— Sir Richard King, KCB, MC; Woodlands Farm House, Woodlands Lane, Cobham, Surrey KT11 3PY (☎ 0372 843 491)

KING, Hon Richard John Rodney; s of Baron King of Wartnaby (Life Peer); *b* 1943; *Educ* Le Rosey (Switzerland); *m* 1985, Monica, da of Erich Boehm, of Boca Raton, Fla, USA; 1 s (b 1986); *Style*— The Hon Richard King; 7612 Covey Chase, Charlotte, North Carolina 28210, USA

KING, Maj-Gen Robert Charles Moss; CB (1955), DSO (1944), OBE (1944); s of Robert Charles Henry Moss King (d 1929); *b* 6 June 1904; *Educ* Clifton, RMA Sandhurst; *m* 1939, Grizel Elizabeth Stuart, *née* Mackay; 2 da; *Career* serv WWII, Brig Burma Malaya Indonesia (despatches), Bde Cdr 1944-47, Dep Dir Mil Operations 1953, GOC Home Cos Dist 1954-56, Maj-Gen 1955, Dir of Quartering War Off 1957-58, ret; dep constable of Dover Castle; *Recreations* shooting, fishing; *Style*— Maj-Gen Robert King, CB, DSO, OBE; Church Place, Eversley Cross, Hants (☎ 732171)

KING, Robert John Stephen; s of Stephen King, of Wolverhampton, and Margaret Digby; *b* 27 June 1960; *Educ* Radley, St John's Coll Cambridge (MA); *Career* conductor/harpsichordist; dir: The King's Consort (baroque orchestra), Consort Records; conductor/dir of over two dozen record on: Hyperion, Pickwick, Erato, Meridian, Consort, ASV; guest dir: Nat Youth Music Theatre, Choir of New Coll Oxford, Euro Baroque Orchestra; concert tours: France, Holland, Belgium, Spain, Italy, Japan, USA, Aust; TV and radio appearances all over Euro and the UK, ed of much 1600-1750 music, keyboard continuo with many leading Br Orchestras incl Acad of Ancient Music and City of London Sinfonia; *Recreations* skiing, cricket, graphic design; *Style*— Robert King, Esq; 2 Salisbury Rd, Ealing, London, W13 9TX (☎ 01 579 6283, 01 566 1278, ›telex‹ 9312 110127 KC G, ›fax‹ 01 567 8824)

KING, Robert Shirley; s of Rev William Henry King, MC, TD, of Trumpington, and Dorothy Sharpe (d 1964); *b* 12 July 1920; *Educ* Alexandra Road Elementary Sch Oldham, Manchester GS, Cambridge Univ (MA); *m* 1, 1947, Margaret, da of Ernest Douglas Costain Siddall (d 1963), of Wallasey; 2 da (Janet b 1950, Rachel b 1953); m 2, 1958, Mary, da of Clifford William Rowell, CBE (d 1962), of Cambridge; 1 s (John b 1961), 2 da (Ruth b 1959, Helen b 1965); *Career* served RAF 1940-45, Corpl, Madagascar, E Africa, ME; Tanganyika Civil Serv 1949-62, sr dist offr; asst sec HO 1962-70 (1985-86), under sec DHSS 1971-80; govr: Chestnut Fndn 1976-83, Bell Educn Tst 1984-89; sec: Working Party on the Rôle and Tables of Social Workers, Nat Inst for Social Work 1980-82, Health Promotion Res Tst 1984-89; cncl memb: Shape 1982-, Br and For Sch Soc 1982-89; chm co-ordinating ctee Save The Children Fund Cambridge Project 1984-88; *Recreations* walking, cycling, gardening, African affairs; *Style*— Robert King, Esq; 3 Nightingale Ave, Cambridge (☎ 0223 248 965)

KING, Roger Douglas; MP (C) Birmingham Northfield 1983-; *b* 26 Oct 1943; *Educ* Solihull Sch; *m* 1973, Jennifer Susan (*née* Sharpe); 2 s, 1 da; *Career* engrg apprentice Br Motoring Corpn 1960-66 (sales rep 1966-74), own mktg business 1974-81; contested (C) Cannock 1974, PPS to Michael Havard, QC, MP, Min of State DOE 1987-; non-exec dir of Nat Express Hldgs Ltd; vice-chm All Pty Motor Indust Gp 1985-, jt sec Commons Tourism Ctee; FIMI; *Recreations* motoring; *Style*— Roger King Esq, MP; House of Commons, London SW1

KING, Hon (John) Rupert Charles; s of Baron King of Wartnaby (Life Peer); twin with Philip *qv*; *b* 1950; *Educ* Harrow; *Style*— The Hon Rupert King; Clawson Lodge, Long Clawson, Melton Mowbray, Leics

KING, Dame Ruth; *née* Railton; DBE (1966); *see*: Railton, Dame Ruth

KING, Stephen William Pearce; s of William Raymond Pearce King, CBE (d 1980), and Edna Gertrude King, *née* Swannock (d 1971); *b* 21 Jan 1947; *Educ* King Edward's Sch Birmingham; *m* 22 Sept 1973, Angela Denise, da of Dennis George Gammon, of Worcester; 2 s (Alexander b 1976, Jeremy b 1978); *Career* princ Stephen King & Co slrs, specialists in child care and matrimonial law; *Recreations* sport, music, charity work, theatre, travelling, meeting people; *Style*— Stephen W P King, Esq; Stephen King & Co, 258 High Street, Erdington, Birmingham B23 6SN (☎ 021 382 8222)

KING, Sir Sydney Percy; OBE (1965), JP (Kesteven 1956); s of James King; *b* 20 Sept 1916; *Educ* Brockley Central Sch; *m* 1944, Millicent Prendergast; 2 da; *Career* alderman Kesteven; chm Trent RHA 1973-82, former dist organiser NUAAW, chm Sheffield Regnl Hosp Bd; memb E Midland Econ Planning Cncl 1965-, chm E Midland Regnl Panel MAFF 1977; memb: Lincs Family Practitioner Ctee 1982-, Leicester Univ Cncl 1980-; Hon LLD: Leicester, Nottingham; kt 1975; *Style*— Sir Sydney King, OBE, JP; 49 Robertson Dve, Sleaford, Lincs (☎ 0529 302056)

KING, Thea; OBE (1985); da of Henry Walter Mayer King, and Dorothea Louise King; *b* 26 Dec 1925; *Educ* Bedford HS, RCM; *m* 1953, late Frederick Thurston; *Career* Sadler's Wells Orch 1950-52, Portia Wind Ensemble 1955-68, London Mozart Players 1956-84; current memb: English Chamber Orch, Melos Ensemble of London, Robles Ensemble; frequent soloist broadcaster and recitalist; prof: RCM 1962-87, Guildhall Sch of Music 1988-; recordings incl works by: Mozart, Brahms, Spohr, Mendelssohn, Bruch, Finzi, Stanford, Blake, Seiber, Lutoslawski; publications: Clarinet Solos

(Chester Woodwind series, 1977), arrangement of J S Bach Duets for Two Clarinets (1979); FRCM, ARCM; *Recreations* cows, pillow-lace; *Style—* Ms Thea King, OBE; 16 Milverton Rd, London NW6 (☎ 01 459 3453)

KING, Rt Hon Thomas Jeremy (Tom); PC (1979), MP (C) Bridgwater March 1970-; s of John H King, JP, of Langford, Somerset; *b* 13 June 1933; *Educ* Rugby, Emmanuel Coll Cambridge; *m* 1960, (Elizabeth) Jane, 3 and yst da of Robert Tilney, CBE, DSO, TD, DL, Lord of the Manor of Sutton Bonington (maternal gs of Sir Ernest Paget, 1 Bt); 1 s, 1 da; *Career* serv Nat Serv in Somerset LI and King's African Rifles (Tanganyika and Kenya), formerly with E S & A Robinson Ltd Bristol (rising to div gen mangr), chm Sale Tilney & Co 1971-79 (dir 1965-1979), vice-chm Cons Parly Indust Ctee 1974, PPS to min Posts and Telecommunications 1970-72, min for Industl Devpt 1972-74; oppn front bench spokesman: Indust 1975-76, Energy 76-79; min state for Local Govt and Environmental Servs DOE 1979-83; sec state: Environment Jan-June 1983, Transport June-Oct 1983, Employment Oct 1983-85, NI 1985-; *Style—* The Rt Hon Tom King, MP; House of Commons, London SW1

KING, Timothy John; s of Wing Cdr John Hall King, of Little Compton, Moreton-in-Marsh, Glos, and Heather Grace, *née* Baden Powell (d 1986); *b* 22 Feb 1946; *Educ* Charterhouse; *m* 28 Aug 1971, Marion Mason, wid of Christopher Parrott, da of Herbert Ingram (d 1979); 1 da (Natasha b 1973), 1 step s (Timothy b 1966), 1 step da (Esther b 1973); *Career* sales dir Bass Sales Ltd 1980-84, sales admin dir Bass Mitchells & Butlers 1984-88, sales dir Belhaven Brewery Co Ltd 1988-; *Recreations* equestrianism, campanology, scouting; *Style—* Timothy King, Esq; Easter Langlee, by Galashiels, Selkirkshire, Scotland (☎ 0896 58588); Belhaven Brewery Co Ltd, Dunbar, East Lothian, Scotland (☎ 0368 62734, car tel 0860 816 433)

KING, Sir Wayne Alexander; 8 Bt (UK 1815), of Charlestown, Roscommon; s of Sir Peter Alexander King, 7 Bt (d 1973); *b* 2 Feb 1962; *Style—* Sir Wayne King, Bt; Church View, Herne St, Herne, Herne Bay, Kent

KING, William Lawrence; s of Ian Lawrence (d 1974), and Maisie, *née* Cooke (d 1988); *b* 29 Dec 1947; *Educ* Oundle, Trinity Hall Cambridge (MA); *m* 24 May 1975, Jane, da of Philip George Wrixon, of Norton Canon, Hereford; 2 s (Edward b 1979, Tom b 1981); *Career* slr, Macfarlanes 1970 (ptnr 1979); memb Ct Worshipful Co of Slrs; *Recreations* beagling; *Clubs* Utd Oxford and Cambridge; *Style—* William King, Esq; Macfarlanes, 10 Norwich St, London EC4A 1BD (☎ 01 831 9222, fax 01 831 9607, telex 296381)

KING OF WARTNABY, Baron (Life Peer, UK 1983), of Wartnaby in Co of Leicestershire; John Leonard King; yr s of Albert John and Kathleen King; *m* 1, 1941, Lorna Kathleen Sykes (d 1969); 3 s (Richard, Philip, Rupert, *qqv*), 1 da (Rachel); m 2, 1970, Hon Isabel Monckton (*see* King of Wartnaby, Baroness), 3 and yst da of 8 Viscount Galway; *Career* chm: Babcock Int plc (formerly Babcock & Wilcox) 1972-, Babcock Int Inc, Br Nuclear Assocs, SKF (UK) Ltd 1976-, R J Dick Inc, Dick Corpn, NEB 1979-81, Br Airways 1981-; dir: First Union Corpn, Nat Nuclear Corpn, 1928 Investmt Tst, Tyneham Investmts Ltd, BFSS Investmts, Mill Feed Hldgs Ltd, Royal Opera House Tst, Royal Ordnance plc, Clogau Gold Mines; chm: City and Industl Liaison Cncl, Alexandra Rose Day 1980-; pres Heathrow branch Royal Aeronautical Soc; MFH: Badsworth 1949-58, Belvoir 1958-72; hon fellow Coke Oven Managers' Assoc 1983; Cdr of Royal Order of the Polar Star 1983, Freeman City of London; FBIM; kt 1979; *Clubs* White's, Pratt's, Brook (New York); *Style—* The Rt Hon the Lord King of Wartnaby; Wartnaby, Melton Mowbray, Leics LE14 3HY; Cleveland House, St James's Sq, London SW1Y 4LN (☎ 01 930 9766)

KING-FARLOW, Charles Roderick; s of Roderick Sydney King-Farlow, of Birmingham, and Alice Frances Joan, *née* Ashley; *b* 16 Feb 1940; *Educ* Eton, Trinity Coll Oxford (MA); *m* 1965, Tessa, da of Robert Lawrence Raikes, of Llanvethrine, nr Abergavenny; 1 s (Joshua Michael b 1971), 1 da (Alice Caroline 1968); *Career* slr, ptnr Pinsent & Co 1969-; cncl memb Birmingham Law Soc 1976-; dir: ISS Servisystem Ltd 1969-, ISS Clorius Ltd 1979-, Exec Resources Ltd 1974-, CW Cheney & Son Ltd 1980-88; chm Cannon Hill Tst Ltd (which manages Midlands Arts Centre Birmingham) 1985-; memb: City of Birmingham Orch Cncl of Mgmnt 1972-80, Friends of Birmingham Museums and Art Gallery Ctee 1972-78, 1983-88; tstee City of Birmingham Orchestral Endowment Fdn 1971-; bd memb City of Birmingham Touring Opera 1987-; contributes to Int Jl of Museum Mgmnt; *Recreations* gardening, fishing, skiing; *Clubs* Oriental; *Style—* Charles King-Farlow, Esq; 8 Vicarage Rd, Edgbaston, Birmingham B15 3ES (☎ 021 455 0902); Post & Mail House, 26 Colmore Circus, Birmingham B4 6BH (☎ 021 200 1050)

KING-HALL, Hon Ann; da of Baron King-Hall (Life Peer, d 1966); *b* 1920; *Style—* The Hon Ann King-Hall; 11 North Side, Clapham Common, SW4 0RF

KING-HALL, Hon Adrianna - Frances Susan; da of Baron King-Hall (Life Peer, d 1966); *b* 11 August 1927; *Educ* Dartington Hall, Frensham Heights, Univ Coll Exeter (BSc), Graduate Inst of Int Affairs Geneva (Lès Sciences Politiques, Int Relns), Yale Univ (master of public health); *Career* asst gen-sec Health Visitors Assoc 1953-56, ed Int Nursing Review 1956-60, exec sec Int Union for Health Educn 1960-62, gen sec Soc for Health Educn 1962-71, dir Int Fedn of Practitioners of Natural Therapies 1978-79; chm and advsr to nat and int voluntary orgns since 1975, UK rep for Project Sunrise (concerned with the redevpt of Darling Harbour area of Sydney, Australia); *Recreations* domestic crafts, gardening; *Style—* The Hon Adrianna King-Hall; Old Barn, Northdown Rd, Woldingham, Surrey CR3 7BD (☎ Woldingham 3197)

KING-HAMILTON, His Hon (Myer) Alan Barry; QC (1954); s of Alfred King-Hamilton (d 1959), of Oxshott Surrey, and Constance Clyde Druiffe (d 1962); *b* 9 Dec 1904; *Educ* Bishop's Stortford GS, Trinity Hall Cambridge (MA),; *m* 1935, Rosalind Irene, da of Dr Abraham Ellis, LRCP, MD; 2 da (Mary, Jane); *Career* serv WWII Sqdn Ldr RAF; rec: Hereford 1954, Gloucester 1956, Wolverhampton 1961; dep chm Oxford County Quarter Sessions 1955, ldr Oxford Circuit 1961, cmmr of Assize 1961 and 1963, legal memb Med Practices Ctee Miny of Health 1961; additional judge Central Criminal Ct 1964, ret 1979, dep circuit judge 1980-84, legal memb ABTA Appeal Bd 1980 memb ctee Bernbeck Housing Assoc 1982, memb Arts and Library Ctee MCC 1985, Tstee Barnet Community Tst 1986, chm Mary Whitehouse Res and Educn Tst 1986, pres Westlon Housing Assoc, pres W London Synagogue 1965-72 and 1975-83, memb Bar Cncl 1956-60, bench Middle Temple 1961; Freeman City of London 1965, Master Worshipful Co of Needlemakers 1969; *Books* And Nothing But the Truth (autobiog 1982); *Style—* His Hon Alan King-Hamilton, QC; c/o RAF Club, 128 Piccadilly, London W1

KING-HARMAN, Col Anthony Lawrence; OBE (1982), DL (Bedfordshire 1987); s of Capt Robert Douglas King-Harman, DSO, DSC, RN (d 1978), and Lily, *née* Moffatt (d 1965); *b* 28 Feb 1918; *Educ* Wellington, RMA Woolwich; *m* 21 Dec 1944, Jeanette Stella, *née* Dunkerley, stepda of Frederick C Guthrie (d 1976), of Cape Province, S Africa; 2 s (Lt-Col (Anthony) William (RA) b 2 May 1946, Michael Charles b 10 Aug 1947); *Career* cmmnd RA 1938, serv Western Desert and Burma (despatches), Staff Coll 1945, CO 39 Regt RA 1959-61, NATO Standing Gp Washington 1963-67, ret 1968; joined Int Staff NATO Brussels 1968, head Def Policy Section, ret 1982; Cmmnr St John Ambulance Bedfordshire 1983-87; OStJ 1987; *Recreations* golf, gardening; *Clubs* Army and Navy, Anglo-Belgian; *Style—* Col Anthony King-Harman, OBE, DL; Ouse Manor, Sharnbrook, Bedford MK44 1PL (☎ 0234 781439)

KING-TENISON, Lady Bridget Honor; da of late 9 Earl of Kingston; *b* 1902; *Style—* Lady Bridget King-Tenison; c/o Barclays Bank, 106 Piccadilly, London W1A 2AB

KINGAN, (Thomas) John Antony; DL Co Down (1965); s of William Sinclair Kingan (d 1946), of Glenganagh, 39 Bangol Rd, Groomsport, Bangor, Co Down, and Catherine Elizabeth Margaret, OBE, JP, *née* Brett; paternal ancestry listed in Burke's Irish family records (1976); *b* 10 May 1923; *Educ* Stowe, Trinity Coll Oxford; *m* 11 Dec 1954, Daphne Marian, da of Rt Hon Sir Norman Stronge, 8th Bt, MC, of Tynan Abbey, co Armagh (assassinated by IRA 1981); 1 s (James Anthony John b 1957); *Career* Lt IG 1943-46, serv Normandy 1944; trainee Messrs J & T Sinclair Belfast 1946-48; farmer 1948-; *Clubs* Cavalry and Guards, Ulster Reform Belfast, Royal Ulster YC Bangor; *Style—* Thomas Kingan, DL; Glenganagh, 39 Bangol Rd, Groomsport, Bangor, Co Down, N Ireland BT19 2JF (☎ 0297 460043)

KINGDOM, Leonard Grantley; s of Thomas Kingdom (d 1957), of Leics, and Amy, (d 1968); *b* 24 June 1919; *Educ* Wyggeston Sch Leicester, King's Coll Cambridge (MA, MB, BChir), St Bartholomew's Hosp; *m* 1, 4 Dec 1943 (m dis 1969), Joyce Elizabeth Mary, da of Sqdn Ldr William Catchpole, AFC (d 1935); 1 s (Richard b 31 March 1946, d 1971), 1 da (Susan b 6 June 1948); m 2, 3 Dec 1969, Susan Elizabeth, da of William King (d 1971), of Bexley; 1 s (William b 8 Dec 1971), 1 da (Sarah b 21 Feb 1976); *Career* Capt RAMC 1943-47, graded surgical specialist BLA 1944; served: Mobile Neurosurgical Unit, Field Surgical Unit (O/C); jr hosp appts at St Bart's Hosp and Royal Free Hosp, demonstrator of anatomy Cambridge Univ 1942, chief asst St Bart's Hosp 1948-52, conslt otologist LCC 1950-64; conslt ENT surgn: Univ Coll Hosp 1952-78, Queen Mary's Hosp for Children 1950-64, St Lukes Hosp for the Clergy 1964-80, Hosp of St John and St Elizabeth 1978-80; now in private practice; memb of ct City Univ 1980-85; Freeman City of London, Liveryman Worshipful Co of Fan Makers (memb of Ct 1967-, Past Master 1979-80), Hon Sec City of London Past Masters Assoc 1980-81; memb Br Assoc of Otolaryngologists 1952; FRSM 1948-, FRCS (Eng); *Recreations* travelling; *Style—* Leonard Kingdom, Esq; Stoneygate, Top Pk, Gerrards Cross, Bucks SL9 7PW (☎ 0753 883615); 19 Cavendish Sq, London W1M 9AB (☎ 01 636 9077/8)

KINGDOM, Thomas Doyle; CB (1959); s of Thomas Kingdom (d 1957); *b* 30 Oct 1910; *Educ* Rugby, King's Coll Cambridge; *m* 1937, Elsie Margaret, da of Leslie Caie Scott, MBE; 2 da; *Career* asst princ Home Civil Serv (Inland Revenue) 1933, controller Govt Social Survey Dept 1967-70, charities VAT advsr Nat Cncl for Voluntary Orgns 1972-; *Style—* Thomas Kingdom, Esq, CB; 2 Grosvenor Rd, Northwood, Middx, HA6 3HJ (☎ Northwood 22006)

KINGERLEE, Gavin John; s of Henry John Kingerlee, of Switzerland, and Constance Mary, *née* Skinner (d 1938); *b* 10 Oct 1936; *Educ* Dragon, Repton; *m* 1967, Margriet Marjan; 1 s (Aidan b 1973), 2 da (Sharon b 1970, Elaine b 1971); *Career* dir: Rodenhurst Properties Ltd, Kingerlee Hldgs Ltd; chm Highcroft Investmt Tst plc; dir Avrelic Plastics Ltd; *Recreations* fishing, swimming, watching, sport; *Clubs* Shark Angling of GB (pres), Kidlington and Gosford Swimming (vice-chm), Hanborough Cricket (pres); *Style—* Gavin Kingerlee, Esq; Straits Cottage, Church Hanborough, Oxford; Aurelia Plastics Ltd, Station Approach, Kidlington, Oxford (☎ 08675 4118 or 2900)

KINGHAM, His Hon Judge James Frederick; s of Charles William Kingham (d 1985), and Eileen Eda, *née* Hughes (d 1986); *b* 9 August 1925; *Educ* Wycliffe Coll, Queens Coll Cambridge (BA, MA), Graz Univ Austria; *m* 1958, Vivienne Valerie Tyrrell, da of Edwin George Brown, of Barnet Herts; 2 s (Simon b 1966, Guy b 1967), 2 da (Sarah b 1960, Emma b 1962); *Career* served WWII RN, Pacific Fleet 1943-47; barr Gray's Inn 1951; memb gen cncl of Bar 1954-58, Bar Cncl sub-ctee Sentencing & Penology, dep rec Nottingham 1970-75, (dep rec 1966-70), circuit judge 1973, liaison judge Bedfordshire 1981-; dep co cmmr scout 1971-80, venture scout ldr Harpenden 1975-86; *Recreations* skiing, climbing, squash, gardening, supporting football; *Clubs* Gray's Inn; *Style—* His Hon Judge James Kingham; Stone Ho, High St, Kimpton, Hitchin, Herts

KINGHAM, Norman Frederick; JP (1959); s of Maj Alfred Kingham (d 1960), and Gertrude Isobel, *née* Neems (d 1971); f in law 'Billy' Williams joined the Army in 1915, and won the MM at the age of 16. He was discharged until he was old enough to rejoin as a volunteer; *b* 5 Dec 1920; *Educ* Convent, Liscard HS, Univ of Liverpool, Columbia Univ NY, Liverpool (Dip Arch); *m* 10 March 1951, Muriel Olive, da of Ch Supt Hugh Herbert Williams (d 1974); 2 s (Paul b 1954, Timothy b 1956); *Career* TA and war serv RE 1937-39, Lance Corp Western Desert 1940 (POW 1941, excaped 1942), UK 1943, Middle East 1944-45; pres: Liverpool Architectural Soc 1969-71, Wallasey Boys Club 1973-; fndr memb and chm Martime Housing Assoc 1963-65, vice-chm bd of govrs Wirrall Coll of Art Design and Adult Studies 1980-82; chm: bldg and environment gp Merseyside C of C 1973-76, Liverpool ctee Br Heart Fndn 1986-, advsy bd Merseyside Branch of the Salvation Army 1982-, Liverpool Branch RIBA; memb: advsy bd Merseyside Branch Manpower Cmmn Services 1976-79; cncl memb: RIBA 1972-74, Merseyside C of C 1973-; chm Birkenhead Ironworks and CSS Alabama Tst 1987-; FRIBA 1975; *Recreations* archaeology, ancient history; *Clubs* Royal Cwlth London, Bluecoat Club (Liverpool), Honorable Soc Knights of the Round Table, Veteran Car of GB, Fortress Study Gp; *Style—* Norman F Kingham, JP; Rock Villa, Wellington Rd, Wallasey, Merseyside L45 2NF (☎ (051) 639 1731); Kingham Knight Associates, Architects, 18 Queen Ave, Castle St, Liverpool (☎ 051 236 3186, fax 051 236 2455)

KINGMAN, Sir John Frank Charles; s of Dr Frank Edwin Thomas Kingman, FRSC (d 1983), and Maud Elsie Kingman *née* Harley (d 1951); *b* 28 August 1939; *Educ* Christ's Coll Finchley, Pembroke Coll Cambridge (MA, ScD); *m* 1964 Valerie, da of Frank Cromwell, OBE, ISO (d 1978); 1 s (John b 1969), 1 da (Charlotte b 1972); *Career* mathematician; prof of Maths & Stats Univ of Sussex 1966-69, prof of Maths

Univ of Oxford 1969-85; chm Sci and Engrg Res Cncl 1981-85; vice chllr Univ of Bristol 1985-; *Clubs* Lansdowne, United Oxford and Cambridge; *Style*— Sir John Kingman; Univ of Bristol, Bristol BS8 1TH (☎ 0272 303960)

KINGS NORTON, Baron (Life Peer UK 1965), of Wotton Underwood, Co Buckingham; Harold Roxbee Cox; s of William John Roxbee Cox (d 1931), of Birmingham, and Amelia, *née* Stern (d 1949); *b* 6 June 1902; *Educ* Kings Norton GS, Imperial Coll London (PhD, fell); *m* 1, 12 July 1927, Doris Marjorie (d 1980), da of Ernest Edward Withers (d 1939), of Northwood; 2 s (Christopher, Jeremy); m 2, 1982, Joan Ruth Pascoe, da of late W G Pack of Torquay; *Career* chm: Landspeed Ltd 1975-, Cotswold Res Ltd 1979-, Berger Jenson & Nicholson Ltd 1967-75, Metal Box Co 1961-67; dir: Dowty Rotol 1968-75, Ricardo & Co (Engrs) 1927 Ltd 1965-77, Br Printing Corpn 1968-77, Hoechst UK 1970-75; pres: Royal Aeronautical Soc 1947-49, Royal Instn 1969-76; chm: Cncl for Scientific & Industl Res 1961-65, Cncl for Nat Academic Awards 1964-71; chllr Cranfield Inst of Technol 1969-; DIC, FIMechE; Hon FRAeS, Hon DSc, Hon DTech, Hon LLD; Medal of Freedom with Silver Palm (USA) 1947; Freeman City of London; Liveryman Guild of Air Pilots and Air Navigators; kt 1953; *Recreations* collecting aeronautical antiquities; *Clubs* Athenaeum, Turf; *Style*— The Rt Hon Lord Kings Norton; Westcote House, Chipping Campden, Glos (☎ 0386 840440)

KINGSALE, 30 Baron (I c 1340, precedence 1397); John de Courcy; Premier Baron of Ireland; s of Lt-Cdr Hon Michael de Courcy, RN (d 1940; s of 29 Baron Kingsale who was fifth in descent from the Lord Kingsale who successfully claimed from George III the hereditary privilege of keeping his hat on in front of the king; his cous and predecessor had also successfully claimed this privilege under William III, though the legend that King John granted the permission first is probably apocryphal), and Joan Reid (d 1967); *b* 27 Jan 1941; *Educ* Stowe, Sorbonne, Salzburg Univ; *Heir* 3 cous twice removed, Nevinson Russell de Courcy; *Career* 2 Lt Irish Guards 1962-65; former: bingo caller, film extra, safari park driver, barman in local pub; occasional broadcaster, plumber, builder and carpenter; chm Strand Publications 1970, Nat Assoc Serv to Realm 1979; dir: D'Olier Grantmesnil & Courcy Acquisitions 1970, Banaid Int (Brisbane) 1987, De Courcy-Daunt (Brisbane) 1987; pres Impex Conslts 1987, patron L'Orchestre de Monde 1987; *Recreations* shooting, palaeontology, venery; *Clubs* Cavalry & Guards';; *Style*— The Rt Hon Lord Kingsale; 1st Floor, Macarthur Chambers, 201 Edward St, Brisbane, Queensland 4000, Australia

KINGSBOROUGH, Viscount; Robert Charles Henry King-Tenison; s and h of 11 Earl of Kingston; *b* 20 Mar 1969; *Style*— Viscount Kingsborough

KINGSBURY, Derek John; CBE (1988); s of Maj A Kingsbury BEM, of Virginia Water, Surrey; *b* 10 July 1926; *Educ* Strodes Secdy Sch Egham, City and Guilds Coll London (BSc); *m* 1; 1 child (and 1 decd); m2, 1980, Sarah; 1 child; *Career* chm 1987 and gp chief exec Fairey Gp and chm of gp subsidiary cos 1982-, non-exec dir Vickers 1981-, dep chief exec Dowty Gp to 1982; memb cncl CBI 1980-86, (chm overseas ctee 1980-84), memb review bd for Govt Contracts 1986-; pres Br Heart Fndn Horse Show 1977-; CEng, FIEE, FCGI, DIC; *Recreations* golf (Capt Aircraft Golfing Soc 1982); *Clubs* MCC, RAC, Beaconsfield GC, St Enodoc GC; *Style*— Derek Kingsbury, Esq, CBE; Fairey Group plc, Cranford Lane, Heston, Hounslow, Middx TW5 9NQ (☎ 01 759 4811)

KINGSBURY, Lady Patricia Mary Charlemont; *née* French; da of 2 Earl of Ypres (d 1958), and his 1 w Olivia Mary, *née* John (d 1934); *b* 6 July 1919; *Educ* privately in Munich and Paris; *m* 24 Jan 1942, Henry Edmund Roland Kingsbury (d 1980), yst s of Gerald Francis Kingsbury, JP (d 1950) (ggs through his mother of 1 Earl of Bradford); 2 s (Philip Charles Orlando b 1944, Gerald Richard Charlemont b 1945); *Career* civil defence 1940-41; dir: Electrolube Ltd, H K (Wentworth) Holdings Ltd, Automation Facilities Ltd, DCS Packaging Ltd; *Recreations* travel, racing; *Style*— Lady Patricia Kingsbury; c/o Lloyds Bank Ltd, 6 Pall Mall, London SW1Y 5NH; Electrolube Ltd, Blakes Rd, Wargrave, Berks (☎ 073 522 3014)

KINGSHOTT, Albert (Leonard); s of Albert Leonard Kingshott, of Ingatestone, Essex, and Katherine Bridge, *née* Connelley; *b* 16 Sept 1930; *Educ* LSE, London Univ (BSc); *m* 10 Aug 1957, Valerie, da of Ronald Simpson (d 1964); 2 s (Adrian b 1980, Brendan b 1982), 1 da (Nicola b 1958); *Career* RAR (FO) 1952-55; fin analyst Br Petroleum Corp 1955-59, economist British Nylon Spinners 1960-62; fin mangr Iraq Petroleum Co 1963-65; tres: Ford of Europe, Ford Motor Co, Ford of Britain 1965-70; fin dir Whitbread Gp 1970-72; md finance British Steel Corp 1972-77, dir int banking div Lloyds Bank plc (dir merchant banking div 1977); exec dir: Europe 1980, Marketing & Planning 1983; dep chief exec 1985 and dir several assoc cos; govr and assoc memb faculty Ashridge Mgmnt Coll; FCIS; *Books* Investment Appraisal (1967); *Recreations* reading, chess, golf; *Style*— Leonard A Kingshott, Esq; 4 Delamas, Beggars Hill, Fryerning, Ingatestone, Essex; Lloyds Bank plc, 71 Lombard St, London EC3P 3BS (☎ 01 626 1500)

KINGSHOTT, Air Vice-Marshal Kenneth; CBE (1971, DFC 1950); s of Walter James Kingshott (d 1958) and Eliza Ann *née* Dale (d 1949); *b* 8 July 1924; *Educ* Edmonton County GS; *m* 15 May 1948, Dorrie Marie Dent (d 1978); 2 s (Mark John Dale b 1953, Guy Rupert Dale b 1956); *Career* RAF officer retired rank Air Vice-Marshal; principal appnts: Chief of Staff Allied Air Forces, Central Region Europe 1977-80, Dep Chief of Staff UK Air 1975-77; *Recreations* golf, fishing; *Clubs* RAF; *Style*— Air Vice-Marshal Kenneth Kingshott, CBE DFC; Tall Trees, Manor Raod, Penn, Bucks HP10 8NY

KINGSLAND, Sir Richard; CBE (1967), DFC (1940); *b* 19 Oct 1916; *Educ* Sydney Boys' HS, RAAF Staff Coll, IDC London; *m* 1943, Kathleen Jewel, da of R B Adams (d 1979); 1 s, 2 da; *Career* serv WWII Pilot 10 Sqdn RAAF 1939-41 UK, cmmnd 11 Sqdn RAAF New Guinea 1942-43, Gp Capt 1943, Dir Air Force Intelligence 1945-46; dir gen of Organisation RAAF 1946-48; mangr Sydney Airport 1948, airline tport pilot 1949, sec Dept of Interior Canberra 1963-70, dir Arts Cncl of Aust 1970-72 , sec Repatriation Dept and Dept of Veterans' Affrs Canberra 1970-81; first chm: cncl of Canberra Sch of Music 1972-75, cncl Canberra Sch of Art 1976-83; hon nat sec Nat Heart Fndn of Aust 1976-, first chm ACT Arts Devpt Bd 1981-83; chm: Cwlth Films Bd of Review 1982-86, Aust Uranium Advsy Cncl 1982-83; dir Australian Bicentennial Authy 1983-, pres bd of mgmnt Goodwin Retirement Villages Inc 1984-87, fndr cncl memb Aust Conservation Fndn 1967-69, memb Nat Cncl of Aust Opera 1983-; kt 1978; *Recreations* reading, looking at paintings; *Clubs* Commonwealth (Canberra), National Pres (Canberra); *Style*— Sir Richard Kingsland, CBE, DFC; 36 Vasey Cres, Campbell, ACT 2601, Australia (☎ 47 8502)

KINGSLEY, Ben; s of Rahimtulla Harji Bhanzi, and Anna Lyna Mary, *née* Goodman; *b* 31 Dec 1943; *Educ* Manchester GS; *Career* actor; RSC 1967-86: title roles incl Hamlet, Othello; National Theatre 1977-78: leading roles incl Mosca in Volpone; films incl: Gandhi, Betrayel, Turtle Diary, Harem, Silas Marner, Maurice, Slipstream, Testimony, Lenin, The Train, Pascali's Island, Without a Clue, Murderers Amongst Us; awards incl: Oscar, BAFTA (twice), Golden Globe (twice), NY Critics, LA Critics, London Standard, Grammy; associate artist RSC; patron and affiliated memb of many charitable organisations; MA Salford 1984; memb: BAFTA 1983, American Acad of Motion Picture Arts and Sciences; PADMA SRI (India) 1985; *Style*— Ben Kingsley, Esq; ICM, 388-396 Oxford St, London W1N 9HE (☎ 01 629 8080)

KINGSLEY, David John; s of Walter John Kingsley, and Margery, *née* Walden; *b* 10 July 1929; *Educ* Southend HS for Boys, LSE (BSc); *m* 1, July 1965 (m dis), Enid Sophia, da of Thomas Jones, MBE (d 1985), of Llandeilo; 2 s (Andrew John b 1966, Paul David b 1967), 2 da (Nichola Sophia b 1962, Nadia b 1964); m 2, May 1968 (m dis), Gillian, da of George Leech (d 1978); m 3, Oct 1988, Gisela Irene, *née* Reichardt; *Career* dir Benton and Bowles Advertising Agency 1961-64, fndr and ptnr Kingsley Manton & Palmer Advertising Agency 1964-78, dir and chm Kimpher Gp Communications Gp 1969-78, ptnr and chm Kingsley & Kingsley Business Consultancy 1974-; dir: King Pubns, Francis Kyle Gallery; chm Stokecroft Arts; chm Inner Action Community Arts Tst, govr LSE (memb standing ctee), memb devpt ctee RCM, hon tres Centre for World Devpt Educn, hon sec The Ireland Fund (UK); contested (L) E Grinstead 1952-54; advsr: to Lab Party and Govt on Communications 1962-70 (SDP 1981-87), to Pres Kaunda Zambia 1974-80, to Mauritius Govt 1977-81; organiser and creator: The Greatest Children's Party in the World for the Int Year of the Child 1980, HM the Queen's 60th Birthday Celebration; FRS, FIPA, ASIAD; *Books* Albion in China (1979); *Recreations* music, books, creating happy public events, travel, art; *Clubs* Reform, RAC; *Style*— David J Kingsley, Esq; 99 Hemingford Rd, London N1 1BY (☎ 01 607 4866); 33 Thornhill Rd, London N1 1HX (☎ 01 609 5770, fax 01 607 8025, car tel 0836 252 805)

KINGSLEY, Ivor; s of Harry Kaminsky (d 1959), and Bertha Kaminsky, *née* Karinski (d 1961); parents were refugees from Russia; *b* 10 August 1933; *Educ* Waterloo Rd Sch, Broughton M/C; *m* 4 Feb 1960, Brenda, da of James Egan, of Bury; 2 s (Mark b 1960, Paul b 1967); *Career* md Kingsley Forester plc until 1986; works in fin; semi ret; *Recreations* golf; *Clubs* Whitefield Golf; *Style*— Ivor Kingsley, Esq; 197-199 Monton Rd, Monton Green, Eccles M30 9PP (☎ 2340 607867)

KINGSLEY, John (Jack) Francis; s of Francis Jeffries Kingsley (d 1930), and Mary, *née* Mary Colomb (d 1944); *b* 17 Sept 1907; *Educ* Bradfield Coll Berks, Trintiy Coll Cambridge (BA); *m* 1 Aug 1940, Helen Cleeve, da of Cecil Cleeve Cox, of Geelong, Victoria, Aust; 3 s (John Cleeve b 18 July 1944, Michael Francis b 16 Aug 1946, Robert Jeremy b 6 Feb 1953), 1 da (Mary Colomb (Mrs Bohham-Carter, JP) b 5 June 1941); *Career* WWII RAFVR PO Initial Trg Wing, Newquay & Scarborough, Flt Lt 221 Gp Calcutta India, Sqdn Ldr GSQ Counter Intelligence Delhi India SEAC 1940-45; Shipping Mangr: Hong Kong 1946, Bangkog Siam 1947 Borneo 1947; rejoined Warner Barnes & Co as provincial mangr Bacolod Negros Phillippines 1949 and Manila Head Office Mangr 1958-63 (ret 1963); hon tres St Luke's Parish Church 1964-74; *Recreations* rowing, riding; *Clubs* Jr Carlton, Hong Kong, Manila; *Style*— J F C Kingsley, Esq; Rockfort, Hindhead, Surrey GU26 6SL

KINGSLEY, Sir Patrick Graham Toler; KCVO (1962, CVO 1950); s of Gerald Kingsley; *b* 1908; *Educ* Winchester, New Coll Oxford; *m* 1947, Priscilla Rosemary, da of Capt A Lovett Cameron; 3 s, 1 da; *Career* serv WWII Queen's Royal Regt; sec and Keeper of the Records Duchy of Cornwall 1954-72 (asst sec 1930-54); *Style*— Sir Patrick Kingsley, KCVO; West Hill Farm, West Knoyle, Warminster, Wilts

KINGSLEY, Stephen Michael; s of Ernest Robert Kingsley, of Cheadle, Cheshire, and Ursula Renate, *née* Bochenek (d 1972); *b* 1 June 1952; *Educ* Cheadle Hulme Sch, Univ of Bristol (BSc); *m* 18 March 1982, Michelle, da of Oscar Solovici (d 1983), of Paris; 1 da (Natalie b 1984), 2 step s (Anthony b 1968, James b 1973); *Career* Arthur Andersen & Co 1973-: mangr 1979-86, ptnr 1986-, head London capital mkts gp 1987-, dir euro regnl capital mkts 1988-; memb tech panel Securities and Investmts Bd 1985-87; FCA; *Books* Managing A Foreign Exchange Department (contrib 1985), Currency Options (contrib 1985); *Recreations* travel, ballet, classical music, current affairs; *Style*— Stephen Kingsley, Esq; 2 Hocroft Ave, London NW2 2EH (☎ 01 794 6542); Arthur Andersen & Co, 1 Surrey St, London WC2R 2PS (☎ 01 836 1200, 01 438 3855, fax 01 831 1133, telex 8812711)

KINGSTON, 11 Earl of (I 1768); Sir Barclay Robert Edwin King-Tenison; 15 Bt (I 1682); Baron Kingston of Rockingham (I 1764), Viscount Kingsborough (I 1766), Baron Erris (I 1800), Viscount Lorton (I 1806); s of 10 Earl of Kingston (d 1948); *b* 23 Sept 1943; *Educ* Winchester, RMA Sandhurst; *m* 1, 1965 (m dis 1974), Patricia Mary, da of E C Killip, of Beoley Lodge, Uttoxeter, Staffs; 1 s, 1 da (Lady Maria Lisette b 1970); m 2, 1974 (m dis 1979), Victoria, da of D C Edmonds, of Northwood, Middx; *Heir* s, Viscount Kingsborough; *Career* late Lt Royal Scots Greys; *Style*— The Rt Hon the Earl of Kingston; c/o Midland Bank Ltd, 47 Ludgate Hill, EC4

KINGSTON, Thomas Archer; s of Leonard James Kingston (d 1982), and Patricia Elisabeth, *née* Clay; *b* 4 Feb 1952; *Educ* Lady Eden's Sch, Highgate Sch, Keble Coll Oxford (MA); *m* 19 April 1980, Margaret, da of Thomas Donnellan, of 5 Horseshoe Crescent, Bath; 3 da (Joanna b 1983, Philippa b 1985, Helen b 1988); *Career* fin dir Mayfair Cateringt Co Ltd 1978-83 (co sec 1975), conslt BTR Mgmnt Servs 1980-83, sr conslt Interactive Incorporated 1983-; hon tres Chipperfield Choral Soc; Freeman City of London 1974, Liveryman Worshipful Co of Vintners 1983; MBIM; *Recreations* music, children's entertainer; *Clubs* Oxford & Cambridge; *Style*— Thomas Kingston, Esq; Briarwood, Langley Rd, Chipperfield Herts WD4 9JP (☎ 09277 63 486); Interactive Inc, 9 Marlin House, Marlins Meadow, Croxley Centre, Watford (☎ 0923 227 777)

KINGTON, Miles Beresford; s of William Beresford Nairn Kington, of Vrondeg Hall, nr Wrexham, and Jean Ann, *née* Sanders; descended from Thomas Kington (d 1857), of Charlton House, Somerset, who m Margaret, yr da and co-heiress of Laurance Oliphant, 8th Lord of Gask (sr line is Kington-Blair-Oliphant, of Ardblair Castle, Perthshire); *b* 13 May 1941; *Educ* Glenalmond, Trinity Coll Oxford (BA); *m* 1, 28 Feb 1964 (m dis), Sarah, da of Robert Paine, of Canterbury; 1 s (Thomas b 1968), 1 da (Sophie b 1966); m 2, 6 June 1987, Caroline, da of Nick Carter, of Knysna, S Africa; 1 s (Adam b 1987); *Career* freelance writer and former asst gardener in Ladbroke Sq; late jazz corresp The Times, double bass player with Instant Sunshine, literary ed

Punch (cr Let's Parler Franglais column) 1973-80; went up Andes for BBC's Great Train Journeys of The World Series (Three Miles High) 1980; humorous columnist for The Times (cr Moreover) 1981-87, since when on The Independent; translator of Alphonse Allais, French humorist; *Books* Miles and Miles, Moreover, Moreover Two, Nature Made Ridiculously Simple, The Franglais Lieutenant's Woman etc; *Recreations* bicycling, drinking, trying to remember if I have signed the Official Secrets Act; *Clubs* Garrick, Ronnie Scott's; *Style—* Miles Kington, Esq; 40 Lower Stoke, Limpley Stoke, Bath BA3 6HR (☎ 022 122 2262)

KINGZETT , Jan Anthony; s of Richard Norman Kingzett, of 18 Sloane Ave, London, and Julia Mary Kingzett; *b* 25 Oct 1955; *Educ* Eton, Trinity Coll Cambridge, (MA);; *Career* res staff J Henry Schroder Wagg Ltd 1977, asst dir Singapore Int Merchant Bankers Ltd 1981, dir Schroder Investmt Magmnt Ltd 1986- ; *Clubs* MCC, Queens; *Style—* Jan Kingzett, Esq; Schroder Investment Management Ltd, 36 Old Jewry, London, EC2R 8BS (☎ 01 382 6000)

KININMONTH, James Wyatt; s of Peter Wyatt Kininmonth, of Tappington Grange, Wadhurst, Sussex, and Priscilla Margaret, *née* Sturge; *b* 26 Sept 1952; *Educ* Harrow, RMA Sandhurst; *m* 19 March 1977, Susie, da of Richard William Griffin, of Norwood, N Carolina, USA; 1 s (Charles b 1985), 2 da (Annabel b 1980, Harriet b 1983); *Career* cmmnd 5 Royal Inniskilling Dragoon Gds 1974, Capt 1977, trans to reserve 1978; dir: Kininmonth Hldgs 1982-85, Kininmonth Reinsur brokers 1982-85; md Kininmonth Lambert Ltd 1987- (dir 1985-); non exec dir: Integrated Security Services 1985-, Edward Lloyd Ltd USA 1985-, Kininmonth Lambert Canada 1987-; memb Lloyds since 1983, Freeman City of London; Liveryman: Worshipful Co of Haberdashers 1982, Worshipful Co of Insurers 1985; *Recreations* shooting, skiing, tennis, golf; *Clubs* City of London; *Style—* J W Kininmonth, Esq; Lampool, Fairwarp, Sussex (☎ 082571 2447); Kininmonth Lambert Ltd, 53 Eastcheap, London EC3P 3HL (☎ 01 283 2000, fax 01 623 4130, telex 8814631)

KININMONTH, Peter Wyatt; s of Alec Marshall Kininmonth, MBE (d 1968); *b* 23 June 1924; *Educ* Sedbergh, Barenose Coll Oxford; *m* 1951, Priscilla Margaret, da of Raymond Wilson Sturge, of Lords Mead, Ashmoore, Dorset; 3 s, 1 da; *Career* Capt WWII; dep chm Lowndes Lambert Gp, chm Kininmonth Lambert Ltd P W Kininmonth Ltd; *Recreations* golf, gardening, opera; *Clubs* Vincents, City of London, Royal and Ancient St Andrews, Royal St Georges, Swinley Forest, Rye, Portmarnock, Old Elm (Chicago); *Style—* Peter Kininmonth Esq; Tappington Grange, Wadhurst, Sussex (☎ 089 288 2186)

KININMONTH, Sir William Hardie; s of John Kininmonth; *b* 8 Nov 1904; *Educ* Dunfermline HS, George Watson's Coll Edinburgh, Edinburgh Coll of Art; *m* 1934, Caroline Eleanor Newsam Sutherland (d 1978); 1 da; *Career* serv WWII RE; Royal Fine Arts Cmmn for Scotland 1952-65; consultant to Sir Rowand Anderson & Ptnrs (architects and planners); pres Royal Scottish Academy 1969-73; PPRSA, FRIBA, FRIAS; kt 1972; *Style—* Sir William Kininmonth; The Lane House, 46a Dick Place, Edinburgh, Scotland EH9 2JB (☎ 031 667 2724)

KINLOCH, Lady; Ann Maud; da of Gp Capt Frank Leslie White, of London; *m* 2 June 1965, as his 3 w, Sir Alexander Kinloch, 12 Bt (d 1982); 1 s (James, *qv*); *Style—* Ann, Lady Kinloch; East Longstone House, Chatton, Nr Alnwick, Northumberland NE66 5PY

KINLOCH, Sir David; 13 Bt (NS 1686), of Gilmerton, East Lothian; s (twin with his sister Ann) of Sir Alexander Davenport Kinloch, 12 Bt (d 1982), by his 2 w, Hilda Anna, da of late Thomas Walker, of Edinburgh; *b* 5 August 1951; *Educ* Gordonstoun; *m* 1, 1976 (m dis 1986), Susan, da of Arthur Middlewood; 1 s (Alexander b 1978), 1 da (Alice b 1976); m 2, 1987, Maureen, da of Robert Carswell; 1 s (Christopher Robert b 1988); *Heir* s, Alexander Kinloch b 31 May 1978; *Career* civil engr; *Style—* Sir David Kinloch, Bt; Gilmerton House, Athelstaneford, North Berwick, East Lothian (☎ 062 082 207)

KINLOCH, David Oliphant; s and h of Sir John Kinloch, 4 Bt; *b* 15 Jan 1942; *Educ* Charterhouse; *m* 1, 1968 (m dis 1979), Susan Minette, da of Maj-Gen Robert Elliott Urquhart, CB, DSO; 3 da; m 2, 1982, 1 s; Sabine de Loës, da of Philippe de Loës, of Geneva, Switzerland; *Career* CA; co director; *Style—* David Kinloch, Esq; House of Aldie, Fossoway, Kinross-shire, Scotland; 29 Walpole St, London SW3 4 QS

KINLOCH, Sir John; 4 Bt (UK 1873), of Kinloch, Co Perth; s of Sir George Kinloch, 3 Bt, OBE (d 1948); *b* 1 Nov 1907; *Educ* Charterhouse, Magdalene Coll Cambridge; *m* 1934, Doris Ellaline, da of late Charles Joseph Head, of Imber Close, Esher, Surrey; 1 s, 2 da; *Heir* s, David Oliphant Kinloch, CA; *Career* Br Miny of War Tport Iran 1942-45; employed by Butterfield & Swire in China and Hong Kong 1931-63, by John Swire & Sons Ltd London 1964-73; *Clubs* New (Edinburgh); *Style—* Sir John Kinloch, Bt; Aldie Cottage, Kinross, Kinross-shire KY13 7QH (☎ 05774 305)

KINLOCH, Tom; TD (1942); s of Tom Kinloch (d 1942), of Wimbledon, and Eva Jarman (d 1972); *b* 4 Jan 1917; *Educ* Westminster Abbey Choir Sch, Rutlish GS Surrey; *m* 1, Carol Ann, da of Philip Pearce (d 1953), of Henley-on-Thames; 1 s (Ian Philip b 1948), 1 da (Carol Ann Fiona b 1950); m 2, 14 July 1972, Diana Elizabeth Beaufoy, da of C J Edmonds, CVO, CBE (d 1979); *Career* Maj Army 1937-46, personnel dept NAAFI 1939, i/c Admin HQ NAAFI ME 1947, Staff mangr UK HQ 1948, personnel mangr 1950 NAAFI HQ Europe, Staff Coll Henley 1953, field appts 1964, regnl mangr E Anglia, regnl mangr C Region, Germany 1967, cmmd supervisor Hong Kong 1970, asst Head of UK (S) 1973, cmmnd supervisor Cyprus 1977, controller Trg 1980-82, sec Friends Queen Mary's Univ Hosp, Roehampton 1982-; *Recreations* golf, cricket; *Clubs* Roehampton Golf and County; *Style—* Tom Kinloch, TD; 1 Rye Walk, Putney, London SW15 6HR (☎ 789 5865); Friends of Queen Marys Hosp, Roehampton Lane SW15 5PN (☎ 789 4536)

KINLOSS, Lady (S Lordship 1602); Beatrice Mary Grenville; *née* Morgan-Grenville; da of Rev the Master of Kinloss (2 s, of Lady Kinloss, 11 holder of title, but he suc er bro in courtesy title); suc grandmother as 12 holder of title 1944; *b* 18 August 1922; *Educ* Ravenscroft Sch Eastbourne; *m* 1950, Greville Stewart Parker, s of Rev Ernest Freeman (changed name with husb to Freeman-Grenville, recognised by Lord Lyon King of Arms 1950); 1 s, 2 da; *Heir* s, Master of Kinloss; *Career* sits as Independent peer in House of Lords; Lady Kinloss's husb, Dr Freeman-Grenville, was with Overseas Civil Serv 1951-64, history prof State Univ of New York 1969-74, and is an author, chiefly of books on African and Islamic history; *Clubs* Royal Cwlth Soc; *Style—* The Rt Hon Lady Kinloss; North View House, Sheriff Hutton, York YO6 1PT (☎ 03477X) 447)

KINLOSS, Master of; Hon Bevil David Stewart Chandos Freeman-Grenville; s and h of Lady Kinloss; *b* 20 June 1953; *Style—* The Master of Kinloss

KINMONT, Dr Patrick David Clifford; MBE (Mil 1945), TD (1946); s of Patrick Kinmont, JP, MD, FRCSE (d 1953), of Newark-on-Trent, and Marie Therèse Clifford (d 1942), of Ennistown, Co Meath; *b* 28 Feb 1916; *Educ* Epsom Coll, King's Coll London, King's Coll Hosp (MD); *m* 25 March 1950, Elizabeth Gladys Matilda, da of Lt Charles West, RM (d 1945), of Corfe Castle; 1 s (John b 1951), 1 da (Philippa b 1953); *Career* War Serv Maj RAMCT, serv Norway and W Desert 1940, Greece 1940-41, (despatches), sr Br offr Stalag 18A Austria 1941-45, CO Bovington Mil Hosp 1945; head of dermatology: Derby Royal Infirmary 1950-73, Univ and Gen Hosp Nottingham 1973-79; consIt dermatologist: and post grad tutor Univ of Kuwait 1979-81, (emeritus) Notts Hosps 1979; visiting lectr Univ of: (Sydney, Adelaide, Melbourne, Perth, Singapore, Dacca, Damascus, Beirut 1967), Chicago 1979, (state) Pennsylvania 1982; memb: NY Acad of Sciences 1987, E Mids Med Appeal Tbnls 1973-88, of bd of dirs The Christian Children's Fund (GB) 1983-; memb hon Dermatologists Assocs (Br, American Irish); former pres Assoc of Dermatologists: Br 1978, N of England 1969, Mids 1970; former pres: E Mids Assoc of Physicians 1966, Derby Med Soc 1972; vice pres RSM Dermatology (sec 1977); FRCP; *Books* Skin Diseases for Beginners (with R B Coles), other dermatological pubns; *Recreations* shooting, fishing; *Clubs* Kildare Street Dublin and Univ Dublin, United Services Notts, Univ Nottingham; *Style—* Dr Patrick Kinmont, MBE, TD; Ermine House, Fulbeck, Lincs NG32 3JT (☎ 0400 72905); 11 Regent St, Nottingham (☎ 0602 474475)

KINMONT, Lady Sophia; *née* Pelham; da of 7 Earl of Yarborough, JP; *b* 15 Oct 1958; *m* 1983, John Kinmont, s of Dr Patrick Kinmont, of Ermine House, Fulbeck, Lincolnshire; *Style—* Lady Sophia Kinmont; 45 Lynette Avenue, London SW4 9HF

KINNAIRD, Lady (Germaine) Elizabeth Olive; *née* Eliot; da of 8 Earl of St Germans, KCVO, OBE (d 1960) and Helen, nee Post; *b* 1911; *m* 1, 1932 (m dis 1940) Thomas James (d 1976), s of Hon Cuthbert James, CBE, MP (s of 2 Baron Northbourne); m 2, 1950 (m dis 1963), Hon (Kenneth) George Kinnaird (d 1973), s of late 12 Lord Kinnaird; *Style—* Lady Elizabeth Kinnaird; New York

KINNAIRD, 13 Lord (S 1682); Graham Charles Kinnaird; Baron Kinnaird of Rossie (UK 1860); s of 12 Lord Kinnaird, KT, KBE (d 1972); *b* 15 Sept 1912; *Educ* Eton; *m* 1, 1938 (m dis 1940), Nadia, da of Harold Augustus Fortington, OBE; m 2, 1940, Diana Margaret Elizabeth, da of late Robert Shuckburgh Copeman, of Roydon Hall, Diss, Norfolk; 1 s decd, 4 da (Hon Mrs Wigan, Hon Anna Kinnaird, Hon Susan, Hon Mary); *Heir* none; *Career* Flying Offr RAFVR, late Lt 4/5 Bn Black Watch (TA); sits as Cons in House of Lords; *Clubs* Brooks's, Pratt's, New (Edinburgh), Boodles, Beefsteak; *Style—* The Rt Hon the Lord Kinnaird; Rossie Priory, Inchture, Perthshire (☎ Inchture 86 246)

KINNAIRD, Hon Mary Clare; *née* Kinnaird; da of 13 Lord Kinnaird; *m* 29 May 1988, John Staib, o s of Edward Staib, of Las Palmas, and the Dowager Countess of Dundonald, *qv*; *Style—* The Hon Mary Kinnaird

KINNAIRD, Hon Susan; da of 13 Lord Kinnaird; *Style—* The Hon Susan Kinnaird

KINNELL, Ian; QC (1987); s of Brian Kinnell (d 1960), and Grace Madeline, *née* Borer (d 1983); *b* 23 May 1943; *Educ* Sevenoaks Sch Kent; *m* 17 March 1970, Elizabeth Jane, da of David Farries Ritchie, of Hereford; 1 s (Alexander Murray b 1978), 1 da (Fiona b 1981); *Career* barr Gray's Inn 1967, SE Circuit, rec 1987-; *Style—* Ian Kinnell, Esq; 7 King's Bench Walk, Tempple, London EC4Y 7DS (☎ 01 583 0404, fax 01 583 0950, telex 887491 KBLAW)

KINNOCK, Rt Hon Neil Gordon; PC (1983), MP (Lab) Islwyn 1983-; s of Gordon Kinnock and Mary, *née* Howells; *b* 28 Mar 1942; *Educ* UC Cardiff; *m* 1967, Glenys Parry; 1 s, 1 da; *Career* MP (Lab) Bedwellty 1970-1983, TGWU sponsored; tutor/organiser WEA 1966-70; former dir Tribune Publications; memb ed bd Lab Res Dept 1974-; PPS to Sec State Employment 1974-75; former memb Select Ctees: Nationalised Industries, Euro Secondary Legislation; memb: BBC Gen Advsy Cncl 1977-, NEC 1978-, Anti-Apartheid Movement; cncl memb Get Britain Out of EEC Campaign; chief oppn spokesman Educn and memb Shadow Cabinet 1979-1983; ldr Labour Party and ldr Oppn 1983-; *Style—* The Rt Hon Neil Kinnock, MP; House of Commons, London SW1

KINNOULL, 15 Earl of (S 1633); Arthur William George Patrick Hay; Viscount Dupplin and Lord Hay (S 1627, 1633, 1697), Baron Hay (GB 1711); s of 14 Earl of Kinnoull (d 1938); *b* 26 Mar 1935; *Educ* Eton; *m* 1961, Gay Ann, da of Sir Denys Colquhoun Flowerdew Lowson, 1 Bt (d 1975); 1 s, 3 da; *Heir* s, Viscount Dupplin; *Career* sits as Conservative in House of Lords; jr Cons whip House of Lords 1966-68; FRICS; sr ptnr Langley Taylor; memb Agricultural Valuers' Assoc; pres: National Cncl on Inland Tport 1964-76, Scottish Clans Assoc 1970; vice-pres Nat Assoc of Parish Cncls 1971; chm Property Owners' Building Soc; cncl memb Royal Nat Mission to Deep Sea Fishermen 1978-; Cons del Cncl of Europe 1983-; memb Royal Co of Archers (Queen's Body Guard for Scotland) 1965-; *Clubs* Turf, Pratt's, White's, MCC; *Style—* The Rt Hon the Earl of Kinnoull; 5 Verulam Bldgs, Grays Inn, London WC1 (☎ 01 242 5038); 15 Carlyle Sq, London SW3; Pier House, Seaview, IOW

KINROSS, 5 Baron (UK 1902); Christopher Patrick Balfour; s of 4 Baron Kinross, OBE, TD, DL, and his 2 w, Helen (d 1969), da of Alan Hog and formerly w of Lt-Col Patrick Perfect; *b* 1 Oct 1949; *Educ* Eton, St Andrews Univ, Edinburgh Univ; *m* 1974, Susan Jane, da of Ian Robert Pitman; 2 s (Hon Alan, Hon Derek Andrew b 1981); *Heir* s, Hon Alan Ian Balfour b 4 April 1978; *Career* Writer to the Signet; *Recreations* pistol and rifle shooting, military vehicle restoration; *Clubs* New (Edinburgh); *Style—* The Rt Hon The Lord Kinross; 11 Belford Place, Edinburgh EH4 3DH

KINROSS, John; s of James Kinross (d 1961); *b* 4 May 1922; *Educ* Co Boys' Sch Windsor; Southall Tech Coll; *m* 1, 1947, Marie (d 1969), da of Arthur Horace Lucas; 1 s, 1 da; m 2, 1972, Eileen Margaret, da of Alfred Seamarks (d 1971), proprietor of Seamarks Coach & Travel Gp, of which Eileen is now chm); 1 step da; *Career* joined Lancer Boss Gp 1959, appointed project dir 1961; received Design Cncl awards 1972 and 1976; dir Seamarks Coach & Travel Gp 1975-; CEng, MIMechE; *Recreations* creative pastimes, conservation and preservation; *Style—* John Kinross Esq; Lancer Boss Group Ltd, Leighton Buzzard, Beds LU7 8SR (T Leighton Buzzard 372031); Papplewick, Oldhill Wood, Studham, Beds LU6 2NF (☎ Whipsnade 872391)

KINROSS, Ruth, Baroness; Ruth Beverley Balfour; da of late William Henry Mill, SSC; *m* 1, Kenneth William Bruce Middleton; m 2, 1972, as his 3 w, 4 Baron Kinross, OBE, TD, DL (d 1985); *Style—* The Rt Hon Ruth, Lady Kinross; 58 India St, Edinburgh EH3 6HD

KINTORE, 12 Earl of (S 1677); Sir James Ian Keith; 3 Bt (UK 1897); Lord Keith of Inverurie and Keith Hall (S 1677), Baron Stonehaven (UK 1925), Viscount Stonehaven (UK 1938); s of 1 Viscount Stonehaven, GCMG, DSO, PC (d 1941), and Lady Ethel Sydney Keith-Falconer, da of late 9 Earl of Kintore, KT, GCMG, PC (she suc bro, 10 Earl 1966, as Countess of Kintore, 11 in line, and d 1974); *b* 25 July 1908; *Educ* Eton, Royal Sch of Mines (London); *m* 1935, Delia, da of late William Lewis Brownlow Loyd, of Upper House, Shamley Green, Guildford; 2 s, 1 da; *Heir* s, Lord Inverurie, Master of Kintore; *Career* changed his name and arms from Baird to Keith by Interlocutor Lyon Court 1967; suc mother as chief of the name of Keith 1974; serv WWII as Maj RM, memb Royal Co of Archers, UK del to Cncl of Europe and Western Euro Union 1954-64, cncllr Grampian Region (chm Water Serv Ctee) 1974-78; Kincardineshire: cllr co cncl 1954-76, DL 1959, convenor 1974-76, Vice-Lt 1965-76; CEng AIStructE; *Clubs* Beefsteak, Rand (Johannesburg S Africa), Caledonian; *Style—* The Rt Hon the Earl of Kintore; Glenton House, Rickarton, nr Stonehaven, Kincardineshire (☎ Stonehaven 63071)

KIRBY, Hon Mrs; Hon Antonia; da of 8 Baron Rendlesham by his 2 w, Clare; *b* 17 Jan 1956; *m* 1981, Hugo Giles Stephen Astley Kirby, s of Giles Kirby, of The Manor House, South Harting, Petersfield, Hants, and Mrs Angela Kirby, of 17 Wetherby Gdns, London SW5; 1 s (Nicholas b 1983), 1 da (Natasha b 1985); *Style—* The Hon Mrs Kirby

KIRBY, Hon Mrs (Cecilia Alice); *née* Clifford; da of 13 Baron Clifford of Chudleigh; *b* 15 Nov 1945; *m* 1968, Capt Nicholas Breakspear Kirby, RN, s of Ronald Ernest Kirby; 1 s, 3 da; *Style—* The Hon Mrs Kirby; Melbury Bubb House, Melbury Bubb, Evershot, nr Dorchester, Dorset

KIRBY, David Donald; s of Walter Donald Kirby (d 1958), and Margaret Irene, *née* Halstead (d 1977); *b* 12 May 1933; *Educ* Royal GS High Wycombe, Jesus Coll Oxford (MA); *m* 1955, Joan Florence, da of Frederick James Dickins; 1 s (William), 1 da (Elizabeth); *Career* dir London & SE Services BR 1982-; (md Sealink UK until 1981; chm Fishguard & Rosslare Railways & Harbours until 1981); *Recreations* singing in choirs, messing about in boats; *Style—* David Kirby, Esq; Waterloo Station, London SE1 8SE (☎ 01 928 5151)

KIRBY, Prof Gordon William; s of William Admiral Kirby (d 1950), of Liverpool, and Frances Teresa, *née* Townson (d 1973); *b* 20 June 1934; *Educ* Liverpool Inst HS, Liverpool Tech Coll, Gonville and Caius Coll Cambridge (MA, PhD, SCD); *m* 4 April 1964 (m dis 1983), Audrey Jean, da of Col C E Rusbridge, of Halse, Somerset; 2 s (Giles Peter b 1968, Simon Michael b 1970); *Career* univ teacher Imperial Coll London 1960-67 (asst lectr 1960-61, lectr 1961-67), prof of organic chemistry Loughborough Univ of Technol 1967-72, regius prof of chemistry Glasgow Univ 1972-; Corday-Morgan Medal and Prize 1969, Tilden Lectureship and Medal 1974-75; memb chemistry ctee SERC 1971-75, chm journals ctee Royal Soc of Chemistry 1981-84; FRSC 1970, FRSE 1975; *Books* Progress in the Chemistry of Organic Natural Products (ed), plus many res papers in journals of the Chemical Soc; *Recreations* hill walking, amateur astronomy; *Style—* Prof Gordon Kirby; Dept of Chem, Univ of Glasgow, Glasgow G12 8QQ (☎ 041 339 8855, ext 4416/4417, telex 777070 UNIGLA)

KIRBY, John; s of Percival Henry Kirby, of 64 Rydal Gdns, Wembley, and Dorothy Alice, *née* Southgate; *b* 31 Oct 1931; *Educ* Harrow GS, Acton Tech Coll, Chelsea School of Pharmacy; *m* (Phyllis) Joy, da of Charles Dodd (d 1975), of 16 Lapstone Gdns, Kenton; 4 da (Susan Elizabeth b 27 July 1956, Caroline Jane b 20 Dec 1957, Sarah Christine b 21 Dec 1958, Rebecca Charlotte b 21 Dec 1962); *Career* community pharmacist: St John's Wood 1956-61, Welwyn Gdn City 1961-; dir: Johns Kelynack Gp of Pharmacies 1962-, Stearns Pharmacies 1969-77, Scotts Pharmacies 1970-77, Focus Ltd (Gifts) 1982-88; chm local professional assoc 1966 and 1983; memb: Pharmaceutical Servs Negotiating Ctee 1982- (nat standing advsy ctee to HMG); former memb govrs; Applecroft Sch, Stanborough Sch; pres Welwyn Hatfield Rotary Club 1983-84, chm Welwyn Gdn Round Table 1971-72; memb: Royal Pharmaceutical Soc 1956-, Inst of Pharmacy Mgmnt 1963; fndr memb Coll of Pharmacy Practice 1985; *Style—* John Kirby, Esq; 2 Elmwood, Welwyn Gdn City, Herts AL8 6LE; 31 Cole Green Lane, Welwyn Gdn City, Herts AL7 3PP (☎ 0707 326043)

KIRBY, John Edward Weston; s of Lt-Col Robert Fry Kirby, DSO, MBE, of The Oak, Beaumont, Clacton-on-Sea, Essex, and Pamela Mary, *née* Weston; *b* 4 Feb 1936; *Educ* Ampleforth, Corpus Christi Coll Oxford (MA); *m* 1, 4 Oct 1963, Teruko Frances (d 1974), da of Rear Adm Yoshio Takahashi, of Tokyo, Japan; 2 s (Patrick b 21 Nov 1966, Peter b 30 June 1974); m 2, 11 Feb 1978, Michiko, da of Junichi Wada of Tokyo Japan; 1 da (Alicia b 21 May 1981); *Career* Bank of England 1959-: fin attache Br Embassy Tokyo 1974-76, advsr Far East and Australasia 1977-83 (W Europe 1983-85), alternate memb EC monetary ctee 1983-85, head Int Div (N America, W Europe and Japan) 1985-88, alternate exec dir Bank for Int Settlements 1985-88, head Int Div (developing countries and int fin insts)1988-; memb UK/Japan 2000 gp; *Books* Business in Japan (contrib, 1980); *Recreations* reading, the arts, cricket; *Clubs* Vincent's; *Style—* John Kirby, Esq; Bank of England, Threadneedle St, London EC2R 8AH (☎ 01 601 4174)

KIRBY, (Phyllis) Joy; *née* Dodd; da of William Charles Dodd (d 1975), of Harrow, and Phyllis Ruby, *née* Champion-Jones; *b* 27 June 1935; *Educ* Preston Manor GS Harrow Middx, Hatfield Poly (BA); *m* John, s of Percival Henry Kirby, of Harrow; 4 da (Susan Elizabeth b 16 July 1956, Caroline Jane (Herring) b 20 Dec 1957, (Sarah Christine) Gaynor b 21 Dec 1958, Rebecca Charlotte b 21 Dec 1962); *Career* teacher 1972-82, dir Johns and Kelynack 1978-, chm Focus Gifts 1983-88; memb: Greenpeace, Friends of the Earth, CND; *Style—* Mrs Joy Kirby; Johns and Kelynack Ltd, 31 Cole Green Lane, Welwyn Garden City, Herts

KIRBY, Paul Michael; s of William Raistrick Kirby (d 1968), and Laura, *née* Topham; *b* 19 Feb 1948; *Educ* Hanson GS Bradford Yorks; *m* 16 Sept 1967, Vivien, da of Jack Longstaff, of 10 Bryanstone Rd, Laisterdyke, Bradford, W Yorks; 1 s (Anthony b 1980), 2 da (Deborah b 1976, Michelle b 1978); *Career* Provident Fin Gp plc: trainee programmer 1966, project mangr (customer accounting systems) 1972, systems devpt mangr ICL 1900 systems 1975, dep md HT Greenwood Ltd 1980, md Practical Credit Servs Ltd 1983, md Car Care Plan (Securites Div) Ltd 1985-; *Recreations* cricket, rugby, football, squash; *Style—* Paul Kirby, Esq; 8 Glenview Close, Nab Wood, Shipley, West Yorks BD18 4AZ (☎ 0274 599877); Car Care Plan (Securities Division) Ltd, Bramley District Centre, Bramley, Leeds, West Yorks LS13 2EJ (☎ 0532 562133, fax 0532 551601, car tel 0836 756150, telex 557316 SAFETY G)

KIRBY, Dr Peter Linley; OBE (1976); *b* 25 June 1924; *Educ* Bede Sch, Durham Univ (BSc, MSc, DSc); *m* 1948, Lilian; 1 s (Paul Kelvin b 1953), 1 da (Pamela Gillian b 1956); *Career* gp dir of res Crystalate Electronics Ltd; dir: Welwyn Strain Measurement Ltd, Strainstall Ltd; visiting prof: Univ of Edinburgh, Univ of Newcastle, Univ of Durham; external examiner Newcastle and Sunderland Poly; vice chm Cncl Durham Univ; chm govrs Durham Business Sch; lectr on microelectronics, advsr UNESCO on electronics; author of over 50 publications on electronics; FInstP, FIEE; *Style—* Dr Peter Kirby, OBE; 14 Woodlands, Gosforth, Newcastle upon Tyne (☎ 091 2857932)

KIRBY, Hon Sir Richard Clarence; s of Samuel Enoch Kirby (d 1972) and Agnes Mary Kirby (d 1972); *b* 22 Sept 1904; *Educ* King's Sch Parramatta, Sydney Univ (LLB); *m* 1937, Hilda Marie, da of Oswald Joseph Ryan (d 1966); 2 da; *Career cchief judge* Cwlth Ct of Conciliation & Arbitration 1956-73, (*judge* 1947), pres Cwlth Conciliation & Arbitration Cmmn 1956-73 (ret), chm Aust Stevedoring Conference 1977; memb Cncl Univ of Wollongong 1978-; pres H E Evatt Memorial Fndn 1980; kt 1961; *see Debrett's Handbook of Australia and New Zealand for further details*; *Style—* The Hon Sir Richard Kirby; The White House, Cudmirrah, via Nowra, NSW 2540, Australia

KIRBY, Roger Ian Paul William; s of Vernon Kirby of Lytham, and Audrey Georgina Kirby; *b* 3 Mar 1953; *Educ* Malvern Coll, Kingston Poly (BA); *m* 1981, Kathryn Warner, da of Lewis L Warner, of USA; 1 da (Molly b 1983); *Career* md Inenco Gp; dir: Industl Energy Costs Ltd 1972-, Inenco Energy Conservation Ltd 1976-, Industl Energy Costs (telecommunications) Ltd 1978, Industl Energy Costs (systems) Ltd 1983-, Inenco Ltd 1984, Inenco Energy Performance Ltd 1985-; *Recreations* sailing, swimming; *Clubs* Ocean Cruising; *Style—* Roger Kirby; East Beach, Lytham, Lancashire; Inenco Group, Vulcan House, Orchard Road, St Annes-on-Sea, Lancs (☎ 0253 728951, telex 677155)

KIRDAR, Nemir Amin; s of Amin Jamil Kirdar (d 1958), and Nuzhet Mohammed Ali Kirdar (d 1982); *b* 28 Oct 1936; *Educ* Baghdad Coll, Univ of the Pacific California (BA), Fordham Univ (MBA), Harvard Univ; *m* 1 Feb 1967, Nada, da of Dr Adnan Shakir; 2 da (Rena b 1968, Serra b 1975); *Career* proprietor Nemir A Kirdar Business Enterprises 1963-69, trainee then asst vice-pres Allied Bank Int NY 1969-73, vice-pres Nat Bank of N America NY 1973-74, vice-pres and head of Gulf div Chase Manhattan Bank NY 1974-81, fndr pres and chief exec offr Arabian Investmt Banking Corpn Bahrain 1982-; fell Sommerville Coll Oxford, memb advsy ctee Georgetown Univ Washington DC; memb: Arab Thought Forum Aman Jordan, North South Round Table Washington DC, World Econ Forum Geneva, Inter-Religious Fndn London, Arab Bankers Assoc London, Centre for Contemporary Arab Studies Georgtown Univ Washington DC; author of several articles in leading business and fin magazines; *Recreations* reading, skiing, windsurfing, tennis, collecting antiques; *Clubs* Marks, Annabels, Les Ambassadeurs, Harry's Bar, Vanderbilts; *Style—* Nemir Kirdar, Esq; Wyldewood, The Bishops Ave, London N2 (☎ 01 458 9438); Investcorp Int Ltd, 65 Brook St, London W1Y 1YE (☎ 01 629 6600, fax 01 499 0371, telex 28430)

KIRK, Lady; Elizabeth Mary; da of Richard Brockbank Graham (d 1957), and Gertrude Anson (d 1987); *b* 9 Jan 1928; *Educ* St Leonards Sch, Somerville Coll Oxford (MA); *m* 1950, Sir Peter Michael Kirk (d 1977; MP (C) Saffron Walden), s of Rt Rev Kenneth Escott Kirk, late Bp of Oxford (d 1954); 3 s; *Career* Countryside Cmmn 1979-87, Eastern Cncl for Sport and Recreation 1982-87, chm Peter Kirk Meml Fund, tstee Byways and Bridleways Tst; memb: regnl advsy ctee Forestry Cmmn 1987, East Anglian regnl ctee Nat Tst 1982-87 (Yorks 1988-); DL Essex 1983-87; *Recreations* fell walking, music, riding; *Clubs* Farmers'; *Style—* Lady Elizabeth Kirk; Manor Farm, Newton on Rawcliffe, Pickering, North Yorks YO18 8QA

KIRKE, Rear Adm David Walter; CB (1967), CBE (1962, OBE 1945); s of Percy St George Kirke (d 1966), and Alice Gertrude (d 1959), da of Sir James Gibson-Craig, 3Bt; *b* 13 Mar 1915; *Educ* RNC Dartmouth; *m* 1, 1936 (m dis 1950), Tessa, da of Capt Patrick O'Connor; 1 s; m 2, 1956, Marion Margaret, da of late Dr James Gibb; 1 s, 1 da; *Career* chief of Naval Aviation Indian Navy New Delhi 1959-62, Flag Offr Naval Flying Trg 1965-68; *Recreations* golf; *Clubs* Army & Navy; *Style—* Rear Adm David Kirke, CB, CBE; Lismore House, Pluckley, Kent (☎ 023 384 439)

KIRKHAM, David John; s of Joseph Edward Kirkham (d 1961), of Chingford, and Doris Evelyn Kirkham; *b* 8 Mar 1947; *Educ* Chingford GS, Lady Lumley's GS; *m* 12 April 1971, Elizabeth Margaret, da of Edward Armstrong Hayes, of Thornton-le-Dale; 1 s (James Edward b 1981), 1 da (Charlotte Mary b 1978); *Career* ptnr Gardiners CA's Scarborough 1974-89 (mangr 1970-74), nat exec ptnr Moore Stephens E Yorks 1988-89 (sr ptnr 1977-79), company sec Co Properties Gp plc 1980-88 (fin dir 1976-88), fin dir and dep chm GA Pindar and Sons Ltd 1988-; dir: Kingsley Res Ltd, Desktop Professional Systems Ltd, Glazebrook Interior Architects; Pan Orient Resources (PTE) Ltd Singapore; tstee consort Hotels UK; roundtable 1972-87, rotary 1988-, Rydale Cons Assoc; FCA 1970, IOD 1988; *Books* Minding Your Own Successful Business (1989); *Recreations* squash, deer stalking; *Clubs* RAC, London; *Style—* David Kirkham, Esq; The High Hall, Thornton-le-Dale, Pickering, N Yorks YO18 7QR (☎ 0751 74 371); Catriona, Roshven, Irine, Lochailort, Fortwilliam, Inverness-shire (☎ 0687 7271); G A Pindar & Son Ltd, 3rd Floor, Pavilion Hse, Scarborough, N Yorks (☎ 0723 354 354, fax 0723 362 339, mobile phone 0836 690 957, telex 527670)

KIRKHAM, Donald Herbert; s of Herbert Kirkham (d 1987), and Hettie, *née* Trueblood; *m* 16 Sept 1960, Kathleen Mary, da of Christopher Lond; 1 s (Richard b 1963), 1 da (Sarah b 1966); *Career* Nat Serv Army 1954-56; The Woolwich Equitable Bldg Soc: joined Lincoln branch 1959, branch mangr Worcester 1963, gen mangr's asst 1967, business prodn mangr 1970, asst gen mangr ops 1972, gen mangr 1976, dep chief gen mangr 1981, appointed to local bd for Scotland and NI 1979-84, memb main bd 1982, chief exec 1986; vice-pres Chartered Bldg Socs Inst 1986 (pres 1981-82), vice-pres Cncl of Inst of Chartered Secretaries and Adminstrators 1984-85; chm Met Assoc of Bldg Socs; tstee Greenwich Festival; Freeman City of London, Liveryman Worshipful Co of Chartered Secretaries and Adminstrators; FCIS 1960, FCBSI 1965, CBIM 1986; *Recreations* boating; *Clubs* IOD; *Style—* Donald Kirkham, Esq; 2 Chaundrye Close, The Court Yard, Eltham SE9 5QB (☎ 01 854 2400, fax 01 316 4204)

KIRKHAM, Hon Mrs (Pamela Vivien); da and co-heiress of Baroness Berners, *qv*; *b* 30 Sept 1929; *m* 1952, Michael Joseph Sperry Kirkham; 2 s, 1 da; *Style—* The Hon Mrs Kirkham; Parwich Lees, Derbyshire

KIRKHILL, Baron (Life Peer UK 1975); John Farquharson Smith; s of

Alexander Findlay Smith; *b* 7 May 1930; *Educ* Robert Gordon's Colls Aberdeen; *m* 1965, Frances Mary Walker Reid; 1 step-da; *Career* lord provost of the City and Royal Burgh of Aberdeen 1971-75, min of State Scottish Office 1975-78, chm North of Scotland Hydro-Electric Bd 1979-82; memb Cncl of Europe 1987-; Hon LLD (Aberdeen Univ 1974); *Style—* The Rt Hon the Lord Kirkhill; 3 Rubislaw Den North, Aberdeen (☎ 0224 314167)

KIRKHOPE, Timothy John Robert; MP (C) Leeds NE 1987-; s of John Thomas Kirkhope, of Newcastle upon Tyne, and Dorothy Buemann, *née* Bolt (d 1973); *b* 29 April 1945; *Educ* Royal GS Newcastle upon Tyne; Coll of Law Guildford; *m* 1969, Caroline, da of Christopher Thompson Maling (d 1975), of Newcastle upon Tyne; 4 s (Justin b 1970, Rupert b 1972, Dominic b 1976, Alexander 1979); *Career* slr, ptnr with Wilkinson Maughan Newcastle upon Tyne, (formerly Wilkinson Marshall Clayton & Gibson) 1977-87, conslt 1987-, cncllr Northumberland 1981-85; memb: Newcastle Airport Controlling Bd 1981 -85, Cons Nat Exec Ctee, Northern Region Health Authy 1982-86; ; *Recreations* swimming, tennis, flying; *Clubs* Northern Counties; *Style—* Timothy Kirkhope, MP; 7 Dewar Close, Collingham nr Wetherby L522 5JR (☎ 0532 492502); 8 Castle Street, Warkworth, Northumberland

KIRKPATRICK, Sir Ivone Elliott; 11 Bt (NS 1685), of Closeburn, Dumfriesshire; s of Sir James Alexander Kirkpatrick, 10 Bt (d 1954); *b* 1 Oct 1942; *Educ* Wellington, St Mark's Coll Adelaide Univ;; *Heir* bro, Robin Kirkpatrick; *Style—* Sir Ivone Kirkpatrick, Bt

KIRKPATRICK, (Jennifer Augustine) Jenny; da of Richard Arthur Seckerson (d 1973), Wallasey, Merseyside, and Olive Frances Maude, née o'Connor; *b* 7 August 1946; *Educ* Oldershaw GS Wallasey, Cheshire Coll of Educn, Univ of Keele Inst of Educn (BEd); *m* 4 April 1969 (m dis 1984), Jack Kirkpatrick; *Career* teacher of english Dunstable Beds 1968-70, head of resources St Albans Herts 1970-75 (head of english 1971-75, sr sixth form tutor 1972-75), dep head Comprehensive London Borough of Barnet 1975-79, gen sec Nat Assoc of Probation Offrs (NAPO) 1979-85, dir Electricity Consumers' Cncl (ECC), nat watchdog for the Electricity Supply ind 1985-88; dir The Paul Hamlyn Fndn 1988-; writer and broadcaster; *Recreations* written and spoken word, public sector policy, anything obsessional-crosswords, bridge, puzzles, horses; *Style—* Jenny Kirkpatrick; 86 Bryanston Ct, George St, London W1 (☎ 01 741 2812)

KIRKPATRICK, Robin Alexander; s of Sir James Alexander Kirkpatrick, 10 Bt, and hp of bro, Sir Ivone Elliott Kirkpatrick, 11 Bt; *b* 19 Mar 1944; *Educ* Wellington; *Style—* Robin Kirkpatrick Esq

KIRKPATRICK, William Brown; s of Joseph Kirkpatrick (d 1961), of Dumfriesshire, and Mary Laidlaw Kirkpatrick, *née* Brown (d 1985); *b* 27 April 1934; *Educ* George Watson's Coll Edinburgh, Strathclyde Univ (BSc Econ), Colombia Univ New York (MSc); *Career* Served Investors in Indust plc 1960-85, chm Findlater Mackie Todd & Co Ltd, dir of other cos;; *Recreations* Scottish paintings, porcelain pigs, current affairs; *Clubs* Caledonian; *Style—* William Kirkpatrick, Esq; 20 Abbotsbury House, Abbotsbury Rd, London W14 8EN (☎ 01 603 3087)

KIRKUP, Prof James Falconer; s of James Harold Kirkup (d 1958), and Mary Johnson (d 1973); descendant of Barone Seymour Kirkup (DNB), Thomas Kirkup (DNB), William Falconer (DNB); *b* 23 April 1918; *Educ* South Shields Secdy Sch, King's Coll Univ of Durham (BA); *Career* lectr and prof at various univs in Britain, Europe, USA and Far East, prof of comparative literature Kyoto Univ of Foreign Studies 1976-88; named Ollave Order of Bards, Ovates and Druids 1974, sponsor Inst of Psychophysical Res Oxford 1970; FRSL; *Books* 20 volumes of poetry, The Sense of the Visit (1985), translator of Kawabata, Simone de Beauvoir Kleist, Pasolini; (autobiog) I of All People; *Recreations* reading, music (jazz and classical), cinema, travel; *Style—* Prof James Kirkup; BM-Box 2780, Br Monomarks, London WC1N 3XX

KIRKWOOD, Archibald Johnston; MP (SLD) Roxburgh and Berwickshire 1983-; s of David Kirkwood, of Glasgow, and Jessie Barclay (d 1980); *b* 22 April 1946; *Educ* Heriot-Watt Univ (BSc); *m* 1972, Rosemary Jane, da of Edward John Chester; 1 s, 1 da; *Career* slr; *Recreations* music, skiing; *Clubs* Nat Lib; *Style—* Archibald Kirkwood, Esq, MP; House of Commons, London SW1

KIRKWOOD, 3 Baron (UK 1951); David Harvie Kirkwood; s of 2 Baron Kirkwood (d 1970, s of 1 Baron, PC, JP, MP Dumbarton Burghs 1922-50, who as David Kirkwood was deported for being the ringleader in a protest against rent increases); *b* 21 Nov 1931; *Educ* Rugby, Trinity Hall Cambridge (MA, PhD); *m* 1965, Judith, da of John Hunt, of Leeds; 3 da (Hon Ruth b 17 Sept 1966, Hon Anne b 24 April 1969, Hon Lucy b 28 July 1972); *Heir* bro, Hon James Kirkwood; *Career* warden Stephenson Hall 1974-79, sr lectr Sheffield Univ 1976-; CEng; *Style—* The Rt Hon the Lord Kirkwood; 56 Endcliffe Hall Ave, Sheffield S10 3EL (☎ 0742 663107)

KIRKWOOD, Eileen, Baroness; Eileen Grace; da of late Thomas Henry Boalch, of Pill, Bristol; *m* 1931, 2 Baron Kirkwood (d 1970); *Style—* The Rt Hon Eileen, Lady Kirkwood; 25 The Dale, Keston, Kent

KIRKWOOD, The Hon Lord Kirkwood Ian Candlish; QC (1970); s of John Brown Kirkwood OBE (d 1964), and Mrs Constance Kirkwood (d 1987); *b* 8 June 1932; *Educ* George Watson's Boys' Coll Edinburgh, Edinburgh Univ (MA, LLB), Univ of Michigan (LLM); *m* 1970, Jill, da of Lt-Cdr Trevor P Scott RN (ret), of Torquay; 2 s (Jonathan b 1973, Richard b 1975); *Career* chm Medical Appeal Tribunal (until 1987); senator Coll of Justice Scotland 1987; *Recreations* tennis, golf, chess; *Style—* The Hon Lord Kirkwood; 58 Murrayfield Ave, Edinburgh, EH12 6AY (☎ (031 337) 3468); Knockbrex Ho, Nr Borgue, Kirkcudbrightshire (☎ Borgue 269)

KIRKWOOD, Hon James Stuart; s of 2 Baron Kirkwood (d 1970), and hp of bro, 3 Baron; *b* 19 June 1937; *Educ* Rugby, Trinty Hall Cambridge; FRICS; *m* 1965, Alexander Mary, da of late Alec Dyson, of Holt, Norfolk; 2 da; *Style—* The Hon James Kirkwood; The Cearne, Kent Hatch, Crockham Hill, Edenbridge, Kent

KIRKWOOD, James William; s of Robert William Cecil Kirkwood, OBE, of 4 Marnabrae, Belsize Rd, Lisburn, NI, and Isobel Margaret, *née* Kerr; *b* 12 Feb 1962; *Educ* Friends' Sch Lisburn NI; *Career* sales exec Forward Tst Gp 1983-; 48 Ir Caps 1981-, 25 GB Caps 1987-, Olympic Gold Medal Seoul 1988, 3 Ir cricketing caps 1983-; *Recreations* all sports, music; *Style—* James Kirkwood, Esq; 11 Greenbank, Lisburn, NI (☎ 08462 87337); Forward Trust Ltd, 5 Donegall Sq South, Belfast, NI (☎ 0232 324 641)

KIRKWOOD, (Iona Mary) Nicole; da of 12 Baron de Fresnes (Fr), and his w, Lady Fiona, *née* Abney-Hastings, *qv*; *b* 30 June 1957; *Educ* Edinburgh Univ (BA); *m* 1982, Timothy John Kirkwood, 2 s of Andrew and Patricia Kirkwood, of Half Acre, Corfe Castle, Dorset; 3 da (Harriet Mary b 1984, Matilda Alice b 1986, Jemima Jane b 1987); *Style—* Mrs Timothy Kirkwood; Straan, Advie, Grantown-on-Spey, Moray

KIRWAN, Ernest O'Gorman; s of E O'G Kirwan, CIE, MD FRCSI (d 1965) and Mary D Therkelsen (d 1974); *b* 6 June 1929; *Educ* Ampleforth, Cambridge Univ (MA, MB, BChir), Middlesex Hosp;; *m* 20 April 1963, Marie Christine, da of Dr J Coakley (d 1954); 3 s (Robert b 1965, Edward b 1967, Patrick b 1969), 1 da (Sarah b 1966); *Career* Capt RAMC 1954-56; civilian conslt to the RN and RAF 1962-; conslt orthopaedic surgn; Royal Nat Orthopaedic Hosp, Univ Coll Hosp 1966-; Br exec memb of Int Soc for the Study of the Lumbar Spine 1984-; exec of the Br Orthopaedic Assoc 1981-84; *Books* publications in medical journals on spinal surgery, pain and hip surgery; FRCS(E) 1960;; *Recreations* sailing, skiing; *Clubs* St Albans Medical Soc; *Style—* Ernest Kirwan, Esq,; 31 Newlands Avenue, Radlett, Herts; 107 Harley St, London W1

KIRWAN, Sir (Archibald) Laurence Patrick; KCMG (1972, CMG 1958), TD (1949); s of Patrick Kirwan; *b* 13 May 1907; *Educ* Wimbledon Sch, Merton Coll Oxford; *m* 1, 1933 (m dis) Joan Elizabeth, da of Capt Hon Wentworth Chetwynd (bro of 8 Viscount Chetwynd, d 1914); 1 da; m 2, 1949, Stella Mary Monck; *Career* serv WWII Intelligence Corps, TARO 1939-57, Hon Lt-Col; dir and sec Royal Geographical Soc 1945-75 (hon vice pres 1981-); ed Geographical Journal 1945-78; memb: Ct of Arbitration Argentine-Chile Frontier Case 1965-68, Sec of State for Transport's Advsy Ctee on Landscape Treatment of Trunk Roads 1968-81, UN Register of fact-finding experts 1968-, memb CT Exeter Univ 1969-80;; *Style—* Sir Laurence Kirwan, KCMG, TD; c/o Royal Geographical Society, 1 Kensington Gore, London SW7

KIRWAN, Brig Rudolph Charles Hogg; DSO (1943), OBE (1940); s of Lt-Gen Sir Bertram Kirwan, KCMG, CB (d 1961), and Helen Margaret Trower, *née* Hogg (d 1971); *b* 22 May 1903; *Educ* Rugby, RMA Woolwich; *m* 4 Oct 1934, Patricia Evelyn Markness, da of Col William (d 1937), of Lovells Ct Marnhull, Dorset; 1 s (James b 9 April 1957), 2 da (Sonia b 22 May 1937, Angela b 23 March 1942); *Career* GSO2 RA 2 Corps 1939, GSO1 5 Div 1940, CO 92 FD Regt 1943, CRA 4 Div, DDMO WO 1946-48, ret 1949; farmer Rignall Farm Bucks 1949-68; chm Great Missenden Cons Assoc 1949-62; *Recreations* tennis, golf; *Clubs* Ashridge GC; *Style—* Brig Rudolph Kirwan, DSO, OBE; Marnhull, Little Hollis, Great Missenden, Bucks (☎ 024 062 552)

KISCH, John Marcus; CMG (1965); s of Sir Cecil Kisch, KCIE, CB (d 1961), and Myra Kisch, *née* Adler (d 1919); *b* 27 May 1916; *Educ* Rugby, King's Coll Cambridge (MA); *m* 1951, Gillian May, da of Sir Kenneth Poyser, KBE, DSO (d 1943); 4 da (Nicola, Cherry (twins), Margaret, Antonia); *Career* serv WWII, Lt RS 8 Army; asst sec Colonial Off 1945-65; 1945-65; MOD 1965-68, Miny of Overseas Devpt 1968-72, planning inspr DOE 1972-79; *Books* William of Ockham (1985); *Clubs* Ski of GB; *Style—* John Kisch, Esq, CMG; 21 Pembroke Sq, London W8 (☎ 01 937 8590); Westwood Dunsford, Surrey (☎ 048 649 252)

KISSIN, Baron (Life Peer UK 1974), of Camden in Gtr London; Harry Kissin; s of Israel Kissin and Reusi, *née* Model; *b* 23 August 1912; *Educ* Basle Univ (LLD); *m* 1935, Ruth Deborah, da of Siegmund Samuel; 1 s, 1 da; *Career* chm: Lewis & Peat Ltd 1961-73, Experanza Int Servs plc 1970-83, Guinness Peat Gp plc 1973-79, Linfood Hldgs 1974-81, Lewis & Peat Hldgs 1982-87; life pres GPG plc (formerly Guinness Peat Gp plc) 1979; dir: Tycon Spa Venice 1974-, Transconinental Servs Gp NV 1982-86; pres Guinness Guinness Mahon Hldgs plc 1988; chm cncl Inst of Contemporary Arts 1968-75, dir Royal Opera House Covent Garden 1973-84, tstee Royal Opera House Tst 1974- (chm 1974-80); govr: Bezadel Acad of Arts & Design 1975-, Hebrew Univ of Jerusalem 1980-; cdr Ordem Nacional do Cruzeiro do Sul (Brazil) 1977, Chevalier Légion d'honneur 1981; 1300 Years Bulgaria Medal 1982; *Clubs* Reform, E India, Devonshire Sports, Public Schs; *Style—* The Rt Hon the Lord Kissin; 32 St Mary at Hill, London EC3P 3AJ (☎ 01 623 3111/9333); House of Lords, London SW1A 0AA

KISTER, Hon Mrs (Jane Elizabeth); *née* Bridge; da of Baron Bridge of Harwich, PC; *b* 1944; *m* 1978, Prof J K Kister; *Style—* The Hon Mrs Kister

KISZELY, Hon Mrs (Arabella Jane); da of 3 Baron Herschell; *b* 1955; *m* 1984, Maj John Panton Kiszely, SG, s of Dr John Kiszely, of Whitefield, Totland Bay, IOW; 1 s (Matthew b 1987); *Style—* Hon Mrs Kiszely

KITAJ, R B; s of Dr Walter Kitaj (d 1982), and Jeanne Brooks Kitaj; *b* 29 Oct 1932; *Educ* Royal Coll of Art; *m* 15 Dec 1983, Sandra Fisher; 2 s (Lem b 1958, Max b 1984), 1 da (Dominie b 1964); *Career* US Army 1955-57; artist; pt/t teacher: Camberwell Sch of Art 1961-63, Slade Sch 1963-67; visiting prof: Univ of California Berkeley 1968, UCLA 1970; one-man exhibitions: Marlborough New London Gallery 1963 and 1970, Marlborough Gall NY 1975 and 1974, LA Co Museum of Art 1965, Stedelijk Museum Amsterdam 1967, Museum of Art Cleveland 1967, Univ of California Berkeley 1967, Galerie Mikro Berlin 1969, Kestner Gesellschaft Hanover 1970, Boymans-van- Beuningen Mus Rotterdam 1970, Cincinnati Art Museum Ohio (with Jim Dine) 1973, Marlborough Fine Art 1977, 1980 and 1985; retrospective exhibitions: Hirshorn Museum Washington 1981, Cleveland Museum of Art Ohio 1981, Kuntshalle Düsseldorf 1982; Hon DLitt London 1982; memb US Inst of Arts and Letters NY 1982, Nat Acad of Design NY 1987; ARA 1984; *Style—* R B Kitaj, Esq; c/o Marlborough Fine Art Ltd, 6 Albemarle St, London W1

KITCHEN, Stanley; s of Percy Inman Kitchen, OBE (d 1963), of Solihull, and Elizabeth, *née* Green (d 1982); *b* 23 August 1913; *Educ* Rugby; *m* 27 Sept 1941, Jean, da of Albert Renwick Craig (d 1950), of Wellington, Salop; 2 da (Jennifer (Mrs Griffin) b 15 July 1942, Susan (Mrs White) b 31 July 1947); *Career* enlisted RASC 1939, 2 Lt 1940, S/Capt WO CPO (FS) 1941, Maj 1942, DADST and ADST Br Army Staff Washington DC USA 1943-46; CA; sec and chief accountant The Br Rollmakers Corpn Ltd Wolverhampton 1946-48, Birmingham ptnr Foster & Stephens 1948-65 (merged with Touche Ross & Co, ptnr 1965-81), chm Step Mgmnt Servs Ltd 1978-85, dir Cobalt (UK) Ltd 1986-; memb cncl Inst of CAs 1966-81 (pres 1976-77), memb ctee Birmingham W Midlands Soc of CAs 1951-81 (pres 1957-58), pres Birmingham CA Students Soc 1962-63; Liveryman Worshipful Co of Chartered Accountants 1977- (Court 1977-85); FCA 1937, FInstD 1980; *Recreations* golf, gardening, travel; *Clubs* Lansdowne, The Birmingham, Birmingham Chamber of Commerce; *Style—* Stanley Kitchen, Esq; 1194 Warwick Rd, Knowle, Solihull, W Midlands B93 9LL (☎ 0564 772 360)

KITCHENER, Hon Mrs Charles; Ursula Hope; da of Capt C M Luck, CMG, DSO, Royal Indian Navy; *m* 1959, Hon Charles Eaton Kitchener (d 1982), yr bro of 3 Earl Kitchener of Khartoum, *qv*; 1 da (Emma Joy b 1963); *Recreations* gardening; *Style—* The Hon Mrs Charles Kitchener; Croylands, Old Salisbury Lane, Romsey, Hants SO5I

KITCHENER OF KHARTOUM AND OF BROOME, 3 Earl (UK 1914); Henry Herbert Kitchener; TD, DL (Cheshire 1972); s of Viscount Broome (d 1928, s of 2 Earl and n of the general who won his reputation at the recapture of Khartoum); suc gf 1937; *b* 24 Feb 1919; *Educ* Winchester, Trinity Coll Cambridge; *Career* Maj RSC (TA), ret; *Clubs* Brooks's; *Style*— The Rt Hon the Earl Kitchener of Khartoum, TD, DL; Westergate Wood, Eastergate, Chichester, W Sussex PO20 6SB (☎ 0243 543061)

KITCHIN, David James Tyson; s of Norman Tyson Kitchin, and Shirley Boyd *née* Simpson; *b* 30 April 1955; *Educ* Oundle, Fitzwilliam Coll Cambridge (MA); *Career* barr Grays Inn 1977; *Recreations* golf, fishing; *Clubs* Walton Heath, Leander, Hawks (Cambridge); *Style*— David Kitchin, Esq; 22 Perrymead St, London SW6 (☎ 01 736 2161); Francis Taylor Building, Temple, London EC4 (☎ 01 353 5657)

KITCHIN, John Blurton; s of Edward Stanhope Kitchin (d 1919), and Florrie Ida Kitchin *née* Blurton (d 1969); *b* 21 Jan 1912; *Educ* Kent Coll Canterbury, St Andrews Univ (BSc);; *m* 1, 5 June 1935, Marjorie Ada (decd), da of Frederick Poulton (d 1962); 2 da (Jenifer b 1937, Carol b 1938); m 2, 26 March 1966, Eileen, da of Wilfred Jackson (decd); *Career* Industl Chemist ICI Ltd Dyestuffs Div 1955-60 industl chemist 1934-55); personnel and production dir Plastics Div 1960-65; ICI (Europa) Ltd dir and deputy chief exec 1965-72, dir Danbrit Chem Copenhagen 1967-72; ret 1972; *Recreations* gardening, cooking; *Clubs* Carlton,; *Style*— John Kitchin, Esq; Eiling Lodge, Drivers End Lane, Codicote, Herts SG4 8TP (☎ 0438 820242)

KITCHING, Henry Alan; s of Noel Kitching, JP (d 1975), and Gladys Nichols (d 1961); *b* 9 Feb 1936; *Educ* Leighton Park Reading, Peddie Inst Hightstown NJ USA; *m* 1988, Ann Margaret, *née* Britton; 2 s; *Career* serv RN Sub-Lt; stockbroker; chm Middlesbrough Warehousing Ltd; dir: Allied Provincial Securities Ltd, ST & H Nominees Ltd, Talstan Nominees Ltd; *Recreations* tennis, shooting, fishing, bridge; *Clubs* Cleveland; *Style*— Alan Kitching, Esq; Angrove House, Catton, North Yorkshire

KITCHING WALKER, Stephen; s of Ernest Smith Walker (d 1965), and Alice Kate (d 1964); *b* 22 April 1923; *Educ* Alcester GS, Gonville and Caius Cambridge (MA); *m* 1, 28 July 1951, Betty Simpson; 1 s (Philip Stephen b 1956), 1 da (Catherine b 1952); m 2, 20 Feb 1971, Yvonne Teresa, da of George Albert Theakston; *Career* Sandhurst 1943, Capt 25 Dragoons, India and Burma; slr 1949; clerk to cmmnrs 1954-, dep coroner 1954-74; fndr pres Pickering & Dist Rotary Club; Paul Harris fell 1988; *Recreations* shooting, tennis, walking; *Style*— Stephen Kitching Walker, Esq; Old Maltongate Farm, Thornton-le-Dale, Pickering, N Yorks (☎ 0751 74435); 8 Market Place, Kirbymoorside, Yorks (☎ 0751 31237)

KITSON, Gen Sir Frank Edward; GBE (1985), KCB (1980), (CBE for gallantry 1972, OBE 1968, MBE 1959), MC and Bar (1955, 1958); s of Vice-Adm Sir Henry Kitson, KBE, CB, by his w Marjorie, *née* de Pass; *b* 15 Dec 1926; *Educ* Stowe; *m* 1962, Elizabeth Janet, da of Col Charles Richard Spencer, OBE, DL; 3 da; *Career* cmmnd 2 Lt Rifle Bde 1946, BAOR 1946-53, served Kenya, Malaya, Cyprus; CO: 1 Bn Royal Green Jackets 1967-69, defence fellow Univ Coll Oxford 1969-70, Cmd 39 Inf Bde NI 1970-72, Cmdt Sch of Infantry 1972-74, RCDS 1975, GOC 2 Div (subsequently Armoured Div) 1976-78, Cmdt Staff Coll 1978-80, Col-Cmdt 2 Bn Royal Green Jackets 1979-87, dep C-in-C UKLF and inspr-gen TA 1980-82, C-in-C UKLF 1982-85, Rep Cmdt RGJ 1982-85, Hon Col Oxford Univ OTC (V) 1982-87, General 1982; ADC Gen to HM The Queen 1983-85; *Books* author of books on war incl: Gangs and Countergangs (1960), Low Intensity Operations (1971), Bunch of Five (1977), Warfare as a Whole (1987); *Style*— Gen Sir Frank Kitson, GBE, KCB, MC; c/o Lloyds Bank, Farnham, Surrey

KITSON, Hon Mrs (Ginette Molesworth); da of 2 Baron Kindersley, CBE, MC (d 1976); *b* 1924; *m* 1, 1945 (m dis 1949), Dominick Moore Sarsfield; 2 s (Simon b 1945, Shaun b 1947); m 2, 1953, Henry James Buller Kitson; *Style*— The Hon Mrs Kitson; Nine Acres, Wallcrouch, Wadhurst, E Sussex

KITSON, Sir Timothy Peter Geoffrey; s of Geoffrey Kitson; *b* 28 Jan 1931; *Educ* Charterhouse, RAC Cirencester; *m* 1959, Diana Mary Fattorini; 1 s, 2 da; *Career* former memb Thirsk RDC & N Riding Yorks CC; formerly farmed in Australia; MP (C) Richmond (Yorks) 1959-83, PPS to Parly Sec Miny of Agriculture 1960-64, Oppn Whip 1967-70, PPS to Edward Heath as PM 1970-74, to same as Ldr of Oppn 1974-75; memb House of Commons Bridge Team in match against Lords 1982; dep chm Provident Financial Gp 1982-83, chm 1983-; dir Leeds Permanent Building Soc 1983-; kt 1974; *Style*— Sir Timothy Kitson; Leases Hall, Leeming Bar, Northallerton, N Yorks (☎ 0677 2180)

KITSON, Hon Verona Vandeleur; OBE (1982, MBE mil 1960), TD; da of 3 Baron Airedale, DSO, MC (d 1958); *b* 28 Sept 1920; *Career* serv WWII as Jr Cdr ATS; Maj WRAC (TA); chm Riding for the Disabled Assoc 1970-82; formerly JP; Liberty of Peterborough; *Recreations* riding; *Style*— The Hon Verona Kitson, OBE, TD; Pasture House, N Luffenham, Oakham, Rutland

KITT, Stanley; s of William Edward Kitt (d 1945), of Blackpool, and Lavinia, *née* Harrington (d 1971); *b* 10 Oct 1910; *Educ* Elementary Sch; *m* 20 Sept 1937, Kathleen, da of Alfred Mitchell (d 1957), of Blackpool; 2 s (Stanley b 1951, Michael b 1960), 4 da (Lavinia b 1940, Kathleen b 1942, Ann b 1945, Susan b 1948); *Career* chm: Daintee Chocolate Confectionary Co (Blackpool) Ltd, Keenlift Ltd, S K Daintee (Hldgs) Ltd, Daintee (Canada) Ltd, Sterling Candy Inc, Clifton Cash & Carry Ltd; *Recreations* gardening; *Clubs* Directors; *Style*— Stanley Kitt, Esq; Green Ridges, 99 Ballam Rd, Lytham St Annes, Lancs FY8 4LF (☎ 0253 735513); Daintee Choc Cfy Co (Blackpool) Ltd, Clifton road, Marton, Blackpool FY4 4QB (☎ 0253 61021-5, telex 67679 DAINTE G, fax 0253 792006)

KITTEL, Gerald Anthony; s of Francis William Berthold Kittel of Faraway, South View Rd, Pinner Hill, Middx and Eileen Winifred, *née* Maybanks (d 1973); *b* 24 Feb 1947; *Educ* Merchant Taylors', Univ of Poitiers (History Diploma), Ealing Poly; *m* 26 April 1975, Jean Samantha *née* Beveridge; 2 s (Ashley b 1976, Christian b 1969), 1 da (Natalie b 1979); *Career* md: Harrison Agency; MInstM; memb Inst of Practioners in Advertising, Int Advertising Assoc; *Recreations* antique furniture collection, squash, tennis; *Clubs* St James, Park Place, Old Merchant Taylors' Society; *Style*— Gerald Kittel, Esq; Valence End, Hosey Hill, French St, Westerham, Kent TN16 1PN; 20 Lime Ct, Gipsy Lane, Putney, London SW15 5RJ; The Harrison Agency, 2/4 Fitzroy St, London W1A 1AT

KITTO, Rt Hon Sir Frank Walters; AC (1983), KBE (1955), PC (1963), KC (1942); s of James Walters Kitto, OBE (d 1955), and Adi Lilian Kitto (d 1927); *b* 30 July 1903; *Educ* N Sydney HS, Sydney Univ (BA, LLB); *m* 1928, Eleanor May (d 1982), da of William Henry Howard (d 1942); 3 da (and 1 decd); *Career* Crown Slr's Off NSW 1921-27, barr NSW 1927, Justice High Ct of Australia 1950-70 (ret), chm Aust Press Cncl 1976-82 (ret), chllr Univ of New England 1970-81 (ret); Hon LLD (Sydney Univ) 1982; Hon DLitt (new England Univ) 1982;; *Style*— The Rt Hon Sir Frank Kitto, AC, KBE, QC; Unit 18, Autumn Lodge Retirement Village, Armidale, NSW 2350, Australia

KITZINGER, Uwe; CBE (1980); *b* 12 April 1928; *Educ* Watford GS, Balliol and New Coll Oxford; *m* 1952, Sheila Helena Elizabeth, *née* Webster; 5 da; *Career* pres union Oxford Univ 1950, Cncl of Europe 1951-56, fell Nuffield Coll 1956-76; fndr ed Jnl of Common Market Studies 1961-; prof Paris Univ 1970-73; advsr to vice pres of EEC Cmmn i/c external rels Brussels 1973-75; dean Euro Inst of Business Admin Fontainebleau 1976-80; dir Oxford Centre for Mgmnt Studies 1980-84; fndr chm Major Projects Assoc 1981-86, pres Int Assoc of Macro Engrg Socs 1987-, Oxfordshire Radio Ltd 1988; cncl memb: RIIA 1976-85; OXFAM 1981-85; pres Templeton Coll Oxford 1984-; Hon LLD 1986; *Books* German Electoral Politics (1960), The Challenge of the Common Market (1961), Diplomacy and Persuasion (1973); *Recreations* sailing (ketch Anne of Cleves); *Clubs* Reform, Royal Thames Yacht, Utd Oxford and Cambridge; *Style*— Uwe Kitzinger, Esq, CBE; Standlake Manor, Witney, Oxon (☎ 086 731 266); La Rivière, 11100 Bages, France (☎ 68 412960)

KLARE, Hugh John; CBE (1967); s of Frederick Klare (d 1973), and Ella Helen Klare (d 1970) came to England from Austria in 1932; *b* 22 June 1916, (Berndorf, Austria); *Educ* Gymnasium Berndorf, Geneva Univ; *m* 18 Sept 1946, Eveline Alice Maria, da of Lt-Col James Dodds Rankin, MBE (d 1965); *Career* Maj (GSO II), served Middle East; dep dir Economic Organisation Div, Control Commn for Germany; criminologist and penologist, dir Howard League for Penal Reform 1950-59 and 1961-71; seconded to Cncl of Europe Strasbourg: dep dir Divn of Crime Problems 1959-61, head Divn of Crime Problems 1971-72; First Sperry & Hutchinson lectr, LSE 1966-, Extra Mural lectr in Criminology, London Univ 1961-71; regular columnist Justice of the Peace 1971-85; memb Parole Bd 1972-74, Glos Probation Ctee 1972-86, chm Tstees, Glos Arthritis Tst 1984-; *Books* Anatomy of Prison (1960), Delinquency and Social Control (1966), People in Prison (1972);; *Style*— Hugh Klare, CBE; 34 Herriots Ct, St George's Crescent, Droitwich Spa, Worcs (☎ 0905 776316)

KLEANTHOUS, Christodoulos Photios; s of Photios Kleanthous (d 1971), and Zenovia Hatgipanayi (d 1977); *b* 1 Mar 1944, (Cyprus); *Educ* Upton House Sch Hackney E London; graduated from Sir John Cass Coll, London Univ 1967 (BSc); *m* 14 Nov 1969, Diana Margaret, da of George Smith ('Gus'-the cartoonist), of Abbotsfield, Fitzroy Rd, Fleet, Hants; 1 s (Andrea George b 1976), 1 da (Anna Zinovia b 1971); *Career* advertising; exec dir McCann-Erickson Advertising Ltd 1972- (bd memb 1979); *Recreations* swimming, hill walking; *Clubs* RAC, Pall Mall; *Style*— Christodoulos Kleanthous, Esq; McCann-Erickson Advertising Ltd, 36 Howland St, London W1A 1AT (☎ 01 580 6690)

KLEEMAN, David George; s of Jack Kleeman (d 1984), and Ruth, *née* Stephany (d 1981); *b* 20 August 1942; *Educ* St Paul's, Trinity Hall Cambridge (MA); *m* 1968, Manuela Rachel, da of Edouard Cori, Avenue de Wagram, Paris; 4 da (Susanna b 1970, Nicole b 1973, Julie b 1974, Jenny b 1978); *Career* dir Spong Hldgs plc, The Bridgend Gp plc; dir: Daman Investment Co (London) Ltd; Daman Financial Services Ltd; slr; conslt to and former sr ptnr of Pickering Kenyou; dir: The English Stage Co; *Recreations* fishing, reading, theatre; *Clubs* MCC; *Style*— David Kleeman, Esq; 141 Hamilton Terrace, London NW8 9QS (☎ 01 624 2335); office - 22 Oldbury Place, London W1M 3AL (☎ 01 935 4160)

KLEEMAN, Harry; CBE (1984); s of Max Kleeman (d 1947); *b* 2 Mar 1928; *Educ* Westminster, Trinity Coll Cambridge; *m* 1955, Avril, da of Dr Maurice Lees (d 1974); 2 s (John, Daniel), 2 da (Jacqueline, Amanda); *Career* chm Kleeman Plastics Gp 1968, former pres British Plastics Fedn; cncl memb British Plastics Federation 1977-85, pres 1979-80; cncl memb CBI representing small firms; chm CBI small firms cncl 1988; former chm: mgmnt ctee of Polymer Engrg Directorate, Plastic Processing EDC of NEDO; Freeman City of London, Liveryman Worshipful Co of Horners (memb Ct); fell Plastics & Rubber Inst (chm 1985-87, memb cncl 1984-); chm Advsy Ctee on Telecommunications for Small Businesses 1986-88; *Recreations* amateur radio, riding; *Clubs* RSA; *Style*— Harry Kleeman, Esq; 41 Frognal, London NW3 (☎ 01 794 3366), High Trees, Friday St, Dorking, Surrey (☎ 0306 730 678)

KLEIN, Bernat; CBE (1973); s of Lipot Klein (d 1964), of Senta, Yugoslavia, and Serena, *née* Weiner (d 1944); *b* 6 Nov 1922; *Educ* Bezalel Sch of Art Jerusalem, Univ of Leeds; *m* 31 March 1951, Margaret Soper; 1 s (Jonathan b 1953), 2 da (Gillian b 1957, Shelley b 1963) ; *Career* designer: Tootal 1948-49, Munrospun 1949-51; chm and md: Bernat Klein Ltd Colourcraft 1962; md: Bernat Klein Ltd 1962-66, Bernat Klein Design Ltd 1966-81; exhibitions: E-SU 1965, Alwyn Gal 1967, O'Hana Gal 1969, Assoc of Arts Gal Capetown, Goodmant Gal Johannesburg and O'Hanna Gal 1972; FCSD; *Publications* Eye for Colour (1966), Design Matters (1976); *Recreations* reading, tennis; *Style*— Bernat Klein, Esq, CBE; High Sunderland, Galashiels (☎ 0750 20730)

KLEINPOPPEN, Prof Hans Johann Willi; s of Gerhard Kleinpoppen (d 1985), and Emmi, *née* Maass; *b* 30 Sept 1928; *Educ* HS W Germany, Univ of Giessen Germany, Univ of Tübingen; *Career* Privat-Dozent Univ of Tübingen 1967, visiting fell and prof Univs of Colorado and Columbia 1967-68; Stirling Univ: prof of experimental physics 1968- head of physics dept 1972-74, dir of Inst of Atomic Physics 1974-81, head of atomic and molecular physics res unit 1981-; fell of Genter for theoretical studies Univ of Miami 1973, visiting prof Univ of Bielefeld 1978-79; chm of various int conferences on atomic and molecular physics; co-ed Monograph Series on Physics of Atoms and Molecules, ed of eleven books on atomic and molecular physics; FRAS 1974, FAmPhysSoc 1972, FInstP 1969, FRSE 1987; *Recreations* music, fine art; *Style*— Prof Hans Kleinpoppen; 27 Kenningknowes Rd, Stirling, Scotland; Atomic and Molecular Physics Research Unit, Univ of Stirling, Stirling, Scotland (☎ 0786 73 171 ext 2067)

KLEINWORT, Joan Nightingale; *née* Crossley; MBE (1945), JP (1951), DL (West Sussex 1983); da of Dr Arthur William Crossley, CMG, CBE, FRS, LLD (d 1927, the first director of Porton Station 1916, researching poison gas), and Muriel (d 1973, having m 2, Col Sir John Wallace Pringle, CB, RE), da of Ralph Lamb, of Liverpool; *b* 3 April 1907; *Educ* St Felix Sch Southwold; *m* 29 Dec 1932, Ernest Greverus Kleinwort (d 1977), 4 s of Sir Alexander Drake Kleinwort, 1 Bt (d 1935); 1 s (Sir Kenneth Drake Kleinwort, 3 Bt, *qv*), 1 da (Gillian Mawdesley (Mrs Warren) b 1937); *Recreations* gardening; *Style*— Mrs Joan Kleinwort, MBE, JP, DL; Heaselands, Haywards Heath, W Sussex (☎ 0444 454181)

KLEINWORT, Sir Kenneth Drake; 3 Bt (UK 1909), of Bolnore, Cuckfield, Sussex; s of Ernest Greverus Kleinwort (d 1977, chm Kleinwort Benson Ltd 1961-66, 2 s of Sir Alexander Kleinwort, 1 Bt, who was ptnr of Kleinwort Sons & Co); succeeded unc, Sir Alexander Kleinwort, 2 Bt, who d 1983; *b* 28 May 1935; *Educ* Eton, Grenoble Univ; *m* 1, 1959, Lady Davina Rose Pepys (d 1973), da of 7 Earl of Cottenham (d 1968); 1 s (Richard b 1960), 1 da (Marina b 1962); m 2, 1973, Madeleine Hamilton, da of Ralph Taylor, of Buenos Aires; 2 s (Alexander b 1975, Michael b 1977), 1 da (Selina b 1981); *Heir* s, Richard Drake Kleinwort; *Career* pres Interalia Leasing LTDA Chile; dir: Heaselands Estates Ltd, Neubar SA Geneva, Trebol Int Corpn USA, Kleinwort Benson Gp plc, Banque Kleinwort Benson SA Geneva, Kleinwort Benson (Europe) SA Brussels; cncl memb WWF Int, Switzerland, cncl memb and tres Wildfowl Tst Slimbridge, memb environment ctee RSA, fell World Scout Fndn Geneva; *Recreations* travel, photography, skiing, shooting, gardening; *Style—* Sir Kenneth Kleinwort, 3 Bt; La Massellaz, 1126 Vaux-sur-Morges, Switzerland; Banque Kleinwort Benson SA, 2 Place du Rhône, Geneva

KLEINWORT, Richard Drake; s and h of Sir Kenneth Kleinwort, 3 Bt, by his 1 w, Lady Davina Pepys; *b* 4 Nov 1960; *Educ* Stowe, Exeter Univ (BA); *Career* banker Deutschebank A G Frankfurt; *Recreations* photography, travel, sports (in general); *Clubs* WWF (1001), World Scout Foundation; *Style—* Richard Kleinwort, Esq; c/o Sir Kenneth Kleinwort, 3Bt, 'La Massellaz' 1111 Vaux-sur-Morges, Vaud, Switzerland

KLIMES, Michal Vladimir; s of Prof Vladimir Klimes of Prague; *b* 9 July 1944; *Educ* Inst of Chem Technol Prague; *m* 1966, Radana Zdena, *née* Egermeyer; 2 children; *Career* gp tech dir Thomas & Green Hldgs Ltd; dir: Fourstones Paper Mills Co Ltd, Thomas Green Ltd; *Recreations* tennis; *Style—* Michal Klimes, Esq; The Cedars, Stratford Drive, Wooburn Green, Bucks (☎ 062 85 26576)

KLOOTWIJK, Jaap; s of Jacob Leendert, of Rotterdam, and Woutrina Johanna Klootwijk, *née* Boer, of Rotterdam; *b* 16 Nov 1932; *Educ* Rotterdam GS, Delft Univ Holland (MSc); *Career* Lieut Royal Netherlands Navy 1956-58; Shell Res Ltd 1958-64, Shell Refining and Marketing Co Ltd 1964-66, E African Oil Refineries Ltd 1967-69, Shell Int Petroleum My BV 1970-73, Shell Refining and Marketing Co Ltd 1974-76, Shell Int Petroleum Co Ltd 1976-79, md Shell Int Gas Ltd 1979-82, md: Shell UK Oil 1983-88, Shell UK Ltd 1983-88; chm: UK Oil Pipelines Ltd 1983-88, The Flyfishers Co Ltd 1985-; FInst Pet 1983; FRSA 1986; *Recreations* deer-stalking, shooting, fishing, reading; *Clubs* The Flyfishers (pres 1985-87); *Style—* Jaap Klootwijk, Esq; Shell-Mex House, Strand, London WC2R 0DX (☎ 01 257 3765, telex 22858 Shell G)

KLUG, Sir Aaron; s of Lazar Klug, of Durban (d 1971), of Bella Silin (d 1932); *b* 11 August 1926; *Educ* Durban HS, Univ of the Witwatersrand (BSc), Univ of Cape Town (MSc), Univ of Cambridge (PhD, ScD); *m* 8 July 1948, Liebe, da of Alexander Bobrow (d 1983), of Cape Town; 2 s (Adam Brian Joseph b 1954, David Rupert b 1963); *Career* Nuffield res fell Birbeck Coll London 1954-57, ldr virus res project 1958-61; Cambridge Univ: molecular biol 1962-, fell Peterhouse 1962-, dir of natural sci studies 1962-85, jt head structural studies 1978-86, dir of laboratory 1986-; awards: Heineken Prize Royal Netherlands Acad 1974, Louisa Gross Horwitz Prize Columbia Univ 1981, Nobel Prize for Chemistry 1982; hon DSc Chicago 1978, Columbia 1978, Dr hc Strasburg 1978, hon Dr Stockholm 1980, hon fell Trinity Coll Cambridge 1983; hon DSc: Witwatersrand 1984, Hull 1985, St Andrews 1987; hon PhD Jerusalem 1984, hon FRCP 1986; (Baly Medal 1987); memb Biochem Soc (Harden Medal 1985), FRS 1969 (Copley Medal 1985); kt 1988; *Recreations* reading, gardening; *Style—* Sir Aaron Klug; MRC Laboratory of Molecular Biology, Hills Rd, Cambridge CB2 2QH (☎ 0223 248011)

KLYBERG, (Charles) John; *see*: Fulham, Bishop of

KNAPMAN, Paul Anthony; s of Frederick Ethelbert Knapman, of Torquay, Devon, and Myra, *née* Smith; *b* 5 Nov 1944; *Educ* Epsom Coll, King's Coll London Univ, St George's Hospital Medical Sch (MB BS, DMJ), Inns of Court Sch of Law (barrister, Gray's Inn); *m* 1970, Penelope Jane, da of Lt-Cdr Michael Cox, of Torquay, Devon; 1 s, 3 da; *Career* medical practitioner and barrister; Surgn Lt RNR 1970; HM coroner Inner West London at Westminster Coroners Ct 1980-; hon lectr medical jurisprudence: St George's, United Hosps of Guy's and St Thomas's, St Mary's, Charing Cross and Westminster, Middx and Univ Coll Hosp; memb Lloyds and company dir; MRCS, LRCP; *Books* The Law and Practice on Coroners (jtly, 3 edn 1985); *Recreations* squash rackets, sailing, shooting; *Clubs* Athenaeum, Royal Torbay Yacht; *Style—* Paul Knapman, Esq; c/o Westminster Coroners Ct, Horseferry Rd, London SW1 (☎ 01 834 6515)

KNAPMAN, Roger Maurice; s of Harry Arthur Blackmore Knapman of North Tawton, Devon and Joan Margo, *née* Densham (d 1970); *b* 20 Feb 1944; *Educ* St Aubyn's Sch Tiverton, All Hallows Sch Lyme Regis, RAC Circencester; *m* 25 March 1967, Carolyn Trebell, da of Sidney George Eastman of Appledore near Bideford, N Devon; 1 s (William b 1970), 1 da (Rebecca b 1971); *Career* chartered surveyor (FRICS 1967); *Recreations* fishing, snooker; *Style—* Roger Knapman, Esq; 31 Tufton Court, Tufton Stret, London SW1; c/o Stroud Conservative Association, Carlton Gardens, London Road, Stroud, Glos

KNAPP, Edward Ronald; CBE (1979); s of Percy Charles Knapp (d 1979), and Elsie Maria, *née* Edwards (d 1978); *b* 10 May 1919; *Educ* Cardiff HS, St Catharine's Coll Cambridge (MA), Harvard Business Sch (AMP); *m* 16 April 1942, Vera Mary, da of Capt William Stephenson, of Cardiff; 2 s (Ian b 1946, William b 1951), 2 da (Vanessa b 1956, Lucille b 1959); *Career* RNVR Lt-Cdr 1940-46, HMS Aurora 1941-44, US Naval Res Est Washington DC 1944-46, Admty 1946; md: British Timken 1969-79 (joined 1946), Timken Europe 1979-84; dir Timken Co USA 1976; rugby capt: Univ of Cambridge 1940-41, Northampton RFC 1948; played for Wales 1940; govr Nene Coll 1948-89, pres Northants RFC 1986-88; *Recreations* gardening, golf, world travel; *Clubs* East India, Northants & County, Hawks Cambridge; *Style—* Ron Knapp, Esq, CBE; The Elms, 1 Millway, Duston, Northampton (☎ 0604 584737)

KNARESBOROUGH, Bishop of, 1986-; Rt Rev Malcolm James Menin; s of The Rev James Nicholas Menin (d 1970) Vicar of Shiplake, Oxon and Doreen *née* Dolamore (d 1967); *b* 26 Sept 1932; *Educ* Dragon Sch, St Edward's, Univ Coll Oxford (MA), Cuddesdon Coll; *m* 11 Oct 1958, Jennifer Mary, da of Andrew Patrick Cullen (d 1966); 1 s (Andrew b 1961), 3 da (Catherine b 1959, Brigid b 1963, Sarah b 1965); *Career* deacon 1957 Portsmouth, priest 1958; asst curate Holy Spirit Southsea 1957-59, asst curate Fareham Hants 1959-62; vicar St Mary Magdalene with St James Norwich 1962-86; rural dean Norwich East 1981-86; hon canon Norwich Cathedral 1982; consecrated Bishop of Knaresborough 1986; *Recreations* carpentry, walking, gardening, photography, wine making; *Style—* The Rt Rev the Bishop of Knaresborough; 16 Shaftesbury Avenue, Leeds LS8 1DT (☎ 0532 664800)

KNATCHBULL, Hon Michael-John Ulick; s of 7 Baron Brabourne, and Countess Mountbatten of Burma, *qqv*; *b* 24 May 1950; *Educ* Gordonstoun, Reading Univ; *m* 1985, Melissa Clare, only da of Judge Sir John Owen, of Bickerstaff House, Idlicote, Shipston-on-Stour, Warwicks; 1 da (Kelly b 1988); *Style—* The Hon Michael-John Knatchbull; 9 Queen's Elm Square, London SW3 6ED

KNATCHBULL, Hon Philip Wyndham Ashley; s of 7 Baron Brabourne and Countess Mountbatten of Burma, *qqv*; *b* 2 Dec 1961; *Educ* Gordonstoun, Kent Univ, London Int Film Sch; *Career* film maker; *Style—* The Hon Philip Knatchbull; Flat 8, 92 Elm Park Gardens, London SW10 9PE

KNEEBONE, Peter Jack Georges; s of John Kneebone (d 1963), of St John's Wood, London, and Léontine Marie Julie Augustine, *née* Marchau (d 1984); *b* 28 April 1923; *Educ* Christ's Coll Finchley, Univ Coll Oxford (MA); *m* 1, 1957 (m dis 1976), Catherine McCallum, da of the late William Shanks; 1 s (Jonathan b 1958), 3 da (Anna (Mrs Pearce) b 1954, Sophie (Mrs Wood) b 1960, Lucy b 1963); m 2, 1976, Francoise, da of the late Pierre Jollant; *Career* Lt RNVR, Br Naval Liaison Offr Italy 1944-45, SW Europe Surrender Cmmn 1945, Naval Broadcasting Rep ME 1945-46; Festival of Britain: asst to dir exhibitions 1948-50, W Euro rep 1950-51; TV prodr BBC 1952-54, co-ordinator postgraduate studies Central Sch of Art and Design 1967-74; graphic designer illustrator and conslt 1952-; major clients incl: NEDO, IOD, Cambridge Univ Press, Arts Cncl of Ireland, Miny Res and Culture (France); design conslt Nat Fund for Crippling Diseases 1969-74; Int Cncl of Graphic Design Assoc: chm Cmmn Int Signs and Symbols 1965-79, del UNESCO 1965-, sec gen 1977-79, pres 1979-81; FCSD, FSTD, FRSA; *Books* Look Before You Elope (1952), Sexes and Sevens (1953), Oiling the Wheels (1957), Signalétique (1980); Co-author: How To Interview (1975), How to Be Interviewed (1980); *Recreations* collecting popular art and artifacts, writing; *Style—* Peter Kneebone, Esq; 27 rue Danton, 93310 Le Pré-Saint-Gervais, France; 5 Lawman Ct, Kew Rd, Richmond, Surrey TW9 3EF

KNEIPP, Hon Sir (Joseph Patrick) George; s of A G Kneipp (decd); *b* 13 Nov 1922; *Educ* Downlands Coll, Univ of Queensland;; *m* 1948, Ada, da of C Cattermole; 2 s, 1 da; *Career* serv WWII; barr Queensland 1950-69, judge of Supreme Court of Queensland 1969-, northern judge 1970-; chllr James Cook Univ of North Qld 1974-; kt 1982; *Style—* The Hon Sir George Kneipp; 20 Kenilworth Ave, Hyde Park, Townsville, Qld 4812, Australia

KNIGHT, Sir Allan Walton; CMG (1960); s of Gustavus Walton Knight (decd); *b* 26 Feb 1910; *Educ* Hobart Tech Coll, Tas Univ; *m* 1936, Margaret Janet, da of Howard Buchanan, MBE; 2 s, 1 da; *Career* chief engr Public Works Dept Tas 1937-46, chief cmmr Hydro-Electric Cmmn Tas 1946-77, cmmr Aust Univs Cmmn 1966-74, cmmr Tasman Bridge Restoration Cmmn 1975-80; Peter Nicol Russell Medal Inst of Engrs Australia 1963, Kernot Memorial Medal Melbourne Univ 1963, Chapman Award Aust Welding Inst 1974; kt 1970; *Style—* Sir Allan Knight, CMG; 64 Waimea Ave, Hobart, Tas 7005, Australia (☎ Hobart 25 1498)

KNIGHT, Andrew Stephen Bower; s of M W B Knight, and S E F Knight; *b* 1 Nov 1939; *m* 1, 1966 (m dis), Victoria Catherine Brittain; 1 s (Casimir); m 2, 1975, Begum Sabiha Rumani Malik; 2 da; *Career* ed The Economist 1974-86, dir Ballet Rambert 1987- (chm 1984-87), dir Tandem Computers Inc 1984-; Daily Telegraph plc: chief exec 1986-, ed-in-chief 1987-; dir Reuters Hldgs plc 1988-; memb cncl: Friends of Covent Garden 1981-, Templeton Coll Oxford 1984-; *Clubs* Brook's, Royal Automobile; *Style—* Andrew Knight, Esq; 181 Marsh Wall, London E14 9SR

KNIGHT, Sir Arthur William; s of Arthur Frederick Knight; *b* 29 Mar 1917; *Educ* Tottenham Co Sch, LSE; *m* 1, 1945, Beatrice, *née* Oppenheim (d 1968); 1 s, 3 da; m 2, 1972, Sheila Whiteman; *Career* chm: Courtaulds 1975-79, Nat Enterprise Bd 1979-80; non-exec dir Dunlop Hldgs 1981-84 (resigned Nov 1984); vice-chm Cncl RIIA until 1986; kt 1975; *Style—* Sir Arthur Knight; Charlton End, Singleton, W Sussex PO18 0HX; Flat 20, Valiant House, Vicarage Crescent, London SW11 3LU (☎ 01 228 3026)

KNIGHT, Brien Walter; s of Edward Alfred Knight, of Sussex, and Winifred, *née* Stolworthy (d 1976); *b* 27 June 1929; *Educ* Woodhouse GS, Sir John Cass, London Univ; *m* 1, 1955, Annette, da of Alfred Scotten (d 1964), of Barnet; 1 s (Darrell b 1963), 4 da (Carolyn b 1961, Judith b 1964, Emma b 1966, Sophie b 1966); m 2, Maria Antoinette (Rita), da of Abraham Van Der Meer (d 1958), of Holland; *Career* dir: Knight Strip Metals Ltd 1951 (chm 1970-), Sterling Springs Ltd 1952-, Knight Precision Wire Ltd 1979- (chm 1979-); Precision Metals NV (Belgium) 1973-; chm Knuway Investmts Ltd 1973-, FIOD; *Recreations* DIY, sailing; *Style—* Brien Knight, Esq; Millview, 3 Hawthorn Grove, Barnet Rd, Arkley, Herts EN5 3JZ; Knuway House, Cranborne Rd, Potters Bar, Herts EN6 3JL

KNIGHT, Capt Christopher Moreton; s of Moreton Thorpe Knight, JP (d 1982), of Cooling Castle, Cliffe, Kent, and Laura, *née* Noble (d 1964); *b* 31 May 1934; *Educ* Felsted, Sir John Cass Coll London (Master Mariner); *m* 26 Nov 1987, Janet Vivien, da of Alfred Arthur Aston (d 1984), of Sidcup, Kent; 1 s (Peter b 1989); *Career* Merchant Navy; dir J P Knight Ltd (tugowners) 1964- (vice-chm 1982-), md J P Knight (offshore) Ltd 1981-; chm Br Tugowners Assoc 1974-76, chm ropes cordage and netting standards ctee and memb chm's advsy panel Br Standards Inst 1981, cncl memb CBI 1982-83; chm Shaftesbury Homes Arethusa 1973-, hon tres Victoria League for Cwlth Friendship 1988, bd memb Cwlth Tst 1989; Freeman City of London 1973, Liveryman Hon Co of Master Mariners 1973, Freeman Worshipful Co of Watermen and Lightemen 1985; memb Nautical Inst 1975; *Recreations* wood carving, bee-keeping; *Clubs* Naval and Military, Cwlth Tst; *Style—* Capt Christopher Knight; 47 St Georges Square, London SW1V 3QN (☎ 01 821 8675); Cooling Castle, Cliffe-at-Hoo, Kent ME3 8DT; 348 High St, Rochester, Kent ME1 1DH (☎ 0634 826 633, fax 0634 829 093, telex 965016)

KNIGHT, Hon Mrs (Elizabeth Angela Veronica Rose); *née* Nall-Cain; da of 2 Baron Brocket (d 1967); *b* 3 May 1938; *m* 1, 1958 (m dis 1969), 6 Marquess of Headfort; 1 s (Christopher b 1959), 2 da (Rosanagh b 1961, Olivia b 1963); m 2, 1970 (m dis 1987), William Murless Knight; 1 s (Peregrine b 1971); *Career* colour cnsllr for Isle of Man; *Style—* The Hon Mrs Knight; Northfield, Kirk Andreas, Isle of Man (☎ 0624 880452)

KNIGHT, Geoffrey Egerton; CBE (1970); s of Arthur Egerton Knight, and Florence Gladys, *née* Clarke; *b* 25 Feb 1921; *Educ* Stubbington House, Brighton Coll Sussex; *m* 1947, Evelyn Bugle; 2 da; *Career* RM 1939-46; joined Bristol Aeroplane Co Ltd 1953, dir Bristol Aircraft Ltd 1956; dir BAC Ltd 1964-77, vice-chm 1972-76; Fenchurch Insur Hldgs Ltd 1979- (chm 1980); dir: GPA Gp Ltd 1976-, Guinness Peat Gp plc

1976- (dep chm 1987), Trafalgar House plc 1980-; *Books* Concorde: the inside story (1976); *Clubs* Boodle's, White's, Turf; *Style*— Geoffrey Knight, Esq, CBE; 33 Smith Terrace, London SW3 (☎ 01 352 5391); Fenchurch Insurance Holdings Ltd, 136 Minories, London EC3N 1QN (☎ 01 488 2388, telex 884442)

KNIGHT, Greg(ory); MP (Cons) Derby North 1983-; s of Albert George Knight, of Leicester, and Isabella, *née* Bell; *b* 4 April 1949; *Educ* Alderman Newton's GS Leicester, Coll of Law Guildford; *Career* slr 1973; Leicester City cllr 1976-79, Leicestershire county cllr 1977-83, former chm Public Protection Ctee, former dir Leicester Theatre Tst Ltd (former chm of fin ctee); pps to David Mellor; Min of State at Foreign Off June 1987-88, pps to Min of Health 1988-; journalist, owns a recording studio; *Books* Westminster Words (1988); *Recreations* arts, especially music; *Style*— Greg Knight, Esq, MP; House of Commons, London SW1

KNIGHT, Maj (Hubert) Guy Broughton; MC (1941); s of Lt-Col F Guy Knight, MC (d 1956), of Aston Hall, Stone, Staffordshire, and Edith Rosmond, *née* Broughton-Adderley (d 1949); *b* 9 April 1919; *Educ* Eton, Sandhurst; *m* 8 July 1944, Hester, da of Arthur Thomas Loyd, OBE (Lord-Lt Berks, d 1944); 2 da (Henrietta Catherine b 15 Dec 1946, Celia Elizabeth (The Lady Vestey) b 11 Oct 1949); *Career* Coldstream Guards 1938-51, Western Desert Campaign 1940-43, (wounded four times), Staff Coll 1944, G2 Ops London Dist 1947-50; gen cmmr Income Tax 1950- (chm 1979-88); farmer; tres NFU 1982-89; former chm Wantage RDC, former memb Oxfordshire CC; *Recreations* shooting, fishing; *Clubs* Whites, Bucks, Pratts; *Style*— Maj Guy Knight, MC; Lockinge Manor, Wantage, Oxfordshire (☎ 0235 833 266); West Lockinge Farm, Wartage, Oxfordshire (☎ 0235 833 275, car tel 0860 527 044)

KNIGHT, Sir Harold Murray; KBE (1980), DSC; s of W H P Knight; *b* 13 August 1919; *Educ* Scotch Coll Melbourne, Melbourne Univ (MCom); *m* 1951, Gwenyth, da of F A Pennington; 4 s, 1 da; *Career* Lt AIF 1940-43, Lt RANVR 1943-45; Cwlth Bank of Australia 1946-55, res & statistics dept Int Monetary Fund 1955-59; govr and chm Reserve Bank of Aust 1975-82 (res economist 1960, asst mangr 1962-64, mangr 1964-68, govr and dep chm 1968-75); dir Western Mining Corpn Ltd; *Style*— Sir Harold Knight, KBE, DSC; 21 Hazelbank Rd, Wollstonecraft, NSW 2065, Australia

KNIGHT, Jeffrey Russell; s of Thomas Edgar Knight (d 1972), of Bristol, and Ivy Cissie, *née* Russell; *b* 1 Oct 1936; *Educ* Bristol Cathedral Sch, St Peter's Coll Oxford (MA); *m* 12 Dec 1959, Judith Marion Delver, da of Reginald Delver Podger (d 1968), of Weston-Super-Mare; 4 da (Ketherine Anne b 1964, Elizabeth Jane b 1967, Emma Frances b 1968, Alison Mary b 1972); *Career* articled clerk Fuller Wise Fisher & Co 1962-66, CA 1966; The Stock Exchange: joined quotations dept 1967, head of dept 1973, dep chief exec 1976, chief exec 1982-; special advsr to Dept of Trade on the EEC; memb CAs Livery Co; FCA, FRSA; *Recreations* cricket, music; *Clubs* Brooks's; *Style*— Jeffrey Knight, Esq; Robin Haye, The Dr, Godalming, Surrey (☎ 048 68 24399); The Stock Exchange, London EC2 (☎ 01 588 2355)

KNIGHT, Dame (Joan Christabel) Jill; DBE (1985, MBE 1964) MP (C) Birmingham Edgbaston 1966-; da of A E Christie (d 1933); *b* 1927,July; *Educ* Fairfield Sch, King Edward GS for Girls Birmingham; *m* 1947, Montague Knight, s of Leslie Knight of Harpole Hall Northampton; 2 s; *Career* lectr, broadcaster; memb Northampton Borough Cncl 1956-66; contested (C) Northampton 1959 and 1964; memb Select Ctee on Race Relations and Immigration 1969-72, chm Cons backbench ctee health and social services 1981-, memb Cncl Europe 1977-, chm Lords and Commons All-Pty Child Protection Gp, pres W Midlands Cons Political Centre 1980-83; dep chm: exec 1922 Ctee, Select Ctee Home Affrs 1980-84; *Style*— Dame Jill Knight DBE, MP; House of Commons, London SW1

KNIGHT, Air Chief Marshal Sir Michael William Patrick; KCB (1983, CB 1980), AFC (1964); s of William and Dorothy Knight; *b* 23 Nov 1932; *Educ* (BA); *m* 1967, Patricia Ann, *née* Davies; 1 s, 2 da; *Career* ADC No 1 Gp RAF Strike Cmd 1980-82, air memb for Supply and Orgn 1983-86; UK mil rep NATO 1986-89, Air ADC to HM The Queen 1986-; pres RAFRU, CSRFU; memb RFU 1977-, cncl memb Taunton Sch 1987-; Hon Dlitt; memb RUSI 1984-87, FRAeS; *Recreations* rugby, other sports, music, writing; *Clubs* RAF; *Style*— Air Chief Marshal Sir Michael Knight, KCB, AFC , ADC; c/o Ministry of Defence, Whitehall, London SW1A 2HB

KNIGHT, Hon Mrs Priscilla; *née* Dodson; da of 2 Baron Monk Bretton, CB (d 1933); *b* 1914; *m* 1935, Maj Claude Thorburn Knight; 1 s (William), 3 da (Patricia, Jane, Sarah); *Style*— The Hon Mrs Knight; Idlehurst, Birch Grove, Horsted Keynes, Sussex RH17 7BT (☎ 082574 224)

KNIGHT, Richard James; s of R W Knight (d 1966), of Cheam Surrey, and Mrs R W Knight, *née* Spire (d 1966); *b* 19 July 1915; *Educ* Dulwich Coll, Trinity Coll Cambridge (MA); *m* 1953, Hilary Marian, da of Rev Frank Wilkinson Argyle (d 1969), of Sevenoaks Kent; 2 s (Richard, John), 1 da (Susan); *Career* housemaster Marlborough Coll Wiltshire 1948-56, headmaster: Oundle Sch Northants 1956-68, Monkton Combe Sch Bath 1968-78, JP; *Recreations* cricket, golf; *Clubs* MCC, Jesters; *Style*— Richard Knight, Esq, JP; Sherwood, 123 Midford Rd, Bath BA2 5RX (☎ 0225 832276)

KNIGHT, (Warburton) Richard; CBE (1987); s of Warburton Henry Johnston Knight (d 1987), and Alice Gweneth Knight; *b* 2 July 1932; *Educ* Trinity Coll Cambridge (MA); *m* 26 Aug 1961, Pamela, da of Leonard Charles Hearmon; 2 s (James, Matthew), 1 da (Sarah); *Career* Nat Serv 2 Lt RAEC 1950-52; teacher in Middx and Huddersfield 1956-62, asst dir for secdy schs Leicester 1967, asst educn offr for secdy schs and for special and social educn in WR 1970, dir of edncn servs Bradford Met DC 1974-; *Recreations* squash, cycling, fell walking, bee keeping; *Clubs* Royal Overseas League; *Style*— Richard Knight Esq, CBE; Thorner Grange, Sandhills, Thorner, nr Leeds, West Yorks; Provincial House, Tyrrel Street, Bradford, West Yorks (☎ 0274 752500)

KNIGHT, (John) Roger; s of Tom Knight (d 1966), of Pier St, Aberystwyth, and Friswyth, *née* Raymond Jones (d 1972); *b* 16 August 1946; *Educ* Littleover Derby; *m* 25 Oct 1980, Wendy Laurena, da of Roy Francis May, of Kynmar, Penn Rd, Chalfont-St-Peter, Gerrads Cross, Bucks; 1 s (Thomas Roger b 1983), 1 da (Lucy Jane b 1985); *Career* computer systems devpt & troubleshooting Cinema Int Corpn Amsterdam 1970-72, freelance computer conslt 1972-79, dir chm and md J computer logic Ltd 1980-89; ctee memb Hereford Business Club, MBCS 1981; *Recreations* cycling, walking, food, rearing ducks and geese; *Style*— Roger Knight, Esq; New Mill, Eaton Bishop, Hereford HR2 9QE (☎ 0981 251 324); Golden Valley Software Factory, New Mills, Eaton Bishop, Hereford HR2 9QE (☎ 0981 251 359, 0432 264 121)

KNIGHT, Dr Roger John Beckett; s of Lt-Cdr John Beckett Knight R N (d 1983) of Bromley, Kent and Alyson Yvonne Saunders, *née* Nunn; *b* 11 April 1944; *Educ* Tonbridge Sch, Trinity Coll Dublin (MA), Univ of Sussex (PGCE), UCL (PhD); *m* 3 Aug 1968 (m dis 1980), Helen Elizabeth, da of Dr William Magowan (d 1980) Hawkhurst, Kent; 2 s (William b 1973, Richard b 1976); *Career* Nat Maritime Museum: Custodian of Manuscripts 1977-81 (dep 1974-77) dep head books and manuscripts 1981-84, head info project gp 1984-86-, head documentation div 1986-88; head collections div 1988-; memb ctee Greenwich Soc, cncl Soc for Nautical Res 1975-79, cncl Navy Records Soc 1975-; FRHistS; *Books* Guide to the Manuscripts in the National Museum (1977, 1980), The Journal of Daniel Paine, 1794-1797 (with Alan Frast 1983), Portsmouth Dockyard in the American War of Independence, 1774-1783 (1986); *Recreations* sailing, cricket, music; *Style*— Dr Roger Knight, Esq; 133 Coleraine Rd, London SE3 7NT (☎ 01 853 1912); National Maritime Museum, Greenwich, London SE10 (☎ 01 858 4422)

KNIGHT, Stephen Charles; s of Reginald Frank Knight, of 32 Grangemill Road, London, and Sheila Ethel Clarice, *née* Jones; *b* 25 Nov 1954; *Educ* Colfe's Sch, Bromley Coll; *m* 30 July 1977, Lesley Joan, da of Haraold Leonard Davison, of 4 Donaldson Rd, London; 1 s (Timothy David Stephen b 1988); *Career* gen mangr mktg and devpt Newcross Bldg Soc 1983-84, vice pres Citibank 1984-87, chm Private Label Mortgage Servs Ltd 1987-; FCBSI 1977, MBIM 1978, MInstM 1979; *Recreations* squash, cricket, freelance writing; *Clubs* Inst of Dirs; *Style*— Stephen Knight, Esq; Jackdaws, Kemnal Rd, Chislehurst, Kent BR7 6LT (☎ 01 467 2239); Brettenham House, 14-15 Lancaster Place, London WC2E 7EB (☎ 01 379 5232, fax 01 379 4078, car tel 0836 773240 and 0836 243659),

KNIGHT, Wilfred Victor Robert; s of Maj Wilfred Knight (d 1972), and Edith Nell, *née* Clarkson; *b* 24 May 1940; *Educ* Watford GS, Bramshill Police Coll, Trinity Coll Cambridge (MA, MPhil); *m* 1, 1963 (m dis); *m* 2, Patricia Ann, *née* Liddiard; 3 s (Robert John b 4 April 1969, Gregory Iain b 6 June 1972, Alistair Grant b 7 Aug 1977); *Career* joined Met Police 1969, progressed through ranks from Detective Constable to Detective Superintendant and Special Br Protection Off (for Hon Harold Wilson PM and Edward Heath PM), served in NI off to four sec's of state, staff offr to various sr police offrs, awarded Bramshill Scholarship to Trinity Coll Cambridge 1977-78 and 1982-83, served with Crime Prevention and Community Rels Branch until 1984, injured and medically ret from force 1985 following injuries received during the miners strike (rank, Detective Superintendant); fndr Robert Gregory Assocs Ltd 1985 (security conslt, designing security systems for Architects and Developers), also acts as tech advsr to TV and Cinema (The Bill, The Sweeney, etc); coach to rowing eights for Cambridge Univ Colls; ARICS; *Recreations* squash, rowing, running; *Clubs* MPAA, CUBC; *Style*— Wilfred Knight, Esq

KNIGHT, William Arnold; CMG (1966), OBE (1954); s of William Knight (d 1953), of Llanfairfecham, and Clara, *née* Maddock (d 1987); *b* 14 June 1915; *Educ* Friars Sch Bangor, Univ Coll North Wales (BA); *m* 1939, Bronwen, da of Evan Parry (d 1914), of Bethesda; 1 s (William), 1 da (Gillian); *Career* Colonial Audit Dept 1958, served in: Kenya 1938-46, Mauritius 1946-49, Sierra Leone 1949-52, Br Guiana 1952-57, Uganda 1957-68; controller and auditor-gen of Uganda 1962-68, cmmr for economy and efficiency Uganda 1969-70; *Recreations* fishing, gardening; *Clubs* East India; *Style*— William Knight, Esq, CMG, OBE; Neopardy Mills, Crediton, Devon (☎ 036 32 2513)

KNIGHT, (Christopher) William; s of Claude Thorburn Knight, of Idlehurst, Birchgrove, Horsted Keynes, Sussex, and The Hon Priscilla, *née* Dodson; *b* 10 April 1943; *Educ* Eton; *m* 6 Sept 1969, Sylvia Caroline, da of H E Jonkheer Emile van Lennep, Ruychrocklaan 444, Den Haag, The Netherlands; 1 s (Christopher Thorburn b 20 Oct 1973), 2 da (Alexa Isobel b 9 Nov 1971, Loui Jane b 15 Oct 1977); *Career* princ mangr The Bank of London and S America Portugal 1982-84; dir: Lloyds Merchant Bank 1985, Lloyds Investmt Mangrs 1987; md Lloyds Bank Fund Mgmnt 1988; memb: Anglo-Netherlands Soc, Anglo-Portuguese Soc; MInstM; *Style*— William Knight, Esq; 82 Lansdowne Rd, London W11 2LS (☎ 01 221 3911); 82 Queen St, London EC4 NI3E (☎ 01 600 4500, 01 283 4169, fax 01 929 2354, car tel 0860 308 982, telex 881 2696)

KNIGHT, William John Langford; s of William Knight, and Gertrude Alice, *née* Wallage; *b* 11 Sept 1945; *Educ* Sir Roger Manwood's Sch Sandwich Kent, Univ of Bristol (LLB); *m* 21 April 1973, Stephanie Irina, da of Lt Col Edward Jeffrey Williams; 1 s (Sam b 1980), 1 da (Sarah b 1977); *Career* Simmons & Simmons Slrs 1967- (ptnr 1973-, i/c Hong Kong office 1979-82); memb cncl: Haydn Mozart Soc, SCAR (sickle cell anaemia relief); memb standing ctee on co law for Law Soc (ldr collective investmt scheme working pty), memb City of London Slrs Co; memb Law Soc, FRSA; *Books* The Acquisition of Private Companies (1975, fifth edn 1989); *Recreations* riding, piano, skiing; *Clubs* Hong Kong; *Style*— W J L Knight, Esq; 14 Dominion St, London EC2M 2RJ (☎ 01 628 2020, fax 01 588 4129, telex 888562)

KNIGHTS, Baron (Life Peer UK 1987), of Edgbaston, Co West Midlands Philip Douglas Knights; CBE (1976, OBE 1971), QPM (1964), DL (1985); s of Thomas James Knights (d 1978), of Ottershaw, Surrey, and Ethel Ginn (d 1963); *b* 3 Oct 1920; *Educ* E Grinstead Co Sch, King's Sch Grantham, Police Staff Coll; *m* 1945, Jean da of James Henry Burman (d 1972); *Career* served WW II with RAF; dep chief constable Birmingham City Police 1970-72 (asst chief constable 1959-70); chief constable: Sheffield and Rotherham 1972-74, S Yorks 1974-75, West Midlands Police 1975-85; memb Aston Univ Cncl 1985-; ctee memb Warwicks CCC 1985-89; tstee Police Fndn 1979-, memb Advsy Cncl Cambridge Inst of Criminology 1986-; Kt 1980; *Recreations* sport, travel, reading; *Style*— The Rt Hon the Lord Knights, CBE, QPM, DL; 11 Antringham Gdns, Edgbaston, Birmingham, B15 3QL

KNILL, Sir John Kenelm Stuart; 4 Bt (UK 1893), of The Grove, Blackheath, Kent; s of Sir (John) Stuart Knill, 3 Bt (d 1973); *b* 8 April 1913; *Educ* Downside; *m* 1951, Violette Maud Florence Martin (d 1983), da of Leonard Martin Barnes, of Durban, S Africa; 2 s; *Heir* s, Thomas Knill; *Career* WWII Lt RNVR 1940-45; canal carrier 1948-54, farmer 1956-63, MOD 1963-77, pres Avon Tport 2000, Assoc Canal Enterprises; vice pres Thames Severn Canal Tst, hon life memb Inland Waterways Assoc; *Clubs* Victory Services; *Style*— Sir John Knill, Bt; Canal Cottage, Bathampton, Avon (☎ 0225 63603)

KNILL, Prof John Lawrence; s of William Cuthbert Knill (d 1983), of S Croydon, and Mary, *née* Dempsey; *b* 22 Nov 1934; *Educ* Whitgift Sch Croydon, Imperial Coll London (BSc, ARCS, PhD, DIC, DSc); *m* 16 July 1957, Diane Constance, da of John Corr Judge (d 1956), of Hagerstown, USA; 1 s (Patrick b 1966), 1 da (Fiona b 1962); *Career* geologist Sir Alexander Gibbs & Ptnrs 1957; London Univ: asst lectr 1957-59, lectr 1959-65, reader 1965-73, prof of engrg geology 1973-, head dept of geology 1979-88; dean Royal Sch of Mines 1980-83; chm Natural Enviroment Res Cncl 1988-; chm Radioactive Waste Mgmnt Advsy Ctee, memb Nature Conservancy Cncl; hon FCGI 1988; FICE 1981, FHKIE 1982, FIGeol 1986; *Books* Industrial Geology (1978); *Recreations* viticulture; *Clubs* Athenaeum; *Style*— Prof John Knill; Highwood Farm, Shaw-cum-Donnington, Newbury, Berks RG16 9LB; Natural Environment Research Council, Polaris Ho, N Star Ave, Swindon, Wilts SN2 1EU (☎ 0793 411 653, fax 0793 411 501, telex 444293)

KNILL, Eve, Lady; Ruth Evelyn; *née* Barnes; da of Archibald Barnes and Amy Frances Atkinson; *b* 25 Oct 1911; *Educ* Newhaven Cncl Sch; *m* 1 (m dis), George Henry Foord; m 2, 1941, as his 2 w, Sir (John) Stuart Knill, 3 Bt (d 1973); 2 s, 1 da; *Career* numerologist; Grand Dame of the Order of St George; *Clubs* RAF; *Style*— Eve, Lady Knill; 7 Barton Close, Berrow, Burnham-on-Sea, Somerset (☎ 78 6955)

KNILL, Thomas John Pugin Bartholomew; s and h of Sir John Kenelm Stuart Knill, 4 Bt; *b* 23 August 1952; *m* 1977, Kathleen Muszynski; *Style*— Thomas Knill Esq

KNIPE, Sir Leslie Francis; MBE; *b* 1913; *Educ* West Monmouth Sch Pontypool; *Career* served WW II, Maj RASC Burma; farmer; pres Cons Pty in Wales (chm 1972-77), Monmouth Cons and Unionist Assoc; *Style*— Sir Leslie Knipe, MBE; Brook Acre, Llanvihangel, Crucorney, Abergavenny, Gwent, Wales (☎ 087 382 348)

KNOCKER, Col Nigel Bedingfield; OBE (1974); s of Gp Capt John Bedingfield Knocker, Angmering-on-Sea, Sussex (d 1958), and Lilian Helen *née* Gibbard (d 1975); *b* 31 August 1930; *Educ* Oakham Sch; *m* 1, 15 Nov 1958, Catriona Jane (d 1979), da of Gen Sir Roderick Mcleod, GBE, KCB, DL, of Surrey (d 1980); 1 s (Jonathan b 1961), 1 da (Fiona b 1963); m 2, 14 March 1981, Angela Grey, da of Maj Gen Sir John Willoughby, KBE, CB of Warminster; *Career* cmmnd The Royal Sussex Regt 1950; served in: Egypt, UK, Germany, Korea, Aust, N Ireland, N Africa, Aden, Gibraltar; CO Desert Regt Sultans Armed Forces Sultanate of Oman 1971-73; def attaché Muscat 1978-80 Cmdt Support Weapons Wing Sch of Inf 1980-82, staff of CDS MOD Oman 1982-85 (ret Army 1985); joined Wiltshire CC 1985, currently county emergency planning offr Wilts; Knight Chevalier (1 class) House of Orange (1954), DSM Oman (1973); *Recreations* tennis, skiing, walking, photography; *Clubs* Army and Navy; *Style*— Col Nigel Knocker, OBE; The Hatch, Seend, Melksham, Wilts SN12 6NW; County Hall, Trowbridge, Wilts (☎ 0380 828 609)

KNOLLYS, Hon Christopher Edward; s of 3 Viscount Knollys; *b* 1964; *Style*— The Hon Christopher Knollys

KNOLLYS, 3 Viscount (UK 1911); David Francis Dudley Knollys; Baron Knollys (UK 1902); s of 2 Viscount Knollys, GCMG, MBE, DFC (d 1966), and Margaret, da of Sir Stuart Coats, 2 Bt; *b* 12 June 1931; *Educ* Eton; *m* 1959, Hon Sheelin Virginia, da of Lt-Col the Hon Somerset Arthur Maxwell, MP (decd), and sis of 12 Baron Farnham; 3 s, 1 da; *Heir* s, Hon Patrick Knollys; *Career* late 2 Lt Scots Gds; *Style*— The Rt Hon the Viscount Knollys; Bramerton Grange, Norwich NR14 7HF (☎ Surlingham 266)

KNOLLYS, (Edward) Eardley; s of Cyprian Robert Knollys (d 1940), of Bath, and Audrey, *née* Hill (d 1957); *b* 21 Nov 1902; *Educ* Winchester, Christ Church Oxford (BA); *Career* painter; private sec to Lord Hambleden 1930-40, art dealer and owner of Storran Gallery 1935-40, Nat Tst agent and rep SW England 1942-57 (ctee memb 1957-72), ctee memb Contemporary Art Soc 1949-64; one-man exhibitions: Marjorie Parr Gallery 1974, Achim Moeller Gallery 1980, Michael Parkin Gallery 1987; *Recreations* travel, music; *Style*— Eardley Knollys, Esq; 16 West Halkin St, London SW1 (☎ 01 235 7456); 33 St Johns Square, London EC1 (☎ 01 251 3715)

KNOLLYS, Hon Michael James George; s of 3 Viscount Knollys; *b* 1968; *Style*— The Hon Michael Knollys

KNOLLYS, Hon Patrick Nicholas Mark; s and h of 3 Viscount Knollys; *b* 11 Mar 1962; *Style*— The Hon Patrick Knollys

KNORPEL, Henry; CB (1982), QC (1988); s of Hyman Knorpel (d 1958), of Guildford Surrey, and Dora, *née* Lukes; *b* 18 August 1924; *Educ* City of London Sch, Magdalen Coll Oxford (BCL, MA); *m* 1953, Brenda, da of Harry Sterling (d 1982), of Wembley, Middx; 2 da (Melanie, Helen); *Career* barr Inner Temple 1947-52; Govt Legal Serv 1952-85: MNI/MPNI 1952-65, Law Cmmn 1965-67, MSS 1967-68, DHSS asst slr 1968-71 (princ asst slr 1971-78, slr 1978-85); lectr in law 1950-, counsel to The Speaker 1985-; *Style*— Henry Knorpel Esq, CB, QC; Conway, 32 Sunnybank, Epsom, Surrey KT18 7DX (☎ 03727 21394); House of Commons, London SW1A 0AA (☎ 01 219 3776)

KNOTT, Sir John Laurence; AC (1981), CBE (1960); s of James Joseph Knott and Helen Mary, *née* Clarke; *b* 6 July 1910; *Educ* Cobram State Sch, Melbourne Univ, Imperial Def Coll London; *m* 1935, Jean Rose, da of Clarence William Milnes; 3 s, 1 da; *Career* company dir; sec Dept of Supply Aust 1959-66, dep high cmmr for Aust in London 1966-69, Freeman City of London 1968, dir-gen Posts & Telegraphs Aust 1969-72 (ret); memb cncl Melbourne Univ 1972-76; chm Scandinavian Pacific Hldgs Ltd; AASA, FCIS, FAIM; kt 1971; *see Debrett's Handbook of Australia and New Zealand for further details*; *Style*— Sir John Knott, AC, CBE; 3 Fenwick St, Kew, Vic 3101, Australia

KNOTT, Air Vice-Marshal Ronald George; CB (1967), DSO (1945), DFC (1944), AFC (1956); s of Capt George Knott (d 1952), and Edith Rose, *née* Anderson (d 1981); *b* 19 Dec 1917; *Educ* Borden GS; *m* 1941, Hermione Violet, da of Col Robert Bernard Phayre (d 1964); 3 s (Terence, Nicholas (decd), Andrew), 1 da (Alexandra); *Career* RAF Dir of Op Requirements MOD 1963-67, Sr Air Staff Offr ME Air Force 1967-70, Air Offr Admin Air Support Cmd 1970-72, ret; *Recreations* wine growing, property restoration; *Style*— Air Vice Marshal Ronald Knott, CB, DSO, DFC, AFC; Pilgrims Cottage, Charing, Ashford, Kent TN27 0DR

KNOTT, (Charlotte) Theresa; JP; da of Maj John Stobart Keith, OBE, of 96 Barton Rd, Newnham, Cambridge, and Joan, *née* Hansell (d 1969); *b* 28 Mar 1940; *Educ* Priors Field Godalming Surrey, Cordon Bleu Cookery Sch Marylebone Lane (Dip Cordon Bleu), Mon Fertile Morges Switzerland; *m* 1968, William Espenett Bayly Knott, s of Lt-Col John Espenett Knott, CMG, DSO; 1 s (Richard John b 3 Feb 1971), 1 da ((Adeline) Louise b 1 Dec 1969); *Career* owner of self-created garden open to the public Glenwhan Gdns Dunragit Stranraer; Magistrate Stranraes Dist Ct, chm Nat Cncl Conservation of Plants in Gdns Dumfries and Galloway; memb: Int Dendrology Soc, Hardy Plant Soc, Scottish Rock Garden Club; Freewoman City of London Freewoman Worshipful Co Skinners; *Recreations* collector of early english water colour drawings, water-colour painting, swimming, gardening, fishing; *Style*— Mrs William Knott, JP; 12 Courtfield House, Baldwin Gdns, Glenwhan House, Dunragit, Stranraer DG9 8PH (☎ 05814 222)

KNOWLES, Sir Charles Francis; 7 Bt (GB 1765), of Lovell Hill, Berkshire; s of Sir Francis Gerald William, 6 Bt (d 1974); *b* 20 Dec 1951; *Educ* Marlborough, Oxford Sch of Architecture (BA, DipArch); *m* 1979, Amanda Louise Margaret, da of Lance Bromley, MChir, FRCS, of Molyneux St, W1; *Heir* kinsman, Peter Knowles; *Style*— Sir Charles Knowles, Bt; Merlin Haven House, Wotton-under-Edge, Glos

KNOWLES, Colin George; s of George William Knowles (d 1977), and Isabelle, *née* Houghton (d 1980); *b* 11 April 1939; *Educ* King George V GS Southport, CEDEP Fontainebleau France; *m* 1981, Lesley Carolyn Angela (Carla), da of Roland Stansfield Stamp, of Devonshire; 1 da (Marguerite Isabella (Daisy) b 1984), by earlier m, 2 da (Emma, Samantha); *Career* co sec and head of public affrs Imperial Tobacco Ltd 1960-80, chm Griffin Assoc Ltd UK 1980-83, dir TWS P R (Pty) Ltd Johannesburg 1984, chm Concept Communications (Pty) Ltd Johannesburg 1983-84, dir of devpt and public affrs Univ of Bophuthatswana 1985-, chm P R Inst of S Africa Bophutatswana regn 1988-; dir: Assoc for Business Sponsorship of the Arts 1975-84 (chm 1975-80), The Bristol Hippodrome Tst Ltd 1977-81, The Bath Archaeological Tst Ltd 1978-81, The Palladian Tst Ltd 1979-81; memb Chllr of Duchy of Lancaster's Ctee of Honour on Business and the Arts 1980-81; Freeman City of London (1974), Liveryman Worshipful Co of Tobacco Pipe Makers and Tobacco Blenders London (1973); MInstM, MIPR, FBIM, FRSA, MPRISA, APR; OStJ; *Recreations* game watching, reading, fishing, shooting; *Clubs* Carlton, MCC, Mafikeng Golf; *Style*— C G Knowles, Esq; Univ of Bophuthatswana, Post Bag X2046, Mmabatho 8681, Rep of Bophuthatswana, Southern Africa (☎ 010 27 1401 21171, telex 3072 BP)

KNOWLES, Sir Leonard Joseph; CBE (1963); s of late Samuel Joseph Knowles; *b* 15 Mar 1916; *Educ* Queen's Coll Nassau, King's Coll London (LLB, BD, Certificate of Honour); *m* 1939, Harriet Hansen Hughes; 2 s; *Career* served WW II RAF radar; barr Gray's Inn 1939, registrar-gen Bahamas 1949-50, MLC Bahamas 1960-63, pres of Senate 1964-72, chief justice Bahamas 1973-78; lay preacher; kt 1974; *Books* Elements of Bahamian Law, My Life, Bahamian Real Property Law; *Clubs* Royal Cwlth Soc; *Style*— Sir Leonard Knowles, CBE; P O Box SS 6378, Nassau, Bahamas

KNOWLES, Hon Mrs; Lorraine Charmian Gabrielle; *née* Carleton; da of 2 and last Baron Dorchester, and Kathleen de Blaquiere, only da of 6 Baron de Blaquiere; *b* 29 Dec 1919; *Educ* Convent of the Sacred Heart Roehampton, St Mary's Sch Calne, RCM; *m* 1947, James Metcalfe Knowles, FRIBA, s of Thomas Greenwood Knowles, of Halifax, Yorks; 1 s (Thomas), 1 da (Elizabeth Coleman); *Career* served WW II: VAD 1939-44, (P10 1944), SOE FANY and Force 136 India and Ceylon 1944-46; former: dist cmmr Chelsea Girl Guides, hon sec Chelsea Soc; ed the FANY Gazette 1976-88, chm West Dean Parish Meeting 1979-88; *Recreations* running family vineyard, free lance writing; *Style*— The Hon Mrs Knowles; 9 St Leonard's Terrace, London SW3; Sheep Pen Cottage, Friston Forest, West Dean, nr Seaford, East Sussex

KNOWLES, Michael; MP (C) Nottingham East 1983-; s of Martin Christopher and Anne Knowles; *b* 21 May 1942,May; *Educ* Clapham Coll; *m* 1965, Margaret Isabel Thorburn; 3 da; *Career* sales mangr; contested (C): Merthyr Tydfil Feb 1974, Brent East Oct 1974; memb: Surbiton constituency exec 1971-, Kingston Cncl 1971- (ldr 1974-), Kingston constituency exec 1974-, London Boroughs Assoc; *Style*— Michael Knowles Esq, MP; 63 Guilford Avenue, Surbiton, Surrey (☎ 01 399 6449)

KNOWLES, Hon Mrs Patricia Janet; *née* Brown; yr da of Baron George-Brown, PC (Life Peer); *b* 1942; *m* 1967, Derek Knowles; *Style*— Hon Mrs Knowles

KNOWLES, Peter Cosby; s of Robert Cosby Knowles (decd) (5 s of 4 Bt) and Phyllis, da of Rev Canon Ward Thomas, of Lorne, Victoria; hp of kinsman, Sir Charles Francis Knowles, 7 Bt; *b* 27 June 1930; *m* 1, 1957 (m dis 1977), Gloria, da of H Oaten, of Melbourne; 1 s, 3 da; m 2, 1977, Jane Winifred, da of B Cooper, of Kenmore, Brisbane; *Style*— Peter Knowles Esq; Namarva, Private Bag, Winton, Qld 4735, Australia

KNOWLES, (George) Peter; s of Geoffrey Knowles, MC, RA (d 1968), of 57 Charlton Rd, Weston-Supermare, and Mabel Evelin, *née* Bowman (d 1958); *b* 30 Dec 1919; *Educ* Clifton, Queens Coll Cambridge (MA, LLM); *m* 2 Oct 1948, (Elizabeth) Margaret, da of John Scott, of East Lilburn, Old Bewick, Alnwick; 1 s (George b 15 Jan 1958), 2 da (Susan (Mrs Architage) b 12 March 1951, Christine (Mrs Gardner) b 29 Nov 1953); *Career* WW11 2 Indian Field Regt RA 1939-45; slr 1948-; legal sec and registrar Archbishop of York, registrar of Convocation of York 1968-86, jt registrar of COE Gen Synod 1970-80, chm York Rent Tbnl; memb: Rent Assesment Ctee, Mental Health Tbnl; former dep coroner for York and coroner for s dist of N Yorks; former sec York branch RSPCA, memb Merchant Adventurers of York; memb Law Soc; *Recreations* fishing, gardening; *Clubs* Yorkshire (York); *Style*— Peter Knowles, Esq; 11 Lang Rd, Bishopthorpe, York

KNOWLES, Brig Royston; CBE (1969); *b* 9 July 1919; *Educ* St John's Sch Fulham, Wandsworth Tech Coll, Regent St Poly (HND); *m* 21 Dec 1946, Christina Joyce; 1 s (Roger Ian b 1947, d 1957), 1 da (Lesley Jane b 1949); *Career* cmmnd 1941, Lt 1 AA Div 1941, Capt 18 Inf Div 1941-45 (Far East POW 1942-45), 1 AA Gp 1946-48, Royal Mil Coll of Sci 1948-50, Maj Admty Estab 1950-53, HQ NORTHAG 1953-55, 3 Armd WKSP REME 1955-56, Miny of Supply 1956-58, OC 37 GW Regt WKSP 1959-60, CO radar branch 1960-63, Col ADEME MOD 1963-66, cmdt 38 Central WRSP REME 1966-69, Brig DDEME Southern Cmd 1969-72, MOD 1972-74; vice pres Inst of Quality Assur 1988-(sec gen 1974-88), academican Int Acad of Quality 1980, cncl memb Euro Orgn For Quality 1987; memb Worshipful Co of Engrs 1984; FIEE 1947, FBIM 1959, FIQA 1974; *Books* Automatic Test Systems and Applications (1975); *Recreations* travel; *Clubs* Army and Navy; *Style*— Brig Royston Knowles, CBE; 30 Acacia Rd, Hampton, Middx TW12 3DS

KNOWLES, Timothy (Tim); s of Cyril William Knowles (d 1966), of Worcester, and Winifred Alice, *née* Hood (d 1965); *b* 17 May 1938; *Educ* Bishop Gore GS Swansea; *m* 30 Sept 1967, Gaynor, da of Edgar Ernest Hallett, of Llandaff, Cardiff; 1 da (Tracy b 1969); *Career* co sec and accoutant Louis Marx & Co Ltd 1960-68, controller Modco Valentite 1968-69, asst md HTV Ltd 1981-86 (co sec 1969-78, fin dir 1975-81), gp md HTV Gp plc 1986-88 (fin dir 1976-86); parly candidate (Cons) Swansea East 1966; memb: S Wales Electricity Bd 1981-82, Welsh Water Authy 1982-; FCA 1960; *Recreations* travel, walking, watching cricket; *Style*— Tim Knowles, Esq; 9 Ger-y-Llan, St Nicholas, Cardiff CF5 6SY (☎ 0446 760726)

KNOWLTON, Richard James; CBE (1983), QFSM (1977); s of Richard John

Knowlton, AM (1918) (d 1981), and Florence May *née* Humby (d 1950); *b* 2 Jan 1928; *Educ* Bishop Wordworth's Sch Salisbury; *m* 1949, Pamela Vera, da of Charles Horne, of Salisbury; 1 s (Richard b 1950); *Career* served 42 Commando RM (Hong Kong, Malta) 1945-48; fireman Southampton FB 1949-59, stn offr Worcester City & Country FB, asst div offr London FB 1963-67, div offr London FB 1967-69, div cdr London FB 1969-71, Firemaster SW Scotland 1971-75, Firemaster Strathclyde FB 1975-84; HM Chief Insp of Fire Services (Scot) 1984-; chm London Branch Inst of Fire Engrs 1969, UK chm Fire Services Nat Ben Fund 1980-81, UK pres Chief & Asst Chief Fire Offrs Assoc 1980-81, Br rep, Cncl Euro Assoc of Prof Fire Brigade Offrs 1979-85, pres Scot Dist Fire Serv Sports & Athletic Assoc 1985-; FBIM, FIFireE; *Style*— James Knowlton, CBE, QFSM; Scottish Home and Health Department, St Andrew's House, Edinburgh EH1 3DE (☎ 031 244 2342)

KNOX, Anthony James (Tony); s of Harry Cooke Knox (d 1979), of Belfast, and Lila Mary Knox; *b* 9 Oct 1949; *Educ* Royal Belfast Academical Inst, Wadham Coll Univ of Oxford (BA, MA), Queens Univ Belfast (MA); *m* 30 March 1972, Marie-Hélène Clotilde, da of Pierre Hubert, of St Gervais, Hte Savoie, France; s da (Jessica b 1975, Chloe b 1980); *Career* radio prodr BBC NI 1975-82, prodr South Bank Show LWT 1982-; *Recreations* fishing; *Clubs* Dromore Anglers; *Style*— Tony Knox, Esq; LWT, London SE1 9LT (☎ 01 261 3788, fax 01 633 0842)

KNOX, Bryce Harry; CB (1986); s of Brice Henry Knox, of London, and Rose, *née* Netty-Yelland; *b* 21 Feb 1929; *Educ* Stratford GS; Nottingham Univ (BA); *m* 1957, Florence Norma, da of George Thomas, of London (d 1958); 1 s (Daniel b 1967); *Career* dep chm Bd of Customs and Excise 1983-88, asst princ HM Customs 1953 (princ 1958), HM Treasy 1963-65, asst sec 1966, seconded to HM Dip Serv, cnsllr off of UK Perm Rep to Euro Communities 1972-74, under sec 1974, cmmr HM Customs and Excise 1975; *Recreations* reading, listening to music, tasting/discussing wine, bridge; *Clubs* Reform, MCC; *Style*— Bryce Knox, CB; 9 Manor Way, Blackheath, London SE3 9EF (☎ 01 852 9404);

KNOX, Col Bryce Muir; MC (1944, and Bar), TD (1947); s of James Knox (d 1960), of Kilbirnie, and Dorothy, *née* Fry (d 1980); *b* 4 April 1916; *Educ* Stowe, Trinity Coll Cambridge (BA); *m* 1948, Patricia Marie, da of Major Herbert James Dunsmuir (d 1971), of Martnaham Lodge, by Ayr; 1 s (James), 1 da (Lucy); *Career* Ayrshire (ECO) Yeo 1939-45, CO 1953-56, Hon Col 1968-71, Queen's Own Yeo 1971-79, Hon Col Ayrshire Yeo Sqdn; chm W & J Knox Ltd 1959-79, vice chm Lindustries Ltd 1979-(dir 1953-79); pres Lowlands TA & VR Assoc 1978-83, memb: Queen's Bodyguard for Scotland, Royal Co of Archers; Lord Lt of Ayr and Arran 1974-, (DL 1953-70, Vice Lt 1970-74), CStJ 1979; *Publications* Historical Notes 152 (Ayrshire Yeomanry), Field Regiment RA (1946), The History of the Eglinton Hunt (1985); *Recreations* country sports; *Style*— Col B M Knox, MC, TD; Martnaham Lodge, by Ayr (☎ 029256 204)

KNOX, (Alexander) David; CMG (1988); s of James Knox (d 1953), and Elizabeth Maxwell, *née* Robertson (d 1961); *b* 15 Jan 1925; *Educ* The Queen's Royal Coll Trinidad West Indies, Univ of Toronto Canada (BA), LSE; *m* 15 July 1950, Beatrice Lily, da of William Benjamin Dunell (d 1963); 1 s (Andrew b 1953), 2 da (Helen b 1954, Julia b 1963); *Career* LSE 1949-63 (reader in economics 1955-63), Int Bank for Reconstruction and Devpt 1963-87 (vice pres 1980-87); *Recreations* walking, tennis, opera; *Clubs* Reform; *Style*— David Knox, Esq, CMG; Knights Barn, Manor Farm Lane, East Hagbourne, Oxfordshire OX11 9ND (☎ 0235 817792)

KNOX, David Laidlaw; MP (C) Staffs Moorlands 1983-; s of John McGlasson Knox (d 1951), of Lockerbie, and Catherine Helen Campbell, *née* Laidlaw; *b* 30 May 1933; *Educ* Lockerbie and Dumfries Acads, London Univ; *m* 1980, Margaret E Maxwell, *née* McKenzie; *Career* economist and mgmnt conslt, contested (C): Birmingham Stechford 1964 and 1966, Nuneaton (by-election) 1967; MP (C) Leek 1970-83, jt-sec Cons Fin Ctee 1972-73, PPS to Sec State Def 1973-74, sec Cons Trade Ctee 1974, vice-chm Cons Pty 1974-75, memb Select Ctee Euro Legislation 1976-; vice-chm: Cons Employment Ctee 1979-80 (sec 1976-79), Cons Gp for Europe 1984-87; memb of the chm's Panel in the House of Commons 1983-; *Style*— David Knox, Esq, MP; House of Commons, London SW1

KNOX, Lady Elizabeth Marianne; er da of 7 Earl of Ranfurly, *qv*

KNOX, Jack; s of Alexander Knox (d 1986), of Kirkintilloch, Scotland, and Jean Alexander Gray, *née* Graham (d 1988); *b* 16 Dec 1936; *Educ* Lenzie Acad, Glasgow Sch of Art (Dip Art); *m* 5 July 1960, Margaret Kyle, da of Walter Duncan Sutherland (d 1973), of Glasgow, Scotland; 1 s (Kyle b 6 April 1964), 1 da (Emily b 13 May 1967); *Career* lectr in art Duncan of Jordanstone Coll of Art Dundee 1965-81, hd of painting studios Glasgow Sch of Art 1981-; Solo exhibitions: 57 Gallery Edinburgh 1961, Scottish Gallery Edinburgh 1966, Richard Demarco Gallery Edinburgh 1969, Serpentine Gallery London 1971, Buckingham Gallery London 1972, Civic Arts Centre Aberdeen 1972, Glasgow Sch of Art 1982, Retrospective 1983; Scottish Arts Cncl 1973 -78, tstee ctee Scottish Nat Gallery of Modern Art 1975-81, govr Duncan of Jordanstone Coll of Art Dundee 1980-83, tstee Scottish Nat Gallery 1982-87, govr Glasgow Sch of Art 1985-88; RSA 1979, RGI 1981 RSW 1987; *Style*— Jack Knox, Esq; 31 North Erskine Park, Bearsden, Glasgow G61 4LY (☎ 041 942 6629); Glasgow Sch of Art, 167 Renfrew St, Glasgow (☎ 041 332 9797)

KNOX, Hon Mr Justice; Sir John Leonard; QC (1979); s of Leonard Needham Knox (d 1956), and Berthe Helene, *née* Knox (d 1981); *b* 6 April 1925; *Educ* Radley, Worcester Coll Oxford (MA); *m* 1953, Anne Jacqueline, da of Herbert Mackintosh; 1 s (Thomas), 3 da (Diana, Catherine, Margaret); *Career* Lt RA 1944-47; barr Lincoln's Inn 1953-85, bencher Lincoln's Inn 1977, attorney-gen Duchy of Lancaster 1984-85, justice of High Ct Chancery Div 1985, judge of Employment Appeal Tribunal 1989; kt 1985; *Style*— The Hon Mr Justice Knox; Royal Cts of Justice, Strand, London WC2

KNOX, Robert William (Bob); s of Jack Dallas Knox (d 1983), of Claygate, Surrey, and Margaret Meikle, *née* Elder; *b* 15 Dec 1943; *Educ* Cranleigh; *m* 10 Feb 1968, Susan Mary, da of Cyril Joseph O'Bryen, of Weybridge, Surrey; 2 da (Julie b 1970, Katharine b 1972); *Career* ptnr Kidsons CAs 1972-, memb London (W End) dist trg bd ICEAW 1984; FCA 1966; *Books* Statements of Source and Application of Funds (1977); *Recreations* occasional golf, bridge, philately; *Style*— Robert W Knox, Esq; Kidsons, Russell Square House, 10-12 Russell Square, London WC1B 5AE (☎ 01 436 3636, fax 01 436 6603, telex 263901)

KNOX, Hon Rupert Stephen; yr s of 7 Earl of Ranfurly, *qv*; *b* 5 Nov 1963; *Style*— Hon Rupert Knox; Albion Chambers East, Broad Street, Bristol, BS1 1DR (☎ 0212 272 144, fax 262569)

KNOX, Hon Sir William Edward; s of Edward Knox (Air Cdr, decd), and Dr Alice Thomas (decd); *b* 14 Dec 1927; *Educ* Melbourne HS; *m* 1956, Doris Alexia Ross; 2 s, 2 da; *Career* MLA Qld (Lib) for Nundah 1957-, sec Parly Lib Party 1960-64, sec Jt Govt Parties 1965, min for Transport 1965-72, chm Qld Road Safety Cncl and memb Aust Transport Advsy Cncl 1965-72, min for Justice and attorney-gen 1971-76, dep ldr Parly Lib Party 1971-76, state tres 1976-78, dep premier and ldr Parly Lib Party 1976-78, min for Health 1978-80, min for Employment and Lab Relations 1980-; ldr Parly Lib Pty 1983-88; chm St John's Cncl Queensland; kt 1979; *Style*— The Hon Sir William Knox, MLA; 1621 Sandgate Rd, Nundah, Qld 4012, Australia (☎ 266 9893)

KNOX-JOHNSTON, Capt William Robert Patrick (Robin); CBE (1969), RD (1978, and Bar); s of David Robert Knox-Johnston (d 1970), and Elizabeth Mary, *née* Cree, of Kent; *b* 17 Mar 1939; *Educ* Berkhamsted Sch; *m* 1962, Suzanne, da of Denis Ronald Singer; 1 da (Sara b 1963); *Career* yachtsman first person to circumnavigate the world non-stop & single handed 14 June 1968-22 April 1969; holder Br Sailing Trans Atlantic Record (10 days, 14 hours, 9 mins) 1986, World Champion Class II multihulls 1985; FRGS 1965; *Books* World of my Own (1969), Sailing (1975), Twilight of Sail (1978), Last but not Least (1978), Bunkside Companion (1982), Seamanship (1986), The BOC Challenge (1986-87), The Cape of Good Hope (1989); *Recreations* sailing; *Clubs* Royal Cruising, Royal Ocean Racing; *Style*— Capt Robin Knox-Johnston, CBE, RD; 26 Sefton St, Putney, London SW15 (☎ 01 789 0465)

KNOX-LECKY, Maj Gen Samuel; CB (1979), OBE (1967); s of John Daniel Lecky (d 1929), of Coleraine, and Mary Thompson, *née* Knox (d 1968); *b* 10 Feb 1926; *Educ* Coleraine Acad, Queen's Univ Belfast (BSc CEng); *m* 18 Oct 1947, Sheila Constance, da of Hugh Jones (d 1951) of Liverpool; 1 s (Paul b 1955), 2 da (Karla b 1949, Jennifer b 1952); *Career* Army 1946-79, cmmnd REME 1946, DEME BAOR and Cmdt SEME as Brig; DMAO (MOD) and Min (DS) Br Embassy Tehran as Maj Gen, Hon Col QUB OTC 1978-83, Col Cmdt REME 1980-86; dir gen Agric Engrs Assoc 1980-88; FIMechE, FIAgE, CBIM; *Recreations* fishing, sailing; *Clubs* Caledonian; *Style*— Maj-Gen Samuel Lecky, CB, OBE

KNOX-PEEBLES, Brian Philip; s of Lt Col George Edward Knox-Peebles, RTR, DSO (d 1969), and Patricia, *née* Curtis-Raleigh; *b* 19 June 1936; *Educ* Wellington Coll, Göttingen Univ W Germany, Brasenose Coll Oxford (MA); *m* 20 Aug 1960, Rose Mary, da of Capt Cyril Telford Latch (RFC WWI, RNVR WWII); 1 s (Brendan b 21 Sept 1965), 3 da (Nina b 16 Nov 1962, Fleur b 3 Feb 1964, Bryonie b 16 Nov 1967); *Career* Daily Mail 1963-64, Evening Standard 1964-65, The Times 1965-67, United Newspapers plc 1967-; dir: Punch Pubns 1968-86 (publisher 1984-86), Bradbury Agnew Ltd 1979-82, United Provincial Newspapers 1981 (gp mktg dir 1974-); dir: Jt Indust Ctee for Nat Readership Surveys, Press Res Cncl, Audit Bureau of Circulations; chm Fin and GPc Press Res Cncl, fndr memb and first pres Int Newspaper Mktg Assoc (Europe); memb: Mktg Soc, Int Advertising Assoc, Newspaper Res Cncl (USA), Mkt Res Soc; FInstD; *Books* The Fleet Street Revolution; *Recreations* cinema, walking, swimming, reading, writing; *Clubs* Hurlingham; *Style*— Brian Knox-Peebles, Esq; 2 Campden House Tce, Kensington Church St, London W8 4BQ (☎ 01 727 9595); Group Marketing Director, United Newspapers plc, 23/27 Tudor St, London EC4 OHR (☎ 01 583 9199)

KNUTSFORD, 6 Viscount (UK 1895); Michael Holland-Hibbert; DL (1977 Devon); also Baron Knutsford, of Knutsford, Co Chester (UK 1888), and 7 Bt (UK 1853); o s of Hon Wilfrid Holland-Hibbert (d 1961; 2 s of 3 Viscount), and Isabel Audrey, *née* Fenwick; s cousin 5 Viscount 1986; *b* 27 Dec 1926; *Educ* Eton, Trinity Coll Camb (BA); *m* 8 May 1951, Hon Sheila Constance Portman, er da of 5 Viscount Portman (d 1942); 2 s (Hon Henry Thurstan, Hon James Edward b 19 May 1967), 1 da (Hon Lucy Katherine b 27 June 1956); *Heir* s, Hon Henry Thurstan Holland-Hibbert b 6 April 1959; *Career* SW regnl dir Barclays Bank 1956-86; memb var ctees Nat Tst 1965-86, memb finance ctee 1986; chm 250th anniversary ctee London Hosp; High Sheriff of Devon 1977-78; *Clubs* Brooks's; *Style*— The Viscount Knutsford, DL; Broadclyst House, Exeter, Devon EX5 3EW (☎ 0392 61244)

KNUTSFORD, Viscountess; Sheila Constance; *née* Portman; er da of 5 Viscount Portman (d 1942); *b* 25 June 1927; *m* 8 May 1951, 6 Viscount Knutsford, *qv*; 2 s, 1 da; *Style*— The Rt Hon the Viscountess Knutsford; Broadclyst House, Exeter EX5 3EW (☎ 0392 61244)

KOECHLIN-SMYTHE, Patricia Rosemary; OBE (1956); da of Capt Eric Hamilton Smythe, MC (d 1945), and Frances Monica Curtoys (d 1952); *b* 22 Nov 1928; *Educ* Pates GS Cheltenham, St Michael's Cirencester; *m* 1963, Samuel Koechlin (d 1985), s of Hartmann Koechlin (d 1961), of Basel Switzerland; 2 da (Monica b 1966, Lucy b 1968); *Career* equestrian; memb Br Show Jumping Team 1947-64, has won numerous prizes incl: Leading Show Jumper of the Year 1949, 1958 and 1962, set Ladies' record for high jump Brussels 1954 (2m 20cm); with Br Equestrian Olympic Team: Stockholm (1956, won Show Jumping Team Bronze Medal, tenth Individual), Rome (1960, tenth Individual); memb World Wildlife Fund Int Cncl and UK Cncl; pres Br Show Jumping Assoc 1982-86; writer; landowner; Freeman: Worshipful Co of Farriers 1955, City of London 1956, Worshipful Co of Loriner 1961, Worshipful Co of Saddlers 1963; *Books* (as Pat Smythe) Jump for Joy: Pat Smythe's Story (1954), Pat Smythe's Book of Horses (1955), One Jump Ahead (1956), Jacqueline Rides for a Fall (1957), Three Jays Against the Clock (1957), Three Jays on Holiday (1958), Three Jays Go to Town (1959), Three Jays Over the Border (1960), Three Jays Go to Rome (1960), Three Jays Lend a Hand (1961), Horses of Places (1959), Jumping Round the World (1962), Florian's Farmyard (1962), Flanagan My Friend (1963), Bred to Jump (1965), Show Jumping (1967), A Pony for Pleasure (with Fiona Hughes, 1969), A Swiss Adventure (1970), Pony Problems (with Fiona Hughes, 1971), A Spanish Adventure (1971), Cotswold Adventure (1972); *Recreations* sport, music; *Style*— Mrs Patricia Koechlin-Smythe, OBE; Sudgrove House, Miserden, nr Stroud, Glos (☎ 028582 360); 1M GL675D Therwiler Str, 83 CH 4104 Oberwil, Switzerland, (☎ 00 41 61 401 2279)

KOELLE, Lady; Elizabeth Anne; da of Sir Philip Henry Devitt, 1 Bt (d 1947, when Btcy became extinct); *b* 1921; *m* 1948, as his 2 w, Vice-Adm Sir Harry Philpot Koelle, KCB (d 1980); 2 da; *Style*— Lady Koelle; Pippins, Longburton, Sherborne, Dorset

KOHNER, Prof Eva Maria; da of Baron George Nicholas Kohner of Szaszberek (d 1944), of Hungary, and Andrea Kathleen, *née* Boszormenyi (d 1985); *b* 23 Feb 1929; *Educ* Baar-Madas Presbyterian Boarding Sch for Girls, Royal Free Hosp Sch of Med London Univ (BSc, MB, BS, MD); *m* 26 April 1961 (m dis 1979), Steven Ivan Warman; *Career* med registrar med ophthalmogy Lambeth Hosp 1963-64, res fell Royal Postgraduate Med Sch Hammersmith Hosp London 1965-68, MRC Alexander Wernher Piggott Meml fell NY 1968-69; Moorfields Eye Hosp and Hammersmith

Hosp: sr registrar and lectr 1970-77, conslt med ophthalmologist 1977-88, prof med ophthalmology (first full-time prof in Britain) 1988-; freelance lectr on treatment of diabetic eye disease by laser (in part instrumental in this treatment now being available to all patients in Britain); MRCP 1963, FRCP 1977; *Books* over three hundred publications in field of retinal vascular disease; *Recreations* art, travel; *Style*— Prof Eva Kohner; 32 Monckton Ct, Strangways Terrace, London W14 8NF

KOLBERT, His Hon Judge Colin Francis; s of Arthur Richard Alexander Kolbert, of Barnet and Barnstaple, and Dorothy Elizabeth, *née* Fletcher; *b* 3 June 1936; *Educ* Queen Elizabeth's Barnet, St Catharine's Coll Cambridge (MA, PhD), St Peter's Coll Oxford (MA, DPhil); *m* 12 Sept 1959, Jean Fairgrieve, da of Stanley Hutton Abson (d 1964), of Friern Barnet; 2 da (Julia Catharine b 1963, Jennifer Sally b 1965); *Career* RA 1954-56, Cambridge Univ OTC (TAVR) 1969-74; called to the Bar Lincoln's Inn 1961; fell and tutor in jurisprudence St Peter's Coll Oxford 1964-68, fell Magdalene Coll Cambridge 1968- (tutor 1969-88), lectr in law Dept of Land Economy Cambridge 1968-88; rec SE circuit 1985-88 (circuit judge 1988-); *Clubs* Hawks' (Cambridge), MCC, Farmers', Cambridge Univ Rugby; *Style*— His Hon Judge Colin Kolbert; Magdalene Coll, Cambridge (☎ 0223 332150); Lamb Building, Temple, London EC4Y 7AS (☎ 01 353 6381, fax 01 583 1786)

KOLTAI, Ralph; CBE (1983); s of Dr med Alfred Koltai, of Budapest, Vienna, Berlin, Brussels (d 1970, London), and Charlotte, *née* Weinstein (d 1987); *b* 31 July 1924; *Educ* Berlin, Central Sch of Arts and Crafts London (Dip Art/Design); *m* 29 Dec 1954 (m dis 1976), Mary Annena, da of the late George Stubbs, of Liverpool; *Career* RASC attached Intelligence Corps served Nuremburg War Crimes Trial and London Interrogation Unit 1944-47; freelance stage designer for Drama Opera and Dance; assoc designer Roy Shakespeare Co 1963-66 and 1976-; first prodn Angelique for London Opera Club 1950; designs for Royal Opera House, Sadlers Wells, Scottish Opera, Nat Welsh Opera Ballet Rambert; RSC prodns incl: The Caucasian Chalk Circle 1962, The Birthday Party 1964, Timon of Athens 1965, Little Murders 1967, Major Barbara 1970, Old World 1976, Wild Oats 1977, The Tempest 1978, Hamlet 1980, Moliere 1982, Cyrano de Bergerac (SWET award) 1983; for Nat Theatre: As You Like It 1967, Back To Methuslah 1969, State of Revolution 1977, Brand (SWET award) 1978, Richard III 1979, Man and Superman 1981; has worked throughout Europe and in Argentine, USA, Canada, Australia; other prodns incl: for ENO Wagners complete Ring Circle 1973, Tannhauser (Sydney) 1973, Fidelio (Munich) 1974, Bugsy Malone 1983, Pack of Lies 1983, vice chm Assoc Br Theatre Designers; BSA; *Recreations* wildlife photography; *Style*— Ralph Koltai, Esq, CBE; c/o MLR 2000, Fulham Rd, London SW10; Unit 52 350-56 Wharf Rd, London N1 (☎ 01 250 3282)

KOMIEROWSKA, Hon Mrs (Katharine Mary); *née* Godley; da of 2 Baron Kilbracken, CB, KC (d 1950); *b* 1923; *Educ* (BSc); *m* 1944, Capt Peter Komierowski; 1 s, 1 da; *Style*— The Hon Mrs Komierowska; 4 Stanley Mansions, Park Walk, SW10

KOOPS, Eric Jan Leendart; s of Leendart Koops, and Daphne Vera, *née* Myhill; *b* 16 Mar 1945; *Educ* Eastbourne Coll, Univ of Lancaster (BA); *m* 1, June 1968 (m dis 1985), Glenys Marie Baker; 1 s (Mark Alexander b 20 Feb 1975), 1 da (Amanda Charlotte b 25 Sept 1972); m 2, 11 Sept 1987, Hon Mary Claire Hogg, da of Baron Hailsham of St Marylebone, KG, CH, *qv*; 1 da (b 17 March 1989); *Career* TA 2 Lt 4/5 KORR 1964-67; investmt banker and dir of several public and private cos in UK and the Benelux; hon dir The Duke of Edinburgh's Award World Fellowship, tstee: The Inst for Policy Res, The Winnicott Clinic of Psychotherapy Charitable Tst; parly candidate (Cons) Wakefield 1974; chm Carlton Club Political Ctee 1984-88; FCA 1971; *Books* Money for our Masters (1970), Airports for the Eighties (1980); *Recreations* travel, cricket; *Clubs* Buck's, Carlton, MCC; *Style*— Eric Koops, Esq; 16 Moreton Place, London SW1V 2NP (☎ 01 834 5615)

KOOPS, Hon Mrs Mary Claire; *née* Hogg; QC (1989); er da of Baron Hailsham of St Marylebone, KG, CH, (Life Peer; disclaimed Viscountcy of Hailsham 1963), and his w, Rt Hon Baroness Hailsham (d 1978), of St Marylebone, *née* Mary Martin; *b* 15 Jan 1947; *Educ* St Paul's Girls' Sch; *m* 11 Sept 1987, Eric Jan Leendart Koops, *qv*, s of Leendart Koops, of Hellingly, Sussex; 1 da (b 17 March 1989); *Career* barr at law 1968; govr Polytechnic of Central London; Freeman of City of London 1981; *Style*— The Hon Mrs Koops, QC; 1 Mitre Court Buildings, Temple, London EC4

KOPPEL, Hon Mrs (Jessica Gwendolen); *née* St Aubyn; da of 3 Baron St Levan (d 1978), and Hon Clementina, Gwendolen Catherine Nicolson, o da of 1 Baron Carnock; sis of Giles St Aubyn, the writer; niece of late Sir Harold Nicolson; *b* 8 Feb 1918; *m* 1939, John Patrick Koppel, late Maj Welsh Gds and former dep chm Courtaulds, s of Percy Alexander Koppel, CMG, CBE (d 1932); 1 s, 2 da; *Career* assoc memb Save the Children Fund, ctee memb Cons Assoc NW Hants; *Recreations* gardening; *Clubs* Army & Navy; *Style*— The Hon Mrs Koppel; Goodworth House, Goodworth Clatford, Andover, Hants (☎ 0264 66539)

KORALEK, Paul George; CBE (1984); s of Mr Ernest Koralek (d 1983), and Alice, *née* Muller; *b* 7 April 1933; *Educ* Aldenham, Architectural Assoc Sch of Arch (AA Dip); *m* 13 Dec 1958, (Audrey) Jennifer, da of Capt Arthur Vivian Chadwick (d 1980); 1 s (Benjamin b 14 July 1967), 2 da (Catherine b 16 March 1961, Lucy b 19 Dec 1962); *Career* ptnr and dir Ahrends Burton & Koralek Architects 1961-; princ works incl: Trinity Coll Dublin (Berkeley Library 1972, Arts Faculty Bldg 1979), residential bldg Keble Coll Oxford 1976, Templeton Coll Oxford 1969-88, Nebenzahl House Jerusalem 1972, warehouse and showroom for Habitat Wallingford, factory for Cummins Engines Shotts, J Sainsbury Canterbury Supermarket 1984, Retail HQ WH Smith Swindon 1985, Kingston Dept Store John Lewis, St Marys Hosp Newport IOW, Heritage Centre Dover, stations for extention Docklands Railway; RIBA 1957, ARA 1986; *Style*— Paul Koralek, Esq, CBE; 3 Rochester Rd, London NW1 9JH (☎ 01 485 9143); Ahrends Burton & Koralek, Unit 1, 7 Chalot Rd, London NW1 8LH (☎ 01 586 3311)

KORNBERG, Prof Sir Hans (Leo); s of Max Kornberg; *b* 14 Jan 1928; *Educ* Queen Elizabeth GS Wakefield, Sheffield Univ; *m* 1956, Monica King; twin s, 2 da (Julia, Rachel); *Career* prof biochem Leicester Univ 1960-75, Sir William Dunn prof biochem Cambridge, fell Christ's Coll Cambridge 1975- (master of Christ's 1982-); a managing tstee Nuffield Fndn 1973-, chm Royal Cmmn Environmental Pollution to 1981; memb: Kuratorium Max-Planck Inst Dortmund 1979-, ARC 1981-85, Advsy Cncl for Applied Res and Devpt 1982-85; FIBiol; Hon DSc: Cincinnati, Warwick, Leicester, Sheffield, Bath, Strathclyde; DUniv Essex; also memb various int academies; pres Br Assoc 1984-85; chm Adv Ctee Genetic Manipulations 1986-; FRSA, FRS 1965; *Clubs* United Oxford and Cambridge Universities; *Style*— Prof Sir Hans Kornberg, FRS; The Master's Lodge, Christ's Coll, Cambridge CB2 3BU

KORNBERG, Justin Anthony; s of late Isaac Eugene Kornberg and Bessie, *née* Nathan; *b* 16 August 1928; *Educ* Bronx HS of Science (USA), Clifton, Trinity Coll Cambridge, Bradford Tech, LSE; *m* 1961, Elizabeth Ann, *née* Oppenheim; 1 s, 2 da; *Career* chm Lister & Co Ltd; memb: cncl Anglo-Israel C of C, Aims the Free Enterprise Orgn, Freedom Assoc Ltd; chm Industl Property Action Gp; chm & fndr of Transpennine; *Recreations* reading, fishing, golf; *Clubs* Athenaeum; *Style*— Justin Kornberg, Esq; 15 Portland Place, London W1N 3AA

KORNICKA, Lady Lepel (Sophia); *née* Phipps; da of 4 Marquess of Normanby, CBE; *b* 1952; *m* 1975, Richard Kornicki; 2 s, 1 da; *Style*— Lady Lepel Kornicka; 15 Castello Ave, London SW15

KOSSOFF, David; s of Louis Kossoff (d 1941), and Anne Kossoff, *née* Shaklovitz (d 1966); *b* 24 Nov 1919; *Educ* Northern Poly (Sch of Architecture & Design); *m* 1947, Jennie, da of Frank Jenkins; 2 s (Simon, Paul (decd)); *Career* commercial artist 1937, draughtsman 1937-38, furniture designer 1938-39, tech illustrator 1939-45, began acting 1943, worked as actor and illustrator 1945-52, as actor and designer 1952-; BBC Repertory Co 1945-51; actg parts incl: Col Alexander Ikonenko in the Love of Four Colonels 1952, Sam Tager in The Shrike 1953, Morry in The Bespoke Overcoat, Tobit in Tobias and the Angel 1953, Prof Lodegger in No Sign of the Dove 1953, Nathan in The Boychik 1954, Mendele in The World of Sholom Aleichen 1955 (Johannesburg 1957), one-man show One Eyebrow Up 1957, Man on Trial 1959, Stars in Your Eyes 1960, The Tenth Man 1961, Come Blow Your Horn 1962, one-man show Kossoff at the Prince Charles 1963 (later called A Funny Kind of Evening), Enter Solly Gold 1970, Cinderella 1971, Bunny 1972; own Bible Storytelling programmes on radio and TV as writer and teller 1964-69; solo performance (stage) As According to Kossoff 1970-, Late Great Paul (anti-drugs performance in shcools) 1981-; has appeared in many films, won Br Acad Award 1956; MSIA, FRSA; *Books* Bible Stories retold by David Kossoff (1968), The Book of Witnesses (1971), The Three Donkeys (1972), The Voices of Masada (1973), The Little Book of Sylvanus (1975), You Have a Minute, Lord? (1977), A Small Town is a World (1979), Sweet Nutcracker (1985); *play* Big Night for Shylock (1968); *Recreations* reading, conversation; *Style*— David Kossoff Esq; 45 Roe Green Close, Hatfield, Herts AL10 9PD (☎ 07072 63475)

KOSTICK, Marjorie (Phyllis); da of Roy Tudball (d 1984), and Annie Elzabeth Webber; *b* 6 Oct 1938; *Educ* London Univ, Exeter Unv (BA), MBIM; *m* 26 Dec 1961, Gerald, s of Nathan Kostic (d 1950); 2 s (Eonor Patrick b 1964, Michael b 1966); *Career* CA; ptnr E Noel Humphreys & Co, Chester, dir Hunter St Fin Services Ltd, ACA, ATII, MBIM; *Clubs* UK Fedn of Business and Professional Women; *Style*— Marjorie Kostick; 14 Walpole St, Chester CH1 2AU (☎ 0244 375789); 6 Hunter St, Chester (☎ 0244 375789, fax 0244 44535)

KRAMER, Prof Dame Leonie Judith; DBE (1983, OBE 1976); da of late A L Gibson; *b* 1 Oct 1924; *Educ* PLC Melbourne, Melbourne Univ (BA), Oxford Univ (DPhil); *m* 1952, Harold Kramer; 2 da; *Career* prof aust literature Sydney Univ 1968- (first woman prof of Sydney Univ), visiting prof in aust studies Harvard Univ, vice-pres (formerly pres) Aust Cncl Educnl Standards 1973-, chm Aust Broadcasting Cmmn 1982-83 (cmmr 1977-82); memb of Universities Cncl 1977-86; dir Australia and New Zealand Banking Gp Ltd 1983-; nat pres Australia-Britain Soc; dir: Western Mining Corpn, Australia Fixed Tsts; chm bd of dirs Nat Inst of Dramatic Art, cmmr Electricity Cmmn of NSW (ELCOM) 1988-, sr fell Inst of Public Affairs (IPA) 1988-, dep chllr Univ of Sydney Senate 1989-; Encyclopedia Britannica Award 1986; Hon DLitt Tasmania 1952 ; Hon LLD: Melbourne Univ, ANU; MACE, FAHA; *Style*— Prof Dame Leonie Kramer, DBE; 12 Vaucluse Rd, Vaucluse, NSW 2030, Australia

KRAUSHAR, Christopher Arthur Anthony; s of Casimir Kraushar (d 1948); *b* 8 Feb 1940; *Educ* St Paul's, Christ's Coll Cambridge (MA); *m* 1963, Alison Margaret, da of Alexander Graham, of Peterborough; 1 s (Robert b 1967), 1 da (Alison b 1964); *Career* md: Gaskell & Chambers Ltd 1980-83, Dreamland Electrical Gp 1983-85, Autonumis Ltd 1985-87, Fordham Bathrooms & Kitchens Ltd 1987-; dir: Perkins Engines Gp 1978-80, MKR Hldgs 1980-83, Hepworth Plastics Ltd 1987-; CEng, FBIM, FID; *Recreations* badminton, squash, windsurfing; *Style*— Christopher Kraushar, Esq; Highfields, 26 Tinacre Hill, Wightwick, nr Wolverhampton, Staffs WV6 8DA (☎ 0902 761053)

KRAUSHAR, Peter Maximilian; s of Casimir Kraushar (d 1948) and Maria Dauksza (d 1960); Polish by origin; *b* 30 August 1934; *Educ* St Paul's Sch, Ch Ch Cambridge (MA); *m* 4 April 1959, Rosalind, da of Dr Harold Pereira (d 1976); 3 s (Mark b 1960, Gregory b 1964, Justin b 1966), 1 da (Joanna b 1962); *Career* chm: KAG Gp Ltd 1969, Mintel 1985, Kag Devpt Ltd 1969, IIS Ltd 1984, Partime Careers Ltd 1980; chm: Mktg Soc 1973-74 and 1974-75; *Books* New Products and Diversification (1977), Practical Business Devpt - What Succeeds What Does Not (1985); *Recreations* bridge, tennis, travel, reading, writing; *Style*— Peter Kraushar, Esq; 2 Lauradale Road, London N2 9LV (☎ 01 883 4736); 7 Arundel St, London WC2 (☎ 01 379 6118)

KREBS, Lady Margaret Cicely; da of J L Fieldhouse, of Wickersley, Yorks; *b* 30 Oct 1913; *Educ* Manchester Univ; *m* 1938, Sir Hans Krebs, FRS, FRCP, Nobel Laureate & sometime prof of Biochemistry at Sheffield & Oxford Univs; 2 s, 1 da; *Career* teaching; *Style*— Lady Krebs; 25 Abberbury Rd, Iffley, Oxford OX4 4ET (☎ 0865 777534)

KREMER, Lady Alison Emily; *née* Balfour; yr da of 3 Earl of Balfour (d 1968); *b* 16 Nov 1934; *m* 8 May 1963, Thomas Kremer, s of Bernard Kremer, of Kolozsvar, Transylvania; 1 s, 2 da; *Style*— Lady Alison Kremer

KRETSCHMER, John Martin; s of Dr Eric Kretschmer (d 1954); *b* 1 April 1916; *Educ* Ottershaw Coll, King's Coll London (BSc); *m* 1943, Noel Mary, da of George Herbert Tapsfield; 2 s (Robin James, Richard Andrew), 1 da (Katharine Anne Dures); *Career* Maj RE; chm: Reed & Mallik Ltd, Reed & Stuart (Pty) Ltd; dir Rush & Tompkins Gp Ltd 1978; memb cncl: Inst CEng 1979, Fedn of CE Contractors; ret 1982; elected memb Engrg Assembly 1985; tres: Mt Everest Fndn, Salisbury, S Wilts Museum Tst; CEng, FICE, FIStructE, FRGS; *Recreations* mountaineering, natural history; *Clubs* Alpine; *Style*— John Kretschmer, Esq; Tower House, Redlynch, Salisbury, Wilts (☎ 0725 20401)

KRIKLER, His Hon Judge Leonard Gideon; s of Maj J H Krikler, OBE, ED (d 1971), of St Brelade Jersey CI, and Tilly (d 1974); *b* 23 May 1929; *Educ* Milton Sch, Bulawayo S Rhodesia; *m* 1955, Thilla (d 1973); m 2, 1975, Lily; 6 s, 2 da; *Career* recorder of Crown Cts 1980-84; *Recreations* drawing, painting; *Style*— His Hon Judge Leonard Krikler; Lambs Bldgs, Temple, London EC4Y 7AS (☎ 01 435 3348)

KRIKORIAN, Gregory; CB (1973); s of Kevork Krikorian (d 1950), of Wembley, and

Christine, *née* Kevorkian (d 1972); *b* 23 Sept 1913; *Educ* Poly Secdy Sch, Lincoln Coll Oxford (BA); *m* 1943, Seta Djirdjirian, da of Souren Garabed (d 1949); 1 da (Tamara Seta); *Career* RAF Intelligence Offr Fighter Cmd 1940-45 (despatches); barr Middle Temple 1939, practised 1945-51; jr Oxford Circuit 1947-, joined slrs office HM Customs & Excise 1957, slr for Customs & Excise 1971-78, ret; *Recreations* gardening, bird watching; *Clubs* Reform, Civil Service; *Style*— Gregory Krikorian Esq, CB; The Coach Ho, Hawkchurch, Axminster, Devon EX13 5TX

KROCH, Henry Justus; CBE (1983, OBE 1968); s of Dr Curt Kroch (d 1960), of Leipzig, and Lilly, *née* Rummelsburg (d 1971); Kroch jr family bank 1870-1940 Leipzig Germany; *b* 28 Oct 1920; *Educ* St Gall & Winterthur Switzerland; *m* 8 March 1956, Margot Emma Natalie, da of late Adolf Kohlstadt; 2 s (Anthony, Ian), 1 da (Margaret (Mrs Cottam)); *Career* AB Electronic Products Gp plc: joined 1951, dir 1957, md 1964, chm and chief exec 1978 (currently pres and non exec dir); former: pres (currently hon pres) Euro Electronic Component Manufacturers Assoc Brussels, chm Electronic Components Bd, cncl memb (currently tstee) Electronic Components Industry Fedn; memb: cncl CBI Wales 1966-77, Welsh Cncl 1968-79; pres Engrg Employers Assoc of S Wales 1969-70, dir Devpt Corpn for Wales 1971-82, chm Inst of Welsh Affairs 1987-; Master Worshipful Co of Scientific Instrument Makers 1987-88, Hon Freeman Borough of Cynon Valley 1987; hon fell and life govr Univ Coll Cardiff, hon fell the Poly of Wales; CIEE, FBIM; Golden Order of Merit State of Salzburg Austria 1986; *Recreations* music, mountains, swimming; *Clubs* East India, Cardiff & County, City Livery, United Wards' of City of London; *Style*— Henry Kroch Esq, CBE; AB Electronic Products Gp plc, Abercynon, Mid Glamorgan CF45 4SF (☎ 0443 740331, telex 498606 ABEC G)

KROLL, Natasha; da of Dr Hermann Kroll (phil) and Sophie *née* Rabinovich; *b* 20 May 1914, (Moscow); *Educ* Berlin HS; *Career* TV and film designer; teacher of window display Reimann Sch of Art London 1936-40; display mangr: Rowntrees Yorks 1940-42, Simpson Piccadilly 1942-55; sr designer BBC TV 1955-66, freelance 1966-; RDI, FSIAD; *Recreations* painting, entertaining; *Style*— Ms Natasha Kroll; 5 Ruvigny Gardens, London SW15 (☎ 01 788 9867)

KROLL, Dr Una Margaret Patricia; da of Brig George Arthur, CB, DSO, MC (d 1970), and Hilda Evelyn Hill, *née* Pediani (d 1965); *b* 15 Dec 1925; *Educ* Malvern Girls' Coll, Cambridge Univ (MA, MB, BChir); *m* 1957, Leopold, s of Bp Leopold Kroll (d 1949), of New York; 1 s (Leopold), 3 da (Florence, Elisabeth, Una); *Career* medical practitioner Missionary Serv in Liberia and Namibia 1953-61, GP (England) 1961-81, community health doctor 1981-, deaconess (C of E) 1970-, memb: Christian Medical Cmmn 1978-85, CRAC (Churches Religious Advsy Cncl to BBC) 1980-85, Gen Synod of C of E (diocese of Chichester) 1980-87; Deacon Church in Wales Dec 1988; *Books* A Signpost to the World (1975), Flesh of my Flesh (1976), Lament for a Lost Enemy (1978), Sexual Counselling (1980), A Spiritual Exercise Book (1985), Growing Older (1988); *Style*— Rev Dr Una Kroll; St Mary's Cottage, Osbarton, Monmouth, Gwent NP5 JE3

KRUSIN, Sir Stanley Marks; CB (1963); *b* 8 June 1908; *Educ* St Paul's Sch, Balliol Coll Oxford; *m* 1, 1937 (w died 1972); 1 s, 1 da; m 2, 1976; *Career* served WW II RAFVR; barr Middle Temple 1932, parly counsel 1953-69, second parly counsel 1970-73; kt 1973; *Style*— Sir Stanley Krusin, CB; 5 Coleridge Walk, London NW11 (☎ 01 458 1340)

KUDLICK, Martin; s of Joseph Kudlick and Raie Kudlick; *b* 27 Dec 1933; *Educ* Westcliff High; *m* 16 Sept 1962, Margaret Helen, da of David Fisher; 1 s (Jonathan b 1970), 2 da Suzanne b 1968, Nicola b 1973); *Career* CA, sr ptnr H W Fisher & Co; *Recreations* walking, jogging, reading, music; *Clubs* Reform; *Style*— Martin Kudlick, Esq; 36 Paines Lane, Pinner, Middx (☎ 01 868 4055); 69/76 Long Acre, London WC2 E9JW (☎ 01 379 3461, fax 01 831 1290)

KUENSSBERG, Nicholas; s of Dr Ekkehard Von Kuenssberg, CBE, of Little Letham, Haddington, East Lothian, and Constance, *née* Hardy; *b* 28 Oct 1942; *Educ* Edinburgh Acad, Wadham Coll Oxford (BA); *m* 27 Nov 1965, Sally, da of Hon Lord Robertson, (Lord of Session), of 13 Moray Place, Edinburgh; 1 s (David b 1971), 2 da (Joanna b 1973, Laura b 1976); *Career* chm Dynacast Int Ltd 1978-; dir: J & P Coats Ltd 1978-, West of Scotland Bd Bank of Scotland 1984-88, South of Scotland Electricity Bd 1984-, Coats Patons plc 1985-, Coats Viyella plc 1986-, Standard Life Assurance Co 1988-; visiting prof Strathclyde Business Sch 1988- (visiting fell 1986-87), govr Queen's Coll Glasgow 1989-; FCIS 1977, FBIM 1978; *Recreations* travel, languages, opera, sport; *Style*— Nicholas Kuenssberg, Esq; 6 Cleveden Drive, Glasgow G12 OSE; Coats Viyella plc, 166 St Vincent St, Glasgow G2 5PA (☎ 041 221 8711, fax 041 248 2512)

KUFFELER, John Philip; s of Capt F de Blocq van Kuffeler of Royal Netherlands Navy, and Stella *née* Hall; *b* 9 Jan 1949; *Educ* Atlantic Coll, Clare Coll Cambridge (MA); *m* 3 April 1971, Lesley, da of Dr EM Callander; 2 s (Hugo b 1974, Alexander b 1979), 1 da (Venetia b 1977); *Career* CA 1973, Peat Marwick Mitchell & Co 1970-77 (assignments UK, Holland, Germany, Egypt) head of corporate fin Grindley Brandts Ltd 1980-82 (mangr 1977-80); Brown Shipley & Co Ltd: dir 1983-, head of corporate fin 1983-, memb exec ctee 1985-, head investmt banking UK and USA 1986-; currently gp chief exec numerous public cos incl: Campbell & Armstrong plc, St Paul's Fin and Investmt Ltd, Lease Mgmnt Servs Ltd; memb ctee Issuing Houses Assoc 1984-88; FCA; *Recreations* fishing, shooting, tennis; *Clubs* Newmarket; *Style*— John de Blocq van Kuffeler, Esq; Park House, Chrishall, Nr Royston, Herts; 24 Chester Row, London SW1 (☎ 01 823 5182); Founders Court, Lothbury, London EC2R 7HE (☎ 01 606 9833, fax 01 606 9833 x 4128, car tel 0860 525 290, telex 886704)

KUIPERS, John Dennis; s of Joannes Kuipers (d 1961), of Holland, and Marion, *née* Sewell (d 1973), of Spain; *b* 9 July 1918; *Educ* St John's Coll Cambridge (MA), Univ of London (MSc), Univ of Amsterdam (DSc), Univ of Strathclyde (LLD); *m* 17 Feb 1940, Johanna Adriana, da of Mackiel Pieter De Roon (d 1968), of Holland; 3 s (Francis b 1941, Adrian b 1944, Richard b 1946); *Career* SOE 2 Lt and Capt 1941-44, Royal Netherlands Army Gen Serv Capt and Maj 1944-45; chm Royal De Betine Co Ltd Holland 1945-65 (dir), memb EEC Indust Fedn 1964-74, pres ESC of EEC 1970-72 (memb 1962-74), vice-pres Fedn of Netherlands Industs 1970-75, chm Foreign Affairs Ctee Cncl of Netherlands Indust Fedns 1970-75, visiting prof Strathclyde Business Sch 1973-78; Kt Order Netherlands Lion (1974), Offr Orante Nassau (1969), Cdr Italian Order of Merit (1972), Cdr Order of Leopold II Belgium (1972), Offr Order of George I Greece (1964); *Books* Resale Price Maintenance in GP 1950; *Recreations* study of art and history, music; *Style*— Dr Dennis Kuipers; Los Algarrobos, PU 106, 03730 Javea, Alicante, Spain (☎ 6 579 1334); 7 Avenue Paul Hymans, (Bte 5) Brussels 1200 (☎ 2 762 7173)

KULUKUNDIS, Eddie (Elias George); s of George Elias Kulukundis (d 1978), and Eugenia, *née* Diacakis; 5 generation shipping family; *b* 20 April 1932; *Educ* Collegiate Sch NY City NY; Salisbury Sch Salisbury Connecticut, Yale Univ; *m* 4 April 1981, Susan Hampshire (actress), *qv*, da of George Kenneth Hampshire (d 1964); *Career* dir: Rethymnis & Kulukundis ltd, 1964-, London & Overseas Freighters plc 1980-86; memb: Lloyd's 1964-, Cncl 1983-85, 1985-89; Baltic Exchange 1959-; govr: Greenwich Theatre Ltd, The Raymond Mander and Joe Mitchenson Theatre Collection Ltd, Royal Shakespeare Theatre, Sports Aid Fndn Ltd (vice-chm 1987-); chm Knightsbridge Theatrical Prodns Ltd 1970-; dir Hampstead Theatre Ltd; memb cncl of mgmnt: Royal Shakespeare Theatre Tst (vice-chm 1983), Traverse Theatre Club; memb exec Cncl SWET; tstee: Salisbury Sch, Conn, Theatres Trust; theatrical producer, London prodns incl (some jtly): Enemy, The Happy Apple, Poor Horace, The Friends, How the Other Half Loves, Tea Party and The Basement (double bill), The Wild Duck, After Haggerty, Hamlet, Charley's Aunt, Straight Up, London Assurance, Journey's End, Small Craft Warnings, A Private Matter, Dandy Dick, The Waltz of the Toreadors, Life Class, Pygmalion, Play Mas, The Gentle Hook, A Litle Night Music, Entertaining Mr Sloane, The Gay Lord Quex, What the Butler Saw, Travesties, Lies, The Sea Gull, A Month in the County, A Room With a View, Too True to Be Good, The Bed Before Yesterday, Dimetos, Banana Ridge, Wild Oats, Candida, Man and Superman, Once a Catholic, Privates on Parade, Gloo Joo, Bent, outside Edge, Last of the Red Hot Lovers, Beecham, Born in the Gardens, Tonight at 8.30, Steaming, Arms and the Man, Steafel's Variations, Messiah, Pack of Lies, Of Mice and Men, The Secret Diary of Adrian Mole Aged 13-3/4, Camille, The Cocktail Party, N Y prodns (jtly): How The Other Half Loves, Sherlock Holmes, London Assurance, Travesties, The Merchant, Players, Once a Catholic; FRSA; *Recreations* theatre; *Clubs* Garrick; *Style*— Eddie Kulukundis, Esq; Winchmore House, 15 Fetter Lane, London EC4A 1JJ (☎ 01 583 2266, telex 8811736 RANDK G, facsimile 01 583 0046) (car ☎ 0836 236806, 0034 219957)

KUT, David; s of Jakob Kut (d 1962), of London , and Frieda Sachs (d 1979); *b* 5 May 1922; *Educ* Adass Real Gymnasium of Berlin Germany, ORT Tech Sch Berlin, Northampton Poly London, Univ of London (BSc); *m* 2 Nov 1952, Seena, da of Itzak Assuschkewitz (d 1950), of London; 1 s (Steven Humphrey b 1959), 1 da (Deborah Helen b 1962); *Career* WWII Aux War Serv; draughtsman Benham and Sons (Engrs) Ltd 1943-46, jr engr Oscar Faber and Ptnrs Consulting Engrs 1946-49, sr engr Powell Duffryn Tech Servs Ltd 1949-54, fndr David Kut and Ptnrs (sr ptnr) 1954-87, conslt 1988-; author: Heating and Hot Water Servs in Buildings (1968), Warm Air Heating (1970), Applied Waste Recycling for Energy Conservation (with G Hare 1981), District Heating and Cooling for Energy Conservation (with R E Diamant, 1981), Dictionary of Applied Energy Conservation (1982), Applied Solar Energy (with G Hare, 1983), Efficient Waste Management (with G Hare 1989); chm professional affairs sub-ctee Engrg Cncl Regnl Orgn Ctee (London Central), past memb of guide Ctee of Inst of Heating and Ventilating Engrs; memb: FIMechE, FCIBS, FCIArb, MInstE, MConsE, CEng; *Recreations* graphology, chess, yoga, tropical fish, swimming; *Style*— David Kut, Esq; 5 Thornton Way, London NW11 6RY (☎ 01 455 7018); David Kut and Ptnrs, Rosebery House, Tottenham Lane, London N8 9BY (☎ 01 348 5171/6, fax 01 340 8926, telex 291347)

KWIATKOWSKI, Lady Barbara; *née* Legge; da of late 7 Earl of Dartmouth; *b* 1916; *m* 1945, Adam Kwiatowski, Lt Polish Army; 4 s; *Career* formerly in First Aid Nursing Yeo; *Style*— Lady Barbara Kwiatkowski; The Bothy, Patshull Park, Wolverhampton, W Midlands

KYLE, James; s of John Kyle (d 1978), of Brocklamont, Ballymena, N Ireland, and Dorothy Frances, *née* Skillen (d 1967); *b* 26 Mar 1925; *Educ* Ballymena Aca, Queen's Univ Belfast (MB, BCh, MCh, DSc); *m* 31 July 1950, Dorothy Elizabeth, da of Alexander Galbraith (d 1945); 2 da Frances b 1952, Maureen b 1956); *Career* lectr in surgery Liverpool Univ 1957, sr lectr Aberdeen Univ 1959, currently sr surgn Aberdeen Royal Infirmary; former chm: BMA rep body 1984-87, Scottish Ctee for Hosp Med Servs 1977-81, Scottish Jt Conslts Ctee, 1984-89 (memb Gen Cncl 1979-); FRCS 1954, FRCSI 1954, FRCSE 1964; *Books* Pye's Surgical Handicraft (1962), Peptic Ulceration (1960), Crohn's Disease (1972), Scientific Foundations of Surgery (1967); *Recreations* skiing, amateur radio GM4CHX, philately; *Clubs* Royal Northern, University; *Style*— James Kyle, Esq; Grianan, 74 Rubislaw, Den North, Aberdeen AB2 4AN (☎ 0224 317 966); Aberdeen Royal Infirmary, AB9 2ZB (☎ 0224 681 818); Grampian Health Board, 1 Alb yn Place, Aberdeen (☎ 0224 589 901)

KYLE, Kenneth Warnock; s of David Warnock Kyle (d 1967), and Erminie Corinaldi, *née* Levy (d 1969); *b* 9 August 1919; *Educ* Jamaica Coll Jamaica; *m* 3 June 1944, Dorothy Joyce, da of James Arthur Best Horton (d 1950); 1 s (Steven b 1950), 1 da (Denise b 1952); *Career* FICA; *Recreations* gardening, bridge; *Style*— Kenneth W Kyle, Esq; 87 Warren Rd, Leigh-on-Sea, Essex SS9 3TT (☎ 0702 557869); 11 Weston Rd, Southend-on-Sea, Essex SS1 1AZ

KYLE, (James) Terence; s of James Kyle (d 1976), of Belfast, and Elizabeth, *née* Cinnamond; *b* 9 May 1946; *Educ* The Royal Belfast Acad Inst, Christ's Coll Cambridge (MA); *m* 17 May 1975, Diana, da of Duncan Sager Jackson, of Buxton; 1 s (Robin b 1984), 2 da (Susan b 1979, Alison b 1981); *Career* ptnr Linklaters & Paines 1979- (asst slr 1972-79); Freeman City of London Slrs Co 1979; memb Law Soc 1972; *Recreations* cricket, squash; *Style*— J T Kyle, Esq; Barrington House, 59-67 Gresham St, London EC2Y 7JA (☎ 01 606 7080, fax 01 606 5113, telex 884349)

KYNASTON, Guy (Onslow Fairfax); TD (1975); s of Unthank Fairfax Kynaston (d 1964), and Ina Louisa, *née* Kidman (d 1973); *b* 8 May 1919; *Educ* Bedford Sch; *m* 16 July 1949, Joyce Winifred Milora, da of Lt-Gen Sir Humfrey Gale KBE, CVO, CB, MC (d 1971); 2 s (James b 1951, Guy b 1955), 1 da (Celia b 1953); *Career* cmmnd Bedford Yeo TA 1938, WWII (Lt) Far East; vice-pres Scottish Employers Cncl for the Clay Industs 1962; *Recreations* foreign travel, tennis, field sports; *Clubs* The Colquhoun (Glasgow); *Style*— Guy Kynaston, Esq, TD; Croxdale Wood House, Croxdale, Co Durham DH6 5JW

KYNGE, Maj (John) Julian; s of Lt Col Sydney John Kynge, MC and bar (d 1950), and Marian Hinchcliffe, *née* Lancaster (d 1977); *b* 15 Jan 1932; *Educ* Canford Sch, RMA Sandhurst, RMC of S Schrivenham; *m* 18 Nov 1961, Augusta Pauline Foster, da of Clifford Hubert Davies, MA, CF, FRGS (d 1980), Canon of York; 1 s (James b 1963), 2 da (Marian b 1962, Madelaine b 1969); *Career* Regular Army Offr, Maj served: Korea, Japan, Malaya, Hong Kong, Cyprus, Aden, Malaysia; farmer and landowner; *Recreations* game shooting, fishing, cricket; *Clubs* Junior, Army and Navy; *Style*— Maj Julian Kynge; Potto Grange, Northallerton, N Yorks, (☎ 0642 700212)

KYRLE POPE, Vice Admiral Sir Ernie John; KCB (1976); s of Cdr Rowland Cecil Kyrle Pope (d 1976), and late Agnes Jessie MacDonald; *b* 22 May 1921; *Educ* RNC Dartmouth; *m* 21 Dec 1968, Phyllis Mary Webber; 5 s (Christopher, Andrew, Nicholas Ernie, Martin, Jonathan); *Career* served WW II HMS Decoy 1962-64, dir Naval Equipment 1964-66, CO HMS Eagle 1966-68, Flag Offr Western Fleet Flotillas 1969-71, COS to C in C Western Fleet 1971-74, cdr Allied Naval Forces S Europe 1974-76, Rear Adm 1969, Vice Adm 1972; pres RN Assoc; *Clubs* Army and Navy; *Style*— Sir Ernie J Kyrle Pope, KCB; Homme House, Much Marcle, Ledbury, Hereford

KYRLE POPE, Rear Adm Michael Donald; CB (1969), MBE (1945), DL (Hertfordshire 1983); s of Cdr Rowland Kyrle Cecil Pope, DSO, OBE, DL, RN (d 1976), of Ledbury Herefordshire, and Mrs Agnes Jessie, *née* Macdonald (d 1968); *b* 1 Oct 1916; *Educ* Wellington Coll; *m* Angela Suzanne, da of Adm Sir Geoffrey Layton, GBE, KCMG, DSO (d 1964), of Rowland's Castle Hants; 1 s (James), 1 da (Emma); *Career* joined RN 1934-70, Submarine Serv, Capt HMS Vanguard 1946-47, Sr Naval Offr Persian Gulf 1962-64, Cdre Intelligence Def Intelligence Staff MOD 1965-67, Rear Adm COS to C-in-C Far East Singapore 1967-69; gen mangr Middle East Navigation Aids Serv (Bahrain) 1971-77, dir Jerusalem and East Mission Tst 1978-; Deans Administrator St Albans Cathedral 1977-80; *Recreations* country interests, sailing; *Clubs* Army & Navy; *Style*— Rear Adm Michael Kyrle Pope, CB, MBE, DL; Hopfields, Westmill, Buntingford, Herts

L

L'ETANG, Dr Hugh Joseph Charles James; s of Dr Joseph Georges L'Etang (d 1966), of London, and Frances Helène Maas (d 1961); *b* 23 Nov 1917; *Educ* Haileybury, St John's Coll Oxford (BA), St Barts Hosp (BM, BCh); *m* 1951, Cecily Margaret, da of Frank Stanley Tinker (d 1923), of Barrowmore Hall, Cheshire; 1 s (Guy), 1 da (Jacqueline); *Career* RAMC 1943-46, RMO 5 Bn Royal Berks Regt, serv Normandy and NW Europe 1944-46 (despatches), RAMC (TA) 1947-55, Lt-Col RAMC 1953-56, OC 167 Field Ambulance (TA); med advsr: N Thames Gas Bd 1948-56, Br Euro Airways 1956-58, Sun Life Assur Soc 1947-55, John Wyeth & Bros Ltd 1958-64 (head of med dept 1964-69); ed: The Practitioner 1973-82 (dep ed 1969-72), Travel Med Int 1982-; ed-in-chief RSM Int Congress & Symposium Series, conslt ed The Physician; memb Royal Utd Servs Inst, Int Inst Strategic Studies, Mil Commentators Circle; hon fell Coll of Physicians of Philadelphia 1985; *Books* The Pathology of Leadership (1969), Fit to Lead? (1980); *Recreations* reading, study of medical aspects of Military and Foreign Affrs; *Clubs* Utd Oxford & Cambridge; *Style—* Dr Hugh L'Etang; 27 Sispara Gardens, West Hill Rd, London SW18 1LG

LA ROCHE, Anthony Philip; TD (1978); s of Philip La Roche (d 1988), and Ruby, *née* Peach; *b* 10 July 1944; *Educ* St Georges Coll, Weybridge, Surrey; *m* 10 Sept 1965, Jane Elizabeth, da of Herbert Custerson, 2 da (Amy Jane b 1972, Sophie Elizabeth b 1979); *Career* TA 1962-82, md: Allen Harvey Ross Ltd 1976-81, Cater Allen Futures Ltd 1981-; dir: Cater Allen Hldgs plc 1982-, London Int Fin Futures Exchange 1984-; *Recreations* swimming, cycling, field sports; *Clubs* City of London; *Style—* Anthony La Roche, Esq, TD; Cater Allen Futures ltd, 1 King William Street, London, EC4N 7AU, (☎ 01 283 7432 fax 01 929 1641)

LA TROBE-BATEMAN, Richard George Saumarez; s of John Salmarez La Trobe-Bateman, of Sark, CI, and Margaret Jane, *née* Schmid; *b* 17 Oct 1938; *Educ* Westminster, St Martins Sch of Art, RCA (MDes); *m* 26 April 1969, Mary Elizabeth, da of Arthur Jolly, JP (d 1984), of Hove; 1 s (Will b 1973), 2 da (Emily b 1971, Alice b 1976); *Career* studied sculpture under Anthony Caro St Martins Sch of Art 1958-61, studied furniture under David Pye RCA 1965-68; exhibited: UK Design Centre, Crafts Cncl, V & A, Br Craft Centre, Contemporary Applied Art; exhibited in: Belgium, Holland, Denmark, Austria, France, USA, Japan; works in public collections incl: V & A, Crafts Cncl, Leeds City Art Collection, Tyne and Wear Art Collection, Shipley Gallery, Portsmouth Gallery Craft Study Centre (Bath); memb Crafts Cncl 1982-86; prof of furniture San Diego State Univ USA 1986-87; work presented to HRH Prince of Wales by Craft Cncl 1984; *Clubs* Contemporary Applied Arts; *Style—* Richard La Trobe-Bateman, Esq; Elm House, Batcombe, Shepton Mallet, Somerset BA4 6AB (☎ 074 985 442)

LABAND, Paul Alexander Kenneth; s of Oliver Ernest Kenneth Laband, MBE, of Glenyra, Earlsferry, Elie, Fife, and Margaret Ann, *née* MacCallum; *b* 15 August 1948; *Educ* Strathallan Sch Forgandenny Perth, Downing Coll Cambridge (BA); *m* 22 Aug 1970, Shelia, da of Albert Russell, of Poole, Dorset; 2 da (Kathryn b 14 June 1974, Caroline b 15 Feb 1977); *Career* stockbroker Simon & Coates 1970-73, asst exec dir Abbey Life 1984-86 (portfolio mangr 1973-84), dep md Abbey Life Investmt Servs Ltd 1989 (dir 1986-88); ASIA; *Recreations* athletics, sailing, singing; *Style—* Paul Laband, Esq; Compton Cottage, 5 Canford Crescent, Canford Cliffs, Poole, Dorset BH13 7NB (☎ 0202 700460); Abbey Life Assurance Co Ltd, 80 Holdenhurst Rd, Bournemouth BH8 8AL (☎ 0202 292373, fax 0202 296816, telex 41310)

LABOUCHERE, Sir George Peter; GBE (1965), KCMG (1951); s of Lt-Col Frank Anthony Labouchere (d 1948), of 15 Draycott Ave, London; *b* 2 Dec 1905; *Educ* Charterhouse, La Sorbonne; *m* 1943, Rachel Katharine, da of Hon Eustace Hamilton-Russell (d 1962, 6 s of 8 Viscount Boyne); *Career* FO 1929, cnsllr Nanking 1946, Buenos Aires 1948; min: Vienna 1950-53, Hungary 1953-55; ambassador to: Belgium 1955-60, Spain 1960-66 (ret); pres Shropshire branch of CPRE; FRSA; *Recreations* shooting, fishing, chinese ceramics, modern art; *Clubs* White's, Brooks's, Beefsteak, Pratt's, Dilettante Soc; *Style—* Sir George Labouchere, GBE, KCMG; Dudmaston, Bridgnorth, Shropshire (☎ 0746 780 351)

LABOVITCH, Carey Elizabeth; da of Neville Labovitch, MBE, and Sonia Deborah, *née* Barney; *b* 20 April 1960; *Educ* Lyçée Française De Londres, St Paul's Girls' Sch London, St Hilda's Coll Oxford (MA); *Career* magazine publisher 1980-; md Cadogan Press Gp Ltd; fndr publisher of Blitz Magazine 1980 and The Magazine Distribution Book 1984; awards for publishing: Guardian Best Graphics Award 1981, Magazine Publishing Entrepreneur of the Year Award (highly commended) 1984; BBC Enterprise Award for Small Businesses 1985; yst ever finalist in Veuve Clicquot/IOD, Businesswoman of the Year Award 1986, judge for Guardian/NUS Student Media Awards 1987 and BBC Enterprise Awards 1987; patron of the Virgin Charitable Fndn; *Recreations* cartooning, cinema, photography, reading; *Style—* Miss Carey Labovitch; 40-42 Newman Street, London W1P 5PA (☎ 01 436-5211, fax 01 436 5290)

LACAMP, Philippe Frederick; s of Philippe Albert Lacamp (d 1982), of Milton Regis, Kent, and Dorothea Jeanette, *née* Barker; *b* 12 Mar 1940; *Educ* City of London Sch; *m* 31 July 1965, Marie-Louise, da of Capt Peter Stephens Impey, of High Barn, Finstall, Worcs; 1 s (Philippe Paul b 5 Feb 1969), 2 da (Melissa b 26 April 1971, Camilla b 18 Dec 1972); *Career* dir Allders Ltd 1973-82, independent conslt 1982-; mangr C of E primary sch, tstee Contacts Charity for Handicapped Children, chm St Mary's Norton Restoration Ctee; Freeman: City of London 1961, Worshipful Co of Blacksmiths 1966; MBCS 1963; *Books* Microcomputers in Retail (1984); *Recreations* singing, piano, tennis, golf; *Clubs* Kent and Canterbury; *Style—* Philippe Lacamp, Esq; Prospect House, High St, Westerham, Kent TN16 1RG (☎ 0959 644 22, fax 0959 644 22)

LACE, John Herbert; s of William Stanley Lace (d 1958), and Helen (d 1985); *b* 12 Sept 1934; *Educ* King Williams Coll; *m* 2 Sept 1961, Ann Morwen; 1 s (Jonathan b 1967), 1 da (Victoria b 1970); *Career* REME 1953-55; currently Maj Engr and Staff Corps RE; md: Babcock Power 1987 (projects dir 1984-87, construction dir 1977-84); *Recreations* golf, aviation; *Clubs* Royal Troon GC; *Style—* John Lace, Esq; Reindene, 86 Kilnford Drive, Dundonald, Kilmarnock, Ayrshire (☎ 0563 850272); Babcock Energy Ltd, 165 Great Dover Street, London SE1 4YB (☎ 01 407 8383, telex: 884151)

LACEY, Nicholas Stephen; s of John Stephen Lacey, of Highgate, London, and Norma, *née* Hayward; *b* 20 Dec 1943; *Educ* Univ Coll Sch, Emmanuel Coll Cambridge (MA), Architectural Assoc London (AADip); *m* 1, 1965 (m dis 1976), Nicola, da of Dr F A Mann; 2 s (Joshua b 1968, William b 1973), 1 da (Olivia b 1970); m 2, 1981, Juliet, da of Dr Wallace Aykroyd, CBE (d 1979); 2 da (Laetitia b 1978, Theodora b 1980); *Career* ptnr: Nicholas Lacey & Assoc Architects 1971-83, Nicholas Lacey Jobst & Ptnrs Architects 1983-; winner: Wallingford Competition 1972, Crown Reach 1977; jt winner Arunbridge 1977; prize winner Paris Opera House Competition 1983; *Recreations* music, theatre, sailing; *Style—* Nicholas Lacey, Esq; Reeds Wharf, Mill St, London SE1 (☎ 01 237 6281); Nicholas Lacey, Jobst & Partners, 66-70 Worship St, London EC2 (☎ 01 247 5971)

LACEY, Timothy John Twyford; s of William Joseph Lacey, of Sunbury on Thames, and Phylis Edith, *née* Thomas; *b* 17 May 1935; *Educ* Downside; *m* 24 March 1962, Anne Patricia, da of Maj Reginald William Henley-Stuart (d 1987), of Hereford; 2 s (Michael b 1963, Christopher b 1965); *Career* chief exec William Lacey Gp and of all subsid cos; *Recreations* golf, farming; *Style—* Timothy Lacey, Esq; Little Wildwood Farm, Wildwood Lane, Cranleigh, Surrey GU6 8JR; Elmbridge House, Elmbridge Lane, Woking, Surrey GU22 9AF (☎ 04862 70474, fax 04862 29451, car 0836 713060)

LACHS, His Hon Judge Henry Lazarus; s of Samuel Lachs (d 1960); *b* 31 Dec 1927; *Educ* Liverpool Inst HS, Pembroke Coll Cambridge; *m* 1959, Dr Edith Lachs, JP, da of Ludwig Bergel; 4 da; *Career* rec of the Crown Ct 1972-79, circuit judge 1979-; regnl chm Mental Health Review Tbnl 1968-79; *Style—* His Hon Judge Lachs; 41 Menlove Gdns West, Liverpool L18 (☎ 051 722 5936)

LACON, Edmund Richard Vere; s and h of Sir Edmund Vere Lacon, 8 Bt; *b* 2 Oct 1967; *Style—* Edmund Lacon, Esq; Milbrook, Holton, St Peter, Halesworth, Suffolk

LACON, Sir Edmund Vere; 8 Bt (UK 1818); s of Sir George Vere Francis Lacon, 7 Bt (d 1980), by his 1 w Hilary; *b* 3 May 1936; *Educ* Woodbridge Sch Suffolk; *m* 1963, Gillian, da of Jack Henry Middleditch, of Wrentham, Suffolk; 1 s, 1 da; *Heir* s, Edmund Richard Vere b 2 Oct 1967; *Career* gen mangr; *Style—* Sir Edmund Lacon, Bt; Milbrook, Holton St Peter, Halesworth, Suffolk (☎ 098 67 2536)

LACROIX, Hon Mrs (Susan Gina); *née* Weinstock; da of Baron Weinstock; *b* 1955; *Educ* Cranbourne Chase, St Hilda's Oxford, LSE; *m* 1980, Laurent Lacroix; *Style—* The Hon Mrs Lacroix

LACY, Ernest Joseph Henry; JP; s of James Herbert Lacy (d 1959), and Amelia Mary, *née* Gilbert (d 1969); *b* 6 Oct 1912; *Educ* Willesden Tech Coll; *m* 24 March 1940, Irene Sara Lynforth, da of John Alfred Pike (d 1934); 2 da (Diane Lynforth Bell b 1941, Jennifer Mary Picklance b 1947); *Career* bldg and public works contractor; chm and md of own business; chm Arun DC 1984 (chm planning and devpt ctee), fin and admin memb Littlehampton Harbour Bd, tstee Arundel Castle; Freeman City of London, memb Worshipful Co of Paviors; FCIOB; *Recreations* local affairs, deep sea fishing, wood carving; *Clubs* City Livery; *Style—* Ernest Lacy, Esq, JP; Seafurl, Second Ave, Felpham, West Sussex PO22 7LJ (☎ 0243 692 157)

LACY, Patrick Bryan Finucane; s of Sir Maurice John Pierce Lacy, 2 Bt (d 1965); and hp to Btcy of bro, Sir Hugh Maurice Pierce Lacy, 3 Bt; *b* 18 April 1948; *Educ* Downside; *m* 1971, Phyllis Victoria, da of Edgar P H James; 1 s, 1 da; *Style—* Patrick Lacy, Esq; 11 Tudor Gdns, Barnes, SW13

LACY-HULBERT, Edward; OBE (1974); s of Charles Edward Lacy Lacy-Hulbert (d 1934), of Warlingham, Surrey, and Haidee Irene, *née* Piguenit (d 1959); *b* 14 Mar 1904; *Educ* Shrewsbury, Univ of Liege with apprenticeship at 'La Societe Anonyme de la Meuse' a Sclessin-Lez-Liege Belgium; *m* 9 March 1935, Gabrielle, da of Gerald Lloyd-Jones (d 1956), of Esher, Surrey, and Donnington, Albrighton; 1 s (David Edward b 1937), 1 da (Sarah b 1941); *Career* Capt 8 Relief Batty 106 Co of London Z AA Batty 1941-45; sales engr: Assoc Equipment Co of Southall 1930-32, dir Lacy-Hulbert & Co Ltd 1933-35 (chm & md 1935-72, ret); pres Br Compressed Air Soc 1938 and 1964-65; chm: Croydon and Sutton local employment ctee 1963-74, Croydon and dist disablement advsy ctee 1958-75; Sykes Lacy-Hulbert Ltd Gp of Cos (now known as Henry Sykes Ltd) 1966-72; memb DHSS SW London Supplementary Benefit Appeals Tbnl 1971-76; cncllr Dorking UDC 9 years (ultimately vice-chm); chm Commercial Union Assur Co Ltd, and Croydon Local Bd 1965-78; yacht and power boat racing until end 1981; since retirement has invented and patented the 'SITIKIT' Seat & Back Support; FRSA, FInstD; *Recreations* sailing; *Clubs* Royal Thames YC, Itchenor SC; *Style—* Edward Lacy-Hulbert, Esq, OBE; Shackerley, Lavant, Chichester, West Sussex (☎ 0243 527399); The Lacy-Hulbert Company, 66 Midhurst Rd, Lavant, Chichester, West Sussex (☎ 0243 527841)

LADAS, Diana M; da of Bertram E Hambro (d 1916), and Margaret C N Boyle, *née* Lubbock (d 1969); gggda of astronomer Sir William Herschel; *b* 8 Feb 1913; *Educ* Downe House Newbury, Girton Coll Cambridge (MA); *m* 1945 (m dis 1952), Alexis, s of Christopher Ladas (d 1935), of Greece; 1 s (Andreas Ladas b 1947); *Career* temp asst princ civil serv during WWII serv: London, Cairo, Athens, Washington DC, New York; vice princ Queens Gate Sch, head mistress Heathfield Sch Ascot, ret 1972; *Style*— Mrs Diana Ladas; 154 Peckham Rye, London SE22 9QH (☎ 01 693 8233)

LADENBURG, Michael John Carlisle; s of John Arthur George Ladenburg, of W Sussex, and Yvonne Rachel Bankier, *née* Carlisle (d 1968); *b* 2 Feb 1945; *Educ* Charterhouse, Christ Church Oxford (MA); *m* 1971, Susan Elizabeth, da of Dr George Denys Laing, of Surrey; 1 s (William b 1980), 2 da (Harriet b 1975, Olivia b 1978); *Career* merchant banker; dir: J Henry Schroder Wagg & Co Ltd 1979-88, Robert Fleming & Co Ltd 1988-; *Recreations* music, sailing, golf, skiing, reading, tennis; *Clubs* Hurlingham, Tandridge GC; *Style*— Michael Ladenburg, Esq; 62 Cloncurry St, London SW6 6DU (☎ 01 736 5605); Robert Fleming & Co Ltd, 25 Copthall Ave, London EC2R 7DR (☎ 01 638 5858)

LAFLIN, Reginald Ernest; s of Sydney Ernest Laflin (d 1975), of The Crescent, Rustington, West Sussex, and Rosie, *née* Nichols (d 1988); *b* 21 Mar 1926; *Educ* Sir Walter St John's Public Sch, Battersea Poly (HNC), Borough Poly (HNC); *m* 28 Sept 1952, (Ruby) Elsie, da of George Francis Brown; 1 s (Michael John), 1 da (Susan); *Career* WWII pilot/navigator in trg RAFVR 1943-45; md APV Paralec Ltd (chief engr APV Paramount Ltd) 1952-75, assoc ptnr Revell Hayward & Ptnrs 1975-78, ptnr EG Phillips Son & Ptnrs 1978-88, ptnr Nordale Assocs 1988-; Ceng, FIEE, FIMechE, FICBSE, FIMechIE, MIM, MConst, FID; *Clubs* Directors; *Style*— Reginald Laflin, Esq; 9 Gorham Ave, Rottingdean, Brighton, E Sussex (☎ 0273 300 106); Noredale Assocs, 51-53 Burney Rd, Greenwich, London SE10 8EX (☎ 01 858 4482, fax 01 858 5876, telex 895 1039)

LAGDEN, Ronald Gordon; s of Reginald Bousfield Lagden, OBE, MC (d 1944), and late Christine, *née* Haig; *b* 4 Sept 1927; *Educ* Marlborough, RMC Sandhurst (Sword of Honour), Harvard, AMP Univ; *m* 1951, Elizabeth Veronica, da of John Kenneth Mathews (d 1972); 2 s, 1 da; *Career* Lt Queen's Own Cameron Highlanders serv Italy; Maconochie Foods 1947-53, Bowater Scott Corpn 1953-63, md Findus Ltd 1963-68, chm and md Quaker Oats Ltd 1968-71 (chm and pres Europe for Quaker Oats Co 1971-85, non exec dir 1985-); non exec dir: WA Baxter & Sons Ltd, Eldridge Pope; chm Caters Int, dir Pagepine Ltd, chm Golf Dept Int (Brussels); *Books* Principles and Practices of Management (jtly); *Recreations* golf, gardening, reading, bridge, family; *Clubs* Royal and Ancient GC, Sunningdale GC, Royal GC de Belgique, Pulborough/ Anglo Belge (Knightsbridge); *Style*— Ronald Lagden, Esq; Spear Hill Cottage, Ashington, Sussex

LAGESEN, Air Marshal Sir Philip Jacobus; KCB (1979, CB 1974); *Career* Air Cdre RAF 1970, SASO Strike Cmd 1972, Air Vice-Marshal 1972, dep cdr RAF Germany 1973-75, AOC No 1 Gp RAF Strike Cmd 1975-78; AOC 18 Gp Northwood 1978-; *Style*— Air Marshal Sir Philip Lagesen KCB; c/o Lloyds Bank, 6 Pall Mall, London SW1

LAIDLAW, Sir Christophor Charles Fraser; s of late Hugh Alexander Lyon Laidlaw; *b* 9 August 1922; *Educ* Rugby, St John's Coll Cambridge; *m* 1952, Nina Mary Prichard; 1 s, 3 da; *Career* BP Co Ltd: dir ops 1971-72, md 1972, dep chm 1980-81; chm BP Oil 1977-81; exec chm ICL plc 1981-84; dir: Commercial Union Assur 1978-83, Barclays Bank Int 1980-, Barclays Bank plc 1981-, Amerada Hess Corpn 1983-, Barclays Merchant Bank Ltd 1984-, Redland 1984-; warden Chandlers' Co 1982; pres German Chamber of Industry and Commerce in UK 1983-; kt 1982; *Style*— Sir Christophor Laidlaw; Bridge House, Putney Bridge, London SW6 3JX

LAIDLAW, Bt-Col John Andrew Mitchell; TD (1949); s of Austin Laidlaw (d 1963); *b* 20 August 1916; *Educ* Malvern; *m* 1943, Sonia (d 1981), da of late P M Haines; 2 da; *Career* 1939-45 serv AA Cmd N W Europe, cmd 118 Reg RA 1945-46, cmd 452 Reg RA 1953-55; DL Essex 1963-84; *Style*— Col John Laidlaw, TD; The Old Stable, Ramsdell Rd, Monk Sherborne, Basingstoke, Hants R626 5HS (☎ 0256 850984)

LAIDLAW, (Henry) Renton; s of Henry Renton Laidlaw, of Broughty Ferry, of Dundee, and Margaret McBeath, *née* Raiker; *b* 6 July 1939; *Educ* James Gillespie's Edinburgh, Daniel Stewart's Coll Edinburgh; *Career* golf corr Evening News Edinburgh 1957-68, news presenter Grampian TV Aberdeen 1968-70, news presenter and reporter BBC Scotland Edinburgh 1970-73, golf corr The London Evening Standard 1973-, ITV golf presenter 1973-, presenter BBC Sport on 2 1985-; *Books* Play Golf (with Peter Alliss), Tony Jacklin: The First 40 Years (with Tony Jacklin), Play Better Golf; *Recreations* theatre-going, playing golf, travelling; *Clubs* Caledonian, Sunningdale GC; *Style*— Renton Laidlaw, Esq; Evening Standard, Derry St, London (☎ 01 938 6000); BBC Sport, Portland Place, London (☎ 01 580 44669 ext 5050)

LAIDLAW, Robin David; s of Alexander Banatyne Stewart Laidlaw (d 1968), and Margaret Alicia, *née* Hutt (d 1981); *b* 8 Oct 1928; *Educ* George Watson's Coll, Heriot Watt Univ; *m* 29 Nov 1951, Noreen Frances, da of Reginald Wilson (d 1979); 1 s (David b 1956), 1 da (Deborah b 1953); *Career* combustion engr; dir: Laidlaw Drew & Co Ltd 1965-, St Serf's Sch Tst 1975- (chm 1967-75); sec Scottish Sailing Assoc 1977-81; CEng, MIMechE; *Recreations* flying (light aircraft, previously Rang gliders and microlights), photography, sailing; *Clubs* Edinburgh Flying, Edinburgh Photographic Society; *Style*— Robin Laidlaw, Esq; The Smiddy, Dalmeny, W Lothian, EH30 9TU; Laidlaw Drew & Co Ltd, Sighthill, Edinburgh EH11 4HG (☎ 031 453 5445; telex: 72609, fax: 031 453 4793)

LAIDLAW THOMSON, Hilary Dulcie; da of Dr Edward Laidlaw Thomson, Surgn Capt RNVR, and Dulcie Elspeth Mary, *née* Redfearn; *b* 9 July 1939; *Educ* international; *m* 26 Oct 1962, Antony Meysey Wigley Severne, s of Charles Edward Severne; 1 s (Charles Edward); *Career* chief exec Media Relations Ltd; *Recreations* gardening, writing, skiing; *Clubs* The White Elephant; *Style*— Ms Hilary Laidlaw Thomson; Media Relations, 125 Old Brompton Rd, London SW7 3RN (☎ 01 835 1000)

LAIGHT, Barry Pemberton; OBE (1970); s of Donald Norman Laight (d 1935), of Durham, and Norah, *née* Pemberton (d 1946); *b* 12 July 1920; *Educ* Johnston Sch Durham, Birmingham Central Techn Coll, Merchant Verturers Techn Coll Bristol, Bristol Univ (MSc); *m* 17 Feb 1951, Ruth da of Alfred Sutro Murton, DCM (d 1975), of Warsash, Hants, 1 s (Timothy b 1952), 1 da (Deborah b 1954); *Career* chief aerodynamicist Bristol Aeroplane Co 1937-52, tech dir Blackburn and General Aircraft 1952-61, dir mil projects Hawker Siddeley Aviation 1961-77, engrg dir Short Bros 1977-82, sec RAeS 1982-85 (pres 1974-76), conslt DTI Vertical Axis Wind Turbines 1985-; memb: NATO Advsy Gp on Aerospace R & D Aircraft Res Assoc, Int Cncl Aeronautical Scis; AERO Mensa; govr Kingston Poly; FEng 1981, FRAes 1955, FIMechE 1983, FInstD 1975, MAIAA 1982; *Recreations* music, mathematics, walking; *Clubs* Athenaeum; *Style*— BP Laight, Esq, OBE; Dunelm, 5 Littlemead, Esher, Surrey, KT10 9PE, (☎ 0372 63216)

LAINE, Cleo - Clementine Dinah (Mrs John Dankworth); OBE (1979); *b* 28 Oct 1927; *m* 1, 1947 (m dis 1958), George Langridge; 1 s; m 2, 1958, John Philip William Dankworth; 1 s, 1 da; *Career* vocalist; *Style*— Miss Cleo Laine, OBE; International Artistes Representation, Regent House, 235 Regent St, WC1 (☎ 01 439 8401)

LAING, Alastair Stuart; CBE (1980), MVO (1959); s of Capt Arthur Henry Laing (d 1943), and Clare May, *née* Ashworth (d 1959); *b* 17 June 1920; *Educ* Sedbergh; *m* 17 July 1946, Audrey Stella, da of Dr Frederick William Hobbs (d 1924); 1 s (Stuart b 1956, d 1961); *Career* WWII Capt 10 Gurkha Rifles IA 1940-46: 3/10 Gurkha Rifles 1941-42, 10 Gurkha Rifles Regtl Centre 1943-44, seconded to civil admin in Bengal 1944-46; dep dir-gen Cwlth War Graves Cmmn 1975-83 (various appts 1947-75); chm Vale of Aylesbury Hunt 1981-87 (jt sec 1970-81); *Recreations* gardening, racing, hunting, history; *Style*— Alastair Laing, Esq, CBE, MVO; Wagtails, Lower Wood End, Nr Marlow, Bucks SL7 2HN (☎ 062 844 481)

LAING, Austen; CBE (1973); s of William Laing (d 1940), of Sunderland, Co Durham, and Sarah Ann Laing (d 1972); *b* 27 April 1923; *Educ* Bede Collegiate Sch Sunderland, Newcastle Univ (BA); *m* 5 July 1945, Kathleen, da of Alfred Pearson, MM (d 1930), of Sunderland; 1 s (Peter b 1952), 1 da (Lesley b 1947); *Career* WWII Lt (A) RNVR 1942-46; econ lectr Durham Univ 1950-56, admin Distant Water Vessels Devpt Scheme 1956-61, dir-gen British Trawlers Fedn Ltd 1962-82; memb ctee of inquiry into veterinary profession 1971-74, cncl Food From Britain 1986-; chm Home-Grown Cereals Authy 1983-; *Recreations* walking; *Clubs* Army and Navy; *Style*— Austen Laing, Esq, CBE

LAING, David Magnus; s of Rev John Magnus Laing (d 1949), and Edith Alice, *née* Marlowe; *b* 22 May 1933; *Educ* St Edward's Sch Oxford, St Edmund Hall Oxford (MA); *m* 1957, Deirdre Ann; 3 da (Philippa b 1957, Louise b 1959, Rosalind b 1960); *Career* mgmnt conslt; dir Mktg Improvements Ltd 1981-; *Recreations* fishing, opera, gardening; *Style*— David M Laing, Esq; Elms, Wisborough Green, W Sussex; 7 Bulstrode St, London W1; 17 Ulster Terrace, Regents Park, London NW1

LAING, Dr Gordon James; ISO (1985); s of James William Laing (d 1941), of Oldham, Lancs, and Mary, *née* Shaw (d 1978); *b* 12 Jan 1923; *Educ* Eltham Coll London, Oldham Hulme GS, Oldham Tech Coll, UMIST, Sussex Univ (MSc), London Univ (PhD); *m* 8 Feb 1975, Frances, d of John Wilson (d 1958); 1 s (Fraser James b 9 Nov 1976); *Career* res engr Nat Gas and Oil Engine Co Ltd until 1949; Miny of Supply 1949: scientific offr 1949, sr scientific offr i/c of an RARDE outstation 1951, princ scientific offr 1955, trials dir overseas ops, sr princ scientific offr 1983, left DCAE 1985; qualified as an NHBC builder and formed Surrey Residential Devpts Ltd; currently exec dir and mgmnt conslt for socs dealing with homeless or incurably sick; Freeman: City of London 1973, Worshipful Co of Bakers 1973; CEng, MIMechE, MIEE 1947, MORS 1970; *Books* Building Scientific Models (1986); *Recreations* tennis, painting; *Style*— Dr Gordon Laing, ISO; 23 Woodend Park, Cobham, Surrey KT11 3BX

LAING, Sir Hector; s of Hector Laing; *b* 12 May 1923; *Educ* Loretto, Jesus Coll Cambridge; *m* 1950, Marian Clare Laurie; 3 s; *Career* WWII Scots Gds 1942-47, demob Capt; chm: United Biscuits Hldgs plc 1972- (dir 1953-64, md 1964-72); dir: Bank of England 1973-, Allied Lyons plc (formerly Allied Breweries Ltd) until 1982; chm: Food and Drink Industs Cncl 1977-79, Scottish Business in the Community 1932, The Lambeth Fund 1983, City and Industl Liaison Cncl 1985, Business in the Community; pres Goodwill 1983; govr: Wycombe Abbey Sch 1981, Nat Inst of Econ and Social Res 1985; jt tres Cons Pty 1988; Hon DUniv Stirling, Hon DUniv Heriot-Watt, hon fell Jesus Coll Cambridge; kt 1978; *Style*— Sir Hector Laing; United Biscuits (Hldgs) plc, Grant House, Syon Lane, Isleworth, Middx TW7 5NN

LAING, Maj Hugh Charles Desmond; s of Capt Hugh Desmond Bertram Laing (d 1953), and Dorothy Linton, *née* Harvey (d 1986); *b* 24 Dec 1931; *Educ* Kings Coll Sch Canada, Millfield, RMA Sandhurst; *m* 2 May 1959, Rosemary, da of Charles Legh Shuldham Cornwall-Legh, CBE, DL; 1 da (Camilla Catherine Harvey b 29 June 1964); *Career* cmmnd 2 Lt Scots Gds 1952, Adj Gds Trg Bn Pirbright, GSO3 16 Ind Parachute Bde, Staff Coll Camberley, GSO2 Int Coord Jt Int Staff Hong Kong, Co Cmd Scots Gds, Sqdn Ldr 22 SAS Regt, GSO2 Br Def Liaison Staff Washington, ret 1973; Sqdn Ldr Duke of Lancaster's Own Yeo 1984-88; called to the Bar Inner Temple 1976, practicing Northern circuit Manchester; pres Scots Gds Assoc Manchester branch; *Recreations* golf, walking, shooting, photography; *Clubs* Special Forces; *Style*— Maj Hugh Laing; Cherry Hall, Cherry Lane, Lymm, Cheshire (☎ 0925 75 5954); Crown Square Chambers, 1 Deans Çt, Manchester (☎ 061 833 9801)

LAING, Dr Ian Geoffrey; s of George Edward Laing and Frances May, *née* Hutton; *b* 15 May 1933; *Educ* Leeds GS, Univ of Leeds (BSc, PhD); *m* 5 April 1958, Una, da of Albert Hannam (d 1982); 2 s (Andrew Nicholas b 1962, Jonathan Richard b 1964); 2 da (Deborah Claire b 1960, Rebecca Sarah b 1967); *Career* dir of health, safety and ecology Ciba-Geigy plc 1986-, tech dir Clayton Aniline Co Ltd 1978-85 (prod dir 1971-77, production mangr 1966-71, memb of bd 1971-), memb Health and Safety Cmmn's Advsy Ctee on Toxic Substances 1978-85; CIA: memb Cncl for Industl Safety, Health and Environmental Control 1985-, Carcinogenic Substances Ctee 1960, chm 1974-86; chm Task Force for Carcinogens Mutagens and Teratagens 1985-; FRSC, FSDC, FBIM; *Recreations* photography, oil and water colour painting, skiing, walking, cycling; *Style*— Dr Ian Laing; Shieldaig, Calrofold Lane, Rainow, nr Macclesfield, Cheshire SK11 0AA (☎ 0625 20552); Ciba-Geigy plc, Hurdsfield Industrial Estate, Macclesfield, Cheshire SK10 2LY (☎ 0624 21933, fax 0625 619637)

LAING, Sir (William) Kirby; JP (Middx 1965), DL (1978); s of Sir John Laing, CBE (d 1978), and Beatrice, *née* Harland (d 1972); *b* 21 July 1916; *Educ* St Lawrence Coll Ramsgate, Emmanuel Coll Cambridge (MA); *m* 1939, Joan Dorothy (d 1981), da of Capt E C Bratt (d 1965); 3 s; m 2, 1986, Isobel Lewis, da of late Edward Wray; *Career* chm Laing Properties plc 1978-87, dir John Laing plc 1939-80; pres: Nat Fedn of Bldg Trades' Employers 1965 and 1967, Inst of Civil Engrs 1974, Royal Albert Hall 1979-; hon fell Emmanuel Coll Cambridge 1983; kt 1968; *Clubs* Naval & Military, Royal Fowey YC; *Style*— Sir Kirby Laing, JP, DL; 133 Page St, London NW7 2ER

LAING, Hon Mrs; Hon Lucy Ann Anthea; *née* Low; da of 1 Baron Aldington, KCMG, CBE, DSO, TD, PC; *b* 1956; *Educ* Cranborne Chase Sch; *m* 1979, Alasdair North Grant Laing; 1 da (Emma Mary b 1980), 2 s (Alexander William b 1982, Frederick Charles b 1985); *Style*— The Hon Mrs Laing; Relugas, Forres, Moray,

Scotland

LAING, Peter Anthony Neville Pennethorne; s of Lt-Col Neville Ogilvie Laing, DSO (d 1950); *b* 12 Mar 1922; *Educ* Eton, Paris Univ; *m* 1958, Penelope Lucinda, da of Sir William Pennington-Ramsden, 7 Bt, of Muncaster Castle, Cumberland; 2 da; *Career* attaché Br Embassy, Madrid 1944-46; int mktg conslt in: Western Europe, US, Caribbean, Latin America; dir ITC Project for UN 1975-; *Style*— Peter Laing, Esq; Sotogrande, Guardiaro, Cadiz, Spain

LAING, Ronald David; s of D P M Laing, and Amelia Laing; *b* 7 Oct 1927; *Educ* Glasgow Univ (MB CHB, DPM); *Career* West of Scotland Neurosurgical Unit 1951, Central Army Psychiatric Unit Netley 1951-52, dept of psychological Med Glasgow Univ 1953-56, Tavistock Clinic 1956-60, Tavistock Inst of Human Relations 1960-, fell Fndns Fund for Res in Psychiatry 1960-67, dir Langham Clinic for Psychotherapy 1962-65, fell Tavistock Inst of Med Psychology 1963-64, princ investigator schizophrenia and family research unit Tavistock Inst 1964-67, chm Philadelphia Assoc 1964-82; *Books incl:* The Divided Self (1960), The Self and Others (1961), The Politics of Experience and the Bird of Paradise (1967), Knots (1970), The Politics of the Family (1971), The Facts of Life (1976), Do You Love Me (1977), Conversations with Children (1978), Sonnets (1979), The Voice of Experience (1982); *Style*— Ronald Laing, Esq

LAIRD, Edgar Ord; CMG (1969), MBE (1958); s of Edgar Balfour Laird (d 1945), of Monifieth, Angus; *b* 16 Nov 1915; *Educ* Rossall, Emmanuel Cambridge; *m* 1940, Heather Lonsdale, da of Arthur Eric Forrest (d 1971); 4 da; *Career* serv E Africa Cmd, WWII Maj Middle E and Far E; AMOCS Uganda and Malaya 1939-58, ret as dep sec PM's Dept Fedn of Malaya 1957; CRO 1958, high cmmr Brunei 1963, dep high Cmmr Nigeria 1965-69, FCO 1969-72, Br Govt rep Assoc States W Indies 1972-75; *Recreations* playing the piano; *Clubs* Royal Cwlth Soc; *Style*— Edgar Laird, Esq CMG, MBE; St Jude's Cottage, 87 Fore St, Topsham, Exeter (☎ 0392 874183)

LAIRD, Endell Johnston; *b* 6 Oct 1933; *Educ* Forfar Academy; *m* 5 Sept 1958, June; 1 s (David b 1965), 2 da (Susan b 1960, Jackie b 1963); *Career* ed in chief and dir Scottish Daily Record & Sunday Mail, chm Scottish Editors Ctee 1986-88, memb D Notice Ctee 1986-; *Recreations* walking, golf, bridge; *Clubs* Bishopbriggs GC, Bishopbriggs Bridge; *Style*— Endell J Laird, Esq; 10 Glenburn Gdns, Bishopbriggs, Glasgow; Daily Record Anderston Quay, Glasgow (☎ 041 242 3353)

LAIRD, Gavin Harry; s of James Laird; *b* 14 Mar 1933; *Educ* Clydebank HS; *m* 1956, Catherine Gillies Campbell; 1 da; *Career* full-time Trade Union Official 1971-; memb: Scottish Industl Devpt Advsy Bd 1975-, exec cncl Amalgamated Union of Engrg Workers 1975-, TUC Gen Cncl 1979-; dir Br Nat Oil Corpn 1976-; *Style*— Gavin Laird, Esq; 24C Castleton Ct, Castleton Drive, Newton Mearns, Glasgow

LAIRD, John; s of John Laird d 1962, and Mary, *née* McGalliard; *b* 16 Mar 1936; *Educ* Oatlands Sch, Royal Coll of Sci and Technol (MSc); *m* 1957, Joan Norma, da of late John Shrigley (d 1981); 1 s (Andrew b 1958), 1 da (Joanna b 1964); *Career* dir Lahoud Engrg Co (UK) Ltd; CEng, FIMarE; *Recreations* music, reading; *Clubs* Naval; *Style*— John Laird, Esq; 1 Hill St, Berkeley Sq, London W1X 7FA (☎ 01 493 1293)

LAIRD, Michael Donald; OBE (1983); s of George Donald Struthers Laird (d 1980), and Catherine Brown Dibley, *née* Tennent; *b* 22 Mar 1928; *Educ* Loretto Sch, Edinburgh Coll of Art ARIBA (Dip Art); *m* 23 March 1957, Hon Kirsty Noel-Paton, da of Baron Ferrier (Life Peer), *qv*; 2 s (Simon b 1958, Stephen b 1962), 1 da (Anna b 1958); *Career* lectr dept of architecture Edinburgh Univ and Coll of Art 1954-57, architect and industl designer Michael Laird & Ptnrs 1954-, MacLaren Fellowship 1956-58; works incl: Edinburgh Univ Central Facilities Bldg, head off Standard Life Assur Co, computer HQ Royal Bank of Scotland; sundry awards: Saltire Soc, Bri Steel, Civic Tst, Stone Fedn, Royal Scottish Acad etc; FRSA (gold medallist 1968), FSIA, FRIAS, RIBA; *Recreations* sailing, skiing, hill walking; *Clubs* New (Edinburgh); *Style*— Michael Laird, Esq, OBE; 22 Moray Place, Edinburgh EH3 6DB (☎ 031 225 5859); Michael Laird and Partners, 5 Forres St, Edinburgh EH3 6DE (☎ 031 226 6991, fax 031 226 2771, telex 72465)

LAIRD, Robert Edward (Bob); s of Robert Laird (d 1975), of Seaford, Sussex, and Esther Margaret, *née* Stoney (d 1976); *b* 25 Dec 1940; *Educ* Aldenham, Harvard; *m* 8 Aug 1964, Mary Theresa, da of Martin Cooke (d 1969), of Galway, Ireland; 2 s (Robert Richard Martin b 1964, Julian Alexander b 1968) 1 da (Caroline b 1971); *Career* various appts Unilever Ltd 1959-76, dir Carnation Foods 1977-80, md Vandemoortele 1980-86, chm Polar Entertainment Gp 1986-88, dir Keith Butters Ltd 1988; cncl memb Coronary Prevention Gp; Freeman: City of London 1984, Worshipful Co of Upholders 1984; MInsTM 1978, FBIM 1980, MIOD 1982; *Recreations* golf, jogging, reading, genealogy; *Clubs* Old Aldenhamians, Harvard Business Sch Club of London, The Sportsman; *Style*— Bob Laird, Esq; 53 Stafford Ct, Kensington High St, London W8 7DW (☎ 01 937 0387); Keith Butters Ltd, Kellett Gate, Spalding, Lincolnshire PE12 6EH (☎ 0775 68831, fax 0775 61618, telex 32646)

LAIRD CRAIG, Hon Mrs (Roxane); *née* Balfour; o da of 2 Baron Balfour of Inchrye, *qv*; *b* 8 Sept 1955; *m* 1978, Adrian Laird Craig; 1 s (Robert Joseph b 1982), 2 da (Mary Ann Josephine b 1984, Alethea Katharine b 1986); *Style*— The Hon Mrs Laird Craig; Libberton House, Libberton, nr Carnwath, Lanarkshire

LAISTER, Peter; s of late Horace Laister; *b* 24 Jan 1929; *Educ* King Edward's Sch Birmingham, Manchester Univ Coll of Technol; *m* 1, 1951, Barbara Cooke; 1 s, 1 da; m 2, 1958, Eileen Alice Goodchild, *née* Town; 1 da; *Career* RAF 1949-51; Esso Petroleum Co 1951-66, gp md Br Oxygen Co Ltd (BOC Int Ltd) 1969-79, Ellerman Lines Ltd 1976-79, chief exec Thorn EMI 1983- (chm 1984-); chm: BOC Fin Corpn (USA) 1974-75, Tollemache & Cobbold Breweries 1978-79, London & Hull Insur Co 1976-79, BMCL 1984- (dir 1976-), Park Hotels plc 1985-, Tower Gp 1985-, Contec plc; dir Mirror Gp Newspapers Ltd 1985-; memb Industl Devpt Advsy Bd 1981-; cncl memb: Industl Soc 1971, UCL 1978 chm Br Fndn for Age Res 1982-; *Recreations* private flying, boating, angling, gardening, photography; *Clubs* Athenaeum; *Style*— Peter Laister, Esq; Thatches, 92 Staines Rd, Wraysbury, Bucks

LAITHWAITE, Prof Eric Roberts; s of Herbert Laithwaite (d 1954), of Kirkham, Lancs, and Florence, *née* Roberts (d 1966); *b* 14 June 1921; *Educ* Kirkham GS, Manchester Univ (BSc, MSc, PhD, DSc); *m* 8 Sept 1951, Sheila Margaret, da of Arthur Haighton Gooddie (d 1981), of Hawkinge, Kent; 2 s (Martin b 1954, Dennis b 1965), 2 da (Helen (Mrs Boam) b 1956, Louise b 1962); *Career* WWII RAF 1941-46 (RAF Farnborough 1943-46); lectr Manchester Univ 1951-64, prof heavy electrical engrg Imperial Coll London 1964-86, (emeritus prof 1986-); pres Assoc for Sci Educn 1970; dir: Linear Motors Ltd 1971-, Londspeed Ltd 1975-, Cotswold Res Ltd; conslt Brian Colquhoun & Ptnrs 1975-; former conslt: Br Rail, Tracked Hovercraft Ltd, GEC, Pilkington Bros; RS SG Brown Award and Medal 1966, fell Univ of Hong Kong 1986; Nikola Telsa Award; TV and radio progs incl: Tomorrow's World, Horizon, The World Around Us, Science Now, Dial a Scientist; CEng, FIEEE, FIEE, FRCA; *Books incl:* Induction Machines for Special Purposes (1966), Propulsion Without Wheels (1966), The Engineer in Wonderland (1967), How to Invent (1970), Engineer Through the Looking Glass (1974), Dictionary of Butterflies and Moths (1981), Invitation to Engineering (1984), Shape is Important (1986), History of Linear Electric Meters (1988); *Recreations* entomology, gardening; *Clubs* Athenaeum; *Style*— Prof Robert Laithwaite; Department of Electrical Engineering, Imperial College, London SW7 (☎ 01 589 5111, ext 5112)

LAJTHA, Prof Laszlo George; CBE (1983); s of Laszlo John Lajtha (d 1963), of Budapest, and Rose Stephanie Emily, *née* Hollos; *b* 25 May 1920; *Educ* Presbyterian HS Budapest, Univ Med Sch Budapest (MD), Exeter Coll Oxford (DPhil); *m* 28 Aug 1954, Gillian MacPherson, da of Dr Alastair Wingate Henderson (d 1985); 2 s (Christopher b 1955, Adrian b 1957); *Career* asst prof physiology Univ of Budapest 1944-46, res assoc haematology Radcliffe Infirmary Oxford 1947-50, head radiobiology laboratory Churchill Hosp Oxford 1951-62, res fell pharmacology Yale Univ USA 1954-55, dir Paterson Inst of Cancer Res Christie Hosp Manchester 1962-83, prof experimental oncology Univ of Manchester 1970-83 (emertius 1983), ed Br Journal of Cancer 1972-82; pres: Br Soc of Cell Biology 1977-80, Euro Orgn for Res and Treatment of Cancer 1979-81; memb: bd govrs Pownall Hall Prep Sch Wilmslow 1972-83, cncl All Saints Sch Bloxham 1986-; hon citizen Texas 1964, hon memb Hungarian Acad of Scis 1983; Hon MD Univ of Szeged Hungary 1980; FRCPath 1973, FRCPE 1980; *Books* Use of Isotopes in Haematology (1961); *Recreations* achaeology, medieval history, baroque music, alpine gardening, bonsai; *Clubs* Athenaum, RN Med; *Style*— Prof Laszlo Lajtha, CBE; Brook Cottage, Little Bridge Rd, Bloxham, Oxfordshire OX15 4PU (☎ 0295 720 311)

LAKE, Sir (Atwell) Graham; 10 Bt (GB 1711), of Edmonton, Middx; s of Capt Sir Atwell Henry Lake, 9 Bt, CB, OBE, RN (d 1972); *b* 6 Oct 1923; *Educ* Eton; *m* 1983, Mrs Katharine Margaret Lister, da of D W Last; *Heir* bro, Edward Geoffrey Lake; *Career* serv in Gilbert & Ellice Mil Forces 1944-45, Col Admin Serv 1945-55, sec to Govt of Tonga 1950-53, Br High Cmmn New Delhi 1966-68, FCO 1969-72; sr tech advsr MOD to 1983, ret; *Recreations* bridge, chess, tennis, skiing; *Clubs* Lansdowne; *Style*— Sir Graham Lake, Bt; Magdalen Laver Hall, Chipping Ongar, Essex

LAKE, John Walter; s of Norman Lake (d 1952), of Derby, and Ella, *née* Mills (d 1984); *b* 7 May 1930; *Educ* Repton; *m* 4 Sept 1959, Anne Patricia, da of Thomas Ash (d 1982), of Derby; 1 s (John Emmerson b 1965); *Career* builders' merchant; chm and md E & J W Lake (Hldgs) Ltd 1979-, E & J W Lake Ltd 1964-; chm Great Central Merchants Ltd 1961-, chm and md J H Thornhill (coal and haulage) Ltd 1964-, chm Brookhouse Johnson Ltd 1975-, Magiglide Leisure Ltd 1975-, N Midland Bldg Supplies 1969-, Belper Bldg Supplies 1980-; Freeman City of London 1982, Liveryman Worshipful Co of Builders' Merchants 1982; FIBM 1969, FInstD 1965, FBIM 1982; *Recreations* squash, tennis, hockey; *Clubs* The Carrington, Derby Hockey; *Style*— John W Lake, Esq; Flower Lillies, Windley, Derbyshire DE5 2LQ (☎ 077 389 455); Lake House, Parcel Terrace, Derby DE1 1LQ (☎ 0332 49083, telex 37131)

LAKE, Terence Edward; s of Walter Joseph Lake (d 1978), and Maud, *née* Ford (d 1951); *b* 26 July 1933; *Educ* East Ham GS for Boys, Leicester Univ (BSc); *m* 11 June 1955, Margaret, da of Gerald Steechman: 2 da (Hazel (Mrs Anwell) b 2 June 1957, Helen (Mrs Kitchingham) b 24 Jan 1959); *Career* Nat Serv 1954-56, Sch of Ammunition Bromley (Sgt ammunition examiner); gp fin controller Elliott Automation 1960-68, commercial dir and md Instrument Maintenance and Erection Co 1968-75, dir Roxby Engrg Ltd 1981-; Liveryman Worshipful Co of Scientific Instrument Makers; *Recreations* reading, gardening, travel, wine; *Style*— Terence Lake, Esq; 7 Lawpings, New Barn, Longfield, Kent DA3 7NH (☎ 04 747 4190); Roxby House, Station Rd, Sidcup DA15 7EJ (☎ 01 300 3393, fax 01 300 4400, telex 896172 ROXBY G)

LAKEMAN, Enid; OBE (1980); da of Horace Bradlaugh Lakeman (d 1962), and Evereld, *née* Simpson (d 1950); *b* 28 Nov 1903; *Educ* Tunbridge Wells Co Sch, Bedford Coll London (BSc); *Career* WAAF 1941-45; memb of staff Electoral Reform Soc 1945- (dir 1960-79, ed conslt 1979-); parly candidate (Lib): St Albans 1945, Brixton 1950, Aldershot 1955 and 1959; *Recreations* travel, gardening, reading; *Clubs* Nat Lib; *Style*— Miss Enid Lakeman, OBE; 37 Culverden Ave, Tunbridge Wells, Kent TN4 9RE (☎ 0892 21674; office: 01 633 0483)

LAKER, Sir Frederick Alfred; *b* 6 August 1922; *Educ* Simon Langton Sch Canterbury; *m* 1, 1946 (m dis 1968), Joan; 1 s (decd), 1 da (Elaine); m 2, 1968 (m dis 1975), Rosemary Black, of S Africa; 2 da; m 3, 1975 (m dis 1982), Patricia Gate, of Oklahoma; 1 s (Freddie Jr b 1978); m 4, 1985, Jacqueline Ann Harvey; *Career* with Short Bros Rochester 1938-40, Gen Aircraft 1940-41, ATA 1941-46, md Aviation Traders Gp 1946-65, md Br Utd Airways 1960-65, chm and md Laker Airways (Int) Ltd 1966-82; established Skytrain Holidays 1983; memb Airworthiness Requirements Bd to 1982, aviation and travel conslt 1982-; Lloyd's underwriter 1964-82; chm Guild of Air Pilots and Air Navigators; hon fell UMIST; Hon DSc City Univ, Hon DSc Cranfield Inst of Technol, Hon LLD Manchester; kt 1978; *Clubs* Jockey, Eccentric, Little Ship; *Style*— Sir Freddie Laker; Furzegrove Farm, Chailey, E Sussex (☎ 082 572 2648)

LAKES, Gordon Harry; CB (1987), MC (1951); s of Harry Lakes (d 1980), and Annie, *née* Butcher (d 1970); *b* 27 August 1928; *Educ* Army Tech Sch Arborfield, RMA Sandhurst; *m* 2 Oct 1950, Nancy, da of Joseph Watters Smith (d 1952); 1 da (Alison b 1953); *Career* cmmnd RA 1948, 39 Medium Regt 1949-50, Lt 1950, 170 Ind Mortar Batty 1950-52, pilot 657 Air Op sqdn RAF 1952-54, Capt 1953, Adj 383 Light Regt RA (DCRH) TA 1954-56, 2 Ind Field Btg RA 1956-58, promoted Maj to command Ghana Recce Sqdn Ghana Army 1958-60, ret 1960; asst govr HM Prison Serv 1961, HM Borstal Feltham 1962-65, asst princ Offrs Trg Sch Leyhill 1965-68, govr HM Remand Centre Thorp Arch 1968-70, Prison Serv HQ 1970, govr class 3 1971, HM prison Pentonville 1974, govr class 2 1975, HM Prison Gartree 1975, prison Serv HQ 1977, govr class 1 1979, asst controller and dep chief inspr of prisons 1982, AUSS and dep dir gen of prison serv 1985, ret 1988; *Recreations* golf, photography; *Style*— Gordon Lakes, Esq, CB, MC; Havelock House, New St, Charfield, Wotton-Under-Edge, Glos GL12 8ES (☎ 0453 842 705)

LAKEY, Prof John Richard Angwin; s of late William Richard Lakey, and late Edith, *née* Hartley; *b* 28 June 1929; *Educ* Morley GS, Sheffield Univ (BSc, PhD); *m* 22 Dec

1955, (Dr) Pamela Janet, JP, da of late Eric Clifford Lancey; 3 da (Joanna, Philippa (Mrs Lewry), Nicola (Mrs King)); *Career* R & D Simon-Carves Ltd 1953, secondment to AERE Harwell 1954-57 and GEC 1957-60, asst prof RNC Greenwich 1960-80 (prof of nuclear sci and Technol 1980-89, dean 1984-86 and 1988-89); visiting lectr Harvard Univ 1984-, hon visiting prof Surrey Univ 1987-, memb Medway Health Authy 1981-; pres: Soc for Radiological Protection 1975-76, Inst of Nuclear Engrs 1987-, Int Radiation Protection Assoc 1988-; vice-pres London Int Youth Sci Fortnight 1988; Freeman City of London, Liveryman of Worshipful Co of Engrs 1988; FInsP 1963, FINucE 1974, FInstE 1988, CEng 1978, CPhys 1985; *Books* Protection Against Radiation (1961), Radiation Protection Measurement - Principles and Practices (1975), Alara Principles Practices and Consequences (1987); *Recreations* yachting, photography, conversation; *Clubs* Athenaeum, Medway YC, RNSA; *Style—* Prof John Lakey; Royal Naval College, Greenwich, London SE10 9NN (☎ 01 858 2154, ext 4108, fax 01 858 2154, ext 4300)

LAKIN, Hon Mrs (Helena Daphne); *née* Pearson; da of 2 Viscount Cowdray, JP, DL (d 1933); *m* 1939, Lt-Col John Lakin, TD, JP, DL, *qv*; 1 s (Michael, b 1955); *Style—* The Hon Mrs Lakin; Hammerwood House, Iping, nr Midhurst, W Sussex (☎ 073 081 3635)

LAKIN, John; TD, JP (West Sussex), DL (West Sussex 1977-); s of Henry Gilbert Lakin (d 1964), of Pipers Hill, Warwicks; *b* 22 Dec 1910; *Educ* Eton, Oxford Univ; *m* 1939, Helena Daphne, *qv*, youngest da of 2 Viscount Cowdray (d 1933); 1 s; *Career* WWII Lt-Col Warwicks Yeo; serv: Persia, Syria, Iraq, El Alamein, Italy; JP Warwicks 1951, DL Warwicks 1950-67; farmer; *Clubs* White's; *Style—* Lt-Col John Lakin, TD, JP, DL; Hammerwood House, Iping, nr Midhurst, W Sussex GU29 0PF (☎ 073 081 3635)

LAKIN, Sir Michael; 4 Bt (UK 1909); s of Sir Henry Lakin, 3 Bt (d 1979); *b* 28 Oct 1934; *Educ* Stowe; *m* 1, 1956 (m dis 1963), Margaret, da of Robert Wallace, of Mount Norris, Co Armagh; m 2, 1965, Felicity, da of Anthony Denis Murphy, of Londiani, Kenya; 1 s, 1 da; *Heir* s, Richard Anthony Lakin b 26 Nov 1968; *Style—* Sir Michael Lakin, Bt; Torwood, Post Office, Rosetta, Natal, S Africa

LAKIN, Noel Oscar Ernest; s of Oscar Dennis Lakin (d 1953), and Beryl Ann, *née* Danert (d 1968); *b* 19 Oct 1924; *Educ* Irish Christian Bros Schs in India; *m* 1958, Aurela Avadney Barbara, da of Thomas William Tristram (d 1968); 3 s (Peter b 1959, Andrew b 1966, Russell b 1968), 3 da (Paula b 1960, Noeline b 1962, Ursula b 1964); *Career* md Taymel 1982 (dep chm Taymel 1985), dir Taylor Woodrow Cons Ltd; *Recreations* tennis; *Style—* Neol Lakin, Esq; Alpha House, Westmount Centre, Delamere Road, Hayes Middx UB4 0HD

LALANDI, Lina Madeleine; OBE 1975; da of late Mikolas Kaloyeropoulos, former dir Byzantine Museum Athens, and the late Toula, *née* Gelekis; *Educ* Athens Conservatoire, privately in England; *Career* first appeared as harpsichord soloist Royal Festival Hall 1954, int career in concert, radio and TV, fndr Eng Bach Fest Tst 1962 (dir 1963-), specialises baroque opera and dance appearances incl: Covent Gdn, Versailles and numerous festivals of music (Granada, Athens, Monte Carlo); Offr Dans L'Ordre des Arts et Des Lettres France 1978; *Recreations* cats, cooking, reading, knitting; *Style—* Mrs Lina Lalandi, OBE; 15 South Eaton Place, London SW1W 9ER (☎ 01 730 5925); English Bach Festival Trust, 15 South Eaton Place, London SW1W 9ER

LAM, Martin Philip; *b* 10 Mar 1920; *Educ* Univ Coll Sch Hampstead, Gonville and Cains Cambridge; *m* 1953, Lisa, *née* Lorenz; 1 s (Stephen), 1 da (Jenny); *Career* WWII 1940-45, Air Formation Signal, Special Forces, Capt Mil Govt Italy; assoc conslt BIS Mackintosh 1979- on loan to Euro cmmn DG XIII 1986-88; 1947-78: Bd of Trade Miny of Materials, Nuffield Fell on aspects of Econ devpt in Latin America, memb UK Delgn to OECD, ldr of Delgn to UNCTAD 1972, under-sec Computer Systems and Electronics DTI; *Style—* Martin Lam, Esq; 22 The Avenue, Wembley, Middx, HA9 9QJ (☎ 01 904 2584); BIS Mackintosh, Napier Rd, Luton

LAMARQUE, Lady Emma Elizabeth Anne; da of 7 Earl of Rosebery, DL; *b* 12 Sept 1962; *m* 1984, William Lamarque, s of late W G Lamarque, of Coxwold, York; 1 s (Victor George b 1986), 1 da (Francesca b 1988); *Style—* Lady Emma Lamarque

LAMB, Lady; Ada Henderson; *née* Langlands; da of James Henry Langlands, JP (decd), of Cunmont, Monikie, By Dundee; *b* 14 Nov 1898; *m* 1923, Lt-Col Sir Thomas Lamb (d 1943); 2 da; *Style—* Lady Lamb; 23 Camperdown St, Broughty Ferry, Dundee DD5 3AA (☎ 0382 79033)

LAMB, Adrian Frank; s of Frank Lamb (d 1981), and Mary Elizabeth Graham, *née* Chambers (d 1977); *Educ* Gateshead GS; *m* 4 May 1974, Jane, da of William Moore, of Stital Farm, Blyth, Notts; 1 s (Richard b 1982), 3 da (Katherine b 1976, Amy b 1978, Jennifer b 1982); *Career* CA Richard Ormond Son & Dunn 1960-65, ptnr Coopers & Lybrand 1975-, seconded to Civil Serv Dept 1970; hon tres Int Fedn of Multiple Sclerosis Socs; FCA 1966; *Books* Analysed Reporting (1977), Internal Avoit in the Civil Service (jtly 1971); *Recreations* tennis, bridge, music, gardening; *Style—* Adrian Lamb, Esq; Lynbury House, Burtons Way, Chalfont St Giles, Bucks HP8 4BP (☎ 024 04 4810); Coopers & Lybrand, Plumtree Court, London EC4A 4HT (☎ 01 583 5000, fax 01 822 4652, telex 887470)

LAMB, Sir Albert Thomas; KBE (1979); CMG (1974); DFC (1945); MBE (1953); s of Reginald Selwyn Lamb (d 1970), and Violet, *née* Haynes (d 1980); *b* 23 Oct 1921; *Educ* Swansea GS; *m* 8 April 1944, Christina Betty, da of Albert Henry Wilkinson (d 1960) ; 1 s (Robin b 1948), 2 da (Elizabeth b 1945, Kathryn b 1959); *Career* RAF 1941-46; FO 1938-41, Rome Embassy 1947-50, Genoa Consulate and GB 1950, Bucharest Legation 1950-53, FO 1953-55, MECAS 1955-57, Bahrain (political residency) 1957-61, FO 1961-65, Kuwait Embassy 1965, political agent in Abu Dhabi 1965-68, chief insptr of Dip Serv 1968-74; ambassador: Kuwait 1974-77, and Norway 1978-80; bd memb BNOC 1981-82, dir Brit Oil plc 1982-88, bd memb Samuel Montagu & Co Ltd 1981-85 (advsr 1985-88), sr assoc Conant & Assocs Ltd, Washington DC 1985-; *Recreations* gardening; *Clubs* RAF; *Style—* James John Chandler Esq

LAMB, Andrew Martin; s of Harry Lamb, of Abergele, Clwyd, and Winifred, *née* Emmott; *b* 23 Sept 1942; *Educ* Werneth Sch Oldham, Manchester GS, Corpus Christi Coll Oxford (MA); *m* 1 April 1970, Wendy Ann, da of Frank Edward Davies, of Shirley, Solihull, Warwicks; 1 s (Richard Andrew b 1976), 2 da (Helen Margaret b 1972, Susan Elizabeth b 1973); *Career* investmt mangr, asst gen mangr MGM Assur 1985-; dir: Triton Petroleum Ltd, MGM Unit Mangrs Ltd, MGM Assur (Tstees) Ltd; musicologist: contrib to Gramophone, The Musical Times, The New Grove Dictionary of Music & Musicians; FIA (1972) AMSIA; *Books* Jerome Kern in Edwardian London (1985); *Recreations* cricket, music, family; *Clubs* Lancashire CCC; *Style—* Andrew Lamb, Esq; 12 Fullers Wood, Croydon, CR0 8HZ; MGM Assurance, 11-15 St Mary at Hill, London EC3R 8EE (☎ 01 623 2577)

LAMB, Hon David Charles; s and h of 2 Baron Rochester, *qv*; *b* 8 Sept 1944; *Educ* Shrewsbury Sch, Univ of Sussex; *m* 9 April 1969, Jacqueline Agnes, yr da of John Alfred Stamp, of Torquay, Devon; 2 s (Daniel b 1971, Joe b 1972); *Career* journalist; *Style—* The Hon D C Lamb; 14 Stamford Rd, Bowdon, Cheshire WA14 2JU (☎ 061 928 9030)

LAMB, Eric Alan; s of Eric Lamb, of the Wirral, and Edna Marjorie, *née* Wright; *b* 3 Mar 1953; *Educ* Park HS Birkenhead, Liverpool Univ (LLB); *m* 5 April 1980, Elizabeth Ann, da of Douglas Gill, of the Wirral; *Career* called to the Bar Lincoln's Inn 1975; *Recreations* boating, tennis; *Clubs* Athenaeum, Liverpool Racquet; *Style—* Eric Lamb, Esq; 1 Exchange Flags, Liverpool (☎ 051 236 7747)

LAMB, Air Vice-Marshal George Colin; CB (1977), CBE (1966), AFC (1947); s of George Lamb, of Wryville, Hornby, Lancs (d 1953), and Bessie Lamb; *b* 23 July 1923; *Educ* Lancaster Royal GS; *m* 1, 1945, Nancy Mary, da of Ronald Godsmark, of Norwich; 2 s; m 2, 1981, Mrs Maureen Margaret Mepham, da of Thomas Bamford (d 1967), of Hounslow, Middx; *Career* asst cmdt RAF Coll Cranwell 1964-65, dep cdr Air Forces Borneo 1965-66, Air Cdre 1968, OC RAF Lyneham 1969-71, Royal Coll of Def Studies 1971-72, dir of control (ops) Nat Air Traffic Serv 1972-74, cdre Southern Maritime Air Region 1974-75, COS No 18 Gp 1975-78; RAF vice-pres Combined Cadet Forces Assoc 1978-, chief exec Badminton Assoc of England 1978-; RFU Ctee 1973-85 (privilege memb RFU 1985); int rugby football referee 1967-72, memb Sports Cncl 1983; chm: Lilleshall Nat Sports Centre 1983, sports ctee Princes Tst 1985; FBIM; *Recreations* rugby union football, cycling, gardening; *Clubs* RAF; *Style—* Air Vice Marshal George Lamb, CB, CBE, AFC; Hambledon, 17 Meadway, Berkhamsted, Herts HP4 2PN (☎ 044 27 2583; office: 0908 568822)

LAMB, Maj Gilbert Wrightson; s of His Hon Percy Charles Lamb, QC (d 1973), of Chislehurst, Kent, and Constance, *née* White (d 1981); *b* 29 April 1924; *Educ* Clifton; *m* 1 Aug 1957, Sarah Geraldine Ruth, da of Ralph Tennyson-d'Eyncourt, MBE, of Bayons Manor, Lincs; 1 s (Matthew Gilbert Peregrine b 1966), 2 da (Joanna Elizabeth b 1958, Emma Harriet b 1961); *Career* WWII enlisted 1943, cmmnd Gren Gds, serv Italy (wounded 1944); Army Staff Coll Camberley 1954, DAA & QMG 1 Gds Bde 1956-58, DAMS London Dist 1960-62, ret 1962; called to the Bar Grays Inn 1962; Formica Ltd 1962-70: gen mangr (Switzerland) 1964-65, gen mangr (India) 1965-68, md 1968-70; dir Inc Soc of Br Advertisers 1971-79, dir public affrs T1 Gp plc 1979-89; Order of Humyau Iran 1958; *Recreations* hunting, gardening; *Clubs* Cavalry and Guards; *Style—* Maj Gilbert Lamb

LAMB, Capt (William) John; CVO (1947, MVO 1936), OBE (1944); s of Sir Richard Amphlett Lamb, KCSI, CIE, ICS (d 1923), and Kathleen Maud, *née* Barry (d 1980); *b* 26 Dec 1906; *Educ* RN Colls Osborne and Dartmouth; *m* 27 Nov 1948, (Lilian) Bridget, wid of Lt Cdr George Stevenson Salt, RN, and da of Frederick Stewart Francis (d 1949), of Thakeham, Sussex; 2 da (Elizabeth Kathleen (Mrs Horn) b 1951, Sarah Bridget (Mrs Fradgley) b 1953), 1 step s (Rear Adm James Frederick George Salt b 1940), 1 step da (Joanna Elizabeth (Lady Spencer-Nairn) b 1937); *Career* cmmnd Sub Lt RN 1928, serv in destroyers Home Fleet 1928-31, qualified gunnery specialist Gunnery Sch 1932-34, serv in cruisers Med and China Fleets 1934-38, Gunnery Sch Staff 1939, staff of C-in-C Med Fleet 1940-42, promoted Cdr 1941, staff of C-in-C Eastern Fleet 1942-44 (despatches 1944), exec offr HMS Vanguard (including Royal Tour to SA) 1944-47, promoted Capt 1947, dep dir Naval Ordnance 1948-50, Capt destroyers 4 Trg Flotilla 1950-52, Capt Supt Admlty Signal and Radar Establishment 1952-54, i/c HMS Cumberland 1955-56, ret 1957; AMBIM 1966, hon life memb BIM 1974, FBIM 1979; *Recreations* sailing, DIY; *Clubs* Naval and Military, Royal Cruising; *Style—* Capt John Lamb, CVO, OBE, RN; Brookway, Rhinefield Rd, Brockenhurst, Hants SO42 7SR (☎ 0590 22309)

LAMB, Katherine Margaret; da of Charles Gordon Wallace, of 31 Charteris Rd, Longnidory, East Lothian, and Emelia Campbell, *née* Stewart; *b* 9 Oct 1952; *Educ* St Georges Sch For Girls Edinburgh, Aberdeen Univ (BSC); *m* 27 Dec 1980, John Crawford, s of William Lamb (d 1980); 1 s (Gordon); *Career* personnel mangr William Thyne 1974-86, dir William Sommerville & Son plc 1986-; *Recreations* golf, skiing, swimming, hill walking; *Clubs* Dundas GC; *Style—* Mrs Katherine Lamb

LAMB, Hon Kenneth Henry Lowry; CBE (1985); s of 1 Baron Rochester, CMG (d 1955); *b* 23 Dec 1923; *Educ* Harrow, Trinity Coll Oxford (MA); *m* 1952, Elizabeth Anne, da of Douglas Arthur Saul (d 1981); 1 s, 2 da; *Career* WWII instr Lt RN 1944-46; pres Oxford Union 1944; sr lectr history and english RN Coll Greenwich 1946-53; BBC 1955-80: head of religious broadcasting 1963-66, sec 1967-68, dir public affrs 1969-77, special advsr broadcasting res 1977-80; sec to Church Cmmrs 1980-85; chm Charities Effectiveness Review Tst 1987-; FRSA; *Recreations* golf, cricket, music; *Clubs* MCC, Nat Lib, Royal Fowey YC, Highgate GC; *Style—* The Hon Kenneth Lamb, CBE; 25 South Terr, London SW7 2TB (☎ 01 584 7904);

LAMB, Sir Larry; *b* 15 July 1929; *Educ* Rastrick GS; *m* Joan Mary Denise, *née* Grogan; 2 s, 1 da; *Career* ed: Daily Mail (Manchester) 1968-69, The Sun 1969-72 and 1975-81 (ed dir 1971-81, dep chm News Gp 1979-81), dep chm and ed-in-chief Western Mail Ltd W Aust 1981-82; ed: The Australian 1982, Daily Express 1983-86; chm Larry Lamb Assocs 1986-; kt 1980; *Recreations* cricket, fell-walking, fishing; *Style—* Sir Larry Lamb; Hoskins Barn, Buckland Rd, Bampton, Oxon OX8 2AA

LAMB, Lady (Margaret) Pansy Felicia; da of 5 Earl of Longford, KP, MVO (ka 1915); *b* 1904; *m* 1928, Henry Lamb, RA, MC (d 1960); 1 s, 2 da; *Style—* Lady Pansy Lamb; 22 Via di San Stefano del Cacco, Rome, Italy

LAMB, Peter John; s of Henry Robert Lamb, of St Ives, Cambs, and Lilly Greensitt (d 1954); *b* 4 July 1944; *Educ* Ramsey Abbey Sch, Coll Mid-Essex Chelmsford (HNC); *m* 1987, Suzanne Beverley, da of Paul Ryder, of Swansea, Wales; 2 s (Jonathan b 1983, Tobias b 1985), 2 da (Nicola b 1966, Alison b 1968); *Career* dir Gyproc Insulation Ltd 1985-, md Insulation Techniques and Materials Ltd 1983-85, md West Anglia Insulation Ltd 1985-; *Recreations* sailing, teaching meditation; *Clubs* Haven Ports YC, Br Meditation Soc; *Style—* Peter Lamb, Esq; Gyprol Insulation, 10 Leather Lane, Braintree, Essex CM7 7UZ (☎ 0376 22713, telex 987804)

LAMB, Richard Anthony; s of Maj Stephen Eaton Lamb, of 30 Redcliffe Sq, London SW10, and Leila Mary, *née* Whyte; *b* 11 May 1911; *Educ* Downside, Merton Coll Oxford (MA); *m* 18 Feb 1948, Daphne, da of Sir Paul Butler, KCMG; 2 s (Richard

Michael b 1952, Peter Stephen b 1954) 2 da (Rosemary Anita b 1951, Penelope Mary b 1956); *Career* 12A (TA) 1939, Capt AFHQ 1943 (Algiers), Maj GSO2 RA with Friuli Italian Div 1943-45; dir Hartley Main Collieries 1939-49; ed: City Press 1966-76, Military History Monthly (formerly War Monthly) 1979-82; memb Cumberland CC 1946-52, Parly candidate: (Lib) Lichfield Gen Election 1945, (C) Stockton on Tees 1950, (Lib) N Dorset 1964-66; *Books* Montgomery in Europe (1983), Ghosts of Peace (1987),Failure Eden Government (1987); *Recreations* lawn tennis, travelling; *Clubs* Hurlingham, Utd Oxford & Cambridge, Nat Lib; *Style*— Richard Anthony Lamb ; Knighton Manor, Broad Chalk, Salisbury, (☎ 0722 780 206)

LAMB, Rev Hon Roland Hurst Lowry; s of 1 Baron Rochester, CMG (d 1955); *b* 1917; *Educ* Mill Hill, Jesus Coll Cambridge; *m* 1943, Vera Alicia, da of Arthur Morse (d 1974), of Edgware, Middx; 1 s, 3 da; *Career* chaplain RAF 1942, Middle E 1944, supt Aberystwyth Eng Methodist circuit 1955-61, Callington 1961, resigned Methodist Miny 1967; gen sec Br Evangelical Cncl 1967-82; *Style*— The Rev the Hon Roland Lamb, MA; Meadowside, 13 Eversleigh Rise, South Darley, Matlock, Derbys DE4 2JW (☎ 0629 732645)

LAMB, Stuart Howard; s of William Lamb, of Fairways, Walton Lane, Wakefield, W Yorks (d 1966), and Ruth Evelyn, *née* Mellor; *b* 21 April 1948; *Educ* Queen Elizabeth GS Wakefield, Leicester Poly; *m* 1, 1969, Gillian Margaret (m dis 1974) da of Robert Stuart Hadfield of Wakefield; 1 s (William b 1970), 1 da (Deborah b 1972); m 2, 1979, Jean Lesley, da of Charles Willey Wagstaff, of Wakefield; 2 da (Ruth b 1981, Charlotte b 1983); *Career* gp chm William Lamb (Hldgs) Ltd, chm and chief exec Gola Lamb Ltd 1984- (dir 1967-); chm: Austin Footwear (Wholesale) Ltd, Gola Sourcing and Licencing Ltd; dep chm Gola Sportswear Int Ltd; *Recreations* sailing, power boating, cruising, water skiing, golf; *Clubs* Wakefield, Woodthorpe GC; *Style*— Stuart Lamb, Esq; Gola Lamb Ltd, Stanley, Wakefield, W Yorks WF3 AAY (☎ 0924 823541, telex 557740, Gola G fax 820299, car ☎ 0860 618490)

LAMB, Hon Timothy Michael; s of 2 Baron Rochester; *b* 1953; *Educ* Shrewsbury, Queen's Oxford; *Style*— The Hon Timothy Lamb

LAMB, Dr Trevor Arthur John; s of Arthur Bradshaw Lamb, and Ruth Ellen, *née* Eales; *b* 7 Dec 1929; *Educ* Wanstead GS Essex, QMC Univ of London (BSc, PhD); *m* 1952, Shirley Isabel, da of Sidney Charles Hubbard (d 1971); 2 s (John b 1957, Martin b 1960), 2 da (Susan b 1960, Karen b 1964); *Career* chm: IMI Bailey Birkett Ltd, IMI Control & Instrumentation Ltd, IMI Fluid Power Int Ltd, IMI Int ltd, Norgreen Martonair Ltd, Norgren Martonair Pacific Ltd (Aust), Norgren Martonair Pty Ltd (Aust), Mecafrance SA (France), Norgren Martonair Europa GmbH (Germany), Conax Buffalo Corpn (USA), Control Components Inc (USA), Norgren Co (USA); exec dir: IMI plc 1974-, IMI Gp Inc 1987-; non exec dir W Canning plc 1979-; CEng, FIMechE; *Recreations* tennis, swimming; *Style*— Dr Trevor Lamb; Mead End, Bushwood Drive, Dorridge, Solihull, W Mids B93 8JL (☎ 0564 773877); IMI plc, PO Box 216, Witton, Birmingham B6 7BA (☎ 021 356 4848, fax 021 356 7916, telex 336771)

LAMBART, Lady Katherine Lucy; *née* Lambart; da of 12 Earl of Cavan, TD, DL; *b* 2 Mar 1955; *Educ* St Mary's Sch Wantage, L'Institut Alpin Videmanette (Alliance Française) Vaud Switzerland; *m* 1978 (m dis 1986), Lorenzo Ruiz Barrero, s of Don Lorenzo Ruiz Jimenez, of Madrid; 1 s (Lorenzo b 1980), 1 da (Natasha b 1982); *Style*— Lady Katherine Lambart; 174 Broomwood Rd, London SW11

LAMBE, Lady; Petra Rachel; changed first name from Lesbia 1966; only da of Sir Walter Orlando Corbet, 4 Bt, JP, DL (d 1910); *b* 27 Jan 1905; *Educ* Downe House Sch; *m* 1, 1927 (m dis 1940), Cdr Victor Ivor Henry Mylius, formerly RN, only s of Henry Mulius, of Villa Olivetta, Lago di Como; 1 s (Andrew); m 2, 1940, Adm of the Fleet Sir Charles Edward Lambe, GCB, CVO (d 1960); 1 s (James, *see* Fairfax-Lucy, Hon Lady), 1 da (Louisa); *Career* vice-chm Women's Cncl; *Recreations* music, gardening, reading, translating; *Style*— Lady Lambe; Knockhill House, St Fort, Newport on Tay, Fife (☎ 0382 542152); 21 Stafford Place, London SW1 (☎ 01 828 3953)

LAMBERT *see also*: Drummond Lambert

LAMBERT, Dr Andrew David; s of David George Lambert, of Toad Hall, Beetley, Norfolk, and Nola, *née* Burton; *b* 31 Dec 1956; *Educ* Hamond's Sch Swaffham, City of London Poly (BA), King's Coll London (MA, PhD); *m* 27 Nov 1987, Zohra, da of Mokhtar Bouznat, of Casablanca, Morocco; *Career* lectr modern int history Bristol Poly 1983-87, conslt dept of history and int affrs RNC Greenwich 1987-88; dir SS Great Britain Project 1989-, cncllr Soc Navy Records 1985; *Books* Battleships in Transition: The Creation of the Steam Battlefleet 1815-1960 (1984 and 1985), Warrior: Restoring The World's First Ironclad (1987), Beyond a Crimean War: British Strategy Against Russia 1853-56 (1989); *Recreations* running, motorcycling; *Clubs* Vintage Motorcycle; *Style*— Dr Andrew Lambert; 47 Fane House, Waterloo Gdns, London E2 9HY

LAMBERT, Sir Anthony Edward; KCMG (1964, CMG 1955); s of Reginald Everitt Lambert (d 1968), of Pensbury House, Shaftesbury, Dorset, and Evelyn Lambert (d 1968); *b* 7 Mar 1911; *Educ* Harrow, Balliol Coll Oxford; *m* 28 April 1948, Ruth Mary, da of Sir Arthur Percy Morris Fleming, CBE (d 1960); 3 da (Jane b 1949, Katherine b 1950, Julia b 1953 d 1958); *Career* entered Foreign Serv 1934; cnsllr: Stockholm 1949 and Athens 1951, min to Bulgaria 1958; Ambassador: Tunisia 1960, Finland 1963, Portugal 1966-70; *Clubs* Brooks's; 16 Kent Hse, 34 Kensington Ct, London W8 5BE (☎ 01 937 7453)

LAMBERT, Barry Unwin; s of Henry Benjamin Lambert (d 1981), and Elsie, *née* Organ (d 1977); *b* 28 Jan 1934; *Educ* The John Lyon Sch, Harrow GS, Br Sch of Osteopathy (DO, MRO); *m* 3 Oct 1959, Penelope Frances, da of Harold David Frearson (d 1982); 3 s (Simon b 1960, Jonathan b 1962, Christopher b 1967); *Career* registered osteopath; chm of the Gen Cncl & Register of Osteopaths 1971-76 and 1983-, memb Osteopathic Educn Fndn cncl of mgmnt 1968-; memb Nat Tst and RSPB; *Recreations* fly fishing, field sports, sailing, wood engraving, wood carving, etching; *Clubs* RSM, Rotary; *Style*— Barry U Lambert, Esq; Fairlead, Chart Lane, Reigate, Surrey (☎ 0737 245500, 0737 245041)

LAMBERT, David John; s of Edward Lambert (d 1959), of London, and Gladys Julia, *née* Coleman (1966); *b* 16 July 1938; *Educ* St Pauls Way Secdy Sch Bow London; *m* 26 Sept 1959, Vera Margaret, da of John Hatcher, BEM (d 1976), of Wilton, Wilts; 1 s (Simon David b 1967), 1 da (Jacqueline Anne (Mrs Fuller) b 1963); *Career* RAPC; trainee estimator Nat Painting Contractors eventually became dir of estimating and survey, chm and md John Ruskin Co Ltd; former pres Horley Lions Club, Friends of Farmfield Hosp; pres Mid Surrey Construction Trg Gp, E Surrey Assoc of Bldg Employers Confedn, former nat pres Nat Fedn of Painting and Decorating Contractors; FICM 1981, FBIM 1982, FFB 1985; *Recreations* rambling, swimming, gardening, reading; *Style*— David Lambert, Esq; Long Melford, 76 Oakwood Rd, Horley, Surrey RH6 7BX (☎ 0293 773 262); John Ruskin Co Ltd, Old Carters Yard, 65B Lumley Rd, Horley, Surrey RH6 7RF (☎ 0293 774521)

LAMBERT, Sir Edward Thomas; KBE (1958), CVO (1957); s of Brig-Gen Thomas Stanton Lambert, CB, CMG (d 1921); *b* 19 June 1901; *Educ* Charterhouse, Trinity Coll Cambridge; *m* 1936, Rhona Patricia Gilmore, da of Harold St George Gilmore (decd), and of Mrs J H Molyneux (decd); 1 s, 1 da; *Career* entered HM Foreign Serv 1926, served at Bangkok, Batavia, Medan, Curacao; FO: consul-gen Geneva 1949-53, Paris 1953-59; *Style*— Sir Edward Lambert, KBE, CVO; c/o Lloyds Bank Ltd, 16 St James's St, London SW1; Crag House, Aldeburgh, Suffolk

LAMBERT, 2 Viscount (UK 1945); George Lambert; TD; s of 1 Viscount, PC (d 1958); *b* 27 Nov 1909; *Educ* Harrow, New Coll Oxford; *m* 1939, Patricia, da of J F Quinn, of London; 1 s (decd), 1 da; *Heir* bro, Hon Michael John Lambert; *Career* serv WWII TA, Lt-Col 1942; MP (Lib Nat) South Molton 1945-50, Torrington (Nat Lib and C) 1950-58; DL (Devon) 1969-70; chm Devon and Exeter Savings Bank 1958-70; chm of govrs Seale-Hayne Agric Coll 1968-70; pres Young Farmers Clubs 1968-70, life vice-pres Nat Fedn of Young Farmers' Clubs 1970-; *Clubs* Carlton, Army & Navy; *Style*— The Rt Hon the Viscount Lambert, TD; Les Fougères, 1806 St Légier, Switzerland (☎ 021 53 1063)

LAMBERT, Hon Grace Mary; da of 1 Viscount Lambert, PC (d 1958); *Style*— The Hon Grace Lambert; 1 St Germans, Exeter, Devon (☎ 74219)

LAMBERT, Sir Greville Foley; 9 Bt (GB 1711); s of Lionel Foley Lambert (d 1934, 4 s of 6 Bt); suc cousin, Sir John Foley Grey, 8 Bt, 1938; *b* 17 August 1900; *Educ* Rugby; *m* 1932, Edith Roma, da of Richard Batson; 3 da; *Heir* kinsman, Peter John Biddulph Lambert; *Style*— Sir Greville Lambert, Bt; Flat 5, Henleydale, Stratford Rd, Shirley, Solihull, W Midlands

LAMBERT, Harry Paul; s of James Lambert (d 1979), of Kent, and Irene, *née* Kennedy; *b* 20 Feb 1944; *Educ* Cholton Tech High, Stockport Coll; *m* 1974, Shan Elizabeth Rose, da of Trevor Watkins, of Kent; 1 s (Mark James Trevor b 1981), 1 da (Katie Elizabeth b 1982); *Career* chm & chief exec The Adscene Gp plc (dir 1974-); dep chm Invicta Radio plc 1984-; dir Assoc of Free Newspaper 1983-; *Style*— Harry Lambert, Esq; Newspaper House, Wincheap, Canterbury, Kent CT1 3YR

LAMBERT, Henry Uvedale Antrobus; s of Roger Uvedale Lambert, MBE (d 1985), of Blechingley, and Muriel, da of Sir Reginald Antrobus, KCMG, CB ; *b* 9 Oct 1925; *Educ* Winchester, New Coll Oxford (MA); *m* 1951, Diana Elsworth, da of Capt Henry Eric Dumbell, Royal Fus (d 1957); 2 s (Michael Uvedale b 1952, Roger Mark Uvedale b 1959), 1 da (Jennifer b 1955); *Career* RN 1939-45, Sub Lt RNVR, later RNR Lt Cmdr (ret); chm Barclays Bank Int Ltd 1979-83 (joined Barclays 1948, dir 1966, vice-chm 1973, dep chm Barclays Bank plc 1979-85), chm: Barclays Bank UK Ltd 1983-85, Sun Alliance & London Insur Gp 1985 (vice-chm 1978-83, dep chm 1983-85), dep chm Agric Mortgage Corpn plc 1977-85 (chm 1985); dir BA 1985-; fell Winchester Coll; *Recreations* fishing, gardening, golf, naval history; *Clubs* Brooks's, MCC; *Style*— Henry Lambert, Esq; The Agricultural Mortgage Corporation plc, AMC House, 27 Camperdown Street, London, E1 8DZ (☎ 01 480 7658, fax 01 481 8363, telex 8814729)

LAMBERT, Sir John Henry; KCVO (1980), CMG (1975); s of Col R S Lambert, MC (d 1976), and Mrs H J F Mills; *b* 8 Jan 1921; *Educ* Eton, Sorbonne, Trinity Coll Cambridge; *m* 1950, Jennifer Ann, da of Sir Robert Urquhart, KBE, CMG; 1 s, 2 da; *Career* served Grenadier Gds 1940-45; entered For Serv 1945: cnsllr Stockholm 1964, commercial cnsllr and consul-gen Vienna 1971-74, min and dep cmdt Br Mil Govt Berlin 1974-77, ambass to Tunisia 1977-81; dir Heritage of London Tst 1981-; chm Channel Tunnel Investmts plc 1986-; Grand Offr Order of Tunisian Repub 1980;; *Clubs* Hurlingham, MCC, Royal St Georges Golf, Sandwich; *Style*— Sir John Lambert, KCVO, CMG; 103 Rivermead Court, London SW6 3SB (☎ 01 731 5007; office: 01 734 8144)

LAMBERT, Hon Margaret Barbara; CMG (1965); da of 1 Viscount Lambert, PC (d 1958); *b* 1906; *Educ* Lady Margaret Hall Oxford, LSE; *Career* serv WWII in Euro Service of BBC; asst ed Br Documents of Foreign Policy 1946-50; lectr in modern history Univ Coll of South West 1950-51; ed-in-chief of German diplomatic archives FO 1951-, lectr in modern history St Andrew's Univ 1956-60; *Style*— The Hon Margaret Lambert, CMG; 39 Thornhill Rd, London N1 (☎ 01 607 2286)

LAMBERT, Hon Michael John; yr s of 1 Viscount Lambert, PC (d 1958); hp of bro, 2 Viscount; *b* 29 Sept 1912; *Educ* Harrow, New Coll Oxford; *m* 5 Sept 1939, Florence Dolores, da of Nicholas Lechmere Cunningham Macaskie, QC; 3 da; *Style*— The Hon Michael Lambert; Casanuova di Barontoli, 53010 5 Rocco a Pilli, Siena, Italy

LAMBERT, Maj Olaf Francis; CBE (1984); s of Walter Lambert (d 1965), of London, and Edith Jemima, *née* Gladstone (d 1963); *b* 13 Jan 1925; *Educ* Caterham Sch, RMA Sandhurst (wartime); *m* 1950, Lucy, da of John Adshead (d 1943), of Macclesfield; 2 s (Simon, Charles), 2 da (Sarah, Harriet); *Career* cmmnd RTR, served NW Europe 7th Armoured Div, and BAOR (ret as Maj 1959), Hon Col Royal Mil Police (TA) 1984; landowner; joined AA 1959, md 1973-77 (dir gen 1977-87, vice-pres 1987-), dir of all associated AA cos up to 1987; dir Mercantile Credit Ltd 1980-85; chm: Br Road Fedn 1987-, AA Friendly Soc 1986-; memb: Standing Jt Ctee RAC, AA, RSAC 1968-87, Int Advanced Motorist Cncl 1965-, Int Touring Alliance (AIT) (world pres 1983-86), Hants Ctee Army Benv Fund, Winchester Cathedral Tst Cncl, Br Horse Soc Devpt Cncl, Freeman City of London; Liveryman Worshipful Co of Coachmakers and Coach Harness Makers, FRSA, CBIM, FIMI; *Recreations* hunting, skiing, walking, music; *Clubs* Army & Navy; *Style*— Maj O F Lambert; Elm Farm, Baybridge, Owslebury, Hampshire

LAMBERT, Patricia; OBE (1980); da of Frederick Burrows (d 1961), and Elsie, *née* Mummery (d 1971); *b* 16 Mar 1926; *Educ* Malet Lambert HS Hull, West Bridgford GS Nottingham; *m* 1949, (m dis 1982), George Richard, s of Richard Palin Lambert (d 1982); 1 s (Warwick b 1954), 1 da (Margaret b 1952); *Career* Nat Consumer Cncl 1978-82, Br Standards Inst 1972- (chm consumer standards advsy ctee, bd memb 1980-86, memb quality assur bd, govr 1986-) advsy ctee on safety of electrical appliances Br Tech Approval Bd 1980-86, Direct Mail Servs Standards Bd 1983- (dir 1986-), vice chm Think campaign 1983, advsy panel UTA 1981, Nat House Building Cncl 1981; *Style*— Patricia Lambert, OBE; 42 Tollerton Lane, Tollerton, Nottingham (☎ 06077 2412)

LAMBERT, Sir Peter John Biddulph; 10 Bt (GB 1711), of London ; o s of John Hugh Lambert (d 1977), and Edith, *née* Davis; suc kinsman Sir Greville Foley Lambert, 9 Bt (d 1988); *b* 5 April 1952; *Educ* Upper Canada Coll, Trent Univ Peterborough (BSc), Univ of Manitoba Winnipeg (MA); *Heir* uncle, Robert William Lambert b 6 June 1911; *Style*— Sir Peter Lambert, Bt; c/o 483 Spadina Rd, Toronto, Canada

LAMBERT, Robert Guy Wilson; CBE (1981); s of Guy William Lambert, CB (d 1983), formerly of Dernasliggan, Leenane, Co Galway, Rep of Ireland, (ggs, through maternal line, of Lady Susan Sherard, da of 5 Earl of Harborough, d 1809, himself bro of 6 Earl who d 1859 when title became extinct), and Nadine Frances Gwendolen MBE, (d 1983), yst da of Wilson Noble of Park Place, Henley-on-Thames; *b* 6 Mar 1921; *Educ* Eton, Magdalene Coll Cambridge (MA); *m* 1950, (Charlotte) Ann, (d 1988), da of Col Ambrose John Rayner Waller (d 1972), of Packwood, Boxted, Colchester, Essex; 1 s (Thomas), (Susan, Anna); *Career* serv WWII, Lt RA: Sicily, Normandy (landing on D-Day), Belgium, Holland; Bank of Eng 1946-61, Euro rep Barclays Gp of Banks 1961-80, pres Br-Swiss C of C in Switzerland 1978-80; *Recreations* sailing, skiing; *Clubs* Bembridge SC; *Style*— Robert Lambert, Esq, CBE; Schnabelsberg, 8840 Einsiedeln, Switzerland (☎ 055 534127)

LAMBERT, Lady; (Edith) Roma; *née* Batson; da of Richard Batson; *m* 15 July 1932, Sir Greville Foley Lambert, 9 Bt (d 1988); 3 da; *Style*— Howard G Pearl Esq; 12 Newborough Rd, Shirley, Solihull, Warwicks

LAMBERT, Thomas Peter; s of Thomas Lambert (d 1938); *b* 7 Oct 1927; *Educ* Stowe, RMA Sandhurst; *m* 1956, Davinia Margaret, *née* Walford; 4 children; *Career* Capt Inniskilling Dragoon Gds; pres Bradford C of C 1975-77, regnl dir Nat West Bank Ltd 1977, jt md John Foster & Son Ltd 1980, chm Wool Industry Res Assoc 1981; *Recreations* shooting, tennis, gardening; *Style*— Thomas Lambert, Esq; The Old Vicarage, S Stainley, Harrogate, N Yorks (☎ 770169)

LAMBERT, Verity Ann; da of Stanley Joseph Lambert, and Ella Corona Goldburg; *b* 27 Nov 1935; *Educ* Roedean, Sorbonne; *Career* ind film prodr 1985-; (co name Cinema Verity Ltd); *Recreations* good books, good food; *Style*— Ms Verity Lambert; Cinema Verity Ltd, The Mill House, Millers Way, 1A Shepherds Bush Rd, London W6 7NA (☎ 01 749 8485)

LAMBIE, Alexander Ogilvie; s of J M S Lambie (decd); *b* 24 Oct 1938; *Educ* Mill Hill Sch, Durham Univ; *m* 1969, Diana Margaret, *née* Owen; 1 da; *Career* md Cammell Laird Shipbuilders Ltd 1979-, chm Cammell Laird (Training) Ltd 1976-; *Style*— Alexander Lambie, Esq; St Nicholas House, Burton, South Wirral, Cheshire

LAMBIE, David; MP (Lab) Cunninghame S 1983-; s of late Robert Lambie, JP (d 1985),; *b* 13 July 1925; *Educ* Ardrossan Acad, Glasgow Univ (BSc, DipEd), Geneva Univ; *m* 1954, Netta May, da of Alexander Merrie (d 1985), of Barnett Court, Saltcoats, Ayr; 1 s, 4 da; *Career* teacher; chm Scottish Lab Pty 1965-66, MP (Lab) Central Ayrshire 1970-1983, memb select ctee on Parly Cmmr for Admin 1974-83, chm select ctee Scottish Affrs 1982-87 (memb 1979-87), sec All Pty Parly Energy Gp; memb Cncl of Europe and Western Euro Union (alternate memb 1987-), USDAW Sponsored, FEIS; *Recreations* watching football; *Clubs* Cunninghame North Labour (Saltcoats); *Style*— David Lambie, Esq, MP; 11 Ivanhoe Drive, Saltcoats, Ayrshire (☎ 0294 64843; office 76844); House of Commons, London SW1 (☎ 01 219 5140)

LAMBOLL, Alan Seymour; JP Inner London 1965; s of Frederick Seymour Lamboll (d 1935), of Frankham, Mark Cross, Sussex, by his w Charlotte Emily; *b* 12 Oct 1923; *Educ* Marlborough; *Career* serv WWII: Royal Signals, E Africa Cmd 1943-47, Capt; dir Slack & Lamboll Ltd 1947-54 (family firm of wine merchants), insur broker with Alexander Howden Stewart Smith (Home) 1954-57; dir: Anglo-Portuguese Agencies Ltd (insur and reinsur agents) 1957-62, Aga Dictating Machine Co Ltd 1962-70, Roger Grayson Ltd (wine merchants) 1971-74, London Investmt Tst Ltd; conslt to Rank Orgn 1970-72; dir Ellinger Heath Western (Underwriting Agencies) Ltd 1974-82; chm S Westminster Petty Sessional Div 1978-80, dep chm City of London Cmmn 1979-82; sheriff City of London 1976-77 (Silver Jubilee year); memb Cncl Toynbee Hall 1958-81, dir City Arts Tst 1962-77, vice-chm Royal Gen Theatrical Fund 1967-; donation govr Christ's Hosp 1971-; Freeman City of London 1947, memb Ct of Assts Worshipful Co of Distillers (master, tercentenary year, 1972-73), hon asst Worshipful Co of Parish Clerks (Master 1975-76); JP Inner London 1965, Supp 1983; FRSA 1970, CStJ 1973; *Recreations* theatre, music; *Clubs* Athenaeum, Garrick, Pratt's; *Style*— Alan Lamboll, Esq; Little Buckden, Iken, nr Woodbridge, Suffolk IP12 2EY (☎ 072 888 530)

LAMBTON, Viscount; (*see*: Durham, Baron)

LAMBTON, Antony Claud Frederick; (Viscount Lambton, by which courtesy title he was known in House of Commons); s of 5 Earl of Durham (d 1970); disclaimed peerages (Earldom of Durham, Barony of Durham and Viscountcy of Lambton) for life 1970; *b* 10 July 1922; *m* 1942, Belinda, da of Maj Douglas Holden Blew-Jones, of Westward Ho, N Devon; 1 s, 5 da; *Heir* to renounced Earldom of Durham, s, Lord (courtesy title of Baron) Durham; *Career* MP (C) Northumberland (Berwick-on-Tweed) 1951-73; PPS to Min of Supply 1954, parly under-sec of state for Def (RAF) 1970-73; *Books* Snow and Other Stories (1983); *Style*— Antony Lambton, Esq; Biddick Hall, Lambton Park, Chester-le-Street, Durham; Lambton Castle, Fence Houses, Durham (☎ Fence Houses 36)

LAMBTON, Lady Elizabeth Mary; *née* Petty-FitzMaurice; yr da of 6 Marquess of Lansdowne, DSO, MVO (d 1936); *b* 1927; *m* 1950, Maj Charles William Lambton (s of Brig-Gen Hon Charles Lambton, DSO, himself 4 s of 2 Earl of Durham); 3 s, 1 da; *Style*— Lady Elizabeth Lambton; The Old Rectory, Calstone, Calne, Wilts (☎ 0249 812149)

LAMBTON, Hon John George; s of 5 Earl of Durham; *b* 1952; *Style*— The Hon John Lambton; Fenton, Wooler, Northumberland (☎ Wooler 12); Lambton Castle, Fence Houses, Durham (☎ Fence Houses 36)

LAMBTON, Lady Lucinda; *née* Lambton; eldest da of Antony Lambton (6 Earl of Durham who disclaimed peerage 1970); *b* 10 May 1943; *m* 1, 16 Jan 1965, Henry Mark Harrod, s of Sir (Henry) Roy Forbes Harrod; 2 s (Barnaby, Huckleberry); m 2, 11 Jan 1986, Sir Edmund Fairfax-Lucy, 6 Bt, of Charlecote Park, Warwick; *Career* photographer, writer, television presenter; television programmes: On the Throne, Animal Crackers, Cabinet of Curiosities; *Books* Vanishing Victorian, Temples of Convenience, Chambers of Delight, Beastly Buildings; *Style*— Lady Lucinda Fairfax-Lucy; Charlcote Park, Warwick

LAMBTON, Lady Mary Gabrielle Anne; da of Antony Lambton; *b* 1954; *Style*— Lady Mary Lambton

LAMBTON, Hon Mrs Monica Dorothy; *née* Brand; da of 3 Viscount Hampden, GCVO, KCB, CMG (d 1958); *b* 3 Mar 1914; *m* 1933, D'Arcy Lambton (d 1938), s of Hon Claud Lambton (decd); 2 children; *Style*— The Hon Mrs Lambton; Saxon House, Shottisham, Woodbridge, Suffolk IP12 3HG (☎ 0394 411322)

LAMMIMAN, Surgn Rear Adm David Askey; LVO (1978), QHS (1987); s of Herbert Askey Lammiman (d 1943), and Lilian Elsie, *née* Park (d 1981); *b* 30 June 1932; *Educ* Wyggeston Sch Leicester, St Bartholomew's Hosp (MB BS, DA, DObstRCOG); *m* 1, 7 Sept (m dis 1984), Sheila Mary, da of Frederick Graham (d 1963); 3 s (Christopher b June 1958, Robert b April 1960, Michael b March 1969), 1 da (Susie b Feb 1967); m 2, 30 Oct 1984, Caroline Dale, da of Francis John Brooks (Lt Cdr RN, ret); *Career* res house offr Redhill County Hosp and St Bartholomew's Hosp 1957-58; joined RN 1959; clinical asst 1966-69: Southampton Gp of Hosps, Alder Hey Children's Hosp, Liverpool/Radcliffe Infirmary Oxford; conslt anaesthetist RN Hosp Malta 1969-71, RN Hosp 1971-73 and 1978-82, RN Hosp Gibralter 1973-75, RN Hosp Plymouth 1975-76; serv in ships: HMS Chaplet 1959, HMS Eagle 1967-68, HMY Britannia 1976-78; dir of med personnel MOD 1982-84; med offr i/c: RN Hosp Plymouth 1984-86, RN Hosp Haslar 1986-88; Surgn Rear Adm (Support Med Servs) 1989; memb Assoc of Anaesthetists 1962, FRCS 1969; *Recreations* fly fishing, golf, tennis; *Clubs* Army and Navy, RN Sailing Assoc (Portsmouth); *Style*— Surgn Rear Admiral David Lammiman, LVO, QHS; c/o National Westmister Bank, St Thomas's Square, Ryde, IOW (☎ 0983 68311); Surgeon Rear Admiral (Support Medical Services), RN Hosp, Haslar, Gosport, Hants PO12 2AA (☎ 0705 584 255 ext 2110, fax 0705 584 255 ext 2128)

LAMOND, James Alexander; JP (Aberdeen), MP (Lab) Oldham Central and Royton 1983-; s of Alexander Lamond (d 1965), of Burrelton, Perthshire; *b* 29 Nov 1928; *Educ* Burrelton Sch, Coupar Angus; *m* 1954, June Rose, da of Joseph Wellburn, of Aberdeen; 3 da; *Career* draughtsman; MP (Lab) Oldham E 1970-83, lord provost and ld-lt of Aberdeen 1970-71; vice-pres World Peace Cncl, tres Br-Soviet Friendship Soc; *Style*— James Lamond, Esq, JP, MP; 15 Belvidere St, Aberdeen (☎ 0224 638074); Flat 7, 26 Medway St, London SW1 (☎ 01 222 1874); House of Commons, London SW1A 0AA (☎ 01 219 4154); 59 Trafalgar St, Oldham (☎ 061 626 1354); office: Bartlam Place, Oldham (☎ 061 620 0118)

LAMOND, William; s of Robert Lamond (d 1973); *b* 26 April 1925; *Educ* Shawlands Acad; *m* 1950, Kathleen Mary; 2 s, 1 da; *Career* CA, fin dir James Finlay plc; *Recreations* golf, bridge; *Clubs* Oriental, Western (Glasgow); *Style*— William Lamond, Esq; Windward, Ferniegair Ave, Helensburgh, Scotland (☎ 0436 5014)

LAMONT, Brig (John) David Alexander; DSO (1945), MBE (1938); s of Capt Rous Milner Limond (d 1912); the name Limond distortion of Le Monde was adopted by forebear in mid-seventeenth century, when, as a supporter of Montrose, he was 'on the run' from covenanters; proper name of Lamont re-adopted by Deed Poll 1919.; *b* 27 July 1907; *Educ* Cheltenham; *m* 12 Sept 1938, Margot, da of John McIntosh McPherson (d 1947); 1 s (Hamish John b 1941, d 1981), 1 da (Jane Margaret b 1946); *Career* RA and staff 1927-59, serv India, UK, Sierra Leone, Germany after N W Europe Campaign, Hong Kong, Pakistan (dir of Artillery 1954-57); ADC to HM The Queen 1958-59; md Edger Investmts (London) 1974-77; che de L'Ordre Leopold I (1945), Belgian Croix de Guerre (1940); *Clubs* Army and Navy; *Style*— Brig David Lamont; White Lodge, Lion Green, Haslemere (☎ 0428 3137)

LAMONT, Norman Stewart Hughson; PC (1986), MP (C) Kingston upon Thames 1972-; s of Daniel Lamont; *b* 8 May 1942; *Educ* Loretto Sch, Fitzwilliam Coll Cambridge; *m* 1971, Alice Rosemary, da of Lt-Col Peter White, of Hall Farm, Thorp Arch, Boston Spa, Yorks; 1 s, 1 da; *Career* PA to Duncan Sandys 1965, CRD 1966-68, N M Rothschild & Sons 1968-79, contested (C) Hull E 1970; chm: Coningsby Club 1970-71, Bow Gp 1971-72; PPS to Arts min 1974; oppn spokesman: Consumer Affrs 1975-76, Industry 1976-79; under-sec state Dept Energy 1979-81; min state: for Industry 1981-83, Dept of Trade and Industry 1983-86; finance sec to Treasury 1986-; *Style*— The Rt Hon Norman Lamont, MP; House of Commons, London SW1

LAMONT OF THAT ILK, Peter; Chief of Clan Lamont; s of Noel Brian Lamont of that Ilk (decd); *b* 1955; *Career* student St Patrick's Coll Manly, NSW, Australia; *Style*— Peter Lamont of that Ilk; St Patrick's College, Darley Rd, Manly, NSW 2025, Australia

LAMPARD, Martin Robert; s of Austin Hugo Lampard (d 1964); *b* 21 Feb 1926; *Educ* Radley, Christ Church Oxford; *m* 1957, Felice, da of John MacLean (d 1944); 3 da; *Career* Sub Lt RNVR North Atlantic; slr 1952, Ashurst Morris Crisp & Co ptnr 1957, sr ptnr 1974; dir: Allied Breweries 1981-, Laird Gp, Canadian Overseas Packaging Industs Ltd, Hambros 1983-; *Recreations* farming in E Anglia, sailing, shooting; *Clubs* Royal Yacht Squadron, Royal Ocean Racing; *Style*— Martin Lampard, Esq; c/o Ashurst Morris Crisp, 7 Eldon Drive, London EC2 (☎ 01 247 7666); 507 Willoughby House, Barbican, London EC2Y 8BN (01-588 4048); Theberton House, Theberton, nr Leiston, Suffolk (☎ 0728 830510)

LAMPERT, Hon Mrs (Jill Mary Joan); 4 da of 3 Baron Acton, CMG, MBE, TD (d 1989); *b* 15 June 1947; *m* 1970, Nicholas Lampert; 2 da; *Style*— The Hon Mrs Lampert; 46 Clarence Road, Moseley, Birmingham B13 9UH

LAMPL, Frank William; s of Dr Otto Lampl (d 1934), and Olga, *née* Jellinek (d Auschwitz 1944); *b* 6 April 1926; *Educ* Tech Univ Brno Czechoslovakia, Faculty of Arch and Engrg; *m* 1948, Blanka, da of Jaroslav Kratochvil (d 1981); 1 s (Thomas b 1950); *Career* emigrated from Czechoslovakia to the UK 1968, exec dir Bovic Construction 1974, md Bovis Int 1978, dir Bovis Ltd 1979, chm Bovis Construction and Bovis Int 1985, exec dir Peninsular and Oriental Steam Navigation Co (P&O) 1985, dir Lehrer McGovern Bovis Inc New York 1986, chm: Bovis (Far E) Ltd 1987; CBIM, FCIOB; *Clubs* RAC; *Style*— Frank W Lampl, Esq; Bovis Ltd, 127 Sloane St, SW1X 9BA (☎ 01 422 3488, telex 919435, fax 01 730 4722, car tel 0860 311309)

LAMPRELL-JARRETT, Peter Neville; s of Reginald Arthur Lamprell-Jarrett (d 1966); *b* 23 June 1919; *Educ* Cliftonville Coll; *m* 1944, Kathleen, da of Percival Francis Furner (d 1973); 2 children; *Career* architect and surveyor 1954-; pres Incorporated Assoc of Architects and Surveyors 1967-68; Freeman City of London 1978, Liveryman Worshipful Co of Wheelwrights; life vice-pres London Caledonian Catholic Assoc; KCSG 1975, KCHS 1974, KASG; Cdr Cross Polonia Restituta (Poland) 1982; FFB, FRSA, FSAScot; *Recreations* painting, fishing, walking, classical music; *Clubs* Royal Cwlth Soc, Lighthouse; *Style*— Peter Lamprell-Jarrett, Esq; Hramsa, Reeds Lane, Sayers Common, Hassocks, W Sussex; Carrick House, Carrick Castle, by Lochgoil, Argyll (☎ 030 13 394); 42 Mall Chambers, Kensington Mall, London W8 4DZ (☎ 01

229 8247)

LAMPSON, Hon Victor Miles George Aldous; s of 1 Baron Killearn, GCMG, CB, MVO, PC (d 1964), by his 2 w Jacqueline (herself da of Marchese Senator Aldo Castellani, KCMG); hp of half-bro, 2 Baron; *b* 9 Sept 1941; *Educ* Eton; *m* 1971, Melita Amaryllis Pamela Astrid, da of Rear Adm Sir Morgan Charles Morgan Giles, DSO, OBE, lately MP Winchester; 2 s, 2 da; *Career* late Capt Scots Gds; *Style—* The Hon Victor Lampson; Franchise Manor, Burwash, Sussex

LAN, Henry Hing-Kam; s of Kim Fa Lan (d 1971), and Sun Yin Lan *née* Chan (d 1987); *b* 9 Nov 1948; *Educ* St Joseph Coll Mauritius; *m* 5 Jan 1977, Christiane, da of Felix Li-Kwet-Liit (Mauritius); 2 s (Oliver b 20 Sept 1979, Nigel b 1 Aug 1983); *Career* CA, ptnr David Rubin & Co; *Recreations* tennis, squash; *Style—* Henry Lan, Esq; 14 Parkfield Gardens, N Harrow, Middx HA2 6JR; David Rubin & Co, Pearl Assurance House, 319 Ballards Lane, N Finchley, London N12 8LY (☎ fax 01 446 2994)

LANCASTER, Bt-Col Aubrey John; TD (1947), DL (Co of London 1955); s of John T Lancaster (d 1979), and Margaret E, *née* Giles (d 1953); *b* 29 May 1915; *Educ* Merchant Taylors'; *m* 1942, Joan Elizabeth, da of Albert W Crofts (d 1969); 2 s, 1 da; *Career* 2 Lt 33 (St Pancras) AA Bn RE (TA) 1937, serv WWII with RA ADGB, War Crimes Cmmn (Norway) 1945-46, Lt-Col cmdg 568 (St Pancras) LAA Regt RA (TA) 1952-55, Bt Col 1955; chm DL Ctee: Deptford 1958-65, Lewisham 1965-; assoc Chartered Insur Inst 1961, insur co official; Freeman City of London 1972; *Recreations* shooting and conservancy; *Style—* Bt-Col Aubrey Lancaster, TD, DL; Spinneys, 22 Condover Pk, Condover, Shrewsbury, Shropshire SY5 7DU (☎ 074 373 674)

LANCASTER, Christopher; s of George Lancaster (d 1959), of Headingley, Leeds, and Grace Evelyn, *née* Foster (d 1974); *b* 10 August 1932; *Educ* Queen Elizabeth GS Wakefield, Trinity Hall Cambridge (MA, LLM); *m* 12 Sep 1959, Aase,da of Kristoffer Böe (d 1965), of Bergen, Norway; 2 s (Stephen b 1960, Richard b 1962), 1 da (Anne-Lise b 1964); *Career* articled clerk Booth and Co 1956-59, asst slr William Henry and Co 1959-60 (ptnr 1960-72), ptnr Willey Hargrave 1972-88 (conslt 1988-), pres Leeds Law Soc 1979-80 (press offr 1972-79); memb: Headingley Rotary 1974-84, Leeds Skyrack Lions Club 1965-69, tstee Grassington Angling Club 1972-85, Law Soc 1959; *Recreations* fly-fishing, England history, jazz piano; *Style—* Christopher Lancaster Esq; Park Lane House, Westgate, Leeds, LS1 2RD (☎ 0532 441 151, fax 0532 436 050, telex 265871)

LANCASTER, Graham; s of Eric Lancaster, of Salford, Gtr Manchester, and Edna, *née* Butterworth; *b* 24 Feb 1948; *Educ* Salford GS, Mid Cheshire Coll (HND); *m* 10 Oct 1971, Lorna Mary, da of William Thomas White (d 1979); *Career* Hawker Siddeley Aviation 1968-69, asst to dir of info and educn The Textile Cncl 1969-70, trg devpt offr Corah Ltd 1971, policy coordinator to pres CBI 1972-77, hd of public affairs ABTA 1977, chm and chief exec Biss Lancaster plc 1978-; memb MInstM, MIPR, FRSA; *Books* The Nuclear Letters (1979), Seward's Folly (1980), The 20 Percent Factor (1987); *Recreations* writing; *Clubs* Groucho's; *Style—* Graham Lancaster, Esq; Biss Lancaster plc, 180 Wardour St, London W1V 3AA (☎ 01 437 7733, fax 01 439 7733, telex 894767 BISSPR G)

LANCASTER, Dame Jean; DBE (1963); da of Richard C Davies, of Blundellsands, Lancs; *b* 11 August 1909; *Educ* Merchant Taylors' Crosby Lancs; *m* 1967, Roy Cavander Lancaster; *Career* dir WRNS 1961-64; *Style—* Dame Jean Lancaster; Greathed Manor, Dormansland, Lingfield, Surrey

LANCASTER, Bishop of (RC) 1985-; Rt Rev John Brewer; s of Eric Winston Brewer (d 1977), of Derbyshire, and Laura Helena Webster (d 1987); *b* 24 Nov 1929; *Educ* Ushaw Coll Durham, Venerable English Coll Rome, Gregorian Univ Rome (STL, JCL, PhL); *Career* vice-rector Ven English Coll Rome 1964-71, auxilliary bishop of Shrewsbury 1971-83, co-adjutor to Bishop of Lancaster 1983-85, bishop of Lancaster 1985-; *Style—* The Rt Rev the Bishop of Lancaster; Bishop's House, Cannon Hill, Lancaster LA1 5NG (☎ 0524 32231)

LANCASTER, John Meredith; s of Dr Zikmund F Foltin, and Alica Foltinova, *née* Polakova; *b* 23 August 1919; *Educ* Komenius Univ Bratislava, Coll of Aeronautical Engrg London, LSE; *m* 12 June 1943, Jean Gertrude, da of Lt-Col George William Thomas Coles, TD; 2 s (Michael John b 1944, David John b 1967), 3 da (Jane Deirdre (Mrs Brentnall) b 1949, Sally Jean (Mrs de Elye Cole) b 1951, Judith Elisabeth b 1953); *Career* RAOC Workshop Univ 6 AA Div 1940-42, cmmnd East Surrey Regt 1943-46, Intelligence Corps 1943, Interserv Topographical Dept 1943-46, Maj GSO2; head of mkt res Riotinto Co Ltd 1947-51, mktg exec Metallo-Chemical Refining Co 1952; The Br Sulphur Corpn Ltd: joined 1953, md 1954-85, chm 1970-; dir CRU Hldgs Co Ltd 1986-; chm: Orlestone Parish Cncl 1961-, Hamstreet Victory Hall 1966-, Hamstreet & Warchorne branch Ashford Cons Assoc 1963- (memb exec ctee); memb: Cncl for the Preservation of Rural England, Romney Marsh Level; Lord of the Manor of Orlestone 1969-; Freeman City of London 1978, Liveryman Worshipful Co of Stationers & Newspaper Makers 1978; memb Fertiliser Soc, Francis New Memorial Medal; *Books* World Survey of Sulphur Resources (1966); *Recreations* swimming, skiing, gardening; *Clubs* Carlton; *Style—* John Lancaster, Esq; Ct Lodge, Orlestone, Ashford, Kent (☎ 0233 732 339); 4 Eccleston Sq, London SW1; 31 Mount Pleasant, London WC1X 0AD (☎ 01 837 5600, fax 01 837 0292, telex 918918 LONDON SULFEX G)

LANCASTER, Vice Adm Sir John Strike; KBE (1961), CB (1958); s of George Henry Lancaster (d 1955), of Plymouth; *b* 26 June 1903; *Educ* King Edward VI Sch Southampton; *m* 1927, Edith Laurie (d 1980), da of late Ernest Robert Jacobs; 2 da; *Career* Rear Adm Personnel, Home Air Cmd 1956-59, Vice Adm 1959, dir-gen of Manpower Admin and Chief Naval Supply and Secretariat Offr 1959-62, ret 1962; *Recreations* gardening; *Style—* Vice Adm Sir John Lancaster, KBE, CB; Moorings, 59 Western Way, Alverstoke, Gosport, Hants PO12 2NF (☎ 0705 584172)

LANCASTER, Noel Brownrigg; s of Thomas William Carruthers Lancaster (d 1938), and Margaret Mary, *née* Callander (d 1964); *b* 25 Dec 1925; *Educ* Nelson Sch, Wigton, Queen Elizabeth GS Penrith; *m* 6 Jan 1955, Elizabeth Susan, da of James Lamb Chalmers (d 1961); 2 s (Ian Callander, David Forbes d 1958), 1 da (Hilary Elizabeth Margaret); *Career* ptnr NB Lancaster & Co CAs; former sec, Cumberland Agric Soc 1961-68; farmer W Mains, Penton, Carlisle; Lord of the Manor of Docker; FCA; *Recreations* golf, fishing, shooting; *Clubs* Powfoot GC, Brampton GC, Carlisle GC; *Style—* Noel B Lancaster, Esq; Little Drawdykes, Whiteclosegate, Carlisle, Cumbria; N B Lancaster & Co, Chartered Accountants, St Cecil Street, Carlisle, Cumbria (☎ 0228 25788)

LANCASTER, Patricia Margaret; da of Vice Adm Sir John Lancaster, CBE, CB, qv, of Moorings, 59 Western Way, Alverstoke, nr Gosport, Hants, and Edith Laurie, *née* Jacobs (d 1980); *b* 22 Feb 1929; *Educ* London Univ (BA), Southampton Univ (PGCE); *Career* teacher St Mary's Sch Calne Wilts 1951-58, housemistress and teacher of english St Swithun's Winchester 1958-62; headmistress St Michaels Petworth 1962-73, headmistress Wycombe Abbey Sch Bucks 1974-88; pres GSA 1980-81; *Recreations* theatre, art galleries; *Style—* Miss Patricia Lancaster; 8 Vectis Rd, Alverstoke, nr Gosport, Hants (☎ 0705 583 189)

LANCELEY, Ian Kenneth; s of Thomas Peter Kenneth Lanceley, of Paignton, Devon, and Barbara Doreen, *née* Allen; *b* 12 Feb 1946; *Educ* Blundell's Sch, Coll of Law; *m* 12 Dec 1980, Valerie, da of Frederick William Kay (d 1987), of Kirby Hill, Richmond, North Yorks; 2 s (Adam b 1981, Charles b 1983); *Career* admitted slr 1971; sr ptnr Freeborough Slack & Co 1985- (ptnr 1977-85);; *Recreations* squash, golf; *Clubs* Roehampton; *Style—* Ian Lanceley, Esq; 14/15 Vernon St, West Kensington, London W14 (☎ 01 602 3474, fax 01 603 7004)

LANCHIN, Gerald; s of Samuel Lanchin (d 1969), of London, and Sara Bernstein (d 1967), of London; *b* 17 Oct 1922; *Educ* St Marylebone GS, LSE (BCom); *m* 1951, Valerie Sonia, da of Charles Lyons (d 1970), of London; 1 s (Michael), 2 da (Wendy, Judith); *Career* HM Forces 1942-46; under-sec Dept of Trade 1971-82; conslt; chm Direct Mail Servs Standards Bd 1983-, memb: cncl Consumers' Assoc 1983-88, Data Protection Tbnl 1985-; vice pres Nat Fedn of Consumer Gps 1984-; *Books* Government and the Consumer (1985); *Recreations* photography, music, walking; *Clubs* Reform; *Style—* Gerald Lanchin, Esq; 28 Priory Gardens, Berkhamsted, Herts HP4 2DS (☎ 0442 875283); Direct Mail Servs Standards Bd, 26 Eccleston St SW1W 9PY (☎ 01 824 8651)

LAND, David; s of Solomon Land (d 1952), and Sarah Land; *b* 22 May 1918; *Educ* Davenant Fndn GS London; *m* 1945, Alexandra Zara, da of Capt A V Levinson, RFC; 2 children; *Career* serv WWII with RASC; impresario and prodr; fndr David Land (Agency) Ltd which introduced Harlem Globetrotters to Europe, personal mangr to Tim Rice and Andrew Lloyd Webber 1969, dep chm Robert Stigwood Gp Ltd 1979; co-productions: Jesus Christ Superstar (NY 1971, London 1972), Joseph and the Amazing Technicolor Dreamcoat (London 1973), Jeeves (London 1975), Evita (with Robert Stigwood, London 1978, Olivier Award and NY 1979, Tony and Drama Desk Awards), Swan Esther (1983); admin Dagenham Girl Pipers 1948-, chm and exec dir Theatre Royal Brighton, chm Young Vic Theatre London; *Recreations* theatre and youth organisations, poker, cricket; *Style—* David Land, Esq; Nevill House, Nevill Rd, Rottingdean, Sussex; Robert Stigwood Group Ltd, 118-120 Wardour St, London W1V 4BT (☎ 01 437 3224)

LAND, Peter Anthony; s of Anthony Land (d 1973), and Barbara Williamson Land, *née* Markland (d 1980); *b* 14 April 1927; *Educ* Bemrose Sch Derby; *m* 1952, Dorothy Jessica, da of Samuel Robert Pritchard; 1 s (Patrick), 2 da (Jane Sally); *Career* cmmn Sherwood Foresters; CA; md Br Tport Hotels 1978-83, md Nat Carriers 1967-77; chief accountant: BR Western Region 1963-67, BTR Industries 1958-63; chm J N Dobbin (Hldgs) Ltd 1980-85; chm Bisham Abbey Nat Sport Centre 1980-84, tstee HRH Princess Christians Hosp 1984-, chm Wycombe Health Authy 1986; *Recreations* travel, cricket, golf (former Capt Derbys Hockey); *Clubs* MCC; *Style—* Peter Land, Esq; South Riding, Bisham Rd, Marlow, Bucks (☎ 06284 2898); 3 Vicarage St, Colyton, Devon EX13 6JR (☎ 0297 52092)

LANDA, Clive Hugh Alexander; MBE (1980); s of Basil Walter Landa, of London, and Alice Applebaum (d 1956); *b* 11 July 1945; *Educ* William Ellis School, Queen's Coll Oxford (MA), London Graduate School of Business Studies (MSc); *m* 1981, Lynda, da of Sidney Henry James Bates (d 1986); *Career* md: Pearl & Dean Gp Ltd, Shepperton Studios Ltd, Air Call Teletext Ltd, Allen Computers Int Ltd; *Recreations* tennis, bridge; *Clubs* Carlton; *Style—* Clive Landa, Esq; Allen House, Station Rd, Egham, Surrey (☎ 0784 37411, car tel 0836 503165)

LANDALE, David William Neil; s of David Fortune Landale (d 1970), and Louisa D M C, *née* Forbes (d 1956), yst da of Charles Forbes of Callander House, Falkirk, Stirlingshire; *b* 27 May 1934; *Educ* Eton, Balliol Coll Oxford (MA); *m* 1961, Norah Melanie, da of Sir Harold Roper, MC, MP (d 1969); 3 s (Peter b 1963, William b 1965, Jamie b 1969 ; *Career* Black Watch Royal Highland Regt 1952-54, Jardine Matheson & Co Ltd 1958-75; Hong Kong, Thailand, Taiwan, Japan (dir 1967-75); dir: Matheson & Co Ltd 1975-, Pinneys Hldgs Ltd 1982-86; chm: T C Farries & Co Ltd 1982-, Timber Growers UK Ltd 1985-87; appointed sec and keeper of Records of The Duchy of Cornwall 1987, dep Lord Lieutenant Nithside and Annandale (Dumfriesshire); *Recreations* all countryside pursuits, theatre, reading (history); *Clubs* Boodle's, Pratt's, New (Edinburgh); *Style—* David Landale, Esq; Duchy of Cornwall, 10 Buckingham Gate, London SW1E 6LA (☎ 01 834 7346; fax 01 931 9541)

LANDAU, Sir Dennis Marcus; s of late Michael Landau, metallurgist; *b* 18 June 1927; *Educ* Haberdashers' Aske's Sch Hampstead; *Career* chief exec Co-op Wholesale Soc, dir Co-op Bank and other assoc Co-op Cos; kt 1987; *Style—* Sir Dennis Landau; Co-operative Wholesale Society Ltd, PO Box 53, New Century House, Manchester M60 4ES (☎ 061 834 1212, telex 667046)

LANDAU, Steven Martin; s of Capt John Joseph Landau of 11 Gay Close London NW2 and Gloria Violet Landau *née* Harvey; *b* 5 Dec 1949; *Educ* Warwick University (MSc); *m* 1977, Kay, da of Detective Inspector Roy Woolley of 25 Denbigh Place Lutterworth, Leics; 2 da (Kelly Elizabeth b 1980, Laura Jane b 1982); *Career* fin controller Levi Strauss N Europe 1978-80, md Herondrive 1985-88 (fin dir 1980-85); md Norfolk Fin 1988-; *Recreations* sport; *Style—* Steven Landau, Esq; Ashburton Hse, Lashbrook Rd, Lower Shiplake, Henley-on-Thames, Oxen RG9 3NX (☎ 073522 2203, car tel 0860 748632)

LANDER, John Hugh Russell; s of Hugh Russell Lander, of IOW, and Maude Louise, *née* Ellis; *b* 25 Feb 1944; *Educ* Sandown GS, Sheffield Univ (BSc), Imperial Coll London (MSC, DIC); *m* 1972, Veronica Eluira, da of Peter Mathew Van Eijk, of Holland; 2 s (Robert b 1976, Edward b 1983), 2 da (Melody b 1975, Annabel b 1982); *Career* exploration dir RTZ Oil & Gas Ltd 1983-, vice-pres Exploration Platt Energy Corp 1983-86; *Recreations* sailing, squash; *Clubs* RAC, Lagos YC; *Style—* John Lander, Esq; 45 Burgh Heath Rd, Epsom, Surrey; RTZ Oil and Gas Ltd, 10 Babmaes St, London W1 (☎ 01 930 6277, telex 8951451)

LANDER, Maxwell; s of Gustave Lander (d 1948); *b* 10 May 1914; *Educ* King Edward's Sch Birmingham; *m* 1939, Helena Margaret, da of Wolf Halon; 1 da (Pamela Marjorie m 1978 Neil Brinkley); *Career* former Col GHQ India Cmd; conslt actuary, jt sr ptnr Duncan C Fraser & Co 1950-84 (ptnr 1984-86), conslt William M Mercer Fraser Ltd 1986-, asst sec Admty 1947-50; pres Nat Assoc of Pension Funds 1981-85; Master Worshipful Co of Actuaries 1986-87; holder of Queen's Silver Jubilee Medal; *Recreations* fast cars, reading, theatre, music, food and wine; *Clubs* RAC, Ferrari Owners'; *Style*— Maxwell Lander, Esq; 1st Floor, 189 Pall Mall House, Tithebarn St, Liverpool L2 2QU (☎ 051 236 9771); Flat 124, 25 Porchester Place, W2 2PF (☎ 01 262 4119); 83 Waterloo Rd, Hillside, Southport, Merseyside PR8 2NW (☎ 0704 67408)

LANDERS, Brian Whitfield; s of William Reginald Harry Whitfield (d 1964), of Bucks, and Gladys Winifred, *née* Widgery (d 1979); *b* 22 Mar 1921; *Educ* City of London Sch; *m* 7 Sept 1943, Elizabeth Joan Marguerite, da of John Pearce of Lynton, Northcroft Rd, Wooburn Green, Bucks (d 1950); 2 da (Valerie Elizabeth b 1947, Rosalind Mary b 1954); *Career* Pilot RAF 1941-46; Fl Lt, Flying Boat Capt with Coastal Cmd; slr, sr ptnr Waterhouse and Co London 1982-86; pres: City of Westminster Law Soc 1977-78, John Carpenter Club 1981-82; chm Castle Baynard Ward Club 1973-74; Liveryman Worshipful Co of Basketmakers 1956-; *Recreations* photography, cricket; *Clubs* MCC, City Livery, John Carpenter (Old Citizens' Assoc); *Style*— Brian W Landers, Esq; Cobbleston, The Glen, Farnborough Park, Kent BR6 8LR (☎ 0689 56209); Waterhouse & Co, 4 St Pauls Churchyard, London EC4M 8BA (☎ 01 236 2333; telex 884217, fax 01 236 8320)

LANDES, Emil; s of Wilhelm Landes (d 1983), of London, and Toni, *née* Held; *b* 13 July 1932; *Educ* Parmiter's Sch, King's Coll London (BDS); *m* 7 Feb 1960, Suzanne Dorrit, da of Paul Fraenkel, of Stockholm, Sweden; 2 s (Anthony b 1963, Jermey b 1966), 1 da (Viveca b 1961); *Career* Flt Lt dental branch RAF 1958-59 (Flying Offr 1957-58); dental surgn St Thomas' Hosp, St Mary's Hosp, currently private practice Harley St; Freeman City of London 1971; GDC 1956, BDA 1956, SAAD 1971, RSM 1974, EDS 1983; *Recreations* golf, tennis, skiing, chess, reading, biographies; *Clubs* RAC, RAF; *Style*— Emil Landes, Esq; Penthouse West, Thornbury Sq, London N6 5YW (☎ 01 281 1843); 22 Harley St, London W1 (☎ 01 637 0491, car tel 0836 248 529)

LANDON, Theodore Luke Giffard; s of Rev Sylvanus Luke Landon (d 1979; his m was Jane Mary Giffard, *see* Halsbury, 3 Earl of), formerly vicar of Marldon, Devon, and Florence Faith Loetitia Trelawny, *née* Lowe (d 1972; her m was Eleanor Salusbury-Trelawny), *see* Sir John Salusbury in Trelawny Bt, *qv*, Mr Landon is the head of the French Huguenot family of Landon, founded in England by Samuel Landon in 1683; *b* 10 Oct 1926; *Educ* Blundell's Sch, London Univ; *m* 1956, Joan, da of Frederic Archibald Parker (d 1977), of Alresford Hants (s of Rev Hon Archibald Parker, sometime rural dean of Wem, Salop, and Hon Maud Bateman-Hanbury, da of 2 Baron Bateman; the dean was 9 s of 6 Earl of Macclesfield); 3 s (Mark b 1958, Philip b 1962, Benjamin b 1967), 2 da (Felicity b 1960, Rohais b 1964); *Career* dep chm and md Terra Nova Insur Co Ltd 1970-79, dep chm C T Bowring Underwriting Hldgs Ltd 1979-83, dir English and American Insur Co Ltd 1982-; memb Lloyd's 1961-; govr Kelly Coll Tavistock 1969-; tstee Huguenot Soc 1973-; *Recreations* history, music, genealogical research; *Clubs* East India, Gresham; *Style*— Theodore Landon, Esq; Three Quays, Tower Hill, London EC3R 6DSD (☎ 01 283 7575); Great Bromley House, Great Bromley, Colchester, Essex CO7 7TP (☎ 0206 230 385)

LANE, Anthony John; s of Eric Marshal Lane, and Phyllis Mary, *née* Hardwick; *b* 30 May 1939; *Educ* Caterham Sch, Balliol Coll Oxford; *m* 1967, Judith Sheila, da of William Herbert Dodson (d 1968); 2 s (Barnaby b 1969, Robin b 1972), 1 da (Lucinda b 1976); *Career* dep dir gen Off of Fair Trading; *Recreations* music; *Style*— Anthony Lane, Esq; Foxbury, East Grinstead, Sussex; Field House, Breams Buildings EC4

LANE, Dr Anthony Milner; s of Herbert William Lane (d 1977), and Doris Ruby, *née* Milner (d 1965); *b* 27 July 1928; *Educ* Trowbridge Boys GS, Cambridge Univ (BA, PhD); *m* 28 Aug 1952 (d 1980), Anne Sophie, da of Isaac Zissman (d 1964); 2 s (Michael b 1964, Mark b 1970), 1 da (Galina b 1961); m 2, 1983, Jill Valerie, *née* Parvin; *Career* chief scientist UKAEA Harwell 1977- (scientist 1953-); FRS 1974; *Recreations* walking; *Style*— Dr Anthony Lane; 6 Walton St, Oxford, OX1 2HG (☎ 0865 56565); UK Atomic Energy Authority (☎ 0235 24141, ext 3247)

LANE, Maj-Gen Barry Michael; CB (1984), OBE (1974, MBE 1965); *b* 10 August 1932; *Educ* Dover Coll; *m* 1 (1956) Eveline Jane, da of Sir Harry Koelle KCB; 1 s (Antony b 1962) 1 d (Eveline d 1986); m 1987 Shirley Ann, da of E V Hanton, Esq; *Career* cmmnd LI 1954; cmd: 1 LI 1972-75, II Arm Bde 1977--78; RCDS 1979; dir Army QM 1981-82; vice QMG 1982-83; GOC S W Dist 1984-87; Col 7 LI 1982-87; *Recreations* cricket, travel, wines; *Clubs* Army and Navy; *Style*— Maj-Gen Barry Lane, CB, OBE; c/o National Westminster Bank, Tadworth, surrey KT20 5AF

LANE, David Goodwin; s of James Cooper Lane (d 1981), of Gloucester, and Joyce Lilian, *née* Goodwin; *b* 8 Oct 1945; *Educ* Crypt Sch Gloucester, King's Coll London (LLB, AKC); *Career* called to the Bar Gray's Inn 1968, rec Crown Ct; memb Royal Soc of St George; Freeman City of London; *Style*— David Lane, Esq; 2 All Saints' Court, Bristol BS1 1JN

LANE, David Neil; CMG (1983); s of A C Lane (d 1974), of Bath, and H M Lane, *née* Tonner (d 1980); *b* 16 April 1928; *Educ* Abbotsholme Sch, Merton Coll Oxford (MA); *m* 1968, Sara, da of C J Nurcombe, MC (d 1988), of Watchet Somerset; 2 da (Harriet b 1969, Victoria b 1973); *Career* HM Foreign (later Diplomatic) Serv 1951-88, Br high cmmr Trinidad and Tobago 1980-85; ambass to the Holy See 1985-88; *Recreations* music; *Clubs* Travellers'; *Style*— David Lane, Esq, CMG; 6 Montague Sq, London W1H 1RA (☎ 01 486 1673)

LANE, Sir David William Stennis Stuart; s of Hubert Samuel Lane, MC; *b* 24 Sept 1922; *Educ* Eton, Trinity Coll Cambridge, Yale; *m* 1955, Lesley Anne Mary, da of Sir Gerard Clauson, KCMG, OBE, former chm Pirelli Ltd and asst under-sec Colonial Off (d 1974); 2 s; *Career* serv WWII RNVR; barr Middle Temple 1955, Br Iron and Steel Fedn 1948-59 (sec 1956), with Shell Int 1959-67; MP (C) Cambridge 1967-76 (had contested Lambeth (Vauxhall) 1964, Cambridge 1966), PPS to Employment Sec 1970-72, parly under-sec Home Off 1972-74; chm: N Kensington Cons Assoc 1961-62, Cmmn for Racial Equality 1977-82, Nat Assoc of Youth Clubs 1982-87; kt 1983; *Recreations* travel, walking, golf; *Clubs* MCC; *Style*— Sir David Lane; 5 Spinney Drive, Great Shelford, Cambridge CB2 5LY (☎ 0223 843437)

LANE, (Sara) Elizabeth; da of Rt Hon Sir Lionel Heald, QC, MP (d 1981), of Chilworth Manor, Surrey and Daphne Constance Heald, CBE; *b* 30 April 1938; *Educ* Heathfield and Paris; *m* 15 May 1963, George Henry MC, s of Ernest Lanyi, of Budapest, Hungary; *Career* dir Seek & Find Ltd 1963-68, advsr on works of art and assoc Baron Martin von Koblitz 1968-78, dir Christie Manson & Woods Ltd 1978-; *Recreations* country pursuits; *Style*— Mrs George Lane; 12 Petersham Place, London, SWY 5PX (☎ 01 584 7840); Christie Mansion Woods Ltd, 8 King St, St James, London SW1 (☎ 01 839 9060)

LANE, Baron (Life Peer UK 1979); Geoffrey Dawson Lane; AFC (1943), PC (1974); s of late Percy Albert Lane; *b* 17 July 1918; *Educ* Shrewsbury, Trinity Coll Cambridge; *m* 1944, Jan, da of Donald Macdonald; 1 s; *Career* served RAF 1939-45, Sqdn Ldr 1942; barr 1946, QC 1962, bencher 1966, dep chm Beds QS 1960-66, rec Bedford 1963-66, judge High Ct of Justice (Queen's Bench) 1966-74, lord justice of appeal 1974-79, Lord of Appealin Ordinary 1979-80, lord chief justice 1980-, hon master of the bench Inner Temple 1980-; Hon DCL Cambridge 1984; kt 1966; *Style*— The Rt Hon the Lord Lane, AFC; Royal Courts of Justice, Strand, London WC2; House of Lords, London SW1

LANE, (formerly Lanyi) George Henry; MC; s of Ernest Lanyi (d 1945), of Budapest, and Theresa, *née* Schweitzer (d 1938); *b* 18 Jan 1915; *Educ* Eotvos Jozsef Foreal Budapest, Univ of London; *m* 1, 1943 (m dis 1956), Hon Miriam Rothschild; 1 s, 3 da; m 2, 15 May 1963, (Sara) Elizabeth, da of Rt Hon Sir Lionel Heald, QC, MP; *Career* cmmnd Buffs served 10 Commando, carried out special ops (small scale raids), captured 1944 (POW); farmer Ashton Wold Peterborough 1946-56; tres De Pontet & Co NY Stock Exchange 1956-61, exec vice-pres Euro Eccn News Agency 1961-86; pres Br Legion Oundle Northants, area chm Cons Pty Soke Peterborough, chm Oundle branch NFU; memb American C of C, MInstM; *Recreations* shooting, skiing; *Style*— George Lane, Esq, MC; 12 Petersham Place, London SW7 5PX, (☎ 01 584 7840)

LANE, (John) Godfrey; s of Vivian Charles Thomas Lane (Wing Cdr 1945, d 1982), of Hale, Cheshire, and Myra Victoria Lane; *b* 5 Jan 1932; *m* 1958, Winifred Lily, da of John Henry Brooks (d 1972); 3 s (Paul Bruce, Gordon Stuart, Michael John); *Career* CA 1954; 2 yr Nat Serv; employed on Internal Audit with Esso 1957-58, fin/distribution dir Abbots Packaging Ltd 1958 (md 1981-86); dir: MacFarlane gp (Clansman) plc, Abbott's Packaging Ltd; FCA; *Recreations* yachting, golf, swimming, ballet; *Clubs* Poole Harbour YC, South Heats GC, Porsche; *Style*— Godfrey Lane, Esq; Abbott's Packaging Ltd, Gordon House, Oakleigh Rd South, New Southgate, London N11 1HL (☎ 01 368 1266)

LANE, John; CB (1981); s of Roger James Iddison Lane (d 1972), and Mary Elizabeth Lily, *née* Roberts (d 1982); *b* 23 Oct 1924; *Educ* John Lyon, Harrow, Univ Coll Hull, LSE (BSc); *m* 1954, Ruth Ann, da of Thomas Victor Crocker (d 1941); 1 s (Robert); *Career* civil servant, under sec Depts of the Environment and Tport 1972-78, dep dir Central Statistical Off 1978-81, dep sec, ret; *Recreations* theatre, music, golf; *Clubs* Civil Service; *Style*— John Lane, Esq, CB; Fern Hill, 67 Mount Ephraim, Tunbridge Wells, Kent

LANE, John Anthony; s of Walter William Lane, of Harrow, Middx, and Phyllis Gwendoline, *née* Jones; *b* 30 June 1946; *Educ* Harrow Co GS; *m* 8 Aug 1970, Joan Elizabeth, da of Harold Burgess, of Harrow, Middx; 2 s (Andrew Michael b 1977, Stuart Christopher b 1981); *Career* CA; sr ptnr Lane & Co; formerly ptnr: Josolyne Layton-Bennett & Co, Arthur Young McClelland Moores & Co, Everett Collins & Loosley; *Clubs* Tring Lions; *Style*— John Lane, Esq; Far Hills, Grove Rd, Tring, Herts HP23 5PA (☎ 044 282 2766); Exchange House, Lake Street, Leighton Buzzard, Beds LU7 8RS (☎ 0525 373 767)

LANE, (Henry) John Noxon; s of Henry Audley Lane (d 1965), and Annie Elizabeth, *née* Larking; *b* 15 Oct 1958; *m* 25 Apr 1959, Maureen Edith, da of Reginald Morris (d 1979); 1 s (Jon b 1967), 3 da (Susan b 1960, Philippa b 1964, Jacky (twin) b 1964); *Career* Nat Serv RM 1947-49; accountant George Hay and Co (ptnr 1956-, sr ptnr 1975-); dir: Stylus Supplies (Mountings) Ltd 1970-, TEE (Heat Treatment) Ltd 1975-; fndr memb Biggleswade Round Table 1954, and Rotary Club 1966; FCA 1953; *Recreations* work and walking; *Style*— John Lane, Esq; Parkside, The Ave, Sandy, Bedfordshire (☎ 0767 80550), Brigham House, 93 High Street, Biggleswade, Bedfordshire (☎ 0767 315 010, fax 0767 318 388)

LANE, Josiah Bowen; s of Josiah Bowen Lane (d 1947), of Sandhills House, Walsall Wood, Staffordshire, and late Harriot Anne, *née* Kircham; *b* 2 Oct 1924; *Educ* Rossall Sch, Clare Coll Cambridge; *m* 30 April 1955, Anita Joy, da of Harold Andrews (d 1974), of 62 Wake Green Road, Moseley, Birmingham; 2 da (Claire b 1956, Fleur b 1959); *Career* WWII RE 1943, cmmnd RE 1945; serv 1945-47: Bombay Sappers and Miners, 401 Field Sqdn 3 Indian Armd Bde (Burma and NW Frontier India); Lane Bros Tar Distillers Ltd 1947- (Lancs Tar Distillers Ltd): dir 1948 (later jt md), chm 1973-; Freeman: City of London, Worshipful Co of Paviors; *Recreations* skiing, watching cricket, shooting; *Clubs* Livery, MCC; *Style*— Josiah Lane, Esq; 24 Bowgreen Rd, Bowdon, Altrincham, Cheshire WA14 3LX; Lancashire Tar Distillers Ltd, Liverpool Rd, Cadishead, Manchester (☎ 061 775 2644, fax 061 776 1077, telex 668620)

LANE, Kenneth Alexander; OBE; s of Lt Alexander William Lane, MBE, RN (d 1970); *b* 20 Mar 1924; *Educ* Winchester, Christ's Coll Cambridge; *m* 1, 1945, Peggy (d 1973), da of Patrick Murphy (d 1942); 3 s, 3 da; m 2, 1975, Delma, da of Walter Garrod, of Kings Lynn; *Career* Admty Scientific Serv 1943-45, Avon Rubber Co 1946-53; English Electric Co 1953 and dir various subsidiaries until 1969, dep md Bowthorpe Hellermann Ltd 1970-72, md Porvair Ltd 1973-75, exec chm Kearney and Trecker Marwin Ltd 1976-81, dir gen The Machine Tool Trades Assoc 1981-85; chm: Kempton Cons Assoc 1979-81, Brighton Cons Assoc 1986-88, Hove Cons Assoc 1988-89; *Clubs* St Stephen's, IOD; *Style*— Kenneth Lane, Esq, OBE; 83 Kingsway Court, Hove, E Sussex BN3 2LR

LANE, Lady; Lettice; da of Sir Charles William James Orr, KCMG (decd); *m* 1941, Sir Allen (Lane Williams) Lane, CH (d 1970); *Style*— Lady Lane; Priory Farm, Beech Hill, Berks

LANE, Margaret; *see*: Huntingdon, Countess of

LANE, Mary; *née* Dunhill; s of Alfred Dunhill (d 1960), and Alice Mary Stapleton (d 1945); *b* 17 Sept 1906; *Educ* St Felix Southwold; *m* 1, 1934, Frank Geoffrey; 2 da (Kay b 1935, Tessa b 1938 (d 1973)); m 2, 1957, Reginald Joseph, s of William Lane (d 1962), of Watford; *Career* dir Alfred Dunhill Ltd 1940-, chm Alfred Dunhill Ltd 1949-65; *Recreations* gardening; *Style*— Mrs Mary Lane; 30 Duke Street, St James SW1 (☎ 499 9566)

LANE, Hon Mrs Miriam Louisa; *née* Rothschild; CBE (1982); eld da of Hon Nathaniel Charles Rothschild (d 1923); sis of 3 Baron Rothschild; granted the rank and precedence of a Baron's da 1938; *b* 5 August 1908; *Educ* privately; *m* 14 Aug 1943 (m dis 1957), Capt George Henry Lane, MC; 1 s, 3 da (1 s and 1 da decd); *Career* serv WWII F O (Def Medal); farmer & biologist (300 Scientific publns); tstee Br Museum 1967-75; visiting prof Biology Royal Free Hosp 1970-74; Romanes lectr 1985; memb: Zoological and Entomological Res Cncl, Marine Biological Assoc, Royal Entomological Soc, Systematics Assoc, Soc for Promotion of Nature Reserves, Publns Ctee ZS; hon fell St Hugh's Oxford, Hon DSC Oxford, Gotenberg, Hull, North Western (Chicago), Leicester, FRS; *Books* Dear Lord Rothschild (1983), Catalogue of the Rothschild collection of fleas (six volumes) (1953-82), The Butterfly Gardener (1983), Atlas of Insect Tissue (1985), Animals and Man (1986); *Recreations* natural history, conservation; *Clubs* Queens, Br Ornithological, Entomological; *Style*— The Hon Mrs Miriam Lane, CBE; Ashton Wold, Peterborough PE8 5LZ (☎ 0832 73575)

LANE, Dr Peter Edward; OBE (1985); s of Harry Edward Lane (d 1961) and Louisa Carrie, *née* Jones (d 1979); *b* 8 Sept 1925; *Educ* Sutton GS Durham Univ (BSc, PhD, CEng, CPhys); *m* 1960, Freda Dorthy, da of Roland Towers Irving, of Cumbria (d 1985); 1 s (Nigel b 1966); 1 da (Nicola b 1964); *Career* (ret) RAF Aircrew War 1983-85, (ret) dir BP Shipping Ltd 1983-85, chief exec dir BP Exploration Co Ltd 1985-, chm Oceaneering Int Servs Ltd 1985-; dir: Trafalgar House Offshore Ltd 1985-, Trafalgar House Oil and Gas Ltd; FInstPet, MIEE; *Recreations* motor cruising, music, reading; *Clubs* Phyllis Court, Henley; Pine Lodge, River Rd, Taplow, Bucks SL6 0BG (☎ 0628 30364)

LANE, Sir Peter Stewart; JP (Surrey 1976); s of Leonard George Lane (d 1950); *b* 29 Jan 1925; *Educ* Sherborne; *m* Doris Florence (d 1969), da of Robert Simpson Botsford (d 1955); 2 da (of whom Rosalie m 2 Baron Trefgarne, *qv*); *Career* serv Sub-Lt RNVR 1943-46; sr ptnr BDO Binder Hamlyn CA 1979-, ptnr int firm BDO Binder & Co; chm Brent Chemicals Int plc; dep chm More O'Ferrall plc; govr Nuffield Nursing Homes Tst; chm Air Travel Tst Ctee; Nat Union of Cons and Unionists Assocs: (vice-chm 1981-83, chm 1983, chm exec ctee 1986-, hon vice-pres 1984-); kt 1984; *Clubs* Boodle's, MCC; *Style*— Sir Peter Lane, JP; Rossmore, Pond Rd, Hook Heath, Woking, Surrey GU22 0JY (☎ 04862 61858); BDO Binder Hamlyn, 8 St Bride St, London EC4A 4DA (☎ 01 353 3020)

LANE, Hon Richard Geoffrey; s of Baron Lane (Life Peer); *b* 1948; *Style*— The Hon Richard Lane

LANE, Robert Charles; s of Sidney Arthur Lane, of Wanstead, London, and Eileen Ethel Anna, *née* Cleave; *b* 29 August 1958; *Educ* Buckhurst Hill HS, Univ Coll London (LLB); *m* 26 April 1986, Margaret Enid, da of Rev Stanley Peter Handley Stubbs, of Brondesbury Park, London; 1 s (Edward b 2 Aug 1988); *Career* asst slr McKenna & Co 1988- (Slaughter and May 1982-88); memb Kensington Soc; Freeman: City of London 1987, Liveryman Worshipful Co of City of London Slrs 1988; memb law soc 1982; *Recreations* opera, watching cricket, rugby; *Clubs* RAC, Bentham; *Style*— Robert Lane, Esq; McKenna and Co, 71 Queen Victoria St, London EC4 (☎ 236 4340, fax 236 4485)

LANE, Terence Maurice; s of Alexander Uriah Lane (d 1927), of Fleet, Hants, and Hilda Rachel, *née* Smith (d 1976); *b* 5 Oct 1918; *Educ* London Univ (BA), Indiana Univ (AB), Coll of Law; *m* 15 Aug 1944, (Bruce) Jacqueline, da of Bruce Alexander Johnston Dunlop, MC; 3 s (Jeremy, Piers, Crispin), 4 da (Litan, Rafael (Mrs Hall), Halcyon (Mrs Day), Meredith (Mrs Sanders)); *Career* RA 1940, cmmnd 2 Lt 1941, seconded 2 Indian Anti-Tank Regt and 28 Mountain Regt RIA 1941, Capt 1944, Maj 1944 (mentioned in despatches); Colonial Admin Serv Tanganyika Territory (now Tanzania) 1946, dist cmmr Chunya Dist 1948, invalided from serv 1949; slr 1953, fndr ptnr Baker & McKenzie 1961, sr ptnr Lane & Ptnrs 1974, ptnr Marks Murase & White NYC 1974; Freeman City of London 1987, Liveryman Worshipful Co Arbitrators 1987; memb Law Soc 1954, FCIArb 1977; *Books* International Licensing Agreements (1973); *Recreations* riding, hunting, racing; *Clubs* Savage, Hampshire Hunt; *Style*— Terence Lane, Esq; Peregrine House, Rake, Liss, Hants (☎ 073089 3138); 46/47 Bloomsbury Square, London WC1A 2RU (☎ 01 242 2626 , fax 01 242 0387, telex 8812495)

LANE FOX, Col Francis Gordon Ward (Joe); DL (W Riding Yorks 1952); s of Claude Ward Jackson (d 1937), of Kingsley Mill, Black Torrington, Beaworthy, Devon, and Una, *née* Wilcox (d 1930); changed name for Jackson by Deed Poll 1937; *b* 14 Oct 1899; *Educ* Eton, RMC Sandhurst; *m* 3 Oct 1929, Hon Marcia Agnes Mary, *née* Lane Fox, da of 1 and last Baron Bingley, PC (d 1947); 2 s (George b 15 May 1931, Richard b 19 Sept 1933), 1 da (Marcia (Mrs Wakeham b 19 Sept 1940); *Career* joined RHG 1919, WWII cmd: Household Cavalry Trg Regt 1941, 43 Reconaissance Regt 1943, Yorks Hussars 1945; ret 1946; pres: Central Yorks Boy Scouts Assoc 1949, W Riding Standing Conf of Nat Voluntary Youth Orgns, Yorks Agric Soc 1961; chm: W Riding Fedn of Young Farmers 1957-60, cncl OStJ for W Riding 1957; Miny of Agric liaison offr for Yorks and Lancs Region 1961; memb: cncl Royal Agric Benevolent Inst, Cncl of Friends of York Min and York Diocesan Bd Diocesan Bd of Fin; fell Woodard Corpn 1948; alderman W Riding of Yorks CC 1955 (cnclr 1949); JP 1948, Vice Lt of the W Riding of Yorks 1968-74; KStJ 1965; Offr Order of the Crown (with palm), Croix de Guerre (with palm) Belgium 1946; *Clubs* Yorkshire (York); *Style*— Col Joe Lane Fox, DL; The Little House, Bramham Park, Wetherby, W Yorks LS23 6LS (☎ 0937 843220)

LANE FOX, Col George Francis; s of Col Francis Gordon Ward Lane Fox, DL (name changed from Jackson 1937), of The Little House, Bramham Park, Wetherby, W Yorks, and Hon Marcia Agnes Mary, *née* Lane Fox (d 1980), da of 1 and last Baron Bingley (d 1947); *b* 15 May 1931; *Educ* Eton, RMA Sandhurst, RMCS Shrivenham; *m* 10 Aug 1962, (Helen) Victoria (d 1980), da of Maj Charles Edward Rodney Duff (ka 1942); 3 s (Nicholas b 1963, James b 1966, Edward b 1976); *Career* joined RHG 1950, RMA Sandhurst 1950-52, RHG 1952-69, Household Cavalry Regt 1953-55, No 1 Gds Independent Co The Parachute Regt 1958-59, RMCS 1962-64, asst mil attaché Paris 1967-69, The Blues and Royals 1969-70, resigned 1970; master Bramham Moor Foxhounds 1970-75 and 1980-82, memb: Woodard Schs Northern Chapter 1975-85, cncl chm Queen Margaret's Sch Escrick York 1981-85, pres CPRE Yorks Lower Dales Branch 1977-, dep pres St John Ambulance for S and W Yorks 1975-; chm: BHS for NW Yorks 1985-, W and S Yorks Playing Fields Assoc 1974-; pres Yorks Agric Soc 1984-85; High Sheriff of W Yorkshire 1975-76; C Eng 1968, MIERE/MIEE 1968, FRSA 1974; *Recreations* horse trials, riding, shooting; *Clubs* Turf; *Style*— Col George Lane Fox; Bramham Park, Wetherby, West Yorkshire, LS23 6ND (☎ 0937 842114 and 0937 844265)

LANE FOX, Hon Mrs Janet; da of 3 Baron Hamilton of Dalzell, MC; *b* 8 Sept 1936; *m* 1960, Richard Sackville Lane Fox, s of Col Francis Gordon Ward Lane Fox, of The Little House, Bramham Park, Wetherby, York; 1 s, 1 da; *Style*— The Hon Mrs Lane Fox; 17 Princedale Rd, London W11 4NW (☎ 01 727 4330); Kingsley Mill, Black Torrington, Beaworthy, Devon (☎ 040 923 209)

LANE FOX, Robin James; s of James Henry Lane Fox, of Middleton Cheney, Oxon, and Anne, *née* Loyd; *b* 5 Oct 1946; *Educ* Eton, Magdalen Coll Oxford (MA); *m* 26 June 1970, Louisa Caroline Mary, da of Maj Charles Farrell, MC, of Cutmill House, Watlington, Oxon; 1 s (Henry b 19 Oct 1974), 1 da (Martha b 10 Feb 1973) ; *Career* fell Magdalen Coll Oxford 1970-73, lectr in classics Worcester Coll Oxford 1974-76, res fell classical and Islamic history Worcester Coll 1976-77, fell and tutor New Coll Oxford 1977-, univ lectr in ancient history 1977-, gardening columnist Finanical Times 1970-, Br Press Award Leisure Journalist of Year 1988; garden master New Coll 1979-; FRSL 1974; *Books* Alexander The Great (1973), Variations On A Garden (1974), Search for Alexander (1980), Better Gardening (1982), Pagan and Christians (1986); *Recreations* gardening, hunting, travelling; *Clubs* Beefsteak; *Style*— Robin Lane Fox, Esq; c/o New College, Oxford (☎ 0865 248 451)

LANESBOROUGH, 9 Earl of (1756); Denis Anthony Brian Butler; TD, JP (Leics 1967), DL (1962); also Baron of Newtown-Butler (I 1715, but eldest s & h usually styled Lord Newtown-Butler) and Viscount Lanesborough (I 1728); s of 8 Earl of Lanesborough (d 1950), by his 2 w Grace, da of Sir Anthony Abdy, 3 Bt; *b* 28 Oct 1918; *Educ* Stowe; *m* 1939 (m dis 1950), Bettyne Ione, da of Sir Lindsay Everard, JP, DL, MP (d 1949); 2 da (1 decd); *Heir* Major Henry Butler; *Career* Lt Leics Yeo 1939, Maj RA (TA) 1945; memb Nat Gas Consumers' Cncl 1973-78, Trent RHA 1974-85; chm Loughborough & Dist Housing Assoc 1978-; *Style*— The Rt Hon Earl of Lanesborough, TD, JP, DL; Alton Lodge, Kegworth, Derby (☎ 0509 672243)

LANG, Prof Andrew Richard; s of Ernest Lang (decd); *b* 9 Sept 1924; *Career* asst prof Harvard Univ 1954-59; physics lectr 1960-66, reader 1966-79, prof of physics University of Bristol 1979-; FRS 1975; *Style*— Prof Andrew Lang; 1B Elton Rd, Bristol BS8 1SJ

LANG, Hon Mrs (Cecilia Alexandra Rose); *née* Alport; JP (Inner London); da of Baron Alport, PC (Life Peer); *b* 3 Sept 1946; *Educ* County High Sch Colchester, Arundel Sch Harare Zimbabwe, Queensgate Sch; *m* 1969, Rev Geoffrey Wilfrid Francis Lang, MA, s of Frederick Lang of Croxley Green, Herts; 1 s, 1 da (Oliver b 1971, Imogen b 1973); *Style*— The Hon Mrs Lang, JP; 6 St Peter's Square, London W6 9AB

LANG, David Louis; s of Howard J Lang and Helen, *née* Grant; *b* 6 Oct 1939; *Educ* Univ of Western Ontario (BA); *m* 1963, Elizabeth Anne Holton; 2 s (Alen b 1969, Douglas b 1970), 2 da (Cynthia Anne b 1964, Catherine Elaine b 1966); *Career* dir: Coopers and Lybrand 1962-66, Bank of Montreal 1966-69, Cochran Murray and Wisener 1969-75, Crang and Ostiguy (Investmt Dealers) 1975-77, Citicorp Int Gp 1977-80, Lloyds Bank Int Ltd 1980-83; vice-pres treasy ops Canadian Imp Bank Gp 1983-88, dir and risk mangr Girozentrale Gilbert Eliott; former memb Bd of Govrs Montreal Childrens Hosp; *Recreations* hunting, fishing, squash; *Clubs* Toronto, Hurlingham; *Style*— David Lang, Esq; Broom Close, Esher, Surrey KT10 9ET

LANG, Lt-Gen Sir Derek Boileau; KCB (1967, CB 1964), DSO (1944), MC (1941), DL (Edinburgh 1978); s of Lt-Col C F G Lang, Indian Army (d 1961), of Whytegates, Church Crookham, Hants; *b* 7 Oct 1913; *Educ* Wellington, RMC Sandhurst; *m* 1, 1942, Morna Helena Casey (d 1953), da of Charles Massy-Dawson, of Sussex; 1 s, 1 da; m 2, 1953 (m dis 1969), Anita Lewis Shields; m 3, 1969, Mrs Elizabeth H Balfour (d 1982); m 4, 1983, Mrs Maartje McQueen, wid of Charles N McQueen; *Career* 2 Lt Cameron Highlanders 1933, Brig 1958, COS Scottish Cmd 1960-61, GOC 51 Highland Div 1962-64, Dir Army Trg, MOD 1964-66, GOC-in-C Scottish Cmd and govr of Edinburgh Castle 1966-69, Lt-Gen 1966, ret 1969; sec Stirling Univ 1970-74, assoc conslt PA Mgmnt Conslts Ltd 1975-83; OStJ; *Recreations* golf, shooting, fishing, music; *Clubs* Hon Co of Edinburgh Golfers, New (Edinburgh), Army & Navy, Muthaiga (Kenya), Sr Golfers; *Style*— Lt-Gen Sir Derek Lang, KCB, DSO, MC, DL; Templeland, Kirknewton, Midlothian EH27 8DJ (☎ 0506 883211)

LANG, Rear Adm (William) Duncan; CB (1981); s of James Hardie Lang (d 1936), of Edinburgh, and Elizabeth Foggo Paterson, *née* Storie (d 1965); *b* 1 April 1925; *Educ* Edinburgh Acad; *m* 1947, Joyce Rose, da of Alfred Henry Weeks (d 1936), of Catford; 1 s (James), 1 da (Celia); *Career* serv WWII RN 1943; pilot in 800, 816 and 825 Sqdns, Flying Instr; Test Pilot, CO 802 Sqdn 1958-59, CO RNAS Lossiemouth 1970-72, COS to Flag Offr Naval Air Cmd 1975-76, Naval ADC to HM The Queen 1978, Mil Dep to Head of Def Sales 1978-81; MOD 1981-86; *Recreations* golf (pres RNGS 1979-85); *Clubs* Army & Navy; *Style*— Rear Adm Duncan Lang, CB; c/o MOD London

LANG, Hugh; s of Hugh Lang (d 1981), of Holmwood, Surrey, and Lilian Maydee, *née* Mackay; *b* 22 Dec 1934; *Educ* St Edmunds Sch Hindhead, Harrow Sch; *m* 11 March 1961, Rosanne Auber, da of Col Richard Quentin Charles Mainwaring (d 1983), of Cortown, Kells, Co Meath Ireland; 2 s (Alistair Hugh b 15 July 1963, James Richard b 13 March 1966); *Career* 2 Lt 5 Royal Inniskilling Dragoon Gds cmmnd 1954, RARO (AER) 1956-65 Maj 1964; ptnr John Prust & Co 1963-70, Laurence Prust & Co 1970-80, non exec dir Wallace Smith Tst Co Ltd 1985; memb Stock Exchange 1962-, chief exec and sec The Stock Exchange Benevolent Fund 1980; govr Crossways Tst Ltd, tstee Poyle Charity; Freeman City of London 1956, Liveryman Worshipful Co of Skinners 1956; *Recreations* shooting, skiing, gardening, wine; *Clubs* The Cavalry & Guards, The City of London; *Style*— Hugh Lang, Esq; Durfold Hatch Cottage, Fisher Lane, Chiddingfold, Surrey GU8 4TF (☎ 0428 79 4286); Stock Exchange, London EC2N 1HP (☎ 01 588 2355)

LANG, Hugh Montgomerie; CBE (1978); s of John Montgomerie Lang; *b* 7 Nov 1932; *Educ* Glasgow Univ (BSc); *m* 1, 1959 (m dis 1981), Marjorie Armour; 1 s, 1 da; m 2, 1981, Susan Lynn Hartley; *Career* REME 1953-55; chm: P-E Int 1980- (dir 1972-, chief exec 1977-), Redman Heenan Int 1982-86 (dir 1981-86), Technol Transfer Series Advsy Ctee 1982-85 (memb 1978-85); dir: Fairey Hldgs 1978-82, UKO Int 1985-6; (non-exec) B Elliott plc 1986-88, Renaissance Hldgs plc 1987-, Siebe plc 1987-), Strong & Fisher (Hldgs) plc 1988-, Co-Rodinated Land and Estates plc 1988-; memb: Business Educn Cncl 1980-81, CBI Industl Policy Ctee 1980-83, Design Cncl 1983- (dep chm 1987-), Engrg Cncl 1984-86; CEng, FIProdE, FIMC, CBIM, FRSA; *Recreations* fishing, gardening, golf, reading; *Clubs* Denham Golf; *Style*— Hugh Lang, Esq, CBE; Mount Hill Farm, Gerrards Cross, Bucks SL9 8SU (☎ Fulmer 2406)

LANG, Ian Bruce; MP (C) Galloway and Upper Nithsdale 1983-; s of James Fulton Lang, DSC; *b* 27 June 1940; *Educ* Lathallan Sch Kincardineshire, Rugby Sch, Sidney

Sussex Coll Cambridge (BA); *m* 1971, Sandra Caroline, da of John Alastair Montgomerie, DSC; 2 da; *Career* contested (C): Central Ayrshire 1970, Glasgow Pollok 1974; MP (C) Galloway 1979-83, asst govt whip 1981-83, lord cmmr Treasy 1983-6; Parly Under Sec of State: Dept of Employment 1986, Scottish Off 1986-7; Min of State Scottish Off 1987-; vice-chm Scottish Cons Pty 1983-6; memb Lloyd's; tstee W of Scotland Tstee Savings Bank 1974-81; dir: Hutchison and Craft Ltd 1975-81, Hutchison and Craft (Underwriting Agents) Ltd 1976-81; dir Glasgow C of C 1978-81; memb Royal Co of Archers (Queen's Body Guard for Scotland) 1974; OStJ 1974; *Clubs* Western (Glasgow), Prestwick GC, Pratt's; House of Commons, London SW1A 0AA

LANG, The Very Rev John Harley; s of Frederick Henry Lang (d 1973), of Rickmansworth, Herts, and Eileen Annie Harley (d 1966); *b* 27 Oct 1927; *Educ* Merchant Taylors', King's Coll London, Emmanuel Coll Cambridge (MA, BD); *m* 1972, Francis Rosemary, da of Reginald Widdowson, of Budleigh, Salterton, Devon; 3 da (Henrietta b 1973, Victoria b 1975, Charlotte b 1977); *Career* curate St Mary's Portsea 1952-54, priest vicar Southwark Cathedral 1957-60, chaplain Emmanuel Coll Cambridge 1960-64, head of religious broadcasting BBC 1972-80 (asst head 1964-72), chaplain to HM The Queen 1977-80, dean of Lichfield 1980-; Hon DLitt Univ of Keele 1988; *Recreations* music; *Clubs* Cavalry and Guards; *Style—* The Very Rev the Dean of Lichfield; The Deanery, Lichfield, Staffs WS13 7LD

LANG, (John) Russell; CBE; s of Charles Russell Lang, CBE (d 1945), and Jessie, *née* Crow (d 1953); *b* 8 Jan 1902; *Educ* Loretto Sch; *m* 1934, Jenny, da of Sir John Train, MD (d 1947); 3 da (Diana b 1934, Patricia b 1936, Jennifer b 1938); *Career* Lt Col 277 Field Regt RA TA 1937; dep chm Weir Gp Ltd 1968-73, chm Weir Housing Corpn 1946-66; pres Scottish Engrg Epilogers 1963-64; *Recreations* hunting, shooting, fishing, golf; *Clubs* Troon and Prestwick Golf; *Style—* J Russell Lang, Esq; Crawford Ct, The Ferns, Tetbury, Glouc (☎ 0666 53227)

LANGDALE, Simon John Bartholomew; s of Geoffrey Ronald Langdale (d 1977), of Tunbridge Wells, and Hilda Joan, *née* Bartholomew; *b* 26 Jan 1937; *Educ* Tonbridge, St Catharine's Coll Cambridge (MA); *m* 30 July 1962, Diana Morjory, da of Roger Wilby Hall, MVO, JP (d 1973), of Glebe House, West Grinstead, Sussex; 2 s (Andrew Rupert b 1964, Mark Simon b 1970), 1 da (Philippa Kate b 1967); *Career* housemaster Radley Coll 1968-73 (master 1959-73); headmaster: Eastbourne Coll 1973-80, Shrewsbury 1981-88; dir educational and gen grants The Rank Fndn 1988-; *Recreations* boks, gardening, golf; *Clubs* East India, Hawks; *Style—* Simon Langdale, Esq; Park House, Culworth, Banbury, Oxon OX17 2AP (☎ 0295 76 222); 12 Warwick Sq, London SW1V 2AA (☎ 01 834 7731)

LANGDON, David; OBE; s of Bennett and Bess Langdon; *b* 24 Feb 1914; *Educ* Davenant GS; *m* 1955, April Yvonne Margaret; 2 s (Ben, Miles), 1 da (Beth); *Career* Sqdn Ldr RAFVR 1945; cartoonist & illustrator; memb of Punch Table, contributor to Punch, New Yorker; official artist to Centre Internationale Audio-Visuel, D'Etudes et de Recherches; *Books* various cartoon collections; *Recreations* golf; *Clubs* RAF; *Style—* David Langdon, Esq, OBE; 46 Albert St, Tring, Herts (☎ 044 282 3070); Punch (☎ 01 583 9199)

LANGDON, (Augustus) John; s of late Rev Cecil Langdon, and Elizabeth Mercer Langdon, MBE; *b* 20 April 1913; *Educ* Berkhamsted Sch, St John's Coll Cambridge (MA); *m* 1; 2 da; m 2, 1949, Doris Edna, *née* Clinkard; 1 s; *Career* chartered surveyor and land agent; asst to J Carter Jonas & Sons Oxford 1936-37 (ptnr 1937-45), supt lands offr Admty 1937-45, regnl land cmmr Miny of Agric 1948-65, dep dir agric land serv Miny of Agric 1965-71, chief surveyor agric devpt and advsy serv MAFF 1971-74, Nat Tst London 1974-76; chm Statutory Ctee on Agric Valuation; memb: gen cncl RICS, Land Agency and Agric Divnl Cncl 1971-75; FRICS, FRSA; *Books* Rural Estate Management (contrib); *Recreations* gardening, walking, collecting; *Clubs* Utd Oxford and Cambridge; *Style—* John Langdon, Esq; Thorn Bank, Long Street, Sherborne, Dorset DT9 3BS

LANGDON, Michael; CBE (1973); s of Henry Birtles (d 1931), of Wolverhampton, and Violet Mary Price (d 1966); *b* 12 Nov 1920; *Educ* Bushbury Hill Sr Boys Sch; *m* 1947, Vera Laura, da of Robert Duffield (d 1958), of Norfolk; 2 da (Christine b 1948, Diana b 1950); *Career* opera singer Royal Opera House 1950-80; sang internationally at Metropolitan Opera: San Francisco, Chicago, Seattle, Los Angeles, Miami, San Diego, Houston, Bueonos Aires, Paris, Aix En Provence, Marselliese, Monte Carlos, Lisbon, Brussels, Zurich, Lausanne, Geneva, Berlin, Stuttgart, Munich, Cologne, Copenhagen, Budapest and Rhodesia; also with Scottish Opera, WNO, Opera North, and Glyndebourne; many performances on BBC radio & TV, also on BBC in full length operas and lieder recitals, dir Nat Opera Studio 1978-87; *Books* Notes From a Low Singer (1982); *Recreations* Association Football, cricket, baseball, reading science fiction; *Style—* Michael Langdon, Esq; 34 Warnham Court, Grand Ave, Hove, Sussex BN3 2NJ (☎ 0273 733120)

LANGDON, Richard Norman Darbey; s of Norman Langdon (d 1959), of Shrewsbury, and Dorothy Hewitt, *née* Darbey; *b* 19 June 1919; *Educ* Shrewsbury Sch; *m* 1 Nov 1944, June Phyllis da of Alec Earnest Dixon (d 1954), of Kingston, Surrey, 2 s (John b 1946, Michael b 1948); *Career* offr RA 1939-46; ptnr Spicer and Pegler 1951-84 (managing ptnr 1971-84, sr ptnr 1976-84); chm: First Nat Fin Corp 1984-, Time Prods plc 1984-, Finlay Packaging plc 1984-, Hammond and Champness Ltd; dep chm Chemring Gp 1984-, dir Rockware Gp plc 1984-; memb cncl Univ of Surrey, tres City and Guilds of London Inst; FCA 1946; *Recreations* gardening, golf, bricklaying; *Clubs* City of London; *Style—* Richard Langdon, Esq; Rough Hill House, Munstead, Godalming, Surrey (☎ 04868 21507

LANGDON, Richard Norman Darbey; s of Norman Langdon (d 1959), of Shrewsbury, and Dorothy Hewitt, *née* Darbey; *b* 19 June 1919; *Educ* Shrewsbury; *m* 1 Nov 1944, June Phyllis, da of Alec Ernest Dixon (d 1954), of Kingston, Surrey; 2 s (John b 1946, Michael b 1948); *Career* offr RA 1939-46; ptnr Spicer and Pegler 1951-84 (managing ptnr 1971-84, sr ptnr 1976-84); chm: Finlay Packaging plc 1984-, Hammond and Champness Ltd 1966-, First Nat Fin Corp 1984-, Time Prods plc 1984-; dep chm Chemring Gp 1984-, dir Rockware Gp plc 1985-; cncl Univ of Surrey, tres City and Guilds London Inst; FCA 1946; *Recreations* sailing, gardening, golf, bricklaying; *Clubs* City of London, Old Salopian; *Style—* Richard Langdon, Esq; Rough Hill House, Munstead, Godalming, Surrey (☎ 048 68 215 07)

LANGE, Leo Stanley; s of Jacob Lange (d 1966), and Gertrude, *née* Wolfowitz (d 1969); *b* 25 July 1931; *Educ* Worcester HS for Boys, Univ of Cape Town (MB ChB, MD); *m* 7 Jan 1962, Natasha, da of Dr Maurice Rose (d 1982); 3 da (Claire b 1963, Annushka b 1967, Tamara b 1968); *Career* conslt neurologist Charing Cross Hosp; contrib various pubns and scientific jls; FRCP; *Books* various pubns, scientific jls; *Recreations* music, sailing; *Clubs* Athenaeum; *Style—* Dr Leo Lange; 17 Harley St£ London W1N 1DA (☎ 01 631 0770)

LANGER, Air Cdre John Francis; CBE (1973), AFC, (1958) DL (Gtr London 1983); s of Cecil Edward Langer (d 1966), and Emma Elizabeth Maud, *née* Tucker (d 1988); *b* 24 June 1925; *Educ* Wimbledon Coll; *m* 1951, Doreen, da of Wilfrid Newland-Hodges; 2 s, 1 da; *Career* served WWII in SE Asia Cmd, Sqdn Cdr No 43 (Fighting Cocks) Sqdn 1957-59, chief instr Central Flying Sch 1962-64, Station Cdr RAF Valley 1970-71, dep dir Air Plans MOD 1972, dir Air Staff Singapore Air Force 1973-75, Flying Trg MOD 1975-79, ret; UK govt advsr on aviation security 1979-1987; vice-chm (Air) TAVR Assoc for Gtr London 1980-1988; aviation security conslt 1987-; rep DL for Hillingdon 1987; *Recreations* cat watching; *Clubs* RAF; *Style—* Air Cdre John Langer, CBE, AFC, DL; 29 Beechwood Ave, Kew, Surrey TW9 4DD (☎ 01 878 3932)

LANGFORD, Bonita (Bonnie); da of Donald Langford, of Twickenham Middx, and Babette, *née* Palmer; *b* 22 July 1964; *Educ* Arts Educnl Sch, Italia Conti Stage Sch; *Career* TV debut Opportunity Knocks 1970 (aged 6); subsequent major TV appearances incl: 3 series Junior Showtime Yorkshire TV 1971-74, 2 series Just William LWT 1976-77, Lena and Bonnie (with Lena Zavaroni) LWT 1978, 2 series The Hot Shoe Show BBC TV 1983-84, Rub-a-dub-tub TVAM 1984, Saturday Starship Central TV 1984, 2 series Dr Who BBC TV 1986-87; West End debut Bonnie Butler in Gone With The Wind Theatre Royal Drury Lane 1972; other West End appearances incl: Baby June in Gypsy, Piccadilly theatre 1973-74; Rumpleteazer in Cats New London Theatre 1981 and 1983, Kate in The Pirates of Penzance Theatre Royal Drury Lane 1982, title role in Peter Pan The Musical Aldwych Theatre 1985, Sally Smith in Me and My Girl Adelphi Theatre 1988-89; major American theatre tour as Baby June in Gypsy 1974-75 (Broadway debut Winter Gardens Theatre 1974); films incl: Bugsy Malone 1975, Wombling Free 1980; numerous Royal Variety Show appearances, first record Just One Kiss 1984; *Style—* Miss Bonnie Langford; c/o The Barry Burnett Organisation Ltd, Suite 42-43 Grafton House, 2-3 Golden Square, London W1 (☎ 01 437 7048)

LANGFORD, Florence, Baroness; Florence Eileen O'Donovan; da of Isaac Shiel, of Dublin; *m* 1922, 7 Baron Langford (d 1952); 1 s (Clotworthy Alexander, b 1923, d 1924); *Recreations* opera, polo; *Style—* The Rt Hon Florence, Lady Langford; 52 Edge Hill Ct, Edge Hill, Wimbledon, London SW19 4LW; Peppard's Castle, Kilmuckridge, Co Wexford

LANGFORD, 9 Baron (I 1800); Col Geoffrey Alexander Rowley-Conwy; OBE (mil 1943), DL (Clwyd 1977); s of Maj Geoffrey Seymour Rowley-Conwy (ka 1915, himself ggs of 1 Baron, who in his turn was 4 s of 1 Earl of Bective, the Earldom of the same now forming one of the subsidiary dignities of the Marquesses of Headfort), of Bodrhyddan, Rhuddlan, Flintshire; suc 2 cous once removed, 8 Baron Langford, 1953; *b* 8 Mar 1912; *Educ* Marlborough, RMA Woolwich, Staff Coll Quetta; *m* 1, 1939 (m dis 1956), Ruth St John, da of late Albert St John Murphy; m 2, 1957, Grete (d 1973), da of late Col E T von Freiesleben, Danish Army; 3 s; m 3, 1975, Susan, da of C Denham; 1 s (Hon Christopher b 1978), 1 da (Hon Charlotte b 1980); *Heir* s, Hon Owain Grenville Rowley-Conwy b 1958; *Career* cmmnd RA 1932, Lt 1935, Capt 1939, Maj 1941, Lt-Col 1945, serv 1939-45, with RA in Singapore (POW escaped), with Indian Mountain Artillery in Burma, DAQMG Berlin Airlift, FASSBERG 1948-49, GSO1 42 Inf Div TA 1949-52, ret 1957, Hon Col 1967; constable of Rhuddlan Castle lord of the manor of Rhuddlan; Freeman City of London; *Clubs* Army and Navy; *Style—* The Rt Hon the Lord Langford, OBE, DL; Bodrhyddan, Rhuddlan, Clwyd LL18 5SB (☎ 0745 590414)

LANGFORD, Ruth, Lady; Ruth St John; da of Albert St John Murphy, of The Island House, Little Island, Co Cork; *m* 1939 (m dis 1956), 9 Baron Langford; *Style—* Ruth, Lady Langford; Somerdale, Midleton, Co Cork, Eire

LANGFORD-HOLT, Lt Cdr Sir John Anthony; s of late Ernest Langford-Holt; *b* 30 June 1916; *Educ* Shrewsbury; *m* 1, 1953 (m dis 1969), Flora Evelyn Innes, da of late Ian St Clair Stuart; 1 s, 1 da; m 2, 1971 (m dis 1982), Betty Ann Maxworthy, of Bexhill-on-Sea; m 3, 1983, Irene, da of David Alexander Kerr; *Career* joined air branch RN 1939, Lt Cdr 1944; MP (C) Shrewsbury 1945-83, sec Cons Parly Labour Ctee 1945-50, jt-sec House of Commons Branch Br Legion 1945-50; memb: Parly and Scientific Ctee, Cwlth Parly Assoc; chm: Anglo-Austrian Soc 1960-63 and 1971-83, Select Ctee Defence 1980-83; Freeman and Liveryman City of London, memb Ct of Worshipful Co of Horners 1967; Austrian Grand Decoration of Honour in Silver with Star, Order of Civic Merit (France); kt 1962; *Clubs* White's, Royal Yacht Sqdn; *Style—* Lt Cdr Sir John Langford-Holt; 2 Woodley Gardens, Lymington, Hants SO41 9LH

LANGHAM, Sir James Michael; 15 Bt (E 1660), TD; s of Sir John Charles Patrick Langham, 14 Bt (d 1972); *b* 24 May 1932; *Educ* Rossall; *m* 1959, Marion Audrey Eleanor, da of Oswald Barratt; 2 s, 1 da; *Heir* s, John Stephen Langham; *Style—* Sir James Langham, Bt; Claranagh, Tempo, Enniskillen, Co Fermanagh, N Ireland

LANGHAM, John Michael; CBE (1976); s of George Langham (d 1951); *b* 12 Jan 1924; *Educ* Bedford Sch, Queen's Coll Cambridge (MA), Admin Staff Coll; *m* 1949, Irene Elizabeth, *née* Morley; 2 s, 1 da; *Career* served RN 1944-46; exec chm Stone Manganese Marine Ltd 1967-, divnl chm Stone-Platt Industs Ltd 1967-81, chm Vacu-Lug Traction Tyres Ltd 1973-, dir BPB Industs Ltd 1976-, chm and md Langham Industs Ltd 1981-; exec bd memb British Standards Inst 1969-76 (dep chm quality assurance cncl 1971-79); memb: CBI cncl 1967-79 (chm CBI prodn ctee 1970-79), gen cncl Engrg Employers Fedn 1974-82 (memb mgmnt bd 1979-82); *Recreations* skiing, sailing, farming; *Clubs* Brooks's, Royal Motor YC; *Style—* John Langham, Esq, CBE; Bingham's Melcombe, Dorchester, Dorset (☎ 0258 880808)

LANGHAM, John Stephen; s and h of Sir James Michael Langham, 15 Bt; *b* 14 Dec 1960; *Style—* John Langham, Esq; Claranagh, Tempo, Enniskillen, Co Fermanagh

LANGHAM, Rosamond, Lady; Rosamond Christabel; MBE (1969); da of Arthur Rashleigh (d 1952), of Killiney, Dublin; *b* 3 July 1903; *Educ* in England with governess at home and music, riding & dancing masters; *m* 1930, Sir John Charles Patrick Langham, 14 Bt (d 1972), s of Sir Herbert Langham, 13 Bt (d 1951); 1 s (15 Bt) Sir James Langham-present Bart; *Career* patron NIGFAS for N Ireland and life long interest in Girl Guides: County Commission for Carlow, Eire, for 21 yrs & for Co Fernanagh N Ireland for 12 yrs; memb of Br Red Cross; medal of Merit from World Chief Guide (Lady BP) in 1959; *Books* All Things Bright and Beautiful (book of poems 1982); *Recreations* gardening, flower arranging, ballroom and folk dancing; *Style—*

Rosamond, Lady Langham; Tempo Manor, Tempo, Enniskillin, Co Fermanagh, N Ireland (☎ 036 554 202)

LANGHORNE, Richard Tristan Bailey; s of Eadward John Bailey Langhorne, MBE, of Chichester, and Rosemary, *née* Scott-Foster; *b* 6 May 1940; *Educ* St Edward's Sch Oxford, St John's Coll Cambridge (BA, MA); *m* 18 Sept 1971, Helen Logue, da of William Donaldson, CB (d 1988); 1 s (Daniel b 22 Nov 1972), 1 da (Isabella b 29 Aug 1975); *Career* lectr in history Univ of Kent 1966-75 (master Rutherford Coll 1971-74), fell St John's Coll Cambridge 1975- (steward 1975-79, bursar 1975-87), dir Centre of Int Studies Univ of Cambridge 1987-; visiting prof sch of int rels Univ of S California 1986; chm Br Int History Assoc 1988; FRHistS 1985; *Books* The Collapse of the Concert of Europe, 1890-1914 (1982), Diplomacy and Intelligence during the Second World War ed (1985); *Recreations* cooking, music, railways; *Clubs* Athenaeum; *Style*— Richard Langhorne, Esq; 15 Madingley Road, Cambridge CB3 0EG (☎ 0223 635 41); Centre of Int Studies, West Rd, Cambridge and St John's Coll, Cambridge CB2 1TP (☎ 0223 335 333/338 641)

LANGLAIS, Hon Mrs (Joanna Harriet Nevill); da of 7 Baron Latymer, *qv*; *b* 1928; *m* 1951, Pierre Langlais; 1 s, 4 da; *Style*— The Hon Mrs Langlais; PO Box 113, North Hartland, Vermont 05052, USA

LANGLANDS, Dr Ross William Duff; s of Ronald Ross Langlands (d 1959), of Dundee, and Mary Duff, *née* Jolly; *b* 1 Nov 1948; *Educ* Kirton HS Dundee, Edinburgh Univ (BSc, MB ChB, MRCGP), East of Scotland Coll of Agric (Dip Tat Rog); *m* 30 June 1973, Diana Elizabeth, da of Ronald Nelson Holton, of Newhall Port, Gifford; 2 s (Alasdair b 1982, Niall b 1983); *Career* gen medical practitioner 1977-; trainer in gen practice 1986; *Recreations* shooting, reading, gardening, good food and wine, opera, German language; *Style*— Dr Ross W D Langlands; Ardlea, Gifford, E Lothian EH41 4JD (☎ 062 081 564); Newton Port Surgery, Haddington, E Lothian EH41 3NF (☎ 062 082 3183)

LANGLANDS, Hon Mrs (Selena Mary); da of 5 Baron Manners, *qv*; *b* 4 Oct 1952; *m* 1974, Maj Christopher Jeremy George Langlands, 1 The Queen's Dragoon Gds, s of Maj Percy Christopher Langlands, of Malta; 1 s, 1 da; *Recreations* hunting, sailing; *Style*— The Hon Mrs Langlands; c/o Messrs Coutts & Co, Chandos Branch, 44O The Strand, London WC2R 0QS

LANGLEY, Maj-Gen Sir (Henry) Desmond Allen; KCVO (1983), MBE (1967); s of Col Henry Langley, OBE; *b* 16 May 1930; *Educ* Eton, RMA Sandhurst; *m* 1950, Felicity, da of Lt-Col K J P Oliphant, MC; 1 s, 1 da; *Career* cmmnd Life Gds 1949; cmd Life Gds 1969-71; Lt-Col cmdg Household Cavalry and Silver Stick-in-Waiting 1972-75, Cdr 4 Gds Armd Bde 1976-77, RCDS 1978, Brig Gen Staff HQ UK Land Forces 1979, GOC London Dist and Maj-Gen cmdg Household Div 1979-83, Cdr British Forces Cyprus and Admin Sovereign Base Areas 1983-85, govr and c in c Bermuda 1988; govr Church Lads' and Church Girls' Bde 1986-; *Style*— Maj-Gen Sir Desmond Langley, KCVO, MBE; Government House, Bermuda

LANGLEY, Edward Noel; s of Edward George Langley (d 1975), of Kings Lynn, and Katie ELizabeth, *née* Wright (d 1981); *b* 28 Dec 1926; *Educ* Gt Yarmouth GS; *m* 9 June 1951, Audrey Alicia Betty, da of Leslie Edward Dugmore (d 1966), of Birmingham; *Career* Sgt RCS (Germany) 1947-48; sales engr Coventry Climax Engines 1950-52, md Isaac Bentley & Co Ltd 1970-85 (sales dir 1962-70), gp md Marston Bentley Gp 1985-; memb: Diecasting Soc, IOD; *Recreations* hiking, sport in general; *Style*— Edward Langley, Esq; Hylo House, Cale Lane, New Springs, Wigan WN2 1JR (☎ 0942 824 242, fax 0942 826 653, car tel 675255, telex 67230)

LANGLEY, (Julian Hugh) Gordon; QC (1983); s of Gordon Thompson Langley (d 1943), and Marjorie, *née* Burgoyne; *b* 11 May 1943; *Educ* Westminster, Balliol Coll Oxford (BA, BCL); *m* 20 Sept 1968, Beatrice Jayanthi, da of Simon Tennakoon (d 1986), of Colombo, Sri Lanka; 2 da (Ramani Elizabeth b 1969, Sharmani Louise b 1972); *Career* called to the Bar Inner Temple 1966, rec 1986; *Recreations* music, sport; *Clubs* Travellers; *Style*— Gordon Langley, Esq, QC; Fountain Court, Temple, London EC4Y 9DH (☎ 01 583 3335, fax 01 353 0329, telex 881 3408 FONLEG G)

LANGLEY, Kenneth William; s of William Thomas Charles Langley (d 1984), of Osmont House, Grove Park, Wanstead, London, and Ada Winifred, *née* Looke (d 1979); *b* 13 Jan 1932; *Educ* East Ham Tech HS, East Ham Tech Coll; *m* 16 March 1957, Daisy Rosina, da of Frederick Charles Parsons (d 1956), of 14 Durell Rd, Dagenham, Essex; 3 da (Gillian b 1959, Susan b 1961, Elizabeth b 1964); *Career* Nat Serv, Sgt RE Egypt and Jordan; memb: Greenwich Chamber of Trade, Kent branch jt consultative ctee for Bldg Indust, CBI, divnl cncl RICS; memb Rotary Club Gravesend; Freeman City of London 1972, Liveryman Worshipful Co of Basketmakers 1977; FRICS 1960, FCIOB 1957, ACIArb 1966; *Recreations* music, reading, golf; *Clubs* City Livery; *Style*— Kenneth Langley, Esq; Pucksdown, Pondfield Lane, Shorne, Kent DA12 3LD (☎ 047482 2240); W M Bryen Langley & Co, 58 Footscray Rd, London SE9 2SU (☎ 01 850 7775, fax 850 6772)

LANGMAN, Lady Iris Pamela Gaskell; *née* Kennard; o da of Capt (Alan) Spencer Gaskell Kennard (d 1951), formerly of Purslow Hall, Craven Arms, Shropshire, and Agatha Frances, *née* Colfox; *b* 1 May 1912; *m* 18 July 1936, Sir John Lyell Langman, 3 and last Bt (d 1985); 3 da (1 decd); *Style*— Lady Langman; The Goslings, Gooseacre Lane, Cirencester, Glos GL7 2DS

LANGMAN, Prof Michael John Stratton; *b* 30 Jan 1935; *Educ* St Pauls, Guys Hosp Med Sch (BSc, MB, MD); *m* Rosemary Ann, JP; 2 s (Nicholas, Benjamin), 2 da (Suzannah, Victoria); *Career* conslt physician, sr lectr, reader in med Nottingham Teaching Hosps 1968-73, Boots prof of therapeutic med Univ of Nottingham Med Sch 1974-87, William Withering prof of med Univ of Birmingham Med Sch 1987-; memb: Ctee on Review of Medicines 1980-86, ctee on Safety of Medicines 1987; MRCP 1960, FRCP 1974, memb Br Soc of Gastroeterology; *Recreations* squash, cricket, opera-going; *Clubs* MCC; *Style*— Prof Michael Langman; Queen Elizabeth hosp, Birmingham B15 2TH (☎ 021 472 1311)

LANGRICK, John Nigel; s of Peter Roland Langrick, of 19 Westfield Lane, S Milford, N Yorks, and Jean Margaret, *née* Wilson; *b* 25 Sept 1956; *Educ* Sherburn HS, Univ of Nottingham (BSc); *Career* CA; Price Waterhouse: Nottingham 1978-82, Brussels 1982-85, Leicester 1985-87; Scarborough Building Soc 1987-; ACA 1982; *Recreations* swimming, genealogy; *Style*— John N Langrick, Esq; 4 The Stoneways, Hutton Buscel, Scarborough (☎ 0723 864797); Scarborough Building Society, PO Box 6, Scarborough (☎ 0723 368155, fax 0723 500322)

LANGRIDGE, Philip Gordon; s of Arthur Gordon, and Elsie Kate, *née* Underhill; *b* 16 Dec 1939; *Educ* Maidstone GS, Royal Acad of Music; *m* 1, 2 Aug 1962, (Margaret) Hilary, da of Rev George Davidson; 1 s (Stephen Maitland b 28 May 1962), 2 da (Anita James b 11 June 1966, Jennifer Mary b 19 Dec 1970); m 2, 6 June 1981, Ann, da of Joseph Eugene Murray, of Dublin; 1 s (Jonathan Philip b 20 Oct 1986); *Career* concert and opera singer (tenor); Debut Glyndebourne Festival 1964, BBC Promenade Concerts 1970; first appearance: in Indomeneo at Angers 1975, at La Scala in Boris Godunov with Abbado 1979; performed in: Indomeneo at Glyndebourne 1983, Boris Godunov Royal Opera Covent Garden, Cosi Fan Tutte at Themet 1985, World Permier of Mask of Oprheus (Birtwistle) ENO 1986, new prodn of Billy Budd (Britten) ENO 1988; sang Aron at Salzburg Fest 1987 and 1988; won a Grammy Award for Moses und Aron (Schonberg) under Solti 1986; served on Music Panel for Arts Cncl of GB; made over 50 records of early, baroque, classical, romantic and modern music; LRAM, GRSM, FRAM, ARAM; *Recreations* collecting watercolours; *Style*— Philip Langridge, Esq; c/o Allied Artists, 42 Montpelier Sq, London SW7 1JZ (☎ 01 589 6243)

LANGRISHE, Hon Lady (Grania Sybil Enid); *née* Wingfield; da of 9 Viscount Powerscourt (d 1973), and Sheila, Viscountess Powerscourt *qv*; sis of 10 Viscount; *b* 25 April 1934; *m* 1955, Sir Hercules Ralph Hume Langrishe, 7 Bt; 1 s, 3 da; *Style*— The Hon Lady Langrishe; Ringlestown House, Kilmessan, Co Meath, Ireland (☎ 010 353 46 25243)

LANGRISHE, Sir Hercules Ralph Hume; 7 Bt (I 1777), of Knocktopher Abbey, Kilkenny; s of Capt Sir Terence Hume Langrishe, 6 Bt (d 1973), of Knocktopher Abbey, Co Kilkenny; *b* 17 May 1927; *Educ* Summer Fields (St Leonards), Eton; *m* 1955, Hon Grania Sybil Enid, *qv*, da of 9 Viscount Powerscourt; 1 s, 3 da (Miranda, Georgina, Atalanta); *Heir* s, James Hercules Langrishe; *Career* 2 Lt 9 Lancers 1947, Lt 1948, ret 1953; *Clubs* Kildare Street and Univ (Dublin); *Style*— Sir Hercules Langrishe, Bt; Ringlestown House, Kilmessan, Co Meath, Ireland (☎ 010 353 46 25243)

LANGRISHE, James Hercules; s and h of Sir Hercules Ralph Hume Langrishe, 7 Bt; *b* 3 Mar 1957; *m* 1985, Gemma, da of Patrick O'Daly, and Rita, *née* Hickey, of Kiltale, Co Meath; 1 s (b 8 April 1988), 1 da (b 1986); *Clubs* Kildare Street and Univ (Dublin); *Style*— James Langrishe, Esq; Ringlestown House, Kilmessan, Co Meath

LANGSTAFF, Brig Henry Spunner; s of Col James William Langstaff, DSO, late RAMC (d 1949), and Dorothy, *née* Ross (d 1948); *b* 24 Oct 1919; *Educ* Cheltenham, RMA Woolwich; *m* 1, 26 Feb 1942 (m dis 1949), Patricia, da of Col J S L Norris, OBE, MC; m 2, March 1953 (m dis 1966), Gillian, da of Col G H Brooks, of Farnham, Surrey; 1 s (James Henry b 1956); *Career* RA WWII UK, Middle East, Italy; Staff Coll 1946, Nat Def Coll (then Jt Services Staff Coll) 1958; Brevet Lt-Col 1958, asst-sec COS Ctee 1959, CO 25 Regt RA 1960-62, Cdr 1 Artillery Bde 1962-65, ret 1966; joined McKinsey & Co Inc 1966, elected ptnr 1971, dir of Professional Staff 1971, London 1966-71 and 1974-, NY 1971-74; *Recreations* fishing, tennis, ornithology; *Clubs* Lansdowne; *Style*— Brig Harry Langstaff; Barrow Hill House, Barrow Hill, Goodworth Clatford, Andover, Hants SP17 7RG (☎ 0264 333404); 74 St James's St, London SW1A 1PS (☎ 01 839 8040, telex 261831, fax 01 930 3780)

LANGTON, Bryan David; CBE (1988); s of Thomas Langton (d 1974), and Doris, *née* Brown (d 1987); *b* 6 Dec 1936; *Educ* Accrington GS, Westminster Tech Coll (Dip Hotel Operation), Ecole Hotelière de la SSA Lausanne (Dip Operation); *m* 23 Sept 1960, Sylva, da of Herman Heinrich Leo Degenhardt, of Richterstrasse 11, Braunschweig, W Germany; 2 da (Suzanne (Mrs Boyette) b 1962, Michele (Mrs Wijegoonaratna) b 1964); *Career* dir Bass plc 1985-; chm Crest Hotels Ltd 1985- (md 1982-88), Bass Horizon Hotels 1985-, Holiday Inns Int 1988-, Toby Restaurants Ltd 1988-; memb: Grand Cncl of Hotel and Catering Benevolent Assoc, exec ctee of Int Hotel Assoc, bd of mgmnt British Hotels, Restaurants and Caterers Assoc; hon fell Manchester Poly 1986; FHCIMA; *Recreations* golf, reading, cricket, theatre, tennis; *Style*— Bryan D Langton, Esq; Westward Lodge, Shilton Road, Burford, Oxon OX8 4PA (☎ 099 382 2599); Bridge Street, Banbury, Oxon OX16 8RG (☎ 0295 52555; fax, 0295 67339; car ☎ 0836 601588; telex, 837294)

LANGTON, Edward Langton; s of Lewis Langton, and Louisa Kate, *née* Levy; *b* 30 Oct 1921; *Educ* City of London Sch; *m* 1 Sep 1949, Joye Amelia, da of Jack Isaacs (d 1962); 1 s (Timothy John b 25 July 1953), 1 da (Louise (Mrs Rawlins) b 26 June 1950); *Career* WWII serv: Flt Lt and Sqdn Navigation Offr RAF 1941-46; CA; sr ptnr Stoy Hayward 1968-85 (ptnr 1951-86); memb exec cncl Horwath and Horwath Int 1975-86 (currently Euro regnl dir); chm: Logitek plc, Oak Hotels plc; Sinclair Goldsmith Hldgs plc: memb exec bd Variety Club of GB, chm Jewish Home and Hosp Tottenham; Liveryman Worshipful Co of Chartered Accountants; FCA; *Recreations* golf, cricket; *Clubs* Hurlingham, RAC, MCC; *Style*— Edward Langton Langton, Esq; Flat 8, 40 Chester Square, London SW1W 9HT (☎ 01 730 1847); 8 Baker St, London W1M 1DA (☎ 01 486 5888)

LANGTON, Lord; James Grenville Temple-Gore-Langton; s and h of 8 Earl Temple of Stowe, *qv*; *b* 11 Sept 1955; *Educ* Winchester; *Style*— Miss Katharine Darroch; c/o The Rt Hon Earl Temple of Stowe, Garth, Outertown, Stromness, Orkney

LANGTON, John Leslie; s of Arthur Lawrence Langton (d 1976), and Sarah Jane, *née* Baker; *b* 23 Nov 1948; *Educ* Roan GS Greenwich; *m* 10 Aug 1979, Raymonde, da of Raymond Glinne, of Gembloux, Belgium 5800; 1 da (Jennifer Marie-Anne b 8 Dec 1983); *Career* Strauss Turnbull & Co 1965-69, Scandinavian Bank Ltd 1970-73, Williams & Glyns Bank 1973-74, Bondtrade in Brussels 1974-77, Morgan Stanley Int 1977-78, exec dir Amex Bank Ltd 1979-80, sr exec dir Orion Royal Bank Ltd 1980-85, exec dir Security Pacific Hoare Govett Ltd 1986-87, md Gintel & Co Ltd 1987-, bd memb AIBD London/Zurich 1981-; memb Oak Lodge Sch Parents Assoc; *Recreations* wine, food, books, backgammon, travel, football; *Style*— John Langton, Esq; 8 Beckenham Road, West Wickham, Kent BR4 0GT (☎ 01 777 1202); Gintel & Co Ltd, 4th Floor Plantation House, 31-35 Fenchurch St, London EC3M 3DX (☎ 01 626 5522, fax 626 9642, telex 6952472)

LANGTON, John Raymond; *b* 28 May 1929; *Educ* Stationers' Co Sch; *m* 4 April 1953, Brenda Olive; 1 s (Toby b 1970), 2 da (Fiona b 1962, Charlotte b 1966); *Career* fndr and md Sun Life Unit Servs Ltd 1980-; ACII 1953; *Style*— John Langton, Esq; 10-12 Ely Place, London EC1N 6TT (☎ 01 242 2905, fax 01 4051326)

LANGTON, Col Roland Stephen; LVO (1953), MC (1945); s of Leslie Langton (d 1952), memb Lloyd's; *b* 1921; *Educ* Radley, Jesus Coll Cambridge; *m* 1948, Pamela Elvira, da of Kenneth Headington, MC (decd), of Paley St, Berks; 3 s, 1 da; *Career* served 1939-45 with Irish Gds, NW Europe 1940-45 (despatches), Palestine (despatches), Egypt, Cyprus, BAOR; psc, jssc; cmd 1 Bn Irish Gds 1961-64, AAG MOD (PS12 Army) 1964-66, sr Army rep Defence Operational Analysis Estab 1966-69; underwriting memb of Lloyd's; dir: Langton Underwriting Agents Ltd, Milestone Underwriting Mgmnt Ltd; memb Ct of Assistants Worshipful Co of Merchant Taylors 1971 (Master 1978), memb Ct of Corpn of Sons of the Clergy; FRSA, FBIM; *Recreations* enjoying retirement; *Clubs* City of London, Leander, London Rowing; *Style*— Col Roland Langton, LVO, MC; Keeper's Cottage, Crowsley Park, Harpsden, Henley-on-Thames, Oxon RG9 4JB (☎ Henley 573698)

LANGTON-LOCKTON, Thomas Langton; eld s of Noel Langton Langton-Lockton, of Teeton Hall, Spratton, Northants (d 1954), and Annie Worsley, *née* Powell (d 1953) (assumed addl surname of Langton by deed poll 1942); gf Charles Langton Lockton (1856-1932) was JP Co Surrey, India Off 1877-81, Clerk House of Commons 1881-1921, well known athelete and rugby footballer; *see* Burke's Landed Gentry 1952 Edn; *b* 23 April 1918; *Educ* Epsom, and Hertford Coll, Oxford (MA); *m* 17 Dec 1943, Leslie Mary, da of Maj Francis Murphy, RA, of Exbourne, Devon; 1 s (John Philip Charles b 13 Feb 1950); *m* 1974 (m dis 1981), Lady Emma Howard, yr da of 12 Earl of Carlisle), 2 da (Vanessa Jane Mary b 15 Sept 1944, Judith Ann b 8 Feb 1947); *Career* Oxford Univ Atheletic Team 1937-39, Br Decathlon Champion 1938 and English Athletic Team (High Hurdles) 1939; cmmnd Devonshire Regt 1940, seriously wounded NW Frontier, Mil Govt Germany 1945; farmer (ret); patron of living of Slapton Northants; *Clubs* Vincents, MCC, E India; *Style*— Thomas Langton-Lockton, Esq; 6 Brown's Close, Uckfield, Sussex (☎ Uckfield 2549)

LANGTRY, (James) Ian; s of Rev Herbert James Langtry (d 1942), and Irene Margaret Langetry, *née* Eagleson; *b* 2 Jan 1939; *Educ* Coleraine Academical Institution, Queen's Univ Belfast (BSc); *m* 1959, (Eileen Roberta) Beatrice, da of James Burnside Nesbitt (d 1957); 1 s (Paul Eacleson b 1960); 1 da (Beatrice b 1965); *Career* asst master Bangor GS 1960-61, lectr Belfast Coll of Technol 1961-66, asst dir Civil Service Cmmn 1966-70; Dept of Education and Science: princ 1970-71, asst sec 1976-82, under sec 1982-87; under sec Dept of Health and Social Security 1987-; *Recreations* golf, sailing; *Clubs* Royal Portrush and West Kent GC; *Style*— Ian Langtry, Esq; Dept of Health and Social Security (☎ 01 703 6380 ext 3489)

LANKESTER, Richard Shermer; s of Richard Ward Lankester (d 1969), and Elsie Marion, *née* Shermer; *b* 8 Feb 1922; *Educ* Haberdashers' Aske's Hampstead Sch, Jesus Coll Oxford (MA); *m* 30 May 1950, Dorothy, da of Raymond Jackson (d 1966), of Worsley, Lancs; 3 s (Simon b 1951, Toby b 1960, Thomas b 1964), 1 da (Ruth b 1955); *Career* serv Hants RHA Regt Italy 1943-45, RA 1942-45, Lt; Dept of Clerk of House of Commons 1947; co-ed The Table 1962-67; clerk of Standing Ctees 1973-75, clerk to Expenditure Ctee 1975-79, registrar of Members' Interests 1976-87; clerk of Select Ctees House of Commons 1979-87; *Style*— Richard Lankester, Esq; The Old Farmhouse, The Green, Boughton Monchelsea, Kent (☎ 0622 43749)

LANSDELL, Dr Norman Rupert Chamberlain; s of Rev Frederick John Lansdell (d 1933), of St James' Vicarage, Hereford, and Alice, *née* Chamberlain (d 1964); *b* 18 Jan 1907; *Educ* Marlborough, Kings Coll London, Kings Coll Hosp (MROS, LRCP); *m* 6 Jan 1934, (Mary) Joyce, da of Frank Fenton (ka 1914); 1 s (Michael John b 1937); *Career* Capt RAMC Med Offr, 4 Bn Oxf and Bucks Lt Infantry, POW 1940-45 (despatches); SHMO Anaesthetist Oxford RHA 1947-77; MRCS, LRCP; *Recreations* gardening, dinghy sailing; *Style*— Dr Norman Lansdell; Toad Hall, Maidens Gr, Henley-on-Thames RG9 6EZ (☎ 049 163422)

LANSDOWNE, 8 Marquess of (GB 1784); Maj George John Charles Mercer Nairne Petty-Fitzmaurice; PC (1964), JP (Perthshire 1950); also Baron Kerry and Lixnaw (I 1295), Earl of Kerry, Viscount Clanmaurice (both I 1723), Viscount FitzMaurice, Baron Dunkeron (both I 1751), Earl of Shelburne (I 1753), Lord Wycombe, Baron of Chipping Wycombe (GB 1760), Earl Wycombe, and Viscount Calne and Calston (both GB 1784); assumption of additional surnames of Petty-Fitzmaurice recognised by decree of Lord Lyon 1947; s of Maj Lord Charles Mercer-Nairne, MVO (ka 1914, himself 2 s of 5 Marquess, sometime Viceroy of India and Foreign Sec), and Lady Violet Mary Elliot Murray-Kynynmound, da of 4 Earl of Minto; suc 7 Marquess (first cousin, who was ka 1944); *b* 27 Nov 1912; *Educ* Eton, Ch Ch Oxford; *m* 1, 1938, Barbara (d 1965), da of Harold Stuart Chase, of Santa Barbara, California; 2 s, 1 da (and 1 decd); m 2, 1969 (m dis 1978), Hon Selina Polly Dawson, da of 1 Viscount Eccles, KCVO, PC; m 3, 1978, Gillian Ann (d 1982), da of Alured Morgan; *Heir* s, Earl of Shelburne; *Career* served WWII Capt Scots Greys & Maj Free French; private sec to Duff Cooper (1 Visc Norwich) when ambass in Paris 1944; 2 Lt Scottish Horse (TA), a lord in waiting to HM The Queen 1957-58, jt parly under-sec state FO 1958-62, min of state Colonial Affairs 1962-64, DL Wilts 1952-73, sec Junior Unionist League for E Scotland 1939; memb Royal Company of Archers (Queen's Body Guard for Scotland); chm Franco-British Soc 1972- (and pres); patron of two livings; *Clubs* Turf, New (Edinburgh); *Style*— The Most Hon the Marquess of Lansdow; Meikleour House, Perthshire (☎ Meikleour 210)

LANSDOWNE, Peter William; s of William Marks Lansdowne (d 1972), and Bessie Maria, *née* Eales; *b* 1 Feb 1938; *Educ* Boys GS Gowerton, Univ Coll Swansea (BSc); *m* 12 July 1963 (m dis) Anna Deborah, da of Howell Vernon David (d 1966); 3 s (Simon b 1966, Nicholas b 1968, Anthony b 1971), 1 da (Amanda b 1964); *Career* sr ptnr Lansdowne and Ptnrs 1973-; vicars warden All Saints Oystermouth; memb Assoc of Consulting Engrs, FIChemE 1979 (former cncl memb and chm S Wales branch), MIWE 1979; *Recreations* cycling; *Clubs* Bristol, Channel Yacht, Rotary; *Style*— Peter W Lansdowne, Esq; 4 Caswell Bay Road, Bishopston, Swansea, SA3 3DD, (☎ 044 128 2442); Lansdowne and Partners, 88-90 Gower Road, Sketty, Swansea, SA2 9BZ (☎ 0792 204 059), fax 0792x 206 766

LANSDOWNE, Polly, Marchioness of; (Selina) Polly Dawson; da of 1 Viscount Eccles, KCVO, PC, *qv*; *b* 1937; *Educ* Sherborne Sch for Girls, London U; *m* 1, 1962 (m dis 1968), Robin Andrew Duthac Carnegie, late Capt Queen's Dragoon Gds; 1 s; m 2, 1969 (m dis 1978), 8 Marquess of Lansdowne; *Style*— Polly, Marchioness of Lansdowne; 7 Bloomfield Terrace, London SW1

LANYON, Brig (Mortimer Cecil) Tim; MBE (1962), MC (1944); s of Maj Louis Frank Lanyon (d 1973), and Celia Louisa Ethel Lanyon; *b* 18 July 1920; *Educ* Wellington Coll, RMA, Woolwich; *m* 6 March 1954, Rachel Mary, da of Cdr the Hon Henry Mitford Amherst Cecil (d 1962); 1 s (Robert Henry Mortimer b 1962), 2 da (Charlotte Yvonne b 1955,f Victoria Clare b 1956); *Career* cmmnd RA 1939, Italy 1943; active operations: France and Belgium 1940, Western Desert 1942-43, NW Europe (D Day to Berlin) 1944-45, Cyprus 1957-58; Brig dir Army Mgmnt Servs 1971-74; appeal dir Army Benevolent Fund 1975-86; *Books* Management in the Armed Forces (jt author, 1977); *Recreations* all country pursuits, gardening; *Clubs* Army and Navy; *Style*— Brig Mortimer Lanyon, MBE, MC; Woodmans Farm House, West Meon, Hants GU32 1JJ (☎ 073086 276)

LAPOTAIRE, Jane Elizabeth Marie; da of Louise Elise Burgess Lapotaire; *b* 26 Dec 1944; *Educ* Northgate GS Ipswich, Bristol Old Vic Theatre Sch; *m* 1 s (Rowan b 1973); *Career* major leading roles with Nat Theatre, Royal Shakespeare Co (over 20 yrs); freelance TV & Film, BBC, ITV, Paramount, MGM UA; PIAF SWET Award Variety Club Award, London Critics Award, Tony Award; Marie Curie BBC TV Emmy & BAFTA nominations 1976; *Recreations* walking, water colours; *Style*— Ms Jane Lapotaire; c/o William Morris Organisation, 147/149 Wardour St, London W1 (☎ 01 434 2191)

LAPPER, Maj-Gen John; s of Col Wilfred Mark Lapper, OBE (d 1976), of Highcliffe, Dorset, and Agnes Lapper, *née* Powner (d 1981); *b* 24 July 1921; *Educ* Wolverhampton GS, King Edward VI Sch Birmingham, Birmingham Univ (MB ChB, DLO); *m* 1948, Dorothy Irene, da of Roland John Simpson, of Staffs; 3 s (Mark, Simon, Matthew); *Career* conslt ENT Surgn (Lt-Col), Br Army served in UK, Germany and Malaya, Hosp Cdr (Col) UK and Germany, dir Med Servs (Col) Hong Kong, inspr of trg (Brig) AMS, dep dir med servs (Brig) UK Land Forces 1973-76, dir medical supply (Brig) UK Jt Service MOD London 1976-77, Med Policy and Plans (Maj-Gen), UK Jt Servs MOD London 1978-80; hosp and med dir Nat Guard Hosp Jeddah 1981-83, med dir Int Hosps Gp (conslt 1988-); chm of cncl Yateley Industs for Disabled; OStJ; FFCM, QHS 1977-80; FBIM; *Recreations* travel, militaria; *Style*— Maj-Gen John Lapper; Holmbush, Old School Lane, Yateley, Camberley, Surrey GU17 7NG; Rocas Del Mar, Mijas Costa, Malaga, Spain

LAPPERT, Prof Michael Franz; s of the late Julius Lappert, of Brno, Czechoslovakia, and the late Kornelie, *née* Beran; *b* 31 Dec 1928; *Educ* Wilson's GS London, Northern Poly London (BSc, PhD, DSc); *m* 14 Feb 1980, Lorna, da of David McKenzie (d 1974), of Senton, Workington; *Career* sr lectr: N Poly London 1955-59 (lectr 1953-55, asst lectr 1952-53), Univ of Manchester Inst Sci and Technol 1961-64 (lectr 1959-61); prof Univ of Sussex 1969- (reader 1964-69); sr fell at Univ of Sussex SERC 1980-85; FRS, FRCS, MACS; *Books* Metal and Metalloid Amides: Syntheses, Structures and Physical and Chemical Properties (with P P Power, A R Sanger, R C Srivastava 1980), Chemistry of Organo-Zirconium and Hafnium Compounds (with D J Cardin, C L Raston 1986); *Recreations* music, theatre, tennis, golf; *Style*— Prof Michael Lappert; 4 Varndean Gardens, Brighton BN1 6WL (☎ 0273 503 661); School of Chemistry and Molecular Sciences, Univ of Sussex, Brighton BN1 9QJ (☎ 0273 678 316)

LAPSLEY, (Alastair Gourlay) Howard; s of Rev Claude William Lapsley, BA, HCF (d 1976), and Florence Lapsley; *b* 20 May 1940; *Educ* Dulwich Coll, Coll of Law; *m* 5 June 1965, Susan Elizabeth, da of Charles Henry Bassingthwaighte (d 1988), of Diss, Norfolk; 1 s (Angus b 1970), 1 da (Catriona b 1972); *Career* slr; dir: J A Gadd Ltd 1975-, Hubdean Ltd 1981-; RAC Motor Sports Assoc Ltd 1986-, Bugatti Owners Club Ltd 1986-; memb Br Motor Sports Cncl 1984-; Br Rally Champion (1300 cc) 1983; *Recreations* motor sport, music, travel; *Clubs* RAC; *Style*— Howard Lapsley, Esq; 8 Horsefair, Chipping Norton, Oxon (☎ 0608 2063, fax 0608 44429)

LAPSLEY, Air Marshal Sir John Hugh; KBE (1969), CB (1966), DFC (1940), AFC (1950); s of Edward John Lapsley (d 1918), and Norah Gladys, *née* Kelly (d 1972); *b* 24 Sept 1916; *Educ* Wolverhampton Sch, RAF Coll Cranwell; *m* 1, 1942, Jean Margaret (d 1979), da of Douglas Tait MacIvor (d 1958), of Gravesend; 1 s, 1 da; m 2, 1980, Mrs Millicent Rees, da of Charles Hubert Beadnell (d 1936), and widow of T A Rees; *Career* RAF 1933, awarded Lord Wakefield scholarship to RAF Coll Cranwell 1936, 1939-45 War (Egypt, UK, France and Germany), Gp Capt 1956, Air Cdre 1961, Dep COS (Air) 2 TAF 1961-62, Air Vice-Marshal 1965, sec to Chiefs of Staff Ctee, MOD 1964-66, Air Marshal 1968, AOC-in-C Coastal Cmd RAF 1968-69, head of British Def Staff, Washington 1970, ret 1973; dir-gen Save the Children Fund 1974-75, dir Falkland Islands R & D Assoc Ltd 1978-83; vice pres The United Kingdom Falklands Islands Ctee 1986; cncllr Suffolk Coastal Dist Cncl 1979-87 (vice chm 1982-83, chm 1983-84); *Recreations* golf, fishing, ornithology; *Clubs* RAF, Aldeburgh GC, Suffolk Fly Fishers'; *Style*— Air Marshal Sir John Lapsley, KBE, CB, DFC, AFC; 149 Saxmundham Road, Aldeburgh, Suffolk IP15 5PB (☎ 072 885 3957)

LAPUN, Sir Paul; *b* 1923; *Educ* Catholic Mission Vunapope; *m* 1951, Lois; 2 s, 1 da; *Career* memb S Bougainville Papua New Guinea House of Assembly 1964-, fndr Pangu Party 1967, ldr 1967-68, dep Parly ldr 1968-; kt 1974; *Style*— Sir Paul Lapun; c/o House of Assembly, Port Moresby, Papua New Guinea

LARCOM, Sir (Charles) Christopher (Royde); 5 Bt (UK 1868); s of Sir Philip Larcom, 4 Bt (d 1967); *b* 11 Sept 1926; *Educ* Radley, Clare Coll Cambridge; *m* 1956, Barbara Elizabeth, da of Balfour Bowen; 4 da; *Career* memb The Stock Exchange London 1959-1987, memb cncl 1970-1980, ptnr Grieveson Grant and Co stockbrokers 1960-1986, fin dir Kleinwort Grieveson 1986; *Recreations* sailing, music; *Clubs* Naval and Military, Cruising Assoc, Ocean Cruising, Itchener SC, Island SC, Blackwater SC; *Style*— Sir Christopher Larcom, Bt; 8 The Postern, Barbican, Wood Street, London EC2Y 8BJ; and 4 Marinacay, PO Box 145, Road Town, Tortola, British Virgin Islands

LARDNER-BURKE, Thomas David; s of Desmond William Lardner-Burke (d 1984), of Zimbabwe, and Alice May, *née* Fraser; f was Min of Justice and Min of Commerce and Ind in Mr Ian Smith's Rhodesian Govt; *b* 9 Dec 1937; *Educ* St Andrew's Coll, Grahamstown S Africa, Brixton Sch of Building; *m* 1966, Virginia Alicia *née* Allison; 3 da (Claire Olivia b 1968, Amanda May b 1969, Katherine Anna b 1975); *Career* chm Building Brokers Ltd 1964; dir: Trac Office Contracts Ltd 1968, Trac Telecom Ltd 1982; chm Anglo Rhodesian Society 1969-80; *Recreations* tennis, travel; *Clubs* Harare, Institute of Directors; *Style*— T D Lardner-Burke, Esq; 15 Lyon Rd, London SW19 2SB (☎ 01 543 4411, car ☎ 233355)

LARGE, Andrew Mcleod Brooks; Maj-Gen Stanley Eyre Large, MBE, of Drumcrannog, Dalbeattie, Kirkcudbrightshire, and Janet Mary, *née* Brooks; *b* 7 August 1942; *Educ* Winchester, Cambridge Univ (BA), Insead Fontainebleu (MBA); *m* 17 June 1967, Susan Mary, da of Sir Ronald Melville, KCB, *qv*; 2 s (Alexander b 1970, James b 1972), 1 da (Georgina b 1976); *Career* Br Petroleum Ltd 1964-71, md Orion Bank Ltd 1971-79, chief exec and dep chm Swiss Bank Corpn Int 1983 (md 1980), gp chief exec and dep chm Swiss Bank Corpn Int 1987, memb exec bd Swiss Bank Corpn 1988; dep chm Int Securities Regulation Orgn 1985-86, chm The Securities Assoc 1986-87, memb cncl Int Stock Exchange 1986-87; *Recreations* skiing, walking, photography, music, weather, sailing, gardening; *Clubs* Brooks's; *Style*— Andrew

Large, Esq; Stokes House, Ham St, Richmond, Surrey (☎ 01 940 2403); Swiss Bank Corpn, Barengasse 16, 8022 Zurich; SBC Investment Banking, Swiss Bank House, 1 High Timber St, London EC4 (☎ 010 41 223 1111, 01 329 0329, telex 887434)

LARGE, Maj-Gen Stanley Eyre (Sandy); MBE (1945); s of Brig David Torquil Macleod Large, RAMC (d 1969), of Edinburgh, and Constance Lucy, *née* Houston (d 1979); *b* 11 August 1917; *Educ* Cheltenham, Gonville and Caius Cambridge, St Thomas's Hosp London (MA, MB BChir, MD); *m* 19 July 1941, Janet Mary, da of Maj A C Brooks, RE (d 1955), of Goudhurst, Kent; 3 s (Andrew b 1942, Duncan b 1948, Stephen b 1949); *Career* cmmnd RAMC 1942; served in WWII in N Africa, Italy, Austria and Greece as regtl mo and with Field Ambulance Units; Staff Coll Camberley 1948, sr course RAMC 1949; served in various mil hosps at home (Hindhead, Aldershot), and abroad (Egypt, Malta, Singapore, Malaya) as sr specialist and later as conslt in med 1950-65, held several sr med admin posts in Cyprus (OC hosp and ADMS), and in BAOR (ADMS Div and DDMS 1 (Br) Corps (Brig)) 1965-75, dir med servs HQ UK Land Forces (in rank of Maj-Gen) 1975-78, ret 1978; dir med servs (1978-83) and conslt in med (1978-87) King Edward VII Hosp, conslt emeritus Midhurst 1987-; hon med advsr The Abbeyfield Stewartry Soc Ltd Kirkcudbrightshire 1987-; FRCPE 1958, FRCP 1975; *Books* King Edward VII Hospital, Midhurst, 1901-1986, A History (1986); numerous contributions to med journals; *Recreations* golf, skiing, photography, travel; *Style*— Maj-Gen Sandy Large, MBE; Drumcrannog, Colvend, Dalbeattie, Kirkcudbrightshire (☎ 055 663 280)

LARKEN, Cmdt Anthea; da of Frederick William Savill, of Winchester, and Nance, *née* Williams; *b* 23 August 1938; *Educ* Stafford Girl's HS; *m* 19 Dec 1987, Rear Adm (Edmund Shackleton) Jeremy Larken, DSO, s of Rear Adm Edmund Thomas Larken, CB, OBE (d 1965), of Yarmouth, IOW; *Career* range assessor WRNS 1956, cmmnd 1960, qualified photographic interpreter 1961, staff LC Singapore (Indonesia Confrontation) 1964-66, qualified WRNS Sec Offr 1967, i/c WRNS offrs trg BRNC Dartmouth 1976-78, RN Staff Coll 1988-89, NATO Mil Agency for Standardisation Brussels 1981-84, Chief Staff Offr (admin) to Flag Offr Plymouth 1985-86, Royal Coll of Def Studies 1987, Dir WRNS ADC to HM The Queen 1988; govr Royal Naval Sch Haslemere, cncl memb King George's Fund for Sailors; *Recreations* theatre, music, reading, home, family and friends; *Clubs* Royal Cwlth Soc; *Style*— Cmdt Anthea Larken, WRNS; c/o The Naval Secretary, MOD, Old Admiralty Building, Spring Gardens, London SW1

LARKEN, Jasper Wyatt Royds; s of Capt Francis Wyatt Rawson Larken (d 1985), of Rushall Manor, Pewsey, Wilts, and Florence Meriel, *née* Royds, (see Burke's Landed Gentry, 18th Edn Vol 1 1965); *b* 12 Sept 1939; *Educ* Winchester; *m* 20 April 1968, Caroline Lucia Marie, da of Stuart West Little, of Fenwick, Old Saybrook, Connecticut, USA; 1 s (Jonathan b 1973), 1 da (Melissa b 1970); *Career* Grenadier Gds 1958-61; md Financial Intelligence UK Ltd 1978-; *Recreations* bridge, hunting, tennis, golf; *Clubs* Boodles, MCC, Berkshire; *Style*— Jasper Larken, Esq; 24 Astell St, London SW3 3RU; The Green, Fifield, Milton-under-Wychwood, Oxon (☎ 01 352 1796); 10 St James Place, London SW1A 1NP (☎ 01 491 8147, fax 01 499 6755, telex 88 3416)

LARKINS, Derrick Alfred; CBE (1987); s of Walter Arthur Larkins (d 1950), and Ada Aelia Larkins (d 1966); *b* 5 July 1926; *Educ* Royal Liberty Sch Romford; *m* 1960, Noël Sarah, da of William White, of Co Meath, Ireland; 1 s (Barry b 1966), 1 da (Trudi b 1968); *Career* WWII served RN Patrol Serv 1943-46; Apex Oilfields Trinidad 1951-54, Ford Motor-Co & Chrysler Motors 1954-61, dep chm (formerly chief accountant and jt md) Lansing Bagnell 1961-; FCMA; *Recreations* gardening, watching sport, music, reading; *Clubs* MCC; *Style*— Derrick Larkins, Esq, CBE; Kneledore, Barn Close, Church Rd, Tadley, Hants RG26 6AU (☎ 07356 4730); Lansing Bagnall Ltd, Basingstoke (☎ 0256x 473131)

LARKINS, Hon Mrs (Miranda); da of Sir Richard Sharples (d 1972), of Government House, Bermuda, and Baroness Sharples, *née* Newall; *b* 26 Nov 1951; *m* 1981, Nicholas John Larkins, s of Dr Nicholas Larkins, of Sydney, Australia; 1 s (Harry b 1985); *Style*— The Hon Mrs Larkins; The Old Rectory, Stoke Wake, Blandford, Dorset

LARLHAM, Christopher; s of Maj Percival Edward Larlham (d 1968), of London, and Cecelia Louise, *née* Farrell; *b* 8 Nov 1949; *Educ* Dulwich Coll; *m* 3 May 1973 (m dis 1984), Caroline Jane, da of Stanley Godfrey, of Ruislip; 3 s (Edward b 1976, Guy b 1978, George b 1980); *Career* slr 1975; article Allibones 1969-75 (merged with Cameron Kemm Nordon 1973), ptnr Cameron Kemm Nordon 1976-80 (merged with Markbys 1980), ptnr Cameron Markby 1980-; hon fixture sec Incogniti CC, capt Saffron Walden Bridge Club; Liveryman Worshipful Co Slrs; memb Law Soc; *Recreations* cricket, bridge, wine; *Clubs* MCC; *Style*— Christopher Larlham, Esq; Sceptre Ct, 40 Tower Hill, London EC3N 4BB (☎ 01 702 2345, fax 01 702 2303, telex 925779 CAMLAW G)

LARMINIE, (Ferdinand) Geoffrey; OBE (1971); s of Ferdinand Samuel Larminie (d 1963), of Dublin, Ireland, and Mary, *née* Willis; *b* 23 June 1929; *Educ* St Andrew's Coll Dublin, Trinity Coll Dublin (BA, MA); *m* 3 April 1956, Helena Elizabeth Woodside, da of late Ralph Coburn Carson, of Inch House, Kilkenny, Ireland; 1 s (Christopher b 8 June 1969), 1 da (Susan b 23 Dec 1963); *Career* asst lectr geology Univ of Glasgow 1954-56, lectr geology Univ of Sydney 1956-60; British Petroleum plc: joined 1960, exploration dept (Sudan, Greece, Canada, Libya, Kuwait, California, NY, Alastea, Thailand), scientific advsr info dept London 1974-75, gen mangr public affrs and info dept 1975-76, gen mangr environmental control centre London 1976-84, external affairs co-ordinator health safety and evnironmental servs 1984-87, ret 1987; dir Br Geological Survey 1987-; memb: Royal Cmmn on Environmental Pollution 1979-83, Natural Envirmonment Res Cncl 1983-87, Cncl RGS 1984- (vice pres 1987-), gen advsy cncl IBA 1980-85, polar res bd Nat Rev Cncl Washington DC 1984-88, bd of mgmnt Inst of Offshore Engrg Heriot-Watt Univ 1981-; pres: Alaska Geological Soc 1969, Soc for Underwater Technol 1987-; govr Bangkok Patana Sch Thailand 1972-74, scientific tstee Bermuda Biological Station for Res; Freeman City of Fairbanks Alaska; Gold Pan Award; FGS, FRSA, FRGS; *Recreations* archaeology, natural history, reading, shooting; *Style*— Geoffrey Larminie, Esq, OBE; British Geological Survey, Keyworth, Nottingham NG12 5GG (☎ 060 77 6111, fax 060 77 6602, telex 378173 BGSKEY G)

LARMINIE, Maj John Charles; s of John Peel Alexander Larminie (d 1958), of Monk Sherborne, Hants, and Alison Yorke, *née* Lyle (d 1978); *b* 12 July 1926; *Educ* Winchester, RMCS; *m* 30 Dec 1950, Carola Anne, da of Brig Thomas Farquaharson Ker Howard (d 1963); 2 s (James b 1952, Oliver b 1953), 2 da (Annabelle b 1958, Penelope b 1961); *Career* Br Army 1944-72, Maj 1 Queen's Dragoon Gds; consulting mechanical engr 1972-; author of several technical and historical books; *Recreations* sailing; *Clubs* Army and Navy, Poole YC; *Style*— Maj John Larminie; Tithe Barn, Lytchett Matravers, Poole, Dorset BH16 6BJ (☎ 092 945 201)

LARMOUR, Sir Edward Noel; KCMG (1977, CMG 1966); s of Edward Larmour; *b* 25 Dec 1916; *Educ* Royal Belfast Academical Inst, Trinity Coll Dublin, Sydney Univ; *m* Agnes Margaret, da of Thomas Bill; 1 s, 2 da; *Career* served Royal Inniskilling Fus and 15 Indian Corps in Burma 1940-46, joined CRO 1948, Br high cmmr in Jamaica and ambassador (non res) to Haiti 1970-73, Br high cmmr for New Hebrides (res in London) 1973, dep under-sec of state FCO 1975-76; *Style*— Sir Edward Larmour, KCMG; 68 Wood Vale, London N10 (☎ 01 444 9744)

LARRECHE, Prof Jean-Claude; s of Pierre Albert Alexis Larreche, of Pau, France, and Odette Jeanne Madeleine, *née* Hau-Sans; *b* 3 July 1947; *Educ* Lyon France (INSA), London Univ (MSc), Fontainebleau France (MBA), Stanford Univ USA (PhD); *m* 10 Sept 1971, Denyse Michèle Joséphine, da of Michel Francis Henri Gros, of Besancon, France; 1 s (Philippe b 1978), 1 da (Sylvie b 1975); *Career* prof of mktg INSEAD 1974-, non-exec dir Reckitt and Colman plc London 1983-, dir Euro strat mktg inst INSEAD 1985-, chm Strat X Veneux France 1985-, bd memb The Mac Gp Boston 1986-; memb: America Mktg Assoc 1973, Inst of Mgmnt Sci 1975; *Recreations* tennis; *Style*— Prof Jean-Claude Larreche; 85 Rue Murger, 77780, Bourron Marlotte, France (☎ 1 64457974); INSEAD, 77305, Fontainebleau, France (☎ 1 60724000, fax 1 60724242, telex 690389 F)

LASCELLES, Hon Alexander; 2 s (but h to courtesy Viscountcy since b in wedlock) of Viscount Lascelles, *qv*; *b* 13 May 1980; *Style*— The Hon Alexander Lascelles

LASCELLES, Viscount; David Henry George Lascelles; s of 7 Earl of Harewood; *b* 21 Oct 1950; *Educ* The Hall Sch, Westminster; *m* 12 Feb 1979, Margaret Rosalind, da of Edgar Frank Messenger; 3 s (Hon Benjamin b 9 Sept 1978, Hon Alexander, Hon Edward b 19 Nov 1982), 1 da (Hon Emily b 23 Nov 1975); *Heir* 2 s (but 1 b in wedlock), Hon Alexander Edgar Lascelles b 13 May 1980; *Style*— Viscount Lascelles; 2 Orme Sq, London W2

LASCELLES, Hon Gerald David; yr s of 6 Earl of Harewood, KG, GCVO, DSO, TD (d 1947), and HRH The Princess Royal (d 1965, da of George V); *b* 21 August 1924; *Educ* Eton; *m* 1, 1952 (m dis 1978), Angela, da of Charles Stanley Dowding (d 1972); 1 s (Henry Ulick b 1953, m 1979 Alexandra Clare Ruth, da of Peter Morton); m 2, 1978, Elizabeth Evelyn, da of Brig Sydney Collingwood, CMG, CBE, MC; 1 s (Martin David b 1962); *Career* pres Br Racing Drivers Club 1964-, dir Silverstone Circuits Ltd and subsidiaries, pres Inst of the Motor Indust 1969-73 and 1975-77; *Recreations* shooting, gardening; *Clubs* RAC; *Style*— The Hon Gerald Lascelles; Cliffordine House, Rendcomb, Cirencester GL7 7ER (☎ 028 583 321)

LASCELLES, Hon James Edward; s of 7th Earl of Harewood, *qv*; *b* 5 Oct 1953; *Educ* Westminster; *m* 1, 4 April 1973 (m dis 1985), Fredericka Ann, da of Prof Alfred Duhrsson, of Majorca; 1 s, 1 da; m 2, 4 May 1985, Lori ("Shadow"), da of J R Lee of Arizona, USA; 1 s, 1 da; *Career* leader of rock groups *Breakfast Band, Cuckoo*; session work and composer; dir Tribal Music Int (tape co, releasing American Indian music); part-time disc jockey at Albuquerque Univ Station; *Style*— The Hon James Lascelles; 1 Orme Lane, London W2 (☎ 01 727 1163)

LASCELLES, Hon (Robert) Jeremy Hugh; s of 7 Earl of Harewood, *qv*; *b* 14 Feb 1955; *m* 1981, Julie, da of Robert Baylis, of Mildenham Mill, Cairnes, nr Worcester; 1 s (Thomas Robert b 1982), 1 da (Ellen Mary b 1984); *Style*— The Hon Jeremy Lascelles

LASCELLES, Hon Mark Hubert; s of 7 Earl of Harewood, *qv*; *b* 5 July 1964; *Style*— The Hon Mark Lascelles

LASDUN, Sir Denys Louis; CBE (1965); s of Norman Lasdun; *b* 8 Sept 1914; *Educ* Rugby, Architectural Assoc; *m* 1954, Susan Bendit; 2 s, 1 da; *Career* served WWII RE; architect; in practice with Peter Softley 1960-; works incl: Royal Coll of Physicians London, Flats 26 St James's Place, Nat Theatre and IBM Central Marketing Centre, South Bank London, EEC HQ for Euro Investmt Bank, Luxembourg design for new Hurva Synagogue Old City Jerusalem; tstee British Museum 1975-85; memb: Academie d'Architecture 1984, Slade ctee Int Acad of Architecture Bulgaria 1986; hon fell American Inst of Architects 1966; Hon DLitt: E Anglia 1974, Sheffield 1978; Accademia Nazionale di San Luca 1984; RIBA Gold Medal 1977; FRIBA; kt 1976; *Books* Architects Approach to Architecture (1965), A Language and a Theme (1976), Architecture in the Age of Sceptisism; *Style*— Sir Denys Lasdun, CBE; 146 Grosvenor Rd, London SW1V 3JY (☎ 01 630 8211, telex 22244)

LASOK, Prof Dominik; s of Alojzy Lasok of Turza (Poland) (d 1956); *b* 4 Jan 1921; *Educ* elementary educn in Poland and Switzerland, Univ of Fribourg (Licence on Droit), Univ of Durham (LLM), Univ of London (PhD, LLD), Polish Univ Abroad (Dr Juris); *m* 7 Aug 1952, Sheila May, da of James Corrigan; 2 s (Paul b 1953, Marc b 1960), 3 da (Pia b 1962, Teresa b 1962, Carmen b 1965); *Career* WWII in Polish Army (cmmnd 1944), served Poland, France and Italy 1939-46 (holds Polish, French and British decorations); employed in indust 1948-51, barr 1954, legal advsr 1954-58, prof of euro law Exeter Univ 1968-86, prof emeritus; vis prof: Williamsburg (1966-67 and 1977), McGill Univ 1976-77, Rennes Univ 1980-81 and 1986, College d'Europe Bruges 1984-86, Aix-Marseille Univ 1986-89, Marmara Univ Istanbul 1987-89; Hon LLD Aix-Marseille 1987; officer dans L'ordre des Palmes academiqes France 1983; *Books* Law and Institutions of the European Communities (1972, 4 edn 1987), The Law of the Economy of the European Communities (1980), The Customs Law of the European Community (1983), Professions and Services in the EEC (1986), Conflict of Laws in the European Community (1987), Polish Faculty Law (1968), Polish Civil Law (1975); *Style*— Prof Dominik Lasok; Reed, Barley Lane, Exeter (☎ 0392 72582); Ground Floor, Lamb Bldg, Temple, London 4Y 7AS

LASS, Jonathan Daniel; s of Jacob Lass, of 57 Southway, London NW11, and Regina Lass, *née* Weinfeld; *b* 22 Feb 1946; *Educ* Univ Coll Sch, Downing Coll Cambridge (MA); *m* 24 March 1985, Andria Mina, da of Mervyn Thal; 1 s (Saul Alexander Yentis); *Career* Herbert Oppenheimer Nathan & Vandyk 1970-75, admitted slr 1972, slr Crawley & De Reya 1975-77, vice pres and legal advsr Citibank NA 1977-86, ptnr Lovell White Durrant (formerly Lovell White & King) 1986-; memb: Law Soc, Int Bar Assoc; *Recreations* history, opera, theatre, art, antiques, swimming, tennis; *Clubs* RAC; *Style*— Jonathan Lass, Esq; 4 North Square, London NW11 (☎ 01 458 5289); 21 Holborn Viaduct, London EC1 (☎ 01 236 0066)

LASSEN-DIESEN, David Peter; s of Sigurd Lassen-Diesen (d 1986), and Mary Margaret, *née* Wright; *b* 30 Jan 1938; *m* 7 Sept 1968, Valerie Jane, da of Joseph John Ive (d 1964); 2 s (David b 1974, Piers b 1977), 1 da (Karen b 1971); *Career* fndr Finance Centre, first money shop business in UK 1967, fndr ptnr Diesen Property Co 1967; dir: Frost Hldgs 1972-74, Konrad Roberts Ltd 1978, Konrad Roberts plc 1985-; *Recreations* golf; *Style—* David P Lassen-Diesen, Esq; Roundwood Hall, Norwood Hill, Horley, Surrey RH6 0HS (☎ 0293 862798, fax 0293 862846, car telephone 0836 289209)

LASSETER, Ronald Sydney Gaston; s of Ronald Edwin Lasseter, of 3 Highfield Place, Coneyhill Rd, Gloucester, and Marcelle, *née* Gondry; *b* 26 May 1947; *Educ* Prince Rupert Sch Wilhelmshaven W Germany, Univ of Exeter (BSc); *m* 1971, Diane, da of Arthur Ronald Ellis, of 5 Whitestones, Cranford Av, Exmouth, Devon; 1 s (Michael b 1975); 1 da (Emma b 1978); *Career* currently md of Pilkington's Tiles Hldgs Ltd and chm of its subsidiaries; FCA; *Recreations* tennis, squash; *Style—* R S G Lasseter, Esq; PO Box 4, Clifton Junction, Manchester M27 2LP (☎ 061 794 2024, telex 667663, fax 061 794 5455)

LAST, Maj-Gen Christopher Neville; OBE (1976); s of Jack Neville Last, and Lorna Kathleen Mary, *née* Goodman; *b* 2 Sept 1935; *Educ* Culford Sch, Brighton Tech Coll; *m* 11 Feb 1961, Pauline Mary, da of Henry Percy Lawton (d 1981); 2 da (Caroline Victoria Neville (Mrs Ludwig) b 3 Aug 1964, Alexandra Louise Neville b 10 June 1969); *Career* Regular Army, Royal Signals troop cdr 1956-67: serv Germany, UK 16 Para Bde, 44 Para Bde, Far East Borneo Campaign 1967, Maj and Cdr 216 Para Signal Sqdn in UK, GS01 Signals HQ BAOR 1973, Cdr Royal Signals NI 1974-76, GS01 Directorate of Combat Devpt MOD 1976, GS01 Directorate of Mil Ops MOD 1977, Col asst dir Long Range Surveillance and Cmd and Control Projects (Army) 1977, Cdr 8 Signal Regt 1980, Brig and Cdr 1 Signal Bde HQ 1 (Br) Corps Germany 1981-83; dir of Mil Cmd and Control Projects (Army) UK 1984, dir of Procurement Policy (special studies) for Chief of Def Procurement 1985, Maj Gen and Vice Master Gen of the Ordnance 1986, mil dep to Head of Def Export Servs 1988; memb CLA, Br Field Sports Soc, Nat Tst; hockey rep Corps Army and Combined Servs; Freeman: Worshipful Co Info Technologists 1988, City of London 1988; *Recreations* shooting, sailing, skiing, ballet; *Clubs* Special Forces; *Style—* Maj Gen Christopher Last, OBE; Military Deputy to Head of Defence Export Services, MOD (Main Building), RMNO 0210, Whitehall, London SW1 (☎ 01 218 3060)

LAST, John William; s of late Jack Last (d 1986), former Dir of Fin Met Police, and Freda Edith, *née* Evans (d 1976);; *b* 22 Jan 1940; *Educ* Sutton GS Surrey, Trinity Coll Oxford (MA); *m* 1967, Susan Josephine, da of John Holloway Farmer, of Knaresborough; 3 s; *Career* head of corporate affrs Littlewoods Orgn (joined 1969) fndr Merseyside Maritime Museum; chm: Walker Art Gallery Liverpool 1977-81, Royal Liverpool Philharmonic Orch 1977-; memb: Arts Cncl 1980-84, Press Cncl 1980-86, Museums Cmmn 1983-; vice-pres Museums Assoc 1983-; tstee: Theatre Museum 1983-86, V&A 1983-6 (also memb advsy cncl), visiting prof in arts Admin City Univ 1985-, vice-chm Northern Ballet Theatre; Freeman City of London 1985, Liveryman Worshipful Co of Barber Surgns 1986; *Recreations* Victoriana, music, swimming; *Clubs* Bluecoat (Liverpool), RAC, RACQUET; *Style—* John Last Esq; 25 Abbey Rd, West Kirby, Wirral, Merseyside L48 7EN; business: 100 Old Hall St, Liverpool L70 1AN (☎ 051 235 2222, fax 051 235 4900)

LASZLO; *see*: de Laszlo

LATEY, Rt Hon Mr Justice; Hon Sir John Brinsmead; MBE (1943), PC (1986); s of William Latey, CBE, QC (d 1976) and Annie (d 1983); *b* 7 Mar 1914; *Educ* Westminster Sch, Ch Ch Oxford; *m* 1938, Betty Margaret, da of Dr Edwyn Henry Beresford of London; 1 s, 1 da; *Career* served WWII MEF and WO; barr Middle Temple 1936, QC 1957; bencher Middle Temple 1964-84; a judge of High Court of Justice (Probate, Divorce and Admty Div, now Family Div) 1965-; chm Lord Chllrs Ctee on Age of Majority 1965-67, dep chm Oxfordshire quarter sessions 1966; kt 1965; *Recreations* golf, fishing, chess, bridge; *Clubs* United Oxford and Cambridge Univs; *Style—* The Rt Hon Mr Justice Latey, MBE; 16 Daylesford Ave, Roehampton, London SW15 5QR (☎ 01 876 6436)

LATHAM, Anthony Michael; s of Hon Francis Charles Allman Latham (d 1959) (s of 1 Baron Latham), and hp of twin bro, 2 Baron; *b* 20 Sept 1954; *Style—* Anthony Latham, Esq

LATHAM, Cecil Thomas; OBE (1976); s of Cecil Frederick James Latham (d 1942) and Elsie Winifred *née* Lewis (d 1959); *b* 11 Mar 1924; *Educ* Rochester Cathedral Choir Sch, King's Sch Rochester; *m* 8 Aug 1945, Ivy Frances, da of Thomas William Fowle (d 1935); 1 s (Martin John b 1954), 1 da (Helen Susan b 1952); *Career* war serv 1942-45; asst clerk Magistrate's Courts: Chatham 1939-42, Maidstone 1945, Leicester 1948-54, Bromley 1954-63; dep clerk to the Justices: Liverpool 1963-5, Manchester 1965-76 (clerk); stipendiary magistrate Greater Manchester (Salford) 1976-; memb: Royal Cmmn on Criminal Procedure 1978-81, Criminal Law Revision Ctee 1981-; Hon MA Manchester Univ 1984; *Books* Stone's Justices' Manual 101-109 editions; fndr ed: Family Law Reports 1980-86, Family Court Reporter 1987-; specialist ed J P Reports 1986-; *Style—* Cecil Latham, Esq, OBE; 19 Southdown Crescent, Cheadle Hulme, Cheshire SK8 6EQ (☎ 061 485 1185); Magistrates' Court, Bexley Square, Salford M3 6DJ

LATHAM, David Nicholas Ramsay; QC (1985); s of Robert Clifford Latham, CBE, of Cambridge, and Eileen Frances, *née* Ramsay (d 1969); *b* 18 Sept 1942; *Educ* Bryanston, Queens' Coll Cambridge (MA); *m* 6 May 1967, Margaret Elizabeth, da of Francis Penrose Forrest, FRCS of 4 Lancaster Drive, Broadstone, Dorset; 3 da (Clare Frances b 2 Aug 1969, Angela Josephine b 23 Jan 1972, (Rosemary) Harriet b 10 Dec 1974); *Career* barr Middle Temple 1964; jnr counsel to the Crown, Common Law 1979- 85; counsel to Dept of Trade in export guarantee matters 1982-85; memb Gen Cncl of the Bar 1986-; memb Judicial Studies Bd 1988-; *Recreations* reading, music, food, drink; *Clubs* Leander; *Style—* David Latham, Esq, QC; The Firs, Church Rd, Sunningdale, Ascot, Berks (☎ 0990 22686); 1 Crown Office Row, London EC4 (☎ 01 353 1801, fax 01 583 1700)

LATHAM, David Russell; s of Russell Latham CBE, MC, JP (d 1967), and Elsa Mary (*née*) Andrews) (d 1980); *b* 9 Nov 1937; *Educ* Rugby; *m* 1963, Susan Elisabeth, da of Charles Alfred (d 1984); 2 s (Jonathan b 1966, Nicholas b 1968); 1 da (Katherine b 1970); *Career* md of James Latham plc; *Recreations* tennis, golf, skiing; *Style—* D R Latham; James Latham plc, Leeside Wharf, Clapton E5 9NG (☎ 01 806 3333)

LATHAM, Derek James; s of James Horace Latham, DFC, of Newark-on-Trent, and Mary Pauline, *née* Turner (d 1974); *b* 12 July 1946; *Educ* King Edward VI GS Retford, Leicester Sch of Architecture, Trent Poly Nottingham; Dip Arch, Dip TP, Dip LD, ALI); *m* 14 Sept 1968, Pauline Elizabeth, da of Philip George Tuxworth, of Lincs; 2 s (Benjamin James b 1974, Oliver James b 1981), 1 da (Sarah Jane b 1972); *Career* Clifford Wearden & Assocs (architects & planners) London 1968-70; housing architect and planner with Derby CC 1970-73; design and conservation offr Derbyshire CC 1974-78; princ Derek Latham and Assocs 1980-; md Michael Saint Devpts Ltd 1984, tech advsr Derbyshire Historic Bldgs Tst 1978, architectural advsr Peak Park Tst 1986, concept co-ordinator Sheffield Devpt Corpn 1987-; external examiner: Leicester Sch of Architecture 1988-, Leicester of Archtectural Conservation Studies 1983-86; memb exec ctee Cncl for Care of Churches 1985-, govr Nottingham Sch of Interior Design 1986-; *Recreations* squash; *Clubs* Duffield Squash and Lawn Tennis; *Style—* Derek J Latham, Esq; Hieron's Wood, Vicarage Lane, Little Eaton, Derby DE3 5EA (☎ 0332 832371); Derek Latham and Associates, St Michaels, Derby DE1 3SU (☎ 0332 365777)

LATHAM, 2 Baron (UK 1942); Dominic Charles Latham; er (twin) s of Hon Francis Charles Allman Latham (d 1959), and his 3 w Gabrielle Monica, *née* O'Riordan (d 1987), and gs of 1 Baron Latham (d 1970); *b* 20 Sept 1954; *Educ* NSW Univ (BEng 1977, MEngSc 1981); *Heir* bro, Anthony Latham; *Career* civil engr with Electricity Cmmn of New South Wales 1979-88; structural engr with Rankine & Hill consulting engrs 1988-; *Recreations* tennis, squash, snooker, electronics, sailboarding; *Style—* The Rt Hon the Lord Latham; PO Box 355, Kensington, NSW 2033, Australia

LATHAM, Hon Mrs Francis; Gabrielle; da of Dr S M O'Riordan; *m* 1951, as his 3 w, the Hon Francis Charles Allman Latham (d 1959, s of 1 Baron Latham); *Style—* The Hon Mrs Francis Latham; 6/226 Rainbow St, S Coogee 2034, Sydney, NSW, Australia

LATHAM, Lady Gwendoline Lucy Constance Rushworth; da of Adm of the Fleet 1 Earl Jellicoe, GCB, OM, GCVO (d 1935); *b* 14 April 1903; *m* 1935, Lt-Col Edward Latham, MC (d 1957); 2 s, 1 da; *Style—* Lady Gwendoline Latham; Oak Knoll, Sunningdale, Berks (☎ Ascot 22842)

LATHAM, James Miles; s of Maj James Francis Latham, TD, JP (d 1966); *b* 24 Jan 1940; *Educ* Haileybury; *m* 1968, Margaret Eleanor, *née* Gray; 2 s; *Career* wood merchant, dir James Latham plc, chm Richard Graefe Ltd; memb cncl: Timber Trade Fedn of UK 1974-, Timber Res and Devpt Assoc 1975-, Assoc of Br Plywood and Veneer Mfrs; *Recreations* golf, gardening, field sports; *Clubs* Royal Worlington, Newmarket Golf; *Style—* James Latham, Esq; Gills Farm, Epping Upland, Essex (☎ 0378 75878); James Latham plc, Leeside Wharf, Clapton, London E5 9NG (☎ 01 806 3333; telex 265670)

LATHAM, Michael Anthony; MP (C) Rutland and Melton 1983-; *b* 20 Nov 1942; *Educ* Marlborough, King's Coll Cambridge, Dept of Educn Oxford Univ; *m* 1969, Caroline Susan, da of Maj T A Terry, RE (d 1971); 2 s; *Career* CRD 1965-67, co-opted memb GLC Housing Ctee 1967-73, memb Westminster City Cncl 1968-71, dir and chief exec House Builders Fedn 1971-73, former memb mgmnt bd Shelter; MP (C) Melton 1974-83, vice chm Cons Parly Environment Ctee 1979-83, hon sec Cons Parly Countryside Sub-Ctee 1979-83; memb: select ctee Energy 1979-82, Public Accounts Ctee 1983-; vice-pres Bldg Socs Assoc, memb Advsy Cncl on Public Records 1985-; *Recreations* cricket fencing, gardening, listening to classical music; *Clubs* Carlton; *Style—* Michael Latham, Esq, MP; House of Commons, London SW1

LATHAM, (Edward) Michael Locks; s of Edward Bryan Latham, CBE (d 1980); *b* 7 Jan 1930; *Educ* Stowe, Clare Cambridge; *m* 1955, Joan Doris, da of Charles Ellis Merriam Coubrough (d 1967); 1 s, 2 da; *Career* chm: Trebartha Estates Ltd, G A Day Timber Centres Ltd, Malcolm Turner Buildings Supplies Ltd, James Latham plc 1973-87 (dir 1987-); pres: Sandringham Assoc of Royal Warrant Holders 1982-83, Fedn of Tropical Timber Trade in EEC 1980-82, Timber Trade Fedn 1984-85; memb exec ctee Nat Cncl of Building Material Prodrs 1985; pres Int Tech Assoc of Tropical Timber; *Recreations* tennis, the countryside, classic cars, books; *Clubs* Launceston GC; *Style—* E Michael Latham, Esq; Trebartha Lodge, Launceston PL15 7PD; James Latham plc, Yate, Bristol BS17 5JX (☎ 0454 315 421, telex 449418)

LATHAM, Air Vice-Marshal Peter Anthony; CB (1980), AFC (1960); s of Oscar Frederick Latham (d 1945), of Birmingham, and Rhoda, *née* Archer; *b* 18 June 1925; *Educ* St Phillip's GS Birmingham, St Catherine's Coll Cambridge; *m* 19 Sept 1953, Barbara Mary, da of Reginald des Landes Caswell (d 1984), of Birmingham; 2 s (Mark b 1958, Phillip b 1960), 6 da (Jane (Mrs Foskett) b 1954, Sarah (Mrs Street) b 1955, Anne (Mrs Lewis) b 1956, Katherine (Mrs Hampden-Smith) b 1959, Margaret b 1962, Josephine b 1965); *Career* joined RAF 1944, served in 26, 263, 614, 247 sqdns 1946-54, cmd III Sqdn (leader Black Arrows Aerobatic Team) 1958-60, MOD jt planning staff 1962-64, cmd NEAF strike and PR wing 1964-66, Gp Capt Ops 38 Gp 1967-69, cmd RAF Tengah, Singapore 1969-71, MOD central staff 1971-73, AOC Offr and Aircrew Selection Centre Biggin Hill 1973-74, SASO 38 Gp 1974-76, dir def ops MOD 1976-77, AOC II Gp 1977-78, Cdre RAF Sailing Assoc 1974-80, pres Assoc of Service Yacht Clubs 1978-81, ret RAF 1981, princ Oxford Air Trg Sch and dir CSE Aviation 1981-85; sr air advsr Short Bros plc 1985-; memb ctee East Wessex TAVR; Liveryman Worshipful Co of Clockmakers Co 1987-; *Recreations* sailing, horology; *Clubs* RAF; *Style—* Air Vice-Marshal P A Latham, CB, AFC; Short Brothers plc, Glen House, Stag Place, Victoria, London SW1E 5AG (☎ 01 828 9838, fax 01 630 8071, telex 24934 and 23383)

LATHAM, Peter Douglas Langdon; s of Lt Col James Douglas Latham TD (d 1985), of Stondon Massey Ho, Nr Brentwood, Essex, and Rosemary Langdon Buckley; *b* 6 Feb 1951; *Educ* Repton, Exeter Univ (BA); *m* 1977, Barbara Frances, da of Frank John Neve, OBE; 2 s (Simon b 1980, Martin b 1982); *Career* dir: James Latham plc 1985-, Richard Graefe Ltd 1977-; chm Latham Timber Centres (Hldgs) Ltd 1983-; pres: Wood Forum 1981-84, High Wymcombe Furniture Mfrs Soc 1984-86; *Recreations* squash, beekeeping, mountaineering; Latham Timber & Building Supplies, Simpton Rd, Bletchley, Milton Keynes MK1 1BB (☎ (0908) 644222, car ☎ 0836 210 154)

LATHAM, Sir Richard Thomas Paul; 3 Bt (UK 1919); s of 2 Bt (d 1955); *b* 1934; *Educ* Eton, Trinity Cambridge; *m* 1958, Marie Louise Patricia, da of Frederick H Russell, of Vancouver, BC Canada; 2 da; *Clubs* Cavalry; *Style—* Sir Richard Latham, Bt; 830 Rockbridge Rd, Santa Barbara, Calif 93108, USA

LATHAM, Robert Sidney; s of Ronald Geoffrey Latham (d 1951), of Ridge Park, Bramhall, Ches, and Doris, *née* Greenhalgh (d 1940); *b* 4 Feb 1929; *Educ* Repton Coll,

Trinity Coll Oxford (MA); *m* 1 June 1963, Suzannah da of Ralph Herbert Lane of Leigh Place, Reigate, Surrey, 3 s (Simon b 1964, Harry b 1964, William b 1967), 1 da (Sophie b 1970); *Career* Nat Serv Ches Regt 1947-49; asst slr Farrer and Co 1956-58, dep slr Nat Tst 1959-64 (slr 1964-89); govr and tstee St Marys Prep and Choir Sch Reigate 1984-; church warden St Philips Reigate 1984-; memb: Law Soc 1956-; *Recreations* allotment, environment; *Style*— Robert Latham, Esq; The Old Granary, Park Lane, Reigate, Surrey RH2 8JX (☎ 0737 242203)

LATHBURY, Lady; Mairi Zoë; *m* 1, Patrick Somerset Gibbs (decd); m 2, 1972, Gen Sir Gerald William Lathbury, GCB, DSO, MBE, DSC (d 1978); *Style*— Lady Lathbury; Casa San Pedro, Gata de Gorgos, Prov Alicante, Spain

LATIEF, Hon Mrs (Annette Yvonne); *née* Curzon; da (by 1 m) of 3 Viscount Scarsdale; *b* 28 Oct 1953; *m* 1979, Capt Hani Talaat Latief, of Cairo; 1 s (Sagi b 1982); *Style*— The Hon Mrs Latief; 7 Dr Ismaiel Ghanem St, Nozha Geddida, Heliopolis, Cairo, Egypt

LATIMER, Sir (Courtenay) Robert; CBE (1958, OBE 1948); s of Sir Courtenay Latimer, KCIE, CSI (d 1944), and Isabel Primrose, *née* Aikman (d 1981); *b* 13 July 1911; *Educ* Rugby, Ch Ch Oxford (MA); *m* 3 Oct 1944, Elizabeth Jane Gordon, da of William Mitchell Smail (d 1971); 1 s (Colin b 1947), 1 da (Penelope b 1953); *Career* Indian Civil Serv/Indian Political Serv 1935-47, HM Overseas Serv 1948-64 (dep high cmmr for Basutoland, Bechuanaland Protectorate and Swaziland 1960-64), min (Territories) in Br Embassy Pretoria 1964-66; registrar Kingston Poly 1964-66; *Recreations* golf; *Style*— Sir Robert Latimer, CBE; Benedicts, Old Avenue, Weybridge, Surrey KT13 0PS (☎ 0932 842381)

LATNER, Prof Albert Louis; s of Harry Latner (d 1971), of Finchley, London, and Miriam, *née* Gordon (d 1978); *b* 5 Dec 1912; *Educ* Imperial Coll (BSc, MSc, ARCS, DIC), Univ of Liverpool (MD, DSc); *m* 3 Sept 1936, Gertrude (d 1986), da of The Rev Sabita Franklin (d 1920), of Newcastle upon Tyne; *Career* RAMC 1941-46; lectr dept physiology Univ of Liverpool 1939-41 (asst lectr 1933-36), sr registrar Br Postgraduate Med Sch 1946-47; Univ of Durham: lectr chem pathology 1947-55, reader med biochem 1955-61; Univ of Newcastle Upon Tyne: prof clinical biochem 1961-78, dir cancer res unit 1967-78; conslt Royal Victoria Infirmary Newcastle Upon Tyne 1947-78; pres Assoc of Clinical Biochem 1961 and 1962, cncl memb Assoc Clinical Pathologists 1967-70; memb: ctee Standards Int Fedn Clinical Chem 1967-70, Br Nat Cmmn for Biochem 1967-77, titular memb Int Union Pure & Applied Chem 1967-73; FRIC 1953, FRCPath 1963, FRCP 1964, hon FNACB USA 1977; *Books* Isoenzymes in Biology and Medicine (with A W Skillen 1968), Clincial Biochemistry (Cantarow and Trumper 1975); *Recreations* photography, gardening; *Clubs* Athenaeum; *Style*— Prof Albert L Latner; Ravenstones, 50 Rectory Rd, Newcastle upon Tyne NE3 1XP (☎ 091 285 8020)

LATOUR-ADRIEN, Hon Sir (Jean Francois) Maurice; s of Louis Constant Emile Adrien (decd); *b* 4 Mar 1915; *Educ* Royal Coll Mauritius, UCL; *Career* chief justice of Mauritius 1970-77; kt 1971; *Style*— The Hon Sir Maurice Latour-Adrien; Vacoas, Mauritius

LATTANAN, Pornlert; s of Gp-Capt Lek Lattanan, and Praphit Lattanan; *b* 13 Nov 1953; *Educ* Assumption Coll Bangkok, Chulalongkorn Univ Bangkok (BSc), Columbia Univ NYC (MBA); *m* 14 Nov 1980, Rinthan, da of Virat Sivakoses; 2 s (Prom b 29 March 1984, Pat b 23 Feb 1986); *Career* Geschaeftsleter Thai Farmers Bank, Hamburg Branch 1983, vice pres and branch mangr Thai Farmers Bank London Branch 1987; *Recreations* tennis, golf; *Clubs* Overseas Bankers; *Style*— Pornlert Lattanan, Esq; 80 Cannon St, London EC4N 6HH (☎ 01 623 4975, fax 2837437, telex 8811173)

LATTER, (Henry) James (Edward); s of Henry Edward Latter, of Horley, Surrey, and Hilda Bessie, *née* Gyford; *b* 19 April 1950; *Educ* Reigate GS, Trinity Hall Cambridge (BA, MA); *m* 27 May 1978, Penelope Jane, da of Douglas Arthur Morris, of Pulborough, Sussex; 1 s (Christopher b 1980), 1 da (Sarah b 1985); *Career* barr Middle Temple 1972; chm disciplinary ctee Potato Mktg Bd 1988; churchwarden Parish of Horley 1982-86; *Recreations* gardening, reading; *Style*— James Latter, Esq; 1 Harcourt Buildings, Temple, London EC4Y 9DA (☎ 01 353 9421, fax 01 353 4170, telex 8956718 CRIPPSG)

LATTO, Dr Douglas; s of David Latto (d 1946), of Dundee, and Christina *née* Gordon (d 1960); *b* 13 Dec 1913; *Educ* St Andrews (MB, ChB, DObst, RCOG, MRCOG); *m* 11 Oct 1945, Dr Edith Monica, da of Capt Arthur Edward Druitt (RAMC); 1 s (Conrad b 1948), 3 da (Christina b 1947, Elizabeth b 1952, Veronica b 1957); *Career* house surgn Dundee Royal Infirmary 1939, house physician Cornelia and E Dorset Hosp Poole 1940, res obstetrician and gynaecologist Derbys Hosp for Women Derby 1940, res surgical offr Birmingham Accident Hosp 1944, casualty offr Paddington Gen Hosp London 1944, asst obstetrics and gynaecology Mayday Hosp Croydon 1945, res obstectrics and gynaecologist Southlands Hosp Shoreham-by-Sea Sussex 1946-49, Nuffield dept of obstetrics and gynaecology Radcliffe Infirmary Oxford 1949-51; chm Br Safety Cncl 1971- (Sword of Honour 1985); Freeman City of London 1988, Liveryman Worshipful Soc of Apothecaries 1988; memb BMA, FRPSL 1975; *Recreations* squash, travelling, gardening, philately; *Clubs* RAC, Rolls-Royce Enthusiasts; *Style*— Dr Douglas Latto; Lethnot Lodge, 4 Derby Road, Caversham, Reading, Berks RG4 0EZ (☎ 0734 472282); 59 Harley St, London W1N 1DD (☎ 01 580 1070)

LATYMER, 8 Baron (E 1431-32); Hugo Nevill Money-Coutts; s of 7 Baron Latymer (d 1987); *b* 1 Mar 1926; *Educ* Eton; *m* 1, 1951, Hon (Penelope) Ann Clare (m dis 1965), da of Thomas Addis Emmet (d 1934) and Lady Emmet of Amberley (Life Peeress); 2 s (Crispin b 1955, Giles b 1957), 1 da (Clare b 1952); m 2, 1965, Jinty, da of Peter Calvert (d 1970); 1 s (Henry b 1967), 2 da (Vera b 1972, Fanny b 1973); *Heir* s, Hon Crispin; *Career* gardener; *Style*— The Rt Hon the Lord Latymer; Vivero Hortus, Santa Maria, Mallorca

LAUCKE, Hon Sir Condor Louis; KCMG (1978); s of Frederick Laucke (d 1957), and late Marie Laucke; *b* 9 Nov 1914; *Educ* Greenock Public Sch, Immanuel Coll Adelaide; *m* 1942, Rose, da of late Jacob Hambour; 1 s, 1 da; *Career* MHA SA (Lib) for Barosa 1956-65, govt whip 1962-65, senator for SA 1967-81, temp chm of Ctees (Senate) 1969-72, ldr Aust Delegation to 57 IPU Conf New Delhi 1969, memb oppn exec 1972-75, jt pres and chm exec ctee Cwlth of Aust Branch Cwlth Parly Assoc 1976-79, pres of the Senate 1976-81, jt pres Aust Nat Gp Inter-Parly Union 1976-81, lt-govr of S Aust 1982; *Style*— The Hon Sir Condor Laucke, KCMG; Bunawanda, Greenock, S Australia 5360 (☎ 085 62 8143)

LAUDER, Col Philip Dalrymple Scott; s of Lt-Col Richard Dalrymple Lauder (d 1961), of Sevenoaks, Kent, and Margaret Hilda May *née* Hickman (d 1983); *b* 22 July 1918; *Educ* Clifton, RMC Sandhurst, Staff Coll Camberley; *m* 8 March 1941, Frances Tertia Elliot, da of Mr Sydney Paterson (d 1950), of Bournemouth; 1 s (Desmond b 1947) 3 da (Gillian b 1942, Brigid b 1944, Joanna b 1954),; *Career* Army 1939-73, CO 11 Hussars 1961-63, Col i/c RAC Records 1963-66, Cdr recruiting and liaison staff 1966-69, Col A HQ BAOR 1969-72, served Western Desert, Germany, Malaya Aden, Kuwait; *Recreations* game shooting, horticulture, arboriculture; *Clubs* Army and Navy; *Style*— Colonel Philip Lauder; Buckhorn Weston, Dorset

LAUDERDALE, Irene, Countess of Lauderdale; Irene Alice May Maitland; *née* Shipton; da of Rev C P Shipton (d 1933), of Halsham, Yorks, by his w Lory (Florence Leslie, d 1962); *b* 1 May 1900; *Educ* Maynard Sch Exeter, St Hilda's Sch Whitby, Battersea Poly; *m* 1940, as his 2 w, 16 Earl of Lauderdale (d 1968); *Books* Of Shoes and Ships and Sealing Wax (poems), of Cabbages and Kings; *Recreations* travel, reading, writing verse, naval history; *Style*— The Rt Hon Irene, Countess of Lauderdale; Flat 11, West Preston Manor, Station Road, Rustington, West Sussex BN16 3AX (☎ 0903 782720)

LAUDERDALE, 17 Earl of (S 1624); Sir Patrick Francis Maitland; 13 Bt (NS 1680); also Lord Maitland of Thirlestane (S 1590), Viscount of Lauderdale (S 1616), Viscount Maitland, and Lord Thirlestane and Boltoun (both S 1624); s of Rev Hon Sydney George William Maitland (d 1946; 2 s of 13 Earl, and gggggg nephew of 2 Earl and 1 Duke of Lauderdale, (the 'L' of Charles II's acronymic CABAL); suc bro, 16 Earl, 1968; f of Lady Olga Maitland, the soc (*see* Hay, Lady Olga); *b* 17 Mar 1911; *Educ* Lancing, Brasenose Oxford; *m* 1936, Stanka, da of Prof Milivoje Lozanitch, of Belgrade Univ; 2 s, 2 da; *Heir* s, Master of Lauderdale, Viscount Maitland; *Career* sits as Cons in House of Lords; journalist 1933-, fndr and sometime ed Fleet Street Letter Serv, sometime ed The Whitehall Letter, war corr The Times (Central Europe) 1939-41, News Chronicle (Pacific 1941-43); MP (C) Lanarkshire (Lanark Div) 1951-59 (resigned whip 1956 in protest at withdrawal from Suez); fndr and chm Expanding Cwlth Gp at the House of Commons 1955-59, re-elected chm 1959, chm House of Lords sub-ctee Energy Tport and Res 1974-79; dir Elf Aquitaine UK Hldgs; pres The Church Union 1956-61; memb (emeritus) Coll Guardians Nat Shrine of Our Lady of Walsingham 1955-; FRGS; *Clubs* New (Edinburgh), RSAC (Glasgow); *Style*— The Rt Hon the Earl of Lauderdale; 12 St Vincent St, Edinburgh (☎ 031 556 5692); 10 Ovington Sq, London SW3 (☎ 01 589 7451)

LAUGHARNE, Richard James; s of James Reginald Laugharne of 49 Langdon Rd, Parkstone, Poole, Dorset, and Anne, *née* Hurst; *b* 22 Sept 1949; *Educ* Poole GS, London Univ (BA); *m* 1972, Carol Anne da of David George Odwell of 23 Broadwater Ave, Parkstone, Poole, Dorset; 2 s (Jonathan David b 1980, Nicholas James b 1983); 1 da (Katharine Angela b 1987); *Career* slr: co dir (legal) of Ideal Homes London Ltd (and Southern and Thames) 1985-, Ideal Homes Solent Ltd 1987; *Style*— R J Laugharne; Southern House, Station Approach, Woking, Surrey

LAUGHLAND, (Graham Franklyn) Bruce; QC (1977); s of Andrew Percy Laughland, of Birmingham (d 1962); *b* 18 August 1931; *Educ* King Edward's Sch Birmingham, Ch Ch Oxford; *m* 1969, Victoria Nicola Christina, da of A S Jarman, of Brighton; 1 s; *Career* barr Inner Temple 1958, standing counsel to the Queen's Proctor 1968-; prosecuting counsel to Inland Revenue (Midland & Oxford circuit) 1973-77; a recorder of Crown Ct 1972-; bencher of the Inner Temple 1985; *Style*— Bruce Laughland, Esq, QC; 4 King's Bench Walk, Temple, EC4 (☎ 01 353 3581); 30 Monmouth Rd, London W2 (☎ 01-229-5045)

LAUGHLAND, Hugh William; s of William Laughland (d 1949), and Eleanor Anne Gordon, (*née* Wildow; *b* 20 Dec 1931; *Educ* Ayr Acad, Manchinton Castle Sch, CA, ATII; *m* 24 Aug 1961, Louise Osborne; 1 s (Brian b 1963), 1 da (Tracy b 1966); *Career* Fleet Air Arm 1954-56; dir Scottish Aviation Ltd 1970-75 (joined 1957), chief exec Scottish Universal Investmt 1976-79; dir: Thames Tilling plc 1981-83 (joined 1980), BTR plc 1983-; jt exec chm Euro Assoc; *Recreations* golf, gardening; *Clubs* Caledonian; *Style*— Hugh Laughland, Esq; Staple, Silvertown House, Vincent Square, London SW1P 2DL (☎ 01 834 38481)

LAUGHLAND, Iain Hugh Page; s of Hugh Norman Wilson Laughland (d 1984), and Morag Laughland; *b* 29 Oct 1935; *Educ* Merchiston Castle Sch; *m* 1972, Ann Stewart, da of Andrew Blackwood Stewart Young, of Belhaven, Troon, Ayrshire, Scotland; 1 s (Andrew Iain Stewart b 1965), 1 da (Rosemary Ann b 1963); *Career* 2 Lt 1 Bn Seaforth Highlanders, serv Egypt, Aden, Gibraltar 1955-56; dir press: Coomberlands 1964-68; Benn Pubns Ltd 1977-87, Farm Holiday Guides Ltd 1981-88; 31 Caps Scotland Rugby XV 1960-64; cpt 1965, record 5 wins Middx Sevens; *Recreations* golf; *Clubs* Rye, Caledonian, London Scottish Football; *Style*— Iain Laughland, Esq; Benn Bros Ltd, Sovereign Way, Tonbridge, Kent TN9 1RW (☎ 0732 364422, fax 0732 361534)

LAUGHTON-SCOTT, Rachel Annabel; da of Martin Alfred Butts Bolton, JP, DL, and Margaret Hazel, *née* Kennaway; *b* 24 August 1957; *Educ* Moreton Hall Sch, Univ of Exeter (BA); *m* 5 Sept 1981, Charles Gilbert Foster Laughton-Scott, s of His Hon Edward Hey Laughton-Scott, QC (d 1978); 1 s (Rory Edward b 6 Dec 1986); *Career* publishing dir Reed Publishing Servs 1985-; *Style*— Mrs Rachel Laughton-Scott; Reed Publishing Services, 7-11 St Johns Hill, London SW11 (☎ 01 228 3344)

LAUNDER, Victor Charles; s of Charles Walter Launder (d 1974), of Carisbrooke, IOW, and Millicent Alice, *née* Missen (d 1986); *b* 13 July 1916; *Educ* Newport IW Co Secdy Sch, Southern Coll of Art Portsmouth, Bristol Univ; *m* 23 July 1955, Audrey Ann, da of Thomas Maynard Vowles (d 1973), of Backwell, nr Bristol; 2 da (Susan b 1956, Robina b 1960); *Career* war serv; aircraft prodn engr Saunders-Roe Ltd 1939-45; architect; lectr Southern Coll of Art Portsmouth 1947-59; vice princ Royal West of England Acad Sch of Architecture 1960-64; sr lectr Sch of Architecture Bristol Univ 1964-81; author; numerous book reviews; ARIBA; *Books* Foundations (1972); *Recreations* walking, cycling, archaeology, photography; *Style*— Victor Launder, Esq; 9 Lower Gurnick Road, Newlyn, Penzance TR18 5QN (☎ 0736 64655)

LAURENCE, Dan H; *b* 28 Mar 1920; *Educ* Hofstra Univ (AB), New York Univ (AM); *Career* WWII radar specialist Fifth AF (USA) 1942-45; served: Aust, New Guinea, Philippines; instr of english NY Univ 1967-70 (assoc prof 1962-67); visiting prof: Indiana Univ 1969, Univ of Texas at Austin 1974-75, Tulane Univ (Andrew Mellon prof in humanities) 1981, Univ of BC 1984; visiting fell Inst for Arts and Humanistic Studies Pennsylvania State Univ 1976, adjunct prof of drama Univ of Guelph 1986- (visiting prof 1983); literary and dramatic advsr estate of George Bernard Shaw 1973-, literary advsr Shaw Festival Ontario 1982- (assoc dir 1988-); John Guggenheim Meml fell

1960, 1961 and 1972, Montgomery fell Dartmouth Coll 1982, assoc memb RADA 1979, Hon Phi Beta Kappa 1967; *Books* Henry James: A Bibliography (with Leon Edel 1957, third edn 1981), Bernard Shaw: A Bibliography (1983), A Portrait of The Author as a Bibliography (1983), Collected Letters of Bernard Shaw (ed of vols 1965, 1972, 1985, 1988), Bernard Shaw Collected Plays with their Prefaces (ed 7 vols 1970-74), Shaw on Dickens (with Martin Quinn 1985); *Style*— Dan Laurence, Esq; The Shaw Festival, Box 774, Niagara-on-the-Lake, Ontario, Canada LOS 1JO (☎ 416 468 2153, fax 416 468 7861)

LAURENCE, John Kellock; TD (1946); s of Robert Peter Gow Laurence (d 1956), and Janetta Maclean, *née* Kellock (d 1939); *b* 8 Oct 1913; *Educ* George Watson's Boys Coll, Edinburgh Univ (BL); *m* 11 Dec 1940, Mary, da of Bartholomew Davison (d 1960); 3 da (Katherine Patricia Ivens, Veronica Gail Trenchard, Pamela Rosamund Morgan); *Career* Capt RA; served: Western Desert, Sicily, Europe; CA, sr ptnr Hays Allan 1976-83; chm: Dencora plc 1981-, KLP plc 1983-; *Recreations* walking, gardening; *Clubs* Caledonian, London Scottish RFC; *Style*— John Laurence, Esq; Cardross House, Church Rd, Ham Common, Richmond TW10 5HG (☎ 01 940 8708)

LAURENCE, Michael; s of Jack Laurence, MBE (d 1960), of 31 Deansway, London N2, and Eveleen, *née* Lewis (d 1988); *b* 18 June 1930; *Educ* Stonyhurst, St Mary's Hosp Med Sch, Univ of London (MB, BS); *m* 12 Sept 1967, Parvin, da of Jamshid Faruhar (d 1969), of Iran; 1 s (Arian b 1968), 2 da (Nicola b 1970, Hotessa b 1973); *Career* RAMC Capt specialist aneasthetics MELF 1955-57; orthopaedic surgn and conslt: Guy's Hosp 1970- (St Olve's Hosp, New Cross Hosp, Lewisham Hosp), Hosp of St John and St Elizabeth; conslt orthopaedic surgn: Hammersmith Hosp 1968-70, Royal Nat Orthop Hosp Stanmore 1968-70; sr lectr inst of orthopaedics London Univ 1968-70, lectr Dept of Surgery Royal Post Graduate Med Sch 1968-70, chm med staff ctee Hosp of St John & St Elizabeth 1982-88; author of many articles papers and chapters in books on the subject of Reconstuctive Joint Surgery in Chronic Arthritis; FRCS; *Recreations* sailing, golf; *Clubs* Island Sailing (Cowes); *Style*— Michael Laurence, Esq; 2 Lyndhurst Terrace, Hampstead NW3 5QA; Billingham Manor, nr Newport IoW PO30 3HE; 106 Harley St, W1N 1AF (☎ 01 486 3131)

LAURENCE, Sir Peter Harold; KCMG (1981, CMG 1976), MC (1944); s of Ven George Laurence (d 1954); *b* 18 Feb 1923; *Educ* Radley, Ch Ch Oxford; *m* 1948, Elizabeth Aïda, da of H C B Way; 2 s, 1 da; *Career* diplomat; political advsr Berlin 1967-69; visiting fell All Souls Coll Oxford 1969-70, cnsllr (commercial) Paris 1970-74; chief inspr Dip Serv 1974-78; ambass Ankara 1980-83, ret; chm: Br Inst of Archaeology at Ankara 1984-, Community Cncl of Devon 1986-, fell Woodard Corpn, chm of govrs Grenville Coll Bideford 1988-; *Clubs* Army and Navy; *Style*— Sir Peter Laurence, KCMG, MC; Trevilla, Beaford, Winkleigh, N Devon EX19 8NS

LAURENSON, James Tait; s of James Tait Laurenson (d 1986), of Seal, Kent, and Vera Dorothy, *née* Kidd (d 1968); *b* 15 Mar 1941; *Educ* Eton, Magdalene Coll Cambridge (MA); *m* 13 Sept 1969, Hilary Josephine, da of Alfred Howard Thompson, DFC, of Eweside House, Cockburnspath, Berwickshire; 1 s (Fergus b 1976); 3 da (Emily b 1972, Marianne b 1974, Camilla b 1978); *Career* banker: dep chm and md Adam & Co Gp plc 1983- formerly Ivory & Sime, investmt managers - joined 1968, partner 1970, dir 1975-83; chm: Tayburn Design Gp 1983; dir: United Scientific Hldgs plc 1971, Japan Assets Tst plc 1983, First Charlotte Assets Tst plc 1983, chm: Nippon Assets Investments SA 1984; Freeman of City of Edinburgh; Memb Court Worshipful Co of Merchants of City of Edinburgh; FCA 1968; *Recreations* tennis, gardening, skiing, shooting, stalking; *Clubs* New (Edinburgh); *Style*— James Laurenson, Esq; Hill House, Kirknewton, Midlothian EH27 8DR (☎ 0506 881990); 22 Charlotte Square, Edinburgh EH2 4DF (☎ 031 225 8484, fax 031 225 5136)

LAURENT, Hon Mrs (Isabelle); da of Baron Lever of Manchester, PC and his 2 w Diane, *née* Bashi; *m* 17 Sept 1988, Dr Antony Laurent (as Antione Laurent author of Cuisine Novelle), er s of the late Jacques Condou and Mme Jacques Bertheau; *Style*— The Hon Mrs Laurent; c/o The Rt Hon Lord Lever of Manchester, House of Lords, London SW1

LAURIE, Sir (Robert) Bayley Emilius; 7 Bt (UK 1834), of Bedford Sq, Middlesex; s of Maj-Gen Sir John Emilius Laurie, 6 Bt, CBE, DSO (d 1983), and Evelyn, Lady Laurie (d 1987); *b* 8 Mar 1931; *Educ* Eton; *m* 1968, Laurelie Meriol Winifreda, da of Sir Reginald Lawrence William Williams (d 1971), 7 Bt, MBE, ED; 2 da (Clare b 1974, Serena b 1976); *Heir* kinsman, Andrew Ronald Emilius Laurie b 1944; *Career* Capt 11 Bn Seaforth Highlanders (TA) 1951-67; Samson Menzies Ltd 1951-58, CT Bowring & Co Ltd 1958-88, dir CT Bowring (Underwriting Agencies) Ltd 1967-83, chm Bowring Membs Agency Ltd 1983-88, dir Murray Lawrence Membs Agency Ltd 1988-; elected memb Lloyd's 1955; *Style*— Sir Bayley Laurie, Bt; The Old Rectory, Little Tey, Colchester, Essex (☎ 0206 210410)

LAURIE, Lt-Col David Alexander St George; OBE (1960), MC (1942); s of Brig Sir Percy Laurie, KCVO, CBE, DSO, JP (d 1962) and Ethel Frances Lawson-Johnston; *b* 30 Mar 1918; *Educ* Canford Sch; *m* 1949 (m dis 1971), Tessa, da of John Gilroy; m 2, 1974, Margaret, da of Col Fitz Hardinge Hancock of Congham Hall, Norfolk; 2 s (Peter b 1951, Nigel b 1962); 1 da (Amanda b 1955); *Career* 1937 2 Lt 9 Queens Royal Lancers, BEF 1939, N Africa 8 Army 1941, Maj 1942, Italy 1944, Palestine 1946, Italy Col Cmdg 1958-60, Cmdt RAC Tactical Sch 1960-62; Gentleman of the Hon Corps of Gentlemen at Arms 1968; Freeman The Worshipful Co of: Saddlers 1964, Merchant Taylors 1985; memb: The Wine Guild of the UK 1975, The Pilgrims 1983; *Recreations* shooting, hunting, polo; *Clubs* Buck's, Pratt's; *Style*— Lt Col D A St G Laurie, OBE, MC; 38 Cadogan Lane, London SW1 (☎ 01 235 2803); Baker's Shaw, Goring Heath, Oxon (☎ 07357 2650)

LAURIE, Richard Thomas; s of Thomas Werner Laurie (d 1944), of 9 Lytton Gro, Putney, London, SW15, and Elizabeth Mary Beatrice, *née* Blackshaw (d 1967); *b* 4 Oct 1935; *Educ* Bradfield Coll; *m* 29 June 1959 (m dis), Susan, da of John Dring, OBE of Fakenham, Norfolk; 2 s (Daniel b 1959, Thomas b 1963), 1 da (Sophie b 1961); *Career* Nat Serv RASC 1954-56 2 Lt; creative dir Brockie Haslam Advertising 1970-81, creative dir and princ Breen Bryan Laurie and Dempsey Advertising 1985-, cncl memb UK Advertising Creative Circle 1982-; memb: of exec ctee Soho Soc 1977-, ed Soho Clarion 1977-; memb of Inst Practitioners in Advertising 1972-81; *Recreations* musician, bandleading, book collecting, magazine editing; *Style*— Richard T Laurie, Esq; 27 Clarendon Drive, Putney, London, SW15 1AW (☎ 01 788 2780); BBL and D, 199 Knightsbridge, London, SW7 1RP (☎ 01 225 1081, fax 589 3247, telex 9419672)

LAURIE, Capt Robert Peter; JP (1974), DL (1979); s of Col Vernon Stewart Laurie, CBE, TD, DL (d 1981), of The Old Vicarage, S Weald, Brentwood, Essex (*see* Burke's Landed Gentry 18th Edn, vol iii), and Mary, 2 da of late Selwyn Robert Pryor, of Plaw Hatch, Bishop's Stortford, Essex; *b* 20 August 1925; *Educ* Eton; *m* 26 Nov 1952, Oonagh Margaret Faber, da of late William Preston Wild, of Warcop Hall, Westmorland; 3 s (Ranald Martin b 1956, Benjamin William b 1959, Andrew Robert b 1963), 1 da (Marian Doone b 1955); *Career* Coldstream Gds 1943-47 (hon Capt); farmer; memb Stock Exchange 1953-87; ptnr Heseltine Powell & Co (then Heseltin Moss & Co) 1953-80; conslt 1980-85; dir Br Empire Securities & Gen Tst plc 1954- (chm 1973-84); govr: Brentwood Sch 1974-, Alleyn's Sch 1984-; chm Essex Assoc of Boys Clubs 1977-86 (pres 1986-), a vice pres Nat Assoc of Boys Clubs 1986-, pres Essex Agric Soc 1986-87; High Sheriff of Essex 1978-79, Vice-Lord Lieut 1958-; chm Essex Co Ctee TAVRA 1987-, cncl memb CGLI 1984-; Master Worshipful Co of Saddlers 1981-82; *Recreations* foxhunting, gardening, reading, attempting to behave; *Clubs* City Livery; *Style*— Capt Robert P Laurie, JP, DL; Heatley's, Ingrave, Brentwood, Essex (☎ 0277 810224)

LAURISTON, His Hon Judge Alexander Clifford; QC (1972); s of Alexander Lauriston, MBE (d 1960); *b* 2 Oct 1927; *Educ* Coatham Sch Redcar, Trinity Coll Cambridge; *m* 1954, Inga Louise, da of E Gregor (d 1987), of Tunbridge Wells; 2 da; *Career* barr Inner Temple 1952, rec Crown Ct 1972-76, circuit judge 1976-; Freeman: City of London 1969, Worshipful Co of Loriners 1969; *Clubs* Berkshire GC, Utd Oxford and Cambridge; *Style*— His Hon Judge Lauriston, QC; 2 Harcourt Buildings, Temple, London EC4

LAURITZEN, Lady Rose Deirdre Margaret; *née* Keppel; raised to rank of an Earl's da 1980; da of Viscount Bury (d 1968), and gda of 9 Earl of Albemarle, MC (d 1979); *b* 11 Dec 1943; *Educ* Heathfield; *m* 1975, Peter Lathrop Lauritzen, s of George Lauritzen, of Chicago; 1 s (Frederick Alexander Mark); *Style*— Lady Rose Lauritzen; Palazzo Da Silva, Cannaregio 1468, Venice, Italy (☎ 715006)

LAUTERPACHT, Elihu; QC (1970); s of Sir Hersch Lauterpacht, QC (d 1960), and Rachel, *née* Steinberg; *b* 13 July 1928; *Educ* Harrow, Trinity Coll Cambridge (MA, LLM); *m* 1, 1955, Judith Maria (d 1970), er da of Harold Hettinger; 1 s (Michael), 2 da (Deborah, Gabriel); m 2, 1973, Catherine Josephine, da of Francis Daly (d 1960); 1 s (Conan b 1980); *Career* bencher Gray's Inn 1983; reader in int law & dir Res Centre for Int Law Cambridge Univ, judge World Bank Admin Tbnl; *Clubs* Athenaeum; *Style*— Elihu Lauterpacht, Esq, QC; Res Centre for Int Law, 5 Cranmer Rd, Cambridge CB3 5BL (☎ 0223 335358)

LAUTERPACHT, Lady; Rachel; da of Michael Steinberg; *m* 1923, Sir Hersch Lauterpacht, QC, (d 1960); *Style*— Lady Lauterpacht; 1 Essex court, Temple, EC4; 6 Cranmer Rd, Cambridge

LAUTI, Rt Hon Toalipi; PC (1979); *b* 1928; *Educ* St Andrew's Coll NZ, Christchurch Teachers' Training Coll NZ; *m* ; 3 s, 2 da; *Career* first PM Tuvalu 1978-; *Style*— The Rt Hon Toalipi Lauti; Office of the Prime Minister, Funafuti, Tuvalu, SW Pacific

LAVAN, Hon Mr Justice; Hon Sir John Martin; s of M G Lavan, KC (d 1925), and Amy Alice Lavan (d 1925); *b* 5 Sept 1911; *Educ* Aquinas Coll Perth, Xavier Coll Melbourne; *m* 1939, Leith, da of W E Harford; 1 s, 3 da; *Career* private law practice 1934-69, memb Barr's Bd WA 1960-69, justice of Supreme Ct of W Aust 1969-, pres Law Soc WA 1964-66, chm Parole Bd WA 1969-76; KStJ, kt 1981; *Style*— The Hon Mr Justice Lavan; 165 Victoria Ave, Dalkeith, WA 6009, Australia

LAVELLE, Roger Garnett; s of Dr Henry Allman Lavelle (d 1955), and Dr Ewelyn Alice Garnett (d 1986); *b* 23 August 1932; *Educ* Leighton Park, Reading; Trinity Hall Cambridge (BA, LLB); *m* 7 Dec 1956, Gunilla Elsa, da of Prof Hugo Odeberg (d 1973); 3 s (Barnaby b 22 March 1962, Richard b 19 March 1967, Edward b 4 May 1972); 1 da (Katharine b 18 July 1959); *Career* dep sec HM Treasury 1985-; special asst (Common Market) Low Privy Seal 1961-63; private sec Chllr of Exchequer 1965-68; under-sec HM Treasury 1975; *Recreations* shopping, gardening; *Style*— Roger Lavelle, Esq; Parliament Street, London SW1

LAVERICK, Peter Michael; s of Cdr Roy Carpenter, and Joyce Margaret Carpenter; *b* 7 June 1942; *Educ* Canford Sch, Sch of Law; *m* 26 Feb 1972, Elaine Ruth, da of Leopold Steckler; 2 da (Helen Tanya b 1973, Elise Mary b 1975); *Career* Capt GS (attached Coldstream Guards) 1968-71; slr 1966, Notary public 1985, ptnr Bellamy Knights & Griffin Worthing; *Recreations* sailing & skiing, former tideway oarsman; *Clubs* RORC, Island Sailing, Ski Club of GB, Martlake Angliaux Boat; *Style*— Peter M Laverick, Esq; North Barn, Poling, W Sussex (☎ (0903) 883205); 23 Warwick Street, Worthing, W Sussex (☎ 0903 210781, fax 0903 37625)

LAVIES, Brig (Austin) Peter; CBE 1959 (OBE 1948); s of Dr Harry Brandreth Lavies, MD (d 1924), of 45 Belgrave Rd, London, and Bridget Edith Alberta *née* Gardiner (d 1959); *b* 3 May 1911; *Educ* Wellington Coll, RMA Woolwich, Clare Coll Cambridge (MA); *m* 4 July 1947, Caroline Joan, da of Vice-Adm Herbert Arthur Buchanan-Wollaston, CMG, RN (d 1975); 2 s (Peter Robin b 1949, Nicholas George b 1951); *Career* RE 1931-64, (Brig) India and Burma; *Recreations* gardening; *Style*— Brig Austin Lavies, CBE; Church Cottage, West Hill, Ottery St Mary, Devon EX11 1UW

LAVIN, Deborah Margaret; da of George E Lavin (d 1987), of Johannesburg, SA, and Laura Kathleen Lavin (d 1987); *b* 22 Sept 1939; *Educ* Roedean Sch Johannesburg SA, Rhodes Univ Grahamstowe SA, Lady Margaret Hall Oxford (BA, Dip Ed, MA); *Career* lectr dept of history Univ of Witwatersrand SA 1962-64, lectr then sr lectr dept of history Queens Univ Belfast 1965-80, princ Trevelyan Coll Univ of Durham 1980-; *Clubs* Royal Cwlth Soc; *Style*— Miss Deborah Lavin; Hickmans Cottages, Cat St, East Hendred, Wantage, Oxon OX12 8JT; Trevelyan College, University of Durham, Elvet Hill Road, Durham DH1 3LN (☎ 091 374 3761)

LAVINGTON, His Hon (Cyril) Michael; MBE (1940), JP (Cornwall 1974); s of Cyril Claude Lavington, of Bristol; *b* 21 June 1912; *m* 1950, Frances Anne (m dis 1968), da of Colson Wintle, MD, JP; MB; 1 s (Peregrine); *Career* served WWII 1939-45 (despatches twice); barr Middle Temple 1936, Western circuit, rec of Barnstaple 1964-71, former dep chm Dorset Wilts and Hants QS; a co ct judge (Circuit 54 1971-72, circuit judge 1972-83), hon rec of Barnstable; *Style*— His Hon Michael Lavington, MBE, JP; 182 St Stephen's Rd, Saltash, Cornwall PL12 4NJ (☎ 0752 843204)

LAVINGTON, Michael Richard; s of Richard Lavington; *b* 21 Feb 1943; *Educ* Whitgift, Cambridge, Columbia Univ New York, Lancaster Univ (BA, MA, PhD); *m* 1966, Clarie June, da of James Watford; 2 da (Susan b 1969, Victoria b 1970); *Career* pres Black Starr & Frost (New York), Kay Jewellers (Alexandria Va); dir: Bowater-Ralli America (1971-74), Ralli Australia (1970-71); *Recreations* theatre, chess, bridge, travel; *Style*— Dr Michael R Lavington; 501 South Fairfax St, Alexandria, Va 22314, USA (☎ business (703) 683 3800)

LAW, Hon Andrew Bonar; s of 1 Baron Coleraine, PC (decd); *b* 1933; *Educ* Rugby, Trinity Coll, Dublin; *m* 1961, Joanna Margarette, da of Raymond Neill, of Fairview, Delgany, Co Wicklow, Ireland; 1 s (Richard Pitcairn Bonar b 1963), 1 da (Charlotte Mary de Montmorency b 1964); *Books* various books on Irish Cartography; *Style—* The Hon Andrew Law; Shankill Castle, Shankill, Co Dublin, Ireland

LAW, Anthony John; s of Victor Frank Law, of London, and Hilda Ellen, *née* Whitaker; *b* 19 April 1940; *Educ* Christ's Coll Blackheath; *m* 18 July 1970, Pamela Ann, da of Stuart Nelson Middleton; 2 da (Alexandra Michelle Jane b 7 Feb 1978, Nicola Anne-Marie b 28 May 1980); *Career* publisher Apollo Magazine, The Int Magazine (art and antiques); chm bd of govrs Christ's Coll Blackheath; memb Inst of Journalists; *Clubs* Rugby; *Style—* Anthony Law, Esq; 10 Strathmore Close, Caterham, Surrey CR3 5EQ (☎ 0883 48082); Apollo Magazine Ltd, 22 Davies Street, London W1Y 1LH (☎ 01 629 3061, fax 01 491 8752)

LAW, Hon Cecil Towry Henry; s of 7 Baron Ellenborough, MC (d 1945); *b* 1931; *Educ* Eton; *m* 1957, (Daphne Mary) Jean, da of Hon Laurence Paul Methuen (d 1970); 1 s, 3 da; *Career* Lt 1 King's Dragoon Gds 1950-52; Lloyd's insur broker 1952; chm Towry Law (Hldgs) Ltd 1958-, and other companies; *Style—* The Hon Cecil Law; 6 Sussex Sq, London W2 2SJ; Towry Law (Holdings) Ltd, Towry Law House, High St, Windsor, Berks SL4 1LX

LAW, Hon Charles Adrian Christian Towry; s of 8 Baron Ellenborough; *b* 7 Nov 1960; *Style—* The Hon Charles Law

LAW, Charles Ewan; s of Robert Charles Ewan Law, DSO, DFC (ret Gp Capt), of Constantine Bay, Cornwall, and Norah, *née* Eaden; *b* 12 August 1946; *Educ* Wrekin Coll, Nottingham Univ (BSc), Manchester Business Sch (MBA); *m* 5 Sept 1970, Clodagh Susan Margaret, da of Lt-Col Eric Steele-Baume, MBE (d 1968); 2 (Huw b 1974, Henry b 1980), 1 da (Angharad b 1972); *Career* metallurgist BSC 1969-71, mangr Utd Int Bank 1973-79, vice-pres Merrill Lynch Inst Bank 1979-81, exec dir First Interstate Ltd 1984-87, non-exec dir Continental Illinois Ltd 1987- (exec dir 1981-84), md Continental Bank 1988-; *Recreations* sailing, theatre; *Clubs* RAC; *Style—* Charles Law, Esq; 162 Queen Victoria St, London EC4V 4BS (☎ 01 860 5153, fax 01 236 3099, telex 946246)

LAW, David Charles; s of Charles Law, of 50 Savage Lane, Sheffield (d 1975), and Florence Gladys Wainwright; *b* 9 Sept 1930; *Educ* King Edward VII Sheffield, BNC Oxford (MA); *m* 25 Jan 1956, Mary, da of Joseph William Senior, of Sheffield (d 1967); 1 s (Richard b 1962), 1 da (Sally b 1956); *Career* slr, sr ptnr David Law & Co Sheffield, exec chm Hallamshire Electric Co Ltd 1972-78; dir: Wigfalls plc 1983-85, Mirenhill Ltd 1985, Gilleyfield Investmts Ltd 1960-, The Chris Fund Ltd 1980-; hon consul for Belgium in Sheffield; sporting records: Oxford full blues track & cross county, Univ 3 Mile and cross-country record, UAU 1 mile champion 1952, world student 1500 m champion 1953, world record 4 x 1500 m relay champion 1953, Br Cwlth record 4 x 1 mile relay, 1 mile finalist BR Empire games 1954; *Recreations* golf, skiing, shooting; *Clubs* Sheffield, Abbeydale Golf, Abersoch Golf; *Style—* David Law, Esq; Dore Lodge, 79 Dore Rd, Sheffield S17 3ND (☎ 0742 366401); David Law & Co Telegraph House, High St, Sheffield S1 1PT (☎ 0742 700 999, telex 54317, fax 0742 739 292, car 0836 250 893)

LAW, Hon Edmund Ivor Cecil; 2 s of 8 Baron Ellenborough; *b* 21 Dec 1956; *m* 1982, Susan, er da of Derek Baker, of 5 Jermyn Close, Cambridge; 2 s (David Chrisotpher b 1984, John Christian b 1986); *Style—* The Hon Edmund Law; 20 Collins Meadow, Hortan, Essex

LAW, George Llewellyn; s of George Edward Law, MC (d 1974), of Maplehurst, Sussex, and Margaret Dorothy, *née* Evans, OBE (d 1980); *b* 8 July 1929; *Educ* Westminster, Clare Coll Cambridge (BA); *m* 26 March 1960, Anne Stewart, da of Arthur Adolphus Wilkinson (d 1974), of Chelsea, London; 1 da (Jane b 1962); *Career* Nat Serv RCS 1948-49; ptnr Slaughter and May (slrs) 1961-67 (joined 1952); exec dir: Morgan Grenfell & Co Ltd 1968-, Morgan Grenfell Gp plc 1971- (vice chm 1987); memb: City of London Slrs Co, The Law Soc; FRSA; *Recreations* opera, ballet, classical music, theatre, art, art history; *Clubs* Brooks's, MCC; *Style—* George Law, Esq; 6 Phillimore Gdns Cl, London W8 7QA (☎ 01 937 3061); Gainsborough Cottage, Cley-next-the-Sea, Holt, Norfolk; 23 Great Winchester St, London EC2P 2AX (☎ 01 588 4545, fax 01 588 5598, telex 8953511 MGLDN G)

LAW, Gordon Malcolm; s of Robert Law, of Sheffield, and Elizabeth Black, *née* Cassells; *b* 7 Nov 1932; *Educ* King Edward VII GS Sheffield, Univ of Sheffield (BA); *m* 31 Aug 1957, Elaine, da of Thomas Whittingham (d 1942); 3 da (Helen b 15 Nov 1959, Mary b 4 Feb 1961, Charlotte b 12 Oct 1965); *Career* Nat Serv 12 Royal Lancers (POW) 1955-57; staff offr Jessop-Saville Ltd Sheffield 1960-62 (graduate trainee 1957-60), gp estab offr Shepherd Bldg Gp Ltd York 1965-70 (personnel offr 1962-65), gen mangr (personnel and trg) Woolwich Equitable Bldg Soc 1976- (personnel mangr 1970-72, asst gen mangr personnel 1972-76); cncl memb: Nat Interactive Video Centre, Nat Cncl for Educnl Technol, Chartered Bldg Socs Inst (CBSI), memb: educn ctee, corporate planning, trg agency learning advsy gp, York Tourist Advsy Bd 1968-70, York Crime Prevention Ctee 1967-70; govr Thames Poly (chm ct of govrs 1985-88), pres York Jr C of C; Freeman City of London, Liveryman Worshipful Co of Distillers; hon FCBSI 1977, hon FBIM 1975, FIPM 1960; *Books* Personnel Policy and Line Management (1974, revised 1983); *Recreations* golf, philately; *Clubs* City Livery, W Kent GC; *Style—* Gordon Law, Esq; 6 Hawthorne Close, Bickley, Bromley, Kent BR1 2HJ (☎ car 0836 231410); Woolwich Equitable Building Soc, Equitable House, Woolwich, London SE18 6AB (☎ 01 467 3861, 01 854 2400, fax 01 316 4204)

LAW, Adm Sir Horace Rochfort; GCB (1972, KCB 1967, CB 1963), OBE (1951), DSC (1941); s of Dr Samuel Horace Law, FRICS, MD (d 1940), of Dublin, and Sybil Mary, *née* Clay; *b* 23 June 1911; *Educ* Sherborne; *m* 13 Dec 1941, Heather Valerie, da of Rev Henry Haworth Coryton (d 1952); 2 s (Robert b 1946, Edward b 1952), 2 da (Philippa b 1942, Deborah b 1948); *Career* joined RN 1929; CO: HMS Duchess 1952, HMS Centaur 1958; Capt Britannia RNC Dartmouth 1960; Rear Adm, Flag Offr Sea Trg 1962, Submarines 1963; Vice Adm Controller of the Navy 1965-70; Adm, C-in-C Naval Home Cmd and First and Princ Naval ADC to HM The Queen 1970-72; ret 1972; chm Hawthorn Leslie 1973-81; pres RINA 1979-81; chm Church Army Bd 1979-86; pres offr Christian Union 1970-86; chm Agnes Weston's Royal Sailors Rest 1958-85; Order of William of Orange 1 cl (Netherlands) 1972; *Style—* Admiral Sir Horace Law, GCB, OBE, DSC; Cowpers, West Harting, Petersfield, Hants (☎ 073 085 511)

LAW, James; QC (Scotland 1970); s of George Law (d 1961), and Isabella Rebecca Law, *née* Lamb (d 1985); *b* 7 June 1926; *Educ* Kilmarnock Acad, Girvan HS, Glasgow Univ (MA, LLB); *m* 1956, Kathleen Margaret, da of Alexander Gibson (d 1984); 2 s (George, Bruce), 1 da (Catriona); *Career* advocate dep 1957-64, memb Criminal Injuries Compensation Bd 1970-, chm Temp Sheriffs' Assoc 1975-; *Clubs* New (Edinburgh), Caledonian (Edinburgh); *Style—* James Law, Esq, QC; 7 Gloucester Place, Edinburgh EH3 6EE (☎ 031 225 2974); Advocates Library, Edinburgh EH1 1RF (☎ 031 226 5071)

LAW, Laurence Arthur; s of Frederick Charles Law, of 29 Jedburgh Gardens, Newcastle upon Tyne and Lilian Boland; *b* 2 June 1937; *Educ* Rutherford GS Newcastle, Open Univ (BA); *m* 1963, Orray; 2 s (Keith b 1965, Anthony b 1968), 2 da (Julie b 1964, Helen b 1970); *Career* div dir Alexander Stenhouse UK Ltd (dir 1974-), pres Newcastle upon Tyne Chartered Insur Inst 1980-81, chm Br Insur Brokers Assoc Northern Region 1981-82; *Recreations* choral singing, music, badminton; *Style—* L A Law, Esq; Alexander Stenhouse UK Ltd, 230 High St, Potters Bar, Herts EN6 5BU (☎ 0707 51222, telex 2987785, fax 0707 46092)

LAW, Capt Hon Rupert Edward Henry; s and h of 8 Baron Ellenborough; *b* 28 Mar 1955; *Educ* Eton; *m* 1981, Hon Grania Boardman, only da of Baron Boardman (Life Peer); 1 s (James Rupert Thomas b 8 March 1983), 1 da (Georgina b 16 Dec 1984); *Career* Maj Coldstream Gds until 1988; Coutts and Co 1988-; *Style—* The Hon Rupert Law; Castle Cottage, 14 Castle Rd, Lavendon, nr Olney, Bucks MK46 4JD (☎ 0234 712639)

LAW-SMITH, Sir (Richard) Robert; CBE (1965), AFC (1943); s of Walter Henry Law-Smith and Agnes Giles (d 1975); *b* 9 July 1914; *Educ* St Edward's Sch Oxford, Adelaide Univ; *m* 1941, Joan, da of Harold Gordon Darling (d 1950); 1 s (decd), 2 da; *Career* chm Aust Nat Airlines Cmmn 1979- (cmmr 1962); dir: Cwlth Aircraft Corpn Ltd 1965-, Blue Circle Southern Cement Ltd 1974-; chm TAA: Chase-NBA Gp Ltd 1980-; kt 1980; *see Debrett's Handbook of Australia and New Zealand for further details*; *Style—* Sir Robert Law-Smith, CBE, AFC; Bolobek, Macedon, Vic 3440, Australia

LAWES, Sir (John) Michael Bennet; 5 Bt; s of Sir John Claude Bennet Lawes, 4 Bt (d 1979); *b* 24 Oct 1932; *Educ* Elizabeth Coll Guernsey; *Style—* Sir Michael Lawes, Bt; c/o Barclays Bank, Lymington, Hants

LAWLER, Geoffrey John; s of Maj Ernest Lawler and Enid Florence Lawler, of Richmond, N Yorks; *b* 30 Oct 1954; *Educ* Colchester Royal GS, Richmond Sch, Hull Univ (BSc); *Career* PR exec 1982-83, dir PR Co 1983, conslt with own PR Co 1987-, vice pres Int Access Inc 1987-; MP (C) Bradford North 1983-87; pres: Hull Univ Students' Union 1976-77, Br Youth Cncl 1984-87, memb cncl UKIAS; *Recreations* cricket, travel; *Style—* Geoffrey Lawler, Esq; Club Centre, Westfield Rd, Leeds LS3 1NQ

LAWLER, Sir Peter James; OBE (1965); *Career* memb Cncl of Order of Aust and Aust Decorations Advsy Ctee, dep sec PM's Dept 1964-72; sec: Dept of Special Min of State 1973-75, Dept of Admin Services 1975-; kt 1981; *Style—* Sir Peter Lawler, OBE; 6 Tennyson Cres, Forrest, ACT 2603, Australia

LAWLOR, Prof John James; s of Albert John Lawlor (d 1938), and Teresa Anne Clare, *née* Knight (d 1954); *b* 5 Jan 1918; *Educ* Ryders Sch, Magdalen Coll Oxford (BA, MA, DLitt); *m* 1, 26 April 1941 (m dis 1979), Thelma Joan, da of Charles Edward Parkes Weeks (d 1964); 1 s (John b 1954), 3 da (Teresa Anne (Mrs Ribgy) b 1945, Judith Mary (Mrs Griffiths) b 1947, Penelope Jane (Mrs Jeffrey) b 1949); m 2, 7 Nov 1984, Prof Kimie Imura, *née* Fukuda; *Career* WW11 The Devonshire Regt 1940-45, cmmnd 1941, Capt 1942-45; asst chief instr Artists' Rifles OCtU 1943-44, serv in Italy with Royal West Kent and Hamps Regts 1944-45, mil govt Austria 1945; lectr in english Brasenose and Trinity Colls Oxford 1947-50, univ lectr in english lit 1949-50, prof english lang and lit Univ of Keele 1950-80, fell Folger Shakespeare Library Washington DC 1962, Ziskind visiting prof Brandeis Univ USA 1966, vis prof Univ Hawaii 1972; pres N Staffs Drama Assoc 1955-72, jt sec advsy ctee for adult educn N Staffs 1957-60; sec gen and tres Int Assoc of Univ Profs of English 1971-; FSA 1966; *Books* The Tragic Sense in Shakespeare (1960), Piers Plowman: An Essay in Criticism (1962), Patterns of Love and Courtesy (1966), To Nevill Coghill From Friends (with W H Auden, 1966); *Recreations* any sort of seafaring; *Clubs* Athenaeum; *Style—* Prof John Lawlor; Penwithian, Higher Fore St, Marazion, Cwll (☎ 0736 711 180); 5-19-7 Arai, Nakano-Ku, Toyko 165 (☎ 03 389 3633)

LAWLOR, Thomas Francis Christopher; s of Thomas Francis Lawlor (d 1976), of Dublin, Rep of Ireland, and Elizebeth Hendrick Lawlor; *b* 17 June 1938; *Educ* Christian Brothers Sch Dublin, Univ Coll Dublin (BA); *m* 1, 21 Sept 1963, Marcia (d 1969), da of late William Carew, of Dublin; m 2, 2 Aug 1971 (m dis 1981), Pauline, da of late Francis Wales, of Stockton-on-Tees; 1 da (Frances b 19 Jan 1971); m 3, 21 June 1982, Ghislaine Ruby Solange, da of Joseph Raymond Labour, of Beau Basin, Mauritius; *Career* bass-baritone opera singer; has sung over 60 operatic roles 1963-71, princ baritone D'Oyly Carte Opera Co touring USA and Canada 1964 1966 1968; debut: Glyndebourne 1971, Kent Opera and Royal Opera House 1972, Opera North 1979, ENO 1975; also performed with New Sadlers Wells Opera, Central City Opera Festival USA 1968, Prom concerts 1968 and 1988, Carnegie Hall NY 1976-86, Singapore Festival of the Arts 1988, Valencia Festival 1988; memb Lions Int, pres Wharfedale Lions Club 1983-84; Hon Citizen Central City Colorado (USA, 1968); *Clubs* Nat Univ of Ireland (London); *Style—* Thomas Lawlor, Esq; 31 Bridge La, Ilkley, W Yorks (☎ 0943 608 913)

LAWRANCE, (June) Cynthia; da of Albert Isherwood Emmett (d 1986), and Ida Emmett; *b* 3 June 1933; *Educ* 9 Schs (Wartime), St Annes Coll Oxford (BA, MA); *m* 27 Jun 1957, Rev David Lawrance, s of David Lawrance; 3 da (Elizabeth b 1958, Mary b 1960, Ruth b 1963); *Career* teacher: Inst Britannique Univ de Paris 1954-57, Br Cncl Cyprus 1957-58, Ahlyyah Sch Amman Jordan 1958-61, Counthill GS Oldham 1962-64; dep headmistress Chadderton GS for Girls 1965-70, headmistress: Broughton HS 1970-74, Harrogate Ladies Coll 1974-; SHA, NAHT, GSA; *Recreations* music, chess, French literature; *Style—* Mrs Cynthia Lawrance; 21 Clarence Drive, Harrogate HG1 2QE (☎ 0423 504050); 5 Cavendish Mansions, Mill Lane, Hampstead, London NW6 1TE;Harrogate Ladies College, Clarence Drive, Harrogate, North Yorkshire HG1 2QG (☎ 0423 504543)

LAWRENCE, Hon Mrs (Christine) Alexandra Canning; da of 5 Baron Garvagh; *b* 20 Sept 1949; *Educ* RNS Haslemere, Guildford Tech Coll; *m* 1971, (m dis 1987), Louis David Lawrence; 2 s (Stafford, Lucas); *Career* arts admin; *Style—* The Hon Mrs

Lawrence; 4 Artesian Rd, London W11

LAWRENCE, Barclay Ronald; s of Ronald George Lawrence, of Norwich, Norfolk, and Beryl Lawrence; *b* 1 Feb 1948; *Educ* Stowe, Univ de Dijon, Univ of Buckingham Univ (BA); *Career* property conslt; *Recreations* racing, cricket, Eton Fives; *Clubs* MCC; *Style*— Barclay Lawrence, Esq; 5 Park Steps, St George's Fields, London W2 2YQ

LAWRENCE, Hon Catherine Dorina Mary; da of 3 Baron Lawrence (d 1947); *b* 1910; *Style*— The Hon Catherine Lawrence; 14 Juxon Close, Chichester, Sussex

LAWRENCE, Christopher Nigel; s of Rev William Wallace Lawrence (d 1979), and Millicent, *née* Atkinson (d 1983); *b* 23 Dec 1936; *Educ* Westborough HS Westcliff-on-Sea, Central Sch of Arts and Crafts London (NDD); *m* 1958, Valerie Betty; 2 s (Adrian, Robin), 2 da (Fay, Verity); *Career* goldsmith, silversmith and industl designer 1968-; one-man exhibitions: Galerie Jean Renet London 1970-71, Hamburg 1972, Goldsmiths' Hall 1973, Ghent 1975, Hasselt 1977; maj cmmns: Br Govt, city livery cos, banks, mfrg cos; judge and external assessor for art colls, specialist in symbolic presentation pieces and limited edns of decorative pieces, industl designer to leading mfrs of cutlery and hollow ware, chm Goldsmiths' Craft Cncl 1976-77, Liveryman Worshipful Co of Goldsmiths 1978-; Jacques Cartier Meml Award for Craftsman of the Year 1960, 1963, and 1967 (unique achievement), TV and radio bdcaster; FTC, FIPG; *Recreations* cruising on family's narrow boat, badminton, carpentry; *Style*— Christopher Lawrence, Esq; 20 St Vincent's Rd, Westcliff-on-Sea, Essex SS0 7PR (☎ 0702 338443); 172 London Road, Southend-on-Sea, Essex SS1 1PH (☎ 0702 344897)

LAWRENCE, Clive Wyndham; s of Lt-Col Sir (Percy) Roland (Bradford), MC and hp to Btcy of bro, Sir David (Roland Walter) Lawrence; *b* 6 Oct 1939; *Educ* Gordonstoun; *m* 1966, Sophia Annabel Stuart, da of Ian Hervey Stuart Black; 3 s; *Career* late Lt Coldstream Gds; *Style*— Clive Lawrence, Esq; Woodside, Frant, nr Tunbridge Wells, Kent TN3 9HW

LAWRENCE, 5 Baron (UK 1869); Sir David John Downer Lawrence; 5 Bt (UK 1858); s of 4 Baron (d 1968) by his 1 w, Margaret; *b* 4 Sept 1937; *Educ* Bradfield; *Style*— The Rt Hon the Lord Lawrence; c/o Bird & Bird, 2 Gray's Inn Sq, London WC1

LAWRENCE, Sir David Roland Walter; 3 Bt (UK 1906); s of Lt-Col Sir (Percy) Roland (Bradford) Lawrence, 3 Bt, MC (d 1950); *b* 8 May 1929; *Educ* Radley, RMC; *m* 1955, Audrey (formerly w of 11 Duke of Leeds), da of Brig Desmond Young, CIE, OBE, MC; *Heir* bro, Clive Wyndham Lawrence; *Career* late Capt Coldstream Gds; *Clubs* Cavalry & Guards; *Style*— Sir David Lawrence, Bt; 28 High Town Rd, Maidenhead, Berks

LAWRENCE, Derek Howard; s of Eric Lawrence (d 1940); *b* 11 Oct 1925; *Educ* Bradfield Coll, Exeter Univ, Faraday House; *m* 1952, Ann Margaret, da of James Percival Bristow of Aldeburgh, Suffolk; 3 s, 1 da; *Career* Lt Royal Signals; DFH, CENG, FIMechE, MIEE; *Style*— Derek Lawrence, Esq; 5 Park Ave, Bedford MK40 2JY (☎ 0234 58950)

LAWRENCE, Edward George; s of Capt Edward Sear Lawrence (d 1964), of Southgate, London, and Mrs Ethel May, *née* Lambert; *b* 26 Feb 1927; *Educ* Edmonton Co GS; *Career* dir Lawrence Bros (Tport) Ltd 1949-77 (ret); memb Heraldry Soc 1952-, life govr Royal Soc of St George 1953 (memb exec cncl for eight years) Silver Staff Usher jubilee serv HM Queen Elizabeth II 1977, wandsman St Paul's Cathedral London 1977-88, usher at wedding of TRH The Prince and Princess of Wales 1981; memb ctee Middx Fedn of Old Grammarian Socs 1955-64, asst dir of ceremonies of Most Venerable Order of St John 1980; Freeman City of London 1959; Liveryman: Worshipful Co of: Carmen 1960, Scriveners 1983; AMInstTA 1947, FFCS 1954, FInstD 1955, FRSA 1963; CStJ 1979; *Recreations* heraldry, deipnosophism, ceremonial, official & academic dress; *Clubs* City Livery, Wig & Pen, Inst of Dirs; *Style*— Edward Lawrence, Esq; 77 Prince George Ave, Southgate, London N14

LAWRENCE, Felicity Jane Patricia; da of Prof Clifford Hugh Lawrence, and Helen Maud, *née* Curran; *b* 15 August 1958; *Educ* Ursuline Convent Wimbledon, St Anne's Coll Oxford (BA); *Career* ed New Health Magazine 1984-86; Daily Telegraph plc: ed Sunday Magazine 1986-88, ed Weekend Magazine 1988-, head of devpt magazines 1988-; *Publications* Additives: Your Complete Survival Guide (ed); *Style*— Ms Felicity Lawrence; Daily Telegraph plc, Peterborough Ct, at South Quay, 181 Marsh Wall E14 9SR (☎ 01 538 5000)

LAWRENCE, George Alexander Waldemar; s of Sir Alexander Waldemar Lawrence, 4 Bt and hp of bro, Sir John Waldemar Lawrence, 6 Bt, OBE; *b* 22 Sept 1910; *Educ* Eton, Trinity Cambridge; *m* 1949, Olga, da of Peter Schilovsky; 1 s, 2 da; *Style*— George Lawrence, Esq; Brockham End, Bath

LAWRENCE, Gordon Charles; s of Alfred Charles Lawrence, and Gertrude Emily, *née* Frost; *b* 2 Mar 1931; *Educ* Isleworth GS; *m* 17 July 1954, Barbara Mary Rees, da of Francis Charles Rees Deacon, MBE (d 1983); 2 s (Simon b 1957, Jonathan b 1963), 1 da (Catriona b 1959); *Career* fin conslt; dir of fin Nat Tst 1977-88; dir: Helena Rubinstein Ltd 1970-74, Schreiber Industries Ltd 1967-70; FCA, FCMA, JDip MA; *Recreations* music, sailing; *Style*— Gordon Lawrence, Esq; The Chantry, Bromham, Wilts (☎ 0380 850294)

LAWRENCE, Sir Guy Kempton; DSO (1943), OBE (1945, DFC 1941); s of Albert Edward Lawrence (d 1951); *b* 5 Nov 1914; *Educ* Marlborough; *m* 1947, Marcia Virginia, da of Prof Harold Clark Powell; 2 s, 1 da; *Career* memb Stock Exchange London 1937-45, chm Findus (UK) Ltd 1967-75; dep chm: Spillers French Hldgs Ltd 1972-75, J Lyons & Co Ltd 1950-75; chm Food and Drink Industs Cncl 1973-77, dir Eagle Aircraft Servs Ltd 1977, chm Eggs Authy 1978-81; kt 1976; *Recreations* Br ski team 1937-38, farming, squash, carpentry; *Clubs* RAF; *Style*— Sir Guy Lawrence, DSO, OBE, DFC; Courtlands, Kier Park, Ascot, Berks (☎ 0990 21074)

LAWRENCE, Henry Richard George; s of George Napier Lawrence, OBE (d 1962), of Southsea, Hants, and Margaret Hilda Noel Neave, *née* Breay; *b* 16 April 1946; *Educ* Westminster Abbey Choir Sch; Haileybury; Worcester Coll, Oxford (BA); *Career* music dir Arts Cncl of GB 1983-; music offr Arts Cncl of GB 1973-83; Overseas Dept Ginn 7 Co Ltd, Educnl Publishers 1968-73; London rep, Cheshire Publishing Pty Ltd 1971-73; *Recreations* the good things in life; *Style*— H R G Lawrence, Esq; 105 Piccadilly, London W1V 0AU (☎ 01 629 9495)

LAWRENCE, Prof (Clifford) Hugh; s of Ernest William Lawrence, (d 1956), of London, and Dorothy Estelle, *née* Mundy; *b* 28 Dec 1921; *Educ* Stationers' Co Sch, Lincoln Coll Oxford (BA, MA, D Phil); *m* 11 July 1953, Helen Maud, da of Felix Curran, of Dublin and Yorks; 1 s (Peter), 5 da (Clare, Margaret, Felicity, Katherine, Julia); *Career* 2 Lt RA 1943, Lt 1944, Capt Beds and Herts 1945, Maj 1945-46; lectr in history Bedford Coll Univ of London 1951-62, prof medieval history Univ of London 1970-87 (reader 1962-70), dean Faculty of Arts Bedford Coll 1975-77, head dept of history Bedford Coll 1980-85; author: St Edmund of Abingdon, a study in Hagiography and History (1960), The English Church and the Papacy in the Middle Ages (1965), Medieval Monasticism, Forms of Religious Life in Western Europe in the Middle Ages (1984), 'The University in Church and State' in History of University of Oxford (vol 1, ed J Catto); memb governing body Westfield Coll 1982-86, vice chm of govrs Heythrop Coll 1988- (memb governing body 1980-), memb Press Cncl 1976-80; FR Hist S 1960, FSA 1985; *Recreations* reading, painting, sightseeing; *Style*— Prof Hugh Lawrence; 11 Durham Road, London, SW20 OQH (☎ 01 946 3820)

LAWRENCE, Ivan John; QC (1981), MP (C) Burton 1974-; s of Leslie Lawrence; *b* 24 Dec 1936; *Educ* Brighton, Hove and Sussex GS, Ch Ch Oxford; *m* 1966, Gloria Helene; 1 da; *Career* barr Inner Temple 1962, Se circuit, rec of the Crown Cts 1987; chm: Cons Parly Legal Ctee, Cons Parly Home Affrs Ctee, All-Pty Jt Parly Barrs Gp; memb: Foreign Select Ctee, Cncl of Justice, Exec 1922 Ctee, Exec Cwlth Parly Assoc (Br Branch); *Style*— Ivan Lawrence, Esq, QC, MP; Dunally Cottage, Lower Halliford Green, Shepperton, Middx (☎ 0932 224692); Grove Farm, Drakelow, Burton-on-Trent, Staffs (☎ 44360)

LAWRENCE, Jeffrey; s of Alfred Silver (d 1957), and Sylvia, *née* Fishgold; *b* 28 Mar 1946; *Educ* Carmel Coll, London Business Sch; *m* 8 April 1971, Vivienne Lesley, da of Clifford Arch (d 1987); 2 da (Faith b 1973, Sarah b 1975); *Career* Merrill Lynch: off mangr 1980-84, md corporate fin servs 1984-87, regnl mangr Scandanavia and Netherlands 1987-89; currently md Merrill Lynch Global Asset Mgmnt; memb ctee and Old Age Home; FInstD ; *Recreations* golf, race horse owner; *Clubs* RAC; *Style*— Jeffrey Lawrence, Esq; Moor Land House, Moor Lane, Sarratt, Herts; 99 Park St, London W1 (☎ 01 499 7812)

LAWRENCE, John; OBE (1974); s of William Lawrence (d 1988), and Nellie, *née* Rhoda Smith (d 1975); *b* 22 April 1933; *Educ* Luton GS, Queens' Coll Cambridge (BA, MA), Indiana Univ (MA); *m* 1, 17 Oct 1964 (m dis 1976), Lorraine, da of Charles Edwin Bertram Cooper; m 2, 1 Oct 1988, Khaw Yew-Mei, da of khaw Kai Boh (d 1971); *Career* Nat Serv RAF 1951-53; Br Cncl offr 1961: various HQ appts 1961-65, regnl rep Sabah 1965-68, rep Zambia 1968-73, rep Sudan 1974-76, rep Malaysia 1976-80, controller Asia & Americs div 1982-86 (dep controller 1980-82), rep Brazil 1987-; *Recreations* walking and talking, simultaneously or otherwise; *Style*— John Lawrence, Esq, OBE; 4 Shearman Rd, Blackheath, London SE3; Swinkle House, Longsleddale, Nr Kendal, Cumbria; British Council SCRN 708/9 BLOCO F Nos 143, Brasilia (☎ 272 3060, fax 061 272 3455, telex 061 1859)

LAWRENCE, John Eugene; s of Ernest Eugene Oliver Lawrence (d 1970), of Welbeck, Long Rd, Canvey Is, Essex, and Irene Muriel, *née* Kynoch; *b* 29 April 1927; *Educ* Brentwood Sch; *m* 15 Set 1955, Vera Edna, da of George Henry Bigsby (d 1976), of Wall Rd, Canvey Is, Essex; *Career* cmmnd RASC (T/Capt) 1945-48; chm Canvey Supply Co Ltd 1970-, md Canvey Wharf Co Ltd 1970-; JP (Essex 1966-76); Freeman City of London, Liveryman Worshipful Co of Builders Merchants (1979); FInstB; *Recreations* boating, skiing; *Style*— John Lawrence, Esq, JP; 40 Chapman Road, Canvey Island, Essex SS8 7QS (☎ 0268 682204, fax 0268 696 724)

LAWRENCE, Air Vice-Marshall John Thornett; CB (1975), CBE (1967, OBE 1961, AFC 1945); s of Tom Lewis Lawrence, JP (d 1970), and Beatrice Mary Sollars (d 1977); *b* 16 April 1920; *Educ* The Crypt Sch Gloucester; *m* 2 June 1951, Hilary Jean, da of Lewis Davis Owen (d 1968); 3 s (Patrick b 1952, Christopher b 1955, Andrew b 1959), 1 da (Tessa b 1964); *Career* RAFVR 1938-, WWII Coastal Cmd 235, 202 and 86 Sqdns, dir staff RAF Flying Coll 1949-53, Cc No 14 Sqdn 1953-55, so 2ATAF Turkey 1956-58, OC Flying RRFU 1958-61, Gp Capt Ops AFME Aden 1962-64, Co RAF Wittering 1964-66, AOC No 3 Gp Bomber Cmd 1967, Student IDC 1968, Dir of Orgn and Admin plans RAF 1969-71, Dir Gen Personnel Mgmnt RAF 1971-73, Air Offr Scot and NI 1973-75, ret April 1975; Rolls Royce Ltd 1975-81, chm SSAFA Glos 1980-, memb cncl SSAFA 1987, memb CNCC Cheltenham Ladies Coll 1976-88 (corporate memb 1976); order of Leopold II Belgium 1945, Croix De Guerre Belgium 1945; *Recreations* golf, bridge; *Clubs* RAF; *Style*— Air Vice-Marshal John Lawrence, CB, CBE, OBE, AFC; Corinium House, Edge, Stroud, Gloucestershire (☎ 0452 813 226)

LAWRENCE, Sir John Waldemar; 6 Bt (UK 1858), OBE (1945); s of Sir Alexander Waldemar Lawrence, 4 Bt (d 1939), and Anne Elizabeth Le Poer, *née* Wynne (d 1948); suc bro, Sir Henry Eustace Waldemar Lawrence, 5 Bt (d 1967); *b* 27 May 1907; *Educ* Eton, New Coll Oxford (MA); *m* 1, 1947, Jacynth Mary, da of Rev F G Ellerton (d 1987); m 2, 1988, Audrey Viola Woodiwiss, w of late John Woodiwiss; *Heir* s, George Alexander Waldemar Lawrence; *Career* with BBC 1940-42 (Euro intelligence offr and subsequently Euro services organiser), press attaché Moscow 1942-45, chm Centre for Study of Religion and Communism (now Keston Coll) 1969-83, pres Keston Coll 1983-; chm Gt Britain-USSR Assoc 1970-85; ed of Frontier 1958-75; *Books* A History of Russia (1960), Russians Observed (1969), The Journals of Honoria Lawrence (with Audrey Woodiwiss 1980), The Hammer & The Cross (1986); *Recreations* walking, argument and reading in ten languages; *Clubs* Athenaeum; *Style*— Sir John Lawrence, Bt, OBE; 24 St Leonards Terrace, London SW3 4QG (☎ 01 730 8033); 1 Naishe's Cottage, Northstoke, Bath BA1 9AT (☎ 0272 326076)

LAWRENCE, Hon Mrs (Louise Eleanor Alice); *née* Canning; yr da of 5 Baron Garvagh; *b* 14 April 1951; *m* 1975, Mark Lawrence; 2 s (Jack Canning b 1982, Rufus Powell b 1986); *Style*— The Hon Mrs Lawrence; Croft House, All Cannings, Devizes, Wiltshire (☎ 038 086 339)

LAWRENCE, Lady; Marjorie Avice; da of Charles Angelo Jones (decd), of Bodney Hall, Norfolk; *m* 1941, Hon Mr Justice (Sir Frederick) Geoffrey Lawrence (d 1967); *Style*— Lady Lawrence; Bridge Farm, Burgess Hill, Sussex

LAWRENCE, Michael Hugh; CMG (1972); s of Hugh Moxon Lawrence, MC (d 1965), of Woldingham, Surrey, and Lilian Nora, *née* Marks (d 1982); *b* 9 July 1920; *Educ* Highgate Sch, Cambridge Univ (MA); *m* 1948, Rachel Mary, da of Humphrey Percival Gamon, OBE (d 1949), of Gt Barrow nr Chester; 1 s (Richard), 2 da (Louise, Catharine); *Career* served IA 1940-45; Indian Civil Serv 1945-56, asst clerk House of Commons 1947, sr clerk 1948, dep princ clerk 1962, clerk of the Overseas Off 1967-72, clerk administrator House of Commons Servs Ctee 1972-76, head of Admin Dept House of Commons 1972-80, memb bd of mgmnt House of Commons 1979-80, sec History of Parl Tst 1959-66, ret 1980; *Recreations* beagling, sea bathing, looking at churches; *Style*— Michael Lawrence, Esq, CMG; 22 Stradbroke Rd, Southwold, Suffolk IP18 6LQ

LAWRENCE, (Walter Nicholas) Murray; s of Henry Walter Neville Lawrence (d 1959), and Sarah Schuyler (d 1947), da of Nicholas Murray Butler who was pres of Columbia Univ in NY and USA Republican vice-pres candidate 1912 (under Taft); *b* 8 Feb 1935; *Educ* Winchester, Trinity Coll Oxford (BA, MA); *m* 29 April 1961, Sally Louise, da of Col Alleyn Becher O'Dwyer (d 1973); 2 da (Sarah Louise, Catherine Jane); *Career* treaty dept CT Bowring & Co Ltd 1957-62, underwriter Harvey Bowring & others 1970-84 (asst underwriter 1962-70); dir: CT Bowring & Co Ltd 1976-84, C T Bowring (underwriting agencies Ltd 1973-84), sr ptnr-Murray Lawrence & Ptnrs 1985-; chm: Murray Lawrence Hldgs Ltd 1988-, Murray Lawrence Members Agency Ltd 1988-, chm Lloyds 1988 and 1989 (ctee memb 1979-82, dep chm 1982 and 1984-87); Liveryman Worshipful Co of Insurers; FCII 1979; *Recreations* golf, opera, travelling; *Clubs* Boodle's, MCC, Royal and Ancient GS (St Andrews), Woking GC, Swinley GS, Royal St George's GS, Rye Golf; *Style*— Murray Lawrence, Esq; Murray Lawrence & Partners, 32 Threadneedle St, London EC2R 8AY (☎ 01 588 7447)

LAWRENCE, Hon Patrick John Tristram; s and h of 4 Baron Trevethin and 2 Baron Oaksey; *b* 29 June 1960; *m* 20 May 1987, Lucinda H, eldest da of Demetri Marchessini, of Wilton Crescent, SW1; 1 da (b 1987); *Clubs* New World; *Style*— The Hon Patrick Lawrence; 20 Aldebert Terrace, London SW8 (☎ 01 582 7502)

LAWRENCE, Dr Peter Anthony; s of Instr Lt Ivor Douglas Lawrence, (RN ret), of Swanage, Dorset, and Joy Frances, *née* Liebert; *b* 23 June 1941; *Educ* Wennington Sch Wetherby Yorks, Cambridge Univ (MA, PhD); *m* 9 July 1971, (Ruth) Birgitta, da of Prof Ake Haraldson (d 1985), of Uppsala, Sweden; *Career* Cwlth (Harkness) fell 1965-67, genetics dept Univ of Cambridge 1967-69, MRC Lab of Molecular Biol Cambridge 1969-; parish cnllr; FRS 1983; *Books* Insect Development (ed 1976); *Recreations* fungi, gardening, golf, theatre, trees; *Style*— Dr Peter Lawrence; 9 Temple End, Gt Wilbraham, Cambridge CB1 5JF (☎ 0223 880505); MRC Laboratory Molecular Biology, Hills Rd, Cambridge CB2 2QH (☎ 0223 248011, fax 0223 213556, telex 81532)

LAWRENCE, Professor Raymond John; s of Herbert Lawrence, (d 1959), of Ruislip, and Nellie Grace, *née* Martin (d 1982); *b* 3 July 1925; *Educ* St Paul's Sch, Pembroke Coll Cambridge (BA, MA), Univ of California Berkeley; *m* 27 Dec 1952, Antonia Victorine, da of Coenraad Jan Graadt Van Roggen (d 1934), of Rotterdam, Holland; 1 da (Caroline Mary b 1959), 1 adopted s (Steven Martin b 1963); *Career* WWII Lt Intelligence Corps served: Philippines, India, Malaya, Singapore, W Germany; mgmnt trainee Unilever Ltd 1950-52, product mangr (Summer County Margarine) Van der Berghs Ltd London 1953-56, PA to MD Savonneries Lever Paris 1956-59, advtg mangr Unilever Aust pty Ltd 1959-62; prof of mktg (first Univ chair in mktg) Univ of Lancaster 1965-88; professor emeritus 1988, FInstM 1988; *Books* Modern Marketing Management (1971); *Recreations* tennis, golf, chess, bridge; *Style*— Prof Raymond Lawrence; Toll Bar Gate, 41 Toll Bar Crescent, Lancaster LA1 4NR (☎ 0524 65059); Department of Marketing, University of Lancaster, Bailrigg, Lancaster LA1 4YX (☎ 0524 65201)

LAWRENCE, Ruth Isabel; da of Frederick Lawrence, of London, and Clare, *née* Rosenblatt; *b* 13 May 1957; *Educ* E Barnet GS, Clare Coll Cambridge Univ (BA); *Career* managing ed Sweet and Maxwell Ltd, 1980-85, publishing mangr Law Soc of Eng and Wales 1986-, (press offr 1985-86); memb: N Barnes Residents Assoc, Hon Soc of Middle Temple; Hon MA Cambridge Univ; *Recreations* flying light aircraft, classical guitar, walking; *Style*— Ms Ruth Isabel; Barnes, London SW13; The Law Society, 113 Chancery Lane, London W12A 1PL (☎ 01 242 1222)

LAWRENCE, Hon Sara Honoria Angel; da of 3 Baron Lawrence (d 1947); *b* 1912; *Style*— The Hon Sara Lawrence; 14 Juxon Close, Chichester, Sussex

LAWRENCE, His Hon Judge Timothy; s of Alfred Whiteman Lawrence and Phyllis Gertrude Lloyd-Jones; *b* 29 April 1942; *Educ* Bedford Sch; *Career* Slrs Dept New Scotland Yard 1967-70, ptnr Caude Hornby and Cox 1970-86 (sr ptnr 1976), rec 1983, circuit judge 1986-; memb: criminal law ctee Law Soc 1978-86, No 13 Area Legal Aid Ctee 1983-86, Judicial Studies Bd 1984-87 (criminal ctee until 1988); chm No 14 Area Duty Slr Ctee 1984-86, pres London Criminal Cts Slrs Assoc 1984-86 (sec 1974-84); *Clubs* Hurlingham; *Style*— His Honour Judge Lawrence; 8 Slaidburn Street, London SW10 0JP

LAWRENCE, Vernon John; s of Douglas Lawrence of Berlin, Germany, and Lilian Cicily, *née* Collings (d 1956); *b* 30 April 1940; *Educ* Dulwich Coll, Kelham Coll; *m* 10 Sept 1960, Jennifer Mary, da of Maj Michael Drewe, MBE, JP (d 1986) of Sidmouth, Devon; 2 s (James b 1964, Jeremy b 1966) 1 da (Sarah b 1961); *Career* studio mangr BBC Radio 1958 (prodr 1963), dir BBC TV 1964 (prodr 1967); programmes incl: Top of the Pops, Lulu, Omnibus, Full House, Cilla; asst head entertainment Yorks TV 1974 (controller 1985); progs incl: Rising Damp, Song by Song, Only when I Laugh, Duty Free, The New Statesman, Bit of a do, Home to Roost; cncl memb BAFTA 1985; *Recreations* walking, fishing, gardening, art; *Style*— Vernon Lawrence, Esq; Yorkshire Television, Television Centre, Leeds LS3 1JS (☎ 0532 438283/01 242 1666, fax 4058062)

LAWRENCE, Sir William Fettiplace; 5 Bt (UK 1867), at Ealing Park, Middx; s of Sir William Lawrence, 4 Bt (d 1986); *b* 23 August 1954; *Educ* King Edward VI Sch Stratford-upon-Avon; *Heir* cousin, Peter Stafford Hayden Lawrence; *Career* asst fin accountant W B Bumpers Ltd, Rockwell Int 1980-81; gen mangr Newdawn & Sun Ltd 1981-; memb: Stratford-on-Avon Dist Cncl 1982-, South Warwickshire Health Authy 1984-, West Midlands Arts Mgmnt Cncl 1984-; *Recreations* horse racing, wine; *Style*— Sir William Lawrence, Bt; The Knoll, Walcote, nr Alcester, Warks B49 6LZ (☎ 078981 303)

LAWRENCE-JONES, Sir Christopher; 6 Bt (UK 1831); s of Cdr Bertram Edward Jones, RN (d 1958), and h of Sir Lawrence Evelyn Jones, 5 Bt, MC, TD (d 1969); *b* 19 Jan 1940; *Educ* Sherborne, Gonville and Caius Cambridge, St Thomas' Hosp (MA, MB, BChir, DIH, FFOM, RCP); *m* 1967, Gail, da of C A Pittar; 2 s; *Heir* s, Mark Christopher Lawrence-Jones b 28 Dec 1968; *Career* industrial med advsr 1967-; ICI Dyestuffs Div 1967-70, BP Co Ltd 1970-73, health and safety exec 1973-75, ICI Paints Div 1975-79, ICI centl med advsr 1979-85, ch med offr ICI plc, Millbank SW1 1985-, CMO ICI plc, chm Medichem; *Recreations* cruising under sail (Yacht 'Seago'); *Clubs* Royal Cruising; *Style*— Sir Christopher Lawrence-Jones, Bt; c/o Coutts & Co, 440, Strand, London, WC24 0QS

LAWRENCE-JONES, David; s of Lawrence Jones (d 1930); *b* 16 August 1919; *Educ* Charterhouse; *m* 1949, Gwynnyth Anne, *née* Logan; 3 s; *Career* Lt RNVR: Home Fleet, Med Fleet (despatches 1942); slr 1949; *Recreations* shooting, fishing; *Clubs* Army & Navy; *Style*— David Lawrence-Jones, Esq; Rettendon Old Hall, Chelmsford, Essex (☎ 0268 733360)

LAWRENCE-MILLS, Rowena Margaret; da of Edward Charles Leader (d 1982), and Blanche Linda, *née* Calcott (d 1979); *b* 14 July 1931; *Educ* North London Collegiate Sch for Girls, UC London (BSc); *m* 3 Sept 1955, John, s of Herbert Harold (d 1964); 1 s (Charles Sebastian b 1966), 1 da (Alexandra Louise b 1968); *Career* chm & chief exec Rowena Mills Assocs Ltd, former economist Metal Box Co Ltd, chm packaging working pty NEDO 1988-, memb ctee of investigation MAFF 1988-, cncllr CBI London Region 1985-88; Freeman City of London, Liveryman Worshipful Co of Plumbers, Fellow Inst of Packaging; writes for major journals, newspapers & TV; *Recreations* work, riding, music, theatre, reading, writing; *Clubs* Naval and Military; *Style*— Mrs Rowena M Lawrence-Mills; Peart Hall, Spaxton, Bridgwater, Somerset TA5 1DA (☎ 027 867 343); 50 Pembroke Rd, Kensington, London W8 6NX; Rowena Mills Associates Ltd, PO Box 594, London W8 7DE (☎ 01 937 4035, fax 01 937 7850)

LAWRENSON, Prof Peter John; s of John Lawrenson (d 1949), of Prescot, and Emily, *née* Houghton (d 1979); *b* 12 Mar 1933; *Educ* Prescot GS, Manchester Univ (BSc, MSc, DSc); *m* 5 April 1958, Shirley Hannah, da of Albert Edward Foster, of Macclesfield; 1 s (Mark b 1958), 3 da (Ruth b 1960, Rachel b 1963, Isobel b 1965); *Career* res engr GEC 1956-61; Univ of Leeds: lectr 1961, reader 1965, prof 1966, head dept of electrical and electronic engrg 1974-84, chm faculty of sci and applied sci 1978-80, chm faculty of engrg 1980-81; chm and chief exec Switched Reluctance Drives Ltd 1980-; dir: Dale Electric Int plc 1988-, Allenwest Ltd 1988-; author of over 120 papers for various sci jnls; awards: Inst Premium IEE 1981, Alfred Ewing Gold Medal Royal Soc and Inst of Civil Engrs 1983, Esso Energy Gold Medal Royal Soc 1985; vice pres IEE 1987-; memb cncl Univ of Buckingham; FIEE 1974, FIEEE 1975, FEng 1980, FRS 1982; *Books* Analysis & Computation of Electric & Magnetic Fields (with K J Binns 1963 and 1973), Per Unit Systems (with M R Harris & J M Stephenson 1970); *Recreations* chess, bridge, squash, walking; *Style*— Prof Peter Lawrenson; Switched Reluctance Drives Ltd, Springfield House, Hyde Terrace, Leeds LS2 9LN; University of Leeds, Leeds LS2 9JT (☎ 0532 332014, 0532 443844, fax 0532 423179, telex 0532 556578)

LAWREY, Keith; JP (Inner London); s of Capt George William Bishop Lawrey, West Meads, Bognor Regis, West Sussex, and Edna Muriel,*née* Gass ; *b* 21 August 1940; *Educ* Colfe's Sch, Birbeck Coll Univ of London (LLB, MSc); *m* 20 Dec 1969, (Helen) Jane, da of James Edward Marriott, MBE, and Betty Evelyn, *née* Church; 2 s (David Keith b 1972, Andrew Charles b 1976), 2 da (Sarah Jane b 1979, Katherine Jane b 1979); *Career* barr Grays Inn, educn offr Plastics and Rubber Inst 1960-68, lectr and sr lectr Bucks Coll of Higher Educn 1968-74, head dept business studies Mid-Kent Coll of Higher and Further Educn 1974-78, sec gen The Library Assoc 1978-84, dean of faculty of business and mgmnt Harrow Coll of Higher Educn 1984-; hon tres Coll of Preceptors 1987-, examiner and assessor; lay preacher Methodist church; Freeman City of London, Liveryman Worshipful Co of Chartered Secretaries and Administrators; FCollP 1980, FCIS 1967;; *Recreations* preaching, sailing, swimming, theatre, gardening,; *Clubs* Dell Quay Sailing, Old Colfeians' Assoc; *Style*— Keith Lawrey, Esq, JP; Harrow College of Higher Education, Northwick Park, Harrow HA1 3TP (☎ 01 864 5422)

LAWRIE, Harold Adrian; s of Alfred Ainslie Lawrie (d 1941), of Edinburgh, and Jean Maxwell Campbell, *née* Cook (d 1932); *b* 2 Oct 1919; *Educ* Winchester, BNC Oxford; *m* 17 July 1948, Betty Mavis, da of Noel Goddard Terry, MBE (d 1980); 3 da (Jean Rachel b 1949, Sandra Jane b 1951, Patricia Anne b 1956); *Career* ADC to Maj-Gen Hakewell-Smith 1943-45; former mangr Burton Rowe Pension Ltd, Lloyds Brokers; farmer; hon sec SSAFA; *Recreations* golf, tennis; *Clubs* Farmers'; *Style*— Harold Lawrie, Esq; Ballinger Grove, Great Missenden, Bucks (☎ 024 06 2417)

LAWRY, Rev (Samuel) John Lockhart; s of Samuel James Lawry (d 1954), of Plympton, Devon, and Susan Lockhart, *née* Newcombe (d 1968); *b* 23 July 1911; *Educ* Repton Sch; CCC (MA), Wells Theol Coll; *m* 28 April 1955, Susan, da of Patrick Lyons Fleming (d 1985), of The Manor House, Sutton Park, Guildford, Surrey; 1 da (Rachel Mary Fleming (Mrs Christopher Arthur) b 1956); *Career* clerk in Holy Orders C of E 1935; chaplain RNVR 1940-47; vicar: St Cuthbert's Portsmouth 1948-57, East Meon Hamps 1957-68; *Clubs* Royal Naval (Portsmouth); *Style*— The Rev S J L Lawry; Broadlands House, Petersfield, Hants GU31 4BA (☎ 0730 62134)

LAWS, Courtney Alexander Henriques; OBE (1987); s of Ezekiel Laws (d 1986), and Agatha, *née* Williams (d 1983); *b* 16 June 1934; *Educ* Lincoln Coll, Nat Coll Youth Workers Leicester, Cranfield Coll Bedford; *m* 7 Sept 1955, Wilhel (Rubie), da of Nikana Brown (d 1962); 1 s (Clive Anthony b 3 Jan 1959), 2 da (Carole Alexandra b 14 March 1964, Claudette Joanna b 13 Oct 1967); *Career* dir Brixton Neighbourhood Community Assoc Ltd 1971-; memb: St Johns Inter Racial Club 1958, W Indian Standing Conf 1959, NCII 1960; involved with Campaign Against Racial Discrimination 1960, memb Works Ctee Peak Freans Biscuit Co 1960-69, shop steward TAWU 1960-70; memb: Central Ctee Br Caribbean Assoc 1960, Assoc Jamaicans 1965, West Indians St Citizens Assoc 1973, consultative ctee ILEA 1975, Cmmnr Racial Equality 1977-80, Consortium Ethnic Minorities 1978, S Eastern Gas Consumer Cncl 1980; memb: Lambeth Cncl for Community Relations 1964, Geneva and Somerleyton Community Assoc 1966; govr Brixton Coll, memb Consultative Cncl City and East London Coll 1975; Order of Distinction Jamaica 1978, Prime Minister of Jamaica Medal of Appreciation 1987; *Recreations* reading, music; *Clubs* Brixton United CC, Oasis Sports and Social, Brixton Domino; *Style*— Courtney A Laws, Esq, OBE; 164 Croxted Rd, W Dulwich, London SE21 8NW; 71 Atlantic Rd, London SW9 8PU (☎ 01 274 0011)

LAWS, Frederick Geoffrey; s of Frederick Roberts Laws (d 1987), and Annette Kirby (d 1975); *b* 1 August 1928; *Educ* Arnold Sch Blackpool, London Univ (LLB); *m* 8 June 1955, Beryl Holt; 2 da (Amanda (Mrs Leslie) b 16 Nov 1957, Diana (Mrs Howers) b 30 Sept 1961); *Career* Nat Serv RA 1947-49; admitted slr 1952; asst solr: Blackpool Corpn 1952-54, Bournemouth Corpn 1955-59, Southend-on-Sea Corpn 1959-71, Town Clerk Southend-on-Sea 1971-84; local ombudsman; capt Thorpe Hall Golf Club 1983, chm Thorpe Hall Golf Club 1984-; Freedom Borough of Southend-on-Sea 1985; memb: Law Soc; *Recreations* golf; *Clubs* Thorpe Hall Golf, Anthenaeum; *Style*— Frederick Laws, Esq; 270 Maplin Way North, Southend-on-Sea, Essex (☎

0702 587 459), Commission for Local Administration in England, 21 Queen Anne's Gate, London SW1H 9BU (☎ 01 222 5622)

LAWSON, Hon Alma; da of 1 Baron Lawson (d 1965); *b* 1920; *Style*— The Hon Alma Lawson

LAWSON, Anthony Raymond; s of Alexander Lawson (d 1965), of Redcroft, Whitefield, Manchester, and Jeanne Alexandra Lawson (d 1968); *b* 26 August 1931; *Educ* Repton; *m* 1, 1955, Anne, da of Dr Walter Martin, MC, of Bury, Lancs; 1 s, 1 da; m 2, 1980, Patricia Jane, da of Dr F Lascelles, MC, of Formby, Lancs; *Career* chm and chief exec Hollas Gp plc; memb: Lloyd's, IOD; FBIM; *Recreations* tennis; *Style*— Anthony Lawson, Esq; Hollas Group plc, Windsor House, Southmoor Rd, Wythenshawe, Manchester (☎ 061 945 3221, telex 669656); Moss Bank Farm, Toft, Knutsford, Cheshire (☎ 0565 2002)

LAWSON, Hon Mrs Carole; *née* Samuel; da of Baron Samuel of Wych Cross (Life Peer) *qv*; *b* 1942; *m* 1963, Geoffrey Clive Henry Lawson (a slr of Supreme Ct 1963-); 2 s; *Style*— The Hon Mrs Lawson; Stilemans, Brighton Rd, Munstead, Godalming, Surrey (☎ 048 68 28782)

LAWSON, Lady Caroline; *née* Lowther; da of 7 Earl of Lonsdale; *b* 11 Mar 1959; *m* 1, 1978 (m dis), Guy Forrester; m 2 (m dis), Steven Hunt; 1 s (George b 1982); m 3, 18 Sept 1987, Charles John Patrick Lawson, s of Sir John Charles Arthur Digby Lawson, 3 Bt, DSO, MC; 1 da (Tess b 1988); *Style*— Lady Caroline Lawson

LAWSON, Charles John Patrick; s and h of Sir John Charles Arthur Digby Lawson, 3 Bt, DSO, MC; *b* 19 May 1959; *Educ* Harrow, Leeds Univ, Royal Agricultural College, Cirencester; *m* 18 Sept 1987, Lady Caroline Lowther, da of 7 Earl of Lonsdale; 1 da (Tessa b 1988); *Style*— Charles Lawson, Esq; 46 High Street, Helmsley, North Yorkshire

LAWSON, Sir Christopher Donald; *b* 1922; *Educ* Magdalen Coll Sch Oxford; *m* 1945, Marjorie Patricia, *née* Bristow; 2 s, 1 da; *Career* served RAF 1941-50 Sqdn ldr; subsequently joined Thomas Hedley Ltd (sales mangr, mktg, personnel), retail sales mangr Cooper McDougal & Co; *Clubs* RAF, MCC, Gloucester RFC, Lillybrook, Doublegate, Thurlstone GC, Country (USA); *Style*— Sir Christopher Lawson; Church Cottage, Great Witcombe, Glos GL3 4TT (☎ 0452 862591); Luggers, S Milton, Devon

LAWSON, Eileen Day; da of Maurice Day (d 1952), of 71 Harley House, London NW1, and Henrietta, *née* Goldstein (d 1975); *b* 12 Dec 1919; *Educ* South Hampstead HS, Lycee de Versailles France, Sorbonne Paris; *m* 21 June 1949, Ernest Lawson, s of Jack Lawson; 1 s (Maurice Day b 26 March 1952), 2 da (Neroli Louise Day b 8 May 1960, Virginia Ann Day (twin)); *Career* chm Fuerst Day Lawson Gp 1956-86; *Style*— Mrs Ernest Lawson; 1 Eaton Mansions, Cliveden Place, London SW1 (☎ 01 730 5788, fax 01 488 9927, telex 887871)

LAWSON, Rear Adm (Frederick Charles William); CB (1971), DSC (1942 and bar 1945); s of Maximillian Leopold Lawson (d 1950), of Freshford, Somerset, and Mary Catherine Lawson (d 1964); *b* 20 April 1917; *Educ* Eastbourne Coll, RN Engrg Coll Keyham Devonport, RNC Greenwich; *m* 1945, Dorothy Mary, da of Dr George Percy Norman (d 1943), of Eastbourne; 1 s (Andrew b 1951), 3 da (Judith b 1946, Penelope b 1947, Belinda b 1956); *Career* RN 1935-72; chief exec Royal Dockyards 1972-75, Flag Offr Medway and Adm Superintendent Chatham 1969-72, Cdre Supt Singapore 1965-69; *Recreations* golf; *Clubs* Bath and County; *Style*— Rear Admiral F C W Lawson, CB, DSC; 20 Woolley St, Bradford on Avon, Wilts (☎ 02216 3234)

LAWSON, Hon Harriet Mary; *née* Lawson; da of 5 Baron Burnham; *b* 1954; *Style*— The Hon Harriet Lawson

LAWSON, Hon Hugh John Frederick; s of 4 Baron Burnham, CB, DSO, MC (d 1963), and hp of bro, 5 Baron Burnham; *b* 1931; *Educ* Eton, Balliol Coll Oxford; *m* 1955, Hilary, da of Alan Hunter, of Huntingtowerfield House, Almondbank, Perthshire; 1 s, 2 da; *Career* Lt Scots Gds (SR) 1952; *Style*— The Hon Hugh Lawson; Woodlands Farm, Beaconsfield, Bucks

LAWSON, Air Vice Marshal Ian Douglas Napier; CB (1965), CBE (1961, DFC 1941 and bar 1943); s of James Lewis Lawson (d 1944), late of Mill Hill, London, and Kirriemuir, Forfar, Scotland, and Ethel Mary, *née* Ludgate (d 1975); *b* 11 Nov 1917; *Educ* Brondesbury Coll, Regent St Polytechnic, RAF Staff Coll, Royal Joint Services Staff Coll, Air Force Flying Coll, FBIM; *m* 1945, Dorothy Joyce Graham, da of Dr Charles Henry Nash (d 1952), of Camberley, Surrey and Ballymartle, Co Cork, Ireland; 1 s , 1 da; *Career* aircraft engr DeHavilland 1934-39; joined RAFVR 1938, Bomber Cmd 1940-41; Middle East 1941-42; (Western Desert Cyrenaica Tunisia-Sicily) 1943-45, Italy (HQ MAAF) Bomber Cmd 1945-46 (despatches 1944, 1945, 1946), Air Miny 1947-49, Tport Cmd OC 10 Sqn 1949-50, Middle E 1950-52, OC 683 Sqdn RAF Kabrit (OC Admin Wing) JSSC 1953, MOD (A1/JIS) 1953-56, RAF Flying Coll 1957, OC 216 Sqdn 1957-58, Tport Cmd 1958-61, OC RAF Lyneham 1961-62, HQ Air Forces Middle E 1962-64, Cmdt RAF Coll Cranwell, Air Vice Marshal 1964-67 (asst chief advsr personnel and logistics MOD 1967-69), ret 1969; gen sales mangr Br Aircraft Corpn 1969-77, Br Aerospace Weybridge Div 1977-81, special dir Gloss Air Hldgs plc 1981-82; chm N Wilts Cons Assoc, Labock Branch Div; AE 1945; FBIH; US Legion of Merit 1944; *Recreations* motor sport, gardening, grandchildren; *Clubs* RAF; *Style*— Air Vice Marshal I D N Lawson

LAWSON, Hon Mrs Irene; da of 1 Baron Lawson (d 1965); *b* 1909; *m* 1935, Charles Frederick Campbell Lawson; 3 da; *Style*— The Hon Mrs Lawson; Dourene, Park Rd North, Chester-le-Street, Co Durham

LAWSON, John Arthur; DFC; s of Charles Lawson (d 1975), of Bognor Regis, Sussex, and May, *née* Holland (d 1978); *b* 19 Oct 1920; *Educ* Dunstable GS; *m* 3 May 1947, Olive Mary, da of Charles Albert Hulford (d 1977); *Career* Flight Lt RAF (bomber cmd) 1941-46; accountant: Electricity Supply 1946-52, accountant (reorganisation) United Yeast Co 1952-55; supervising consultant (Mgmnt) Associated Industrial Consultants (INBUCON) 1955-66; dir: Carrington & Dewhurst plc 1966-70, Reed Internat Ltd 1970-79, Tavener Rutledge plc 1979-86, Butler & Tanner Ltd 1981-, (chm of Exec Bd as well as dir on Governing Bd); non exec dir: Lawrence-Allen Ltd 1986-, Rubery Owen (Hldgs) Ltd 1984-, Abacus Municipal Ltd 1983-; Fell Assoc of Corporate Treasurers, Assoc Inst Mgmnt Accountants, MIMC, FID; *Recreations* golf, swimming; *Style*— John A Lawson, Esq, DFC; Manor Stables Cottage, Great Somerford, Chippenham, Wilts SN15 5EH; The Selwood Painting Works, Frome, Somerset, BA11 1NF (☎ 0373 51500, telex 449967, fax 0373 51333)

LAWSON, Col Sir John Charles Arthur Digby; 3 Bt (UK 1900), of Weetwood Grange, Headingley-cum-Burley, W Riding of Yorkshire, DSO (1943), MC (1940); s of Maj Sir Digby Lawson, 2 Bt, TD, JP (d 1959), and Iris Mary Fitzgerald (d 1941); *b* 24 Oct 1912; *Educ* Stowe, RMC, Staff Coll Camberley; *m* 1, 17 March 1945 (m dis 1950), Rose (d 1972), da of David Cecil Bingham (d 1914); m 2, 22 Dec 1954, Tresilla Anne Eleanor, da of late Maj Eric Buller Leyborne Popham, MC, of Downes, Crediton; 1 s; *Heir* s Charles John Patrick Lawson, *qv*; *Career* 2nd Lt 11th Hussars (PAO) 1933, served in Palestine 1936 (despatches), seconded Trans/Jordan Frontier Force 1939-40, Western Desert 1940-43 (wounded despatches 3), Temp Lt Col 1943 as Gen Montgomery apptd advsr on armoured reconaissance to Gen Patton N Africa 1943 (wounded), US Marine Staff Course Quantico Virginia 1944-, Personal Liaison Offr to Gen Montgomery at 21st Army GP N France 1944-, cmdg Inns of Court Regt 1944-46, ret 1947, Col 11th Hussars (PAO) 1965-69, Col R Hussars 1969-72; chm Fairbairn Lawson Ltd and subsidiary cos 1968-79, memb cncl Univ of Leeds 1972-79; US Legion of Merit 1943; *Recreations* golf, gardening, country pursuits; *Clubs* Cavalry, Army and Navy, MCC; *Style*— Col Sir John Lawson, Bt, DSO, MC; El Bodon, Calle Castilla 3, Sotogrande (Cadiz) Spain

LAWSON, Maurice Day; s of Ernest Lawson, of St John's Wood, and Eileen, *née* Day; *b* 26 Mar 1952; *Educ* Harrow, Exeter Coll Oxford (MA), Harvard Business Sch; *m* 14 Sept 1985, Charlotte Mary Clare, da of Sir William Godfrey Agnew, KCVO, of Pinehurst, South Ascot, Berks; 1 da (Eloise Ruth b 1987); *Career* commodity trader; dir and chief exec: Fuerst Day Lawson Ltd, Union Merchants Overseas Ltd, Fuerst Day Lawson Citrus Ltd, Fuerst Schneider Chemicals Ltd, R Verney & Co Ltd; *Recreations* tennis, squash, sailing; *Clubs* RAC, Royal Motor Yacht, Sandbanks; *Style*— Maurice Lawson, Esq; 42 Holland Park Avenue, London W11 3QY (☎ 01 229 1346, telex 887871, fax 01 488 9927); Fuerst Day Lawson Holdings Ltd, St Clare House, 30-33 Minories, London EC3N 1LN

LAWSON, Hon Mrs Miranda Jane; *née* Newall; da of 2 Baron Newall; *b* 25 Feb 1959; *m* 31 May 1986, Timothy Guy Lawson, son of Derek C Lawson, of Sherbourne, Warwick; 1 s (George Thomas Guy b 1987); *Style*— The Hon Mrs Lawson; The Pointed House, Meeting House Lane, Brant Broughton, Lincoln LN5 0SH

LAWSON, (Hon) Sir Neil; QC (1955); s of Robb Lawson (decd); *b* 1908; *Educ* Hendon County Sch, London Univ; *m* 1933, Gweneth Clare, da of late Sidney Wilby, FCA (decd), of Leicester; 1 s, 1 da; *Career* served with RAFVR 1940-45; barrister Inner Temple 1929, bencher 1961, law commissioner 1965-71, a judge of High Court (Queen's Bench Div) 1971-83, ret; kt 1971; *Style*— Sir Neil Lawson, QC; 30a Heath Drive, Hampstead, London NW3 (☎ 01 794 2585)

LAWSON, Rt Hon Nigel; PC (1981), MP (Cons Blaby 1974-); s of Ralph Lawson, and Joan Elisabeth, *née* Davis; *b* 11 Mar 1932; *Educ* Westminster, Christ Church Oxford; *m* 1, 1955 (m dis 1980), Vanessa Mary Addison, *née* Salmon; 1 s, 3 da; m 2, 1980, Thérèse Mary Maclear; 1 s, 1 da; *Career* Sub-Lt RNVR 1954-56; memb editorial staff Financial Times 1956-60, city editor Sunday Telegraph 1961-63, editor The Spectator 1966-70; contested (C) Eton and Slough 1970, opposition whip 1976-77, opposition spokesman on Treasy and Economic Affairs 1977-79, financial sec to the Treasy 1979-81, Energy sec 1981-83, Chancellor of the Exchequer 1983-; special advsr Cons HQ 1973-74, chm Coningsby Club 1963-64, vice chm Cons Political Centre Nat Advsy Ctee 1972-75; *Style*— The Rt Hon Nigel Lawson, PC, MP; 11 Downing St, London SW1; The Old Rectory, Stoney Stanton, Leics

LAWSON, Gen Sir Richard George; KCB (1980), DSO (1962, OBE 1968); s of John Lawson, and Florence Rebecca Lawson; *b* 24 Nov 1927; *Educ* St Alban's Sch, Birmingham Univ; *m* 1956, Ingrid, da of Dr Sture Nikolaus Montelin, of Sweden (d 1979); 1 s; *Career* served with UN peacekeeping force Zaire 1962 when he rescued Belgian priest from 800 rebels armed only with a swagger-stick (DSO); CO Independent Sqdn Royal Tank Regt Berlin 1963-64, GSO 2 MOD 1965-66, COS S Arabian Army 1967, CO 5 Royal Tank Regt 1968-69, Cdr 20 Armoured Bde 1972-73, Asst Military Dep to Head of Defence Sales 1975-77, GOC 1 Armd Div 1977-79, GOC N Ireland 1979-82, Gen 1982, C-in-C Allied Forces N Europe 1982-84; Col Cmdt Royal Tank Regt 1980-82; Order of Leopold (Belgium) 1962, Kt Cdr Order of St Sylvester (Vatican) 1962; kt 1979; *Books* Strange Soldiering (1963), All The Queen's Men (1967), Strictly Personal (1972); *Recreations* sailing, writing; *Clubs* Army and Navy; *Style*— Gen Sir Richard Lawson, KCB, DSO, OBE

LAWSON, Richard Henry; s of Sir Henry Brailsford Lawson, MC, of Churchmead, Pirbright, Surrey (d 1980), and Lady Mona Lawson, *née* Thorn; *b* 16 Feb 1932; *Educ* Lancing; *m* 1958, Janet Elizabeth, da of Hugh Govier, of Shere, Nr Guildford, Surrey; 3 s (Anthony b 1966, Charles b 1969, Philip b 1972), 1 da (Sally d 1975); *Career* jt sr ptnr W Greenwell & Co 1980-86; memb: Stock Exchange 1959, Cncl of Stock Exchange (dep chm 1985-86), dep chm Security Assocs 1986; chm: Greenwell Montagu Stockbrokers Ltd 1987, Smith Kee Cucle Ltd 1987; *Recreations* golf, tennis, walking, birdwatching, skiing; *Clubs* Naval and Military; *Style*— Richard Lawson, Esq; Cherry Hill, Burrows Lane, Gromshall, Surrey GU5 9QE; Greenwell Montagu Stockbrokers, 117/118 Old Broad St, London EC2 (☎ 01 588 1673, telex 925363)

LAWSON, Lady Grant; Virginia; da of Sidney Butler Dean (decd), of St Paul, Minnesota, USA; *m* 1940, Col Sir Peter Grant Lawson, 2 Bt (d 1973); *Style*— Lady Grant Lawson; Dorridge Farm, Fordingbridge, Hants

LAWSON JOHNSTON, Hon (George) Andrew; s of 2 Baron Luke, KCVO, TD; *b* 1944; *Educ* Eton; *m* 1968, Sylvia Josephine Ruth, da of Michael Richard Lloyd Hayes; 3 s, 1 da; *Career* designer and engraver of glass; *Style*— The Hon Andrew Lawson Johnston

LAWSON JOHNSTON, Hon Arthur Charles St John; s and h of 2 Baron Luke, KCVO, TD, by his w Barbara, da of Sir FitzRoy Hamilton Anstruther-Gough-Calthorpe, 1 Bt; *b* 13 Jan 1933; *Educ* Eton, Trinity Coll Cambridge (BA 1954); *m* 1, 6 Aug 1959 (m dis 1971), Silvia Maria, da of Don Honorio Roigt, former Argentine Ambass at The Hague; 1 s, 2 da; m 2, 1971, Sarah Louise, da of Richard Hearne, OBE; 1 s; *Career* art dealer, farmer; ccllr Beds 1966-70 (chm of Staffing Ctee 1967-70), High Sheriff of Beds 1969-70, pres of Nat Assoc of Warehouse-Keepers 1960-78; cmmr St John Ambulance Bde in Beds 1972-85; cmdr St John Ambulance Beds 1985-; KStJ, OStJ; *Recreations* shooting, fishing; *Style*— The Hon Arthur Lawson Johnston; Odell Manor, Beds MK43 7BB (☎ Bedford 720416)

LAWSON JOHNSTON, Hon Hugh de Beauchamp; TD (1951), DL (Beds 1964); s of 1 Baron Luke, KBE (d 1943), by his w Hon Edith Laura St John (d 1941), da of 16 Baron St John of Bletso; *b* 7 April 1914; *Educ* Eton, Chillon Coll, Corpus Christi Cambridge; *m* 1946, Audrey Warren, da of Col Frederick Warren Pearl (decd); 3 da; *Career* Capt 5 Bn Bedfordshire Regt (TA Reserve); with Bovril Ltd 1935-71 (finally as chm), chm Tribune Investmt Tst Ltd 1950-86, Pitman Ltd (chm to 1981); chm of ctees United Soc for Christian Literature 1949-82; High Sheriff Beds 1961-62; *Style*— The Hon Hugh Lawson-Johnston, TD, DL; Flat 1, 28 Lennox Gdns, SW1 (☎ 01 584 1446); Woodleys Farmhouse, Melchbourne, Bedfordshire (☎ 0234 708282)

LAWSON JOHNSTON, Hon Ian (Harry) Henry Calthorpe; s of 2 Baron Luke, KCVO, TD; *b* 1938; *Educ* Harrow; *m* 1970, Lady (Pamela) Lemina Gordon, da of 12 Marquess of Huntly; 1 s, 1 da; *Clubs* Boodle's; *Style*— The Hon Harry Lawson Johnston; Coombe Slade Farm, Brailes, Banbury, Oxon OX15 5AF

LAWSON JOHNSTON, Lady (Pamela) Lemina; *née* Gordon; da of 12 Marquess of Huntly; *b* 1942; *m* 1970, Hon Ian Henry Calthorpe Lawson Johnston; 1 s, 1 da; *Style*— Lady Lemina Lawson Johnston; Coombe Slade Farm, Brailes, Banbury, Oxon OX15 5AF

LAWSON JOHNSTON, Hon Olive Elizabeth Helen; *née* Lawson-Johnston; eldest da of 1 Baron Luke, KBE (d 1943), and Hon Edith Laura (d 1941), 5 da of 16 Baron St John of Bletso; *b* 22 Jan 1904; *m* 18 Dec 1934 (m annulled 1936), Frederick Lothair Lawson Johnston (d 1963), s of W E Lawson Johnston, of 29 Wilton Crescent, London SW1; *Career* Sr Cmdt ATS 1938-40, 2 Officer WRNS 1941-45; *Style*— The Hon Olive Lawson-Johnston; Shona Beag, Station Rd, Dirleton, North Berwick, E Lothian (☎ 0620 3176)

LAWSON JOHNSTON, Hon (Laura) Pearl; OBE (1946), JP ((Beds 1941-84), DL (1976)); da of 1 Baron Luke, KBE (d 1943); *b* 18 August 1916; *Career* county pres St John Ambulance Brigade 1971-, cdr 1981-; High Sheriff of Bedfordshire 1985-86; OStJ; *Recreations* race horse breeder; *Style*— The Hon Pearl Lawson Johnston, OBE, JP, DL; Woodleys Stud House, Melchbourne, Beds MK44 1AG (☎ 0234 708 266)

LAWSON JOHNSTON, Hon Philip Richard; 4 and yst s of 2 Baron Luke, KCVO, TD; *b* 20 Nov 1950; *Educ* Eton; *m* 1977, (Saskia) Moyne, da of Terence George Andrews, MBE; 3 s (incl twins), 1 da; *Career* glass engraver; *Style*— The Hon Philip Lawson Johnston; The Garden Studio, 22 Cathcart Rd, London SW10

LAWSON-RODGERS, (George) Stuart; s of George Henry Roland Rogers, CBE (d 1983), of Bournemouth, and Mary Lawson (d 1983); *b* 23 Mar 1946; *Educ* Buckingham Coll Harrow Middx, LSE (LLB Hons); *m* 19 July 1969, Rosalind Denise, da of Lt Dennis Ivor Leach, of Bournemouth; 1 s (Dominic b 1971), 1 da (Lucy b 1972); *Career* asst boundary cmmr Boundary Cmmn (Parly) for England and Wales 1981, ad hoc appt asst boundary cmmr Local Govt Boundary Cmm for England and Wales 1983, appt to Panel of Chairmen of Structure Plan Examinations in Public Dept of Enviorment 1984, asst rec 1986, appt to Panels of Legal Assessors to GMC and Gen Dental Cncl; memb local Horticultural Soc; memb Hon Soc Gray's Inn, memb RCA; *Recreations* gardening, reading; *Style*— Stuart Lawson-Rodgers, Esq; Lamb Building, Temple, London (☎ 01 353 6701, fax 353 4686, telex 261511)

LAWSON-TANCRED, Andrew Peter; s and h of Sir Henry Lawson-Tancred, 10 Bt, of Boroughbridge, Yorkshire and Jean Veronica, *née* Foster (d 1970); *b* 18 Feb 1952; *Educ* Eton Coll, Univ of Leeds; *Career* barr at Law, Hon Soc of the Middle Temple; *Recreations* flying; *Style*— Andrew Lawson-Tancred, Esq; 1 Cristowe Rd, London SW6 3QF; Molinare Visions plc, Craven House, 34 Fouberts Place, London W1V 2BH (☎ 01 439 2244, telex 299200)

LAWSON-TANCRED, Sir Henry; 10 Bt (E 1662), JP (WR Yorks 1967); s of Maj Sir Thomas Selby Lawson-Tancred, 9 Bt (d 1945); *b* 1924; *Educ* Stowe, Jesus Coll Cambridge; *m* 1, 1950, Jean Veronica (d 1970), da of Gerald Robert Foster (d 1962); 5 s, 1 da; *m* 2, 1978, Susan Dorothy Marie-Gabrielle, da of late Sir Kenelm Cayley, 10 Bt, and formerly w of Maldwin Drummond; *Heir* s, Andrew Peter Lawson-Tancred; *Career* served with RAFVR 1942-46; *Style*— Sir Henry Lawson-Tancred, Bt, JP; Aldborough Manor, Boroughbridge, Yorks (☎ 0423 322716)

LAWSON-TURNER, Wilberforce; s of Arthur Lawson-Turner (d 1959), of Maitlands, Chapel-en-le-Frith, Derbys, and Alice Ewart, *née* Pearson (d 1974); *b* 21 April 1918; *Educ* Buxton Coll; *m* 1951, Felicity Marion, da of William Reader; 2 s (Simon b 31 Aug 1956, Guy b 17 May 1953); *Career* RNR Naval Communications Offr 1940-46; dir Surbiton Aircraft Weybridge Surrey 1949-; Liveryman Worshipful Co of Playing Card Makers 1962; *Recreations* flat racing, bridge; *Style*— Wilberforce Lawson-Turner, Esq; Wild Acre, Broad Lane, Hale, Ches WA15 ODG

LAWTON, Charles Henry Huntly; s of Philip Charles Fenner Lawton CBE, DFC, and Emma Letitia Gertrude Lawton, *née* Stephenson; *b* 17 April 1946; *Educ* Westminster Sch; *m* 21 April 1979, Sarah Margaret, da of The Rev Christopher Lambert; 1 s (Timothy b 1982), 1 da (Hermione b 1984); *Career* slr, head legal dept RT2 Corpn plc 1985-; *Recreations* walking, reading, fishing; *Clubs* White's; *Style*— Charles Lawton, Esq; 26 Abingdon Villas, London W8 (☎ 01 937 9148); 6 St James's Square, London SW1 (☎ 01 930 2399)

LAWTON, Rt Hon Sir Frederick Horace; PC (1972), QC (1957); s of William John Lawton, OBE; *b* 21 Dec 1911; *Educ* Battersea GS, CCC Cambridge; *m* 1937, Doreen, da of Richard John Maker Wilton (d 1979), of Bodmin, Cornwall; 2 s; *Career* WWII London Irish Rifles 1939-41; judge of the High Ct 1961-72, lord justice of appeal 1972-86; chm: standing ctee for Criminal Law Revision 1977-86, advsy ctee on Legal Educn 1976-86, pres British Acad of Forensic Scis 1964; kt 1961; *Style*— The Rt Hon Sir Frederick Lawton, PC, QC; 2 Harcourt Bldgs, Temple, London EC4 (☎ 01 353 3720); Mordryg, Stoptide Rock, Nr Wadebridge, Cornwall (☎ 020 886 3375); No 1, The Village, Skelton, York (☎ 0904 470441)

LAY, Patrick William; s of William Henry Lay (d 1984), of Cockfosters, Enfield, and Ellen Louise, *née* Cole (d 1972); *b* 24 July 1930; *Educ* Edmonton Co GS; *m* 24 Dec 1955, Lois, da of Robert Henry Thornton-Berry (d 1987), of Bristol; 1 da (Karen b 1956); *Career* Nat Serv RN; fin jounalist: Lloyds List Shipping Gazette 1954-56, Reuters 1956-59, Times 1959-61, Evening News; dep fin ed Daily Mirror, dir fin pr co Shareholder Relations (An PR) 1970-74, fin journalist Daily Mail 1974-76, fin ed Daily Express 1983-86 (dep fin ed 1976-83), city ed Sunday Express 1986-; *Recreations* cricket, walking, weimaraner dogs; *Clubs* MCC; *Style*— Patrick Lay, Esq; Didgenere Lodge, Epping Rd, Roydon, Essex, CM19 5DB (☎ 027979 2258); Sunday Express, Fleet St (☎ 01 353 8000)

LAY, Richard Neville; s of Edward John Lay, of Banstead, Surrey, and Nellie, *née* Gould (d 1987); *b* 18 Oct 1938; *Educ* Whitgift Sch; *m* 12 Sept 1964, 1 s (Martin Richard Forbes b 1969), 1 da (Melaine St Clair b 1965); *Career* chartered surveyor; ptnr Debenham Tewson & Chinnocks 1965-87, chm Debenham Tewson & Chinnocks Hldgs plc and subsid cos 1987-; surveyor to the Armourers' & Brasiers' Co 1983-, memb West End bd Sun Alliance and London Insur Gp, tstee Tate Gallery Fndn; FRICS; *Recreations* gardening; *Clubs* RAC; *Style*— Richard Lay, Esq; 1 Eaton Gate, Eaton Square, London SW1; 44 Brook St, London W1 (☎ 01 408 1161, telex 22105, fax 01 491 4593)

LAYARD, Prof (Peter) Richard Grenville; s of John Willoughby Layard (d 1974), and Doris, *née* Dunn (d 1973); *b* 15 Mar 1934; *Educ* Eton, Cambridge Univ (BA), LSE (MSc); *Career* 2 Lt 4 RHA 1953-54, RA 1952-54; sch teacher LCC 1959-61, sr res fell Robbins Ctee Higher Educn 1961-64; LSE: dep dir higher educn res unit 1964-74, lectr 1968-75, head centre lab econs 1974-, reader 1975-80, prof econs 1980-; memb Univ Grants Ctee 1985-89, chm exec ctee Employment Inst until 1986 and chm 1987-; fell Econometric Soc; *Books* More Jobs, Less Inflation (1982), How to Beat Unemployment (1986), Restoring Europe's Prosperity (with O Blanchard and R Dornbusch 1986) Microeconomic Theory (1978, reissued 1987), The Performance of the British Economy (with R Dornbusch 1987); *Recreations* walking; *Style*— Prof Richard Layard; 18 Provost Rd, London NW3 4ST (☎ 01 722 6347); Centre for Lab Econs LSE, Houghton St, London WC2A 2AE (☎ 01 405 7686, fax 01 242 0392)

LAYCOCK, Lady; Angela Clare Louise; yr da of Rt Hon William Dudley Ward, PC (d 1946, gn of 1 Earl of Dudley), and Winifred May, *née* Birkin, later Marquesa de Casa Maury (d 1982); *b* 1916; *m* 24 Jan 1935, Maj-Gen Sir Robert Edward Laycock, KCMG, CB, DSO, Royal Horse Guards (d 1968), s of Brig-Gen Sir Joseph Laycock, KCMG, DSO, TD, JP, DL, by Katherine, formerly w of 6 Marquess of Downshire and da of Hon Hugh Hare, 4 s of 2 Earl of Listowel, KP; 2 s (Joseph William (decd), Benjamin Richard), 3 da (Tilly Jane m Sidney Davis, Emma Rose m Richard Temple, Katherine Martha m David Mlinaric, *qv*); *Career* former CC and JP Notts; DStJ; *Style*— Lady Laycock, JP; La Canada Real, Sotogrande, (PA) Cadiz, Spain

LAYCOCK, Lady; Hilda Florence; da of Christopher Ralph Carr; *m* 1931, Sir Leslie Laycock, CBE, JP, company dir (d 1981); 2 s; *Style*— Lady Laycock; The Gables, Rayleigh Rd, Harrogate, N Yorks (☎ 0423 66219)

LAYCOCK, Mrs Peter; Patricia; da of Kenneth Richards, of NSW; *b* 20 Jan 1914; *m* 1, 1932 (m dis 1937), as his 1 w, 9 Earl of Jersey; 1 da (Lady Caroline Ogilvy); m 2, 1937, Maj Robin Filmer-Wilson (k 1944); 1 s, 1 da; m 3, 1953, Lt-Col Peter Laycock (d 1978); *Style*— Mrs Peter Laycock; 80 Eaton Sq, London SW1

LAYDEN, Sir John; JP (1965); s of Thomas Henry Layden (d 1961), of 7 Millicent Square, Maltby, Rotherham, South York, and Annie, *née* Peach (d 1959); *b* 16 Jan 1926; *Educ* Maltby Hall Sch, Sheffield Univ; *m* 26 March 1949, (Dorothy) Brenda, da of James McLean (d 1949), of Manor House, Maltby, Rotherham, South York; 2 s (John b 13 March 1956, Keith b 18 Oct 1959); *Career* chm Assoc Met Authys, ldr Rotherham Met Borough Cncl, vice-pres Br Section Int Univ Lacal Authys; Freeman City of London 1988, Kt 1988; *Recreations* watching football, reading; *Style*— Sir John Layden, JP; Rotherham Met Borough Cncl, The Civic Suite, Elliott House, Frederick Street, Rotherham S60 1QW (☎ 0709 823 580, fax 0709 371 597, car tel 0836 508 292)

LAYFIELD, Sir Frank Henry Burland Willoughby; QC (1967); s of Henry Layfield (d 1960); *b* 9 August 1921; *Educ* Sevenoaks Sch; *m* 1965, Irene Partricia, da of Capt J D Harvey, RN; 1 s, 1 da; *Career* barrister 1954; chm: Inquiry into Greater London Plan 1970-72, Ctee of Inquiry into Local Govt Finance 1974-76; a recorder of the Crown Court 1979-, govt inspector on Inquiry into Sizewell B Nucelar Power Station; bencher Gray's Inn 1974, hon fellow Coll of Estate Mgmnt 1981, hon fellow Incorporated Soc of Valuers and Auctioneers, Lincoln Land Inst Gold Medal 1983; ARICS; kt 1976; *Style*— Sir Frank Layfield, QC; 2 Mitre Court Bldgs, Temple, London EC4 (☎ 01 583 355); Grove House, Beckley, Oxford

LAYLAND, Hon Mrs Sheila Hamnett; da of Baron Hamnett (Life Peer); *b* 24 July 1933; *Educ* Levenshulme HS, City of Portsmouth Training Coll; *m* 1962, Eric Layland; 1 s, 1 da; *Style*— The Hon Mrs Layland; 31 Sevenoaks Ave, Heaton Moor, Stockport, Cheshire (☎ 061 432 8083)

LAYMAN, Rear-Adm Christopher Hope; DSO (1982), LVO (1977); s of Capt HFH Layman, DSO, RN, and Elizabeth Layman, *née* Hughes; *b* 9 Mar 1938; *Educ* Winchester; *m* 15 Aug 1964, Katharine Romer, da of Capt Stephen Romer Ascherson, RN (d 1955); 1 s (James b 1965), 1 da (Alexandra b 1969); *Career* joined RN 1956, specialised communications and electronic warfare 1966; cmd: HMS Hubberston 1968-70, cmd HMS Lynx 1972-74, exec offr HM Yacht Britannia 1976-78, Capt 7 Frigate Sqdn 1981-83, cmd HMS Argonaut 1981-82, cmd HMS Cleopatra 1982-83, cmd HMS Invincible 1984-86, cdr Br Forces Falkland Islands 1986-87, asst dir (CIS) Int Mil Staff NATO HQ 1988-; *Recreations* fishing, archaeology; *Clubs* New (Edinburgh); *Style*— Rear-Adm CH Layman, DSO, LVO; c/o Drummonds, 49 Charing Cross, London, SW1A 2DX

LAYTE, James Douglas; s of George Douglas Layte (d 1978), and Phyllis Joan, *née* Bullock; *b* 29 July 1951; *Educ* Monkton Combe Sch Bath, Tabor Acad Marion Mass USA, Univ of East Anglia (BA); *m* 16 June 1974, Caroline Clare Gage, da of late Peter Bruce Gage Miller, of Norwich; 2 s (Samuel b 1974, Henry b 1979); *Career* antique and fine art dealer; memb vetting ctee Fine Art and Antiques Fair Olympia 1980-; *Recreations* gardening, travel; *Style*— James D Layte, Esq; Waterfall Cottage, Mill St, Swanton Morley, Norfolk; 3 Fish Hill, Holt, Norfolk

LAYTON, Hon Christopher Walter; s of 1 Baron Layton, CH, CBE (d 1966); *b* 31 Dec 1929; *Educ* Oundle, King's Coll Cambridge; *m* 1, 1952 (m dis 1957), Anneliese Margarethe, da of Joachim von Thadden, of Hanover; 1 s, 1 da; m 2, 1961, Margaret Ann, da of Leslie Moon; 3 da; *Career* dir Computer Electronics, Telecommunications and Air Transport Equipment Manufacturing, Directorate-General of Internal Market and Industrial Affairs, Commission of the European Communities 1973-; *Style*— The Hon Christopher Layton; Directorate-General of Internal Market & Industrial Affairs, Commission of the European Communities, 200 rue de la Loi, 1049 Brussels, Belgium; Ave Albert Lancaster, 95B, 1080 Brussels, Belgium

LAYTON, Dr Clive Allan; s of Peter Eric Layton (d 1979), and Joan, *née* Sims; *b* 17 April 1944; *Educ* City of London Sch, King's Coll London, St George's Hosp Med Sch London (MB, BS); *m* 2 April 1971, Helen MacLean, da of William Paxton (d 1953); 2 da (Charlotte b 1972, Sarah b 1974); *Career* sr registrar in cardiology The London Hosp 1972-77; conslt cardiologist Nat Heart and Chest Hosps The London Chest Hosp 1977-, NE Thames Regnl Health Authy 1977-; non exec dir Medihome Ltd; contrib to pubns on cardiology and intensive care, serving memb Ctee of Essex Hunt Branch of Pony Club; former memb English Fencing Team; Br Schs, Public Schs and Br Junior Fencing Champion; MRCP 1969; *Recreations* equestrian activities; *Style*— Dr Clive Layton; 22 Upper Wimpole St, London W1M 7TR (☎ 01 486 8961, fax 01 486 7918, car tel 0836 289 087, telex 23621 CARDIO G)

LAYTON, Lt-Col Hon David; MBE (1946); s of 1 Baron Layton, CH, CBE (d 1966), and Eleanor Dorothea (d 1959), da of Francis Beresford Plumptre Osmaston; uncle and hp of 3 Baron Layton, *qv*; *b* 5 July 1914; *Educ* Gresham's Sch Holt, Trinity Coll Cambridge; *m* 1, 1939, Elizabeth, da of Rev Robert Millar Gray, of Hampstead; 2 s, 1 da; m 2, 1972, Joy Parkinson; *Career* 2 Lt RE 1939; md Incomes Data Services; *Style*— Lt-Col the Hon David Layton, MBE; 18 Grove Terrace, Highgate Rd, London NW5

LAYTON, Dr Denis Noel; s of Reginald Frank Layton (d 1966), of Banstead, Surrey, and Ida Mary, *née* Pinker (d 1976); *b* 29 Dec 1925; *Educ* City of London Freemen's Sch, Imperial Coll London (PhD, MSc); *m* 12 July 1958, Margaret Alison, da of Richard Kestell Floyer (d 1975), of Mayfield; 2 da (Frances b 1961, Hilary b 1963); *Career* Nat Serv Capt REME 1946-48; various appts GKN Group 1952-62; dir: Mountford (GKN Gp) 1962-76 (md 1967-76), Hoskins & Horton plc 1978-82; chm CSM Plating Ltd 1979-; chm DTI Ctee on Corrosion 1975-78, memb DTI Ctee for Industl Technols, pres Inst of Metal Finishing 1988-; FBIM, FIMF, MInstP; *Recreations* campanology, music; *Style*— Dr Denis Layton; CSM Plating Ltd, Heath Mill Lane, Birmingham B9 4AP

LAYTON, Lady; Dorothy Rose Layton; *née* Cross; da of Albert Luther Cross, of Rugby; *m* 1938, 2 Baron Layton (d 1989); 1 s (3 Baron, *qv*), 1 da (Hon Mrs Jennings, *qv*); *Career* JP Middx 1954-67; *Style*— The Rt Hon Dorothy, Lady Layton; 6 Old Palace Terrace, Richmond Green, Richmond, Surrey TW6 1NB (☎ 01 940 0834)

LAYTON, 3 Baron (UK 1947); Geoffrey Michael Layton; o s of 2 Baron Layton (d 1989); *b* 19 July 1947; *Educ* St Paul's, Stanford Univ Calif, Univ of Southern Calif; *m* 1, 1969 (m dis 1971), Viviane, da of François P Cracco, of Louvain, Belgium; m 2, 1989, Caroline Jane, da of William Thomas Mason, of Fairford, Glos, and formerly w of Adm Spyros Soulis, of Athens; *Heir* uncle, Hon David Layton, MBE, *qv*; *Style*— The Rt Hon the Lord Layton; c/o House of Lords, London SW1

LAZARUS, Sir Peter Esmond; KCB (1985), CB (1975); s of Kenneth Michaelis Lazarus (d 1961), of London, and Mary Rebecca, *née* Halsted (d 1982); *b* 2 April 1926; *Educ* Westminster, Wadham Coll Oxford; *m* 1950, Elizabeth Anne Marjorie, da of Leslie H Atwell, OBE, of London (d 1971); 3 s (Richard, Stephen, James); *Career* perm under sec Dept of Tport 1982-85, bd memb Civil Aviation Authy 1986-, dir Manchester Ship Canal Co 1986-, chm Ctee for Monitoring Agreements on Tobacco Advtg and Sponsorship, Bde Cmdt Jewish Lads and Girls Bde, vice pres Anglo Jewish Assoc, tstee Channel Ferry Disaster Fndn, chm Lib Jewish Synagogue; *Recreations* music, reading; *Clubs* Athenaeum; *Style*— Sir Peter Lazarus, KCB, CB; 28 Woodside Ave, London N6 4SS (☎ 01 883 3186)

LAZENBY, David William; s of George William Lazenby, of Walton-on-Thames, Surrey, and Jane, *née* Foster; *b* 13 Oct 1937; *Educ* Canford Sch Dorset, Battersea Coll of Technol, Imperial Coll London (DIC), City Univ London (Dip, CU); *m* 2 Sept 1961, Valerie Ann, da of Lewis Edward Kent, OBE (d 1972); 1 s (Jonathan b 22 Jan 1965), 1 da (Andrea b 23 Feb 1965); *Career* chm Andrews Kent & Stone consulting engrs 1983- (joined 1962, ptnr 1972); civil and structural engrg work includes: Nat Library of Wales, Merchant Navy Coll, E Sussex County Hall; vice pres IStructE, chm Br Standards Inst Construction Codes Ctee, visitor to Building Res Estab; FICE, FIStructE, MAssocCE; *Books* co-author of 1936/85 Structural Steelwork for Students (jtly 1985), Structural Mechanics for Students (1984), Cutting for Construction (1978); *Recreations* travel, tennis, opera, good food and wine; *Style*— David W Lazenby, Esq; Paddock Hse, Bennett Way, West Clandon, Guildford, Surrey (☎ 0483 223 104); Andrews Kent & Stone, 1 Argyll St, London W1V 2DH (☎ 01 437 6136, fax 01 437 1035, telex 291585)

LE BAILLY, Vice-Adm Sir Louis Edward Stewart Holland; KBE (1972), CB (1969, OBE 1952, DL (Cornwall 1982)); s of Robert Francis Le Bailly; *b* 18 July 1915; *Educ* RN Coll Dartmouth, RN Engrg Coll Devonport (CEng); *m* 1946, Pamela Ruth, da of Rear-Adm Charles Pierre Berthon; 3 da; *Career* joined RN 1929, served WWII, Cdr British Navy Staff and naval attaché Washington DC 1967-69, dir Serv Intelligence MOD 1970, ret 1972; dir-gen of Intelligence MOD 1972-75; cncl memb: Inst for Study of Conflict, The Pilgrims; FIMechE, MIMarE, FInstPet; *Clubs* Naval and Military; *Style*— Vice-Adm Sir Louis Le Bailly, KBE, CB, OBE, DL; Garlands House, St Tudy, Bodmin, Cornwall

LE BRUN, Lady Carina Doune; *née* Brudenell-Bruce; 2 da (yr da by 1 m) of 8 Marquess of Ailesbury and his 1 w, Edwina Sylvia de Winton, da of Lt-Col Sir Edward Wills, 4 Bt; *b* 13 Jan 1956; *Educ* Lawnside; *m* 1982, Anthony Le Brun, only s of Basil Le Brun, of Beauchamp, St John, Jersey, and Mrs Elaine Le Brun, of Le Douet, St John, Jersey; *Career* pottery decorator; *Style*— Lady Carina Le Brun; Beauchamp, St John, Jersey, Channel Islands; Jersey Pottery, Goray, Jersey

LE BRUN, Christopher Mark; s of John Le Brun, BEM, QSM, RM (d 1970), of Portsmouth, and Eileen Betty, *née* Miles; *b* 20 Dec 1951; *Educ* Southern GS Portsmouth, Slade Sch of Fine Art (DFA), Chelsea Sch of Art (MA); *m* 31 March 1979, Charlotte Eleanor, da of Gp Capt Hugh Beresford Verity, DSO, DFC, of Richmond, Surrey; 1 s (Luke J H b 1984), 1 da (Lily G V b 1986); *Career* artist; one man exhibitions incl: Nigel Greenwood Gallery London (1980, 1982, 1985), Gillespie-Laage-Salomon Paris 1981, Sperone Westwater NY (1983, 1986, 1988), Fruitmarket Gallery Edinburgh 1985, Arnolfini Gallery Bristol 1985, Kunsthalle Basel 1986, DAAD Galerie Berlin 1988, Galerie Rudolf Zwirner Cologne 1988; gp exhibitions incl: Nuova Imagine Milan Triennale 1980, Sydney Biennale 1982, New Art Tate Gallery London 1983, 'An International Survey of Recent Painting and Sculpture' Museum of Modern Art NY 1984, 'The British Show' toured Australia and NZ 1985, Paris Biennale 1985, San Francisco Biennale 1985, Venice Biennale 1982 and 1984, 'Falls the Shadow' Recent British and European Art Hayward Gallery London 1986, 'Twelve British Artists' Kunstlerhaus Vienna 1986, 'Current Affairs, British Art of the 1980's' Museum of Modern Art: Oxford, Budapest, Warsaw, Prague 1987; 'Avant Garde in the Eighties' LA County Museum LA 1987, British Art of the 1980's' Liljevalchs Museum Stockholm 1987, 'The British Picture' LA Louver Gallery LA 1988, 'New British Painting' Cincinnati Museum and American tour 1988-89; awards and cmmns: prizewinner John Moores Liverpool Exhibitions 1978 and 1980, Calonste Gulbenkian Fndn Printmakers Commission Award 1983, designer 'Ballet Imperial' Royal Opera House Covent Garden 1984, DAAD Fellowship Berlin 1987-88; *Style*— Christopher Le Brun, Esq; c/o Nigel Greenwood Gallery, 4 New Burlington St, London W1X 1FE (☎ 01 434 3795)

LE CARRÉ, John - David John Moore Cornwell; s of Ronald Cornwell; *b* 19 Oct 1931; *Educ* Sherborne, Berne Univ, Lincoln Coll Oxford; *m* 1, 1954 (m dis 1971), Alison Ann Veronica Sharp; 3 s; m 2, 1972, Valerie Jane Eustace; 1 s; *Career* former schoolteacher Eton, Foreign Service 1960-64; novelist; *books include*: The Spy Who Came In From The Cold (1963), Tinker, Tailor, Soldier, Spy (1974) (TV series), Smiley's People (1980) (TV series), The Little Drummer Girl (1983), A Perfect Spy (1986); *Style*— David Cornwell, Esq; John Farquharson Ltd, 162-168 Regent St, London W1R 5TB

LE CHEMINANT, Air Chief Marshal Sir Peter de Lacey; GBE (1978), KCB (1972, DFC 1943, and bar 1951); s of Col Keith Le Cheminant, TD, of Guernsey, CI, by his w Blanche Etheldred Wake Clark; *b* 17 June 1920; *Educ* Elizabeth Coll Guernsey, RAF Coll Cranwell; *m* 1940, Sylvia, da of J van Bodegom (d 1963); 1 s, 2 da; *Career* joined RAF 1939, Cmdt Joint Warfare Establishment 1968-70, asst chief of Air Staff (Policy) 1972, memb Permanent Military Deputies Gp gen Treaty Orgn 1972-74, vice-chief of Defence Staff 1974-76, dep C-in-C Allied Forces Central Europe 1976-79, Lt-govr and C-in-C Guernsey 1980-85; *Recreations* golf, sailing; *Clubs* RAF; *Style*— Air Chief Marshal Sir Peter Le Cheminant, GBE, KCB, DFC; La Madeleine de Bas, Ruette de La Madeleine, St Pierre du Bois, Guernsey, Channel Islands

LE FANU, Hon Mrs (Juliet Louise); *née* Annan; yr da of Baron Annan, OBE; *b* 7 Jan 1955; *Educ* Francis Holland, King's Coll Cambridge (MA); *m* 4 April 1987, Dr James Richard Le Fanu, 2 s of Richard Le Fanu, of 166 Cloudesley Road, London N1; *Career* publisher with Pantheon Books New York City USA; *Style*— The Hon Juliet Annan; 24 Grafton Square, London SW4 0DB

LE FANU, Mark; s of Adm of the Fleet Sir Michael Le Fanu (d 1970), and Prudence, *née* Morgan (d 1980); *b* 14 Nov 1946; *Educ* Winchester, Univ of Sussex (BA), Coll of Law; *m* 1976, Lucy Rhoda, da of John Cowen (d 1982), of Bisley, Stroud, Glos; 3 s (Thomas b 1980, Matthew b 1982, Caspar b 1986), 1 da (Celia b 1985); *Career* Lt RN 1964-73; slr McKenna & Co 1973-78; memb Soc of Authors 1979- (gen sec 1982-); *Recreations* canals, sailing, rough travelling; *Style*— Mark Le Fanu, Esq; 25 St James's Gardens, London W11 4RE (☎ 01 603 4119); Soc of Authors, 84 Drayton Gardens, London SW10 9SB (☎ 01 373 6642)

LE FLEMING, Isabella, Lady; Isabella Annie Fraser; da of late James Craig, of Manaia, Taranaki, NZ; *m* 24 March 1921, Sir Frank Thomas Le Fleming, 10 Bt (d 1971); 3 s; *Style*— Isabella, Lady Le Fleming; Rydal Lovat, Aurora Road, Manaia, Taranaki, New Zealand

LE FLEMING, Morris John; s of Maj Morris Ralph Le Fleming (d 1969), of Durham, and Mabel, *née* Darling (d 1980); *b* 19 August 1932; *Educ* Tonbridge Sch, Magdalene Coll Cambridge (BA); *m* 27 Aug 1960, Jenny Rose, da of Reginald McColvin Weeks, of Bristol; 1 s (Daniel b 1963), 3 da (Emma b 1961, Bridget b 1965, Alice b 1969); *Career* Nat Serv 2 Lt RA 1951-52, Capt TA 1952-61; slr 1958; asst slr: Worcestershire CC 1958-59, Middx CC 1959, Nottinghamshire CC 1959-63; asst clerk Lincolnshire CC 1963-69; Hertfordshire CC: dep clerk 1969-73, county sec 1973-79, chief exec 1979-, clerk to the Lieutenanty 1979-, clerk to the Magistrates Cts Ctee 1979-, sec to the Probation Ctee 1979-; memb Educn 2000 mgmnt ctee Letchworth 1986-, Prince's Youth Business Tst Reg Bd 1987; CBIM; *Recreations* theatre, family history, gardening, architecture; *Style*— Morris Le Fleming, Esq; Swangleys Lane, Knebworth, Herts SG3 6AA (☎ 0438 813 152); County Hall, Hertford (☎ 0992 555 600, telex 81272 HERBKS)

LE FLEMING, Noveen, Lady; Noveen Avis; da of C C Sharpe, of Rukuhia, Hamilton, New Zealand; *m* 28 April 1948, Sir William Kelland Le Fleming, 11 Bt (d 1988); 3 s, 4 da; *Style*— Noveen, Lady Le Fleming; 6 Kopane Road, Palmerston North, New Zealand

LE FLEMING, Sir Quentin John; 12 Bt (E 1705), of Rydal, Westmorland; s of Sir William Kelland Le Fleming, 11 Bt (d 1988); *b* 27 June 1949; *m* 26 June 1971, Judith Ann, da of C J Peck, JP, of Ashhurst, Manawatu, NZ; 2 s (David Kelland, Andrew John b 4 Oct 1979), 1 da (Josephine Kay b 31 July 1973); *Heir* s, David Kelland Le Fleming b 12 Jan 1976; *Style*— Sir Quentin Le Fleming, Bt; 147 Stanford Street, Ashhurst, Manawatu, New Zealand

LE GALLAIS, Lady; Juliette; da of Lt-Col P A Forsythe, KRRC (decd); *m* 1947, Sir Richard Lyle Le Gallais (d 1983); 2 s; *Style*— Lady Le Gallais; 506 Hawkins House, Dolphin Square, London SW1V 3LX

LE MARCHANT, Sir Francis Arthur; 6 Bt (UK 1841); s of Sir Denis Le Marchant, 5 Bt (d 1987), and Elizabeth Rowena Worth; *b* 6 Oct 1939; *Educ* Gordonstoun, Royal Acad Schs; *Heir* kinsman, Michael Le Marchant b 1937; *Career* painter; *Style*— Sir Francis Le Marchant, Bt

LE MARCHANT, Lady; Lucinda Gaye; *née* Leveson Gower; o da of Brig Hugh Nugent Leveson Gower (ggggs of Adm Hon John Leveson-Gower, yr s of 1 Earl Gower), of Tilford, and his 1 w, Avril Joy, *née* Mullens; *b* 12 Nov 1935; *m* 5 May 1955, Sir Spencer Le Marchant (d 1986); 2 da; *Style*— Lady Le Marchant; 29 Rivermill, Grosvenor Rd, London SW1 (☎ 01 821 9191); The Saltings, Yarmouth, Isle of Wight (☎ 0983 760223)

LE MARECHAL, Robert Norford; s of Reginald Le Marechal (d 1976), of Southhampton, and Margaret, *née* Cokely; *b* 29 May 1939; *Educ* Taunton's Sch Southampton; *m* 21 Dec 1963, Linda Mary, da of Noel Stanley Williams (d 1983), of Ludlow; 2 da (Kate b 1969, Rebecca b 1971); *Career* Sgt RAEC 1958-60; joined Exchequer and Audit Dept 1957: sr auditor MOD 1971-76, chief auditor DOE 1976-1980, dep dir of audit 1980-83, dir of policy and planning NAO 1984-86, asst auditor gen 1986-; *Recreations* reading, gardening ; *Style*— Robert Le Marechal, Esq; 62 Woodcote Hurst, Epsom Surrey (☎ 03727 21291); National Audit Office, Buckingham Palace Road, Victoria, London (☎ 01 798 7390)

LE MASURIER, Sir Robert Hugh; DSC (1942); s of William Smythe Le Masurier (d 1955); *b* 29 Dec 1913; *Educ* Victoria Coll Jersey, Pembroke Coll Oxford; *m* 1941, Helen Sophia Sheringham; 1 s, 2 da; *Career* serv in 1939-45 war, slr gen Jersey 1955-58, attorney gen 1958-62, bailiff of Jersey 1962-74, a judge of Guernsey Ct of Appeal 1964-; kt 1966; *Style*— Sir Robert Le Masurier, DSC; 4 La Fantasie, Rue Du Huquet, St Martin, Jersey, CI

LE PARD, Geoffrey; s of Desmond Allen Le Pard, Silver Crest, Silver St, Sway, Lymington, and Barbara Grace, *née* Francis; *b* 30 Nov 1956; *Educ* Purley GS, Brockenhurst GS, Bristol Univ (LLB); *m* 19 May 1984, Linda Ellen, da of Leslie Jones, of 42 Ruskin Rd, Costessey, Norwich; *Career* articled clerk Corbould Rigby & Co 1979-81, ptnr Freshfields 1987- (asst slr 1981-87); memb City of London Slrs Co;

Recreations cricket, rugby, squash, theatre, good food; *Clubs* Law Soc RFC, Dulwich CC, Tulse Hill and Honor Oak Squash; *Style*— Geoffrey Le Pard, Esq; Grindall Ho, 25 Newgate St, London EC1 (☎ 01 606 6677, fax 01 329 6022)

LE POER TRENCH, Brinsley; *see*: Clancarty, Earl of

LE POER TRENCH, (Nicholas) Richard Power; s of Hon Power Edward Ford Le Poer Trench (decd) (yst s of 5 Earl of Clancarty); hp of unc, 8 Earl; *b* 1 May 1952; *Educ* Westminster Sch, Ashford GS, Plymouth Polytechnic; *Style*— Richard Le Poer Trench, Esq; 36 Pinner Road, Sheffield S11 8UH

LE QUESNE, Sir (John) Godfray; QC (1962); 3 s of Charles Thomas Le Quesne, QC (d 1954), of London and Jersey, and Florence Elizabeth Eileen, *née* Pearce Gould (d 1977); bro of Sir Martin and Prof Leslie, *qqv*; *b* 18 Jan 1924; *Educ* Shrewsbury, Exeter Coll Oxford (MA); *m* 6 April 1963, Susan Mary, da of Rev Thomas Woodman Gill; 2 s, 1 da; *Career* barr Inner Temple 1947, admitted to bar of St Helena 1959; dep chm Kesteven Lincs QS 1963-71, judge of Cts of Appeal of Jersey and Guernsey 1964-, Rec of Crown Ct 1972-; chm Monopolies and Mergers Cmmn 1975-87; chm Cncl of Regent's Park Coll Oxford 1958-87; resumed practice 1988; Dato Order of the Crown of Brunei 1978; kt 1980; *Recreations* music, railways, walking; *Style*— Sir Godfray Le Quesne, QC; 1 Crown Office Row, Temple, London EC4 7HH (☎ 01 583 9292, telex 8953152)

LE QUESNE, Prof Leslie Philip; CBE (1984); 2 s of Charles Thomas Le Quesne, QC (d 1954), and (Florence Elizabeth) Eileen (d 1977), 3 da of Sir Alfred Pearce Gould, KCVO, FRCS; bro of Sir Martin and Sir Godfray, *qqv*; *b* 24 August 1919; *Educ* Rugby, Exeter Coll Oxford (DM, MCh); *m* 1969, Pamela Margaret, da of Dr Archibald Fullerton, MC (d 1972), of Batley, Yorks; 2 s (Thomas b 1973, William b 1975); *Career* prof of surgery Middx Hosp and dir Surgical Studies Dept 1963-84, dep vice chllr and dean faculty of medicine London Univ 1980-84; medical awards administrator Commonwealth Scholarship Cmmn 1984-; FRCS; *Recreations* fishing, sailing; *Clubs* Reform; *Style*— Prof Leslie Le Quesne, CBE; 8 Eton Villas, London NW3 4SX (☎ 01 722 0778); work: John Foster House, 36 Gordon Square, London WC1 OPF (☎ 01 387 8572)

LE QUESNE, Sir (Charles) Martin; KCMG (1974); s of Charles Thomas Le Quesne, QC (d 1954); bro of Sir Godfray and Prof Leslie, *qqv*; *b* 10 June 1917; *Educ* Shrewsbury, Exeter Coll Oxford; *m* 1948, Deidre Noel Fisher; 3 s; *Career* entered Foreign Office 1946; ambass to: Republic of Mali 1961-64, Algeria 1968-71; dep under-sec FCO 1971-74, high cmmr Nigeria 1974-76; memb of the States of Jersey 1978-; *Style*— Sir Martin Le Quesne, KCMG; Beau Desert, St Saviour, Jersey, CI (☎ (0534) 22076)

LEA, His Honour Judge Christopher Gerald; MC; yst s of late George Percy Lea, and Jocelyn Clare, *née* Lea, of Franche, Kidderminster, Worcs; *b* 27 Nov 1917; *Educ* Charterhouse, RMC Sandhurst; *m* 1952, Susan Elizabeth, da of Maj Edward Pendarves Dorrien Smith; 2 s, 2 da (1 decd); *Career* barr Inner Temple 1948; memb: Assistance Bd Appeal Tribunal Oxford Area 1961-63, Mental Health Review Tbnl 1962-68 and 1983-, met magistrate 1968-72, dep chm Berks QS 1968-71, circuit judge 1972-; *Style*— His Hon Judge Christopher Lea, MC; Simms Farm House, Mortimer, Reading, Berks (☎ 0734 332 360)

LEA, Lady Diana Silva; *née* Thompson; only da of James Howard Thompson, MIME, of Coton Hall, Bridgnorth, Shropshire, and Gladys, *née* Yates; *m* 1, 1945 (m dis 1947), Capt Guy William Bannar-Martin, IA; m 2, 1950, as his 2 wife, Sir Thomas Claude Harris Lea, 3 Bt (d 1985); *Style*— Diana, Lady Lea

LEA, Lt-Gen Sir George Harris; KCB (1967), CB (1964, DSO 1957, MBE 1950); s of George Percy Lea (d 1961), and Jocelyn Clare, *née* Lea (d 1974); *b* 28 Dec 1912; *Educ* Charterhouse, RMC Sandhurst; *m* 1948, Pamela Elizabeth, da of Brig Guy Lovett-Tayleur (d 1969); 1 s, 2 da; *Career* cmd 2 Inf Bde Gp 1957-60, Dep Mil Sec 1960-62, Maj-Gen 1962, GOC 42 Div and NW Dist 1962-63, cmd Forces N Rhodesia and Nyasaland 1964, dir of ops Borneo and cdr Br Forces Borneo 1965-66, head Br Def Staff Washington 1967-70, Lt-Gen 1967, ret 1970; chm Eagle Star Tst Co Jersey and Guernsey until 1988; Order of Stia Negara Brunei (1957); *Recreations* previously private flying; *Clubs* Army & Navy; *Style*— Lt-Gen Sir George Lea, KCB, DSO, MBE; Les Ruisseaux Lodge, St Brelade, Jersey, CI

LEA, Harold Rodney; DFC (1945); s of Albert Lea (d 1967), of Fordingbridge, Hants, and Elsie, *née* Tattersall (d 1934); *b* 31 Mar 1922; *Educ* King's Norton GS Birmingham; *m* 1, 16 March 1946, Pamela Alice, da of late John Leicester, of Ashtead, Surrey; m 2, 2 June 1951, Ruby, da of Rueben Tallon, of Storth, Milnthorpe, Cumbria; 1 s (Timothy John b 1959), 1 da (Suzanne Elizabeth b 1954); *Career* WWII joined RAFVR 1940, Fighter Cmd Flt Lt served: N Africa, Malta, Sicily, Italy, Holland, Belgium; instr: Central Gunnery Sch RAF 1944, Fighter Ldrs Sch RAF 1945-46; served RAF Korean War; joined Br Euro Airways (attaining cmd) 1964; hi-jacked 1975 on a flight Manchester to London; ret 1976; flew photographic aircraft for Arthur Gibson specialising in air to air photography; chm and pres West Berks Cons Assoc 1979-85; Queen's Commendation for Valuable Serv in the Air 1976; *Recreations* gardening, golf, reading; *Clubs* Penina GC (Algarve, Portugal); *Style*— Harold Lea, Esq, DFC; Casa Dos Bunkers, Falfeira, Portelas, 8600 Lagos, Algarve, Portugal (☎ Lagos 082 63937)

LEA, Vice-Adm Sir John Stuart Crosbie; KBE (1979); s of Lt Col Edward Heath Lea, IA (d 1947), by his w Aileen Beatrice Hawthorne (d 1973); *b* 4 June 1923; *Educ* Shrewsbury, RNEC Keyham; *m* 1947, Patricia Anne, da of William Martin Thoseby (d 1955); 1 s, 2 da; *Career* joined RN 1941, Capt 1966, dir of Naval Admin Planning 1970-71, Cdre HMS Nelson 1972-75, Rear-Adm 1975, asst chief of Fleet Support 1976-77, dir gen Naval Manpower and Trg 1977-80, Vice Adm 1978, ret; chm GEC Marine and Industl Gears Ltd 1980-87; chm: Portsmouth Naval Heritage Tst 1983-87, Hayling Is Hort Soc 1982, Regular Forces Employment Assoc 1987; Master Worshipful Co of Plumbers 1988; *Recreations* walking, gardening; *Style*— Vice Adm Sir John Lea, KBE; Springfield, 27 Bright Lane, Hayling Island, Hants (☎ 070 5 463801)

LEA, Sir (Thomas) Julian; 4 Bt (UK 1892); s of Sir Thomas Claude Harris Lea, 3 Bt (d 1985) and his 1 w, Barbara Katharine, OBE, JP (d 1945), da of Albert Julian Pell, JP, DL; *b* 18 Nov 1934; *Educ* Stowe, RNC Dartmouth, RNC Greenwich; *m* 1970, Gerry Valerie, da of late Capt Gibson Clarence Fahnestock, USAF; 3 s (Thomas William b 1973, Alexander Julian b 1978, Oliver David Pell b 1983), 2 da (Rebecca Barbara b 1972, Henrietta Katharine b 1976); *Heir* s, Thomas William b 1973; *Career* Lt RN 1952-58; merchant banker; dir: Mfrs Hanover Ltd 1975-81, Bank of America Int 1981-83; dep chief exec Midland Bank Project Fin Ltd 1983-84; fndr Lea Fin Servs 1986, dir J R Commodities Ltd 1987, Stewart Clark Mktg Ltd 1989, landowner; *Recreations* singing, music, shooting, sailing, fishing; *Style*— Sir Julian Lea, Bt; Bachelors Hall, Hundon, Sudbury, W Suffolk CO10 8DY (☎ 044086 236)

LEA, Philip; s of Herbert James Lea (d 1932), and Elizabeth, *née* Maskery; *b* 28 July 1915; *Educ* Sandbach Sch Cheshire; *m* Oct 1940, Vera Nadine (d 1986), da of Albert Cope (d 1969); 1 s (John Edward), 1 da (Anne Arden (Mrs Borrowdale)); *Career* chm and md Morning Foods Ltd North Western Mills 1942-; dir: H J Lea & Sons, P J Lea Consulting Services Ltd, Mornflake Oats Ltd, Wheelock Estates Ltd, Trustlea Ltd, Walter Brown & Sons Lts, Assoc of Cereal Food Manufacturers; engrg consit UK Agric Supply Trade Ass Trade Assoc; life govr Nat Inst of Agricultural Botany Cambridge; Freeman of City of London, memb Worshipful Co of Farmers; *Recreations* shooting, golf, boar hunting; *Clubs* Farmers', City Livery, RAC; *Style*— Philip Lea, Esq; Calveley Court, Tarporley, Cheshire (☎ 027 073 222); St Petrock's, Marine Drive, Llandudno (☎ 0492 77367); Morning Foods Ltd, North Western Mills, Crewe, Cheshire CW2 6HP (☎ 0270 213261, fax 0270 500291, telex 36548)

LEA, Robert Francis Gore; OBE (1942); s of Sir (Thomas) Sydney Lea, 2 Bt (d 1946), of Dunley Hall, nr Stourport, Worcs, and Mary Ophelia, *née* Woodward; *b* 22 Jan 1906; *Educ* Lancing, Clare Coll Cambridge (BA, MA); *m* 1, 5 March 1936, Valerie Josephine (d 1948), da of Lt Sir James Henry Domville 5 Bt; 1 da (Annabel Clare Ophelia b 1945); m 2, 3 May 1956, Susan, da of John Greenwood, of Dorset; 1 s ((Francis) Rupert Chad Lea b 1957); *Career* Aux Airforce 600 City of London F Sqdn 1930, enlisted 1939, served at Hornchurch Battle of Br, Siege of Malta 1941-42, Wing-Cdr 1943 (despatches); Lloyds of London 1928-36, commercial dir Aero-Res Ltd Duxford 1955-60 (joined 1937), md CIBA Duxford 1960 (jt md and dep chm 1963), chm TECHNE Ltd 1975-88; amateur breeder of roses, created the gardens at Duxford Mill opens for charity six times a year; fell Woodand Corpn 1939-56; *Recreations* gardening, shooting, fishing; *Style*— Robert Lea, Esq, OBE

LEACH, Allan William; s of Frank Leach (d 1938), of Rotherwick Hants, and Margaret Ann, *née* Bennett (d 1973); *b* 9 May 1931; *Educ* Watford GS, Loughborough Coll, Open Univ (BA, DPA); *m* 1962, Betty, da of William George Gadsby, of Bramcote, Notts; 1 s (William b 1967), 1 da (Sarah b 1969); *Career* county librarian Bute 1965-71, burgh librarian Ayr 1971-74; dir of Library Servs Kyle and Carrick 1974-82; dir gen and librarian Nat Library for the Blind 1982-, memb Standing Ctee IFLA Section of Libraries for the Blind 1983- (chm 1985-87); *Recreations* people, music, the countryside; *Style*— Allan Leach, Esq; 4 Windsor Rd, Hazel Grove, Stockport, Cheshire SK7 4SW (☎ 061 483 6418); Nat Library for the Blind, Cromwell Rd, Bredbury, Stockport, Cheshire SK6 2SG (☎ 061 494 0217)

LEACH, Clive William; s of Stanely Aubrey Leach, of Kessingland, Suffolk, and Laura Anne, *née* Robinson; *b* 4 Dec 1934; *Educ* Sir John Leman Sch, Beccles Suffolk, Birmingham Univ; *m* 1, 25 October 1958, 3 s (Christopher b 1959, Stuart b 1961, Adrian b 1964); m 2, 25 September 1980, Stephanie Miriam, da of Patrick McGinn, of Newlands Rd, Sidmouth, Devon; 1 s (Damian b 1981); *Career* md Yorks TV Ltd, chm Yorks TV Enterprises Ltd; played first class cricket for Warwicks 1955-57, also for Durham and Bucks counties; *Recreations* golf, travel, entertaining; *Clubs* Harwood Downs Golf, Warwickshire County Cricket, Bucks County Cricket, Clermont, MCC; *Style*— C W Leach, Esq; Yorkshire Television Ltd, 32 Bedford Row, London WC1

LEACH, Frank; s of George Manley Leach (d 1954), and Ethel Leach (d 1968); *b* 1 May 1935; *Educ* Wirral GS, London Univ (BA); *m* 1959, Marion, da of Reginald Edwards (d 1975); 2 s; *Career* chartered sec; gp sec The Cunard S/S Co Ltd 1968-74; dir: Br Lion Films Ltd 1974-76, Thorn EMI Screen Entertainment 1977-86, Weintraub Entertainment 1987-; *Recreations* painting, gardening; *Style*— Frank Leach, Esq; 11 Upton Quarry, Langton Green, Tunbridge Wells, Kent (tel 089 286 2733); Weintraub Entertainment, 167/9 Wardour St, London W1 (☎ 01 439 1790)

LEACH, Adm of the Fleet Sir Henry Conyers; GCB (1978), KCB (1977); s of Capt John Caterall Leach, MVO, DSO, RN (ka 1941), and Evelyn Burrell, *née* Lee (d 1969); *b* 18 Nov 1923; *Educ* RNC Dartmouth and Greenwich; *m* 15 Feb 1958, Mary Jean, da of Adm Sir Henry William Urquhart McCall, KCVO, KBE, CB, DSO (d 1980); 2 da (Henrietta b 1959, Philippa b 1964); *Career* joined RN 1937, Capt 1961, dir Naval Plans 1968-70, Rear Adm 1971, asst chief Naval Staff (Policy) 1971-73, Vice Adm 1974, Flag Offr First Flotilla 1974-75, vice-chief of Defence Staff 1976-77, Adm 1977, C-in-C Fleet and Allied C-in-C Channel and Eastern Atlantic 1977-79, chief of Naval Staff and First Sea Lord 1979-82, Adm of the Fleet 1982, first and princ Naval ADC to the Queen 1979; chm St Dunstan's 1983-; pres Sea Cadet Assoc 1984-; chm Royal Navy Club 1986-; pres Regal Naval Benevolent Soc 1983-; vice-pres SSAFA 1984-; naval pres Offrs Assoc 1984-; chm cncl: King Edward VII Hospital 1987-; Freeman of City of London 1982, memb Shipwrights' Co and Merchant Taylors' Co; *Recreations* fishing, shooting, gardening, repairing antique furniture; *Clubs* Farmers'; *Style*— Adm of the Fleet Sir Henry Leach, GCB, KCB; Wonston Lodge, Wonston, Winchester, Hants (☎ 0962 760327)

LEACH, Peter Timothy Lionel; s of Lt-Col Lionel Robert Henry Gerald Leach, MC, DL, of Benington Park, Stevenage, Herts, and Joan Mary, *née* Rochford; *b* 2 Oct 1945; *Educ* Ampleforth; *m* 1972, Stephanie, da of Geoffrey Haig Pike (d 1981), 2 s (Robert b 1974, Mark b 1980); 2 da (Emma b 1973, Sarah b 1977); *Career* CA dir Joseph Rochford Gp 1983; *Recreations* field sports; *Style*— P T L Leach, Esq; Wormley House, 82 High Rd, Wormley, Broxbourne, Herts (☎ 0992 466324)

LEACH, Maj Robert (Robin) Francis; s of late Maj Robert Wild Leach, and Jocelyn Mary, *née* Hudson (d 1979); *b* 25 May 1926; *Educ* Marlborough, RMA Sandhurst; *m* 13 Feb 1954, Christine Rosemary, da of Robert Christopher Giles, of Terwick Hill, Rogate, Sussex; 2 s (Robert Charles b 1957, Andrew Christopher b 1963), 1 da (Frances Columbel b 1955); *Career* WWII cmmnd 3 Kings Own Hussars served: Palestine, UK, Germany; Capt: GSO3 11 Armd Div HQ, staff 23 Armd Bde TA; instr RMA Sandhurst; Maj: staff mil ops branch MOD, HQ Aldershot dist; cmd sqdn 4/7 Royal Dragoon Gds Catterick, ret Maj 1963; memb mgmnt Kimberley Clarke consumer div 1963-65; Time-Life Int: Life Magazine 1965-70, advertising dept Time Magazine London 1970-76, mangr Time M East (also Scotland and Ireland) 1977-83; dir C W Assocs Ltd Int Media Reps 1983-89; memb Int Advertising Assoc 1965-83; pres Pirbright Br Legion, cncllr (also church warden and vice chm) Pirbright PCC; former master Sandhurst Beagles; *Recreations* golf, tennis, travel, shooting, hunting; *Clubs* Cavalry Guards, Worplesdon GC; *Style*— Maj Robin Leach; Greengates, The Green, Pirbright, nr Woking, Surrey (☎ 04867 2215); C W & Associates Ltd, 1/2 Rutland Gdns, London SW7 1BX (☎ 01 584 8588)

LEACH, Dr Rodney; s of Edward Leach (d 1951), of Thornton Clevelys, Lancs, and Alice Matthews, *née* Marcroft; descendent of one of the Rochdale Pioneers who founded the Worldwide Co-operative movement; *b* 3 Mar 1932; *Educ* Baines GS, Poulton de Fylde Lancs, Birmingham Univ (BSc, PhD); *m* 1958, Eira Mary, da of David Arthur Tuck (d 1975), of Caterham, Surrey; 3 s (Michael, Stephen, Alan), 1 da (Alison); *Career* ptnr McKinsey & Co Inc 1970-74, exec dir P & O Steam Navigation co 1974-85; chm: P & O Euro Tport Servs Ltd 1974-85, P & O Cruises Ltd 1980-85; chief exec and md VSEL Consortium plc 1985-, chm and chief exec Vickers Shipbuilding and Engrg Ltd 1986-; Freeman City of London, Liveryman Worshipful Co of Carmen; FRINA, FIIM, FInstM; *Recreations* sailing, reading, gardening, fell walking; *Clubs* RAC, Royal Yachting Assoc; *Style*— Dr Rodney Leach; Cleeve Howe, Windermere, Cumbria LA23 1AS; Vickers Shipbuilding and Engineering Ltd, Barrow-in-Furness, Cumbria LA14 1AF (☎ 0229 23366, telex 65411)

LEACH, Sir Ronald George; GBE (1976); s of William T Leach; *b* 1907; *Educ* Alleyns; *m* Margaret Alice, da of Henry Binns; *Career* dep fin sec Miny of Food 1939-46; memb: Departmental Ctee on Flooding 1953, Ctee of Inquiry into Shipping 1967; chm: Standard Chartered Bank (CI) Ltd, Standard Chartered Trust Co (CI) Ltd; Consumers Ctee for GB 1957-66, sr ptnr Peat Marwick Mitchell & Co Chartered Accountants 1966-77, pres Inst of Chartered Accountants 1979-80; dir: Samuel Montagu & Co, 1977-80, Banque Nationale de Paris Ltd 1977-80, Samuel Montagu & Co (Jersey) Ltd 1980-87, Int Investment Tst of Jersey Ltd, Ann St Brewery; Govett America Endevour; kt 1970; *Style*— Sir Ronald Leach, GBE; La Rosière, Mont de la Rosière, St Saviour, Jersey (☎ 0534 77039); Limeuil, Dordoyne, France;

LEACH, Stephen Michael Joseph; s of Lt Col Lionel Robert Henry Gerald Leach MC, JP, of Benington Park, Stevenage, Hert, and Joan Mary, *née* Rochford, MD; *b* 5 Nov 1947; *Educ* Ampleforth; *m* 24 July 1976, Sarah Margaret Young, da of Maj Edward Young Dobson (d 1972), 1 s (Timothy b 1979), 2 da (Rebecca b 1978, Katie b 1982); *Career* slr; sec Woodbridge Rotary Club, clerk Oxford Tstees; memb: Law soc memb: Law soc 1973; Provincial Notaries soc; *Recreations* fishing, shooting; *Style*— Stephen Leach, Esq; 28 Church Street, Woodbridge, (☎ 0394 385161 fax 0394 380134

LEACHMAN, Jack Ramsay; s of William Thomas Leachman (d 1985), of Colwyn Bay, and Grace, *née* Stamper (d 1979); *b* 14 Jan 1924; *Educ* Northampton Town & Co Sch; *m* 26 Sept 1949, (Isobel) Patricia, da of Henry McIntyre Whent (d 1949); 1 s (Robert), 2 da (Sara, Emma); *Career* WWII Fl Lt RAF Saudi Arabia 1943-47; brewer Bass plc 1951-86 (dir 1975-86), dir Grinkle Park Estate 1984-; memb Sail Trng Assoc; Freeman City of London 1981; Diplomate Inst of Brewing; *Recreations* shooting, fishing, cricket; *Clubs* MCC, Boodles; *Style*— Jack Leachman, Esq; Pear Tree Cottage, Egton Bridge, Whitby, N Yorks YO21 1UZ (☎ 0947 85219); Grinkle Pk Estate, Loftus, Saltburn, Cleveland (☎ 0287 40515)

LEADBITTER, Edward; MP (Lab) Hartlepool 1964-; s of Edward Leadbitter of Easington, Co Durham; *b* 18 June 1919; *Educ* State Sch, Teachers' Training Coll; *m* 1940, Phyllis Irene Mellin; 1 s, 1 da; *Career* cmmnd Royal Artillery 1941, served WW II; teacher; memb W Hartlepool Borough Cncl, organizer of Exhibition on History of Lab Movement 1956; chm: PLP Transport Gp 1978-, PLP Ports Gp 1978-, Anglo-Tunisian Parly Gp 1977-; memb House of Commons Chairmen's Panel 1980-; sponsored Registration of Children's Homes Bill 1981 successfully; hon freeman Borough of Hartlepool 1981; *Style*— Edward Leadbitter, Esq, MP; 30 Hylton Rd, Hartlepool, Cleveland

LEAF, Ian Andrew; s of Walter Murray Leaf Esq, FCIS, and Norma Leaf (*née* Asquith); *b* 29 Nov 1953; *Educ* Univ College Sch London, Business Sch London (BA (Hons) Business Studies); FAAI; *m* 1, 12 Sept 1976, Sandra Gillian, da of John; 1 s (Jarrod b 1980); 1 da (Marisa b 1978); m 2, 16 Dec 1984, Caroline Lesley, da of Michael (d 1973); 1 s (Harrison b 1986); *Career* Br Petroleum Co Ltd Mgmnt Trainee, Rapport Int Gp chm 1975-82, Symbol Int plc Gp-chm 1980-87 (ret 1986); Liveryman Worshipful Co of Coachmakers and Coach harness Makers; *Recreations* flying, sailing, hunting, piano, guitar, computers, tennis, squash, skiing; *Clubs* Royal Naval, City Livery; *Style*— Ian Leaf, Esq

LEAF, Robert Stephen; People of Today; s of Nathan Leaf, and Anne, *née* Feinman; *b* 9 August 1931; *Educ* Univ of Missouri (Bacherlor of Journalism, MA); *m* 8 June 1958, Adele Renee; 1 s (Stuart Leaf b 4 June 1961); *Career* Burson-Marsteller Int 1957-: vice pres 1961, exec vice pres 1965, pres 1968, chm 1985; writer of various trade and business publications for: USA, Europe, Asia; speaker on PR marketing and communications in W and E Europe (incl Russia), Asia (incl China), Australia, N and S America; memb folowing assocs: Int PR, PR consulting (former bd memb), Int Advertising, Foreign Press; memb: PR Soc of America, Inst of PR; *Recreations* tennis, travel, theatre; *Clubs* Hurlingham; *Style*— Robert Leaf, Esq; 3 Furescroft, George St, London W1 (☎ 01 262 4846); 24-28 Bloomsbury Way, London WC1A 2PX (☎ 01 831 6262, fax 01 430 1033, telex 267531)

LEAHY, Sir John Henry Gladstone; KCMG (1981), CMG (1973); s of William Henry Gladstone Leahy (d 1941), and Ethel, *née* Sudlow (d 1967); *b* 7 Feb 1928; *Educ* Tonbridge, Clare Coll Cambridge (BA), Yale (MA); *m* 1954, Elizabeth Anne, da of John Hereward Pitchford, CBE, *qv*; 2 s, 2 da; *Career* serv RAF 1950-52; entered FO 1952, head of chancery Tehran 1965-68, FCO 1968, head Personnel Servs FCO 1969, head news dept FCO 1971-73, cnsllr and head of chancery Paris 1973-75, asst under sec state on loan to NI Off 1975-77, asst under sec state FCO 1977-79, ambass SA 1979-82, dep under sec state (Africa and ME) FCO 1982-84, high commr Aust 1984-88; memb ct Skinners' Co; *Recreations* travel, reading, tennis, golf; *Clubs* Oxford & Cambridge, Lords Taverners; *Style*— Sir John Leahy, KCMG, CMG; Manor Stables, Bishopstone, Seaford, E Sussex BN25 2UD (☎ 0323 898898)

LEAKE, Prof Bernard Elgey; s of Norman Sidney Leake (d 1963), and Clare Evelyn, *née* Walgate (d 1970); *b* 29 July 1932; *Educ* Wirral GS Bebington, Liverpool Univ (BSc, PhD), Bristol Univ (DSc); *m* 23 Aug 1956, Gillian Dorothy, da of Prof Charles Henry Dubinson, CMG, 5 s (Christopher b 1958, Roger b 1959, Alastair b 1961, Jonathan b 1964, Nicholas b 1966); *Career* Leverhulme res fell Liverpool Univ 1955-57, lectr in geology Bristol Univ 1957-68, res assoc Berkeley California 1966, reader in geology Bristol Univ 1968-74, prof and head dept of geology Glasgow Univ (hon keeper of geological collections Hunterian Museum Glasgow 1980-85 (pres 1986-88), tres Geological Soc London 1980-85; FRSE 1976, FGS 1956; *Books* Catalogue of analysed calciferous Amphiboles (1968), over 100 res papers & maps especially of connemara, Western Ireland; *Clubs* Geological Soc; *Style*— Prof B E Leake; Geology Dept, University of Glasgow, Glasgow G12 8QQ

LEAKER, Dudley Roberts; s of Charles Henry Leaker (d 1941), and Mabel Gwendoline Leaker (d 1967); *b* 22 Dec 1920; *Educ* Dynevor Sch Swansea, Welsh and RWA Schs of Architecture UCL, Strathclyde Univ; *m* 12 June 1945, Mary Venn (Molly), da of Sydney James (d 1958); 1 s (David Charles b 1949), 3 da (Margaret (Mrs Halstead) b 1947, Jane (Mrs Smith) b 1953, Patricia (Mrs Eynon) b 1956); *Career* Civil Def; architect on bomb-damaged cities: Bristol, Plymouth, Coventry 1945-52; sr architect Stevenage New Town 1952-56; chief architect and planner: Cumbernauld New Town 1962-70, Warrington New Town 1970-75; architectural advsr and exec dir Milton Keynes New City 1975-78, hon res fell Open Univ 1979-84, exchange prof of architecture Pennsylvania State Univ 1981-82, chm int study gp invited to Tokyo by Japanese govt 1985, sr ind inspr at major public inquiries 1978-, head of team winning Reynolds Award for community architecture, and various other architectural awards; chm: Int Working Party on New Towns 1976-87, bd of tstees Inter Action (Milton Keynes) 1976-78; external examiner Strathclyde and Sheffield Univs; memb bd: Oxford Citizen's HSG Assoc 1978-85, S Shrops Rural HSG Assoc 1988-; hon life memb Int Fedn of HSG & Planning, fndr memb Cottage Theatre Cumbernauld; JP Dunbartonshire 1968-75; FRIBA 1952, FRIAS 1958, memb ISOCARP 1962; *Books* New Towns in National Development (1980), New Towns Worldwide (1985); *Recreations* painting, music, travel; *Style*— Dudley Leaker, Esq; Anchorsholme, Heighway Lane, All Stretton, Shrops SY6 6HN (☎ 0694 722095)

LEAKEY, Dr David Martin; s of Reginald Edward Leakey (d 1969), of Redhill, Surrey, and Edith Doris, *née* Gaze (d 1974); *b* 23 July 1932; *Educ* Imp Coll London (BSc, PhD, DIC); *m* 31 Aug 1957, Shirely May, da of George Clifford Webster (d 1968), of Bridlington, Yorks; 1 s (Graham Peter b 1967), 1 da (Pamela Susan b 1961); *Career* chief scientist Br Telecom 1986-; dir: Fulcrum Telecommunications Ltd 1985-, Mitel Inc Canada 1986-; dep engr-in-chief Br Telecom 1969-84, tech dir GEC Telecoms Ltd 1969-84; Liveryman Worshipful Co of Engrs; Freeman City of London; FEng, FIEE, FCGI; *Recreations* horticulture; *Style*— Dr David Leakey; British Telecom Centre, 81 Newgate St, London EC1A 7AJ (☎ 01 356 5315, telex 883051)

LEAKEY, Dr Mary Douglas; *née* Nicol; da of Erskine Edward Nicol (d 1926), and Cecilia Marion Elizabeth, *née* Frere; *b* 6 Feb 1913; *Educ* privately; *m* 1936, Dr Louis Seymour Bazett Leakey, FBA (d 1972), s of Canon Henry Leakey (d 1940); 3 s; *Career* archaeologist; former dir of research Olduvai Gorge Excavations; Hon DSc Witwatersrand 1965, Hon DSocSc Yale 1976, Hon DSc Chicago 1981, Hon DLitt Oxford 1982; FBA, FSA, FRAI, Mem US Nat Ac Sc; Hon DSc Cambridge 1987; *Recreations* reading, game watching; *Clubs* Women's Univ Club; *Style*— Dr Mary Leakey; c/o National Museum, Box 30239, Nairobi, Kenya

LEAMY, Stuart Nigel; s of Charles Kitchener Leamy, of 13 Buckingham Gdns, E Molesey, Surrey, and Constance Patricia, *née* Buckingham; *b* 9 July 1946; *Educ* Christ's Hosp Pembroke Coll, Oxford (BA 1968, MA 1972); *m* 31 July 1971, Carol Juliet, da of Donald Thomson (d 1949); 2 s ((Charles) Edmund b 1975, Selwyn b 1977); *Career* Charted Accountant (FCA); md: Auguste Noël Ltd, 1987; dir: Fitch & Son Ltd 1980, Hampton Pool Ltd 1984; *Recreations* swimming, watching cricket, medieval history; *Style*— S N Leamy; 39 Barnham St, London SE1 2UX (☎ 01 407 4011, telex 919700, fax 01 403 1135)

LEAN, Sir David; CBE (1953); s of Francis William le Blount (decd) and Helena Annie Tangye; *b* 25 Mar 1908; *Educ* Leighton Park Sch Reading; *m* 1; 1 s; m 2, 1949 (m dis 1957), Ann Todd (actress); m 3, 1960 (m dis 1978), Mrs Leila Markar; *Career* film dir: In Which We Serve (co-director with Noël Coward), This Happy Breed, Blithe Spirit, Brief Encounter, Great Expectations, Oliver Twist, The Passionate Friends, Madeleine, The Sound Barrier, Hobson's Choice, Summer Madness, The Bridge on the River Kwai (US Academy Award 1957), Lawrence of Arabia (US Academy Award 1963), Dr Zhivago, Ryan's Daughter, Passage to India (1984); kt 1984; *Style*— Sir David Lean

LEAPMAN, Hon Mrs; Hon Anne Cynthia Veronica Tempest; da of 2 and last Viscount Plumer (d 1944); *b* 22 April 1921; *m* 19 July 1952, John Frederick Martyn Leapman, s of Lt-Col H M Leapman, of Hove, Sussex; 3 da (Joanna b 1953, Emma b 1956, Sarah b 1961; *Style*— The Hon Mrs Leapman; 4 Upper King's Cliff, St Helier, Jersey

LEAR, Lt-Col Donald Jeffrey; s of William George Lear (d 1957), of Marine Gate, Rottingdean, Sussex, and Gladys Edith, *née* Othen (d 1984); *b* 18 Dec 1922; *Educ* Chigwell Sch Essex; *m* 12 Feb 1955, Penelope Helena, da of Charles Thomas Fitzgerald Pearson (d 1955), of Edinburgh; 4 s (Robin b 1957, Andrew b 1960, Christopher b 1966, Simon b 1969); *Career* Indian Army (16 Punjab Regt), serv in 4 Indian div in N Africa and Italy (Cassino) and Peshawar (NW Frontier of India), Adj 4 BN 16 Punjab Regt in Italy and India 1944-46, transferred to 2 Bn KOSB Peshawar 1946; asst ADC to Gov of NW Frontier (in Peshawar), Brig Maj 28 Cwlth Brig in Korea 1950-51, Army Staff Col 1952, Adj/KOSB in Malaya 1957, Adj 4 Bn the KOSB (TA) in Galashiels 1958, RAF Staff Coll 1959, GSO2 Intelligence Singapore Dist 1962-64, Chief Intelligence Offr (Lt-Col) to Dir of Ops in Borneo War 1964-65, GSOI in Directorate of Army Security 1965-69, passed Polish Exam 1969, naval and mil attaché Warsaw Poland 1969-71, security liaison offr in Directorate of Army Security 1971-77; re-engaged as ret offr (civil servant) 1978, as advsr on computer security in directorate of Army Security, chief intelligence and security offr in HQ SE Dist Aldershot 1979-88; chm Rowledge Rose Show 1979-; memb Policy Ctee 4 Indian Div Offrs' Assoc; *Recreations* shooting, fishing, gardening, beekeeping, vine growing; *Clubs* Royal Aldershot Offrs'; *Style*— Lt-Col Donald Lear, Esq; Long Valley, Echo Barn Lane, Wrecclesham, by Farnham, Surrey

LEARMOND, Hon Mrs Virginia Mary; da of Baron Marshall of Leeds (Life Peer); *b* 1949; *Educ* Queen Margaret's Sch York, Cygnets House London; *m* 1972, Nigel James Alexander Learmond; 1 s (Alexander Marshall b 1978), 1 da (Marissa Virginian Stuart b 1973); *Career* teacher; FRSA; *Recreations* music, theatre; *Style*— The Hon Mrs Learmond; 52 Marryat Rd, Wimbledon SW19

LEARMONT, Maj-Gen John Hartley; CBE (1980, OBE 1975); s of Capt Percy Hewitt Learmont, CIE (d 1983) of Curry Rivel Somerset and Doris Orynthia, *née* Hartley (d 1982); *b* 10 Mar 1934; *Educ* Fettes Coll, RMA Sandhurst; *m* 2 Mar 1957, Susan, da of Thomas Jefferson Thornborrow, FRICS, (d 1971) of Penrith; 3 s (Mark b 7 Jan 1958, Richard John 8 June 1960, James Jefferson b 9 Feb 1967); *Career* cmmnd RA 1954, Instr RMA 1960-63, student Staff Coll 1964, served 14 Fld Regt, Staff Coll and 3 RHA 1965-70, MA to C-in-C BAOR 1971-73, CO 1 RHA 1974-75 (despatches

1974), HQ BAOR 1976-78, cdr 8 Fld Force 1979-81, Dep Cdr Cwlth Monitoring Force Rhodesia 1979-80, student RCDS 1981, Chief of Mission Br C-in-C Mission to Soviet Forces in Germany 1982-84, Cdr Artillery 1 (Br) Corps 1985-87, Chief of Staff UKLF 1987-88, Cmdt Staff Coll Camberley 1988-, Col Cmdt Army Air Corps 1988-; FBIM; *Recreations* fell walking, all sport, theatre; *Clubs* Naval and Military

LEAROYD, Lady Mary Sarah-Jane Hope; da of 3 Marquess of Linlithgow, MC; *b* 25 May 1940; *Educ* Heathfield Ascot, Paris; *m* 1967 (m dis 1978), Michael Gordon Learoyd; 1 s (Jeremy b 1971); *Style*— Lady Sarah-Jane Learoyd

LEARY, Brian; QC; s of late A T Leary, and late M C, *née* Bond; *b* 1 Jan 1929; *Educ* Kings Sch Canterbury, Wadham Coll Oxford (MA); *m* 14 April 1965, Myriam Ann, da of late Kenneth Bannister, CBE, of Mexico City; *Career* barr Middle Temple 1953, sr prosecuting counsel to Crown 1971-78 (jr 1964-71), master of the bench 1986; *Recreations* travel, sailing, growing herbs; *Style*— Brian Leary, Esq, QC; East Farleigh Ho, East Farleigh, Kent (☎ 0622 272 95); 5 Paper Bldgs, Temple EC4 (☎ 01 583 6117)

LEASK, Lt-Gen Sir Henry Lowther Ewart Clark; KCB (1970, CB 1967), DSO (1945), OBE (1957, MBE 1945); s of Rev James Leask, rector of Scruton, Yorks, and Margaret Ewart Leask; *b* 30 June 1913; *m* 1940, Zoë de Camborne, da of Col William Patterson Paynter, DSO, RHA (d 1958), of Dogmersfield Lodge, Odiham, Hants; 1 s, 2 da; *Career* 2 Lt Royal Scots Fusiliers 1936, served WWII (India, Med and Italy), GSO 1942, Bde Maj Inf Bde 1943, 2 i/c (later CO) 8 Bn Argyll and Sutherland Highlanders 1944-45, CO 1 Bn London Scottish 1946-47, Gen Staff Mil Ops WO 1947-49, instr Staff Coll 1949-51, CO 1 Bn Parachute Regt 1952-54, Cmdt Tactical Wing Sch of Inf 1957-58, Cdr Inf Bde 1958-61, Brig 1961, idc 1961, dep mil sec to sec state for war 1962-64, Col Royal Highland Fusiliers 1964-69, Col Cmdt Scottish Inf 1968, GOC 52 Lowland Div 1964-66, Maj-Gen 1964, dir Army Trg MOD 1966-69, Lt-Gen 1969, GOC Scotland 1969-72, govr of Edinburgh Castle 1969-72, ret; *Recreations* shooting, fishing; *Clubs* New (Edinburgh), Hurlingham, Carlton; *Style*— Lt-Gen Sir Henry Leask, KCB, DSO, OBE; 9 Glenalmond House, Manor Fields, London SW15 (☎ 01 788 6949)

LEASK OF LEASK, Madam Anne Meredith Gordon Fleming; 22 Chief of Clan Leask; da of Alexander Leask Curr, univ lectr; suc Alexander Graham Leask of that Ilk 1968; *b* 1915; *Educ* Lonsdale Sch for Girls Norwich, Univ of London (BA), Sorbonne, Univ of Colorado (MA, PhD); *Career* instr, Univ of Colorado, asst and assoc prof Univ of Toledo (Ohio) and Kalamazoo Coll (Michigan), prof Cedar Cres Coll (Pennsylvania), lectr Inst of Adult Educn Norwich; personally involved with Clan Leask Soc and membs worldwide and with charitable orgns; Chev de l'Ordre des Palmes Acad́emiques; *Books* La Littéerature Française Contemporaine (1970), French Grammar, Spanish Grammar, The Leasks (1980); *Recreations* dramatics, music, swimming; *Style*— Madam Leask of Leask; 1 Vincent Rd, Sheringham, Norfolk; Leask, Aberdeenshire

LEASON, (Catherine Constance) Jean; *née* Hamilton; da of William Claud Hamilton (d 1982, who started the first official hosp and prison library servs), and Kathleen Mary Hamilton, *née* Pendrich (d 1944); *b* 7 July 1924; *Educ* Durham Girls' County Sch; *m* 9 Aug 1947, Dennis Brigham, da of Stanley Brigham Leason (d 1981), of Dorset; 1 s (Mark b 1958), 2 da (Linda b 1950, Penelope b 1953); *Career* Leeds General Infirmary SRN; chm, hon sec and fndr Dorking Branch of Leukaemia Res Fund; *Style*— Mrs Jean *Recreations* cooking, gardening, burmese cats, choral singing; Leason; 24 Upper Rose Hill, Dorking, Surrey RH4 3EB (☎ 0306 882752)

LEASOR, (Thomas) James; s of Richard Leasor, (d 1959), of Erith, Kent, and Christine, *née* Hall (d 1949); *b* 20 Dec 1923; *Educ* City of London Sch, Oriel Coll Oxford (BA, MA); *m* 1 Dec 1951, Joan Margaret, da of Capt Roland S Bevan (d 1968), of Crowcombe, Somerset; 3 s (Jeremy b 1953, Andrew b 1956, Stuart b 1958); *Career* WWII vol Royal E Kent Regt 1942, cmmnd 2 Lt Royal Berks Regt 1944; served 1 Lincolns: Burma, India, Malaya, ret Capt 1976: ed staff London Daily Express 1948-55, magazine conslt Geo News Ltd (later IPC) 1955-59, co fndr and dir Elm Tree Books, underwriting memb Lloyds; FRSA; *Books* author of 30 books incl the Jason Love series of suspense books; also: The Red Fort (1954), War at the Top (1959), Hess, The Uninvited Envoy (1962), Singapore The Battle that Changed the World (1968), Green Beach (1975), Open Secret (1983), Ship of Gold (1984), Tank of Serpents (1986); *Recreations* walking dogs, swimming, vintage sports cars; *Clubs* Garrick; *Style*— James Leasor, Esq; Swallowcliffe Manor, Salisbury, Wilts SP3 5PB; C Do Zimbro, Praia da Luz, Lagos, Algarve, Portugal

LEATHAM, Michael Gurney; Nigel Clere Leatham, OBE (d 1939), and Eileen Edith, *née* Riley; *b* 23 Dec 1922; *Educ* Ampleforth; *m* 15 Feb 1952, Frida Monica, da of René Charles Roughtion (d 1973); *Career* HM Forces 1940-48, Royal Indian Artillary, SOE, SEAC, Burma, China Malaya, Mil Govt Italy and Austria 1946-48, Lt-Col; md Bulova UK Ltd 1968-71, dir and gen mangr Klarcrete Ltd 1971-74; chm Monmouth Cons Assoc 1978-81, Gwent Nat Tst Assoc 1982-85, Kymin Restoration Appeal 1986-88; *Recreations* antiquities, long distance walking, bird-watching, bridge, gardening; *Style*— Michael Leatham, Esq; Millbrook Cottage, Penrhos, nr Raglan, Gwent NP5 2DE (☎ 0291 690909)

LEATHAM, Philip William; s of Maj Patrick Magor Leatham (d 1950), and Hon Cecily, *née* Berry (d 1976), da of 1 Baron Buckland (d 1928 when title extinct); bro Simon Leatham, *qv*; *b* 30 August 1946; *Educ* Eton, Magdalene Coll Cambridge; *m* 1971, Hon Rowena Margaret, *née* Hawke, *qv* da 9 Baron Hawke; 1 s (Patrick b 1974), 1 da (Arabella b 1976); *Career* chartered accountant; *Recreations* riding, shooting; *Clubs* Boodle's; *Style*— Philip Leatham, Esq; Burleigh Hall, Stroud, Glos

LEATHAM, Hon Mrs (Rowena Margaret); *née* Hawke; da of 9 Baron Hawke; *b* 1948; *Educ* Hatherop Castle Sch; *m* 1971, Philip William Leatham, *qv*; 2 s, 1 da; *Style*— The Hon Mrs Leatham; Burleigh Hall, Brimscombe, Glos

LEATHAM, Simon Patrick; eldest s of Maj Patrick Magor Leatham (d 1951), and Hon Cecily Eveline, *née* Berry (d 1976), da of 1 and last Baron Buckland (d 1928); bro of Philip Leatham, *qv*; *b* 9 Nov 1944; *Educ* Eton, Trinity Coll Cambridge; *m* 25 April 1967, Lady Victoria Diana, *née* Cecil, da of 6 Marquess of Exeter (d 1982); 1 s (Richard b 1971), 1 da (Miranda b 1969); *Career* chartered accountant; chief exec Oceanic Finance Corpn Ltd 1982-; *Clubs* Boodles; *Style*— Simon P Leatham, Esq; Burghley Ho, Stamford, Lincolnshire PE9 3JY (☎ 0780 63 131); Flat 18, Chelsea Ho, St Lowndes St, London SW1X 9JE (☎ 01 245 6366); Albermarle Ho, 1 Albermarle St, London (☎ 01 491 4294, telex 8812315 OCFIN G)

LEATHAM, Lady Victoria Diana; *née* Cecil; da of 6 Marquess of Exeter, KCMG, and 2 w, Diana, da of Hon Arnold Henderson, OBE (d 1933, 5 s of 1 Baron Faringdon, CH); *b* 1947; *m* 1967, Simon Patrick Leatham, *qv*; 1 s, 1 da; *Career* mangr Burghley House, dep dir Sotheby's, presenter of tv progs on stately homes; *Style*— Lady Victoria Leatham; Burghley House, Stamford, Lincs (☎ 0780 63131)

LEATHART, Air Cdre James Anthony; CB (1960), DSO (1940); s of Percival Wilson Leathart (d 1952), ent surgn, of Overacres, Alnmouth, Northumberland, and Margaret Ellen, *née* Beazley (d 1974); *b* 5 Jan 1915; *Educ* St Edwards Sch Oxford, Liverpool Univ; *m* 4 July 1939, Elaine Lance, da of Reginald Radcliffe, of School Lane, Birkenhead; 2 s (Anthony b 1944, Robin b 1948), 1 da (Judith b 1940); *Career* fndr memb 610 Co of Chester Aux Sqdn 1936-37, No 3 Flying Trg Sch RAF 1937, CO during Battle of Br No 54 (F) Sqdn 1937-40 (despatches), directorate of Air Tactics Air Miny 1940-41 HQ Fighter Cmd 1941, Temporary CO No 406 (NF) Sqdn RCAF 1941, Air Tactics HQ RAF ME Cairo 1941-42, CO No 89 NF Sqdn Western Desert 1942-43 (despatches), Admin Plans HQ 84 Gp 1943, personal SO and pilot to C in C Allied Euro AF 1944, Dep/SASO No 85 Gp 1944-45, CO 148 Wing (4 Mosquito NF Sqdns) 1945, dir staff RAF Staff Coll 1945-48, Air Staff No 66 Gp 1948-50, Jt Servs Staff Coll 1950, air rep Jt Intelligence Staff (3 servs M15, M16) 1950-53, Ops Controller Northern Sector Fighter Cmd; CO: Air Def Ops Centre HQ Fighter Cmd 1955-57, RAF N Coates (RAF Guided Weapon Def Station) 1957-58; SASO No 12 Gp 1958-60, dir Operational Requirments Air Miny 1960-62, retd 1960; *Recreations* fly-fishing, motor sport; *Clubs* RAF; *Style*— Air Cdre James Leathart, CB, DSO; Wortley Farmhouse, Wotton under Edge, Glos (☎ 0453 842312)

LEATHER, Sir Edwin Hartley Cameron; KCVO (1975), KCMG (1974), MP (C) Somerset N 1950-64; s of Harold H Leather, MBE; *b* 1919; *Educ* Trinity Coll Sch Ontario, RMC Kingston Ontario; *m* 1940, Sheila Alexie, da of A H Greenlees; 2 da; *Career* dir Hogg Robinson and Capel-Cure Ltd and subsidiary cos 1946-64, pres Inst of Mktg 1963-67, dir William Baird and Co Ltd 1966-73, chm Nat Union of Cons Assocs 1969-70, govr and C-in-C Bermuda 1973-77, dir N M Rothschild (Bermuda) 1978-, and others; broadcaster and author; hon FRSA, hon LLD Bath 1975, hon citizen Kansas City, medal of merit Royal Canadian Legion; Gold medal, Nat Inst of Social Sciences NY; KStJ 1973; kt 1962; *Books* The Vienna Elephant, The Mozart Score, The Duveen Letter; *Recreations* travel, reading, music; *Clubs* Royal Bermuda YC, Canadian (New York), York (Toronto), Hamilton (Ontario); *Style*— Sir Edwin Leather, KCMG, KCVO; Chelsea, Inwood Dr, Paget, Bermuda (☎ 809 236 0240); 130 St Joseph's Drive, Hamilton, Canada L8N 2E8 (☎ 416 527 1917)

LEATHERLAND, Baron (Life Peer UK 1964); Charles Edward Leatherland; OBE (1951), JP (Essex 1944), DL (Essex 1963); s of John Edward Leatherland (d 1945), of Churchover, Warwicks; *b* 18 April 1898; *Educ* Birmingham; *m* 1922, Mary Elizabeth (d 1987), da of Joseph Henry Morgan, of Shareshill, Staffs; 1 s (Hon John, *qv*), 1 da (Hon Mrs Irene Richards); *Career* sits as Labour peer in House of Lords; served WW I Co Sgt-Maj Royal Warwicks Regt, Somme and Ypres (MSM and despatches), army of occupation Bonn; vice-chm Essex CC 1952-55 and 1958-60 (chm 1960-61, chm Finance Ctee 1952-55 and 1958-60); tres and memb Essex Univ Cncl 1961-73; memb: Basildon Dvpt Corpn 1967-71, Monopolies Cmmn to consider newspaper mergers 1969; hon Doctor of the Univ (DU) Essex; won both Prince of Wales's Gold Medals for essays on economic subjects 1923 and 1924; *Books* Book of the Labour Party (part author); *Recreations* formerly fox hunting, now walking; *Style*— The Rt Hon the Lord Leatherland, OBE, MSM, JP, DL; 19 Starling Close, Buckhurst Hill, Essex (☎ 01 504 3164)

LEATHERLAND, Hon John Charles; s of Baron Leatherland, OBE (Life Peer) *qv*; *b* 2 July 1929; *Educ* Brentwood; *m* 1954, Esther, da of Mrs Dora Steckman, of London; 2 da; *Style*— The Hon John Leatherland; 4 Manor Way, Chingford Hatch, London E4 6NW (☎ 01 529 0347)

LEATHERS, Hon Christopher Graeme; s and h of 2 Viscount Leathers, *qv*; *b* 31 August 1941; *Educ* Rugby; *m* 1964, Maria Philomena, da of Michael Merriman, of Charlestown, Co Mayo; 1 s (James Frederick b 1969), 1 da (Melissa Maria b 1966); *Style*— The Hon Christopher Leathers; Sunhill, Mold Rd, Bodfari, Denbigh, Clwyd LL4 BDP

LEATHERS, 2 Viscount (UK 1954); Frederick Alan Leathers; also Baron Leathers (UK 1941); s of 1 Viscount Leathers, CH, PC (d 1965); *b* 4 April 1908; *Educ* Brighton Coll, Emmanuel Cambridge; *m* 1, 1940 (m dis 1983), Elspeth Graeme, da of Sir Thomas Alexander Stewart, KCSI, KCIE (d 1964); 2 s (Hon Christopher, Hon Jeremy *qqv*), 2 da (Hon Mrs Arthur Centner b 1944, Hon Mrs Thomas Chadbon b 1974); m 2, 1983, Mrs Lorna Barnett, widow of A A C Barnett; *Heir* s, Hon Christopher Graeme Leathers; *Career* chm Missions to Seamen; memb Baltic Exchange; former chm of various shipping and cement cos; former dir Nat Westminster Bank (outer London regn); FRPSL, FRSA, MInstPet; *Clubs* RAC; *Style*— The Rt Hon the Viscount Leathers; Park House, Chiddingfold, Surrey GU8 4TS (☎ 042 879 3222)

LEATHERS, Hon Jeremy Baxter; s of 2 Viscount Leathers, *qv*; *b* 11 April 1946; *Educ* Rugby, Trinity Coll Dublin; *m* 1969, Fiona Lesley, eldest da of late George Stanhope Pitt, of Rowbarns Manor, Horsley, Surrey; 1 da (Fern Griselda b 1979); *Style*— The Hon Jeremy Leathers

LEATHERS, Hon Leslie John; s of 1 Viscount Leathers, CH, PC (d 1965); *b* 25 Nov 1911; *Educ* Brighton Coll; *m* 1937, Elizabeth Stella, da of Thomas Stanley Nash (d 1964); 2 s (Michael b 1938, David b 1942), 1 da (Mrs Wilfried Bischoff, *qv*); *Career* Lt-Col (AQMG); Staff Coll 1943; slr 1934; memb Cncl London Chamber of Commerce 1955-65; gen cmmr of income tax 1958-75; memb Worshipful Co of Coachmakers and Coach Harness Makers; *Clubs* Brooks's, Hurlingham, Rand (Johannesburg); *Style*— The Hon L J Leathers; Middleton Park, Middleton Stoney, nr Bicester, Oxfordshire OX6 8SQ

LEAVER, Sir Christopher; GBE (1981), JP (Inner London); s of Dr Robert Leaver, and Audrey, *née* Kerpen; *b* 3 Nov 1937; *Educ* Eastbourne Coll; *m* 1975, Helen Mireille Molyneux Benton; 1 s (Benedict), 2 da (Tara, Anna); *Career* cmmnd RAOC 1956-58, Hon Col 151 (Gtr London) Tport Regt RCT (V) 1983-88, Hon Col Cmdt RCT 1988-; chm: Russell & McIver Gp (wine merchants), Thames Line plc 1987-; dir: Bath & Portland Gp plc 1983-85, Thermal Scientific plc 1985-88; chm London Tourist Bd 1983-, dep chm Thames Water Authy 1983-; memb cncl RBKC 1970-73, memb ct of common cncl Ward of Davygate City of London 1973 (Alderman 1974-), Sheriff City of London 1979-80, memb Cmmn of Lt for City of London 1982, Lord Mayor London 1981-82, HM Lieutenant City of London 1982; Chm Young Musicians Symphony

Orchestra 1979-81; vice pres: Euro Acad GB 1982-, cncl Mission to Seamen 1983-, Nat Playing Fields Assoc 1983-, Bridwell Royal Hosp 1983-; govr: Christs' Hosp Sch 1975-, City of London Girls Sch 1975-78, City Univ 1978-(chllr 1981-82), City of London Freemen's Sch 1980-81, Music Therapy Tst 1981-; hon memb GSM 1982-, tstee London Symphony Orchestra 1983-; bd memb Brixton Prison 1975-78, church warden St Olave's Hart St 1975-; Church Cmmr 1982-, memb fin ctee London Diocesan Fund 1983-88, almoner tstee St Paul's Cathedral Choir Sch Tst, cncl memb Eastbourne Coll 1988-; Freeman Worshipful Co of Watermen and Lightermen; Hon Liveryman: Worshipful Co of Framers, Worshipful Co of Environmental Cleaners 1982-, Master Worshipful Co of Carmen 1987-88; KStJ 1982; Hon DHus City Univ 1982; FRSA, FCIT; *Style—* Sir Christopher Leaver, GBE, JP; The Rectory, St Mary-at-Hill, London EC3R 8EE (☎ 01 283 3575)

LEAVER, Prof Christopher John; s of Douglas Percival Leaver (d 1978), and Elizabeth Constance, *née* Hancock; *b* 31 May 1942; *Educ* Lyme Regis GS, Imp Coll London (BSc, DIC, PhD); *m* 8 Oct 1971, Anne, da of Prof Hastings Dudley Huggins (d 1970); 1 s (Tristan), 1 da (Anya); *Career* Fulbright Scholar Purdue Univ USA 1966-68, sci offr ARC Plant Physiology Unit Imperial Coll 1968-69; prof at Plant Molecular Biology Univ of Edinburgh 1986- (SERC sr res fell 1985-, reader 1980-86, lectr 1969-80); tstee John Innes Inst 1987-, T H Huxley Gold Medal Imp Coll 1970, Tate and Lyle Award Phytochem Soc of Europe 1984; EMBO 1982, FRS 1986, FRSE 1987, ARCS; *Recreations* walking and talking in Upper Coquetdale; *Style—* Prof Christopher Leaver; Dept of Botany, The Kings Buildings, University of Edinburgh, Edinburgh EH9 3JH (☎ 031 667 1081, ext 3304)

LEAVER, Colin Edward; s of Edward Roy Leaver, of West Wittering, West Sussex, and Freda Eleanor, *née* Toogood; *b* 25 May 1958; *Educ* Haywards Heath GS, Lincoln Coll Oxford (MA); *m* 10 May 1986, Maria Victoria, da of John Hutton Simpkins, of Alicante, Spain; 1 da (Chirstina b 1987); *Career* Simmons & Simmons: articled clerk 1980-82, asst slr 1982-86, ptnr 1986-; *Recreations* hockey, philately, aviation; *Style—* Colin Leaver, Esq; The Coppice, Birtley Rise, Bramley, Nr Guilford, Surrey; 14 Dominion St, London EC2M 2RJ (☎ 01 628 2020, fax 01 588 4129, telex 888 526 SIMMON G)

LEAVER, Hon Mrs Margaret; *née* Cavendish; da of 6 Baron Waterpark (d 1949); *b* 1907; *m* 1934, Wallace Thomas Leaver (d 1972); 2 da (Mrs Peter Wiggins b 1938, Elizabeth b 1942); *Style—* The Hon Mrs Leaver; St Benets, Beech Hill, Bridge, Canterbury, Kent

LEAVETT, Alan; s of George Leavett, Gosport, Hants (d 1952), and Mabel Dorothy, *née* Witts, (d 1976); *b* 4 May 1924; *Educ* Gosport County Sch, Southampton, UCL (BA); *m* 9 Oct 1948, Jean Mary, da of Arthur Charles Albert Wanford, ISO, of Bristol; 3 da (Judith b 1950, Antonia b 1952, Phillida b 1958); *Career* memb: Rural Devpt Cmmn 1981-, Woodspring DC 1986-, vice pres: Action with Communities in Rural England (ACRE) 1987-, Miny of Aircraft Prodn RAE 1943-46, HM Customs and Excise 1947-49, HM Foreign Serv 1949-61 (Rio de Janeiro 1950-53, Bangkok 1955-59, UK perm del to ECAFE 1958-59), Cabinet Off 1961-63, Miny of Housing and Local Govt DOE 1963-73, Civil Serv Selection Bd 1973-74, under-sec for Rural Affairs DOE 1974-81, gen sec Avon Wildlife Tst 1981-84, vice-chm Avon Community Cncl 1981-; memb: Cncl of World Wildlife Fund (UK) 1982-86, exec ctee, European Cncl for the Village and Small Town (ECOVAST) 1984-86; *Recreations* book collecting; *Style—* Alan Leavett, Esq; Darenth House, St Martins, Long Ashton, Bristol BS18 9HP (☎ 0272 392876)

LEAVETT-SHENLEY, John; s of Ernest Leavett-Shenley (d 1974); *b* 21 May 1930; *m* 1961, Alison Yvonne, da of Cdr The Hon Henry Cecil, OBE (d 1962, 4 s of Baroness Amherst of Hackney, OBE, by her husb Col Lord William Cecil, CVO, who in his turn was 3 s of 3 Marquess of Exeter); 2 s, 1 da; *Career* Welsh Gds 1948-53; farmer and forester; pres Devon Cattle Breeders Soc 1978, High Sheriff of Hamps 1985-86; *Recreations* racing, shooting, fishing; *Clubs* Cavalry & Guards, Welsh Guards; *Style—* John Leavett-Shenley, Esq; The Holt, Upham, nr Southampton, Hants SO3 1HR (☎ 048 93 3452)

LEAVEY, John Anthony; *b* 3 Mar 1915; *Educ* Mill Hill Sch, Trinity Hall Cambridge (BA); *m* 1952, Lesley, da of Rt Hon Sir Benjamin Ormerod; *Career* WWII Maj 5 Royal Inniskilling Dragoon Gds; MP (Cons) Heywood and Royton 1955-64; business dir; *Recreations* fishing; *Clubs* Army and Navy; *Style—* John Leavey, Esq; 30 Pembroke Gardens Close, London W8 6HR

LEBERL, Geoffrey Albert; s of Francis Albert Leberl, and Nancy Reay, *née* Harrison; *b* 23 August 1943; *Educ* Archbp Tenisons GS; *m* 18 June 1966, Pauline, da of Redvers Buller Percy Mee; 1 s (Martin b 1970), 1 da (Samantha b 1967); *Career* dir Leberl Advertising Ltd 1965-; MIPA; *Recreations* half marathon running, badminton, swimming, gardening, music, theatre; *Clubs* Norwood Sports & Social; *Style—* Geoffrey A Leberl, Esq; c/o 143 Regent Street, London W1R 8DQ (☎ 01 734 4521, fax 01 437 4845)

LEBUS, Hon Mrs (Christina); da of 2 Baron Strathalmond, CMG, OBE, TD (d 1976); *b* 1954; *m* 1974, Timothy Andrew Lebus; 1 s (David b 1983); *Style—* The Hon Mrs Lebus; 70 Ellerby St, London SW6 6EZ

LEBUS, John Edward Louis; s of Louis Solomon Lebus (d 1983), and Edith Anne, *née* Mannheim (d 1978); *b* 28 May 1932; *Educ* Montezuma Mountain Sch Calif USA, Canford, Pembroke Coll Cambridge (MA); *m* 15 Dec 1956, Jane Penelope, da of Lionel Livingstone, OBE (d 1962); 3 s (Simon b 1957, Matthew b 1959, Andrew b 1961), 1 da (Amanda Suzanne b 1964); *Career* md: Kitchen Range Foods Ltd, Common Mktg Ltd; dir Hernitage Projects Ltd, vice pres Br Frozen Food Food Fedn; vice chm Cambridge Symphony Orch; *Clubs* HAC; *Style—* John Lebus, Esq; Cokenach House, Barkway, Royston, Herts SG8 8DL; Kitchen Range Foods Ltd, Bar Hill, Cambridge CB3 8EX (☎ 0954 80078, telex 818202)

LECHMERE, Sir Berwick Hungerford; 6 Bt (UK 1818), JP (Worcs 1966); s of Capt Sir Ronald Berwick Hungerford Lechmere, 5 Bt (d 1965), and Constance, *née* Long; the estate of Severn End at Hanley Castle, formerly known as Lechmere's Place has been in the family since 11th century; Nicholas Lechmere, chancellor of Duchy of Lancaster for Life 1717 cr. Baron Lechmere 1721, *dsp* 1727; *b* 21 Sept 1917; *Educ* Charterhouse, Magdalene Coll Cambridge; *m* 1, 24 May 1952 (m annulled 1954), Susan Adele Mary, o child of late Cdr George Henry Maunsell-Smyth, RN; m 2, 17 Nov 1954, Norah Garrett, eldest da of late Lt-Col Christopher Garrett Elkington, DSO, DL, of The Moat House, Cutnall Green, Worcs; *Heir* kinsman, Reginald Anthony Hungerford Lechmere; *Career* High Sheriff Worcs 1962, vice Lord-Lt Hereford and Worcester 1977- (DL 1972); FICS; CStJ (1980); *Style—* Sir Berwick Lechmere, Bt, JP, HM Vice Lord-Lt for Hereford & Worcester; Church End House, Hanley Castle, Worcester (☎ 068 46 2130)

LECHMERE, Reginald Anthony Hungerford; s of Anthony Hungerford Lechmere (d 1954, 3 s of 3 Bt); hp of kinsman, Sir Berwick Hungerford Lechmere, 6 Bt; *b* 24 Dec 1920; *Educ* Charterhouse, Trinity Hall Cambridge; *m* 1956, Anne Jennifer, da of late A C Dind, of Orbe, Switzerland; 3 s (Nicholas b 1960, Adam b 1962, Mark b 1966), 1 da (Jennifer b 1959); *Career* formerly Capt 5 Royal Inniskilling Dragoon Gds; antiquarian bookseller; *Style—* Reginald Lechmere, Esq; Primeswell, Evendine Lane, Colwall, nr Malvern, Worcs (☎ 0684 40 340)

LECKY, Ian Cecil Hamilton Browne; s of Capt Halton Stirling Lecky, CB, AM, RN (d 1940), and Agnes, *née* Close (d 1976); *b* 16 Dec 1924; *Educ* RN Coll Dartmouth; *Career* WWII 1942-44 Midshipman (later Sub Lt) RN; served Med: HMS Emerald, HMS Rodney, HMS Quail; admitted slr 1949, airline pilot Br United Airways 1955-66, slr private practice 1967-, ptnr Batchelors, asst rec Crown Ct; memb Law Soc 1949; *Recreations* flying, sub aqua diving, under water photography; *Style—* Ian Lecky, Esq; 22 Andsell Terr, Kensington, London W8 5BY; Batchelors, The Outer Temple, 222-225 Strand, London WC2R 1BG (☎ 01 353 5134, fax 01 353 2766, telex 262 363)

LEDERMAN, Colin Stuart; s of Morris Lederman, of London, and Rachel, *née* Baroness Iglitski (d 1988); *b* 4 Mar 1937; *Educ* City of London Sch; *m* 15 May 1960, Jill, da of Capt Maxwell Lincoln (d 1985), of London; 1 s (Martin David b 1962), 1 da (Meryl Ruth b 1965); *Career* CA; ptnr: Frank Dymond & Co London 1965-69, Backhouse Young Partnership (formerly B & E Backhouse) 1970-88; dir: Loggia Ltd Film distributors 1987-, Atlantis Devpt Corpn Ltd 1988-; former del Bd of Deps for Br Jews; Lord of the Manor of Ashton, ACA 1962, FCA 1969, MBIM 1987; *Recreations* golf, badminton; *Style—* Colin Lederman, Esq; P O Box 1433, London NW4 1TZ (☎ 01 203 6727, fax 01 203 7502, car tel 0836 739 697)

LEDERMAN, Geoffrey Lewis Harry; s of David Lederman (d 1945), and Sylvia Doris, *née* Langbart; *b* 9 July 1929; *Educ* Whittinghame Coll; *m* 29 April 1963, Olivia, da of Frederick Russell (d 1978); 2 da (Amanda (Mrs Pinder) b 1965, Caroline b 1968); *Career* memb London 1954 ptnr Smith Bros 1960-73, (joined 1951), jt exec Smith New Court plc 1987- (dir 1973-87); memb Stock Exchange; *Recreations* cricket, squash, tennis, golf; *Clubs* MCC, RAC, Incogniti, Annabels; *Style—* Geoffrey Lederman, Esq; 145 Hamilton Terrace, London NW8 (☎ 01 624 4986); Smith New Court plc, Chetwynd House, 24 St Swithins Lane, EC4 8AE (☎ 01 626 1544, car tel 0836 286339)

LEDERMAN, Paul; s of François Lederman (Belgian Médaille Commémorative de la Guerre with 2 crossed swords), of 99 Penshurst Gdns, Edgware, Middx, and Elena, *née* Attias; *b* 2 August 1942; *Educ* Lycée Français, London, Finchley Co Grmr, London Univ, and Birklands Mgmnt Centre (DMS); *m* 1, 16 Dec 1973 (m dis 1983), Nichole Marie, da of Henri Deparmentier (d 1972); 2 s (Henry b 1976, David b 1979); m 2, 20 oct 1985, Barbara, da of Simon Dove, of 81 Grove End Gdns, NW8; *Career* CA (1968), sole practitioner 1977-; prop P L Advertising 1976-82, mgmnt conslt 1976-80; dir: Skyparks Ltd 1982-, Elena Chocolates Ltd (fnd by mother) 1984-86, md Skylinks Ltd, exec Airline 1985-; Freeman: Guild of Air Pilots and Air Navigators 1965-, City of London 1967-; lectr in Accountancy Camb, Postgrad Centre and Hatfield & Middx Polys 1978-81; memb Economic Res Cncl 1981; patented aero engine 1982; DMS, FCA, FBIM, MInstPI; *Recreations* music, countryside, former private pilot; *Clubs* The Gardens Kensington, Elstree Aero; *Style—* Paul Lederman, Esq; 18 Wheatley Close, Hendon, London NW4 4LG (☎ 01 203 5513, 01 203 7243); Skylinks Ltd, 108 New Bond St, London W1Y 9AA (☎ 01 499 9195, telex 262690 NHBS, fax 01 499 7517)

LEDERMANN, Dr Erich Kurt; s of Dr William Ledermann (d 1949) of 3 Church Crescent, London N10 and Charlotte *née* Apt (d 1981); *b* 16 May 1908; *Educ* Univ of Berlin (MD), Univ Freiburg, Heidelberg Univ, Royal Infirmary Edinburgh (LRCP & S Ed, LRFPS Glas, FRCPsych Dip FFHom); *m* 21 June 1941, Marjorie Alice, da of Herbert Francis Smith (d 1938) of Harpenden, Herts; 1 s (David b 1942), 1 da (Elizabeth b 1944); *Career* med practitioner, conslt physician at Royal London Homoeopathic Hosp, ret 1974; conslt psychiatrist, Marlborough Day Hosp, ret 1974, physician, Nature Cure Clinic, London W1; *Recreations* writing, walking; *Style—* Dr Erich Ledermann; 13 Ardwick Road, London NW2; 97 Harley Street, London W1 (☎ 01 935 8774); National Westminster Bank, 280 Finchley Road, London NW3)

LEDGER, Christopher John Walton; Queens Commendation For Brave Conduct 1965; s of Peter Walton Ledger, of Truro, Cornwall, and Barbara Nancy, *née* Eve; *Educ* The Nautical Coll Pangbourne Berks; *m* 1, 21 April 1971 (m dis 1973); m 2, 17 Sept 1977, Gillian Penelope, da of Col Paul Heberden Rogers (d 1972); 1 s (James Walton Herberden b 17 July 1981), 1 da (Nicola Kate b 10 Aug 1978); *Career* RM cmmnd 2 Lt 1962, Cdr Offr 43 1964, Cdr Offr 4J, OC Reece TP 1965-66, AT VRM Poole 1966-67, OC HMS Bulwark 1967-69, Adj Poole 1969-72, ATT HQ Cdr Offr Forces 1972-74, Queens Commendation for Brave Conduct 1965; Shell UK Ltd: joined 1974, pa mangr Expro 1976-77 (dir of pa 1981-84), seconded chief exec World Energy Business, Films & Educnl Serv 1978-81, chief exec The Phoenix Initiative 1986-; chm Broom Water Assoc; Liveryman Worshipful Co of Grocers' 1972; FRSA, FInstPet; *Recreations* sailing, shooting; *Clubs* Royal Cornwall YC, Special forces; *Style—* Christopher Ledger, Esq; The willows, 29 Broom Water, Teddingrow, Middx TW11 9Q5 (☎ 01 977 3451); The Phoenix Initiative, 82 New Cavendish St, London W1M 8AD (☎ 01 580 5588, car phone 0836 703150)

LEDGER, Frank; OBE (1985); s of Harry and Doris Ledger; *b* 16 June 1929; *Educ* London Univ (BSc); *m* 1953, Alma, *née* Moverley; 2 s; *Career* student apprentice Leeds Corp Electricity Dept 1947, station mangr Cottam 1965, gp mangr Midlands Region 1968, dir computing 1980, dir operations 1981; memb bd for prodn CEGB 1986-; *Style—* Frank Ledger, Esq; CEGB, 15 Newgate Street, London EC1 (☎ 01 634 6673)

LEDGER, Sir Frank (Joseph Francis); s of late Edson Ledger; *b* 29 Oct 1899; *Educ* Perth Boys' Sch; *m* 1923, Gladys Muriel, da of late Charles Oliver Lyons; 1 s, 2 da; *Career* pres J & E Lodger Pty Ltd, J & E Ledger Sales Pty Ltd, Ledger Electrics Pty Ltd, chm Winget Moxey Pty Ltd, governing dir Ledger Investmts, chm S Aust Insurance Co (WA), dir Lake View & Star Ltd, Chamber of Manufacturers Insurance Co, A R C Engrg Co WA, chm W Aust Govt Industl Devpt Advsy Ctee, past pres W Aust chamber of Manufacturers, pres WA Trotting Assoc, past pres Royal Cwlth Soc, vice-pres Aust Trotting Cncl; kt 1963; *Style—* Sir Frank Ledger; 2 The Esplanade,

Peppermint Grove, W Australia

LEDGER, Dr Philip Stevens; CBE (1985); s of Walter Stephen Ledger (d 1986), of Bexhill-on-Sea, and Winifred Kathleen, *née* Stevens; *b* 12 Dec 1937; *Educ* Bexhill GS, King's Coll Cambridge (MA, MusB); *m* 15 Apr 1963, Mary Erryl, *née* Wells; 1 s (Timothy b 1964), 1 da (Katharine b 1966); *Career* master of music Chelmsford Cathedral 1962-65, dir of music UEA 1965-73 (dean Sch of Fine Arts and Music 1968-71), conductor Cambridge Univ Musical Soc 1973-82, dir Music and Organist Kings Coll Cambridge 1974-82, princ Royal Scottish Acad of Music and Drama 1982-; Hon LLD Strathclyde Univ 1987, Hon RAM 1984; FRCM 1983, FRCO; *Recreations* swimming, theatre-going; *Clubs* Athenaeum; *Style—* Dr Philip Ledger, CBE; Royal Scottish Academy of Music and Drama, 100 Renfrew Steet, Glasgow G2 3DB (☎ 041 332 4101, fax 041 332 8901)

LEDINGHAM, Dr John Gerard Garvin; s of John Ledingham (d 1970) of 47 Ladbroke Square, London W11, and Dr Una Christina *née* Garvin (d 1965); *b* 19 Oct 1929; *Educ* Rugby, New Coll Oxford (MA, DM), Middx Hosp Med Sch London Univ (BM, BCH); *m* 3 March 1962, Elaine Mary, da of Richard Glyn Maliphant (d 1977), of Cardiff; 4 da (Joanna b 1963, Catherine b 1964, Clare b 1968, Sarah b 1971); *Career* Nat Serv 2 Lt RA 1949-50; registrar in med Middx Hosp London 1960-62 (house offr 1957-58), sr registrar Westminster Hosp London 1963-65, visiting fell Columbia Univ NY 1965-66, conslt physician Utd Oxford Hosps 1966-74, May reader in Med Univ of Oxford 1974-; tstee: Nuffield Prov Hosps Tst, Oxford Hosp Devpt and Improvement Fund, Oxford Hosps Servs and Devpt Tst; memb: Supra Regnl Servs Ctee Dept of Health, Animal Procedures Ctee of Home Sec; chm MRS; examiner in med Univs of: Glasgow, Oxford, London, Southampton, Sheffield; examiner RCP; formerly: hon sec/hon tres Assoc of Physicians of GB and Ireland, pres Hypertension soc, Censor RCP, fell New Coll Oxford 1974; FRCP 1971; *Books* Oxford Textbook of Medicine (1 edn 1983, 2 edn 1987), contrib various med/sci journals; *Recreations* music, golf, reading; *Clubs* Vincents (Oxford); *Style—* Dr John Ledingham; Nuffield Department of Clinical Medicine, John Radcliffe Hospital Oxford OX3 9DU (☎ 0865 817640)

LEDLIE, John Kenneth; OBE (1977); s of Reginald Cyril Bell Ledlie, (d 1966), and Elspeth Mary, *née* Kaye (d 1982); *b* 19 Mar 1942; *Educ* Westminster Brasenose Coll Oxford (MA); *m* 27 Nov 1965, Rosemary Julia Allan, da of Francis Glen Allan (d 1974); 3 da (Rebecca b 1969, Kate b 1971, Joanna b 1973); *Career* UK delgn to NATO Brussels 1973-76, head def section 19 MOD 1983, chief PR MOD 1985-87, under sec MOD 1987; fell centre for int affrs Harvard Univ 1987-88; *Recreations* cricket, tennis, squash, ornithology, hill-walking, opera; *Clubs* Royal Cwlth Soc; *Style—* John Ledlie, Esq; c/o Ministry of Defence, London, Whitehall, London SW1A 2HB (☎ 01 218 7812)

LEDWARD, Lady Jane Annabelle; *née* Howard; da of 12 Earl of Carlisle; *b* 1947; *m* 1, 1968 (m dis 1977), John David Vaughan Seth-Smith, only s of Lt-Cdr David Keith Seth-Smith, RN; 1 da (Gemma b 1972); m 2, 1983, Rodney S Ledward, s of late Arthur Ledward; *Style—* Lady Jane Ledward

LEDWARD, Rodney Spencer; s of Arthur Ledward (d 1984), of Stone, Staffs, and Beatrice Maud, *née* Pritchard (d 1986); *b* 30 June 1938; *Educ* Alleynes GS, Univ Manchester (BSc, MPS), Univ Liverpool (MB, CHB), Univ Nottingham (DM); *m* 26 Aug 1983, Lady Jane Annabelle Howard, er da of 12 Earl of Carlisle, MC, and formerly wife of John D V Seth-Smith; 1 s (Bertie Arthur Ruthven b 7 Nov 1985); *Career* obstetrician and gynaecologist, med educator and local radio broadcaster; conslt SE Kent Health Dist 1980-, NHS and private practice, chm and md Tutorial Systems Int; dean Ross Univ Med Sch NY, FRSM, FRCOG, FRCS, MRSH; *Books* Drug Treatment in Obstetrics (1984), Drug Treatment in Gynaecology (1986), Hand Book of Obstetrics and Gynaecology (1986); *Recreations* swimming, riding; *Clubs* Mosimann Knightsbridge, RSM; *Style—* Rodney Ledward, Esq; Beaulieu, The Riviera, Sandgate CT20 3AB (☎ 0303 40104); Flat 71, Christian Warehouses, 8 Shad Thames, London SE1 7YJ; Consulting Rooms: St Saviours Hosp Hythe (☎ 0303 265 581); Chaucer Hosp Canterbury (☎ 0227 455 466); 144 Harley St, London (☎ 01 935 0023); London Bridge Hosp (☎ 01 403 488)

LEDWIDGE, Sir (William) Bernard John; KCMG (1974), CMG (1964); s of Charles Bernard Arthur Ledwidge (d 1945); *b* 9 Nov 1915; *Educ* Cardinal Vaughan Sch, King's Coll Cambridge, Princeton Univ USA; *m* 1, 1948 (m dis 1970), Anne, da of George Henry Kingsley (d 1959); 1 s, 1 da; m 2, Flora, da of André Groult (d 1967); *Career* entered India Office 1939, Indian Army 1941-46, NW Frontier, relinquished Police Complaints Bd 1982; FO 1948, first sec Kabul 1952-56, political advsr Br Mil Govt Berlin 1956-61, Cnsllr FO 1961, head of Western Dept FO 1963-65, min Paris 1965-69; ambass: Finland 1969-72, Israel 1972-75; chm UK Ctee for UNICEF 1976-, memb Police Complaints Bd 1977; *Books* Frontiers (1980), Des Nouvelles de la Famille (1981), De Gaulle (1982), De Gaulle et les Americains (1984), Sappho la Premiere Voix de Femme (1987); *Clubs* Travellers (London and Paris) MCC; *Style—* Sir Bernard Ledwidge, KCMG, CMG; 54 rue de Bourgogne, 75007 Paris France (☎ 705 8026); 19 Queen's Gate Terrace, SW7 (☎ 01 584 4132)

LEE, (Edward) Adam Michael; s of His Hon Judge Michael Lee, DSC (d 1983), of The Manor Farm House, Easton, Winchester, and Valerie Burnett Georges, *née* Drake-Brockman; *b* 29 June 1942; *Educ* Winchester, Christ Church Oxford (MA); *m* 5 July 1975, Carola Jean, da of Capt Frederick Le Hunt Anderson, of Standen Manor Farm, Hungerford, Berks; 2 s ((Frederick) Edward Machonchy b 1977, (James) Michael Maconchy b 1981); *Career* barr Middle Temple 1965; trainee Glyn Mills & Co 1964; Williams & Glyn's Bank: sr planner 1969, dep dir city div 1974, dir Holts branches 1978; local dir Child & Co 1977, asst gen mangr Royal Bank of Scotland 1985, gp devpts dis Adam & Co 1988-; investmt advsr RAF Central Fund, conslt Humberts Landplan; dep chm Kent Opera; tstee: Chelsea Opera Gp, Southern pro Art Orchestra; published articles in Three Banks Review, Royal Bank of Scotland Review, Humberts Commentary; Freeman City of London, Liveryman Worshipful Co of Dyers 1984; FCIB 1981; *Recreations* fly fishing, food, travel, opera; *Clubs* Travellers', Rye GC, Chathan Dining (memb ctee); *Style—* Adam Lee, Esq; The Farm, Northington, Alresford, Hants SO24 9TH (☎ 0962 732 205); 42 Pall Mall, London SW1Y 5JG (☎ 01 839 4615, fax 01 839 5994, telex 25338)

LEE, Sir Arthur James; KBE (1966, CBE 1959), MC (and Bar); s of late Arthur James Lee, and late Katherine Maud Lee; *b* 30 July 1912; *Educ* Collegiate Sch of St Peter's; *m* 1945, Valerie Scanlan; 3 s, 1 da; *Career* served WW II; Nat pres RSL Aust 1960-74 (state pres 1954-60), pres War Veterans' Home Myrtle Bank SA 1967-; dir: Lee's Hotels Ltd; *see Debrett's Handbook of Australia and New Zealand for further details*; *Clubs* Seaton GC, Adelaide Oval Bowling; *Style—* Sir Arthur Lee, KBE, MC; 2 Arthur St, Toorak Gdns, S Australia 5065

LEE, Barbara Mary; MBE (1968); da of Canon Dudley Westerman Lee (d 1964), of The Vicarage, Tanworth-in-Arden, Warwicks, and Isabel Mary, *née* Fellows of and Albury Park, Guildford, Surrey; *b* 30 July 1920; *Educ* Sch of St Mary and St Anne Abbots Bromley, Staffs; *Career* 2 Offr WRNS 1944-47; orthoptist; princ orthoptist: Sch of Orthoptics Moorfields Eye Hosp 1954-84, Coventry and Warwicks 1947-54; *Recreations* travel; *Style—* Miss Barbara Lee, MBE; 35 Weiss Rd, Putney, London SW15 1DH (☎ 01 789 1771)

LEE, Charles Barnaby; s of Capt RA Lee, DFC, of The Manor House, Byfleet, Surrey, and BJ Lee; *b* 22 Oct 1943; *Educ* Tonbridge; *m* 1 Oct 1970, Meryan Patricia Louise, da of Maj PTV Leith (d 1969); 3 da (Melissa b 23 Aug 1974, Catriona b 26 June 1976, Alice b 30 Oct 1952); *Career* ptnr (later dir) RA Lee Fine Arts Ltd, md Ronald A Lee plc; chm Grosvenor House Antiques Fair 1983, First Int Art Fair Johannesburg SA 1984, pres BADA 1981-83, ctee memb Burlington House Fair; co-prodr and res Br Clocks 1600-1850 (film); Freeman City of London, memb Worshipful Co of Clockmakers 1973 (steward 1980); *Clubs* Garrick, Bucks, Bembridge SC; *Style—* Charles Lee, Esq; 80 Thurleigh Rd, London SW12 8UD (☎ 01 499 6266, 01 629 5600); 1-9 Bruton Place, Mayfair, London W1X 7AD (☎ fax 01 629 2642)

LEE, Christopher Frank Carandini; s of Lt-Col Geoffrey Trollope Lee (d 1941), and Contessa Estelle Marie Carandini (d 1981); m descends from one of the six oldest Italian families, created Count 1184 and granted Arms Emperor Charlemagne by Emperor Frederick Barbarossa; *b* 27 May 1922; *Educ* Eton, Wellington Coll; *m* 1961, Birgit, da of Richard Emil Kroencke (d 1982); 1 da (Christina b 1963); *Career* served WW II RAF 1941-46, Flt-Lt, Intelligence and Special Forces, W Desert, Malta, Sicily, Italy and Central Europe (despatches 1944); actor (entered film indust 1947), author, singer; appears in over 160 feature films worldwide incl: Moulin Rouge, Tale of Two Cities, Dracula, Rasputin, The Devil Rides Out, Private Life of Sherlock Homes, The Wicker Man, The Three Musketeers, The Four Musketeers, Man with a Golden Gun, To the Devil a Daughter, Airport 77, The Far Pavilions, 1941, The Return of Captain Invincible, The Desputation (TV), Round the World in 80 Days (TV), The Return of Musketeers; also theatre, opera and TV; Off Arts Sciences et Lettres (France 1974); *Books* Christopher Lee's X Certificate (1975), Archives of Evil (1975), Tall, Dark and Gruesome (1977); *Recreations* golf, travel, languages, opera; *Clubs* Buck's, Special Forces, MCC, RAC, Hon Co Edinburgh Golfers, Travellers (Paris); *Style—* Christopher Lee, Esq; c/o James Sharkey, 15 Golden Sq, London W1 (☎ 01 434 3801)

LEE, Prof David John; s of Douglas Lee (d 1987) and Mildred Amy *née* Checkley (d 1955); *b* 28 August 1930; *Educ* Chislehurst & Sidcup Co GS, Univ of Manchester (BSC Tech), Imperial Coll London (DIC); *m* 6 Dec 1957, Helga, *née* Bass; 1 s (Graham b 1961), 1 da (Caroline b 1960); *Career* Nat Serv RE 1950-52; Lt Col Engr & Tport Staff Corps RE (TA) 1982 (Maj 1978); chm G Maunsell & Ptnrs 1984- (joined 1955, ptnr 1966, managing ptnr 1978-84); dir Maunsell Int Gp; visiting prof: Imp Coll London, Univ of Newcastle upon Tyne; Freeman City of London, Liveryman Worshipful Co of Engrs; F Eng 1980, FICE 1966, FIStructE 1968 (pres 1985-86); *Books* Theory and Practice of Bearings and Expansion Joints for Bridges (1971), contrib Civil Engineering Reference Book, many papers in learned jnls; *Clubs* East India; *Style—* Prof David Lee; G Maunsell & Partners, Yeoman House, 63 Croydon Road, Penge, London SE2O 7TP (☎ 01 778 6060, fax 01 659 5568, telex 946171)

LEE, Air Chief Marshal Sir David John Pryer; GBE (1969, KBE 1965, CBE 1947), CB (1953); s of John Lee (d 1955), and Gertrude Ethel Lee (d 1964), of Bedford; *b* 4 Sept 1912; *Educ* Bedford Sch, RAF Coll Cranwell; *m* 1938, Denise, da of Louis Hartoch (d 1934), of Bedford; 1 s, 1 da; *Career* joined RAF 1930, served WW II, Cmdt RAF Staff Coll Bracknell 1962-64, air memb for Personnel 1965-68, UK Mil Rep NATO 1968-71, ret 1971; chm Grants Ctee RAF Benevolent Fund 1971-88, dir Utd Servs (tstee 1972-88), chm exec ctee Nuffield Tst for Armed Forces 1975-, pres Corps of Commissionaires 1984-88; *Books* Flight From the Middle East (1980), Eastward (1983), Never Stop the Engine When Its Hot (1983), Wings in the Sun (1989); *Recreations* golf; *Clubs* RAF; *Style—* Air Chief Marshal Sir David Lee, GBE, CB; Danemore Cottage, Danemore Lane, South Godstone, Surrey (☎ 0342 893162)

LEE, David Stanley Wilton; DL (1984); s of Col Kenneth C Lee, TD (d 1964); *b* 17 Sept 1933; *Educ* Uppingham, Queens' Coll Cambridge; *m* June 1957, Jennifer Ann, da of Col John P Hunt, TD (d 1971); 3 s, 2 da; *Career* dir Arthur Lee & Sons 1965-; non-exec dir: Halifax Building Soc 1977-, Iron Trades Insurance 1978-; chm: SSAFA Sheffield, cncl of Order of St John for S and W Yorkshire; past Master Co of Cutlers in Hallamshire, Sheffield; *Recreations* golf, shooting, fishing, farming; *Clubs* The Club (Sheffield), Farmers'; *Style—* David Lee, Esq, DL; Arthur Lee & Sons plc, PO Box 54, Meadow Hall, Sheffield S9 1HU (☎ 0742 437272, fax 0742 439782, telex 54165 CROWN G)

LEE, Sir (Henry) Desmond (Pritchard); s of Rev Canon Henry Burgass Lee (d 1951), and Ida Marian, *née* Pritchard (d 1963); *b* 30 August 1908; *Educ* Repton, CCC Cambridge (MA); *m* 1935, Elizabeth, da of Col Arthur Crookenden (d 1962); 1 s, 2 da; *Career* lectr in Classics Cambridge 1937-48; Miny of Home Security 1940-44; headmaster: Clifton 1948-54, Winchester 1954-68; chm Headmaster's Conference 1959-60 and 1967; memb Secdy Schs Examination Cncl and Schools Cncl 1952-68; pres Hughes Hall Cambridge 1974-78; Hon LittD Nottingham, life fell CCC Cambridge; kt 1961; *Recreations* philosophy, carpentry; *Clubs* East India, Devonshire Sports, Public Schools; *Style—* Sir Desmond Lee; 8 Barton Close, Cambridge CB3 9LQ (☎ 0223 356553)

LEE, Hon Mrs Doris; da of Baron Williams of Barnburgh, Life Peer (d 1967); *b* 1916; *m* 1939, Robert Kesteven Lee (d 1967); *Style—* The Hon Mrs Lee; 346 Thorne Rd, Doncaster

LEE, Edward David; s of Walter George Lee (d 1974), and Annie Rosina, *née* Wriggle; *b* 23 Dec 1947; *Educ* Southend HS for Boys, Coll of Law; *m* 10 May 1971 (m dis 1986), Janet Laurie, da of Jack Cyril Mitchell, of Southend-on-sea, Essex; 1 s (Matthew Mitchell b 13 May 1978), 1 da (Michelle Alexandria b 10 June 1976); *Career* slr to the cncl Rochford DC 1984- (princ legal asst 1980-84), ptnr Wiseman Lee Marshall of Essex 1985-; tres Southend on Sea, Playbos Ctee sec Abbeyfield Rochford and Dist Soc Ltd; memb: Crouch Valley Housing Assoc (formerly chm), Horse Riding Working Pty Rochford DC; FInstLEx 1967, memb Law Soc 1977; *Recreations* musician; *Style—* Edward Lee, Esq; 4 Newhall, Ashingdon Rd, Ashingdon, Essex (☎

0702 549 313)

LEE, Geoffrey; OBE (1980); s of Clifford Lee, of Bolton, Lancs, and Florence Lee (d 1988); *b* 7 Jan 1931; *Educ* Sunning Hill Sch, Lords Commercial Coll Bolton; *m* 1955 (m dis 1986), Shirley, *née* Massey; 2 da (Janet b 1958, d 1981, Caroline b 1956); *Career* insurance and investmt broker; dir: B & C Insurance Brokers Ltd Lloyds Brokers, North West Business Promotions Ltd; underwriting memb Lloyds; pres Altrincham & Dist C of C & Trade 1965 (tres 1963, chm 1964, memb exec ctee 1960-81); memb Appeals Tbnl for Miny of Pensions & Nat Insur 1961-64, chm Assoc of Insur Brokers NW Area (memb nat exec ctee 1968-70), vice-chm NW Industl Cncl 1973-87 (ctee memb 1968-); Altrincham & Sale Cons Assoc: tres 1969-75, vice pres 1975-83, patron 1983-; memb exec ctee Knutsford Constituency Cons Assoc 1975-77; memb: Northern exec ctee French C of C 1982-87, Cons Manchester Action Ctee 1988-; ABIBA; *Recreations* weight training, keeping fit; *Clubs* Valley Lodge Country, Wilmslow Cheshire; *Style*— Geoffrey Lee, Esq, OBE; Mode Cottage, Church Lane, Mobberley, Cheshire WA16 7RA (☎ 0565 873485); B & C Insurance Brokers Ltd, Station House, Stamford, New Road, Altrincham, Cheshire WA14 1EP (☎ 061 928 3483)

LEE, Brig Sir (Leonard) Henry; CBE (1964, OBE 1960); s of Henry Robert Lee (d 1969), of Southsea, Hants, and Nellie, *née* Randall; *b* 21 April 1914; *Educ* Portsmouth GS, Southampton Univ; *m* 1949, Peggy Metham; *Career* served WWII BEF, Maj Royal Scots Greys (despatches 1945), Lt-Col 1954, Chief of Intelligence to Dir of Ops of Malaya 1957-60, Col naval and mil attaché Saigon 1961-64, Chief of personnel and admin Allied Land Forces Centl Europe (France) 1964-66, Brig Chief of Intelligence Allied Forces Centl Europe (Netherlands) 1966-69, ret 1969; dep dir Cons Party Bd of Fin 1970-; kt 1983; *Recreations* gardening, golf; *Clubs* Kingswood Golf; *Style*— Brig Sir Henry Lee, CBE; Fairways, Sandy Lane, Kingswood, Surrey (☎ 0737 832577); Conservative Party Central Office, 32 Smith Sq, London SW1 (☎ 01 222 9000)

LEE, James Giles; s of John Lee, CBE, and Muriel, *née* Giles; *b* 23 Dec 1942; *Educ* Trinity Coll Glenalmond, Glasgow Univ, Harvard Univ; *m* 1966, Linn, *née* MacDonald; 1 s, 2 da; *Career* conslt McKinsey & Co 1969-80, dep chm and chief exec Pearson Longman 1980-83; chm: Penguin Publishing Co 1980-84, Longman Gp 1980-84; dep chm: Westminster Press 1989-84, Financial Times 1980-84, Yorks TV 1982-85; dir S Pearson & Son 1981-84; chm Goldcrest Films and TV 1981-85 (chief exec 1983-85), Direct Broadcasting by Satellite Consortium 1986-87; dir Boston Consulting Gp Ltd 1987-; *Books* Planning for the Social Services (1978), The Investment Challenge (1979); *Recreations* photography, travelling, sailing; *Clubs* Reform, Harvard (NY USA); *Style*— J G Lee, Esq; Meadow Wood, Penshurst, Kent (☎ Penshurst 870309); Devonshire House, Mayfair Place, London W1X 5FH (☎ 01 493 3222, telex 28975, fax 01 499 3660)

LEE, Maj-Gen James Stuart; MBE (1970); s of George Lee (d 1974), and Elizabeth, *née* Hawkins (d 1955); *b* 26 Dec 1934; *Educ* Normanton GS, Univ of Leeds (BA), King's Coll London (MA); *m* 21 Mar 1960, (Alice) Lorna, da of James Leonard Powell (d 1988); 1 s (James b 29 Dec 1964); *Career* educn offr UK trg units Catterick 1959-64, mil trg offr Beaconsfield 1964, RMCS and Staff Coll 1964-65; DAQMG HQ: Cyprus Dist 1966, NEARELF 1967; SO2 MOD 1968-70, DAA & QMG HQ NEARELF 1970-, GSO2 HQ FARELF 1970-71, OC offr trg wing Beaconsfield 1971-74, gp educn offr Rheindahlen 1974-75, chief educn offr NE Dist 1976-78, head offr educn branch 1978-79, SO1 trg hq UKLF 1979, Col Chief Inspr res 1980-82, cdr educn HQ BAOR 1983-87, dir army educn 1987-; pres Leeds Univ Union 1958-59, res assoc Int Inst of Strategic Studies 1982-83, dep co cmmr Br Scouts Western Europe 1983-87, tstee and sec Gallipoli Meml Lecture 1987-, pres Army Canoe Union 1987-, pres Army Chess 1987-; memb: bd of mgmnt Nat Fndn for Educnl Res 1987-, Nat Advsy Ctee Duke of Edinburgh's Award 1987-, Cncl Scout Assoc 1988-; FRSA 1987; *Recreations* theatre, boats; *Style*— Maj-Gen Stuart Lee, MBE; c/o Royal Bank of Scotland, Holt's Branch, Kirkland House, Whitehall, London SW1

LEE, Jeremy Charles Roger Barnett; s of Lt Cdr Charles Alexander Barnett Lee, RNR (d 1982), of Phyllis Kathleen Mary, *née* Gunnell (d 1986); *b* 10 July 1944; *Educ* Bristol Cathedral Sch; *m* 4 April 1972 (m dis 1983), Patricia Margaret, *née* Coleridge; 3 da (Veryan Georgina Coleridge b 1974, Isobel Mary b 1977, Caroline Sybella b 1978); *Career* RM: 2 Lt 1962, Troop Cdr 40 Commando serving in Malaya and Sabah 1964-65, Lt 1965, co cdr Sultan's Armed Forces Muscat and Oman 1967-69, Adj (later co cdr) 40 Commando serving in NI Cyprus during Turkish invasion 1972-74, Capt 1973, invalided 1976; slr 1978, sr ptnr Symes Robinson & Lee 1983-; area tres Crediton Cons Assoc 1980-, chm Coldridge Brushford and Nymet Rowland Cons Assoc 1981-; rugby player: Capt RM 1971, RN 1971, Exeter FC 1965-67 and 1969-72; memb: Law Soc, Anglo Omani Soc; Sultan's Bravery Medal 1968; *Recreations* tennis, fox-hunting, walking, gardening, cycling; *Clubs* Army and Navy; *Style*— Jeremy Lee, Esq; Frogbury, Coldridge, Nr Crediton, Devon (☎ 03635 484); Symes Robinson and Lee, Manor Office, North Street, Crediton, Devon (☎ 03632 5566)

LEE, John Desmond (Des); s of Ernest Wilson Lee (d 1988), of Doncaster, and Sarah, *née* Murphy (d 1958); *b* 18 Jan 1942; *Educ* Belmont Abbey Hereford, Doncaster Tech Coll; *m* 30 April 1964, Susan, da of Eric Bott (d 1974), of Doncaster; 1 s (Ryan b 18 March 1970), 1 da (Tracy b 25 April 1967); *Career* computer supervisor NCB 1960-65, computer servs mangr Centre File 1965-67, sr mangr GMS Rowntree Ltd 1967-81, mgmnt servs controller Brooke Bond Oxo Ltd 1981-86, gp head of systems and communications Lloyds of London 1986-, chm IBM Computer Users Assoc 1979-81 (hon life pres), memb Butler Cox Fndn Advsy Bd, int conf speaker on info technol, former memb York 65 Round Table; Freeman Worshipful Co of Info Technologists 1987, City of London 1987; FBCS 1981, FIDPM 1978; *Recreations* tennis, motor racing; *Style*— Des Lee, Esq; York and Weybridge; Lloyds of London, Lime St, London EC3 7HA (☎ 01623 7100, ext 6152, fax 01 626 2389, car tel 0860 365 055, telex 987321 LLOYDS G)

LEE, John Michael Hubert; s of Victor Lee (d 1978), of Wentworth, Surrey, and Reneé Annette, *née* Harburn (d 1960); *b* 13 August 1927; *Educ* Reading Sch, Christ Coll Cambridge (MA), SOAS London Univ; *m* 16 July 1960, Margaret Ann, da of James McConnell Russell, ICS; 1 s (Julian b 1968), 1 da (Joanna b 1963); *Career* HM Colonial Serv Gold Coast (Ghana) 1951-58 (cadet dist cmmr Transvolta Togoland 1951-52, asst sec Accra 1952-53, asst govt agent Koforidua 1953, sec to Regnl Off Prov Cmmn 1953-54, asst govt agent Kibi 1954-55, govt agent Kofiridua and Akuse 1955-58, princ asst sec Accra 1958); on staff BBC 1959-65; called to the Bar Middle Temple, in practice Midland circuit 1965-; MP (Lab): Reading 1966-70, Handsworth 1974-79; Parly candidate (Lab) Reading 1964, chm W Midland Gp of London MPs 1974-75; memb Parly Ctee on Obsolete Legislation; *Recreations* gardening, watching cricket and tennis, reading; *Clubs* Royal Overseas League; *Style*— J M H Lee, Esq; 2 Dr Johnson's Building, Temple, London EC4Y 7YR (☎ 01 353 5371)

LEE, John Preston; TD (1969); s of George Thomas Lee (d 1982), and Margaret Preston; maternal gf Hubert Preston, former ed of Wisden; *b* 4 Oct 1934; *Educ* Emanuel Sch; *m* 16 Sept 1961, Jeanette Mary, da of John William Arthur Knapman (d 1975), of Salters Heath, Sevenoaks, Kent; 1 da (Vivienne b 1966); *Career* Capt RA 1952-54, TA 1954-71; area mangr Midland bank plc Guernsey CI; dir: Midland Bank Tst Corpn Guernsey Ltd 1981-, Thomas Cook Guernsey Ltd 1981-, Midland Bank Nominees Guernsey Ltd 1981-, Griffin Insur Ltd 1987-, Thai Investmt Fund Ltd (1988), Automotive Fin Insur Ltd (1988); FCIB (1985); *Recreations* yachting; *Clubs* United (Guernsey), Royal Channel Island YC, Guernsey YC; *Style*— John Lee, Esq, TD; La Girouette, Rue de la Mare, St Andrews, Guernsey, CI; Midland Bank plc, Box 31, St Peter Port, Guernsey, CI (☎ 0481 24201)

LEE, John Robert Louis; MP (C) Pendle 1983-; s of Basil Lee (d 1983) and Miriam (d 1982); *b* 21 June 1942; *Educ* William Hulme's GS Manchester; *m* 1975, Anne Monique, *née* Bakirgian; 2 da; *Career* founding dir Chancery Consolidated Ltd Investmt Bankers, political sec to Rt Hon Robert Carr (now Lord Carr of Hadley) 1974, contested (C) Manchester (Moss Side) Oct 1974, dir Paterson Zochonis (UK) Ltd 1975-76, vice-chm NW Conciliation Ctee Race Relations Bd 1976-77, MP (C) Nelson and Colne 1979-1983, PPS to Kenneth Baker (min state Info Technol) 1981-83, PPS to Rt Hon Cecil Parkinson (sec state Trade and Indust) June-Oct 1983, under-sec state for Def Procurement (following Ian Stewart's promotion during reshuffle caused by Rt Hon Cecil Parkinson's resignation) Oct 1983-, under sec state Dept of Employment 1987, min for Tourism; chm Nat Youth Bureau 1981-83; *Style*— John Lee, Esq, MP; House of Commons, London SW1 (☎ 01 219 4002)

LEE, His Honour Judge; John Thomas Cyril Lee; s of Cyril Lee (d 1974), and Dorothy Lee (d 1985), of Leadon Bank, Ledbury; *b* 14 Jan 1927; *Educ* Holly Lodge GS, Emmanuel Coll Cambridge (MA, LLB); *m* 1956, Beryl, da of John T Haden (d 1959); 1 s, 3 da; *Career* served HM Forces 1945-48, Royal W African Frontier Force; barr Gray's Inn 1952, chm various tribunals, circuit judge (Midland and Oxford) 1972-; *Recreations* golf; *Clubs* Union & County, Worcester Golf & Country; *Style*— His Honour Judge Lee; The Red House, Upper Colwall, Malvern, Worcs

LEE, Julian Francis Kaines; s of Dr Terence Joseph Lee, and Dr Gwen Elizabeth, *née* Kaines (d 1974); *b* 17 July 1945; *Educ* Worth Abbey; *m* 1, Sept 1970 (m dis 1975), Maria, da of William Cecil Diver (d 1986); m 2, 6 Sept 1975, Lesley Jane Merzies, da of George William Rumford; 2 s (Simon b 1978, Marcus b 1986), 3 da (Charlotte b 1979, Georgina b 1981, Arabella b 1983); *Career* ptnr Tansley Witt & Co 1975-78, ptnr Arthur Anderson & Co 1978-82, dir and chief operating offr of Phibro Solomon Ltd 1984-86, jt md Br and Cwlth Holdgs Ltd 1987-88 (dir 1986-87), chief exec The Bricom Gp Ltd 1988-; FCA 1975, ACA 1969; *Recreations* family, farming, reading; *Clubs* Brooks's, RAC; *Style*— Julian Lee, Esq; Ford House, Ashurst, Sussex; The Bricom Group Ltd, Milton Heath House, Dorking, Surrey RH4 3NB (☎ 0306 740445, fax 0306 740529, telex 858756 BRICOM G)

LEE, (Harry) Lincoln; s of Harry Lee (d 1965), of Cheshire, and Florence Catherine, *née* Harrison (d 1980); *b* 7 Jan 1922; *Educ* Stockport GS; *m* 6 July 1945, Helen Hunter, da of Charles Hunter McCallum (d 1958), of West Dulwich; 3 s (Neil b 1948, Nicholas b 1950, Dougal b 1959); *Career* RAF pilot 1940, cmmd 1941 (demob 1946); capt BSAA 1947 (then BOAC, pilot 1946), master air pilot 1965, regnl tech dir Int Air Tport Assoc N Atlantic and N America 1968 (joined 1965), aviation conslt and author 1988-; served on numerous aviation ctees and panels both Br and Int; Freeman City of London 1966, Upper Freeman Guild of Air Pilots and Air Navigators; FRIN 1974; *Books* Three-Dimensioned Darkness (1962), Torwolf the Saxon (1988); *Clubs* RAF; *Style*— Lincoln Lee, Esq; 7 Saxon Gdns, Taplow SL6 ODD (☎ 0628 20826, 0628 24005)

LEE, Malcolm Kenneth; QC (1983); s of Thomas Marston Lee (d 1972), of Birmingham, and Fiona Margaret, *née* Mackenzie; *b* 2 Jan 1943; *Educ* King Edward's Sch Birmingham, Worcester Coll Oxford (MA 1965); *m* 16 May 1970, (Phyllis) Anne Brunton, da of Andrew Watson Speed, of Bromsgrove, Worcs; 3 s (Oliver b 1973, Dominic b 1974, Adrian b 1977), 4 da (Phyllis b and d 1972, Lydia b 1976, Flora b 1979, Georgina b 1981); *Career* Lt 268 Regt (RA) TA 1965-69; barr Inner Temple 1967; practised Midland Circuit 1967-71, Midland and Oxford Circuit 1972-; jr cnsl to DHSS 1979-83; dep chm Agric Land Tribunal, E Midland area and Midland area 1978-; rec Crown Ct 1980-; *Recreations* squash, tennis, walking, reading; *Clubs* Edgbaston Priory; *Style*— Malcolm Lee, Esq, QC; 24 Estria Rd, Edgbaston, Birmingham B15 2LQ (☎ 021 440 4481); 4 Fountain Ct, Steelhouse Lane, Birmingham B4 6DR (☎ 021 236 3476)

LEE, Nicholas (Nick) John; s of Percy Horatio Lee, and Vera Maud, *née* West; *b* 14 August 1942; *Educ* Colchester Royal GS; *m* 17 Sept 1966, Wendy Elizabeth, da of Norman Frederick White (d 1968); 1 s (Simon John b 19 Feb 1969), 1 da (Sarah Jayne b 15 Nov 1967); *Career* Arthur Goddard and Co 1959-68 (qualified as CA 1964); Jardine Insur Brokers (formerly Pickford Dawson and Holland Ltd) 1968-: joined as accountant and progressed to co sec and fin dir; memb St Osyth PCC; FCA 1969; *Recreations* golf, tennis, skiing; *Clubs* Royal Oversea's League; *Style*— Nick Lee, Esq; 31 St Clairs Rd, St Osyth, Clacton-on-Sea, Essex (☎ 0255 821163); Jardine Insur Brokers Ltd, PO Box 861, 91-99 New London Rd, Chelmsford, Essex CM2 OPL (☎ 0245 490949, fax 0245 491664)

LEE, Paul Anthony; s of Wilfred Lee (d 1970), of Manchester, and Anne, *née* Molyneux; *b* 26 Jan 1946; *Educ* Central GS Manchester, Clare Coll Cambridge (MA, LLB); *m* 16 Sept 1977, Elisabeth Lindsay, da of Maj Geoffrey Robert Taylor, of Manchester; 2 s (Jonathan b 1980, William b 1985), 1 da (Antonia b 1983); *Career* slr; ptnr Addleshaw Sons & Latham Manchester; dir: Robert H Lowe plc 1985- (dep chm 1986), Davies & Metcalfe plc 1986, Whitwham & Co Wines Ltd 1977-, Pugh Davies & Co Ltd 1976-, Royal Exchange Theatre Co 1986-, Leaf Properties Ltd (chm) 1986-, Welcomebranch Ltd 1987-; chm Patron and Assocs Manchester City Art Gallery; *Recreations* the arts, travel, tennis, wine; *Clubs* Oxford and Cambridge, St James's Manchester, Real Tennis and Racquets Manchester; *Style*— Paul A Lee, Esq; Riverbank Cottage, Stanton Avenue, W Didsbury, Manchester M20 (☎ 061 434 6971); Dennis House, Marsden Street, Manchester M2 1JD (☎ 061 832 5994, car telephone 0860 615729)

LEE, Peter Gavin; s of Lt Cdr John Gavin Lee, RNVR, of Burygate, Felsted, Essex, and late Helena Frances, *née* Whitehead; *b* 4 July 1934; *Educ* Midhunt GS, Wye Coll; *m* 27 April 1963, Caroline Mary, da of Cdr EN Green, RN (d 1976); 2 s (William Gavin b 1964, Jonathan Campbell b 1966), 1 da (Olivia Alice b 1969); *Career* RA Nat Serv 1953-55; chartered surveyor Strutt & Parker 1957-, (sr ptnr 1979-), chm Anglo American Liason ctee Wethersfield USAF; govr Felsted sch; Freeman City of London 1977, Liveryman Worshipful Co of Chartered Surveyors 1977; FRICS; *Recreations* pilot, country pursuits, vintage cars and aircraft; *Clubs* Boodles; *Style—* Peter Lee, Esq; Fanners, Great St Waltham, Essex CM3 1EA (☎ 0245 360 470); 13 Hill St, London W1 (☎ 01 629 7282, fax 01 495 3176)

LEE, Samuel George; s of George Alles Lee (d 1966), and Nancy, *née* Moore; *b* 16 Oct 1939; *Educ* Rossall; *m* 12 May 1965, Jennifer Anne Nye, da of Rev J A K Nye, of Lytham St Annes; 2 s (Matthew Everett b 1968, Joseph James b 1970); *Career* slr 1963, dep coroner Blackpool and Fylde Dist 1964; *Recreations* squash, reading, watching rugby; *Style—* Samuel G Lee, Esq; The Croft, 7 St Clements Avenue, Blackpool FY3 8LT (☎ 0253 31990); John Budd & Co, 283 Church Street, Blackpool FY1 3PG (☎ 0253 26557)

LEE, Rev Terence; s of (John) Denis Lee, FCCA (d 1967), of Newcastle-upon-Tyne, and Kathleen, *née* Meakin; *b* 5 Dec 1946; *Educ* Barnard Castle Sch Co Durham, Oxford NSM Course; *m* 1 Jan 1972, Susan Anne, da of Kenneth Spence, of Leyburn, N Yorks; 1 s (James Denis b 1975), 1 da (Victoria Anne b 1973); *Career* practised as a CA: Newcastle-upon-Tyne 1971-73, Gallon Lee and Co 1971-76, Haines Watts 1978-84; ptnr Feltons Chartered Accountants (Harley Street and Windsor) 1984-; chm Thames Valley Soc of CAs 1985-; trained under the Oxford Non Stipendiary Ministry Ct 1980-83, ordained deacon 1983 and priest 1984; asst priest: Calcot Reading 1983-86, Burghfield Saint Mary the Virgin Oxon 1986-88; ACA 1971, FCA 1976 ; *Recreations* singing solo tenor, shooting, fishing, riding, squash, eating, cooking; *Clubs* Athenaeum; *Style—* The Rev Terence Lee; 45 Christchurch Road, Reading, Berks RG2 7AN; 12 Sheet Street, Windsor, Berks SL4 1BG (☎ 0753 840111, fax 0753 850028); 55 Welbeck St, London W1

LEE, Thomas Albert; s of Thomas Ernest Lee (d 1978), of Kensington, and Harriet Elizabeth *née* Halesworth; *b* 2 Feb 1901; *Educ* Surrey Co GS, RAF Coll Cranfield, Kenya Univ Nairobi; *m* 27 July 1958, Nancy Marie Terese, da of John Augustus Hope (d 1957), of Ireland; 2 s (Gerald b 1962, Nathan (twin, still born); *Career* RAF 1950-56; md: Rocke Int Ltd 1968-71, Lee Engrg Ltd 1971-; memb Cons Pty; memb Royal Aeronautical Soc; *Recreations* motor racing; *Clubs* RAC; *Style—* Thomas Lee, Esq; Lee Rebels Beech, Portnall Rise, Wentworth, Surrey GU25 4JZ (☎ 09904 3256); Lee Engineering Ltd, Sky Business Park, Thorpe, Surrey TW20 8RF, (☎ 0784 71166, fax 0784 71160, telex 928475)

LEE, Col Sir William Allison; OBE (1945), TD (1948), DL (1965) Co Durham; s of Samuel Percy Lee (d 1939), of Darlington, and Florence Ada, *née* Short (d 1944); *b* 31 May 1907; *Educ* Queen Elizabeth GS Darlington; *m* 1, 1933, Elsa Norah (d 1966), da of Thomas Hanning (d 1943); m 2, 1967, Mollie Clifford, da of Sir Cuthbert Whiteside (d 1968); *Career* served in Royal Signals 1935-53, TA Col 150 and 151 Inf Bdes 1953-58; chm: Newcastle Regnl Hosp Bd 1970-73, Northern Regnl Health Authy 1973-78; ret Branch Mangr-Guardian Royal Exchange Assur Gp; High Sheriff 1978, pres Darlington SSAFA, memb St John Cncl Co Durham; OStJ 1980; kt 1975; *Recreations* beagling, gardening; *Style—* Col Sir William Lee, OBE, TD, DL; Candle House, Feetham, Richmond, North Yorks (☎ Richmond 0748 86207); The Woodlands, Woodland Rd, Darlington, Co Durham (☎ 0325 462318)

LEE OF NEWTON, Baroness; Amelia; *née* Shay; da of William Shay; *m* 1938, Baron Lee of Newton, PC (Life Peer) (d 1984); 1 da (Hon Mrs Rodney Flint, *qv*); *Style—* The Rt Hon Lady Lee of Newton; 52 Ashton Road, Newton-le-Willows, Merseyside, EA12 0AE

LEE-BARBER, Rear-Adm John; CB (1959), DSO (1940) and Bar (1941); s of Richard Lee-Barber (d 1960); *b* 16 April 1905; *Educ* RN Colls Osborne, Dartmouth; *m* 1939, Suzanne Claude (d 1976), da of Col Albert Le Gallais, ADC, MC; 2 da; *Career* joined RN 1919, served 1939-45 in HMS Griffin, Opportune and King Alfred Co, St James 1946-47, sr off Reserve Fleet Harwich 1948-49, Naval Attaché Chile 1950-52, CO Agincourt and Capt D4 1952-54, Cdre Inshore Flotilla 1954-56, Adm Supt H M Dockyard Malta 1957, ret 1959, Polish Cross of Valour 1940; *Style—* Rear-Adm John Lee-Barber CB,DSO; Ferry House, The Quay, Wivenhoe, Essex (☎ Wivenhoe 2592)

LEE-BROWNE, Col Martin Shaun Lee; OBE (1974), TD, DL; s of Denis William Lee-Browne (d 1960) of Cirencester, and Freda Rosamund Austin (d 1974); *b* 17 Oct 1931; *Educ* Leighton Park Sch, Reading; Emmanuel Coll, Cambridge; *m* 14 Sept 1957, Diana Frances, da of Dr Geoffrey Richard Ford of Dartford, Kent; 3 s (Jeremy b 1960, Patrick b 1964, Rupert b 1966); 1 da (Alison b 1962); *Career* Col TA (ret 1981), Dep Col The Glos Regt; slr, sr ptnr Wilmot & Co, dir Clements (Watford) Ltd 1985-; chm Western Wessex TAVR Assoc 1982, vice chm Cncl of TAVR Assocs 1987-; *Recreations* music, sailing; *Clubs* Army and Navy; *Style—* Col M S Lee-Browne; Park Farm House, Fairford, Glos GL7 4JL (☎ 0285 712102)

LEE-STEERE, Sir Ernest Henry; KBE (1978, CBE 1963), JP; s of Ernest Augustus Lee-Steere (d 1959); *b* 22 Dec 1912; *Educ* Hale Sch Perth, St Peter's Coll Adelaide; *m* 1942, Jessica Margaret, da of Frank Venn; 2 s, 3 da; *Career* Capt Army/Air Liaison Gp AIF, SW Pacific Area 1944-45; co dir and pastoralist; pres: Pastoralists & Graziers Assoc WA 1959-72, Nat Tst WA 1962-72; Lord Mayor of Perth 1972-78, memb Met Regnl Planning Authy 1972-78 and Perth Regnl Tport Coordinating Ctee 1972-78; chm: City Building Soc to 1980, Aust Mutual Provident Soc WA bd 1962, dir princ bd 1962-84, chm Heytesbury Hldgs Ltd 1976-82, Katanning Hldgs to 1986; chm: Paragon Resources NL, Central Kalgoorlie Gold Mines NL, Griffen Coal Mining Co, Perth Building Soc to 1984; chm WA Turf Club 1963-84 *see Debrett's Handbook of Australia and New Zealand for further details*; *Style—* Sir Ernest Lee-Steere, KBE; 26 Odern Crescent, Swanbourne, W Australia 6010 (☎ 09 3842929)

LEE-STEERE, Gordon Ernest; s of Charles A Lee-Steere (ka 1940), of Jayes Park, Ockley, Surrey, and Patience Hargreaves, *née* Pigott-Brown; *b* 26 Dec 1939; *Educ* Eton, Trinity Coll Cambridge (MA); *m* 14 July 1966, Mary Katharine, da of Lt-Col Innes Stuart of Ethie Mains, of Inverkeilor, Angus; 1s (James b 1976), 3 da (Henrietta b 1969, Lucinda b 1971, Marina b 1973); *Career* mgmnt conslt Deloitte Robson Morrow 1968-74, pres Country Landowners Assoc 1987; chm Surrey branch CPRE 1982-, dist cncllr Mole Valley 1983-, parish cncllr Ockley 1976-, chm of govrs Sondes Place Sch Dorking; MIMC, MBCS; *Recreations* country; *Clubs* Boodles, Farmers; *Style—* Gordon Lee-Steere, Esq; Jayes Park, Ockley Surrey, RH3 5RA (☎ 030 670 223); Country Landowners Association, 16 Belgrave Sq, London SW1X 8PQ (☎ 01 235 0511), fax 01 235 4696

LEECE, Geoffrey Robert; s of Robert Sydney Leece (d 1984), and Edith Leece, *née* Stevenson; *b* 1 Dec 1931; *Educ* Alsop HS, Prescot GS; *m* 16 May 1973, Janet Kate, da of Colin McCaig (d 1982); 2 s (Stuart b 1975, Alastair b 1977); *Career* sr ptnr Pannell Kerr Forster CA Liverpool 1970-; FCA 1954; *Recreations* golf, watching Everton FC; *Clubs* Athenaeum Liverpool, Huyton and Prescot GC, Heswall GC; *Style—* Geoffrey R Leece, Esq; Thornhill, Briardale Road, Willaston, south Wirral, L64 1TD; 52 Mount Pleasant, Liverpool L3 5UN (☎ 051 708 8232)

LEECH, His Honour Robert Radcliffe; s of Edwin Radcliffe Leech (d 1947); *b* 5 Dec 1919; *Educ* Monmouth, Worcester Coll Oxford; *m* 1951, Vivienne Ruth, da of A J Rickerby; 2 da; *Career* served WWII Border Regt (despatches twice) 1940-44; barr Middle Temple 1949, dep chm Cumberland QS 1966, co ct judge 1970, circuit judge 1971-86, hon rec City of Carlisle 1985-86; *Recreations* sailing, golf; *Clubs* Oriental, Border and Co (Carlisle); *Style—* His Honour Robert Leech; Scaur Hse, Cavendish Terrace, Stanwix, Carlisle CA3 9ND (☎ 0228 21946)

LEECH, William Charles; CBE (1980); s of Albert William Leech; *b* 15 July 1900; *m* 1947, Ellen Richards; 2 da; *Career* served WWI RFC; fndr: William Leech plc 1932 (dir 1940-, pres 1975-), Northern Homes and Estates Ltd 1933- (shareholders are: Br and For Buble Soc, Church Missionary Soc, Methodist Missionary Soc, Salvation Army, Soc for Promoting Christian Knowledge); fndr registered charities: William Leech Fndn Ltd 1960-, The William Leech Property Tst Ltd 1960-, William Leech (Investmts) Ltd 1960 (also pres); Hon DCL Newcastle 1975; *Style—* William Leech, Esq, CBE; High House, Morpeth, Northumberland NE16 2YU (☎ 0670 513364); William Leech plc, 1/3 City Rd, Newcastle upon Tyne, PO Box 1, NE99 1PG (☎ 0632 329954); Northern Homes & Estates Ltd, 4 St James St, Newcastle upon Tyne NE1 4NG

LEEDS, Archdeacon of; *see*: Comber, Ven Anthony James

LEEDS, Aubrey; s of William Henry Leeds (d 1947, gs of 2 Bt), and Mary (d 1956), el da of James Fyfe-Jamieson, of Renfrews; hp of cous Sir Christopher Leeds, 8 Bt, *qv*; *b* 4 August 1903; *m* 1933, Barbara, only child of J Travis, of Lightcliffe, Yorks; 1 s (Antony b 1937), 2 da (Mrs John Nation b 1936, Sharman b 1953); *Career* rubber planter; *Recreations* angling; *Clubs* 22; *Style—* Aubrey Leeds, Esq; 17 Atwood Avenue, Kew Gardens, Surrey (☎ 01 876 2038)

LEEDS, Sir Christopher Anthony; 8 Bt (UK 1812), of Croxton Park, Cambs; s of Maj Geoffrey Hugh Anthony Leeds (d 1962, yr bro of 6 Bt) by his w Yolande Therese Barre, *née* Mitchell (d 1944); suc cous, Sir Graham Mortimer Leeds, 7 Bt, in 1983; *b* 31 August 1935; *Educ* King's Sch Bruton, LSE (BSc Econ), Univ of S California (MA); *m* 1974 (m dis 1980), Elaine Joyce, da of late Sqdn Ldr Cornelius Harold Albert Mullins; *Heir* cous, Aubrey Leeds, *qv*; *Career* asst master: Merchant Taylors' Sch 1966-68, Christ's Hosp 1972-75, Stowe 1978-81; sr lectr Univ of Nancy II; author, memb Soc of Authors; *Publications include* Political Studies (1968, third edn 1981), European History 1789-1914 (1971, second edn 1980), Italy under Mussolini (1972), Management and Business Studies (with R S Stainton and C Jones, 1974, third edn 1983) World History-1900 to the present day (1987), Peace and War (1987), L'humour Anglais (1989); *Recreations* tennis, modern art, travel; *Clubs* Lansdowne; *Style—* Sir Christopher Leeds, Bt; 6 Hurlingham Manor, 14 Manor Way, Eastcliffe, Bournemouth, Dorset; 7 Rue de Turique, 54000 Nancy, France (☎ 83 96 43 838); c/o 45A High Street, Wimbledon Village, London SW19 5AU; Université de Nancy II, BP 33 97, 54015 Nancy, France

LEEMING, Charles Gerard James; s of Gerard Paschal de Pfyffer Leeming, of Field Dalling Hall, Holt, Norfolk, and Joan Helen Mary (d 1954), da of Edmund Trappes-Lomax (d 1927, *see* Burke's Landed Gentry 1952); *b* 4 May 1936; *Educ* Ampleforth Coll, York; *Career* slr 1959; ptnr Wilde Sapte London 1963, (sr ptnr 1987); chm banking sub ctee London Law Soc; memb Lloyds Co of Watermen and Lightermen of the River Thames, Freeman Worshipful Co of Slrs; *Recreations* sailing, music, art, books, bee-keeping, collecting electronic gadgets; *Clubs* Little Ship, Cruising Assoc; *Style—* Charles Leeming, Esq; Picton House, 45 Strand-on-the-Green, Chiswick, London W4 3PB (☎ 01 994 0450); Wilde Sapte, Queensbridge House, 60 Upper Thames St, London EC4V 3BD (☎ 01 236 3050, telex 887793, fax 01 236 9624)

LEEMING, David Roger; s of Stanley James Robert Leeming and Ada; *b* 29 August 1947; *Educ* Felsted Sch, Clare Coll Cambridge (MA Mechanical Science); *m* 18 May 1974, Geraldine Margaret, da of Antony Duke Coleridge; 2 s (Robert b 1978, Toby b 1981); *Career* chm: Platignum plc (managing) 1985 (chm) and all subsidiary and assocs; *Style—* David Leeming, Esq; PO Box 1, Royston, Herts (☎ 0763 44133)

LEEMING, Ian; QC (1988); s of FLt Lt Thomas Leeming (d 1981), of Preston, Lancs, and Lilian, *née* Male; *b* 10 April 1948; *Educ* Catholic Coll Preston, Manchester Univ (LLB); *m* 26 May 1973, Linda Barbara, da of Harold Cook, of Walton-le-Dale, Preston, Lancs; 1 s (Charles b 1985), 2 da (Lucinda b 1976, Angela b 1981); *Career* called to the Bar Gray's Inn 1970, Lincoln's Inn (Ad Eundem), Northern circuit 1971, in practice at the Chancery and Commercial Bars 1971-, fndr memb Northern Soc of Cons Lawyers (vice chm 1985-), asst rec 1986, chm of Heaton Cons 1986-88, former pt/t lectr in law Univ of Manchester; *Recreations* squash, real tennis, occasional racquets; *Clubs* Carlton, Manchester Tennis and Racquets; *Style—* Ian Leeming, Esq, QC; 11 Stone Bldgs, Lincoln's Inn, London; Crown Square Chambers, 1 Dean's Ct, Crown Square, Manchester (☎ 01 404 5055, 061 833 9801)

LEEMING, Jan (Mrs Steenson); da of Ivan Terrence Atkins, MBE, of Nailsworth, Glos, and Hazel Louise Wyatt, *née* Haysey; *b* 5 Jan 1942; *Educ* St Joseph's Convent GS, Abbey Wood Kent; *m* 1, 10 April 1980 (m dis July 1986), Patrick Geoffrey s of Rev Canon Ronald Lunt, of Ledbury, Herefordshire; 1 s (Jonathan Patrick Geoffrey b 18 May 1981); m 2, 8 Aug 1988, John Eric Steenson; *Career* TV newsreader and presenter, TV announcer NZ 1962, first woman TV newsreader Sydney Aust 1963, theatre actress 1963-66, childrens TV presenter Tom Tom BBC; presenter: Women Only and Report West HTV West 1970-76, Pebble Mill at One and various outside broadcast specials 1976-80; announcer Radio 2, newsreader BBC 1980-87, compere Eurovision Song Contest 1982, contrib holiday articles to Travelling Magazine; newsreader of the Year 1981 and 1982, TV Personality of the Year 1982; vice pres: Thames Valley Hospice, Story of Christmas Appeal - Cheyne Centre for Spastics; memb: Bristol Cancer Help Centre, Stars Orgn for Spastics, Business in the Community; memb Guild of Freemen City of London 1988; *Books* Working in Television (1980), Simply Looking Good (1984); *Style—* Miss Jan Leeming; c/o James

Kelly, IMG The Pier House, Strand-on-the-Green, Chiswick, London W4 3NN (☎ 01 994 1444, fax 01 994 9606, telex 267486)

LEEMING, John Coates (Jack); s of late James Arthur Leeming, and Harriet Leeming (d 1950); *b* 3 May 1927; *Educ* Chadderton GS Lancs, St John's Coll Cambridge (MA); *m* 1, 14 April 1949, Dorothy, da of late Joseph Carter; 2 s (Barry b 1950, Peter b 1959); m 2, 7 Dec 1985, Cheryl Elise Kendall, da of Adam Mitchell Gillan (d 1979); *Career* teacher 1948-50, HM Customs and Excise 1950-56, HM Treasy 1958-67, World Bank Washington DC 1967-70, Civil Serv Dept 1970-75, cmmr of Customs & Excise 1975-78, DTI 1978-86, dir gen Br Nat Space Centre 1987-88, space conslt 1988-; golf capt RAC Woodcote Park 1988; *Recreations* golf; *Clubs* RAC; *Style—* Jack Leeming, Esq; 9 Walnut Close, Epsom, Surrey KT18 5JL (☎ 03727 25397); 4 Astral House, Maunsel St, London SW1P 2EA (☎ 01 630 9243)

LEEPER, (Thomas William) Brian; s of Richard Leeper, of W Byfleet; bro of Desmond Leeper, *qv*; *b* 16 June 1927; *Educ* Downside, Magdalene Coll Cambridge; *m* 1951, Edreen Diana, da of Capt Edric Lyte; 4 s (Patrick b 1953, Michael b 1955, James b 1957, Timothy b 1965), 2 da (Mrs Andrew Bruce b 1952, Jennifer b 1959); *Career* dir LEP Gp Ltd 1970- (non exec 1986); student of Homeopathy at Inst of Alternative Med; *Recreations* horticulture, herbalism, photography; *Clubs* Cavalry & Guards; *Style—* Brian Leeper, Esq; Bonners, Hambledon, Godalming, Surrey

LEEPER, (Richard John) Desmond; s of Richard Leeper, of W Byfleet; bro Brian Leeper, *qv*; *Career* chm and md LEP Gp Ltd; *Style—* Desmond Leeper, Esq; LEP Gp Ltd, Sunlight Wharf, Upper Thames St, London EC4

LEES, Sir (William) Antony Clare; 3 Bt (UK 1937); s of Sir William Hereward Clare Lees, 2 Bt (d 1976); *b* 14 June 1935; *Educ* Eton, Magdalene Coll Cambridge (BA); *m* 1986, Joanna Olive Crane; *Style—* Sir Antony Lees, Bt

LEES, Col Brian Musson; LVO (1979), OBE (1978); s of John Lees (d 1978), and Margaret *née* Musson (d 1942), of Tanworth; *b* 9 Oct 1931; *Educ* Queen Elizabeth GS Tamworth, Leeds Univ (BA); *m* 1963, Diana Caroline, da of John Harold Everall; 2 da (Diana b 1964, Alexia b 1966); *Career* Cmmnd KOYLI 1954; served: Kenya (Mau Mau campaign), Cyprus (EOKA campaign), Arabian Peninsula (S Yemen emergency); CO 5 Bn LI 1971-73, Def Attaché Jedda 1975-79, Def Intelligence Staff MOD 1979-82, Head Br Def Intelligence Liaison Staff Washington 1982-84, Defence Attaché Muscat 1984-1986, ret 1987; Middle East conslt; *Books* The Al Sa'ud, Ruling Family of Saudi Arabia (1980); *Recreations* music, gardening, reading; *Clubs* Army & Navy, MCC, Royal Soc for Asian Affairs; *Style—* Col B M Lees, LVO, OBE; The Old Rectory, Kenley, Shropshire SY5 6NH (☎ 069 44 281); 74 Leith Mansions, Grantully Rd, London W9 1LJ (☎ 01 289 7559)

LEES, His Honour Judge; Charles Norman; s of Charles Lees; *b* 4 Oct 1929; *Educ* Stockport Sch, Univ of Leeds; *m* 1961, Stella (d 1987), da of Hubert Swann; 1 da (Rosemary); *Career* barr Lincoln's Inn 1951, a dep chm Cumberland quarter sesions 1969-72, rec of Crown Ct 1972-80, circuit judge 1980-, legal chm of Disciplinary Ctee of the Potato Mktg Bd 1965-80, memb Mental Health Review Tribunal Manchester Region 1971-80, chm 1977-80; *Style—* His Honour Judge Lees; 1 Deans Court, Crown Sq, Manchester 3

LEES, Christopher James; s and h of Sir Thomas Edward Lees, 4 Bt; *b* 4 Nov 1952; *Educ* Eton, Edinburgh Univ; *m* 1977 (m dis), Jennifer, da of John Wyllie, of Newton Stewart Wigtownshire; *Career* farmer; County Cncllr; *Style—* Christopher Lees Esq; Cuzenage, Foxhills Road, Lytchett Matravers, Poole, Dorset

LEES, David Bryan; s of Rear Adm Dennis Marescaux Lees, CB, DSO (d 1973), and Daphne May, *née* Burnett; *b* 23 Nov 1936; *Educ* Charterhouse; *m* 1961, Edith Mary, da of Brig Ronald Playfair St Vincent Bernard, MC, DSO (d 1943); 2 s, 1 da; *Career* served Nat Serv 2 Lt RA; fin dir Guest Keen Nettlefolds plc 1981- (gp md 1987-), chm and chief exec GKN plc, memb Audit Cmmn 1983-; memb Governing Body Shrewsbury Sch; FCA; *Recreations* golf, music; *Clubs* MCC; *Style—* David Lees, Esq; GKN plc, P O Box 55, Redditch, Worcs B98 0TL

LEES, Lady; Dorothy Gertrude; da of Francis Alexander Lauder; *m* 1930, Sir William Hereward Clare Lees, 2 Bt (d 1976); *Style—* Lady Lees

LEES, Helen, Lady; Helen Agnes Marion; da of Charles C Chittick (decd), and widow of Thomas Orr Gibb; *m* 1927, Sir Arthur Henry James Lees, 5 Bt (d 1949); *Style—* Helen, Lady Lees; 3 Valsayn Ave, Valsayn Park, Curepe, Trinidad

LEES, John Cathcart; s of John Rutherford D'Olier-Lees (decd); descends from Sir John Lees 1 Bt successively Usher of Black Rod, Sec of State for War and sec to PO in Ireland d 1811, hp of kinsman, Sir Thomas Harcourt Ivor Lees, 8 Bt, *qv*; *b* 12 Nov 1927; *m* 1957, Wendy Garrold, da of Brian Garrold Groom (decd), of Edinburgh; 2 s (John b 1961, James b 1963); *Career* formerly Lt 12 Bn Border Regiment and SAS Regiment (Artists Rifles) TA; *Style—* John Lees, Esq; 5 Pound Close, Ringwood, Hants

LEES, Dr Kenneth; s of Noel Darwin Lees (d 1974), and Doris Lees (d 1947); *b* 19 Mar 1927; *Educ* Audenshaw GS (BSc), Univ of London (PhD); *m* 1 Sept 1951, Mary Eastwood, da of Arthur Horrabin (d 1943), 2 s (Roderic b 1956, Nicholas b 1960), 2 da (Amanda b 1958, Rebecca b 1965); *Career* chemist Wool Industs Research Assoc 1946-60 (mangr 1960-69); tech dir: London Textile Testing House Ltd 1969-86, Wool Testing Servs Int Ltd 1973-77, Quality Control Int Ltd 1977-80 (md 1980-); dir: ICCH Pension Fund 1983-85, Wood Testing Servs NZ 1977-85; *Recreations* tennis, badminton, squash, gardening, mountain walking; *Style—* Dr Kenneth Lees; Game Cottage, Pollards Park, Nightingales Lane, Chalfont St Giles, Bucks; Gaw House, Alperton Lane, Wembley, Middlesex HA0 1WU (telex 25658, fax 01 997 9723)

LEES, Michael Edward; s of Robert Edward (d 1940), of The Vicarage, Thornton-Le-Kylde, Lancs, and Gladys Mary, *née* Prescott (d 1985); *b* 28 Oct 1937; *Educ* St Edmund's Sch Canterbury, Gonville and Caius Coll, Cambridge (BA, MA); *m* 15 Jan 1966, Jill Virginia, da of Raymond Cawthorne, of The Chalet, Croft Meadow, Sampford Brett, Somerset; 2 s (Andrew b 1970, Richard b 1973); *Career* Royal Army Educnl Corps 1958-76, Maj Scotland 1959-64, Aden 1964-67, London 1967-71, ANZUK Force Singapore 1971-74, Winchester 1974-76; corp security exec The Plessey Co plc 1979-; *Recreations* offshore sailing, travel, walking, gardening; *Clubs* Royal Lymington Yacht; *Style—* Michael Lees, Esq; Rye Gate, East End, Lymington, Hants (☎ 0590 65232); The Plessey Co plc, Grange Rd, Christchurch, Dorset (☎ 0202 486344, telex 418417)

LEES, Air Vice-Marshal Robin Lowther; CB (1985), MBE (1962); s of Air Marshal Sir Alan Lees, KCB, CBE, DSO, AFC (d 1973), of Newbury, Berks, and Norah Elizabeth, *née* Thompson (d 1974); *b* 27 Feb 1931; *Educ* Wellington, RAF Cranwell; *m* 1966, Alison, da of Lt Col Cuthbert Benson Carrick, MC, TD, JP (d 1966), of Newcastle upon Tyne; 3 s (Timothy, Anthony, Edward); *Career* RAF 1949-86, Air Offr Admin RAF Support Cmd and Head of RAF Admin Branch 1982-86 (AVM); chief exec Br Hotels Restaurants and Caterers Assoc 1986-; rep Hants Combined Servs and RAF at squash, rep RAF at tennis and Cambs at hockey; *Recreations* lawn tennis, real tennis, squash, rackets, golf; *Clubs* All England Lawn Tennis, Jesters, RAF; *Style—* Air Vice-Marshal Robin Lees, CB, MBE; c/o Barclays Bank Ltd, 6 Market Place, Newbury, Berks; 40 Duke St, London W1M 6HR (☎ 01 499 6641)

LEES, Air Marshal Sir Ronald Beresford; KCB (1961, CB 1946), CBE (1943), DFC (1940); s of John Thomas Lees, of Adelaide; *b* 27 April 1910; *Educ* St Peter's Coll Adelaide; *m* 1931, Rhoda Lillie, da of Arthur Pank, of Adelaide; 1 s, 1 da; *Career* joined RAF 1931, air ADC to HM the King 1943-52, to HM the Queen 1952-53, Asst Chief of Air Staff (Ops) 1955-58, SASO Fighter Cmd 1958-60, dep ch of Air Staff 1960, Air Marshal 1961, C-in-C RAF Germany 1963-65, ret 1966; grazier; *Style—* Air Marshal Sir Ronald Lees, KCB, CBE, DFC; Jelbra, RMB 367 Via Albury, NSW 2640, Australia

LEES, Sir Thomas Edward; 4 Bt (UK 1897), JP (1951) Dorset; s of Col Sir John Victor Elliott Lees, 3 Bt, DSO, MC (d 1955); *b* 1925; *Educ* Eton, Magdalene Coll Cambridge; *m* 1949, Faith Justin, JP (1963) Dorset, da of Gaston Jessiman; 1 s, 3 da (Sarah b 1951, Mrs Martin Green b 1954, Elizabeth b 1957); *Heir* s, Christopher James Lees; *Career* served with RAF 1943-45, High Sheriff of Dorset 1960; *Recreations* sailing; *Clubs* Royal Cruising; *Style—* Sir Thomas Lees, Bt, JP; Post Green, Lytchett Minster, Dorset (☎ Lytchett Minster 2317)

LEES, Sir Thomas Harcourt Ivor; 8 Bt (UK 1804), of Blackrock, Dublin; s of Sir Charles Archibald Edward Ivor Lees, 7 Bt (d 1963); *b* 6 Nov 1941; *Heir* kinsman, John Cathcart D'Olier Lees, *qv*; *Style—* Sir Thomas Lees, Bt

LEES, William; CBE (1971), TD (1962 bar 1968); s of Maj William Lees (d 1986), and Elizabeth, *née* Massey (d 1962); *b* 18 May 1924; *Educ* Queen Elizabeth Blackburn, Victorian Univ Manchester (MB ChB, DPH); *m* 4 Oct 1947, (Winifred) Elizabeth, da of Robert Archibald Hanford (d 1964), of Cheshire; 3 s (William b 1948, John b 1953, Christopher b 1959); *Career* RAMC 1948-50, TA 1950-71: Col Cmdg 257 Gen Hosp TA 1966-71, Col Cmdt NW sector ACF 1971-77; lectr gynaecologist St Mary Hosp Manchester 1950-59, sr princ med offr Miny of Health DHSS 1959-81 (under sec 1977-81), conslt advsr Med Manpower and Post Graduate Educn SW Thames RHA 1981-87; chm Dacorum Cancer Relief and McMillan Fund; Hon Physician HM The Queen 1970-72; Liveryman Worshipful Co of Apothecaries; O St J 1968; FROCG 1964, MFCM 1973; *Recreations* golf, music, travel; *Clubs* Athenaeum St Johns; *Style—* Dr William Lees, CBE, TD; 13 Hill Park Hill, Berkhamsted, Herts HP4 2NH (☎ 0442 863010)

LEES-MILNE, James; s of George Crompton Lees-Milne (d 1949), of Crompton Hall, Lancashire, and Wickhamford Manor, Evesham, Worcs, and Helen Christina, *née* Bailey; *b* 6 August 1908; *Educ* Eton, Magdalen Coll Oxford, Grenoble Univ; *m* 19 Nov 1951, Alvilde, da of late Lt-Gen Sir Tom Molesworth Bridges, KCB, KCMG, DSO, former wife of 3 Viscount Chaplin; *Career* 2 Lt Irish Gds 1940-41 (invalided); private sec to 1 Baron Lloyd 1931-35, staff at Reuters 1935-36, on staff Nat Tst 1936-66, advsr on historic buildings Nat Tst 1951-66; FRSL 1957, FSA 1974; *Books* The National Trust (ed 1945), The Age of Adam (1947), National Trust Guide: Buildings (1948), Tudor Renaissance (1951), The Age of Inigo Jones (1953), Roman Mornings (Heinemann Award, 1956), Baroque in Italy (1959), Baroque in Spain and Portugal (1960), Earls of Creation (1962), Worcestershire: A Shell Guide (1964), St Peter's (1967), English Country Houses: Baroque 1685-1714 (1970), Another Self (1970), Heretics in love (1973), Ancestral Voices (1975), William Beckford (1976), Prophesying Peace (1977), Round the Clock (1978), Harold Nicolson (vol 1 1980, vol II 1981, Heineman Award 1982), Images of Bath (with David Ford 1982), The Country House (1982), Caves of Ice (1983), The Last Stuarts (1983), Midway on the Wanes (1985), The Enigmatic Edwardian (1986), Some Cotswold Country Houses (1987), Venetian Evenings (1988); *Recreations* walking; *Clubs* Brooks's; *Style—* James Lees-Milne, Esq; Essex House, Badminton GL9 1DD (☎ 045 421 288)

LEES-SPALDING, Rear-Adm Ian Jaffery; CB (1973); s of Frank Souter Lees-Spalding (d 1970); *b* 16 June 1920; *Educ* Blundells; *m* 1946, June Sandys Lyster, da of Maj Warren Lyster Sparkes, of Devon; 2 da; *Career* joined RN 1938, awarded commendation 1940, joined submarines 1945, chief staff offr (tech) to C-in-C Fleet and inspr gen Fleet Maintenance 1971, ret 1974, ADC 1971; admin London Int Film Sch 1975-79; *Books* Macmillan and Silk Cut Nautical Almanac (ed), Macmillan and Silk Cut Yachtsman's Handbook (ed); *Recreations* sailing, travel, gardening; *Clubs* Army and Navy; *Style—* Rear Adm Ian Lees-Spalding, CB; St Olaf's, Wonston, Winchester, Hants SO21 3LP (☎ 0962 760249)

LEESE, Arthur; s of Henry Leese (d 1969), and Edith Mabel Leese, *née* Baker (d 1952); *b* 4 May 1931; *Educ* Battersea GS 1942-47; *m* 18 July 1959, Marian, da of Walter Thomas Bryant, of 19 Birch Close, Stowupland, Stowmarket, Suffolk; 1 s (Simon b 1967), 1 da (Sarah b 1971); *Career* dir: Columbia Pictures Corpn Ltd 1980-, Columbia Pictures Video Ltd 1982-, Colgems Productions Ltd since 1983, Coca-Cola Hldgs (UK) Ltd 1983-; *Recreations* reading, walking, fishing; *Style—* Arthur Leese, Esq; 53 Chieveley Drive, Tunbridge Wells, Kent TN2 5HQ (☎ 0892 30706); 19/23 Wells St, London W1P 3FP (☎ 01 580 2090, telex 263392, fax 01 580 7696)

LEESE, Sir John Henry Vernon; 5 Bt (UK 1908); s of Vernon Francis Leese, OBE (d 1927), 2 s of 1 Bt; suc kinsman, Sir Alexander William Leese, 4 Bt, 1979; *b* 7 August 1901; *Style—* Sir John Leese, Bt

LEESON, Ian Arthur; s of Alister Curtis Leeson, of Heathfield, Chilworth, Nr Southampton, Hamps, and Nancy Avis Louise, *née* Cayzer; *b* 13 Mar 1937; *Educ* Rugby, Univ Coll Oxford (MA); *m* 7 Aug 1965, (Eileen) Margaret, da of Col Anderson Kirkwood Tennent, OBE (d 1971); 2 da (Sally b 1968, Patricia b 1971); *Career* CA, ptnr Ernst and Whinney 1970-; FCA 1964; *Recreations* golf, tennis; *Clubs* Woking GC, St Georges Hill Lawn Tennis; *Style—* Ian Leeson, Esq; Talana, Esher Close, Esher, Surrey (☎ 0372 66683); c/o Ernst and Whinney, Becket House, 1 Lambeth Palace Road, London SE1 7EU (☎ 01 928 2000, fax 01 928 1345)

LEFEVRE, Frank Hartley; s of chalres Wilson Lefevre of 3 Harlaw Terrace, Aberdeen, and Ethil Edith, *née* Hartley (d 1956); *b* 4 Dec 1934; *Educ* Robert Gordon's Coll Aberdeen, Aberdeen Univ (MA, LLB); *m* 20 Aug 1960, Hazel, da of Magnus Harper Gray (d 1981), of 30 Albert Terrace, Aberdeen; 1 s (Paul b 1964), 2 da (Tracey b 1961, Julie b 1966); *Career* slr & advocate in Aberdeen; firm of Lefevre & Co; dir: Quantum Claims Compensation Specialists Ltd, conslt in law Albervic Ltd

1968-; Notary Public; former pres Grampian Squash Racquets Assoc; *Recreations* golf, squash racquets, musical appreciation; *Clubs* Royal Northern & Univ, Royal Aberdeen GC, Aberdeen Sportsmans, Aberdeen Squash Racquets, Sloan; *Style*— Frank Lefevre, Esq; Braco Lodge, 11 Rubislaw Den North, Aberdeen; 8 Rubislaw Terrace, Aberdeen (☎ 0224 644411, telex: LANDCO 7333)

LEFEVRE, Garry Ernest Grant; s of Maj Jack Ernest Lefevre, of Zimbabwe, and Irene Kathleen, *née* Osborne; *b* 6 May 1938; *Educ* Clifton Sch SA, Kingston Coll; *m* 4 April 1977, Inge, da of Hans Rosted (d 1985), of Copenhagen Denmark; 1 da (Tanya b 1 March 1980); *Career* RAF 1958-60; audit mangr Price Waterhouse 1965-70, controller Morgan Guarantee Tst 1970-73, fin dir Interdan 1973-77, mangr TSB Gp 1977-81, Nationwide Building Soc 1982-86; dir 1986-: Meteor Hldgs, Bunzl Pulp & Paper Sales, Meteor Mercantile, Toysplus, Intermega, Giltra (Denmark); FCCA 1965; *Recreations* golf, bridge; *Clubs* Wentworth GC; *Style*— Garry Lefevre, Esq; Hillside, Gorse Hill Lane, Wentworth, Surrey (☎ 09904 2440)

LEFF, Prof Gordon; s of Solomon Elvin Leff (d 1983), of London, and Eva, *née* Gordon; *b* 9 May 1926; *Educ* Summerhill Sch Leiston Suffolk, Minchenden Sch Southgate London, King's Coll Cambridge (BA, PhD, Litt D); *m* 20 Jun 1953 (m dis 1979), Rosemary Kathleen, da of Charles Fox (d 1987), of Sawston, Cambridge; 1 s (Gregory b 1959); *Career* fell King's Coll Cambridge 1955-59, lectr Manchester Univ 1956-65, reader York Univ 1966-69, prof of history York Univ 1969-88; *Books* Bradwardine and the Pelagians (1957), Medieval Thought (1958), Gregory of Rimini (1961), The Tyranny of Concepts (1961), Richard Fitzralph (1963), Heresy in the Later Middle Ages 2 Vols (1967), Paris and Oxford Universities in the 13 and 14 Centuries (1968) History and Social Theory (1969), William of Ockham (1975), The Dissolution of The Medieval Outlook (1976); *Recreations* walking, cricket watching, music; *Clubs* MCC; *Style*— Prof Gordon Leff; The Sycamores, 12 The Village, Strensall, York YO3 5XS (☎ 0904 490 358)

LEGARD, Christopher John Charles; s and h of Sir Charles Thomas Legard, 15 Bt, *qv*, and Elizabeth (who m 2, 1988, Patrick M L Hibbert-Foy), da of John M Guthrie; *b* 19 April 1964; *Educ* Eton Coll; *m* 1986, Miranda, da of Fane Gaffney, of Hurworth, Co Durham; *Career* accountant; *Recreations* skiing, shooting, photography; *Style*— Christopher Legard, Esq; 155 King St, Cottingham, North Humberside HU16 5QQ (☎ Hull 842464)

LEGG, Barry Charles; s of Henry Wellman Legg, of Hucclecote, Glos, and Elfreda, *née* Thorp; *b* 30 May 1949; *Educ* Sir Thomas Rich's GS Gloucester, Manchester Univ; *m* 16 March 1974, Margaret Rose, da of Roy Stewartson, of Roath Park, Cardiff; 1 s (George Alexander b 27 Nov 1987), 2 da (Victoria Rose b 21 Jan 1981, Elizabeth Fiona b 12 Sept 1984); *Career* CA, Courtaulds Ltd 1971-76, Coopers & Lybrand 1976-78, exec dir Hillsdown Hldgs plc 1978-; memb Westminster City Cncl 1978 (chm fin ctee 1986, chief whip Cons gp 1983); Parly candidate (Cons) Bishop Auckland 1983; FCA 1975, ATII 1976; *Recreations* cricket; *Clubs* Glos Co Cricket, Glos Exiles; *Style*— Barry Legg, Esq; 22 Chapel Street, London SW1 7BY (☎ 01 235 4944); Hillsdown Holdings Plc, Hilldown House, 32 Hampstead High Street, London NW3 1QD (☎ 01 794 0677)

LEGGATT, Hon Mr Justice; Hon Sir Andrew Peter; s of Capt Peter W R C Leggatt, DSO, RN (d 1983), of Odiham, Hants, and (Dorothea Joy), *née* Dreyer; *b* 8 Nov 1930; *Educ* Eton, King's Coll Cambridge (MA); *m* 17 July 1953, Gillian Barbara (Jill), da of Cdr C P Newton, RN, of Petersfield, Hants; 1 s (George b 1957), 1 da (Alice b 1960); *Career* served Rifle Bde 1949-50 and TA 1950-59; barr Inner Temple 1954; QC 1972; Recorder of Crown Ct 1974-82; High Ct Judge 1982-; memb: Bar Cncl 1971-82 (chm 1981-82), Top Salaries Review Body 1979-82; kt 1982; *Recreations* listening to music, personal computers; *Clubs* MCC; *Style*— The Hon Mr Justice Leggatt; Royal Cts of Justice, Strand, London WC2A 2LL (☎ 01 936 6635)

LEGGATT, Sir Hugh Frank John; s of Henry Alan Leggatt (d 1951), of London, and Beatrice Grace, *née* Burton (d 1934); *b* 27 Feb 1925; *Educ* Eton, New College Oxford; *m* 1953, Jennifer Mary, da of Paul Hepworth (d 1964); 2 s (Charles b 1954, Martin b 1955); *Career* joined Leggatt Bros 1946 (ptnr 1952, sr ptnr 1962); pres Fine Art Provident Inst 1960-63, chm Soc of London Art Dealers 1966-70, memb Museums & Galleries Cmmn 1983-; hon sec Heritage in Danger 1974; kt 1988; *Recreations* the arts; *Clubs* Whites; *Style*— Sir Hugh Leggatt; Flat 1, 10 Bury St, St James's, London SW1Y 6AA (☎ 01 839 4698); 17 Duke St, St James's, London SW1Y 6DB (☎ 01 930 3772)

LEGGE, Lady Charlotte; da of 9 Earl of Dartmouth; *b* 16 July 1963; *Style*— Lady Charlotte Legge

LEGGE, Hon Henry; s of 9 Earl of Dartmouth; *b* 1968; *Style*— The Hon Henry Legge

LEGGE, Hon Rupert; s of 9 Earl of Dartmouth and Countess Spencer, *qv*; *b* 1 Jan 1951; *Educ* Eton, Ch Ch Oxford (MA); *m* 1984, Victoria, da of Lionel Edward Bruce Ottley, of Tichborne Park Cottage, Alresford, Hants; 1 s (Edward Peregrine b 1986), 1 da (Claudia Rose b 1989); *Career* barr Inner Temple 1975; *Books* The Children of Light (1986); *Style*— The Hon Rupert Legge; Hamswell House, nr Bath BA1 9DG

LEGGE-BOURKE, Hon Mrs (Elizabeth Shân Josephine); *née* Bailey; LVO; da of 3 Baron Glanusk, DSO (d 1948), and Margaret (who later m 1 Viscount De L'Isle, *qv*); *b* 10 Sept 1943; *m* 2 June 1964, Capt William Nigel Henry Legge-Bourke, er s of Sir Harry Legge-Bourke, KBE, DL, and Lady Legge-Bourke; 1 s (Harry b 1972 page of honour to HM The Queen 1984-87), 2 da (Alexandra b 1965, Zara (Mrs R Dray) b 1966); *Career* lady-in-waiting to HRH The Princess Royal 1978-; pres: Welsh Cncl of Save the Children Fund, Brecon and Radnor NSPCC; chief cadet offr for Wales, St John's Ambulance Bde; *Style*— The Hon Mrs Legge-Bourke; Penmyarth, Glanusk Park, Crickhowell, Powys NP8 1LP (☎ 0873 810230)

LEGGE-BOURKE, Lady; (Catherine) Jean; da of Col Sir Arthur Grant of Monymusk, 10 Bt, CBE, DSO (d 1931); *b* 18 August 1917; *m* 1938, Maj Sir Harry Legge-Bourke, KBE, MP, DL (d 1973, *see* Peerage Earl of Dartmouth); 2 s (William m Hon Elizabeth, *née* Bailey, *qv*; Heneage b 1948 m Maria Clare *née de Sá-Carneiro: 1 s, 1 da), 1 da (Victoria, qv)*; *Style*— Lady Legge-Bourke; Flat 2, 121 Dovehouse St, London SW3 6JZ (☎ 01 352 5911)

LEGGE-BOURKE, Victoria Lindsay; LVO (1986); da of Maj Sir Harry Legge-Bourke, KBE, DL, MP (d 1973), and Lady Legge-Bourke, *qv*; *b* 12 Feb 1950; *Educ* Benenden, St Hilda's Coll Oxford; *Career* dir Junior Tourism Ltd 1974-81; lady-in-waiting to HRH The Princess Royal 1974-86; extra lady-in-waiting to HRH The Princess Royal 1986-; special asst American Embassy London 1983-89; *Style*— Miss Victoria Legge-Bourke, LVO; 21 Eccleston Square, London SW1V 1NS (☎ 01 834 0978); c/o Price Investment Corporation, 1 West Armour Boulevard, Kansas City, Missouri 64111, USA

LEGGE-BOURKE, William Nigel Henry; er s of Sir Harry Legge-Bourke, KBE, DL, MP (d 1973), and (Catherine) Jean, *née* Grant of Monymusk (*see* Lady Legge-Bourke); *b* 12 July 1939; *Educ* Eton, Magdalene Coll Camb (MA); *m* 2 June 1964, Hon Elizabeth Shân Josephine Bailey, LVO, da of 3 Baron Glanusk, DSO (d 1948) (*see* Hon Mrs Legge-Bourke); 1 s (Harry Russell b 1972), 2 da (Alexandra Shân b 1965, Zara Victoria b 1966, m 1985, Capt R Plunkett-Ernle-Erle-Drax); *Career* cmmnd Royal Horse Guards (The Blues) 1959, Capt and Adjt, ret 1968; memb Int Stock Exchange; ptnr Grieveson Grant & Co 1974-86; dir Kleinwort Benson Securities Ltd 1986-; memb Cncl of ISE 1988-; memb Representative Body of the Church in Wales; chm Finance Ctee, The Scout Assoc; *Recreations* country sports; *Clubs* White's, City of London; *Style*— William Legge-Bourke, Esq; Penmyarth, Glanusk Park, Crickhowell, Powys NP8 1LP (☎ 0873 810230); 8 Kensington Mansions, Trebovir Road, London SW5 9TF; Kleinwort Benson Securities Ltd, 20 Fenchurch Street, London EC3P 2DB (☎ 01 623 8000)

LEGGETT, Sir Clarence Arthur Campbell; MBE (1943); s of Arthur James Leggett (d 1968), and Daisy Ethel Leggett (d 1975); *b* 24 July 1911; *Educ* Sydney Univ (MB, BS), Qld Univ (MS, MA); *m* 1939, Avril Olga, da of Robert Lester Bailey (d 1968); 1 s, 2 da; *Career* sr surgeon Princess Alexandra Hosp Brisbane 1956-68, vice-pres Royal Australasian Coll of Surgns 1964-65, hon consulting surgn Princess Alexandra Hosp 1968-75; landowner; kt 1980; *Recreations* horse sport and breeding; *Style*— Sir Clarence Leggett, MBE; 217 Wickham Terrace, Brisbane, Qld 4000, Australia

LEGGETT, Keith Arnold; s of Jack Eric Leggett, of 22 Danes Close, Kirkham, Preston, Lancashire, and Marian Lois, *née* Perkins; *b* 18 Mar 1940; *Educ* Monkton Combe Sch, Cloverley Hall Whitchurch Salop; *m* 4 Sept 1964, Sonja Ruth, da of Marco Fortune Gareh, of 14 Linden Avenue, Thornton Cleveleys, Fylde; 3 s (Stephen b 1966, Oliver b 1968, Robert b 1972); *Career* Estate Agent, Valuer, Surveyor and Auctioneer; princ N Routledge & Co, Sale Cheshire 1964-87; residential sales dir Nationwide Anglia Beresfords Estate Agents 1987-; past chm: Sale and District Round Table, Manchester Branch of Incorporated Soc of Valuers and Auctioneers, Sale Festival of Sport and Drama; FSVA, FCIArb, FRVA; *Recreations* golf, specialist ceramic collecting, antiques; *Clubs* Hale Golf, N Cheshire 41; *Style*— Keith Leggett, Esq; The Ridge, York Drive, Bowdon, Altrincham, Cheshire WA14 3HF (☎ 061 941 2997); Charter Buildings, 9 Ashton Lane, Sale, Cheshire M33 1WT (☎ 061 973 6248, fax 061 456 5545, car ☎ 0860 813 644)

LEGGOTT, (James Peter) Bruce; s of Walter Leggott (d 1980), and Miriam Moss, *née* Weston (d 1966); *b* 1 Nov 1950; *Educ* Monkton Combe Sch, Shuttleworth Agric Coll; *m* 28 Dec 1974, Elizabeth Maltby, da of Cncllr Ronald Hubert Fielding, of Courcelle, 35 Windmore Ave, Potters Bar, Herts; 1 s (Thomas b 1980), 1 da (Claire b 1981); *Career* farmer; ptnr in W Leggott & Son (family business) 1974-, agric instr in Kenya (vol service overseas) 1971-73; church warden SS Peter & Paul Algarkirk Boston 1979-; chm Lincs and S Humberside Farming and Wildlife Advsy Gp 1984-; *Recreations* sailing, skiing, photography; *Clubs* Ski (GB); *Style*— Bruce Leggott, Esq; Manor Farm, Burtoft, Boston, Lincs PE20 2PD (☎ 0205 460283)

LEGH, Charles Francis; s of Cdr Ralph Armitage Broughton, RN (d 1975), and Cynthia Combermere Broughton Legh, OBE (d 1983), of Adlington Hall; assumed surname of Legh in lieu of patronymic 1940; Legh family have lived at Adlington Hall since 1315 (*see* Burke's Landed Gentry 1952; cadet line cr Bt 1611 and Baron 1643, extinct 1786, 2 cr 1839, *see* Peerage, Alice Leigh cr. Duchess of Dudley for Life 1644 *dspm* 1669); *b* 2 Feb 1922; *Educ* Stowe, Trinity Coll Cambridge; *m* 24 Sept 1954 (m dis 1974), Jane Mary Chaworth, da of Fergus Munro Innes, of Surrey; 1 s (Robert b 1955, d 1962), 1 da (Camilla b 1960); *Career* served 2 KE VII own Gurkha Rifles 1942-46; served in India and Burma; broker Lloyds 1954-67, underwriting memb Lloyds 1956-; historic house and landowner; *Recreations* gardening, historical research; *Clubs* Arts; *Style*— Charles F Legh, Esq; Adlington Hall, Macclesfield, Cheshire SK10 4LF (☎ 0625 829508)

LEGH, Hon David Piers Carlis; s of 4 Baron Newton; *b* 21 Nov 1951; *Educ* Eton, RAC Cirencester; *m* 1974, Jane Mary, da of John Roy Wynter Bee, of Heather Hills, West End, Woking, Surrey; 2 s (Hugo b 1979, Thomas b 1984), 1 da (Charlotte Mary b 1976); *Career* chartered surveyor; ptnr John German chartered surveyors; FRICS, MRAC; *Clubs* Farmers; *Style*— The Hon David Legh; Cubley Lodge, Ashbourne, Derbys (☎ 033 523 297); The Rotunda, High Street, Burton-on-Trent (☎ 0283 42051)

LEGH, Hon Richard Thomas; s and h of 4 Baron Newton; *b* 11 Jan 1950; *Educ* Eton, Ch Ch Oxford; *m* 1978, Rosemary Whitfoot, da of Herbert Clarke, of Eastbourne; 1 s; *Style*— The Hon Richard Legh; 101 Eton Rise, Eton College Rd, London NW3

LEGRAIN, Gérard, Marie, Francois; s of Jean Legrain (d 1985), and Marie Hélène *née* Merica (d 1962); *b* 16 April 1937; *Educ* Ecole St Louis de Gonzague, Sorbonne, Faculté de Droit Instit d' Etudes Politiques, Ecole Nationale d'Aministration Paris; *m* 1969, Katrin Ines, da of Harald Tombach, of Altadena, California, USA; 2 s (Philippe b 1973, Pierre b 1980), 1 da (Milli b 1976); *Career* Sub Lt 27 and 15 Batallions de Chasseurs Alpins 1962; Citibank Paris 1965, NY 1967, Mexico City 1969; vice-pres Citicorp Int Bank Ltd London 1972; md Int Mexican Bank Ltd London 1974; *Recreations* skiing, swimming, tennis; *Clubs* Hurlingham; *Style*— Gérard Legrain, Esq; Intermex, 29 Gresham Street, London EC2V 7ES (☎ 01 600 0880, fax 01 6009891, telex 881 017)

LEHANE, Maureen Theresa (Mrs Peter Wishart); da of Christopher Lehane (d 1970), of London, and Honor, *née* Millar; *Educ* Queen Elizabeth's Girls' GS Barnet, Guildhall Sch Music and Drama; *m* 26 May 1966, Peter Wishart (d 1984); *Career* concert and opera singer; studied under: Hermann Weissenborn, John and Aida Dickens; debut Glyndebourne 1967; speciality Handel, numerous leading roles with Handel opera socs in: England, America, Poland, Sweden, Germany; numerous master classes on the interpretation of Handel's vocal music; title roles in: Handel's Ariodante Sadlers Wells 1974, Peter Wishart's Clytemnestra London 1974, Purcell's Dido and Aeneas Netherlands Opera 1976, castrato lead JC Bach's Adriano London 1982, female lead Hugo Cole's The Falcon Somerset 1983, Peter Wishart's The Lady of the Inn Reading Univ 1984; festival appearances incl; Stravinsky Festival Cologne, City of London, Aldeburgh, Cheltenham, Three Choirs, Bath, Oxford Bach, Göttingen Handel Festival; tours incl: N America, Australia, Far East, Middle East; visits incl: Holland, Belgium, Berlin, Lisbon, Poland, Rome, Warsaw; recordings incl: Bach, Haydn,

Mozart, Handel (Cyrus in first complete recording Belshazzar); tv appearances incl: BBC, ABC Australia, Belgian TV; regular appearances promenade concerts; memb jury int singing comp s'Hertogenbosch Festival Holland 1982-; *Books* Songs of Purcell (co ed Peter Wishart); *Recreations* cooking, gardening, reading; *Style*— Miss Maureen Lehane; Bridge House, Great Elm, Frome, Somerset BA11 3NY

LEHMAN, Hon Mrs (Karen Jean); da of 9 Viscount Doneraille (d 1983), and Melva, Viscountess Doneraile, *qv*; *b* 1955; *m* 1977, R Lehman; *Style*— The Hon Mrs Lehman

LEHMANN, Prof (Andrew) George; s of Andrew W Lehmann (d 1970), of London, and M Grisel, *née* Bissett (d 1982); *b* 17 Feb 1922; *Educ* Dulwich, Queen's Coll Oxford (MA, D Phil); *m* 31 Jan 1942, Alastine Mary, da of Kenneth Norman Bell (d 1952, of Oxford; 2 s (Max b 1945, Martin b 1947), 1 da (Miranda d 1954); *Career* lectr Manchester Univ 1945-51, prof French Studies Reading Univ 1951-68, hon prof Warwick Univ 1968-78, prof Euro Studies Hull Univ 1978-83, rank prof Euro Studies Buckingham Univ 1983-88 (emeritus 1988-); *Books* The Symbolist Aesthetic in France (1950,1967), Sainte-Beuve (1963), The European Heritage (1984); *Clubs* Athenaeum; *Style*— Prof George Lehmann; Westway Cottage, W Adderbury, Oxon (☎ 0295 810 272)

LEHMANN, Rosamond Nina; CBE (1982); da of Rudolph Chambers Lehmann; sis of John Lehmann; *Educ* privately, Girton Coll Cambridge; *m* 1, 1923 (m dis 1928), 2 Viscount Runciman of Doxford (then Walter Runciman); m 2, 1928 (m dis 1944), as his 1 w, Wogan Philipps (later 2 Baron Milford); 1 s (Hon Hugo Philipps), 1 da (Sarah, d 1958 having m the poet and novelist Patrick J Kavanagh); *Career* novelist, books include Dusty Answer, The Weather in the Streets, A Sea-Grape Tree (1982); *Style*— Miss Rosamond Lehmann, CBE; 70 Eaton Sq, SW1

LEICESTER, 6 Earl of (UK 1837); Anthony Lovel Coke; also Viscount Coke (UK 1837); s of Lt the Hon Arthur Coke (2 s of 3 Earl); suc first cous 1976; *b* 11 Sept 1909; *Educ* Gresham's Sch Holt; *m* 1, 1934 (m dis 1947), Moyra (d 1987), da of Douglas Crossley; 2 s, 1 da; m 2, 1947, Vera (d 1984), da of Herbert Haigh, of Salisbury, Rhodesia (now Zimbabwe); m 3, 1985, Elizabeth Hope, da of Clifford Arthur Johnstone, of Kiswani, Addo, CP, S Africa; *Heir* s, Viscount Coke; *Career* served WWII RAF; rancher, farmer retired; *Style*— The Rt Hon the Earl of Leicester; Hillhead, Pendeen Crescent, Plettenberg Bay, Cape Province 6600, S Africa; PO Box 544, Plettenberg Bay 6600, RSA (☎ 04457 32255)

LEICESTER, 4 Bishop of, 1978-; Rt Rev Cecil Richard Rutt; CBE (1973); patron of eighty-five livings, the provostship and residentiary canonries of St Martin's Cathedral, the Archdeaconries of Leicester and Loughborough, and twenty-one Hon Canonries. The present Diocese was founded by Act of Parliament Nov 1926, but an earlier Diocese of Leicester was in existence from about 680 to 874, during which period at least nine Bishops occupied the See; s of Cecil Rutt and Mary Hare, *née* Turner; *b* 27 August 1925; *Educ* Kelham Theological Coll, Pembroke Coll Cambridge (MA); *m* 1969, Joan Mary Ford; *Career* served RNVR 1943-46; ordained priest 1952, rector St Michael's Seminary (Oryu Dong, Seoul, Korea) 1965-66, bishop of Taejon 1968-74 (asst Bp 1966-68), Bishop Suffragan of St Germans and hon canon St Mary's Cathedral Truro 1974-79; bard of Gorsedd of Cornwall, Cornwhylen 1976; Hon DLitt Confucian Univ Seoul 1974; ChStJ 1978; Order of Civil Merit (Peony Class) Korea 1974; *Books* Korean Works and Days (1964), An Anthology of Korean Sijo (1970), The Bamboo Grove (1971), Three Virtuous Women (translation) 1974; *Clubs* United Oxford and Cambridge; *Style*— The Rt Rev the Bishop of Leicester; Bishop's Lodge, 10 Springfield Rd, Leicester LE2 3BD (☎ 0533 708985)

LEICESTER, Lady; Marthe; da of Louis de Miéville de Rossens; *m* 1930, as his 2 w, Sir Peter Fleming Frederic Leicester, 8 Bt (d 1945); *Style*— Lady Leicester; Shearwater, Downderry, Cornwall

LEICESTER, Archdeacon of; see: The Ven Robert David Silk

LEIFLAND, HE Leif; GCVO; The Swedish Ambassador; s of Sigfrid Leifland (d 1970), and Elna Jonson (d 1985); *b* 30 Dec 1925; *Educ* Univ of Lund (LLB); *m* 1954, Karin Kristina, da of Gustaf Abard, (d 1982); 1 s (Karl), 2 da (Christina, Eva); *Career* joined Swedish Miny of Foreign Affrs 1959; served: Athens 1953, Bonn 1955, Stockholm 1958; Washington 1961, Stockholm 1964, Washington 1970, Stockholm 1975; perm under-sec of State 1977-82; ambass London 1982; Grand Cross of: Austria, Finland, Fed Rep of Germany, Iceland, Rep of Korea, Mexico, Spain, Yugoslavia; *Style*— HE the Ambass of Sweden; 27 Portland Place, W1; 11 Montagu Place, W1H 2AL (☎ 01 724 2101)

LEIGH, Hon Benjamin Chandos; s of 4 Baron Leigh, TD (d 1979), and Anne Hicks Beach (d 1977); *b* 24 Oct 1942; *Educ* Eton, Mons OCS; *m* 1979, Jennifer Vivian, da of late Capt Peter Winser, and formerly w of Hon Richard Henry Strutt, el s 4 Baron Belper; 1 da (Samantha Jane Hazel b 1980), 2 step-children (*see* Lord Belper); *Career* Lt 11 Hussars (PAO) 1960-65; *Recreations* racing, shooting; *Clubs* Turf; *Style*— The Hon Benjamin Leigh; Little Rissington House, Little Rissington, Cheltenham, Glos GL54 2NB

LEIGH, Hon Camilla Anne; only da of 5th Baron Leigh; *b* 1962; *Style*— The Hon Camilla Leigh

LEIGH, Hon Christopher Dudley Piers; er s (but only one by 1 w) & h of 5 Baron Leigh; *b* 20 Oct 1960; *Style*— The Hon Christopher Leigh; Fern Farm, Adlestrop, Moreton-in-the-Marsh, Gloucs

LEIGH, Christopher Humphrey de Vero; s of Wing Cdr Humphrey de Verd Leigh, OBE, DFC, AFC (d 1981), and Johanna Emily, *née* Whitfield Hayes; *b* 12 July 1943; *Educ* Harrow; *m* 18 July 1970, Frances Raymonde, da of Col Raymond Henry Albert Powell OBE, MC; *Career* called to the Bar 1967, Recorder of the Crown Ct 1985; *Recreations* travel; *Style*— Christopher Leigh, Esq; Dennetts, Broughton, Stockbridge, Hants SO20 8AD (☎ 0794 301 387); 1 Paper Buildings, Temple, London EC4Y 7EP (☎ 01 353 3728)

LEIGH, Edward Julian Egerton; MP (C) Gainsborough and Horncastle 1983-; s of Sir Neville Leigh, KCVO, *qv*, and Denise Yvonne, *née* Branch; *b* 20 July 1950; *Educ* Oratory Sch, Lycée Francaise de Londres, Durham Univ; *m* 25 Sept 1984, Mary, eldest da of Philip Henry Russell Goodman, of 21 Upper Phillimore Gardens, London W8, and Sophie (Sonia), o da of late Count Vladimir Petrovitch Kleinmichel, CVO; 1 s (b 1988), 2 da; *Career* barr; former: pres Durham Union Soc, chm Durham Univ Cons Assoc; dir Coalition for Peace through Security, chm Nat Cncl for Civil Defence; memb ULC 1977-81; *Clubs* Carlton; *Style*— Edward Leigh, Esq, MP; House of Commons, London SW1

LEIGH, Geoffrey Norman; s of Morris, and Rose Leigh; *b* 23 Mar 1933; *Educ* Haberdashers' Aske's Sch, Univ of Michigan; *m* 1976, Sylvia, *née* King; 5 children; *Career* industrialist; chm: Allied London Properties plc, Sterling Homes Hldgs Ltd, Wetenhall Cooper Ltd; memb: int advsy bd The American Univ 1983-, advsy cncl Prince's Youth Business Tst 1985-; sponsor Dartford City Technol Coll 1988-; *Clubs* Carlton, Royal Automobile, Savile, Hurlingham; *Style*— Geoffrey Leigh, Esq; 26 Manchester Sq, London W1A 2HU (☎ 01 486 6080)

LEIGH, 5 Baron (UK 1839); John Piers Leigh; s of 4 Baron Leigh (d 1979), and Anne, da of Ellis Hicks Beach (nephew of 1 Earl St Aldwyn); *b* 11 Sept 1935; *Educ* Eton, Oriel Coll Oxford, London Univ; *m* 1, 1957 (m dis 1974), Cecilia Poppy, da of late Robert Cecil Jackson; 1 s (Hon Christopher, *qv*), 1 da (Hon Camilla, *qv*) (and 1 da decd); m 2, 1976 (m dis 1982), Susan, da of John Cleave, of Whitnash, Leamington Spa; 1 s (Hon Piers b 1979); m 3, 1982, Lea, o da of Col Harry Noel Havelock Wild and Violet, yst da of Henry Selby-Lowndes, formerly w of Lt Col Brian Gustavus Hamilton-Russell (*see* Peerage, Viscount Boyne, by whom she had 1 s (Henry b 1969) and 1 da (b 1976)); *Heir* s, Hon Christopher Dudley Piers Leigh; *Style*— The Rt Hon the Lord Leigh; Stoneleigh Abbey, Kenilworth, Warwickshire (☎ 0926 52116/57766)

LEIGH, John Roland; s of Adam Dale Leigh (d 1978); *b* 11 Mar 1933; *Educ* Winchester, King's Coll Cambridge; *m* 1957, Rosemary Renée, da of late Capt Gordon Furze, MC; 1 s, 3 da; *Career* merchant banker; ptnr Rathbone Bros & Co 1963-; dir Greenbank Tst Ltd 1969-81, Albany Investment Tst plc 1979-; chm Blackburn Diocesan Bd of Finance Ltd 1976-; *Clubs* Flyfishers', Athenaeum (Liverpool); *Style*— John Leigh, Esq; Robin Hood Cottage, Blue Stone Lane, Mawdesley, Ormskirk, Lancs (☎ 0704 822641)

LEIGH, Prof Leonard Herschel; s of Leonard William Leigh (d 1976), of Edmonton, Canada, and Lillian Mavis, *née* Hayman (d 1965); *b* 19 Sept 1935; *Educ* Strathcona HS Edmonton Canada, Univ of Alberta (BA, LLB), Univ of London (PhD); *m* 17 Dec 1960, Jill Diane, da of George Gale (d 1986); 1 s (Matthew b 1967), 1 da (Alison Jane b 1965); *Career* cmmnd Royal Canadian Artillery 1955, transferred Kings Own Calgary Regt 1959, res 1962; barr, private practice Alberta 1958-60, advsy counsel Dept of Justice Canada 1960-62, prof of criminal law LSE 1982- (asst lectr 1964-65, lectr in law 1965-71, reader 1971-82), visiting prof Queens Univ Kingston Ontario 1973-74; UK corres; La Revue de Science Criminelle (Paris), La Revue de Droit Penal et de Criminologie (Belgium); UK chm: Int Assoc of Penal Law 1986-, Université de l'Europe 1986-, pt/t conslt to govts of: Canada, Quebec, Alberta; admitted to bar: Alberta 1958, NW Territories 1960; *Books* The Criminal Liability of Corporations in English Law (1969), Northey & Leigh, Introduction to Company Law (4 ed 1987), Police Powers in England and Wales (2 ed 1985), Strict and Vicarious Liability (1982), Leigh and Edey, Companies Act 1981 (1982), A Guide to the Financial Services Act 1986 (with others 1986); *Recreations* music, walking; *Style*— Prof Leonard Leigh; Rowan Cottage, 20 Woodside Ave, Beaconsfield, Bucks HP9 1JJ (☎ 0494 672 787); Law Dept, London Sch of Economics and Political Science, Horghton St, Aldwych WC2 2AE (☎ 01 405 7686)

LEIGH, Hon Michael James; s of 4 Baron Leigh, TD (d 1979); *b* 1945; *Educ* Eton, Keble Coll Oxford; *m* 1972 (m dis 1980), Cherry Rosalind, da of late David Long-Price; *Style*— The Hon Michael Leigh

LEIGH, Sir Neville Egerton; KCVO (1980, CVO 1967); s of Capt Cecil Egerton Leigh (d 1930); *b* 4 June 1922; *Educ* Charterhouse, abroad; *m* 1944, Denise, da of C D Branch, MC (d 1977), of Paris, France; 2 s (Edward J E Leigh, MP, *qv*), 1 da; *Career* served in RAFVR 1942-47; barr Inner Temple 1948, legal asst Treasury Solicitor's Dept 1949-51, sr clerk Privy Cncl Off 1951-65, dep clerk of the Privy Cncl 1965-74, clerk 1974-84; pres Br Orthoptic Soc 1984-; tstee: Dept Tst for Young Disabled, Royal Home and Hosp Putney 1985-; conslt Royal Coll of Nursing 1985-88; govr Sutton's Hosp in Charterhouse 1986-, ret; public memb Press Council 1986-88; *Style*— Sir Neville Leigh, KCVO; 11 The Crescent, Barnes, London SW13 (☎ 01 876 4271)

LEIGH, Hon Rebecca Moraigh Eveleigh; da of 7 Baron Burgh; *b* 17 Dec 1959; *Educ* St Margaret's Exeter; *Style*— The Hon Rebecca Leith; Achany House, By Lairg, Sutherland IB27 4EB; 66 Cumberland Road, Spike Island, Bristol BS1 6UF

LEIGH, Richard Henry; s of Eric Leigh (d 1982), and his 1 w, Joan Fitzgerald Lane (d 1973), eldest da of M C L Freer; hp to unc Sir John Leigh, 2 Bt; *b* 11 Nov 1936; *Educ* England and Switzerland; *m* 1, 1962 (m dis 1977), Barbro Anna Elizabeth, eldest da of late Stig Carl Søebastian Tham, of Sweden; m 2, 1977, Chérie Rosalind, eldest da of D D Dale, of La Blanchie, Cherval, France, and widow of A Reece, RMS; *Style*— Richard Leigh, Esq; Trythall Vean, Madron, nr Penzance, Cornwall

LEIGH, Hon William Rupert; 2 s of 4 Baron Leigh; *b* 13 Sept 1938; *Educ* Eton, RMA Sandhurst; *m* 1965, Priscilla Elizabeth, da of late Lt Cdr E F P Cooper, o Markree Castle, Collooney, Co Sligo, Ireland; 3 s (James b 1967, Edward b 1968, Richard b 1974) (and 1 s decd); *Career* Lt 11 Hussars (served Aden, NI), ret 1962; estate agent 1965-66; stud owner; *Style*— The Hon William Leigh; Lower Farm, Adlestrop, Moreton-in-Marsh, Glos (☎ 060 871 228)

LEIGH FERMOR, Hon Mrs (Joan Elizabeth); *née* Eyres Monsell; da of 1 Viscount Monsell, GBE (d 1969); *b* 7 Feb 1912; *m* 1, 1939 (m dis 1947), William John Rayner, CBE; m 2, 1968, Patrick Michael Leigh Fermor, DSO, OBE, *qv*; *Style*— The Hon Mrs Leigh Fermor; c/o Messrs John Murray, 50 Albemarle St, London W1

LEIGH FERMOR, Patrick Michael; DSO (1944), OBE (Mil 1943); s of Sir Lewis Leigh Fermor, OBE, FRS, DSc, and Muriel Eileen, *née* Ambler; *b* 11 Feb 1915; *Educ* King's Sch Canterbury; *m* 1968, Hon Joan, *née* Eyres-Monsell, *qv*; *Career* served WW II Irish Gds, Intelligence Corps, in Greece and Germany, Maj 1943; dep dir Br Inst Athens 1936; author; corresponding memb Athens Acad; hon citizen Herakleion Crete; *Books* The Travellers Tree (1950), A Time to Keep Silence (1953), The Violins of St Jacques (1953), Mani (1958) Roumeli, A Dime of Gifts, Between the Woods and the Water (1986); *Recreations* travel; *Clubs* Travellers', White's, Pratt's, Beefsteak, Special Forces; *Style*— Patrick Leigh Fermor, Esq, DSO, OBE; c/o Messrs John Murray, 50 Albemarle St, London W1

LEIGH PEMBERTON, Jeremy; s of late Robert Douglas Leigh Pemberton, MBE, MC, JP, and late Helen Isabel, *née* Payne-Gallwey; bro of Rt Hon Robin Leigh Pemberton, qv; *b* 25 Nov 1933; *Educ* Eton, Magdalen Coll Oxford (MA), INSEAD Fontainebleau (MBA); *m* 1, 30 May 1968 (m dis 1980), Mary, da of John Ames, of Boston, Mass; 1 s (Richard b 13 Dec 1971); m 2, 3 June 1982, Virginia Marion, da of Sir John Curle, KCVO, CMG, qv; *Career* Nat Serv Grenadier Gds 1952-54, cmmnd 2 Lt 1953; Brooke Bond Liebig 1957-69 (finally gp mktg controller), md W & R Balston

Gp 1973-74 (gp mktg controller and corporate planner 1970-73), md Whatman Reeve Angel plc 1974-; chm: Mid Kent Water Co, Kent Co Crematorium plc; dir: London & Manchester Gp plc, Fleming Fledgeling Investment Tst plc, Kent Econ Devpt Bd, TD Bailey Products Ltd, Genzyme (UK) Ltd, SE Region Girobank; CBI: memb Nat Cncl, memb econ and fin policy ctee, memb fin and gen purposes ctee, fndr chm Kent area ctee (later chm SE Regnl Cncl); visiting prof in mktg at INSEAD 1965-70, pres INSEAD Int Alumni Assoc 1962-66; pres Kent branch Inst of Mktg 1988-89, chm fin ctee Kent Branch Red Cross, SE memb Nat Employers' Liaison Ctee, memb rates consultative ctee Kent CC, tstee: Understanding Indust Tst, Lord Cornwallis Meml Fund; govr Mid Kent Coll of Higher and Further Educn; FInstD; *Recreations* opera, fishing; *Style*— Jeremy Leigh Pemberton, Esq; Hill House, Wormshill, Sittingbourne, Kent ME9 OTS; Whatman Reeve Angel plc, Springfield Mill, Maidstone, Kent ME14 2LE (☎ 0622 692 022, fax 0622 691 425)

LEIGH-PEMBERTON, Rt Hon Robin (Robert); PC (1987); s of Capt Robert Leigh-Pemberton, MBE, MC (d 1964), and Helen Isabel, *née* Payne-Gallwey (d 1985), gs of Sir Edward Leigh Pemberton, KCB, JP, DL, sometime MP for E Kent and n of 1 and last Baron Kingsdown; *b* 1 Jan 1927; *Educ* Eton, Trinity Coll Oxford; *m* 1953, Rosemary, da of Lt-Col David Forbes, MC (ka 1943), and Diana (d 1982; who m 2, 1946, 6 Marquess of Exeter who d 1981), gda of 1 Baron Faringdon; 5 s (John b 1955; James b 1956, Edward b 1959, Thomas b 1961, William b 1964); *Career* late Lt Gren Gds, served Palestine 1946-48; barr 1954, practised in London and SE Circuit 1954-60, chm Nat West Bank 1977-83 (dir 1972-83, dep chm 1974); dir: Birmid Qualcast 1966-83 (dep chm 1970, chm 1975-77), Redland Ltd 1972-83, Equitable Life Assur Soc 1979-83; memb: Kent CC 1963-77 (chm 1972-75), NEDC 1982-; pro-chllr Kent Univ 1977-83; govr Bank of Eng 1983-; Lord-Lieut of Kent 1982- (DL 1970, vice lord-lieut 1972-82); Hon DCL Kent 1983; hon master of the Bench Inner Temple 1983; seneschal of Canterbury Cathedral 1983-, hon fell Trinity Coll Oxford 1984; KStJ 1983; *Recreations* country life; *Clubs* Brooks's, Cavalry & Guards; *Style*— The Rt Hon Robin Leigh-Pemberton; Bank of England, Threadneedle St, London EC2R 8AH (☎ 01 601 4444)

LEIGH-SMITH, (Alfred) Nicholas Hardstaff; s of Lt-Col Alfred Leigh Hardstaff Leigh-Smith, TD, DL (d 1978), of Stanwell Moor, Middx, and Marguerite Calvert, *née* Calvert- Harrison (d 1983); *b* 21 Dec 1953; *Educ* Epsom Coll, Leeds Univ (LLB); *Career* barr Lincoln's Inn 1976, dep clerk Bromley Justices 1985; *Recreations* rugby union football, clay pigeon shooting, reading, walking; *Style*— Nicholas Leigh-Smith, Esq; 163 Elborough St, London SW18 (☎ 01 874 1217); 3-4 John St, Penmachno, North Wales; The Court House, South St, Bromley BR1 1RD (☎ 01 466 6621, fax 01 466 6214)

LEIGHTON, Henry Gerard Mather; s of Wilfrid Leighton (d 1967), of Burnett, Somerset, and Margaret, *née* Mather; *b* 15 August 1932; *Educ* Winchester, Corpus Christi Coll Oxford (MA); *m* 5 June 1982, Amanda Juliet, da of Brig Cedric George Buttenshaw, CBE, DSO, of Worton, Nr Devizes, Wiltshire; 1 s (Henry b 1984), 1 da (Alice b 1985); *Career* CA; ptnr Grace Darbyshire & Todd, Bristol 1959-68; dir: Tyndall Gp Ltd & Subsidiaries 1962-86, Gateway Securities Ltd 1965-77; chm Jordan Gp Ltd 1985- (dir 1968-); hon tres Bristol and Gloucs Archaeological Soc 1971-; chm: Bristol Diocesan Advsy Ctee for Care of Churches 1974-, Somerset Record Soc 1977-; dep chm: W of England Tst Ltd 1982- (dir 1972-), Wells Cathedral Fabric Ctee 1987-; FSA; *Recreations* gardening, hunting, archaeology; *Clubs* Travellers; *Style*— Gerard Leighton, Esq; Hassage Manor, Faulkland, nr Bath, Somerset (☎ 037 387 449); 21 St Thomas St, Bristol (☎ 0272 299292)

LEIGHTON, Ian; s of James Horsburgh Leighton, and Kathleen, *née* Paton; *b* 2 Sept 1954; *Educ* Madras Coll St Andrew, Kirkcaldy Tech Coll (BArch), Liverpool Univ (BA Hons); *m* 20 Aug 1977, Joan, da of Robert Porter; 1 s (David b 1982), 1 da (Christine b 1980); *Career* chartered architect; ptnr in own practice specialising in technol consultancy and defects investigation; previous appointments have included res asst Liverpool Univ Sch of Architecture 1975; memb RIBA Merseyside Branch Ctee 1985-87, Liverpool Architectural Soc Cncl 1987-88, Liverpool Regnl Jt Consultative Ctee for Bldg; RIBA 1981; *Recreations* badminton; *Style*— Ian Leighton, Esq; 15 Ennis Rd, Liverpool L12 9JD

LEIGHTON, Kathleen, Lady; Kathleen Irene Linda; da of Maj Albert Ernest Lees, of Rowton Castle, Shrewsbury; *m* 1932, Col Sir Richard Tihel Leighton, 10 Bt, TD (d 1957); 1 s (Sir Michael, 11 Bt, *qv*), 3 da (Mrs Edward Bonner-Maurice b 1932, Judy b 1937, Mrs David Treasure b 1938 m dis 1985); *Style*— Kathleen, Lady Leighton; The Spawns, Shrewsbury

LEIGHTON, Sir Michael John Bryan; 11 Bt (E 1693); s of Col Sir Richard Tihel Leighton, 10 Bt, TD (d 1957); *b* 8 Mar 1935; *Educ* Stowe, RAC, Cirencester, Tabley House Agric Sch; *m* 1974 (m dis 1980), Amber Mary Ritchie; *Career* photographer of wild life; ornithologist; *Recreations* panel 'A' gun dog judge, cricket, tennis, golf, writing poetry, cooking; *Clubs* MCC; *Style*— Sir Michael Leighton, Bt; Loton Park, nr Shrewsbury, Shropshire (☎ 074 378 232)

LEIGHTON, Ronald; MP (Lab) Newham North East 1979-; s of Charles Leighton; *b* 24 Jan 1930; *Educ* Monteagle and Bifrons Sch Barking; *m* 1951, Erika Wehkin; 2 s; *Career* chm: Labour Common Market Safeguards Ctee, chm House of Commons Select Ctee on Employment; *Style*— Ronald Leighton, Esq, MP; House of Commons, London SW1

LEIGHTON OF ST MELLONS, 2 Baron (UK 1962); Sir John Leighton Seager; 2 Bt (UK 1952); s of 1 Baron, CBE (d 1963), and Marjorie, Lady Leighton of St Mellons *qv*; *b* 11 Jan 1922; *Educ* Caldicott Sch, Leys Sch Cambridge; *m* 1, 31 Oct 1953, Elizabeth Rosita (d 1979), o da of late Henry Hopgood, of Cardiff; 2 s (Hon Robert b 1955, Hon Simon b 1957), 1 da (Hon Carole b 1958) (and 1 d decd); m 2, 1982, Ruth Elizabeth, wid of John Hopwood; *Heir* s, Hon Robert William Henry Leighton Seager; *Career* dir: Principality Bldg Soc, Watkin Williams & Co; former chm Cardiff & Bristol Channel Shipowners Assoc, former dir W H Seager & Co Ltd; *Recreations* gardening, photography, being educated by my grandchildren; *Style*— The Rt Hon the Lord Leighton of St Mellons; 346 Caerphilly Road, Cardiff

LEIGHTON OF ST MELLONS, Marjorie, Baroness; Marjorie; JP (Monmouthshire); da of William Henry Gimson, of Breconshire; *m* 1921, 1 Baron Leighton of St Mellons (d 1963); 2 s (2 Baron, *qv*, Hon Douglas b 1925), 2 da (Hon Mrs Edmonds b 1923, Hon Mrs Peniston b 1928); *Career* freeman City of London, Hon Freedom of Shipwrights' Co; *Style*— The Rt Hon Marjorie, Lady Leighton of St Mellons, JP

LEINSTER, Maj 8 Duke of (I 1766); Gerald FitzGerald; Premier Duke, Marquess and Earl in the Peerage of Ireland, also Baron of Offaly (I *ante* 1203 restored 1554), Earl of Kildare (I 1316), Viscount Leinster of Taplow (GB 1747), Marquess of Kildare, Earl of Offaly (both I 1761), and Baron Kildare (UK 1870); s of 7 Duke of Leinster (d 1976, descended from common ancestors of (1) The Earls of Plymouth, (2) Giraldus Cambrensis the medieval historian, (3) the Earls of Desmond (now extinct), (4) the hereditary Knights of Glin and Kerry and the (extinct) White Knight, (5) the Marquesses of Lansdowne, and his 1 w May, *née* Etheridge (d 1935); *b* 27 May 1914; *Educ* Eton, Sandhurst; *m* 1, 17 Oct 1936 (m dis 1946), Joane, eldest da of late Maj Arthur McMorrough Kavanagh, MC; 2 da (Lady Rosemary Wait b 1939, Lady Nesta Tirard b 1942), and 1 decd; m 2, 12 June 1946, Anne, yr da of Lt-Col Philip Eustace Smith, MC TD; 2 s (Marquess of Kildare, *qv*, Lord John b 1952); *Heir* s, Marquess of Kildare, *qv*; *Career* served WW II with 5 Royal Inniskilling Dragoon Gds (wounded in Normandy); master: N Kilkenny foxhounds 1937-40, W Percy foxhounds 1945-46, Portman foxhounds 1946-47; *Recreations* shooting, fishing; *Style*— Major His Grace the Duke of Leinster; Kilkea House, Wilcote Lane, Ramsden, Oxon OX7 3BA (☎ 099 386 585)

LEINSTER, Dowager Duchess of; Vivien Irene; da of Thomas Albert Felton (d 1957), and his w Lilian Adshead; *b* 19 Feb 1920; *m* 1, 1937 (m dis 1965), George William Conner; 1 s; m 2, 1965, as his 4 w, 7 Duke of Leinster, Premier Duke, Marquess and Earl of Ireland (d 1976); *Career* pres All Ireland Distress fund 1975-76, Gift Shop admin Help the Aged 1976, founder-pres of the charity Stress 1976; *Style*— Her Grace the Dowager Duchess of Leinster; 26 The Albemarle, Marine Parade, Brighton, East Sussex BN2 1TX (☎ 0273 680827)

LEIPER, Dr John; MBE (1945), TD (1962); s of J W K Leiper (d 1939), of Liverpool, and Georgina Pauline, *née* Black (d 1946); *b* 2 June 1912; *Educ* Liverpool Univ (MB, ChB 1936, DPH 1939); *m* 11 May 1940, (Mary) Elizabeth, da of G A Whitaker (d 1942), of IOM; s (John Keith b 1950), 2 da (Georgina b 1941, Jennifer b 1946); *Career* Maj CO 1 Field Hygiene Section RAMC 1940-45; co med offr Health Cumberland CC 1960-73; area med offr Cumbria Health Authority 1973-77; QHP 1971-73; chm Cumbria Alcohol Advsy Service (CADAS) 1980; Branch Med Offr Cumbria BRCS; FFCM 1971; *Recreations* gardening, cathedral sidesman, cathedral guide ; *Style*— Dr John Leiper, MBE, TD; Foxdale, Plains Rd, Wetheral, Carlisle CA4 8LE (☎ 0228 60514)

LEISHMAN, Hon Mrs (Marista Muriel); da of 1 Baron Reith, KT, GCVO, GBE, CB, TD (d 1971); *b* 10 April 1932; *Educ* St George's Ascot, St Andrews Univ (MA); *m* 1960, Rev Robert Murray Leishman, MA, chaplain to Royal Edinburgh (Psychiatric) Hosp, lectr New Coll Edinburgh; 1 s (Mark b 1962), 3 da (Iona b 1963, Martha b 1965, Kirsty b 1969); *Career* Head of Education Nat Tst for Scotland 1978-86; dir The Insite Tst for Staff Training in Heritage Properties 1987-; FRSA 1988; *Recreations* music, writing, painting, walking; *Style*— The Hon Mrs Leishman; Hunter's House, 508 Lanark Rd, Edinburgh EH14 5DH (☎ 031 453 4716)

LEITCH, Alexander Park (Sandy); s of Donald Leitch (d 1949), of Blairhall, Fife, and Agnes Smith, *née* Park; *b* 20 Oct 1947; *Educ* Dunfermline HS; *m* 22 March 1970, Valerie Beryl, da of Douglas Hodson; 3 da (Fiona b 1971, Joanne b 1973, Jacqueline b 1975); *Career* chief systems designer Nat Mutual Life 1969, Hambro Life 1976 (bd dir 1981), md Allied Dunbar 1988; govr Stonar Sch; MBCS 1966; *Recreations* tennis, books; *Style*— Sandy Leitch, Esq; The Old Rectory, Kington St Michael, Chippenham, Wilts SN14 6NZ (☎ 024 975 330); Allied Dunbar, Swindon SN1 1EL (☎ 0793 514 514, car tel 0836 212 494)

LEITCH, Sir George; KCB (1975, CB 1963), OBE (1945); er s of late James Simpson Leitch and Margaret Leitch; *b* 5 June 1915; *Educ* Wallsend GS, King's Coll, Durham Univ; *m* 1942, Edith Marjorie, da of late Thomas Dawson Maughan; 1 da; *Career* served WW II (despatches), Brig 1946; entered Civil Service 1947, dep under-sec state MOD 1965-72, sec (procurement exec) 1972-74, chief exec (perm sec) 1974-75, ret; chm: Short Brothers 1976-83, standing advsy ctee on Trunk Rd Assessment 1977-80; *Style*— Sir George Leitch, KCB, OBE; 10 Elmfield Rd, Gosforth, Newcastle-upon-Tyne (☎ 091 284 6559); Black Brae, Port Charlotte, Islay, Argyll (☎ 049 685 430)

LEITCH, Jonathan Andrew; OBE (1988); s of Andrew Macintosh Leitch (d 1953), of Buenos Aires, Argentina, and Beryl Roscoe, *née* Allen (d 1951); *b* 31 Mar 1932; *Educ* Charterhouse, Cranfield (MSc); *m* 27 Feb 1954, Barbara, da of late William Louis Lovell; 1 s (Jamie b 1958), 2 da (Lesley b 1956, Joanna b 1963); *Career* apprentice engr Rolls Royce Ltd 1950-55, Bristol Aircraft Ltd 1957, mfrg mangr Bristol Guided Weapons Div 1965, works mangr Opperman Gears Ltd 1966, dir BAC Guided Weapons Div 1978, dep managing dir BAC Weapons Div 1980, operations dir BAC Dynamics Div 1988; various offices Local Cons Assocs; *Recreations* historic vechiles, aeromodelling, travel; *Clubs* VCC, VMCC, BMFA, and others; *Style*— Jonathan Leitch, Esq, OBE; The Coach House, 16B High St, Brampton, Cambs PE18 8TG (☎ 0480 51622); BAC (Dynamics) Ltd, Six Hills Way, Stevenage, Herts (☎ 0438 312 422 ext 3257, telex 825125/825126)

LEITH, Hon (Alexander) Gregory Disney; s and h of 7 Baron Burgh; *b* 16 Mar 1958; *m* 1984, Catharine Mary, da of David Parkes; 2 s (Alexander James Strachan b 1986, Benjamin David Willoughby b 1988); *Style*— The Hon Gregory Leith; 28 High Street, Nettlebed, Henley-on-Thames, Oxon

LEITH, Hon John Barnabas; s of 6 Baron Burgh (d 1959); *b* 27 Dec 1947; *Educ* Wellington Coll, Exeter Univ, Birmingham Univ; *m* 1970, Erica Jane, da of David M Lewis, of Winchester; 2 s (Alexander David Kalimat b 1973, Thomas Magnus Abad b 1976), 1 da (Angharad Jane b 1977); *Style*— The Hon John Leith; 24 Gardiner Close, Abingdon, Oxon OX14 3YA (☎ 0235 35224)

LEITH, Lady; (Rhoda) Mary; da of late Leonard Asquith, of Brook House, Cleckheaton, Yorks; *b* 2 August 1894; *Educ* private; *m* 1954, as his 2 w, Sir Alexander Leith, MC, 1 and last Bt (d 1956); *Style*— Lady Leith; Larchfield Manor, Leadhall Lane, Harrogate, N Yorks (☎ 0423 879240)

LEITH, Hon Patrick Simon Vincent; s of 7 Baron Burgh; *b* 1964; *Style*— The Hon Patrick Leith

LEITH, Prudence Margaret; da of Stewart Leith (d 1961), of Johannesburg, SA, and Margaret, *née* Inglis; *b* 18 Feb 1940; *Educ* St Mary's Sch Johannesburg, Univ of Cape Town, Sorbonne Paris (Cours de la Civilisation Francaise); *m* 1974 (Charles) Rayne Kruger (author); 1 s (Daniel b 1974), 1 da (Li-Da b 1974); *Career* restaurateur, caterer, author, journalist; fndr: Leith's Good Food 1961, Leith's Restaurant 1969,

Prudence Leith Ltd 1972, Leith's Sch of Food and Wine 1975, Leith's Farm 1976; dir: Br Tport Hotels Ltd 1977-83, Travellers-Fare 1977-85, BR Bd 1980-85 (part-time memb), Prudence Leith Ltd (md) 1972-, Leith's Good Food Ltd 1961-, Leith's Restaurant Ltd 1969-, Leith's Promotions Ltd 1975-, Leith's Farm Ltd 1976-, Location (Kensington) Ltd, Ettington Park Hotel plc 1984-87, Argyll Gp plc, Safeway plc (non-exec); cncl memb: Food From Britain 1983-87, Museum of Modern Art 1984; appeared in: 26-part TV series (cookery) on Tyne-Tees TV, Best of Br BBC TV, The Good Food Show, Take 6 Cooks; memb: Econ Devpt Ctee for the Leisure & Tourism Industs, Nat Trg Task Forces Dept of Employment 1989; *Books* written 11 cookery books between 1972 and 1987; *Recreations* riding, tennis, old cookbooks; *Clubs* Groucho, Forum; *Style—* Prue Leith; 94 Kensington Park Rd, London W11 2PN (☎ 01 221 5282)

LEITH-BUCHANAN, Barbara, Lady; Barbara Deane; da of Willard Phelps Leshure, of Springfield, Mass; *b* 28 Feb 1904; *Educ* Emme Willard Sch Troy NY, New England Conservatory of Music Boston; *m* 16 Sept 1933, Sir George Hector Macdonald Leith-Buchanan, 6 Bt (d 1973); *Recreations* music, gardening, youth welfare; *Style—* Barbara, Lady Leith-Buchanan; Drummakill, Alexandria, Dunbartonshire (☎ 038 983 232)

LEITH-BUCHANAN, Sir Charles Alexander James; 7 Bt (1775); s of John Wellesley MacDonald Leith-Buchanan (d 1956); suc kinsman Sir George Hector MacDonald Leith-Buchanan, 6 Bt (d 1973); *b* 1 Sept 1939; *m* 1962 (m dis 1987), Marianne, da of Col Earle Wellington Kelly; 1 s, 1 da; *Heir* s, Gordon Kelly McNicol Leith-Buchanan b 18 Oct 1974; *Career* pres Utd Business Machines Ind 1978; *Style—* Sir Charles Leith-Buchanan, Bt; 7510 Clifton Road, Clifton, Virginia 22024, USA

LEMAITRE, Jean-Conrad; s of Bernard Lemaitre, of 69 Ave Georges Mandel, 75016 Paris, France, and Marie Rose, *née* De Witt; *b* 5 June 1943; *Educ* Ecole Superieure de Commerce Paris, INSEAD (MBA); *m* 1 Oct 1970, Isabelle, da of Baron Hubert de Turckheim, of Rue Chalgrin, Paris 75016; 1 s (Amaury b 18 June 1978), 1 da (Geraldine b 4 April 1974); *Career* Res Lt French Navy 1968-70; account offr Banque NSM 1970-73; corporate head Paris branch Chemical Bank 1973-77, head corporate northern and southern Europe (Chemical Bank NY), head Nordic div Chemical Bank London 1980-82, dep gen mangr Spain Chemical Bank Madrid 1982-86, head int private banking (Europe, N America) Chemical Bank London 1986-89; Knight of St Johanni's Von Spital Zu Jerusalem Order Germany 1977; *Clubs* Automobile de France, RAC; *Style—* Jean-Conrad Lemaitre, Esq; 15 Halsey St, London SW3; Chemical Bank House, 180 Strand, London WC2R 1EX, (☎ 01 380 5452)

LEMAN, Richard Alexander; s of Dennis Alexander George Leman, and Joyce Mabyn, *née* Pickering; *b* 13 July 1959; *Educ* Gresham's Sch Holt; *Career* hockey player; Bronze Medal Olympic Games (LA) 1984; Silver Medal: World Cup (London) 1986, European Cup (Moscow) 1987; Gold Medal Olympic Games (Seoul) 1988; *Recreations* golf; *Clubs* E Grinstead Hockey; *Style—* Richard Leman, Esq; Dartel House, 2 Lumley Road, Horley, Surrey (☎ 0293 785633, fax 0293 772053)

LEMKIN, James Anthony; CBE (1986); s of William Lemkin, CBE, of Old Oak Cottage, Wherwell, Hants, and Rachel Irene, *née* Faith (d 1958); *b* 21 Dec 1926; *Educ* Charterhouse, Merton Coll Oxford (MA); *m* 23 Nov 1960, Joan Dorothy Anne, da of Thomas Casserley (d 1945), of Wellington, NZ; 2 s (Robert b 1961, David b 1968), 2 da (Judith b 1966, Alix b 1968); *Career* served RN 1945-48; admitted solr 1953; ptnr Field Fisher Waterhouse (and predecessors) 1959- ; memb GLC 1973-86 (chm legal and parly ctee 1977-78, chm scrutiny ctee 1978-81, Con spokesman on police 1981-82, opposition chief whip 1982-86); chm Bow Gp 1952, 1956 and 1957; tres Soc of Con Lawyers 1978-82 and 1985-88 ; govr: Westfield Coll London Univ 1970-83, Royal Marsden Hosp 1984; Cmwlth Inst 1985- ; parly candidate; (Con and NL) Chesterfield 1959, (L) Cheltenham 1964; Law Soc; *Books* Ed Race and Power (1956); *Recreations* cricket umpiring, fishing; *Clubs* Athenaeum, Carlton; *Style—* James A Lemkin, Esq, CBE; Field, Fisher and Martineau, Lincoln House, 296-302 High Holborn, London, WC1V 7JL (☎ 01 831 9161)

LEMMON, Mark Benjamin; s of Edmund Lemmon (d 1984), of 27 Childs Hall Rd, Gt Bookham, and Mary Patricia, *née* Bryan; *b* 15 April 1952; *Educ* Wimbledon Coll, Univ Coll London (BA), LSE (MSc); *m* 8 Aug 1980, Anna, da of Prof Tamas Szekely, of Budapest; 2 da (Esther b 1981, Patricia b 1985); *Career* Touche Ross, Grindlays Bank, Guinness Mahon, sr corporate mangr Hong Kong and Shanghai Banking Corpn; Freeman City of London, memb Billingsgate Ward Club; FCA 1978, ATII 1979, ACIB 1982; *Recreations* squash, skiing, opera; *Clubs* Wimbledon Squash and Babminton; *Style—* Mark Lemmon, Esq; 7 Devonshire Sq, London EC2M 4HN (☎ 01 626 0566)

LEMON, Sir (Richard) Dawnay; CBE (1958), QPM; s of Lt-Col Frederick Joseph Lemon, CBE, DSO (d 1952); *b* 1912; *Educ* Uppingham, RMC; *m* 1939, Sylvia Marie, da of Lt-Col L W Kentish, of Burnham, Bucks; 1 s, 2 da (1 decd); *Career* joined W Yorks Regt 1932; Metropolitan Police 1934-37, Leics Constabulary 1937-39; chief constable: E Riding Yorks 1939-42, Hants 1942-62, Kent 1962-74; kt 1970; *Recreations* golf; *Clubs* Naval, Military; *Style—* Sir Dawnay Lemon, CBE, QPM; Rosecroft, Ringwould, nr Deal, Kent (☎ 030 45 67 554)

LEMON, Roy; s of Leslie George Lemon, of Poole, Dorset, and Aubrey May *née* Weller; *b* 31 Mar 1946; *Educ* Royal GS Guildford (LLB); *m* 22 March 1969, Barbara Denise, da of Herbert David Jackson, of Leeds, Yorks; 2 s (Benedict Mathew b 31 May 1975, Luke Kitson b 10 Feb 1987), 1 da (Rebecca Kate b 16 July 1977); *Career* Barr Gray's Inn 1970; *Recreations* sailing and other displacement activities; *Style—* Roy Lemon, Esq; Devereux Chambers, Devereux Ct, Temple, London, WC2R 3JJ, (☎ 01 353 7534, fax 01 353 1724)

LEMOS, Costas George; s of George Constantine Lemos (d 1985), of London, and Chrysanthi, *née* Lemos (d 1979); *b* 2 Jan 1937; *Educ* St Paul's, Pembroke Coll Cambridge (BA); *m* 3 April 1985, Catherine (Kitty), da of Alexander N Vernicos, of Athens; 1 step s (John b 8 Oct 1970), 2 step da (Alexandra b 11 Oct 1975, Marina b 12 June 1972); *Career* co fndr and ptnr Poseidon Shipping Agencies 1964 (partnership dis 1970), fndr Lemos Maritime Co Ltd 1970-; *Recreations* travelling and reading, own antiquarian book collection; *Clubs* Annabel's; *Style—* Costas Lemos, Esq; Lemos Maritime Co Ltd, 107 Fleet St, London EC4 (☎ 01 583 8441)

LEMPRIERE-ROBIN, Brig Raoul Charles; OBE (1956); s of Capt Charles Harold Robin (ka 1917), and Yvonne, da and heiress of Jurat Reginald Raoul Lempriere, CBE, of Rosel Manor, Jersey (she m 2, 1931, Lt-Col Christopher J M Riley, MC, and d 1948) (*see* Burke's Landed Gentry, 18 edn, vol iii); *b* 6 Sept 1914; *Educ* Eton, Univ Coll Oxford (MA); *m* 6 Jan 1955, Sheelagh, da of Lt-Col Charles Edgar Maturin-Baird, of Langham, Colchester; 1 da (Emma b 1965); *Career* cmmnd Coldstream Gds 1935, served in BEF 1939, Madagascar, India, Italy, Malaya, M East and Jordan (ret as Brig 1966); memb States of Jersey 1969-78; seigneur de Rosel, Jersey; Hereditary Butler to HM The Queen in Jersey; *Recreations* gardening, sailing; *Clubs* White's; *Style—* Brig Raoul Lempriere-Robin, OBE; Rosel Manor, Jersey (☎ 0534 52611)

LENG, Gen Sir Peter John Hall; KCB (1978, CB 1975), MBE (1962), MC (1945); s of J Leng; *b* 9 May 1925; *Educ* Bradfield Coll; *m* 1 (m dis), Virginia Rosemary Pearson; 3 s, 2 da; m 2, 1981, Mrs Flavia Tower, da of Lt-Gen Sir Frederick Browning, KCVO, DSO (d 1965), and Dame Daphne du Maurier, DBE (d 1989); *Career* cmmnd 1944, served WWII, Cdr Land Forces NI 1973-75, Dir Mil Operations MOD 1975-78, Cdr 1 (Br) Corps 1978-80, Master-Gen of the Ordnance 1981-83, ret; Col Cmdt: RAVC 1976, RMP 1976; *Style—* Gen Sir Peter Leng, KCB, MBE, MC; 409 Hawkins House, Dolphin Sq, London SW1V 3LX

LENG, Virginia Helen Antoinette; MBE (1986); da of Col Ronald Morris Holgate (d 1980), and Heather Alice Mary, *née* Rice; *b* 1 Feb 1955; *Educ* abroad, Bedgebury Park Goudhurst Kent; *m* 7 Dec 1985 (m dis 1989), Hamish Peter Leng, s of Gen Sir Peter Leng, KCB, MBE, MC, *qv*; *Career* Equestrian; Three Day Event wins inc: Jr Euro Champion 1974, Mini Olympics 1975, Euro Championships (team gold) 1981, World Championships (team gold) 1982, Euro Championships (team silver) 1983, Olympic Games (team silver) 1984, Euro Championships (team gold) 1985, World Championships (team gold) 1986, Olympic Games (team silver) 1988; won Burghley 1983, 1984, 1985, 1986; won Badminton 1985; individual Euro Champion 1985, 1987; World Champion 1986; Olympics (Individual Bronze 1984,1988), dir P and N Co; involved in Riding for Disabled; *Recreations* swimming, skiing, sunning, sightseeing; *Style—* Mrs Virginia H A Leng, MBE; Ivyleaze, Acton Turville, Badminton, Avon (☎ 045421 681)

LENNARD-JONES, Prof John Edward; s of Sir John Lennard-Jones, KBE (d 1954), of The Clock House, Keele, Staffs, and Kathleen Mary, *née* Lennard; *b* 29 Jan 1927; *Educ* King's Coll Choir Sch Cambridge, Gresham's Sch Holt, Corpus Christi Coll Cambridge (MA, MD), UCH Med Sch London; *m* 19 Feb 1955, Verna Margaret, da of Ebenezer Albert Down (d 1960); 4 s (David b 1956, Peter b 1958, Andrew b 1960, Timothy b 1964); *Career* memb MRC Gastroenterology Res Unit Centl Middx Hosp 1963-65, conslt physician UCH 1965-74, prof of Gastroentology London Hosp Med Coll 1974-87, conslt gastroenterologist St Mark's Hosp London 1965-, emeritus prof; Sir Arthur Hurst Lecture Br Soc of Gastroenterology 1973, Humphrey Davy Rolleston Lecture RCP 1977, Schorstein Lecture London Hosp Med Coll 1987; chm med ctee St Mark's Hosp; Br Soc of Gastrenterology: hon sec 1965-70, memb cncl 1965-, pres 1983; memb cncl RCP (chm Gastroenterology Ctee 1985-89), vice-chm Nat assoc for Colitis and Crohn's disease 1987-; circuit steward Wembley and Golders Green Methodist Circuit; FRCP 1968; *Books* Clinical Gastroentology (jtly 1968); *Recreations* ornithology, golf, gardening; *Style—* Prof John Lennard-Jones; 55 The Pryors, East Heath Rd, London NW3 1BP (☎ 01 435 6990); St Mark's Hosp, City Rd, London EC1V 2PS (☎ 01 253 1050)

LENNON, Dennis; CBE (1968), MC (1942); s of John Joseph Lennon (d 1978), and Eleanor, *née* Farrell (d 1974); *b* 23 June 1918; *Educ* Merchant Taylors', UC London; *m* 3 Sept 1947, Else Bull, da of Bjarna Bull Anderssen, of Bergen, Norway; 3 s (Christopher b 1950, Nicolas b 1952, Peter b 1956); *Career* WWII Maj Royal Engr (despatches 1940); first armed Div France 1940, 7 armed Div N Africa Alamein to Tunis, Italy, Sth to Nth 6 Armed Div, taken prisoner in St Valery and escaped through France, Spain to Gibraltar; architect private practice; Main Chalcot Estate Camden, Ridgeway Hotel Lusaka, RST HQ Building Lusaka, Royal Opera House (conslt for 10 years, incl: 6 State Galas), Hotels and Restaurants for J Lyons, Jaeger thirty shops, Harrow Sch, Shepherd Churchill Hall; co-ordinator and principle designer of: the interior design of Queen Elizabeth 2, Glyndeborne set for Richard Strauss 'Capriccio', Leeds Castle, Ritz Hotel, Stafford Hotel, Docklands Ind Estate, Commercial Union Main Executive Floors, Sainsburys HQ, Rothschild HQ, The Arts Club Dover St, planning permission for Criterion site Piccadilly; FRIBA, FSIA, FRSA; *Recreations* the arts; *Clubs* Savile, Royal Thames Yacht; *Style—* Dennis Lennon, Esq, CBE, MC; Hamper Mill, Watford, Herts (☎ 0923 34445); 3 Fitzhardinge St, London W1 (☎ 01 935 1181)

LENNOX; *see*: Gordon Lennox

LENNOX, Michael James Madill; s of Rev James Lennox, of 30 Hazel Beck, Cottingley Bridge, Bingley, Yorks, and May Ester, *née* Rosenthal; *b* 11 Sept 1943; *Educ* St John's Sch Leatherhead; *m* 4 May 1948, Ingrid Susan Elizabeth, da of Ronald Ewart Binns; 1 s (Timothy b 6 Dec 1974), 1 da (Rebecca b 6 Oct 1972); *Career* CA; Armitage & Norton, Bradford 1961-68; Price Waterhouse (Montreal) 1968-70, asst controller Honeywell Ltd, Toronto 1970-73; European business planning controller Honeywell Europe (Brussels) 1973-78, dir of finance Eaton Ltd (Bedford) 1978-85, dir Cutler Hammer: Euro Ltd, Nigeria Ltd 1978-85; gp fin dir C P Roberts & Co Ltd, Potters Bar; dir: C P Roberts & Co Ltd 1985-88, gp fin dir Central Trailer Rentco Ltd; FCA; *Recreations* tennis, squash, skiing; *Style—* Michael Lennox, Esq; 34 Church End, Renhold, Bedford MK41 0LU (☎ 0234 771209); Roberts House, Station Close, Potters Bar, Herts (☎ 707 51277)

LENNOX COOK, John Mortimer; s of Arthur Lennox Cook (d 1942), of New Malden, Surrey, and Gladys Louisa, *née* Chapman (d 1942); *b* 13 June 1923; *Educ* King's Coll Sch Wimbledon, Trinity Coll Oxford (MA); *m* 3 Sept 1966, Ann, da of Kenric Cambridge Pryor, MBE; 2 da (Sara Ann b 29 Sept 1967, Cathy Emma b 12 Nov 1970); *Career* RAF, invalided out; schoolmaster Bilton Grange nr Rugby 1947-50, Victoria Coll Cairo 1953-54, sr tutor Bell Sch of Languages 1955-62, fndr Lennox Cook Sch of English 1962-84; novelist and travel writer; played Rugby Football for Harlequins, Oxford Univ, Warwicks; *Books* The World Before Us (1955), The Lucky Man (1956), No Language but a Cry (1958), Six Great Travellers (1960), A Feeling of Disquiet (1973), The Bridge (1976), The Manipulator (1979), Under Etna (1983); *Recreations* most games; *Clubs* Vincents (Oxford); *Style—* John Lennox Cook, Esq; Coachman's Cottage, 35a Grange Rd, Cambridge CB3 9AU (☎ 0223 68 480)

LENNOX-BOYD, Hon Benjamin Alan; s and h of 2 Viscount Boyd of Merton; *b* 21 Oct 1964; *Educ* Millfield; *Style—* The Hon Benjamin Lennox-Boyd; Wiveliscombe, Saltash, Cornwall

LENNOX-BOYD, Hon Charlotte Mary; da of 2 Viscount Boyd of Merton; *b* 16 April 1963; *Educ* Cheltenham Ladies' Coll, UCL; *Style—* The Hon Charlotte Lennox-Boyd; 9 Eland Rd, London SW11

LENNOX-BOYD, Hon Christopher Alan; s of 1 Viscount Boyd of Merton, CH, PC, DL (d 1983), and Patricia, Viscountess Boyd of Merton, *qv*; bro of 2 Viscount Boyd of Merton, *qv*, and Hon Mark Lennox-Boyd, MP, *qv*; *b* 22 July 1941; *Educ* Eton, Ch Ch Oxford; *Books* Axel Herman Haig, The Victoria Vision of the Middle Ages (co-author); *Clubs* Carlton, Brooks's; *Style*— The Hon Christopher Lennox-Boyd

LENNOX-BOYD, Hon Mark Alexander; MP (C) Morecambe and Lonsdale (1979-83); s of 1 Viscount Boyd of Merton, CH, PC, DL (d 1983), and Patricia, Viscountess Boyd of Merton, *qv*; bro of 2 Viscount Boyd of Merton and Hon Christopher Lennox-Boyd, *qqv*; *b* 4 May 1943; *Educ* Eton, Ch Ch Oxford; *m* 1974, Mrs Arabella Lacloche, o da of Piero Parisi, of Rome; 1 da (Patricia Irene b 1980); *Career* barr Inner Temple 1968; PPS to chllr of Exchequer (Rt Hon Nigel Lawson) 1983-84; govt whip 1984-; *Style*— The Hon Mark Lennox-Boyd, MP; House of Commons, London SW1

LENOX-CONYNGHAM, Charles Denis; s of Capt Alwyn Douglas Lenox-Conyngham, RN, of Benenden, Kent, and Margaret Cecilia, *née* Clear; *b* 24 Jan 1935; *Educ* Winchester, Magdalen Coll Oxford (MA), Wharton Sch of Business Admin, Univ of Pennsylvania; *m* 15 April 1972, Helga Gerrit, da of Lt.-Gen Hans von Liebach (d 1966), of Berlin; 1 s (Patrick b 1972), 1 da (Laura b 1974); *Career* cmmnd Royal Hussars (2nd Lieut) served Germany 1954-56; md Blue Funnel Line 1970, exec dir: Ocean Transport & Trading 1972-85, md: Price & Pierce 1985; chm and chief exec Sealink (UK) Ltd 1985-; *Recreations* gardening, tennis, squash, skiing; *Clubs* RAC; *Style*— Charles Lenox-Conyngham, Esq; Yew Tree House, Benenden, Kent TN17 3EJ (☎ 0580 240 630); Sealink UK Ltd, 20 Upper Ground, London SE1 9PF (☎ 01 928 6969, telex: 914028, fax: 928 1469)

LENT, Martin Victor; s of Lt Eric Lent, of Pinner, Middx, and Tina, *née* Koten; *b* 18 June 1954; *Educ* John Lyon Sch Harrow-on-the-Hill; *m* 16 Sept 1979, Melanie Ruth, *qv*, da of Cyril Searle, of London; *Career* Malvern & Co 1973-77, Emile Woolf and Assocs 1977-79, Premier Clay Litho Ltd 1979-80, Crocodile 1980-81, chm Pamplemousse 1982-; ACA, FCA 1981; *Recreations* tennis, skiing, theatre, gourmand, travel, reading; *Clubs* Vanderbilt, Stocks, Ragdale Health; *Style*— Martin Lent, Esq; The Tower, Well Rd, Hampstead, London NW3; Pamplemousse, 22 St Pancras Way, Camden Town, London NW1 1LH (☎ 01 387 8797, fax 01 387 0320, telex 295383 PAMPLE G)

LENT, Melanie Ruth; da of Cyril Searle, of Woodford, Essex, and Ita, *née* Bursztyn; *b* 31 August 1958; *Educ* Caterham Co Sch Essex, London Sch of Fashion, Ravensbourne Coll of Art (BA); *m* 16 Sept 1979, Martin Lent, *qv*; *Career* designer: Polly Peck plc 1979-80, Fitrite 1980-81; design dir Pamplemousse 1982-; *Recreations* linguistics, aerobics, travel; *Clubs* Ragdale Health; *Style*— Mrs Melanie Lent; The Tower, Well Rd, Hampstead, London NW3; Pamplemousse, 22 St Pancras Way, Camden Town, London NW1 1LH (☎ 01 387 8797, fax 01 387 0320, telex 295383 PAMPLE G)

LENTON, (Aylmer) Ingram; s of Albert Lenton (d 1981), and Olive Lenton; *b* 19 May 1927; *Educ* Leeds GS, Magdalen Coll Oxford, Leeds Univ; *m* 1951, Ursula Kathleen, da of Cyril Henry Brownlow King (d 1964); 1 s, 2 da; *Career* md S African Nylon Spinners 1964-66; dir ICI Fibres 1966-67; md John Heathcoat & Co 1967-75; chm: Bowater UK Paper Co 1976-78, Bowater UK Ltd 1979-81, chm John Heathcoat & Co (Hldgs) Ltd 1984; md Bowater Corpn 1981-84 (dir 1979-); chm and md Bowater Industries plc 1984-87; dep chm Watts Blake Bearne & Co plc 1988 and dir 1987-; Atkins Hldgs Ltd 1987, Crown Agents 1987, Chapman Industries plc, Scopa Gp plc 1988; chm Compass Group Ltd; Worshipful Co of Stationers and Newspaper Makers; *Recreations* golf, fencing, walking, fishing; *Clubs* Inst of Dirs; memb Court of Assts; *Style*— Dr A I Lenton

LENTON, John Robert; s of Rev Robert Vincent Lenton, vicar of Lacock, Wilts; *b* 13 May 1946; *Educ* Prince of Wales Sch Nairobi, Exeter Coll Oxford, Harvard Business Sch; *m* 1967, Ann Cathrine; 1 s, 1 da; *Career* specialist in fin mktg; Int Factors Ltd: dir sales and mktg 1976, dir operations 1977, dir sales and mktg 1979; sr vice-pres (Euro Operating Centre and Customer Services) American Express 1988- (vice pres fin and travel 1982-86, vice pres and gen mangr N Europe 1986-88); *Recreations* skiing, choral singing, treble recorder; *Style*— John Lenton, Esq; 25 Wilbury Ave, Hove, Sussex (☎ 0273 28429; office 0273 693555)

LENYGON, Bryan Norman; s of Maj Frank Norman Lenygon, of Highfield, Bells Yew Green, E Sussex, and Marjorie Winifred, *née* Healey; *b* 6 May 1932; *Educ* London Univ (MA, LLB); *m* 27 Oct 1967, Diana Jane, da of Betty Patricia Baxter, of Hingham, Norfolk; 2 da (Fiona b 1957, Sally b 1961); *Career* barr Gray's Inn; Gen Cmmr City of London, Freeman City of London; FCA, FCIS, ATII; *Recreations* tennis; *Clubs* City of London, City Livery; *Style*— Bryan Lenygon, Esq; Highfield, Bells Yew Green, E Sussex TN3 9AP (☎ 089 275 343)

LEON, Alexander John; s and h of Sir John Ronald Leon, 4 Bt; *b* 3 May 1965; *Educ* Bryanston; *Career* music prodn asst; *Recreations* skiing, watersports, tennis, cricket; *Style*— Alexander Leon, Esq; 8 Markham St, London SW3 (☎ 01 589 2230)

LEON, Dowager Lady; Alice Mary; da of late Dr Thomas Holt; *b* 10 Sept 1919; *Educ* Queen Ethelburga's Sch Harrogate; *m* 1947, as his 3 w, Sir Ronald George Leon, 3 Bt (d 1964); *Career* served FANY 1941-46; *Style*— Dowager Lady Leon; 83 Lexham Gdns, London W8

LEON, Sir John Ronald; 4 Bt (UK 1911); s of Sir Ronald George Leon, 3 Bt (d 1964), and his 1 w, Dorothy Katharine, (the actress Kay Hammond) (d 1980), da of Cdr Sir Guy Standing, KBE (d 1937), and who m 2, Sir John Clements, CBE, *qv*; *b* 16 August 1934; *Educ* Eton, Byam Shaw Sch of Art; *m* 1, 1961 (m dis 1972), Jill, da of Jack Melford, actor; 1 s; m 2, 1984, Sarah, da of Bryan Forbes, film dir; 1 s (Archie b 1986), 1 da (India b 1985); *Heir* s, Alexander John Leon, *qv*; *Career* 2 Lt KRRC 1953-55; actor (John Standing); artist (watercolours); *Style*— Sir John Leon, Bt; 98 Ebury St, SW1

LEON, Ronald; s of Capt Alec Leon (D 1973), and Capt Perla Glucksmann (d 1970); *b* 11 Dec 1931; *Educ* Arnold Sch Blackpool, Royal Tech Coll Salford; *m* 19 Nov 1971, Susana, da of Alberto Mamrud, of Buenos Aires, Argentina; 2 s (Nick b 1972, Andrew b 1974); *Career* Army Cadet Force 1943-50; regnl mangr Latin America Werner Mgmnt Consits NY 1960-73; dir: Int Business Devpt 1973-76, Visa Int Inc San Francisco California 1973-76; md Occidental Petroleum's subsidaries Mexico and Venezuela 1976-80; chm: Oxy Metal Industs GB Ltd 1980-84, EFCO Ltd 1984-; vice-chm Br Industl Furnace Constructors Assoc; ATI, ARTCS; *Recreations* hiking; *Style*— Ronald Leon, Esq; Sefton, The Hockering, Woking, Surrey (☎ 04862 60292); Efco Ltd, Forsyth Rd, Sheerwater, Woking, Surrey GU21 5RZ (☎ 04862 26433, fax 04862 73818, telex 859465)

LEONARD, Hon Derek John; s of Baron Leonard (Life Peer, d 1983); *b* 1956; *Career* ptnr Leonard Cheung and Co, slrs; *Style*— The Hon Derek Leonard

LEONARD, Baroness; Glenys Evelyn; da of Ernest Kenny; *m* 1945, Baron Leonard, OBE (Life Peer, d 1983); 1 s, 1 da; *Style*— The Rt Hon the Lady Leonard; 19 Queen Anne, Cardiff

LEONARD, Rt Rev and Rt Hon Graham Douglas; *see*: London, Bishop of

LEONARD, His Honour Judge; James Charles Beresford Whyte; s of late Hon James Weston Leonard, KC, of Johannesburg; *b* 1905; *Educ* Clifton, Ch Ch Oxford; *m* 1939, Barbara Helen, da of Capt William Incledon-Webber (d 1938), of Buckland House, Braunton, N Devon; 2 s, 1 da; *Career* barr Inner Temple 1928, rec of Walsall 1951-64, bencher 1961; dep chm: Oxfordshire QS 1962-71, County and Inner London QS and Middx QS 1965-72; circuit judge 1972-79, judge of Mayor's and City of London Ct 1973-79; junior counsel min: Agriculture, Fisheries and Food, Forestry Cmmn, Statutory Ctee Pharmaceutical Soc of GB 1962-65; *Style*— His Hon Judge James Leonard; Cross Trees, Sutton Courtenay, Oxon (☎ 0235 848)

LEONARD, Hon Mr Justice; Hon Sir (Hamilton) John Leonard; s of Arthur Leonard; *b* 28 April 1926; *Educ* Dean Close Sch Cheltenham (govr 1987-), BNC Oxford; *m* 1948, Doreen, yr da of late Lt-Col Sidney Parker, OBE; 1 s, 1 da; *Career* served Coldstream Gds (Capt) 1944-47; barr Inner Temple 1951, cmmr Central Criminal Ct 1969-71, dep chm Surrey QS 1969-71, QC 1969; Crown Court recorder 1972-78, circuit judge 1978-81, high court judge Queen's Bench 1981-; presiding judge Wales and Chester circuit 1982-86, Common Serjeant City of London 1979-81; memb: Gen Cncl Bar 1970-74, Judicial Studies Bd 1979-82; cncl memb Hurstpierpoint Coll 1975-82, Liveryman Worshipful Co of Plaisterers; HM Lt City London 1980-81; former chm Criminal Bar Assoc; kt 1981; *Style*— The Hon Mr Justice Leonard; Royal Courts of Justice, Strand, London WC2A 2LL

LEONARD, John Thirlestane; CBE (1984); o s of John Gifford Leonard, of Oxhey Cottage, Oxhey Woods, Northwood, Middx; *b* 10 July 1922; *Educ* Rugby; *m* 1946, Gabrielle Mary, MBE; 3 s, 2 da; *Career* CM 1941-46, Lt RNVR; chm Carless Capel and Leonard plc; vice-pres: London Chamber of Commerce and Industry 1984, Inst of Petroleum 1985-88; CBIM; *Recreations* yachting, gardening, reading; *Clubs* Naval, Royal Solent Yacht (Cdre), Little Ship; *Style*— John Leonard, Esq, CBE; c/o Carless Capel & Leonard plc, 90 Long Acre, London WC2E 9RD (☎ 01 836 1577)

LEONARD, (James) Nigel Robert; s of Norman Arthur Leonard, of Limpsfield Chart, Surrey, and Patricia Jessie, *née* Barrett; *b* 23 Mar 1952; *Educ* Forest Sch, RCM; *Career* operatic bass; work at ENO incl: Aida and Damnation of Faust 1980, Fidelio and Tosca 1981, The Flying Dutchman and Boris Godunov 1982, Don Carlos and The Magic Flute 1983, Rigoletto and Mazeppa 1984, Faust and the Mastersingers 1985, Don Giovanni and Parsifal 1986, Akhnaten and Queen of Spades 1987, La Bohéme and King Lear 1988-89; Simone Boccanegra Royal Opera House 1980; notable roles incl: Sarastro in The Magic Flute, Zaccariah in Nabucco, King Philip in Don Carlos, Fiesco in Simone Boccanegra; TV appearances incl: Rigoletto, Lady Macbeth, Akhnaten, Mary Stuart; ARCM; *Recreations* sailing, collecting fountain pens, bridge; *Clubs* Players Theatre; *Style*— Nigel Leonard, Esq; 2 Lower Chart Cottages, Chart Lane, Brasted Chart, nr Westerham, Kent TN16 1LN (☎ 0959 62847); c/o English Nat Opera, St Martins Lane, London WC2; FLat 2, 24 Sutherland St, London SW1

LEONARD-WILLIAMS, Air-Vice Marshal Harold Guy; CB (1966), CBE (1946), DL Somerset (1976); s of Rev Bennet Guyon Leonard-Williams (d 1956), of Tavistock and Margaret Haigh (d 1970); *b* 10 Sept 1911; *Educ* Lancing, RAF Coll Cranwell, RAF Staff Coll; *m* 11 Sept 1937, Catherine Estelle, da of George Arthur Munroe Levett, of Packington Hall (d 1940); 1 da (Ann Catherine b 1944); *Career* RAF, 58 Sqdn and 208 Sqdn 1932-36, No 17 signals course 1936-37, various signals appts 1938-63 (incl D Sigs AM, despatches 1940), chm Br Jt Communications Bd, Co No 1 Radio Sch, chief Electronics Off Fighter Command, dir-gen of Manning (RAF) Air Force Dept 1966-68, ret 1968; warden St Michaels Cheshire Home 1968-72, memb Somerset CC 1973-85 (chm 1978-83); chm Exmoor Nat Park 1978-85; chm Somerset Tst for Nature Conservation Appeal; Legion of Merit (Offr) USA; *Recreations* gardening, DIY; *Clubs* RAF; *Style*— Air Vice-Marshal H G Leonard-Williams, CB, CBE, DL; Open Barrow, Barrows Park, Cheddar, Somerset BS27 3AZ (☎ 0934 842474)

LEROY-LEWIS, David Henry; s of Stuyvesant Henry LeRoy-Lewis (d 1956); *b* 14 June 1918; *Educ* Eton; *m* 1953, Cynthia Madeleine, da of Cdr John Christian Boldero, DSC, RN (d 1984), of Bridport, Dorset; 3 da (Jennifer (Mrs Herford), Zara (Mrs Webb), Victoria (Mrs Meakin); *Career* former chm Akroyd & Smithers Ltd 1976-81, dep chm The Stock Exchange London 1973-76 (cncl memb 1961-81), chm TR North America Investmt Tst plc 1974-88, dep chm Touche Remnant & Co 1981-88 (dir 1974-88); non-exec chm: R P Martin plc 1981-85, Henry Ansbacher Hldgs plc 1982-88; dir: TR Industl & Gen Tst 1967-88, TR Tstees Corpn plc 1973-88; TR Energy plc 1980-; memb IOD; FCA; *Clubs* MCC, Naval and Military; *Style*— David LeRoy-Lewis, Esq; Stoke House, Stoke, Andover, Hants SP11 0NP (☎ 026 473 548)

LESEBERG, Michael; s of Lt Walter Leseberg (ka 1944) of Hamburg, and Karla, *née* Menge (d 1977); *b* 16 Feb 1940; *Educ* Germany Bus Studies; *m* 27 Sept 1962, Traute, da of Johannes Plueschau, of Hamburg; 3 da (Birte b 1964, Petra b 1966, Katja b 1968); *Career* dir: Orimex Handelsgesellschaft MBH Hamburg 1969, Gilbert J McCaul (overseas) Ltd 1977, London Potato Futures Assoc 1983 (formerly chm), London Commodity Exchange Ltd 1984-87, Baltic Int Freight Futures Exchange 1985; md Gilbert J McCaul Ltd 1987 (overseas 1988); cncl memb AFBD 1984-86; Stour Valley Music Soc; memb Baltic Exchange; *Recreations* music, tennis; *Style*— Michael Leseberg, Esq; Bridge House, 4 Borough High St, London, SE1 9QZ, (☎ 01 378 1415, fax 378 1126)

LESLIE, Sir (Colin) Alan Bettridge; s of Rupert Colin Leslie, and Gladys Hannah, *née* Bettridge; *b* 10 April 1922; *Educ* King Edward VII Sch Lytham, Merton Coll Oxford (MA); *m* 1, 1963, Anne Barbara *née* Coaters (d 1982); 2 da; m 2, 1983, Jean Margaret (Sally), widow of Dr Alan Cheatte; *Career* cmmnd RSF 1941-46; slr Stafford Clark & Co 1948-60; head of legal dept and co sec BOC Gp (formerly BOC Int previously Br Oxygen Co) 1960-83; pres Law Soc 1985-86 (vice-pres 1984-86); kt 1986; *Recreations* fishing; *Clubs* United Oxford and Cambridge Univ; *Style*— Sir Alan Leslie; Tile Barn Cottage, Alfriston, East Sussex (☎ 0323 870 388); 36 Abingdon Rd, London W8 (☎ 01 937 2874); Foreign Compensation Commission, 134 Buckingham Palace Rd, London SW1W 95A

LESLIE, Capt Alastair Pinckard; TD; s of Hon John Wayland Leslie (s of 19 Earl of

Rothes); *b* 29 Dec 1934; *Educ* Eton; *m* 1963, Rosemary, da of Cdr Hubert Wyndham Barry, RN; 1 s (David b 1967), 2 da (Fiona b 1965, Ann b 1973); *Career* Capt Royal Scots Fusiliers (TA); md Willis Faber & Dumas (Agencies) Ltd 1976-85, dir A P Leslie Underwriting Agency Ltd and other Lloyds underwriting agencies; dir Utd Goldfields NL until 1988, memb Royal Co of Archers (Queen's Body Guard for Scotland); *Recreations* fishing, stalking, shooting; *Clubs* Boodle's, Pratt's; *Style*— Capt Alastair Leslie, TD; Seasyde House, Errol, Perthshire (☎ 082 12 500); 7 Wallgrave Rd, London SW5 0RL (☎ 01 373 3875); Office: Wakefield House, 41 Trinity Square EC3N 4DJ (☎ 01 488 3382)

LESLIE, Hon Alexander John; s of 21 Earl of Rothes; *b* 1962; *Educ* Eton; *Career* wine trade, insurance broking, conference organisation; *Style*— The Hon Alexander Leslie; Flat B, 25 Bolton Gardens, London SW5

LESLIE, David Carnegie; Baron of Leslie; o s of David Brown Leslie (d 1985), of Aberdeen, and Ethel Watson, *née* Kenn; *b* 1 Feb 1943; *Educ* Aberdeen GS, Scott Sutherland Sch of Architecture (Dip Arch 1969); *m* 7 June 1967, Margaret, da of Roderick Allen Stuart (d 1970), of Aberdeen; 2 da (Angela Elizabeth b 1970, Yvonne Margaret b 1972); *Career* ptnr Leslie Castle by Insch; restorer of ruined Leslie Castle, ancestral home of the Leslies; Freeman of City of London 1987, Burgess of Trade Aberdeen 1979, Burgess of Guild Aberdeen 1984; RIBA 1974, ARIAS 1979, FSA (Scot) 1981; KSG 1984; *Recreations* skiing, shooting, gardening, genealogy; *Clubs* Conservative; *Style*— The Much Honoured Baron of Leslie; Leslie Castle, Leslie, by Insch, Aberdeenshire (☎ 0464 20869)

LESLIE, Desmond Arthur Peter; s of Sir (John Randolph) Shane Leslie, 3 Bt (d 1971), and hp of bro Sir John Norman Ide Leslie, 4 Bt; *b* 29 June 1921; *Educ* Ampleforth, Trinity Coll Dublin; *m* 1, 1945, Agnes, o da of Rudolph Bernauer, of Budapest, Hungary; 2 s, 1 da; m 2, 1970, Helen Jennifer, da of late Lt-Col E I E Strong, of Wiveliscombe, Som; 2 da; *Career* Flt Sgt RAF; composer, author, film producer, discologist; musical compositions: The Living Shakespeare (an album of 12 LPs of electronic music for Macbeth, Hamlet, Othello, Midsummer Night's Dream, The Tempest, Julius Caesar, Antony and Cleopatra, Measure for Measure, King Lear, Richard III, Henry V); film music: The Day the Sky Fell In, Dr Strangelove, Yellow Submarine, Death of Satan, also numerous library music pieces for Joseph Weinberger; produced and dir films; The Missing Princess, Stranger at My Door; author of: Careless Lives, Pardon My Return, Angels Weep, Hold Back the Night, The Amazing Mr Lutterworth, The Jesus File, The Daughters of Pan; humour: How Britain Won the Space Race, Susie Saucer and Ronnie Rocket; *Books* Flying Saucers Have Landed (1,000,000 copies sold; 21 translations to other languages); *Recreations* building cross country courses, falling off horses, teasing evil minded officials, investigating spiritualist and psychic phenomena; *Style*— Desmond Leslie, Esq; Castle Leslie, Gaslough, co Monaghan, Ireland

LESLIE, (Hubert) Graham; s of Hubert John Leslie, artist (d 1976); *b* 24 May 1917; *Educ* Rugby; *m* 1946, Patricia, da of George Hayward (d 1965); 1 s, 1 da; *Career* served WWII RAF in UK, Egypt, Sudan, Palestine; with Royal Bank of Scotland 1935-77; *Publications* The Descendants of Henry David Leslie (1983); *Recreations* DIY, photography; *Style*— Graham Leslie, Esq; 15 Tushmore Lane, Crawley, W Sussex RH10 2JZ (☎ 0293 22370)

LESLIE, James Francis; TD (1974), JP (Co Antrim 1967), DL (Co Antrim 1973); s of Seymour Argent Sandford Leslie, CMG, DL (d 1953), and Eleanor Mary, *née* Stuart; *b* 19 Mar 1933; *Educ* Eton, Queen's Coll Cambridge (MA); *m* 16 June 1956, (Patricia) Elizabeth Jane, da of Col William Anderson Swales, OBE, MC, TD (d 1955); 2 s (James b 1958, John b 1960), 1 da (Rosejane b 1964); *Career* cmmnd N Irish Horse (TA) 1963, Maj (Sqdn-Ldr) Royal Yeo (V) 1968; colonial serv (dist offr) Tanganyika 1956-59; farmer 1960-; pres local branch Royal Br Legion; memb: Royal Forestry Soc, Royal Ulster Agricultural Soc; High Sheriff of Co Antrim 1967, Vice-Lt 1983; *Recreations* shooting, fishing; *Style*— James Leslie, Esq, TD, JP, DL; Leslie Hall, Ballymoney, Co Antrim BT53 6QL

LESLIE, Lord; James Malcolm David Leslie; s and h of 21 Earl of Rothes; *b* 4 June 1958; *Educ* Eton; *Style*— Lord Leslie; 8 Kinnoul Rd, London SW6

LESLIE, Capt Sir John Norman Ide; 4 Bt (UK 1876); s of Sir (John Randolph) Shane Leslie, 3 Bt (d 1971), and Marjory Mary Ide (d 1951); branch of Earls of Rothes; *b* 6 Dec 1916; *Educ* Downside, Magdalene Coll Cambridge (BA); *Heir* bro, Desmond Arthur Peter Leslie, of Castle Leslie, Glaslough, Co Monaghan; *Career* serv WWII, Irish Gds (POW 1940-45); artist, ecologist, restorer of old buildings; Kt of Honour and Devotion SMO Malta, Kt Cdr Order of St Gregory the Great; landowner (900 acres), previous to Irish land act 1910 fortynine thousand acres; *Recreations* ornithology, forestry; *Clubs* Travellers', Circolo della Caccia (Rome); *Style*— Capt Sir John Leslie, Bt; 19 Piazza in Piscinula, Rome 00153, Italy

LESLIE, Hon John Wayland; s of 19 Earl of Rothes (d 1927); *b* 16 Dec 1909; *Educ* Stowe, CCC Cambridge; *m* 1932, Coral Angela, da of George Henry Pinckard, JP (d 1950), of Combe Court, Chiddingfold, Surrey, and of 9 Chesterfield St, Mayfair; 1 s, 1 da; *Career* served WWII, RAFVR, Fl-Lt (invalided 1943); memb Royal Co of Archers (Queen's Body Guard for Scotland); Liveryman Worshipful Co of Clothworkers; *Recreations* fishing, shooting; *Clubs* Boodle's; *Style*— The Hon John Leslie; Guildford House, Castle Hill, Farnham, Surrey GU9 7JG (☎ 0252 716975)

LESLIE, Peter Evelyn; s of Patrick Holt Leslie (d 1972), of Oxford, and Evelyn de Berry; *b* 27 Mar 1931; *Educ* Dragon Sch Oxford, Stowe, New Coll Oxford; *m* 1975, Charlotte, da of Sir Edwin Arthur Chapman-Andrews, KCMG, OBE (d 1979); 2 step s (Francis, Mathew), 2 step da (Alice, Jessica); *Career* cmmnd Argyll and Sutherland Highlanders 1951, served 7 Bn (TA) 1952-56; dep chm Barclays Bank 1987- (gen mangr 1973-76, dir 1980, chm gen mangr and md 1985-88, chm exec ctee Br Bankers Assoc 1978-79; govr: Nat Inst of Social Work 1973-83, Stowe Sch 1983-; chm: Exports Guarantee Advsy Cncl 1987- (Advsy Cncl 1978-81), Overseas Devpt Inst 1988-, Queen's Coll 1989; Cwlth Devpt Corp 1989-; *Recreations* natural history, historical research; *Style*— Peter Leslie, Esq; 54 Lombard St, London EC3

LESLIE, Richard Andrew; s of Cyril Leslie, of Middx, and Rozella, *née* Keen; *b* 24 April 1954; *Educ* Kingbury HS, Morehead State Univ Kentucky, USA (MBA); *m* 7 Aug 1982, Margaret Elizabeth, da of Colston Henry Harrison, of Bristol, Avon; *Career* CA, proprietor of R A Leslie & Co; Middx Co: tennis player 1970-87, squash player 1976-78; twice Capt England Snr Tennis Team, formerly Br under 18 and 21 doubles champion; *Recreations* tennis, squash, snooker; *Clubs* Lansdowne, formerly All England Club Wimbledon; *Style*— Richard A Leslie, Esq; The Old School House, Tormarton, nr Badminton GL9 1HZ (☎ 045 421 370); car phone 0836 590122

LESLIE, Robin; s of Lt-Col John Leslie (d 1965), of Kings Lynn; *b* 6 Nov 1924; *Educ* Eton; *m* 1, 1949, Susan Mary, yr da of Maj-Gen James Francis Harter, DSO, MC (d 1960); 2 da (Sarah b 1950, Belinda b 1952); m 2, 1983, June Rose, da of Lt-Gen Frederick George Beaumont Nesbitt, CVO, CBE, MC (d 1972); *Career* served WW II Capt; fruit farmer; dir: Home Grown Fruits Ltd 1969-73, Colchester Oyster Fishery Ltd; *Recreations* golf, gardening; *Clubs* White's; *Style*— Robin Leslie, Esq; Glebe House, Langham, Colchester, Essex (☎ 0206 322131)

LESLIE, (Percy) Theodore; heir to btcy of Leslie of Wardis and Findrassie (NS 1625); succession, as 10 Bt, pending at time of going to press; s of (Frank Harvey) Leslie (d 1965; ggs of Sir John Leslie, 4 Bt, who assumed the title in 1800, after a period of dormancy), and Amelia Caroline (d 1918), da of Alexander Russon; *b* 19 Nov 1915; *Educ* London, privately; *Career* engineer British Aerospace, ret 1980; Freeman City of London 1978; FSA (Scot); KASG; *Recreations* chess, gardening, visiting places of historic interest; *Style*— Theodore Leslie, Esq; c/o National Westminster Bank, 5 Market Place, Kingston-upon-Thames, Surrey

LESLIE, Thomas Gerard; s of Thomas Leslie, JP (d 1985), and Ellen Slaven *née* McAllister (d 1976); *b* 11 August 1938; *Educ* St Joseph's Coll Dumfries, Mons Officer Cadet Sch Aldershot; *m* 12 June 1982, Sonya Anne, da of Leslie John Silburn (d 1980); 1 s (Thomas b 1985); *Career* Nat Serv, Scots Gds 1958, cmmnd Argyll and Sutherland Highlanders 1959, Lt HAC RARD; various exec posts Canada Dry (UK) Ltd, Booker McConnell Ltd, Thos de la Rue; adjt The Corps of Commissionaries; memb The Company of Pikemen and Musketeers HAC; Freeman City of London 1974; FSA (Scot) 1980; KASG 1983; chm London Caledonian Catholic Assoc 1983-87; *Recreations* shooting, heraldry, genealogy; *Style*— Thomas Leslie, Esq; 3 Crane Court, Fleet St, London EC4A 2EJ (☎ 01 353 1125)

LESLIE MELVILLE, Lady Elizabeth (Eliza); *née* Compton; da of 6 Marquess of Northampton, DSO (d 1978), and Virginia Lucie Hussey, *née* Heaton; *b* 7 Dec 1944; *m* 1968 (Ian) Hamish Leslie Melville, s of Maj Michael Ian Leslie Melville, of Bridgelands, Selkirk; 2 s (James Ian b 1969, Henry Bingham b 1975); *Clubs* Turf; *Style*— Lady Eliza Leslie Melville; Lochluichart Lodge, by Garve, Ross-shire

LESLIE MELVILLE, Hon Alan Duncan; s of 13 Earl of Leven and 12 of Melville, KT (d 1947); *b* 1928; *Educ* Eton; *Career* Capt Rifle Bde 1954, ret 1956; *Style*— The Hon Alan Leslie Melville; Fingask, Kirkhill, Inverness

LESLIE MELVILLE, Hon Archibald Ronald; yr s of 14 Earl of Leven and (13 of) Melville; hp to er bro, Lord Balgonie; *b* 15 Sept 1957; *Educ* Gordonstoun; *m* 4 April 1987, Julia Mary Greville, yr da of Basil Fox, of 32 Pembroke Gdns, W8; *Career* 2 Lt Queen's Own Highlanders to 1981, Lt 1981, Lt RARO 1982; *Style*— The Hon Archibald Leslie Melville; Glenferness House, Nairn, Scotland IV12 5UP

LESLIE MELVILLE, Hon George David; s of 13 Earl of Leven and 12 of Melville, KT (d 1947); *b* 13 May 1924; *Educ* Eton, Trinity Coll Cambridge; *m* 1955, Diana Mary, da of Brig Sir Henry Houldsworth, KBE, DSO, MC (d 1963); 1 s, 1 da; *Career* late Rifle Bde, served 1942-45 (wounded 1945), Maj Black Watch TA, chartered land agent, FRICS; *Recreations* shooting, skiing; *Clubs* Naval and Military; *Style*— The Hon George Leslie Melville, JP; Inneshewen, Aboyne, Aberdeenshire AB3 5BH

LESLIE MELVILLE, (Ian) Hamish; o s of Maj Michael Leslie Melville, TD, DL, s of Lt-Col Hon Ian Leslie Melville (4 s of 11 Earl of Leven and 10 Earl of Melville), and Cynthia, da of Sir Charles Hambro, KBE, MC; *b* 22 August 1944; *Educ* Eton, Ch Ch Oxford (BA, MA); *m* 1968, Lady Elizabeth Compton, yr da of 6 Marquess of Northampton; 2 s (James b 1969, Henry b 1975); *Career* chm: Jamestown Investmts Ltd, Central Capital Ltd, Capel-Cure Myers Capital Mgmnt Ltd; *Clubs* Turf, White's, Pratt's; *Style*— Hamish Leslie Melville, Esq; Lochluichart Lodge, by Garve, Ross-shire (☎ 09974 242)

LESLIE MELVILLE, Lady Jean Elizabeth; da of 13 Earl of Leven and 12 of Melville, KT (d 1947); *b* 1921; *Style*— Lady Jean Leslie Melville; Pathways, Sedgeberrow, Evesham, Worcs WR11 6UF

LESSELS, Norman; s of John Clark Lessels (d 1981) of Edinburgh, and Gertrude Margaret Ellen, *née* Jack; *b* 2 Sept 1938; *Educ* Melville Coll, Edinburgh Acad; *m* 1, 31 Dec 1960, Gillian Durward, *née* Clark (d 1979); 2 s (Alasdair b 1963, James b 1967 d 1979), 1 da (Sarah b 1965 d 1979); m 2, 27 Jan 1981, Christine, da of George Stevenson Hitchman (d 1971), of Gullane, E Lothian; *Career* admitted CA 1961; ptnr: Ernst Whinney (and predecessor firms) 1962-80, Chiene and Tait CA 1980-; non exec dir: Anderson Strathclyde plc 1973, Standard Life Assur Co (chm 1988) 1978-, Scottish Eastern Investment Tst plc 1980-, Bank of Scotland 1988-, Companies House Steering Bd, Scottish Homes, ICAS (pres 1987-88); *Recreations* golf, music, bridge; *Clubs* New Edinburgh, Hon Co of (Edinburgh) Golfers, R & A, Bruntsfield Links Golfing Soc; *Style*— Norman Lessels, Esq; 11 Forres St, Edinburgh EH3 6BJ (☎ 031 225 5596); 3 Albyn Place, Edinburgh EH2 4NQ (☎ 031 225 7515, fax 031 220 1083, telex 72687)

LESSER, Dr Jeffrey; s of Louis Lesser (d 1952), of Hampstead, and Gaby, *née* Katz (d 1974); *b* 18 Feb 1927; *Educ* City of London (Corpn Scholar), London Univ (MB BS, BDS (Lond) LDS, RCS Eng); *m* 13 Nov 1955, Sheila, da of Mark Goldstein (d 1980) of Horsmonden, Kent; 2 s (Adam b 1958, Jeremy b 1962); *Career* Capt RAMC; physician, dental surgeon; past chm: Univ London J Students Union, Univ London J Graduates, Alpha Omega Int; *Recreations* squash; *Style*— Dr Jeffrey Lesser; The Maverns, 4 Hill Crescent, Totteridge (☎ 01 445 8280); 82 Harley Street, London W1 (☎ 01 636 7170)

LESSER, Leslie Hugh; s of Isaac Lesser (d 1960); *b* 7 Jan 1934; *Educ* Westcliff High Sch; *m* 1956, Joyce; 1 s (Guy Fenton), 1 da (Vivien Adele); *Career* dir: Greenfields Leisure Ltd, Greenfield Milletts Int Ltd Hong Kong, Rheilffordd Llyn Padarn Cyfyngedig, vice-chm Southend United Football Club Ltd; Freemason; FCA; *Recreations* golf, fishing, Shakespearean theatre; *Style*— Leslie Lesser, Esq; 130 Rivermill, SW1; 17 Burlescoombe Rd, Thorpe Bay, Essex

LESSING, Charlotte; da of George Fainstone, and Helene Peretz; *b* 14 May 1924; *Educ* Henrietta Barnet Sch, Univ of London Extension Course (Dip Eng Lit); *m* 25 May 1948, Walter Lessing; 3 da (Diana b 1953, Judith b 1954, Nicola b 1957); *Career* writer of short stories, travel articles, features and occasional broadcaster; ed-in-chief: Good Housekeeping 1987- (ed 1973-87, dep ed 1964-73), Country Living 1985-86; ed conslt 1988-; ed of the Year Award, Periodical Publisher Assoc 1983; *Recreations* travel, wine; *Clubs* Groucho; *Style*— Mrs Charlotte Lessing; 2 Roseneath Rd, London SW11 6AH (☎ 01 228 0708); National Magazine Co, 72 Broadwick St, W1 (☎ 01 439

7144)

LESSING, Doris May; da of Alfred Cook, and Emily Maude, *née* McVeagh; *b* 22 Oct 1919; *m* 1, 1939 (m dis 1943), Frank Charles Wisdom; 1 s (John), 1 da (Jean); m 2, 1945 (m dis 1949), Gottfried Anton Nicholas Lessing; 1 s (Peter); *Career* author; recipient: Mondello Prize (Italy) 1946, Somerset Maugham Award 1954, Prix Media 1976, Austrian State Prize for Euro Lit 1981, Shakespeare Prize Hamburg 1982, WH Smith Lit Award 1986, Grinzane Cavour (Italy-Foreign Fiction) 1989; memb Nat Inst Arts and Letters, Inst Cultural Res; *Books* The Grass is Singing (1950), Children of Violence (five vols, 1951-69), The Golden Notebook (1962), Briefing for a Descent into Hell (1971), The Summer Before Dark (1973), The Memoirs of a Survivor (1975), Canopus in Argos, Archives (5 vols 1979-83), The diaries of Jane Somers (Diary of a Good Neighbour 1983 and If the Old Could..1984, published under pseudonym Jane Somers), The Good Terrorist (1985), The Fifth Child (1988); short stories incl: African Stories (two vols), This was the Old Chief's Country, and The Sun Between Their Feet, and collected stories (two vols), To Room 19, and The Temptation of Jack Orkney; non-fiction incl: The Wind Blows Away our Words... and other Documents Relating to the Afghan Resistance (1987), Prisons We Choose to Live Inside (1986); essays incl: A Small Personal Voice (1974); poetry incl: Fourteen Poems (1959); one play: Play with a Tiger 1962; *Style*— Mrs Doris Lessing; c/o Jonathan Clowes Ltd, 22 Prince Albert Rd, London NW1 7ST

LESTER, Anthony Paul; QC (1975); s of Harry Lester (d 1984), of London, and Kate, *née* Cooper-Smith; *b* 3 July 1936; *Educ* City of London Sch, Trinity Coll Cambridge (BA), Harvard Law Sch (LLM); *m* 29 July 1971, Catherine Elizabeth Debora, da of Michael Morris Wassey (d 1969), of London; 1 s (Gideon b 1972), 1 da (Maya b 1974); *Career* 2 Lt RA 1956; barr Lincolns Inn 1963 (bencher 1985), memb Northern Ireland Bar (QC) and Irish Bar; rec S Eastern circuit 1987; special advsr to; Home Sec 1974-76, standing Cmmn on Human Rights in NI 1975-77; chm: bd of govrs James Allens Girls Sch, Interights (Int Centre for Legal Protection of Human Rights); tstee Runnymede Tst, govr LSE Science; Hon Visiting Prof of Law UCL; CIArb; *Books* Justice in the American South (1964), Shawcross and Beaumont on Air Law (ed jtly, third edn 1964), Race and Law (jtly 1972); contrib British Nationality, Immigration and Race Relations, in Halsbury's Laws of England (fourth edn 1973), The Changing Constitution (ed Powell and Oliver 1985); *Recreations* walking, sailing, golf, water colours; *Clubs* Garrick, RAC; *Style*— Anthony Lester, Esq, QC; 2 Hare Court, Temple, London EC4Y 7BH (☎ 01 583 1770, fax 01 583 9269, telex 27139 LINLAW)

LESTER, James Theodore; MP (C) Broxtowe 1983-; s of Arthur Ernest and Marjorie Lester; *b* 23 May 1932; *Educ* Nottingham HS; *m* 1953, Iris; 2 s; *Career* MP (C) Beeston Feb 1974-83, oppn whip 1975-79, parly under sec state Employment 1979-81, fndr memb CARE (Cons Action to Revive Employment), dep chm all party gp on Overseas Devpt; *Style*— James Lester, Esq, MP; 4 Trevose House, Orsett Street, London SE11

LESTER, Richard; s of Elliott Lester (d 1951), of Pennsylvania, USA, and Ella Young Lester (d 1969); *b* 19 Jan 1932; *Educ* William Penn Charter Sch, Univ of Pennsylvania (BA); *m* 1956, Deirdre Vivian, da of Sqdn Ldr Frederick James Smith (d 1970); 1 s (Dominic), 1 da (Claudia); *Career* tv dir: CBS (USA 1951-54), AR (dir TV Goon shows 1956); directed The Running, Jumping and Standing Still Film (Academy award nomination, 1st prize San Francisco Festival 1960); film dir; feature films directed: It's Trad, Dad (1962), Mouse on the Moon (1963), A Hard Day's Night (1964), The Knack (1964, Grand Prix Cannes Film Festival), Help (1965, Best Film Award and Best Dir Award Rio de Janeiro Festival), A Funny Thing Happened on the Way to the Forum (1966), How I won the War (1967), Petulia (1968), The Bed Sitting Room (1969, Gandhi Peace Prize Berlin Film Festival), The Three Musketeers (1973), Juggernaut (1974, Best Dir Award Teheran Film Festival), The Four Musketeers (1974), Royal Flash (1975), Robin and Marian (1976), The Ritz (1976), Butch and Sundance: the early days (1979), Cuba (1979), Superman II (1981), Superman III (1983), Finders Keepers (1984), awarded Grand Prize Avoriaz Festival 1977; Order of Academy of Arts and Letters (France) 1973; *Style*— Richard Lester, Esq; Courtyards, River Lane, Petersham, Surrey; Courtyard Films Ltd, Twickenham Studios, St Margarets, Middlesex, TW1 2AW (☎ 01 892 4477)

LESTOCK REID, Lt Cdr Christopher Gordon; OBE (1985), DL (Northumberland 1971); s of Claud Lestock Reid (d 1954), and Dorothea Joan Steward Taylor (d 1959); *b* 12 Oct 1920; *Educ* Pangbourne Nautical Coll; *m* 1946, Alwine, da of Col Richard Straker, OBE, MC (d 1949); 1 da (Joanna); *Career* served in RN 1938-55; farmer; MFH 1965-67; county cmmr Northumberland Scouts 1968-76, chief cmmr of England Scout Assoc 1976-85; *Clubs* Northern Counties; *Style*— Lt Cdr Christopher Lestock Reid, OBE, DL; Low Angerton House, Hartburn, Morpeth, Northumberland (☎ 067 072 230); c/o Coutts & Co, 440 Strand, London WC2

LESTOR, Joan; MP (L) Eton and Slough 1966-; *b* 1931,Vancouver; *Educ* Blaenavon Secdy Sch (Monmouth), William Morris Secdy Sch Walthamstow, London Univ; *m* ; 1 s, 1 da (both adopted); *Career* nursery sch teacher 1959-66, memb LCC 1962-64; Parly Under-Sec of State Dept of Education and Science 1969-70 & 1975-76, memb Labour Party NEC 1967-82 (chm 1977-78), parly under-sec of state FCO 1974-75, co-chm Jt Ctee Against Racism 1978-, chm Int Ctee Labour Party 1978-; oppn front bench spokesman Women's Rights & Welfare 1981-; *Style*— Miss Joan Lestor, MP; 59 Magdalen Rd, SW18; House of Commons, SW1

LETANKA, Lady Christina; *née* Gathorne-Hardy; da of 4 Earl of Cranbrook, CBE; *b* 1 May 1940; *m* 1967, Stanley Edward Letanka; 1 s (Peter Edward b 1974), 2 da (Stella Dorothy b 1968, Florence Ruth b 1969); *Style*— Lady Christina Letanka; Pepsal End, Pepperstock, nr Luton, Beds LU1 4LH (☎ 0582 23861)

LETCHER, (Robert) Peter; s of Henry Percival Letcher, of St Ives House, Ringwood, Hants, and Catherine Jessie, *née* Harris (d 1980); *b* 12 August 1924; *Educ* Radley; *m* 1, 22 Aug 1947 (m dis 1955), Patricia Enid, da of Eugene Baerselman; m 2, 27 July 1957, Virginia Rose Lou da of Gurth Kemp Fenn-Smith; 2 s (Piers b 15 Aug 1960, Peregrine b 20 Nov 1961); *Career* Lt Gren Guards 1944, King's Co N W Europe (despatches, wounded) Capt Control Cmmn 1945, ADC to Regnl Cmmr N Rhine and Westphalia 1946-47; slr 1948; ptnr Letcher & Son; NP; chm Industl Tribunals 1976-79, dir Valagro SA; *Recreations* skiing, shooting, racing, photography; *Clubs* Army and Navy; *Style*— Peter Letcher, Esq; Honeypound, Martin, Fordingbridge, Hants SP6 3LR (☎ 072 589 389); Letcher & Son, 24 Market Place, Ringwood, Hants BH24 1BS (☎ 0425 471 424, fax 0425 470 917, telex 41124 G)

LETHBRIDGE, John Francis Buckler Noel; s and h of Sir Thomas Periam Hector Noel Lethbridge, 7 Bt; *b* 10 Mar 1977; *Educ* Ravenswood Devon, Wilken Park Bucks; *Recreations* running, swimming; *Style*— John Lethbridge, Esq; Lloyds House, Honeymead, Simonsbath, Minehead, Somerset

LETHBRIDGE, Sir Thomas Periam Hector Noel; 7 Bt (UK 1804); s of Sir Hector Wroth Lethbridge, 6 Bt (d 1978), and Diana Evelyn Noel; *b* 17 July 1950; *Educ* Milton Abbey, RAC Cirencester; *m* 1976, Susan (Suzie) Elizabeth, da of Lyle Rocke, of Maryland; 4 s (John b 1977, Edward b 1978, Alexander b 1982, Henry b 1984), 2 da (Georgina b 1980, Rachel b 1986); *Heir* s, John Francis Buckler Noel Lethbridge; *Career* art dealer in sporting subjects of 1700 to date, int agent for distinguished retail names; *Clubs* Farmer's, Turf, Raffle's; *Style*— Sir Thomas Lethbridge, Bt; 164 Ashley Gdns, Emery Hill St, London SW1

LETLEY, Peter Anthony; s of Sidney Charles Letley (d 1978), of Woodbridge, Suffolk, and Ruby, *née* Berry; *b* 11 Nov 1945; *Educ* Woodbridge Sch Suffolk, St John's Coll Oxford (BA); *m* 21 March 1970, (Alice) Emma Campbell, da of Lt-Col Campbell K Finlay, of W Ardhu, Isle of Mull, Argyll; 1 s (Alfred Thomas b 4 Sept 1988); *Career* joined Hong Kong Bank Gp 1974; Wardley Ltd: Head of Lending Dept 1974-78, dir overseas ops and dir 1978-82, jt md Aust 1982-83; chief exec Hong Kong Int Trade Fin Ltd (London) 1983-86; fin dir: James Capel Bankers Ltd 1986-87 (md 1987-88), James Capel & Co 1988-; *Recreations* theatre, opera, reading; *Clubs* Hong Kong Jockey; *Style*— Peter Letley, Esq; 24 Princedale Rd, London W11 4NJ (☎ 01 229 1398); James Capel and Co, James Capel House, 6 Bevis Marks, London EC3A 7JQ (☎ 01 621 0011, telex 888866)

LETTS, Anthony Ashworth; s of Leslie Charles Letts, of Old Swaylands, Penshurst, Kent (d 1984), and Elizabeth Mary, *née* Gibson (d 1971); John Letts (gggf) founded Diary Publishing Business in 1796 as stationer, first Diary 1812, co still family controlled; *b* 3 July 1935; *Educ* Marlborough, Magdalene Coll Cambridge (MA); *m* 15 Sept 1962, Rosa Maria, da of Avvocato Aminta Ciarrapico, of Rome, Italy (d 1985); 1 s (Philip Leslie b 1966), 1 da (Adalgisa b 1965); *Career* Nat Serv 1954-56 Lt; md Charles Letts & Co Ltd 1965, chm Charles Letts (Hldgs) Ltd 1977; dir: Charles Letts & Co Ltd 1963, Charles Letts Scotland Ltd 1978, Charles Letts Gp Servs 1978, Letts of London (USA) 1978, Letts of London Pty (Australia) 1986, Mascot Developments 1984; *Recreations* tennis, sailing, hill walking, theatre; *Clubs* Hurlingham; *Style*— A A Letts, Esq; Fairlight, Kingston Hill, Kingston-upon-Thames, Surrey KT2 7LX (☎ 01 546 5757); Charles Letts (Hldgs) Ltd, 77 Borough Rd, London SE1 1DW (☎ 01 407 8891, telex 884498 LETTS G, fax 01 403 6729)

LETTS, John Campbell Bonner; OBE (1980); s of (Christian) Francis Campbell Letts, of Oakley Hall, Cirencester, Glos (d 1963), and Eveleen Frances Calthrop, *née* Bonner (d 1969); *b* 18 Nov 1929; *Educ* Haileybury, Jesus Coll Cambridge (BA); *m* 21 Sep 1957, Sarah Helen, da of E Brian O Rorke, RA; 3 s (Robert b 1959, Matthew b 1961, Daniel b 1963) 1 da (Vanessa b 1966); *Career* Penguin Books 1959, J Walter Thompson 1960-63, Sunday Times Publications 1964-66, gen mangr Book Club Assoc 1966-69, mktg dir Hutchinson 1969, jt chm (ed and mktg dir) Folio Soc 1971-87; fdr and chm Nat Heritage 1972, tstee and memb ctee Euro Museums Tst, tstee Museum of Empire and Cwlth Tst, fdr and chm The Trollope Soc 1987-; FRSA; *Poetry* A Little Treasury of Limericks (1973); *Recreations* walking in Scotland, reading visiting museums, gardening; *Clubs* Reform; *Style*— John Letts, Esq, OBE; 83 West Side, Clapham Common, London SW4 (☎ 01 228 9448); The Trollope Society, 9a North St, London SW4 0HN (☎ 01 720 6789/ 924 1146)

LETTS, John Martin; s of Leslie Charles Letts (d 1985) (direct desc of John Letts first diary publisher), and of Elizabeth Mary, *née* Gibson (d 1972); *b* 15 Feb 1934; *Educ* Marlborough; *m* 6 March 1964, Eileen Patricia, da of Brig D W McConnel, of Hawick, Roxburghshire; 2 s (Charles b 1965, Anthony b 1966, d 1976), 1 da (Diana b 1971); *Career* pres dirships inc: Charles Letts (Hldgs) Ltd, College Valley Estates, Charles Letts (Scot) Ltd (chm), huntsman Bolebroke Beagles 1956-63, master and huntsman Eastern Counties Otterhounds 1958-63, master and huntsman College Valley Foxhounds 1964-82, master and huntsman College Valley Foxhounds (Nth Northumberland) 1982-; *Recreations* foxhunting, fishing, gardening; *Style*— Martin Letts, Esq; Hethpool, Wooler, Northumberland; Thornybank Estate, Dalkeith, Lothian, Scotland

LEUCH, Werner; s of Ulrich Leuch, of Appenzell, Switzerland and Aline, *née* Baenziger (d 1984); *b* 8 Dec 1937; *Educ* ATZ Zurich (BSc); *m* 1963, Barbara Helen Elise, da of Alfred Mottet of Gossau, Switzerland; *Career* Maj Swiss Air Force 1981; md BMARC 1977-; vice-chm Swiss Economical Cncl; govr The Kings Sch Grantham; *Recreations* skiing, swimming, fishing, shooting; *Style*— Werner Leuch, Esq; Harlaxton Close, Harlaxton Rd, Grantham, Lincs (☎ 0476 65792); BMARC, Springfield Rd, Grantham, Lincs NG31 7JB (☎ 0476 65577, telex 37635)

LEUCHARS, Hon Mrs Gillian Wightman; *née* Nivison; da of 2 Baron Glendyne (d 1967); *b* 1931; *m* 1953, Maj-Gen Peter Raymond Leuchars, CBE (*qv*); 1 s; *Style*— The Hon Mrs Leuchars; 5 Chelsea Sq, London SW3

LEUCHARS, Maj-Gen Peter Raymond; CBE (1966); s of Raymond Leuchars and Helen Inez Leuchars, *née* Copland-Griffiths (d 1979); *b* 29 Oct 1921; *Educ* Bradfield Coll; *m* 1953, Gillian Wightman, da of 2 Baron Glendyne (d 1967), of E Grinstead, Sussex; 1 s (Christopher); *Career* cmmnd in Welsh Guards 1941, serv NW Europe and Italy 1944-45, Adj 1 Bn Welsh Guards Palestine 1945-48; Bde Maj 4 Bde Germany 1952-54, GSO 1 (Instr) Staff Coll Camberley 1956-59, GSO1 HQ 4 Div BAOR 1960-63, cmd 1 Bn Welsh Guards 1963-65, Princ SO to Dir of Ops Borneo 1965-66, cmd 11 Armd Bde BAOR 1966-68, cmd Jt Operational Computer Projects Team 1969-71, Dep Cmdt Staff Coll Camberley 1972-73, GOC Wales 1973-76, Col The Roy Welch Fus 1974-84; pres Gds Golfing Soc 1977-, cmmr-in-chief St John Ambulance 1978-80 and 1985-86, chief cdr St John Ambulance 1981-89; Order of Istiqlal (Jordan) 1946; KStJ 1978; *Recreations* golf, shooting, travel, photography; *Clubs* Royal and Ancient Golf, Sunningdale Golf (capt 1975); *Style*— Maj-Gen Peter Leuchars, CBE; 5 Chelsea Sq, London SW3 6LF (☎ 01 352 6187); 1 Grosvenor Cres, London SW1X 7EF (☎ 01 235 5231)

LEUTHOLD, Rudolph; s of Eugen Albert Leuthold (d 1981), of Zurich, and Anna, *née* Wild; *b* 10 May 1949; *Educ* Gymnasium Zurich (Baccalaureate), Univ of Geneva (Lic Ès Sciences Economiques), McGill Univ Montreal (MBA); *Career* vice pres Morgan Guaranty Tst NY 1981-, md JP Morgan Investmt Inc 1984-; memb Soc of Investmt Analysts 1978; *Recreations* music, theatre, literature, skiing; *Clubs* Royal Automobile; *Style*— Rudolph Leuthold, Esq; J P Morgan Investment Management Inc, 83 Pall Mall, London SW1 5ES (☎ 01 839 4145, fax 01 839 3115/3117, telex 8954543)

LEVEN AND MELVILLE, 14 Earl of Leven and 13 of Melville (S 1641); Alexander Robert Leslie Melville; also Lord Melville of Monymaill (S 1616), Lord Balgonie (S 1641), Viscount Kirkaldie, and Lord Raith, Monymaill and Balwearie (both S 1690); s of 13 Earl of Leven and (12 of) Melville, KT (d 1947), and Lady Rosamond Foljambe (da of 1 Earl of Liverpool); *b* 13 May 1924; *Educ* Eton; *m* 1953, Susan, da of late Lt-Col Ronald Steuart-Menzies of Culdares; 2 s, 1 da; *Heir* s, Lord Balgonie; *Career* vice-pres Highland Dist TA, 2 Lt Coldstream Gds 1943, Capt 1947, DL (1961) Co of Nairn; chm Cairngorm Chairlift Co; late ADC to Gov-Gen NZ; pres Br Ski Fedn 1981-85; convener Nairn Co Cncl 1970-74; chm bd of govs Gordonstoun Sch 1971-; *Recreations* shooting, skiing, fishing; *Clubs* New (Edinburgh); *Style—* The Rt Hon the Earl of Leven and Melville, DL; Glenferness House, Nairn, Scotland (☎ Glenferness 202)

LEVENE, Sir Peter Keith; KBE (1989); s of Maurice Pierre Levene (d 1970), and Rose Levene; *b* 8 Dec 1941; *Educ* City of London Sch, Univ of Manchester (BEcon); *m* 1966, Wendy Ann, da of Frederick Fraiman; 2 s, 1 da; *Career* dir: Utd Sci Hldgs plc 1968-85 (chm 1982-85), UK Nat Armaments 1988-; chief of def procurement MOD 1985-, vice-chm Def Mfrs Assoc 1983-, chm IEPG (Euro) Nat Armaments Dirs 1989-; personal advsr to sec state for def 1984-; govr: City of London Sch for Girls 1984-85, City of London Sch 1985-, Sir John Cass Primary Sch 1985-; vice-pres City of London Red Cross; memb: Ct HAC, bd of mgmnt London Homes for the Elderly; common cnclr Ward of Candlewick 1983-84; Alderman Ward of Portsoken 1984-; JP City of London 1984-; *Recreations* skiing, swimming, watching association football, travel; *Clubs* Guildhall, City Livery; *Style—* Sir Peter Levene, KBE; Ministry of Defence, Main Building, Whitehall, London SW1A 2HB (☎ 01 218 2928)

LEVENE, Victor; s of George Levene and Rose, *née* Tencer; *b* 20 Feb 1939; *Educ* Latymer Upper Sch, UCL (LLB); *m* 1, (m dis); 2s (Adam b 1971, Gideon b 1972), 1 da (Nadia b 1968); m 2, 1980 Jacqueline Anne, da of Clarence Perry; 1 s (Nicolas b 1981); *Career* Middle Temple 1961; in practice both civil and criminal spheres 1961-; *Recreations* cinema, philately, numismatics; *Clubs* BFI; *Style—* Victor Levene, Esq; 2 Mitre Court Buildings, Temple, London EC4Y 7BX (☎ 01 353 1353, fax 01 353 8188)

LEVENTHAL, Colin David; *b* 2 Nov 1946; *Educ* London Univ (BA); *Career* slr 1971; head of copyright BBC to 1981; head of programme acquisition Channel Four TV 1981-86; dir of programme acquisition and sales Channel Four TV 1987-; *Recreations* film, television, theatre; *Style—* Colin Leventhal, Esq; Channel Four TV Co Ltd, 60 Charlotte St, London W1 (☎ 01 631 4444)

LEVENTHORPE, Richard Christopher; s of Col Graham Sidney Leventhorpe, DSO (d 1963), and Dorothy, *née* Leyland (d 1965); *b* 19 June 1927; *Educ* Eton, King's Coll Cambridge (BA); *m* 14 Jan 1959, Penelope, da of Cdr Ross Leonard William Moss (d 1960); 3 s (John b 1961, Adrian b 1963, Thomas b 1965), 1 da (Susan b 1959); *Career* Lt Coldstream Gds serv Palestine (despatches); dir: Four Leaf Farm Supplies Ltd 1976-79, Devon Gp Feeds 1976-82; memb House of Keys 1986; *Recreations* shooting, gardening; *Style—* Richard Leventhorpe, Esq; Hillberry Manor, Little Mill, Onchan, IOM (☎ 0624 29542); Govt Bldgs, Bucks Rd, Douglas (☎ 0624 26262)

LEVER, Hon Bernard Lewis; s of Baron Lever (Life Peer, d 1977), by his w Ray, *see* Baroness Lever; n of Baron Lever of Manchester (Life Peer); *b* 1 Feb 1951; *Educ* Clifton, Queen's Coll Oxford (MA); *m* 1985, Anne Helen, da of Patrick Chandler Gordon Ballingall, MBE, of Seaford, E Sussex; *Career* barr Middle Temple 1975, co-fndr of SDP in NW 1981, contested (SDP) Manchester Withington 1983; *Recreations* walking, music, skiing; *Clubs* Vincent's; *Style—* The Hon Bernard Lever; 28 St John St, Manchester 3 (☎ 061 834 8418)

LEVER, Sir (Tresham) Christopher Arthur Lindsay; 3 Bt (UK 1911); s of Sir Tresham Joseph Philip Lever, 2 Bt, FRSL (d 1975); *b* 9 Jan 1932; *Educ* Eton, Trinity Coll Cambridge (MA); *m* 1, 1970 (m dis 1974), Susan Mary, da of late John A Nicholson, of Crossmolina, Co Mayo; m 2, 1975, Linda Weightman McDowell, da of late James Jepson Goulden, of Tennessee, USA; *Heir* none; *Career* Lt 17/21 Lancers 1950; Peat, Marwick, Mitchell & Co 1954-55, Kitcat & Aitken 1955-56, dir: John Barran & Sons Ltd 1956-64; author; patron Rhino Rescue Tst 1985- (tstee 1986-), cncl Soc for the Protection of Animals in N Africa 1986-88; conslt Zoo Check Tst 1984-; tstee: Int Tst for Nature Conservation 1980 (vice-pres 1986-), Migraine Tst 1983-; chm African Fund for Endangered Wildlife (UK) 1987-, chm: Br Tst for Ornithology National Centre Appeal 1986; memb: cncl Br Tst for Ornithology 1988-, Skin Disease Res Fund Appeal Ctee 1988-; patron Skin Treatment and Res Tst 1988-; chm Lever Tst 1988-; hon life memb Brontë Soc 1988; *Books* Goldsmiths and Silversmiths of England (1975), The Naturalized Animals of the British Isles (1977; paperback edition 1979); Wildlife '80: the World Conservation Yearbook (contrib 1980), Evolution of Domesticated Animals (contrib 1984), Naturalized Mammals of the World (1985), Beyond the Bars: The Zoo Dilemma (contrib 1987), Naturalized Birds of the World (1987), Accent on Animals (contrib 1989); *Recreations* nature conservation, fishing, golf; *Clubs* Buck's; *Style—* Sir Christopher Lever, Bt; Newell House, Winkfield, Windsor, Berks SL4 4SE (☎ 0344 882604)

LEVER, Pamela Lady; Clodagh Pamela; da of Lt-Col the Hon Malcolm Bowes-Lyon, CBE (d 1957), and formerly w of Lord Malcolm Avondale Douglas-Hamilton, OBE, DFC (d 1964); *b* 15 July 1908; *m* 1962, as his 2 w, Sir Tresham Joseph Philip Lever, 2 Bt (d 1975); *Style—* Pamela, Lady Lever; Lessudden, St Boswells, Roxburghshire

LEVER, Jeremy Frederick; QC (1972); s of Arnold Lever (d 1980), and Elizabeth Cramer, *née* Nathan; *b* 23 June 1933; *Educ* Bradfield, Univ Coll Oxford, Nuffield Coll Oxford, All Souls Coll Oxford (MA); *Career* 2 Lt RA (E African Artillery) 1952-53; barr Gray's Inn 1957 bencher 1985; pres Oxford Union Soc 1957, tstee 1972-77 and 1988-; dir (non exec): Dunlop Hldgs Ltd 1973-80, Wellcome Fndn Ltd 1983-; govr Berkhamsted Schs 1985-; fell All Souls Coll Oxford 1957- (sub-warden 1982-84, sr dean 1988-); memb cncl and ctee of mgmnt Br Inst of Int and Comparative Law; *Books* The Law of Restrictive Trading Agreements (1964), Chitty on Contracts (ed 1961, 1968, 1972, 1977); *Recreations* mountain walking, music; *Clubs* Garrick; *Style—* Jeremy Lever, Esq, QC; 59 Doughty St, London WC1N 2LS (01 831 0351); All Souls College, Oxford OX1 4AL (☎ 0865 279379); Gray's Inn Chambers, Gray's Inn, London WC1R 5JA (☎ 01 405 7211, fax 01 405 2084, telex 8954665 VB STLX G, ref KQC)

LEVER, John Kenneth; s of Kenneth Lever, and Doris Lever; *b* 24 Feb 1949; *Educ* Dane Secdy Sch Ilford; *m* 1983, Christine Ann, da of John Wilkinson; 1 da; *Career* cricketer, played for England in 20 Test Matches; *Clubs* Eccentric, Wanstead GC; *Style—* John Lever, Esq; c/o Essex CCC, New Writtle St, Chelmsford, Essex

LEVER, Paul Ronald Scott; s of Thomas Denis Lever, of Conningsby House, Sandygate, Sheffield, and Mary Barclay, *née* Scott; *b* 9 Dec 1940; *m* 23 Sept 1964, Elisabeth Barbra, da of Sir Richard Hughes, Bt (d 1970), of Rivelin Cottage, Hollow Meadows, Sheffield; 1 s (Christopher Mark b 17 July 1965), 2 da (Alison Clare b 25 Feb 1967, Catherine Elisabeth b 17 June 1969); *Career* md Tower Housewares (subsidiaries of TI Gp) 1979-83, chm darius Industl Investmts 1983-86, md Crown Paints Div (subsidiary of Reed Int) 1986-88, vice-chm Clarich Investmts Ltd 1987-, md Crown Berger Europe Ltd 1988- (chm Ireland 1988-); chm: Curpinol Ltd 1988-, Williams Euro Consumer Prodns Div (subsidiaries of Williams Hldgs plc) 1989-; Int Mgmnt Centre Europe: industl fell Mktg and business policy 1984, industl prof strategic mgmnt 1986, elected master teacher 1987, elected cncl memb 1988; memb ed bd Mgmnt Digest 1987; *Recreations* listening to classical music, watching cricket, fishing, shooting; *Style—* Paul Lever, Esq; Crown Berger Europe Ltd, Crown House, Hollins Rd, Darwen, Lancs BB3 OBG (☎ 0254 74951, fax 0606 40583, car 0836 382157, telex 63150)

LEVER, Baroness; Ray Rosalia; JP (Manchester); da of Dr Leonard Levene (d 1971), of Leicester, by his w Yetta (d 1965); *b* 23 Sept 1916; *Educ* Cheltenham Ladie's Coll; *m* 1939, Baron Lever (Life Peer, d 1977), s of Bernard Lever (d 1942); 1 s, 1 da; *Style—* The Rt Hon the Lady Lever, JP; 9 Plowley Close, Didsbury, Manchester M20 8DB (☎ 061 445 3456)

LEVER OF MANCHESTER, Baron (Life Peer UK 1979); (Norman) Harold Lever; PC (1969); s of late (Hyman) Bernard Lever, and Bertha Lever, of Manchester; *b* 15 Jan 1914; *Educ* Manchester GS, Manchester Univ; *m* 1 (m dis), Ethel Samuels; m 2, 1 March 1945, Betty (d 1948), da of Myer Woolfe, and formerly w of Monty Featherman; 1 da; m 3, 1962, Mrs Diane Zihlka, da of late Saleh Bashi, of Geneva; 3 da; *Career* sits as Lab Peer in House of Lords; barr Middle Temple; MP (L) Manchester Exchange 1945-50, Manchester Cheetham 1950-74, Manchester Central 1974-79; jt parly under-sec of state, Dept of Economic Affairs 1967, fin sec to the Treasy 1967-69, paymaster gen 1969-70, chm Public Accounts Ctee 1970-73, tres Socialist Int 1971-73, chllr Duchy of Lancaster 1974-79; dir: Guardian and Manchester Evening News 1979-, Singer & Friedlander 1984-; memb House of Lords Bridge Team in match against Commons chm Jt Ctee on Art and Antiques Trade and Auction Houses 1982-85, memb Franks Ctee on Falklands 1982; London Interstate Bank Ltd, chm Britannia Arrow Hldgs plc, dir memb of the Int Advsy Bd of the Creditanstalt Bankverein; govr: LSE, Manchester Univ, chm English-Speaking Union; chm of Tstees of Royal Acad Tst, 1981-87, Tstee Royal Opera House 1974-82; *Style—* The Rt Hon the Lord Lever of Manchester, PC; House of Lords, SW1

LEVERHULME, 3 Viscount (UK 1922); Sir Philip William Bryce Lever; 3 Bt (1911), KG (1988), TD, JP; also Baron Leverhulme (UK 1917); s of 2 Viscount (d 1949), by his 1 w, Marion; *b* 1 July 1915; *Educ* Eton, Trinity Coll Cambridge; *m* 1937, Margaret Ann (d 1973), da of John Moon, of Tiverton, Devon; 3 da (Hon Mrs Susan Pakenham, Hon Mrs Apsion, Hon Mrs Heber-Percy); *Career* advsy dir Unilever Ltd; lord-lt for City and County of Chester 1949-; Hon Col Queen's Own Yeo 1979- and RAC, TAVR 1972-; memb Nat Hunt Ctee 1961 (steward 1965-68), dep sr steward Jockey Club 1970-73, sr steward 1973-76; chllr Liverpool Univ 1980-; pres NW Tourist Bd 1982-; FRCS; KStJ; *Clubs* Boodle's, Jockey; *Style—* The Rt Hon the Viscount Leverhulme, KG, TD, JP; Thornton Manor, Thornton Hough, Wirral, Merseyside (☎ 051 336 4834); Flat 6, Kingston House East, Princes Gate, Kensington, London SW7 1LJ (☎ 01-589-9322); Badanloch, Kinbrace, Sutherland

LEVESON, Lord; Granville George Fergus Leveson Gower; s and h of 5 Earl Granville, MC; *b* 10 Sept 1959; *Career* a page of honour to HM Queen Elizabeth, the Queen Mother 1973-; *Style—* Lord Leveson

LEVESON GOWER, Hon Niall James; s of 5 Earl Granville, MC; *b* 24 August 1963; *Style—* The Hon Niall Leveson Gower

LEVEY, Lady Melissa Geraldine Florence; *née* Bligh; da (by 3 w) of 9 Earl of Darnley (d 1955); *b* 1945; *m* 1965, Don Manuel Torrado y de Fontcuberta (d 1980); 1 s (Manuel Ivo b 1966), 2 da (Maria Melissa b 1968, Victoria Irene b 1973); m 2, 1985, Rev Colin Russell Levey; *Style—* Lady Melissa Levey; The Rectory, Elmley Lovett, Droitwich, Worcs WR9 0PU (☎ 0299 250255)

LEVEY, Sir Michael Vincent; LVO (1965); s of O L H Levey and Gladys Mary Milestone; *b* 8 June 1927; *Educ* Oratory Sch, Exeter Coll Oxford; *m* 1954, Brigid Brophy, *qv*; 1 da; *Career* serv Army 1945-48; asst keeper Nat Gallery 1951-66, dir 1973-86; Slade Prof of Fine Art Cambridge 1963-64, hon fellow Exeter Coll Oxford 1973; FBA, FRSL; kt 1980; *Books* 14 vols non-fiction; 3 vols fiction; *Style—* Sir Michael Levey; Flat 3, 185 Old Brompton Rd, London SW5 0AN (☎ 01 373 9335)

LEVEY, Hon Mrs (Moyra Christine); *née* Wilson; da of Baron Wilson of Radcliffe (d 1983); *b* 5 Feb 1943; *Educ* Stand GS Whitefield, Birmingham U; *m* 1964, Dr Arthur Crowther (d 1979); 2 da (Katherine, Caroline); m 2, 1983, Joseph Levey (d 1985); *Recreations* badminton, golf, bridge; *Style—* The Hon Mrs Levey; Acre Lane, Cheadle Hulme, Cheshire

LEVI, Prof Peter (Chad Tigar); s of Herbert Simon Levi (d 1956), of Ruislip, Middlx, and Edith Mary Tigar (d 1973); *b* 16 May 1931; *Educ* Beaumont Oxford (MA); *m* 31 Mar 1977, Deirdre, da of Hon Dennis Craig, MBE (d 1971), of Bath; *Career* tutor and lectr Campion Hall Oxford 1965-76, lectr in classics Christ Church Oxford 1979-82, prof of poetry Univ of Oxford 1984-89; fell St Catherine's Coll 1977-; author numerous volumes of poetry and some prose incl: poetry The Gravel Ponds (1960), Water Rock and Sand (1962), The Shearwaters (1985), Fresh Water Sea Water (1966), Ruined Abbeys (1968), Life is a Platform (1971), Death is a Pulpit (1971), Collected Poems (1976), Five Ages (1978), Private Ground (1981), The Echoing Green (1983), Shakespeare Birthday (1985); prose: Beaumont (1961), The Lightgarden of the Angel King (1973), In Memory of David Jones (1975), The Noise Made By Poems (1976), The Hill of Kronos (1980), The Flutes of Autumn (1983), A History of Greek Literature (1985), The Frontiers of Paradise (1987), To The Goat (1988), Life and Times of Wm Shakespeare (1988); thrillers: The Head in the Soup (1979), Grave Witness (1985), Knit One Drop One (1987); translations: The Psalms (1976), Marko the Prince (1983), The Holy Gospel of St John (1985); memb FSA, FRSL; *Recreations* a little quiet touring, visiting small museums; *Clubs* Beefsteak; *Style—* Prof Peter Levi; St Catherines Coll, Oxford

LEVIN, (Henry) Bernard; s of late Phillip Levin and Rose, *née* Racklin; *b* 19 August 1928; *Educ* Christ's Hosp, LSE (BSc); *Career* journalist; author; *Style—* Bernard

Levin, Esq; c/o Curtis Brown Ltd, 162-168 Regent St, London W1

LEVINE, Sir Montague (Bernard); s of Philip Levine (decd); *b* 15 May 1922; *Educ* RCS in Ireland, RCP in Ireland; *m* 1959, Dr Rose Gold; 1 s, 1 da; *Career* gen practitioner; dep coroner Inner S London, clinical tutor in gen practice St Thomas' Hosp 1972-; author; kt 1979; *Books* Interparental Violence and its Effect on Children; *Style*— Sir Montague Levine; Gainsborough House, 120 Ferndene Rd, Herne Hill, SE24 (T 01 274 5554)

LEVINE, Sydney; s of Rev Isaac Levine (d 1957), of Bradford, and Miriam, *née* Altman (d 1967); *b* 4 Sept 1923; *Educ* Bradford GS, Leeds Univ (LLB); *m* 29 March 1959, Cécile Rona, da of Joseph Rubinstein (d 1987), of Dublin; 3 s (Iain David b 1960, Simon Mark b 1962, Colin Philip b 1964), 1 da (Emma Rachel b 1969); *Career* called to the Bar Inner Temple 1952, rec of the Crown Crt 1975; *Recreations* acting and directing in amateur theatre, gardening, marathon running; *Style*— Sydney Levine, Esq; 2A Primley Park Road, Alwoodley, Leeds 17 (☎ 0532 683769); Broadway House, 9 Bank St, Bradford 1 (☎ 0274 722560, fax: 0274 370708)

LEVINGE, Jane, Lady; Jane Rosemary; *née* Stacey; *m* 1976, as his 2 w, Maj Sir Richard Vere Henry Levinge, 11 Bt, MBE (d 1984); *Clubs* Naval; *Style*— Jane, Lady Levinge; Abbey Lodge, Rectory Lane, Itchen Abbas, Hants

LEVINGE, Sir Richard George Robin; 12 Bt (I 1704), of High Park, Westmeath; s of Sir Richard Vere Henry Levinge, 11 Bt, MBE (d 1984), and his 1 w, Barbara, da of George Jardine Kidston, CMG; *b* 18 Dec 1946; *m* 1, 1969, Hilary Jane, da of Dr Derek Mark, of Wingfield, Bray, Co Wicklow; 2, 1979, Donna Maria d'Ardia Caracciolo, da of HE Prince Frederico Caracciolo, of Grange Rd, Rathfarnham, co Dublin; *Style*— Sir Richard Levinge, Bt; Clohamon House, Bunclody, Co Wexford

LEVY, Allan Edward; s of Sidney Levy, and Mabel, *née* Lewis; *b* 17 August 1942; *Educ* Bury GS, Hull Univ (LLB), Inns of Ct Law Sch; *Career* called to the Bar Inner Temple 1969, South Eastern Circuit; memb cncl of Justice, speaker at Seventh Int Congress on Child Abuse in Rio de Janeiro 1988; *Books* Wardship Proceedings (1 edn 1982, 2 edn 1987), Custody and Access (1 edn 1983), Adoption of Children (with J F Josling, 10 edn 1985); *Recreations* travel, reading; *Clubs* Reform; *Style*— Allan E Levy, Esq; 1 Temple Gardens, Temple, London, EC4Y 9BB (☎ 01 353 3737, fax 01 583 0018)

LEVY, Sir Ewart Joseph Maurice; 2 Bt (UK 1913), JP (Leics 1934); s of Sir Maurice Levy, 1 Bt, DL, JP (d 1933); *b* 10 May 1897; *Educ* Harrow; *m* 1932, Hylda Muriel (d 1970), da of Sir Albert Levy (d 1937); 1 da; *Career* Royal Pioneer Corps 1940-45 (despatches), Lt-Col 1944; High Sheriff Leics 1937; *Clubs* Reform; *Style*— Sir Ewart Levy, Bt, JP; Welland House, Weston-by-Welland, Market Harborough, Leics

LEVY, George Joseph; s of Percy Levy (d 1967); *b* 21 May 1927; *Educ* Oundle; *m* 1952, Wendy Yetta, da of Philip Blairman (d 1972); 1 s, 3 da; *Career* chm H Blairman & Sons Ltd 1965- (dir 1955), pres Br Antique Dealers Assoc 1974-76; chm: Grosvenor House Antiques Fair 1978-79, Somerset House Art Treasures Exhibition 1979, Friends of Kenwood 1979-, Burlington Fine Art and Antique Dealers Fair 1980-82, London Historic House Museums Liaison Gp English Heritage 1985; memb cncl Jewish Museum 1978; *Recreations* photography, theatre, tennis; *Style*— George Levy, Esq; 27 Oakhill Ave, London NW3 (☎ 01 495 1730)

LEVY, Dr Paul; s of Hyman Solomon Levy (d 1980), of Kentucky USA, and Mrs Shirley Singer Meyers; *b* 26 Feb 1941; *Educ* Univ of Chicago (BA, MA), Univ Coll London, Harvard Univ (PhD), Nuffield Coll Oxford; *m* 1977, Penelope, da of Clifford Marcus (d 1952); 2 da (Tatyana b 1981, Georgia b 1983); *Career* journalist and lapsed don; food and wine ed The Observer 1980-, frequent broadcaster on radio and TV; tstee Strachey Tst; FRSL; *Books* Out to Lunch (1986), The Official Foodie Handbook (with Ann Barr, 1984), G E Moore and the Cambridge Apostles (1977, new edn 1989), The Shorter Strachey (ed with Michael Holroyd, 1980, new edn 1989); *Recreations* being cooked for, drinking better wine; *Clubs* Groucho, Wednesday; *Style*— Paul Levy, Esq; c/o The Observer, Chelsea Bridge House, Queenstown Rd, London SW8 4NN (☎ 01 350 3466)

LEVY, Philip Grenville; s of Sydney George Levy, of London, and Ella-Mary *née* Jacob (d 1952); *b* 11 Sept 1946; *Educ* Clifton, Manchester Univ (LLB); *m* 16 July 1972, Sheila Michell, da of Ian Baxter, of London; 1 s (James b 1980), 1 da (Tania b 1977); *Career* barr Inner Temple Gray's Inn; chm Harrow SDP 1986-87; elected memb Harrow Police and Community Consultative Ctee 1987-; *Recreations* bridge, music; *Style*— Philip Levy, Esq; 11 South Square, Grays Inn, London WC1 (☎ 01 831 6974)

LEVY, Victor Raphael; s of Moise Edward Joseph Levy, and Thelma, *née* Goide; *b* 14 April 1951; *Educ* UCS, Univ of Manchester (BSc); *Career* tax ptnr Arthur Andersen and Co; FCA, FTII; *Style*— Victor Levy, Esq; Arthur Anderson & Co, 1 Surrey St, London WC2R 2PS (☎ 01 438 3473, fax 01 831 1133, telex 8812711)

LEWANDO, Sir Jan Alfred; CBE (1968); s of Maurice Lewando, of Manchester, and Eugenie, *née* Goldsmid; *b* 31 May 1909; *Educ* Manchester GS, Manchester Univ; *m* 1948, Nora, da of William Slavouski; 3 da; *Career* serv WWII: Br Army Staff Washington DC and Br Min of Supply Mission 1941-45, Lt-Col 1943; joined Marks & Spencer Ltd 1929, dir 1954-70; chm Carrington Viyella Ltd 1970-75; pres Br Textile Confedn 1972-73; dir: Heal and Son Hldgs Ltd 1975-82, Bunzl Gp 1976-86, W A Baxter & Sons Ltd 1975-, Johnson Industs Inc (USA) 1976-85; Royal Worcester Spode Ltd 1978-79; memb: Br Overseas Trade Bd 1972-77, European Trade Ctee 1973-83; memb Br Nat Export Cncl 1969-71; chm Appeal Ctee Br Inst Radiology 1979-84; vice-pres Transport Tst 1973-; vice-chm Clothing Export Cncl 1966-70; CBIM, FRSA; Companion Textile Inst 1972; Legion of Merit (USA) 1946; kt 1974; *Style*— Sir Jan Lewando, CBE; Davidge House, Knotty Green, Beaconsfield, Bucks (☎ Beaconsfield (049 46) 4987)

LEWEN, John Henry; CMG (1977); s of Carl Henry Lewen (d 1968), and Alice, *née* Mundy (d 1983); *b* 6 July 1920; *Educ* Christ's Hosp, King's Coll Cambridge (MA); *m* 1945, Emilienne Alette Julie Alida, da of Robert Leon Cesar Galant (d 1958); 3 s (Michael, Stephan, Nigel); *Career* Royal Signals 1940-45, Capt; HM Dip (formerly Foreign) Serv 1946-79; serv: Lisbon, Rangoon, Rio de Janeiro, Warsaw, Rabat; consul-gen Jerusalem 1967-70; Dip Serv inspr 1970-73; seconded to Cncl of Ministers EEC 1973-75; ambass Maputo (Mozambique) 1975-79; OStJ 1969; *Recreations* singing, sailing, history; *Style*— J H Lewen, Esq, CMG; 1 Brimley Rd, Cambridge CB4 2DQ (☎ 0223 359101)

LEWER, Michael Edward; QC (1983); s of Lt-Col Stanley Gordon Lewer (d 1985), of Ashtead, Surrey, and Jeanie Mary, *née* Hay (d 1980); *b* 1 Dec 1933; *Educ* Tonbridge, Oriel Coll Oxford (MA); *m* 1965, Bridget Mary, da of Harry Anderson Clifford Gill (d 1980), of Buckland, Surrey; 2 s (William b 1966, Simon b 1969), 2 da (Natasha b 1967, Louise b 1977); *Career* barr Gray's Inn 1958, rec 1983; memb Criminal Injuries Compensation Bd 1986; *Clubs* Western, Glasgow; *Style*— Michael Lewer, Esq, QC; 99 Queens Drive, London N4; Whitehouse Cottage, Horham, Suffolk; Farrars Bldg, Temple, London EC4

LEWERS, Very Rev Benjamin Hugh; s of Dr H B Lewers, DSO, OBE (d 1950), of Ilfracombe, Devon, and Coral Helen Lewers; *b* 25 Mar 1932; *Educ* Sherborne, Selwyn Coll Cambridge (MA); *m* 1957, Sara, da of Cyprian Claud Blagden; 3 s (Timothy, Michael, Thomas); *Career* Nat Serv 2 Lieut The Devon Regt; ordained: deacon 1962, priest 1963; curate St Mary Northampton 1962-65, priest i/c Church of The Good Shepherd Hounslow 1965-68, industl chaplain Heathrow Airport 1968-75, vicar Newark 1975-80, rector 1980-81, provost Derby 1981-; *Recreations* cricket, gardening, music, wine, rug making; *Style*— The Very Rev the Provost of Derby; The Provost's House, 9 Highfield Rd, Derby DE3 1GX (☎ 0332 42971); Cathedral Office, St Michael's House, Queen St, Derby DE1 3DT (☎ 0332 41201)

LEWES, Bishop of 1977-; Rt Rev Peter John Ball; s of Thomas James Ball (Capt WWI, d 1966), of Eastbourne, and Kathleen Obena, *née* Bradley-Morris (d 1980); *b* 14 Feb 1932; *Educ* Lancing, Queens' Coll Cambridge (MA), Wells Theol Coll; *Career* ordained: deacon 1956, priest 1957; curate Rottingdean Chichester 1956-58, novice Society of the Sacred Mission 1958-60, prior Community of the Glorious Ascension 1960-77, licence to officiate Birmingham 1965-66, priest i/c Hoar Cross Lichfield 1966-69, licence to officiate Bath and Wells 1969-77, canon and prebendary Chichester 1977-; fell Woodard Corpn 1961-88; memb Advsy Cncl for Religious Ctees 1980-; govr: Wellington Coll 1986-, Radley Coll 1987-, Eastbourne Coll 1978-; select preacher Univ of Oxford 1988; Cambridge Blue for squash 1954; *Recreations* squash, music; *Style*— The Rt Rev the Bishop of Lewes; The Rectory, Litlington, Polegate, E Sussex BN26 5RB (☎ 0323 870387)

LEWIN, Hon Jonathan James; yr s of Adm of the Fleet Baron Lewin, KG, GCB, LVO, DSC; *b* 20 May 1959; *Educ* Merchant Taylors', Trinity Coll Cambridge (BA); *Career* musician and writer; rock music critic for local BBC radio station; *Recreations* music, writing; *Style*— The Hon Jonathan Lewin

LEWIN, Adm of the Fleet Baron (Life Peer UK 1982), of Greenwich, in Greater London; Terence Thornton Lewin; KG (1983), GCB (1976, KCB 1973), LVO (1959), DSC (1942); s of E H Lewin (d 1963); *b* 19 Nov 1920; *Educ* Judd Sch Tonbridge; *m* 1944, Jane, da of Rev Charles James Branch Evans (d 1956); 2 s, 1 da; *Career* RN 1939, serv WWII Home and Med Fleets (despatches); cmd: HMS Corunna 1955-56, HMY Britannia 1957-58; Capt 1958; cmd: HMS Urchin 1962, HMS Tenby 1963, Dartmouth Trg Sqdn 1962-63, HMS Hermes 1966-67; Rear Adm 1968; asst chief of Naval Staff (Policy) MOD 1968-69, Flag Offr second in cmd Far E Fleet 1969-70, Vice-Adm 1970, vice-chief of Naval Staff 1971-73, Adm 1973, C-in-C Fleet, Allied C-in-C Channel and C-in-C Eastern Atlantic Area 1973-75, C-in-C Naval Home Cmd 1975-77, chief of Naval Staff and First Sea Lord 1977-79, Adm of the Fleet 1979, chief of Def Staff 1979-82; Naval ADC to HM The Queen 1967-68, Flag ADC to HM The Queen 1975-77 and first and princ ADC 1977-79; chm of tstee Nat Maritime Museum 1981-87, er bro Trinity House 1975; pres Br Schs Exploring Soc, pres Shipwrecked Mariners Soc; hon Freeman Skinners' Co and Shipwrights' Co; Hon DSc City Univ; *Style*— Adm of the Fleet the Rt Hon the Lord Lewin, KG, GCB, LVO, DSC; House of Lords, London SW1

LEWIN, Hon Timothy Charles Thornton; er s of Adm of the Fleet Baron Lewin, KG, GCB, LVO, DSC; *b* 1947; *Style*— The Hon Timothy Lewin; c/o Adm of the Fleet the Rt Hon the Lord Lewin, KG, GCB, LVO, DSC, House of Lords, London SW1

LEWINSOHN, Max Robert; *b* 12 Oct 1946; *m* Joan Krystyna, 3 children; *Career* dep chm Dominion Int Gp plc, chm Southwest Resources plc, dep chm Top Value Industs plc; FCA, ATII; *Recreations* tennis, skiing, windsurfing; *Style*— Max Lewinsohn, Esq; Dominion International Group plc, Dominion House, 49 Parkside, Wimbledon, London SW19 5NB (☎ 01 946 5522, fax 01 947 4770)

LEWIS, HE Sir Allen Montgomery; GCMG (1979), GCVO (1985), GCSL (1986); s of George Ferdinand Montgomery Lewis (decd), and Ida Louisa, *née* Barton; *b* 26 Oct 1909; *Educ* St Mary's Coll St Lucia, London (LLB); *m* 1936, Edna Leofrida, da of Thomas Alexander Theobalds (decd); 3 s, 2 da; *Career* barr St Lucia 1931, Middle Temple 1946; MLC St Lucia 1943-51; actg Puisne judge Windward and Leewards Islands 1955-56, QC 1956, cmmr for reform and revison of laws St Lucia 1954-58; judge: Fed Supreme Ct 1959-62, Br Caribbean Ct of Appeal 1962, Ct of Appeal Jamaica 1962-67 (actg pres Ct of Appeal 1966, actg chief justice Jamaica 1966); chief Justice WI Assoc States Supreme Ct 1967-72; chm Nat Dvpt Corpn St Lucia 1972-74; govr of St Lucia 1974-79, govr-gen of St Lucia 1979-80 and 1982-87; chllr Univ of the WI 1975-89; Hon LLD UWI 1974; KStJ 1975; kt 1968; *Publications* Revised Edition of Laws of St Lucia (1957); *Recreations* gardening, swimming; *Clubs* St Lucia Yacht, St Lucia Golf; *Style*— HE Sir Allen Lewis, GCSL, GCMG, GCVO, QC; Beaver Lodge, The Morne, Castries, St Lucia (☎ 27285)

LEWIS, Adm Sir Andrew (Mackenzie); KCB (1971); s of late Rev Cyril F Lewis, of Gilston, Herts, and Effie M, *née* Mackenzie; *b* 24 Jan 1918; *Educ* Haileybury; *m* 1943, Rachel Elizabeth (d 1983), da of Vice-Adm Eustace La Trobe Leatham, CB (d 1935); 2 s (Christopher, David); *Career* Capt RN 1955, C-in-C Naval Home Cmd 1972-74, ADC to HM the Queen 1972-74, DL (1975) Essex, Lord Lt Essex 1978-; *Clubs* Brooks's; *Style*— Adm Sir Andrew Lewis, KCB; Coleman's Farm, Finchingfield, Essex CM7 4PE

LEWIS, Anthony Jonas; *Career* memb Stock Exchange 1950; dir and sr ptnr Smith Bros plc, chm Smith NC plc; *Style*— Anthony Lewis, Esq; Ashley House, 11 Rivercourt Rd, London W6 9LD (☎ 01 748 2753); Smith New Court plc, Chetwynd House, 24 St Swithins Lane, London EC4N 8AE (☎ 01 626 1544)

LEWIS, Anthony Meredith; s of Lt-Col GVL Lewis (d 1985), and Mrs G Lewis, *née* Fraser, of Twickenham, Middx; *b* 15 Nov 1940; *Educ* Rugby, St Edmund Hall Oxford (MA); *m* 26 July 1970, Ewa Maria Anna, da of Stanislaw Strawinski (d 1980); 1 s (Alexander Edward Meredith (Beetle) b 1 Oct 1976), 1 da (Antonina Kathryn (Nina) b 18 Sept 1981); *Career* articled clerk and slr Freshfields 1964-70, sr ptnr Joynson-Hicks 1986-(ptnr 1971-86); chm parish cncl 1982-85; memb Law Soc; *Recreations* shooting, skiing, tennis, cricket; *Style*— Anthony Lewis, Esq; 10 Maltravers St, London WC2R 3BS (☎ 01 836 8456, fax 01 379 7196, telex 268014 JHICKS G)

LEWIS, Hon Antony Thomas; JP (1979); s of 3 Baron Merthyr, KBE, PC (d 1977), and Violet, *née* Meyrick; *b* 4 June 1947; *Educ* Eton, Univ of Wales (LLM); *m* 1974, Mary Carola Melton, da of Rev Humphrey John Paine; *Career* barr Inner Temple 1971; lectr in law Univ Coll Cardiff 1976-; *Style—* The Hon Antony Lewis, JP; The Skreen, Erwood, Builth Wells, Powys; Dept of Law, University Coll, Cardiff

LEWIS, Sir (William) Arthur; s of George Ferdinand Lewis, of Castries, St Lucia, W Indies, by his w Ida Louisa, *née* Barton; bro of Sir Allen Lewis (*qv*); *b* 23 Jan 1915; *Educ* St Mary's Coll Castries, LSE; *m* 1947, Gladys Isabel, da of William Jacobs of Grenada; 2 da; *Career* lectr LSE 1938-47; Stanley Jevons Professor of Political Economy at Univ of Manchester 1948-1959; vice-chllr Univ of West Indies 1960-63, prof of economics and int affairs Princeton Univ 1963-68; James Madison prof of political economy, Princeton Univ 1968-; kt 1963; *Style—* Sir Arthur Lewis; Woodrow Wilson School, Princeton University, Princeton, New Jersey, USA

LEWIS, Arthur William John; s of J Lewis (d 1958); *b* 1917; *Educ* Elementary Sch, Borough Poly; *m* 1940, Lucy Ethel, da of J Clack (d 1956); 1 da; *Career* formerly trade union official Nat Union of Gen and Municipal Workers, MP (L) W Ham (Upton) 1945-50, W Ham (N) 1950-74, Newham (NW) 1974-83; *Style—* Arthur Lewis, Esq; 1 Doveridge Gdns, Palmers Green, N13

LEWIS, Dr Barry Winston; s of Alfred Lewis (d 1967), of Essex, and Winifred Alice, *née* Doggett (d 1984); *b* 31 Mar 1941; *Educ* Hornchurch GS, UCH Med Sch (MB BS, DCH); *m* 1, 17 April 1962 (m dis 1982), Rosemary Agnes, da of James Bryant Petter (d 1988); 1 s (Timothy John Barry b 1962), 1 da (Catherine Rosemary b 1964); m 2, 24 June 1982, Josephine Caroline, da of Robert William Cunningham (d 1987), of Swansea; 1 s (Hugo Frederick b 1987, d 1988); *Career* conslt paediatrician London 1973-, chm London Children's and Women's Hosp 1987-(dir 1981-); fell Hunterian Soc (1983); BPA (1973, memb cncl 1979-82), BMA, FRSM, FRCP; *Recreations* shooting, horses (racing and breeding), cricket; *Clubs* RSM; *Style—* Dr Barry Lewis; Bungeons Farm, Barking, Suffolk IP6 8HN (☎ 0449 721 992); 17 Wimpole St, London W1M 7AD (☎ 01 486 0044, car tel 0836 271 020)

LEWIS, His Honour Bernard; s of late Solomon Lewis, and Jeannette Lewis; *b* 1 Feb 1905; *Educ* Trinity Hall Cambridge (MA); *m* 1934, Harriette, da of late I A Waine, of Dublin, London and Nice; 1 s (Bryan Timothy Brendan); *Career* barr Lincoln's Inn 1929, co ct judge 1966, circuit judge 1972-80; *Recreations* revolver shooting, bricklaying; *Clubs* Reform, Ham & Petersham Rifle & Pistol, Aula, Cambridge Soc; *Style—* His Hon Bernard Lewis; Trevelyan House, Arlington Rd, St Margarets, Twickenham, Middx (☎ 01 892 1841)

LEWIS, Bernard Walter; CBE (1973), JP (Essex 1970); s of Walter Watson Lewis (d 1949), of Lincoln, and Florence Teresa, *née* Greenbury (d 1979); *b* 24 July 1917; *Educ* Lincoln Sch, Manchester Univ; *m* 12 May 1943, Joyce Ilston, da of James Issac Storey (d 1932), of Rothbury, Northumberland; 1 s (John Michael b 6 Aug 1947), 1 da (Susan Joan Ilston b 29 June 1945); *Career* joined King's Own Regt 1940, RASC 1941, Capt 1942, Maj 1943, serv Middle E 1940-46; chm and md Green's Flour Mills Ltd 1955-; chm: Edward Baker Hldgs Ltd 1983-, Finance Bd Cons Pty 1966-75, Flour Advsy Bureau 1979-; pres Nat Assoc of Br and Irish Millers 1985-86; chm: Dengie and Maldon Essex bench 1970-88, Maldon Harbour Cmmrs 1978-; Gen Tax Cmmr 1957-; memb: fin bd Cons Pty 1966-75, bd of govrs Plume Sch 1968-83; Liveryman Worshipful Co of Bakers 1973; *Recreations* travel, gardening; *Clubs* RAC, United and Cecil, Essex; *Style—* Bernard Lewis, Esq, CBE, JP; Roughlees, 68 Highlands Drive, Maldon, Essex (☎ 0621 52981); Greens Flour Mills Ltd, Station Rd, Maldon, Essex CM9 7LE (☎ 0621 52696, fax 0621 54525, telex 987111)

LEWIS, Brian Geoffrey Marshall; s of Col Geoffrey Archibald Ernest Lewis (d 1977), of Tunbridge Wells, and Joan Isabel, *née* Stratford; *b* 1 Dec 1943; *Educ* Bethany Sch Goudhurst; *m* 29 June 1974, Elizabeth Jane, da of John Alexander Miller, of Heathfield, Sussex; 3 da (Sarah Isabel b 2 Aug 1976, Anna Charlotte, Claire Victoria twins b 10 April 1979); *Career* exec positions H J Heinz Ltd and Canada Dry (UK) Ltd; md Heron Cruisers Ltd Kent, dir Stanton Asset Mgmnt Kent; *Recreations* motor sports, point-to-point, eventing; *Style—* Brian Lewis, Esq; Stanton Asset Mgmnt Ltd, Stanton Hse, Romford Rd, Pembury, Kent TN2 4AY (☎ 089 282 5454, fax 089 282 2482, telex 94013002 LEAS G)

LEWIS, Prof Clifford Thomas; s of Arthur Charles Lewis, of Newport, Gwent (d 1975), and Florence Lewis, *née* Golding (d 1973); *b* 29 August 1923; *Educ* Newport HS, Queens' Coll Cambridge (MA), Imperial Coll London (PhD); *m* 19 July 1949, (Ada) Joan Lewis, da of George Augustine Willey, of Newport, Gwent (d 1964); 1 s (Julian b 12 Feb 1956), 1 da (Rosalind b 1958); *Career* Imperial Coll London: lectr insect physiology 1955-65, sr lectr 1965-74, reader 1974-78; Royal Holloway Coll (later Royal Holloway and Bedford new Coll): prof of zoology 1978-88, vice princ 1981-85, emeritus prof 1988-; visiting prof: UCLA Calfornia 1975, Ghana 1976, La Trobe Australia 1986; *Recreations* painting, sculpture, fell-walking; *Clubs* Athenaeum; *Style—* Prof Clifford Lewis; 9 Silwood Close, Ascot, Berks

LEWIS, Clive Hewitt; s of Sqdn Ldr Thomas Jonathen Lewis, OBE, AE, of Sway Wood Paddock, Mead End Rd, Sway, Hants, and Margrarita Eileen, *née* De Brule (d 1987); *b* 29 Mar 1936; *Educ* St Peter's Sch York; *m* 7 July 1961, Jane Penelope (Penny), da of Rowland Bolland White (d 1970), of Carr Lane, Sandal, Wakefield, Yorks; 2 s (Simon Nicholas Hewitt b 1962, Mark Hewitt b 1966), 1 da (Victoria (Jane) b 1968); *Career* Pilot Officer RAF 1956-58, Lt 40/41 Royal Tank Regt (TA) 1958-62; sr ptnr Clive Lewis and Ptnrs 1963-, dir St Modwen Properties plc 1985-, bd memb Merseyside Devpt Corp 1986-, chm RICS Journals Ltd 1987-, dir Surveyors Hldgs Ltd 1987-, pres gp divn RICS 1989-(sr vice-chm 1988-89); pres Land Aid Charitable Tst, worldwide FIABCI, Totteridge cc; Northern Co's Sprint Champion 1957, Cheshire Co Athlete; Freeman City of London 1983, Freeman Worshipful Co of Chartered Surveyors; FRICS 1961, FSVA 1980; *Recreations* cricket, tennis; *Clubs* Totteridge CC, MCC, Forty Club; *Style—* Clive Lewis, Esq; Oakhurst, 7 Totteridge Common, London N20 8LL (☎ 01 445 5109); 8/9 Stratton St, London W1X 5FD (☎ 01 499 1001, car tel 0860 327 127)

LEWIS, David; s of Leonard Lewis (d 1945), of London, and Clara, *née* Tauber (d 1974); *b* 2 June 1924; *m* 24 June 1951, Esther Elizabeth Ruth, da of Joseph Benjamin, of London; 3 s (Julian, Simon, Ben (twin)), 2 da (Debbie, Rachel (twin)); *Career* WWII navigator RAF Bomber Cmd 1943-47; CA; chm Lewis Tst Gp Ltd 1956-; FCA 1950-; *Recreations* flying, skiing, sailing; *Style—* David Lewis, Esq; Chelsea House, West Gate, Ealing, London W5 (☎ 01 998 8822)

LEWIS, David Gwynder; s of Gwynder Eudaf Lewis (d 1963), of Bryn-y-Groes, Sketty, Swansea, and Gwyneth, *née* Jones (d 1979); *b* 31 August 1942; *Educ* Rugby; *m* 2 July 1966, Susan Joyce, da of Andrew Agnew, of Crowborough; 1 s (George b 1972), 1 da (Alexandra b 1969); *Career* Warrant Offr TA C Battery Hon Artillery Co; banker Hambros Bank Ltd 1961- (dir 1979), md Hambro Pacific Hong Kong 1974-82, pres Hambro America New York 1982-85, dir Hambro Countrywide plc and other Hambro Gp Cos; ACIOB 1967; *Recreations* fishing, music, shooting; *Clubs* Turf, RAC, Madison Square Garden (NY); *Style—* D G Lewis, Esq; 57 Victoria Rd, London W8 5RH (☎ 01 937 2277); Hambros Bank Ltd, 41 Tower Hill, London EC3N 4HA (☎ 01 480 5000, fax 01 702 9827, car ☎ 0836 290027, telex 883851)

LEWIS, Col David Henry; OBE (1954), TD (1948), DL (Staffs 1958); s of David Lewis, JP (d 1942), of Cannock, Staffs; *b* 23 Feb 1914; *Educ* King Edward's HS Birmingham, St John's Coll Cambridge; *m* 1943, Denise Esmé, da of Col William John Beddows, MC, TD, JP, DL (d 1962), of Ackleton House, nr Wolverhampton; 2 da (Patricia m 1975 Jonathan Harvie, Elaine m 1981 Martin Hall); *Career* serv WWII, RA, France, BEF, RWAFF BAOR (despatches); engr; *Recreations* fishing, sailing; *Clubs* Army & Navy; *Style—* Col David Lewis, OBE, TD, DL; Ash Cottage, Corfton, nr Craven Arms, Shropshire (☎ 058 473 638)

LEWIS, David John; s of Eric John Lewis, of Nuneaton, Warks, and Vera May, *née* Heath (d 1981); *b* 18 Oct 1942; *Educ* King Edward VI GS; *m* 5 Aug 1967, Vyvian Christine Dawn, da of Eric Hutton Stewart (d 1981), of Coventry; 2 da (Sophie b 1972, Anna b 1975); *Career* qualified CA 1966; Pannell Kerr Forster: Belize 1967-70, Barbados 1970-75 (ptnr 1972), Leeds 1975 (ptnr 1976, sr ptnr and chm 1986); memb: Leeds Jr C of C 1978-83, Otley Round Table 1980-83 (pres 1988), ctee W Yorks Soc of CAS 1982 - (tres 1982-85, sec 1985-); pres CAS Student Soc of Leeds 1984-85, govr Prince Henry's GS Otley 1988-; FICA 1966; *Clubs* Leeds, Leeds Taverners; *Style—* David Lewis, Esq; 1 Craven Park, Menston, Ilkley, W Yorks LS29 6EQ; Pannell Kerr Forster, Pannell House, 6 Queen St, Leeds LS1 2TW (☎ 0532 443 541, fax 0532 445 560)

LEWIS, David Wyn; s of Albert Brinley Lewis, of Newcastle-under-Lyme, Staffs, and Eiluned Gwynedd, *née* Hughes; *b* 1 Nov 1944; *Educ* High Storrs GS, Univ of Sheffield (BArch); *m* 10 July 1971, Meirlys; 1 s (Steffan Gwynedd b 1972), 1 da (Bethan Rhiannon b 1975); *Career* architect and interior designer; pres Sheffield and S Yorks Soc of Architects 1982-84; princ of David Lewis Associates 1978- (specialising large industl buildings, housing devpts, public houses and listed buildings); ARIBA 1971; *Recreations* antiques, gardening; *Style—* David Lewis, Esq; Delf View House, Eyam, Sheffield S30 1QW

LEWIS, Dr Dennis Aubrey; s of Joseph Lewis and Minnie *née* Coderofsky; *b* 1 Oct 1928; *Educ* Latymer Upper Sch Hammersmith, Chelsea Coll, London Univ (BSc, PhD); *m* 10 Nov 1956, Gillian Mary da of George Arthur Bratby, 2 s (Ian Andrew); *Career* serv RAF 1947-49; res chemist ICI Plastics Div 1956-68 (intelligence mangr 1968-81), dir ASLIB (The Assoc for Information Mgmnt) 1981-; CBI rep Br Library Advsy Cncl 1976-80, memb Br Cncl Library Advsy Ctee 1981-; cncllr Welwyn Garden Urban Dist 1968-74, Welwyn Hatfield Dist 1974 - (chm cncl 1976-77); fndr Welwyn Hatfield cncl of voluntary serv 1968-, pres Welwyn Hatfield Mencap soc 1981-, fndr pres Welwyn Garden City Chamber of Trade and Commerce 1984-86; FInstInfSci (1982); *Recreations* walking, trying to avoid gardening, admiring old churches; *Style—* Dr Dennis Lewis; ASLIB, Information House, 26/27 Boswell St, London, WC1N 3JZ (☎ 01 430 2671 fax 01 430 0514

LEWIS, Derek Compton; s of Kenneth Compton Lewis (d 1982), of Zeal Monachorum, Devon, and Marjorie Buick; *b* 9 July 1946; *Educ* Wellington, Queens' Coll Cambridge (MA), London Business Sch (MSc); *m* m, 26 April 1969, Louise, da of Dr D O Wharton (d 1986), of Colwyn Bay, North Wales; 2 da (Annabel b 1983, Julia b 1984); *Career* dir Granada Gp plc; *Clubs* Caledonian; 36 Golden Square, London W1R 4AH

LEWIS, Derek William Richard; s of percy William Lewis, of Worcs, and Edith, *née* Wisdom (d 1941); *b* 6 July 1936; *Educ* King's Sch Worcester; *m* 16 April 1963, Hedwig Albertine, da of Karl Kamps, of St Arnold, Rheine, W Germany; 2 s (Thomas b 1964, Ron b 1968), 1 da (Stephanie b 1967); *Career* RAEC 1957-59; The Hereford Times 1953-61, The Press Assoc 1961-62; BBC 1962-: seconded head of news Radio Zambia Lusaka 1966-68, TV news 1968; dep ed: 1970-74: The World at One, PM, The World This Weekend; ed 1974-76: The World Tonight, Newsdesk, The Financial World Tonight; ed 1976-88: The World at One (Radio Programme of the year 1976 and 1979), PM, The World this Weekend (Best Current Affairs Programme 1983); dir Skan Film Prodns Int Ltd, md Diplomatic News Servs 1988-; cncl memb The Royal Albert Hall; assoc memb For Press Assoc in London; *Recreations* music, assoc football, exploring US Nat Parks; *Clubs* Norwegian, Castaways, Ritz; *Style—* Derek Lewis, Esq; 4 Campbell Rd, London, W7 3EA (☎ 01 567 2478); BBC Radio News, Broadcasting Hse, London, W1A 1AA

LEWIS, His Hon Judge Esyr Gwilym; QC (1971); s of Rev Thomas William Lewis (d 1946), of Stamford Hill, London, and Mary Jane May, *née* Selway (d 1974); *b* 11 Jan 1926; *Educ* Mill Hill, Trinity Hall Cambridge (MA, LLB); *m* 1957, Elizabeth Anne Vidler, da of William Origen Hoffmann, of Bassett Southampton; 4 da (Emma, Clare, Alice, Charlotte); *Career* Intelligence Corps 1944-47; circuit judge (official referee) 1984; memb Criminal Injuries Compensation Bd 1977-84, bencher Gray's Inn 1978, ldr Wales & Chester Circuit 1978-80; *Recreations* watching rugby football; *Clubs* Garrick; *Style—* His Hon Judge Esyr Lewis, QC; 2 South Sq, Gray's Inn, London WC1R 5HP (☎ 01 405 5918); Law Cts, Strand, London

LEWIS, Prof Geoffrey; s of Ashley Lewis (d 1971), of London, and Jeanne Muriel, *née* Sintrop (d 1960); *b* 19 June 1920; *Educ* Univ Coll Sch Hampstead, St John's Coll Oxford (BA, MA, D Phil); *m* 26 July 1941, Raphaela Rhoda, da of Reuben Bale Seideman; 1 s (Jonathan b 1949), 1 da (Lalage b 1947, d 1976); *Career* WWII RAF pilot 1940-41, radar 1941-45; Oxford Univ: lectr in Turkish 1950-54, sr lectr in Islamic Studies 1954-64, sr lectr in Turkish 1964-86, prof of Turkish 1986-87; visiting prof: Robert Coll Istanbul 1959-68, Princeton Univ 1970-71 and 1974, UCLA 1975, Br Acad Leverhulme Turkey 1984; fell of St Antony's Coll Oxford 1961-87 (sub warden 1984-85, sr tutor 1985-87): memb Br Turkish Mixed Cmmn 1975-; Dr (Honoris Causa) Univ of the Bosphorus Istanbul 1986; memb Turkish Language Soc 1953, FBA 1979; Turkish Govt Cert of Merit 1973; *Books* Plotiniana Arabica (1959), Albucasis on Surgery and Instruments (1973), The Book of Dede Korkut (1974), Turkish Grammer (1988); *Recreations* bodging, etymology; *Style—* Prof Geoffrey Lewis; 25 Warnborough Rd, Oxford; Le Baousset, 06500 Menton, France

LEWIS, Geoffrey David; s of David Lewis (d 1973), of Brighton, E Sussex, and

Esther Grace, *née* Chatfield (d 1978); *b* 13 April 1933; *Educ* Varndean Sch Brighton, Univ of Liverpool (MA); *m* 7 July 1956, Frances May, da of Frederick John Wilderspin (d 1959), of Hove, E Sussex; 3 da (Jennifer b 1958, Heather b 1959, Esther b 1971); *Career* asst curator Worthing Museum and Art Gallery 1950-60, dep dir and keeper of antiquities Sheffield City Museum 1960-65; dir: Sheffield City Museums 1966-72, Liverpool City Museums 1972-74, Merseyside County Museums 1974-77, museum studies Univ of Leicester 1977-; pres: Yorks and Humberside Fedn of Museums and Art Galleries 1969-70, NW Fedn of Museums and Art Galleries 1976-77, Museums Assoc 1980-81, Int Cncl of Museums 1983-89; advsr at various times to: UNESCO, Egyptian Antiquities Orgn, Assoc of Met Authorities; FMA 1966, FSA 1969; *Books* Manual on Curatorship (co-ed with J M A Thompson et al, second edn 1986), An History of the Museums Association (1989); *Recreations* reading, writing, walking, computing; *Style—* Geoffrey Lewis, Esq; 4 Orchard Close, Wolvey, Kinckley, Leics LE10 3LR (☎ 0455 220708); Univ of Leics, Dept of Museum Studies, 105 Princess Rd South, Leics LE1 7LG (☎ 0533 523962, fax 0533 522200, telex 347250 LEICUN G)

LEWIS, Geoffrey Maurice; s of Sidney Lewis (d 1977), of Edghill, Vicarage Rd, Minehaead, Somerset, and Helen, *née* Redwood (d 1988); *b* 11 July 1929; *Educ* Taunton Sch, Trinity Hall Cambridge (MA); *m* 27 Aug 1960, Christine Edith, da of Lt-Col AD May, of The Barn, Weden Hall, Wendens Ambo, Essex; 1 s (Gregory b 1969), 3 da (Joanna b 1961, Sophie b 1964, Penelope b 1965); *Career* Nat Serv 2 Lt RA 1948-9; slr 1955; sr ptnr Hong Kong Off Herbert Smith 1983-86 (ptnr Herbert Smith 1960); seconded advsr securities legislation Hong Kong Govt 1988; memb Int Bar Assoc 1975; *Books* Lord Atkin (1983); *Recreations* music, walking, watching football; *Clubs* Garrick; *Style—* Geoffrey Lewis, Esq; Wenden Hall, Wendens Ambo, Saffron Walden, Essex CB11 4JZ (☎ 0799 40 744); Watling Ho, 35 Cannon St, London EC4M 5SD (☎ 01 489 8000, fax 01 236 5733, telex 886633)

LEWIS, Maj-Gen (Alfred) George; CBE (1969); s of late Louis and Edith Lewis; *b* 23 July 1920; *Educ* St Dunstan's Coll, King's Coll London; *m* 11 April 1946, Daye Neville, da of late Neville Greaves Hunt; 2 s (David b 1947, Graham b 1949), 2 da (Ruth (Mrs Kernohan) b 1953, Valerie b 1967); *Career* serv WWII: India, Burma, Malaya, Africa, Germany; cmd 15/19 The King's Royal Hussars 1961-63, dir Def Ops Requirements Staffs MOD 1967-68, Dep Cmdt RMCS 1968-70, dir gen Fighting Vehicles and Engrg Equipment MOD 1970-73; md Alvis Ltd 1973-80 (dep chm 1980-82); dep chm Self Changing Gears Ltd 1980-82; co sec: Leyland Vehicles Ltd 1980-82, Bus Mfrs Hldgs 1980-82; staff dir BL plc 1982-84; ret 1984; chm Rowington Branch Royal Br Legion; memb: Coventry Branch Army Benevolent Fund, ctee Warwickshire Branch Order of St John; *Recreations* gardening, golf, shooting; *Clubs* Cavalry and Guards'; *Style—* Maj-Gen George Lewis, CBE; c/o Nat Westminster Bank, Sydenham, London

LEWIS, Dr Gerwyn Elidor David; s of David Lewis (d 1912), of New Scotland Yard, and Gwenllian Anne Lewis, *née* Davies (d 1944); *b* 2 Dec 1912; *Educ* Royal Masonic Sch, LSE (BSc, PhD, DipEd); *m* 1945, Eluned, da of Dr Frances Knoyle (d 1940) of London; 2 da (Megan b 1949, Rhiannon b 1955); *Career* Colonial Serv 1937-62, PRO War Tax Dept Singapore 1940, POW (Singapore, Thailand, Burma) 1942-45; state emergency info offr (Pahang) Malaysia 1949-51; headmaster Victoria Inst Kuala Lumpur 1955-62, asst dir educn in Fed of Malaysia 1952-53; author of more than 40 textbooks, maingly geographical for use in Malaysia, Singapore, Australia, W Africa, Kenya; FRGS; *Recreations* rugby, exploring; *Clubs* Reform, London Welsh Rugby; *Style—* Dr Gerwyn E D Lewis; 3 Newton Grove, Bedford Park, London W4 1LB (☎ 01-994-3399)

LEWIS, Hon Mrs; Hilary Zaraz; *née* Morris; da of 1 Baron Morris of Kenwood (d 1954); *b* 1932; *m* 1964, Ronald Graham Lewis (b 5 June 1919, educ London Univ); 1 s (Ross Graham, m 1974 Carol), 1 da (Mrs (Beryl Anne) John Badger); *Recreations* bridge; *Style—* The Hon Mrs Lewis; Zaraz, Littlewick Green, Maidenhead, Berks (☎ 062 882 3183)

LEWIS, Hugh Wilson; s of Cdr Hubert Thomas Lewis, OBE, RN (ret), of Midford Rd, Combe Down, Bath, Avon, and Gwyneth, *née* Ridgway; *b* 21 Dec 1946; *Educ* Clifton, Birmingham Univ (LLB); *m* 2 Dec 1972, Philippa Jane, da of Lt-Col John Rose Terry (d 1988), of Ensworthy, Gidleigh, Chagford, Devon; 3 s (Edward b 1973, Thomas b 1975, Christopher b 1984), 1 da (Katharine b 1979); *Career* called to the Bar Middle Temple 1970; memb: Western circuit, Family Law Bar Assoc; *Recreations* walking Dartmoor, fly fishing, skiing, surfing; *Clubs* Devon and Exeter Inst Exeter, Ski Club of GB; *Style—* Hugh Lewis, Esq; 26 Southernay East, Exeter (☎ 55777 431005, fax 412007); Creaber Cottage, Gidleigh, Chagford, Devon

LEWIS, His Honour Judge; Sir Ian Malcolm; QC (1961); *b* 14 Dec 1925; *Educ* Clifton, Trinity Hall Cambridge (MA, LLM, LLD); *m* 1955, Marjorie, da of W G Carrington, of Cleethorpes, Lincs; 1 s; *Career* barr Middle Temple 1951, justice of Supreme Ct of Nigeria 1966-72, circuit judge 1973-, pres Mental Health Appeal Tbnl for Restricted Category Patients 1983-; memb cncl Bristol Univ 1979-, memb cncl Clifton Coll 1975- (chm 1981-84); kt 1964; *Style—* His Honour Judge Sir Ian Lewis, QC; 10 Southfield Rd, Westbury-on-Trym, Bristol BS9 3BH

LEWIS, Ian Talbot; s of Cyril Frederick Lewis, CBE, and Marjorie, *née* Talbot; *b* 7 July 1929; *Educ* Marlborough; *m* 1, 1962, Patricia Anne, da of Rev William Dalrymple Hardy (d 1982), 2 s (James b 1964, Charles b 1966); m 2, 1986, Susan Lydia, da of Henry Alfred Sargant, of Putney, London; *Career* Nat Serv KOH and QOH followed by AER Serv (Capt) 1952-61; under-sec (Legal) Treasy Slrs Off, memb of Law Cmmn Working Gp on Commonhold 1986-87; pres Blackheath FC (RU) 1985-88, hon vice-pres Blackheath CC; ctee memb Marlburian Club 1984-87; Liveryman Worshipful Co of Merchant Taylors; *Recreations* sport, countryside, theatre, reading, films; *Clubs* Cavalry and Guards, MCC, Blackheath FC (RU), Piltdown GC; *Style—* Ian Lewis, Esq; 15 Elystan Court, 121 Howards Lane, Putney SW15 (☎ 01 785 6727); South Cottage, Fordcombe, Tunbridge Wells, Kent (☎ 089 274 413); Queen Annes Chambers, 28 Broadway, London SW1 (☎ 01 210 3030)

LEWIS, Prof Sir Jack; *b* 13 Feb 1928; *Educ* Barrow GS, London Univ (BSc, DSc), Nottingham Univ (PhD), Manchester Univ (MSc), Cambridge Univ (MA, ScD); *m* 1951, Elfreida Mabel Lamb; 1 s, 1 da; *Career* lectr: Sheffield Univ 1954-56, Imperial Coll London 1956-57, lectr/reader UCL 1957-61; prof of chem Manchester Univ 1961-67, UCL 1967-70, Cambridge Univ 1970-; warden Robinson Coll Cambridge 1975-; Firth visiting prof Sheffield Univ 1967; memb: SRC Polys Ctee 1973-79, SRC Sci Ctee 1975-80, SRC Sci Bd 1975-79, Univ Grants Ctee for Physical Sciences 1975-80, jt ctee SERC/SSRC 1979-; SERC Cncl 1980-86, cncl Royal Soc 1982-84, Nato Sci Ctee; chm: Royal Cmmn on Environmental Pollution 1985-, DES visiting Ctee to Cranfield Inst 1984-; pres Royal Soc of Chem 1986-; Hon DUniv: Open 1982, Rennes 1980; Hon DSc: East Anglia 1983, Nottingham 1983, Birmingham 1988, Leicester 1988; FRS, FRIC, FRSA; *Style—* Prof Sir Jack Lewis; Warden's Lodge, 4 Sylvester Rd, Cambridge (☎ 0223 602 22); Univ Chemical Laboratory, Lensfield Rd, Cambridge (☎ 0223 664 99)

LEWIS, Hon John Frederick; s of 3 Baron Merthyr, KBE, PC (d 1977); *b* 30 Dec 1938; *Educ* Eton, St John's Coll Cambridge; *m* 1966, Gretl, twin da of Lt-Col J W Lewis-Bowen; 1 s, 2 da; *Career* organiser Citizens' Advice Bureau; *Recreations* DIY; *Clubs* Island Sailing; *Style—* The Hon John Lewis; 1 Cedar Hill, Carisbrooke, Newport, IOW (☎ 0983 522014)

LEWIS, John Henry James; s of Leonard Lewis, QC, of East Park House, Newchapel, Nr Lingfield, Surrey, and Rita Jeanette, *née* Stone; *b* 12 July 1940; *Educ* Shresbury, UCL (LLB); *m* 30 Nov 1984, Susan Mary Frances, da of Maj Robert Ralph Merton, of The Old Rectory, Burghfield, Berks; 2 da (Daisy Leonora Frances b 1 Jan 1985, Lily Charlotte Frances b 23 Feb 1986); *Career* slr; ptnr Lewis Lewis & Co 1965-85, conslt Jaques & Lewis 1985-; chm: Blakeney Hldgs Ltd, Cliveden Hotel Ltd; vice chm John D Wood & Co plc; dir: The Brent Walker Gp plc, GR (Hldgs) plc; chm Attingham Summer Sch Tst 1988; Freeman City of London, memb Worshipful Co of Gunmakers 1984-; memb Law Soc; *Recreations* sculpture, architecture, tennis, swimming, shooting; *Clubs* Brooks's; *Style—* John Lewis, Esq; 5 West Eaton Place, London SW1 (☎ 01 235 1052); 243/247 Pavilion Rd, London SW1X 7BP (☎ 01 730 5420, fax 01 730 6608, car tel 0836 211165)

LEWIS, Maj John Henry Peter Sebastian Beale; s of Maj Peter Beale Lewis, MC (d 1961), and Mary Evelyn Louise Piers, *née* Dumas (d 1970); *b* 7 July 1936; *Educ* Eton; *m* 21 Dec 1971, Mary Virginia, da of Charles Barstow Hutchinson (d 1978); 2 s (Rupert Henry Alexander b 1974, Antony Rhydian b 1977); *Career* Maj 11 Hussars (PAO) 1955-69; dir: Br Bloodstock Agency plc 1976-; dir: Lower Burytown Farm 1983-; dir: Nawara Stud Co 1985-; rode over 25 winners under Jockey club rules; represented GB in Bobsleigh; *Clubs* Calvalry and Guards', MCC; *Style—* Maj J Lewis; British Bloodstick Agency plc, 16/17 Pall Mall, London SW1 (☎ 01 839 3393, telex 27403, car ☎ 0836 283109)

LEWIS, Jonathan Malcolm; s of Harold Lewis, of London, and Rena, *née* Goldser; *b* 27 Mar 1946; *Educ* Harrow Co Sch for Boys, Downing Coll Cambridge (BA, MA); *m* 4 July 1971, Rosemary, da of Lewis Mays (d 1971); 2 s; *Career* slr 1971, ptnr jt hd of co/commercial dept D J Freeman & Co 1974- (asst slr 1971-74), insolvency practitioner 1986-, columnist (City Comment) Law Soc Gazette 1983-, lectr and author on various legal topics; involved in the Scout movement; memb: Law Soc 1971, Int Bar Assoc 1981; Freeman Worshipful Co of Slrs; *Recreations* walking, theatre, family; *Style—* Jonathan Lewis, Esq; D J Freeman & Co, 43 Fetter Lane, London EC4A 1NA (☎ 01 583 4055, fax 01 353 7377, telex 894579)

LEWIS, Keith William; CB (1981); s of Ernest John Lewis (d 1985), of Adelaide, S Aust, and Alinda Myrtle Lewis, *née* Edge; *b* 10 Nov 1927; *Educ* Adelaide HS, Univ of Adelaide (BE Civil), Imperial Coll Univ of London (DIC); *m* 1958, Alison Bothwell, da of Malcolm Granger Fleming, OBE, of Bulawayo, Zimbabwe; 2 da (Victoria, Elizabeth); *Career* prof engr; permanent head Engrg and Water Supply Dept 1974-, River Murray cmmr representing S Aust 1982-; chm: S Aust Water Resources Cncl 1976-, Aust Water Res Advsy Cncl 1985-, Murray Darling Freshwater Res Centre 1986-, Pipelines Authy SA 1987-; memb: State Planning Authy 1974-82, Electricity Tst of S Aust 1974-84, Aust Water Resources Cncl Standing Ctee 1974-87, S Aust Urban Land Tst 1984-, S Aust Natural Gas Task Force 1987-, Amdel Ltd Bd 1984-; FIE (Aust), FAIM; *Recreations* tennis, golf, ornithology, skiing; *Clubs* Adelaide, Kooyonga Golf; *Style—* Keith Lewis, Esq, CB; 24 Delamere Ave, Netherby, S Aust 5062; Energy Planning Exec, Level 19, 30 Wakefield St, Adelaide 5000 (☎ 08 226 5500, fax 01 226 5523)

LEWIS, Sir Kenneth; DL (Rutland 1973); s of William Lewis (d 1977), and Agnes, *née* Bradley (d 1980); *b* 1 July 1916; *Educ* Jarrow Central Sch, Edinburgh Univ; *m* 1948, Jane, da of Samuel Pearson; 1 s, 1 da; *Career* serv WWII; memb Lloyd's; contested (C): Newton 1945 and 1950, Ashton-under-Lyne 1951, MP (C) Rutland and Stamford 1959-83 and Stamford and Spalding 1983-87; chm Cons Back Bench Labour Ctee 1963-64; chm and chief exec Business and Holiday Travel Ltd; *Clubs* Carlton, RAF, Pathfinders; *Style—* Sir Kenneth Lewis, DL; 96 Green Lane, Northwood, Middx (☎ Northwood 23354); Redlands, Preston, Uppingham, Rutland (☎ Manton (057 285) 320); Business and Holiday Travel Ltd, 49 Lambs Conduit St, London WC1 (☎ 01 831 8691)

LEWIS, Lady; Lesley Lisle; *née* Smith; da of Frank Lisle Smith (d 1974), and Dorothy Sutcliffe (d 1973); *b* 4 July 1924; *Educ* St Hildas Collegiate Sch Dunedin NZ, Sch of Physiotherapy Dunedin NZ; *m* 1959, Prof Sir Anthony Carey Lewis, CBE (d 1983, princ Royal Academy of Music 1968-82); *Recreations* golf, gardening; *Style—* Lady Lewis; High Rising, Holdfast Lane, Haslemere, Surrey (☎ 0428 3920)

LEWIS, Hon Mrs (Lucia Anne); *née* FitzRoy Newdegate; er da of Cdr Hon John Maurice FitzRoy Newdegate, RN (d 1976), and sis of 3 Viscount Daventry, *qv*; raised to the rank of a Viscount's da 1988; *b* 28 Mar 1920; *m* 4 July 1942, Maj Timothy Stuart Lewis, *qv*; 1 s (decd), 1 da (Caroline Anne, m Sir Frederick Douglas David Thomson, 3 Bt, *qv*); *Style—* The Hon Mrs Lewis; 29 Charlotte Square, Edinburgh EH2 4HA

LEWIS, Lynn Alexander Mackay; s of Victor Lewis (d 1982), of London , latterly of Malta, and Maysie, *née* Mackay; *b* 23 August 1937; *Educ* Elizabeth Coll Guernsey, Trinity Kandy Sri Lanka; *m* 23 May 1959, Valerie Elaine, da of Harry Procter, of London; 1 s (Lindon b 1961), 1 da (Carol b 1959); *Career* fndr Corby News 1961, Rome bureau chief Sunday Mirror 1966-68, reporter and presenter BBC TV Nationwide 1969-74, fndr and md Nauticalia Ltd 1974 (chm 1988-); chm Marine Trades Assoc 1986-, cncl memb Br Marine Indust Fedn 1986-, dir Nat Boat Shows Ltd 1988-; *Recreations* cricket, bridge; *Style—* Lynn Lewis, Esq; Riverbank House, Shepperton-on-Thames, Middx (☎ 0932 220 794); Nauticalia Ltd, Ferry Works, Shepperton-on-Thames, Middx (☎ 0932 244 396, fax 0932 241 679, mobile tel 0860 716 114, telex 8814255 (NAUTIC)

LEWIS, Mark Robin Llewelyn; s of Gp Capt Howard Llewelyn Lewis, and Joan Blodwen, *née* Williams; *b* 6 Nov 1953; *Educ* Millfield, Exeter Coll Oxford (BA); *m* 29 June 1974, Fay Catherine, da of Patrick Alfred Tester; *Career* Allen & Overy: articles 1976-78, admitted slr 1978, asst slr 1978-81 and 1982-85, ptnr 1985-; asst slr

Cunningham John & Co 1981-82; memb City of London Slrs Co; memb Law Soc; *Recreations* golf, cycling, walking, reading; *Style—* Mark Lewis, Esq; 9 Cheapside, London EC2V 6AD (☎ 01 248 9898, fax 01 236 2192)

LEWIS, Martyn John Dudley; s of Thomas John Dudley Lewis (d 1979), of Coleraine, NI, and Doris *née* Jones; *b* 7 May 1945; *Educ* Dalriada GS Ballymoney NI, Trinity Coll Dublin (BA); *m* 20 May 1970, Elizabeth Anne, da of Duncan Carse, of Fittleworth, Sussx; 2 da (Sylvie b 11 May 1975, Kate b 24 July 1978); *Career* TV journalist, presenter and newsreader: presenter BBC Belfast 1967-68, journalist and broadcaster HTV Wales 1968-70, joined ITN 1970, set up and ran ITN's Northern Bureau Manchester 1971-78; newsreader and foreign corr ITN: News at Ten, News at 5.45 1978-86; ITN reports 1970-86 incl: Cyprus War, Seychelles Independence, Fall of Shah of Iran, Soviet Invasion of Afghanistan, Vietnamese Boat People; co-presenter: ITV gen election programmes 1979 and 1983, ITV Budget programmes 1981-84, wrote and produced Battle for the Falklands video, wrote and presented The Secret Hunters documentary (TVS), joined BBC as presenter One O'Clock News 1986, presenter Nine O'Clock News 1987-; BBC documentaries: MacGregor's Verdict, Royal Tournament, Great Ormond Street - A Fighting Chance, Princess Anne - Save The Children, Help is There, Indian Summer; vice-pres Cancer Relief MacMillan Nurses, chm PR ctee London Fedn of Boys Clubs, patron Utd Response, tstee Drive for Youth, tstee Adopt a Student, memb exec ctee Stars Orgn for Spastics; memb Tidy Br Gp Policy Advsy Ctee; *Books* And Finally (1984); *Recreations* photography, tennis, good food; *Style—* Martyn Lewis, Esq; BBC TV News, BBC TV Centre, London W12 7RJ (☎ 01 576 7779, fax 01 749 7534)

LEWIS, (Patricia) Mary; da of late Donald Leslie Cornes, of Lythwood Farm, Bayston Hill, Nr Shrewsbury, Shrops, and Eleanor Lillian, *née* Roberts; *Educ* Stonehurst Sch Shrewsbury, St Margaret's Yeaton Peverey Shropshire, Shrewsbury Sch of Art, Camberwell Sch of Arts and Crafts (BA), Central Sch of Art Middx Poly; *m* 17 Aug 1974 (m dis), Garth David Lewis, s of David Lewis; *Career* graphic designer; creative dir and founding ptnr Lewis Moberly Design Conslts (specialists in packaging design) 1984-; memb 1989 Design and Art Direction Exec Ctee; design awards incl: 6 Clio Gold Award for Int Packaging Design, Design and Art Direction Gold Award for Outstanding Design 1988, Design and Art Direction Siver Award for the Most Outstanding Packaging Range 1988; juror: BBC Design Awards 1987, Design and Art Direction Awards, Assoc of Illustrators Awards; work exhibited: London, Los Angeles, Japan, NYC; memb Chartered Soc of Designers; *Recreations* design; *Style—* Ms Mary Lewis; 33 Gresse St, London WIP 1PN (☎ 01 580 9252, fax 01 255 1671, telex 0836 200 996)

LEWIS, Michael AP Gwilym; QC (1975); s of Rev Thomas William Lewis (d 1946), of London, and Mary Jane May, *née* Selway (d 1975); *Educ* Mill Hill, Jesus Coll Oxford (MA); *m* 3 s (Meyric b 1962, Gareth b 1964, Evan b 1966), 1 da (Bronwen b 1960); *Career* cmmnd RTR 1952-53; called to the Bar Gray's Inn 1956, memb of Senate 1976-9, bencher Gray's Inn 1986-; churchwarden Wootton Kent; *Style—* Michael Lewis, Esq, QC; 3 Hare Ct, Temple, London EC4

LEWIS, Maj-Gen (John) Michael Hardwicke; CBE (1970); s of Brig Sir Clinton Gresham Lewis (d 1978), of London, and Lilian Eyre, *née* Wace (d 1962); five generations of the Lewis family have been distinguished professional artists; *b* 5 April 1919; *Educ* Oundle, RMA Woolwich; *m* 1943, Barbara Dorothy, da of Louis Alexander Wright (d 1955), of Storrington; 3 s (Stephen, James, Clive); *Career* served WWII RE 1939-45, in Europe and Far E, Brevet Lt-Col 1958, Instr Jt Servs Staff Coll 1961-63, Imperial Def Coll 1966, asst chief of staff (Ops) HQ Northern Army Gp 1968-70, head of intelligence Supreme Headquarters Allied Powers in Europe 1972-75, Maj-Gen 1972, ret 1975; lectr for Nat Assoc of Decorative & Fine Arts Soc; *Books* Michiel Marieschi (Venetian artist) 1710-1743 (1967), John Frederick Lewis, RA 1805-1876 (1978); *Style—* Maj-Gen Michael Lewis, CBE; Bedfords Farm, Frimley Green, Camberley, Surrey GU16 6HE (☎ Deepcut 835188)

LEWIS, Neville Julian Spencer; s of Raymond Malcom Lewis (d 1980), of Llanishen, Cardiff, and Constance Margaret, *née* Jones; *b* 17 Mar 1945; *Educ* Radley, Pembroke Coll Oxford (MA); *m* 14 July 1967, Caroline Joy, da of Robin Homes (d 1987), of Oare, Wiltshire; 1 s (David b 1978), 1 da (Miranda b 1974); *Career* barr; Pty candidate (Lib) Paddington Feb and Oct 1974; *Books* Guide to Greece (1977), Delphi and the Sacred Way (1987); *Clubs* Nat Lib; *Style—* Neville Spencer Lewis, Esq; 20 South Hill Park Gardens, London NW3; 12 Kings Bench Walk, Temple, London EC4 (☎ 01 353 5892)

LEWIS, Nigel Wickham; s of Henry Wickham Lewis, and Marjorie, *née* Greene; *b* 3 Jan 1936; *Educ* Gayhurst Sch Gerrards Cross Bucks, Greshams' Sch Holt Norfolk, Clare Coll Cambridge (MA); *m* 21 Oct 1961, Chloe Elizabeth, da of John Hershell Skinner; 1 s (Tristram b 1967), 2 da (Derryn b 1964, Venetia b 1969); *Career* graduate apprentice and design engr Vickers-Armstrongs (Aircraft) Ltd 1958-62, sr engr Glacier Metal Co Ltd 1962-68, mgmnt conslt McKinsey & Co Inc 1968-72, md Security Control Engrg Ltd 1972-76, dir and chief industl advsr 3i plc 1977-; Liveryman Worshipful Co of Cordwainers; CEng, MIMechE, MBCS; *Recreations* lawn tennis, real tennis, garden supression, music; *Style—* Nigel Lewis, Esq; Cadsden House, Princes Risborough, Aylesbury, Bucks HP17 0NB (☎ 08444 3020); 3i plc, 31 Homer Rd, Solihull, West Midlands B91 3QA (☎ 021 711 3131, fax 021 711 2020, telex 337786)

LEWIS, Peter Daniel Nicolas David; s of R C Lewis, TD, of Shere, Surrey, and Miriam Lorraine, *née* Birnage; *b* 14 Oct 1957; *Educ* Westminster; *Career* day centre dep warden Age Concern Westminster 1976-79, mangr London Business Sch Bookshop 1979-82, ptnr London Town Staff Bureau 1982- (taken over by Burns Anderson Recruitment plc 1988), currently md London Town Staff Bureau and subsid dir Burns Anderson Recruitment plc; memb Inst of Employment Conslts 1984; *Recreations* driving, flying, Africa, bridge; *Style—* Peter Lewis, Esq; 2 Dealtry Rd, London SW15 (☎ 01 780 1699); 19 Broad Ct, London WC2B 5QN (☎ 01 836 0627, fax 01 836 1997)

LEWIS, Lt-Col Hon Peter Herbert; 2 s of 3 Baron Merthyr, KBE, PC (d 1977); *b* 25 Mar 1937; *Educ* Eton; *m* 1974, Caroline Monica, da of Erik Cadogan, JP, of Wasperton Hill, Barford, Warwicks (gs of Capt Hon Charles Cadogan, 4 s of 4 Earl Cadogan) by his w Caroline, da of Count Hans Wachtmeister (there are two creations of Count for this family, which was ennobled in 1578; one by Charles XI of Sweden 1687; the other by Frederick William III of Prussia in 1816), of Malmö, Sweden; 1 da (Amanda Caroline b 1977); *Career* formerly Maj 15/19 Hussars; Lt-Col cmdg 9/12 Royal Lancers (Prince of Wales's) to 1982; Hon Corps to Gentlemen at Arms 1988; *Style—* Lt-Col the Hon Peter Lewis; The Old Rectory, Chilfrome, Dorchester, Dorset

LEWIS, Peter Tyndale; s of Oswald Lewis (d 1966), of Beechwood, Highgate, MP for Colchester 1929-45, and Frances Merriman Cooper; gf founded John Lewis, Oxford St in 1864, uncle John Spedan Lewis founded John Lewis Partnership 1929; *b* 26 Sept 1929; *Educ* Eton, Christ Church Oxford (MA); *m* 22 July 1961, Deborah Anne, da of Sir William Collins, CBE (d 1976), of St James's Place, London SW1; 1 s (Patrick b 1965), 1 da (Katharine b 1962); *Career* Nat Serv Coldstream Gds 1948-49; chm John Lewis Partnership since 1972, Retail Distributors' Assoc 1972; barr Middle Temple 1956; joined John Lewis Ptnrship 1959; Cncl Indust Soc 1968-79; Design Cncl 1971-74; govr: NIESR 1983-, Windlesham Ho Sch 1979-; tstee Bell Educn Tst 1987-; CBIM, FRSA; *Recreations* golf; *Clubs* MCC; *Style—* Peter Lewis, Esq; John Lewis Partnership plc, Oxford St, London W1A 1EX (☎ 01 637 3434 Ext 6117)

LEWIS, (Arthur) Raymond; s of Harold Arthur Lewis (d 1981) of 8 Moorlands, Wilderness Rd, Chislehurst, Kent and Gladys Nellie *née* Thompson; *b* 13 Oct 1933; *Educ* Tonbridge; *m* 13 Sept 1957, Anne Margaret Elizabeth, da of John Christie Wishart, MBE (d 1977) of 86 Widmore Rd, Bromley, Kent; 1 s (Andrew b 1961), 1 da (Katharine b 1962); *Career* Pilot Offr RAF 1952-54; CA; dir: Frazer Nash Gp Ltd (and subsidiaries), Salamander Property Gp Ltd (and subsidiaries); *Recreations* swimming, music, gardening, reading, gourmet eating; *Clubs* The White Elephant; *Style—* Raymond Lewis, Esq; 'Hilltop', Ruxley Crescent, Claygate, Esher, Surrey KT10 0TX (☎ 0372 62543); Frazer Nash Group Limited, Randalls Way, Leatherhead, Surrey KT22 0TX (☎ 0372 379717, fax: 0372 377879, telex: 929947G

LEWIS, Rev Canon Robert Hugh Cecil; s of Herbert Cecil Lewis, OBE (Capt Welsh Regt, d 1967), and Olive Francis, *née* Marsden (d 1980); *b* 23 Feb 1925; *Educ* Swansea GS, Manchester GS, New Coll Oxford (BA, MA), Westcolt House; *m* 15 July 1948, Joan Dorothy, da of Ernest Gordon Hickman (Maj Cheshire Regt, d 1970); 1 s (David b 15 June 1949), 1 da (Ruth b 17 Nov 1952); *Career* Nat Serv 1942-47, PO RAFVR 1945, Flying Offr 1946, Flt Lt 1947; ordained: deacon 1952, priest 1953; curate: St Mary Crumpsall 1952-54, St James New Bury 1954-56; incumbent: St Peter Bury 1956-63, St George Poynton 1963-; rural dean: Stockport 1972-84, Cheadle 1984-86; hon canon Chester Cathedral 1973-, Chaplain to HM the Queen 1987; county ecumenical offr for Cheshire 1986-; *Style—* The Rev Canon Robert Lewis; The Vicarage Poynton Stockport Cheshire SK12 1AF

LEWIS, Hon Robin William; OBE (1988); 4 s of 3 Baron Merthyr, KBE, PC (d 1977); *b* 7 Feb 1941; *Educ* Eton, Magdalen Coll Oxford; *m* 28 April 1967, Judith Ann, o da of (Vincent Charles) Arthur Giardelli, MBE, of Pembroke, Dyfed; 1 s, 1 da; *Career* Cwlth Devpt Corpn 1964-66; Alexa Aluminium Ltd 1967-68; Westminster Bank Ltd 1968-72; Devpt Corpn for Wales 1972-82; md Novametrix Medical Systems Ltd; High Sheriff of Dyfed 1987-88; chm Gen Advsry Cncl of Independent Broadcasting Authority 1989-; *Style—* The Hon Robin Lewis, OBE; Orchard House, Llanstephan, Carmarthen, Dyfed SA33 5HA (☎ 026 783 254)

LEWIS, Roger St John Hulton; s of Dr John Edward Lewis, of Beaupre, Jersey, Channel Islands and Ann, *née* Hulton; *b* 26 June 1947; *Educ* Eton; *m* 1973, Vanessa Anne, da of late Michael A England, and Mrs J A Lawrence, of Scotland Hall, Stoke by Nayland; 3 s (Harry b 1975, Alexander b 1977, James b 1981); *Career* CA with Peat Marwick Mitchell & Co in London and Spain 1970; joined Crest Homes plc as gp accountant 1972; dir Crest Homes 1973, (md 1975); dir Crest Nicholson Gp 1979; gp chief exec 1983; *Style—* Roger Lewis, Esq; Ashford Farm House, Stoke D'Abernon, Surrey (☎ 0932 62025); Crest Nicholson plc, Crest House, Station Rd, Egham, Surrey (☎ 0784 38771)

LEWIS, Roland Peter; s of Peter Oliver Lewis, and Lily May, *née* Rice; *b* 11 Mar 1951; *Career* CA; dir Resort Hotels plc; *Recreations* skiing, windsurfing, flying; *Style—* Roland P Lewis, Esq; West House, Kingston Gorse, Sussex; Lewis & Co, 20 Springfield Rd, Crawley, Sussex (☎ 0293 542244, fax 510566, car phone 0860 614767)

LEWIS, Roland Swaine; s of William James Lewis (d 1937), of Tyrwaun, Ystalyfera, W Glam, and Constance Mary, *née* Adeney; *b* 23 Nov 1908; *Educ* Epsom Coll, St John's Coll Cambridge, St George's Hosp London (MA, MB, BChir); *m* 21 Dec 1936, Mary Christianna (d 1988), da of Alexander Milne (d 1948); 1 da ((Christianna) Victoria); *Career* Maj RAMC as otolaryngologist 1939-45, serv: Britain, Sudan, Western Desert and Italy; otolaryngologist to King's Coll Hosp 1946-73, Norwood & Dist Hosp 1948-73, Mount Vernon Hosp 1948-74; memb Br Assoc Otolaryngologists; MRCS 1932, LRCP 1932, FRCS 1934, FRSM 1946; *Books* Essentials of Otolaryngology (contributed 1967), Diseases of the Ear, Nose and Throat (contributed 1971); *Recreations* fishing, ornithology, hill walking; *Style—* Roland Lewis, Esq; 88 Maida Vale, London W9 1PR (☎ 01 624 6253); Aberdar, Cwrt-y-Cadno, Pumpsaint, Llanwrda, Dyfed SA1 9YH

LEWIS, Ronald Howard; MP (Lab) Carlisle 1964-; s of Oliver Lewis; *b* 16 July 1909; *Educ* Elementary Sch, Cliff Methodist Coll; *m* 1937, Edna, da of Arthur Cooke, of Pleasley, Mansfield; 2 s; *Career* served in H M Forces Aug 1940-46; CC (1949) Derbyshire; pres Pleasley Co-op Soc; *Style—* Ronald Lewis, Esq, MP; 22 Alandale Ave, Langwith Junction, nr Mansfield, Notts (☎ (0623) 742460)

LEWIS, Stephen John; s of Douglas John Lewis, of Codsall, Staffs, and Dorothy Pauline, *née* Shaw; *b* 8 Mar 1948; *Educ* Wolverhampton GS, Balliol Coll Oxford (BA); *Career* Phillips & Drew: ptnr 1980-85, dir Securities Ltd 1985-88, md Fifth Horseman Pubns Ltd 1988-; *Recreations* antiquities; *Clubs* Reform ; *Style—* Stephen Lewis, Esq ; 17 Solar Ct, Etchingham Park Rd, London N3 2DZ (☎ 01 349 1439)

LEWIS, (John) Stuart; s of John Charles Lewis, OBE, JP, of 34 Moss Close, Pinner, Middx, and Kathleen Gertrude Clara, *née* Pennick (d 1973); *b* 9 Mar 1944; *Educ* Downer GS; *m* 19 July 1969, Bridget Margaret, da of Eric Billingham Nash (d 1987); 2 s (James b 1971, Edward b 1983), 1 da (Anna b 1973); *Career* ptnr Fielding Newson-Smith & Co 1975, first vice pres Drexel Burnam Lambert Inc 1986 (vice-pres 1980), md Private Fund Mngrs Ltd 1988, chm Musicale plc; memb Broad St Ward Club; Freeman City of London; FCIS 1974; *Recreations* shooting, tennis, opera, reading, travel; *Clubs* City of London; *Style—* J Stuart Lewis, Esq; Greenaway House, Rose Lane, Wheathampstead, Herts AL4 8RA (☎ 05 8283 2132)

LEWIS, Terence; MP (Lab) Worsley 1983-; s of Andrew Lewis; *b* 29 Dec 1935; *m* 1958, Audrey, da of William Clarke; *Style—* Terence Lewis Esq, MP; House of Commons, London SW1

LEWIS, Thomas Loftus Townshend; CBE (1975); s of A Neville Lewis, RP (d 1973), of Stellenbosch, Cape, SA, and Theodosia, *née* Townshend (d 1978); *b* 27 May

1918; *Educ* Diocesan Coll Rondesbosch S Africa, St Paul's, Cambridge Univ (BA), Guy's Hosp (MB, BChir); *m* 27 Nov 1946, (Kathleen) Alexandra Ponsonby Lewis, da of late Wentworth W T Moore; 5 s (John, Anthony, Robert, Charles, Richard); *Career* WWII, Capt RAMC serv Italy and Greece 1944-45; obstetric and gynaecological surgn; Guy's Hosp 1948-83, Chelsea Hosp for Women 1950-83, Queen Charlottes Maternity Hosp 1952-83; hon conslt Br Army 1973 (now emeritus), pres Obstetric Section RSM 1980-81; memb Bd of Dirs Pte Patients Plan Ltd; played rugby for Guy's Hosp, Middex Co, London Counties 1945-48, travelling res for England (full back) 1948-49; Freeman City of London, Liveryman Apothecaries Soc; FRCS Eng, FRCOG (vice pres 1975-78); *Books* Progress in Clinical Obstetrics and Gynaecology (1964), Ten Teachers Obstetrics (15 ed due 1990), Ten Teachers Gynaecology (15 edn 1989), French's Index of Differential Diagnosis (12 edn 1985); *Recreations* golf, windsurfing, skiing, dingy sailing, collecting wine; *Clubs* Royal Wimbledon Golf; *Style*— Thomas Lewis, Esq, CBE; 13 Copse Hill, Wimbledon, London SW20 0NB (☎ 01 946 5089); Parkside Hospital, Wimbledon, London SW19 (☎ 01 946 4202)

LEWIS, Timothy Stuart; s of Col William Herbert Lewis, DSO, MC (d 1966), and Kathleen Campbell Naylor (Dallas) (d 1982); *b* 26 Nov 1921; *Educ* Cheltenham, RMA Sandhurst; *m* 4 July 1942, Hon Lucia Anne, da of Cdr the Hon John Maurice FitzRoy Newdegate (d 1976), of Arbury Hall, Nuneaton; 1 s (Michael b 1943 d 1963), 1 da (Caroline b 1946, m Sir David Thomson, 3 Bt); *Career* Coldstream Gds 1941-47 (NW Europe 1944-45), Roy Scots Greys 1947-52; Scottish and Newcastle Breweries 1964-78, Securities Tst of Scotland 1975- (chm 1985-); *Recreations* shooting, fishing, golf; *Clubs* Hon Company of Edinburgh Golfers (Capt 1978-80); *Style*— Timothy Lewis, Esq; 29 Charlotte Square, Edinburgh EH2 4HA (telex 72505/MCCO G)

LEWIS, Trevor Oswin; CBE (1983), JP (Dyfed 1969); suc as 4 Baron Merthyr (UK 1911) in 1977, but disclaimed Peerage for life, and does not use his title of Bt (UK 1896); s of 3 Baron Merthyr, KBE, PC, TD (d 1977); *b* 29 Nov 1935; *Educ* Eton, Magdalen Coll Oxford; *m* 18 April 1964, Susan Jane, da of A J Birt-Llewellin; 1 s, 3 da (Lucy b 1967, Elizabeth b 1970, Jessamy b 1972); *Heir* to Btcy and disclaimed Barony, s, David Trevor Lewis b 21 Feb 1977; *Career* memb: Dept of Transport Landscape Advsy Ctee 1968, Countryside Cmmn 1973-83; *Style*— Trevor Lewis, Esq, CBE, JP; Hean Castle, Saundersfoot, Dyfed (☎ 0834 812222)

LEWIS OF NEWNHAM, Baron (Life Peer UK 1989), of Newnham in the Co of Cambridgeshire; Sir Jack Lewis; *b* 13 Feb 1928; *Educ* Barrow GS, London Univ (BSc, DSc), Nottingham Univ (PhD), Manchester Univ (MSc), Cambridge Univ (MA, ScD); *m* 1951, Elfreida Mabel, *née* Lamb; 1 s, 1 da; *Career* sits as an Independent in the House of Lords; lectr: Sheffield Univ 1954-56, Imperial Coll London 1956-57, lectr/reader Univ Coll London 1957-61; prof of chemistry: Manchester Univ 1961-67, Univ Coll London 1967-70, Cambridge Univ 1970-; warden Robinson Coll Cambridge 1975-; Firth Visiting Prof Sheffield Univ 1967; memb: SRC Poly Ctee 1973-79, SRC Sci Ctee 1975-80, SRC Sci Bd 1975-79, Univ Grants Ctee for Physical Scis 1975-80, jt ctee SERC/SSRC 1979-, SERC Cncl 1980-86, cncl Royal Soc 1982-84, Nato Sci Ctee; chm: Royal Cmmn on Environmental Pollution 1985-, DES visiting Ctee to Cranfield Inst 1984-; pres Royal Soc of Chemistry 1986-; Hon DUniv: Open 1982, Rennes 1980; Hon DSc: E Anglia 1983, Nottingham 1983; FRS, FRIC, FRSA; kt 1982; *Style*— The Rt Hon Lord Lewis of Newnham, FRS; Warden's Lodge, 4 Sylvester Rd, Cambridge (☎ 0223 60222); University Chemical Laboratory, Lensfield Rd, Cambridge (☎ 0223 66499)

LEWIS-BOWEN, His Honour Judge; Thomas Edward Ifor; s of Lt-Col J W Lewis-Bowen and Kathleen, *née* Rice (d 1981); *b* 20 June 1933; *Educ* Ampleforth, St Edmund Hall Oxford; *m* 1965, Gillian, da of the late Reginald Brett, of Puckington, Somerset; 1 s, 2 da; *Career* barr Middle Temple 1958, rec of Crown Ct 1974-80, circuit judge (Wales and Chester) 1980-; *Style*— His Honour Judge Lewis-Bowen; Clynfyw, Boncath, Dyfed (☎ 023 974 236); 4 Asquith Court, Swansea, W Glamorgan SA1 4QL (☎ 0792 473736)

LEWISHAM, Viscount; William Legge; s and h of 9 Earl of Dartmouth by Raine, now Countess Spencer; *b* 23 Sept 1949; *Educ* Eton, Christ Church Oxford, Harvard Business Sch; *Career* contested (C) Leigh Lancs 1974, Stockport South 1974; FCA; *Style*— Viscount Lewisham; The Manor House, Chipperfield, King's Langley, Herts

LEWISOHN, His Honour Judge; Anthony Clive Leopold Lewisohn; s of John Lewisohn (d 1939); *b* 1 August 1925; *Educ* Stowe, Trinity Coll Oxford; *m* 1957, Lone Ruthwen Jurgensen; 2 s; *Career* serv Oxfordshire & Bucks LI 1946-47, Lt; barr Middle Temple 1951, circuit judge 1974-; *Style*— His Hon Judge Lewisohn; Brackenhurst, Fairoak Lane, Oxshott, Surrey

LEWISOHN, Oscar Max; s of Max Lewisohn (d 1973), of Copenhagen, Denmark, and Jenny Lewisohn, (d 1984); *b* 6 May 1938; *Educ* Sortedam Gymnasium Copenhagen, Denmark; *m* 1, 4 Aug 1962, Louis Madeleine (d 1985), da of Henry Grunfeld, of London; 3 s (Mark b 1963, Richard b 1965, James b 1970), 1 da (Anita b 1967); m 2, 24 Oct 1987, Margaret Ann, da of Don Paterson, of Wellington, NZ; *Career* joined SG Warburg & Co Ltd 1962 (exec dir 1969, dep chm 1987), dir SG Warburg Gp plc 1985; life govr Imperial Cancer Res Fund; *Recreations* music; *Style*— Oscar Lewisohn, Esq; 1 Finsbury Ave, London EC2M 2PK (☎ 01 606 1066)

LEWTHWAITE, Brig Rainald Gilfrid; CVO (1975), OBE (1974), MC (1943); s of Sir William Lewthwaite, 2 Bt, JP (d 1933), and hp of bro, Sir William Anthony Lewthwaite, 3 Bt; *b* 21 July 1913; *Educ* Rugby, Trinity Coll Cambridge; *m* 1936, Margaret Elizabeth, MBE, da of Harry Edmonds (d 1982), of NY, USA; 2 s, 1 da (1 da decd); *Career* 1939-45 War in ME and NW Europe, former Brig Scots Gds; mil attaché 1964 and def attaché Br Embassy Paris 1964-68, Cabinet Off 1952-55, NATO HQ Paris 1961-64, ret 1968; dir Protocol Hong Kong 1969-76; *Recreations* country life; *Style*— Brig Rainald Lewthwaite, CVO, OBE, MC; Earls Cottage, 14 Earls Walk, London W8 6LP

LEWTHWAITE, Sir William Anthony; 3 Bt (UK 1927); s of Sir William Lewthwaite, 2 Bt, JP (d 1933), and Beryl Mary Stopford (d 1970), *née* Hickman; *b* 26 Feb 1912; *Educ* Rugby, Trinity Coll Cambridge (BA); *m* 1936, Lois Mairi, da of Capt Struan Robertson Kerr-Clark (ka 1915; bro of 1 Baron Inverchapel, GCMG, PC), and Lady Beatrice Minnie Ponsonby Moore (d 1966, having m 2, 1941, 1 Lord Rankeillour, PC; she was da of 9 Earl of Drogheda); 2 da (Catherine Jane b 1954, m 1986 William Tobias Hall and 1 da decd); *Heir* bro, Brig Rainald Gilfrid Lewthwaite, CVO, OBE, MC; *Career* served Grenadier Gds 1943-46; slr 1937; memb: cncl Country Landowners Assoc 1948-64, ctee Westminster Law Soc 1964-73; *Recreations* forestry; *Style*— Sir William Lewthwaite, Bt; 73 Dovehouse St, London SW3 (☎ 01 352 7204/3)

LEY, Sir Francis Douglas; 4 Bt (UK 1905), MBE (1961), TD, JP (Derbys 1939), DL (1957); s of Maj Sir Henry Gordon Ley, 2 Bt (d 1944); *b* 1907; *Educ* Eton, Cambridge; *m* 1931, Violet Geraldine, da of Maj Gerald Johnson, of Foston, Derbys; 1 s, 1 da; *Heir* s, Ian Francis Ley; *Career* chm: Ley's Malleable Castings Co Ltd, Ewart Chainbelt Co Ltd, Ley's Foundries & Engrg Ltd; High Sheriff Derbys 1956; *Style*— Sir Francis Ley, Bt, MBE, DL, TD; Pond House, Shirley, Derby (☎ 0335 60327)

LEY, Ian Francis; s and h of Sir Francis Douglas Ley, 4 Bt, MBE, TD; *b* 12 June 1934; *Educ* Eton; *m* 1957, Caroline Margaret, da of Maj George H Errington, MC, of Rhodesia (now Zimbabwe); 1 s, 1 da; *Career* formerly chm: Ley's Foundries & Engrg, Ley's Malleable Castings, Ewart Chainbelt Co, Beeston Boiler Co (Successors) Ltd, W Shaw & Co (ret 1982 on takeover of the gp); chm S Russell & Son Ltd 1983-; *Recreations* tennis, shooting; *Clubs* White's, Buck's; *Style*— Ian Ley, Esq; 23 Bywater St, London SW3 (☎ 01 584 4125); Fauld Hall, Tutbury, Staffs (☎ 0283 812266)

LI, Choh-Ming; Hon KBE (1973, Hon CBE 1967); s of Kanchi Li, and Mewching Tsui; *b* 17 Feb 1912; *Educ* Univ of California Berkeley; *m* 1938, Sylvia Chi-Wan Lu; 2 s, 1 da; *Career* dir Center for Chinese Studies Univ of California 1951-63 (prof emeritus 1974-), founding vice-chllr The Chinese Univ of Hong Kong 1964-78; memb Soc of Berkeley Fellows 1981-; *Books* Economic Development of Communist China (1959), The Statistical System of Communist China (1962), The Li's Chinese Dictionary (1980); *Style*— Choh-Ming Li, Esq, KBE; 81 Northampton Ave, Berkeley, California 94707, USA

LIARDET, Maj-Gen Henry Maughan; CB (1960), CBE (1945, OBE 1942), DSO (1945), DL (Sussex, later W Sussex 1965); s of Maj-Gen Sir Claude Liardet, KBE, CB, DSO, TD, DL (d 1966), of Ballsdown, Chiddingfold, Surrey, and Dorothy, *née* Hopper (d 1968); *b* 27 Oct 1906; *Educ* Bedford Sch; *m* 25 Feb 1933, Joan Sefton, da of Maj Guy Sefton Constable, MC, JP (d 1935), of Warningcamp House, Arundel, W Sussex; 3 s (Guy Francis b 1934, Timothy William b 1936, Andrew John b 1939); *Career* cmmnd 106 (Lancs Hussars) Bde RHA (TA) 1924; regular cmmn RTC 1927 serv: UK, India, Egypt; Staff Coll 1939, WO, GHQ M East, Cdr Tank regt 7 Armd Div Western Desert, GSO1 10 Armd Div Alamein 1942, 1943-45 served Palestine, Iraq and Italy, 2 i/c admin Kent Dist UK 1946, 2 i/c 6 Armd Bde Italy and Palestine 1946-48, Brig RAC M East 1948-50, Co 8 RTR 1950, various staff appts WO, Co 23 Armd Bde 1952-54, Imperial Def Coll 1956, COS Army Staff Br Jt Servs Mission Washington DC 1951-58, dir gen fighting vehicles WO 1958-61, dep master gen of the ordnance WO 1961-64, ret 1964; ADC to HM The Queen 1956-58, Col Cmdt RTR 1961-67; W Sussex CC: memb for Arundel 1965-70, Alderman 1970-74; pres Royal Br Legion Sussex Cncl 1965-78, chm W Sussex SSAFA 1965-85; *Recreations* shooting, gardening; *Clubs* Army and Navy, Sussex; *Style*— Maj-Gen Henry Liardet, CB, CBE, DSO, DL; Warningcampt House, nr Arundel, W Sussex BN18 9QY (☎ 0903 882 533)

LIBBY, Dr Donald Gerald; s of Herbert Lionel Libby (d 1958), and Minnie, *née* Green (d 1986); *b* 2 July 1934; *Educ* RMA Sandhurst, Univ of London (BSc, PhD); *m* 1, 13 May 1961, Margaret Elizabeth Dunlop (d 1979), da of John Kennedy Dunlop McLatchie; 1 da (Fiona b 1966); m 2, 26 March 1982, June, da of Collin George Belcher, of Newmarket, Suffolk; *Career* Dept of Educn and Science: princ scientific offr 1967-72, princ 1972-74, asst sec 1974-80, asst under-sec of state planning and int rels branch 1980-82, architects bldg and schs branch 1982-86, further and higher educn branch 1986-; CEng, MIEE; *Recreations* music, rowing, tennis; *Style*— Dr Donald Libby; Lygon Cottage, 26 Wayneflete Tower Ave, Esher, Surrey KT10 8QG; Dept of Education and Science, Elizabeth House, York Rd, London SE1 7PH (☎ 01 934 9927)

LIBRACH, Dr Israel Mayer; s of Maurice Librach (d 1952), of 9 Brookvale Drive, Belfast, and Annie, *née* Bogen (d 1940); *b* 23 Nov 1914; *Educ* Royal Belfast Academical Inst, Queen's Univ Belfast (MB, BCH, BAO, DPH), Univ of London (DCH England); *m* 12 April 1945, Enid Mina, da of Arthur Lewis (d 1967), of 23 The Chase, London SW4; *Career* med supt City Isolation Hosp Nottingham 1945-47, lectr in hygiene Univ Coll Nottingham 1945-47, asst med offr of health Nottingham 1945-47, physician Chadwell Heath Hosp Ilford 1948-83, conslt for smallpox DHSS 1960-; chm Ilford Med Soc, ctee memb Barking and Havering branch BMA, lectr and examiner St John's Ambulance and Br Red Cross, memb Ilford and Barking Med Advsy Ctee; Freeman City of London 1966, Liveryman Worshipful Soc of Apothecaries 1968; Hon MRCGP 1986, Hon MFCH 1989; memb BMA 1938, FRSM 1942, fell Med Soc of London 1952; *Recreations* antiquarian, gardening, book collecting; *Clubs* Royal Soc of Medicine; *Style*— Dr Israel Librach; 2 Fauna Close, Chadwell Heath, Romford, Essex RM6 6AS (☎ 01 590 9727)

LICHFIELD, Dean of; *see*: Lang, Very Rev John Harley

LICHFIELD, 97 Bishop of, 1984-; Rt Rev Keith Norman Sutton; the see of Lichfield was founded by Oswy, King of Mercia in 656; in 1075 it was removed to Chester, in 1102 to Coventry, and finally to its original foundation at Lichfield; patron of one hundred and thirty-four livings, the canonries and prebends in his cathedral and the archdeaconries of Stafford, Salop and Stoke-upon-Trent; s of Norman and Irene Sutton; *b* 23 June 1934; *m* 1963, Edith Mary Jean Geldard; 3 s, 1 da; *Career* curate St Andrew's Plymouth 1959-62, chaplain St John's Coll Cambridge 1962-67, tutor and chaplain Bishop Tucker Coll Mukono Uganda 1968-73, princ Ridley Hall Cambridge 1973-78, bishop of Kingston-upon-Thames 1978-83; select preacher Univ of Cambridge 1987; admitted House of Lords 1989; chm: bd of govrs Queen's Coll Birmingham 1987-, bd of mission and unity of the Gen Synod 1989-; memb: admin cncl Royal Jubilee Tst, African RC Conf; *Books* The People of God (1982); *Recreations* Russian literature, baroque music, walking, travel in France and Africa; *Style*— The Rt Rev the Bishop of Lichfield; Bishop's House, The Close, Lichfield, Staffs WS13 7LG

LICHFIELD, 5 Earl of (UK 1831); (Thomas) Patrick John Anson; also Viscount Anson and Baron Soberton (both UK 1806); s of Lt-Col Viscount Anson (d 1958, s and h of 4 Earl, who he predeceased) by his 1 w Anne Ferelith Fenella (d 1980, having m 1950 HH Prince George of Denmark, CVO, who d 1986), da of Hon John Bowes-Lyon (s of 14 Earl of Strathmore and bro of HM Queen Elizabeth The Queen Mother); suc gf 1960; *b* 25 April 1939; *Educ* Harrow, RMA Sandhurst; *m* 1975 (m dis 1986), Lady Leonora Mary Grosvenor, da of 5 Duke of Westminster, TD, and sis of Duchess of Roxburghe; 1 s, 2 da (Lady Rose Meriel Margaret b 1976, Lady Eloise Anne Elizabeth b 1981); *Heir* s, Viscount Anson; *Career* served in Grenadier Gds 1959-62 (Lt); photographer; fell: Royal Photographic Soc, The Br Inst of Professional Photographers; *Books* The Most Beautiful Women (1981), Lichfield on Photography (1981), A Royal Album (1986), Lichfield on Travel Photography (1986), Not The Whole Truth (autobiography), Unipart Calendar Books (1985), Creating the Unipart

Calendar (1983), Hotfoot to Zabriskie Point (1985); *Recreations* arboriculture; *Clubs* White's; *Style*— The Rt Hon the Earl of Lichfield; Shugborough Hall, Stafford (☎ 0889 881454); studio: 133 Oxford Gdns, London W10 6NE (☎ 01 969 6161, fax 01 960 6494)

LICHT, Leonard Samuel; s of Bernhard Licht (d 1982), and Hilde Licht; *b* 15 Mar 1945; *Educ* Christ's Coll Finchley; *m* 1973, Judith, da of Albert Grossman (d 1980); 1 s, 1 da; *Career* investmt banker; dir Mercury Fund Mangrs 1974; vice-chm and dir: Mercury Asset Mgmnt Gp Ltd 1985, Mercury Asset Mgmnt plc 1987; dep chm and dir Mercury Warburg Investmt Mgmnt Ltd 1986, chm Channel Islands and Int Investmt Tst Ltd 1988, dir Keystone Investmt Tst plc 1988; *Recreations* philately, tennis, eighteenth century pottery; *Clubs* Brooks's; *Style*— Leonard Licht, Esq; 35 Stormont Rd, Highgate, London N6 4NR; office: 33 King William St, London EC4R 9AS

LICKLEY, Sir Robert Lang; CBE (1973); *b* 19 Jan 1912; *Educ* Dundee HS, Univ of Edinburgh, Imperial Coll (fell 1973); *Career* formerly: prof of aircraft design Coll of Aeronautics Cranfield, md Fairey Aviation Ltd; md Hawker Siddeley Aviation Ltd 1960-76 (asst md 1965-76), head Rolls Royce support staff NEB 1976-79; Hon DSc Strathclyde 1976; FRSE, FEng, FRAeS, FIProdE, Hon FIMechE, Hon MSME; kt 1984; *Style*— Sir Robert Lickley, CBE; Foxwood, Silverdale Ave, Walton-on-Thames, Surrey KT12 1EQ (☎ 0932 225 058)

LICKORISH, Adrian Derick; s of Leonard John Lickorish, CBE, of 46 Hillway, Highgate, London N6, and Maris, *née* Wright; *b* 29 Oct 1948; *Educ* Highgate Sch, Univ of London (LLB, LLM); *m* 16 May 1987, Vivien Mary, da of John Bernard Gould, of Wirswall Hall, Whitchurch, Shrops; *Career* slr 1974; ptnr: Durrant Piesse 1981, Lovell White Durrant 1988; memb Law Soc; *Recreations* farming, shooting, fishing, mil history; *Clubs* Royal Over-seas League; *Style*— Adrian Lickorish, Esq; Woodhouse Farm, Avening, Gloucs; 73 Cheapside, London EC2 (☎ 01 236 0066)

LICKORISH, Leonard John; CBE (1975); s of Adrian Joseph Lickorish (d 1957), and Josephine, *née* Rose (d 1953); *b* 10 August 1921; *Educ* St Georges Coll Weybridge, UCL (BA); *m* 1945, Eileen Maris (d 1983); 1 s (Adrian); *Career* serv WWII RAF 1941-46, Fl-Lt; gen mangr Br Travel Assoc 1963-69, dir gen Br Tourist Authy 1970-86; chm: Euro Travel Cmmn 1984-86, Exhibition Indust Fed Ctee 1987; hon vice-chm Euro Travel Cmmn and sec Euro Tourism Action Gp 1987, dir of studies (tourism) Royal Inst of Public Admin 1987, external examiner Univ of Strathclyde 1987; Order of the Crown of Belgium 1967; *Books* The Travel Trade (1958), Reviews of UK Statistical Sources, Tourism (1975), Marketing Tourism (1989) and numerous int pubns; *Recreations* gardening, sailing, walking; *Clubs* Royal Automobile, Royal Overseas League; *Style*— Leonard Lickorish, Esq, CBE; 46 Hillway, London N6 6EP (☎ 01 340 8920)

LIDBURY, Sir John (Towersey); s of John Lidbury (d 1950); *b* 25 Nov 1912; *Educ* Owen's Sch; *m* 1939, Audrey Joyce, da of Harold Wigzell; 1 s, 2 da; *Career* joined Hawker Aircraft Ltd 1940 (dir 1951, md 1959, chm 1961-77), dep chm and chief exec Hawker Siddeley Aviation Ltd 1959-77; chm: Hawker Siddeley Dynamics Ltd 1971-77, High Duty Alloys Ltd 1978-79 (dep chm 1970-78), Carlton Industs plc 1981-83 (dir 1978-81); vice-chm Hawker Siddeley Gp plc 1970-83 (dir 1960-83, dep md 1970-81); dir: Hawker Siddeley Int Ltd 1963-83, Invergordon Distillers (Hldgs) plc 1978-83, Smiths Industs plc 1978-; JP Kingston-upon-Thames 1952-62, pres Soc of Br Aerospace Cos Ltd 1969-70; FRAeS, CBIM; kt 1971; *Style*— Sir John Lidbury; c/o Hawker Siddeley Group plc, 18 St James's Sq, London SW1Y 4LJ (☎ 01 930 6177)

LIDDELL, Hon Mrs (Anna); *née* Kinnaird; 2 da of 13 Lord Kinnaird, *qv*; *b* 18 Dec 1952; *m* 3 Sept 1988, Edward Henry (Harry) Liddell, eld s of Thomas Liddell, of Dormans Corner, Lingfield, Surrey; *Style*— The Hon Mrs Liddell; 97 Narbonne Ave, London SW4

LIDDELL, (Andrew) Colin MacDuff; WS (1980); s of Ian Donald MacDuff Liddell, WS (d 1976), and Barbara, *née* Dixon; descendent of MacDuffs of Strathbraan, Perthshire; *b* 21 June 1954; *Educ* Cargilfield Sch Edinburgh, Fettes, Balliol Coll Oxford (BA), Univ of Edinburgh (LLB); *m* 11 Aug 1979, Katrina Louise, da of Dr Kenneth Terence Gruer, MC, of Edinburgh; 2 da (Iona Michelle b 1983, Bryony Marsali b 1985); *Career* slr, ptnr Messrs J & H Mitchell, Pitlochry and Aberfeldy 1981; sr pres Speculative Soc of Edinburgh 1983-84, sec Highland Perthshire Devpt Co Ltd 1985-; govr Cargilfield Sch Edinburgh 1985- (vice-chm 1987-); *Recreations* skiing, windsurfing, hillwalking, curling; *Style*— Colin Liddell, Esq, WS; Messrs J & H Mitchell WS, 51 Atholl Rd, Pitlochry PH16 5BU (☎ 0796 2606, fax 0796 3198)

LIDDELL, Douglas Gerard; s of Gen Sir Clive Liddell, KCB, CMG, CBE, DSO (d 1956), and Hilda Jessie Bissett, *née* Kennedy; *b* 2 Sept 1919; *Educ* Wellington, Peterhouse Cambridge; *m* 1 March 1940, Doreen Joyce, *née* Ducker; 3 da (Anita, Serena, Simone); *Career* serv WWII, Maj; md Spink & Son Ltd; *Recreations* reading, theatre, music, cricket; *Clubs* Oxford & Cambridge Univ; *Style*— Douglas Liddell, Esq; Three Oaks, Bramlands Lane, Woodmancote, Henfield, W Sussex (☎ 0273 49 2758); Spink & Son Ltd, 5-7 King St, St James's, London SW1 6QS (☎ 01 930 7888, telex 916711)

LIDDELL, Hamish George Macduff; WS (1949); s of Buckham William Liddell (d 1950), and Katharine, *née* MacDuff (d 1957); *b* 20 Feb 1924; *Educ* Cargilfield Sch Edinburgh, Fettes, Balliol Coll Oxford (BA), Univ of Edinburgh (LLB); *m* 9 Jul 1965, Mary Elizabeth, da of Leslie George Milliken (d 1981); 1 s (Duncan b 1969), 1 da (Diana b 1971); *Career* WWII Lt Black Watch & KAR served E Africa, India, Burma 1943-46; practising slr 1949-; memb Scottish Sports Cncl 1972-76, pres Scottish Nat Ski Cncl 1973-78 (chm 1963-73), hon life memb Br Ski Fedn, invitation life memb SCGB; awarded Queen's Jubilee Medal 1977; *Recreations* field sports, skiing, sailing; *Style*— Hamish Liddell, Esq; 51 Atholl Rd, Pitlochry (☎ 0796 2606)

LIDDELL, Helen Lawrie; da of Hugh Reilly, of Falkirk, Stirlingshire, and Bridget, *née* Lawrie; *b* 6 Dec 1950; *Educ* Univ of Strathclyde (BA); *m* 22 July 1972, Dr Alistair Henderson, s of Robert Liddell, of Coatbridge, Lanarks; 1 s (Paul b 1979), 1 da (Clare b 1985); *Career* head econ dept Scottish TUC 1971-75 (asst sec 1975-76), econ corr BBC Scotland 1976-77, Scottish sec the Lab Pty 1977-88, dir personnel and pub affrs Scottish Daily Record and Sunday Mail (1986) Ltd 1988-; parly candidate E Fife 1974, cabinet rep Int Women's Year Ctee 1975, memb Nat Jl Cncl for Academic Salaries and Awards 1974-76; *Recreations* writing, walking; *Style*— Mrs Helen Liddell; Glenisla, Main Rd, Langbank, Renfrewshire, Scotland PA14 6XP (☎ 047 554 344); Largiemore, Argyll; Scottish Daily Record and Sunday Mail (1986) Ltd, Anderston Quay, Glasgow G3 8DA (☎ 041 242 3331, fax 041 204 0703, telex 778277)

LIDDELL, Mark Charles; s of Peter John Liddell, DSC (d 1979), of Moorhouse Hall, Carlisle, Cumbria, and Priscilla, *née* Downes; *b* 19 Sept 1954; *Educ* Ampleforth; *m* 21 July 1979, Hon Lucy Katherine, da of 6 Viscount Knutsford, *qv*; 1 s (James b 23 Jan 1987), 1 da (Katherine b 4 June 1983); *Career* Lloyds broker 1974-81; dir: Lycetts (Cumbria) Ltd 1981-87, Lycetts (Insur Brokers) Ltd 1987-, Lycetts (Fin Servs) Ltd 1987-; memb of Lloyds 1981; *Recreations* shooting, cricket, snooker; *Clubs* Northern Counties; *Style*— Mark Liddell, Esq; Cumrew House, Cumrew, Carlisle, Cumbria CA4 9DD; Lycetts, Milburn House, Dean St, Newcastle upon Tyne NE1 1PP (☎ 091 232 1151, fax 091 232 1873)

LIDDELL, Hon Thomas Arthur Hamish; s and h of 8 Baron Ravensworth; *b* 27 Oct 1954; *m* 1983, Linda, da of H Thompson, of Hawthorn Farm, Gosforth, Newcastle-upon-Tyne; *Style*— The Hon Thomas Liddell

LIDDELL-GRAINGER, David Ian; DL (1962); Baron of Ayton (territorial); s of Capt Henry H Liddell-Grainger, JP, DL (d 1935), of Ayton Casle, Berwicks, and Lady Muriel Felicia Vere, *née* Bertie (d 1981, da of 12 Earl of Lindsey and Abingdon); *b* 26 Jan 1930; *Educ* St Peter's Coll Adelaide SA, Eton, Univ of London; *m* 1957 (m dis 1982), Anne, da of Col Sir Henry Abel Smith, KCMG, KCVO, DSO, DL, of Barton Lodge, Windsor, Berks, and Lady May Cambridge (da of 1 Earl of Athlone and HRH Princess Alice, gda of Queen Victoria through the Queen's 4 s, the Duke of Albany); 4 s (Ian Richard Peregrine b 1959, Charles Montague b 1960, Simon Rupert b 1962, Malcolm Henry b 1967), 1 da (Alice Mary b 1964); issue by Lady (Christine) de la Rue; 2 s (David Henry b 1983, Maximilian b 1985); *Career* Scots Gds 1948-50; property developer and farmer; cncllr 1958-73, has served on Scottish Gas Council and cncls of: RNLI, Scottish Scout Assoc, Nat Tst for Scotland, Royal Agric Soc of England, Scottish Landowners Fedn; dep chm Timber Growers UK 1985-88, memb regnl advsy ctee Forestry Cmmn, area cmmr for Scouts in Borders; underwriting memb Lloyd's; hospitaller Order of St John (Scotland) 1977-82, KStJ, Grand Master Mason of Scotland 1969-74, memb Queen's Bodyguard for Scotland (Royal Co of Archers) 1955-83; FSA; *Recreations* shooting, gliding, model engineering, history; *Clubs* New (Edinburgh), MCC; *Style*— David Liddell-Grainger, Esq, DL; Ayton Castle, Berwicks TD14 5RD (☎ 08907 81 212)

LIDDERDALE, Sir David William Shuckburgh; KCB (1975); s of late Edward Wadsworth Lidderdale; *b* 30 Sept 1910; *Educ* Winchester, King's Coll Cambridge; *m* 1943, Lola, da of late Rev Thomas Alexander Beckett; 1 s; *Career* serv The Rifle Bde (TA) 1939-45 War, active serv N Africa, Italy; asst clerk House of Commons 1934, clerk of the House 1974-76; hon vice-pres Assoc of Secs-Gen of Parl (Inter-Parly Union); *Publications* The Parliament of France (1951); *Clubs* Travellers', MCC, Pilgrim Soc; *Style*— Sir David Lidderdale, KCB; 46 Cheyne Walk, London SW3

LIDDIARD, Michael Richard; s of Richard England Liddiard, CBE, of Oxford Lodge, Wimbledon SW19, and Constance Lily, *née* Rock; *b* 15 Nov 1946; *Educ* Oundle, Univ of Exeter (BA), London Business Sch; *m* 14 March 1970, Judith Elizabeth Best, da of Wing Cdr Frederick John Edward Ison, DFC, RAF (d 1978); 1 s (James Stratton b 1973), 1 da (Amanda Brooke b 1975); *Career* C Czarnikow Ltd 1970-: dir 1981, vice-chm 1983, dir Czarnikow Hldgs 1984-; dir Lion Mark Hldgs 1983-; memb: cncl Assoc of Futures Brokers and Dealers 1986, RCH Bd (part of ICCH) 1987-; Freeman City of London 1970, Ct Asst Worshipful Co Haberdashers 1987 (Liveryman 1971); *Recreations* tennis, shooting; *Clubs* Carlton, Hurlingham, RAC, Roehampton; *Style*— Michael Liddiard, Esq; 5 Edwardes Pl, Kensington, London W8 6LR (☎ 01 603 0199); C Czarnikow Ltd, 66 Mark Lane, London EC3P 3EA (☎ 01 480 9300, fax 01 480 9500, car 0836 221 011)

LIDDIARD, Richard England; CBE (1977); s of Edgar Stratton Liddiard, MBE (d 1963), and Mabel Audrey, *née* Brooke (d 1968); *b* 21 Sept 1917; *Educ* Oundle, Worcester Coll Oxford (MA); *m* 16 Oct 1943, Constance Lily, da of Sir William Rook (d 1958); 1 s (Michael Richard b 1946); 3 da (Susan Millicent b 1949, Diana Brooke b 1951, Penelope Jane b 1954); *Career* WWII RCS 1939-46 (despatches 1944), Temp Lt-Col 1945 head of Ceylon Signal Corps; C Czarkikow Ltd 1946 (dir 1948, chm 1958-74); chm: Sugar Assoc of London 1960-78, Br Fedn of Commodity Assocs 1963-71 (vice-chm 1971-77), London Commodity Exchange 1972-75, Czarkikow Gp 1974-84, Lion Mark hldgs 1983-88 (dep chm 1988-); memb ctee of Invisible Exports 1966-67; Silver Jubilee Medal 1977; Master Worshipful Co of Haberdashers 1977-78; Polish MC 1942; *Recreations* walking, reading; *Clubs* RAC; *Style*— Richard Liddiard, Esq, CBE

LIDDIARD, Ronald; s of Tom Liddiard (d 1954), and Gladys Marion, *née* Smith (d 1970); *b* 26 July 1932; *Educ* Canton HS Cardiff, Coll of Advanced Technol and Commerce Cardiff, Inlogov Univ of Birmingham; *m* 7 Sept 1957, June Alexandra, da of James George Ford; 2 da (Angela J b 1959, Clare A b 1961); *Career* socl worker: Cardiff 1960-61, Bournemouth 1961-64; chief admin offr welfare servs Co borough of Bournemouth 1964-70; dir of socl servs: City of Bath 1971-74, Birmingham 1974-85; mgmnt and soc admin conslt pilot (air tport) 1985-, chm Lamond Ltd; dir Prospect Hall Coll for Disabled, govr Bluescoat Sch Birmingham; memb: Assoc Dir of Socs Servs 1971; *Books* chapters in: Innovations in the Care of the Elderly (1984), Self Care and Health in Old Age (1986); *Recreations* flying instruction, travel, wines, writing; *Style*— Ronald Liddiard, Esq; Whitefriars, Portway, Alvechurch, Worcs B48 74P (☎ 0564 826235)

LIDDLE, Hon Mrs (Caroline Agnes Morgan); *née* Thomson; da of Baron Thomson of Monifieth, PC; *b* 1954; *m* 1, 1977 (m dis 1981), Ian C Bradley; m 2, 1983, Roger Liddle; *Style*— The Hon Mrs Liddle

LIDSTER, Felicity; da of Harold Roberts (d 1981), of Monk Bretton, Barnsley, and Winifred, *née* Beaumont; *b* 7 May 1952; *Educ* Broadway GS, Huddersfield Poly (BSc); *m* 9 Feb 1970, Eric James Lidster, s of James Henry Lidster, of Stocksbridge, Sheffield; 2 s (Harvey James b 1970, Anthony John b 1972), 1 da (Charlotte Marie b 1982); *Career* dir: E J Lidster & Sons Ltd 1983, E J Lidster (Construction) Ltd 1984, Barnsley Mini-Skips Ltd 1983, Fellmoor Ltd 1985; *Recreations* hockey, squash; *Style*— Mrs Eric Lidster; Arunden House, Lund Lane, Burton Grange, Barnsley, S Yorks (☎ 0226 289859 298484, car tel 0860 614952)

LIDSTONE, John Barrie Joseph; s of Arthur Richard Francis Lidstone (d 1930) and Lillian May, *née* Teppett (d 1973); *b* 21 July 1929; *Educ* Presentation Coll Reading, Univ of Manchester, (RAF Educn Officers' Course); *m* 1957, Primrose Vivien, da of Vincent Russell (d 1947), of Derby; 1 da (b 1960); *Career* Nat Serv RAF 1947-48; English master Repton 1949-52; Shell-Mex and BP Gp and assoc cos 1959-62, dep md Vicon Agric Machinery Ltd 1962-63, dir and gen mangr Mktg Selections Ltd 1969-72; Mktg Improvements Gp: joined 1965, dir 1968-, dir and gen mangr 1972-74, dep md

1974-88, dep chm 1988-; non-exec dir: Kalamazoo plc, N Hants Tst Co Ltd, St Nicholas Sch Fleet Educnl Tst Ltd; UK Mgmnt Consultancies Assoc: memb 1978-88, vice chm 1985-86, chm 1986-87; memb nat exec ctee Inst of Mktg 1985-; voted top speaker on Mktg in Europe 1974, Dartnell lecture tours USA 1978-82; articles contrib to: The Times, Daily Telegraph, Financial Times, Observer, Sunday Times, Sundey Telegraph, Long Range Planning, International Mgmnt, Marketing, Marketing Week, Mgmnt Today; Freeman City of London, Liveryman Worshipful Co of Marketors; memb BAFTA, FIMC, FBIM, FIOD, FInstM, MIPM; *Films and Video*: technical advsr and script writer: The Persuaders (1975), Negotiating Profitable Sales (1979), Training Salesmen on the Job (1981, won highest award for creative excellence at US Industl Film Festival 1982), Marketing for Managers (1985), Marketing To-Day (1985), Reaching Agreement and Interviewing (1987, 1988);; *Books* Training Salesmen on the Job (1975, 2 edn 1986, translated into French, German, Spanish, Swedish), Recruiting and Selecting Successful Salesmen (1976, 2 edn 1983), Negotiating Profitable Sales (1977, made into two part film by Video Arts 1979), Motivating your Sales Force (1978), Making Effective Presentations (1985), The Sales Presentation (jtly 1985), Profitable Selling (1986), Marketing Planning for the Pharmaceutical Industry (1987); *Recreations* writing, cricket, golf; *Clubs* Naval, N Hants GC, BAFTA; *Style*— John B J Lidstone, Esq; Marketing Improvements Gp plc, Ulster House, 17 Ulster Terrace, Regent's Pk, London NW1 4PJ (☎ 01 487 5811, telex 299723 MARIMP G, fax 01 935 4839)

LIESNER, Hans Hubertus; CB (1980); s of Curt Liesner, and Edith, *née* Neumann; *b* 30 Mar 1929; *Educ* German Schs, Univ of Bristol (BA), Nuffield Coll Oxford; *m* 1968, Thelma; 1 s (Jeremy), 1 da (Raina); *Career* teaching appts 1955-70: LSE, Emmanuel Coll, Univ of Cambridge; under sec HM Treasy 1970-76, chief econ advsr and dep sec DTI 1976- ; *Recreations* gardening, walking, skiing, cine photography; *Style*— Hans Liesner, Esq. CB; Dept of Trade and Industry, 1 Victoria St, London SW1H 0ET (☎ 01 215 4258)

LIFFORD, 9 Viscount (I 1781); (Edward) James Wingfield; also Baron Lifford (I 1768); s and h of 8 Viscount Lifford (d 1987), and Alison Mary Partricia, *née* Ashton; *b* 27 Jan 1949; *Educ* Aiglon Coll Switzerland; *m* 1976, Alison, da of Robert Law, of Turnpike House, Withersfield, Suffolk; 1 s (James Thomas b 1979), 1 da (Annabel Louise b 1978); *Heir* s, James Thomas b 26 Sept 1979; *Career* stockbroker; dir Cobbold Roach Ltd; *Recreations* country sports; *Clubs* Boodles; *Style*— The Rt Hon Viscount Lifford; Field House, Hursley, nr Winchester, Hants SO21 2LE

LIFFORD, Mary, Viscountess (Alison) Mary Patricia; *née* Ashton; 2 da of Thomas Wingrave Ashton, of The Cottage, Hursley, nr Winchester; *b* 17 Feb 1910; *Educ* private; *m* 16 Jan 1935, Alan William Wingfield Hewitt, 8 Viscount Lifford (d 1987); 1 s (9 Viscount b 1949), 3 da (Hon Mrs Swann, Hon Mrs Warburton, Hon Mrs Henderson); *Style*— Mary, Viscountess Lifford; The Barn, Hursley, Winchester, Hants (☎ Hursley 75515)

LIGGINS, Sir Edmund Naylor; TD; s of Arthur William Liggins; *b* 21 July 1909; *Educ* King Henry VIII Sch Coventry, Rydal Sch; *m* 1952, Celia Jean, da of William Henry Lawrence; 3 s, 1 da; *Career* slr 1931, Liggins & Co Slrs; pres Law Soc 1975-76; kt 1976; *Recreations* travel, cricket, rugby, football, squash, rackets; *Clubs* MCC, Army and Navy; *Style*— Sir Edmund Liggins, TD; Hareway Cottage, Hareway Lane, Barford, Warwicks CV35 8DB (☎ 0926 624246); Liggins & Company, 150 Station Rd, Balsall Common, W Midlands CV7 7FF

LIGHTBODY, Hon Mrs (Charlotte Hazell); *née* Pym; er da of Baron Pym (Life Peer), *qv*; *b* 2 July 1950; *m* 1984, Ian Lightbody, s of P R Lightbody; 1 s (Thomas Hugh b 1986), 1 da (Helena Rosamund b 1988); *Style*— The Hon Mrs Lightbody; School House, Liverpool College, Mossley Hill, Liverpool 18 8BE

LIGHTBODY, Ian Macdonald; CMG (1974); s of Thomas Paul Lightbody (d 1932), and Dorothy Marie-Louise, *née* Cooper (d 1969); *b* 19 August 1921; *Educ* Queen's Park Sch, Univ of Glasgow (MA); *m* 1954, Noreen Robson, da of Capt Thomas Herbert Wallace, OBE, MC (d 1967), of Dromore, Co Down; 3 s (Nigel, Donald, Bruce), 1 da (Heather); *Career* war serv India and Far East 1942-45, Capt; Colonial Admin Serv Hong Kong: joined 1945, dist cmmr New Territories 1967-68, def sec 1968-69, cmmr for resettlement 1971, sec for housing and chm Hong Kong Housing Authy 1973-77, sec for admin 1977-78, chm Hong Kong pub serv cmmn 1978-80; MLC, MEC, ret from Hong Kong 1980; memb Arun DC 1983; *Recreations* tennis, hill walking; *Clubs* Hong Kong, Royal Hong Kong Jockey; *Style*— Ian Lightbody, Esq, CMG; Two Stacks, Lake Lane, Barnham, W Sussex PO22 0AD

LIGHTBOWN, David Lincoln; MP (C) Staffs S E 1983-; *b* 30 Nov 1932; *Career* former md W Midlands Engrg Gp of Cos until entry into Parly, appt govt asst whip 1986, Lord Cmmr HM Treasy 1987; memb: Staff CC, Lichfield Dist Cncl; *Style*— David Lightbown Esq, MP; House of Commons, London SW1

LIGHTERNESS, Tony (Thomas John); s of Thomas Charles Lighterness (d 1980), of Wimborne, Dorset, and Eleanor Mary Jones (d 1986); *b* 20 Jan 1932; *Educ* Royal Liberty Sch Gidea Park Essex; *m* 21 Feb 1959, Margaret; 1 s (David b 1961), 3 da (Elizabeth b 1959, Catherine (twin) b 1959, Janine b 1963); *Career* The RTZ Corpn plc; FCIS, FCT; *Recreations* skiing, cycling, photography; *Clubs* RAC, St James'; *Style*— Tony Lighterness, Esq; 6 St James Sq London SW17 4LD (☎ 01 930 2399, telex 24639)

LIGHTFOOT, George Cecil; CBE (1968), DL (Suffolk 1970); s of Ernest William Lightfoot (d 1943); *b* 25 Mar 1906; *Educ* Cheltenham, Wadham Coll Oxford; *m* 1935, Ghetal Angelita Emerson, da of Arnold Herschell; 1 s (James Cecil Emerson, *qv*, 1 da; *Career* slr, clerk E Suffolk CC, ret 1971; *Recreations* golf, painting; *Clubs* Woodbridge GC; *Style*— George Lightfoot, Esq, CBE, DL; Penrith House, Woodbridge, Suffolk

LIGHTFOOT, James Cecil Emerson; s of George Cecil Lightfoot, of Woodbridge, Suffolk, and Ghetal Angelita, *née* Herschell; *b* 16 Nov 1949; *Educ* Charterhouse Univ of Oxford; *m* 7 Jan 1977, Hilary Pleydell, da of Robert Cecil Crowhurst, of Newmarket, Suffolk; 2 s (George William b 1980, Harry Robert b 1988), 1 da (Rosalie Pleydell b 1983); *Career* admitted slr, started own practice 1973, currently sr ptnr Lightfoot and O'Brien Marshall; *Recreations* sports; *Style*— James Lightfoot, Esq; Spaldings Barn, Hall Lane, Framsden, Stowmarket, Suffolk IP14 6HU; Lightfoot and O'Brien Marshall, 69 The Thoroughfare, Woodbridge, Suffolk IP12 1AH (☎ 03943 6336, fax 0394 380098, telex 987116 LITLAW)

LIGHTFOOT, His Hon Judge (George) Michael; s of Charles Herbert Lightfoot (d 1941), of Leeds, and Mary, *née* Potter (d 1974); *b* 9 Mar 1936; *Educ* St Michael's RC Coll Leeds, Exeter Coll Oxford (MA); *m* 20 July 1963, Dorothy, da of Thomas Miller (d 1977), of Rosecroft Farm, Loftus, Cleveland; 2 s (John b 1970, David b 1977), 2 da (Catherine b 1968, Anne b 1973); *Career* Nat Serv 1955-57, York and Lancaster Regt, Intelligence Corps; schoolmaster 1962-66; called to Bar Inner Temple 1966, practised NE circuit 1967-86, rec of Crown Ct 1985-86, apptd a circuit judge NE circuit 1986-; pres; MENCAP Leeds, Leeds Friends of the Home Farm Tst; *Recreations* cricket and sport in general, reading; *Clubs* Lansdowne, Catenian Assoc, City of Leeds Circle; *Style*— His Hon Judge Lightfoot; 4 Shadwell Park Close, Leeds LS17 8TN (☎ 0632 665673)

LIGHTHILL, Sir (Michael) James; s of Ernest Balzar Lighthill; *b* 23 Jan 1924; *Educ* Winchester, Trinity Coll Cambridge; *m* 1945, Nancy Alice Dumaresq; 1 s, 4 da; *Career* Lucasian Prof of mathematics Univ of Cambridge 1969-79, provost of UCL 1979-89 (hon fell 1982); awarded gold medal by Inst of Mathematics and Its Applications 1982; kt 1971; *Style*— Sir James Lighthill; University College London, Gower St, London WC1

LIGHTON, Lt-Col Sir Christopher Robert; 8 Bt (I 1791), of Merville, Dublin, MBE (1945), JP (Somerset); s of Sir Christopher Lighton, 7 Bt, JP, DL (d 1929); *b* 1897; *Educ* Eton, RMC; *m* 1, 1926 (m dis 1953), Rachel Gwendoline, da of Rear Adm Walter S Goodridge, CIE (d 1929); 2 da; m 2, 1953, Horatia Edith (d 1981), da of A T Powlett; 1 s, 2 da; m 3, 1985, Eve, da of late Rear Adm Alexander Mark-Wardlaw, and wid of Maj Stopford Ram; *Heir* s, Thomas Lighton b 1954; *Career* served in Great War 1914-18 with KRRC, re-employed 1939-45 on staff; *Style*— Lt-Col Sir Christopher Lighton, Bt, MBE, JP; Fairview, Dirleton, E Lothian

LILFORD, 7 Baron (GB 1797); George Vernon Powys; s of Robert Horace Powys (d 1940, gggs of 2 Baron Lilford), by his w Vera Grace; suc 6 Baron (2 cous twice removed) 1949; *b* 8 Jan 1931; *Educ* St Aidan's Coll Grahamstown SA, Stonyhurst; *m* 1, 1954 (m dis), Mrs Eveline Bird; m 2, 1957 (m dis 1958), Anuta, da of L F Merritt, of Johannesburg; m 3, 1958 (m dis 1961), Norma Yvonne, da of V Shell, of Johannesburg; m 4, 1961 (m dis 1969), Muriel, *née* Cooke; 2 da; m 5, 1969, Margaret, da of Archibald Penman (d 1983), of Roslin, Midlothian; 1 s, 2 da (Hon Sarah b 1971, Hon Hannah b 1974); *Heir* s, Hon Mark Vernon Powys b 16 Nov 1975; *Recreations* golf, cricket; *Style*— The Rt Hon the Lord Lilford; Le Grand Câtelet, St John, Jersey, CI (☎ 0534 63871)

LILL, John Richard; OBE (1978); s of G R Lill; *b* 17 Mar 1944; *Educ* Leyton County HS, Royal Coll Music; *Career* concert pianist, soloist with leading orchestras, worldwide TV and radio appearances, prof Royal Coll Music, winner of Int Tchaikowsky competition Moscow 1970; *Recreations* amateur radio, chess, psychic research; *Style*— John Lill Esq, OBE; c/o Harold Holt Ltd, 134 Wigmore St, W1 (☎ 01 935 2331)

LILLEY, Prof Geoffrey Michael; OBE (1981); s of Morland Michael Dessau Lilley (d 1946), and Emily Lilley (d 1977); *b* 16 Nov 1919; *Educ* Isleworth GS, Imperial Coll; *m* 1948, Leslie Marion, da of Leonard Frank Wheeler, of Cranfield, Beds; 1 s (Michael b 1957), 2 da (Grete b 1950, Elisabeth b 1953); *Career* served RAF 1935-36; prof of: experimental fluid mechanics Coll of Aeronautics 1962, aeronautics and astronautics Univ of Southampton 1964-82 (prof emeritus 1982-); memb Noise Advsy Cncl (chm Noise from Air Traffic) 1970-80; *Recreations* walking, chess, opera and ballet; *Clubs* Athenaeum; *Style*— Prof Geoffrey Lilley, OBE; Highbury, Pine Walk, Chilworth, Southampton SO1 7HQ (☎ 0703 769109); Dept of Aeronautics and Astronautics, University of Southampton, Southampton SO9 5NH (☎ 0703 595000, ext 2325)

LILLEY, Peter Bruce; MP (C) St Albans 1983-; *b* 1943; *Educ* Dulwich, Clare Coll Cambridge; *Career* energy industs investmt advsr; contested (C) Haringey Tottenham Oct 1974, former chm Bow Gp; sec Cons Backbench Energy Ctee 1983-84, memb Treasy Select Ctee 1983-84, PPS to min of state for Local Govt 1984, PPS to Chllr of Exchequer 1985-, econ sec to Treasy 1987- FInstPet 1978; *Books* Delusions of Incomes Policy (with Samuel Brittan); *Style*— Peter Lilley, Esq, MP; House of Commons, London SW1

LILLICRAP, Dr David Anthony; s of Albert Ernest Lillicrap (d 1984), and Margaret, *née* Baldwin (d 1958); *b* 26 Oct 1930; *Educ* St Edwards Sch Oxford, St Edmund Hall Oxford, Guy's Hosp London (BM, BCh, MA); *m* 15 June 1967, Gwyneth Frances, da of Philip Lister Roberts (d 1987); 3 s (Stephen b 1958, Richard b 1964, Peter b 1965), 1 da (Susan b 1960); *Career* sr registrar med Guy's Hosp 1962-66, res fell John Hopkins Hosp Baltimore 1964-65, conslt physician Thanet Dist Hosp 1966-, conslt endocrinolist Canterbury Hosp Kent 1966-; memb: Margate Rotary, Dist Health Authy Canterbury Thanet; FRCP 1974; *Recreations* squash, dinghy sailing, bridge; *Style*— Dr David Lillicrap; 29 Princes Gdns, Cliftonville, Magate, Kent CT9 3AR (☎ 0843 292 335); Thanet Dist Gen Hosp, Margate, Kent (☎ 0843 225 544)

LILLINGSTON, Lady Vivienne Margaret Nevill; da of 5 Marquess of Abergavenny, KG, OBE; *b* 15 Feb 1941; *m* 1962, Alan Lillingston, s of Capt Luke Theodore Lillingston (ka Normandy Invasion Aug 1944); 2 s (Luke b 1963, Andrew b 1972), 2 da (Georgina b 1965, Sophie b 1968); *Style*— Lady Vivienne Lillingston; Mount Coote, Kilmallock, Co Limerick, Ireland (☎ 063 98111)

LILLIS, Anthony Percival Noel; s of late Capt Percival Joseph Lillis; *b* 25 Dec 1916; *Educ* King Edward V1 GS Totnes; *m* 1940, Beryl, nee Bruton; 2 da; *Career* Lt RNVR, serv Med, N Africa, Italy, Pacific; dir H J Heinz Co Ltd 1966-70; *Recreations* sailing, motoring; *Clubs* IOD; *Style*— Anthony Lillis, Esq; Underdean House, Blakeney, Glos (☎ 0594 510236); Severn Valley Woodworks Ltd, Blakeney, Glos (☎ 0594 510217)

LILLY, Prof Malcolm Douglas; s of Charles Victor Lilly (d 1977), and Amy, *née* Gardner; *b* 9 August 1936; *Educ* St Olave's GS, UCL (BSc, PhD), Univ of London (DSc); *m* 19 Sept 1959, Sheila Elizabeth, da of George Frederick Andrew Stuart (d 1973); 2 s (Andrew Stuart b 14 Nov 1966, Duncan Stuart b 12 May 1968); *Career* RNVR 1953-54, Nat Serv RN 1954-56; prof biochem engrg UCL 1979- (lectr 1963-72, reader 1972-79), dir Whatman Biochems 1968-71, visiting prof Univ of Pennsylvania USA 1969, chm Int Orgn for Biotechnol and Bioengrg 1972-80, cncl memb Soc of Gen Microbiology 1979-83-, memb Br Gas Res Ctee 1982-, dir Inst Biotechnol Studies 1983, visiting res fell Merck Sharp and Dohme USA 1987, bd memb Public Health Lab Serv 1988, fell UCL 1988-; govr St Olaves GS Orpington Kent, observer SE Gp Inst of Advanced Motorists, registered referee Kent Co FB Assoc; FIChemE 1980, FEng 1982; *Books* Fermentation and Enzyme Technology (jtly 1979); *Recreations* advanced motoring, sailing, swimming; *Style*— Prof Malcolm Lilly; Collingwood, 8 Tower Rd, Orpington, Kent BR6 0SQ (☎ 0689 217 62); Dept of Chemical and Biochemical Engineering, Univ Coll London, Torrington Place, London WC1E 7JE (☎ 01 380 7368, fax 01 388 0808)

LILLY, Michael Hugh; s of Archibald Hugh Rendall Lilly, of Mount Agar, Carnon Downs, Truro, Cornwall, and Beryl Calenda, *née* Pryor (d 1986); *b* 11 Mar 1951; *Educ* Hardyes Sch Dorset, Oxford Sch of Architecture (Dip Arch); *m* 20 Sept 1980, Penelope Sarah Jane, da of Ronald Horace Cranton, of Steeple Leaze Farm, Steeple, Dorset; 2 s (James b 1983, Alexander b 1985); *Career* scholarship awarded by Worshipful Co of Carpenters to study in Philadelphia USA 1978, design tutor (p/t) Plymouth Sch of Architecture 1980-83, ptnr John Crowther & Assocs Truro 1983-; chm Cornwall Branch Assoc of Conslt Architects; memb: exec ctee Truro Civic Soc, educn ctee Carpenters Co; Freeman City of London, Liveryman Worshipful Co of Carpenters 1982; RIBA 1978; *Recreations* travel, windsurfing, walking, art; *Style—* Michael Lilly, Esq; Clifden, Carnon Donns, Truro, Cornwall TR3 6LE (☎ 0872 863 942); c/o John Crowther & Assoc, 26/28 Charles St, Truro, Cornwall TR1 2PH (☎ 0872 755 44, fax 0872 401 54)

LIMB, Christopher; s of William Herbert Limb, of Lymm, and Dora *née* Clayton; *b* 12 Mar 1953; *Educ* Lymm GS, Univ of Liverpool (LLB); *m* 31 July 1976, Gilian May, da of John Ernest Heady, of Chester; 2 s (Timothy b 1984, Joseph b 1986); *Career* called to the bar Gray's Inn 1975, practising Manchester; chm: Lymm-Meung Twin Town Soc, Lymm Rushbearing Ctee; co-organiser Lymm Jr Music Festival; memb: Salford Choral Soc, Bar Cncl, Manchester Medico Legal Soc; *Books* legal articles in New Law Jl; *Recreations* music, French, my children; *Style—* Christopher Limb, Esq; 6th Floor Sunlight House, Quay St, Manchester M3 3LE

LIMBU, Capt Rambahadur; VC (1965); s of Tekbir Limbu (d 1949), and Tunimaya Limbu (d 1952); *m* 1, Tikamaya (d 1966); 2 s; m 2, 1967, Punimaya, da of Lachuman Rai, of Nepal; 2 s (and 1 s decd); *Career* VC for gallantry against Indonesians in Borneo; 10 Princess Mary's Own Gurkha Rifles 1957, Capt Dipakbahadur Gurung (Gurkha Tport Regt); HM The Queen's Gurkha Orderly Offr 1983-84; *Style—* Capt Rambahadur Limbu, VC; Ex 10th PMO Gurkha Rifles, HQ, Gurkha Reserve Unit, PO Box 420, Bandar Seri Begawan 1904, Brunei Darussalam

LIMERICK, 6 Earl of (I 1803); Patrick Edmund Pery; KBE (1983), DL (W Sussex 1988); also Baron Glentworth (I 1790; from 1834 the gs and h of 1 Earl was designated 'Viscount' Glentworth, now the style of the eldest s and h), Viscount Limerick (I 1800), and sits as Baron Foxford (UK 1815); s of 5 Earl of Limerick, GBE, CH, KCB, DSO, TD (d 1967), by his w Angela, GBE, CH, DStJ (da of Lt-Col Sir Henry Trotter, KCMG, CB); *b* 12 April 1930; *Educ* Eton, New Coll Oxford; *m* 1961, Sylvia Rosalind, *qv*; 2 s (Viscount Glentworth, Hon Adrian b 1967), 1 da (Lady Alison b 1964); *Heir* s, Viscount Glentworth, *qv*; *Career* Sits as Cons Peer in House of Lords, parly under-sec state Dept of Trade and Indust 1972-74; Kleinwort Benson Gp plc: dir 1967-72 and 1974-85, dep chm 1985-87; dir: T R Pacific Investmt Tst plc 1976-, Brooke Bond Gp plc 1981-84, The De La Rue Co plc 1983-; chm BOTB 1979-83, govrs City of London Poly 1984-; chm: Br Invisible Export Cncl 1984-, Polymeters Response Int Ltd 1988-; pres Inst of Export 1983-, vice-pres Assoc of British C of Cs (pres 1974-77); *Recreations* skiing, mountaineering; *Style—* The Rt Hon the Earl of Limerick, KBE, DL; Chiddinglye, W Hoathly, E Grinstead, W Sussex (☎ 0342 810214); 30 Victoria Rd, London W8 (☎ 01 937 0537)

LIMERICK, Countess of; Sylvia Rosalind Pery; er da of Brig Maurice Stanley Lush, CB, CBE, MC, and Diana Ruth, *née* Hill; *b* 7 Dec 1935; *Educ* St Swithun's Sch Winchester, LMH Oxford; *m* 22 April 1961, 6 Earl of Limerick, *qv*; 2 s, 1 da; *Career* vice-chm Fndn for the Study of Infant Deaths 1971-; pres: UK Ctee for UN Children's Fund 1972-79, Nat Assoc for Maternal and Child Welfare 1973-84; memb: Ctee of Mgmnt Inst of Child Health 1976-, cncl and ctee of mgmnt King Edward's Hosp Fund 1977-81 and 1985-, Kensington Chelsea and Westminster Area Health Authy 1977-82; pres Health Visitors Assoc 1984-, chm Br Red Cross 1985-; *Books* Sudden Infant Death: patterns, puzzles and problems (jtly, 1985); *Recreations* skiing, music; *Style—* The Rt Hon the Countess of Limerick; 30 Victoria Rd, London W8 5RG (☎ 01 937 0573); Chiddinglye, W Hoathly, E Grinstead, W Sussex RH19 4QT (☎ 0342 810214)

LIMERICK AND KILLALOE, Bishop of 1985-; Rt Rev Edward Flewett Darling; s of Ven Vivian W Darling, BD (Archdeacon of Cloyne, d 1965), and Honor Frances Garde, *née* Flewett (d 1984); *b* 24 July 1933; *Educ* Cork GS, Midleton Coll, St John's Sch Leatherhead, Trinity Coll Dublin (BA, MA); *m* 2 Aug 1958, (Edith Elizabeth) Patricia, da of Very Rev A W M Stanley Mann (Dean of Down, d 1968); 3 s (David b 1960, Colin b 1961, Philip b 1963), 2 da (Alison b 1966, Linda b 1968); *Career* curate: St Luke's Belfast 1956-59, St John's Orangefield Belfast 1959-62; incumbent St Gall's Carnalea Bangor Co Down 1962-72, rector St John's Malone Belfast 1972-85; *Books* A Child is Born (1966), Choosing the Hymns (1984); *Recreations* music, gardening; *Style—* The Rt Rev the Bishop of Limerick and Killaloe; Bishop's House, N Circular Rd, Limerick, Ireland (☎ 061 51532)

LINACRE, Sir (John) Gordon Seymour; CBE (1979), AFC (1943), DFM (1941); s of John James Linacre (d 1957), of Norton Woodseats, Sheffield; *b* 23 Sept 1920; *Educ* Firth Park GS Sheffield; *m* 1943, Irene Amy, da of Alexander Gordon (d 1946); 2 da; *Career* serv RAF WWII; former: chm and dir of Press Assoc, pres Newspaper Soc; chm Yorks Post Newspapers Ltd 1983- (md 1965-83), dep chm United Newspapers Ltd 1983- (formerly chief exec 1981-88), dir Yorkshire TV, chm Opera North; former pres Fédération Internationale des Editeurs de Journaux et Publications 1984-88; kt 1986; *Recreations* golf, country walking; *Clubs* Leeds, Headingley Taverner, Alwoodley GC; *Style—* Sir Gordon Linacre, CBE, AFC, DFM

LINCOLN, Sir Anthony Handley; KCMG (1965, CMG 1958), CVO (1957); s of John Bebrouth Lincoln, OBE (d 1938); *b* 2 Jan 1911; *Educ* Mill Hill Sch, Magdalene Coll Cambridge; *m* 1948, Lisette Marion, da of late A E Summers, of Buenos Aires; *Career* formerly cnsllr Br Embassy Copenhagen, ambass to Venezuela 1064-69; *Clubs* Brooks's, Reform; *Style—* Sir Anthony Lincoln, KCMG, CVO

LINCOLN, Hon Mr Justice; Hon Sir Anthony Leslie Julian; s of Samuel Lincoln; *b* 7 April 1920; *Educ* Highgate, Queen's Coll Oxford (MA); *Career* served WW II in Somerset LI and RA 1941-45; barr Lincoln's Inn 1949, QC 1968, rec of Crown Ct 1974-79, judge of the High Court of Justice family div 1979-; chm Harrison Homes for the Elderly; kt 1979; *Style—* The Hon Mr Justice Lincoln; Upper Woodford, Salisbury, Wilts

LINCOLN, 18 Earl of (E 1572); Edward Horace Fiennes-Clinton; er s of Edward Henry Fiennes-Clinton (ka 1916), and Edith Annie, *née* Guest (d 1965); suc his kinsman 10 and last Duke of Newcastle and 17 Earl of Lincoln (d 1988); *b* 23 Feb 1913; *m* 1, 1940, Leila Ruth, *née* Millen (d 1947); 1 s (Hon Edward Gordon), 1 da (Lady Patricia Elrick, *qv*); m 2, 3 Dec 1953, Linda Alice, *née* O'Brien; *Heir* s, Edward Gordon Fiennes-Clinton, *qv*; 73 Picton Rd, Bunbury, W Australia 6230

LINCOLN, Frederick; s of F Lincoln, of Warlingham, Surrey, and Mary J, *née* Stevenson (d 1979); *b* 6 Oct 1927; *Educ* Croydon Poly, Regent St Polytec, Sch of Architecture; *m* 30 Aug 1952, Frances Joan Ninette, da of Horace J Minshull, CBE (d 1963); 1 s (Paul b 1959), 1 da (Clare b 1957); *Career* chartered architect in private practice; formerly sr architect and asst to Sir William Atkins 1957-60 on Berkeley Nuclear Power Station; architect: Ford Tractor Plant Basildon 1962, SGS-Fairchild Falkirk 1966; CBI award; FRIBA; *Recreations* gardening, travel, vintage cars, industrial archeology, France; *Clubs* VSCC; *Style—* Frederick Lincoln, Esq; Woldingham, Surrey (☎ 088 385 2223)

LINCOLN, His Hon Dr John Francis; AM; s of John Lincoln (d 1916); *b* 30 July 1916; *Educ* Newington College Aust, Balliol Coll Oxford; *m* 1952, Joan Alison, da of Harold Robert Lionel Scott (d 1977); 1 s, 1 da; *Career* Maj served India, Singapore, Palestine; barr Lincoln's Inn, DJAG 1946-47 actg judge Supreme Ct of New South Wales 1967, judge Dist Ct of New South Wales 1968-, dep-chllr Macquarie Univ 1976-, chllr Diocese of Newcastle NSW 1978-; formerly Mayor of N Sydney 1956-58, NSW state tres Lib Pty of Aust 1966-68; chm: Parole Bd of NSW 1984-, N Sydney Community Hosp 1962-, Northolm GS; hon LLD; hon sec Order of Australia Assoc NSW 1986-88 (vice-pres 1988-); *Recreations* swimming; *Style—* His Hon Dr John Lincoln, AM; Stone Lodge, 30-34 Stanley St, St Ives NSW 2075, Australia

LINCOLN, 70 Bishop of (1072), 1986-; Rt Rev Robert Maynard Hardy; see founded from two more ancient ones (Lindisfarn at Sidnacester and Middle Angles at Leicester, united in one diocese under see of Leicester; the new entity was firstly removed to Dorchester and secondly, after the conquest, to Lincoln); patron of 154 livings and 21 alternately and by turns or jointly, the Canonries, Precentorship, Chancellor-ship, Sub-Deanery, and the Archdeaconries of Stow, Lincoln and Lindsey, also Prebendal stalls in the Cathedral; s of Harold and Monica Mavie Hardy; *b* 5 Oct 1936; *Educ* Queen Elizabeth GS Wakefield, Clare Coll Cambridge (MA); *m* 1970, Isobel Mary, da of Charles Burch; 2 s, 1 da; *Career* deacon 1962, priest 1963, asst curate All Saints and Martyrs Langley Manchester 1962, fell and chaplain Selwyn Coll Cambridge 1965, vicar All Saints Borehamwood 1972, priest-in-charge Aspley Guise 1975, course dir St Albans Diocese Ministerial Trg Scheme 1975, incumbent of United Benefice of Aspley Guise with Husborne Crawley and Ridgmont 1980, bishop suffragan of Maidstone 1980-86, bishop to HM Prisons 1985-; Hon Fell Selwyn Coll Cambridge 1986; *Recreations* walking, gardening, reading; *Style—* The Rt Rev the Bishop of Lincoln; Bishop's House, Eastgate, Lincoln LN2 1QQ (☎ 0522 534701)

LINDA, Lady Isobel Mackenzie; da of Countess of Cromartie (d 1962); *b* 1911; *m* 1947, Capt Oscar Linda; *Style—* Lady Isobel Linda; Assynt House, Evanton, Ross (☎ 0349 830602)

LINDENBAUM, Dr David Edward; s of Dr Konrad Lindenbaum, of Hendon (d 1958), and Sybil Mary, *née* Thorpe (d 1972); *b* 7 July 1936; *Educ* St Pauls, Univ Coll Oxford (MA, BM, BCh), St Mary's Hosp London (DMRD); *m* 4 March 1967, Kathleen Mary, da of Alec Davies Saxon (d 1962), of Wilmslow, Cheshire; 2 s (Roderic James Edward b 1972, Charles Peter b 1975), 1 da (Joanne Sarah b 1969); *Career* sr registrar Manchester Royal Infirmary, hon prosector RCS, res neurosurgical registrar Gt Ormond St Hosp for Sick Children, conslt radiologist Gen Hosp Northampton 1973-; fell Manchester Med Soc, memb Br Inst Radiology and Br Med Ultrasound Soc; FFR 1972, FRCR 1975; *Recreations* fly fishing, trout and salmon, sailing; *Clubs* Royal Ocean Racing, Oxford Univ YC, Oxford Med Graduates; *Style—* Dr David Lindenbaum; The Coach House, Old Northamptonshire NN6 9RJ (☎ 0604 781214 0604 34700); General Hospital, X-Ray Dept, Northampton NN1 5BD (☎ 0604 34700)

LINDESAY-BETHUNE, Hon John Martin; s of 14 Earl of Lindsay; *b* 27 Nov 1929; *Educ* Eton, Trinity Hall Cambridge; *m* 1, 1953 (m dis 1976), Enriqueta Mary Jeanne, da of Peter Koch de Gooreynd; 3 s, 1 da; m 2, 1977, Jean Maxwell, da of Brig Eric Brickman, and formerly w of Stephen John Younger; *Career* former Lt Scots Gds; md J Walter Thompson Gp Ltd 1975-81, chm Westminster C of C 1980-82; *Style—* The Hon John Lindesay-Bethune; Muircambus, Elie, Leven, Fife KY9 1HD (☎ 033 334 200)

LINDGREN, Hon Graham Alastair; s of Baron Lindgren (Life Peer, d 1971); *b* 25 July 1928; *Educ* Welwyn Garden City GS; *m* 1953, Gwendolyne Mary, da of late A W Miller, of Coleford, Glos; 1 s (Derek, b 1969); *Style—* The Hon Graham Lindgren; 43 Westly Wood, Welwyn Garden City, Herts (☎ 0707 326706);

LINDISFARNE, Archdeacon of; *see*: Bowering, Ven Michael Ernest

LINDLEY, Sir Arnold Lewis George; s of George Dilnot Lindley (d 1927), and Charlotte, *née* Hooley (d 1946); *b* 13 Nov 1902; *Educ* Woolwich Poly; *m* 1, 1927, Winifred (d 1962), da of Francis Cowling, of Somerset; 1 s, 1 da; m 2, 1963, Phyllis, da of Walter Burns, of Lincoln; *Career* chm GEC Ltd 1961-64 (vice chm 1959, md 1961-62); chm Engrg Indust Trg Bd 1964-74, vice chm Motherwell Bridge (Hldgs) Ltd 1965-84, dir General Advsrs Ltd; chm Cncl of Engrg Insts 1971-73, memb Design Cncl 1972-74; pres: Int Electrical Assoc 1963-65, Inst of Mechanical Engrs 1968-69; consulting mechanical and electrical engr, conslt to Govt for various engrg projects; Hon DSc: City 1969, Aston 1969, London 1970; kt 1964; *Recreations* golf; *Style—* Sir Arnold Lindley; Heathcote House, 18 Nab Lane, Shipley, W Yorks (☎ 0274 598484)

LINDLEY, Dr Bryan Charles; CBE 1982; s of Wing Cdr Alfred Webb Lindley (d 1988), of Lichfield, and Florence, *née* Pratten (d 1975); *b* 30 August 1932; *Educ* Reading Sch, UCL (BSc, PhD); *m* 2 May 1987, Dr Judith Anne, da of Robert Heyworth, of Bramhall; 1 s ((John) Julian b 1960); *Career* Nat Gas Turbine Estab 1954-57, Hawker Siddeley Nuclear Power Co Ltd 1957-59, Int Res & Dept Co Ltd and CA Parsons Nuclear Res Centre 1959-65, mangr R&D div CA Parsons & Co Ltd 1965-68, chief exec and md ERA Technol Ltd (chm: ERA Patents Ltd, ERA Autotrack Systems Ltd) 1968-1979, dir of technol Dunlop Hldgs plc (dir Dunlop Ltd, chm: Thermal Conversions (UK) Ltd, Soilless Cultivation Systems Ltd, Dunlop Solaronics Div, Dunlop Bioprocesses Ltd) 1979-85, dir technol & planning BICC Cables Ltd (chm Optical Fibro; dir: Thomas Bolton & Johnson Ltd) 1985-88; dir RAPRA Technol Ltd 1985-, chief exec Nat Advanced Robotics Res Centre 1989-; memb: ACARD 1980-86, Materials Advsy Gp DTI 1984; fell UCL 1979; FIMechE 1968, FIEE 1968, FInstP 1969, FPRI 1980; *Recreations* music, photography, walking, skiing, sailing; *Clubs* IOD; *Style—* Dr Bryan Lindley, CBE; 1 Edgehill Chase, Wilmslow, Cheshire, SK9 2DJ, (☎ 0625 523323)

LINDLEY, Raymond Peter; s of Frederick George Lindley, by his w Edith Elizabeth, *née* Evans (d 1979); *b* 26 May 1929; *m* 1953, Lilian May, *née* Scales; 1 da; *Career* insur broker, ret; former dir: Reed Stenhouse UK Ltd 1969-85, Reed Stenhouse Ltd 1979-85; conslt to various cos and slrs; FCII; *Recreations* flyfishing, music, collecting porcelain; *Style*— Peter Lindley, Esq; Springrove House, Redwings Lane, Pembury, Tunbridge Wells, Kent (☎ 089 282 2172)

LINDNER, Dr Gerhard; *b* 26 Feb 1930; *Educ* Leipzig Univ; *m* Edletraut; 2 s; *Career* entry into Dip Serv 1956; cncllr: Czechoslovak Socialist Republic 1964, Finland 1965-68; head Trade Mission (Denmark) 1970-74; ambass: GDR (Australia) 1977-81, GDR UK and GB and NI; holder of several awards and medals; *Recreations* sport, classical music; *Style*— Dr Gerhard Lindner, Esq

LINDOP, David Harry; s of Col Carl Arthur Boys Lindop (d 1968); *b* 17 July 1928; *Educ* Sedbergh, Univ of Birmingham; *m* 1952, Heather Margaret Murray, *née* Lambert; 3 s; *Career* chm and md FJ Whittle Metal Prodns Ltd 1973-83; Freeman City of London, Liveryman and Asst Worshipful Co of Founders; CEng; *Recreations* golf, gardening; *Clubs* Little Aston GC; *Style*— David Lindop, Esq; 147 Hill Village Rd, Four Oaks, Sutton Coldfield, W Midlands B75 5JH (☎ 021 308 3163)

LINDOP, Sir Norman; DL (Hertford 1989); s of Thomas Cox Lindop, of Stockport, Cheshire, and May Lindop; *b* 9 Mar 1921; *Educ* Northgate Sch Ipswich, Queen Mary Coll London (MSc); *m* 1974, Jenny Caroline Quass; 1 s; *Career* chemistry lectr Queen Mary Coll 1946, asst dir examinations Civil Serv Cmmn 1951; sr chemistry lectr Kingston Coll of Technol 1953-57 (head of chem and geology dept 1957-63); princ: SW Essex Tech Coll and Sch of Art 1963-66, Hatfield Coll of Technol 1966-69; dir Hatfield Poly 1969-82, princ Br Sch of Osteopathy 1982-; chm: Hatfield Philharmonic Soc 1970-82, ctee of Dirs of Polys 1972-74, cncl for Professions Supplementary to Medicine 1973-81, cncl of Westfield Coll London 1983-, Home Off Data Protection Ctee 1976-78, DES Public Sector Validation Enquiry 1984-85, Br Library Advsy Cncl 1986-, vice-chm steering gp responsible for planning new inst to replace New Univ of Ulster and Ulster Poly 1982-84; memb: US-UK Educnl Fulbright Cmmn 1971-81, SRC 1974-78, GMC 1979-84; fell: Queen Mary Coll London Univ 1976, Hatfield Poly 1983, Coll of Preceptors; Hon DEd Cncl for Nat Academic Awards 1982; FRSA, FRSC kt 1973; *Clubs* Athenaeum; *Style*— Sir Norman Lindop, DL; The British Sch of Osteopathy, 1-4 Suffolk St, London SW1Y 4HG (☎ 01 930 9254/8)

LINDQVIST, Andrew Nils Gunnar; s of Kjell Gunnar Lindqvist, of Nether Langleys, Tharston, Norwich, and Joan Bernice Kathleen, *née* Skingley; *b* 7 May 1943; *Educ* Gresham's, Trinity Hall Cambridge (MA); *m* 4 Sept 1971 (m dis), Sonia Frances, da of Sqdn-Ldr Alfred Basil Charles, MBE (d 1984); 2 da (Hanna b 1980, Annika b 1982); *Career* barr 1968, memb area Legal Aid Ctee 1983; Friend and Volunteer First Mate Ocean Youth Club; *Recreations* sailing, tennis, hockey, languages; *Clubs* Norfolk (Norwich); *Style*— Andrew Lindqvist, Esq; Mill Farm, Deopham, Wymondham, Norwich (☎ 0953 851 434); Octagon House, 19 Colegate, Norwich NR3 1AT (☎ 0603 623 186, fax 0603 760 519)

LINDSAY, Lady Amabel Mary Maud Yorke; da of 9 Earl of Hardwicke (d 1974); *b* 2 April 1935; *m* 16 Dec 1955, Hon Patrick Lindsay (d 1986); 3 s, 1 da; *Style*— Lady Amabel Lindsay; 12 Lansdowne Rd, London W11 (☎ 01 727 6006); Folly Farm, Hungerford, Berks (☎ 0488 82790)

LINDSAY, Hon Mrs (Audrey Lavinia); *née* Lyttelton; da of 9 Viscount Cobham, KCB, TD (d 1949); *m* 21 June 1950, David Edzell Thomas Lindsay (d 1968); 2 s (1 decd), 1 da; *Style*— The Hon Mrs Lindsay; Poplar Cottage, Fore St Hill, Budleigh Salterton, Devon (☎ 039 54 5244)

LINDSAY, Hon Mrs Bronwen Mary; *née* Scott-Ellis; da of 8 Baron Howard de Walden and (4 Baron) Seaford (d 1946); *b* 1912; *m* 1933, Hon James Louis Lindsay, *qv*, s of 27 Earl of Crawford and Balcarres; *Style*— The Hon Mrs Lindsay

LINDSAY, Lady Clare Rohais Antonia Elizabeth; *née* Giffard; da of 3 Earl of Halsbury, and his 2 w, Elizabeth Adeline Faith, da of late Maj Harry Crewe Godley, DSO; *b* 23 June 1944; *m* 27 Oct 1964, Col Oliver John Martin Lindsay; 2 s (Sir Martin Alexander Lindsay of Dowhill, 1 Bt, CBE, DSO, Mark (now Mark Gifford-Lindsay) b 1968), 2 da (Victoria (Mrs Gregory Wheatley) b 1967, Fiona b 1972); *Style*— Lady Clare Lindsay; Brookwood House, Brookwood, nr Woking, Surrey GU24 0NX

LINDSAY, Crawford Callum Douglas; QC (1987); s of Douglas Marshall Lindsay, and Eileen Mary Lindsay; *b* 5 Feb 1939; *Educ* Whitgift Sch Croydon, St John's Coll Oxford (BA); *m* 1963, Rosemary Gough; 1 s, 1 da; *Career* barr 1961, rec SE circuit 1982-; *Style*— Crawford Lindsay, Esq, QC; 6 King's Bench Walk, Temple, EC4Y 7DR (☎ 01 353 9901)

LINDSAY, 15 Earl of (S 1633); David Bethune Lindesay-Bethune; also Lord Lindsay of the Byres (S 1445), Lord Parbroath (S 1633), Viscount Garnock, and Lord Kilbirnie, Kingsburn and Drumry (both S 1703); s of 14 Earl of Lindsay (d 1985), by his w, Marjorie (*see* Dowager Countess of Lindsay); *b* 9 Feb 1926; *Educ* Eton, Magdalene Coll Cambridge; *m* 1, 1953 (m dis 1968), Hon Mary Clare Douglas Scott Montagu, da of 2 Baron Montagu of Beaulieu (d 1929); 1 s, 1 da; m 2, 1969, Penelope Georgina, da of late Anthony Crommelin Crossley, MP (only s of Sir Kenneth Crossley, 2 Bt), and formerly wife of Maj Henry Ronald Burn-Callander, MC; *Heir* s, Viscount Garnock; *Career* Scots Gds 1943-45, US & Canadian Railroads 1948-50, former dir Carpets Int Gp Servs Ltd, Crossley-Karastan Carpet Mills Ltd, Crossley-Karastan Carpet Mills Ltd Canada, dir Festiniog Railway Co Ltd, patron Servern Valley Railway (Hldgs) Ltd, chm Romney Hythe and Dymchurch Light Rly Co 1976-, Sallingbury Ltd 1977-; dir: Abbey Life Insur Co of Canada 1964-, Bain Dawes Ltd (Northern) 1978-81; vice-chm N American Advsy Gp BOTB 1973-87, vice-pres Tport Trust 1973-; chm: Br Tourist Authy 1975-81, Br Carpets Manufacturers Assoc Export Cncl 1976-85, Air Tport Users Ctee 1983-85; memb Royal Co Archers (Queen's Body Gd for Scotland) 1960-; *Clubs* Boodle,s; *Style*— The Rt Hon the Earl of Lindsay; Combermere Abbey, Whitchurch, Salop (☎ 094 870 287); Coates House, Upper Largo, Fife (☎ 033336 429)

LINDSAY, Maj-Gen (Courtenay Traice) David; CB (1963); s of Courtenay Traice Lindsay (d 1915), and Charlotte Editha, *née* Wetenhall (d 1956); *b* 28 Sept 1910; *Educ* Rugby, RMA Woolwich; *m* 31 Oct 1934, Margaret Elizabeth, da of William Pease Theakston, MBE (d 1937), of Lawrence Ct, Huntingdon; 2 s (John b 1936, Michael b 1938); *Career* cmmnd 2 Lt RA 1930, served WW11 1939-45, Col memb Ordanace Bd, Brig sr mil offr Royal Armament R & D Estab 1955-58, dir of munitions Br staff Washington 1958-60, Maj-Gen dir-gen of artillery WO 1961-64, ret 1964; *Recreations* golf; *Clubs* Rye GC; *Style*— Maj-Gen David Lindsay, CB; Huggits Farm, Stone-on-Oxney, Tenterden, Kent TN30 7JT (☎ 023 383 383)

LINDSAY, Hon Erica Susan; da of 2 Baron Lindsay of Birker; *b* 1942; *Educ* Canberra HS Australia, Sch of Int Serv, American Univ Washington DC, LMH Oxford; *Style*— The Hon Erica Lindsay; 6812 Delaware St, Chevy Chase 15, Maryland, USA (☎ 656 4245); Gillbank, Boot, Holmrook, Cumberland

LINDSAY, Hugh; *see*: Hexham and Newcastle, Bishop of

LINDSAY, Hon James Francis; s and h of 2 Baron Lindsay of Birker; *b* 29 Jan 1945; *Educ* Canberra HS, Geelong GS Victoria, Bethesda-Chevy Chase HS, Univ of Keele, Univ of Liverpool; *Career* formerly lectr dept of physics Tunghai Univ Taichung Taiwan Repub of China; second sec Australian Embassy Santiago Chile 1973-76; first sec: Vientiane Laos 1979-80, Dhaka Bangladesh 1982-83, Caracas Venezuela 1986-; *Recreations* hiking, mountaineering, tennis; *Style*— The Hon James Lindsay; Australian Foreign Service, Dept of Foreign Affairs, Canberra, ACT, Australia

LINDSAY, Sir James Harvey Kincaid Stewart; s of Arthur Harvey Lindsay (d 1970), and Doris Kincaid Lindsay (d 1944); *b* 31 May 1915; *Educ* Highgate Sch; *m* Marguerite Phyllis Bondville; 1 s, 1 da by previous m; *Career* devpt conslt; formerly: chm and md The Metal Box Co of India Ltd, pres Assoc C of C and Indust of India; tstee Inst of Family and Environmental Res 1971, pres Inst of Cultural Affrs Int Brussels 1981-, convenor Int Exposition of Rural Devpt (sponsored by four UN agencies and the Inst of Cultural Affrs Int) 1981-86; life memb All India Mgmnt Assoc; CBIM, FInstM; kt 1966; *Recreations* music; *Clubs* East India, IOD; *Style*— Sir James Lindsay; Christmas Cottage, Lower Shiplake, Oxfordshire RG9 3LH (☎ 073 522 2859)

LINDSAY, Hon James Louis; s of 27 Earl of Crawford and (10) Balcarres (d 1940); *b* 16 Dec 1906; *Educ* Eton, Magdalen Coll Oxford; *m* 26 April 1933, Hon Bronwen Mary Scott Ellis, *qv*, da of 8 Baron Howard de Walden; 3 s (Hugh John Alexander b 1934, Alexander Thomas b 1936, Stephen James b 1940), 1 da (Julia Margaret b 1941),; *Career* formerly Maj KRRC, served WW II; contested Bristol SE 1950 and 1951, MP (C) N Devon 1955-59; *Style*— The Hon James Lindsay

LINDSAY, James Martin Evelyn; s and h of Sir Ronald Lindsay of Dowhill, 2 Bt; *b* 1968; *Style*— James Lindsay, Esq

LINDSAY, Dr John Maurice; CBE (1979), TD (1946); s of Matthew Lindsay (d 1969), of 32 Athole Gdns, Glasgow, and Eileen Frances, *née* Brock (1954); *b* 21 July 1918; *Educ* Glasgow Acad, Scottish Nat Acad of Music; *m* 3 Aug 1946, Aileen Joyce, da of Evan Ramsay Macintosh Gordon (d 1973); 1 s (Niall Gordon Brock b 1957), 3 da (Seona Morag Joyce b 1949, Kirsteen Ann b 1951, Morven Morag Joyce b 1959); *Career* poet, author, broadcaster, music critic and environmentalist; drama critic Scottish Daily Mail 1946-47, music critic The Bulletin 1946-60, ed Scots Review 1949-50; Border TV: programme controller 1961-62, prodn controller 1962-64, features exec and chief interviewer 1964-67; dir The Scottish Civic Tst 1967-83 (conslt 1983-), hon sec-gen Europa Nostra 1982-; Hon DLitt Glasgow 1982; Hon FRIAS; *Books* poetry: The Advancing Day (1940), Perhaps Tomorrow (1941), Predicament (1942), No Crown for Laughter: Poems (1943), The Enemies of Love: Poems 1941-45 (1946), Selected Poems (1947), Hurlygush: Poems in Scots (1948), At the Wood's Edge (1950), Ode for St Andrew's Night and Other Poems (1951), The Exiled Heart: Poems 1941-56 (1957), Snow Warning and Other poems (1962), One Later Day and Other Poems (1964), This Business of Living (1969), Comings and Goings: Poems (1971), Selected Poems 1942-72 (1973), The Run from Life (1975), Walking Without an Overcoat: Poems 1972-76 (1977), Collected Poems (1979), A Net to Catch the Winds and Other Poems (1981), The French Mosquitoes' Woman and Other Diversions and Poems (1985); prose: A Pocket Guide to Scottish Culture (1947), The Scottish Renaissance (1949), The Lowlands of Scotland: Glasgow and the North (third edn 1979), Robert Burns, The Man, His Work, The Legend (third edn 1980), Duncan: The Gem of the Clyde Coast (1954), The Lowlands of Scotland: Edinburgh and the South (third edn 1979), Clyde Waters: Variations and Diversions on a Theme of Pleasure (1958), The Burns Encyclopaedia (third edn 1980), Killochan Castle (1960), By Ton Bonnie Banks: A Gallimaufry (1961), Environment: A Basic Human Right (1968), Portrait of Glasgow (second edn 1981), Robin Philipson (1977), History of Scottish Literature (1977), Lowland Scottish Villages (1980), Francis Geroge Scott and the Scottish Renaissance (with Anthony F Versting, 1980), The Buildings of Edinburgh (second edn 1987), Thank You for Having Me: a personal memoir (with Dennis Hardley, 1983), Unknown Scotland (1984), The Castles of Scotland (1986), Count All Men Mortal - A History of Scottish Providence 1837-1987 (1987), Victorian and Edwardian Glasgow (with David Bruce, 1987), Edinburgh Then and Now (1987); other work: Poetry Scotland One, Tow, Three (1943, 1945 and 1946), Sailing Tomorrow's Seas: An Anthology of New Poems (1944), Modern Scottish Poetry: An Anthology of the Scottish Renaissance 1920-45 (with Fred Urquhart, fourth edn 1986), No Scottish Twilight: New Scottish Stories (1947), Selected Poems of Sir Alexander Gray (1948), Poems, by Sir David Lyndsay (with Hugh McDiarmid, 1948), Poetry Scotland Four (with Helen Cruickshank, 1949), Selected Poems of Marian Angus (1950), John Davidson: A Selection of his Poems (with Edwin Morgan and George Bruce, 1961), Scottish Poetry One to Six 1966-72 (with Alexander Scott and Roderick Watson), The Eye is Delighted: Some Romantic Travellers in Scotland (1970), Scottish Poetry Seven to nine (with R L MAckie, 1974, 1976 and 1977), Scotland: An Anthology (1974), As I Remember (1979), The Discovery of Scotland (second edn 1979), Scottish Comic Verse 1425-80 (1980), A Book of Scottish Verse (third edn 1983); *Recreations* enjoying compact disc collection, walking, seeking out, sailing on paddle-steamers; *Style*— Dr Maurice Lindsay, CBE, TD; 7 Milton Hill, Milton, Dumbarton, Scotland G82 2TS (☎ 0389 61500)

LINDSAY, Hon Mary Muriel; da of 2 Baron Lindsay of Birker; *b* 1951; *Educ* Chevy Chase Elementary and HS, Bethesda and Leland Junior HS, Case-Western Reserve Univ Cleveland USA; *Style*— The Hon Mary Lindsay

LINDSAY, Col Oliver John Martin; yr s of Sir Martin Alexander Lindsay of Dowhill, 1 Bt, CBE, DSO (d 1981), and his 1 w, Joyce Emily, *née* Lindsay; *b* 30 August 1938; *Educ* Eton, RMA Sandhurst, Staff Coll Camberley, Nat Def Coll Latimer; *m* 27 Oct 1964, Lady Clare Rohais Antonia Elizabeth Giffard, da of 3 Earl of Halsbury; 1 s (Mark Oliver Giffard b 1968), 2 da (Victoria Louise Elizabeth Louise (Mrs Gregory Wheatley) b 1967, Fiona Emily Margaret b 1972); *Career* cmmnd Grenadier Gds 1958, served in W Africa, Cyprus, Hong Kong and Europe, and on staff in Rhodesia, Ottawa and London; memb Royal Co of Archers (Queen's Body Guard for Scotland); lectr (in particular on Far Eastern events 1940-45), historian and author; memb bd of govrs: Cwlth Tst, Victoria League; memb Woking Church Synod; MBIM 1975, FRHistS 1984; *Books* The Lasting Honour - The Fall of Hong Kong 1941 (1978), At the Going

Down of the Sun - Hong Kong and South East Asia 1941-45 (1981), A Guard's General - the Memoirs of Sir Allan Adair (ed, 1986); *Recreations* tennis, writing; *Clubs* Boodle's, Royal Cwlth Soc; *Style*— Col Oliver Lindsay; Brookwood House, Brookwood, nr Woking, Surrey GU24 ONX

LINDSAY, Patrick Alexander Richard; s of Lt-Col Michael Egan Lindsay, DSO, DL (d 1957), of Scotland, and Elsie Catherine Harriet, *née* Riddiford (d 1951); *b* 1 April 1917; *Educ* Harrow, Clare Coll Cambridge (MA Law); *m* 9 Sept 1944, Dagmar Natalie Oliveira, da of Dudley Oliveira Davies, of Las Palmas, Grand Canary; 2 s (Michael b 1947, Jonathan b 1956), 2 da (Delia b 1945, Anthea b 1949); *Career* war serv: Sudan Def Force, Nuba bat 8 Army N Africa 1941-43, MS to GOC Troops Sudan 1943-44, Major DAAG HQ Khartoum; dist cmmr Sudan Political Servs 1939-49; United Africa Co 1949-67, personnel dir Port of London Authy 1967-70, ptnr Tyzack & Ptnrs 1970-81; formerly: FBIM, FIPM; *Recreations* golf, gardening; *Clubs* memb: RAC, Royal & Ancient GC; *Style*— Patrick Lindsay, Esq; Windfall, W Orchard, Shaftesbury, Dorset

LINDSAY, Robert Keith; s of Robert Lindsay (d 1978); *b* 15 Nov 1936; *Educ* Lancing, Magdalene Coll Cambridge; *m* 1961, Elisabeth, *née* Smith; 2 s, 1 da; *Career* dir Tennant Trading Ltd 1974-79, md New Metals and Chemicals Hldgs Ltd 1979-; CEng, FICemE; *Recreations* squash, gardening; *Clubs* Inst of Directors, Wilderness Squash; *Style*— Robert Lindsay, Esq; Russell House, Station Rd, Otford, Sevenoaks, Kent (☎ 09592 2352); office: Abbey Chambers, Highbridge St, Waltham Abbey, Essex (☎ 0992 711111)

LINDSAY, Hon Thomas Martin; MBE (1946); s of 1 Baron Lindsay of Birker, CBE (d 1952); *b* 5 Mar 1915; *Educ* Sidcot Sch, Edinburgh Univ; *m* 1, 1939 (m dis 1951), Denise Theresa, da of Gerald Albert Vaughan; 2 s, 1 da; m 2, 1951 (m dis 1961), Felicitas, da of Dr Martin Lange; 2 s; m 3, 1961, Erica, da of Maj Eric Thirkell-Cooper; 2 s; *Career* served 1939-45 War (despatches), Maj Sherwood Rangers; *Style*— The Hon Thomas Lindsay, MBE; rue de Toulouse 17, 1040 Brussels, Belgium

LINDSAY OF BIRKER, 2 Baron (UK 1945); Michael Francis Morris Lindsay; s of 1 Baron Lindsay of Birker, CBE (d 1952); *b* 24 Feb 1909; *Educ* Gresham's, Balliol Coll Oxford; *m* 1941, Hsiao Li, da of Li Wen-chi, of the Chinese Army, of Lishih, Shansi; 1 s, 2 da; *Heir* s, Hon James Francis Lindsay; *Career* served with 18 Gp Army N China 1942-45; sinologist and economist; economics lectr at Yenching Univ Peking 1937; press attaché British Embassy, Chunking 1940; visiting lectr Harvard Univ 1946-47, lectr Univ Coll Hull 1948-51, rdr Australian Nat Univ Canberra 1951-59; former prof of far eastern studies American Univ Washington DC (now Prof Emeritus); *Style*— The Rt Hon the Lord Lindsay of Birker; 6812 Delaware St, Chevy Chase, Maryland 20815, USA (☎ 301 656 4245)

LINDSAY OF DOWHILL, Hon Lady; Hon Loelia Mary Ponsonby; da of 1 Baron Sysonby, GCB, GCVO (d 1935); *b* 1902; *m* 1, 20 Feb 1930 (m dis 1947), as his 3 w, 2 Duke of Westminster (d 1953); m 2, 1 Aug 1969, as his 2 w, Sir Martin Alexander Lindsay of Dowhill, 1 Bt, CBE, DSO (d 1981); *Style*— The Hon Lady Lindsay of Dowhill; The Old Vicarage, Send, Woking, Surrey

LINDSAY OF DOWHILL, Sir Ronald Alexander; 2 Bt (UK 1962), of Dowhill, Co Kinross; s of Sir Martin Lindsay of Dowhill, 1 Bt, CBE, DSO (d 1981) by 1 w, Joyce, da of Maj the Hon Robert Hamilton Lindsay, s of 26 Earl of Crawford; Sir Ronald is 23 in derivation from Sir William Lindsay of Rossie, 1 of Dowhill (b 1350) uncle of 1 Earl of Crawford. The coat of arms of Adam 5 of Dowhill d 1544 is shown in the Armorial of his Kinsman, Sir David Lindsay of the Mount, Lyon King of Arms. Adam had a Crown Charter of confirmation of his barony of Crambeth called Dowhill in 1541. Earlier such charters were in 1353 by David II, in 1397 by Robert III and in 1447 by James II. Dowhill Castle and the estates were sold by James 12 Laird in the 1740s. His three sons, Martin, James and William were involved in the losing side in the 1745 Jacobite Rising. The 1 Bt Sir Martin was Solihull's first MP (1945-62). He led the longest self-supporting sledge journey of 1050 miles across Greenland in 1934 (see Guinness Book of Records). In 1944-45 he cmd the 1 Bn The Gordon Highlanders in 16 ops in NW Europe. This Bn led the Siegfried line break through, not far from where in 1814 Sir Martin's ggf Col Martin Lindsay CB led the bayonet charge which broke through the French defences at Merxem when cmd the 78 Regt (the Seaforths); *b* 6 Dec 1933; *Educ* Eton, Worcester Coll Oxford (MA); *m* 1968, Nicoletta, yr da of Capt Edgar Storich (d 1985), Royal Italian Navy; 3 s (James b 1968, Hugo b 1970, Robin b 1972), 1 da (Lucia b 1974); *Heir* s, James Martin Evelyn Lindsay; *Career* Lt Grenadier Gds 1952-54; insur exec 1958-, dir Oxford Members' Agency Ltd 1989-; chm Standing Cncl of the Baronetage, vice-chm Anglo-Spanish Soc; memb Queen's Body Gd for Scotland (Royal Co of Archers); FCII; *Style*— Sir Ronald Lindsay of Dowhill, Bt; Courleigh, Colley Lane, Reigate, Surrey RH2 9JJ (☎ 0737 243290)

LINDSAY-FYNN, Adrian; s of Sir Basil Lindsay-Fynn (d 1988), and Marion Audrey Ellen, *née* Chapman; *b* 12 April 1948; *Educ* Charterhouse; *m* 5 July 1974, Penelope Jean, da of Dennis Ward, of 4 Lyall Mews, London SW1; 3 s (James b 1975, Hugo b 1978, Alexander b 1981); *Career* Farmer, landowner; dir: ALFCO Investmt Ltd 1983, Mortimer Machinery 1976, Carrollstown Estate Ltd 1974; *Recreations* shooting, sailing, tennis; *Clubs* Royal Irish Yacht; *Style*— Adrian Lindsay-Fynn, Esq; Carrollstown, Trim, Co Meath, Republic of Ireland (☎ Trim 31421) (car ☎ 0860 333 783)

LINDSAY-FYNN, Nigel; s of Sir Basil Lindsay-Fynn (d 1988), and Marion Audrey Ellen, *née* Chapman; *b* 4 May 1942; *Educ* Charterhouse, Oriel Coll Oxford (MA); *m* 12 May 1971, Helene Vanda Mary, da of Bill Wilson-Pemberton, of London; 1 s (Piers b 1975), 2 da (Miranda b 1978, Eleanor b 1981); *Career* chm Int Express Co Ltd, dir private family cos; chm Exeter Nuffield Hosp, tstee Exeter Cathedral Preservation Tst, cncl memb and chief steward Devon Co Agric Assoc; *Clubs* Buck's, Garrick, Kildare St and University Dublin; *Style*— Nigel Lindsay-Fynn, Esq; Lee Ford, Budleigh Salterton, Devon EX9 7AJ (☎ 03954 5894, fax 03954 6219, telex 42689)

LINDSAY-HOGG, Sir Edward William; 4 Bt (UK 1905); s of Sir Lindsay Lindsay-Hogg, 1 Bt (d 1923), suc n, Sir William Lindsay-Hogg, 3 Bt, 1987; *b* 23 May 1910; *m* 1, 18 Nov 1936 (m dis 1946), Geraldine Mary, da of Edward Martin Fitzgerald; 1 s; m 2, 30 Oct 1957, Kathleen Mary, da of James Cooney, of Carrick-on-Suir, Co Tipperary, and wid of Capt Maurice Cadell, MC; *Heir* s Michael Edward Lindsay-Hogg b 5 May 1940; *Clubs* St Stephen's Green (Dublin); *Style*— Sir Edward Lindsay-Hogg, Bt; c/o Michael Lindsay-Hogg, Esq, 9 Fitzwilliam Place, Dublin 2, Republic of Ireland

LINDSAY-HOGG, Marie, Lady; Marie Teresa; *née* Foster; da of late John Foster, of St Helens, Lancashire; *m* 1987, as his 2 w, Sir William Lindsay Lindsay-Hogg, 3 Bt (d 1987); 1 step da; 7B Atherton Street, London SW11

LINDSAY-MacDOUGALL OF LUNGA, Colin John Francis; s of John Stewart Lindsay-MacDougall of Lunga, DSO, MC (ka 1943), and Shiela Marion, *née* Sprot; *b* 21 July 1939; *Educ* Radley; *m* 11 Feb 1961 (m dis 1979), Hon Frances Phoebe, da of Capt Hon Anthony Phillimore (ka 1943), of Cappid Hall, nr Henley on Thames, Oxfordshire; 3 s (James, Lucian, Aidan); 2 da (Antonia, Johanna); *Career* Nat Serv 2 Lt Queen's Own Hussars; landowner; *Recreations* sailing, riding, skiing, arts; *Clubs* Glasgow Art; *Style*— Colin Lindsay-MacDougall of Lunga; Lunga, Ardfern, Argyll (☎ 08 525 237); Lunga Estate, Argyll PA31 8QR (☎ 08 525 237, fax 085 25 639)

LINDSAY-SMITH, Iain-Mór; s of Edward Duncanson Lindsay-Smith (d 1951); *b* 18 Sept 1934; *Educ* High Sch of Glasgow, London Univ Extension Dip Course; *m* 1960, Carol Sara, da of Edward Philip Paxman (d 1948); 1 s (Sholto); *Career* cmmnd 1 Bn Cameronians (Scottish Rifles) 1953-55 W Germany, 6/7 Bn 1955-63; journalist, Scottish Daily Record 1951-57, Daily Mirror 1957-60, featured Daily Mail 1968-71 (for corr, for ed 1960-70), dep ed Yorkshire Post 1971-74, ed Glasgow Herald 1974-77, exec ed The Observer 1977-84; publisher Lloyd's List', dep md Lloyds of London Press Ltd, dir Lloyds of London Press Ltd, dir Lloyd's of London Press Inc USA 1984-; dir Lutine Pubns Ltd; dir Mercury Theatre Colchester; memb of ct Univ of Essex 1985-; memb Little Horkesley Parish Cncl 1986-, memb little Horkesley PCC 1987; *Recreations* shooting, windsurfing, highland bagpipes, gardening; *Clubs* Travellers'; *Style*— Iain-Mór Lindsay-Smith, Esq; Lloyd's of London Press, 1 Singer St, London EC2A 4LQ (☎ 01 250 1500, telex 987321 Lloyds G)

LINDSEY, Wing Cdr Ian Walter; s of Walter Richard Lindsey (d 1966), of Bromley, and Christine, *née* Gosman (d 1981); *b* 7 May 1946; *Educ* Univ of Nottingham (BA, M Phil); *m* 1971, Janet, da of Sydney Hewitt; 2 s (Gordon b 1973, Robert b 1979), 1 da (Alison b 1972); *Career* cmmnd RAFVR(T) 1967 (Flying Offr 1969, Flt-Lt 1973, Sqdn-Ldr 1983, Wing-Cdr 1984, retd 1988), OC Herts/Bucks Wing ATC; mktg exec Williams and Glyns Bank 1971-75, sr lectr Harrow Coll 1975-77, conslt to Price Cmmn 1977-78, asst gen mangr TSB Trustcard Ltd 1978-83, dir: Save and Prosper Gp Ltd 1983-, Robert Fleming 1988-; tres: Nat Assoc of Local Cncls, ATC Central and E Region; FCIB 1980 (memb Centl Cncl); *Recreations* flying; *Clubs* Halton House; *Style*— Wing Cdr Ian Lindsey; 3 Kinderscout, Liverstock Green, Herts HP3 8HW (☎ 0442 212 420); Save and Prosper Group Ltd, 1 Finsbury Ave, London EC2M 2QY (☎ 01 588 1717, fax 01 247 5006, car tel 0860 226 707, telex 883838 SAVPRO G)

LINDSEY AND ABINGDON, 14 and 9 Earl of (E 1626 & 1682); Richard Henry Rupert Bertie; also Baron Norreys of Rycote (E 1572); s of Lt-Col Hon Arthur Michael Bertie, DSO, MC (d 1957), and Aline Rose, *née* Arbuthnot-Leslie (d 1948); suc cousin 13 Earl of Lindsey and (8 of) Abingdon 1963; *b* 28 June 1931; *Educ* Ampleforth; *m* 1957, Norah Elizabeth Farquhar-Oliver, da of late Mark Oliver, OBE, and Norah (d 1980), da of Maj Francis Farquhar, DSO, 2 s of Sir Henry Farquhar, 4 Bt, JP, DL; 2 s (Lord Norreys, Hon Alexander Michael Richard b 8 April 1970), 1 da (Lady Annabel Frances Rose b 11 March 1969); *Heir* s, Lord Norreys b 6 June 1958; *Career* sits as Conservative Peer in House of Lords; served with Scots Guards 1950 and Royal Norfolk Regt 1951-52, Lt; insurance broker and underwriting memb of Lloyd's 1958; High Steward of Abingdon 1963; Pres The Friends of Abingdon 1982; company director 1965; chm: Dawes & Henderson (Agencies) Ltd 1988, Anglo-Ivorian Soc 1974-77 (vice-pres 1978-); *Recreations* country pursuits; *Clubs* Pratt's, Turf, White's, Puffin's (Edinburgh); *Style*— The Rt Hon the Earl of Lindsey and Abingdon; Gilmilnscroft, Sorn, Mauchline, Ayrshire KA5 6ND (☎ 0290 51246); 3 Westgate Terrace, London SW10 9BT

LINDSLEY, David Middleton; s of Richard Middleton Lindsley (d 1960), of Valebrooke, Sunderland, Co Durham, and Ethel Muriel, *née* Greig; *b* 8 Mar 1936; *Educ* The Leys Sch Cambridge; *m* 20 Aug 1960, Elizabeth Anne Dickinson, da of Dr William Athelstane Dickinson Oliver (d 1964), of Belgrave, Coxhoe, Co Durham; 1 s (David) James Middleton b 1971), 2 da ((Elizabeth) Suzanne Middleton b 1963, (Alice) Elspeth Middleton b 1967); *Career* slr, pres Sunderland Law Soc 1986-87; dir: Vedra Shipping Co Ltd 1976-, United and Gen Tst Ltd 1977-, Bright and Galbraith Ltd 1977-, Vale Trust Ltd 1977-; *Recreations* shooting; *Clubs* The Club (Sunderland); *Style*— David Lindsley, Esq; Springfield House, Fremington, Richmond, North Yorkshire (☎ 0748 84432); 52 John St, Sunderland, Tyne and Wear (☎ 091 5652421)

LINE, Prof Maurice Bernard; s of Bernard Cyril Line (d 1978), of Bedford, and Ruth Florence, *née* Crane (d 1936); *b* 21 June 1928; *Educ* Bedford Sch, Exeter Coll Oxford (BA, MA); *m* 12 April 1954, Joyce, da of Walter Gilchrist (d 1953), of Paisley; 1 s (Philip b 1955), 1 da (Jill b 1957); *Career* sub librarian Univ of Southampton 1954-65, dep librarian Univ of Newcastle upon Tyne 1965-68; librarian: Univ of Bath 1968-71, Nat Central Library 1971-73; dir gen: lending div Br Library 1974-85, sci tech and indust Br Library 1985-88 (conslt 1988-); prof assoc Univ of Sheffield 1980-, visiting prof Univ of Loughborough 1987-; memb Br Library Bd 1974-88; author of 14 books, 230 articles in learned jls, 40 res reports; Hon DLitt Heriot-Watt Univ 1980, Hon DSc Univ of Southampton 1988; FLA 1954, Hon Fla 1987, FBIM 1980, FRSA, FIInfSci 1975 ; *Recreations* tennis, walking, music listening, theatre; *Style*— Prof Maurice Line; 10 Blackthorn Lane, Burn Bridge, Harrogate, N Yorks HG3 1NZ (☎ 0423 872984, car tel 0423 872984)

LINEKER, Gary Winston; s of Barry Lineker, of 9 Coverdale Rd, The Meadows, Wigston, Leicester, and Margaret Patricia Morris, *née* Abbs; *b* 30 Nov 1960; *Educ* City of Leicester Boys GS; *m* 5 July 1986, Michelle Denise, da of Roger Edwin Cockayne, of 1 Brickman Close, Forest Farm, Forest East, Leicester; *Career* professional footballer, debut Leicester City 1979, transfrd to Everton 1985, represented England in the 1986 World Cup Mexico (leading goal scorer), FC Barcelona 1986-; *Recreations* cricket, golf; *Clubs* MCC; *Style*— Gary Lineker, Esq; 16-26 Paseo Sagrero, B-S Bel Parc, Santjust Desvern, Barcelona, Spain; Futbol Club Barcelona, Nou Camp Stadium, Aristides Maillol, Barcelona, Spain (☎ 3309411, telex 51804 FCBXE)

LINES, David John Vincent; s of William Henry Lines, of Hayes, Kent, and Marjorie Florence Helen, *née* Wood (d 1973); *b* 9 Nov 1935; *Educ* City of London Sch, City of London Coll (MBIM); *m* 8 April 1963 (m dis 1978), Patricia Ann, da of Charles Quested-Drayson (d 1975), of Addington, Surrey; 2 da (Deborah Karen Louise b 1967, Rebecca Sally Jane b 1970); *Career* indust chemist Standard Telephones and Cables 1952-59, conslt OW Roskill 1959-61, sales conslt Bary Wiggins (pt of BP) 1961-64, sales dir Reece Machinery Co 1964-; former hon chm Clothing Inst, chm Br Assoc of Clothing Machinery Mfrs; chm Badminton Club and local soc club; Freeman: City of London 1959, Worshipful Co of Bakers; MInst Pet, MBIM, FCTI, MBInstPKG;

Recreations badminton, country dancing; *Clubs* Conservative; *Style*— David Lines, Esq; 113 Whyteleaf Rd, Caterham on the Hill, Surrey CR3 5EG (☎ 0883 46118); Reece Machinery Co Ltd, 32-38 Leman St, London E1 8EZ (☎ 01 481 2835, fax 01 480 7485, telex 887663)

LINES, (Roy) Nicholas; MBE (1943); s of William Edward Lines (d 1945), of Hillesden, Bucks, and Helen Elizabeth, *née* Hellings (d 1960); *b* 11 Sept 1914; *Educ* Royal Latin Sch Buckingham, Worcester Coll Oxford (MA); *m* 12 July 1944, (Edith) Mary, da of Joseph Allum (d 1922), of Stanton St John, Oxford; 2 s (Nicholas b 1953, Thomas b 1954), 3 da (Diana b 1946, Susan b 1947, Margaret b 1950); *Career* ICS 1937-47, Colonial Admin Serv N Rhodesia 1947-51, Cwlth Devpt Corpn 1952-74 (London, Nigeria, Carribean); memb Bucks CC 1977-85, chm Social Servs Ctee 1980-85; fndr memb Nat Schizophrenia Fellowship (chm 1984-87), tres and churchwarden Latimer 1963-81; *Recreations* gardening, photography, politics; *Clubs* Royal Cwlth Soc; *Style*— Nicholas Lines, Esq, MBE; 21A Chenies Ave, Little Chalfont, Amersham, Bucks HP6 6PP (☎ 024 04 2443)

LINES, Richard Stuart; s of Harold Thomas Lines, Wing Cdr RAF (d 1954), of Purley, and Mimi Kathleen Lee, *née* Bailey (d 1983); *b* 4 August 1936; *Educ* Seaford Coll Petworth Hants, RN; *m* 20 June 1959, Janet Marion Boyes, da of Percy Clifford Stronach; 2 s (Simon Richard b 1962, Timothy James b 1965); *Career* Air Crew Lt RN; chm and chief exec MTM plc 1986- and dir subsid and assoc cos (incl jt ventures with ICI plc 1967-78, mktg exec prior to 1967); chm bd of govrs Teeside Poly; *Recreations* golf, swimming, walking; *Style*— Richard Lines, Esq; MTM plc, Rudby Hall, Hutton Rudby, Yarm, Cleveland TS15 0JN (☎ 0642 701078, telex 58365, fax 0642 700667, car tel 0860 615625)

LINFORD, David; s of Albert Louis Linford, of Hatherton, Comberford Rd, Tamworth, Staffs (d 1976), and Olive Leonie, *née* Harston (d 1968); *b* 29 May 1934; *Educ* King Edward VII's Sch Bath, QEI GS Tamworth Staffs; *m* 29 Dec 1961, Barbara, da of Eric Whitehouse of Woodend, Old Penkridge Rd, Cannock, Staffs; *Career* chm and md: F & E V Linford Ltd 1967- (and its subsidiaries), Linford-Bridgeman Ltd 1985-; dir of Presco (Hldgs) Ltd 1975-; *Recreations* hockey, int rotary, historic bldgs; *Style*— David Linford, Esq; The Kennels, Upper Longdon, Rugeley, Staffs (☎ 0543 491230); F & E V Linford Ltd, Park Rd, Cannock, Staffs (☎ 0543 466566)

LING; *see*: de Courcy Ling

LING, Arthur George; s of George Frederick Ling (d 1957); *b* 20 Sept 1913; *Educ* Christ's Hosp, UCL; *m* 1939, Marjorie, da of Robert John Tall (d 1962); 1 s (Peter), 3 da (Anna, Judith, Frances); *Career* planning offr London CC 1943-55, sr lectr dept of town planning London Univ 1947-55, city architect and planning offr Coventry 1955-64, prof of architecture and planning Nottingham 1964-69, project mangr UN Habitat Project Physical Perspective Plan for Libya 1977-80; private practice Arthur Ling & Assocs Architects & Town Planners 1965-; vice-pres RIBA 1963-64, pres Royal Town Planning Inst 1968-69, pres Cwlth Assoc of Planners 1970-75; memb Sports Cncl 1967-71; fell of UCL; *Books* Master Plan for Runcorn New Town; Urban and Regional Planning and Development in the Commonwealth; *Style*— Arthur Ling, Esq; The Old Rectory, Howell, Sleaford, Lincs (☎ 0529 60412)

LING, Maj-Gen Fergus Alan Humphrey; CB (1958), CBE (1964), DSO (1944), DL (1969); s of John Richardson Ling (d 1938), of Bath, and Mabel, *née* Pratchitt (d 1948); *b* 5 August 1914; *Educ* Stowe, RMC Sandhurst; *m* 20 March 1940, Sheelah Phyllis, da of William Godfrey Molyneux Sarel (d 1950), of Berks; 2 s (Anthony b 1941, Philip b 1946), 3 da (Virginia b 1948, Elizabeth and Diana b 1950); *Career* cmd 2/5 Bn Queen's Royal Regt Italy 1944, directing staff Staff Coll Camberley 1951-53, cmd 5 Bn Queen's Royal Regt 1954-57, asst mil sec WO 1957-58, Cdr 148 Inf Bde (TA) 1958-61, Dep Adj-Gen Rhine Army 1961-65, Gen Offr cmd 54 E Anglian Div (TA), Cdr E Anglian 1965-67, GOC Eastern Dist 1967-69, ret; dir: Caffin Hldgs Ltd 1969-72, Lundi Appeal 1969, founding admin dir Inst for the Study of Conflict 1970-72, def conslt ISC 1972-82; chm Surrey TAVR Assoc 1973-78, vice-chm SE TAVR Assoc 1973-78 (chm 1978-79), Dep Col The Queen's Regt 1969-73, (Col 1973-77); vice Lord-Lieut Surrey 1973-82; *Recreations* grand children, gardening; *Clubs* Royal Cwlth Soc; *Style*— Maj-Gen Fergus A H Ling, CB, CBE, DSO, DL; Mystole Coach House, nr Canterbury, Kent (☎ 0227 738496); Shepherd House, Netherwasdale, nr Seascale, Cumbria (☎ 0940 6312)

LING, Prof Robin Sydney Mackwood; s of William Harold Godfrey Mackwood Ling (d 1973), of Keighley W Yorks, and Margaret Mona, *née* Price (d 1979); *b* 7 Sept 1927; *Educ* Shawnigan Lake Sch, Vancouver Island Br Columbia, Univ of Oxford (MA, BM, Bch), St Mary's Hosp London; *m* 18 Sept 1956, Mary, da of Capt W F Steedman, MC (d 1959); 2 da (Jennifer b 1959, Katherine b 1962); *Career* former conslt orthopaedic surgn; Royal Infirmary Edinburgh, Princess Margaret Orthopaedic Hosp Edinburgh; sr conslt orthopaedic surgn Princess Elizabeth Orthopaedic Hosp Exeter; hon prof at bio-engrg Univ of Exeter, immediate past press Br Orthopaedic Assoc, pres Br Orthopaedic Res Soc 1979-80; visiting prof: Louisiana State Univ 1983, Univ of Arizona 1985, Chinese Univ of Hong Kong (1985), R&E Univ of California 1986, Baylor Univ Texas 1986; memb: Int Hip Soc, SICOT; Lt Sir John Charnley Meml Lectr Univ of Liverpool 1986, Pridie Meml lectr Univ of Bristol 1987; pubns: incl numerous papers in leading med and scientific jls on hip surgery, implant fixation, properties of biomaterials; *Recreations* sailing; *Clubs* Royal Ocean Racing, Royal Dart YC, Royal Soc of Med; *Style*— Prof Robin S M Ling; Lod Cottage, The Lane, Dittisham, nr Dartmouth, Devon T96 0HB (☎ 080 422 451); 2 The Quadrant, Wonford Rd, Exeter EX2 4LE (☎ 0392 37070)

LINGARD, Lady Caroline Flower; da of 16 Earl of Buchan (d 1984), and Christina, Countess of Buchan, *qv*; *b* 29 June 1935; *m* 26 Feb 1963, John Robin William Lingard; 2 da; *Style*— Lady Caroline Lingard; Semley Grange, Shaftesbury, Dorset

LINGARD, James Richard; s of Walter Wadsworth Lingard, and Emily, *née* Watson; *b* 7 June 1936; *Educ* Dulwich, UCL (LLB); *m* 7 Sept 1963, Maureen Winifred (d 1985), da of George Henry Ball; 3 s (Andrew b 1964, Peter b 1967, Christopher b 1971); *Career* slr Supreme Ct 1959-, ptnr Norton Rose 1972-, insolvency practitioner 1987-, dir Jt Insolvency Examination Bd 1988-; contrib Encyclopaedia of Forms and Precedents; chm: City of London Law Soc Banking Sub-Ctee, Jt Law Soc Bar Banking Sub Ctee; Freeman City of London; memb Law Soc 1959; *Books* Corporate Rescues and Insolvenices (1986), Banking Security Documents (2 edn 1988); *Recreations* writing, snooker; *Clubs* Law Soc; *Style*— James Lingard, Esq; Norton Rose, Kempson House, Camomile St, London EC3A 7AN (☎ 01 283 2434, fax 01 588 1181, telex 883652)

LINGENS, Michael Robert; s of Dr Friedrich Otto Lingens, of Stuttgart, W Germany, and Karin Thielen, *née* Weber; *b* 15 May 1957; *Educ* St Edmunds Sch Canterbury, Trinity Coll Oxford (MA); *Career* slr, ptnr Woodham Smith, chm Bow Gp 1984-85; cncllr London Borough of Hammersmith and Fulham (dip liaison offr), parly candidate (C) Bolsover 1987; *Books* The SDP A Critical Analysis, Beveridge and The Bow Group Generation, Winning on Welfare; *Recreations* real tennis, racquets; *Clubs* Coningsby, The Queens, Carlton; *Style*— Michael Lingens, Esq; 8 Hauteville Ct Gdns, Stamford Brook Ave, London W6 0YF (☎ (home) 01 748 4693; (business) 01 242 0801)

LINGWOOD, David Frederick; s of Frederick Joseph Lingwood, of Bedford, England, and Grace Ann, *née* Clark (d 1986); *b* 5 May 1946; *Educ* Royal GS Newcastle Upon Tyne, Univ of Newcastle; *Career* PA to md Theatres Consolidated, house mangr for Sadlers Wells Opera London Coliseum, gen mangr Watford Civic Theatre Tst, admin dir Unicorn Theatre, admin Actors Co, asst exec prodr Robert Stigwood Orgn; gen mangr: Mermaid Theatre London, Shaftesbury Theatre London; asst gen mangr Royal Albert Hall; theatre mangr: Duchess Theatre 1987, Queens Theatre 1987, London Palladium 1988-; *Recreations* music, theatre, swimming, gardening; *Style*— David Lingwood, Esq; 28 Ennismore Ave, Chiswick, London W4 1SF (☎ 01 747 1441); London Palladium, Argyll St, London W1A 3AB (☎ 01 734 6846)

LINKIE, William Sinclair; s of Peter Linkie, of Edinburgh (d 1961), and Janet Black, *née* Sinclair; *b* 9 Mar 1931; *Educ* George Heriots Sch Edinburgh; *m* 24 Dec 1955, Elizabeth Primrose Marion, da of William Reid (d 1957), of Inverness; 1 s (David b 1962), 1 da (Rosalind b 1958); *Career* Inland Revenue Scotland 1952-: HM Inspr of Taxes 1961, princ inspr i/c Centre I 1975, dist insp Edinburgh 5 1982, controller 1983-; elder Church of Scotland; *Recreations* choral singing, golf; *Style*— William Linkie, Esq; Lauriston House, 80 Lauriston Place, Edinburgh EH3 9SL (☎ 031 229 9344)

LINKLATER, Peter Stronach; s of Dr James Thomas Parker Linklater (d 1981), and Hilda Cuthbert, *née* Marr; *b* 7 Jan 1924; *Educ* Oundle, Clare Coll Cambridge, Lincoln's Inn; *m* 16 July 1949, Pauline Elizabeth, da of Duncan Hardwick (d 1955); 3 da (Catriona b 1950, Sarah b 1954, Victoria b 1957); *Career* Capt Scots Gds 1944-47, cmd Ceremonial Gd Nuremburg 1945; mangr patents & licensing Shell Int 1955-81; dir: Shell Chemical UK 1961-67, (personnel) Shell UK 1967-79; exec vice-chm Shell Res 1975-78; memb: CBI Cncl 1969-72, Emloyment Policy Ctee 1972-78, NEDO ctee large construction sites 1970-78; chm ed ctee Chemistry & Indust 1965-80, indust advsr Churchill Coll Cambridge 1966-; chm: The Windsor Meeting (biannual) at St George's House Windsor Castle 1980-, CRAC (Careers Res and Advsy Centre) Cambridge 1984-, World Conf Coop Educn Programme Edinburgh 1985, Friends of Lewes (Civic Soc) 1970-; indust fell Churchill Coll Cambridge 1980-82; indust memb: Advsy Ctee Adult and Continuing Educn 1978-84 (ACACE), Advsy Bd Res Cncls (ABRC) Post Graduate Awards 1981-83, Univ Grants Ctee (UGC) Continuing Educn 1982-84; introduced and edited Education and the World of Work - Positive Partnerships (1987); *Recreations* opera, archaeology, walking; *Clubs* Garrick, Caledonian; *Style*— Peter S Linklater, Esq; The Gables, Southover High St, Lewes, E Sussex BN7 1JA (☎ 0273 473872); Birch Cottage, Aboyne, Aberdeenshire (☎ 0339 2251)

LINLEY, Viscount; *see* Royal Family section

LINLITHGOW, 4 Marquess of (UK 1902); Sir Adrian John Charles Hope; 12 Bt (NS 1698); also Earl of Hopetoun, Viscount Aithrie, Lord Hope (all S 1703), Baron Hopetoun (UK 1809), and Baron Niddry (UK 1814); o son of 3 Marquess of Linlithgow, MC (d 1987), and his 1 w Vivien, *née* Kenyon-Slaney (d 1963); *b* 1 July 1946; *Educ* Eton; *m* 1, 9 Jan 1968 (m dis 1978), Anne Pamela, eld da of Arthur Edmund Leveson, of Hall Place, Ropley; Hants; 2 s (Earl of Hopetoun, Lord Alexander b 3 Feb 1971); m 2, 1980, Peta Carol, da of Charles Victor Ormonde Binding, of Congresbury, Somerset; 1 s (Lord Robert b 17 Jan 1984), 1 da (Lady Vivienne b 16 April 1981); *Heir* s, Earl of Hopetoun, *qv*; *Style*— The Most Hon the Marquess of Linlithgow; Hopetoun House, South Queensferry, West Lothian EH30 9SL; 123 Beaufort St, London SW3

LINLITHGOW, Marchioness of Judith; *née* Lawson; da of late Stanley Matthew Lawson, of Cincinnati, Ohio, USA; *m* 1 (m dis), John Symonds Radway; m 2, 21 Jan 1960, as his 2 w, Lt-Col Esmond Charles Baring, OBE (d 1963); m 3, 18 Feb 1965, as his 2 w, 3 Marquess of Linlithgow, MC (d 1987); *Style*— The Most Hon Judith, Marchioness of Linlithgow; 11 Cheyne Place, London SW3

LINNELL, David George Thomas; CBE (1987); s of George Linnell, and Marguerite, *née* Gardener; *b* 28 May 1930; *Educ* Leighton Park Sch, Reading; *m* 11 March 1953, Margaret Mary, da of Robert John Paterson; 1 s (Mark David b 1955), 1 da (Claire Elizabeth b 1958); *Career* md Thomas Linnell and Sons Ltd 1964-75, chief exec Linfood Hldgs Ltd 1975-81, chm Spar Food Hldgs 1975-79, pres inst of Grocery Distribution 1980-82; chm: Eggs Authy 1981-86, Neighbourhood Stores PLC 1983-87, Brunning Gp plc 1987-; memb: CBIM 1978, FIGD 1977; *Clubs* Carlton; *Style*— David Linnell, Esq, CBE; The Old Rectory, Titchmarsh, Kettering, Northants; PO Box 47, Kettering, Northants NN14 3DZ (☎ 08012 2912)

LINNELL, David Gerald; s of Rev Gerald Hislop Linnell (d 1944), and Enid Marion, *née* Anderson (d 1974); descendant of John Linnell, landscape artist (1792-1882); *b* 29 Dec 1934; *Educ* Christ's Hosp, Royal Tech Coll Salford; *m* 1985, Ann Nora, da of John Edwin Palmer; 2 s, 1 da by previous m and 1 step s, 1 step da; *Career* former chm and md Cableform Gp Ltd 1973-86; former memb: NW Indust Devpt Bd, electrical engrg sub-ctee of Machines and Power Ctee of Science and Engrg Res Cncl 1985-87, electrical tech ctee of Mech & Engrg Ctee of Elec Engrg Req Bd 1980-84; PR conslt The March Consulting Gp Ltd; *Recreations* gardening, reading, photography, travel; *Style*— David Linnell, Esq; Heatherbank, 67 Gilbraltar Lane, Haughton Green, Manchester M34 1PY

LINNETT, Dr Michael Joseph; OBE (1975); s of Joseph Linnett (d 1967), of Leicester, and Dora Alice Linnett; *b* 14 July 1926; *Educ* Wyggeston GS for Boys, St Bartholomew's Hosp; *m* 1950, Marianne Patricia; da of Aubrey Dibdin, CIE (d 1958); 2 da (and 1 s decd); *Career* house physician: St Bartholomew's Hosp 1949, Evelina Children's Hosp 1950; jr registrar St Bartholomew's 1955, GP 1957-; chm of cncl RCGP 1976-79, memb Medicines Cmmn 1976-; apothecary to TRH The Prince and Princess of Wales 1983-; FRCGP; *Style*— Dr Michael Linnett, OBE; 82 Sloane St, London SW1X 9PA (☎ 01 245 9333); 37 Ashcombe St, London SW6 3AW (☎ 01 736 2487)

LINTHWAITE, Peter John Nicholas; s of John Linthwaite, ISO, of Johannesburg, SA, and June Margaret Fiennes, *née* Nicoll; *b* 3 Dec 1956; *Educ* Bedford Modern Sch, New Coll Oxford (BA); *m* 18 Sept 1982, Gillian Deborah, da of Rei Oblitas, OBE, ED; *Career* vice pres Bank of America NT SA London and Hong Kong 1978-86, Standard Chartered Bank Hong Kong 1986-87, dir Tranwood Earl and Co Ltd 1987-; *Recreations* cricket, skiing, bridge, ballet; *Clubs* MCC, RAC; *Style—* Peter Linthwaite, Esq; 123 Sloane St, London SW1X 9BW (☎ 01 730 3412, fax 01 730 5770, car tel 0836 627509, telex 932016)

LINTOTT, Sir Henry John Bevis; KCMG (1957); *m* 1940, Margaret Orpen; 1 da; *Career* entered Civil Serv 1932, under-sec Bd of Trade 1946, dep sec-gen Orgn for Euro Econ Co-Operation 1948-56, dep under-sec of state Cwlth Rels Off 1956-63, Br high cmmr in Canada 1963-68; co dir; *Style—* Sir Henry Lintott, KCMG; 12 Willow Walk, Cambridge (☎ Cambridge 312410)

LINTOTT, Robert Edward; s of Charles Edward Lintott (d 1981), and Doris Mary, of Maidenhead, Berks; *b* 31 Mar 1989; *Educ* Cambridgeshire HS, Trinity Coll Cambridge (MA); *m* 26 Jul 1958, Mary Alice, da of Canon Frank Hope Scott (d 1971), of Hull; 3 s (Mark b 1959, John b 1961, Benedict b 1965); *Career* Nat Serv PO RAF 1951-52; Esso Petroleum Co/Esso UK 1955-86: dir logistics 1979-81, dir mktg 1981-83, md 1983-86; chief exec The Coverdale Orgn Ltd 1987-, dir Matthew Hall Engrg (Hldgs) Ltd 1987-; memb cncl: Royal borough Windsor and Maidenhead 1987- (vice chm leisure servs ctee 1988-), Manchester Bus Sch; chm: exec ctee Fndn for Mgmt Educn, Oxford Summer Business Sch; CBIM, FInstPet; *Recreations* vintage motoring, cricket; *Clubs* RAF, MCC; *Style—* Robert Lintott, Esq; Huish Barton, Watchet, Somerset TA23 0LU (☎ 0984 402 08); La Queyrie Basse, Tremolat 24510, France; 1 Gordon Cottages, Lock Lane, Maidenhead, Berks; The Coverdale Organisation Ltd, Dorland House, 14-16 Regent St, London SW1 (☎ 01 925 0099, fax 01 491 7636, telex 295956 CTLCOVG)

LIPFRIEND, His Hon Judge Alan; s of Israel Lipfriend (d 1931), and Sarah Lipfriend (d 1970); *b* 6 Oct 1916; *Educ* Central Fndn Sch London, Queen Mary Coll London (BSc); *m* 1948, Adele Burke; 1 s; *Career* design staff Hawker Aircraft Ltd 1939-48; barr Middle Temple 1948, pres Appeal Tbnl (England and Wales) under Wireless and Telegraphy Act (1949) 1971-73, circuit judge 1973-, memb Parole Bd 1978-81; govr Queen Mary Coll 1981-, govr and tstee Central Fndr Sch 1985-, fell Queen Mary Coll 1987; *Recreations* theatre, sport; *Clubs* RAC; *Style—* His Hon Judge Lipfriend; 27 Edmunds Walk, London N2 OHU (☎ 01 883 4420)

LIPMAN, Dr Harald Martin; s of Dr Isaac Lipman (d 1955), and Dr Rachel, *née* Caplan (d 1964); *b* 10 Dec 1931; *Educ* City of London Sch, UCH (MB, BS, DCH); *m* 19 April 1959, Nahid, da of Jacoub Sahim, of USA; 1 s (Marc b 1963), 1 da (Amanda b 1961); *Career* dir Small Wonder Ltd 1965-, med advsr Transcare Int 1977-87, cnslt physician Repub of the Sudan 1980-87, regnl med advsr Br Embassy Moscow 1987; chm Moscow Med Assoc; memb: GB-USSR Assoc, Iran Soc, Tibet Soc, Med Soc for study of Venereal Diseases; memb Worshipful Soc of Apothecaries, Freeman City of London; MRCGP, FRSM; *Recreations* skiing, tennis; *Clubs* City Livery; *Style—* Dr Harald Lipman; FCO (Moscow), King Charles St, London SW1A 2AH

LIPMAN, Vivian David; CVO (1978); s of Samuel N Lipman, MBE (d 1946), and Cecelia, *née* Moses (d 1932); *b* 27 Feb 1921; *Educ* Colet Ct, St Paul's, Magdalen Coll and Nuffield Coll Oxford (MA, DPhil); *m* 21 June 1964, Sonia Lynette (d 1987); 1 s (Anthony b 1971); *Career* Royal Signals and Intelligence Corps 1942-45; asst princ Miny of Health 1947, under sec DOE; dir Ancient Monuments and Historic Bldgs 1978, pres Jewish Historical Soc of England 1965-67 (vice-pres), hon res fell Univ Coll London, chm exec ctee Architectural Heritage Fund, memb Redundant Churches Fund; FSA, FRHistS; *Books* Local Government Areas (1949), Social History of the Jews in England (1954), A Century of Social Service (1959), Jews of Mediaeval Norwich (1967), Three Centuries of Anglo-Jewish History (ed, 1961), The Age of Moses Montefiore (with Sonia Lipman,1985); *Recreations* reading detective stories; *Clubs* Athenaeum; *Style—* Vivian Lipman, Esq, CVO; 9 Rotherwick Rd, London NW11 7DG (☎ 01 458 9792)

LIPPINCOTT, Hon Mrs Caroline; da of Baron Seebohm (Life Peer); *b* 1940; *Educ* Oxford; *m* 1, 1962 (m dis 1967), Roger John Smith; m 2, 1974, Walter H Lippincott; 1 s (Hugh b 1982), 1 da (Sophie b 1978); *Career* writer; *Style—* The Hon Mrs Lippincott; 1 River Knoll Drive, Titusville, NJ 08560, USA

LIPSCOMBE, Eric Richard; s of Eric Wilfred Lipscombe (d 1965), and Frances Selina Emma, *née* Cowdrey (d 1985); *b* 23 June 1938; *Educ* Churchers Coll Hants; *m* 5 March 1966, Rosemary Christine Frances, da of Maj Harold Ernest White (d 1978); 1 s (Guy b 1968), 2 da (Sophie b 1970, Emily b 1975); *Career* Nat Serv 1960-62, Asst Adj to Sch of Military Engrg; dir Teradata Europe Ltd, chm Teradata UK Ltd, dir Teradata Deutschland GMBH, Teradata France SA; non-exec chm: Euro Mktg Conslts, Data Processing People (Hldgs) Ltd; fndr chm and md Computer Peripherals Ltd and subsidiaries 1979-84, dir Micro Business Systems plc 1984-86; Hants Rugby player, memb Richmond FC 1962-66; CEng, MICE; *Recreations* sport, music; *Clubs* East India; *Style—* Eric R Lipscombe, Esq; Bridgend House, Ockham, nr Ripley, Surrey (☎ 0483 222007); Tredata Europe Ltd, The Albany Works, Thames Ditton, Surrey (☎ 01 398 9121)

LIPTON, Stuart Anthony; s of Bertram Green, of London, and Jeanette Lipton; *b* 9 Nov 1942; *Educ* Berkhamsted Sch; *m* 16 June 1966, Ruth Kathryn, da of Harry Marks (d 1987), of London; 2 s (Elliot Steven b 17 March 1969, Grant Alexander b 20 Jan 1975), 1 da (Sarah Joanna b 15 June 1971); *Career* dir: Sterling Land Co 1971-73, First Palace Securities Ltd 1973-76; md Greycoat plc 1976-83, advsr to Hampton Site Co for Sainsbury Bldg Nat Gallery 1985; memb: advsy bd dept of construction mgmnt Univ of Reading 1983-, property advsy gp DOE 1986-, mil bldgs ctee MOD 1987-, cncl Br Property Fedn 1987-; tstee Whitechapel Art Gallery 1987-, cmmr Royal Fine Art Cmmn; memb: cncl ICA 1986-, bd Nat Theatre 1988-, advsy bd RA 1987, governing bd Imperial Coll 1987-; RIBA; *Recreations* architecture, crafts, art and technology, wine; *Style—* Stuart Lipton, Esq; Lansdowne House, Berkeley Sq, London W1X 6BP (☎ 01 495 7575)

LIPWORTH, (Maurice) Sydney; s of Isadore Lipworth (d 1966), of Johannesburg, SA, and Rae, *née* Sindler (d 1983); *b* 13 May 1931; *Educ* King Edward VII Sch Johannesburg, Univ of Witwatersrand Johannesburg (BCom, LLB); *m* 1957, Rosa, da of Bernard Liwarek (d 1943); 2 s (Bertrand, Frank); *Career* dep chm Allied Dunbar Assur plc (formerly Hambro Life Assur plc) 1984- (dir 1971-, jt md 1980-84); chm: Allied Dunbar & Co plc, Allied Dunbar Unit Tsts plc 1985- (md 1983-85); dir: J Rothschild Hldgs plc 1984-, BAT Industs plc 1985; memb Monopolies and Mergers Cmmn 1981- (chm 1988-); tstee Philharmonic Orchestra 1982-, govr Sadler's Wells Tst 1986-;; *Recreations* tennis, music, theatre; *Clubs* Queens; *Style—* Sydney Lipworth, Esq; Allied Dunbar Assurance plc, 9/15 Sackville St, London W1X 1DE (☎ 01 434 3211)

LIRONI, Mark Creig; *b* 3 Oct 1937; *Educ* Bell Baxter HS Cupar, Edinburgh Coll of Art, Univ of Strathclyde Glasgow (Dip, TP); *m* 13 May 1961, Marjory; 2 s (Stephen b 1963, Graham b 1964), 2 da (Kathryn b 1966, Joanna b 1980); *Career* architect; fndr ptnr Cobban and Lironi (architects, planning conslts and engrs) 1973-; dir: Cobban & Lironi 1987-, Dumbarton Stabilisers Ltd 1987, Hotels Devpt Consortium Ltd 1985; 1984; Suil Scotland Ltd 1981; *Recreations* golf; *Clubs* Cathkin Braes GC; *Style—* Mark C Lironi, Esq; Cobban & Lironi, Park House, Park Circus Place, Glasgow G3 6AN (☎ 041 333 9466)

LIS, David George; s of Henry George Lis, of Penrith, Cumbria, and Irene Isabel Lis (d 1965); *b* 8 Feb 1950; *Educ* Queen Elizabeth GS Penrith Cumbria, Newcastle-Upon-Tyne Poly (HND); *m* 1, 10 June 1972 (m dis 1986), Patricia Ann, da of William Stredwick, of Yarm, N Yorks; 3 da (Emily b 1976, Katie b 1978, Sophie b 1981); m 2, Patricia Margaret, da of Ronald Teasdale (d 1980); 1 da (Stephanie b 1988), 1 step s (Ben b 1977), 1 step da (Nicola b 1980); *Career* investmt analyst NatWest Bank 1972-79; fund mangr: Carliol Investmt Tst 1979-80, Target Unit Tst Mangrs 1980-84; investmt dir Baltic Tst Mangrs 1985, md Windsor Tst Mangrs and Windsor Investmt Mgmnt 1985-; *Recreations* golf, tennis, skiing, gardening; *Clubs* Lansdowne, Hadley Wood GC; *Style—* David Lis, Esq; 57 Crescent West, Hadley Wood, Herts EN4 0EQ (☎ 01 440 3469); Windsor House, 83 Kingsway, London WC2B 6SD (☎ 01 831 7373, fax 01 405 7472)

LISBURNE, 8 Earl of (I 1776); Capt John David Malet Vaughan; also Viscount Lisburne and Baron Fethard (I 1695); the eld s & h appears to have been styled Lord Vaughan since 1776; s of 7 Earl of Lisburne (d 1965); *b* 1 Sept 1918; *Educ* Eton, Magdalen Coll Oxford; *m* 1943, Shelagh, da of late T A Macauley, of Montreal, Canada; 3 s; *Heir* s, Viscount Vaughan; *Career* 2 Lt Welsh Gds 1939, Capt 1943, served 1939-45 War; barr Inner Temple; dir: S Wales regnl bd Lloyds Bank Ltd 1978-, Nationwide/Anglia Bldg Soc (Welsh bd); pres Wales Cncl for Voluntary Action, memb exec ctee AA 1981-; *Clubs* Buck's, Pratt's, Turf; *Style—* The Rt Hon the Earl of Lisburne; Cruglas, Ystrad Meurig, Dyfed (097 45 230)

LISLE, 7 Baron (I 1758); John Nicholas Horace Lysaght; s of Horace George Lysaght (d 1918), and Alice, da of Sir John Wrixon-Becher, 3 Bt; gs of 6 Baron (d 1919); *b* 10 August 1903; *m* 1, 1928 (m dis 1939), Vivienne (d 1948), da of Rev M Brew; m 2, 1939, Marie, da of A D Purgold, of Salop; *Heir* n, Patrick Lysaght; *Style—* The Rt Hon the Lord Lisle; 4 Bramerton St, London SW3

LISSER, Hon Mrs June Lisette May; da of 2 Baron May (d 1950); *b* 1929; *Educ* St Paul's; *m* 1958, Raymond Charles Lisser; 1 s; *Style—* The Hon Mrs Lisser; 6H Hyde Park Mansions, London NW1; School House, Stanton, Broadway, Worcs

LIST; *see*: Appleyard-List

LISTER, Anthony Charles Bramham; s of David Bramham Lister (d 1980), and Monica Joan, *née* Russell; *b* 31 August 1939; *Educ* Sutton Valence Sch Kent, Coll of Estate Mgmnt St Albans Grove London; *m* 1 June 1963, Susan Kitty, da of (Harold) Norman Funnell, of Gt Paddock Farm, Challock, Ashford, Kent; 3 s (Giles Anthony Bramham b 12 Jan 1966, Timothy Norman Bramham (twin) b 12 Jan 1966, Guy Bramham b 16 Oct 1968); *Career* Geering and Colyer Chartered Surveyors: equity ptnr 1972, head residential agency Black Horse Agencies 1988 (memb bd mgmnt 1982); RICS: chm Kent jr orgn 1972-72, memb ctee Kent branch 1973-74; chm: Ashford Chamber of Trade 1974, Challock & Holash branch Cons Assoc 1975-80, Maidstone and Dist Estate Agents Assoc 1981; Freeman City of London 1961, Liveryman Worshipful Co of Leathersellers 1964 (Freeman 1961, 3 Warden 1988-89); AMBIM 1968, FRICS 1970; *Recreations* sheep farming, golf, sailing, tennis; *Clubs* Rye GC, Whitstable GC; *Style—* Anthony Lister, Esq; Dean Ct, Westwell, Ashford, Kent TN25 4NH (☎ 0233 712924); Black Horse Agencies Geering & Polyer, 31 Castle St, Canterbury, Kent CT1 2QD (☎ 0227 457253)

LISTER, David; s of Frank Charles Lister (d 1973), of Grimsby, and Doris May Lister; *b* 18 April 1930; *Educ* Humberston Fndn Sch Cleethorpes, Downing Coll Cambridge (BA, MA); *m* 6 Sept 1956, Margaret, da of Herbert Walter Crampin, OBE (d 1974), of Grimsby; 2 s (Richard b 1961, Mark b 1965), 1 da (Frances b 1958); *Career* Nat Serv RAF 1948-50; Wilkin and Chapman Slrs Grimsby: articled clerk 1953, asst slr 1956, ptnr 1962-; legal sec (formerly sec) Grimsby and Cleethorpes Church Extension Soc 1963-, chm S Humberside Marriage Guidance Cncl 1969-73, lay chm Grimsby and Cleethorpes Deanery Synod 1970-71, pres Grimsby and Cleethorpes Law Soc 1979-80, pres Rotary Club Cleethorpes 1986-87, chm The Flag Inst 1983-, vice pres Br Origami Soc 1988- (chm 1972-75); memb Law Soc; *Recreations* heraldry and flags, paperfolding, study of playing cards, Arthurian literature and history, folklore, old roses, swimming; *Style—* David Lister, Esq; Candletrees, 21 Vaughan Avenue, Grimsby (☎ 0472 692033); New Oxford House, PO Box 16, Osborne St, Grimsby, S Humberside DN31 1HE (☎ 0472 358234)

LISTER, Geoffrey Richard; s of Walter Lister (d 1949), and Margot, *née* Callaghan; *b* 14 May 1937; *Educ* St Bede's GS Bradford; *m* 26 Jan 1962, Myrtle Margaret, John Cooper (d 1942); 1 s (Jonathan Paul b 27 July 1963), 2 da (Caroline Jane b 12 Oct 1967, Christina Margaret b 25 April 1975); *Career* articled clerk 1955-60, qualified CA 1960, data processing equipment salesman Burrough Machines 1960-63; Bradford & Bingley Bldg Soc: asst accountant and computer mangr 1965-70, chief accountant 1970-73, asst dep gen mangr 1973-80, gen mangr & dep chief exec 1980-84, chief exec 1985-; sch govr: Nab Wood GS, Beckford GS; pres Bingley & Dist Scouts; FCA 1960, CBIM 1987, FCBSI 1988; *Recreations* walking, swimming, shooting; *Clubs* Bradford & Bingley Rugby Union FC, Shipley GC; *Style—* Geoffrey Lister, Esq; Mandalay, Longwood Hall, Longwood Ave, Bingley, W Yorks (☎ 0274 562276); Bradford & Bingley Bldg Soc, Main St, Bingley, W Yorks (☎ 0274 568111)

LISTER, Dr Herbert Keith Norton; s of Maj Herbert Victor Lister (d 1984), of Saxon Lodge, Seaford, Sussex, and Kathleen, *née* Norton (d 1965); *b* 5 Dec 1922; *Educ* Eastbourne Coll, Queens' Coll Cambridge (BA, MA); *m* 1, 6 May 1950 (m dis 1979), Esther, da of Cdr Godfrey Wigram-Arkwright, DSO (d 1953), of Youngsbury, Ware, Herts; 2 s (John b 1954, Tom b 1956), 2 da (Jane (Mrs Allen) b 1951, Sarah (Mrs Brown) b 1952); m 2, 25 June 1980, Caroline, da of Lislie Thomas Laurence (d 1975), of Porlock, Somerset; 1 s (Christoher b 1982), 1 da (Lucie b 1979); *Career* medic Capt and Temp Maj TA 1952; GP: Harlow Essex 1951-60, Minehead and Porlock Somerset 1960-83; asst surgn Minehed Hosp 1960; county MO Br Red Cross Essex Div 1952, fndr memb ctee Pony Riding for the Disabled, chm Abbeyfield Porlock Soc, vice-chm and govr St Dubricius Sch Porlock; memb ctee: St Margarets Hospice Taunton, Abbeyfield Withcare Taunton; published several articles on gardening 1985-89; MRCS, LRCP; memb: RHS, Int Camellia Soc, Int Dendroligical Soc; *Recreations* gardening, tennis; *Style—* Dr Herbert Lister; Dhap Knap, Porlock, Weir, Somerset TA24 8PA (☎ 0643 862364)

LISTER, John; CBE (1987); s of Thomas Henry Lister (d 1959), and Florence May, *née* Holdsworth (d 1988); *b* 26 Feb 1931; *Educ* Sir William Turner's Sch Redcar, King's Coll London (BSc); *m* 31 Dec 1955, Catherine Ferguson, da of James Mackay (d 1979); 1 s (John b 26 Dec 1956), 4 da (Janet b 4 Jan 1958, Mhairi b 10 April 1959, Kathrynn b 3 March 1961, Anne b 20 Aug 1962); *Career* Flying Offr tech branch RAF 1954-57; chm ICI Fibres 1978-87 (gen mangr planning 1976-78, dep chm petrochemicals 1972-76), chm Br Shipbuilders 1987-; Freeman: Worshipful Co of Farriers 1981, Worshipful Co of Shipwrights 1989; MRSC, CBIM; *Clubs* RAF, Yorkshire CCC; *Style—* John Lister, Esq, CBE; 10 Simon Close, London W11 (☎ 01 229 4854); 197 Knightsbridge, London (☎ 01 581 1393)

LISTER, Raymond George; s of Horace Lister (d 1971), and Ellen Maud Mary, *née* Arnold; *b* 28 Mar 1919; *Educ* Cambridge and County HS for Boys, St John's Coll Sch Cambridge; *m* 1947, Pamela Helen, da of Frank Bishop Brutnell; 1 s, 1 da; *Career* author, artist, co dir; dir: George Lister & Sons Ltd 1941-, John P Gray & Sons Ltd 1978-83; pres: Royal Soc of Miniature Painters Sculptors and Gravers 1970-80, Architectural Metalwork Assoc 1975-77; chm bd of govrs Fedn of British Artists 1976-80; fell Wolfson Coll Cambridge, Liveryman Worshipful Co of Blacksmiths' 1957- (memb ct of assts 1980-); a syndic Fitzwilliam Museum Cambridge 1981-; *Publications* Prints and Printmaking (1984), The Letters of Samuel Palmer (1974), Samuel Palmer and 'The Ancients' (1984), The Paintings of Samuel Palmer (1985), The Paintings of William Blake (1986), Samuel Palmer: His Life and Art (1987), Catalogue Raisonné of the Works of Samuel Palmer (1988); *Clubs* Athenaeum, Sette of Old Volumes; *Style—* Raymond Lister, Esq; Windmill House, Linton, Cambridge CB1 6NS (☎ 0223 891248)

LISTER, Prof (Margot) Ruth Aline; da of Dr Werner Bernard Lister, of Manchester, and Daphne, *née* Carter; *b* 3 May 1949; *Educ* Moreton Hall School, Univ of Essex (BA), Univ of Sussex (MA); *Career* dir Child Poverty Action Gp 1979-87 (legal res offr 1971-75, asst dir 1975-77, dep dir 1977-79), prof applied social studies Univ of Bradford 1987-; memb mgmnt ctee Bradford CAB; Hon LLD Univ of Manchester 1987; *Books* Supplementary Benefit Rights (1974), Welfare Benefits (1981), plus numerous chapters in books and pamphlets; *Recreations* walking, meditation, tai chi, reading, music, women's gp; *Style—* Prof Ruth Lister; 26 Lynton Drive, Bradford BD9 5JT; Dept of Applied Social Studies, Univ of Bradford, W Yorks BD7 1DP (☎ 0274 733 466 ext 8258, fax 0274 305 340)

LISTER, Dame Unity Viola; *née* Webley; DBE (1972, OBE 1959); da of Dr Arthur Sydney Webley (d 1931), and Viola, *née* Hockley (d 1938); *b* 19 June 1913; *Educ* St Helen's Blackheath, Sorbonne; *m* 1940, Samuel William Lister, s of Victor Edward Lister (d 1954); *Career* memb London CC 1949-65 (dep chm 1963-64), int vice-chm European Union of Women 1963-69, (memb exec 1965-), memb Inner London Advsy Ctee on Appt of Magistrates; chm: Nat Union of Cons and Unionist Assocs 1970-71, Women's Nat Advsy Ctee (Cons) 1966-69; memb exec: European Movement 1970-, Cons Gp for Europe 1970-; chm Horniman Museum 1967-, govr Royal Marsden Hosp 1957-83; *Recreations* music, languages, walking, gardening, history; *Clubs* St Stephen's, Europe House; *Style—* Dame Unity Lister, DBE; 32 The Court Yard, Eltham, London SE9 5QE (☎ 01 850 7038)

LISTER-KAYE, Sir John Philip Lister; 8 Bt (UK 1812), of Grange, Yorkshire; s of Sir John Christopher Lister Lister-Kaye, 7 Bt (d 1982), by his 1 w, Audrey Helen (d 1979), da of Edwin James Carter, of Westbury-on-Trym, Glos; descended from Sir John Kaye, Knight, of Woodsome, Yorkshire living in 1066, and Sir John Kaye of Woodsome created Baronet in 1641 by Charles I, also Lord Mayor of York; This Baronetcy became extinct through illegitimacy in 1810 and Sir John Lister-Kaye of Grange was re-created Baronet in 1812 for services to George III; Sir John Lister-Kaye of Grange 3rd Baronet was groom-in-waiting to Edward VII; *b* 8 May 1946; *Educ* Allhallows Sch; *m* 1, 1972, Sorrel Deirdre, da of Count Henry Noel Bentinck, s of Capt Count Robert Charles Aldenburg-Bentinck (Mediatised Count of the Holy Roman Empire), a descendant of Hon William Bentinck, s of 1 Earl of Portland; 1 s, 2 da (twins); m 2, 17 Feb 1989, Mrs Lucinda Anne Baillie, eld da of Robin Law, of Withersfield, Suffolk; *Heir* s, John Warwick Noel Lister-Kaye b 10 Dec 1974; *Career* naturalist, author, lectr, farmer; dir of Aigas Field Centre Ltd 1977-, fndr dir Scottish Conservation Charity The Aigas Tst 1980-; chm Scottish Advsy Ctee RSPB 1986-; memb int ctee The World Wilderness Fndn 1983, recipient of Wilderness Soc Gold Award for Conservation 1984; *Books* The White Island (1972), Seal Cull (1979), The Seeing Eye (1980); *Recreations* breeding horses and highland cattle; *Clubs* Farmers', Caledonian; *Style—* Sir John Lister-Kaye, Bt; Aigas House, Beauly, Inverness (☎ 0463 782729; Grange Estate Co Office, 782443)

LISTER-KAYE, Margaret, Lady; Margaret Isabelle; da of Lt-Col Barnaby Duke, TD, JP (d 1959), of Martinstown, Dorchester; *Educ* Sherborne Lady's Coll; *m* 1, 1940, late Rex Lovelace; 1 s (d 1981), 2 da; m 2, 1980, as his 2 w, Sir John Christopher Lister Lister-Kaye, 7 Bt (d 1982); 1 step s (Sir John Lister-Kaye, Bt), 1 step da; *Books* Where Have all the Cowslips Gone? Bishopsgate Press (one chapter); *Recreations* hunting, sailing, gardening; *Style—* Margaret, Lady Lister-Kaye; Hawthorne Cottage, Rectory Rd, Piddlehinton, Dorchester, Dorset (☎ 030 04 229)

LISTON, Prof David Joel; OBE (1972, MBE 1944); s of Edward Lichtenstein (d 1937), of Salford Lancs, and Hannah, *née* Davis (d 1962); *b* 27 Mar 1914; *Educ* Manchester GS, Wadham Coll Oxford (MA); *m* 29 Aug 1939, Eva Carole (d 1987), da of Robert Kauffman (d 1942), of London; 1 s (Edward Robin b 30 Oct 1947), 2 da (Veronica Joan b 29 May 1943, Valerie Ann b 14 Sept 1946); *Career* RCS TA 1938; WWII serv 1939-: cmmnd 2 Lt RCS posted 137 Divnl Signals 1940, Capt 1941-42, Maj i/c 137 Armed Bde Signal Sqdn, 2 i/c 8 Corp Signals, serv Normandy, France, Belgium, Holland, Germany, 2 i/c 43 Div Signals (despatches 1944), demobbed 1945; Metal Box Co: mgmnt trainee 1937, economic advsr head info and statistics div, head plastics div, md; asst dir Manchester Business Sch 1966-69, industl advsr to govt 1969-72, pro-rector (subsequently visiting prof) PCL; currently: visiting prof and memb cncl European Business Sch, educnl advsr BOTB; memb current affrs ctee (formerly govt) Eng Speaking Union, pres Winchester City SLD; FRSA, FSS, FIOD, CIEX; *Books* The Purpose and Practice of Management (1971), Education and Training for Overseas Trade (1973), Business Studies Languages and Overseas Trade (1986), The Invisible Economy (1988); *Clubs* Nat Lib, IOD; *Style—* Prof David Liston, OBE; 15 Twyford Ct, Northlands Drive, Winchester, Hants SO23 7AL (☎ 0962 66087); European Business Sch, Regents Coll, Inner Circle, Regents Pk, London, NW1 4NS (☎ 01 487 7400)

LISTON, (Edward) Robin; s of David Joel Liston, OBE, of 15 Twyford Ct, Northlands Drive, Winchester, Hants, and Eva Carole, *née* Kauffmann (d 1987); *b* 30 Oct 1947; *Educ* Bryanston Sch Dorset, Mercersburg Acad PA USA, Univ of Kent (BA); *m* 6 July 1969 (m dis 1987), Judith Margaret, da of Frederick Tye, CBE, of 6 Downing Close, Sutton, Macclesfield, Ches; 2 da (Rebecca b 1970, Victoria b 1974); *Career* dist ed Kent Messenger 1969-70, asst ed Benn Bros 1970-72; assoc dir: Forman House PR Ltd 1972-79, Welbeck PR Ltd 1981-84; dir: Cary Byoir Ltd 1984-86, Hill & Knowlton Ltd 1986-88; jt md Buckmans PR Ltd 1988-; *Recreations* music, films, railways, suburban architecture; *Style—* Robin Liston, Esq; 26 Southern Rd, London, N2 9JG (☎ 01 883 7314); Buckmans Ltd, 1 Bedford St, London, WC2E 9HD (☎ 01 836 8866)

LISTOWEL, 5 Earl of (I 1822); William Francis Hare; GCMG (1957), PC (1946); also Baron Ennismore (I 1800), Viscount Ennismore and Listowel (I 1816, usually shortened to Viscount Ennismore when used as courtesy title for eldest s and h), and Baron Hare of Convamore (UK 1869, which sits as); s of 4 Earl (d 1931), by his w Hon Freda Vanden-Bempde-Johnstone (da of 2 Baron Derwent); er bro of Lord (1 Viscount) Blakenham and unc of Lord (3 Earl of) Iveagh; *b* 28 Sept 1906; *Educ* Magdalene Coll Cambridge; *m* 1, 1933 (m dis 1945), Judith, da of Raoul de Marffy-Mantuano, of Budapest; 1 da (Lady Grantley); m 2 1958 (m dis 1963), Stephanie Sandra Yvonne, da of Sam Wise, of Toronto, and formerly w of Hugh Currie; 1 da; m 3, 1963, Pamela, da of Francis Day, of Croydon, and formerly w of John Read; 2 s, 1 da; *Heir* s, Viscount Ennismore; *Career* memb LCC 1937-58; late Lt Intell Corps; parly under-sec of state India Off 1944-45, also dep ldr House of Lords 1944-45 (Lab whip 1941-44); sec state: India 1947, Burma 1947-48; min state Colonial Affrs 1948-50, jt parly sec Min Agric & MAFF 1950-51; govr-gen Ghana 1957-60; chm Ctees House of Lords 1965-76; *Style—* The Rt Hon The Earl of Listowel, GCMG, PC; 10 Downshire Hill, London NW3 (☎ 01 431 3327)

LITCHFIELD, Dame Ruby Beatrice; DBE (1981, OBE); *Career* tstee Adelaide Festival Centre 1971-, dir (first woman appointed) Festival City Broadcasters Ltd 1975-; honoured for services to the performing arts and to the community; *Style—* Dame Ruby Litchfield, DBE; c/o Liberal Party of Australia, 234 George St, Sydney, NSW 2000, Australia

LITHERLAND, Robert Kenneth; MP (Lab) Manchester Central (by-election) Sept 1979-; s of Robert Litherland and Mary, *née* Parry; *b* 1930; *Educ* N Manchester HS for Boys; *m* 1953, Edna; 1 s, 1 da; *Style—* Robert Litherland, Esq, MP; 32 Darley Avenue, Didsbury, Manchester M20 8YD

LITHGOW, Sir William James; 2 Bt (UK 1925), of Ormsary, Co Argyll, DL (Renfrewshire 1970); s of Sir James Lithgow, 1 Bt, GBE, CB, MC, TD, JP, DL (d 1952); *b* 10 May 1934; *Educ* Winchester; *m* 1, 1964, Valerie Helen (d 1964), da of Denis Herbert Scott, CBE (d 1958); m 2, 1967, Mary Claire, da of Col F M Hill, CBE, of East Knoyle, Wilts; 2 s, 1 da; *Heir* s, James Frank Lithgow b 13 June 1970; *Career* shipbuilder and farmer; chm: Lithgows Ltd 1959-84, Scott-Lithgow Drydocks Ltd 1967-78; vice-chm Scott Lithgow Ltd 1968-78; dir: Bank of Scotland 1962-, Landcatch Ltd 1981-, Lithgows Pty Ltd 1972-; memb: Br Ctee Det Norske Veritas 1966-, exec ctee Scottish Cncl Devpt and Indust 1969-85, Scottish regnl cncl of CBI 1969-76, Clyde Port Authy 1969-71, W Central Scotland Plan Steering Ctee 1971-74, gen bd Nat Physical Labour 1963-66, Greenock Dist Hosp Bd 1961-66, Scottish Milk Mktg Bd 1979-83; chm Iona Cathedral Tstees Mgmnt Bd 1979-83, memb cncl Winston Churchill Meml Tst 1979-83, hon pres Students Assoc, memb ct Univ of Strathclyde 1964-69; Hon LLD Strathclyde 1979, memb Queen's Body Guard for Scotland (Royal Co of Archers); *Recreations* rural life, invention, photography; *Clubs* Oriental, Western, Royal Scottish Automobile (Glasgow); *Style—* Sir William Lithgow, Bt; Ormsary, Lochgilphead, Argyllshire (☎ Ormsary 252); Drums, Langbank, Renfrewshire (☎ 606)

LITMAN, Dr Gloria Klein; da of Emil Klein (d 1963), and Sadie Epstein (d 1982); *b* 10 April 1936; *Educ* Hunter Coll New York City (BA), North Texas State Univ (MSc), Univ of London (PhD); *m* 4 Dec 1954, Armand Charles Litman, s of Charles Louis Litman (d 1987); 2 s (David b 1957, Jonathan b 1960); *Career* sr lectr Inst of Psychiatry 1987, hon conslt psychologist Maudsley Hosp, clinical res psychologist Addiction Res Unit; *Recreations* bridge, yoga; *Style—* Dr Gloria Litman; 22 Stafford Terrace, London W8 7BH (☎ 01 937 9267)

LITTLE, Capt Alec Haines; CBE (1973); s of Cdr Henry Alexander Kettle Little (d 1932), of Middx, and Dorothy Mainwaring (d 1968); *b* 28 August 1920; *Educ* Lucton Sch, RN Engrg Coll Keyham; *m* 1945, Pamela Ruby, da of Col Richard Perry William Bolt (d 1957); 1 s, 1 da; *Career* served 1939-45 War in Atlantic, Indian and Pacific Oceans; chief staff offr (tech) to Flag Offr Medway 1968-70; dir of quartering RN 1970-73; welfare officer to Met Police 1973-83; MIMechE, FIMarE, FInstPet; *Recreations* tennis, squash, golf, gardening; *Clubs* Naval and Military; *Style—* Capt Alec Little, CBE, RN; Pepys Cottage, 5 The Close, Brambridge Park, Kiln Lane, Nr Eastleigh, Hants SO5 7HT (☎ 0962 712532)

LITTLE, Hon Sir Douglas Macfarlan; s of John Little; *b* 23 July 1904; *Educ* Wangoom State Sch, Scotch Coll, Ormond Coll Melbourne Univ; *m* 1931, Ida Margaret, da of Edward Chapple; *Career* served in 1939-45 War; barr and slr Victoria 1929, QC 1954, judge of Supreme Court Victoria 1959-74; kt 1973; *Style—* The Hon Sir Douglas Little; 1/74 Serrell St, East Malvern, Melvourne, Victoria 3145, Australia

LITTLE, George Noel Lincoln; s of Douglas Lincoln Little (d 1961), of N Yorks, and Joan, *née* Arnold (d 1960); *b* 5 Jan 1928; *Educ* The Elms Malvern, Uppingham; *m* 10 Sept 1954, June Helen, da of Ian Maitland Milne (d 1964), of Guildford, Surrey; 2 da (Ann Louise b 1956, Amelia b 1958); *Career* Capt RA 1946-48, RA (TA) 1948-53; chm David Little & Co Ltd 1976, proprietor Malt House Co (off supplies); *Style—* George N L Little, Esq; Lane Farm Guilsfield, Welshpool, Powys SY21 9DH (☎ 0938 5282); 2 Boot St, Welshpool, Powys SY21 7SA (☎ 0938 5005/0938 5080)

LITTLE, Lt-Col John Ernest; MC (1944), DL (Warwicks 1988-); s of Noel Ernest Little (d 1954), of Lane House, Compton, Winchester, and Frances Catherine, *née*

Eden (d 1974); *b* 8 June 1922; *Educ* Marlborough; *m* 23 May 1953, Nancy Elizabeth, da of Joseph William Smith; 1 s (William b 1958), 2 da (Catherine b 1955, Georgina b 1967); *Career* memb Warwicks CC 1979-85 (chm educn ctee 1981-85), chm Stratford-on-Avon Cons Assoc 1975-80; memb cncl Warwick Univ 1982-(chm: careers bd 1986-, building ctee 1987-); *Recreations* shooting, fishing; *Clubs* Army & Navy; *Style*— Lt-Col John Little, MC, DL; Newbold Pacry Hall, Warwick (☎ 0926 651270)

LITTLE, John Noel; s of Ronald Little (d 1974), and Margaret Elizabeth, *née* Thompson; *b* 25 Dec 1935; *Educ* Stockton-on-Tees GS; *m* 1961, Mavis, da of James Sydney Ord (d 1960); 1 s (Mark), 1 da (Elaine); *Career* Lloyds and Scottish plc 1957-84 (exec dir 1973-84), md Lloyds and Scottish Finance Ltd 1969-84; chm: Fin Houses Assoc 1980-82, Investor Homes plc, Tamaris plc, Lease & Fin Servs Ltd, Stortext (Scotland) Ltd, J W Galloway Ltd, Scotbeef Ltd; dir: Barry D Trentham Ltd, Hatrick-Bruce Construction Ltd, Caledonian Tst plc; dep chm London Fiduciary Tst plc; FID; *Recreations* cricket, hockey, tennis, golf, bridge; *Clubs* RAC, Royal Burgess Golfing Soc, The Grange; *Style*— John N Little, Esq; Dunosdale, 22 Cammo Cres, Edinburgh EH4 8DZ

LITTLE, Most Rev Thomas Francis; *see*: Melbourne (RC) Archbishop of

LITTLEALES, Paul Cade; s of Henry William Littleales (d 1986), of Sidmouth, Devon, and Marie Alice, *née* Cade (d 1984); *b* 8 Feb 1932; *Educ* Canford, Luton Poly; *m* 6 June 1962, Sallie Ann, da of Jack Thomas Joice (d 1968), of Fakenham, Norfolk; 2 s (Lawrence Henry b 1964, Andrew Paul b 1965); *Career* mech engr; chm and md: Trinity Motors Ltd 1962-84, Green's Garage Gp 1968-84; fin and engrg conslt 1984-; memb of Lloyds 1978-; *Recreations* riding, hunting; *Clubs* Eccentric; *Style*— Paul C Littleales, Esq; The Gate House, Limpsfield Common, nr Oxted, Surrey (☎ 0883 722104)

LITTLECHILD, Prof Stephen Charles; s of Sydney Littlechild, of Wisbech, and Joyce, *née* Sharpe; *b* 27 August 1943; *Educ* Wisbech GS, Univ of Birmingham (BCom), Stanford Univ, Northwestern Univ, Univ of Texas at Austin (PhD), Univ of California at Los Angeles; *m* 1 Aug 1975, Kathleen (d 1982), da of Charles T Pritchard; 2 s (Harry b 1978, Richard b 1980), 1 da (Elizabeth b 1976); *Career* Harkness fell Stanford Univ 1965-67, sr res lectr Graduate Centre for Mgmnt Studies Birmingham 1970-72, prof applied econ Univ of Aston 1973-75, prof of commerce and head dept industl econ and business studies Univ of Birmingham 1975-; visiting prof: New York Univ, Stanford Univ, Chicago Univ, Virginia Poly 1974-80; memb: Monopolies and Mergers Cmmn 1983-, ACORD 1987-; advsr UK Govt on privatisation of BT, BAA, water and electricity; *Books* Operational Research for Managers (1977), Fallacy of the Mixed Economy (1978), Elements of Telecommunications Economics (1979), Energy Strategies for the UK (with KG Vaidya, 1982), Regulation of British Telecoms Profitability (1983), Economic Regulation of Privatised Water Authorities (1986); *Recreations* genealogy; *Style*— Prof Stephen Littlechild; University of Birmingham B15 5TT (☎ 021 414 6689)

LITTLEFAIR, Henry (Harry) George Peter; s of Bernard Littlefair, of York (d 1975), and Ellen Littlefair *née* Houghton (d 1961); *b* 6 Feb 1931; *Educ* Ratcliffe Coll, Leicester; *m* 9 Aug 1960, Mary Edith, da of Sydney Fryer Monkman, of York (d 1980); 2 s (Nicholas b 1962, Dominic b 1964); *Career* imvestmt mangr: vice-chm Allied Dunbar Unit Tst 1986-; md: A D Unit Tst 1983-86 (dep md 1975-83); *Recreations* philately, music, chess, walking; *Style*— Harry Littlefair, Esq; 4 Fallowfield Close, Emmer Green, Reading, Berkshire RG4 8NQ (☎ 0734 475993); Allied Dunbar Unit Trusts plc, 9-15 Sackville Street, London W1X 1DE

LITTLEJOHN, Alistair George; s of James Davidson Littlejohn (d 1970); *b* 17 Feb 1935; *Educ* Aberdeen GS, Aberdeen Univ (BScEng); *m* 1962, Mairwen Lloyd, da of Capt Henry Lloyd Jones (d 1971); 1 s, 1 da; *Career* civil engr; dir: Cementation Building Ltd, Trollope & Colls Ltd; *Clubs* Eccentric, IOD; *Style*— Alistair Littlejohn, Esq; Harlyn, 14 Hempstead Lane, Potten End, Berkhamsted, Herts (☎ Berkhamsted 3706); office: Trocol House, 25 Christopher St, London EC2 (☎ 01 377 2500)

LITTLER, Lady; Cora; *née* Goffin; *m* 1933, Sir Emile Littler (d 1985); 2 da; *Career* actress; *Style*— Lady Littler; c/o Mrs J Manners, 55 Spencer Park, London SW18 2SX

LITTLER, Sir (James) Geoffrey; KCB (1985, CB 1981); s of James Edward Littler (d 1961), of Manchester, and Evelyn Mary Taylor; *b* 18 May 1930; *Educ* Manchester GS, Corpus Christi Coll Cambridge (BA); *m* 20 Sept 1958, Shirley, da of Sir Percy William Marsh, CSI, CIE, of Dorchester-on-Thames, Oxfordshire; 1 s (Peter b 1967); *Career* civil servant: second perm sec (fin), HM Treasy 1983-; joined Civil Serv in Colonial Office 1952, Treasy 1954; chm Working Party 3 of OECD 1985-, Euro Community Monetary Ctee 1987-; *Recreations* music, reading, travelling; *Clubs* Reform; *Style*— Sir Geoffrey Littler, KCB; HM Treasy, Parliament Street, London SW1P 3AG

LITTLER, Lady; Shirley; da of Sir Percy Marsh, CSI, CIE (d 1969), of Dorchester-on-Thames, Oxon, and Joan Mary, *née* Beecroft (d 1972); *b* 8 June 1932; *Educ* Headington Sch Oxford, Girton Coll Cambridge (BA, MA); *m* 20 Sept 1958, Sir (James) Geoffrey Littler, KCB, *qv*; 1 s (Peter b 1967); *Career* asst princ HM Treasy 1953, princ 1960; asst sec Prices and Incomes Bd (NBPI) 1969; sec to V and G Tbnl of Enquiry 1971, Home Office 1972; asst under sec of state: Broadcasting Dept Home Office 1978, Immigration and Nationality Dept Home Office 1981; dir of admin IBA 1983 (dep dir gen 1986); FRSA 1988, MRTS, RIPA; *Recreations* reading, history; *Style*— Lady Littler; c/o Independent Broadcasting Authority, 70 Brompton Road, London SW3 1EY (☎ 01 584 7011, telex 24345)

LITTLETON, Hon Mrs (Aileen Mary); *née* Fitzherbert; er da of 14 Baron Stafford (d 1986); *b* 29 Mar 1953; *m* 1980, Antony Robin Walhouse Westby Littleton (changed his surname from Perceval to Littleton by Royal Licence 1971), son of Robert Westby Perceval, by his wife, Hon Joanna Ida Louise, da of 5 Baron Hatherton; 1 s (Thomas Alastair Westby b 1986), 1 da (Katrina b 1983); *Style*— The Hon Mrs Littleton; Old Walls, Hannington, nr Basingstoke, Hants

LITTLETON, Hon Hester Mary Modwena; da of 4 Baron Hatherton (d 1944); *b* 1912; *Career* 1939-45 with WTS/FANY; *Style*— The Hon Hester Littleton; Pitt Manor Cottage, Winchester, Hants (☎ 4898)

LITTLETON, Hon Jonathan Lloyd; s of 6 Baron Hatherton (d 1973), and his 2 w, Mary, Lady Hatherton, *qv*; *b* 17 July 1949; *m* 1970, Maxine Elizabeth, da of Alistair Brough Mills; 2 s (Alexander, Jonathan), 2 da (Rosalind, Melissa); *Style*— The Hon Jonathan Littleton; Eatonbrook House, Rushbrook, Church Stretton, Shropshire

LITTLETON, Hon Moonyeen Meriel; da of 6 Baron Hatherton (d 1973), and his 1 w, Nora Evelyn, *née* Smith (d 1955); *b* 1933; *Style*— The Hon Moonyeen Littleton; c/o Hassan Hafer St no5, Saray El Qubba, Cairo, Egypt

LITTLETON, Hon Richard Brownlow; s of 6 Baron Hatherton (d 1973), and his 2 w, Mary, Lady Hatherton, *qv*; *b* 17 July 1949; *m* 1975 (m dis), Shirley Margaret Adamson; 1 s (Ian b 1981), 1 da (Kirsty 1985); *Career* Nat Tst warden i/c Aderley Estates and Hare Hill Estates; *Style*— The Hon Richard Littleton; Foresters Lodge, Nether Alderley, Macclesfield, Cheshire

LITTLEWOOD, James; CB (1973); s of Thomas Littlewood (d 1930), of Royton, Lancs, and Sarah Jane, *née* Penhall (d 1967); *b* 21 Oct 1922; *Educ* Manchester GS, St John's Coll Cambridge (MA); *m* 9 Aug 1950, Barbara, da of Harry Shaw (d 1958), of Blackburn, Lancs; 2 s (David b 1955, Peter b 1957), 1 da (Pamela b 1953); *Career* enlisted Army 1942, cmmnd KORR, WWII serv India and Burma, transferred W Yorks Regt (later HQ 17 Indian Div 1945), Wingate's second campaign 1944, 17 Ind Div campaign 1945, Capt; Civil Serv: admin class 1947, HM Treasy 1947-67 (seconded Cabinet Off 1955), transferred Dept for Nat Savings 1967 (dir of savings 1972), ret 1981; *Recreations* golf, bridge; *Clubs* Utd Oxford and Cambridge Univ, Barton-on-Sea GC; *Style*— James Littlewood, Esq, CB; 3 Smugglers Lane South, Highcliffe, Christchurch, Dorset BH23 4NF (☎ 0425 275 649)

LITTLEWOOD, John Nigel; s of George Littlewood, and Diana Mary, *née* Wallis; *b* 11 April 1935; *Educ* Lutterworth GS, Farnborough GS, New Coll Oxford (MA); *m* 29 Sept 1962, Rosemary Underwood; 2 s (William, Richard); *Career* Nat Serv RN 1954-56; Read Hurst-Brown Stockbrokers 1959-75 (ptnr 1964-75), ptnr Rowe & Pitman stockbrokers 1975-86, dir S G Warburg Gp plc 1986-; FSIA; *Recreations* cinema, gardening, golf, music, reading, writing; *Clubs* North Hants GC; *Style*— John Littlewood, Esq; Mavins Ct, Greenhill Rd, Farnham, Surrey; S G Warburg Gp plc, 1 Finsbury Ave, London EC2M 2PA (☎ 01 606 1066)

LITTMAN, Jeffrey James; s of Louis Littman (d 1981), of Edmonton, Middx, and Sarah (Sadie), *née* Coberman (d 1974); *b* 19 Feb 1943; *Educ* Latymer Sch Edmonton, St Catharine's Coll Cambridge (MA); *m* 20 March 1975, Sandra Lynne, da of David Kallman (d 1975), of NY; 2 da (Amanda, Léonie); *Career* ldr mgmnt gp dept of computing and control Imp Coll London; barr Middle Temple 1974, Midlands and Oxford circuit; *Recreations* history; *Style*— Jeffrey Littman, Esq; 4 Verulam Buildings, Gray's Inn, London WC1R 5LW (☎ 01 405 6114, fax 01 831 6112)

LITTMAN, Mark; QC (1961); s of Jack Littman (d 1963), and Lilian, *née* Rose ; *b* 4 Sept 1920; *Educ* Owens Sch, LSE (BSc), Queens Coll Oxford (MA); *m* 18 Sept 1965, Marguerite, da of Tyler Lamkin, of Monroe, Louisiana, USA; *Career* Lt RN 1941-46; barr Middle Temple 1947, practice 1947-67 and 1979, master of bench 1971, master tres Middle Temple 1988; dep chm Br Steel Corpn 1976-79; dir: RTZ, Burtons, Granada; former dir: Commercial Union, Br EnKalon; Amerada Hess (US); memb Royal Cmmn Legal Servs 1976-79; *Clubs* Reform, Garrick, Oxford & Cambridge, Century (New York); *Style*— Mark Littman, Esq, QC; 79 Chester Square, London SW1 (☎ 01 730 2973); 12 Grays Inn Sq, London WC1 (☎ 01 405 8654)

LIVENS, Leslie John Philip; s of Lt Leslie Francis Hugh Livens (d 1981), of London, and Betty Livens; *b* 13 Dec 1946; *Educ* Wimbledon County Secdy Sch; *m* 3 Aug 1968, Carole Ann, da of Henry William Todd, of London; 1 s (Stephen b 1970), 1 da (Clare b 1972); *Career* ed and conslt ed Taxation Practitioner (Jl of Inst of Taxation) 1974-; former ed: Tax Planning Int, Fin Times, World Tax Report, Review of Parliament; managing ed Butterworths Tax Books 1977-81, taxation conslt Rowland Nevill & Co (now Moores Rowland) 1981-83, ptnr Moores Rowland 1983-; ATII 1972, AITI 1983; *princ publications*: Moores & Rowland's Tax Guide (1982-87), Share Valuation Handbook (1986), Daily Telegraph Tax Guide (1987), Daily Telegraph Personal Tax Guide (1988); *Recreations* music, writing, walking, family; *Style*— Leslie Livens, Esq; Clifford's Inn, Fetter Lane, London EC4A 1AS (☎ 01 831 2345, fax 01 831 6123, telex 886504)

LIVERMORE, Sir Harry; s of Jack Livermore; *b* 1908; *Educ* Royal GS Newcastle-upon-Tyne, Durham Univ; *m* 1940, Esther, da of Samuel Angelman; *Career* slr 1930; vice pres Royal Liverpool Philharmonic Soc (former chm), Everyman Theatre Liverpool and Merseyside Arts Assoc; chm Royal Ct Theatre and Arts Tst Ltd; Lord Mayor of Liverpool 1958-59; kt 1973; *Style*— Sir Harry Livermore; 18 Burnham Rd, Liverpool L18 6JU

LIVERPOOL, Archdeacon of; *see*: Spiers, Ven Graeme Hendry Gordon

LIVERPOOL, 6 Bishop of (cr 1880) 1975-; Rt Rev David Stewart Sheppard; s of Stuart Sheppard (d 1937), and Barbara Sheppard (d 1983); *b* 6 Mar 1929; *Educ* Sherborne, Trinity Hall Cambridge (MA); *m* 1957, Grace, da of Rev Bruce Raymond Isaac; 1 da (Jenny); *Career* Nat Serv 2 Lt Royal Sussex Regt 1947-49; ordained: deacon 1955, priest 1956; curate St Mary's Islington 1955-57, warden and chaplain Mayflower Family Centre Canning Town 1957-69, bishop suffragan of Woolwich 1969-75, bishop of Liverpool 1975-; Hon LLD Liverpool 1981; *Books* Parson's Pitch (1964), Built as a City (1974), Bias to the Poor (1983), Better Together (1988); *Recreations* painting, cricket (played for Sussex 1947-62, England 1950-63, Cambridge Univ 1950-52), reading, gardening, music; *Style*— The Rt Rev the Bishop of Liverpool; Bishop's Lodge, Woolton Park, Liverpool L25 6DT Church House, 1 Hanover St, Liverpool L1 3DW (☎ 051 708 9480)

LIVERPOOL, Dean of; *see*: Walters, Very Rev (Rhys) Derrick Chamberlain

LIVERPOOL, 10 Archbishop of (RC, 1911 by Letters Apostolic 'Si qua est' of Pius X) 1976-; Most Rev Derek John Harford Worlock Derek John Harford Worlock; also Metropolitan of Northern Province with Suffragan Sees, Hexham, Lancaster, Leeds, Middlesbroug, Salford and Hallam; s of Capt Harford Worlock and Dora, *née* Hoblyn; *b* 4 Feb 1920; *Educ* St Edmund's Coll Ware; *Career* ordained 1944, curate Kensington 1944-45, private sec to archbishop of Westminster 1945-64, dean of Stepney 1964-65, bishop of Portsmouth 1965-76, translated Liverpool 1976; *Books* Seek Ye First (1950), Give Me Your Hand (1977), Better Together (1988); *Style*— His Grace the Archbishop of Liverpool; Archbishop's House, 87 Green Lane, Mossley Hill, Liverpool L18 2EP (☎ 051 722 2379)

LIVERPOOL, 5 Earl of (UK 1905); Edward Peter Bertram Savile Foljambe; also Baron Hawkesbury (UK 1893) and Viscount Hawkesbury (UK 1905); s of Capt Peter George William Savile Foljambe (ka Italy 1944, gn of 4 Earl of Liverpool who d 1969 and who was ggs of half-bro of the nineteenth century PM), and Elizabeth Joan, *née* Flint (who m 2, Maj Andrew Gibbs, MBE, TD, *qv*); *b* 14 Nov 1944; *Educ* Shrewsbury, Perugia Univ Italy; *m* 29 Jan 1970, Lady Juliana Noel, *qv*, da of 5 Earl of Gainsborough; 2 s; *Heir* s, Viscount Hawkesbury; *Clubs* Turf, Pratt's; *Style*— The Rt Hon the Earl of Liverpool; The Grange Farm, Exton, nr Oakham, Leics (office 078086

555)

LIVERPOOL, Countess of; Lady Juliana Mary Alice; *née* Noel; da of 5 Earl of Gainsborough; *b* 1949; *m* 1970, 5 Earl of Liverpool, *qv*; 2 s; *Style—* The Rt Hon the Countess of Liverpool; The Grange Farm, Exton, nr Oakham, Leics

LIVERSEDGE, Richard Lorton; s of Lt-Col John Ridler Liversedge (d 1968), of Fawke House, Sevenoaks, Kent, and Grace Evelyn Liversedge (d 1982); *b* 31 August 1940; *Educ* Tonbridge, London Hosp Dental Sch (BDS), London Hosp Med Coll (MB BS); *m* 28 Oct 1972, Jennifer Jane, da of John Hurrel Robertson, of Johannesburg, SA; 1 s (Dominic b 1974), 2 da (Annabel b 1975, Belinda b 1979); *Career* registrar London Hosp 1970-72 (house surgn 1968-69), sr registrar Royal Dental Hosp and St Georges Hosp 1972-77; conslt maxillo facial surgn: Middx Hosp 1977-89, Barnet Gp of Hosps 1977-; responsible for various surgical instrument innovations; winter sportsman (luge); winner Br Luge Champs 1971; Winter Olympics: represented GB Grenoble 1968, capt Sapporo 1972, capt Innsbruck 1976; pres Br Racing Toboggan Assoc 1972-; chm Med Ctee Fedn Internationale de Luge de Course 1972-, memb med ctee Br Olympic Assoc 1976-; Freeman City of London 1968, Liveryman Worshipful Co of Skinners 1977; FDS RCS (Edinburgh) 1971, FDS RCS (England) 1972; *Recreations* Luge, cresta run, moto polo; *Clubs* St Moritz Tobogganing; *Style—* Richard Liversedge, Esq; Oak Cottage, 117 Flaunden, Hertfordshire HP3 0PB (☎ 0442 833 047); Flat 1, 43 Wimpole St, London W1M 7AF (☎ 01 935 7909)

LIVESAY, Vice Adm Michael Howard; s of William Lindsay Livesay (d 1982), of Bishop Auckland, Co Durham, and Margaret Elenora Chapman Steel (d 1974); *b* 5 April 1936; *Educ* Ackland Hall GS Middlesborough, HMS Britannia, RNC Dartmouth; *m* 8 Aug 1959, Sara, da of Dr Arthur Vivian House, of Bicester, Oxon; 2 da (Harriet b 1962, Georgia b 1964); *Career* joined RN 1952, trg appts 1954-57, cmmnd 1957, qualified aircraft direction specialist 1959, direction offr HMS Hermes and HMS Aisne, Fighter Direction Sch and 893 Naval Air Sqdn 1959-66; cmd: HMS Hubberston 1966-68, HMS Plymouth 1970-72; Capt 1975-77, Fishery Protection and Mine Counter Measures 1975-77, first CO HMS Invincible 1979-82, dir Naval Warfare 1982-84; Flag Offr Sea Trg 1984-85; asst chief Naval Staff 1986-88, Flag Offr Scotland and NI 1989; *Recreations* gliding, sailing, skiing, gardening; *Clubs* Army and Navy, Royal Yacht Sqdn; *Style—* Vice Adm Michael Livesay; c/o Naval Secretary, Old Admiralty Building, MOD, London SW1

LIVESEY, Bernard Joseph Edward; s of Joseph Augustine Livesey (d 1965), of Hatch End, Middx, and Marie Gabrielle, *née* Caulfield; *b* 21 Feb 1944; *Educ* Cardinal Vaughan Sch London, Peterhouse Cambridge (MA, LLB); *m* 25 Sept 1971, Penelope Jean, da of Samuel Walter Harper, of Slindon, W Sussex; 2 da (Sarah b 6 June 1973, Kate b 21 Aug 1977); *Career* barr Lincoln's Inn 1969, rec of Crown Ct 1987; *Recreations* listening to music, gardening, bell ringing; *Style—* Bernard J E Livesey, Esq; 2 Crown Office Row, Temple, London, EC4 (☎ 01 353 1365)

LIVESEY, Geoffrey Colin; MBE (1968); *b* 21 Dec 1943; *m* 1969 (m dis 1982), Elisa Jane Pullen; 2 s; *Career* joined FCO 1962, second sec and vice-consul Abidjan 1977-81, vice-consul for Niger and Upper Volta 1981-83, first sec FCO 1983-; *Recreations* squash, tennis; *Style—* Geoffrey Livesey, Esq, MBE; 21 Villiers Rd, Kingston-upon-Thames, Surrey (☎ 01 541 0649); Foreign and Commonwealth Office, London SW1 (☎ 01 233 5412)

LIVESEY, Robert; s of Stanley Livesey (d 1960), and Mable, *née* Heigh; *b* 23 August 1938; *Educ* Grace Ramsden GS, Huddersfield Coll of Technol; *m* 28 Oct 1961, Joan, da of Clifford Ledgard; 4 s (Stephen Alan b 1962, David Andrew b 1964, Graham Michael b 1967, Jonathan Robert b 1973); *Career* chartered measurement and control technologist; chm and fndr Chemitrol Process Equipment Ltd 1977-; Fisher Process Equipment Ltd 1972-77; MIMC; *Recreations* restoration of medieval buildings; *Style—* Robert Livesey, Esq; Chainhurst Farm, Hunton Rd, Marden, Kent; Cook Lubbock House, St Faith's St, Maidstone, Kent

LIVESEY, Rodger Charles; s of Roland Livesey; *b* 19 June 1944; *Educ* Downing Coll Cambridge (MA); *m* 29 May 1972, Pat; 2 s (Matthew b 1974, Graham b 1979), 1 da (Caroline b 1977); *Career* md Security Pacific Hoare Govett Ltd 1976-88, gen mangr Tokai Int Ltd 1988-, chm W Hampton Ltd 1987-; Freeman City of London, Liveryman Worshipful Co of Actuaries; FIA; *Style—* Rodger Livesey, Esq; 60 West Common, Harpenden, Herts AL5 2LD (☎ 0582 767 527); Tokai Int, 14 Finsbury Sq, London (☎ 01 638 6030, fax 01 588 5875)

LIVINGSTON, Air Vice-Marshal Graham; QHS (1985); s of Neil Livingston (d 1977), and Margaret Anderson, *née* Graham, of Bo'ness, West Lothian; *b* 2 August 1928; *Educ* Bo'ness Acad, Edinburgh Univ (MB, ChB, DPH, DIH); *m* 1, 11 Nov 1953 (m dis 1968), Catherine Law; 1 s (Graham b 1955), 2 da (Jennifer b 1957, Catriona b 1959, d 1961); m 2, 19 June 1970, Carol Judith Palmer; 1 s (David b 1972), 1 da (Sara Jane b 1971); *Career* RAF med offr, flying stations N Ireland 1952-4, sr med offr RAF El Hamra, Abyad, Egypt 1954-55; GP 1956-57; sr med offr: RAF Lindholme 1958-60, RAF Honington 1960-62; post grad Edinburgh Univ 1962-63, sr med offr RAF Laarbruch Germany 1963-66, RAF Coll Cranwell 1966-70, registrar RAF Hosp Cosford 1970, CO RAF IHMT Halton 1971, registrar TPMRAF Hosp Akrotiri Cyprus 1972-74; CO RAF Hosp: Cosford 1974-76, Wegberg Germany 1976-9; dep dir med personnel & orgn MOD 1979-80; Air Cdre 1980, dep princ med offr Strike Cmd 1981-3; princ med offr: RAF Germany 1983-4, RAF Support Cmd 1984-; Air Vice-Marshal 1984; MFCM 1974, MFOM 1981, FBIM 1986; *Recreations* golf, skiing, caravanning; *Clubs* RAF, Ashridge GC; *Style—* Air Vice-Marshal Graham Livingston, QHS; Chimanimani, Tom's Hill Road, Aldbury, Tring, Hertfordshire HP23 5SA; Headquarters, RAF Support Command, Royal Air Force, Brampton, Huntingdon, Cambs (☎ 0480 52151, ext 6535)

LIVINGSTON BOOTH, (John) Dick; OBE (1975); s of Julian Livingston Booth (d 1962), of Hadlow, Tonbridge, Kent, and Grace Marion, *née* Swainson (d 1962); *b* 7 July 1918; *Educ* Melbourne GS, Sidney Sussex Coll Cambridge (MA); *m* 1, 1 Nov 1941, Joan Ashley (d 1976), da of Ashley Tabrum, OBE (d 1952); 2 s (Timothy b 3 May 1943, Michael b 12 Dec 1946), 1 da (Fiona b 21 Feb 1960); m 2, Audrey Betty Hope Harvey, da of Sqdn Ldr James Haslett (ka 1916); *Career* War Serv 1940-43 T/Capt RA, instr 212 HAC OCTU RHA RWAFF; Colonial Admin Serv Nigeria 1943-57, perm sec Min of Local Govt E Nigeria 1956-57; dir Charities Aid Fndn 1957-81; charity cnslt 1981-; chm: Europhil Tst 1986-87, Legislation Monitoring Serv for Charities 1981-; patron Int Standing Conf on Philanthropy 1987-; lay reader C of E 1955-83; FRGS 1949; *Books* Directory of Grant-Making Trusts (bi-annual 1968-), Charity Statistics (annual 1978-), Trusts and Foundations in Europe (1971), Report on Foundation Activity (1977); *Recreations* travel; *Clubs* Garrick, Royal Cwlth; *Style—* Dick Livingston Booth, Esq, OBE; Trulls Hatch IV, Rotherfield, E Sussex TN6 3QL (☎ 0892 853 205); 221 Bahia Dorada, Estepona, Malaga, Spain (☎ 052 801 338)

LIVINGSTONE, David Willmott; CBE; s of late George Blair Livingstone; *b* 3 Feb 1926; *Educ* Haberdashers' Aske's, Ch Ch Oxford; *m* 1950, Jane Margaret; 1 s, 3 da; *Career* Sub Lieut RNVR; dep chm and md Albright & Wilson Ltd (md 1972, dep chm and md 1977), dir IMI Ltd, vice-pres Chemical Industries Assoc (CIA), memb Econ Devpt for Chemical Industry, memb cncl CBI; life govr Birmingham Univ, hon tres-govr Fircroft Coll Birmingham; *Recreations* squash, golf, reading, music; *Clubs* Athenaeum, Edgbaston Priory, Edgbaston GC; *Style—* David Livingstone, Esq, CBE; 87 Harborne Rd, Edgbaston, Birmingham (☎ 021 454 2087)

LIVINGSTONE, Ian Lang; s of John Lang Livingstone, of 23 Cunningham Street, Motherwell, and Margaret Steele, *née* Barbour (d 1982); *b* 23 Feb 1938; *Educ* Hamilton Acad, Glasgow Univ (BL); *m* 30 March 1967, Diane, da of Frank Hales, of 199 Inner Promenade, Lytham St Annes; 2 s (Andrew b 1968, Gordon b 1970); *Career* slr; dir: Scotland West Bd Tstee Savings Bank 1985, Motherwell Enterprise Tst 1983-, Glendale Homes (Strathclyde) Ltd, Bowmere Properties Ltd, Clydesdale Building Services Ltd; chm: Interchase Ltd, Motherwell Enterprise Devpt Co Ltd; dir and chm Motherwell FC 1973-87, chm Hamilton and Dist Solicitors Property Centre 1980-84; hon pres: Motherwell Cons Asoc 1981-, Motherwell Utd YMCA, Motherwell Co of St Andrew's Ambulance Corps; hon slr Dalziel HS Memorial Tst; Notary Public 1962; *Recreations* golf, music; *Clubs* Motherwell Conservative; *Style—* Ian Livingstone, Esq; Roath Park, 223 Manse Road, Motherwell ML1 2PY (☎ 0698 53750); Ballantyne & Copland, Solicitors, Torrance House, Knowetop, Motherwell (☎ 0698 66200, fax 0698 69387)

LIVINGSTONE, Jack; s of Harry Livingston, of Southport, and Ruth, *née* Kaye; *b* 27 April 1934; *Educ* Ackworth Sch, King's Coll London; *m* 5 June 1963, Janice Vivienne, da of Lt Sidney Jeffrey Manson, of Salford, Manchester; 1 s (Terence b 1966), 2 da (Joanna b 1964, d 1978, Vanessa b 1970); *Career* Sr Aircraftsman 2 Tactical Force RAF, serv Germany; chm London Scottish Bank plc; memb Deposit Protection Bd, involved with: Jewish Blind Soc, Centl Br Fund, Brookvale for the Mentally Handicapped; memb: Patrons and Assocs Manchester City Art Gallery, NW ctee The Lord Taverners; *Recreations* tennis, bridge; *Clubs* IOD; *Style—* Jack Livingstone, Esq; London Scottish Bank plc, Arndale House, Arndale Centre, Manchester M4 3AQ (☎ 061 834 2861, fax 061 834 2536, car tel 0836 618151, telex 669004)

LIVINGSTONE, Lady Elisabeth; (Jeanne-Doreen); *née* Fox-Strangways; da of 8 Earl of Ilchester (d 1970), by his w Laure, *née* Mazaraki; *b* 22 Jan 1931; *m* 1, 1958 (m dis 1969), Peter Skelton; 1 da (Caroline); m 2, 1977, John Livingstone, s of Thomas Livingstone (d 1986), of Orchard Way, Woolavington, Somerset; *Career* french language tutor 1960-; princ of Personality and Modelling Course (Devon) 1982-; *Style—* Lady Elisabeth Livingstone; 1 St Anthony, Higher Woodfield Rd, Torquay, Devon

LIVINGSTONE, Ken; MP (Lab) Brent East 1987-; s of Robert Moffat and Ethel Ada Livingstone; *b* 17 June 1945; *Educ* Tulse Hill Comprehensive Sch, Philippa Fawcett Coll of Education; *m* 1973 (m dis 1982), Christine Pamela Chapman; *Career* memb (Lab) GLC for Norwood 1973-77, Hackney North 1977-81, for Paddington 1981-86, leader GLC 1981-86; *Style—* Ken Livingstone, Esq, MP; House of Commons, London SW1A 0AA

LIVINGSTONE-LEARMONTH, (Lestock Harold) George; s of Lestock Brian Livingstone-Learmonth, of Park Farm, Pinkney, Malmesbury, Wilts, and Nancy Douglas, *née* Roffey (d 1950); *b* 4 July 1942; *Educ* Radley, Edinburgh Univ (BSc), Univ of Capetown (MBA); *m* 1, 4 June 1966, Diana, da of Col C K Hill-Wood; 1 s (Alexander b 1969); m 2, 28 Sept 1973, Katherine, da of T R D Kebbell; 2 s (Edward b 1974, Maxwell b 1977); *Career* dir: Beralt Tin and Wolfram 1973-80, Ayer Hitam Tin 1976-77, Aokam Tin 1977-80, Tongkah Harbour 1977-78, Amalgamated Tin Mines of Nigeria 1977-80, Gopeng Consolidated 1978-80, New Court Natural Resources 1982-86; md: Insituform Gp Ltd 1987, Hampton Gold Mining Areas plc 1980-86; *Recreations* boxing, photography, woodwork; *Clubs* Hurlingham, IOD; *Style—* George Livingstone-Learmonth, Esq; 23 Perrymead St, London SW6 3SN

LIVINGSTONE-LEARMONTH, John Christian; s of Lt-Col Lennox John Livingstone-Learmonth, DSO, MC (d 1988), and Nancy Winifred, *née* Wooler; *b* 30 Oct 1950; *Educ* Eton, Univ of York (BA); *m* 13 Dec 1986, (Elizabeth) Fiona, da of A J Stewart-Liberty, MC, of The Lee, Buckinghamshire; 1 s (Edward b 1988); *Career* SA mktg offr James Buchanan and Co 1975-83, sr ptnr Livingstone Communication 1987; Distinguished Visitor to Miami; *Books* The Wines of the Rhône (1978); *Recreations* the turf, fishing, association football, travel in south america, wine tasting & writing; *Clubs* Turf, Fox House; *Style—* John Livingstone-Learmonth, Esq; Livingstone Communication, New House, 67/69 Hatton Garden, London EC1 (☎ 01 405 0336, fax 01 831 8593)

LIYANAGE, Chris; s of Wilmot Porambe Liyanage (d 1971), and Valerie *née* Rupasinghe; *b* 26 May 1939; *Educ* Royal Coll Colombo Sri Lanka, Univ of Ceylon (BSc), Univ of Surrey (MSc), Cranfield Sch of Mgmnt (MBA); *m* 6 July 1968, Dr Priya, da of Edmund Dias (d 1985), of Sri Lanka; 2 s (Priyantha b 31 Dec 1970, Rohantha b 28 Dec 1973), 1 da (Chrisanthi b 14 Nov 1971); *Career* Lt Ceylon Engrs Regt Sri Lankan Army 1964, Capt 1968; WS Atkins & Ptnrs Epsom 1970-72, Santa Fe Engrg Ltd 1978-80, Worley Engrg Ltd 1980-85, Kvaerner Engrg A/S Norway 1985-88, project mangr Brown & Root Vickers Ltd 1989-; CEng, MICE, MIMarE, MBIM; *Recreations* squash, cricket, golf; *Clubs* RAC (Pall Mall & Woodcote); *Style—* Chris Liyanage Esq; 19 Links Rd, Epsom, Surrey, KT17 3PP, (☎ 0372 729075); c/o Brown & Root Vickers Ltd, 125 High St, Colliers Wood, London SW19 2JR (☎ 01 540 8300 fax 01 543 1799 telex 8812671 BRRTLN G)

LLAMBIAS, Douglas Ernest John; s of Ernest Llambias (d 1943), and Hilda, *née* Peat (d 1984); *b* 13 Nov 1943; *Educ* De La Salle Sch London; *m* 25 June 1984, Renée; 1 s by previous m (Damian Heathcote Jotham b 1971); *Career* CA; taxation specialist Arthur Andersen 1968-70, chm Douglas Llambias Assocs Ltd 1982- (md 1970), chm and chief exec The Business Exchange Gp 1984-, dir Murlen Ltd 1985-, chm Reform Club Econ & Current Affairs Gp 1980-; memb cncl ICA; *Recreations* badminton, wines; *Clubs* Reform, RAC; *Style—* Douglas Llambias, Esq; 410 Strand, London WC2 (☎ fax 01 930 1041)

LLEWELLEN PALMER, Hon Mrs; Hon Veronica; *née* Saumarez; da of late 5 Baron de Saumarez; *b* 1915; *m* 1945, Brig Anthony William Allen Llewellen Palmer,

DSO, MC, King's Dragoon Gds; *Career* VAD attached RAF 1940-43, ATS 1943-45; *Clubs* Cavalry and Guards'; *Style*— The Hon Mrs Llewellen Palmer; Clos du Menage, Sark, Channel Islands

LLEWELLIN, Rt Rev (John) Richard Allan; *see*: St Germans, Bishop of

LLEWELLIN, (John) Stephen; s of John Charles Llewellin, of Guernsey, CI, and Lilian, *née* Jenkins (d 1968); *b* 31 Oct 1938; *Educ* Cheltenham, Harper Adams Agric Coll; *m* 28 July 1961, Christine Irene, da of John Stanley Crewe (d 1955); 2 s (Richard b 1962, Peter b 1967); *Career* farmer and co dir; chm and md Little Haven Farms Ltd 1968-74; dir: Coastal Cottages Ltd, Celtic Sea Supply Base Ltd 1972-80, Barnlake Engrg Ltd 1972-80, Celtic Haven Ltd 1972-80; *Recreations* sailing, swimming; *Clubs* Lloyds of London; *Style*— Stephen Llewellin, Esq; Mill Race, Little Haven, Haverfordwest, Pembs SA62 3UH; Little Haven Farms Ltd, Fenton, Little Haven (☎ 0437 781 291)

LLEWELLIN DAVIES, Rev Dr Lawrence John David; s of Rev Canon Llewellin Davies (d 1948), of The Rectory, Narberth, Dyfed, and Elizabeth Anne, *née* Williams (d 1947); reverted surname to Llewellin Davies, the family name in the 18C, by deposition 1984; *b* 26 June 1916; *Educ* St David's Coll Sch Lampeter Dyfed, Jesus Coll Oxford (BA, MA), Dip Ed (Oxon), Univ of Bonn (DTheol); *m* 29 Dec 1949, Eileen May, da of late Harry Onion; 1 da (Elizabeth Anne (Mrs E A Kirkby) b 1951); *Career* ordained St Davids Cathedral: deacon 1939, priest 1940; curate Narberth Dyfed 1939-48, officiating chaplain RAF 1942-44, chaplain Royal Marines Sch of Signalling 1944-46, chaplain RN Arms Depot Trecwn Dyfed 1947-48, TA CCF 1947-48, chaplain RAF (Extended Serv Cmmn) 1948-57, princ 2 Tactical Air Force Moral Leadership Sch Cologne W Germany 1953-57, dean of chapel and head Divinity Hall Herschel High Sch Slough 1959-80; sec gen: Schs Cncl for the Ordained Ministry 1970-80, BHS; FRSPB; *Recreations* riding, gardening, protection of local ennvironment; *Style*— The Rev Dr Llewellin Davies; Deans Lodge, Hollybush Hill, Stoke Poges, Slough, Berks SL2 4PZ (☎ 028 16 2495)

LLEWELLYN *see also*: Seys Llewellyn

LLEWELLYN, Anthony David; s of William Henry Llewellyn (d 1977), of Rickmansworth, Herts, and Ida Elsie, *née* Davies (d 1980); *b* 23 Mar 1940; *Educ* Watford GS; *m* 23 May 1967, Jacqueline Hilary, da of William Frederick Curtis, of Croydon, Surrey; 2 da (Felicity b 1973, Lucinda b 1975); *Career* tax ptnr Touche Ross & Co CAs 1972-, memb bd of mgmnt and fin and gen purposes ctee London Sch of Hygiene and Tropical Med 1988-; ACIB 1963, FTII 1969, ACA 1970, FCA 1977; *Recreations* tennis, skiing, bridge; *Style*— Anthony Llewellyn, Esq; Kingswood, Parkfield, Sevenoaks, Kent TN15 OHX; Touche Ross and Co, Hill House, 1 Little New St, London EC4A 3TR (☎ 01 936 3000, fax 01 583 8517, telex 884739 TRLNDN G)

LLEWELLYN, Hon Lady; Hon Christine Saumarez; da of 5 Baron de Saumarez (d 1969); *b* 1916; *m* 1944, Lt-Col Sir Henry (Harry) Morton Llewellyn, 3 Bt, CBE, DL, *qv*; *Career* serv WWII WRNS; *Style*— The Hon Lady Llewellyn; Ty'r Nant, Llanarth, Nr Raglan, Gwent NP5 2AR

LLEWELLYN, David St Vincent; s and h of Sir Harry Morton Llewellyn, 3 Bt, CBE, and Hon Christine Saumarez, yr da of 5 Baron de Saumarez; *b* 2 April 1946; *Educ* Eton, Aix-en-Provence; *m* 15 March 1980 (m dis 1987), Vanessa Mary, da of Lt Cdr Theodore Bernard Peregrine Hubbard; 2 da (Olivia b 1980, Arabella b 1983); *Career* ctee pres Club Royale of Geneva 1980-; *Recreations* foxhunting, wildlife preservation; *Clubs* Club Royal, Geneva; *Style*— David Llewellyn, Esq; 27 Hill Street, London W1 (☎ 01 493 1977, telex 881 3271 GECOMS-G)

LLEWELLYN, Prof David Thomas; s of Alfred George Llewellyn, of Gillingham, Dorset, and Elsie Elizabeth, *née* Frith; *b* 3 Mar 1943; *Educ* William Ellis GS, LSE (BSc); *m* 19 Sept 1970, Wendy Elizabeth, da of Henry Cecil James, MM (d 1973); 1 s (Mark b 15 Aug 1972, Rhys b 18 Dec 1978); *Career* economist: Unilever MV Rotterdam 1964-65, HM Treasy 1965-68; lectr Univ of Nottingham 1968-73, economist IMF Washington 1973-76, prof money and banking Loughborough Univ 1976- (head dept of economics 1980-); chm Loughborough Univ Banking Centre 1985-, conslt economist Butler Harlow Veda Till 1989-; memb: London Bd Halifax Bldg Soc 1986-, ed bd Banking World 1984-; former conslt The World Bank, occasional memb Bank of England Panel of Econ Conslts; *Books* International Financial Integration (1980), Framework of UK Monetary Policy (1983), Regulation of Financial Institutions (1985), Evolution of British Financial System (1986);; *Recreations* boating, cooking, DIY, gardening, travel; *Style*— Prof David T Llewellyn; 8 Landmere Lane, Ruddington, Nottingham NG11 6ND (☎ 0602 216 071); Dept of Economics, Loughborough Univ, Loughborough, Leics (☎ 0509 222 700, fax 0509 610 813, telex 34319)

LLEWELLYN, Sir David Treharne; 3 s of Sir David Richard Llewellyn, 1 Bt (d 1940), and Magdalene Anne, *née* Harries (d 1966); *b* 17 Jan 1916; *Educ* Eton, Trinity Coll Cambridge (MA); *m* 18 Feb 1950, Joan Anne, OBE, da of Robert Henry Williams; 2 s, 1 da; *Career* served 1939-45 War, fusilier Royal Fusiliers, Capt Welsh Gds NW Europe; MP (C) Cardiff North 1950-59, parly under-sec of state Home Off 1951-52, resigned; former memb Broadcasting Cncl for Wales; journalist; kt 1960; *Books* Nye the Beloved Patrician, The Adventures of Arthur Artfully, The Racing Book of Quotations (jtly with Nick Robinson); *Style*— Sir David Llewellyn; The Glebe, Yattendon, nr Newbury, Berks

LLEWELLYN, David Walter; CBE (1983); s of Eric Gilbert Llewellyn and Florence May Llewellyn; *b* 13 Jan 1930; *Educ* Radley; *m* 1, 1955 (m dis 1985), Josephine Margaret Buxton; 3 s; m 2, Tessa Caroline Sandwith; *Career* cmmnd RE 1952; jt md Llewellyn Mgmnt Servs Ltd and other cos in the Llewellyn Gp 1953-; industl advsr to Min Housing and Local Govt 1967-68; pres Joinery and Timber Contractors' Assoc 1976-77; chm: nat contractors' gp of Nat Fedn of Building Trade Employers 1977, Building Regulations Advsy Ctee 1977-85; dep chm Nat Building Agency 1977-82; Lloyd's underwriter 1978-; govr St Andrew's Sch Eastbourne 1966-78; tstee Queen Alexandra Cottage Homes Eastbourne 1973-; Master Worshipful Co of Tin Plate Workers (Wire Workers) 1985; pres Chartered Inst of Building 1986-87; *Recreations* the use, restoration and preservation of historic vehicles; *Clubs* Reform, The Devonshire (Eastbourne), Bentley Drivers; *Style*— David Llewellyn, Esq, CBE; Coopers Cottage, Chiddingly, nr Lewes, E Sussex (☎ 0825 872 447); Walter Llewellyn & Sons Ltd, 16/20 South St, Eastbourne, East Sussex (☎ Eastbourne 0323 21300, telex 877 213)

LLEWELLYN, Graham David; *b* 22 Sept 1921; *Career* gp chief exec Sotheby Parke Bernet 1982-83, gp sr vice-pres Sotheby Hldgs Inc 1983-; *Style*— Graham D Llewellyn, Esq; Sotheby's, 34-35 New Bond St, London W1A 2AA (☎ 01 408 5423, telex 24454 SPBLON-G, fax 01 409 3100)

LLEWELLYN, Sir Henry Morton (Harry); 3 Bt (UK 1922), of Bwllfa, Aberdare, Glamorgan, CBE (1953, OBE Mil 1945), DL (Monmouthshire 1952); s of Sir David Richard Llewellyn, 1 Bt, (d 1940); suc bro, Sir Rhys Llewellyn, 2 Bt (d 1978); *b* 18 July 1911; *Educ* Oundle, Trinity Hall Cambridge (MA); *m* 1944, Hon Christine, da of 5 Baron de Saumarez (d 1969); 2 s (David St Vincent and Roderic Victor, *qqv*), 1 da (Anna Christina); *Heir* s, David St Vincent Llewellyn; *Career* joined Warwickshire Yeo 1939; ME Staff Coll 1942; GSO2 8 Army 1943 (despatches twice), GSO1 21 Army gp 1943-44; chm Davenco (Engrs) Ltd, pres Whitbread Wales Ltd, dir Chepstow Racecourse Co Ltd, pres British Equestrian Federation; pres British Show Jumping Assoc 1967-69, memb Nat Hunt Ctee 1946- (steward 1948-50), Jockey Club 1969; riding Ego, came 2 Grand Nat 1936, and 4 1937; chm sports Council for Wales; vice-chm Civic Tst for Wales; chm Nationwide Building Soc Wales; formerly chm C L Clay & Co (Coal Exporters), Norths Navigation Collieries Ltd, Welsh reg B Eagle Star Insurance, Lloyds Bank reg B; dir TWW 1958-68 JP 1953-67, High Sheriff Monmouthshire 1966; memb UK Cncl World Wide Fund for Nature 1985-; fell Royal Inst for the Protection of Birds 1987; Grand Prix des Nations (Equestrian) Gold Medal, Olympic Games, Helsinki 1952; Bronze Medal, London 1948; Royal Humane Soc Medal 1956; *Style*— Sir Harry Llewellyn, Bt, CBE, DL; Ty'r Nant, Llanarth, nr Raglan, Gwent NP5 2A

LLEWELLYN, Lady Honor Morvyth Malet; *née* Vaughan; JP (Dyfed); da of 7 Earl of Lisburne (d 1965); *b* 1919; *m* 1943, Maj (William Herbert) Rhidian Llewellyn, MC, DL, *qv*; *Career* sub-visitor St David's Coll Lampeter; *Style*— Lady Honor Llewellyn, JP; 4 St Omer Rd, Guildford, Surrey GU1 2DB

LLEWELLYN, Rev John Francis Morgan; LVO (1981); s of Canon David Leonard John Llewellyn (d 1966); *b* 4 June 1921; *Educ* King's Coll Sch Wimbledon, Pembroke Coll Cambridge, Ely Theological Coll; *m* 1955, Audrey Eileen, da of Frederick James Binks; *Career* served WWII; chaplain and asst master King's Coll Sch Wimbledon 1952-58, headmaster Cathedral Choir Sch and minor canon St Paul's Cathedral 1958-74, sacrist and warden of Coll of Minor Canons 1968-74, priest in ordinary to HM The Queen 1970-74 (formerly dep), chaplain of the Chapel Royal of St Peter ad Vincula within HM Tower of London 1974-, chaplain of the City Solicitors Co 1974-, sub-chaplain Order of St John of Jerusalem 1970-74, sr officiating chaplain 1974-; chaplain of Builders' Merchants Co 1986-; *Books* The Tower of London: Its Buildings and Institutions (contrib 1978), The Chapels in the Tower of London (1987); *Clubs* Cavalry and Guards, Hawks (Cambridge); *Style*— The Rev John Llewellyn, LVO; Chaplain's Residence, HM Tower of London, London EC3N 4AB

LLEWELLYN, Sir Michael Rowland Godfrey; 2 Bt (UK 1959), of Baglan, JP (West Glamorgan 1984), DL (West Glamorgan 1982), vice Lord-Lieutenant (West Glamorgan 1986), Lord Lieutenant (West Glamorgan 1987); s of Col Sir (Robert) Godfrey Llewellyn, 1 Bt, CB, CBE, MC, TD, JP, DL (d 1986); *b* 15 June 1921; *Educ* Harrow; *m* 1, 24 Sept 1946 (m dis 1951), Bronwen Mary (d 1965), da of Sir (Owen) Watkin Williams-Wynn, 8 Bt; m 2, 1 Dec 1956, Janet Prudence, da of Lt-Col Charles Thomas Edmondes, JP, DL, of Bridgend, Glamorgan; 3 da; *Career* Capt (Hon Maj) Grenadier Gds (Reserve); High Sheriff West Glamorgan 1980-81; pres: West Glamorgan Scout Cncl 1987-, West Glamorgan Branch SSAFA 1987-; Swansea Business Club 1985-88; CStJ, chm W Glamorgan St John Cncl 1967-79, (vice-pres 1979-88, pres 1988-), pres Swansea branch British Legion 1987-; *Recreations* shooting, gardening; *Style*— Sir Michael Llewellyn, Bt, JP; Glebe House, Penmaen, nr Swansea, West Glamorgan SA3 2HH (☎ 0792 371 232)

LLEWELLYN, Maj (William Herbert) Rhidian; MC, DL (Dyfed); 4 s of Sir David Richard Llewellyn, 1 Bt, (d 1940); *b* 8 July 1919; *Educ* Eton, RMC; *m* 1943, Lady Honor, JP, *qv*; *Career* Capt Welsh Gds 1941, served 1939-45 (despatches), Maj 1945, CC Cardiganshire 1961-70, High Sheriff 1967-68, memb Welsh Hosps Bd 1964-70, memb ct of govrs Nat Library of Wales 1967-68, memb T&AF Assoc Cardiganshire 1961-68, memb Wales and Monmouthshire TA&AVR Assoc 1968-70, memb Cardiganshire Agric Exec Ctee 1968-72; *Style*— Maj Rhidian Llewellyn, MC, DL; 4 St Omer Rd, Guildford, Surrey GU1 2DB

LLEWELLYN, Roderic Victor (Roddy); 2 s of Sir Harry Llewellyn, 3 Bt, CBE, and Hon Christine Saumarez, yr da of 5 Baron de Saumarez; *b* 9 Oct 1947; *Educ* Shrewsbury, Aix-en-Provence, Merrist Wood Agric Coll; *m* 1981, Tatiana, da of Paul Soskin (d 1975), the film producer; 3 da (Alexandra b 1982, Natasha b 1984, Rose-Anna b 1987); *Career* landscape designer, gardening conslt to Oracle (ITV information service, for London area) 1982-83, author and journalist; gardening corr for The (Daily) Star 1981-86, gardening presenter for TV 'Greenfingers' 1984-85; *Books* Town Gardens (1981); Beautiful Backyards (1985), Water Gardens (1987); *Recreations* philately, jig-saw puzzles; *Style*— Roddy Llewellyn, Esq; 112 Abbeville Rd, Clapham Park, London SW4 9LU (☎ office: 01 627 2965); Maritime House, Old Town, London SW4 0JP (☎ 01 627 2965)

LLEWELLYN, Timothy David; s of Graham David Llewellyn, of Chislehurst, Kent, and Dorothy Mary Driver; *b* 30 May 1947; *Educ* St Dunstan's Coll, Magdalene Coll Cambridge; *m* 1, 8 Aug 1970, Irene Sigrid Mercy, da of Sigurd Henriksen, of Copenhagen, Denmark; 1 s (Kristian b 1975); m 2, 9 Sept 1978, Elizabeth, da of Prof Mason Hammond, of Cambridge, Mass, USA; *Career* md Sotheby's 1984- (dir 1974-), chm The Friends of the Courtauld Inst 1986-, Miny of Culture and Fine Arts of the People's Republic of Poland, Order of Cultural Merit 1986; *Recreations* music, fishing, travel; *Clubs* Brooks's, Queen's; *Style*— Timothy D L Llewellyn, Esq; 3 Cranley Mansion, 160 Gloucester Rd, London SW7 4QF (☎ 01 373 2333); Sotheby's, 34-35 New Bond St, London W1A 2AA (☎ 01 493 8080, telex 24454 SPBLON G)

LLEWELLYN JONES, His Hon Ilston Percival; s of Rev Louis Cyril Francis Jones (d 1968), and Gertrude Ann, *née* Edmunds (d 1974); *b* 15 June 1916; *Educ* St John's Sch Leatherhead; *m* 3, 1963, Mary Eveline; 1 s from earlier marriage (Nigel Llewellyn b 1943); *Career* cmmnd RA, WWII serv to 1942; admitted slr 1938, Slrs Dept New Scotland Yard 1942-48, Devon County prosecutor 1952-56, clerk N Devon Justices 1956-62, rec 1973-78, circuit judge 1978-88, Parole Bd 1975-79; *Recreations* golf, music; *Clubs* Burnham and Berrow GC, Royal Porthcawl GC; *Style*— His Hon Ilston P Llewellyn Jones; Stonecroft, The Hayes, Cheddar, Somerset BS27 3HP (☎ 0934 743524)

LLEWELLYN SMITH, Prof Christopher; s of John Clare Llewellyn Smith, of

Tettenhall Cottage, W Bagborough, Somerset, and Margaret Emily Frances, *née* Crawford; *b* 19 Nov 1942; *Educ* Wellington, New Coll Oxford (BA, DPhil); *m* 10 Sept 1966, Virginia, *née* Grey; 1 s (Caspar Michael b 24 Jan 1971), 1 da (Julia Clare 2 Nov 1968); *Career* Royal Soc Exchange fell Lebedev Inst Moscow 1967-68, fell theoretical studies div Cern Geneva 1968-70, res assoc Stanford Linear Accelerator Centre (SLAC) Stanford California 1970-72, staff memb theoretical studies div Cern Geneva 1972-74; St John Coll Oxford: fell 1974-, lectr 1974-80, reader 1980-87, prof 1987-, chm of physics 1987; FRS 1984; *Style*— Prof Christopher Llewellyn Smith; 3 Wellington Place, Oxford OX1 2LD (☎ 0865 57145); Clarendon Laboratory, Oxford (☎ 0865 272370/1, fax 0865 272400, telex 83154 CLAROX G)

LLEWELLYN SMITH, Dr Michael John; s of John Clare Llewellyn Smith, and Margaret Emily Frances, *née* Crawford; *b* 25 April 1939; *Educ* Wellington, New Coll Oxford (BA), St Antony's Coll Oxford (DPhil); *m* 8 April 1967, Colette, da of Georges Gaulier (d 1979), of France; 1 s (Stefan Gregory b 1970), 1 da (Sophie Alexandra b 1971); *Career* cultural attaché Moscow 1973-75; first sec Br Embassy Paris 1976-77, cnsllr Athens 1980-83, head of soviet dept FCO 1985-87, min Paris Embassy 1988-; author; *Books* The Great Island - A Study of Crete (1965), Ionian Vision - Greece in Asia Minor 1919-22 (1983); *Clubs* Royal Cwlth Soc; *Style*— Dr Michael Llewellyn Smith, CMG; Foreign and Commonwealth Office, King Charles St, London SW1A 2AH

LLEWELLYN-JONES, John Everard; s of Dr John Llewellyn-Jones (d 1976), of Honan, W Mersea, Essex, and Dr Joan, *née* Hannaford; *b* 3 August 1943; *Educ* Allhallows Sch, Kings Coll London Univ (BSc), Dept Educn Cambridge Univ; *m* 4 Jan 1969, Marianne, da of Leendert Been, of Tanjabuurt 16, 8806 KW, Achlum, Friesland, Netherlands; 1 s (David b 1976), 1 da (Céline b 1974); *Career* biology master Soham GS, second year ldr City of Ely Coll, head biology Chalvedon Sch; meetings organiser and sec Basildon Natural History Soc, vice-chm Friends Southend Museums, memb Conchological Soc GB and Ireland; *Books* Cambridge Vertebrate Cut-Out series: Fish, Amphibian, Reptile, Bird, Mammal (1984), An Introductory Study of some aspects of Pollution (1984), Body Plans, Animals from the Inside (1986), Biokeys (1988); *Recreations* natural history; *Style*— John Llewellyn-Jones, Esq; 22 Grasmere Rd, Thundersley, Essex SS7 3HF (☎ 0268 759268)

LLEWELLYN-SMITH, Elizabeth Marion; CB (1986); da of John Clare Llewellyn Smith, of Bagborough, Somerset, and Margaret Emily Frances , *née* Crawford; *b* 17 August 1934; *Educ* Christ's Hosp, Girton Coll Cambridge (BA 1956) ; *Career* govt serv; Bd of Trade 1956, dep dir gen of Fair Trading 1982-87, dep sec Dept of Trade & Industry 1987-; dir Euro Investmt Bank 1987-; *Clubs* Utd Oxford and Cambridge Univ; *Style*— Miss Elizabeth Llewellyn-Smith, CB; 1 Charlwood Road, Putney, London SW15 1PJ (☎ 01 789 1572); DTI, Kingsgate House, 66-74 Victoria St, London SW1E 6SW (☎ 01 215 8358)

LLEWELYN; *see*: Dillwyn-Venables-Llewelyn

LLEWELYN, Desmond Wilkinson; s of Ivor Llewelyn (d 1930), of Newport, Gwent and Mia, *née* Wilkinson (d 1942); *b* 12 Sept 1914; *Educ* Radley, RADA; *m* 16 May 1938, Pamela Mary, da of Charles William Rivers Pantlin (d 1978); 2 s (Ivor b 1949, Justin b 1952); *Career* actor; joined Artists Rifles 1939, OCTU RMC Sandhurst 1939-40, cmmnd Royal Welch Fusiliers 1940, joined 1 Bn 1940, POW Germany 1940-45; in repertory Oxford Playhouse 1939, first appearance on TV 1939; plays incl: Golden Eagle, Spiders Webb; TV incl Follyfoot; Films incl: Cleopatra, 14 James Bond films in the character of "Q"; *Recreations* gardening; *Clubs* Farmers; *Style*— Desmond Llewelyn, Esq; Linkwell, Old Town, Bexhill on Sea, East Sussex

LLEWELYN, John William Howard; s of Maj Howard William Jones Llewelyn, MC (d 1987), of Llangynidr, Powys, and Gladys May, *née* Marshally; *b* 2 May 1939; *Educ* Harrow, Brasenose Coll Oxford; *m* 1, 18 March 1967, Priscilla Caroline, da of Thomas Arthur Rickard, of The Old Rectory, Rushock, Worcs; 2 s (Hugo b 1971, Benjamin b 1974), 2 da (Virginia b 1969, Joanne b 1979); m 2, 10 May 1984, Diana Mary, da of Timothy Hallinan (d 1970), of Co Cork; *Career* Lt The Shropshire Yeo 1961-66; slr 1966; asst dep coroner for Powys 1978-; under sheriff Brecknock 1979-85; *Recreations* fishing, shooting, sailing, golf, oenology; *Clubs* Cavalry and Guards'; *Style*— John W H Llewelyn, Esq; Lower Castleton, Clifford, Herefordshire (☎ 04973 591); 4 The Bulwark, Brecon, Powys (☎ 0874 4422, fax 0874 611303)

LLEWELYN DAVIES, Hon Harriett Lydia Rose; da of Baron Llewelyn-Davies (Life Peer, d 1981); *b* 1955; *Style*— The Hon Harriett Llewelyn Davies; 2 Carpenter's Yard, Park St, Tring, Herts

LLEWELYN-DAVIES OF HASTOE, Baroness (Life Peer UK 1967); Patricia; PC (1975); da of C P Parry; *b* 16 July 1915; *Educ* Liverpool Coll Huyton, Girton Coll Cambridge; *m* 1943, Baron Llewelyn-Davies (Life Peer, d 1981); 3 da; *Career* sits as Lab Peer in Lords; temp administrative civil servant 1940-51, Parly Cmmd (L) 1951-60; dir Africa Educnl Tst 1960-69, chm Gt Ormond St Hosp for Sick Children until 1969; a Baroness in waiting to HM The Queen 1969-70; oppn dep chief whip House of Lords 1972, oppn chief whip 1973-74, capt of The Gentlemen at Arms and govt chief whip 1974-79, oppn chief whip 1979-82, princ dep chm Ctees House of Lords 1982-86, chm Lords' Euro Communities Select Ctee 1982-86; chm Women's Nat Cancer Control Ctee 1972, dep speaker House of Lords 1986-; hon fell Girton Coll Cambridge 1978; *Style*— The Rt Hon the Lady Llewelyn-Davies of Hastoe, PC; Flat 15, 9-11 Belsize Grove, London NW3 4UU (☎ 01 586 4060)

LLOYD, Angus Selwyn; s of Selwyn Lloyd (d 1935), of Great Dixtor, Northiam, Sussex, and Elaine Mary, *née* Beck; *b* 12 July 1935; *Educ* Charterhouse; *m* 12 Jan 1961, Wanda Marian, da of Raymond Davidson, of 5 Devonshire Place, London W1; 3 s (James, Christopher, Richard), 2 da (Virginia, Philippa); *Career* Nat Serv 1954-55, 2 Lt 15/19 The Kings Royal Hussars (serv Malaya 1955); dir: Nathaniec Lloyd & Co (printers) 1956-63, Oscar & Peter Johnson Ltd (fine art dealers) 1963-81, Sealproof Ltd (textile proofing) 1973-; chm: Henri-Lloyd Ltd (textile mfrs) 1963-85, Craig- Lloyd Ltd (property) 1971-, Burlington Gallery Ltd (fine art/print dealers) 1979-, Burlington Paintings Ltd (fine art/print dealers) 1984-; tstee Albany Piccadilly 1967-, Charterhouse in Southwork 1962- (chm tstees 1979-82); Freeman: City of London, Worshipful Co of Stationers & Newspapermakers; *Recreations* golf; *Clubs* The Royal St Georges GC (Sandwich) (capt 1985), The Birkshire (capt 1978) The Royal West Norfolk, The Royal and Ancient (House), Swinley Forest, Pine Tree GC USA; *Style*— Angus Lloyd, Esq; East Ct, Beech Ave, Effingham, Surrey (☎ 0372 58111); Burlington Paintings Ltd, 12 Burlington Gdns, London W1X 1LG (☎ 01 734 9984, fax 01 494 3770)

LLOYD, Rt Hon Lord Justice; Rt Hon Sir Anthony John Leslie; DL (E Sussex 1983); s of Edward John Boydell Lloyd, of Little Bucksteep, Dallington, Sussex; *b* 9 May 1929; *Educ* Eton, Trinity Coll Cambridge; *m* 1960, Jane Helen Violet, da of C W Shelford, of Chailey Place, Lewes, Sussex; *Career* Nat Serv 1 Bn Coldstream Gds 1948; barr Inner Temple 1955, QC 1967, attorney-gen to HRH The Prince of Wales 1969-77, high ct judge (Queen's Bench) 1978-84, lord justice of Appeal 1984-; former memb Top Salaries Review Body, memb Criminal Law Revision Ctee 1981-, chm Civil Serv Security Apeals Panel 1982-, memb Parole Bd 1983-84; chm Glyndebourne Arts Tst 1975, dir RAM 1979-; chm Chichester Diocesan Bd of Fin 1972-76; kt 1978; *Style*— The Rt Hon Lord Justice Lloyd, DL; Ludlay, Berwick, E Sussex (☎ 0323 870204); 68 Strand-on-the-Green, London W4 (☎ 01 994 7790)

LLOYD, Anthony Joseph; MP (Lab) Stretford 1983-; *b* 25 Feb 1950; *Educ* Nottingham Univ, Manchester Business Sch; *m* Judith Lloyd; 1 s, 3 da; *Career* Univ lecturer, memb Trafford Dist Cncl 1979-84; *Clubs* West Indian Sports & Social, Stretford Ex-Servicemans, Stretford Trades & Labour; *Style*— Anthony Lloyd, Esq, MP; House of Commons, London SW1A 0AA

LLOYD, Barrie Otway; s of Arthur Balfour Lloyd (d 1963), and Elma Minnie, *née* Curnow; *b* 1 July 1940; *Educ* Fettes; *m* 18 Sept 1965, Ailsa Anne Grace, da of William Hector Stephenson; 1 s (James Rupert Samuel b 30 May 1972), 1 da (Kirstie Jane b 28 Feb 1969); *Career* admitted slr 1964, ptnr White & Leonard 1967-80, currently ptnr Masons; memb: City of London Slrs Co, Law Soc; *Recreations* cricket, golf, fishing, skiing; *Clubs* MCC, Worplesdon GC; *Style*— Barrie Lloyd, Esq; 4 Beech Lawn, Guildford, Surrey GU1 3PE; 10 Fleet St, London EC4Y 1BA (☎ 01 583 9990, fax 01 353 9745, telex 8811117)

LLOYD, (William Arnold) Bill; s of George Arthur Lloyd (d 1940), of Sheffield, and Margaret Caroline, *née* Plymouth (d 1959); *b* 5 August 1914; *Educ* Sheffield Sch of Art; *m* 25 April 1953, Vera Elizabeth, da of William George Webb (d 1942), of London; 3 s (Graham Martin b 1954, Adrian b 1956, Robert Michael b 1964); *Career* TA 1938-46 Capt; jnd PO as boy, Head of Br PO Telecommunication Sales Trg Centre, chief sales Supt London 1961, Trg Devpt Advsr African and Pacific 1961-82 ret; conslt; Hon Fell Univ of S Pacific; FBIM; *Recreations* cricket, water polo, rugby

LLOYD, Dr Brian Beynon; CBE (1983); s of David John Lloyd (d 1951), of Menai Bridge, Anglesey, and Olwen, *née* Beynon (d 1974); *b* 23 Sept 1920; *Educ* Newport HS, Winchester, Balliol Coll Oxford (BA, MA, DSc); *m* 1949, Reinhild Johanna, da of Dr Karl Wilhelm Engeroff (d 1951), of Bad Godesberg, W Germany; 4 s (Thomas, Martyn, Brian and Owen (twins)), 3 da (Megan and Olwen (twins), Lucy); *Career* registered as conscientious objector 1941, tech asst Oxford Nutrition Survey 1941 (res asst 1943-46), pres Jr Common Room Balliol 1941-42, chm Undergraduate Rep Cncl Oxford Univ 1942, biochemist: SHAEF Nutrition Survey Gp Leiden Holland, Düsseldorf Germany 1945-46; Magdalen Coll Oxford: fell by examination in Physiology 1948-52, by special election 1952-70, sr tutor 1963-64, vice-pres 1967-68, emeritus fell 1970; chemist Lab of Human Nutrition, Univ demonstrator and lectr in Physiology Univ of Oxford 1948-70, sr proctor 1960-61, dir Oxford Poly 1970-80, memb: Advsy Cncl on Misuse of Drugs 1978-81, visiting physiologist NY 1963, pres section I 1964-65, section X 1980, Br Assoc for the Advancement of Science (rep in Ceylon 1959, Russia 1964), chm of govrs Oxford Coll of Technol 1963-69, chm: CNAA Health and Med Servs Bd 1975-80, Oxford-Bonn Soc 1973-81, Oxford Mgmnt Club 1979-80, Health Educn Cncl 1979-82 (memb 1975-82), Oxford Gallery Ltd 1968-, Trumedia Study Oxford Ltd 1985-, Pullen's Lane Assoc 1985; pres Oxford Poly Assoc 1984-; *Books* Gas Analysis Apparatus (various Patents, 1960), The Regulation of Human Respiration (jt ed, 1962), Cerebrospinal Fluid and the Regulation of Respiration (jt ed 1965); articles in physiological and biochemical journals on vitamin C, human respiration, blood gases and exercise; *Recreations* klavarskribo, Correggio, analysis of athletic records, slide rules, ready reckoners, round tables, home computing; *Style*— Dr Brian B Lloyd, CBE; High Wall, Pullen's Lane, Oxford OX3 0BX (☎ Oxford 63353)

LLOYD, Christopher; s of Nathaniel Lloyd, OBE (d 1933), of Great Dixter, Northiam, Rye, E Sussex, and Daisy, *née* Field (d 1972); *b* 2 Mar 1921; *Educ* Rugby, King's Coll Cambridge (MA), Wye Coll London (BSc); *Career* asst lectr in decorative hort Wye Coll 1950-54, fndr Nursery in Clematis and unusual Plants at Family Home Great Dixter 1954; author Victoria Medal of Hon RHS, memb RHS; *Pubications:* The Mixed Border (1957), Clematis (1965, revised 1977), Foliage Plants (1973), The Well Tempered Garden (1970), Shrubs and Trees for Small Gardens (1965), Gardening on Chalk and Lime (1969), Hardy Perennials (1967), The Well Chosen Garden (1985), The Adventurous Gardener (1985), The Year at Great Dixter (1987); *Recreations* music, walking, entertaining friends at Great Dixter, cooking; *Style*— Christopher Lloyd, Esq; Great Dixter, Northiam, Rye, E Sussex TN31 6PH

LLOYD, Christopher; s of Rev Hamilton Lloyd, of Litchfield, Hants, and Suzanne, *née* Moon; *b* 30 June 1945; *Educ* Marlborough, Christ Church Oxford (BA, MA, BLtt); *m* 7 Oct 1967, (Christine Joan) Frances, da of George Henry Reginald Newth (d 1978), of Whitchurch, Hants; 4 s (Alexander b 1970, Benedict b 1972, Oliver b 1973, Rupert b 1980); *Career* asst curator pictures Christ Church Coll Oxford Univ 1967-68; dept Western Art Ashmolean Museum Oxford: print room asst 1968, departmental asst 1969, asst keeper 1972-88; surveyor of the Queen's pictures 1988-; fell Villa I Tatti Florence (Harvard Univ) 1972-73, visiting res curator early Italian painting Art Instit Chicago 1980-81; FRSA; *Books* Art and Its Images (1975), A Catalogue of the Earlier Italian Paintings in the Ashmolean Museum (1977), Camille Pissarro (1980), A Catalogue of the Drawings by Camille Pissarro in the Ashmolean Museum (1980), The Journal of Maria Lady Callcott 1827-28 (1981), Camille Pissarro (1981), Dürer to Cézanne: Northern European Drawings from the Ashmolean Museum (1982), Impressionist Drawings from British Collections (1986), Catalogue of Old Master Drawings at Holkham Hall (1986), contrib Studies on Camille Pissarro (ed C Lloyd, 1986); *Recreations* real tennis, theatre, music; *Style*— Christopher Lloyd, Esq; 179 Woodstock Rd, Oxford OX2 7NB (☎ 0865 59133); The Royal Collection, Stable Yard House, St James Palace, London SW1A 1JR (☎ 01 930 4832)

LLOYD, Clive Hubert; AO (1985), OJ (1985), OR, OB (1986); s of Arthur Christopher Lloyd (d 1961), and Sylvia Thelma Lloyd; *b* 31 August 1944; *Educ* Fountain, Chatham HS Georgetown Guyana; *m* 11 Sept 1971, Waveney, *née* Benjamin; 1 s (Jason Clive b 15 June 1981), 2 da (Melissa Simone b 22 Feb 1974, Samantha Louise b 26 Jan 1976); *Career* clerk Georgetown Hosp 1960-66; cricketer; began career with Demarara CC Georgetown 1959, debut for Guyana 1963, first test match for the WI 1966, initial first class century 1966, played for Haslingden CC in the Lancs League 1967, first played for Lancs CCC 1969 (capt 1981-84 and 1986), capt WI

1974-78 and 1979-85; scored over 25,000 runs incl 69 centuries during career; dir Red Rose Radio plc 1987-, exec promotions offr Project Fullemploy 1987-; pt/t memb Cmmn for Racial Equality; memb: Sickle Cell Anemia Soc, Cwlth Soc for the Deaf; *Books* Living for Cricket (with Tony Cazier), Clive Lloyd the Biography (with Trevor McDonald); *Style*— Clive Lloyd, Esq; Waverley, 296 Styal Rd, Meald Green, Cheadle, Cheshire; Harefield Home for the Elderley, Harefield Drive, Wilmslow, Cheshire (☎ 0625 522371, fax 061 437 8177)

LLOYD, Maj-Gen Cyril; CB (1948), CBE (1944, OBE 1943), TD (1945) and 2 bars; s of late A H Lloyd; *b* 1906; *Educ* Brighton GS, London and Cambridge Univs; *Career* Sussex Territorials (RA) 1929-39, Gen Staff Canadian Army 1940-42 (despatches, OBE), dep chief of Staff 21 Army Gp 1943-45, Invasion of Europe (despatches, CBE) 1944-45, dir-gen Army Educn and Training 1945-49; lectr and teacher, former res worker in sci; former memb numerous educn and trg cncls; dir-gen City and Guilds of London Inst 1962-67, conslt 1968- (dir 1949-62); chm Associated Examining Bd for GCE 1970-77, pres 1978-; chm: Ctee on Scientific Library Servs, govrs Crawley Coll of Further Educn; vice-pres Crawley Planning Gp, chief offr Cwlth Tech Trg Week 1961, tres 1963 Campaign for Educn, memb Cncl for Educnl Advance; tstee: Edward James Fndn, Industl Trg Fndn, pres Roffley Park Mgmnt Inst, govr Imperial Coll 1950-70, memb Delegacy of City and Guilds Coll 1950-70, hon exec princ West Dean Coll 1969-72, chartered physicist, Liveryman Worshipful Co of Goldsmiths', Freeman City of London; FInstP, FRSA, FRGS, MRST; *Publications* (booklets) British Services Education (1950), Human Resources and New Systems of Vocational Training and Apprenticeship (1963); contributions to journals; *Recreations* the countryside, sailing, traditional crafts; *Clubs* Athenaeum; *Style*— Maj-Gen Cyril Lloyd, CB, CBE, TD; The Pheasantry, Colgate, Horsham, W Sussex

LLOYD, David Alan; s of Dennis Herbert Lloyd, of Leigh-on-Sea, Essex, and Doris, *née* Renshaw; *b* 3 Jan 1948; *Educ* Southend HS; *m* 14 Dec 1972, Veronica Jardine, da of Maj Cochran Kirkwood MacLennan, MBE (d 1984); 1 s (Scott b 1975), 2 da (Camila b 1979, Laura b 1981); *Career* tennis player, semi-finalist Wimbledon Doubles (with J Paish) 1973, Br Davis Cup Team 1973-82; opened: David Lloyd Slazenger Raquet club Hestow 1982, David Lloyd Sports and Health Club Raynes Pk 1989; runs 4 tennis clubs (2 Spain, 2 Portugal); BBC Radio Commentator, ITV Tennis Commentator; launched Slater Tennis Fndn (sponsorship and coaching scheme for young players) with J Slater 1986; Freeman City of London 1985; *Recreations* golf; *Clubs* All England Lawn Tennis, Foxhills, Stage Soc; *Style*— David Lloyd, Esq; Appletree Cottage, 12 Leys Rd, Oxhsott, Surrey KT22 OQE (☎ 0372 842150); David Lloyd Racquet Club, Southall LAne, Heston, Middx (☎ 01 573 0143)

LLOYD, (John) David; s of Sir Thomas Ingram Kynaston, GCMG, KCB (d 1968), and Bessie Nora, *née* Mason; *b* 20 Sept 1929; *Educ* Stowe, Trinity Hall Cambridge (MA); *m* 1961, Elizabeth Caroline, da of Lt-Col Walter George Hingston, of Ramsbury, Wilts; 1 s, 2 da; *Career* 2 Lt KRRC 1948-50; memb Stock Exchange 1958, memb Stock Exchange Cncl 1971-78; sr ptnr L Messel & Co stockbrokers 1979-86; exec dir Shearson Lehman Int 1986-88, ret; *Recreations* shooting, travel; *Clubs* City of London, Hawkes, Greenjacket; *Style*— David Lloyd, Esq; Amberden Hall, Widdington, nr Saffron Walden, Essex CB11 35T (☎ 0799 40 402)

LLOYD, David Mark; s of Maurice Edward Lloyd (d 1988), and Roma Doreen, *née* Morgan (d 1958); *b* 3 Feb 1945; *Educ* Felsted Sch, Brentwood Sch Essex, Barenose Coll Oxford (MA); *m* 30 Oct 1982, Jana, da of Karel Tomas (d 1980); 1 s (Mark b 1983), 1 da (Katie b 1985), 1 step s (Tom b 1976); *Career* ed: The Money Programme 1980-82, Newsnight 1982-83, 60 Minutes 1983-84, Breakfast Time 1984-86; sr commissioning ed new and current affairs Channel 4 1986-; *Recreations* cricket, golf, music, photography; *Style*— David Lloyd, Esq; Channel 4, 60 Charlotte St, London W1 (☎ 01 927 8759)

LLOYD, Hon Davina Margaret; da of 2 Baron Lloyd, MBE; *b* 13 Mar 1943; *Style*— The Hon Davina Lloyd; Clouds Hill, Offley, Hitchin, Herts (☎ Offley 350); 11 Morpeth Mansions, Morpeth Terrace, London SW1 (☎ 01 834 2342)

LLOYD, Rev Father Denys David Richard; s of Richard Norman Lloyd, of 7 Whitfield Hill, Kearsney, Dover, Kent, and Grace Enid, *née* Appleton; *b* 28 June 1939; *Educ* Brighton Coll, Trinity Hall Cambridge (MA), Univ of Leeds (MA); *Career* asst curate St Martin's Rough Hills Wolverhampton 1936-67, professed memb of the Community of the Resurrection Mirfield 1969, tutor Coll of the Resurrection Mirfield 1970-75, assoc lectr dept of theol and religious studies Univ of Leeds 1971-, vice princ Coll of the Resurrection Mirfield 1975-84, princ 1984-; *Recreations* walking, domestic architecture; *Style*— The Rev Father Denys Lloyd, CR; College of the Resurrection, Mirfield, W Yorks WF14 OBW (☎ 0924 490 441)

LLOYD, (Gabriel) Frederic Garnons; OBE (1969), JP (North Westminster 1969); s of Rev William Wellesley Gordon Lloyd (d 1947), of St Leonards-on-Sea, Sussex, and Minna Lucy Margaret, *née* Greenstreet (d 1958); *b* 1 July 1918; *Educ* Sandrock Hall Hastings, St Leornard Coll of Music; *m* 16 June 1945, Valerie, da of Rev John Buchanan Fraser (d 1944), of St Catherines, Nottingham; 2 s (William, Hugh); *Career* regnl dir Arts Cncl (N Midlands) 1943-50, dir Festival of 6B Oxford 1950-51, gen mangr D'Oyly Carte Opera and Tst, gen mangr Savoy Theatre and dir Savoy Hotel Entertainments 1951-82, pres Theatre Mangrs Assoc 1967-70 (life vice pres 1982); govr: Royal Academy of Music 1965 (chm 1980-84, vice pres 1984), Royal Gen Theatrical Fund 1960 (vice pres 1986); chm Nottingham Co Music Ctee, govr Sadlers Wells Theatre, warden Queens Chapel of the Savoy, convener Diocese of Moray Ross and Caithness; memb: Royal Choral Soc, Royal Philharmonic Orchestra, Scottish Opera Cncl, Malcolm Sargent Cancer Fund for Children, Central City Opera Denver USA; Freeman City of London 1961, Liveryman Worshipful Co of Musicians 1960; hon citizen: Denver 1953, Texas 1973; hon FRAM 1970, hon memb RCM 1976; *Books* The D'Oyly Carte Years (with Robin Wilson, 1984); *Recreations* music, gardening, fishing, reading; *Clubs* Garrick, MCC, Harvard (Boston USA); *Style*— Frederic Lloyd, Esq, OBE, JP; Blaen-Y-Glyn, West Park, Strathpeffer, Ross-shire, Scotland 1V 14 9BT (☎ 099 7 21429)

LLOYD, Frederick John; CBE (1977); s of Frederick James Lloyd (d 1952); *b* 22 Jan 1913; *Educ* Ackworth Sch York, Univ of Liverpool; *m* 1942, Catherine Johnson, da of Cecil Herbert Parker (d 1942); 1 s, 1 da; *Career* chief operating mangr London Red Buses 1961-65, chief commercial and planning offr London Tport 1965-69, dir-gen W Midlands Passenger Tport Exec 1969-78; chm Road Tport Indust Trg Bd 1978-83; FIA; *Clubs* Birmingham Rotary, Whittingham Barracks GC; *Style*— Frederick Lloyd, Esq, CBE; 8 Cliveden Coppice, Sutton Coldfield, W Midlands (☎ 021 308 5683)

LLOYD, Prof Geoffrey Ernest Richard; s of William Ernest Lloyd (d 1975), of London, and Olive Irene Neville, *née* Solomon; *b* 25 Jan 1933; *Educ* Charterhouse, King's Coll Cambridge (BA, MA, PhD); *m* 14 Sept 1956, Janet Elizabeth, *née* Lloyd, da of Edward Archibald Lloyd (d 1978), of Paris, France; 3 s (Adam b 1957, Matthew b 1962, Gwilym b 1963); *Career* Nat Serv Intelligence Corps 2 Lt/actg capt; Cambridge: fell King's Coll 1957-89, univ asst lectr classics 1965-67, (univ lectr 1967-74), prof of in ancient phiosophy and sci 1983-, (sr reader 1974-83); Master of Darwin Coll Cambridge 1989-; Bonsall prof Stanford Univ 1981, Sather Prof of Classics California Univ (Berkeley) 1984; fell Royal Anthropological Soc 1970, FB 1983; *Books* Polarity and Analogy (1966), Aristotle The Growth and Structure of his Thought (1968), Early Greek Science (1970), Greek Science After Aristotle (1973), Hippocratic Writings (ed 1978), Aristotle on Mind and the Senses (ed 1978), Magic Reason and Experience (1979), Science Folklore and Ideology (1983), The Revolutions of Wisdom (1987); *Recreations* travel; *Style*— Prof Geoffrey Lloyd; 2 Prospect Row, Cambridge, CB1 1DU (☎ 0223 335970)

LLOYD, Herbert Merlin; s of Leoline Oscar Lloyd (d 1945), of Elder House, Brigend, Glamorgan, and Annie, *née* Tanner (d 1926); *b* 29 Oct 1912; *Educ* Brigend Co GS, Cardiff Univ Coll, Open Univ (BA); *m* 30 Aug 1939, Dilys Bonnie, da of Idris Evan Davies (d 1957), of Austin Friars, Porthcawl, Glamorgan; 3 s (Jonathon Kendal b 29 Oct 1947, Brian Edwin b 9 March 1950, Peter Fraser b 19 Dec 1953); *Career* serv 77 Welsh HAA Regt 242 Battery TA 1937; cmmnd 1940, air def of GB, Staff Capt Far E 1942-45, (despatches, TA decorations) demob 1946; admitted slr 1937, former under sec Law soc, former PR offr Port of London Authy, sr PR cnsllr Young & Rubicam 1975-76; md: Image Aust 1976-78, Compton Assocs (UK) Ltd 1978-80; sec Wake Field and Tetley Tsts, Northcott Fndn, Tower Hill Devpt Tst; fndr memb and vice chm Cardiff Literary Soc 1946, Br Acad of Forensic Sci, fndr memb & tstee World Wildlife Fund, pres Inst of PR 1968-69, fell inst of PR; Freeman City of London 1957, Liveryman Worshipful Co of Slrs 1957; memb Int Bar Assoc, FRSA, fell Chartered Inst of Tport; *Books* Public Relations (1963), The Legal Limits of Journalism (1965); *Clubs* Reform, Highgate Golf; *Style*— Herbert Lloyd, Esq ; 49 Barnes Ct, Station Rd, New Barnet, Herts EN5 1QY (☎ 01 440 2087) Tower Hill Improvement Tst 33B Station Rd, New Barnet, Herts EN5 1PH (☎ 01 441 7706)

LLOYD, Dame Hilda Nora; DBE (1951); da of late John Shufflebotham, of Birmingham; *b* 1891; *Educ* King Edward's Sch Birmingham, Birmingham Univ; *m* 1, 1930, Bertram Lloyd (d 1948); m 2, 1949, Baron Rose; *Career* emeritus prof of obstetrics and gynaecology Birmingham Univ and Utd Birmingham Hosp; pres Royal Coll of Obstetricians and Gynaecologists 1949-52; *Style*— Dame Hilda Lloyd, DBE; Broome House, Clent, Worcs

LLOYD, Sir Ian Stewart; MP (C) Havant 1983-; s of Walter John Lloyd (d 1973), and Euphemia Craig Lloyd (d 1971), of Natal, SA; descended from Tudor Trevor (d 948) and his w, Angharad, da of Hywel Dda, King of Wales; *b* 30 May 1921; *Educ* Michaelhouse Natal, Witwatersrand Univ, King's Coll Cambridge, Admin Staff Coll Henley; *m* 1951, Frances Dorward, da of Hon William Addison, CMG, OBE, MC, DCM (d 1966), of Salisbury, Rhodesia; 3 s; *Career* SA Air Force 1941-45, RAFVR 1945-49, econ advsr Central Mining Corpn 1949, dir and gp econ advsr (former head res dept) Br Cwlth Shipping Co 1956-83; pres Cambridge Union; MP (C): Portsmouth Langstone 1964-74, Havant and Waterloo 1974-83; memb UK delgn Cncl of Europe and WEU 1968-72, memb Select Ctee Sci and Technol 1970-79, chm All-Pty Ctee Info Technol 1979-87, chm Select Ctee Energy 1979-, chm advsy bd Parly Off for Sci and Technol 1988-; kt 1986; *Books* Rolls Royce: The Growth of a Firm (Vol I), The Years of Endurance (Vol II), The Merlin at War (Vol III); *Recreations* sailing (yacht 'Shemalier'); *Clubs* Brooks's, Royal Yacht Sqdn; *Style*— Sir Ian Lloyd, MP; House of Commons, London SW1A 0AA

LLOYD, Illtyd Rhys; s of John Lloyd (d 1971), of Cwmafan Neath, and Melvina Joyce, *née* Rees (d 1973); *b* 13 August 1929; *Educ* Port Talbot (Glan Afan) Co GS, Swansea UC Univ of Wales (BSc, MSc, DipEd, DipStat, hon Fell); *m* 1955, Julia, da of David John Lewis (d 1951), of Pontyberem, Dyfed; 1 s (Steffan), 1 da (Catrin); *Career* RAF (Educn Branch) 1951-54, Flt Lt; second maths master Howard Sch for Boys Cardiff 1954-57; head of maths dept Pembroke GS 1958-59, dep headmaster Howardian HS 1959-63; Her Majesty's Inspectorate: HMI 1964-71, staff inspr 1972-82, chief inspr (Wales) 1982-; hon fell Univ of Wales; *Recreations* walking; *Style*— Illtyd Lloyd, Esq; 134 Lake Rd East, Roath Park, Cardiff (☎ 755296); Welsh Off, Cathays Park, Cardiff CF1 3NQ (☎ 823431)

LLOYD, Baroness; Lady (Victoria) Jean Marjorie Mabell; *née* Ogilvy; da of 12 Earl of Airlie, KT, GCVO, MC, and Lady Alexandra Coke, da of 3 Earl of Leicester; *b* 21 Sept 1918; *m* 1942, 2 Baron Lloyd, MBE (d 1985, when the peerage became extinct); 2 da (and 1 s decd); *Style*— The Rt Hon The Lady Lloyd; Clouds Hill, Offley, Hitchin, Herts (☎ Offley 350)

LLOYD, Jeffrey Hywel; s of Gwillym Hywel Lloyd (d 1966), of S Glamorgan, and Olwen Menai, *née* Williams (d 1987); *b* 9 June 1946; *Educ* Barry GS, UMisT (LLB); *m* 23 Oct 1976, Pauline Margaret, da of Benjamin Albert Jones, of Mountain Ash; 2 s (Adam b 1979, Simon b 1983); *Career* slr; *Recreations* walking, badminton, chess; *Style*— Jeffrey H Lloyd, Esq; 39 Porth-y-Castell, Barry, S Glamorgan; 87 Holton Rd, Barry (☎ 741919)

LLOYD, Jeremy William; s of Maj-Gen Richard Eyre Lloyd CB, CBE, DSO of Lymington, Hants and Gillian, *née* Patterson; *b* 19 Dec 1942; *Educ* Eton, Pembroke Coll Cambridge (MA), Harvard Business Sch (MBA); *m* 2 Sept 1966, Britta Adrienne, da of Alfred de Schulthess of Geneva, Switzerland; 1 s (Adrian b 1979), 3 da (Tara b 1971, Bettina b 1975, Antonia b 1985); *Career* barr Middle Temple; with Hill Samuel & Co; subsidiary dir London & Co Securities Bank 1971-72, dir Mfrs Hanover Property Servs Ltd 1973-81, dir James Capel Bankers Ltd 1982-87; sr mangr Hong Kong & Shanghai Banking Corpn 1982-; *Recreations* tennis, skiing; *Style*— Jeremy Lloyd, Esq; Hong Kong & Shanghai Banking Corpn, 7 Devonshire Square, London EC2M 4NH (☎ 01 626 0566)

LLOYD, Hon Joanna Elizabeth; da of Baron Selwyn-Lloyd (Life Peer) (d 1978); *b* 1952; *Style*— The Hon Joanna Lloyd

LLOYD, John Andrew; s of Kenneth Lawrence Lloyd, JP, of Cheltenham, Glos, and Pamela Oriette, *née* Clarke; *b* 28 Mar 1951; *Educ* Cheltenham GS, Berks Coll of Educ, London Univ Inst of Educ; *Career* teacher: Ashe Hall Sch Etwall Derbyshire 1972-74, Park Place Sch Henley Oxon 1974-79; press and pubns offr: Nat Children's Home 1980-83, Nat Assoc of Boys' Clubs 1983-88; freelance journalist and writer

1973-, formerly polo corr Daily Telegraph, The Independent UK ed Polo Int; assoc Coll of Preceptors 1976; *Books* The Debrett Season (polo chapter, 1981), The Action Bunch Handbook (1983), The Polo Annual (1985), The Pimm's Book of Polo (1989); *Recreations* swimming, theatre, reading; *Clubs* Wig and Pen, Naval; *Style*— John Lloyd, Esq; The Old School House, The Green, Calne, Wilts SN11 8DJ (☎ 0249 814888); Centaur House, 25 London Rd, Calne, Wilts SN11 0AA (☎ 0249 816309)

LLOYD, John Wilson; s of Dr Ellis Lloyd, of Swansea (d 1964), and Dorothy Wilcoxon, *née* Smith; *b* 24 Dec 1940; *Educ* Swansea GS, Clifton, Christ's Coll Cambridge (BA, MA); *m* 25 March 1967, Buddug, da of Rev J D Roberts, of Caernarfon, Gwynedd; 2 s (Huw b 1973, Geraint b 1973), 1 da (Sarah b 1968); *Career* asst princ HM Treasy 1962-67 (private sec to Fin Sec 1965-67), princ successively HM Treasy, CSD and Welsh Off 1967-75 (private sec to Sec of State for Wales 1974-75), dep sec Welsh Off 1988- (asst-sec 1975-82, under-sec and princ establishing offr 1982-86, under-sec Housing Health and Social Serv Gp 1986-88); *Recreations* golf, squash, swimming; *Style*— John Lloyd, Esq; Welsh Office, Cathays Park, Cardiff CF1 3NQ (☎ 825111)

LLOYD, Professor June Kathleen; da of Arthur Cresswell Lloyd MBE, (d 1957), and Lucy Bevan, *née* Russell, BEM; *b* 1 Jan 1928; *Educ* Royal Sch Bath, Univ of Bristol, (MB, ChB, MD), Univ of Durham (DPH); *Career* trg posts in medicine 1951-65 at Bristol, Oxford, Newcastle, Birmingham; Inst of Child Health London: sr lectr 1965-69, reader 1969-74, prof 1974-75; prof St George's Med Sch 1979-85; Nuffield prof of child health Univ of London 1985-; FRCP 1969; *Recreations* cooking, walking; *Style*— Prof June Lloyd; Inst of Child Health, 30 Guilford St, London W21 N1EH (☎ 01 242 9789)

LLOYD, Kerry Edward; s of Edward George Frederick Lloyd, of Portsmouth, and Olive Mary, *née* Wurr; *b* 24 May 1951; *Educ* Kingston Sedcy Modern Sch Portsmouth, Portsmouth Coll of Art and Design (Dip Art and Design); *m* 1, 19 Sept (m dis 1985), (Barbara) Denise Mary, da of Donald Smaldon; 2 da (Rosy b 5 Sept 1976, Sophie b 6 Oct 1978); m 2, 21 Oct 1985, Melanie Jane, da of Lt Frederick Hind; *Career* dir and creative dir Golley Slater and Ptnrs 1987-; *Recreations* sailing, walking, cooking; *Style*— Kerry Lloyd, Esq; The Mill House, Tintern, Chepstow, Monmouthshire NP6 6TQ (☎ 0291 689510); Golley Slater and Ptnrs Ltd, 9-11 The Hayes, Cardiff (☎ 0222 388621)

LLOYD, Hon Laura Blanche Bridget; da of 2 Baron Lloyd, MBE; *b* 7 Mar 1960; *Style*— The Hon Laura Lloyd; 4 Patience Road, London SW11

LLOYD, Leslie Geoffrey; s of Geoffrey Llewellyn Lloyd, of Cradley, Worcs, and Rita Louise, *née* Palfrey; *b* 28 June 1940; *Educ* Worcester Royal GS; *m* 18 May 1968, Jenifer Elizabeth, da of col Walter Sowden North CBE, of Rake, Hants; 2 s (Thomas 1 Feb 1971, John 25 June 1972), 1 da (Katharine 10 Sept 1969); *Career* head of mgmnt servs Bank of Eng 1988- (joined 1957, asst chief cashier 1977-80, sr advsr Commodities and Futures Mkts 1980-84, The Auditor 1984-88); organist Milland Church Hamps; MBCS; *Recreations* music, philosophy; *Style*— Leslie Lloyd, Esq ; The Loke, Rake, Liss, Hants; Bank of England, Threadneedle Str, London EC2R

LLOYD, Lloyd; s of David Herbert Llooyd, and Rachel Dilys, *née* Davies; *b* 12 Feb 1930; *Educ* City of London Sch, Trinity Coll Cambridge, King's Coll London (LLM); *Career* called to Bar Gray's Inn 1973; cncl memb Hon Soc of Cymmrodorion; AIArb 1976; *Recreations* music, theology, art, travel, welsh, literature; *Style*— Lloyd Lloyd, Esq; 3 Archery Fields House, Wharton St, London WC1X 9PN (☎ 01 837 4727); Queen Elizabeth Bldg, Temple, London EC4 (☎ 01 353 9153, fax 01 583 0126, telex 262762 INREM G)

LLOYD, Nicholas Markley; *b* 9 June 1942; *Educ* Bedford Modern Sch, St Edmund Hall Oxford (MA), Harvard Univ; *m* 1; m 2, 1979, Eve Pollard; 3 s, 1 da; *Career* dep ed Sunday Mirror 1980-82, ed Sunday People 1982-84, dir Mirror Gp 1982-84; ed News of the World Jan 1984-85; dir News Gp Newspapers 1985-; *Style*— Nicholas Lloyd, Esq; News Group Newspapers, 30 Bouverie St, London EC4 (☎ 01 353 3030)

LLOYD, Patrick John; s of Edmund Commeline Lloyd (d 1936), of Pitsworthy, Exford, Som; *b* 20 Mar 1925; *Educ* Clifton, Magdalene Coll Cambridge (MA); *m* 1956, Margaret, da of Claude Douglas-Pennant (d 1955, gs of 1 Baron Penrhyn); 1 s (John Philip b 1960), 1 da (Phyllida Christian b 1957); *Career* Capt RA; wine merchant; master of wine 1961; *Recreations* hunting, shooting; *Style*— Patrick Lloyd, Esq; Valaford, West Anstey, South Molton, Devon EX36 3PW (☎ 039 84 258)

LLOYD, (George) Peter; CMG (1965), CVO (1983); er s of Sir Thomas Ingram Kynaston Lloyd, GCMG, KCB (d 1968), and Bessie Nora, *née* Mason; *b* 23 Sept 1926; *Educ* Stowe, King's Coll Cambridge; *m* 1957, Margaret, da of Dr Eugene Harvey, of Bermuda; 2 s, 1 da; *Career* served Lt KRRC 1945-48, dist offr Kenya 1951-60, colonial sec Seychelles 1961-66, chief sec Fiji 1966-70, def sec Hong Kong 1971-74, dep govr Bermuda 1974-81, govr Cayman Islands 1982-87; *Style*— Peter Lloyd, Esq, CMG, CVO; Watch House, 13 Fort Hamilton Dr, Pembroke, HM 19 Bermuda (☎ 29581301)

LLOYD, Peter Robert Cable; MP (C) Fareham 1979-; s of David and late Stella Lloyd; *b* 12 Nov 1937; *Educ* Tonbridge, Pembroke Coll Cambridge (MA); *m* 1967, Hilary Creighton; 1 s, 1 da; *Career* former mktg mangr Utd Biscuits, chm Bow Gp 1972-73; former ed Crossbow; sec Cons Parly Employment Ctee 1979-81, vice-chm European Affrs Ctee 1980-81; PPS to Min State NI 1981-82, to Sec State Educn and Sci 1983-84; Govt whip 1984-; Lord Cmmr of the Treasy Oct 1986-; *Style*— Peter Lloyd, Esq, MP; House of Commons, SW1

LLOYD, Reginald Arthur Harris; TD (1980, and clasp), DL (Shropshire 1979); s of Rev Richard Harris Lloyd (d 1952); *b* 24 Jan 1913; *Educ* Hull GS, Scarborough Coll; *m* 1946, Maureen, da of John Thelwall Salusbury (d 1946); 4 s, 1 da; *Career* Shropshire CC: cncllr 1961, vice chm 1977, chm 1981-85; gen cmmr of taxes 1975-78; head off mgmt Sun Alliance & London until 1973 (ret); chm Bylaw (Ross) Ltd 1987; memb: Telford Devpt Corpn 1977-, bd Ironbridge Gorge Museum Tst 1985-, Bell Concord Educnl Tst 1983-; govr Shrewsbury Sch 1968-88; Man Cncl W Midland Regnl Investmt Tst 1985-; vice-chm W Mercia Police Authy 1985-; pres Shropshire Assoc of Parish and Town Cncls 1984-; pres Shropshire CPRE; chm: Shropshire Army Cadet League 1965-, Packwood Haugh Prep Sch Shropshire 1963-88; tstee Hereford Cathedral Appeal 1984, pres Shrewsbury and Alcham Cons Assoc 1988-; *Recreations* riding, tennis, fishing; *Clubs* Carlton, MCC; *Style*— Reginald Lloyd, Esq, TD, DL; Acre Batch, Lower Wood, All Stretton, Shropshire SY6 6LG (☎ 069 45 233)

LLOYD, Sir Richard Ernest Butler; 2 Bt (UK 1960), of Rhu, Co Dunbarton; o s of Maj Sir (Ernest) Guy (Richard) Lloyd, 1 Bt, DSO, DL (d 1987), and Helen Kynaston, *née* Greg (d 1984); *b* 6 Dec 1928; *Educ* Wellington, Hertford Coll Oxford (MA); *m* 6 June 1955, Jennifer Susan Margaret, er da of Brig Ereld Boteler Wingfield Cardiff (d 1988), CB, CBE of Easton Ct, nr Ludlow, Shropshire; 3 s; *Heir* s, Richard Timothy Butler Lloyd b 12 April 1956; *Heir* s, (Richard) Timothy Butler Lloyd b 12 April 1956; *Career* former Capt Black Watch, mil serv Malaya 1947-49; banker; exec then dir Glyn Mills & Co 1952-70, chief exec Williams & Glyn's Bank 1970-78, chm Hill Samuel Bank Ltd 1989- (dep chm 1978-80, dep chm and chief exec 1980-87, jt chm 1987-88); Freeman City of London 1964, Liveryman Worshipful Co of Mercers 1965, memb Guild of Freemen of Shrewsbury 1978; CBIM, FCIB; *Recreations* fishing, gardening, walking; *Clubs* Boodle's; *Style*— Sir Richard Lloyd, Bt; Sundridge Place, Sundridge, Sevenoaks, Kent TN14 6DD (☎ 0959 63599); 100 Wood St, London EC2P 2AJ (☎ 01 628 8011, fax 01 726 4671, telex 888822)

LLOYD, Richard Hey; s of Charles Yates Lloyd (d 1969), and Ann, *née* Hey (d 1952); *b* 25 June 1933; *Educ* Rugby, Jesus Coll Cambridge; *m* 29 Dec 1962, (Teresa) Morwenna, da of Rev Oliver Leonard Willmott; 4 da (Emma b 1964, Julia b 1967, Catharine b 1969, Olivia b 1971); *Career* sub organist Salisbury Cathedral 1957-66; organist: Hereford Cathedral 1966-74, Durham Cathedral 1974-85; dep headmaster Salisbury Cathedral Sch 1985-88; *Recreations* reading, cricket, music, enjoying the countryside; *Style*— Richard Lloyd, Esq; Refail Newydd, Pentraeth, Anglesey LL75 8YF (☎ 024 870 220)

LLOYD, Robert Andrew; s of Inspr William Edward Lloyd (d 1963), and May, *née* Waples; *b* 2 Mar 1940; *Educ* Southend HS, Keble Coll Oxford (MA), London Opera Centre; *m* 22 Feb 1964, Sandra Dorothy, da of Douglas Watkins; 1 s (Marcus b 1965), 3 da (Anna b 1966, Candida b 1969, Alice b 1973); *Career* Instr Lt RN 1962-65; civilian tutor Bramshill Police Staff Coll 1966-68; freelance singer, writer and broadcaster; princ bass: Sadlers Well's Opera 1969-72, Royal Opera 1972-83; major opera appearances: Covent Garden, La Scala Milan, Metropolitan Opera, Paris Opera, Munich, Vienna, San Francisco; frequent broadcaster on radio and TV, Films: Parsifal (Artificial Eye), 6 Foot Cinderella (BBC), Blackbeard's Castle (BBC); *Recreations* sailing, hill walking; *Clubs* Garrick; *Style*— Robert Lloyd, Esq; Harrison Parrott Ltd, 12 Penzance Place, London W11 (☎ 01 229 9166)

LLOYD, Capt Robert Edmund; DSC and Bar 1944, DL (Somerset 1974); s of Edmund Commeline Lloyd (d 1931), of Pitsworthy Farm, Exford, Minehead, Somerset, and Violet Emily, *née* Hooper (d 1966); *b* 10 Mar 1916; *Educ* RNC Dartmouth; *m* 2 Jan 1941, Marjorie Russell, da of William Alexander Broom, JP (d 1954), of Campbeltown, Argyllshire; 2 s (Derek b 1942, Brian b 1946); *Career* Midshipman 1934-35: HMS Hood, HMS Renown, HMS Norfolk; serv 1937-40 in destroyers: HMS Basilisk, HMS Codrington, HMS Brazen; qualified anti-submarine specialist 1940, Atlantic and Med escort duties HMS Keppel 1941-42, HMS Affleck Atlantic and Channel 1944-45 (despatches three times during WWII), Fleet Anti-Submarine Offr Med 1946-48, qualified Torpedo Anti-Submarine Sch (later staff) and 1 Cruiser Sqdn 1948-53; Cdr 1953-57: Naval Air Warfare Div Admty, RN Staff Course Greenwich, RN Air Station Brawdy; Capt Staff TAS Offr Home Fleet 1958, asst dir Underwater Weapons Admty 1958-61, Naval Attaché Athens and Tel Aviv 1961-63, dir Seamen and Gen Trg Admty 1963-65, Capt HMS Vernon (Torpedo Anti-Submarine Sch Portsmouth) 1965-67, ret 1967; cncllr Dulverton and West Somerset DC 1967-80; *Clubs* Naval & Military; *Style*— Capt R E Lloyd, DSC, DL, RN; Pitsworthy Farm, Exford, Minehead, Somerset (☎ 064383 260)

LLOYD, Shirley; da of Trevor Emlyn Williams, of 1 Neville Rd, Porthcawl, Mid Glamorgan, and Elsie, *née* Jones (d 1974); *b* 7 Dec 1934; *Educ* Porthcawl Secdy Mod; *m* 12 Oct 1968, Robert David Lloyd, s of Robert Denis Lloyd, of 3 Fairfax Cres, Porthcawl, Mid Glamorgan; *Career* md: P E Thomas Ltd 1971-76 (dir 1966-71), P E Thomas (Porthcawl) Ltd 1976-82; dir P E Thomas (Precision) Ltd 1984-; divnl cmmr Girl Guides, sec Porthcawl Civic Festival Ctee; vice-pres: Porthcawl Disabled Gp, Porthcawl Rugby Club; memb Porthcawl Chamber of Trade; *Style*— Mrs Shirley Lloyd; P E Thomas (Precision), Glan Rd, Porthcawl CF36 5DF (☎ 065 671 3555)

LLOYD, Simon Croil; s of Lt-Col R C Lloyd, DSO, MC, TD (d 1972), of Denbigh, and Joan, *née* Tate (d 1980); *b* 10 Mar 1925; *Educ* Stowe; *m* 28 April 1951, Diana Nesta, da of Henry Robertson (d 1976), of Gwynedd; *Career* serv 1943-49 The Rifle Bde, Capt 1946; High Sheriff Denbighshire 1964; jt MFH Flint and Denbigh 1961-67 and 1985-; hon showyard dir Denbighshire and Flintshire Agric Soc 1962-; *Recreations* hunting, shooting, breeding and showing hunters; *Style*— Simon Lloyd, Esq; Garn, Denbigh, Clwyd LL16 5BW (☎ 074 574 610)

LLOYD, Hon Mrs (Thelma Margaret Leighton); *née* Seager; da of 1 Baron Leighton of St Mellons, CBE (d 1963); *b* 6 Nov 1923; *Educ* Queenswood Sch, London Univ; *m* 1, 1951 (m dis 1981), Michael Edmonds; 1 s, 2 da; m 2, 1983, Joseph Evan Lloyd; *Career* magistrate 1962-68, psychiatric social worker; *Recreations* swimming, exploring, talking with friends; *Style*— The Hon Mrs Lloyd; Penarth, S Glam

LLOYD, Thomas (Tom); s of Thomas Lloyd (d 1969), and Dr Alice Margaret, *née* Ramsden; *b* 26 April 1946; *Educ* Wellington, Liverpool Univ (BA); *m* 20 April 1974 (sep); 1 s (Owen Anthony b 14 Nov 1981), 1 da (Katherine b 22 Feb 1980); *Career* ed Financial Weekly 1983-; *Books* Dinosaur and Co Studies in Corporate Evolution (1984), Managing Knowhow (jtly 1987); *Recreations* walking, reading, writing; *Style*— Tom Lloyd, Esq; 14 Greville St, London, EC1N 8SB (☎ 01 405 2288, fax 01 8312625)

LLOYD, Brig Thomas Ifan; CBE (1957), DSO (1944), MC (1940); s of Rev David Lloyd (d 1921), of Weston-super-Mare, Somerset; *b* 1903; *Educ* Westminster, RMA; *m* 1927, Irene Mary, da of Prof A Fullerton, CB, CMG, (d 1932); 1 s, 1 da; *Career* 2 Lt RE 1923, serv WWII, dep engr-in-chief WO 1955-57, Brig 1955, ret 1957; hon founder-pres Railway Conversion League; *Style*— Brig Thomas Lloyd, CBE, DSO, MC; 24 Grove Rd, Merrow, Guildford, Surrey

LLOYD, Thomas Owen Saunders; s of Maj John Audley Lloyd, MC, of Court Henry, Carmarthen, and (Mary Ivy) Anna *née* Owen; *b* 26 Feb 1955; *Educ* Radley, Downing Coll Cambridge (MA); *m* 7 Nov 1987, (Christabel) Juliet (Anne), da of Maj David Harrison-Allen (d 1976), of Cresselly nr Pembroke; *Career* slr, publisher and author; dir and co sec The Golden Grove Book Co 1987-; tstee Br Historic Bldgs Tst 1986- (chm 1987); memb: Historic Bldgs Cncl for Wales, Nat Tst Ctee for Wales, ctee Save Britain's Heritage; *Books* The Lost Houses of Wales (1986); *Clubs* Lansdowne; *Style*— Thomas Lloyd, Esq; Freestone Hall, Cresselly, Kilgetty, Dyfed SA68 0SX (☎ 0646 651493); Golden Grove House, 10 Quay Street, Carmarthen, Dyfed (☎ 0267 236350)

LLOYD, Hon Mrs Victoria Mary; *née* Ormsby-Gore; da of 5 Baron Harlech, KCMG, PC (d 1985); *b* 1946; *m* 1972, Julian Richard Leslie Lloyd; 1 s, 2 da; *Style*— The Hon

Mrs Lloyd; The Glebe, Leixlip, Co Kildare, Eire

LLOYD, Maj William Rhys (Bill); s of Lt Col Sir John Conway Lloyd, MC, JP, DL (d 1954), of Dinas, and Marion Clive, *née* Justice (d 1962); *b* 25 Jan 1909; *Educ* Radley; *m* 24 April 1927, Lucy Pamela, da of Ernest Baxter (d 1942); 1 s (John Richard Conway b 1941), 1 da (Lavinia Madeleine b 1944); *Career* WWII cmmnd S Wales Borderers, serv N Africa and Italy (despatches) 1940-45; stockbroker; ptnr: Keith, Bayley & Rigg 1937-69, Hoare Govett 1969-75; High Sheriff Brecon 1965 being sixth memb of family to serve (ancestor Thomas Lloyd ap Meredith was Ld-Lt Brecon 1545); *Recreations* fishing; *Clubs* Naval and Military; *Style—* Maj William Lloyd; Abercynrig, Brecon, Powys LD3 7AQ (☎ 087 486 204)

LLOYD DAVIES, DR Alan Trevor; s of Trevor L Davies (d 1962) of Reigate Surrey, and Doris Madeleine, *née* Morris; *b* 30 Dec 1935; *Educ* King's Coll Choir Sch Cambridge, Malvern Coll, King's Coll London, Westminster Med Sch and Univ of London (MB BS); *m* 4 April 1964, Rosalind Frances, da of Oliver Seadon Naylor, of Walton-on-Thames; 3 da (ceri Henrietta b 1966, Sophie Sian b 1968, Megan Frances b 1972); *Career* house surgn: Westminster Hosp 1962, Redhill Gen Hosp 1963; res obstetrics offr St Teresa's Hosp 1964-65, civilian med practitioner 4 Field Ambulance 1965-68, GP 1968-, hosp practioner in geriatrics 1987-; former pres Andover Rotary Club, former sec Hants Branch Salmon and Trout Assoc, memb Waynflete Singers 1969, dir Goodworth Singers 1975-; memb BMA, MRCS, LRCP; *Recreations* fly fishing, game fishing, choral singing, golf; *Style—* Dr Alan Lloyd Davies; Godewirda, St Anns Close, Goodworth Clatford, Andover, Hants SP11 7RW (☎ 0264 52 983); 35 High Street, Andover, Hants (☎ 0264 61 424)

LLOYD GEORGE, Hon Robert John Daniel; s of 3 Earl Lloyd-George of Dwyfor; *b* 13 August 1952; *Educ* Eton, Univ Coll Oxford; *m* 1978, Kim, da of Carl Fischer of New York; 1 s (Richard b 1983), 1 da (Alice b 1987); *Style—* The Hon Robert Lloyd George

LLOYD GEORGE, Hon Sara Gwenfron; da of 3 Viscount Tenby; *b* 1957; *Style—* The Hon Sara Lloyd George

LLOYD GEORGE, Hon Timothy Henry Gwilym; s and h of, 3 Viscount Tenby; *b* 19 Oct 1962; *Educ* Downside, Univ Coll of Wales Aberystwyth; *Style—* The Hon Timothy Lloyd George; Triggs, Crondall, nr Farnham, Surrey

LLOYD GEORGE OF DWYFOR, 3 Earl (UK 1945); Owen Lloyd George; also Viscount Gwynedd (UK 1945); s of 2 Earl Lloyd George of Dwyfor (d 1968, s of the celebrated PM 1916-22) and his 1 w, Roberta, da of Sir Robert McAlpine, 1 Bt; *b* 28 April 1924; *Educ* Oundle; *m* 1, 1949 (m dis 1982), Ruth Margaret, da of Richard Coit (d 1960); 2 s, 1 da; m 2, 1982, (Cecily) Josephine (who m 1, 1957, as his 2 w, 2 Earl of Woolton, who d 1969; m 2, 1969 (m dis 1974), as his 2 w, 3 Baron Forres, who d 1978), er da of Sir Alexander Gordon Cumming, 5 Bt, MC (d 1939); *Heir* s, Viscount Gwynedd; *Career* Capt Welsh Gds 1942, serv 1944-45 in Italy; carried the Sword of State at investiture of HRH The Prince of Wales, Caernarvon Castle 1969; underwriting memb of Lloyd's; memb Historic Buildings Cncl for Wales 1971-; pres Channel Tunnel Assoc; memb ct Nat Museum of Wales; *Clubs* White's, Pratt's, City of London; *Style—* The Rt Hon the Earl Lloyd George of Dwyfor; 47 Burton Court, Chelsea, London SW3 4SL; The Hall, Freshford, Bath BA3 6AJ

LLOYD HUGHES, David; s of Trevor Lloyd Hughes, of 10a Kingsley Ave, Leeds, and Isabella Mary, *née* Buchan (d 1954); *b* 12 August 1941; *Educ* Leeds GS; *m* 1965, Jean Mary, da of William Kenny (d 1945); 1 s; *Career* fin dir and co sec Stylo plc and dir of each of its trading subsids; FCA;; *Style—* David Lloyd Hughes, Esq; Stylo plc, Stylo House, Apperley Bridge, Bradford BD10 0NW (☎ 0274 617761, telex 517050, fax 0274 616111); 5 Hollin Gdns, Leeds LS16 5NL (☎ 0532 758478)

LLOYD JONES, David Elwyn; MC (1946); s of Daniel Lloyd Jones (d 1974), of Aberystwyth, and Blodwen, *née* Evans (d 1953); *b* 20 Oct 1920; *Educ* Ardwyn GS Aberystwyth, Univ Coll of Wales Aberystwyth (BA); *m* 23 July 1955, Mrs Elsie Winifred Gallie, wid of Dr Ian Gallie Dean, da of Prof Robert Peers, CBE, MC (d 1972), of Nottingham; 1 steps; *Career* WWII OCTU 1941-42, cmmnd (Sandhurst) Indian Army 1942, serv 1 Bn Assam Regt Burma Campaign 1942-46 (Maj 1945); Dept of Educn and Sci (formerly Miny of Educn): asst princ 1947-49, princ 1949-60, asst sec dep account gen 1961-68, under sec (head Higher and Further Educn Branch for non Univ sector) 1969-80, seconded princ private sec to Chllr of the Duchy of Lancaster 1960-61; memb cncl: Royal Acad of Dancing 1980-, RCM 1981-, Froebel Educnl Inst 1981-; FRCM 1988; *Recreations* music, Indian history, playing golf, watching cricket; *Clubs* MCC, Roehampton, Royal Cwlth; *Style—* David E Lloyd Jones, Esq, MC; 5 Playfair Mansions, Queen's Club Gardens, London W14 9TR (☎ 01 385 0586)

LLOYD MOSTYN *see also*: Mostyn

LLOYD OF HAMPSTEAD, Baron (Life Peer UK 1965); Dennis Lloyd; QC (1975); s of Isaac Lloyd (d 1975), co dir, of 22 Stourcliffe Close, London W1, and Betty, *née* Jaffa (d 1965); *b* 22 Oct 1915; *Educ* Univ Coll Sch, Univ Coll London (LLB), Gonville and Caius Coll Cambridge (BA, MA, LLD); *m* 15 Sept 1940, Ruth Emma Cecilia, da of late Carl Tulla; 2 da (Naomi Katharine (Hon Mrs Hodges) b 1946, Corinne Deborah (Hon Mrs Newman) b 1951); *Career* serv RA 1939-41 and RAOC WWII, Capt DADOS, liaison offr Free French Forces in Syria and Lebanon; barr Inner Temple 1936; in practice in London 1937-39 and 1946-82; reader in english law Univ Coll London 1947-56; Quain Prof of Jurisprudence 1956-82, now emeritus; head of dept of law Univ Coll 1969-82; memb: Law Reform Ctee 1961-82, European Communities Ctee 1973-79 and 1984-; chm: Nat Film and Television Sch 1970-88, Br Film Inst 1973-76 (govr 1968-76), Br Screen Advsy Cncl 1985-, Cncl of Univ Coll Sch 1971-79; Fell Univ Coll London, Fell Ritsumeikan Univ Kyoto Japan 1978 and Hon LLD 1987; *Books* Unincorporated Associations (1938), Rent Control (2 edn 1955), Public Policy (1953), Business Lettings (1956), Introduction to Jurisprudence (5 edn 1985), Idea of Law (1964, revised edns 1968-87); *Publications incl*: Introduction to Jurisprudence (5th Edn 1985), Idea of Law (8th revised impression 1987); *Recreations* painting, listening to music, modern Greek; *Clubs* Athenaeum, RAC; *Style—* The Rt Hon the Lord Lloyd of Hampstead, QC; Faculty of Laws, University College, London WC1

LLOYD OF KILGERRAN, Baron (Life Peer UK 1973); Rhys Gerran Lloyd; CBE (1953), QC (1961), JP (Surrey 1953); s of James Griffith Lloyd (d 1940), of Kilgerran, Dyfed, and Mary Lloyd (d 1972); *b* 12 August 1907; *Educ* Sloane Sch, Selwyn Coll Cambridge (MA), London Univ (BSc); *m* 1940, Phyllis Mary, da of Ronald Shepherd, JP (d 1953), of Chilworth, Southampton; 2 da; *Career* sits as Lib in House of Lords; serv WWII as scientific researcher; barr Gray's Inn 1939, Middle Temple 1955; specialist in Patent, Trade Mark and Copywright Law; contested Anglesey (Lib) 1959, pres Welsh Lib Pty 1971-74, UK Lib Pty 1973-74, jt tres 1977-84; Lib whip and delegate WEU and Cncl of Europe 1973-75; pres: Inst of Patentees and Inventors 1975-, Mobile Radio Users Assoc 1986-, ASLIB 1988-, Bembridge Sch 1980-; memb: House of Lords Select Ctee on Sci and Technol 1977-83, EEC Ctee on Sci and Technol; hon sec Parly Ctee on Information Technol 1979-; dir: Strayfield Int Ltd, Morgan Marine Ltd; chm: Educn Tst, Brantwood (John Ruskin) Tst, Fndn for Sci and Technol 1983-, Bracondale Properties Ltd; dep pres Victoria League, former vice-chm Cwlth Parliamentarians Assoc; Freeman City of London, former Master Worshipful Co of Tallow Chandlers; dep chm Parly Energy Parl Gp tres Franc Br Gp; hon fell: Selwyn Coll Cambridge 1971-, Inst Structural Engrg 1988-; landowner; *Books* Kerly on Trade Marks (7 and 8 edns), Halsbury Laws of England (3 edn), Trade Marks and Design, various pamphlets; *Clubs* Reform, Royal Cwlth, City Livery, Nat Lib, Utd Wards'; *Style—* The Rt Hon the Lord Lloyd of Kilgerran, CBE, QC, JP; 15 Haymeads Drive, Esher, Surrey KT10 9EX; Brantwood, Coniston, Cumbria

LLOYD OWEN, Maj-Gen David Lanyon Lloyd; CB (1971), DSO (1945), OBE (1954), MC (1942); s of Capt Reginald Charles Lloyd Owen, OBE, RN (d 1945); *b* 10 Oct 1917; *Educ* Winchester, RMC Sandhurst; *m* 18 Oct 1947, Ursula Evelyn, da of Evelyn Hugh Barclay (d 1956), of Colney Hall, Norwich; 3 s; *Career* 2 Lt The Queen's Royal Regt 1938, serv WWII, LRDG 1941-45; mil asst to High Cmmr in Malaya 1952-53, GOC Cyprus Dist 1966-67 and NEARELF 1967-69, Maj-Gen 1966, pres Regular Commissions Bd 1969-72; ret 1972; chm Br Assoc for Shooting and Conservation 1979-85; Cross of Merit Kt SMO Malta 1946; author; *Books* The Desert My Dwelling Place (1957), Providence Their Guide (1980); *Style—* Maj-Gen David Lloyd Owen, CB, DSO, OBE, MC; Violet Bank, Swainsthorpe, Norwich NR14 8PR (☎ 0508 470468)

LLOYD RICHARDS, Hon Mrs (Joyce); *née* Taylor; da of Baron Taylor of Gryfe (Life Peer); *b* 14 Mar 1948; *Educ* Hutcheson's Girls' GS Glasgow, Strathclyde Univ; *m* 1, 1969, Alan Begbie; 1 s (Alasdair b 1970), 1 da (Caroline b 1972); m 2, 1982, John Huw Lloyd Richards; *Style—* The Hon Mrs Lloyd Richards; 19 Kessington Drive, Bearsden, Glasgow (☎ 041 942 1454)

LLOYD WEBBER, Andrew; s of William Southcombe Lloyd Webber, CBE (d 1982, dir London Coll Music, musical dir Westminster Central Hall London), and Jean Hermione, *née* Johnstone; *b* 22 Mar 1948; *Educ* Westminster, Magdalen Coll Oxford, Guildhall Sch of Music, RCM; *m* 1, 24 July 1971 (m dis 1983), Sarah Jane Tudor, *née* Hugill; 1 s (Nicholas b 1979), 1 da (Imogen b 1977); m 2, 22 March 1984, Sarah, da of Grenville Geoffrey Brightman, of Bournemouth; *Career* composer: Joseph and the Amazing Technicolour Dreamcoat (1968), Jesus Christ Superstar (1970), Jeeves (1975), Evita (1976), Tell Me on a Sunday (1980), Cats (1981), Song and Dance (1982), Starlight Express (1984), The Phantom of the Opera (1986); orchestral/choral works: Requiem (1985), Variations (1985), Evita Suite (1988); film scores: Gumshoe (1971), The Odessa File (1974); prodr of: Daisy Pulls It Off (1983), The Hired Man (1984), Lend Me a Tenor (1986); Awards: Tony 1980, 1983 (twice), 1988, Drama Desk 1971/80/83, Grammy 1984/86, Triple Play ASCAP 1988; *Recreations* architecture; *Style—* Andrew Lloyd Webber, Esq; The Palace Theatre, Shaftesbury Ave, London W1V 8AY

LLOYD WEBBER, Julian; s of William Southcombe Lloyd Webber, CBE (d 1982), and Jean Hermione, *née* Johnstone; *b* 14 April 1951; *Educ* Westminster Under Sch, Univ Coll Sch, RCM; *m* 1974, Celia Mary, da of Dr James Rollo Ballantyne; *Career* UK debut Queen Elizabeth Hall London 1972, USA debut Lincoln Centre NY 1980, debut with Berlin Philharmonic Orch 1984; has performed with all maj Br orchs and toured the USA, Germany, Holland, Africa, Bulgaria, Czechoslovakia, S America, Spain, Belgium, France, Scandinavia, Portugal and Australia; tour: Singapore and Japan 1986, Japan and Korea 1988; has made first recordings of works by: Benjamin Britten, Frank Bridge, Frederick Delius, Gustav Holst, Joaquin Rodrigo, Ralph Vaughan Williams; Gold and Silver discs for Variations 1978, Spanish Miny of Culture award for recording of Joaquin Rodrigo's Concierto Como Un Divertimento 1982, Winner 'Best British Classical Recording' for Elgar Cello Concerto 1987; ARCM; *Books Incl:* The Classical Cello (1980), The Romantic Cello (1981), The French Cello (1981), 6 pieces by Frank Bridge (1982), The Young Cellist's Repertoire Books 1, 2 & 3 (1984), Holst Invocation (1984), Vaughan Williams Fantasia on Sussex Folk Tunes (1984), Travels with My Cello (1984), Song of the Birds (1985), Recital Repertoire for Cellists (1986); *Recreations* turtle keeping, topography (especially Br); *Style—* Julian Lloyd Webber, Esq; c/o Kaye Artists Management, 250 Kings Rd, London SW3 6NR (☎ 01 376 3456, telex 266102)

LLOYD-DAVIES, Capt (Cromwell) Felix (Justin); DSO (1950), DSC (1944); s of Dr John Lloyd-Davies, MRCS, LRCP, JP (d 1937), and Esther Ann, *née* Evans (d 1962); *b* 22 Sept 1903; *Educ* RNC Osborne and Dartmouth; *m* 8 March 1941 (m dis 1952), Rachel Mary, da of Maj the Hon A V Agar Robartes, MC, later Viscount Clifden (d 1980); 1 da (Ann b 1942 (Mrs Colin Victor Kennett Williams); *Career* RN Capt; serv WWII: Mediterranean, Atlantic, D Day, SEA; CO to force receiving Japanese surrender of Singapore 1945, Korean War Capt HMS Ceylon, Cmd W Coast Blockade Force; chief of plans to Adm Mountbatten when C in C Allied forces Mediterranean 1953-54; int sales exec Hawker Siddely Gp 1955-70; memb Bray Parish Cncl 1971-87, chm Bray Preservation Soc 1971-86; *Recreations* sailing, swimming; *Clubs* Naval & Military, Royal Naval and Royal Albert YC, Royal Naval Sailing Assoc, Phyllis Ct (Henley); *Style—* Capt Felix Lloyd-Davies, DSO, DSC, RN; 48 Braybank, Old Mill Lane, Bray, Berkshire SL6 2BH (☎ 0628 21946)

LLOYD-DAVIES, (John) Robert; CMG (1953); s of John Robert Lloyd-Davies (d 1971), of Muswell Hill, London, and Nellie Louise, *née* Wilson (d 1928); *b* 24 Mar 1913; *Educ* Highgate, Oriel Coll Oxford (MA), Univ of Freiburg-im-Breisgau; *m* 1, 6 Feb 1943, Margery (d 1978), da of Maj William McClelland (d 1918); 1 s (Peter Russell b 18 Nov 1943), 1 da (Virginia Mary b 9 March 1947); m 2, 19 June 1982, Grace, *née* Williams, wid of Frederick Reynolds II, of Bethesda, MD, USA; *Career* Lt RNVR 1942-45; sr Civil Servant and memb of HM Dip Serv; private sec to Sir Thomas Phillips, KCB (Employment Dept) 1940, labour cllr HM Embassies Paris (1956-60) and Washington DC (1972-73), princ Trg Serv Agency 1973-77; pt/t teacher Working Men's Coll London 1970-, Inst for Learning in Retirement American Univ Washington DC 1987-; *Recreations* keyboard music (baroque and modern); *Clubs* Utd Oxford and Cambridge Univ; *Style—* Robert Lloyd-Davies, Esq, CMG; 59 Elm Park

Court, Pinner, Middx HA5 3LL (☎ 01 866 9526)

LLOYD-DAVIS, Glynne Christian; s of Col G St G Lloyd-Davis (d 1956), and Daphne Mary, *née* Barnes; *b* 9 Mar 1941; *Educ* St Paul's, Ealing Tech Coll, Royal Sch of Mines (London Univ); *m* 20 April 1963, Dorothy Helen, da of Michael Felix O'Shea, of Toowong, Brisbane, Queensland, Australia; 1 s (Simon b 1966), 1 da (Sarah b 1964); *Career* chartered sec; assist sec The RTZ Corp plc 1976; dir subsidiary cos; FCIS; *Recreations* reading, walking, sketching; *Style—* Glynne Lloyd-Davis, Esq; Forge Cottage, Whitehill, Ospringe, Faversham, Kent; 6 St James's Square, London SW1Y 4LD (☎ 01 930 2399, telex 24639)

LLOYD-EDWARDS, Capt Norman; RD (1971) and Bar (1980); s of Evan Stanley Edwards (d 1986), of Cardiff, and Mary Leah, *née* Lloyd (d 1977); *b* 13 June 1933; *Educ* Monmouth Sch, Quakers Yard GS, Bristol Univ (LLB); *Career* Capt RNR, cmding offr HMS Cambria, S Wales Div RNR 1981-84; slr; memb Cardiff City Cncl 1963-87, dep lord mayor 1973-74, chapter clerk Llandaff Cathedral 1975-, ptnr Cartwrights 1960-; ADC to HM The Queen 1984; lord mayor of Cardiff 1985-86; BBC Cncl Wales 1987-; chm Nat Res Trg Cncl 1984-, chm Cardiff Festival of Music 1981-; vice Lord Lt South Glamorgan 1986-; OStJ 1983, KStJ 1988, Prior for Wales 1989; *Recreations* music, gardening, table talk; *Clubs* Army & Navy, Cardiff & Co; *Style—* Capt Norman Lloyd-Edwards, RD, VL, RNR; Hafan Wen, Llantrisant Rd, Llandaff, Cardiff CF5 2PU (☎ 0222 566107); 36 West Bute St, Cardiff (☎ 0222 465959, fax 0222 480006)

LLOYD-HUGHES, Sir Trevor Denby; s of Elwyn Lloyd-Hughes (d 1969), of Dwygyfylchi, Penmaenmawr, and Lucy, *née* Denby (1960); *b* 31 Mar 1922; *Educ* Woodhouse Grove Sch, Jesus Coll Oxford (MA); *m* 1, 9 May 1950, (m dis 1971), Ethel Marguerite Durward (dec'd) da of the late John Ritchie of Bradford; 1 s (Richard b 1954), 1 da (Katherine b 1951); m 2, 18 May 1971, Marie-Jeanne, da of Marcel Moreillon of Geneva, Switzerland; 1 s (decd), 1 da (Annabelle b 1971), 1 adopted da (Nammon b 1969 in Thailand); *Career* asst inspr Taxes 1947-48, freelance journalist 1949; political corr: Liverpool Echo 1950, Liverpool Daily Post 1951-64, press sec to PM 1964-69, chief info advsr to Govt 1969-70, int cnslt in public affairs 1971-; involved in many charitable, religious and environmental activities; memb Circle of Wine Writers 1961-(chm 1972-73); FBIM, FIOD; kt 1970; *Recreations* yoga, golf, travel, walking; *Clubs* Reform, Mossiman's (Belfrey), Wellington; *Style—* Sir Trevor Lloyd-Hughes, KB; Llawenydd, Eford Gyffylog, Eglwysbach, Near Colwyn Bay, Clywd LL28 5TU (☎ 0492 650 050, fax 0492 650 639)

LLOYD-JONES, David Mathias; s of Harry Vincent Lloyd-Jones, and Margaret Alwyna, *née* Mathias; *b* 19 Nov 1934; *Educ* Westminster, Magdalen Coll Oxford (BA); *m* 23 May 1964, Anne Carolyn, da of Brig Victor Whitehead, of 2160 Lakeshore Dr, Montreal; 2 s (Gareth b 1966, Simon b 1968), 1 da (Vanessa b 1964); *Career* conductor, with Royal Opera House Covent Garden 1959-60, chorus master and conductor New Opera Co 1961-64, freelance conductor engagements with: BBC, WNO, Scottish Opera; asst music dir Sadlers Wells Eng Nat Opera 1972-78, artistic dir Opera North 1978-; ed original version of Mussorgsky's Boris Godunov 1974; published full score Gilbert and Sullivans' The Gondoliers 1983; trans: Eugene Onegin, Boris Godunov, The Queen of Spades, The Love for Three Oranges; hon D Mus Leeds; *Style—* David Lloyd-Jones, Esq; 9 Clarence Rd, Horsforth, Leeds (☎ 0532 584 490); Opera North, Grand Theatre, Leeds LS1 6NZ (☎ 0532 439 999)

LLOYD-JONES, His Hon David Trevor; VRD (1952); s of Trevor Lloyd-Jones (d 1933), of Holywell, and Ann, *née* Hughes Roberts (d 1977); *b* 6 Mar 1917; *Educ* Holywell GS; *m* 1, 1942 (m dis 1949), Mary Violet (d 1980), da of Frederick Barnardo, CIE, CBE; m 2, 1958, Anstice Elizabeth (d 1981), da of William Perkins; m 3, 1984 Florence Mary, da of William Fairclough (d 1979); 1 s (Martyn), 2 da (Margaret, Ceridwen); *Career* WWII Lt Cdr RNVR Atlantic Pacific; barr Gray's Inn 1951; dep chm Caernarvonshire Quarter Sessions 1960-66; chm 1970-72, HM circuit judge 1972-88; *Recreations* golf, music; *Clubs* Army and Navy, Royal Dornoch GC; *Style—* His Hon David Lloyd-Jones, VRD; 29 Curzon Park North, Chester

LLOYD-JONES, Prof (Peter) Hugh (Jefferd); s of Brevet Maj William Lloyd-Jones, DSO (d 1963 late Capt of Invalids Royal Hosp Chelsea), and Norah Leila, *née* Jefferd (d 1953); *b* 21 Sept 1922; *Educ* Westminster, Lycee Francais du Royaume Univ, Christ Church Oxford (MA); *m* 1, 30 July 1953 (m dis 1981), Frances Elizabeth, da of RHB Hedley; 2 s (Edmund b 1958, Ralph b 1960), 1 da (Antonia b 1962); m 2, 26 March 1982, Prof Mary Lefkowitz, da of Harold Rosenthal ; *Career* 2 Lt Intelligence Corps, serv India 1942, Capt 1944, demob 1946; fell Jesus Coll Cambridge 1948-54, lectr Univ of Cambridge 1952-54 (asst lectr 1950-52), fell and EP Warren Praelecter in Corpus Christi Coll Oxford 1954-60, regius prof Greek Univ of Oxford, student of Christ Church Oxford 1960-89, corresponding memb: Acad of Athens, American Acad of Arts and Scis, Rheinisch-Westfalische Akedemie, Accademia di Letteratura Archelogia e Belle Arti Naples; hon PhD Univ Tel Aviv 1982, hon DH Chicago Univ 1970; *Books* The Justice of Zeus (1971 2 edn 1983), Blood for the Ghosts (1982), Supplementum Helenisticum (with P J Parsons 1983), with N G Wilson: Sophoclis Fabulae (with N G Wilson 1989), Sophoclea (1989), Collated Academic Papers (1989); *Recreations* cats, remembering old cricket; *Clubs* Utd Oxford and Cambridge; *Style—* Prof Hugh Lloyd-Jones; Marlborough Rd, Oxford OX1 4LS; 15 West Riding, Wellesley, Massachusetts, 02181 (☎ USA 617 237 2212)

LLOYD-JONES, Mary; da of John Francis Elkington (d 1984), of Harrow-on-the-Hill, and Jennie Ada Sybil, *née* Tucker (d 1984); *b* 2 August 1931; *Educ* St Mary's Sch Baldslow St Leonards-on-Sea E Sussex, Hampstead Business and Secretarial Coll; *m* 2 May 1959, Col John Lloyd-Jones (d 1982), s of Capt Robert Lloyd-Jones (d 1959), of Ealing, London W5; 3 s (Jeremy b 1960, Adam b 1965, Tomas b 1968), 1 da (Vanessa b 1962); *Career* Guildford Borough Cncl: cncllr 1979-, Mayoress 1986-87, Dep Mayoress 1987-88; chm Housing and Health Ctee 1987- (vice-chm 1983-87); tstee Yvonne Arnaud Theatre; memb: Ct of Univ of Surrey, W Surrey and NE Hants Health Authy, vice-pres Guildford-Freiburg Soc; *Recreations* music, theatre, swimming, watching sport; *Clubs* Yvonne Arnaud Theatre; *Style—* Mrs Mary Lloyd-Jones; White Lodge, Wentworth Crescent, Ash Vale, Aldershot GU12 5LE (☎ 0252 26587); Associated Examining Board, Stag Hill House, Guildford GU2 5XJ (☎ 0483 506506 ext 2213, fax 0483 300152)

LLOYD-JONES, Robert (Bob); s of Robert Lloyd-Jones, (d 1950), of Caernarvon, N Wales, and Edith May, *née* Hughes (d 1954); *b* 30 Jan 1931; *Educ* Wrekin Coll, Queens' Coll Cambridge (MA), Harvard Business Sch; *m* 9 June 1958 (m dis 1977), Morny Downer; 2 s (Ashley Paul b 8 June 1961, Alasdair Guy b 12 Feb 1966), 1 da (Sarah Louise (Mrs Britton) b 14 Oct 1962); *Career* Lt RN 1956-59; patent attorney Shell Int 1959-62, head legal and licensing BTR Indus Ltd 1962-64, dir (Woolmark) Int Wool Secreteriat 1964-71, pa chm and export dir Schachenmayr Germany 1971-77; dir gen Br Textile Employers Assoc 1977-81, Retail Consortium 1981-83; dir gen Brick Dvpt Assoc 1984-, dir Fedn Euro des Fabricants de Tuiles et de Briques 1984-; friend: Roy Acad, Tate Gallery; govr Ccll for Distributitive Trades 1982-84, fndr chm Nat Retail Trg cncl 1982-84; memb: FRSA ; *Recreations* golf, tennis, squash, chess, travel, arts, reading, music; *Clubs* Lansdowne, Royal Birkdale, Rye, Liphook, Formby GC, Royal Ascot Tennis, IOD; *Style—* Bob Lloyd-Jones, Esq; Newell Cottage, Winkfield, Windsor, Berks SL4 4SE (☎ 0344 883 054): Woodside House, Winkfield, Windsor, Berks SL4 2DX (☎ 0344 885651, fax 0344 890129, car 0860363314, telex 847840)

LLOYD-ROBERTS, George Edward; s of George Charles Lloyd-Roberts (d 1986), of Cheyne Place, London, and Catherine Ann, *née* Wright; *b* 21 Mar 1948; *Educ* Gordonstoun, London Univ (MSc); *m* 2 Aug 1969, Elizabeth Anne, da of Horace Edward Kenworthy, of Cork, Eire; 1 s (Henry b 1977), 1 da (Sophie b 1975); *Career* underwriter GE Lloyd-Roberts Synd 1976, (fndr) Lloyds Non Marine Assoc 1986-, Lloyds Solvency and Security 1987-; *Recreations* running, riding, reading; *Style—* George Lloyd-Roberts, Esq; Lloyd's, Lime St, London (☎ 01 623 7100)

LLOYD-ROBERTS, Dr Robert Edmund; TD (1972); o s of Richard Lloyd Roberts (d 1939), of Pinner, Middx, and Margaret Sarah Lloyd-Roberts, *née* Evans (d 1987); representative of a cadet branch of the ancient house of Nannau, N Wales, derived from the Princes of Powys (*see* Burke's Landed Gentry, 18 edn, vol II, 1969); *b* 22 July 1925; *Educ* Merchant Taylors', St Thomas's Hosp (MB BS Lond 1951, MRCS Eng, LRCP Lond 1951); *m* 2 July 1955, Elizabeth, yr da of Dr Mandale Byers (d 1923), of Mowhan House, Co Armagh, and St Anne's-on-Sea, Lancs (the Byers of Mowhan descend from the Byres of Coates, Scotland); 2 s (Richard b 1956, Meyrick b and d 1958), 2 da (Arabella b 1959, Sophia b 1963); *Career* princ in general med practice 1957-; visiting med offr Nunnery Fields Hosp and Mount Hosp, Canterbury; med offr Christ Church Coll and St Edmund's Sch Canterbury; chm War Pensions and Industl Injuries Med Bds, DHSS; local med advsr Med Advsy Serv, Civil Serv Dept; med examiner Insur Cos, Br Red Cross Soc etc; in attendance on HH Pope John Paul II at his visit to Canterbury Cathedral 29 May 1982; Lt-Col RAMC RARO formerly TA; DADMS 44 (Home Counties) Divn TA 1962-67; CO 144 Field Ambulance RAMC(V) and SMO 44 Parachute Bde (V) 1969-73; hon tres Airborne Med Soc 1973-83; OStJ 1967; FRSM; memb: Br Geriatric Soc, Dist Gen Practitioner Ctee, Canterbury Police Advsy Ctee; *Recreations* history, heraldry, genealogy, membership of various socs; *Clubs* Army & Navy, Kent and Canterbury (Canterbury); *Style—* Dr Robert Lloyd-Robertts, TD; Plas Glanafon, Talybont, Merioneth, Gwynedd; Longport House, 8 Longport, Canterbury, Kent; King's Bridge, Canterbury, Kent CT1 2AX (☎ 0227 463128)

LLOYD-WILLIAMS, Lt Cdr Huw Ceiriog; s of Tomos Lloyd-William (d 1963), of Derigaron, Tregaron, Dyfed, and Elizabeth, *née* Evans-Jones (d 1945); *b* 8 Feb 1928; *Educ* Tragaron Co Sch, Open Univ (BA); *m* 7 Dec 1968, (Celia) Anne, da of John Williams (d 1983), of Riverside, Tregaron; 2 s (Tomos b 1971, Daniel b 1972), 1 da (Laisa b 1973); *Career* joined RN 1944, Dartmouth Coll (Upper Yardsman) 1951-52, Greenwich 1952 (Sub Lt), Fleet Appts 1952-67, Staff Coll 1964, Flag offr ME Staff 1963-65, Admty 1965-67, resigned 1967; Nationwide Building Soc 1970-87: branch mangr Aberystwyth 1971-74, regnl mangr Wales 1974-87, memb Welsh regnl bd 1987-; dep chm Corinthian Construction & Devpt Co 1987-; candidate (Lib) Cardiganshire 1968-70; memb: bd Housing Corpn 1983-, cncl Nat Museum of Wales, cncl St Davids Univ Coll Lampeter; *Recreations* golf; *Clubs* Cardiff and Co Radyr GC; *Style—* Lt Cdr Huw Lloyd-Williams, RN; Plaz Trefilan, Lampeter, Dyfed, Rhiwbina, Cardiff, (☎ 0570 470 814); c/o Cotinthian Construction & Development Co, Haywood House, Dunfries Place, Cardiff CF1 4BA, (☎ 0222 378252 fax 0222 382380)

LLOYD-WORTH, Hon Mrs Frances Patricia; da of 3 Baron Tollemache (d 1955); *b* 1908; *m* 1949 (m dis 1964), Charles Edward Lloyd-Worth; *Style—* The Hon Mrs Frances Lloyd-Worth

LOACH, Mr Kenneth Charles (Ken); s of John Loach (d 1974), and Vivien Nora, *née* Hamlin; *b* 17 June 1936; *Educ* King Edward VI Sch Nuneaton, St Peter's Coll Oxford (BA); *m* 17 July 1962, Lesley, da of William Leslie Ashton (d 1967); 3 s (Stephen b 1963, Nicholas b 1965, James b 1969), 2 da (Hannah b 1967 Emma b 1972); *Career* film dir: Up The Junction 1965, Cathy Come Home 1966, Poor Cow 1967, Kes 1969, Family Life 1971, Days of Hope 1975, The Price of Coal 1977, The Gamekeeper 1979, Black Jack 1979, Looks and Smiles 1981, Which Side Are You On? 1984, Fatherland 1986, The View from the Woodpile 1988; *Style—* Ken Loach, Esq; c/o Judy Dalsh Assoc, 83 Eastbourne Mews, London W2 6LQ (☎ 01 262 1101)

LOADER, Sir Leslie Thomas; CBE (1980); s of Edward Robert Loader (d 1963), of Southampton, and Ethel May, *née* Tiller (d 1966); *b* 27 April 1923; *Educ* Bitterne Park Sch, Bournemouth Coll, LSE; *m* 1, 27 April 1957 (m dis 1980), Jennifer Jane, *née* Pickering; 3 da (Melanie Susan (Mrs Loader-Pittams) b 18 Jan 1959, Katharine Lucy (Mrs Cledwyn) b 14 Oct 1961, Anna Victoria (Mrs Loader-Easton) b 10 Feb 1964); m 2, 26 Nov 1981, Elizabeth; *Career* cmmnd Hants Regt (now Royal Hants Regt), active serv Italy; co chm (ret); cncllr (C) Southampton City Cncl 1947-59, Parly candidate (C) Southampton Itchen 1955, nat union exec Cons Pty 1969-76; chm: Southampton Cons Fedn 1964-72, Wessex Area Cons Pty 1972-75 (vice chm 1969-72), Swaythling Housing Soc 1975-83 (currently pres); fndr chm and currently pres: Rotary Club of Bitterne, Woolston Housing Soc 1962-83; pres Eastleigh Cons Assoc, memb Southampton and SW Hants Health Authy, chm Wessex Body Scanne Appeal 1980-83, tstee Wessex Med Sch Tst 1983-86; Freeman City of London, Liveryman Worshipful Co of Painter Stainers; kt 1987; *Books* various articles on politics and housing; *Clubs* Carlton; *Style—* Sir Leslie Loader, CBE; (☎ 04893 3551)

LOADER, Neil John; s of Charles Tyrle Loader (d 1986), of Chadwell Heath, and Emily Florence Loader; *b* 9 Sept 1929; *Educ* Brentwood Sch Essex; *m* 1 April 1960, Delphine Ann, da of Charles Stanley Dunlop (d 1986), of Brentwood; 2 s (Stuart b 1963, Phillip b 1964), 1 da (Susan b 1961); *Career* Nat Serv RNVR 1949-50; UK sales dir Monsanto Chems Ltd, md Leader Chemicals & Plastics Ltd 1973-; Freeman Worshipful Co of Needlemakers; *Recreations* golf, walking, bird watching; *Clubs* MCC, Old Brentwoods; *Style—* Neil Loader, Esq; 13 Headley Chase, Warley, Brentwood, Essex (☎ 0277 219 965); Loader Chemicals & Plastics Ltd, 2 Gresham Rd, Brentwood, Essex (☎ 0277 260 820, fax 0277 561 590, car tel 0836 622 805, telex

99337)

LOANE, Most Rev (Sir) Marcus Lawrence; KBE (1976); s of Kenneth Owen Archibald Loane (d 1963), and Flora Gwendoline Loane (d 1963); *b* 14 Oct 1911; *Educ* King's Sch Parramatta, Sydney Univ (MA); *m* 1937, Patricia Evelyn Jane Simpson; 2 s, 2 da; *Career* deacon 1935, priest 1936, chaplain AIF 1941-43, canon of St Andrew's Cathedral Sydney 1949-58, princ Moore Theological Coll 1954-58, Bishop-Coadjutor of Sydney 1958-66, Archbishop of Sydney 1966-82, Primate of Australia 1978-82 (ret); *see Debrett's Handbook of Australia and New Zealand for further details*; *Style*— The Most Rev Marcus Loane, KBE; Box Q 190, Queen Victoria Post Office, York St, Sydney, NSW 2000, Australia

LOANE, (Simon Folliott) Warren Thomas Barton; DL (Co Fermanagh 1972); s of Simon Christopher Loane (d 1940), of Crocknacrieve, Enniskillen, NI, and Mildred Penelope Matilda, *née* Barton (d 1971); *b* 16 August 1920; *Educ* Portora Royal Sch; *m* 4 Aug 1955, (Heather Everina) Anne, da of Capt David Alexander Mackey (d 1986), of Crocknacrieve; 1 s (Charles b 14 Nov 1956), 1 da (Erica b 30 April 1959); *Career* farmer; dir and vice-chm Ulster Wools 1970-, dir and chm Ulster Wool and Farm Supplies 1981-; exec memb Ulster Farmers' Union 1945-76 (cncl memb 1944-, fndr memb and former chm Fermanagh branch), fndr memb N memb N Fermanagh Gp ctee 1951 (chm 1951-76); chm: Ulster Wool Growers, NI regnl ctee Br Wool Mktg Bd 1987- (memb 1959-), cncl memb Royal Ulster Agric Soc 1969-73, tstee Agric Res Inst for NI 1963-86, dir UK Wool Growers Fedn 1977-83, chm mgmnt ctee Irvinestown and Dist Attested Sales 1982-, exec ctee memb Ulster Agric Orgns Soc 1962-65, dir and vice-chm Ulster Wool GP 1981-; vice-chm and fndn memb Western Educn and Library Bd 1973-85, chm Library and Info Servs Cncl NI 1983-85, memb Br Library Advsy Cncl 1984-85, Gen Synod Church of Ireland 1972- (memb bd of educn 1989); dist cmmr of Scouts 1957-62; govr Duke of Westminster HS 1975-; vice-chm of govrs Enniskillen Collegiate Sch 1983- and Enniskillen HS 1982-; memb: Enniskillen RDC 1965-67 Fermanagh CC 1967-73 (chm planning ctee 1968-73, fndr memb and chm museum ctee 1969-73); memb Fermanagh DC 1985- (chm planning ctee); vice-pres (later pres) Ballinamallard Young Unionists 1963-73; exec ctee memb Fermangh Unionist Assoc 1981-: memb Fermanagh and S Tyrone Unionist Cncl 1981- (exec memb 1985-); *Recreations* outdoor pursuits, genealogy, local history; *Clubs* Fermanagh; *Style*— Warren Loane, Esq, DL; Crocknacrieve, Enniskillen, NI (☎ 0365 81 214)

LOBANOV-ROSTOVSKY, Prince John; s of Prince Constantine Lobanov-Rostovsky, of Hove; *m* 1956 (m dis 1980), Princess Roxane Bibica Rosetti (*see Bibica Rosetti, Princess Raoul*); 2 s, 1 da; *Style*— Prince John Lobanov-Rostovsky

LOBANOV-ROSTOVSKY, Princess Roxane; *née* Bibica-Rosetti; da of Prince Raoul Bibica Rosetti and Dorothy, *née* Baroness Acton (*see* Princess Raoul Bibica Rosetti); *b* 3 Oct 1932; *Educ* St George's Ascot, Carlton Univ Ottawa; *m* 1956 (m dis 1980), Prince John Lobanov-Rostovsky, yr s of Prince Constantine Lobanov-Rostovsky, of Hove; 2 s (Prince Paul b 1956, Prince Dimitry b 1962), 1 da (Princess Helena b 1964); *Career* watercolourist and sculptor, memb Soc of Women Artists; *Style*— Princess Roxane Lobanov-Rostovsky; Swallowdale, 67 Woodruff Ave, Hove, Sussex BN3 6PJ

LOBB, Eric; s of William Hunter Lobb (d 1916), and Betsy, *née* Smerdon (d 1956); family Bootmaking business founded 1849; *b* 3 Mar 1907; *Educ* UCS Hampstead, Pembroke Coll Oxford (MA); *m* 1949 (m dis), Miss Denby; 1 s (Edward), 1 da (Alice); *Career* private in the Home Guard; master bootmaker; chm and md John Lobb Ltd; pres West End Master Bootmakers Assoc; holds Royal Warrants for: HM the Queen, HRH the Duke of Edinburgh, HRH the Prince of Wales; Jubilee Medal; *Books* The Last Shall Be First, History of John Lobb, Bootmaker, by Brian Dobbs; *Recreations* small farming, laughter and the love of friends; *Clubs* Little Ship; *Style*— Eric Lobb, Esq; Newlands, Radlett, Herts WD7 8EH (☎ Radlett 6311), 9 St James's Street, SW1 A1ET (☎ 01 930 3664/5)

LOBB, Howard Leslie Vicars; CBE (1952); s of Hedley Vicars Lobb (d 1950); *b* 9 Mar 1909; *Educ* privately, Regent Street Poly Sch of Architecture; *m* 1949, Charmian Isobel, da of Charles Oliver Callcott Reilly, MBE (d 1970); 3 s; *Career* sr ptnr Howard Lobb Ptnrship 1950-74, chm Cncl for Architecture, Town Planning and Building Res of The Festival of Br, and later controller of Construction of the South Bank Exhibition 1951; architect Br Pavilion, Brussels Expo 1958, gold medal award; architect for numerous schools, nuclear and oil fired stations, motorway serv areas, offs, flats and other bldgs; chm Architects' Benevolent Soc 1952-89 (vice-pres), memb cncl RYA 1977-80; chm Solent Protection Soc 1982-; FRIBA, CEng, AIStructE, FRSA; *Recreations* sailing, model railways, painting; *Clubs* Arts, Royal Corinthian YC (vice cdre 1960-63), Royal Lymington YC, Tamesis (cdre 1954-57); *Style*— Howard Lobb, Esq, CBE; Shallows Cottage, Pilley Hill, Pilley, Lymington, SO41 5QF (☎ Lym 77595)

LOBBENBERG, (John) Peter; s of Hans Lobbenberg (d 1955), and Annemarie, *née* Rabl (d 1971); *b* 12 Sept 1939; *Educ* Leighton Park Sch, Oriel Coll Oxford (MA); *m* 14 Dec 1969, Naomi, da of Ronald Green (d 1985); 1 s (David b 1971); 1 da (Anna b 1974); *Career* CA; ptnr in Clark Whitehill, chm Electronic Machine Co plc; dir Br Uralitc plc; govr The Purcell Sch; *Style*— Peter Lobbenberg, Esq; Clark Whitehill, 25 New Street Square, London EC4A 3LN (☎ 01 353 1577, telex 887422, fax 01 583 1720)

LOBLE, George Frederick; JP (1967 Gateshead); s of Frederick Loble (d 1956), and Elsa, *née* Fried (d 1982); *b* 25 Sept 1926; *Educ* Rutherford Coll of Technol Newcastle-upon-Tyne, Regent St Poly London (HNC); *m* 12 April 1953, Eve Marion, da of Frederick Heinemann, of London; 1 s (Peter Frederick b 1958), 1 da (Monica Frances b 1955); *Career* chm and md Loblite Ltd 1965-, memb ctee of mgmnt of various local charities 1960-, chm Gateshead Cncl of Social Service 1965-75, govr Special Schools in Gateshead 1965-, tstee John Haswell Housing Tst 1965-, pres Rotary Club of Gateshead 1968-69, tstee Rotary Club 50 Anniv Tst (Gateshead) 1971-, memb: Tech Ctees of Br Electrical Apparatus Mfrs Assoc 1976-, memb Tech Ctees of the Br Standards Inst 1980-; dep chm Juvenile Bench, Gateshead CEng, MIMechE, MIQA, FInstPet, MInstD, FRSA; *Recreations* mountain walking, skiing, photography, voluntary organisations; *Style*— George Loble, Esq, JP; 5 Kenton Ave, Newcastle-upon-Tyne NE3 4JB (☎ 091 285 2547); Loblite Ltd, Third Ave, Team Valley Trading Estate, Gateshead, Tyne & Wear NE11 0QQ (☎ 091 487 8103, telex 537358 LOBLIT G)

LOBO, Hon Sir Rogerio (Roger) Hyndman; CBE (1978, OBE 1972), JP; s of Dr P J Lobo and Branca Helena, *née* Hyndman; *b* 15 Sept 1923; *Educ* Escola Central Macao, Seminario de S Jose Macao, Liceu Nacional Infante Dom Henrique Macao, La Salle Coll Hong Kong; *m* 1947, Margaret Mary, *née* Choa; 5 s, 5 da; *Career* chm P J Lobo & Co Ltd Hong Kong 1950-; kt 1985 for public servs in Hong Kong; *Style*— Sir Roger Lobo, CBE; Woodland Heights, E1, 2 Wongneichong Gap Rd, Hong Kong

LOCH, Hon Allegra Helen; da of 3 Baron Loch (d 1982), and his 4 w, Sylvia Barbara (who m 3, 1984, Richard G P Hawkins), da of Alexander Gordon Beauchamp Cameron, of Delmahoy, Midlothian, and formerly w of Christopher Beauchamp-Wilson; *b* 14 Oct 1982; *Style*— Hon Allegra Loch

LOCH, Hon Sara Nan; only surviving child of 4 Baron Loch, MC, by his 1 w, Rachel; *b* 25 Oct 1949; *Style*— The Hon Sara Loch

LOCH, 4 Baron (UK 1895); Spencer Douglas Loch; MC (1945); yr s of 2 Baron Loch, CB, CMG, DSO, MVO (d 1942), and Lady Margaret Compton, o da of 5 Marquess of Northampton; suc bro, 3 Baron Loch, 1982; *b* 12 August 1920; *Educ* Wellington, Trinity Coll Cambridge; *m* 1, 1948, Hon Rachel (d 1976), da of Baroness Lucas of Crudwell and Dingwall (9 and 12 holder of Baronies respectively) and Gp Capt Howard Lister Cooper, AFC, RAF; 1 da (and 2 s decd); m 2, 1979, Davina Julia, formerly w of Sir Richard James Boughey, 10 Bt, and da of FitzHerbert Wright and Hon Doreen, *née* Wingfield, only da of 8 Viscount Powerscourt; *Career* serv Maj Gren Gds NW Europe 1944-45; barr Lincoln's Inn 1948; *Clubs* Beefsteak, Cavalry and Guards'; *Style*— The Rt Hon the Lord Loch, MC; Lochluichart by Garve, Ross; Bratton House, Westbury, Wilts

LOCHRANE, (Francis Henry Alastair Julian) John; s of Charles Damien Lochrane, MD, FRCS(E), FRCOG (d 1956), of Derby, and Phoebe Sybil Mansel, *née* Porter, MBE; *b* 11 June 1919; *Educ* Ampleforth, Christ Church Oxford (MA); *m* 10 Sept 1955, Rosemary, da of Clarence Edward Victor Buxton, MC (d 1973), of Limuru, Kenya; *Career* serv 4 Bn Seaforth Highlanders 1939-45 (POW 1940-45) Germany; Maj 11 Bn Seaforth Highlanders (TA) 1947-60; insur broker H Clarkson (Insur) Ltd, dir H Clarkson & Co (Midlands) Insur Ltd 1954-66; memb of LLoyds; cncllr Derbyshire, ret; *Recreations* fishing; *Clubs* Army & Navy; *Style*— John Lochrane, Esq; The Corner House, Mapleton, nr Ashbourne, Derbyshire (☎ 033 529 267)

LOCK, (George) David; s of George Wilfred Lock (d 1943); *b* 24 Sept 1929; *Educ* Haileybury, Queens' Coll Cambridge (MA); *m* 1965, Ann Elizabeth, da of Sidney Harold Biggs; 4 s, 1 da; *Career* Br Tabulating Co Ltd (now ICL) 1954-59, Save & Prosper Gp Ltd 1959-69, American Express 1969-74, Private Patients Plan 1974-85 (md 1975-85); dir plan for active retirement Frizzell Insur and Fin Servs Ltd 1986-; sec Frizzell Fndn 1988-; memb RSM; Freeman Worshipful Co of Barber Surgns; memb RSM,; *Recreations* bridge, music, entertaining, family activities; *Style*— David Lock, Esq; Plan for Active Retirement, Frizzell House, County Gates, Poole, Dorset BH13 6BH (☎ 0202 292333); Buckhurst Place, Horsted Keynes, W Sussex RH17 7AH (☎ Danehill (0825) 790599)

LOCK, Lt Cdr Sir (John) Duncan; s of Brig-Gen F R E Lock, DSO; *b* 5 Feb 1918; *Educ* RNC Dartmouth; *m* 1947, (Alice) Aileen Smith (d 1982); 3 da; *Career* serv regular offr in RN 1931-58, WWII: Battle of the Atlantic, Norwegian and N African campaigns, Pacific War, Normandy and Anzio landings; farmed family estate in Somerset 1958-61; specialist in magnetic compasses Admiralty Compass Observatory 1961-83; memb: Lloyd's, Eton RDC 1967-74; chm Bucks branch RDC Assoc 1969-74, memb S Bucks Dist Cncl 1973-; chm: S Bucks Dist Cncl 1985-87, Assoc of Dist Cncls of England and Wales 1974-79 (chm Bucks branch 1974-); Br rep Cncl of Local and Regnl Auths of Europe 1979-, Local Auths Mgmnt Servs and Computer Ctee 1981-1986, rep Body for England 1976-; kt 1978; *Recreations* gardening, shooting; *Style*— Lt Cdr Sir Duncan Lock, RN; Fen Ct, Oval Way, Gerrards Cross, Bucks SL9 8QD (☎ 0753 882467)

LOCK, Dr Stephen Penford; s of Wallace Henry Lock (d 1968), and Edith Mary Bailey; *b* 8 April 1929; *Educ* City of London Sch, Queens' Coll Cambridge, St Bartholomew's Hosp (MA, MD, MSc); *m* 1955, Shirley Gillian, da of Edwin Walker; 1 s (Adam), 1 da (Imogen); *Career* ed Br Med Journal; offr first class White Rose of Finland; *Recreations* trying to learn Russian and the harpsichord; *Clubs* Athenaeum; *Style*— Dr Stephen Lock; 115 Dulwich Village, London SE21 7BJ (☎ 01 693 6317); BMA House, Tavistock Sq, London WC1H 9JR

LOCK-NECREWS, John Ernest; s of William Ernest Necrews (d 1982), and Mary Constance, *née* Lock (d 1987); *b* 30 August 1939; *Educ* Bridgend GS, Univ of Wales (Dip Arch); *m* 3 Jan 1978, Daphne, da of Maj Stanley Dickinson, of Cardiff; 1 s (Christian b 1979); *Career* CA; jt chm Hoggett Lock-Necrews plc; chm Central Branch Soc of Architects Wales 1981-82 (cncl memb 1974-82); architectural awards: Prince of Wales, Civic Tst, Times/RICS, Cardiff 2000, Lord Mayors civic award; guest speaker on architectural conservation UNESCO World Congress Basle 1983; ARIBA, AC Inst Arb, FFB; *Recreations* golf, skiing, painting; *Clubs* Carlton, Cardiff and Co, Royal Porthcawl GC; *Style*— John E Lock-Necrews, Esq; Bishopsgate, Howells Crescent, Llandaff, Cardiff; Trafalgar House, Waterloo Place, London (☎ 01 930 7996, car ☎ 0860 702861)

LOCKE, (Harry) Brian; s of Henry William Locke (d 1982) of New Earswick, York, and Mary *née* Moore (d 1972); *b* 28 May 1924; *Educ* Bootham Sch York, Imperial Coll London; *m* 1, 19 Feb 1949, (m dis 1974), Margaret Beven, da of Thomas William King (d 1962), of Barnet; 1 s (Richard b 28 March 1961), 3 da (Sarah b 1 July 1952 (Mrs Watson), Frances b 20 Jan 1954, Judith b 22 April 1958); m 2 3 Jan 1976, Marie Patricia Keegan, 1 step s (Michael b 18 July 1962); *Career* WWII serv Friends Ambulance Unit 1942-46; chem engr: Johnson Matthey Ltd 1948-49, Kestner Evaporator Ltd 1949-50, Miny of Power 1950-58, NCB 1958-65; mangr indus chemistry NRDC 1965-78, md Combustion Systems Ltd 1974-78; dir: Formed Coke Ltd 1975-78, Cadogan Cnslts, int energy mgmnt 1978-; Electrolysis Energy Ltd 1979-83, Chemplant Stainless Ltd 1980-84; dep chm Cadogan Mgmnt Ltd 1989-, (chm 1984-88); special serv UN Agencies as coal specialist 1980-; received: Melchett Award Design & Indus Assoc 1987, spl award Inst Energy 1987; memb Econ & Social Affairs ctee UN Assoc; memb for Br The Club of Rome, govr Paddington Coll, memb cncl Inst of Energy, memb exec The Watt Ctee on Energy, memb low grade coal ctee World Energy Conference, chm chemical engrg & fuel technol dept liaison ctee Sheffield Univ, hon advst Int Soc for Educn Information Japan, hon sec Design & Technol Educn Assoc, vice-pres & hon sec Old Centralians The Imperial Coll Engrg Alumus Assoc, memb Br Standards Inst (chm ctee Assessing Thermal Performance of Boilers) Freeman City of London 1984, Liveryman Worshipful Co of Engrs 1984; FCGI 1987, FIChemE 1948, FInstE 1953, FIGasE 1966, FIOD 1974, MConsE 1985;

Books Industrial Fuel Efficiency (Annually 1957-85), Modern Motoring Handbook (Annually 1959-82), Coal (Jointly 1965); *Recreations* Bentleys, Nat Tst, silver, origins of thought; *Clubs* Athenaeum, Royal Automobile; *Style*— Brian Locke, Esq; Cadogan Consultants, Court House, Bisley, Glos GL6 7AA (☎ 0452 770 010, fax 0452 770 058); Cardogan Consultants, 37a Cadogan Str, London, SW3 2PR (☎ 01 589 9778); Cadogan Management Ltd, London House, 53-54 Haymarket, London, SW1Y 4PR (☎ 01 930 4241, fax 01 930 6993, telex 8950049 CADOGN G)

LOCKE, John Howard; CB (1984); s of Percy John Howard Locke and Josephine Alice, *née* Marshfield; *b* 26 Dec 1923; *Educ* Hymers Coll Hull, Queen's Coll Oxford (MA); *m* 1948, Eirene Sylvia Sykes; 2 da (Diana, Imogen); *Career* MAFF 1945-65; under-sec: Cabinet Off 1965-66, Miny of Transport 1966-68, Dept of Employment and Productivity 1968-71; dep-sec Dept of Employment 1971-74, dir Health & Safety Exec 1975-83; chm Nat Examination Bd in Occupational Safety and Health 1986-; *Recreations* mountain walking, gardening, squash; *Style*— John Locke, Esq, CB; 4 Old Palace Terrace, The Green, Richmond-on-Thames, TW9 1NB (☎ 01 940 1830); Old Box Trees, East Preston, Sussex (☎ 0903 785 154)

LOCKET, David Frank; s of late Frank Barton Locket, and Phyllis Jesie, *née* Lawson; *b* 29 June 1940; *Educ* Haileybury ISC Hertford, Battersea Coll of Technol; *m* 24 Sept 1966, (Ingegerd) Christina, da of Ake Bontell, of Sweden; 1 s (Martin Frank b 1970), 1 da (Annicka Louise b 1972); *Career* Savoy Hotel London, Strand Hotels London 1972-78, catering mgr Anchor Hotels London 1978-83, md LMS (Conslts) Ltd 1983; ctee memb Veteran Car Club GB; clerk to Master Innholders Assoc; Freeman City of London 1973; FHCIMA, MCFA; *Recreations* veteran cars, fishing, shooting, clocks; *Style*— David Locket, Esq; Pinecrest, Northdown Rd, Woldingham, Surrey CR3 7AA (☎ 088 385 3681)

LOCKETT, His Hon Judge Reginald; s of George Alfred Lockett and Emma, *née* Singleton; *b* 24 June 1933; *Educ* Ashton-in-Makerfield GS, Manchester Univ, London Univ; *m* 1959, Edna, *née* Lowe; 1 s, 1 da; *Career* slr 1955, asst coroner Wigan 1963-70, dist and Co Ct registrar Manchester 1970-81, rec Crown Ct 1978-81, circuit judge Northern circuit 1981-; vice-pres Boys Bde 1978- (dist pres NW 1973-), lay reader C of E; memb Co Ct Rule Ctee 1985-, co-ed Butterworths Family Law Services; *Style*— His Hon Judge Lockett; c/o Sessions House, Lancaster Rd, Preston

LOCKHART *see also*: Sinclair-Lockhart

LOCKHART; *see*: Macdonald Lockhart

LOCKHART, Brian Alexander; s of John Arthur Hay Lockhart and Norah, *née* Macneil, of Quadrant Rd, Glasgow; *b* 1 Oct 1942; *Educ* Glasgow Acad, Glasgow Univ (BL); *m* 1967, Christine Ross, da of James B Clark, of Ayr; 2 s, 2 da; *Career* slr; ptnr Robertson Chalmers & Auld 1964-79; sheriff: N Strathclyde 1979-81, Glasgow and Strathkelvin 1981-; *Recreations* fishing, golf, squash, family; *Clubs* Royal Scottish Automobile; *Style*— Brian Lockhart, Esq; 18 Hamilton Ave, Glasgow (☎ 041 427 1921); Sheriff Court, Glasgow (☎ 041 429 8888)

LOCKHART, (Harry) Eugene, Jr; s of Harry Eugene Lockhart, Sr, of Austin, Texas, USA, and Gladys Cummings Lockhart (d 1982); *b* 4 Nov 1949; *Educ* Univ of Virginia (BS, MBA)J; *m* 8 June 1974, Terry, da of Frederick Bon Jasperson, of Washington DC, USA; 1 s (Andrew Jasperson b 13 July 1977), 3 da (Julia Cummings b 9 Oct 1979, Victoria MacLaren b 15 Sept 1984, Charlotte Carson b 9 April 1987); *Career* md Nolan Norton and Co 1980-82, gp dir C T Bowring and Co 1982-85, md First Manhattan Bank 1985-87, chief exec ops and dir Midland Bank 1987-, dep chm Thomas Cook Gp; FCA; *Recreations* tennis, golf, running, skiing, photography, riding; *Clubs* St Georges Hill, Liphook, Vanderbilt; *Style*— Eugene Lockhart, Esq, Jr; 29 Kensington Gate, London W8 (☎ 01 584 3792); Road Farm, Churt, Surrey; Poultry, London EC2 (☎ 01 260 7358)

LOCKHART, Frank Roper; s of Clement Lockhart, of Braithwell, Yorks, and Betsy Lockhart, *née* Roper (d 1981); *b* 8 Dec 1931; *Educ* King Edward VI GS, Retford, Doncaster GS, Leeds Univ (LLB); *m* 5 Aug 1957, Brenda Harriett, da of Cyril Johnson (d 1985), of Greenways, Woodlands, nr Doncaster; 1 s (John Michael Roper b 1961), 1 da (Jeanette Anne b 1959); *Career* slr ptnr with Jefferies slrs; Rec 1985; chm Industl Tbnls 1983; chm Soc Security tbnls 1970-; *Recreations* golf, tennis, squash; *Clubs* Thorpe Hall GC; *Style*— Frank R Lockhart, Esq; Jefferies, slrs, 41, Victoria Ave, Southend-on-Sea, Essex (☎ 0702 332311, telex 885353, fax 332807)

LOCKHART, Geoffrey John Charles; s of George Arthur Lockhart (d 1961), of Christchurch, Hants, and Margaret Helen, *née* Sutton (d 1982); *b* 16 April 1926; *Educ* Truro Cathedral Sch; *m* 19 Feb 1960, Dodie Mary, da of John Walter Cooper (d 1958), of Brighton; 2 da (Juliet Caroline b 1963, Joanna Helen b 1964); *Career* CA; dir of several local family cos, ptnr Bland Fielden 1965 (sr ptnr 1982-); cncl memb: for E Anglia ICAEW 1977, Assoc of Accounting Technicians 1980- (pres 1985-86); chm of govrs St Mary's Sch Colchester 1970, FCA; *Recreations* cricket, golf, gardening, reading, sport generally; *Clubs* MCC; *Style*— Geoffrey Lockhart, Esq; Chandlers, Nayland, Colchester, Essex CO6 4LA (☎ 0206 262617); 18 Sir Isaacs Walk, Colchester CO1 1JL (☎ 0206 48811)

LOCKHART, Ian Stuart; s of Rev Prebendary Douglas Stuart Mullinger Lockhart (d 1983) and Hilda Mary, *née* Walker; *b* 9 Nov 1940; *Educ* Rugby, Clare Coll Cambridge (MA); *m* 30 Nov 1974, Rosanna, da of Capt Edward Hugh Cartwright of The White House, Osmington, Weymouth, Dorset; *Career* admitted slr 1967; ptnr Peake & Co 1969-; dir Wynnstay Properties plc and assoc cos; govr St Mary's Sch Wantage; ctee memb Clergy Orphan Corpn, memb Ct of Assts Corpn of The Sons of The Clergy; memb Worshipful Co of Tylers & Brick Layers Livery 1974; *Clubs* Athenaeum; *Style*— Ian S Lockhart, Esq; 9 Marlborough Hill, London NW8 0NN; c/o Peake & Co, 7-9 St James's St, London SW1A 1EE (☎ 01 839 6171, fax 01 930 3933, telex 25987)

LOCKHART, James Duncan; s of James Jackson Lockhart (d 1974); *b* 3 Oct 1933; *Educ* HS of Glasgow, Glasgow Univ; *m* 1964, Joyce, da of Harold Walter Oakley (d 1955); 2 da; *Career* Capt Army; md Tport Devpt Gp Ltd 1979-; *Style*— James Lockhart, Esq; c/o Transport Development Gp Ltd, Windsor House, 50 Victoria St, London SW1H 0NR

LOCKHART, Maj Simon Foster Macdonald; assumed surname of Lockhart, in lieu of Macdonald, by declaration 1946 on succeeding to estates of Lee, Carnwath and Dryden; s of John Ronald Moreton Macdonald (d 1921), of Largie Castle, Tayinloan, Argyllshire; *b* 1916; *Educ* Winchester, Magdalen Coll Oxford; *m* 1942, Ella Caitriona, da of Seton Gordon, of Upper Duntulm, Portree; 3 s, 1 da; *Career* serv WWII with The Lovat Scouts, Italy (wounded), Maj 1946, Lanarkshire Yeo (TA) 1947-49; DL (1950) JP (1950) Lanarkshire; dir Lawrie & Symington (Auctioneers) Ltd, Medwin sands, Largia Worklands; *Books* Seven Centuries-A History of the Lockharts of Lee and Cornwath, To My Pocket-A Personal Cash Book of an 18th Century Scottish Laird; *Recreations* gardening; *Style*— Maj Simon Macdonald Lockhart; Dunsyre House, Dunsyre, Lanark (☎ 089 981 260); Lee and Carnwath Estates, Estate Office, Carnwath, Lanark (☎ 055 584 273)

LOCKHART OF THE LEE, Angus Hew; recognised as Chief of the Name Lockhart by The Lord Lyon 1957; s of Maj Simon Foster Macdonald Lockhart of the Lee and Ella Catriona Gordon; *b* 17 August 1946; *Educ* Rannoch Sch Perths, N of Scotland Coll of Agric; *m* 1970, Susan Elizabeth, da of Hon William Normand (d 1967), s Baron Normand (Life Peer d 1962), and Hon Mrs William Norman *qv*; 1 s, 1 da; *Career* landowner; *Recreations* shooting, water-skiing, renovating cottages; *Clubs* New (Edinburgh); *Style*— Angus Lockhart of the Lee; Newholm, Dunsyre, Lanark ML11 8NQ (☎ 0968 82254); Lee and Carnwath Estates, Estate Office, Carnwath, Lanark (☎ 0555 840273)

LOCKHART-BALL, Hugh Frederick; s of Lt Cdr Alfred Ernest Ball, RN (d 1965), and Margaret Daphne, *née* Lockhart; *b* 18 April 1948; *Educ* Sedbergh, Birmingham Sch of Architecture, City of Birmingham Sch of Art and Design; *m* 1 April 1972 (m dis), Godelieve Antoinette; 1 s (Simon Hugh b 1976), 1 da (Amelia b 1979); *Career* architect; princ Lockhart-Ball Assoc 1981-, chm London Energy Gp 1983-; ctee memb UK section of Int Solar Energy Soc 1984-, cncl memb S London Soc of Architects 1979-, chm Tooting Traders Assoc 1986-; former pres Rotary Club of Tooting 1986; *Recreations* sketching, reading, photography, building, jazz and blues, wine and food; *Style*— Hugh Lockhart-Ball, Esq; 934 Garratt Lane, London SW17 0ND (☎ 01 767 6955, office 01 672 1056, fax 01 767 9401)

LOCKHART-MUMMERY, Christopher John; QC (1986); s of Sir Hugh Evelyn Lockhart-Mummery KCVO, (d 1988), of Duns House, Hannington, Basingstoke, Hants, and Elizabeth Jean, *née* Crerar (d 1981); *b* 7 August 1947; *Educ* Stowe, Trinity Coll Cambridge; *m* 4 Sept 1971, Elizabeth Rosamund, da of Neil Patrick Moncrieff Elles, of 75 Ashley Gardens, London, SW1; 1 s (Edward b 1975), 2 da (Clare b 1973, Alice b 1980); *Career* barr, QC 1986; *Books* specialist ed: Hill and Redman's Law of Landlord and Tenant (1973); *Recreations* fishing, gardening, opera; *Style*— Christopher J Lockhart-Mummery, Esq, QC; 52 Argyll Road, London, W8 7BS (☎ 01 937 1289); 2 Paper Bldgs, Temple, London, EC4 (☎ 01 353 5835, fax 01 583 1390, car tel 0860 353 348)

LOCKHART-MUMMERY, Hon Mrs (Elizabeth) Rosamund; *née* Elles; da of Baroness Elles (Life Peer) and Neil Patrick Moncrieff Elles; *b* 15 May 1947; *Educ* St Andrew's Univ (MA), Courtauld Inst, London Univ (MA); *m* 1971, Christopher John Lockhart-Mummery; 1 s, 2 da; *Style*— The Hon Mrs Lockhart-Mummery; 52 Argyll Rd, London W8 (☎ 01 937 1289)

LOCKHART-MURE, Thomas Ochterlon (Tom); s of Dr Thomas Valiant Lockhart-Mure (d 1925), and Isabella Dodds McGown (d 1941); *b* 25 August 1904; *Educ* Edinburgh Acad; *m* 18 July 1936, Sheila, da of John MacKinnon (d 1938); 3 s (Peter Thomas b 1941, John Kevin b 1945, James Edward b 1937, d 1965); *Career* Maj KAR serv Abyssinian Campaign (despatches); Cmd HQ Inspectorate of Mechanical Tport; ptnr Manchester Airways (A Barnstorming Co) 1923; dir: Kenyan Co rep General Motors prods 1924-, Airspray Kenya; former pres: AA of E Africa, Areo Club of E Africa; conslt Caspair Air Charter; *Recreations* rugby, hockey, cricket; *Clubs* Mt Kenya Safari, Mombasa, Nairobi, Aero (E Africa); *Style*— Tom Lockhart-Mure, Esq; Mawingo, Benenden, Cranbrook, Kent (☎ 0580 241722)

LOCKLEY, Ven Dr Harold; s of Harry Lockley (d 1936); *b* 16 July 1916; *Educ* Hinckley GS, London Univ (BA, BD, MTh), Westcott House Cambridge, Nottingham Univ (PhD); *m* 1947 Ursula Margaret Anneliese, da of Rev Dr Hans Wedell (d 1964); 3 s; *Career* deacon 1946, priest 1947, chaplain and lectr Loughborough Coll 1946-51, vicar of S Wigston 1951-58, residentiary canon and chllr of Leicester Cathedral 1958-63, vicar All Saints Leicester 1963-77, examining chaplain to Bishop of Leicester 1951-79, diocesan dir of training 1951-83, proctor in Convocation 1960-80, archdeacon of Loughborough 1963-86, archdeacon emeritus 1986-; postgraduate res Univ of Cambridge; *Recreations* walking, foreign travel, antiquarian interests; *Clubs* Leicestershire (Leicester); *Style*— The Ven Dr Harold Lockley; Emmanuel Coll, Cambridge CB2 3AP; 7 Dower House Gardens, Quorn, nr Loughborough, Leicestershire, LE12 8DE

LOCKWOOD, Arthur William; s of William Storm Lockwood (d 1971); *b* 11 May 1924; *Educ* Denstone Coll Staffs; *m* 1948, Heather, da of Maj William Rogerson, OBE, MC (d 1961); 1 s, 2 da; *Career* landowner and farmer; memb Lloyd's, chm Castle Hill Hldgs Ltd; master Burton Hunt 1959-; *Recreations* hunting, yachting (yacht TSDY 'Island Fox'); *Clubs* Carlton, RSrnYC; *Style*— Arthur Lockwood, Esq; Coach House, Spridlington, Lincoln (☎ 0673 61057); 6-7 Castle Hill, Lincoln (☎ 0522 22243)

LOCKWOOD, Baroness (Life Peer UK 1978); Betty; DL (W Yorks); da of late Arthur Lockwood; *b* 22 Jan 1924; *Educ* Eastborough Girls' Sch, Ruskin Coll Oxford; *m* 1978, Lt-Col Cedric Hall (d 1988), s of late George Hall; *Career* sits as Lab Peer in House of Lords; Yorks regnl women's offr Lab Pty 1952-67, chief woman offr and asst nat agent Lab Pty 1967-75, chm Equal Opportunities Cmmn 1975-83, chm EEC Advsy Ctee on Equal Opportunities for Women and Men 1982-83; pres Birkbeck Coll London Univ 1983-, memb: Advtg Standards Authy Cncl 1983-, Leeds Devpt Corpn 1988-; memb cncl: Univ of Bradford 1983- (pro-chllr 1988-), Univ of Leeds 1985-; hon fell: UMIST, Birbeck Coll; Hon DLitt Univ of Bradford, Hon DLL Univ of Strathclyde 1985; *Clubs* Soroptimist Int; *Style*— The Rt Hon the Lady Lockwood, DL; 6 Sycamore Drive, Addingham, Ilkley, W Yorks LS29 0NY (☎ 0943 831098)

LOCKWOOD, Graham Henry; s of Henry George Lockwood, of Ipswich, and Doris Evelyn, *née* Dawson; *b* 16 June 1935; *Educ* Carlisle GS; *m* 20 Oct 1962, Eileen Joyce, da of Arthur Dawkes; 2 da (Elaine b 1967, Fiona b 1970); *Career* actuary; exec dir Eagle Star Gp 1984- (gen mangr 1980-84); Freeman Worshipful Co of Actuaries; FIA 1964; *Recreations* music, squash, walking; *Style*— Graham Lockwood, Esq; Eagle Star Gp, 60 St Mary Axe, London EC3A 8BA (☎ 01 929 1111, fax 01 626 1266)

LOCKWOOD, Sir Joseph Flawith; *b* 14 Nov 1904; *Career* chm EMI Ltd 1954-74; dir: Nat Res Devpt Corpn 1951-67, Smith's Industs Ltd 1959-79, Beecham Gp 1966-75, Hawker Siddeley Gp 1964-77, Racecourse Hldgs Tst Ltd 1969, United Racecourses, Laird Gp Ltd 1970-, Young Vic Co (chm 1974-75); memb: Industl Reorgn Corpn 1966-71 (chm 1969-71), cncl Imperial Soc of Knights Bachelor, Arts Cncl 1965-70; chm: Royal Ballet Sch Endowment Fund and Govrs 1960-78, Royal Ballet Sch 1960-78, The Royal Ballet 1971-85; vice-pres Central Sch of Speech and

Drama 1968-; CIEE; kt 1960; *Clubs* Carlton; *Style*— Sir Joseph Lockwood; c/o Lockwoods Foods Ltd, Bridge Rd, Long Sutton, Spalding, Lincs PE12 9EQ

LOCKYER-NIBBS, John Brian; s of Gerald Norman Henry Lockyer-Nibbs (d 1978), and Ella Nora Cook; *b* 1 July 1934; *Educ* St Paul's; *m* Diana, da of Bernard Murray Davis, of Cobham, Surrey; 2 da (Caroline Alison b 20 May 1963, Vanessa Anne b 16 Aug 1965); *Ccreer* CA; cncllr Guildford Borough 1983-87, cncl chm Normandy Parish; *Recreations* horses in various activities; *Style*— John Lockyer-Nibbs, Esq; South Lodge, Westwood, Normandy, Guildford, Surrey (☎ 0483 811092); Welbeck House, High St, Guildford, Surrey (☎ 0483 503059, telex 859643 (PAY DAY), fax 0483 66761)

LODER, Hon Christina Anne; da of 3 Baron Wakehurst, *qv*, and Ingeborg Krumbholz-Hess (d 1977); *b* 13 Dec 1959; *Educ* Millfield, RCA London (MDes); *Clubs* No.2 Brydges Place; *Style*— The Hon Christina Loder; No.2 Brydges Place, Covent Garden, London WC1 (☎ 01 836 1436)

LODER, Edmund Jeune; s and h of Sir Giles Rolls Loder, 3 Bt; *b* 26 June 1941; *Educ* Eton; *m* 1966 (m dis 1971), Penelope Jane, da of Ivo Forde; 1 da; *Career* FCA; *Style*— Edmund Loder, Esq; Eyrefield Lodge, The Curragh, Co Kildare

LODER, Sir Giles Rolls; 3 Bt (UK 1887), JP (Sussex), DL (W Sussex 1977); s of Capt Robert Egerton Loder (ka 1917); suc gf, Sir Edmund Giles Loder, 2 Bt, 1920; *b* 1914; *Educ* Eton, Trinity Coll Cambridge (MA); *m* 1939, Marie, only da of Capt Bertram Hanmer Bunbury Symons-Jeune (d 1963), of Runnymede Hse, Old Windsor; 2 s; *Heir* s, Edmund Jeune Loder; *Career* serv 98 Surrey and Sussex Yeo Field Bde RA, 2 Lt 1935, Lt 1938; memb Horsham RDC 1947-68 (chm 1963-68), High Sheriff Sussex 1948-49; memb cncl Royal Horticulture Soc VMH 1951-85; *Recreations* horticulture, yachting; *Clubs* Royal Yacht Squadron (Cowes); *Style*— Sir Giles Loder, Bt; Ockenden House, Cuckfield, Haywards Heath, Sussex

LODER, Hon James David Gerald; s of 2 Baron Wakehurst, KG; *b* 1928; *Educ* Geelong C of E GS Victoria, Trinity Coll Cambridge; *Career* Coldstream Gds RARO; barr Inner Temple 1953; OStJ; *Style*— The Hon James Loder; 3l Lennox Gdns, SWI

LODER, Lady (Jean Arnot); *née* Maxwell; da of G Arnot Maxwell, QC; *m* 1924, Sir Louis Francis Loder (d 1972); *Style*— Lady Loder; 20 Hillcrest Ave, Kew, Victoria, Australia 310l

LODER, Hon Robert Beauclerk; s of 2 Baron Wakehurst, KG; *b* 24 April 1934; *Educ* Eton, Trinity Coll Cambridge (MA); *m* 1973, Josette, da of Joseph Bromovsky, of Otmanach, Pischeldoff, Karnten, Austria; 1 s (Jan), 1 da (Nell); *Career* farmer 1966-; dir: Transcontinental Servs Gp NV 1970- (formerly Esperanza Ltd), Precious Metals Tst 1981-, Sheringham Hldgs Ltd 1982-; chm Mental Health Fndn 1982-; *Clubs* Beefsteak, Buck's; *Style*— The Hon Robert Loder; 14 Ladbroke Grove, London W11; Curtis Brown, 162-168 Regent St, London W1 (☎ 01 437 9700)

LODER, Hon Timothy Walter; s and h of 3 Baron Wakehurst, *qv*, and Ingeborg Krumbholz-Hess (d 1977); *b* 28 Mar 1958; *Educ* Millfield; *m* 1987, Susan E Hurst; *Style*— The Hon Timothy Loder; 26 Wakehurst Rd, London SW11 6BY

LODER-SYMONDS, Roderick (Roddy) Francis; s of Brig Robert Guy Loder-Symonds, DSO, MC (d 1945), of Three Chimneys, Heytesbury, Warminster, Wilts, and the late Merlin Audrey Houghton Brown, *née* Allen; *b* 16 Nov 1938; *Educ* Radley, Royal Agric Coll Cirencester; *m* 20 July 1987, Caroline Anne, da of Cdr Mel Beebee (d 1988), of Womaston House, Presteigne, Powys; 2 s (Robert b 1971, James b 1974), 1 da (Sacha b 1968); *Career* ptnr Strutt & Parker 1976- (joined 1973); chm: Farmers' Club 1976, Kent Branch Country Landowners' Assoc 1985-86, Canterbury Farmers' Club 1984; bd memb East Kent Enteprise Agency 1986-; FRICS 1976; *Style*— Roddy Loder-Symonds, Esq; Denne Hill Farm, Womenswold, Canterbury, Kent CT4 6HD (☎ 0227 831203); Strutt & Parker, 2 St Margaret's St, Canterbury, Kent CT1 2TP (☎ 0227 451123)

LODGE, Dr Brian Robert William; s of Bertram Hugh Cleverly Lodge (d 1967), of 10 the Vale, Golders Green, London NW11, and Gwendolin Olive Theodosia, *née* Burford (d 1963); *b* 15 May 1925; *Educ* Univ Coll Sch Hamstead, London Hosp Med Sch (MRCS, LRCP); *m* 15 Dec 1954, Kathleen, da of Ernest Herbert Fox (d 1951), of Bunwell, Norfolk; *Career* temp conslt physician in geriatric medicine Utd Oxford Hosps and Oxford Regnl Hosp Bd 1965-71, conslt physician in geriatric and psychogeriatric medicine Leics Dist Health Authy 1971-, chm specialist planning gp (elderly and severly mentally impaired) Mental Health Unit Leics Health Authy, memb exec ctee Age Concern Leics, vice chm MINK Hinckley, Leics; memb: exec ctee Br Assoc for Services to the Elderly (BASE) 1988; steering gp for quadruple support for dementia Hinckley Leics Health Authy, Br Geriartrics Soc; Health and Social Serv Jl Jt Care Award 1983; FRSM; *Books* Coping With Caring Mind (1981), Living Well Into Old Age Kings Fund (jtly 1986), Handbook of Mental Disorders In Old Age (1988); *Recreations* walking, theatre, concerts, books; *Style*— Dr Brian Lodge; Carlton Hayes Hosp, Narborough, Leics LE9 5ES (☎ 0533 863481)

LODGE, Bubble; da of David Albert Ainley Lodge, of York and Judith Anne, *née* Pennicard; *b* 24 May 1964; *Educ* Queen Margaret's Sch Escrick Park York, Bretton Hall Coll W Bretton, Leeds Univ (BA); *Career* admin and VIP host Nat Student Drama Festival Swansea 1985, co-organiser Nat Symposium of Youth Theatres Nottingham 1985, box off and co mangr Nat Student Theatre Co Edinburgh Festival 1985, first female asst mangr Stoll Moss Theatres (The London Palladium, Her Majesty's Theatre, Victoria Palace Theatre) 1986, house mangr The Globe Theatre, gen mangr The Theatre Comedy Co Ltd Shaftesbury Theatre 1988, exec dir Springboard Theatre Co 1988; Young Cons Assoc York 1981-83; teaching linguistically disadvantaged children 1982, Roteracy Club 1982-84, external affairs off Bretton Hall Coll SU 1984-85; *Recreations* swimming, skiing, riding, dance, theatre, art, piano; *Clubs* Friend of the Br Theatre, Hon Memb: The Theatre; *Style*— Miss Bubble Lodge; Holmefield Court, Belsize Grove, London NW 3TT; Rowancourt, Grantham Drive, York YO2 4TZ; The Theatre of Comedy Co Ltd, The Shaftesbury Theatre, Shaftesbury Ave, London WC2H 8DP (☎ 01 379 3345, fax 01 240 0961)

LODGE, (John) Gordon; s of Abraham Gordon Lodge (d 1944), and Ivy, *née* Robertshaw; *b* 9 May 1944; *Educ* Bradford GS; *m* 3 Oct 1967, Diana Maureen, da of Nelson George Harrison, of 5 Langley Grove, Binsley, West York; 2 s (Alastair b 1973, James b 1977); *Career* Bradford & Bingley Bldg Soc: joined 1961, devpt mangr 1976-79, regnl mangr 1979-82, asst gen mangr personnel & trg 1982-87, gen mangr devpt of branch & agency network 1987-; pres Bradford GS, tres Shipley GC, your Cottingley Sch, dir Beckfoot Estate Co; FBIM 1980-, memb Bldg Soc Inst 1964; *Recreations* golf, bridge, climbing, fell walking; *Clubs* Shipley GC; *Style*— Gordon Lodge, Esq; Bradford & Bingley Building Soc, Main St, Binsley, West Yorks (☎ 0274 56 8111)

LODGE, Jane Ann; da of John Humphrey Lodge (d 1984), of York, and Marian, *née* Smith; *b* 1 April 1955; *Educ* Mill Mount GS York, Univ of Birmingham (BSc); *m* 2 July 1983, Anthony (Tony) John Borton, s of Reginal Aubrey Borton (d 1980), of Rugby; 1 s (John Aubrey b 1988); *Career* Touche Ross & Co Birmingham: trainee accountant 1973, qualified 1976 ptnr 1986; ctee memb Birmingham & W Midlands Soc of Chartered Accountants 1987-(chm Young Chartered Accountants Gp 1986-88); Univ of Birmingham: memb cncl 1986-, pres guild of graduates 1987-88, memb strategy planning and resources ctee 1987; ACA 1976; *Recreations* cookery, tapestry, golf; *Style*— Ms Jane Lodge; Touche Ross & Co, Kensington House, 136 Suffolk St, Queensway, Birmingham B1 1LL (☎ 021 631 2288, fax 021 631 4512, telex 338876 TRBHAM G)

LODGE, John Stuart; s of Edmund Roy Lodge (d 1961); *b* 30 April 1938; *Educ* Cranbrook Sch Sydney; *m* 1962, Peta, da of Sir Albert Robinson, KBE; 1 s, 2 da; *Career* Lt Far East 1958-59; int security specialist; *Recreations* hunting, tennis; *Clubs* Brooks's; *Style*— John Lodge, Esq; 20 Cadgan Lane, London SW1; Daglingworth Place, Cirencester, Glos GL7 7HU

LODGE, Oliver Raymond William Wynlayne; s of Oliver William Foster Lodge (d 1955), of Cud Hill House, Upton St Leonard's, Glos (s of late Sir Oliver Joseph Lodge and Winifred, *née* Wynlayne (d 1922) only da of late Sir William Nicholas Atkinson; *b* 2 Sept 1922; *Educ* Bryanston, King's Coll Camb (MA); *m* 17 Oct 1953, Charlotte, da of Col Arthur Davidson Young, CMG (d 1938), of St Margaret's, Twickenham; 1 s (Oliver b 1957), 2 da (Victoria b 1955, (Elizabeth) Lucy b 1960); *Career* Royal Fus 1942; barr Inner Temple 1945, practised Chancery Bar 1945-74, admitted *ad eundem* Lincolns Inn 1949, bencher 1973; perm chm Industl Tbnls 1975-80 (regnl chm 1980-); memb: Bar Cncl 1952-56 and 1967-71, Supreme Ct Rules Ctee 1968-71; gen cmmr of Income Tax Lincoln's Inn 1983-; *Recreations* walking, bell-ringing, reading history; *Clubs* Garrick; *Style*— Oliver Lodge, Esq; Southridge House, Hindon, Salisbury, Wilts; office: Central Off of the Industl Tbnls, 93 Ebury Bridge Rd, London SW1 (☎ 01 730 9161)

LODGE, Sir Thomas; s of James Lodge (d 1936), of Sheffield; *b* 25 Nov 1909; *Educ* Sheffield Univ; *m* 1940, Aileen, da of James Corduff, of Co Donegal; 1 s, 1 da; *Career* medical practitioner (ret); consultant radiologist United Sheffield Hospitals 1946-74; clinical lectr Sheffield Univ 1963-66; kt 1974; *Books* Recent Advances in Radiology (6th edn 1979); *Clubs* Royal Society of Medicine; *Style*— Sir Thomas Lodge; 46 Braemore Court, Kingsway, Hove, E Sussex BN3 4FG (☎ 0273 724371)

LOEFFLER, Frank; s of Ernst Loeffler (d 1967), and Bianka Klein, *née* Breitmann; *b* 21 Jan 1931; *Educ* Mill Hill, Gonville and Caius Coll Cambridge, London Hosp Med Coll (MB, BChir, FRCS, FRCOG); *m* 10 Aug 1958, Eva, da of Sir Ludwig Guttmann (d 1981), of High Wycombe and Aylesbury; 1 s (Mark b 1961), 2 da (Clare b 1959, Juliet b 1964); *Career* conslt: Central Middlesex Hosp 1967-68, St Mary's Hosp W2 1968-, Queen Charlotte's Hosp 1982-; ed British Journal of Obstetrics & Gynaecology 1973-80; memb Ctee on Safety of Medicines 1987-; memb Cncl Royal Coll of Obstetricians and Gynaecologists 1987-; *Recreations* sailing, skiing, theatre, music, tennis; *Clubs* Aldeburgh Yacht, Holland Park LTC; *Style*— Frank Loeffler, Esq; 25 Lansdowne Crescent, London W11 2NS (☎ 01 221 1662); St Mary's Hospital, London W2 (☎ 01 725 6666); 86 Harley St, W1 (☎ 01 486 2966)

LOEHNIS, Anthony David; CMG (1988); s of Cdr Sir Clive Loehnis, KCMG, RN (ret), and Rosemary, da of Hon Robert Ryder (ka 1917, s of 2 Earl of Harrowby, KG, PC, and Lady Mary Cecil, da of 2 Marqess of Exeter); *b* 12 Mar 1936; *Educ* Eton, New Coll Oxford, Harvard Univ; *m* 7 Aug 1965, Jennifer, da of Sir Donald Anderson; 3 s; *Career* with FCO to 1966; Schroder Wagg 1967-, assoc dir Bank of England 1980-81, exec dir 1981-; *Style*— Anthony Loehnis, Esq, CMG; Haughton House, Churchill, Oxon; Bank of England, Threadneedle St, London EC2

LOEWENSTEIN-WERTHEIM-FREUDENBERG, Prince Rupert Ludwig Ferdinand zu; also Count von Loewenstein-Scharffeneck; s of Prince Leopold zu Loewenstein-Wertheim-Freudenberg (d 1974; of the family of mediatised Princes, title of Bavarian Prince conferred 1812, stemming from the morganatic marriage of Elector Palatine Friedrich I (d 1476), with Klara Tott, of Augsburg; Counts of HRE 1494, recreated Loewenstein Scharffeneck 1875), and Countess Bianca Fischler von Treuberg; *b* 24 August 1933; *Educ* St Christopher's Letchworth, Magdalen Coll Oxford (MA); *m* 1957, Josephine Clare, da of Capt Montague Lowry-Corry (d 1977, gggs of 2 Earl Belmore) by his 1 w, Hon Mary Biddulph, yr da of 2 Baron Biddulph; 2 s (Prince Rudolf Amadeus b 1957, Prince Konrad Friedrich b 1958), 1 da (Princess Maria Theodora Marjorie b 1966); *Career* financial advsr, formerly merchant banker; Kt of Honour and Devotion SMO Malta 1980, Bailiff Grand Cross of Justice Constantine Order of St George, pres Br Assoc; *Recreations* music; *Clubs* Beefsteak, Boodle's, Buck's, Portland, Pratt's, White's; *Style*— Prince Rupert zu Loewenstein-Wertheim-Freudenberg; Pertersham Lodge, River Lane, Richmond, Surrey TW10 7AG (☎ 01 940 4442); Rupert Loewenstein Ltd, 2 King Street, London SW1Y 6QL (☎ 01 839 6454; telex, 291367 FINANZ; fax, 01 930 4032)

LOEWENTHAL, Lady; Anne June; da of James Stewart, MB (d 1961), of Maitland, NSW, and Ethel, *née* Humphries; *b* 1 Nov 1921; *Educ* Maitland Girls' High Sch, Library Sch Public Library of NSW; *m* 1944, Sir John Loewenthal, CMG, ED, FRCS, FRACS, FACS, sometime Prof and Chm Sydney Univ Surgery Dept (d 1979), son of A M Loewenthal, of Sydney (d 1945); 2 s (Andrew, Hugh), 2 da (Elspeth, Merran); *Career* Daily Telegraph Library 1940, Public Library of NSW 1941; VAD and Australian Army plc 1942-44; Bd of Sydney Home Nursing Service 1970-82, Divnl Cncl Red Cross Soc NSW 1982; hon life memb Australian Red Cross 1987; *Recreations* gardening, reading; *Clubs* Queens; *Style*— Lady Loewenthal; 82 Bendooley St, Bowral, NSW 2576 (☎ 048 61 1172); 8/45 Wharf Rd, Birchgrove, NSW 2041 (☎ 02 810 1277)

LOFTHOUSE, Geoffrey; JP (Pontefract 1970), MP (Lab) Pontefract and Castleford 1978-; s of Ernest Lofthouse (d 1935), and Emma Lofthouse (d 1944); *b* 18 Dec 1925; *Educ* Featherstone Primary and Secondary Schs, Whitwood Tech Coll, Leeds Univ; *m* 1946, Sarah, da of Joesh Thomas Onions; 1 da; *Career* Manpower Office NCB 1964-70, personnel mangr NCB Fryston 1970-78; memb: Pontefract Borough Dist Cncl 1962-74, Wakefield Metropolitan Dist Cncl 1974-79; MIPM 1984; *Books* autobiography A Very Miner MP (1986); *Recreations* rugby league, cricket; *Style*— Geoffrey Lofthouse, Esq, JP, MP; 67 Carlton Crest, Pontefract, W Yorkshire (☎ 0977 704

275); House of Commons, London SW1A 0AA (☎ 01 219 5133)

LOFTHOUSE, Reginald George Alfred; *b* 30 Dec 1916; *m* 1939, Ann Bernardine, *née* Bannan; 3 da; *Career* chief surveyor MAFF 1973-76, vice-chm Standing Conference on Countryside Sports 1988- (convener 1978-88), advsr Nature Conservancy Cncl 1978-82; memb bd of govrs Coll of Estate Mgmnt 1963-84 (chm 1972-77, res fell 1980-, hon fell 1985), memb cncl Reading Univ; chm advsy ctee Centre for Agricl Strategy 1982-; FRICS; *Clubs* Athenaeum, MCC; *Style*— Reginald Lofthouse, Esq; c/o College of Estate Management, Whiteknights, Reading, Berks (☎ 0734 861101)

LOFTHOUSE, Ronald William; s of William Lofthouse (d 1940), and Gladys Lofthouse (d 1985); *b* 13 Nov 1928; *Educ* Bootle GS, Bootle Tech Coll; *m* Rita, da of Richard Cooke (d 1944); 1 s (Neil b 8 July 1964), 1 da (Sandra b 13 Mar 1961); *Career* served MN, Lt (SP) RNVR 1951; trg advsr American Can C 1972-76 (works mangr 1966-72), md DKS Packaging 1979- (works dir 1976-79); chm: Merseyside Trg cncl, S Sefton C of C; dir S Sefton Enterprise Agency; FITD, FInstD; *Clubs* Conservative; *Style*— Ronald Lofthouse, Esq; 1 Rymers Gn, off Old Town Lane, Freshfield, Formby (☎ 070 48 71889); 62-70 Litherland Rd, Bootle, Merseyside (☎ 051 922 2656, fax 051 933 0547, car 0836 272016, telex 628484)

LOFTHOUSE, Stephen; s of Harry Lofthouse (d 1980), and (Janet) Mary Hume Scott, *née* Fraser; *b* 23 Mar 1945; *Educ* Tauntons GS, Univ of Manchester (BA, MA); *Career* res assoc Univ of Manchester 1968, lectr (later sr lectr) Manchester Poly 1969-72, lectr Manchester Business Sch 1972-75, dir Grade 10 Industs Assistance Cmmn Australia 1975, conslt Price Cmmn 1976-77, assoc Capel-Cure Myers 1977-83, sr exec James Capel and Co 1983-85, dir (later md) James Capel Fund Mangrs (formerly James Capel Int Asset Mgmnt) 1985-; non exec dir: James Unit Tst Mgmnt Ltd 1988-, Wardley Investmt Serv Ltd 1988-; *Books* numerous articles published in acad and professional jls; *Style*— Stephen Lofthouse, Esq; 4 North Several, London SE3 0QR (☎ 01 318 7132); 6 Bevis Marks, London EC3A 7JQ (☎ 01 621 0011, fax 01 621 0426, telex 9413578)

LOFTUS, Viscount; Charles John Tottenham; s and h of 8 Marquess of Ely; *b* 2 Feb 1943; *Educ* Trinity Coll Sch Port Hope Ont, Ecole Internationale de Genève, Toronto Univ (MA); *m* 1969, Judith Marvelle, da of Dr J J Porter of Calgary, Alberta, Canada; 1 adopted s (Andrew b 1973), 1 adopted da (Jennifer b 1975); *Heir* bro, Lord Timothy Tottenham, *qv*; *Career* head of Dept of French Strathcona-Tweedsmuir Sch Calgary, Alberta; *Style*— Viscount Loftus; 1424 Springfield Place SW, Calgary, Alberta, T2W OY1 Canada

LOFTUS, Ian William Townshend; s of Col Oliver St John Loftus (d 1980), of Hillcroft House, Hardington Mandeville, Somerset, and Edna Minnie Clare, *née* Davies (d 1986); *b* 4 July 1937; *Educ* Cheam Sch, Wellington Coll, Cambridge Univ (MA); *m* 9 May 1969, Elizabeth Antoinette, da of Harold Birchmore Harrison (d 1982), of Grove House, Utkinton, Tarporley, Cheshire; 1 s (Alexander b 1972); *Career* res scientist Shell (UK) 1961-66; bloodstock breeder; *Recreations* racing, tennis; *Style*— Ian Loftus, Esq; Bookham Stud, Bishopsdown, Sherborne, Dorset DT9 5PL (☎ 096 321 248)

LOFTUS, John Michael; s of Donald Loftus, of 4 Hemmant Way, Gillingham, Beccles, Suffolk, and Jean, *née* Hockney; *b* 4 Dec 1952; *Educ* Woodbridge Sch Suffolk, Univ of Sheffield (BSc); *Career* slr, NP, clerk to the Lowestoft Charity Bd 1987-, ptnr Norton Peskett and Forward; *Recreations* running, gardening, cycling, camping, walking; *Style*— John Loftus, Esq; Keld House, The Street, Hulver, Beccles, Suffolk NR34 7UE (☎ 050 276 257); Norton Peskett & Forward, 148 London Road North, Lowestoft (☎ 0502 565146, fax 0502 515941); Norton, Peskett & Forward, 55A High Street, Leiston, Suffolk (☎ 0728 832250, fax 0728 832246)

LOGAN, Andrew David; s of William Harold Logan, of The Leys, Witney, Oxford, and Irene May, *née* Muddimer; *b* 11 Oct 1945; *Educ* Lord Williams's GS Thame, Burford GS Oxon, Oxford Sch of Architecture (Dip Arch 1970); *Career* sculptor and artist; Alternative Miss World Events: 1972, 1973, 1975, 1978, 1981, 1985; 1986; Biba's Sculpture Garden 1974, Goldfield, Exhibition Whitechapel Art Gallery 1976, Egypt Revisited Sand and Light Spectacular Super Tent Clapham Common 1978, Trigon-Graz Austria 1979, Goddesses Exhibition at Commonwealth Inst London 1983; Henley Arts Festival, The Book Show, The Cylinder Gallery London 1984, Galactic Forest Exhibition, Functional Art Gallery, Los Angeles & Limelight Club New York 1985, Galactic Forest Exhibition Chicago, Daily Mail Ideal Home Exhibition Living Art Pavilion Arts Council, Glass Sculpture Exhibition Singapore 1986, Monuments & Music Exhibition, Botanical Gardens, Rome; designer: Wolfy, Ballet Rambert London 1987, Bastet, Sadler's Wells Royal Ballet 1988; Andrew Logan's Alternative Miss World nos 1-7 1972-87; *Style*— Andrew Logan, Esq; The Glasshouse, Melior Place, London SE1 3PQ

LOGAN, Capt Brian Ewen Weldon; s of Sir Ewen Reginald Logan, and Edith Frances, *née* Molony; *b* 13 Jan 1906; *Educ* RNC Osborne, Dartmouth; *m* 17 Oct 1933, Mary, da of Sir Herbert Ernest Fass, KGMB, CB; 1 s (David b 1943), 1 da (Shirley b 1934); *Career* Fleet Air Arm Capt of HMS Ocean, org dir Air Trg, Admiralty Man Overseas Scholarships; CBI; *Recreations* crosswords, squash, tennis, golf, rowing; *Style*— Capt Brian E W Logan; Woodmancote, Linchmere, Haslemere, Surrey GU27 3NQ (☎ 72 3195)

LOGAN, David Brian Carleton; s of Capt Brian Ewen Weldon Logan, RN, of Linchmere, Surrey, and Mary, *née* Fass; *b* 11 August 1943; *Educ* Charterhouse, Univ Coll Oxford (MA); *m* 4 March 1967, Judith Margaret, da of Walton Adamson Cole (d 1963); 2 s (Matthew b 1970, d 1988, James b 1976), 1 da (Joanna b 1968); *Career* Dip Serv 1965-: third sec (later second sec) Ankara 1965-69, private sec to Parly Under Sec of State for Foreign and Cwlth Affrs 1970-73, first sec UK Mission to the UN 1973-77, FCO 1977-82, cnsllr head of chancery and consul-gen Oslo 1982-85, head of personnel ops dept FCO 1986-88; sr assoc memb St Antony's Coll Oxford 1988-; *Recreations* music, reading, sailing, tennis; *Clubs* Royal Ocean Racing, Roehampton; *Style*— David B C Logan, Esq; c/o Foreign & Commonwealth Off, King Charles St, London SW1

LOGAN, Sir Donald Arthur; KCMG (1977), CMG (1965); s of Arthur Alfred Logan (d 1967), and Louise Anne Bradley; *b* 25 August 1917; *Educ* Solihull; *m* 1957, Irène Jocelyne Angèle, da of Robert Everts, sometime Belgian Ambass to Madrid; 1 s, 2 da; *Career* served WW II RA; entered Diplomatic Service 1945, ambassador Guinea 1960-62, cnsllr Paris 1964-70, ambassador Bulgaria 1970-73, dep perm rep N Atlantic Cncl 1973-75, perm leader of UK Delegation to UN Conference on Law of the Sea 1976-77, leader UK Delegation to Conference on Marine Living Resources of Antarctica 1978-80; dir Great Britain/East Europe Centre 1980-87; chm St Clare's Coll Oxford 1984-; chm Jerusalem and East Mission Trust Ltd 1980-; *Clubs* Brooks's, RAC; *Style*— Sir Donald Logan, KCMG; 6 Thurloe St, London SW7 2ST (☎ 01 589 4010)

LOGAN, James; OBE (1988); s of John Logan, and Jean, *née* Howie; *b* 28 Oct 1927; *Educ* Robert Gordon's Inst Aberdeen; *m* 27 Dec 1958, Anne, da of Duncan Brand; 1 s (Jeremy b 1959), 1 da (Judith b 1961); *Career* sr scientific staff Macaulay Inst 1981, appeal admin Aberdeen Maritime Museum, dir Scotland The What? revue co; fndr and chm of Friends & Aberdeen Art Gallery and Museums, chm and dir Vol Serv Aberdeen, vice chm Scottish Arts Cncl 1984-88, memb Arts Cncl GB 1984-88; CChem, MRIC; *Recreations* theatre going; *Style*— James Logan, Esq, OBE; 53 Foutainhall Rd, Aberdeen (☎ 0224 646914)

LOGAN, Lady Janet Colville; da of John McIntyre; *m* 1920, Sir William Marston Logan, KBE, CMG (d 1968); *Style*— Lady Logan; Ann St, Gatehouse-of-Fleet, Kircudbrightshire

LOGAN, Vincent Paul; *see*: Dunkeld, Bishop of

LOGAN-SALTON, Maurice Highton Ekegren; s of Ivor Logan Assheton-Salton, of Cornwall, and Tora Ulla Margaretha Assheton-Salton, *née* Ekegren; *b* 2 Feb 1952; *Educ* Canford Sch, Durham Univ, Teesside Poly (Dip SW, CQSW); *Career* local authy social worker 1973-87; estates mangr Francome Ltd (nursing homes) 1988-; author Monday Club Policy Paper Juvenile Crime 1984; campaigner for reduction in custody for young offenders, supporter of CHEs (community homes with educn) and the equivalent training-schs of N Ireland and former List D Schs of Scotland, as spokesman for Monday Club Law and Order Ctee 1984-, tres Durham Univ Union Soc 1972-73; *Recreations* conservationist; *Style*— Maurice Logan-Salton, Esq; The Lodge, Llanarth Ct, Llanarth, Raglan, Gwent NP5 2YD (☎ 0873 840 200); 43 Falmouth Rd, Heaton, Newcastle-upon-Tyne NE6 5NS (☎ 091 2659992)

LOGERES; *see*: de Logeres

LOGUE, Christopher; s of John Dominic Logue (d 1951), and Florence Mabel, *née* Chapman (d 1981); *b* 23 Nov 1926; *Educ* Portsmouth GS, Prior Park Coll Bath,; *m* 1985 Rosemary Hill; *Career* writer, actor, Private Eye columnist; *Books* Ode to the Dodo: Poems 1952-78, War Music: an Account of Book 16-19 of Homer's Iliad; ed: The Children's Book of Comic Verse (1979), The Bumper Book of True Stories (1981), The Oxford Book of Pseuds (1983), Sweet and Sour: an Anthology of Comic Verse (1983), The Children's Book of Children's Rhymes (1986), trans Baal, The Seven Deadly Sins 1986, Bertold Brecht 1986; *screenplays*: Professor Tucholsky's Facts (poem used as screenplay of animated film by Richard Williams 1963), The End of Arthurs Marraige (music by Stanley Myers dir Ken Loach 1965), Savage Messiah (dir Ken Russell 1972), Crusoe (with Walon Green dir Caleb Deschanel 1988); *Clubs* The Hotsy Totsy (Ghent); *Style*— Christopher Logue; 41 Camberwell Grove, London SE5 8JA (☎ 01 703 0874)

LOGUE, John Lindsay; s of Arthur Logue (d 1952), and Mary Logue (d 1966), of Lytham House, Lytham St Annes, Lancs; *b* 3 April 1930; *Educ* Manchester GS, Manchester Univ; *m* 1967 (m dis 1977), Vivienne Louise, da of Patrick Wayland Warner (d 1970); 1 da (Lisa); *Career* engr, company dir and mgmnt conslt; chm and md SAP Ltd (engrg co), chm BMK Carpets May 1982-, previously dep md Bowyers Food Gp; memb Worshipful Co of Pattenmakers; *Recreations* golf, sailing (yacht 'Vaquero'), cricket; *Clubs* Royal Ocean Racing, Royal Thames YC, Royal Gourock YC, Royal Southern YC, St James's, Minchinhampton Golf; *Style*— John Logue, Esq; Amberley Court, Amberley, Glos GL5 5AE; Monkton Hall, Troon, Ayrshire; Eildon Hall, St Boswells, Roxburghshire, SAP Ltd, Chalford Industrial Estate, Brimscombe, Stroud, Glos (☎ 0453 884144); BMK Ltd, Kilmarnock, Ayrshire (☎ 0563 21100);

LOISEAU, Hon Mrs (Eliza); da of Baron Hutchinson of Lullington, *qv*; *b* 1941; *m* 1974, Pierre Loiseau; *Style*— The Hon Mrs Loiseau; Les Bouleaux, 2 Rue de Gazet, Seine Port, 77 France

LOKOLOKO, Sir Tore; GCMG (1977), OBE; s of Loko Loko Tore; *b* 21 Sept 1930; *Educ* Sogeri High Sch, Papua New Guinea; *m* 1950, Lalahaia Meakoro; 4 s, 6 da; *Career* govr-gen of Papua New Guinea 1977-83; *Style*— Sir Tore Lokoloko; Government House, Port Moresby, Papua New Guinea (☎ (25) 9366)

LOMAS, Alfred; MEP (Lab) London NE 1979-; s of Alfred Lomas; *b* 30 April 1928; *Educ* St Pauls Elem Sch Stockport, various further educnl estabs; *Career* political sec London Co-op 1975-79; *Style*— Alfred Lomas, Esq, MEP; 23 Hatcliffe Close, London, SE3 9UE (☎ 01 852 5433)

LOMAX, Hon Mrs (Elizabeth Margaret); *née* Brand; da of 3 Viscount Hampden, GCVO, KCB, CMG (d 1958); *b* 1911; *m* 1935, Cecil Lomax (d 1988); 3 da; *Style*— The Hon Mrs Lomax; Codicote Mill, Hitchin, Herts (☎ 0438 820206)

LOMER, Richard Godfrey; MC; s of Lt-Col Godfrey Lomer, RHA, DSO (d 1952), and Mavis Mary, *née* Garrett (d 1979); inherited (1965) Ballinacor, Rathdrum, Co Wicklow, the ancestral home of the Lomer/St Albans fam from his c Capt W D O Kemmis; *b* 22 April 1922; *Educ* Cranleigh Coll; *m* Patricia Katharine Mary, da of Sir Richard Lewis, KGMG, CB, CBE (d 1965); 2 s; *Career* WW II enlisted (age 17) Royal Berks 1939, cmmnd Coldstream Guards served 1940-46, wounded Normandy (despatches); recalled War Office (ERE list) 1950-56; qual slr 1949, sr ptnr Lomer & Co 1956-75; dir diverse cos; farms Ballinacor Estate 1965-; tres (under Sir Keith Joseph) Mulberry Housing Assn (the pioneer housing assn); memb mgmnt ctee and tstee WWF; fell World Pheasant Assn, Wildfowl Tst; Merchant Taylor and Freeman City of London; *Recreations* conservation, military history; *Style*— Richard Lomer, Esq; Manor Farm, Chantry, Frome, Somerset; Ballinacor Estates, Ballinacor, Rathdrum, Co Wicklow, Rep of Ireland

LONDESBOROUGH, Ann, Baroness; (Elizabeth) Ann; *née* Sale; da of late Edward Little Sale, ICS, and formerly w of late Thomas Chambers Windsor Roe, CBE; *b* 28 April 1916; *Educ* Headington Sch Oxford; *m* 15 June 1957, as his 2 w, 8 Baron Londesborough, TD (d 1968); 1 s (9 Baron); *Style*— The Rt Hon Ann, Lady Londesborough; 31 Lyttelton Rd, Droitwich, Worcs

LONDESBOROUGH, Jocelyn, Baroness; Jocelyn Helen; da of late Lt-Cdr Hugh Duppa Collins, RN; *m* 1952, as his 3 w, 7 Baron Londesborough (d 1967); *Style*— The Rt Hon Jocelyn, Lady Londesborough; Anchor Cottage, Bembridge, IOW (☎ 0983 872216)

LONDESBOROUGH, 9 Baron (UK 1850); Richard John Denison; s of 8 Baron Londesborough, TD, AMICE (d 1968, gs of Lord Albert Denison, *née* Conyngham, 2 s of 1 Marquess Conyngham), by his 2 w Ann; *b* 2 July 1959; *Educ* Wellington Coll, Exeter Univ; *m* 26 Sept 1987, Rikki, da of J E Morris, of Bayswater, W2; *Style*— The

Rt Hon the Lord Londesborough; Edw Cottage, Aberedw, Powys

LONDON, Archdeacon of; *see*: Cassidy, Ven George Henry

LONDON, 130 Bishop of 1981-; Rt Rev and Rt Hon Graham Douglas Leonard; PC (1981); patron of one hundred and sixty livings and eighteen alternately with others, all Prebendal stalls, Archdeaconries of Londons, Middx, Hampstead, Hackney and Northolt, the Precentorship, the Chancellorship and the Treasureship; the See of London has existed since the first introduction of Christianity into Britain. Restitutus, Bishop of London, was present at the Council of Arles in AD 314, and signed the decrees; s of Rev Douglas Leonard; *b* 8 May 1921; *Educ* Monkton Combe Sch, Balliol Coll Oxford, Westcott House Cambridge; *m* 1943, (Vivien) Priscilla, da of late Dr Swann, fell of Gonville and Caius Coll Cambridge; 2 s; *Career* served WW II Oxford & Bucks LI as Capt; ordained 1948, Archdeacon Hampstead, Bp Suffragan of Willesden 1964-73; bishop of Truro 1973-81, delegate to fifth Assembly WCC Nairobi 1975; chm Gen Synod Bd for Social Responsibility 1976-83, dean of HM's Chapel Royal 1981-, prelate Order of the British Empire 1981-; hon master of Bench of Middle Temple 1981-; chm: Churches Main Ctee 1981-, Jerusalem and Middle East Church Assoc 1981-, Bd of Educn and National Soc 1983-89; church cmmr; episcopal canon St George's Cathedral Jerusalem 1981-; *Style*— The Rt Rev and Rt Hon the Lord Bishop of London; London House, 8 Barton St, London SW1 3NE (☎ 01 222 8661)

LONDON, John Frederick; s of Eric Horton London, MBE, of Bexhill-on-Sea, and Doris Emma, *née* Browning; *b* 17 Nov 1934; *Educ* Tonbridge Sch; *m* 6 Oct 1962, Merrill Anne, da of Alfred Edward James Prior (d 1967), of Sevenoaks, 1 s (James b 8 Nov 1964), 2 da (Anne-Louise b 27 Oct 1967, Sally b 3 Aug 1969); *Career* Nat Serv 1953-54; Bank of England 1954-69, First Nat Bank of Boston 1959-72, Quin Cope Ltd (formerly Gerald Quin Cope and Co Ltd) 1972-: asst dir, dir, md, chm; pres Sevenoaks and Dist Assoc of Mental Health 1962-79, chm Sevenoaks Dist Scout Cncl 1971-88; memb: Sevenoaks Urban DC 1959-62 and 1963-74 (chm 1970-71), Sevenoaks Town Cncl 1974- (Mayor 1974-75 and 1988-89); *Recreations* sailing, gardening; *Style*— John London, Esq; 18 Knole Way, Sevenoaks, Kent TN13 3RS (☎ 0732 456327); 150 Leadenhall St, London EC3V 4SD (☎ 01 626 1674, telex 8813939)

LONEY, Keith Edward; s of William Edward Loney (d 1977), of Yeovil, Somerset, and Marjorie Maud Rose Miles; *b* 16 Nov 1935; *Educ* King's Sch Bruton, Univ of London (LLB); *m* 1971, Valerie Elizabeth, da of Percy Arthur Stuttard (d 1977), of Purley, Surrey; *Career* Royal Signals 1954-57, Cyprus 1955-56; barr Lincoln's Inn 1972, Inst of CA in England and Wales (fell 1972), Br Insur Assoc 1966-85 (asst sec 1971, dep sec 1975), Assoc of Br Insurers 1985 (dep chief exec 1987); Freeman City of London 1959, Liveryman The Worshipful Co of Butchers 1960; hon tres Old Brutonian Assoc, memb Hon Artillery Co; *Recreations* swimming, travel; *Clubs* Lansdowne; *Style*— Keith Loney, Esq; Aldermary House, Queen St, London EC4N 1TT (☎ 01 248 4477, telex 937035)

LONG, Alan C (Tom); s of Joseph F Long, of Leigh-on-Sea, Essex, and Dorothy, *née* Swinfen (d 1982); *b* 29 June 1930; *Educ* Westcliff HS, Exeter Univ (BA); *m* 4 Jan 1958, Joyce (Jo), da of William Fielding (d 1975); 1 s (Andrew b 1963), 2 da (Susan b 1959, Caroline b 1960); *Career* Intelligence Corps 1948-50; BAT Industs plc 1953-: fin dir 1983-, personnel dir 1988-; Freeman Rio de Janeiro 1980; ACIS 1962; *Recreations* golf, bridge, gardening; *Clubs* MCC, Wentworth GC; *Style*— A C Long, Esq; Bat Industries plc, Windsor House, Victoria St, London SW1H ONL (☎ 01 222 7979)

LONG, Brian; s of Harry Long (d 1955), and Doris Long (d 1977); *b* 30 August 1932; *Educ* Hanson GS Yorks; *m* 29 Dec 1956, Joan Iris, da of Charles Eric Hoggard, of Huggate, Yorks; 2 s (Nigel b 10 Feb 1959, Gareth b 15 Jan 1962); *Career* qualified co sec 1953, with Int Computers and Tabulators Ltd 1955-65, joined Honeywell Ltd 1965 (divnl dir 1969), md Honeywell Information Systems Ltd 1978, memb Honeywell Advsy Cncl 1978, vice pres Honeywell Inc 1981, vice chm Honeywell Ltd 1985 (chief exec 1986), chm and chief exec Honeywell Bull Ltd (now Bull H N Informations Systems Ltd) 1987, dir Bull SA of France 1987; bd memb Nat Computing Centre (NCC) 1970-71, memb Indust Ctee Help the Aged 1988; Freeman City of London 1987, memb Co of Information Technologists 1987; FIOD 1970, CBIM 1987, MBCS 1987, FCIS 1988; *Recreations* golf, music, theatre; *Clubs* RAC; *Style*— Brian Long, Esq; Bull H N Information Systems Ltd, Computer House, Great West Road, Brentford, Middx TW8 9DH (☎ 01 568 9191, fax 01 568 9191 ext 2305, telex 284534, car tel 0836 719319)

LONG, Hon Mrs ((Anne) Cathrine); *née* Parnell; eldest da of 8 Baron Congleton, *qv*; *b* 1956; *Educ* St Mary's Calne, Trinity Coll of Music London; *m* 1980, (Michael) Robin Long; 2 s (Richard Per b 1981, Willum b 1984); *Style*— The Hon Mrs Long; Pear Tree Cottage, Ebresbourne, Salisbury, Wilts

LONG, Christopher John; s of John Frederick Lawrence Long (d 1986), and Joan Ethel, *née* Murphy; *b* 16 Feb 1944; *Educ* Netteswell Comprehensive Sch, Harlow, Queens' Coll Cambridge (MA); *m* 13 Dec 1969, Lesley Anne, *née* Hatcher, JP; 2 s (Stuart b 1976, Stephen b 1979), 1 da (Deborah b 1972); *Career* md CLA Ltd (Rutland Tst plc gp) 1987-, ptnr CJ Long & Co CAs 1981, md Christopher Long & Assocs Ltd 1984-87, dir Omeha Int Ltd 1986-87, mangr Midland Bank Int 1975-76, vice-pres Continental Illinois London 1981-84; *Recreations* choral music, jazz, gardening; *Style*— Christopher Long, Esq; Alsa Wood House, Stansted, Essex CM24 8SU (☎ (0279 813111, fax 816564); Rutland House, Rutland Gardens, London SW7 1BX (☎ 01 225 3391, fax 225-1364)

LONG, (Adrian) Douglas; s of Harold Edgar Long (d 1951), of Fulham, London, and Kate, *née* Sawyer (d 1958); *b* 9 Feb 1925; *Educ* Wandsworth Sch; *m* 12 March 1949, Barbara, da of Ernest Wellstead (d 1948), of Southfields, London; 1 s (Mark); *Career* Home Gd 1942, India and Burma (255 Indian Tank Bde 14 Army) 1943-47, cmmnd 1944 Royal Deccan Horse, 2 Lt 43 Cavalry, Lt Probyns Horse 5 KEO Lancers, ret as Capt; reporter Daily Record 1947-57, Scottish ed Daily Herald 1958, news ed/features ed Daily Herald and Sun 1959-68, gen mangr Oldhams Newspapers Ltd 1969-71, dep chief exec Mirror Gp Newspapers Ltd 1971-80, dir Daily Record and Sunday Mail Ltd 14974-84, chm Syndication International 1976-83, chief exec Mirror Gp 1980-84, conslt Surrey Business Enterprise Ltd 1985, md and co fndr The Independent Newspaper Publishing plc 1986, memb Press Cncl Newspapers Publishers Assoc 1986-88, chm and co-fndr Sunday Newspaper Publishing plc (The Sunday Correspondant) 1988-memb Cwlth Press Union, FInstD, FRSA; *Recreations* swimming, tennis, racing, golf, theatre; *Clubs* RAC, Sandown Park, Cuddington GC (social); *Style*— Douglas Long, Esq; 3 Garbrand Walk, Ewell, Epsom, Surrey (☎ 01 394 1323)

LONG, Hon James Richard; s and h of 4 Viscount Long; *b* 31 Dec 1960; *Style*— The Hon James Long

LONG, Hon Mrs; Jean; da of Baron Douglas of Cleveland (d 1978); *b* 1928; *m* 1952, Garry Long, FCIS; *Style*— The Hon Mrs Long; 8 The Avenue, Hatch End, Pinner, Middlesex

LONG, Jeremy Paul Warwick; s of Ronald Walter Long, of Warwick, and Gwendolen Dorothy Long; *b* 24 Mar 1953; *Educ* Warwick Sch, Exeter Coll Oxford Univ (MA); *Career* gp fin dir Mecca Leisure Gp 1980-; FCA; *Recreations* tennis, theatre, cinema, skiing; *Style*— Jeremy Long, Esq; Mecca House, 76 Southwark St, London SE1 (☎ 01 928 2323)

LONG, Hon John Hume; s of 3 Viscount Long; *b* 1930; *Educ* Harrow; *m* 1967 (m dis 1969), Averil Juliet, da of Henry Stobart; 1 da; *Style*— The Hon John Long; Swyre Farm Cottage, Aldsworth, Glos

LONG, Martyn Howard; s of Victor Frederick Long, of Hove, Sussex, and Dorothy Maud, *née* Lawrence; *b* 1 May 1933; *Educ* Univ Coll Sch London, Merrist Wood Agric Coll Surrey; *m* 4 Oct 1958, Veronica Mary Gascoigne, da of James Edward Bates (d 1952); 4 da (Helen b 1959, Maria b 1961, Samantha b 1965, Rosalind b 1969); *Career* Nat Serv RAF 1952-54; farmer 1949-85, dir of family firm, chm Mid-Downs Health Authy W Sussex 1981- (former hon tres); chm E Grinstead Cons Assoc 1972-75; memb: E Sussex CC 1970-74, Cuckfield RDC 1972-74, Mid Sussex DC 1973-79, W Sussex CC 1973- (current chm policy and resources ctee), Assoc of CC's 1979-, W Sussex Area Health Authy 1973-77, SW Thames Regnl Health Authy 1980-81; chm ACC Soc Servs 1982-88 (formerly vice chm); *Recreations* magic (assoc memb Inner Magic Circle with Silver Star); *Clubs* Farmers, Whitehall; *Style*— Martyn Long, Esq; Mid-Downs Health Authy, Haywards Heath, W Sussex (☎ 0444 441666)

LONG, Hon Mrs Meriel (Davina); *née* Edwardes; o da of Capt the Hon (Hugh) Owen Edwardes (d 1937), 2 s of 6 Baron Kensington; sis of 8 Baron and was raised to rank of Baron's da by Royal Warrant 17 May 1982; *b* 19 April 1935; *m* 1972, (David) Andrew Long; 2 s; *Style*— The Hon Mrs Long; Hill House, Filmore Hill, Privett, Alton, Hants GU34 3NX (☎ 073088 321)

LONG, 4 Viscount (UK 1921); Richard Gerard Long; s of 3 Viscount Long, TD, JP, DL (d 1967); *b* 30 Jan 1929; *Educ* Harrow; *m* 1, 2 March 1957 (m dis 1984), Margaret Frances, da of Ninian Frazer; 1 s, 1 da (and 1 decd); m 2, 1984, Catherine Patricia Elizabeth Mier Woolf, da of Charles Terrence Miles-Ede, of S Africa; *Heir* s, Hon James Long, b 31 Dec 1960; *Career* The Wilts Regt 1947-49; pres Bath and Wilts Gliding Club, vice-pres Wilts Royal Br Legion; oppn whip 1974-79, lord-in-waiting 1979-; *Recreations* shooting, gardening; *Style*— The Rt Hon the Viscount Long; House of Lords, London SW1

LONG, (William Ivers) Roland; s of George Roland Long (d 1967), and Margaret, *née* Smith; *b* 18 Feb 1947; *Educ* Roy Belfast Acad Inst Belfast; *m* 17 Apr 1971, Jennifer Mary, da of Patrick Raymund Devin Carmichael, of Bournemouth (d 1985); 1 s (Jeremy b 1977), 1 da (Deborah b 1974); *Career* dir AV Browne Advertising 1967-72, chm Armstrong Long Advertising Ltd 1972-83, chm The RLA Group Ltd 1984-; chm NI branch Inst of Marketing 1981-82; MInstM 1972, FBIM 1982, MIPA 1987; *Style*— Roland Long, Esq; The RLA Group Ltd, Burlington Arcade, Old Christchurch Rd, Bournemouth, Dorset BH1 2HZ (☎ 0202 297755, fax 0202 26149)

LONG, Hon Sarah Victoria; da of 4 Viscount Long; *b* 1958; *Career* art conslt ptnr of Long and Ryle Art Int London, Midlands Contemporary Art based in Birmingham; *Recreations* reading, travel; *Style*— The Hon Sarah Long; The Garden House, Turleigh, Bradford on Avon, Wilts

LONG, William Casson; s of Capt Clifford Long (d 1974), and Bessie, *née* Casson (d 1952); *b* 25 August 1923; *Educ* Sedbergh, St John's Coll Cambridge; *m* 14 June 1947, Joan Cantrill, da of Maj Norman Feather, MC (d 1971); 1 s (James Duncan Clifford b 1952), 1 da (Elspeth Jane Baty b 1949); *Career* 2 Lt RA 1942 (Capt 1945, Hon rank of Capt granted on demob 1947), Burma Command 14th Army 1944-46; CA Public Practice 1952-88, memb Ins Taxation 1955, sr ptnr Long and Co CA's (ret 1988); ACA 1931, FCA 1952, ATII 1955; *Recreations* gardening, fly-fishing, woodcarving, ornithology, motor sport; *Clubs* Keighley RUFC, Kilnsey Anglers; *Style*— William Long, Esq; 132 Banks Lane, Riddlesden, Keighley, W Yorks BD20 5PQ

LONGBOTHAM, Maj Samuel; JP, DL (Ross and Cromarty 1964); s of George Longbotham, of Elgin, Morayshire, and Elizabeth, *née* Monks; *b* 19 Mar 1908; *Educ* Elgin, Glasgow; *m* 1941, Elizabeth Rae, da of Donald Davidson (d 1960), of Glasgow; 2 s, 1 da; *Career* served RA and Intelligence Corps 1940-46, cmmnd 1944; Maj Lovat Scouts, TA (RA) 1952-60; Maj North Highland ACF 1968-75; Ld-Lt Islands Area Western Isles 1975-83; ret md Stornoway Gazette Ltd, Stornoway, Isle of Lewis; *Recreations* angling, gardening, walking; *Style*— Maj Samuel Longbotham, JP, DL; 25 Lewis St, Stornoway, Isle of Lewis PA87 2JW (☎ Stornoway (0851) 2519)

LONGBOTTOM, Charles Brooke; s of William Ewart Longbottom (d 1943); *b* 22 July 1930; *Educ* Uppingham Sch; *m* Anita, da of Giulio Trapani; 2 da; *Career* barr Inner Temple; contested (C) Stockton on Tees 1955, MP (C) York 1959-66, pps to Chllr of Duchy of Lancaster 1961-63; chm: Ariel Fndn 1960-, Austin & Pickersgill Shipbuilders Sunderland 1966-72, A & P Appledore Ltd 1970-78, Seascope Hldgs Ltd 1970-82, Seascope Shipping Ltd 1970-86; dir: Henry Ansbacher Hldgs plc, Henry Ansbacher & Co, Ansbacher Guernsey Ltd 1982-86; memb: general advsy cncl BBC 1965-75, Community Relations Cmmn 1968-70; pt/t memb bd of Br Shipbuilders, chm Acorn Healing Tst; *Style*— Charles Longbottom, Esq; 66 Kingston House North, Princes Gate, London SW7

LONGCROFT, James George Stoddart; s of Reginald Stoddart Longcroft (d 1969), and Annie Mary, *née* Thompson (d 1972); *b* 25 Oct 1929; *Educ* Wellington; *m* 1963, Valerie Sylvia, da of Air Cdre Ellacott Lyne Stephens Ward CB, DFC, RAF ret; 3 s (Dominic b 1966, Christopher b 1971, Nicholas b 1975), 1 da (Juliet b 1970); *Career* sr ptnr Longcrofts CA; chm Tricentrol Ltd (oil exploration and prodn) 1979-81, Tricentrol plc 1981-88; dir various Tricentrol subsidiaries; Master Worshipful Co of Founders 1977-78; FCA, FInstPet, FBIM, FRSA; *Recreations* skiing, tennis; *Clubs* City of London, HAC; *Style*— James Longcroft, Esq; Chalet Tournesol, 3780 Gstaad, Switzerland (☎ 030 45416, fax 030 45418); Longcrofts Chartered Accountants, Longcroft House, Victoria Avenue, Bishopsgate, London EC2 (☎ 01 623 6626, fax 01 623 4997, telex 915074) (☎ 01 623 6626, telex 915074, fax 01 623 4997)

LONGDEN, Sir Gilbert James Morley; MBE (Mil 1944); s of Lt-Col James Morley Longden and Kathleen Morgan; *b* 16 April 1902; *Educ* Haileybury, Emmanuel Coll Cambridge (MA, LLB) Sorbonne; *Career* serv WWII with Durham LI, 2 Div and 36 Div in Burma Campaign; slr 1927; sec ICI (India) Ltd 1930-38; contested (C) Morpeth

1945, MP (C) SW Herts 1950-74; UK del: Cncl of Europe 1953, XII and XIII Sessions of the UN 1957-58; kt 1972; *Books* A Conservative Philosophy (1947), One Nation (jtly 1950), Change is Our Ally (1954), A Responsible Society (1959), One Europe (1969); *Clubs* Brooks's, Hurlingham; *Style—* Sir Gilbert Longden, MBE; 89 Cornwall Gdns, London SW7 4AX (☎ 01 584 5666)

LONGDEN, Henry Alfred; s of late Geoffrey Appleby Longden and Marjorie Mullins; *b* 8 Sept 1909; *Educ* Oundle, Univ of Birmingham; *m* 1935, Ruth, da of Arthur Gilliat, of Leeds; 1 s, 4 da; *Career* mining engr; dir: Blackwell Colliery Co 1940-, Briggs Collieries 1941-, New Hucknall Colliery Co 1941; chm W Mids NCB 1960- (prodn dir NE dir 1948-), chm and chief exec Cementation Co 1961-70, dir Trafalgar House 1970-76, ret; *Recreations* rugby, cricket, tennis, shooting, fishing, sailing; *Style—* Henry Longden, Esq; Raeburn, Northdown Rd, Woldingham, Surrey CR3 7BB (☎ 088 385 2245)

LONGE, Desmond Evelyn; MC (1944), DL (Norfolk 1971); s of late Rev John Charles Longe, of Spixworth Park, Norfolk; *b* 8 August 1914; *Educ* Woodbridge; *m* 1944, Isla, da of Richard Moore Bell (d 1953), of London; 1 s, 1 da; *Career* served with Sharp Shooters Co of London Yeo 1936-38; Royal Norfolk Regt 1940-46 (W Africa, Middle East, Far East and N W Europe); SOE (Croix de Guerre avec Palme 1944); dir Norwich Union Insurance Gp 1958-81 (chm 1964-81); chm D E Longe & Co and East Coast Grain Ltd 1962-82; dir: BR Eastern Region 1969-70, BR London Midland Region 1971-74, BR London & SE Region 1975-77, BR Property 1978-82, Eastern Counties Newspapers 1977-82, Anglia TV 1970-82; church cmmr 1970-76, High Sheriff Norfolk 1975-76; *Recreations* fishing, travel; *Clubs* MCC, Norfolk Co; *Style—* Desmond Longe, Esq, MC, DL; Woodton Grange, Bungay, Suffolk (☎ 050 844 260)

LONGE, Nicholas; s of Lt Col Roland Bacon Longe, of Hasketon Lodge, Woodbridge, Suffolk, and Diana, *née* Hastings; *b* 20 Mar 1938; *Educ* St Peter's Court Harrow; *m* 14 March 1970, Julia Victoria, da of Maj David Arthur Peel, MC (ka 1944); 2 s (William b 1972, David b 1975); *Career* Sub Lt RN 1957-59; farmer; PE Consulting Gp Ltd 1968-73, dir Brook House Investmts Ltd; memb Apple and Pear Devpt Cncl, dir Kingdom Mktg Scheme (chm 1980-82), chm Museum of E Anglian Life; High Sheriff of Suffolk 1984-85; Freeman: City of London, Worshipful Co of Fruiterers; *Recreations* sailing, sport, reading; *Clubs* Naval and Military; *Style—* Nicholas Longe, Esq; Hasketon Manor, Woodbridge, Suffolk; Grange Farm, Hasketon, Woodbridge, Suffolk (☎ 047 335 610)

LONGFIELD, Richard Lewis; s of John Longfield, OBE, and Mary Lyon, *née* Waddell; *b* 2 Nov 1939; *Educ* Marlborough Coll, Trin Dublin (BA); *m* Felicity Laura, da of Alex Miller, of Straidarran, N Ireland; 1 s (Edward), 2 da (Onnalee, Shauna); *Career* oil co exec, mangr of Govt Relations Shell UK Ltd, dir Gateway to India; *Recreations* photography, golf, gardening, fishing; *Style—* Richard L Longfield, Esq; The Old Rectory, Weston Patrick, Hants; 11 Rouseden Street, Camden; Shell UK Ltd, Shell-Mex House, Strand, London WC2

LONGFORD, Countess of; Elizabeth; CBE (1974); da of late Nathaniel Bishop Harman, FRCS, and Katherine, *née* Chamberlain; *b* 30 August 1906; *Educ* Headington Sch Oxford, Lady Margaret Hall Oxford; *m* 1931, Hon Francis Pakenham, 7 Earl of Longford; 4 s, 3 da (1 da decd); *Career* author (as Elizabeth Longford and Elizabeth Pakenham); lectr for WEA and univ extension lectr 1929-35, contested (Lab) Cheltenham 1935, Oxford 1950, candidate for King's Norton, Birmingham 1935-43, memb Rent Tribunal Paddington and St Pancras 1947-54, tstee Nat Portrait Gallery 1968-78; memb: Advsy Cncl V&A Museum 1969-75, Advsy Bd Br Library 1976-, (vice-pres 1982); vice-pres London Library 1983; Hon DLitt (Sussex 1970); FRSL; *Books* Jameson Raid (reprinted 1982); *Biographies include* Victoria RI (James Tait Black Prize), Wellington (2 vols; Yorkshire Post Prize for vol I), The Royal House of Windsor, Churchill, Byron, Wilfrid Scawen Blunt, The Queen Mother, Elizabeth R (1983); Memoir: The Pebbled Shore (1986); *Style—* The Rt Hon the Countess of Longford, CBE; Bernhurst, Hurst Green, E Sussex (☎ Hurst Green 248); 18 Chesil Court, Chelsea Manor St, London SW3 (01 352 7794)

LONGFORD, 7 Earl of (I 1785); Francis Aungier Pakenham; KG (1971), PC (1948); also Baron Longford (I 1756), Baron Silchester (UK 1821), Baron Pakenham (UK 1945); sits as Baron Pakenham; s of 5 Earl of Longford, KP, MVO (ka 1915), by his w, Lady Mary Julia Child-Villiers (d 1933, da of 7 Earl of Jersey); suc bro, 6 Earl, 1961; *b* 5 Dec 1905; *Educ* Eton, New Coll Oxford; *m* 1931, Elizabeth, CBE (*see* Countess of Longford), da of Nathaniel Bishop Harman, FRCS; 4 s, 3 da (Lady Antonia Fraser/Pinter, Mrs Alexander Kazantzis, Lady Rachel Billington, and 1 da decd); *Heir* s, Thomas Pakenham; *Career* sits as Labour peer in Lords; lord-in-waiting to HM 1945-46, parly under-sec of state for War 1946-47, Chllr of Duchy of Lancaster 1947-48, min of Civil Aviation 1948-51, first lord of the Admty May-Oct 1951 and lord privy seal 1964-65, sec of state for the colonies 1965-66, again lord privy seal 1966-68; chm: Nat Youth Employment Cncl 1968-71, Sidgwick & Jackson 1970-; *Clubs* Garrick; *Style—* The Rt Hon The Earl of Longford, KG, PC; Bernhurst, Hurst Green, East Sussex (☎ 058 086 248); 18 Chesil Court, Chelsea Manor St, SW3 (☎ 01 352 7794)

LONGLAND, Sir David Walter; CMG (1973); s of David Longland (d 1954), and Marie Ann, *née* McGriskin (d 1948); *b* 1 June 1909; *Educ* Brisbane State Primary Sch, Qld State Commercial HS; *m* 1935, Ada Elizabeth, da of Edward Harrison Bowness (d 1950); 1 s, 1 da; *Career* govt admin: fifty years' crown service in Depts of: Educn, Treasury, Premier's Immigration, Works; chm Pub Service Bd and Qld's first Parly cmmr for Admin Investigations (Ombudsman), ret 1979; pres Qld Spastic Welfare League (chm of dirs), hon exec dir Qld Art Gallery Fndn; kt 1977; *Recreations* reading, gardening; *Clubs* Rotary of Qld (Brisbane); *Style—* Sir David Longland, CMG; Elimbari, Unit 1, 39 Wambool Street, Bulima Heights, Qld 4171, Australia

LONGLAND, Sir Jack Jack (John Laurence); eld s of Rev Ernest Harry Longland (d 1956), of Cambridge, and Emily Rose (d 1952), eld da of Sir James Crockett, of Dallington Lodge, Northampton; *b* 26 June 1905; *Educ* King's Sch Worcester, Jesus Coll Cambridge (MA); *m* 1934, Margaret Lowrey, da of Arthur Harrison (d 1936), of Durham (sr ptnr of Harrison and Harrison, builders of the organs of Westminster Abbey, Albert Hall, King's Coll Cambridge, Royal Festival Hall); 2 s, 2 da; *Career* by-fellow Magdalene Coll Cambridge 1927-29, lectr Durham Univ 1930-36, educn offr and later dir Community Serv Cncl for Durham Co 1936-40, dep educn offr Hertfordshire 1940-42, co educn offr Dorset 1942-49, dir of educn Derbyshire 1949-70; broadcaster for 40 years; pres Alpine Club 1974-76, pres Br Mountaineering Cncl, pres Climbers' Club, Cambridge Univ Mountaineering Club (memb Mount Everest Expdn 1933); devpt cmmr 1946-76, Royal Cmmn of Local Govt 1966-69, Countryside Cmmn 1966-72, vice-chm Sports Cncl 1970-74; kt 1970; *Recreations* mountaineering, rugby, pole-vault (four times regnl champion); *Clubs* Savile, Alpine, Climbers', Achilles, Hawks; *Style—* Sir Jack Longland; Bridgeway, Bakewell, Derbyshire (☎ 062 981 2252)

LONGLEY, Adrian Reginald; s of Evelyn Longley (d 1956), and Mary Anastasia, *née* Thompson (d 1962); *b* 27 Sept 1925; *Educ* Winchester, Trinity Coll Cambridge (MA); *m* 14 Dec 1957, Sylvia Margaret, da of Capt George Keith Homfray Hayter (d 1968); 3 da (Anne b 1959, Joanna b 1960, Melissa b 1963); *Career* mil serv Rifle Bde (A/Capt) served M East 1944-47; admitted slr 1959; Freshfields 1959-69, White Brooks and Gilman 1970-72; legal advsr Nat Cncl for Voluntary Orgns 1972-; memb: Goodman Ctee 1974-76, cncl L'Orchestre du Monde (Orchestra of the World) 1988; *Recreations* music, walking, foreign travel; *Clubs* Royal Cwlth, Cavalry & Guards, MCC; *Style—* Adrian R Longley, Esq; 7 Kersley St, London SW11 4PR (☎ 01 223 7515); 26 Bedford Square, London WC1B 3HU (☎ 01 636 4066)

LONGLEY, Michael; JP (1984); s of Sir Norman Longley, KBE, DL, of Crawley, W Sussex, and Dorothy Lillian, *née* Baker; *b* 23 July 1929; *Educ* Clifton, Brighton Tech Coll; *m* 24 Sept 1955, Rosemary, da of Walter Jackson (d 1968); 2 s (Julian Philip b 1957, James Christopher b 1959, d 1977); *Career* dir: James Longley Hldgs Ltd 1961-, James Longley & Co Ltd 1967-, James Longley Properties Ltd 1981-, Longley Freeholds Ltd 1979-, Longley Devpts 1961-, WG Boyce Ltd 1967-, Romanbury Investmt Ltd 1961-, Forumcrown Ltd 1980-, Rocatelle Ltd 1980-, James Longley Enterprises Ltd 1976, Towgreen Ltd 1980-, Canningford Ltd 1978- (Investmts Ltd 1983-), Reigate Securities Ltd 1985-, Sackville Trading Est Magmnt Ltd 1984-, St Barnabas Ct Mgmnt Co Ltd 1986-; FCIOB 1980; Freeman City of London, Liveryman Worshipful Co of Armourers and Brasiers 1963; *Recreations* gardening, ornithology, natural history, property speculation; *Style—* Michael Longley, Esq, JP; Isle of Thorns, Lewes Rd, Chelwood Gate, Haywards Heath, West Sussex RH17 7DE; James Longley (Hldgs) Ltd, East Park, Crawley, West Sussex RH10 6AP (☎ 0293 561212 Ext 2230, direct line 0293 564230, fax 0293 564564)

LONGLEY, Peter; s of Sir Norman Longley, CBE, DL, and Dorothy Lilian Baker; *b* 28 July 1927; *Educ* Clifton; *m* 1954, da of Sidney Brittain (d 1974); 1 s (Robert b 1960), 2 da (Elizabeth b 1956, Alison b 1958); *Career* building contractor; dir: James Longley & Co Ltd 1961-87, James Longley (Hldgs) Ltd 1969-; chm: Clayton House (Toc H) Crawley Ltd, The Longley Tst; dir: Brighton West Pier Tst, BEC Pension Tstees Ltd, Southern Industl History Centre; pres Crawley Boys' Club; vice-pres Sussex Assoc of Boys' Clubs, memb SE Regnl Cncl CBI; Liveryman Worshipful Co of Armourers and Brasiers; FRSA; Fell Chartered Inst Bldg; *Style—* Peter Longley, Esq; Lackenhurst, Brooks Green, Horsham, W Sussex; Longley House, East Park, Crawley, W Sussex (☎ 0293 561212)

LONGMAN, Lady Elizabeth Mary; *née* Lambart; er da of Field Marshal 10 Earl of Cavan, KP, GCB, GCMG, GCVO, CBE (d (1946), of Cavan, and Joan, Countess of Cavan, DBE (d 1976); *b* 16 Oct 1924; *m* 1949, Mark Frederic Kerr Longman (d 1972), 5 s of Henry Kerr Longman (d 1972), of Wildwood, Pyrford, Surrey; 3 da; *Career* bridesmaid at wedding of HM The Queen 1947; dir The Fine Art Soc plc, tstee Harrison Homes; *Recreations* gardening; *Style—* Lady Elizabeth Longman; The Old Rectory, Todenham, Moreton-in-Marsh, Glos; 1/58 Ruthland Gate, London SW7 (☎ 01 581 1230); The Fine Art Society, 148 New Bond St, London W1

LONGMAN, (James Edward) Ford; s of George Lewis Ernest Longman, and Alice Lizzie Mary (d 1954); *b* 8 Dec 1928; *Educ* Watford GS, Birkbeck Coll London (BSc), Leeds Univ; *m* 22 May 1954, Dilys Menai, da of Reginald Wilfred Richard Hunt (d 1972); 2 s (Jonathan b 1955, Richard b 1962), 3 da (Sarah b 1957, Rachel b 1960, Margaret b 1965); *Career* RAF Radar/Wireless Sch and Educn Branch 1947-49; Miny of Health, Bd of Control and Off Min for Science 1949-62; hon sec Watford and DC of Churches and Lay Preacher 1950-62; asst dir Joseph Rowntree Memorial Tst, sec J R M Housing Tst, clerk to Joseph Rowntree Schs 1962-70; dir Yorks (Regnl) Cncl of Social Serv 1970-75, sec seven other Regnl Bodies; hon sec Yorks Arts Assoc 1970-76; chm Yorks CSS 1967-70; sometime memb of ten Govt Ctees on social services and penal matters, inc ctee on serv overseas; Lord Chllr's Advsy Ctee on Crown Cts (NECCT) and Bd of HM Borstal Wetherby (chm); conslt in Social Planning to Govt of W Berlin and UNESCO; chm All-Pty United World Tst for Educn and Res, exec memb Nat Peace and NCSS; memb Yorks and Humberside Regnl Econ Planning Cncl (and three of its four working gps 1965-72); jt fndr of St Leonard's Housing Assoc, York Abbeyfield Soc, Regnl Studies Assoc, founded Community Devpt Tst to tackle unmet needs in social res and social serv 1968 (dir 1968-76); HM Inspr of Community Educn 1975-83; Co Cllr N Yorks and shadow chm of public Protetion cteey; Parly Candidate (Lib/SDP Alliance) Selby 1987; memb Soc of Friends (Quakers) 1958-; *Recreations* painting, gliding, reading, renovating historic bldgs (with wife, restored Healaugh Priory 1981-86), writing; *Style—* James Longman, Esq; Whitbygate House, Thornton-le-Dale, N Yorks YO18 7RY (☎ 0751 74609)

LONGMAN, Peter Martin; s of Denis Martin Longman, of Som, and Mary Joy, *née* Simmonds (d 1977); *b* 2 Mar 1946; *Educ* Huish's Sch Taunton, Univ Coll Cardiff (BSc), Univ of Manchester (Drama); *m* 22 May 1976, Sylvia June, da of John Lancaster Prentice, of E Sussex; 2 da (Tania Louise b 1978, Natalie Therese b 1981); *Career* housing arts offr Arts Cncl GB 1969-78 (fin dept 1968-69), dep dir Crafts Cncl 1978-83, sec Museums & Galleries Cmmn 1984- (dep sec 1983-84); sec working party reports on: Trg Arts Admins (Arts Cncl 1971), Area Museum Cncls and Servs (HMSO 1984), Museums in Scot (HMSO 1986); memb: Arts Centres Panel Gtr London Arts Assoc 1981-83, bd of Caryl Jenner Prodns Ltd (Unicorn Theatre for Children) 1983-87, Cncl Textile Conservation Centre Ltd 1983-, co-opted bd Scot Museums Cncl 1986-; FRSA 1989; *Recreations* discovering Britain, listening to music; *Style—* Peter Longman, Esq; Museums & Galleries Cmmn, 7 St James's Sq, London SW1Y 4JU (☎ 01 839 9341, fax 01 930 2058)

LONGMORE, Andrew Centlivres; QC (1983); s of Dr John Bell Longmore (d 1973), of Shrewsbury, and Virginia Albertina, *née* Centlivres; *b* 25 August 1944; *Educ* Winchester, Lincoln Coll Oxford (MA); *m* 17 Oct 1979, Margaret Murray, da of Dr James McNair (d 1980), of Milngavie, Glasgow; 1 s (James Centlivres b 1981); *Career* barr Middle Temple 1966; memb Bar Cncl 1982-85, chm Law Reform Ctee 1987-; *Books* co-ed MacGillivray and Parkington, Law of Insurance (6 edn 1975, 7 edn 1981, 8 edn 1988); *Recreations* fell-walking; *Style—* Andrew Longmore, Esq, QC; 7 Kings Bench Walk, Temple, London EC4 (☎ 01 583 0404)

LONGMORE, Prof Donald Bernard; s of Bernard George Longmore, of Wolverley, Sandown Rd, Sandwich, Kent, and Beatrix Alice, *née* Payne; *b* 20 Feb 1928; *Educ*

Solihull Sch, Guys Hosp Med Sch (MB, BS), Baylor Univ Texas, Univ of Texas, The London Hosp; *m* 2 April 1956, Patricia Christine Greig, da of Arthur Hardman Spindler (d 1984), of Bray on Thames, Berks; 3 da (Annabel b 1958, Juliet b 1959, Susan b 1962); *Career* Guy's Hosp: house appts 1953, jr lectr in anatomy 1954; surgical resident Baylor Univ Texas 1956-58, surgical registrar London Hosp 1958-59, sr registrar Middx Hosp 1960-61, lectr in surgery St Thomas' Hosp 1962-63, conslt Nat Heart Hosp 1963-83, dir magnetic resonance unit Brompton Hosp 1983-, cardiac surgn and memb Britains first heart transplant team, co fndr Coronary Artery Disease Res Assoc (memb bd of mgmnt), hon sr lectr Univ of London; LRCP, FRCS, FRCSE, memb Br Inst Radiology; *Books* over 250 scientific pubns incl: Spare Part Surgery (1968), Machines in Medicine (1969), The Heart (1970), The Current Status of Cardiac Surgery (1975), Modern Cardiac Surgery (1978), Towards Safer Cardiac Surgery (1981); *Recreations* sailing, skiing; *Clubs* Royal Yacht Sqdn, Utd Hosps SC; *Style—* Prof Donald Longmore; Whitemayes, Chertsey Lane, Staines TW18 3LQ (☎ 0784 452436); 9 Crowsport, Hamble, Hants; Aldebaran, Flaine, France; Magnetic Resonance Unit, 30 Britten St, Chelsea SW3 6NN (☎ 01 351 5773, fax 01 351 4986)

LONGMORE, Lady; Enid Marjory; da of Col Murray Ray de Bruyne James, CMG (d 1939), and Ethel Westrop (d 1968); the Westrops came from Westphalia to England in the reign of King John as hired mercenaries; *b* 1 Mar 1905; *Educ* Mrs Dudley Harvey's Sch Aldeburgh, Sorbonne; *m* 1, 1935, Lt-Col Geoffrey Hadden Bolster, OBE (ka 1944); m 2, 1960, Air Chief Marshal Sir Arthur Murray Longmore, GCB, DSO (d 1970); *Career* served WW II SOE Mil Intelligence; travel lectr; FRGS; *Style—* Lady Longmore

LONGMORE, Lady Felicity Ann; da of 1 Earl Wavell; *b* 1921; *m* 1947, Maj Peter Maitland Longmore, MC, (RA); 1 s (and 1 s decd), 2 da; *Career* Co Cllr W Sussex 1981-; chm Social Services Ctee 1985-; *Style—* Lady Felicity Longmore; Bramleys, Funtington, Chichester

LONGMORE, Hon Mrs (Jean Mary); only da of 2 Baron Forres (d 1954), of Glenogil, Scotland; *m* 28 April 1941, Wing Cdr (William) James Maitland Longmore, CBE (d 1988), 2 s of Air Chief Marshal Sir Arthur Murray Longmore, GCB, DSO (d 1970); 3 da (Virginia, Carolyn, Jennifer); *Style—* The Hon Mrs Longmore; Cross Lane Cottage, Stake lane, Ashton, Bishops Waltham, Hants SO3 1FL (☎ 048 93 2794)

LONGMORE, (Charles John) Nigel; DL (Herts 1971); s of Brig John Alexander Longmore, CB, CBE, TD, DL (d 1973), and Marguerite Madeleine, *née* Chapman Mathews; *b* 2 April 1933; *Educ* Harrow; *m* 1973 (m dis 1983), Celia Jane, *née* Walker; 1 da (Alexandra b 26 March 1975); *Career* admitted slr 1960; sr ptnr Longmores Hertford 1969; Dep Sheriff for Co of Herts 1960-69, Under Sheriff for Co of Herts 1969-; clerk to HM Cmmrs of Taxes for Hertford and Stevenage Divns 1965-; dep coroner 1986-; co cmmr, subsequently co cdr, now co pres St John Ambulance Bde for Herts; KStJ 1980, CStJ 1975, OStJ 1949; life govr Haileybury and Imperial Service Coll 1966-; pres Herts Agric Soc 1979-80 i/c; *Recreations* painting, shooting, fishing; *Clubs* Arts, Chelsea Arts; *Style—* Nigel Longmore, Esq, DL; Longmores, Solicitors, 24 Castle Street, Hertford SG14 1HP (☎ 0992 586781)

LONGRIGG, John Stephen; CMG (1972), OBE (1963); s of Brig Stephen H Longrigg, OBE (d 1979), and Florence, *née* Anderson (d 1977); *b* 1 Oct 1923; *Educ* Rugby, Magdalen Coll Oxford (BA); *m* 1966, Ann, *née* O'Reilly; 2 s (Stephen, Harry), 1 da (Hannah); *Career* WWII 1942-45, The Rifle Bde, Lt (despatches); HM Diplomatic Serv 1948-82, Paris, Baghdad, Berlin, Dakar, Johannesburg, Pretoria, Washington, Bahrain, Hong Kong, ret; admin Common Law Inst of Intellectual Property 1983-88; *Recreations* golf; *Clubs* Reform, Royal Blackheath GC, Littlestone GC; *Style—* John Longrigg, Esq, CMG, OBE; 2 The Cedars, 3 Westcombe Park Rd, Blackheath, London SE3 7RE (☎ 01 858 1604)

LONGRIGG, Roger Erskine; s of Brig Stephen Hemsley Longrigg, OBE D Litt of Chancellor House, Tunbridge Wells (d 1979) and Florence Amy, *née* Anderson (d 1974); *b* 1 May 1929; *Educ* Bryanston Sch, Magdalen Coll, Oxford (BA); *m* 20 July 1957, Jane Catherine, da of Capt Marcus Beresford Chichester of Compton Chamberlyne, Wilts (d 1985); 3 da (Laura b 1958, Frances b 1961, Clare b 1963); *Career* entered army 1947, cmmnd Buffs 1948, demob 1949; joined TA 1952, Capt 1955; *Books* author of over 50 published books (pseudonyms inc Rosalind Erskine, Ivor Drummond, Laura Black); novels inc: High Pitched Buzz (1956), Daughters of Mulberry (1961), The Paper Boats (1965), The Desperate Criminals (1972), Bad Bet (1981); non fiction inc: The History of Horse Racing (1972), The History of Foxhunting (1975), The English Squire and His Sport (1977); *Recreations* trout fishing, painting; *Clubs* Brooks's, Pratt's; *Style—* Roger Longrigg, Esq; Orchard House, Crookham, Hampshire (☎ 0252 850333)

LONGSDON, Anthony Ernest Cross; s of Ernest Morewood Longsdon (d 1940), of Little Longstone, and Esther Chappé, *née* Cross (d 1956); family living at Little Longstone 1807-; *b* 12 Mar 1911; *Educ* Shrewsbury, Pembroke Coll Cambridge (BA); *m* 23 Sept 1936, Hilda Dearmer, da of John Cawley (d 1924), of Buxton; *Career* mining engr Frepia Yugoslavia 1933-36; civil engr J Mowlem 1936-46; farming 1946-; *Recreations* fishing; *Style—* Anthony Longsdon, Esq; The Manor, Little Longstone, nr Bakewell, Derbyshire (☎ 062 987 215)

LONGSDON, Lt Col (Robert) Shaun; s of Wing Cdr Robert Cyril Longsdon, of Crickhowell, Powys, and Evadne Lloyd, *née* Flower; *b* 5 Dec 1936; *Educ* Eton; *m* 19 Dec 1968, Caroline Susan, da of Col Michael Colvin Watson, OBE, MC, TD, DL, of Barnsley, Gloucs; 3 s (James b 1971, Rupert b 1972, Charles b 1975), 1 da (Laura b 1983); *Career* Regular Army Offr 1955-81; princ mil appts: Lt Col, mil assist (GSO1) to the Chief of Gen Staff 1975-77, CO 17/21 Lancers 1977-79, directing staff (GSO1 DS) Nat Def Coll 1979-81; dir of PR Knight Frank & Rutley 1981-; ensign of the Queen's Body Gd of the Yeomen of the Guard 1985-, Col 17/21 Lancers 1988; govr Royal Shakespeare Co 1982-; *Recreations* field sports; *Clubs* White's, Cavalry and Guards, Pratt's; *Style—* Lt-Col Shaun Longsdon; Southrop Lodge, Lechlade, Glous GL7 3NU (☎ 036 785 2841); 20 Hanover Square, London W1R 0AH

LONGSTAFF, Bernard; s of Joseph Longstaff (d 1980), of Wade House, Dewsbury, and Agnes Longstaff (d 1975); *b* 14 April 1939; *Educ* St Paulinus RC Sch Dewsbury, Dewsbury Tech Sch, Wakefield Tech Coll; *Career* md and chm Elco Power Plant Ltd (British Overseas Trade Bd's export award for small mfrg businesses 1982; Queen's Award for Export 1983); md S & B Longstaff Ltd; *Recreations* tennis, horses, farming, swimming; *Style—* Bernard Longstaff, Esq; Elco Power Plant Ltd, Station Rd, Tadcaster, N Yorks (☎ (0937) 835834); Langdale House, York Rd, Malton, N Yorks (☎ (0653) 5021)

LONGSTAFF, Wilfred; s of Thomas Longstaff (d 1980), and Phoebe Alice Calvert, *née* Rain; *b* 10 Dec 1931; *Educ* Tottenham Tech Coll, Northern Poly (dip Arch); *m* 1 Aug 1959, Stephanie Maria, da of John Joseph Macken (d 1958); 2 s (Wilfred b 1960, David b 1961); *Career* RE Corpl, served Cyprus and Egypt; chartered architect in private practice 1983-, chief architect Courage Eastern Ltd 1975-80; ARIBA, FFAS; *Recreations* golf; *Clubs* Goring & Streatley Golf; *Style—* Wilfred Longstaff, Esq; 7 Cambrian Way, The Orchard, Calcot, Reading, Berkshire RG3 7DD (☎ Reading 419152)

LONGUËIL; *see*: de Longuëil

LONGWELL, Dennis Charles; s of Charles Longwell, San Diego, California, USA, and Viola, *née* Nelson; *b* 30 August 1941; *Educ* Evanston HS Evanston Illinois USA, Harvard Univ (BA), Stanford Business Sch Stanford USA (MBA); *m* 13 June 1964, Ashby, da of George Houghton Haslam, of Charlottesville, Virginia, USA; 2 s (John b 14 Sept 1970, David b 7 Dec 1972); *Career* US Army 1963-65: Lieut and ADC to Cmdg Gen Transportation Sch; The Chase Manhattan Bank: joined as credit trainee 1962, relationship mangr 1967, asst tres 1968, second vice pres 1969, vice pres 1970, asst sec to Mgmnt Ctee 1971, pres Chase Manhattan Bank of Centl NY (Syracuse) 1972-76, div exec Banks Corporate Industries Sector 1976, gp exec 1977, country mangr UK 1982, sr vice pres 1981, area exec for Europe Africa and M East; chm American Banks Assoc of London 1986-88, memb bd of govrs and managing cncl Ditchley Fndn; *Recreations* golf, sailing, boating and travel; *Clubs* Bucks Club, Annabel's, Harry's Bar, Sky Club of New York city; *Style—* Dennis Longwell, Esq; The Chase Manhattan Bank, NA Woolgate House, Coleman Street, London EC2P 2HD (☎ 01 726 5200, fax 01 726 7639, telex 8813137)

LONGWILL, Col John Alexander Rankin; s of Matthew Rankin Longwill (d 1983), of Plymouth, and Winifred Lilian, *née* Sleath; *b* 5 Sept 1939; *Educ* Liverpool Coll, Liverpool Univ Med Sch (MB, ChB), DTM and H London (DTM and H, DCH), RCOG London (DObst); *m* 5 Jan 1973, Say Fah, da of Shu Pi Chu (d 1965), of Singapore; 2 s (Toby b 1975, Andrew b 1979), 2 da (Sarah b 1973, Katie b 1977); *Career* British Army; cmmnd 1962, Capt RMO regular army Aden 1966-67; Maj SMO: Trucial Oman Scouts 1968-70, Anzuk FMC Singapore 1971-73, Minden Baor 1974-77; Lt Co anaesthetist: BMH Belfast 1980, QEMH Woolwich 1980-83; detached anaesthetist: mine field surgical team Belize 1981, mily wing MPH Belfast 1982; cmdg offr BMG Falkland Islands 1983-84 (FMA), SMO Tutong Brunei 1984-87 (Royal Brunei Armed Forces, loan serv), Col SMO Hereford (HQ R Divn) BAOR 1987-; MRCGP 1971, BMA 1964; GSM Brunei 1985, Royal Brunei Armed Forces Jubilee Medal 1986; *Recreations* bloodhounds, photography, fishing; *Clubs* RAMC Mill Bank, The Bloodhound; *Style—* Col John Longwill; MRS, Bassingburn Barracks, Royston, Herts

LONGWORTH, Dr Ian Heaps; s of Joseph Longworth (d 1968), of Bolton, Lancs, and Alice, *née* Heaps (d 1961); *b* 29 Sept 1935; *Educ* King Edward VII Lytham, Peterhouse Cambridge (MA, PhD); *m* 27 Sept 1967, Clare Marian, da of Maurice Edwin Titford (d 1967), of Croydon; 1 s (Timothy b 1975), 1 da (Alison b 1978); *Career* asst keeper dept of british and medieval antiquities Br Museum 1963-69, keeper dept of prehistoric and romano british antiquities Br Museum 1973- (asst keeper 1969-73); memb Ancient Monuments Bd for England 1977-84, chm Area Archaeological Advsy Ctee for NW England 1978-79; Publications: Durrington Walls - Excavations 1966-68 (with G J Wainwright 1971), Collared Urns of the Bronze Age in GB and Ireland (1984), Prehistoric Britain (1985), Catalogue of the Excavated Prehistoric and Romano British Material in the Greenwell Collection (with I A Kinnes 1985), Archaeology in Britain since 1945 (ed with J Cherry, 1986), Excavations at Grimes Graves Norfolk 1972-76 (contrib, 1988); FSA 1966 (sec 1974-80; vice pres 1985-88); *Clubs* MCC; *Style—* Dr Ian Longworth; 2 Hurst View Rd, S Croydon, Surrey CR2 7A6 (☎ 01 688 4960); Dept of Prehistoric and Romano - British Antiquities, British Museum, London WC1B 3DG (☎ 01 323 8293)

LONSDALE, 7 Earl of (UK 1807); Sir James Hugh William Lowther; 8 Bt (GB 1764); also Viscount and Baron Lowther (GB 1797); s of Viscount Lowther (d 1949, er s of 6 Earl); suc gf 1953; *b* 3 Nov 1922; *Educ* Eton; *m* 1, 1945 (m dis 1954), Tuppina Cecily (decd), da of Capt C H Bennett (decd); 1 s, 1 da; m 2, 1954 (m dis 1962), Hon Jennifer Lowther, da of Maj the Hon Christopher William Lowther (decd) (himself s of 1 Viscount Ullswater); 1 s, 2 da; m 3, 1963, Nancy Ruth Stephenson, da of Thomas Cobbs (decd), of Pacific Palisades, Cal, USA; 1 s; m 4, 1975, Caroline Sheila, da of Sir Gerald Gordon Ley, 3 Bt, TD; 1 s, 1 da; *Heir* s, Viscount Lowther; *Career* 1939-45 War with RAC and as Capt E Riding Yeo (despatches); structural engrg 1947-50, farmer, forester and dir of associated and local cos in Cumberland and Westmorland and of Border Television; memb The Sports Cncl 1971-74, English Tourist Bd 1971-75; pres Cumberland and Westmorland NPFA; CBIM, FRSA; *Clubs* Brooks's, Turf; *Style—* The Rt Hon the Earl of Lonsdale; Askham Hall, Penrith, Cumbria CA10 2PF (☎ 09312 208)

LONSDALE, Yvonne Muriel; *née* Perry; da of John Edgar Perry (d 1954), of Stourbridge, Worcs, and Josephine Margaret, *née* Edwards (d 1973); *b* 8 Oct 1916; *Educ* Roedean, Institut Heubi Lausanne Switzerland; *m* 11 Aug 1945 (m dis 1974), Richard Thomas Henry Lonsdale, DSO, MC (d 1988), s of Robert Lonsdale (d 1946), of Carrick-on-Shannon, Eire; 2 s (Clive b 1947, Hugh b 1959), 1 da (Julia b 1950); *Career* WWII serv Emergency Med Serv 1939-42, Red Cross 1940-45, RAF 1942-45; *Recreations* horse racing, walking; *Clubs* New Cavendish, WI; *Style—* Mrs Yvonne M Lonsdale; Pear Tree Cottage, Amport, nr Andover, Hants SP11 8AE (☎ 0264 710566)

LOOKER, Sir Cecil Thomas; s of Edward William Looker (decd), of Sydney; *b* 11 April 1913; *Educ* Fort St High Sch, Sydney Univ; *m* 1941, Jean Leslyn, da of Ernest Edward Withington (decd), of Melbourne; 1 s, 2 da; *Career* private sec to PM (Rt Hon St Robert Menzies) 1939-41; ptnr Ian Potter & Co 1953 (sr ptnr 1967-76); chm Stock exchange of Melbourne 1966-72; pres Aust Assoc Stock Exchanges 1968-71; dir PNG Devpt Bank 1966-74; memb Immigration Planning Cncl 1968-74; ctee memb Stock Exchange of Melbourne 1962-78 (chm 1966-72); chm Australian United Corpn Ltd (Group); dep chm Ansett Tport Industs Ltd; chm Plessey Pacific Pty Ltd; dir: Southern Cross Properties Ltd, Herald Devpt Ltd; kt 1969; *Clubs* Australian, RACV; *Style—* Sir Cecil Looker; 26 Thormey St, N Balwyn, Victoria, Australia (☎ 857 9316)

LOPES, Hon George Edward; yr s of 2 Baron Roborough, *qv*; *b* 22 Feb 1945; *Educ* Eton, RAC Cirencester; *m* 1975, Hon Sarah Violet Astor, da of 2 Baron Astor of Hever (d 1984); 1 s, 1 da; *Style—* The Hon George Lopes; Gnaton Hall, Yealmpton, Plymouth, Devon PL8 2HU

LOPES, Hon Henry Massey; s and h of 2 Baron Roborough; *b* 2 Feb 1940; *Educ* Eton; *m* 1, 1968 (m dis 1986), Robyn Zenda Carol, da of John Bromwich, of Point Lonsdale, Victoria, Aust; 2 s (Massey b 1969, Andrew b 1971), 2 da (Katie b 1976, Melinda b 1978); m 2, 1986, Sarah Anne Pipon, da of Colin Baker of Peter Tarn, Devon; 1 da (Emily b 1987); *Career* landowner; *Style*— The Hon Henry Lopes; Bickham House, Roborough, Plymouth (☎ 0822 852742)

LORAM, Vice-Adm Sir David Anning; KCB (1979), LVO (1957); s of John Anning Loram (d 1969), and Jessie Eckford, *née* Scott (d 1961); *b* 24 July 1924; *Educ* RNC Dartmouth; *m* 1, 1958 (m dis 1981), Fiona (*née* Beloe); 3 s; m 2, 1983, Diana, da of Timothy Carlton Keigwin MC (d 1987), of The Old Vicarage, West Anstey, N Devon; *Career* RN: served WWII, ADC to Govr-Gen NZ 1946-48, equerry to HM The Queen 1954-57, flag offr Malta and NATO Cdr SE Med and Cdr Br Forces 1973-75, Cmdt Nat Def Coll 1975-77, Dep Supreme Allied Cdr Atlantic 1977-80; a gentleman usher to HM The Queen 1982-; *Recreations* fishing; *Style*— Vice Adm Sir David Loram, KCB, LVO; The Old Vicarage, West Anstey, South Molton, N Devon (☎ 039 84 529)

LORD, Alan; CB (1972); s of Frederick Lord; *b* 12 April 1929; *Educ* Rochdale, St John's Coll Cambridge; *m* Joan; 2 da; *Career* former cmmr Inland Revenue and second perm sec Treasury; dir Allied Breweries, md Dunlop Hldgs 1980- (md Dunlop Int 1978-), dir Bank of England 1983-; *Style*— Alan Lord, Esq, CB; Mardens, Hildenborough, Tonbridge, Kent (☎ Hildenborough 832268)

LORD, David Gerald; s of Lt Cdr Cuttbert Edward Lord RN (ret) of Petersfield, Hamps and Nancy Muriel, *née* Gibson; *b* 14 Dec 1947; *Educ* Repton, Trinity Coll Dublin (BA); *m* 2 Sept 1978, (Diana) Jennifer, Herbert Louis Benjamin; 1 s (Benjamin Edward b 1979), 2 da (Philippa Katherine, Jessica Rachel); *Career* with First Nat Bank in Dallas 1971, Chase Manhattan Bank NA (London), exec dir Continental Illinois Ltd (Tokyo) 1983 (joined London off 1973, assoc dir 1980), md First Interstate Capital Mkts Ltd (formerly Continental Illinois) 1987- (joined 1984); *Recreations* sailing, skiing, golf; *Clubs* Boodles Oriental; *Style*— David Lord, Esq; 30 Old Park Avenue, London SW1R (☎ 01 675 1700); Stanhoe Norfolk; 6 Agar Street, London WC2 (☎ 01 379 5915, telex 947161)

LORD, Lady; Doris; *née* Jones; da of Ernest Jones, of Sheffield; *b* 1928; *m* Sir Percy Lord (d 1968); *Style*— Lady Lord; 10 Yewlands Drive, Fulwood, Preston

LORD, Graham John; s of Harold Reginald Lord, OBE (d 1969), of Beira Mozambique, and Ida Frances, *née* McDowall (d 1966); *b* 16 Feb 1943; *Educ* Falcon Coll Essexvale Bulawayo Rhodesia, Churchill Coll, Cambridge (BA); *m* 12 Sept 1962, Elizabeth Jane, da of John Carruthers (d 1976), of Littleport, Cambs; 2 da (Mandy b 1963, Kate b 1966); *Career* ed Varsity Cambridge 1964; Reporter: Cambridge Evening News 1964, Sunday Express 1965 (lit ed 1969-, launched Sunday Express Book of the Year Award 1987-); Lambourn parish cncllr 1983-87, vice chm Newbury Mencap 1982-88, chm Eastbury Poor's Furje Charity 1983-88, sub-ctee W Berks Cons Assoc Exec 1985-88, Newbury Dist cncllr 1985-87; *Books* Marshmallow Pie (1970), A Roof Under Your Feet (1973), The Spider and The Fly (1974), God and All His Angels (1976), The Nastradomus Horoscope (1981), Time Out Of Mind (1986); *Recreations* tennis; *Style*— Graham Lord, Esq; Sunday Express, 121 Fleet St, London EC4P 4JT (☎ 01 353 8000)

LORD, His Honour Judge; John Herent; s of Sir Frank Lord, KBE, DL, JP (d 1974); *b* 5 Nov 1928; *Educ* Manchester GS, Merton Coll Oxford (MA); *m* 1959, June Ann, da of George Caladine (d 1969); 3 s; *Career* barr Inner Temple 1951, jr of Northern Circuit 1952, asst recorder of Burnley 1971, a recorder of Crown Ct 1972-78, a circuit judge 1978-; *Recreations* photography, shooting, boating ('MC Overlord'); *Clubs* Leander, St James's (Manchester); *Style*— His Honour Judge Lord; Three Lanes, Greenfield, Oldham, Greater Manchester (☎ 045 77 2198)

LORD, John William; s of William James Lord (d 1970), and Bessie Maria, *née* Watkins, of 54 St Albans Close, Gravesend, Kent; *b* 28 May 1931; *Educ* Gravesend GS for Boys; *m* 28 April 1956, Patricia Jane, da of Maj Frank Palmer (d 1979); 3 s (David b 1964, Richard b 1966, Peter b 1971); *Career* Nat Serv RAF 1953-55; articled clerk MacIntyre Hudson and Co 1948-53, CA, audit mangr Evnas Fripp Deed and Co 1955-57, tax mangr Midgley Snelling and Co 1957-60, sr ptnr Carley and Co 1983- (mangr 1961, ptnr 1962-); dir and sec Gravesend Masonic Hall Co Ltd, memb Assoc of Ex Round Tablers; FCA 1953, ATII 1962; *Recreations* golf, tennis, gardening; *Clubs* Mid Kent Golf; *Style*— John Lord, Esq; Lark Rise, Pondfield Lane, Shorne, nr Gravesend, Kent DA12 3LD; 8 Overcliffe, Gravesend, Kent DA11 OHJ (☎ 0474 569032, fax 0474 320410)

LORD, Michael Nicholson; MP (C) Suffolk Central 1983-; s of John Lord and Jessie, *née* Nicholson; *b* 17 Oct 1938; *Educ* Christs Coll Cambridge (MA); *m* 1965, Jennifer Margaret, *née* Childs; 1 s, 1 da; *Recreations* golf, sailing, trees; *Clubs* Farmers; *Style*— Michael Lord, Esq, MP; House of Commons, London SW1

LORD, Richard Thomas Geoffrey; s of Sam Lord; *b* 29 Mar 1934; *Educ* Giggleswick Sch, Univ of Leeds; *m* 1959, Elizabeth Logie, *née* Forrester; 1 s, 2 da; *Career* chartered textile technologist; Scapa Gp plc 1955-84 (dir 1976-84), dir Lancashire Enterprises Ltd 1985-; business conslt; pres Chorley Cons Assoc 1988- (chm 1985-88); *Recreations* golf, local politics, old maps; *Clubs* District & Union (Blackburn), Pleasington Golf; *Style*— Richard Lord, Esq; Cuerden Lodge, Bamber Bridge, Preston PR5 6AU (☎ 0772 35326)

LORD, William Burton Housley; CB (1979); s of Arthur James Lord (d 1931); *b* 22 Mar 1919; *Educ* King George Sch Southport, Univ of London (MSc), Trinity Coll Cambridge (MA); *m* 1942, Helena Headon, da of Douglas Jaques (d 1957); 2 da; *Career* WWII as Capt South Lancashire Regt serv Middle East, North Africa; inventor of radio proximity fuse; head of metallurgy AWRE 1958, asst chief sci advsr MOD 1964-68, dep chief scientist Army 1968-71, dir-gen of Estabs Resources & Progs MOD 1971-76, dir Royal Armament R & D Estab 1976-79, conslt scientist; *Recreations* walking, various water sports, amateur radio; *Style*— William Lord, Esq, CB; Linden Mews, The Mount, Reading RG1 5HL

LORENZ, John Antonin (Tony); s of Hans Viktor Lorenz (d 1985), and Catherine Jesse Cairns, *née* James; *b* 4 Mar 1944; *Educ* Stamford Sch, Trinity Coll Dublin (BBS); *m* 24 Feb 1968, (Jennifer) Bernice, da of Lancelot James Harper, of Angmering-on-Sea; 1 s (Simon b 1976), 2 da (Martha b 1977, Zoë b 1979); *Career* Ford Motor Co 1966-67, Hoare Govett 1967-68, PA Mgmnt Cnslts 1968-73, First Nat Hldgs 1973-75, Charterhouse Gp 1975-77, Equity Capital for Indust 1977-86; co-fndr and managing ptnr ECI Ventures 1986-; co-fndr and chm Br Venture Capital Assoc 1984-85, co-fdr and bd memb Euro Venture Capital Assoc 1987-; memb NEDO working gps: Corporate Venturing 1986-87, Tourism and Leisure 1988-89; visiting fell Cranfield Inst Tech; F Inst M 1980, bd memb Proned, tstee Education 2000; *Books* Venture Capital Today (1985, 1989), Small Business and Entrepreneurship (1988); *Recreations* travel, writing, riding, skiing; *Clubs* Lansdowne, LBS Alumni; *Style*— Tony Lorenz, Esq; Greenacre, Beacon Hill, Penn, Bucks HP10 8NJ (☎ 049 481 2248) ECI Ventures, Brettenham House, Lancaster Place, London WC2E 7EN (☎ 01 606 1000, fax 01 240 5050)

LORETTO, Denis Crofton; s of Cecil Rupert Loretto, MM (d 1976), of Belfast, and Violet Florence, *née* Walker; *b* 7 April 1936; *Educ* Royal Belfast Academical Inst; *m* 17 March 1960, (Margaret) Wilma, da of William Alexander Campbell (d 1986), of Belfast; 1 s (Timothy 1961), 1 da (Angela b 1964); *Career* Cornhill Insur 1953-: branch underwriter Belfast 1953-59, head off underwriter London 1959-62, branch supt Belfast 1962-72, asst branch mangr Belfast 1972-74, branch mangr Belfast 1974-81, div mangr underwriting head off 1981-86, asst gen mangr Guildford 1986-; dir: Trafalgar Insur plc 1988, Br Reserve Insur plc 1988; memb The Northern Ireland Ptnrship; Belfast city cncllr 1977-81; FCII 1961; *Recreations* walking, photography; *Style*— Denis Loretto, Esq; 107 Lower Road, Fetcham, Leatherhead, Surrey KT22 9NQ (☎ 0372 53276); 57 Ladymead, Guildford, Surrey GU1 1DB (☎ 0483 68161, fax 0483 3009 52, telex 859383)

LORIMER, Sir (Thomas) Desmond; KB; s of Thomas Berry Lorimer (d 1952); *b* 20 Oct 1925; *Educ* Belfast Tech HS; *m* 1957, Patricia Doris, da of Ernest Samways; 2 da; *Career* chm: Lamont Hldgs plc 1973, Northern Bank Ltd 1985-, Northern Ireland Housing Exec 1970-75; chm Indust Devpt Bd for NI 1982-85; pres Inst of CAs in Ireland 1968-69, ptnr Deloitte Haskins and Sells (ret 1974); dir: Ruberoid plc 1972-, Distillers Gp plc 1986-; fell of Inst of Chartered Accountants in Ireland; Hon DSc; *Recreations* gardening, golf; *Clubs* Carlton, Royal Co Down Golf, Royal Belfast Golf; *Style*— Sir Desmond Lorimer; Windwhistle Cottage, 6A Circular Road West, Cultra, Holywood, Co Down BT18 0AT (☎ 02317 3323)

LORIMER, Patrick James; s of Lt-Cdr J T Lorimer, DSO, DL, of the Upper Church, Barr, Girvan, Ayrshire, and Judith Eileen, *née* Hughes Onslow; *b* 1 Oct 1946; *Educ* Willington, Magdalene Coll Cambridge (MA, Dip A); *m* 25 Sept 1976, (Julia) Caroline, da of Patrick Pringle (d 1974); 2 s (James b 7 May 1979, William b 23 Dec 1980), 1 da (Cressida b 14 April 1984); *Career* qualified architect 1972, fndr own practice ARP Architects London 1974-; capt ice hockey team Cambridge Univ 1968; Freeman City of London, Liveryman Worshipful Co of Loriners 1979; memb RIBA, ARCUK; *Recreations* shooting, fishing, building; *Style*— Patrick Lorimer, Esq; 13 Hanley Rd, London N4 (☎ 01 263 2706); 31 Oval Rd, London NW1 (☎ 01 485 0991, fax 01 482 4622)

LORNE, Marquess of; Torquhil Ian Campbell; only s and h of 12 Duke of Argyll; *b* 29 May 1968; *Career* page of honour to HM The Queen 1981-83; *Style*— Marquess of Lorne

LOSINSKA, Kathleen Mary; *née* Conway; OBE (1986); da of James Henry Conway (d 1941), and Dorothea Marguerite Hill (d 1977); da of Charles Hill, of the Connaught Rangers 1880-91; *b* 5 Oct 1924; *Educ* Selhurst GS; *m* 1942, Stanislaw, s of Franciszek Losinski and Helena Dekutowska (d 1949); 1 s (Julian); 2 gs (Stefan and Zygmunt) 1 gd (Zoe); *Career* entered Civil Serv 1939, Off of Population Censuses and Surveys, mgmnt memb Cncl of Civil Serv Unions (previously chm of cncl), vice-pres Civil and Public Servs Assoc; govr Ruskin Coll Oxford, cncl memb Peace through NATO; work for: Christian Trade Union Movement, Solidarnosc Polish Trade Unions; Gen Cncl memb TUC; Nuclear Energy Review Cmmr (TUC); Cavalier Order Odrodzemia Polski 1987; *Recreations* journalism, writing, music, history, archaeology; *Clubs* Civil Service; *Style*— Mrs Kate Losinska, OBE; 45 Rectory Park, Sanderstead, South Croydon, Surrey; Civil and Public Services Assoc, 215 Balham High Road, London SW17 (☎ 01 672 1299)

LOSS, Joe - Joshua Alexander (Joe); LVO (1984), OBE (1978); s of Israel and Ada Loss; *b* 22 June 1909; *Educ* Jewish Free Sch Spitalfields, Trinity Coll of Music, London Coll of Music; *m* 1938, Mildred Blanch Rose; 1 s, 1 da; *Career* band leader; former silent film accompanist, formed his own orch Astoria Ballroom 1930, became youngest Br band leader at age 20, first broadcast 1934, won 14 Carl Alan Awards; theme tune In the Mood; Freeman City of London 1979; *Style*— Joe Loss, Esq, LVO, OBE; Morley House, Regent St, London W1R 6QH (☎ 01 580 1212)

LOTEN, Alexander William; CB (1984); s of late Alec Oliver Loten, and Alice Maud Loten; *b* 11 Dec 1925; *Educ* Churcher's Coll Petersfield, CCC Cambridge (BA); *m* 1954, Mary Diana Flint; 1 s, 1 da; *Career* served WWII, RNVR 1943-46; engr: Rolls-Royce Ltd Derby 1950-54, Benham & Sons Ltd London 1954-58; Air Miny Work Directorate 1958-64; MPBW: sr engr 1964-70, superintending engr (mechanical design) 1970-75; dir of Works (Civil Accommodation) Property Servs Agency 1975-81, pres CIBS 1976-77, under-sec DOE and dir Mech and Electrical Engrg Services PSA 1981-85; *Style*— Alexander Loten, Esq, CB; Mansers Farm, Nizels Lane, Hildenborough, Tonbridge, Kent, TN11 8NX (☎ 0732 833204)

LOTHIAN, 12 Marquess of (S 1701); Peter Francis Walter Kerr; KCVO (1983), DL (Roxburghshire 1962); also Lord Newbottle (S 1591), Lord Jedburgh (S 1622), Earl of Lothian, Lord Ker of Newbattle (*sic*) (both S 1631), Earl of Ancram (1633), Viscount of Briene, Lord Ker of Newbottle, Oxnam, Jedburgh, Dolphinstoun and Nisbet (all S 1701), and Baron Ker of Kersheugh (UK 1821); s of Capt Andrew William Kerr, JP, RN (d 1929), and cous of 11 Marquess (d 1940); *b* 8 Sept 1922; *Educ* Ampleforth, Ch Ch Oxford; *m* 1948, Antonella (fndr pres Women of the Year Luncheon), da of Maj-Gen Sir Foster Reuss Newland, KCMG, CB (d 1943), and Mrs William Carr, of Ditchingham Hall, Norfolk (d 1986); 2 s, 4 da; *Heir* s, Earl of Ancram, MP; *Career* Lt Scots Gds 1943; jt parly sec Miny of Health April-Oct 1964; a lord-in-waiting to HM the Queen 1972-73; chm of cncl Scottish Red Cross 1976-86; Lord Warden of the Stanneries and keeper of Privy Seal of Duke of Cornwall 1977-83; memb Royal Company of Archers (Queen's Body Guard for Scotland); FRSA; kt SMO Malta; *Recreations* music; *Clubs* Boodle's, Beefsteak, New (Edinburgh); *Style*— The Most Hon the Marquess of Lothian, KCVO, DL; 54 Upper Cheyne Row, London SW3; Monteviot, nr Jedburgh, Roxburghshire (☎ 083 53 288); Melbourne Hall, Derby (☎ 033 16 2163)

LOTT, David Charles; s of Air Vice-Marshal Charles George Lott, CB, CBE, DSO, DFC, and Evelyn Muriel, *née* Little; *b* 8 May 1940; *Educ* Alhallows Sch, RAF Coll Cranwell; *m* 1, 5 June 1965 (m dis 1982), Elfriede; 2 s (Simon b 1966, Dieter b 1969); m 2, Kathryn Elizabeth; 1 da (Katie b 1986); *Career* RAF Coll Cranwell 1958-61, 17

Sqdn RAF Wildenrath 1961-64, ADC to AOC 23 Gp 1964-66, Hunter Pilot 208 54 Sqdn 1966-70, Deputy Flight Cdr 20 Sqdn Harriers 1970-74, Flight Cdr 1 Sqdn RAF Wittering 1974-78; Queens Commendation for Valuable Servs in the Air 1976; airline capt Britannia Airways; *Recreations* ski-ing, shooting, Jaguar cars; *Style*— Capt David Lott; 91 Silver End Rd, Haynes, Beds

LOTT, Felicity Ann Emwhyla; da of John Albert Lott, and Iris Emwhyla, *née* Williams; *b* 8 May 1947; *Educ* Pate's Girls GS Cheltenham, RHC London Univ (BA), Royal Acad of Music (LRAM); *m* 1, 22 Dec 1973 (m dis 1982), Robin Mavesyn Golding; m 2, 19 Jan 1984, Gabriel Leonard Woolf, s of Alec Woolf; 1 da (Emily b 19 June 1984); *Career* opera singer, debut Magic Flute ENO 1975; princ appearances: ENO, Glyndebourne, Covent Garden, WNO, SNO, Paris Opera, Brussels, Hamburg, Chicago, Munich Strauss Festival 1988; recordings: EMI, Decca, Harmonia Mundi Chandes, Deutsche, Gramphon Hyperion; sang at Royal Wedding 1986, patron New Sussex Opera; Hon DMus Sussex Univ 1989; *Recreations* reading, gardening; *Style*— Ms Felicity Lott; c/o Lies Askonas Ltd, 186 Drury Lane, London WC2B 5RY (☎ 01 405 1808)

LOTT, Air Vice-Marshal (Charles) George; CB (1958), CBE (1954), DSO (1940), DFC (1940); s of Charles Lott, and Beatrice Josephine Lott; *b* 28 Oct 1906; *Educ* Portsmouth Jr Tech Sch; *m* 23 July 1936, Evelyn Muriel, da of Frederick Little (d 1940); 2 s (David Charles b 1940, Jeremy Keith b 1947), 1 da (Jennifer Ann b 1937); *Career* aircraft apprentice RAF Halton 1922-25, cmmnd 1933, CO 43 Sqdn 1939-40, dir of trg USA 1944-45, chief instr Empire Flying Sch 1948-49, dir Air Def SHAPE 1955-57, cmdt Sch of Land/Air Warfare 1957-59, ret 1959; *Clubs* RAF; *Style*— Air Vice Marshal George Lott; Glen Waverley, Hooke Hill, Freshwater, IOW PO40 9BG (☎ 0988 755146)

LOUDON, Dr John Duncan Ott; OBE (1988); s of James Alexander Law Loudon (d 1931), of 10 Harrison Rd, Edinburgh, and Florence Ursula Marguerita, *née* Ott (d 1985); *b* 22 August 1924; *Educ* Wyggeston GS, Univ of Edinburgh (MB, ChB); *m* 10 Sept 1963, Nancy Beaton, da of Alexander John Mann (d 1967), of Avoch, Rosshire; 2 s (Alasdair John b 7 April 1956, Richard Donald b 8 Oct 1957); *Career* RAF Med Branch 1948-50; conslt obstetrician and gynaecologist Eastern Gen Hosp Edinburgh 1960-87, sr lectr Univ of Edinburgh 1962-87; VP RCOG 1981-84, memb GMC 1986-; FRCS (Ed) 1954, FRCOG 1972 (memb 1956); *Recreations* golf, gardening, travel, food and drink; *Style*— Dr John Loudon; Thorncroft, 94 Inverleith Place, Edinburgh EH3 5PA (☎ 031 552 1327)

LOUDON, Lady Prudence Katharine Patton; JP (Kent); 5 da of Adm of the Fleet 1 Earl Jellicoe (d 1935), and Florence Gwendoline, *née* Cayzer (d 1964); *b* 30 August 1913; *Educ* North Foreland Lodge Broadstairs; *m* 22 Dec 1936, Francis William Hope Loudon (d 1985), s of James Hope Loudon (d 1952), of Olantigh, Kent; 1 s, 2 da; *Recreations* sketching; *Style*— Lady Prudence Loudon, JP; Little Olantigh, Wye, nr Ashford, Kent (☎ 0233 812916)

LOUDOUN, Maj Gen Robert Beverley; CB (1983), OBE (1965); s of Robert Alexander Loudoun (d 1968), of Northwood, Middx, and Margaret Anne Homewood (d 1960); *b* 8 July 1922; *Educ* Univ Coll Sch London; *m* 1950, Audrey Olive, da of William Pearson Stevens (d 1976), of Dublin, Ireland; 2 s (Steven, Robin); *Career* enlisted RM 1940, war serv Italy, Yugoslavia, post war serv in Far East, Med, America, Caribbean, CO 40 Commando 1967-69, Brig UK Commandos 1969-71, Maj Gen RM Trg 1971-75; chm Jt Shooting Ctee for GB 1977-82, dir The Mental Health Fndn 1978-; Rep Col Cmdt RM 1983-84; Freeman City of London 1979, memb Guild of Freeman 1982-; *Recreations* sport (spectator); *Clubs* Army & Navy; *Style*— Maj Gen Robert Loudoun, CB, OBE; 2 Warwick Drive, Putney, London SW15 6LB (☎ 01 789 1826); The Mental Health Fndn, 8 Hallam St, London W1N 6DH (☎ 01 580 0145)

LOUGHBOROUGH, Archdeacon of; *see*: Jones, Ven (Thomas) Hughie

LOUGHBOROUGH, Derek Ralph; *b* 5 Mar 1927; *Educ* Clark's Coll; *m* 1 Sept 1951, Hazel Hilda; 2 s (Martin b 1959, Andrew b 1964); *Career* RN 1945-47; joined Sun Life Assur Soc 1943-77 (mangr 1969), sec PO Insur Soc 1977-78, dir Lautro Ltd 1986-; London Borough of Croydon: cncllr 1974-, chm educn ctee 1978-88, Mayor 1988-89; ACII 1952, APMI 1977, MBIM 1977; *Recreations* walking, photography; *Style*— Derek Loughborough, Esq; 45 Cheston Ave, Croydon CR0 8DE (☎ 01 777 5583)

LOUGHNAN, Kenneth Francis Manly; s of Col William F M Loughnan, MC, and Eileen Mary,*née* Manly; *b* 28 Feb 1925; *Educ* Beaumont, Trinity Coll Oxford (MA); *m* 1978, Susan, da of Maj Geoffrey Huskisson, DSO, MC; 1 da; *Career* Lt 8 KRI Hussars 1945-47, Capt City of London Yeo 1952-57; admitted slr 1952, ptnr Triggs Turner & Co Guildford 1954-; dir: Tindle Newpapers Ltd, County Sound plc, and others; chm St John Cncl for Surrey 1986-, C St J; *Style*— Kenneth Loughnan, Esq; Old Langham Farm, Lodsworth, nr Petworth, W Sussex GU28 9DA

LOULOUDIS, Hon Mrs (Madeleine Mary); *née* Dillon; 4 but 3 survg da (twin) of 20 Viscount Dillon (d 1979); *b* 29 Oct 1957; *m* 4 March 1989, Leonard Constantine Louloudis, o s of Constantine Louloudis; *Style*— The Hon Mrs Louloudis; 17 The Porticos, 374 King's Rd, London SW3 (☎ 01 352 1584)

LOUP, Michael Douglas Trollope; s of Brig Gerald Davies Loup, MC (d 1962), of London, and Marjorie Kennedy, *née* Trollope (d 1940); *b* 19 May 1929; *Educ* Stowe; *m* 25 March 1956 (m dis 1974), (Lorna) Diana, da of James King (d 1962); 3 s (Richard b 7 March 1958, Nicholas b 28 May 1960, Mathew b 14 Dec 1968); m 2, 1976, Mary, *née* Smith (d 1981); *Career* cmmnd and served 2 Royal Tank Regt 1948; slr; ptnr Boodle Hatfield 1957-; pres City of Westminster Law Soc 1973, memb cncl Law Soc 1975-83, non-exec dir Grosvenor Estate Hldgs-; govr Stowe 1987-; memb Law Soc 1956 ; *Recreations* golf, cricket, reading, English and French countryside; *Clubs* Boodle's, Buck's, MCC; *Style*— Michael Loup, Esq; 43 Brook St, London W1Y 2BL (☎ 01 629 7411, fax 01 629 2621, telex 261414)

LOUSADA, Sir Anthony Baruh; s of Julian George Lousada (d 1945); *b* 4 Nov 1907; *Educ* Westminster, New Coll Oxford; *m* 1, 1937 (m dis 1960), Jocelyn, da of late Sir Alan Herbert, CH; 1 s, 3 da; m 2, 1961, Patricia, da of late Charles McBride, of USA; 1 s, 1 da; *Career* admitted slr 1933; Miny of Econ Warfare 1939-44; memb: cncl Royal Coll of Art 1952-79 (hon fell 1957, sr fell 1967, vice-chm 1960-72, tres 1967-72, chm 1972-79), ctee Contemporary Art Soc 1955-71 (vice-chm 1961-71), cncl Friends of Tate Gallery 1958- (hon tres 1960-65, chm 1971-77); tstee Tate Gallery 1962-69 (vice-chm 1965-67, chm 1967-69), conslt Stephenson Harwood (slrs) 1973-81 (ptnr 1935-73); kt 1975; *Recreations* painting, the arts, travel; *Clubs* Garrick; *Style*— Sir Anthony Lousada; The Tides, Chiswick Mall, London W4 (☎ 01 994 2257)

LOUSADA, Peter Allen; 2 s of Air Commodore Charles Rochford Lousada, DL (d 1988), and Elizabeth, *née* Shaw; *b* 30 Mar 1937; *Educ* Epsom Coll; *m* 13 Oct 1962, Jane, da of Lt Col Donald Gillmor (d 1972); 2 s (Toby b 1963, James b 1965), 1 da (Sarah b 1965); *Career* Nat Serv, Flying Offr RAF, G D Pilot Canada & 61 Sqdn; vice-pres: Canada Dry Corpn and subsidiaries 1979-, Cadbury Beverages Europe 1987-; *Recreations* golf, fishing; *Clubs* RAF, Woburn Golf; *Style*— Peter A Lousada, Esq; Well Cottage, Bow Brickhill, nr Milton Keynes, Bucks MK17 9JU (☎ 0908 72186); Cilcambach, Eglyswgn, Dyfed; 1-11 Hay Hill, London W1X 7LF (☎ 01 493 3961)

LOUTH, Baroness Ethel May; da of Walter John Gallichen, of Jersey; *m* 1927, 15 Baron Louth (d 1950); *Style*— The Rt Hon Ethel, Lady Louth; Gardone Cottage, Hormfield Drive, St Brelade, Jersey, CI

LOUTH, 16 Baron (I 1541); Otway Michael James Oliver Plunkett; s of 15 Baron (d 1950); *b* 19 August 1929; *Educ* Downside; *m* 1951, Angela, da of William Cullinane, of Jersey; 3 s, 2 da; *Heir* s, Hon Jonathan Plunkett; *Style*— The Rt Hon the Lord Louth; Les Sercles, La Grande Piece, St Peter, Jersey

LOUTIT, John Freeman; CBE (1957); s of John Freeman Loutit (d 1950), and Margaret, *née* Gould (d 1971); *b* 1910; *Educ* Guildford GS W Aust, Melbourne Univ Aust, St John's Coll Oxford; *m* 1941, Thelma, da of J Thelwall Salusbury (d 1946), of Kimcote, Leics; 1 s, 2 da; *Career* dir: S London Blood Supply Depot 1940-47, Radiobiology Unit Med Res Cncl Harwell 1947-69, external staff Med Res Cncl 1969-75; visitor Radiobiology Unit 1975-88; Hon VMD Stockholm, Hon DSc St Andrews; DM, FRCP, FRS; Offr Order of Orange Nassau 1952; *Recreations* gardening, cooking; *Style*— Dr John Loutit, CBE; Lyking, 22 Milton Lane, Steventon, Oxon OX13 6SA (☎ 0235 831279)

LOVAT, Sheriff Leonard Scott; s of Charles Lovat (d 1959), and Alice, *née* Hunter (d 1973); *b* 28 July 1926; *Educ* St Aloysius Coll Glasgow, Univ of Glasgow (BL); *m* 1960, Elinor Frances, da of Joseph Alexander McAlister (d 1979); 1 s (Andrew), 1 da (Judith); *Career* sr asst procurator fiscal of Glasgow and Strathkelvin 1976; Sheriff of South Strathclyde Dumfries and Galloway at Hamilton 1978-; Cropwood Fell Cambridge Univ 1971; *Recreations* music, mountaineering, bird-watching; *Clubs* Alpine; *Style*— Sheriff L S Lovat; 38 Kelvin Ct, Glasgow G12 0AE (☎ 041 357 0031); Sheriff Ct, Almada St, Hamilton (☎ 0698 282957)

LOVAT, Master of; Simon Augustine Fraser; s and h of 15 Lord Lovat, DSO, MC; *b* 1939; *Educ* Ampleforth; *m* 1972, Virginia, da of David Grose, of 49 Elystan St, SW3; 2 s, 1 da; *Career* Lt Scots Gds 1960; *Style*— Master of Lovat; Beaufort Castle, Beauly, Inverness-shire

LOVAT, 15 Lord (S 1458-64); Simon Christopher Joseph Fraser; DSO (1942), MC (1942), TD (1945), JP (Inverness-shire 1944), DL (1942); 24 Chief of Clan Fraser of Lovat; *de facto* 15 Lord, 17 but for the attainder; Baron Lovat of Lovat (UK 1837); s of 14 Lord Lovat, KT, GCVO, KCMG, CB, DSO, TD (d 1933), by his w Hon Laura Lister, herself da of 4 Baron Ribblesdale; er bro of Rt Hon Sir Hugh Fraser, MP (decd); bro-in-law of Sir Fitzroy Maclean, 1 Bt; bro-in-law and cous of 5 Earl of Eldon; *b* 9 July 1911; *Educ* Ampleforth, Magdalen Coll Oxford; *m* 1938, Rosamond, da of Sir Henry John Delves Broughton, 11 Bt (d 1942); 4 s, 2 da; *Heir* s, Master of Lovat; *Career* sits as Conservative in House of Lords; 2 Lt Lovat Scouts 1930, Brig 1944, served with Commandos 1941; proprietor of around 190,000 acres; jt parly under-sec of state Foreign Office 1945; Officier de la Légion d'Honneur, Croix de Guerre (France); Norwegian Cross; Order of Suvarov (Soviet Union); Papal Order of St Gregory with Collar; Kt Sov Mil Order of Malta; Hon LLD: Simon Fraser BC, Antigonish NS; OStJ, CStJ; *Style*— The Rt Hon the Lord Lovat, DSO, MC, TD, JP, DL; Balblair House, Beauly, Inverness-shire

LOVE, Prof Andrew Henry Garmany; s of Andrew Love (d 1976), of Ballymagee, Bangor, Co Down, and Martha, *née* Fleming (d 1981); *b* 28 Sept 1934; *Educ* Bangor Endowed Sch, Queens Univ Belfast (BSc, MB, MCh, BAO, MD); *m* 29 May 1963, Margaret Jean, da of William Stuart Lennox, (d 1987); 1 s (Anthony W G b 24 Oct 1967); *Career* Queens Univ Belfast: prof of Gastroenterology 1977-83, prof of medicine 1983-, dean of med faculty 1981-86; Ulster Boys Golf Champion 1952, Irish Amateur Gold Champion 1956, memb bd of govrs Campbell Coll, chm res ctee Ulster Cancer Fndn; chm central med advsy ctee DHSS NI, memb Eastern Health Socl Servs Bd, pres Euro Assoc of Med Deans; FRCP 1973, FRCPI 1973; Gastroenterology, Tropical Diseases, Nutrition; *Recreations* riding, sailing; *Clubs* East India, Devonshire Sports, Royal Ulster YC; *Style*— Prof Andrew Love; The Lodge, New Rd, Donaghadee, Co Down BT21 ODU (☎ 0247 883507); Dept Medicine, QUB, Institute of Clinical Science, Grosvenor Road, Belfast BT12 6BJ (☎ 0232 240503 ext 2707, fax 0232 230788 ext 3020, telex 747578 QUB MEDG)

LOVE, Heather Beryl; da of the late John Sydney Love, and Joyce Margaret, *née* Cracknell; *b* 17 Nov 1953; *Educ* Mayfield Sch Putney; 1 s (Matthew Paul Hodges b 1982); *Career* publishing dir IPC Magazines (Woman's Journal, Marie Claire) 1988- (publisher 1988, assoc publisher 1985, gp publicity mangr 1981, publicity mangr 1980); memb: Nat Sm Bore Rifle Assoc; *Recreations* pistol shooting, interior design, work; *Style*— Miss Heather Love; No 2, Hatfields, London SE1 (☎ 01 261 5508, fax 01 261 4277)

LOVE, Prof Philip Noel; CBE (1983); s of Thomas Love, of Aberdeen, and Ethel, *née* Philip; *b* 25 Dec 1939; *Educ* Aberdeen GS, Univ of Aberdeen (MA, LLB); *m* 21 Aug 1963, Isabel Leah, da of Innes Mearns, of Aberdeen; 3 s (Steven b 1965, Michael b 1967, Donald b 1969); *Career* princ Campbell Conon & Co Slrs Aberdeen 1963-74 (conslt 1974-), vice-princ Univ of Aberdeen 1986- (prof conveyancing and professional practice of law 1974-, dean faculty of law 1979-82), pt/t memb Law cmmn 1986-, vice-pres Scottish Law Agents Soc 1970, Law Soc Scotland 1981-82 (memb cncl 1975-86, vice pres 1980-81), local chm Rent Assessment Panel Scotland 1972-, memb rules cncl Ct of Session 1968-, chm Grampian Med Ethical Ctee 1984-, hon Sheriff of Grampian Highland & Islands 1978-, chm Aberdeen Home for Widowers Children 1971-, pres Aberdeen GS Former Pupils Club 1987-88, tstee Grampian & Islands Family Tst 1988-; advocate in Aberdeen 1963-; memb Law Soc of Scotland 1963-; *Recreations* rugby (golden oldies variety now), keep fit, FRS (Aberdeen); *Clubs* New (Edinburgh); *Style*— Prof Philip N Love; Univ of Aberdeen, King's Coll, Old Aberdeen AB9 2UB (☎ 0224 272414, fax 0224 487048, telex 73458 UNIABN G)

LOVE, Robert Malcolm; s of Robert Love, of Paisley, Scotland, and Mary, *née* Darroch; *b* 9 Jan 1936; *Educ* Paisley GS, Glasgow Univ (MA), Washington Univ St Louis; *Career* short serv cmmn Flt Lt Educn Branch RAF 1959-62; actor and dir numerous English rep theatres 1962-66, prodr TV drama Thames TV 1966 -75;

prodns incl: Public Eye, The Rivals of Sherlock Holmes, The Mind of Mr J G Reeder, Van der Valk, Frontier, Moody and Pegg; freelance TV prodr 1975-79, controller of drama Scottish TV 1979-; prodns incl: House on the Hill, Skin Deep, City Sugar, Northern Lights, Taggart, Extras, The Steamie, Winners and Losers; govr Scottish Theatre Co 1981-87, visiting lectr media studies Stirling Univ 1986-, memb ctee BAFTA Scotland 1987-; memb: Royal TV Soc; *Recreations* music, theatre, foreign travel, books, railway history; *Style*— Robert Love, Esq; Scottish Television plc, Cowcaddens, Glasgow G2 3PR (☎ 041 332 9999, fax 041 332 6982)

LOVEDAY, Bt-Col George Arthur; TD (1952); s of Arthur Frederick, OBE (d 1968); *b* 13 May 1909; *Educ* Winchester, Magdalen Oxford, Hon Sch Modern Languages; *m* 1, 1935, Sylvia Mary, da of Antony Edmund Gibbs (d 1924); 2 s; m 2, 1967, Penelope Elton (Dugdale), da of Cyril Grant Cunard (d 1914); *Career* Maj RA Northwest Europe 1944-45, Brevet Col RA (TA) 1956; memb London Stock Exchange 1945, dep chm The Stock Exchange 1971-73, chm 1973-75, ret 1975; *Recreations* golf, gardening; *Clubs* Boodles; *Style*— Bt-Col George Loveday, TD; Bushton Manor, Wooton Bassett, Swindon

LOVELACE, Countess of; Manon Lis; da of Axel Sigurd Transo, of Copenhagen, Denmark, and wid of Baron von Blixen Finecke; *m* 1951, as his 2 w, 4 Earl (d 1964); *Style*— The Rt Hon The Countess of Lovelace; Torridon House, Torridon, Ross-shire

LOVELACE, 5 Earl of (UK 1838); Peter Axel William Locke King; also Lord King, Baron of Ockham (GB 1725), and Viscount Ockham (UK 1838); s of 4 Earl (d 1964, seventh in descent from the sis of John Locke, the philosopher); through his paternal grandmother, Lady Edith Anson, the present Lord Lovelace is 2 cous once removed of Lord (5 Earl of) Lichfield; *b* 26 Nov 1951; *Educ* privately; *Heir* none; *Style*— The Rt Hon the Earl of Lovelace; Torridon House, Torridon, Ross-shire (☎ 228)

LOVELL, Sir (Alfred Charles) Bernard; OBE (1946); s of Gilbert Lovell; *b* 31 August 1913; *Educ* Kingswood GS, Bristol Univ; *m* 1937, Mary Joyce Chesterman; 2 s, 3 da; *Career* served with Telecommunications Research Estab MAP 1939-45; prof Radio Astronomy Manchester Univ 1951-80, Emeritus 1980-; founder and dir Nuffield Radio Astronomy Laboratories Jodrell Bank 1945-81; pres: Royal Astronomical Soc 1969-71, British Assoc 1974-75, Master Worshipful Co of Church Musicians 1986-87; Cdr Order of Merit (Poland) 1975; FRS 1955; kt 1961; *Books Incl:* The Story of Jodrell Bank (1968), In the Centre of Immensities (1975), Emerging Cosmology (1981), The Jodrell Bank Telescopes (1985), Voice of the Universe (1987); *Clubs* Athenaeum; *Style*— Sir Bernard Lovell, OBE; The Quinta, Swettenham, Cheshire (☎ Lower Withington 0477 71254); Jodrell Bank, Cheshire (☎ 0477 71321)

LOVELL-DAVIS, Baron (Life Peer UK 1974), of Highgate; Peter Lovell-Davis; s of William Lovell Davis (d 1974), and Winifred Mary (d 1954); *b* 8 July 1924; *Educ* Christ's Finchley, King Edward VI GS Stratford-on-Avon, Jesus Coll Oxford (BA, MA); *m* 1950, Jean, da of Peter Foster Graham (d 1948); 1 s, 1 da; *Career* sits as Labour peer in Lords; memb bd Cwlth Dept Corpn 1978-84, London Consortium 1978-, md Central Press Features Ltd 1950-70; dir newspaper & printing cos 1950-70; chm: Davis & Harrison Ltd 1970-73, The Features Syndicate Ltd 1971-74; a lord in waiting to HM The Queen 1974-75, parly under-sec of state Dept of Energy 1975-76; chm: Lee Cooper Licensing Ltd 1983-, Pettifor Morrow Assocs Ltd 1986-; memb Islington Dist Health Authy 1982-85, tstee Whittington Hosp Academic Centre 1980-, vice-pres YHA 1978-; *Recreations* industrial archaeology, aviation, inland waterways, bird-watching, walking; *Style*— The Rt Hon the Lord Lovell-Davis; 80 North Rd, Highgate, London N6 4AA (☎ 01 348 3919)

LOVELOCK, Sir Douglas Arthur; KCB (1979, CB 1974); s of late Walter Lovelock, and Irene Lovelock; *b* 7 Sept 1923; *Educ* Bec Sch London; *m* 1961, Valerie Margaret Lane; 1 s, 1 da; *Career* joined Treasy 1949, asst under-sec (personnel) MOD 1971-72 (previously with Minys of Technol and Aviation Supply), DTI 1972-74; dep sec: Trade, Indust, Prices & Consumer Protection Depts 1974-77, chm bd of Customs & Excise 1977-83, Civil Servs Benevolent Fund 1980-, first Church Estates Cmmr 1983-, gov Whitgift and Trinity schs 1986-; *Style*— Sir Douglas Lovelock, KCB; The Old House, 91 Coulsdon Rd, Old Coulsdon, Surrey (☎ 07375 55211)

LOVELOCK, James Ephraim; s of Tom Arthur Lovelock (d 1957); *b* 26 July 1919; *Educ* Strand Sch Brixton, Manchester, London; *m* 1942, Helen Mary, da of David Manson Hyslop (d 1967) 2 s, 2 da; *Career* scientist formerly staff memb Nat Inst for Medical Research 1941-61, prof Baylor Coll of Medicine, Texas 1961-64; pres Marine Biology Assocn 1986-; FRS; *Recreations* growing trees, mathematical puzzles; *Style*— James Lovelock, Esq, FRS; Coombe Mill, St Giles on the Heath, Launceston, Cornwall

LOVERIDGE, Sir John Henry; CBE (1964, MBE 1945); s of Henry Thomas Loveridge, and Vera Lilian Loveridge; *b* 2 August 1912; *Educ* Elizabeth Coll Guernsey, Caen Univ; *m* 1946, Madeleine Melanie, da of Eugene Joseph C M Tanguy; 1 s, 1 da; *Career* RAFVR 1954-59; barr Middle Temple 1950, advocate Royal Court of Guernsey 1951, bailiff of Guernsey 1973-82 (dep 1969-73, attorney-gen 1960-69, slr-gen 1954-60), appeal judge Jersey 1974-82; KStJ 1980; kt 1975; *Clubs* Royal Guernsey GC; *Style*— Sir John Loveridge, CBE; Kinmount, Sausmarez Rd, St Martin's, Guernsey, CI (☎ 0481 38038)

LOVERIDGE, Sir John Warren; JP (West Central Division 1963); s of Claude Warren Loveridge (d 1956), and Emilie Warren, *née* Malone (d 1954); *b* 9 Sept 1925; *Educ* St John's Coll Cambridge (MA); *m* 1954, Jean Marguerite, da of C E Chivers, of Devizes, Wilts; 3 s (Michael, Steven, Robert), 2 da (Amanda, Emma); *Career* head of family businesses; princ St Godric's Coll 1954-; farmer; Parly candidate (C) Aberavon 1951, contested Brixton (LCC) 1952; MP (C): Hornchurch 1970-74, Upminster 1974-83; memb: Parly Select Ctee on Expenditure, Gen Purposes Sub-Ctee, Procedure Ctee; chm Cons Small Business Ctee 1979-83; memb Hampstead Borough Cncl 1953-59, tres and tstee Hampstead Cons Assoc 1959-74, pres Hampstead and Highgate Cons Assoc 1986-; vice pres: Greater London Area Cons Assoc 1984-, Nat Cncl for Civil Protection (formerly Civil Defence); pres Axe Cliff GC; Liveryman Worshipful Co of Girdlers; FRAS, FRAgS, RIIA; kt 1988; *Books* Moving Forward: Small Businesses and the Economy (jt author), God Save the Queen (1981), Hunter of the Moon (1983), Hunter of the Sun (1984); *Recreations* painting, poetry, historic houses, shooting; *Clubs* Bucks, Carlton, Hurlingham; *Style*— Sir John Loveridge, JP; Bindon Manor, Axmouth, nr Seaton, Devon EX12 4AS (☎ 0297 21234); The White House, 82 Fitzjohn's Ave, London NW3 (☎ 01 435 2684)

LOVETT, Ian Nicholas; s of Frederick Lovett, of Croydon, Surrey, and Dorothy Evelyn, *née* Stanley; *b* 7 Sept 1944; *Educ* Selhurst GS, Univ of Wales, BA (Hons); *m* 3 May 1969, Patricia Lesley; 2 da (Emma b 1977, Sophie b 1979); *Career* md Dunbar Bank plc 1984-; FCIB 1982; *Recreations* cricket; *Clubs* MCC; *Style*— Ian N Lovett, Esq; Dunbar Bank plc, 9 Sackville St, London W1X 1DE (☎ 01 437 7844, telex 28300 ALLIED G)

LOVETT, Martin; *b* 3 Mar 1927; *Educ* RCM; *m* 1950, Suzanne *née* Rozsa; 1 s (Peter Sandor b 1955), 1 da (Sonia Naomi 1951); *Career* Cellist of Amadeus Quartet 1947-1987; D Univ York, D Mus London; memb: FRSA, Hon memb RAM; Grosses Verpienst Kreuz (Germany), Ehrenkreuz Für Kunst and Wissenschafft (Austria); *Style*— Martin Lovett, Esq, OBE; 24 Redington Gdns, NW3 7RX (☎ 01 794 9898); 5 Coastal Rd, Angmering-On-Sea, W Sussex 1BN 1SJ

LOVICK, Peter Alan; s of Peter George Lovick (d 1953), and Dora Evelyn, *née* Elvidge; *b* 23 Jan 1928; *Educ* City of London Coll; *m* 14 July 1961, Shirley Georgina, da of Edward Duffin (d 1956); 1 da (Susan Caroline b 1963); *Career* dir: Bleichroder Bing & Co Ltd (Lloyds brokers) 1965-69, Ropner Insurance servs 1969-72; Benfield Lovick Rees & Co Ltd: dir 1972-88, chm underwriting agencies Ltd 1980- (chm Holdings Ltd 1984-88); dir Bell & Clements Ltd 1984-, dir Benfield Bell & Clements Ltd 1985-; Liveryman Worshipful Co of Carmen; FCIB, FLustD; *Recreations* fine wine and food, ecology, conservation; *Clubs* Carlton, RAC, City of London; *Style*— Peter Lovick, Esq; 35 Chalkwell Esplande, Westcliff-on-Sea, Essex; Old Forge House, Thorington St, Stoke by Wayland, Suffolk; 5M Portland Mansions, Chiltern St, London W1 (☎ 0702 347 041); Chesterfield House, 26-28 Fenchurch St, London EC3 (☎ 01 626 5432)

LOVILL, Sir John Roger; CBE (1983), DL (E Sussex 1983); s of Walter Thomas Lovill and Elsie, *née* Page; *b* 26 Sept 1929; *Educ* Brighton Hove and Sussex GS; *m* 1958, Jacqueline, *née* Parker; 2 s, 1 da; *Career* chm exec cncl CCA 1983-86; kt 1987; *Style*— Sir John Lovill, CBE, DL; CCA, Eaton House, 66a Eaton Sq, London SW1W 9BH (☎ 01 235 1200)

LOW; *see*: Morrison-Low

LOW, Alistair James; s of James Grey Low (d 1973), and Elsie Georgina, *née* Holden; *b* 2 August 1942; *Educ* Dundee HS, St Andrews Univ (BSc); *m* 30 Aug 1966, Shona Petricia, da of John Galloway Wallace, OBE, of Edinburgh; 2 s (John b 1970, Hamish b 1972), 1 da (Katharina b 1977); *Career* ptnr Duncan C Fraser & Co 1968-86, dir William M Mercer Fraser Ltd 1986-; chm: championship ctee, Royal & Ancient GC 1986-88; FFA 1967; *Recreations* golf, skiing; *Clubs* Royal & Ancient GC, Hon Co of Edinburgh Golfers New; *Style*— Alistair Low, Esq; Thornfield, Erskine Lane, Gullane, East Lothian; William M Mercer Fraser Ltd, Hobart House, 80 Hanover St, Edinburgh, Lothian (☎ 031 226 2477)

LOW, Hon Charles Harold Stuart; s and h of 1 Baron Aldington, KCMG, CBE, DSO, TD, PC; *b* 22 June 1948; *Educ* Winchester, New Coll Oxford, INSEAD; *Career* dir Grindlays Bank; gen mangr Deutshe Bank London; *Style*— The Hon Charles Low; 9 Warwick Sq, London SW1; Deutshe Bank, 6 Bishopsgate, London EC2 (☎ 01 283 4600)

LOW, Prof Donald Anthony; s of late Canon Donald Low and Winifred, *née* Edmunds; *b* 22 June 1927; *Educ* Haileybury, ISC, Univ of Oxford (MA, DPhil); *m* 1952, Isobel Snails; 1 s, 2 da; *Career* lectr (later sr lectr) Makerere Coll Univ Coll of E Africa 1951-58; fell (then sr fell) in history Res Sch of Social Sciences ANU 1959-64; fndg Dean of Sch of African & Asian Studies and Prof of History Univ of Sussex 1964-72; Smuts Prof of the History of the Br Cwlth 1983- and dir internat studies Univ of Cambridge 1985-; pres of Clare Hall 1987-; FAHA, FASSA; *Books* The Mind of Buganda (1971), Lion Rampant (1973) and numerous articles on international history; *Style*— Prof Donald Low; Clare Coll, Cambridge

LOW, Ernest; s of Rev Eli Ernest Low (d 1978), of Melbourne, Australia, and Rose Anna *née* Kwan (d 1983); *b* 19 Jan 1927; *Educ* St James's Sch Calcutta, Univ of Hong Kong (BSc), City and Guilds Coll Imperial Coll London (DIC); *m* 5 Sept 1959 (m dis 1984), Elizabeth, da of Dr Christopher William Lumley Dodd (d 1972), of Haywards Heath, Sussex; 1 s (Christopher b 31 Jan 1961, d 7 Dec 1971), 1 da (Alison b 1 Oct 1962); *Career* Sr Eng: Wimpey Central Laboratory 1954-57, Binnie & Ptnrs 1957-59; mangr of site Investigation Div of Marples Ridgway Ltd 1959-70; ptnr Low and Parsons Brown cnslt engrs 1969-77, Low and Ptrns Hong Kong (conslt engrs) 1976-; dep chm Civil Div of Hong Kong Inst of Engrs 1978-80, chm Hong Kong Branch CIArb 1980-82; memb: Ctee on Arbitration of the Hong Kong Law Reform Cmmn 1980-82, cncl CIArb 1988-; arbitrator on lists of: CIArb, pres Inst of Civil Engrs, pres Inst of Br Architects, Hong Kong Int Arbitration Centre, FIDIE Euro Int Contractors, and others; Liveryman of the Worshipful Co of Painter Stainers 1973, Liveryman of the Worshipful Co of Arbitrators 1981; FICE 1968, FASCE 1969, FCIArb 1971, MConSE 1975; *Recreations* golf, oratorios, opera, reading and others; *Clubs* Carlton, St Stephens and Constitutional (Hong Kong); *Style*— Ernest Low, Esq; c/o Cheng & Partners, 2015 Hang Lung Centre, Paterson St, Hong Kong (☎ 852 5 224779, fax 852 5 8106223); 60 Carlton Mansions, Randolph Avenue, London W9 1NR (☎ 01 925 0066, fax 01 930 8004)

LOW, Roger L; s of Niels L Low, of USA, and Mary Margaret Low; *b* 29 Jan 1944; *Educ* Columbia Coll, Columbia Univ (AB), Wharton Grad Sch of Fin and Commerce, Univ of Pennsylvania (MBA); *m* 1967, Helen Webster, da of Bates W Bryan, of USA; 1 s, 1 da; *Career* 1 Lt US Marine Corps, served Vietnam; Drexel Burnham & Co 1971-75, vice pres Salomon Bros 1975-81; md: Dean Witter Reynolds Overseas 1981-84, Bear Stearns & Co 1984-; *Recreations* marathon running, skiing; *Clubs* St Anthony Hall (NYC); *Style*— Roger L Low, Esq; Bear Stearns Int Ltd, 9 Devonshire Sq, London EC2M 4YL (☎ 01 626 5301)

LOW, William; CBE (1984), JP (1971); s of William Low (d 1957); *b* 12 Sept 1921; *Educ* Merchiston Castle Edinburgh; *m* 1949, Elizabeth Ann Stewart, *née* Sime; 2 s; *Career* Maj IA 1943-45; textile mfr, chm Don & Low (Hldgs) Ltd, memb CBI Scottish Cncl, vice-chm Assoc of British Cs of C, vice-pres Scottish Cncl Devpt and Indust; chm: Dundee Heritage Tst 1984, UBI (Understanding Br Indust) Scotland Advsy Ctee 1985; CBIM 1983; *Recreations* shooting, fishing, golf; *Clubs* Naval and Military, Royal and Ancient St Andrews; *Style*— William Low, Esq, CBE, JP; Herdhill Ct, Kirriemuir, Angus (☎ 0575 72215); Don & Low (Hldgs) Ltd, St James Rd, Forfar, Angus DD8 2AL (☎ 0307 65111, telex 76552 DONLOW G)

LOWCOCK, Andrew Charles; s of Eric Lowcock, of Quarry Bank House, Styal, Wilmslow Ches, and Elizabeth, *née* Kilner; *b* 22 Nov 1949; *Educ* Malvern, New Coll Oxford (MA); *m* 1, 14 Aug 1976 (m dis 1985), Patricia Anne, da of Emlyn Roberts; m

2, 7 Sept 1985, Sarah Elaine, da of Robert Edwards, of Quinton Lodge, Ditchling, Sussex; 1 s (Robert Charles b 24 Feb 1988); *Career* barr Middle Temple 1973, Northern circuit; *Recreations* music, princ timpanist Stockport Symphony Orchestra, cricket, theatre; *Clubs* Whicker Soc, Stockport Garrick Theatre; *Style*— Andrew Lowcock, Esq; 28 St John St, Manchester M3 4DJ (☎ 061 834 8418)

LOWE, His Hon Judge; David Bruce Douglas Lowe; s of Douglas Gordon Arthur Lowe, QC (d 1981, Olympic Gold Medallist 800m 1924 and 1928), and Karen Lowe; *b* 3 April 1935; *Educ* Winchester, Pembroke Coll Cambridge; *m* 1, 1 s, 1 da; m 2, 1978, Dagmar, da of Horst Bosse (d 1972); 1 s, 3 da; *Career* prosecuting counsel to Dept of Trade 1975-83, rec of the Crown Ct 1980-83, circuit judge S Eastern Circuit 1983-; *Recreations* tennis, music; *Clubs* Hawks (Cambridge); *Style*— His Hon Judge Lowe; The Crown Ct at Middlesex Guildhall, Broad Sanctuary, London SW1P 3BB

LOWE, Air Chief Marshal Sir Douglas Charles; GCB (1977, KCB 1974, CB 1971), DFC (1943), AFC (1946); s of John William Lowe (d 1970); *b* 14 Mar 1922; *Educ* Reading Sch; *m* 1944, Doreen Elizabeth, da of Ralph Henry Nichols (d 1952); 1 s, 1 da (Frances, m 1974 Hon Christopher Russell Bailey, *qv*); *Career* entered RAF 1940, Air Vice-Marshal 1970, Air Marshal 1973, AOC 18 Gp 1973-75, controller of aircraft MOD 1975-82, ADC to HM The Queen 1978-83, chief of Defence Procurement 1982-83; chm Mercury Communications Ltd 1984-; dir: Rolls Royce Ltd 1983, Royal Ordnance 1984; *Style*— Air Chief Marshal Sir Douglas Lowe, GCB, DFC, AFC; 90 Long Acre, London WC2E 9NP (☎ 01 836 2449, telex 28846)

LOWE, Lady Elisabeth Olive; da of 5 Earl Cairns; *b* 1944; *m* 1965, Capt Martin Ralph Lowe; 1 s; *Style*— Lady Elisabeth Lowe; Castle End, Ross-on-Wye

LOWE, Geoffrey Colin; s of Colin Roderick Lowe (d 1964), and Elsie Winifred Lowe, *née* Garton (d 1962); *b* 7 Sept 1920; *Educ* Reigate GS; *m* m 1, 10 April 1948, Joan (d 1985), da of James Stephen (d 1940); 1 da (Alison Barbara b 1956); m 2, 18 June 1988, Jean Marion (formerly Bailey), da of Otho Stopher Wigginton (d 1970); *Career* WWII cmmnd RAFVR Fl/Lt (served M E Flying Control Sch Heliopolis Egypt) 1941-46; GPO 1937-39, Exchequer and Audit Dept 1939-47, princ Miny of Civil Aviation 1950-54 (asst princ 1947-50, pvt sec to perm sec 1950), princ Colonial Office 1954-57, princ Miny Tport and Civil Aviation 1957-61, civil air attaché SEA 1961-64; asst sec: Miny of Aviation 1964-68, BOT 1968-71; cnsllr Br Embassy Washington 1971- 74, under sec DOI 1974-80, aviation conslt 1980-88; memb: exec ctee Essex Voluntary Assoc for the Blind 1985-, All Saints Church (hon tres 1985-88), Bancrofts Decorative and Fine Arts Soc; chm Greenholme Residential Home for the Blind 1986-; *Recreations* theatre, crossword puzzles; *Style*— Geoffrey Lowe, Esq; 13 Highwood, Sunset Avenue, Woodford Green, Essex IG8 OSZ (☎ 01 504 7035); 11124 Popes Head Road, Fairfax, Virginia, USA

LOWE, Harry Frederick; OBE (1984); s of Harry Lowe (d 1963), Supt of Police, Kidderminster Dist, and Mary Jane Giles; *b* 31 May 1925; *Educ* Aston Univ (BSc); *m* 9 July 1948, Patricia Mary, da of Ernest Davies (d 1941); *Career* Engr md Brintons Ltd; chm Brintons Telford Ltd; dir Brintons Pty Ltd Australia; memb Regnl & Nat Cncl CBI, Govr Kidderminster Coll 1980-87; FTI, FIMechE, FIProdE; *Recreations* gardening; *Style*— Harry F Lowe, OBE; Brintons Ltd, PO Box 16, Kidderminster (☎ 0562 820000)

LOWE, Lady Helen Suzanne; *née* Macaskie; da of Sandys Stuart Macaskie, slr; *m* 1971, as his 2 w, Sir Francis Lowe, 3 Bt (d 1986); *Style*— Lady Lowe; 4 New Sq, Lincoln's Inn, London WC2 (☎ 01 242 8508); Bagwich, Godshill, Isle of Wight

LOWE, Michael John; JP (1975); s of Joseph (d 1980), and Gladys May Howells (d 1978); *b* 6 Jan 1936; *Educ* Wolverhampton Municipal GS; *m* 11 July 1959, Janet Emily, da of Frank Poppitt Clemson; 2 s (Phillip b 1963, David b 1966); *Career* RCS 1941-42, 2 Lt RA 1942, served E Surrey Regt seconded to Somali Scouts 1944-46, ret Capt; instr in history Princeton Univ 1952-53, asst lectr (later lectr) in American history UCL 1953-63, Commonwealth Fund American Studies 1957, visiting prof Berkeley 1960-61 (Jefferson Meml lectr 1971), visiting prof Ghana 1966, Chicago 1969, fell Center for Advanced Study in Behavioural Sciences Stanford California 1969; Cambridge Univ: reader in American history and govt 1963-78, fell Churchill Coll 1968-78, vice master 1975-78, memb cncl of senate 1970-74; guest scholar Woodrow Wilson Int Center Washington 1978-79, visiting prof Peking 1984; Oxford Univ: Rhodes prof of American history and visits and fell of St Catherine's Coll 1979-; memb Amnesty Int; Hon Fell Historical Soc of Ghana 1967; Jersey Prize Princeton Univ 1953, Ramsdell Prize Southern Hist Assoc USA 1960 FBA 1985, FRHists; *Recreations* hockey, squash; *Clubs* Shifnal, Telford; *Style*— Michael Lowe, Esq, JP; The Manor House, Admaston, Shropshire TF5 0AD (☎ 0952 641239); Bank House, 66 High St, Dawley, Telford, Shropshire TF4 2HD (☎ 0952 505896, fax 0952 507788, telex 35191 TRALOW G)

LOWE, Neville Henry; s of Henry Lee Lowe (d 1974), and Dorothy, *née* Hesketh; *b* 28 Oct 1933; *Educ* Merchant Taylors' (Moor Park), Law Socs Sch of Law; *m* 30 March 1959, Ruth Margaret, da of James George Ernest Turner (d 1975); 1 s (Justin Henry b 1966), 1 da (Fiona Ruth b 1962); *Career* slr; ptnr Heckford Norton & Co, Slrs, Letchworth, Royston and Stevenage 1962-66, sr ptnr Mooring Aldridge & Haydon (Bournemouth and Poole), and Aldridge Myers until 1984, dist registrar of High Ct and County Ct Registrar (Bournemouth and Poole) 1984-, Assistant Rec 1989-, NP (sole practitioner); former memb Bd Western Orchestral Soc Ltd (Bournemouth Symphony Orchestra); pres Bournemouth & District Law Soc 1977-78; Freeman Merchant Taylors' Co and City of London since 1980; *Recreations* squash, fishing, ancestral research, opera; *Style*— Neville H Lowe, Esq

LOWE, Robson; s of John Boyd Lowe (d 1950); *b* 7 Jan 1905; *m* 1928, Winifred (d 1972); 2 da; *Career* philatelist (founded business 1920), publisher 1930-, auctioneer 1937- (merged with Christie's Int 1980); ed The Philatelist 1933-89; chm expert ctee British Philatelic Assoc 1941-65, philatelic advsr National Postal Museum 1964-, pres Br Philatelic Fedn 1979-81, pres Postal History Soc 1986; exposed: 1937 Coronation forgeries, 1953 Sperati forgeries, 1980 Gee-Ma forgeries; *Books* Encyclopaedia of Empire Postage Stamps, Handstamps of the Empire, The British Postage Stamp, The Codrington Correspondence, The Lazara Correspondence, St Vincent (with J L Messinger), Waterlow Die Proofs (with Colin Fraser); *Recreations* postal history, postage stamps, writing; *Clubs* East India, Devonshire, Sports and Public Schools; *Style*— Robson Lowe, Esq; c/o East India Club, 16 St James Sq, London SW1 (☎ 01 930 1000); St Cross, Bodorgan Rd, Bournemouth (☎ 0202 25150); office: 10 King St, St James's, London SW1Y 6QT (☎ 01 930 5287, telex 895 0974)

LOWE, Sir Thomas William Gordon; 4 Bt (UK 1918); s of Sir Francis Reginald Gordon Lowe, 3 Bt (d 1986), and Franziska Cornelia Lanier, da of Siegfried Steinkopf; *b* 14 August 1963; *Educ* Stowe, LSE (LLB), Jesus Coll Cambridge (LLM); *Heir* bro, Christopher Francis b 1964; *Career* barr Inner Temple; Inner Temple Queen Elizabeth II Silver Jubilee Scholarship 1987; articles in legal periodicals; *Style*— Sir Thomas Lowe, Bt; 8 Seymour Walk, London SW10

LOWE-McCONNELL, Dr Rosemary Helen; da of Harold Newton Lowe, OBE (d 1970), of Liverpool, and Mary Birditt, *née* Bradford (d 1976); *b* 24 June 1921; *Educ* Howell's Sch Denbigh, Univ of Liverpool (BSc, MSc, DSc); *m* 31 Dec 1953, Richard Bradford McConnell (d 1986), s of Richard George McConnell (d 1942), of Ottawa; *Career* biologist, Freshwater Biological Assoc 1942-45, Overseas Res Serv at East African Fisheris Res Organisation Uganda 1947-53, freelance biologist on UNDP, FAO missions, lectr Makerere Univ Uganda, postgraduate study Univ of Salford; served numerous UN Bodies; memb tropical gp Br Ecological Gp; memb (formerly vice pres) Linnean Soc of London; *Books* Speciation Tropical Environment (1969), Fish Communities in Tropical Freshwaters (1975), Ecological Studies in Tropical Fish Communities (1987); *Recreations* travel, bird & fish watching (natural history); *Clubs* Cwlth Soc; *Style*— Dr Rosemary Lowe-McConnell; Steatwick, Streat, nr Hassocks, West Sussex (☎ 0273 890479)

LOWEIN, John Charles; CBE (1987); s of Authur Edmund Lowein (d 1950), of Cowes, IOW, and Kathleen Minnie, *née* Yates (d 1982); *b* 4 Feb 1924; *Educ* Pangbourne; *m* 24 March 1951, Pamela Fay, da of Thomas Christopher Ratsey (d 1965); 2 s (Miles, Robert), 1 da (Victoria); *Career* Midshipman RNR HMS Sheffield 1941-43, Sub Lt then Lt HMS King George V 1943-46, HMS Duke of York 1946-47; asst sec: TB Hall & Co Ltd 1949, Vacuum Oil Co Ltd 1950; Mobil Oil Co Ltd: credit and collections mangr 1952-59, exec asst NY 1959-62, planning and supply mangr Mobil Oil Co Ltd 1962-66, fin and planning dir 1966-68, mktg dir 1968-70, vice pres Mobil Seriyu Tokyo 1970-74, planning dir europe Mobil Europe Inc 1974-78, exec vice pres europe 1978-80, chm and chief Mobil Oil Co Ltd 1980-87; chm IOW Devpt Bd 1988, tstee Jubilee Sailing Tst 1985; FCIS 1950; *Recreations* sailing; *Clubs* RYS, RNSA, ISC, DWSC, RAC; *Style*— John Lowein, Esq, CBE; 4 Colnebridge Close, Staines TW18 4RZ; 2 Melbourne Place, Queens Rd, Cowes, IOW; IOW Development Board, Samuel Whites Board Room, Medina Rd Cowes, IOW (☎ 0983 200 222, fax 0983 297 242)

LOWELL, Lady Caroline Maureen; *née* Hamilton-Temple-Blackwood; er da of 4 Marquess of Dufferin and Ava (ka 1945); *b* 16 July 1931; *m* 1, 9 Dec 1953 (m dis 1957), Lucian Michael Freud, the painter, *qv*; m 2, 15 Aug 1959 (m dis), Israel Citkowitz (d 1974); 3 da (1 decd); m 3, 1972, Robert Lowell playwright and poet (d 1977); 1 s; *Books* fiction: Corrigan, Goodnight Sweet Ladies, For All that I Found There, The Stepdaughter, Great Granny Webster; cookery book: Darling, You Shouldn't Have Gone To So Much Trouble; reportage books: On The Perimeter, In The Pink; *Style*— Lady Caroline Lowell; 80 Redcliffe Sq, London SW10

LOWEN, David Travers; s of Norman Frederick Lowen, of Southgate, London, and Beatrice, *née* Dannell; *b* 20 June 1946; *Educ* Queen Elizabeth's GS Barnet, Emmanuel Coll Cambridge (MA); *m* 23 May 1970, Jennifer, da of Sqn Ldr Leonard Durston, of Tipton St John, Devon; 1 s (James Cybranet b 1 May 1973), 1 da (Amy Lys b 15 Jan 1976); *Career* prodr and ed; economist NatWest Bank 1967-68; Kent Messenger 1968-71, Southern Television 1971-74, Westward Television 1974-77; feature programmes Yorkshire Television 1977-; memb: Yorkshire Ctee, Lord's Taverners, Forty Club, Yorks Ctee Royal Television Soc; *Books* Stay Alive (with Eddie McGee, 1979), Fighting Back: A Woman's Guide to Self-Defence (1983); *Recreations* cricket, bird-watching, horse-racing; *Style*— David Lowen, Esq; Yorkshire Television, TV Centre, Leeds LS3 1JS (☎ 0532 438 283)

LOWIN, Rex James; s of Haydn Leslie Lowin (d 1971), and Madge Ruth, *née* Lamb; *b* 16 Nov 1945; *Educ* Luton GS, Imperial Coll London Univ (MPhil, BSc, DIC, ARCS), Cranfield Inst of Technol (MBA); *m* 20 July 1968, Susan Annette, *née* Gibbs, da of Charles Thomas Gibbs (d 1983); 3 s (Simon b 1970, Guy b 1976, Julian b 1978), 1 da (Anastasia 1972); *Career* md: Plessey Microwave Ltd 1983-88, Plessey Three-Five Gp Ltd 1988-; dir Marplex SA (France) 1984-; *Style*— Rex Lowin, Esq; 19 Lower Rd, Milton Malsor, Northants (☎ 0604 858605): Wood Burcote Way, Burcote Rd, Towcester, Northants (☎ 0327 52828, telex 312428)

LOWIS, Lt-Col John William Anson; s of Reginald Fendall Lowis (d 1962), and Elizabeth Huntly Muir Coldstream (d 1954); *b* 27 Sept 1908; *Educ* Sherborne Sch, RMC Sandhurst; *m* 21 Feb 1940, Muriel Florence Mary, da of Herbert William Robinson (d 1931); 1 s (Iain b 1942), 1 da (Rosemary b 1941); *Career* cmmnd Army 1928, joined Gurkha Rifles 1929, NW Frontier 1930-31, S Waziristan Scouts (despatches) 1937-40; served Iraq, Syria, Iran, Italy 1941-45; Regimental Centre India 1946-47, ret 1948; since ret active in local affairs: ACF, CD, TAVR Ctee, Dist Cncl; pres Dist Cncls Assoc for Scotland 1966-68; *Recreations* outdoor sports; *Clubs* Army and Navy; *Style*— Lt-Col John W A Lowis; Fauhope, Melrose, Roxburghshire, Scotland (☎ Melrose 2157)

LOWNDES, Rosemary Morley; da of Henry Vaughan Lowndes (d 1951), of Oxton, Cheshire, and Patricia, *née* Watts; *b* 20 Sept 1937; *Educ* Moreton Hall Shrops, Liverpool Coll of Art (BA); *m* 23 Oct 1975, (Trevor Courtney) Jones, s of William Jones (d 1978), of The White Lodge, Caversham, Berks; 1 s (Simon Geoffrey b 30 Oct 1977); *Career* graphic designer, writer and illustrator with Claude Kailer; 46 childrens books incl: Make Your Own World of Christmas, Make Your Own History of Costume, Make Your Own World of Theatre, Make Your Own Noah's Ark, Make Your Own Victorian House, The Market, An Edwardian Album; designer for china and stationery; oil-painting exhibitions incl one man shows in: Paris, Deauville, Honfleur, London, Oxford, Chicago; dir Heritage Ptnrs Tapestries; FCSD 1976; *Recreations* opera, ballet; *Style*— Miss Rosemary Lowndes; 132 Tachbrook St, London SW1 (☎ 01 834 5273)

LOWREY, Air Cmdt Dame Alice; DBE (1960), RRC (1954); da of William John Lowrey and Agnes; *b* 8 April 1905; *Educ* Yorkshire Training Sch, Sheffield Royal Hosp; *Career* joined PMRAFNS 1932; served in Iraq and Aden; principal matron HQ, Middle East Air Force and Far East Air Force 1956-58, HQ Home Command and Technical Training Cmmd 1958-59, Air Cmdt 1959, matron-in chief PMRAFNS 1959-63 (ret), Offr Sister OStJ 1959; *Style*— Air Cmdt Dame Alice Lowrey, DBE, RRC; 5 Snowdrop Drive, Springfield, Attleborough, Norfolk NR17 2PP

LOWRIE, Tony Carmel; s of Vincent Lowrie, of Rhodesia and SA (d 1988), and Gwendoline, *née* Stephens; *b* 24 Mar 1942; *Educ* Llewellyn HS N Rhodesia, RMA

Sandhurst; *m* 3 Nov 1969, Liv Torill, s of Torbjon Ronningen; 1 s (Alexander Christian b 27 Jan 1975), 1 da (Louise Therese (twin) b 27 Jan 1975); *Career* Cadet Rhodesian Army 1960-62, 2 Lt Platoon Cdr Middx Regt, Lt support platoon Queen's Regt, Capt 10 PMO Gurkha Rifles cmdg support company, Maj 1/2 Gurkha Rifles Cmdg C company; bd dir of Hoare Govett stockbrokers 1986- (trainee 1973, devpt Asian equity saks, ptnr 1978-, dir of Hoare Govett Asia, hd of SE Asia devpt Singapore), chm Hoare Govett Int Securities 1988-, bd dir Security Pacific Hoare Govett; non-exec dir: J D Weatherspoon, City Wine Bars; non-exec Superchalet Ltd; memb London Stock Exchange 1984 ; *Recreations* rugby, golf, tennis, skiing; *Clubs* Blackheath, The Addington, The Oriental; *Style—* Tony Lowrie, Esq; 7 Orchard Drive, Blackheath, London SE3 (☎ 01 852 0652); Hoare Govett Ltd, Security Pacific House, 4 Broadgate, London EC2M 7LE (☎ 01 374 1256/01 601 0101, fax 01 256 9961, telex 297801)

LOWRY, (Edward) Frederick Blair; s of Henry Lowry (d 1973), and Evelyn Lowry (d 1970); *b* 27 Jan 1936; *Educ* Cambell Coll Belfast, Dublin Univ (BA, LLB); *m* 19 July 1961, (Flora) Elisabeth, da of Austin Fulton (d 1986); 3 s (David b 1963, John b 1966, Andrew b 1969), 1 da (Catherine b 1962); *Career* CA in practice 1965-67, co sec Ulster Hosiery Ltd 1967-70, dir Berks Int (UK) Ltd 1970-75; md: Lee Div of VF Corpn (UK) Ltd 1975-81, Berks Hosiery (UK) Ltd 1982-; chm Br Branded Hosiery Gp 1988-; FCAI; *Recreations* golf, sailing, gardening, photography; *Style—* Frederick Lowry, Esq; Berkshire Hosiery (UK) Ltd, Donaghadee Rd, Newtownards, Belfast BT23 3QR (☎ and telex 0247 813 461, fax 0247 816 345)

LOWRY, Sir John Patrick (Pat); CBE (1978); s of John McArdle Lowry; *b* 31 Mar 1920; *Educ* Wyggeston GS, LSE (BComm); *m* 1952, Sheilagh Davies; 1 s, 1 da; *Career* served WWII HM Forces, joined Engrg Employers Fedn (dir 1965-70); British Leyland 1970-81; chm ACAS 1981-87, mediator between govt and unions in NHS dispute 1982; former memb: UK employers delegn to ILO, ct of inquiry Grunwick dispute 1977; pres Inst of Personnel Mgmnt 1987; CPIM, CBIM; kt 1985; *Style—* Sir Pat Lowry, CBE; Ashfield, Snowdenham Links Rd, Bramley, Guildford (☎ 893289)

LOWRY, Hon Margaret Ina; da of Baron Lowry (Life Peer); *b* 1956; *Style—* The Hon Margaret Lowry

LOWRY, Her Hon Judge Noreen Margaret (Nina); *née* Collins; da of John Edmund Collins, MC (d 1971), of Sway, Hants, and Hilda Grace, *née* Gregory (d 1985); *b* 6 Sept 1925; *Educ* Bedford HS, Univ of Birmingham (LLB); *m* 1, 25 March 1950 (m dis 1962), Edward Lucas, s of late Edward Walker Gardner, of Preston, Lancs; 1 s (Stephen b 15 May 1956), 1 da (Sally b 2 Oct 1953); m2, 24 April 1963, Richard John Lowry; 1 da (Emma b 25 Nov 1964); *Career* called to the Bar Grays Inn 1948, practised as Miss Nina Collins, appointed Metropolitan Stipendiary Magistrate 1967, memb Criminal Law Revision Ctee 1975, appointed Circuit Judge 1976; *Recreations* theatre, travel; *Style—* Her Honour Judge Lowry; Central Criminal Ct, Old Bailey, London EC4M 7EH (☎ 01 248 3277)

LOWRY, His Hon Judge Richard John; QC (1968); s of Geoffrey Charles Lowry, OBE, TD (d 1974), of Ham, Surrey, and Margaret Spencer, *née* Fletcher-Watson (d 1976); *b* 23 June 1924; *Educ* St Edward's Sch Oxford, University Coll Oxford (BA,MA); *m* 24 April 1963, Noreen Margaret (Nina), da of John Edmond Collins, MC (d 1971), of Sway, Hants; 1 da (Emma b 25 Nov 1964); *Career* enlisted RAF 1943, cmmnd and qualified as pilot 1944, Gp Staff Offr 228 Gp India 1945, Fl Lt 1946; called to Bar Inner Temple 1949 (bencher 1977), memb Bar Cncl 1965-69, dep chm Herts QS 1968, rec Crown Ct 1972-, circuit judge 1977-, memb Home Off Advsy Ctee on Penal System 1972-77; *Recreations* theatre, swimming; *Clubs* Garrick, RAC, Vincents, Leander; *Style—* His Hon Judge Richard Lowry, QC; Central Criminal Court, Old Bailey, London EC4M 7EH (☎ 01 248 3277)

LOWRY, Capt Robert Hugh; DL; s of Cdr R G Lowry, RN (d 1975), of Glasgdrummond, Annalong, Co Down, and Mary Langton, *née* Montgomery (d 1982); *b* 6 Oct 1932; *Educ* Kings Sch Canterbury, RMA Sandhurst; *m* 11 Oct 1958, Angela Adine, da of Lt Cdr K Woods, RN (ka 1940); 2 s (Nicholas b 1961, Peter b 1964), 1 da (Joanna b 1969); *Career* cmmnd RIF 1954, served: Kenya 1954-55, ADC GOC NW Dist 1956-57, Tripoli 1959, Adj Armagh Depot 1959-60, Germany 1962-63, ret 1963; farmer family estate since 1964; pres: fivemiletown branch Royal Br Legion, Clogher Valley Scouts Ctee, Clogher Valley Agri Soc, bd of Ulster Tst for Nature Conservation; vice chm Fermanagh Harriers Hunt Club; memb of synod and church vestry; *Recreations* riding, shooting; *Clubs* Naval and Military, 94 Piccadilly, Tyrone County (Omagh); *Style—* Capt Robert Lowry, DL; Blessingbourne, Fivemiletown, Co Tyrone, N Ireland (☎ 03655 21221)

LOWRY, Baron (Life Peer UK 1979); Robert Lynd Erskine; PC (1974), PC (NI 1971); s of William Lowry (Rt Hon Mr Justice Lowry (d 1949), and Catherine Hughes (d 1947), da of Rev R J Lynd, DD; *b* 30 Jan 1919; *Educ* Royal Belfast Academical Institution, Jesus Coll Cambridge (MA); *m* 1945, Mary Audrey (d 1987), da of John Martin (d 1979); 3 da; *Career* served WW II N Africa Royal Irish Fusiliers 1940-46, Maj, Hon Col TA Bn; barr NI 1947, QC (NI) 1956, high court judge 1964; chm NI Constitutional Convention 1975; Lord Chief Justice of N Ireland 1971-88; Lord of Appeal in Ordinary 1988-; hon bencher: Middle Temple 1973, King's Inns Dublin 1973; hon fell Jesus Coll Cambridge; kt 1971; *Recreations* golf, showjumping; *Clubs* Royal and Ancient (St Andrews), MCC, Army and Navy; *Style—* The Rt Hon the Lord Lowry; White Hill, Crossgar, Co Down, NI (☎ 0396 830397); House of Lords

LOWRY-CORRY, Frederick Henry; s of Lt-Col Sir Henry Charles Lowry-Corry (decd), and Betty, da of Col Douglas Proby (decd), who assumed surname Proby by Royal Licence 1904 in lieu of patronymic Hamilton (n of 1 Duke of Abercorn); *b* 23 Dec 1926; *Educ* Eton; *m* 1949, Hon Rosemary Diana Lavinia, da of 2 Viscount Plumer; 2 s; *Career* Lt RN (ret); *Style—* Frederick Lowry-Corry Esq; Edwardstone Hall, Boxford, Suffolk

LOWRY-CORRY, Hon Mrs; Rosemary Diana Lavinia; *née* Plumer; 3rd and yst da of 2 and last Viscount Plumer, MC (d 1944); *b* 29 Jan 1929; *m* 1949, Frederick Henry Lowry-Corry, *qv*; *Style—* Hon Mrs Lowry-Corry; Edwardstone Hall, Boxford, Suffolk (☎ 210233)

LOWSLEY-WILLIAMS, David; TD (1968), JP (Gloucestershire 1966), DL (1974); s of Maj Philip Savile Lowsley-Wiliams, TD (d 1986) and Ida Moira, *née* Carrol-Leahy (d 1979); *b* 14 August 1933; *Educ* Eton, RAC Cirencester; *m* 14 April 1958, Rona Helena, da of Maj Angus McCorquodale (da 1940, late of Coldstream Gds); 1 s (George b 1959), 2 da (Caroline b 1962, Joanna b 1963); *Career* nat serv 11 Hussars 1954-56, Royal Gloucestershire Hussars 1956-71, Wessex Yeo 1971-76 (CO 1973-76), SW Dist Staff 1976-79, Col TA, chm Gloucestershire TAVRA 1983-; farmer, historic house owner, chm Tetbury NFU 1960-63, cncl memb Historic Houses Assoc 1983-, steward Stratford on Avon Races, memb Gloucestershire Police Authy; *Recreations* golf, squash, skiing, travel; *Clubs* RAC; *Style—* David Lowsley-Williams, Esq; Chavenage, Tetbury, Glos (☎ 0666 52329)

LOWSLEY-WILLIAMS, Lady (Caroline Moira) Fiona; *née* Crichton-Stuart; da of 5 Marquess of Bute (d 1956); *b* 1941; *m* 1959, Capt Michael Lowsley-Williams, 16/5 Lancers; 4 s; *Style—* Lady Fiona Lowsley-Williams; Guadacorte, Estacion de San Roque, Cadiz, Spain

LOWSLEY-WILLIAMS, Hon Mrs Olivia; *née* Bootle-Wilbraham; da of 6 Baron Skelmersdale, DSO, MC (d 1973), and Ann (d 1974), da of Percy Quilter and gda of Sir Cuthbert Quilter, 1 Bt; *b* 31 Dec 1938; *m* 29 July 1961 (m dis 1975), Anthony John Hoole Lowsley-Williams, 2 s of Maj Francis Saville Hoole Lowsley-Williams, 16/5 Lancers, and gs of Sir Paul Makins, 2 Bt, JP; 3 s (Richard b 1962, Sebastian b 1964, Benjamin b 1968); *Career* Interior Designer; *Style—* The Hon Mrs Olivia Lowsley-Williams; 24 Comyn Road, London SW11 1QD

LOWSON, Hon Lady; Hon Ann Patricia; da of 1 Baron Strathcarron (d 1937); *b* 1919; *m* 1936, Sir Denys Colquhoun Flowerdew Lowson, Bt (d 1975); 1 s (Sir Ian, *qv*), 2 da; *Career* OStJ; *Style—* The Hon Lady Lowson; Oratory Cottage, 33 Ennismore Gdns Mews, London SW7

LOWSON, Sir Ian Patrick; 2 Bt (UK 1951), of Westlaws, Co Perth; s of Sir Denys Colquhoun Flowerdew Lowson, 1 Bt (d 1975), and Hon Lady Lowson, *qv*; *b* 4 Sept 1944; *Educ* Eton, Duke Univ USA; *m* 1979, Tanya Theresa H Du Boulay, da of Raymond F A Judge; 1 s, 1 da; *Heir* s, Henry William Lowson b 10 Nov 1980; *Career* OStJ; *Clubs* Boodle's, Pilgrims, Brook (New York); *Style—* Sir Ian Lowson, Bt; 23 Flood St, London SW3

LOWTHER, Hon Charles Alexander James; s of 7 Earl of Lonsdale; *b* 1978; *Style—* The Hon Charles Lowther; Askham Hall, Penrith, Cumberland

LOWTHER, Lt Col Sir Charles Douglas; 6 Bt (UK 1824), of Swillington, Yorks; s of Sir William Guy Lowther, 5 Bt, OBE, DL (d 1982, himself 4 in descent from Sir John Lowther, 1 Bt, whose er bro was cr Earl of Lonsdale), and Grania, Lady Lowther, *qv*; *b* 22 Jan 1946; *Educ* Winchester; *m* 1, 1969 (m dis 1975), Melanie Pensee FitzHerbert, da of late Roderick Christopher Musgrave; m 2, 1975, Florence Rose, da of late Col Alexander James Henry Cramsie, OBE, of Ballymoney, Co Antrim; 1 s, 1 da (Alice Rose b 1979); *Heir* s, Patrick William Lowther b 15 July 1977; *Career* Lt-Col cmdg the Queens Royal Irish Hussars; *Recreations* field sports, travel; *Clubs* Cavalry and Guards; *Style—* Lt Col Sir Charles Lowther, Bt; Erbistock Hall, nr Wrexham, Clwyd

LOWTHER, Grania, Lady; Grania Suzanne; yst da of Maj Archibald James Hamilton Douglas-Campbell, OBE (decd), of Blythswood, Renfrew, by his w, Hon Anna Leonora Beatrice, *née* Butler Massy, da of 5 Baron Clarina by his 2 w; *b* 1919; *m* 1939, Sir William Lowther, 5 Bt, OBE, DL, KStJ (d 1982); 1 s (6 Bt), 1 da (Grizelda b 1948, m 1968 Capt Timothy Bell, Scots Gds; 1 s and 1 da); *Style—* Grania, Lady Lowther; Erbistock Hall, nr Wrexham, Clwyd (☎ 0978 780144)

LOWTHER, Viscount; Hugh Clayton Lowther; s and h of 7 Earl of Lonsdale; *b* 27 May 1949; *m* 1971, Pamela Middleton; *Style—* Viscount Lowther; Parkside, Lowther, Penrith, Cumbria

LOWTHER, Hon James Nicholas; s of 7 Earl of Lonsdale; *b* 1964; *Style—* The Hon James Lowther; Askham Hall, Penrith, Cumberland

LOWTHER, Col John Luke; CBE (1983, JP 1984); s of Col John George Lowther, CBE, DSO, MC, TD (d 1977), of Guilsborough Ct, Northampton, and Lilah Challotte Sarah, *née* White (d 1976); 1st recorded Lowther Baronet Sir Hugh Lowther 1250-1317; *b* 17 Nov 1923; *Educ* Eton, Trinity Coll Oxford (MA); *m* 21 Feb 1952, Jennifer Jane, da of Col J H Bevan, CB (d 1978); 1 s (Hugh b 1956), 2 da (Sarah b 1954, Lavinia b 1958); *Career* served Kings Royal Rifle Corps 1942-47, NW Europe Capt ; worked for Singer Machine Co, USA 1949-51, md: own manufacturing co 1951-60; dir: Equitable Life Assurance Soc 1960-76; farmer 1960; Northants County Cncl 1970-84 (ldr of the Cncl 1977-81); High Sheriff 1971-, Dep Lieutenant 1977, hon Colonel The Royal Anglian Regt (Northamptonshire) 1986; Lord Lieut and Custos Rotulorum of Northamptonsire 1984-; KStJ; *Recreations* shooting, countryman; *Clubs* Boodle's; *Style—* Col John Lowther, CBE, JP; Guilsborough Ct, Northampton NN6 8QW (☎ 0604 740289)

LOWTHER, Hon Mrs Anthony; Lavinia; *née* Joyce; only child of Thomas H Joyce (decd), of San Francisco, USA; *m* 1958, Capt the Hon Anthony George Lowther, MBE, who d 1981 (raised to the rank of an Earl's son 1954), and yr bro of 7 Earl of Lonsdale; 1 s, 3 da; *Style—* Hon Mrs Anthony Lowther; Whitbysteads, Askham, Penrith, Cumbria

LOWTHER, Lady Marie-Louisa; da of 7 Earl of Lonsdale; *b* 1976; *Style—* Lady Marie-Louisa Lowther; Askham Hall, Penrith, Cumberland

LOWTHER, Maurice James; s of James Lowther (d 1983), of Carnforth, Lancs, and Margaret Agnes Hind (d 1986); *b* 14 Sept 1926; *Educ* Lancaster Royal GS, Queen's Univ Belfast (BSc); *m* 1, 1 Nov 1947 (m dis 1976), Audrey Margaret, da of George Holmes (d 1979), of Belfast; 3 da (Anne, Valerie, Pamela); m 2, 1977, Dr Rachel Shirley Lloyd, da of Lt Cdr William F Hood (d 1980), of Handcross, Sussex; *Career* Capt RE 1944-48; md Newcastle and Gateshead Water Co 1971-86 (non exec dir 1988-), non exec dir Stanley Miller plc 1983-; nat pres Inst of Water Engrs and Scientists 1980-81, Nat chm Water Cos Assoc 1984-87, (vice pres 1987-); founding dir Water Aid (third world charity) 1981-; chm Br Inst of Mgmnt Tyne and Wear 1973-75, govr Lancaster Royal GS 1982-; Freeman City of London, Liveryman Worshipful Co of Plumbers; Int Medal American Waterworks Assoc; FICE 1962, FIWES 1967, CBIM 1986; *Recreations* fell walking, angling, beekeeping; *Clubs* National, Northern Counties (Newcastle-upon-Tyne); *Style—* Maurice Lowther, Esq; The Old Schoolhouse, Wall Village, Hexham, Northumberland (☎ 043 481 660); Water Companies Assoc, Gt College St, Westminster

LOWTHER, Lady Miranda; *née* Lowther; er da of 7 Earl of Lonsdale, and his 2 w, Hon Jennifer Lowther (who later married Flt Lt William Edward Clayfield, DFC), younger da of late Hon Christopher William Lowther (only s of 1 Viscount Ullswater, PC, GCB); *b* 1 July 1955; *m* 1978, Martin Dunne; separated 1983 and resumed surname of Lowther by deed poll; *Career* carpenter; proprietor L M L Components; *Style—* Lady Miranda Lowther; L M L Components, Beemill Garage, Ribchester, nr Longridge, Lancs (☎ 025 484 728)

LOWTHER, Hon Mrs Timothy; Susan Ann; *née* Smallwood; da of Capt Leonard Stephen Smallwood, of Jersey, CI, and Mrs Beryl Low, of Jersey; *m* 1977, as his 2 w, Hon Timothy Lancelot Edward Lowther (d 1984), yr s of 6 Earl of Lonsdale (d 1953), by his 2 w, Sybil Beatrix (d 1966), only child of late Maj-Gen Edward Feetham, CB, CMG, of Farmwood, Ascot; 1 da (Melinda Clare b 1978); *Career* social worker, ret; *Style—* Hon Mrs Timothy Lowther; Ivystone House, Rue De La Croix, St Clements, Jersey, CI

LOWTHER, Hon William James; s of 7 Earl of Lonsdale; *b* 1957; *Style—* The Hon William Lowther; Askham Hall, Penrith, Cumberland

LOWY, Kurt; s of Bedrich Lowy (d 1959), of London, and Marie, *née* Gutmann; *b* 28 Dec 1919, (North Czechoslovakia); *Educ* GS, Prague Univ Metallurgical Chemistry; *m* 4 Nov 1945, Blanche Ellaine, da of Isaac Pack (ka 1941); 3 da (Michele b 1948, Arlene b 1951, Stephanie b 1958); *Career* Sergeant Home Guard and Anti-Aircraft Battery 1940-44; md Denham & Morely Overseas 1968-73; chm and md JVC (UK) Ltd 1973-83 (chm 1983-); *Clubs* Institute of Directors; *Style—* Kurt Lowy, Esq; 23 Cranbourne Gardens, London NW11 0HS (☎ 01 209 0181); JVC (UK) Ltd, Eldonwall Trading Estate, Priestley Way, London NW2 7BA (☎ 01 450 3282, fax 01 450 8218, telex 919215)

LOWY, Stanley Robert; MBE (1984), JP (1969); s of Frank Lowy (d 1969), of 74 Purley Bury Ave, Purley, Surrey, and Violet, *née* Rien (d 1982); *b* 20 May 1932; *Educ* Dulwich Coll, Imperial Coll, London Univ (BSc) ACGI; *m* 16 Oct 1954, Ann, da of Stanley Churchill Whitbread (d 1984), of Old Ct, Ridgewood, E Sussex; 1 da (Gillian b 1956), 2 s (Richard b 1958, Edward b 1962); *Career* co dir: Unicorn Products Ltd 1958-, Gunn & Moore Ltd 1971-, Sports Feathers Ltd 1958-, Br Sports & Allied Industs Ltd 1963; chm: Croydon Bench 1980-82, SE London Magistrates Cts Ctee 1982-86, Croydon Magistrates Cts Ctee 1986-; pres Fedn of Br Mfrs of Sports and Games 1970-71, vice-pres Euro Sports Trade Fedn 1975-85, tstee Sports Trade Benevolent Fund 1984-, memb Br Educn Cncl 1980-83; *Recreations* gardening, hill walking, music; *Clubs* MCC; *Style—* Stanley Lowy, Esq, MBE, JP; The Coppice, Beech Ave, Sanderstead, Surrey CR2 0NL; Drimlee, Inveraray, Argyll (☎ 0499 2085); 119-121 Stanstead Rd, London SE23 1HJ (☎ 01 291 3344, fax 01 699 4008, telex 896124)

LOXAM, John Gordon; s of John Loxam (d 1986), of The Barn, Sellet Mill, Whittington, Carnforth, Lancs, and Mary Elizabeth, *née* Rigby (d 1966); *b* 26 April 1927; *Educ* Lancaster Royal GS, Royal Veterinary Coll Edinburgh; *m* 7 June 1950, Margaret Lorraine, da of James Edward Smith (d 1970), of 20 Sharpes Ave, Lancaster, Lancs; 1 s (Richard b 1955, d 1977), 1 da (Stephanie b 1952); *Career* state veterinary serv MAFF; VO 1953, DVO 1963, DO Agric Devpt and Advsy Serv 1971, DRVO 1971, RVO 1976, ACVO 1979, DVFS 1983, ret 1986; gen veterinary practice 1949-53; BVA: memb cncl 1959-71, ctee chm 1963-67, hon sec Lincolnshire and Dist Div 1958-63; ASVO: hon sec 1963-66, pres 1966-67; sr vice pres COEs Standing Ctee on the Welfare of Animals kept for Farming Purposes 1979-80; elected to cncl of VBF 1986, hon sec 1987-; pres Old Lancastrians Club 1988-89; MRCVS 1949; *Recreations* gardening, dog walking, golf, accommodating grand-daughters; *Clubs* Farmers, Stowmarket GC (Suffolk); *Style—* John Loxam, Esq; Riverside, Chelsworth, Ipswich, Suffolk IP7 7HU (☎ 0449 740619)

LOXDALE, Peter Alasdair; s of Hector Alasdair Robert Loxdale, and Hilary Kathleen Ross, *née* Steen; *b* 21 Nov 1959; *Educ* Radley, Welsh Agric Coll Aberystwyth; *Career* farmer 1981-, dir Aberystwyth Marina Ltd 1988-, memb Cardiganshire exec ctee of CLA 1987-, chm Aberystwyth and Dist Rifle and Pistol Club 1984-, pres Llanilar and N Cardiganshire Agric Soc 1987-; *Recreations* shooting; *Style—* Peter A Loxdale, Esq; Castle Hill, Llanilar, Aberystwyth, Dyfed (☎ 097 47 202)

LOY, (Francis) David Lindley; s of Archibald Loy (d 1968) of Sheringham, Norfolk and Sarah Eleanor (d 1967) *née* Lindley; *b* 7 Oct 1927; *Educ* Repton, Corpus Christi Coll Cambridge (BA); *m* 28 Aug 1954, Brenda Elizabeth, da of William Henry Walker of 11 Moorland Garth, Strensall, York; 3 da (Sarah b 1958, Alexandra b 1960, Phillida b 1967); *Career* RN 1946-8; barr 1952, practised North Eastern circuit 1952-72, rec N circuit 1972; stipendiary magistrate: City of Leeds 1972-79, at Leeds 1974-; crown ct recorder 1983-; hon sec Soc of Provincial Stipendiary Magistrates; *Recreations* walking, reading, English history; *Clubs* Leeds; *Style—* David Loy, Esq; 4 Wedgewood Drive, Roundhay, Leeds LS8 1EF; 14 The Avenue, Sheringham, Norfolk; Magistrates Room, Town Hall, Leeds LS1 1NY (☎ 0532 459653)

LOYD, Christopher Lewis; MC (1943), JP (Berks 1950), DL (Berks 1954); s of Arthur Thomas Loyd, OBE, JP (d 1944), of Lockinge, Wantage, and Dorothy, *née* Willert (d 1966); *b* 1 June 1923; *Educ* Eton, King's Coll Cambridge (MA); *m* 13 Dec 1957, Joanna, da of Capt Arthur Turberville Smith Bingham, of Milburn Manor, Malmesbury, Wilts; 2 s (Thomas Christopher b 1959, James William b 1966), 1 da (Harriet Sara b 1962); *Career* served 1942-46, Capt Coldstream Gds; High Sheriff of Berks 1961; chartered surveyor; tstee Wallace Collection 1973-; FRICS 1955 (ARICS 1952); *Clubs* Boodle's, Jockey; *Style—* Christopher Loyd, Esq, MC, JP, DL; Lockinge, Wantage, Oxfordshire OX12 8QL (☎ 0235 833265)

LOYD, Sir Francis Alfred; KCMG (1965, CMG 1961), OBE (1954, MBE 1951); s of Maj A W K Loyd, Royal Sussex Regt; *b* 5 Sept 1916; *Educ* Eton, Trinity Coll Oxford (MA); *m* 1, 1946, Katharine (d 1981), da of Lt-Col S C Layzell, MC, of Kenya; 2 da; m 2, 1984, Monica, widow of Lt Col C R Murray Brown, DSO, Royal Norfolk Regt; *Career* served WW II E Africa; district offr Kenya 1939, private sec to Govr Kenya 1942-45; consul Mega (Ethiopia) 1945; commissioner for Swaziland 1964-68; chm Oxfam Africa Ctee 1979-85; *Style—* Sir Francis Loyd, KCMG, OBE; 53 Park Rd, Aldeburgh, Suffolk (☎ 072 885 2478)

LOYD, Julian St John; CVO (1979), DL (1983); s of Gen Sir Charles Loyd, of Mettingham Pines, Bungay, Suffolk (d 1973), and Moyra, *née* Brodrick (d 1982); *b* 25 May 1926; *Educ* Eton, Magdalene Coll Cambridge (MA); *m* 20 October 1960, Mary Emma, da of Sir Christopher Steel, of Southrop Lodge, Southrop, Lechlade, Gloucs (d 1973); 1 s (Charles b 1963); 2 da (Alexandra b 1961, Mary Rose b 1967); *Career* Coldstream Gds 1944-45; ptnr Savills 1955-64; Agent to HM The Queen at Sandringham 1964-; FRICS 1958; *Recreations* fishing, shooting; *Clubs* Army and Navy; *Style—* J Loyd, Esq; Laycocks, Sandringham, King's Lynn (☎ 0485 40581); The Estate Office, Sandringham, King's Lynn (☎ 0553 772675)

LOYD, Peter Haig; s of Wilfrid Haig Loyd (d 1971), of 36 Chester Square, London SW1, and later of Oakhill, Seaview, IOW, and Emily Charlotte Eileen Loyd, MBE, *née* Oakeley (d 1978); *b* 9 Oct 1922; *Educ* Eton; *m* 1, 8 April 1950 (m dis 1957), Suzanne, da of late Eric McLeod Duncan, of The Croft, The Leigh, nr Cheltenham, Glos; 1 s (William b 6 June 1955), 2 da (Julie b 30 April 1952, Penelope b and d 8 May 1954); m 2, 26 Aug 1961, Rosemary (Rosie) Joan, elder da of late Dr John Hay Moir, of Worplesdon, Surrey 1 s (Anthony (Tony) b 5 Feb 1963), 1 da (Sophie b 10 June 1969); *Career* RM: probationary 2 Lt 1941, Lt 1943, Actg Capt 1943, Adj and Troop Cdr 42 Commando 1943-45, OC HMS Nigeria 1945-47, ADC Maj Gen Portsmouth 1947-49, Inf Trg Centre 1950-51, Capt and Troop Cdr 42 Commando 1952-53; seconded 1 Malay Regt 1955-56, ret 1957; plastics div ICI 1958-61, BTR Indust 1961-66, Industl Soc 1966-74, dir Br Inst of Mgmnt 1974-84; offshore yachtmaster 1976, neighbourhood watch area co-ordinator Hampstead Garden Suburb 1988-, vice chm Hampstead Garden Suburb Residents Assoc 1988; FMS 1966-84, FBIM 1974-, FIIM 1979-84; *Recreations* sailing, carpentry, DIY; *Clubs* Royal Naval Sailing Assoc; *Style—* Peter Loyd, Esq; 12 Meadway, Hampstead Garden Suburb, London NW11 7JS (☎ 01 455 4543)

LOYDEN, Edward; MP (Lab) Liverpool Garston 1983-; s of Patrick Loyden of Liverpool; *b* 3 May 1923; *Educ* Friary Elementary Sch, TUC educn courses, Nat Cncl of Lab Colls; *m* 1924, Rose Ann; 1 s, 2 da (1 da decd); *Career* former port worker and memb Mersey Docks and Harbour Bd (Marine) 1946-74, memb Liverpool: City Cncl 1960-74, CC Met 1973-; TGWU sponsored, MP (Lab) Liverpool Garston Feb 1974-1979,; *Style—* Edward Loyden Esq, MP; 456 Queens Drive, Liverpool L4 8UA

LOYN, Prof Henry Royston; s of Henry George Loyn (d 1939), of Cardiff, and Violet Monica, *née* Thomas (d 1987); *b* 16 June 1922; *Educ* Cardiff HS, Univ of Wales (BA, MA, DLitt); *m* 14 July 1950, Patricia Beatrice, da of Capt Richard Selwyn Haskew, OBE (d 1959), of Harpenden and London; 3 s (Richard Henry b 1951, John Andrew b 1954, Christopher Edward b 1958); *Career* Univ Coll Cardiff: asst lectr 1946-49, lectr 1949-61, sr lectr 1961-66, reader 1966-69, dean 1968-70, prof 1969-74, established chair of medieval history 1974-77, dean 1975-76; prof and head of dept Westfield Coll London Univ 1977-86 (vice princ 1980-86); pres: Historical Assoc 1976-79, Soc for Medieval Archaeology 1983-86; vice pres Soc of Antiquaries 1983-86, memb Ancient Monuments Bd for England 1982-84; pres: Glarmorgan History Soc 1975-77, Cardiff Naturalists Soc 1975-76; memb St Albans Abbey Res Ctee; FRHistS 1958, FSA 1968, FBA 1979; *Books* Anglo-Saxon England and The Norman Conquest (1962), Norman Conquest (1965), Norman Britain (1966), Alfred The Great (1967), A Wulfstan MS (1971), The Reign of Charlemagne (1975), The Vikings in Britain (1977), Medieval Britain (1977), The Governance of England Vol 1 (1984); *Recreations* natural history; *Clubs* Athenaeum; *Style—* Prof Henry Loyn; 25 Cunningham Hill Rd, St Albans, Herts AL1 5BX (☎ 0727 51456) Westfield College, University of London, Kidderpore Avenue, London NW3 (☎ 01 435 7141)

LOYN, Dr William George Grenville; ERD (1968), TD (1980); s of George Morris Loyn (d 1951), of Bronant, and Jane Maria Rees (d 1978); *b* 10 May 1924; *Educ* Tregaron County Sch, Middx Hosp Med Sch (MB, BS); *m* 2 Sept 1950, Elizabeth Magery, da of Fred Gent, CBE (d 1972), of Pinhoe, Exeter; 1 s (David b 1954), 2 da (Monica b 1951, Joanna b 1956); *Career* Col RAMC (TA), RARO; conslt anaesthetist: Whittington Hosp London 1956-80, Bronglais Hosp Aberystwyth 1980-86; OStJ, Hon Col 203 (Welsh) Gen Hosp RAMC (TA); FFARCS 1981; *Recreations* walking, gardening, genealogy; *Style—* Dr William G G Loyn, ERD, TD; Llechwedd, Banc-y-Darren, Aberystwyth, Dyfed SY23 3JE (☎ 0970 828913)

LUARD, (David) Evan Trant; s of Col Trant Bramston Luard, DSO, RM, by his w Helen, wid of Capt Charles Cockburn and da of Laman H Evans, of Cobham, Kent; *b* 31 Oct 1926; *Educ* Felsted, King's Coll Cambridge; *Career* author on int rels; served FO (Hong Kong and Peking) 1950-56, fell St Antony's Coll Oxford 1957-, Oxford city cncllr 1958-61; MP (Lab) Oxford 1966-70 and Oct 1974-79' parly under-sec FCO 1969-70 and 1976-79, del UN Gen Assembly 1967-68, contested (SDP) Oxford West and Abingdon 1983; with Oxfam 1980-84, memb U Sec Gen's Ctee on Restructing of UN 1975-76, EEC Devpt Cmmrs advsy ctee of experts 1981-83; *Books* The United Nations: How it Works and What it Does (1978), Socialism Without the State (1979), A History of the United Nations (1982), War in International Society (1987), Conflict and Peace in the Modern International System (second ed 1988); *Recreations* music, gardening; *Style—* Evan Luard, Esq; 35 Observatory St, Oxford (☎ 0865 513302); St Antony's College, Oxford (☎ 0865 59651)

LUARD, Hon Mrs (Philippa Mary Agnes Joan); da of 9 Viscount Chetwynd (d 1965); *b* 1930; *m* 1959, Maj John Anthony Hawtrey Luard; 1 s, 1 da; *Career* chm: Access and Rights of Way Policy Ctee, Br Horse Soc; *Style—* The Hon Mrs Luard; Maidenford, Goodleigh, nr Barnstaple, Devon EX32 7NG

LUBBOCK, Sir Alan; s of Frederic Lubbock (d 1927, 6 s of Sir John William Lubbock, 3 Bt, and yr br of 1 Baron Avebury); *b* 13 Jan 1897; *Educ* Eton, King's Coll Cambridge; *m* 1918, Helen Mary, *née* Bonham-Carter (d 1987); 2 s; *Career* RA 1915-19 and 1939-45, Maj; chm: Hants CC 1955-67, CC Assoc 1965-69; pro-chllr Univ of Southampton 1967-83; kt 1963; *Clubs* Oxford and Cambridge; *Style—* Sir Alan Lubbock; Adhurst St Mary, Petersfield, Hants

LUBBOCK, Christopher William Stuart; s of late Capt Rupert Egerton Lubbock, RN (3 s of Henry Lubbock, JP, DL, himself 2 s of Sir John Lubbock, 3 Bt and yr bro of 1 Baron Avebury); *b* 4 Jan 1920; *Educ* Charterhouse, BNC Oxford; *m* 1947, Hazel Gordon, *née* Chapman; 1 s, 1 da; *Career* Lt RNVR 1939-45; Master of the Supreme Court of Judicature (appointed 1970); *Clubs* Pratt's; *Style—* Christopher Lubbock, Esq; New Barn House, Great Horkesley, Essex (☎ 0206 271207)

LUBBOCK, Hon Mrs Helen Anne Boyd; yr da of 1 and last Baron Boyd-Orr, CH, DSO, MC (d 1971), and Elizabeth Pearson, *née* Callum; *b* 12 May 1919; *m* 7 July 1939, David Miles Lubbock (sometime md James Simpson & Son, of Peterhead), yr s of Maj Geoffrey Lubbock (himself n of 1 Baron Avebury), by his w Marguerite (wid of Sir Charles Tennant, 1 Bt, whose 2 w she was and by whom she was mother of (Margaret) Lady (w of 2nd Baron) Wakehurst, Baroness Elliot of Harwood, and the late (Nancy) Lady (w of 1st Baron) Crathorne); 3 s (Geoffrey b 1946, John b 1948, Kenneth b 1950), 1 da (Ann b 1941); *Career* sculptor; *Style—* The Hon Mrs Lubbock; Newton of Stracathro, Brechin, Angus DD9 7QQ (☎ Edzeli 294)

LUBBOCK, Joseph Guy; s of Brig-Gen G Lubbock, CMG, DSO (d 1955), of Glebe House, Westerham, Kent, and Lettice Isabell, *née* Mason (d 1978); *b* 20 May 1915; *Educ* Eton, Trinity Coll Cambridge (BA); *m* April 1941, Ruth Cecilia, da of Quintin Edward Gurney, of Bawderwell Hall, Norfolk; 3 da (Jennifer b 1942, Catherine b 1949, Lucinda b 1948); *Career* RE 1939-45; tech dir Drayton-Southern Ltd, ret 1963; chm Royal Br Legion Waldingfield Dist 1969-75; memb Art Workers Guild; IStructE; *Books*

Art and the Spiritual Life (1967), Aspects of Art and Science (1969), Reflections from the Sea (1971), Light and the Mind's Eye (1974), Perceptions of the Earth (1977), From Garden to Galaxy (1980), The Sphere of Rocks and Water (1983), From the Snows to the Sea (1986); *Recreations* sailing, ornothology, world travel; *Clubs* Carlton; *Style—* Joseph Lubbock, Esq; High Elms, Waldringfield, Woodbridge, Suffolk IP12 4QR (☎ 047 336 603)

LUBBOCK, Hon Lyulph Ambrose Jonathan Mark; s and h of 4 Baron Avebury, *qv*, and his 1 w, Kina Maria, *née* O'Kelly de Gallagh; *b* 15 June 1954; *Educ* St Olaves GS, Univ of Birmingham (BSc); *m* 1977, Susan Carol, da of Kenneth Henry MacDonald, of Cliffsea Cottage, 10 Sunridge Close, Swanage, Dorset; 1 s (Alexander Lyulph Robert b 17 Jan 1985), 1 da (Vanessa Adelaide Felicity b 1983); *Career* local govt offr Computer Dept; *Recreations* golf, astronomy; *Style—* The Hon Lyulph Lubbock; 12 Fox Close, Orpington, Kent (☎ Farnborough 57268)

LUBBOCK, Hon Maurice Patrick Guy; 2 s of 4 Baron Avebury, *qv*, and his 1 w, Kina Maria, *née* O'Kelly de Gallagh; *b* 5 Nov 1955; *Educ* BSc; *m* 1982, Diana Rivia Tobin; *Career* ACGI, MIMechE, CEng; *Style—* The Hon Maurice Lubbock

LUBBOCK, Hon Victoria Sarah Maria; da of 4 Baron Avebury; *b* 1959,April; *m* 1983, Alan Binnie; 2 s (Archie b 1983, Alastair b 1985); *Career* freelance fin journalist; contested (Lib) Hackney Borough Cncl 1982; *Style—* The Hon Victoria Lubbock; 225 Evering Rd, London E5 8AL

LUBRAN, Jonathan Frank; s of Prof Michael Lubran, of LA, California, and Avril Roslyn, *née* Lavigne; *b* 27 April 1948; *Educ* Bedales, Univ of Chicago (BA), Cambridge (Dip, PhD); *Career* investmt advsr Crown Agents for Overseas Govts 1979-80; md: Royal Bank of Canada Investmts Mgmnt Int 1980-88, Bankers Tst Investmt Ltd 1988-; former tres Crisis at Christmas, memb London Project Ctee Nat Art-Collections Fund 1977-88; *Recreations* opera, theatre, antiques, swimming, photography; *Clubs* Brooks's, Hurlingham; *Style—* Jonathan Lubran, Esq; 129 Studdridge St, London SW6 3TD (☎ 01 731 0048); Bankers Tst, 1 Appold St, London EC2A 2HE (☎ 01 726 4141, 01 982 2637, fax 01 982 3397, telex 883341)

LUCAS, Sir Cyril Edward; CMG (1956); s of Archibald Lucas (d 1970); *b* 30 July 1909; *Educ* Hull GS, Univ of Hull; *m* 1934, Sarah Agnes, da of Henry Alfred Rose; 2 s, 1 da; *Career* head of dept of oceanography, Univ of Hull 1942-48; entered Civil Serv 1948; dir fishery research in Scotland, Dept of Agric and Fisheries for Scotland 1948-70; memb: Cncl for Scientific Policy 1969-70, Natural Environment Res Cncl 1970-78; FRS; kt 1976; *Style—* Sir Cyril Lucas, CMG; 16 Albert Terrace, Aberdeen (☎ Aberdeen 0224 645568)

LUCAS, Brig Frederick John; CBE (1984); s of Frederick Victor Lucas (d 1977), of London, and Mary Lois, *née* Heath; *b* 15 April 1932; *Educ* Credon Secdy Sch London, Scottish Business Sch Univ of Strathclyde (Dip Mgmnt Studies); *m* 8 Feb 1961, Virginia Isabella Elliott, da of James Robertson Hastie, of Invergordon; 3 s (Lance b 1962, Clive b 1963, Adam b 1964); *Career* cmmnd 1951, asst dir Royal Pioneers MOD 1979-81, dir Pioneers BAOR 1982-84, dir Army Pioneers 1983-85, Hon Col Cmdt Royal Pioneers 1988-; dist gen mangr Central Birmingham Health Authy 1985-86, dir Beacon Estates 1989; memb Harwich Cons Soc, sec Harwich and Dovercourt branch Cons Assoc; Cons candidate Essex CC elections 1989; hon life memb Deutsche Angestellten-Gewerkschaft 1983; *Recreations* work; *Clubs* Lansdowne; *Style—* Brig Frederick Lucas, CBE; Old Swan House, King's Head St, Harwich, Essex CO12 3EE (☎ 0255 240 652)

LUCAS, Capt (Paul) Henry; s of Henry Lucas, and Alice Cowie; *b* 21 Mar 1962; *Educ* St George's Coll Zimbabwe; *Career* Capt QOH; served Berlin, Kenya, Falkland Islands, Jordan, Cyprus, W Germany; involved property devpt Africa and Europe, fndr Ranchco Ranching; *Recreations* polo, downhill skiing; *Clubs* Cavalry and Guards; *Style—* Capt Henry Lucas; c/o Lloyd's Bank, 115 Victoria Road, Aldershot, Hampshire GU11 1JQ; Schloss Bredebeck, The Queen's Own Hussars, BFPO 30

LUCAS, Prof Ian Albert McKenzie; CBE (1977); s of Percy John Lucas (d 1970), and Janie Inglis Hamilton (d 1984); *b* 1 July 1926; *Educ* Clayesmore Sch, Reading Univ (BSc), McGill Univ (MSc); *m* 20 Dec 1950, Helen Louise, da of Ernest Struban Langerman (d 1930), of S Africa; 1 s (Michael Ian b 27 Feb 1952), 2 da (Karen Elizabeth b 25 March 1953, Catherine Helen b 17 July 1967); *Career* lectr Harper Adams Agric Coll 1949-50, princ sci offr (formerly sci offr, sr offr) Rowett Res Inst Aberdeen 1950-61, DSIR res fell Ruakura Res Station NZ 1957-58, prof of agric Univ Coll N Wales 1961-77, princ Wye Coll Univ of London 1977-88; memb: Br Soc Animal Prodn, Agric Educn Assoc, RAS, Royal Welsh Agric Soc; FRAgs 1972, FIBiol 1978, hon memb Br Cncl 1987; *Recreations* sailing; *Clubs* Farmers; *Style—* Prof Ian Lucas, CBE; Valley Downs, Brady Rd, Lyminge, Folkestone, Kent CT18 8DU (☎ 0303 863 053)

LUCAS, Hon Ivor Thomas Mark; CMG (1980); 2 s of 1 Baron Lucas of Chilworth (d 1967); *b* 25 July 1927; *Educ* St Edward's Sch Oxford, Trinity Coll Oxford; *m* 1954, Christine Mallorie, twin da of Cdr A M Coleman, OBE, DSC, RN (d 1981); 3 s; *Career* served with RA; entered Dip Serv 1951, formerly dep high cmmr Kaduna Nigeria; cnsllr Copenhagen 1972-75, head Middle East Dept FCO 1975-79; ambass to: Oman 1979-81, Syria 1982-84; asst sec-gen Arab-Br C of C 1985-87; memb cncl Royal Soc for Asian Affrs 1988-, memb central cncl Royal Over-Seas League 1988-; *Books* Handbook to the Middle East (contrib 1988); *Recreations* music, cricket, tennis, scrabble; *Clubs* Royal Commonwealth Soc, Royal Over-Seas League; *Style—* The Hon Ivor Lucas, CMG

LUCAS, Jeremy Charles Belgrave; s of Percy Belgrave Lucas CBE, DSO, DFC of London, and Jill Doreen, *née* Addison; *b* 10 August 1952; *Educ* Stowe, Pembroke Coll Cambridge (MA); *m* 4 Sept 1976, Monica Dorothea Lucas; 2 s (Christopher b 1981, Timothy b 1984) ; *Career* slr Denton Hall and Burgin 1974-78; merchant banker Morgan Grenfell & Co Ltd 1978- (dir 1986-); *Recreations* tennis, golf; *Clubs* Royal West Norfolk Golf; *Style—* Jeremy Lucas, Esq; Morgan Grenfell & Co Ltd, 23 Great Winchester St, London EC2P 2AX (☎ 01 588 4545)

LUCAS, Michael Stewart; s of William Lucas (d 1980), of Gt Totham, Essex, and Muriel Blanche, *née* Ginn; *b* 8 July 1947; *Educ* Fryerns GS Basildon Essex; *m* 1 Aug 1970, Letitia Marie, da of Thomas Ralph Auchincloss, of The Grange, Stanningfield, Bury St Edmunds, Suffolk; 2 s (Stewart, Charles), 2 da (Catherine, Antonia); *Career* ptnr RJ Lester & Sons 1970-76, ind surveyor 1977-86, dir Bristol Oil & Minerals plc 1986-88, chm BOM Hldgs plc 1988-, dir KCA Drilling plc 1987-; FRICS 1969; *Recreations* polo, hunting, skiing; *Style—* Michael Lucas, Esq; Rivenhall Park, Rivenhall, Essex 5 Old Queen St, London SW1 (☎ 01 233 0533, fax 01 499 6056)

LUCAS, Nigel David; s of Joseph Lucas (d 1986), of Purley, Surrey, and Dorothy Mary, *née* Collier; *b* 14 May 1941; *Educ* Whitgift Sch, Westminster Hotel Sch; *m* 1, 19 Sept 1970, Linda Elisabeth (d 1979), da of Sidney Alfred Stanton (d 1972); 2 da (Sarah b 1973, Catherine b 1974); m 2, 5 May 1982, Janette Muriel, da of Harold Stanley Vian-Smith; *Career* restaurateur and wine wholesaler; dir Castle Inn Ltd 1964-; memb: Hotel Catering and Institutional Mgmnt Assoc, Cooking and Food Assocn; Freeman City of London 1983; *Recreations* family and home; *Style—* Nigel D Lucas, Esq; Withers, Chiddingstone, Edenbridge, Kent TN8 7AE (☎ (0892) 870694); Castle Inn, Chiddingstone, Edenbridge, Kent TN8 7AH (☎ (0892) 870247)

LUCAS, Peter William; s of William George Lucas, of Bradford Abbas, Dorset, and Jose Mabel, *née* House; *b* 12 April 1947; *Educ* Foster's Sch Sherborne, Harrow Coll (Dip M); *m* 10 June 1972, Gail da of John Small (d 1983), of Camberley, Surrey; 1 s (James Peter William b 1981), 2 da (Zoe b 1978, Joanna b 1984); *Career* mktg dir Lyons Tetley Ltd 1978-84, md Foodcare Ltd 1984-85, princ The Mktg Dept 1985-, managing ptnr Mappin Parry Lucas 1988-; chm bd govrs Watlington CPS; memb Mktg Soc 1980, MIGD 1985, FCIM 1987; *Recreations* shooting, gardening; *Style—* Peter Lucas, Esq; Clare Hill Cottage, Pyrton, Oxford OX9 5AX; 20 High Street, Watlington, Oxford OX9 5PY (☎ 049 161 3366, fax 049 161 2934, car tel 0836 288 621)

LUCAS, Hon Rachel Ann; da of 2 Baron Lucas of Chilworth; *b* 1963; *Educ* BA; *Career* public affrs political res 1986-88, foreign language teaching 1988-; *Recreations* travel; *Clubs* Royal Overseas; *Style—* The Hon Rachel Lucas; The Lord Lucas of Chilworth, House of Lords, London SW1A 0AA

LUCAS, Hon Simon William; s and h of 2 Baron Lucas of Chilworth; *b* 6 Feb 1957; *Educ* Univ of Leicester (BSc); *Career* computer systems engr, geophysicists (S America, Pakistan); *Style—* The Hon Simon Lucas

LUCAS, Stephen Ralph James; s and h of Sir Thomas Edward Lucas, 5 Bt; *b* 11 Dec 1963; *Educ* Wellington, Edinburgh Univ; *Style—* Stephen Lucas Esq

LUCAS, Sir Thomas Edward; 5 Bt (UK 1987); s of Ralph John Scott Lucas (decd), late Coldstream Gds, gs of 1 Bt, and Dorothy (d 1985), da of H T Timson; *b* 16 Sept 1930; *Educ* Wellington, Trinity Hall Cambridge; *m* 1, 1958, Charmian Margaret (d 1970), da of late Col James Stanley Powell; 1 s; m 2, 1980, Mrs Ann J Graham Moore; *Heir* s, Stephen Lucas; *Career* engr, scientist, writer, conslt, co dir 1952-; memb European Cmmn, int cos future world mkt studies 2010; FBIM; FRSA; *Recreations* books, cars, gardens, horses, mountains, music, painting, planes, travel; *Clubs* Athenaeum, Ski Club of GB; *Style—* Sir Thomas Lucas, Bt; Sir T E Lucas & Partner (London), Shermans Hall, Dedham, Essex CO7 6DE (☎ 0206 323 506, telex 94011352)

LUCAS, Hon Timothy Michael; 2 s of 2 Baron Lucas of Chilworth; *b* 13 Sept 1959; *Educ* Lancing Coll, Univ of Surrey (BSc); *Style—* The Hon Timothy Lucas; Connaught Lodge, 59 Brownhill Rd, Chandlers Ford, Hants

LUCAS OF CHILWORTH, 2 Baron (UK 1946); Michael William George Lucas; s of 1 Baron Lucas of Chilworth (d 1967, sometime Lord in Waiting to George VI and parly sec to min of Transport), by his w Sonia (d 1979), da of Marcus Finkelstein, of Latvia; *b* 26 April 1926; *Educ* Peter Symonds Sch Winchester, Luton Tech Coll; *m* 1955, Ann-Marie, only da of Ronald Buck, of Southampton; 2 s, 1 da; *Heir* s, Capt Hon Simon William Lucas; *Career* sits as Cons peer in House of Lords; served with Royal Tank Regt 1943-47; pres: League of Safe Drivers 1976-80, Inst of Tport Admin 1980-83; vice-pres Royal Soc for Prevention of Accidents 1980-; UK delegate N Atlantic Assembly 1981-83 and 1988; memb: cncl Inst of Motor Industry 1971-75, RAC Public Policy Ctee 1981-83, and 1988, House of Lords Select Ctee Sci and Technol 1980-83, House of Lords Euro Communities Ctee 1987-; lord in waiting (govt whip) 1983-84; parly under sec of state Trade and Industry 1984-87; govr Churcher's Coll Petersfield 1984-; TEng (CEI), FIMI, FIOTA; *Style—* The Rt Hon the Lord Lucas of Chilworth

LUCAS OF CRUDWELL, Baroness (10 holder of E Barony of 1663) and Lady Dingwall (6 holder of S Lordship 1609); Anne Rosemary; *née* Cooper; da of Baroness Lucas also Lady Dingwall (d 1958, 12 holder of Lordship but for the attainder of 1715 whereby her ggggg unc, the Jacobite 2 Duke of Ormonde, was stripped of all Scottish and English honours) and Gp Capt Howard Lister Cooper (d 1972); co-heiress to Barony of Butler (abeyant since death in 1905 of her great unc, 7 and last Earl Cowper); *b* 28 April 1919; *m* 1950, Maj Hon Robert Jocelyn Palmer, MC, JP, s of 3 Earl of Selborne, CH, PC; 2 s, 1 da; *Heir* s, Hon Ralph Matthew Palmer; *Style—* The Rt Hon the Lady Lucas of Crudwell, and Dingwall; The Old House, Wonston, Winchester, Hants (☎ Winchester 760323)

LUCAS-TOOTH, Hon Mrs Caroline; da of 1 Baron Poole, CBE, TD, PC; *b* 1934; *m* 1955, Hugh John Lucas-Tooth, s of Sir Hugh Vere Huntly Duff Munro-Lucas-Tooth, 1 Bt; *Style—* The Hon Mrs Lucas-Tooth; 44 Queens Gate Gdns, SW7; Parsonage Farm, East Hagbourne, Didcot, Berks

LUCAS-TOOTH, Sir (Hugh) John; 2 Bt (UK 1920); s of Sir Hugh Vere Huntly Duff Munro-Lucas-Tooth of Teananich, 1 Bt (d 1985), and Laetitia Florence, OBE (d 1978), er da of Sir John Ritchie Findlay, 1 Bt, KBE; *b* 20 August 1932; *Educ* Eton, Balliol Coll Oxford; *m* 1955, Hon Caroline Poole, er da of 1 Baron Poole; 3 da; *Heir* cousin, James Lingen Warrand b 6 Oct 1936; *Career* late Lt Scots Gds; dir of various cos including Lazard Investmts Ltd; *Clubs* Brooks's; *Style—* Sir John Lucas-Tooth, Bt; 21 Faroe Rd, London W14; Parsonage Farm, E Hagbourne, Didcot, Oxon

LUCE, Rt Hon Richard Napier; MP (C) Shoreham 1974-, PC (1986); s of Sir William Luce, GBE, KCMG, (d 1977) and Margaret, da of Adm Sir Trevelyan Napier, KCB; *b* 14 Oct 1936; *Educ* Wellington, Christ's Coll Cambridge; *m* 5 April 1961, Rose Helen, da of Sir Godfrey Nicholson, 1 Bt, 2 s (Alexander b 1964, Edward b 1968); *Career* Nat Serv served Cyprus; dist offr Kenya 1960-62, former mangr Gallaher and Spirella Co (GB); parly candidate contested (C) Hitchin 1970, MP (C) Arundel and Shoreham 1971-74, pps to Min Trade and Consumer Affrs 1972-74, oppn whip 1974-75, oppn spokesman Foreign and Cwlth Affrs 1977-79; FCO: parly under-sec 1979-81, min state 1981-82 (resigned over invasion of Falkland Islands), re-appointed min state June 1983-; appt min for the Arts and min of State Privy Cncl Office Sept 1985; *Style—* The Rt Hon Richard Luce, MP; House of Commons, London SW1

LUCKES, Richard James; s of Norman James Luckes, of Spain, and Phyllis Edna, *née* Perry; *b* 9 Dec 1945; *Educ* St Georges Tunbridge Wells, Weston-s-Mare GS, Leeds Univ (LLB); *m* 18 Oct 1969, Mary Penelope, da of Douglas Aldwys Humphries, of Weston-s-Mare, Burma Star; 3 da (Anna b 1974, Julia, Sally b (twins) 1975); *Career* slr of Supreme Ct 1969-, NP 1980-, former memb Saffron Walden Round Table, tstee

Saffron Walden Medics (formerly Accident Gp); memb: Leeds Univ Law Graduates Assoc, Cambs and Dist Law Soc, Prov Notaries Soc, Sd Benevolent Assoc, Law Soc AIJA 1980; *Recreations* golf, tennis, motoring; *Clubs* Saffron Walden Golf, Great Chesterford Country, Saffron Walden Rotary; *Style*— Richard Luckes, Esq; 18 Hill St, Saffron Walden, Essex (☎ 0799 22636, fax 0799 513282)

LUCKHAM-DOWN, Melvyn Raymond; s of Sydney Claude Luckham-Down (d 1958), of The Glen, Plympton, Devon, and Florence Gard, *née* Oatey (d 1957); *b* 20 August 1926; *Educ* Plymouth Coll, London Univ and Royal Dental Hosp (LDS, RCS); *m* 3 April 1954, Margaret Gwendoline, da of John Rees Davies (d 1950), of The Tonn, Llandovery, Wales; 2 s (John b 1956, Edwin b 1965), 1 da (Sarah b 1959); *Career* cmmnd Devonshire Regt 1944, Capt GSO3 Greece 1948, Maj RADC 1955-59; dental surgn and co dir; Freeman City of London 1977, Liveryman Worshipful Co of Wheelwrights; memb: Marine Biolgical Assoc, Fedn Dentaire Internationale, American Dental Assoc; *Recreations* fly fishing, golf, shooting, orchid growing; *Style*— Melvyn Luckham-Down, Esq

LUCKHOO, Hon Sir Edward Victor; QC (Guyana 1965); s of Edward Alfred Luckhoo, OBE (d 1965); bro of Sir Lionel A Luckhoo, *qv* and Evelyn Maud, *née* Mungalsingh (d 1975); *b* 24 May 1912; *Educ* Queen's Coll Guyana, St Catharine's Coll Oxford (BA); *m* 1981, Maureen, da of John Mitchell Moxlow (resides in Yorkshire); *Career* barr Middle Temple 1936, chllr and pres Ct of Appeal Guyana 1968-77; high cmmr for Guyana to India and Sri Lanka 1977-83; chm: Customs Tarrif Tbnl 1954-56, Judicial Serv Cmmn in Guyana 1968-76, Honours Advsy Cncl of Guyana 1970-76; pres Guyana Bar Assoc 19653-60; memb: Municipal Cncl of Georgetown 1946, exec bd of UNESCO 1983-; represented Guyana: on the Caribbean Cncl of Legal Educn 1970-75, at the Cwlth Law Conference in New Delhi 1977; Order of Roraima Guyana 1976; kt 1970; *Clubs* Georgetown Cricket; *Style*— Hon Sir Edward Luckhoo, QC; 17 Lamaha St, Georgetown, Guyana (☎ 58399); office: Whitehall Chambers, Croal Street, Georgetown (☎ 59232)

LUCKHOO, Hon Sir Joseph Alexander; s of Joseph Alexander Luckhoo, KC (d 1949), by his w Clara Irene Luckhoo (d 1966); *b* 8 June 1917; *Educ* Queen's Coll British Guiana, UCL; *m* 1964, Leila Patricia, da of David Dudistil Singh, of New Jersey, USA; 3 s, (Joseph b 1965, Philip b 1968, Jeremy b 1970), 1 da (Elizabeth b 1972); *Career* barr Middle Temple 1944, puisne judge British Guiana 1956; chief justice: Br Guiana 1960-66, Guyana 1966-67; judge Court of Appeal Jamaica 1967-76; reserve judge Bahamas Court of Appeal 1978-81; judge Turks and Caicos Islands Court of Appeal 1978-82, pres 1982-; Bahamas Court of Appeal 1981-82, pres 1982-89; judge Belize Court of Appeal 1987-; ed Br Guiana Law Reports 1956-58, Br Guiana Section of West Indian Reports 1958-60, Jamaica section of West Indian Reports 1968-70; kt 1963; *Recreations* watching sport (principally tennis, baseball and hockey); *Style*— The Hon Sir Joseph Luckhoo; 31 Aldenham Crescent, Don Mills, Ontario M3A 1S3, Canada

LUCKHOO, Sir Lionel Alfred; KCMG (1969), CBE (1962), QC (Guyana 1954); s of late Edward Alfred Luckhoo, OBE; bro of Hon Sir Edward V Luckhoo, *qv*; *b* 2 Mar 1914; *Educ* Queen's Coll Guyana; *m* Sheila Chamberlin; 2 s, 3 da; *Career* barr Middle Temple 1940; MLC 1947-52, memb State Cncl 1953-54, MEC 1955-57, min without portfolio 1955-57; high cmmr for Guyana in the UK 1966-70; ambass for Guyana and Barbados to Paris Bonn and the Hague 1967-70; ambass of Guyana to Venezuela 1970-72; private law practice 1972- (holds record as world's most successful advocate with 236 successful defences in murder cases); *Style*— Sir Lionel Luckhoo, KCMG, CBE, QC; Lot 1, Croal St, Georgetown, Guyana

LUCKIN, (Peter) Samuel; s of Geoffrey Grimston Luckin (d 1986), of High Easter, Nr Chelmsford, Essex, and Muriel Bessie, *née* Need (d 1962); *b* 9 Mar 1938; *Educ* Felsted Sch Essex; *Career* Nat Serv cmmnd Essex Regt 1956-58, platoon cdr BAOR; press aide for Rt Hon Edward Heath CCO 1960's, dep head P/R for Brewers' Soc 1970's Owner Sam Luckin Assoc Surrey 1980-, served on Bd of Mgmnt of Ashridge Mgmnt Coll Assoc 1982-85; memb IPR cncl 1989-, Residents Assoc, active with the Camberley Soc; MIPR; *Recreations* swimming, jogging, theatre, mgmnt devpt, IPR events; *Clubs* Farmers Club, MCC; *Style*— Samuel Luckin, Esq; 13 Belmont Mews, Camberley, Surrey GU15 2PH (☎ 0276 61928)

LUCKOCK, Lt Col (Tomas) Peter; MC (1944); s of Capt Edward Henry Mortimer (d 1963), of Taunton, Somerset, and Muriel Harriet, *née* Christy (d 1976); *b* 23 Sept 1911; *Educ* Eton, RMA Sandhurst; *m* 3 Feb 1940, Elizabeth Margaretta, da of Brig-Gen Frederick Gore Anley (d 1936), of Bolney, Sussex; 2 s (Geoffrey b 1944, Robert b 1952), 1 da (Angela b 1941); *Career* cmmnd Somerset Light Infantry 1931; regular Army Offr 1931-53; WWII Italy (MC 1944); military attaché Br Embassy, Addis Ababa, Ethiopia 1953; awarded Insignia of Cdr of Order of Star of Ethiopia by Emperor Haile Sellassie 1954; *Style*— Lt Col Peter Luckock MC; Mill Cottage, Mill Lane, Bourton, Dorset

LUCY; *see*: Fairfax-Lucy

LUCZYC-WYHOWSKI, Hon Mrs (Oriel Annabelle Diana Skeffington); da of 13 Viscount Massereene and Ferrard; *b* 6 Feb 1950; *Educ* Downham, Tunbridge Wells Tutors, La Sorbonne; *m* 1971, Dominik Albin Thomas, s of Stanislaus Luczyc-Wyhowski, of Dalcove, Roxburgh; 2 da; *Style*— The Hon Mrs Luczyc-Wyhowski; Greenedge House, Badlesmere Lees, Nr Faversham, Kent

LUDBROOK, Michael Sydney; *b* 31 Oct 1944; *m* (m dis); 1 s (James Michael b 1982), 3 da (Claudia Jane b 1976, Gemma Elizabeth b 1977, Hannah Penelope b 1979); *Career* chm Mecca Int 1986, joint md Mecca Leisure Gp plc 1986; md: Mecca Leisure Ltd 1981, Warner Holidays 1985-87; dir: Tiffany Prodns Ltd 1986, Mecca Dancing 1977, Mecca Scotland Ltd; *Recreations* tennis; *Clubs* Groucho's; *Style*— Michael S Ludbrook, Esq

LUDDINGTON, Sir Donald Collin Cumyn; KBE (1976), CMG (1973), CVO (1974); s of Norman John Luddington; *b* 18 August 1920; *Educ* Dover Coll, St Andrews Univ (MA); *m* 1945, Garry Brodie, da of Alexander Buchanan Johnston; 1 s, 1 da; *Career* WWII served KOYLI and RAC; Hong Kong Govt 1949-73: dist cmmr 1969-71, sec for home affrs 1971-73; high cmmr Western Pacific 1973-74, govr Solomon Islands 1974-76; chm Public Servs Cmmn Hong Kong 1977-78, cmmr Ind Cmmn against Corruption Hong Kong 1978-80, ret; *Style*— Sir Donald Luddington, KBE, CMG, CVO; The Firs, Little Lane, Easingwold, York

LUDDINGTON, Gary Anthony Cluer; s of Anthony William Davey Luddington, of Thurlestone, Devon; *b* 20 Feb 1946; *Educ* Brockenhurst GS, Cambridge Univ (MA); *m* 1, 1968; 1 s (Thomas James b 11 Jan 1972);l 1 da (Victoria Louise b 31 July 1970); m 2, 1978, Diana Elizabeth Parkinson, *née* Turnbull; 1 step s (Rufus Joseph b 1972), 1 step da (Clair Elizabeth b 1966); *Career* brand mangr: Beecham 1968-70, Warner Lambert 1970-72; marketing mangr Mars Confectionery 1972-77, md ATV Licensing 1977-79, mktg dir Carlsberg UK 1979-82, md Letraset UK 1982-83, mktg dir Guinness Brewing 1983-87, world wide gp mktg dir Utd Distillers Gp 1987-89; exec dir Norman Broadbent Int 1989-; *Recreations* shooting, sailing, golf; *Style*— G Luddington, Esq; Norman Broadbent Int, 65 Curzon St, London (☎ 0491 579203)

LUDLOW, Lady Margaret Maud; *née* Abney-Hastings; da of Countess of Loudoun, *qv* and her 3 husb, Peter Abney-Hastings; *b* 10 Feb 1956; *m* 1977, Brian Peter Ludlow; 1 s (Thomas William b 1983), 2 da (Kathleen b 1981, Iona b (twin) 1981); *Style*— Lady Margaret Ludlow

LUDLOW, Michael Basil; s of late George Rex Ludlow; *b* 1 Oct 1928; *Educ* Prior Park Coll Bath; *m* 1958, Anne, da of late William F P Bull; 1 s, 1 da (1 da decd 1987); *Career* md Devenish Redruth Brewery Ltd, dir J A Devenish plc (ret 1985); chm Falmouth Harbour Cmmrs; memb Cornwall Valuation Panel Appeal Ctee chm Assoc of Cornish Boys Club; *Recreations* sailing, gardening; *Clubs* Royal Cornwall YC; *Style*— Michael Ludlow, Esq; The Bluff, Restronguet Hill, Mylor, Falmouth, Cornwall TR11 5ST (☎ 0326 73785)

LUDLOW, Michael Richard; s of Sir Richard Robert Ludlow (d 1956), and Katharine Guthrie, *née* Wood; *b* 30 Mar 1933; *Educ* Rugby, Trinity Coll Oxford (MA); *m* 1, 6 Jan 1962 (m dis 1968), Prunella Evelyn Mary, *née* Truscott (now Mrs Clarke); 1 s (Richard Simon b 17 May 1964), 1 da (Anna Mary b 30 Nov 1966); m 2, 31 Oct 1969, Diane April, da of Rowland Wright MBE (d 1960), of Bishops Park Rd, London; 2 da (Zehra Jane b 20 March 1972, Fiona Katharine b 30 Jan 1976); *Career* Nat Serv 1951-52, jr under offr Royal Welsh Fus, cmmnd 2 Lt Queens Regt 1952, seconded to Sierra Leone Regt 1952 (trg offr), Lt N Staffs Regt TA 1952-54; slr 1959, sr ptnr Beak & Co Slrs 1982- (ptnr 1965-82); Freeman of City of London 1987, Worshipful Co of Arbitrators 1987; FCIArb 1983, memb Law Soc 1959-; *Books* Fair Charges (1982); *Recreations* dreaming about past cricket, hockey and rugby exploits; *Clubs* Reform, Vincents (Oxford), Grannies CC; *Style*— Michael Ludlow, Esq; Garrick House, 27-32 King St, Covent Garden, London WC2E 8JD (☎ 01 240 3474, fax 01 240 9110, telex 912072)

LUFF, Graham Oliver; s of John Graham Luff; *b* 7 Sept 1923; *Educ* Swansea GS; *m* 1946, Jeanne Iris; 2 da; *Career* dir Betec plc 1984- (former gp md Bifurcated Eng Ltd), Graphic Types Ltd, former chm prod engrg Research Assoc, fndr and chm Black and Luff Ltd; *Recreations* painting, gardening; *Clubs* RAF; *Style*— Graham Luff, Esq; Bishop's Orchard, Dobbins Lane, Wendover, Bucks HP22 6BP (☎ 0296 622389); National-Westminster Bank, High St, Wendover, Bucks

LUFF, Richard William Peter; s of William Victor Luff (d 1962), and Clare, *née* Wieland (d 1968); *b* 11 June 1927; *Educ* Hurstpierpoint, Coll of Estate Mgmnt; *m* 23 Sept 1950, Betty Hazel, da of Alan Chamberlain (d 1970); *Career* Lt RA UK and India 1945-48; city surveyor Corpn City of London 1975-84, dir: Br Telecom Pty 1984-87, bd memb cmmn for the New Towns 1987-, memb LRT Property Bd 1987- (dep chm 1988-); pres Local Authy Valuers Assoc 1978; pres: RICS 1982-83, Assoc Owners City Properties 1987-; Master Worshipful Co of Chartered Surveyors 1985-86; FRICS; *Books* (jtly): Furniture in England, The Age of the Joiner, many articles in Antique Collector and Country Life; *Recreations* studying, lecturing, antique furniture, country houses; *Clubs* MCC; *Style*— Richard Luff, Esq; Blossoms, Broomfield Park, Sunningdale, Ascot, Berks SL5 0JT

LUFF, Robert Charles William; s of Robert Hill Luff (d 1955), and Ethel Maud Luff (d 1976); *b* 7 July 1914; *Educ* Bedford Modern Sch; *Career* served WWII Gordon Highlanders (India and Burma), Maj; underwriting memb Lloyd's 1961; vice-pres and tstee Cystic Fibrosis Res Tst; tstee: Brompton Hosp Adolescent and Adult Cystic Fibrosis Dept, Asthma Res Cncl, Phillip Zorab Scoliosis Res Fund, Gordon Highlanders Regtl Tst, Manton Charitable Tst; pres: Scarborough Ctee of Br Heart Fndn, Scarborough div St John Ambulance; dir: Cystic Fibrosis Res Investmt Tst 1981-85 (chm 1985-86), Hammersmith Palais Ltd 1955-61, Euro Sports Promotions Ltd Empress Hall 1952-60; chm: Beryl Evetts & Robert Luff Animal Welfare Tst Ltd, Robert Luff Fndn Ltd, Robert Luff Hldgs Ltd gp of companies controlling Royal Hotel (Scarborough) Ltd, Futurist Light & Sound Ltd, Luff Light & Sound Ltd, John Tiller Schs of Dancing, Robert Luff Ltd, Robert Luff Plays Ltd; impresario responsible for the promotion of all the Black and White Minstrel Show presentations in West End, recognized in the Guinness Book of Records as longest running musical prodn; FID; *Recreations* golf; *Clubs* RAC, Army and Navy; *Style*— Robert Luff, Esq; 294 Earls Court Rd, London SW5 9BB (☎ 01 373 7003)

LUFT, His Hon Arthur Christian; CBE (1988); s of Ernest Christian Luft (d 1962), and Phoebe Luft (d 1977); *b* 21 July 1915; *Educ* Bradbury Cheshire; *m* 1950, Dorothy, da of Francis Manley (d 1936); 2 s (Peter, Timothy); *Career* served RA and REME 1940-46; advocate Manx Bar 1940, HM Attorney Gen IOM 1973, HM second deemster (HC Judge) 1974, HM first deemster, clerk of the rolls and dep govr IOM 1980-88; memb: legislative cncl of IOM 1988-, Dept of Local Govt and Environment 1988-; chm: Criminal Injuries Compensation Tbnl 1975-80, Prevention of Fraud Investmts Act Tbnl 1975-80, Licensing Appeal Ct 1975-80, Tynald Ceremony Arrangements Ctee 1980-88, IOM Income Tax Cmmrs 1980-88; pres: Manx Deaf Soc 1975-, IOM Cricket Club 1980-; *Recreations* theatre, watching cricket, reading, gardening; *Clubs* Ellan Vannin, IOM Automobile; *Style*— His Hon Arthur Luft, CBE; Leyton, Victoria Rd, Douglas, Isle of Man (☎ 0624 21048)

LUGG, (Herbert Kenneth) Michael; s of Reginald Lugg (d 1969), of Ryde, and Winifred Agnes, *née* Stuart; *b* 7 April 1934; *Educ* Ryde Sch, Isle of Wight, London Univ (BSc); *m* 22 July 1961, Valerie Dean, da of Maurice William Alfred Jacobs (d 1987); 1 da (Sarah b 1965); *Career* civil engr: agent Bridgwater Bros (PWC) 1962-64, engr Shell Mex & BP 1964-73, mangr retail engrg BP Oil 1973-78, engrg mangr BP Oil 1978-; govr Ryde Sch 1987- (vice chm 1987); *Recreations* concert, theatre going, classic sports cars, walking, gardening; *Style*— Michael Lugg, Esq; The Merrick, Tarn Rd, Hindhead, Surrey GU26 6TP (☎ 042 873 6883); BP Oil, BP House, Breakspear Way, Hemel Hempstead, Herts HP2 4UL (☎ 0442 225719)

LUKE, Hon Mrs; (Oenone) Clarissa; *née* Chaplin; only da of 3 and last Viscount Chaplin (d 1981), by his 1 w, Alvilde, da of Lt-Gen Sir Tom Molesworth Bridges, KBE, KCMG, DSO, LLD (whose unc was Robert Bridges, the poet laureate); *b* 12 April 1934; *m* 1958, Michael Charles Deane Luke, yr s of Sir Harry Charles Luke, KCMG; 1 s (Igor b 1965), 3 da (Chloe b 1959, Oenone b 1960, Cressida b 1961);

Style— The Hon Mrs Luke; Flat 6, 22 Eaton Sq, London SW1 (☎ 01 235 1841)

LUKE, Hon Sir Emile Fashole; KBE (1969, CBE 1959); s of late Josiah Thomas Steven Luke; *b* 19 Oct 1895; *Educ* Wesleyan Methodist HS, Fourah Bay Coll Sierra Leone; *m* 1929, Sarah Christina Jones (decd); 2 s, 1 da; *Career* barr 1925-43, puisne judge Sierra Leone 1954-59, actg chief justice 1957-59, justice of the Court of Appeal 1960-61 and 1967; speaker of the House of Representatives Sierra Leone 1968-73; *Style*— Hon Sir Emile Luke, KBE; 85 Motor Rd, Wilberforce, P O Box 228, Freetown, Sierra Leone (☎ Freetown 30602)

LUKE, 2 Baron (UK 1929); Ian St John Lawson-Johnston; KCVO (1976), TD (1949), JP (Beds 1939), DL (1938); s of 1 Baron Luke, KBE, JP (d 1943), and Hon Edith Laura (d 1941), da of 16 Baron St John of Bletso; *b* 7 June 1905; *Educ* Eton, Trinity Cambridge; *m* 4 Feb 1932, Barbara, da of Sir FitzRoy Hamilton Anstruther-Gough-Calthorpe, 1 Bt, JP (d 1957); 4 s; 1 da; *Heir* s, Hon Arthur Charles St John Lawson-Johnston; *Career* life-pres Electrolux Ltd 1978-; chm: Gateway Bldg Soc 1978-86, Bovril Ltd 1943-70; dir Ashanti Goldfields Corpn Ltd; former dir: Lloyds Bank, IBM UK, vice-pres Nat Playing Fields Assoc 1977- (late chm); chm governing body of Queen Mary Coll Univ of London 1963-82, memb Int Olympic Ctee 1951-88 (hon memb 1988-); pres: Inst of Export 1973-83, London C of C 1952-55; late MFH Oakley Hunt; one of HM's Lts for City of London; CStJ; *Clubs* Carlton; *Style*— The Rt Hon Lord Luke, KCVO, TD, JP, DL, HM Lieut for City of London; Odell Castle, Odell, Beds (☎ 0234 720 240)

LUKE, Peter Ambrose Cyprian; MC (1944); s of Sir Harry Luke, KCMG (d 1969), and Joyce Evelyn, *née* Fremlin (d 1973); *Educ* Eton, Byam Shaw Sch of Art, Atelier Andre Lhote Paris; *m* 1, late Carola Peyton Jones; m 2, Lettice Granshaw (m dis); 1 s (Harry d 1985), 1 da (Giana); m 2, 23 Nov 1963 (Mary Pamela) June, da of Lt-Col W V Tobin (d 1969); 2 s (Anthony, Ormody); 3 da (Anna, Oonagh, Rasario); *Career* WWII Rifle Bde 1939-46 served: Middle East, Italy, NW Europe; writer dramatist and dir; sub ed Reuters News Desk 1946-47, wine trade 1947-57; ABC TV: story ed 1958-62, ed The Bookman 1962-63, ed Tempo (arts programme) 1963-64; drama prodr BBC TV 1963-67; dir: Hadrian VII (Abbey Theatre Dublin) 1970, Edwards-Mac Liammoir (Dublin Gate Theatre Co) 1977-80, Rings for a Spanish Lady (Gaeity Theatre Dublin) 1978; writer of stage plays: Hadrian VII (Antionette Perry Award nomination 1968-69), Proxopera (adaption) 1979, Married Love (translation) 1985, Yerma (by Frederico Garcia Lorca) 1987; produced TV play Silent Song (BBC TV, Prix Italia 1967); wrote and directed TV plays: Anach Cuan (BBC TV) 1967, Black Sound Deep Song (BBC TV) 1968; author TV plays: Small Fish are Sweet 1958, Pig's Ear with Flowers 1960, Roll on Bloomin' Death (with William Sanson) 1961, A Man on Her Back 1965, Devil a Monk Would Be 1966, Honour Profit and Pleasure 1985; hon memb Hermandad de Das Hermanas Sevilla Spain; OStJ 1940; *Books* Sisyphus and Reilly (autobiography, 1972), Enter Certain Players Edwards - Mac Liammoir 1928-78 (ed 1978), Paquito and the Wolf (1981), Telling Tales: selected short stories (1981), The Other Side of the Hill, a novel of the Peninsular War (1984), The Mad Pomegranate and the Praying Mantis Adventure in Andalusia (1985); translated from Spanish: Yerma (by Frederico Garciá Lorca), Rings for a Spanish Lady (by Antonio Gala; writer of many short stories); *Recreations* attending bull-fights, growing citrus fruit; *Style*— Peter Luke, Esq, MC; Calle Fuente de la Cruz, 28-30 Jimena de la Frontera, Cadiz, Spain

LUKE, (William) Ross; s of Maj Hamish Galbraith Russell Luke TD, JP (d 1970), and Ellen Robertson Boyd *née* Mitchell; *b* 8 Oct 1943; *Educ* Stowe Sch; *m* 16 May 1970, Deborah Jacqueline, da of Derek John Gordon; 3 da (Alison b 1973, Kirstene b 1974, Victoria b 1978); *Career* CA 1968; dir: Appleton Hldgs plc 1986, The Mar Agency Ltd 1981, Vehicle Crime Prevention 1983; hon sec London Scottish RFC; Met Police Commendation 1983; *Recreations* rugby football, squash; *Clubs* London Scottish Rugby FC; *Style*— Ross Luke, Esq; 105 Palewell Park, London SW14 8JJ (☎ 01 876 9228); 139 King St, London W6 9JG (car tel 0836 523594)

LUMLEY, Henry Roberts Lane; s of Edward Lumley Lumley (d 1960), and Kathleen Agnew, *née* Wills (d 1978); *b* 29 Dec 1930; *Educ* Eton Coll, Cambridge MA; *m* m, 7 Oct 1959, Sheena Ann, da of Air Vice-Marshal Somerled Douglas MacDonald, CB, CBE, DFC; 2 s (Peter b 1960, Robert b 1965); 1 da (Julia b 1962); *Career* insur broker; chm Edward Lumley Hldgs Ltd 1986 (joined 1974); dir: Edward Lumley & Sons Ltd, Lloyd's Brokers 1956, Lumley Corp Ltd Aust 1974; *Clubs* East India; *Style*— Henry Lumley, Esq; Lumley House, 43/51 St Mary Ave, London EC3A 8AL (☎ 01 283 5266, fax 01 220 7559, telex 888224)

LUMLEY, Joanna Lamond (Mrs Stephen Barlow); da of Major James Rutherford Lumley, 2/6 Gurkha Rifles, of Cranbrook Kent and Thyra Beatrice Rose Weir, FRGS; *b* 1 May 1946; *Educ* Army Sch Kuala Lumpar, St Mary's Baldslow Sussex; *m* 1, 1970 (m dis 1971), John Jeremy Lloyd; m 2, 23 Oct 1986, Stephen William, s of George William Barlow of Witham, Essex; 1 s (James b 16 Oct 1967); *Career* actress; films incl: On Her Majesty's Secret Service 1968, The Breaking of Bumbo 1970, The Satannic Rites of Dracula 1973, The Trial of the Pink Panther 1982, The Curse of the Pink Panther 1982; plays incl: Don't Just Lie There Say Something 1971, Private Lives 1981, Noel and Gertie 1983, Hedda Gabler 1984, Blithe Spirit 1986, An Ideal Husband 1987; TV incl: The New Avengers, Sapphire and Steel The Glory Boys, Mistrial's Daughter; patron: Speedwell Tst, Friedrich's Ataxia Gp, Farm Africa; FRGS 1982;; *Books* Peacocks and Commas (1984); *Recreations* reading, painting, travelling, rejoicing, collecting junk; *Style*— Miss Joanna Lumley; MLR, 200 Fulham Rd, London SW10 (☎ 01 351 5442)

LUMLEY, John Adrian; s of Thomas Lumley (d 1983), and Patience, *née* Henn Collins (d 1987); *b* 29 May 1942; *Educ* Eton, Magdalene Coll Cambridge (MA); *m* 14 June 1969, Catita, da of Hans Lieb (d 1959), of Algeciras, Spain; 1 s (Joshua b 1970), 2 da (Eliza b 1973, Olivia b 1981); *Career* Christie's (Christie, Manson & Woods Ltd): joined 1964, dir 1969; memb Kent and E Sussex regnl ctee Nat Tst 1981-87; Liveryman Worshipful Co of Goldsmiths 1984; *Clubs* Brooks's; *Style*— John Lumley, Esq; Court Lodge, Egerton, Ashford, Kent (☎ 023 376 249); Christie's, 8 King St, London SW1 (☎ 01 839 9060)

LUMLEY, Richard Edward Walter; er s of Edward Lumley Lumley (d 1960), and Kathleen Agnew, *née* Wills (d 1978); respective fndrs of the Edward Lumley Hall at the RCS of England (opened by H M Queen 1954), and of Kathleen Lumley Coll Univ of Adelaide S Aust (opened 1969); *b* 7 July 1923; *Educ* Eton; *m* 1953, Josephine Mary, da of Dr F Melville Harvey, MC (d 1935), of St Mary's Hosp Paddington and of Montivideo; 3 s (Edward d 1955, John, Christopher), 5 da (Sarah, Caroline, Astrid, Emma, Susan); *Career* served Coldstream Gds WWII Capt; underwriting memb of Lloyd's 1944-, chm: Edward Lumley & Sons Ltd 1980-85 (dir 1951-88 chm and md 1960-85), Edward Lumley & Sons (underwriting agencies) Ltd 1971-88, Edward Lumley Hldgs Ltd 1974-85 (dir 1974-); dir Lumley Corpn Ltd Aust 1974-; patron RCS of England, memb of cncl Br Aust Soc; *Recreations* family pursuits, walking in country, skiing; *Clubs* Boodles, Cavalry & Guards, East India & Devonshire, MCC, Berkshire GC, Cook Soc; *Style*— Richard Lumley, Esq; Roundwood, Sunninghill Rd, Windlesham, Surrey GU20 6PP (☎ 0276 72337); Lumley House, 43/51 St Mary Axe, London EC3A 8AL (☎ 01 621 0688)

LUMLEY, Viscount; Richard Osbert Lumley; s and h of 12 Earl of Scarbrough; *b* 18 May 1973; *Heir* bro, Hon Thomas Lumley; *Style*— Viscount Lumley

LUMLEY-SAVILE, Hon Henry Leoline Thornhill; s of 2 Baron Savile, KCVO (d 1931), and hp of bro, 3 Baron; *b* 2 Oct 1923; *Educ* Eton; *m* 1, 1946, Presiley June (m dis 1951), da of Maj G H E Inchbald; 1 s; m 2, 1961, Caroline Jeffie (d 1970), da of Peter Clive; m 3, 1972, Margaret Ann (nee Phillips), wid of Peter Bruce; 3 s (triplets b 1975); *Career* served with Grenadier Gds (wounded), demobilized 1947; *Clubs* White's; *Style*— The Hon Henry Lumley-Savile; 9 King's Road, Richmond, Surrey TW10 6NN

LUMSDEN, Sir David James; s of Albert Lumsden (d 1985), and Vera, *née* Tate (d 1980); *b* 19 Mar 1928; *Educ* Cambridge Univ (PhD, MA, MusB); *m* 1951, Sheila Gladys, da of George Daniels; 2 s (Stephen, Andrew), 2 da (Jennifer, Jane); *Career* fell and organist New Coll Oxford 1959-76, princ Royal Scottish Acad of Music and Drama Glasgow 1976-82, Royal Acad of Music London 1982-; kt 1985; *Recreations* hill walking, reading, friends; *Style*— Sir David Lumsden; 47 York Terrace East, London NW1 4PT; Royal Acad of Music, Marylebone Rd, London NW1

LUMSDEN, Edward Gabriel Marr; s of Edward Gabriel Lumsden of Barons Court, London W14 and Isobel, *née* Dyker; *b* 4 July 1946; *Educ* Hampton GS, Westminster Hotel Sch (Nat Dip in Hotelkeeping and Catering); *Career* area mangr Truman Taverns 1980-81, dir and gen mangr Arden Taverns 1981-83, tied trade dir Drybroughs of Scotland 1983-86, innkeeper dir Truman Ltd May 1986-Oct 1986; innkeeper ops dir Watney Co Reid & Truman 1986-; FHCIMA, FCFA, FRSH, MBIM, MBII, FInstD; *Recreations* travel, gastronomy, the arts; *Style*— Edward Lumsden, Esq; Sunny Bank, North Side, Steeple Aston, Oxon OX5 3FE (☎ Steeple Aston 40546); The Old Brewery, St Johns Road, Isleworth, Middlesex TW7 6PS (☎ 01 876 3434, telex: 935051)

LUMSDEN, Ian George; s of James Alexander Lumsden, MBE, of Bannachra, By Helensburgh, Dunbartonshire, and Sheila, *née* Cross; *b* 19 Mar 1951; *Educ* Rugby, Corpus Christi Coll Cambridge (BA), Edinburgh Univ (LLB); *m* 22 April 1978, Mary Ann, da of Maj Dr John William Stewart Welbon, of Cornwall; 1 s (Richard d 1984), 1 da (Sarah d 1986); *Career* ptnr Maclay Murray and Spens 1980- (trainee and asst slr 1974-78) asst slr Slaughter and May London 1978-80; memb Law Soc of Scotland, Royal Faculty of Procurators; *Recreations* golf, shooting; *Clubs* New (Edinburgh), Prestwick GC; *Style*— Ian Lumsden, Esq; The Myretoun, Menstrie, Clackmannanshire FK11 7EB (☎ 0259 61453); Maclay Murray and Spens, Hogarth House, 43 Queen Street, Edinburgh EH2 3NH (☎ 031 226 5196, fax 031 226 3174, 031 225 9610, telex 727238 VINDEX)

LUMSDEN, James Alexander; MBE (1945), TD (1962), DL (Dunbartonshire 1966); s of Sir James Robert Lumsden, CBE (d 1970), and Henrietta Macfarlane, *née* Reid (d 1985); *b* 24 Jan 1915; *Educ* Cargilfield Sch, Rugby, CCC Cambridge (BA), Glasgow Univ (LLB); *m* 21 June 1947, Sheila, da of Malcolm Cross (d 1919), of Glasgow; 3 s (James b 1948, Ian b 1951, Michael b 1952); *Career* WWII RA (AA) 1939-46, demobbed Maj 1946; TA 1937-62; ptnr Maclay Murray & Spens (Slrs) Glasgow 1947-82; chm: Burmah Oil plc 1971-75 (dir 1957-76), Murray Int Investmt Tst 1971-85 (dir 1967-85), Scottish Provident Inst 1977-83 (dir 1968-85); dir: Weir Gp plc 1957-84, Bank of Scotland 1958-85, William Baird plc 1959-84; pres (formerly chm) Dumbarton Cons Assoc, gen cmmr of income tax West Dumbarton, cncl memb Friends of Loch Lomand, elder and tres Luss Parish Church; life memb: Merchants House of Glasgow, Incorpn of Weavers in Glasgow; memb Law Soc of Scotland; *Recreations* shooting, fishing, country pursuits; *Clubs* New (Edinburgh), Western (Glasgow), Caledonian; *Style*— James Lumsden, Esq, MBE, TD, DL; Bannachra, by Helensburgh, Dunbartonshire (☎ 038 985 653)

LUMSDEN, Prof Keith Grant; s of Robert Sclater Lumsden (d 1964), of Bathgate, and Elizabeth, *née* Brow; *b* 7 Jan 1935; *Educ* The Academy Bathgate, Edinburgh Univ (MA), Stanford Univ California (PhD); *m* 21 July 1961, Jean Baillie, da of Capt Kenneth Macdonald, MC (d 1962), of Armadale; 1 s (Robert Alistair Macdonald b 1964); *Career* Stanford Univ: instr dept of econs 1960-63, assoc prof Graduate Sch of Business 1968-75 (asst prof 1964-67), prof econs Advanced Mgmnt Coll 1971-; res assoc Stanford Res Inst 1965-71, visiting prof econs Heriot-Watt Univ 1969, academic dir Sea Tport Exec Programme 1984-, currently affiliate prof econs INSEAD France; dir: Stanford Univ Conf RREE 1968, Econ Educn Project 1969-74, Behavioral Res Laboratories 1970-72, Capital Preservation Fund Inc 1971-75, Nielsen Engrg Res Inc 1972-75, Hewlett-Packard Ltd 1981-; currently dir The Esmee Fairbaim Res Centre; memb: American Econ Assoc Ctee on Econ Educn 1978-81, advsy cncl David Hume Inst 1984-; numerous articles in professional jls, creator of various softwear systems; *Books* The Free Enterprise System (1963), The Gross National Product (1964), International Trade (1965), Microeconomics: A Programmed Book (with R E Attiyeh and G L Bach new edn 1981), Macroeconomics: A Programmed Book (with RE Attiyeh and GL Bach new edn 1981), New Developments in the Teaching of Economics (ed 1967); *Recreations* tennis, deep sea sports, fishing; *Clubs* Waverley Lawn Tennis & Squash; *Style*— Prof Keith Lumsden; 40 Lauder Road, Edinburgh EH9 1UE (☎ 031 667 1612); The Esmee Fairbaim Research Centre Heriot-Watt University, Riccarton, Edinburgh EH14 4AS (☎ 031 451 3090, fax 031 451 3002)

LUMSDEN-COOK, Anthony James; s of James Alexander Lumsden-Cook, MB, CHB, DLO (d 1977), of Durban, Natal, S Africa, and Mary Kathleen, *née* Bennion ; *b* 23 August 1935; *Educ* Stowe Sch RAC; *m* 1, 1959 (m dis), Christine, da of Oswald Rissen (d 1958); 2 s (Mark Alexander Rowe b 28 Oct 1961, Sean Anthony b 6 June 1960), 1 da (Julie Clare b 16 July 1960); m 2, 3 Feb 1973, Carol Marie, da of Col Clinton Kearny, USAF (d 1976); 1 s (James Justin b 23 Oct 1975); *Career* serv HAC 1957-59; dir Swann & Everett Ltd 1967-72, md Alexander Howden & Swann 1973-76, chm Anthony Lumsden & Co 1977-84 (also chm of subsidiary cos), dir Wigham Poland Hldgs Ltd 1984-86, dep chm Sedgwick Marine Ltd 1985-86; proprietor Continental

Villas and Sloan Travel 1987-, ptnr Lumsden Leche Ptnrship (int estate agents) 1987-; underwriting memb Lloyds 1959-; FBIM (1975), FCIB (1972); *Recreations* Concours D'Elegance cars, swimming; *Clubs* Caledonian RAC, Hurlingham, City of London Tanglin (Singapore), Singapore town; *Style*— Anthony Lumsden-Cook, Esq; 29 Pembroke Gardens Close, London W8 6HR (☎ 01 602 6381); 33 Great Tew, Oxon OX 75AL (☎ 060 883 444); Continental Villas, Eagle House, 58 Blythe Rd, Londn W14 OHA (☎ 01 371 1313, fax 01 602 4165, telex 918054 Villas G, car phone 0836 204 313)

LUNCH, John; CBE (1975), VRD (1965); s of Percy Valentine Lunch (d 1974), and Amy, *née* Somerville (d 1960); *b* 11 Nov 1919; *Educ* Roborough Sch Eastbourne; *m* 1943 Joyce Barbara, da of Arnold Basil O'Connell Clerke (d 1959); 2 s; *Career* Lt Cdr RNR 1940-69 (ret), served WW II Crete, Malta convoys, N Africa, Sicily D-Day, Atlantic convoys; Col (TA) Engr and Tport Staff Corps RE 1971-; in business in City 1946-48; asst md Tokenhouse Securities Corp Ltd 1947, and dir several cos; Br Tport Cmmn, 1948-61, road and rail tport and ancillary businesses; PLA, 1961; dir of finance, also dir of commerce, 1966; asst dir-gen, responsible docks and harbour 1969; dir-gen PLA and bd memb 1971-76; chm: Comprehensive Shipping Gp 1973-75, Transcontinental Air Ltd 1973-75; cncl: memb ICAEW 1970-77, RNLI: memb ctee of mgmnt 1977- (vice-pres 1987-, pres Hayling Island Station 1978-88, fndr Manhood Branch 1976, hon art advsr 1981; Freeman City of London; court memb Worshilful Co of Watermen's 1976-; FCA, FCIT (memb 1973-76), FInstM, CBIM, FRSA, hon FInst FF (pres 1972-73); *Recreations* sailing (yacht 'Lively'), art; *Clubs* Army and Navy, Press, Itchenor Sailing; *Style*— John Lunch, Esq, CBE, VRD; Twittens, Itchenor, Chichester, W Sussex PO20 7AN (☎ 0243 512105); 97A York Mansions, Prince of Wales Drive, London SW11 4BN (☎ 01 622 8100)

LUND, Anthony Marling; s of Lt-Gen Sir Otto Lund, KCB, DSO, and Margaret Phyllis Frances, *née* Harrison; *b* 24 Sept 1929; *Educ* Eton; *m* 1 Sept 1967, Sophie, da of Count Soumarokoff-Elston (d 1970), of London; 2 da (Tatiana b 1969, Anna Maria b 1970); *Career* 2 Lt 11 Hussars (PAO) 1948-49; assoc: Kulm Leob and Co NY 1952-59, Int Fin Corp Washington DC 1958-61; vice pres then ptnr/md: Kuhn Loeb and Co, Lehman Bros Kuhn Loeb Inc, Shearson Lehman Bros; chief exec EBC Amro Bank Ltd 1986-88; *Clubs* White's; *Style*— Anthony Lund, Esq; 10 Devonshire Square, London EC2 (☎ 01 621 0101, fax 01 623 9309, telex 8811001)

LUND, Rodney Cookson; s of Arthur Lund (d 1975), and Doris, *née* Bond; *b* 16 June 1936; *Educ* Wallasey GS, Liverpool Univ (BCom); *Career* Lt RAPC 1957-59; Evans Medical 1959, Carreras Rothmans 1960-64, ptnr Urwick Orr & Ptnrs 1964-66 and 1969-73, md The Mace Voluntary Gp 1966-69, vice-chm Produce Importers Alliance 1966-69, exec dir Rank Radio Int 1973-75, exec dir British Sugar 1976-82, exec dir Woolworth Hldgs 1982-86; chm: Nat Bus Co 1986, chm Short Bros plc; CBIM; *Recreations* travel, opera, cooking; *Style*— R C Lund, Esq; 18 Billing Rd, Chelsea SW10 9UL (☎ 01 352 2641)

LUNN, Rt Rev David Ramsay; *see*: Sheffield, Bishop of

LUNN, (Henry) Fletcher; s of Henry Gerrard Lunn (d 1957), and Isobel Elizabeth, *née* Young (d 1979); *b* 7 June 1916; *Educ* Berkhampsted Sch, Guys Hosp Med Sch, London Univ (MB, BS, BSc); *m* 6 July 1940, Agnes Rosalind, da of Rev William John Wright (d 1945), of Calcutta, E Horsley, Surrey and Wimborne, Dorset; 1 s (Peter Granger b 1945), 3 da (Christine b 1941, Rosalind b 1943, Patricia b 1951); *Career* WWII Maj RAMC, served RMO and DADMS 4 Br Div Home and CMF 1940-44; surgn 103 Gen Hosp Italy and Greece 1944-46, conslt surgn Church Missionary Hosp Cairo 1948-53, sr registrar St Helier Hosp Carshalton 1953-55, sr casualty offr Peace Memorial Hosp Watford 1955-57, conslt surgn and sr lectr Makerere Coll Uganda 1957-65, sr lectr in clinical physiology Guys Hosp 1965-73, conslt surgeon Isle of Arran Hosps 1973-81, pt/t clinical asst Geriatric Day Hosp Frenchay 1981-84, memb Glos Community Health Cncl 1985-87; appts in RCS incl: Sir Halley Stewart Res Fell 1946-47, Arris & Gale lectrships 1947 and 1952, Hunterian prof 1968; FRCS; *Books* many article in medical press on inguinal hernia, tropical surgery, medical ethics, heat balance in intensive care; *Recreations* small holding, church activities; *Style*— Henry Lunn, Esq; c/o Lloyds Bank, High Street, Lydney, Glos GL15 5DW

LUNN, Jonathan William Peter; s of Cecil Peter Lunn, and Eileen, *née* Smith; *b* 14 June 1955; *Educ* St John's Sch Leatherhead, Hull Univ (BA), London Comtemporary Dance Sch; *m* 1979 (m dis 1985); *Career* dancer: Mantis 1980, Siobhan Davies & Dancers 1981, London Contemporary Dance Theatre 1981-; choreographer LCDT: Wild Life Dung 1986, Hang Up 1987, Bottom's Dream 1988, Shift 1988; choreographer: Ballet Gulbenkian (Lisbon) Movimento Para Uma Tela 1988, LCDS Exchanges 1986, Love Let Loose 1987, Free Will 1988; *Style*— Jonathan Lunn, Esq; 17 Highbury Terrace, London N5 (☎ 01 354 5108); LCDT, 16 Flaxmam Terrace, London WC1 (☎ 01 387 0324)

LUNN, (George) Michael; s of John Lunn (d 1969), of Edinburgh, and May, *née* Hope (d 1971); *b* 22 July 1942; *Educ* Kelvinside Acad Glasgow, Glasgow Univ (BSC Agric), Heriot-Watt Univ (Dip Brewing); *m* 27 Aug 1971, Jennifer, da of John Burgoyne, of Glasgow; 3 s (Stuart b 17 Jan 1974, Jamie b 27 July 1978, Alexander b 18 March 1981); 1 da (Victoria b 11 Jan 1976); *Career* Lt RNR 1956-66; md Whyte & Mackay Distillers Ltd Glasgow; dir: Dalmore Distillers Distillers Ltd, Scottish and Universal Investmts Ltd; dir cncl of Scotch Whisky Assoc, Kelvinside Acad War Meml Tst; fndr memb Glasgow Action Ctee; govr Kelvinside Acad Glasgow; memb cncl The Queen's Coll Glasgow; *Recreations* golf, sailing, tennis; *Clubs* IOD, Buchanan Castle Golf; *Style*— Michael Lunn, Esq; Whyte & Mackay Distillers Ltd, Dalmore House, 296/298 St Vincent St, Glasgow G2 5XR (☎ 041 248 5771, fax 041 221 9667, telex 778552)

LUNN, Peter; CMG (1957), OBE (1951); s of Sir Arnold Lunn, the father of ski racing, and Lady Mabel Northcote, sis of 3 Earl of Iddesleigh; *b* 15 Nov 1914; *Educ* Eton; *m* 1939, Hon Antoinette (d 1976), only da of 15 Viscount Gormanston; 3 s, 3 da; *Career* former Capt British Ski Team; FO 1947-1972: served Vienna, Berne, Germany, Bonn, Beirut, FCO 1967-72; author; *Books* The Guinness Book of Skiing (1983); *Recreations* skiing; *Clubs* SCGB; *Style*— Peter Lunn Esq, CMG, OBE; c/o The Ski Club of Great Britain, 118 Eaton Square, London SW1W 9AF

LUNT, Capt David Broughton; TD; s of Willougby Broughton Lunt (d 1960), of Birmingham, and Fanny Elizabeth Victoria Owen (d 1950); *b* 10 Feb 1909; *Educ* Bromsgrove Sch, Birmingham Univ; *m* 16 Aug 1956, Marjorie Joyce, da of Reginald Percy Davies (d 1974), and Birmingham; *Career* Major TA 1938-, BEF 1940, served Western Desert, M East 1942- (despatches); chm and md Nathaniel Mills Ltd 1946-76; ret; *Recreations* gardening, fishing, golf; *Style*— Capt David B Lunt, TD; Broughton House, Cliff Terrace, Budleigh, Salterton, Devon EX9 6JY (☎ 03954 3046)

LUNT, Maj-Gen James Doiran; CBE (1964, OBE 1958); s of Brig Walter Thomas Lunt, MBE (d 1977), of Camberley, Surrey, by his w Archilles Cameron, *née* Dodd (d 1975); *b* 13 Nov 1917; *Educ* King William's Coll IOM, RMC Sandhurst; *m* 1940, Muriel Jessie, da of Albert Henry Byrt, CBE, of Bournemouth (d 1964); 1 s, 1 da; *Career* 2 Lt Duke of Wellingtos's Regt 1937, served: Burma Rifles 1939-42, Arab Legion 1952-55, Fedn Regular Army Aden 1961-64, chief of staff Contingencies Planning SHAPE 1968-70, Vice-Adj-Gen MOD 1970, Maj-Gen, ret 1972; Col 16/5 Queen's Royal Lancers 1975-80; fell and domestic bursar Wadham Coll Oxford 1973-83 (emeritus fell 1983-); author; FRGS, FRHistS; Hon MA Oxon; Order of Independence (Jordan) 1956, Order of South Arabia (1965); *Books Incl:* Charge to Glory (1961), From Sepoy to Subedar (1970), Imperial Sunset (1981), Glubb Pasha (1984), Hussein of Jordan (1989); *Recreations* writing, flyfishing; *Clubs* Cavalry and Guards, Flyfishers; *Style*— Maj-Gen James Lunt, CBE; Hill Top House, Little Milton, Oxon OX9 7PU (☎ 084 46 242)

LUPTON, Prof Thomas; s of Thomas Lupton (d 1956), and Jane, *née* Vowell; *b* 4 Nov 1918; *Educ* Elem Sch, Ruskin Oxford, Oriel Coll Oxford, Univ of Manchester; *m* 1, 1942, Thelma Chesney; 1 da; m 2, 1963 (m dis 1987), Constance Shirley, da of Sydney Herbert Wilson (d 1949); 1 s, 1 da; *Career* Corpl RE; prof of industl rels Univ of Leeds 1964-66, prof of orgn behaviour Manchester Business Sch 1966; dep dir Manchester Business Sch 1967, dir 1977-83; *Books* several on mgmnt subjects; *Recreations* golf, talking, writing; *Style*— Prof Thomas Lupton; 667 Burnage Lane, Manchester M19 1RT (☎ 061 431 6880)

LURGAN, 5 Baron (UK 1839); John Desmond Cavendish Brownlow; OBE (1950); s of Capt the Hon Francis Cecil Brownlow (d 1932; 3 s of 2 Baron Lurgan); suc 1 cous, 4 Baron Lurgan, 1984; *b* 29 June 1911; *Educ* Eton; *Heir* none; *Career* Lt-Col Grenadier Gds, ret; *Style*— The Rt Hon the Lord Lurgan, OBE; Pennington House, Lymington, Hants

LURGAN, Baroness; (Florence) May Brownlow; *m* 1, Eric Cooper (decd), of Johannesburg, S Africa; m 2, 1979, 4 Baron Lurgan (d 1984); *Style*— The Rt Hon the Lady Lurgan; PO Box 18161, Dalbridge 4014, Natal, S Africa

LUSCOMBE, Prof David Edward; s of Edward Dominic (d 1987), of 3 Ridgeview Road, London N20, and Nora, *née* Cowell; *b* 22 July 1938; *Educ* Finchley Catholic GS, King's Coll Cambridge (BA, MA, PhD, LittD); *m* 20 August 1960, Megan, da of John Richard Phillips (d 1967); 3 s (Nicholas b 1962, Mark b 1964, Philip b 1968), 1 da (Amanda b 1970); *Career* fell King's Coll Cambridge 1962-64: fell, lectr and dir of studies in history Churchill Coll Cambridge 1964-72; prof medieval history Univ of Sheffield 1972- (head Dept of History 1973-76; 1978-84, dean faculty of Arts 1985-87; vice pres Société Int l'Etude de la Philosophie Médiévale 1987-; memb: FBA 1986, FSA 1984, FR Hists 1970; *Books* The School of Peter Abelard (1969); Peter Abelard's Ethics (1971); co-ed: Church and Government in the Middle Ages (1976), Petrus Abaelardus 1079-1142 (1980), D Knowles, The Evolution of Medieval Thought (1988); Cambridge Studies in Medieval Life and Thought (advsy ed 1983-88, gen ed 1988-); *Recreations* exercising a spaniel, cricket; *Style*— Prof David Luscombe; Department of History, The University, Sheffield 2TN 3DE (☎ 0742 768555, ext 6362, fax 07422 739826, telex 547216 UGSHEF G)

LUSH, Christopher Duncan; CMG (1983); s of Eric Duncan Thomas Lush (d 1980); *Educ* Sedbergh, Magdalen Coll Oxford; *m* 1967, Marguerite Lilian, da of Frederick William Bolden (d 1975); *Career* barr 1953-59; asst legal advsr FO 1959-62, first sec West Berlin 1962-66, FO (later FCO) 1966-69, Amman 1969-71, cnsllr FCO 1971-73, Canadian Nat Def Coll 1973-74, Paris 1974-78, Vienna 1978-82, ambass to Cncl of Europe Strasbourg 1983-86, Euro Campaign for North South Awareness 1986-88, War Crimes Inquiry 1988; govr Br Inst of Human Rights 1988; *Clubs* Travellers'; *Style*— Christopher Lush, Esq, CMG; UK Delegation, 18 Rue Gottfried, Strasbourg, France (☎ 350078)

LUSH, Denzil Anton; s of Dennis John Lush, of 4 Tudor Close, Penarth, S Glamorgan, and Hazel June, *née* Fishenden (d 1979); *b* 18 July 1951; *Educ* Devonport HS Plymouth UCL (BA, MA), Coll of Law Guildford, CCC Cambridge (LLM); *Career* slr 1978; ptnr Anstey and Thompson slrs 1985-; author numerous articles in learned jls; licensed as reader (Wells Cathedral 1982) for utd benefice of E Harptree, W Harptree and Hinton Blewett (Diocese of Bath and Wells); memb Law Soc; *Recreations* supporting Plymouth Argyle FC and Somerset CCC; *Clubs* Exeter and County; *Style*— Denzil Lush, Esq; 3 Pennsylvania Park, Exeter, EX4 6HB; 5 Barnfield Crescent, Exeter EX1 1RF (☎ 0392 438011, fax 0392 75176)

LUSH, Hon Sir George Hermann; s of J F Lush; *b* 5 Oct 1912; *Educ* Carey GS, Ormond Coll Melbourne Univ; *m* 1943, Winifred Betty, da of E S Wragge; 3 da; *Career* former cmmr Overseas Telecommunications Cmmn; chm Vic Bar Cncl 1964-66, QC 1957, pres Aust Bar Assoc 1964-66, judge Supreme Court of Vic 1966-83; chllr Monash Univ Victoria Australia 1983-; chm Ormond Coll Cncl 1981-; kt 1979; *Style*— The Hon Sir George Lush; 37 Rochester Rd, Canterbury, Vic 3126, Australia

LUSH, Brig Maurice Stanley; CB (1944), CBE (1942), MC (1916 and bar 1917); s of Hubert S Lush; *b* 1896; *Educ* Tonbridge, RMA Woolwich; *m* 1930, Diana Ruth, da of Charles Alexander Hill; 1 s, 2 da; *Career* served in RA WWI; Sudan Political Service 1919-41, Sudan Agent Cairo 1935-38, govr Northern province 1938-41; WWII served as Brig (despatches); chief civil affairs offr Ethiopia, Madagascar, Tripolitania, exec cmmr Allied Control Cmmn Italy; chief Middle East Int Refugee Orgn 1946-51; rep Shell (Libya), md Shell Pakistan 1952-59; dep chm Neptune ctee Nat Trust 1963-68; vice-pres Br and Foreign Bible Soc; *Clubs* Athenaeum; *Style*— Brig Maurice Lush, CB, CBE, MC; 3 Carlton Mansions, Holland Park Gdns, London W14 (☎ 01 603 4425)

LUSH, Peter Maurice; s of Bernard Simeon Lush, of Holmside, South Walk, Middleton-on-Sea, Sussex, and Judy Adele, *née* Markham; *b* 19 April 1939; *Educ* Brighton Coll; *m* 1 (m dis), Cynthia, *née* Leslie-Bredée; m 2 (m dis), Peggy, *née* Gough; m 3, 3 Oct 1964, Lyn, da of Eyre Fitzgerald Massy (d 1970); 1 s (Jonathan Charles b 11 July 1966), 1 da (Amanda Lyn Geraldine b 18 Aug 1967); *Career* account dir Ogilvy & Mather advtg agency 1958-72, jt md Knight Keeley Ltd 1972-74, conslt TCCB 1988- (PR and mktg mangr 1974-87); England cricket tour mangr: B team to Sri Lanka 1986, Aust (Ashes retained) 1986-87, World Cup in India and Pakistan 1987, Pakistan 1987, NZ 1988; Sussex jr squash champion 1957; *Recreations* cricket, golf; *Clubs* MCC, Old Brightonians, Sonning GC; *Style*— Peter Lush, Esq; Dunmore, Holmemoor Dr, Sonning, Reading, Berks RG4 OTE (☎ 0734 693 735); TCCB, Lord's

Ground, London NW8 8QZ (☎ 01 286 4405, fax 01 289 5619, telex 24462 TCCB G)

LUSHINGTON, Sir John Richard Castleman; 8 Bt (GB 1791), of South Hill Park, Berkshire; s of Sir Henry Edmund Castleman Lushington, 7 Bt (d 1988); *b* 28 August 1938; *Educ* Oundle; *m* 21 May 1966, Bridget Gillian Margaret, o da of Col John Foster Longfield, of Knockbeg, Saunton, N Devon; 3 s; *Heir* s, Richard Douglas Longfield Lushington b 29 March 1968; *Career* mgmnt trg consult, trading as MAST (Eastern), a memb of the MAST Orgn; *Style*— Sir John Lushington, Bt; Standen, Longbottom, Seer Green, Bucks

LUSHINGTON, Pamela, Lady; Pamela Elizabeth Daphne; *née* Hunter; er da of late Maj Archer Richard Hunter, of Hare Hatch Grange, Twyford, Berks; *m* 2 Oct 1937, Sir Henry Edmund Castleman Lushington, 7 Bt (d 1988); 1 s (Sir John, 8 Bt, *qv*), 2 da (Caroline Elizabeth b 1942, Penelope Daphne b 1945); Carfax, Crowthorne, Berks (☎ 0344 2819)

LUSTY, Sir Robert Frith; s of late Frith Lusty, of Shrewsbury, by his w Winifred Hobbs; *b* 7 June 1909; *Educ* Soc of Friends Co-educnl Sch Sidcot; *m* 1, 1 Sept 1939, Joan Christie (d 1962), da of late Archibald Brownlie, of Glasgow; m 2, 7 Nov 1963, Eileen Mary, wid of Dr Denis Carroll, and da of late Dr George Phocian Barff; *Career* Messrs Hutchinson & Co 1928-35; co-fndr (with Michael Joseph) and editorial and prodn mangr of Michael Joseph Ltd 1936, resigned as vice-chm 1956; chm and md Hutchinson Publishing Gp 1956-73, ret; govr BBC 1960-68 (vice-chm 1966-68); kt 1969; *Books* Bound to be Read (autobiography, 1975); *Style*— Sir Robert Lusty; Broad Close, Blockley, Moreton-in-Marsh, Glos GL56 9DY (☎ (0386) 700335)

LUTON, Elizabeth Mary; da of Alan David Luton, and Elaine Mary, *née* Harris; *b* 8 April 1958; *Educ* City of London Sch For Girls, The London Coll of Secs; *Career* sec and PA: Weatherall Gran and Smith 1977-81, Longbarr Devpts Ltd 1981-82, Future Tech Systems Ltd 1982, devpt surveyor Longback Devpts Ltd 1982-84, dir The Rutland Gp 1984-; Freeman Worshipful Co of Painters and Stainers 1987; *Recreations* walking, reading, skiing, gardening, cooking; *Clubs* The American; *Style*— Miss Elizabeth Luton; The Rutland Group, 11 Upper Brook St, London W1Y 1PB (☎ 01 499 6616, fax 01 408 1459, telex 23143 UBSLON G)

LUTTMAN-JOHNSON, Hon Mrs; Hon Barbara Amy; *née* Sclater-Booth; 2 da of 3 Baron Basing (d 1969); *b* 5 April 1926; *m* 27 April 1961, Peter Michell Luttman-Johnson; 1 s, 2 da; *Style*— The Hon Mrs Luttman-Johnson; Woodmancote, Lodsworth, Petworth, W Sussex

LUTTMAN-JOHNSON, Peter Michell; TD; s of Frederic Michell Luttman-Johnson (d 1967), of Crouchland, Plaistow, W Sussex, and Janet Maud *née* Horne (d 1954); *b* 21 Nov 1919; *Educ* Winchester; Trinity Oxford (MA); *m* 27 April 1961, The Hon Barbara Amy, da of John Limbrey Robert Sclater-Booth, 3 Baron Basing, of Basing Byflete, TD, DL (Dorset), of The Malt House, Gillingham, Dorset; 1 s (William Michell b 1963), 2 da (Anne Elizabeth b 1962, Catherine Mary b 1966); *Career* 2/Lt to Capt, 15/19 K R Hussars and GHQ Liaison Regt (Phantom), France and Germany 1939-45, Lieut to Lieut-Col, Army Phantom Signal Regt TA 1946-64; dir Allen Harvey & Ross Bill-brokers 1946-63; farmer and memb Chichester DC 1971; High Sheriff of W Sussex 1978-89, Master Worshipful Co of Clothworkers 1985-86; *Recreations* shooting; *Clubs* Garrick, Cavalry and Guards, MCC; *Style*— Peter Luttman-Johnson, Esq, TD; Woodmancote, Lodsworth, Petworth, W Sussex GU28 9DA (☎ Lodsworth 212)

LUTTRELL, Lady Elizabeth Hermione; da of 12 Earl Ferrers (d 1954), by his w Hermione Justice (d 1969, da of A Noel Morley); *b* 3 Dec 1923; *Educ* Downe House-Newbury; *m* 1959, John Fownes Luttrell (d 1985), s of Hugh Courtenay Fownes Luttrell (d 1918); 1 s (Robert Hugh Courtenay Fownes b 1961); *Career* served with WRNS; held various secretarial posts until marriage; *Recreations* arts, architecture, gardening, travel, music; *Style*— Lady Elizabeth Luttrell; Waterwynch, Itchen Abbas, nr Winchester, Hants SO21 1AX

LUTTRELL, John Henry Fownes; s of Claude Mohun Fownes Luttrell (d 1941), and Edith Rose, *née* Leigh; *b* 29 Dec 1919; *Educ* Bryanston; *m* 1, 27 Nov 1948 (m dis), Eleanor Sarah Joy, da of Sir Philip Francis Cunningham Williams, Bt (d 1958); 1 da (Charlotte b 1954); m 2, 28 Sept 1968, Beryl Mary, da of Robert Sare Hickman (d 1968); 4 step s (David Phillips b 1947, James Phillips b 1949, Charles Phillips b 1951, Peter Phillips b 1955); *Career* banker (ret 1973); *Recreations* hunting, gardening; *Style*— John H F Luttrell, Esq; Pheasant Hill House, Kemble, Cirencester GL7 6AW (☎ (0285) 770288)

LUTTRELL, Col (Geoffrey) Walter Fownes; MC (1945), JP (Somerset 1961); s of Geoffrey Luttrell (d 1957), of Dunster Castle (which until recently had been in the Luttrell family's possession from 1375) and Alys, da of Rear-Adm Walter Bridges, of Trewalla, Victoria, Australia; *b* 2 Oct 1919; *Educ* Eton, Exeter Coll Oxford; *m* 1942, Hermione Hamilton, da of Capt Cecil Gunston, MC (decd) (er bro of Sir Derrick Gunston, 1 Bt), and Lady Doris Hamilton-Temple-Blackwood, da of 2 Marquess of Dufferin and Ava; *Career* served with: 15/19 King's Royal Hussars 1940-46, N Somerset Yeo 1952, Lt-Col 1955; Somerset: DL 1958, high sheriff 1960, vice Ld-Lt 1968-78, Ld-Lt 1978-; memb Nat Parks Cmmn 1962-66, liaison offr Miny Ag 1965-71; memb: SW Electricity Bd 1969-78, Wessex Regnl Ctee Nat Tst 1970-85; regnl dir Lloyds Bank 1972-83, memb University Grants Cmmn 1973-76, pres Royal Bath and West Show Soc 1982-83; Hon Col: 6 Bn Light Infantry 1977-87, Somerset ACF 1982-; KSRJ 78; *Recreations* fishing, gardening; *Clubs* Cavalry and Guards; *Style*— Col Walter Luttrell, MC, JP; Court House, East Quantoxhead, Bridgwater, Somerset TA5 1EJ (☎ 027 874 242)

LUTYENS, Mary; da of Sir Edwin Lutyens, OM, KCIE, PRA, the celebrated architect (particularly of New Delhi) and Lady Emily Lytton, da of 1 Earl of Lytton (s of the novelist Bulwer Lytton) by Edith (da of Hon Edward Villiers, yr bro of 4 Earl of Clarendon, the Victorian Foreign Sec); sis of Elisabeth Lutyens (decd), the composer, and aunt of 4 Viscount Ridley and Rt Hon Nicholas Ridley, MP, *qqv*; *b* 31 July 1908; *Educ* Queen's Coll London and abroad; *m* 1, 1930 (m dis 1945), Anthony Sewell (decd); 1 da (Amanda, b 1935, m John Pallant); m 2, 1945, Joseph Gluckstein Links, OBE, s of Calman Links; *Career* writer of fiction and of works on the Lyttons, Ruskin, Venice and Krishnamurti; FRSL; *Style*— Miss Mary Lutyens; 8 Elizabeth Close, Randolph Avenue, London W9 1BN (☎ 286 6674)

LUTYENS, Richard David; *b* 1 July 1948; *Educ* Rugby Sch, St Edmund Hall Oxford; *m* 9 Oct 1971, Mary Ann July Phyllis; 3 da (Tanya b 1975, Alice b 1980, Camilla b 1985); *Career* exec dir SG Warburg and Co Ltd 1972-82, exec vice pres Utd Gulf Investmt Co (Bahrain) 1982-84, vice pres Goldman Sachs Int 1984-85, md: Merrill Lynch Europe Ltd 1985-88, Merrill Lynch Capital Mkts (NY) 1985-88; *Style*— Richard D Lutyens, Esq; 53 Clarendon Rd, London, W11 4JD (☎ 01 727 0577); Campbell Lutyens & Co, 4 Clifford St, London, W1X 1RB (☎ 01 439 7191, fax 01 437 0153, telex 21888 CAMLUT G)

LUXMOORE, Edmund; DL (Durham 1978); s of Allan Aylmer Luxmoore, DL (d 1969); *b* 21 Sept 1914; *Educ* Stowe, Trinity Coll Cambridge; *m* 1946, Diana Jean, MBE, da of John Methuen Coote, OBE (d 1967, 2 s of Sir Algernon Coote, 12 Bt); 2 s (Michael, Richard), 1 da (Elizabeth Macdonald); *Career* Fl Lt RAF, Gibralter and N Africa; slr (ret), under-sheriff Co Durham and Co Cleveland (Durham deputy with his father 1937-65 and solely since 1965, and of Cleveland since formation); company dir; *Books* Deer Stalking (1980); *Recreations* shooting, fishing, stalking; *Clubs* Oxford and Cambridge, Durham County (chm), Yorkshire Fly Fishers'; *Style*— Edmund Luxmoore, Esq, DL; Staindrop Hall, Staindrop, Darlington, Co Durham (☎ 0833 60331); Crackenthorpe Hall, Appleby-in-Westmorland, Cumbria (☎ 0930 51409); Tom-Na-Moine, Roybridge, Inverness (☎ Spean Bridge 558)

LUXMOORE, Michael John; s of Edmund Luxmoore, of Staindrop Hall, Staindrop, Darlington, and Diana Jean Luxmoore, *née* Coote; *b* 5 April 1948; *Educ* Harrow Sch, Trinity Coll Cambridge (MA); *m* 1, 28 April 1973, Margaret Rosemary (m diss); 2 s (Andrew b 1976, Jamie b 1979), m 2, 3 Dec 1988, Ann Dalrymple-Smith; *Career* slr; deputy under sheriff County of Durham; dir Middleton Hall Ltd 1984-; *Recreations* fell running; *Clubs* Swaledale Outdoor; *Style*— Michael Luxmoore, Esq; 42 Frenchgate, Richmond, N Yorks DL10 7AG (☎ 0748 3283)

LYALL, Eric; CBE; s of late Alfred John Lyall, of Essex, and Alice Amelia, *née* Jackson (d 1982); *b* 12 May 1924; *Educ* Chigwell, King's Coll Cambridge; *m* 1952, Joyce, da of late Sydney Edward Smith; 1 s (Alexander); *Career* formerly slr, ptnr Slaughter and May, former ptnr Guinness Mahon; chm: Rocla GB Ltd, Br Hartford Fairmont Ltd, Clark Nickolls & Coombs plc, Frewen Educnl Tst; dir: Letchworth Garden City Corpn, Australian Mutual Provident Soc (UK) Bd, Lockton Devpts plc, gen cmmr Income Tax; *Recreations* philately, tennis, medieval history; *Clubs* Oriental, City of London, MCC; *Style*— Eric Lyall, Esq, CBE; Riders Grove, Old Hall Green, Ware, Herts (☎ 0920 821370)

LYALL, Gavin Tudor; s of Joseph Tudor Lyall, and Agnes Ann, *née* Hodgkiss; *b* 9 May 1932; *Educ* King Edward VI Sch Birmingham, Pembroke Coll Cambridge (BA, MA); *m* 4 Jan 1958, Katharine Elizabeth, da of Alan Drummond Whitehorn, MA (d 1980); 2 s (Bernard b 1964, John b 1967); *Career* RAF pilot 1951-53; journalist Picture Post, BBC TV, Sunday Times until 1963; chm Crime Writers' Assoc 1966-67; memb Air Tport Users' Ctee 1979-85; (hon conslt 1985-); author; *Books* 11 thriller/espionage titles, incl: The Secret Servant (1980), The Conduct of Major Maxim (1982), The Crocus List (1985), Uncle Target (1988); *Recreations* model making, cartooning; *Clubs* RAF, Groucho, Detection; *Style*— Gavin Lyall, Esq; 14 Provost Rd, London NW3 (☎ 01 722 2308)

LYALL, Ian Alastair; DSC (1944), VRD (1952), DL (Dumbartonshire 1963); s of William Lyall, MRINA (d 1937); *b* 16 Mar 1917; *Educ* Hillhead HS Glasgow; *m* 1947, Eileen Patricia, da of Capt Bennett, HAC (1918); 1 da; *Career* Lt Cdr RNR; shipping co chm and md 1968-80; pres Glasgow C of C 1978-79; chm: Port Employers Assoc 1970-80, Nat Dock Labour Bd (Clyde) 1978-80; *Recreations* sailing, shooting, fishing; *Clubs* Royal Northern and Clyde Yacht, Clyde Cruising, Western, Glasgow; *Style*— Ian Lyall, Esq, DSC, VRD, DL; Rimsdale, Helensburgh, Dunbarton (☎ 0436 3976)

LYALL GRANT, Maj-Gen Ian Hallam; MC 1944; s of Col Henry Frederick Lyall Grant, DSO (d 1958); *b* 4 June 1915; *Educ* Cheltenham, Gonville and Caius Coll Cambridge; *m* 1951, Mary Jennifer, da of Norman Moore (d 1980); 1 s, 2 da; *Career* joined Army 1935, Cmdt Royal Sch of Mil Engrg 1965-67, DQMG MOD 1967-70; Civil Serv dir gen Supply Co-Ordination 1970-75; gemmologist; *Recreations* sailing (yacht 'Starfire'), travel, gemmology;; *Clubs* Naval and Military; *Style*— Maj-Gen Ian Lyall Grant, MC; Kingswear House, Kingswear, Dartmouth, Devon TQ6 0BX

LYBURN, (Andrew) Drew Usherwood; s of Andrew Lyburn (d 1969), of Edinburgh, and Margaret Scott Glass (d 1988); *b* 16 August 1928; *Educ* Melville Coll, Edinburgh Univ (MA); *m* 25 July 1958, Joan Ann, da of Eric Stevenson (d 1975), of Edinburgh; 3 s (Andrew b 1960, Colin b 1962, Iain b 1967), 1 da (Fiona b 1974); *Career* RAF Flying Offr Cyprus 1954-56; actuary: Scottish Widows Fndn 1949-54 and 1956-57, Confed Life Toronto 1957-59, Standard Life Montreal 1959-65 (Edinburgh) (gen mangr admin 1985-), memb Occupational Pensions Bd 1982-, vice-pres Faculty of Actuaries 1987-; chm: Cairn Petroleum Oil and Gas Ltd 1987-88, Melville Coll Tst 1983-86; FFA (1957), fell: Pensions Mgmnt Inst 1976, Canadian Inst of Actuaries 1965; Assoc Soc of Actuaries of America 1957; *Recreations* golf, gardening, squash, hill walking; *Clubs* Bruntsfield Links, Golfing Soc, Edinburgh, RAF London; *Style*— Drew Lyburn, Esq; 4 Cumlodden Ave, Edinburgh EH12 6DR (☎ 031 337 7580); 3 George St, Edinburgh EH2 2X2 (☎ 031 245 7002, fax 031 245 7266)

LYCETT, Maj Michael Hildesley Lycett; CBE (1987); s of Rev Norman Lycett (d 1963), of East Dean, Sussex, and Ruth Edith, *née* Burns-Lindow (d 1965); *b* 11 Dec 1915; *Educ* Radley, Merton Coll Oxford; *m* 1, 4 Feb 1944, Moira Patricia Margaret (d 1958), da of Maj Norman Martin, CBE; 1 da (Anthea Theresa b 6 June 1954); m 2, 12 Oct 1959, Lady June Wendy Lycett, JP, da of 5 Earl of Yarborough, MC (d 1948); *Career* Maj Royal Scots Greys 1935-47 served: Palestine, Greece, Western Desert, Italy, Germany; md: Rhodesian Insurances Ltd 1949-61, Wright Deen Lycett Ltd Newcastle-upon-Tyne 1961-73, Lycett Browne-Swinburne & Douglas Ltd (chm 1973-76); chm B S and D (underwriting agents) 1976, dir B S and D (Cumbria) Ltd; govr and chm exec ctee Bernard Mizeki Schs 1959-61 (London tstee 1961-), MFH Tynedale Hunt 1975-77; chm Morpeth Div Cons Assoc 1966-72, parly candidate (C) Co Durham 1981-83, pres Northumbria Euro Constituency, former memb Cons Nat Exec and GP Ctees, chm Cons Northern Area 1985-87; *Recreations* politics, field sports, looking things up, writing rhymes; *Clubs* Cavalry and Guards, Pratts, Boodles, Northern Counties; *Style*— Maj Michael Lycett, CBE; West Grange Scots Gap, Morpeth, Northumberland NE61 4EQ (☎ 067 074 662)

LYCETT, Lady (June) Wendy; *née* Pelham; da of 5 Earl of Yarborough, MC (d 1948), and co-heiress to Baronies of Fauconberg and Conyers (*see* Lady Diana Miller); *b* 6 June 1924; *m* 12 Oct 1959, Maj Michael Hildesley Lycett CBE, late Royal Scots Greys, s of late Rev Norman Lycett; 1 adopted da (the er child of Lady Wendy's sis, Lady Diana Miller, *qv*); *Career* late 3 offr WRNS, jt master Tynedale Hunt 1974-77; JP; *Clubs* Cavalry and Guards'; *Style*— Lady Wendy Lycett; West Grange, Scots Gap, Morpeth, Northumberland (☎ 067 074 662)

LYCETT GREEN *see also*: Green

LYDDON, (William) Derek Collier; CB (1984); s of late A J Lyddon, CBE, and E E Lyddon; *b* 17 Nov 1925; *Educ* Wrekin Coll, UCL; *m* 1949, Marian Louise Kaye, *née* Charlesworth, da of late Prof J K Charlesworth, CBE; 2 da; *Career* dep chief architect and planning offr Cumbernauld Devpt Corpn 1962, chief architect and planning offr Skelmersdale Devpt Corpn 1963-67, chief planning offr Scottish Devpt Dept 1967-85; pres Int Soc of City and Regnl Planners 1981-84; Hon DLitt Heriot Watt 1981; hon prof Heriot Watt Univ; visiting prof Univ of Strathclyde; hon fell: Univ of Edinburgh, Duncan Jordanstone Coll; chm: environment and planning ctee of Econ and Social Res Cncl 1986-87, Edinburgh Old Town Ctee for Conservation and Renewal, mgmt ctee Edinburgh Sch of Environmental Design; govr Edinburgh Coll of Art; *Style*— Derek Lyddon, Esq, CB; 38 Dick Place, Edinburgh EH9 2JB (☎ 031 667 2266)

LYDEKKER, Brig Richard Neville Wolfe; CBE (1976); s of Rev Neville Wolfe Lydekker (d 1956), of Sussex, and Sylvia Gwendolen, *née* Palmer (d 1970); descendant of Rev Gerrit Leydecker who presented the Petition of American Loyalists to King George III in 1782 before emigrating to England; *b* 7 May 1921; *Educ* Sherborne; *m* 25 March 1947, Margaret Julia Mary, da of Rev Canon Lionel Edward Lydekker (d 1973), of Bucks; 1 da (Elizabeth b 1955); *Career* cmmnd RA 1941, psc 1952, jssc 1959, serv WWII N Africa and Italy, cmd RA Regt Malaya and Borneo 1963-65, staff Strategic Reserve 1967-72, Dep QMG UK Land Forces 1972-74, dir MOD (Army Dept) 1974-76, ret; regnl organiser Army Benevolent Fund 1977-; *Recreations* field sports, cricket; *Clubs* Army and Navy; *Style*— Brig Richard Lydekker, CBE; Hatherden, nr Andover, Hants (☎ 0264 475 221); Bulford Camp, Salisbury, Wilts (☎ 0980 3371 ext 2337)

LYE, David Beresford; s of Capt Herbert Beresford Lye (d 1971), of 31 Brockhill Rd, Hythe, Kent, and Edith Hope, *née* Luly; *b* 24 Nov 1930; *Educ* Dover Coll; *m* 2 March 1957, Rosemary Ann, da of Graham Charles Sevier Hills (d 1985), of 2 Ingleside House, Shorncliffe Rd, Folkestone, Kent; 2 s (Christopher b 1962, Patrick b 1963 d 1971), 2 da (Susan b 1958, Alison b 1959); *Career* mil serv: GHQ ME Land Forces; CA 1957; established (with others) early commercial (pirate) radio station to attract audiences of all age gps; md Estuary Radio Ltd (Radio 390) 1967- (dir 1965); appeal ct case of Lye (All England law reports 1967) is leading authy on territorial waters; chm Romney Hythe & Dymchurch Light Railway Co 1968-72; FCA; *Recreations* motoring, travel; *Clubs* Royal Automobile; *Style*— David Lye, Esq; Swallowfield, Pelham Gardens, Folkestone, Kent CT20 2LE (☎ 0303 52371); 34 Cheriton Gardens, Folkestone, Kent CT20 2AX (☎ 0303 51742, fax 0303 580391)

LYELL, Alastair Hew Roderick (Toby); s of Gp Capt Angus Chambers Lyell (decd), and Ida Angela Bryant, *née* Smith (d 1978); *b* 15 Mar 1926; *Educ* Radley; *m* 11 Feb 1967, Jane, da of Gen Richard Charles Woodroffe (d 1965), of Bembridge, Isle of Wight; 3 step s; *Career* WWII Capt Scots Gds Germany 1944-47 ; Lloyds broker 1947, memb of Lloyds 1955; Forestry Indust 1968-; cncl memb N E Royal Forestry Soc (past chm); memb: Timber Growers UK N Cncl, Int Dendrology Soc 1969-; *Recreations* fishing, shooting, arboriculture; *Clubs* White's, Pratts; *Style*— Toby Lyell, Esq; Pallinsburn, Cornhill-on-Tweed, Northumberland TD12 4SG

LYELL, Maj Andrew; DFC (1945); s of Col David Lyell CMG, CBE, DSO (d 1940), of Logie Kirriemuir, Angus, and Kathleen Constance, *née* Briggs (d 1934); *b* 22 July 1912; *Educ* Marlborough, Trinity Hall Cambridge (LLB); *m* 6 Feb 1943, Diana, da of Sir (Herbert George) Donald Cory 2 Bt (d 1935); 2 da (Vivien b 1944, Clementina b 1949); *Career* WWII 1939-45, Queen's Own Dorset Yeomanry 1939, Air Observation Post (currently the Army Air Corps) 1940, 1943 formed 658 (AOP) Squadn CO/CO till after 1945; barr (ret); non-exec dir of a number of public cos (ret); memb Inner Temple; Croix de Guerre (France 1944); *Books* Memoirs of an Air Observation Post Officer (1985); *Recreations* gardening, fishing, shooting; *Clubs* RAF; *Style*— Maj Andrew Lyell, DFC; Wester Auchleuchrie, by Forfar, Scotland (☎ 030786 201)

LYELL, 3 Baron (UK 1914); Sir Charles Lyell; 3 Bt (UK 1894), DL (Angus); s of Capt 2 Baron Lyell, VC, Scots Guards (ka 1943, VC awarded posthumously), and Sophie, *née* Trafford (whose family, of Wroxham Hall, Norfolk were a cadet branch of the Traffords now represented by the de Trafford Bts), whose mother was Lady Elizabeth Bertie, OBE, yst da of 7 Earl of Abingdon; *b* 27 Mar 1939; *Educ* Eton, Christ Church Coll Oxford; *Heir* none; *Career* 2 Lt Scots Gds 1957-59; CA; oppn whip House of Lords 1974-79, a lord in waiting (Govt Whip) 1979-84; memb Queen's Body Guard for Scotland (Royal Co of Archers); parly under sec of state NI Office 1984-; *Clubs* White's, Pratt's. Turf; *Style*— The Rt Hon the Lord Lyell; Kinnordy House, Kirriemuir, Angus (☎ 0575 72848); 20 Petersham Mews, Elvaston Place, London SW7 (☎ 01 584 9419)

LYELL, Hon Lady Katharine; da of 1 Viscount Runciman of Doxford (d 1949), and Hilda, *née* Stevenson (d 1956); *b* 1909; *Educ* St Leonard's Sch St Andrews, Girton Coll Cambridge; *m* 1, 23 Oct 1931, 4 Baron Farrer (d 1954); m 2, 24 Sept 1955, Sir Maurice Legat Lyell (d 1975); *Career* JP County of Hertford 1954-79,; chm of Dacorum Magistrates 1976-79; *Recreations* hunting (Master of the Aldenham Harriers 1956-83); *Style*— The Hon Lady Lyell; Puddephats Farm, Markyate, Herts

LYELL, Malcolm Charles Alastair; s of Angus Chambers Lyell, MC (d 1960), of Church Farm House, Chippenham, Ely, Cambs and Ida Angela Bryant Smith (d 1972);; *b* 9 Jan 1922; *Educ* Westminster Sch, Univ Coll of N Wales (BSc Forestry), Kings Coll London (BSc Botany); *m* 22 April 1949, Mary Patricia Rosamunde, da of Douglas Horsford Wilmer (d 1973), of Hucklesbrook Cottage, Gorley, Nr Fordingbridge, Hants; 2 da (Caroline b 1952, Harmony b 1955); *Career* TARO (invalided 1941); dir Westley Richards 1948-56, md Westley Richards (Agency) Co 1956-60, md Holland & Holland 1960-84, dep chm 1984-87, ret 1989; Knight Commander of Order of the Star of Honour of Ethiopia (1987); *Recreations* big game shooting, fishing, gardening, photography; *Clubs* Buck's, Flyfishers, Shikar Club of GB; *Style*— Malcolm Lyell, Esq; c/o Drummond Bank, 49 Charing Cross, London SW1A 2DX; c/o Holland & Holland, 33 Bruton Street, London W1 (☎ 01 499 4411)

LYELL, Michael George Rudinge; s of George Drummond Lyell (d 1957), of Petersfield, Addington Park, Surrey, and Freda Adela, *née* Martin (d 1975); *b* 14 April 1924; *Educ* Charterhouse, Architectural Assoc London (Dipl Arch Hons); *m* 1, 26 Oct 1946 (m dis), Jean Mary Agnes, da of James Anderson (d 1950), of Mossside Park, Glasgow; 3 s (Nicholas b 1950, Jeremy b 1952, Jonathan b 1956), 1 da (Joanna b 1954); m 2, 30 Dec 1988, Berit, da of Harald Wildhagen (d 1980); *Career* RAF 1942-46, Flying Offr, Navigator/Wireless Operator; architect, sr ptnr Michael Lyell Assocs 1954-84 (conslt 1984); FRIBA, ARCUK; *Recreations* golf; *Clubs* Sunningdale GC; *Style*— Michael Lyell, Esq; 4 Onslow Gdns, London SW7 3LX (☎ 01 584 1297); 16 Yeomans Row, London SW3 9AJ (☎ 01 589 7273, fax 01 225 2431, telex 917084 MILARC)

LYELL, Sir Nicholas Walter; QC (1980), MP (C) Mid-Bedfordshire 1983-; s of Hon Mr Justice Maurice Legat Lyell (d 1975), and his 1 w, Veronica Mary, *née* Luard (d 1950); *b* 12 Dec 1938; *Educ* Stowe, Ch Ch Oxford (MA), Coll of Law; *m* 2 Sept 1967, Susanna Mary, da of Prof Charles Montague Fletcher, CBE, MD, FRCP, FFCM, *qv*; 2 s (Oliver b 1 July 1971, Alexander b 8 Dec 1981), 2 da (Veronica b 8 May 1970, Mary-Kate b 5 March 1979); *Career* nat serv with RA 1957-59, 2 Lt 1957; with Walter Runciman & Co 1962- 64; barr Inner Temple 1965, bencher 1986; in private practice in London 1965-86; recorder of the Crown Court 1985; jt sec Constitutional Ctee 1979; pps to Attorney Gen 1979-86; parly under sec of state (Social Security) DHSS 1986-87; Solicitor Gen 1987-; chm Soc of Cons Lawyers 1985-86 (vice chm 1982-85); vice chm BFSS 1983-86; Freeman of the City of London 1964, memb Worshipful Co of Salters; kt 1987; *Recreations* gardening, drawing, shooting; *Clubs* Brooks's; *Style*— Sir Nicholas Lyell, QC, MP; 1 Brick Court, Temple, London EC4Y 9BY (☎ 01 583 0777); House of Commons, London SW1A 0AA (☎ 01 219 3000)

LYELL, Baroness; Sophie Mary; da of Maj Sigismund William Joseph Trafford, JP, DL (d 1953), of Wroxham Hall, Norfolk and Honinton Hall, Grantham and of Lady Elizabeth Bertie, OBE (d 1987), da of 7 Earl of Abingdon (d 1928); *b* 10 Feb 1916; *m* 1938, 2 Baron Lyell, VC (ka 1943, serving with Scots Guards); 1 s (3 Baron, *qv*); *Career* ccllr Angus 1943-65; *Style*— The Rt Hon the Lady Lyell; Kinnordy, Kirriemuir, Angus DD8 5SR (☎ (0575) 72848); 20 Petersham Mews, London (☎ 01 584 9419)

LYES, Jeffrey Paul; s of Joseph Leslie Lyes, of Daventry, Northants, and Rose Mary Anne, *née* Harris; *b* 19 April 1946; *m* 5 Oct 1968, Jan, da of John Armstrong, of Oxford; 2 da (Sarah b 1974, Julia b 1977); *Career* journalist United Newspapers 1963-69, news ed Heart of Eng Newspapers 1969-71, exec Hertford PR 1971-73, asst press and PR offr Thames Valley Police 1973-78; dir: Lexington Int PR 1978-81, Good Relations Gp plc 1985-86, Good Relations Corp Communications 1986-87, Good Relations Ltd 1987-88; memb of MIPR 1977, FBIM 1985, FInstD 1988; *Recreations* motor yacht cruising; *Style*— Jeffrey Lyes, Esq; Good Relations Ltd, 59 Russell Sq, London WC1B 4HJ (☎ 01 631 3434, fax 01 631 1399, telex 265903)

LYGO, Adm Sir Raymond Derek; KCB (1977); s of Edwin Lygo; *b* 15 Mar 1924; *Educ* Ilford Co HS, Clarke Coll Bromley; *m* 1950, Pepper Van Osten, of the USA; 2 s, 1 da; *Career* served RN 1942-78, vice-chief and chief of Naval Staff 1975-78; with the Times 1940; Br Aerospace: md Hatfield/Lostock div 1978-79, chief exec and chm Dynamics Gp 1980-82, main bd memb 1980, md 1983-86, chief exec 1986-; chm Royal Ordnance 1987-88, chm various cos; FRAeS, CBIM, FRSA; *Clubs* RN, RAYC, RAC, Les Ambassadeurs; *Style*— Adm Sir Raymond Lygo, KCB; British Aerospace plc, 11 Strand, London WC2N 5JT

LYGON, Hon Mrs Richard; Patricia Janet; *née* Norman; da of late Rev T K Norman; *m* 1939, Hon Richard Edward Lygon (d 1970), yr son of 7 Earl Beauchamp (d 1938); 2 da (Lettice Patricia Mary b 1940, Rosalind Elizabeth b 1946); *Style*— Hon Mrs Richard Lygon; Pyndar House, Hanley Castle, Worcester

LYLE, Hon Mrs (Elizabeth); *née* Sinclair; yr da of 1 Viscount Thurso, KT, CMG, PC (d 1970), of Thurso Castle, Caithness, by his w, Marigold, da of Col James Stewart Forbes; *b* 5 June 1921; *Educ* Kensington HS, Oxford Univ; *m* 1942, Lt Col Archibald Michael Lyle, youngest s of Sir Archibald Lyle, 2 Bt; 3 da (Veronica b 1943, Janet b 1944, Sarah b 1963), and 1 da decd; *Style*— The Hon Mrs Lyle; Riemore Lodge, Dunkeld, Perths (☎ (035 04) 205)

LYLE, Sir Gavin Archibald; 3 Bt (UK 1929), of Glendelvine, Co Perth; s of Capt Ian Archibald de Hoghton Lyle (ka 1942), s of 2 Bt; suc gf, Col Sir Archibald Moir Park Lyle, 2 Bt, MC, TD, 1946; *b* 14 Oct 1941; *m* 1967 (m dis 1985), Susan Cooper; 5 s, 1 da; *Heir* s, Ian Abram Lyle b 25 Sept 1968; *Career* estate mangr; farmer; co dir; *Style*— Sir Gavin Lyle, Bt; Glendelvine, Caputh, Perthshire

LYLE, (Robert) Ian; s of Sgt Isaac Lyle (d 1954), of Edinburgh, and Margaret Mary, *née* Henderson; *b* 18 August 1949; *Educ* Heath Clark GS, Newcastle Univ (BA), Cranfield Business Sch (MBA); *m* 10 June 1978, Leslie Mary, da of Reginald John Halcomb (d 1982), of Worcs; 1 da (Fiona Clare b 1987); *Career* Whitbread plc 1978-83, visiting prof Ohio USA 1980, md Mary Quant Ltd 1983-; dir WWF, WFN; MBIM 1982, memb Mktg Soc; *Recreations* walking, cricket, squash; *Style*— Ian Lyle, Esq; Mary Quant Ltd, 3 Ives Street, London SW3 2NE (☎ 01 584 8781, fax 01 589 9443, telex 923185 MQ LDN)

LYLE, Lt Col (Archibald) Michael; DL (1961, JP 1950; s of Col Sir Archibald Moir Park Lye, 2 Bt of Glendelvine, MC TD, JP, DL (d 1946) of Glendelvine, Murthly, Perthshire and Dorothy de Hoghton (d 1967), eldest da of Sir James de Hoghton 11 Bt (1611); *b* 1 May 1919; *Educ* Eton, Trinity Coll Oxford (MA); *m* 18 July 1942, Hon Elizabeth Sinclair, da 1 Viscount Thurso (Sir Archibald Sinclair 4 Bt 1786) (d 1970) of Thurso Castle, Thurso, Caithness; 4 da (Veronica b 1943, Janet b 1944, Diana b 1946 (d 1972), Sarah b 1963); *Career* Black Watch 1939-45 (wounded Normandy 1944 discharged with wounds 1946); Lt Col The Scottish Horse RAC (TA) 1953-5; chm T & AF Assoc Perthshire 1959-64; memb Royal Co of Archers (Queens Bodyguard for Scotland); hon attaché Rome 1938-9; ccnclr; Perthshire 1945-74, Tayside Reg 1974-9; vice Lord Lieut of Perth & Kinross 1984; chm Perth Coll of FE 1981-; company dir, farmer; *Recreations* fishing, shooting, music; *Clubs* Royal Perth, Puffin's (Edinburgh), MCC; *Style*— Lt Col Michael Lyle, DL, JP; Riemore Lodge, Dunkeld, Perthshire (☎ (03504) 205)

LYLE, Robert Arthur Wyatt; s of Robert David Lyle Lyle and Irene Joyce Lyle, *née* Francis (d 1984); uncle Sir Woodrow Wyatt, *qv*; *b* 5 May 1952; *Educ* Eton, Oriel Oxford (MA); *Career* fndr dir Berry Palmer & Lyle Ltd; worldwide corr for China Int Econ Conslts Beijing; md BPL (China) Ltd; memb Lloyds; landowner (ptnr Bonython Estate); *Recreations* hurdles (co-owner racehorses), travel; *Clubs* Whites, City of London, Marylebone Cricket; *Style*— Robert Lyle Esq; 20 Princes Gate Mews, London SW7 2PS; Bonython Manor, Cury, Helston, Cornwall (☎ 0326 240234); Berry Palmer & Lyle Ltd, 69-70 Mark Lane, London EC3R 7HY (☎ 01 265 1921)

LYLE, Robert David Lyle; changed name by deed poll 1949 as result of inheriting family estate; s of Robert Harvey Lyle Wyatt; er bro of Lord Wyatt of Weeford, *qv*; *b* 20 Mar 1915; *Educ* Eastbourne Coll; *m* 1945, Irene Joyce, *née* Francis (d 1984); 1 s, 1 da; *Career* Maj RASC, served WWII Eighth Army, Desert Campaign (despatches); former memb London Stock Exchange; chm Cornish Spring Water Co Ltd; memb cncl: Br Diabetic Assoc, The Duchy Hosp Cornwall; High Sheriff Cornwall 1984-85; vice-pres Br Diabetic Assocn; chm Tstees Lanlivery Tst; *Recreations* travel, golf; *Clubs*

Landsdowne, Marylebone Cricket, Mullion Golf (pres); *Style*— Robert Lyle, Esq; Bonython Manor, nr Helston, Cornwall (☎ 0326 240234); Fax 0326 240478

LYLES, John; CBE (1987), DL (West Yorkshire 1987); s of P G Lyles (d 1958), of Dewsbury, and Alice M M Lyles, *née* Robinson (d 1968); *b* 8 May 1929; *Educ* Giggleswick, Leeds Univ (BSc); *m* 1953, Yvonne, da of G F Johnson (d 1954), of Waddesdon; 2 s (Jonathan, Christopher), 2 da (Jane, Anne); *Career* chm S Lyles plc, non exec dir Hillards plc 1984-87; High Sheriff West Yorkshire 1985-86; magistrate Dewsbury 1968-; memb Yorkshire and Humberside CBI 1983-85; *Recreations* gardening, travel, photography; *Style*— John Lyles, Esq, CBE, DL; c/o S Lyles plc, Jilling Ing Mills, Earlsheaton, Dewsbury, Yorks (☎ 0924 463161, telex 55303)

LYLES, Sam; CBE (Jan 1981); s of Percy George Lyles (d 1958), of Alderman, 'Cheriton', Carlton Grange, Batley, and Alice Maud Mary, *née* Robinson (d 1968); *b* 12 Sept 1920; *Educ* Giggleswick Sch; *m* 18 April 1945, Audrey Jean, da of Sir Walter Ward JP, CBE (d 1959), of Lynn Wood, Alexandra Rd, Pudsey; 2 s (Jeremy b 1946, Timothy b 1951), 3 da (Veronica b 1953, Rosemary b 1953 (twins), Jenifer b 1946 d 1972); *Career* dep chm non-exec S Lyles plc; formerly dir and chm S Lyles Sons and Co Ltd, Carpet Yarn Mfrs; pres Dewsbury Constituency Con Assoc 1987; vice-chm Batley & Spen Con Assoc; chm Charles Jones Ct Batley, Royal Br Legion Housing Assoc; pres Dewsbury C of C 1958; fndr pres Dewsbury and Dist Jr C of C 1959; chm: Dewsbury and Dist Hosp Mgmnt Cmmn 1968, Kirklees Area Health Authy 1973-82, Kirklees Family Practitioner Ctee 1975-87, Dewsbury Dist Health Authy 1982-86; pres: Rotary Club of Dewsbury, Woollen Yarn Spinners Assoc; memb Wool Textile Delegation; *Recreations* travel; *Style*— Sam Lyles, CBE; Fieldhurst, Liversedge, W Yorks WF15 7DD (☎ 0924 402048)

LYMBERY, His Hon Judge Robert Davison; QC (1967); s of Robert Smith Lymbery (d 1981), of West Wittering Sussex, and Louise Lymbery, *née* Barnsdale (d 1968); *b* 14 Nov 1920; *Educ* Greshams, Pembroke Coll Cambridge (MA), (fndn exhibitioner Harmsworth Law Scholar); *m* 1952, Pauline Anne, da of Maj John Reginald Tuckett (d 1981), of Knebworth Herts; 3 da (Carole, Sarah, Jane); *Career* serv WWII 1940-46, cmmnd 1941 Maj Royal Tank Regt, ME, Italy, Greece; barr Middle Temple 1949, practiced Midland Circuit 1949-71, rec Grantham 1965-71, chm Bedfordshire and Rutland Quarter Sessions, circuit judge 1971; Freeman City of London 1983; *Recreations* various; *Clubs* Hawks (Cambridge); *Style*— His Hon Judge Robert Lymbery; c/o Central Criminal Ct, London EC4

LYMINGTON, Viscountess; Julia; *née* Ogden; only da of W Graeme Ogden, DSC (decd), and Sheila Faber; *m* 1, Peter Robin Kirwan-Taylor; m 2, as his 3 w, 1974, Viscount Lymington (d June 1984), s of 9 Earl of Portsmouth (d Sept 1984); 1 s (Charles), 2 da (Antonia, Laura); *Style*— Viscountess Lymington

LYMINGTON, Viscount; Oliver Henry Rufus Wallop; s and h of 10 Earl of Portsmouth, *qv*; *b* 22 Dec 1981; *Style*— Viscount Lymington

LYNAM, Desmond Michael; s of Edward Lynam, and Gertrude Veronica, *née* Malone; *b* 17 Sept 1942; *Educ* Varndean GS Brighton, Brighton Bus Coll; *m* 1965 (m dis 1974), Susan Eleanor, *née* Skinner; 1 s (Patrick); *Career* in insur and freelance journalism until 1967; local radio reporter 1967-69, reporter presenter and commentator BBC Radio 1969- 78; presenter and commentator BBC TV Sport 1978- (inc Grandstand Cwlth and Olympic Games, World Cup); pres The Holiday Programme; TV Sports Pres of the Year (TV and Radio Industries Club) 1985, 1986, 1988; dir CPR Ltd 1978-; *Publications* Guide to Commonwealth Games (1986), 1988 Olympics (1988); *Style*— Desmond Lynam, Esq; c/o John Hockey Associates, 106/110 Brompton Rd, London SW3 1JJ (☎ 01 581 5522)

LYNCH, Alan Russell; s of Stanley Benjamin (d 1967), and Lilian Ivy Moffett (d 1976); *b* 29 Dec 1936; *Educ* Christs Hosp Sch, Guy's Hosp (Univ of London) (BDS); *m* 29 Dec 1959, Margaret, da of Dr Theodore Parkman, of Hastings, Sussex; *Career* house surgn Queen Victoria Hosp (E Grinstead) 1962, gen dental practice 1963-72, assistenarzt Katharinen Hosp (Stuttgart) 1968; orthodontist in private practice 1972-; *Recreations* sailing, skiing, music, forestry; *Style*— Alan R Lynch, Esq; 78 Clifton Hill, London NW8; Pattendens Farm, Broad Oak Brede, nr Rye, E Sussex; 31 Queen Anne Street, London W1M 9FB (☎ 01 580 2786)

LYNCH, Barbara; da of Sgt Francis Vincent Lynch, of St Mary in the Marsh, Kent, and Maureen Dorothy, *née* Hartley; *b* 3 June 1953; *Educ* Simon Langton GS Canterbury, Univ of Essex (BA); *Career* Sales Mangr (braille and books) Royal Nat Inst for the Blind 1978-79, appeal dir Marie Stopes Centenary Appeal 1979-81, nat appeals dir The Samaritans 1981-86, devpt dir Scottish Opera 1986-, tstee Arches Charitable Tst; memb Inst Charity Fundraising Dirs 1981-; *Recreations* photography, opera, theatre; *Style*— Ms Barbara Lynch; 61 Inverness Terrace, London W2; 40 Derby St, Glasgow (☎ 041 334 3401); Scottish Opera, 39 Elmbank Crescent, Glasgow G2 (☎ 041 248 4567)

LYNCH, Dr Barry Andrew; s of Andrew Lynch, and Eileen, *née* O'Gara; *b* 20 Feb 1952; *Educ* Salford GS, Univ of St Andrews (BSc), Univ of Manchester (MB, ChB); *Career* house offr Manchester Royal Infirmary and Univ Hosp of Manchester 1977-78; BBC Wales: radio prodr 1978-82, TV prodr 1982-87, hd of features and documentaries 1987-; *Books* Don't Break Your Heart - All You Need to Know About Heart Attacks and How to Avoid Them (1987), The BBC Diet (1988), BBC Healthcheck (1989); *Style*— Dr Barry Lynch; 16 Prospect Drive, LLandaff, Cardiff CF5 2HN (☎ 0222 561 978); BBC Broadcasting Ho, Llandaff, Cardiff CF5 2YQ (☎ 0222 564 888)

LYNCH, Lady; Leah Brigid; da of Thomas Joseph O'Toole (decd); *Educ* St Ann's Ladies Coll Victoria Aust, Coll of Occupational Therapy Univ of Melbourne Aust (Dip Occupnl Ther); *m* 1958, Rt Hon Sir Phillip Lynch, KCMG, PC (d 1984); 3 s; *Career* dir and co sec Denistoun Pty Ltd 1983-; dir Aarque Systems Pty Ltd 1984-87; dir corporate PR Federal Pacific Hotels and Casinos 1988-; social sec Young Lib Movement 1956, Young Lib Rep on State Exec 1957; memb Bd of Dirs Micro-Surgery Unit St Vincent's Hosp Melbourne Aust; patron: Mt Eliza branch Save the Children Fund, Red Cross; *Recreations* art, gardening, tennis, golf, antiques collecting; *Clubs* Peninsula Golf, Daveys Bay Yachting; *Style*— Lady Lynch; The Moorings, 6 Denistoun Avenue, Mt Eliza, Vic 3930, Australia

LYNCH, Prof Thomas Dawson; s of Andrew Lynch (d 1969), and Elizabeth Lynch, *née* Dawson (d 1961); *b* 14 June 1924; *Educ* Sacred Heart AC Glasgow; *m* 3 Feb 1951, Anne (d 1980), da of Charles Edward Dean (d 1965); 4 da (Anne b 1954, Elizabeth b 1955, Catherine b 1957, Frances b 1959), 2 s (Thomas b 1952, Michael b 1966); *Career* CA; ptnr Ernst & Whinney 1955-83; visiting prof Taxation Glasgow Univ 1982; dir: West Highland Woodlands 1983, Redburn Property Co Ltd 1983; lectr, author of articles and books on taxation; chm St Andrews Hosp, Airdrie, Lanarkshire 1986-; *Recreations* forestry, gardening, walking, book collecting; *Clubs* Royal Scottish Automobile Glasgow, Royal Scots Edinburgh; *Style*— Professor Thomas D Lynch, Esq

LYNCH-BLOSSE, Lady Elizabeth; da of Thomas Harold Payne, of Welwyn Garden City; *m* 1950, Sir David Edward Lynch-Blosse, 16 Bt (d 1971); 1 s, 2 da; *Style*— Elizabeth, Lady Lynch-Blosse; c/o Lloyds Bank, High St, Moreton-in-Marsh, Gloucs

LYNCH-BLOSSE, Gp Capt (Eric) Hugh; OBE (1952); s of Maj Cecil Eagles Lynch-Blosse (d 1966), by his 1 w Dorothy Delahaize, *née* Ouvry (d 1963); hp of kinsman, Sir Richard Hely Lynch-Blosse, 17 Bt; *b* 30 July 1917; *Educ* Blundells Sch, RAF Coll; *m* 1946, Jean Evelyn, da of Cdr Andrew Robertson Hair, RD, RNR (d 1965); 1 s (David), 1 da (Valerie), and 1 da decd (Fiona); *Career* served RAF 1935-67, POW 1941-45, Gp Capt; standards engr Rank Xerox 1969-74, sec Wyedean Tourist Bd and mangr Tourist Info Centre Ross on Wye 1974-80, ret; *Books* Wartime Memories from Newnham; *Clubs* RAF; *Style*— Hugh Lynch-Blosse, Esq, OBE; 17 Queens Acre, Newnham, Glos GL14 1DJ (☎ 0594 516 335)

LYNCH-BLOSSE, Sir Richard Hely; 17 Bt (I 1622), of Castle Carra, Galway; s of Sir David Edward Lynch-Blosse, 16 Bt (d 1971), by his w Elizabeth, *née* Payne; *b* 26 August 1953; *Educ* Welwyn Garden City, Royal Free Hosp Sch of Medicine London Univ (MB BS); *m* 1976, Cara Lynne, only da of George Longmore Sutherland, of St Ives, Cambs; 2 da (Katy b 1983, Hannah b 1985); *Heir* kinsman, (Eric) Hugh Lynch-Blosse, OBE, *qv*; *Career* med practitioner, short serv cmmn with RAMC 1975; LRCP, MRCS, DRCOG, MRCGP; *Recreations* shooting, sailing, racquet sports; *Style*— Sir Richard Lynch-Blosse, Bt; The Surgery, Clifton Hampden, Oxon OX14 3EL

LYNCH-ROBINSON, Dominick Christopher; s and h of Sir Niall Bryan Lynch-Robinson, 3 Bt, DSC; *b* 30 July 1948; *m* 28 Nov 1973, Victoria, da of Kenneth Weir, of 37 Stokesay Rd, Sale, Manchester; 1 s (Christopher Henry Jake b 1 Oct 1977), 1 da (Anna Elizabeth Seaton b 19 July 1973); *Career* creative dir advertising agency; *Style*— Dominick Lynch-Robinson Esq; Palmers Hill House, Burghclere, Newbury, Berks

LYNCH-ROBINSON, Sir Niall Bryan; 3 Bt (UK 1920), of Foxrock, Co Dublin, DSC (1941); s of Sir Christopher Henry Lynch-Robinson, 2 Bt (d 1958), and Dorothy Mary Augusta, *née* Warren (d 1970); *b* 24 Feb 1918; *Educ* Stowe; *m* 30 March 1940, Rosemary Seaton, er da of Capt Harold John Eller (d 1929), 1 s, 1 adopted da (Anthea Lucy b 1956); *Heir* s, Dominick Christopher Lynch-Robinson; *Career* Sub Lt RNVR 1939, Lt 1940; chm Leo Burnett Ltd 1969-78; memb exec ctee Nat Marriage Guidance Cncl 1960-1986; Croix de Guerre 1944; *Recreations* flyfishing, gardening, caravanning; *Style*— Sir Niall Lynch-Robinson, Bt, DSC; The Old Vicarage, Ampfield, Romsey, Hants SO51 9BQ

LYNDON-SKEGGS, Andrew Neville; s of Dr Peter Lyndon-Skeggs, of Valley House, Preston Candover, Hants, and June Angela, *née* Reid; *b* 10 Jan 1949; *Educ* Rugby, Magdalene Coll Cambridge; *m* 8 April 1972 (m dis); 2 da (Vanessa b 1975, Tessa b 1979); *Career* master and tstee Cambridge Univ Drag Hunt 1968-71; chm Westbrook Property Devpts Ltd; *Recreations* stalking, hunting, fishing, skiing, gardening; *Clubs* Travellers; *Style*— Andrew Lyndon-Skeggs, Esq; Westbrook House, Holybourne, Alton, Hants (☎ 0420 83244/87539, fax 0420 89535, car ☎ 0836 220633)

LYNE, Air Vice-Marshal Michael Dillon; CB (1968), AFC (1943, and two bars 1947 and 1955), DL (1973); s of Robert John Lyne (d 1943), and Ruth Walton, *née* Robinson (d 1952); *b* 23 Mar 1919; *Educ* Imperial Serv Coll, RAF Coll Cranwell; *m* 1943, Avril Joy, da of Lt Col Albert Buckley, CBE, DSO (d 1965), of Liverpool; 2 s (Peter, Roderic), 2 da (Justine, Barbara); *Career* joined RAF 1937, served Fighter Cmd (Dunkirk, N Atlantic, catapult fighters on merchant ships, and M E) 1939-46, Air Cdre 1961, air attaché Moscow 1961-63, Cdr RAF Coll Cranwell 1963-64, Air Vice-Marshal 1965, AOC 23 Gp 1965-67, sr RAF instr IDC 1968-69, dir-gen RAF Trg MOD 1970-71, ret 1971; sec Diocese of Lincoln 1971-76, fndr Lincs Micro Soc; led world's first formation aerobatics by jet aircraft (Vampires of 54 Sqdn) at an int display Brussels 1947; pres: 54 Sqdn Assoc, Lincoln branch of Save the Children Fund, Grantham Constituency Lib Assoc; vice-pres: Old Cranwellian Assoc, RAF Gliding Assoc, RAF Motor Sport Assoc; *Recreations* cruising, photography, writing; *Clubs* RAF, Cruising Assoc, Royal Mersey YC; *Style*— Air Vice-Marshal Michael Lyne, CB, AFC, DL; 9 Far Lane, Coleby, Lincoln LN5 0AH (☎ 0522 810468)

LYNN, Jonathan Adam; s of Dr Robin Lynn, of London, and Ruth Helen, *née* Eban; *b* 3 April 1943; *Educ* Kingswood Sch Bath, Pembroke Coll Cambridge (MA); *m* 1 Aug 1967, Rita Eleonora Merkelis, da of Alex Jucys; 1 s (Edward b 19 Oct 1973); *Career* writer and dir; actor in repertory, Leicester, Edinburgh and Bristol Old Vic, and on West End stage; TV actor: Barmitzvah Boy 1975, The Knowledge 1979, Outside Edge 1982, Diana 1984; artistic dir Cambridge Theatre Co 1977-81 (produced 42 prodns and directed over 20); London dir incl: The Glass Menagerie 1977, The Gingerbread Man 1977, The Unvarnished Truth 1978, Songbook 1979 (SWET and Evening Standard Awards for Best Musical; re-titled The Moony Shapiro Songbook for Broadway Prodn 1981), A Little Hotel On The Side (NT 1984), Jacobowski and the Colonel (NT 1986), Three Men on a Horse (NT 1987 Olivier Award for Best Comedy), Budgie 1988; company dir at NT 1986-; TV writer incl: Yes Minister 1980-82, Yes Prime Minister 1986- (with co-author Anthony Jay received BAFTA Writers Award, Broadcasting Press Guild Award (twice), Pye Television Writers Award (twice), Ace Award - Best Comedy writing on US cable tv, Special Award from The Campaign For Freedom of Information); film scriptwriter: The Internecine Project 1974, Micks People 1982 (also dir), Clue (also dir) 1986; TV dir Smart Guys (NBC TV pilot); Hon MA Univ of Sheffield; *Books* (with Anthony Jay): The Complete Yes Minister, Yes Prime Minister vols 1 and 2, A Proper Man (1976); *Recreations* working; *Style*— Jonathan Lynn, Esq; 36 Meadway, London NW11 6PJ (☎ 01 455 7476, fax 01 455 1871)

LYNN, Dame Vera Margaret; DBE (1975, OBE 1969); da of Bertram Welch, and Annie, *née* Martin; *b* 20 Mar 1917; *Educ* Brampton Rd Sch East Ham; *m* 1941, Harry Lewis; 1 da (Virginia Penelope Ann); *Career* singer; dir Channel Contemporary Radio; Forces' Sweetheart in WW II, toured Egypt, India, Burma 1944; over 12,000,000 copies of record Auf Wiederseh'n sold; pres Printers' Charitable Corpn 1980; *Recreations* gardening, painting, needlework, knitting; *Style*— Dame Vera Lynn, DBE

LYNTON, Prof Norbert Casper; s of Dr Paul Lynton, (d 1974), and Amalie Christiane, *née* Lippert; *b* 22 Sept 1927; *Educ* Douai Sch, Birkbeck Coll London Univ (BA), Courtauld Inst (BA); *m* 1, 1 Oct 1949 (m dis 1968), Janet Mary, da of Henry Braid Irving; 2 s (Jeremy b 1957, Oliver b 1959); m 2, 3 May 1969, Sylvia Anne, *née*

Towning; 2 s (Thomas b 1970, Peter b 1973); *Career* lectr history of art and architecture Leeds Coll of Art 1950-61, head of dept of art history and gen studies Chelsea Sch of Art 1961-70 (previously sr lectr), dir of exhibitions Arts Cncl of GB 1970-75, visiting prof of history of art Open Univ 1975, prof of history of art Univ of Sussex 1975- (dean of Sch of Euro Studies 1985-88); London corr of Art Int 1961-66, Art critic on The Guardian 1965-70; tstee Nat Portrait Gallery 1985-; memb Assoc of Art Historians 1977-; *Books* Paul Klee (1964), The Modern World (1968), The Story of Modern Art (1980, 1989), Looking at Art (1981), Looking into Paintings (jtly 1985); *Style—* Prof Norbert Lynton; Univ of Sussex, Falmer, Brighton BN1 9QN (☎ 0273 606 755)

LYON, Prof Christina Margaret; da of Edward Arthur Harrison, of Liverpool, and Kathleen Joan, *née* Smith; *b* 12 Nov 1952; *Educ* Wallasey HS for Girls, UCL (LLB); *m* 29 May 1976, Adrian Pirrie Lyon, s of Alexander Ward Lyon, of London; 1 s (David Edward Arandall b 8 July 1985), 1 da (Alexandra Sophie Louise b 5 Jan 1984); *Career* slr Bell & Joynson Liscard Wallasey Merseyside 1975-77; lectr in law faculty: Univ of Liverpool 1977-80, Univ of Manchester 1980-86 (sub-dean 1986); head of sch of law Univ of Keele 1988- (prof of law and head dept of law 1986-); Dr Barnardo's Res Fellowship 1987-89; pres N Staffs Relate Marriage Guidance 1987-, ind memb Merseyside Children's Secure Accommodation Panel 1988-; memb: Law Soc 1977, Soc of Pub Teachers of Law 1977; *Books* Cohabitation Without Marriage (1983), The Law of Residential Homes and Day Care Extablishments (1984), Bitterworths Family Law Encyclopaedia; *Recreations* tennis, opera, theatre, foreign travel, writing; *Style—* Prof Christina Lyon; Dept of Law, Sch of Law, Univ of Keele, Keele, N Staffs ST5 5BG (☎ 0782 621111 ext 3713, fax 0782 613847, telex 36113 UNKLIB G)

LYON, Clive; s of Lt Col Ivan Lyon DSO, MBE, The Gordon Highlanders (ka 1944), and Gabrielle Anna Georgina, *née* Bouvier (d 1978); *b* 12 Sept 1941; *Educ* Harrow, Selwyn Coll Cambridge (MA), Cirencester; *m* 29 March 1967, Madeline Rosa Edith, da of Maj Herbert Frederick Brudenell Foster, TD, of Park House, Drumoak, Aberdeenshire; 2 s (Charles Henry b 1971, Francis James Edward b 1974); *Career* Subaltern Offr Gordon Highlanders 1964-67, active serv, Borneo 1965-66; exec Consolidated Goldfields 1967-73, farmer 1975-88; *Recreations* reading, collecting books, walking; *Style—* Clive Lyon, Esq; The Old Rectory, Stanfield, Dereham, Norfolk (tel: 0328 700224)

LYON, Donald Stewart; s of Alexander Lyon (d 1969), of London; and Dorothy Elizabeth, *née* Tomlinson (d 1986); *b* 27 June 1934; *Educ* Goring Hall, King Edward VII Nautical Coll, Univ of London; *m* 27 June 1956, Marie Pauline, da of Walter Alfred Greenfield (d 1980); *Career* MN Offr Shell (cadet to chief offr) 1951-62; Inchcape Gp 1962-73: gen mangr (previously asst) M E, dir and vice-pres jt venture Incape/Canadian Pacific Canada; Thorn EMI Gp 1977-82: dir AFA Minerva Ltd, chm overseas cos within gp; md Voith Engrg Ltd 1982-; memb: Bahrain Soc, Anglo Omani Soc; Freeman City of London 1974, Liveryman Honourable Co of Master Mariners; FInstD; *Recreations* squash; *Clubs* Oriental; *Style—* Capt Donald Lyon; Voith Engrg Ltd, Ambassador House, Brigstock Rd, Thornton Heath, Surrey CR4 7JG (☎ 01 684 3600, fax 01 684 9635)

LYON, Lady Mary; *née* Charteris; da of 11 Earl of Wemyss (d 1937); *b* 1895; *m* 1, 1915, Algernon Walter Strickland (d 1938); m 2, 1943, Maj John George Lyon, RA; *Style—* Lady Mary Lyon; Apperley Ct, Gloucs

LYON, Michael Edmund; s of Harry Limnell Lyon (d 1969), of Hillam Hall, S Milford, Yorks, and Lois Marjory, *née* Sharpe (d 1975); *b* 10 Oct 1916; *Educ* Uppingham; *Career* Capt Queens Own Yorks Dragoons: BEF 1939-40, MEF 1942 (POW 1942-45); chm and md Lyon & Lyon plc 1948-86; dir: Yorks Tar Distillers 1969-75, Tees Towing Co Ltd 1970-84, Br Marine Mutual Insur Assoc Ltd 1965-80; JP (Pontefract) 1961-83, High Sheriff W Yorks 1976-77; govr The Kings Sch Pontefract 1970-86; memb The Merchants of the Staple of Eng 1968- (Mayor of the Staple 1978-79); ARINA; *Recreations* shooting, skiing, sailing; *Style—* Michael Lyon, Esq; Cedar House, Ackworth, W Yorks WF7 7EQ (☎ 0977 704910)

LYON, Maj Gen Robert; CB (1976), OBE (1964, MBE 1960); s of David Murray Lyon (d 1943), and Bridget, *née* Smith (d 1925); *b* 24 Oct 1923; *Educ* Ayr Acad; *m* 15 Jan 1951, Constance Margaret, da of Colin Gordon (d 1963); 1 s (David b 21 April 1953), 1 da (Melanie Jane (Mrs Manton) b 6 June 1957); *Career* cmmnd A & SH 1943; serv: Italy, Palestine, Egypt, Greece; transfrd and regular cmmn RA 1947, 19 Field Regt BAOR, 3 RHA Libya, F Sphinx Battery 7 Para RHA M E, instr Mons OCS,GSO 1 ASD 2 MOD 1962-65; CO 4 Light Regt: Borneo (despatches), UK, Germany; Brig CRA 1 Armd Div 1967-69, Imperial Def Coll 1970, dir operational requirements MOD 1971-73, Maj-Gen dir RA 1973-75, GOC SW Dist 1975-78, ret 1978; Col Cmdt RA 1976-; pres Army Hockey Assoc 1974-76; chm: Army Golf Assoc 1977-78, RA Cncl of Scotland 1984-; memb: Lothian Territorial Assoc 1980-, Offrs Assoc Scotland 1980-; bursar Loretto Sch 1979-; memb exec ctee: Ind Schs Bursars Assoc 1981-85, Ind Schs Info Serv (Scotland) 1988-; cmmr Queen Victoria Sch Dunblane 1984-; dir: Edinburgh Mil Tattoo plc 1988-, Braemar Civic Amenities Tst 1986-; ctee memb Musselburgh Conservation Soc 1987-; MBIM 1978, FBIM 1981; *Recreations* golf, fishing, skiing, writing; *Clubs* New (Edinburgh), Hon Co of Edinburgh Golfers; *Style—* Maj Gen Robert Lyon, CB, OBE; Woodside, Braemar, Aberdeenshire (☎ 03383 667); Linkfield Cottage Musselburgh, E Lothian, (☎ 031 665 2380); Loretto Sch, Musselburgh, E Lothian, (☎ 031 605 2825)

LYON, (Colin) Stewart Sinclair; s of Col Colin Sinclair Lyon, OBE, TD (d 1967), and Dorothy Winstanley, *née* Thomason; *b* 22 Nov 1926; *Educ* Liverpool Coll, Trinity Coll Cambridge (MA); *m* 9 Aug 1958, Elizabeth Mary Fargus, da of Oliver Fargus Richards (d 1946); 4 s (Richard b 1959, Julian b 1961, Ian b 1962, Alistair b 1963), 1 da (Catherine b 1962); *Career* chief exec Victory Insur Co Ltd 1974-76, dir and chief actuary Legal and Gen Assur Soc Ltd 1976-85, gp chief actuary Legal and Gen GP plc 1985-87 (dir and gen fin mangr 1980-87); dir: Lautro Ltd 1987-, The Cologne Reinsurance Co Ltd 1987-, Aetna Int (UK) Ltd 1988-; vice-pres Br Numismatic Soc 1971- (pres 1966-70); dir: Disablement Income Gp 1984-, City of Birmingham Touring Opera Ltd 1987-; memb Occupational Pensions Bd 1979-82, pres Inst of Actuaries, memb Inquiry into Provison for Retirement 1983-85, tstee Ind Living Fund 1988;Sanford Saltus Gold Medallist 1974 Freeman City of London, memb Worshipful Co of Actuaries 1984; FIA 1954; *Books* Coinage in Tenth-Century England (with C E Blunt and B H I H Stewart, 1988); *Recreations* numismatics, music; *Clubs* Actuaries; *Style—* Stewart Lyon, Esq; Cuerdale, White Lane, Guildford, Surrey GU4 8PR (☎ 0483 573 761)

LYON, Thomas Stephen; s of Clifford Alexander Lyon (d 1962), and Felicia Maria Maximiliana, *née* Rosenfeld; *b* 26 Nov 1941; *Educ* Univ Coll Sch, Wadham Coll Oxford (MA), LSE (LLM); *m* 1971, Judith Elizabeth Jervis, da of Joseph Globe, of Toronto, Canada; 3 s (Edmund b 1971, Charles b 1973, Roger b 1974); *Career* Woodham Smith Borradaile and Martin 1962-68, Berwin & Co 1968-70, Berwin Leighton 1970-; memb City Slrs Co; *Recreations* bicycling up hills, music; *Clubs* United Oxford and Cambridge; *Style—* Thomas Lyon, Esq; 24 Denewood Rd, London N6 (☎ 01 340 0846); Fernlea, Redmire, Leyburn, N Yorks (☎ 0969 22776); Adelaide House, London Bridge, London EC4R 9HA (☎ 01 623 3144, fax 01 623 4416)

LYON, (Thomas Redshaw Spring) Tom; CBE (1978), TD bar 1949 and 1955; s of Robert Lyon (d 1944), of Woodleigh Ave, Friern Barnet, N11, and Julia Gertrude, *née* Spring (d 1975); *b* 6 Nov 1919; *Educ* Tollington Sch; *m* 21 Sept 1954, Grace, da of Jesse Hedley Hayes, of N Finchley, N12; 1 da (Jane Elizabeth Redshaw b 1956); *Career* London Scottish (TA) 1938, cmmnd Sherwood Foresters 1941, Staff Off Chitral 1942, Burma 1943, Supp Serv Off to Govt of India fin dept, war zones 1943-44, Bde Maj 8 Indian Div 1944-45, ret 1946; rejoined London Scottish 1947, 2 ic 1959, chm Regtl Assoc; chm: various cos Clam-Brummer Gp, Reliance Adhesive Co Ltd, Br Paste Co Ltd, London Adhesive Co Ltd, Martis Paints Ltd, Martin Chemicals Ltd, Capital Paints Ltd, Thomas Smith & Co Ltd; *Recreations* shooting, riding, swimming, country pursuits; *Clubs* Caledonian; *Style—* T R S Lyon, CBE, TD; Bedwell End, Essendon, Herts AL9 6HL (☎ 07072 61238); Clam-Brummer Ltd, Bradfield Rd, E16

LYON-DALBERG-ACTON, Hon Edward David Joseph; 4 s of 3 Baron Acton, CMG, MBE, TD (d 1989); *b* 4 Feb 1949; *Educ* Univ of York (BA), Univ of Cambridge (PhD); *m* 1972, Stella Marie, da of Henry Conroy, of 8 Stirling Rd, Bolton; 2 da; *Career* sr lectr in history Univ of Manchester; *Books* Alexander Herzen and the role of the intellectual revolutionary (1979); Russia: the present and the past (1986); *Recreations* tennis, bridge, racing; *Style—* The Hon Edward Lyon-Dalberg-Acton; 24 Moss Lane, Sale, Cheshire M33 1GO (☎ 061 973 0128); Dept of History, University of Manchester, Manchester M13 9PL (☎ 061 275 3105)

LYON-DALBERG-ACTON, Hon Joan Henrica Josepha Mary Clare; da of 2 Baron Acton, KCVO (d 1924); *b* 7 August 1915; *Style—* The Hon Joan Lyon-Dalberg-Acton; 602 Park West, Edgware Rd, London W2

LYON-DALBERG-ACTON, Rev Hon John Charles; 2 s of 3 Baron Acton, CMG, MBE, TD (d 1989); *b* 26 Jan 1943; *Educ* Gregorian Univ Rome; *Career* prof of dogmatic theology Westminster Diocesan Seminary; *Style—* The Rev the Hon John Lyon-Dalberg-Acton; Westminster Diocesan Seminary, 28 Beaufort St, London SW3

LYON-DALBERG-ACTON, Hon John Charles Ferdinand Harold; o s and h of 4 Baron Acton, *qv*; *b* 19 August 1966; *Educ* Winchester, Balliol Coll Oxford; *Style—* The Hon John Lyon-Dalberg-Acton

LYON-DALBERG-ACTON, Hon Margaret Mary Teresa; 6 da of 2 Baron Acton, KCVO (d 1924); *b* 27 May 1919; *Style—* The Hon Margaret Lyon-Dalberg-Acton; 602 Park West, London W1

LYON-DALBERG-ACTON, Hon Peter Hedley; 5 and yst s of 3 Baron Acton, CMG, MBE, TD (d 1989); *b* 27 Mar 1950; *Educ* Cirencester Agric Coll; *m* 1981, Annie Sinclair; 1 s (Simon); *Style—* The Hon Peter Lyon-Dalberg-Acton; Dancing Dicks, Witham, Essex

LYON-DALBERG-ACTON, Hon Robert Peter; 3 s of 3 Baron Acton, CMG, MBE, TD (d 1989) ; *b* 23 June 1946; *Educ* St George's Coll Salisbury S Rhodesia; *m* 1974, Michele Daniele, da of Henri Joseph Laigle, of Paris; 3 s (Christopher Richard Henri b 1977, Patrick John b 1979, William Benjamin b 1986); *Career* stud mangr; *Recreations* bridge, tennis; *Style—* The Hon Robert Lyon-Dalberg-Acton; Rutland House, Saxon Street, Newmarket, Suffolk; Dalham Hall Stud, Duchess Drive, Newmarket, Suffolk

LYON-SMITH, David; s of Dr George Lyon Lyon-Smith (d 1954), and Violet Mary, *née* Bovill (d 1974); *b* 19 Jan 1926; *Educ* Wellington, Christ's Coll Cambridge (BA); *m* 26 Aug 1961, Diana Caroline, da of Cdr Thomas Stanley Lane Fox-Pitt, OBE (d 1985), of Devon; 2 s (George Thomas b 1962, William Harry b 1964), 1 da (Katherine Diana b 1963); *Career* organist Christs Coll Cambridge 1944, slr, chapter clerk Exeter Cathedral 1959-64, registrar of Archdeaconry of Exeter 1959-65; master: Stoke Hill Beagles 1952-63, m E Devon Foxhounds 1963-66 and 1968-69; govr All Hallows Sch 1976-89; *Recreations* music, country sports; *Style—* David Lyon-Smith, Esq; Chapple, Gidleigh, Chagford, Devon (☎ 064 73 2200)

LYONS, Bernard; CBE (1964), JP (Leeds 1960), DL (Yorks W Riding 1971); s of S H Lyons, of Leeds; *b* 30 Mar 1913; *Educ* Leeds GS; *m* 1938, Lucy, da of Wilfred Hurst, of Leeds; 3 s, 1 da; *Career* chm and md UDS Gp Ltd 1972-82, (pres 1983-); memb Leeds City Cncl 1951-65; chm: Leeds Judean Youth Club 1955-70, Swarthmore Adult Educn Centre Appeal 1957-60, City of Leeds Audit sub-ctee 1959-63, Yorks and NE Conciliation Ctee Race Relations Bd 1968-70; jt-chm Leeds branch Cncl of Christians and Jews 1955-60, hon life pres Leeds Jewish Rep Cncl 1960-; memb: ct and cncl Leeds Univ 1953-58, Cmmn for Community Relations 1970-72, Govt Advsy Ctee on Retail Distribution 1970-76; Hon LLD Leeds 1973; *Books* The Thread is Strong (1981), The Narrow Edge (1985); *Recreations* farming, forestry, travel, writing; *Style—* Bernard Lyons, Esq, CBE, JP, DL; Upton Wood, Fulmer, Bucks SL3 6JJ (☎ 02816 2404)

LYONS, Hon Deborah; da of Baron Lyons, of Brighton (d 1978); *b* 1965; *Style—* The Hon Deborah Lyons

LYONS, Edward; QC (1974); s of Albert Lyons (d 1950), of Leeds, and Sarah, *née* Sellman; *b* 17 May 1926; *Educ* Roundhay Sch Leeds, Univ of Leeds (LLB); *m* 4 Sept 1955, Barbara, da of Alfred Katz (d 1972), of London; 1 s (John Adam b 1959), 1 da (Jane Amanda b 1961); *Career* served RA 1944-48, interpreter in Russian Br Control Cmmn Germany 1946-48; barr 1952, Crown Ct rec 1972-, bencher Lincolns Inn 1983-; MP (Lab) Bradford E 1966-74, Bradford W 1974-81 and MP (SDP) Bradford W 1981-83, pps Treasy 1969-70, chm PLP Home and Legal Affrs Gps 1977-79, parly spokesman SDP Home and Legal Affrs 1981-83, SDP Nat Ctee 1984-; *Recreations* history, walking, opera; *Style—* Edward Lyons, Esq, QC; 4 Primley Park Lane, Leeds LS17 7JR (☎ 0532 685351); 59 Westminster Gdns, Marsham St, London SW1P 4JG (☎ 01 834 1960); 4 Brick Court, Temple, London EC4Y 9AD (☎ 01 353 1492); 6 Park Sq, Leeds LS1 2NG (☎ 0532 459763)

LYONS, Hamilton; s of late Richard Lyons, and late Annie Cathro, *née* Thom; *b* 3 August 1918; *Educ* Gourock HS, Greenock HS, Univ of Glasgow; *m* 1943, Jean Cathro Blair; 2 s; *Career* Sheriff of N Strathclyde (formerly Renfrew and Argyll, and Ayr and Bute) 1968-1984; *Style—* Hamilton Lyons, Esq; 14 Cloch Rd, Gourock,

Inverclyde PA19 1AB (☎ 0475 32566)

LYONS, Sir (Isidore) Jack; CBE (1967); s of Samuel Henry Lyons (d 1958), and Sophia, *née* Niman (d 1969); *b* 1 Feb 1916; *Educ* Leeds GS; *m* 1943, Roslyn Marion, da of Jacob Rosenbaum; 2 s, 2 da; *Career* dir UDS Gp 1955-80, life tstee Shakespeare's Birthplace 1967, tstee LSO Tst 1970- (chm 1971, hon memb LSO 1973), chm FCO US Bicentennial Arts Ctee 1973-76, memb cultural advsy ctee UNESCO 1973-, UK and Europe advsr Bain & Co (of Boston and London) 1981-87, sr ptnr Sir J Lyons & Co; memb advsy ctee Britain Salutes NY 1982-83, chm First Computer Ltd 1983-84, dir Bain Capital Fund Boston Mass USA 1984-87, chm JE London Properties Ltd 1987, JLC (London) Ltd 1986-; tstee Heslington Fndn for Music and Assoc Arts 1987-; Hon FRAM 1973, D Univ York 1975; kt 1973; *Style*— Sir Jack Lyons, CBE; Blundell House, 2 Campden Hill, London W8 7AD; International Investments, 30 Ledbury Rd, Kensington, London W11 2SH (☎ 01 229 9481)

LYONS, Sir James Reginald; JP (Cardiff 1966); s of James Lyons (d 1968), and Florence Hilda Lyons (d 1951); *b* 15 Mar 1910; *Educ* Howard Gdns HS, Cardiff Tech Coll; *m* 1937, Mary Doreen, da of Thomas Alfred Fogg (d 1936); 1 s (Colin); *Career* served WW II Royal Tank Regt 1940-46; civil serv 1929-65; Cardiff City Cncl: cllr 1949-58, Alderman 1958-74, Dep Lord Mayor 1966-67 Lord Mayor 1968-69; memb: Wales Tourist Bd 1951-72, BBC Wales; airport mangr Cardiff Airport 1954-75; chm and govr: De La Salle Sch, St Illtyds Coll 1955-, Univ Coll Cardiff 1955-70: (local govt offr 1965-75, co dir 1977-); assessor under Race Rels Act 1976, pres Welsh Games Cncl, chm Cardiff Hort Soc 1962-; chm and dir Park Lodge Property Co; JP 1966, memb Norfolk Ctee 1968; holder of Silver Acorn for Scouts; OStJ, KCSG; kt 1969; *Recreations* rugby, all outdoor games; *Clubs* Cardiff Athletic; *Style*— Sir James Lyons, JP; 101 Minehead Ave, Sully, S Glam, Wales (☎ 0222 530403)

LYONS, Jeremy Nicholas Michael; s of Michael Joseph Lyons (d 1970), and Barbara Virginia Berry, *née* Van Den Bergh; *b* 20 Dec 1949; *Educ* Worth Abbey Sch Sussex, Sorbonne Paris; *Career* Lloyds: broker 1971, memb 1978; currently dir J Lyons Conslts Ltd retained by Tyser and Co at Lloyds, dir Vistaero Internat SA Spain; memb: Game Conservancy Soc, Chelsea Cons Assoc, Lloyds Wine Soc, Lloyds Motor Club; Freeman: City of London 1981, Worshipful Co of Insurers 1982; *Style*— Jeremy Lyons, Esq; 12 Wallgrave Rd, London SW5 0RL; Villa Vistaero, Competa, Malaga, Spain; Lloyds, Lime St, London EC3 (☎ 01 623 6262, 01 623 7100 ext 4671, fax 01 621 9042, telex 883907)

LYONS, Sir John; *b* 23 May 1932; *Educ* St Bede's Coll Manchester, Christ's Coll Cambridge (BA, Dip Ed, PhD, LittD) ; *m* 1959, Danielle Jacqueline Simonet; *Career* lectr in comparative linguistics SOAS of London 1957-61, lectr in gen linguistics Univ of Cambridge and fell Christ's Coll 1961-64, prof of gen linguistics Univ of Edinburgh 1964-76, prof of linguistics Sussex Univ 1976-84 (pro-vice-chllr 1981-84); master Trinity Hall Cambridge 1984-, hon fell Christ's Coll Cambridge 1985-, hon memb Linguistic Soc of America 1978, Docteur des Lettres (Honoris Causa) Univ Cath de Louvain 1980, Hon DLitt: Univ of Reading 1986, Univ of Edinburgh 1988;FBA 1973; kt 1987; *Books* Structural Semantics (1963), Psycholinguistics Papers (ed with R J Wales, 1966), Introduction to Theoretical Linguistics (1968), Chomsky (1970), New Horizons in Linguistics (1970), Semantics 1 and 2 (1977), Language and Linguistics (1980), Language, Meaning and Context (1980); *Style*— Sir John Lyons; Master's Lodge, Trinity Hall, Cambridge CB2 1TJ

LYONS, John Gerald; s of Arthur John Lyons (d 1977), and Elizabeth Caroline, *née* Braybrooke Webb (d 1973); *b* 14 Jan 1926; *Educ* WHSS Guildhall Schs of Music, RMC Sandhurst, City Univ (LR); *m* 1, 26 March 1949, Jean Hutcheon-Horne Smith (d 1980); 2 s (Russell b 11 May 1950, Stuart b 9 Oct 1951); m 2, 29 May 1983, Susan, da of Robert Cuffel; *Career* cmmnd Northamptonshire Regt Grenadier Gds; lectr and examiner in: physiological optics, anatomy, binocular vision, orthoptics, ocular pathology, ocular pharmacology; papers published and res in: fixation disparity, glaucoma & tonometry, binocular vision, visual inhibition and clinical studies; in practice Whipps Cross Hosp Chigwell; Freeman City of London, Liveryman Worshipful Co of Spectacle Makers; SMSA, FBCO, FBOA, HD, DOrth, DCLR, FSMC, FAAO; *Recreations* offshore sailing, music (cello), astrophysics, anthropology; *Clubs* City Livery, CLYC, HYC; *Style*— John Lyons, Esq; 55 Romford Rd, Chigwell, Essex IG7 4QS (☎ 01 500 5402)

LYONS, John Trevor; s of Sir Rudolph Lyons, and Lady Jeanette Lyons, *née* Dante; *b* 1 Nov 1943; *Educ* Leeds GS, Univ of Leeds (LLB); *m* 7 Sept 1969, Dianne Lucille, da of Geoffrey Saffer; 3 s (Alan b 1971, James b 1973, Benjamin b 1974); *Career* slr; ptnr J Lester Lyons & Falk; *Style*— John T Lyons, Esq; 140 Alwoodley Lane, Leeds LS17 7PP (☎ 0532 674575); 7 Park Sq, Leeds LS1 2LS (☎ 0532 450406, fax 0532 422169)

LYONS, Jonathon Edward; s of Sir Jack Lyons, CBE, of Blundell House, 2 Campden Hill, London, and Lady Roslyn Marion Lyons; *b* 1 May 1951; *Educ* Carmell Coll; *m* 30 Dec 1975, Miriam, da of Simon Djanogly (d 1977), of Geneva, Switzerland; 2 s (Jacob b 1976, Simon b 1980), 1 da (Deborah b 1983); *Career* exec sales Alexandra Ltd Leeds 1968-71, chief exec John David Mansworld Ltd 1971-89, ptnr Int Investmts Ltd 1978-, chief exec H Alan Smith Ltd 1983-85, dir JLC Ltd London 1986, jt chief exec JE London Properties Ltd 1988-, private investmt conslt Jonathon E Lyons & Co 1988-; dir: Britimpex Ltd Canada, Art Leasing Inc Canada; memb ctee: Cons Industl Fund, RMC, RAM; jt chm Hyde Park ctee Central Br Fund 1975-80; FInstD, memb FIMBRA; *Clubs* Carlton, IOD; *Style*— Jonathon E Lyons, Esq; 35 Loudoun Rd, St Johns Wood, London NW8, (☎ 01 624 7733); Chalet Emeroude, 1837 Chateau D'Oex, Switzerland; 30 Ledbury Rd, Kensington, London W11 (☎ 01 229 9481 fax 01 229 9229 car phone 0836 200 683)

LYONS, (Andrew) Maximilian; s of Dennis John Lyons, CB, of Summerhaven, Gough Rd, Fleet, Hants, and Elizabeth Dora Maria, *née* Müller Haefliger; *b* 16 Jan 1946; *Educ* Queen Marys GS Basingstoke, Brixton Sch of Bldg (Dip Arch); *m* 16 June 1983, Katherine Jane (Kate), da of Brig John Joseph Regan; 1 s (Shaun b 1984), 1 da (Rosalie b 1986); *Career* sr ptnr Lyons & Sleeman & Hoare architects 1974; winner of: Euro Architectural Heritage Award 1974, Br Cncl of Shopping Centres Award 1987, Euro Cncl of Shopping Centre Award 1988, City Heritage Award of London 1988, Silver Jubilee Cup RTPI 1988, other environmental and design awards; RIBA 1974; *Recreations* sailing, shooting, walking; *Style*— Maximilian Lyons, Esq; School Lane House, School Lane, Ewshot, Farnham, Surrey GU10 5BN; Old Threshing Barn, E Prawle, Kingsbridge, S Devon (☎ 0252 850222); 82 Park St, Camberley, Surrey GU15 3NY (☎ 0276 692266, fax 0276 692207)

LYONS, Hon Rodney Max; s of Baron Lyons of Brighton (Life Peer, d 1978), and Laurie Adele; *b* 27 May 1941; *Educ* St Paul's, Magdalen Coll Oxford (BA, post-grad CertEd); *m* 1963, Cory Frances, da of Dr William Owen Hassall, of the Manor House, Wheatley, Oxford; 1 s, 1 da; *Career* county advsr for English Devon LEA 1974-82, head of Dept of Arts and Humanities Exeter Coll 1982-86, dir of Coll Servs Exeter Coll 1986-88, princ Taunton's Coll Southampton 1989-; *Recreations* visiting peace camps; *Clubs* Campaign for Nuclear Disarmament; *Style*— The Hon Rodney Lyons; 9 Abbotts Crt, Park Rd, Winchester, Hants, (☎ 0962 52024); Taunton's Coll, Highfield Rd, Southampton

LYONS, His Honour Sir Rudolph; QC (1953); er s of G Lyons (d 1966), of Leeds; *b* 5 Jan 1912; *Educ* Leeds GS, Univ of Leeds (LLB); *m* 1936, Jeanette, yr da of Philip Dante, of Leeds; 1 s, 2 da; *Career* barr Gray's Inn 1934; rec: Sunderland 1955-56, Newcastle-upon-Tyne 1956-61, Sheffield 1961-65, Leeds 1965-70, Liverpool 1970-71; bencher 1961, ldr NE circuit 1961-70, slr-gen Durham 1961-65; cmmr: Centl Criminal Ct 1962-70, of Assize Newcastle-upon-Tyne 1969; attorney-gen County Palatine of Durham 1965-70, circuit judge Manchester N circuit 1972-82 (ret); hon rec: Liverpool, Manchester 1977-; memb ct Manchester Univ Gen Cncl Bar, pres ctee Cncl Circuit Judges 1974; Hon LLD Leeds 1982; kt 1976; *Style*— His Honour Sir Rudolph Lyons, QC; 8 Brookside, Alwoodley, Leeds LS17 8TD (☎ 0532 683274)

LYONS, Russell John Stewart; s of John Gerald Lyons, and Jean Hutcheon Horne, *née* Smith; *b* 11 May 1950; *Educ* Forest Sch, City Univ Graduate Sch (MBA); *m* 1, May 1970 (m dis 1986), Yvonne Noelly; 1 da (Caroline Jane b 26 Oct 1982); m 2, 1 June 1987, Margaret Roberta, da of Col George Lennie, MBE; *Career* dep md Nippon Int 1977, md Icon Int 1980, dir sales and mktg Torch Computers plc 1981 (fndr shareholder), chm Mgmnt Innovation Gp 1983-, md XAT software 1985; FCA 1973 and 1978, memb CMI 1975; *Recreations* sailing, waterskiing, riding, playing several musical instruments; *Clubs* Public Schs, East India; *Style*— Russell Lyons, Esq; Century House, Pluckley Rd, Charing, Kent (☎ 023371 3512; 9 New Rd, Rochester Kent (☎ 0634 814931, fax 0634 815878)

LYONS, Stuart Randolph; *Career* chm and chief exec Royal Doulton Ltd; *Style*— Stuart Lyons, Esq; Minton House, London Rd, Stoke-on-Trent, Staffs ST4 7QB (☎ 0782 744766)

LYONS, Terence Patrick; s of Maurice Peter Lyons (d 1978), of Pevensey Bay, Sussex, and Maude Mary Elizabeth, *née* O'Farrell (d 1958); *b* 2 Sept 1919; *Educ* Wimbledon Coll, King's Coll London, LSE; *m* 11 June 1945, Winifred Mary, da of James Basil Ward Normile (d 1965), of Sutton, Surrey; 2 da (Moira Teresa b 16 Nov 1947, Celia Mary b 19 May 1952); *Career* Gunner RA and Offr Cadet IA 1940-41, 2 Lt Indian Armd Corps (attached RIASC) 1941-46, Capt 1942; head staff dept Unilever Ltd 1948-54, chief personnel offr Philips Industs (Croydon) 1954-60, gp personnel mangr Ilford Ltd 1960-66, dir of personnel Staveley Industs Ltd 1966-69, exec dir (personnel) Williams & Glyn's Bank 1969-82, dir Industl Trg Serv 1983-, conslt 1983-; pres Inst of Personnel Mgmnt 1981-73; memb: Monopolies & Mergers Cmmn 1975-81, MSC 1981-82; chm: Fedn of London Clearing Bank Employers 1976-78, CBI Educ and Trg Ctee 1976-77, CBI Manpower Servs Advsy Panel 1975-82; memb CBI Educn Fndn cncl 1974-86, Open Univ Cncl 1980-; CIPM, FCIB; *Books* The Personnel Function in a Changing Envirnoment (second edn 1985); *Recreations* golf, sailing, bridge, music; *Clubs* Army and Navy, Wilderness GC, Royal Eastbourne GC, Chipstead SC; *Style*— Terence Lyons, Esq; Winter Ride, 2 Rosefield, Kippington Rd, Sevenoaks, Kent

LYONS, Thomas Colvill Holmes (Toby); s of Robert Henry Cary Lyons, of Cilwych Hse, Builch, Powys, and Dorothy Joan Garnons Lyons; *b* 8 Mar 1937; *Educ* Harrow, Oriel Coll Oxford (MA); *m* 1, 17 July 1965 (m dis 1971), Heather Mary Meryies Forbes; 1 s (David b 1968), 1 da (Sophia b 1966); m 2, 3 June 1972 (Gwendolin) Frances, da of Col W D Gosling, TD, DL; 2 da (Kate b 1975, Annabel b 1976); *Career* cmmnd Royal Welch Fus 1956-58 (TA 1958-69); admitted slr 1965; Linklaters & Paines 1964-66, Allen & Overy 1966-69, md Minster Tst Ltd 1973; dir: Minster Assets plc 1976, Tillshare plc 1984, Monument Oil & Gas plc 1984; chm R & J Hadlee Fine Art plc 1985; Asst Worshipful Co of Tinplate Workers; memb Law Soc 1965; *Recreations* shooting, water sports, winter sports; *Style*— Toby Lyons, Esq; Hole Farm, Stansted, Essex CM24 8TJ

LYONS, Hon William; s of Baron Lyons of Brighton (d 1978); *b* 1945; *m* 1963, Petra Deanna, da of William Tibble; *Style*— The Hon William Lyons; 15 Lower Town, Sampford, Peverell, Devon

LYSAGHT, Patrick James; s of late Horace James William Lysaght (bro of 6 Baron Lisle); hp to Barony of Lisle; *b* 1 May 1931; *Educ* Shrewsbury; *m* 1957, Mary Louise, da of late Lt-Col Geoffrey Riginald Devereux Shaw, and formerly w of Euan Guy Shaw-Stewart (now 10 Bt); 2 s, 1 da; *Career* late Lt Gren Gds; *Style*— Patrick Lysaght, Esq; 52 Wardo Ave, London SW6

LYSTER, Peter Haggard; s of Lionel Charles Lyster (d 1980), of Apps, Stock, Essex, and Avice Dorothy, *née* Haggard (d 1986); bro of Rae Lionel Haggard Lyster, *qv*; *b* 17 Nov 1934; *Educ* Marlborough; *m* 1967, Gillian Barbara, da of Sir Arthur John Grattan-Bellew, CMG, QC (d 1985); 1 s (Thomas), 2 da (Grania, Anna); *Career* former 2 Lt 11 Hussars; former Capt City of London Yeo; ptnr Wed Durlacher Mordaunt & Co 1962-86; memb: Stock Exchange 1956, Cncl of Stock Exchange; joint-master Meynell Foxhounds 1972-76; *Recreations* Hunting, fishing; *Clubs* Cavalry and Guards; *Style*— Peter Lyster, Esq; Little Chishill Manor, Royston, Herts (☎ 0763 838238)

LYSTER, Rae Lionel Haggard; s of Lionel Charles Lyster (d 1980), of Apps, Stock, Essex, and Avice Dorothy, *née* Haggard (d 1986); *b* 24 August 1931; *Educ* Bradfield, Trinity Coll Cambridge (BA); *m* 24 May 1958, Julia Elizabeth, da of Charles Humphrey Scott Plummer, of Mainhouse, Kelso, Roxburghshire; 1 s (Nicholas b 8 March 1959), 2 da (Amanda b 29 May 1961, Lucy b 23 May 1963); *Career* 2 Lt Royal Scots Greys (2 Dragoons) 1951-52, Capt Ayrshire (ECO) Yeo 1952-62; ptnr Cazenove & Co 1961-; govr and hon tres Reed's Sch Cobham Surrey, chm and tstee The Perry Watlington Tst Essex; Freeman of City of London; *Recreations* fishing, shooting, golf; *Clubs* Boodle's, City of London; *Style*— Rae Lyster, Esq; Malting Green House, Layer De La Haye, Colchester, Essex CO2 OJE (☎ 0206 34354); Cazenove & Co, 12 Tokenhouse Yard, London EC2R 7AN (☎ 01 588 2828, fax 01 606 9205, telex 886758)

LYTHALL, Basil Wilfrid; CB (1966); s of Frank Herbert Lythall (d 1969), of Kingswinford, Staffs, and Winifred Mary Carver (d 1953); *b* 15 May 1919; *Educ* King Edward's Sch Stourbridge, Christ Church Oxford (MA); *m* 1942, Mary Olwen, da of Simon Dando (d 1980), of Wall Heath, W Midlands; 1 s (David); *Career* occasional res conslt; asst dir Physical Res Admlty 1957-58, dep chief scientist Admlty Surface

Weapons Establishment 1958-60, first chief scientist Admlty Underwater Weapons Establishment 1960-64, chief scientist RN and memb Admlty Bd Def Cncl 1964-78, dep controller of Navy, Res and Devpt 1964-71, dep controller establishments and res procurement exec MOD 1971-78, dir Saclant ASW Res Centre La Spezia Italy 1978-81; tstee Nat Maritime Museum 1974-80, chm CORDA Policy Bd chm Sema Gp 1985-; *Recreations* walking, sculpting, music; *Style*— B W Lythall, Esq, CB; 48 Grove Way, Esher, Surrey KT10 8HL (☎ 01 398 2958)

LYTHGOE, Joseph; s of Adam Lythgoe (d 1946), of Wigshaw Grange, Culcheth, Warrington, and Mary Elizabeth, *née* Leather; *b* 11 August 1922; *Educ* Ashton-In-Makerfield GS; *m* 3 Sept 1948 (m sep), Catherine Crompton, *née* Brooks; 1 s (David b 1954); *Career* served RCS 1941-46; landowner; chm & md Adam Lythgoe Ltd Fertilizer mfrs 1949-; chm Ches branch Cncl for the Protection of Rural Eng; *Recreations* restoration of Rural Economy, Landscape conservation; *Clubs* Farmers, Warrington; *Style*— Joseph Lythgoe, Esq; Swinhoe Hse, Culcheth, Warrington WA3 4NH (☎ 092 576 4106)

LYTTELTON, Hon Christopher Charles; s of 10 Viscount Cobham, KG, GCMG, GCVO, TD, PC (d 1977), and Elizabeth Alison, *née* Makeig-Jones; *b* 23 Oct 1927; *Educ* Eton; *m* 1976, Tessa Mary, da of Col Alexander George Jeremy Readman, DSO (d 1973); 1 s (Oliver b 1976), 1 da (Sophie b 1978); *Career* chief exec Nivison Cantrade Ltd (stockbrokers); *Recreations* gliding, cricket; *Clubs* MCC, Booker GC,; *Style*— The Hon Christopher Lyttelton; 28 Abbey Gdns, London NW8 9AT; NCL Investments Ltd, 9-12 Basinghall St, London

LYTTELTON, Hon Deborah Clare; da of 2 Viscount Chandos (d 1980); *b* 1963; *Style*— The Hon Deborah Lyttelton; The Vine, Sherborne St John, Basingstoke, Hants

LYTTELTON, Hon Laura Katherine; da of 2 Viscount Chandos (d 1980); *b* 1950; *Educ* Cranborne Chase Sch, St Anne's Oxford, Univ of London; *Style*— The Hon Laura Lyttelton; The Vine, Sherborne St John, Basingstoke, Hants

LYTTELTON, Hon Matthew Peregrine Antony; s of 2 Viscount Chandos (d 1980), and hp of bro, 3 Viscount; *b* 21 April 1956; *Educ* Eton, Trinity Coll Cambridge; *Style*— The Hon Matthew Lyttelton; The Vine, Sherborne St John, Basingstoke, Hants

LYTTELTON, Hon Nicholas Adrian Oliver; s of 1 Viscount Chandos, KG, DSO, MC, PC (d 1972); *b* 1937; *Educ* Eton, Magdalen Coll Oxford; *m* 1960, Margaret, da of Sir Harold Hobson, CBE; 1 s, 1 da; *Career* prof of modern history: Reading Univ 1976-78, John Hopkins Univ Centre Bologna 1978-; fell: All Souls Coll Oxford 1960-69, St Antony's Coll Oxford 1969-75; *Style*— The Hon Nicholas Lyttelton

LYTTELTON, Hon Nicholas Makeig; 4 and yst s of 10 Viscount Cobham, KG, GCMG, GCVO, TD, PC (d 1977); *b* 3 Jan 1951; *Educ* Shiplake Court Oxon; *m* 1980, June Carrington; *Style*— The Hon Nicholas Lyttelton; 30 Paulton's Sq, London SW3

LYTTELTON, Hon Richard Cavendish; s of 10 Viscount Cobham, KG, GCMG, GCVO, TD, PC (d 1977); *b* 1949; *Educ* Eton; *m* 1971, Romilly, da of Michael Barker; 1 da (May); *Style*— The Hon Richard Lyttelton; 22 Baskerville Rd, London SW18

LYTTON, Lady Caroline Mary Noel; da of 4 Earl of Lytton, OBE (d 1985), and Clarissa, *née* Palmer; *b* 1947; *Educ* St Mary's Shaftesbury, Univ of Birmingham, Sir John Cass Sch of Art; *Career* arts admin; admin: Prussia Cove Music, Metal Smith; *Recreations* travel, reading; *Style*— Lady Caroline Lytton; 113 Plimsoll Rd, London N4 2ED

LYTTON, Countess of; Clarissa Mary; *née* Palmer; da of Brig-Gen Cyril Eustace Palmer, CB, CMG, DSO; *m* 1946, 4 Earl of Lytton (d 1985); *Style*— Clarissa, Countess of Lytton; Keeper Knight's, Crawley, Sussex, RH10 3PB

LYTTON, 5 Earl (UK 1880); Sir John Peter Michael Scawen Lytton; also Viscount Knebworth (UK 1880), 18 Baron Wentworth (E 1529), and 6 Bt (UK 1838); s of 4 Earl of Lytton; *b* 7 June 1950; *Educ* Downside, Univ of Reading; *m* 1980, Ursula, da of Anton Komoly, of Vienna; 1 s (Viscount Knebworth b 7 March 1989), 1 da (Lady Katrina b 1985); *Heir* s, Philip Anthony Scawen, Viscount Knebworth b 9 March 1989; *Career* ptnr Permutt Brown & Co 1983-; ARICS; *Style*— The Rt Hon the Earl of Lytton; New Buildings Place, Dragons Green, Horsham, Sussex

LYTTON, Lady Lucy Mary Frances; da of 4 Earl of Lytton, OBE; *b* 29 Jan 1957; *Educ* St Teresa's Minehead, Sacred Heart Convent Woldingham; *Career* engrg draughtsman; *Style*— Lady Lucy Lytton

LYTTON, Hon (Thomas) Roland Cyril Lawrence; s of 4 Earl of Lytton, OBE (d 1985); *b* 10 August 1954; *Educ* St Teresa's Minehead Worth Downside; *Career* farmer and engr; *Recreations* DIY; *Style*— The Hon Roland Lytton; Bratton Ct, Minehead, Somerset

LYTTON, Sandra, Countess of; Rosa Alexandrine Fortel; *m* 1924, as his 2 w, 3 Earl of Lytton, OBE, Legion of Honour (d 1951); 1 da; *Style*— The Rt Hon Sandra, Countess of Lytton; 8 Rue du Val de Grace, Paris, France

LYVEDEN, Dowager Baroness; Ada; da of late Arthur Hodgkinson, of Accrington; *m* 1, 1910, Richard Springate; m 2, 1925, as his 2 w, 3 Baron Lyveden (d 1926); *Career* actress (Lynda Martell); *Style*— The Rt Hon the Dowager Baroness Lyveden

LYVEDEN, Baroness Gladys; *m* 1, late John Cassidy; m 2, 1957, as his 2 w, 5 Baron Lyveden (d 1973); *Style*— The Rt Hon Gladys, Lady Lyveden; Day's Bay, nr Wellington, NZ

LYVEDEN, 6 Baron (UK 1859); Ronald Cecil Vernon; s of 5 Baron Lyveden (d 1973); *b* 10 April 1915; *m* 1938, Queenie Constance, da of Howard Ardern; 3 s; *Heir* s, Hon Jack Leslie Vernon; *Style*— The Rt Hon the Lord Lyveden; 20 Farmer St, Te Aroha, NZ (☎ 410)

M

MAAN, Bashir Ahmed; JP (1968), DL (Glasgow 1982); s of Choaudhry Sardar Khan Maan, of Village Maan, Gujranwala Pakistan, and Hayat Begum Maan (d 1975); *b* 20 Oct 1926; *Educ* DB HS, Qila Didar Singh, Panjab Univ; *m* (m dis); 1 s (Tariq Hassan), 3 da (Rashda Begum, Hanna Bano, Aalya Maaria); *Career* involved in struggle of Pakistan 1943-47, organized rehabilitation of refugees from India in Maan and surrounding areas 1947-48; emigrated to UK, settled in Glasgow 1953, fndr sec Glasgow Pakistan Social and Cultural Soc 1955-65 (pres 1966-69), memb exec ctee Glasgow City Lab Pty 1969-70, vice-chm Glasgow Community Rels Cncl 1970-75, cncllr Glasgow City Corpn 1970-75, magistrate City of Glasgow 1971-74, vice-chm Glasgow Corpn Police Ctee 1971-74 (chm 1974-75); memb: Nat Road Safety Ctee 1971-74, Scottish Accident Prevention Ctee 1973-75, BBC Immigrant Programmes Advsy Ctee 1972-80; convenor Pakistan Bill Action Ctee 1973, contested (Lab) E Fife Parly Constituency 1974, pres Standing Conference of Pakistani Orgns in the UK and Eire 1974-77, police judge City of Glasgow 1974-75, cncllr City of Glasgow District Cncl 1975-84, dep chm Cmmn for Racial Equality 1977-80, memb Scottish Gas Consumer Cncl 1978-81, baillie City of Glasgow 1980-84, memb Gtr Glasgow Health Bd 1981-, fndr chm Scottish Pakistani Assoc 1984-, judge City of Glasgow District Cts; chm Strathclyde Community Relations Cncl 1986-; vice chm (chm mgmnt ctee) Glasgow Int Sports Festival Ltd 1987-; govr Jordanhill Coll of FE 1987-; *Recreations* reading, golf; *Clubs* Douglas Park; *Style—* Mr Bashir Maan JP, DL; 20 Sherbrooke Ave, Glasgow G41 4PE (☎ (041 427) 4057)

MABANE, Baroness; Stella Jane; da of late Julian Duggan, of Buenos Aires; *m* 31 March 1944, as his 2 wife, 1 and last Baron Mabane, KBE, PC (d 1969); *Style—* The Rt Hon Lady Mabane; 11 Stanhope Gdns, SW7

MABBS, Alfred Walter; CB (1982); eldest s of James Alfred Mabbs (d 1975), of Eton Wick, and Amelia Emily Mabbs (d 1985); *b* 12 April 1921; *Educ* Hackney Downs Sch; *m* 1942, Dorothy, da of George Lowley; 1 s (John); *Career* keeper of public records 1978-82; pres Int Cncl on Archives 1980-82; *Style—* Alfred Mabbs, Esq, CB; 14 Acorn Lane, Cuffley, Herts EN6 4JE (☎ 0707 873660)

MABEY, Bevil Guy; CBE (1985); s of Guy Mabey (d 1951), and Madeline Johnson (d 1957); *b* 16 April 1916; *Educ* Tonbridge Sch, Cambridge (MA); *m* 4 Oct 1947, June Penelope, da of Brig Cecil Herbert Peck, DSO, MC; 1 s (David b 1961), 5 da (Bridget Ann b 1949, Isabel Denise b 1950, Christine b 1954, Juliet b 1955, Fiona b 1965); *Career* cmmnd Royal Corps Signals 1939, RASC 1940-46, Maj, France, N Africa, Italy, Yugoslavia, Greece; chm: Mabey Hldgs Ltd, Mabey & Johnson Ltd, Mabey Hire Co Ltd, Fairfield-Mabey Ltd, Mabey Construction Co Ltd, Beachley Property Ltd; Freeman City of London, Worshipful Co of Vinters; *Recreations* rowing, skiing, riding, golf, carpentry, bricklaying; *Clubs* Leander, London Rowing; *Style—* Bevil G Mabey, Esq, CBE; Mabey Holdings, Floral Mile, Twyford, Reading RG10 9SQ (☎ 073 522 3921, telex 848 649 Mabey TG, fax 073 522 3941)

MABON, Rt Hon Dr (Jesse) Dickson; PC (1977); s of Jesse Dickson Mabon and Isabel Simpson, *née* Montgomery; *b* 1 Nov 1925; *Educ* schools in Cumbrae and Kelvinside; *m* 1970, Elizabeth Sarah, da of Major William Victor Zinn (sometime pncpl ptnr W V Zinn & Associates, consulting engrs); 1 s; *Career* formerly in coalmining industry, journalism (with Scottish Daily Record); MP (Lab and Co-op 1955-81, SDP 1981-83) Greenock 1955-74, Greenock and Port Glasgow 1974-83 (fought Bute and N Ayrshire (Lab) 1951, Renfrewshire W (Lab and Co-op) 1955; jt parly under-sec Scotland 1964-67, min of state Scottish Office 1967-70, dep oppn spokesman Scotland 1970-72, min of state for Energy 1976-79; chm UK Labour Ctee for Europe 1974-76, Scottish PLP 1972-73 and 1975-76, fndr chm PLP Manifesto Gp 1974-76, pres European Movement 1975-76; memb: Cncl Europe 1970-72 and 1974-76, WEU Assembly 1970-72 and 1974-76; visiting physician Manor House Hosp London; fellow Faculty of History of Medicine, Soc of Apothecaries; FInstPet, FRSA; freeman City of London; *Style—* The Rt Hon Dr J Dickson Mabon; 57 Hillway, London N6 6AD

MAC INNES, Archibald; CVO (1977); s of Duncan Mac Innes (d 1987), of Gourock, and Catherine, *née* Mac Donald (d 1970); *b* 10 April 1919; *Educ* Kirkcudbright Acad, Royal Tech Coll Glasgow; *m* 10 June 1950, Nancey Elizabeth (d 1976), da of Alec Blyth (d 1958), of Wivenhoe; 1 s (Duncan John b 1955), 2 da (Morag Catherine b 1951, Fiona Margaret b 1960); *Career* Scotts Shipbuilding and Engrg Co Greenock 1938-45, chief mech engr HMOCS N Nigeria 1945-59; WO: cmd works offr Gibraltar 1959-63, supt engr Southern Cmd Wilton 1963-64; supt engr MPBW Bristol 1964-68, cmd works offr DOE Germany 1968-72, dir London regn PSA 1972-79, conslt planning inspr DOE 1980-; CEng, FIMechE, FBIM; *Recreations* fishing, shooting, golf, rugby supporter; *Clubs* Civil Service, Salisbury RFC, High Post GC; *Style—* Archibald Mac Innes, Esq, CVO; New Ho, Lower Rd, Homington, Salisbury SP5 4NG (☎ 072 277 336)

MACADAM, (Elliott) Corbett; s of Sir Ivison Macadam, KCVO, CBE (d 1974), of Runton Old Hall, Cromer, Norfolk, and Caroline, *née* Corbett; *b* 29 August 1942; *Educ* Eton, Trinity Coll Cambridge (BA), INSEAD Fontainebleau (MBA); *m* 17 Dec 1977, (Alexandra) Camilla, da of Maj Trevor Binny, of Little Wenham Hall, Colchester; 3 s (Harry b 1979, John b 1981, James b 1988); *Career* dir: Kleinwort Benson Ltd 1977-84 (mangr and other positions 1965-77), Baring Bros and Co Ltd 1984-; *Clubs* Brooks's; *Style—* Corbett Macadam, Esq; 23 Redburn St, London SW3; Runton Old Hall, Cromer, Norfolk; Baring Bros & Co Ltd, 8 Bishopsgate, London EC2 (☎ 01 283 8833, telex 883662)

McADAM, Sir Ian William James; OBE (1957); s of William James McAdam; *b* 15 Feb 1917; *Educ* Plumtree Sch Rhodesia, Edinburgh Univ (MB, ChB); *m* 1, 1939 (m dis 1961), Lettice Gibson; 1 s, 2 da; m 2, 1967, Lady (Pamela) Hunt (who previously m as his 1 w Sir David W S Hunt, *qv*, sis of Sir Peter B Medawar, *qv*); *Career* consulting surgn: Uganda 1946-72, Kenya 1962-72; prof of surgery Medical Sch Makerere Univ Coll Uganda 1959-72; conslt Nat Insts of Health (Bethesda, Maryland, USA) 1973-74; FRCS, FRCSE; kt 1966; *Recreations* golf; *Style—* Sir Ian McAdam, OBE; PO Box 166, Plettenberg Bay, Cape Province, 6600 S Africa (☎ 04457 8850); Knysna Hospital, Main Rd, Knysna, Cape Province, SA

MCADAM, Prof Keith Paul William James; s of Sir Ian William James McAdam, OBE, KBE, and (Lettice Margaret) Hrothgaarde, *née* Gibson (now Mrs Bennett); *b* 13 August 1945; *Educ* Prince of Wales Sch Nairobi Kenya, Millfield, Clare Coll Cambridge (MA, MB, BChir), Middx Hosp Med Sch; *m* 27 July 1968, Penelope Ann, da of Rev Gordon Charles Craig Spencer; 3 da (Karen, Ruth, Cheyrl); *Career* house physician and house surgn Middx Hosp London 1969-70; sen house offr appts London: Royal Northern Hosp 1970-71, Brompton Hosp 1971-72, Royal Nat Hosp 1972-73; lectr Inst of Med Res Papua New Guinea 1973-75, med res cncl travellilng fellowship Nat Cancer Inst 1975-76, visiting scientist Nat Inst of Health Bethesda Maryland USA 1976-77, asst prof Tufts Univ Sch of Med Boston USA 1977-81, assoc prof New England Med Centre Boston USA 1982-84, Wellcome prof of tropical medicine London Sch of Hygiene and Tropical Med 1984-, hon physician Hosp for Tropical Diseases Bloomsbury Health Authy 1984-; memb med advsy bds: Br Cncl, Br Leprosy Relief Assoc, Wellcome Trust; chief med offr MRC, expert advsr to House of Commons Soc Servs Ctee enquiry into AIDS 1987; FRSTM 1973, FRCP 1985; *Recreations* cricket, squash, tennis, skiing; *Clubs* MCC; *Style—* Prof Keith McAdam; Oakmead, 70 Luton Lane, Redbourn, Herts AL3 7PY; Dept of Clinical Sciences, London Sch of Hygiene & Tropical Med, Keppel St, London WC1E 7HT (☎ 01 636 8636, fax 01 436 5389, telex 8953474)

MACADAM, Sir Peter; s of Francis Macadam (d 1981), of Buenos Aires, and Marjorie Mary, *née* Browne (d 1984); *b* 9 Sept 1921; *Educ* Buenos Aires Argentina, Stonyhurst Coll Lancs; *m* 1949, Ann, da of Eric Methven Musson; 3 da; *Career* gp chm BAT Industries Ltd 1976-82 (ret, joined gp 1946), dir National Westminster Bank plc 1978-84; chm Libra Bank plc 1984-; pres Hispanic and Luso Brazilian Cncls (Canning House) 1982-87; Hon FBIM, FRSA; kt 1981; *Clubs* Naval & Military; *Style—* Sir Peter Macadam; Layham Hall, Layham, nr Hadleigh, Suffolk IP7 5LE (☎ 0473 822137); Libra Bank plc, 140 London Wall, London EC2

McAFEE, Patrick John; s of John McAfee, and Maud O'Donnell, *née* Lynas (d 1979); *b* 25 May 1940; *Educ* Portora Royal Sch, Trinity Coll Dublin (MA); *m* 2 March 1979, Jane Greer, da of Prof W L J Ryan, of Dublin; 1 da (Clare Jane b 1982); *Career* banker; dir Morgan Grenfell & Co Ltd 1973-; *Recreations* sailing, shooting; *Clubs* Royal St George Yacht; *Style—* Patrick J McAfee, Esq; c/o Morgan Grenfell & Co Ltd, 23 Gt Winchester St, London EC2P 2AX (☎ 01 588 4545)

MCALISTER, Michael Ian; s of S McAlister, CBE (d 1972), of Walton-on-Thames, Surrey, and Jessie Anne, *née* Smith; *b* 23 August 1930; *Educ* St John's Coll Oxford (MA); *m* 1, 4 July 1953 (m dis 1984), (Crystal) Patricia, da of John David Evans (d 1958), of Sao Paulo, Brazil; 4 s (Richard b 1 June 1956, Peter b 5 Dec 1957, Sam b 29 July 1963, James b 17 March 1979), 3 da (Maureen b 9 June 1954, Carolyn b 25 Jan 1960, Emma b 19 May 1972); m 2, 2 June 1984, Elizabeth Anne, da of Louis Hehn, of Hatfield Peverel, Chelmsford, Essex; *Career* Nat Serv Army 1949-51, Acting-Capt Intelligence Corps 1951, (MI8) Austria (BTA 3); articled clerk Price Waterhouse & Co 1954-58, private and fin sec HRH Duke of Windsor KG 1959-61, md Ionian Bank Tstee Co 1961-69, chm Slater Walker Securities (Australia) 1969-72, pres Australian Stock Exchanges 1972-75, Knight Int plc Chicago 1975-78, corporate planning dir Cluff Resources plc 1979-; chm Woking Cons Assoc 1967-68; ACA 1959, FCA 1969; *Recreations* carpentry, DIY, travel; *Clubs* RAC; *Style—* Michael McAlister, Esq; c/o Cluff Resources plc, 58 St James St, London SW1A 1LD (☎ 01 493 8272, fax 01 493 6791, telex 24352)

McALISTER, Maj-Gen Ronald William Lorne; CB (1977), OBE (1968, MBE 1958); s of Col Ronald James Frier McAlister, OBE (d 1963), of Edinburgh, and Mrs Nora Ford Collins, *née* Prosser; *b* 26 May 1923; *Educ* Sedbergh; *m* 25 Jan 1964, Sally Ewart, da of Dr Gordon King Marshall (d 1974), of Broadstairs, Kent; 2 da (Angela Frances b 15 May 1965, Caroline Jane b 14 Sept 1966); *Career* OCTU Bangladore 1942, cmmnd QAO Gurkha Rifles 1942, Adj 1/3 Gurkha Rifles Burma 1945 (despatches), 10 Gurkha Rifles 1948, Adj 2/10 Gurkha Rifles 1949-52 (despatches), instr Sch of Infantry Warminster 1952-55, Staff Coll 1962, asst sec Chiefs of Staff Ctee MOD 1962-65; CO 1/10 Gurkha Rifles: Borneo 1966 (despatches), Hong Kong 1967; instr Jr Servs Staff Coll 1968, CO Berlin Infantry Bde 1968-71, Canadian Nat Def Coll 1971-72, exercise controller to UK Cs-in-C 1972-74, Maj Gen Bde of Gurkhas and Dep Cdr Hong Kong Land Forces 1975-77, ret 1977; bursar Wellesley House Prep Sch Broadstairs 1977-88, chm Buckmaster Memorial Home for Ladies Broadstairs 1983-, capt Royal St Georges GC Sandwich 1989; *Books* Bugle and Kukri Vol 2(1986); *Recreations* golf, gardening; *Clubs* Army & Navy, Senior Golfers Soc; *Style—* Maj-Gen Ronald McAlister, CB, OBE; The Chalet, 41 Callis Court Rd, Broadstairs, Kent

McALISTER, William Harle Nelson; s of Flying Offr William Nelson (d 1940), and Marjorie Isobel, *née* McIntyre; *b* 30 August 1940; *Educ* St Edwards Sch Oxford, Univ Coll London (BA); *m* 1968 (m dis 1985), Sarah Elizabeth; 2 s (Daniel b 1969, Benjamin b 1977), 2 da (Leila b 1970, Alix b 1972); *Career* dir Almost Free Theatre 1968-72, dep dir Inter-Action Tst 1968-72, fndr dir Islington Bus Co 1972-77; dir: Battersea Arts Centre 1976-77, Sense of Ireland Festival 1980-; bd dir London Int Theatre

Festival 1983, chm: for the Arts IT 82 Ctee 1982, Recreational Tst 1972-; co-fndr Fair Play for Children 1974-75, advsr Task Force Tst 1972-74; tstee: Circle 33 Housing Tst 1972-75, Moving Picture Mime Tst 1978-80, Shape (Arts for the Disadvantaged) 1979-81; govr Holloway Adult Educn Inst 1974-76; memb: ct RCA 1980-, Br Delgn to Ministerial Conference on cultural policy Bulgaria 1980, Br Cultural Delgn China 1982; *Books* Community Psychology (1975), EEC and the Arts (1978); articles on arts policy; *Recreations* angling, tennis, travel; *Style—* William McAlister, Esq; 151c Grosvenor Ave, London N5 (☎ 01 226 0205); Institute of Contemporary Arts, Nash House, The Mall, London SW1 (☎ 01 930 0493)

McALLISTER, John Brian; s of Thomas McAllister (d 1979), and Jane, *née* McCloughan; *b* 11 June 1941; *Educ* Royal Belfast Academical Instn, Queen's Univ Belfast (BA); *m* 1966, Margaret Lindsay, da of William Walker (d 1964), of Belfast; 2 da (Lynne b 1970, Barbara b 1972); *Career* civil servant 1964; asst princ Dept of Educn (NI) 1968 (dep princ 1969, princ 1971), princ NI Info Serv 1973, asst sec Dept of Educn (NI) 1976, sr asst sec Dept of Educn (NI) 1978 (dep sec 1980), dep sec Dept of Finance (NI) 1983, under sec Dept of Environment (NI) 1985, dep chief exec Industrial Dvpt Bd NI 1985 (chief exec 1986); *Recreations* family holidays, watching sport; *Clubs* NI Civil Serv; *Style—* John McAllister, Esq; c/o Industrial Devpt Bd for NI, IDB House, 64 Chichester St, Belfast, Northern Ireland BT1 4JX (☎ 0232 233233, telex 747025)

McALPINE, (Robert Douglas) Christopher; CMG (1967); s of Dr Archibald Douglas McAlpine, MBE, FRCP (d 1981), and Elizabeth Meg, *née* Sidebottom (d 1941); *b* 14 June 1919; *Educ* Winchester, New Coll Oxford (MA); *m* 4 Dec 1943, Helen Margery Frances, da of Capt Astley Cannan(d 1934); 2 s (David b 1949, Robert b 1953), 2 da (Christine b 1944 (d 1944), Sarah b 1946); *Career* WWII cmmnd midshipman RNVR 1939, fighter pilot Fleet Air Arm 1941-44, demobbed as temp Lt 1946; Dip Serv 1946-69: FO 1946-47, asst private sec to Sec of State 1947-49, second sec (later first sec) Bonn High Commn 1949-52, FO 1952-54, Lima 1954-56, Moscow 1956-59, FO 1959-62, dep consul gen and cnsllr NYC 1962-65, cnsllr Mexico City 1965-69; ptnr and dir Baring Bros & co Ltd 1969-79, non exec dir Horace Clarkson plc 1980-87; chm Tetbury branch: Royal Br Legion, RNLI; cncllr Tetbury Town Cncl 1987-; Cdr Peruvian Order of Merit; *Recreations* sailing, tennis, golf; *Clubs* United Oxford & Cambridge Univ; *Style—* Christopher McAlpine, Esq, CMG

McALPINE, Hon David Malcolm; s of Baron McAlpine of Moffat (Life Peer); *b* 1946; *m* 1971, Jennifer Anne, da of Eric Hodges, of Chart Cottage, Fawley Green, Henley-on-Thames; 1 s, 2 da; *Career* dir Sir Robert McAlpine & Sons; *Style—* The Hon David McAlpine

McALPINE, Lady; Kathleen Mary; late da of Frederick Best; *m* 1, Charles Bantock Blackshaw; m 2, 1965, as his 2 w, Sir Thomas McAlpine, 4 Bt (d 1983; *see* McAlpine of Moffat, Baron); *Style—* Lady McAlpine; The Manor House, Stanford-in-the-Vale, nr Faringdon, Oxon

McALPINE, Kenneth; DL (Kent 1976); s of Sir Thomas Malcolm McAlpine, KBE (d 1967), and Maud Dees (d 1969); *b* 21 Sept 1920; *Educ* Charterhouse; *m* 1955, Patricia Mary, da of Capt Francis William Hugh Jeans, CVO, RN (d 1968); 2 s; *Career* Flying Offr RAFVR; dir: Newarthill Ltd, Sir Robert McAlpine & Sons Ltd; High Sheriff Kent 1973-74; govr Royal Hosp of St Bartholomew 1972-74; owner Lamberhurst Vineyards; FRAeS; *Clubs* Royal Yacht Sqdn, Air Squadron; *Style—* Kenneth McAlpine Esq, DL; The Priory, Lamberhurst, Kent TN3 8DS

McALPINE, Hon Mary Jane; da of Baron McAlpine of West Green (Life Peer), *qv*, by his 1 w, Sarah Alexandra, da of Paul Hillman Baron (decd); *b* 1965; *Style—* The Hon Mary McAlpine

McALPINE, Sir Robin; CBE (1957); assumed forename of Robin in lieu of Robert by deed poll 1939; s of Sir (Thomas) Malcolm McAlpine, KBE (d 1967); *b* 18 Mar 1906; *Educ* Charterhouse; *m* 1, 1939, Nora Constance Perse (d 1966); m 2, 1970, Mrs Philippa Nicolson (d 1987), da of Sir Gervais Tennyson D'Eyncourt, 2 Bt (d 1971); *Career* chm: Sir Robert McAlpine & Sons (civil engrs) 1967-77, Newarthill Ltd 1972-77; pres Fedn of Civil Engrg Contractors 1966-71; racehorse breeder; kt 1969; *Style—* Sir Robin McAlpine, CBE; Aylesfield, Alton, Hants; 40 Bernard St, London WC1N 1LG

McALPINE, Hon Victoria Alice; da of Baron McAlpine of West Green (Life Peer), *qv*, by his 1 w, Sarah Alexandra, da of late Paul Hillman Baron; *b* 1967; *Style—* The Hon Victoria McAlpine

McALPINE, Hon William Hepburn; eld s of Baron McAlpine of Moffat (Life Peer) and the late Ella Mary Gardner; heir to father's Baronetcy; *b* 12 Jan 1936; *Educ* Charterhouse; *m* 1959, Jill Benton, da of Lt-Col Sir Peter Fawcett Benton Jones, 3 Bt, OBE (d 1972); 1 s (Andrew), 1 da (Lucinda); *Career* Life Guards 1954-56; dir: Sir Robert McAlpine & Sons Ltd 1959-, Newarthill plc 1977-, Turner & Newall plc 1983-; chm Railway Heritage Tst 1985-; FRCE, FCIT; *Recreations* railway and transport preservation, horse racing; *Clubs* Garrick, Caledonian; *Style—* The Hon William McAlpine; Fawley Hill, Fawley Green, Henley-on-Thames RG9 6JA (☎ 0491 571373); 40 Bernard St, London WC1N 1LG (☎ 01 837 3377, telex 22308); 10 Kinnerton Yard SW1

McALPINE OF MOFFAT, Baron (Life Peer UK 1979), of Medmenham in the Co of Buckinghamshire; Sir (Robert) Edwin; 5 Bt (UK 1918) of Knott Park, Co Surrey; s of William Hepburn McAlpine (d 1951); suc to Baronetcy of bro, Sir Thomas McAlpine (d 1983); *b* 23 April 1907; *Educ* Oundle; *m* 1, 1930, Ella Mary Gardner (d 1987), da of James Garnett, formerly of Vancouver; 3 s, 1 da; m 2, 15 Jan 1988, Mrs Nancy Hooper, wid of Robert Hooper; *Heir* (to Baronetcy only) s, Hon William McAlpine; *Career* sits as a Conservative in House of Lords; ptnr Sir Robert McAlpine & Sons Ltd 1928-, chm Greycoat London Estates 1978-; kt 1963; *Clubs* Garrick, Buck's, Caledonian, Jockey; *Style—* The Rt Hon the Lord McAlpine of Moffat; Benhams, Fawley Green, nr Henley-on-Thames, Oxon; office: 40 Bernard St, London WC1N 1LG (☎ 01 837 3377)

McALPINE OF WEST GREEN, Baron (Life Peer UK 1984), of West Green in the Co of Hampshire; Hon (Robert) Alistair; s of Baron McAlpine of Moffat (Life Peer), *qv*; *b* 14 May 1942; *Educ* Stowe; *m* 1, 1964 (m dis 1979), Sarah Alexandra, da of Paul Hillman Baron; 2 da; m 2, 1980, Romilly, o da of A T Hobbs, of Cranleigh, Surrey; 1 da (Skye b 1984); *Career* joined Sir Robert McAlpine & Sons Ltd 1958, dir George Weidenfeld Holdings Ltd 1975-83; vice pres: Friends of Ashmolean Museum 1969-, Gtr London Arts Assoc 1971-77, Euro League of Econ Cooperation 1975- (tres 1975-75); tres Euro Democratic Union 1978-; dir: ICA 1972-73, Theatre Investmt Fund 1981- (chm 1985-); vice chm Contemporary Arts Soc 1973-80; memb: Arts Cncl of GB 1981-82, Friends of V and A Museum 1976-, cncl British Stage Co 1973-75; tstee Royal Opera House Tst 1974-80; govr: Polytechnic of the South Bank 1981-82, Stowe Sch 1981-84; *Recreations* the arts, horticulture, aviculture, agriculture; *Clubs* Garrick, Carlton, Buck's, Beefsteak, Pratts, Weld (Perth, W Aust); *Style—* The Rt Hon the Lord McAlpine of West Green; West Green House, Hartley Wintney, nr Basingstoke, Hants

MacANDREW, Hon Christopher Anthony Colin; s and h of 2 Baron MacAndrew; *b* 16 Feb 1945; *Educ* Malvern; *m* 1975, Sarah Helen, da of Lt-Col Peter Hendy Brazier, of Nash Ct Farmhouse, Marnhull, Dorset; 1 s, 2 da; *Style—* Hon Christopher MacAndrew; Hall Farm, Archdeacon Newton, Darlington (☎ Darlington 462246)

MacANDREW, 2 Baron (UK 1959); Colin Nevil Glen MacAndrew; s of 1 Baron MacAndrew, TD, PC (d 1979), and his 1 wife, Lilian Cathleen, *née* Curran; *b* 1 August 1919; *Educ* Eton, Trinity Coll Cambridge; *m* 15 Sept 1943, Ursula Beatrice, yr da of Capt Joseph Steel, of Kirkwood, Lockerbie, Dumfriesshire; 2 s, 1 da; *Heir* s, Hon Christopher Anthony Colin MacAndrew; *Career* serv WWII; *Style—* The Rt Hon Lord MacAndrew; Dilston House, Aldborough St John, Richmond, Yorks (☎ 032 754 272)

MacANDREW, Hon Nicholas Rupert; s of 2 Baron MacAndrew; *b* 12 Feb 1947; *Educ* Eton; *m* 1975, Victoria Rose, da of George Patrick Renton, of Isington Close, Alton, Hants; 1 s, 2 da; *Style—* Hon Nicholas MacAndrew; The Old Chapel, Greywell, Odiham, Hampshire RG25 1BS (☎ 025671 2390)

McANDREW, Nicolas; s of Robert Louis McAndrew; *b* 9 Dec 1934; *Educ* Winchester Coll; *m* 1960, Diana Leonie, *née* Wood; 3 children; *Career* Capt Black Watch (Army) Kenya 1954-55, memb of the Inst of Chartered Accountants of Scotland since 1962; md NM Rothschild & Sons; *Recreations* shooting, fishing, golf, skiing; *Clubs* City of London, Swinley Forest Golf; *Style—* Nicolas McAndrew Esq; The Worthys, Martyr Worthy, Winchester, Hants (☎ (0962) 882149); 36 Fabian Rd, London SW6 (☎ 01 381 1924; off: 01 280 5401)

MACARA, Sir (Charles) Douglas; 3 Bt (UK 1911), of Ardmore, St Anne-on-the-Sea, Co Lancaster; s of Sir William Cowper Macara, 2 Bt (d 1931), and Lilian Mary, *née* Chapman (d 1971); *b* 19 April 1904; *Educ* Fettes; *m* 20 Nov 1925 (m dis 1945), Quenilda Mary, da of late Herbert Whitworth, of St Anne's-on-Sea, Lancs; 1 s (decd); 2 da; *Heir* bro, Hugh Kenneth Macara; *Style—* Sir Douglas Macara, Bt

McARDLE, Carrie Burnett; s of Denis James McArdle, of Lake Cottage, Rake Manor, Milford, Surrey, and Kathleen Burnett; *b* 7 June 1957; *Educ* St Catherines Sch, Bramley, Surrey; *Career* editor Promotions, Over 21 Magazine 1979-; assoc editor Living Magazine 1983-, dep editor Woman's Journal 1987-; *Recreations* reading, writing, walking, entertaining; *Style—* Carrie McArdle; 19 Dale Street, Chiswick, London WL1; Woman's Journal, IPC Magazines, Kings Reach Tower, Stamford Street, London SE1

McARDLE, Rear-Adm Stanley Lawrence; CB (1975), LVO (1952), GM (1953), JP (Wilts 1977); *b* 1922; *m* 1, 1945, Joyce, *née* Cummins; 1 da; m 2, 1962, Jennifer, *née* Goddard; 1 da; *Career* joined RN 1939, served WW II, Capt 1963, Rear-Adm 1972, Flag Offr Porstmouth 1973-75, ret 1973; *Recreations* sailing; *Style—* Rear-Adm Stanley McArdle, CB, LVO, GM, JP; Barn Ridge Cottage, Farley, Salisbury, Wilts

MACARTHUR, Brian Roger; s of S H MacArthur (d 1971), of Ellesmere Port, Cheshire and Marjorie; *b* 5 Feb 1940; *Educ* Brentwood Sch, Helsby GS, Leeds Univ (BA MA (hon open); *m* 22 Aug 1975, Bridget da of Nicholas Rosevear Trahair of The Croft, South Milton, Kingsbridge, South Devon; 2 da (Tessa b 1976, Georgina b 1979); *Career* educn correspondent The Times 1967-70, ed The Times Higher Educ Supplement, 1971-76, exec ed The Time 1981-82, dep ed The Sunday Times 1982-84; ed: The Western Morning News 1984-85, Today 1985-86; exec ed Sunday Times 1987-; *Recreations* family, gardening, reading; *Clubs* Garrick; *Style—* Brian MacArthur, Esq; 50 Lanchester Road, London N6 4TA (☎ 01 883 1855); The Sunday Times, PO Box 481, Virginia Street, London E1 9BD (☎ 01 822 9801, fax: 822-9658)

MacARTHUR, Ian; OBE (1988); s of Lt-Gen Sir William MacArthur, KCB, DSO, MD, DSc, FRCP, KHP (d 1964), and Marie Eugénie Thérèse, *née* Antelme; *b* 17 May 1925; *Educ* Cheltenham, Queen's Coll Oxford (MA); *m* 1957, Judith Mary, da of Francis Gavin Douglas Miller (d 1955); 4 s (Niall, Duncan, Ruaidhri, Gavin), 3 da (Jane, Anne, Lucy); *Career* serv with RN and RNVR 1943-46, Ordinary Seaman RN 1943, Lt RNVR 1946; MP (C) Perth and E Perthshire 1959-74; lord cmmr of the Treasy and Govt, scottish whip 1963-64; oppn scottish whip 1964-65; oppn spokesman on Scottish Affrs 1965-70; oppn front bench 1965-66 and 1969-70; vice-chm Cons Pty in Scotland 1972-75; dir Br Textile Confedn 1977-89; former dir of admin J Walter Thompson Co Ltd; FRSA; Gold Cross of Merit Polish Govt in exile 1971; King's Badge 1944; *Clubs* Naval, Puffin's (Edinburgh); *Style—* Ian MacArthur, Esq, OBE; 15 Old Palace Lane, Richmond, Surrey; 24 Buckingham Gate, London SW1

McARTHUR, Dr Thomas Burns (Tom); s of Archibald McArthur (d 1967), of Glasgow, and Margaret Dymock Dow, *née* Burns (d 1986); *b* 23 August 1938; *Educ* Woodside Secdy Sch Glasgow, Univ of Glasgow (MA), Univ of Edinburgh (MLitt, PhD); *m* 30 March 1963, Fereshteh, da of Habib Mottahedin, of Teheran, Iran; 1 s (Alan b 30 April 1970), 2 da (Meher b 11 Nov 1966, Roshan b 16 Nov 1968); *Career* 2 Lt Offr Instr RAEC 1959-62; educn offr: Depot the Royal Warwickshire Regt, Depot the Mercian Bde; asst teacher Riland-Bedford Boys HS Sutton Coldfield Warwicks 1962-64, head of eng dept Cathedral and John Cannon Sch Bombay India 1965-67, visiting prof Bharatiya Vidya Bhavan Univ of Bombay 1965-67, dir of studies Extra Mural Eng Language Courses Univ of Edinburgh 1972-79, assoc prof of eng Université du Québec à Trois - Rivières Quebec Canada 1979-83; editor: English Today: The International Review of the English Language 1984-, The Oxford Companion to the English Language 1987-; conslt to: Collins, Longman, Chambers, Cambridge Univ Press, WHO, Henson Int TV (the Muppets), Govt of Quebec, Century Hutchinson, Oxford Univ Press; fndr memb and tutor Birmingham Yoga Club 1963, schs lectr and pres offr Bombay Soc of Prevention of Cruelty to Animals (BSPCA) 1965-67, chm Scottish Yoga Assoc 1977-79, co-chm Scots Language Planning Ctee 1978, memb editorial bd International Journal of Lexicography 1988-, numerous broadcasts BBC Eng by Radio (World Serv); *Books* Building English Words (1972), Using English Prefixes and Suffixes (1972), Using Compound Words (1972), A Rapid Course in English for Students of Economics (1973), Using Phrasal Verbs (1973), Collins Dictionary of English Phrasal Verbs and Their Idioms (with Beryl T Atkins 1974), Learning Rhythm and Stress (with Mohamed Heliel 1974), Using Modal Verbs (with Richard Wakely 1974), Times, Tenses and Conditions (with John Hughes 1974),

Languages of Scotland (co-ed with A J Aitken 1979), Longman Lexicon of Contemporary English (1981), A Foundation Course for Language Teachers (1983), The Written Word: A Course in Controlled Composition (books 1 and 2 1984), Worlds of Reference: Lexicography, Learning and Language from the Clay Tablet to the Computer (1986), Understanding Yoga: A Thematic Companion to Yoga and Indian Philosophy (1986), Yoga and the Bhagavad-Gita (1986), Unitive Thinking: A Guide to Developing a More Integrated and Effective Mind (1988); *Recreations* reading, television, walking, cycling, travel; *Style—* Dr Tom McArthur; 22-23 Ventress Farm Court, Cherry Hinton Road, Cambridge CB1 4HD (☎ 0223 245934)

MACARTNEY, Sir John Barrington; 6 Bt (I 1799), of Lish, Armagh; s of John Barrington Macartney d 1951, and Selina, *née* Koch; and nephew of 5 Bt (d 1960); *b* 1917; *m* 1944, Amy Isobel Reinke; 1 s; *Heir* s, John Ralph Macartney *qv*; *Career* dairy farmer; *Style—* Sir John Macartney, Bt; 37 Meadow St, North Mackay, Queensland 4740, Australia

MACARTNEY, John Ralph; s and h of Sir John Barrington Macartney, 6 Bt; *b* 1945; *m* 1966, Suzanne Marie Fowler, of Nowra, NSW; 4 da; *Career* Petty Officer RAN (ret); teacher (head of dept) ACT Inst of TAFE; *Style—* John Macartney Esq; PO Box 589, Quean Beyan, NSW 2620, Australia

MACASKILL, John Harry; s of John Macaskill (d 1981), and Nancy Love, *née* Mills (d 1963); *b* 13 Feb 1947; *Educ* Oundle, Nottingham Univ (BA); *m* 11 May 1974, Gwyneth June, da of Ralph Herbert Keith Evers, of Four Winds, Westward Ho, N Devon; 3 s (James b 6 Sept 1979, Robert b 1 Oct 1981, Sandy b 9 May 1985); *Career* ptnr Slaughter and May 1979- (articled clerk 1970-72, slr 1972-79); Freeman City of London 1985, Liveryman The Solicitor's Co 1985; memb Law Soc 1972; *Recreations* walking, gardening, sheep dog trials; *Clubs* City Livery; *Style—* John H Macaskill, Esq; 35 Basinghall St, London EC2V 5DB (☎ 01 600 1200, fax 01 726 0038, telex 883486)

MACASKILL, Ronald Angus; s of Angus Duncan Macaskill, and Elsie Broadbridge, *née* Tosh; *b* 21 April 1947; *Educ* King's College Sch Wimbledon, King's Coll Univ of London (BSc AKC), The City Univ (MSc); *m* 6 Aug 1977, Irmgard Elisabeth, da of Heinrich Matthias Hinterstein, of Poysdorf, Austria; 2 da (Elisabeth Ann b 6 Aug 1981, Alexandra Jane b 15 Apr 83); *Career* mktg exec: Dynamit Nobel (UK) Ltd 1969-71, Macaskill Gp 1971- (dir 1975-); memb: ctee local branch World Ship Soc, Admiralty Ferry Crew Assoc, ctee Mitcham Job Concern, Farringdon Ward Club; vice pres Rotary Club of Mitcham; Freeman of the City of London 1978, Liveryman Worshipful Co of Blacksmiths 1978 (sec Craft ctee 1987-); MBIM 1970, FInst SMM 1979; *Recreations* skiing, swimming, ship modelling, photography; *Clubs* City Livery; *Style—* Ronald Macaskill, Esq; 41 The Gallop, Sutton, Surrey SM2 5RY (☎ 01 643 7743); Macaskill Engineering Ltd, Forval Close, Mitcham, Surrey CR4 4NE (☎ 01 640 7211, fax 01 640 9411, telex 885721 ASKMAC)

MACAULAY, Anthony Dennis; s of Dennis Macaulay, of Wakefield, W Yorks, and Frances, *née* Frain; *b* 15 Nov 1948; *Educ* Queen Elizabeth GS Wakefield, Keble Coll Oxford; *m* 8 Oct 1978, Dominica Francisca, da of Dr Henri Compernolle, of Bruges, Belgium; 1 s (Thomas b 29 March 1985), 2 da (Laura b 20 April 1983, Rosemary b 4 Oct 1987); *Career* articled clerk/slr Biddle & Co 1971-75, asst slr Wilkinson Kimbers & Staddon 1975-77, ptnr Herbert Smith 1983- (asst slr 1977-83) sec to Panel on Take-overs and Mergers 1983-85; chm Tudor Branch Finchley and Friern Barnet Con Assoc 1977-83, memb Law Soc; memb Worshipful Co of Slrs 1987; *Books* Take-Overs, Mergers and Acquisitions For Butterworths Handbook of UK Corporate Finance (1988); *Recreations* tennis, skiing, music, cooking, family; *Clubs* Cumberland LTC; *Style—* Anthony Macaulay, Esq; Watling House, 35 Cannon St, London EC4M 5SD (☎ 01 489 8000, fax 01 329 0426, telex 886633)

MACAULAY, Lady Marjorie Slinger; *née* Gill; *m* 1930, Sir Hamilton Macaulay, CBE (d 1986); 1 da; *Style—* Lady Macaulay; The Cottage, Harpers Rd, Ash, Surrey (☎ (0252) 26721)

McAULAY, (John) Roy Vincent; QC (1978); Dr John McAulay, of West Wickham, Kent and Marty, *née* Kuni; *b* 9 Sept 1933; *Educ* Whitgift Sch, Queens' Coll Cambridge (MA); *m* 1970, Ruth Kathleen, da of Alexander Smith, of Sevenoaks Kent; 1 s (Gavin b 1972), 1 da (Charlotte b 1975); *Career* recorder 1975, legal assessor to General Medical Council; *Style—* Roy McAulay, Esq, QC; 5 Montpelier Row, Blackheath, London SE3; office: 1 Harcourt Buildings, Temple, London EC4

MACAULAY OF BRAGAR, Baron (Life Peer 1989), of Bragar, Co Ross and Cromarty; Donald Macaulay

MACAULEY, Hon Mrs; Diana Phyllis; *née* Berry; yst da of 1 Viscount Camrose (d 1954), and Mary Agnes, *née* Corns (d 1962); *b* 1924; *m* 7 April 1948, William Perine Macauley, s of late Timothy Alfred Macauley, of Montreal, Canada; 3 s, 3 da; *Style—* Hon Mrs Macauley; Ballyward House, Blessington, Co Wicklow

McAULIFFE, Thomas Vincent; s of William McAuliffe (d 1940); *b* 19 July 1935; *Educ* Presentation Brothers Coll Cork; *m* 1959, Audrey Ann, da of Robert Malyon; 2 s; *Career* chm: Argos Distributors Ltd 1979-82, Modern Merchandise Ltd; *Recreations* golf, rugby; *Clubs* Harpenden Common Golf, Porters Park Golf; *Style—* Thomas McAuliffe, Esq; Modern Merchandise Ltd, Bennett House, 1 High St, Edgware, Middx (☎ 01 951 0311, telex 917791 MODERN); Glenanaar, 15 West Common Grove, Harpenden, Herts (☎ 058 27 64777)

McAVOY, Sir (Francis) Joseph; CBE (1969); s of William Henry McAvoy (d 1930), and Hanorah Catherine, *née* McGrath (d 1934); *b* 26 Feb 1910; *Educ* Good Samaritan Convent Innisfail, St Joseph's Coll Qld, Nudgee Coll; *m* 1936, Mary Irene, da of James Henry Doolan, of Bowen, Q'land, Aust; 4 s (Joseph, Vincent, William, Michael), 1 da (Mary); *Career* Nudgee Capt of 1st XV, XI, IV (tennis) 1929; Innisfail Dist Cane Growers Exec 1949-82, Qld Cane Growers Cncl 1952-82 (chm 1963-82) pres Nat Farmers Union 1966-68, vice-pres Int Fedn Agric Producers 1972-75, Nat Farmers rep on Aust Immigration Advsy Cncl 1964-72, memb Aust Metric Conv Bd 1970-78; landowner; kt 1976; *Recreations* lawn bowls; *Clubs* Innisfail Rotary (life memb), Innisfail 5th Johnstone, East Brisbane Bowls; *Style—* Sir Joseph McAvoy, CBE; PO Box 95, Innisfail, Qld 4860, Australia (☎ 070 633724)

McAVOY, Thomas McLaughlin; MP (Lab and Co-op) Glasgow Rutherglen 1987-; D of Edward McAvoy (d 1985), and Frances McLaughlin McAvoy (d 1982); *b* 14 Dec 1943; *Educ* St Columbkilles PS and Jr Secdy Sch; *m* 1968, Eleanor Kerr, da of William Kerr, of 21 Burnhill St, Rutherglen, Glasgow; 4 s (Thomas b 1969, Michael b 1971, Steven b 1974, Brian b 1981); *Career* regnl cncllr Strathclyde 1982-87; *Style—* T M McAvoy, Esq, MP; 82 Snaefell Ave, Burnside, Rutherglen, Glasgow (☎ 01 219 5009)

McBAIN OF McBAIN, James Hughston; chief of Clan McBain; his father was recognised as chief by Lord Lyon 1959; s of Hughston Maynard McBain of McBain (d 1984), and Margaret, *née* Keith; *b* 1928; *m* Margaret, *née* Stephenson; *Style—* James McBain of McBain; 7025 North Finger Rock Place, Tucson, Arizona, USA

McBEAN, Angus Rowland; s of Clement Phillip James George McBean (d 1920), and Irene Sara, *née* Thomas; gf William McBean walked barefoot from Inverness to Abertillary, Monmouthshire, where he later became Mayor, and built up a prosperous coal mining centre - now virtually defunct; *b* 8 June 1904; *Educ* Monmouth GS; *m* May 1925, Helina Wood; *Career* free-lance photographer; has held exhibitions all over the world; *Books* Angus McBean (1982), Masters of Photography (1985); *Recreations* photography, antique collecting, interior decorating; *Style—* Angus McBean, Esq; Flemings, High Street, Debenham, Suffolk (☎ 0728 860422)

MacBEAN, Dr Ian Grant; CBE (1986); s of William Charles MacBean (d 1977) and Isabel Clara *née* Haro; *b* 30 Sept 1931; *Educ* Highgate Sch, Imperial Coll London (PhD, BSc, DIC, ACGI); *m* 28 July 1956, Joan Annie, da of George Rowell of Alton Hants; 3 da (Diane b 1961, Valerie b 1963, Judith b 1968); *Career* md GEC-Marconi Ltd; FEng, FIEE, CEng; *Recreations* golf, gardening, bridge, DIY; *Style—* Ian MacBean Esq, CBE; GEC-Marconi Ltd, The Grove, Stanmore, Middx (☎ 01 954 2311)

McBEATH, Hon Mrs; Janet Mary; *née* Blades; da of 1 Baron Ebbisham, GBE (d 1953); *b* 1916; *m* 1952, Rear Adm John Edwin Home McBeath, CB, DSO, DSC, DL (d 1982); 1 s, 1 da; *Style—* The Hon Mrs McBeath; Woodbury, 9 Annandale Dr, Lower Bourne, Farnham, Surrey GU10 3JD

MACBETH, George Mann; s of George MacBeth, and Amelia Morton Mary, *née* Mann; *Educ* New Coll Oxford; *m* 1, 1955 (m dis 1975), Elizabeth Browell, *née* Robson; m 2, 1982, Lisa St Aubin de Téran;15; *Career* BBC 1955-76: prodr overseas talks dept 1957, prodr talks dept 1958; ed: Poets Voice 1958-65, New Comment 1959-64, Poetry Now 1965-76; Geoffrey Faber Memorial Award (jointly) 1964, Cholmondly Award, (jointly) 1977; *Books* Poems: A From of Words (1954), The Broken Places (1963), A Doomsday Book (1965), The Colour of Blood (1967), The Night of Stones (1968), A War Quartet (1969), The Burning Cone (1970), Collected Poems 1968-70 (1971), The Orlando Poems (1971), Shrapnel (1973), A Poets your (1973), In the Hours Waiting For the Blood to Come (1975), Buying a Heart (1978), Poems of Love and Death (1980), Poems from Oby (1982), The Long Darkness (1983), The Cleaver Garden (1986); prose poems: My Scotland (1975), prose: The Transformation (1975), The Samurai (1975), The Survivor (1977), The Seven Witches (1978), The Born Loser (1981), A Kind of Treason (1982), Annu's Book (1983), The Lion of Pescara (1984), Dizzy's Woman (1986), Anthologies The Penguin Book of Sick Verse (1963): (with J Clemo and E Lucie-Smith) Penguin Modern Poets VI (1964), The Penguin Book of Animal Verse (1965), Poetry 1900-1965 (1967), The Penguin Book of Victorian Verse (1968), The Falling Splendour (1970), The Book of Cats (1976), Poetry 1900- 1975 (1980), Poetry for Today (1984): Childrens Books: Jonah and the Lord (1969), The Rectory Mice (1982), The Story of Daniel (1986); autobiography: A Child of the War (1987); *Recreations* japanese swords; *Style—* George MacBeth, Esq; Moyne Pk, nr Tuam, County Galway, Ireland

MacBETH, George Mann; s of Lt George MacBeth (ka 1941), of Broomhill, Sheffield, and Amelia Morton Mary, *née* Mann (d 1948); *b* 19 Jan 1932; *Educ* King Edward VII Sch Sheffield, New Coll Oxford (MA); *m* 1, 6 Aug 1955 (m dis 1975), Prof Elizabeth Browell, *née* Robson; m 2, 1982, Lisa St Aubin de Téran; 1 s (Alexander Morton George b 30 Sept 1982); *Career* author; BBC 1955-76, prodr overseas talks dept 1957, talks dept 1957, talks dept 1958; ed: Poet's Voice 1958-65, New Comment 1959-64, Poetry Now 1965-76; jt awards: Geoffrey Faber Memorial 1964, Cholmondeley 1977; FRSL; *Books* poetry: A Form of Words (1954), The Broken Places (1963), A Doomsday Book (1965), The Colour of Blood (1967), The Night of Stones (1968), The Burning Cone (1970), Collected Poems 1958-70 (1971), Shrapnel (1973), In The Hours Waiting for the Blood to Come (1975), Buying a Heart (1978), Poems of Love and Death (1980), The Long Darkness (1983), The Cleaver Garden (1986); prose: The Transformation (1975), The Samurai (1975), The Survivor (1977), The Seven Witches (1978), The Born Losers (1981), A Kind of Treason (1982), The Lion of Pescara (1984), Dizzy's Woman (1986), A Child of the War (autobiography 1987); children's books: Jonah and the Lord (1969), The Rectory Mice (1982), The Story of Daniel (1986); anthologies: The Penguin Book of Sick Verse (with J Clemo and E Lucie-Smith 1963), The Penguin Book of Animal Verse (1965), The Penguin Book of Victorian Verse (1968), The Book of Cats (1976), Poetry for Today (1984); *Recreations* collecting Japanese swords; *Clubs* London Library; *Style—* George MacBeth, Esq; Moyne Park, nr Tuam, Co Galway, Ireland; c/o Giles Gordon, Anthony Sheil Assoc, 43 Doughty St, London WC1N 2LE (☎ 01 405 9351)

McBRATNEY, George; s of George McBratney (d 1977), of Comber, Co Down, NI, and Sarah Jane, *née* Bailie (d 1965); *b* 5 May 1927; *Educ* Coll of Technol Belfast, Northampton Coll for Advanced Technol, London Univ (BSc), Queen's Univ Belfast (DipEd); *m* 5 Aug 1949, Margaret Rose Patricia (Trissie), da of the late John Robinson, of Melbourne, Aust; 1 s (Stephen George b 15 Aug 1954); *Career* apprentice fitter/draughtsman Harland and Wolff 1943-47, teacher Comber Trades Prep Sch 1947-54, princ Coll of Technol Belfast 1984- (lectr and sr lectr 1954-67, asst to princ 1967-69, vice princ 1969-84); memb: NI Manpower Cncl, cncl Lambeg Industl Res Assoc, Business and Technician Educn Cncl (London), cncl NI branch IME; memb: CEng, FIMechE 1971; *Books* Mechanical Engineering Experiments (with W R Mitchell vols I and II 1962, with T G J Moag, vol III 1964), Science for Mechanical Engineering Technicians (with T G J Moag 1966); *Recreations* gardening, reading, charitable work; *Style—* George McBratney, Esq; 16 Glencregagh Drive, Belfast BT6 ONL (☎ 0232 796123); Coll of Technology, Coll Sq East, Belfast (☎ 0232 327244)

McBRIDE, John Carlisle; s of Vice Adm Sir William McBride, KCB, CBE (d 1959), and Juanita, *née* Franco; *b* 11 Mar 1930; *Educ* Radley, RNC Greenwich; *m* Priscilla Reynolds; 2 s (Alexander b 1969, Nathaniel b 1971); *Career* regular cmmn RN 1948-55; mktg dir Sunday Times 1962-66, fndn Media Expenditure Analysis Ltd 1967; md: Hulton Technical Press 1973-82, AGB Publications 1982; dir AGB Research plc; *Style—* John C McBride, Esq; 11 Chalcot Square, London NW1; AGB Publications Ltd, Audit House, Field End Road, Eastcote, Middx (☎ 01 868 4499)

MacCABE, Michael Murray; s of Brian Farmer MacCabe, and Eileen Elizabeth Noel, *née* Hunter (d 1984); *b* 20 Nov 1944; *Educ* Downside, Lincoln Coll Oxford; *m* 8 Aug 1969, Olga Marie (d 1985); 1 s (James Hunter b 1970), 1 da ((Alexandra) Kate b 1973); *Career* admitted slr 1969, managing ptnr Freshfields 1985- (ptnr 1974-)

managing ptnr Freshfields Paris 1981-84, dir Slrs Indemnity Mutual Insur Assoc Ltd 1986-; memb City of London Slrs Co; FRSA; *Recreations* fishing, painting; *Style—* Michael MacCabe, Esq; Freshfields, Whitefriars, Fleet St, London EC4

MacCABE, Patrick Farmer; s of James MacCabe (d 1918), and Katharine, *née* Harwood (d 1967); *b* 26 Jan 1909; *Educ* Christ's Coll Finchley; *Career* WWII cmmnd 7 Gurkha Rifles serv Burma and India 1941-46 (despatches), Staff Coll Quetta 1944, Bde Maj 48 Indian Inf Bde 1945-46; joined John Swire & Sons Ltd and stationed Hong Kong, China, Japan 1935-66; dir Butterfield and Swire (Japan) Ltd 1962-66; *Recreations* gardening, walking, sailing, fishing; *Clubs* Royal Ocean Racing, Hong Kong; *Style—* Patrick F MacCabe, Esq; Mullins' Mead, Donhead St Mary, Shaftesbury, Dorset (☎ 074 788 432)

McCABE, Sarah Frances; *née* McGrath; da of Patrick McGrath (d 1960), and Mary, *née* Murray (d 1926); *b* 28 Feb 1913; *Educ* Notre Dame HS Glasgow, Univ of Glasgow (MA), Univ of Oxford (BLitt); *m* 11 April 1942, Edward McCabe, OBE, s of Edward McCabe (d 1946); 1 da (Mary Margaret b 1948); *Career* criminologist; formerly of the centre for criminological res Univ of Oxford (currently hon assoc memb), memb Parole Bd for Eng and Wales 1981-84, former memb mgmnt ctee inst for judicial admin Univ of Birmingham, memb bd of mgmnt centre for police studies Univ of Exeter, emeritus fell Leverhulme Tst 1985-87; memb: The Howard League, Justice, Br Soc of Criminology; *Recreations* gardening, walking, reading detective stories; *Style—* Mrs Sarah McCabe; 1 Stoke Place, Old Headington, Oxford OX3 9BX (☎ 0865 61659)

McCAFFREY, Sir Tom (Thomas Daniel); s of William P McCaffrey; *b* 20 Feb 1922; *Educ* Hyndland Secdy Sch, St Aloysius Coll Galsgow; *m* 1949, Agnes Campbell Douglas; 2 s, 4 da; *Career* served WWII RAF; Scottish Office 1948-61, chief info offr Home Office 1966-71, press sec 10 Downing St 1971-72, dir Info Servs Home Office 1972-74, head of news dept FCO 1974-76, chief of staff to Rt Hon James Callaghan, MP 1979-80 (his chief press sec when he was PM 1976-79), chief asst to Rt Hon Michael Foot, MP 1980-; kt 1979; *Style—* Sir Tom McCaffrey; Balmaha, The Park, Great Bookham, Surrey (☎ Bookham 54171)

McCALL, Charles James; s of William McCall (d 1947), of Edinburgh, and Kathleen Keith (d 1925); *b* 24 Feb 1907; *Educ* Edinburgh Univ, Edinburgh Coll of Art; *m* 1945, Eloise Jerwood, da of Fred Ward (d 1970), of London; *Career* Capt RE 1940-46; artist; first one-man show Leicester Galleries 1950; other exhibitions incl: Victor Waddington Dublin 1951, Duveen Graham Galleries NY 1955-57, Ash Barn 1965, 1969 and 1973, Klinkoff Montreal 1958-60, Nevill C'bury and Bath 1972, Belgrave Gallery 1975-77, BBC TV 1975, Arts Cncl 1972, Edmonton Art Gallery Canada, Pattersons 1988; pictures collected by: Lord Ezra, Christopher Tugendhat, John Keffer, Mark Sharman, Michael Spicer MP, Sir David Mitchell MP, William Home, HRH Princess Michael of Kent; FRSA, FBA; *Recreations* music, literature, travel; *Style—* Charles McCall, Esq; 1a Caroline Terrace, London SW1W 8JS (☎ 01 730 8737)

McCALL, Christopher Hugh; QC (1987); s of Robin Home McCall, CBE, of Bernina, Northbrook Avenue, Winchester, and Joan Elizabeth, *née* Kingdon; *b* 3 Mar 1944; *Educ* Winchester, Magdalen Coll Oxford (BA); *m* 20 June 1981, Henrietta Francesca, da of Adrian Leslie Sharpe, of Trebetherick, N Cornwall; *Career* barr Lincoln's Inn 1966; second jr counsel to Inland Revenue in Chancery Matters 1977-87, jr counsel to HM Attorney-Gen in Charity Matters 1981-87; jt hon tres Barristers' Benevolent Assoc 1981-86; *Recreations* glass, music, travel; *Clubs* RAC, Leander; *Style—* C H McCall, Esq, QC; 29 Burgh Street, London N1 (☎ 01 226 4702); 7 New Square, Lincoln's Inn, London WC2A 3QS (☎ 01 405 1266)

McCALL, David Slesser; CBE (1988); s of Patrick McCall (d 1987), of Norwich, and Florence Kate Mary, *née* Walker; *b* 3 Dec 1934; *Educ* Robert Gordon Coll Aberdeen, Aberdeen Univ; *m* 6 July 1968, (Lois) Patricia, da of Ernest Lonsdale Elder, FEIS (d 1985), of Glasgow; *Career* Nat Serv RAF 1959-60; accountant Grampian Television Ltd 1961-68; Anglia Television Ltd: co sec 1968-76, dir 1970, chief exec 1976-86; gp chief exec 1986-; gp chief exec Anglia TV Gp plc 1986-, fndr dir Channel Four Television Co Ltd 1981-85; chm Independent Television Assoc 1986-88, dir Br Satellite Broadcasting Ltd 1987-; hon vice-pres Norwich City FC 1988; dir eastern advisory bd Nat Westminster Bank 1988; pres Norfolk & Norwich C of C 1988 (vice pres 1984, dep pres 1986); MICAS 1958, FRTS 1988, CBIM 1988; *Recreations* golf, tennis, skiing, soccer, travel; *Clubs* Norfolk (Norwich); *Style—* David McCall, Esq; Woodland Hall, Redenhall, Harleston, Norfolk IP20 9QW (☎ 0379 854442); Anglia House, Norwich, Norfolk NR1 3JG (☎ 0603 615161, fax 0603 623081, telex 97424, car ☎ 0836 235 285)

McCALL, Hon Mrs; (Gillian Patricia Denman); da of 5 Baron Denman, CBE, MC; *b* 1944; *m* 1971, William K McCall; 2 s, 1 da; *Style—* The Hon Mrs McCall; Upper Old Park Farm, Farnham, Surrey

McCALL, John Armstrong Grice; CMG (1964); s of Rev Canon James George McCall (d 1954), of St Andrews, and Mabel Lovat Armstrong (d 1917); gggs of John McCall of Glasgow, one of fndrs of Thistle Bank in 1761; *b* 7 Jan 1913; *Educ* Glenalmond, St Andrews Univ (MA), Cambridge; *m* 1951, Kathleen Mary, DL (Tweeddale 1987-), da of Arthur Clarke (d 1936); *Career* colonial admin service (HMOCS) Nigeria 1936-67 (Class I 1956, Staff Grade 1958), chm Mid West Nigerian Corpn 1966-67, asst chief admin offr East Kilbride Devpt Corpn 1967-77, Scottish rep Exec Ctee Nigeria Br C of C 1977-88; memb: panel Industl Tribunals (Scotland) 1972-74, central cncl Britain Nigeria Assoc 1983-; gen sec for Scotland Royal Overseas League 1978-80, sec West Linton Community Cncl 1980-83; *Recreations* golf, walking; *Clubs* Caledonian, Royal & Ancient (St Andrews), Royal Overseas League (Hon Life Memb); *Style—* J A G McCall, Esq, CMG; Burnside, W Linton, Scotland EH46 7EW (☎ 0968 60488)

McCALL, John Kingdon; s of Robin Home McCall, CBE, of Winchester, and Joan Elizabeth, *née* Kingdon; *b* 28 July 1938; *Educ* Winchester; *m* 20 April 1963, Anne Margaret, da of Dr Harry Kirby Meller, MBE (d 1965); 2 s (Patrick b 1964, William b 1971), 1 da (Claire b 1966); *Career* slr; ptnr Freshfields 1969-, seconded to head of legal dept The Br National Oil Corpn 1976-79, sr res ptnr Freshfields NY 1983-87, chm Int Bar Assoc's Section on Energy and Natural Resources Law 1988-; memb; Law Soc, Int Bar Assoc; *Recreations* real tennis, road running, sea birds; *Clubs* Racquet and Tennis (NY); *Style—* John K McCall, Esq; Freshfields, Grindall House, 25 Newgate St, London EC1A 7LH (☎ 01 606 6677, fax 01 248 3487)

MCCALL, Sir (Charles) Patrick Home; MBE (1944), TD (1946); s of Charles William Home McCall, CBE (d 1958), and Dorothy Margaret, *née* Kidd; *b* 22 Nov 1910; *Educ* St Edward's Sch Oxford; *m* 1934, Anne, da of late Samuel Brown, of Sedlescombe, Sussex; 2 s, 1 da; *Career* served WWII ADOS SEAC; slr 1936; last clerk of the peace Lancs 1960-71, clerk of the CC 1960-72, clerk of the Lieutenancy Lancs 1960-74; kt 1971; *Recreations* gardening, walking, swimming, travel; *Style—* Sir Patrick McCall, MBE, TD; Auchenhay Lodge, Corsock, by Castle Douglas, Kirkcudbrightshire, Scotland DG7 3HZ (☎ 064 44 651)

McCALL, Robert Henry; s of William McCall (d 1937), and Anna Laurie (d 1937); *b* 15 Nov 1931; *Educ* Woodside Sr Secdy Sch Glasgow; *m* 4 Sept 1954, Grace da of George Robinson (d 1958); 2 s (Laurie Allan b 1956, Roderick Robert (b 1960); *Career* whiskey broker/distiller; dir: Whyte & Mackay Distiller Ltd (parent company), Dalmore Whyte & Mackay Ltd, Whyte & Mackay Ltd, W & S Strong Ltd, Hay & Macleod Ltd, The Tomintoul-Glenlivet Distillery Ltd, Fettercairn Distillery Ltd, Jarvis Halliday & Co Ltd, Lycidas (109); *Recreations* golf, snooker, horse racing; *Clubs* Glasgow Golf; *Style—* Robert McCall, Esq; 20 Herries Road, Glasgow, Scotland G41 4DF (☎ 041 423 4683); Whyte & Mackay Distillers Limited, Dalmore House, 296/298 St Vincent Street, Glasgow G2 5RG (☎ 041 248 5771, fax: 041 221 1993)

McCALL, Robin Home; CBE (1976, OBE 1969); s of Charles William Houe McCall, CBE (d 1958), of Chislehurst, Kent, and Dorothy Margaret, *née* Kidd (d 1966); *b* 21 Mar 1912; *Educ* St Edwards Sch Oxford, Law Soc Sch London; *m* 9 Oct 1937, Joan Elizabeth, da of H F Kingdon (d 1922), of Woking; 2 s (John Kingdon, Christopher Hugh, QC, *qv*), 1 da (Elizabeth, Mrs Peternal Wells, MBE); *Career* RAFVR 1941-46, Sqdn Ldr (D Day Normandy i/c 15083 Night Fighter GC Station), ret 1946; admitted slr 1935, asst slr Bexhill, clerk Hastings and Bristol Corpns, dep Town Club Hastings 1947-48, town clerk of the peace City of Winchester 1948-72; sec AMA 1973-76; memb various govt ctees, govr St Swithuns Sch Winchester 1977-87, memb North Hants Hosp Ctee 1969-72, sole contributor "Local Government" Halsbury Laws of England (4 Edn 1980); Hon Freeman City of Winchester; memb Law Soc; *Recreations* gardens, mountains; *Clubs* Alpine; *Style—* Robin McCall, Esq, CBE; Bernina, Northbrook Ave, Winchester, Hants (☎ 0962 54 101)

McCALL, William; s of Alexander McCall, and Jean Corbet, *née* Cunningham; *b* 6 July 1929; *Educ* Dumfries Acad, Ruskin Coll Oxford; *m* 3 Sept 1955, Olga Helen, da of William Brunton; 1 s (Martin b 1960), 1 da (Ruth b 1957); *Career* civil serv 1946-52, TLIC 1954-58, gen sec Inst of Professional Civil Servants 1963- (asst sec 1958-63), vice chm Civil Serv Nat Whitley Cncl 1983 (memb 1963-), Hon Tres Parly and Sci Ctee 1976-80, memb Ctee of Inquiry into Engrg Profession 1977-79, memb: (pt/t) Eastern Electricity Bd 1977-86, TUC Gen Cncl 1984-, Ct Univ of London 1984-; *Style—* William McCall, Esq; Foothills, Gravel Path, Berkhamstead, Herts HP4 2PF (☎ 0442 864794); Institution of Professional Civil Servants, 75-79 York Road, London SE1 7AQ (☎ 01 928 9951, fax 928 5996, telex 881 4818)

McCALLUM, Anthony Colin; s of Colin McCallum and Serena Enid, *née* Tylden; *b* 8 Mar 1947; *Educ* Radley Coll; *m* 16 June 1972, Lady Charlotte Mary Cathcart, yr da of Maj-Gen 6 Earl Cathcart, CB, DSO, MC, *qv*; 2 s (Charles Colin b 1973, Anthony James b 1977), 1 da (Sophia Charlotte b 1975); *Career* Capt The Queen's Dragoon Gds 1966-76, served Aden, W Germany, Berlin, N Ireland, Argentina; dir CT Bowring Reinsur Ltd 1986; insur broker and underwriter Lloyds; *Style—* Anthony McCallum, Esq; Week Green Farm, Froxfield, Petersfield, Hants; CT Bowring & Co, Tower House, London EC3

McCALLUM, Hon Mrs (Celia Yvonne Lovett); *née* de Villiers; da of Baron de Villiers, of Wynberg, Cape Town, S Africa; *b* 7 Nov 1942; *Educ* Herschel Claremont Cape Town, Univ of Cape Town, Royal Northern Hosp London; *m* 1, 23 March 1968 (m dis), Robin Hastings Sancroft Beck, s of (Harold) Hastings Beck, of St James, SA, and Mrs G G Denoon, of Rondebosch Cape Town, SA; 2 s, 1 da; m 2, 1979, Alan McCullam; 1 da; *Style—* Hon Mrs McCallum

McCALLUM, Lady Charlotte Mary; *née* Cathcart; yr da of 6 Earl Cathcart, CB, DSO, MC, *qv*; *b* 29 Oct 1951; *Educ* Woldingham; *m* 16 June 1972, Anthony Colin McCallum, *qv*; 2 s, 1 da; *Style—* Lady Charlotte McCallum; Week Green Farm, Froxfield, Hants

McCALLUM, (Andrew) Graham Stewart; CBE (1975); s of H G McCallum (d 1975); *b* 1 April 1926; *Educ* Glenalmond, Pembroke Coll Oxford (MA); *m* 1952, Margaret; 2 s, 1 da; *Career* pres John Swire & Sons (Japan) Ltd 1972-78; dir: John Swire & Sons Ltd 1979-88 (advsr 1988-), James Finlay plc 1979-; chm: British C of C in Japan 1975-76, Japan Assoc 1979-; *Recreations* golf, tennis; *Clubs* Royal Ashdown Golf; *Style—* Graham McCallum, Esq, CBE; Medleys Farm, High Hurstwood, nr Uckfield, E Sussex (☎ 082 581 2470); John Swire & Sons Ltd, 59 Buckingham Gate, London SW1

McCALLUM, Prof (Robert) Ian; CBE (1987); s of Charles Hunter McCallum (d 1958), and Janet Lyon, *née* Smith (d 1980); *b* 14 Sept 1920; *Educ* Dulwich, Guy's Hosp and London Univ (MD, DSc); *m* 28 June 1952, Jean Katherine Bundy, da of Sir James Rögnvald Learmonth, KCVO, CBE (d 1967), of Edinburgh; 2 s (James b 1958, Andrew b 1966), 2 da (Helen b 1956, Mary b 1963); *Career* Rockefeller travelling fell USA 1953-54; Univ of Newcastle upon Tyne: reader in industl health 1962-81, prof of occupational health and hygiene 1981-85; conslt Inst of Occupational Med Edinburgh 1985-; chm Decompression Sickness Panel MRC 1982-85 (memb 1962-), ed Br Journal of Industl Med 1972-79, memb Advsy Ctee on Pesticides 1975-87; pres: Soc of Occupational Medicine 1979-80, Br Occupational Hygiene Soc 1983-84; Hon Conslt Br Army 1980-85, dean Faculty of Occupational Med RCP London 1984-86; FRCP London 1970, FFOM 1979, FRCP Edinburgh 1985; *Recreations* gardening; *Clubs* RSM, Edinburgh Univ Staff; *Style—* Prof Ian McCallum; 4 Chessel's Ct, Canongate, Edinburgh EH8 8AD (☎ 031 556 7977); Inst of Occupational Medicine, Roxburgh Place, Edinburgh EH8 9SU (☎ 031 667 5131)

MCCALLUM, Ian Stewart; s of John Blair McCallum (d 1972), and Margaret Stewart, *née* Hannah; *b* 24 Sept 1936; *Educ* Kingston GS; *m* 1, 26 Oct 1957 (m dis 1984), Pamela Mary, da of James Herbert Shave; 1 s (Andrew Stewart b 12 Sept 1958), 2 da (Sheila Anne (Mrs Curling) b 8 July 1960, Heather Jean (Mrs Dury) b 26 June 1963); m 2, 15 Sept 1984, Jean, da of Patrick Wittingstall, of 94 Oakwood Rd, Bricket Wood, Herts; 2 step da (Michelle b 6 Feb 1971, Donna b 8 May 1974); *Career* Highland LI 1954-56; Eagle Star Insur Co Ltd 1953-54 and 1956-58, FE Wright & Co 1958-63, A Clarkson Hume Ltd 1963-68, currently sr sales mangr Save & Prosper Gp Ltd (joined 1968); mayor Woking BC 1976-77 (ldr 1972-76 and 1978-81, dep ldr 1981-84), pres Woking Swimming Club 1977-84, hon vice pres Woking cons AISM 1976-; chm assoc of DCs 1979-84 (ldr 1976-79); vice chm: UK Steering Ctee on Local Authy Superannuation 1974-84, Standing Ctee Local Authorites & the Theatre 1977-81, The Sports Cncl 1980-86; memb: Consultative Cncl on Local Govt Fin 1975-84, Local

Authorites conditions of Serv Advsy Bd 1978-84, cncl for Business & the community 1981-84, Audit Cmmn 1983-86, Health Promotion Res Tst 1983-; LIA; *Recreations* swimming, jogging, walking, reading; *Style—* Ian McCallum, Esq; 5 Minters Orchard, Maidstone Rd, St Marys Platt, nr Sevenoaks, Kent TN15 8QJ (☎ 0732 886 653); Save & Prosper Gp Ltd, Alhambra House, 20 Charing Cross Rd, London WC2H 0AG (☎ 01 930 3275)

McCANCE, (John) Neill; s of Henry Bristow McCance, CBE (d 1977), and Francis May McCance (d 1976); the family has been involved in banking and the linen industry in NI since early eighteenth century; John McCance was MP for Belfast 1835; *b* 6 August 1928; *Educ* Radley, Lincoln Coll Oxford MA; *Career* barr Inner Temple; stockbroker with Vickers da Costa Ltd 1954-86; memb: Stock Exchange 1955, Cncl of Stock Exchange 1982-84 (Cncl's Membership, Settlement Servs and Disciplinary Ctees); dir Worldwide Special Fund NV; dep chm Allside Asset Management Co Ltd 1986; *Recreations* shooting, fishing, travel, music; *Clubs* Brooks's, 1900; *Style—* Neill McCance, Esq; Flat 8, 6 Tedworth Sq, London SW3 4DY; Allside Asset Management Co Ltd, 7 Old Park Lane, London W1Y 3LJ. (☎ 01 629 2714 telex, 295554)

McCANN, Charles Graham; s of Charles McCann, of 25 Dunwan Ave, Glasgow, and Mary, *née* Graham; *b* 19 Sept 1941; *Educ* St Mungo's Acad Glasgow, Glasgow Univ (LLB); *m* 5 Oct 1963, Jacqueline Phillis, da of Maj Montague James Rendel, of West Byfleet, Sussex; 2 da (Pamela Margaret b 1969, Penelope Sue b 1971); *Career* slr, procurator fiscal depute in Kilmarnock 1976-78, previously immigration offr with Home Office; *Recreations* numismatics (recognised expert in Scottish coins); *Clubs* London Scottish (serving memb 1960-63); *Style—* Charles McCann, Esq; Shoreham, Bellevue Rd, Prestwick (☎ 75628); McCann Graha, Slrs, 6 Portland Rd, Kilmarnock (☎ 20328)

McCANN, Christopher Conor; s of Noel McCann, and Katharine Joan, *née* Sultzberger; *b* 26 June 1947; *Educ* Downside, Clare Coll Cambridge (MA); *m* 1 June 1974, Merlyn Clare Winbolt, da of Dr Francis Lewis, of Osborne House, Falloden Way, Bristol; 1 s (Edward), 2 da (Kate, Eleanor); *Career* Price Waterhouse and Co 1969-73, asst dir Barclays Merchant Bank 1973-82, sr vice-pres Barclays Bank plc NY 1983-87; dir: County Natwest Ventures Ltd 1987-, County Natwest Ltd 1987-; non exec dir: Aynsley Gp Ltd 1988-, Redifon Hldgs Ltd 1988-; FCA 1969, ACIB 1978; *Recreations* skiing, sailing, travel; *Style—* Christopher McCann, Esq; 10 Lonsdale Sq, London N1 1EN; St Andrews East, Bedchester, Dorset (☎ 01 607 8546); County Natwest Ltd, Drapers Gardens, 12 Throgmorton Avenue, London EC2P 2ES (☎ 01 826 8646, fax 01 638 1615, telex 882121)

McCANN, Keith; s of George McCann; *b* 27 Sept 1931; *Educ* Queen Mary Coll London Univ; *m* 1955, Ina Lucy, da of Samuel Rostron; 2 da (Corrie, Kirstie); *Career* chm: AEI Clabes Ltd, Transmission & Distribution Int Ltd, BSc (Eng), MIEE, MIMECHE, MIEEE, FBIM, CEng; *Recreations* flying; *Clubs* Stapleford Essex, Newcastle Flying Clubs; *Style—* Keith McCann, Esq; Springs, Sandy Hill Lane, Weybourne, Holt, Norfolk NR25 7HW

MCCANN, Michael Denis; s of Walter McCann, of The Cottages, Toft-Newton, Lincs, and May, *née* Tindall; *b* 31 Mar 1948; *Educ* Greatfields Sch Yorks, Hull Univ (BSc); *m* 28 June 1975, Anne Jennifer, da of Wing-Cdr Alan James Bannister (ret), of Nightingale Cottage, Rickmansworth, Herts; 1 da (Penelope Olivia); *Career* gp tres: Grand Met plc 1988-, Trafalgar House plc 1986-88, Ford Motor Co Ltd 1983-86, Ford of Europe Inc 1970-83; dir: Grand Met Fin plc 1988-, Grand Met Investmts Ltd 1988-, Grand Met Int Fin plc 1988-, Grand Met Hotel and Catering Ltd 1988-, Cappoquin Securities Ltd 1988-, Rachel Securities 1988-, Stag Insur Co Ltd, City Corp Tres Cnslts Ltd; Fell Assoc of Corp Treasurers 1983; *Recreations* shooting, fishing, rugby; *Clubs* RAC; *Style—* Michael McCann, Esq; Giffords Farm, Rettendon, Essex (☎ 0261 710 383); 11/12 Hanover Sq, London W1A 1DP (☎ 01 629 7488, fax 01 408 1246, car tel 0860 746 870, telex 299606)

McCARRAHER, Hon Mrs; Belinda Jane; *née* Siddeley; only da of 3 Baron Kenilworth (d 1981); *b* 11 Jan 1950; *Educ* Downham Sch; *m* 1, 1971 (m dis 1974), Christopher Aston James; m 2, 1982, David Ian McCarraher, s (step) of His Hon Judge McCarraher, VRD, *qv*; *Career* gift shop owner in Richmond; *Recreations* relaxing with friends and decorating our Home; *Style—* The Hon Mrs McCarraher; Silver Coppers, College Road, Epsom, Surrey (☎ 03727 20601)

McCARRAHER, His Hon Judge David; VRD (1964); s of Colin McCarraher (d 1960); *b* 6 Nov 1922; *Educ* King Edward VI Sch Southampton, Magdalene Coll Cambridge; *m* 1950, Betty, *née* Haywood; 2 da, 1 step s (*see* Hon Mrs McCarraher), 1 step da; *Career* WWII Indian Ocean NW Europe, Capt RNR 1969, CO Solent Div (HMS Wessex) 1969-72, ADC to HM The Queen 1972-73; barr Lincoln's Inn practising West Circuit 1948-52, slr 1955, recorder Crown Ct 1979-84, circuit judge 1984-; *Recreations* family, golf, sailing; *Clubs* Stoneham Golf, Royal Naval Sailing Association, Naval; *Style—* His Hon Judge McCarraher, VRD; Guildhall Broad St, Bristol BS1 2HL

McCARTER, Keith Ian; s of Maj Peter McCarter (d 1971), of Edinburgh, and Hilda Mary, *née* Gates; *b* 15 Mar 1936; *Educ* The Royal HS of Edinburgh, Edinburgh Coll of Art (DA); *m* 5 Jan 1963, Brenda Maude Edith, da of James A Schofield (d 1974), of Langley, Bucks; 1 s (Andrew Keith b 1968), 1 da (Alix-Jane b 1966); *Career* Nat Serv RA 1954-56; sculptor; primarily involved in architectural and landscaped situations; numerous cmmns incl: Ordnance Survey HQ Southampton 1967, Lagos Nigeria 1974, Wingate Centre City of London 1980, Goodmans Yard City of London 1982, 1020 19th Street Washington DC 1983, American Express Bank City of London 1984, Guys Hosp NCC London 1986, Royal Exec Park NY 1986, Evelyn Gdns London 1987, London Docklands 1988; works in private collections world-wide; FRSA 1970; *Recreations* music, literature, beach combing; *Clubs* Farmers; *Style—* Keith McCarter, Esq; Ottermead, Church Rd, Great Plumstead, Norfolk NR13 5AB (☎ 0603 713001)

MacCARTHY, Charles Joseph Finnin; s of Thomas J MacCarthy, FJI (d 1949), and Sarah A, *née* O'Connor (d 1955); *b* 23 May 1912,, Kenmare, Co Kerry; *Educ* Presentation Coll Cork, Univ Coll Cork (MComm); *m* 1942, Elizabeth, *née* O'Donovan; 3 s, 3 da; *Career* Irish Def 1939-46 (Area Ops Offr 1942-45), gp Sec Dwyer Gp Cork 1958-72, currently dir Guardian Securities Ltd; pres Assoc of CAs (Irish Region) 1974, Bd of Visitors Nat Museum of Ireland 1974-87; Cork City Public Library Ctee 1974-, chm Cork Archives Inst 1981-; PC; *Recreations* antiquary; *Clubs* Army; *Style—* Charles MacCarthy Esq; 10 Carrigduhb Estate, Blackrock Rd, Cork, Ireland (☎ 021 961 242)

McCARTHY, Daniel Peter Justin; TD (1978, clasp 1984); s of Thomas Joseph McCarthy, GM, of Bootle, and Margaret Mary Josephine, *née* Bowden; *b* 4 July 1939; *Educ* St Mary's Coll Crosby, Aberdeen Univ (MB, ChB), Coll of Law London; *m* 1977, Dr Bronwen Elizabeth Knight Teresa, da of Richard Knight Evans, of Wimbledon; 5 s (Oliver, Richard (twins), Simon, Philip, Nicholas); *Career* MO 4 (V) Bn Royal Green Jackets 1982-88, Maj RAMC (TA); barr Inner Temple 1978; medical practitioner; HM dep coroner: City of London 1979-88, Inner West London 1980-; divnl surgn St John Ambulance; med offr Royal Home and Hosp at Putney; Freeman City of London 1975, Liveryman Worshipful Soc of Apothecaries 1974; kt Sovereign Military Order of Malta 1985; FSAScot; Cross of Merit with Swords 1988; *Recreations* running, jumping, standing still; *Clubs* Cavalry and Guards, Green Jackets; *Style—* Dr D P J McCarthy, TD; 23 Grandison Road, London SW11 6LS; 328 Clapham Rd, London SW9 9AE (☎ 01 622 2006)

McCARTHY, David; s of John Francis McCarthy, of 2 Watercall Ave, Styvechale, Coventry, Warwickshire, and Ivy Eileen, *née* Davies; *b* 27 Jan 1942; *Educ* Ratcliffe Coll Syston Leics, Birmingham Univ (LLB); *m* 25 Oct 1970, Rosemary Ruth, da of Raeburn Gray Norman, of 35 Reddings Rd, Moseley, Birmingham; 2 s (Gavin Stephen b 19 Feb 1972, Nicholas James b 17 May 1974); *Career* articled with Wragge & Co Slrs Birmingham; joined Coward Chance 1976 (ptnr 1978); dir: Mithnas Ltd, Minthas Nominees Ltd, St George's Hill Residents Assoc Ltd; memb City of London Law Soc Company Law sub-ctee;; *Recreations* fly fishing, tennis, cricket, books; *Clubs* Richmond Cricket, St George's Hill Tennis, Loch Achonachie Angling; *Style—* David McCarthy, Esq; La Pineta, East Rd, St George's Hill, Weybridge, Surrey; Royex House, Aldermanbury Sq, London EC2V 7LD (☎ 01 600 0808)

MacCARTHY, Fiona; da of Lt-Col Gerald MacCarthy (d 1943), and Yolande, *née* de Belabre; *b* 23 Jan 1940; *Educ* Wycombe Abbey Sch, Oxford Univ (BA); *m* 19 Aug 1966, David, s of Colin Mellor (d 1969); 1 s (Corin b 1966), 1 da (Clare b 1970); *Career* dir of exhibitions: Homespun Highspeed Sheffield City Art Galleries 1979, Omega Workshops Decorative Arts of Bloomsbury Crafts Cncl 1984, Eye For Indust Victoria and Albert Museum 1987; hon fell Royal Coll of Art London 1989, Royal Soc of Arts Bicentenary Medal 1987; *Books* All Things Bright and Beautiful (1972), The Simple Life: C R Ashbee in the Cotswolds (1981), British Design since 1880 (1982), Eric Gill (1989); *Style—* Ms Fiona MacCarthy; Broom Hall, Broomhall Rd, Sheffield S10 2DR (☎ 0742 664 124)

McCARTHY, Mary; da of Roy Winfield McCarthy (d 1918), and Therese Preston McCarthy (d 1918); ggf Simon Manly Preston was Col of a Union Regt in the US Civil War, gf Harold Preston was framer of the first Workman's Compensation Act in the USA; *b* 21 June 1912; *Educ* Annie Wright Seminary Tacoma Washington, Vassar Coll (AB); *m* 1961, James Raymond West, s of Frank Raymond West (d 1964); 1 s (Reuel); *Career* writer; Doctor of Law Univ of Aberdeen 1979; Vassar Coll President's Distinguished Visitor Medal 1982, Offr French Order of Arts and Letters 1983, Nat Medal for Literature 1984, Edward McDowell Medal for Outstanding Contribution to Literature 1984; DLitt: Syracuse Univ 1973, Univ of Hull 1974, Bard Coll 1976, Bowdoin Coll 1981, Univ of Maine Orono 1983; Stevenson Chair of Literature Bard Coll 1986-; *Books* The Company She Keeps (1942), The Oasis (1949), The Groves of Academe (1952), A Charmed Life (1955), Venice Observed (1956), Memories of a Catholic Girlhood (1957), The Stones of Florence (1959), On the Contrary (1961), The Group (1963), Birds of America (1971), The Mask of State: Watergate Portraits (1974), The Seventeenth Degree (1974), Cannibals and Missionaries (1979), Ideas and the Novel (1980), Occasional Prose (1985), How I Grew (1987); translator: Simone Weil The Iliad (1947), Rachel Bespaloff On the Iliad (1948); *Clubs* Cercle de l'Union Interalliée (Paris); *Style—* Ms Mary McCarthy; 141 rue de Rennes, 75006 Paris, France (☎ 45 48 10 92); Castine, Maine 04421 (☎ 207 326 8239)

McCARTHY, Terence David; s of Patrick Terence McCarthy and Sheila Mary BA, *née* Jackson; *b* 5 May 1954; *Educ* Haileybury, Oxford Univ (MA); *Career* managing editor The Coat of Arms; Bluemantle Pursuivant of Arms 1983-; Freeman City of London; divnl pres Essex St John Ambulance; *Recreations* painting, reading, generally trying to avoid ignorance in the arts; *Clubs* Norfolk; *Style—* Terence McCarthy, Esq, Bluemantle Pursuivant of Arms; The Old Vicarage, Cornish Hall End, Finchingfield, Essex (☎ 079 986 368) College of Arms, Queen Victoria St, London EC4V 4BT (☎ 01 236 2749/01 248 2762)

McCARTHY, Baron (Life Peer UK 1975); William Edward John McCarthy; s of Edward McCarthy; *b* 30 July 1925; *Educ* Ruskin Coll Oxford, Merton & Nuffield Colls Oxford Univ; *m* 1957, Margaret, da of Percival Godfrey; *Career* formerly worker in men's outfitters and clerk; lectr industrial rels Oxford Univ, res dir Royal Cmmn on Trade Unions and Employers Assocs 1965-68, fell Nuffield Coll and Oxford Mgmnt Centre 1969-, chm Railway Staff Nat Tribunal 1974-86; dir Harland & Wolff Ltd 1976-86, special cmmr Equal Opportunities Cmmn 1977-79; oppn spokesman (Lords) Employment 1983-; *Recreations* theatre, ballet, gardening; *Clubs* Reform; *Style—* The Rt Hon the Lord McCarthy; 4 William Orchard Close, Old Headington, Oxford (☎ 0865 62016)

McCARTNEY, Gordon Arthur; s of Arthur McCartney (d 1987), and Hannah, *née* Seel; *b* 29 April 1937; *Educ* Grove Park GS Wrexham; *m* 1, 23 Jul 1960 (m dis 1987), Ceris Isobel Davies; 2 da (Heather Jane b 11 April 1963, Alison b 6 Dec 1965); m 2, 26 March 1988, Wendy Ann Vyvyn, da of Sidney Titman; *Career* slr 1959, chief exec Delyn Borough Cncl Clwyd 1974-81, sec Assoc of DCs 1981-, co sec Local Govt Int Bureau 1988-, dir Nat Tport Tokens Ltd 1984-; *Recreations* music, gardening, cricket; *Clubs* Middx CCC, Northants CCC; *Style—* Gordon McCartney, Esq; 33 Duck Street, Elton, Petersborough, Cambs PE8 6RQ (☎ 08324 659); 203 Frobisher House, Dolphin Sq, London SW1 (☎ 01 630 8207); 9 Buckingham Gate, London SW1E 6LE (☎ 01 828 7931, fax 01 828 6948)

McCARTNEY, Hugh; s of John McCartney, of Glasgow; *b* 1920; *Educ* John Street Sr Secdy Sch, Royal Tech Coll Glasgow; *m* 1949, Margaret, da of Fred MacDonald, of Kirkintilloch, Glasgow; 1 s, 2 da; *Career* ILP 1934-36, joined Lab Pty 1936; memb Kirkintilloch Town Cncl 1955-1970, ccnclr Dunbartonshire 1965-70; MP (Lab): Dunbartonshire (East) 1970-74, Dunbartonshire Central 1974-1983, Clydebank and Milngavie 1983-87; *Style—* Hugh McCartney, Esq; 23 Merkland Drive, Kirkintilloch, Glasgow G66 3PG

McCARTNEY, (James) Paul; MBE (1965); s of late James McCartney, of Liverpool, and the late Mary Patricia, *née* Mohin; *b* 18 June 1942; *Educ* Liverpool Inst; *m* 13 April 1969, Linda Louise, da of Lee Eastman, of New York City; 1 s (James b 1977), 1 da (Mary b 1969), 2 step da (Stella b 1961, Heather b 1962); *Career* joined first group, the Quarrymen, and started writing songs with John Lennon 1956; formation of the

Beatles 1960; first Beatles recordings issued in Germany 1961: Please Please Me gave group their first British No 1, She Loves You cemented their success 1963; first triumphant American tour 1964; Royal Command Performance and release of first film A Hard Day's Night 1964; single I Want to Hold Your Hand became the biggest selling British single ever, with worldwide sale of 15,000,000; release of second film Help 1965; last ever Beatles public performance in San Francisco Aug 1966 Eleanor Rigby and Paperback Writer are the group's single hits; release of Sergeant Pepper's Lonely Hearts Club Band album, as well as Penny Lane/Strawberry Fields Forever 1967; formation of Apple Corps 1968; release of third film, the cartoon Yellow Submarine and their only double album, The Beatles (better known as The White Album) 1968; group play live for the last time together on the roof of the Apple building in London 1969; fourth and final film, Let It Be, released 1970; dissolution of Apple sees the break-up of the Beatles; forms MPL group of cos and releases his debut solo album McCartney 1970; released second solo album Ram and formed Wings 1971; returned to live work 1972; appeared in own TV special James Paul McCartney 1973; Wings toured UK and Australia 1975; Wings first American tour resulted in a triple album Wings Over America 1976; Mull of Kintyre became best selling single ever in UK and received Ivor Novello award for this achievement 1977; released a new album London Town, and a compilation Wings Greatest Hits 1978; honoured by the Guiness Book of Records with a Triple Superlative Award, for sales of 100,000,000 albums, 100,000,000 singles and as holder of 60 gold discs, making him the most successful popular music composer ever 1979; presented with a unique Rhodium Disc by the minister of the Arts; released Wings Rockshow film from 1976 US tour 1981; released acclaimed Tug of War album 1982; Pipes of Peace album released 1983; Give My Regards to Broad Street released 1984; performed Let It Be at Bob Geldof's Live Aid concert to 1.5 billion people 1985; released 15th solo album Press To Play and returned to concert stage for special Royal Command concert The Prince's Trust, in the presence of TRH The Prince and Princess of Wales 1986; Hon DUniv (Sussex) 1988; *Style—* Paul McCartney, Esq; c/o MPL Communications Ltd, 1 Soho Square, London W1V 6BQ

McCARTNEY, Robert; OBE (1968), QPM (1962); s of Arthur McCartney (d 1970); *b* 15 August 1912; *Educ* Queen Elizabeth's GS Blackburn; *m* 1937, Marjorie, *née* Grayston; 1 s, 1 da; *Career* Lancashire Constabulary 1932-54, dep chief constable of Monmouthshire 1955-58, chief constable of Herefordshire 1958-67, dep govr of HM Tower of London 1968-71; OStJ 1962; *Recreations* golf, lectures for charities; *Style—* Robert McCartney, Esq, OBE, QPM; 11 Weatherby Gdns, Hartley Wintney, Basingstoke, Hants (☎ 025 126 2045)

McCAULEY, Air Marshal Sir John Patrick Joseph; KBE (1955, CBE 1943), CB (1950); s of John Alfred McCauley (d 1919), and Sophia, *née* Combes (d 1953); *b* 18 Mar 1899; *Educ* St Joseph's Coll Sydney, RMC Duntroon, Melbourne Univ (BCom); *m* 1925, Murielle Mary, da of John Patrick Burke (d 1934); 1 s, 2 da; *Career* Dep Chief of Air Staff 1942-44 and 1946-47, Air OC Eastern Area 1949-53, Chief of Air Staff RAAF 1954-57, Air Marshal 1955, ret; fed pres Air Force Assoc 1964; *see Debrett's Handbook of Australia and New Zealand for further details*; *Style—* Air Marshal Sir John McCauley, KBE, CB; 10 Onslow Gdns, Greenknowe Ave, Elizabeth Bay, Sydney, NSW 2011, Australia (☎ 358 1257)

McCAW, Hon Sir Kenneth Malcolm; s of late Mark McCaw; *b* 8 Oct 1907; *Career* slr 1933-65, barr 1965-, MLA NSW (Lib) for Lane Grove 1947-75, QC 1972, attorney-gen of NSW 1965-75; kt 1975; *Style—* The Hon Sir Kenneth McCaw; Woodrow House, Charlish Lane, Lane Cove, NSW 2066, Australia (☎ 358 1257)

MCCLATCHEY, Dr Samuel Jones; s of Thomas McClatchey (d 1946), and Emily, *née* Jones (d 1975); *b* 13 June 1916; *Educ* Royal Belfast Academical Inst, Queens Univ Belfast (MB, BCh, BAO, DPH, MFCM) Univ Athletic Blue; *m* 2 April 1942, Patricia Kathleen (d 1981), da of Frederick Allen (d 1948); 3 da (Judith b 5 Sept 1944, Diana b 8 March 1948, Lindsay b 16 May 1951); *Career* WWII Sqdn Ldr RAF, station MO Northolt 1943-44, Sqdn MO 137 Sqdn 2 TAF Normandy landings 1944-45, sr MO RAAE Boscombe Down 1945-46; MO of Health New Windsor 1950-74 (presented at Ct Windsor Castle 1952), community physician and MO environmental health East Berks 1975-86; currently: med referee to Crematoria, mangr Mental Health Cmmn to Cardinal Clinic Windsor; hon tres Soc Community Med 1976-83; memb: Royal Br Legion, RNLI; parish cncllr; BMA, MFCM; *Recreations* yachting, ocean cruising; *Clubs* Pathfinder (RAF), Leander, Windsor Constitutional, RFYC; *Style—* Dr Samuel McClatchey; Cluain-na-Slige, Thames St, Sonning-on-Thames, Berkshire (☎ 0734 693 197)

McCLEAN, Professor (John) David; s of Maj Harold McClean (d 1983), of Prestbury, Cheshire, and Mabel, *née* Callow (d 1981); *b* 4 July 1939; *Educ* Queen Elizabeth GS Blackburn, Magdalen Coll Oxford (BA, BCL, MA, DCL); *m* 10 Dec 1966, Pamela Ann, da of Leslie Arthur Loader (d 1959), of Yeovil, Somerset; 1 s (Michael b 1969), 1 da (Lydia b 1972); *Career* lectr Sheffield Univ 1963-68 (sr lectr 1968-73, prof 1973-), visiting lectr Monash Univ 1968 (visiting prof 1978); lay vice-pres Sheffield diocesan Synod 1982-, memb gen Synod 1970-, vice chm House of Laity 1979-85 (chm 1985-), Crown Appts Cmmn 1977-87; *Books* Legal Context of Social Work (1975, 2 edn 1980), Recognition of Familty Judgments in the Commonwealth (1983); co-author: Criminal Justice and the Treatment of Offenders (1969), Defendants in the Criminal Process (1976), Shawcross and Beaumont on Air Law (4 edn 1977), Dicey and Morris, the Conflict of Laws (10 edn 1980, 11 edn 1987); *Recreations* detective fiction; *Clubs* RCS; *Style—* Prof David McClean; 6 Burnt Stones Close, Sheffield S10 5TS (☎ 0742 305794); Faculty of Law, The University, Sheffield S10 2TN (☎ 0742 768555, ext 6754)

McCLEAN, Richard Arthur Frank; s of Donald Stuart McClean (d 1959), and Marjory Cathleen, *née* Franks; *b* 5 Dec 1937; *Educ* Marlborough; *m* 29 Aug 1959, Janna, da of Eric Constantine Doresa; 1 s (Paul b 23 Sept 1962); 2 da (Lucinda b 27 June 1961, Philippa b 23 July 1966); *Career* joined ad dept Financial Times 1955, ad dir Financial Times 1974, apptd to the Bd of the Financial Times 1977, mktg dir Financial Times 1979, md Financial Times (Marketing), md Financial Times (Europe) 1981; dir: Financial Times Gp Ltd 1984, The Financial Times Ltd 1977, FT Business Information Ltd 1984, St Clements Press Ltd 1981, The Financial Times (Europe) Ltd 1978, Westminster Press Ltd 1986; *Recreations* golf, tennis; *Clubs* Garrick, Royal St Georges Golf; *Style—* Richard McClean, Esq; Catherinehams, Grove Heath, Ripley, Surrey (☎ 0483 224050); The Financial Times Ltd, Bracken House, 10 Cannon St, London EC4P 4BY (☎ 01 248 8000)

MCCLEARY, Benjamin Ward; s of George William McCleary, of Asheville, N Carolina, and Nancy *née* Grim; *b* 9 July 1944; *Educ* St Mark's Sch, Princeton Univ (AB); *m* 1, 6 May 1967 (m dis 1977), Deirdre Stillman Marsters; 1 s (Benjamin Pierce b 6 May 1970), 1 da (Katherine Chase b 1 Sept 1972); m 2, 15 Oct 1983, Jean, da of Henry G Muchmore, of New Vernon NJ USA; *Career* Lt US Navy 1966-69; vice pres Chemical Bank 1969-81, sr vice-pres Lehman Brothers 1981-84, md Shearson Lehman Brothers 1984-; *Recreations* sailing, skiing; *Clubs* Dunes; *Style—* Benjamin W McCleary, Esq; 114 E 90th Street, New York NY 10128 (☎ 212 831 5461); Shearson Lehman Hutton Inc, World Financial Centre, New York NY 10285-1700 (☎ 212 298 6425)

McCLELLAN, Col Sir Herbert Gerard Thomas; CBE (1979, OBE 1960), TD (1955), JP (City of Liverpool 1968), DL (Merseyside 1974, Lancs 1967-74); s of late George McClellan and Lillian, *née* Fitzgerald; *b* 24 Sept 1913; *m* 1939, Rebecca Ann Nancy (d 1982), da of Michael Desforges; 1 s (Anthony George), 3 da (Mary Colette, Mrs Ann Winifred Walsh, Mrs Petra Clare Plant); *Career* served WWII Loyal N Lance Regt, Royal Regt of Artillery, London Irish Rifles RUR, served M East, N Africa, Italy (wounded, despatches), cmd 626 (Liverpool Irish) HAA Regt (RA, TA), 470 (3 W Lancs) RA TA 1955-60, County Cmdt W Lancs Army Cadet Force 1961-66; vice-chm and md: Vernons Tst Corpn, Vernons Finance Corpn, Vernons Insur Brokers; dir Vernons Orgn; md Competition Mgmnt Servs 1977-82; ret 1982; chm Intro Merseyside Ltd 1988-; memb: TAVR Assoc W Lancs 1955-66 (vice-chm 1966-68), N W England & IOM 1968-70 (vice-chm 1970-75, chm 1975-79); former memb Liverpool City Cncl (Childwall Ward); govr: Archbishop Whiteside SM St Brigid's High Sch, 1961-, Christ's Coll Liverpool 1962-69, St Mary's Primary Sch Little Crosby 1986-; chm: Liverpool (Liverpool European) Cons Constituency Cncl 1978-84, Merseyside West European CCC 1984-85; pres Merseyside West European CCC 1985-; vice-pres: Merseyside County Soldiers, Sailors & Airmens Assoc 1975-, Churchill Cons Club, Wavertree 1976-; pres Halewood Cons Club 1981-88; memb: North West Area Cons Assoc 1971-, The Nat Union of Cons and Unionist Exec Ctee 1982-87, Mabel Fletcher Tech Liverpool 1969- (chm Govrs 1971-86); vice-pres The Liverpool Sch of Tropical Med 1987-; High Sheriff Merseyside 1980-81; FInstAM; kt 1986; *Clubs* Athenaeum (Liverpool), Army & Navy; *Style—* Col Sir Gerard McClellan, CBE, TD, JP, DL; 13 Ince Blundell Hall, Ince Blundell, Liverpool L38 6JN (☎ 051 9292269)

McCLELLAN, John Forrest; s of John McClellan (d 1978), of Caledonian Place, Aberdeen, and Hester Strathmore, *née* Niven (d 1954); *b* 15 August 1932; *Educ* Aberdeen GS, Aberdeen Univ (MA); *m* 22 Dec 1956, Eva Maria, da of Otto Pressel (d 1967), of Churchfields, 37 The Ridgeway, Fetcham, Nr Leatherhead, Surrey; 3 s (James b 1957, Nicholas b 1960, Tommy b 1963), 1 da (Rose b 1965); *Career* Nat Serv Army 1954-56, 2 Lt Gordon Highlanders 1955-56, seconded to Nigeria Regt Royal West African Frontier Force 1955-56; entered Civil Serv 1956; Scottish Educn Dept: asst princ 1956-59, princ 1960-68, asst sec 1969-77; Scottish Office: private sec to Perm Under Sec of State 1959-60, asst under sec of state 1977-80; civil serv fell Glasgow Univ 1968-69, under sec Indust Dept for Scotland 1980-85, ret Civil Serv 1985; dir Scottish Int Educn Tst 1986-; memb mgmnt ctee Hanover Housing Assoc Scotland 1986-; Hon Fell Dundee Inst of Technol 1988; *Recreations* walking, vegetable gardening; *Clubs* Royal Scots; *Style—* John McClellan, Esq; Grangeneuk, West Linton, Peeblesshire EH46 7HG (☎ 0968 60502); 22 Manor Place, Edinburgh (☎ 031 225 1113)

McCLELLAND, HE Douglas; AC (1987); s of Alfred McClelland (d 1969), and Gertrude Cooksley (d 1962); *m* 1 s, 2 da; *Career* sen for NSW in Australian Parliament 1962-87, min for media 1972-75, special min of state 1975, dep ldr of opposition in Senate 1977, dep pres of the Senate 1981-83, pres of the Senate 1983-87; Aust high cmmr in London 1987; *Recreations* rugby league, theatre, films, reading; *Clubs* City Tattersalls Sydney (life memb), St George Leagues, Sydney, Garrick, London; *Style—* HE Mr D McClelland; Australian High Commission, The Strand, London

McCLELLAND, Prof (William) Grigor; s of Arthur McClelland (d 1966), of Newcastle upon Tyne and Jean, *née* Grigor (d 1966); *b* 2 Jan 1922; *Educ* Newcastle Prep Sch, Leighton Park Sch, Balliol Coll Oxford (MA); *m* 1946, Diana Avery, da of William Harold Close, of Hampstead; 2 s, 2 da; *Career* md Laws Stores Ltd 1949-65 and 1978-85 (chm 1966-85); dir Manchester Business Sch 1965-77, prof business admin Manchester Univ 1967-77; dep chm Nat Computing Centre 1966-68; chm: Washington Devpt Corpn 1977-, EDC for the Distributive Trades 1980-84 (memb 1965-70); memb: Consumer Cncl 1963-66, Econ Planning Cncl (Northern Region) 1965-66, IRC 1966-71, NEDC 1969-71, SSRC 1971-74, Northern Industl Devpt Bd 1977-86; tstee: Joseph Rowntree Charitable Tst 1956- (chm 1965-78), Anglo-German Fndn for the Study of Indust Soc 1973-79; govr nat inst of econ and social research Leighton Park Sch 1952-60 and 1962-66; memb Friends Ambulance Unit 1941-46; MBA Manchester Univ, Hon DCL Durham; CBIM; *Publications* Studies in Retailing (1963), Costs and Competition in Retailing (1966), And a New Earth (1976), Quakers Visit China (ed 1957), Journal of Management Studies (ed 1963-65); *Recreations* walking, tennis, skiing; *Style—* Prof Grigor McClelland; 66 Elmfield Rd, Gosforth, Newcastle-upon-Tyne NE3 4BD

MCCLELLAND, Melvyn John; s of Hugh McClelland, of 4 South Walk, W Wickham, Kent BR4 9JA, and Winifred Dilys, *née* Hughes; *b* 6 Nov 1941; *Educ* St Dunstan's Coll Catford (BEng), Liverpool Univ; *m* 1, 1965, Kathleen Elaine (dec), da of Ferdinand Barrington Da Costa Greaves, of Liverpool; 1 s (Ian Hugh b 1970), 1 da (Jennifer Jane b 1976); m 2, 6 March 1982, Susan, da of Edward J Hudson (d 1976), of Brighton; 1 da (Amy Alexandra b 1983); *Career* chartered engr, design dir Ricardo Consulting Engrs Ltd (d 1982); CEng, FIMechE; *Recreations* bridge, badminton, genealogy; *Style—* M J McClelland, Esq; Riversdale, The Paddock, Shoreham-by-Sea, W Sussex BN4 5NW (☎ 0273 461260); Ricardo Consulting Engineers, Bridge Works, Shoreham-by-Sea, W Sussex BN4 5FG (☎ 0273 455611, telex 87383, fax 0273 464124)

McCLELLAND, Dr Richard (stage name Richard Leech); s of Herbert Saunderson McClelland (d 1953), of 18 Palmerston Park, Dublin, and Isabella Frances, *née* Leeper (d 1963); *b* 24 Nov 1922; *Educ* Haileybury Coll, Trinity Coll Dublin (BA, BAO, BCL, MB); *m* 1, 28 Jan 1950, Helen Hyslop, *née* Uttley (d 1971); 2 da (Sarah Jane b 15 Jan 1952, Eliza b 3 June 1954); m 2, 27 June 1975, (Margaret) Diane, *née* Pearson; *Career* house surgn and house physician Meath Hosp Dublin 1946; actor; theatre incl: All My Sons 1948, The Lady's not for Burning 1949, Relative Values 1950, No Other Verdict 1954, Uncertain Joy 1955, Subway in the Sky 1956, A Man for All Seasons 1960, Dazzling Prospect 1961, Cyder with Rosie 1963, The Rt Hon Gentleman 1964, Horizontal Hold 1967, The Cocktail Party 1968, Whose Life Is It Anyway (Savoy Theatre) 1979-81); TV incl: Jane Eyre, The Gold Robber, The Doctors, Barchester Chronicles, Smiley's People; films incl: Dam Busters, Night to Remember, Ice Cold in Alex, The Young Churchill, Gandhi, Handful of Dust, The Shooting Party; wrote column Doctor in the Wings in World Medicine 1968-83; dir Rocks Country Wines Ltd 1985-; *Books* How To Do It (1979), TCD Anthology (1945); *Recreations* bricklaying, cinematography, gardening; *Clubs* Garrick; *Style—* Dr Richard McClelland; 27 Claylands Rd, London SW8 1NX (☎ 01 735 1678); Loddon Park Farm, Twyford, Berks; Rocks Country Wines Ltd, Loddon Park Farm, New Bath Rd, Twyford, Berks (☎ 0734 342 344)

McCLENAGHAN, Lt-Col (Frank) Worsfold; JP (Hants 1954), DL (Hants 1972); s of Rev George Richard McClenaghan (d 1950), of Stockton Hall, Beccles, Suffolk, and Amy Margaret, *née* Mayo (d 1926); *b* 6 July 1910; *Educ* Marlborough, Clare Coll Cambridge (MA), Yale Univ USA; *m* 12 Dec 1945, Elizabeth, da of Allon Dawson (d 1928), of Leathley Grange, Otley, Yorks; 2 da (Elizabeth b 1946, Virginia b 1950); *Career* Gunner RA (TA) 1938, cmmnd 2 Lt 1939, Capt 1941, Maj 1942, Lt-Col 1943; farmer; High Sheriff Hants and IOW 1971; *Recreations* shooting; *Clubs* Special Forces, Hampshire (Winchester), Elizabeth (New Haven USA); *Style—* Lt-Col Worsfold McClenaghan, JP, DL; Westfield House, Highclere, Newbury, Berks (☎ 0635 253067)

MACCLESFIELD, Archdeacon of; *see*: Gaisford, Ven John Scott

MACCLESFIELD, 8 Earl of (GB 1721); George Roger Alexander Thomas Parker; JP (Oxon 1955), DL (1965); also Lord Parker, Baron of Macclesfield, Co Chester (GB 1716) and Viscount Parker (GB 1721); s of 7 Earl of Macclesfield (d 1975), and Lilian Joanna Vere, *née* Boyle (d 1974); *b* 6 May 1914; *Educ* Stowe; *m* 18 June 1938, Hon Valerie Mansfield, o da of 4 Baron Sandhurst, OBE (d 1964); 2 s; *Heir* s, Viscount Parker; *Career* Lt RNVR, served WW II; *Style—* The Rt Hon the Earl of Macclesfield, JP, DL; Shirburn, Watlington, Oxon

MACCLESFIELD, Countess of; Hon Valerie; *née* Mansfield; da of 4 Baron Sandhurst, OBE (d 1964); *b* 25 Dec 1918; *m* 18 June 1938, 8 Earl of Macclesfield; *Career* chm CC Oxon 1970; *Style—* The Rt Hon The Countess of Macclesfield; Shirburn Castle, Watlington, Oxon

McCLINTOCK, Surgeon Rear-Adm Cyril Lawson Tait; CB (1974), OBE (1964); s of Lawson Tait McClintock (d 1918); *b* 2 August 1916; *Educ* Epsom, Guys Hosp; *m* 1966, Freda Margaret, da of Robert Jones (d 1956); 2 step s; *Career* joined RN Medical Servs 1940, served WW II, Cmdg Medical Advsr to C-in-C Naval Forces S Europe 1969-71, medical offr-in-C RN Hosp Malta 1969-72, medical offr-in-C RN Hosp Haslar 1972-75, medical offr C-in-C Naval Home Cmd 1972-75, ret; conslt in ENT Bermuda 1976-85; *Recreations* cricket, history; *Clubs* Army and Navy, MCC; *Style—* Surgn Rear-Adm Cyril McClintock, CB, OBE; 5 Ambleside Ct, Alverstoke, Hants (☎ 0705 503648)

McCLINTOCK, David; TD; s of Rev Edward L L McClintock (d 1961), of Glendaragh, Crumlin, Co Antrim, and Margaret Katharine, *née* Buxton (d 1974); f descended from, *inter alia*, John Foster, Lord Oriel, last speaker of the Irish House of Commons, mother from Sir Thomas Fowell Buxton, "The Liberator" (of the slaves) and Mrs Elizabeth Fry, the prison reformer; *b* 4 July 1913; *Educ* Harrow, Trinity Coll Cambridge (MA); *m* 6 July 1940, (Elizabeth) Anne, da of late Maj Victor J Dawson, of Miserden, Glos; 2 s (Andrew David b 1944, Hugh John b 1947), 2 da (Alison Ruth (Mrs Johnson) b 1941, Joanna Margaret (Mrs Chisholm) b 1949); *Career* WWII offr Hertfordshire Yeo RA TA 1938, Lt-Col 1944; KH News-letter 1938-46; Coal Utilisation Cncl 1951-73; pres: Botanical Soc of the Br Isles 1971-73, Kent Field Club 1978-80, Ray Soc 1980-83; vice-pres: Kent Tst for Nature Conservation 1963-, Heather Soc 1960-, Linnean Soc 1971-74; chm: Wild Flower Soc 1981-, Cncl Int Dendrology Soc 1979-, Nat Tst 1980-84, vice chm RHS Scientific Ctee 1981-; Veitch Gold Medal RHS 1981; FCA, FLS; *Books* Pocket Guide to Wild Flowers (with R S R Fitter 1956, supplement 1957), Natural History of the Garden of Buckingham Palace (jtly, 1964), Companion to Flowers (1966), Wild Flowers of Guernsey (1975; supplement 1987), Wild Flowers of the Channel Islands (1975, with J Bichard), Joshua Gosselin of Guernsey (1976), Guernsey's Earliest Flora (1982); *Recreations* natural history, gardening, music; *Style—* David McClintock, Esq, TD; Bracken Hill, Platt, Sevenoaks, Kent TN15 8JH (☎ 0732 884102)

McCLINTOCK, Sir Eric Paul; s of Robert Emanuel (d 1979), and Ada Marion, *née* Whitton; *b* 13 Sept 1918; *Educ* De La Salle Coll Armidale, Sydney Univ; *m* 1942, Eva Trayhurn, da of Edgar Lawrence (d 1956); 2 s, 1 da; *Career* Dept Navy Supply Off 1936-46, Depts of Commerce, Agric & Trade Canberra 1947-61; investmt banker; chm: Yuills Aust Ltd, McClintock Assocs Ltd, Yal Font Ltd, O'Connell St Assoc, Williams Brot Engrg Pty Ltd, fell Aust IOD, cncllr Aust Inst of Mgmnt; vice pres: Royal Life Saving Soc NSW, Inst of Public Affrs; kt 1981; *Style—* Sir Eric McClintock; 16 O'Connell St, Sydney, NSW 2000, Australia (☎ 233 5733)

McCLINTOCK, Nicholas Cole; CBE (1979); s of Col Robert Singleton McClintock, DSO (d 1969), of Brakey Hill, Godstone, Surrey, and Mary Howard, *née* Elphinstone (d 1965); *b* 10 Sept 1916; *Educ* Stowe, Trinity Coll Cambridge (BA, MA); *m* 3 Sept 1953, Pamela Sylvia, da of Maj Rhys Clavell Mansel (d 1968), of Smedmore, Corfe Castle, Dorset; 2 s (Alexander b 1959, Michael b 1960), 2 da (Sylvia b 1954, Elizabeth b 1962); *Career* WWII cmmnd RA 1938-45 served Dunkirk, cmd 1 Field Batty final Burma Campaign 1945; Northern Nigeria: Col admin serv 1946-62: private sec to govr 1949-50, clerk to exec cncl Northern Region 1950-53, actg res Kano Province and pres Bornu Province 1958-62; KStJ 1968 (dep sec gen Order of St John 1963-68, sec gen 1968-81); sec Dorset Historic Churches Tst 1984-, chm Aidis Tst 1988-; Freeman City of London 1981; *Clubs* Army & Navy; *Style—* Nicholas McClintock, Esq, CBE; Lower Westport House, Wareham, Dorset (☎ 092 95 3252)

McCLINTOCK-BUNBURY, Hon Hermione Jane; da of 4 Baron Rathdonnell (d 1959); *b* 11 August 1943; *Style—* The Hon Hermione McClintock-Bunbury; Lisnavagh, Rathvilly, Co Carlow; c/o Wright, Stephenson & Co Ltd, PO Box 1895, Wellington, New Zealand

McCLINTOCK-BUNBURY, Hon Pamela Rosemary; da of 4 Baron Rathdonnell (d 1959); *b* 30 July 1948; *Educ* Lawnside Gt Malvern Worcs, Millfield; *Career* sculptor, painter; *Style—* The Hon Pamela McClintock-Bunbury; Calle Marbella 4, Benehavis, Malaga, Spain

McCLUNE, Rear Adm (William) James; CB (1978); s of James McClune, MBE (d 1952); *b* 20 Nov 1921; *Educ* Foyle Coll, Queen's Univ Belfast, Birmingham Univ (MSc); *m* 1953, Joan Elizabeth Symes, da of Albert Prideaux (d 1952); 1 s (James), 1 da (Bridget); *Career* radar offr RNVR 1941-47, CSO (engrg) to C-in-C Fleet 1976-78; chm of tstees Royal Sailors' Rests; Admty govr RN Benevolent Tst; chm: Christian Alliance Tst Corpn, consultative cncl SW Electricity, mgmnt ctee, RNLI; *Recreations* sailing; *Clubs* Royal Cwlth Soc, Royal Naval and Royal Albert YC; *Style—* Rear Adm James McClune, CB; Harlam Lodge, Lansdown, Bath, Avon (☎ 0225 311748); 7 Theed St, London SE1 (☎ 01 928 2720)

McCLURE, Wing Cdr Charles George Buchanan; AFC (1944), AE (1944), DL (1976); s of Judge George Buchanan McClure (d 1955, cmmr at Old Bailey), and Doris Elizabeth, *née* Tydd; *b* 20 April 1916; *Educ* Winchester, Trinity Coll Oxford, de Havilland Tech Sch; *m* 1943, Helen Margaret Gilloch, da of Maj John Whyte, MBE; 1 s, 1 da; *Career* Wing Cdr RAF 1945, chief test pilot RAE Farnborough 1945-46, ops offr Miny of Civil Aviation 1946, head of flight Cranfield Coll of Aeronautics 1949, prof of flight Cranfield Inst of Technol 1973; CEng, FRAeS; *Recreations* golf, gardening; *Clubs* RAF, Leander; *Style—* Wing Cdr Charles McClure, AFC, AE, DL; The Shrubbery, Aspley Guise, Milton Keynes MK17 8HE (☎ 0908 583126)

McCLURE FISHER, David Anthony; s of Douglas McClure Fisher, of Northwood, Middx, and Mary Margaret, *née* Haley; *b* 4 Mar 1939; *Educ* Tonbridge; *m* 30 Dec 1961, Lesley Carol, da of William Henry Chester-Jones (d 1971); 1 s (Duncan b 1964), 1 da (Joanna b 1968); *Career* md HRGM Automotive Insur Servs Ltd 1984-, md Greyfriars Admin Servs Ltd 1984-, Hogg Robinson Gardner Mountain Insur Brokers Ltd; FCII, FInstD, FCIS, FBIIBA, MIMI; *Recreations* golf, bridge; *Clubs* Moor Park GC; *Style—* D A McClure Fisher, Esq; 1 Station Hill, Reading, Berks (☎ 0734 391221, car tel 0836 222943)

McCLUSKEY, Hon Catherine Margaret; da of Baron McCluskey, QC (Life Peer); *b* 1962; *Career* further educn lectr; *Style—* The Hon Catherine McCluskey

McCLUSKEY, Hon David Francis; s of Baron McCluskey, QC; *b* 1963; *Educ* St Augustines HS, Napier Coll Edinburgh; *Career* software engr; *Recreations* photography, golf; *Clubs* Edinburgh Univ Staff; *Style—* The Hon David McCluskey

McCLUSKEY, Baron (Life Peer UK 1976); John Herbert McCluskey; QC (Scotland 1967); s of F J McCluskey (d 1961), of Edinburgh; *b* 12 June 1929; *Educ* St Bede's GS Manchester, Holy Cross Acad Edinburgh, Edinburgh Univ (Vans Dunlop Scholar); *m* 1956, Ruth Friedland, of Manchester; 2 s, 1 da; *Career* advocate 1955, advocate-depute 1964, sheriff princ of Dumfries and Galloway 1973-1974, slr gen for Scotland 1974-79, senator of the Coll of Justice in Scotland 1984; BBC Reith lectr 1986; Hon LLD Dundee 1989; *Books* Law, Justice and Democracy (1987); *Style—* The Rt Hon the Lord McCluskey; Ct of Session, Parliament Square, Edinburgh (☎ 031 225 2595); 5 Lansdowne Crescent, Edinburgh EH12 5EQ (☎ 031 225 6102)

McCLUSKEY, Hon John Mark; s of The Rt Hon Lord McCluskey, QC, of Edinburgh, and The Lady McCluskey, *née* Friedland; *b* 21 July 1960; *Educ* George Watson's Coll, Aberdeen Univ, The Napier Coll; *m* 1986, Judith Karen, *née* Fernie; 1 da (Kate Louise b 2 Jan 1988); *Career* contract's executive: Ferranti plc (Ferranti Defence Systems Ltd), Display Systems Dept, South Gyle Edinburgh (☎ (031 314 8148); *Recreations* golf, swimming; *Style—* Mark McCluskey; 20 Redford Avenue, Edinburgh EH13 0BU

McCOLGAN, Elizabeth; *née* Lynch; da of Martin Lynch, of Dundee, and Elizabeth, *née* Fearn; *b* 24 May 1964; *Educ* St Vincents De Paul PS, St Saviours HS Dundee, Ricks Coll Idaho, Univ of Alabama; *m* 3 Oct 1987, Peter Conor, s of Thomas McColgan, of Strabane, NI; *Career* sports devpt offr Dundee DC; Gold Medallist 10000m Cmwlth Games 1986, Silver medallist world and country champs 1986, Silver Medallist 10000m 1988, UK 5000m champion 1988, Grand Prix winner 3000/5000m 1988, world record holder 5000m and 10 000m on roads, Euro 10000 record holder, Br and Scottish 5000m and 10 000m record holder; granted Freedom of Tuscaloosa Alabama 1986; *Recreations* cooking, cinema, crosswords, my dogs; *Style—* Mrs Elizabeth McColgan; Formentera, Husbandtown Monikie, Dundee, Scotland (☎ 082 623 506); 353 Clepington Rd, Dundee, Scotland (☎ 0382 231 41)

MacCOLL, David Ferguson; MC; *Career* chm Corrie MacColl & Son Ltd, dir: Anglo-American Corpn Sdn Bhd Singapore, Anglo-American Corpn (M) Sdn Bhd Malaysia, Imperial Commodities Corpn USA, LM Fischel & Co Ltd, NV Deli Maatschappij Rotterdam, Windmill Windows (Aust) Pty Ltd Australia; *Style—* David MacColl Esq, MC; Corrie MacColl & Son Ltd, Dunster House, Mincing Lane, EC3R 7AX

MCCOLL, Ian; CBE (1983); s of John McColl (d 1947), of Glasgow, and Sarah Isabella McColl (d 1968), of Bunessan, Isle of Mull; descends from the McColls of Mull; *b* 22 Feb 1915; *Educ* Hillhead High Sch Glasgow; *m* 1968, Brenda, da of Thomas McKean (d 1949), of Glasgow; 1 da (Elaine b 1970); *Career* served RAF WW II in air crew Coastal Cmd 202 Sqdn (despatches 1945); chm Scottish Express Newspapers Ltd 1975-82, dir Express Newspapers 1971-82; ed: Daily Express 1971-74, Scottish Daily Express 1961-71 (joined 1933); former memb: Press Cncl, Gen Assembly Bd of Publications; vice-pres Newspaper Press Fund 1981-; memb IOJ, former sec NUJ Glasgow Branch; contested (Lib) Dumfries-shire 1945, Greenock 1950; former Session Clerk Sandyford-Henderson Meml Church of Scotland and former memb Presbytery of Glasgow and Synod of Clydesdale; chm: media div Cwlth Games (Scotland) 1986, Saints and Sinners Club of Scotland 1981; *Style—* Ian McColl, Esq, CBE; 12 Newlands Rd, Glasgow G43 2JB

McCOLL, Prof Ian; s of Frederick George McColl (d 1985), of Dulwich, and Winifred Edith, *née* Murphy (d 1984); *b* 6 Jan 1933; *Educ* Hutchesons' GS Glasgow, St Paul's, London Univ (MB BS, MS); *m* 27 Aug 1960, Dr Jean Lennox, da of Arthur James McNair (d 1964), of London; 1 s (Dr Alastair James b 1961), 2 da (Caroline Lennox b 1963, Mary Alison b 1966); *Career* hon conslt surgn Br Army 1982-; jr hosp appts 1958-67: Barnet, St Marks, St Peters, Gt Ormond Street, Putney, St Olaves; res fell Harvard Med Sch 1967, reader in surgery and sub dean St Bart's Hosp Med Coll 1967-71, dir of surgery Guy's Hosp 1971-85-, conslt advsr to BBC; pres Mildmay Mission Hosp, bd of govrs Dulwich Coll Prep Sch, govr at large for England American Coll of Surgns, chm govt working pty for the Artificial Limb and Wheelchair Serv, vice-chm Special Health Authy Disablement Servs; Liveryman Worshipful Cos of: Barbers, Apothecaries; FRCS, FACS, FRCSE; *Books* Intestinal Absorption in Man (jtly, 1976); *Recreations* forestry; *Clubs* Athenaeum; *Style—* Prof Ian McColl; Dept of Surgery, Guy's Hospital, London SE1 9RT (☎ 01 407 7600)

McCOMB KING, Yvonne Muriel Renee; *née* Jones; OBE (1977); da of Lt Col Percy David Jones, MC, DCM, ED (d 1979), Berthe Gilaine Bracke (d 1971); *b* 23 Nov 1920; *Educ* State Commercial HS; *m* 1, 1946, John Franklyn McComb (d 1972), s of Lt Frank McComb (d 1978); 2 s, 1 da; m 2, 1984, Malcolm George King; *Career* Wing

Cmdt Women's Air Trg Corps (voluntary orgn); public rels dir McComb 1976-, PR conslt Royal Flying Doctor Serv of Aust (Queensland section) 1973-, fed vice-pres Lib Pty Aust 1974-79, state pres (Queensland) 1976-80, fndr/pres Home Mgmnt Advsy Serv 1972-; patron Amnesty Int (Queensland) 1978-, tstee Aust War Meml Canberra 1978-83, dir Queensland Ballet Co 1981-84, dir Later Years Ltd 1981-; tstee Later Years Fndn 1983-; life memb Lib Pty Queensland; life memb Young Lib Mvment; *Recreations* music, politics, theatre, travel; *Clubs* United Serv, Univ of Queensland Staff; *Style—* Mrs Yvonne McComb King, OBE; Galileo Tower, 22 Mullens St, Hamilton, Brisbane, Queensland, Australia (☎ 2683061); 7 Gainsborough, 50 Upper Pitt St, Kirribilli, NSW 2061 (☎ 957 5287)

MCCOMBE, Richard George Bramwell; s of Barbara Bramwell McCombe, *née* Bramwell (d 1969); *b* 23 Sept 1952; *Educ* Sedbergh, Downing Coll Cambridge (MA); *m* 1 (m dis 1986), m 2, 1986, Carolyn Sara, da of Robert Duncan Birrell, of Chart Rising, Ballards Lane, Limpsfield, nr Oxted, Surrey; 1 s (Duncan b 4 Apr 1987); *Career* called to the Bar Lincoln's Inn 1975; first jr counsel to Dir Gen of Fair Trading 1987- (second jr counsel 1982-87); sec London section Old Sedberghian Club; memb: Senate Inns of Ct and Bar Cncl 1981-86, Bar Cncl ctees 1986- (chm Young Barristers Ctee 1983-84); *Recreations* various sporting interests, travel; *Clubs* RAC, MCC, London Scottish FC; *Style—* Richard McCombe, Esq; 13 Old Square, Lincoln's Inn, London WC2A 3UA, (☎ 01 404 4800 fax 01 405 4267)

McCONNACHIE, Charles Petrie; CBE; s of David McConnachie (d 1937); *b* 28 June 1906; *m* 1935, Levia; 1 s; *Career* mining company dir 1946, ret 1966; *Clubs* Royal Cwlth Soc; *Style—* Charles McConnachie Esq, CBE; 48 Albert Rd, Dumfries DG2 9DL (☎ 0387 52191)

McCONNEL, Brig David William; OBE (1952); s of Capt Frederic Bradshaw McConnel (d 1941), of Sunnyside, Melrose, Roxburghshire, and Francis Elizabeth, *née* Pringle (d 1962); *b* 6 June 1913; *Educ* Winchester; *m* 1, 17 Nov 1938 (m dis 1951), Patricia Enid Auriol, da of Capt Turner; 1 s (Ian b 1942), 2 da (Sarah (Sally, Mrs Allday) b 1941, Eildon (Mrs Letts) b 1944); m 2, 2 April 1986, Rosemary Margaret, *née* Allison; *Career* KOSB: cmmnd (TA) 1932, (Reg) 1935, cmd 2 Bn Burma 1944, depot 1949-52, 1 Bn 1954-57, Brig 1960, ret 1964; chief army recruiting offr Scotland 1964-68; chm Scottish ctee Nat Soc for Cancer Relief 1964-78, sec Scottish Field Sports Soc 1968-78; *Style—* Brig David McConnel, OBE; Ravensbourne, Douglas Rd, Melrose, Roxburghshire TD6 9QT (☎ 089 682 2440)

McCONNELL, David Joseph; s of James Francis McConnell and Florence *née* Wilson; *b* 8 June 1936; *Educ* Belfast Royal Acad, Univ Br Columbia (BSc); *m* 27 Dec 1975, Alison, da of Capt Peter Knight Mantell, of 37 Selborne Close, Petersfield, Hants; 3 s (Peter b 1978, Ian b 1979, Jason b 1981); *Career* insur exec, chief exec Preferred Assur Co (1982-), previously Lloyds underwriter; *Recreations* golf, gardening, travel; *Style—* David McConnell, Esq; Kingsbarton, 16 Huntsmead, Alton, Hants GU34 2SE; Preferred Assurance Co, 349 London Road, Camberley

MCCONNELL, Prof (James) Desmond Caldwell; s of Samuel David McConnell (d 1976), of Magheragall, NI, and Cathleen, *née* Coulter; *b* 3 July 1930; *Educ* Wallace HS Lisburn, Queens Univ Belfast (BSc, MSc), Cambridge Univ (MA, PhD); *m* 14 July 1956, Jean Elspeth, da of John Jackson Ironside (d 1975), of Wimborne, Dorset; 1 s (Craig b 1 July 1957), 2 da (Deirdre b 19 May 1959, Elspeth b 3 Nov 1960); *Career* Cambridge Univ: demonstrator in Mineralogy 1955-60, lectr in mineralogy 1960-72, fell of Churchill Coll 1962-82, reader in mineralogy 1972-82, Schlumberger/Cambridge res hd of rock physics dept 1983-86, extraordinary fell of Churchill Coll 1983-87; prof physics & chemistry of minerals Oxford Univ 1986-; FRS 1987; *Books* Principles of Mineral Behaviour (with Andrew Putnis, 1980); *Recreations* choral singing, vernacular architecture; *Style—* Prof Desmond McConnell; 8 The Croft, Old Headington, Oxford OX3 9BU (☎ 0865 69100); Dept of Earth Sciences, Parks Rd, Oxford (☎ 0865 272 043)

McCONNELL, Hon Mrs; Hon Elizabeth Millicent; da of 2 Viscount Selby (d 1923); *b* 1917; *m* 1948, Clarence Henry Quentin McConnell (d 1972); 1 s, 1 da; *Style—* The Hon Mrs McConnell; PO Box 43148, Nairobi, Kenya

McCONNELL, John; s of Donald McConnell, (d 1982), and Enid, *née* Dimberline (d 1967); *b* 14 May 1939; *Educ* Borough Green Secdy Mod Sch Kent, Maidstone Coll of Art Kent (Nat Dip); *m* 1 March 1963, Moira Rose, da of William Allan Macgregor; 1 s (Sam b 20 Feb 1966), 1 da (Kate b 1 Feb 1969); *Career* designer; own practice 1963-74, co-fndr Face Photosetting 1967; dir: Pentagram 1974, Faber and Faber 1983, Clarks of England Inc 1987 awards D and A D President's Award for outstanding contrib to design 1985, memb: PO Stamp Advsy Ctee, CNAA; *Books* Pentagram Papers (ed 1975-), Living By Design (jtly, 1978), Ideas on Design (jtly, 1986); *Recreations* cookery, home restoration; *Clubs* Groucho; *Style—* John McConnell, Esq; 40 Bassett Rd, London W10 9JL (☎ 969 2014); Pentagram Design Ltd, 11 Needham Rd, London W11 2RP (☎ 229 3477, fax 727 9932, telex 8952000 PENTA G)

McCONNELL, Joyce Marion; OBE (1976); da of Lawrence Joseph Smith, of Sydney, Aust (d 1928); *b* 21 August 1916; *Educ* N Sydney Girls' HS, Sydney Univ; *m* 1939, Hugh Graham Douglas McConnell; 2 s, 2 da; *Career* Queen's Jubilee Medal 1977, hon life vice-pres Nat Cncl of Women of Aust 1979-; memb: Nat Women's Advsy cncl 1978-80, 1982-84, Nat Women's Consultative Cncl 1984-; pres Nat Cncl of Women of Aust 1973-78; *Recreations* gardening, golf; *Clubs* Royal Canberra GC, Women's Int; *Style—* Mrs Hugh McConnell, OBE; 95 Stonehaven Cres, Deakin, ACT, Australia (☎ 81 2458)

McCONNELL, Rt Hon Robert William Brian; PC (N Ireland 1964); s of Alfred Edward McConnell (d 1963), 2 s of Sir Robert John McConnell, 1 Bt; *b* 1922; *Educ* Sedbergh, Queen's Univ Belfast (BA, LLB); *m* 1951, Elisabeth Joyce, da of late Samuel Agnew; 2 s, 1 da; *Career* barr NI, MP S Antrim, N Ireland Parl 1951-68; pres Industl Ct 1968-; *Style—* Rt Hon Robert McConnell; Aughnahough, Lisburn, Co Antrim

McCORKELL, Col Michael William; OBE (1964), TD (1954), JP (1980), DL (1962);; s of Capt B F McCorkell, of Templeard Culmore, Co Londerry (d 1957), Eileen Miller (d 1984); *b* 3 May 1925; *Educ* Aldenham; *m* 1950, Aileen Allen (OBE 1975), da of Lt-Col E B Booth, of Darver Castle, Dundalk, Co Louth (d 1962); 3 s (John b 1952, David b 1955, Barry b 1959); 1 da (Mary b 1951); *Career* 16/5 Lancers 1943-47; Maj North Irish Horse 1951, Lt-Col 1961 cmd North Irish Horse TA, ret 1964, TAVR Col NI 1971-74, Bt-Col 1974; Pres TA & VR 1977-; ADC to HM The Queen 1972, High Sheriff 1961, Lieut Co Londonderry 1975; *Recreations* fishing, shooting; *Clubs* Cavalry and Guards; *Style—* Col Michael W McCorkell; Ballyarnett, Londonderry, N Ireland (☎ 0504 351239)

McCORKELL, (Henry) Nigel Pakenham; s of Capt Barry Henry McCorkell (d 1984), and Nina Florence Kendal, *née* Gregory; *b* 9 Jan 1947; *Educ* Wellington Coll, City of London Poly; *m* m, 12 Sept 1973, Lesley Joan, da of Ernest Rowley, of Southwold, Suffolk; 1 s (Marcus b 1981), 2 da (Clare b 1975, Emma b 1977); *Career* CA; trained Thornton Baker 1968-72; fin dir: KCA Int plc 1977-78, FR Gp plc 1981-83, Meggitt Hldgs plc 1983-, The Microsystems Gp plc 1984- (non-exec); asst divnl dir Nat Enterprise Bd 1979-81; FCA; *Recreations* golf; *Clubs* MCC; *Style—* Nigel McCorkell, Esq; 6 Poole Road, Wimborn, Dorset BH21 1QE (☎ 0202 841141, fax 0202 841222)

MacCORKINDALE, Simon Charles Pendered; s of Gp Capt Peter Bernard MacCorkindale, OBE, and Gilliver Mary, *née* Pendered, of 8 Pettitts Lane, Dry Drayton, Cambridge; *b* 12 Feb 1952; *Educ* Haileybury Coll; *m* 1, 10 July 1976 (m dis), Fiona Elizabeth Fullerton, da of Brig Bernard Victor Hilary Fullerton, RAPC; m 2, 5 Oct 1984 Melody George, da of Norman Alfred George, of 19 Braybank, Bray, Berks; *Career* actor, prod and dir; *Films* incl: Juggernaut (1974), Road to Mandalay (1977), Death on the Nile (1977), The Riddle of the Sands (1978), The Quartermass Conclusion (1978), Cabo Blanco (1979), The Sword and the Sorcerer (1982), Jaws 3D (1982-83), Stealing Heaven (1987: also produced); films for TV incl: Jesus of Nazareth (1975), Visitor from the Other Side (1980), The Mansions of America (1980-81), Obsessive Love (1983); TV series Falcon Crest 1984-86; dir: Int Prodns Ltd 1986-, Amy Int Prodns Inc 1984-; memb: dirs Guild of America, acad of motion pictures arts and scis, the British Acad of Film & TV arts; *Recreations* tennis, skiing, music, photography; *Clubs* St James; *Style—* Simon MacCorkindale, Esq; Amy International Productions Ltd, Lee International Studios, Shepperton, Middx (☎ 09328 62611, 078 481 3131, fax 09328 68989)

McCORMACK, Most Rev John; *see*: Meath, Bishop of

McCORMACK, Mark Hume; *b* 6 Nov 1930; *Educ* Princeton Univ, William and Mary Coll, Yale Univ; *m* Nancy Breckinridge; 2 s, 1 da; m 2, 1986, Betsey Nagelson; *Career* admitted Ohio Bar 1957; fndr pres and chief exec Int Mgmnt Gp 1962- (handles personalities in int entertainment and sporting world, also handled the Pope's visit to Great Britain 1982); commentator for televised golf; publisher Golf Int, Tennis World; author The World of Professional Golf (1967); *Recreations* golf; *Style—* Mark McCormack, Esq

MCCORMACK, Thomas; CBE (1980), MBE (1959); s of John McCormack (d 1930); *b* 13 Mar 1911; *Educ* De la Salle Armidale NSW, St Joseph's Coll Nudgee Qld Aust; *m* 1963, Yvonne, da of Archibald Sargeant (decd), of Brisbane; 1 s, 2 da; *Career* slr of Supreme Ct of Qld 1934, pres Australian Rugby Union Football 1955-61, pres Qld Rugby Union Football 1949-62; *Recreations* rugby, horseracing; *Clubs* Qld Rugby, Queensland Turf, Tattersalls (Brisbane); *Style—* Thomas McCormack Esq, CBE, MBE; 48 Oriel Rd, Clayfield, Brisbane, Queensland, Australia (☎ 262 4937)

McCORMICK, (George) Donald King; s of Thomas Burnside McCormick (d 1944), of Clwyd, and Lily Louise, *née* King (d 1970); *b* 9 Dec 1911; *Educ* Oswestry Sch; *m* 1, 1934 (m dis 1947), Rosalind Deirdre, da of Maj G Buchanan Scott, of Horsham; m 2, Sylvia Doreen (d 1960), da of Henry Thomas Cade, of Stamford; 1 s (Anthony Stuart b 1947); m 3, 4 Oct 1963, Eileen Dee, da of Charles Deacon (d 1933), of Romsey, Hants; *Career* served RN 1941-46, combined opns, Lt RNVR; ed Gibraltar Chronicle 1946, foreign corr Kemsley Newspapers, NW Africa 1946-49, Cwlth corr 1949-59, foreign mangr Sunday Times 1963-73, (asst foreign manager 1959-63); author (pen-name Richard Deacon); *Books* The Mask of Merlin: A Critical Biography of David Lloyd George (1963), Pedlar of Death: A Biography of Sir Basil Zaharoff (1966), Madoc & The Discovery of America (1966), Who's Who in Spy Fiction (1977), William Caxton: The First English Editor (1976), With My Little Eye: Memoirs of A Spy-Hunter (1982), "C": A Biography of Sir Maurice Oldfield (1985), The Cambridge Apostles (1985); *Style—* Donald McCormick, Esq; 8 Barry Court, 36 Southend Road, Beckenham, Kent BR3 2AD (☎ 01 650 9476)

MCCORMICK, Peter David Godfrey; s of Ronald Godfrey McCormick, of Harrogate, N Yorks, and Paulina, *née* Salzman; *b* 27 June 1952; *Educ* Ashville Coll, Harrogate, King's Coll, London Univ (LLB); *m* 16 May 1981, Kathryn Mary, da of Jack Gill, of Halifax, W Yorks; 1 s (Guy James Godfrey b 1982), 1 da (Charlotte Alix b 1985); *Career* slr; sr ptnr McCormicks, Leeds and Harrogate; pres Law Soc King's Coll London 1971-72; *Recreations* music, sport, Leeds UFC, wining, dining; *Clubs* Wig and Pen; *Style—* Peter McCormick, Esq; Morcar Hill Farm, Barrowby Lane, Kirkby Overblow, nr Harrogate, N Yorks (☎ 886612); McCormicks, Oxford House, Oxford Row, Leeds LS1 3BE (☎ 0532 460622, fax 0532 467488)

McCORMICK, Sean Robert; s of Lt-Col Robert McCormick, of Windsor, Berks, and Lettitia *née* Worsley; *b* 1 May 1950; *Educ* Alexandra GS Singapore, Chard Sch Somerset; *m* 22 Nov 1977, Zandra, da of Frederick William Hollick; 1 s (Liam b 1978), 1 da (Katy b 1984); *Career* Actg Pilot Offr RAF, aircrew trg RAF Henlow; assoc dir broadcast buying mangr Leo Burnett advtg agency 1970-76, sr media mangr R H Kirkwood & Co advtg agency 1976-78, dep md BBDO UK (formerly SJIP/BBDO, previously media dir and ptnr SJIP advtg agency 1978-84, ptnr and bd account dir Horner Collis & Kirwan 1984, fndr ptnr Juler McCormick West 1987, fndr dir and maj shareholder Good Business Ltd; *Recreations* motor racing, go karting, rugby, cricket, family life; *Clubs* BARC, RAC; *Style—* Sean McCormick, Esq; Windyridge, High Park Avenue, East Horsley, Surrey KT24 5DF; 28-29 Southampton Street, Covent Garden, London WC2 7JA (☎ 01 379 6399; car ☎ (0836) 236883; fax 01 240 7045)

McCORQUODALE, Alastair; er (but sole surviving) s of Maj Kenneth McCorquodale, MC, TD (himself 1 cous of 1 and last Baron McCorquodale of Newton); *b* 5 Dec 1925; *Educ* Harrow; *m* 1947, Rosemary, er da of Maj Herbert Broke Turnor, MC, JP, DL and Lord of the manors of Stoke Rochford, Little Ponton and Colsterworth (gs of Lady Caroline, *née* Finch Hatton, eld da 10 Earl Winchilsea, by his w Lady Enid, *née* Vane, er da of 13 Earl of Westmorland, CBE, JP, and wid of Hon Henry Vane, eld s of 9 Baron; 1 s (Neil b 10 April 1951, *Educ* Harrow, *m* Lady Sarah, *née* Spencer), 1 da (Mrs Geoffrey Von Cutsem, *qv*); *Career* chm McCorquodale & Co Ltd; dir: Br Sugar Corpn Ltd, McCorquodale & Blades Tst Ltd, McCorquodale (Scotland) Ltd, Guardian Royal Exchange Assur 1983-; *Style—* Alastair McCorquodale, Esq; McCorquodale & Co Ltd, 15 Cavendish Sq, London W1M GHT (☎ 01 637 3511)

McCORQUODALE, Hon Mrs; (Charlotte) Enid; da of 1 Baron Luke, KBE (d 1943), and Laura (d 1942); *b* 13 Oct 1910; *m* 1933, George McCorquodale (d 1979), s of Norman McCorquodale (d 1937); 1 s (Hamish, *qv*), 3 da (Mrs Hugh Wilbraham b 1935,

Mrs Simon Biddulph (*see* Peerage Baron Buddulph), Mrs Charles Barnett); *Style*— The Hon Mrs McCorquodale; Broadoak Manor, Broadoak End, Hertford, Herts; Duncan Lodge, Rannoch, Perth (☎ 088 23 230)

McCORQUODALE, Hamish Norman; s of George McCorquodale (d 1979), and the Hon Mrs Charlotte Enid McCorquodale, *qv*; *b* 6 Feb 1945; *Educ* Harrow, AMP Harvard (BsA 1985); *m* 27 July 1985, Mary Anne, da of Capt Peter Cookson, of Pennshill, Lower Slaughter, Cheltenham, Glos; 1 da (Caroline b 1987); *Career* fin dir of Hambro Countrywide plc with dirs of various subsid 1982-86, dir McCorquodale plc and many subsid; ACA 1968-, FCA 1978; *Recreations* shooting, fishing, deer stalking; *Clubs* Boodles, Pratts; *Style*— Hamish McCorquodale, Esq; 43 Abbotsbury Close, London W14 (☎ 01 603 9988); Wilsons Corner, 1-5 Ingrave Road, Brentwood, Essex CM15 8TB (☎ 0277 264466)

McCORQUODALE, Ian; s of Hugh McCorquodale, MC, and Barbara Cartland, *qv*; bro Countess Spencer, *qv*; *b* 11 Oct 1937; *Educ* Harrow, Magdalene Coll Cambridge; *m* Anna, *née* Chisholm; 2 da; *Career* former commercial and export mangr Br Printing Corpn; chm: Debrett's Peerage Ltd, Corporate Broking Servs Ltd; ptnr Cartland Promotions 1976-; dir Royal Exchange Art Gallery; *Recreations* fishing, shooting, gardening, tennis; *Clubs* Boodles, Whites; *Style*— Ian McCorquodale, Esq; 112 Whitehall Ct, London SW1

McCORQUODALE, Lady (Elizabeth) Sarah Lavinia; *née* Spencer; da (by 1 m) of 8 Earl of Spencer, MVO, JP, DL, *qv*; sis of HRH The Princess of Wales (*see* Royal Family); *b* 19 Mar 1955; *Educ* West Heath Sevenoaks, Le Vieux Chalet Château d'Oex Switzerland; *m* 1980, Neil Edmund, s of Alastair McCorquodale, *qv*, and Rosemary, *née* Turnor, da of Lady Enid Vane (da of 13 Earl of Westmorland); 1 s (George b 1984), 1 da (Emily b 1983); *Style*— Lady Sarah McCorquodale; Stoke Rochford, Grantham, Lincs

McCOSH, James; DL (Ayr and Arran 1982); s of Thomas McCosh (d 1983), of Ayr, and Evelyn Ann McCosh; *b* 28 August 1948; *Educ* Wellington Coll, Dundee Univ (LLB); *m* 1973, Sheila Joan, da of John Bertie Thomas Loudon; 2 s; *Career* slr; *Recreations* golf, shooting, curling; *Clubs* Prestwick GC; *Style*— James McCosh, Esq, DL; Kaimhill, 10 Bowfield Rd, West Kilbride, Ayrshire (☎ 0294 822752); Messrs J & J McCosh, Clydesdale Bank Chambers, Dalry, Ayrshire (☎ 029 483 2112)

McCOSH OF HUNTFIELD, Lt Cdr Bryce Knox; JP (Lanark); s of Robert McCosh of Hardington, OBE, MC, WS, JP (d 1959), and Agnes Dunlop Knox; *b* 30 Mar 1920; *Educ* Loretto; *m* 1948, Sylvia Mary (Lady of the Manors of Dacre, Dalemain and Barton, Patterdale and Martindale in the Co of Cumberland), da of Edward William Hasell of Dalemain, JP, DL (d 1972); 3 s; *Career* Lt Cdr RNVR; WWII 1939-46 served: Atlantic, Channel, Far East; formerly with Linen Thread Co, dir W J Knox Ltd and others, sr ptnr SM Penney & Macgeorge stockbrokers (Glasgow, Edinburgh and London) 1956-76, hon pres Cncl Thistle Fndn; formerly: dir Target Tst Mangrs (Scotland) Ltd, Rachan Investmts Ltd, farmer, ret; memb Royal Co of Archers (Queen's Body Guard for Scotland), chm Biggar Museum Tst, Church of Scot Session Clerk; *Recreations* shooting; *Style*— Lt Cdr Bryce McCosh, JP; Huntfield Estate Off, Biggar ML12 6NA, Scotland (☎ 20208); Dalemain Estate Off, Dacre, Penrith, Cumbria (☎ 085 36 223, 085 36 450)

McCOUBREY, Hon Mrs (Anne Lynd); *née* Lowry; da of Baron Lowry (Life Peer); *b* 1952; *m* Neville McCoubrey; 1 s, 2 da; *Style*— The Hon Mrs McCoubrey

McCOWAN, Hon Mr Justice; Sir Anthony James Denys McCowan; s of John McCowan, MBE, of Georgetown, Br Guiana; *b* 12 Jan 1928; *Educ* Epsom, BNC Oxford; *m* 1961, Sue, da of Reginald Harvey, of Braiseworth Hall, Tannington, Suffolk; 2 s, 1 da; *Career* barr 1951, QC 1972, ldr SE circuit 1978-81, rec Crown Ct 1972-81, High Ct judge (Queen's Bench) 1981-; bencher Gray's Inn 1980, memb Parole Bd 1982-84, memb Crown Ct Rule Ctee 1982-88; *Style*— The Hon Mr Justice McCowan; c/o Royal Cts of Justice, Strand, London WC2A 2LL

McCOWAN, David William Cargill; s of Sir David James Cargill McCowan, 2 Bt (d 1965); hp of bro, Sir Hew Cargill McCowan, 3 Bt; *b* 28 Feb 1934; *m* ; 1 s (David b 1975); *Style*— David McCowan Esq; Auchendennan Farm, Arden, by Alexandria, Dunbartonshire G83 8RB (☎ 038 985 277)

McCOWAN, Sir Hew Cargill; 3 Bt (UK 1934); s of Sir David James Cargill McCowan, 2 Bt (d 1965); *b* 26 July 1930; *Heir* bro, David William Cargill McCowan; *Style*— Sir Hew McCowan, Bt; Auchenheglish, Alexandria, Dunbartonshire

McCOWAN, Hon Mrs (Mary Walkden); da of 1 and last Baron Walkden (d 1951); *b* 1907; *m* 1924, Duncan Matheson McCowan (d 1969); 1 s, 1 da; *Style*— The Hon Mrs McCowan

McCOWEN, Hon Mrs (Philippa Ursula Maud); *née* Baillie; 2 da of 3 Baron Burton by his 1 w; *b* 1951; *m* 1980, Ian McCowen; 2 s (Ewan b 1981, Christopher Richard b 1983); *Style*— Hon Mrs McCowen; c/o Rt Hon Lord Burton, Dochfour, Inverness, Scotland

McCRACKEN, John Strachan; CBE (1986); s of Robert Ralston McCracken (d 1959), and Susan Dorian Strachan; *b* 5 July 1930; *Educ* Beath HS, Edinburgh Univ (BSc); *m* 1954, Margaret Boswell Smith (d 1984), da of George Allan Buchan (d 1961); 2 da (Margaret b 1955, Susanne b 1957), 1 s (Ralston b 1959); *Career* Lt RN 1953-56; IBM UK Ltd 1956; dir: IBM Communications 1985-, IBM Scotland and N England 1980-85, Int Business Machines Ltd 1980-86, IBM UK Ltd 1986-, Scott Lighgow Ltd 1984-, Scottish Nat Orch 1985-, Scottish Endeavour Trg 1983-85; bd memb: Scottish Devpt Agency 1980-86, BR Rail (Scotland) 1984-; chm exec cncl Scottish Business in the Community 1982-86; tstee: Nat Museums of Scotland 1985-, Soc of Scottish Artists 1984-; cncl memb: Edinburgh Festival 1985-, Scottish Enterprise Fndn 1981-85, Scottish Graduate Enterprise 1981-85; *Recreations* golf, art, music, cricket; *Clubs* Caledonian, Bruntsfield Links, MCC, New (Edinburgh); *Style*— John S McCracken, Esq, CBE; Lins Mill, Newbridge, Midlothian (☎ 031 333 1666); 48 Millbank SW1; IBM, South Bank, London SE1 (☎ 01 928 1777)

McCRAE, Ian Robert; s of John McCrae (d 1974), of Glasgow, and Marion Isabella, *née* Provan-Logan (d 1962); *b* 13 May 1932; *Educ* The HS of Glasgow, The Scottish Hotel Sch; *Career* personnel dir Waldorf Hotel London 1960-64, gen mangr Excelsior Hotel Manchester 1964-66, proprietor Auchen Castle Hotel Beattock Dumfriesshire 1966-76, constable to Nat Tst for Scotland 1980-87; chm: British Spas Fedn, Ross & Cromarty Tourist Bd, Ross & Cromarty Heritage Soc; Highland memb Nat Tst for Scotland; warden St Annes' Episcopal church Strathpeffer; supporter Malcolm Sargeant Career Fund for Children; memb: Incorpn of Wright Glasgow, The Grand Antiquity Soc Glasgow; *Recreations* music, walking, gardening; *Style*— Ian McCrae, Esq; Eden Cottage, Jamestown, Strathpeffer Ross-Shire IV14 9ER (☎ 0997 219341)

McCRAE, William; s of James Farrell McCrae, and Rose Ann, *née* McGeachie; *b* 10 Oct 1934; *Educ* Holyrood Sr Secdy Sch Glasgow, Glasgow Univ (BSc, Phd); *m* 15 April 1966, Carole Elizabeth, da of Henry Douglas Rose (d 1985); 2 da (Catherine Alexandra b 1971, Jennifer Elaine b 1973); *Career* Glasgow Univ Air Sqdn (RAFVR), Student Pilot Officer 1957-59; res chm Lederle Labs Pearl River USA 1961-64, ICI fell and NATO fell Univ of Cambridge 1964-66, res chm and admin Syntex Labs Palo Alto USA 1966-71, dep gen mangr licensing Wilkinson Match plc, dir technol transfer PA Mgmnt Conslts Ltd 1978-80, conslt NEB and Celltech 1980-81, co-fndr and non exec dir Bioclone Ltd, co-fndr and md Cambridge Life Scis plc 1981-; dir: Biotechnol Int Ltd, Cambridge Biosensor Technol Ltd, Wadefile Ltd, Ab-Ag Laboratories Ltd, Oxford Life Scis Ltd; *Recreations* golf; *Style*— William McCrae, Esq; 19 Meadow Walk, Great Abington, Cambridge CB1 6AZ (☎ 0223 892294); Cambridge Life Sciences plc, Cambridge Science Park, Milton Road, Cambridge CB4 4GN (☎ 0223 354144)

McCRAITH, Col Patrick James Danvers; MC (1943), TD, DL (Notts 1965); s of Sir Douglas McCraith (d 1952); *b* 21 June 1916; *Educ* Harrow; *m* 1946, Hon Philippa Mary Ellis, yr da of 1 and last Baron Robins KBE, DSO (d 1962), of Rhodesia and Chelsea; 1 s (Michael b 1949), 1 da (Mrs Patrick Lort-Phillips); *Career* 2 Lt Sherwood Rangers Yeo 1935-, WWII 1939-45 served N Africa and NW Europe (wounded thrice), raised and cmd Yeo patrol Long Range Desert Gp 1940-41; cmd Sherwood Rangers Yeo 1953-57, Bt-Col 1958, Hon Col B (Sherwood Rangers Yeo Sqdn) The Royal Yeo 1968-79; slr 1939, Notary Public 1946; High Sheriff Nottinghamshire 1963; *Recreations* most field sports, skiing; *Clubs* Special Forces, Nottingham Utd Serv (Nottingham); *Style*— Col Patrick McCraith MC, TD, DL; Cranfield House, Southwell, Notts (☎ 0636 812129)

McCRAITH, Hon Mrs; Philippa Mary Ellis; *née* Robins; da of 1 and last Baron Robins (d 1962); *b* 19 Sept 1923; *m* 16 Feb 1946, Col Patrick James Danvers McCraith, MC, TD, DL, s of late Sir Douglas McCraith, of Normanton Grange, Notts; 1 s, 1 da; *Style*— The Hon Mrs McCraith; Cranfield Ho, Southwell, Notts

McCRAY, Sir Lionel Joseph; s of Joseph Burney McCray (d 1926), and Lady (Florence Mary) McCray (d 1937); *b* 29 August 1908; *Educ* Brisbane GS; *m* 1942, Phyllis Coralie, da of late Harry Howell Burbank; 1 s, 1 da; *Career* company dir; memb Mfrg Industs Advsy Cncl 1967-73, chm State Govt Advsy Ctee on Youth Grants 1967-, senate memb Queenland Univ 1972, tstee Spina Bifida Assoc 1972-, memb: State Cncl Inst of Public Affairs 1976-, state ctee The Queen's Silver Jubilee Appeal for Young Australians 1977-; dir: Aust Utd Foods, Campbell Bros Ltd, Crusader Oil NL, Kennedy Taylor Ltd, Sedgwick Pty Ltd (Qld Bd); kt 1978; *see Debrett's Handbook of Australia and New Zealand for further details*; *Style*— Sir Lionel McCray; 12 Blair Lane, Ascot, Qld 4007, Australia (☎ 262 2095)

McCREA, Sir William Hunter; s of Robert Hunter McCrea (d 1956), of Chesterfield, and Margaret, *née* Hutton (d 1963); *b* 13 Dec 1904; *Educ* Chesterfield Sch, Trinity Coll Cambridge Univ (MA, PhD, ScD), Göttingen Univ; *m* 1933, Marian Nicol Core, da of Thomas Webster, JP (d 1939), of Edinburgh; 1 s (Roderick), 2 da (Isabella, Sheila); *Career* WWII Flt Lt RAFVR (trg branch) 1941-45, temp princ offr Admty 1943-45; prof of mathematics: Queen's Univ Belfast 1936-44, Royal Holloway Coll London 1944-66; prof of astronomy Sussex Univ 1966-72 (emeritus prof 1972-); pres: Royal Astronomical Soc 1961-63, Mathematics Assoc 1973-74; FRS 1952; Freeman City of London 1988; kt 1985; *Books* Relativity Physics (1935), Analytical Geometry of Three Dimensions (1942), Physics of the Sun and Stars (1950), Royal Greenwich Observatory (1975); *Recreations* walking, travel; *Clubs* Athenaeum; *Style*— Sir William McCrea; 87 Houndean Rise, Lewes, Sussex BN7 1EJ (☎ 0273 473296); Astronomy Centre, Univ of Sussex, Brighton BN1 9QH (☎ 0273 606755, telex 877159 UNISEX G)

McCREA, Rev (Robert Thomas) William; MP (UDUP) Mid-Ulster 1983-; s of Robert Thomas McCrea, and Sarah Jane, *née* Whann; *b* 6 August 1948; *Educ* Cookstown HS, Theological Hall Free Press Church of Ulster; *m* 25 June 1971, Anne Shirley, da of George McKnight (d 1983), of Rathfriland, Co Down; 2 s (Ian b 1976, Stephen b 1978), 3 da (Sharon b 1973, Faith b 1979, Grace b 1980); *Career* memb NI Assembly 1982-85; dist cncllr 1973- (chm 1977-81); gospel singer (recording artist) received 2 silver, 2 gold and 1 platinum disc for record sales; dir Daybreak Recordings Co; *Recreations* riding; *Style*— The Rev Robert McCrea, MP; 10 Highfield Road, Magherafelt, Co Londonderry, N Ireland BT45 5JD (☎ 0648 32664, fax 0648 32035)

McCREDIE, Ian Forbes; OBE (1984); s of John Henry McCredie, and Diana, *née* Harris; *b* 28 Dec 1950; *Educ* Harvey GS, Churchill Coll Cambridge (MA); *m* 20 March 1976, (Katharine) Lucy, da of Sir Robert John Frank, 3 Bt (d 1987), of Reading; 1 s (James b 1981), 1 da (Alexandra b 1983); *Career* diplomat; Br Embassy Copenhagen 1985-; *Recreations* squash, jazz, food and drink; *Style*— Ian McCredie, Esq, OBE

McCRICKARD, Don; s of Peter McCrickard (d 1975), and Gladys Mary McCrickard (d 1982); *b* 25 Dec 1936; *Educ* Hove GS, LSE, Univ of Malaya; *m* 7 May 1960, Stella May, da of Walter Edward Buttle, RN (d 1984); 2 da (Sarah Jane b 1961, Lucy Gail b 1965); *Career* chief exec UK (later Far East) American Express Co 1975-83, md Utd Dominions Tst Ltd; chm: UDT Bank Ltd, Swan Nat Ltd, Barnet Enterprise Tst Ltd 1986-; dir: Tst Card Ltd 1983, Hill Samuel Gp plc 1987-; chief exec TSB Bank plc 1989- (dep gp md TSB Gp plc 1987-, chief exec banking 1987-), md TSB Commercial Hldgs Ltd; *Recreations* golf, tennis, theatre; *Clubs* RAC; *Style*— Don McCrickard, Esq; 25 Milk St, London EC2V 8LU (☎ 01 606 7070)

MacCRINDLE, Robert Alexander; QC; s of Fergus R MacCrindle (d 1965), of Ayrs, and Jean, *née* Hill (d 1976); *b* 27 Jan 1928; *Educ* Girvan HS, King's Coll London (LLB), Gonville and Caius Coll Cambridge (LLM); *m* 1959, Pauline Dilys, da of Mark S Morgan, of Berks; 1 s (Guy), 1 da (Claire); *Career* Flt Lt RAF 1948-50; memb Bars of Eng and Hong Kong, bencher of Gray's Inn; conseil juridique; ptnr Shearman & Sterling New York; memb Roy Cmmn on Civil Liability; fell of American Coll of Trial Lawyers; *Recreations* golf; *Clubs* Univ (NY); *Style*— R A MacCrindle, Esq, QC; 88 Ave de Breteuil, 75015 Paris (☎ 33 1 4567 1193); 21 Avenue George V, 75008 Paris (☎ 33 1 4723 5548)

McCRINDLE, Robert Arthur; MP (C) Brentwood and Ongar 1974-; s of late Thomas Arthur McCrindle, of Girvan, Ayrs; *b* 1929; *Educ* Allen Glen's Coll Glasgow; *m* 1953, Myra, da of James P Anderson, of Glasgow; 2 s; *Career* dir: Langham Life Assur Co 1972-76, Hogg Robinson plc 1987-, M & G Assur Gp; chm: Cometco Ltd 1972-78, City Bond Storage plc, Parly Aviation Gp; dir Worldmark Travel Ltd 1978-82; PPS to Min of State Home Off 1974, advsr to Br Caledonian Airways, conslt to Br Insur Brokers

Assoc; memb select ctees on: Trade and Indust 1983-87, Tport 1988-; MP (C) Billericay 1970-74; *Style*— Robert McCrindle, Esq, MP; 26 Ashburnham Gdns, Upminster, Essex (☎ 040 22 27152)

McCRIRRICK, (Thomas) Bryce; CBE; s of Alexander McCrirrick (d 1969), and Janet, *née* Tweedie (d 1986); *b* 19 July 1927; *Educ* Galashiels Acad, Heriot Watt Coll, Regents St Poly (DSc); *m* 1953, Margaret, da of Walter Yates (d 1984); 3 s (Forbes b 1954, Alastair b 1959, Stuart b 1963); *Career* RAF 1946-49; BBC: engr-in-charge TV studios 1963-69, head of studio planning dept 1969-70, chief engr Radio 1970-71, conslt and dir engrg 1978-87 (asst dir 1971-76, dep dir 1976-78); pres SERT 1081-85, vice pres IERE 1985, pres IEE (dep pres 1986-88); FIEE, FRTS;; *Recreations* ski-ing, theatre; *Style*— Bryce McCrirrick, Esq; Oakwood, Knightsbridge Rd, Camberley, Surrey GU15 3TS (☎ 0276 65309)

McCRYSTAL, Damien Peter Adam Doyle; s of Cal C McCrystal, of 94 Totteridge Lane, London N20, and Stella Maris, *née* Doyle; *b* 23 Mar 1961; *Educ* Christ's Coll Finchley; *Career* dep ed: Advertiser North London GP, PR Week; city corr London Evening Standard, asst city ed Today, city ed The Sun, presenter What the Papers Say, columnist Punch; *Style*— Damien McCrystal, Esq; 2 Grove Park, Camberwell, London SE5 (☎ 01 733 7100)

McCUE, Ian Roderick; s of John McCue, and Frances Mary McCue, *née* Quantrill; *b* 24 May 1937; *Educ* Gravesend Tech Sch, London Tech Coll (HNC); *m* 1 April 1961, Stella Kathleen, da of Henry Battle; 2 da (Jane b 1964, Sara b 1965), 1 s (Sean b (decd)); *Career* engr and Indutrialist; dir: Peek Hldgs plc 1987, CEO Sarasta Technol plc 1982-; co fndr md Sarasota Automation Ltd 1966-, pres Automation Inc USA 1978-85; FBIM, FID; *Recreations* power boating, flying, photography; *Clubs* American (London), The Field (Sarasota, Florida, USA); *Style*— Ian R McCue, Esq; St Jacques House, St Jacques St, Peter Portm Guernsey, Channel Islands (☎ 22306, fax 0481 27374)

McCULLAGH, Dr Anthony Graham; s of Dr Graham Patterson McCullagh (d 1957), and Margaret Janet, *née* Dick; *b* 5 July 1947; *Educ* Kings Coll Choir Sch Cambridge, Epsom Coll, Queen's Coll Cambrige (BA), St Barth's Hosp London (MB BCh); *m* 29 May 1971, Lucy Ann, da of George Horace Alphonse Pearce, of Eastbourne; 1 s (Edward b 1985), 1 da (Hannah Margaret b 1983); *Career* princ in GP Lakeside Health Centre Thamesmead London SE2 1980-, clinical lectr in GP Guys Hosp London 1980-, forensic med examiner (police surgn) 1987-; memb: local med ctee Greenwich and Bexley 1986, Post Grad Educn Sub Ctee 1989, SE London Trainer Selection Ctee for GPs 1989; Freeman Worshipful Soc of Apothecaries; BMA; *Books* Endocrinology, common medical diseases in practise (jtly, 1985); *Recreations* sailing; *Clubs* Frobisher SC; *Style*— Dr Anthony McCullagh; Lakeside Health Centre, Thamesmead, London SE2 9UQ (☎ 01 310 3281)

McCULLOCH, Hon Mrs (Cecily Mary Clare); *née* Cornwallis; el da of 3 Baron Cornwallis, OBE, DL (by his 2 w); *b* 23 Oct 1954; *m* 1980, Ian McCulloch; 1 s (Ruari Alexander Fiennes b 27 March 1982); *Style*— The Hon Mrs McCulloch; c/o 25b Queen's Gate Mews, London SW7

MacCULLOCH, Malcolm John; s of William MacCulloch (d 1976), of Macclesfield, Chesire, and Constance Martha, *née* Clegg; *b* 10 July 1936; *Educ* Kings Sch Macclesfield, Univ of Manchester (MB ChB, DPM, MD); *m* 1, 14 July 1962 (m dis 1975), Mary Louise, da of Ernest Sutcliffe Beton (d 1987), of Norwich; 1 s (Thomas Alistair b 1965), 1 da (Louise Elizabeth Mary b 1968); m 2, 24 Sept 1975, Carolyn Mary, da of Sqdn Ldr (William) Alan Walker Reid, of London; 2 da (Sarah Caroline b 1976, Sophie Isabel 1978); *Career* conslt child psychiatrist Cheshire 1966-67, lectr child psychiatry and subnormality Univ of Birmingham 1967-70, sr lectr psychiatry Univ of Liverpool 1970-75, sr princ med offr DHSS London 1975-79, med dir Park Lane Hosp Liverpool 1979-; WHO conslt 1977-79, visiting prof forensic psychiatry Toronto 1987-89, advsr in forensic psychiatry Ontario Govt 1987-; author of numerous pubns in professional jls; FRCPsych 1976; *Books* Homosexual Behaviour: Therapy and Assessment (1971), Human Sexual Behaviour (1980) ; *Recreations* music, golf, horse riding, inventing; *Style*— Dr Malcolm MacCulloch; 10 Abbotsford Rd, Blundellsands, Merseyside L23 6UX (☎ 051 924 4989); Park Lane Hosp, Park Lane, Maghull, Merseyside (☎ 051 520 2244 Fax 051 526 6603)

McCULLOCH, Rt Rev Nigel Simeon; *see*: Taunton, Bishop of

McCULLOCH, Robert Brownlie; s of Robert McCulloch (d 1969); *b* 13 Dec 1939; *Educ* Victoria Drive and Hyndland Schs, Glasgow Univ; *m* 1964, Lilias Stewart, *née* Cuthbertson; 1 s, 1 da; *Career* CA; fin dir GTE Sylvania (UK) Ltd and princ subsids 1976-85 (sec and chief accountant Bridon Engrg Ltd 1973-76, plant accountant Leyland Nat Co Ltd 1971-73, co sec Smith & McLaurin Ltd 1966-71), mfrg controller euro lighting div GTE Sylvania Inc (USA) 1982-84, fin dir and co sec Carter & Parker Ltd and subsids 1985-; FBIM, FInstD; *Recreations* tennis, badminton, gardening; *Style*— Robert McCulloch, Esq; 27 Dalesway, Tranmere Park, Guiseley, W Yorks (☎ 0943 79080, office 0943 72264, telex 51234 WENDY G)

McCULLOUGH, John; s of Henry Christie McCullough, of Belfast, and Jessie, *née* Niven (d 1978); *b* 23 Mar 1949; *Educ* Portsmouth Poly (MSc, PhD); *m* 25 Mar 1971, Geraldine Mabel, da of Gerald Thomas Gardner of Belfast; 1 s (Alexander b 1982), 2 da (Katherine b 1979, Eleanor b 1985); *Career* conslt engr (various appts in N Ireland, England and Scotland), ptnr Hancox & Ptnrs 1982-88, dir Rendel Hancox Ltd Glasgow 1988-; chm Scottish region Inst of Energy 1984-85; CEng 1980, FIMechE 1986, EurIng 1988; *Recreations* music, walking, swimming; *Clubs* Royal Overseas League; *Style*— Dr John McCullough; Kinnoul, Kilmacolm, PA13 4DZ (☎ 050587 2895); Rendel Hancox Ltd, 42 Kelvingrove Street, Glasgow G3 7RZ (☎ 041 332 4153, fax 041 331 1285, telex, 778913)

MCCUNN, Peter Alexander; CBE (1980); s of Alexander McCunn (d 1958), and Ida May, *née* Bailey (d 1938); *b* 11 Nov 1922; *Educ* Mexborough GS, Univ of Edinburgh; *m* 1 Feb 1943, Margaret, da of George William Prescott (d 1981); 3 s (Robert Alexander b 10 Nov 1948, Gerald Peter b 25 March 1950, Neil Andrew b 9 Jan 1952, d 1981); *Career* WWII enlisted and cmmnd W Yorks Regt 1942, served Royal Norfolk Regt 1942-44, wounded Normandy 1944, Capt S Lancs Regt 1944-46; Cable and Wireless: joined 1947, exec dir 1969, md and dep chm 1977-81, dep chm 1981-82, ret 1982 continuing pt/t until 1984; dir External Communications Ltd: Nigerian 1969-72, Sierra Leone 1969-72, Trinidad and Tobago 1972-77, Jamaica Int 1972-77; dir: Cable and Wireless Hong Kong Ltd 1981-84, Mercury Communications Ltd 1981-84; *Recreations* music, gardening, reading, crosswords; *Clubs* Exiles Twickenham; *Style*— Peter McCunn, Esq, CBE; 14 Lime Walk, Pinkneys Green, Maidenhead, Berks (☎ 0628 74308)

McCUNN, Peter Alexander; CBE (1980); s of Alexander McCunn (d 1958), and Ida May, *née* Bailey (d 1938); *b* 11 Nov 1922; *Educ* Mexborough GS, Edinburgh Univ; *m* 1943, Margaret, da of George William Prescott (d 1981); 2 s (and 1 s decd); *Career* Capt W Yorks Regt, served with Royal Norfolk Regt in Normandy; dep chm and gp md Cable & Wireless plc, ret 1982; *Recreations* music, gardening, reading; *Clubs* Exiles, Twickenham; *Style*— Peter McCunn, Esq, CBE; 14 Lime Walk, Pinkneys Green, Maidenhead, Berks (☎ 0628 24308)

McCURLEY, Anna Anderson; da of George Gemmell, and Mary, *née* Anderson; *b* 18 Jan 1943; *Educ* Glasgow HS for Girls, Glasgow Univ (MA), Jordanhill Coll of Educ (Dip Secdy Educ), Strathclyde Univ; *m* (m dis); 1 da; *Career* MP (C) Renfrew W and Inverclyde 1983-87; *Style*— Mrs Anna Anderson McCurley, MP; c/o 4 Lochview, Great Western Road, Glasgow

McCURRACH, David Fleming; OBE; *b* 2 August 1911; *Educ* (BL, LLD); *m* Margaret Jack; 2 da; *Career* US Bank of England rep 1941-46, memb UK Treasy Delgn Washington 1943-46, md and chm Alliance Tst Co and Second Alliance Tst Co, ret; dir Scottish Mortgage & Tst plc (ret.); *Style*— David McCurrach, Esq, OBE; Westoun, Wardlaw Gardens, St Andrews, Fife

McCUSKER, Sir James Alexander; *b* 2 Dec 1913, ; *Educ* Perth Modern Sch W Aust; *m* Mary, *née* Martindale; 3 children; *Career* WWII 1939-45 Sgt 1 Armd Div; Cwlth Bank of Aust (sen branch mangr in Perth until 1959, chm State Ctee of Inquiry into Rates ad Taxes 1980), fndr Town and Country Permanent Bldg Soc 1964 (chm 1964-83); fell Aust Inst of Valuers; kt 1983 for servs to the financial and housing industries; *Style*— Sir James McCusker; 195 Brookdale St, Floreat Park, W Australia 6041

McCUSKER, James Harold; MP (UU) Upper Bann 1983-; s of James Harold McCusker (d 1947), of Lurgan; *b* 7 Feb 1940; *Educ* Lurgan Model Sch, Lurgan Coll and Strawmills Coll Belfast; *m* 1965, Jennifer Leslie Mills; 3 s; *Career* primary sch teacher 1962-64, secdy sch teacher 1964-68, trg offr McLaughlin & Harvey Ltd 1968-69, Goodyear 1969-1973, prodn mangr Goodyear Tyre & Rubber Co 1973-74;,sec and whip Ulster Unionist Pty 1975-76, MP (UU) Armagh 1974-1983, elected to NI Assembly Oct 1982, dep ldr Unionist Assembly Pty; *Style*— James Harold McCusker Esq, MP; 33 Seagoe Rd, Portadown, Craigavon BT63 5HW (☎ 0762 333876); 25 Vincent Sq, London SW1 (☎ 01 821 7036)

McCUTCHEON, Dr (William) Alan; s of William John McCutcheon (d 1978), of Bangor, Co Down, NI, and Margaret Elizabeth, *née* Fullerton (d 1987); *b* 2 Mar 1934; *Educ* Royal Belfast Academical Inst, Queens Univ of Belfast (BA), pt/t univ study (MA, PhD); *m* 30 June 1956, Margaret, da of John Craig (d 1974), Belfast, NI; 3 s (Patrick b 23 Feb 1961, Conor b 4 May 1963, Kevin b 21 Sept 1965); *Career* geography teacher Royal Belfast Academical Inst 1956-62, dir Survey of Indust Archaeology Govt of NI 1962-68, Ulster Museum Belfast 1977-82 (keeper of technol and local history 1968-77), teacher (geography specialist) Ditcham Park Sch 1986-, visiting teacher Glenalmond Coll 1984 and 1986, chm Historic Monuments Cncl NI 1980-85; memb: jt ctee Industl Archaeology NI 1981-85, Malcolm Ctee on Regnl Museums in NI 1977-78, Indust Archaeology Ctee Cncl for Br Archaeology 1981-85; FRGS 1958, FSA 1970, MRIA 1983; *Books* The Canals of the North of Ireland (1965), Railway History in Pictures-Ireland Vol 1 (1970), Vol 2 (1971), Wheel and Spindle - Aspects of Irish Industrial History (1977), The Industrial Archaeology of Northern Ireland (1980); *Recreations* music, reading, poetry, travel, photography, swimming, hill walking; *Style*— Dr Alan McCutcheon; 3 Coxes Meadow, Petersfield, Hampshire GU32 2DU (☎ 0730 65366)

McDERMID, Ven Norman George Lloyd Roberts; s of the Rev Lloyd Roberts McDermid (d 1975), of Greystones, Bedale, and Annie, *née* Harrison (d 1966); *b* 5 Mar 1927; *Educ* St Peter's York, St Edmund Hall Oxford (BA, MA), Wells Theol Coll; *m* 29 July 1953, Vera, da of Albert John Wood (d 1957), of Park View, Kirkby Overblow, Harrogate; 1 s (Nigel Lloyd b 1957), 3 da (Katherine Jane b 1954, Helen Sarah b 1959, Angela Mary b 1963); *Career* RN 1944-47; curate of Leeds 1951-56, vicar of Bramley Leeds 1956-64, rector Kirkby Overblow 1964-80, rural dean Harrogate 1977-83, vicar Knaresborough 1980-83, hon canon of Ripon Cath 1972-, archdeacon of Richmond 1983-; stewardship advsr: Ripon diocese 1964-76, Bradford & Wakefield diocese 1973-76; church cmmr 1978-83; memb: C of E Pensions Bd 1972-79, Assets Ctee and Gen Purposes Ctee 1978-83, exec ctee Control Bd of Fin 1985-, Redundant Churches Fund 1977-; chm: House of Clergy Ripon Diocese 1982-, Ripon Diocesan Bd of Finances 1988-; *Recreations* church buildings, investment, gardens; *Clubs* Nat Lib; *Style*— The Ven the Archdeacon of Richmond; 62 Palace Road, Ripon, Yorks (☎ 0765 4342)

MacDERMOT, The; Sir Dermot; KCMG (1961), CBE (1947); Prince of Coolavin; s of Charles Edward, The MacDermot, Prince of Coolavin (d 1947); suc bro as Chief 1979; the Mac Dermots possessed substantial territory in Roscommon, Sligo and Mayo. Charles MacDermot (Cathal Roe) Chief and Prince of Moylurgh, lost part of his patrimony and was removed to Coolavin by Cromwell. The Rt Hon Hugh MacDermot, PC, QC (d 1904) Slr Gen of Ireland 1886 (Attorney Gen 1892) 1 styled Prince of Coolavin; *see* Burkes Irish Family Records 1976; *b* 14 June 1906; *Educ* Stonyhurst, Trinity Coll Dublin; *m* 19 May 1934, Betty, da of Joseph William Steel, of Hong Kong; 3 s (Niall, Hugh b 1938, Conor b 1945); *Heir* s, Niall Anthony MacDermot b 25 April 1935; *Career* UK FO 1929-65; min to Romania 1954-56; ambass-: Indonesia 1956-59, Thailand 1961-65; *Clubs* Kildare St, Univ; *Style*— The MacDermot, Prince of Coolavin, KCMG, CBE; Mullans, Dunlavin, Co Wicklow, Eire

McDERMOTT, Dermot St John; s of Lionel St John McDermott (d 1981), and Margaret Isabel, *née* Axworthy (d 1984); *b* 4 July 1939; *Educ* Douai Sch, Balliol Coll Oxford (MA), Cornell Univ NY (MBA); *m* 1, 16 Feb 1963, Sally Ann Hay, da of Gp Capt Arthur Hay Donaldson, DSO, DFC, AFC (d 1980); 2 da (Georgina b 1964, Arabella b 1968); m 2, 20 Dec 1984, Helen, da of George Dennis Leinster, of Madrid, Spain; *Career* dir: Esso Nederland BV 1980-83, Esso UK plc 1985-87, Trafalgar House plc 1987-, chm Cunard Line Ltd 1988-; *Style*— Dermot McDermott, Esq; 1 Berkeley St, London W1A 1BY (☎ 01 499 9020)

McDERMOTT, Sir (Lawrence) Emmet; KBE (1972); s of O J McDermott; *b* 6 Sept 1911; *Educ* St Ignatius Coll Riverview, Univ of Sydney, NW Univ Chicago; *m* 1939, Arline Beatrice, da of Hagon William Albertus, of Sydney, Aust (d 1940); 1 s, 1 da; *Career* hon consulting dental surgn Royal Prince Alfred Hosp 1942, bd of control Utd Dental Hosp 1960-79 (pres 1967-79), dental bd of NSW 1967-79, pres Australian

Dental Assoc (NSW 1960-61); cllr Aust Dental Assoc 1962-66; memb: state cncl Lib Pty of NSW, Sydney Cove Redevelopment Authy 1971-76; vice-pres Australia-Br Soc (NSW) 1972-77; dir City Mutual Life Assur Soc Ltd 1970 (dep chm 1972); Lord Mayor of Sydney 1969-72, cllr Sydney CC 1973 (chm 1976, dep chm 1975); *Recreations* golf, bowls, swimming; *Clubs* Royal Sydney GC, Elanora Country, Australia Jockey; *Style—* Sir Emmet McDermott, KBE; 20 Carnarvon Rd, Roseville, NSW 2069, Australia (☎ 46 2086)

MACDERMOTT, The Rt Hon Lord Justice John Clarke; er s of Baron MacDermott, MC, PC, of Belmont (Life Peer d 1979), and Lady MacDermott *qv*; *b* 9 May 1927; *Educ* Campbell Coll, Belfast, Trinity Hall, Cambridge BA, Queens Univ Belfast; *m* 1953, Margaret Helen, da of Hush Dales (d 1935); 4 da (Helen b 1954, Anne b 1956, Janet b 1958, Gillian b 1959); *Career* barr (Inner Temple and NI) 1949; QC (NI) 1964; Judge of High Ct (NI) 1973; Lord Justice of Appeal 1987; kt 1987; *Recreations* golf; *Clubs* The Royal Belfast Golf; *Style—* The Rt Hon Lord Justice John Macdermott; 6 Tarawood, Holywood BT18 0HS; The Royal Courts of Justice, Belfast

MacDERMOTT, Baroness; Louise Palmer; o da of Rev John Corry Johnston, of Dublin; *b* 7 Mar 1902; *Educ* Dublin HS, Trinity Coll Dublin; *m* 26 June 1926, Baron MacDermott, MC, PC (d 1979); 2 s (Rt Hon Lord Justice MacDermott *qv*, Rev Hon Robert *qv*), 2 da; *Style—* The Rt Hon Lady MacDermott; Glenburn, 8 Cairnburn Rd, Belfast BT4 2HR

McDERMOTT, Patrick Anthony; MVO (1972); s of Patrick J McDermott, of Belfast (d 1966), and Eileen, *née* Lyons, of Cork; *b* 8 Sept 1941; *Educ* Clapham Coll London; *m* m 1 1963 (m dis) Patricia Hunter-Naylor; 2 s (Jeremy b 1967, Justin b 1970); m 2 1976, Christa, da of Emil Herminghaus, of Krefeld, W Germany; 2 s (Nicholas b 1977, Christian b 1981); *Career* joined FO 1960, Mexico City 1963, attache UK Delgn to UN 1966, vice-consul Belgrade 1971, FO 1973, second sec Bonn 1973, first sec Paris 1976, FO 1979, HM consul-gen W Berlin 1984-, FO 1988-; Freeman City of London 1986; *Recreations* clocks, gardening; *Style—* Patrick McDermott, Esq, MVO; c/o Foreign Office, Downing St, London SW1A 2AH

MacDERMOTT, Rev the Hon Robert William Johnston; yr son of Baron MacDermott, MC, PC (Life Peer, d 1979), and Lady MacDermott, *qv*; *b* 25 Mar 1934; *Educ* Campbell Coll Belfast, Trinity Hall Cambridge (BA), New Coll Edinburgh (BD), Assembly's Coll Belfast, Yale Univ Divinity Sch (STM); *Career* ordained 1962; *Style—* The Rev the Hon Robert MacDermott; The Manse, Quay Rd, Ballina, Co Mayo, Republic of Ireland

MACDIARMID, Hon Mrs; (Lucinda Mary Joan); *née* Darling; da of 2 Baron Darling; *b* 23 Dec 1958; *m* 4 Sept 1982, Rory P A Macdiarmid, o s of late Col Peter Macdiarmid; 2 s (George b 1985, Fergus b 1987); *Style—* Hon Mrs Macdiarmid; 69 Haldon Rd, London SW18 5QF

MacDONALD, Sheriff Alistair Archibald; s of James MacDonald (d 1984), and Margaret, *née* McGibbon (d 1947); *b* 8 May 1927; *Educ* Broughton Sch Edinburgh, Univ of Edinburgh (MA, LLB); *m* 1949, Jull, da of Sir Robert Russell (d 1972); 1 s (Ian b 1957), 1 da (Catriona b 1964); *Career* serv Army 1945-48; called to Scottish Bar 1954; Sheriff of Grampian, Highland and Islands at Lerwick and Kirkwall; DL of Shetland; kt of the Equestrian Order of the Holy Sepulchre of Jerusalem; *Clubs* Royal Northern; *Style—* Sheriff Alistair MacDonald; West Hall, Ness of Sound, Lerwick, Shetland; Hall Cottage, Burray, Orney W, 110 Nicolson St, Edinburgh; Sheriff Cts, Lerwick, Shetland

MACDONALD, His Hon Judge Angus Cameron; s of Hugh Macdonald, OBE (d 1971), of Ravensden Bedford, and Margaret Cameron, *née* Westley; *b* 26 August 1931; *Educ* Bedford Sch, Trinity Hall Cambridge (MA); *m* 1956, Deborah Anne, da of John Denny Inglis, DSO, MC and Bar, JP (d 1976), of Oban, Argyle; 3 da (Deborah, Sarah, Fiona); *Career* Lieut RA (TA) 1951-57; barr Gray's Inn 1955, resident magistrate Nyasaland Govt 1957-60, crown counsel and sr state counsel Nyasaland/Malawi Govt 1960-67, practised NE Circuit 1967-79; *Recreations* singing, shooting, fishing; *Clubs* Northern Counties Newcastle upon Tyne; *Style—* His Hon Judge Angus Macdonald; Blàran, Kilnihver, By Oban, Argyll (☎ 085 22 246)

MACDONALD, Angus John; s of Colin Macdonald (d 1966, and Jean Livingstone; *b* 20 August 1940; *Educ* Allan Glen's Sch Glasgow; *m* 7 Sept 1963, Alice; 2 da (Jean b 1965, Rowan b 1967); *Career* dir of programmes Scottish TV 1985-, fndr chm Edinburgh Int TV Festival 1977, viewers' ombudsman on Channel 4 Right to Reply programme 1982-, prodr, presenter and dir Granada TV 1967-85; visiting prof film and media studies Univ of Stirling; author; *Books* Victorian Eyewitness, Early Photography; *Recreations* visual arts, music, literature, sport; *Clubs* Reform, RAC, Glasgow Art; *Style—* Angus Macdonald, Esq; Scottish television, Cowcaddens, Glasgow G2 3PR (☎ 041 332 9999)

MACDONALD, Angus Stewart; CBE, DL; *Educ* Conon Primary Sch, Gordonstoun; *m* 2 June 1969, Janet Ann, da of Air Cdre Duncan Somerville; 3 s (Angus, Stewart, Duncan); *Career* dir: Scottish English and Welsh Wool Growers, Reith & Anderson Dingwall, Wonderland Wool Ltd, Wool Growers (GB) Ltd, Gordonstoun Sch, Aberlour Sch; bd memb: British Wool Market Bd, Highlands and Islands Devpt Bd; The Queen's Body Guard for Scotland (Royal Co of Archers); FRAgs; *Style—* Angus Macdonald, Esq, CBE, DL; Torgorm, Conon Bridge, Dingwall, Ross-shire (☎ (0349) 61365)

MACDONALD, Angus William; s of William MacDonald, of Isle of Lewis, and Mary Ann; *b* 18 Feb 1951; *Educ* Nicolson Inst Stornoway, Strathclyde Univ Glasgow; *m* 3 July 1987, Joyce, da of Duncan Munro (d 1986), of Stornoway; *Career* slr, ptnr Macdonald Maciver & Co Notary Public (Scotland) 1987; chm Gaelic Drama Assoc 1985-; *Recreations* amature drama; *Style—* Angus W MacDonald, Esq; 14A Cross St, Stornoway, Isle of Lewis (☎ 0851 2685); 20 Francis St, Stornoway, Isle of Lewis (☎ 0851 4343)

MACDONALD, Hon Mrs; (Margaret) Anne; *née* Boot; 3 da of 2 and last Baron Trent, KBE (d 1956), and Margaret Joyce, *née* Pyman; *b* 31 July 1920; *m* 1, 29 June 1940 (m dis 1948), Maj John Edward Jocelyn Davie, MC, Derbys Yeo, yr s of late Lt-Col Bertie George Davie, of Stanton Manor, Rowsley, Derbys; 1 s (Simon b 1941), 1 da (Mrs Robin d'Abo); 2, 12 May 1949, Air Vice-Marshal Somerled Douglas Macdonald, CB, CBE, DFC (d 1979), s of late Dr David Macdonald, of Kilmichael, Glen Urquhart, Inverness; *Style—* Hon Mrs Macdonald; Thane, Kintbury, Berks (☎ (0488) 58067)

MacDONALD, Gen Sir Arthur Leslie; KBE (1978, OBE 1953), CB (1968); s of Arthur Leslie MacDonald (d 1947), and Margaret Annie MacDonald (d 1960); *b* 30 Jan 1919; *Educ* The Southport Sch Queensland, RMC Duntroon, Staff Coll Camberley UK, IDC UK; *m* 1940, Joan Bevington, da of Sidney Brady (d 1945); 1 da; *Career* Vice-Chief Gen Staff 1973-75, Chief Gen Staff 1975-77, Chief of Def Force Staff 1977-79 (ret); dir: Carricks Ltd 1980-86, Gas Corpn of Queensland Ltd 1983-; Col Cmdt Royal Aust Regt 1981-85, memb of the Def Review Ctee 1981-82; *see Debrett's Handbook of Australia and New Zealand for further details*; *Clubs* Queensland (Brisbane); *Style—* Gen Sir Arthur MacDonald, KBE, CB; 14 Meiers Rd, Indooroopilly, Qld 4068, Australia (☎ 07 870 2375)

McDONALD, Air Marshal Sir Arthur William Baynes; KCB (1958, CB 1949), AFC (1935), DL (Hants 1965); s of Dr William Maclauchlan McDonald (d 1950), of Antigua, WWI, and Hilda Ellen, *née* Edwards (d 1960); *b* 14 June 1903; *Educ* Antigua GS, Epsom Coll, Peterhouse Cambridge (MA, CEng); *m* 1928, Mary Julia, da of Dr Ronald Gray, of Hindhead, Surrey; 2 s, 2 da; *Career* joined RAF 1924, served WW II (despatches four times), Gp Capt 1941, Air Cdre 1943, Air Vice-Marshal 1952, Air Marshal 1958, C-in-C Pakistan Air Force 1956, AOC-in-C Tech Trg Cmd 1958, air memb for personnel 1959-61, ret 1962; FRAeS; *Recreations* sailing (yachts: 'Bachante', 'Mollymawk'); *Clubs* RAF Sailing Assoc (Adm), RAF, Royal Lymington YC; *Style—* Air Marshal Sir Arthur McDonald, KCB, AFC, DL; 9 Dancell's Walk, Lymington, Hants (☎ 0590 73843)

MACDONALD, Col Charles Benson; OBE (1960), TD (1950); s of Charles James Macdonald (d 1955), and Edith Macdonald (d 1968); *b* 18 May 1917; *Educ* Ratcliffe Coll Leicester; *m* 1, 1940, Dorothy Mary (d 1974), da of Reginald James Hebbert (d 1961); m 2, 1974, Kathleen Louisa Rawson, da of Leonard Rawson Bethell (d 1970); 3 s, 2 da and 1 step s; *Career* TA 1938-62, served Iraq, Syria, Lebanon, N Africa, India, Burma, Lt-Col 1957, Col 1960, ret 1962; Sheffield City cllr 1965-71, No 3 Hosp Mgmnt Ctee 1962-70, pres Sheffield Chamber of Trade 1974-75, md Bain Dawes (Sheffield) Ltd 1976-81 (chm 1981-82, conslt 1983-87); memb Lloyd's 1977; *Recreations* golf, fishing, bee-keeping; *Clubs* Sheffield, Army & Navy; *Style—* Col Charles Macdonald, OBE, TD; c/o Bain Clarkson Ltd, New Oxford House, Barkers Pool, Sheffield S1 2HB (☎ 0742 755185); Creagan, Saltergate Lane, Bamford, Sheffield S30 2BE (☎ 0433 51328)

MACDONALD, David Cameron; s of James Fraser Macdonald, OBE, of Umtali, Zimbabwe, and Anne Sylvia, *née* Hutcheson; *b* 5 July 1936; *Educ* St George's Sch Harpenden, Newport GS; *m* 1, 1968, Melody Jane, da of Ralph Vernon Coles; 2 da (Nancy b 1969, Jessica b 1972), m 2, 1983, Sally Anne, da of William Rodger, Invercargill, NZ; 1 s (Hamish b 1984) 1 da (Laura b 1987); *Career* 2 Lt RA Germany 1954; slr Slaughter & May 1961, dir Hill Samuel & Co Ltd 1968 (dep chm 1979, dir Hill Samuel Gp), chm and chief exec Antony Gibbs 1980, sr advsr Credit Suisse First Boston 1983, advsr to HMG on Upper Clyde Shipbuilding Crisis 1971; chm: Issuing Houses Assoc 1975-77, Bath and Portland Gp plc 1983-85, Pittard Garnar plc 1984-; dir gen Panelon Takeovers and Mergers 1977-79; dir: Coutts and Co 1980-, Sears plc 1981-, Merivale Moore plc 1985-; memb Br Tourist Authy 1971-82, tstee of London City Ballet Tst 1982-1987; *Recreations* fishing, music; *Style—* David Macdonald, Esq; Sweetapples Farmhouse, Martin Fordinbridge, Hants (☎ (072 589) 368); 2A Great Titchfield Street, London W1 (☎ 01 322 4954)

McDONALD, David Wylie; CMG (1978), JP (1972); s of William McDonald (d 1956), of 16 Pitkerro Road, Dundee, and Rebecca Wilkinson, *née* Wylie (d 1964); *b* 9 Oct 1927; *Educ* Harris Acad Dundee, sch of architecture Dundee Coll of Art (DA); *m* 1951, Eliza Roberts, da of David Low Steele (d 1955), of 56 Loons Road, Dundee; 2 da (Mairi, Fiona); *Career* mil serv Black Watch (RHR); architect Gauldie Hardie Wright & Needham Dundee, architect architectural off Public Works Dept Hong Kong 1955 (sr architect 1964, chief architect 1967, govt architect 1970, princ govt architect 1972); dir: bldg devpt 1973, public works 1974; sec for lands and works 1981 (ret 1983); memb Cwlth Pty Assoc; former chm: town planning bd, devpt progress ctee, lands and works conf; former memb: legislative cncl, fin ctee, public works sub ctee, public works vetting ctee, land devpt planning ctee, Hong Kong Housing Authy; former dir: Mass Tport Railway Corpn, Hong Kong Ind Estate Corpn, Ocean Park Ltd; former cncl memb: Hong Kong Red Cross, Girl Guides Assoc, Hong Kong Housing Soc; tstee Scottish Tst for the Physically Disabled, memb ctee Margaret Blackwood Housing Assoc; hon memb Worshipful Co of Lorimars 1977; Meml Prize 1950, City CorpnDesign Prize 1953, Silver Jubilee Medal; *Recreations* drawing, painting, calligraphy; *Clubs* Hong Kong (chm 1977), Royal Hong Kong Jockey; *Style—* David Wylie McDonald, Esq; Northbank, Backmuir of Liff, by Dundee, Scotland DD2 5QT (☎ 0382 580483)

MACDONALD, Eleanor Catherine; MBE; da of Frederick William Macdonald (d 1959), and Frances Catherine, *née* Glover (d 1958); *b* 1 Sept 1910; *Educ* Woodford Sch Croydon, London Univ (BA); *Career* WWII MOI and Security Serv 1939-45; fencing prof 1939 (1st woman to become Maître d'Armes de L'Academie d'Epee de Paris); Unilever: dir several subsid cos 1947-69; princ owner mgmnt and trg consultancy 1969-; fndr: Women in Mgmnt, 300 Gp; *Publications* numerous articles on staff devpt; books incl: Live by Beauty, The Successful Secretary, Nothing by Chance; *Recreations* gardening, bird watching; *Clubs* RIIA, RSA; *Style—* Eleanor Macdonald; 4 Mapledale Ave, Croydon, Surrey CR0 5TA (☎ 01 654 4659)

MACDONALD, Hon Mrs (Elspeth Ruth); yst da of 2 Baron Craigmyle (d 1944), and Lady Margaret Cargill, *née* Mackay (d 1958), eldest da of 1 Earl of Inchcape, GCSI, GCMG, KCIE; *b* 17 Feb 1921; *m* 12 Sept 1945, Archibald James Florence Macdonald, JP (d 1983), er s of late Dr G B D Macdonald, of The Oaks, 61 Frognal, NW3; 2 s (Michael b 1947, Ian b 1950); *Style—* Hon Mrs Macdonald; 22 Heath Drive, Hampstead, London NW3

McDONALD, Lady; Ethel Marjorie; da of Theodore Crawford, MC, by his w Sarah Anne Mansfield; *m* 1937, Sir Alexander McDonald, DL, sometime chm Distillers' Co (d 1981); 2 s, 2 da; *Style—* Lady McDonald; 6 Oswald Rd, Edinburgh EH9 2HF (☎ (031 667) 4246)

MacDONALD, Prof (Simon) Gavin (George); s of Simon MacDonald (d 1967), of 34 Moat St, Edinburgh, and Jean Hogarth, *née* Thompson (d 1974); *b* 5 Sept 1923; *Educ* George Heriot's Sch, Edinburgh Univ (MA), St Andrews Univ (PhD); *m* 22 Oct 1948, Eva Leonie, da of Kurt Austerlitz (d 1929), of Breslau, Germany; 1 s (Neil b 1950), 1 da (Carolyn b 1954); *Career* jr sci offr RAE Farnborough 1943-46; lectr Univ of St Andrews 1948-57; sr lectr: Univ Coll of the WI 1957-62, Univ of St Andrews 1962-67, Univ of Dundee 1967-73; dean of Sci 1970-73, vice princ 1974-79, prof physics 1974-78; chm bd of dirs Dundee Rep Theatre 1975-, Fedn of Scottish Theatres 1978-80;

convener Scottish Univ Cncl on Entrance 1976-82 (dep convener 1972-76, memb 1970), dep chm UCCA 1983- (convener tech ctee 1979-83, convener fin and gen purposes ctee 1983-); FInstP 1958, FRSE 1973; *Books* Problems in General Physics (1967), Physics for Biology and Premedical Students (1970, 1975), Physics for the Life and Health Sciences (1975); *Recreations* bridge, golf, writing; *Clubs* Royal Commonwealth; *Style—* Prof Gavin MacDonald; 10 Westerton Ave, Dundee DD5 3NJ (☎ 0382 786 92)

MACDONALD, His Hon George Grant; s of Patrick Thompson Tulloch MacDonald (d 1966), and Charlotte Primrose, *née* Rintoul (d 1978); *b* 5 Mar 1921; *Educ* Kelly Coll Tavistock, Bristol Univ (LLB); *m* 1967, Mary Dolores, *née* Gerrish; *Career* RN 1941-46, Lt RNVR Western Approaches Corvettes, Frigates, and Minesweeping; barr 1947, Western circuit; dep chm Dorest QS 1969, rec of Barnstaple 1971, circuit judge 1972-87, ret; *Recreations* sailing, chess, bridge; *Clubs* Clifton (Bristol); *Style—* His Hon George MacDonald; Flat 1, Minterne House, Dorchester, Dorset DT2 7AX

MACDONALD, 8 Baron (I 1776); Godfrey James Macdonald of Macdonald; JP (1976), DL (1986); Chief of the Name and Arms of Macdonald; s of 7 Baron Macdonald, MBE (d 1970); 3 Baron m 1803 Louisa Maria La Coast, natural da HRH Duke of Gloucester (issue b before m succeeded to Bosville MacDonald, Bt *qv*); *b* 28 Nov 1947; *Educ* Belhaven Hill Sch Dunbar, Eton; *m* 14 June 1969, Claire (Glenfiddich's 1982 Writer of the Year), eld da of Cdre Thomas Noel Catlow, CBE, RN; 1 s (Hon Godfrey Evan Hugo Thomas b 24 Feb 1982), 3 da (Hon Alexandra Louisa b 1973, Hon Isabella Claire b 1975, Hon Meriel Iona b 1978); *Heir* s, Hon Godfrey Macdonald of Macdonald; *Career* pres Royal Scottish Country Dance Soc 1970-73, memb Inverness CC 1970-75, tstee and memb exec ctee Clan Donald Lands Tst 1970-, vice convener Standing Cncl of Scottish Chiefs 1974-, memb of Skye and Localsh Dist cncl 1975-83 (chm fin ctee 1979-83), chm Skye and Lochalsh Local Health Cncl 1978-80; memb Highland Health Bd 1980-; *Clubs* New (Edinburgh); *Style—* The Rt Hon Lord Macdonald; Kinloch Lodge, Isle of Skye (☎ 047 13 214)

MacDONALD, Sir Herbert George deLorme; KBE (1967, OBE 1948), JP (Jamaica); s of late Ronald MacDonald, JP, of Christiania, Jamaica; *b* 23 May 1902; *Educ* Wolmers Boys' Sch, NE HS Philadelphia USA; *Career* clerical and planting activities 1919-1943; published *Sportsman* magazine with Sir Arthur Thelwell, CBE (decd); pres Jamaica Olympic Assoc 1940-44 and 1956-58, pres W Indies Olympic Assoc 1958-61; pres organising ctee: IX Central American and Caribbean Games 1962, 8 Br Empire and Cwlth Games 1966; chm Nat Sports Ltd 1960-67; *Clubs* Constant Spring Golf; *Style—* Sir Herbert MacDonald, KBE, JP; 1 Liguanea Row, Kingston 6, Jamaica (☎ 927 8213)

MACDONALD, Prof Ian; s of Ronald Macdonald, CBE, MC (d 1983), and Amy Elizabeth, *née* Stutz (d 1965); *b* 22 Dec 1921; *Educ* Lancaster Royal GS, Univ of London and Guy's Hosp (MB BS, PhD, MD, DSc); *m* 1, 2 Feb 1946 (m dis 1980), Nora Patricia; 2 s (Graham b 1949, Peter b 1952), 1 da (Helen b 1961); m 2, 10 Aug 1980, Rose Philomena; *Career* RAMC 1946-48; Guy's Hosp: prof of applied physiology 1967-89, head dept of physiology 1977-89; pres Nutrition Soc 1980-83, chm Br Nutrition Fnd 1985-87, memb food additives & food advsy ctee MAFF 1977-86, pres joint WHO/FAO expert ctee on dietary carbohydrates 1986; memb med sub ctee Br Olympic Assoc, cncl London Sports Med Inst; Freeman: City of London 1967, Worshipful Co of Apothecaries 1967; memb American Soc of Clinical Nutrition; FIBiol;; *Books* ed: Effects of Carbohydrates on Lipid Metabolism (1973), Metabolic Effects of Dietary Carbohydrates (1986), Sucrose (1988); *Recreations* walking, DIY; *Style—* Prof Ian Macdonald; Hillside, Fountain Dr, London SE19 1UP (☎ 01 607 3055); Physiology Dept, UMDS, Guy's Hosp, London SE1 9RT (☎ 01 407 6500, ext 3391)

MacDONALD, Ian Alexander; QC (1988); s of Ian Wilson MacDonald (d 1989), of Gullane, E Lothian, and Helen, *née* Nicholson; *b* 12 Jan 1939; *Educ* Glasgow Acad, Cargilfield Sch Edinburgh, Rugby, Clare Coll Cambridge (MA, LLB); *m* 1, 20 Dec 1968 (m dis 1977), Judith Mary, da of William Demain Roberts of Stockport, Cheshire; 2 s (Ian b 3 July 1970, Jamie b 25 Sept 1972); m 2, 12 Oct 1978, Jennifer, da of Roy Hall, of Grimsby, S Humberside; 1 s (Kieran b 17 Oct 1979); *Career* called to the Bar Middle Temple 1963, Astbury Scholar 1962-65, lectr in law Kingston Poly 1968-72, sr legal writer and res conslt Income Data Servs 1974-80, pres Immigration Law Practitioners' Assoc 1984-, memb editorial advsy bd Immigration and Nationality Law and Practice Journal; memb: SE Circuit, Criminal Bar Assoc, Admin Law Bar Assoc; chm independent Inquiry into Racial Violence in Manchester Schs 1987-88; *publications*: Race Relations and Immigration Law (1969), Race Relations - The New Law (1977), The New Nationality Act (with NJ Blake 1982), Immigration Law and Practice (second edn 1987); *Recreations* swimming, squash, reading; *Clubs* Cumberland LTC; *Style—* Ian Macdonald, Esq, QC; 2 Garden Ct, Temple, London EC4Y 9VL (☎ 01 353 1633, 01 353 4621)

MACDONALD, Prof Ian Grant; s of Douglas Grant Macdonald (d 1964), and Irene Alice, *née* Stokes; *Educ* Winchester, Trinity Coll Cambridge (BA, MA), Oxford Univ (MA); *m* 31 July 1954, Margareitha Maria Lodewijk, da of Rene Van Goethem (d 1982); 2 s (Alexander b 1955, Christopher b 1957), 3 da (Catherine b 1959, Helen b 1959, Nicola b 1963); *Career* nat serv Rifle Bd 1947-49; asst princ and princ MoS 1952-57, asst lectr Univ of Manchester 1957-60, lectr Univ of Exeter 1960-63, fell and tutor in mathematics, Magdalen Coll Oxford 1963-72, Fielden prof pure mathematics Queen Mary Coll, Univ of London 1976-87, Emeritus 1987; memb FRS 1979; *Books* Algebraic Geometry: Introduction to Schemes (1968), Introduction to Commutative Algebra (with M F Atiyah 1969), Spherical on a Group of p-adic type (1972), Symmetric Functions and Hall Polynrmials (1979); *Style—* Prof Ian Macdonald; 8 Blandford Avenue, Oxford OX2 8DY (☎ 0865 515373); School of Mathematical Sciences, Queen Mary College, London E1 4NS (☎ 01 975 5473)

MacDONALD, Hon Mrs (Jacaranda Fiona); yr da of 2 Viscount Craigavon (d 1974); *b* 8 Jan 1949; *m* 1972 (m dis 1982), Dudley Francis MacDonald; 1 s (Toby James Francis b 1975), 1 da (Rose Carole b 1978); *Career* co dir; graphology student; *Recreations* tennis, scrabble; *Clubs* Riverside; *Style—* Hon Mrs Macdonald; 23 Kelso Place, London W8 (☎ 01 937 6056)

MACDONALD, Dr James Stewart; s of Kenneth Stewart Macdonald (d 1959), of Mauritius and Perth, and Mary Janet, *née* McRorie; *b* 11 August 1925; *Educ* Sedbergh, Univ of Edinburgh (MB, ChB, DMRD); *m* 19 Oct 1951, Dr Catherine Wilton Drysdale, da of John Drysdale, CBE (d 1979), of Kuala Lumpur, Malaya and Perthshire; 2 s (Kenneth John Stewart, Murdo James Stewart); *Career* RAMC Maj 2 i/c 23 Para Field Ambulance 1952; asst radiologist St Thomas's Hosp London 1959-62, Royal Marsden Hosp: conslt radiologist 1962-85, dir diagnostic X ray dept 1978-85, bd of govrs 1967-82 (vice chm 1975-82); hon sr lectr Inst of Cancer Res 1966-85, teacher in radiology Univ of London 1966-85; memb: ctee of mgmnt Inst of Cancer Res 1969-82, London ctee Ludwig Inst for Cancer Res 1971-85; appeals sec Duke of Edinburgh's Award Scheme (Perth and Kinross) 1986-88, chm Timber Growers UK (E of Scotland) 1988-; memb BMA, FRSM, FRCPE, FRCR; *Books* contrib to numerous books and scientific jls on radiology of cancer; *Recreations* shooting; *Clubs* Army & Navy; *Style—* Dr J S Macdonald; Darquhillan, Gleneagles, Auchterarder, Perthshire PH3 1NG (☎ 0764 62476)

MACDONALD, Hon Janet Anne; da of 7 Baron Macdonald, MBE (d 1970); *b* 2 Nov 1946; *Style—* Hon Janet Macdonald; Armadale Castle, Isle of Skye

MACDONALD, Hon Mrs; Jennifer; *née* Renwick; 2 da of 1 Baron Renwick, KBE (d 1973), and his 1 w, Dorothy Mary, *née* Parkes; *b* 20 Mar 1932; *m* 1, 18 Nov 1954 (m dis 1967), Anthony Duncan Rowe, 3 s of late George Duncan Rowe, of Herons Court, Yateley, Hants; 1 s (Giles b 1956), 1 da (Antonia b 1959); m 2, 1973 (m dis 1978), Roy Philip Arthur; m 3, 1978, Robert Ian MacDonald; *Style—* Hon Mrs Macdonald; Gullet Farm, South Pool, Kingsbridge, S Devon; Flat 11, 40 Chester Sq, London SW1

MACDONALD, Hon Mrs Joan Marguerite; *née* Lord; da of 1 and last Baron Lambury (d 1967), and Ethel Lily, *née* Horton; *b* 10 July 1927; *m* 1, 4 April 1951 (m dis 1965), Miles Lucas Breeden, s of late Carl Breeden; 1 s (Guy b 1953), 1 da (Gail b 1956); m 2, 1966, Angus James Macdonald; *Style—* Hon Mrs Macdonald; 113 Century Court, St John's Wood Rd, NW8

MACDONALD, John Grant; MBE (1962); s of John Nicol MacDonald (d 1969), and Margaret, *née* Vasey (d 1977); *b* 26 Jan 1932; *Educ* George Heriot's Sch, NDC Latimer; *m* 5 Feb 1955, Jean, da of John Kenneth Kyle Harriosn (d 1972); 1 s (Iain b 1959), 2 da (Margaret, Fiona); *Career* HM Armed Forces 1950-52; HM FO now Dip Serv 1949-: Berne 1954-59, third sec Havana 1960-62, second then first sec (commerce) Lima 1966-71, parly clerk FCO 1972-75, first sec (commerce) and head of trade promotion section Washington 1975-79, head of chancery Dhaka 1980-81, head of chancery and HM Consul Bogota 1981-84, cnsllr FCO 1985-86, HM Ambassador to Paraguay 1986-; *Recreations* travel, photography, swimming; *Clubs* Naval an Military, Royal Over-Seas League; *Style—* John G MacDonald, Esq, MBE; c/o Foreign and Commonwealth Office, London SW1A 2AH

MacDONALD, John Grant; s of John William MacDonald (d 1985), of 14 Park Ct, Bishopbriggs, Glasgow, and Jessie, *née* Grant; *b* 20 May 1933; *Educ* Allan Glen's Sch Glasgow, Univ of Strathclyde; *m* 30 March 1968, Ione Margaret, da of Melvyn Philip Bremer, JP (d 1977), of Lake Farm, Waverley, NZ; 1 da (Fiona b 5 March 1970); *Career* Nat Serv RAF 1959-61 serv Malaya and Singapore; worked in London with Sir Basil Spence 1961-65, registered architect 1963, worked with Garner Preston & Strebel 1965-66, directorate of devpt DOE 1966-73, private practice 1973-; chm Andover Town Twinning Assoc 1977-78, pres Andover Chamber of Trade Commerce and Indust 1978-79, chm Central Hants Branch RIBA 1987-89; ARIBA 1965; *Recreations* sailing; *Style—* John MacDonald, Esq; Thorsby, 2 Humberstone Rd, Andover, Hants SP10 2EJ (☎ 0264 51277), Russell Hse, 40 East St, Andover, Hants SP10 1ES (☎ 0264 24068)

MACDONALD, Kenneth Carmichael; CB (1983); William Thomas and Janet Millar Macdonald; *b* 25 July 1930; *Educ* Hutcheson's GS, Glasgow Univ (MA); *m* 1960, Ann Elizabeth Pauer; 1 s, 2 da; *Career* dep under-sec of state MOD (Procurement Executive) 1980-84, (Resources and Programmes) 1985-88; Second Perm Sec MOD 1988-; *Recreations* golf; *Style—* Kenneth Macdonald, Esq, CB; Ministry of Defence, London SW1

MACDONALD, Hon Kenneth Lewis; yr s of 1 Baron Macdonald of Gwaenysgor, KCMG, PC, JP (d 1966), and Mary, *née* Lewis (d 1967); hp to Barony *qv*, Lord MacDonald of Gwaenysgor; *b* 3 Feb 1921; *m* 1952, Maureen Margaret, o da of David Watson-Allan (d 1984); 2 da (Mrs David Waldron b 1954, Laura b 1966); *Career* served 1940-46 with RAFVR; private sec and ADC to Govr and C-in-C Newfoundland Canada 1946-50, dir of Cos, conslt; *Recreations* reading, bridge, walking; *Style—* Hon Kenneth Lewis MacDonald,; Fir Trees, Frog Lane, Balsall Common, West Midlands CV7 7FP

McDONALD, Dr (Edward) Lawson; s of late Charles Seaver McDonald, of London, and late Mabel Deborah, *née* Osborne; *b* 8 Feb 1918; *Educ* Felsted, Clare Coll Cambridge, Middx Hosp, Harvard Univ; *m* 1953 (m dis 1972), (Ellen) Greig, *née* Rattray; 1 s (James b 16 June 1956); *Career* WWII Surgn Lt RNVR served N Atlantic and Normandy Campaigns 1939-45; asst med dept Peter Bent Brigham Hosp Boston Mass and res fell Harvard Univ 1952-53, Rockefeller travelling fell 1952-53, asst dir Inst of Cardiology Univ of London 1955-66; conslt cardiologist: London Hosp 1960-78, Nat Heart Hosp 1961-83, King Edward VII Hosp for Offrs London 1968-88, King Edward VII Hosp Midhurst 1970-; hon conslt cardiologist Nat Heart Hosp 1983-; memb: bd of govrs Nat Heart and Chest Hosps 1975-82, cncl Br Heart Fdn 1975-83; advsr Malaysian Govt; vis lectr: Univs and Cardiac Socs in Europe, N and S America, China and USSR; St Cyres lectr 1966, Charles A Berns Meml lectr Albert Einstein Coll of Med NY 1973, 5 World Congress of Cardiology Souvenir Orator and Lectr's Gold Medallist 1977; FRCP, int fell Cncl on Clinical Cardiology; memb: Br Cardiac Soc, Assoc of Physicians GBI, American Heart Assoc, Italia Soc of Cardiology, Pakistan Cardiac Soc, Revista Portuguesa de Cardiologia; fell American Coll of Cardiology; Order of the Crown of Jahore 1980; *Books* Medical and Surgical Cardiology (jtly 1969), Very Early Recognition of Coronary Heart Disease (ed 1977); *Recreations* art, skiing, mountain walking, sailing; *Style—* Dr Lawson McDonald; 9 Upper Wimpole St, London W1M 7TD (☎ 01 935 7101)

MACDONALD, (Donald) Lewis; s of Donald Macdonald, of Brue, Isle-of-Lewis, and Catherine *née* Maclean; *b* 22 Sept 1942; *Educ* Clydebank HS, Univ of Glasgow (BSc), Chelsea Coll of Sci & Technol; *m* 22 Aug 1969, Christina MacMillan (Christine), da of Donald Roderick Martin, of Lurebost, Isle-of-Lewis; 3 da (Kay b 1972, Nina b 1974, Anne b 1978); *Career* Cadet Pilot RAFVR Glasgow Univ Air Sqdn 1960, cmmnd actg Pilot Offr 1963; sr student 1964; quality assurance mangr Racal-BCC Wembley 1973-74 (prdn planning mangr 1968-73), prdn mangr Racal Datacom Salisbury (1974-78), prdn dir Racal Consec Salisbury 1978-82, md Racal Acoustics Wembly & Watford 1982-89, memb: Lond NW Euroconstituency Businessmen Club (The Europe Club), Lapwwing Flying Gp Denham Aerodrome; MIEE 1974; *Recreations* oil painting, photography, flying, cycling; *Style—* Lewis Macdonald, Esq; Lincoln Lodge, Chalfont Lane, Chorleywood, Rickmansworth, Herts (☎ 09278 4807); Racal Acoustics Ltd,

Beresford AVe, Wembley, Middx (☎ 44 (0) 1 903 1444, fax 44 (0) 1 908 1253, telex 926288)

McDONALD, Hon Mrs; (Margaret Joan); da of Baron Fraser of Lonsdale (d 1974); *b* 1920; *m* 1939, Arthur Edward McDonald; *Style*— THe Hon Mrs McDonald; Tal Marruxa, Safi, Malta

MACDONALD, Michael Stanley; s of Stanley Roche Macdonald (d 1958), and Elsie Roche, *née* Nichols; *b* 12 Sept 1923; *Educ* Churchers Coll Petersfield, Cranleigh Sch; *m* 27 Sept 1947, Cynthia Mary, da of Horace Winstone Harrison (d 1959); 1 s (Martin Stanley Harrison b 1951), 2 da (Michele Annette Cynthia (Mrs Foot) b 1949, Penelope Mary (Mrs Hughes) b 1952); *Career* WW II RAF 1941-46, AC2 Wireless operator, cmmnd PO (Intelligence), served in India and Burma 1942-45, Flt Lt ADC to AOC Malaya 1945-46; md Taylors Eagle Brewery and Austine Cravers 1946-51, md Carlsberg Sales Ltd 1951-74, md Carlsberg Distributors Ltd 1974-81; Carlsberg Brewery Ltd: sales dir 1981-85, md 1985-88, non-exec dir 1988-; church warden St Winifreds Harrogate 1964-74; JP City of Manchester 1965-71 and Harrogate 1971-74; Freeman City of London, Liveryman Worshipful Co of Distillers; Knight of the Danebrau (Denmark); *Recreations* golf, tennis, swimming, gardening; *Clubs* RAF; *Style*— Michael Macdonald, Esq; Carlsberg Brewery Ltd, Bridge St, Northampton NN1 1PD (☎ 0604 234333)

McDONALD, Dr Oonagh; MP (Lab) Thurrock July 1976-; da of Dr McDonald; *b* 21 Feb 1938; *Educ* Roan Sch for Girls Greenwich, E Barnet GS, King's Coll London (PhD); *Career* former philosophy lectr Bristol Univ, sociology lectr, schoolmistress; Parly candidate (Lab): Glos S Feb and Oct 1974; PPS to chief sec Treasy 1977-79; memb: Lab NEC industl policy sub-ctee 1976-, finance and econ affrs sub-ctee 1978-; oppn front bench spokesman: Defence and Disarmament 1981-Nov 1983, Treasy and econ affrs Nov 1983-; *Style*— Dr Oonagh McDonald, MP; Ho of Commons, SW1A 0AA (☎ 01 219 3415/01 940 5563)

MACDONALD, Peter Cameron; DL (West Lothian 1987-); s of Sir Peter George MacDonald WS, JP, DL, (d 1983), of 18 Hermitage Drive, Edinburgh, and Lady Rachel Irene, *née* Forgan; *b* 14 Dec 1937; *Educ* Loretto, East of Scotland Coll of Agric (Dip Agric); *m* 2 Aug 1974, Barbara Helen, da of David Ballantyne, of Peebles; 2 step s (David Drimmie b 1964, Patrick Drimmie b 1967); *Career* farmer 1961-; dir J Dickson & Son Gunmakers 1968-, memb cncl Blackface Sheepbreeders Assoc 1970-74; Scottish Landowners Fedn: memb cncl 1976-85, convener 1985-88, chm countryside review gp 1988-; memb: Pentland Hills Advsy Ctee 1975-78, Pentland Hills Rural Land Mgmnt Gp 1977-84, West Lothian Countryside Advsy Ctee, West Lothian Regn Countryside Ctee 1978-81, Forth River Purification Bd 1979-87; dir Royal Highland Agric Soc of Scotland 1985, vice chm Pentland Hills Regnl Park Consultative Ctee 1987-88; *Recreations* fishing, shooting, golf; *Clubs* Hon Company of Edinburgh Golfers; *Style*— Peter Macdonald, Esq, DL; Colzium Farm, Kirknewton, Midlothian EH27 8DH (☎ 0506 880607)

MACDONALD, The Captain of Clanranald (c 1380); Ranald Alexander Macdonald of Clanranald; 24 Chief of Clanranald; s of Capt Kenneth Macdonald, DSO (d 1938), of Inchkenneth and Gribune; suc kinsman Angus Macdonald, Capt of Clanranald 1944; *b* 27 Mar 1934; *Educ* Christ's Hospital; *m* 1961, Jane, da of Ivar Campbell-Davys, of Llandovery; 2 s (Ranald b 1963, Andrew b 1966), 1 da (Catriona b 1972); *Heir* s, Ranald (Og Angus) Macdonald, yr of Clanranald, b 17 Sept 1963; *Career* fndr, chm and md Tektura Wallcoverings, chm Br Contract Furnishing Assoc 1975-76; memb Standing Cncl Scottish Chiefs 1957-; pres Highland Soc London 1988- (dir 1959-80); vice-pres Caledonian Catholic Assoc London; exec chm Clan Donald Lands Tst 1978-80; chm Museum of Isles 1980; Kt of Justice Constantinian Order of St George 1982; *Recreations* off-shore sailing, fishing; *Clubs* Turf, White's, Pratts, Beefsteak, Puffin's, New (Edinburgh); *Style*— The Captain of Clanranald; Wester Lix House, Killin, Perthshire (☎ 056 72 651); 70B Pavillion Rd, London SW1X 0ES (☎ 01 581 5967); Tektura Ltd, 4-10 Rodney St, London N1 9JH (☎ 01 837 8000, telex 269931)

McDONALD, Hon Lord; Robert Howat McDonald; MC (1944); s of Robert Glassford McDonald (d 1965), of Paisley, Renfrew; *b* 15 May 1916; *Educ* John Neilson Inst Paisley, Glasgow Univ (MA, LLB); *m* 1949, Barbara, da of John Mackenzie, of Ross-shire; *Career* served WWII Maj NW Europe, KOSB (despatches); advocate 1946, QC 1956, sheriff Ayr & Bute 1966-71, pres Industl Tbnl Scotland 1971-73, senator Coll Justice (Scottish Lord of session with title Lord McDonald) 1973-; *Clubs* New (Edinburgh); *Style*— The Hon Lord McDonald, MC; Parliament House, Edinburgh

MACDONALD, Vice Adm Sir Roderick Douglas; KBE (1978, CBE 1966); s of late Douglas Macdonald and Marjorie; *b* 25 Feb 1921,Java; *Educ* Fettes; *m* 1, 1943 (m dis 1980), Joan, da of Adm of the Fleet Sir Algernon Usborne Willis, GCB, KBE, DSO; 2 s (and 1 s decd); m 2, 1980, (Cynthia) Pamela (Mary), da of Humphrey Ernest Bowman, CMG, CBE (d 1965), and sis of Paul Humphrey Armytage Bowman, *qv*; formerly w of Rear Adm Josef Bartosik, CB, DSC, RN; *Career* entered RN 1939, served WW II, served Cyprus 1957 (despatches), cmd Naval Forces Borneo 1965-66 (CBE), Vice Adm 1966, ADC to HM The Queen 1973, COS to C-in-C Naval Home Cmd 1973-76, COS Allied Naval Forces S Europe 1976-79; artist with several one-man exhibitions 1979-; vice-pres 1976-85 and fell Nautical Inst; pres Skye Highland Games, tstee Clan Donald Lands Trust; ygr bro Trinity Ho; *Clubs* Caledonian, Royal Naval Sailing Assoc, Royal Scottish Pipers Soc; *Style*— Vice Adm Sir Roderick Macdonald, KBE; Ollach, Braes, Isle of Skye, Scotland

MACDONALD, Hon Mrs (Rosemary); *née* Brooke; da of 1 Viscount Alanbrooke, KG, GCB, OM, GCVO, DSO (d 1963), and Jane Mary Richardson (d 1925); *b* 25 Oct 1918; *m* 13 July 1945, Capt Ronald Alastair Macdonald, RA, s of Robert Mcdonald, of Liverpool; 2 s (Alastair b 1947, Ian b 1952), 1 da (Janey b 1949); *Style*— The Hon Mrs Macdonald; Bottom Farm, Berkhamsted, Herts

MACDONALD, Trevor John; s of Francis John MacDonald, of 31 Orchard Gardens, Hove, E Sussex, and Violet Eveleigh, *née* Taverner; *b* 15 April 1933; *Educ* Brighton Hove and Sussex GS, Hertford Coll Oxford (MA); *Career* Nat Serv Bombardier RA 1955-57; with Br Iron and Steel Fedn 1957-67 (until nationisation), Br Steel Corpn 1967-88 (until privatisation), asst to chm Br Steel plc 1988-; reader C of E; *Style*— Trevor MacDonald, Esq; 31 Orchard Gardens, Hove, E Sussex (☎ 0273 771228); British Steel plc, 9 Albert Embankment, London SE1 7SN (☎ 01 735 7654, fax 01 387 1142, telex 916061)

McDONALD, Hon Sir William John Farquhar; s of John Nicholson McDonald (d 1964), and Sarah McInnes (d 1941); *b* 3 Oct 1911; *Educ* Scotch Coll Adelaide; *m* 1935, Evelyn Margaret, da of August Koch; 2 da (Sandra, Jacqulyn); *Career* AIF S W Pacific WWII, Capt 1943; MLA Vic (Lib) for Dundas 1947-52 and 1955-70, speaker Legislative Assembly 1955-67, tstee Shrine of Remembrance 1955-70, min for Lands, Conservation and Soldier Settlement 1967-70, tstee Royal Agric Soc; kt 1958; *Recreations* golf, tennis, shooting; *Clubs* Naval and Military, Australian, Melbourne; *Style*— The Hon Sir William McDonald; Brippick, 102 St Georges Rd, Toorak, Vic 3142, Australia (T 241 5839)

MACDONALD OF CLANRANALD, Ranald Alexander; *see*: Clanranald, Capt of

MACDONALD OF GWAENYSGOR, 2 Baron (UK 1949); Gordon Ramsay Macdonald; s of 1 Baron, KCMG, PC (d 1966), and Mary, *née* Lewis (d 1967); *b* 16 Oct 1915; *Educ* Upholland GS, Manchester Univ; *m* 6 May 1941, Leslie Margaret, da of John Edward Taylor, of Rainford, Lancs; 3 da; *Heir* bro, Hon Kenneth Lewis Macdonald *qv*; *Career* served 1940-46 with RA, Maj GSO; joined Bd of Trade 1946; UK trade cmmr Australia 1947-53; md Tube Investments (Export) Ltd 1953-64; chief exec UK Operations Hayek Engineering (AG Zurich), Ferro Metal & Chemical Co, Satra Consultants (UK); *Style*— The Rt Hon Lord Macdonald of Gwaenysgor; c/o House of Lords, London SW1

MACDONALD OF MACDONALD, Hon (Alexander Donald) Archibald; yr s of 7 Baron Macdonald, MBE (d 1970); *b* 3 Sept 1953; *Educ* Eton, Magdalene Coll Cambridge; *Style*— Hon Archibald Macdonald of Macdon; Armadale House, Isle of Skye, Scotland

MACDONALD OF SLEAT; *see*: Bosville Macdonald

MACDONALD OF TOTE, Maj John Lachlan; DL; s of Col Kenneth Lachlan Macdonald of Tote and Skeabost, DSO (d 1938), and his 2 wife, Margaret Elinor, *née* Caldwell; *b* 22 Dec 1919; *Educ* Ampleforth, Trinity Coll Cambridge; *m* 2 June 1961, Mary Imogen, o da of Richard Gerald Micklethwait, TD, of Ardsley House, Barnsley, Yorks; 2 s, 1 da; *Heir* s, Charles Lachlan b 9 July 1964; *Career* served in Lovat Scouts and GHQ Liaison Regt in Faroes, N Africa and Europe 1939-46; memb CC Inverness 1955-64, govr N of Scotland Agric Coll 1959-61; dir Electro Devices Ltd 1962-84; *Clubs* New (Edinburgh); *Style*— Maj John Macdonald of Tote, DL; Tote House, Skeabost Bridge, Isle of Skye (☎ (047 032) 203); 50 Chelsea Park Gdns, London SW3 (☎ 01 352 1925)

MACDONALD ROSS, George; s of John MacDonald Ross, CBE, of London, and Helen Margaret, *née* Wallace; *b* 11 Nov 1943; *Educ* Mill Hill Sch, St Catharine's Coll Cambridge (MA); *m* 24 June 1974, (Margaret) Lynne Ross, da of Elwyn Chubb, of Cardiff; *Career* asst lectr in philosophy Univ of Birmingham 1969-72, res fell in history and philosophy of sci Univ of Leeds 1972-73, (lectr in philosophy 1973-88, sr lectr in philosophy 1988-); chm Nat Ctee for Philosophy, hon sec Br Soc for the History of Philosophy, pres of Leibniz Assoc, memb cncl Royal Inst of Philosophy, memb ctee Leibniz-Gesellschaft; *Books* Leibniz (1984); *Recreations* conviviality, bricolage, walking; *Style*— George MacDonald Ross, Esq; 10 Ashwood Villas, Leeds LS6 2EJ (☎ 0532 755 961); Department of Philosophy, The University, Leeds LS2 9JT (☎ 0532 333 283, fax 0532 336 017, telex 556 473 UNILDS G)

MacDONALD-BARKER, Anthony William; s of William Hector MacDonald-Barker, of Croxley Green, Herts, and Sylvia Gwendoline Ada, *née* Rollings; *b* 18 May 1943; *Educ* Merchant Taylors'; *Career* chemicals trader LS Raw Materials Ltd 1972-75, sales mangr (pharmaceutical div) Intercity Chemicals Ltd 1976-77; sales dir Harbottle (Pharmaceuticals) Ltd 1978- (specialising import-export trade with China); FIEx 1984; *Recreations* most sports, especially cricket (player), football (spectator), horseracing (owner in syndicate), music, travel, philately; *Clubs* Old Merchant Taylors' Soc; *Style*— Anthony MacDonald-Barker, Esq; 29a Chingford Ave, Chingford, London E4 6RJ (☎ 01 529 6054); Harbottle (Pharmaceuticals) Ltd, Seabright Hse, 72-76 River Rd, Barking, Essex IG11 0DY (☎ 01 594 4074/9617, fax 01 591 8563, telex 897933/ 897788)

MACDONALD-BUCHANAN, (Alexander) James; s of Maj Sir Reginald Narcissus Macdonald-Buchanan, KCVO, MBE, MC, DL (d 1981), and Hon Catherine Buchanan (d 1987), o da of 1 Baron Woolavington; bro of Capt John Macdonald-Buchanan, *qv*; *b* 21 April 1931; *Educ* Eton; *m* 26 April 1960, Elizabeth Vivian, da of Hon Hugh Adeane Vivian Smith, MBE (d 1978) (3 s 1 Baron Bicester), of Souldern Manor, Bicester, Oxon; 4 s (Hugh b 1961, James b 1963, Nicholas b 1967, (Charles) Alexander b 1970); *Career* Nat Service Scots Gds (Capt); dir: Macdonald-Buchanan Tstees Ltd, James Buchanan & Co Ltd, Colonial Mutual Life Assur Soc Ltd; High Sheriff Northants 1972; *Clubs* White's, Turf; *Style*— James Macdonald-Buchanan, Esq; Strathconon, Muir of Ord, Ross-shire (☎ 09977 245); 57 Cadogan Lane, London SW1X 9DT (☎ 01 235 3907)

MACDONALD-BUCHANAN, Capt John; MC (1945), DL (Northants 1978); s of Sir Reginald Macdonald-Buchanan, KCVO, MBE, MC, DL (d 1981), and Hon Catherine Buchanan (d 1987), da of 1 Baron Woolavington; bro of Alexander Macdonald-Buchanan, *qv*; *b* 15 Mar 1925; *Educ* Eton, RMC; *m* 1, 3 Nov 1950 (m dis 1969), Lady Rose Fane, o da of 14th Earl of Westmorland (d 1948); 1 s (Alastair b 1960), 2 da (Fiona b 1954, Serena b 1956); m 2, 1969, Jill Rosamonde, o da of Maj-Gen Cecil Benfield Fairbanks, CB, CBE (d 1980), and former w of Maj Jonathan Salusbury-Trelawney (ggs of Sir William S-T, 10 Bt); 2 da (Kate b 1970, Lucy b 1972); *Career* 2 Lt Scots Gds 1943, serv 1944-45 NW Europe, Malaya 1948-50, Capt 1948, ret 1952; High Sheriff Northants 1963-64; sr steward of Jockey Club to 1982 (steward 1969-72), memb Horserace Betting Levy Bd 1973-76; *Clubs* Turf, White's; *Style*— Capt John Macdonald-Buchanan, MC, DL; The Stone House, Lower Swell, Stow-on-the-Wold, Glos (☎ (0451) 30622); 22 Cadogan Place, SW1 (☎ 01 235 8615)

MACDONALD-SMITH, Maj-Gen Hugh; CB (1977); s of Alexander Macdonald-Smith (d 1966), and Ada Macdonald-Smith (d 1972); *b* 8 Jan 1923; *Educ* Birmingham Univ (BSc); *m* 1947, Désirée, da of Arthur Evelyn Williamson (d 1942), of London; 1 s (Alexander), 1 da (Judy); *Career* cmmnd REME 1944, served India 1945-48, Singapore 1956-58, BAOR 1961-63 and 1966-67, Maj Gen 1975, dir gen Electrical and Mechanical Engrg (Army) 1975-78; dir Telecommunication Engrg & Mfrg Assoc 1980-87, ret 1987; *Recreations* golf, photography, gardening; *Style*— Maj-Gen Hugh Macdonald-Smith, CB; c/o Lloyds Bank Ltd, 21 Stepney St, Llanelli

MacDONELL OF GLENGARRY, Air Cdre (Aeneas Ranald) Donald; CB (1964), DFC (1940); Hereditary 22 Chief of Glengarry, 12 Titular Lord MacDonell; eld s of Maj Aeneas Ranald MacDonell of Glengarry, CBE (d 1941), of Swanage, Dorset (*see* Burke's Landed Gentry, 18 edn, vol III), and Dorah Edith, *née* Hartford (d 1935); *b* 15

Nov 1913; *Educ* Hurstpierpoint Coll, RAF Coll Cranwell; *m* 1, 14 Oct 1940 (m dis 1972), Diana Dorothy (d 1980), da of Lt-Col Henry Richard Keane, CBE (d 1938), of Belleville House, Cappoquin, Co Tipperary; 2 s ((Aeneas) Ranald Euan (Younger of Glengarry) b 1941, (Colin) Patrick b 1946), 1 da (Lindsay Alice (Mrs Brian Cuthbertson) b 1947); m 2, 9 March 1973, Lois Eirene Frances, da of Rev Gerald Champion Streatfeild (d 1988), of Winchester, Hants; 1 s (James Donald of Scotus b 1974), 1 da (Penelope Lois b 1976); *Career* cmmnd Pilot Offr RAF 1934, No 54 (F) Sqdn 1934-36, seconded to Fleet Air Arm 1936 (Fleet Fighter Pilot); Flying Instr 1938, Sqdn Ldr Air Min 1939, Offr Cmdg No 64 Spitfire Sqdn 1940-41, POW 1941-45, War Cabinet Off (Wing Cdr) 1946-47, Chief Flying Instr RAF Coll Cranwell 1949-50; Air Cdre, Air Attaché Moscow 1956-58; Cmdt No 1 Initial Trg Sch 1959-60; dir Mgmnt and Work Study MOD 1960-64; ret 1964; Mngr Operational Res, Constructors John Brown 1964-67; Personnel Mngr CITB 1967-73; head of industl dept, Industrial Soc 1973-77; ptnr John Courtis & Ptnrs 1977-80; ret; memb Standing Cncl of Scottish Chiefs; tstee: Clan Donald Lands Tst, Finlaggan Tst, Invergarry Castle Tst; vice-pres Ross & Cromarty Branch of Soldiers', Sailors' and Airmens' Families Assoc; AMBIM, FIWSP; *Recreations* bird watching, reading, writing; *Clubs* RAF; *Style*— Air Cdre Donald MacDonell of Glengarry, CB, DFC; Elonbank, Castle St, Fortrose, Ross-shire IV10 8TH (☎ 0831 20121)

McDONNELL, Lady Alice Angela Jane; da of 9 Earl of Antrim; *b* 5 Dec 1964; *Style*— Lady Alice McDonnell

McDONNELL, His Hon Denis Lane; OBE (Mil) 1945; s of David John Joseph McDonnell (d 1938), and Mary Nora, *née* Lane (d 1970); *b* 2 Mar 1914; *Educ* Christian Bros Coll Cork, Ampleforth Coll, Sidney Sussex Coll, Cambridge (MA); *m* 10 Sept 1940, Florence Nina, da of Lt-Col Hugh Thomas Ryan, DSO (d 1936), of Cork; 4 da (Margaret b 1943, Aileen b 1946 (decd), Patricia b 1948, Mary b 1957), 1 s (Hugh b 1949, decd); *Career* WWII RAFVR 1940-45 served in UK and Europe, Wing Cdr; called to bar Middle Temple 1936, practised 1938-40 and 1946-67, master rec 1965, co ct judge 1967-71, circuit judge 1972-86; hon sec cncl HM Circuit Judges 1979-83; (pres 1985); memb Inst of Aribrators; *Recreations* golf, gardening; *Clubs* Pildown GC, Ryegg GC, Woking GC, Royal Cinque Ports GC; *Style*— His Hon Denis L McDonnell, OBE

McDONNELL, Lady Flora Mary; da of 9 Earl of Antrim; *b* 7 Nov 1963; *Style*— Lady Flora McDonnell

McDONNELL, Hon Hector John; s of 8 Earl of Antrim (d 1977), and Angela, Countess of Antrim, *qv*; *b* 1 Mar 1947; *Educ* Eton, Christ Church Oxford; *m* 1969 (m dis 1974), Catherine Elizabeth, da of Ronald Chapman, of Buttermilk Hall, Brill, Bucks; 1 s (Conquitto Angus b 1972), 1 da (Hannah b 1971); *Career* painter, exhibited London, Dublin, Paris, Vienna, Brussels, Munich, Stuttgart, Lyons (one-man shows); won Darmstädter Kunstpreis 1978, maj retrospective in Matildenhöhe, Darmstadt 1981; master of Hounds 1966-69; *Publications* Ballad of William Bloat (1982), The Ould Orange Flute (1983), The Night Before Larry was Stretched (1984); *Recreations* bloodsports, travelling; *Style*— The Hon Hector McDonnell; 14 Moore St, London SW3 (☎ 01 581 4445); Mill House, Glenarm, Co Antrim (☎ 554)

McDONNELL, Hon James Angus; MBE (1946); s of 7 Earl of Antrim (d 1932); *b* 1917; *Educ* Eton; *m* 1939, Jeanne Irene, da of Col Stanley Leonard Barry, CMG, CBE, DSO, MVO, DL, JP, *see* Baronetage Barry; 1 s (Sorley James b 1940), 1 da (Louisa b 1946); *Career* 2 Lt 5 Bn Royal Norfolk Regt 1939; *Style*— The Hon James McDonnell; 36 Farley Ct, Melbury Rd, London W14

McDONNELL, John Beresford William; QC (1984); s of Beresford Conrad McDonnell (d 1960), and Charlotte Mary, *née* Caldwell (d 1981); *b* 26 Dec 1940; *Educ* City of London Sch, Balliol Coll Oxford (MA), Harvard Law Sch (LLM); *m* 3 Feb 1968, Susan Virginia, da of Wing Cdr Hubert Mortimer Styles, DSO (d 1942), and Audrey Elizabeth (now Lady Richardson); 2 s (Conrad b 1971, William b 1973), 1 da (Constance b 1975); *Career* first sec Dip Serv, asst private sec to Sec of State 1970, Cons Res Dept 1966-69; fell: Hackness, American Political Sci Assoc Congressional 1964-66; *Recreations* sculling; *Clubs* London Rowing; *Style*— John McDonnell, Esq, QC; 20 Brompton Square, London SW3 2AD (☎ 01 584 1498); office: 1 New Square, Lincoln's Inn, London WC2A 3SA (☎ 01 405 0884, fax 01 831 6109, telex 295257 NITPIK G)

McDONNELL, Hon Randal Alexander St John; s and h of 9 Earl of Antrim; *b* 2 July 1967; *Style*— The Hon Randal McDonnell

McDONNELL OF THE GLENS, The Count Randal Christian Charles Augustus Somerled Patrick; s of The Count and 24 Chief Robert Jarlath Hartpole Hamilton McDonnell of the Glens (d 1984), of 5 Longford Terr, Monkstown, Dublin, and his 2 w, The Countess McDonnell of the Glens, *née* Una Kathleen Dolan; descent from Ian Mor McDonnell, 2 s of John Lord of the Isks and Margaret, da of King Robert II of Scotland, who m Heiress of the Glens, of Antrim, *see* Burkes Peerage Earl of Antrim (who descend from s 5 Chief), and Irish Family Records 1976; f suc kinsman the 23 Chief (ka 1941); 19 Chief cr Bt 1872, dsp 1875; *b* 19 August 1950; *Educ* Stonyhurst, Trinity Coll, Dublin and the Kings Inns, Dublin; *Heir* bro, Count Peter Martin Ignatius Laurence David Colla Hamilton McDonnell; *Career* 25 chief Clandonald S of Antrim (Gaelic patronymic "McIan Mor") lord of the Glens of Antrim; Count of the Holy Roman Empire (which title, created in the preceeding generation passed to the heirs male of the 1st Count in 1766); kt SMOM (1971); *Recreations* opera, ballet, rugby, polo, parties, history; *Style*— The Count Randal McDonnell of the Glens; Roseville Lodge, Shankill, Co Dublin, Ireland (☎ 824635)

McDOUGALL, Alexander Francis Sebastian; s of Capt Ian Alexander McDougall, RM (d 1984), of Emsworth, Hants, and Dr Margaret Joan, *née* Francis (d 1982); *b* 20 Nov 1960; *Educ* Portsmouth GS, Chichester Coll; *m* 30 Aug 1986, Deborah Sara, da of Vincent Christopher Finn, of Lavant, West Sussex; 1 s (Maximilian b 27 May 1988); *Career* dir: Haborn Ltd 1986, N R Resources SDNBHD 1987, Senikah SDNBHD 1987, Haborn France Sarl 1987, Pacol Ltd (Gp) 1988, Pacol Futures Ltd 1988, Pacol Rubber & Latex 1988; *Recreations* water and snow skiing, tai chi, collector of veteran cars; *Clubs* RAC, Emsworth SC; *Style*— Alexander McDougall, Esq; Croft Cottage, Almshouse Common, Petworth Rd, Haslemere, Surrey (☎ 0428 3692); Pacol Ltd, St Dunstan's House, 201 Borough High St, London SE1 (☎ 01 488 2333, fax 01 481 4893, telex 888 712)

MacDOUGALL, Sir (George) Donald (Alastair); CBE (1945, OBE 1942); s of Daniel Douglas MacDougall (d 1929), and Beatrice Amy Miller (d 1954); *b* 26 Oct 1912; *Educ* Shrewsbury, Balliol Coll Oxford (MA); *m* 1, 1937 (m dis 1977), Bridget Christabel, da of George Edward Bartrum; 1 s, 1 da; m 2, 1977, (Laura) Margaret (hon fell and former fell and tutor in economics Somerville Coll Oxford (MA), Hon LLD Nottingham, conslt NEDO), da of George Edward Linfoot (d 1988), and formerly w of Robert Lowe Hall (later Baron Roberthall); 2 step-da see Lord Roberthall; *Career* economist; fell Wadham Coll Oxford 1945-50 (hon fell 1964-), fell Nuffield Coll 1947-64 (hon fell 1967-); Winston Churchill's Statistical Branch 1939-45 and 1951-53; econ dir NEDO 1962-64, dir-gen Dept of Econ Affairs 1964-69, head Govt Econ Serv and chief econ advsr HM Treasury 1969-73, chief econ advsr CBI 1973-84; pres Royal Econ Soc 1972-74; Hon LLD Strathclyde, Hon LittD Leeds, Hon DSc Aston; FBA; kt 1953; *Books Incl:* The World Dollar Problem (1957), Studies in Political Economy (2 vols, 1975), Don and Mandarin: Memoirs of an Economist (1987); *Recreations* fishing; *Clubs* Reform; *Style*— Sir Donald MacDougall, CBE; 86A Denbigh St, Westminster, London SW1V 2EX (☎ 01 821 1998)

McDOUGALL, Douglas Christopher Patrick; s of Patrick McDougall (b 1950), and Helen McDougall (d 1980); *b* 18 Mar 1944; *Educ* Edinburgh Acad, Christ Church Oxford (MA); *m* 4 June 1986, Carolyn Jane, da of Baron Griffiths, MC, PC (life peer), *qv*; 1 da (Fiona b 1987); *Career* investmt mangr and ptnr Baillie Gifford & Co 1969 (sr ptnr 1989-), dir (non exec) IMRO 1987; *Clubs* New (Edinburgh), City of London; *Style*— Douglas McDougall, Esq; 26 Edwardes Sq, London W8 (☎ 01 603 9233); Ballie Gifford & Co, 6 Lancaster Place, London WC2

MacDOUGALL of MacDOUGALL, Madam; Coline Helen Elizabeth; 30 Chief of Clan MacDougall; el da of Col The MacDougall of MacDougall, CMG, 29 Chief, of Dunollie Castle (d 1953), and Colina Edith, *née* MacDougall (d 1963); *b* 17 August 1904; *Educ* St James W Malvern; *m* 25 April 1949, Leslie Grahame Thomson (assumed name MacDougall 1953), FRIBA, RSA, PPRIAS, FSA, o s of Patrick William Thomson, of Edinburgh; *Career* late 2 Offr WRNS, Fleet Air Arm; occupied with Clan MacDougall membs & overseas societies; *Recreations* gardening, painting, hill walking; *Style*— Madam MacDougall of MacDougall; Dunollie Castle, Oban, Argyll

MCDOWALL, David Buchanan; s of Angus David McDowall (d 1957), and Enid Margaret, *née* Crook; *b* 14 April 1945; *Educ* Monkton Combe Sch, RMA Sandhurst, St John's Coll Oxford (MA, MLitt); *m* 19 April 1975, Elizabeth Mary Risk, da of Dr John McClelland Laird; 2 s (Angus b 1977, William b 1979); *Career* subaltern RA 1965-70; Br Cncl (Bombay, Baghdad & London) 1972-77, UNRWA 1977-79; writer (for adults and children), specialist in M East affairs and conslt to NGOs 1980-; received The Other Award (for the Palestinians) 1987, Palestine Red Crescent soc Humanitarian Service Award 1982; *Books* Lebanon - A Conflict in Minorities (1983), The Kurds (1985), The Palestinians (children's book 1986), The Palestinians (Minority Rights Gp 1987), The Spanish Armada (1988), An Illustrated History of Britain (1989), Palestine and Israel: The Uprising and Beyond (1989); *Style*— David McDowall, Esq; 29 Marlborough Road, Richmond, Surrey TW10 6JT (☎ 01 940 3911)

MacDOWALL, Dr David William; s of William MacDowall (d 1944), of West Derby, Liverpool, and Lilian May, *née* Clarkson (d 1961); *b* 2 April 1930; *Educ* Liverpool Inst HS, Corpus Christi Coll Oxford (BA, MA, DPhil), Br Sch at Rome; *m* 21 June 1962, Mione Beryl, da of Ernest Harold Lashmar (d 1969), of Hinderton, Berkhamsted, Herts; 2 da (Sophie b 1965, Tara b 1968); *Career* Royal Signals: 2 Lt 1951-53, 2 Lt (TA) 1953, Lt (TA) 1956; asst keeper dept coins and medals Br Museum 1956-60, princ Min Educn 1960-65; Univ Grants ctee: princ 1965-70, asst sec 1970-73; master Univ Coll and hon lectr classics, ancient history and oriental studies Univ of Durham 1973-78; dir Poly N London 1980-85 (asst dir 1979), chm soc S Asian Studies 1983-; conslt: OECD 1962, 1964, 1966, UNESCO 1977 and 1978; hon tres Royal Numismatic Soc 1966-73, memb ed bd Numismatic Chronicle 1966-, hon sec Soc Afghan Studies 1972-82; Barclay Head Prize Ancient Numismatics Univ of Oxford 1953 and 1956, Medallist Associacion Numismatica Espanola 1964, Nelson Wright Medallist Numismatic Soc India 1974, corresponding memb Istituto Italiano per il Medio ed Estremo Oriente 1986; FRNS 1952, FRAS 1958, FSA 1960; *Books* Coin Collections, Their Preservation, Classification and Presentation (1978), The Western Coinages of Nero (1979); *Recreations* travel, antiquities, photography, natural history, genealogy; *Clubs* Athenaeum; *Style*— Dr David MacDowall; Admont, Dancers End, Tring, Herts HP23 6JY

McDOWALL, Keith Desmond; CBE (1988); s of William Charters McDowall (d 1941), of Croydon, Surrey, and Edna Florence, *née* Blake (d 1988), of Banstead, Surrey; *b* 3 Oct 1929; *Educ* Heath CLark Sch Croydon Surrey; *m* 1; 2 da (Clare Hamilton (Mrs Reid), Alison Ross (Mrs Dodson)); m 2, 30 April 1988, Brenda Dean; *Career* Nat Serv RAF 1947-49; journalist 1946-67: Daily Mail 1955-67 (indust ed London 1962-67); dir of info various govt depts 1969-78: Bd of Trade, Dept of Econ Affrs, Home Off, Housing and Local Govt, N Ireland Off, Dept of Employment; dep dir gen Confedn of Br Indust 1986-88 (dir of info 1981-86); conslt on public affrs and govt relations 1988-; FRSA; *Recreations* sailing, golf; *Clubs* Reform, Medway YC, South Herts GC; *Style*— Keith McDowall, Esq, CBE; 42 Gibson Square, Islington, London N1 0RB

MacDOWEL, Hon Mrs; (Angela Christine); *née* Hazlerigg; da of 2 Baron Hazlerigg, MC, and Patricia, *née* Pullar; *b* 22 Dec 1946; *m* 31 May 1969, Timothy Effingham MacDowel, o son of Lt-Col Horace St George MacDowel, of Fulbrook House, Burford, Oxon; 2 s; *Style*— Hon Mrs MacDowel; C 60 Bellevue Court, 41 Stubbs Rd, Hong Kong

McDOWELL, Eric Wallace; CBE (1982); s of Martin Wallace McDowell (d 1968), of Belfast, and Edith Florence, *née* Hillock (d 1974); *b* 7 June 1925; *Educ* Royal Belfast Academical Inst; *m* 24 June 1954, Helen Lilian, da of William Montgomery (d 1951), Belfast; 1 s (Martin b 11 Nov 1959), 2 da (Kathleen b 24 Jan 1958, Claire b 25 March 1964); *Career* WWII serv 1943-46; qualified CA 1948; ptnr Wilson Hennessey & Crawford 1952-73, sr ptnr in Belfast Deloitte Haskin & Sells 1980-85 (ptnr 1973-80); dir: NI Transport Hldg Co 1971-74, Spence Bryson Ltd 1986-89, TSB NI plc 1986-; memb: advsy ctee NI Central Investmt Fund for Charities 1975- (chm 1980-), NI Econ Cncl 1977-83, Industl Devpt Bd for NI 1982- (chm 1986-), Broadcasting Cncl for NI 1983-86; memb: exec ctee Relate Marriage Guidance 1981-, Presbyterian Church in Ireland (trustee 1983-), Abbeyfield Belfast Soc (tres 1986-); chm bd govrs Royal Belfast Academical Inst 1986 (formerly govr 1959, chm 1977); FCA 1957, FInst CA Ireland 1968-77 (pres 1974-75); *Recreations* current affairs, music & drama, foreign travel; *Clubs* Ulster Reform (Belfast), Royal Overseas; *Style*— Eric McDowell, Esq, CBE; Beechcroft, 19 Beechlands, Belfast BT95HU (☎ 0232 668 771)

McDOWELL, George Roy Colquhoun; *Career* exec chm George H Scholes & Co;

CEng, FIEE; *Style—* G R C McDowell Esq; c/o George H Scholes & Co Ltd, Wylex Works, Wythenshawe, Manchester (☎ 061 998 5454)

McDOWELL, Sir Henry McLorinan; KBE (1964, CBE 1959); s of John McDowell, and Margaret Elizabeth Bingham; *b* 10 Dec 1910; *Educ* Witwatersrand Univ, Queen's Coll Oxford, Yale Univ; *m* 1939, Norah Douthwaite; 1 s, 1 da; *Career* served WWII 1 Bn N Rhodesia Regt; entered Colonial Serv 1938, sec Fed Treasy Rhodesia and Nyasaland 1959-63; chm Zimbabwe bd Barclays Bank Int 1969-79; chllr Rhodesia/ Zimbabwe Univ 1971-82; *Style—* Sir Henry McDowell, KBE; 2 Donne Ct, Burbage Rd, London SE24

McDOWELL, Johanna Susan; da of Vincent Bernard Lena (d 1979), and Ethel Florence, *née* Watkins; *b* 31 Jan 1952; *Educ* Olton Ct Convent Solihill, Twickenham Coll of Technol; *Career* advtg exec; bd dir Brookes & Vernons 1986-, lectr in advtg; *Recreations* bridge, theatre, dinner parties; *Clubs* Edgbaston Priory; *Style—* Mrs Johanna McDowell; 22 South St, Harborne B17 0DB; Brookes & Vernons, 109 Hagley Rd, Edgbaston (☎ 021 455 9481)

McDOWELL, (Charles William) Michael; *b* 11 Feb 1928; *Educ* Huntingdon GS, UCL (BSc); *m* Audrey Diana; 1 s (Robert), 3 da (Sally Anne (Mrs Muir), Julie (Mrs Lloyd), Marion (Mrs Cook)); *Career* public works dept Tanganyika 1951, sr engr Howard Humphreys & Sons 1958-62 (res engr 1954-56), dep res engr London CC 1956-58, princ and fndr M McDowell & Ptnrs 1963, sr ptnr M McDowell Co Partnership 1976-88, princ Engrg Disputes Servs 1988-; cncllr London Borough of Sutton 1968-74; chm Met Centre; 1 PHE: memb 1972, memb cncl 1973-87, pres 1982-83; cncl memb IWEM 1987-88, dir Water Pollution Control Fedn 1986, dir Ciria 1988-, chm Br Standard Sewerage Clay Pipes; Freeman City of London 1980, memb Worshipful Co of Paviors 1980, Master Guild of Water Conservators 1988-; FICE 1955, FIHT 1958, FCIArb 1963, hon FIWM 1988; *Recreations* veteran athletics; *Clubs* Ranelagh Harriers and Veterans Athletic; *Style—* Michael McDowell, Esq; 13 Gilhams Ave, Banstead, Surrey SMY 1QL (☎ 01 394 1573, fax 01 394 1864)

MacDUFF, Alistair Geoffrey; s of Alexander MacDonald MacDuff (d 1985), and Iris Emma, *née* Gardner; *b* 26 May 1945; *Educ* Ecclesfield GS, nr Sheffield, LSE (LLB), Sheffield Univ (LLM); *m* 27 Sept 1969, Susan Christine, da of Ronald David Kitchener, of Salthouse, Norfolk; 2 da (Karen b 1971, Jennifer b 1972); *Career* called to the Bar Lincoln's Inn 1969; rec Crown Ct 1987; former local ward chm of Lib Pty; *Recreations* golf, association football, collecting (and drinking) wine; *Clubs* Hendon GC, Economicals AFC; *Style—* Alistair MacDuff, Esq; The Owls, 84 Northumberland Rd, New Barnet, Herts (☎ 01 449 1816); Devereux Chambers, Devereux Court, London WC2 (☎ 01 353 7534, fax 01 353 1724)

MACDUFF, Earl of; David Charles Carnegie; s and h of 3 Duke of Fife, *qv* (*see* Peerage, Royal Family Section); *b* 3 Mar 1961; *Educ* Eton, Pembroke Coll Cambridge (MA), RAC; *m* 1987, Caroline Anne, o da of Martin Bunting; *Career* stockbroker, formerly with Cazenove & Co, now with Ben Lawrie Ltd; memb Worshipful Co of Clothworkers, Freeman of City of London 1987; *Style—* Earl of Macduff

MacECHERN, Gavin MacAlister; s of Dugald MacAlister MacEchern and Diana Mary *née* Body; *b* 7 Mar 1944; *Educ* Tonbridge; *m* 9 Nov 1972, Sarah Alison, da of Eric Walker (d 1949); 3 da (Georgina b 1976, Tanya b 1978, Christina b 1981); *Career* slr 1967; md Int Offshore Investmts, Bermuda 1970-72, fndr shareholder and dir Arlington Securities plc 1980-; *Recreations* hunting, skiing, shooting, tennis; *Clubs* Brooks's, Royal Southern YC; *Style—* Gavin MacEchern, Esq; Burdocks, Fairford, Glos; Arlington Securities plc, 1 Brewer's Green Buckingham Gate, London SW1 (☎ 01 629 1822) A9753, car ☎ 0836 244493)

McELHERAN, John; s of Joseph Samuel McElheran (d 1971), and Hilda, *née* Veale (d 1986); *b* 18 August 1929; *Educ* Archbishop Holgate's GS York, St Edmund Hall Oxford (BA); *m* 1956, Jean Patricia, da of Fred Durham, of Woodham Walter, Essex (d 1967); 1 s (Richard b 1960), 2 da (Alison b 1962, Catherine b 1964); *Career* asst slr Leather Prior & Son Norwich 1959-67 (ptnr 1962-; sr legal asst Land Cmmn Newcastle-upon-Tyne 1971-83, sr legal asst (asst slr 1974-) DTI and successor dept, under sec (legal) MAFF; *Recreations* photography; *Clubs* Civil Serv; *Style—* John McElheran, Esq; 55 Whitehall, London SW1

McELROY, Vernon William; s of Stanley Cowan McElroy (d 1980), and Emily McElroy, *née* Clark (d 1980); *b* 28 Mar 1934; *Educ* James Watt Tech Sch Smethwick Staffs; *m* 1, 1957, (m dis), Dorothy, da of late Robert Audin; 2 da (Julie b 1963, Susan b 1969); m 2, 1975, Sylvia Evelyn, da of late Lewis Hodge; 2 s (Niall b 1978, Iain b (twin) 1978); *Career* Nat Serv Lt RE and Intelligence Corps 1958-60; chartered surveyor and chartered town planner; ptnr Goddard & Smith 1965-71, property controller The Rank Orgn 1971-75 (md Rank Property Devpts 1971-73, jt md Rank City Wall 1973-75); dir: estate mgmnt Cambridge Univ 1975-87, Aquila Investmts Ltd 1984-, Foxhollow Ltd 1976-; property dir Unex Gp 1987-; fell St Johns Coll Cambridge 1977-87, cncl memb and tres Cambridge Forum for the Construction Indust 1980-; *Recreations* DIY, local affairs; *Clubs* Dartmouth House, 1970; *Style—* Vernon McElroy, Esq; Foxhollow, 15 High St, Orwell, Royston, Herts SG8 5QN (☎ 0223 207707); UNEX House, Church Lane, Stetchworth, Newmarket, Cambridge CB8 9TN (☎ 063876 8144)

McENERY, John Hartnett; s of Maurice Joseph McEnery (d 1934), and Elizabeth Margaret, *née* Maccabe (d 1958); *b* 5 Sept 1925; *Educ* St Aloysius Coll Glasgow, Glasgow Univ (MA); *m* 24 Sept 1977, (Lilian) Wendy, da of George Reginald Gibbons (d 1976); *Career* WWII RA 1943-47 (Staff Capt HQ Burma Cmd 1946-47); Civil Service 1949-64; first sec UK Delgn to NATO Paris 1964-66, cnsllr Br Embassy Bonn 1966-69, regnl dir (under sec) Yorks and Humberside Regn DTI 1972-76, under sec (Concorde and nat compensation div) DTI 1977-81; author, conslt and conceptual analyst 1981-; *Books* Manufacturing Two Nations (1981), Towards a New Concept of Conflict Evaluation (1985); *Recreations* travel, military history; *Clubs* Hurlingham; *Style—* John McEnery, Esq; 56 Lillian Road, London SW13 9JF (☎ 01 748 8658)

McENERY, Peter Robert; s of Charles McEnery (d 1981), and Ada Mary Brinson McEnery; *b* 21 Feb 1940; *m* 1978; 1 da; *Career* actor; roles incl: Rudge in Next Time I'll Sing to You (Criterion 1963), Konstantin in The Seagull (Lyric 1964), Edward Glover in Made in Bangkok (Aldwych 1986), Trigolin in The Seagull (Lyric 1975); dir: Richard III (Nottingham 1971), The Wound (Young Vic 1972); films: Tunes of Glory (1961), The Victim (1961), The Moonspinners (1963), Entertaining Mr Sloane (1970); TV: Clayhanger (1976), The Aphrodite Inheritance (1979), The Jail Diary of Albie Sachs (1980), Japanese Style 91982), The Collectors (1986), The Mistress (1986); assoc artist with RSC; *Recreations* steam railway preservation, skiing; *Style—* Peter McEnery, Esq

McENTEE, Peter Donovan; CMG (1978), OBE (1963); s of Ewan Brooke McEntee (d 1947), and Caroline Laura Clare, *née* Bayley (d 1949); *b* 27 June 1920; *Educ* Haileybury; *m* 1945, Mary Elisabeth, da of George Sheriff Sherwood (d 1956); 2 da (Carol, Bridget); *Career* WWII 1939-45, Maj KAR; HM Overseas Civil Serv 1946-63; dist cmmr, ret as princ Kenya Inst of Admin; FCO: first sec 1963, Lagos 1964-67, serv Whitehall 1967-72, consul gen Karachi 1972-75, govr and C-in-C Belize 1976-80; memb of cCncl and exec ctee Royal Cwlth Soc for the Blind; *Recreations* music, reading, natural history; *Clubs* Royal Overseas League; *Style—* Peter McEntee, Esq, CMG, OBE; Woodlands, Church Lane, Danehill, E Sussex RH1T 7EU (☎ 0825 790574)

McEVOY, David Dand; QC (1983); s of David Dand McEvoy (d 1988), of Stevenston, Ayrshire, and Ann Elizabeth, *née* Breslin; *b* 25 June 1938; *Educ* Mount St Mary's Coll, Lincoln Coll Oxford (BA); *m* 6 April 1974, Belinda Anne, da of Lt-Col Thomas Argyll Robertson, OBE, of Pershore, Worcs; 3 da (Alice b 1978, Louise b 1979, Isabella b 1984); *Career* 2 Lt The Black Watch (RHR) 1957-59, served Cyprus 1958; barr Inner Temple 1964, dep circuit judge 1977, rec Crown Ct 1979-; *Recreations* golf, fishing; *Clubs* Caledonian, Blackwell GC; *Style—* David McEvoy, Esq, QC; Chambers Court, Longdon, Tewkesbury, Glos GL20 6AS (☎ 068 481 626); 2 Fountain Court, Steelhouse Lane, Birmingham 4 (☎ 021 236 3882)

McEVOY, Air Chief Marshal; Sir Theodore Newman; KCB (1956, CB 1951), CBE (1945, OBE 1941); s of Rev Cuthbert McEvoy (d 1944), of Watford, Herts, and Margaret Kate, *née* Ulph; *b* 21 Nov 1904; *Educ* Haberdashers' Aske's Sch, RAF Coll Cranwelll; *m* 17 Sept 1935, Marian Jane Benson, da of William A E Coxon (d 1956), of Cairo; 1 s, 1 da; *Career* joined RAF 1923, served WWII, AOC 61 Gp 1947-50, ACAS (trg) 1951-53, COS Allied Air Forces Central Europe 1956-59, Air ADC to HM The Queen 1959-62, air sec Air Miny 1959-62, ret; *Recreations* glass engraving, gardening; *Clubs* RAF; *Style—* Air Chief Marshal Sir Theodore McEvoy, KCB, CBE; Hurstwood, West Drive, Aldwick Bay Estate, Bognor Regis PO21 4LZ

McEWAN, Surgn Capt Alan; OBE (1977); s of Norman McEwan (d 1972), of Darnick, Melrose, and Ethel Maud, *née* Stanley (d 1983); *b* 20 Dec 1928; *Educ* Dollar Acad, Edinburgh Univ (LRCP, LRCS, LRFPts); *m* 29 March 1963, Caroline Mary, da of Lt-Col Roderick Dillwyn Sims (d 1965), 2 s (Angus b 1964, Alistair b 1967); *Career* RN 1957, Royal Naval Hosp Haslar 1957-59, MO HMS Troubridge 1959-61, infectious disease unit RN Hosp Haslar 1961-62, RA Med Coll Millbank 1962-63, Fleet MO S Atlantic and S American on C-in-C Staff Cape Town S Africa, Admty Med Bd London 1965-67; Base MO: HMS Tamar Hong Kong 1965-67, Polaris base HMS Neptune Faslane Scotland 1969-72, HMS Tamar Hong Kong 1972-73, staff and med dir Gen London 1973-75, staff and med dir and dep dir med personnel and advsr in gen practice to RN 1975-77, dir of postgrad studies Inst of Naval Med Alverstoke Hants 1977-79, Surgn Lt 1957-62, Surgn Lt Cdr 1962-68, Surgn Cdr 1968-77, Surgn Capt 1977, voluntary ret 1979; OStJ 1977; res MO HM Tower of London 1979; med advsr: Financial Times 1980-, Booker plc 1980-, Int Wool Secretariat 1980-, Goldman Sachs 1981-, Channel Four TV 1981-, Charles Barker Gp 1985-, Total Oil Marine 1985-; memb Scottish Int Rugby Squad 1954-55, (played for Edinburgh Univ, Melrose, Cooptimists, South & Scotland); hon med advsr SSAFA HQ London, memb exec ctee Forces Help Soc & Lord Roberts Workshops, med examiner in first aid St John Ambulance; former memb: Med Cncl Hong Kong 1967-69 and 1972-73, Gen Practice Advsy Ctee, Postgraduate Cncl for Med Educn England and Wales 1974-79; Freeman City of London 1980, Liveryman Worshipful Co of Curriers 1980; FRSM 1973, MFCM 1977, FRCGP 1978, fell Med Soc of London 1980; *Recreations* golf, cricket, rugby; *Clubs* Whites, Army & Navy, Berkshire GC, MCC, London Scottish RFC; *Style—* Surgn Capt Alan McEwan, OBE; HM Tower of London EC3 (☎ 01 481 1880); 8 Wellington Rd, Hampton Hill, Middx (☎ 01 977 6170); 107 Harley St, London W1 (☎ 01 935 9463)

McEWAN, Geraldine; da of Donald McKeown, and Norah, *née* Burns; *b* 9 May 1932; *Educ* Windsor County Girls' Sch; *m* 1953, Hugh Percival Cruttwell, *qv*; 1 s (Gregory), 1 da (Claudia); *Career* actress; RSC 1956, 1958 and 1961, Nat Theatre Co 1965-71, 1980-81 and 1983-84, A Lie of The Mind Royal Court Theatre 1987, Lettice and Lovage Globe Theatre 1988-89; TV: The Prime of Miss Jean Brodie 1977, L'Elegance 1982, The Barchester Chronicles 1983; Mapp and Lucia 1985-86; dir As You Like It for the Renaissance Co Phoenix Theatre 1988; Henry V (film) 1989; *Style—* Geraldine McEwan; c/o Marmont Mgmnt Ltd, 302-308 Regent St, London W1

McEWAN, Ian Russell; s of Maj David McEwan, of Ash, Hants, and Rose Violet Lilian Moore; *b* 21 June 1948; *Educ* Woolverston Hall Sch, Sussex Univ (BA), Univ of E Anglia (MA); *m* 1982, Penelope Ruth, da of Dennis Allen, of Lewes, Sussex; 2 s (William b 1983, Gregory b 1986), 2 step da (Polly b 1970, Alice b 1972); *Career* author; began writing 1970; FRSL 1982; *Books* First Love, Last Rites (1975), In Between The Sheets (1978), The Cement Garden (1978), The Comfort of Strangers (1981), The Imitation Game (1981), Or Shall We Die? (1983), The Ploughman's Lunch (1985), The Child in Time (1987); films: Last Day of Summer (1984), Sour Sweet (1989); *Style—* Ian McEwan, Esq; c/o Jonathan Cape, 32 Bedford Sq, London WC1B 3EL

McEWAN, Robin Gilmour; QC; s of Ian Gilmour McEwan (d 1976), and Mary McArthur Bowman McEwan; *b* 12 Dec 1943; *Educ* Paisley GS, Univ of Glasgow (LLB, PhD); *m* 1973, Sheena, da of Stewart Francis McIntyre (d 1974); 2 da (Stephanie b 1979, Louisa b 1983); *Career* Sheriff of Lanark 1982-88, Sherrif of Ayr 1988-; *Recreations* golf; *Clubs* New (Edinburgh), Hon Co of Edinburgh Golfers; *Style—* Robin McEwan, Esq, QC; Sheriff Ct, Ayr KA7 1DR (☎ 268474)

McEWEN, Lady; Brigid Cecilia; *née* Laver; only da of James Laver, CBE (d 1975), and Veronica Turleigh, actress; *m* 1954, Sir Robert Lindley McEwen, 3 Bt (d 1980); 2 s (4 and 5 Bts), 3 da (and 1 da decd); *Style—* Lady McEwen of Marchmont; Polwarth Crofts, Duns, Berwickshire TD10 6YR

McEWEN, Cecilia; *née* Countess von Weikersheim; da of HSH Franz, 2 Prince (*Fürst*, Austrian cr of Emperor Franz Josef 1911 for Carl 2 Baron von Bronn, s of HSH Prince Carl of Hohenlohe-Langenburg (*see* Burke's Royal Families of the World Vol 1, Mediatized Section) and Marie Dorothea, *née* Grathwohl, *suo jure* Baroness von Bronn) Weikersheim, of Fox House, Faringdon, Oxon (d 1983), and HSH Princess Irma zu Windisch- Graetz (d 1984); *b* 28 Oct 1937; *m* 1960, Alexander Dundas McEwen (b 16 May 1935, formerly Queen's Own Cameron Highlanders), 4 s of Sir John McEwen, 1 Bt, JP, DL; 2 s (Alexander b 1962, Hugo b 1965), 1 da (Sophie b

1961); *Career* Dame of the Order of Knights of Malta; MFH Eglington Ayrshire Scotland; *Style—* Mrs Alexander McEwen; Bardrochat, Colmonell, Ayrshire KA26 05G

MACEWEN, Ian Lilburn; s of Gordon Lilburn MacEwen (d 1960), and Sybil Maud, *née* Inglis (d 1976); *b* 15 Sept 1905; *Educ* Trinity Coll Glenalmond; *m* 1, 1937, Penelope (d 1970), da of Lt-Col Astley Jackson (d 1951); 3 s (Peter b 1940, Alastair b 1947, James b 1951); m 2, 1977, Yvonne, da of Alexander John Cassavetti; *Career* overseas merchant 1923-70; dir: The Borneo Co Ltd 1957-66, Incheape Co Ltd 1966-70, Chartered Bank 1957-70, Norwich Union 1972-80; *Recreations* golf, shooting; *Clubs* Royal and Ancient GC; *Style—* Ian MacEwen, Esq; Highfield, The Paddocks, Cowden, nr Edenbridge, Kent (☎ 034 286 860)

McEWEN, Sir John Roderick Hugh; 5 Bt (UK 1953), of Marchmont, Co Berwick, and Bardrochat, Co Ayr; yr s of Sir Robert Lindley McEwen, 3 Bt, (d 1980) and Lady (Brigid) McEwen, *qv*; suc bro, Sir James Francis Lindley, 4 Bt, 1983; *b* 4 Nov 1965; *Educ* Ampleforth, UCL; *Heir* cousin, Adam Hugo McEwen, b 9 Feb 1965; *Style—* Sir John McEwen, Bt; Whiteside, Greenlaw, Berwicks

McEWIN, Hon Sir (Alexander) Lyell; KBE (1954); s of Alexander Lyell McEwin (d 1927), and Jessie Smilie, *née* Ferguson (d 1951); *b* 29 May 1897; *Educ* Prince Alfred Coll; *m* 1921, Dora Winifred, da of late Mark Williams; 4 s, 1 da; *Career* former farmer; MLC SA for Northern Dist 1934-75, chm advsy bd of agric S Australian 1935-37 (memb 1930), chief sec and min of Health and Mines SA 1939-65; chm: S Aust Rifle Assoc 1948-83, Cwlth Cncl State Rifle Assoc 1959-62 (memb 1952-62), Royal Caledonian Soc (SA) 1959-68, Adelaide Highland Games 1960; ldr of oppn Legislative Cncl 1965-67, pres of Legislative Cncl 1967-75 (ret); *Recreations* rifle shooting, bowls; *Style—* The Hon Sir Lyell McEwin, KBE; 93 First Ave, St Peters, S Australia 5069 (☎ 423 698)

MACEY, Rear Adm David Edward; CB (1984); s of Frederick William Charles Macey (d 1978), of Strood, Kent, and Florence May, *née* Macey (d 1986); *b* 15 June 1929; *Educ* Sir Joseph Williamson's Mathematical Sch Rochester, Britannia RNC Dartmouth; *m* 1, 1958, Lorna Therese (d 1976), er da of His Honour Judge Oliver William Verner (d 1957); 1 s (Hugo), 1 da (Anna); m 2, 1982, Fiona Beloe, o da of Vice Adm Sir William Beloe, KBE, CB, DSC (d 1966); 3 step s; *Career* RNC Dartmouth, Midshipman 1948, (cruisers, carriers, destroyers 1950-63) Cdr 1963, American Staff Coll 1964, Cdr RNC Dartmouth 1970, Capt 1972, Directorate Naval Plans 1972-74, RCDS 1975; Dir: RN Staff Coll 1976-78, Naval Manpower 1979-81; ADC to HM the Queen 1981, Rear Adm 1981, Dep Asst Chief of Staff (Operations) Staff of the Supreme Allied Cdr 1981-84, ret; receiver gen Canterbury Cathedral 1984-, gentleman usher of the Scarlet Rod 1985; *Recreations* walking, cricket, cooking; *Clubs* MCC; *Style—* Rear Adm David Macey, CB; Petham Oast, Garlinge Green, Canterbury, Kent CT4 5RT (☎ 0227 70291); The Receiver General, Cathedral House, The Precincts, Canterbury, Kent CT1 2EG (☎ 0227 762862)

MACEY, Air Vice-Marshal Eric Harold; OBE (1975); s of Harold F Macey, and Katrina Macey (d 1981); *b* 9 April 1936; *Educ* Shaftesbury GS; *m* 1957, Brenda Ann, da of Frederick Tom Spencer Bracher (d 1983); 1 s (Julian b 1958); 1 da (Sharon b 1963); *Career* AOC and Cmdt RAF Coll, Cranwell 1985-87; asst chief of the Defence Staff (policy and nuclear) 1987-; *Style—* Air Vice-Marshal Eric Macey, OBE; Ministry of Defence, Main Building, Whitehall, London (☎ 01 218 3157)

MACEY, Roger David Michael; s of Eric Hamilton Macey, and Margaret Maria, *née* Newman; *b* 15 Nov 1942; *Educ* St Mary's Coll Ireland; *m* 18 April 1970 (sep 1987), Julie Elizabeth, da of John Everard Mellors, of Mount Eliza, Melbourne, Aust; 2 s (Jonathan b 20 April 1972, Giles b 25 May 1976); *Career* dir: Wm Brandts Sons & Co (insur) Ltd 1972-76, PS Mossé & Ptnrs Ltd 1977-83; non exec dir: J Jackson & Ptnrs Ltd 1975-76, P S Mossé Life & Pensions 1977-83, George Miller Underwriting Agencies Ltd 1977-86; md Macey Williams Ltd 1976-, memb Lloyds 1974-; *Recreations* shooting, golf, tennis, horse racing; *Clubs* Carlton, City of London; *Style—* Roger Macey, Esq; 2 Gonville House, Manor Fields, Putney, London SW15 (☎ 01 788 9864); Macey Williams Ltd, 10 New St, London EC2M 4TP (☎ 01 623 4344, fax 01 929 0414, car 0836 730644, telex 896618)

McFADYEAN, Colin; s of Sir Andrew McFadyean (d 1974), and Lady Dorothea Emily; gs of Sir John McFadyean (d 1941), pres RVC and fndr of modern veterinary science; *b* 21 Sept 1914; *Educ* Rugby, Brasenose Coll Oxford; *m* 1, 1940 (m dis 1960), Marion, da of Herbert Gutmann (d 1942), 2 da (Andrea b 1949 d 1983, Melanie b 1950); m 2, 16 June 1960, Mary, da of Sir Ian Malcolm (d 1944); *Career* WWII Lt Cdr RNVR 1939-45; admitted slr 1946, ptnr Slaughter and May 1951-82; chm section on business law at Int Bar Assoc 1974-76; dir: Charles Ede Ltd 1970-, David Carritt Ltd 1974-, Artemis Fine Arts Ltd 1974-; *Recreations* travel, gardening; *Style—* Colin McFadyean, Esq; 30 Queen's Grove, London NW8 6HJ (☎ 01 722 4728)

McFADYEAN, Colin William; s of Capt Angus John McFadyean, MC (ka 1944), and Joan Mary Irish; *b* 11 Mar 1943; *Educ* Plymouth Coll, Bristol GS, Loughboro' Coll of Educn (DLC), Keele Univ (Advanced Dip Ed); *m* 29 Aug 1970, Jeanette Carol, da of James A T Payne; 1 s (Ian Robert b 1974); *Career* rugby player, sports commentator; PE teacher 1965-67, PE lectr 1967-72, PE sr lectr 1972-74, dep dir Nat Sports Centre Lilleshall 1974-78, chief coach Jubilee Sports Centre Hong Kong 1979-82, housemaster Dulwich Coll 1983-85, dir gen Nat Playing Fields Assoc 1987-87, Croydon Educn Authy 1988-; memb Hong Kong Cncl for Recreation and Sport 1980-82; *Recreations* golf, tennis; *Clubs* Br Sportsman's, England Rugby Internationals, Moseley Football (vice pres); *Style—* Colin McFadyean, Esq; Springhall, 55 Woodland Way, West Wickham, Kent BR4 9LT

McFADZEAN, Hon (Gordon) Barry; s of Baron McFadzean (Life Peer); *b* 14 Feb 1937; *Educ* Winchester, Christ Church Oxford; *m* 1, 1968 (m dis 1972), Julia Maxine, da of Sir Max Dillon, of Sydney, NSW, Aust; 2 da; m 2, 1984, Diana Rosemary, yst da of late Sam Waters, of Norfolk; *Career* Nat Serv 2 Lt RA 1955-57; CA 1963; dir of various merchant banks 1964-85, exec dir S G Warburg & Co Ltd (Merchant Bankers 1975-78, exec chm Corporate Advsy Partnership Ltd 1986-; *Recreations* music, theatre; *Clubs* Boodles, City of London, Melbourne (Melbourne), Australian (Sydney); *Style—* The Hon Barry McFadzean; c/o 3/57 Earls Ct Square, London SW5 9DG (☎ 01 373 6971)

McFADZEAN, Baron (Life Peer UK 1966); William Hunter McFadzean; KT (1976); s of Henry McFadzean (d 1918), of Reyburn, Stranraer, Wigtownshire, and Agnes Wylie Hunter (d 1960); *b* 17 Dec 1903; *Educ* Stranraer Acad and HS, Glasgow Univ; *m* 1933, Eileen, da of Arthur Gordon, of Blundellsands, Lancs; 1 s (Hon Gordon b 1937), 1 da (Hon Mrs Robin Donald b 1942), 1 adopted da (Mrs Riehl b 1941); *Career* BICC: dir 1945-73, chm 1954-73, hon life pres; chm BIC Construction Co Ltd 1952-64, dir and chm BIC (Submarine) Cables Ltd 1954-73, dir and dep chm Canada Life Assur Co of GB Ltd 1971-82 (dir 1982-84); dir: Canada Life Assur Co (Canada) 1969-79 (hon dir), Canadian Imperial Bank of Commerce 1967-74 (dir emeritus, int advsy cncl memb 1976-83), Midland Bank Ltd 1959-81 (dep chm 1968-77), Midland Bank Tst Co Ltd 1959-67; dep chm: Nat Nuclear Corpn Ltd 1973-80, dir and dep chm: RTZ/BICC Aluminium Hldgs Ltd 1967-73, Canada Life Unit Tst Mangrs Ltd 1971-82 (dep chm 1982-84); chm Standard Broadcasting Corpn (UK) Ltd 1972-79 (hon life pres 1979-86, dir Canada 1973-80); dir and chm Home Oil (UK) Ltd 1972-78 (dir Canada 1972-78), chm Scurry Rainbow (UK) Ltd 1974-78; pres: FBI 1959-61, Br Electrical Power Convention 1961-62; memb: ct Br Shippers' Cncl 1964 (pres 1968-71), advsy ctee for Queen's Award to Indust 1965-67 (chm Review Ctee 1970); fndr chm: Export Cncl for Europe 1960-64, Br Nat Export Cncl 1964-66 (pres 1966-68); Cdr Order of Dannebrog Denmark 1964, (Grand Cdr 1974), Grande Oficial da Ordem do Infante Dom Henrique Portugal 1972; kt 1960; *Recreations* gardening, golf, travel; *Clubs* MCC, Carlton; *Style—* The Rt Hon the Lord McFadzean, KT; 16 Lansdown Crescent, Bath BA1 5EX (☎ 0225 335487); 114 Whitehall Ct, London SW1A 2EP (☎ 01 930 3160)

McFADZEAN OF KELVINSIDE, Baron (Life Peer UK 1980), of Kelvinside in the Dist of City of Glasgow; Francis Scott; *b* 26 Nov 1915; *Educ* Glasgow Univ, LSE; *m* 1938 (sep), Isabel McKenzie Beattie; 1 da (married to Baron Marsh, *qv*); *Career* War Serv 1940-45 (Col), Malayan Govt 1945; Bd of Trade 1938, (tres 1939), Colonial Devpt Corpn 1949, md Royal Dutch/Shell 1964-76, chm Shell Tport and Trading 1972-76 (dir 1964-86); chm: Shell Int Marine Ltd 1966-76, Shell Canada Ltd 1970-76, Shell Petroleum Co Ltd 1972-76 (dir 1964-86); dir: Shell Oil Co 1972-76, Beecham Gp Ltd 1974-86, Coats Patons Ltd 1979-; chm: Br Airways 1976-79, Rolls Royce Ltd 1980-83; Cdr Netherlands Order of Orange Nassau 1975; hon fell LSE; kt 1975; *Style—* The Rt Hon the Lord McFadzean of Kelvinside; c/o House of Lords, Westminster, London SW1

McFALL, John; s of John McFall (d 1974), and Jean McFall *née* Cleary (d 1979); *b* 4 Oct 1944; *Educ* St Patrick's HS, Dumbarton (BSc, BA, MBA); *m* 11 Oct 1969, Ward, da of Peter Ward (d 1981); 3 s (John b 1970, Gerard b 1972, Kevin b 1981); 1 da (Elaine b 1975); *Style—* John McFall; 14 Oxhill Rd, Dumbarton (☎ 0389 31437)

McFARLAND, Anthony Basil Scott; er s and h of Sir John Talbot McFarland, 3 Bt, TD; *b* 29 Nov 1959; *Educ* Marlborough, Trinity Coll Dublin (BA); *m* 28 Oct 1988, Anne Margaret, 3 da of Thomas Kennedy Laidlaw, of Somerton, Castleknock, Co Dublin; *Career* exec Thompson T Line plc, Price Waterhouse; ACA; *Recreations* tennis, rugby, skiing; *Style—* Anthony McFarland, Esq; 31 Walham Grove, London SW6

McFARLAND, Sir John Talbot; 3 Bt (UK 1914), of Aberfoyle, Co Londonderry, TD; s of Sir Basil Alexander Talbot McFarland, 2 Bt, CBE, ERD (d 1986), and Annie Kathleen, *née* Henderson (d 1952); *b* 3 Oct 1927; *Educ* Marlborough, Trinity Coll Oxford; *m* 5 March 1957, Mary Scott, da of Dr Scott Watson (d 1986), of Carlisle Place, Londonderry; 2 s (Anthony Basil Scott, Stephen Andrew John b 23 Dec 1968), 2 da (Jane (Mrs Gailey) b 11 Dec 1957, Fiona Kathleen b 1 Feb 1964); *Heir* s, Anthony Basil Scott b 29 Nov 1959; *Career* Capt RA (TA), Capt (RCT) 1962; memb Londonderry Co Borough Cncl 1955-69, High Sheriff Co Londonderry 1958, DL Londonderry 1962-82 (resigned), High Sheriff City of The Co of Londonderry 1965-67; memb North West HMC 1960-73, jt chm Londonderry & Foyle Coll 1976; chm: Lanes Business Equipment Ltd, (Businesses sold), Robert C Malseed & Co Ltd, McFarland Farms Ltd; dir: Londonderry Gaslight Co Ltd, conslt Londonderry and Lough Swilly Railway Co (chm 1978-81); chm J T McFarland Hldgs; *Recreations* golf, shooting; *Clubs* Kildare and Univ, Northern Counties; *Style—* Sir John McFarland Bt, TD; Dunmore House, Carrigans, Lifford, Co Donegal, N Ireland; Lanes Business Equipment Ltd, 51/53 Spencer Rd, Londonderry, N Ireland (☎ 0504 47326)

MACFARLANE, Andrew Elliott; s of Louis Livingstone Macfarlane, of Kingsdene, Tadworth, Surrey, and Doris Joan, *née* Elliott; *b* 16 Oct 1956; *Educ* King's Sch Canterbury, Selwyn Coll Cambridge (MA); *Career* cmmnd 1976 TAVR, Maj cmdg 200 (Sussex Yeo) Field Bty 100 Field Regt RA (v); CA; Coopers & Lybrand 1977-85, Ernst & Whinney 1985- (ptnr corporate finance dept 1987-); ACA; *Recreations* squash, riding, skiing, Territorial Army; *Style—* Andrew Macfarlane, Esq; Ernst & Whinney, Becket House, 1 Lambeth Palace Rd, London SE1 7EU (☎ 01 928 2000, fax 01 928 0467)

MACFARLANE, Sir George Gray; CB (1965); s of John Macfarlane (d 1938), and Mary Knox Macfarlane (d 1933); *b* 8 Jan 1916; *Educ* Airdrie Acad, Glasgow Univ (BSc), Dresden Technische Hochschule (DrIng); *m* 1941, Barbara Grant, da of Thomas Thomson (d 1947); 1 s, 1 da; *Career* scientist; Telecom Res Estab Malvern 1939-60, dep dir Nat Physical Laboratory 1960-62, dir Royal Radar Estab 1962-67, controller Res Miny of Technol 1967-71, controller R & D Establishments MOD 1971-76; memb: PO Bd 1978-81, bd of tstees Imp War Museum 1978-86, NEB 1980-82, NRDC 1981-82, Br Technol Gp, 1982-85, Br Telecom Bd 1981-87; kt 1971; *Recreations* walking, gardening; *Clubs* Athenaeum; *Style—* Sir George Macfarlane, CB; Red Tiles, Orchard Way, Esher, Surrey (☎ 0372 63778)

MACFARLANE, Iain; s of David Macfarlane (d 1984), of Giffnock, Glasgow, and Jean Gibson, *née* Condie; *b* 6 Sept 1932; *Educ* Jordanhill Coll Sch Glasgow; *m* 4 Sept 1960, Sheila Marian, da of Alexander James Ironside (d 1980), of Giffnock, Glasgow; 1 s (Ronald b 1964), 1 da (Heather b 1962); *Career* sales mangr The Wrigley Co Ltd UK 1968-70; md: The Wrigley Co (EA) Ltd Nairobi Kenya 1974-78 (mktg mangr 1970-73), Wrigley Taiwan Ltd Taipei Taiwan 1978-79; area gen mangr (int) Wm Wrigley Jr Co Chicago USA 1981- (mktg mangr 1979-81); chm Confectoners Benevolent Fund (Cornwall & Devon branch), memb Buckland Monarchorum Parish Church Devon; MIOD 1988;; *Recreations* golf, bird shooting; *Clubs* Yelverton GC; *Style—* Iain Macfarlane, Esq; The Wrigley Co Ltd, Estover, Plymouth, Devon PL6 7PR, (☎ 0752 701107, fax 0752 778850, telex 45543)

McFARLANE, Sir Ian; s of Stuart Gordon McFarlane, CMG, MBE, and Mary Grace McDermott; *b* 25 Dec 1923; *Educ* Melbourne GS, Harrow, Sydney Univ (BSc, BE); *m* 10 Nov 1956, Ann Shaw, da of M A Shaw, of Saltlake City; 1 s (John b 1961), 2 da (Jennifer b 1958, Sharon b 1959); *Career* Served RANVR WWII; dir Morgan Stanley & Co 1976-80 (assoc 1949-59) memb Sydney Stock Exchange 1959-64, ptnr Minnet T J Thompson and Ptnrs, dep chm Magellan Petroleum 1964-70; dir: Trans City Discount 1960-64, Consolidated Rutile Ltd 1964-68, Int Pacific Corpn 1967-73, Aust Gen Insur

Co Ltd 1968-74, Mercantile Mutual Insur Co Ltd 1969-74, Concrete Construction Pty Ltd 1972-74, Int Pacific Aust Investmt Pty Ltd 1972-73; chm and md Southern Pacific Petroleum NL and Central Pacific Minerals NL 1968-, chm Trans Pacific Consolidated Ltd 1964-; fell Christs Coll Cambridge 1987, fndr Sir Ian McFarlane Travelling Professorship in Urology 1980, hon positions in various Aust Hosps; life govr Royal Prince Alfred Hosp Sydney 1982, chm Royal Brisbane Hosp Fndn 1985; kt 1984; *Recreations* tennis, swimming; *Clubs* Australian, Royal Sydney Golf, Queensland, Univ (NY), Cwlth (Canberra), Royal Motor YC (NSW); *Style—* Sir Ian McFarlane; 40 Wentworth Road, Vancluse, NSW 2030; Southern Pacific Petroleum NL, Lufthansa House, 143 Macquarie Street, Sydney NSW 2000 (☎ (02) 241 1621)

MCFARLANE, Dr James Sinclair; CBE (1986); s of John Mills McFarlane (d 1959), and Hannah, *née* Langtry (d 1969); *b* 8 Nov 1925; *Educ* Manchester GS, Emmanuel Coll Cambridge (MA, PhD); *m* 31 March 1951, Ruth May, da of William Wallace Harden (d 1974); 3 da (Mary b 1952, Lucy b 1954, Joanna b 1959); *Career* ICI Ltd 1949-53, tech mangr and sales dir Henry Wiggin & Co Ltd 1953-69, chm and md Smith-Clayton Forge Ltd (GKN) 1969-76, md Garringtons Ltd (GKN) 1976-77, main bd dir GKN plc 1979-82, dir gen Engrg Employers' Fedn 1982-89; CEng, FIM, CBIM; *Recreations* music; *Clubs* Utd Oxford and Cambridge, Caledonian; *Style—* Dr James McFarlane, CBE; The Ct House, Atch Lench, Evesham, Worcs WR11 5SP (☎ 0386 870225)

MACFARLANE, Sir James Wright; JP (Renfrew 1940), DL (Renfrew 1962); s of James Colquhoun Macfarlane, OBE, MIEE, of Braehead, Glasgow; *b* 2 Oct 1908; *Educ* Allan Glen's Sch Glasgow, Royal Coll of Science and Technol, Glasgow Univ (PhD); *m* 1937, Claire, da of George Ross, of Glasgow; *Career* Lt-Col TA (ACF) ret; dir Macfarlane Engineering Co 1926-73; md Cathcart Investment Co 1964-; convenor County of Renfrew 1967-73; pres Assoc of C C in Scotland 1969-71; memb: Royal commission of the Police 1970-71, Holroyd Dept. Cttee on the Fire Service; kt 1973; *Style—* Sir James Macfarlane, JP, DL; 2 Sandrigham Court, Newton Mearns, Glasgow, Scotland G77 5DT

MCFARLANE, John; s of John McFarlane, of Dumfries, Scotland, and Christina Campbell (d 1976); *b* 14 June 1947; *Educ* Dumfries Acad, Edinburgh Univ (MA), Cranfield Sch of Mgmnt (MBA); *m* 31 Jan 1970, Anne, da of Rev Fraser Ian MacDonald Dumfries (d 1983), of Scotland; 3 da (Kirsty b 14 March 1976, Rebecca b 17 March 1979, Fiona b March 18 March 1983); *Career* Ford Motor Co 1969-74; Citicorp 1975-: sr relationship mangr 1975, dir Euro trading centre 1978, dir personnel 1980, vice pres treasy 1983, md Citicorp Investmt Bank Ltd 1987, md Citicorp Scrimgeour Vickers Ltd 1988; dir Blackheath Concert Halls, memb of ct Cranfield Inst of Technol; *Recreations* music; *Style—* John McFarlane, Esq; Citicorp Scrimgeour Vickers Ltd, PO Box 200, Cottons Centre, Hays Lane, London SE1 2QT (☎ 01 234 2424, fax 01 234 5413, telex 885171/886004)

MACFARLANE, John Caldwell; *b* 5 Dec 1930; *Educ* Glasgow Acad, Strathclyde Univ (Formerly RCST); *m* Anita, *née* Beard 2 s, 1 da; *Career* chartered engr; CBIM vice-pres UK Cummins Engine Co Inc USA (mfr of diesel engines), memb English Industl Estates Corpn; md Cummins Engine Co Ltd (UK Subsidiary), dir Lloyds Register Quality Assur Ltd 1985; Queens Award CECL; Darl Div; Dav Div; FEng, FIME, FIPE; *Recreations* golf, skiing, swimming; *Clubs* RAC, RSAC, Caledonian; *Style—* John Macfarlane, Esq; Cummins Engine Co Ltd, Yarm Rd, Darlington, Co Durham DL1 4PW (☎ 0325 460606)

MACFARLANE, Jonathan Stephen; s of William Keith Macfarlane (d 1987), and Pearl Hastings, *née* Impey; *b* 28 Mar 1956; *Educ* Charterhouse, Oriel Coll Oxford (MA); *m* 7 May 1983, Johanna Susanne, da of John Mordaunt Foster (d 1988); 1 s (David b 1988); *Career* slr 1980, ptnr Macfarlanes 1985; *Clubs* Leander; *Style—* Jonathan Macfarlane, Esq; 10 Norwich St, London EC4A 1BD (☎ 01 831 9222, fax 01 831 9607, telex 296381)

MACFARLANE, (David) Neil; MP (Cons Sutton and Cheam Feb 1974-); s of Robert and Dulcie Macfarlane, of Yelverton, S Devon; *b* 7 May 1936; *Educ* Bancroft's Sch London; *m* 1961, June Osmond, er da of John King, of Somerset; 2 s, 1 da; *Career* Lt 1 Bn Essex Regt 1955-58, Capt RA 265 LAA TA 1959-69; Essex cricketer 1952-56, capt YA XI; Shell Mex & BP 1959-74; parly candidate: East Ham North 1970, Sutton & Cheam (by-election) 1972; sec: Cons Greater London members, Cons sports ctee, Cons energy ctee; memb all-pty select ctee Sci and Technol; parly under-sec state: DES 1979-81, Sport 1981-85, parly under-sec state DOE 1981-85; dep Arts Min 1979-81; capt parly Golfing Soc; vice pres PGA European Tour; kt 1988; *Books* Politics and Sport (1986); *Recreations* golf; *Clubs* Caledonian, MCC, Essex CCC, Huntercombe GC, Wentworth GC, Harlequins RFC, Sunningdale GC, Walton Heath GC; *Style—* Sir Neil Macfarlane, MP; 48 Benhill Ave, Sutton, Surrey (☎ 01 642 3791); c/o House of Commons, London SW1A 0AA (☎ 01 219 3404)

MACFARLANE, Sir Norman Somerville; s of Daniel Robertson Macfarlane (d 1985), and Jessie Lindsay, *née* Somerville (d 1975); *b* 5 Mar 1926; *Educ* High Sch of Glasgow; *m* 1953, Marguerite Mary, da of John Johnstone Campbell, of 17 Norwood Drive, Whitecraigs; 1 s (Hamish), 4 da (Fiona, Gail, Marjorie, Marguerite); *Career* cmmnd RA; chm and md Macfarlane Gp (Clansman) plc; chm: Guinness plc, American Tst plc, The Fine Art Soc plc; dir: Clydesdale Bank plc, Gen Accident Fire & Life Assur Corpn plc, Edinburgh Fund Mangrs plc; dir: Glasgow C of C 1976-79, Scottish Nat Orch 1977-82, Third Eye Centre 1978-81; former pres: Company of Stationers of Glasgow, Stationers Assoc of GB and Ireland, Glasgow HS Club; former memb Royal Fine Art Cmmn for Scotland, memb Scottish CBI Cncl 1975-81, pres Royal Glasgow Inst of the Fine Arts 1976-87, govr Glasgow Sch of Art 1976-87, bd memb Scottish Devpt Agency 1979-87, memb Glasgow Univ Ct 1980-88, vice chm Scottish Ballet 1983-87; scottish patron The Nat Arts Collections Fund, chm of govrs The HS of Glasgow, tstee Nat Heritage Memorial Fund, chm Glasgow Action, hon vice pres Glasgow Bn Boys Bde; underwriting memb Lloyd's of London; NACF Hon FRIAS 1984; Hon LLD: Strathclyde 1986, Glasgow 1988; Hon RSA 1987 Hon RGI 1987; kt 1982; *Clubs* Royal Scottish Automobile, Glasgow Art, Glasgow Golf; *Style—* Sir Norman Macfarlane; 50 Manse Road, Bearsden, Glasgow; office: Macfarlane GP (Clansman) plc, Sutcliffe Rd, Glasgow G13 1AH (☎ (041 959) 3396)

MACFARLANE, Maj-Gen William (Bill) Thomson; CB (1981); s of James MacFarlane (d 1966), and Agnes Boylan (d 1970); *Educ* 2 Dec 1925; *m* 16 July 1955, Helen Dora (Dr), da of The Rev Leonard Nelson Meredith (d 1976); 1 da (Christina b 22 July 1957); *Career* chief of staff UK Land Forces 1975-78; dir Public Relations (Army) 1973-75; cdr Corps Royal Signals Germany 1972-73; cabinet offr Secutariat 1970-72; cdr 1 Div HQ and Signal Regt Germany 1967-70; Mil Asst to C in C Far East Land Forces 1964-66; cdr 16 Parachute Brig Sig Sqn 1961-63; served Europe, Near, Mid and Far East theatres 1946-1981; Army Offr (ret), co dir consultant; chm Citicare Co Ltd, and consultant admin 1984; operations dir Hong Kong Resort Co Ltd, Hong Kong 1981-84; Col Comdt Royal Signals 1980-85; chief joint services liaison offr Br Forces Germany 1978-81; *Recreations* golf; *Clubs* Naval and Military, Piccadilly; *Style—* Maj Gen William Macfarlane, CB; Colts Paddock, Aveley Lane, Farnham, Surrey (☎ (0252) 714951); Sion Coll, Victoria Embankment, London EC4 (☎ 01 353 7983)

McFARLANE OF LLANDAFF, Baroness (Life Peer UK 1979), of Llandaff in Co of South Glamorgan; Jean Kennedy; da of James McFarlane (d 1963); *b* 1 April 1926; *Educ* Howell's Sch Llandaff, Bedford and Birkbeck Colls London Univ; *Career* dir of educn Inst of Advanced Nursing Educn London 1969-71, sr lectr in nursing Dept of Social and Preventive Medicine Manchester Univ 1971-73, sr lectr and head Dept of Nursing Manchester Univ 1973-74, chm English National Bd for Nursing, Midwifery and Health Visiting 1980-83, prof and head Dept of Nursing Manchester Univ 1974; and memb with War Graves Cmmn (former memb Royal Cmmn on NHS); Hon DSc Ulster 1981, Hon DEd (CNAA) 1984; SRN, SCM, FRCN; *Books* The Proper Study of the Nurse (1970), The Practice of Nursing Using the Nursing Process(1982); *Recreations* photography, walking, music, travel; *Clubs* Royal Cwlth; *Style—* The Rt Hon the Lady McFarlane of Llandaff; 5 Dovercourt Ave, Heaton Mersey, Stockport, Cheshire; Department of Nursing, Univ of Manchester, Manchester M13 9PT

MacFARQUHAR, Prof Roderick Lemonde; s of Sir Alexander MacFarquhar, *qv*; *b* 2 Dec 1930, Lahore; *Educ* Fettes, Keble Coll Oxford (BA), Harvard Univ (AM); *m* 1964, Emily Jane, da of Dr Paul W Cohen, of New York; 1 s (Rory b 1971), 1 da (Larissa b 1968); *Career* Nat Serv 2 Lt; China specialist Daily Telegraph 1955-61, ed The China Quarterly 1959-68, reporter BBC's Panorama 1963-64, MP (Lab) 1974-79, co presenter BBC World Servs 24 Hours 1979-80, prof of govt Harvard Univ 1984-, dir Fairbank Centre for E Asian Res Harvard Univ; fell: Res Inst on Communist Affairs and E Asian Inst Columbia 1969, Royal Inst of Int Affairs 1971-74, Woodrow Wilson Int Centre for Scholars Washington DC, Leverhulme Res, Force Fndn Res Grant, Rockefeller Fndn Res Grant; *Recreations* reading, travel, listening to music; *Style—* Prod Roderick MacFarquhar; 378 Broadway, Cambridge, MA 02139, USA

McFERRAN, (John) Christopher Herdman; s of Lt-Col John Rowan Addison McFerran, DL, JP (d 1969), of Camus, Strabane, Co Tyrone, and Iona Mary, OBE, *née* Herdman; *b* 16 April 1937; *Educ* St Edward's Sch Oxford; *m* 15 June 1963, Elizabeth Murray, da of Cdre Ian Murray Nicoll Mudie, MBE, RN (d 1985), of Chilbolton, Hants; 1 s (Nicholas John Mudie b 28 July 1971), 1 da (Sarah Frances Mary b 9 Oct 1966); *Career* Lt Northern Irish Horse (TA) 1956-62, TARO 1962; proprietor and md Carpex (NI) Ltd Belfast 1972-, co dir Herdman's Ltd Sion Mills 1980; govr Rockport prep Sch Craigavad 1974-; memb Textile Inst 1967-; *Recreations* sailing; *Clubs* Royal North of Ireland YC (cdre); *Style—* Christopher McFerran, Esq; The Priory, Marino, Holywood, Co Down BT18 0AH (☎ 02317 3108); Carpex (NI) Ltd, East Bread St, Belfast BT4 1AN (☎ 02324 52611, fax 02324 52805)

MCFETRICH, Charles Alan; s of Cecil McFetrich, OBE (d 1988), of 8 Belle Vue Drive, Sunderland, Tyne & Wear, and Kathleen Margaret, *née* Proom; *b* 15 Dec 1940; *Educ* Oundle, Magdalene Coll Cambridge (MA); *m* 25 March 1970 (m dis), Patricia Lois, da of Mr McNeall; 2 s (Daniel Ross 1974, Nicholas William (twin) b 1974), 1 da (Anna Louise b 1973); *Career* CA 1966; student accountant Graham Proom & Smith 1959-61 and 1964-66; Deloitte Haskins & Sells: joined 1966, conslt 1968-73, conslt ptnr 1973-80, seconded under sec industl devpt unit Dept Indust, ops ptnr 1983-84, managing ptnr UK 1985-; IMC 1969, FCA 1979; *Recreations* gardening, theatre, reading; *Clubs* Gresham; *Style—* Alan McFetrich, Esq; 78 Blackheath Park, London SE3 0ET (☎ 01 852 2072); Deloitte Haskins & Sells, 128 Queen Victoria St, London EC4P 4JX (☎ 01 248 3913, fax 01 248 3623, telex 894941)

McGAREL GROVES, Anthony Robin; s of Col Robin Jullian McGarel Groves, OBE, of Lymington, Hampshire, and Constance Morton, *née* Macmillan; *b* 7 Oct 1954; *Educ* Eton, Bath Univ (BSc); *m* 16 Dec 1978, Ann Candace, da of Jack Dawes, of Ross on Wye, Herefordshire; *Career* chartered accountant Deloitte Hastings and Sells 1981; currently working as Investmt mngr The Kuwait Investmt Off; *Recreations* shooting, skiing, theatre, bridge, politics; *Clubs* Lansdowne, Ski; *Style—* Anthony R McGarel Groves, Esq; Clapton Road, Woodburn Moor, Buckinghamshire HP10 0NH; St Vedast House, 150 Cheapside, London EC2 6ET (☎ 01 606 8080)

McGAREL-GROVES, Col Robin Jullian; OBE (1966); s of Lt Col Edward Jullian McGarel-Groves, DSO, MC Scots Gds (d 1977), of Capetown, S Africa, s of Col JEG Groves CMG (d 1967, chm Groves & Whitnall Brewery), Manchester and Hon Mrs Norah Evelyn (d 1932); *b* 6 June 1920; *Educ* Eton; *m* 19 June 1949, Constance Morton Macmillan, da of H M Macmillan of Ferniegair (d 1957), of Helensburgh, Dumbartonshire, Scotland; 4 s (Hugh Macmillan Jullian b 1952, Anthony Robin b 1954, Richard Evelyn b 1956, James Roderick b 1959); *Career* cmmnd RM 1938, War Serv: HMS Devonshire 1940-42, HMS Sheffield 1942-43, HMS Diomede 1943, HMS Enterprise 1943-44, HMS Jamaica 1944, HMS Venerable 1944-47; 42 Commando RM 1948-50, Naval Intelligence Div 1950-52 (Capt BM), Staff of Supreme Cdr Atlantic Norfolk Virginia USA 1952-58, RN Staff Course 1958-59 Maj RM, 2 i/c 45 Commando RM 1961-62, Aden, Kuwait, MOD London-Dir of Def Op Plans Brig, ret 1970; dir Mgmnt Consults Assoc 1970-76; *Clubs* Special Forces; *Style—* Col Robin McGarel-Groves, OBE; Battramsley House, Boldre, Lymington, Hants SO41 8ND (☎ Lyminton 72249)

McGARRIGLE, Colin Sinclair; s of Dr Robert Percival McGarrigle (d 1976), of York, and Mrs Jessie Elizabeth, *née* Altman (d 1988); *b* 15 August 1941; *Educ* Radley, Trinity Coll Dublin (MA), Univ of Leeds (Graduate Cert Educn); *m* 1, 3 Sept 1966 (m dis 1975), (Jennifer) Julia Leila, da Lt-Col K E Boome (d 1974), of Geneva, Switzerland; 1 s (Giles b 1970), 2 da (Sophie b 1967, Tessa b 1974); m 2, Morag Muriel Ferguson Cowling, da of John Wiley (d 1969), of Hartlepool; *Career* 2 Lt The Green Howards 1965; headmaster Bramcote Sch Scarborough 1968-83, headmaster Queen Margaret Sch Escrick York 1983-; memb Yorks Gentlemens CC; IAPS 1968, SHA 1983, GSA 1983; *Recreations* golf, jazz, gardening; *Clubs* Knights of the Campanile; *Style—* Colin McGarrigle, Esq; Wold Cottage, Langton Rd, Norton, Malton, N Yorkshire (☎ 0635 692026); Queen Margaret's Sch, Escrick Park, York YO4 6EU (☎ 0904 87261)

McGARRITY, James Forsyth; CB (1981); s of James McGarrity (d 1977), and

Margaret *née* Davidson (d 1976); *b* 10 April 1921; *Educ* Bathgate Acad, Glasgow Univ (MA, BSc, MEd); *m* 1951, Violet Smith Gunn da of John Philp (d 1957); 1 s (Forsyth), 1 da (Gillian); *Career* 5 Lt (A) RNVR 1943-46; HM sr chief inspr of schs (Scotland) 1973-81; *Recreations* golf, gardening, bridge; *Style—* James McGarrity Esq, CB; 30 Oatlands Park, Linlithgow (☎ 0506 84 3258)

McGEACHIE, Daniel; s of David McGeachie (d 1969), of Arbroath, and Jessie McGeachie; *b* 10 June 1935; *Educ* Arbroath HS; *m* 16 Jan 1962, Sylvia, *née* Andrew; 1 da (Fiona b 1964); *Career* Nat Serv 1953-55; journalist Scotland and Fleet St 1955-60, foreign corr (Africa) Daily Express 1960-65, parly corr (later dip and political corr) Daily Express 1965-75, UK political advsr to Conoco 1975-77, dir of Conoco (UK) Ltd and gen mangr govt and public affrs; cncl memb Indust & Parliament Tst, memb Parliamentary Energy Studies Gp; *Clubs* Reform; *Style—* Daniel McGeachie, Esq; 27 Hitherwood Drive, Dulwich, London SE19 1XA (☎ 01 670 5546); Conoco (UK) Ltd, Park St, London W1Y 4NN (☎ 01 408 6608)

McGEE, Darryll St John; s of Henry John McGee (d 1966), and Jessie Adelene, *née* Guvv (d 1976); *b* 15 Nov 1939; *Educ* Emanuel Sch, King's Coll Cambridge (BA Hons); *m* 12 Sept 1979, Christine Mary, da of Arthur Castle; 3 s (Daeron, Charles, Tim); *Career* bd memb: Finicisa SA Portugal 1981-86, Nurel SA Spain 1981-86, ICI Fibres 1981-88; chm Cantex Fabrics Ltd 1981-86; memb: Nuffield Hosp Local Advsy Ctee, N Yorks Indust Advsy Panel, bd of govrs Harrogate Int Festival; *Recreations* skiing, sailing, tennis; *Style—* Darryll McGee, Esq; ICI plc, Chemicals & Polymer, The Heath, Runcorn, Cheshire WA7 4QF (☎ 0928 514 444)

McGEE, Darryll St John; s of Henry John McGee (d 1966); *b* 15 Nov 1939; *Educ* Emanuel Sch London, King's Coll Cambridge; *m* 1979, Christine Mary, *née* Castle; 3 s; *Career* dir ICI Fibres Ltd, chm Camtex Fabrics Ltd; *Recreations* squash, skiing, politics; *Style—* Darryll McGee, Esq; 52 The Oval, Harrogate, N Yorks

McGEOCH, Vice Adm Sir Ian Lachlan Mackay; KCB (1969, CB 1966), DSO (1943), DSC (1943); s of L A McGeoch of Dalmuir; *b* 26 Mar 1914; *Educ* Pangbourne, Edinburgh Univ (MPHil); *m* 1937, Eleanor Somers, da of Rev Canon Hugh Farrie; 2 s, 2 da; *Career* joined RN 1932; Flag Offr: Scotland & NI 1968-70, Submarines 1965-67; Adm pres RNC Greenwich 1964-65; memb: Royal Co Archers (Queen's Body Guard for Scotland) 1969-, White Ensign Assoc (Cncl); tstee Imperial War Museum 1977-87; ed The Naval Review 1973-80, ed dir Naval Forces 1980-83; dir Midar Systems Ltd; co-author with Gen Sir John Hackett: The Third World War: a Future History (1978), The Third World War; the Untold Story (1982); pres RNVR Club (Scotland) 1981-; *Clubs* Royal Yacht Sqdn, Army & Navy; *Style—* Vice-Adm Sir Ian McGeoch, KCB, DSO, DSC; c/o Coutts & Co, Chandus Branch, 440 Strand, London WC2R 0QS

MCGEOUGH, Prof Joseph Anthony; s of Patrick Joseph McGeough (d 1982), of Stevenston, Ayrshire, and Gertrude, *née* Darroch (d 1975); *b* 29 May 1940; *Educ* St Michael's Coll Irvine, Glasgow Univ (BSc, PhD), Aberdeen Univ (DSc); *m* 12 Aug 1972, Brenda, da of Robert Nicholson, of Newcastle upon Tyne; 2 s (Andrew b 1974, Simon b 1977), 1 da (Elizabeth b 1975); *Career* res demonstrator Leicester Univ 1966, sr res fell Queensland Univ 1967, res metallurgist Int R & D Ltd 1968-69, sr res fell Strathclyde Univ 1969-72; Aberdeen Univ: lectr 1972-77, sr lectr 1977-80, reader in engrg 1980-83; regius prof engrg and head dept mechanical engrg Edinburgh Univ 1983-, industl fell sci and engrg res cncl Royal Soc 1987-89; chm coll cncl Dyce Acad 1980-83, memb tech advsy ctee Scottish Centre Agric Engrg 1987-, hon pres Lichfield Sci and Engrg Soc 1988-89, chm Edinburgh and SE Scotland panel Inst Mechanical Engrs 1988-, hon vice pres Aberdeen Univ Athletics Assoc 1981-; numerous Scottish Co AAA and universities athletic championship awards; FIMechE, FIProdE, MIM, companion Inst Chem Engrs; *Books* Principles of Electrochemical Machining (1974), Advanced Methods of Machining (1988), section on Nonconventional Machining: Encyclopaedia Britannica (1987); *Recreations* walking, athletics; *Style—* Prof Joseph McGeough; 39 Dreghorn Loan, Colinton, Edinburgh EH13 0DF (☎ 031 441 1302); Dept of Mechanical Engineering, University of Edinburgh, King's Buildings, Edinburgh EH9 3JL (☎ 031 661 1081 ext 3350, fax 031 667 7938, telex 727442 UNIVED G)

McGEOWN, Prof Mary Graham; CBE (1985); da of James Edward Mc Geown, of Prospect Hall, Aughagallon, Lurgan, NI, and Sarah Graham, *née* Quinn; *b* 19 July 1923; *Educ* Lurgan Coll, Queen's Univ Belfast (MB, BAO, MD, PhD); *m* 1 Sept 1949, (Joseph) Maxwell Freeland (decd), s of Herbert Freeland (d 1982); 3 s (Peter b 1956, Mark b 1957, Paul b 1961); *Career* house physician Royal Victoria Hosp Belfast 1947-48, house offr Royal Belfast Hosp for Sick Children 1948; asst lectr: biochemistry Queen's Univ Belfast 1949-50, pathology Queen's Univ Belfast 1950-55; grantee MRC 1953-56, res fell Royal Victoria Hosp Belfast 1956-58, conslt nephrologist Belfast Hosps 1962-88, physician in admin charge renal unit Belfast City Hosp 1968-88, chm UK Transplant Mgmnt Ctee 1983-; med advsr to NI Kidney Res Fund 1972-88 (patron 1988-), prof fell Queen's Univ 1988-; memb American Soc Artificial Internal Organs; hon memb: Renal Assoc (pres 1983-86, hon tres 1986-), Ulster Med Soc (pres 1986-87), Assoc Physicians Br & Ireland, Br Transplantation Soc, American Soc Artificial Internal Organs, SA Renal Assoc; FRCP, FRCPE, memb Royal Cwlth Soc; author of numerous articles/chapters on calcium metabolism, kidney diseases treatment, kidney transplantation; *Books* Clinical Management of Electrolyte Disorders (1983); *Recreations* gardening, genealogy; *Style—* Prof Mary McGeown, CBE; 14 Osborne Gardens, Belfast BT9 6LE (☎ 0232 669 918); Dept Medicine, Univ Floor Tower, Belfast City Hospital, Belfast BT9 7AB (☎ 0232 329 241, ext 2963)

McGHIE, James Marshall; QC (1983); s of James Drummond McGhie (d 1970), and Jessie Eadie Bennie (d 1975); *b* 15 Oct 1944; *Educ* Perth Acad, Edinburgh Univ; *m* 1968, Ann Manuel, da of Stanley Gray Cockburn (d 1982); 1 s (Angus b 1975), 1 da (Kathryn b 1983); *Career* advocate Scots Bar; advocate-depute 1983-86; pt/t chm Medical Appeal Tbnls 1987; *Style—* James M McGhie, Esq, QC; 3 Lauder Rd, Edinburgh (☎ 031 667 8325); Parly House, Edinburgh (☎ 031 226 2881)

McGIBBON, Lewis; s of Lewis McGibbon (d 1973), of Newcastle-upon-Tyne, and Norah Rebecca, *née* Duggan; *b* 8 Oct 1931; *Educ* Wallsend GS; *m* 12 Sept 1955, Pauline, da of John Walter Haywood (d 1977), of Newcastle-upon-Tyne; 2 s (David b 21 June 1957, Keith b 16 Oct 1961), 2 da (Susan (Mrs King) b 20 Aug 1960, Gillian b 31 July 1965); *Career* Nat Serv RAF 1955-57; CA; Church & Co Ltd 1960-65, ptnr Grant Thornton 1965-70; currently self employed non-exec dir and chm various cos; former local Magistrate, memb Northampton Health Authy, ctee memb Northants GC (former ctee memb Northants CCC); FCA 1959, played cricket for Northumberland CCC 1950-56 and 1957-59 (against Australian Cricket XI 1956);; *Recreations* golf, bridge; *Style—* Lewis McGibbon, Esq; Green Close, Church Brampton, Northampton

MCGILL, Lewis Sinclair; s of Samuel McGill (d 1953), and Margaret Lewis, *née* Burns; *b* 8 April 1939; *Educ* Forfar Acad, Univ of Strathclyde (MBA); *m* 31 March 1965, Ann Mackintosh, da of John Mitchell (d 1967); 2 s (Colin John b 7 March 1966, Michael Scott b 2 Feb 1968); *Career* Royal Bank of Scotland 1956-: asst gen mangr southern region 1980-81, gen mangr southern region 1981-84, gen mangr strategic planning 1985-86, exec dir int 1986-, exec dir UK banking 1989-; FIBScot; *Recreations* music, sport; *Clubs* Denham GC, Luffnes GC, Gerrards Cross Tennis; *Style—* Lewis McGill, Esq; Caol Ila, Blackpond Lane, Farnham Royal, Slough SL2 3ED Bucks (☎ 02814 4396); The Royal Bank of Scotland plc, 67 Lombard St, London EC3P 3DL (☎ 01 623 4356, fax 01 623 6609)

McGILL, Robert Hampton Robertson; s of William McGill (d 1956); *b* 22 Mar 1913; *Educ* Oundle Sch, Cambridge Univ; *m* 1936, Amelia May, da of Sir David Robertson, former MP for Caithness and Sutherland (d 1970); 1 da (Rosemary Nichol); *Career* Maj Scottish Horse, 4 years with SOE; ptnr Turner Peacock (Slrs), exec and fin dir Power Securities and Balfour Beatty Gp 1956-70, dir (and for 2 yrs chm) Nigerian Electricity Supply Co Ltd 1971-80, chm KCA Drilling Gp Ltd 1974-76, chm Inst of Laryngology 1976-79; *Recreations* golf, fishing, swimming; *Clubs* City of London, Army and Navy, Royal St George's Golf Club, Hawks Club (Cambridge),; *Style—* Robert McGill Esq; Little Ct, Sandwich, Kent (☎ (030 461) 7280)

McGILLYCUDDY OF THE REEKS, The, (Mac Giolla Chuda) Richard Denis Wyer McGillycuddy; suc 1959; s of John Patrick, The McGillycuddy of The Reeks (d 1959), and Elizabeth Margaret, The Madam McGillycuddy of The Reeks; *b* 4 Oct 1948; *Educ* Eton, Aix en Provence; *m* 1984, Virginia Lucy, eld da of Hon Hugh Waldorf Astor, of Folly Farm, Sulhamstead, Reading, Berks, *qv*; 1 da (Tara b 1985); *Heir* cousin, Donough McGillycuddy b 1939; *Career* chm: Chelsea Green Ltd 1981-, Figurehead Ltd 1981-; *Recreations* motor-racing, reading; *Clubs* Pratt's; *Style—* The McGillycuddy of the Reeks

McGIVERN, Eugene; s of James McGivern (d 1981), of Belfast, NI, and Eileen, *née* Dickie; *b* 15 Sept 1938; *Educ* St Colman's Sch, St Mary's GS Belfast; *m* 1 Feb 1960, Teresa, da of Owen Doran, of Lurgan, NI; 2 s (Christopher b 1963, Nicholas b 1971), 1 da (Annette b 1961); *Career* joined Inland Revenue 1955; on secondment sec to Min of State (now Baroness White, *qv*) Welsh Off 1967-69, under sec Inland Revenue 1986- (asst sec 1973); chm mgmnt ctee Cwlth Assoc of Tax Admins 1982-86; govr John Fisher Sch Purley 1979- (chm 1985-86); *Recreations* reading, gardening (if unavoidable); *Style—* Eugene McGivern, Esq; c/o Board of Inland Revenue, Somerset House, Strand, London (☎ 01 438 6622)

MCGLADDERY, Joseph Raymond; s of Joseph McGladdery (d 1946), and Margaret McGladdery (d 1983); *b* 28 May 1927; *Educ* Methodist Coll Belfast, Queens Univ Belfast (BSc); *m* 31 March 1967, Ann Pitcairn, da of John Reekie (d 1982); 1 s (Joseph John); *Career* involved construction Carrington Power Station nr Manchester 1949 and i/c various projects NI 1950-58, a dep chief engr Durgapur Steelworks in W Bengal 1959-60 (costing 120m the largest single Br contract abroad at that time), rep London conslts i/c of first major construction project in Danakil Desert Ethiopa 1961-62; fndr McGladdery & Ptnrs 1962- (responsible for numerous civil and structural engrg projects in UK); FIEI 1970, FICE 1973, MConsE 1974, FCIArb 1974, FIStructE 1975, FIHT 1975, FIWEM 1987; *Style—* Joseph McGladdery, Esq; The Cottage, 43A Malone Park, Belfast BT9 6EL (☎ 0232 669 734); McGladdery and Partners, Consulting Civil and Structural Engrs, 64 Malone Avenue, Belfast BT9 6ER (☎ 0232 660682, 669078)

McGLASHAN, John Reid Curtis; CBE (1974); s of John Adamson McGlashan (d 1961), and Emma Rose May, *née* Curtis (d 1986); *b* 12 Dec 1921; *Educ* Fettes, Christ Church Coll Oxford (Rugby Blue); *m* 9 Aug 1947, Dilys Bagnall, da of Oliver Buxton Knight (d 1950); 1 s (John b 1949), 2 da (Jill b 1951, Julie b 1955); *Career* RAF Bomber Cmd 1940-45 (POW 1941-45); HM Dip Serv 1953-79: Baghdad 1955-57, Tripoli 1963-65, Madrid 1968-70, cnsllr FCO 1970-79, ret; *Style—* John McGlashan, Esq, CBE; Allendale, Clayton Rd, Selsey, W Sussex PO20 9BD (☎ 0243 602 019)

MacGLASHAN, Maureen Elizabeth; da of Kenneth MacGlashan (d 1967), and Elizabeth, *née* Elliott; *b* 7 Jan 1938; *Educ* Luton Girls HS, Girton Coll Cambridge (BA, LLM); *Career* Dip Serv 1961-: third sec (later second sec) HM Embassy Tel Aviv 1964-67, first sec (later head of chancery) E Berlin 1973-75, UK rep EEC Brussels 1975-77, Home Civil Serv 1977-82, cnsll HM Embassy Bucharest 1982-85, asst dir Res Centre for Int Law Cambridge 1985-; ASIL 1986, ILA (Br Section) 1986, BIICL; *Style—* Miss Maureen MacGlashan; 5 Cranmer Rd, Cambridge CB3 9BL

McGLASHAN, Prof Maxwell Len; s of Leonard Day McGlashan (d 1969), of Greymouth, NZ, and Margaret Cordelia, *née* Bush (d 1985); *b* 1 April 1924; *Educ* Greymouth NZ Schs, Canterbury Univ Coll Christchurch NZ (BSc, MSc), Univ of Reading (PhD, DSc); *m* 15 Jan 1947, Susan Jane, da of Col Hugh Edward Crosse, MC, OBE, of Patoka, Hawkes Bay, NZ (d 1962); *Career* sr lectr in chem Canterbury Univ Coll NZ 1953 (asst lectr 1946-48, lectr 1948-53), reader in chem Univ of Reading 1961-94 (Sims Empire Scholar 1949-52, lectr 1954-61), prof of physical chem Univ of Exeter 1964-74, prof of chem and head dept of chem UCL 1974-; Cmmn on Physicochemical Symbols Terminology and Units: memb 1963-65, vice chm 1965-67, chm 1967-71; chm interdivisional ctee on nomenclature and symbols Int Union of Pure and Applied Chem 1971-76; memb: Metrication Bd 1969-80, Comité Consultatif des Unités (metre Convention) 1969-, external memb Br Gas Res Ctee 1979-, tstee Ramsay Meml Fellowships Tst 1982- (chm advsy cncl 1975-), ed Jl of Chemical Thermodynamics 1969-; FRCS 1962; *Books* Physicochemical Quantities and Units (second edn 1971), Chemical Thermodynamics (1979); *Recreations* alpine climbing, theatre; *Clubs* Athenaeum, Swiss Alpine; *Style—* Prof Maxwell McGlashan; 9 Camden Sq, London NW1 9UY (☎ 01 267 1583); Dept of Chemistry, Univ Coll London, 20 Gordon St, London WC1H 0AJ (☎ 01 380 7451, fax 01 380 7463)

McGONIGAL, Christopher Ian; s of Maj H A K McGonigal, MC (d 1963), of Beverley, E Yorks, and Cora, *née* Bentley (d 1946); *b* 10 Nov 1937; *Educ* Ampleforth Coll, CCC Oxford (MA); *m* 28 Sept 1961, (Sara) Sally Ann, da of Louis David Mesnard Fearnley Sander (d 1975); 3 s (Dominic b 1962, Gregory b 1967, Fergus b 1969), 1 da (Alice b 1964); *Career* slr 1965, slr Hong Kong 1981; Coward Chance: asst slr 1965-68, ptnr 1969-87, sr litigation ptnr 1972-79, sr resident ptnr M East 1979-83, sr litigation ptnr 1983-87; jt sr litigation ptnr Clifford Chance 1987-; memb Lamberhurst Local History Soc; memb Worshipful Co of Slrs 1972; *Recreations* local history, gardening, walking; *Style—* Christopher McGonigal, Esq; Sandhurst Farm, Clayhill Road, Lamberhurst, Kent TN3 8AX (☎ 0892 890595); Clifford Chance, Black Friars

House, 19 New Bridge Street, London (☎ 01 353 0211, fax 01 489 0046, telex 887847)

McGONIGAL, Lady; Patricia; *née* Taylor; only da of Robert Taylor; *m* 1941, Rt Hon Sir Ambrose McGonigal, PC, MC (d 1979); 2 s, 2 da; *Style—* Lady McGonigal; Bishops Ct Hse, Bishops Ct, Co Down

McGONNIGILL, Hon Mrs (Jean Brown) Kirkwood; da of 1 Baron Kirkwood, PC (d 1955); *b* 1917; *m* 1943, William Henderson McGonnigill; 3 da; town cncllr; *Style—* The Hon Mrs McGonnigill; Dryleaze, Wotton-under-Edge, Glos

McGOUGH, Roger Joseph; *b* 9 Nov 1937; *Educ* St Mary's Coll Liverpool, Hull Univ (BA, Cert Ed); *Career* poet; fell of poetry Univ of Loughborough 1973-75, writer-in-residence Western Aust Coll of Advanced Educn Perth 1986; *poems* In the Glassroom (1976), Holiday on Death Row (1979), Summer with Monika (1978), Waving at Trains (1982), Melting into the Foreground (1986); selected poems (1989); children's: The Great Smile Robbery (1983), Sky in the Pie (1983), The Stowaways (1986), Noah's Ark (1986) Nailing the Shadow (1987), An Imaginary Menagerie (1988), Helen Highwater (1989), Counting by Numbers (1989); *Clubs* Chelsea Arts; *Style—* Roger McGough, Esq; c/o Peter, Fraser & Dunlop, 5th Floor, The Chambers, Chelsea Harbour Lots Rd, London SW10 0XF

McGOWAN, Hon Annabel Kate Cory; da of 3 Baron McGowan; *b* 1965; *Style—* The Hon Annabel McGowan

McGOWAN, Dowager Lady; Carmen; da of Sir (James) Herbert Cory; *m* 1937, 2 Baron McGowan (d 1966); 3 s, 2 da; *Style—* The Rt Hon the Dowager Lady McGowan; Bragborough Hall, Daventry, Warwickshire (☎ 0788 890210)

McGOWAN, Hon Catriona Carmen Harriet; da of 2 Baron McGowan (d 1966); *b* 8 Jan 1953; *Style—* The Hon Catriona McGowan

McGOWAN, Hon Mrs; (Arabella) Charlotte; *née* Eden; da of Baron Eden of Winton (Life Peer); *b* 1 August 1960; *m* 1983, Hon Mungo McGowan, *qv*; *Style—* The Hon Mrs McGowan; Bragborough Hall, Daventry, Northants

McGOWAN, Hon Dominic James Wilson; s of 2 Baron McGowan (d 1966); *b* 26 Nov 1951; *Educ* Bradfield Coll; *Style—* The Hon Dominic McGowan; Bragborough Hall, Braundston, Daventry, Northants

McGOWAN, 3 Baron (UK 1937); Duncan Cory McGowan; s of 2 Baron McGowan (d 1966), and Carmen, da of Sir Herbert Cory, 1 Bt, JP, DL; *b* 20 July 1938; *Educ* Eton; *m* 1962, Lady Gillian Angela Pepys, da of 7 Earl of Cottenham (d 1968); 1 s, 2 da; *Heir* s, Hon Harry John Charles McGowan b 23 June 1971; *Career* ptnr Panmure Gordon & Co 1971-; *Clubs* Boodle's; *Style—* The Rt Hon the Lord McGowan; 12 Stanhope Mews East, London SW7 (☎ 01 370 2346); Highway Ho, Lower Froyle, Alton, Hants (☎ 0420 22104)

McGOWAN, Hon Emma Louise Angela; da of 3 Baron McGowan; *b* 1963; *Style—* The Hon Emma McGowan

McGOWAN, Frankie (Mrs Peter Glossop); *Educ* Notre Dame HS, Poly of Central London; *m* 27 March 1971, Peter Glossop; 1 s (Tom b 28 Dec 1973), 1 da (Amy b 8 May 1977); *Career* journalist and feature writer; Evening News 1970-73, freelance 1983-85, co-ordinating ed Woman's Journal 1985-86, asst ed Sunday Mirror 1986-87, ed New Woman 1988-; *Recreations* family life; *Style—* Ms Frankie McGowan; New Woman, Murdoch Magazines, Kings House, 8-10 Haymarket, London SW1Y 4BP (☎ 01 839 8272, fax 01 925 0721)

McGOWAN, Baroness; Lady Gillian Angela; *née* Pepys; da of late 7 Earl of Cottenham; *b* 1941; *m* 1962, 3 Baron McGowan; 1 s, 2 da; *Style—* The Rt Hon the Lady McGowan

MacGOWAN, Hon Mrs Jane Alice Camilla; *née* Casey; da of Baron Casey, KG, GCMG, CH, DSO, MC, PC (Life Peer, Govr-Gen of Australia 1965-69, d 1976), and Ethel, AC (d 1983), da of Maj-Gen Sir Charles Snodgrass Ryan, KBE, CB, CMG; *b* 7 Oct 1928; *m* 12 March 1955 (m dis 1981), Murray Wynne Macgowan, s of Clifford Glover Macgowan, of Melbourne; 1 s, 3 da; *Style—* Hon Mrs Macgowan; 5 Darley Pla, Darlinghurst, NSW 2021, Australia

McGOWAN, John Peter; s of Peter McGowan, of Motherwell, Scotland, and Jean Findlay; *b* 3 June 1943; *Educ* OLHS, Scottish Coll of Commerce; *m* 1964, Rebecca, da of John Cox (d 1986), of Holytown, Scotland; 1 s (J Paul b 1971), 1 da (Mhairi b 1967); *Career* md AAF Ltd, gp chief exec Wheway plc; *Recreations* golf, sailing; *Clubs* RAC, 1837; *Style—* John P McGowan, Esq; Tithe Barn, Salwarpe, Worcestershire; Trinity Court, Newton Rd, Great Barr, Birmingham (☎ 021 357 9474, fax 021 358 1568, telex 336159)

McGOWAN, Hon Mungo Alexander Cansh; s of 2 Baron McGowan (d 1966), and Carmen, *née* Cory; *b* 10 Dec 1956; *Educ* Eton, RAC; *m* 1983, Hon (Arabella) Charlotte, *qv*, da of Baron Eden of Winton (Life Peer); 1 s (b 21 June 1985); *Career* Landowner; *Style—* The Hon Mungo McGowan; Bragborough Hall, Daventry, Northants

MCGRADY, Alexander Hughes; TD (1946); s of Clement Alexander McGrady (d 1947), of Dundee, and Kate Giffen, *née* Fairweather (d 1952) ; *b* 14 April 1916; *Educ* Merchiston castle Edinburgh; *m* 3 April 1946, (Vivian) Jytte, da of Gunnar Victor Hartman (d 1957), of Copenhagen; 1 s (Hamish b 1950), 2 da (Susan (Mrs Coles) b 1947, Lou (Mrs Howard) b 1952); *Career* 2 Lt 76 (Highland) Field Regt RA TA 1939 served BEF France and Belgium 1940, seconded RAF 1942; Flt Lt 26 Sqdn RAF 1944-45 served: Normandy, Holland, Germany (despatches 3 times); Capt: 276 (Highland) Field Regt RA TA 1947, 666 (Scottish) Air OP Sqdn RAuxAF 1950; Bell & Sime plc (Formerly Bell & Sime Ltd): joined 1933, dir 1947-81, md and alternate chm 1951-81, ret 1981; *Recreations* motoring; *Clubs* Bentley Drivers; *Style—* Alexander McGrady, Esq, TD; Brackenbrae, West Ferry, Dundee DD5 1RX (☎ 0382 79732)

MCGRADY, MP Edward Kevin; s of late Michael McGrady, of Downpatrick, and Lillian, *née* Leatham; *b* 3 June 1935; *Educ* St Patricks Downpatrick; *m* 6 Nov 1959, Patricia, da of Willia Swail; 2 s (Jerome, Conaill), 1 da (Paula); *Career* ptnr MB McGrady & Co CA and insur brokers; Downpatrick Urban Dist Cncl: cncllr 1961-73, chm 1964-73; Down Dist Council: cncllr 1973-, Chm 1974, 1976, 1978; memb South Down: 1973-74, 1987-, NI Convention 1975, NI Assembley 1982-86; min co-ordination NI Exec 1974; SDLP: 1 chm 1970-72, chief whip 1975-; chm: Down Regnl Museum 1981-, Jobspace NI ltd 1985-; FCA, ACA; *Recreations* gardening, walking, ancient monuments, choral music; *Style—* Edward McGrady, Esq, MP; Constituency Off, 14A Scotch St, Downpatrick, Co Down, N Ireland (☎ 0396 612 882)

MCGRATH, Anthony Charles Ormond; s of Patrick Anthony Ormond McGrath, MC, TD (d 1988), of Southwater, Sussex, and Eleanor Mary Howard, *née* Horsman; *b* 10 Nov 1949; *Educ* Worth Abbey Sch, Univ of Surrey (BSc); *m* 20 July 1974, Margaret Mary, da of Capt William Arthur Usher, RN (d 1959), of Painswick; 1 s (Thomas b 21 Aug 1978), 1 da (Philippa b 20 Nov 1980); *Career* Deloitte Haskins & Sells 1971-76, Baring Brothers & Co Ltd 1976-, (dir 1984-); non exec dir W & FC Barham & Sons Ltd 1987-, non exec memb Br Standards Inst Quality Assurance Bd 1986-; FCA 1974; *Style—* Anthony McGrath, Esq; Baring Brothers & Co Ltd, 8 Bishopsgate, London EC2N 4AE (☎ 01 283 8833, fax 01 283 2224, telex 883622)

McGRATH, John Peter; s of John Francis McGrath (d 1986), and Margaret McCann (d 1985); *b* 1 June 1935; *Educ* Alyn GS Mold Clwyd, St John's Coll Oxford; *m* 1962, Elizabeth, da of Sir Hector Maclennan (d 1978); 2 s (Finn b 1966, Daniel b 1968), 1 da (Kate b 1979); *Career* playwright, theatre dir, writer of screen plays for films and tv, tv dir; artistic dir: 7:84 Theatre Co (England), 7:84 Theatre Co (Scotland); *Books* Over 36 plays performed, many published; writer of over 20 film screenplays and tv plays; poems, songs published and performed; *Style—* John McGrath, Esq; c/o Margaret Ramsay, 14A Goodwins Ct, St Martins Lane, London WC2 (☎ 01 240 0691)

McGRATH, Dr Patrick Gerard; CB (1981), CBE (1971); s of Patrick McGrath (d 1960), of Glasgow, and Mary, *née* Murray (d 1924); *b* 10 June 1916; *Educ* St Aloysius' Coll Glasgow, Univ of Glasgow (MB, ChB), Univ of Edinburgh (Dip Psych); *m* 1949, Helen Patricia O'Brien, 3 s (Patrick, Stephen, Simon), 1 da (Judith); *Career* Lt Col RAMC (Emergency Cmmn), served in UK, Gibraltar, India, Burma, China, Malaya, Maj 2i/c, 80 Ind Para FLD AMB 1944-45; hon Lt Col RAMC; registered med practitioner and conslt psychiatrist; physician supt Broadmoor Hosp 1956-81; fndn fell R C Psych 1971 (vice-pres 1978-80, hon fell 1981); memb: Mental Health Review Tbnl 1960-84, Parole Bd 1982-85; *Books* contrib to various books on forensic psychiatric subjects; *Recreations* golf, bridge; *Clubs* RSM, East Berks Golf; *Style—* Dr Patrick McGrath, CB, CBE; 18 Heathermount Drive, Crowthorne, Berks RG11 6HN

McGRATH, Peter William; s of Maj William Patrick McGrath (d 1960), of Salisbury Wilts, and Winifred Clare Fill (d 1966); *b* 19 Nov 1931; *Educ* Boroughmuir Sch Edinburgh, London Univ (BSc); *m* 20 March 1954, Margaret Irene, da of Leonard S Page (d 1973), of Hartley Wintney, Hants; 1 s (Nicholas John), 3 da (Jennifer, Caroline, Melanie); *Career* Nat Serv RA 1950-51; fin mangr Ford (Germany) 1967-69, controller of fin BR bd 1969-72, fin dir Nat Freight Corp 1972-77, fin and systems dir Truck and Bus Div BL 1977-78, md Leyland Int 1978, chm and md BL Components Ltd 1978-80, gp md Rotaflex plc 1980-82, UK ops dir Stone Int Ltd 1982-86, vice chm Emess plc 1987-; *Recreations* sailing, opera; *Clubs* Medway Yacht; *Style—* Peter McGrath, Esq; St Leonard's Forest Ho, Horsham, W Sussex RH13 6HX (☎ 0293 835 19); 20 St James St, London SW1 (☎ 01 321 0127, fax 01 925 2734, car tel 0836 701 175)

MacGREEVY, Hon Catriona Mary; *née* Shaw; da of 3 Baron Craigmyle; *b* 30 Oct 1958; *m* 7 June 1986, Brian I P MacGreevy, s of late Dr Brian MacGreevy; 1 s (b 1987); *Style—* The Hon Mrs Catriona MacGreevy; 1 Manson Mews, London SW7

MacGREGOR, Alastair Rankin; s of Alexander MacGregor, of 8 Terregles Drive, Glasgow, and Anna, *née* Neil; *b* 23 Dec 1951; *Educ* Glasgow Acad, Edinburgh Univ, New Coll Oxford (MA); *m* 21 Feb 1982, Rosemary Alison, da of Ralph Trevor Kerslake; 1 s (James b 13 June 1984), 1 da (Martha b 5 Jan 1989); *Career* called to Bar Lincoln's Inn 1974, practicing London; *Style—* Alastair MacGregor, Esq; Florian's, West Green, Hartley Wintney, Hants RH27 9JW (☎ 01 583 2000, fax 01 503 0118/353 8958, telex 889109 Essex G)

MCGREGOR, Rev Alistair Gerald Crichton; QC (1982), WS (1965); s of James Reid McGregor, CB, CBE, MC (formerly Capt and Perm Under-Sec of State at WO, d 1985), and Dorothy Janet, *née* Comrie (d 1979); *b* 15 Oct 1937; *Educ* Charterhouse, Pembroke Coll Oxford (BA), Edinburgh Univ (LLB), New Coll Edinburgh Univ (BD); *m* 7 Aug 1965, Margaret Dick, da of David Jackson Lees, of 22 Primrose Bank, Edinburgh; 2 s (D James b 1969, Euan R b 1973), 1 da (Elizabeth b 1970); *Career* slr 1965, advocate 1967; standing jr counsel to: Queen's and Lord Treasurers remembrancer 1976, Scottish Home and Health Dept 1978, Scottish Devpt Dept 1979; clerk to Court of Session Rules Cncl 1974, temporary sheriff 1984-86; minister N Leith Parish Church Edinburgh 1987-; sec Barony Housing Assoc Ltd 1973-83; chm: Family Care Inc 1983-88, Discipline Ctee of Potato Mkting Bd; Church of Scotland Elder 1967-86; memb Faculty of Advocates 1967; *Recreations* squash, tennis, swimming; *Clubs* Edinburgh University Staff, Edinburgh Sports; *Style—* The Rev Alistair McGregor, QC, WS; 22 Primrose Bank Rd, Edinburgh EH5 3JG (☎ 031 551 2802); 1A Madeira Place, Leith, Edinburgh (☎ 031 553 7378)

McGREGOR, Hon Alistair John; 2nd s of Baron McGregor of Durris (Life Peer); *b* 1950; *Style—* The Hon Alistair McGregor; c/o Far End, Wyldes Close, NWII 7JB

McGREGOR, Dr Angus; s of Dr William Hector Scott McGregor (d 1989), of Mickleton, Glos, and Dr Olwen May Richards (d 1967); *b* 26 Dec 1926; *Educ* Solihull Sch, Cambridge Univ (MA, MD), Liverpool Univ (DPH); *m* 14 Apr 1951, May Bridget, da of Peter Burke Birr, (d 1967) of Ireland; 1 da (Catherine b 1963); *Career* RAMC: Lt 1951, Capt 1952: GP 1953, asst MOH Chester 1954-56, dep MOH Hull 1958-65, MOH and Port MO Southampton 1965-74, dist community physician E Dorset 1964-79, regnl MO W Mids RHA 1979-88, ret 1988; visiting prof Univ of Keele 1988-; FFCM 1973, FRCP 1986, FRSA 1986; *Books* Disciplining and Dismissing Doctors in the NHS (with Burbury T 1988), and contributions to various med jnls; *Recreations* piano; *Clubs* Royal Over-Seas League; *Style—* Dr Angus McGregor; 4 Meon Close, Upper Quinton, Stratford Upon Avon CV37 8SX (☎ 0789 720863)

MacGREGOR, Lady; Dorothy Constance; da of John Henry Scarlett, of Jamaica; *m* 1926, Sir Colin MacGregor (d 1982), sometime Chief Justice Jamaica; 1 s (Gordon), 1 da (Elizabeth); *Style—* Lady MacGregor; Garth, Knockpatrick, Manchester, Jamaica

MACGREGOR, Sir Edwin Robert; 7 Bt (UK 1828), of Savile Row, Middlesex; s of Sir Robert James McConnell Macgregor, 6 Bt (d 1963); *b* 4 Dec 1931; *Educ* Univ of British Columbia; *m* 1, 1952 (m dis 1981), Margaret Alice Jean, da of Arthur Peake, of Haney, BC, Canada; 2 s (1 decd), 2 da; m 2, 1982, Helen Linda Herriott; *Heir* s, Ian Grant Macgregor; *Career* assoc dep min of state for Thompson-Okanagan and Kootenay responsible for Crown Lands, Provincial Govt BC Canada; *Style—* Sir Edwin Macgregor, Bt; 6136 Kirby Rd, RR3, Sooke, BC V0S 1N0, Canada

McGREGOR, Dr Gordon Peter; s of William Arthur Kenney McGregor (d 1976), of Horfield, Bristol, and Mary Aloysius, *née* O'Brien (d 1978); *b* 13 June 1932; *Educ* St Brendan's Coll Bristol, Bristol Univ (BA), Univ of Africa (M Ed), Univ of Sussex (D Phil); *m* 10 Aug 1957, Jean Olga, da of William Henry Thomas Lewis (d 1984), of New Tredegar, Gwent; 3 da (Clare b 1958, Helen b 1962, Fiona b 1963); *Career* Flying Offr

RAF (Educn Branch) 1953-56; asst master: Worcester Coll for the Blind 1956-59, Kings Coll Budo Uganda 1959-63, lectr in English Language Makerere Univ Uganda 1963-66; Univ of Zambia: sr lectr in educn 1966-68, reader and head of dept of educn 1968-69, prof of educn 1970; princ: Bishop Otter Coll Chicester Sussex 1970-80, Coll of Ripon and York St John 1980-; writer for: Times Higher Educn Supplement, Church Times, Univs Quarterly, PNEU Journal; memb: nat cmmn UNESCO 1983-86, voluntary sector consultative cncl for Higher Educn 1985-88, bd of Nat Advsy Body for Higher Educn 1986-88; memb: York Dist Health Authy 1982-86, Ct Univ of York, Ct Univ of Hull; Hon D Litt Ripon Coll Wisconsin USA 1986; FRSA 1976; *Books* King's Coll, Budo The First Sixty Years (1967), Educating the Handicapped (1967), English for Education? (1968), Teaching English as a Second Language (1970), English in Africa (1971), Bishop Otter College and Policy for Teacher Education, 1839-1980 (1981); *Recreations* literature, theatre, music, swimming, travel, writing; *Style*— Dr Gordon McGregor; Hollyhocks, High St, Selsey, West Sussex (☎ 0904 623 745); The College of Ripon and York St John, Lord Mayor's Walk, York YO3 7EX (☎ 0904 656 771)

McGREGOR, Hon Gregor Wheate; 3 s of Baron McGregor of Durris (Life Peer); *b* 1952; *m* 1978, Wendy Elizabeth, da of Sydney Carlisle, of Yorkshire; *Style*— The Hon Gregor McGregor; c/o Far End, Wyldes Close, NWI 7JB

MacGREGOR, Sir Ian; *b* 21 Sept 1912; *Educ* George Watson's Coll Edinburgh, Hillhead High Sch Glasgow, Glasgow Univ; *m* Sibyl, *née* Spencer; 1 s, 1 da; *Career* chm and chief exec Amax Inc 1966-77 (hon chm 1977-82), dep chm BL Ltd 1977-80, ptnr Lazard Frères & Co New York 1978-, pres Int C of C 1978, chm and chief exec Br Steel Corpn 1980-83, chm NCB 1983-; kt 1986; *Style*— Sir Ian MacGregor; c/o Hobart House, Grosvenor Place, London SW1 (☎ 01 235 2020)

McGREGOR, Prof Sir Ian Alexander; CBE (1968, OBE 1959); s of John McGregor (d 1945), of Cambuslang, Lanarkshire, and Isabella, *née* Taylor (d 1974); *b* 26 August 1922; *Educ* Rutherglen Acad, and St Mungo Coll of Med, Glasgow (LRCP Ed, LRCS Ed, LRFPS Glas); *m* 30 Jan 1954, Nancy Joan, da of Frederick Herbert Small (d 1968), of Mapledurham, Oxfordshire; 1 s (Alistair b 1956), 1 da (Lesley b 1957); *Career* Capt RAMC 1946-48, served Palestine, (despatches); scientific staff MRC 1949-84, Human Nutrition Res Unit 1949-53, dir MRC Labs Gambia W Africa 1954-73, head Lab for Tropical Community Studies Nat Inst for Med Res 1944-77, dir MRC Labs Gambia 1978-80, MRC external staff at Liverpool Univ 1981-84, visiting prof Liverpool Univ at Liverpool Sch of Tropical Med; memb: WHO Advsy Panel of Malaria 1960-, MRC Tropical Med Res Bd 1975-77 and 1981-83, cncl of Liverpool Sch of Tropical Med 1982-; pres Royal Soc of Tropical Med and Hygiene 1983-85, chm WHO Expert Ctee on Malaria 1985-; memb Cncl Royal Soc 1985-87; Chalmers Medal of Royal Soc Tropical Med and Hygiene 1963, Stewart Prize in Epidemiology of BMA 1971, Darling Fndn Medal and Prize of WHO 1974, Laveran Medal of Soc de Pathologie Exotique de Paris 1983, Fred Soper lectr American Soc of Tropical Med and Hygiene 1983, Heath Clark lectr London Sch of Hygiene and Tropical Med 1983-84; hon memb: American Soc of Tropical Med and Hygiene 1984, Br Soc for Parasitology 1988-; Hon LLD Aberdeen Univ 1983, hon DSc Glasgow Uni v 1984; MRCP, FRCP, FFCM, FRS, FRSE, hon FRCP&S (Glasgow); kt 1982; *Recreations* ornithology, fishing, travel; *Clubs* Royal Society of Medicine; *Style*— Sir Ian McGregor, CBE; The Glebe House, Greenlooms, Hargrave, Chester CH3 7RX (☎ 0829 40973); Liverpool Sch of Tropical Medicine, 3 Pembroke Place, Liverpool L3 5QA (telex 627095)

MACGREGOR, Ian Grant; s & h of Sir Edwin Robert Macgregor, 7th Bt; *b* 22 Feb 1959; *Style*— Ian Macgregor Esq

McGREGOR, Dr James Stalker; *b* 30 Oct 1927; *Educ* Dumfries Acad, Royal Tech Coll Glasgow (ARTC), Glasgow Univ (BSc, CEng); *m* 1953, Iris; 1 s; *Career* chm Honeywell Ltd 1981-, md Honeywell Control Systems Ltd 1971-87, chm Honeywell advsy cncl 1981-; Hon LLD Strathclyde Univ, MIMechE, CBIM; *Recreations* golf; *Style*— Dr James McGregor, Esq; Honeywell Ho, Charles Sq, Bracknell, Berks (☎ Bracknell 424555, telex 847064))

McGREGOR, Lady; Jean; da of William Martin, of Penarth, Glam; *m* 1931, Air Marshal Sir Hector Douglas McGregor, KCB, CBE, DSO (d 1973); *Style*— Lady McGregor; Bull's Cottage, Old Bosham, W Sussex

MacGREGOR, Rt Hon John Roddick Russell; OBE (1971), PC (1985), MP (C) S Norfolk Feb 1974-; s of late Dr N S R MacGregor, of Shotts; *b* 14 Feb 1937; *Educ* Merchiston, St Andrews Univ, King's Coll London; *m* 1962, Jean Dungey; 1 s, 2 da; *Career* univ admin 1961-62; former chm: Fedn of Univ Cons & Unionist Assocs, Bow Gp; first pres Cons and Christian Democratic Youth Community, with New Society and Hill Samuel (dir 1973-79); special asst to PM 1963-64, CRD 1964-65, head of Ldr of Oppn's Private Off 1965-68, oppn whip 1977-79, lord cmmr Treasy 1979-81, parly under-sec Trade and Indust with responsiblity for small businesses 1981-83, min state Agric Fish and Food 1983-85, chief sec Treasy 1985-87, min of Agric Fish and Food 1987-; *Recreations* opera, gardening, travel, conjuring; *Style*— The Rt Hon John MacGregor, OBE, MP; House of Commons, London SW1A 0AA

MACGREGOR, His Hon John Roy; s of Charles George McGregor, of Jamaica and New York (d 1914); and Amy Lilla Isabelle, *née* Green (d 1962); *b* 9 Sept 1913; *Educ* Bedford Sch; *Career* 1939-46, RA, Middle East and pow; 1950-61 RA (TA) and SAS (TA), Maj; barr (Gray's Inn) 1939; dep chm Cambs QS 1967-71; rec 1972-74; legal assessor to Gen Optical cncl 1972-74; hon rec of Margate 1972-79; circuit judge 1975-87; vice-pres Clan Gregor Soc; *Clubs* Special Forces; *Style*— His Hon John Macgregor; Nether Gaulrig, Yardley Hastings, Northampton NN7 1HD (☎ 060 129 861)

MacGREGOR, Hon Mrs; Hon Louisa; *née* Saumarez; only da of 6 Baron de Saumarez; *b* 7 Mar 1955; *m* 4 Sept 1982, Duncan W MacGregor, only s of Alasdair MacGregor, of Tregaer Mill, Monmouth; *Style*— Hon Mrs MacGregor; c/o Shrubland Vista, Coddenham, Ipswich, Suffolk

MacGREGOR, (Robert) Neil; s of Alexander Rankin MacGregor, and Anna Fulton Scobie, *née* Neil; *b* 16 June 1946; *Educ* Glasgow Acad, New Coll Oxford, Ecole Normale Supérieure Paris, Univ of Edinburgh, Courtauld Inst of Art; *Career* memb Faculty of Advocates Edinburgh 1972, lectr in history of art and architecture Univ of Reading 1976, ed Burlington Magazine 1981-86, dir Nat gallery 1987-; *Style*— Neil MacGregor, Esq; The National Gallery, Trafalgar Sq, London WC2N 5DN (☎ 01 839 3321)

McGREGOR, Peter; s of Peter McGregor (d 1977), of Altafearn, Kames, Argyll, and Margaret Thomson, *née* McAuslan; *b* 20 May 1926; *Educ* Cardiff HS, Univ of Birmingham, LSE (BSc); *m* 4 Sept 1954, Marion Edith Winifred, da of Herbert Thomas Downer (d 1974), of Cardiff; 1 s (Iain Peter b 1955), 1 da (Fiona Janet b 1958); *Career* mangr Ferranti Ltd 1950-74, gen mangr Power Div 1970-74; dir: Industrie Elettriche di Legnano (Italy) 1970-74, dir gen Export Gp for Constructional Industs 1984-, Oxford Univ Business Summer Sch 1972 (memb Steering Ctee 1974-79); sec gen Anglo-German Fndn for the Study of Industrial Soc 1974-80; industrial dir (dep sec) Nat Econ Devpt Off 1980-84, assoc dir Corp Renewal Assocs Ltd 1988-; industl advsr to the Lib Pty; memb königswinter Conf Steering Ctee 1975-, hon tres Anglo-German Assoc 1978-; FRSA, FIEE, CEng; FBIM; Comp I Prod E; *Recreations* gardening, walking, listening to music, sailing, reading; *Clubs* Caledonian; *Style*— Peter McGregor, Esq; EGCI, Kingsbury House, 15/17 King Street, St James's, London SW1Y 6QU (☎ 01 930 5377)

MACGREGOR, Capt Randal Alasdair; s of Maj Dunnchadh Tearlach Macgregor, ERD (d 1974), and Nighean, *née* Fraser; *b* 17 Nov 1945; *Educ* Gordonstoun, Tunbridge Wells Art Coll, Dorset Coll of Agric (ABM); *m* 29 April 1978, Sarah Brigid, da of Maj Nigel Damer Marten, of Dorchester, Dorset; 2 da (Morag b 1978, Malvena b 1982); *Career* Capt Royal Scots Greys: Libya, Oman, Trucal States; ret 1972; farmer; numerous overseas directorships 1974-; *Recreations* shooting, polo, all outdoor sports; *Clubs* Manx Sailing and Cruising; *Style*— Capt Randal A Macgregor; Higher Came, Dorchester, Dorset; Ballacooley Farm, Ballaugh, Isle of Man

MACGREGOR, Susan Katriona (Sue); da of Dr James McWilliam MacGregor FRCP, FRCP(E), DPM, of Cape Town, S Africa, and Margaret, *née* MacGregor; *b* 30 August 1941; *Educ* Herschel Sch Cape Town; *Career* programme presenter S African Broadcasting Corpn 1962-67; BBC radio reporter (World at One, PM, World this Weekend) 1967-72; presenter BBC Radio 4: Woman's Hour 1972-87, Today 1985-, Conversation Piece (occasional series); dir Municipal Journal Ltd; FRSA; *Recreations* theatre, cinema, skiing; *Style*— Ms Sue MacGregor; c/o BBC, London W1A 1AA (☎ 01 927 5566)

MACGREGOR, Thomas Robert; s of Thomas Low Macgregor (d 1953); *b* 28 Jan 1916; *Educ* Rugby, Clare Coll Cambridge (MA); *m* 1, 1940, Vivien (d 1988), da of Dr L W Sharp (d 1953); 1 s, 1 da; m 2, 1988, Elizabeth Jane Balfour-Melville, da of late Michael Waterhouse, MC; *Career* serv WWII Lt RA (Japanese POW 1942-45); mangr The Scottish Investmt Tst 1953-80, dir 1969-81; chm The Scottish Mortgage & Tst plc 1976-84 (dir 1964-86); *Recreations* golf, fishing, ornithology, gardening; *Clubs* Hawk's, Hon Co of Edinburgh Golfers; *Style*— Thomas Macgregor, Esq; Hazards, N Berwick, E Lothian (☎ 0620 2628)

McGREGOR, Hon William Ross; eld s of Baron McGregor of Durris (Life Peer); *b* 1948; *Educ* Haberdashers' Aske's Sch, Univ Coll London; *m* 1981 (separated 1987), Ann Holms MacGregor; 1 s (William Oliver James); *Style*— The Hon William McGregor; 6, Dura Park, Woodside, Glenrothes, Fife KY7 5EF

MCGREGOR OF DURRIS, Baron (Life Peer UK 1978); Oliver Ross McGregor; s of William McGregor (decd); *b* 25 August 1921; *Educ* Worksop Coll, Univ of Aberdeen, LSE; *m* 1944, Nellie Weate; 3 s; *Career* sits as SDLP peer in Ho of Lords; chm Forest Philharmonic Orchestra, chm Advertising Standards Authy 1980-, pres Nat Cncl for One Parent Families, pres Nat Assoc of Citizens Advice Bureaux, 1981-87; prof of social instns in the Univ of London 1964-85, head of dept of Sociology at Bedford Coll 1964-77; joint dir Rowntree Legal Res Unit 1966-85, independent tstee of Reuters 1984-, chm Reuters Founders Share Co, 1987-; *Clubs* Garrick; *Style*— The Rt Hon Lord McGregor of Durris; Far End, Wyldes Close, London NW11 7JB (☎ 01 458 2856); Advertising Standards Authy, Brook Ho, 2/16 Torrington Place, London, WC1E 7HN (☎ 580 5555)

MacGREGOR of MacGREGOR, Brig Sir Gregor; 6 Bt (GB 1795), of Lanrick, Co Perth; 23 Chief of Clan Gregor; s of Capt Sir Malcolm MacGregor of MacGregor, 5 Bt, CB, CMG, JP, DL, RN (d 1958), and Hon Gylla Rollo, OBE (d 1980), sis of 12 Lord Rollo; *b* 22 Dec 1925; *Educ* Eton; *m* 8 Feb 1958, Fanny, o da of Charles Hubert Archibald Butler, of Newport, Essex, sometime High Sheriff for that county; 2 s; *Heir* s, Capt Malcolm Gregor Charles MacGregor of MacGregor, yr; *Career* Scots Gds, serv 1939-45, Palestine 1947-48, Malaya 1950-51, Borneo 1965; Staff Coll Course 1960; Jt Servs Staff Coll 1965; cmd 1 Bn Scots Gds 1966-69, Br Liaison Offr US Army Inf Centre 1969-71, Col 'A' Recruiting HQ Scotland 1971, Lt-Col cmdg Scots Gds 1971-74; def and mil attaché Br Embassy Athens 1975-78; cmd Lowlands 1978-80; ADC to HM The Queen 1979; memb Royal Grand Master Mason of Scotland 1988-; Co of Archers (Queen's Bodyguard for Scotland); *Clubs* Pratt's, New (Edinburgh); *Style*— Brig Sir Gregor MacGregor of MacGregor, Bt; Bannatyne, Newtyle, Angus PH12 8TR (☎ 082 85 314)

MacGREGOR of MacGREGOR, YOUNGER, Capt Malcolm Gregor Charles; s and h of Brig Sir Gregor MacGregor of MacGregor, 6 Bt, and Fanny MacGregor of MacGregor, *née* Butler; *b* 23 Mar 1959; *Educ* Eton; *m* 8 Oct 1988, Cecilia Margaret Lucy, er da of Sir Ilay Campbell of Succoth, 7 Bt; *Career* Capt Scots Gds, serv Hong Kong, NI, UK; *Recreations* travel, photography, tennis; *Style*— Malcolm MacGregor of MacGregor, younger; Bannatyne, Newtyle, Angus PH12 8TR (☎ 08285 314)

McGRIGOR, Sir Charles Edward; 5 Bt (UK 1831), of Campden Hill, Middx; DL (Argyll and Bute); s of Lt-Col Sir Charles Colquhoun McGrigor, 4 Bt, OBE (d 1946), and Amabel Caroline, *née* Somers-Cocks (d 1977); Sir James McGrigor, 1 Bt, KCB, was dir-gen Army Med Dept for thirty-six years and three times Lord Rector of Marischal Coll Aberdeen; *b* 5 Oct 1922; *Educ* Eton; *m* 7 June 1948, Mary Bettine, da of Sir Archibald Charles Edmonstone, 6 Bt (d 1954), of Duntreath Castle, Blanefield, Stirlingshire; 2 s (James b 19 Oct 1949, Charles b 7 Aug 1959), 2 da (Lorna b 18 Feb 1951, Kirsty b 3 Feb 1953); *Heir* s, James Angus Rhoderick Neil McGrigor; *Career* 2 Lt Rifle Bde 1942, Capt 1943, served in N Africa and Italy (despatches); ADC to HRH The Duke of Gloucester, KG 1945-47 (Australia and England); memb Royal Co of Archers (Queen's Body Gd for Scotland); Exon of the Queen's Bodyguard of Yeomen of the Gd 1970-85; vice-pres and memb ctee of management RNLI; convenor Scottish Lifeboat Cncl, Dep Lt for Argyll and Bute; *Recreations* fishing, gardening; *Clubs* New (Edinburgh); *Style*— Sir Charles McGrigor, Bt, DL; Upper Sonachan, by Dalmally, Argyll (☎ 08663 229)

McGRIGOR, James Angus Rhoderick Neil; s and h of Sir Charles Edward McGrigor, 5 Bt; *b* 19 Oct 1949; *m* Caroline, da of late Jacques Roboh, of Paris; 1 da (Sibylla b 1988); *Style*— James McGrigor Esq

McGRIGOR, Peter Muir; s of Alexander Muir McGrigor (d 1963), of Ryland Lodge,

Dunblane, Perthshire, Scotland, and Eileen Margaret, *née* Denny (d 1976); *b* 13 Sept 1927; *Educ* Uppingham Public Sch; *m* 8 Aug 1959, Rosemary Ann, da of Col Cecil Charters Spooner, DSO (d 1953); 2 s (Neil b 1961, Kenneth b 1963); *Career* supt of tea plantations African Highlands Produce Co Ltd Kenya 1948-60; memb Lloyds Underwriters 1978-; *Recreations* yachting, travel, gardening; *Clubs* Royal Lymington Yacht, Sloane; *Style—* Peter McGrigor, Esq; Normandy Mead, Woodside, Lymington, Hampshire (☎ (0590) 73001)

McGUCKIAN, John Brendan; s of Brian McGuckian (d 1967), of Ardverna, Cloughmills, Ballymena, and Pauline, *née* McKenna; *b* 13 Nov 1939; *Educ* St McNissis Coll Garrontower, Queen's Univ of Belfast (BSc); *m* 22 Aug 1970, Carmel, da of Daniel McGowan, of Pharis, Ballyveeley; 2 s (Brian b 1972, John b 1981), 1 da (Breige b 1977); *Career* chm Cloughmills MFG Co 1967-; dir: Ulster TV plc 1970-, Munster & Leinster Bank 1972-, Allied Irish Bank plc 1976-, Harbour GP Ltd 1978-, Aer Lingus plc 1979-84, Unidare plc 1987-, Irish Ferries plc 1988-; memb Derry Devpt Cmmn 1968-71, pro chllr Queens Univ Belfast 1987-, Laganside Corpn 1988-; *Style—* John B McGuckian, Esq; Ardverna, Cloughmills, Ballymena (☎ 0265 63 692); Lisgoole Abbey, Culkey, Enniskillen; 1 Ballycregagh Rd, Cloughmills, Ballymena (☎ 0265 63 692, fax 0265 63 754, telex 747603)

McGUFFOG, John Lee; s of Capt Donald McGuffog, of Rose Cottage, Little Bookham St, Little Bookham, Surrey, and Ethel Mary, *née* Lee; *b* 18 August 1945; *Educ* Wallington GS; *m* 1, 1971 (m dis 1976), Patricia Anne White; m 2, 6 March 1978, Penelope Jayne, da of Philip Gordon Lee, of Selve Cottage, Monksilver, Somerset; 1 da (Charlotte b 21 Feb 1979); *Career* surveyor 1963-, qualified chartered auctioneer 1968, chief surveyor Leonard W Cotton & Ptnrs 1969; Mann & Co (estate agents): joined 1972, dir 1975, chm commercial div 1985; main bd dir Countrywide Surveyors Ltd 1988-; memb Cranleigh and Dist Round Table 1978-86; memb City Owls (promoted by Worshipful Co of Chartered Surveyors); ARVA 1969, FRICS 1976, ACIArb 1979; *Recreations* fishing; *Clubs* Fernfell; *Style—* John McGuffog, Esq; Hillfield, Amlets Lane, Cranleigh, Surrey; Countrywide Surveyors Ltd, Cavendish House, Goldsworth Rd, Woking, Surrey (☎ 04862 22256, fax 0483 756 229, car tel 0836 263 823)

McGUINNESS, Maj-Gen Brendan Peter; CB (1986); s of Bernard McGuinness; *b* 26 June 1931; *Educ* Mount St Mary's Coll (psc, reds); *m* 1968, Ethne Patricia Kelly; 1 s, 1 da; *Career* despatches Borneo 1966, Brig Royal Regt of Artillery 1975, GOC Western Dist 1983-; *Style—* Maj-Gen B P McGuinness, CB; c/o Ministry of Defence, Whitehall, London SW1

McGUINNESS, Dennis; s of William McGuinness, of Glasgow, and Jane Ross Henderson, *née* Hannah; *b* 20 Nov 1943; *Educ* Holyrood Secdy Sch; *m* 15 Sept 1964, Maureen Campbell, da of Andrew Gaughan (d 1972); 1 s (Dennis William Andrew b 1965), 2 da (Annjanette b 1966, Elaine b 1968); *Career* chm: Bremner plc, Carswell Ltd, Child and Family Tst; memb Stock Exchange 1973-; *Recreations* golf, swimming, football, horse racing; *Clubs* Bonnyton GC; *Style—* Dennis McGuinness, Esq; The Rannoch, Peel Rd, Thorntonhall, Glasgow G74 5AG; Carswell Ltd, Stock Exchange House, 7 Nelson Mandela Place, Glasgow G2 1BU (car ☎ 0836 705248)

McGUINNESS, Col James Hugh; TD (1951); s of William McGuinness (d 1929), of Birkenhead, and Ethel Christina, *née* Sellars (d 1946); *b* 7 June 1918; *Educ* Birkenhead Sch; *Career* cmmnd TA 1937, serv WWII with 4 Bn Cheshire Regt (2/Lt to Maj) France and Flanders 1940; short serv cmmn RA 1947-50 (Palestine, Egypt and Cyrenaica), re-joined TA 1952, cmd 4 Bn Cheshire Regt 1956-59, Dep Cdr 124 Inf Bde 1960-63; ret fund raising conslt; *Publications* The First Hundred Years (story of 4th Bn Cheshire Regt) (1959); articles in various journals; *Recreations* walking, beagling, reading, writing; *Clubs* Royal Over-Seas; *Style—* Col James McGuinness, TD; Oliveira do Mondego, 3360 Penacova, Portugal (☎ 039 45394)

McGUINNESS, James Joseph; *see*: Nottingham, Bishop of (RC)

McGUIRE, Michael Thomas Francis; MP (Lab) Makerfield 1983-; s of Hugh McGuire; *b* 3 May 1926; *Educ* St Joseph's Elementary Sch; *m* 1954, Marie, da of P J Murphy; *Career* coal miner; full-time Trade Union branch sec 1957-64; joined Lab Pty 1951; PPS to Min of Sport 1974-77; memb Cncl of Europe 1977-; WEU 1977-; MP for Ince 1964-1983; *Recreations* rugby league, Irish folk music; *Style—* Michael McGuire Esq, MP; 8 Elm Grove, Eccleston Park, Prescot, Lancs

McHALE, Henry; s of Henry McHale (d 1980); *b* 12 Sept 1934; *Educ* Queens' Cambridge; *Career* barr, dir of Grundy (Teddington) Gp Ltd, Envopak Ltd; FCA; *Recreations* golf, tennis, field sports; *Clubs* Carlton; *Style—* Henry McHale Esq; 44 Cadogan Sq, London SW1

MacHALE, Joseph Patrick; s of Seamus Joseph MacHale, MB, FRCS, and Margaret Mary, *née* Byrne (d 1982); *b* 17 August 1951; *Educ* Ampleforth, Queen's Coll Oxford (MA); *m* 28 Feb 1981, Maryann, da of Rear Adm David Dunbar-nasmith, CB, DSC; 2 s (Henry b 1983, Martin b 1986), 1 da (Laura b 1985); *Career* Price Waterhouse 1973-78, qualified CA 1976; joined JP Morgan Inc 1979: sr vice pres Morgan Guaranty Tst 1986-, md JP Morgan Securities Ltd 1987-; memb: FCA 1978; *Clubs* Brooks's; *Style—* Joseph MacHale, Esq; 5 Elms Rd, London SW4

MACHARG, John Maitland; s of Walter Simpson Macharg (d 1945), of Glasgow, and Isabella Ure Elder, *née* Orr (d 1979); *b* 22 May 1928; *Educ* Glasgow HS, Strathallan Sch, Glasgow Univ (MA); *m* 10 July 1961, Madeline, da of Sidney Yates (d 1978), of Weeke, Winchester; 2 s (Walter b 1962, Richard b 1964), 1 da (Mary Anne b 1965); *Career* Nat Serv 1947-49 (2 Lt RAEC BAOR); gen mangr and actuary Scottish Provident Inst 1970-88, dir Scottish Provident 1981-88, chm The Assoc Scottish Life Off 1980-82, pres The Faculty of Actuaries 1985-87; FFA 1954, CBIM 1987; *Recreations* golf, skiing, gardening, hill walking; *Clubs* New (Edinburgh), Caledonian, Murrayfield GC; *Style—* John Macharg, Esq; Champery, 215 Braid Rd, Edinburgh EH10 6NY (☎ 031 447 4105); 6 St Andrew Square, Edinburgh EH2 2YA (☎ 031 556 9181, telex 72631 SCOPRO, fax 031 558 2486)

McHARG, Bt-Col William Wilson; OBE (1960), MC (1944), TD (1954), DL (Ayr 1970); s of Alexander McHarg (d 1956); *b* 29 August 1918; *Educ* Irvine Royal Acad, Glasgow Univ; *m* 1947, Janet, *née* Gommer; 1 s, 1 da; *Career* Maj MEF, CMF, TA 1938-46 and 1947-61, Col; slr; racecourse mangr and clerk of the course; *Clubs* Ayr County; *Style—* Bt-Col William McHarg, OBE, MC, TD, DL; 29 Earls Way, Doonfoot, Ayr, Ayrshire (☎ 0292 41350)

MACHIN, David; s of Lt Cdr Noel Percy Machin, RN, ret, of Las Palmas, Canary Island (d 1977), and Joan Evelyn Hildige (d 1959); *b* 25 April 1934; *Educ* Sunningdale Sch Berks, Eton, Trinity Coll Cambridge (BA); *m* 8 June 1963, Sarah Mary, da of Col William Alfred Chester-Master, DL, of Norcote House, Cirencester, Glos (d 1963); 2 da (Georgina b 1964, Alice b 1966); *Career* Nat Serv 1952, 2 Lt Welsh Gds served UK & Egypt; publisher's ed and literary agent William Heinemann Ltd and Gregson & Wigan Ltd 1957-68, ptnr A P Watt & Son 1968-70, dir Jonathan Cape Ltd 1970-78, gen sec of the Soc of Authors 1978-81, md The Bodley Head Ltd 1981-87; under tres elect Grays Inn 1989, vice chm Hammersmith Democrats 1988-; *Recreations* reading, walking; *Clubs* Garrick; *Style—* David Machin; 53 Westwick Gardens, London W14 0BS (☎ 01 603 4000)

MACHIN, Edward Anthony; QC (1973); s of Edward Arthur Machin (d 1958), of Finchley, London, and Olive Muriel, *née* Smith (d 1980); *b* 28 June 1925; *Educ* Christ's Coll Finchley, New Coll Oxford (BCL MA); *m* 1953, Jean Margaret, da of Reginald McKanna (d 1972), of Epsom; 2 s (Timothy, Christopher), 1 da (Anna); *Career* Vinerian law scholar 1950, Tan red student 1950, Cassel scholar 1951; barr rec Crown Ct 1976, judge cts of Appeal of Jersey and Guernsey 1988; *Recreations* music, sailing ('Kasta Loss'), languages; *Clubs* Bar Yacht; *Style—* Anthony Machin Esq, QC; Strand End, Strand, Topsham, Exeter (☎ 0392 87 7992); 1 Paper Buildings, Temple, London EC4 (☎ 01 583 7355)

McHUGH, Christopher John Patrick; s of Stanley Thomas McHugh, and Ann Agnes McHugh, *née* Maher; *b* 3 April 1945; *Educ* St John's RC Sch, City of Bath Tech Coll; *m* 9 Jan 1971, Frances Merla, da of Harry Stewart Townsend; 1 s (Daniel Thomas b 1972), 3 da (Georgina Ann b 1973, Annabel Carolyn b 1976, Claudia Jane b 1984); *Career* sr ptnr Chris McHugh & Co Financial Servs, dir St Lawrence Tst Ltd; *Recreations* most sports, horses, show jumping; *Clubs* BSJA, Conservative Assoc; *Style—* Chris McHugh, Esq; Burnt Ash House, Cirencester Road, Chalford, Stroud, Glos GL6 8PE; Willow Court, Beeches Green, Stroud, Glos GL5 8BJ (☎ (04536) 70606, telex 43198 SWAGGY, fax 04536 70600)

McILROY, Hon Mrs; (Elizabeth Mary); da of 2 Baron Rochester; *b* 1951; *m* 1974, Thomas Meredith McIlroy; 3 s; *Style—* The Hon Mrs McIlroy

McILROY, Harry (Alexander); Baron di Novara; *b* 17 May 1940; *Educ* Swinton Coll; *m* 1971, Winifred; 1 s (Nicholas Henry Christopher), 1 da (Catherine Harriet); *Career* chm and owner Unico Gp Ltd, memb Int Financial Futures Exchange (Bermuda), underwriting memb of Lloyd's; Freeman City of London; Liveryman Worshipful Co of: Basketmakers, Marketers, FRSA, FInstM; *Clubs* Carlton, City Livery, E India; *Style—* Harry McIlroy Esq; 16 St Jame's Sq, London SW1

MCILWAIN, Alexander Edward; CBE (1985); s of Edward Walker McIlwain (d 1974), of Aberdeen, and Gladys Edith, *née* Horne; *b* 4 July 1933; *Educ* Aberdeen GS, Univ of Aberdeen (MA, LLB); *m* 14 July 1961, Moira Margaret, da of William Kinnaird (d 1951), of Aberdeen; 3 da (Karen b 5 March 1963, Shona b 6 Feb 1967, Wendy b 17 March 1969); *Career* Lt RCS 1957-59; dist prosecutor Hamilton 1975-76 (burgh prosecutor 1967-75), dean Soc of Slrs Hamilton and Dist 1981-83, hon sheriff Sherriffdom of South Strathclyde, Dumfries and Galloway at Hamilton 1981-(temporary sherriff 1984-, sr ptnr Leornards (slrs), Hamilton 1984-), WS 1985-; sec Lanarkshire Scout Assoc 1967-81, chm Lanarkshire Scout Area 1981-; hon memb American Bar Assoc 1983-, memb Lanarkshire Health Bd 1981-, pres Law Soc of Scotland 1983-84, memb central advsy ctee on JP's 1985-, chm Legal Aid Central Ctee 1985-87; memb: Scout Cncl 1986-, review ctee Scottish Legal Aid Bd 1987-; SSC 1966; *Recreations* gardening, reading, listening to music; *Clubs* New Edinburgh; *Style—* A E McIlwain, Esq, CBE; Craigievar, Bothwell Rd, Uddingston, Glasgow (☎ 0698 813 368); Leonards, 133 Cadzow St, Hamilton (☎ 0698 457 313)

McILWRAITH, Dr George Robert; s of Alexander Herd McIlwraith (d 1971), of Ruislip, Middx, and Kathleen Joan, *née* Heaton; *b* 15 July 1941; *Educ* Merchant Taylors Sch NorthWood, Univ of St Andrews (MB, ChB, MRCP); *m* 24 July 1982, Isabel Margaret, da of Harry Jack Manwaring (d 1988), of Collier St, Marden, Kent; 1 s (Harry Alexander b 1987); *Career* various jr appts in UK Hosps, asst prof of internal med, pulmonary div Univ of Michigan Med Sch USA 1979-80, conslt physician Maidstone Dist Hosps 1981-; memb: Br Thoracic Soc, Br Geriatric Soc; FRCP 1988;; *Books* Chapters, Papers & Articles on Cardiological and Respiratory Medical Matters; *Style—* Dr George McIlwraith; Noah's Ark Farmhouse, East Sutton Road, Headcorn, Ashford, Kent TN27 9PS (☎ 0622 891278); The Maidstone Hospital, Hermitage Lane Barming, Maidstone, Kent (☎ 0622 29000)

McINDOE, Lady Felicity Aileen Ann; *née* Stopford; 3 da of 8 Earl of Courtown, OBE, TD (d 1975) (but sole da by his 2 w (*see* Countess of Courtown)); *b* 17 Dec 1951; *m* 1, 1977 (m dis 1981), Leslie Edward Archer-Davis; resumed name Stopford; m 2, 1982, (John) Andrew Barr McIndoe; 1 s (Harry b 1985); *Style—* Lady Felicity McIndoe; 9 Franche Ct, London SW17 (☎ 01 946 9872)

McINERNEY, Hon Sir Murray Vincent; QC 1957; s of Patrick McInerney; *b* 11 Feb 1911; *Educ* C B C Pretoria, Xavier Coll, Newman Coll Melbourne Univ; *m* 1, 1939, Manda (d 1973), da of F Franich; 2 s, 5 da; m 2, 1975, Frances *née* O'Gorman, wid of P V Branagan; *Career* Lt RANVR 1942-45; barr 1935, chm Vic Bar Cncl 1962, 1963; pres Vic Amateur Athletic Assoc1978-82; dep pres Courts-Martial Appeal Tbnl 1959-65; vice-pres Law Cncl of Aust 1964-65; judge of Supreme Ct of Vic 1965-83 (ret); kt 1978; *Recreations* reading, watching cricket, tennis, atheletics, football; *Clubs* Australian (Melb), Melbourne Cricket, Celtic (Vic), RACV, West Brighton, ESSOIGN (Melb), LTAVic; *Style—* The Hon Sir Murray McInerney, QC; 7 Chatfield Ave, Balwyn, Vic 3103, Australia

MacINNES, Hamish; OBE (1980), BEM (1965); s of Duncan MacInnes, of Gourock, Renfrewshire (d 1987), and Catherine, *née* MacDonald (d 1967); *b* 7 July 1930; *Educ* Gatehouse of Fleet Public Sch; *Career* writer, mfr, advsr on films and mountain rescue; designer: mountain rescue stretchers (used internationally), first all metal ice axe, terodactyl climbing tools; dep ldr Everest SW Face Expedition 1975 (taken part on 20 other expeditions to various parts of the world), special advsr to BBC and feature films in many countries, hon pres Search and Rescue Dog Assoc, former pres Alpine Climbing Gp, ldr Glencoe Mountain Rescue Team, hon memb Scottish Mountaineering Club; Hon DSc Univ of Aberdeen 1988, Hon dir Leishman Res Laboratory, LLD Univ of Glasgow; *Style—* Hamish MacInnes, Esq, OBE, BEM; Achnacone, Glencoe, Argyll (☎ 08552 258)

MacINNES, Hon Mrs (Janitha Stormont); *née* Craig; er da of 2 Viscount Craigavon (d 1974); *m* 1965, Gordon Robert MacInnes, ICSA, ACIB, er s of Robert Wood MacInnes, of Ruislip, Middx; 3 da Avila b 1967, Córdova b 1971, Jimena b 1975); *Style—* The Hon Mrs MacInnes; 44 Kings Rd, Richmond, Surrey TW10 6NW

McINNES, Sheriff John Colin; s of Ian Whitton McInnes (d 1976), of Cupar Fife, and

Lucy Margaret, *née* Wilson; *b* 21 Nov 1938; *Educ* Cargilfield Sch Edinburgh, Merchiston Castle Sch Edinburgh, Brasenose Coll Oxford (BA), Edinburgh Univ (LLB); *m* 6 Aug 1966, Elisabeth Mabel, da of Hugh Royden Neilson, of Kelso, Roxburghshire; 1 s (Ian b 1969), 1 da (Iona b 1972); *Career* 2 Lt 8 RTR 1956-58, Lt Fife and Forfar Yeo Scottish Horse TA 1958-64; advocate in practice Scottish bar 1963-72, tutor Edinburgh Univ 1964-72, dir R Mackness & Co Ltd 1963-70, chm Fios Gp Ltd 1970-72, memb St Andrews Univ Ct 1983-; Sheriff: Lothians and Peebles 1973-74, Tayside Central and Fife 1974-; chm Fife Family Conciliation Serv 1988-; *Recreations* fishing, shooting, skiing, gardening, photography; *Style—* Sheriff John McInnes; Parkneuk, Blebocraigs, Cupar, Fife KY15 5UG; Sheriff Ct, Cupar, Fife (☎ 0334 52121); Sheriff Ct, Perth (☎ 0738 20546)

MACINNES, Keith Gordon; CMG (1984); s of Kenneth Lionel MacInnes CBE, and Helen; da of Sir (Archibald) Douglas Gordon, CIE (d 1966); *b* 17 July 1935; *Educ* Rugby, Trinity Coll Cambridge (MA); *m* 1, 1966 (m dis 1980), Jennifer Anne Fennell; 1 s (Alexander b 1970), 1 da (Francesca b 1968); m 2, 8 March 1985, Mrs Hermiane Ann Felicity Pattinson, 2 step s (Kyle b 1968, Rupert b 1970); *Career* diplomat; ambassador to the Philippines; *Recreations* bridge, chess, golf, tennis; *Clubs* Manila Polo, Manila Golf and Country; *Style—* Keith Macinnes, Esq, CMG; c/o FCO (Manila), King Charles St, London SW1A 2AH

MacINNES, Keith Gordon; CMG (1984); s of Kenneth Lionel MacInnes, CBE, and Helen, *née* Gordon; *b* 17 July 1935; *Educ* Rugby, Cambridge (BA); *m* 1, 1966 (m dis 1980), Jennifer Anne Fennell; 1 s (Alexander b 1970), 1 da (Francesca b 1968); m 2, 1985, Hermione Pattinson; *Career* HM Dip Serv, ambass Manila 1987-; *Recreations* chess, bridge, walking; *Style—* Keith MacInnes, Esq, CMG; FCO, King Charles St, London SW1 (☎ 01 270 3000)

MCINROY, Alan Roderick; s of Charles Alan McInroy (d 1932), of St Mary's Tower, Birnam, Perthshire, and Marjory, *née* Walford (d 1981); *b* 6 June 1920; *Educ* Loretto Sch Musselburgh, Hertford Coll Oxford; *m* 6 Jan 1966, Daphne Eileen Wells, da of Sir Eric Weston (d 1976), of The Manor, Moreton Pinkney, Northants; *Career* RA served ME 1940-42, Italy (POW) 1942-43, Germany (POW) 1943-45, Palestine 1946-48; ptnr Scott-Moncrieff Thomson & Shiells CA 1953-59, mangr American Tst Ltd 1959-69, md Edinburgh Fund Mangrs plc 1969-84; chm: McInroy & Wood Ltd 1986-, New Tokyo Investmt Tst Ltd, chm Edinburgh Oil & Gas plc; dir: Noble Grossart Hldgs Ltd, ITEK Fondsenbeheer NV; chm Haddington Citizens Advice Bureau 1983-88; MICA 1951, memb Soc Investmt Analysts 1963; *Recreations* golf, music; *Clubs* New (Edinburgh), Hon Co of Edinburgh Golfers, Club de Golf Valderrama (Spain); *Style—* Alan McInroy, Esq; Muirfield Green, Gullane, East Lothian EH31 2EG (☎ 0620 843 287)

MACINTOSH, Alexander James; s of Edward Hyde Macintosh, CBE (d 1970) of Rebeg House, Kirkhill, Invernesshire, and Doreen O'Hara *née* Cross; *b* 5 Oct 1931; *Educ* Stowe, Trinity Coll Cambridge (MA); *m* 12 June 1965, Jane Wigham, da of Michael Finch Wigham Richardson (d 1988), of Downton, Wiltshire; 2 s (Jonathan b 1968, Marcus b 1970); *Career* cmmnd Seaforth Highlanders 1950; numerous directorships inc: Cunard Steam Ship Co plc and subsidiaries 1985-, Associated Container Transportation Ltd and subsidiaries 1985-, The Port of London Authority 1980-, Ellerman Gp Ltd 1987-, HLL Shipping Agencies Ltd 1988-, Gen Cncl of British Shipping Ltd 1987-, British Shipping Fedn Ltd 1987-, Ben Line Containers Ltd 1987-, H E Moss & Co Ltd 1987-; *Recreations* country pursuits; *Style—* Alexander Macintosh, Esq; 29 Richborne Terrace, London SW8 1AS (☎ 01 735 4399); Cunard Ellerman Ltd, 12-20 Camomile Street, London EC3A 7EX (☎ 01 283 4311, fax 01 283 1767, telex 884771/2)

MCINTOSH, David Angus; s of Robert Angus McIntosh, of Scotland, and Monica Joan Sherring, *née* Hillier; *Educ* Selwood Co Sch Frome Somerset; *m* 14 Sept 1968, Jennifer Mary, da of Jack Dixon of Mill Hill, London; 2 da (Sarah Alison b 1973, Louise b 1978); *Career* clerk Ames Kent & Rathwell Somerset, articled clerk Davies Arnold Cooper 1964, admitted slr 1968, sr ptnr Davies Arnold Cooper 1976 (ptnr 1968); served on various Law Soc Working Parties concerned with Reform and Admin of Civil Law; Freeman City of London, Liveryman Blacksmiths Co; memb Law Soc of England and Wales, Int Bar Assoc, Int Assoc of Def Cncl, CIArb; *Books* regular contributor to legal, insurance, and pharmaceutical journals; *Recreations* golf, fitness; *Clubs* Chigwell Golf, Barbican Health and Fitness Centre, City Livery; *Style—* David McIntosh, Esq; Spareleaze Lodge, 1 Spareleaze Hill, Loughton, Essex; 12 Bridewell Place, London EC4V 6AD (☎ 01 353 6555, fax 01 353 0574, telex 262894)

McINTOSH, Lady; Doris Hutchinson Pow; *m* 1934, Sir Alister Donald McIntosh, KCMG (d 1978); l s; *Style—* Lady McIntosh; ll Wesley Rd, Wellington, New Zealand

McINTOSH, Douglas Moul; CBE (1961); s of Simon McIntosh (d 1957), and Jane McIntosh (d 1959); *b* 27 Sept 1909; *Educ* Dundee Harris Academy, St Andrews Univ (BSc, MA, PhD), Edinburgh Univ (BEd); *m* 1939, Jean Blair, da of John Paterson (d 1956), farmer, of Balfron; *Career* fell Br Psychological Soc; dir of educn Fife 1944-66, princ Moray House Coll of Ed 1966-74; Hon LLD: New Brunswick 1965, Dundee 1975; FRSE, FEIS; *Books* Promotion from Primary to Secondary Education, Scottish Council for Research in Education (1948), Scaling of Teachers Marks and Estimates (1949), Educational Guidance and the Pool of Ability (1959), Statistics for the Teacher (1963); *Recreations* golf; *Style—* Douglas McIntosh, Esq, CBE; Tigh an Droma, 22 Balwearie Gdns, Kirkcaldy, Fife, Scotland (☎ 0592 260895)

MACINTOSH, Dr Farquhar; CBE (1982); s of John Macintosh (d 1938), of Elgol, Isle of Skye, and Kate Ann, *née* Mackinnon (d 1975); *b* 27 Oct 1923; *Educ* Portree HS Skye, Edinburgh Univ (MA), Glasgow Univ (DipEd); *m* 19 Dec 1959, Margaret Mary Inglis, da of James Inglis Peebles (d 1965); 2 s (John James, Kenneth Donald), 2 da (Ann Mary, Ailsa Kate); *Career* joined RN 1944, cmmnd Sub Lt RNVR 1944, serving in the Far East; teacher in history Greenfield Jr Secdy Sch Hamilton 1951-52, history master Glasgow Acad 1953-59, princ teacher of history Inverness Royal Acad 1959-62, headmaster Portree HS 1962-66, rector Oban HS (headmaster) 1967-72, rector Royal HS Edinburgh 1972-; regular contributor: The Times Educnl Supplement Scot, The Scotsman, The Glasgow Herald; memb: Skye Hosps Bd of Mgmnt 1963-66, Oban Hosps Bd of Mgmnt 1968-72, Aberdeen Coll of Educn Governing Body 1961-66, Jordanhill Coll of Educn Glasgow 1967- (chm 1970-72), Highlands and Islands Devpt Consultative Cncl 1965-82 (chm educn sub ctee 1968-82); sec Gaelic Soc of Inverness 1960-62; chm: Scot Assoc for Educnl Mgmnt and Admin 1980-83, Scot Examination Bd 1977-, Sch Broadcasting Cncl Scot 1980-85; DLitt Heriot Watt Univ 1980, FEIS Conferred by Educnl Inst of Scotland 1970; memb: Educ Inst of Scot, Headmasters' Conference, Headmasters' Assoc of Scot, Scot History Soc; *Recreations* hill-walking, sea-fishing, Gaelic; *Clubs* Rotary (Murrayfield-Cramond); *Style—* Dr Farquhar Macintosh, CBE; 12 Rothesay Place, Edinburgh, EH3 7SQ (☎ 031 225 4404); The Royal High School, East Barnton Ave, Edinburgh EH4 6JP (☎ 031 3362261)

McINTOSH, Hon Francis Robert; er s of Baron McIntosh of Haringey (Life Peer), *qv*; *Educ* Highgate Wood Sch London; *Style—* The Hon Francis McIntosh

McINTOSH, Ian Alexander Neville; s of Alexander McIntosh, of 57 Haworth Road, Bradford, W Yorks BD9 6LH, and Marie Josephine, *née* Lester; *b* 24 Sept 1938; *Educ* Bradford GS, Edinburgh Univ (MA); *m* 26 June 1965, Gillian Mary Sophia, da of Harold John Cropp (d 1984); 1 s (Angus b 15 June 1975), 1 da (Fiona b 3 June 1971); *Career* Armitage & Norton 1959-63, Coopers & Lybrand 1963-69, dep chief exec Samuel Montagu & Co Ltd 1969-; Liveryman Worshipful Co of Goldsmiths; FCA 1963; *Recreations* golf, tennis; *Clubs* MCC, Mid Herts GC; *Style—* Ian McIntosh, Esq; 10 Lower Thames Street, London EC3R 6AE (☎ 01 260 9301, fax 01 623 5512)

McINTOSH, Vice Adm Sir Ian Stewart; KBE (1973, MBE 1941), CB (1970), DSO (1944), DSC (1942); s of Alexander James McIntosh (d 1973), of Melbourne, Aust; *b* 11 Oct 1919; *Educ* Geelong GS; *m* 1943, Elizabeth Rosemary, da of Albert Henry Rasmussen, of Aalesund, Norway; 3 s, (1 da decd); *Career* joined RN 1938, Capt 1959, Rear Adm 1968, dir-gen Weapons (Naval) MOD 1969-70, Vice Adm 1970, dep CDS (Operational Requirements) MOD 1970-73 (ret), conslt Alexander Hughes and Assocs 1973-78; *Style—* Vice Adm Sir Ian McIntosh, KBE, CB, DSO, DSC; 19 The Crescent, Alverstoke, Hants

McINTOSH, Hon Philip Henry Sargant McIntosh; s of Baron McIntosh of Haringey (Life Peer), *qv*, and Naomi Ellen Sargant (*see* Prof Naomi McIntosh); *b* 1964; *Educ* Highgate Wood Sch London, Kingston Poly (BA); pres Kingston Poly Students Union 1987-88; pres Kingston Polytechnic Students Union 1987-88; *Style—* The Hon Philip McIntosh

MACINTOSH, Sir Robert Reynolds; s of Charles Nicholson Macintosh, of Timaru, NZ; *b* 17 Oct 1897; *Educ* Waitaki NZ, Guy's Hosp (MA, DM, DA); *m* 1, 1925, Rosa Marjorie (d 1956), da of William Henderson, of London; m 2, 1962, Dorothy Ann, da of Robert William Manning, of Exmouth; *Career* Nuffield prof anaesthhetics Oxford Univ 1937-65; former hon conslt anaesthetics RAF (Air Cdre); FRCSE, on Hon FFARCS, hon fell RSM, Hon FRCDG, kt 1955; *Style—* Sir Robert Macintosh; 326 Woodstock Rd, Oxford

McINTOSH, Sir Ronald Robert Duncan; KCB (1975, CB 1968); s of Thomas Steven McIntosh, and Christina Jane McIntosh; *b* 26 Sept 1919; *Educ* Charterhouse, Balliol Coll Oxford; *m* 1951, Doreen Frances, only da of Cdr Andrew MacGinnity, of Frinton-on-Sea, Essex; *Career* served MN WWII; joined BOT 1947, under-sec 1963-64, dep-under sec of state DEA 1966-68, dep sec Cabinet Off 1968-70; dep sec: Employment 1970-72, Treasy 1972-73; dir-gen NEDO and memb NEDC 1973-77; chm APV plc 1982- (dep chm 1981); dir: S G Warburg, Foseco, London & Manchester Gp; memb cncl CBI 1980-; Hon DSc (Aston) 1977; FRSA, CBIM; *Style—* Sir Ronald McIntosh, KCB; 24 Ponsonby Terrace, London SW1 (☎ 01 821 6106); APV plc, 2 Lygon Place, London SW1W 0JR

McINTOSH OF HARINGEY, Baron (UK 1982), of Haringey in Gtr London; Andrew Robert McIntosh; s of Prof Albert William McIntosh and (Helena Agnes) Jenny Britton; *b* 30 April 1933; *Educ* Haberdashers' Aske's Hampstead Sch, Royal GS High Wycombe, Jesus Coll Oxford (MA), Ohio State Univ; *m* 1962, Naomi Ellen Sargant (*see* Lady McIntosh), da of Thomas Sargant, OBE, JP (d 1988), of London N6, and previously w of Peter Joseph Kelly; 2 s; *Career* memb Hornsey Borough Cncl 1963-65, memb Haringey Borough Cncl 1964-68; chm: Market Res Soc 1972-73, Assoc for Neighbourhood Cncls 1974-80; memb GLC for Tottenham 1973-83; ldr GLC oppn 1980-81, dep chm IFF Res Ltd 1988- (md 1965-81, chm 1981-88), chm SVP UK Ltd 1983-; chm Fabian Soc 1985-86; *Style—* The Rt Hon the Lord McIntosh of Haringey; 27 Hurst Avenue, London N6 5TX (☎ 01 340 1496)

McINTOSH OF HARINGEY, Baroness; Prof Naomi Ellen Sargant; da of Thomas Sargant, OBE, JP (d 1988), of London N6; *b* 10 Dec 1933; *Educ* Friends Sch Walden, Bedford Coll London Univ; *m* 1, 1954, Peter Joseph Kelly; 1 s (David); m 2, 1962, Andrew Robert McIntosh (Baron McIntosh of Haringey, *qv*); 2 s (Francis, Philip); *Career* pro vice-chllr Student Affairs The Open Univ 1974-78, prof of applied social res 1978-81; chm Nat Gas Consumers Cncl 1977-80; memb: Nat Consumer Cncl 1978-, Cmmn on Energy and Environment 1978-; pres Nat Soc for Clean Air 1981-, sr cmmng editor (education) Channel Four TV 1981-; *Recreations* gardening, photography; *Style—* The Rt Hon the Lady McIntosh of Haringey; 27 Hurst Avenue, London N6 5TX (☎ 01 340 1496); c/o Channel Four Television, 60 Charlotte St, London W1P 2AX (☎ 01 631 4444, telex 892355)

MACINTYRE, Angus Donald; s of Francis Peter Macintyre, OBE (d 1944), and Evelyn Mary Josephine, *née* Synott (d 1956); *b* 4 May 1935; *Educ* Wellington, Hertford Coll Oxford, St Antony's Coll Oxford (MA, D Phil); *m* 5 Sept 1958, Joanna Musgrave, da of Sir Richard Harvey, 2 Bt (d 1978), of Chisenbury Priory, Pewsey, Wilts; 2 s (Benedict Richard Pierce, Magnus William Lachlan), 1 da (Katherine Cressida Eve); *Career* Lt Coldstream Gds 1953-55; official fell and tutor in modern history Magdalen Coll Oxford (univ lectr 1963-, vice-pres 1981-82, actg pres 1987), ed English Historical Review 1978-86; chm Thomas Wall Tst 1971-, govr Wolverhampton GS 1985-, chm of govrs Magdalen Coll Sch Oxford 1987-; FRHistSOC 1972; *Books* The Liberator: Daniel O'Connell and the Irish Parlimentary Party (1965), Daniel O'Connell: Portrait of a Radical (contrib 1984), Magdalen College and the Crown (contrib 1988); *Recreations* cricket, book collecting; *Clubs* MCC; *Style—* Angus Macintyre, Esq; 8 Linton Rd, Oxford; Achaglachgach, By Tarbert, Argyll; Magdalen College, Oxford

MACINTYRE, Charles Edward Stuart; s of John Macintyre (d 1978), and Mary, *née* Agnew; *b* 13 Feb 1932; *Educ* Priory GS Shrewsbury; *m* 28 June 1956, Barbara Mary, da of William Abley (d 1969); 3 da (Sarah (Mrs Garratt) b 10 April 1957, Ruth b 30 March 1958, Jane b 23 May 1963); *Career* dir and gen mangr Heart of England Building Soc 1983-; pres Coventry Centre Building Soc's Inst; FCBSI 1969; *Recreations* sport; *Style—* Charles Macintyre, Esq; Merrywood, Hampton-on-the-Hill, Warwick CV35 8QR (☎ 0926 492766) (☎ 0926 492766); Heart of England Building Soc, 22-26 Jury St, Warwick CV34 4ET (☎ 0926 496111)

MACINTYRE, Prof Iain; s of John MacIntyre (d 1954), of Tobermory, Mull, and Margaret Fraser Shaw (d 1967), of Stratherick, Inverness; *b* 30 August 1924; *Educ* Jordanhill Coll Sch Glasgow, Glasgow Univ (MB, ChB), London Univ (PhD, DSc); *m* 14 July 1947, Mabs Wilson, da of George Jamieson (d 1951), of Largs, Ayrshire; 1 da

(Fiona Bell b 1953); *Career* Royal Post Grad Med Sch: dir dept of chem pathology and endocrine unit 1982-(prof of endocrine chem 1967-82); memb Hammersmith and Queen Charlottes Health Authy 1982-, Br Post Grad Fedn Central Academic Cncl 1983-, Bd of Studies in Medicine London Univ, Bd of Studies in Pathology London Univ; Gairdner Int Award Toronto 1967, Hon MD Turin Univ 1985; MCRPath (fndr memb) 1963, MRCP 1969, FRCPath 1971, FRCP 1977; *Recreations* tennis, chess; *Clubs* Athenaeum, Queen's, Hurlingham; *Style—* Professor Iain MacIntyre; Great Broadhurst Farm, Broad Oak, Heathfield, Sussex TN21 8UX (☎ 0435 883 515); Dept of Chemical Pathology, Royal Postgraduate Medical School, Du Cane Rd, London W12 0NN (☎ 01 740 322, fax 01 740 6680)

McINTYRE, Ian James; s of Hector Harold McIntyre (d 1978), of Inverness, and Annie Mary Michie (d 1979); *b* 9 Dec 1931; *Educ* Prescot GS Lancs, St John's Coll Cambridge (BA, MA), Coll of Europe Bruges; *m* 24 July 1954, Leik Sommerfelt, da of Benjamin Vogt (d 1970), of Kragero, Norway; 2 s (Andrew James, Neil Forbes), 2 da (Anne Leik, Katharine Elspeth); *Career* Nat Serv cmmnd Intelligence Corps; writer and broadcaster; BBC: current affrs talks prodr 1957-59, ed At Home and Abroad 1959-60, mgmnt trg orgnr 1960-61, broadcasting contract 1970-76; controller: Radio 4 1976-78, Radio 3 1978-87; prog servs offr ITA 1961-62, dir of info and res Scottish Cons Centl Off Edinburgh 1962-70; contested Roxburgh, Selkirk and Reebles (Cons) gen election 1966, pres of Cambridge Union 1953; *Books* The Proud Doers (1968), Words (1975); *Recreations* walking, swimming, gardening; *Clubs* Cambridge Union, Beefsteak; *Style—* Ian McIntyre, Esq; Spylaw House, Newlands Avenue, Radlett, Herts WD7 8EL (☎ 0923 853532)

McINTYRE, Very Rev Prof John; CVO (1985); s of John Clark McIntyre and Annie McIntyre, of Bathgate; *b* 20 May 1916; *Educ* Bathgate Acad, Edinburgh Univ (MA, BD, DLitt); *m* 1945, Jessie, da of William Buick, of Coupar, Angus; 2 s, 1 da; *Career* prof of systematic theol St Andrews Coll Sydney 1946-56, princ St Andrews Coll Sydney 1950-56, prof Divinity Edinburgh Univ 1956-86, princ New Coll and dean Faculty of Divinity Edinburgh Univ 1968-74, acting princ and vice-chllr Edinburgh Univ 1973-74 and 1979, dean Order of Thistle 1974-89; chaplain to HM The Queen in Scotland 1975-86, extra chaplain 1974-75, 1986-, moderator Gen Assembly of Church of Scotland 1982; Hon DHL College of Wooster Ohio 1983, Hon DD Glasgow Univ 1961, Hon Dr Edinburgh Univ 1987; *Books* St Anselm and His Critics (1954), The Christian Doctrine of History (1957), In the Love of God (1962), The Shape of Christology (1966), Faith, Theology and Imagination (1987); *Style—* The Very Rev Prof John McIntyre, CVO; 22/4 Minto St, Edinburgh EH9 1RQ (☎ 031 667 1203); Univ of Edinburgh, New College, Mound Place, Edinburgh EH1 2LX (☎ 031 225 8400)

McINTYRE, Air Cdre Kenneth John; CB (1958), CBE (1951), JP (Dorset 1967), DL (Dorset 1983); s of William S McIntyre (d 1950), of Abbots Leigh, Somerset; *b* 1908; *Educ* Blundell's, RMC Sandhurst; *m* 1936, Betty Aveley, da of Col Percie C Cooper (d 1958), of Dulwich; *Career* cmmnd R Tank Corps 1928, RAF 1934, served WWII (France, Belgium, UK), Gp Capt 1947, HQ MEAF 1948-50, IDC 1951, SHAPE NATO Paris 1952-54, Air Cdre 1955, dir of Policy (Air Staff) Air Miny 1955, ret 1958; CC Dorset 1967, chm 1981-; *Clubs* RAF; *Style—* Air Cdre Kenneth McIntyre, CB, CBE, JP, DL; East Penthouse, 57 Branksome Ct, Canford Cliffs, Poole, Dorset

MACINTYRE, Malcolm Valentine Strickland; s of Donald George Frederick Wyville Macintyre, RN, DSO, DSC (d 1981), and Monica Josephine Clifford Rowley, da of Roger Walter Strickland (descended in the sr line of Strickland of Sizergh Castle, Westmorland); f Capt Donald Macintyre was famous U-boat hunter in WWII, f's great uncle Lt-Gen Donald Macintyre raised the 4th Gurkhas and won VC, ggf Gen John Macintyre also served in Indian Army in Madras Artillery; gf Maj-Gen Donald Macintyre served in 2nd and commanded 4th Gurkhas; *b* 5 Nov 1942,; *Educ* Ampleforth; Luton Coll of Technol (HND) Mechanical Engineering; *m* 22 Feb 1969, Lesley Winifred, da of Leslie Donald Brown (d 1961); 1 s (Donald Malcolm Macintyre 1970); *Career* appinted dir PLYSU plc 1981; *Recreations* dog breeding and training; *Style—* Malcolm V S Macintyre; Cedarbrook, Lower Dean, Huntingdon, Cambs, PE18 0LL; Plysu plc, Woburn Sands, Bucks (☎ 0908 582311)

McINTYRE, Michael Mackay (Mike); MBE (1988); s of Prof (William) Ian Mackey McIntyre, of Shandon, Helensburgh, Strathclyde, and Ruth Dick, *née* Galbraith; *b* 29 June 1956; *Educ* Hermitage Acad Helensburgh, Strathclyde, Glasgow Univ (BSc); *m* 29 Aug 1980, Caroline Maria, da of Gerald Albert Abraham, of Stert, nr Devizes, Wilts; 1 s (Angus b 28 Jan 1985), 1 da (Gemma b 24 June 1987); *Career* yachtsman, Int Finn Class: Br Champ 1981, 1983, 1984, Euro Champ 1984, 7 Olympic Games 1984; Int Star Class: Br Champ 1988, Olympic Gold Medalist 1988; AMIEE; *Style—* Mike McIntyre, Esq, MBE; 21 West Dean, nr Salisbury, Wilts SP5 1JB (☎ 0794 409 60); Orbitel Mobile Communications Ltd, The keytech Centre, Ashwood Way, Basingstoke, Hants (☎ 0256 843 468, fax 0256 843 207, car tel 0836 707 848)

MCINTYRE, Prof Neil; s of John William McIntyre (d 1986), of Ferndale, Mid Glamorgan, and Catherine Elizabeth, *née* Watkins; *b* 1 May 1934; *Educ* Porth Co Sch for Boys, King's Coll London and King's Coll Hosp Med Sch (BSc, MB, BS, MD); *m* 3 Sept 1966, Wendy Ann, da of Wing Cdr Richard Kelsey (ret) of Southwold, Suffok; 1 s (Rowan b 1969), 1 da (Waveny b 1968); *Career* MRC travelling fellowship Mass Gen Hosp and Harvard Med Sch USA 1966-68, hon conslt Royal Free Hosp; Royal Free Hosp Sch of Med: sr lectr in med 1968-73, reader in med 1973-78, clinical sub dean 1976-80, prof of med 1979-83, prof and chm dept of med 1983-; Freeman City of London, Liveryman Worshipful Co Apothecaries , sec MRS 1972-77; FRCP 1972; *Books* The Problem Orientated Medical Record (1979), Lipids and Lipoproteins (1989); *Recreations* golf, photographing medical statues; *Clubs* Athenaeum; *Style—* Prof Neil McIntyre; 20 Queenscourt, Wembley, Middx HA9 7QV (☎ 902 2751); Department of Medicine, Royal Free Hospital, Pond St, London NW3 2QG (☎ 794 0500 x 3969; 01 435 0186)

MCINTYRE, Dr Robert Douglas; s of John Ebenezer McIntyre (d 1961), of Edinburgh, and Catherine Campbell, *née* Morison (d 1961); *b* 15 Dec 1913; *Educ* Hamilton Acad, Daniel Stewart Coll, Edinburgh Univ (MB, ChB), Glasgow Univ (DPH); *m* 11 Sept 1954, Letitia Sarah, *née* MacLeod; 1 s (John Douglas b 21 Sept 1959); *Career* area conslt chest physician Stirlingshire 1951-79, hon conslt Stirling Royal Infirmary 1978-; Scottish Nat Pty: MP Motherwell & Wishaw 1945, chm 1948-56, pres 1958-80; contested: Motherwell & Wishaw 1950, Perth and E Perthshire 1951, 1955, 1959, 1964, West Stirlingshire 1966, 1970, Stirling Burgh's (by election 1971 gen election Feb and Oct 1974), Euro election Mid Scotland & Fife 1979; memb univ ct Univ of Stirling 1967-75 and 1979-88 (chllrs assessor 1979-88), memb Stirling Town Cncl 1957-75 (hon tres 1958-64), provost 1967-75; Hon DUniv Univ of Stirling; Freeman Royal Burgh of Stirling, Fell Scottish Cncl; *Recreations* sailing; *Clubs* Scottish Arts, Stirling County; *Style—* Dr Robert McIntyre; 8 Gladstone Place, Stirling (☎ 0786 73456)

MacINTYRE, Robert Hamilton (Sandy); s of Robert Hamilton MacIntyre (d 1964), of 4 Bede House, Manor Fields, London SW15, and Doris, *née* Bateman (d 1978); *b* 2 Mar 1932; *Educ* St Pauls; *m* 3 March 1956, Jean-Anne, da of James Pizzey (d 1975); 2 s (Robert b 1965, Richard b 1967), 2 da (Lisbeth-Anne b 1959, Amanda b 1961); *Career* mil serv as sergeant RAPC; ptnr MacIntyre Hudson (CA), dir: Surrey Building Soc, Bruce & Ford Ltd; FCA; *Recreations* motoring, motor sport, swimming; *Clubs* Leander RC, Thames RC; *Style—* Sandy MacIntyre, Esq; 87 Copse Ave, West Wickham, Kent BR4 9NW; 26/28 Ely Place, London EC1N 6RL (fax 01 405 4786)

McIVOR, Rt Hon (William) Basil; PC (1971); s of Rev Frederick McIvor (d 1968) and (Elizabeth) Lilly *née* Dougan (d 1972); *b* 17 June 1928; *Educ* Methodist Coll Belfast, Queen's Univ Belfast (LLB), Lincoln's Inn; *m* 3 Jan 1953, (Frances) Jill (*qv*), da of late Cecil Reginald Johnston Anderson, of Lisburn, NI; 2 s (Jonathan, Timothy), 1 da (Jane); *Career* barr NI 1950, pres magistrate 1974, MP (Ulster Unionist) Larkfield NI Parly 1969, Min of Community Relations NI 1971-72, memb (UU) for S Belfast, NI Assembly, 1973-5; Min Educ NI 1974; govr Campbell Coll 1975- (chm 1983), fndr and chm of govrs and dirs of Lagan Coll (the first purposely designed integrated RC and Protestant Sch in NI); *Recreations* music, gardening, golf; *Clubs* Royal Commonwealth Soc; *Style—* The Rt Hon Basil McIvor; Larkhill, 98 Spa Road, Ballynahinch, Co Down (☎ (0238) 563534)

McIVOR, Ian Walker; s of William Walker McIvor, of Worsley, Manchester (d 1986), and Susannah, *née* Glover; *b* 19 Jan 1944; *Educ* Worsley HS, Bolton Inst, London Univ (LLB); *m* 16 Sept 1969, Patricia Wendy, da of Harry Blackhurst Swift of Caephilly, South Wales; 1 s (Andrew Walker b 1977), 4 da (Helen b 1970, Rachel b 1971, Caroline b 1974, Joanne b 1984); *Career* AVR 2 Kings Regt OTC 1966-68; barr Inner Temple 1973, head of chambers 1977-; memb Catenian Assoc; *Recreations* golf, swimming, walking, DIY; *Clubs* Heald Green; *Style—* Ian McIvor, Esq; 38 Framingham Rd, Brooklands, Sale, Cheshire M33 3SG (☎ 061 962 8205); Courtletts House, 38 King St West, Manchester (☎ 061 833 9628)

McIVOR, (Frances) Jill; da of Cecil Reginald Johnston Anderson (d 1956), of Lisburn Co Antrim, and Frances Ellen, *née* Henderson (d 1978); *b* 10 August 1930; *Educ* Lurgan Coll, Queen's Univ Belfast (LLB); *m* 1953, Rt Hon William Basil McIvor (*qv*); 2 s (Jonathan, Timothy), 1 da (Jane); *Career* asst librarian (law) QUB 1954-55, tutor in legal res Law Faculty QUB 1965-74, editorial staff NI Legal Qtly 1966-76, librarian Dept of Dir of Public Prosecutions 1977-79, memb Gen Dental Cncl 1979- chm Lagan Valley Regnl Park Ctee 1984- (memb 1975-), memb: N Ireland IBA 1980-86, Ulster Countryside Cmmn 1984-, Fair Employment Agency 1984-, Lay Panel Juvenile Court 1976-77, GDC 1979-; barr NI 1980; exec Belfast Voluntary Welfare Soc 1981-88, bd memb: Cooperation North 1987-, NI advsy ctee Br Cncl 1987-, memb hon sec's advsy panel on Community Radio 1985-6; chm Ulster NZ Tst 1987-, bd of visitors QUB 1988-, chm EGSA (Educnl Guidance Serv for Adults) 1988-; *Publications* Irish Consultant (and contrib) Manual of Law Librarianship (1976), Elegentia Juris: selected writings of F H Newark (ed 1973), Chart of the English Reports (new edn 1982); *Recreations* gardening, beekeeping; *Clubs* Royal Commonwealth Soc, Royal Overseas League; *Style—* Mrs Jill McIvor; Larkhill, 98 Spa Road, Ballynahinch, Co Down (☎ 0238 563534)

MACK, Prof Alan Osborne; s of Arthur Joseph Mack (d 1957), and Florence Emily, *née* Norris; *b* 24 April 1918; *Educ* Westbourne Pk Sch, Univ of London, Royal Dental Hosp (LDS, FDS), Durham Univ (MDS); *m* 19 June 1943, Marjorie Elizabeth, da of Charles Edward Westacott; 2 s (Peter John b 1945, Ian Robert b 1948), 1 da (Susan Elizabeth (Mrs Shinaco) b 1953); *Career* Flt Lt RAF dental branch 1943-47; civil conslt in prosthetic dentistry RAF 1978-88; house surgn Royal Dental Hosp 1942-43, demonstrator Royal Dental Hosp 1948 (asst dir and sr lectr 1949-56), prof dental prosthetics Univ of Durham 1956-67 (Univ of London 1967-81); examiner RCS Univs of: Manchester 1957, Leeds 1961, Glasgow 1961, Liverpool 1965, London 1965, Edinburgh 1968, Lagos Nigeria 1970, Singapore and Khartoum 1977, Benghazi 1978; examination visitor for Gen Dental Cncl, advsr Univ of Malaya, memb bd of faculty RCS 1959, pres Br Soc for Study of Prosthetic Dentistry 1963, p/t conslt Stoke Mandeville Hosp and John Radcliffe Hosp 1976, visiting prof Univ of Singapore 1981; memb Br Dental Assoc 1942-; *Books* Full Dentures (1971); *Recreations* gardening, pottery; *Style—* Prof Alan Mack; Home Farm, London Rd, Aston Clinton, Bucks HP22 5HG (☎ 0296 630 522)

MACK, Donald; OBE (1972); s of Peter Mack (d 1951), and Rebecca, *née* Ross (d 1986); *b* 6 August 1924; *Educ* St John's Coll London; *m* 11 June 1949, June Moyra, da of Joseph Moss Baker (d 1966); 1 s (Christopher Peter b 1955), 1 da (Linda Suzanne b 1951); *Career* dir: M & W Mack Ltd 1948 (chm and chief exec 1985-), Nat Inst Fresh Produce 1975-85, master Worshipful Co of Fruiterers; *Recreations* reading, music, golf; *Style—* Donald Mack, OBE; 43 North Street, Chichester, West Sussex PO19 1NF (☎ (0243) 787646, telex 86568, fax (0243) 775795)

MACK, Keith Robert; s of David Stanley Mack (d 1986), and Dorothy Ivy *née* Bowes; *b* 2 Mar 1933; *Educ* Edmonton County Sch; *m* 23 Jan 1960, Eileen Mary, da of William Owen Cuttell (d 1978); 2 s (Barry b 1962, Bevin b 1964), 4 da (Penny b 1966, Hazel, Heather (twins b 1967, Beth b 1970); *Career* RAF Pilot 1951-58; Civilian Air Traffic Control Officer, Scottish and Oceanic Air Traffic Control Centre, 1960-67; RAF Staff Coll, Bracknell 1968; NATS HQ, 1969-71; ATC Watch Supervisor, Scottish ATCC, 1972-73; CAA Chief Officer, Cardiff Airport, 1974; NATS HQ, 1975-76; ATC Watch Supervisor, London ATCC, 1977; NATS Depty Director of Control (Airspace Policy), 1978-79; Superintendent, London ATCC, 1980-82; Depty Controller, NATS, 1983-84; Gp dir, memb of the Bd of the Civil Aviation Authy and Controller, National Air Traffic Services, 1985; *Recreations* DIY house refurbishment, cycling, walking, photography, music; *Style—* Robert Mack, Esq; National Air Traffic Services, CAA House, 45-59 Kingsway, London WC2B 6TE (☎ 01 379 7311 ext 2772)

McKAIG, Adm Sir (John) Rae; KCB (1973), CBE (1966); s of Sir John Bickerton McKaig, KCB, DSO (d 1962); *b* 24 April 1922; *Educ* Loretto; *m* 1945, Barbara Dawn, da of Dr Frank Marriott, MC; 2 s, 1 da; *Career* joined RN 1939, served WW II, Rear-Adm 1968, Asst Chief Naval Staff Ops Requirements 1968-70, Vice-Adm 1970, Flag Offr Plymouth & Port Adm Devonport, Cdr Central Sub Area E Atlantic & Cdr

Plymouth Sub Area Channel 1970-73, Adm 1973, UK mil rep to NATO 1973-75, ret 1976; memb Royal Patriotic Fund Corpn 1978-, dep chm and chief exec Gray Mackenzie & Co 1980-, exec dir Inchcape plc 1981-86; *Recreations* sailing, shooting, fishing; *Clubs* RYS Army and Navy; *Style*— Adm Sir Rae McKaig, KCB, CBE; Hill Ho, Hambledon, Hants

McKANE, Leonard Cyril; MBE (1945); s of Cyril McKane (d 1978), of Guernsey, and Alice Mary, *née* Falla (d 1950); *b* 8 April 1920; *Educ* Elizabeth Coll Guernsey, Pembroke Coll Oxford; *m* 24 June 1941, (Eleanor) Catharine, da of Rev Bernard James Harris (d 1951); 3 s (Christopher b 1946, Richard b 1947, Andrew b 1953), 1 da (Caroline b 1951); *Career* WW II Lt-Col Intelligence Corps, served in M East, Italy and Austria 1940-46; joined FO 1946; served in Melbourne, Paris, Singapore; cncllr Washington 1973-76, ret 1980; *Recreations* genealogy, gardening, travel; *Style*— Leonard C McKane, Esq, MBE; The Old Bakehouse, Ampney St Peter, Cirencester, Glos GL7 5SH (☎ 0285 85294)

McKANE, Prof William; s of Thomas McKane (d 1964), and Jemima, *née* Smith (d 1957); *b* 18 Feb 1921; *Educ* Univ of St Andrews (MA) Univ of Glasgow (MA, PhD, DLitt); *m* 3 July 1952, Agnes Mathie, da of James Howie, (d 1973) of South Fergushill, Ayrshire; 3 s (Tom b 15 May 1953, James b 8 July 1956, William b 4 May 1966), 2 da (Ursula b 22 Jan 1959, Christina b 20 March 1963); *Career* RAF 1941-45; sr lectr in Hebrew Univ of Glasgow 1965 (asst lectr 1953), prof of Hebrew and Oriental Languages 1968, dean Faculty of Divinity 1973-77 Univ of St Andrews, foreign sec Soc for Old Testament Study 1981-86, (pres 1978), princ St Mary's Coll St Andrews 1982-86; Univ Blue Football St Andrews 1948; Burkitt Medal of Br Acad for distinguished work in biblical studies 1985; Min Church of Scot; DD (Honoris Causa) Univ of Edinburgh 1984; FRAS 1957, FBA 1980, FRSE 1983; *Books* I and II Samuel (1963), Prophets and Wise Men (1965), Proverbs: A New Approach (1970), Jeremiah 1-25. International Critical Commentary (1986), Studies in the Patriarchal Narratives (1979), Selected Christian Hebraists (1989); *Recreations* walking including hill walking; *Clubs* Royal and Ancient (St Andrews); *Style*— Prof William McKane; 51 Irvine Cres, St Andrews, Fife KY16 8LG (☎ 0334 73797); St Mary's Coll, St Andrews Fife KY16 9JU (☎ 0334 76161)

MACKANESS, Barry Samuel; s of Arthur William Mackaness (d 1961), of Gilmorton, Leics, and Ivy Alice Akehurst (d 1986); *b* 12 Dec 1928; *Educ* Cheltenham; *m* 1955 (m dis 1977), Caroline, da of G Trestrail Morton (d 1977), of Fritwell; 2 s (Shaun b 1955, Peter b 1958); *Career* in the wine trade; *Recreations* racing pigeons; *Clubs* Cavalry and Guards'; *Style*— Barry Mackaness, Esq; Upper House, N Aston, Oxfordshire

MACKANESS, James; DL (Northamptonshire 1984); s of John Howard Mackaness, *qv* ; *b* 6 Feb 1945; *Educ* Millfield, RAC Cirencester; *m* 1972, Susan, da of Harold Pike, of Frinton-on-Sea, Essex; 1 s (Oliver b 1975), 1 da (Louise b 1973); *Career* md A J Mackaness Ltd; dir: Landowners Farmers and Traders 1930, various family cos; chm St John Cncl for Northampton, govr St Andrews Hosp Northampton 1987; CStJ 1982; *Recreations* foxhunting; *Clubs* Northampton and County; *Style*— James Mackaness, Esq, DL; The Old Rectory, Church Brampton, Northampton NN6 8AU (☎ 0604 842386)

MACKANESS, John Howard; er s of Alfred James Mackaness (d 1964), of Little Billing, Northampton, and Florence May, *née* Pepper (d 1964); family history from 1465 recorded College of Arms; granted armorial bearings 1960; *b* 11 Oct 1915; *Educ* Oakham Sch, Wye Coll, London Univ; *m* 28 Sept 1940, Marjorie, da of Cecil Stanley Andrews (d 1953); 4 s (Sam *qv*, James *qv*, Simon b 5 Feb 1949, Mark *qv*); *Career* fndr and life pres Mixconcrete (Hldgs) plc; dir: A J Mackaness Ltd, Billing Aquadrome Ltd; gen cmmr Income Tax 1965-69; memb Northants CC 1961-70; master of Pytchley Hunt 1968-71, Royal Warrantholder as Maker and Supplier of Charcoal to HM The Queen; landowner; *Books* Boughton Hall (1969), 600 Years with the Mackaness Family in Northamptonshire (1982); *Recreations* hunting, shooting, walking, travel; *Style*— John Mackaness, Esq; The Dower, Boughton Hall, Northampton (☎ (0604) 843221); Rudding Arch, Harrogate (☎ (0423) 879604)

MACKANESS, Mark; 4 and yst s of John Howard Mackaness, of The Dower, Boughton Hall, *qv*; *b* 20 Jan 1952; *Educ* Oundle, RAC Cirencester; *m* 1985, Nicola Louise, da of William Henry Lax, of Kirkby Chase, Kirkby Overblow, Harrogate, N Yorks; *Career* land agent, dir: A J Mackaness Ltd, Billing Fin Ltd, Billing Aquadrome Ltd, Neaveford Ltd, Rudding House Ltd; FRICS; *Recreations* skiing, shooting,; *Clubs* Farmers'; *Style*— Mark Mackaness, Esq; Home Farm, Harrington, Northants; A J Mackaness Ltd, The Estate Office, Orchard Hill, Little Billing, Northampton NN6 9QX (☎ 0604 412822)

MACKANESS, Sam; eldest s of John Howard Mackaness, of The Dower, Boughton, Northampton, and Marjorie, *née* Andrews; descended from John Mackernes, of Thingdon (later Finedon), Northants, whose will was dated 14 Oct 1515 (*see* Burke's Landed Gentry, 18 Edn, vol II, 1969); *b* 17 Mar 1943; *Educ* Oundle, Lycée Jaggard Switzerland, Shuttleworth Agric Coll; *m* 4 May 1968, Karen Marie, o da of Cecil Featherstone, of Poplars House, Rothersthorpe, Northampton; 1 s (Paul b 8 April 1972), 1 da (Shena b 26 May 1969); *Career* shooting, fishing, skiing; *Clubs* Farmers'; *Style*— Sam Mackaness, Esq; Preston Deanery Hall, Northampton NN7 2DX (☎ 0604 870913); Billing Aquadrome Ltd, Little Billing, Northampton NN3 4DA (☎ 0604 408181)

MACKARNESS, Simon Paul Richard; TD (1980); s of Peter John Coleridge Mackarness TD, of Petersfield, Hants, and Torla Frances Wedd, *née* Tidman; *b* 10 Sept 1945; *Educ* Portsmouth GS, Bristol Univ (BA); *m* 9 Dec 1978, Diana, da of Dr Lewis MacDonald Reid, MC (d 1978); 1 s (Daniel b 198), 1 da (Louise b 1981); *Career* Capt Royal Signals on RARO; slr 1970, sr ptnr MacKarness & Lunt; memb Law Soc; *Recreations* amateur dramatics, motorcycling; *Style*— Simon Mackarness, Esq, TD; 16 High Street, Petersfield, Hants (☎ 0730 65111, fax 0730 67994)

MACKAY, Hon Alan John Francis; 2 s of 2nd Earl of Inchcape (d 1939), by his 1 w, Joan (d 1933), da of Rt Hon Lord Justice Moriarty; *b* 6 Sept 1919; *Educ* Eton, Trinity Coll Cambridge; *m* 1, 3 Jan 1945 (m dis 1946), Janet Mary, yst da of Frederick Wallis, of Elvendon Priory, Goring-on-Thames; m 2, 30 June 1948 (m dis 1953), Sonia Cecilia Helen, yst da of Capt James Richard Tylden, of Milstead Manor, Kent, and of Lady Tower, of Sway, Hants; 2 da (Siobhan b 1949, Kristina b 1951); m 3, 7 July 1955, Countess Lucie Catinka Christiane Julie, only da of Count Curt Ludwig Haugwitz-Hardenberg-Reventlow, of Korinth, Fyn, Denmark, and former w of late John Patrick Douglas-Boswell; 3 step s; *Career* served with: Cameronians 1939-40, Mercantile Marine 1941-46; *Clubs* Naval & Military, Union (Sydney), Royal Sydney Golf, Eccentric, Lansdowne; *Style*— Hon Alan Mackay; Enterkine, Annbank, Ayrshire (☎ (0292) 520223); Fairybridge, Oughterard, Co Galway, Ireland (☎ (091) 82223); Skyttegaarden, Korinth, 5600 Faaborg, Fyn, Denmark (☎ (09) 65 10 03)

McKAY, Maj-Gen Alexander Matthew; CB (1975); s of Colin McKay (d 1977), of Vancouver, Canada, and Ann McKay (d 1979); *b* 14 Feb 1921; *Educ* RN Dockyard Sch, Portsmouth Poly; *m* 1949, Betty Margaret, da of George Lee, of London; 1 s (Andrew), 1 da (Fiona), (1 da decd); *Career* serv WWII DEME (Army) 1942-75 (despatches twice), Palestine, Malaya, (Maj-Gen); chm Stocklake Hldgs plc 1975-87, memb ASME sec Inst of MechE Engrg 1976-87; FEng, FIMechE, FIEE, FRSE; *Recreations* flyfishing, gardening, restoring antique furniture; *Style*— Maj-Gen Alexander McKay, CB; Church Cottage, Martyr Worthy, Nr Winchester SO21 1DY (☎ 096 278 339)

MACKAY, Baron (and Hon) Alexander William Rynhard; 2 s of 12 Lord Reay (d 1921), and Baroness Maria Johanna Bertha Christina Van Dedem (d 1932); *b* 7 Dec 1907; *Career* dir Bank of the Netherlands; *Style*— Baron Alexander Mackay; De Lindelaan, 76 Schapendrift, Blaricum (NH), Netherlands

MACKAY, Capt Alistair Stuart; s of William Mackay (d 1985), of Surrey, and Myra, *née* Freer; *b* 26 Oct 1954; *Educ* Emanuel Sch London, Oxford Air Trg Sch; *m* 7 July 1983; 2 da (Fiona Victoria, Morag Rachel); *Career* RAF cmmn Gen Duties Branch; airline captain; memb Aberdeen Mountain Rescue Assoc, mountain advsr to Scout Assoc; Freeman: City of London 1984, Worshipful Co of Air Pilots and Air Navigators 1980; FBIM, FInstD, MRIN; *Recreations* mountaineering, fishing, shooting; *Clubs* RAF; *Style*— Capt Alistair Mackay; Upper Walden, Horsewood Rd, Bridge of Weir, Renfrewshire, Scot; Caprice, 25 Westhall Pk, Warlingham, Surrey (☎ 0505 612909)

McKAY, Allen; MP (Lab) Barnsley W and Penistone 1983-; s of Fred McKay (d 1980), and Martha Anne McKay; *b* 5 Feb 1927; *Educ* Hoyland Kirk Balk Secdy Mod Sch; *m* 1949, June, da of Clifford Simpson (d 1964); 1 s; *Career* clerical and steel works 1941-45, mineworker 1945-47, mining electrical engr 1947-65, asst manpower offr NCB Barnsley 1966-78 (industl res trainee 1965-66); JP Barnsley 1971, (Lab) MP for Penistone 1978-83, oppn whip 1982; *Style*— Allen McKay Esq, MP; 24 Springwood Rd, Hoyland, Barnsley, S Yorks S74 0AZ (☎ 0226 743418); House of Commons, London SW1 (☎ 01 219 4026)

MacKAY, Andrew James; MP (C) Berks E 1983-; s of Robert James, and Olive Margaret MacKay; *b* 27 August 1949; *Educ* Solihull; *m* 1975, Diana Joy Kinchin; 1 s, 1 d; *Career* ptnr Jones MacKay & Croxford, estate agents 1974-; MP (C) Birmingham, Stechford March 1977-79; dir Birmingham Housing Industs Ltd 1975-83; PPS to Tom King (Sec of State for NI) 1986-; sec of Cons Parly Foreign Affairs Ctee 1984-86; *Recreations* golf, squash; *Clubs* Berks GC, Aberdoury GC; *Style*— Andrew MacKay, Esq, MP; House of Commons, London SW1 (☎ 01 219 4109)

McKAY, Sheriff Archibald Charles; s of Patrick McKay, of Agolagh, Co Antrim (tenant of Sir George White, the hero of Ladysmith d 1957), and Catherine, *née* McKinley (d 1962); *b* 18 Oct 1929; *Educ* Knocknacarry Co Antrim, St Aloysius' Glasgow, Glasgow Univ (MA, LLB); *m* 1956, Ernestine Maria Theresa, da of Ernest Tobia, of Glasgow (d 1934); 1 s (Timothy), 3 da (Frances, Ernestine, Oonagh); *Career* Nat Serv, Lt RASC 1955-56; Sheriff of Glasgow and Strathkelvin 1979-; *Recreations* flying light aircraft, amateur radio, tennis; *Style*— Sheriff Archibald McKay

McKAY, Lady; Beverley; widow of Jack Hylton, impresario; *m* 1973, as his 2 w, Sir Alex (Alick Benson) McKay, KBE (d 1983, sometime dir, dep chm and md News Int); 1 step s, 2 step da; *Recreations* skiing, tennis; *Clubs* Queens, Royal Wimbledon Golf, Eagle (Gstaad); *Style*— Lady McKay; 97 Swan Court, Chelsea Manor Street, London SW3 5RY

MacKAY, Hon Mrs; Cynthia; *née* Vansittart; da of 1 Baron Vansittart (d 1957); *b* 31 Dec 1922; *Educ* Heathfield, Ascot; *m* 1, 9 Jan 1942 (m dis 1954), Frederick Crocker Whitman, s of Malcolm D Whitman; 3 s, 1 da; m 2, 25 Nov 1955, Edward Hart MacKay, s of Dr Edward Hart Mackay; 2 s; *Style*— Hon Mrs MacKay; 2655 Clay St, San Francisco, California 94115, USA (☎ 415 346 5625)

MACKAY, Baron Donald Theodore; s of Baron Daniel Mackay (d 1962, s of Baron Theodoor Mackay, unc of 12 Lord Reay, by Baroness Juliana Anna van Lynden, da of Baron Constantijn van Lynden), and his 1 w, Helene, *née* Hommel; British subject; *b* 23 Feb 1910; *m* 1, 6 Dec 1939 (m dis 1945), Jonkvrouwe Alexandra Frederica, da of Jonkheer Bonifacius Christiaan de Savornin Lohman; m 2, 26 Sept 1945 (m dis 1978), Kathleen, da of Percy Shaw Pearce; 1 s (Baron Niall Mackay b 1956, m 3, 1985, Jennifer Mary, da of Hugh Butcher), 1 da (Baroness Moira Mackay b 1952); *Career* Lt-Cdr (executive) Royal Netherlands Navy, served WW II with RN (submarines); LRCP, LRCS Edin, LRFP&S Glas 1951; *Style*— Baron Donald Mackay; Tigh A Chnuic, 15 Kintulavig, Leverburgh, Isle of Harris, Outer Hebrides PA83 8TX (☎ 085 982 200)

MACKAY, Hon Fergus James Kenneth; s and h of Viscount Glenapp; *b* 9 July 1979; *Style*— Hon Fergus Mackay

MACKAY, Sir (George Patrick) Gordon; CBE (1962); s of Rev Adam Mackay, BD (d 1931), and Katie Forrest, *née* Lawrence (d 1918); *b* 12 Nov 1914; *Educ* Aberdeen U (MA); *m* 1954, Margaret Esmé, da of Christopher John Martin (d 1948); 1 s, 2 da; *Career* gen mangr East African Railways and Harbours 1961-64; World Bank: 1965-71, consultant 1971-73, dep dir 1974-75, dir 1975-78; memb Bd of Crown Agents 1980-82; OStJ 1964; kt 1966; *Recreations* golf; *Clubs* Nairobi; *Style*— Sir Gordon Mackay, CBE; Well Cottage, Sandhills, Brook, Surrey GU8 5UP (☎ 042 879 2549)

McKAY, Graham; s of Tom McKay (d 1985), of St Bees, Cumbria, and Dora Frances, *née* Graham (d 1950); *b* 11 July 1935; *Educ* Whitehaven GS, King's Coll London (LLB); *m* 24 Feb 1968, Christine Taylor, da of Charles Elijah Farnworth, of St Bees, Cumbria; 1 s (James Graham b 1973), 1 da (Sarah Louise b 1971); *Career* slr 1959; cmmr for oaths 1966, chm Social Security Appeals Tbnls 1971; pres W Cumbria Law Soc 1985; memb Law Soc 1959; *Recreations* music; *Style*— Graham McKay, Esq; Abbey House, St Bees, Cumbria CA27 0DY (☎ 0946 822462); PO Box 1, 44 Duke St, Whitehaven, Cumbria CA28 7NR (☎ 0946 692194, fax 0946 62686)

McKAY, Lady; Honor E; da of W Deans; *m* 1934, Sir Charles Holly McKay, CBE (d 1972); *Style*— Lady McKay; 2 Banfield St, Ararat, Victoria, Australia 3377

MACKAY, Ian Stuart; s of Rev Gordon Ernest Mackay, of Adelaide, Australia, and Sylvia Viola Dorothy, *née* Spencer (d 1975); *b* 16 June 1943; *Educ* Kearsney Coll, Bothas Hill, Natal, S Africa; London Univ (MB, BS), Royal Coll of Surgeons; *m* 1, 11 May 1968 (m dis), Angela, da of Eric Gascoigne-Pees; 1 s (Angus b 1971), 1 da (Fiona b 1972); m 2, 4 Sept 1981, Mrs Madeleine Hargreaves (*née* Tull); 1 da (Antonia b

1982); *Career* conslt Ear, Nose and Throat Surgeon Charing Cross Hosp and Brompton Hosp; Hon Sr Lectr Rhinology, Inst of Laryngology and Otology; Hon Lectr Cardiothoracic Inst, Univ of London; jt ed Scott-Brown's Otolaryngology: Rhinology Volume; Hon Tres, European Acad Facial Surgery; contributor on Rhinoplasty to Smith's Operative Surgery; FRCS; *Clubs* Royal Society of Medicine, Royal Coll of Surgeons; *Style*— Ian S Mackay, Esq; The Traverse, Bull Lane, Gerrards Cross, Bucks; 55 Harley Street, London W1N 1DD (☎ 01 580 5070)

MACKAY, Hon James; o s of Baron Mackay of Clashfern (Life Peer); *b* 1958; *Educ* Cambridge Univ (MA), Edinburgh Univ (MB, ChB); *Career* medicine, hon Regnl and res fell Univ Dept of Clinical Surgery Univ of Edinburgh; *Style*— Dr Hon James Mackay; 123 Nicolson Street, Edinburgh, EH8 9ER

MACKAY, Hon James Brooke; s of Baron Tanlaw (Life Peer) and his 1 wife Joanna Susan, *née* Hirsch; *b* 12 June 1961; *Style*— Hon James Mackay

MACKAY, Hon James Jonathan Thorn; yr s of 3 Earl of Inchcape and his 1 wife Aline Thorne (Pixie), *née* Pease; *b* 28 May 1947; *Educ* Eton, Trinity Coll Cambridge (MA); *m* 1970, Mary Caroline, er da of Peter Joyce, of Becklands Farm, Whitchurch-Canonicorum, Dorset; 1 s, 1 da; *Style*— Hon James Mackay; 34A Dorset Square, London NW1 6QJ

McKAY, Sir James Wilson; JP (Edinburgh 1972), DL (Edinburgh 1972); s of John McKay; *b* 12 Mar 1912; *Educ* Dumfermline HS, Portobello Secdy Sch Edinburgh; *m* 1942, Janette K A Urquhart; 3 da; *Career* served WW II Lt RNVR; insur broker; md John McKay (Insur) Ltd Edinburgh, Lord Lieut of the Co of the City of Edinburgh 1969-72, Lord Provost of Edinburgh 1969-72; kt 1971; *Style*— Sir James McKay, JP, DL; 11 Cammo Gdns, Edinburgh, Scotland EH8 8EJ (☎ (031 339) 6755)

MACKAY, Dr John; s of William Mackay (d 1952), of Nottingham, and Eliza, *née* Kellock (d 1952); *b* 23 June 1914; *Educ* Mundella Sch Nottingham, Univ Coll Nottingham, Merton Coll Oxford (BA, DPhil); *m* 7 Aug 1952, Margaret, da of Alexander John Ogilvie (d 1937), of Edinburgh; 2 s (William b 1953, Andrew b 1960), 2 da (Elspeth b 1955, Mary b 1957); *Career* Ordinary and Able Seamen RN 1940-42, Sub Ltd RNVR 1942-45, Temp Instr Lt RN 1945-46; travelling sec Student Christian Movement 1936-38, english lectr St John's Diocesan Trg Coll York 1938-40 and 1946, res Merton Coll Oxford 1946-48, asst master Merchant Taylors' Sch Crosby 194-54, second master Cheltenham Coll 1954-60, headmaster Bristol GS 1960-75; chm HMC 1970; *Recreations* gardenening, reading, watching cricket; *Clubs* East India; *Style*— Dr John Mackay; The Old Post Office, Tormarton, Badminton, Avon GL9 1HU (☎ 0454 21243)

McKAY, Sir John Andrew; CBE (1966), QPM (1968); s of Denis McKay (d 1946), of Woodburn Ave, Blantyre, Glasgow, and Jane Dismore McKay (d 1958); *b* 28 Nov 1912; *Educ* Motherwell, Univ of Glasgow (MA); *m* 1, 1947, Gertrude Gillespie, *née* Deighan (d 1971); 2 da; m 2, 1976, Mildred Grace Kilday, da of Dr Emil Stern, of Empire Ct, Grass Valley, California, USA; *Career* joined Met Police 1935, seconded to Mil Govt in Italy and Austria 1943-47 (Lt-Col), asst and dep chief constable Birmingham 1953-58, chief constable Manchester 1959-66, HM inspr of Constabulary 1966, HM chief inspr of Constabulary for England and Wales 1970-72; OStJ 1963; Hon MA Manchester 1966, hon fell Manchester Poly 1972; kt 1972; *Style*— Sir John McKay, CBE, QPM; 7357 Oak Leave Drive, Santa Rose, Calif 95409, USA

McKAY, Dr John Henderson; CBE (1987), DL (Edinburgh 1988); s of Thomas Johnstone McKay (d 1956), of 16 Letham Grove, Pumpherston, Midlothian, and Patricia Madeleine, *née* Henderson (d 1986); *b* 12 May 1929; *Educ* West Calder HS, Open Univ (BA); *m* 8 Feb 1964, Catherine Watson, da of William Middleton Taylor, (d 1968) of 21 Crewe Grove, Edinburgh; 1 s (Ewen b 1969), 1 da (Charis b 1965); *Career* Nat Serv RA 1950-52, gunner UK and Far East; Customs & Excise 1952-85; Lord Provost of Edinburgh 1984-88, chm Edinburgh Int Festival Soc 1984-88, co-chm Edinburgh Mil Tattoo 1984-88; cnclr Royal Caledonian Hort Soc 1974-77 and 1984-88 (vice pres, sec and tres 1988-); *Recreations* golf, gardening; *Clubs* Lothianburn Golf; *Style*— Dr John McKay, CBE, DL; 2 Buckstone Way, Edinburgh EH10 6PN (☎ 031 445 2865)

MACKAY, John Jackson; L......; s of Jackson Mackay and Jane, *née* Farquharson; *b* 15 Nov 1938; *Educ* Glasgow Univ (BSc, Dip Ed); *m* 1961, Sheena, da of James Wagner (d 1963); 2 s, 1 da; *Career* former head maths dept Oban HS; MP (C) Argyll 1979-83, Argyll and Bute 1983-87; PPS to George Younger as Sec of State for Scotland Feb-April 1982, parly under-sec of state Scottish Office (with responsibility for health and social work) from April 1982; Health Social Work and Home Affairs 1985-86, Education Agriculture and Fisheries (1986-87), chief exec Scottish Cons Pty 1987-; *Recreations* fishing, sailing; *Style*— John Mackay, Esq; Innishail, 51 Springkell Drive, Pollokshields, Glasgow G41 4EZ (☎ 041 427 5356)

MACKAY, Lady Lucinda Louise; *née* Mackay; did not assume husband's surname on marriage; da of 3 Earl of Inchcape and Aline, *née* Pease (now Thorn Rolle), da of Sir Richard Pease, 2 Bt (d 1970), of Richmond, Yorks; *b* 13 Dec 1941; *Educ* Chatelard Sch, Edinburgh Univ (MA), Edinburgh Coll of Art, Central Sch of Art and Design; *m* 1983, (m dis 1987), David Wilson Bogie, s of late R T Bogie, of Edinburgh; *Career* formerly schoolmistress in comprehensive sch; painter; *Recreations* Scrabble, poetry, bridge, theatre, letter writing, skiing, looking for spoonerisms, riding, philosophy, music, making friends, dancing (classical, ballet, ballroom, Scottish), sewing, embroidery, home cooking; *Clubs* New (Edinburgh), Edinburgh Univ Staff, Scottish Arts; *Style*— Lady Lucinda Mackay; c/o 24 Rutland Sq, Edinburgh 1

MACKAY, Neil Douglas Malcolm; s of Gp Capt Malcolm Bruce Mackay (d 1971), and Josephine Mary, *née* Brown (d 1965); *b* 28 August 1939; *Educ* Loretto; *m* 10 May 1969, Frances Sarah, da of Lt-Col Claude Dudgeon van Namen, of Gaunt Cottage, Wargrave, Berks; 2 s (Loudon b 1971, Rory b 1982), 2 da (Kirsty b 1973, Lorna b 1976); *Career* Lt RA BAOR; Merchant Banker, asst dir Lazard Bros & Co Ltd 1974 (exec dir 1979, md 1987); non-exec dirships: Trident Gp Printers Ltd 1974-79, R E AG Crossland Ltd 1975-78, Hadson Oil (UK) Ltd 1981-86, Hadson Petroleum Internat plc 1981-86, Aaronite Gp plc 1983-86, etc; *Recreations* bridge, tennis; *Clubs* Hurlingham; *Style*— Neil D M Mackay, Esq; 21 Moorfields, London EC2P 2HT (☎ 01 588 2721)

MACKAY, Peter; s of John Swinton MacKay, of Kinloch, Perthshire, and Patricia May, *née* Atkinson (d 1976); *b* 6 July 1940; *Educ* Glasgow HS, Univ of St Andrews (MA); *m* 29 Aug 1964, Sarah White, da of Reginald White Holdich, of Cherry Burton, East York; 1 s (Andrew), 2 da (Elspeth, Sally); *Career* teacher Kyogle HS NSW Aust 1962-63, asst princ Scottish Off 1963, princ private sec to Sec of State of Scotland Rt Hon Gordon Campbell MC and Rt Hon William Ross MBE 1973-75, head manpower and orgn div SO 1975-78, Nuffield Travelling fell (Canada, Aust, NZ) 1978-79, head local govt div SO 1979-83, seconded dir Scotland Manpower Servs Cmmn 1983-85, under sec: Dept of Employment 1985-86, Scottish Educn Dept 1987- (responsible for further and higher educn arts and sport); *Recreations* high altitudes and latitudes, climbing, sea canoeing, sailing, tennis; *Clubs* Clyde Canoe, Lothian Sea Kayak; *Style*— Peter Mackay, Esq; 6 Henderland Rd, Edinburgh EH12 6BB (☎ 031 337 2830); New St Andrews Ho, Edinburgh EH1 3SY (☎ 031 556 8400, telex 727 301)

MACKAY, Hon Rebecca Alexandra; da of Baron Tanlaw (Life Peer) and his 1 wife Joanna Susan, *née* Hirsch; *b* 17 Oct 1967; *Style*— Hon Rebecca Mackay

MACKAY, Hon (Shona) Ruth; da of Baron Mackay of Clashfern (Life Peer); *b* 1968; *Educ* St Margaret's Sch Edinburgh; *Career* veterinary student; *Style*— Hon Ruth Mackay; 19/11 East Parkside, Edinburgh EH16 5XN

McKAY, William Robert; s of William Wallace McKay (d 1987), of Edinburgh, and Margaret Halley Adamson, *née* Foster; *b* 18 April 1939; *Educ* Trinity Acad Leith, Univ of Edinburgh (MA); *m* 28 Dec 1962, Margaret Muriel, da of Eric Millard Bellwood Fillmore, OBE, of Bexhill upon Sea; 2 da (Catriona b 4 Mar 1967, (twin) Elspeth (Mrs Sagar); *Career* dept of the clerk of the House of Commons since 1961; clerk Scottish Affrs Ctee 1971-74 and 1979-81, princ clerk fin ctees 1985-87, sec House of Commons Cmmn 1981-84, sec Public Accounts Cmmn 1985-87, Clerk of the Jnls 1987-; Interim Clerk Designate Scottish Assembly 1978 ; *Books* (ed) Erskine May's Private Journal 1883-86 (1984), Mr Speaker's Secretaries (1986), Clerks in the House of Commons a biographical list 1363-1989 (1989), (ed) Observations Rules and Orders (1989); *Recreations* living on Coll; *Style*— William McKay, Esq; 26 Earl St, Cambridge CB1 1JR; Lochana' Bhaigh, Isle of Coll, Argyll House of Commons, London SW1A OAA

MACKAY OF CLASHFERN, Baron (Life Peer UK 1979); James Peter Hymers Mackay; PC (1979); s of James Mackay (d 1958); *b* 2 July 1927; *Educ* George Heriot's Sch Edinburgh, Edinburgh Univ, Trinity Cambridge; *m* 1958, Elizabeth Gunn Hymers, da of D D Manson; 1 s, 2 da; *Career* advocate 1955, QC Scot 1965; sheriff principal Renfrew and Argyll 1972-74, vice-dean Faculty of Advocates 1973-76, dean 1976-79; cmmr Northern Lighthouses 1975-84; part-time memb Scottish Law Cmmn 1976-79; dir Stenhouse Hldgs Ltd 1976-78; memb Insurance Brokers' Registration Council 1978-79; lord advocate of Scotland 1979-84, lord of session 1984-85, and lord of appeal in ordinary 1985-89, Lord Chllr Oct 1987-; Hon LLD Dundee 1983, Hon LLD Edinburgh 1983; Hon LLD Strathclyde 1985; Hon LLD Aberdeen 1987; Hon fell Institute Taxation 1983; FRSE 1984; hon FICE 1989; *Clubs* New (Edinburgh); *Style*— The Rt Hon Lord Mackay of Clashfern, PC; House of Lords, London SW1R 0PW

MACKAY-LEWIS, Hon Mrs (Virginia Charlotte Angela); *née* Campbell; da of 3 Baron Colgrain, and his 1 w Veronica Margaret, *née* Webster; *b* 19 Oct 1948; *m* 1973, Maj Jonathan Charles Mackay-Lewis; 2 s (James Edward b 1978, George Mungo Pyne b 1984), 1 da (Gemma Elizabeth b 1977); *Style*— Hon Mrs Mackay-Lewis; c/o Coutts & Co, 1 Cadogan Pl, London SW1

MACKAY-TALLACK, Sir Hugh; s of late E H Tallack, of Cringleford, Norfolk, and Deborah Lyle Mackay, niece of 1 Earl of Inchcape; *b* 1912; *Educ* Kelly Coll Devon, Heidelberg Univ; *Career* 17 Dogra Regt (Middle East and Burma) 1939-43, private sec to C-in-C ALFSEA 1943-44, mil sec to supreme allied cdr SEAC (Adm of the Fleet Earl Mountbatten of Burma) 1945-46; former chm: Macneill & Barry Ltd, Kilburn & Co Ltd (Inchcape Gp) Calcutta; former govr State Bank of India and dir of various Indian cos; chm India Tea Assoc 1954-55, pres Ross Inst of India 1951-64, memb Indian Bd of Trade 1962-63, pres Bengal C of C and Indust and Assoc Cs of C of India 1962-63, exec dep chm Inchcape & Co Ltd 1964-77, chm The Capital and Nat Trust Ltd, dep chm The Standard Chartered Bank Ltd to 1983, memb Fedn of Commonwealth Chambers of Commerce1; kt 1963; *Clubs* White's, City of London, Oriental, Bengal (Calcutta), Turf (Calcutta), Tollygunge (Calcutta); *Style*— Sir Hugh Mackay-Tallack; 47 South Street, Mayfair, London W1

McKEAN, Charles Alexander; s of John Laurie McKean, of Glasgow, and Nancy Burns, *née* Lendrum; *b* 16 July 1946; *Educ* Fettes Coll Edinburgh, Univ of Bristol (BA); *m* 18 Oct 1975, Margaret Elizabeth, da of Mervyn Yeo, of Cardiff; 2 s (Andrew Laurie b 1978, David Alexander b 1981); *Career* ed London Architect 1970-75; RIBA: London regnl sec 1968-71, Eastern regnl sec 1971-79, projects offr Community Architecture and Industl Regeneration 1977-79; sec and tres RIAS 1979-, architectural corr Scotland on Sunday 1988- (The Times 1977-83), memb exhibitions panel Scottish Arts Cncl 1980-83, dir Workshops and Artists Studios Ltd 1980-85, sec to the RIAS Hill House Tst 1979-82, tstee Thirlestane Castle Tst 1983-, memb environment and town planning ctee The Saltire Soc 1984-85, memb advsy cncl for the Arts in Scotland 1985-88; currently cncl memb: Architectural Heritage Soc of Scotland and Charles Rennie Mackintosh Soc; Architectural Journalist of the Year 1979 and 1983, Bldg Journalist of the Year, RSA Bossom Lecture 1986; FRSA 1978, FSA Scotland 1983; *Books* London 1981 (1970), Modern Buildings in London 1965-75 (with Tom Jestico, 1975), Living over the Shop (1976), Battle of Styles (with David Atwell, 1976), Funding the Future (1977), Fight Blight (1977), An Outine of Western Architecture (jtly, 1980), Architectural Guide to Cambrige and East Anglia since 1920, Edinburgh - an illustrated architectural guide (1982), Dundee - an illustrated introduction (with David Walker, 1984), Stirling and the Trossachs (1985), The Scottish Thirties (1987), The District of Moray (1987); *Clubs* Scottish Arts; *Style*— Charles McKean, Esq; 10 Hillpark Rd, Edinburgh EH4 (☎ 031 226 2753); The Royal Incorporation of Architects in Scotland, 15 Rutland Sq, Edinburgh EH1 2BE (☎ 031 229 7205)

McKEAN, Douglas; CB (1977); s of Alexander McKean (d 1962), of Enfield, and Irene Emily, *née* Ofverberg (d 1980); *b* 2 April 1917; *Educ* Merchant Taylors', St John's Coll Oxford (MA); *m* 6 Juny 1942, Anne, da of Roger Clayton (d 1954), of Riding Mill, Northumberland; 2 s (Robert b 1944, Andrew b 1948); *Career* Civil Serv: princ WO 1947-49, HM Treasy 1949-77 (asst sec 1956-62, under sec 1962-77, loan to DOE 1970-72); dir Agric Mortgage Corpn 1978-87; dep sec Centl Bd of Fin C of E 1978-83, tstee Irish Sailors and Soldiers Land Tst 1980-, govr Whitelands Coll Roehampton 1984-, churchwarden parish church of St Andrew Enfield 1987-; *Books* Money Matters - A Guide to the Finances of The Church of England (1987); *Recreations* mountain walking; *Clubs* Utd Oxford and Cambridge; *Style*— Douglas McKean, Esq, CB; The Dower House, Forty Hill, Enfield, Middlesex EN2 9EJ (☎ 01 363 2365)

MCKEAN, Lorne; da of Lt Cdr J A H McKean, RN (d 1981), and Beatrice Blance Mowbray *née* Bellairs; *b* 16 April 1939; *Educ* Elmhurst Ballet Sch, Guildford Art Sch, Royal Acad Schs; *m* 7 Nov 1964, Edwin John Cumming, s of Edwin Russell; 2 da

(Rebecca 21 January 1966, Tanya 25 April 1968); *Career* artist; public and large works include: A A Milne memorial London Zoo Bear Club Winnie, Shearwaters Sheawater House Richmond, Willoughby House Fountain Richmond, Girl and the Swan Reading Herons Thames Water Authy Reading Osprey Fountain Greenwich Connecticut USA Great Swan Great Swan Alley EC2; equestrian and Horse Sculptures: H R H Prince Philip on his polo pony, H M the Queens personal Silver Wedding Gift to her husband, Prince Charles on polo pony Pans Folly, John Pinches International Dressage Trophy, Galoubet French show jumping stallion, Pony series for Royal Worcester Porcelain, Troy Royal Worcester; portraits include: The late Lord Salisbury Hatfield House, Sir Michael Redgrave The late H R H Prince William of Gloucester The Earl of Lichfield televised for portrait series, H M The Queen Drapers Hall and R H H T; FRBS 1968; *Recreations* animals; *Style—* Miss Lorne McKean; Lethendry, Polecat Valley, Hindhead, Surrey GU26 6BE (☎ 042 813 5655)

McKEE, Maj Sir (William) Cecil; ERD (1945), JP (Belfast 1957); s of W B McKee; *b* 13 April 1905; *Educ* Methodist Coll, Queen's Univ Belfast; *m* 1932, Florence Ethel Irene Gill; 1 da; *Career* served WW II RA; estate agent; Lord Mayor of Belfast 1957-59; Hon LLD Queen's U Belfast; KStJ; kt 1959; *Style—* Maj Sir Cecil McKee, ERD, JP; 250 Malone Rd, Belfast, N Ireland (☎ 0232 666979)

McKEE, Ian Arthur; MBE (1973); s of Rev John McKee (d 1960), of 37 Lyford Rd, London SW18, and Irene Mary, *née* Sainsbury (d 1962); *b* 14 April 1916; *Educ* Taunton Sch, Trinity Coll of Music; *m* 21 Aug 1954, Jessie Stephen, da of Edward Poole; 1 s (James b 27 Aug 1965), 1 da (Melissa b 23 Nov 1963); *Career* cmmnd KOSB 1942, Capt 1943 QM and Adj 5 Northants Regt; J Curwen & Sons Ltd 1934, educn mangr Hutchinson & Co 1950, educn rep Methuen 7 Co Ltd 1954, mangr educn dept Methuen Publishers 1958, chm Educn Publishers Exhibition Ctee 1965-68, sales dir Methuen Educnl Ltd 1966, chm Book Devpt Cncl Overseas Exhibition Ctee 1972-76, vice-chm Methuen Educnl Ltd 1974-83, conslt Educnl Publishers Supplies Ctee 1983-; hon sec 78 Div Battleaxe Club 1947-, life govr Taunton Sch 1940-; chm Crawley Branch Winchester Cons Assoc 1987-89, vice-chm Hants branch Mental Health Fndn 1987-, memb Winchester Co Music Festival Ctee 1978-; *Style—* Ian McKee, Esq, MBE; 5 Park Ave, Winchester, Hants SO23 8DJ (☎ 0962 60992)

McKEE, His Hon Judge John; RD (1968), QC (1974); s of Frank McKee (d 1980), and Mollie, *née* Millar; *b* 18 May 1933; *Educ* Strathallan Sch Scotland, Queen's Univ Belfast (BA, LLB); *m* 1962, Annette, da of W Howard Wilson (d 1957); 2 s, 1 da; *Career* RNR 1952-73, Lt-Cdr: barr NI 1960, barr Middle Temple 1971, sr barr NI 1974, barr Republic of Ireland King's Inns 1975; chm UK Delgn to CCBE 1979-81; pres: Industl Tbnls NI 1981-89, Industl Ct NI 1981-89; *Recreations* golf; *Clubs* Ulster Reform (Belfast), Royal County Down GC; *Style—* His Hon Judge John McKee, QC

McKEE, Dr William James Ernest; QHP (1987); s of John Sloan McKee (d 1974), of Pontefract, Yorks, and Annie Emily *née* McKinley (d 1971); *b* 20 Feb 1929; *Educ* Queen Elizabeth's Wakefield, Trinity Coll Cambridge (BA, MA, MB, BChit, MD), Queens Coll Oxford, The Radcliffe Infirmary; *m* Josée, da of Francis James Tucker (d 1975), of Cardiff; 3 da (Jennifer b 1958, Katherine b 1963, Fiona b 1971); *Career* Nat Serv RAF Educn Serv 1947-49; clinical and res hosp appts 1952-61, community med appts with London RGB's 1961-69, sr admin MO Liverpool Regnl Hosp Bd 1969-74; regnl MO: Mersey RHA 1974-76, Wessex Regnl Health authy (regnl med advsr) 1976-; memb: Hunter Working Party on the Future Arrangements for Med Admin and Public Health in the NHS 1972-73, sec of State's Advsy Ctee on the Application of Computing Sci to Med and the NHS 1973-76; chm jt Liason Ctee for Health Serv Boundary Reorganisation in Met Co of Merseyside 1974, memb: Cncl for Postgrad Med Educn (Eng and Wales) 1975-85, bd of faculty of med Southampton Univ 1976-; chm working pty to Review Health Serv Policy for the Mentally Handicapped in Wessex 1978, memb DHSS advsy ctee on Med Manpower Planning 1982-85, chm Eng Regnl Med Offrs 1984-86, UK Med rep to Hosp Ctee of the EEC 1985-, memb DHSS jt planning advsy ctee 1985-, hd UK delegation to Hosp Ctee of EEC 1988; LRCP, MRCS 1955, FFCM 1972; *Books* contributor to many medical jls on various subjects; *Recreations* fly fishing, golf; *Style—* Dr William McKee, QHP; Morningdale, 22A Bereweeke Ave, Winchester, Hants SO22 6BH (☎ 0962 61369); Wessex Regional Health Authority, Romsey Rd, Winchester, Hants (☎ 0962 63511)

MacKELLAR, Jean Elizabeth; da of Edward Gosset Green-Emmott (d 1976), and Violet Mary, *née* Turner (d 1973) *see* Burke's Landed Gentry 18 edn Vol II, Green Emmott of Emmott Hall; Lady of the Manor of Rawdon; *b* 17 Jan 1935; *Educ* Hatherop Castle; *m* 14 Sept 1962, Maj Peter Malcolm Kerr MacKellar, s of Lt-Col John Gray MacKellar, DSO, OBE, DL (d 1975); 1 s (Peter Douglas Edward Emmott b 1967), 1 da (Kathryn Mary Emmott b 1964); *Style—* Mrs Peter MacKellar; Eden House, Warren Rd, Liss, Hants (☎ 0730 895 191)

McKELLEN, Ian Murray; CBE (1979); s of Denis Murray McKellen (d 1964), of Bolton, Lancs, and Margery Lois, *née* Sutcliffe (d 1952); *b* 25 May 1939; *Educ* Wigan GS, Bolton Sch, St Catharine's Coll Cambridge (BA) ; *Career* actor; first professional appearance A Man For All Seasons at Belgrade Theatre Coventry 1961, first London appearance A Scent of Flowers at Duke of York's 1964; Nat Theatre at the Old Vic 1966, Richard II for Prospect Theatre Co 1968; fndr memb Actors' Co 1971-73: performances incl: Ruling The Roost, 'Tis Pity She's a Whore (Edinburgh Festival) 1972, Knots, The Wood Demon (Edinburgh Festival) 1973; RSC 1976-78, performances incl: Dr Faustus, King John 1975, Romeo and Juliet, The Winter's Tale, Macbeth, Pillars of the Community (SWET Award 1977), The Alchemist (SWET Award 1978); Bent (Royal Court and Criterion; SWET Award) 1979, Amadeus, New York 1980-81 (Tony Award), Cowardice, Ambassadors 1983; Nat Theatre 1984-86: Venice Preserv'd, Wild Honey, Coriolanus; assoc dir NT: The Duchess of Malfi, The Real Inspector Hound, The Critic, The Cherry Orchard; one-man USA tour Acting Shakespeare 1987; Henceforward (Vaudeville) 1988-89, Othello (Iago) RSc 1989; Films incl: Priest of Love, Plenty, Scandal (1988) tv: Walter 1982, Walter and June 1983; hon fell St Catharine's Coll Cambridge 1985, hon LLD Nottingham 1989; *Style—* Ian McKellen, Esq, CBE; James Sharkey Assoc, 15 Golden Sq, London W1R 3AG (☎ 01 434 3801 -6, telex 295 251 ISA Long

McKELVEY, Air Cdre John Wesley; CB (1969), MBE (1944); s of Capt John Wesley McKelvey, of Enfield, Middx (d 1939), and Emily Francis Louisa *née* Milsted (d 1976); *b* 25 June 1914; *Educ* Enfield Central Sch, RAF Aircraft Apprentice; *m* 13 Aug 1938, Eileen Amy, da of John Charles Carter, of Enfield (d 1968); 2 s (John b 1943, d 1969, Michael b 1944); *Career* fighter cmd 1932-38, cmmmd 1941 (Eng branch), served Egypt, Syria, Iraq, Bomber Cmd 1939-45, OC Air Miny Manpower Res Unit 1945-47, OC Air Miny Servicing and Devpt Unit 1947-49, RAF Staff Coll 1949; engr duties: FEAF 1949-52, HQ Bomber Cmd 1952-54; Jt Servs Staff Coll Latimer 1954, OC no 60 Maitenance Unit 1954-56, sr tech SO: HQ no 19 GP 1956-57, Task Force Grapple Christmas Is 1957-59; sr air SO HQ no 24 gp 1959-62, dep dir of intelligence (tech) 1962-64, dir aircraft and asst attache def res devpt Bri Embassy Washington DC 1964-66, AO Wales and Cmdt RAF St Athan 1966-69, ret 1969; sec appeals RAF Benevolent Fund 1970-79; MRAeS 1967, CEng 1968; *Recreations* bowls, gardening; *Clubs* RAF; *Style—* Air Cdre John McKelvey, CB, MBE; Inchmerle, 19 Greensome Drive, Ferndown, Winbourne, Dorset BH22 8BE (☎ 0202 894464)

McKELVEY, William; MP (Lab) Kilmarnock and Loudoun 1983-; *b* 1934,July; *Educ* Morgan Acad, Dundee Coll of Technol; *m* 2 s; *Career* former full-time union official, memb Dundee City Cncl, joined Lab Pty 1961, MP Kilmarnock 1979-1983; sponsored by AUEW; *Style—* William McKelvey, Esq, MP; 41 Main Street, Kilmaurs, Ayrshire

MacKENNA, Sir Brian (Bernard Joseph Maxwell); *b* 12 Sept 1905; *Career* barr Inner Temple 1932, QC (KC) 1950, master of the bench Inner Temple 1958, judge High Ct of Justice (Queen's Bench Div) 1961-77; kt 1961; *Style—* Sir Brian MacKenna; 2 Paper Buildings, Temple, London EC4 (☎ 01 353 2123)

MCKENNA, David; CBE (1967), OBE 1946, MBE 1943); s of Rt Hon Reginald McKenna (d 1943), and Pamela Margaret, *née* Jekyll (d 1943); *b* 16 Feb 1911; *Educ* Eton, Trinity Coll Cambridge (BA, MA); *m* 4 April 1934, Lady Cecilia Elizabeth, da of 9 Earl of Albemarle, MC (d 1979); 3 da (Miranda (Mrs Villiers), Primrose (Mrs Arnander), Sophia); *Career* WWII RE Capt 1939, Maj 1942, Lt-Col 1944 Transportation Serv Iraq, Turkey, India, Burma; London Passenger Tport Bd: 1934-39, 1946-55, Br asst gen mangr S Regn 1955-61, chief commercial offr HQ 1962, gen mangr S Regn 1963-68, bd memb full time 1968-76 (pt/t 1976-78); dir Isles of Scilly Steamship Co 1976-, memb Dover Harbour Bd 1969- 80, vice-pres Royal Coll of music 1980 (cncl memb 1946-); chm: Govrs of Sadlers Wells 1962-76, Bach Choir 1968-76 (memb 1934-76); FCIT (pres 1972); Commandeur de l'Ordre Nationale du Merite France 1974; *Recreations* music, sailing; *Clubs* Brooks's, Royal Cornwall YC; *Style—* David McKenna, Esq, CBE; Rosteague, Portscatho, Truro, Cornwall TR2 5EF (☎ 087 258 346)

MacKENNA, (Edward) Peter; s of Edward Timothy MacKenna (d 1932), and Mary Anne, *née* Walden (d 1969); *b* 4 May 1926; *Educ* Trinity Coll Dublin (MA); *m* 1964, Joanne, da of K Photios Hatzi, of Athens; 1 s (Edward b 1967) 1 da (Jane b 1971); *Career* Navigator RAF 1943-47; economist with IMF 1951-54, mangr ops planning Ford Int 1954-60, Int Fin Corpn (Washington) 1960-63, md Mitchell Cotts 1982-87; cncl memb Belgo-Luxembourg C of C in GB; *Recreations* sport; *Style—* Peter MacKenna, Esq; Paridae House, Fishers Wood, Sunningdale, Berks (☎ 0990 23217); Mitchell Cotts Group Ltd, Cotts House, Camomile St, London EC3A 7BJ (☎ 01 283 1234)

MCKENNA, Virginia Anne (Mrs William Travers); da of Terence Morell McKenna (d 1948), and Anne-Marie, *née* Oakeley; *b* 7 June 1931; *Educ* Herschel Capetown SA, Herons Ghyll Horsham, Central Sch of Speech and Drama; *m* 1, (m dis 1954), Denholm Elliot; m 2, 19 Sept 1957, William Inglis Lindon Travers, s of William Halton Lindon Travers, qv, (d 1966); 3 s (William Morrell Lindon b 4 Nov 1958, Justin McKenna Lindon b 6 Mar 1963, Daniel Inglis Lindon b 27 Feb 1967), 1 da (Louise Annabella Lindon b 6 July 1960); *Career* actress; theatre: season Old Vic 1955-56, The Devils 1961, Beggars Opera 1963, A Little Night Music 1976, The King and I (SWET Award best musical actress), Hamlet RSC 1984; films: The Cruel Sea 1952, Carve Her Name With Pride (Belgian Prix Femina) 1957, Born Free (Variety Club Award best actress) 1964, Ring of Bright Water, A Town Like Alice (Academy Award best actress); tv: Romeo and Juliet (Best Actress Award ITV) 1955, Passage to India 1965, The Deep Blue Sea 1974, Cheap in August; fndr dir Zoo Check Charitable Tst 1984; patron: Elizabeth Fitzroy Homes, Slade Centre, Dorking Operatic Soc, World Family, Dorking Hospice Homecare, Crusade; pres Beauty Without Cruelty UK, tstee Elsa Wild Animal Appeal; Freman City of Houston Texas 1966; *Books* On Playing with Lions (with Bill Travers), Some of my Friends have Tails, Beyond the Bars (jt ed and jt author); *Recreations* reading, travelling, gardening; *Clubs* Chelsea Arts; *Style—* Miss Virginia McKenna; Zoo Check Charitable Tst, Coldharbour, Surrey RH5 6HA (☎ 0306 712 091)

MACKENZIE; *see*: Muir Mackenzie

MACKENZIE, Sir (Alexander George Anthony) Allan; 4 Bt (UK 1890), of Glen Muick, Aberdeenshire; s of Capt Allan Keith Mackenzie (ka 1916), by Hon Alexandra L E, da of 1 Viscount Knollys, GCB, PC, and nephew of 3 Bt, DSO, MVO (d 1944); *b* 4 Jan 1913; *Educ* Stowe; *m* 24 Aug 1937, Marjorie, da of A F McGuire, of Alberta, Canada; 4 da; *Heir* cousin, James William Guy Mackenzie; *Career* memb Royal Canadian Mounted Police 1932-37; page of honour to King George V; enlisted Calgary Highlanders 1939, Lt Seaforth Highlanders of Canada 1941, Capt Black Watch of Canada, ret 1961; *Style—* Sir Allan Mackenzie, Bt; RRI, Cobble Hill, Vancouver Island, BC, Canada

MACKENZIE, Angus Alexander; s of Kenneth Mackenzie (d 1958), of Drumine, Gollanfield, Inverness-shire, and Christina, *née* Mackinnon (d 1966); *b* 1 Mar 1931; *Educ* Inverness Royal Acad, Edinburgh Univ; *m* 31 March 1959, Catherine, da of Murdo Maclennan (d 1971), of Sand Gairloch Ross-shire; 1 da (Margaret Jane b 1960); *Career* Nat Serv RAF 1955-57; qualified CA 1955, own practice 1961-; currently: sr ptnr Angus Mackenzie & Co Inverness, local dir Eagle Star Insur Co Ltd, dir PLM Helicopters Ltd; chm Highland Gp Riding for the Disabled Assoc, sec and tres Highland Field Sports Fair, vice-chm Highland Club Inverness; MICAS 1955; *Recreations* shooting, stalking, hill walking, and gardening; *Clubs* Highland Inverness; *Style—* Angus Mackenzie, Esq; Tigh-An-Allt, Tomatin, Inverness-shire (☎ 08082 270); Redwood, 19 Culduthel Rd, Inverness (☎ 0463 235353, fax 0463 235171)

MACKENZIE, Lady Anne Mildred Ismay; *née* Fitzroy; o da of 10 Duke of Grafton (d 1970), and his 1 wife Lady Doreen Maria Josepha (d 1923), 2 da of 1 Earl Buxton, GCMG; *b* 7 August 1920; *m* 19 April 1947, Maj Colin Dalzell Mackenzie, MBE, MC, DL, *qv*; 2 s, (Alastair (d 1951), Philip), 3 da (Caroline, Laura, Harriet); *Recreations* gardening; *Clubs* Turf, Lansdowne; *Style—* Lady Anne Mackenzie; Farr House, Inverness; Bergh Apton Manor, Norwich

MACKENZIE, Brig Charles Baillie; DSO (1944), OBE (1950); s of Theodore Charles Mackenzie (d 1951), of Druim, Inverness, and Margaret Irvine, *née* Wilson (d 1962); *b* 29 Dec 1909; *Educ* Fettes, RMC Sandhurst; *m* 18 March 1938, Nancy Veronica (d 1962), da of George Francis Dalziel, WS, of Sydney Lodge, Whitehouse

Loan, Edinburgh; 1 s (Angus b 1951), 2 da (Anne (Mrs Lawrie) b 1939, Biddy (Mrs Lewis) b 1940); *Career* cmmnd Queen's Own Cameron Highlanders 1930, Lt 1942; WWII serv: 1 Liverpool Scottish, 5 Scottish Parachute Bn, HQ 1 Airborne Div, HQ 44 Indian Airborne Div; WO (Dept of Air), 4/5 Camerons (TA), Col WO (AG2), Brig 154 Highland Bde (TA) 1954-57, dep Cdr Lowland Div 1957-59; sec City of Glasgow TA Assoc and Lowland TAVR Assoc 1959-74; *Recreations* fishing, shooting; *Clubs* Western (Glasgow); *Style—* Brig Charles Mackenzie, DSO, OBE; 16 Grendon Ct, Snowdon Pl, Stirling (☎ 0786 50618)

MACKENZIE, Charles William Taaffe Munro; s of John Hugh Munro Mackenzie and Eileen Louise Agate *née* Shanks; *b* 3 Feb 1956; *Educ* Eton, Oxford Univ (MA); *m* 17 July 1981, Emma, da of Thomas Lyon Liddell of Dormans Corner, Dormansland, Surrey; 2 s (Charles Alexander Munro b 1983, Kenneth Thomas Munro b 1986); *Career* dir: Scottish English and European Textiles plc, Hugewelcome Ltd, formerly dir: London and Northern Gp plc (1985-87); *Recreations* music, travel, field sports; *Style—* Charles Mackenzie, Esq; Essex Hall, Essex Street, London WC2

McKENZIE, Dr Christopher Gurney; s of Benet Christopher McKenzie (d 1984), and Winifred Grace, *née* Masterman (d 1984); *b* 3 Jan 1930; *Educ* Douai Sch, London Univ (MB, BS); *m* 12 Oct 1963, Barbara Mary Kinsella, da of James Quirk (d 1983); 2 s (James b 1966, Richard b 1972), 1 da (Caroline b 1964); *Career* nat serv in Dental branch RAF (Flt Lt) 1953-55; Maj RAMC (Sr Specialist Surgery) 1967-70; conslt Clinical Oncology Hammersmith Hosp, sr lectr Royal Postgrad Med Sch 1974-, hon conslt: St Mary's Hosp Paddington, the Central Middlesex Hosp; LDS, RCS 1951, MB BS (London) 1960, FRCS 1962, DMRT 1972, FRCR 1974; *Books* author of many articles and chapters on med subjects; *Recreations* sailing, opera; *Clubs* Cruising Assoc; *Style—* Dr Christopher G McKenzie; 61 Mount Avenue, Ealing W5 1PN (☎ 01 997 3452); Dept of Clinical Oncology, Hammersmith Hospital (☎ 01 740 3061)

MACKENZIE, Maj Colin Dalzell; MBE (1945), MC (1940, DL Inverness-shire 1976); s of Lt-Col (Douglas William) Alexander Dalziel Mackenzie, CVO, DSO (d 1955); *b* 23 Mar 1919; *Educ* Eton, RMC; *m* 19 April 1947, Lady Anne Mildred Ismay FitzRoy (*qv*), da of 10 Duke of Grafton; 2 s (1 decd), 3 da; *Career* page of honour to HM King George V 1932-36; joined Seaforth Highlanders 1939, ret 1950; ADC to Viceroy of India 1945-46; dep mil sec to Viceroy of India 1946-47; CC 1950 Inverness-shire; memb Royal Co of Archers (Queen's Body Guard for Scotland); vice-Lt Inverness-shire 1986; *Recreations* shooting, fishing; *Clubs* Turf, New (Edinburgh), Pratt's; *Style—* Maj Colin Mackenzie, MBE, MC, DL; Farr House, Inverness (☎ 08083 202)

MACKENZIE, Colin John; s of John Mackenzie, and Edith vanan *née* Murray; *b* 18 Jan 1955; *Educ* Craigbank Sch, Stow Coll Glasgow; *m* 26 March 1982, Hazel, da of Frank Neil Walker; 1 s (Struan b 22 June 1986), 1 da (Kirsty b 20 April 1984); *Career* md Hifi Corner (Edinburgh) Ltd 1972-; dir: Eastaura Ltd 1983-, Bill Hutchinson Hifi Ltd 1983-85; md Hifi Corner (Glasgow) Ltd 1984-, chief exec Hifi Experience plc 1988- (dir 1985), md James Kerr & Co Ltd 1986-; mgmnt conslt Kerr, mccosh Ltd 1988-; memb mgmnt ctee Br Audio Dealers Assoc 1987-89, organiser annual Scottish Hifi Exhibition 1976-; PRO Tranent and Elphinstone Community Cncl; *Style—* Colin MacKenzie, Esq; Ar Dhachaidh, Viewforth Gardens, Tranent, East Lothian EH33 1DQ (☎ 0875 613 409); Unit 2, 172 The Lane, Easter Rd, Edinburgh (☎ 031 652 1885, fax 031 652 1436)

MACKENZIE, Colin Scott; DL (Western Isles 1975); s of Colin Scott Mackenzie (d 1971), of Stornoway, and Margaret Sarah Tolmie; inter alia celebrated 100 yrs (unbroken) in 1984 as Public Prosecutors in Stornoway; *b* 7 July 1938; *Educ* Nicolson Inst Stornoway, Fettes Coll Edinburgh, Univ of Edinburgh (BL); *m* 1966, Christeen Elizabeth Drysdale, da of William McLauchlan (d 1968), of Tong, Isle of Lewis; *Career* slr 1960; procurator fiscal Stornoway 1969-, clerk to the Lieutenancy 1974-, Vice Lord-Lt Western Isles 1984-, dir Harris Tweed Assoc Ltd 1979, Capt Army Cadet Force, elected cncl memb of Law Soc of Scotland 1985-, Kirk elder 1985; *Recreations* fishing, boating, travel; *Clubs* RSAC Glasgow, New Edinburgh; *Style—* C Scott Mackenzie, Esq, DL; Park Ho, Matheson Rd, Stornoway (☎ 0851 2008, office: 0851 3439)

MACKENZIE, Rear Adm David John; CB (1983); s of David Mackenzie (d 1950), and Alison Walker, *née* Lawrie; *b* 3 Oct 1929; *Educ* Cargilfield Sch Edinburgh, RNC; *m* 1965, Ursula Sybil, da of Cdr Ronald Hugh Balfour, RN; 2 s (David, Alastair), 1 da (Rachel); *Career* joined RN cadet 1943-47, Midshipman 1947-48, Sub Lt 1950-51, Lt 1951-59; Lt Cdr 1959-65, promoted Cdr 1965, Exec Offr HMS Glamorgan 1965-67, Cdr Sea Trg 1967-70, CO HMS Hermione 1971, promoted Capt 1972, CO HMS Phoenix 1972-74, Capt F8 HMS Ajax 1974-76, dir Naval Equipment 1976-78; CO HMS: Blake 1978-79, Hermes 1979-80; promoted Rear Adm 1981; Flag Offr Gibraltar 1981-83; ret 1983; dir Atlantic Salmon Tst 1985-; landowner; *Recreations* shooting, fishing; *Clubs* New (Edinburgh); *Style—* Rear Adm John Mackenzie, CB; Atlantic Salmon Tst, Moulin Pitlochry, Perthshire (☎ 0796 3439)

McKENZIE, Justice Donald Cameron Moffat; s of John McKenzie (d 1975), of Perth, and Jessie Cameron Creelman, *née* Moffat; *b* 3 Mar 1934; *Educ* St Ninian's Cathedral Sch, Balhousie Boys' Sch, Perth Commercial Sch; *m* 29 June 1967, Patricia Janet, da of Ernest Russell Hendry (d 1974), of Dundee; 2 d (Alison b 1968, Evelyn b 1972); *Career* accountant Trinity Coll Glenalmond 1966-70, bursar Corpn of High Sch Dundee 1970-80; ccncllr, magistrate, social worker convener, health convener of Perth 1971-75; ccncllr Perth and Kinross 1971-75; Justice District Ct 1975; estate factor of Pitlochry Estate Tst 1980; govr Dundee Coll of educn; dir R Dundee Instn for Blind; capt Soc of High Constables; memb: Justices Ctee, Prison Visiting Ctee; OStJ (1978); FInst Admin Accountants (1976); FBIM; *Recreations* rifle shooting, cricket, music; *Style—* Justice Donald McKenzie; Balnacraig, Moulin, Pitlochry, Perths (☎ 0796 2591, Pitlochry Estate Office ☎ 0796 2114)

MacKENZIE, Rt Hon (James) Gregor; PC (1977),; s of James MacKenzie (d 1984), and Mary, *née* Wood (d 1972); *b* 15 Nov 1927; *Educ* Queens Park Sch, Royal Tech Coll, Glasgow Univ Sch of Soc Studies; *m* 1958, Joan Swan, da of John Campbell Provan; 1 s, 1 da; *Career* joined Lab Pty 1944, contested (Lab) Kinross and Perths 1959, Aberdeenshire E 1950, MP Rutherglen 1964-87, PPS to Rt Hon James Callaghan 1965-70, shadow oppn spokesman Posts and Telecommunications 1970-74, Min of State Indust 1975-76 (parly under-sec 1974-75), Min of State Scottish Off 1976-79; JP Glasgow 1962; *Style—* The Rt Hon Gregor MacKenzie; 3/2 Nether Graigwell, Edinburgh EH8 8DR

MACKENZIE, (James William) Guy; s of Lt-Col Eric Dighton Mackenzie, CMG, CVO, DSO (d 1972), and Elizabeth Kathrine Mary, *née* Innes; hp of cousin, Sir (Alexander George Anthony) Allan Mackenzie, 4 Bt, CD; *b* 6 Oct 1946; *Educ* Stowe; *m* 1972, Paulene Patricia Simpson; 1 da; *Style—* Guy Mackenzie Esq; 1 Molerun, Pheasant Drive, High Wycombe, Bucks

MACKENZIE, Vice Adm Sir Hugh Stirling; KCB (1966, CB 1963), DSO and bar (1942, 1943), DSC (1945); 3 s of Dr Theodore Charles Mackenzie (d 1951), of Inverness; *b* 3 July 1913; *Educ* Cargilfield Sch, RNC Dartmouth; *m* 10 Aug 1946, Helen Maureen, er da of Maj John Edward Mountague Bradish-Ellames (d 1984); 1 s, 2 da; *Career* joined RN 1927, serv WWII submarines, Capt 1951, Rear Adm 1961, Flag Offr Submarines 1961-63, Chief Polaris Exec 1963-68, Vice Adm 1964; ret Royal Navy 1968; chm: Navy League 1969-74, Atlantic Salmon Tst 1979-83 (dir 1969-79); CBIM; *Recreations* the country; *Clubs* Naval & Military; *Style—* Vice Adm Sir Hugh Mackenzie, KCB, DSO, DSC; Sylvan Lodge, Puttenham, nr Guildford, Surrey (☎ 0483 810 368)

MACKENZIE, Col Ian; TD (1943); s of Alexander Mackenzie (d 1930), of Edinburgh, and Margaret Hay (d 1965); *b* 14 Mar 1904; *Educ* Merchiston Castle Sch, Edinburgh Univ (BSc); *m* 14 Jan 1930, Katharine Drummond, da of Major Thomas Drummond Wilson, MC (d 1950), of Edinburgh; 1 s (John b 1934), 2 da (Ann b 1931, Rosemary b 1937); *Career* Cmmnd as 2 Lt Royal Corps of Signals (TA) 1924; appointed: Maj 2 i/c 15 Scottish Divnl Signals 1939, CO 4 Corps Signal Regt 1941 serving in UK, Iraq, India, Burma until 1944, DCSO (Assam) on Staff of CSO 14 Army 1944, Cmdt Ceylon Signal Corps 1945; md Mackenzie & Moncur Ltd 1945 (personally appointed Royal Warrant Holder 1949); fndr and chm British Assoc of Retired Persons 1969-; Lord Dean of Guild of The City & Royal Burgh of Edinburgh 1972; *Recreations* shooting, fishing, golf, photography, horticulture, music; *Style—* Col Ian Mackenzie, TD

MACKENZIE, Lady Jean; *née* Leslie; da of 20 Earl of Rothes (d 1975); *b* 26 August 1927; *m* 26 April 1949, Roderick Robin Mackenzie, s of Capt Roderick Kilgour Mackenzie (d 1937); *Style—* Lady Jean Mackenzie; Kingfisher House, Ampfield, Hants

MACKENZIE, John Alexander Hugh Munro; s of John Mackenzie of Mornish, *qv*, and Eileen Louise Agate, *née* Shanks; *b* 16 August 1953; *Educ* Eton, Corpus Christi Coll Oxford; *Career* barr 1976; dir: Tace plc 1981-, Scottish Eng and Euro Textiles plc 1983-; chm and md Sloane Graphics Ltd 1987-; dir: London and Northern GP plc 1985-87, Kenneth Mackenzie (Hldgs) Ltd 1988-, Justunit Ltd 1988-; memb Worshipful Co of Merchant Taylors, Freeman City of London 1975; *Recreations* racing, reading, all field sports, opera; *Clubs* Vincent's (Oxford); *Style—* John Mackenzie, Esq; 21 Upper Mall, London W6 9TA (☎ 01 748 5139); Essex Hall, Essex St, London WC2R 3JD (☎ 01 836 9261, fax 836 4859, car tel 0860 391 955)

McKENZIE, John Cormack; s of William Joseph McKenzie and Elizabeth Frances Robinson; *b* 21 June 1927; *Educ* St Andrew's Coll, Trinity Coll Dublin (MA, MAI), Queen's Univ Belfast (MSc); *m* 1954, Olga Caroline; 3 s, 1 da; *Career* civil engr: McLaughlin & Harvey, Sir Alexander Gibb & Ptnrs 1946-48; asst lectr Queen's Univ Belfast 1948-50; Edmund Nuttal Ltd 1950-82 (dir 1967-82); chm Nuttall Geotechnical Services Ltd 1967-82; md Thomas Telford Ltd 1982-; sec: Inst of Civil Engrs 1982-, Cwlth Engrs Cncl 1983-; FEng, FICE; *Publications* Research into some Aspects of Soil Cement (1952), Engineers: Administrators or Technologists? (1971), Civil Engineering Procedure (3rd edn, 1979); *Recreations* philately, collecting ancient pottery, climbing; *Clubs* Athenaeum; *Style—* John McKenzie, Esq; The Institution of Civil Engineers, 1 Great George Street, London SW1P 3AA (☎ 01 222 7722, telex 935637 ICEAS G)

McKENZIE, Julia Kathleen; da of Albion James Jeffrey McKenzie (d 1970), of Enfield, Middx, and Kathleen Maudie, *née* Rowe; *b* 17 Feb 1942; *Educ* Tottenham County Sch, Guildhall Sch of Music and Drama; *m* 9 Sept 1972, Jerry Harte (formally Gerald Carl Hjert), s of Carl Hjert (d 1983), of USA; *Career* actress; has made over 25 West End appearances, notably: Guys and Dolls (SWET Award Best Actress), Woman in Mind (Evening Standard Best Actress), Follies (Critics Award Best Actress); TV series, Fresh Fields (2 Awards), numerous plays and musical specials; dir: Stepping Out, Steel Magnolias; govr Research Into Ageing; Hon Fell Guildhall Sch of Music and Drama 1984; *Books* Clothes Line (1988); *Recreations* cooking; c/o April Young, 2 Lowndes Street, London SW1X 9GT (☎ 01 259 6488/9)

MACKENZIE, Lady (Sibell Anne) Julia; *née* Mackenzie; has resumed use of maiden name; er da (by 1 m) of 4 Earl of Cromartie, *qv*; *b* 15 Feb 1934; *m* 1, 16 June 1953 (m dis 1961), Francis Edward Lascelles-Hadwen, er s of late Edward Hubert Lascelles Hadwen, Levant Consular Service; 1 s (James b 1957), 1 da (Georgina b 1959); m 2, 1974, Apputhurai Jeyarama Chandran; 1 da (Anita b 1977); *Style—* Lady Julia Mackenzie

MACKENZIE, Keith Roderick Turing; OB E(1983), MC (1944); s of Roderick Henry Turne Mackenzie (d 1956), and Elizabeth, *née* Dalzell; *b* 19 Jan 1921; *Educ* Uppingham, RMC Sandhurst; *m* 2 Aug 1949, Barbara Kershaw, da of William Miles (d 1958); 2 s (Miles b 1953, Angus b 1965), 2 da (Jane b 1951, Susannah b 1961); *Career* cmmnd 2/6 Gurkha Rifles 1940, acting Lt-Col Bn Cdr 1944, ret (Maj) 1942; joined Burmah-Shell Oil Storgae and Distribution Co of India 1947 (held sr appointments of sales operations and staff mgmnt), sales mangr Shell Co of Rhodesia 1965 (ret 1966), sec Royal and Ancient GC St Andrews 1967 (ret 1983); pres The Golf Fndn 1984-; *Recreations* golf, gardening; *Clubs* Royal & Ancient GC of St Andrews, Royal St Georges, Royal Cinque Ports, Royal Porthcall, Royal Calcutta, Pine Valley (USA), Atlanta Athletic, various GC's; *Style—* Keith Mackenzie, Esq, OBE, MC; Easter Edenhill, Kennedy Gdns, St Andrews, Fife, Scot (☎ 0334 73581)

MACKENZIE, Kenneth Edward; CMG (1970); s of Alexander Edward Mackenzie, of Dundee and Calcutta; *b* 28 April 1910; *Educ* India, Australia, Scotland, England, Univ Coll London (BSc); *m* 1935, Phyllis Edith, da of Francis Hamley Fawkes, of Prestbury, Glos; 1 s; *Career* engrg indust 1926-29, Inst Civil Engrs 1933-34, Dept Overseas Trade 1934-36; Br Embassy Brussels 1936-40; interned Germany 1940-41, Br Embassy Tehran 1942-45; trade cmmr: India 1946-48, Malaya 1949-53, asst sec Bd of Trade 1953-66, cllr Br Embassy Stockholm 1966-70, (investmt cncllr 1973), investmt cncllr Br Embassy Copenhagen 1974-75, conslt on Inward Investmt to Dept of Indust 1974-75; *Style—* Kenneth Mackenzie, Esq, CMG; 11 St James Close, Pangbourne, Berks RG8 7AP

MacKENZIE, Kenneth John; s of Capt John Donald MacKenzie, Merchant Marine (d 1967), of Milngavie, Dunbartonshire (d 1967), and Elizabeth Pennant Johnston, *née* Sutherland (d 1985); *b* 1 May 1943; *Educ* Birkenhead Sch, Pembroke Coll Oxford (BA, MA), Stanford Univ California (AM); *m* 3 Sept 1975, Irene Mary, da of William Ewart

Hogarth (d 1947), of Mayfield, Paisley, Renfrewshire; 1 s (John b 1977); 1 da (Mary b 1979); *Career* asst princ Scottish Home & Health Dept 1965-70; priv sec to Jt Parly Under-Sec of State Scottish Off 1969-70; princ: Regional Devpt Divn Scottish Off 1970-73, Scottish Educn Dept 1973-77; Civil Service fell: Downing Coll Cambridge 1972, dept of politics Univ of Glasgow 1974-75; princ priv sec to Sec of State for Scotland 1977-79; asst sec Scottish Econ Planning Dept 1979- 83; asst sec Scottish Off Fin Divn 1983-85; princ Fin offr Scottish Off 1985-88; Under Sec Scottish Home & Health Dept 1988-; Session Clerk St Cuthbert's Parish Ch Edinburgh 1979-; pres Edinburgh Civil Serv Dramatic Soc 1971-74, 1976-77 and 1982-85; *Clubs* Nat Lib; *Style—* Kenneth MacKenzie, Esq; Scottish Home and Health Department, St Andrew's House, Edinburgh EH1 3DE (☎ 031 244 2133)

MacKENZIE, Kenneth William Stewart; CMG (1958), CVO (1975; s of William Stewart MacKenzie (d 1950), of Cleckheaton, Yorks; *b* 30 July 1915; *Educ* Whitcliffe Mount GS Cleckeaton, Downing Coll Cambridge (MA); *m* 1939, Kathleen Joyce, da of John Douglas Ingram, of Dewsbury, Yorks; 1 s, Peter b 8 Oct 1942, 1 da, Ann b 17 Feb 1940); *Career* entered Colonial Serv Basutoland 1938, asst sec 1940, Mauritius 1944, Kenya 1948; sec to Treasy Kenya 1955, min for Fin Kenya 1959-62; MLC Kenya 1955-62, ret 1962; princ Colonial Off 1963, HM Treasy 1966, asst sec DOE 1970, ret 1975; dir of studies Royal Inst of Public Administration (Overseas Unit) 1976-; *Recreations* reading, gardening, travel; *Clubs* Nairobi; *Style—* Kenneth MacKenzie Esq, CMG, CVO; Beaumont, 28 Greenhurst Lane, Oxted, Surrey (☎ Oxted 0883 713848)

MACKENZIE, Lady; Lilian; *née* MacSween; da of Malcolm MacSween; sis of Sir Compton's 2 w, Christina MacSween (d 1963); *m* 1965, as his 3 w, Sir (Edward Montague) Compton Mackenzie, OBE (d 1972); *Style—* Lady Mackenzie; 31 Drummond Pla, Edinburgh

McKENZIE, Michael; s of Robert McKenzie, of Brighton, and Kitty Elizabeth, *née* Regan (d 1985); *b* 25 May 1943; *Educ* Varndean GS Brighton; *m* 19 Sept 1964, Peggy Dorothy, da of Thomas Edward William Russell, of Heathfield, E Sussex; 3 s (Justin Grant b 31 May 1968, Gavin John b 28 April 1971, Jamie Stuart b 14 Jan 1977); *Career* barr Middle Temple 1970, dep clerk of the Peace Middx Quarter Sessions 1970-72, dep courts admin Middx Crown Ct 1972-73, cts admin NE Circuit (Newcastle) 1974-79, clerk of the Centl Criminal Ct 1979-84, dep circuit admin SE Circuit 1984-86, asst registrar Ct of Appeal Criminal Div 1986-88, Master of the Crown off (Queens Coroner and Attorney, Registrar of Criminal Appeals, Registrar of Cts Martial Appeal Ct) 1988-; Freedom City of London 1979; *Recreations* Northumbrian stick dressing, fell walking, shooting; *Style—* Michael McKenzie, Esq; Selwyns Wood Hse, Cross in Hand, E Sussex (☎ 04352 2357); Royal Cts of Justice, Strand, London WC2A 2LL (☎ 01 936 6108, fax 01 936 6900)

MACKENZIE, Michael Philip Uvedale Rapinet; s of Brig MR Mackenzie, DSO (d 19850, of Mayfield, Sussex, and Vivienne, *née* Price; *b* 1937, '; *Educ* Downside, Lincoln Coll Oxford ; *m* 1966, Jill, da of Charles Foweraker Beckley, of Chislehurst, Kent; 1 s (William b 1966), 1 da (Elizabeth b 1970); *Career* Utd Biscuits plc 1966-86: prodn dir of various businesses 1974- 83, md DS Crawford Bakeries 1983-86; dir gen Food and Drink Fedn; FRSA 1988, FIFST 1989; *Clubs* Travellers; *Style—* Michael Mackenzie, Esq; Ebony Cottage, Ebony, nr Tenterden, Kent TN30 7HT; Food & Drink Federation, Catherine St, London WC2B 5JJ

MACKENZIE, Sir Robert Evelyn; 12 Bt (NS 1673), of Coul, Ross-shire; s of Sir Arthur George Ramsay Mackenzie, 11 Bt, JP, DL (d 1935); *b* 15 Feb 1906; *Educ* Eton, Trinity Coll Cambridge; *m* 1, 28 June 1940, Mrs Jane Adams-Beck (d 1953), da of Maurice Beck, of Saltwood, Hythe, Kent; m 2, 5 April 1963, Elizabeth, da of Renard Pearth, of Pittsburgh, USA; *Heir* kinsman, Peter Douglas MacKenzie; *Career* Capt Gen List 1939, Maj Intelligence Corps 1942; 1 sec Br Embassy Paris 1945, FO 1947, Br Embassy Washington 1948; memb Lloyd's 1932-71; *Clubs* Brooks's; *Style—* Sir Robert Mackenzie, Bt; 44 Chester Square, London SW1

MACKENZIE, Robert Stephen; s of Brig Frederick Stephen Ronald Mackenzie, OBE (d 1981), and Daphne Margaret, *née* Jickling; *b* 12 Nov 1947; *Educ* Radley, RMA Sandhurst; *m* 24 Mar 1973, Amanda Clair, da of Lt Cdr Richard John Beverley Sutton; 1 s (Rupert b 1982), 1 da (Emily b 1977); *Career* serv Queens Royal Irish Hussars; Allied Lyons 1978, dir Hall and Woodhouse and Badger Inns 1983, md 1984; *Recreations* riding; *Style—* Robert Mackenzie, Esq; Northfield House, Todber, Sturminster, Newton, Dorset (☎ 0258 820269); Badger Inns, The Brewery, Blandford, Dorset (☎ 0258 51462, fax 0258 59528, car tel 0865 239741)

MACKENZIE, Sir Roderick Mcquhae; 12 Bt (NS 1703), of Scatwell, Ross-shire; s of Capt Sir Roderick Edward François McQuhae, CBE, DSC (d 1986); *b* 17 April 1942; *Educ* Sedbergh, King's Coll London, St George's Hosp (MB BS, MRCP (UK), FRCP (C), DCH); *m* 1970, Nadezhda (Nadine), da of Georges Frederick Leon Schlatter, Baron von Rorbas, of Buchs-K-Zurich, Switzerland; 1 s (Gregory Roderick McQuhae b 1971), 1 da (Nina Adelaida b 1973); *Heir* s Gregory; *Style—* Sir Roderick Mackenzie, Bt; 2431 Udell Rd, Calgary NW, Alberta, Canada T2N 4H4

MACKENZIE CROOKS, Air Vice-Marshal Lewis; CBE (1964, OBE 1951); s of David Mackenzie Crooks, MB (d 1953); *b* 20 Jan 1909; *Educ* Epworth Coll Rhyl, Liverpool Univ (MB, ChB, ChM); *m* 1936, Mildred, da of Albert John Gwyther (d 1938); 2 s, 1 da; *Career* enlisted RAF 1935, serv WWII Far E, ME and Europe, surgn RAF 1935-71; conslt advsr in orthopaedics 1965-71, locum conslt in orthopaedics in Cornwall 1970-, SW Regnl Hosp Bd 1971-; *Recreations* golf, gardening; *Clubs* Revose Golf and Country; *Style—* Air Vice-Marshal Lewis Mackenzie Crooks, CBE; Trelawney, Harlyn Bay, Padstow, Cornwall PL28 8SF (☎ 0841 520 631)

MACKENZIE OF GAIRLOCH; *see*: Inglis of Glencorse

MACKENZIE OF MORNISH, John Hugh Munro; s of Lt-Col John Munro Mackenzie of Mornish, DSO, JP, Military Knight of Windsor (d 1964), of Henry VIII Gateway, Windsor Castle and Etheldreda Henrietta Marie *née* Taaffe (d 1965); The Mornish branch of the Mackenzie Clan and direct male descendants of the ancient feudal Barons of Kintail, chiefs of the Mackenzie Clan through the Mackenzies of Gairloch and the Mackenzies of Letterewe; *b* 29 August 1925; *Educ* Edinburgh Acad, Loretto Sch, Trinity Coll Oxford (MA), Hague Academy of Int Law, Inns of Ct Law Sch, McGill Univ Montreal; *m* 20 June 1951, Eileen Louise Agate, da of Alexander Shanks, OBE, MC (d 1965); 5 s (John b 1953, Charles b 1956, Kenneth b 1961, d 1984, Cristin b 1959, James b 1966), 1 da (Catriona b 1952); *Career* serv Army 1942-47, Capt The Royal Scots (Royal Regt); war serv: Europe, 1 KOSB, A Co, 9 Bde, 3 Inf Div (despatches, certs of gallantry), Far E HQ Allied Land Forces SE Asia and HQ Ceylon Army Cmd, Staff Capt Mil Sec's Branch; HM Guard of Honour Balmoral 1946, HQ 3 Auto Aircraft Div 1946-47, GSO III; Harmsworth Law Scholar Middle Temple 1950, called to Bar Middle Temple 1950; trainee Utd Dominions Tst, legal asst Estates Dept ICI Ltd 1951; Hudson's Bay Scholar 1952-53; buyer ICI 1953-54, co sec and legal advsr Truberised (GB) Ltd and Assoc Cos 1955-56, GP dvpt offr Aspro-Nicholas Ltd 1956-57, Knitmaster Hldgs 1957, formed Grampian Hldgs Ltd (mangr and sec) 1958, md 1960, dep chm and md London and Northern Gp Ltd 1962; chm: Tace plc 1967-, Scottish English and European Textiles plc 1969-, London and Northern Gp plc 1962-87, Pauling plc 1976-87, Goring Kerr plc since 1983; eight Queen's Awards for Export won by Gp Cos; FRSA, FBIM, Member of Worshipful of Farmers; *Recreations* opera, bridge, shooting, fishing, field sports; *Clubs* Royal Automobile, Royal Scots (Edinburgh), New (Edinburgh); *Style—* John Mackenzie of Mornish; Mortlake House, Vacarage Rd, London SW14 8RN; Scaliscro Lodge, Uig, Isle of Lewis; Shellwood Manor, Leigh, Surrey; Scottish English & European Textiles plc, and Tace plc, Essex Hall, Essex Street, London WC2R 3JD (☎ 01 836 9261)

McKENZIE SMITH, Ian; s of James McKenzie Smith (d 1977), of Aberdeen, and Mary, *née* Benzie; *b* 3 August 1935; *Educ* Robert Gordon's Coll Aberdeen, Gray's Sch of Art Aberdeen (DA), Hospitalfield Coll of Art Arbroath; *m* 3 April 1963, Mary Rodger, da of John Fotheringham; 2 s (Patrick John b 8 Aug 1966, Justin James b 4 Feb 1969), 1 da (Sarah Jane b 5 Jan 1965); *Career* educn offr Cncl of Industl Design Scottish Ctee 1963-68, dir Aberdeen Art Gallery and Museums 1968-89, City arts offr City of Aberdeen 1989-; memb: Scottish Arts Cncl, Scottish Museums Cncl, Nat Heritage Scottish GP, Scottish Sculpture Workshop; govr: Edinburgh Coll of Art, Robert Gordon Inst of Technol Aberdeen; RSA 1987, PRSW 1981/8, FRSA 1973, FSS 1984, FMA 1987, FSA Scotland 1970; *Clubs* Royal Northern (Aberdeen); *Style—* Ian McKenzie Smith, Esq; 70 Hamilton Place, Aberdeen (☎ 0224 644531); Aberdeen Art Gallery, Schoolhill, Aberdeen (☎ 0224 646333, fax 0224 641985, telex 73366)

MACKENZIE-STUART, Baron (Life Peer UK 1988), of Dean in the City and County of Edinburgh Alexander John Mackenzie Stuart; s of Prof Alexander Mackenzie Stuart, KC (d 1935), and Amy Margaret, er da of John Reid Dean, of Aberdeen; *b* 18 Nov 1924; *Educ* Fettes, Sidney Sussex Coll Cambridge (BA, hon fell 1977), Edinburgh Univ (LLB); *m* 1952, Anne Burtholme, da of late J S L Millar, WS, of Edinburgh: 4 da; *Career* served RE 1942-47 (T/Capt 1946); admitted Faculty of Advocates 1951; QC (Scot) 1963; Keeper of the Advocates Library 1970-72; Standing Jr Counsel: Scottish Home Dept 1956-57, Inland Revenue in Scotland 1957-63; Sheriff-Princ of Aberdeen, Kincardine and Banff 1971-72; a senator of the College of Justice in Scotland (as Hon Lord Mackenzie Stuart) 1972-73; judge of the Court of Justice European Communities Luxembourg 1972-84 (pres 1984-88); govr Fettes Coll 1962-72; hon bencher: Middle Temple 1978, King's Inn Dublin 1983; hon memb Soc of Public Teachers of Law 1982; hon prof Collèe d'Europe Bruges 1974-77; Hon DUniv Stirling 1973; Hon LLD: Exeter 1978, Edinburgh 1978, Glasgow 1981, Aberdeen 1983, Cambridge 1987, Birmingham 1988; awarded Prix Bech for servs to Europe 1989; *Books* Hamlyn Lectures: The European Communities and the Rule of Law (1977); articles in legal publications; *Recreations* collecting; *Clubs* Athenaeum, New (Edinburgh); *Style—* The Rt Hon Lord Mackenzie-Stuart; 7 Randolph Cliff, Edinburgh EH3 7TZ; Le Garidel, Gravières, 07140 Les Vans, France

MACKENZIE-WELTER, Lady Gilean Frances; *née* Blunt Mackenzie; da of 4 Earl of Cromartie, by his 1 w, Dorothy Porter, da of G B Downing, of Kentucky, USA; *b* 25 Feb 1936; *m* 30 Oct 1959 (m dis 1973), René Eugene Welter, o s of late Prof Georges F Welter, of Montreal, Canada, Consul-Gen for Luxembourg; 1 s (Michael b 1964), 1 da (Nadine b 1960); *Career* fndr Scots Int; *Style—* Lady Gilean Frances Mackenzie-Welter; 52 South Edwardes Sq, London W8

McKEOWN, John Wilson; s of John McKeown, and Sarah, *née* Black; *b* 17 April 1950; *Educ* Royal Belfast Academic Instn, Christ's Coll, Cambridge (MA); *m* Lynn Fennah; 1 s (Christopher William John b 7 Aug 1983); 1 da (Rachel Sara Louise b 2 April 1978); *Career* dir Ind Coope Ltd; md Ind Coope & Allsopp Ltd; dir Ind Coope Burton Brewery; *Recreations* sport, politics; *Style—* John McKeown, Esq; 1 Swithland Lane, Rothley, Leicester (☎ 0533 302480); Ind Coope & Allsopp, 119 Loughborough Rd, Leicester (☎ 0533 663663)

McKEOWN, Kenneth Charles; CBE (1973), DL (Durham 1982); s of Robert James Brown McKeown, and Sarah, *née* Black Owens (d 1948); *b* 31 Oct 1912; *Educ* Royal Academical Inst Belfast, Queen's Univ Belfast (MB, MCh, BAO); *m* 1940, Edith Joan, da of Cdr Alfred Charles Waugh, OBE, RN (d 1946); 2 s (Kenneth b 1944, Christopher (twin) b 1944); *Career* surgn emergency med serv sector 9 King's Coll Hosp London during London Blitz WW II, Maj RAMC surgn specialist 82 Gen Hosp Middle E Forces 1944-45, Lt-Col offr i/c Surgical Div 97 Gen Hosp Land Forces Greece 1945-46, offr i/c Surgical Div Cmd Hosp 19 Gen Hosp MEF 1946-47, Hon Lt-Col RAMC 1947; former sr conslt surgn: Darlington Memorial Hosp, Friarage and Rutson Hosps (Northallerton), Hosp of St John of God; former advsr in surgery and surgical tutor RCS England, hon sr conslt surgn Darlington Memorial Hosp, conslt surgn Hosp of St John of God (Scorton, Richmond, N Yorks); memb: central health servs cncl DHSS and its standing med advsy ctee 1971-76, Central Cncl for Postgraduate Med Educn 1970-75, Bd of Science and Educn BMA; Hunterian Prof RCS 1972, (coll lectr 1974); Fraser lectr Univ of Glasgow 1977, Digby Meml lectr Hong Kong 1978, Bennet lectr Trinity Coll Dublin 1983, Ernest Miles Meml Lectr for Br Assoc of Surgical Oniology; Gimbernat Prize Barcelona 1983; past pres and memb Moynihan Surgical Club; FRSM, fell Assoc of Surgns in GB and Ireland, FRCS (Eng), FRCS (ED); *Publications* The Medical Effects of Nuclear War (co-author, 1983); chapters in surgical textbooks and journals on oesophageal cancer, peptic ulcer and general surgical topics; *Recreations* gardening, fishing, travel; *Clubs* Queen's Univ (London); *Style—* Kenneth McKeown Esq, CBE, DL; The Lodge, Tees View, Hurworth Place, Darlington, Co Durham (☎ 0325 720287); 39 Stanhope Rd, Darlington, Co Durham (☎ 0325 462593)

McKERN, Leo Reginald; AO 1983; s of Norman Walton McKern (d 1969), of Sydney, and Vera Martin (d 1971); two McKern bros migrated to Sydney from Limerick (McKern printing works) in 1864; *b* 16 Mar 1920; *Educ* Sydney Technical HS; *m* 9 Nov 1946, Joan Alice (Jane Holland, actress), da of late Joseph Southall; 2 da (Abigail b 1955, Harriet b 1964); *Career* engrg apprentice 1935-37, served AIF (Corp Engrs) 1940-42; actor: 1st appearance Metropolitan Theatre Sydney (amateur) 1943, arrived England 1946, stage work inc: Love's Labour's Lost, She Stoops to Conquer, Hamlet, Old Vic New Theatre 1949; Feste in Twelfth Night (re-opening of Old Vic Theatre

1950), Bartholomew Fair, Henry V (1951), Merry Wives of Windsor, Electra, The Wedding, King Lear, etc; Shakespeare Memorial Theatre Australian and NZ tour 1953: Iago in Othello, Touchstone in As You Like It, Glendower and Northumberland in Henry IV pt 1; Stratford Season 1954: Ulysses in Troilus and Cressida, Grumio in Taming of the Shrew, Quince in A Midsummer Night's Dream, Friar Lawrence in Romeo and Juliet; Toad in Toad of Toad Hall, Prince's Theatre 1954, etc; Big Daddy in Cat on a Hot Tin Roof, Aldwych 1958, etc; dir The Shifting Heart, Duke of York's 1959, Rollo (title rọle), Strand 1959, the Common Man in A Man for all Seasons, Globe 1960, etc, Thomas Cromwell in A Man for all Seasons, Anta Theatre, NY 1961; last season at Old Vic 1962-63: Peer Gynt, The Alchemist, Othello; Volpone (title rôle), Garrick 1971; Melbourne Theatre Co 1971, Adelaide Festival (best actor); Shylock in The Merchant of Venice, Oxford Playhouse 1973, etc, Uncle Vanya (title rôle), Royal Exchange Manchester 1978, Crime and Punishment, Rollo, 1980, etc; has appeared in over 30 films, inc: Murder in the Cathedral, A Man for all Seasons, Ryan's Daughter, The French Lieutenant's Woman, Travelling North; TV appearances inc: King Lear, Monsignor Quixote, Rumpole of the Bailey (series 1977-) (best TV series award 1984), The Master Builder; best actor award Montreal Film Festival 1987; *Publications* Just Resting (memoir) 1983; *Recreations* sailing, photography, travel; *Style—* Leo McKern, Esq, AO; Barclays, 211/213 Banbury Rd, Oxford OX2 7HH; ICM Ltd, 388/396 Oxford St, London W1N 9HE (☎ 01 629 8080)

MACKERRAS, Sir (Alan) Charles MacLaurin; CBE (1974); s of Alan Patrick Mackerras (d 1973), and Catherine Brearcliffe (d 1977); *b* 17 Nov 1925; *Educ* Sydney GS Aust, NSW Conservatorium of Music Aust, Acad of Music Prague; *m* 1947, Helena Judith, da of Frederick Bruce Wilkins (d 1961); 2 da; *Career* musicians, staff conductor Sadler's Wells Opera 1948-54, princ conductor BBC Concert Orch 1954-56, first conductor Hamburg State Opera 1966-70, musical dir English Nat Opera 1970-77, princ guest conductor ENO 1978-, chief conductor Sydney Symphony Orch 1982-85, chief guest conductor Royal Liverpool Philharmonic Orch 1985-87, musical dir Welsh Nat Opera 1987-; FRCM 1987; kt 1979; *Style—* Sir Charles Mackerras, CBE; 10 Hamilton Terrace, London NW8 9UG (☎ 01 286 4047)

McKERRON, Dr Colin Gordon; s of Sir Patrick Alexander Bruce McKerron, KCMG (d 1964), and Marjorie Kennedy, *née* Rettie (d 1975); *b* 8 Sept 1934; *Educ* Rugby, London Univ (MB, BS 1958); *Career* RAMC 1960-62; travelling fell John Hopkins Hosp Baltimore USA 1966-67; conslt physician: Kings Coll Hosp 1969-85, Greenwich Health Dist 1975-85; hon conslt physician King's Coll Hosp; former examiner in med RCP; regnl advsr RCP (SE Thames Regnl Health Authy) 1979-82; FRCP 1972; *Books* papers on thyroid disease, endocrinology and med educn; *Recreations* gardening, walking, music; *Clubs* Lansdowne; *Style—* Dr Colin G McKerron; Brook Cottage, Dennington, Woodbridge, Suffolk IP13 8JH (☎ 072875 209); 148 Harley St, London W1 (☎ 01 637 4177)

McKERROW, Matthew; s of George Edward McKerrow (d 1940), and Margaret Carlton, *née* Robb (d 1967); *b* 3 Mar 1919; *Educ* Loretto; *m* 2 April 1971, Kirsteen Marian Simpson, da of Rev James Victor Logan; 1 s (Matthew James b 1973), 1 da (Alice Jane b 1975); *Career* dir Hi-Fi Corner Edinburgh Ltd 1972-86; farmer; *Recreations* shooting, skiing, walking; *Style—* Matthew McKerrow, Esq; Addinston, Lauder TD2 6QZ (☎ 057 85 275)

MACKESON, Hon Lady; Camilla Margaret; *née* Keith; da of Baron Keith of Castleacre (Life Peer); *b* 7 Mar 1947, (twin); *m* 22 July 1968 (m dis 1972), Sir Rupert Henry Mackeson, 2 Bt; *Style—* Hon Lady Mackeson; 5 Pembroke Gardens, London W8; Apt 36E, 1365 York Ave, New York 10021, USA

MACKESON, Sir Rupert Henry; 2 Bt (UK 1954), of Hythe Co, Kent; s of Brig Sir Harry Ripley Mackeson, 1 Bt (d 1964); *b* 16 Nov 1941; *Educ* Harrow, Trinity Coll Dublin; *m* 22 July 1968, (m dis 1972), Hon Camilla Margaret, da of Baron Keith of Castleacre; *Career* Capt RHG, ret 1968; *Clubs* White's; *Style—* Sir Rupert Mackeson, Bt

MACKESON-SANDBACH, Ian Lawrie; s of Capt Lawrie Mackeson-Sandbach (d 1984), of Caerllo, Llangernyw, Clwyd, and Geraldine, *née* Sandbach; *b* 14 June 1933; *Educ* Eton, Univ of New Brunswick; *m* 6 May 1967, Annie Marie, da of J M G Van Lanschot (d 1983), of S Hertogen Bosch, Netherlands; 4 da (Antoinette b 1969, Sara b 1970, Louise b 1973, Megan b 1976); *Career* Lt WG, Emergency Res 1952-57; md France Fenwick Ltd 1969-75, dir Demerara Co Ltd 1969-76, chief exec Ernest Notcutt Gp ltd 1976-82, chm Hafodunos Farms Ltd 1982; memb bd of gen purposes Utd Grand Lodge of Eng 1978-, memb cncl Grand Charity 1988-; govr Christs Hosp (Horsham) cmmr Crown Estate Paving Cmmn 1974 (chm 1983); Liveryman Worshipful Co of: Grocers, Insurers; memb Inst Fire Engrs 1960; *Recreations* shooting, fishing; *Clubs* Boodles, Pratts, Royal St Georges (Sandwich); *Style—* Ian Mackeson-Sandbach, Esq; 20 Hanover Terr, Regents Park, London NW1; Maesol, Llangernyw, Clwyd; Sir John Lyon House, 5 High Timber St, Upper Thames St, London EC4V 3LE (☎ 01 248 4931, fax 01 402 6390)

MACKIE, Charles Gordon; TD (1945), DL (1985); s of Capt Charles Gordon Stewart Mackie, OBE (d 1965), of St Ann's, by Brechin, Angus, and Gertrude Irvine Mackie (d 1946); *b* 19 Mar 1916; *Educ* Harrow, St John's Coll Oxford (MA); *m* 5 May 1945, Margaret Georgina Koebel (Peggy), da of Maj Frederick Ernest Koebel, DSO (d 1940), of Chudleigh, Devon; 1 s (Alexander b 1946), 2 da (Mary b 1953, Sally b 1958); *Career* cmmnd 2 Lt 7 Bn Argyll and Sutherland Highlanders 51 Highland Div TA 1938, served France 1939-40 (wounded, despatches), Capt 1941, 8 Army 1941-42 serv: N Africa, Sicily, Italy; Europe 1944 (wounded), invalided out 1945; Stewarts & Lloyds 1937-67: trainee 1937-39, mangr London City off 1953, asst md Stanton Ironworks Ltd (subsid) 1956, md Stanton & Staveley Ltd (subsid) 1962, chm and md Stanton & Staveley Ltd and dir Stewarts & Lloyds 1964-67; dir tubes div Br Steel Corpn 1967-78; chm: Shanks & McEwan Ltd 1978-81, Booth Int Ltd 1979-82; tres Univ of Nottingham 1982- (cncl memb 1962-); gen cmmr of income tax 1960-; *Recreations* shooting, fishing, skiing, golf; *Clubs* Carlton; *Style—* Charles Mackie, Esq, TD, DL

MACKIE, Clive David Andrew; s of David Hugh Mackie (d 1978), of Hampton Court, and Lilian Edith, *née* Claughton; *b* 29 April 1929; *Educ* Tiffin Sch Kingston-on-Thames; *m* 20 Dec 1953, Averil Mary Amy, da of John Alfred Ratcliff (d 1974); 1 s (Duncan b 1957), 3 da (Louise b 1958, Rosalind b 1963, Nina b 1967); *Career* CA; dir Grundy Gp Teddington 1961-67, dir and sec D Sebel & Co Ltd 1967-70, asst sec Poly of the S Bank 1970-73, sec gen Inst of Actuaries 1983- (dep sec 1973-78, sec 1978-83); FCA, FRS; *Recreations* music (post 1780), cricket, carpentry, countryside; *Clubs* Reform, Kent CCC; *Style—* Clive Mackie, Esq; Withermere, Burwash, E Sussex TN19 7HN (☎ 0435 88247); Staple Inn Hall, London WC1V 7QJ (☎ 01 242 0106, fax: 01 405 2482)

MACKIE, (William) Denis Grenville; s of (William) Grenville Mackie, of The Lodge, Lissanoure, Loughuile, Cloughmills, Co Antrim, and Constance Beatrice, *née* Rodden (d 1981); *b* 10 Sept 1934; *Educ* Shrewsbury; *m* 23 April 1960, Susannah, da of Bernard Dixon (d 1983), of Pampisford Place, Pampisford, Cambs; 2 s (Alastair b 15 March 1963, Peter (twin) b 15 March 1963), 1 da (Caroline b 1961); *Career* dir James Mackie and Sons Ltd Belfast (and Hldgs) 1968-77, dir Robert Mccalmont and Co Ltd Belfast 1968-83, md Lissanoure Farms Ltd Co Antrim 1969-, non exec dir Strand Spinning Co Belfast 1977-; memb Co Antrim Jury Bursay Ctee; High Sheriff Co Antrim 1979; *Clubs* Ulster Reform (Belfast); *Style—* Denis Mackie, Esq; Lissanoure, Loughguile, Cloughmills, Co Antrim, NI (☎ 026 564 471)

MACKIE, Hon George Yull; 3 and yst s of Baron John-Mackie (Life Peer); *b* 19 April 1949; *Style—* The Hon George Mackie; The Bungalow, Harold's Park Farm, Nazeing, Essex

MACKIE, Gordon; s of Lavens Mathewson Mackie (d 1966), and Marion Klara Gabrielle, *née* Dorndorf; Mackie family is a sept of MacKay (Clan Aodh); *b* 1 Jan 1937; *Educ* Merchiston Castle; *m* 1, 18 July 1963, Elizabeth Ann, da of Cecil Gordon Falloon, of Millicent House, Sallins, Co Kildare; 1 s (Timothy Gordon b 1965); 2 da (Catriona Ann b 1964, Grania Esther b 1967); m 2, 23 Aug 1985, Ruth Alison, da of Hubert Allan Hall, of 33 Lislunnan Rd, Kells, Co Antrim; 2 da (Alexandra Helen b 1987, Sarah Margot b 1988); *Career* dir James Mackie & Sons Ltd 1968; chm and chief exec James Mackie & Sons Ltd 1981; CIMechE 1982; FRSA 1984; CTextFTI 1986; *Recreations* aviation, sub-aqua, skiing, shooting, apiculture; *Style—* Gordon Mackie, Esq; Ladyhill, 18 Ladyhill Rd, Antrim, Co Antrim BT41 2RF (☎ 08494 63051); James Mackie & Sons Ltd, Albert Foundary, Springfield Rd, PO Box 149, Belfast, NI BT12 7ED (☎ 0232 327771)

MACKIE, James Campbell Stephen; s of Prof John Duncan Mackie (d 1978) CBE, MC, LLD, prof of scottish history and literature Glasgow Univ, and Cicely Jean, *née* Paterson (d 1976); *b* 1 Oct 1926; *Educ* Charterhouse, New Coll Oxford (MA); *m* 1951, Margaret Pamela Daphne Moore, da of late Maj Hugh King, Seaforth Highlanders, MC; 4 s (Alexander b 1952, Hugh b 1956, Simon b 1960, Tobias b 1964); 1 da (Miranda b 1962); *Career* serv RM 1944-47, NW Europe; HM Overseas Civil Serv 1951-59, Malaya (asst sec PM Dept), dir Corn Exchange Co 1975-80, dir gen Grain & Feed Trade Assoc 1972-; sec: Cattle Food Trade Assoc 1965-72, Liverpool Cotton Assoc 1960-65; chm: Gayswood Branch of C and Unionist Assoc 1965-73 and 1976-83, (Farnham Div 1973-76); pres SW Surrey Cons Assoc 1988 (vice chm 1984), vice pres Haslemere Hockey Club 1988-; *Recreations* photography, tennis, hockey, history, antiques, dogs, reading, travelling; *Clubs* Caledonian, Farmers'; *Style—* James C Mackie, Esq; c/o The Grain & Feed Trade Assoc, Baltic Exchange Chambers, 24 St Mary Axe, London EC3A 8EP (☎ 01 283 5146, telex 886984, fax 6264449)

MACKIE, Hon Jeannie Felicia; da of Baron Mackie of Benshie (Life Peer); *b* 1953; *Style—* The Hon Jeannie Mackie; c/o Ballinshoe, Kirriemuir, Angus, DD8 5Q9

MACKIE, Hon John Maitland; s of Baron John-Mackie (Life Baron); *b* 1944; *m* 1984, Janet Ann; 1 da (Louise (b 1985); *Style—* The Hon John Mackie; Fairview, Harold's Park Farm, Nazeing, Essex EN9 2SF

MACKIE, Sir Maitland; CBE (1965), JP (Aberdeen 1959); s of Maitland Mackie and bro of Baron Mackie of Benshie and of Baron John-Mackie; *b* 16 Feb 1912; *Educ* Aberdeen GS, Aberdeen Univ; *m* 1, 1935, Isobel Ross (d 1960); 2 s, 4 da; m 2, 1963, Pauline M Turner; *Career* farmer 1932-; lord-lt Aberdeenshire 1975-87: chm Jt Advsy Cttee Scot Farm Bldgs Investigation Unit 1963-75, Aberdeen Milk Mktng Bd 1965-82, Peterhead Bay Mgmnt Co 1975-86; memb Bd Scot Cncl Devpt and Indust 1975-82 and chm Oil Policy Ctee 1975-82; chm Aberdeen Branch, OStJ 1977-; chm Aberdeen Cable Servs Ltd 1983-87; *Style—* Sir Maitland Mackie, CBE, JP; High Trees, Inchmarlo Rd, Banchory (☎ Banchory 03302 4274)

MACKIE, Dr Margaret Alison; CMG (1975); da of David Ross Mackie (d 1937); *b* 6 Nov 1910; *Educ* Presbyterian Ladies' Coll Melbourne, Univ of Melbourne; *Career* med practitioner, obstetrician and gynaecologist, in-patient gynaecologist Queen Victoria Memorial Hosp Melbourne 1952-59, in-patient obstetrician Royal Women's Hosp Melbourne 1959-70, conslt obstetrician 1970-; *Recreations* photography, gardening, travel; *Clubs* Lyceum, Royal Auto, Soroptomist Int of Chisholm; *Style—* Dr Margaret Mackie, CMG; Unit 2/11 Albany Rd, Toorak, Victoria, Australia (☎ 822 7556)

MACKIE, Sheila Gertrude (Mrs R Fenwick-Baines); da of James Watt Bell Mackie (d 1968), and Edna Irene, *née* Watson; *b* 5 Oct 1928; *Educ* Durham HS, King Edward VII Sch of Art Newcastle-upon-Tyne, Durham Univ (BA); *m* 3rd Aug 1967, Robert Fenwick-Baines, s of Albert Baines; 1 s (James Alastair b 1970), 1 da (Anneliese b 1969); *Career* head art dept Consetts S-Sch 1950-82; occasional lectr Sunderland Coll of Art and lectr numerous art socs; artistic advsr Bertam Mills Circus 1950s-60s; artist-illustrator pubns incl: Adventure in Glides Garden (with Terri Le Guerre, 1979), The Great Seasons (with David Bellamy, 1980), The Mouse book (with David Bellamy, 1982), Lindisfarne-the Cradle Island (with Magnus Magnusson, 1984), Beowulf (with Magnus Magnusson and Julian Glover, 1987), The Wanderer (with Michael Cronin and Charlton Heston, 1989); work in Roy Collection, exhibited RA and RSA; one man shows in London and provinces; *Style—* Miss Sheila Mackie; Hoddington Oaks, Spa Grounds, Shotley Bridge, Consett, Co Durham DH8 0TN (☎ 0207 503 065)

MACKIE, (John) Stuart; s of Norman Frederic Mackie (d 1956), of Halifax, and Mary, *née* Rushworth (d 1976); *b* 12 Mar 1933; *Educ* Sowerby Bridge GS, Sheffield Univ (Dip Arch); *m* 3 Aug 1957, Elsie, da of William Breeden, of Ashton under Lyne; 1 s (Robin Jonathan b 1964), 1 da (Amanda Lauren b 1958); *Career* RE 1955-57, serv Germany and Cyprus; chartered architect, ptnr private practice; chm: RIBA Teeside Branch 1957-76, RIBA Northern Regn 1978-79, RIBA Housing Advsy Gp 1982-; cncl memb: Aruck 1982-, RIBA 1981-; sec Teeside Civic Soc, dir Cleveland Bldgs Preservation Tst; *Recreations* travel, photography; *Style—* Stuart Mackie, Esq; 15 Spring Hill, Welbury, Northallerton, N Yorks (☎ 060 982 453); Hugh Wilson & Lewis Womersley, 2 Vaughan Street, Linthorpe Road, Middlesborough (☎ 0642 232333)

MACKIE OF BENSHIE, Baron (Life Peer UK 1974); George Yull Mackie; CBE (1971), DSO (1944), DFC (1944), LLD (1982); s of Maitland Mackie, OBE, LLD and bro of Baron John-Mackie and Sir Maitland Mackie; *b* 10 July 1919; *Educ* Aberdeen GS, Aberdeen Univ; *m* 1, 1944, Lindsay Lyall (d 1985), da of Alexander Sharp, OBE, of Aberdeen; 3 da (and 1 s decd); m 2, 29 April 1988, Jacqueline, widow of Andrew

Lane; *Career* serv WWII Bomber Cmd; farmer 1945-; chm Mackie Yule & Co, Caithness Glass Ltd 1966-85; Caithness Pottery Co, Benshie Cattle Co; rector Dundee Univ 1980-83; MP (Lib) Caithness & Sutherland 1964-66; stood for Parl (Lib) Angus S 1959 & (for Euro Parl) Scotland NE 1979; chm Scot Lib Pty 1965-70; chm Land & Timber Servs Ltd 1986-; Lib spokesman House of Lords: Devolution, Agriculture, Scotland, Indust; memb: parly assembly of Cncl of Europe 1986-, Western Euro Union 1986-; pres Scottish Lib Pty until 1988 (became SLD); *Recreations* golf, tennis, shooting; *Clubs* Garrick, Farmers', RAF, Nat Lib; *Style—* Rt Hon Lord Mackie of Benshie, CBE, DSO, DFC; Ballinshoe, Kirriemuir, Angus (☎ 0575 73466)

MACKILLIGIN, Robert Guy Walter; MC (1944, and bar 1945); s of late Hector Rennie Mackilligin; *b* 11 Oct 1918; *Educ* Charterhouse, Camborne Sch of Mines; *m* 1949, Daphne Gwendoline, *née* Cooper; 3 da; *Career* serv WWII 51 Highland Div RA 1939-46; petroleum engr Shell Int Petroleum Co Ltd 1946-53, mangr Shell Int Co Ltd 1954-73; Exec Div Bisichi Mixing plc 1974-, chm Dragon Mkts Ltd 1984-; *Recreations* genealogy, gardening, ornithology; *Style—* Robert Mackilligin, Esq, MC; Walnut Tree Cottage, Woodlands, Pembury Rd, Tunbridge Wells (☎ 0892 30392 and 01 236 3539)

McKIM, Robert Kenyon; MBE (1964); s of Maj William McKim (d 1958), and Ethel Marjorie, *née* Hanson (d 1985); *b* 29 Oct 1929; *Career* mil serv Infantry (2 Lt) 1947-49; purchasing mangr (aircraft industry) 1969-86; Dep Mayor of Wakefield 1956-57; parly candidate (C) Sowerby 1959 and 1964; *Recreations* genealogy; *Style—* Robert McKim, Esq, MBE; Trendle, Sherborne, Dorset DT9 3NT (☎ 0935 81 2173)

McKIMMIE, John Hedley; s of Dr John McKimmie (d 1983), and Dr Patricia Lucy Frances, *née* Heaton; *b* 24 April 1948; *Educ* Gordonstoun, Glasgow Univ; *m* 10 July 1971, Jacqueline Ann; 1 s (Andrew b 1977), 1 da (Rosie b 1975); *Career* chm and chief exec Parkway Gp plc 1987-; fin dir WCRS Group 1982-87; CA; *Recreations* family, golf, hockey, animals; *Clubs* Wentworth Golf, West Hill Golf, Woking Hockey; *Style—* John H McKimmie, Esq; Windlecote House, Heath House Rd, Worplesdon Hill, nr Woking Surrey GU22 0RD (☎ 04867 3153); Parkway Group plc, 25/27 Farringdon Rd, London EC1 (☎ 01 404 4044)

MacKINLAY, Sir Bruce; CBE (1970); s of Daniel Robertson MacKinlay (d 1920), and Alice Victoria, *née* Rice; *b* 4 Oct 1912; *Educ* Scotch Coll Perth; *m* 1943, (Erica) Ruth, da of Jerold Fleming (d 1938); 2 s; *Career* co dir; pres WA Employers' Fedn 1974-75, chm WA IOD 1975-77, dir Whittakers Ltd 1975-, pres Confed of WA Indust 1976-78, employers' rep Int Lab Conf Geneva 1977; chm (WA) Chamber of Mfrs Insur Ltd 1977-, Keep Australia Beautiful (WA) 1981 (cllr 1970); cllr Aust Cncl on Population & Ethnic Affairs 1981, past former Fremantle Rotary Club; kt 1978; *see Debrett's Handbook of Australia and New Zealand for further details*; *Style—* Sir Bruce MacKinlay, CBE; 9B Melville St, Claremont, W Australia 6010

MACKINLAY MACLEOD, Michael John; s of John MacKinlay MacLeod, of Manor Farm, Elmley Castle, Pershore, Worcs, and Dorothy Rule, *née* MacFarlane (d 1975); *b* 2 Oct 1935; *Educ* Eton, Pembroke Coll Cambridge, RAC Cirencester; *m* 1, 1958 (m dis 1966), Sandra Elizabeth, da of the late Lt Col Alister Maynard, MBE; 3 s (Torquil b 1959, Jocelyn b 1961, Caspar b 1963); m 2, 14 Feb 1967, (Pamela) Dawn, da of late Hugh Nicholas Charrington; 1 s (Euan b 1970), 2 da (Emma b 1967, Iona b 1971); *Career* Lt Grenadier Gds, Capt Ayrshire Yeo; shipbroker Balitic Exchange, shipbuilding Redheads; ship mangr: H Hogarth & Sons antiques, R Harrington London, H W Keil & Sons Broadway; currently farming Scotland and Worcs; memb: W Midlands Agric Forum, cncl S W Regnl Unionist Pty; AICS; *Recreations* country sports; *Clubs* Pratts', Farmers, Union & Country (Worcester); *Style—* Michael MacKinlay MacLeod, Esq; The Old Vicarage, Overbury, Tewkesbury, Glos GL20 7NT (☎ 038 689 510)

MacKINLAY MacLEOD, Michael John; s of John MacKinlay MacLeod, of Worcs, and Dorothy Rule, *née* MacFarlane (d 1975); *b* 2 Oct 1935; *Educ* Eton, Pembroke Coll Cambridge, RAC Cirencester; *m* 1, 17 May 1958 (m dis 1966), Sandra Elizabeth, da of late Lt-Col Alister Maynard, MBE; 3 s (Torquil b 1959, Jocelyn b 1961, Caspar b 1963); m 2, 14 Feb 1967, Pamela Dawn, da of late Hugh Nicholas Charrington; 1 s (Euan b 1970), 2 da (Emma b 1967, Iona b 1971); *Career* Lt Grenadier Gds, Capt Ayrshire (ECO) Yeomanry; shipping Baltic Exchange London; Redheads Tyne; ship mangr; H Hogarth and Sons Glasgow; antiques business London & Broadway Worcs; farmer Scotland and Worcs, branch chm CLA 1987; memb: S W Regn Cncl Unionists, W Midlands Agric Forum; AICS; *Recreations* shooting; *Clubs* Pratt's, Farmer's; *Style—* Michael MacKinlay MacLeod, Esq; The Old Vicarage, Overbury, Tewkesbury, Glos GL20 7NT (☎ 038689 510)

McKINNA, John Gilbert; CMG (1978), CBE (1967), DSO (1945), LVO (1963), ED (1947); s of Rev John McKinna (d 1964); *b* 11 Dec 1906; *Educ* Prince Alfred Coll, Adelaide Univ; *m* 1937, Elizabeth Mary, da of Col Sydney Edwin Beach (d 1933); 2 da; *Career* Brig WW II; gen mangr Quarry Industs Ltd 1949-56, hon ADC to Govr Gen 1953-56; cmmr of police South Australia 1957-72; pres Royal Automobile Assoc of SA 1975-78; pres St John Cncl for SA 1983-85; memb Aust Inst Mining and Metallurgy; Fell Aust Inst of Management; *Clubs* Adelaide, Naval, Military and Air Force (SA); *Style—* John McKinna, Esq, CMG, CBE, DSO, LVO, ED; 12 McKenna St, Kensington Park, S Australia 5068 (☎ 31 4604)

McKINNON, David Douglas; s of John McKinnon (d 1957), and Margaret Douglas (d 1963); *b* 18 July 1926; *Educ* Stirling HS, Glasgow Univ (BSc); *m* 1960, Edith June, da of Edward Fairful Kyles (d 1942); 1 s, 2 da; *Career* asst Maths Dept Glasgow Univ 1946-48; pres Faculty of Actuaries 1979-81; gen mangr and actuary Scottish Mutual Assur Society 1982- (formerly dep gen mangr; dir 1981-); pres Falkirk Bn the Boys Bde 1972-77, vice-chm Church of Scotland Tst 1984-89, memb Church of Scotland Assembly Cncl 1987-, chm Assoc Scottish Life Offices 1988-89, memb Bd Assoc of Br Insurers 1988-; FFA, FIMA; *Recreations* golf; *Clubs* Western (Glasgow); *Style—* Douglas McKinnon Esq; Kinburn, 4 Carronvale Rd, Larbert, Stirlingshire FK5 3LZ (☎ 0324 562373); Scottish Mutual Assur Soc, 109 St Vincent St, Glasgow 2 (☎ 041 248 6321, telex 777145)

McKINNON, Ian; s of John McKinnon, of Ayr, and Mary Kissell Dunlop, *née* Logan; *b* 6 Dec 1944; *Educ* Ayr GS, Newbattle Abbey Dalkeith; *m* 11 Nov 1972, Maureen Margaret, da of James McLeod (d 1947), of Wick, Caithness; 1 s (Robert James b 1984); *Career* exec mangr BMW GB Ltd 1970-75; dir FH Peacock Ltd 1976-; FIMI, FBIM; ; *Recreations* golf, gardening, theatre, opera; *Clubs* W Hill Golf, Brookwood, Sloane; *Style—* Ian McKinnon, Esq; Morar, Hillcrest Rd, Camberley Surrey GU15 1LF; FH Peacock Ltd, 219/22 Balham High Rd, London SW17 7BL (☎ 01 672 1271, car tel 0860 358 021)

MACKINNON, Cdre Neil Alexander; s of Donald de Burg d'Arcy, and Edith Mary, *née* Orr (d 1932); *b* 20 Sept 1906; *Educ* Geelong GS, Royal Australian Naval Coll (Kings Medal); *m* 17 Jan 1936, Rachel Frances, da of Rev John Hilton Molesworth (d 1921), of Norfolk; 2 s (Peter b 1938, John b 1941), 1 da (Fiona b 1946); *Career* Royal Australian Navy 1920-60, dir: Communications RAN 1946-48, Intelligence RAN 1949-51; cmd: HMAS Steuart 1943-44, HMAS Warramunga 1944, HMS Apollo 1952-53; Imp Def Coll 1954; cdre sit pf Trg FND 1955-56, Australian Naval representative Utc 1956-60; US Legion of Merit (Degree of Offr) 1944; *Recreations* golf; *Clubs* Army and Navy, MCC; *Style—* Cdre Neil A MacKinnon; The Old Fox, Lewknor, Oxon OX9 5TL (☎ 0844 51822)

MACKINNON, Hon Mrs (Patricia Ann); *née* Souter; da and co heiress of 25 Baron Audley; *b* 10 August 1946; *m* 1969, Carey Leigh Mackinnon; 1 s, 1 da; *Style—* The Hon Mrs Mackinnon; Scollops, Oast, Ide Hill, Sevenoaks, Kent

MACKINNON, Hon Mrs; (Patricia Clare); da of 1 Baron Glentoran, OBE, PC (d 1950); *b* 1919; *m* 1940, Lt Cdr Adam McLeod Mackinnon, RN; 2 s, 3 da; *Style—* The Hon Mrs Mackinnon; The Cottage Inn, Maidens Green, Winkfield, Windsor, Berks

MACKINNON, Dame (Una) Patricia; DBE (1977, CBE 1972); da of Ernest Thomas Bell, MLA, of Brisbane (d 1930, family arrived in Australia 1807) and Pauline Eva Bell (d 1970, family arrived in Australia 1865); *b* 24 July 1911; *Educ* St Margaret's C of E Sch Brisbane (LTCL, LRSM); *m* 1936, Alistair Scobie Mackinnon (d 1983), s of Lauchlan Mackinnon (d 1933), of Toorak, Vic; 1 s, 1 da; *Career* housewife; memb Ctee of Mgmnt Royal Children's Hosp Melbourne 1948-79 (pres 1965-79, chm Bd of Res 1967-84), memb bd Mayfield Centre Melbourne 1979-83, dir Child Accident Prevention Fndn of Australia 1979-, Coronation Medal 1952, Queen's Silver Jubilee Medal 1977; *Recreations* gardening, reading (history and biographies); *Clubs* Alexandra (Melbourne); *Style—* Dame Patricia Mackinnon, DBE; 5 Ross Street, Toorak, Vic 3144, Australia

McKINNON, Warwick Nairn; s of His Honour Judge Neil Nairn McKinnon (d 1988), of Purley, Surrey, and Janetta Amelia, *née* Lilley; *b* 11 Nov 1947; *Educ* King's Coll Sch Wimbledon, Christ's Coll Cambridge (MA); *m* 29 July 1978, Nichola Juliet, da of David Alan Lloyd, of Limpsfield, Surrey; 1 s (Rory b 1981), 1 da (Kirsty b 1982); *Career* barr Lincoln's Inn 1970, SE circuit; *Recreations* cricket, golf, opera; *Style—* Warwick McKinnon, Esq; Queen Elizabeth Bldgs, Temple, London EC4Y 9BS

MacKINNON OF MacKINNON, The; Anne Gunhild MacKinnon; da of Alasdair Neil Hood MacKinnon of MacKinnon (d 1983), 37 Chief of Clan Fingon (MacKinnon); suc father as 38 Chief; *b* 13 Feb 1955; *Educ* Badminton Sch Bristol, St Loyes Sch of Occupational Therapy (Dip of Occupational Therapy); *m* 1981, Allan; 2 s (Andrew b 1982, Robert b 1985); *Career* occupational therapist Somerset Hosps 1976-88; *Style—* The MacKinnon of MacKinnon; 16 Durleigh Rd, Bridgwater, Somerset TA6 7HR

MACKINNON OF MACKINNON, Lt-Col Ian Kroyer; yr s of Cdr Arthur Avalon MacKinnon of MacKinnon, OBE, RN (d 1964), 36 Chief of Clan MacKinnon, of Charity Acre, Pilgrims Way, Hollingbourne, Kent, and Gunhild, *née* Kroyer (d 1946); er bro Alasdair Neil Hood Mackinnon, 37 Chief of Clan MacKinnon (d 1983); *b* 8 Oct 1929; *Educ* Wellington, RMA Sandhurst; *m* 1 Jan 1955, Joanna Eileen, er da of Capt Sir Robert William Stirling-Hamilton, 12 Bt, JP, DL (d 1982); *Career* cmmnd Queen's Own Cameron Highlanders 1950; served with 1 Bn in Tripoli, Canal Zone and Austria 1950-53; Depot Camerons, Inverness 1953-56; 1 Bn in Malaya, Aden and Dover 1956-59; Adjt 4/5 Bn Queen's Own Cameron Highlanders (TA), Inverness 1959-61; staff appt HQ Land Forces, Hong Kong 1961-63; Trg Maj St Andrews Univ 1964-65; 1 Bn Queen's Own Highlanders (Seaforth and Camerons) Osnabrück and Berlin 1965-66; staff appt HQ Highland Div and Dist Perth 1966-68; 1 Bn Queen's Own Highlanders (2 i/c) Edinburgh and Sharjah 1968-71; HQ BAOR DAMS 1971-73; staff appt HQ Dir of Inf, Warminster 1973-76; Lt-Col 1976; cmd Scottish Inf Depot, Bridge of Don, Aberdeen 1976-79; cmdt Stanford Trg Area, Thetford, Norfolk 1979-84; ret 1984; regnl sec Norfolk and Suffolk CLA 1985-; fndr chm Breckland Gp, Norfolk Naturalists' Tst; memb Centre Ctee (Norfolk) The National Tst; *Recreations* shooting, gardening; *Style—* Lt-Col Ian MacKinnon of MacKinnon; Little Breck House, 4 Trenchard Crescent, Watton, Norfolk IP25 6HR (☎ 0953 883139)

MACKINTOSH, Anthony Robert Kilgour (Tony); s of Philip Kilgour Mackintosh, of Five Ashes, Sussex, and Beryl Ada, *née* Brodie; *b* 15 June 1943; *Educ* Brighton Hove and Sussex GS, Hertford Coll Oxford (MA); *m* 21 Oct 1967, Barbara Dorothy, da of Thomas Fox; 3 s (Julian b 1970, Alastair b 1971, Jonathan b 1975); *Career* exec Br Petroleum Co 1965-71, dir Wood Mackenzie & Co Ltd 1984-86 (ptnr 1976-84, oil analyst 1972-76), dir Hill Samuel Bank Ltd 1986-; *Recreations* chess, bridge, golf, reading; *Clubs* Utd Oxford and Cambridge Univ; *Style—* Tony Mackintosh, Esq; 3 North Hill, London N6 (☎ 01 340 4984); Hill Samuel Bank Ltd, 100 Wood St, London EC2P 2AJ (☎ 01 628 8011, fax 01 588 5292)

MACKINTOSH, Colin Richard; s of Euan Bracebridge Mackintosh (d 1979), of Birmingham, and Enid Mary Lucy, *née* Harris; *b* 19 June 1953; *Educ* Blackfriars Llanarth, George Dixon GS Birmingham, Birmingham Univ (LLB); *m* 18 June 1977, Jani Elizabeth Mary, da of Kenneth Townsend; 3 da (Elizabeth b 1980, Lucy b 1982, Alice b 1987); *Career* barr Inner Temple 1976 M & O Circuit, memb Hon Soc of the Inner Temple, M & O Circuit, memb Hon Soc of the Inner Temple; *Recreations* reading, walking, fishing, family; *Style—* CR Mackintosh, Esq; 3 Fountain Court, Steelhouse Lane, Birmingham B4 6DR (☎ 021 236 5854)

MACKINTOSH, Hon Diana Mary; da of 2 Viscount Mackintosh of Halifax (d 1980); *b* 14 Sept 1947; *Educ* Riddlesworth Hall, Harrogate Coll; *Career* children's nursing; *Style—* The Hon Diana Mackintosh

MACKINTOSH, Lady Fiona Eve Akua; *née* Hare; da of 5 Earl of Listowel, GCMG, PC, and his 2 w, Stephanie Sandra Yvonne, *née* Wise; *b* 24 Feb 1960; *m* 5 Sept 1987, Christopher G G Mackintosh, s of Charlach Mackintosh, of Calgary, Alberta, Canada; *Style—* Lady Fiona Mackintosh

MACKINTOSH, Hon Graham Charles; s of 2 Viscount Mackintosh of Halifax (d 1980), and Gwynneth *née* Gledhill hp of bro, 3 Viscount; *b* 12 Mar 1964; *Educ* The Leys Sch, Univ of Newcastle upon Tyne (BSc), Coll of Estate Mgmnt, Univ of Reading; *Career* surveyor; *Recreations* cricket, golf, tennis, swimming, hockey, squash; *Clubs* E India, MCC, Artist's, Morton's; *Style—* The Hon Graham Mackintosh; 39 Rowallan Road, Fulham, London SW6 6AF (☎ 01 385 0796)

McKINTOSH, His Honour Judge Ian Stanley; s of Herbert Stanley McKintosh (d 1975), of Cranford Ct, Chester; *b* 23 April 1938; *Educ* Leeds GS, Exeter Coll Oxford (MA); *m* 2 Sept 1967, (Alison) Rosemary, da of Kenneth Blayney Large of Inglenook

Cottage, Erlestoke, Wilts; 2 s (Edward b 1970, William b 1975), 1 da (Alexandra b 1972); *Career* serv RAF UK and Germany 1957-59; slr 1966, dep circuit judge 1976-81, recorder Crown Ct 1981-89; circuit judge 1989-, slrs dept New Scotland Yard 1966-68, private practice 1969-89; chm Swindon Branch of Stonham Housing Assoc, memb of SW Legal Aid Area Local General and Area Appeals Ctees 1970-89; *Recreations* family, cricket, sailing, rowing, talking; *Clubs* MCC, XL, Bowmoor Sailing; *Style*— His Hon Judge McKintosh; c/o The Courts of Justice, Edward St, Truro, Corwall

MACKINTOSH, (John) Malcolm; CMG (1975); s of Dr James Macalister Mackintosh, MD (d 1966); *b* 25 Dec 1921; *Educ* Mill Hill, Edinburgh Acad, Glasgow Univ; *m* 1946, Elena, da of late Capt Philip Grafov; 1 s, 1 da (and 1 s decd); *Career* serv WWII: ME, Italy and Balkans, Lt Br Army Allied Control Cmmn Bulgaria 1944-46; programme organiser BBC Overseas Serv 1948-60, res offr FCO 1960-68, asst sec Cabinet Off 1968-87, ret; author; *Recreations* walking, climbing; *Clubs* Garrick; *Style*— Malcolm Mackintosh, Esq, CMG; 21 Ravensdale Ave, London N12 9HP (☎ 01 445 9714)

MACKINTOSH, Lady; (Mary) Yolande Bickford; JP (W Sussex 1968), DL (W Sussex 1982); only da of Leonard William Bickford Smith (3 s of Sir George John Smith, VD, JP, DL); *b* 21 June 1919; *Educ* Downe House, London Univ (BSc); *m* 1, Dr John Clegg (decd); m 2, 1962, as his 2 w, Capt Sir Kenneth Lachlan Mackintosh, KCVO, RN (d 1979), sometime Yeoman Usher of The Black Rod and sec to the Lord Great Chamberlain, also Serjeant-at-Arms House of Lords; 1 s (and 2 s decd), 1 da; *Style*— Lady Mackintosh, JP, DL; The Garden House, Slinfold, Horsham, W Sussex

MACKINTOSH OF HALIFAX, 3 Viscount (UK 1957); Sir (John) Clive Mackintosh; 3 Bt (UK 1935); s of 2 Viscount Mackintosh of Halifax, OBE, BEM (d 1980, whose f was head of the Mackintosh confectionery manufacturers), by his 2 w, Gwynneth, *see* Viscountess Mackintosh of Halifax; *b* 9 Sept 1958; *Educ* The Leys Sch, Oriel Coll Oxford (MA); *m* 1982, Elizabeth, only da of late D G Lakin, and Mrs F E G Melener, of Esher; 2 s (Hon Thomas Harold George b 1985, Hon George John Frank b 24 Oct 1988); *Heir* s, Hon Thomas Harold George Mackintosh b 8 Feb 1985; *Career* CA with Price Waterhouse; pres Oxford Univ Cons Assoc 1979; sits as Cons in House of Lords; ACA; *Recreations* cricket, golf, bridge; *Clubs* Carlton, MCC; *Style*— The Rt Hon the Viscount Mackintosh of Halifax; House of Lords, SW1

MACKINTOSH OF HALIFAX, Gwynneth, Viscountess; Gwynneth Charlesworth; da of Charles Gledhill, of Halifax; *m* 1956, as his 2 w, 2 Viscount Mackintosh of Halifax, OBE, BEM (d 1980); 2 s (3 Viscount, Hon Graham Mackintosh); *Style*— The Rt Hon Gwynneth, Viscountess Mackintosh of Halifax; The Old Hall, Barford, Norwich NR9 4AY (☎ Barnham Broom 271)

MACKINTOSH OF MACKINTOSH, The; Lt Cdr Lachlan Ronald Duncan; OBE (1972), JP, DL (Inverness-shire 1965), RN; 30 Chief of the Clan Mackintosh; s of Vice-Adm Lachlan Donald Mackintosh of Mackintosh, CB, DSO, DSC (d 1957); *b* 27 June 1928; *Educ* Elstree, RN Dartmouth; *m* 1962, Mabel Cecilia Helen (Celia), da of Capt Hon John Bernard Bruce, RN (d 1971); 1 s (John b 1969), 2 da (Louisa b 1962, Bridget b 1966) (and 1 da decd); *Heir* s, John Lachlan, b 1969; *Career* Flag Lt to First Sea Lord 1951, specialised in communications 1954, served in HMY Britannia 1957, ret 1963; chm Highland Exhibitions Ltd 1964-84; vice-pres Scottish Cons and Unionist Assoc 1969-71; CC Inverness-shire 1970-75, Vice-Lt 1971-85; regnl cllr Highland Region 1974-; Lord Lt Lochaber Inverness, Badenoch & Strathspey 1985-; *Clubs* Naval & Military, Highland (Inverness); *Style*— The Mackintosh of Mackintosh, OBE, JP, RN; Moy Hall, Tomatin, Inverness (☎ 080 82 211)

MCKISSOCK, Sir Wylie; OBE (1946); s of Alexander Cathie McKissock; *b* 27 Oct 1906; *Educ* City of London Sch, London Univ (MB, MS), St George's Hosp (MS); *m* 1934, Rachel Madeline, da of Leonard Martin Jones; 1 s, 2 da; *Career* consulting neurological surgn in London 1936-71: Nat Hosp WC1, Hosp for Sick Children Great Ormond St, Nat Hosp WC1, Queen Sq Hosp, St George's Hosp; surgn i/c: EMS Head Centre, Atkinson Morley's Hosp, Leavesden Hosp 1939-45; MS, FRCS, FRSM, Hon FRCR; kt 1971; *Style*— Sir Wylie McKissock, OBE; Camus na Harry, Lechnaside, Gairloch, Wester Ross (☎ 044 583 224)

MACKLEN, Victor Harry Burton; CB; s of Harry Macklen (d 1965), of Brighton, Sussex, and Annie Clara, *née* Hayward (d 1972); *b* 13 July 1919; *Educ* Varndean Secdy Sch Brighton, King's Coll London (BSc); *m* 22 Sept 1950, Scylla Ursula Irene, da of Henry Hope Fellows (d 1924); *Career* Capt Army Operational Res Gp 1943, Capt GHQ Cairo 1943-44, special Operational Res Gp WO and Air Miny 1944, Maj sci advsr staff WO 1944-45, Lt Col GSO1 Sci 2 WO 1945-49; princ sci offr: sci 2 WO 1949, operational res section HQ BAOR 1950-54; dep chief sci offr Chief Sr Advr's Staff MOD 1954-58 (sr princ sci offr 1954-58), head of tech secretariat rector gp UKAEA 1960-64, dep dir tech ops reactor gp UDAEA 1964-67, asst chief sci advsr (Nuclear) MOD 1967-69, dep sec and dep chief advsr Projects and Nuclear MOD 1969-79, special advsr to chm Dynamics Gp BAe 1980-81, personal advsr to chm Br Telecom 1981-87; chm Hartlip Parish Cncl 1983-, pres Sittingbourne and Milton Regis Branch Royal Br Legion; FRSA; *Clubs* Army & Navy; *Style*— Victor Macklen, Esq, CB; Stepp House, The Street, Hartlip, Sittingbourne, Kent ME9 7TH (☎ 0795 842 591)

MACKLEY, (John) Geoffrey; s of George Edward Mackley (d 1961), of College Rd, Ripon, and Lilian, *née* Spetch (d 1985); *b* 12 June 1928; *Educ* Ripon GS, Emmanuel Coll Cambridge (BA); *m* 20 Aug 1955, Jennifer Constance Sharland, da of Gordon Jack Sharland Wood, MBE (d 1984), of Oxton, Notts; 2 s (George b 1956, Jonathan b 1961), 2 da (Fay b 1958, Karen b 1963); *Career* Kenya admin serv 1951-65; incl offr i/c Masai tribe Moran; dist cmmnr Eldoret & Embu dists; dep civil sec Coast Regn Mombasa; regnl chief offr: Housing Corp UK 1965-81, N Manchester and Leeds; first hon sec Didsbury Civic Soc 1966-72; conslt Almhouse Charities in the North 1981-87; *Recreations* beekeeping, forestry, gardening, golf, squash; *Clubs* Hawks Cambridge, Chapel Allerton Tennis & Squash, Bedale & Aloha (Spain) Golf, Bedale Sports; *Style*— Geoffrey Mackley, Esq; Hunton Mill, Bedale, N Yorks DL8 1LU (☎ 0677 50287)

MACKLEY, Ian Warren; CMG (1989); s of Harold William Mackley (d 1973), and Marjorie Rosa Sprawson, *née* Warren; *b* 31 Mar 1942; *Educ* Ardingly Coll; *m* 1, 9 Nov 1968 (m dis 1988), Jill Marion, da of Frank Saunders (d 1955); 3 s (Jonathan b 1970, Nicholas b 1973, Christopher b 1983); m 2, June 1989, Sarah Anne, da of John Churchley; *Career* FO: entered 1960, 3 sec Br Embassy Saigon 1963, asst private sec Min of State 1967; 2 sec 1968, Br High Commn Wellington NZ 1969, 1 sec 1972; FCO 1973; Br High Commn New Delhi 1976; FCO 1980; seconded to ICI 1982; 1984 cnsllr, dep head of UK Delgn to CDE Stockholm; charge d'aFfaires, Br Embassy Kabul Afghanistan; pres Kabul Golf and Country Club; *Recreations* golf; *Style*— Ian Mackley, Esq, CMG; c/o FCO, King Charles St, London SW1A 2AH

MACKLIN, Sir Bruce Roy; OBE (1970); s of Hubert Vivian Macklin, of Adelaide, S Aust (d 1973), and Lillian Mabel, *née* Roy (d 1978); *b* 23 April 1917; *Educ* St Peter's Coll (Adelaide), St Mark's Coll, Adelaide Univ; *m* 1944, Dorothy, da of late George Potts, of Tynemouth, Northumberland; 2 s (David b 1946, Christopher b 1950), 1 da (Annabel b 1954); *Career* aircrew RAAF 1940-45, Flt-Lt, serv UK and SE Asia; former sr ptnr Thomas Sara Macklin & Co CAs, ret 1969; hon consul in SA for Germany 1968-; chm: Homestake Gold of Australia Ltd, GRE Insur Ltd, Standard Chartered Bank Australia Ltd; Dir Boral Ltd, Grundfors Pumps Pty Ltd, Queen ElizabethII Silver Jubilee Tst for Young Australians, Macquarie Textiles Pty Ltd; cncl memb: Australian Opera, Australian Elizabethan Theatre Tst; pres Associated C of C of Commerce of Australia 1967-69, ldr of Australian govt mission to Papua-New Guinea 1971; a fndr Adelaide Festival of Arts (chm bd of govrs 1972-78); Cdr's Cross Order of Merit West Germany 1978; FCA, ACA; kt 1981; *see Debrett's Handbook of Australia and New Zealand for further details*; *Recreations* music, gardening; *Clubs* Adelaide, Naval Military & Air Force Club of SA; *Style*— Sir Bruce Macklin, OBE; Rothe Rd, Echunga, S Australia 5153 (☎ 388 8180); 45 Grenfell St, Adelaide, S Australia 5000 (☎ 237 5300)

MACKLIN, David Drury; CBE (1989); s of (Laurence) Hilary Macklin, OBE (d 1969), of Wendens Ambo, Essex and Alice Dumergue, *née* Tait (d 1977); *b* 1 Sept 1928; *Educ* Felsted, St John's Coll Cambridge; *m* 23 July 1955, Janet, da of Alastair MacNaughton Smallwood (d 1985), of Uppingham; 4 s (Alan Drury, Simon Andre, Alastair Jeremy, Adrian Roger); *Career* asst slr: Coward Chance and Co 1954-56, Warwicks CC 1956-61, Devon CC 1961-67 (asst clerk 1967-69); dep clerk Derbys CC 1969-73; chief exec: Lincs CC 1973-79, Devon CC 1979-88, ret 1988; *Recreations* golf, sailing, bird watching; *Clubs* Hawks, Exeter Golf and Country; *Style*— David Macklin, Esq, CBE; Randolls, Victoria Rd, Topsham, Exeter, Devon EX3 0EU (☎ 0392 873 160)

MACKLIN, Peter Richard (Charlie); s of Lt Col P H Macklin, OBE (d 1976), and Joan Elizabeth, *née* Butcher, of Springfield, Hazlebury Bryan, Sturminster Dorset; *b* 1 April 1946; *Educ* Wellington, Durham Univ (BA); *m* 21 Aug 1971, Pamela Adele, da of A F Plant Jnr, of Washington DC, USA; 3 s (Andrew b 1974, Jonathan b 1977, Christopher b 1981); *Career* slr Clifford Turner 1971-76, ptnr Freshfields 1979-, deptl managing ptnr Property Dept 1986-; Worshipful Co of Slrs; memb Law Soc; *Recreations* family, opera, exploration; *Clubs* Maldon GC; *Style*— Peter Macklin, Esq; 53 Matlock Way, New Malden, Surrey KT3 3AT (☎ 942 5033); Walden House, 17-24 Cathedral Place, London EC4M 7JA (☎ 01 606 6677, fax 01 329 6022, telex 263396)

MACKNESS, Ronald Arthur; s of Albert Mackness (d 1971), of Finchley, and Alice Mary, *née* Skipp (d 1977); *b* 28 June 1921; *Educ* Holloway Sch, LSE (BSc); *m* 5 June 1943, Mary Elizabeth, da of Horace Frank Bird (d 1972), of Akeley; 4 s (Anthony b 1944, Ian b 1950, Andrew b 1953, Robin b 1957), 1 da (Jennifer b 1946); *Career* RAF Flying Offr: S D ME 1942-43, S D Adj Edinburgh VAS 1943-45; dep chief offr: Pig Indust Devpt Authy 1967-69 (de chief 1960-67); dep dir gen Meat and Livestock Cmmn 1967-86; sr agric economist Univ of Cambridge 1946-60; Freeman City of London 1968, Liveryman Worshiipful Co of Butchers 1968; *Recreations* gardening, tennis; *Clubs* Farmers, Royal Agric Soc of England; *Style*— Ronald Mackness, Esq; Wolfrest, Leewood Rd, Dunblane, Perthshire FK15 0DR (☎ 0786 823442)

MACKNIGHT, Dame Ella Annie Noble; DBE (1969); da of late Conway Macknight, of Albury, NSW; *b* 7 August 1904; *Educ* Toorak Coll, Janet Clarke Hall Melbourne Univ (MD); *Career* hon consult gynaecologist and obstetrician Queen Victoria Hosp Melbourne 1935-64 (vice-pres 1965-71, pres 1971-77);; *Style*— Dame Ella Macknight, DBE; 692 Toorak Rd, Malvern, Vic 3144, Australia

McKNIGHT, Ronald; s of Harry McKnight (d 1975), of Cheshire, and Jane, *née* Marsland (d 1977); *b* 7 June 1923; *Educ* Hazel Grove County Boys' Sch, Stockport Tech Coll (C&G, C&J); *m* 19 June 1943, Eileen Hilda, da of Albert Norcott (d 1952), of Hazel Grove, Cheshire; 2 s (Graham Alexander b 1948, Robert Stuart b 1957), 3 da (Judith Denise b 1944, Linda Diane b 1946, Jane Elizabeth b 1956); *Career* RAF Corpl Technician Atlantic and Far East; former md (now chm) Second City Shopfitters Ltd; dir Gram Holdings; pres Fedn of Master Builders Manchester and Dists; chm: Hazel Grove Community Assoc, Hazel Grove Carnival Assoc; Stockport South Police Liaison Panel; memb: NW regnl cncl FMB, fedn rep on the BATJIC Nat Jt Apprentice Trg Cncl; *Recreations* camping and caravaning, folk dancing; *Clubs* life memb RAFA, British Legion, fndr memb SDP; *Style*— Ronald McKnight, Esq; 152 Buxton Road, Hazel Grove, Cheshire (☎ 061 483 3318); Second City Shopfitters Ltd, Maxron House, Green Lane, Romiley, Stockport SK6 3JQ (☎ 061 406 6666, fax 061 406 6144)

MACKRELL, Keith Ashley Victor; s of Henry George Mackrell (d 1967), of Romsey, Hants, and Emily Winifred Jesse Mackrell (d 1972) of Romsey, Hants; *b* 20 Oct 1932; *Educ* Peter Symonds Sch Winchester, LSE (BSc); *m* 20 Feb 1960, June Yvonne, *qv*; 1 s (Ashley b 1961), 3 da (Elliot b 1956, Kim b 1958, Lee b 1961); *Career* RAF Flying Offr 1953-55; dir: Cope Allman Int 1977-86, Shell Int 1977-; memb int advsy cncl East-West Centre Honolulu; MICD 1977, CBIM; *Clubs* Hurlingham; *Style*— Keith Mackrell, Esq; 34 Inner Park Rd, Wimbledon, London SW19 6DD (☎ 01 788 7826); Shell International Petroleum Co Ltd, Shell Centre, London SE1 7NA (☎ 01 934 5226, fax 01 934 4284)

MACKSEY, Maj Kenneth John; MC (1944); s of Henry George Macksey (d 1949), and Alice Lillian, *née* Nightingall (d 1972); *b* 1 July 1923; *Educ* Goudhurst Sch for Boys; *m* 22 June 1946, (Catherine Angela) Joan, da of Thomas Henry Little (d 1967); 1 s (Andrew b 1949), 1 da (Susan b 1947); *Career* enlisted RAC 1941, cmmnd from Sandhurst 141 Regt RAC (The Buffs), transferred RTR 1946, various regtl and staff appts Army Staff Coll 1956, ret maj 1968; mil historian; dep ed Purnell's History of the Second and First World War, conslt Canadian Army with task of writing tactical instructional manuals in form of novels (the 'Clash' series) 1981-; fndr and vice-chm Beaminster Sports Assoc, memb Beaminster Town Cncl 1973-84, vice-chm Dorset Local Cncls Assoc 1983-85; *Books* incl: The Shadow of Vimy Ridge, Afrika Korps, Guinness Book of Tank Facts and Feats, The Guinness History of Land Warfare, Kesselring: the Making of the Luftwaffe, The Tanks 1945-75, History of the Royal Armoured Corps 1914-75, First Clash, The Guinness History of Sea Warfare, The Tank Pioneers, Guderian Panzer-General, Technology in War, Godwin's Saga, Military Errors of World War II, Tank Versus Tank; *Recreations* umpiring ladies hockey; *Style*— Maj Kenneth Macksey, MC; Whatley Mill, Beaminster, Dorset DT8 3EN (☎

0308 862321)

MACKWORTH, Cdr Sir David Arthur Geoffrey; 9 Bt (GB 1776), RN (ret); s of Vice Adm Geoffrey Mackworth, CMG, DSO (d 1952), 5 s of 6 Bt; suc n, Sir Harry Llewellyn Mackworth, 8 Bt, CMG, DSO, 1952; *b* 13 July 1912; *Educ* Farnborough Sch Hants, RNC Dartmouth; *m* 1, 1941 (m dis 1971), Mary Alice, da of late Harry Grylls; 1 s; m 2, 1973, Beryl Joan, former w of late E H Sparkes, da of late Pembroke Henry Cockayn Cross; *Heir* s, Digby John Mackworth; *Career* joined RN 1926, served On HMS Eagle and HMS Suffolk 1939-45, Cdr 1948; naval advsr to dir of guided weapon res and devpt Miny of Supply 1945-59, ret; *Clubs* Royal Naval (Portsmouth), Royal Ocean Racing, Royal Naval Sailing Assoc, Royal Yacht Sqdn; *Style—* Cdr Sir David Mackworth, Bt, RN; 36 Wittering Rd, Hayling Island, Hants (☎ 0705 464085)

MACKWORTH, Digby John; s and h of Sir David Arthur Geoffrey Mackworth, 9 Bt; *b* 2 Nov 1945; *Educ* Wellington; *m* 1971, Antoinette Francesca, da of Henry James McKenna, of Ilford, Essex; *Career* former Lt, AAAC in Malaysia and Vietnam; with Iranian Helicopters Ltd; *Style—* Digby Mackworth Esq; PO Box 2898, Tehran, Iran

MACKWORTH-PRAED, Humphrey Winthrop; MBE (1988); s of Lt Col Cyril Winthrop Mackworth-Praed, OBE (d 1974), of Castletop, Burley, Ringwood, Hants, and Edith Mary Henrietta, *née* Stephenson Clarke; *b* 30 Nov 1919; *Educ* Eton, Trinity Coll Cambridge; *m* 3 June 1947, Penelope, da of Maj Gen RHD Tompson, CB, CMG, DSO (d 1937); 2 S (Nicolas b 1951, Mark b 1955), 3 da (Sheila b 1948, Margaret b 1949, Vanessa b 1959); *Career* WWII, Euro Theatre, RE capt 1942, Maj 1945 (despatches twice); stockjobber London Stock Exchange Francis & Praed 1947-72 (sr ptnr 1966-72), conservation offr Nat Tst Southern regn 1972-84, ecology conslt 1985-; memb: Nat Tst Headley Heath Local Mgmnt Ctee 1953-89 (hon sec 1954-85, chm 1985-89), Surrey Wildlife Tst 1963-88 (chm 1983-86), regnl advisy ctee SE England Conservancy Forestry Commn 1967-85 (chm 1980-85), Bedgebury Pinetum Advsy Ctee 1974- (chm 1985-); FRES 1938; *Recreations* conservation and forestry; *Clubs* Travellers; *Style—* Humphrey Mackworth-Praed, Esq, MBE

MACKWORTH-YOUNG, Lady Eve(lyn); *née* Leslie; da of 20 Earl of Rothes (d 1975), and Beryl, Countess of Rothes (*née* Dugdale); *b* 11 Mar 1929; *m* 1949, (Gerard) William Mackworth Mackworth-Young (d 1984), s of Gerard Mackworth Mackworth-Young (d 1965); 4 da; *Style—* Lady Eve Mackworth-Young; Fisherton Mill, Fisherton de la Mere, Warminster, Wilts BA12 0PZ (☎ 098 56 246)

MACKWORTH-YOUNG, Lady Iona Sina; *née* Lindsay; da of 29 Earl of Crawford and (12 of) Balcarres; *b* 10 August 1957; *Educ* Univ of Edinburgh (MA); *m* 1983, Charles Gerard Mackworth-Young, s of Sir Robin Mackworth-Young, GCVO, *qv*; 1 da (Rose Bettina Natalie b 1987); *Career* art historian; asst curator: Exhibitions Print Room Windsor Castle 1982-84, Drawing Dept Fogg Art Museum 1984-86; *Recreations* paper marbling, bookbinding; *Style—* Lady Iona Mackworth-Young; 18 The Chase, London SW4 0NH

MACKWORTH-YOUNG, Sir Robert (Robin) Christopher; GCVO (1985, KCVO 1975, CVO 1968, MVO 1961); s of Gerard Mackworth-Young, CIE (d 1965; s of Sir (William) Mackworth Young, KCSI, himself 3 s of Sir George Young, 2 Bt, by Susan, da of William Mackworth-Praed and sis of Winthrop MP, the MP and poet); *b* 12 Feb 1920; *Educ* Eton, King's Coll Cambridge; *m* 1953, Helen Rosemarie, da of Werner Charles Rudolf Aue (d 1978), of Menton, France; 1 s (Charles Gerard, m Iona *qv* da of 29 Earl of Crawford); *Career* serv RAFVR as Sqdn Ldr UK, ME, Normandy; For Serv 1948-55, dep librarian Windsor Castle 1955-58, librarian and asst keeper The Queen's Archives 1958-85, librarian emeritus to HM The Queen 1985-; *Recreations* music, skiing, electronics; *Clubs* Roxburghe; *Style—* Sir Robin Mackworth-Young, GCVO; c/o Baring Bros & Co Ltd, 8 Bishopsgate, London EC2

MACLACHLAN, George Styles; s of Samuel Greenlees Rome, of Bentfield, Gullane, E Lothian; assumed surname of Maclachlan 1948; *b* 1921; *Educ* Rugby, Univ of Cambridge; *m* 7 Feb 1948, Marjorie Susan Mary Maclachlan of Maclachlan, Chief of the Clan of Maclachlan *qv*, da of (John) Maclachlan of Maclachlan, 23 of that Ilk (d 1942); 3 s, 3 da; *Career* served 1940-46 with Argyll and Sutherland Highlanders; *Style—* George Maclachlan Esq; Castle Lachlan, Strathlachlan, Argyl (☎ Strachur 244)

McLACHLAN, Gordon; CBE (1967); s of Gordon McLachlan (d 1946), of Leith, and Mary Thomson, *née* Baird; *b* 12 June 1918; *Educ* Leith Acad, Univ of Edinburgh (BComm); *m* 17 Feb 1951, (Monica) Mary, da of Nevill Alfred Malcolm Griffin; 2 da (Katrina Mary (Kirstie) b 19 March 1958, Tessa Anne b 17 Dec 1961); *Career* RNVR 1939-46, Gunnery Specialist 1943-46; apprentice accountant Edinburgh Corpn 1935-39 (accountant 1946-48), NW Met Regn Hosp Bd 1948-53, asst dir (fin) Nuffield Fndn 1953-55, sec accountant ed Nuffield Prov Hosp Tst 1955-86; memb of various official ctees Miny Health; Hon LLD Birmingham 1977, Hon Fell RCGP 1978; memb Inst Med of the Nat Acad of Sciences Washington DC 1974-; FCA 1947; *Recreations* reading, theatre, rugby footbal; *Clubs* Caledonian; *Style—* Gordon McLachlan, Esq, CBE; 95 Ravenscourt Road, London W6 OUJ (☎ 01 748 8211)

McLACHLAN, John James; s of William McLachlan (d 1980), of Birkenhead, and Helen, *née* Duffy; *b* 28 August 1942; *Educ* Rock Ferry HS Cheshire; *m* 24 Sept 1966, Heather Joan, da of George Smith (d 1975), Heswell; 1 s (Alexander b 4 Jan 1975), 1 da (Deborah b 19 Feb 1972); *Career* CA, Poulson & Co Liverpool 1960-66, Norwest Holst Liverpool 1966-67, Martins Bank Barclays Bank Tst Co 1967-74, Br Rail Pension Funds 1974-84, Reed Int plc 1984-88, Utd Friendly Insurance plc 1988-; FCA 1966, AMSIA 1969; *Recreations* squash; *Style—* John McLachlan, Esq; Mountwood, Middlings Rise, Sevenoaks, Kent TN13 2NS (☎ 0732 457865); United Friendly Insurance Plc, 42 Southwark Bridge Rd, London SE1 9HE (☎ 01 928 5644, fax 01 261 9077, telex 8813953)

McLACHLAN, Peter John; OBE (1983); s of Rev Dr H J McLachlan, of Sheffield, and Joan Dorothy Hall (d 1979); gf Dr H McLachlan historian, author of many historical books, prof of Hellenistic Greek at Manchester Univ; *b* 21 Dec 1936; *Educ* Magdalen Coll Sch, Queen's Coll Oxford (MA); *m* 1965, Gillian Mavis, da of John Christopher Lowe (d 1985); 2 da (Heather b 1967, Fiona b 1969); *Career* admin trainee Miny of Fin NICS 1959-62, admin Nat Youth Orchestra of GB 1962-65 and 1966-70, pa to chm of IPC 1965-66, Cons Res Dept 1970-72, exec dir Watney & Powell Ltd 1972-73, unionist memb S Antrim in NI Assembly 1973-75, gen mangr S H Watterson Engrg 1975-77, jt md Ulster Metalspinners Ltd 1976-77, projects mangr Peace by Peace Ltd 1977-79, sec Peace People Charitable Tst 1977-79, chm Community of The Peace People 1978-80; fndr chm: NI Fedn of Housing Assocs 1976-78, Belfast Improved Houses Ltd 1975-81 (ctee memb 1975-), ctee memb Lisnagarvey Housing Assoc Ltd 1977-; memb: The Corrymeela Community 1975-, admin cncl Royal Jubilee Tsts 1975-82, NI Projects Tst 1977-87; chm NI Peace Forum 1980-82; vice-chm: NI Hospice Ltd 1981-, Gulbenkian Advsy Ctee on Community Work 1978-81; gen sec Belfast Voluntary Welfare Soc 1980-86, dir Bryson House 1986-, cncl memb Children's Community Holidays 1982-85, exec ctee memb NI Children's Holiday Scheme 1982-85, chm Dismas House 1983-87 (ctee memb 1983-), presenter BBC Street Corner (Community Action programme) 1983-86; memb: Min's Advsy Ctee on Community Work 1982-84, Min's Advsy Ctee on Personal Social Services 1984-88, exec ctee NI Chest, Heart & Stroke Assoc 1982-85, Bd of Visitors HM Prison Maghaberry 1986 (dep-chm 1987-, chm 1989-); tstee Buttle Tst 1987-, Anchor Tst 1987-; Hon Sec NI Fedn Victims' Support Scheme 1983; vice-chm Victim Support UK 1988- (cncl memb 1987-), hon tres Lisburn VSS 1986-, fndr ctee memb NI Conflict and Mediation Assoc 1986-; UK Eisenhower fell 1986; *Recreations* piano playing, singing, mountain walking, conservation; *Style—* Peter McLachlan, Esq, OBE; 82 Moira Road, Hillsborough, Co Down, N Ireland BT26 6DY (☎ 0846 683497); Bryson House, 28 Bedford St, Belfast BT2 7FE (☎ 0232 325835)

MACLACHLAN OF MACLACHLAN, Madam; Marjorie Susan Mary; Lady of the Barony (territorial) Strathlachlan, Chief of the Clan of Maclachlan; da of John Maclachlan of Maclachlan, 23 of that Ilk (d 1942); *b* 1920; *Educ* Oxenfoord Castle, Abbots Hill; *m* 1948, George Styles Rome, *qv* (assumed surnmane of Maclachlan); 3 s, 3 da; *Heir* s, Euan John Rome-Maclachlan, yr of Maclachlan b 1949; estate mangr and farmer on Maclachlan estate; *Style—* Madam Maclachlan of Maclachlan; Castle Lachlan, Strathlachlan, Strachur, Cairndow, Argyll

MACLAGAN, Michael; CVO (1988); s of Sir Eric Maclagan, KCVO, CBE, former dir V&A Museum (himself s of William Dalrymple Maclagan, former Archbishop of York, and his w Augusta, da of 6 Viscount Barrington) and Helen Elizabeth, in her turn da of Hon Frederick Lascelles (2 s of 4 Earl of Harewood); *b* 14 April 1914; *Educ* Winchester, Christ Church Oxford (MA); *m* 1, 7 Sept 1939 (m dis 1946), Brenda, da of late Lt-Col F D Alexander, CBE, of Red House, Whissendine, Rutland ; 1 s (David b 1940); m 2, Jean Elizabeth Brooksbank, o child of Col W B Garnett, DSO, of Clogher, Co Tyrone, NI; 1 s (Andrew Story b 1958, d 1984), 2 da (Ianthe Mary b 1952, Helen Margaret b 1954); *Career* joined TA (Oxford Univ OTC) 1937, WWII served 16/5 Lancers, Maj GSO II WO; Univ of Oxford: lectr Christ Church 1937-39, fell Trinity Coll 1939-81 (emeritus fell 1981-), sr proctor 1954-55, fell Winchester Coll 1975-89; visiting prof Univ of S Carolina 1974, tstee Oxford Union and former sr librarian; memb: Oxford City Cncl 1949-74, Oxford Diocesan Advsy Ctee 1948- (chm 1961-85); Lord Mayor of Oxford 1970-71; memb Worshipful Co of Scriveners (Master1988-89); OStJ 1952; FSG, FHS, FSA, FRHistS; Slains Pursuivant 1948-70, Portcullis Pursuivant 1970-80, Richmond Herald of Arms 1980-89; *Books* Richard de Bury: Philobiblon (ed, 1960), Clemency Canning (Wheatley Gold Medal, 1962), City of Constantinople (1968), Lines of Succession (with Jiři Louda, 1981); *Recreations* real tennis, wine, walking; *Clubs* Pratt's, Cavalry & Guards, City Livery; *Style—* Michael Maclagan, Esq, CVO; 20 Northmoor Rd, Oxford, OX2 6UR (☎ 0865 58536)

MCLAGGAN, Murray Adams; JP, DL (Mid Glamorgan 1982); s of Sir John Douglas McLaggan, KCVO, (d 1968), of Daws Wood, Frensham, Surrey, and Elsa Violet, *née* Adams (d 1987); *b* 29 Sept 1929; *Educ* Winchester, New Coll Oxford (MA); *m* 1959, Jennifer Ann, da of Robert Iltyd Nicholl, of Merthyr Mawr Ho, Bridgend; 2 s, 1 da; *Recreations* work; *Style—* Murray McLaggan, Esq, JP, DL; Merthyr Mawr House, Bridgend, Mid Glamorgan (☎ 0656 652038)

McLAREN, Hon (Henry) Charles; s and h of 3 Baron Aberconway, *qv*; *b* 26 May 1948; *Educ* Eton, Sussex Univ (BA); *m* 1981, Sally Ann, yr da of late Capt Charles Nugent Lentaigne, RN, of Hawkley Place, Hawkley, Liss, Hants, and formerly w of Philip Charles Bidwell; 1 s (Charles Stephen b 27 Dec 1984), 1 da (Emily b 1982), and 1 step s (Alex b 1975); *Style—* The Hon Charles McLaren; Sailing Barge Repertor, St Mary's Churchyard, London SW11

McLAREN, Hon Christopher Melville; s of 2 Baron Aberconway, CBE (d 1953); *b* 1934; *Educ* Eton, King's Coll Cambridge; *m* 1973, Jane Elizabeth, da of James Barrie; 1 s (Robert Melville b 1974), 1 da (Lara Jane Christabel b 1976); *Career* business conslt; *Recreations* gardening, walking; *Style—* The Hon Christopher McLaren; 31 Upper Addison Gdns, London W14 8AJ

MACLAREN, Deanna; *née* Bullimore; da of Leonard Albert William Bullimore (d 1977), and Dorothy Maude, *née* Austrin; *b* 4 Feb 1944; *Educ* Wallington Co GS; *m* 1, 1965, Patrick Alexander Moffat Maclaren; m 2, 1974, Michael Dennis Godfrey; m 3, 1987, Nicholas Kent; *Career* author: journalist and broadcaster; contrib to: The Guardian, Woman, Ideal Home, Family Circle; *Books* Little Blue Room (1974), The First of all Pleasures (1975), Dagger in the Sleeve (1979), Your Loving Mother (1983); non-fiction: The Single File, How to Live Alone, and Like It; *Recreations* tennis, opera, gardening; *Clubs* Network; *Style—* Ms Deanna Maclaren; 22 Cromwell Ave, Highgate, London N6 5HL

MACLAREN, Derek Anthony Ewen; s of late John Ewen Maclaren; *b* 19 Jan 1925; *Educ* Cranbrook, Sydney Univ; *m* 1951, Pamela Ann, da of Harold Miller; 2 s, 1 da; *Career* dir PA Int Consulting Services Ltd 1971, chm PA Computers and Telecommunications 1976-83, dir PA Holdings Ltd 1982-; memb: Computing Services Assoc Cncl 1975-76, CSERB 1976-78; FIMC; *Recreations* history, Tudor architecture, skiing; *Clubs* Hurlingham; *Style—* Derek Maclaren Esq; The Manor House, West Coker, Somerset (☎ (093 586) 2646); 13 Wetherby Gdns, London SW5 0JW (☎ 01 373 8330); PA Holdings Ltd, Rutland House, Rutland Gdns, Knightsbridge, London SW7 1BY (☎ 01 584 7000, telex 27874)

McLAREN, (George William) Derek; s of Thomas George McLaren, of Eldon Lee, Ormiston Gardens, Melrose, Scotland, and Davina Siddis (d 1982); *b* 21 Nov 1934; *Educ* Galashiels Acad; *m* 1, 7 June 1958 (m dis 1987), Marjory Watt, da of Robert McInnes (d 1981), of Edinburgh; 2 s (Roger b 1960, Angus b 1962), 1 da (Fay (Mrs Thom) b 1964); m 2, 12 Aug 1988, Waltraud, da of Fritz Loges (d 1975), of W Germany; *Career* Nat Serv RAMC 1953-55; mangr Theodore Hamblin Ltd 1963-68; md Silhouette Fashion Frames Ltd 1975-; chm: Optical Frame Importers Assoc 1980;, Optical Info Cncl 1988-; cncl memb: Fedn of Mfrg Opticians, Assoc of Br Dispensing Opticians, involved with the Fight for Sight Charity; Freeman City of London 1980, Liveryman Worshipful Co of Spectacle Makers 1982; FBDO 1956, FInstD 1981, MBIM 1980; *Recreations* gardening, antique restoring, reading; *Clubs* City Livery; *Style—* Derek McLaren, Esq; 25 Dartmouth Park Ave, London NW5 1JL (☎ 01 485 2467); Silhouette Fashion Frames Ltd, 70-72 Old St, London EC1V 9AN (☎ 01 251 3661, fax 01 608 2239, telex 24795)

MACLAREN, Lady Edith Huddleston Griffiths; da of Countess of Loudon (d 1960); co-heiress to the Baronies of Botreaux, Stanley and Hastings; *b* 1925; *m* 1947, Maj David Kenneth Maclaren; 2 s; *Style*— Lady Edith Mclaren

MacLAREN, Sir Hamish Duncan; KBE (1951), CB (1946), DFC and bar (1918); s of Rev Peter MacLaren (d 1952), and Constance Hamilton (d 1945); *b* 7 April 1898; *Educ* Fordyce Acad, Edinburgh Univ (BSc); *m* 1926, Lorna Cecily, da of Dr Reginald Bluett, MC (d 1943); 1 s, 1 da; *Career* serv WWI Flt Lt RAF; electrical engr; dir of electrical engrg The Admiralty 1945-60 (asst dir 1940-45); pt/t memb London Electricity Bd 1960-68; Croix de Guerre avec Palme 1918; *Recreations* music, reading; *Style*— Sir Hamish MacLaren, KBE, CB, DFC and bar; 104 Heath Rd, Petersfield, Hants (☎ 0730 4562)

McLAREN, Ian Francis; OBE (1959); s of Alexander Morrison McLaren (d 1951); *b* 30 Mar 1912; *Educ* Melbourne Univ; *m* 1941, Eileen Adele, da of John Henry Porter (d 1971); 3 s, 1 da; *Career* Lt RANVR (New Guinea and Philippines); chartered accountant 1945-; MP Victorian Parliament 1945-47 and 1965-79, dep speaker 1964-69; *Style*— Ian McLaren, Esq, OBE; 237 Waverley Rd, East Malvern, Victoria 3145, Australia (☎ 01 211 6897)

McLAREN, Hon Michael Duncan; s of 3 Baron Aberconway, *qv*; *b* 29 Nov 1958; *Educ* Eton, Christ's Coll Cambridge; *m* 1985, Caroline Jane, er da of Air Chief Marshal Sir (William) John Stacey, KCB, CBE (d 1981), of Winchester, and his w, Frances Jean, da of Prof Lawrence William Faucett, of USA; 1 s (Angus John Melville b 1987); *Career* barr Middle Temple; *Recreations* travel, music, gardening; *Style*— The Hon Michael McLaren; 1 Maids of Honour Row, The Green, Richmond, Surrey (☎ 01 940 5968)

McLAREN, Lady Rose Mary Primrose Paget; *née* Paget; da of 6 Marquess of Anglesey, GCVO (d 1947); *b* 1919; *m* 1940, Hon John Francis McLaren (d 1953); 2 da (Victoria (Mrs Jonathan Taylor) b 1945, Harriet (Mrs Hugh Geddes) b 1949); *Style*— Lady Rose McLaren; Old Bodnod, Eglwysbach, Colwyn Bay, North Wales LL28 5RF

McLAREN, Hon Mrs; (Rosemary Jean); da of 2 Baron Kinross, KC; *b* 1910; *m* 1, 1934 (m dis 1958), Alec M Mitchell; 1 s, 3 da; m 2, 1958, Robert Monteath McLaren (d 1969); *Style*— The Hon Mrs McLaren; 7B Gloucester Sq, Edinburgh EH3

MacLAREN OF MacLAREN, The; Donald MacLaren of MacLaren and Achleskine; s of late Donald MacLaren of MacLaren; suc his father 1966 as Chief of Clan Labhran; *b* 1954; *m* 1978, Maida Jane, da of late Robert Paton Aitchison, of Markinch, Fife; 2 s (Donald b 1980, Florian Robert b 1981); 1 da (Iona Margaret b 1987); *Heir* s, Donald MacLaren of Maclaren, yr.; *Style*— The MacLaren of MacLaren

MACLAURIN, Sir Ian Carter; s of Arthur George Maclaurin, and Florence Eveline, *née* Bott (d 1970); *b* 20 August 1937; *Educ* Malvern; *m* 25 March 1960, Ann Margaret, da of Edgar Ralph Collar (d 1968); 1 s (Neil Ralph Charter b 1966), 2 da (Fiona Margaret (Mrs Archer) b 1962, Gillian b 1964); *Career* Nat Serv RAF Fighter Cmd 1956-58; Tesco plc: first co trainee 1959, memb bd 1970, md 1973, chm 1985; non exec dir: Enterprise Oil plc 1984, Guiness plc 1986; memb Save The Children Fund commerce and indust ctee; Freeman city of London 1981, memb Worshipful Co of Carmen 1982; D Phil (Stirling) 1987; MInstDirs 1984, FRSA 1986, FInstM 1987; Kt 1989; *Recreations* golf; *Clubs* MCC, RAC; *Style*— Sir Ian MacLaurin; Tesco PLC, Tesco Housse, Delamare Road, Cheshunt, Waltham Cross, Herts EN8 9SL (☎ 0992 32222, fax 0992 30794)

McLAY, Alastair John; s of David Bird McLay (d 1964), of Dundee and Troon, Ayrshire, and Nora Oakeshott, *née* Henderson; *b* 7 May 1928; *Educ* Fettes Coll, St Andrew's Univ (BSc); *m* 19 March 1954, Augusta Michie Neilson (Lolo), da of James Neilson (d 1948), of Malaysia, and Gullane, E Lothian; 1 s (James b 1956); *Career* Nat Serv RAF 1951-53, Flying Offr 54 Sqdn; consulting engr; ptnr Clarke Nicholls & Marcel London 1966-81, st ptnr A J McLay & Ptnrs Glasgow 1981-; deacon convener Trdes House of Glasgow 1979-80; Freeman City of Glasgow 1949, memb Incorpn of Skinners Glasgow (deacon 1973); CEng 1955, FICE 1977, MConsE 1977; *Recreations* golf, sailing; *Clubs* Glasgow GC, Roycl and Ancient GC, Clyde Cruising; *Style*— Alastair McLay, Esq; 7 Pk Circus Pl, Glasgow G3 6AH (☎ 041 332 1984, fax 041 332 8614)

MACLAY, Hon Angus Grenfell; s of 2 Baron Maclay, KBE (d 1969); *b* 11 August 1945; *Educ* Winchester, RAC Cirencester; *m* 1970, Hon (Elizabeth) Victoria Baillie (d 1986), da of 3 Baron Burton; 2 s (Robert, Fergus), 1 da (Sarah); *Recreations* shooting, skiing; *Style*— The Hon Angus Maclay; Gledswood, Melrose, Roxburghshire (☎ 089682 2234)

MACLAY, Hon David Milton; 2 s of 2 Baron Maclay, KBE (d 1969), and Nancy Margaret, *née* Greig; *b* 21 Mar 1944; *Educ* Winchester; *m* 29 Nov 1968, Valerie, da of late Lt-Cdr J P Fyfe, of Kinkell, St Andrews, Fife; 1 s; *Style*— The Hon David Maclay; 12 Langton St, London SW10

MACLAY, Hon Mrs Walter; Dorothy; da of late William Lennox, WS, of Edinburgh, and Georgina Mary Lennox (d 1947); *b* 21 Oct 1901; *Educ* Harrogate Coll; *m* 26 April 1928, Hon Walter Symington Maclay, CB, OBE, MD (d 1964), 4 s of 1 Baron Maclay (d 1951); 3 s, 1 da; *Style*— The Hon Mrs Walter Maclay; 40 Kensington Sq, London W8 5HP

MACLAY, 3 Baron (UK 1922); Sir Joseph Paton Maclay; 3 Bt (UK 1914); s of 2 Baron Maclay, KBE (d 1969); *b* 11 April 1942; *Educ* Winchester; *m* 1976, Elizabeth, da of George Buchanan, of Pokataroo, NSW; 2 s, 1 da; *Heir* s, Hon Joseph Paton Maclay b 6 March 1977; *Career* md: Denholm Maclay Ltd 1970-83, Triport Ferries Mgmnt 1975-83, Denholm Maclay Offshore Ltd 1976-83; dir: Milton Shipping 1970-83, Br Steamship Short Trades Assoc 1976-83, N of England Protection & Indemnity Assoc 1978-83; md Milton Timber Servs Ltd 1984-, chm Scottish branch Br Sailors Soc 1979-81, vice-chm Glasgow Shipowners & Shipbrokers Benevolent Assoc 1982-83; DL Renfrewshire 1986-; *Recreations* gardening, fishing; *Clubs* Western; *Style*— The Rt Hon Lord Maclay; Duchal, Kilmacolm, Renfrewshire (☎ 050 587 2255)

MACLAY, Nancy, Baroness; Nancy Margaret; da of Robert C Greig, of Hall of Caldwell, Uplawmoor, Renfrewshire; *m* 1936, 2 Baron Maclay, KBE (d 1969); 3 s, 2 da; *Style*— The Rt Hon Nancy, Lady Maclay; Milton, Kilmacolm, Renfrewshire (☎ 050 587 2131)

MACLEAN, Charles Andrew Bourke; s of Sir Robert Maclean, KBE, DL, *qv*, of South Branchal Farm, Bridge of Weir, Renfrewshire, and Vivienne Beville Bourke; *b* 31 Jan 1945; *Educ* Harrow, Trinity Coll Dublin (MA); *m* 1972, Moya Clare, da of Cdr T A Pack-Beresford, MBE, RN, of The Tansey, Baily, Co Dublin, Eire (d 1981); 1 s (Robert b 1979), 2 da (Tara b 1975, Georgina b 1976); *Career* dep chm and chief exec Stoddard Hldings plc 1982- (previously md A F Stoddard & Co Ltd); *Recreations* forestry, shooting, skiing; *Clubs* Western (Glasgow); *Style*— Charles Maclean Esq; Carruth, Bridge of Weir, Renfrewshire PA11 3SG (☎ 0505 87 2189); Stoddard Holdings plc, Glenpatrick Works, Elderslie, Renfrewshire PA5 9UJ (☎ 0505 21121, telex 77 237)

MACLEAN, Baron (Life Peer UK 1971); Sir Charles Hector Fitzroy Maclean; 11 Bt (NS 1631), KT (1969), GCVO (1971), KBE (1967), PC 1971), JP (Argyll 1955); 27 Chief of Clan Maclean; 2 but only surviving s of Maj Hector Fitzroy Maclean, Scots Gds, himself eldest s of Sir Fitzroy Maclean, 10 Bt, KCB, JP, DL; *b* 5 May 1916; *Educ* Canford; *m* 7 June 1941, Elizabeth, er da of Francis Thomas (Frank) Mann, of Milton Lilbourne, Wilts; 1 s, 1 da; *Heir* (to Btcy only) s, Hon Lachlan Maclean; *Career* served WWII Maj Scots Gds; lord chamberlain of HM Household 1971-85, lord high cmmr to Gen Assembly of Church of Scotland 1985-, perm lord in waiting, chief steward Hampton Court 1985-, chllr Royal Victorian Order 1971-; Lord-Lieut Argyll and Bute 1954-, lt Royal Co Archers (Queen's Body Gd for Scotland); pres Argyll T&AFA; HM high cmmr to Gen Assembly of Church of Scotland 1985-; memb: Cncl RZS, RASE; former chief scout Cwlth; patron of various charities; author of children's books; Royal Victorian Chain 1984; *Clubs* Puffin's, Pratt's, Cavalry and Guards', Royal Highland YC (Oban), Royal Commonwealth Soc (memb Cncl); *Style*— The Rt Hon The Lord Maclean, KT, GCVO; Duart Castle, Isle of Mull (☎ Craignure 309); Hampton Court Place, East Molesey KT8 9AR (☎ 01 943 4400)

McLEAN, Colin; CMG (1977), MBE (1964); s of late Dr L G McLean; *b* 10 August 1930; *Educ* Fettes, St Catharine's Coll Cambridge; *m* 1953, Huguette Leclerc; 1 s, 1 da; *Career* joined Diplomatic Serv 1964, cnsllr Oslo 1977-81, head Trade Rels and Export Dept FCO 1981-83, high cmmr Uganda 1983-86, UK Permanent Rep to Council of Europe (with rank of Ambassador) 1986-; *Style*— Colin McLean, Esq, CMG, MBE; c/o FCO, King Charles St, London SW1

MCLEAN, David Colin Hugh; s of Colin McLean, CBE (d 1972), of Humbletoft, Dereham, Norfolk, and Elizabeth Penelope, *née* Marchant (d 1976); *b* 24 May 1922; *Educ* Harrow, Trinity Coll Cambridge (MA); *m* 3 Nov 1962, Deborah, da of Lt Col WV Packe, DSO (d 1947), of Elmfield, Bromley Common, Kent; 2 s (Alan b 1963, Hugh b 1965); *Career* REME 1943-47, DADME serv Malaya Cmd ret as Maj; engr; res engr Sir Alexander Gibb & Ptnrs 1947-53, tech dir Hunting Tech Servs 1953-58, dir Lamson Industs Ltd 1951-77; chm NE River Purification Bd 1986- (memb 1982-), memb Don Dist Salmon Fishery Bd 1978- (former chm), cncllr Grampian Regnl Cncl 1978-; CEng, MICE 1951; *Recreations* shooting, fishing, photography, ornithology; *Style*— David McLean, Esq; Littlewood Park, Alford, Aberdeenshire AB3 8PR

MACLEAN, David John; MP (C) Penrith and The Border 1983-; s of John Maclean, and Catherine Jane Maclean; *b* 16 May 1953; *Educ* Fortrose Acad, Univ of Aberdeen (LLB); *m* 1977, Jay(alaluna) Dawn Gallacher; *Career* Lt 2/51 Highland Volunteers 1976-79; *Style*— David Maclean Esq, MP; House of Commons, London SW1A OAA (☎ 01 219 6494)

MACLEAN, Donald Buchanan; s of Donald Maclean, MBE (d 1949); *b* 3 Feb 1924; *Educ* Queen's Park Glasgow; *m* 1954, Isabella Forrester, da of Sir John Henderson; *Career* CA, fin dir HD Symons & Co Ltd 1966-1986; *Recreations* golf, fishing, bridge, reading; *Clubs* Inst of Dirs; *Style*— Donald Maclean Esq; Dolphin Den, Den Close, Beckenham, Kent (☎ 01 650 8428)

MACLEAN, Sir Donald Og Grant; s of Maj Donald Og Maclean, OBE, MC (d 1974), of Dalnabo, Crieff, and Margaret, *née* Smith (d 1972); *b* 13 August 1930; *Educ* Morrison's Acad Crieff, Heriot-Watt Univ; *m* 11 Jan 1958, Muriel (d 1984), da of Charles Giles (d 1972), of Newcastle-upon-Tyne; 1 s (Donald b 1962), 1 da (Fiona b 1960); *Career* Nat Serv RAMC 1952-54; ophthalmic optician (optometrist) practising in Edinburgh, Newcastle-upon-Tyne, Perth and Ayr 1963-; chm Ayr Constituency Assoc (C) 1971-75, chm W of Scotland area cncl SCUA 1977-79, pres SCUA 1983-85, dep chm Scottish Cons Pty 1985-; elder of Church of Scotland; former chm: SW Scotland AOP, Local Optical Ctee; former pres W Highland Steamer Club; former memb Local Tport Users Consultative Ctee; Freeman: City of London 1987, Worshipful Co of Spectacle Makers 1986; FBOA, FBCO; kt 1985; *Recreations* photography, reading; *Clubs* Royal Scottish Automobile (Glasgow); *Style*— Sir Donald Maclean; Dun Beag II, Woodend Rd, Alloway, Ayrshire; J Rusk (Opticians), 59 Newmarket St, Ayr KA7 1LL (☎ 0292 262530)

McLEAN, Sir Francis Charles; CBE (1953, MBE 1945); s of Michael McLean; *b* 6 Nov 1904; *Educ* Birmingham Univ (BSc); *m* 1930, Dorothy Blackstaffe; 1 s, 1 da; *Career* chief engr Psychological Warfare Div SHAEF 1943-45; dir of engrg BBC 1963-68 (dep chief engr 1952-60, dep dir 1960-63); chm BSI Telecommunications Industry Standards Ctee 1960-77; dir Oxley Dvpts 1961-; kt 1967; *Style*— Sir Francis McLean, CBE; Greenwood Copse, Tile Barn, Woolton Hill, Newbury, Berks (☎ 0635 253583)

MACLEAN, Gordon Hector; s of Lt-Col Norman George Maclean (d 1975), ex cmmr of Colonial Police, and Katherine Emily, *née* Scott (d 1977); *b* 30 June 1932; *Educ* Bedford Sch, Univ of the Witwatersrand and Johannesburg (BArch 1955); *m* 5 Sept 1959, Heather (d 1984), da of Donald Graham (d 1983); 2 s (Angus b 1960, Donald b 1962), 1 da (Jane b 1965); *Career* architect; sr ptnr Murray Ward & Ptnrs (chartered architects); ARIBA 1957, FRIBA 1970; *Recreations* music, philately; *Style*— Gordon Maclean, Esq; 162 High Rd, Bushey Heath, Hertfordshire (☎ 01 950 3745); Murray Ward & Partners, 1 Heddon St, Piccadilly, London W1 (☎ 01 439 9774, telex 21530, fax 494 3250)

MACLEAN, Vice Adm Sir Hector Charles Donald; KBE (1962), CB (1960), DSC (1941), JP (Norfolk 1963), DL (Norfolk 1977); s of Capt Donald Charles Hugh Maclean, DSO, Royal Scots (d 1909), and Gwendoline Katherine Leonora, *née* Hope (ggggda of 1 Earl of Hopetoun); *b* 7 August 1908; *Educ* Wellington; *m* 1933, Opre, da of late Capt William Geoffrey Vyvyan, Royal Welsh Fus; 1 s, 2 da; *Career* joined RN 1926, served WWII, Rear Adm 1958, Vice Adm 1960, ret 1962; *Style*— Vice Adm Sir Hector Maclean, KBE, CB, DSC, JP, DL; Deepdale Old Rectory, Brancaster Staithe, King's Lynn, Norfolk (☎ 048 521 210281)

MACLEAN, Iain Donald; s of Capt Donald Maclean, of Toke Warren, Warren Way, Folkestone, Kent, and Leokadia Osko; *b* 2 August 1949; *Educ* Milton Sch, Goldsmith's Coll London; *m* 16 Aug 1975, Briony Susan Aldersey, da of Cdr Noel Hugh Aldersey Taylor, RN (ret), of Locks Coppice, Rowlands Castle; 2 s (Andrew James Donald b 1977, James Hugh Alexander b 1983), 1 da (Iona Felicity Odette b 1988); *Career* controller J Walter Thompson 1970-74, sculptor 1974-75, copywriter Harrison Cowley

Advertising 1975-76, mktg mangr The Franklin Mint 1977-78, mktg dir Spink 1978-82, assoc creative dir Ogilvy Mather Direct 1983-85, fndr Dewar Coyle Maclean (creative dir) 1986-; 12 awards in UK, Europe and USA for creativity; memb: Hartfield and Withyhall Hort Soc, Hartfield Cons Assoc, NSPCC, Coleman's Hatch Church; *Recreations* advertising, writing, sculpture, painting, gardening; *Clubs* The Fifty; *Style—* Iain Maclean, Esq; Hill House, Upper Hartfield, E Sussex (☎ 0342 82 2429); 25 Sherton St, London WC2; DCM, 197 Wardour St, London W1 (☎ 01 379 0170, fax 01 240 9805)

McLEAN, Ivor Drury; s of late George, and late Gwendoline McLean; *b* 4 August 1921; *Educ* St Paul's; *m* 1964, Jacqueline Ann, *née* Binns; 1 s; *Career* Maj Middx Regt 1940-46, serv Europe and Mid E; dir Mallinson-Denny Ltd 1975-85, ret 1985; memb Kingston and Malden Cons Assoc Coombe Ward Ctee; FCA; *Recreations* golf, gardening, travel, local politics; *Clubs* Coombe Wood Golf; *Style—* Ivor McLean, Esq; Harewood Cottage, Kingston Vale, London SW15 3RN;

MacLEAN, Hon J Angus; DFC, CD, PC (1957); s of late George, and Sarah Maclean; *b* 15 May 1914; *Educ* Summerside HS, Univ of BC, Mount Allison Univ (BSc); *m* 1952, Gwendolyn Esther Burwash; 2 s (Allan, Robert), 2 da (Jean, Mary); *Career* serv RAF 1939-47, Wing Cdr 1943; farmer; MP (Fed Govt Canada) 1951-76, min of Fisheries 1957-63; ldr of Progressive Cons Pty for PEI 1976-81; former memb: PEI Energy Corpn, sr Advsy Bd, Maritime Provinces Educn Fndn, United Servs Offrs Club Charlottetown, RCAF Assoc; former vice-pres CPA Assoc; MLA for PEI 1979-81, ret; OStJ 1982; Hon LLD; Mt Allison Univ (1958) and WPEI (1985); *Recreations* birdwatching, photography; *Clubs* Utd Servs Offrs'; *Style—* The Hon J Angus MacLean, PC, DFC, CD; Lewes, RR3, Belle River, Prince Edward Island COA 1BO, Canada (☎ 902 962 2235)

McLEAN, John Alexander Lowry; QC (1974); s of John McLean (d 1969), and Phoebe Jane Bowditch (d 1975); *b* 21 Feb 1921; *Educ* Methodist Coll, Queen's Univ Belfast (LLB); *m* 1950, Diana Elisabeth (d 1986), da of S B Boyd Campbell, MC (d 1971); 1 s (Simon), 2 da (Jane, Sara); *Career* served WWII Intelligence Corps 1943-47, NW Europe 1944-45, Rhine Army 1945-47; barr NI 1949, asst sec NI Supreme Ct and private sec to LCJ of NI 1956-, perm sec NI Supreme Ct (princ sec to LCJ 1979-), clerk of the Crown for NI 1966, under tres Inn of Ct of NI 1966; *Clubs* Royal Cwlth Soc; *Style—* John A L McLean, Esq, QC; 24 Marlborough Park South, Belfast BT9 6HR (☎ 0232 667330); Lifeboat Cottage, Cloughey, Co Down BT22 1HS (☎ 024 77 71313); Royal Cts of Justice, Belfast (☎ 0232 235111)

MACLEAN, Maj John Kenneth Charles; s of Alan Murdoch Maclean (d 1981), and Muriel Jeanette, *née* McAdam; *b* 11 Jan 1945; *Educ* Eastbourne Coll, Univ of Leicester; *m* 26 July 1980, Diana Clare, da of Maj Gen B Aubrey Coad (d 1980), of Nurstead House, Devizes; 2 s (Christopher Charles Aubrey b 1982, William Alan Hamilton b 1986); *Career* cmmnd RCS 1966, Troop Cdr Germany, Singapore 1966-71 cmd Royal Signals Motor Cycle Display Team 1972-73, Regtl cnm Staff Appt 1973-78, cmd 63 SAS Signal Sqdn V 1979-82; MOD appt 1982-84; dir of mktg - Unisys Corpn; *Books* Military Computer Market Europe (1987); *Recreations* tennis, sailing; *Clubs* Royal Ocean Racing; *Style—* Maj John Maclean; Georgian House, Eastbridge, Crondall, Surrey (☎ 0252 850 699); Unisys Europe Africa Division, Bakers Ct, Bakers Rd, Uxbridge MX (☎ 0895 37 137)

MACLEAN, John Robert; DL (Moray 1987); s of Cdr Hugh Chapman Maclean, JP, DL, RN (d 1973), of Westfield House, and Sylvia Louise Radford, *née* Boase; *b* 24 May 1951; *Educ* Blairmore Sch, Milton Abbey Sch; *m* 12 Jan 1979, da of Evelyn Hubert-Powell (d 1985), of Mayfield, Sussex; 1 s (Hugh Charles b 8 May 1984), 2 da (Charlotte Louise b 19 Jan 1982, Anastasia Mary b 18 Sept 1986); *Career* Mons Offr Cadet Sch 1971, cmmnd Queens Own Highlanders, 1971-73 serving Germany, NI and Canada, trg offr Scottish Int Depot Edinburgh 1973-75; 1975-77: Germany, Belize, UK, NI; ret Lt 1977; chm Elgin branch Earl Haig Fund; ctee memb: Highland branch Scottish Landowners Fedn, Moray War Veterans; memb of the Royal Co of Archers (Queens Bodyguard of Scotland); *Recreations* shooting, tennis, golf, farming; *Clubs* Army and Navy; *Style—* John Maclean, Esq; Westfield House, nr Elgin, Moray, Highlands (☎ 0343 7308)

MACLEAN, Maj Hon Lachlan Hector Charles; s and h (to Btcy only) of Baron Maclean, KT, GCVO, KBE (Life Peer); *b* 25 August 1942; *Educ* Eton; *m* 1966, Mary Helen, da of William Gordon Gordon, of Lude, Blair Atholl, Perthshire; 2 s, 2 da (1 decd); *Career* Maj Scots Gds; *Style—* Maj the Hon Lachlan Maclean; Arngask House, Glenfarg, Perthshire

MACLEAN, Lowry Druce; s of Ian Albert Druce Maclean, and Diana Futvoye, *née* Mardsen-Smedley (d 1979); *b* 22 July 1939; *Educ* Eton, Pembroke Coll Cambridge (MA); *m* 1966, Anne Francis, da of Henry Crawford (d 1967), of USA; 2 s, 1 da; *Career* dir: Karastan Inc 1970-72, John Crossley & Sons Ltd 1972-79, Wesleyan & Gen Assur Soc 1987-; chm Tomkinsons plc 1986- (gp chief exec 1979-); *Clubs* Lansdowne House; *Style—* Lowry Maclean, Esq; The Pound, Old Colwall, Gt Malvern, Worcs (☎ 0684 40426); Tomkinsons plc, PO Box 11, Duke Place, Kidderminster, Worcs (☎ 0562 745 771)

McLEAN, (James) Norman; s of Donald Cameron McLean, JP, of Ayr, and Mary Williamson, *née* Mutch; *b* 30 Nov 1939; *Educ* Ayr Acad, Glasgow Sch of Art (certificate in architecture), Edinburgh Coll of Art (Dip Arch); *m* 23 July 1966, Sheila May, da of Ernest Sheriff Colman (d 1961); 2 s (Harvey b 1969, Russell b 1972); *Career* Architect; snr ptnr McLean Gibson & Assocs, dir Calterra Dvpts Ltd; memb of Cncl Glasgow Inst of Architects 1978-89; Royal Incorpn of Architects Scotland 1986-87; MRIBA 1967, FRIAS 1985; *Recreations* golf, music, current affairs; *Clubs* Prestwick GC, Royal Scottish Automobile; *Style—* J Norman McLean, Esq; 20 Cathcart St, Ayr KA7 1BJ

McLEAN, Peter Standley; CMG (1985), OBE (1965); s of William McLean (d 1961), and Alice, *née* Standley; *b* 18 Jan 1927; *Educ* King Edward's Sch Birmingham, Wadham Coll Oxford (MA); *m* 1954, Margaret Ann, da of Richard Henry Minns (d 1967); 2 s (Iain b 1957, Alistair b 1964), 2 da (Fiona b 1955, Catriona b 1962); *Career* Lt 15/19 King's Royal Hussars 1946-48; Uganda Govt 1951-65 perm sec Min of Planning & Economic Devpt; asst sec Overseas Devpt Admin, FCO 1965-80; Min UK perm rep to UN FAO, Rome 1980-85; *Recreations* water-colour painting, DIY; *Style—* Peter S McLean, Esq; 17 Woodfield Lane, Ashtead, Surrey KT21 2BQ (☎ 03722 78146)

MacLEAN, Ranald Norman Munro; QC (1977); s of John Alexander MacLean, of Duart, 12 Eriskay Rd, Inverness, and Hilda Margaret Lind, *née* Munro; *b* 18 Dec 1938; *Educ* Fettes, Cambridge Univ (BA), Edinburgh Univ (LLB), Yale Univ (LLM); *m* 21 Sept 1963, Pamela Ross, da of prof Allan Dawson Ross, of London (d 1982); 3 s (Fergus Ranald b 1970, Donald Ross b 1972, 1 s decd); 1 da (Catriona Joan b 1967); *Career* called to Scottish Bar 1964; advocate-depute 1972-75, Home advocate-depute 1979-82; memb: Cncl on Tbnls 1985- (chm Scottish Ctee), Scottish Legal Aid Bd 1986-; *Recreations* hill walking, Munro collecting; *Clubs* Scottish Arts, New (Edinburgh); *Style—* Ranald N M MacLean, Esq, QC; 12 Chalmers Crescent, Edinburgh EH9 1TS (☎ 031 667 6217); Advocates Library, Parliament House, Edinburgh (☎ 031 226 5071)

MACLEAN, Sir Robert Alexander; KBE (1973), DL (Renfrewshire (1970); s of Andrew Johnston Maclean, JP (d 1924); *b* 11 April 1908; *Educ* Glasgow HS; *m* 1938, Vivienne Neville, da of Capt Bertram Walter Bourke, JP (ka 1915), and half sis of Eileen, Countess of Mount Charles; 2 s, 2 da; *Career* chm Scottish Ctee Cncl of Industl Design 1949-58, regnl controller (Scot) Bd of Trade 1944-46, dir Nat Freight Corpn 1969-72; memb: Export Cncl for Europe 1960-64, Br Nat Export Cncl 1966-70; chm: Scottish Industl Estates Corpn 1955-72, Scottish Exports Ctee; pres Glasgow C of C 1956-58, chm Cncl of Scottish C of C 1960-62, pres Assoc of British C of C 1966-68, dir Norwich Union Insur Bd Gp, hon pres Stoddard Carpets Ltd and assoc cos; Hon LLD Glasgow Univ 1973; CStJ 1975; FRSA, CBIM; kt 1955; *Recreations* golf, fishiing; *Clubs* Carlton; *Style—* Sir Robert Maclean, KBE, DL; South Branchal Farm, Bridge of Weir, Renfrewshire PA11 3SJ

McLEAN, (John David) Ruari; CBE (1973), DSC (1943); s of John Thomson McLean (d 1962), of Oxford, and Isabel Mary Ireland (d 1958); *b* 10 June 1917; *Educ* Dragon Sch Oxford, Eastbourne Coll; *m* 1945, Antonia Maxwell, da of Dr Henry George Carlisle, MD, of Heswall Ches; 2 s (David, Andrew), 1 da (Catriona); *Career* RN, Lt RNVR 1940-45, Atlantic, SE Asia; typographer; fndr ptnr Rainbird McLean Ltd 1951-58, hon typographic advsr HM Stationery Off 1966-80; tstee Nat Library of Scotland 1981; Croix de Guerre (France) 1941; *Books* Modern Book Design (1958), Victorian Book Design (1963, revised edn 1972), Jan Tschichold, Typographer (1975), Magazine Design (1969), Manual of Typography (1980); *Clubs* New (Edinburgh), Double Crown (pres 1971); *Style—* Ruari McLean, Esq, CBE, DSC; Pier Cottage, Carsaig, Isle of Mull PA70 6HD (☎ 06814 216)

MACLEAN, Hon Mrs (Sarah Elizabeth Cameron); eldest da of 3 Baron Rowallan; *b* 5 April 1949; *m* 17 April 1968, (Lachlan) Roderick Maclean, er s of Maj Gordon Maclean, of London; 2 da ; *Style—* The Hon Mrs Maclean; Fairoak Cottage, Stratfield Saye, Reading RG7 2EA

MACLEAN, Lady Sarah Elizabeth Jane; *née* Finch-Knightley; da of 11 Earl of Aylesford; *b* 14 July 1950; *Educ* Abbot's Hill Hemel Hempstead; *m* 1974, Angus Nigel Garnet Maclean, s of Maj Lachlan Gordon Maclean, MC, 11 of Hynish; 2 s (Angus Charles, Ian Andrew); *Style—* Lady Sarah Maclean; c/o Child & Co, Fleet St, London EC4

MACLEAN OF DUNCONNEL, Sir Fitzroy Hew Maclean; 1 Bt (UK 1957), of Dunconnel, Co Argyll; CBE (Mil 1944); 15 Hereditary Keeper and Captain of Dunconnel; s of Maj Charles Maclean, DSO (whose paternal grandmother was Elizabeth, ggda of 5 Duke of Beaufort, while his paternal great grandmother was da of 2 Earl of Hopetoun); *b* 11 Mar 1911; *Educ* Eton, King's Coll Cambridge; *m* 1946, Hon Veronica, *née* Fraser, 2 da of 14 Lord Lovat and wid of Lt Alan Phipps (gggs of 1 Earl of Mulgrave, f of 1 Marquess of Normanby); 2 s; *Heir* s, Charles Maclean, yr of Dunconnel; *Career* Brig cmdg Br Mil Mission to Yugoslav Partisans 1943-45; formerly with For Serv, Queen's Own Cameron Highlanders and SAS (Hon Col 23 Special Air Serv Regt Vols 1984-88); MP (C) Lancaster 1941-59, Bute and N Ayrshire 1959-74; parly under-sec and fin sec WO 1954-57; Croix de Guerre France, Order of Kutuzov USSR, Partisan Star 1 Class Yugoslavia, Yugoslav Order of Merit 1969, order of the Yugoslav Star with Ribbon 1981; *Clubs* White's, Pratt's, Puffin's (Edinburgh), New (Edinburgh); *Style—* Sir Fitzroy Maclean of Dunconnel, Bt, CBE; Strachur House, Argyll (☎ 036 986 242)

MACLEAN OF DUNCONNEL, Hon Lady; Veronica Nell; da of 15 Lord Lovat (and 17 but for the attainder) KT, GCVO, KCMG, CB, DSO, TD (d 1933); *b* 1920; *m* 1, 1940, Lt Alan Phipps, RN (d 1943); 1 s, 1 da; m 2, 1946, Brig Sir Fitzroy Hew Royle Maclean, 1 Bt, CBE, *qv*; 2 s; *Style—* The Hon Lady Maclean of Dunconnel; Strachur House, Argyll

MACLEAN, YR OF DUNCONNEL, Charles Edward; s and h of Sir Fitzroy Hew Maclean of Dunconnel, 1 Bt, CBE, *qv*; *b* 31 Oct 1946; *Educ* Eton, New Coll Oxford; *m* 1986, Deborah, da of Lawrence Young, of Chicago; 1 da (Margaret Augusta b 1987); *Books* Island at the Edge of the World, The Wolf Children, The Watcher; *Style—* Charles Maclean, yr of Dunconnel; Strachur House, Argyll

McLEAVY, Hon Frank Waring; s of Baron McLeavy (Life Peer); *b* 1925; *Educ* Wirral GS, Liverpool Univ, Leeds Univ; *m* 1954, Verena, da of Emil Lüsher, of Unterkulm, Switzerland; *Style—* The Hon Frank McLeavy

McLEAVY, Hon Mrs Douglas; Janet Elizabeth; da of Harry Ogden; *b* 14 Jan 1934; *Educ* Bingley GS, St Osyth's Coll; *m* 1958, Hon Douglas John McLeavy (d 1969), s of Baron McLeavy (Life Peer, d 1975); 1 s (Mark b 1969), 1 da (Ruth b 1964); *Career* school mistress; *Style—* The Hon Mrs Douglas McLeavy; 40 Ruskin Drive, Morecambe, Lancs

McLEAVY, Baroness; Mary; *née* Waring; da of late George Waring, of Rock Ferry, Birkenhead; *m* 1924, Baron McLeavy (Life Peer, d 1976); *Style—* The Rt Hon The Lady McLeavy; 9 Sheridan Terrace, Whitton Ave West, Northolt, Middx

MacLEHOSE OF BEOCH, Baron (Life Peer UK 1981), of Beoch in the District of Kyle and Carrick and of Victoria in Hong Kong; Sir (Crawford) Murray MacLehose; KT (1983), GBE (1976, MBE 1946), KCMG (1971, CMG 1964), KCVO (1975), DL (Ayr and Arran 1983); s of Hamish A MacLehose and Margaret Bruce, *née* Black; *b* 16 Oct 1917; *Educ* Rugby, Balliol Coll Oxford; *m* 1947, Margaret Noël, da of Sir (Thomas) Charles Dunlop, TD, JP, DL (d 1960), of Doonside, Ayrshire, and Elfrida, *née* Watson (whose mother was Ernestine, da of Ernest Slade and gda of Gen Sir John Slade, 1 Bt); 2 da (Hon Mrs Wedgwood, Hon Mrs Sandeman, *qqv*); *Career* serv WWII as Lt RNVR; joined Foreign Serv 1947 (later FO, then FCO, also seconded to CRO), served Hankow, FO, Prague, Wellington, Paris; princ private sec to Foreign Sec 1965-67; ambass: Vietnam 1967-69, Denmark 1969-71; govr and C-in-C Hong Kong 1971-82 (political advsr with rank of cnsllr 1959-63); dir Nat Westminster Bank 1983-; chm: Scottish Tst for the Physically Disabled, Margaret Blackwood Housing Assoc, SOAS; pres GB China Centre; KStJ 1972; *Clubs* Athenaeum, New (Edinburgh); *Style—* The Rt Hon the Lord MacLehose of Beoch,

KT, GBE, KCMG, KCVO, DL; Beoch, Maybole, Ayrshire (☎ 0655 83114)

McLELLAN, Prof David Thorburn; s of Robert Douglas (d 1973), and Olive May, *née* Bush; *b* 10 Feb 1940; *Educ* Merchant Taylors', St John's Coll Oxford (BA, MA, DPhil); *m* 1 July 1967 (m dis 1978), Annie, da of André Brassart; 2 da (Gabrielle b 8 Nov 1968, Stephanie b 8 May 1970); *Career* Univ of Kent: sr lectr in politics 1970-75 (lectr 1966-70), prof of political theory 1975; visiting prof State Univ of NY 1969, visiting fell Indian Inst of Advanced Study Simla 1970; *Books* The Young Hegelians and Karl Marx (1969), Marx before Marxism (1970), Karl Marx: The Early Texts (1971), Marx's Grundrisse (1971), The Thought of Karl Marx (1971), Karl Marx: His Life and Thought (1973), Marx (1971), Engels (1977), Karl Marx: Selected Writings (1977), Marxism after Marx (1980), Karl Marx: Interviews and Recollections (1983), Marx: The First Hundred Years (ed 1983), Karl Marx: The Legacy (1983), Ideology (1985), Marxism: Selected Texts (ed 1987), Marxism and Religion (1987); *Style—* Prof David McLellan; 13 Ivy Lane, Canterbury, Kent (☎ 0227 463 579); Eliot Coll, Univ of Kent, Canterbury (☎ 0227 764 000)

MACLELLAN, Ian David; s of Maj Henry Crawford Maclellan, MBE, TD, of Walton-on-the-Hill, Surrey, and Daphne Loya, *née* Taverner; *b* 21 Feb 1948; *Educ* Sherborne, Cranfield Business Sch (MBA); *m* 29 Aug 1974, Maja Ursula, da of Dr Hans Schaschek, of Weinheim, W Germany; 1 s (Henry b 1983), 1 da (Kirstin b 1980); *Career* public co dir and CA; jt md and fin dir Ibstock Johnsen plc (and subsids in UK), dir Glen Gery Corpn USA, chm Price & Pierce Gp Ltd; FCA; *Recreations* shooting, tennis; *Style—* Ian D Maclellan, Esq; Wormleighton Grange, nr Leamington Spa, Warwickshire CV33 0XJ (☎ 029577 334); Lutterworth House, Lutterworth, Leics (☎ 04555 3071)

MacLELLAN, Maj Gen (Andrew) Patrick Withy; CB (1981), MBE (1964); s of Kenneth MacLellan (d 1981), and Rachel Madeline, *née* Withy (d 1979); *b* 29 Nov 1925; *Educ* Uppingham; *m* 1954, Kathleen Mary, da of Capt Robert Armstrong Bagnell (d 1969), of Hindhead; 1 s (Ian), 2 da (Fiona, Diana (twins)); *Career* cmmnd Coldstream Gds 1944; serv Palestine, N Africa, Egypt, Germany, DAA and QMC 7 Gds Bde Gp 1958-59, mil asst to Chief of Def Staff (Adm of the Fleet Earl Mountbatten of Burma) 1961-64, instr Staff Coll Camberley 1964-66, GSO1 (plans) Far E Cmd Gds 1966-67, CO 1 Bn Coldstream Gds 1968-70, Col GS Near E Land Forces 1970-71, RCDS 1973, dep cdr and COS London Dist 1974-77, pres Regular Commns Bd 1978-80; Govr and Keeper of the Jewel House HM Tower of London 1984-89; Freeman: City of London, Worshipful Co of Watermen and Lightmen of the River Thames; Liveryman Worshipful Co of Fletchers; Chevalier de la Légion d'Honneur 1960; *Clubs* White's, Pratt's; *Style—* Maj-Gen Patrick MacLellan, CB, MBE; c/o Bank of Scotland, 38 Threadneedle St, London EC2P 2EM; Queen's House, HM Tower of London, London EC3N 4AB (☎ 01 709 0765)

MacLELLAN, Sir (George) Robin Perronet; CBE (1969), JP (Dunbartonshire 1973); s of George Aikman MacLellan (d 1966); *b* 14 Nov 1915; *Educ* Ardvreck Sch Crieff, Clifton, Ecole de Commerce Lausanne; *m* 1941, Margaret, da of Dr Berkeley Robertson (d 1941); 1 s; *Career* serv WWII Sgt-Maj RA (invalided out 1941); mfr, export salesman, finally chm George MacLellan Hldgs 1964-76; dep chm Br Airports Authy 1965-74; dir: Scottish Nat Tst plc 1970-85, Nationwide Building Soc 1971-84, Br Tourist Authy 1974-80; memb advsy bd BR (Scotland) 1976-81; dep chm Nat Tst for Scotland 1980-85; chm Scottish Tourist Bd 1974-80, chm Bield (Sheltered Housing Tst) 1983-87, pres The Old Cliftonian Soc 1983-85; Melville Retirement Homes Ltd (dir Edinburgh 1984-); FRCPS (Glasgow); kt 1980; *Recreations* angling, swimming, keeping friendships in good repair; *Clubs* Western (Glasgow), RNVR (Glasgow),; *Style—* Sir Robin MacLellan, CBE, JP; 11 Beechwood Court, Bearsden, Glasgow, Scotland G61 2RY (☎ 041 942 3876)

McLELLAND, (James) Forrest; TD (1953), JP (1970); s of James Forrest McLelland (d 1942), of Northfield, Bearsden, Glasgow, and Janet MacDairmid, *née* Carmichael (d 1978); *b* 13 Nov 1919; *Educ* Glasgow Acad, Fettes Coll Edinburgh; *m* 15 June 1979, Helen Elizabeth (d 1985), da of late George Mailer; *Career* WWII Maj TA UK Western Desert, Italy 1939-46; chm Browntee plc 1980-85, pres Timber Res and Devpt Assoc 1985-, chm St Rollox Indust Devpt Enterprise Ltd Glasgow; chm Glasgow Academical Club 1969-71, Elder New Kilpatrick Parish Church, dir of ceremonies Priory of Scotland, Order of St John 1985-; chm govrs Glasgow Academy 1985-, KStJ 1988; deacon Incorporation of Wrights in Glasgow 1959; FIWSc; *Recreations* rugby football, walking; *Clubs* Western (Glasgow), RNVR (Glasgow), St John's; *Style—* Forrest McLelland, Esq, TD, JP; 34 Coloquhoun Dr, Bearsden, Glasgow G61 4NQ (☎ 041 942 5959)

McLENNAN, Sir Ian Munro; KCMG (1979), KBE (1963, CBE 1956); s of R McLennan; *b* 30 Nov 1909; *Educ* Scotch Coll Melbourne, Melbourne Univ (B Elec Eng); *m* 1937, Dora, da of J Robertson; 2 s, 2 da; *Career* cadet engr The Broken Hill Pty Co Ltd 1933 (md 1967-71, chm 1971-77); chm: Jt War Prodn Ctee 1956-69, Def (Indl) Ctee 1969-75, BHP-GKN Hldgs 1970-78, Tubemakers of Australia Ltd 1973-79, ANZ Banking Gp Ltd 1977-82, Interscan Aust Pty Ltd 1978-84, Elders IXL Ltd 1980-85, Queen Elizabeth II Jubilee Appeal and Tst 1977-81, Melbourne Univ Engrg Sch Fndn 1983-87; dir ICI Aust Ltd 1976-79; pres: Aust Academy of Technological Sciences 1976-83 (fndn pres 1983-), Australia Japan Business Co-operation Ctee 1977-85; cncllr RASV 1978-; memb: Int Cncl Morgan Guaranty Tst Co NYC 1973-79, CSIRO Advsy Cncl 1978-81, Gen Motors Aust Advsy Cncl 1978-82; FTS, FAA, Hon D Dng Melbourne and Newcastle 1968, Hon DSc Wollongong 1978, Hon LLD Melbourne 1987, Hon DSc Deakin 1988; *Style—* Sir Ian McLennan, KCMG, KBE; Apt 3, 112-120 Walsh St, South Yarra, Victoria 3141, Australia

MACLENNAN, Robert Adam Ross; MP (Lab until 1981, when joined SDP) Caithness & Sutherland 1966-; s of Sir Hector Maclennan (d 1978, sometime chm Advsy Ctee on Distinction Awards, an obstetrician & gynaecologist, and twice Lord High Cmmr to the General Assembly of the Church of Scotland), by his 1 w, Isabel, *née* Adam; *b* 26 June 1936; *Educ* Glasgow Acad, Balliol Coll Oxford, Trinity Coll Cambridge, Columbia Univ NY; *m* 1968, Helen, wid of Paul Noyes, and da of Judge Ammi Cutter, of Cambridge, Mass; 1 s, 1 da, 1 step s; *Career* barr 1962; cwlth affrs sec 1967-69, pps to Min without portfolio 1969-70, additional oppn spokesman Scottish Affrs 1970-71, Def 1971-72, parly under-sec Prices and Consumer Protection 1974-79, memb Commons Public Accounts Ctee 1979-; oppn spokesman on For Affrs 1979-80; SDP spokesman: Agric 1981-87, on Home & Legal Affrs 1983-87; elected ldr of the SDP 1987-, Democrats spokesman Home Affrs 1988-; *Recreations* theatre, music, books, 2800 square miles of constituency; *Clubs* Brooks's; *Style—* Robert Maclennan, Esq, MP; Hollandmake, Barrock, Caithness (☎ 084 785 203); 74 Abingdon Villas, London W8 (☎ 01 937 5960)

MacLENNAN OF MacLENNAN, Ronald George; 34 Chief of Clan MacLennan, recognised by Lord Lyon 1978; descended from 33 Chief, Ruaridh Domnull Ban MacLennan who was famed for his valour at the Battle of Auldearn 1645; s of George Mitchell MacLennan (d 1981), of Loanhead, Midlothian, and Helen, *née* Ames; *b* 1925; *Educ* Boroughmuir Secdy Sch Edinburgh, Copenhagen DPE; *m* 1970, Margaret Ann, da of Donald John MacLennan, of Dores Inverness; 1 s, 2 da (Kirsteen Ruth, Lorna Louise); *Heir* s, Ruairidh Donald George MacLennan of MacLennan younger b 1977; *Career* mil serv 1942-47, Europe, Africa, Burma, Col; teacher-lectr 1949-82, Royal HS Edinburgh 1949-51, Sch of Physiotherapy Glasgow 1952-54, Coll of Physical Educn Fredensborg Denmark 1955-56, Ullapool 1970-82; recognised as Chief of Clan MacLennan by Lord Lyon 1978; *Books* History of MacLennans 1978, 'MacLennan-Logan Glowing Embers' 1987; *Style—* Ronald MacLennan of MacLennan; The Old Mill, Dores, Inverness IV1 2TR (☎ 0463 75 228)

MACLEOD, Sheriff, CBE (1987) Angus; CBE (1967); s of Alexander MacLeod (d 1945), of Glendale, Isle of Skye, and Flora, *née* MacPherson (d 1962); *b* 2 April 1906; *Educ* Hutchesons Boys GS Glasgow, Univ of Glasgow (MA, LLB); *m* 25 June 1936, (Jane) Winifred (d 1977), da of Sir Robert Bryce Walker, CBE, LLD, DL, JP; 3 s (Donald Ian Kerr b 1937, Neil Alistair b 1942, Euan Roderick b 1944); *Career* slr qualified 1929, qualified asst legal practice Glasgow 1929-34; depute fiscal 1934-42: Dunfermline, Glasgow, Edinburgh (sr depute Edinburgh); procurator fiscal: Dumfries 1942-52, Aberdeen 1952-55, Edinburgh 1955-71; temp sheriff Scot 1973-77, chm VAT Appeals Trib 1974-77; memb: (fndr memb) cncl Law Soc Scot 1967-73, grant ctee Sheriff Ct 1963-67; pres: PTA, Dumfries Acad 1949-50, Maxwellton Bowling Club Dumfries 1948-49; memb Stair Soc 1948- (memb cncl 1958-61); *Recreations* reading, walking; *Style—* Sheriff Angus MacLeod; 7 Oxford Terr, Edinburgh EH4 1PX (☎ 031 332 5466)

MACLEOD, Dr Calum Alexander; s of Rev Lachlan Macleod (d 1966), of Glenurquhart, and Jessie Mary Morrison (d 1970); *b* 25 July 1935; *Educ* Nicolson Inst Stornoway, Univ of Aberdeen (MA, LLB); *m* 21 July 1962, Elizabeth Margaret, da of David Davidson (d 1973), of Inverness; 2 s (Allan b 1966, David b 1968), 1 da (Edythe b 1972); *Career* Nat Serv 2 Lt RAEC; ptnr Paull & Williamsons (advocates) Aberdeen 1964-80; chm: Aberdeen Petroleum plc 1982-, Harris Tweed Assoc 1984-, North of Scotland Investmt Co plc 1986-, FS Assur 1987-; dep chm: Grampian TV plc 1982-, Scottish Eastern Investmt Tst plc 1988-; dir Aberdeen bd Bank of Scotland 1980-; chllr's assessor Aberdeen Univ 1979-; chm: Robert Gordon's Coll 1981-, Satro North Scotland 1986-; memb: White Fish Authy 1973-80, North of Scotland Hydro-Electric Bd 1976-84; Highlands and Islands Devpt Bd 1984-; vice chm Scottish Cncl of Independent Schs 1988-; Hon LLD Aberdeen Univ 1986; memb Law Soc of Scotland 1958, FInstD 1982; *Recreations* golf, music, travel, reading; *Clubs* Royal Northern, Royal Aberdeen GC, Nairn GC; *Style—* Dr Calum MacLeod; 6 Westfield Terr, Aberdeen AB2 4RU (☎ 0224 641614); Royfold House, Hill of Rubislaw, Anderson Dr, Aberdeen AB2 6GZ (☎ 0224 208110, fax 0224 208120)

McLEOD, Sir Charles Henry; 3 Bt (UK 1925), of the Fairfields, Cobham, Surrey; s of Sir Murdoch Campbell McLeod, 2 Bt (d 1950), and Susan, *née* Whitehead (d 1964); *b* 7 Nov 1924; *Educ* Winchester; *m* 5 Jan 1957, Anne Gillian (d 1978), 3 da of late Henry Russell Bowlby, of London; 1 s, 2 da; *Heir* s, James Roderick Charles McLeod; *Clubs* Brooks's; *Style—* Sir Charles McLeod, Bt; c/o Brooks's, 60 St James's St, London SW1

MACLEOD, Air Vice Marshal Donald Francis Graham; CB (1977), QHDS (1972); s of Alexander Macleod (d 1967), of Stornoway, Isle of Lewis, Scotland, and Isabella Macleod (d 1975); *b* 26 August 1917; *Educ* Univ of St Andrews (LDS); *m* 1 Nov 1941, Marjorie Eileen, da of late William Davidson Gracie, of Glamis Rd, Dundee, Scotland; 1 s (Ronald b 1944), 1 da (Gael b 1947); *Career* RAF: joined dental branch as Flying Offr 1942, serv W Africa (Apapa, Lagos) 1943-44, Cranwell 1944, Harley St London 1945; RAF Hosps: Cosford 1945-50, Aden 1950-52, Wroughton 1952-59; specialist in oral surgery RAF Hosp: Wegberg Germany 1959-62, Ely Cambs 1962-65; Gp-Capt conslt RAF Hosp Aden 1965-67, conslt oral surgery RAF Hosp Ely 1967-72, Air Cdre princ dental offr Strike Cmd 1972-73, Air Vice-Marshal dir RAF dental branch 1973-76; private practice 1940-41, Aberdeen Public Health Authy 1941-42; Ely and Dist Probus Soc: fndr memb 1982, vice-chm 1982, chm 1983; Royal Humane Soc Resuscitation Award 1937; FDS, RCS (Ed) 1955; *Recreations* golf, gardening, outdoor pursuits; *Clubs* Royal Worlington & Newmarket GC; *Style—* Air Vice Marshal D F G Macleod, CB, RAF; 20 Witchford Rd, Ely, Cambs CB6 3DP (☎ 0353 663164)

MacLEOD, Duncan James; CBE (1986); s of Alan Duncan MacLeod, of Skeabost, Isle of Skye (ka Sicily 1943), and Joan Nora Paton (*née* de Knoop); *b* 1 Nov 1934; *Educ* Eton; *m* 14 June 1958, Joanna, da of Samuel Leslie Bibby, CBE, DL, of Villans Wyk, Headley, Surrey (d 1985); 2 s (Alan Hamish b 1959, Charles Alasdair b 1961), 1 da (Davina b 1965); *Career* CA 1958, ptnr Brown Fleming & Murray (now Ernst & Whinney) 1960; dir: Bank of Scotland 1973, Scottish Provident Institution 1976-, The Weir Gp plc 1976; memb Scottish Industl Devpt Advsy Bd 1980-, (chm 1989-), Scottish Tertiary Educ Advsy Cncl 1985-87; *Recreations* golf, shooting, fishing; *Clubs* Western, Glasgow Prestwick GC, Royal and Ancient, MCC; *Style—* Duncan J MacLeod, Esq, CBE; Monkredding House, Kilwinning, Ayrshire KA13 7QN (☎ 0294 52336); Savoy Tower, 77 Renfrew St, Glasgow G2 3BZ (☎ 041 333 9699, telex 779367, fax 041 332 4963)

MacLEOD, Hon Eva Mary Ellen; da of Baron MacLeod of Fuinary, MC (Life Peer); *b* 1950; *Style—* The Hon Eva MacLeod; 23 Learmonth Terrace, Edinburgh 4

McLEOD, Sir Ian George; JP (1977); s of George McLeod; *b* 17 Oct 1926; *Educ* Kearsney Coll Natal, Natal Univ; *m* 1950, Audrey; 2 da; *Career* md EDP Servs Computer Bureau 1964-; memb bd SE Electricity Bd 1983-; chm: Croydon Central Cons Assoc 1973-76, Greater London Area Conservatives 1981-84; memb Nat Union Exec Ctee Conservative Pty 1974-84; ACIS; kt 1984; *Clubs* Carlton, MCC; *Style—* Sir Ian McLeod, JP

McLEOD, James Roderick Charles; s and h of Sir Charles Henry McLeod, 3 Bt; *b* 26 Sept 1960; *Style—* James McLeod, Esq

MACLEOD, Dr John Alasdair Johnston; DL (Western Isles 1979-); s of Dr Alexander John Macleod, OBE (d 1979), of Lochmaddy, and Dr Julia Parker, *née* Johnston; *b* 20 Jan 1935; *Educ* Lochmaddy Sch, Nicolson Inst Stornoway, Keil Sch Dumbarton, Univ of Glasgow (MB, ChB); *m* 4 Nov 1972, Lorna, da of Dr Douglas Ian

Ferguson, of The Cottage, Station Rd, Winterbourne Down, nr Bristol; 2 s (Alasdair Ian b 1974, Torquil John b 1979), 1 da (Elizabeth Jane b 1975); *Career* Temp Actg Sub Lt RNVR 1957-59; jr hosp posts Glasgow and London 1963-70, RMO and sr registrar Middx London 1970-72, GP Isle of N Uist 1973-, examing offr DHSS 1973-, med offr Lochmaddy Hosp 1974-, Admty surgn and agent 1974-, local med offr 1974-; non exec dir Olscot Ltd 1969-; visiting prof dept of family med Univ of N Carolina; memb: N Uist Highland Gathering, N Uist Angling Club, Scandinavian Village Assoc; sec Western Isles Local Med Ctee 1977-; author of various articles and papers on isolated gen practise within the NHS; memb Western Isles Advsy Ctee on JPs 1985-; memb: BMA, RCGP; fell RSM; *Recreations* promoting Western Isles, time-sharing, arboriculture, writing; *Clubs* RNVR (Scotland), Highland; *Style—* Dr A J Macleod, DL; Tigh-na-Hearradh, Lochmaddy, Isle of N Uist, Western Isles PA82 5AO (☎ 08763 224)

MACLEOD, John Francis Matheson (Jeff); s of Dr Ian Matheson Macleod (d 1963), of Inverness, and Annie Frances, *née* Sime (d 1977); *b* 24 Jan 1932; *Educ* Inverness Royal Acad, Geo Watson's Coll, Univ of Edinburgh (MA, LLB); *m* 15 April 1958, Alexandra Catherine, da of late Donald Macleod, of Tarbert Harris; 1 s (Ian Diarmid Skene b 1959); *Career* slr (Scotland), dean Faculty of Slrs of the Highlands; cncl memb Law Soc of Scotland formerly chm: Highland regn of Scottish Lib Pty, Crofters Cmmn 1978-86; vice-chm Broadcasting Cncl for Scotland; contested (Lib): Moray & Nairn 1964, Western Isles 1966; *Clubs* Royal Scots (Edinburgh); *Style—* Jeff Macleod, Esq; Bona Lodge, Aldourie, by Inverness; Messrs Macleod & MacCallum, Solicitors, 28 Queensgate, Inverness (☎ 0463 239 393, fax 0463 222 879)

MacLEOD, Hon John Maxwell Norman; s of Baron MacLeod of Fuinary, MC (Life Peer) and h to father's Btcy only; *b* 23 Feb 1952; *Educ* Gordonstoun; *Style—* The Hon John MacLeod; Fuinary Manse, Loch Aline, Morven, Argyll

MacLEOD, Maj Loudown Henry Davenport; s of Dr Loudoun Hector Bright Macleod (d 1974), of the MacLeod of Raasay, and Gladys Louisa Amy, *née* Davenport (d 1973); *b* 24 Feb 1919; *Educ* Wellington; *m* 11 Nov 1943, Katharine Adair (d 1982), da of Rev William Francis Adair Stride; 3 s (Malcolm b 1944, Ian b 1946, Francis b 1955); *Career* entered RM 1937 and ret (Maj) 1964, served Atlantic and Med; *Recreations* salmon, fishing, golf; *Clubs* Army & Navy; *Style—* Maj Loudoun H D Macleod; Fernshaw, Fridays Hill, Haslemere (☎ 0428 52193); 8 Ossemsley Manor, Ossemsley, Christchurch, New Milton (☎ 0425 622422)

McLEOD, Margaret Henderson; OBE (1980); s of Andrew Kerr McLeod (d 1947), and Helen Dunsire, *née* Nicol (d 1945); *b* 24 July 1919; *Educ* Nyewood and Chichester (Dip Soc (Lond)); *Career* chief nursing offr E Sussex Co Cncl 1962-69; public health nursing offr Dept of Health 1969-76; dep chief nursing offr Dept of Health and Soc Security 1976-80; chm Little Black Bag Housing Assoc 1966-; SRN, SCM, Queen's Nurse HV (cert); *Recreations* photography, walking; *Clubs* Royal Coll of Nursing; *Style—* Ms Margaret McLeod, OBE; 19 Delves Way, Ringmer, Lewes, Sussex BN8 5JU (☎ 0273 812169)

MacLEOD, Hon Neil David; s of Baron MacLeod of Fuinary, MC (Life Peer); *b* 25 Dec 1959; *Style—* The Hon Neil MacLeod

MACLEOD, Nigel Ronald Buchanan; QC (1979); s of Donald Macleod (d 1956), and Katie Ann Buchanan Macleod; *b* 7 Feb 1936; *Educ* Wigan GS, Christ Church Oxford (MA, BCL); *m* 1966, Susan Margaret; 1 s (Alasdair b 1968), 1 da (Victoria b 1972); *Career* Nat Serv RAF 1954-56; barr Gray's Inn 1961, asst cmmr Boundary Cmmn for England 1981-84, rec Crown Ct 1981-; *Recreations* walking, dinghy sailing; *Style—* Nigel Macleod, Esq, QC; The Start, Start Lane, Whaley Bridge, Derby (☎ 0663 32732); 127 Santa Monica, Av du Pacifique, Cap d'Agde, Herault, France; 2 Paper Buildings, Temple, EC 4Y (☎ 01 353 5835, telex 885358 TEMPLE G, fax 01 583 1390)

MacLEOD, Sheriff Princ Norman Donald; QC (Scot 1986); s of Rev John MacLeod, of Edinburgh, and Catherine Mullen, *née* Macritchie (d 1939); *b* 6 Mar 1932; *Educ* Mill Hill, George Watson's Boys' Coll, Edinburgh Univ, Oxford Univ; *m* 1957, Ursula Jane, da of George Herbert Bromley, of Inveresk, Midlothian (d 1982); 2 s (Ian b 1959, Patrick b 1963), 2 da (Catriona b 1960, Johanna b 1964); *Career* passed advocate 1956, Colonial Serv dist Offr and crown counsel 1957-64, sheriff of Lanarkshire at Glasgow (subsequently sheriff of Glasgow and Strathkelvin) 1967-86; sheriff princ of Glasgow and Strathkelvin 1986-; visiting prof Strathclyde Univ; *Recreations* gardening, sailing; *Style—* Sheriff Princ Norman D MacLeod, QC; Calderbank, Lochwinnoch, Renfrewshire PA12 4DJ (☎ 0505 843 340); Sheriff Principal's Chambers, Sheriff Court of Glasgow and Strathkelvin, 1 Carlton Place, Glasgow G5 9DA (☎ 041 429 8888)

McLEOD, Robert; s of Robert Frew McLeod (d 1973), and Marion McLeod; *b* 1 Oct 1928; *Educ* Alloa Academy and Royal Tech College (Glasgow); *m* 1954, Agnes Myrtle, da of David George; 1 s, 1 da; *Career* dep chm Scottish Business Gp 1979-; md, Scottish Business Group 1987; *Recreations* gardening, travel, golf; *Style—* Robert McLeod, Esq; Rozelle, 4 Briarhill Ave, Dalgety Bay, Fife KY11 5UR (☎ 0383 823 200); Carron House, 114/116 George St, Edinburgh (☎ 031 226 7491)

MacLEOD, (Hugh) Roderick; s of Neil Macleod, and Ruth, *née* Hill; *b* 20 Sept 1929; *Educ* Bryanston, St John's Coll Cambridge; *m* 1958, Josephine Seager Berry; 2 s, 1 da; *Career* chm and chief exec Lloyd's Registrar of Shipping 1983-; dir: Lloyd's Registrar Techn Servs Inc, Lloyd's Registrar Indl Servs (Insur) Inc, Lloyd's Registrar Inspection Ltd, Lloyd's Registrar (Overseas) Ltd, Lloyd's Register Espana SA, Lloyd's Register of Shipping (ASBL) Belgium, Rontgen Technische Dienst, Lloyd's Register of Shipping Tst Corpn Ltd, The Monks Investmt Tst plc, Murray Electronics plc; jt md Ben Line Steamers 1964-82, dir Scottish Equitable Life Assur Soc, chm Br Railways (Scottish) Bd 1980-82, pt/t memb Br Railways Bd 1980-86; *Recreations* outdoor pursuits, music; *Style—* Roderick MacLeod, Esq; 14 Dawson Place, London W2; Lloyd's Register of Shipping, 71 Fenchurch St, London EC3 (☎ 01 709 9166)

MacLEOD, Lady (Rosemary Theodora Hamilton); *née* Wills; da of Frederick Noel Hamilton Wills (d 1927), 3 s of 1 Bt Dulverton; *b* 1913; *m* 1938, Sir John MacLeod, TD (late Capt Queen's Own Cameron Highlanders (d 1984)); 2 s, 3 da; *Style—* Lady MacLeod; Bunkers Hill, Farmington, Northleach, Glos

McLEOD, Thomas Symington; s of Prof James Walter McLeod, OBE, FRS (d 1978), and Jane Christine, *née* Garvie (d 1953); *b* 5 Oct 1919; *Educ* Leeds GS, Trinity Hall Cambridge (MA 1947); *m* 12 Aug 1941, Marion Boyd, da of Duncan McNicol Thomson (d 1951); 2 s (Hugh b 1944, Peter b 1946), 2 da (Alison b 1950, Elizabeth b 1954); *Career* served WW II 1941-45 Capt RM, Africa, Italy, France, Belgium, Holland (despatches); chartered electrical engr, tech mangr The Plessey Co plc 1952-79, dir Design Technol 1979-85; cncl memb and chm Social Security Ctee CBI 1974-81; chm: Tech and Vocational Educn Initiative Dorset 1986-; C Eng, FIEE 1968; *Books* The Management of Research, Development and Design in Industry (1 edn 1969, 2 edn 1988), Research and Development, Industrial (Encyclopedia Britannica, 15 edn); *Recreations* golf, fly fishing, bridge, chess, skiing; *Style—* Thomas McLeod, Esq; Little Woolgarston Cottage, Corfe Castle, Dorset (☎ 0929 480536)

MACLEOD, Hon Torquil Anthony Ross; s of Baroness Macleod of Borve; *b* 20 Feb 1942; *Educ* Harrow; *m* 1967 (m dis 1973), (Elizabeth) Meriol, da of Brig Arthur Pelham Trevor, DSO (d 1984); 1 s (Iain b 1970); *Style—* The Hon Torquil Macleod

MACLEOD MATTHEWS, Alistair Francis; OBE (1970), JP (Bucks 1971); s of Capt Reginald Francis Macleod Matthews; *b* 12 April 1921; *Educ* St Paul's, Christ Church Oxford; *m* 1956, Elizabeth Marina Addenbrooke, da of Lt-Col Gordon Spencer Marston, DSO, MC, (RE), of Chalfont St Giles; 2 s; *Career* served as Lt-Col Gen Staff Med; former asst gen mangr BP; dir: Br Gas Corpn 1975-84, Volvo Petroleum UK Ltd, Leyland Bus Gp; memb: Royal Institution, Scottish Industl Devpt Bd 1972-87; companion Inst of Gas Engrs; former High Sheriff Bucks; *Recreations* shooting, fishing, historical research; *Clubs* Royal Scottish Automobile; *Style—* Alistair Macleod Matthews, Esq, OBE, JP; 29 Carlisle Place, London SW1 (☎ 01 828 2032); Achnacarnin, Culkein, Sutherland (☎ 057 15 262); The Manor House, Chenies, Herts (☎ 02 404 2888)

MACLEOD OF BORVE, Baroness (Life Peeress UK 1971); Evelyn Hester; *née* Blois; JP (Middx 1955), DL (Gtr London 1977); da of Rev Gervase Vanneck Blois (d 1961, yst s of Sir John Blois, 8 Bt, DL) and Hon Hester Pakington, da of 3 Baron Hampton; *b* 19 Feb 1915; *Educ* Lawnside Gt Malvern; *m* 1, 1937, Mervyn (ka 1940), s of Alwyne Humfrey-Mason, JP, formerly of Foxley Manor Malmesbury and Necton Hall Norfolk; m 2, 1941, Rt Hon Iain Macleod, PC, MP (d 1970), s of Dr Norman Macleod, of Isle of Lewis; 1 s, 1 da; *Career* sits as Cons in House of Lords; memb IBA 1972-76; chm: Nat Gas Consumers Cncl 1972-77, Nat Assoc League of Hosp Friends 1976-85 (pres 1985-); memb Parole Bd 1977-81, govr Queenswood Sch 1977-85, pres Nat Assoc of Wids 1976-, co-fndr and pres of charity of single homeless Crisis at Christmas, tstee Attle Meml Fndn 1980-; *Recreations* family, music, conservation; *Style—* The Rt Hon the Lady Macleod of Borve, JP, DL; Luckings Farm, Coleshill, Amersham, Bucks (☎ 024 03 5158)

MacLEOD OF FUINARY, Baron (Life Peer UK 1967); Sir George Fielden MacLeod; 4 Bt (UK 1924), MC (1917); 2 s of Sir John MacLeod, 1 Bt, JP, DL, sometime MP Glasgow Centl and Glasgow Kelvingrove (d 1934), and Edith Fielden, of Nutfield; suc n, 3 Bt, 1944; *b* 17 June 1895; *Educ* Winchester, Oriel Coll Oxford (BA), DD Edinburgh Univ; *m* 1948, Lorna Helen Janet (d 1984), da of Rev Donald MacLeod, of Balvonie of Inshes, Inverness; 2 s, 1 da; *Heir* (to Btcy only) s, Hon John Maxwell Norman MacLeod; *Career* serv WWI, Capt 1917; min of St Cuthbert's Edinburgh 1926-30 and of Govan Old Parish Church 1930-38, ldr of Iona Community 1938-67; select preacher Cambridge Univ 1943 and 1963; chaplain to HM The Queen in Scotland 1956-65, extra chaplain 1965-; moderator of Gen Assembly Church of Scotland 1957-58; *Clubs* New (Edinburgh); *Style—* The Very Rev Lord MacLeod of Fuinary, MC; 23 Learmonth Terrace, Edinburgh EH4 1PG (☎ (031 332) 3262)

MacLEOD OF GLENDALE, Donald Alexander; er s of Col Colin Sherwin MacLeod of Glendale, OBE, TD (d 1977), of Kilchearan, South Oswald Rd, Edinburgh, and Margaret Drysdale Robertson, *née* Campbell (d 1987); head of a cadet branch descended from Iain Borb MacLeod, 6 Chief of MacLeod (d ca 1442), which acquired Glendale in the 17 cent (*see* Burke's Landed Gentry, 18 edn, vol I, 1965); *b* 23 Jan 1938; *Educ* Edinburgh Acad, Pembroke Coll Cambridge (BA); *m* 10 Dec 1963, Rosemary Lilian Abel, da of Abel Edward Randle (d 1951), of Gnosall, Shropshire; 2 s (Rory b 1965, Alasdair b 1971), 2 da (Katrina b 1967, Fiona b 1970); *Career* 2 Lt Queen's Own Cameron Highlanders 1956-58; entered FO 1961, Br Embassy Rangoon 1962-66, Cwlth Off (priv sec to Miny of State) 1966-69, 1 sec Br High Cmmn Ottawa 1969-73, FCO 1973-78, head of chancery Br Embassy Bucharest 1978-81, commercial cnsllr Br High Cmmn Singapore 1981-84, dep high cmmr Br High Cmmn Barbados 1984-87, head of protocol dept, FCO 1987-; *Recreations* hill-walking; *Clubs* Utd Oxford and Cambridge Univ; *Style—* Donald MacLeod of Glendale; Kinloch Follart, by Dunvegan, Isle of Skye IV55 8WQ

MacLEOD of MacLEOD, John; s of Capt Robert Wolrige-Gordon, MC; suc grandmother Dame Flora MacLeod of MacLeod, DBE, 1976, as Chief of Clan MacLeod; *b* 10 August 1935; *Educ* Eton; *m* 1, 1961, Drusilla Mary, da of Sebastian Shaw, actor; m 2, 1973, Melita, da of Duko Kolin, of Sofia, Bulgaria; 1 s (Hugh b 1973), 1 da (Elena b 1977); *Heir* s, Hugh Magnus b 1973; officially recognised in the name of MacLeod of MacLeod, Yr, by decree of Lyon Ct 1951; officially recognised in the name of Macleod of MacLeod, Yr, by decree of Lyon Court 1951; *Style—* John MacLeod of MacLeod; Dunvegan Castle, Isle of Skye

McLEOD-BAIKIE, Ian; s of David George McLeod-Baikie (d 1963), and Winifred May, *née* McNicol; *b* 13 Dec 1921; *Educ* Perth Acad, Univ of Glasgow (LRCP, LRFPS), Univ of Edinburgh (LRCS); *m* 27 Aug 1949, Sylvia Rosemary, da of John Smith, MBE (d 1978), of Lancs; *Career* conslt orthopaedic surgn, ret 1984; hon conslt surgn St Anthony's Hosp N Cheam Surrey and Holy Cross Hosp Haslemere Surrey; chm Pembs Branch Cncl for Protection of Rural Wales; *Recreations* gardening, sailing, photography, history; *Clubs* Naval; *Style—* Ian McLeod-Baikie, Esq; The Forge, Landshipping, nr Norberth, Pembrokeshire SA67 8BG (☎ 083485 279)

MacLEOD-SMITH, Alastair MacLeod; CMG (1956); s of Robert Arthur Smith (d 1950), and Catherin Ethel Welsh, *née* Kellner (d 1977); *b* 30 June 1916; *Educ* Wells House Malvern Wells, Ellesmere Coll Salop, Queens' Coll Oxford (BA); *m* 18 Aug 1945, Ann, da of George Francis Langdale Circuitt (d 1966); 1 s (Geoffrey Langdale b 1953), 1 da (Catherine Amanda Gilbert b 1955); *Career* Colonial Admin Serv; Nigeria 1939-49, econ and fin advsr Windward Islands 1949-52, fin sec Western Pacific High Cmmn 1952-57, fin sec Sierra Leone 1957-61; joined Selection Tst 1961 (dir 1975-80), ret, conslt Nat Westminster Bank 1980-82; *Recreations* golf; *Clubs* Utd Oxford and Cambridge Univs, Knole Park GC (Sevenoaks); *Style—* Alastair MacLeod-Smith, Esq, CMG; Roughetts Lodge, Coldharbour Lane, Hildenborough, Kent TN11 9JX (☎ 0732 833239)

McLINTOCK, (Charles) Alan; s of Charles Henry McLintock (d 1947), and Charlotte Alison, *née* Allan (d 1971); *b* 28 May 1925; *Educ* Rugby; *m* 1955, Sylvia Mary, da of George Foster Taylor (d 1968); 1 s, 3 da; *Career* chartered accountant; sr ptnr K M G Thomson McLintock 1982-87 (ptnr 1954-87); chm: Woolwich Equitable Bldg Soc,

Ecclesiastical Insur Off plc; Govett Atlantic Investmt Tst plc, Govett Oriental Investmt Tst plc, Govett Strategic Investmt Tst plc, dir: Nat West Bank plc, M & G Gp plc; chm governing body Rugby Sch 1988- (vice-chm 1984-88, memb 1973); memb court London Univ 1987-; *Recreations* music, family life; *Clubs* Army and Navy; *Style—* Alan McLintock, Esq; The Manor House, Westhall Hill, Burford, Oxon (☎ 099 382 2276); 74/78 Finsbury Pavement, London EC2A 1JD (☎ 01 236 8000)

McLINTOCK, Hon Mrs (Carla Ann); da of Adm of the Fleet Baron Hill-Norton, GCB (Life Peer); *b* 14 Nov 1943; *Educ* St Mary's Sch Calne; *m* 1, 1966, Christopher Thomas Jowett; 2 s; m 2, 1974, Thomson Graeme McLintock, MBE, s of Charles Henry McLintock, OBE (d 1946); *Style—* The Hon Mrs McLintock; Old Beith House, Milland, Liphook, Hampshire (☎ 042876 589)

McLINTOCK, Jean, Lady; Jean; da of late Robert Traven Donaldson Aitken, of Newcastle, New Brunswick, Canada; *m* 1929, Sir Thomson McLintock, 2 Bt (d 1953); *Style—* Jean, Lady McLintock; c/o Peter T. McLintock, Esq, Springfield, Penicuik, Midlothian

MCLINTOCK, Sir Michael William; 4 Bt (UK 1934), of Sanquhar, Co Dumfries; s of Sir William Traven McLintock, 3 Bt (d 1987); *b* 13 August 1958; *Style—* Sir Michael McLintock, Bt; 8 Grove Place, Dixons Hill Rd, Welham Green, Herts AL9 7DG

McLOUGHLIN, Donald; OBE (1977); s of James Archibald McLoughlin (d 1951); *b* 13 Mar 1926; *Educ* Perth Modern Sch W Aust, Univ of W Aust; *m* 1960, Elizabeth Anne, da Philip Charles Hagan; 1 s (decd), 7 da; *Career* Flt Lt RAAF Aust and Pacific Ocean; private legal practice W A 1951-56; magistrate Fiji 1956-63; slr-gen Fiji 1963-71; legal conslt: Papua New Guinea 1972-75, Fiji 1971-80; legal advsr to Govt of Pitcairn Island Colony 1964-80, fisheries advsr 1980; *Recreations* swimming, fishing, boating; *Clubs* Swan Yacht (Fremantle WA); *Style—* Donald McLoughlin, Esq, OBE; 8 James Rd, Swanbourne, W Australia 6010 (☎ 09 384 7042)

McLURE, Donald Niven Allen; s of Alexander McLure (d 1934), and Helen Russell McLure; *b* 20 Mar 1926; *Educ* Dollar Acad, Brasenose Coll Oxford (MA); *m* 1956, Rosemary, da of James E Mardon (d 1973); 4 da; *Career* Capt RA (attached Indian Mountain Artillery) India 1943-47; dir: Beecham Gp plc 1957-86, London Buses Ltd 1986-, United Distillers plc 1987-; dep chm Wessex Water Authy 1986-; chm: Arthur Bell and Sons plc 1986-, Int Laboratories Ltd 1987; memb: Gen Advsy Cncl of Independent Broadcasting Authy 1986-, Cncl of Inc Soc of Br Advertisers 1976- (former pres); vice-pres Propriety Assoc of GB 1981-; FInstM; *Clubs* Lansdowne; *Style—* Donald McLure, Esq; Woodpeckers, Alleyns Lane, Cookham Dean, Berks SL6 9AD;

MACLURE, Elspeth, Lady; Elspeth King; da of Alexander King Clark (d 1918), of Wykeham Hatch, W Byfleet, and Katharine Margaret Elizabeth Mainwaring, *née* Knocker (d 1927); *b* 31 Jan 1908; *Educ* Versailles France; *m* 1929, Sir John Maclure, 3 Bt, OBE (d 1980), s of Col Sir John Edward Stanely Maclure, 2 Bt (d 1938); 2 s (Sir John Maclure, 4 Bt, Patrick Maclure), 1 da (Mrs (Elspeth) Michael Matthews); *Style—* Elspeth, Lady Maclure; Flat 2, 25 Christchurch Rd, Winchester, Hants SO23 9SU (☎ 0962 54147)

MACLURE, John Mark; s and h of Sir John Robert Spencer Maclure, 4 Bt, and Jane Monica, *née* Savage; *b* 27 August 1965; *Educ* Winchester; *Career* stockbroker; *Recreations* cricket, soccer, tennis, squash, shooting, swimming; *Clubs* Lansdowne, Berkeley Square Cottons, London Bridge City; *Style—* John Maclure, Esq; 205 Queenstown Rd, Battersea, London SW8; Croftinloan, Pitlochry, Perthshire; Wild Goose Cottage, Gooseham, Morwenstow, Bude, N Cornwall (office ☎ 01 638 4010)

MACLURE, Sir John Robert Spencer; 4 Bt (UK 1898), of The Home, Whalley Range, nr Manchester, Co Palatine of Lancaster; s of Lt-Col Sir John Maclure, 3 Bt, OBE (d 1980), and Elspeth, Lady Maclure, *qv*; *see also* Maj-Gen Michael Matthews; *b* 25 Mar 1934; *Educ* Winchester; *m* 26 Aug 1964, Jane Monica, da of late Rt Rev Thomas Savage, Bishop of Zululand and Swaziland; 4 s; *Heir* s, John Mark Maclure b 27 Aug 1965; *Career* 2 Lt KRRC 2 Bn, BAOR 1953-55, Lt Royal Hants Airborne Regt TA; asst master Horris Hill 1955-66 and 1974-78; teacher: NZ 1967-70, St Edmund's Hindhead 1971-74; headmaster Croftinloan Sch 1978-; DIP IAPS; *Clubs* MCC, Royal and Ancient Golf; *Style—* Sir John Maclure, Bt; Croftinloan School, Pitlochry, Perthshire (☎ 0796 2057); Wild Goose Cottage, Gooseham, Morwenstow, Bude, N Cornwall

MACLURE, (John) Stuart; CBE (1982); s of Hugh Seton Maclure (d 1967), of Highgate, London, N6, and Berth Lea, *née* Hodge (d 1948); *b* 8 August 1926; *Educ* Highgate Sch, Christs Coll Cambridge (MA); *m* 8 Sept 1951, (Constance) Mary, da of Alfred Ernest Butler, of Fulbrook, Burford, Oxon (d 1962); 1 s (Michael b 1952), 2 da (Mary b 1957, Clare b 1962); *Career* Sub Lt RNVR 1946-47; ed trainee The Times 1950, reporter The Times Educnl Supplement 1951-54; ed; Education 1954-69, The Times Educnl Supplement 1969-; hon fell: Sheffield Poly, Coll of Preceptors; FRSA; *Books* Educational Documents England and Wales 1816 to present day (ed 1965-86), A Hundred Years of London Education (1970), Educational Development and School Building 1945-1973 (1984), Education Re-Formed (1988); *Recreations* golf, bridge; *Clubs* MCC; *Style—* Stuart Maclure, Esq, CBE; 109 College Rd, Dulwich, London SE21 7HN (☎ 01 693 3286); The Times Educational Supplement, Priory Hse, St John's La, London EC1M 4BX (☎ 01 253 3000, fax 01 608 1599, telex 24460)

McLUSKEY, Andrew Herbert; s of Very Rev James Fraser McLuskey (Moderator of Church of Scotland 1983-84), and Irene Calaminus (d 1959); *b* 26 Sept 1947; *Educ* Broughty Ferry Eastern Sch, Glasgow Acad, Latymer Upper Sch, Univ of East Anglia (BA hons); *m* 1 April 1972, Rosemary, da of Andrew Murphy (d 1980); 1 s (Howard b 1977), 1 da (Emily b 1975); *Career* lectr; Hastings Coll of Further Educn 1971-73, Harrow Coll of Further Educn 1973-75; teacher: Berufsbildende Schule Burgsteinfurt, W Germany 1976-77, St Aldate's Coll 1978-82; lectr in history Reading Coll of Technol 1982-88; chm W Reading SDP 1984-85, ctee memb Limehouse Gp (SDP) 1984-88; theological student Mansfield Coll Oxford (studying for miny of United Reform Church) 1988-; *Recreations* rowing, choral singing; *Clubs* Wallingford Rowing; *Style—* Andrew McLuskey, Esq; 124 The Meadway, Reading RG3 4AL (☎ 0734 421707); Reading College of Technology, Kings Rd, Reading (☎ 0734 583501)

McMAHON, Andrew; s of Andrew and Margaret McMahon; *b* 1920; *Educ* Dist Sch Govan; *m* 1944; 1 s, 1 da; *Career* boilermaker; MP (Lab) Glasgow Govan 1979-83; memb Glasgow Dist Cncl 1973-79; chm Scottish Arab Friendship Assoc, Br-Iraqi Friendship Assoc; *Recreations* youth work, care and comfort for elderly; *Style—* Andrew McMahon, Esq; 21 Morefield Road, Govan, Glasgow G51 4NG

McMAHON, Sir Brian Patrick; 8 Bt (UK 1817); s of Sir (William) Patrick McMahon, 7 Bt (d 1977); *b* 9 June 1942; *Educ* Wellington, Wednesbury Tech Coll (BSc); *m* 1981, Kathleen Joan, da of late William Hopwood; *Heir* bro, Shaun Desmond McMahon; *Career* AIM; *Style—* Sir Brian McMahon, Bt; 157B Wokingham Road, Reading, Berks RG6 1LP

MACMAHON, Brian Sean; s of Gerard MacMahon (d 1962), of Dublin, and Mary, *née* Coughlan; *b* 3 April 1938; *Educ* Terenure Coll Dublin; *m* 1, 18 Sept 1961 (m dis 1977), Una Mary, da of Bernard Egan (d 1953), of Dublin; 2 s (Gerard b 1965, Cormac b 1967), 2 da (Cara b 1962, Niamh b 1964); m 2, 17 Dec 1983, Colleen Jean, da of Harry Harbottle, of Bristol; *Career* Irish Pensions Tst Dublin 1955-72, pension fund mangr Allied-Lyons Pension Fund 1973-82, gp pensions exec BET plc 1982-; memb cncl Pensions Mgmnt Inst 1981-85, vice chm Nat Assoc of Pension Funds 1989 (cncl memb 1983-); *Recreations* golf, cricket, theatre; *Clubs* Bristol and Clifton GC; *Style—* Brian MacMahon, Esq; BET plc, Stratton House, Piccadilly, London W1X 6AS (☎ 01 629 8886, fax 01 499 5118, telex 299573 BETCL G)

McMAHON, Sir Christopher William; *b* 10 July 1927; *Educ* Melbourne GS, Univ of Melbourne, Magdalen Coll Oxford; *m* 1, 1956, Marion Kelso; 2 s; m 2, 1982, Alison Braimbridge; *Career* fell and economics tutor Magdalen Coll Oxford 1960-64; Bank of England: advsr 1964, advsr to the govrs 1966-70, exec dir 1970-80, dep govr 1980-; kt 1986; *Style—* Sir Christopher McMahon; Bank of England, Threadneedle St, London EC2 (☎ 01 601 4444)

McMAHON, Shaun Desmond; s of Sir (William) Patrick McMahon, 7 Bt (d 1977); h to Btcy of bro, Sir Brian Patrick McMahon, 8 Bt; *b* 29 Oct 1945; *Educ* Wellington Coll; *m* 1971, Antonia Noel, da of Antony James Adie, of Rowington, Warwicks; *Style—* Shaun McMahon Esq; 28 Mathew Rd, Claremont, Cape Town, S Africa

McMAHON, Rt Hon Sir William; GCMG (1977), CH (1972), PC (1966); s of William Daniel McMahon; *b* 23 Feb 1908; *Educ* Sydney GS, St Paul's Coll, Sydney Univ Australia (BEc, LLB); *m* 1965, Sonia Rachel Hopkins; 1 s, 2 da; *Career* served WWII Aust Army Lt 1 Inf Bn; slr Allen Allen & Hemsley; MHR (Lib) for Lowe NSW Aust 1949-82, min for Navy and Air 1951-54, min for Social Servs 1954-56, acting min for Trade 1956, actg min in Charge CSIRO 1956, min for Primary Indust 1956-58, actg min for Labour and Nat Serv 1958-66, actg min for Nat Dvpt 1959, actg min for Territories 1961, acting attorney gen 1960-61, tres Cwlth of Aust 1966-69, min for External Affairs 1969-71, prime minister of Australia 1971-72; memb bd of govrs IMF and World Bank 1966-69, chm bd of govrs Asian Dvpt Bank 1968-69, led Aust delegations to Bangkok, Djarkarta, Wellington, Tokyo, Manila and Saigon 1970, attended Cwlth Prime Ministers' Conference Singapore 1971; *Recreations* squash, swimming; *Clubs* Australian, AJC, Melbourne, Union; *Style—* The Rt Hon Sir William McMahon, GCMG, CH, PC; 100 William St, Sydney, NSW 2011, Australia

MacMANAWAY, Maj (James) Peter Alexander; ERD (1943); s of Lt-Col Richard Thomas Ringwood MacManaway, OBE (d 1945), of 7 Warren Fields, Stanmore, Middx; and Zelma Norah Kathleen MacManaway (d 1985); *b* 26 Dec 1919; *Educ* Imperial Service Coll Windsor (now rejoined with Haileybury); *m* 3 Nov 1945, Joyce, da of Harold Tout Tilley (d 1940), of Haileybury, Purley Way, Purley, Surrey; 2 da (Rosemary b 30 Oct 1948, Heather b 18 March 1950); *Career* serv: BEF in France and Belgium, Dunkirk 1939-40, UK Counter Invasion Duties 1940-42, 1 Army N Africa, Italy and Austria 1942-48, UK 1948-50, Korea 1950-52, BAOR Germany 1952-55, Suez Operation 1956, UK 1957-59; Supplementary Cmmn 1938-44, Reg Cmmn 1944, promoted Major 1945; area mangr Planned Giving Ltd 1959-64, dir Jt Anglican Missionary Exhibition (Task 6) 1964-68, mktg Fnd purchasing offr Nat Westminster Bank 1968-80, fin offr Trident Tst 1980-81, The Duke of Edinburgh's Award Int Head Office 1981-85; memb Dunkirk Veterans Assoc; Freeman City of London 1982, Liveryman Worshipful Co of Carmen 1982; King Leopold III; *Recreations* bowls & snooker; *Clubs* City Livery, Sion Coll (London), Drive Bowls (Hove), Past Rotarians (Hove & Brighton); *Style—* Maj Peter MacManaway, ERD; 16 St Aubyns, Hove, E Sussex BN3 2TB (☎ 0273 29 289)

McMANNERS, Prof the Rev John; s of Rev Canon Joseph McManners (d 1975), and Ann Marshall (d 1979); *b* 25 Dec 1916; *Educ* Univ of Oxford (BA), Univ of Durham (Dip Theol) Univ of Oxford (D Litt); *m* 27 Dec 1951, Sarah Carruthers, da of George Errington (d 1956); 2 s (Joseph Hugh b 9 Dec 1952, Peter John b 9 June 1958), 2 da (Helen b 28 Feb 1953, Ann b 22 June 1961); *Career* WWII 2 Lt Royal Northumberland Fusiliers 1940; First Bn Royal Northumberland Fusiliers: platoon cdr, co second in cmd, adjutant; Maj GSO II 210 Br Liaison Unit (Greek Mission) 1943; fell and chaplain St Edmund Hall Oxford 1948-56, prof hist Univ of Tasmania 1956-59, prof European history Univ of Sydney 1959-66, professorial fell All Souls Coll Oxford 1965-66, prof of history Univ of Leicester 1967-72, Regius Prof of ecclesiastical history and Canon of Christchurch Univ of Oxford 1972-84, fell and chaplain All Souls Coll Oxford 1984-, directeur d'Études associé École Pratique des Hautes Études Paris 1980-81; Wolfson Literary Prize 1981; tstee Nat Portrait Gallery 1970-78, Doctrine Commn of C of E 1978-82; Univ of Durham (D Litt 1984); Fell Aust Acad of Humanities 1970, FRHistS 1971, FBA 1978; Offr of the Royal Order of King George of the Hellenes; *Books* French Ecclesiastical Society under the Ancien Regime: a Study of Angers (1960), Lectures on European History 1789-1914: Men, Machines and Freedom (1966), The French Revolution and the Church (1969), Church and State in France 1870-1914 (1972), Death and The Enlightenment (1981); *Recreations* tennis; *Style—* Prof the Rev John McManners; All Souls College, Oxford OX1 4AL (☎ 0865 279 368)

MacMANUS, His Hon Judge; John Leslie Edward; QC (1976), TD (1945); s of Edward Herbert MacManus (d 1979), of Hove, and Hilda Smith, *née* Colton (d 1962); *b* 7 April 1920; *Educ* Eastbourne Coll; *m* 18 July 1942, Gertrude Mary Frances (Trudy), da of Bernard Koppenhagen (d 1952); 2 da (Frances Mary Theresa b 6 July 1950, Georgina Anne b 6 Oct 1956); *Career* TA 1939, RA 1939-45, served M East, Italy, Crete, Yugoslavia, Maj 1945, called to bar Middle Temple 1947, dep chm E Sussex QS Sessions 1965- 71; county ct judge 1971, circuit judge 1972; *Recreations* gardening, travel; *Style—* His Hon Judge Leslie MacManus, TD, QC; c/o Circuit Administrator, South Eastern Circuit, 18 Maltravers St, London WC2R 3EU

McMANUS, Richard Brian; s of Michael Mansley McManus (d 1982), and Margaret, *née* Davison; *b* 15 Mar 1956; *Educ* Huddersfield New Coll, Jesus Coll Oxford (BA); *m* 9 Sept 1978 (m dis 1983), Susan Mary; *Career* mgmnt conslt: Proctor & Gamble 1977-80 (mktg), Johnson & Johnson 1980-82 (business devpt), INSEAD 1982-83 (MBA), BCG 1984-86; md: First Res 1987-; First Europe 1988-; *Recreations* skiing, cycling, theatre, travelling; *Clubs* Beaujolais; *Style—* Richard McManus, Esq; 44 Upham Pk Rd, Chiswick (☎ 01 994 1980); business: (☎ 01 747 4054, fax 01 747

3969)

McMASTER, (Thomas) Brown; s of Thomas McMaster, of Newlands, Glasgow, and Isabella Hastings, *née* Cameron; *b* 24 Feb 1949; *Educ* Hillhead HS Glasgow; *m* 28 June 1972, Jean Darroch, da of Joseph Darroch Barrett, of Kilbarchan, Renfrewshire; 3 s (Thomas Craig b 1973, Scott Cameron b 1975, John Barrett b 1978), 1 da (Jill Brown b 1985); *Career* md Thomas McMaster & Son Ltd 1974; chm Scottish Region Nat Fed of Roofing Contractors 1986-87; pres: Glasgow and West of Scotland Master Slaters Assoc 1978-79, Slate Trade Benevolent Assoc 1979, Newlands Lawn Tennis Club 1979-88; FIOR; *Recreations* tennis, golf; *Clubs* Newlands Lawn Tennis, Pollok Golf; *Style—* Brown McMaster, Esq; Hatton House, 50 Langside Drive, Newlands, Glasgow G43 2QT; 23 Crow Road, Partick, Glasgow G11 7RU (☎ 041 339 7272)

McMASTER, Hughan James Michael; s of William James Michael McMaster (d 1976), and Emily *née* Hacquoil; *b* 27 July 1927; *Educ* Christ's Coll Finchley, Regent St Poly (Dip in Architecture); *m* (m dis); 1 s (Malcolm b 1961), 2 da (Jean b 1954, Celia b 1959); *Career* served in RAF as electrician, India and Far East 1946-48; architect; T P Bennet & Son 1951-55, Gollins Melvin Ward & Ptnrs 1955-61; joined Civil Serv: Navy Works Dept 1961-69, Whitehall Devpt Gp, dir home est mgmnt and directorate of civil accommodation 1969-76, def works (procurement exec and overseas 1976-80), chief architect and dir of works of the Home Off 1980-87; ret 1987; ARIBA 1951, FRSA 1988; *Recreations* skiing, mountaineering, swimming, music; *Style—* Hughan McMaster, Esq; 104 Breton House, Barbican, London EC2Y 8DQ

McMICHAEL, Prof Andrew James; s of Sir John McMichael, of 2 North Square, London, and Sybil Eleanor, *née* Blake (d 1965); *b* 8 Nov 1943; *Educ* St Paul's, Gonville and Caius Coll Cambridge (BA, MA), St Mary's Hosp Medical School (MB, B Chir); *m* 12 Oct 1968, Kathryn Elizabeth, da of Capt Alexander Alfred Cross, MBE, of The Old Smithy Cottage, Whittonditch, Ramsbury, Wiltshire; 2 s (Hamish b 1973, Robert b 1982), 1 da (Fiona b 1971); *Career* MRC clinical res prof of immunology Nuffield Dept of Medicine Univ of Oxford 1982- (Wellcome sr fell in clinical science 1977-79, lectr 1979-82), Fell Trinity Coll Oxford 1982-; memb: Scientific ctee Cancer Res Campaign 1986-88, systems bd MRC 1987-, AIDS steering ctee MRC 1988-; FRCP 1985; *Books* Monoclonal Antibodies in Clinical Medicine (ed 1981), Leucocyte Typing III, White Cell Differentiation Antigens (ed 1987); *Recreations* windsurfing, walking, reading; *Style—* Prof Andrew McMichael; Institute of Molecular Medicine, John Radcliffe Hospital, Oxford (☎ 0865 752336)

McMICHAEL, Sir John; s of James McMichael (d 1933), and Margaret, *née* Sproat; *b* 25 July 1904; *Educ* Kirkcudbright Acad, Edinburgh Univ (MD); *m* 1, 1942, Sybil Eleanor (d 1965), da of Francis Blake; 4 s; m 2, 1965, Dr Sheila M Howarth, wid of Prof E P Sharpey-Schafer; *Career* emeritus prof of Med London Univ; served on: MRC 1949-53, Wellcome Tst 1960-77, Univ Grants Med Advsy Ctee 1964-72; dir Br Post-Graduate Med Fedn 1966-71; chm cncl Br Heart Fndn 1966-72; pres World Congress of Cardiology 1970; FRS, FRCP, FRCPE; kt 1965; *Style—* Sir John McMichael; 2 North Sq, London NW11 7AA (☎ 01 455 8731)

McMICHAEL, Hon Dr (Paquita Mary Joanna); *née* Florey; da of Baron Florey (Life Peer) (d 1968); *b* 26 Sept 1929; *m* 1955, John McMichael, s of Dr Gerald Joseph Wylde McMichael (d 1958), of 255 Woodstock Rd, Oxford, and Farchynys Fach, Bontddu, Merioneth; 2 s (1 decd); *Style—* The Hon Dr McMichael; 12 Craigleith Gdns, Edinburgh EH4 3JW

MCMICHAEL-PHILLIPS, William James; s of William James Phillips (d 1982), of Edinburgh, and Mary Jane, *née* Sneddon (d 1983); *b* 17 Mar 1934; *Educ* George Heriot's Sch Edinburgh; *m* 1, 12 Aug 1957, Fleming (d 1981), da of James Mckinel McMichael (d 1982), of Lochmaben Dumfriesshire; 2 s (Scott b 1961, d 1961, James b 1962), 1 da (Danielle b 1966); m 2, 4 Oct 1982, Laura Teresa, da of Valtiero Bertonesi, of La Spezia, Italy; *Career* cmmnd 2 Lt RA 1952-54, cmmnd Lt RA (TA) 1954-57; dir 1969-72: John Newbould & Son Ltd Bradford, Arthur Davy & Son Ltd Sheffield, Sunblest Bakeries Ltd Sheffield; regnl gen mangr Associated Dairies Ltd Leeds 1972-78; currently dir: Sorbie Cheese Co Ltd (chm 1981-82, 1985-86), Assoc Co-op Dairies Ltd, Southern Co-op Dairies Ltd, United Co-op Dairies Ltd; gp gen mangr Milk Gp Co-op Wholesale Soc Ltd, chm English Butter Mktg Co Ltd (vice-chm 1982-88); vice pres EEC Advsy Ctee on Milk and Milk Products 1982-, memb Economic Ctee for Food and Drink Manufacturing Indust 1985-(chm sector working gp milk and milk products 1985-), pres Dairy Trade Fedn 1987-89 (vice pres 1982-87); MCIM 1960; *Recreations* badminton, reluctant gardener; *Style—* James McMichael-Phillips, Esq; Co-Operative Wholesale Soc Ltd, Milk Group, PO Box 53, New Century House, Manchester M60 4ES (☎ 061 834 1212, fax 061 832 0430, telex 667046)

MACMILLAN, Hon Adam Julian Robert; s of Viscount Macmillan of Ovenden (Rt Hon Maurice Macmillan, d 1984), and Katharine, Viscountess Macmillan of Ovenden, *qv*; *b* 21 April 1948; *Educ* Eton, Univ of Strasbourg; *m* 1982, Sarah Anne Mhuire, yr da of late Dr Brian MacGreevy, of London; 2 da (Sophia Elizabeth Katherine b 1985, Alice Charlotte Rose b 1987); *Style—* The Hon Adam Macmillan

McMILLAN, Alan Austen; CB (1986); s of Allan McMillan (d 1967), and Nellie Mabel, *née* Austin (d 1983); *b* 19 Jan 1926; *Educ* Ayr Acad, Glasgow Univ; *m* 25 June 1949, Margaret Forbes Park, da of Malcolm Moncur (d 1957); 2 s (Alan b 1953, Malcolm b 1955), 2 da (Fiona b 1959, Alison b 1963); *Career* WWII serv 52 Div 4/5 RSF Western Front 1944-45, Sgt instr RAEC 1946-47; admitted slr 1950, slr to Sec of State for Scotland 1955-87, div slr 1968, seconded to Cabinet Off Constitution Unit 1977-78, dep slr 1982, slr to Sec of State for Scotland and to HM Treasy in Scotland 1984-87, ret 1987; *Recreations* hill walking, reading, music, theatre; *Style—* Alan McMillan Esq, CB; 28A Polwarth Terr, Edinburgh (☎ 031 337 1451)

MACMILLAN, Alexander Ross; s of Donald Macmillan (d 1975), and Johanna, *née* Ross (d 1973); *b* 23 Mar 1922; *Educ* Tain Royal Acad; *m* 17 June 1961, Ursula Miriam, da of Edwin Grayson (d 1975); 2 s (David b 1964, Niall b 1966), 1 da (Alexandra b 1962); *Career* WWII Corpl RAF 1942-46, (despatches 1945); banker 1938-87; chief gen mangr Clydesdale Bank plc 1971-82, (dir 1974-87); dir: Caledonian Applied Technol plc 1982-87, Highland North Sea Ltd 1982-, Highland Deephaven 1982-, John Laing plc 1982-86, Radio Clyde plc 1982-, Scottish Devpt Fin Ltd 1982-, Martin Black plc 1983-85, Kelvin Technol Devpt 1984-, First Northern Corporate Fin Ltd 1983-87, Wilsons Garage Co (Argyll) Ltd 1987-, Wilsons Fuels Ltd 1987-, EFT Gp plc 1987-, Balmoral Gp Ltd 1988-; chm Nat House Building Cncl (Scotland) 1982-1988; dir High Sch of Glasgow 1979-; memb Court Univ of Glasgow 1980-; *Recreations* golf; *Clubs* Killermont Glasgow; *Style—* Alexander Macmillan, Esq; 16 Ledcameroch Rd, Bearsden, Glasgow G61 4AB (☎ 041 942 6455, 041 943 0606)

McMILLAN, (William) Bill; s of Edward McMillan (d 1975), of Lanarkshire, and Agnes Conway (d 1979); *b* 11 Jan 1929; *Educ* Ayr Acad, Royal Tech Coll, Glasgow Univ; *m* 1, 26 Aug 1950 (m dis), Sheila Hallett; 2 s (Ian William b 1955, Neil David b 1960); m 2, Moira, da of Austin Damer; 1 da (Hannah Kathy b 30 Nov 1988); *Career* joined Standard Telephones & Cables (ITT) 1955 as researcher (press relations mangr), PR mangr Br Standards Inst 1963-65, princ scientific offr Miny of Technol 1965-68, mangr public affairs Assoc of Br Pharmaceutical Indust; dir of information: Chemical Indust Assoc 1973-83, UK Atomic Energy Authy 1983-88; sec gen Assoc Européenne des Producteurs d'Acides Gras (APAG) Brussels; *Books* numerous technical articles in New Scientist and elsewhere, The Role and Place of the Chemical Industry in Europe (cmmnd by UN 1982); FRSM; *Recreations* music, skiing; *Style—* Bill McMillan, Esq; 36 Hill House Close, Turners Hill, W Sussex RH10 4YY (☎ 0342 716315); APAG, 250 Avenue Louise, Bte 111, B-1050 Bruxelles (☎ 02 648 82 90)

MACMILLAN, Hon David Maurice Benjamin; s of Viscount Macmillan of Ovenden (Rt Hon Maurice Macmillan, d 1984), and Katharine, Viscountess Macmillan of Ovenden, *qv*; *b* 1957; *Educ* Harrow; *Clubs* Brooks, Turf; *Style—* The Hon David Macmillan; Flat 3, 12 Bramham Gardens, London SW5

McMILLAN, Rev Monsignor Donald Neil; s of Daniel McMillan (d 1942), and Mary Cameron, *née* Farrell (d 1951); *b* 21 May 1925; *Educ* St Brendan's Coll Bristol, Prior Park Coll Bath, Oscott Coll Sutton Coldfield; *Career* Army Chaplain 1951-81, BAOR 1961-63, 1966-68, 1975-77, Middle East 1956-59, 1968-70, E Africa 1961, Far East 1952-55, Princ RC Chaplain and Vicar Gen (Army) MOD 1977-81; ordained priest Diocese of Clifton 1948; curate: Bath 1948-49, Gloucester 1949-51, Taunton 1951; parish priest St Augustine's Gloucester 1981-85, St Teresa's Bristol 1985-86, St Nicholas Winchcombe 1986-; Prelate of Honour 1977; *Recreations* walking, reading; *Clubs* Army and Navy, Challoner; *Style—* The Rev Monsignor Donald McMillan; St Nicholas Presbytery, Chandos St, Winchcombe, Glos GL54 5HX (☎ 0242 602412)

MACMILLAN, Sir (Alexander McGregor) Graham; s of James Orr Macmillan (d 1961), of Glasgow, and Sarah Dunsmuir, *née* Graham (d 1952); *b* 14 Sept 1920; *Educ* Hillhead HS Glasgow; *m* 1947, Christina Brash, da of Robert Brash Beveridge, of Glasgow; 2 s (Alistair b 1948, Donald b 1956), 2 da (Janie b 1950, Catriona b 1955); *Career* govr Leeds GS 1968-75, dir Scottish Cons Pty 1975-84, dir M & P Fin Servs 1984- (chm 1986 and 1988), chm Mid Anglian Enterprise Agency 1986 (govr 1987, chm 1988); memb Tport Users' Consultative Ctee for Eastern England 1987-; kt 1983; *Recreations* fishing, watching cricket and rugby; *Clubs* St Stephen's Constitutional; *Style—* Sir Graham Macmillan; 46 Crown St, Bury St Edmunds, Suffolk IP33 1QX (☎ 0284 704443)

MacMILLAN, Sir Kenneth; *b* 11 Dec 1929; *m* 1974, Deborah Williams; *Career* choreographer; former dancer Royal Ballet; princ choreographer Royal Ballet 1977-; works include Romeo and Juliet, The Song of The Earth, Manon, Elite Syncopations, Mayerling, Gloria, Isadora; kt 1983; *Style—* Sir Kenneth MacMillan; c/o Royal Opera House, Covent Garden, London WC2

MACMILLAN, Michael Muirdon; s of Donald Uilleam Macmillan (d 1981), of Castlehill, Conon Bridge, Ross-shire, Scotland, and Catherine Aird, *née* McIntosh; *b* 14 Mar 1941; *Educ* Univ of St Andrews (MA), Univ of Edinburgh (LLB); *m* 18 Sept 1965, Maureen, da of Felix Hoey (d 1983), of Oban, Argyll; 2 s (Peter Donald b 1966, Paul Felix b 1969), 2 da (Lucy Eileen b 1967, Anna Catherine b 1972); *Career* admitted as Scottish slr 1966; sr ptnr in own firm 1977- (specialising in civil and criminal ct work); lectures, tutors and broadcasts on legal topics; memb Law Soc of Scotland's Future of the Profession Ctee; joined Lab Party 1969, active at all levels in the Pty; contested (Lab) Ross, Cromarty and Skye Constituency, General Election 1987; *Recreations* talking, dry stone dyking, curling; *Clubs* Keir Hardie; *Style—* Michael Macmillan, Esq; Old Ferintosh, Drummondreach, Conon Bridge, Ross-shire (☎ 0349 87228); 87-89 High St, Alness Ross-Shire, Scotland (☎ 0349 883338)

MACMILLAN, Robert Hugh; s of Hugh Robert Munro Macmillan (d 1934), the gs of John bro of Daniel fndr of Macmillan the publishers; *b* 27 June 1921; *Educ* Felsted Sch, Emmanuel Coll Cambridge; *m* 1950, Anna Christina, da of Christian Roding, of Amsterdam (d 1935); 1 s, 2 da; *Career* Fl Lt RAF 1945; chartered engr; asst prof MIT 1950, prof of mech engrg Univ of Wales 1956, dir Motor Indust Res Assoc 1964, prof of vehicle design CIT 1977-82, dean of engrg CIT 1979-82, NADFAS lectr 1985, guide to Winslow Hall and Ascott Bucks 1985; memb univ cncl Loughborough 1965-82 and 1988-; *Books* Symmetry (1977), Vehicle collisions (1983); *Recreations* music, painting, philately; *Clubs* RAF, RAC, Royal Philatelic Soc, Royal Soc of Arts; *Style—* Robert Macmillan, Esq; Woodgate, Aspley Heath, Woburn Sands, Bucks (☎ 0908 584 011)

MACMILLAN, Roderick Alan Fitzjohn; s of John Armour Macmillan (d 1939), and Margery Babington O'Cock, *née* Hill (d 1975); *b* 2 May 1928; *Educ* Winchester, New Coll Oxford (MA); *m* 27 Sept 1952, Brenda Courtenay, da of Courtenay Walter Snook (d 1986); 2 s (Jeremy b 1957, Bruce b 1963), 1 da (Sally b 1954); *Career* RA 1946-48, 2 Lt 1947; elected memb Lloyds 1965, dir Leslie & Godwin (Underwriting) Ltd 1973-1985; active underwriter: Syndicate 80 1973-88, Syndicate 843 1977-86; dir RAF Macmillan & Co Ltd 1976-; chm Rickmansworth & West Hyde Branch Royal Br Legion 1986-; Liveryman Worshipful Co of Insurers 1982, Freeman Worshipful Co of Watermen and Lightermen 1989; ACII 1952, FIOD 1986; *Recreations* golf, rowing (Olympic Games 1952); *Clubs* City of London, Beaconsfield GC, Thames RC; *Style—* Roderick Macmillan, Esq; 14 The Readings, Chorleywood, Rickmansworth, Herts WD3 5SY; RAF Macmillan & Co Ltd, Corn Exchange Bldgs, 52/57 Mark Lane, London EC3R 7NE (☎ 01 480 6825, fax 01 702 3303)

McMILLAN, Col Thomas; TD (1946); s of Thomas McMillan (d 1971), and Sarah Whitehead, *née* McGowan (d 1951); *b* 18 June 1912; *Educ* Oundle; *m* 11 July 1936, Barbara Fitzmaurice Kendrick (d 1970); 2 da (Susan Catherine b 1939, Elizabeth Jean b 1946); *Career* mil serv RE (TA) 1932-51, WWII served BEF France, Western Desert and Italy (despatches); civil engr Tarmac Gp of Cos (dir and vice-chm) 1934-61, dir Peter Lind Ltd 1961-70; Liveryman Worshipful Co of Paviors; *Recreations* golf, travel; *Clubs* Naval and Military, Royal and Ancient Golf (St Andrews), Rye Golf, Little Aston Golf; *Style—* Col Thomas McMillan, TD

MACMILLAN, Rev William Boyd Robertson; s of Robert Macmillan (d 1953), and Annie Simpson, *née* Machattie; *b* 3 July 1927; *Educ* Royal HS Edinburgh, Univ of Aberdeen (MA, BD); *m* 22 Aug 1962, Mary Adams Bisset, da of Donald Bisset Murray (d 1974); *Career* RN 1946-48; parish min: St Andrews Bo'ness 1955-60, Fyvie 1960-67, Bearsden (South) 1967-78, St Mary's Dundee 1978-; moderator Presbytery of Dumbarton 1976-77, convenor Bd of Practice and Procedure and convenor of Assembly Arrangements C of S 1984-88, chaplain in ordinary to HM the Queen in Scotland 1988-; chaplain: Dundee DC, Guildry Incorpn of Dundee, HS of Dundee; sr chaplain Sea Cadet Corps, memb: exec cncl Scottish Veterans' Assoc, Scottish Church Soc, Church Serv Soc; *Recreations* golf, stamp collecting, reading; *Style—* The Rev William Macmillan; Manse of Dundee, 371 Blackness Rd, Dundee DD2 1ST, (☎ 0382 69406); Dundee Parish Church (St Mary's), Nethergate, Dundee DD1 4DG, (☎ 0382 26271)

MACMILLAN, William Sillars (Bill); s of William Macmillan (d 1979), of Surrey, and Marion Horne Dunlop, *née* Canning (d 1970); *b* 12 Jan 1936; *Educ* Paisley GS, Univ of Glasgow; *m* 22 Dec 1962 (m dis 1987); 2 s (David Richard b 1963, Robert William b 1965); *Career* Nat Serv RAF, Corp instr in Airborne Wireless 1956-58; Leo Computers 1958-62, Burroughs Machines 1962-64, Schweppes 1964-66, M & G Unit Tst 1966, Rank Orgn 1966-69, fndr dir and chm Macro 4 plc 1968-86; FBCS; *Books* Simply Blue (1985); *Recreations* golf, bridge, piloting light aircraft, motoring; *Style—* W S Macmillan, Esq; 13 Highwoods, Harestone Lane, Caterham-on-the-Hill, Surrey CR3 6AL (☎ 0883 40016)

MACMILLAN, Sir (James) Wilson; KBE (1976, CBE 1962, OBE 1951); *b* 1906; *m* Beatrice Woods; *Career* former min of Educn Health and Housing in Br Honduras; governing dir Macmillan Bros; pres: Br Red Cross, Boy Scout Assoc; *Style—* Sir Wilson Macmillan, KBE; 3 St Edward St, Belize City, Belize

MACMILLAN OF MACMILLAN AND KNAP, George Gordon; s of Gen Sir Gordon Holmes Alexander MacMillan, KCB, KCVO, CBE, DSO, MC (d 1986), of Finlaystone, Langbank, Renfrewshire, and Marian, *née* Blakiston-Houston, OBE; *b* 20 June 1930; *Educ* Eton, Trinity Coll Cambridge (MA), Univ of Strathclyde; *m* 2 Sept 1961, (Cecilia) Jane, da of Capt Arthur Rushworth Spurgin, IA (d 1934); 3 s (Arthur Gordon b 29 July 1962, Richard Anthony b 30 Dec 1963, d 1985, Malcolm James b 30 June 1967); *Career* teacher Wellington Coll 1953-63, lectr in religious knowledge Trinity Coll Toronto 1963-64, lectr in religious studies Bede Coll Durham 1965-74; currently self-employed and owner of small estate with historic house and garden open to the public; memb cncl of mgmnt Quarrier's Village Renfrewshire, chm Renfrew West Cons Assoc, elder Langbank Church of Scotland; *Recreations* garden-tending, making small structures; *Style—* George Macmillan of MacMillan and Knap; Finlaystone, Langbank, Renfrewshire PA14 6TJ (☎ 047 554 285)

MACMILLAN OF OVENDEN, Katherine, Viscountess of; Hon Dame Katharine Margaret Alice Macmillan; *née* Ormsby-Gore; DBE (1974); da of 4 Baron Harlech, KG, GCMG, PC (d 1964); *b* 4 Jan 1921; *m* 1942, Rt Hon Maurice Victor Macmillan, PC, MP, (Viscount Macmillan of Ovenden, d 1984), s of 1 Earl of Stockton, *qv*; 3 s (and 1 s decd), 1 da; *Career* vice-chm Cons Pty 1968-71; *Style—* Katharine, Viscountess Macmillan of Ovenden, DBE; 9 Warwick Sq, London SW1 (☎ 01 834 6004)

McMILLAN-SCOTT, Edward Hugh Christian; MEP (York (C) 1984); s of Walter Theodore Robin McMillan-Scott, and Elizabeth Maud Derrington Hudson; *b* 15 August 1949; *Educ* Blackfriars Sch Llanarth Raglan Mon, Blackfriars Sch Laxton Corby, Exeter Tech Coll; *m* 1972, Henrietta Elizabeth Rumney, da of Richard Derrington Mogridge Hudson, of Bristol Avon; 2 da (Lucinda b 1973, Arabella b 1976); *Career* tour dir in Europe, Africa, USSR 1968-75; pr exec then parly conslt 1976-84, political advsr Falkland Islands Govt London Off 1983-; *Clubs* St Stephens Constitutional; *Style—* Edward McMillan-Scott, MEP; Wick House Farm, Wick, Pershore, Worcs WR10 3NU; European Parliament, 97 Rue Belliard, Brussels 1040, Belgium (☎ 010 322 234 2438)

McMINN, Alexander (Alex); JP (Merseyside 1972); s of William Edward Blanchard McMinn, and Sara, *née* Bird; *b* 12 Dec 1932; *Educ* Liverpool Collegiate Scis, Inst of Med Laboratory Scis Liverpool Univ Centre; *m* 18 Aug 1956, Kathleen Frances, da of Arthur Rannard; 2 da (Helen b 1961, Fiona b 1964); *Career* princ lectr in med scis Liverpool Poly 1968-72; educn advsr: WHO Geneva 1972-84, UN Econ Cmmn for Europe 1984-85; exec dir Int Assoc for Med Scis 1982-88; chief exec: Health Manpower Servs Ltd 1984-88, Athena Try Int 1988-; chm Vocational Guidance Assoc UK 1985-; dir: Diagnostic Int Trg and Recruitment Ltd 1984-, Merseyside Vocational Servs 1985-, Heriot Business Servs Ltd 1987-; hon sr lectr dept of int community health Liverpool Sch of Tropical Med 1985-, conslt in health care Univ of N Carolina USA, conslt in med educn for numerous govts and int orgns 1972-, cncl memb Univ Coll of Ajman UAE 1988-, educn and trg advsr St John's Ambulance Assoc; memb: tst Merseyside Christian Youth Camps 1970-, educn and trg ctee Merseyside Chamber of Trade 1986-; FRSM, MIBiol 1964, CBiol, fell Inst of Med Laboratory Scis 1955; Medal of the Cncl of Europe; *Books* Training Medical Laboratory Technicians (1975), Design of Competency Based Curricula for Health Workers (1984); *Recreations* watersports, playing organ; *Clubs* Athenaeum (Liverpool); *Style—* Dr Alex McMinn, JP; 10 St Bedes Close, Old Mill Hill, Ormskirk, Lancs; Athena Training International, Mast House, Derby Rd, Merseyside L20 1EA (☎ 051 994 1991, 051 944 1559, car tel 0836 251351, telex 626273 HERIOT G)

McMORRAN, William George; s of Donald Hanks McMorran, RA, RIBA (d 1965), and Margaret, *née* Cox; *b* 30 April 1953; *Educ* Univ of Newcastle-upon-Tyne (BA Hons); *m* 9 Aug 1980, Janet Felicity, da of Hugh Forbes Arbuthnott, MA (d 1982); 2 s (Donald b 1983, Roland b 1985); *Career* private architect; sr ptnr William G McMorran Architects; Dip Arch, RIBA; *Style—* William McMorran, Esq; 46 Holmewood Road, London SW2 3RR (☎ 01 674 9777)

McMULLEN, Fergus John; s of John Christopher McMullen, of Westmill, nr Buntingford, Herts, and Cecily Rose, *née* Pearson-Rogers; *b* 2 Nov 1958; *Educ* Harrow RAC, Cirencester; *m* 4 Sept 1982, Clare Margaret, da of Maj Ivan Straker, of Edinburgh; 2 s (Rory James b 6 July 1985, Hugo George b 4 June 1987); *Career* sales and mktg exec The Hertford Brewery (family owned and run business); memb Br Field Sports Assoc; *Recreations* shooting, fishing, cricket, golf; *Style—* Fergus McMullen, Esq; Flint Cottage, Wendens Ambo, Saffron Walden, Essex CB11 4UL (☎ 0799 412 69); The Hertford Brewery, 26 Old Cross, Hertford, Herts (fax 0992 500 729)

McMURTRIE, (Robert) Peter (Lax); VRD; s of Donald Scott Anderson McMurtrie (d 1962), and Margaret Isobel Stratton McMurtrie (d 1962, int hockey and lacrosse player for England); *b* 24 Mar 1926; *Educ* Marlborough, St John's Coll Cambridge (MA); *m* 1953, Margaret Jane, da of Lt-Col Lancelot Edwin Lax Wright; 3 da; *Career* Lt Cdr RNVR 1943-46; dir Plantation Hldgs 1978-79, exec dir Phicom Ltd 1979-82 (non-exec dir 1982-87); md: Fractional HP Motors Ltd 1964-67, Hills (Patents) Ltd 1967-74, Southern Instrument Hldgs 1974-76, Consumer & Video Hldgs Ltd 1976-78; chm: Imhof-Bedco Standard Products Ltd, Imhof-Bedco Special Products Ltd 1976-82, I-B Precision Engrg Ltd 1978-82, Skinners (Electro-Platers) Ltd 1978-82, I-B Gerard SA (France) 1978-82; chm and chief exec offr: Elbar Indust plc 1983-85, Viewplan plc 1987-88; non-exec dir Intergrad 1983-88, non-exec chm Scientese Ltd 1986-87; lay memb Slrs Disciplinary Tbnl Law Soc 1986-, dir Christian Children's Fund of GB 1987-; *Recreations* shooting, gardening, countryside; *Clubs* Naval; *Style—* R P L McMurtrie, Esq, VRD; St Ibbs Bush, nr Hitchin, Herts (☎ 0462 32146)

McMURTRIE, Gp Capt Richard Angus; DSO (1940), DFC (1940); s of Radburn Angus McMurtrie (d 1961), of Edinburgh, and Ethel Maud, *née* Wilkins (d 1927); *b* 14 Feb 1909; *Educ* Newcastle-upon-Tyne Royal GS, RAF Staff Coll, RN War Coll Greenwich; *m* 1, 2 Nov 1931, Gwenyth Mary (d 1958), da of Rev Herbert James Philpott (Lt-Col); m 2, 1963, Laura, da of William H Gerhardi, of Smolensk; *Career* 2 Lt 72 Bde RA (TA) Newcastle Upon Tyne 1927-29, PO RAF No 2 FTS Digby 1930, No 2 AC Sqdn Manston 1931-32, Fl Offr 1932, No 442 Flight HMS Furious (later 822 Sqdn 1933-), RAF Cranwell (E & W Sch) 1933-35, Flt Lt 1935, Flying Boat Pilot's course RAF Calshot 1935-36 (No 201 Flying Boat Sqdn 1938), Sqdn Ldr Cmd No 2 Recruits Sub-depot RAF Linton-on-Ouse unitl 1939, 2 i/c No 269 (GR) Sqdn RAF Abbotsinch, WWII (despatches thrice), RAF Wick and Iceland, Wing Cdr i/c Sqdn 1940, HQ18 GP 1941, CO RAF Sumburgh 1942-43, Gp Capt 1942, Coastal Cmd 1943, Tport Cmd Air Miny Whitehall HQ 1944, Station Cdr RAF Stoney Cross Hants 1945, fndr No 61 Gp RAF Reserve Cmd 1946, Br Jt Servs Mission Washington DC 1946-49, Cmd Cardington 1949-52, HQ No 1 Gp RAF 1952-54, HQ Supreme Cmd Atlantic NATO 1954-56, HQ Coastel Cmd Northwood 1957-59, ret 1959; *Recreations* sailing; *Clubs* RAF Yacht (Hon Life Member), Royal Cornwall Yacht; *Style—* Gp Capt Richard A McMurtrie; Rose in Vale Farm, Constantine, Falmouth TR11 5PU (☎ 0326 40338)

McMURTRY, HE R (Roy); High Commissioner for Canada; QC (1970); s of late Roland Roy McMurtry, and Doris Elizabeth, *née* Belcher; *b* 31 May 1932; *Educ* St Andrew's Coll Ontario, Trinity Coll Univ of Toronto, Osgoode Hall Law Sch (LLB); *m* 18 April 1957, Ria-Jean, da of late Dr Harry Macrae, of Toronto, Ontario; 3 s (Jimmy, Harry, Michael), 3 da (Janet, Jeanie, Erin); *Career* ptnr Benson McMurtry Percival and Brown 1958-75, elected Ontario legislative 1975 (re-elected 1977, 1981), slr gen Ontario 1978-82 (att-gen 1975-78); high cmmr for Canada to GB 1985-; hon chm (past pres Big Brothers of Metropolitan Toronto, nat dir St Leonard's Soc of Canada, past chm Ontario Folk Arts Cncl, former vice-chm Ontario Coll of Art; hon LLD; Univ of Ottawa (1983), Law Soc of Upper Canada (1984); hon freedom City of London (1986); *Recreations* painting, skiing, tennis; *Clubs* Albany, Garrick, Hurlingham, Badminton & Racquet; *Style—* HE Mr Roy McMurtry, QC; Canadian High Commission, 1 Grosvenor Square, London W1 (☎ 01 629 9492)

MACNAB, Brig Sir Geoffrey Alex Colin; KCMG (1962, CMG 1955), CB (1951); s of late Brig-Gen Colin Macnab, CMG, and Beatrice Bliss; *b* 23 Dec 1899; *Educ* Wellington, RMC Sandhurst; *m* 1930, Norah Cramer-Roberts (d 1981); *Career* first cmmn Royal Sussex Regt, instr Small Arms Sch Hythe 1925-28, Capt Argyll and Sutherland Highlanders 1931, Staff Coll Camberley 1930-31, GSO 3 WO 1933-35, BM 10 Inf Bde 1935-38, mil attaché Prague and Bucharest 1938-40, served War of 1939-45, campaigns Western Desert, Greece, Crete, Brig 1944, mil mission Hungary 1945, DMI ME 1945-47, mil attaché Rome 1947-49, Paris 1949-54, ret; sec Govt Hospitality Fund 1957-68; *Clubs* MCC, Army and Navy; *Style—* Brig Sir Geoffrey Macnab, KCMG, CB; Stanford House, Stanford, Ashford, Kent (☎ 030 381 2118)

MACNAB, Hon Mrs; (Sarah Margaret); da of 10 Lord Polwarth, TD; *b* 1944; *m* 1977, John Alexander Hamish Macnab of Barravorich; 2 da; *Style—* The Hon Mrs Macnab; c/o Bank of Scotland, 16/18 Piccadilly, London W1

MACNAB OF MACNAB, Hon Mrs (Diana Mary); *née* Anstruther-Gray; er da of Baron Kilmany, PC, MC, JP, DL (Life Peer d 1985), and Monica Helen Anstruther-Gray, OBE, JP, *née* Lambton (d 1985); *b* 16 June 1936; *m* 11 April 1959, James Charles Macnab of Macnab (The Macnab, *qv*); 2 s (James William Archibald b 1963, Geoffrey Charles b 1965), 2 da (Virginia Mary (Mrs Fyffe) b 1960, Katharine Monica b 1968); *Career* chm Scotland's Gardens Scheme; *Style—* The Hon Mrs Macnab of Macnab; West Kilmany House, Cupar, Fife KY15 4QW (☎ 082 624 247)

MACNAB OF MACNAB (THE MACNAB), ; James Charles Macnab of Macnab; 23 Chief of Clan Macnab; eldest s of Lt-Col James Alexander Macnabb, OBE, TD (*de jure* 21 Chief), of Bramerton St, Chelsea, and Ursula Walford, *née* Barnett (d 1979); suc great unc, Archibald Corrie Macnab of Macnab, CIE (*de facto* 22 Chief) 1970; *b* 14 April 1926; *Educ* Radley, Ashbury Coll Ottawa; *m* 11 April 1959, Hon Diana Mary Anstruther-Gray (*see* Hon Mrs Macnab of Macnab); 2 s, 2 da; *Heir* s, James William Archibald Macnab of Macnab, yr, b 22 March 1963; *Career* RAF 1944, Scots Gds 1944-45, Lt Seaforth Highlanders 1945-48, Capt Seaforth Highlanders (TA) 1960-64; asst then dep supt Fedn of Malaya Police 1948-57; memb: Western Dist Cncl of Perthshire 1961-64, Perth and Kinross Jt County Cncl 1964-75, Central Regnl Cncl 1978-82; memb Royal Co of Archers (Queen's Bodyguard for Scotland); JP Perthshire 1968-75 and Stirling 1975-86; *Clubs* New (Edinburgh), Puffin's (Edinburgh); *Style—* The Macnab; West Kilmany House, Kilmany, Cupar, Fife KY15 4QW (☎ 082 624 247)

MACNAGHTEN, Angus Iain Jacques; s of Capt Angus Charles Rowley Stewart Macnaghten, Lt Black Watch (ka 1914); collateral branch of the Macnaghten Baronets of Bushmills House, Co Antrim, and Hazel, *née* Irwin (d 1956); *b* 29 May 1914; *Educ* Eton, Trinity Coll Cambridge (BA); *m* 1 May 1957, Daphne (d 1984), da of Horace Nettleship Soper (d 1956); 1 adopted da (Fiona b 1962); *Career* served in Intelligence Corps 1940-46, Maj, (despatches); Gold Staff Offr at Coronation of HM Queern Elizabeth II; served in British Cncl 1946-67; author; *Recreations* gardening, walking; *Style—* Angus Macnaghten, Esq; New Mile Cottage, Ascot, Berks SL5 7EX (☎ 0990 21081)

MACNAGHTEN, Magdalene, Lady; Magdalene; da of late Edmund Fisher; *m* 1926, Sir Antony Macnaghten, 10 Bt (d 1972); *Style—* Magdalene, Lady Macnaghten; Dundarave, Bushmills, Co Antrim

MACNAGHTEN, Sir Patrick Alexander; 11 Bt (UK 1836), of Bushmills House, Co Antrim; s of Sir Antony Macnaghten, 10 Bt (d 1972); *b* 24 Jan 1927; *Educ* Eton, Trinity Coll Cambridge; *m* 1955, Marianne, da of Dr Eric Schaefer, of Cambridge; 3 s; *Heir* s, Malcolm Francis Macnaghten; *Career* ret project mangr Cadbury Schweppes plc; *Style—* Sir Patrick Macnaghten, Bt; Dundarave, Bushmills, Co Antrim, NI BT57 8ST;

MACNAGHTEN, Robin Donnelly; s of Sir Henry Pelham Wentworth Macnaghten (d 1949); *b* 3 August 1927; *Educ* Eton, King's Coll Cambridge; *m* 1961, Petronella Gerturde Anne Card; 2 adopted s, 1 adopted da; *Career* asst Mackinnon Mackenzie & Co Bombay 1949-54, asst master Eton Coll 1954-65 (housemaster 1965-74), headmaster Sherborne 1974-88; author; *Recreations* gardening, walking; *Clubs* Royal Western India Turf; *Style—* Robin Macnaghten Esq; Prospect House, Tisbury, Wilts (☎ 0747 870355)

McNAIR, Archibald Alister Jourdan; s of Donald McNair (d 1975); *b* 16 Dec 1919; *Educ* Blundell's Sch Tiverton; *m* 1954, Catherine Alice Jane, da of John Fleming (d 1947), of Barraghcore, Kilkenny, Ireland; 1 s, 1 da; *Career* chm: Mary Quant Gp 1955-88, Thomas Jourdan plc 1971-88, dir City & Capital Hotels plc 1986-, chm TPI Corpn plc 1988-; *Recreations* tennis, fruit farming, chess, carving wood; *Clubs* Turf; *Style—* Archie McNair, Esq; c/o Coutts & Co, 440 Strand, London WC2N 5LJ

McNAIR, Douglas Fenn Wyndham; s of A W McNair, CSI, OBE (d 1965), and Elizabeth Eva Dawn, *née* Griffith (d 1965); *b* 29 Jan 1914; *Educ* Cheltenham, Christ's Coll Cambridge (MA); *m* 15 April 1944, Rosemary Dew, da of Capt A E Monro, RN (d 1958); 2 s (Duncan b 1945, Bruce b 1946), 2 da (Rosamund b 1952, Anne b 1986); *Career* F Perkins Ltd (diesel engine mFrs): joined 1935, service mangr 1946- 51, export sales dir 1951-60, dep mktg dir 1962-63, dir Perkins Outboard Motors Ltd and Perkins Gas Turbines 1960-62; Charles Churchill Ltd Tube Investmts 1963-76: md V L Churchill & Co Ltd, divnl dir T I machine tool div, chief exec tport serv equipment operation; MInst Export 1955-62, CEng, MSAE, FIMechE 1964; *Recreations* classic car restoration and use; *Clubs* Caledonian; *Style—* Douglas McNair, Esq; Beaworthy House, Beaworthy, Devon EX21 5AB (☎ 040 922 501)

McNAIR, Hon Duncan James; s and h of 2 Baron McNair; *b* 26 June 1947; *Educ* Bryanston; *Style—* The Hon Duncan McNair

McNAIR, 2 Baron (UK 1955); (Clement) John McNair; s of 1 Baron McNair, CBE, QC (d 1975); *b* 11 Jan 1915; *Educ* Shrewsbury, Balliol Coll Oxford; *m* 1941, Vera, da of Theodore J Faithfull; 2 s, 1 da; *Heir* s, Hon Duncan James McNair; *Career* served in Tunisia and Italy 1940-46, Maj RA; sits as Lib peer (dep whip) in House of Lords; author; memb Gen Advsy Cncl IBA 1978-83; substitute memb Cncl of Europe and WEU 1979-85; chm ME Subctee Br Refugee Cncl; *Style—* The Rt Hon the Lord McNair; House of Lords, Westminster, London SW1

McNAIR, Hon Josephine Margaret; da of 2 Baron McNair; *b* 1949; *Style—* The Hon Josephine McNair

McNAIR, Prof Philip Murray Jourdan; s of Donald McNair (d 1975), of The Old Grammar Sch, Cirencester, Gloucs, and Janie Grace, *née* Jourdan (d 1970); *b* 22 Feb 1924; *Educ* Blundell's Sch Tiverton, Ch Ch Oxford (MA, DPhil, PhD Cantab); *m* 3 Feb 1948, May, da of Arthur Thomas Aitken (d 1926), of Edinburgh; 1 da (Philippa (Pippa) b 1949); *Career* WWII 1942-48: Queen's Royal Regt, Claims Cmmn, RAEC; served: Italy, Austria, Belgium, Germany; lectr in Italian: Univ of Leeds 1954-61, Bedford Coll London 1961-63, Cambridge Univ 1963-74 (fell Darwin Coll 1965-74, dean Darwin Coll 1965-69); visiting prof Univ of California (Berkeley) 1970, Serena prof and head of dept of Italian Univ of Birmingham 1974-, Barlow lectr on Dante Univ of London 1979; hon pres Birmingham Univ Christian Union 1980-89, church warden St John's Church Harborne Birmingham 1978-81 (elder 1978-88), lay chm Edgbaston Deanery Synod Diocese of Birmingham 1978-87, hon pres Dante Alighieri Soc (Birmingham) 1976-89, govr Malvern Coll 1977-86; *Books* Peter Martyr in Italy: An Anatomy of Apostasy (1967, Italian edn 1971); *Recreations* music, painting, foreign travel, gardening; *Style—* Prof Philip McNair; The Elms, 33 Edgbaston Park Rd, Birmingham B15 2RS; Linnett Hill, 213 Huntingdon Rd, Cambridge CB3 0DL (☎ 021 454 2980); Dept of Italian, The University of Birmingham, P O Box 363, Birmingham B15 2TT (☎ 021 414 5931)

McNAIR, Hon William Samuel Angus; s of 2 Baron McNair; *b* 1958; *Style—* The Hon William McNair

McNAIR SCOTT, Hon Mrs (Camilla Birgitta); *née* Davidson; da (twin) of 2 Viscount Davidson by 1 w; *b* 17 Feb 1963; *m* 14 May 1988, Simon Guthrie McNair Scott, s of Thomas McNair Scott; *Style—* The Hon Mrs Camilla McNair Scott

McNAIR-WILSON, Sir (Robert) Michael Conal; MP (C) Newbury 1974-; s of Dr Robert McNair Wilson; bro of Patrick McNair-Wilson, MP, *qv*; *b* 12 Oct 1930; *Educ* Eton; *m* 1974, Deidre, wid of C Granville, and da of Philip Tuckett; 1 da; *Career* 2 Lt Royal Irish Fus 1948, serv Jordan, Suez Canal, Gibraltar; farmer Hants 1950-53, dir Sidney-Barton Ltd (public rels conslts) 1961-79, currently pub affrs conslt Gresham Consultancy; MP (C) Walthamstow E 1969-74, chm Cons Aviation Ctee 1972-74, dep chm All Pty Air Safety Gp 1979-; PPS to Min of Agric 1979-83; memb Select Ctee on Members' Interests, Educn Sci and the Arts; kt 1988; *Recreations* gardening, riding; *Style—* Sir Michael McNair-Wilson, MP; House of Commons, London SW1

McNAIR-WILSON, Patrick Michael Ernest David; MP (C) New Forest 1968-; s of Dr Robert McNair-Wilson, of Lyndhurst, Hants; bro of Sir (Robert) Michael McNair-Wilson, MP, *qv*; *b* 28 May 1929; *Educ* Eton; *m* 1953, Diana Evelyn Kitty Campbell, da of Hon Laurence Methuen-Campbell (d 1970, s of 3 Baron Methuen); 1 s, 4 da; *Career* conslt; MP (C) for Lewisham W 1964-66, PPS to Min for Tport Indust DOE 1970-74, oppn front bench spokesman on energy 1974-76, chm Jt Lords and Commons Select Ctee on Private Bill Procedure 1987-; *Recreations* pottery, photography; *Style—* Patrick McNair-Wilson, Esq, MP; House of Commons, London SW1

McNALLY, Jack Reginald Moore; MBE (1963), JP (Fife 1965); *b* 15 Dec 1916; *m* 1939, Lena; *Career* Lt Home Guard; author; engr Dental Mfg, Telephone Mfg Co; with Sunvic Controls Ltd, Electrothermal Engrg Ltd; md Beckman Instruments Ltd 1963-76 (chm 1976-80), dir Beckman Int Operations; chm: Beckman Instruments (Hldg) Ltd 1970-80, Scientific Documentation Centre Ltd 1960-, Vivian Industries Ltd 1960-, Triad Tech & Indust Servs Ltd 1980-, Kineticon Ltd 1983; memb: CBI (London) Regnl Devpt and Euro Ctee, Fife Region Health Bd 1975-85, Glenrothes Devpt Corpn Bd 1975-85; pastmaster Worshipful Co Scientific Inst Makers (London); Queen's Award to Industry (Export) 1975; FSCCM, FIWM, FBIM, FAEEE, IOD, FRSA; *Clubs* City Livery, RAC; *Style—* Jack McNally, Esq, MBE, JP

McNALLY, Peter Joseph Deane; s of Gp Capt Patrick John McNally, of Marlow, Bucks, and Mary Deane, *née* Outred; *b* 16 Mar 1933; *Educ* Stonyhurst; *m* 1, 1956 (m dis 1960), Mary B Gardiner; 1 da (Joanna b 1957); m 2, 3 March 1969, Edmée Maria, da of Egon Carmine del Sasso, of Estaplatz, Vienna, Austria; 2 s (Alexis b 1970, Markus b 1972); *Career* CA 1955-; exec dir: LWT (Hldgs) plc 1976-, London Weekend Television 1972-, Ind TV Pubns Ltd 1973-, Co of Designers plc 1987-, Countries Properties plc Westminster 1986, non exec Claridge Assoc Ltd 1973-, underwriter at Lloyd's; FCA; *Recreations* fishing, shooting, skiing, tennis, bridge; *Clubs* RAC, Hurlingham; *Style—* Peter McNally, Esq; 1 Elthiron Rd, London SW6; Wildmoor, Sherfield-on-Loddon, Hants; Kent House, London SE1 (☎ 01 261 3148)

McNALLY, Thomas; s of John Patrick McNally (d 1982), and Elizabeth May (d 1982); *b* 20 Feb 1943; *Educ* Coll of St Joseph Blackpool, Univ Coll London (BSc); *m* 28 Aug 1970, Eileen Isobel, da of Thomas Powell, of Dumfries, Scot; *Career* asst gen sec the Fabian Soc 1966-67, vice pres NUS 1966-67, res Lab Party HQ 1967-69, Int Sec Lab Party 1969-74, political advsr to For and Cwlth Sec 1974-76, political advsr to PM (hd of political off 10 Downing St) 1976-79; public affrs advsr (GEC, Pilkington, Granada Retailers etc), hd of public affairs Hill and Knowlton 1987; Lab MP for Stockport S 1979-83, joined SDP 1981; memb: Select Ctee Indust and Trade 1979-83, Fed Exec SLD 1987-; *Recreations* watching sport, reading political biographies; *Clubs* RCS; *Style—* Thomas McNally, Esq; Hill and Knowlton, 5-11 Theobalds Rd, London WC1X 8SH (☎ 01 405 8755, fax 01 405 0295, telex 264100 HILNOL G)

McNAMARA, (Joseph) Kevin; MP (Lab) Hull North 1983-; s of Patrick McNamara, of Liverpool; *b* 5 Sept 1934; *Educ* St Mary's Coll Crosby, Hull Univ (LLB); *m* 1960, Nora, da of John Jones, of Warrington; 4 s, 1 da; *Career* former lecturer in law Hull Coll of Commerce and head History Dept St Mary's GS Hull; MP Hull North 1966-74, Kingston-upon-Hull Central 1974-83, pps to min without portfolio 1969-70, oppn front bench spokesman Def and Disarmament 1982-87; shadow Sec of State for NI 1987; chm PLP NI Gp, sec TGWU Parly Gp, memb League Against Cruel Sports,; *Style—* Kevin McNamara Esq, MP; 145 Newland Park, Hull, East Yorkshire HU5 2DX (☎ 0482 448170)

McNAUGHT, His Honour Judge; John Graeme; s of Charles William McNaught (d 1955), and Isabella Mary McNaught (d 1969); *b* 21 Feb 1941; *Educ* King Edward VII Sch Sheffield, Queen's Coll Oxford (MA); *m* 1966, Barbara Mary, da of George Rufus Smith (d 1961); 2 s, 1 da; *Career* barr Gray's Inn 1963, practising Western circuit; Recorder 1981-87, Circuit Judge 1987-; *Style—* His Honour Judge McNaught; Ryton Ho, Lechlade, Glos (☎ 0367 52286)

McNAUGHTAN, David Pringle; s of James McNaughtan, of Glasgow, and Helen Duff, *née* Pringle; *b* 6 Mar 1950; *Educ* High Sch of Glasgow, Univ of Strathclyde (BA); *m* 26 June 1980, Anne Patricia, da of Michael Joseph Harrington, of St John's Hosp, St John's Hill, London; 1 s (James Alexander b 1984); 1 da (Eleanor Rose b 1985); *Career* Investmt Banker, Deltec Securities (UK) Ltd 1981; Deltec Banking Corp Ltd 1986; May & Hassell plc 1985 (resigned 1986); *Recreations* gardening; *Clubs* City of London, Travellers'; *Style—* David P McNaughtan, Esq; Watergate, Wadhurst, East Sussex TN5 6QD (☎ 089288 3069); 4 Clifton Street, London EC2A 4BT (☎ 01 377 5005, fax 01 377 9559, telex 883306)

MACNAUGHTON, The Hon Mrs Elizabeth Margaret; da of 3 Baron Wrenbury, and Penelope Sara Frances, *née* Fort; *b* 31 May 1964; *Educ* St Andrews Sch Eastbourne, St Leonards-Mayfield Sch Mayfield, Inst of Sci and Technol, Univ of Manchester; *m* 30 April 1988, Capt Andrew Murray Macnaughton, (The Argyll and Sutherland Highlanders), elder s of R M Macnaughton, of Edinburgh; *Career* devpt scientist corporate res div Amersham Int plc; *Recreations* reading, walking, country life, travel; *Style—* The Hon Mrs Macnaughton; Corner Cottahge, 1 The Strand, Quainton, nr Aylesbury, Bucks HP22 4AF

MacNAUGHTON, Hon Mrs; Liza Jane; *née* Pearson; da of 3 Viscount Cowdray; *b* 30 Mar 1942; *Educ* Cheltenham Ladies' Coll, Brondesbury-at-Stocks, Paris, Madrid; *m* 1967, Malcolm MacNaughton; 1 s, 1 da; *Style—* The Hon Mrs MacNaughton; 1302 Canada Rd, Woodside, Calif 94062, USA

MACNAUGHTON, Prof Sir Malcolm Campbell; KB (1986); s of James Hay Macnaughton (d 1951), and Mary Robieson Hogarth (d 1954); *b* 4 April 1925; *Educ* Glasgow Acad Sch, Univ of Glasgow (MB, ChB, MD); *m* 26 April 1955, Margaret-Ann, da of William Boyd Galt, of Glasgow; 2 s (Graham, Torquil); 3 da (Jane, Gillian, Jennifer); *Career* prof of obstetrics and gynaecology Univ of Glasgow 1970-; pres Royal Coll of Obstetricians & Gynaecologists London 1984-87; kt 1986; *Recreations* fishing, curling, walking; *Clubs* Glasgow Academical, West of Scotland Football, Royal Scottish Automobile; *Style—* Sir Malcolm Macnaughton; 15 Boclair Rd, Bearsden, Glasgow G61 2AF (☎ 041 942 1909); Dept of Obstetrics & Gynaecology Royal Infimary, 10 Alexandra Parade, Glasgow (☎ 041 552 8316)

MacNEACAIL OF MacNEACAIL AND SCORRYBREAC, Iain (formerly Ian Norman Carmichael Nicolson of Scorrybreac); Chief of the Highland Clan MacNeacail; recognised by the Lord Lyon in the name Iain MacNeacail of MacNeacail and Scorrybreac 18 May 1988; eldest s of late Norman Alexander Nicolson of Scorrybreac; *b* 19 June 1921; *Educ* Scotch Coll Tasmania; *m* 1946, Pamela Savigny, da of Philip Oakley Fysh; 1 s; *Heir* s, Philip John Lyne Nicolson; *Career* served WW II 1939-45; grazier and company dir; *Style—* Iain MacNeacail of MacNeacail and Scorrybreac; PO Box 420, Ballina, NSW 2478, Australia

McNEAL, Hon Mrs (Julia); da of Baroness Gaitskell (Life Peeress); *b* 1939; *Educ* Somerville Coll Oxford; *m* 1969, George Peter McNeal; *Style—* The Hon Mrs McNeal; 35 Newstead Rd, London SE12

MCNEANY, Kevin Joseph; s of Bernard Joseph McNeany, of Keady, Co Armagh, and Mary Christina, McDonnell; *b* 10 April 1943; *Educ* St Patricks Coll Armagh, Queens Univ Belfast (BA), London Univ, Manchester Univ; *m* 1 Aug 1968 (m dis 1985), Christine, da of Stephen McNulty; 2 s (Matthew Ciaron b 1970, Myles Anthony b 1986); *Career* teacher: St Pauls Sch Lurgan Co Armagh 1964-66, Corpus Christi Sch Leeds 1966-68; lectr: Kitson Coll Leeds 1968-70, Southport Tech Coll 1970-73, Wythenshawe Coll Manchester 1973-77; co-fndr (with Christine McNeany 1972) md and chief exec Nord Anglia Int (Hldgs) Ltd (formerly Nord-Anglia Int) 1977-; *Recreations* walking, cycling, tennis; *Style—* Kevin McNeany, Esq; Ridge Park, 32 Bramhall Park Rd, Bramhall, Cheshire SK7 3JN (☎ 061 439 2563); Broome House, 152 Palatine Road, West Didsbury, Manchester M20 8QH (☎ 061 434 7475, fax 061 434 3565)

McNEE, Sir David Blackstock; QPM (1975); s of John McNee; *b* 23 Mar 1925; *Educ* Woodside Sr Secdy Sch Glasgow; *m* 1952, Isabella Hopkins; 1 da; *Career* dep chief Constable Dunbartonshire 1968-71; chief constable: Glasgow 1971-75, Strathclyde 1975-77; cmmr Metropolitan Police 1977-82; memb Air Safety Review Ctee Br Airways 1982-85, advsr to chm Br Railways 1982-85; dir: Clydesdale Bank 1982-, Fleet Hldgs 1983-86, Trusthouse Forte 1983-, Plextel Int Ltd; Caledonian, Naval (Life memb); chm: Integrated Security Systems 1985, Clyde Publishing Ltd 1987-; non-exec chm Scottish Express Newspapers 1983-; pres: Nat Bible Soc of Scotland, Royal Life Saving Soc UK; hon vice-pres Boys' Bde, patron Scottish Motor Neurone Disease Assoc; Freeman City of London; FBIM; CStJ; kt 1978; *Style*— Sir David McNee, QPM; Scottish Express Newspapers, Park House, Park Circus Place, Glasgow 3

MACNEE, (Daniel) Patrick; s of Daniel Macnee (d 1952), of Lambourn, Berks, and Dorothea Mary Henry, BEM (d 1985), niece of 13 Earl of Huntingdon); *b* 6 Feb 1922; *Educ* Eton; *m* 1, Nov 1942 (m dis 1956), Barbara Douglas; 1 s (Rupert b 1948), 1 da (Jennifer b 1951); m 2, April 1965 (m dis 1968), Kate Woodrille; m 3 Feb 1988 Baba Sekerley, *née* Majos de Nagyzsenye; *Career* actor; served WWII: Sub-Lt HMS Alfred (Offrs' Trg Sch nr Brighton) 1942, Royal Naval Coll Greenwich 1943, MTB Flotilla 1943, 1 Lt 1944, demobbed 1946; Long Service Medal, Atlantic Medal; actor; Films incl: The Life and Death of Colonel Blimp 1942, Hamlet 1948, The Elusive Pimpernel 1950, Scrooge 1951, Battle of the River Plate 1956, Les Girls 1957, Incense for the Damned (US: Bloodsuckers) 1970, Mr Jericho 1970, Matt Helm 1975, King Solomon's Treasures 1976, Sherlock Holmes in New York 1976, Battlestar Galactia 1979, The Sea Wolves 1980, The Howling 1981, This is Spinal Tap 1983, A View to a Kill 1984, Shadey 1984, Waxworks 1988, The Chill Factor 1988, The Lobster Man From Mars 1988; TV incl: The Avengers 1960-69, Alfred Hitchcock presents, Dial M For Murder, Thriller, Columbo, For The Term of his Natural Life; over 150 stage appearances; memb: Palm Springs Youth Centre, Palm Springs Opera Guild; Freedom of Filey Yorks 1962, Freedom of City of Macon Georgia 1985; Variety Club of GB Jt TV personality of the Year Award (with Honor Blackman) 1963, Straw Hat Award (NY) 1975, Golden Camera Award (Berlin) For Air Safety From the Administrator of the Federal Airway Administration Washington DC; *Books* Blind In One Ear (autobiography) 1988; *Recreations* nude tennis, reading, chatting with pretty women, praying, musing; *Style*— Patrick Macnee, Esq; c/o Kenneth Earle, London Mgmnt, 235-241 Regent St, London W1A 2JT (☎ 01 493 1610)

McNEICE, Sir Thomas Percy Fergus; CMG (1953), OBE (1947); s of Canon W G McNeice (d 1968), and Mary Masterston (d 1943); *b* 16 August 1901; *Educ* Bradford GS, Keble Coll Oxford (MA); *m* 1947, Yuen Peng Loke, da of Dr Loke Yew, CMG (d 1917), of Kuala Lumpur; 1 s (Anthony), 1 da (Janis); *Career* entered Colonial Serv (Malaya) 1925; Capt Straits Settlement Volunteer Force (POW 1942-45); pres Singapore City Cncl 1949-55, ret 1956; kt 1956; *Clubs* Royal Cwlth Soc; *Style*— Sir Percy McNeice, CMG, OBE; 12 Jalan Sampurna, Singapore 1026

McNEIL, Lady; Barbara Jessie; da of Percy Stuart Turner (d 1944), and Laura Beatrice Cowley (d 1967); *b* 7 Jan 1915; *Educ* Wimbledon; *m* 1939, Sir Hector McNeil, CBE (d 1978); 1 s, 1 da; *Career* hon pres Motor Neurone Disease Assoc; *Recreations* gardening, tapestry, foreign languages; *Style*— Lady McNeil; Bramber, St George's Hill, Weybridge, Surrey (☎ 0932 48484)

MACNEIL OF BARRA, The; Ian Roderick Macneil of Barra; 46 Chief of Clan Macneil; s of Robert Lister Macneil of Barra, of Kisimul Castle, Isle of Barra (d 1970), and Kathleen Gertrude Metcalf Macneil (d 1933); *b* 20 June 1929; *Educ* Scarborough Sch, Vermont Univ (BA), Harvard Univ (LLB); *m* 1952, Nancy Carol, da of James Tilton Wilson, of Ottawa, Canada; 2 s, 1 da (and 1 s decd); *Heir* s, Roderick Macneil, yr of Barra b 1954; *Career* Lt US Army 1951-53, Army Res 1950-69; prof Cornell Law Sch Ithaca NY 1959-72 and 1974-76, visiting prof faculty of law Univ Coll Dar-es-Salaam Tanzania 1965-67, visiting prof of law Duke Univ 1970-71, prof of law and memb centre for advanced studies Univ of Virginia 1972-74, Ingersoll prof law Cornell 1976-80; visiting fell: Univ of Oxford 1979, Univ of Edinburgh 1978 (1979 and 1987); Wigmore prof of law Northwestern Univ 1980-, Braucher visiting prof of law Harvard Univ 1988-89; author; *Recreations* tennis; *Clubs* New; *Style*— The Macneil of Barra; Kisimul Castle, Isle of Barra (☎ 087 14 300); 357 E Chicago Avenue, Chicago, Illinois 60611, USA

McNEILL, Cameron Alastair; s of Albert William McNeill, of Newbury, Berks, and Elizabeth, *née* Kelly; *b* 25 Mar 1958; *Educ* Christ's Hosp, Pembroke Coll Oxford (BA); *m* 10 Aug 1981, Shirley Anne Eileen, da of Ernest Edward Hance; *Career* dir: Barclays De Zoete Wedd ltd 1986-, Barclays De Zoete Wedd Capital Mkts Ltd 1986-, Ebbgate hldgs Ltd 1986-; md Oxford Tech Systems 1986- (dir 1983); memb Bank of Eng Ad Hoc Swaps Ctee; *Clubs* United Oxford and Cambridge Univ; *Style*— Cameron McNeill, Esq; Ebbgate House, 2 Swan Lane, London EC4R 3TS (☎ 01 623 2323, fax 01 623 4709)

McNEILL, Hon Mr Justice; Hon Sir David Bruce McNeill; s of late Ferguson McNeill and Elizabeth Bruce; *b* 6 June 1922; *Educ* Rydal Sch, Merton Coll Oxford, BCL, MA; *m* 1949, Margaret Lewis; 1 s, 3 da; *Career* barr Lincoln's Inn 1947, lectr in Law Liverpool Univ 1948-58, Recorder of Blackburn 1969-71, QC 1966, Crown Ct Recorder 1972-78, ldr N Circuit 1974-78, High Ct Judge Queen's Bench 1979-; chm Senate Inns of Ct 1977-78 and memb 1975-82; memb Bar Cncl 1968-72, memb Restrictive Practices Ct 1981-, Presiding Judge 1980-84; hon memb American and Canadian Bar Assocs; Hon LLD Liverpool 1982; kt 1979; *Style*— The Hon Mr Justice McNeill; Royal Courts of Justice, Strand, London WC2

McNEILL, Prof John; s of Thomas McNeill (d 1972), of Edinburgh, of Helen Lawrie, *née* Eagle (d 1984); *b* 15 Sept 1933; *Educ* George Heriot's Edinburgh, Univ of Edinburgh (BSc, PhD); *m* 29 July 1961, Bridget Mariel, da of Paul Winterton; 2 s (Andrew Thomas b 1964, Douglas Paul b 1966); *Career* asst lectr then lectr dept of agric botany Univ of Reading 1957-61, lectr dept of botany Univ of Liverpool 1961-69, sr res sci biosystematics res inst Agric Canada Ottawa 1977-81 (res sci 1969-77), prof and chm dept of biology Univ of Ottawa Canada 1981-87, Regius keeper Royal Botanic Garden Edinburgh 1987-, author of numerous sci papers and reports; pres; Biological Cncl of Canada 1986-87 (vice-pres 1984-86), Canadian Cncl of Univ Biology (chm 1984-85, vice-pres 1983-84); exec memb Int Union of Biological Sci 1985-88, admin of fin Int Assoc of Plant Taxonomy 1987- (cncllr 1981-87); memb 15 sci socs; *Books* Phonetic and Phylogenetic Classification (ed with V H Heywood, 1964), Grasses of Ontario (with W G Dore, 1980), The Genus Atriplex in Canada (with I J Bassett et al, 1983), International Code of Botanical Nomenclature (adopted 1981, jt ed 1983), International Code of Botanical Nomenclature (adopted 1987, jt ed 1987); *Style*— Prof John McNeill; Royal Botanic Garden, Edinburgh EH3 5LR (☎ 031 552 7171, fax 031 552 0382)

McNEILL, Maj-Gen John Malcolm; CB (1963), CBE (1959, MBE 1942); s of Brig-Gen Angus John McNeill, CB, CBE, DSO, TD (d 1950), of Acre, Palestine, and Lilian Vaughan Barron (later Findlay); *b* 22 Feb 1909; *Educ* Imperial Serv Coll Windsor, RMA Woolwich; *m* 24 Nov 1939, Helen Barbara Christine, da of Col C H Marsh, DSO; 2 da (Sheila b 1940, Jean b 1944); *Career* 2 Lt RA 1929; WWII served: Western Desert, Sicily, Italy, NW Europe, Burma; cmd 1 regt RHA 1948-51, student Imperial Def Coll 1952, dep sec Chiefs of Staff Ctee MOD 1953-55, cmd 2 Div RA 1955-58, cmdt sch of Artillery 1959-60, Cdr Br Army Staff and mil attaché Washington DC 1960-63, Col Cmdt RA 1964-74, princ staff offr to sec of state for Cwlth Relations 1964-69, ADC to HM the Queen 1958-60; *Recreations* field sports; *Clubs* Army and Navy, English Speaking Union; *Style*— Maj-Gen John McNeill, CB, CBE; Hole's Barn, Pilton, Shepton Mallet, Somerset BA4 4DF (☎ 074989 212)

McNEILL, Peter Grant Brass; s of William Arnott McNeill (d 1973), and Lillias Philips, *née* Scrimgeour (d 1980); *b* 3 Mar 1929; *Educ* Hillhead HS Glasgow, Morrison's Acad Crieff, Glasgow Univ (MA, LLB, PhD); *m* 1959, Matilda Farquhar; 1 s (Angus), 3 da (Christian, Morag, Katrina); *Career* barr Scotland 1956, hon sheriff substitute of Lanarkshire, and of Stirling, Clackmannan and Dumbarton 1962, standing jr counsel to Scottish Devpt Dept (Highways) 1964, advocate depute 1964; Sheriff of: Lanarkshire (later Glasgow and Strathkelvin) at Glasgow 1965, Lothian and Borders at Edinburgh 1983; *Books* Balfour's Practicks (ed 1962-63), An Historical Atlas of Scotland c400-c1600 (ed jtly 1975), Adoption of Children in Scotland (2 edn 1986), legal and historical articles in: Juridicial Review, Scots Law Times, Glasgow Herald, Encyclopaedia Britannica; *Recreations* legal history, gardening, bookbinding; *Style*— Dr Peter McNeill, QC; c/o Sheriff Ct, Lawnmarket, Edinburgh EH1 2NS (☎ 031 226 7181)

McNICOL, Prof George Paul; s of Martin Wilkinson McNicol (d 1956), and Elizabeth Straiton Harper (d 1973); *b* 24 Sept 1929; *Educ* Hillhead HS Glasgow, Glasgow Univ (MD, PhD); *m* 1959, Susan Moira, da of Gilbert Benjamin Ritchie (d 1969); 1 s, 2 da; *Career* hon conslt physician Makerere Univ Coll Med Sch Nairobi 1965-66, appts in Glasgow Teaching Hosps and Glasgow Univ 1952-81, chm bd Faculty Med Leeds Univ 1978-81, prof Med and hon consulting physician Leeds Gen Infirmary 1971-81, princ Aberdeen Univ 1981-; memb local Aberdeen bd Bank of Scotland 1983-, chm of govrs Rowett Res Inst 1981-, chm med advsy ctee Ctee of Vice-Chllrs and Princs 1985-, memb Ctee for Int Co-op in Higher Educn (CICHE) Br Cncl 1985-, memb cncl Assoc of Cwlth Univs 1988-; FRSE, FRSA, FRCP, FRCPG, FRCPE, FRCPath, Hon FACP; *Recreations* skiing, sailing; *Clubs* Caledonian, Athenaeum, Royal Northern and Univ (Aberdeen); *Style*— Prof George McNicol; The Chanonry Lodge, 13 The Chanonry, Old Aberdeen, AB2 1RP; Univ of Aberdeen, Regent Walk, Aberdeen AB9 1FX (☎ 0224 272134)

MACNICOL, Ian Duncan Robertson; s of Maj Duncan Cowan MacNicol (d 1969), and Ethel Margaret, *née* Blanch (d 1976); *b* 25 August 1943; *Educ* Fettes, Royal Agric Coll Cirencester; *m* 11 May 1974, Adel Jean, da of Richmond Noel Richmond-Watson, of Wakefield Lodge, Potterspury, Northants; 2 s (Charles b 1 Sept 1980, George b 9 Feb 1983), 2 da (Arabella b 24 Aug 1976, Catherine b 6 June 1978); *Career* current dir: GC & FC Knight Ltd, Yeovil Livestock Auctioneers, Dorchester Livestock Mrt, Barnham Broom plc, Raynham Workshops; former tstee Game Conservancy, former chm Norfolk branch CLA; currently: chm taxation ctee CLA (memb cncl), memb cncl Royal Agric Soc, chm bd govrs Astley Primary Sch, govr Beeston Hall Sch, chm Stody Parish Cncl; FRICS; *Recreations* country pursuits; *Clubs* White's, Farmer's; *Style*— Ian MacNicol, Esq; Stody Lodge, Melton Constable, Norfolk NR24 2EW (☎ 0263 860 254); Stody Estate Office, Melton Constable, Norfolk (☎ 0263 860 572)

McNULTY, Lady Sarah Lillian; *née* Lowry-Corry; da of 7 Earl Belmore (d 1960); *b* 31 Mar 1945; *Educ* Manor House Armagh N Ireland, Florence Italy; *m* 1979, Gary McNulty; *Style*— Lady Sarah McNulty; 4131 County Rd 103, Carbondale, 81623 Colorado, USA

MACONACHIE, Martin Osbert; CBE (1984); s of Sir Richard Roy Maconachie, KBE, CIE (d 1962), of Hants, and Joan, *née* Lethbridge (d 1975); *b* 18 Mar 1925; *Educ* Winchester, Univ Coll Oxford; *m* 21 Oct 1950, Evelyn (d 1985), da of Raymond Molloy Kateley (d 1948); 2 s (Simon b 1955, Paul b 1957 (decd)), 1 da (Amanda b 1958); *Career* WWII Lt Coldstream Gds NW Europe; Overseas Civil Serv Nigeria 1948-62, asst sec Cabinet Off Lagos 1960-61, MOD 1962-85, cncl memb Sussex Assoc for the Blind; *Recreations* fishing, gardening, travel; *Clubs* Lansdowne; *Style*— Martin O Maconachie, CBE; 3 Kings Close, Bexhill-on-Sea, E Sussex TN4O 1QT (☎ 0424 225786)

McPARTLIN, Sheriff; Noel; s of Michael Joseph McPartlin, of Galashiels (d 1955), and Ann *née* Dunn (d 1978); *b* 25 Dec 1939; *Educ* Galashiels Acad Edinburgh Univ MA, LLB; *m* 10 July 1965, June Anderson, da of David Anderson Whitehead, of 14 Lennox Av, Stirling (d 1961); 3 s (Simon b 1970, Guy b 1972, Donald b 1982), 3 da (Alison b 1966, Diana b 1967, Julia b 1979); *Career* advocate 1976, slr 1964-76; sheriff Grampian Highland and Islands at Peterhead and Banff 1983-; *Recreations* country life; *Clubs* Elgin; *Style*— Sheriff McPartlin; Sheriff Court, Elgin

McPETRIE, Sir James Carnegie; KCMG (1966, CMG 1961), OBE (1953); s of James Duncan McPetrie (d 1948); *b* 29 June 1911; *Educ* Madras Coll St Andrews, St Andrews Univ (MA), Jesus Coll Oxford (MA); *m* 1941, Elizabeth Howie; 1 da; *Career* served WWII RA; barr Middle Temple 1938; legal advsr: Colonial Off 1960-66, Cwlth Off 1966-68, Foreign and Cwlth Off 1968-71, ret; temp memb legal staff DOE 1972-75; chm UNESCO Appeals Bd 1973-79; *Style*— Sir James McPetrie, KCMG, OBE; 52 Main Street, Strathkinness, St Andrews, Fife, Scotland KY16 9SA (☎ 033 485235)

MACPHAIL, Bruce Dugald; s of Dugald Ronald Macphail; *b* 1 May 1939; *Educ* Haileybury, Balliol Coll Oxford, Harvard Business Sch; *m* 1963, Susan Mary (d 1975), da of late Col T Gregory, MC, TD; 3 s; *Career* dir Sterling Guarantee Tst 1969-74, md Town & City Properties Ltd 1976-; FCA; *Style*— Bruce Macphail Esq; 13 West Heath Rd, London NW3 (☎ 01 435 9412)

MACPHAIL, Sheriff; Iain Duncan; s of Malcolm John Macphail, of Edinburgh, and Mary Corbett Duncan (d 1973); *b* 24 Jan 1938; *Educ* George Watson's Coll, Univ of Edinburgh (MA), Univ of Glasgow (LLB); *m* 1970, Rosslyn Graham Lillias, da of Edward John Campbell Hewitt, TD, of Edinburgh; 1 s (David b 1973), 1 da (Melissa b 1977); *Career* admitted to Faculty of Advocates 1963, practising bar Scotland 1963-73, Faulds fell in law Univ of Glasgow 1963-65; lectr in evidence and procedure: Univ of Strathclyde 1968-69, Univ of Edinburgh 1969-72; extra advocate-depute 1973; Sheriff of: Glasgow and Strathkelvin (formerly Lanarkshire) 1973-81, Tayside, Centl and Fife at Dunfermline and Alloa 1981-82, Lothian and Borders of Linlithgow 1982-; chm Scottish Assoc for the Study of Delinquency 1978-81; *Books* The Law of Evidence of Scotland (1979), Evidence (1987); *Recreations* music, theatre, reading, writing; *Clubs* New (Edinburgh); *Style*— Sheriff Macphail; c/o Sheriff Ct House, Ct Square,

Linlithgow EH49 7EQ (☎ 0506 842922)

MACPHAIL, Ian Angus Shaw; s of Robert Shaw MacPhail (d 1938), and Edith Hadden (d 1968); *b* 11 Mar 1922; *Educ* Grays Sch of Art Aberdeen (Dip Graphic Design); *m* 1, 1943 (m dis 1948), Armorel Davie; 1 da (Diana); m 2, 12 March 1951, Michal Hambourg, da of Mark Hambourg; *Career* RAF 1940-43; asst music controller ENSA 1944-46, asst music dir Arts Cncl 1946-52, publicity dir Dexion Ltd 1952-58, dir Greenway Advsy Serv 1958-60, pr conslt Brewers Soc 1960-61, dir-gen World Wildlife Fund (UK) 1961-67, chief info offr Arthur Guinness Son & Co Ltd 1967-69, conslt in communications 1970; broadcaster BBC Far Eastern Serv, European rep Fund for Animal Welfare, govr Brathay Hall Tst; hon PR advsr: Fauna Preservation Soc, Nat Assoc for Gifted Children; former chm pr ctee Royal Soc for the Prevention Accidents, memb Soc of Industl Artists; ed: You and the Theatre, You and the Opera, English Music 1200-1750, Dexion Angle, Good Company, World Wildlife News; lectr to: Publicity and Rotary Clubs, schs, tech colls, univs, HM Prisons and borstals, womens socs; graphic designer (responsible for prodn supervision of publicity): eight Coronation concerts at the Royal Festival Hall, third congress Int Assoc of Gerontology, jt metallurgical socs meeting in Europe, house-style and literature World Wildlife Fund, first world conf on Gifted Children; FIPR 1970; *Books* You and the Orchestra (1948), Birdlife of Britain and Europe (1977); *Recreations* ornithology, music, poetry; *Clubs* Savile, Wig and Pen; *Style—* Ian MacPhail, Esq; 35 Boundary Rd, St John's Wood, London NW8 0JE (☎ 01 024 3535, telex, 957 471 IFAW SXG, fax, 01 624 9358)

MACPHERSON, Hon Mrs (Alexandra Grace); *née* Baring; 2 da of 5 Baron Northbrook, *qv*; *b* 4 Feb 1957; *Educ* St Mary's Sch Wantage; *m* 1981, (Philip) Strone (Stewart) Macpherson, s of late G P S Macpherson CBE, TD, of The Old Rectory, Aston Sandford, Bucks; 1 s (Philip b 1985); *Style—* The Hon Mrs Macpherson; 8 Holland Park Mews, London W11

MACPHERSON, Hon Andrew Charles James; s of 2 Baron Strathcarron; *b* 1959; *Style—* The Hon Andrew Macpherson; Otterwood, Beaulieu, Hants SO4 7YS (☎ 0590 612334)

MACPHERSON, Angus John; s of Lt Archibald Norman MacPherson, RN, of Commonwood, Bearsted, Kent, and Joan Margaret, *née* Backhouse; *b* 17 Mar 1953; *Educ* Stowe, Pembroke Coll Cambridge (MA); *m* 14 Aug 1982, Anne Louise Felicity, da of Capt Edward Morton Barford, of Lilac Cottage, Bowlhead Green, Godalming, Surrey; 1 s (William Archibald b 19 March 1988), 1 da (Eloise Isobel b 5 Jan 1985); *Career* barr Inner Temple 1977, practises SE circuit; *Recreations* tennis, scottish history, cooking; *Clubs* Lansdowne; *Style—* Angus MacPherson, Esq; 44 Kyrle Rd, London SW11 (☎ 01 228 3816); 1 Harcourt Buildings, Temple, London EC4 (☎ 01 353 2214)

MACPHERSON, Archibald Ian Stewart; s of Sir Thomas Stewart Macpherson (d 1949), and Helen, *née* Cameron (d 1976); *b* 10 August 1913; *Educ* Edinburgh Acad, Fettes, Univ of Edinburgh (MB, ChB, ChM), Columbia Univ New York; *Career* RAMC 1942-47, Maj surgical specialist 1943-45, Lt-Col and offr i/c surgical div 31 BGA 1946, served in N Africa, Sicily, Italy, Austria, hon conslt surgn to Army in Scotland 1976-81; Univ of Edinburgh: Crichton res scholar 1940-42, clinical tutor 1940-42, 1947-52, sr lectr 1954-78; Rockefeller fell Columbia Presbyterian New York 1948-49, conslt surgn: Royal Edinburgh Infirmary 1954-78, Royal Edinburgh Hosp 1954-78, Leith Hosp 1958-66; pres Vascular Surgical Soc 1976-77, vice-pres RCSE(a) 1976-79 (memb of cncl); Univ of Edinburgh: capt rugby XV 1935-36, capt cricket XI 1935, capt fencing 1935-36; Scottish cricket int 1934-35; chm Clan Macpherson Assoc 1969-73 (currently hon vice-pres), pres Graduates' Assoc Univ of Edinburgh 1972-75, chief Gaelic Soc of Inverness 1984-85, vice-pres Royal Celtic Soc, Clan Chattan Assoc; FRCSE 1940, FRSE 1962, memb Vascular Surgical Soc 1964, hon memb Surgical Res Soc; *Books* The Spleen (1973); *Recreations* golf, fishing, highland history; *Clubs* New Club (Edinburgh), Hon Company of Edinburgh Golfers; *Style—* A I S Macpherson, Esq; 18 Grange Terr, Edinburgh EH9 2LD (☎ 031 667 1169); Speyville, Newtonmore, Inverness-shire PH20 1AR (☎ 054 03 224)

MacPHERSON, Colin; s of Ian MacPherson (d 1984), of Broughton, and Anne Elizabeth, *née* McLean; *b* 17 Feb 1927; *Educ* Trinity Coll Cambridge (BA); *m* 1, 1951 (m dis), Christian Elizabeth Randolph; 2 s (Andrew b 1955, Francis b 1961), 1 da (Caroline b 1953); m 2, June 1981, Judith Margaret, da of Capt Henry M Denham, CMG; *Career* accountant; former sr ptnr Smith & Williamson, former chm Smith & Williamson Securities; dir: Chichester Estates Co 1971-, Guide Dogs for the Blind Assoc 1964 (chm 1987), Keystone Investmt Co plc 1975, Kleinwort Barrington Ltd 1975, Lazard Far Eastern Exempt Fund 1977, Smith & Williamson Securities 1970 (chm 1970-86), Smith & Williamson Unit Tst Mangrs 1985 (chm 1985), Smith & Williamson Tst Corpn 1986, Sun Life Assur Soc plc 1968 (vice-chm 1987), Sun Life Pension Mgmnt 1982, Sun life Unit Assur Ltd 1979, Sun Life Corpn plc 1986; *Recreations* skiing, shooting, golf, gardening; *Clubs* City, Oriental; *Style—* Colin MacPherson, Esq; Flat 3, 17 Redcliffe Square, London SW10 (☎ 01 373 8612); The Mill, Droxford, Hampshire SO3 1QS; No 1 Riding House Street, London W1A 3AS (☎ 01 637 5377, telex 25187, fax Group 3 01 631 0741)

MACPHERSON, Donald Charles; s of Donald Hugh Macpherson (d 1947), and Hilda Mary Pulley (d 1952); *b* 3 Jan 1932; *Educ* Winchester; *m* 1962, Hilary Claire; *Career* former Capt Black Watch; exec dir Co Natwest Ltd; dir: Co Natwest Ltd, Judy Farquharson Ltd; *Recreations* art collection, golf, tennis, travel; *Style—* Donald Macpherson Esq; 28 Campden Hill Square, London W8 7JY (☎ 01 727 8292); Willow Cottage, East Lavington, nr Petworth, West Sussex (☎ 07986 266); County Natwest Limited, Drapers Gardens, 12 Throgmorton Ave, London EC2P 2ES

MacPHERSON, Ewen Cameron Stewart; s of G P F MacPherson (d 1981), and Elizabeth Margaret Cameron, *née* Smail; *b* 19 Jan 1942; *Educ* Fettes Coll Edinburgh, Queens' Coll Cambridge (MA), London Business Sch (MSc); *m* 1982, Laura Anne, da of 5 Baron Northbrook, *qv*; 2 s (James b 25 Oct 1983 George b 27 Nov 1985); *Career* rep Massey Fergusson (Export) Ltd 1964-68, various appointments ICFC 1970-, dir and memb exec ctee 3i plc (formerly Investors in Industry) 1982-; *Recreations* gardening, sailing, vintage motor cars; *Clubs* City of London, Caledonian; *Style—* Ewen Macpherson, Esq; Denham Leys, Quainton, nr Aylesbury, Bucks HP22 4AL (☎ 029675 227); 91 Waterloo Rd, London SE1 8XP (☎ 01 928 7822, fax 01 928 0058)

MACPHERSON, Ian; s of William Rodger, RAF (ka 1940), and Isobel, *née* Laing (d 1976); *b* 25 Mar 1936; *Educ* Morrison's Acad Crieff,; *m* 6 Aug 1960, Margaret (Greta); 1 s (Ian b 24 Aug 1969), 1 da (Karen b Karen b 20 Aug 1966); *Career* CA 1961, ptnr W Greenwell & Co 1967-73, dir various cos 1973-76, vice pres Mfrs hanover Tst 1976-79, dep chief exec Br Linen Bank 1982-88 (dir 1979-88), chief exec Watson & Philip plc 1988, currently non-exec dir Low & Bonar plc and Martin Currie Unit Tsts Ltd; dep chm Br Olympic Appeal 1987-88; FInstD; *Recreations* golf, reading, gardening; *Style—* Ian Macpherson, Esq; c/o Watson & Philip plc, Blackness Rd, Dundee DD1 9PU (☎ 0382 27501)

MACPHERSON, Hon Ian David Patrick; s and h of 2 Baron Strathcarron; *b* 31 Mar 1949; *Style—* The Hon Ian Macpherson; Otterwood, Beaulieu, Hants (☎ 334)

McPHERSON, Dr James Paton (Pat); OBE (1987); s of David Robb McPherson (d 1974), of Dundee, and Georgina Watt, *née* Dunbar (d 1969); *b* 9 July 1916; *Educ* Dundee HS; *m* 7 March 1942, Muriel Stewart, da of Stewart Finlay Anderson (d 1948), of Dundee; *Career* RAF Air Sea Rescue 1941-46; chm: Wright Health Gp Ltd, Walter D Watt and Co Ltd, Drug Devpt (Scot) Ltd; dir: Abbey Nat Bldg Soc (Scottish bd) 1981-87, Dundee Indust Assoc; covener of fin and memb of ct Univ of Dundee, vice-chm Tenorus Tayside, former pres Rotary Club of Dundee, ctee memb The Malcolm Sargent Cancer Fund for Children (Dundee Ctee); JP, Cmmnr of Taxes; LLD Univ of Dundee 1986; MInst Dirs; *Recreations* golf; *Clubs* Rosemount, Gleneagles Golf; *Style—* Dr Pat McPherson, OBE; Mylnfield House, Invergowrie, Dundee, Scotland DD2 5EH (☎ 082 622 360); Wright Health Gp Ltd, Kingsway West, Dundee, Scotland DD2 3QD (☎ 0382 833 866, fax 0382 811 042, telex 76443)

MACPHERSON, John Hannah Forbes; CBE (1983); s of John Hannah Macpherson (d 1942), of Glasgow, and Anne Hicks, *née* Watson (d 1976); *b* 23 May 1926; *Educ* Glasgow Acad, Merchiston Castle Sch; *m* 1959, Margaret Graham, da of Robert Roxburgh, of Glasgow (d 1957); 1 s (John b 1972); *Career* Sub Lieut RNVR 1943-47; apprentice CA Wilson Stirling & Co (subsequently Touche Ross & Co) 1947-49 (ptnr 1956), 1956, ret 1986; chm: Glasgow Jr C of C 1965, Scottish Industl Estates Corpn 1972, Irvine Devpt Corpn 1976, Glasgow Opportunities Enterprise Tst 1983, Scottish Mutual Assur Soc 1985, TSB Scotland plc 1984, Glasgow Action 1985; pres Glasgow C of C 1980; dir: TSB Gp plc 1985, Scottish Business in the Community 1985, Scottish Met Property plc 1986, Utd Dominions Tst Ltd 1986; memb: Prince and Princess of Wales Hospice, Merchants House of Glasgow, The Scottish Civic Tst; OStJ 1980; *Recreations* gardening, reading; *Clubs* East India, Western (Glasgow) RNVR (Scotland); *Style—* John Macpherson, Esq, CBE; 16 Collylinn Rd, Bearsden, Glasgow G61 4PN (☎ 041 942 0042); TSB Scotland plc, Henry Duncan House, 120 George St, Edinburgh EH2 4TS (☎ 031 225 4555)

MACPHERSON, Sir Keith Duncan; s of late Duncan Macpherson; *b* 12 June 1920; *Educ* Scotch Coll Melbourne; *m* 1946, Ena McNair; 3 s, 2 da; *Career* chm The Herald & Weekly Times Ltd: joined 1938, sec 1959-64, assist gen mangr 1965-67, dir 1974, chief exec 1975 chm 1977; chm Aust Newsprint Mills Hldgs Ltd 1978- (vice-chm 1976-78), Tasman Pulp & Paper Co Ltd 1977-78, chm W Aust Newspapers Ltd 1981- (dir 1970), dir Davies Bros Ltd 1975-, chm Qld Press Ltd 1983-; dir Gordon and Gotch Ltd 1985-, chm Tstees Reuters Ltd 1984-; FASA; kt 1981; *Style—* Sir Keith Macpherson; 24 Balwyn Rd, Canterbury, Vic 3126, Australia

MACPHERSON, Hon Mrs (Laura Anne); *née* Baring; er da of 5 Baron Northbrook; *b* 12 June 1952; *m* 1982, Ewen C S, eld s of late G P S Macpherson, of The Old Rectory, Aston Sandford, Bucks; 2 s; *Style—* The Hon Mrs Macpherson; 61 Holland Park Mews, London W11

MACPHERSON, Norman (Croumbie); CBE (1980), WS; s of Sir Norman Macgregor Macpherson (d 1947), of Edinburgh, and Adelaide Jean Hunter-Craig (d 1938); *b* 21 Mar 1910; *Educ* Merchiston Castle Sch, Emmanuel Coll Cambridge (BA); *m* 11 June 1936, Irene Betty, da of Ralph Heasman (d 1927), of Sussex; 3 s (Robert Norman b 1937, Ralph Erskine b 1949, Michael Croumbie b 1949), 1 da (Jane Harriet (Mrs Steel) b 1941); *Career* served WWII BEF, GHQ, Arrass France 1939, then HQ Scottish Cmd & UK, Maj; slr in Scotland to the Admty Bd MOD 1948-85; *Recreations* reading, walking, painting; *Clubs* New (Edinburgh); *Style—* N Croumbie Macpherson, CBE, WS; Viewfield Coach House, 1 Stable Lane, Edinburgh EH10 5ET (☎ 031 447 1185)

MACPHERSON, Hon Mrs; Sarah Catherine; *née* Conolly-Carew; yr da of 6 Baron Carew, CBE; *b* 6 Nov 1944; *m* 5 March 1966, Ian Arthur Cluny Macpherson, s of late Maj Arthur Clarence Macpherson, of N Devon; 1 s, 2 da; *Style—* The Hon Mrs Macpherson; Bratton Farm, Chittlehampton, North Devon EX37 9QH (☎ (07694) 231)

MACPHERSON, (Ronald) Thomas Stewart; CBE (1967), MC (1943, and 2 bars 1944 and 1945), TD (1960), DL (Gtr London 1977); 5 s of Sir (Thomas) Stewart Macpherson, CIE (d 1949), of Newtonmore, Inverness-shire, and Helen (d 1976), er da of Rev Archibald Borland Cameron, of Edinburgh; bro of 1 Baron Drumalbyn, cous of 15 Earl of Kinnoull and 2 Baron Strathcarron, *qqv*; *b* 4 Oct 1920; *Educ* Cargilfield Fettes, Trinity Coll Oxford (MA); *m* 1953, Jean Henrietta, yst da of David Butler-Wilson, of Alderley Edge, Cheshire; 2 s, 1 da; *Career* Queen's Own Cameron Highlanders 1939, cmmnd serv WW II: Scottish Commando, parachutist (POW 1941-43), Maj 1943 (despatches); TA 1947-67; 21 SAS (Artists), co 1 Bn London Scottish, Col TAVR London Dist 1964-67; chm Louis T Leonowens Ltd (Thailand, Singapore, Malaysia, Indonesia) 1972-82, Mallison-Denny Gp 1980-82 (joined William Mallinson & Sons Ltd 1948, md Mallinson-Denny 1967-81); former chm cos in Aust and USA; dir: Transglobe Expedition Ltd 1976-83, Brooke Bond Gp 1981-82, Birmid Qualcast plc 1982-88 (chm), Scottish Mutual Assur Soc 1982-, NCB 1983-86, C H Industls plc 1983-, Cosmopolitan Textile Co Ltd 1983- (chm); memb cncl CBI (past chm London and SE regn, memb pres's City Advsy Bd); memb: Ctee on Invisible Exports 1982-85, Scottish Cncl for Devpt and Indust, Steering bd Univ of Strathclyde 1980-85; chm: cncl London C of C 1980-82 (vice-pres 1982-), Allstate Reins Co Ltd 1983-, Employment Conditions Abroad Ltd; Nat Employers Liaison Ctee for Vol Res Forces 1986; dir: New Scotland Insur 1986-, TSB Scotland 1986-; chm Boustead plc 1986-, London advsr Sears Roebuck & Co 1984-, chm Assoc of British Cs of C 1986-88; govr Fettes Coll, pres Achilles Club 1981; memb Royal Co of Archers (Queen's Bodyguard for Scotland); High Sheriff Gtr London 1983-84, Dep Lt Gtr London 1972-; memb Worshipful Co of Dyers (prime warden 1985-86); Chev de la Légion d'Honneur, Croix de Guerre (2 palms and star); FRSA, FBIM; *Recreations* fishing, shooting, outdoor sport, squash, modern languages, Oxford Univ and London Scottish rugby player, Oxford Univ and Mid-Surrey hockey player, Oxford blue athletics (and Scottish Int); *Clubs* Hurlingham, MCC; *Style—* Thomas Macpherson, Esq, CBE, MC, TD; 27 Archery Close, London W2 2PN (☎ 01 262 8487); Balavil, Kingussie, Inverness-shire (☎ 054 02 470)

MACPHERSON OF CLUNY (AND BLAIRGOWRIE), Hon Mr Justice; Hon Sir

William Alan Macpherson of Cluny (Cluny Macpherson); TD (1965), QC (1971); 27 Chief of the Clan Macpherson; s of Brig Alan David Macpherson of Cluny-Macpherson, DSO, MC (d 1969), and Catherine Richardson Macpherson (d 1967); *b* 1 April 1926; *Educ* Wellington Coll, Trinity Coll Oxford (MA); *m* 27 Dec 1962, Sheila McDonald, da of Thomas Brodie (d 1979), of Edinburgh; 2 s (Alan Thomas b 8 Oct 1965, James Brodie b 5 June 1972), 1 da (Anne b 10 Nov 1963); *Heir* s, Alan Macpherson yr of Cluny b 1965; *Career* Capt Scots Gds 1944-47, Lt-Col 21 SAS Regt (TA) 1962-65, Hon Col 21 SAS 1983-; barr Inner Temple 1952, bencher 1978; Crown Ct rec 1971; judge of the High Ct of Justice (Queen's Bench Divn) 1983; presiding judge Northern Circuit 1984-88; Hon Memb Northern Circuit 1987; memb Royal Co of Archers (Queen's Body Gd for Scotland) 1977; govr Royal Scottish Corpn; pres London Scottish Football Club 1977-79; kt 1983; *Recreations* golf, fishing, rugby football; *Clubs* Caledonian, Highland Soc of London, London Scottish Football (pres 1972-79), Blairgowrie Golf; *Style*— The Hon Mr Justice Macpherson of Cluny, TD, QC; Royal Courts of Justice, Strand, London WC2

MACPHERSON OF DRUMOCHTER, 2 Baron (UK 1951); (James) Gordon Macpherson; JP (Essex 1961); s of 1 Baron (d 1965), and Lucy (d 1984), da of Arthur Butcher; *b* 22 Jan 1924; *Educ* Wells House Malvern, Loretto; *m* 1, 1947, (Dorothy) Ruth (d 1974), da of Rev Henry Coulter (decd), of Bellahouston, Glasgow; (1 s decd), 2 da; m 2, 1975, Catherine Bridget, only da of Dr Desmond MacCarthy, of Brentwood; 1 s, 2 da (Hon Jennifer b 1976, Hon Anne b 1977); *Heir* s, Hon James Anthony Macpherson b 27 Feb 1979; *Career* served with RAF 1941-46; memb: cncl of London C of C 1958, exec ctee of W India Ctee 1959 (dep chm 1971, chm 1973); fndr chm and patron Br Importers Confedn 1972-; chm Godron Macrobin (Insur) Ltd; chm and md of Macpherson, Train and Co Ltd, Food and Produce Importers and Exporters; chm A J Macpherson & Co Bankers; memb Cncl E Euro Trade Cncl 1969-72; chief Scottish Clans Assoc London 1972-74; Freeman: City of London 1969, Worshipful Co of Butchers 1969; memb Essex Magistrates' Cts Ctee 1974-75, dep chm Brentwood Bench 1972; govr Brentwood Sch 1970-, hon game warden for the Sudan 1974; landowner (10,000 acres grouse, deer and salmon, with 1000 farming); Fell: Royal Entomological Soc, FZS, FRSA; *Recreations* shooting, fishing, orchids; *Clubs* Boodle's; *Style*— The Rt Hon the Lord Macpherson of Drumochter, JP; Kyllachy, Tomatin, Inverness-shire (☎ Tomatin (08082) 212); Macpherson House, 69-85 Old St, London EC1 (☎ 01 253 9311)

MACPHERSON OF PITMAIN, (Michael) Alastair Fox; 17 Sr Chieftain of Clan Macpherson; s of Stephen Marriott Fox (d 1971), of Surrey, and Margaret Gertude Macpherson of Pitmain; *b* 17 Dec 1944; *Educ* Haileybury, Magdalene Coll Cambridge (BA Law); *m* 10 June 1972, Penelope Margaret, da of Frederick William Birkmyre Harper (d 1977), of Oxon; 2 s (Alexander b 1976, Charles b 1980), 1 da (Isabella); *Heir* s, Alexander Macpherson, yr of Pitmain; *Career* slr 1971; ptnr Ashurst, Morris, Crisp, slrs, of Broadgate House 1974; non exec dir: Smith & Nephew plc 1986-, Johnson Fry plc 1987-, Thomas Jourdan plc 1987- ; *Recreations* golf, cricket, fishing, ballet; *Clubs* Oxford and Cambridge, Hurlingham; *Style*— Alastair Macpherson of Pitmain, Esq; 58 Luttrell Avenue, Putney, London SW15 6PE (☎ 01 788 1812); Achara House, Duror of Appin, Argyll (☎ 063 174 262)

MACPHERSON-GRANT, Lady; (Evelyn) Nancy Stopford; da of Maj Edward Spencer Dickin (d 1969), and Mrs Norah Grace Eden, *née* Stopford (d 1966); *b* 3 Oct 1915; *m* 1937, Maj Sir Ewan George Macpherson-Grant, 6 Bt (d 1983, when the Baronetcy becamse extinct), s of George Bertram Macpherson-Grant, MBE; 1 da (Clare); *Style*— Lady Macpherson-Grant; Pitchroy Lodge, Blacksboat, Ballindalloch, Banffshire AB3 9BQ (☎ 08072 208)

McPHIE, John Kent; TD and Clasp (1945); s of John Kent McPhie (d 1919), and Sarah Paterson Duncan (d 1956); *b* 8 Nov 1918; *Educ* Glasgow Acad; *m* 1943, Elsie May; 1 s, 1 da; *Career* cmmnd TA 1936, served overseas (Europe) WWII, Lt-Col RASC, (despatches); dir: Johnson & Johnson (GB) Ltd, Johnson & Johnson (Dressings) Ltd, Johnson & Johnson (Ireland) Ltd, Johnson & Johnson (Pty) Ltd 1957-63, Permacel Ltd, MAC Marketing Servs Ltd (md) 1963-64, Robinson & Sons Ltd (exec) 1964-82, Robinson-Eirecot Ltd 1965-82, Edward Taylor Ltd 1965-82, Pressure Sealed Plastics Ltd 1968-82; vice-chm Toilet Preparations Fedn 1961-62, vice-pres and chm Mfrs' Section Proprietary Articles Trade Assoc 1961-62; chm: Surgical Dressings Mfrs Assoc 1970-73, Assoc of Sanitary Protection Mfrs' 1976-80, Disposable Baby Napkin Mfrs' Assoc 1977-81; memb govrs Euro Disposables and Nonwovens Assoc 1981-82, hon life memb Euro Surgical Dressings Mfrs' Assoc 1982-; Inst of Marketing: chm: Royal Counties Branch 1956-57 (pres 1964-65, nat vice-chm 1959-62, nat chm 1962-63), Contact Gp Euro Insts of Marketing 1963-64, Nat Fellowship Panel 1968- (hon fell 1978); fndr memb Guild of Marketers, master Worshipful Co of Marketers 1983-84; elder of Utd Reform Church, vice-pres High Peak Hunt Club; *Recreations* marketing, hunting; *Clubs* Army and Navy; *Style*— John McPhie, Esq; Hanover Cottage, Eaton Hill, Baslow, Bakewell, DE4 1SB (☎ 024 688 2142)

MACPHIE, (Charles) Stewart; s of Charles Macphie (d 1970), and Hilda Gladys, *née* Marchant (d 1978); *b* 22 Sept 1929; *Educ* Rugby; *m* 12 April 1958, Elizabeth Margaret Jill, da of Charles George Michael Pearson (d 1977); 1 s (Alastair b 1961), 1 da (Fiona b 1959); *Career* chm Macphie of Glenbervie, dir N of Scotland Hydro Electric Co; farmer, ptnr Glenbervie Home Farm; memb Scottish Cncl of CBI 1981-87, chm of govrs Oxenfoord Castle Sch Midlothian, former chm Bakery and Allied Trades Assoc, cncl memb Food Mfrg Res Assoc Leatherhead; tstee Kincairdineshire Jubilee Tst, pres of appeal Bakers Benevolent Assoc; *Recreations* estate management, travel, reading, theatre; *Clubs* New (Edinburgh), Caledonian; *Style*— Stewart Macphie, Esq; Knock Hill House, Glenbervie, Kincardineshire (☎ 056 94 259); Macphie of Glenbervie, Glenbervie, Kincardineshire (☎ 056 94 641, telex 73589, fax 05694 677)

McQUAID, Dr James; s of James McQuaid (d 1981), and Brigid, *née* McDonnell (d 1988); *b* 5 Nov 1939; *Educ* Christian Brothers Sch Dundalk, Univ Coll Dublin (BEng), Jesus Coll Cambridge (PhD), Nat Univ of Ireland (DSc); *m* 17 Feb 1968, Catherine Anne, da of Dr James John Hargan (d 1988), of Rotherham; 2 s (James Benedict b 1968, Martin Hargan b 1971), 1 da (Fiona Catherine b 1969); *Career* graduate engr apprentice Br Nylon Spinners Ltd 1961-63, princ sci offr Safety in Mines Res Estab 1972-78 (sr res fell 1966-68, sr sci offr 1968-72), dir Safety Engrg Laboratory 1980-85 (dep dir 1978-80), res dir Health and Safety Exec 1985-; CEng, MIMechE 1972, FIMinE 1986; *Recreations* model engineering, ornamental turning, industrial archaeology; *Clubs* Athenaeum; *Style*— Dr James McQuaid; 61 Pingle Rd, Sheffield, S Yorks S7 2LL (☎ 0742 365349); Health and Safety Executive, Broad Lane, Sheffield, S Yorks S3 7HQ (☎ 0742 768141)

MACQUAKER, Donald Francis; s of Thomas Mason Macquaker (d 1979), of Brae of Auchemdrare by Ayr, and Caroline Bertha Floris Macquaker (d 1983); (gf Sir Thomas, fndr Royal Samaritan Hosp for Women Glasgow); *b* 21 Sept 1932; *Educ* Winchester, Trinity Coll Oxford (MA), Glasgow Univ (LLB); *m* 9 Jan 1964, Susan Elizabeth, da of William Archibald Kay Finlayson (d 1969); 1 da (Diana b 1965), 1 s (Charles b 1968); *Career* farmer landowner and slr; ptnr TC Young & Son, Glasgow 1957-; memb: (later vice-chm) bd of mgmnt Royal Maternity Hosp 1965-74, chm: Gtr Glasgow Health Bd 1983-87 (convenor fin ctee 1973-83), Common Servs Agency Scottish Health Serv 1987-; dir Lithgows Ltd 1987-; *Recreations* shooting, fishing, gardening; *Clubs* Western Glasgow, Western Meeting Ayr, Leander, Henley; *Style*— Donald Macquaker, Esq; Blackbyres, by Ayr KA7 4TS (☎ 0292 41088); 30 George Square, Glasgow G2 1LH

McQUARRIE, Sir Albert; s of Algernon Stewart McQuarrie (d 1955), and Alice Maud Sharman (d 1961); *b* 1 Jan 1918; *Educ* Highlanders Acad Greenock, Greenock HS, Strathclyde Univ; *m* 1945, Roseleen (d 1986), da of Hugh McCaffery (d 1960); 1 s (Dermot Hugh Hastings, producer/dir Scottish TV); *Career* HM Forces 1939-45; chm and md A McQuarrie & Son (GB) Ltd 1946-; hon patron N E Junior FA; MP (C) Aberdeenshire E 1979-83; conslt Bredero plc 1979-; The Challoner Club Ltd London 1982-; freedom of City of Gibraltar 1982; former MP (C) East Aberdeenshire 1979-83, Banff and Buchan 1983-87; kt 1987; *Recreations* golf, bridge, soccer, horticulture; *Clubs* RSAC, Turriff Golf, The Challoner; *Style*— Sir Albert McQuarrie; 33 Castlebay Court, Larks, Ayrshire KA30 8DS (☎ 0475 686614)

MACQUEEN, Professor John; s of William Lockhead Macqueen (d 1963), of 92 Hermiston Rd, Springboig, Glasgow E2, and Grace Palmer, *née* Galloway (d 1983); *b* 13 Feb 1929; *Educ* Hutchesons' GS, Glasgow Univ (MA), Christ's Coll Cambridge (BA, MA); *m* 22 June 1953, Winifred Wallace, da of Wallace McWalter, (d 1979), of 114 Maxwellton Road, Calderwood, East Kilbride; 3 s (Hector b 1956, Angus b 1958, Donald b 1963); *Career* PO, Flying Offr RAF 1954-56; asst prof Washington Univ St Louis Missouri USA 1956-59, lectr Univ of Edinburgh 1959-63 (masson prof 1963-71, dir Sch of Sco Studies 1969-88, prof Sco Lit 1971-88, endowment fell 1988-); DLitt National Univ of Ireland 1985; *Books* St Nynia (1961), Robert Henryson (1967), Ballattis of Luve (1970), Allegory (1970), Progress and Poetry (1982), Numerology (1985), The Rise of the Historical Novel (1988); *Recreations* walking, reading, music, casual archaeology; *Clubs* Scottish Arts, University Staff (Edinburgh); *Style*— Professor John Macqueen; 12 Orchard Toll, Edinburgh, EH4 3JF; Slewdonan, Damnaglaur, Drummore, Stranraer, Wigtownshire DG9 9QN (☎ 031 332 1488); School of Scottish Studies, Unversity of Edinburgh, 27 George Square, Edinburgh EH8 9LD (☎ 031 667 1011)

McQUEEN, Dr Norman John; s of William Wood McQueen (d 1968), of Lennoxtown, and Isabella Neilson Richmond (d 1967); *b* 11 July 1914; *Educ* Glasgow HS, Glasgow Univ (MB, ChB); *m* 17 Sept 1943, Jean, da of Col Reginald Winnington Fanshawe, CMG (d 1926); 2 s (Iain b 1945, William Gordon b 1946), 2 da (Anne b 1944, Kirsteen b 1954); *Career* Maj Indian Med Service, surgical specialist, India, Burma, Ceylon (despatches 1942); med practitioner, MRCGP (1953), hon memb (ex pres) Glasgow Univ Medico-Clinical Soc, asst surgn Out Patient Dept Royal Infirmary Glasgow; *Recreations* sailing; *Clubs* Royal Highland Yacht; *Style*— Dr Norman McQueen; Achnacladach, Appin, Argyll PA38 4BQ (☎ 063173 378)

MCQUIGGAN, John; MBE (1955); s of John McQuiggan (d 1937), of Liverpool, and Sarah Elizabeth, *née* Sim (d 1960); *b* 24 Nov 1922; *Educ* St Edward's Coll Liverpool; *m* 17 June 1950, (Doris)Elsie, da of Gilbert Henry Hadler (d 1973), of Bromley; 3 s (Tony b 8 March 1956, Simon b 21 July 1959, David b 29 April 1963), 1 da (Sarah b 13 Sept 1961); *Career* Dominions Office 1940-42, CRO 1947-50, admin offr Canberra 1950-54, 2 sec and consul Lahare and Dacca 1954-57, 1 sec (inf) Lahare and Peshawar 1957-58, dep dir UK inforserv in Australia 1958-61; dir Br Info servs: E Nigeria 1961-64 (concurrently 1 sec Kigali Rwanda) Uganda 1964-69; FCO London 1969-73, HM Consul Chad (London based) 1970-73, dep HC and Cnsllr Lusaka Zambia 1973-76; ret (own request) HM Dip Serv 1976; princ John McQuiggan Assoc 1976-78, exec dir UK S Africa Trade Assoc 1978-86, dir-gen Br Indus Ctee on S Africa 1986; princ John McQuiggan Assoc 1986-; FIOD; pubns: num contribs to Trade & Economic Jls; *Recreations* tennis, carpentry, craftwork (wood); *Clubs* Royal Overseas League London; *Style*— John McQuiggan, Esq, MBE; 7 Meadowcroft, Bickley, Kent BR1 2JD (☎ 01 467 0075)

MacQUITTY, James Lloyd; OBE (1983), QC (NI); s of James MacQuitty, of Bangor, Co Down, and Henrietta Jane, *née* Little; *b* 2 Nov 1912; *Educ* Campbell Coll Belfast, Methodist Coll Belfast, St Catherine's Coll Oxford (MA), Trinity Hall Cambridge (MA, LLM); *m* 1941, Irene Frances, da of Nicholas Alexander Miller McDowell, of Belfast; *Career* memb English Bar and Bar of NI; chm NI of: Compensation Appeals Tbnl, Compensation Tbnl for Loss of Employment through Civil Unrest, Wages Cncls; chm: Ulster TV 1977-83, Ulster Folk and Tport Museum 1976-85; memb Industl Injuries Advsy Cncl 1960-86; Hon LLD Queen's Univ Belfast 1987; *Recreations* swimming; *Clubs* Carlton, Royal Ulster Yacht; *Style*— J L MacQuitty, Esq, OBE, QC; 10 Braemar Park, Bangor, Co Down BT20 5HZ (☎ 0247 454420)

MacRAE, (Alastair) Christopher Donald Summerhayes; CMG; s of Dr Alexander MacRae and Dr Grace MacRae; *b* 3 May 1937; *Educ* Rugby, Lincoln Coll Oxford, Harvard; *m* 1963, Mette Willert; 2 da; *Career* served RN 1956-58, joined CRO 1962; served: Dar es Salaam 1963-65, ME Centre for Arab Studies Lebanon 1965-67, Beirut 1967-68; FCO 1968-70; first sec and head of chancery Baghdad 1970-71, Brussels 1972-76; (granted temp leave from FCO) Euro Cmmn Brussels 1976-78; ambass: Gabon 1978-80, (non-res) Sao Tomé and Principé 1979-80; head W Africa Dept FCO 1980-83, ambass Chad (non res) 1982-83; political cnsllr and head of chancery Paris 1983-87; min head of Br Interests Section Swedish Embassy Tehran 1987; *Clubs* Royal Cwlth Soc; *Style*— Christopher MacRae, Esq, CMG; FCO, King Charles St, London SW1

McRAE, Frances Anne; *née* Cairncross; da of Sir Alec (Alexander Kirland) Cairncross, KCMG, *qv*; *b* 30 August 1944; *Educ* Laurel Bank Sch Glasgow, St Anne's Coll Oxford (MA); *m* 1971, Hamish McRae, qv, 2 da; *Career* staff memb: The Times 1967-69, The Banker 1969, The Observer 1970- 73, The Guardian (economics correspondent 1973-81), ed women's page 1981-84, Br ed The Economist 1984-89, environmental ed The Economist 1989; memb SRRC Economics Ctee 1972-76, Newspaper Panel Monopolies Cmmn 1973-80, cncl of Royal Economic Soc 1980-85, Inquiry into Br Housing 1984-

85; hon tres Nat Cncl for One Parent Families 1980-83; tstee Kennedy Meml Tst 1974-, non exec dir Prolific Group 1988-;; *Books* Capital City (with Hamish McRae, 1971), The Second Great Crash (with H McRae, 1973), The Guardian Guide to the Economy (1981), Changing Perceptions of Economic Policy (1981), The Second Guardian Guide to the Economy (1983); *Style*— Mrs Frances McRae; 6 Canonbury Lane, London N1 2AP (☎ 01 359 4612)

McRAE, Hamish Malcolm Donald; s of Donald Barrington McRae (d 1980), and Barbara Ruth Louise, *née* Budd; *b* 20 Oct 1943; *Educ* Fettes Coll Edinburgh, Trinity Coll Dublin (BA); *m* 20 Sept 1971, Frances Anne, qv, da of Sir Alec Cairncross, KCMG, of Oxford; 2 da (Isabella b 1977, Alexandra b 1979); *Career* dep ed The Banker 1971-72, ed Euromoney 1972-74, fin ed The Guardian 1975-; Fin Journalist of the Year 1979; *Books* Capital City: London as a Financial Centre (with Frances Cairncross, 1973); *Style*— Hamish McRae, Esq; The Guardian, 119 Farringdon Rd, London EC1

MACRAE, James Norman; s of Col William Donald Macrae, MC, TD, and Mary Robertson, *née* Crowther; *b* 5 July 1940; *Educ* Loretto Sch; *m* 1 Oct 1977, Miranda Jane, da of Sir Dugald Leslie Lorn Stewart of Appin, KCVO, CMG (d 1984); *Career* 15 (Scottish) Bn The Para Regt 1959-65 and 1967-69, 21 SAS Regt (Artists Rifles) 1965-67, 23 SAS Regt 1975-77, A/Maj W(HSF) Co 3/51 Highland Volunteers 1986-; CA; dir Arbuckle Smith & Co Ltd 1971-76; gp fin dir and co sec Arbuckle Smith Gp 1976-; *Recreations* riding, yachting, skiing, TA, amateur stage; *Clubs* Royal Northern and Clyde YC; *Style*— James N Macrae, Esq; Burnside Cottage, Gartocharn, Dunbartonshire G83 8SD (☎ 038 283 430); Arbuckle Smith & Co Ltd, 91 Mitchell Street, Glasgow G1 3LS (☎ 041 248 5050, telex 778212)

MacRAE, (Merelina) Mary Phyllis; DL (Suffolk 1984); er da of Capt (John) Duncan George MacRae (d 1966), and Lady Phyllis MacRae, *qv*; *b* 20 August 1922; *Educ* Downham, Brilliamont Lausanne; *Career* served in ATS 1942-46; dir MacRae Farms Ltd; pres Suffolk Agric Assoc 1987; memb Suffolk CC (chm 1984-86); *Style*— Miss Mary MacRae, DL; Hatchery House, Little Mill Lane, Barrow, Bury St Edmunds, Suffolk IP29 5BT (☎ 0284 810442, business ☎ 0284 810300)

MacRAE, Lady Phyllis; *née* Hervey; yr da of 4 Marquess of Bristol, MVO (d 1951), and Alice Frances Theodora, *née* Wythes (d 1957); *b* 30 Nov 1899; *m* 9 Nov 1921, Capt (John) Duncan George MacRae, Seaforth Highlanders (d 1966), only s of Lt-Col John MacRae-Gilstrap (who assumed the additional name Gilstrap under the will of his wife's paternal uncle, Sir William Gilstrap, 1 Bt); 1 s (John) and 1 s decd, 2 da ((Merelina) Mary Phyllis, *qv*, Jean m 1949 13 Earl of Northesk); *Career* ATS 1939-46, Co Cdr 1940-48; dir MacRae Farms Ltd; *Style*— Lady Phyllis MacRae; Hatchery House, Little Mill Lane, Barrow, Bury St Edmunds, Suffolk IP29 5BT (☎ 0284 810442)

MACRAE, Col Robert Andrew Alexander Scarth; MBE (1953), JP (1975), DL (Orkney 1946); s of Robert Scarth Farquhar Macrae, CIE CBE (d 1926) of Grindelay, Orphir, Orkney, and Beatrix Reid, *née* McGeoch (d 1970); *b* 14 April 1915; *Educ* Lancing, RMC Sandhurst; *m* 7 June 1945, Violet Maud, da of Walter Scott MacLellah (d 1959) of Edinburgh; 2 s (Christopher b 1948, Malcolm b 1956); *Career* cmmnd 2 Lt Seaforth Highlanders 1935, served BEF 1940; (POW); active service NW Europe 1940-45 (despatches) Korea 1952-53, Kenya 1953-54, Col 1963 ret 1968; farmer; memb: Orkney CC l1970-74, Orkney Islands Cncl 1974-78; vice chm: Orkney Hosp Bd 1971-74, Orkney Health Bd 1974-79; Lord Lt 1972- (vice Lt 1967); *Recreations* sailing; *Clubs* New (Edinburgh), Army & Navy, Puffins; *Style*— Col Robert Macrae, MBE JP; Grindelay, Orphir, Orkney (☎ 085 681 228); Binscarth Farms, Orkney

McRAE, Stuart Neil; s of Max Harvey McRae, and Vivienne Blanche Rosemary, *née* Lewin; *b* 23 June 1939; *Educ* Diocesan Coll, Cape Town, S Africa; Univ of Witwatersrand (BA); *m* 24 June 1961, Joyce Rowena, da of Arthur Breeze-Carr (d 1968); 3 da (Fiona Jane b 1965, Louise Mary b 1967, Caroline Anne b 1970); *Career* md Reader's Digest Assoc Ltd 1986-, dir Reader's Digest: (Ireland) Ltd, AB Sweden; dir: Drive Pubns Ltd, Nine Colt Ltd, Periodical Publishers Assoc 1987-, Save the Children Fund (Sales) Ltd 1987- (chm SCF Trading Ctee); pres Assoc of Mail Order Publishers 1986; *Recreations* squash, tennis, dinghy sailing; *Clubs* Lansdowne; *Style*— Stuart McRae, Esq; Readers Digest Assn Ltd, 25 Berkeley Square, London WI (☎ 01 629 8144)

MacRAE, Hon Mrs; Hon Susan Mary; *née* Southwell; da of 6 Viscount Southwell (d 1960); *b* 1926; *m* 1951, Keith Francis MacRae; 2 s; *Style*— The Hon Mrs MacRae; 27 Dennis Rd, Slacks Creek, via Brisbane

MacRAE OF BALLIMORE, John Duncan Hervey; 24 Constable of Eilean Donan Castle, suc his f, as 2 of Ballimore 1966; s of Capt John Duncan George MacRae of Ballimore (d 1966), and Lady Phyllis Hervey, yr da of 4 Marquess of Bristol; *b* 11 Jan 1925; *Educ* Eton; *m* 1950, Marigold Elizabeth, o da of late George Henry Tritton, of Lyons Hall, Great Leighs, Essex; 5 da; *Style*— John MacRae of Ballimore; Nairnside House, by Inverness; Eilean Donan Castle, Ross-shire

MACREADY, Sir Nevil John Wilfrid; 3 Bt (UK 1923), of Cheltenham, Co Gloucester; CBE (1983); s of Lt-Gen Sir Gordon Nevil Macready, 2 Bt, KBE, CB, CMG, DSO, MC (d 1956); *b* 7 Sept 1921; *Educ* Cheltenham, St John's Oxford; *m* 1949, Mary, da of Sir (John) Donald Balfour Fergusson, GCB (d 1963); 1 s, 3 da; *Heir* s, Charles Nevil Macready; *Career* served RA 1942-47, Staff Capt 1945; BBC Europ Serv 1947-50, md Mobil Oil Co Ltd 1975-85; pres: Royal Warrant Holders' Assoc 1979-80, Inst of Petroleum 1980-82; chm: Crafts Cncl 1984-, Horseracing Advsy Cncl 1986-; tstee V & A Museum 1985-; *Clubs* Boodle's, Naval and Military, Jockey (Paris); *Style*— Sir Nevil Macready, Bt, CBE; The White House, Odiham, Hants RG25 1LG (☎ 0256 70 2976)

MacROBERT, (John Carmichael Thomas) Michael; s of Capt John MacRobert (d 1947), of Lismore, Millikenpark, Renfrewshire, and Jessie Simpson, *née* MacCuaig; *b* 26 April 1918; *Educ* Rugby, Cambridge Univ (MA), Glasgow Univ (LLB); *m* 16 Sept 1947, Anne Rosemary, da of Kenneth MacKay Millar, of Hill House, Paisley; 1 s (David John Carmichael b 1953), 2 da (Fiona Garwood b 1949, Susan Walker b 1951); *Career* 80 Field Regt RA TA, 125 OCTU Filey 1939, 2 Lt 10 Field Regt RA BEF 1940, India 1942, Egypt 1943, Assam and Burma 1944 (despatches), 80 Field Regt 1946 BAOR, 402 Anti-tank Regt RA TA and 402 A & SH Mortar Regt 1947; slr; ptnr MacRobet Son & Hutchinson 1948, cncl memb Law Soc of Scotland 1965-77, Hon Sheriff 1969, ret 1987; chm Paisley Cons Assoc, hon pres Paisley South Cons Assoc; cncl memb Nat Tst for Scotland, Clyde Estuary Amenity Cncl; tstee Scottish Civic Tst, hon sec Paisley Abbey Surroundings Ctee; *Recreations* sailing, country sports; *Clubs* Western (Glasgow); *Style*— Michael MacRobert, Esq; Failte Colntraive, Argyll; 21 Carriage Hill, Paisley, (☎ 070084 239, 041 8893425)

MACRORY, Henry David; s of Sir Patrick Macrory, of Walton-on-the-Hill, Surrey, and Lady Marjorie Elizabeth, *née* Lewis; *b* 15 Dec 1947; *Educ* Westminster, Kent Univ (BA); *m* 4 April 1972, Janet Carolyn, da of Henry James Potts; 1 s (David b 1985), 2 da (Julia b 1978, Caroline b 1980); *Career* reporter Kent Messenger 1969-72; Sunday Express 1972-: reporter 1972-79, political columnist 1979-83, asst ed 1983-; *Style*— Henry Macrory, Esq; Sunday Express, Ludgate House, 245 Blackfriars Rd, London SE1 (☎ 01 928 8000, fax 01 633 0244)

MACRORY, Sir Patrick Arthur; s of Lt-Col F S N Macrory, DSO, DL (d 1956); *b* 21 Mar 1911; *Educ* Cheltenham, Trinity Coll Oxford (MA); *m* 1939, Elizabeth, da of Rev J F O Lewis (d 1960); 3 s; *Career* serv WWII; barr Middle Temple 1937; joined Unilever 1947 (sec 1956, dir 1968, ret 1971); memb NI Devpt Cncl 1956-64; gen tres Br Assoc for Advancement of Sci 1960-65; memb ctee: Inquiry into Indust Representation 1971-72, Preparation of Legislation 1974-75; chm Confedn of Ulster Socs 1974, (pres 1980-83); dep pres cncl Cheltenham Coll 1980-83; kt 1972; *Style*— Sir Patrick Macrory; Amberdene, Walton-on-the-Hill, Tadworth, Surrey (☎ 073 781 3086)

McSHANE, Ian David; s of Henry McShane, of Manchester, and Irene, *née* Cowley; *Educ* Stretford GS Leeds, RADA; *m* 30 Aug 1980, Gwendolyn Marie, da of Claude Humble; 1 s (Morgan b 7 July 1974), 1 da (Kate b 18 April 1970); *Career* actor; films incl: The Wild and the Willing 1962, The Battle of Britain 1968, If its Tuesday this must be Belgium 1969, Villain 1971, Sitting Target 1972; Exposed 1984, Torchlight 1986; theatre (West End): The Glass Menagerie 1965, Loot 1966, The Promise 1967 (also on Broadway); theatre (Los Angeles): As You Like It 1979, Betrayal 1983, Inadmissable Evidence 1985; TV: Jesus of Nazareth, Wuthering Heights, Disraeli, Whose Life Is It Anyway, Lovejoy, Dallas, War and Remembrance, The Letter; memb: BAFTA, Acad of Motion Picture Arts and Sciences; *Style*— Ian McShane, Esq; Duncan Heath Associates Ltd, Paramount House, 162-170 Wardour St, London

McSHINE, Hon Sir Arthur Hugh; s of Arthur Hutton McShine, CBE (d 1948); *b* 11 May 1906; *Educ* Queen's Royal Coll Trinidad; *m* 1945, Dorothy Mary Vanier; 1 s, 1 da; *Career* barr Middle Temple 1931, judge of the Supreme Ct Trinidad and Tobago 1953-62, justice of appeal 1962-68, chief justice Trinidad and Tobago 1968-71, acting govr-gen Trinidad and Tobago 1970 and 1972; Order of Trinity Cross (Trinidad and Tobago); kt 1969; *Style*— Hon Sir Arthur McShine; 6 River Rd, Maraval, Port-of-Spain, Trinidad

MacTAGGART, Lady; Irene; da of late Ferdinand Richard Holmes Meyrick; *m* 1, 1939 (m dis 1954), 6 Earl of Craven (d 1965); m 2, 1961, Sir Andrew MacTaggart (d 1978); *Style*— Lady Irene MacTaggart; Clatfields, Marsh Green, Edenbridge, Kent (☎ 0732 2819)

MACTAGGART, Sir John Auld; 4 Bt (UK 1938), of Kings Park, City of Glasgow; s of Sir Ian (John) Auld Mactaggart, 3 Bt (d 1987), and Lady Belhaven and Stenton (*see* Belhaven and Stenton, Lord); *b* 21 Jan 1951; *Educ* Shrewsbury, Trinity Coll Cambridge; *m* 1977, Patricia, da of late Maj Harry Alastair Gordon, MC; *Career* chartered surveyor; dir Centl and City Hldgs, chm Western Heritable Investmt Co Ltd, dir of property cos; memb Thames Valley Housing Soc Ltd, dir Scottish Ballet; FRICS; *Clubs* Annabel's, Argyllshire, Gathering, MCC; *Style*— Sir John Mactaggart, Bt; Ardmore House, Ardtalla Estate, Islay, Argyll; 55 St James's St, London SW1 (☎ 01 491 2948)

MacTAGGART, Air Vice-Marshal William Keith; CBE (1976, MBE 1956); s of Duncan MacTaggart (d 1947), of Glasgow, and Marion Winifred *née* Keith (d 1988); *b* 15 Jan 1929; *Educ* Aberdeen GS, Aberdeen Univ (BSc Eng); *m* 1, 30 July 1949 (m dis 1977), Christina Carnegie, da of James Geddes (d 1974), of Aberdeen; 1 s (Alan b 26 May 1954), 2 da (Carol b 24 March 1950, Shelagh b 23 April 1952); m 2, 9 Sept 1977, Barbara Smith Brown, da of Adm Stirling P Smith (d 1977); 1 step da (Carolyn b 12 June 1957); *Career* cmmnd RAF 1949, Engr Offr/Pilot 1949-70, Gp Capt and OC RAF Newton 1971, Air Cdre and dir of air armament MOD (PE) 1973, RCDS 1977, Air Vice-Marshal and vice pres Ordnance Bd 1978 (pres 1978-80); dep chm Tomash Hldgs Ltd 1980-84; md MPE Ltd 1984-; CEng 1965, FIMechE 1973, FRAeS 1974, FBIM 1978; *Recreations* music, travel, reading; *Clubs* RAF; *Style*— Air Vice-Marshal W MacTaggart, CBE; MPE Ltd, Cobbs Wood, Ashford, Kent TN23 1EB (☎ 0233 23404, telex 965227, fax 0233 41777)

MacTHOMAS OF FINEGAND, Andrew Patrick Clayhills; o s of Capt Patrick Watt MacThomas of Finegand (d 1970), and Elizabeth Clayhills-Henderson, of Invergowrie, Angus; suc f 1970 as 19 Chief of Clan MacThomas; *b* 28 August 1942; *Educ* St Edward's Sch Oxford; *m* 1985, Anneke Cornelia Susanna, da of Mr and Mrs A Kruyning-van Hout, of Heesch, The Netherlands; *Heir* s, Thomas David Alexander MacThomas, yr of Finegand (b 1987); *Career* Public Affairs, Barclays Bank; memb Standing Cncl of Scottish Chiefs; pres Clan MacThomas Soc; FSA (Scot); *Recreations* Travel, promoting the clan; *Style*— Andrew MacThomas of Finegand; c/o Clan MacThomas Society, 19 Warriston Avenue, Edinburgh EH3

McTIERNAN, Rt Hon Sir Edward Aloysius; KBE (1951), PC (1963); s of Patrick and Isabella McTiernan; *b* 16 Feb 1892; *Educ* Marist Brothers' HS Sydney, Sydney Univ (BA, LLB); *m* 1948, Kathleen, da of Sidney Lloyd; *Career* admitted to Bar NSW 1917, MLA for NSW 1920-27, attorney-gen 1920-22 and 1925-27, lectr in Law Sydney Univ 1927, MHR 1928-30, judge of High Ct 1930-76; *Style*— The Rt Hon Sir Edward McTiernan, KBE; 36 Chilton Parade, Warrawee, Sydney, NSW 2074, Australia

MacVICAR, Rev Kenneth; MBE, DFC, TD; s of Angus John MacVicar (d 1973), of Southend, Argyll, and Marjorie, *née* McKenzie (d 1965); *b* 25 August 1921; *Educ* Campbeltown GS, St Andrews Univ (MA); *m* 4 Sept 1946, Isobel Guild, da of Johnston Reid McKay, of Glasgow; 3 s (Angus John b 1947, Kenneth Johnston McKay b 1948, Cameron William b 1953), 1 da (Jean Helen b 1961); *Career* Flt Cdr, RAF pilot Burma Campaign 1942-45; minister of religion, parish of Kenmore & Lawers 1950-; *Recreations* golf; *Clubs* Taymouth Castle GC; *Style*— The Rev Kenneth MacVicar, MBE, DFC, TD; Manse, nr Kenmore, Aberfeldy, Perthshire (☎ 088 73 218)

McVIE, John; WS; s of John McVie, OBE, MSM (d 1967), and Jessie Gordon, *née* Hunter; *b* 7 Dec 1919; *Educ* Royal HS Edinburgh, Edinburgh Univ (LLB); *m* 14 July 1943, Lindsaye Woodburn Mair; 1 s (John Gordon b 1945), 1 da (Fiona Jean Richmond Sheldon b 1948); *Career* Capt 7/9 Btn The Royal Scots 1940-46 (despatches); signals offr UK and North Western Europe; convener of ctee for Restoration of the Choir and Transepts of St Mary's Church Haddington; Hon Sheriff of Lothian & Borders at

Haddington Sheriff Court; sr ptnr McVies WS slrs Haddington; town clerk of Royal Burgh of Haddington 1951-75; *Recreations* fishing, golf, travel; *Clubs* Royal Scots, Edinburgh Univ Staff; *Style*— John McVie, Esq, WS; Ivybank, Haddington, East Lothian (☎ 062 082 3727); McVies WS, 47/48 St Haddington

McVITTIE, John Bousfield; s of Brig Arthur Bousfield McVittie , OBE (d 1976), and Valerie Florence, *née* Crichton; *b* 9 April 1943; *Educ* Radley, Selwyn Coll Cambridge (MA); *m* 25 Sept 1971, Jane Elizabeth, *née* Hobson; 2 da (Clare, Amy); *Career* md Privatbanken Ltd 1984-87, sr vice-pres and gen mangr First Interstate Bank of California 1981-; Freeman: City of London 1969, Worshipful Co of Clothworkers 1974; *Recreations* skiing, tennis; *Clubs* Pembroke Tennis (hon sec); *Style*— John McVittie, Esq; 72 Scarsdale Villas, London W8 6PP (☎ 01 937 8926); 6 Agar St, London WC2H 4HN (☎ 01 836 3560)

McWATTERS, George Edward; s of Lt-Col George Alfred McWatters, 81 Pioneers, IA (d 1955), and Christina Ellen Mary, *née* Harvey (d 1977), gd of John Harvey, the Bristol wine merchant; *b* 17 Mar 1922; *Educ* Clifton; *m* 1, 7 Dec 1946, Margery Neilson (d 1959), da of David Robertson; m 2, 21 July 1960, Joyce Anne Matthews; 1 s (Christopher George b 19 Aug 1962); *Career* chm: John Harvey & Sons 1956-66, HTV West 1969-88 and HTV Ltd 1986-88; dir Martins Bank 1960-70; memb: Automobile Assoc Ctee 1962, CBI Grand Cncl 1970-82; chm: Appeal Ctee Avon Wildlife Tst 1982, St John Cncl Avon 1983; vice-chm Bristol & West Bldg Soc 1985-; govr Clifton Coll 1958-; city cllr Bristol 1949-53, JP (Bristol 1960-67), JP (Marylebone 1969-71), High Sheriff Cambs 1979; master of Soc of Merchant Venturers Bristol 1986-87; Hon Freeman: City of Bristol 1955, City of London 1948, Worshipful Co of Vintners 1948; *Recreations* walking, swimming, reading; *Clubs* Buck's, MCC; *Style*— George McWatters, Esq; Burrington House, Burrington, Bristol BS18 7AD (☎ 0761 62291)

McWATTERS, Dr the Hon Veronica; *née* Stamp; da of 2 Baron Stamp (d 1941), and Katharine, Baroness Stamp (d 1985); *b* 25 May 1934; *Educ* Queenswood Sch Hatfield, Royal Free Hosp Med Sch London; *m* 1961, Richard Alfred Hugh McWatters, s of Sir Arthur Cecil McWatters, CIE (d 1966); 1 s, 2 da; *Career* doctor (MRCS, LRCP), former house offr Royal Free Hosp and Stamford and Rutland Hosp; pt/t GP Bristol; *Recreations* bee keeping; *Clubs* Br Bee Keepers Assoc; *Style*— Dr the Hon Veronica McWatters; The Grove, Dundry, Bristol, Avon BS18 8JG (☎ 0272 641334); Hartcliffe Health Centre, Bristol

McWHIRTER, Norris Dewar; CBE (1980); s of William McWhirter (md Associated Newspapers and Northcliffe Newspapers Gp); er twin brother of Ross McWhirter (killed 1975), Norris's co-fndr and ed of Guinness Book of Records (1954-86); *b* 12 August 1925; *Educ* Marlborough, Trinity Coll Oxford (MA); *m* 1957, Carole (d 1987), da of George Eckert; 1 s, 1 da; *Career* dir Gieves plc 1972-, Guinness Superlatives Ltd 1954- (md 1954-76), chm Wm McWhirter & Sons 1955-86; fndr and chm Redwood Press; former sports (athletics) correspondent Observer, Star, BBC Olympic commentator (radio 1952-56, TV 1960-72); chm Freedom Assoc; contested (C) Orpington 1964 and 1966; sports cncl 1970-74; *Books* Guinness Book of Records (252 editions in 31 languages 59 million sales), Guinness Book of Answers, Ross-Story of a Shared Life; *Recreations* family tennis, skiing, watching athletics and rugby; *Clubs* Caledonian, Achilles, Vincent's; *Style*— Norris McWhirter, Esq, CBE; c/o Guinness Publications Ltd, 33 London Rd, Enfield EN2 6DJ (☎ 01 367 4567)

MCWHIRTER, Prof Robert; CBE (1963); s of Robert McWhirter (d 1944), of Ballantrae, Ayrshire, Scotland, and Janet Ramsay, *née* Gairdner (d 1947); *b* 8 Nov 1904; *Educ* Glasgow Univ (MB ChB), Cambridge Univ (DMRE); *m* 26 June 1937, Susan Muir, da of William Mac Murray (d 1938), of 40 Kelvinside Gardens, Glasgow; 1 s (William b 18 May 1939); *Career* cancer res fell Holt Radium Inst Manchester 1933-34, chief asst x-ray dept St Bartholomews Hosp London 1934-35, prof med radiology Edinburgh Univ 1946-70 (lectr 1935-46); pres: radiology section RSM 1956-57, Scottish Radiological Soc 1957-58, Medical and Dental Defence Union 1959-, Radiotherapists Visiting club 1965-69, RCR 1966 -69; chm standing cancer ctee Scottish Health Servs Cncl 1962-70, Nat Soc Cancer Relief Scotland 1963-70, conslt adviser organsiation of radiotherapy servs (govts of Australia, S Africa, Nigeria, Rep of Ireland); awards incl: Liston Victoria Jubilee Prize RCS Edinburgh 1941, Twinning Meml Medal Royal Coll of Radiologists 1943, Fndn lecture Mayo Clinic USA 1948, Caldwell Meml Lecture, Montreal, America, Roentgen Ray Soc 1963; hon memb American Radium Soc 1948, hon fell RCR of Australia 1954 hon memb American Coll of Radiologists 1964, hon FFR RCS Ireland 1967; hon memb radiologist Soc: France 1967, Italy 1968; FRCS 1932, FRCR 1939, FRCP 1965; fell Royal Soc of Edinburgh; *Books* British Surgical Practice (contrib vol 2 1948), British Practice in Radiotherapy (contrib 1955), Frontiers of Radiotherapy (contrib 1970); *Recreations* ornithology and golf; *Clubs* Edinburgh Univ Staff, Bruntsfield Links GC; *Style*— Prof Robert McWhirter, CBE; 2 Orchard Brae, Edinburgh EH4 1NY (☎ 031 332 5800)

MacWILLIAM, Very Rev (Alexander) Gordon; s of Andrew George MacWilliam (d 1940), of Conwy, Gwynedd, and Margaret, *née* Davies; *b* 22 August 1923; *Educ* Queen Elizabeth GS, Univ of Wales (BA), Univ of London (BD, PLD); *m* 28 June 1951, Catherine Teresa, da of John Bogue, of Britannia Terrace, Valley, Holyhead, Gwynedd; 1 s (Andrew John b 1957); *Career* minor canon Bangor Cathedral 1949-55, rector Llanfaethlu Gwynedd 1955-58, head dept of theol Trinity Coll Carmarthen 1984-85, visiting prof Central Univ of Iowa USA, dean of St Davids Cathedral 1984-; *Recreations* travel, classical music; *Style*— The Very Rev Gordon MacWilliam; The Deanery, Haverfordwest, Dyfed (☎ 0437 720202)

McWILLIAM, Jillian; MBE (1988); da of Herbert McWilliam, of Preston, Lancs, and Mabel Harwood, *née* Harrison; *b* 17 Nov 1946; *Educ* Ashton-on-Ribble Secdy Sch, Elizabeth Gaskell Coll (Dip Ed); *m* 28 Sept 1979, Geoffrey Michael Lee, s of Percy John Lee (d 1977), of Flamstead, Herts; *Career* mktg dir Bejam 1987-88, PR dir Iceland Frozen Foods plc 1989-, currently broadcaster; memb Inst Home Economics; *Books* 7 cookery books on freezing and microwave cooking; *Recreations* cooking, reading, gardening; *Style*— Miss Jillian McWilliam, MBE; Adelaide Cottage, Common Rd, Studham, nr Dunstable, Beds (☎ 0582 873 214); Iceland Frozen Foods plc, Honeypot Lane, Stanmore, Middx (☎ 01 952 8311, fax 01 952 3577, telex 21776 ICELAND)

McWILLIAM, John David; MP (Lab) Blaydon 1979-; s of Alexander and Josephine McWilliam; *b* 16 May 1941; *Educ* Leith Acad, Heriot-Watt Coll, Napier Coll of Science and Technol; *m* 1965, Lesley Mary Catling; 2 da; *Career* Post Office engr; *Style*— John McWilliam, Esq, MP; House of Commons, London SW1

MADDEN, Lt-Col Brian John George; DSO (1941); s of Lt-Col Gerald Hugh Charles Madden (d of wounds 1915), and Mabel Lucy MacPherson Grant (d 1951); *b* 16 Dec 1908; *Educ* Wellington Coll RMC Sandhurst; *m* 11 Jan 1969, Mary, da of Percy Middleton-Evans (d 1922); *Career* Lt Col cmmnd The Black Watch 1928, served WW II in Dunkirk, N Africa, Italy, NW Europe, Cdr: 6 Black Watch 1943-44 (wounded), 5/7 Gordon Highlanders 1945, 6 Black Watch 1946 until they were disbanded, ret on med grounds 1947; asst supt Middx Hosp 1948-51, chief admin offr St Helier Gp of Hosps 1951-74; govr of the Royal Star and Garter Home for Disabled Servicemen 1974-84; *Recreations* classical music, chess, light verse, ball games, P G Wodehouse novels; *Clubs* Highland Brigade; *Style*— Lt-Col Brian Madden, DSO; Gaelen House, Bovingdon, Herts (☎ 0442 832 287); Royal Bank of Scotland, Kirkland House, 22 Whitehall, London

MADDEN, Adm Sir Charles Edward; 2 Bt (UK 1919), of Kells, Co Kilkenny; GCB (1965); s of Adm of the Fleet Sir Charles Edward Madden, 1 Bt, GCB, OM, GCVO, KCMG (d 1935), and Constance Winifred (d 1964), yst da of Sir Charles Cayzer, 1 Bt, of Gartmore; *b* 15 June 1906; *m* 1942, Olive, da of late George Winchester Robins, of Caldy, Ches; 1 da; *Heir* bro, Lt-Col John Wilmot Madden, MC; *Career* joined RN 1920, WWII served HMS Warspite (despatches) and HMS Emperor (despatches); chief of Naval Staff NZ 1953-55, naval ADC to HM The Queen 1955, C-in-C Plymouth 1959-62, Adm 1961, C-in-C Home Fleet and Eastern Atlantic 1963-65, ret 1965; chm Royal Nat Mission to Deep Sea Fishermen 1971-81, tstee Nat Maritime Museum 1968 (chm 1972-77), chm Standing Cncl of the Baronetage 1975-77; Vice Lord Lt (Gtr London) 1969-82; *Clubs* Arts; *Style*— Adm Sir Charles Madden, Bt, GCB; 21 Eldon Rd, London W8 (☎ 01 937 6700)

MADDEN, Rear-Adm Colin Duncan; CB (1966), CBE (1964), MVO (1954), DSC (1940 and bar 1944); s of Archibald Maclean Madden, CMG (d 1928); *b* 19 August 1915; *Educ* R N Coll Dartmouth; *m* 1943, Agnes Margaret, da of H K Newcombe, OBE (d 1949), of W Sussex and Canada; 2 da; *Career* joined RN 1928, world wide war serv at sea, Naval Attaché Rome 1955, dir Navigation and Direction Admty 1961, Rear Adm 1965, sr naval memb directing staff IDC 1965-67, formerly Cdr (N) HM Yacht Britannia, Capt HMS Crossbow, HMS Albion; dir Nat Trade Devpt Assoc 1967, Brewers Soc 1969-82; *Recreations* sailing, gardening, embroidery, tapestry; *Clubs* Army and Navy, Royal Cruising; *Style*— Rear-Adm Colin Madden, CB, CBE, LVO,; c/o Army & Navy Club, 36 Pall Mall, London SW1Y 5JN

MADDEN, Lt-Col John Wilmot; MC (1943); s of Adm of the Fleet Sir Charles Edward Madden, GCB, OM, GCVO, KCMG, DCL (d 1935); h to Btcy of bro, Sir Charles Edward Madden, 2 Bt, GCB; *b* 20 Dec 1916; *m* 1941, Beatrice Catherine, JP, da of late W A Sievwright, WS, of St Andrews, Fife; 2 s, 1 da; *Career* Lt-Col (ret) RA, Burma 1944 (despatches); chm Warminster and Westbury RDC 1969-72; *Style*— Lt-Col John Madden, MC; Little Queen Oak, Fantley Lane, Bourton, Dorset SP8 5AL (☎ Bourton 840351)

MADDEN, Maxwell Francis; MP (Lab) Bradford West 1983-; s of George Francis Leonard Madden, and Rene Frances Madden; *b* 29 Oct 1941; *Educ* Lascelles Secdy Mod Sch, Pinner GS; *m* 1972, Sheelagh Teresa Catherine Howard; *Career* journalist: E Essex Gazette, Tribune, Sun, Scotsman; Br Gas Corpn press and info offr; MP (Lab) Sowerby Feb 1974-79; dir of publicity Lab Pty 1979-, front bench oppn spokesman Health and Social Security Nov 1983- March 1984; *Recreations* fishing; *Style*— Maxwell Madden, Esq, MP; House of Commons, London SW1A 0AA

MADDEN, Michael; s of John Joseph Madden (d 1978), and Mary Ann, *née* Donnelly; *b* 14 Jan 1937; *Educ* St Illtyds Coll Cardiff Wales, LSE (BSc); *m* 27 Feb 1960, Patricia Margaret, *née* Gaspa, da of Charles Gaspa of Cliftonville, Kent; 2 s (Simon Jude b 1960, Stephen Paul b 1964); 1 da (Alison Maria b 1962); *Career* asst gen mangr Moscow Narodny Bank Ltd 1966-68 (economic advsr 1959-66), gen mangr First Nat Fin Corpn Ltd 1968-70, md Exim Credit Mgmnt Conslts Ltd 1971-76, exec dir Standard Chartered Merchant Bank Ltd 1977-86, dir Standard Chartered Merchant Bank Hldgs 1984, md Standard Chartered Merchant Bank Ltd 1986, gen mgr Standard Chartered Bank 1987-88, and chief exec Standard Chartered Export Fin Ltd 1987-88; non-res conslt: 1BRD (World Bank) Washington, FAO (Investmt centre) Rome, UNCTAD Geneva; *Recreations* rugby football, gardening, writing; *Clubs* Reform, IOD, Overseas Bankers; *Style*— Michael Madden, Esq; 16 Wolsey Rd, Moor Park, Herts HA6 2HW (☎ 09274 26767)

MADDISON, Roger Robson; s of Ralph Robson Maddison (d 1943), and Ethel Daisy, *née* Smith; *b* 15 July 1929; *Educ* Dulwich Coll, Cambridge Univ (MA) ; *m* m 1, 1954, (m dis 1975) Christine Elizabeth, *née* Fulljames; 2 s (Patrick James Robson b 1959, Timothy Paul Robson b 1963), 1 da (Vivien Mary b 1956); m 2 Sara Caroline da of Arthur Geoffrey Howland-Jackson, MBE; *Career* slr; sr ptnr Knapp-Fishers (Westminster) 1980-83; sr ptnr Baldocks (Guildford) 1984-; memb Law Soc .; *Recreations* golf, tennis, music, gardening; *Clubs* Worplesdon GC, St Georges Hill LTC; *Style*— Roger Maddison, Esq; Rydal House, East Horsley, Surrey (☎ 048 65 2377); 59 Quarry St, Guildford, Surrey (☎ 0483 573 303)

MADDOCK, John Henry; s of Charles Maddock (d 1957), of Preston, and Sarah Ann, *née* Theobald (d 1954); *b* 20 Dec 1906; *Educ* The Catholic Coll Preston; *m* 12 April 1941, Julia, da of John Lewis-Murphy (d 1959), of Lincs; 5 s (Thomas b 1942, Charles b 1944 (decd), Peter b 1945, Edward b 1948 (decd), Roger b 1950); *Career* fruit importer; memb Liverpool Fruit Exchange 1946-59; md: Radford Products Ltd 1941-44, Charles Maddock Ltd 1946-59; *Recreations* collecting french antique paper weights, japanese prints, gardening; *Style*— John Maddock, Esq; The Chase, High Knott, Arnside, via Carnforth, Cumbria (☎ 0524 761732)

MADDOCK, Thomas Patrick; s of John Henry Maddock, of The Chase, High Knott, Arnside, Cumbria, and Julia, *née* Murphy; *b* 5 Mar 1942; *Educ* Downside; *m* 15 July 1972, Carmen, da of Royston St Noble (d 1971), of Barcelona, Spain; 2 s (Royston b 1975, William b 1978); *Career* Lt Duke of Lancaster's Own Yeo (TA); owner and dir The Tom Maddock Gallery Barcelona 1968-, dir Charles Maddock Ltd; *Recreations* riding, tennis, swimming; *Clubs* Real Club de Polo (Barcelona), Sloane; *Style*— Thomas Maddock, Esq; Ganduxer 136, 2o2a 08022 Barcelona Spain; Casanova, Vilanova del Valles Prov de Barcelona Spain; The Chase, High Knott Rd, Arnside, Cumbria (☎ 343 418 3975); TOM MADDOCK Gallery, Aribau 306, 08006 Barcelona, Spain (☎ 343 201 2687, fax 343 203 3512)

MADDOCKS, Bertram Catterall; s of His Hon George Maddocks (d 1980), and Harriet Mary Louisa *née* Day (d 1983); *b* 7 July 1932; *Educ* Malsis Hall Nr Keighley Yorkshire; Rugby Sch; Trinity Hall, Cambridge MA; *m* 13 June 1965, Angela Vergette, da of Michael Leetham Forster, of Aughton, Lancashire; 2 s (Jeremy b 1954, Jolyon b 1969); 1 da (Cindy b 1967); *Career* 2 Lieut RA 1951; Duke of Lancaster's own Yeomary TA 1956-67; *Recreations* real tennis, lawn tennis, skiing, bridge; *Clubs* Manchester Tennis and Racquet, Queens; *Style—* Bertram Maddocks, Esq; Moor Hall Farm Aughton Lancashire (☎ 0695 421601); St James's Chambers, 68 Quay St, Manchester (☎ 061 834 7000)

MADDOCKS, Sir Kenneth Phipson; KCMG (1958, CMG 1956), KCVO (1963); s of Arthur P Maddocks (d 1957); *b* 8 Feb 1907; *Educ* Bromsgrove Sch, Wadham Oxford; *m* 1, 1951, Elnor Radcliffe (d 1976), da of Sir E John Russell, OBE, FRS (d 1965); m 2, 1980, Patricia Josephine, *née* Hare Duke, wid of Sir George Mooring, KCMG; *Career* HMOCS; civil sec Northern Region Nigeria 1955-57, dep govr 1957-58, actg govr Northern Region Nigeria 1956 and 1957, govr and C-in-C Fiji 1958-63, dir and sec East Africa and Mauritius Assoc 1964-69; KStJ; *Recreations* gardening; *Clubs* Royal Cwlth Soc; *Style—* Sir Kenneth Maddocks, KCMG, KCVO; 11 Lee Rd, Aldeburgh, Suffolk IP15 5HG (☎ 072 885 3443)

MADDOCKS, Rt Rev Bishop Morris Henry St John; s of Rev Canon Morris Arthur Maddocks (d 1953), and Gladys Mabel, *née* Sharpe; *b* 28 April 1928; *Educ* St John's Sch Leatherhead, Trinity Coll Cambridge, Chichester Theological Coll; *m* 1955, Anne, da of late William Oliver Miles; *Career* nat serv as 2 Lt RASC; curate: St Peter's Ealing 1954-55, St Andrew's Uxbridge 1955-58; vicar: Weaverthorpe, Helperthorpe and Luttons Ambo 1958-61, St Martin-on-the-Hill Scarborough 1961-71; bishop suffragan of Selby 1972-83; hon asst bishop: Diocese of Bath and Wells 1983-87; Diocese of Chichester 1987-; chm of Churches Cncl for Health and Healing 1982-85 (co-chm 1975-82), advsr to the Archbishops of Canterbury and York for the Ministry of Health and Healing 1983-; co-fndr (with wife) of Acorn Christian Healing Tst; FRSM 1988; *Books* The Christian Healing Ministry (1981), The Christian Adventure (1983), Journey to Wholeness (1986), A Healing House of Prayer (1987), Twenty Questions About Healing (1988); *Recreations* walking, gardening, music; *Clubs* Army and Navy; *Style—* The Rt Rev Morris Maddocks; St Mary's, Burrswood, Groombridge, Nr Tunbridge Wells, Kent TN3 9PY (☎ 0892 863637 ext 221, 04203 8121/2); Acorn Christian Healing Trust, Whitehall Chase, Bordon, Hampshire GU35 OAP

MADDOX, Sir (John) Kempson; VRD (1948); s of Sidney Harold Maddox (d 1941), and Mabel Adeline Maddox (d 1945); *b* 20 Sept 1901; *Educ* N Sydney Boys' HS, Sydney Univ (MB, ChB, MD); *m* 1940, Madeleine, da of Hugh J Scott (d 1931); 1 s, 1 da; *Career* Surgn Cdr RANR Pacific Area and Aust 1939-45; conslt physician: Royal Prince Alfred Hosp Sydney, Royal Hosp for Women Sydney, Gosford Dist Hosp; formerly pres: NSW Branch Br Med Assoc, Int Soc of Cardiology, Asian Pacific Soc of Cardiology, Cardiac Soc of Aust and NZ; Chevalier de l'Ordre de la Santé Publique (France) 1961, Comendador Orden Hispolito Unanue (Peru) 1968, kt 1964; *Style—* Sir Kempson Maddox, VRD; 8 Annandale St, Darling Point, NSW 2027, Australia (☎ 32 1707)

MADDRELL, Geoffrey Keggen; s of Capt Geoffrey Douglas Maddrell (d 1975) of Port Erin, IOM, and Barbara Mary Maddrell; *b* 18 July 1936; *Educ* King Williams Coll, Isle of Man; Corpus Christi Coll Cambrige (MA); Columbia Univ New York (MBA); *m* 12 Oct 1964, Winifred Mary Daniel, da of Fank Dowell Jones (d 1984) of St Asaph, Clwyd; 2 s (Paul b 1965, Michael b 1971), 1 da (Siân b 1966); *Career* Lt Parachute Regiment 1955-57; Shell Int Petroleum (1960-69); dir Bowater Corp 1978-86; chief exec: Tootal Gp plc 1986-; *Recreations* running, golf; *Clubs* Rowany Golf; *Style—* Geoffrey Maddrell, Esq; Summerhill, 16 Meadlay, Esher, Surrey (☎ 0372 68694); Tootal Group plc, Spring Gardens, Manchester (☎ 061 831 7777)

MADDRELL, (Alan) Lester; s of Capt Stanley Taubman Maddrell, of Colby, IOM, and Sylvia, *née* Leece; *b* 20 Feb 1944; *Educ* King William's Coll IOM; *m* 26 March 1966, Diana Mary, da of Arthur Fallows Tate (d 1984), of Douglas, IOM; 2 s (Richard b 1975, Alan b 1976), 2 da (Tania b 1974 (decd), Stephanie b 1987); *Career* slr 1971-; dep co prosecuting slr Gloucs 1977-80, HM coroner for the Cheltenham Dist of Gloucs; *Recreations* family; *Style—* Lester Maddrell, Esq; 70 Bournside Rd, Cheltenham, Glos GL51 5AH (☎ 0242 528 167); Lester Maddrell & Co, 25 Imperial Square, Cheltenham GL50 1QZ (☎ 0242 514 000, fax 0242 226 575)

MADEL, William David; MP (C) S W Bedfordshire 1983-; s of William R Madel (d 1975), and Eileen Madel; *b* 6 August 1938; *Educ* Uppingham, Keble Coll Oxford (MA); *m* 1971, Susan Catherine, da of Lt-Cdr Hon Peter Carew, RN (ret); *Career* advertising exec; memb Bow Gp Cncl 1966-67; MP (C) Bedfordshire South 1970-83, pps to jt parly under-secs of state Def 1973-74, pps to min state Def 1973-74, chm Cons Parly Educn 1983-85; *Style—* David Madel Esq, MP; 120 Pickford Rd, Markyate, Herts

MADGE, James Richard; CB (1975); s of James Henry Madge (d 1975), and Elisabeth, *née* Self; *b* 18 June 1924; *Educ* Bexhill GS, Eggars GS Alton, New Coll Oxford (BA); *m* 1955, Alice June Annette (d 1975), da of Maj Horace Reid (d 1974), of Jamaica; 2 da (Dinah, Miranda); *Career* Pilot RAFVR 1942-46, Flying Offr ME; entered Civil Serv 1947, Miny of Civil Aviation and Tport & DOE, princ private sec to: Lord Cherwell 1950-51, Ernest Marples 1960-61; dep sec 1974, seconded to be chief exec and bd memb Housing Corpn (ret 1984); church warden St Mary Abbots Kensington; *Recreations* furniture making, tennis; *Style—* Richard Madge, Esq, CB; 56 Gordon Place, Kensington, London W8 4JF

MADIGAN, Sir Russel Tullie; OBE (1970); s of late Dr Cecil Madigan; *b* 22 Nov 1920; *Educ* Adelaide Univ (ME, LLB); *m* 1, 1942, Margaret Symons (decd); 4 s, 1 da, m 2, 1982, Satsuko Tamura; *Career* dep chm CRA Ltd, chm APV Asia Pacific, dir: APV Hldgs plc, Nat Commercial Union Ltd, chm Aust Mineral Fndn, pres Aust Inst of Int Affrs, tres Aust Academy of Technol Sciences; formerly chm Hamersley Hldgs Ltd, dir: Rio Tinto Zinc plc, Comalco Ltd, chm: Australian-Japan Fndn, Pacific Basin Econ Cncl, pres Aust Inst of Mining and Metallurgy; FSASM, FTS; kt 1981; *Style—* Sir Russel Madigan, OBE; 60 Broadway, East Camberwell, Vic 3126, Australia

MADOCKS, John Edward; CBE (1965, MBE 1956), DL (Notts 1978); s of Sidney George Robert Madocks (d 1935); *b* 14 Mar 1922; *Educ* King Edward VI Sch Lichfield, Birmingham Univ; *m* 1945, Jessica Kinross, da of Andrew Davidson (d 1939); 1 s, Ida; *Career* served WWII, Europe and Middle East, Maj; HMOCS, perm sec 1946-65; bursar of Nottingham Univ 1965-87; dir ATV Network Ltd 1979-81, chm East Midlands bd Centl Independent Television; region bd memb BR (London Midland) 1979-; memb E Midlands Economic Planning Cncl 1975-79; chm Notts Economic Planning Forum 1980-82; nat chm Assoc of Br Chambers of Commerce 1980-82; county rep Royal Jubilee Tsts 1976-86; *Recreations* books, pictures, sport; *Clubs* Royal Commonwealth; *Style—* John Madocks, Esq, CBE, DL; 7 Middleton Cres, Beeston, Nottingham (☎ 0602 256592);

MAEGRAITH, Prof Brian Gilmore; CMG (1968), TD (1972); s of Alfred Edward Maegraith (d 1952), of Adelaide, Aust, and Louise, *née* Gilmore (d 1938); *b* 26 August 1907; *Educ* St Peters Collegiate Sch Aust, Univ of Adelaide (MB BS), Oxford (BSc, MSc, DPhil, MA); *m* 18 June 1934, Lorna Elsie, da of Edgar Langley (d 1956), of Adelaide, Aust; 1 s (Michael Patrick b 21 April 1937); *Career* Capt 43 Wessex RE TA 1932-39; Maj liason unit public health RAF (France) 1939-40, Maj Pathologist Forces Sierra Leone, and Lt-Col asst dir Pathology West Afica Cmmd (West Africa) 1940-42; Lt-Col WO: biological res serv, Malasia res unit (Oxford), discharged 1945; res: meningococcal meningitis Dunn Sch of Pathology 1931-35, pathophysiology 1935-39; fell Exeter Coll Oxford Univ 1934-40, demonstrator and sr lectr 1936-44, dean Sch of Med Oxford Univ 1938-44, vice pres Liverpool Sch of Tropical Med 1975- (dean of Sch 1946-75, prof tropical med 1944-72); RAF: conslt in tropical med 1945-72, hon conslt in tropical med 1972-; conslt/advsr various UK and Foreign bds and ctees (WHO: India, Thailand, S E Asia); pres (local) Int Friendship League 1970-88, pres Royal Soc Tropical Med 1969-71, memb tropical med res bd Miny of Overseas Devpt, fndr memb W African Cncl for Tropical Res, co-fndr Faculty Tropical of Med; DSc Siriraj-Bangkok 1966, emeritius MD Athens Univ 1972, hon fell London Sch Hygeine & Tropical Med 1976, hon fell of various int tropical med socs; FRCP (London 1956, Edinburgh 1956, Aust 1970); Tritiborn Exacted Order White Elephant (Thailand 1983); *Books* Clinical Tropical Medicine (1989), One World (Health Clark lectures, London Univ 1943), Exotic Diseases in Practice (1968), Tropical and Mediteranean Diseases (1963), Pathological Progresses in Malaria (1948); *Recreations* music, writing, odd-jobs; *Clubs* Athenaeum; *Style—* Prof Brian Maegraith, CMG, TD; 23 Eaton Rd, Cressington Park, Liverpool L19 0PN (☎ 051 4271133); School Tropical Medicine, Pembroke Place, Liverpool L3 5QA (☎ 051 7089393)

MAFFEY, Hon Christopher Alan; s of 2 Baron Rugby; *b* 20 Feb 1955; *m* 1, 1977 (m dis 1981), Barbara Anne, da of Guthrie Stewart, of Auckland, NZ; m 2, 1982, Kathryn, da of V Rutherford of Waiuku, NZ; 2 s (Aaron b 1983, Leigh b 1984); *Career* farmer; pres Manukau Peninsula Play Centre; *Recreations* fishing, building; *Clubs* Awhitu Social Club; *Style—* The Hon Christopher Maffey; Kemps Rd, RD4 Waiuku, New Zealand

MAFFEY, Hon Mark Andrew; yst s of 2 Baron Rugby; *b* 7 June 1956; *Educ* Harrow, Ecole de Commerce Neuchâtel Switzerland; *m* 16 July 1983, Angela Mary, da of Derek J Polton, of Draycote, Rugby; 1 s (Thomas Henry), 1 da (Georgina Louise); *Career* gen mgmnt; Liveryman Worshipful Co of Saddlers; *Recreations* shooting, fishing; *Style—* The Hon Mark Maffey; Grove Farm Flat, Frankton, Rugby, Warwicks

MAFFEY, Hon Robert Charles; 2 (but eldest surviving) s & h of 2 Baron Rugby; *b* 1951; *m* 1974, Anne Penelope, da of David Hale, of Somerden, Chiddingstone, Kent; 2 s; *Style—* The Hon Robert Maffey; Grove Farm Cottage, Frankton, Rugby

MAFFEY, Hon Selina Penelope; da of 2 Baron Rugby, of Grove Farm, Frankton, nr Rugby, Warks, and Lady Rugby, *née* Bindley; *b* 15 Nov 1952; *Educ* Hawnes Sch Beds; *m* 1 da (Angelica Helena b 1986); *Career* farmer, tropical fruit and cattle, landowner; *Style—* The Hon Selina Maffey; McDougal Road, Julatten, Queensland 4880, Australia

MAFFEY, Hon Simon Chelmsford Loader; s of 1 Baron Rugby, GCMG, KCB, KCVO, CSI, CIE (d 1969); *b* 1919; *Educ* Rugby; *m* 1949, Andree Norma (m dis 1962), da of George Middleton; 1 da; *Career* Lt Coldstream Gds 1937, served 1939-42, served MN 1942-45; *Style—* The Hon Simon Maffey

MAGAN, George Morgan; s of Brig William Morgan Tilson Magan, CBE, and Maxine, *née* Mitchell; *b* 14 Nov 1945; *Educ* Winchester; *m* 1972, Wendy Anne, da of Maj Patrick Chilton, MC; 2 s (Edward b 1975, Patrick b 1984), 1 da (Henrietta b 1977); *Career* merchant banker; dir: J O Hambro Magan & Co Ltd, Asprey plc, WCRS Gp plc, CCA Pubns plc; govr Hawtrey's Sch; FCA; *Clubs* Royal Yacht Squadron, Turf, Boodle's; *Style—* George Magan, Esq; J O Hambro Mgan & co Ltd, 30 Queen Anne's Gate, London SW1 (☎ 01 222 2020); St Michael's House, Nr Tonbridge, Kent

MAGAREY, Sir (James) Rupert; s of Dr Rupert Eric Magarey (decd); *b* 21 Feb 1914; *Educ* St Peter's Coll Adelaide, St Mark's Coll Adelaide Univ (MB, BS); *m* 1940, (Catherine) Mary, da of William Gilbert (d 1969); 1 s, 2 da (and 1 decd); *Career* Lt-Coll RAMC AIF, served Aust, Palestine, N Africa, New Guinea, New Britain; surgn and visiting surgical specialist Queen Elizabeth Hosp Adelaide 1958-; FRCS, FRACS, FRACGP; kt 1980; *Style—* Sir Rubert Magarey; 78 Kingston Terrace, N Adelaide, S Australia 5006 (☎ (267) 2159)

MAGEE, Bryan; s of Frederick Magee; *b* 12 April 1930; *Educ* Christ's Hosp, Lycée Hôche Versailles, Keble Coll Oxford (MA), Yale; *m* 1954 (m dis), Ingrid Söderlund; 1 da; *Career* writer, critic and broadcaster; hon sr res fell in the history of ideas Univ King's Coll London 1984-; music critic for numerous pubns 1959-; formerly: columnist The Times, drama critic The Listener; Silver Medallist Royal Television Soc 1978, pres Critics' 1983-84 (cncl memb 1975-) judge Evening Standard Opera Award 1973-84, former visiting fell All Souls and lectr in Philosophy at Balliol Coll Oxford, pres Edinburgh Univ Philosophy Soc 1987-88, govr Ditchley Fndn 1979- (cncl memb 1982-) hon fell QMC 1988, parly candidate (Lab) Mids Beds 1959 and 1960, MP Leyton (Lab until 1982, Ind Lab 1982, SDP 1982-83); *Books* Crucifixion and Other Poems (1951), Go West Young Man (1958), To Live in Danger (1960), The New Radicalism (1962), The Democratic Revolution (1964), Towards 2000 (1965), One in Twenty (1966), The Television Interviewer (1966), Aspects of Wagner (1968 and Revised ed 1988), Modern Br Philosophy (1971), Popper (1973), Facing Death (1977), Men of Ideas (1978), The Philosophy of Schopenhauer (1983), The Great Philosophers (1987); *Recreations* music, theatre, travel; *Clubs* Beefsteak, Brooks's, Garrick, Savile; *Style—* Bryan Magee, Esq; 12 Falkland House, Marloes Rd, London W8 (☎ 01 937 1210)

MAGGS, Air Vice-Marshal William Jack; CB (1967), OBE (1943); s of Frederick Wilfrid Maggs (d 1959), and Hilda Lilian Marguerite Maggs (d 1914); *b* 2 Feb 1914; *Educ* Bristol GS, St John's Oxford (MA); *m* 1940, Margaret Grace, da of Thomas Liddell Hetherington (d 1975); 1 s, 1 da; *Career* joined RAF 1939, Air Vice-Marshal 1967; served WWII in UK, N Africa, Sicily, Italy; sr staff offr RAF Maintenance Cmd 1967-69; official fell and domestic bursar Keble Oxford 1969-77, emeritus fell Keble Coll 1981-; govr Bristol GS 1979; *Recreations* golf, gardening; *Clubs* RAF; *Style—* Air Vice-Marshal William Maggs, CB, OBE, MA; No 7 The Spindlers, Church St, Old Kidlington, Oxford OX5 2YP (☎ 086 75 3139)

MAGINNIS, Ken Wiggins; MP (UU) Fermanagh and S Tyrone 1983-; s of Gilbert Maginnis (d 1974), of Dungannon, and Margaret Elizabeth Wiggins (d 1984); *b* 21 Jan 1938; *Educ* Royal Sch Dungannon, Stranmills TTC Belfast; *m* 1961, Joy, da of Herbert

Moneymore (d 1976); 2 s (Stewart b 1963, Steven b 1971), 2 da (Gail b 1964, Grainne b 1969); *Career* UDR 1970-81 (cmmnd 1972, Maj), princ sch teacher 1966-82; Dungannon DC 1981-; NI Assembly 1982-86; chm Security & Home Affrs Ctee 1983-1986; memb select ctee on Def; party spokesman on security Ulster Unionist Pty; memb Ulster Defence Reg 1970-81; Commissioned 12/3/72; Major; *Clubs* Army & Navy; *Style*— Ken Maginnis, Esq, MP; House of Commons, London SW1

MAGNAY, John Christopher Frederick; s of Maj Frederick Alexander Magnay, MVO, of Sulgrave Manor, Oxon (d 1961), and his w Rosalinda Minna , da of Robert Charles Donner (d 1926), of Sulgrave Manor (and his w Hon Maude Celestina (d 1952), da of 26 Baron Dunboyne); *b* 10 Jan 1936; *Educ* Eton, RMA Sandhurst; *m* 29 May 1970, Gabriele Renate Helene, da of Georg von Posern, formerly of Waltersdorf, Thuringia; 2 s (Charles b 1971, Michael b 1973), 2 da (Caroline b 1975, Diana b 1977); *Career* Grenadier Gds 1954-68, Gds Para Co Borneo 1966, ret Maj; stockbroker Albert E Sharp London Office;; *Recreations* riding, country pursuits; *Clubs* Turf, Pratts; *Style*— John C F Magnay, Esq; Sulgrave House, nr Banbury, Oxon (☎ 0295 76242)

MAGNIAC, Rear Adm Vernon St Clair Lane; CB (1961); s of Maj Francis Arthur Magniac (d 1951), and Beatrice Caroline, *née* Davison; *b* 21 Dec 1908; *Educ* Clifton; *m* 1947, Eileen Eleanor, da of Herbert William Witney (d 1951); 1 s, 1 da (and 1 da decd); *Career* joined RN 1926, served WW II, HMS Renown 1940-43, Mediterranean, SE Asia Cmd, combined ops India 1943-45, HM Dockyards Chatham, Malta and Devonport 1945-50, Capt 1952, Rear Adm 1959, ret 1962; *Recreations* golf, fishing; *Style*— Rear Adm Vernon Magniac, CB; Marlborough, Yelverton, Devon (☎ 0822 852076)

MAGNUS, Alan Melvyn; s of Norman Alexander Magnus, and Mimi, *née* Folkson; *b* 31 August 1938; *Educ* Sir George Monoux GS, Worcester Coll Oxford (MA), Coll of Law; *m* 25 Nov 1962, Judith Sophia, da of Sidney Sack (d 1987), 2 s (Adrian b 1963, Brian b 1966), 1 da (Tina 1968); *Career* head co and commercial branch legal dept NCB 1973-87, D J Freeman & Co Slrs 1987-; jt tres Reform Synagogues of GB 1988-; memb: City of London Slrs Co 1988, Law Soc 1963, Freeman City of London 1988;; *Recreations* scuba diving, opera, ballet, music; *Clubs* Coal Industry Soc; *Style*— Alan Magnus, Esq; 84 Holders Hill Rd, Hendon, London NW4 1LN (☎ 01 346 1941); D J Freeman & Co, 43 Fetter Lane, EC4A 1NA (☎ 01 583 4055, nt 01 583 2373, fax 01 353 7377, telex 894579)

MAGNUS, Sir Laurence Henry Philip; 3 Bt (UK 1917), of Tangley Hill, Wonersh, Co Surrey; s of Hilary Barrow Magnus, TD, QC (d 1986), and Rosemary, *née* Masefield; suc unc, Sir Philip Magnus-Allcroft, 2 Bt (d 1988); *b* 24 Sept 1955; *Educ* Eton, Christ Church Oxford; *m* 1983, Jocelyn Mary, eldest da of Robert Stanton; 1 s (Thomas Henry Philip b 1985), 1 da (Iona Alexandra b 1988); *Heir* s, Thomas Henry Philip Magnus b 1985; *Career* exec dir Samuel Montagu & Co Ltd merchant bankers; memb Bow Gp; *Recreations* fishing, reading, hill walking; *Style*— Sir Laurence Magnus, Bt; 24 Milson Rd, London W14 OLJ

MAGNUS, Samuel Woolf; QC (1964); s of Samuel Woolf Magnus (d 1910), and Elizabeth, *née* Sachs (d 1958); *b* 30 Sept 1910; *Educ* private, UCL (BA); *m* 7 June 1938, Anna Gertrude, da of Addlph Shane (d 1958), of Cardiff; 1 da (Patricia Ruth (Mrs Anthony Morris) b 11 Feb 1943); *Career* WWII 1939-46, cmmnd RAOC served Egypt and Palestine; barr Gray's Inn 1937, practised London 1937-59, ptnr legal firm N Rhodesia 1959-64, legal conslt 1964; MP: N Rhodesia 1964, Zambia 1964-68, puisne judge Zambia High Ct 1968, justice of appeal Zambia 1971, cmmr for Compensation Cmmn 1977-83; tres Assoc of Liberal Lawyers, memb Cncl London Lib Pty, pres N Hendon Lib Assoc until 1959; contested (Lib) Central Hackney 1945, pres Westminster E Rotary Club 1980, memb exec ctee Friends of Westminster Hosp, chm Law Parly and GP Ctee Bd of Deputies of Br Jews 1979-83; FCIArb 1987; *Books* Companies Act 1947 (with M Estrin 1947), Companies: Law and Practice (with M Estrin 1948, 1978, supplement 1981), Advertisement Control (with R M Lyons 1949), Magnus on Leasehold Property (Temporary Provisions), Act 1951 (1951), Magnus on Landlord Tenant Act 1954 (1954), Magnus on Housing Repairs and Rents Act 1954 (1954), Kinght's Annotated Housing Acts 1958 (with F E Price 1958), Magnus on Housing Finance (with Tovell 1960), Compaines Act 1967 (with M Estrin 1967), Magnus on the Rent Act 1968 (1968), Magnus on Business Tenancies (1970), Magnus on the Rent Act 1977 (1978), Butterworths Company Forms Manual (1988); *Style*— Samuel Magnus, Esq, QC; 33 Apsley Hse, Fincheley Rd, St John's Wood, London NW8 0NX (☎ 01 586 1679)

MAGNUS-ALLCROFT, Lady; Jewell; *née* Allcroft; o da of Herbert John Allcroft (d 1911), of Stokesay Court, and Margaret Jane (who m 2, 1917, Brig-Gen John Guy Rotton, CB, CMG, and d 1946), o da of Gen Sir William Russell, 2 Bt, CB; *b* 26 Jan 1907; *m* 14 July 1943, Sir Philip Montefiore Magnus-Allcroft, 2 Bt, CBE (d 1988); *Career* welfare Offr ATS 1943-45; co vice-chm Br Legion Women's Section; *Clubs* Ladies' Carlton, Shropshire County; *Style*— Lady Magnus-Allcroft; Stokesay Ct, Onibury, Shropshire (☎ 058 477 372)

MAGNUSSON, Magnus; s of Sigursteinn Magnusson (d 1982), of Edinburgh, and Ingibjrg, *née* Sigurdardottir (d 1983); *b* 12 Oct 1929; *Educ* The Edinburgh Acad, Jesus Coll Oxford (MA); *m* 30 June 1954, Mamie, da of John Baird (d 1945), of Rutherglen, Glasgow; 2 s (Siggy b 1961, d 1973, Jon b 1965), 3 da (Sally b 1955, Margaret b 1959, Anna b 1960); *Career* journalist and broadcaster; Scottish Daily Express 1953-61, asst ed The Scotsman 1961-68; presenter many BBC TV and Radio programmes incl: Mastermind, Chronicle, Tonight, Mainly Magnus, BC: The Archaeology of the Bible Lands, Vikings!, Pebble Mill at One, Living Legends, Personal Pursuits, Current Account, All Things Considered, Landlord or Tenant - A View of Irish History; rector Edinburgh Univ 1975-78, fndr chm Scottish Churches Architectural Heritage Tst 1978, chm Ancient Monuments Bd for Scotland 1981-, tstee Nat Museums of Scotland 1985-, pres RSPB 1985-, memb UK ctee for Euro Year of the Environment 1987; Hon DHc Edinburgh Univ 1978, Hon DUniv York Univ 1981; FSA Scot 1974, FRSE 1980, FRSA 1983, Hon FRIAS 1987; Knight of the Order of the Falcon Iceland 1975, Knight Cdr 1986; *Books* Introducing Archaeology (1972), Viking Expansion Westwards (1973), Viking Hammer of the North (1976), BC: The Archaeology of the Bible Lands (1977), Vikings! (1980), Treasures of Scotland (1981), Lindisfarne (1984), Iceland Saga (1987); *Recreations* reading; *Style*— Magnus Magnusson, Esq; Blairskaith House, Balmore-Torrance, Glasgow G64 4AX (☎ 0360 20226)

MAGOR, Maj (Edward) Walter (Moyle); CMG (1960), OBE (1956, MBE 1947), DL (Cornwall 1974); s of Edward John Penberthy Magor (d 1941), and Gilian Sarah (d 1971), da of Canon W Westmacott; *b* 1 June 1911; *Educ* Marlborough, Magdalen Coll Oxford (MA), Magdalene Coll Cambridge (BA); *m* 15 Aug 1939, Daphne Davis (d 1972), 2 da of Hector Robert Lushington Graham (d 1960); 2 da; *Career* Maj, cmmnd 1932, The Poona Horse IA served 1934-47, RARO 10 Royal Hussars 1949-61; Indian Political Serv 1937-39 and 1943-47; Colonial Serv Kenya 1947-61: perm sec Miny of Def 1954, sec to the Cabinet 1958; Home Civil Service BOT 1961, asst sec 1964, ret 1971; High Sheriff Cornwall 1981; pres: Cornwall Garden Soc 1982-84, Royal Cornwall Agric Assoc 1983; Medaille de la Belgique Reconnaissante 1961; CStJ 1978 (OStJ 1975); *Recreations* gardening; *Clubs* Army & Navy; *Style*— Maj Walter Magor, CMG, OBE, DL; Lamellen, St Tudy, Bodmin, Cornwall PL30 3NR (☎ 0208 850207)

MAGUIRE, Air Marshal Sir Harold John; KCB (1966, CB 1958), DSO (1946), OBE (1949); s of Michael Maguire, of Maymooth, Ireland, and Harriette, *née* Warren; *b* 12 April 1912; *Educ* Wesley Coll, Trinity Coll Dublin; *m* 1940, Mary Elisabeth, da of George Wild, of Dublin; 1 s, 1 da; *Career* joined RAF 1933, served WWII, Gp Capt 1950, Air Cdre 1958, Air Vice-Marshal 1960, SASO Far East Air Force 1962-64, asst CAS (Intelligence) 1964-65, dep CDS (Intelligence) 1965-68, Air Marshal 1966, ret RAF 1968; dir-gen Intelligence MOD 1968-72; dir Commercial Union Assur Co 1975-82 (political and economic advsr 1972-79); Freeman City of London 1978, Liveryman Worshipful Guild of Airpilots and Navigators 1978; chm cncl of Offrs' Pension Soc 1974-84; *Clubs* RAF; *Style*— Air Marshal Sir Harold Maguire, KCB, DSO, OBE; c/o Lloyds Bank, 6 Pall Mall, London SW1

MAGUIRE, Robert Alfred; OBE (1983); s of Arthur Maguire (d 1950), of London, and Rose Lilian, *née* Fountain (d 1986); *b* 6 June 1931; *Educ* Bancroft's, The Architectural Assoc Sch of Arch (AA Dip); *m* 1, 6 Aug 1955 (m dis 1978), Robina Helen, da of Robert Finlayson; 4 da (Susan b 1956, Rebecca b 1958, Joanna b 1960, Martha b 1963); m 2, 26 Oct 1982, Alison Margaret, da of George Marshall Mason, of Henley-on-Thames; *Career* bldgs ed Architects' Jl 1954-59, private architectural practice 1956-, ptnr Robert Maguire and Keith Murray 1959-; most important works incl: St Pauls' Church Bow Common London 1959, Trinity Coll Oxford extensions 1965, student village, Stag Hill Ct Surrey Univ 1969; comp winners incl: extensions Magdalen Coll Oxford 1975, Kindertagesstate Berlin-Kreuzberg 1983, extensions Pembroke Coll Oxford 1986, visitor centre Chepstow Castle 1986, extensions Worcester Coll Oxford 1988; also bldgs in Cathedral Precinct for King's Sch Canterbury 1975-86; Surveyor of the Fabric to St George's Chapel Windsor Castle 1975-87, head of dept of architecture Oxford Poly 1976-86; churchwarden, St Lawrence's Church S Weston Oxon; RIBA 1953, FRSA 1984; *Books* Modern Churches of the World (1963); *Recreations* sailing, growing sub-tropical fruits; *Style*— Robert Maguire, Esq, OBE; South Weston Cottage, South Weston, Tetsworth, Oxon OX9 7EF (☎ 084 428 262); Cortijo Pepe Pedro, Pago de Sarja, Competa, Malaga, Spain; 104 High St, Thame, Oxon OX9 3DZ (☎ 084 421 7373, fax 084 421 6846); 21 St John's Rd, Richmond, Surrey TW9 2PE

MAHER, Terence; s of John Maher (d 1954), and Bessie; *b* 20 Dec 1941; *Educ* Burnsley GS, Univ of Manchester (LLB); *m* 4 Sept 1965 (m dis 1983); 2 da (Catherine Helen b 1971, Elizabeth Jane b 1972); *Career* met stipendiary magistrate 1983-, chm Inner London Juvenile Ct, asst recorder of the Crown Ct; memb edl bd Jl of Criminal Law; *Recreations* reading, walking, travel; *Clubs* Frewen (Oxford), 41 (Chipping); *Style*— Terence Maher, Esq; c/o Old Street Magistrates Court, Old Street, London EC1

MAHER, Terence Anthony (Terry); s of Herbert Maher (d 1978); *b* 5 Dec 1935; *Educ* Xaverian Coll Manchester; *m* 1960, Barbara, da of Dr Franz Greenbaum (d 1961); 3 s (Nicholas b 1960, Anthony b 1962, Jeremy b 1964); *Career* chm Pentos plc; dir various subsid and associated cos; *Recreations* skiing, tennis; *Style*— Terry Maher, Esq; 33 Clarence Terr London NW1 4RD; Pentos plc, New Bond St House, 1 New Bond St, London W1Y 0SB (☎ 01 499 3484, fax 01 629 9413)

MAHLER, Prof Robert Frederick; s of Dr Felix Mahler (d 1959), of London, and Olga, *née* Lowy; *b* 31 Oct 1924; *Educ* Edinburgh Acad, Edinburgh Univ (BSc, MB, ChB); *m* 13 June 1951, Maureen, da of Horace Calvert (d 1963), of Dublin; 2 s (Graeme, Brian); *Career* Sqdn Ldr RAF Med Branch 1949-51; res fell Harvard Univ 1956-58, reader Guy's Hosp London 1958-66; prof: Univ of Indiana 1962-63, Univ of Wales 1966-79; visiting prof Stockholm 1976-77, physician Clinical Res Centre Harrow 1979-; ed Jl of RCP 1987; FRCP (London) 1963, FRCP (Edinburgh) 1963;; *Recreations* opera, theatre, music, watching rugby; *Clubs* RSM; *Style*— Prof Robert Mahler; Royal Coll of Physicians, St Andrews Place, Regents Park, London NW1 4LE (☎ 01 935 1174)

MAHON, Sir (John) Denis; CBE (1967); s of John FitzGerald Mahon (d 1942), 4 s of Sir W Mahon 4 Bt, and Lady Alice Evelyn Browne (d 1970), da of 5th Marquess of Sligo; *b* 8 Nov 1910; *Educ* Eton, Ch Ch, Oxford Univ (MA); *Career* art historian; tstee Nat Gallery 1957-64 and 1966-73, memb advsy panel Nat Arts Collection Fund 1975; specialist on 17 century painting in Italy and has notable collection; has long campaigned for fiscal measures to encourage support from private individuals for art galleries and museums; memb ctee of the Biennial Exhibitions at Bologna, Italy; awarded: Medal for Benemeriti della Cultura (1957), Archiginnasio d'Oro City of Bologna (1968), Serena Medal for Italian Studies Br Acad (1972), elected Academico d'Onore, Clementine Acad Bologna (1964), Corresp Fell Accad Raffaello, Urbino (1968); Deputazione di Storia Patria per le provincie di Romagna (1969); Ateneo Veneto (1987); Hon Citizen, Cento (1982), Hon DLitt Newcastle (1969); FBA 1964; kt 1986; *Books* Studies in Seicento Art and Theory (1947), Mostra dei Carracci, Catalogo critico dei Disegni (1956, 1963), Poussiniana (1962), Catalogues of the Mostra del Guercino (Dipinti 1968, Disegni 1969); The Drawings of Guercino in the collection of HM The Queen at Windsor Castle (with N Twiner 1988); contrib: Actes of Colloque Poussin (1960), Friedlaender Festschrift (1965), Problemi Guardeschi (1967), I Dipinti del Guercino (conslt to Luigi Salermo 1988); numerous articles, especially on Caravaggio and Poussin in art-historical periodicals inc: Apollo, The Art Bulletin, The Burlington Magazine, Gazette des Beaux Arts, Art de France, Commentori, Paragone, Zeitschrift fur Kunstwissenschaft; collaborated in compilation of catalogues raisonnés of many exhibitions incl: Italian Art in Britain (Royal Academy 1960), Artists in 17th Century Rome (London 1955), L'Ideale Classico dei Seicento in Italia (Bologna 1962), Omaggio al Guercino (Cento 1967); *Style*— Sir Denis Mahon, CBE; 33 Cadogan Square, London SW1X 0HU (☎ 01 235 7311, 01 235 2530)

MAHON, Lady; Roma Irene Maxtone; da of Maxtone Lockhart Mailer (d 1948), of Tanganyika, and Helen May Gibson Mailer (d 1971); *b* 7 Mar 1914; *m* 1938, Sir Gerald

Mahon (d 1982, sometime chief justice Zanzibar and chm Med Appeal Tbnls under Industl Injuries Acts); 2 s; *Style—* Lady Mahon; The Plough House, Stratton Audley, Bicester, Oxon

MAHON, Suzanne, Lady; Suzanne; *née* Donnellan; da of late Thomas Donellan, of Pirbright, Surrey ; *m* 1958, as his 2 w, Sir George Edward John Mahon, 6 Bt (d 1987); 1 da (Sarah Caroline b 1959); *Style—* Suzanne, Lady Mahon; 7 Waltham Terrace, Blackrock, Co Dublin, Ireland (☎ 0001 880473)

MAHON, Col William Walter; 7 Bt (UK 1819), of Castlegar, Co Galway; s of Sir George Edward John Mahon, 6 Bt (d 1987), and his 1 w, Audrey Evelyn (d 1957), da of Walter Jagger; *b* 4 Dec 1940; *Educ* Eton; *m* 20 April 1968, Rosemary Jane, yr da of late Lt-Col Michael Ernest Melvill, OBE, of The Old Manse, Symington, Lanarkshire; *Heir* s, James William Mahon b 29 Oct 1976; *Career* Irish Gds 1960-; *Recreations* shooting, badge collecting, water colours; *Clubs* Army and Navy; *Style—* Col Sir William Mahon, Bt; Clare House, Goose Rye Rd, Worplesdon, Guildford, Surrey GU3 3RQ

MAHONEY, Eric; s of John Mahoney (d 1948), and Dorothy Maxey, *née* Appleby; *b* 2 April 1945; *m* 1 June 1968, Iris; 1 s (Simon b 1970), 2 da (Jane b 1973, Lucy b 1979); *Career* md Br Credit Tst Ltd 1986- dir Bank of Ireland Br Hldgs Ltd, exec dir Citibank Savings 1986- (business dir 1984); FBIM; *Recreations* horse racing, golf; *Clubs* RAC; *Style—* Eric Mahoney, Esq; British Credit House, High St, Slough, Berks (☎ 0753 73211, car tel 0836 297810)

MAHONY, David Arthur; s of Albert Robert Mahony (d 1972), and Vera May, *née* Williamson; *b* 10 Feb 1944; *Educ* Hatfield Sch, Univ of York (BA), London Business Sch (MSc); *m* 2 Jan 1977, Adrienne Mahony, da of Capt Iain Kerr (d 1944); 1 s (Iain James Albert), 2 da (Catriona Jane, Antonia Brickell); *Career* chm: Harland Simon Gp plc, Craton Lodge & Knight plc, Barwell Int Ltd, Cavendish Automation Ltd: dir: Applied Holographic plc, Continental Microwave Hldgs plc, Holders Technol plc; FRSA 1980; *Recreations* shooting, fishing, golf; *Clubs* Carlton; *Style—* David Mahony, Esq; 41 Towerhill, London EC3N 4HA (☎ 01 480 5000)

MAHONY, Lieut Dominic John Grehan; s of Cdr John Grehan Mahony, RN, of Alverstoke, Hampshire, and Josephine Diana, *née* Foulds; *b* 26 April 1964; *Educ* Millfield, LSE (BSc), RMA Sandhurst; *Career* cmmd Lt LG 1987, Troop Ldr CVR Windsor 1987-; Br under 20 epée fencing champion 1984, Br jr under 21 modern pentathlon champion 1984-85, Br epée team champion 1983-85, Br Univ epée champion 1984, Br epée champion 1986, Army epée champion 1987 (1984-85), later Servs epée champion 1987-88; modern pentathlon: World Bronze team medallist 1987, Olympic Bronze team medallist 1988; *Clubs* Cavalry and Guards; *Style—* Lieut Dominic Mahony; Combermere Barracks, Windsor (☎ 0753 855 606); The Life Guards, Combermere Barracks, Windsor, Berks (☎ 0753 868 222)

MAHONY, Stephen Dominic Patrick; s of Dermot Cecil Mahony, of Cork, Ireland, and Kate, *née* O'Neill; *b* 3 Mar 1956; *Educ* Ampleforth, Oxford (MA); *m* 15 July 1983, Lucinda Margaret Ann, da of Maj Donald Struan robertson, of Winkfield Plain Farm, Winkfield, Windsor, Berks; 1 s (Dermot b 16 Nov 1988), 1 da (Caroline b 3 May 1987); *Career* Citibank NA 1977-82, exec dir SBCI Swiss Bank Corpn Investmt Banking Ltd 1986-88 (joined 1982); *Clubs* Chelsea Arts; *Style—* Stephen Mahony, Esq; 40 Lilyville Rd, London SW6 5DW (☎ 01 736 3628)

MAIDEN, Ian Arthur; s of Arthur Maiden (d 1977), of Southport, and Jessie, *née* Henshall; *b* 26 Nov 1933; *Educ* Malvern Coll; Royal Agric Coll, Cirencester; *m* 8 June 1963, Annette Stella Jean (m dis 1987); 1 s (Daniel b 1970), 2 da (Angela b 1965, Emma b 1966); *Career* chm and chief exec Arthur Maiden Ltd and assoc cos; *Recreations* offshore sailing; *Clubs* Royal Ocean Racing, Royal Thames YC; *Style—* Ian A Maiden, Esq; 38 Old Church St, Chelsea, London SW3 (☎ 01 352 3941); Quay Flat, Fisherman's Quay, Lymington, Hampshire (☎ 0590 77611); 14 Half Moon St, London W1Y 7RA (☎ 01 629 3333, fax 01 491 7326, telex 262963, car tel 0836 273856, and Yacht Fanfare 0860 342556)

MAIDMENT, Dr Susan Rachel; da of Peter Elman, of Jerusalem, Israel, and Frances, *née* Tuckman; *b* 15 Feb 1944; *Educ* South Hampstead HS for Girls, London School of Economics (LLB, LLM), Univ of Keele (LLD); *m* 16 Aug 1969, Dr Richard Anthony Maidment, s of Harold St Clair Maidment (d 1971), of London; 1 s (Adam b 1973), 2 da (Alice b 1971, Eleanor b 1980); *Career* barr Lincolns Inn 1968, lectr law Univ of Bristol 1967-70, sr lectr law Univ of Keele 1970-84, practising barr 1984; *Books* Child Custody and Divorce (1984); *Style—* Dr Susan Maidment; 36 Gondar Gardens, London NW6 1HG (☎ 01 794 1630); 4 Brick Crt, Temple, London EC4 (☎ 01 353 5392)

MAIDSTONE, Viscount; Daniel James Hatfield Finch Hatton; s and h of 16 Earl of Winchilsea; *b* 7 Oct 1967; *Style—* Viscount Maidstone

MAIDSTONE, Bishop of 1987-; Rt Rev David James Smith; s of Stanley James Smith (d 1965), and Gwendolen Emie, *née* Nunn (d 1960); *b* 14 July 1935; *Educ* Hertford GS, King's Coll London (AKC); *m* 2 Dec 1961, Mary Hunter, da of Eric John Moult (d 1970); 1 s (Christopher b 1966), 1 da (Rebecca b 1965); *Career* asst curate: All Saints Gosforth 1959-62, St Francis High Heaton 1962-64, Longbenton 1964-68; vicar: Longhirst with Hebron 1968-75, St Mary Monkseaton 1975-81, Felton 1982-83; archdeacon of Lindisfarne 1981-87; *Style—* The Rt Rev the Bishop of Maidstone; Bishop's House, Pett Lane, Charing, Ashford, Kent TN27 ODL (☎ 023 371 2950)

MAILE, David Grenville; s of John William Kingsley Maile (d 1952), and Vera Christine, *née* Hancock; *b* 24 April 1927; *Educ* Mill Hill Sch, Emmanuel Coll Cambridge (MA); *m* 18 July 1953, Suzanne Mary Courtney, da of Herbert Charles Derham (d 1976); 1 s (Nigel b 1955), 2 da (Alison b 1958, Sarah b 1963); *Career* Staff Sgt RE 1948; ecclesiastical craftsman; Freeman City of London 1969, Liveryman of the Glaziers Co; *Recreations* walking, golf, music, bridge; *Clubs* Kent and Canterbury; *Style—* David G Maile, Esq; Brookmans End, Plough Lane, Upper Harbledown, Canterbury CT2 9AR (☎ 0227 61296 and 66055)

MAILE, Nigel Kingsley; s of David G Maile, of Canterbury, Kent, and Suzanne Mary *née* Derham; *b* 4 Sept 1955; *Educ* Mill Hill Sch, Hatfield Poly ; *m* 19 Oct 1985, Julia Eileen, da of Cdr John E Hommert of Rowland Castle, Hants; *Career* CA Spicer & Oppenheim 1977-82, fin dir Bartle Bogle Hegarty (advtg agency) 1982-; ACA 1982; *Recreations* golf, walking, motorcycling; *Style—* Nigel Maile, Esq; Manor Way, Potters Bar, Herts (☎ 0707 55622); Bartle Bogle Hegarty Ltd, 24-27 Great Pulteney St, London W1R 3DB (☎ 01 734 1677, fax 01 437 3666)

MAIN, His Hon Judge John Roy Main; QC (1974); s of Alfred Charles Main (d 1968); *b* 21 June 1930; *Educ* Portsmouth GS, Hotchkiss Sch USA, Brasenose Oxford; *m* 1955, Angela de la Condamine, da of Robert William Home Davies (d 1970); 2 s, 1 da; *Career* Lt RNR; barr Inner Temple 1954, memb special panel Tport Tbnl 1970-76, dep chm IOW Quarter Sessions 1971, recorder Crown Court 1972-76, circuit judge 1976-; *Recreations* walking, boating, gardening, music; *Style—* His Honour Judge Main, QC; 4 Queen Anne Drive, Claygate, Surrey KT10 0PP (☎ 0372 66380)

MAIN, Sir Peter Tester; ERD (1964); s of Peter Tester Main (d 1977), of Aberdeen, and Esther Paterson, *née* Lawson (d 1955); *b* 21 Mar 1925; *Educ* Robert Gordon's Coll Aberdeen, Aberdeen Univ (MB, ChB, MD), RCP; *m* 1, 13 May 1952, Dr Margaret Fimister (d 1984), da of Thomas William Tweddle (d 1952); 2 s (Lawson Fimister b 16 Feb 1953, Gerald Peter b 5 Oct 1957), 1 da (Jennifer Marjory (Mrs Shilton) b 26 June 1955)); m 2, 13 Dec 1986, May Heatherington Anderson, *née* McMillan; *Career* Lt-Col RAMC (AER); The Boots Co: joined 1957, dir of res 1968, dir 1973-85, vice-chm 1980-81, chm 1981-85; govr Henley Mgmnt Coll 1983-86, memb NEDC 1984-85; memb Scottish Health Servs Policy Bd 1985-88; dir: W A Baxter & Sons Ltd 1985-, John Fleming & Co Ltd 1985-; chm Inveresk Res Int 1985-; dir Scottish Devpt Agency 1986-; memb Univ of Aberdeen Devpt Tst 1987-, chm Grentown Heritage Tst 1987-; Hon LLD Aberdeen 1986; FRCPE 1982, CBIM 1978; kt 1985; *Recreations* fishing, shooting, Scottish music; *Clubs* Naval & Military, Flyfishers'; *Style—* Sir Peter Main, ERD; Lairig Ghru, Dulnain Bridge, Grantown-on-Spey, Highland PH26 3NT (☎ 047 985 264)

MAINDS, Hon Mrs (Veronica Mary); *née* Addington; elder da of 7 Viscount Sidmouth; *b* 1944; *Educ* St Mary's Convent, S Ascot Berkshire; *m* 1982, Allan (Sam) Mainds, of Bishopstone, Bucks, eld s of George Mainds; 1 da (Phillipa); *Career* teacher (BEd); *Style—* The Hon Mrs Mainds; 41 Bramham Gdns, London SW5 0HG

MAINE-TUCKER, Neville; s of Geoffrey Maine-Tucker (d 1978), and Alfreda Marian St Clair Robson (d 1985); *b* 15 April 1926; *Educ* St Bees Sch, Christ Coll Brecon; *m* 26 July 1961, Joyce Edna Pandora, da of Michael Cedric Cooper; 1 s (Simon b 1965), 2 da (Amanda b 1962, Melanie b 1963); *Career* Army 1944-48 Royal Signals 1948-51, TA Lt 22 Cheshire Regt; holiday property developer 1959-87, civil engr 1948-57, boat & caravan industry 1957-59; dir: W H Main-Tucker Ltd 1983-87, St Clair Investmts Ltd 1973-87; *Recreations* shooting, vintage motoring, sailing; *Clubs* RAC; *Style—* Neville Maine-Tucker, Esq; 2 Gendroc House, Barrack Lane, Truro TR1 2DS (☎ 0872 73137)

MAINES, James Dennis; s of late Arthur Burtonwood Maines, and Lilian Maines,*née* Carter; *b* 26 July 1937; *Educ* Leigh GS, City Univ (BSc); *m* 15 Oct 1960, Janet Enid, da of late Percy Kemp; 3 s (Stephen, Christopher, Daniel); *Career* joined RSRE (formerly RRE) Malvern 1956: scentific offr 1960, head guided weapons optics and electronics gp 1981, head microwave and electro optics gp 1983; head sensors electronic warfare and guided weapons ARE Portsdown 1984, dep dir (weapons) RAE 1986, dir gen guided weapons and electronics MOD (PE) 1988; FIEE, CEng; *Books* Surface Wave Filters (contrib 1977), more than 30 pubns in learned jls; *Recreations* sailing, cricket, squash, painting, gardening, car restoration; *Style—* Dennis Maines, Esq; MOD (PE), c/o Ministry of Defence, Whitehall, London SW1A 2HB

MAINGARD DE LA VILLE-ES-OFFRANS, Sir (Louis Pierre) Rene; CBE (1961); s of Joseph René Maingard de la Ville-es-Offrans (d 1956), and Véronique, *née* Hugnin (d 1969); *b* 9 July 1917; *Educ* St Joseph's Coll, Royal Coll of Mauritius, Business Trg Corp London; *m* 1946, Marie Hélène Françoise, da of Sir Philippe Raffray, CBE, QC (d 1975); 3 da (Catherine, Anne, Sophie); *Career* served WWII RAF Fighter Cmd 131 and 165 Sqdn 1939-45; chm De Chazal du Mée Assocs Ltd, chm and md Rogers & Co Ltd 1948-82; chm: Colonial Steamships Co Ltd 1948-, Mauritius Steam Navigation Co Ltd 1964, Mauritius Portland Cement Co Ltd 1960-, Mauritius Molasses Co Ltd 1968-, New Mauritius Dock Co Ltd 1948-, Utd Docks Ltd 1960-; dir: Mauritius Commercial Bank Ltd 1956-, The Anglo-Mauritius Assur Soc Ltd; consul for Finland in Mauritius 1957-83, Order of the White Rose Finland 1973; kt 1982; *Recreations* golf, fishing, boating; *Clubs* Dodo, Mauritius Turf; *Style—* Sir René Maingard de la Ville-ès-Offrans, CBE; De Chazal Du Mée Associates Ltd, PO Box 799, Port Louis, Mauritius (☎ 08 7923, telex 4417 COLYB)

MAINI, Sir Amar Nath; CBE (1953, OBE 1948); s of Nauhria Ram Maini, of Nairobi; *b* 31 July 1911; *Educ* Govt Indian Sch Nairobi, LSE; *m* 1935, Ram Saheli Mehra (d 1982); 2 s; *Career* dep chm Kenya Broadcasting Corpn 1962-63, speaker E African Central Legislative Assembly 1961-67, min commerce and indust Uganda 1958-61, former pres Central Cncl Indian Assocs Uganda and dep chm Uganda Electricity Bd; first mayor Kampala 1950-55, former advocate High Cts Uganda and Kenya; kt 1957; *Clubs* The Reform; *Style—* Sir Amar Maini, CBE; 55 Vicarage Rd, E Sheen, London SW14 8RY (☎ 01 878 1497)

MAIR, Alexander; MBE (1968); s of Charles Meston Mair (d 1968), and Helen, *née* Dickie (d 1969); *b* 5 Nov 1922; *Educ* Sch of Accountancy Glasgow; *m* 7 Aug 1953, Margaret Isobel Gowans, da of John Rennie (d 1955); *Career* RAC 1943-47, 3 Carabiniers 1944-47, served in India, Burma; chief accountant Bydand Industl Hldgs 1956-60; Grampian TV: co sec 1961-70, dir 1967, chief exec 1970-87; dir: Ind TV News 1978-87, TV Times 1975-87; chm: RGIT Offshore Survival Centre Ltd 1988-, Clifton Collier Advertising Ltd 1987-; pres: Aberdeen C of C 1989-, Royal Northern and Univ Club 1984-85; chm Aberdeen Int Football Festival 1981-; memb: Aberdeen Airport Users Ctee 1978-, Working Gp Grampian Intiative 1987-, Aberdeen 2000 Gp 1987-; assoc Chartered Inst of Mgmnt Accountants, FRTS, FRSA; *Recreations* skiing, golf, gardening; *Clubs* Royal Northern and Univ Club, Royal Aberdeen GC; *Style—* Alexander Mair, Esq, MBE; Ravenswood, 66 Rubislaw Den South, Aberdeen AB2 6AX (☎ 0224 638914)

MAIR, Antony Stefan Romley; s of John Mair, MBE, (d 1971), of Hill House, Surley Row, Caversham, Berks, and Marie Justine Antoinette, *née* Bunbury; *b* 27 Dec 1946; *Educ* Reading Sch (BA, MA), Magdalen Coll Oxford; *Career* slr; chm mgmnt ctee Holman Fenwick and Willan 1987-88 (ptnr 1979, joined 1976); ptnr Stephenson Harwood 1988-; govr St Stephen's RC Sch Shepherds Bush London; Freeman of City of Oxford 1975; memb: Br Horse Soc, Law Soc; IBA; *Recreations* dressage, gardening; *Style—* Antony Mair, Esq; One St Paul's Churchyard, London EC4 (☎ 01 329 4422, fax 606 0822, telex 886789 SHSPC G)

MAIR, Prof (William) Austyn; CBE (1969); s of Dr William Mair (d 1968), of London, and Catharine Millicent, *née* Fyfe (d 1966); *b* 24 Feb 1917; *Educ* Highgate Sch, Clare Coll Cambridge (BA, MA); *m* 15 April 1944, Mary Woodhouse, da of Rev Christopher Benson Crofts (d 1956); 2 s (Christopher b 1945, Robert b 1950); *Career* RAF (Tech Branch) cmmnd Pilot Offr 1940, released from serv Sqdn Ldr 1946, attached to Royal Aircraft Estab 1940-46; dir fluid motion lab Univ of Manchester

1946-52, Francis Mond prof of aeronautical engrg Univ of Cambridge 1952-83, (head of engrg dept 1973-83), fell Downing Coll 1953-83 (hon fell 1983-), emeritus prof of aeronautical engrg 1983-; FRAeS 1952, FEng 1984; *Clubs* Utd Oxford & Cambridge Univ; *Style*— Prof Austyn Mair, CBE; 74 Barton Rd, Cambridge CB3 9LH (☎ 0223 350137)

MAIR, Hon Mrs; Elizabeth Smith; da of 1 Baron Kirkwood, PC (d 1955); *b* 1908; *m* 1944, John Archibald Dugald Mair, ARIBA; 1 s, 2 da; *Style*— The Hon Mrs Mair; Shieldaig, 12 Iain Rd, Bearsden, Dunbartonshire

MAIRS, Raymond John; s of David Mairs, of Co Antrim, and Susan Elizabeth, *née* Colvin (d 1978); *b* 15 August 1951; *Educ* Bauyclare HS, Queen's Univ Belfast (BSc, Dip Arch); *m* 6 Aug 1976, Carol Jean Ruth, da of Neville Arthur Ginn, of Co Antrim; 2 da (Rachel Ruth b 1981, Rebecca Ann b 1985); *Career* architect, fish farmer; private practice 1978, ptnr Mairs & Wray 1979-; memb RSUA Housing Ctee 1985-86; *Style*— Raymond J Mairs, Esq; Glen Oak House, Crumlin BT29 4BW (☎ 08494 23172); Mairs & Wray Architects, 1 Nutts Corner Rd, Crumlin BT29 4BW (☎ 08494 52975)

MAIS, Baron (Life Peer UK 1967); Alan Raymond Mais; GBE (1973, OBE 1944), ERD (1958), TD (1944), JP (City of London 1962), DL (Kent 1976, Co of London subsequently Gtr London 1951-76); s of late Capt Ernest Mais, of Mornington Court, Kensington; *b* 7 July 1911; *Educ* Banister Court Hants, Coll of Estate Mgmnt Univ of London; *m* 1936, Lorna Aline, da of Stanley Aspinall Boardman, of Addiscombe, Surrey; 2 s, 1 da; *Career* sits as Lib peer in House of Lords (1981-, previously Lab); 2 Lt Royal West Kent Regt 1929, RE 1931-70, Lt City of London Regt 1963; Lord Mayor of London 1972-73 (first Lab Lord Mayor); memb Court of City Univ 1973; pres London C of C & Industry 1975-78; memb Cwlth Scholars Cmmn 1978; past pres London Master Builders' Assoc; memb Govt Ctees for Works and Bldgs Emergency Orgn; vice-pres Inst of Structural Engrs; formerly with Richard Costain, late chm Trollope & Colls; cmmr of Income Tax 1972-81; alderman Walbrook Ward 1962-69, Sheriff 1969-70; dir Royal Bank of Scotland 1969-81; chm Peachey Property Corpn 1977-81; memb Freeman Worshipful Co of: Marketers' 1977 (Master 1983), Cutlers' (Master 1966-67), Paviors' (Master 1974-75); hon degree Univ of Ulster; Hon DS City Univ; FICE, FRICS, KStJ; *Style*— The Rt Hon Lord Mais, GBE, ERD, TD, JP, DL; Griffins, Sundridge Ave, Bromley, Kent (☎ 01 460 9896)

MAIS, Sir (Robert) Hugh; s of Robert Stanley Oliver Mais (d 1947), and Edith Catherine, *née* Ashley (d 1974); *b* 14 Sept 1907; *Educ* Shrewsbury, Wadham Coll Oxford (MA); *m* 1938, Catherine (d 1987), da of James Pearson Pattinson (d 1945); 1 s; *Career* served WWII RAF, Wing Cdr; barr Inner Temple 1930; chllr of the Diocese of Manchester 1948-71, Carlisle 1950-71, Sheffield 1950-71; co court judge: W London 1958-60, Marylebone 1960-71, dep chm Berks QS 1964-71, cmmr of assizes SE circuit 1964 and 1967, Oxford circuit 1968 and 1969, NE circuit 1971, bencher Inner Temple 1971, High Court judge (Queen's Bench) 1971-82, ret; memb Winn Ctee Personal Injuries Litigation; hon fell Wadham Coll Oxford 1971; kt 1971; *Recreations* fishing, golf; *Style*— Sir Hugh Mais; Ripton, Streatley-on-Thames, Berks (☎ 0491 872397)

MAIS, Hon Jonathan Robert Neal; s of Baron Mais, GBE (Life Peer); *b* 1954; *Educ* Hurstpierpoint Coll, City of London Coll of Commercial Law; *m* 1978, Frances Louise, da of Robert Mark Barrington Brown (decd); *Style*— The Hon Jonathan Mais; Griffins, Sunbridge Avenue, Bromley, Kent

MAIS, Hon Richard Jeremy Ian; s of Baron Mais, OBE (Life Peer); *b* 2 Nov 1945; *Educ* Stowe Sch, Ewell Tech Coll; *m* 1972, Janice, da of Ralph Dean, of Hurley, Berks; 1 s (Alexander b 1975), 2 da (Vanessa b 1977, Lydia b 1981); *Career* property developer; md Clarke Nickolls & Coombs PLC, chm: Becontree Est Ltd; Altbarn Properties Ltd, CNC Properties Ltd, Waterden Surveys Ltd, CNC Devpts Ltd, CNC Benfleet Ltd, Philpot Mgmnt Ltd, Beacontree Plaza Ltd, CNC Delaware Inc, CNC California Investmts Inc; MCIOB, FIOD; *Recreations* tennis, motor sport, badminton, DIY; *Clubs* Br Automobile Racing; *Style*— The Hon Richard Mais; Clarke Nickolls & Coombs PLC, Beacontree House, 33 High St, Sunninghill Ascot, Berks SL5 9NR (☎ 0990 28721) 79 Seal Hollow Rd, Sevenoaks, Kent (☎ 0732 454886)

MAISNER, Air Vice-Marshal Alexander (Aleksander); CB (1977), CBE (1969), AFC (1955); s of Henryk Maisner (d 1943), and Helene Anne, *née* Brosin (d 1959); *b* 26 July 1921; *Educ* High Sch and Lyceum Czestochowa Poland, Warsaw Univ; *m* 1946, Mary, da of O R Coverley (d 1958); 1 s, 1 da; *Career* War Serv Polish Artillery and Polish AF, joined RAF 1946, DSD RAF Staff Coll, CO RAF Seletar, asst Cmdt RAF Coll Cranwell, ret as dir gen Personnel Mgmnt 1977; personnel exec Reed Int Ltd 1977-82; govr Shiplake Coll 1978-; pres of Polish AF Assoc 1982-; dir Indust and Parly Tst 1984-1987; *Recreations* reading, gardening; *Clubs* RAF; *Style*— Air Vice-Marshal Alexander Maisner, CB, CBE, AFC; c/o Lloyds Bank, 1 Reading Rd, Henley-on-Thames, Oxon RG9 1BR

MAITLAND, Lady Caroline Charlotte Militsa; da of 17 Earl of Lauderdale; *b* 18 Nov 1946; *Educ* Queen's Gate Sch London, SS Mary and Anne Abbots Bromley Rugeley, Lycée Français de Londres, London Univ; *Career* teacher 1970-77; *Recreations* song and dance; *Style*— Lady Caroline Maitland; 12 St Vincent St, Edinburgh (☎ 031 556 5692)

MAITLAND, David Henry; CVO (1988); s of George Maitland (d 1959), of London, and Mary Annie. *née* Levy (d 1977); *b* 9 May 1922; *Educ* Eton, King's Coll Cambridge; *m* 21 June 1955, Judith Mary, da of Patrick Hugh Gold (d 1976), of London; 3 da (Jessica b 1957, Lucy b 1957, Rebecca b 1964); *Career* served 1 Bn Oxford and Bucks LI 1943-47, Capt and Adjt 1945-47; chief exec Save & Prosper Gp 1965-81; chm Unit Tst Assoc 1973-75; memb City Capital Market Ctee 1974-84; tstee Lord Mayor Treloar Coll 1984-; memb: Royal Cmmn for 1851 Exhibition 1983-, cncl of Duchy of Lancaster 1977-87; chm Inst of Psychiatry 1985-; memb Bethlem Royal Hosp and Maudsley Hosp SHA 1982-; FCA 1950; *Recreations* golf, gardening; *Clubs* City of London; *Style*— David Maitland, Esq, CVO; St Paul's House, Upper Froyle, Alton, Hants (☎ 0420 22183)

MAITLAND, Sir Donald James Dundas; GCMG (1977), CMG (1967), OBE (1960); s of Thomas Douglas Maitland, and Wilhelmina Sarah Dundas; *b* 16 August 1922; *Educ* George Watson's Coll Edinburgh, Edinburgh Univ (MA); *m* 1950, Jean Marie, da of Gordon Young (d 1969); 1 s, 1 da; *Career* served WWII M East India and Burma in Royal Scots and Rajputana Rifles; served Foreign Serv (later Dip Serv) 1947-80: in Amara, Baghdad, dir MECAS Lebanon 1956-60, Cairo, head News Dept FO 1965-67, ambass Libya 1969-70, chief press sec 10 Downing St 1970-73, ambass and perm UK rep UN 1973-74 and EEC 1975-79, dep under-sec FCO 1974-75, dep to perm under-sec FCO 1979-80; perm under-sec Dept Energy 1980-82, ret 1982; govt dir Britoil 1983-85, dir Slough Estates 1983-; chm: UK ctee World Communications Year 1983, Ind Cmmn for World-Wide Telecommunications Devpt 1983-85; dir Northern Engrg Industs 1986-, dep chm IBA 1986-89, memb Cwlth War Graves Cmmn 1983-87, advsr to Br Telecom 1985-86; chm Health Educn Authy 1989-; kt 1973; *Recreations* hill-walking, music; *Style*— Sir Donald Maitland, GCMG, CMG, OBE; Murhill Farm Ho, Limpley Stoke, Bath BA3 6HH (☎ 022 122 3157)

MAITLAND, Lady Elizabeth Sylvia; da of Viscount Maitland (ka 1943); *b* 1943; *Career* granted 1953, title, rank and precedence of an Earl's da which would have been hers had her father survived to succeed to Earldom of Lauderdale; *Style*— Lady Elizabeth Maitland; 11 Boundary Close, Woodstock, Oxford

MAITLAND, Helena, Viscountess; Helena Ruth; *née* Perrott; da of Col Sir Herbert Charles Perrott, 6 and last Bt, CH, CB (d 1922), and Ethel Lucy, *née* Hare (d 1939); *b* 14 August 1912; *m* 29 Oct 1936, Ivor Colin James, Viscount Maitland (s and h of 15 Earl of Lauderdale, ka 1943 predeceasing his f); 3 da (Lady Mary Biddulph, Lady Anne Eyston, Lady Elizabeth Maitland, all raised to rank of Earl's da); *Career* OStJ; *Recreations* fishing, gardening; *Style*— Helena, Viscountess Maitland; Flat E, 34 Cadogan Sq, London SW1 (☎ 01 584 9920); Park House, Makerstoun, nr Kelso, Roxburghshire (☎ 057 36 248)

MAITLAND, Viscount; Ian Maitland; The Master of Lauderdale,; s and h of 17 Earl of Lauderdale; *b* 4 Nov 1937; *Educ* Radley, Brasenose Oxford (MA); *m* 27 April 1963, Ann Paule, da of Geoffrey B Clarke, of London; 1 s, 1 da; *Heir* s, Master of Maitland; *Career* Lt RNR 1963-73; has held various appts in mfrg industry, regnl mangr N Africa Int Banking Div Nat Westminster Bank Ltd 1975-; memb The Queen's Body Guard for Scotland (Royal Co of Archers); *Recreations* sailing, photography; *Clubs* Royal Ocean Racing; *Style*— Viscount Maitland; 150 Tachbrook St, London SW1

MAITLAND, Master of; Hon John Douglas Maitland; s and h of Viscount Maitland; *b* 29 May 1965; *Style*— Master of Maitland

MAITLAND, Lady; Lavender Mary Jex; da of late Francis William Jex Jackson, of Kirkbuddo, Forfar; *m* 1951, Maj Sir Alexander Keith Maitland, 8 Bt (d 1963); *Style*— Lady Maitland; Burnside, Forfar, Angus

MAITLAND, Neil Kenneth; s of Col John Kenneth Maitland, MBE, MC, DL, JP (d 1972), of Hertingfordbury, Herts, and Jean Redman, *née* Collingridge, MBE; *b* 26 Dec 1929; *Educ* Sedbergh Sch Canada, Winchester Coll; *m* 21 Jan 1961, Gillian (d 1988), da of Gerald Leonard Forsteen Bird, (d POW 1944); 1 s (James b 1962), 1 da (Elizabeth b 1968); *Career* Nat Serv 2 Lt RA 1948-49; md Ridgways Ltd Tea & Coffee Merchants 1968; Master Worshipful Co of Girdlers 1979-80, chm London Fedn of Boys' Clubs 1983-, dir Inst of Child Health; *Recreations* golf, gardening; *Clubs* Royal Ashdown Forest GC, Army and Navy; *Style*— Neil K Maitland, Esq; Barnsden House, Duddleswell, nr Uckfield, Sussex TN22 3DB (☎ 082 572 2426)

MAITLAND, Lady (Helen) Olga; *née* Maitland; elder da of 17 Earl of Lauderdale, *qv*; *b* 23 May 1944; *Educ* Sch of St Mary and St Anne Abbots Bromley, Lycée Francais de Londres; *m* 19 April 1969, Robin William Patrick Hamilton Hay, s of William Reginald Hay, of Mapperley, Nottingham; 2 s (Alastair b 1972, Fergus b 1981), 1 da (Camilla b 1975); *Career* former trainee reporter with Fleet St News Agency, Blackheath and Distict Reporter; former sec Br Embassy Mexico City; journalist Sunday Express 1967-, reporter and columnist; memb Islington S and Finsbury Cons Assoc (memb exec ctee Chelsea Young Cons 1960, YC rep on Brompton Ward); memb Bow Gp 1970-; fndr and chm Families for Def 1983;, chm Br Red Cross Westminster Christmas Fair 1983-; memb Euro Union of Women; nominated UN Media Peace Prize 1983; vice chm WHY campaign against offensive weapons 1987-; conslt ILEA Holborn & St Pancras, parly candidate (C) Bethnal Green & Stepney 1987; patron: Stoke Park Tst for Handicapped, Rainbow Tst Holidays for the Disabled; *Recreations* theatre, travel painting; *Style*— Lady Olga Maitland; 21 Cloudesley St, London N1 (☎ 01 837 9212); Mill Farm, Wighton, Wells-next-the-sea, Norfolk (☎ 032 872 666) Sunday Express, Fleet St, London EC4 (☎ 01 353 8000 ext 3678, 01 353 1656)

MAITLAND, Sir Richard John; 9 Bt (UK 1818), of Clifton, Midlothian; s of Maj Sir Alexander Maitland, 8 Bt (d 1963); sixth in descent from Gen Hon Sir Alexander Maitland, 1 Bt, 5 s of 6 Earl of Lauderdale); *b* 24 Nov 1952; *Educ* Rugby, Exeter Univ, Edinburgh Sch of Agriculture; *m* 1981, Carine, er da of J St G Coldwell, of Somerton, Oxford, by his w Mrs R A Coldwell, of Llandovery; 1 s (Charles b 1986), 1 da (Alice Emma b 1983); *Heir* s, Hon Charles Alexander b 1986; *Career* farmer; memb Royal Co of Archery (Queen's Body Guard for Scotland); *Recreations* skiing, shooting, fishing, travel; *Style*— Sir Richard Maitland, Bt; Burnside, Forfar, Angus

MAITLAND, Hon Mrs (Rosemary Ethel Coupar); JP (Glos 1973); yr da of 1 and last Baron Abertay (d 1940), and Baroness Abertay (d 1983); *b* 26 Jan 1931; *Educ* Crofton Grange, Brillant Mont (Lausanne, Switzerland); *m* 1952, John Stuart Maitland, s of Lt-Col John Kenneth Maitland, MC, TD, JP, DL; 3 s (John Andrew Charles b 1954, Robin Neil b 1958, Angus Kenneth b 1963), 1 da (Fiona Romaire b 1961); *Style*— The Hon Mrs Maitland, JP; The Grange, Park Lane, Stancombe, Dursley, Glos GL11 6AY

MAITLAND, Rev the Hon Sydney Milivoye Patrick; s of 17 Earl of Lauderdale, *qv*; *b* 23 June 1951; *Educ* Eton, Edinburgh Univ (BSc), Strathclyde Univ (DipTP); *m* 1974, (Dorothy) Eileen, da of A R Bedell, of Kirbymoorside, N Yorks; *Career* town planner; made deacon in Scottish Episcopal Church 1986, ordained priest in Scottish Episcopal Church 1987, hon priest-in-charge, St Georges Sandbank St Maryhill Glasgow; MRTPI; *Recreations* sailing, photography; *Clubs* Loch Ard SC; *Style*— The Rev the Hon Sydney Maitland; 14 Kersland St, Glasgow G12 8BL

MAITLAND BIDDULPH, Hon William Ian Robert; yr s of 4 Baron Biddulph (d 1988), bro and hp of 5 Baron, *qv* ; *b* 27 Mar 1963; *Educ* Loretto; *Career* wine merchant; *Recreations* shooting, fishing, tennis, hockey, walking, cooking, wine making, gardening; *Style*— The Hon William Maitland Biddulph

MAITLAND PARKS, Hon Sarah Caroline; da of Viscount Maitland; *b* 1964; *Educ* St Paul's Girls' Sch, Durham Univ (Trevelyan Coll) BA; *m* 5 Nov 1988, Stuart George Parks; *Style*— The Hon Sarah Maitland Parks

MAITLAND SMITH, Geoffrey; s of Philip John Maitland Smith, of Ramsden Heath, Billericay, Essex, by his w Kathleen, *née* Goff; *b* 27 Feb 1933; *Educ* Univ Coll Sch London; *m* m; children; *Career* chartered accountant; chm Sears plc 1978- (chief exec 1978-88, dir 1971-), dir Asprey & Co 1980- (the Bond Street jewellers, in which Sears has a 25 percent stake); chm: Br Shoe Corpn 1978-, Selfridges 1978-, Garrard & Co 1978-, Mappin & Webb 1978-; dir: Courtaulds plc 1983-, Imperial Gp plc 1984-86; chm: Central Ind Television plc 1983-85, dir: Midland Bank plc 1986-; chm: Mallett plc

1986; chm of Cncl of Univ Coll Sch London 1987; hon vice pres Inst of Marketing 1987-; memb Royal Acad Advsy Bd 1986-, fin devpt bd NSPCC 1985-; Freeman Worshipful Co of Gardners; *Recreations* opera; *Clubs* Cripplegate Ward; *Style—* Geoffrey Maitland Smith, Esq; 40 Duke St, London W1A 2HP (☎ 01 408 1180)

MAITLAND-CAREW, Hon Gerald Edward Ian; yr s of 6 Baron Carew, CBE, *qv*; name changed to Maitland-Carew by deed poll 1971; *b* 28 Dec 1941; *Educ* Harrow; *m* 1972, Rosalind Averil, da of Lt-Col Neil Hanning Reed Speke, MC; 2 s, 1 da; *Career* 2 Lt 15/19 Hussars 1961, Capt 1965, formerly ADC to GOC 44 Div Dover, Castle; memb the Queens Body Guard for Scotland, The Royal Co of Archers 1978; elected memb the Jockey Club 1987, chm Fauderdale Hunt 1979-; *Clubs* Cavalry, New; *Style—* The Hon Gerald Maitland-Carew; Thirlestane Castle, Lauder, Berwickshire

MAITLAND-MAKGILL-CRICHTON; *see*: Crichton

MAITLAND-ROBINSON, Hon Susannah Jane; *née* Henderson; da of 3 Baron Faringdon; *b* 1963; *m* 1986, Aidan James, s of Joseph Maitland-Robinson, of St Lawrence, Jersey; 1 da (Joanna Alice b 1987); *Style—* The Hon Susannah Maitland-Robinson

MAITLIS, Peter Michael; s of Jacob J Maitlis (d 1987) and Judith *née* Ebel (d 1985); *b* 15 Jan 1933; *Educ* Hendon Co GS, Birmingham Univ (BSc), London Univ (PhD, DSc); *m* 19 July 1959, Marion da of Herbert Basco (d 1977); 3 da (Niccola b 1963, Sally b 1965, Emily b 1970); *Career* asst lectr Univ of London, 1956-60, Fulbright fell Cornwall Univ 1960-61, res fell Harvard Univ 1961-62; McMaiter Univ Hamilton Canada: asst prof 1962-64, assoc prof 1964-67, prof 1967-72; prof of inorganic chem Sheffield Univ 1972-, fell Alfred P Sloan Fndn (USA) 1968-70, EWR Steacie Prize (Canada) 1971, RSC Medallist (UK) 1981, Tilden lectr 1979, Sir Edward Frankland lectr (UK) 1984; pres Dalton div RSC 1984-86 chm Serc Chemistry ctee 1985-88, various offs in RSC (Royal Society of Chemistry); FRS, FRSC; *Books* The Organic Chemistry of Palladium (Vols 1 & 2 1971); incl res paper in various chemistry jls; *Recreations* travel, music, reading; *Style—* Prof Peter Maitlis

MAJOR, Christopher Ian; s of Edward Richard Major, of Friar's Cliff, Dorset and Audrey Yvonne, *née* Beardmore; *b* 14 June 1948; *Educ* Kingston GS, Wadham Coll Oxford (MA); *m* 19 Aug 1972, Susan Fenella, da of Harry Morrison Kirton (d 1984); *Career* slr 1973; ptnr: Lovell, White & King 1979-88, Lovell White Durrant 1988-; memb Worhsipful Co Slrs 1974; memb: Law Soc of England & Wales - 1973, Int Bar Assoc 1979, American Bar Assoc 1981, American Arbitration Assoc 1981; *Recreations* tennis; *Style—* Christopher Major, Esq; 73 Cheapside, London EC2V 6ER (☎ 01 236 0066, fax 01 236 0084, telex 919014)

MAJOR, The Rt Hon John; MP (C) Huntingdon 1983-, PC (June 1987); s of Thomas Major (d 1963), and Gwendolyn Major (d 1970); *b* 29 Mar 1943; *Educ* Rutlish; *m* 1970, Norma Christine Elizabeth, da of Norman Johnson (d 1945); 1 s, 1 da; *Career* sr exec Standard Chartered Bank plc to 1979; assoc Inst of Bankers; MP (C) Huntingdonshire 1979-83; PPS to Min of State, Home Office 1981-, asst govt whip 1983-84; Lord Cmmr of Treasury 1984-85; parly under-sec of state DHSS 1985-86, min for Social Security 1986-87, chief sec to the Treasury June 1987-; *Style—* The Rt Hon John Major, MP; House of Commons, London SW1A 0AA

MAKA, Lady Isabella Augusta; da of 6 Earl of Gosford, OBE; *b* 17 Jan 1950; *m* 1979, Tevita T Maka; 1 s (Charles Nicholas b 1980); *Style—* Lady Isabella Maka; PO Box 1234, Nuku' Alofa, Tonga

MAKEPEACE, John; OBE (1988); s of Harold Alfred Smith (d 1967), of Woad House, Fenny Compton, Leamington Spa, Warwicks, and Gladys Marjorie, *née* Wright; *b* 6 July 1939; *Educ* Denstone Coll Staffs; *m* May 1963 (m dis 1978), Ann, da of William Sutton; m 2, 3 Dec 1984, Jennifer Moores, da of Harry Brinsden; *Career* teacher Birmingham Educn Authy 1959-62; dir: Farnborough Barn Ltd (subsequently John Makepeace Ltd) 1963-, The Parnham Tst (charitable educnl tst) 1977-, Sch for Craftsment in Wood 1977, Hooke Forest (Construction) Ltd 1984-, Hooke Forest Ltd 1984, Hooke Park Coll for Advanced Mfrg in Wood 1989; memb: Crafts Cncl 1972-77; Liveryman Worshipful Co fo Furniture Makers 1977; FCSD 1975, FBIM 1986; *Clubs* Royal Overseas League, Farmers; *Style—* John Makepeace, Esq, OBE; Parnham House, Beaminster, Dorset DT8 3NA (☎ 0308 862204)

MAKER, Daljit Singh; s of late Kishan Singh Maker (d 1961), and Daya Kaur Maker; *b* 21 Jan 1954; *Educ* Brighton Coll; *Career* fund mangr James Capel Stockbrokers 1974-78, dir Savory Milln Stockbrokers (fund mangr 1978-84, ptnr 1984), dir Parrish Stockbrokers 1988; memb Int Stock Exchange; *Recreations* squash, tennis, skiing; *Clubs* Hampstead Cricket; *Style—* Daljit Maker, Esq; Parrish Stockbrokers, 4 London Wall Buildings, London Wall EC2 (☎ 01 638 1212)

MAKEY, Arthur Robertson; s of Arthur Frank Makey (d 1968), of Dover, and Lily, *née* Findlay (d 1964); *b* 3 June 1922; *Educ* Dover GS, King's Coll, Charing Cross Hosp Med Sch (MB BS, MS); ; *m* 19 March 1947, Patricia Mary, da of Iion Victor Cummings (d 1984), of Canford Cliffs, Dorset; 2 s (David b 1949, John b 1955), 1 da (Margaret b 1951); *Career* RAFVR Med Serv, served in India 1946-48; conslt surgn cardiothoracic: Charing Cross Hosp 1955, W Middex Univ Hosp 1975-, Colindale Hosp 1967-85; civil conslt thoracic surgery RAF 1985-, sr examiner in surgery Univ of London 1968-86; chm Ct of Examiners RCS 1980; external examiner surgery: Univ of Malaysia 1981 and 1982, Univ of Khartoum 1985; official visitor for RCS and Physicians to Univ of Khartoum 1984; Kitchener Scholar; FRCS ; *Books* chapters in med books; *Recreations* golf, music, gardening; *Clubs* Royal Midsurrey Golf; *Style—* Arthur R Makey, Esq; 2 Beverley Close, Barnes, London SW13 0EH (☎ 01 876 7347); Charing Cross Hospital, London W6 8RF (☎ 01 748 2040)

MAKGILL, Hon Diana Mary Robina; LVO (1983, MVO 1971); da (by 1 m) of 12 Viscount of Oxfuird, *qv*; *b* 4 Jan 1930; *Educ* Strathcona Lodge Sch Vancouver Island BC Canada; *Career* ceremonial offr Protocol Dept FCO 1961-, hon steward of Westminster Abbey 1978-; Order of Star of Afghanistan 1971, Order of the White Rose of Finland 1969, Order of the Sacred Treasure of Japan 1971, Order of Al Kawkab of Jordan 1966; *Recreations* riding, reading, gardening; *Style—* The Hon Diana Makgill, LVO; Clouds Lodge, E Knoyle, nr Salisbury, Wilts; 15 Iverna Court, Iverna Gdns, London W8 (☎ 01 937 2234, off 01 210 6381)

MAKGILL, Master of Oxfuird; Ian Arthur Alexander; s and h of 13 Viscount of Oxfuird; *b* 1969; *Style—* The Master of Oxfuird

MAKGILL CRICHTON MAITLAND, Maj John David; s of Col Mark Edward Makgill Crichton Maitland, CVO, DSO, DL, JP (d 1972), of The Island House, Wilton, Salisbury, Wilts; *b* 1925; *Educ* Eton; *m* m 1, 1954, Jean Patricia (d 1985), da of Maj-Gen Sir Michael Creagh, KBE, MC (d 1970), of Salisbury, Wilts; 1 s, 1 da; m 2, 1987, Mary Ann Vere Curzon, *née* Ogilvy, widow of Capt James Quintin Curzon (d 1986); *Career* serv 1944-57 with Gren Gds, Temp Maj 1952, ret 1957 with rank of Capt (Hon Maj); DL (Renfrewshire 1962), Vice-Lt 1972, Lord-Lt of Renfrewshire 1980-; *Clubs* Turf, Puffins, MCC; *Style—* Maj John David Makgill Crichton Maitland; Houston House, by Johnstone, Renfrewshire PA6 7AR (☎ 0505 612 545)

MAKIN, John Beverley; s of William Makin (d 1983), of Ottershaw, Surrey, and Helen, *née* Southern (d 1980); *b* 28 Feb 1937; *Educ* Kingston GS; *m* 6 Oct 1969, Alicia Jane, da of Gordon Edward Fairclough, of Weybridge, Surrey; 3 s (Andrew b 1975, Alex b 1980, Stephen b 1983); *Career* assoc ed Motoring News 1960, ed Cine Camera 1960-63 formerly (asst ed), Parker PR 1963-67, chm IH Pubns 1967-77 (formerly md), dep chief exec Adgroup 1977-81, dir Dewe Rogerson 1982-; memb Br Assoc of Industl Eds 1966: nat chm 1973-74, fell 1976, chm of senate 1984-87; *Books* A Management Guide to House Journals (1970); *Recreations* cooking, bridge, golf; *Clubs* RAC; *Style—* John Makin, Esq; Easter Cottage, Wrens Hill, Oxshott, Surrey (☎ 0372 843 516); Dewe Rogerson Ltd, 3 1/2 London Wall Bldgs, London Wall, London EC2M 5SY (☎ 01 638 9571)

MAKINS, Hon Christopher James; s and h of 1 Baron Sherfield, GCB, GCMG; *b* 23 July 1942; *Educ* Winchester, New Coll Oxford; *m* 1975, Wendy Cortesi; *Career* HM Dip Serv 1964-74; fell All Souls' Coll Oxford 1963; *Style—* The Hon Christopher Makins; 3034, P St NW, Washington DC, USA

MAKINS, Hon Dwight William; s of 1 Baron Sherfield, GCB, GCMG, and Alice, *née* Davis; *b* 2 Mar 1951; *Educ* Winchester, Christ Church Oxford; *m* 1983, Penelope Jane, da of Donald R L Massy Collier; *Career* dir: John Govett & Co, Berkeley Govett Ltd, Macarthy plc; *Recreations* shooting; *Style—* The Hon Dwight Makins; Beaurepaire Ho, Sherborne St John, Basingstoke, Hants;

MAKINS, Jean, Lady; Jean; da of Capt Lord Arthur Vincent Hay (decd); *m* 1932, Lt-Col Sir William Vivian Makins, 3 Bt (d 1969); *Style—* Jean, Lady Makins; Martyrwell, Cheriton, Alresford, Hants

MAKOWER, (Arthur) Denis; s of Walter Makower, OBE (d 1945), and Dorothy Lois, *née* Drey (d 1977); *b* 6 Oct 1917; *Educ* St Paul's, Trinity Coll Cambridge (MA); *Career* scientist Miny of Supply 1940-45, scientist Lobitos Oilfield Ltd 1945-50, dir of scientific control Nat Coal Bd 1977-82 (scientist 1950-60, asst dir of scientific control 1960-66, dep dir of scientific control 1966-77); *Recreations* technical writing, golf, chess, bridge; *Clubs* Wildernesse Golf, Utd Oxford and Cambridge; *Style—* Denis Makower, Esq; Flat 2, Hollington, 73 Bradbourne Park Rd, Sevenoaks, Kent TN13 3LH (☎ 453621)

MAKOWER, Peter; s of Anthony Makower, (d 1984), of London, and Sylvia Evelyn, *née* Chetwynd; *b* 12 Sept 1932; *Educ* Westminster, Trinity Coll Cambridge (MA), The Poly Regent St (Dip Arch), UCL (Dip Town Planning); *m* 20 Aug 1960, Katharine, da of John Howarth Paul Chadburn, MBE, of London; 2 s (Andrew b 1961, Timothy b 1965), 1 da (Mary b 1963 (d 1979)); *Career* RE 1951-56, architect and town-planner, on staff of Frederick Gibberd & Ptnrs 1959-82, and Chapman Taylor Ptnrs 1982-85, in practice as Peter Makower Architects and Planners 1985-; FRIBA; MRTPI; *Style—* Peter Makower, Esq; Peter Makower Architects and Planners, 13 Tideway Yard, Mortlake High St, London SW14 8SN (☎ 01 392 1488, fax 01 878 1807)

MALAN, Mrs Daniel; Dorothy Elise; *née* Henry; da of Henry James Raymond (d 1954, s of Evelyn, da of Sir John Pelly, 2 Bt, by his 1 w Johanna), and Josine Elise Françoise Du Toit (d 1970), of a family of Huguenot origin; *b* 31 August 1908; *m* (Daniel) François Malan, s of Jacobus Du Toit Malan and n of Dr Malan, sometime PM of SA; 1 s (James b 1941), 1 da (Françoise b 1948, m Gert Bezuidenhout); *Style—* Mrs Daniel Malan; 42 Paradise Rd, Newlands 7700, Cape Town, S Africa

MALCOLM, Alastair Richard; s of Colin Ronald Malcolm (decd); *b* 20 Oct 1947; *Educ* Eton, New Coll Oxford; *m* 1971, Elizabeth Anne, da of Edward Wilfred George Joicey-Cecil; 2 s; *Career* barr Inner Temple 1971; *Recreations* shooting, country pursuits; *Style—* Alastair Malcolm Esq; Hart Hill Farm, Woodfalls, Salisbury, Wilts

MALCOLM, Hon Mrs (Annabel Mary Adelaide); *née* Norrie; da of 1 Baron Norrie, GCMG, GCVO, CB, DSO, MC (d 1977); *b* 23 Dec 1945; *Educ* Downham Herts, Blois France; *m* 16 April 1988, Ian R Malcolm, s of late C R Malcolm, of Newent, Glos; *Style—* The Hon Annabel Norrie; 124 Swan Court, Chelsea Manor St, SW3

MALCOLM, Sir David Peter Michael; 11 Bt (NS 1665), of Balbedie and Innertiel, Co Fife; s of Maj Sir Michael Albert James Malcolm, 10 Bt (d 1976); *b* 7 July 1919; *Educ* Eton, Magdalene Coll Cambridge (BA); *m* 6 June 1959, Hermione, da of Sir David Home, 13 Bt; 1 da; *Heir* kinsman, Lt-Col Arthur William Alexander Malcolm, CVO; *Career* Scots Gds 1939-46, Maj; CA; former dir James Capel & Co; former memb: Stock Exchange 1956-80, Stock Exchange Cncl 1971-80; memb: Queen's Bodyguards for Scotland (Royal Co of Archers); *Clubs* New (Edinburgh), Hon Co of Edinburgh Golfers; *Style—* Sir David Malcolm, Bt; Whiteholm, Whim Road, Gullane, Scotland

MALCOLM, Dugald; CMG (1966), CVO (1964), TD (1945); s of Maj-Gen Sir Neill Malcolm, KCB, DSO (d 1953), and Angela Malcolm (d 1930); *b* 22 Dec 1917; *Educ* Eton, New Coll Oxford (MA); *m* 22 June 1957, Patricia Anne, wid of Capt Peter Atkinson Clarke (killed 1944), da of late Gilbert Gilbert-Lodge; 2 da (Anne (Mrs Carpenter) b 1943, Helen (Mrs Whittow) b 1962); *Career* Argyll & Sutherland Highlanders (Territorial Cmmn) 1939, discharged wounded 1945; HM Dip Serv: Lima, Bonn, Seoul 1945-57, HM Vice-Marshal of the Dip Corps 1957-65, ambass Luxembourg 1966-70, Panama 1970-74; Min Holy See 1975-77; Freeman Worshipful Co of Fishmongers; *Clubs* Boodle's, Brook's, Travellers; *Style—* Dugald Malcolm, Esq, CMG, CVO, TD

MALCOLM, George John; CBE (1965); s of George Hope Malcolm, and Johanna, *née* Brosnahan; *b* 28 Feb 1917; *Educ* Wimbledon Coll, Balliol Coll Oxford (MA, BMus), RCM; *Career* musician; master of the cathedral music Westminster Cathedral 1947-59 (trained unique boys' choir for which Benjamin Britten wrote Missa Brevis), now mainly harpsichordist pianist and conductor; winner Cobbett Medal Worshipful Co of Musicians 1960, hon fell Balliol Coll Oxford 1966; Hon DMus Sheffield 1978; hon RAM 1961, FRCM 1974, Hon FRCO 1988; Papal Knight of the Order of St Gregory the Great 1970; *Style—* George Malcolm, Esq, CBE; 99 Wimbledon Hill Rd, London SW19 7QT; c/o Harold Holt Ltd, 31 Sinclair Rd, London W14 0NS (☎ 01 603 4600, fax 01 603 0019, telex 22339 Hunter G)

MALCOLM, Kathleen, Lady; Kathleen; da of late Cdr George Jonathan Gawthorne, RN, (decd), and formerly w of James Melvin; *m* 1947 (as his 2 w), Maj Sir Michael Albert James Malcolm, Scots Guards, 10 Bt (d 1976); *Clubs* Cavalry & Gds; *Style—* Kathleen, Lady Malcolm; 11 Onslow Square, London SW7 3NJ

MALCOLM, (Thomas) Neil (Carmichael); s of Robert Malcolm (d 1983), and Janet Irene, *née* Carmichael; *b* 1 Sept 1938; *Educ* HS of Stirling, Univ of Glasgow; *m* 30 Sept 1967, Kay Donnet, da of John Donnet Anderson; 1 s (Colin b 1977), 2 da (Susan b 1968, Victoria b 1971); *Career* CA, sr ptnr Macfarlane Gray 1967-; memb tax practice ctee Inst of CAs of Scotland; tres: Allan Pk Sth Church of Scotland 1971-, Stirling GC 1977-; CA, FCCA, FSA Scotland; *Recreations* golf, squash, tennis, hill walking; *Clubs* Stirling GC, Stirling Lawn Tennis and Squash, Stirling and County, Rotary of Stirling; *Style—* Thomas Malcolm, Esq; 26 Snowdon Place, Stirling FK8 2JN (☎ 0786 75975); 6 Viewfield Place, Stirling FK8 1NR (☎ 0786 51745)

MALCOLM-BROWN, Tessa; da of Bernard Dixon (d 1983), of Pampisford, Cambridge, and Olive Marie, *née* Watts; *b* 23 July 1937; *Educ* Chatelard Sch Les Avants Montreux Switzerland; *m* 26 July 1958 (dis 1979), James Anthony Gerard Malcolm-Brown, s of William Isbister Malcolm-Brown, of Harpenden; 3 s (Charles Barry b 13 Dec 1961, Guy James b 15 Nov 1963 (decd), Mark b 19 May 1965); *Career* dir: Dixon Int Ltd 1979, Dixon Int Gp Ltd 1984, Sealmaster Ltd 1968, SK Bearings Ltd 1979, The Dixon Malt Co Ltd 1979, (chm and md all cos 1984) md and chm Intumescent Seals Ltd 1980-;; *Recreations* breeding arabian horses, carriage driving, piano; *Clubs* Br Driving Soc (horse carriages), Arab Horse Soc; *Style—* Mrs Tessa Malcolm-Brown; Pampisford Court, Pampisford Cambridge (☎ 0223 832795); Pampisford, Cambridge (☎ 0223 832851, telex 81664 Dixon G, fax 837215)

MALDEN, Aubrey Dicken; s of Peter James Malden, of Chiswick, London, and Marie Roselyn, *née* Clarke; *b* 7 Nov 1949; *Educ* Fowey Sch Cornwall, Ealing Sch of Art London; *m* 24 Sept 1983, Veronika Susan, da of Horst Max Schneider (d 1979), of Johannesburg SA; *Career* fndr memb Craton Lodge & Knight New Product Devpt Consultancy London 1973-79, gp head of J Walter Thompson Brussels 1979-80; creative dir and bd memb Ogilvy & Mathers Brussels 1980-82 Johannesburg 1982-87, creative dir and bd memb Ash Gupta Communications: Clio Awards for TV work, radio & Print work, other awards for print, TV, and Radio; involved in Prince's Tst Charity, memb The Creative Forum; *Recreations* rugby, squash, fishing; *Style—* Aubrey Malden, Esq; Ash Gupta Communications, 9 Coates Cres, Edinburgh EH3 7AL (☎ 031 225 9587, fax 031 225 9588, telex 72346); 8 Rosehall Place, Haddington, Scotland

MALDEN, Viscount; Frederick Paul de Vere Capell; s and h of 10 Earl of Essex; *b* 29 May 1944; *Educ* Skerton Boys' Secdy Sch, Lancaster Royal GS, Didsbury Coll of Educn, N Sch of Music; *Career* acting head teacher Marsh Co Jr Sch 1974-77; head teacher Cockerham C of E Sch 1979-81; i/c Pastoral Care, Curriculum Devpt and Music at Skerton County Primary Sch Lancaster 1981-; LLCM (teacher's dip), ALCM, FRSA, ACP; *Recreations* classical music; *Style—* Viscount Malden; Lindisfarne, Pinewood Ave, Brookhouse, Lancaster, Lancs

MALE, David Ronald; s of Ronald Male (d 1963), of Worthing, and Gertrude, *née* Simpson (d 1946); *b* 12 Dec 1929; *Educ* Aldenham Sch; *m* 6 June 1959, Mary Louise, da of Rex Powis Evans, of St Albans; 1 s (James b 1964), 2 da (Sarah b 1962, Charlotte b 1966); *Career* 2 Lt RA 1948-49; memb: bd dirs Building Centre 1970-80, Govt Construction Panel 1973-74; RICS: memb gen cncl 1976-, pres quantity surveyors dival cncl 1977-78, sr vice-pres 1988-; sr ptnr Gardiner & Theobald 1979- (ptnr 1960); memb Econ Devpt Cncl for Bldg 1982-86, chm Commercial Bldgs Steering Gp 1984-88; govr Aldenham Sch 1974-, pres Old Aldenhamian Soc 1986-; MCC: memb ctee 1984-, chm estates sub-ctee 1984-; Freeman City of London 1961, Liveryman Worshipful Co Painter-Stainers 1961-, Master Worshipful Co Chartered Surveyors 1984-85 (memb ct 1977-85); ARICS 1954, FRICS 1964; *Recreations* opera, ballet, lawn tennis, real tennis, golf; *Clubs* Boodle's, Garrick; *Style—* David Male, Esq; Pollards Farm, Kinsbourne Green, Harpenden, Herts AL5 3PE (☎ 058 27 60532); 6 Bowland Yard, Kinnerton St, London SW1X 8EE (☎ 01 245 6084); 49 Bedford Sq, London WC1B 3EB (☎ 01 637 2468, fax 01 636 3185, car tel 0860 544 601, telex 24410)

MALET, Col Sir Edward William St Lo; 8 Bt (GB 1791), of Wilbury Wiltshire; OBE (1953); s of Lt-Col Sir Harry Charles Malet, 7 Bt, DSO, OBE, JP (d 1931), and Mildred Laura, da of Capt Henry Stephen Swiney; *b* 27 Nov 1908; *Educ* Dover Coll, Christ Church Oxford (MA); *m* 1935, Baroness Benedicta (d 1979), da of Baron Wilhelm von Maasburg, of Vienna; 1 s, 2 da; *Heir* s, Harry Douglas St Lo Malet; *Career* gazetted 8 KRI Hussars 1932, serv Palestine 1935-36, and N Africa (despatches) 1937-42, Capt 8 Hussars 1938; attached Br Embassy Anakara 1942-44, active serv France, Belgium, Holland, Germany 1944-45, sr control offr Brunswick Kreis Gp 1946-47, chief civil affrs offr Suez Canal Zone 1951-55, ret 1955; pres Bridgwater Div Cons Assoc 1959-66; High Sheriff Somerset 1966-67; *Clubs* Cavalry and Gds; *Style—* Col Sir Edward Malet, Bt, OBE; Chargot, Luxborough, Watchet, Somerset (☎ Washford 371)

MALET, Harry Douglas St Lo; s and h of Sir Edward William St Lo Malet, 8 Bt, OBE; *b* 26 Oct 1936; *Educ* Downside, Trinity Coll Oxford; *m* 28 Aug 1967, Julia Gresley, da of Charles Harper, of Perth, W Australia; 1 s (Charles Edward St Lo); *Career* late Queen's Royal Irish Hussars; JP; *Style—* Harry Malet, Esq, JP; Langham Farm, Luxborough, Watchet, Somerset

MALET, Hon Mrs (Margaret Cherry); da of 2 Baron Wigram, MC; *b* 24 April 1942; *m* 1972, Lt-Col Greville J W Malet, OBE; 1 s (Charles b 1976), 1 da (Henrietta b 1978); *Style—* The Hon Mrs Malet; The Walled Ho, Hatherop, Cirencester, Glos GL7 3NA

MALIA, (John) David; s of Austin Patrick Malia, and Hilda Elizabeth, *née* Mallan (d 1974); *b* 31 Jan 1947; *Educ* St Cuthberts GS; *m* 1 (m dis 1982), Marie; 1 s (Aidan b 12 Dec 1976); m 2, 20 Sept 1986, Agnes, da of James O'Brien (d 1966); *Career* chm BUMA Engrg Co Ltd 1981 (dir 1973, jt md 1975, md 1979); patron Ellingham Hall Sch, cncllr Tosson PCC; *Recreations* viniculture, opera, photography; *Style—* David Malia, Esq; The Pele Tower, Whitton, Rothbury, Northumberland NE65 7RL (☎ 0669 20410); BUMA Engineering Co Ltd, Robson St, Newcastle upon Tyne NE6 1NB (☎ 091 265 9088, fax 091 265 1259, telex 537886 BUMA G)

MALICKI, Janusz Maciej; s of Malicki Marian (d 1970), of Poland, Naleczow, and Malicka Helena, *née* Majdylo (d 1971); *b* 11 August 1929; *Educ* Secdy Sch Naleczow, Merchant Secdy Sch Lublin, Central Sch of Planning and Stats (MSc); *m* 27 Nov 1955, Irena Wanda, da of Wolski Konstanty (d 1939), of Poland, Jablonowo; 1 s (Donald b 1960), 1 da (Maryla (Mrs Ostrowska) b 1956); *Career* various positions Nat Bank of Poland 1950-63, expert Int Bank for Econ Cooperation Moscow 1964-68, dir of dept Bank Handlowy W Warszawie SA Warsaw 1968-72, mangr int relations Int Bank for Econ Cooperation 1973-75, md and gen dir Int Investmt Bank Moscow 1976-81, dir and gen mangr Bank Handlowy N Warsawie SA London 1985 (vice pres bd of mgmnt Warsaw 1981-85); memb: Overseas Bankers Club, Lombard Assoc; Polonia Restituta, Knight's Cross, Cross of Merit, Cold Class, Cross of Merit, Silver Class; *Style—* Janusz Malicki, Esq; Bank Handlowy W Warszawie SA, 4 Coleman St, London EC2R 5AS (☎ 01 606 7181, fax 01 726 4902, telex 8811681)

MALIM, Christopher John; CBE (1969); s of Frederick Blagden Malim (d 1966), master Haileybury Coll 1911-21, master Wellington 1921-37, and Amy Gertrude, *née* Hemmerde (d 1960); *b* 14 Sept 1911; *Educ* Wellington, Corpus Christi Coll Oxford (MA); *m* 1, 30 Nov 1939, Naomi, da of Waldemar Max de Paula (d 1972); 2 s (Adrian b 1941, Andrew b 1943); m 2, 20 Jan 1959, Audrey, da of Quiller Orchardson Gilbey Gold (d 1972); m 3, 24 May 1975, Barbarie, da of Col W E C Terry (d 1959); *Career* 1 Bn 43 Oxon and Bucks LI 1943, WO 1941, GSO2 PM Jt Planning Staff 1942-43, GSO1 plans HQ SE Asia Cmd 1943-45, Col 1945; chm: Moorfields Eye Hosp 1957 (govr 1955-69), Pantechnicon (Seth Smith Bros Ltd) 1976-86, Hampstead Garden Suburb Tst 1967-69, London Post-Grad Ctee 1968-69; govr London Hosp 1970-78, memb cncl King Edward's Hosp Fund for London 1969, Borough of Kensington 1953-59, cncl memb Law Soc 1959-68, dir Westminster Fire Off (Sun Alliance W End Branch) 1960-83, tstee of Wellington Coll Tst Funds 1979; appointed Upper Warden Worshipful Co of Scriveners 1988; CBE 1969; FRSA 1968; *Recreations* music, real tennis, country life; *Clubs* Carlton, MCC; *Style—* Christopher Malim, Esq, CBE; 45 Whitelands House, Cheltenham Terr, London SW3 (☎ 01 730 3520); Shepherds Cottage, Greys Green, Henley-on-Thames, Oxon (☎ 049 17 235)

MALIM, Rear Adm Nigel Hugh; CB (1971), LVO (1960), DL (1970); s of John Charles Malim, MBE (d 1957), and Brenda Stirling, *née* Robinson (d 1973); *b* 5 April 1919; *Educ* Weymouth Coll, RN Engrg Coll Plymouth, RNC Greenwich; *m* 6 Sept 1944, Moonyeen Maureen Ogilby, da of Capt William Edmund Maynard, DL (d 1926); 2 s (Jeremy b 1945, Timothy b 1957), 1 da (Marquita b 1953); *Career* special entry cadet RN 1936, HMS Manchester 1940-42, HMS Norfolk 1942-43, HMS Jamaica 1945-47, staff RNEC 1948-50, Admty 1956-58 (1951-54), HMS Triumph 1954-56, HM Yacht Britannia 1958-60, dist overseer Scotland 1960-62, dep dir Marine Engrg 1962-65, IDC 1966, Capt RNEC 1967-69, CSO (T) to C in C Western Fleet 1967-69; md Humber Graving Dock & Engrg Co Ltd 1972-82, chm Assoc Western Euro Shiprepairers 1982-86; Lincoln Cathedral: memb preservation cncl 1985, chm fabric cncl 1985; *Recreations* gardening, sailing; *Clubs* RNSA, Royal Ocean Racing; *Style—* Rear Adm Nigel Malim, CB, LVO, DL; The Old Vicarage, Caistor, Lincoln LN7 6UG (☎ 0472 851 275)

MALIN, Dr Stuart Robert Charles; s of Cecil Henry Malin (d 1968), and Eleanor Mary, *née* Howe; *b* 28 Sept 1936; *Educ* Royal GS High Wycombe, King's Coll London (BSc), Univ of London (PhD, DSc); *m* 30 March 1963, Irene, da of Frederick Alfred Saunders, of Polegate, Sussex; 2 da (Jane b 1966, Rachel b 1969); *Career* Royal Greenwich Observatory Herstmonceux: asst experimental offr 1958-61, scientific offr 1961-65, sr scientific offr 1965-70; Cape observer Radcliffe Observatory SA 1963-65, visiting scientist Nat Center Atmospheric Res USA 1969; Inst Geological Scis Herstmonceux and Edinburgh: prin scientific offr (individual merit) 1976-81, head geomagnetism unit 1981-82; Green Scholar Scripps Inst Oceanography USA 1981, visiting prof dept physics and astronomy UCL 1983-, head dept astronomy and navigation Nat Maritime Museum 1982-88, mathematics dept Dulwich Coll 1988-; pres Jr Astronomical Soc, vice-pres Maidstone Astronomical Soc, churchwarden St Margaret's Church Lee; FRAS 1961, FInstP 1971, CPhys 1985; *Books* The Greenwich Meridian (with C Stott 1984), Spaceworks (with C Stott 1985), The Planets (1987), Stars, Galaxies and Nebulae (1989); *Recreations* croquet, clocks; *Clubs* RAS; *Style—* Dr Stuart Malin; 30 Wemyss Rd, Blackheath, London SE3 0TG (☎ 01 318 3712); Dulwich Coll, Dulwich, London SE21 7LD (☎ 01 693 5271)

MALINS, Humfrey Jonathan; MP (C) Croydon NW 1983-; s of Rev Peter Malins and Lilian Joan Malins, of Greenwich; *b* 31 July 1945; *Educ* St John's Sch Leatherhead, Brasenose Coll Oxford (MA); *m* 1979, Lynda Ann; 1 s (Harry b 1985), 1 da (Katherine b 1982); *Career* slr; pps to Home Office Min 1987-; *Recreations* rugby football, golf, gardening; *Clubs* Vincents (Oxford), W Sussex GC; *Style—* Humfrey Malins Esq, MP; Highbury, Westcott Street, Westcott, Surrey (☎ Dorking 0306 885554); work: Old Gun Court, North St, Dorking, Surrey (☎ 0306 881256)

MALLABY, Sir Christopher Leslie George; KCMG (1988); s of Brig A W S Mallaby, CIE, OBE (ka 1945), and Margaret Catherine, *née* Jones; *b* 7 July 1936; *Educ* Eton, King's Coll Cambridge (BA); *m* 1961, Pascale, da of Francois Thierry-Mieg, of Paris; 1 s (Sebastian b 1964), 3 da (Emily b 1967, Julia b 1971, Charlotte b 1972); *Career* entered Hm Dip Serv 1959, Moscow Embassy 1961-63 and 1975-77, first sec Berlin 1966-69; dep dir Br Trade Devpt Off (NY) 1971-74; head of: Arms Control & Disarmament Dept FCO 1977-79, E Euro and Soviet Dept 1979-80, Planning Staff 1980-82; min Bonn 1982-85, dep sec Cabinet 1985-87, ambass to Fed Rep of Germany 1988-; *Recreations* fishing, reading, travel; *Clubs* Beefsteak; *Style—* Sir Christopher Mallaby, KCMG; c/o FCO, London SW1

MALLABY, Lady; Elizabeth Greenwood; *née* Brooke; da of Hubert Edward Brooke, and Helen Honey; *b* 12 Nov 1911; *m* 1, J W D Locker, OBE (decd); m 2, 1955, Sir (Howard) George (Charles) Mallaby, KCMG, OBE (d 1978); *Recreations* painting, gardening; *Style—* Lady Mallaby; Mill End, Dunwich Rd, Bylthburgh, Suffolk IP19 9LY (☎ 050 270 273)

MALLALIEU, Ann; QC (1988); da of Sir William Mallalieu (d 1980), and Lady Harriet Rita Mallalieu, *née* Tinn; *b* 27 Nov 1945; *Educ* Holton Park Girls GS Wheatley Oxon, Newham Coll Cambridge (MA, LLM); *m* 1979, Timothy Felix Harold Cassel, QC s of Sir Harold Cassel, Bt, QC; 2 da (Bathsheba b 1981, Cosima b 1984); *Career* barr Inner Temple 1970, rec 1985-; first woman pres Cambridge Union Soc; *Recreations* horses, sheep, reading poetry; *Style—* Miss Ann Mallalieu, QC; Studdridge Farm, Stokenchurch, Bucks; 6 Kings Bench Walk, Temple EC4 (☎ (583) 0410)

MALLALIEU, Lady; Betty Margaret Oxley; da of Dr Pride, late of Bridlington and gda of J W Oxley (decd), of Leeds; *m* 1934, Sir Edward Lancelot (Sir Lance) Mallalieu, QC (d 1979); *Style—* Lady Mallalieu; c/o Hempsons (Slrs), 33 Henrietta St, Strand, London WC2E 8NH

MALLALIEU, Lady; Harriet Rita Riddle Tinn; *m* 1945, Sir Joseph Percival William Mallalieu (d 1980); *Style—* Lady Mallalieu; Village Farm, Boarstall, Aylesbury, Bucks (☎ Brill 454)

MALLENDER, Neil Alan; s of Ron Mallender and Jean Elizabeth; *b* 13 August 1961; *Educ* Beverley GS E Yorks; *m* 1983, Caroline, da of Peter Russel; *Career* professional cricketer; *Recreations* golf, watching rugby league; *Style—* Neil Mallender Esq; c/o Northants CCC

MALLET, John Valentine Granville; s of Sir Victor Alexander Louis Mallet, GCMG, CVO (d 1969), and Christiana Jean (Peggy), *née* Andreae (d 1984); bro of Philip Louis Victor Mallet, *qv*; *b* 15 Sept 1930; *Educ* Winchester, Balliol Coll Oxford (BA); *m* 1958, Felicity Ann, da of Ulick Basset; 1 s (Hugh Thurstane Victor Ulick); *Career* cmmnd Intelligence Corps, temp Lt Trieste Security Off (1949-50); ceramics and works of art dept Sotheby & Co 1955-62, keeper dept of ceramics V & A 1976- (asst keeper 1962-76, sec advsy cncl 1967-73); Prime Warden Ct of Assts, Fishmongers Co 1983-84 (memb of Ct 1970-); FRS, FRSA; *Books* various articles and reviews on ceramics; *Recreations* tennis; *Clubs* Brooks's; *Style—* John Mallet, Esq

MALLET, Hon Mrs (Laura); *née* Aitken; da of Sir Max Aitken, 2 Bt, DSO, DFC (d 1985; 2 Baron Beaverbrook who disclaimed title 1964), by his 3 w, Violet, da of Sir Humphrey de Trafford, 4 Bt, MC; sis of 3 Baron Beaverbrook; *b* 18 Nov 1953; *m* 1984, David Victor Mark Mallet, s of Sir Victor Mallet, GCMG, CVO (d 1969); 1 s (David Sonny Victor Maxwell b 1984); *Style—* The Hon Mrs Mallet; Oakwood Farm, Oakwood, nr Chichester, Sussex

MALLET, Philip Louis Victor; CMG (1980); s of Sir Victor Alexander Louis Mallet GCMG, CVO (d 1969), and Christiana Jean, *née* Andreae (d 1984); descended from Jacques Mallet du Pan, chronicler of the French Revolution; *b* 3 Feb 1926; *Educ* Winchester, Balliol Coll Oxford (BA); *m* 1953, Mary Moyle Grenfell, da of Rev Granville William Borlase (d 1953); 3 s (James, Stephen, Victor); *Career* HM Dip Serv (ret); high cmmr Guyana, non-resident ambass Suriname 1978-82; *Clubs* Brooks's; *Style—* Philip Mallet Esq, CMG; Wittersham Ho, Wittersham, Kent TN30 7ED (☎ 07977 238)

MALLETT, Michael John; s of Albert William Mallett (d 1972); *b* 14 Dec 1931; *Educ* Devonport HS Plymouth, Penzance; *m* 1956, Joan Barbara, *née* Ayre; 1 s, 2 da; *Career* ptnr Noel Lewis & Co (Liverpool) 1957-60; sec James Neill Hldgs Ltd 1960, dir corporate devpt 1970, dep chief exec 1974, chm and chief exec Neill Tool Gp Ltd 1981, chm and md Neill Tools 1981-83, exec dir James Neill Hldgs plc 1983-84; chm Radio Hallam Ltd 1979-, Record Hldgs plc 1985-; dep chm TT Gp plc 1984-; chm: Ayre Mallett & Co Ltd 1960-, Girobank plc ne regnl bd 1985-, Yorks and Humberside Independent Radio Ltd 1987-; dir: Viking Radio Ltd 1987-, Bradford Community Radio Ltd 1987-, chm: Andionics Ltd 1987-, Coated Electrodes Int 1988-, Smith Indust Serv Gp Ltd 1988-; memb Yorks & Humberside regnl cncl CBI 1979-81, nat cncl CBI 1979-, econ and fin policy ctee CBI 1982-88; Master Co of Cutlers in Hallamshire 1978-79; memb Accounting Standards Ctee 1982-; FCA (pres); Sheffield & Dist Soc of Chartered Accountants; *Recreations* riding, reading; *Style—* Michael Mallett Esq; 106 Ivy Park Rd, Sheffield, S Yorks S10 3LD (☎ 0742 305166)

MALLIN, Very Rev; Dean Stewart Adam Thomson; s of George Garner Mallin (d 1976), of Melville View, Lasswade, Midlothian, and Elizabeth, *née* Thomson, (d 1949); *b* 12 August 1924; *Educ* Lasswade Secdy Sch, Coates Hall Theol Coll Edinburgh; *Career* ordained: deacon 1961, priest 1962; precentor Inverness Cath 1961- 64, itinerant priest for the Diocese 1964-68, priest i/c St Peter and The Holy Rood Thurso and rector St John the Evangelist Wick 1968 -77, canon Inverness Cath 1974, rector St James the Great Dingwall and St Anne's Strathpeffer 1977, dean Moray Ross and Caithness 1983- (synod clerk 1981-83); memb: Co of the Servants of God, St John Assoc of Scotland Highland Branch, Rotary Club of Dingwall (former pres); hon memb Royal Br Legion Thurso Caithness (Communication USA Caithness) Unit 1971-77; exec memb Ross and Cromarty Cncl: on Alcohol, of Voluntary Serv; chapalin Dingwall Acad; *Recreations* gardening, music, travel; *Style—* The Very Rev the Dean of Moray, Ross and Caithness; The Parsonage, 4 Castle St, Dingwall, Ross-shire (☎ 0349 62204)

MALLINCKRODT, George Wilhelm Gustav; s of Arnold Wilhelm von Mallinckrodt (d 1982), of 8110 Riegsee, nr Murnau, W Germany, and Valentine, *née* von Joest; *b* 19 August 1930; *Educ* Schule Schloss Salem, Hamburg Business Sch; *m* 31 July 1958, Charmaine Brenda, da of Helmut Schroder (d 1967), of Dunlossit, Isle of Islay; 2 s (Philip b 1962, Edward b 1965), 2 da (Claire b 1960, Sophie b 1967); *Career* joined J Henry Schroder Banking Corpn NY 1954, exec chm Schroders plc London 1984-, chm and chief exec Schroders Inc NY 1983-, chm J Jenry Schroder Bank A G (Zurich) 1984-, chm and pres Schroder Int Ltd 1984-; dir: Schroder Australia Hodgs Ltd Sydney 1984-, Wertheim Schroder & Co Inc NY 1986-, J Henry Schroder Wagg & Co Ltd London 1967-, Singapore Int Merchant Bankers Ltd 1988-, N M UK Ltd 1986-, Euro Arts Fndn Ltd 1986-, Euris Paris 1987-; memb of Euro advsy ctee McGraw-Hill Inc NY 1986-; vice-pres German Chamber of Indust & Comm in UK 1974-, pres German YMCA in London 1971-; CBIM 1986, FRSA 1986; Cross of Order of Merit German Federal Republic 1986; *Recreations* shooting, skiing, gardening, classical music, reading; *Clubs* River (NY); *Style—* George Mallinckrodt, Esq; Schroders plc, 120 Cheapside, London EC2V 6DS (☎ 01 382 6000, fax 01 382 6878, telex 885029)

MALLINSON, Anthony William; s of Stanley Tucker Mallinson, of Bury St Edmunds, Suffolk (d 1955), and Dora Selina, *née* Burridge (d 1960); f was 2 s of Sir William Mallinson, 1 Bt, of Walthamstow, the fndr of William Mallinson & Sons Ltd, timber merchants, now part of the Mallinson-Denny Gp; *b* 1 Dec 1923; *Educ* Marlborough, Gonville and Caius Coll Cambridge (BA, LLM); *m* 20 April 1955, Heather Mary, da of Thomas Arthur Mansfield Gardiner (d 1950); *Career* Army 1943-47, Maj RA Europe and India; admitted slr 1951; ptnr Slaughter and May 1957-86; (sr ptnr 1984-86); slr to the Fishmongers' Co 1964-86, hon legal advsr Accounting Standards Ctee 1982-86; cncl memb section on business law Int Bar Assoc 1984, memb London Bd of Bank of Scotland 1985; dir Stratton Investmt Tst plc 1986, Morgan Grenfell Asset Mgmnt Ltd 1986; chm Cinematograph Films Cncl 1973-76, memb exec Ctee Essex CCC 1986; *Recreations* sport watching, (principally cricket), reading; *Clubs* MCC; *Style—* Anthony Mallinson, Esq; 15 Douro Place, London W8 5PH (☎ 01 937 2739)

MALLINSON, Michael Heathcote; s of Reynold Heathcote Mallinson (d 1970), of Skateshill Farm, Chalford, Glos and Beatrice Maud *née* Butt (d 1978); *b* 17 Sept 1934; *Educ* Marlborough; *m* 9 Aug 1958, Audrey, da of Lt-Col Frank Clifford Arnold, of Hillcrest, 11A Avenue Rd, Belmont, Surrey; 1 s (Matthew Frank Heathcote b 1964); *Career* RA 1953-55, 2 Lt 1954; chartered surveyor Prudential Assur Co 1955-80, property dir and chief surveyor Prudential Portfolio Mangrs Ltd 1985- (jt chief surveyor 1981-85); vice pres Cncl of the Br Property Fedn 1988-89 (memb 1984-); memb: Cmmn for the New Towns 1986-, Property Advsy Gp to the DOE 1985-88; govr South Bank Poly 1986-; FRICS 1960; *Recreations* music, gardening, walking; *Style—* Michael Mallinson, Esq; Chelston, Guildford Rd, Chobham, Surrey (☎ 09905 8720); Princeton House, 271/3 High Holborn, London WC1V 7EE (☎ 01 548 6620, fax 01 548 6999, telex 8811 419)

MALLINSON, Sir William John; 4 Bt (UK 1905), of Walthamstow, Co Essex; s of Sir (William) Paul Mallinson, 3 Bt (d 1989), and his 1 w, Eila Mary, *née* Guy; *b* 8 Oct 1942; *Educ* Charterhouse; *m* 1968 (m dis 1978), Rosalind Angela, da of Rollo Hoare; 1 s (William James), 1 da (Kate Sophia b 1972); *Heir* s, William James Mallinson b 22 April 1970; *Style—* Sir William Mallinson, Bt; 1 Hollywood Mews, London SW10 9HU

MALLON, Seamus; MP (SDLP Newry & Armagh 1986-); s of Francis Patrick Mallon (d 1969), of Markethill, Armagh, and Jane, *née* O'Flaherty (d 1965); *b* 17 August 1936; *Educ* Abbey GS Newry, St Mary's Coll of Educn Belfast; *m* 22 June 1964, Gertrude Cora, da of Edward Cush, of 1 Moy Rd, Armagh; 1 da (Orla b June 1969); *Career* headmaster St Jame's PS Markethill 1960-73; memb: Armagh DC 1973-, NI Assembly 1973-74, NI Convention 1975-76, Irish Senate 1982, New Ireland Forum 1983-84, House of Common Select Ctee on Agric 1986; Humbert Summer Sch Peace Prize 1988; *Recreations* golf, angling, landscape painting; *Clubs* Challoner; *Style—* Seamus Mallon, Esq, MP; 5 Castleview, Markethill, Armagh (☎ 0861 551 555); House of Commons, Westminster SW1A 0AA (☎ offices: 01 219 3000, 0861 526 800, 0396 679 33)

MALLOWAN, Lady; Barbara Parker; *m* 1977, as his 2 w, Sir Max Mallowan, CBE (d 1978); *Style—* Lady Mallowan; Thames Cottage, Castle Lane, Wallingford, Oxon

MALLOWS, Surgn Rear Adm (Harry) Russell; s of Harry Mallows (d 1953), of Martock Somerset, and Amy, *née* Law (d 1941); *b* 1 July 1920; *Educ* Wrekin Coll, Christ's Coll Cambridge (MA, MD), Univ of London (DPH); *m* 1942, Rhona Frances, da of William Christopher Wyndham-Smith, of Patagonia Argentina; 1 s (Richard), 2 da (Robin, Bryony); *Career* RN, serv Home, Med & Far E Cmds 1946-77; house physician Wellhouse Hosp Barnet & Royal N Hosp Holloway, sr med advsr Shell Int Petroleum Co Ltd 1977-85; QHP 1974-77; FFOM, FFCM, DIH; CStJ 1976; *Recreations* music, travel; *Style—* Surgn Rear Adm Russell Mallows; Chesters, 1 Shear Hill, Petersfield, Hants GU31 4BB

MALMESBURY, Countess of; Hon Diana Claudia Patricia; *née* Carleton; da of 2 and last Baron Dorchester; *b* 1912; *m* 1932, 6 Earl of Malmesbury; *Style—* The Rt Hon the Countess of Malmesbury

MALMESBURY, Bishop of 1983-; Rt Rev Peter James Firth; s of Atkinson Vernon Firth (d 1952), of Stockport, Cheshire, and Edith, *née* Pepper (d 1967); *b* 12 July 1929; *Educ* Stockport GS, Emmanuel Coll Cambridge (BA, MA, DipEd), St Stephens House Oxford; *m* 27 Aug 1955; Felicity Mary, da of late Longworth Allan Wilding, of Oxford; 2 s (Julian b 8 Jan 1961, Matthew b 10 Aug 1966), 3 da (Gabriel 23 Oct 1958, Susannah b 12 Nov 1962, Linda Hennessy (fostered since 1974) b 17 Feb 1967); *Career* asst curate St Stephens Barbourne Worcs 1955-58, priest i/c Ascension Church Malvern Link 1958-62, rector St George's Abbey Hey Gorton Manchester 1962-66, asst prodr and organiser Religious Progs BBC Bristol 1967-83; winner Int Radio Award Seville Festival 1975; chm Public Enquiry into Swindon Rail Closure 1985 (with John Garnett and Lord Scanlon); *Books* Lord of the Seasons (1978); *Recreations* photography, music, TS Eliot, Manchester Utd; *Style—* The Rt Rev the Bishop of Malmesbury; 7 Ivywell Rd, Bristol BS9 1NX (☎ 0272 685 931)

MALMESBURY, 6 Earl of (GB 1800); William James Harris; TD (1944) and two clasps, JP (Hants 1950), DL (Hants 1983); also Baron Malmesbury (GB 1788) and Viscount Fitzharris (GB 1800); s of 5 Earl of Malmesbury, JP, DL (d 1950, gn of 3 Earl, who d 1889, having been sec state for Foreign Affrs and Lord Keeper of the Privy Seal); 1 Earl was last to be created in the GB Peerage (three days before the Union with Ireland), he had previously been sent in 1794, as a special envoy to Brunswick, to negotiate the marriage between Princess Caroline and the future George IV; *b* 18 Nov 1907; *Educ* Eton, Trinity Coll Cambridge (MA); *m* 1932, Hon Diana Carleton, da of 2 and last Baron Dorchester, OBE (d 1963); 1 s (James), 2 da (Sylvia, Nell); *Heir* s, Viscount FitzHarris; *Career* serv Royal Hants Regt (TA); a gold staff offr at Coronation of King George VI; surveyor; chm Hants CLA 1954-56, personal liason offr Min of Agric SE Region 1958-64, chm Hants Agric exec ctee 1959-67, dir Mid-Southern Water Co 1961-78; Official Verderer of the New Forest 1966-74; DL 1957-60, Vice Ld-Lt Southampton Co 1960-73, Ld-Lt and Custos Rotulorum of Hants 1973-83; Hon Col 65 Signal Regt 1959-66 and Hon Col 2 Bn Wessex Regt 1970-73; KStJ; ARICS; *Recreations* rural life, sailing, working a labrador, travel; *Clubs* Royal Yacht Sqdn (vice cdre 1971-78); *Style—* The Rt Hon the Earl of Malmesbury, TD; Greywell Hill, nr Basingstoke, Hants RG25 1DB (☎ 0256 702033)

MALONE, Christopher Kevin; s of Stanley Malone (d 1973), and Beryl Marguerite, *née* Fletcher (d 1982); *b* 20 June 1947; *Educ* St John's Coll Southsea; *m* 7 July 1973, Pamela Ann, da of James W Bird, of 57 Southbrook Rd, Havana; 1 s (Timothy James b 1978), 1 da (Rebecca Suzanne b 1980); *Career* practising CA; *Recreations* sailing, history, trams, honorary audits, politics; *Clubs* various (mainly sailing); *Style—* Christopher Malone, Esq; 91 Red Barn Lane, Fareham, Hampshire PO15 6HE (☎ 0329 288 060)

MALONE, Hon Mr Justice; Hon Sir Denis Eustace Gilbert; s of Sir Clement Malone, OBE, QC; *b* 24 Nov 1922; *Educ* St Kitts-Nevis GS, Wycliffe Coll Glos, Lincoln Coll Oxford (BA); *m* 1963, Diana, *née* Traynor; *Career* serv RAF 1942-46; barr Middle Temple 1950, slr-gen Barbados 1958-61, puisne judge: Belize 1961-65, Trinidad and Tobago 1966-74; chief justice Belize 1974-79, puisne Judge Bahamas 1979-; *Style—* The Hon Mr Justice Malone; c/o The Supreme Court, P O Box N8167, Nassau, Bahamas

MALONE, (Peter) Gerald; s of Peter Andrew Malone and Jessie Robertson Ritchie Malone, of Glasgow; *b* 21 July 1950; *Educ* Aloysius Coll, Glasgow Univ (MA, LLB); *m* 1981, Anne Scotland, da of William Blyth, of Edinburgh; *Career* slr; MP (C) Aberdeen S 1983-87; PPS to Parly Under Secs of State Dept of Energy 1985, asst govt whip 1986-87; *Recreations* opera, music; *Clubs* Royal Northern & Univ, Glasgow Arts; *Style—* Gerald Malone, Esq; 32 Albyn Lane, Aberdeen (☎ 0224 571779)

MALONE, (John) Malcolm; s of James Edward Malone (d 1968), of Theydon Bois, Essex, and Margaret, *née* Swinney; *b* 4 Oct 1945; *Educ* St Clement Danes, Bancrofts; *m* 29 July 1967, Marjorie Elizabeth Ann, da of Maj George Shaw Browne, of Ipswich, Suffolk; 1 s (Jonathan b 1969), 1 da (Miranda b 1968); *Career* slr; ptnr in Malone and Wells, dir Carr-Gomm Soc (E Anglia) Ltd; *Recreations* sailing, botany; *Style—* Malcolm Malone, Esq; 13 Vicarage Rd, Cromer, Norfolk NR27 9DQ; Shipden Cottage, 7 High St, Cromer, Norfolk NR27 9HG (☎ 0263 514049/0263 572774, fax 0263 514167)

MALONEY, Michael John; JP (1975); s of John William Maloney, of Eastbourne, and Olive Lois, *née* Morriss; *b* 26 July 1932; *Educ* St Albans Sch, Trinity Coll Oxford (MA); *m* 1960, Jancis Anne, da of Felix Robert Ewing, of Shrewsbury; 1 s (Patrick b 1971), 1 da (Bridget b 1974); *Career* 2 Lt RWAFF 1955-57; May & Baker Ltd 1957-58; asst master Shrewsbury Sch 1958-66, sr sci master, house master and dep headmaster Eastbourne Coll 1966-72; headmaster: Welbeck Coll 1972-85, Kamuzu Acad Malawi 1986-; *Books* Advanced Theoretical Chemistry (co ed with DEP Hughes); *Recreations* antique furniture restoration; *Style*— Michael Maloney, Esq, JP; Kamuzu Academy, PO Box 1, Mtunthama, Malawi

MALOY, Paul John; s of William J Maloy, of the USA, and late Theresa, *née* O'Reilly; *b* 29 Jan 1947; *Educ* Georgetown Univ (BSFS), New York Univ (MBA); *m* 2 da; *Career* Mfrs Hanover Tst: mgmnt trainee 1968-71, asst tst offr 1971-72, asst sec 1972-73, asst vice pres 1973-76, vice pres 1976-82, sr vice pres Energy Div 1982-, asst md London 1984-86 (later md), hd of London Branch 1986-; *Style*— Paul Maloy, Esq; Manufacturers Hanover Trust Co, 7 Princes St, London EC2P 2LR (☎ 01 315 6000, fax 01 315 6400)

MALPAS, Prof James Spencer; s of Tom Spencer Malpas (d 1972); *b* 15 Sept 1931; *Educ* Sutton Co GS, St Bart's Hosp London Univ, Oxford Univ; *m* 1957, Joyce May, da of Albert Edward Cathcart (d 1962); 2 s; *Career* Flt Lt RAF; prof of med oncology St Bartholomew's Hosp London Univ, dir Imperial Cancer Res Fund Unit of Med Oncology, dep dir (clinical) Imperial Cancer Res Fund 1986; conslt physician St Bartholomew's Hosp, dean Med Coll 1969-72; asst registrar RCP 1975-80, vice-pres Med Coll 1987; *Recreations* skiing, sailing, history, painting, travel; *Style*— Prof James Malpas; 36 Cleaver Square, London SE11 4EA (☎ 01 735 7566)

MALPAS, (John) Peter Ramsden; s of A H Malpas (d 1942), and E N E D, *née* Gledhill; *b* 14 Dec 1927; *Educ* Winchester, New Coll Oxford (MA); *m* 10 Mauy 1958, Rosamund Margaret, da of R J Born (d 1984), of Chiswick, London; 3 s (Simon b 1959, David b 1962, Johnny b 1965); *Career* Lt RB serv India and UK 1946-48; commercial asst Imperial Chemical Industs 1951-55, Chase Henderson & Tennant Stockbrokers 1956-58; Paribas Quilter Securities (formerly Quilter; Goodson, previously Quilter & Co): joined 1959, dep sr ptnr and chm 1983-87; dir Penny & Giles Int 1988; hon tres Royal Hosp and Home Putney, memb ctee Friends of Templeton Coll Oxford, tstee Devpt Tst for Young Disabled; memb Stock Exchange 1961-88; *Recreations* skiing, walking, sailing, the arts; *Clubs* Carlton, Itchenor SC, Ski GB; *Style*— Peter Malpas, Esq; St Christophers, W Strand, W Wittering, Sussex (☎ 01 878 2623); Penny and Giles Int, 8 Airfield Way, Christchurch, Dorset

MALPAS, Robert; CBE (1976); s of Cheshyre Malpas (d 1962), and Louise Marie Marcelle, *née* Boni (d 1984); *b* 9 Sept 1927; *Educ* Taunton Sch, St Georges Coll Buenos Aires, King's Coll Durham Univ (BSc); *m* 30 June 1956, Josephine, da of Leslie James Dickenson (d 1982); *Career* main bd dir ICI 1975-78, pres and chief exec offr Halcon Int Corpn USA 1978-82, bd memb and md BP plc 1983-89; chm designate Power Gen (one of successor cos to CEGB) 1989-; non exec dir: BOC plc, Eurotunnel, Baring plc; chm LINK, the DTI business HEI initiative, pres Soc of Chem Indust 1988-89, vice-pres Fellowship of Engrg; memb: Cncl of Indust and Higher Educn, cncl of CEST; Hon doctorate Univ of Surrey 1986, Univ of Loughborough 1985; fell N London Poly 1988; FEng, FIMechE, FIChemE, FIMatH; Order of Civil Merit (Spain) 1968; *Recreations* music, sport, opera; *Clubs* RAC London, Mill Reef Antigua, The River New York; *Style*— Robert Malpas, Esq, CBE; 2 Belgrave Mews West, London SW1X 8HT (☎ 01 235 3924)

MALTBY, Antony (Tony) John; JP (1980), DL (1984); s of Gerald Charles Maltby (d 1971), of Heathfield E Sussex, and Emily Norah Maltby (d 1981); *b* 15 May 1928; *Educ* Clayesmore Sch, St John's Coll Cambridge (MA); *m* 1959, Jillian (Jill) Winifred, da of N F Burtof Dover Kent; 4 da (Claire, Anita, Katrina, Lucy); *Career* teacher Dover Coll 1951-58, head of history and housemaster Pocklington Sch 1958-68, headmaster Trent Coll 1968-88; *Recreations* travel, squash; *Clubs* Hawks (Cambridge), E India Sports; *Style*— Tony Maltby, Esq, JP, DL; Little Singleton Farm, Great Chart, Ashford, Kent TN26 1JS (☎ 0233 629397)

MALTBY, Colin Charles; s of George Frederick Maltby, MC, and Dorothy Maltby; *b* 8 Feb 1951; *Educ* George Heriot's Sch Edinburgh, King Edward's Sch Birmingham, Christ Church Oxford (MA, MSc); *m* 1983, Victoria Angela Valerie, da of Paul Guido Stephen Elton; 2 da (Lorna b 1976, Katherine b 1986); *Career* pres Oxford Union 1973; chm Fedn of Cons Students 1974-75; merchant banker; asst dir Kleinwort Benson Investmt Mgmnt 1982-, dir: Kleinwort Benson (ME) EC 1983-84, Kleinwort Benson Investmt Mgmnt Ltd 1984-, Banque Kleinwort Benson SA 1985-; *Recreations* curiosity; *Style*— Colin Maltby, Esq; 1222 Vesenaz, Switzerland; Banque Kleinwort Benson SA, 2 Place du Rhone, 1204 Geneva, Switzerland (☎ 022 21 22 33)

MALTBY, John Newcombe; CBE (1988); s of Air Vice-Marshal Sir Paul Copeland Maltby, KCVO, KBE, CB, DSO, AFC, DL (d 1971); *b* 10 July 1928; *Educ* Wellington, Clare Coll Cambridge; *m* 1956, Lady Sylvia Veronica Anthea, da of 6 Earl of Malmesbury; 1 s, 2 da; *Career* chm: Burmah Oil 1983-, Dover Harobur Bd 1989-; dir DRG plc, Harrisons & Crosfield plc, UKAEA; *Recreations* history, sailing, gardening; *Clubs* Naval & Military; *Style*— John Maltby Esq; Broadford Ho, Stratfield Turgis, Basingstoke, Hants RG27 0AS

MALTBY, Lady Sylvia Veronica Anthea; *née* Harris; da of 6 Earl of Malmesbury, TD; *b* 17 May 1934; *Educ* Croft House Dorset; *m* 1956, John Newcombe Maltby, CBE, s of late Air Vice-Marshal Sir Paul Copeland Maltby, KCVO, KBE, CB, DSO, AFC, DL; 1 s, 2 da; *Style*— Lady Sylvia Maltby; Broadford Ho, Stratfield Turgis, Basingstoke, Hants

MALTBY, Lady; Winifred Russell; *née* Paterson; da of late James H Paterson, of 6 Moray Place, Edinburgh; *b* 23 Nov 1894; *Educ* St George's Ascot; *m* 1921, Air Vice-Marshal Sir Paul Copeland Maltby, KCVO, KBE, CB, DSO, AFC, DL (d 1971); 2 s, 1 da; *Style*— Lady Maltby; Heatherside, Nately Scures, Basingstoke, Hants

MALTWOOD, Derek Ryder; s of Ryder Gardyne Maltwood (d 1988), and Nancy Kathleen, *née* Lewis (d 1983); *b* 2 May 1938; *Educ* Radley, Pembroke Coll Cambridge; *m* 1, 27 Sept 1965, Lesley; 1 s (Bruce b 1968), m 2, 16 Sept 1972, Margaret; 1 s (Damien b 1975); *Career* memb Stock Exchange 1968; chm Hoare Govett Channel Islands; Jersey Gen Investmt Tst Ltd 1985; chm Jersey Branch Inst of Dirs 1984-87; dep for St Mary 1987; *Recreations* gardening, travel, DIY; *Clubs* United, IOD, RAC; *Style*— Deputy Derek R Maltwood; Greenfields, Rue de Bel Air, St Mary, Jersey CI (☎ 0534 61907); PO Box 1, Westaway Chambers, 39 Don St, St Helier, Jersey, CI (☎ 0534 35111)

MALVERN, 3 Viscount (UK 1955); Ashley Kevin Godfrey Huggins; s of 2 Viscount Malvern (d 1978); *b* 26 Oct 1949; *Heir* unc, Hon (Martin) James Huggins; *Style*— The Rt Hon the Visount Malvern

MALVERN, John; s of Harry Ladyman Malvern, CBE (d 1982) of Cookham and Doreen *née* Peters; *b* 3 Oct 1937; *Educ* Fettes, Univ of London and The London Hosp (MB BS, BSc); *m* 10 July 1965, Katharine Mary Monica, da of Hugh Guillebaud (d 1958), of Marlborough; 1 s (James b 1977), 2 da (Susan b 1966, Joanna b 1969); *Career* conslt obstetrician Queen Charlottes Hosp 1973, conslt gynaecologist Chelsea Hosp for Women 1973-, hon sr lectr Inst of Obstetrics and Gynaecology 1973-, memb of cncl: RCOG 1977-83, 1987-, BPA 1987-, Centl Manpower Ctee 1981-84; memb academic bd of Royal Postgraduate Med Sch; chm: academic gp Inst of Obstetrics and Gynacology 1986-88, Blair Bell Res Soc, Int Continence Soc, Gynaecological Visiting Soc and Fothergill Club; examiner for MRCOG: Univs of London Liverpool Manchester, Khartoum Central Midwives Bd, Professional and Linguistics Assessment Bd; pres Queen Charlotte's Hosp Dining Club; Liveryman Worshipful Co of Apothecaries; FRCS (Ed), FRCOG; FRSM (pres obstetrics and gynaecology); *Books* various publications on urogynaecology; *Recreations* wine tasting, Chinese ceramics, travel; *Clubs* RSM, Hurlingham; *Style*— John Malvern, Esq; 30 Roedean Crescent, Roehampton, London SW15 5JU (☎ 01 876 4943); 84 Harley St, London W1 (☎ 01 636 2766)

MALVERN, Viscountess; Patricia Margery; da of Frank Renwick-Bower, of Durban; *m* 1949, 2 Viscount Malvern (d 1978); *Style*— The Rt Hon Viscountess Malvern; c/o Standard Bank, Cecil Sq, Salisbury, Zimbabwe

MALYN, (Richard) Anthony; OBE (1958), JP County of Oxford (1979-); s of late Rev Richard Henry Malyn, and Margretta Louisa, *née* Davies (d 1965); *b* 30 Mar 1914; *Educ* Rossall, St Peter's Coll Oxford (MA); *m* 9 Jan 1946, Joyce Mary, da of William Frederick Dent (d 1942); *Career* WW II seconded KAR (A/Capt) 1940-43 served Abyssinian campaign; Colonial Administrative Service Uganda 1936-58, dist offr 1938-53, seconded E African Govrs Conference 1943-46, asst chief sec then perm sec Miny of Educn of Health Uganda 1953-58; asst registrar Oxford Univ 1961-81; fell St Peter's Coll; *Recreations* watching sport, gardening; *Clubs* Vincent's Oxford; *Style*— Anthony Malyn, Esq, JP; Moat Cottage, Stratton Audley, Bicester, Oxon (☎ 08697 322)

MAMBA, HE Senator Hon George Mbikwakhe; GCVO (hon) (1987); s of Ndzabatebelungu Mamba, of Swaziland and gs of Chief Bhokweni, and Getrude Mtwalose *née* Thwala; *b* 5 July 1932; *Educ* Betani Misson Sch, Newhaven Misson Sch, Cambridge Inst of Educn, Nairobi Univ; *m* 1960, Sophie Sidanda, da of Johanes Mapamula Nsibande (d 1987); 3 s (Ndumiso b 1961, Subusiso b 1963, Phuthumile b 1964), 2 da (Pholile b 1967, Muzi b 1971); *Career* head teacher Makhonza Mission Sch 1956-60, teacher Kwaluseni Central Sch 1961-66, head teacher Enkamheni Central Sch 1966-67, insp of Schs 1969-71, welfare/aftercare offr 1971-72, cnsllr Swaziland High Cmmn Nairobi 1972-77; High Cmmr London 1978-; field cmnr Swaziland Boy Scots Assoc 1967-68, chief cnsllr of Order of Sobhuza II 1987; *Style*— HE Senator Hon George M Mamba; 64 Alyestone Ave, London NW6 (☎ 01 459 3372); Swaziland High Commission, 58 Pont St, London SW1

MAMO, Sir Anthony Joseph; OBE (1955); s of Joseph Mamo (d 1928), and Carla, *née* Brincat (d 1931); *b* 9 Jan 1909; *Educ* Archibishop's Seminary, Royal Univ of Malta (BA, LLD); *m* 1939, Margaret, da of Carmelo Agius (d 1943); 1 s (John), 2 da (Josephine, Monica); *Career* prof of criminal law Malta Univ 1943-57, attorney-gen (Malta) 1954-56; QC (Malta) 1957, chief justice and pres of Ct of Appeal Malta 1957-71; pres Constitutional Ct (Malta) 1964-71; pres Ct of Criminal Appeal 1967-71; govr-gen Malta 1971-74; pres Republic of Malta 1974-76; KStJ 1969; kt 1960; *Recreations* reading; *Clubs* Casino (1853); *Style*— Sir Anthony Mamo, OBE; 49 Stella Maris St, Sliema, Malta GC (☎ 330708)

MANASSEI DI COLLESTATTE, Hon Mrs Susan Barbara; *née* Addington; da of 7 Viscount Sidmouth; *b* 1945; *m* 1965 (m dis 1975), Count John Paul James Alessandro Camillo Manassei di Collestatte, s of Count Alessandro Manassei di Collestatte and Lady Maryel de Wichfield, nee Drummond, da of 16 Earl of Perth and Hon Angela Constable-Maxwell, da of 11 Lord Herries of Terregles; 1 s, 1 da; *Style*— The Hon Mrs Susan Manassei di Collestatte; 27 Ellerby St, London SW6

MANATON, John Westacott; s of William Alfred Westacott Manaton, and Linda Maud, *née* Townsend; *b* 10 Jan 1926; *Educ* Dulwich, Downing Coll Cambridge; *m* 23 June 1951, Mavis June, da of Frederick George Langton (d 1959), of Dartford, Kent; 1 da (Gillian Clare b 15 May 1964); *Career* Fleet Air Arm RN 1945-47; Lt Inns of Ct Regt and 3/4 Co of London Yeo (Sharpshooters) TA; Royal Exchange Assur 1947-51, Legal & Gen Assur Soc Ltd 1951-56, Canada Life Assur Co Ltd 1956-59, Scottish Provident Inst 1959-63, pensions mangr Nat Mutual Life Assoc of Australasia Ltd 1964-67; gen mangr (UK) Swiss Life Insur and Pension Co 1967-89; Freeman City of London 1980, Liveryman Worshipful Co of Actuaries 1980; AIA 1968, FPMI 1976; *Recreations* sailing (yachtmaster); *Clubs* Little Ship; *Style*— John Manaton, Esq; 2 Blair Drive, Sevenoaks, Kent TN13 3JR (☎ 0732 458528); Swiss Life Insurance and Pension Co, 101 London Rd, Sevenoaks, Kent (☎ 0732 450161, fax 0732 463801)

MANCE, Lady; Joan Erica Robertson; *née* Baker; *m* 1940, Sir Henry Mance (d 1981, chm of Lloyd's 1968-72, md Lloyd's Life 1971-81 and dep chm and tres Lloyd's Register Shipping 1979-81); 1 s, 3 da; *Style*— Lady Mance; 6 West Heath Lodge, Branch Hill, Hampstead, London NW3 7LU (☎ 01 435 7703)

MANCE, Jonathan Hugh; QC (1982); s of Sir Henry Stenhouse Mance (d 1981), and Lady Joan Erica Robertson *née* Baker; *b* 6 June 1943; *Educ* Charterhouse, Univ Coll Oxford (LLB); *m* 26 May 1973, M/s Mary Howarth Arden, QC, da of Lt-Col Eric Cuthbert Arden (d 1973); 1 s (Henry b 1982), 2 da (Abigail b 1976, Jessica b 1978); *Career* barr; *Recreations* tennis, music, languages; *Clubs* Cumberlan LTC; *Style*— Jonathan Mance Esq, QC; 7 King's Bench Walk, Temple, London EC4Y 7DS (☎ 01 583 0404, telex: 88791 KBLAW, fax: 01 583 0950)

MANCERA, Rafael Joaquin; s of Rafael Mancera, of Mexico City, and Guadalupe de Arrigunaga de Mancera; *b* 19 August 1956; *Educ* Universidad Iberoamericana, Northwestern Univ (MBA); *m* 3 July 1982, Katherine, da of Vaden Fitton, of Hamilton Ohio, USA; 1 s (Eduardo b 1988), 2 da (Katherine b 1985, Luisa b 1987); *Career* vice pres Banco Nacional de Mexico 1977-85, dep md Int Mexican Bank Ltd 1985- (seconded by Banco Nacional de Mexico); *Recreations* squash, classical music; *Style*— Rafael Mancera, Esq; 29 Gresham St, London EC2V 7ES (☎ 01 600 0880, fax 01 600 9891, telex 881 1017)

MANCHESTER, Andrea, Duchess of; Andrea; *née* Joss; da of Cecil Alexander Joss, of Johannesburg; *m* 1, G J W Kent; m 2, 1978, as his 2 w, 11 Duke of Manchester (d 1985); *Style—* Her Grace Andrea, Duchess of Manchester; PO Box 24667, Karen, Kenya

MANCHESTER, 12 Duke of (GB 1719); Angus Charles Drogo Montagu; also Baron Kimbolton (E 1620) and Earl of Manchester (E 1626, cr three days after Charles I's coronation); s of 10 Duke, OBE (d 1977; himself tenth in descent from the 2 Earl of Manchester, a Parly Cdr in the Great Rebellion, being Cromwell's immediate superior at Marston Moor) and his 1 w, Nell; suc bro, 11 Duke (d 1985); *b* 9 Oct 1938; *Educ* Gordonstoun; *m* 1961 (m dis 1970), Mary Eveleen, da of Walter Gillespie McClure, of Geelong, Vic, Australia; 2 s, 1 da; m 2, 1971 (m dis 1985), Diane Pauline, da of Arthur Plimsaul, of Wimborne, Dorset; m 3, 27 Jan 1989, Mrs Ann-Louise Bird, da of Dr Alfred Butler Taylor, of Cawthorne, S Yorkshire; *Heir* s, Viscount Mandeville; *Career* business conslt; pres and patron The Duke's Tst; *Recreations* golf; *Style—* His Grace the Duke of Manchester; House of Lords, Westminster, London SW1

MANCHESTER, Elizabeth, Duchess of; Elizabeth; da of Samuel C Fullerton, of Miami, Oklahoma; *m* 1, W W Crocker; m 2, 1969, as his 2 w, 10 Duke of Manchester (d 1977); *Style—* Her Grace Elizabeth, Duchess of Manch; PO Box 303, Pebble Beach, California 93953, USA; Ca Vendramin, 13 Giudecca, 30123 Venice, Italy (☎ 5207 746)

MANCHESTER, 9 Bishop of (cr 1847), 1979-; Rt Rev Stanley Eric Francis Booth-Clibborn; s of Eric Booth-Clibborn and Lucille; *b* 20 Oct 1924; *Educ* Highgate Sch, Oriel Coll Oxford (MA), Westcott Ho Cambridge; *m* 1958, Anne Roxburgh, da of late Prof W R Forrester, 2 s, 2 da; *Career* serv WWII RA and Royal Indian Artillery, temp Capt; curate of Heeley, Diocese of Sheffield, of the Arrercliffe Parishes; trg offr Christian Cncl Kenya 1956-63, ed-in-chief E African Venture Christian Papers (Target and Lengo) 1963-67, ldr Lincoln City Centre Team Miny 1967-70, vicar of Great St Mary's Cambridge 1979, bishop of Manchester 1979-, moderator of Movement for the Ordination of Women in C of E to 1982; memb Int Affairs Ctee Br Cncl of Churches 1968-79, leader BCC delgn to Namibia 1982; *Recreations* tennis, reading, listening to music; *Clubs* Royal Cwlth Soc; *Style—* The Rt Rev the Bishop of Manchester; Bishops Ct, Bury New Rd, Manchester M7 OLE (☎ 061 792 2096/1779)

MANDELSON, Hon Mrs (Mary Joyce); da of Baron Morrison of Lambeth (Life Peer; d 1965); *b* 1921; *m* 1, 1941 (m dis 1948), Horace Williams (afterwards The Hon Horace Williams), s of Baron Williams of Barnburgh (Life Peer); m 2, 1948, George Mandelson (d 1988); 2 s; *Style—* The Hon Mrs Mandelson; 12 Bigwood Rd, London NW11

MANDER, Sir Charles Marcus; 3 Bt (UK 1911), of the Mount, Tettenhall, Co Stafford; s of Maj Sir Charles Mander, 2 Bt, TD, JP, DL (d 1951), and Monica Claire, *née* Cotterell (d 1963); *b* 22 Sept 1921; *Educ* Eton, Trinity Coll Cambridge; *m* 1945, Maria Dolores Beatrice, da of Alfred Brödermann (decd), of Hamburg (d 1923); 2 s, 1 da; *Heir* s, Charles Nicholas Mander; *Career* serv WWII, Capt Coldstream Gds; dir: Mander Bros Ltd 1948-58, Headstaple Ltd 1976, Arlington Securities (chm 1976-82, dep chm 1982-83); chm London & Cambridge Investmts Ltd; underwriting memb of Lloyd's; High Sheriff Staffs 1962; Liveryman Fishmongers Co; *Recreations* yachting, shooting, music; *Clubs* Boodle's, Royal Thames Yacht; *Style—* Sir Charles Mander, Bt; Little Barrow, Moreton-in-Marsh, Glos (☎ 0451 30265); 6 Greville Ho, Kinnerton St, London SW1 (☎ 01 235 1669)

MANDER, David Charles; s of Alan Mander, of 5 Charlecote, Warwicks, and Muriel Betty, *née* Whitemann (d 1975); *b* 16 April 1938; *Educ* Wrekin Coll Salop, Univ Birmingham (LLB); *m* 6 Sept 1962, Elizabeth Ann, da of Frederick William Thorn; 2 s (Philip James b 1964, Nicholas David b 1967), 1 da (Charlotte Louise b 1972); *Career* slr sr ptnr Mander Hadley & Co Slrs; dir Warwicks Law Soc Ltd 1969-; cncl memb: Warwicks Law Soc (sec 1969-72), Birmingham Law Soc 1972-80, The Law Soc for constituency of W Midlands W Mercia and Welsh Marshes 1980; chm: Law Soc Indemnity Insur Ctee 1986-87, Coventry diocesan Tstees 1985-; dir and chm Slrs Indemnity Fund Ltd 1987-; Freeman City of Coventry; *Recreations* golf, fell walking; *Clubs* The Law Soc Chancery Lane WC2; *Style—* David C Mander, Esq; Whitestitch House, Great Packington, Nr Meriden, Warwickshire CV7 7JW (☎ 0676 22362); Mander Hadley & Co, 1 The Quadrant, Coventry CV1 2DW (☎ 0203 631212, fax 0203 633131, telex 312290)

MANDER, John; VRD (1964); s of Thomas Goddard Mander, OBE, JP (d 1959), of 10 Park Lane, Sheffield, and Edith Alice Ruth, *née* Bland (d 1987); *b* 5 August 1924; *Educ* Dean Close Sch Cheltenham, Emmanuel Coll Cambridge (MA, MB, BChir); *m* 24 July 1957, Mary Josephine (d 1968), da of Cornelius Clifford (d 1961), of Ballard, Tralee, Co Kerry; 2 s (Philip b 1960, Brian b 1964), 2 da (Jane b 1961, Maria (Mrs Coveney) b 1962); *Career* Surgn Lt RNVR 1949, lectr aviation med Gosport 1950-51, Surgn Lt Cdr 1965, ret 1977-; house offr 1948-54: UCH, Queen Charlotte's Hosp, Soho Hosp for Women; registrar St Thomas' Hosp 1955-56, sr registrar Chelsea Hosp for Women and Queen Charlotte's Hosp 1956-60, clinical asst Royal Marsden Hosp and St Paul's Hosp, conslt obstetrician and gynaecologist York 1960-; FRSM, FRCS 1958, FRCOG 1969; *Recreations* sailing, tennis, walking; *Clubs* Naval, Yorkshire, Island Cruising; *Style—* John Mander, Esq, VRD; 99 Station Rd, Upper Poppleton, York (☎ 0904 794447); 28 High Petergate, York (☎ 0904 32983)

MANDER, His Hon Judge Michael Harold; s of Elisha Harold Mander, of Cumberland (d 1984), and Ann, *née* Moores (d 1960); *b* 27 Oct 1936; *Educ* Workington GS, The Queen's Coll, Oxford, MA (Oxon); *m* 6 Aug 1960, Jancis Mary, da of The Rev Charles William Dodd of Eaton Constantine (d 1974); *Career* RA 2nd Lt 1955-57; slr 1963-72; barr (Inner Temple) July, 1972; in practise Birmingham 1972-85, asst recorder 1982-85; dep chm of Agric Lords Tbnl 1983-85; CJ 1985-; *Recreations* life under the Wrekin; *Clubs* East India, Wrekin Rotary (Hon memb); *Style—* His Honour Judge M H Mander; Garmston, Eaton Constantine, Shrewsbury, SY5 6RL (☎ (0952) 89 288)

MANDER, Michael Stuart; s of James Charles Stuart Mander (d 1974), and Alice Patricia Mander (d 1964); *b* 5 Oct 1935; *Educ* Tonbridge Sch, Hackley New York; *Career* publisher; chm and chief exec Thomson Info Servs Ltd 1985-86; chm Int Thomson Publishing Ltd 1984-86; dir Int Thomson Org plc 1983-86 Thomson Directories 1983-, Hill Samuel & Co Ltd; vice-chm Advertising Assoc 1983-87; pres Nat Advertising Benevolent Soc 1985-1986, vice pres Periodical Publishers Assoc 1985-, chm Market Anaylsis and Information Database Systems Ltd; IOD 1976; *Recreations* sailing (yacht 'Mon Tour'), skiing, golf; *Clubs* Royal Southern Yacht, Royal Wimbledon Golf; *Style—* Michael Mander, Esq; 41 Rivermill, Grosvenor Rd, London SW1V 3JN (☎ 01 821 9651); Hill Samuel & Co Ltd, 100 Wood St, London EC2P 2AJ (☎ 01 628 8011)

MANDER, (Charles) Nicholas; s and h of Sir Charles Marcus Mander, 3 Bt; *b* 23 Mar 1950; *Educ* Downside, Trinity Coll Cambridge (Scholar MA); *m* 1972, Karin Margareta, da of Gustav Arne Norin (d 1985), of Stockholm; 4 s, 1 da; *Career* co dir (various publishing, educnl land and property devpt cos); farming, holiday cottages and forestry, Lloyd's underwriter 1972; fndr ptnr of Mander Portman Woodward (private tutors) in Kensington; liveryman Fishmongers' Co; proprietor of Owlpen, a Tudor Manor House (reputed to have oldest garden in England) 1974-; fndr dir Alan Sutton Publishing Ltd 1976-; *Recreations* humane letters and arts, conversation, dreaming; *Clubs* Boodle's; *Style—* Nicholas Mander, Esq; Owlpen Manor, nr Dursley, Gloucs GL11 5BZ (☎ 0453 860261, telex 43690 OWLPEN G)

MANDL, George Thomas; s of Dr Gottfried Mandl (d 1941); *b* 8 August 1923; *Educ* Secdy Schs in Czechoslovakia and Switzerland, Sir George Monoux GS London, Prague Univ; *m* 14 April 1987, Uschi, da of Ernst Klingberg; *Career* active serv France 1944-56; chm: Thomas & Green Hldgs Ltd and subsidiary cos, Fourstones Paper Mill Co Ltd, Papierfabrik Netstal AG Switzerland, GT Mandl & Co A/S Denmark; dep chm: Linthesa Hldg AG, Linthkraft AG Switzerland; dir Indupa NV Belgium; ct memb Stationers' Co; Paper Indust Gold Medal 1981; Medal of Merit (Military Divn) of Czechoslovakia 1945; *Books* 300 Years in Paper (1985); *Recreations* skiing, collecting books and manuscripts, paper making history; *Clubs* City Livery; *Style—* George Mandl, Esq; 2 The Orchard, Town Lane, Wooburn Green, High Wycombe, Bucks HP10 0PP (☎ 06285 25051); CH-8754 Netstal, Switzerland (☎ 058 61 3836); Thomas & Green Holdings Ltd, Soho Mill, Wooburn Green, High Wycombe, Bucks HP10 0PP (☎ 06285 22881, fax 06285 31450, telex 847580 Thomas G)

MANDLEBERG, (Charles) John; s of Brig Lennard Charles Mandleberg, CBE, DSO, MC, TD (d 1975), of Lochinver, Sutherland, and Marjorie Helen, *née* Craig (d 1975); *b* 22 Jan 1922; *Educ* Harrow Sch, New Coll Oxford (MA, BSc); *m* 28 Dec 1945, Felicity Joyce, da of Meyrick Frederick Legge Beebee, of Walton Radnorshire; 1 s (Charles Andrew b 1950), 1 da (Alison Mary b 1953); *Career* Capt RA 1942-46 N Africa, Italy, Greece; dir: Reads Ltd 1966-75 (md 1970-75), Distributive Indust Trg Bd 1976-83; chm: Reads and Drums Ltd 1968-75, Reads Ltd 1984-88; church warden; memb of Middlewich Deanery Synod; FRSC; CChem; fellow Scottish Business Educn Cncl (Scotbec); chm Cheshire Beagle Hunt 1974-; vice-chm Cheshire County BFSS; *Books* Topics in Modern Chemistry (1964), papers in JCS, Phil Mag, J Inorg Nucl Chem Patents etc; *Recreations* field sports; *Clubs* Whites; *Style—* John Mandleberg, Esq; Ruloe House, Cuddington, Northwich, Cheshire CW8 2TW (☎ 0606 F52284)

MANDUCA, Paul Victor Sant; s of Victor Sant Manduca of Weybridge, Surrey and Elizabeth (d 1960); *b* 15 Nov 1951; *Educ* Harrow, Hertford Coll Oxford (BA); *m* 1982, Dr Ursula, da of Edmund Vogt of Jollenbeck, nr Bielefeld W Germany; 2 s (Mark b 1983, Nicholas b 1988); *Career* md Tr Indus and General plc 1986 (takeover 198, resigned), dir TR Tstees Corpn plc 1986, dir Clydesdale JT plc (resigned 1989), vice-chm Touche Remnant Hldgs 1987-; *Recreations* golf, squash ; *Clubs* Wentworth, Landsdowne; *Style—* Paul Manduca, Esq; 54 Brompton Sq, London SW3 (☎ 01 584 3987); Mermaid House, 2 Puddle Dock, London EC4 (☎ 01 236 6565, fax 01 248 9756, telex 885703)

MANGEOT, Fowke Jean André; s of André Louis Mangeot (d 1970), of 21 Cresswell Place, London SW10, and Olive Summerley Rede, *née* Fowke (d 1969); *b* 18 April 1911; *Educ* Westminster; *m* 20 Nov 1954, (Erica) June Leslie, da of Gp-Capt Eric Mackay Murray, DSO, MC (d 1954), of Inches, Battledown, Cheltenham, Glos; 1 s (Andrew Rede Fowke b 15 Nov 1955), 1 da (Louise Rose Everest b 18 July 1958); *Career* Home Gd 1942-44; Price Waterhouse & Co: articled clerk 1928-33, qualified CA 1933-38; mgmnt conslt Prodn Engrg Ltd 1938-47, chief accountant Dowty Equipment Ltd 1947-49, (commercial dir 1949-62), jt md Elliot-Flight Automation Ltd 1962-70, fin dir GEC Avionics Ltd 1970-76; hon tres Aldenburgh GC; ACA 1933, AIPE 1948, companion Royal Aeronautical Soc 1953, FCA 1960; *Recreations* squash, tennis, sailing, golf, reading; *Clubs* Rye GC, Aldeburgh GC; *Style—* Fowke Mangeot, Esq; The Crows Nest, North End Ave, Thorpeness, Leiston, Suffolk IP16 4PD (☎ 0728 452042)

MANGHAM, Maj-Gen (William) Desmond; CB (1978); s of Lt-Col William Patrick Mangham (d 1973), and Margaret Mary, *née* Donnachie (d 1965); *b* 29 August 1924; *Educ* Ampleforth Coll; *m* 1960, Susan, da of Col Henry Brabazon Humfrey (d 1964); 2 s (Mark b 1962, Benedict b 1971), 2 da (Catherine b 1965, Marie b 1966); *Career* 2 Lt RA 1943, served India, Malaya 1945-48, BMRA 1 Div Egypt 1955, staff HQ ME, Cyprus 1956-58, instr Staff Coll Camberley and Canada 1962-65, OC 3 Regt RHA 1966-68, Cdr RA 2 Div 1969-70, RCDS 1971, COS 1 Br Corps 1972-74, GOC 2 Div 1974-75, VQMG MOD 1976-79; Col Cmdt: RA 1979; RHA 1983; dir of the Brewers' Soc 1979; *Recreations* shooting, golf, tennis; *Clubs* Army & Navy; *Style—* Maj-Gen Desmond Mangham, CB; Redwood House, Woolton Hill, Nr Newbury, Berks (☎ 0635 253460); The Brewers' Soc, 42 Portman Square, London W1H 0BB (☎ 01 486 4831, telex 261948, fax: 01 935 3991)

MANGOLD, Tom - Thomas Cornelius; s of Dr Fritz Mangold (d 1957), and Dorothea Stephanie Mangold (d 1986); *b* 20 August 1934; *Educ* Dorking GS; *m* 1972, Valerie Ann Hare, da of Keith Dean (d 1979); 3 da (Sarah b 1965, Abigail b 1975, Jessica b 1979); *Career* served RA BAOR; with Sunday Mirror 1958-62, Daily Express 1962-64; reporter: BBC TV News 1964-70, BBC TV current affairs and several investigative documentaries 1970-76; television reporter BBC TV Panorama 1976-; *Books* The File on the Tsar (co-author, 1976), The Tunnels of Cu Chi (co-author 1985); *Recreations* reading, writing, playing blues harmonica; *Style—* Tom Mangold, Esq; c/o BBC TV, Lime Grove, London W12 7RJ (☎ 01 743 8000)

MANGRIOTIS, Hon Mrs (Anne Margaret); da of Maj Sir Arthur Lindsay Grant, 11 Bt (ka 1944), and Baroness Tweedsmuir of Belhelvie (Life Peeress d 1978); *b* 1937; *Educ* Lady Margaret Hall Oxford; *m* 1965, Nicolas Mangriotis; 2 s; *Style—* The Hon Mrs Mangriotis; 57 Ypsilantou St, Athens, 140 Greece

MANKIEWICZ, Joseph Leo; s of Prof Frank Mankiewicz (d 1941), and Johanna, *née* Blumenau (d 1943); *b* 11 Feb 1909; *Educ* Columbia Univ (BA), Yale Univ; *m* 1, 1939, Rosa Stradner (d 1958); 2 s, (1 s by previous m); m 2, 1962, Rosemary Helen Joan, da of Hubert John Matthews, Archdeacon of Hampstead 1950-62 (d 1971); 1 da (Alexandra Kate); *Career* writer, film dir 1929-; pres of Screen Dirs Guild (1950); first awards for both direction and screenplay Motion Picture Academy 1949 and 1950, screen dir awards 1949 and 1950, Br Film Academy 1950, NY Critics Award 1950; dir La Bohème for Metropolitan Opera 1952; Films include; Philadelphia Story, Woman of the Year, Julius Caesar, Keys of the Kingdom, A Letter to Three Wives, All About Eve, Suddenly Last Summer, Guys and Dolls, Sleuth; *Retrospectives* Cinemathèque Française (1967), Br Film Institute (1960 and 1982); *author* All About Eve (screenplay, 1951), More About All About Eve (colloquy, 1972); Erasmus Award, City of Rotterdam, 1984; D W Griffith Award, Dirs Guild of America 1986; Alexander Hamilton Medal Columbia Coll NYC 1986; Golden Lion Award Venice Film Festival 1987; Retrospective Hommage Cinematheque Français 1987; Cinemateque Municipale Retrospective City of Luxembourg 1987; Cdr Order of Merit (Italy) 1965; assoc fell Yale Univ; Chevalier de la Legion d'Honneur (France) 1988; *Recreations* theatrical history, golf, travel; *Clubs* Bedford GC and Tennis (NY); *Style—* Joseph Mankiewicz, Esq; 491 Guard Hill Rd, RFD 1, Bedford, New York 10506, USA

MANKIN, Robert Michael; s of James William Mankin (d 1969), of Coventry, and Margaret Florence, *née* Lewin; *b* 21 Nov 1936; *Educ* The Coventry Sch; *m* 29 Sept 1968, Megan Christine, da of Arthur Samuel Frank Langridge, of Bournemouth; 1 s (James b 1977), 1 da (Elizabeth b 1972); *Career* CA 1959 (RSA silver medal 1956); dir: Bridport Gundry plc 1978-81, Datafit Ltd 1985-, Dillon Technol Ltd 1985-, Microscribe Ltd 1986-, March Med plc 1987-, Curran Gp Ltd 1987-, Cotton Commercial Ltd 1988-, David Lunan Ltd 1986-87, Percell Gp Ltd 1985-87; *Recreations* walking, reading, crosswords, social events; *Style—* Robert Mankin, Esq; Oaklawn, 1 Childs Hall Close, Gt Bookham, Leatherhead, Surrey KT23 3QE (☎ 0372 57838, car ☎ 0836 239 539)

MANKTELOW, Rt Rev Michael Richard John; *see*: Basingstoke, Bishop Suffragan of

MANLEY, Brian William; s of Gerald William Manley (d 1950), of Eltham, London, and Ellen Mary, *née* Scudder (d 1965); *b* 30 June 1929; *Educ* Shooters Hill GS, London Univ, Woolwich Poly (BSc), Imperial Coll (DIC); *m* 1 May 1954, Doris Winifred, da of Alfred Dane (d 1966), of Eltham, London; 1 s (Gerald b 1958), 1 da (Susan b 1955); *Career* RAF 1947-49; Mullard Res Laboratories 1954-68, commercial gen mangr Mullard Ltd 1971-75; md: Pye Business Communications Ltd 1975-77, TMC Ltd 1977-82, Philips Data Systems Ltd 1979-82; gp md Philips Business Systems 1980-83, chm and md MEL Def Systems 1983-86, dir for telecommunications defence electronics & res Philips Electronic & Assoc Industs Ltd 1983-87; chm: AT&T Network Systems (UK) Ltd 1986-, Pye Telecommunications Ltd 1984-87; pres Telecommunications Engrg & M/rg Assoc 1985-86, vice-pres Inst of Electrical Engrs 1988-; cncl memb Inst of Manpower Studies 1986-, memb exec ctee Nat Electronics Cncl 1986-88, memb NEDO ctee Info Technol 1982-85, police scientific devpt ctee Home Off; represented England in swimming 1947-50; FInstP 1967, FIEE 1974, Fellowship of Engineering 1984; *Recreations* swimming, walking, gardening; *Clubs* Naval and Military; *Style—* Brian Manley, Esq; Hopkins Crank, Ditchling Common, Sussex (☎ 0 4446 3734) AT&T Network Systems (UK) Ltd, Swindon Rd, Malmesbury, Wilts SN16 9NA (☎ 0666 822 861)

MANLEY, Bruce; s of Maj William Arthur Reginald Ivor Manley (d 1973), of Bacton, Hereford, and Gwendoline Deidamia, *née* Trewhella; *b* 1 Oct 1940; *Educ* Downside; *m* 1, 28 Oct 1968 (m dis 1975), Alison Dudley Ward; 2 s (Edward b 1969, Dominic b 1970); *m* 2, 18 Nov 1978, Charlotte Mary Frances, o da of Cdr John Harford Stanhope Lucas-Scudamore, DL, RN, of Kentchurch Court, Hereford, and Lady Evelyn Patricia Mary, *née* Scudamore-Stanhope, da of 12 Earl of Chesterfield; 1 s (Harry b 1979); *Career* md Bacton Stud and farms; dir Probiotics Int Ltd; *Recreations* horseracing; *Style—* Bruce Manley, Esq; The Old Rectory, Bacton, Hereford HR2 OAP; Bacton Stud, Bacton, Hereford HR2 OAP (fax 0981 240 660, telex 35783 BACTON)

MANLEY, Ivor Thomas; CB (1984); s of Frederick Stone and Louisa Manley; *b* 4 Mar 1931; *Educ* Sutton HS Plymouth; *m* 1952, Joan Waite; 1 s, 1 da; *Career* entered Civil Serv 1951; princ: Miny of Aviation 1964-66, Miny of Technol 1966-68; private sec to: Rt Hon Anthony Wedgwood Benn 1968-70, Rt Hon Geoffrey Rippon 1970; princ private sec to Rt Hon John Davies 1970-71, asst sec Dept of Trade and Industry 1971-74, princ estab offr Dept of Energy 1974-78, under sec Atomic Energy Div 1978-81, memb UKAEA 1981-86; dep sec Dept of Energy 1981-87 and Dept of Employment 1987-; *Style—* Ivor Manley, Esq, CB; 28 Highfield Ave, Aldershot, Hants GU11 3BZ (☎ (0252) 22707)

MANN, Alexander Rupert; *qv*; s and h of Sir Rupert Edward Mann, 3 Bt; *b* 6 April 1978; *Style—* Alexander Mann Esq

MANN, David Francis Chadwick; s of William Frank Mann (d 1969), of London, and Clara Mann (d 1971); *b* 10 June 1924; *Educ* Alleyn's Sch Dulwich, LSE (MSc); *m* 8 May 1947, Daphne, da of Sidney Bonny (d 1958), of Rochester, Kent; 2 s (Michael b 1950, Robert b 1952), 1 da (Margaret b 1950); *Career* Army 1943-45, Capt Royal Army Educnl Corps 1945-47, Army Emergency Reserve of Offrs 1947-69; ICI Ltd 1947-64 (latterly admin servs mangr agric div), Milk Mktg Bd 1964-84 (dir of admin, personnel and admin dir, latterly gp personnel dir); memb Industl Tbnls for England and Wales 1983-, vice pres Inst of Admin Mgmnt 1971-(chm 1969-71), chm of employers (alternating chm of cncl) Nat Jt Cncl for the Dairy Indust 1977-84, jt UK rep to ILO meeting on Food Industs 1978; chm (former sec and tres) The New Church Orphanage; memb: cncl exec and fin ctees The Industl Soc 1967-84 (chm and tstee pension fund 1984-), CBI SE Cncl 1980-84, Surrey Area Manpower Bd 1982-85, Merton and Sutton Health Authy 1986-, cncl (former pres, later chm) Swedenborg Soc; FInstAM 1960, FBIM 1977, FIPM 1982; *Books* Effective Adminstration (1967); *Recreations* walking, writing; *Clubs* Athenaeum, Nat Lib; *Style—* David Mann, Esq; Ashdown, Four Acres, Cobham, Surrey KT11 2EB (☎ 0932 62391)

MANN, David William; s of William James Mann (d 1966) of Trimley Saint, Mary, Suffolk and Mary Ann *née* Bloomfield (d 1987); *b* 14 June 1944; *Educ* Felixstowe County GS, Jesus Coll Cambridge (BA 1966, MA 1971); *m* 29 June 1969, Gillian Mary, da of Rev David Emlyn Edwards (d 1978) of Felixstowe, Suffolk; 2 s (Richard b 1972, Edward b 1975); *Career* computing systems conslt; CEIR (UK) Ltd (now SD-Scicon plc) 1966-69, joined Logica plc on its formation 1969 (mangr conslt 1971, mangr Advanced Systems Div 1972, dir Advanced Systems Gp 1976, md Logica Ltd 1979, (chm 1982), dep md and head of ops, Logica plc 1986 (md 1987); memb Cncl Br Computer Soc, memb Co of Info Technologists; *Recreations* walking, skiing, golf; *Style—* David Mann, Esq; Theydon Copt, Forest Side, Epping, Essex CM16 4ED; 64 Newman Street, London W1A 4SE (☎ 01 637 9111, fax: 01 637 0719)

MANN, Lady; Evelyn Aimée; da of Charles Richard Hughes (decd); *m* 1958, as his 2 w, Sir James Gow Mann, KCVO (d 1962); *Style—* Lady Mann; 23 Chapel St, SW1

MANN, Dr Felix Bernard; s of Leo William Mann (d 1956), and Caroline Lola Mann (d 1985); *b* 10 April 1931; *Educ* Shrewsbury Ho, Malvern Coll, Christ's Coll Cambridge, Westminster Hosp; *m* 1986, Ruth Csorba Von Borsai; *Career* doctor; fndr of the Med Acupuncture Soc; *Books* Acupuncture; the Ancient Chinese Art of Healing (2 edn, 1971), The Meridians of Acupuncture (1964), Atlas of Acupuncture (1966), Acupuncture; cure of many diseases (1971), Scientific Aspects of Acupuncture (1977), Textbook of Acupuncture (1987); *Recreations* walking in the countryside; *Clubs* RSM; *Style—* Dr Felix Mann; 15 Devonshire Place, London W1N 1PB (☎ 01 935 7575)

MANN, Dr Frederick (Francis) Alexander; CBE 1980; s of Richard Mann and Ida *née* Oppenheim; *b* 11 August 1907; *Educ* Univs of: Geneva, Munich, Berlin (Dr Jur), London (LLD); *m* 1933, Eleonore *née* Ehrlich (d 1980); 1 s 2 da; *Career* asst Berlin Faculty of Law 1929-33, int law conslt London 1933-46, admitted slr 1946; conslt Herbert Smith & Co 1984- (ptnr 1957 - 83); memb: legal div Allied Control Cncl Berlin 1946, Lord Chancellors Standing Ctee on Place of Payment Cncl of Europe 1968-71; lectr: Acad of Int Law at the Hague (1959, 1964, 1971 and 1984) and at num Univs in England, Austria, Belgium, Germany, Switzerland, Japan, and USA; hon prof: Univ of Birmingham 1985-87, Univ of Bonn 1960-; fell Br Acad 1974, hon Dr Jur: Kiel 1978, Zurick 1983; Alexander von Humboldt Prize 1984; Grand Cross of Merit W Germany 1977 (with Star 1982); *Books* The Legal Aspect of Money (1938, 1953, 1982), Studies in International Law (1973), Foreign Affairs in English Courts (1986); num articles on int law and monetary law in Eng and foreign jnls;; *Recreations* music, walking; *Clubs* Athenaeum; *Style—* Dr Francis Mann, CBE; Flat 4, 56 Manchester St, London W1 M5PA (☎ 01 487 4735)

MANN, (Francis) George; CBE (1983), DSO (1942), MC (1941); s of Capt Francis Thomas Mann (d 1964; 3 s of Sir Edward Mann, 1 Bt who was chm of Mann Crossman & Paulin, and of Brandon's Putney Brewers), and Enid Agnes, *née* Tilney; *b* 6 Sept 1917; *Educ* Eton, Pembroke Coll Cambridge (BA); *m* 1949, Margaret Hildegarde, *née* Marshall Clark; 3 s (Simon, Richard, Edward), 1 da (Sarah); *Career* served WWII Scots Gds (wounded); dir: Mann Crossman and Paulin, Watney Mann, Watney Mann and Truman Brewers 1946-77; non exec dep chm Extel Gp 1980-87; (dir 1977-87); Middlx CCC: first played 1937, capt 1948-49, pres 1983-88; captained England: SA 1948-49 NZ 1949; chm: Test and County Cricket Bd 1978-83, Cricket Cncl 1983;; *Clubs* MCC (pres 1984-85); *Style—* George Mann, Esq, CBE, DSO, MC; Great Farm House, West Woodhay, Newbury, Berks RG15 0BL (☎ 04884 243)

MANN, Cdr Graham Hargrave; s of Cdr Edgar H Mann (d 1969), and Wenonah Mann; *b* 26 June 1924; *Educ* RNC Dartmouth; *m* 1959, Carol Mary, da of Victor Leslie Seyd; 3 da; *Career* joined RN 1941; served: Atlantic, Arctic, Med, Korea; Capt HMS Crossbow 1960-62, ret Cdr 1962; head private client dept and ptnr Grieveson Grant & Co stockbrokers 1967-1986, conslt Binder Hamlyn CAs; *Recreations* yachting (helmsman 1958 Americas Cup Challenger 'Sceptre'; Olympic Yachting Teams: 1956, 1960, 1964), book collecting; *Clubs* Royal Yacht Sqdn; *Style—* Cdr Graham Mann, RN; 30, Stanley Rd, Lymington, Hampshire SO41 9SG (☎ 0590 74271); 138 Rivermead Court, London SW6 3SA (☎ 01 736 2263)

MANN, Jessica D E; da of Dr F A Mann, CBE, of London, and Eleonore, *née* Ehrlich (d 1980); *b* 13 Sept 1937; *Educ* St Paul's Girls' Sch, Newnham Cottage Cambridge (MA), Univ of Leicester (LLB); *m* 1 July 1959, Prof A Charles Thomas, s of D W Thomas (d 1959), of Cornwall; 2 s (Charles Richard Vivian b 1961, Martin Nicholas Caleb b 1963), 2 da (Susanna Charlotte Elizabeth b 1966, Lavinia Caroline Alice b 1971); *Career* writer and journalist; memb: Carrick dist Cncl 1972-78, Cornwall Area Health Authy 1976-78, Industl Tbnls 1977-86, SW Regnl Health Authy 1979-84, Med Practices Ctee 1982-87, Cornwall Family Practitioner Ctee 1985-; *Books* A Charitable End (1971), Mrs Knox's Profession (1972), The Only Security (1973), The Sticking (1974), Captive Audience (1975), The Eighth Deadly Sin (1976), The Stink of Death (1978), Funeral Sites (1982), No Man's Island (1983), Grave Goods (1985), A Kind of Healthy Grave (1986), Deadlier than the Male (1981); *Style—* Ms Jessica Mann; Lambessow, St Clement, Cornwall (☎ 0872 72980)

MANN, John Frederick; s of Frederick Mann (d 1972), and Hilda Grace *née* Johnson; *b* 4 June 1930; *Educ* Poole and Tavistock GS, Oxford Univ (MA), Univ of Birmingham; *m* 30 July 1966, Margaret, da of Herbert Frederick Moore, of Bridlington, Yorks; 1 s (David John b 6 Dec 1971), 1 da (Susan Margaret b 6 March 1970); *Career* Nat Serv RAF 1949-50; asst educn offr Essex CC 1965-67, dep educn offr Sheffield City Cncl 1967-78, sec Schools Cncl for Curriculum and Examination 1978-83, dir of educn London Borough of Harrow 1983-88, educn cnslt London Boroughs of Harrow and Camden 1988-; JP Sheffield Bench; memb: Nat Tst, Br Educn Mgmnt and Admin Soc; hon fell: Sheffield City Poly 1979, Coll of Preceptors 1986; FBIM, FRSA; *Books* Education (1979), Chapters in Education Administration (1988), Life & Death of Schools Council (1985), Chapters in Education Administration (1988); *Recreations* local history, theatre, writing; *Style—* John Mann, Esq; 109 Chatsworth Rd, London NW2 4BH (☎ 01 459 5419)

MANN, Hon Mr Justice; Sir Michael; QC (1972); s of Adrian Mann, CBE; *b* 9 Dec 1930; *Educ* Whitgift, King's Coll London (LLB, PhD); *m* 1957, Jean Bennett, MRCVS; 2 s; *Career* barr Gray's Inn 1953, bencher 1980, part-time legal asst FO 1954-56, law lectr LSE 1957-64 (asst lectr 1954-57), jr counsel to Land Cmmn 1967-71, Crown Ct recorder 1979-82, high ct judge 1982-88, Lord Justice of Appeal 1988-; inspector Vale of Belvoir Coal Inquiry 1979-80; fell Kings Coll 1984; kt 1982; *Books* (ed jtly) Dicey, Conflict of Laws, (7 ed 1957); Dicey & Morris, Conflict of Laws (8 ed 1967 to 10 ed 1980); *Clubs* Athenaeum; *Style—* The Hon Mr Justice Mann; Royal Cts of Justice, London WC2A 2LL

MANN, Rt Rev Michael Ashley; s of late Herbert George Mann and Florence Mary *née* Kelsey, MBE (d 1950); *b* 25 May 1924; *Educ* Harrow, RMC Sandhurst, Wells Theol Coll, Harvard Business Sch (AMP); *m* 25 June 1949, Jill Joan, da of Maj Alfred Jacques (d 1960), of Thanet; 1 s (Capt Philip Ashley Mann, 1 The Queen's Dragoon Gds, b 1 Aug 1950, ka 13 April 1975), 1 da (Dr Elizabeth Mann b 22 Aug 1950); *Career* 1 King's Dragoon Gds, served Italy 1943-44, Greece 1944-45, Middle East 1945, Palestine 1945-46, Capt 1945, Maj 1945; Colonial Admin Serv Nigeria 1946-55; ordained 1957, curate Newton Abbot 1957-59; vicar: Sparkwell 1959-62, Christ Church Port Harcourt 1962-67; dean Port Harcourt Social and Industl Project 1963-67, home sec Missions to Seamen 1967-69, canon Norwich Cathedral 1969-73 (vice-dean 1971-73), Bishop of Dudley 1973-76; Dean of Windsor, Domestic Chaplain to HM The Queen, Register of the Order of the Garter 1976-; tstee: Imperial War Museum,

Army Museums Ogilby Tst; cmmr Royal Hosp Chelsea, chm Friends Nat Army Museum, govr Harrow Sch (chm 1980-88); CBIM, FRSA; *Books* A Particular Duty, A Windsor Correspondence, And They Rode On, China 1860, Some Windsor Sermons; *Recreations* military history; *Clubs* Cavalry and Guards; *Style—* The Rt Rev Michael Mann; Lower End Farm Cottage, Eastington, Northleach GL54 3PN (☎ 0451 60 767); The Deanery, Windsor Castle, Berks SL4 1NJ (☎ 0753 865 561)

MANN, Patricia (Mrs Pierre Walker); *née* Mann; da of Charles Alfred Mann (d 1986), of Westcliff-On-Sea, Essex, and Marjorie Lilian, *née* Heath; *b* 26 Sept 1937; *Educ* Clifton HS for Girls, Bristol; *m* 23 June 1962, Pierre George Armand Walker, s of Lt Thomas George Walker (d 1969), of Paris and London; 1 da (Lucy b 26 June 1965); *Career* ed Consumer Affs 1974-; J Walter Thompson Co Ltd 1959-: int vice pres 1981-, head of external affrs J Walter Thompson Gp (UK) 1981-; dir: Woolwich Equitable Bldg Soc 1983-, UK Centre Econ and Enviromental Devpt 1984-, Valor plc 1985- (now Yale & Valor plc); memb: Cncl Ind Schs Careers Orgn 1983-86, Food Advsy Ctee 1986-, Gas Consumers Cncl 1986- (Nat Gas Consumer Cncl 1981-86), Kingman Ctee Enquiry Teaching of English 1987; govt Cam Educnl Fndn 1971-77; memb: cncl Advertising Standards Authy 1973-86, cncl Nat Advertising Benevolest Soc 1973-77, Awards Nomination Panel Royal TV Soc 1974-78, cncl Brunel Univ 1976-86 (memb ct 1976-); gov Admin Staff Coll Henley 1976-; FIPA 1966, FCAM 1979, CBIM 1986; *Recreations* word games; *Clubs* Reform, Women's Advertising London; *Style—* Miss Patricia Mann; J Walter Thompson Co Ltd, 40 Berkeley Sq, London W1X 6AD (☎ 01 629 9496, fax 01 493 8432 and 01 493 8418, telex 22871 JWT LDN 6)

MANN, Philip Ashley; TD (with Bar); s of Herbert George Mann (d 1955), and Mary, *née* Kelsey (d 1950); *b* 7 May 1919; *Educ* Harrow; *m* 1, 21 June 1941, Marjorie Elizabeth Eldridge (d 1979); 3 s (Christopher Ashley b 1942, Peter Ashley 1948, Alexander Ashley 1955); 1 da (Jennifer Ashley b 1944); m 2, 7 May 1980, Mary Paterson Scott; *Career* war serv 1939-46; 2 Lt The Middlesex Regt (DCO) TA 1937; Regtl Serv 1939-42; GSO III ALO & HQ Home Forces 1952-44; Staff Coll 1944; GSO 2 Carrier Born ALO & WO 1944-46; TA 1946-50; Rank Maj; dir and chm Mann Gp of Shipping & Tport Cos 1954; pres Fedn Int Des Voitures Anciennes 1972-77; *Recreations* philately, vintage motoring; *Clubs* Army and Navy, Vintage Sports Car (past pres); *Style—* Philip Mann, Esq; Riverside House, High St, Woolwich, London SE18 (☎ 01 854 8822)

MANN, (Thomas) Richard Edward; s of Thomas Conrad Mann, and Eileen Olive Mary, *née* Barrett (d 1979); *b* 6 May 1936; *Educ* Malvern Coll, Universite de Grenoble; *m* 28 April 1962, Josephine, da of Joseph Rex Pearson; 2 s (James b 1963, Andrew b 1964); *Career* brewery dir: Tamplins 1963-69, Mann Crossman and Paulin 1965-69, Watney Combe Reid 1968-69; dir: Watney Mann (London and Home Cos) Ltd 1969-77, Watneys (London) Ltd 1969-78; md: Watneys Southern Ltd 1969-81, Grand Metropolitan Community Servs Tst 1981-; *Recreations* skiing, golf, gardening, game shooting; *Clubs* Ski Club of GB, Seaford GC; *Style—* Richard Mann, Esq; Litlington Place, Litlington, Nr Polegate, E Sussex (☎ 0323 870330; Grand Metropolitan Community Servs Tst, 1 Gloucester Mansions, Gloucester Place, Brighton (☎ 0273 570170)

MANN, (Leslie) Roy; OBE (1980); s of Sidney Mann (d 1953), of Birmingham, and Gwendoline, *née* Rowney (d 1973); *b* 23 April 1929; *Educ* King Edward's Sch Birmingham, Univ of Birmingham (BSc); *m* 3 Sept 1955, Moira Jean, da of William Sim (d 1943), of Whitecraigs, Renfrewshire; 2 s (Alastair b 1956, Geoffrey b 1962), 1 da (Linda Strachan b 1959); *Career* chm: Northern Region CBI 1979-81, NE Industl Devpt Bd 1982-87, NE Open Learning Network 1984-88, Victor Products plc 1984-88 (dir of subsidiary companies), Northern Devpt Co Ltd 1986-88; ret 1988; *Recreations* numismatology, canal travel and history; *Style—* Roy Mann, Esq, OBE; Riverside, Wyre Piddle, Pershore, Worcestershire WR10 2JD (☎ 0368 556327)

MANN, Sir Rupert Edward; 3 Bt (UK 1905), of Thelveton Hall, Thelveton, Norfolk; s of Edward Charles Mann, DSO, MC (d 1959), and great nephew of Sir John Mann, 2 Bt (d 1971); *b* 11 Nov 1946; *Educ* Malvern; *m* 1974, Mary Rose, da of Geoffrey Butler, of Cheveley Cottage, Stetchworth, Newmarket, Suffolk; 2 s (Alexander, William); *Heir* s, Alexander Rupert Mann; *Career* farmer; *Clubs* Norfolk, MCC; *Style—* Sir Rupert Mann, Bt; Billingford Hall, Diss, Norfolk (☎ 0379 740314)

MANN, Lady; Yvonne Ella; da of William Stanley Stanton (decd), of Melbourne; *Educ* Tintern C of E GS, Melbourne Univ; *m* 1940, Hon Mr Justice (Sir Alan Harbury) Mann, MBE, QC (d 1970); *Career* slr Victoria 1938; chm UNICEF Papua New Guinea, memb cncl UNICEF Aust 1966-69, dir YWCA; memb cncl Tintern CEGGS 1950-57; exec ctee memb: Aust Asian Assoc of Victoria 1973-76, cncl memb Emily McPherson Coll Melbourne 1971-79; cncl memb Frenkston Mornington Peninsula Hospice Gp 1984-85; *Clubs* Frenkston Golf, The Peninsula Country, Canadian Bay Boat; *Style—* Lady Mann; Harbury, 69 Charles St, Mount Eliza, Victoria 3930, Australia

MANNERS, Lady Charlotte Louisa; da of 10 Duke of Rutland, CBE,; *b* 1947; *Style—* Lady Charlotte Manners; Belvoir Castle, Grantham (☎ Knipton 246); Haddon Hall, Derbyshire (☎ (062 981) 14)

MANNERS, Lord Edward John Francis; s of 10 Duke of Rutland, CBE, *qv*; *b* 29 May 1965; *Educ* Eton Coll, Edinburgh Univ; *Recreations* skiing, flying, fieldsports; *Style—* Lord Edward Manners; Belvoir Castle, Grantham, Lincs

MANNERS, Prof Gerald; s of George William Wilson Manners (d 1964), and Louisa Hannah, *née* Plumpton; *b* 7 August 1932; *Educ* Wallington Co GS, St Catharine's Coll Cambridge (MA); *m* 1, 11 July 1958 (m dis 1982), Anne, *née* Sawyer; 1 s (Christopher Winslow b 24 Oct 1962), 2 da (Carolyn Jarvis b 16 Jan 1961, Katharine b 26 April 1967); m 2, 11 Dec 1982, Joy Edith Roberta, *née* Turner; 1 s (Nicholas Robert b 12 May 1985); *Career* Nat Serv Flying Offr RAF 1955-57; UCL: lectr in geography 1957-67, reader in geography 1967-80, prof of geography 1980-; visiting scholar Resources for the Future INC Washington DC 1964-65, visiting fell Harvard-MIT Jt Center for Urban Studies 1972-73; govr Sadler's Wells Fndn 1978- (chm of Govrs 1986-); memb: central governing body City Parochial Fndn 1977 (chm estate ctee 1987-), Location of Offices Bureau 1970-80, SE Econ Planning Cncl 1971-79; specialist advsr to House of Commons Select Ctee on Energy 1980-; FRGS, MIBG, FRSA, FBIEE; *Books* Geography of Energy (1964), South Wales in the Sixties (1964), Changing World Market for Iron Ore (1971), Spatial Policy Problems of the British Economy (1971), Minerals and Man (1974), Regional Development in Britain (1974), Coal in Britain (1981), Office Policy in Britain (1986); *Recreations* music, dance, theatre, walking; *Style—* Prof Gerald Manners; 105 Barnsbury St, London N1 1EP (☎ 01 607 7920); University College London, Gower St, London WC1E 6BT (☎ 01 387 7050)

MANNERS, Lord John; s of 9 Duke of Rutland (d 1940); *b* 1922; *Educ* Eton, New Coll Oxford; *m* 1957, Mary Diana, da of Lt-Col L Geoffrey Moore, DSO (decd); 1 s, 2 da; *Career* 2 Lt Life Gds 1941; High Sheriff Leics 1973-74; *Clubs* Pratt's, White's; *Style—* Lord John Manners; Haddon Hall, Derbyshire (☎ 062 981 2014); Reservoir Cottage, Knipton, Grantham, Lincs (☎ 047 682 225)

MANNERS, Hon Willie - John Hugh Robert; s and h of 5 Baron Manners by his w Jennifer; *b* 5 May 1956; *m* 1983, Lanya Mary Jackson, da of late Dr H E Heitz, and Mrs Ian Jackson, and step da of Ian Jackson; 1 da (Harriet Frances Mary b 9 July 1988); *Career* slr; *Recreations* gardening, riding, shooting; *Clubs* Pratts; *Style—* The Hon Willie Manners; 14 North Ripley, Avon, nr Christchurch, Dorset

MANNERS, 5 Baron (UK 1807); John Robert Cecil Manners; s of 4 Baron Manners, MC, JP, DL (d 1972, himself ggs of 1 Baron, who was in his turn 5 s of Lord George Manners-Sutton, 3 s of 3 Duke of Rutland, KG), by his w Mary, twin da of Rt Rev Lord William Gascoyne-Cecil, DD, 65 Bishop of Exeter and 2 s of 3 Marquess of Salisbury, the Cons PM; *b* 13 Feb 1923; *Educ* Eton, Trinity Oxford; *m* 1949, Jennifer Selena, da of Stephen Fairbairn (whose w Cynthia was gggda of Sir William Arbuthnot, 1 Bt); 1 s, 2 da; *Heir* s, Hon John Hugh Robert Manners; *Career* joined RAFVR, Flying offr 1942, Fl Lt 1944; slr to Supreme Ct 1949, ptnr Osborne Clarke & Co (Slrs) Bristol; Official Verderer of the New Forest 1983-; *Clubs* Brooks's; *Style—* The Rt Hon The Lord Manners; Wortley Ho, Wotton-under-Edge, Glos (☎ 3174)

MANNERS, Lady; Kathleen Mary; da of James Miller Johnson, of Newcastle, NSW; *m* 1927, as his 2 w, Rear-Adm Sir Errol Manners, KBE (d 1953); *Style—* Lady Manners; Flat 53, 17 Wylde St, Potts Point, Sydney, NSW

MANNERS, Baroness; Mary Edith; da (twin) of the Rt Rev Lord William R Gascoyne Cecil, Bishop of Exeter (d 1936); *b* 1900; *m* 1921, 4 Baron Manners, MC (d 1972); 3 s, 1 da; *Style—* The Rt Hon Mary, Lady Manners; 1 Cranwell Close, Bransgore, Christchurch, Hants BH23 8HY

MANNERS, Hon Richard Neville; 2 s of 4 Baron Manners (d 1972); *b* 1924; *Educ* Eton; *m* 1945, Juliet Mary, da of Col Sir Edward Hulton Preston, 5 Bt, DSO, MC (decd); 3s, 1 da; *Style—* Hon Richard Manners; Cromer Hall, Norfolk

MANNERS, (Arthur Edward) Robin; s of Arthur Geoffrey Manners, and Betty Ursula Joan, *née* Rutter (d 1972); *b* 10 Mar 1938; *Educ* Winchester, Trinity Hall Cambridge; *m* 22 Oct 1966, Judith Mary, da of Lt-Col Francis William Johnston, MBE, of The Old Steading, Berkhamsted, Hertfordshire; 2 s (George b 1968, Richard b 1970); *Career* 2 Lt 10 Royal Hussars 1956-58, Maj Staffordshire Yeo 1958-68; Bass plc: joined 1961, dir 1983, chm Bass Brewing/Bass Malting 1983, Personnel dir 1984 ; *Recreations* golf, tennis, shooting, gardening, skiing; *Clubs* Cavalry and Guards'; *Style—* Robin Manners, Esq; The Old Croft, Bradley, Stafford ST18 9EF

MANNERS, Lord Roger David; s of 9 Duke of Rutland (d 1940); *b* 1925; *m* 1965, Finola St Lawrence, only da of T E Daubeney; 2 da; *Career* 2 Lt Grenadier Gds 1944; *Clubs* Pratts, Whites; *Style—* Lord Roger Manners; Marsh End Farm, Heddington, Calne, Wiltshire

MANNERS, Lady (Helen) Teresa Margaret; da of 10 Duke of Rutland, CBE; *b* 11 Nov 1962; *Style—* Lady Teresa Manners

MANNERS, Hon Thomas Jasper; s of 4 Baron Manners, MC (d 1972); *b* 1929; *Educ* Eton; *m* 1955, Sarah, er da of Brig Roger Peake, DSO, OBE (d 1959), of Little Missenden, Bucks; 3 s; *Career* dir Scapa Gp, Lazard Bros, Legal & Gen Gp, Mercantile Credit, Davy Corpn, Govett Oriental Investmt Tst; *Recreations* shooting, fishing; *Clubs* Whites, Pratts; *Style—* The Hon Thomas Jasper Manners; The Old Malt House, Ashford Hill, Newbury, Berks; 9 Cadogan Sq SW1

MANNING, Graham Ralph; s of James William Manning (d 1974), of Chelmsford, Essex, and Daisy Maud, *née* Warren; *b* 4 June 1943; *Educ* Chelmsford Tech HS; *m* 29 Sept 1966, Barbara, da of Cyril Alfred Burrough (d 1979), of Bradford; 2 s (James 1973, John 1978), 1 da (Joanne 1971); *Career* trainee CA 1960-66 Longcrofts, qualified CA 1966, supervisor Deloitte Haskins & Sells Montreal 1966-69, ptnr Buzzacott & Co 1970-79 (Mangr 1969-70); ptnr: McNally Manning & Co Ipswich 1979-83, Manning Hilder & Girling Ipswich 1983-; memb ICEAW; *Recreations* sailing, books, paintings; *Style—* Graham Manning, Esq; 16a Falcon St, Ipswich IP1 1SL (☎ 0473 599 84, fax 0473 599 88)

MANNING, Dr Jane Marian; da of Gerald Manville Manning (d 1987), of Norwich, and Lily, *née* Thompson; *b* 20 Sept 1938; *Educ* Norwich HS, Royal Acad of Music (GRSM, LRAM, ARCM), Scuola Di Canto Cureglia Switzerland; *m* 24 Sept 1966, Anthony Edward, s of Edward Alexander Payne, of London (d 1958); *Career* int career as soprano concert singer; London debut 1964, more than 250 world premieres, regular appearances in leading halls and festivals, Brussels Opera 1980, Scottish Opera 1978, numerous tours of Aust, NY debut 1981, first BBC broadcast 1965 (over 300 since), numerous recordings incl Messiaen Song Cycles; visiting prof Mills Coll Oakland California: 1981, 1983, 1986; visiting lectr: Harvard Univ, Stanford Univ, Princeton Univ, Yale Univ, York Univ, Cambridge Univ, Durham Univ; vice pres Soc for the Promotion of New Music, chm Nettlefold Festival Tst, exec ctee memb New MacNaghten concerts, ctee memb Musicians Benevolent Fund; Hon DUniv York Univ 1988; memb ISM, SPNM, FRCM 1984; *Books* New Vocal Repertory (1986); *Recreations* cinema, cookery, ornithology; *Style—* Dr Jane Manning; 2 Wilton Square, London N1 3DL (☎ 01 359 1593); 7 Park Terrace, Upperton Rd, Tillington, nr Petworth, W Sussex

MANNING, Patrick John Mannes (Paddy); s of Col Francis James Manning, TD, of Heathstock Cleeve, Wiveliscombe, Somerset, and Sarah Margaret, *née* Jenkins; *b* 16 July 1940; *Educ* Downside Sch, RMA Sandhurst; *m* 19 April 1986, Sally Gail, da of Maj Jeremy Green, of Bickmarsh Hall, Bideford-on-Avon, Warwicks; 1 da (Charlotte b 1987); *Career* Lt 4/7 Royal Dragoon Gds 1961-64, Royal Yeo 1965-72; stockbroker Laurence Keen & Gardner 1965-70, dir Charles Barker City Ltd 1970-80; dir of PR 1981-84, dir St James PR Ltd; hon PR advsr The Br Cwlth Ex-Servs League; MIPR 1974; *Recreations* shooting, opera; *Clubs* Cavalry and Guards; *Style—* Paddy Manning, Esq; Inglewood, Lower Wardington, Banbury, Oxfordshire; 49 Breer St, London, SW6 3HE; St James Public Relations, 4 Red Lion Ct, Fleet St, London, EC4A 3EB (☎ 01 583 2525, fax 01 583 2533)

MANNINGHAM-BULLER, Hon Elizabeth Lydia; 2 da of 1 Viscount Dilhorne, PC; *b* 14 July 1948; *Educ* Benenden Sch, LMH Oxford; *Style—* The Hon Elizabeth

Manningham-Buller

MANNINGHAM-BULLER, Hon James Edward; er s and h of 2 Viscount Dilhorne; *b* 20 August 1956; *Educ* Harrow, Sandhurst; *m* 4 May 1985, Nicola Marion, eldest da of Sven Mackie (d 1986), of Ballydugan House, Downpatrick, Co Down; *Career* Capt Welsh Guards 1976-84; Lloyd's Broker: Stewart Wrightson Surety & Specie Ltd 1984-86, Gibbs Hartley Cooper Ltd 1986-89; insurance broker McGuire Insurances Ltd; *Recreations* shooting, skiing; *Clubs* Pratts; *Style*— Capt The Hon James Manningham-Buller; Ballydugan House, Downpatrick, Co Down

MANNINGHAM-BULLER, Hon Mervyn Reginald; s of 2 Viscount Dilhorne; *b* 1962; *Style*— The Hon Mervyn Manningham-Buller

MANNINGS, William Anthony; s of William Edward Mannings (d 1965), of Claverton Down, Bath, and Helena Mary, *née* Stoffels (d 1961); *b* 2 Sept 1930; *Educ* King Edward Sch Bath; *m* 1 June 1957, June, da of Albert Edward Hill (d 1955), of Bath; *Career* Nat Serv Fleet Air Arm RN 1948-50; chm G Mannings and Sons Ltd 1965-, ptnr JW Knight and Son 1965-, dir Fred Daw Garden Centre (Bath) 1975- and (Trowbridge) 1980-, chm Lloyd Blackmore Ltd 1984-, chm Bath Investmt and Bldg Soc 1984-; pres Bath GC 1988-89 (capt 1962); govr King Edwards Sch Bath 1983-; FFB; *Recreations* golf; *Clubs* Bath GC; *Style*— William Mannings, Esq; Byfield, Winsley, Bradford on Avon, Wilts BA15 2HW (☎ 022122 2220); Oxford House, Combe Down, Bath, Avon (☎ 0225 837 955, fax 0225 834 385)

MANNION, Rosa; da of Patrick Anthony Mannion, of 16 Moorside Rd, Crosby, Liverpool, and Maria, *née* MacGregor; *b* 29 Jan 1962; *Educ* Seafield GS Crosby Liverpool, Royal Scottish Acad of Music and Drama (BA, RSAMD), with Patricia Boyer Kelly; *m* 13 July 1985, Gerard McQuade, s of Michael McQuade, of Cardonald, Glasgow; *Career* opera singer; debut L'Elisir d'Amore Scottish Opera 1984, princ Soprano Scottish Opera 1984-86, Buxton Festival 1986 and 1987; debut: Edinburgh Festival with Scottish Nat Orch 1985, ENO as Sophie in Der Rosenkavalier 1987, Glyndebourne Festival as Konstanze in Die Entführung aus dem Serail (sung first performance at 5 hours notice) 1988, Wigmore Hall 1988; winner Scottish Opera Int Singing Competition 1988, finalist Luciano Pavarotti Singing Competition 1985; *Recreations* tennis, swimming, cooking; *Style*— Ms Rosa Mannion; 23 Prospect Place, Epsom, Surrey (☎ 0372 723937); Lies Askonas, 186 Drury Lane, London (☎ 01 405 1809/1808)

MANS, Keith Douglas Rowland; MP (C) Wyre 1983-; s of Maj Gen Rowland Spencer Noel Mans, CBE, of Ivy Bank Cottage, Vinegar Hill, Off Barnes Lane, Milford on Sea, Hants, and Violet Ellen Mans, *née* Sutton; *b* 10 Feb 1946; *Educ* Berkhamsted Sch, RAF Coll Cranwell, Open Univ (BA); *m* 19 Aug 1972, Rosalie Mary, da of J McCann, of 22 Ullet Rd, Liverpool 8 (d 1977); 1 s (David, b 9 Sept 1982); 2 da (Louise, b 5 Nov 1980, Emma b 6 May 1986); *Career* former Flt Lt RAF; serv UK, Germany, Malta, Cyprus and Malaya; formerly Central Buyer for Electronics for John Lewis Ptnrship; former dep ldr New Forest DC (Dist cncllr 1983-87); memb House of Commons Select Ctee on the Environment, sec Cons Aviation Ctee; sch govr 1984-87; memb Royal United Servs Inst for Def Studies 1965; *Recreations* flying; *Clubs* Army and Navy, RAF; *Style*— Keith D R Mans, Esq, MP; House of Commons, London SW1A 0AA (☎ 01 219 6334/3436)

MANS, Maj-Gen Rowland Spencer Noel; CBE (1971, OBE 1966, MBE 1956); s of Thomas Frederick Mans (d 1954), of Bispham, Lancs, and May Frances, *née* Seigenberg (d 1975); *b* 16 Jan 1921; *Educ* Surbiton GS, RMC Sandhurst; *m* 6 Jan 1945, Veed Ellen, da of Frank Sutton (d 1951), of Southampton; 3 s (Keith b 1946, Mark b 1955, Lance b 1957); *Career* WWII Queens Royal Regt and Kings African Rifles 1939-45, Maj, serv E Africa, Madagascar, Palestine M East, Far East, Canada, Queen's Royal Regt 1939-76, Regtl and Staff appts 1945-69, Col, Cdr Aldershot A/ GOC SE District, Brig, brig dir Personnel Servs 1972-73, dir Mil Assistance Off 1973-76, Maj-Gen, Col Queen's Regt 1978-83; conslt Stewart Wrightson (now Willis Faber) 1976-, mil advsr Def Manufacturers Assoc 1976-, UK Assoc Burdeslaw Ltd (USA) 1988-; co cncllr Hampshire 1984-; pres New Forest Cons Assoc 1984-87; Freeman City of London; Knight Cdr: Dannebrog (Denmark) 1983, Orange & Nassau (Netherlands) 1983; *Books* Canada's Constitutional Crisis (1978), articles for jls in UK and USA; *Recreations* writing, gardening; *Clubs* Army and Navy, Royal Lymington YC; *Style*— Maj-Gen Rowley Mans, CBE; Ivy Bank Cottage, Vinegar Hill, Milford-on-Sea, Hants (☎ 0590 43982)

MANSEL, Rev Canon James Seymour Denis; KCVO (1979, MVO 1972), FSA; s of Edward Mansel, FRIBA (d 1941), of 17 Clarendon Sq, Leamington and Muriel Louisa Mansel (d 1956); *b* 18 June 1907; *Educ* Brighton Coll, Exeter Coll Oxford (MA); *m* 1942, Ann Monica Waterhouse (d 1974), 1 da; *Career* sub-dean of HM Chapels Royal, dep clerk of the Closet, sub-almoner and domestic chaplain to HM the Queen 1965-79, extra chaplain to HM the Queen 1979-; canon and prebendary of Chichester Cathedral 1971-81, canon Emeritus 1981-, asst priest St Margarets Westminster 1980, St M priest vicar Westminster Abbey 1983-; JP City of Winchester 1950-56, Inner London Cmmn 1964; FSA; CStJ; *Clubs* Athenaeum; *Style*— The Rev Canon James Mansel, KCVO; 15 Sandringham Ct, Maida Vale, London W9 1UA (☎ 01 286 3052)

MANSEL, Maj John Clavell; DL (Dorset 1974); s of Maj Rhys Clavell Mansel (d 1969), of Ropley Manor, Hants, and Sylvia Nina, *née* Campbell (d 1944); *b* 9 Jan 1917; *Educ* Eton, Ch Ch Oxford (MA); *m* 11 Aug 1945, Damaris Joan, da of Robert Hyde Hyde-Thomson (d 1970), of 36 Victoria Rd, London W8; 2 s (Richard b 1949, Philip b 1951), 1 da (Lavinia b 1946); *Career* enlisted 1 Bn RB 1938, 2 Motor Trg Bn and 10 RB 1939-41, 1 RB W Desert 1941-42, Capt 1942, HQ Persia Area and RAF Levies Iraq 1943-44, 10 RB Italy 1944-45, Staff Coll 1945-46, Maj 1946, GHQ MELF and HQ BTE 1946-49, 1 RB UK 1953-54, Green Jacket Depot Winchester 1954-56, 9 Trg Regt RE Cove 1956-58, ret 1958; pres: Wareham Dist Twinning Assoc 1978-88; Corfe Castle Branch Royal Br Legion 1977-, Corfe Castle Branch S Dorset Cons Assoc 1974-, Dorset Wildfowlers Assoc 1970-87; chm Dorset Historic Churches Tst 1974-84; memb for Kimmeridge of Wareham and Purbeck Dist Cncl 1958-74; High Sheriff of Dorset 1968-69, JP Wareham Div 1961-82 (chm 1980-82); *Recreations* general country living, occasional shooting; *Style*— Maj John Mansel, DL; Smedmore, Kimmeridge, Wareham, Dorset BH20 5PG (☎ 0929 480717)

MANSEL, Sir Philip; 15 Bt (E 1622), of Muddlescombe, Carmarthenshire; s of Sir John Philip Ferdinand Mansel, 14 Bt (d 1947); *b* 3 Mar 1943; *Educ* Grosvenor Coll Carlisle, Carlisle GS; *m* 24 Aug 1968, Margaret, da of Arthur Docker; 1 s, 1 da (Nicol); *Heir* s, John Philip Mansel b 19 April 1982; *Career* fell Inst of Sales Mgmnt; md Eden-Vale Engrg Co Ltd; *Style*— Sir Philip Mansel, Bt; 4 Redhill Drive, Fellside Park, Whickham, Newcastle upon Tyne

MANSEL LEWIS, David Courtenay; JP (1969); s of Charlie Ronald Mansel Lewis (d 1960), and Lillian Georgina (d 1982), da of Sir Courtenay Warner, 1 Bt; *b* 25 Oct 1927; *Educ* Eton, Keble Coll Oxford (MA); *m* 1953, Lady Mary, *qv*; 1 s, 2 da; *Career* Welsh Gds 1946-49, Lt 1948 RARO; High Sheriff Carmarthen 1965 (DL 1971, HM Lt 1973-74), Lord-Lt Dyfed 1979- (HM Lt 1974-79); KStJ; *Recreations* sailing (yacht 'Nandhi'), music; *Clubs* RYS, Lansdowne, Cruising Assoc; *Style*— David Mansel Lewis, Esq, JP, HM Lord Lt of Dyfed; Stradey Castle, Llanelli, Dyfed SA15 4PL (☎ 0554 774626); 53 New Rd, Llanelli, Dyfed (☎ 0554 773059)

MANSEL LEWIS, Lady Mary Rosemary Marie-Gabrielle; *née* Montagu-Stuart-Wortley; OBE (1983), JP (1974); da of 3 Earl of Wharncliffe (d 1953), and Lady Maud Lilian Elfrida Mary (d 1979), eldest da of 7 Earl Fitzwilliam; goddaughter of Princess Royal (decd); *b* 11 June 1930; *Educ* Heathfield; *m* 1953, David Courtenay Mansel Lewis, *qv*; 1 s (Patrick Charles Arhchibald b 1953), 2 da (Catherine Maud Leucha b 1956, Annabel Elfrida b 1962) 1 s, 2 da; *Clubs* Lansdowne; *Style*— Lady Mary Mansel Lewis, OBE, JP; Stradey Castle, Llanelli, Dyfed SA15 4PL (☎ 0554 774626)

MANSELL, Gerard Evelyn Herbert; CBE (1977); s of Herbert Goodinge Mansell, of Paris (d 1968), and Anne Marie Lintz (d 1985); *b* 16 Feb 1921; *Educ* Lycée Hoche Versailles, Lycée Buffon Paris, Ecole Libre des Sciences Politiques Paris, Chelsea Sch of Art London (Nat Dip in Design); *m* 1956, Diana Marion, da of Roland Crichton Shearr, of Burnham Market, Norfolk; 2 s; *Career* WWII 1940-46 (despatches), Royal Norfolk Regt and Durham LI, served Western Desert, Sicily, NW Europe; intelligence staff offr 50 Div and 8 Corps (Maj); joined BBC Euro Serv 1951, controller Radio 4 and music programme BBC 1965-69, dir of programmes Radio BBC 1970-71, md external broadcasting BBC 1972-80, dep dir-gen BBC 1977-80; chm: communications advsy ctee UK Nat Cmmn for UNESCO 1983-85, Friends of UNESCO 1986-87, CNAA, Br Ctee for Journalists in Europe, Jt Advsy Ctee for Trg of Radio Journalists 1981-87, New Hampstead Garden Suburb Tst 1984-; govr Falmouth Sch of Art and Design 1988-; French Croix de Guerre 1944; FRSA; *Books* Tragedy in Algeria (1961), Let Truth be Told (1982); *Style*— Gerard Mansell, Esq, CBE; 46 Southway, London NW11

MANSELL, Peter William; s of Douglas Vivian Mansell, Esq, of Hampshire, and Dorothy Wellington Mansell, *née* Peer; *b* 21 July 1955; *Educ* Queen Mary's Coll, Basingstoke; King's Coll Cambridge (MA); *m* 20 June 1979, Carolyn, da of Norman John Dredge, Esq, of Essex; 1 s (Stephen b 1986); *Career* md and actuary Royal Life Insur Int Ltd; FIA; *Style*— Peter Mansell, Esq, MA; Royal Life International, Bridge House, Castletown, Isle of Man (☎ 0624 824151, telex 627848 RYLINT, fax 0624 824405)

MANSELL-JONES, Richard Mansell; s of Arnaud Milward Jones, of Carmarthen (d 1964), and Winifred Mabel *née* Foot (d 1978); n of prof P Mansell-Jones (ed of the Oxford Book of French Verse); *b* 4 April 1940; *Educ* Queen Elizabeth's, Carmarthen, Private Tuition, Worcester Coll Oxford (MA); *m* 30 June 1971, Penelope Marion, da of Maj Sir David Hawley, BT, of Tumby Lawn, Boston, Lincolnshire; *Career* CA, memb Stock Exchange; dir Brown Shiply & Co Ltd 1974 (dep chm 1984) dir Brown Shipley Hldgs plc 1984, dir Barr and Wallace Arnold Tst plc 1984, dep chm J Bibby & Sons plc 1987 (dir 1978); *Recreations* art, music; *Clubs* Overseas Bankers; *Style*— Richard Mansell-Jones, Esq; Founders Court, Lothbury London EC2R 7HE (☎ 01 606 9833)

MANSELL-MOULLIN, Michael; s of Sqdn Ldr Oswald Mansell-Moullin (d 1964), and Mary Bagott Mansell-Moullin, *née* Green; *b* 8 Oct 1926; *Educ* St Edwards Sch Oxford, Jesus Coll Cambridge (MA, DIC); *m* 17 May 1969, Marion Elizabeth, da of Capt R L Jordan RN (d 1988); 1 s (David b 1972), 1 da (Jenny Melissa b 1976); *Career* Capt RE India & Pakistan 1944-49; chief hydrologist Binnie & Ptnrs consulting engrs 1959-69, conslt hydrologist UK and Int 1970-; fndr and pres-elect Br Hydrological Soc 1983-85; *Publications* contrib leading scientific jls on water resources and hydrological subjects; companion ICE, MIWEM, FRGS; *Recreations* sailing, hill walking, woodwork; *Clubs* Bosham Sailing; *Style*— Michael Mansell-Moullin, Esq; Old Hatch, Lower Farm Rd, Effingham, Surrey KT24 5JL (☎ 0372 52 672)

MANSER, Michael John; s of Edmund George Manser (d 1971), and Augusta Madge, *née* Bonell (d 1987); *b* 23 Mar 1929; *m* 1953, Dolores Josephine, da of Isadore Bernini; 1 s (Jonathan), 1 da (Victoria); *Career* Nat Service RE, Staff Capt; chartered architect; pres RIBA 1983-85, memb cncl RSA; archtectural awards: Civic Tst Award, Civic Tst Commendation, Euro Heritage Year Award, DOE Commendation for Good Design in Housing, Steel Award Commendation, RIBA Award Commendation; architectural journalism, radio & tv; RIBA, Hon FRAIC; *Recreations* home, garden, books, music, walks, boats (Amadeus); *Clubs* Brooks's; *Style*— Michael Manser, Esq; Morton House, Chiswick Mall, London W4 2PS; Manser Assocs, Bridge Studios, Hammersmith Bridge, London W6 9DA

MANSER, Paul Robert; s of Bob Manser, and Margaret, *née* Rubinstein; *b* 27 Mar 1950; *Educ* Eltham Coll, Warwick Univ (BA); *m* 28 July 1972, Lindy, da of Harry Myers; 2 s (Nicolas b 19 June 1981, Edward b 18 Feb 1983); *Career* slr: ptnr Berwin Leighton 1981-86, ptnr Hammond Suddards 1988-; memb Law Soc; *Recreations* tennis, photography, music books; *Style*— Paul Manser, Esq; Martin Ho, Long Causeway, Adel, Leeds LS16 8EF (☎ 0532 613 629); Josephs Well, Hanover Walk, Leeds LS3 1AB (☎ 0532 450 845, fax 0532 426 868, car tel 0860 416 036, telex 55365)

MANSERGH, Vice-Adm Sir (Cecil) Aubrey Lawson; KBE (1953), CB (1950), DSC (1915); s of Ernest Lawson Mansergh (d 1934); *b* 7 Oct 1898; *Educ* RNC Osborne, RNC Dartmouth; *m* 1, 1928, Helen Rayner Scott (d 1967); 1 s (and 1 s decd); m 2, 1969, Dora Mary Clarke; *Career* joined RN 1914, served WW I, Capt 1938, served WW II, Rear Adm 1948, Flag Offr Second Cruiser Sqdn Home Fleet 1950-51, Vice Adm 1951, pres RNC Greenwich 1952-54, ret; *Style*— Vice-Adm Sir Aubrey Mansergh, KBE, CB, DSC; 102 High St, Rottingdean, Sussex BN2 7HF (☎ 0273 32213)

MANSERGH, Capt Michael Cecil Maurice; s of Adm Sir Maurice James Mansergh, KCB, CBE (d 1966), Ch of Staff to Allied Naval C-in-C, Expeditionary Force for invasion of Normandy (responsible for naval planning 'Overlord'), 5 Sea Lord, C-in-C Plymouth, by his wife, Violet Elsie (d 1983), da of late Bernard Hillman; ggs of James Mansergh (d 1905), Pres Inst of Civil Engrs; *b* 12 August 1926; *Educ* RNC Dartmouth, psc and War Coll; *m* 10 March 1956, Margaret Jean, da of Bernard Howell Cameron Hastie (d 1981); 2 s (Robert b 1957, Michael b 1959), 1 da (Penelope b 1963); *Career* RN 1940, serv WWII supporting Russian convoys 1944, HMS Berwick, Far East and Pacific Fleets 1944-45, HMS Howe, Quality, Illustrious, qualified gunnery and air weapons; serv: HMS Mauritius, Jutland, Agincourt, Triumph, Centaur, Peregrine (RNAS Ford), Heron (RNAS Yeovilton), Fulmar (RNAS Lossiemouth) 1957-58; 2 in cmd 1966-68; Naval Staff MoD 1968-69, Capt 1969, Naval Asst to Ch of Fleet Support 1969, Queen's Harbourmaster Plymouth 1972-73, cmdg offr Gunnery Sch HMS Excellent 1974-76, ADC to HM The Queen 1978; vice-pres Admty Interview Bd 1976-79, Naval asst to Naval Sec 1979-82; FBIM 1970, FRHS; *Recreations* gardening, swimming, golf, rough shooting; *Clubs* Army and Navy, Lyme Regis Golf; *Style—* Capt Michael Mansergh, CBE, RN; Cothayes, Whitchurch Canonicorum, Bridport, Dorset DT6 6RH (☎ Chideock 89261)

MANSFIELD, Colin Eric; Emergency Reserve Decoration ERD (1958); s of Donald Haddon Mansfield (d 1979) of Bishops Stortford and Doris Lydia *née* Hallett (d 1981); *b* 28 May 1929; *Educ* Bishops Stortford Coll, Northampton Poly and evening class (various); *m* 8 Feb 1956, Mary Winifred; 2 s (David Johnathan b 1959, Peter James b 1967), 2 da (Joanna Mary b 1961, Sarah Jane b and d 1966; *Career* maj Royal Engrs 1957-65; dir Trollope & Colls Ltd 1972-86 (md 1985-6); md Trollope & Colls Mgmnt 1981-4 (dep chm 1986-); Freeman City of London: memb Carpenters Co; pres The Concrete Soc 1987-88; *Recreations* church work, golf, drama, gardening; *Style—* Colin Mansfield, Esq; 1 Dang O'Coys Rd, Bishops Stortford, Herts (☎ 0279 54520); 25 Christopher St, London (☎ 01 377 2500)

MANSFIELD, Eric Harold; s of Harold Goldsmith Mansfield (d 1959), and Grace, *née* Phundt (d 1924); *b* 24 May 1923; *Educ* St Lawrence Coll Ramsgate, Trinity Hall Cambridge (MA, ScD); *m* 1, 1947 (m dis 1973), Mary Ola Purves Douglas; 2 s, 1 da; m 2, 1974, Eunice Lily Kathleen Shuttleworth-Parker; *Career* Royal Aircraft Estab: dep chief sci offr 1967-80, chief sci offr (individual merit) 1980-83; memb cncl Royal Soc 1977-78; visiting prof Univ of Surrey; FRS, FEng, FRAeS, FIMA; *Books* Bending and Stretching of Plates (1964, 2 edn 1989); Bridge: The Ultimate Limits (1986); *Recreations* bridge, palaeontology, snorkelling; *Style—* Prof Eric Mansfield, FRS; Manatoba, Dene Close, Lower Bourne, Farnham, Surrey GU10 3PP (☎ 0252 713558)

MANSFIELD, Vice Adm Sir (Edward) Gerard (Napier); KBE (1974), CVO (1981); s of Vice Adm Sir John Maurice Mansfield, KCB, DSO, DSC (d 1949); *b* 13 July 1921; *Educ* RNC Dartmouth; *m* 1943, Joan Worship, da of Cdr John Byron, DSC (decd); 2 da; *Career* joined RN 1935, serv WWII, Capt 1959, Rear Adm 1969, sr naval memb Directing Staff IDC 1969-70, Flag Offr sea Trg 1971-72, Vice Adm 1972, Dep Supreme Allied Cdr Atlantic 1973-75, ret; chm Assoc of RN Offrs' Cncl 1975-86; memb admin cncl Royal Jubilee Tsts 1978-82; chm 'Operation Raleigh' 1984; *Recreations* golf, gardening; *Clubs* Army and Navy; *Style—* Vice-Adm Sir Gerard Mansfield, KBE, CVO; White Gate House, Heath Lane, Ewshot, Farnham, Surrey GU10 5AH (☎ 0252 850325)

MANSFIELD, Hon Guy Rhys John; s and h of 5 Baron Sandhurst, DFC; *b* 3 Mar 1949; *Educ* Harrow, Oriel Coll Oxford (MA); *m* 1976, Philippa St Clair, da of Digby Everard Verdon-Roe, of Le Cannet, France; 1 s (Edward James b 12 April 1982), 1 da (Alice Georgina b 4 Feb 1980); *Career* barr Middle Temple 1972; *Recreations* cricket; *Clubs* Leander, MCC; *Style—* The Hon Guy Mansfield; 1 Crown Office Row, London EC4Y 7HH

MANSFIELD, Prof Peter; s of Sidney George Mawsfield (d 1966), of 87 Kemble House, Lambeth, London, and Rose Lilian, *née* Turner (d 1985); *b* 9 Oct 1933; *Educ* William Penn Sch Dulwich and Peckham, QMC London (BSc, PhD); *m* 1 Sept 1962, Jean Margaret, da of Edward Francis Kibble (d 1972), of Peckham, London; 2 da (Sarah Jane b 1967, Gillian Samantha b 1970); *Career* Nat Serv RASC 1952-54; res assoc Univ of Illinois USA 1962-64; Univ of Nottingham 1964-79: lectr, sr lectr, reader; sr res visitor Max Planck Inst for Med Res Heidelberg Germany 1971-72, prof of physics Univ of Nottingham 1979-, pres Soc of Magnetic Resonance in Med 1987-88, fell QMC, London 1987; gold medal Soc of Magnetic Resonance in Med 1982, gold medal and prize Royal Soc Wellcome Fndn 1984, Duddell medal and prize Inst of Physics 1988, Sylvanus Thompson medal Br Inst of Radiology 1988, Euro Workshop Trophy Euro Soc of Magnetic Resonance in Med and Biology 1988; FRS 1987; *Books* NMR Imaging in Biomedicine (with P G Morris, 1982); *Recreations* languages, walking, DIY; *Style—* Prof Peter Mansfield; 68 Beeston Fields Drive, Bramcote, Notts; Dept of Physics, Univ of Nottingham, Univ Pk, Nottingham NG7 2RD (☎ 0602 484848, ext 2830, fax 0602 229 792, telex 37346 UNINOT G)

MANSFIELD, Sir Philip Robert Aked; KCMG (1984, CMG 1973); s of Philip Theodore Mansfield (d 1975); *b* 9 May 1926; *Educ* Winchester, Pembroke Coll Cambridge; *m* 1953, Elinor, da of Dr Burtis Russell MacHatton (d 1959), of USA; 2 s (Adrian, Humphrey); *Career* WWII Lt Grenadier Gds 1944-47; Sudan Political Serv Equatoria Province 1950-54; Dip Serv: Addis Ababa, Singapore, Paris, Buenos Aires; cnsllr and head Rhodesia dept FCO 1969-72, Royal Coll Def Studies 1973, cnsllr and head of chancery 1974-75, dep high cmmr Nairobi 1976, asst under-sec of state FCO 1976-79, ambass and dep perm rep to the UN 1979-81, ambass to the Netherlands 1981-84; conslt: Rank Xerox, BPB Industs; *Recreations* birdwatching, tree planting, cooking; *Clubs* Royal Cwlth Soc; *Style—* Sir Philip Mansfield, KCMG; Gill Mill, Stanton Harcourt, Oxford, (☎ 0993 702554)

MANSFIELD AND MANSFIELD, 8 Earl of (GB 1776 and 1792); William David Mungo James Murray; JP (Perth & Kinross 1975), DL (1980); also Lord Scone (S 1605), Viscount Stormont (S 1621), Lord Balvaird (S 1641); hereditary keeper of Bruce's Castle of Lochmaben; s of 7 Earl of Mansfield, JP, LL (d 1971, whose family were long the owners of Robert Adam's neo-classical Kenwood; Lord Mansfield is sixth in descent from the bro of the celebrated Lord Chief Justice and 1 Earl who was Alexander Pope's 'silver-tongued Murray'), and Dorothea (d 1985), da of Hon Sir Lancelot Carnegie, GCVO, KCMG, (2 s of 9 Earl of Southesk, by his 2 w); *b* 7 July 1930; *Educ* Wellesley Ho, Eton, Ch Ch Oxford; *m* 19 Dec 1955, Pamela Joan, da of Wilfred Neill Foster, CBE; 2 s (Viscount Stormont, Hon James b 7 June 1969), 1 da (Lady Georgina b 10 March 1967); *Heir* s, Viscount Stormont, *qv*; *Career* Lt Scots Gds Nat Serv 1949-50; barr 1958-71; First Crown Estate Cmmr 1985-; dir Gen Accident Fire & Life Assur Corpn and numerous cos 1972-79 and 1985-; oppn front bench spokesman in the House of Lords 1975-79; min state: Scottish Office 1979-83, NI Office 1983-84; memb Br delgn to Euro Parliament 1973-75; Hon Sheriff Perth 1974; chm Historic Houses Assoc Scotland 1976-79; pres: Scottish Assoc of Boys' Clubs 1976-79, Fédération des Associations de Hasse de l' Europe 1977-79; Royal Scottish Country Dance Soc 1977-; *Clubs* Turf, White's, Pratt's, Beefsteak; *Style—* The Rt Hon the Earl of Mansfield and Mansfield, JP, DL; Scone Palace, Perthshire (☎ 0738 51115)

MANSFIELD COOPER, Sir William; s of late William Ellis Cooper, and late Georgina Caroline Cooper; *b* 20 Feb 1903; *Educ* Univ of Manchester; *m* 1936, Edna Mabel, da of late Herbert Baker; 1 s (Christopher); *Career* asst lectr and lectr Univ of Manchester 1938-49, (prof of industl law 1949-70, registrar 1945-52, vice-chllr 1956-70, emeritus prof 1970-); CStJ 1970; kt 1963; *Recreations* gardening, bird watching; *Clubs* Athenaeum; *Style—* Sir William Mansfield Cooper; Flat 32, The Chestnuts, West St, Godmanchester, Cambs

MANSON, Alexander Reid; s of Capt Alexander Manson (d 1965) of Kilblean, Oldmeldrum Inverurie, Aberdeenshire, and Isobel, *née* Reid, MBE (d 1985); *b* 2 Sept 1931; *Educ* Robert Gordons Coll Aberdeen, N of Scotland Coll of Agrig (Dip Ag); *m* 29 May 1957, Ethel Mary, da of Robert Philip (d 1980), of Hillfoot, Strichen; 1 s (Alexander b 1961), 2 da (Anne b 1958, Lesley b 1960); *Career* fndr chm Aberdeen Beef & Calf Ltd 1962, chm Buchan Meat Producers Ltd 1982 (joined 1968), pres Sco Agric Orgn Soc Ltd 1986-89, vice pres Fed of Agric Co Operatives (UK) Ltd 1988-, dir Sco Beef Devpts ltd 1988-; tstee Plunkett Fndn Oxford 1977-, memb Meat & Livestock Cmmn 1986-;chm Oldmeldrum Sports ctee 1971-75 (memb 1955-82); memb Oldmeldrum Town Cncl 1960-65; *Recreations* golf, shooting and conservation, bird watching; *Clubs* Farmers, Royal Northern and Univ; *Style—* Alexander Manson, Esq; Kilblean, Oldmeldrum, Inverurie, Aberdeenshire AB5 ODN (☎ 065 122 226); Buchan Meat Ltd, Markethill, Turriff, Aberdeenshire AB5 7HW (☎ 0888 63751, fax 0888 62751, car telephone 0836 700 694, telex 73328)

MANSON, Finian Paul Louis; s of Stephen Louis Manson, of 66 Burnaby Gardens, London, and Grainne Caitlin Manson (Dempsey); *b* 8 Mar 1950; *Educ* Chiswick GS, Poly of the South bank, Cranfield Business Sch MBA, FCCA; *Career* chm and md Thomas Christy Ltd; dir: Michael Denham Ltd, Medicam Laboratories Ltd, Marna Christina Ltd, Thomas Christy (SA) Ltd, Thomas Christy (Australia) Ltd, Christy Cosmetics Ltd, Christy (GB) Ltd; *Style—* Finian Manson, Esq; Christy Estate, North Lane, Aldershot, Hants GU12 4QP (☎ 0252 29911, telex 858196)

MANSON, Ian Stuart; s of David Alexander Manson (d 1973), of Halifax, Calderdale, and Elsie May, *née* Newton (d 1985); *b* 15 Mar 1929; *Educ* Heath GS Halifax, Clare Coll Cambridge (BA); *m* 11 Sept 1957, Pamela, da of John Horrocks-Taylor (d 1949), of Halifax; 3 s (Andrew b 1959, Simon b 1962, David b 1964); *Career* Nat Serv 1948-49; asst prosecuting slr: Bradford 1956-57, Birmingham 1960-66; prosecuting slr: Southampton 1957-58, Portsmouth 1958-60, W Mids Police Authy 1966-74; chief prosecuting slr W Mids CC 1974-86, Chief Crown Prosecutor W Mids 1986, ex-warden Kings Norton Parish Church, pres Soc Yorkshirefolk in Birmingham, memb Birmingham Medico-Legal Soc; former pres Prosecuting Slrs Soc Eng and Wales, cncl memb Birmingham Law Soc; memb: The Law Soc 1976, Birmingham Law Soc 1978; *Recreations* reading, music, gardening; *Style—* Ian Manson, Esq; The McLaren Building, Dale End, Birmingham B4 7NR (☎ 021 233 3133, fax 021 233 2499)

MANT, Prof Arthur Keith; s of George Arthur Mant (d 1967), and Elise Muriel Slark (d 1960); *b* 11 Sept 1919; *Educ* Denstone Coll, London Univ (MD, BS); *m* 1947, Heather Olive Emma, da of John William Smith (d 1974); 2 s, 1 da; *Career* serv RAMC, Maj; emeritus prof of forensic med Guy's Hosp Univ of London 1974-84 (formerly res fell, lectr, reader in dept of forensic med), hon conslt in forensic med King's Coll Hosp 1967, visiting lectr in forensic med St Mary's Hosp 1955; FRCP, FRCPath, DMJPath; *Books* Forensic Medicine (1960), Modern Trends in Forensic Medicine (1973), Taylors Principles & Practice of Medical Jurisprudence (13 edn 1984); *Recreations* orchid culture, fishing; *Style—* Prof A Keith Mant; Linn Cottage, 29 Ashley Drive, Walton-on-Thames, Surrey (☎ 0932 225005)

MANT, Sir Cecil George; CBE (1955); s of George Frederick Mant, of London, and Beatrice May Mant; *b* 24 May 1906; *Educ* Trinty County Sch, Hornsey Sch of Art, Northern Poly Sch of Architecture; *m* 1940, Hilda Florence, da of Horace Kingsley Knowles, of London; 3 da; *Career* entered HM Off of Works 1928, dir-gen of Works 1960-63 (dep dir-gen 1950-60), controller-gen Miny of Public Bldgs and Works 1963-67; conslt to Corpn of London and project co-ordinator for Barbican Arts Centre 1972-83; memb cncl London Assoc for the Blind 1970-; memb ct of assts Guild of Freemen of City of London 1972-; kt 1964; *Clubs* Naval; *Style—* Sir Cecil Mant, CBE; 44 Hamilton Ct, Maida Vale, London W9 1QR (☎ 01 286 8719)

MANT, John; OBE (1986); s of Charles Arthur Mant (d 1969), of Bath, and Hilda Ada Louise, *née* Landor (d 1969); *b* 23 May 1920; *Educ* King Edward VI Sch Bath; *m* 2 Jan 1943, Barbara Joan, da of William George Wolfe (d 1968), of Bath; 1 s (Charles b 1951), 3 da (Elizabeth b 1948, Sarah b 1955, Helen b 1962); *Career* HM Army 1940-46: Home Forces 1940-42, Middle East and Sicily 1943, France, Belgium, Holland and Germany 1944-45, Capt; admitted slr 1949, ptnr in private practice 1953-86, conslt Withy King and Lee Slrs Bath 1986-88; pres Bath Law Soc 1979-80, assoc of South Western Law Soc 1982, govr Salisbury and Wells Theological Coll 1982-89; fndr chm Wansdyke Constituency Cons Assoc 1983-85 (pres 1986-); memb House of Laity Gen Synod of the C of E 1975-80; *Recreations* gardening, walking, for travel; *Style—* J C B Mant, OBE; Bassett Barn, Claverton, Bath, Avon BA2 7BG (☎ 0225 69692)

MANTHORP, Rev (Brian) Robert; s of Alan Roy Manthorp (d 1972), of Framlingham, Suffolk, and Stella, *née* Butcher; *b* 28 July 1934; *Educ* Framlingham Coll Suffolk, Pembroke Coll Oxford (BA, MA), Westcott House Cambridge, Coll of Teachers of the Blind (Dip); *m* 8 Aug 1954, Jennifer Mary, da of Vernon Rosewarne Caradine, (d 1985), East Preston, Sussex; 3 s (Christopher b 1955, Stephen b 1958, Jonathan b 1964), 1 da (Helen b 1963); *Career* Instr Lt RN 1955-58; ordained priest Guildford 1961, asst master and chaplain Charterhouse Surrey 1958-65, head of english and housemaster Lawrence Coll Murree W Pakistan and Aitchison Coll Lahore W Pakistan 1965-70, head of english Oakbank Sch Keighley W Yorks 1970-73; headmaster: Holy Trinity Sch Halifax W Yorks 1973-80, Worcester Coll for the Blind 1980-; chm of govrs Bishop Perowne HS Worcs 1986-, vice chm Warnocke Ctee Independent Schs Jr Cncl 1982-; fell Coll of Preceptors 1985; *Books* Fifty Poems for Pakistan (1971); *Recreations* sport, sketching; *Clubs* East India; *Style—* The Rev Robert Manthorp; The Brew House, High St, Chipping, Campden, Glos; The Headmaster's House, Worcester College for the Blind, Worcester WR5 2JX (☎ 0905 763 933)

MANTON, 3 Baron (UK 1922); Joseph Rupert Eric Robert Watson; DL (Humberside 1980); s of 2 Baron Manton, JP (d 1968), by his 1 w Alethea (d 1979, da of Col Philip Langdale, OBE, and gggda of 17 Baron Stourton); *b* 22 Jan 1924; *Educ* Eton; *m* 1951, Mary Elizabeth, twin da of Maj T D Hallinan (decd); 2 s, 3 da; *Heir* s, Hon Miles Ronald Marcus Watson; *Career* joined Army 1942, Lt Life Gds 1943, transferred 7 (QO) Hussars 1951, Capt, ret 1956; sr steward Jockey Club 1982-85, former Jockey Club representative on Horserace Betting Levy Bd 1970-75, former gentleman rider (won 130 Nat Hunt races and Point to Points 1947-64); landowner, farmer, race horse owner; *Clubs* Jockey, White's; *Style—* The Rt Hon the Lord Manton, DL; Houghton Hall, Sancton, York (☎ 0430 873234)

MANWARING, Randle Gilbert; s of George Ernest Manwaring (d 1939), of London, and Lilian, *née* Gilbert; *b* 3 May 1912; *Educ* London Univ, Keele Univ (MA); *m* 9 Aug 1941, Betty Violet, da of Herbert Percy Rout (d 1986), of Norwich; 3 s (David b 1944, Michael b 1946, Christopher b 1949), 1 da (Rosemary b 1942); *Career* joined RAFVR 1940, cmmnd RAF 1941, cmd various sqdns RAF Regt as founding offr 1943-45, Wing Cdr all units of RAF Regt in Burma (approx 3,500 men) 1945, demob Wing Cdr 1945; dir (later md) CE Heath & Co Ltd 1964-71, first md CE Heath Urquhart & Co Ltd 1966-71; dir: Excess Life Assur Co 1967-75, Excess Insur Co 1975-78; vice chm Midland Bank Insur Servs Ltd 1974-77 (first md 1972-74); chm govrs: Luckley - Oakfield Sch 1972-83, Northease Manor Sch 1972-84; chm Uckfield Probus Club 1989-, pres Soc of Pension Conslts 1968-70, dep chm Corpn of Insur Brokers 1970-71; memb: Chichester Deanery and Diocesan Synods, Bishop's Cncl; Churchwarden St Peters-Upon- Cornhill, reader Diocese of Chichester 1968-, vice-pres Crusaders Union; FSS 1970, FPMI 1971; *Books* The Heart Of This People (1954), A Christain Guide to Daily Work (1963), Run Of The Downs (1984), From Controversy To Co-Existance (1985), 10 Volumes of Poetry Culminating In Collected Poems (1986); *Recreations* music, reading, following cricket; *Clubs* RAF; *Style—* Randle Manwaring, Esq; Marbles Barn, Newick, East Sussex BN8 4LG (☎ 082572 3845)

MAPLES, John Cradock; MP (C) Lewisham W 1983-; s of Thomas Cradock and Hazel Mary Maples; *b* 22 April 1943; *Educ* Downing Coll Cambridge, Harvard Business Sch; *m* 1986, Jane; *Style—* John Maples, Esq, MP; Ho of Commons, London SW1A 0AA (☎ 01 219 6373)

MAR, Lady Janet Helen of; da of 30 Earl of Mar; *b* 31 Jan 1946; *Educ* St Andrews Univ; *m* 1969, Lt-Cdr Laurence of Mar (formerly Laurence Duncan McDiarmid Anderson, Winton Castle, East Lothian) recognized in surname of Mar by warrant of Lord Lyon 1969; 2 da (Elizabeth b 1970, Catherine b 1971); *Style—* Lady Janet of Mar; c/o Midland Bank, 26 Biggin Street, Dover, Kent CT16 1BJ; Princes Ct, Brompton Rd, SW3

MAR, Countess of (31 holder of S Earldom *ab initio*, before 1114); **Margaret**; *née* of Mar; also Lady Garioch (an honour originally held together with the ancient territorial Earldom of Mar; holder of Premier Earldom of Scotland by date (the oldest peerage in the Br Isles); the predecessors of the original Earls of Mar were Mormaers of Mar in pre-feudal Scotland, long before the term 'Earl' came to be used; maintains private offr-of-arms (Garioch Pursuivant); da of 30 Earl of Mar (d 1975), and Millicent Mary Lane, *née* Salton; *b* 19 Sept 1940; *Educ* Lewes County GS for Girls Sussex; *m* 1, 1959 (m dis 1976), Edwin Noel of Mar (recognised in surname 'of Mar' by Warrant of the Lord Lyon 1969), s of Edwin Artiss; 1 da (Lady Susan Helen, Mistress of Mar, b 31 May 1963); m 2, 1976, John (also recognised in the surname 'of Mar' by Warrant of Lord Lyon 1976), s of Norman Salton; m 3, 1982, John Henry Jenkin, MA(Cantab), LRAM, FRCO, ARCM, s of William Jenkin, of Hayle, Cornwall; *Heir* da, Mistress of Mar; *Career* holder of Premier Earldom of Scotland; British Telecom sales superintendent to 1982; patron Dispensing Doctors' Assoc; lay memb Immigration Appeals Tbnl; patron Worcester Branch of the National Back Pain Assoc; *Recreations* gardening, painting, interior decoration; *Style—* The Rt Hon the Countess of Mar; St Michael's Farm, Great Witley, Worcester WR6 6JB

MAR, Mistress of; Lady Susan Helen; *née* of Mar; da of Countess of Mar in her own right (31 holder of S Earldom) by her 1 husb Edwin Artiss (later 'of Mar'); *b* 31 May 1963; *Educ* Kidderminster HS for Girls, Christie Coll Cheltenham; *Style—* Mistress of Mar; 72 Oakwood Rd, London NW11 (☎ 01 455 3111)

MAR AND KELLIE, 13 and 15 Earl of (S 1565, 1619); John Francis Hervey Erskine; JP (Clackmannanshire 1971); also Lord Erskine (S 1426), Baron Erskine of Dirletowne (*sic* as stated by The Complete Peerage, S 1604), and Viscount of Fentoun and Lord Dirletoun (S 1619, whereby Lord Mar and Kellie is premier Viscount of Scotland); also Hereditary Keeper of Stirling Castle; s of Lord Erskine, GCSI, GCIE (d 1953), and Lady Marjorie Hervey (d 1967), (er da of 4 Marquess of Bristol); suc gf, 12 Earl, KT, 1955; *b* 15 Feb 1921; *Educ* Eton, Trinity Cambridge; *m* 24 April 1948, Pansy Constance, OBE, CStJ, JP, da of Gen Sir Andrew Nicol Thorne, KCB, CMG, DSO (d 1970); 3 s, 1 da; *Heir* s, Lord Erskine; *Career* serv 1939-45 War, Maj 1950, ret 1954; chm T and AF Assoc Clackmannanshire 1961-68; scottish rep peer 1958-63; CCllr (1955-75); chm Forth Conservancy Bd 1957-68; Lord-Lt Clackmannanshire 1966- (DL 1954, Vice-Lt 1957-66); elder Church of Scotland 1958-; memb Royal Co of Archers (Queen's Body Guard for Scotland); farmer; KStJ 1966; *Clubs* New (Edinburgh); *Style—* The Rt Hon the Earl of Mar and Kellie, JP; Claremont House, Alloa, Clackmannanshire FK10 2JF (☎ 0259 212020)

MAR AND KELLIE, Countess of; Pansy Constance; OBE (1984), JP (1971); da of Gen Sir Andrew Thorne, KCB, CMG, DSO (d 1970), and Hon Margaret Douglas Pennant (d 1967), da of 2 Baron Penrhyn; *b* 16 Dec 1921; *Educ* privately; *m* 24 April 1948, 13 and 15 Earl of Mar and Kellie, *qv*; 3 s, 1 da; *Career* serv WWII, subaltern ATS, UK; chm: Youth-at-Risk Advsy Gp 1968-, Scottish Standing Conference Voluntary Youth Orgns 1978-81 (SCANVYO); hon pres Girls' Bde Scotland 1979-, pres UK Ctee UNICEF 1979-84, pres JMB Devpt Trg 1985-87, Scottish chm Int Year of the Child (IYC) 1979; Elder of the Church of Scotland 1977-; CStJ 1983 (OStJ 1977); *Recreations* walking, family outings; *Clubs* New (Edinburgh), Univ Women's; *Style—* The Rt Hon the Countess of Mar and Kellie, OBE, JP; Claremont House, Alloa, Clackmannanshire FK10 2JF (☎ 0259 212020)

MARA, Rt Hon Ratu Sir Kamisese Kapaiwai Tuimacilai; GCMG (1983), KBE (1969, OBE 1961), PC (1973); *b* 13 May 1920; *Educ* Sacred Heart Coll NZ, Otagu Univ NZ, Wadham Coll Oxford (MA); *m* 1951, Adi Lady Lala Mara; 3 s, 5 da; *Career* MLC Fiji 1953-, MEC 1959-61, prime minister of Fiji 1970-, hereditary high chief of the Lau Islands; *Style—* The Rt Hon Ratu Sir Kamisese Mara, GCMG, KBE; 6 Berkeley Crescent, Domain, Suva, Fiji

MARAIS, Walter; s of Col John Jacob Marais, of Cape Town, S Africa, and Maude, *née* Miller (d 1933); *b* 26 Jan 1931; *Educ* Wynberg Boys' HS, Univ of Cape Town (BCom); *m* 21 July 1956, Barbara Jean, da of Dr Boyd Franklin Brown (d 1976); *Career* chm and owner Marwalt Ltd; memb Lloyd's, ctee memb Int Steel Trades Assoc, life memb Game Conservancy; Freeman City of London, memb Worshipful Co of Gunmakers; *Recreations* shooting, tennis, squash, gardening; *Clubs* Brooks's, The Landsdowne, Marks and Annabels; *Style—* Walter Marais, Esq; Garden House, Cornwall Gardens, London SW7; Marlborough, Wilts;

MARANGOS, Anthony C; s of John Anthony Marangos, and Peggy D, *née* Swinden; *b* 9 July 1943; *Educ* Stone Ho, Cheltenham Coll; 1 s (Nicholas b 1972), 2 da (Natacha b 1987, Alexandra b 1987); *Career* serv HAC 2Lt; md: Cartier Ltd 1984, ACD Markitins 1981-84, Laura Ashley 1974-81; Young and Rubican; cncl memb: French C of C, Bond St Assoc; Freeman City of London; *Recreations* riding, tennis, clocks; *Clubs* Brooks, RTYC; *Style—* Anthony Marangos, Esq; Cartier Ltd, 175 New Bond St, London W1 (☎ 01 493 6962)

MARCH, Sir Derek Maxwell; KBE (1988), CBE (1982), OBE (1973); s of Frank George March, (d 1963), of Plymouth, and Vera Winifred, *née* Ward; *b* 9 Dec 1980; *Educ* Devonport HS for Boys, Birkbeck Coll London; *m* 4 June 1955, Sally Annetta, da of Alfred Riggs, (d 1964), of Walsall, Staffs; 1 s (Michael b 1956), 2 da (Judith b 1957, Sarah b 1959); *Career* joined HM Dip Serv 1949, Nat Serv ICAF 1949-51, For Off 1951, Br Embassy Bonn 1955, HM vice consul Hanover 1957, asst trade cmmnr Salisbury 1959, HM consul Dakar 1962, first sec For Off 1964, first sec Rawalpindi 1968, first sec Peking 1971, first For and Cwlth Off 1974, cnsll Dept of Trade 1975, sr Br trade cmmnr Hong Kong 1977, cnsllr Dept of Indust 1982, Br high cmmnr Kampala 1986; *Recreations* cricket, golf, reading, history; *Clubs* East India, MCC, Hong Kong; *Style—* Sir Derek March; Soke House, The Soke, Alresford Hants SO24 9DB (☎ 0962 732558); British High Commission Kampala, c/o Foreign Commonwealth Office, King Charles St, London SW1A 2AH (☎ 257054, telex 61202 KAMPALA)

MARCH AND KINRARA, Earl of; Charles Henry Gordon Lennox; DL (W Sussex 1975); s and h of 9 Duke of Richmond and (4 of) Gordon, *qv*; *b* 19 Sept 1929; *Educ* Eton, William Temple Coll Rugby; *m* 1951, Susan Monica, da of Col Cecil Grenville-Grey, CBE, by his w, Monica, da of Ernest Morrison-Bell, OBE; 1 s, 4 da; *Heir* s, Lord Settrington, *qv*; *Career* late 2 Lt KRRC; CA; chm: Goodwood Gp of Cos 1969-, John Wiley & Sons Ltd 1985-, Ajax Insu (Hldgs) Ltd 1987-; memb: House of Laity Gen Synod 1960-80, central and exec ctee World Cncl Churches 1968-75; church cmmr 1962-75; chm: Bd for Mission and Unity Gen Synod 1968-77; House of Laity Chichester Diocese 1976-79, Chichester Cathedral Tst 1985-; pres: Voluntary & Christian Serv 1982-; vice-chm Archbishops' Cmmn on Church and State 1966-70, memb W Midlands Regnl Econ Planning Cncl 1965-68, chm tstees Sussex Heritage Tst 1978-, pres Sussex Rural Community Cncl 1973-; vice-pres SE England Tourist Bd 1974-; chm: Rugby Cncl of Social Serv 1961-68, Dunford Coll (YMCA) 1969-82; tres Sussex Univ 1979-82, (chllr 1985-); hon tres and dep pres HHA 1975-86, chm CORAT 1970-87; pres S of England Agric Soc 1981-82; chm Assoc of Int Dressage Event Organisers 1987-, pres Br Horse Soc 1976-78, dir CGA 1975-; Medal of Honour Br Equestrian Fedn 1983; CBIM 1982, FCA; *Style—* The Rt Hon the Earl of March and Kinrara, DL; Goodwood Ho, Chichester, W Sussex PO18 OPY (☎ home 0243 774760; office: 774107)

MARCH PHILLIPPS DE LISLE, Hon Aubyn Cecilia; *née* Hovell-Thurlow-Cumming-Bruce; da of 8 Baron Thurlow, KCMG; *b* 1958; *Educ* Westonbirt School, Exeter Univ; *m* Frederick March Phillipps de Lisle; 1 s James b 1987; *Career* Mktg Conslt; *Recreations* reading, skiing, theatre, stalking, painting; *Style—* The Hon Mrs Frederick March Phillips; Quenby Hall, Leics

MARCHANT, Sir Herbert Stanley; KCMG (1963), CMG (1957, OBE 1946); s of Ernest Joseph Marchant (d 1928); *b* 18 May 1906; *Educ* Perse Sch, St John's Coll Cambridge (MA); *m* 1937, Diana, da of Cornelius Selway, CVO, CBE (d 1948); 1 s; *Career* asst master Harrow 1928-39; entered Foreign Off 1940, consul-gen Düsseldorf 1955-57, San Francisco 1957-60, ambass Cuba 1960-63, Tunisia 1963-66; assoc dir Inst of Race Rels 1966-68, Br memb UN Ctee for Elimination of Racial Discrimination 1970-74; *Books* Scratch a Russian (1936), His Excellency Regrets (1980); *Style—* Sir Herbert Marchant, KCMG, OBE; 5 Kensington Park Gdns, London W11 (☎ 01 727 9788)

MARCHANT, Philip Lester; s of Frederick Marchant (d 1984), of Theydon Bois, Essex, and Marjorie Marchant, *née* Fuller; *b* 7 Sept 1944; *Educ* King's Coll Taunton; *m* 30 Nov 1968, Helen Shirley, da of Stanley Lawrence Middleton, of Melbourne, Australia; 3 s (Simon b 1972, James b 1974, Robert b 1979); *Career* co dir: Marchant Manufacturing Co Ltd 1975-, Castle St Devpts Ltd 1981-, Haverhill Trg Servs Ltd 1986-; *Recreations* golf; *Clubs* IOD; *Style—* Philip L Marchant, Esq; Camps Hall, Castle Camps, Cambridgeshire CB1 6TP (☎ 079 984265); Marchant Manfc Co Ltd, Piperell Way, Haverhill, Suffolk CB9 8QW (☎ 0440 705351)

MARCHWOOD, 3 Viscount (UK 1945); Sir David George Staveley Penny; 3 Bt (UK 1933); also Baron Marchwood (UK 1937); s of 2 Viscount Marchwood, MBE (d 1979), and Pamela, *née* Colton Fox; *b* 22 May 1936; *Educ* Winchester; *m* 1964, Tessa Jane, da of Wilfred Francis Norris, of Chiddingfold, Surrey; 3 s (Hon Peter, Hon Nicholas b 1967, Hon Edward b 1970); *Heir* s, Hon Peter George Worsley Penny b 8 Oct 1965; *Career* 2 Lt, Royal Horse Gds (The Blues) in UK and Cyprus 1955-57; former dir of various cos in Cadbury Schweppes Gp, now with Moët & Chandon (London) Ltd; *Recreations* cricket, shooting, racing; *Clubs* White's, Twelve, MCC; *Style—* The Rt Hon the Viscount Marchwood; Filberts, Aston Tirrold, nr Didcot, Oxon (☎ 0235 850386); 5 Buckingham Mews, London SW1 (☎ 01 828 2678)

MARCKUS, Hon Mrs (Rachel); *née* King; o da of Baron King of Wartnaby (Life Peer); *b* 1945, ; *m* 1, 1968 (m dis 1974), Michael Gibson; 2, 1980 (m dis 1985), Guy Henry René Bondonneau, of Paris; 3, 1987, Melvyn Marckus; *Style—* The Hon Mrs Marckus; 25 Waterford Road, London SW6 2DJ

MARCOW, Hon Mrs; Hannah Olive; da of 1 Baron Marks of Broughton (d 1964); *b* 1918; *m* 1, 1941, Dr Alec Lerner, now of Savyon, Israel (m dis 1959); 1 s (Joel David b 1942, m 1982 Deborah, da of C Travers, of Woking), 2 da (Diana b 1947, Maureen b 1952); m 2, 1960, Gerald William Harold Marcow; *Style—* The Hon Mrs Marcow; Hotel de Paris, Monte Carlo, Monaco

MARCUS, Frank Ulrich; s of Frederick James Marcus (d 1963), of London, and Gerda, *née* Marcuse (d 1981); *b* 30 June 1928; *Educ* Bunce Ct Sch Kent and Shropshire, St Martins Sch of Art; *m* 8 July 1951, Jacqueline Ruth, da of Philip Silvester (d 1979), of London; 1 s (Paul b 1954), 2 da (Joanna b 1956, Julia b 1961); *Career* playwright and critic; plays: The Formation Dancers (1964), The Killing of Sister George (1965), Cleo (1965), Studies of the Nude (1966), Mrs Mouse Are You Within (1968), Notes on a Love Affair (1971), Beauty and the Beast (1975); numerous other plays for TV and Radio; Translations of: Schnitzler, Molnar, Hauptmann, Kaiser; drama critic: London Magazine 1965-68, Sunday Telegraph 1968-78; TV critic on Plays

Internat 1983-, former memb Drama Panel of Arts Cncl; memb Soc of Authors, hon life memb Critics Circle; *Recreations* cats; *Style—* Frank Marcus, Esq; 8 Kirlegate, Meare, Glastonbury, Somerset BA6 9TA (☎ 045 86 398); c/o Margaret Ramsay Ltd, 14 Goodwins Court, St Martins Lane, London WC2N 4LL (☎ 01 240 0691)

MARCUS, Martin Alan; s of Sydney Marcus; *b* 12 Jan 1948; *Educ* Wanstead Co HS; *m* 1971, Cheryl Natalie, da of Dr Benjamin Green; 2 s; *Career* dep chm and jt md Queens Moat Houses plc; tstee and tres British SLE Aid Gp; FCA; *Recreations* golf, tennis, badminton, table tennis; *Clubs* Abridge GC, Woodford GC, Woodford Wells Crostyx and Tennis; *Style—* Martin Marcus, Esq; 25 Linden Cres, Woodford Green, Essex; Queens Moat Houses plc, Queens Court 9-17, Eastern Rd, Romford, Essex, RM1 3NG

MARDON, Lt-Col John Kenric La Touche; DSO (1945), TD (1943), JP (1948) Somerset, DL (1962); s of Evelyn John Mardon (d 1958), and Maud Mary (d 1950); *b* 29 June 1905; *Educ* Clifton Coll, Christ's Coll Cambridge (MA); *m* 1933, Dulcie Joan, da of Maj-Gen Kenneth Marten Body, CB, CMG, OBE (d 1973); 2 s, 1 da; *Career* 2 Lt Royal Devon Yeo 1925, Maj 1938, served WW II, Lt Col 1942, NW Europe 1944-45 (despatches); chm Mardon Son & Hall Ltd 1962-69; High Sheriff Somerset 1956, Vice-Lord Lt Avon 1974-80; dir Bristol & West Bldg Soc 1969-82; govr Clifton Coll 1957; master Soc of Merchant Venturers Bristol 1959-60; pres YMCA Bristol 1969-79; *Recreations* shooting, lawn tennis, squash rackets (rep Cambridge v Oxford 1925); *Clubs* Bath & County; *Style—* Lt-Col Kenric Mardon, DSO, TD, JP, DL; 4 Rivers Street, Bath, Avon BA1 2PZ (☎ 0225 337725)

MAREK, Dr John; MP (Lab) Wrexham 1983-; *b* 24 Dec 1940; *Educ* King's Coll London (BSc, PhD); *m* 1964, Anne, da of R H Pritchard; *Career* lectr in applied mathematics Univ Coll Wales Aberystwyth 1966-83; *Style—* Dr John Marek, MP; 44 Percy Rd, Wrexham, Clwyd (☎ 0978 264152); House of Commons, London SW1A 0AA

MARETT, Lady; Piedad; da of Vicente Sanchez Gavito, of Mexico City; *m* 1935, Sir Robert Marett, KCMG, OBE, Seigneur of Franc Fief, Jersey (feudal title of Norman origin held by Marett family since seventeenth century), sometime Br Ambass to Peru and pres Policy Advsy Ctee States of Jersey (d 1981); 1 da (Suzanne Elizabeth m 1968); *Style—* Lady Marett; Mon Plaisir, St Aubin, La Haule, Jersey (☎ 0534 34577)

MARFFY, Hon Mrs (Pelline Margot); *née* Lyon-Dalberg-Acton; eldest da of 3 Baron Acton, CMG, MBE, TD (d 1989) ; *b* 24 Dec 1932; *m* 30 June 1953, Laszlo de Marffy von Versegh, s of Elemer de Marffy von Versegh; 7 s (1 decd), 1 da; *Style—* The Hon Mrs Marffy; Ealing Farm, PO Box 29, Umvukwes, Zimbabwe

MARGADALE, 1 Baron (UK 1964); John Granville Morrison; TD (1944), JP (Wilts 1936), DL (Wilts 1983); s of Hugh Morrison, MP, JP, DL (d 1931), and Lady Mary Leveson-Gower (d 1934, 2 da of 2 Earl Granville by his 2 w Castalia, yst da of Walter Campbell of Islay); *b* 16 Dec 1906; *Educ* Eton, Magdalene Coll Cambridge; *m* 1928, Hon Margaret Esther Lucie Smith, JP (d 1980), da of 2 Viscount Hambleden (d 1928); 3 s (James, Charles, Peter, *qqv*), 1 da (Mary, *qv*); *Heir* s, Maj Hon James Ian Morrison, TD, DL; *Career* serv WWII with Royal Wilts Yeo (M East), Hon Col Royal Wilts Yeo, RAC (TA) 1960-72 and Royal Yeo; Cmdt Yeomanries to 1972; master South and W Wilts foxhounds 1932-65; JP Wilts 1933 (high sheriff 1938, DL 1950-69) and Argyll, Lord Lt Wilts 1969-81; MP (C) Salisbury 1942-64, chm 1922 Ctee 1955-64; pres Br Field Sports Soc 1980-; KStJ; *Recreations* hunting, shooting, fishing, racing; *Clubs* Pratt's, White's, Turf, Jockey; *Style—* The Rt Hon the Lord Margadale, TD, JP, DL; Eallabus, Bridgend, Islay, Argyll (☎ 049 681 223); Fonthill Ho, Tisbury, Salisbury, Wilts SP3 5SA (☎ 0747 870202); 55 Westminster Gardens, London

MARGESSON, 2 Viscount (UK 1942); Francis Vere Hampden Margesson; s of 1 Viscount, PC, MC (d 1965, whose mother was Lady Isabel Hobart-Hampden, JP, 3 da of 7 Earl of Buckinghamshire); *b* 1922; *Educ* Eton, Trinity Coll Oxford; *m* 1958, Helena Backstrom, of Oulu, Finland; 1 s, 3 da; *Heir* s, Hon Richard Francis David Margesson; *Career* late ADC to Govr Bahamas, dir Thames & Hudson Publications Inc of N Y; Sub-Lt RNVR 1942-45; info offr Br Consulate-Gen N Y 1964-70; *Style—* The Rt Hon the Viscount Margesson; Stone Ridge, New York, NY 12484, USA

MARGESSON, Hon Jane Henrietta; da of 2 Viscount Margesson; *b* 20 Oct 1965; *Style—* The Hon Jane Margesson

MARGESSON, Hon Rhoda France; s of 2 Viscount Margesson; *b* 31 May 1962; *Style—* The Hon Rhoda Margesson

MARGESSON, Hon Richard Francis David; s and h of 2 Viscount Margesson; *b* 25 Dec 1960; *m* Susan, *née* Beresford-Peirse; 1 da (Lucy b 1986); *Style—* The Hon Richard Margesson

MARGESSON, Hon Sarah Helena; da of 2 Viscount Margesson; *b* 18 Oct 1963; *Style—* The Hon Sarah Margesson

MARGETSON, Sir John William Denys; KCMG CMG 1986, 1979; s of The Very Rev W J Margetson (d 1946), and Marian, *née* Jenoure (d 1937); *b* 9 Oct 1927; *Educ* Blundell's, St John's Coll Cambridge (MA); *m* 1963, Miranda, da of Sir William Coldstream; 1 s (Andrew b 1965), 1 da (Clare b 1967); *Career* Lt Life Gds 1947-49; Colonial Serv 1951-60, dist offr Tanganyika (private sec to govr 1956-57); Dip Serv 1960-87: The Hague 1962-64, speech writer to for sec Rt Hon George Brown MP 1966-68, head of Chancery Saigon 1968-70, seconded to Cabinet Secretariat 1971-74; head of Chancery UK Delegation to NATO 1974-78, ambass Vietnam 1978-80, seconded to MOD as sr civilian instr Royal Coll of Def Studies 1980-82, ambass and dep perm rep UN NY 1982-84, pres UN Tsteeship Cncl 1983-84, ambass Netherlands 1984-87; dir John S Cohen Fndn 1988-, chm Royal Sch of Church Music 1988-, chm Foster Parents Plan (UK) 1988-; *Recreations* music, the arts; *Clubs* Brooks's; *Style—* Sir John Margetson, KCMG; c/o Coutts & Co, 1 Old Park Lane, London W1Y 4BS

MARGRETT, David Basil; s of Basil Stanley Margrett, of Yelverton, Devon, and Kathleen Hilda Nellie, *née* Hayter; *b* 25 Oct 1953; *Educ* Plymouth Poly; *m* 15 March 1985, Pauline Annette, da of Donald Lowe; 1 s (Charles); *Career* dir Lowndes Lambert UK Ltd 1982 (md 1986), dir Lowndes Lambert Gp Ltd 1987; ACII; *Style—* David Margrett, Esq; 98 Priory Gardens, Highgate, London N6 5QT; Lowndes Lambert House, 53 Eastcheap, London EC3P 3HL (☎ 01 283 2000, fax 01 283 1927)

MARGRIE, Victor Robert; CBE (1984); s of Robert Margrie, of London, and Emily Miriam, *née* Corbett; *b* 29 Dec 1929; *Educ* Southgate Co GS, Hornsey Sch of Art (now Middx Poly, NDD, ATD); *m* 1955 Janet Margrie; 3 da (Joanna b 19 Oct 1959, Kate b 26 Dec 1961, Miriam b 10 Sept 1963); *Career* own workshop 1952-71, pt/t teaching London Colls of Art and Design 1952-56, head of ceramics and sculpture Harrow Sch of Art 1956-71 (fndr studio pottery course 1963); solo exhibitions Crafts Centre of GB (now Contemporary Applied Arts): 1964, 1966, 1968; prof RCA 1984-85; studio potter, critic and teacher 1985-; external advsr: dept of ceramics Bristol Poly 1987-, Goldsmiths' Coll London Univ 1989-; sec Crafts Advsy Ctee 1971-77, dir Crafts Cncl 1977-84; memb: advsy cncl Victoria and Albert Museum 1979-84, ctee for art and design CNAA 1981-84, fine art advsy ctee Br Cncl 1983-86, UK nat cmmn UNESCO 1984-85; govr Loughborough Coll of Art and Design 1984-, memb craft initiative Gulbenkian Fndn 1985-; memb: Craftsmen Potters Assoc 1960, Int Acad of Ceramics 1971, FCSD 1975; *Books* contrib: Europaischt Keramik Seit 1950-79 (1979), Oxford Dictionary of Decorative Arts (1975), Lucie Rie (1981); *Recreations* cooking; *Style—* Victor Margrie, Esq, CBE; Bowlders, Doccombe, Moretonhampstead, Devon TQ13 8SS (☎ 0647 40264)

MARJORIBANKS, Sir James Alexander Milne; KCMG (1965, CMG 1954); s of Rev Thomas Marjoribanks of that Ilk, DD (d 1947); *b* 29 May 1911; *Educ* Edinburgh Acad, Edinburgh Univ (MA), Strasbourg Univ; *m* 1936, Sonya Patricia Stanley Alder (d 1981); 1 da; *Career* HM Dip Serv 1934-71, asst under-sec of state FCO 1962-65, ambass to EEC, Euro Atomic Energy Community and ECSC 1965-71; dir The Distillers Co 1971-76; chm Scotland in Europe 1979-; vice-pres Scottish Cncl (dvpt and indust) 1971-83; governing memb Inveresk Res Fndn 1979-; Europe Medal 1973; *Recreations* mountaineering; *Clubs* Scottish Mountaineering, New (Edinburgh); *Style—* Sir James Marjoribanks, KCMG; 13 Regent Terr, Edinburgh, Scotland EH7 5BN (☎ 031 556 3872); Lintonrig, Kirk Yetholm, Kelso, Roxburghshire, Scotland TD5 8PH (☎ 057 382 384)

MARK, Dr James; MBE (1942); s of John Mark (d 1962); bro of Sir Robert Mark, *qv*; *b* 12 June 1914; *Educ* William Hulme's GS Manchester, Trinity Coll Cambridge, Univ of Munich and Münster; *m* 1941, Mary Trewent, da of Alfred Rowland (d 1937); 3 s, 2 da; *Career* Intelligence Corps 1940-46; asst sec HM Treasy 1950-64, under-sec Miny of Overseas Devpt 1965-74; jt ed Theology 1976-83; *Recreations* reading, writing, walking, music; *Style—* Dr James Mark, MBE; 6 Manorbrook, London SE3 9AW (☎ 01 852 9289)

MARK, (John) Richard Anthony; s of John Mark, and Dorothy, *née* White; *b* 20 Jan 1946; *Educ* Clifton, Magdalene Coll Cambridge (MA); *m* 1, 30 Sept 1972 (m dis 1979), Angela Mary, da of Jeffrey Holroyd; 1 s (James b 1975), 1 da (Clare b 1973); m 2, 31 March 1983, Diane Virginia, *née* Roberts; 1 da (Isabel b 1986); *Career* Peat Marwick Mitchell & Co 1967-73, Br Linen Bank 1973-77, Carolina Bank Ltd (now Panmure Gordon Bankers Ltd) 1977-; FCA 1970; *Style—* Richard Mark, Esq; 108 Somerset Rd, London SW19 (☎ 01 947 1496); Panmure Gordon, 14 Moorfields Highwalk, London EC2 (☎ 01 638 4010)

MARK, Sir Robert; GBE (1977), QPM (1965); s of John Mark (d 1962); bro of James Mark, *qv* and Louisa, *née* Hobson (d 1982); *b* 13 Mar 1917; *Educ* William Hulme's GS Manchester, MA (Oxon) 1971; *m* 1941, Kathleen Mary, da of William Leahy (d 1977); 1 s (Christopher), 1 da (Christina); *Career* served WW II RAC, Maj, NW Europe 1942-47; chief constable of Leicester 1957-67, dep cmmr London Met Police 1968-72, cmmr 1972-77; Dimbleby TV Lect 1973; dir Phoenix Assur Co 1977-85, chm Forest Mere Ltd 1978-, govr and memb admin bd Corps of Commissionaires 1977-86, dir Control Risks Ltd 1979-87; KStJ 1977; Hon LLM Leicester 1967, Hon DLitt Loughborough 1976, Hon LLD Manchester 1978; Hon LLD Liverpool 1978; kt (1973); *Publications* Policing a Perplexed Society (1977), In the office of Constable (1978); *Style—* Sir Robert Mark, GBE, QPM; Esher, Surrey KT10 8LU

MARKHAM, Alfred Langton; s of John Hatton Markham (d 1960); *b* 19 Feb 1923; *Educ* Haberdashers' Aske's Sch Hampstead, London Polytechnic (BSc); *m* 1948, Marian Audrey Lyon; 5 children (1 decd); *Career* plant mangr Common Cars 1953-56, md Chubb & Sons Lock & Safe Co 1970-75, dir Chubb & Sons 1974-85; *Recreations* gardening; *Clubs* MCC; *Style—* Alfred Markham, Esq; Windy Ridge, Grubbins Lane, Speen, Aylesbury, Bucks (☎ 024 028 229)

MARKHAM, Betty, Lady; (Frederica) Betty Cornwallis (Crawford); da of late Hon Christian Edward Cornwallis Eliot, OBE; *m* 1942, as his 3 w, Sir Charles Markham, 2 Bt (d 1952); *Style—* Betty, Lady Markham; P O Box 583, Mbabane, Swaziland

MARKHAM, Sir Charles John; 3 Bt (UK 1911), of Beachborough Park, Newington, Kent; s of Sir Charles Markham, 2 Bt (d 1952); *b* 2 July 1924; *Educ* Eton; *m* 1949, Valerie, da of Lt-Col E Barry-Johnston, of Kenya; 2 s, 1 da; *Heir* s, (Arthur) David Markham; *Career* served 1943-47, Lt 11 Hussars (despatches); MLC Kenya 1955-60; KStJ; *Clubs* Cavalry; *Style—* Sir Charles Markham, Bt; PO Box 42263, Nairobi, Kenya (☎ 891 182)

MARKHAM, (Arthur) David; s and h of Sir Charles John Markham, 3 Bt; *b* 6 Dec 1950; *m* 1977, Carolyn, da of Capt Mungo Park, of The Lodge, Carraig Breac, Baily, Co Dublin; 2 da; *Style—* David Markham Esq; PO Box 42263, Nairobi, Kenya

MARKHAM, (Arthur) Geoffrey; s of Col Frank Stanley Markham (d 1978), of Huddersfield, and Emma Woodhouse, *née* Spurr (d 1983); *b* 27 Sept 1927; *Educ* Giggleswick Sch Leeds Univ (LLB); *m* 26 Sept 1959, Patricia, da of John James Holliday (d 1935) of Barnsley, Yorks; 1 s (Jonathan b 1962), 1 da (Sarah b 1966); *Career* admitted slr 1949, sr ptnr Raley and Pratt Barnsley 1967-; chm Soc Security Appeal Tribunal 1981-; Historian; memb Law Soc 1949-; *Books* Woolley Hall, The Historical Development of a Country House (1979); *Recreations* reading, writing, music, freemasonry, gardening; *Style—* Geoffrey Markham, Esq; Petwood House, Woolley, Wakefield WF4 2JJ (☎ 0226 382495); 5 Regent St, Barnsley S70 2EF (☎ 0226 733777, fax 0226 731829)

MARKHAM, Rev Canon Gervase William; s of Algernon Augustus Markham, Bishop of Grantham (d 1949), of Stoke Rectory, Grantham, and Winifred Edith, *née* Barne; *b* 7 Nov 1910; *Educ* Bramcote Sch Scarborough, Winchester Coll, Trinity Coll Cambridge (MA); *m* 29 Aug 1945, Barbara Mary Dalziel, da of Rev Bennet M Banks (d 1953), of Barnham Broom Rectory, Norwich; 1 s (Frederick C T b 6 July 1949), 2 da (Victoria K (Mrs V Singh) b 10 July 1952, Frances W (Mrs N Dennys) b 8 Feb 1954); *Career* Chaplain to the Forces 1940-45, 8 Army N Africa 1942, Sicily 1943, Normandy 1944; schoolmaster Bishop Gobat Sch Jerusalem 1932-34, student Westcott House Cambridge 1934-36; ordained (Durham Cathedral): deacon 1936, priest 1937; curate Bishopwearmouth Parish Church Sunderland, domestic chaplain to Bishop of Durham 1939; vicar: St Stephen's Burnley 1945, Grimsby 1952, Morland 1965-84; hon canon: Lincoln Cathedral 1955, Carlisle Cathedral 1972; fndr: Morland Choristers' Camps, Morland Festival of Village Choirs; *Recreations* book collecting, gardening, dry stone-walling; *Style—* The Rev Canon Gervase Markham; Morland House, Morland,

Penrith, Cumbria (☎ 09314 657)

MARKHAM, (Frank) Richard Gordon; s of Maj Sir Frank Markham, MP, DL (d 1975), of Leighton Buzzard, Beds, and Lady Frances, *née* Lawman; *b* 18 Mar 1939; *Educ* Bedford Modern Sch, Nat Foundry Coll; *m* 27 Sept 1969, Hazel Jean, da of PF Martin, of Dunstable, Beds; 1 da (Katharine Frances Elizabeth b 10 Sept 1978); *Career* apprentice Foundry Equipment Ltd 1957-64, ptnr Markham Robinson Planning Conslts 1964-85, land mangr Black Horse Agencies Estate Agents 1985-88, ptnr Malcolm Reay & Co Estate Agents 1988-; cncllr Leighton-Linslade UDC (chm planning ctee 1964-74, vice-chm 1974-75), chm South Beds DC 1975-76 (chm planning ctee 1975), vice chm planning ctee South Oxfordshire cncl 1985 (memb 1984-); *Recreations* driving of horses, golf; *Style—* Richard Markham, Esq; Home Farm, Henton, Chinnor, Oxford OX9 4AH (☎ 0844 51369); Malcolm Reay & Co, Ipsden House, Oxford Rd, Stokenchurch, Bucks H14 3SX (☎ 024 026 4273, fax 024 026 5219)

MARKING, Sir Henry Ernest; KCVO (1978), CBE (1969), MC (1944); s of Isaac Marking; *b* 11 Mar 1920; *Educ* Saffron Walden GS, UCL; *Career* served WWII Sherwood Foresters (N Africa, ME, Italy); slr 1948; asst slr BEA 1949 (chief exec 1964-72, chm 1971-72); memb bd: BOAC 1971-72, BA 1971-80 (md 1972-76, dep chm 1972-77); chm: Br Tourist Authy 1977-85 (memb bd 1969-77), Carreras Rothmans 1979-85, Rothmans (UK) Ltd 1985-86; dir Barclays Int Ltd 1978-86, memb bd Rothman Int plc 1979-; CRAeS, FCIT, FBIM; *Clubs* Reform; *Style—* Sir Henry Marking, KCVO, CBE, MC; 6A Montagu Mews North, London W1H 1AH

MARKOVA, Dame (Lilian) Alicia Marks; DBE (1963, CBE 1958); da of Arthur Tristman Marks and Eileen Barry; *b* 1 Dec 1910; *Career* Diaghilev's Russian Ballet Co 1925-29, Rambert Ballet Club 1931-34, Vic-Wells Ballet Co 1933-35, Markova-Dolin Ballet Co 1935-37, Ballet Russe de Monte Carlo 1938-41, Ballet Theatre USA 1941-46, co-fndr and prima ballerina Festival Ballet 1950-51: Br prima ballerina assoluta; guest prima ballerina: La Scala, Milan 1956, Buenos Aires 1952, Royal Ballet 1953 and 1957, Royal Danish Ballet 1955, Festival Ballet 1958 and 1959; guest appearances at Metropolitan Opera Ho New York 1952, 1953-54, 1955, 1957, 1958; vice-pres Royal Acad of Dancing 1958-; dir Metropolitan Opera Ballet 1963-69; guest prof: Royal Ballet Sch 1973-, Paris Opera Ballet 1975, Australian Ballet Sch 1976; prof of Ballet and Performing Arts College-Conservatory of Music Univ of Cincinnati 1970-; govr Royal Ballet 1973-; pres London Ballet Circle 1980-; BBC series Markova's Ballet Call 1960, Masterclass BBC2 1980; Queen Elizabeth II Coronation Award, Royal Acad of Dancing 1963; Hon DMus: Leicester 1966, East Anglia 1982; prof Yorkshire Ballet Seminars 1975-; pres: All England Dance Competition 1983-, London Festival Ballet 1986-, Arts Educnl Schs 1984-; *Books* Giselle and I (1960), Markova Remembers (1986); *Style—* Dame Alicia Markova, DBE; c/o Royal Ballet School, London W14

MARKS, Hon Mrs; (Adrianne Barbara Ellis); da of Baron Stone, MB (Life Peer) (d 1986), and Beryl Florence, *née* Bernstein (d 1989); *b* 1934; *m* 1957, Clive M Marks; *Style—* The Hon Mrs Marks; 39 Farm Ave, London NW2

MARKS, Bernard Montague; OBE (1984); s of Alfred Marks (d 1942), and Elizabeth Marks (d 1972); *b* 11 Oct 1923; *Educ* Highgate, Imperial Coll, London Univ; *m* 11 Oct 1956, Norma Delphine, da of Jack Renton (d 1972); 2 s (Nicholas b 1952, Stephen b 1959); *Career* md (later chm) Alfred Marks Bureau Gp of Cos 1946-84, since when life pres; memb Equal Opportunities Commn 1984-85, vice chm (later chm) Fedn of Personnel Services 1965-69 and 1973-82; *Recreations* bridge, golf, skiing; *Clubs* St George's Hill GC; *Style—* Bernard Marks, OBE; Cossyns, Albury Rd, Burwood Park, Walton-on-Thames, Surrey KT12 5DY

MARKS, Dr John Henry; s of Lewis Myer Marks (d 1960), and Rose, *née* Goldbaum (d 1986); *b* 30 May 1925; *Educ* Tottenham County GS, Univ of Edinburgh (MB, ChB, MD, DObstRCOG); *m* 17 June 1954, Shirley Evelyn, da of Alic Nathan, OBE (d 1988); 1 s (Richard), 2 da (Helen, Laura); *Career* Capt RAMC 1949-51; house physician and surgn Wembley Hosp 1948-49, sr house offr obstetrics St Martin's Hosp Bath 1951-52; clinical asst dermatology: Barnet Gen Mount Vernon, Wat Gen Hosps; trainee asst 1952-53, asst GP 1953-54, GP Borehamwood 1954-, cncl chm BMA 1984-; memb Herts CC Health Ctee, chm Herts Exec Cncl 1971-74; memb: GMC 1979-84, Standing Med Advsy Ctee 1984-; MRCGP 1959, FRCGP 1975; *Recreations* modern British postal stamps, medical politics, walking, gardening; *Style—* Dr John Marks; Brown Gables, Barnet Lane, Elstree, Herts WD6 3RQ (☎ 01 953 7687); 121 Theobald St, Borehamwood, Herts WD6 4PU (☎ 01 953 3355, fax 01 207 4928)

MARKS, Paul; s of Sidney Marks OBE, Brecon Hse, The Close, Totteridge; *b* 16 Sept 1935; *Educ* Acton GS; *m* 1960, Patricia Susan; 2 children; *Career* chief exec & chm M Y Hldgs plc (consumer products & packaging materials); vice-pres English Table Tennis Association; cncl memb Br Toy & Hobby Manufacturers Assoc; *Recreations* tennis, table tennis; *Style—* Paul Marks, Esq; Hertsedge, Pine Grove, Totteridge, London N20

MARKS, Pauline; da of Jacob Noskeau, (d 1984), and Bessie, *née* Zenftman (d 1971); *b* 20 Oct 1935; *Educ* S Hampstead HS; *m* 2 May 1954, Martin Marks, s of Samuel Sidney Marks; 1 s (Stephen Harold b 17 Aug 1964), 1 da (Alison Rachel (Mrs Hirsch) b 24 Nov 1961); *Career* md Pauling Marks Direct Marketing; chm: B Telecom 1 Int Telmarketing Conference, Telecom Australia Int Telemarketing Conference, chm Audiotext plc 1985; MInstM; *Books* The Telephone Marketing Book (1984),; *Recreations* reading, family; *Clubs* IOD; *Style—* Mrs MM Marks; 3 Oldfield Mews, London N6 (☎ 01 341 4633); Pembroke House, Compsbourne Rd, London N8 (☎ 01 341 5656, fax 01 340 3269, car tel 0836 215046)

MARKS, Hon Simon Richard; only s and h of 2 Baron Marks of Broughton; *b* 3 May 1950; *Educ* Eton, Balliol Coll Oxford; *m* 1982, Marion, only da of Peter F Norton, of the Azores; 1 da (Miriam b 1983); *Style—* The Hon Simon Marks; c/o Michael Ho, Baker St, London W1

MARKS OF BROUGHTON, 2 Baron (UK 1961); Michael Marks; s of 1 Baron Marks of Broughton, sometime chm and jt md Marks & Spencer (d 1964), by his w Miriam, sis of Joseph Edward Sieff (Hon Pres of M & S), and late Baron Sieff (Life Peer, who m (the first) Lord Marks of Broughton's sis) and aunt of Baron Sieff of Brimpton; *b* 27 August 1920; *Educ* St Paul's, CCC Cambridge; *m* 1, 1949, Ann Catherine (m dis 1958), da of Maj Richard James Pinto, MC; 1 s, 2 da; m 2, 1960, Helene (m dis 1965), da of Gustav Fischer; *Heir* s, Hon Simon Richard Marks; *Style—* The Rt Hon Lord Marks of Broughton; Michael Ho, Baker St, W1

MARLAND, Paul; MP (C) Gloucestershire W 1979-; s of Alexander Marland by his w Elsa May Lindsey; *b* 19 Mar 1940; *Educ* Gordonstoun, Trinity Coll Dublin; *m* 1 1965 (m dis 1983), Penelope Anne Barlow; 1 s, 2 da; m 2, 1984, Caroline Anne Rushton; *Career* farmer; worked with Hopes Meal Windows 1964, London Press Exchange 1965-66; jt PPS to Hon Nicholas Ridley as financial sec Treasury and Jock Bruce-Gardyne as economic sec to Treasury, 1981-83, PPS to Rt Hon Michael Jopling as min of Agric 1983-1986; 1986- Agricultural Select Ctee; *Clubs* Boodles; *Style—* Paul Marland Esq, MP; Ford Hill Farm, Temple Guiting, Cheltenham, Glos (☎ 045 15 232)

MARLAND, Ross Crispian; s of John Marland (d 1988), and Sylvia, *née* Norris; *b* 17 August 1940; *Educ* Stamford Sch, RNC Dartmouth, UCL (LLM, Dip Air and Space Law); *m* 23 Oct 1965, (Daphne Mary) Virginia, da of Brig William Hugh Denning Wakely (d 1979); 1 s (Timothy b 27 July 1970), 1 da (Lavinia b 22 Sept 1974); *Career* graduated RNC actg Sub Lt 1961, No 1 Flying Trg Sch HMS Heron 1961-63, transfd RAF PO 1963, No 2 Air Navigation Sch 1963, No 1 Advanced Navigation Sch flying offr 1964, visual bombing course Canberra OCU 1964-65, Flt Lt No 3 Sqdn Germany 1966-70, jt servs warfare course 1968, radar navigation and bombing sch Vulcan OCU 1970, 50 Sqdn UK 1970-73, jr cmd and staff sch 1973, Flt Cdr jt air reconnaisance and intelligence centre 1973-79; called to the Bar Inner Temple 1975, in practice 1979-81; dir: Int Insur Servs Ltd 1981-87, Airclaims Insur Servs 1987-; memb: Bar Assoc Commerce Finance and Indust, Aust Aviation Law Assoc; memb ctee: Asia Pacific Lawyers Assoc, Air Law Gp, Royal Aeronautical Soc, Air Law Gp; lectr Chartered Inst Insur Studies; memb Huntingdon Cons Club; MRIN 1973, MRAeS 1982, ACIArb 1984; *Recreations* salmon fishing, equestrian sports; *Clubs* RAF; *Style—* Ross Marland, Esq; 84 East Hill, Wandsworth, London SW18 2HG (☎ 01 870 6893); Winterfold, The Village, Orton Longeville, Peterborough, Cambs; Airclaims Insur Services Ltd, Cardinal Point, Newall Rd, Heathrow Airport (London), Hounslow TW6 2AS (☎ 01 897 1066, fax 01 897 0300, telex 934679)

MARLAR, Robin Geoffrey; s of Edward Alfred Geoffrey Marlar MBE (d 1976), and Winifred, *née* Stevens; *b* 2 Jan 1931; *Educ* Magdalene Coll Cambridge (BA); *m* m 1, 1955, Wendy, da of J S Dumersque; 2 s (John b 1957, James b 1964), 4 da (Sarah b 1959, Kate b 1962, Anna-Jane b 1966, Tammy b 1968); m 2, 1980, Gillian, da of Baron Taylor of Hadfield (Life Peer), *qv*; *Career* founder Marlar International (Head Hunters) 1971; cricket correspondent Sunday Times 1970-; capt Cambridge Univ Cricket (Capt) 1953, Sussex 1955-59; Cons Candidate Bolsover 1959, Leicester NE (by-election) 1962; *Books* History of Cricket, English Cricketers Trip to USA 1859, Decision against England; *Recreations* sport, music, gardening; *Clubs* Garrick, MCC; *Style—* Robin Marlar, Esq; 14 Grosvenor Place, London SW1X 7HH (☎ 01 235 9614)

MARLBOROUGH, 11 Duke of (E 1702); John George Vanderbilt Henry Spencer-Churchill; JP (Oxon 1962), DL (1974); also Baron Spencer (E 1603), Earl of Sunderland (E 1643), Baron Churchill of Sandridge (E 1685), Earl of Marlborough (E 1689), Marquess of Blandford (E 1702), Prince of the Holy Roman Empire (1704), and Prince of Mindelheim (1705, cr of the Emperor Joseph); s of 10 Duke of Marlborough (d 1972), by his 1 w, Hon Alexandra Cadogan, CBE, da of Viscount Chelsea and gda of 5 Earl Cadogan, KG; *b* 13 April 1926; *Educ* Eton; *m* 1, 1951, Susan Mary (m dis 1960, she m 1962 Alan Cyril Heber-Percy), da of Michael Charles St John Hornby, of Pusey Ho, Berks, by his w Nicolette (da of Capt Hon Cyril Ward, MVO, RN, 5 s of 1 Earl of Dudley); 1 s, 1 da (and 1 s decd); m 2, 1961, Mrs Tina (Athina) Livanos (m dis 1971, she d 1974), da of Stavros G Livanos, of Paris, and formerly w of Aristotle Onassis (decd); m 3, 1972, (Dagmar) Rosita (Astri Libertas), da of Count Carl Ludwig Douglas (decd); 1 s (Lord Edward b 1974), 1 da (Lady Alexandra b 1977) (and 1 s decd); *Heir* s, Marquess of Blandford; *Career* proprietor of Blenheim Palace, said to be England's largest domestic bldg and one of the masterpieces of Sir John Vanbrugh; formerly Capt Life Gds to 1953; chm: Martini & Rossi Ltd 1979-, London Paperweights Ltd; pres: Thames and Chilterns Tourist Bd 1974-, Oxon Assoc Boys' Clubs, Oxon CLA 1978-; former Oxon ccllr; memb House of Lords Bridge Team in match against Commons 1982; dep pres Nat Assoc Boys' Clubs; pres: Sports Aid Fndn (Southern Area) 1981; Oxfordshire Branch SSAFA 1977; Oxford United Football Club 1975; hon vice-pres Football Assoc 1959; *Clubs* White's, Portland; *Style—* His Grace the Duke of Marlborough, JP, DL; Blenheim Palace, Woodstock, Oxon (☎ 0993 811666); 1 Shepherd's Place, Upper Brook St, London W1 (☎ 01 629 7971)

MARLBOROUGH, Laura, Duchess of; (Frances) Laura; da of Capt Hon Guy Lawrence Charteris (d 1967, 2 s of 11 Earl of Wemyss, and unc of Baron Charteris of Amisfield) by his 1 w, Frances Tennant, niece of 1 Baron Glenconner and Margot Asquith; *b* 10 August 1915; *Educ* governesses; *m* 1, 14 Nov 1933 (m dis 1942), 2 Viscount Long (ka 1944); 1 da (Sara, Hon Mrs Morrison; *qv*); m 2, 25 Feb 1943 (m dis 1954), 3 Earl of Dudley; m 3, 13 June 1960, Michael Temple Canfield (d 1969); m 4, 1972, as his 2 w, 10 Duke of Marlborough (d 1972); *Career* trained as a nurse; cmdt Red Cross Hosp at Himley Hall, Dudley; owned and ran material and antique shops; awarded two campaign medals and Médaille de Reconnaissance Francaişe (for work with Free French); *Books* Laughter from a Cloud (autobiography 1980); *Recreations* int show jumping, gardening and writing, antiques, decorating; *Style—* Her Grace Laura, Duchess of Marlborough; c/o Coutts & Co, 16 Cavendish Sq, London W1 (☎ 01 935 3006 and Chalfont St Giles (024 07) 2141)

MARLER, Christopher John Sydney; s of Maj Leslie Sydney Marler, OBE, TD (d 1981), of Bolebec House, Whitchurch, Bucks , and Doris Marguerite, *née* Swaffer, JP for Bucks; *b* 22 Feb 1932; *Educ* Stowe, RAC Cirencester; *m* 22 Sept 1957, Shirley Carolyn, da of Lewis Edward van Moppes (d 1983), of Theale, Berks; 1 s (James Christopher Sydney b 1962), 2 da (Julie Carolyn b 1959, Serena Rose b 1965); *Career* pedigree cattle breeder and zoo owner; chm Whaddon Estates Ltd (property and investmnt co); Liveryman Worshipful Co of Merchant Taylors' 1955, Freeman City of London 1955; fell: Zoological Soc of London, Linnean Soc; *Recreations* racing, travel, animal photography; *Style—* Christopher J S Marler, Esq; Overbrook House, Weston Underwood, Olney, Bucks (☎ 0234 711451)

MARLER, Dennis Ralph Greville; s of Greville Sidney Marler (d 1952), and Ivy Victoria, *née* Boyle; *b* 15 June 1927; *Educ* Marlborough; *m* 11 June 1952, Angela, da of Harold Cann Boundy, of Putney; 1 s (Timothy b 1957), 1 da (Melanie b 1955); *Career* Lt 2 Bn Royal Lincs Regt 1945-48, served in Palestine (MELF); chm Capital & Counties plc 1985- (md 1969-85); pres Br Property Fedn 1983-84; Freeman of City of London, memb Court of Merchant Taylors' Co; FRICS 1969, CBIM, FRSA; *Recreations* reading, golf, travel; *Clubs* Royal Thames YC, St Stephen's Roehampton, St Enodoc GC ; *Style—* Dennis Marler, Esq; c/o Capital & Counties plc, St Andrew's House, 40 Broadway, London SW1H 0BU (☎ 01 222 7878); 13 Whaddon House, William Mews, London SW1X 9HG (☎ 01 245 6139)

MARLEY, 2 Baron (UK 1930); Maj (Godfrey) Pelham Leigh Aman; s of 1 Baron, DSC, JP, DL, under-sec of state War Off in Ramsay Macdonald's 1930-31 Govt (d 1952), by his w Octable (d 1969), da of Sir Hugh Gilzean-Reid, DL, of Tenterden Hall, Hendon, Middx; *b* 6 Sept 1913; *Educ* Bedales, Grenoble Univ; *m* 1956, Catherine Doone, da of late Frank Angwyn Beal ; *Heir* none; *Career* film producer 1933-75; 2 Lt RM 1939; served 1939-45 War, Acting Maj 1944; sits as Conservative in Ho of Lords; *Recreations* travel; *Clubs* Royal Automobile; *Style—* The Rt Hon the Lord Marley; 104 Ebury Mews, London SW1 (☎ 01 730 4844)

MARLING, Sir Charles William Somerset; 5 Bt (UK 1882), of Stanley Park and Sedbury Park, Co Gloucester; s of Lt-Col Sir John Stanley Vincent, 4 Bt, OBE (d 1977); *b* 2 June 1951; *Educ* Harrow; *m* 1979, Judi P, adopted da of Thomas W Futrille, of Sunningdale; 2 da (b 1982 and 1984); *Clubs* White's, Chelsea Arts; *Style—* Sir Charles Marling, Bt; The Barn, The Street, Eversley, Hants

MARLOW, Antony Rivers; MP (C) Northampton N 1979-; s of the late Major Thomas Keith Rivers Marlow, MBE, RE, and the late Beatrice Nora, *née* Hall; *b* 17 June 1940; *Educ* Wellington, RMA Sandhurst, St Catharine's Coll Cambridge; *m* 1962, Catherine Louise Howel, nee Jones; 3 s, 2 da; *Career* serv Army 1958-69; mgmnt conslt 1969-79; *Clubs* Spencer Working Mens; *Style—* Tony Marlow Esq, MP; House of Commons, London SW1A 0AA

MARLOW, Kingsley Hamnett; s of Walter Marlow RN (d 1930), and Nora Marlow, *née* Bakewell; *b* 6 June 1930; *Educ* Western Park Sch Leicester, Leicester Polytechnic (BA); *m* 1977, Mary Mackinnon, da of Harold Noel Hamilton Barlow Waldie, Maj (ret), of Langholm, Dumfriesshire, Scotland (d 1985); *Career* man dir EX-Cell-O Corp 1983- (finance dir and co sec 1974-82, co sec and financial controller 1964-74); dir: Ex-Cell-O Mulhead Ltd 1984-, LETG Ltd 1978-81, Pure-Pak Ltd 1972-84; govr Charles Keene Coll of FE Leicester 1980-83; companion British Inst of Mgmnt 1983- (memb cncl 1981-83, memb finance ctee 1980-83, chm East Midlands Branch Area Ctee 1980-83); memb: E Midlands Regnl Bd BIM 1984-, Nat Economic Devpt Office Professional Mgmnt Ctee 1985-, BR Assoc for Shooting and Conservation, Inland Waterways Assoc; *Recreations* fishing, shooting, woodword, philatelist, numismatist, gardening; *Style—* Kingsley Marlow, Esq; EX-Cell-O Corporation, PO Box 133, Hastings Rd, Leicester LE5 OHT (☎ 0533 768181)

MARLOW, Hon Mrs (Teresa); *née* Sackville-West; da (by 1 m) of 6 Baron Sackville; *b* 1954; *m* 1979, (Alastair) Rupert Marlow, s of Capt C N Marlow, RN, of Greenhill Ho, Upper Westwood, Wilts; 1 s (Sebastian b 1985), 2 da (Julia 1982, Rebecca b 1983); *Style—* The Hon Mrs Marlow

MARPER, (William) John; s of Ronald Marshall Marper, of Saltburn, and Caroline, *née* Jarville; *b* 9 Dec 1946; *Educ* Sir William Turners Sch; *m* 12 Dec 1976, Maureen Ann, da of Henry Pullen, of Eastbourne; *Career* CA; Charles Barker Gp 1972-77, vice-pres Citicorp 1977-85, dir ANZ Merchant Bank 1985-; FCA, memb stock exchange; *Recreations* tennis, english literature; *Style—* John Marper, Esq; 20 Upbrook Mews, London W2 (☎ 01 258 3483); ANZ Merchant Bank, 65 Holborn Viaduct, London EC2 (☎ 01 489 0021, fax 01 796 4641)

MARPLES, Baroness; Ruth; da of F W Dobson, JP, FSA (decd), of Nottingham; *m* 1956, as his 2 w, Baron Marples, PC (Life Peer) (d 1978); *Style—* The Rt Hon Lady Marples; 33 Eccleston St, SW1

MARQUAND, Prof David Ian; s of Rt Hon Hilary Marquand, PC (d 1972), and Rachel Eluned, *née* Rees; *b* 20 Sept 1934; *Educ* Emanuel Sch, Magdalen Coll Oxford, St Antony's Coll Oxford, Univ of California Berkeley; *m* 12 Dec 1959, Judith Mary, da of Dr Morris Reed, of London; 1 s (Charles b 1962), 1 da (Ruth b 1964); *Career* Nat Serv RAF 1952-54; leader writer The Guardian 1959-62, res fell St Antony's Coll Oxford 1962-64, lectr in sch of social studies Univ of Sussex 1964-66; MP (Lab) Ashfield 1966-67; PPS to: Min of Works 1966-67, Min of Overseas Devpt 1969-79; Br delegate to Cncl of Europe and WEU Assemblies 1970-73, chief advsr European Cmmn Brussels 1977-78; prof of contemporary hist and politics Univ of Salford 1978-; jt ed The political Quarterly 1987-; chm High Peak SDP 1981-82 and 1987-88, pres High Peak SLD 1988-; memb: Nat ctee SDP 1981-88, Policy ctee SLD 1988-; FRHistS 1986; *Books* Ramsay MacDonald (1977), Parliament for Europe (1979), European Elections and British Politics (with David Butler, 1981), John MacKintosh on Parliament and Social Democracy (ed, 1982), The Unprincipled Society (1988); *Recreations* walking, listening to music; *Style—* Prof David Marquand; 2 Buxworth Hall, Buxworth, Stockport, SX12 7NH (☎ 06633 2319); Dept of Politics and Contemporary History, University of Salford, Salford, M5 4WT (☎ 061 736 5843)

MARQUES, Reginald William David; JP; s of Charles Albert Marques, MBE (d 1967); *b* 9 Dec 1932; *Educ* Tonbridge, Queens' Coll Cambridge (MA); *m* 1965, Janet Isabel; 3 s; *Career* 2 Lt, Royal Engrs; md Concrete Utilities Ltd 1979-; played rugby for England and Br Lions; sailed on 'Sovereign' in America's Cup 1964; CEng, MIPLE, MCIBS; *Clubs* Harlequins, Br Sportsman's; *Style—* Reginald Marques Esq; Cockhamsted, Ware, Herts (☎ 027 974 312); Concrete Utilities Ltd, Great Amwell, Ware, Herts SG12 9TA (☎ 0920 2272)

MARQUIS, James Douglas; DFC (1945); s of James Charles Marquis, ISM (d 1983), and Jessica Amy, *née* Huggett (d 1988); *b* 16 Oct 1921; *Educ* Shooters Hill Sch Woolwich; *m* 8 Jan 1945, Brenda Eleanor, da of Robert Reyner Davey, of Blackpool, Lancashire; 2 s (Peter b 1947, David b 1953); *Career* RAF 1941-46, Pilot Offr 1942, Flying Offr 1943, Sqdn Navigation Offr 177 Sqdn 1943-44, Flt Lt 1944, Gp Navigation Offr 224 Gp 1944, Navigation Offr AHQ Malaya 1945-46, Sqdn Ldr 1945 (RAF First Class Navigation Warrant 1945), local govt 1946-56, New Town devpt 1957-81, md Irvine Devpt Corpn 1972-81; *Recreations* growing bonsai, water colour painting; *Clubs* RAF, Scottish Bonsai Assoc; *Style—* James Marquis, Esq, DFC; Vibelyng, 3 Knoll Park, Ayr KA7 4RH (☎ 0292 42212)

MARQUIS, Dr Robert Macfie; MBE (1946); s of Capt Edward Marquis (d 1931), of Birkenhead, and Elsie Jean, *née* Anderson (d 1947); *b* 9 Jan 1917; *Educ* Abbotsholm Sch Derbyshire, Univ of Edinburgh (MB, ChB); *m* 11 Dec 1943, Mary Herndon, da of Major Roy Wilson Potter (d 1943), of London; 1 s (Edward b 1950), 2 da (Jane b 1945, Anna b 1948); *Career* RMO Parachute Regt NW Europe 1944-45, DADMS 6 Airborne Div Palestine 1946; conslt physician Dept of Cariodology Royal Infirmary of Edinburgh 1964-79, cardiologist Royal Hospital of Sick Children Edinburgh 1966-79, dir Rose, Thomson, Young (underwriters) Ltd Lloyds of London 1982-; cncl memb: RCPE 1966-71, Br Cardiac Soc 1966-70, Assoc of European Paediatric Cardiologists 1966-71, Br Heart Fndn 1967-71; tstee RCPE 1967-87; patron St Columba's Hospice (Edinburgh) 1967-, elder Ch of Scotland Howgate Ch Midlothian 1958-80; Brit Rep Monospeciality Cardiology, Union of Europ Med Specialists 1974-; memb exec ctee SE Cambridgeshire Cons Assoc 1980-; FRCPE; *Books* Heart Disease in the Newborn (ed, vol 2 1979); numerous scientific papers in learned jls on: congenital heart dis, cardiac surgery, heart dis and pregnancy; *Recreations* gardening, English and French literature, cooking, history, walking, tennis; *Clubs* Univ Staff (Edinburgh); *Style—* Dr R M Marquis, MBE; Park House, Balsham, Cambridge CB1 6DJ

MARR, Allan James; CBE (1965); s of William Bell Marr (decd), s of 1 Bt; hp of kinsman, (Sir) Leslie Marr (2 Bt); *b* 6 May 1907; *Educ* Oundle, Durham Univ; *m* 1935, Joan de Wolf, da of John Ranken, of Sunderland; 1 s, 2 da; *Career* chm Sir James Laing & Sons Ltd and dir Assoc Cos 1960-73 (dir 1933-73), dir and chm EGS Ltd; chm Cncl of Br Ship Res Assoc 1965-73; former pres: Shipbuilding Conference, NEC Inst of Eng Shipbuilders; *Style—* Allan Marr Esq, CBE; Dalesford, Thropton, Morpeth, Northumberland NE65 7JE

MARR, John; s of Harry Needham Marr, of Manchester, and Harriet Constance, *née* Portwood; *b* 7 Mar 1946; *Educ* Doncaster GS; *m* 15 April 1972, Caroline Anne, da of David Cowan, of Stockport; 1 s (Richard b 23 March 1985), 2 da (Victoria b 18 Oct 1978, Jessica 3 Feb 1981); *Career* accountant Mather and Platt 1964-69, investmt mangr Co Operative Insur Soc 1969-73; Charterhouse Tilney (formerly Tilney and Co) Stockbrokers: res investmt analyst 1973-, dir 1986; underwriter Lloyds of London 1987; ACIS 1969, ASIA 1970, FCCA 1970, memb Stock Exchange 1976; *Recreations* squash, cricket, vintage cars; *Clubs* Liverpool Racquet, Yorks CCC; *Style—* John Marr, Esq; Sea Lawn, 14 Westcliffe Rd, Birkdale, Southport PR8 2BN (☎ 0704 68283); Charterhouse Tilney, Royal Liver Building, The Pier Head, Liverpool L3 1NY (☎ 051 236 6000, fax 051 236 6000 ext 273)

MARR, (Sir) Leslie Lynn; (2 Bt, UK 1919, of Sunderland, Co Palatine of Durham); does not use title; s of Col John Lynn Marr, OBE, TD (decd), s of 1 Bt; suc gf, Sir James Marr, 1 Bt, CBE, JP; *b* 14 August 1922; *Educ* Shrewsbury, Pembroke Cambridge (MA); *m* 1948 (m dis 1956), Dinora Delores Mendelson; 1 da (adopted); m 2, 1962, Lynn Heneage; 2 da (Joanne b 1963, Rebecca b 1966); *Heir* kinsman, Allan James Marr, CBE; *Career* Pilot Offr RAF 1942, Flight Lt; artist (painter and draughtsman); *Publications* 'From my Point of View' (1978); *Style—* Leslie Marr, Esq; c/o Lloyds Bank, Holt, Norfolk

MARR, Lindsay Grigor David; s of Grigor Wilson Marr (d 1986), and Linda Grace,*née* Sergeant; *b* 14 Sept 1955; *Educ* The Perse Sch, Gonville and Caius Coll Cambridge (BA, MA); *Career* slr 1981; Freshfields: articled 1979-81, asst slr 1981-87, ptnr 1987-; Freeman City of London Slrs Co 1988; memb The Law Soc; *Recreations* reading, music, golf, squash; *Style—* Lindsay Marr, Esq; 39 Broad Lane, Hampton, Middlesex TW12 3AL,(☎ 01 979 0517); Walden House, 17-24 Cathedral Place, London EC4M 7JA, (☎ 01 979 0517, fax 01 329 6022)

MARR-JOHNSON, Hon Mrs (Diana Julia); *née* Maugham; da of 1 Viscount Maugham (d 1958); *m* 1932, Kenneth Marr-Johnson (d 1986); 3 s (Frederick b 1936, Simon b 1938, William b 1945); *Books* seven novels; *Style—* The Hon Mrs Marr-Johnson; Flat 3, 14 Onslow Sq, London SW7 3NP

MARR-JOHNSON, Frederick James Maugham; s of Kenneth Marr-Johnson (d 1986), and Hon Diana Julia, *née* Maugham, da of 1 Viscount Maugham; *b* 17 Sept 1936; *Educ* Winchester, Trinity Hall Cambridge (MA); *m* 26 March 1966, Susan, da of Maj R P H Eyre, OBE (d 1982); 1 s (Thomas b 30 Sept 1966), 1 da (Rachel b 27 May 1969); *Career* Nat Serv RN 1955-56, Midshipman RNVR; called to the Bar Lincolns Inn 1962, rec 1986-; *Recreations* sailing, skiing; *Style—* Frederick Marr-Johnson, Esq; 59 Perrymead St, London SW6 3SN (☎ 01 731 0412); Farrar's Building, Temple, London EC4Y 7BD (☎ 01 583 9241, fax 01 583 0090)

MARRACK, Rear Adm Philip Reginald; CB (1979); s of Capt Philip Marrack, RN (d 1955), and Annie Kathleen Marrack, *née* Proud; *b* 16 Nov 1922; *Educ* Eltham Coll, Royal Naval Engrg Coll; *m* 1954, Pauline Mary, da of Charles Haag (d 1938); 2 da (Claire, Philippa); *Career* war service Atlantic & Mediterranean, Naval Offr, 8 appointments at sea in surface ships and submarines; 5 other appointments in shore establishments and MOD; ret 1981; dir: Naval Ship Production MOD 1974-77, Dockyard Production and Support MOD 1977-81; specialist in Engrg and Submarines; *Recreations* trout and salmon fishing, viticulture; *Style—* Rear-Adm Philip Marrack, CB; c/o Barclays Bank, Princess Street, Plymouth

MARRE, Sir Alan Samuel; KCB (1970, CB 1955); s of Joseph Marre (d 1953); *b* 25 Feb 1914; *Educ* St Olave's GS, Trinity Hall Cambridge (MA); *m* 1943, Romola Mary, da of Aubrey John Gilling (d 1952); 1 s, 1 da; *Career* entered Civil Serv 1936, second perm sec DHSS 1968-71, ret; parliamentary cmmr: Administration (Ombudsman) 1971-76, Health Serv 1973-76; ex-officio memb Cncl on Tribunals 1971-76, vice chm advsy ctee on Distinction Awards for Conslts 1979-85; tstee Whitechapel Art Gallery 1977-84, chm Crown Housing Assoc 1978-, ctee memb Friends of the Hebrew Univ of Jerusalem 1980-, gen govr Br Nutrition Fndn 1981- (chm 1983-85), chm Rural Dispensing Ctee 1983-87, pres The Maccabaeans 1982-; *Recreations* reading, walking; *Clubs* Athenaeum, MCC; *Style—* Sir Alan Marre, KCB; 44 The Vale, London NW11 8SG (☎ 01 458 1787)

MARRETT, Dr (Henry) Rex; s of Dr Henry Norman Marrett (d 1961), and Florence Dering, *née* Mathew-Lanove (d 1944); *b* 25 Oct 1915; *Educ* Felsted, St Bart's Hosp; *m* 25 Oct 1940 (Diana) Jacqueline, da of Philip Henry Marsh; 2 s (Norman b 1942, Roger b 1944); *Career* WWII Lt RAMC 1943, Capt 1944, Maj 1944-46, specialist anaesthetist Euro Campaign with Field Surgical unit, inventor of the Marrett Anaesthetic Apparatus at the request of the Army 1945; jr anaesthetist St Bart's Hosp 1941-43, conslt anaesthetist Coventry 1947-79, inventor Medrex Apparatus for Dental Anaesthesia; fndr memb Hickman Anaesthic Soc; hon memb: History of Anaestesia Soc, Assoc Dental Anaesthists; capt Coventry GC 1974, Essex Co hockey colours 1939; MRCS, LRCP FFARCS; memb RSM, Assoc of Anaesthetists; *Recreations* engineering, golf, gardening; *Style—* Dr Rex Marrett; 7A The Firs, Kenilworth Rd, Coventry CV5 6QD (☎ 0203 74706)

MARRIAN, Lady Emma Clare; da of 6 Earl Cawdor; *b* 15 Mar 1958; *m* 1983, David Marrian, s of Peter Marrian, of Nairobi; 2 s (Jack Alexander Wolf b 1985, Hunter James b 1988); *Style—* Lady Emma Marrian; 15 Callow St, London SW3

MARRIOTT; *see*: Smith-Marriott

MARRIOTT, Douglas Haig; MC (1944); s of William George Marriott (d 1954), and Maida Amy, *née* Babbage (d 1966); descendant of Adm M de Ruyter (Amsterdam) who sacked Chatham Naval Base in 1667; *b* 20 Dec 1918; *Educ* Ardingly Coll, Sussex; *m* 1, 5 April 1947, Margaret Anne, da of Frederick Goddard (d 1962); 2 s (Graham b 1948,

David b 1953); m 2, 11 March 1982, Ann Penelope, da of Geoffrey Holmes Glenny, of Beckenham, Kent; 1 step s (Richard b 1966), 2 step da (Joanna b 1962, Katheryn b 1964); *Career* Capt Kent Yeomanry 1939-45, Iceland, Europe; architect, FRIBA, created practice 1963 of Douglas Marriott, Worby and Robinson London, Provinces and overseas; notable bldgs: Vickers Millbank Tower (London's first tower block), United Nations Maritime Organisation HQ London, Nat Farmers Union HQ London; also architects to DOE inc: Houses of Parliament, Westminster Bank, Trinity House, Watneys Brewery, J Sainsbury, Electricity Cncl, Legal & General, Provident Mutual, Br Rail, Borough Cncls, Australian High Cmmn, Post Office, Sun Life, Trafalgar House, BOC Gp, Church Cmmnrs, and many others; on Court of Worshipful Co of Carpenters (Livery Co London); Capt Sundridge Park GC 1960-61; *Recreations* sailing, golf, oil painting, photography, travel, politics; *Clubs* Royal Southern Yacht, Naval (Little Ships), Sundridge Park GC, City Livery; *Style*— Douglas Marriott, Esq, MC; 2 Old Rectory, Church Rd, Offham, Kent ME19 5NY (☎ 0732 847559); 1 Westminster Bridge Rd, London SE1 7PL (telex 8954526 DMWR G, fax 01 928 1593)

MARRIS, David Drummond; s of Adam Denzill Marris, CMG (d 1983); *b* 5 May 1942; *Educ* Winchester; *m* 1978, Clare Katrina, *née* Mayers; *Career* 2 Lieut 3 Green Jackets, The Rifle Bgde; banker; local dir Barclays Bank Ltd Manchester 1977-82 (Chelmsford 1973-77); Caribbean dir Barclays Int 1982-83; sr Caribbean dir Barbados Barclays Bank plc 1983-87; Regional Dir Luton Region 1987-; *Recreations* country pursuits, sailing, music; *Clubs* Boodle's; *Style*— David Marris, Esq; Flat 10, 54 Redcliffe Square, London SW10

MARRON, (Joseph) Ronald; s of Joseph Marron, Acklam, Middlesborough, Cleveland, and Elsie Marron, *née* Harding; *b* 20 Jan 1935; *Educ* St Richards RC; *m* 1955, Audrey, da of Thomas Dowson, of Cleveland County Cleveland; 3 s (Ronald, Craig, Jason), 3 da (Carol, Susan, Tracy); *Career* gen sec Assoc Metal Workers Union; *Style*— Ronald Marron, Esq; 92 Deansgate, Manchester 3

MARS-JONES, Hon Mr Justice; Hon Sir William Lloyd; MBE (1945); s of Henry Mars Jones, of Denbighshire; *b* 4 Sept 1915; *Educ* Denbigh County Sch, Univ Coll of Wales at Aberystwyth (LLB), St John's Cambridge (BA); *m* 1947, Sheila Cobon; 3 s; *Career* WWII Lt Cdr RNVR; barr 1941, QC 1957, dep chm Denbighshire QS 1962-68; rec: Birkenhead 1959-65, Swansea 1965-68, Cardiff 1968-69; High Ct judge (Queen's Bench) 1969-, presiding judge Wales & Chester circuit 1971-75; memb: Home Off inquiry into Allegations against Metropolitan Police Offrs 1964, Home Sec's advsy cncl on Penal System 1966-68; pres N Wales Arts Assoc 1976-, tres Gray's Inn 1982; pres: Univ Coll of N Wales Bangor 1983-, Univ Coll of Wales Aberystwyth 1987-88, London Welsh Tst 1989-; Hon LLD Univ Coll Wales; kt 1969; *Style*— The Hon Mr Justice Mars-Jones, MBE; Royal Courts of Justice, Strand, London WC2

MARSDEN, Andrew Guy; s of Flt Lt Geoffrey Ansdell Marsden, DFC, of Egmont House, Darley, Harrogate, N Yorks, and Margaret Jean, *née* Furniss; *b* 6 August 1953; *Educ* Monkton Combe Sch, Pembroke Coll Oxford (MA); *Career* called to the Bar Middle Temple 1975, memb S E circuit; in practice: Colchester, Norwich, Ipswich 1977-; patron Acorn Villages Mistley Home for Mentally Handicapped, organist Church of Holy Innocents Lamarsh Essex, memb Kelvedon Singers; *Recreations* historical vocal recordings, architecture, singing; *Clubs* United Oxford and Cambridge; *Style*— Andrew Marsden, Esq; Little Gables, Lamarsh, Bures, Suffolk (☎ 0787 227054); 53 North Hill, Colchester, Essex (☎ 0206 572756, fax 0206 562447); 3 Princes St, Ipswich, Suffolk, Wensum Chambers, Wensum St, Norwich; 4 Paper Buildings, Temple, London EC4

MARSDEN, Lady; Joyce Winifred; da of William Alfred and Beatrice Ellen Chote, of Wellington, NZ; *m* 1958, as his 2 w, Sir Ernest Marsden, CMG, CBE, MC, FRS (d 1970); *Style*— Lady Marsden; 104 Winara Ave, Waikanae, Wellington, New Zealand

MARSDEN, Sir Nigel John Denton; 3 Bt (UK 1924), of Grimsby, Co Lincoln; s of Sir John Denton Marsden, 2 Bt (d 1985); *b* 26 May 1940; *Educ* Ampleforth; *m* 1961, Diana Jean, da of Air Marshal Sir Patrick Hunter Dunn, KBE, CB, DFC, *qv*; 3 da (Lucinda Ann b 1962, Rose Amanda b 1964, Annabel Juliet b 1968); *Heir* bro, Simon N L Marsden Esq, *qv*; *Career* self employed gardener; *Recreations* walking, family, countryside pursuits; *Style*— Sir Nigel Marsden, Bt; 1 Grimsby Rd, Waltham, Lincs

MARSDEN, Rear-Adm Peter Nicholas; s of Dr James Pickford Marsden (d 1977), and Evelyn Holman (d 1970); *b* 29 June 1932; *Educ* Felsted Sch; *m* 12 Oct 1956, Jean Elizabeth, da of Cdr J H Mather, DSO, VRD, RNVR (d 1957); 2 s (James b 1957, Jonathan b 1960), 1 da (Joanna b 1963); *Career* dir Fleet Supply Duties Div MOD 1980-81; Cdre Admiralty Interview Bd 1983-85; sr naval memb Directing Staff Records 1985-88; *Recreations* beagling, golf; *Style*— Rear-Admiral Peter Marsden; Royal Coll of Defence Studies, 27 Belgrave Sq, London SW1

MARSDEN, Simon Neville Llewelyn; yr s of Sir John Denton Marsden, 2 Bt (d 1985); hp of bro, Sir Nigel John Denton Marsden, 3 Bt, *qv*; *b* 1948; *Educ* Ampleforth, Sorbonne Univ Paris; *m* 1, 1970 (m dis), Catherine Thérèsa, da of Brig James Charles Windsor-Lewis, DSO (decd); m 2, 1984, Caroline Stanton; 1 da (Skye Atalanta b 24 Feb 1988); *Career* photographer, collections in Victoria and Albert Museum, Getty Museum California, and author; *Books* In Ruins (The Once Great Houses of Ireland) (1980), The Haunted Realm (Ghosts, Witches and other Strange Tales) (1986), Visions of POE (1988); *Style*— Simon Marsden, Esq; The Presbytery, Hainton, Lincoln LN3 6LR

MARSDEN, Hon Mrs; Vere Mary; da of Hon Conrad Adderley Dillon (d 1901), and sister of 19 Viscount Dillon, CMG, DSO (d 1946); *m* 1911, Reginald Edward Marsden (d 1960); 3 s, 3 da; *Style*— The Hon Mrs Marsden; Bishopsgate Pla, Englefield Green, Egham, Surrey (☎ Egham 3034)

MARSDEN, William; s of Christopher Alexander Marsden, and Ruth, *née* Kershaw (d 1970); *b* 15 Sept 1940; *Educ* Winchester, Lawrenceville Sch USA, Trinity Coll Cambridge (MA), Univ of London (BSc); *m* 19 Sept 1964, Kaya; 1 s (Thomas Alexander b 16 Jan 1970), 1 da (Inge Katharine b 29 July 1966); *Career* third sec UK Delgn to NATO Paris 1964-66, second sec Rome Embassy 1966-69, seconded asst to gen mangr Joseph Lucas Ltd 1970, first sec and cultural attaché Moscow Embassy 1976-79, asst head Euro community dept FCO 1978-81, cnsllr UK Representation to the EEC Brussels 1981-85, head E African dept FCO and cmmr Br Indian Ocean Territory 1985-88, ambass to Costa Rica (concurrently non-resident ambass to nicaragua) 1989-; Freeman: City of London 1967, Worshipful Co of Grocers 1967; MBIM; *Style*— William Marsden, Esq; c/o Foreign and Commonwealth Office, London SW1 A 2AH

MARSDEN-SMEDLEY, Robert Andrew Huntsman; s of Andrew Bethell Marsden-Smedley, of The Glebe House, Bayton, Nr Kidderminister, Worcs DY14 9LT, and Lavina Ann, *née* Lea; *b* 3 Jan 1962; *Educ* Stowe, North Worcestershire Coll (Business Studies); *Career* Leslie & Godwin Aviation Insur Brokers 1983-87, Investmt Insur Int Managers Ltd 1987-88, Lloyd Thompson Ltd 1988-; *Recreations* skiing, shooting, motorsports; *Clubs* RAC; *Style*— Robert Marsden-Smedley, Esq; 33 Novello St, London SW6 4JB (☎ 01 731 3479); Lloyd Thompson Ltd, 14 Lovat Lane, London EC3R 8DT (☎ 01 623 5616, fax 01 623 4033, telex 885671)

MARSH, Alan James; s of James Alfred Leonard Marsh, of 10 Caple Ct, Albany Rd, St Leonards-on-Sea, Sussex, and Grace Maud, *née* Weller (d 1985); *b* 26 August 1929; *Educ* Colfes GS, Christ Church Oxford (MA); *m* 1, 28 Dec 1957 (m dis 1984), Ingrid Hilma Elizabet, da of Nils Areskog (d 1977), of Kalmar, Sweden; 1 s (Neil b 4 Aug 1959), 1 da (Caroline b 27 Oct 1961); m 2, Joanna Maud, da of Brig Bertram Edward Lionel Burton, CBE (d 1976), of Uckfield, Sussex; *Career* Lt 4 RTR 1952-54; Metal Box Co 1954-61, mangr corporate strategy div PA Int Mgmnt Conslts 1961-71, gp fin dir Revertex Chemicals Ltd 1971-80, exec dir Midland Montagu Ventures 1980-; Freeman City of London, Liveryman Worshipful Co of Gold and Silver Wire Drawers; FCMA 1966, FCT 1978, MIMC 1963; *Recreations* sailing, golf; *Clubs* Royal Corinthian YC; *Style*— Alan Marsh, Esq; Flat 8, 11 Lindfield Gardens, Hampstead, London NW3 6PX (☎ 01 435 8427); 7 The Belvedere, Burnham-on-Crouch, Essex; 10 Lower Thames St, London EC3R 6AE (☎ 01 260 0312, fax 01 220 7265, car tel 0836 582 815, telex 887213)

MARSH, Alan John Scott; s of Reginald John Marsh, MA, Cantab, and Vera Kathleen Marsh; *b* 1 Nov 1936; *Educ* Charterhouse and Coll Estate Mgmt London; *m* 3 Nov 1962, Pamela Mary, da of Albert Edward White, of Eastbourne; 2 da (Caroline b 1963, Nicola b 1965); *Career* md and chief exec Toyota (FB) Ltd 1986-; md IMC Belgium 1984-85; gen sales mangr Austin Morris Div 1974-75, Fleet Sales dir Leylandcars 1975-77, regnl dir Leyland Int 1977-78, dir Service Rover Triumph 1978-79, sales and marketing dir Toyota (FB) Ltd 1979-84; *Recreations* motoring, sport, sailing; *Style*— Alan Marsh, Esq; Toyota (FB) Ltd, The Quadrangle, Redhill, Surrey RH1 1PX (☎ 0737 768585)

MARSH, Alexander James; s of James Robertson Marsh, of London, and Clara *née* Rakos (d 1984); *b* 18 Jan 1946; *Educ* Univ Coll Sch London (BSc), Univ of Newcastle Upon Tyne (BSc); *m* 29 June 1968, Elspeth Mary Russell, da of Joseph Russell Cameron of Newcastle Upon Tyne; 3 s (Nicholas b 1971, Alasdair b 1974, Stephen b 1980); *Career* Swan Hunter shipbuilders ltd: gen mangr Wallsend Shipyard 1976-80, shipbuilding dir 1980-83, dep md 1983-84, md 1984-86, jt md 1986-87, chief exec 1987-; chief exec Swan Hunter Ltd 1987-(jt md 1986-87), dir Maravia Int Ltd 1987-; memb Cncl NE Coast Inst Engrs & Shipbuilders 1987-; MRINA 1974, MIMarE 1974, CEng 1976; *Recreations* vintage sports cars, sailing, travel, wine, sheep farming; *Style*— Alexander Marsh, Esq; Swan Hunter Ltd, Wallsend, Newcasle Upon Tyne, NE28 6EQ (☎ 0912 628921, fax 091 234 0707, telex 53151)

MARSH, Hon Andrew; er son of Baron Marsh, PC (Life Peer), by his 1 w; *b* 1950; *Style*— Hon Andrew Marsh; c/o Rt Hon Lord Marsh, PC, 27 Crossfields Rd, London NW3

MARSH, Barbara Elizabeth; JP (Shropshire 1969); da of John Watson (d 1965), of St Helens, Lancs, and Elizabeth, *née* Burrows (d 1987); *b* 3 July 1931; *Educ* Cowley Girls GS, London Univ (BSc), Birmingham Univ (PhD); *m* 1 April 1958, (George) Eric Marsh, s of Richard George Marsh, of Newport, Shropshire; 3 s (Andrew b 1958, Stephen b 1961, Piers b 1963), 1 da (Fiona b 1967); *Career* demonstrator Kings Coll Newcastle 1956-57, lectr St Helen Tech Coll 1957-58, teacher Adams GS Newport 1959-60, non exec bd memb Midlands Electricity Bd 1984-; memb: Cncl on Tbnls 1977-84, Roskill Ctee on Fraud 1984-86; vice chm Shropshire CC 1981-85 (cncllr 1964-), memb Exec Assoc of CC, former chm Area Manpower Bd for Shropshire, vice pres Nat Inst of Adult Continuing Educn, memb Industl Tbnl, dep church warden St Nicholas Church Newport; *Recreations* dabbling; *Style*— Mrs Barbara Marsh; Middle Farm, Chetwynd Aston, Newport, Shropshire

MARSH, (Graham) Barrie; s of Ernest Heaps Marsh (d 1983), of 102 Victoria Court, Birkdale, Southport, and Laura Greenhalgh, *née* Bancher; *b* 18 July 1935; *Educ* Loughborough GS, Liverpool Univ (LLB); *m* 5 April 1961, Nancy, da of Leslie Herbert Smith (d 1984), of 146 Cropston Rd, Anstey, Leicester; 1 s (Peter James b 1962), 2 da (Susan Nancy b 1964, Caroline Judith b 1966); *Career* nat serv with RASC 1957-59; slr 1957; nat chm Young Solicitors' Gp of Law Soc 1975; pres: Liverpool Law Soc 1978-79, Solicitors' Disciplinary Tribunal 1988-; chm Mersyside Chamber of Commerce and Industry 1984-86; pres Liverpool Publicity Assoc 1980; chm Radio City plc 1988-; Belgian Consul in Liverpool; FRIA; *Books* Employer and Employee (3 edn 1989); *Recreations* hill walking, golf, bird watching; *Clubs* Liverpool Racquet, Anglo-Belgian (London); *Style*— Barrie Marsh, Esq; Calmer Hey, Benty Heath Lane, Willaston, South Wirral L64 1SA (☎ 051 327 4863); Mace & Jones, 19 Water Street, Liverpool L2 0RP (☎ 051 236 8989, fax 051 227 5010)

MARSH, The Ven Bazil Roland; s of The Ven Wilfred Carter Marsh (d 1921), of Devil's Lake, N Dakota, and Mary Jean, *née* Stott (d 1925); *b* 11 August 1921; *Educ* State Schs in Calgary Alberta and Williston and Devil's Lake N Dakota, Coll Secdy Sch Swindon Wilts, Common Weal Secdy Sch Swindon, Leeds Univ, Coll of the Resurrection Mirfield Yorks; *m* 25 Aug 1946, Audrey Joan, da of Owen George Oyler (d 1979), of Brookman's Park, Hatfield, Herts; 3 s (Nicholas b 1947, Charles b 1952, David b 1956), 1 da (Katherine b 1962); *Career* asst curate: Cheshunt Herts 1944-46, St John Baptist Coventry 1946-47, St Giles Reading 1947-51; rector St Peter's Townsville Queensland Aust 1951-56, vicar St Mary Northampton 1956-64, rector St Peter Northampton 1964-, canon Peterborough Cathedral 1964-, archdeacon of Northampton 1964-; *Recreations* walking, gardening, architectural history; *Clubs* Royal Commonwealth Soc; *Style*— The Ven the Archdeacon of Northampton; 11 The Drive, Northampton, NN1 4RZ (☎ 0604 714015)

MARSH, Brian Peter; s of Albert Edward Marsh (d 1980), and Maud Elisabeth, *née* Holman; *b* 28 Feb 1941; *Educ* Sutton Valence Sch; *m* Aleksandra Barbara, *née* Waclawik; 1 s (Rupert b 1973), 2 da (Natalie b 1976, Antonia b 1988); *Career* chm Nelson Hurst & Marsh (Hldgs) Ltd and 40 other cos 1979-; snr tstee Marsh Christian Tst; govr Dummer Acad; *Recreations* swimming, writing; *Clubs* Authors; *Style*— Brian P Marsh, Esq; Flat 7, 30 Onslow Gardens, London SW7 (☎ 584 6056); 1 Seething Lane, London EC3

MARSH, Hon Christopher; yr s of Baron Marsh by his 1 w; *b* 1960; *Style*— The Hon Christopher Marsh; Blackfen, Sidcup, Kent

MARSH, David John; s of Harry Cheetham Marsh, of Solihull Warwickshire (d 1979), and Florence, *née* Bold; *b* 2 Nov 1936; *Educ* Leeds GS, Merton Coll Oxford (MA); *m* 26 May 1962, Hilary Joy, da of Edwin Leslie Pitt, of Tetbury, Glos; 1 s (Nigel b 1966), 2 da (Carole b 1963, Rowena b 1965); *Career* admitted slr 1961, ptnr Wragge & Co Slrs 1963-, dir Marla Tube Fittings Ltd 1965-, dir and sec Fownes Hotels plc 1985-; memb Law Soc 1961; *Recreations* sport, travel, wine, food; *Clubs* Midland Sporting; *Style—* David Marsh, Esq; Lenchwick House, Lenchwick, nr Evesham, Worcs WR11 4TG (☎ 0386 2451); Wragge & Co, Bank House, 8 Cherry St, Birmingham B2 5JY (☎ 021 632 4131, fax 021 643 2417, telex 338728 WRAGGE G)

MARSH, Eric Morice; s of Frederick Morice Marsh (d 1970), of Carnforth, Lancs, and Anne, *née* Leigh; *b* 25 July 1943; *Educ* The Abbey Sch Fort Augustus Inverness-shire Scotland, Courtfield Catering Coll Blackpool, Lancs (Nat Dip Hotelkeeping & Catering); *m* 2 Sept 1968, Elizabeth Margaret, da of John (Jack) Lowes, of Macclesfield, Cheshire; 2 s (Andrew Paul b 4 Aug 1969, Christopher Simon b 5 July 1974), 2 da (Erika Louise b 26 Oct 1971, Lucy Anne b 4 Aug 1982); *Career* student Hotel Sch 1960-63, stagiare George V Hotel Paris 1964-65, trainee the Dorchester 1965-68, asst mangr Royal Lancaster 1969-73, dir and gen mangr NewLing Ward Hotels Ltd 1973-75, tenant Cavendish Hotel Chatsworth Estate 1975-; md: Paludis Ltd (trading as Cavendish Hotel) 1975-, Cavendish Aviation; pt/t lectr Sheffield Poly, occasional contribs to professional publns; memb Catholic Church Fin Ctee, co-ordinator ctee Neighbourhood Watch; memb ctee: Br Areobatics Assoc, Br Hotels Restaurants & Caterers Assoc; memb Inst Advanced Motorists, MinstM; *Recreations* collection of fine art, aviation(aerobatics), distance running; *Style—* Eric Marsh, Esq; Cavendish Hotel, Baslow, Derbys DE4 1SP (☎ 024 688 2311); Paludis Ltd, Baslow, Derbys DE4 1SP (☎ 024 688 2311, fax 024688 3464, car phone 0836 587 690, telex 547150 CAVTEL G)

MARSH, Baroness; Hon Felicity Carmen Francesca; da of Baron McFadzean of Kelvinside (Life Peer); *b* 26 April 1946; *Educ* St Paul's Girls' Sch, SOAS (BA in Japanese); *m* 1979, as his 3 w, Baron Marsh, *qv*; *Career* investment analyst/portfolio mangr Robert Fleming 1974-79, asst vice-pres Rowe Price-Fleming Int Inc 1979-81, dir Mannington Mgmnt Servs Ltd 1982-; *Books* Japanese Overseas Investment - The New Challenge (1983), Japan's Next Export Success: The Financial Services Industry (1986); *Recreations* oriental antiques, classic cars, windsurfing, photography; *Style—* The Hon Lady Marsh; Lloyds Bank Ltd, South Bank Branch, 2 York Rd, London SE1

MARSH, Frederick Oliver; *b* 13 Sept 1925; *Educ* Regent St Poly (Dip Mgmt Studies); *Career* capt Royal Berks Regt, demobed 1948; chm and md Winton-Smith (Foods) Ltd 1964-74, princ Marsh Business Servs 1974-; mktg conslt: UN Agency (ITC UNCTAD GATT) 1978-86, Helsinki Sch of Econs 1984-; vice-chm Royal Aero Club 1977-82, vice-pres Fedn Aeronautique Internationale 1982-; Br Air Racing champion 1977-82, winner Duke of Edinburgh Trophy for Formula Air Racing 1972 and 1976; FAI Tissandier Dip 1978, Order of Merit World Aerospace Educn Orgn 1985; Liveryman Worshipful Co Butchers 1962; FBIM 1970; *Books* The Market for New Foods and Beverages in Europe (1986, re-written 1988); *Recreations* air sport, painting, travel, scottish dancing; *Clubs* Navel & Military, Royal Aero; *Style—* Frederick Marsh, Esq; 40 Buckingham Gate, London SW1E 6BS; Suite 4, 40 Buckingham Gate, London SW1E 6BS (☎ 01 834 6983, fax 01 222 7471, telex 28604 MONREF G)

MARSH, Gordon Victor; s of The Venerable Wilfred Carter Marsh (d 1931), of Devil's Lake, North Dakota, USA, and Rosalie Marsh (d 1947); *b* 14 May 1929; *Educ* The Coll and Cwlth GS's Swindon Wilts, Keble Coll Oxford (MA), Sloan Business Sch Cornell Univ, USA; *m* 13 June 1959, Millicent, da of Christopher Thomas Rowsell (d 1959); 1 s (Richard Marsh b 1960), 1 da (Susan Marsh b 1961); *Career* RAF PO personnel selection branch 1947-49; dep sec United Cardiff Hosps 1960-65, dep sec and house govr St Georges Hosp 1965-72, admin and sec bd of govrs Univ Coll Hosp 1972-74, area admin Lambeth Southwark and Lewisham Area Health Authy (teaching) 1974-82, dep health serv cmmr for England Scot and Wales 1982-; chm Trelawn Mgmnt Ctee of Richmond Fellowship 1970-83, memb advsy bd coll of occupational Therapist 1974-, memb various working parties concerned with med ethics, Wandsman and hon sec of congregation St Paul's Cathedral, memb cncl NAHA 1979-82, vice chm Assoc of Chief Admins of Health Authorities 1980-82; FIHSM 1964, RSM; *Recreations* gardens and gardening, music; *Clubs* United Oxford and Cambridge Universities; *Style—* Gordon Marsh, Esq; Springwater, St Lucian's Lane, Wallingford OX10 4ER (☎ 0491 36 660); Office of Health Service Commissioner, Church House, Gt Smith St, SW1P 3BW (☎ 01 276 2089)

MARSH, Capt John; CBE (1977); s of Arthur Frank Marsh (d 1953), of Cheam, Surrey, and Doris Evelyn, *née* Dabbs; *b* 23 August 1932; *Educ* Epsom Coll, St Johns Coll Cambridge (MA); *m* 12 April 1958, Margaret Hilda, da of Eric William Beresford Brailey (d 1977), of Fremington, Devon; 2 s (Jonathon b 1961, Nigel b 1964); *Career* cmmnd RN 1954, Cdr 1968, Staff of Saclant Norfolk, UA, USA 1972, HMS Ark Royal 1975, RN Sch of Meteorology and Oceanography 1977, Capt 1978, Staff of Saceur Belgium 1979, Staff of Cincfleet Northwood and UK 1982, dir naval oceanography and meteorology MOD London 1985, Chief Naval Instr Offr 1986; dir Int toga Project Off World Meteorological Orgn Geneva Switzerland 1987; vice-chm Royal Br Legion Swiss Branch; memb: Anglo Swiss Club of Geneva, Br Residents Assoc; *Recreations* bridge, music, walking; *Style—* Capt John Marsh, CBE; Overton Hse, Queen Camel BA22 7NG; 38B Les Landes, 1299 Crans, Vaud, Switzerland (☎ 010 41 22 621 877); World Meteorological Orgn, CP No 5, CH 1211, Geneva 20 (☎ 010 41 22 734 6400)

MARSH, Laurie Peter; s of Davis Marsh; *b* 23 Oct 1930; *Educ* Perse Sch, Cambridge Univ; *m* 1961 (m dis); 1 s, 2 da; *Career* md LP Marsh Properties Ltd 1958-, md John Laurie & Co Ltd 1961-64, jt md English Property Corpn 1965-70, chm and chief exec Intereuropean Properties Ltd (formerly Tigon Gp) 1969-, merged with Assoc Communications Corpn 1979, dir ACC 1979-; chm and chief exec: Laurie Marsh Gp, Soundalive Tours plc, Laurie Marsh Consultants Ltd, and others 1980-; *Recreations* travel, theatre, music, literature; *Style—* Laurie Marsh, Esq; Laurie Marsh Group Ltd, 30 Grove End Rd, London NW8 9LJ (☎ 01 289 6081); 244 East 48th St, New York 10017

MARSH, Prof Paul Rodney; s of Harold Marsh, of Bournemouth, Dorset, and Constance, *née* Miller; *b* 19 August 1947; *Educ* Poole GS, LSE (BSc), London Business Sch (PhD); *m* 13 Sept 1971, Stephanie Beatrice, da of Mark Simonow, of London; *Career* systems analyst: Esso Petroleum 1968-69, Scicon 1970-71; London Business Sch 1974-; Bank of England res fell 1974-85, dir Sloan Fellowship Programme 1980-83; Centre for Mgmnt Devpt: dir, non exec dir 1984-, prof of mgmnt & fin 1985-, memb governing body 1986-, faculty dean 1987-; author of numerous pubns on corporate fin and investmt mgmnt in: Jnl of Fin, Jnl of Fin Econs, Mgmnt Fin, Jnl of the Inst of Actuaries, Res in Mktg, The Investmt Analyst, Long Range Planning; memb CBI task force on City-Indust relationships 1986-88; exec ctee memb Br Acad of Mgmnt; memb: Euro Fin Assoc, American Fin Assoc; *Books* Cases in Corporate Finance (1988), Managing Strategic Investment Decisions (1988), The HGSC Smaller Companies Index (1988); *Recreations* gardening; *Style—* Prof Paul Marsh; 52 Vivian Way, London N2 0HZ (☎ 01 444 6462); London Business Sch, Sussex Place, Regents Park, London NW1 4SA (☎ 01 262 5050, fax 01 724 7875, telex 27461 LONDISKOL)

MARSH, Peter Dudley; s of Dudley Graham Marsh (d 1969), of Canterbury, and Norah Marion *née* Wacher (d 1974); *b* 16 Feb 1926; *Educ* Dulwich, St Johns Coll Hurstpierpoint, Edinburgh Univ, Sch of Architecture, Canterbury Coll of Art; *m* 1, 18 Aug 1949, June, *née* Saxby (d 1969); 2 s (Richard b 1957, Jonathan b 1961), 1 da (Anne Crouch b 1953); m 2, 23 May 1970, Valerie, da of Charles Alfred Williams (d 1983); 1 s (Henry b 1977); *Career* Univ Short Course (Admty) 1944, cmmnd Sub Lt RNVR 1945, HMS Drake (Gunnery Sch) 1945, GCO HMS Savage 1945, GCO HMS Zodiac GCO 1947; architect in private practice 1952-, surveyor to the fabric Canterbury Cathedral 1969-; chm: Cathedral Architects Assoc 1984-87, Canterbury Branch RIBA 1969; memb tech sub ctee Euro Cathedrals Assoc 1986-; pres Rotary Club of Dover 1970; memb: Canterbury Conservation Advsy Ctee, Ecclesiastical Architects and Surveyors Assoc; fell Soc of Antiquaries of London, govr Kent Inst of Art and Design; Freeman City of London, Liveryman Worshipful Co of Masons 1978; ARIBA 1953, FSA 1982; *Recreations* bee keeping; *Style—* Peter Marsh, Esq; Little Watersend, Temple Ewell, Dover, Kent CT15 7EP (☎ 0304 822022)

MARSH, Peter Waller; s of Major Michael John Waller Marsh (d 1983) of Parkside, Lime St, Burton Lazars, Leics, MC TD (Cantab), and Kathleen, *née* Harrison (d 1983); *b* 19 April 1950; *Educ* Oakham Public Sch; *m* 11 Oct 1985, Kay, da of Edward Hewitt, of Somerby, Leics, 1 s (Michael John Robert b 16 June 1982); *Career* slr (1974), licenced conveyancer (1986); *Recreations* wine appreciation; *Clubs* Aries Melton Mowbray, Leics; *Style—* Peter Waller, Esq; Pembroke Chambers, 4 Avenue Road, Grantham, Lincs (☎ 0476 68922)

MARSH, Baron (Life Peer UK 1981); Richard William; PC (1966); s of William Marsh, of Belvedere, Kent; *b* 14 Mar 1928; *Educ* Jennings Sch Swindon, Ruskin Coll Oxford; *m* 1, 1950 (m dis 1973), Evelyn Mary, da of Frederick Andrews, of Southampton; 2 s; m 2, 1973, Caroline Dutton (d 1975); m 3, 1979, Felicity, da of Baron McFadzean of Kelvinside, *qv*; *Career* health servs offr Nat Union of Public Employees 1951-59; memb Clerical and Admin Whitley Cncl for Health Serv 1953-59; MP (L) Greenwich 1959-71; memb nat exec Fabian Soc; jt parly sec Miny of Labour 1964-65; Miny of Technol 1965-66, Miny of Power 1966-68; chm: Br Railways Bd 1971-76, Br Iron and Steel Consumers' Cncl to Jan 1983, Lee Cooper Licensing Servs, Lee Cooper plc 1982-88, Newspaper Publishers Assoc 1976-, (pt/t) TV-AM 1983-84; Mannington Mgmnt Servs Ltd; dep chm Lopex plc; dir: China and Eastern Investmt Tst (Hong Kong) 1987-, Bali Hldgs Co 1986, Imperial Life of Canada (Toronto) 1984; kt 1976; *Recreations* Reform, Buck's; *Style—* The Rt Hon the Lord Marsh, PC; Newspaper Publishers' Assoc Ltd, 34 Southwark Bridge Rd, London SE1 9EU (☎ 01 928 6928)

MARSH, Robin Lewis; s of Charles Edward Marsh (d 1969), of Westminster London, and Elsie May, *née* Peckham (d 1986); *b* 20 July 1939; *Educ* Henry Thornton Sch London, Christs Coll Cambridge (MA); *m* 26 Oct 1963, Suzette Fay, da of Frederick William Cockerton (d 1988) of Petersfield, Hants; 1 s (Charles Timothy Cockerton b 1980), 3 da (Claire Louise Cockerton b 1965, Annabel Lucy Cockerton b 1968, Camilla Sophie Cockerton b 1972); *Career* CA; articles clerk Fuller Wise Fisher 1958-60 and 1963-65; md Br Rare Earth Ltd 1966-69; chm and chief exec: CT Gp Ltd 1970-85, Wills Gp plc 1985-87; chm Marsh & Co Ltd 1987-; non exec dir various cos; memb ctee: Cons, Bramley Sch, Residents Assoc; memb IOD Freeman City of London 1968, Liveryman Worshipful Co Butchers 1969; Assoc ICEAW 1964, FCA 1975, FRGS; *Recreations* shooting, fishing, skiing, antique map collecting, travel, golf; *Style—* Robin Marsh. Esq; Marsh & Co Ltd, PO Box 47, Tadworth, Surrey KT20 7SZ (☎ 073 781 2920, fax 073 781 3113)

MARSH, Roger Edward; s of Albert Edward Marsh (d 1980), of Bickley, Kent, and Maud Elizabeth, *née* Holman; *b* 5 Mar 1945; *Educ* Sutton Valence Sch, Cranbrook USA; *m* 12 Sept 1968 (m dis 1989), Susan Louise, da of Alfred Gabriel Chase, of Bexhill-On-Sea; 1 s (Nicholas b 22 Feb 1971); *Career* entered Lloyd's 1963 with Sir Wm. Garthwaite Ins, elected underwriting memb Lloyds 1966, Tyser & Co: ptnr 1975 (sr ptnr 1988), various directorships within gp (UK & overseas); memb St Helen's PCC Bishopsgate c 1981-84, chm Lloyds Wine Soc; *Recreations* wine, books (antiquarian), music, shooting, tennis, cricket; *Clubs* City Univ, MCC, Harlequins FC, Les Ambassadeurs; *Style—* Roger Marsh, Esq; 10/23 Queen's Gate Gdns, London SW7 (☎ 01 589 1938); Tyser & Co, Ellerman House, 12/20 Camomile St, London EC3 (☎ 01 623 6262)

MARSH, Simon Peter; s of Peter Ridge Marsh TD, DL, of Peartree House, 23 Shireburn Rd, Formby, Liverpool L37 1LR, and Kathreen Mary Reynolds; *b* 19 Mar 1941; *Educ* Packwood Haugh, Uppingham, Oriel Coll Oxford Univ (MA); *m* 1, 29 June 1963, Kate Adair Halsey; 1 s (Peter Halsey b 1968), 2 da (Virginia Reynolds b 1964, Caroline Elizabeth Ridge b 1965); m 2, 24 April 1984, Ursula Fantasia; *Career* chief exec Peter Marsh & Sons Ltd; dir: Peter Marsh Packaging Ltd, Sedgebest Ltd, Club Caribbean Jamaica; *Recreations* national hunt horseracing, co sponsor the Peter Marsh Chase at Haydock Park; *Style—* Simon Marsh, Esq; Coomb Cottage, Charlton, Malmesbury, Wilts SN16 9DR (☎ 0666 823563); 47 Canal St, Bootle, Liverpool L20 8AE (☎ 051 922 1971, telex 628291, 051 922 3804)

MARSHALL; *see*: Johnson-Marshall

MARSHALL, Alan John; s of Arthur Edward Marshall, ISO, of 129 Harlington Rd, Hillingdon, Middx, and Hilda May,*née* Sloss (d 1988); *b* 31 Dec 1927; *Educ* William Morris Central Sch; *m* 2 Sept 1950, Dorothy Margaret, da of Arthur Vernon, of Highams Park; 1 s (Chistopher Alan b 1957), 1 da (Caroline Jane b 1955); *Career* Nat Serv RAF; keeper Guildhall City of London; magistrate Inner London Bench 1975-, cncllr Epping Forest DC 1982-86, dep pres Essex Co Bowls; Freeman City of London, Liveryman Worshipful Co of Scriveners; *Recreations* Flat Green Bowls; *Clubs* Bread Street Ward; *Style—* Alan Marshall, Esq; The Keeper, The Guildhall, London

MARSHALL, Alan Ralph; s of Ralph Marshall (d 1931), of London, and Mabel, *née* Mills; *b* 27 July 1931; *Educ* Beckenham Techn Sch, London Univ (Ac, Dip, Ed), Eastern Washington Univ (M Ed), London Univ (M Phil), Stanford Univ California (MA); *m* 19 Feb 1959, Caterina, da of Luigi Gattico (d 1971), of Pallanza Italy; 1 s (Roy Luigi b 1966), 1 da (Dilva b 1961); *Career* RAF Air Photographic Intelligence 1950-51; teaching posts in Eng and USA 1954-62, sr lectr Shoreditch Coll Surrey 1962-68, visiting prof Eastern Washington State Coll 1964-65, Field dir Sch Cncl Project Technol 1970-71, course team chm Open Univ 1972-75; Des: HM Insp 1977-82, HM Staff Inspr Secdy Educ 1983-85, HM Chief Insp Teacher Educn 1985-; FRSA; *Books* School Technology in Action (Ed, 1975), International Dictionary of Education (with Page & Thomas, 1977-); *Recreations* theatre, travel, reading; *Style—* Alan Marshall, HMI; Des, Elizabeth House, York Rd, London, SE1 7PH (☎ 01 934 9806)

MARSHALL, Alexander Badenoch; *b* 31 Dec 1924; *Educ* Glenalmond & Worcester Coll Oxford (MA); *m* 1961, Mona; 2 s, 1 da; *Career* served WW II RNVR; chm Commercial Union Assur Co plc 1983-, vice chm The Boots Co plc, chm The Maersk Co Ltd, Bestobell plc 1979-85; dir Royal Bank of Canada; *Style—* Alexander Marshall Esq; Crest House, Woldingham, Surrey Commercial Union Assurance Co plc, St Helen's, 1 Undershaft, London EC3P 3DQ (☎ 01 283 7500)

MARSHALL, Alfreda, aka Fredda Brilliant; da of Mordechai (d 1946), of Melbourne Aust, and Roselle Wartezki (d 1947); *b* 7 April 1908; *Educ* Gymnasium Poland; *m* 1935, Herbert P J Marshall (prof Emeritus), s of P C Marshall (d 1957); *Career* sculptress 1932-; actress and singer USA 1930-33, actress and script writer London 1937-50; works include Nehru, Krishna Menon, Paul Robeson, Herbert Marshall, Mahatma Gandhi (a maquette of which is in The Queen's Collection, St George's Chapel, Windsor), Indira Gandhi, Carl Albert, Sir Maurice Bowra, Duncan Grant, Lord Elwyn-Jones, Sir Isaac Hayward, Tom Mann, Dr Delyte Morris; exhibitions in London include Royal Acad, Royal Watercolour Soc, Whitechapel Art Gallery, India House, St Paul's Cathedral, etc; other exhibitions in Melbourne, Moscow, New Delhi, Bombay and Washington; FRSA; *Books* Biographies in Bronze (1986), Women in Power (1987); *Recreations* singing, composing, lyricist; *Style—* Ms Fredda Brilliant; 1204 Chautauqua St, Carbondale, Illinois 62901, USA (☎ 618 549 4569)

MARSHALL, Sir Arthur Gregory George; OBE (1948), DL (Cambs 1968); s of David Gregory Marshall, MBE (d 1942), and Maude Edmunds, *née* Wing (d 1931); *b* 4 Dec 1903; *Educ* Tonbridge, Jesus Coll Cambridge (MA); *m* 1931, Rosemary Wynford (d 1988), da of Marcus Dimsdale (d 1918); 2 s, 1 da; *Career* chm and md Marshall of Cambridge (Engrg)' 1942-; joined Garage Co of Marshall (Cambridge) Ltd 1926, established Aircraft Co now Marshall of Cambridge (Engrg) Ltd 1929-; chm Aerodrome Owners Assoc 1964-65; memb: Air Cadet Cncl 1951-59 and 1965-76, advsy cncl on Technol 1967-70; High Sheriff of Cambs and Isle of Ely 1969-70; Hon Old Cranwellian 1979; Companion of Royal Aeronautical Soc 1980; kt 1974; *Recreations* flying (pilot's licence since 1928), Cambridge Athletics Blue, Olympic Team Reserve 1924; *Clubs* RAF, Hawks (Cambridge); *Style—* Sir Arthur Marshall, OBE, DL; Horseheath Lodge, Linton, Cambridge CB1 6PT (☎ 0223 891318); Marshall of Cambridge (Engrg) Ltd, Airport Works, Newmarket Rd, Cambridge CB5 8RX (☎ 0223 61133, telex 81208)

MARSHALL, Arthur Stirling-Maxwell; CBE (1986, OBE 1978); s of Victor Stirling-Maxwell Marshall (d 1941), of Edinburgh, and Jeannie Theodora, *née* Hunter (d 1971); *b* 29 Jan 1929; *m* 1, 25 Dec 1955, Eleni (d 1969), da of Panagiotis Kapralos (d 1946), of Athens, Greece; 1 s (John b 1958), 2 da (Jeannie b 1956, Anna b 1957); *m* 2, 14 Aug 1985, Cheryl Mary, da of Desmond Hookens, of Madras, India; 1 da (Christina b 1988), 1 step s (Lionel b 1974), 2 step da (Suzanne b 1972, Margaret b 1973); *Career* FO 1959, ME Centre for Arab Studies Lebanon 1959-61, political offr Bahrain 1961-64, registrar HBM Ct for Bahrain 1961-64, attache Br Embassy Athens 1964-67, second sec Br Embassy Rabat Morocco 1967-69, first sec Br High Cmmn Nicosia Cyprus 1970-75 (formerly second sec), first commercial sec Br Embassy Kuwait 1975-79, dep Br high cmmr Southern India 1979-83, cnsllr Br Embassy Kuwait 1983-85, Br ambassador People's Democratic Republic of Yemen 1986-89 (ret Jan 1989); *Recreations* nature, music; *Clubs* Oriental; *Style—* Arthur Marshall, Esq, CBE; 147 Highbury Grove, London N5 1HP

MARSHALL, Sir Colin Marsh; s of Marsh Edward Leslie Marshall, and Florence Mary Marshall; *b* 16 Nov 1933; *Educ* Univ Coll Sch Hampstead; *m* 1958, Janet Winifred, da of John Cracknell; 1 da; *Career* Orient Steam Navigation Co 1951-58; gen mangr Hertz Corpn (UK, Netherlands & Belgium) 1962-64 (joined co 1958, gen mangr Mexico 1959-60, asst to pres NY 1960, gen mangr UK 1961-62); regnl mangr and vice-pres Avis Inc (Europe 1964-66, Europe & Middle East 1966-69, int 1969-71), pres and chief exec Avis Inc NY 1976-79 (exec vice-pres and chief operating offr 1971-75, pres and chief operating offr 1975-76), co-chm Avis Inc 1979-81; exec vice-pres Norton Simon Inc 1979-81, dir and dep chief exec Sears Hldgs plc 1981-83, chief exec and bd memb BA 1983-; bd memb: BTA, South Bank, Grand Met plc; kt 1987; *Recreations* tennis, skiing; *Clubs* Queen's; *Style—* Sir Colin Marshall; Head Office, Speedbird House, PO Box 10, London Airport (Heathrow), Hounslow, Middx TW6 2JA (☎ 01 759 5511, telex 8813983)

MARSHALL, David; MP (Lab) Glasgow, Shettleston 1979-; *b* 7 May 1941; *Educ* Larbert, Denny and Falkirk High Schs; Woodside Sr Secondary Sch; *m* 1968, Christina; 2 s, 1 da; *Career* joined Lab Pty 1962, memb TGWU, former Labour Party Organiser for Glasgow; chm Manpower Ctee, Convention of Scottish Local Authorities; memb Select Ctee Scottish Affairs 1981-83, Select Ctee on Tport 1983-, sec Scottish Labour MPs 1981-; chm PLP Tport Ctee 1987-; put Solvent Abuse (Scotland) Act 1983 through Parliament; *Recreations* gardening; *Style—* David Marshall, Esq, MP; 32 Enterkin St, Glasgow G32 7BA (☎ (041 778) 8125); House of Commons, London SW1A 0AA (☎ 01 219 5134)

MARSHALL, (Andrew) David (Michael Greagh); s of Andrew Harold Marshall (d 1970), of London, and Brenda Medlicott, *née* Massy; *b* 6 Sept 1954; *Educ* King's Coll Sch Wimbledon, Merton Coll Oxford (MA); *m* 19 March 1983, Jill Francesca, da of Laurence Duval Merreywether, of Harrogate; 1 s (Andrew b 1988), 1 da (Cicely b 1987); *Career* barr Lincoln's Inn 1981; cncl memb Soc for Computers and Law 1987-; *Style—* David Marshall, Esq; 3 Paper Buildings, Temple, London EC4Y 7EU (☎ 01 353 1182, fax 01 583 2037)

MARSHALL, Sir Denis Alfred; s of late Frederick Herbert, and Winifred Mary Marshall; *b* 1 June 1916; *Educ* Dulwich Coll; *m* 1, 1949, Joan Edith, *née* Straker (d 1974); 1 s; *m* 2, 1975, Jane, *née* Lygo; *Career* WWII cmmnd XX The Lancashire Fusiliers 1939, served India and Burma (Maj) 1940-45, slr 1937; ptnr Barlow Lyde & Gilbert 1949-83 (conslt 1983-); memb: cncl Law Soc 1966-86 (vice-pres 1980, pres 1981-82), Insur Brokers Registration Cncl 1979-, Criminal Injuries Compensation Bd 1982-; memb cncl FIMBRA 1986-; kt 1982; *Recreations* sailing (yacht 'Turtledove of Mersea'); *Clubs* Naval & Military, Lloyd's YC, Royal Dartmouth YC; *Style—* Sir Denis Marshall; Redways, Warfleet Rd, Dartmouth, South Devon TQ6 9BZ; work: Beaufort Hse, 15 St Botolph St, London EC3A 7NJ, (☎ 01 247 2277, telex 887249 G)

MARSHALL, Dr Edmund Ian; s of Harry Marshall, and Koorali Etrenne, *née* Rowlands (d 1975); *b* 31 May 1940; *Educ* Humberstone Fndn Sch, Magdalen Coll Oxford, Liverpool Univ (PhD); *m* 1969, Margaret Pamela, da of John Frederick Antill, of New Southgate, London; 1 da; *Career* univ teacher 1962-66, memb Wallasey Co Borough Cncl 1963-65, joined Lab Pty 1967, mathematician in industry 1967-71, MP (Lab) Goole 1971-83; PPS to: NI sec 1974-76, Home sec 1976-79; oppn whip 1982-83; lectr in mgmnt sci Univ of Bradford 1984-; joined SDP 1985; *Books* Parliament and the Public (1982); *Recreations* music, word games; *Clubs* Yorkshire CC; *Style—* Dr Edmund Marshall; 14 Belgravia Rd, Wakefield, W Yorks WF1 3JP

MARSHALL, Dr Geoffrey; s of Leonard William Marshall (d 1953) and Kate, *née* Turner (d 1961); *b* 22 April 1929; *Educ* Arnold Sch Blackpool, Manchester Univ (BA, MA), Glasgow Univ (PhD); *m* 10 Aug 1957, Patricia Anne Christine, da of Edward Cecil Woodcock (d 1988), of Oxford; 2 s (David b 1962, Stephen Edward b 1967); *Career* res fell Nuffield Coll Oxford 1955-57, fell and praelector The Queen's Coll Oxford 1957-, Andrew Dixon White visiting prof Cornell Univ 1985-; memb Oxford City Cncl 1964-74, Sheriff City of Oxford 1970-71; FBA 1970; *Books* Parliamentary Sovereignty and the Commonwealth 1957, Police and Government 1965, Constitutional Theory 1971, Constitutional Conventions 1986; *Recreations* squash; *Style—* Dr Geoffrey Marshall; The Queen's Coll, Oxford

MARSHALL, Geoffrey Wyndham; s of Wyndham J Marshall, of Reepham, Norfolk, and the late Gwendoline May Burdick Marshall; *b* 5 Mar 1937; *Educ* KES Birmingham, Jesus Coll Oxford, Harvard Business Sch (MBA); *m* 1960, Sally Rose, da of the late Thomas Barton Gerard; 2 s (Andrew b 1965, Julian b 1969), 1 da (Miranda b 1964); *Career* shoemaker; dir: Somervell Brothers Ltd 1972-75, Bally Shoe Factories (Norwich Ltd) and Bally Shoe Co Ltd 1975-, Bally London Shoe Co Ltd, Russell and Bromley Ltd 1984-, Paper Shops (East Anglia) Ltd 1987-; gp md Bally Group UK Ltd 1979-; head of mkt region 3 Bally Int AG Zurich, pres Norwich and Norfolk C of C and Industy 1981-83, chm Norwich Enterprises Agency Tst, pres Norwich Footwear Mfrs Assoc 1983-84; memb Br Footwear Manufacturers Fedn 1987-88; trade warden Worshipful Co of Pattenmakers 1984-86 (Renter Warden 1987-88, Upper Warden 1988-89); chm Theatre Royal Norwich Tst; *Recreations* squash, gardening, travel, music; *Clubs* United Oxford and Cambridge; *Style—* Geoffrey Marshall, Esq; Salle Place, Reepham, Norfolk NR10 5SF (☎ 0603 870638); Wells House, 79 Wells St, London W1P 4JL (☎ 01 631 4222, telex 261105)

MARSHALL, Dr (Frank) Graham; s of Frank Marshall, of Wyke Manor, Gillingham, Dorset, and Vera, *née* Barker; *b* 28 Mar 1942; *Educ* W Bridgford GS, Birmingham Univ (BA), Nottingham Univ (PhD); *m* 10 July 1965, Patricia Anne, da of Thomas Leonard Bestwick, of Nottingham; 2 s (Stephen James b 1967, David Edward b 1971), 1 da (Anne-Marie b 1969); *Career* Royal Signals and Radar Estab (MOD) Malvern 1969-80; cnsllr Sci and Technol Br Embassy Tokyo 1980-82; md: Plessey Res Roke Manor Romsey 1982-87; tech dir: Plessey Naval Systems Ltd, Templecombe 1987-; FIEE; *Recreations* country hobbies, electronic projects; *Style—* Dr Graham Marshall; Wilkinthroop House, Templecombe, Somerset BA8 0DH (☎ 0963 70551, telex 46108)

MARSHALL, James; MP (Lab) Leicester S Oct 1974-; *b* 13 Mar 1941; *Educ* Sheffield City GS, Leeds U; *m* 1962, Shirley, da of W Ellis; 1 s, 1 da; *Career* oppn spokesman Home Affrs 1982-, asst govt whip 1977-79, fought Leicester S Feb 1974 Gen Election, Harborough 1970 Gen Election; former memb Leeds & Leicester Cncls; *Style—* James Marshall Esq, MP; Flat 15, The Woodlands, 31 Knighton Rd, Leicester (☎ 708237)

MARSHALL, (John) Jeremy Seymour; s of Edward Pope Marshall (d 1983), of Truro, Cornwall, and Nita Helen, *née* Seymour; *b* 18 April 1938; *Educ* Sherborne, New Coll Oxford (MA); *m* 20 July 1962, Valiette Anne, da of (Archibald) Donald Butterley (d 1957), of Leicester; 1 s (Simon b 1965), 1 da (Sarah b 1964, Anna b 1971); *Career* Nat Serv Lt Royal Signals 1956-58; Wiggins Teade 1962-64, Riker Laboratories 1964-67, CIBA Agrochems 1967-71, Hanson 1971-87; md: Dufaylite Devpts Ltd 1971-76, SLD Olding Ltd 1976-79; chief exec: industries Ltd 1979-86, Imp Foods Ltd 1986-87, BAA plc 1987-; FBIM; *Recreations* tennis, squash, skiing; *Clubs* Army and Navy; *Style—* Jeremy Marshall, Esq; Willow House, Bourne, Cambridge CB3 7SQ; BAA plc, 130 Wilton Rd, London SW1 (☎ 01 932 6707)

MARSHALL, Prof John; s of James Herbert Marshall, and Bertha, *née* Schofield; *b* 16 April 1922; *Educ* Thornleigh Coll Bolton, Univ of Manchester (MB, ChB, MD, DSc); *m* 9 Oct 1946, (Margaret) Eileen, da of Albert Hughes (d 1937), of Unionville, Pennsylvania, USA; 2 s (Michael John, Christopher John) 3 da (Patricia Mary, Mo Lin Cecilia, Catherine Ann); *Career* Lt-Col RAMC 1949-51; sr lectr Edinburgh Univ 1954-56; Univ of London: reader in neurology 1956-71, prof 1971-87, dean Inst of Neurology 1982-87, emeritus prof 1987; memb Attendance Bd 1978- (chm 1982-); memb Assoc of Br Neurologists 1954, Assoc of Physicians 1956; Aenbrugger Medal Univ of Raz (1983); *Books* Management of Cenebrovasular Diseae (1965), Planning for a Family (1965), The Infertile Period (1969); *Recreations* walking, gardening; *Style—* Prof John Marshall; 203 Robin Hood Way, London SW20 0AA (☎ 01 942 5509)

MARSHALL, John Alexander; CB (1982); s of James Alexander Marshall (d 1981), of Edgware Middx, and Mena Dorothy, *née* Finch; *b* 2 Sept 1922; *Educ* Hackney Downs Sch; *m* 1947, Pauline Mary, da of Victor Holden Taylor (d 1971), of Ickenham Middx; 6 s (Adrian, Stephen, Philip, Christopher, Nicholas, James); *Career* civil servant; entered HM Treasury 1946; sometime asst PS to Hugh Gaitskell and R A Butler (Chancellors of the Exchequer), PS to Reginald Maudling (Economic Secretary to the Treasy), under-sec i/c Public Expenditure 1972-, under-sec Cabinet Office 1974-77, dep sec NI Off 1977-82, ret from Civil Serv 1982; gen sec Distressed Gentlefolk's Aid Assoc 1982-; *Recreations* literature, music; *Style—* John Marshall Esq, CB; 48 Long Lane, Ickenham, Middx (☎ 672020); Vicarage Gate House, Vicarage Gate, Kensington, London W8 4AQ (☎ 01 229 9341)

MARSHALL, John Leslie; MP(C) Hendon South 1987, MEP (EDG) London North 1979-; s of Prof William Thomas Marshall (d 1975), of Glasgow, and Margaret Ewing Marshall; *b* 19 August 1940; *Educ* Glasgow Acad, St Andrews Univ (MA); *m* 1978,

Susan Elizabeth, da of David Spencer Mount, JP, of The Dower House, Petham, Kent; 2 s (William b 1979, Thomas b 1982); *Career* lectr in economics Aberdeen Univ 1966-70; stockbroker, ptnr Carr Sebag & Co 1979-1982, assoc memb Kitcat & Aitken 1982-83, ptnr Kitcat & Aitken 1983-; ACIS; *Recreations* spectator sports, theatre, bridge; *Clubs* Carlton, Middlesex Cricket; *Style—* John Marshall Esq, MP, MEP; 28 Sherwood Rd, London NW4 1AD (☎ 01 203 4322); Kitcat & Aitken, The Stock Exchange, London EC2

MARSHALL, Rt Hon Sir John Ross; GBE (1974), CH (1973), PC (1966); s of Allan Marshall (d 1930), of Wellington, NZ; *b* 5 Mar 1912; *Educ* Whangarei Boys' HS, Otago Boys' HS, Victoria Univ Wellington NZ (BA, LLM); *m* 1944, (Jessie) Margaret Livingston; 2 s, 2 da; *Career* served WWII Maj NZEF; MP (Nat) for Mt Victoria 1946-54, for Karori 1954-75; chm Nat Dvpt Cncl for NZ 1969-72, PM of New Zealand 1972, leader of Oppn 1972-74; visiting fell Victoria Univ Wellington 1975-85 (lectr in law 1948-51); Hon LLD; *see Debrett's Handbook of Australia and New Zealand* for further info; *Recreations* golf, tennis, trout fishing, reading; *Clubs* United Servs Offrs', Wellington, Wellington GC; *Style—* Rt Hon Sir John Marshall, GBE, CH; 22 Fitzroy St, Wellington, New Zealand (☎ 736 631)

MARSHALL, Margaret Anne (Mrs Graeme Davidson); *née* Marshall; *b* 4 Jan 1949; *Educ* Stirling HS, Royal Scottish Acad of Music and Drama; *m* 25 March 1970, Graeme Griffiths King Davidson; 2 da (Nicola b 19 Nov 1974, Julia b 29 Dec 1977); *Career* int opera singer; First prize Munich Int Festival 1974; concert appearences: Florence, Covent Gdn, Hamburg, Koln, Frankfurt, La Scala, Milan, Vienna, Salzburg; numerous recordings; *Recreations* skiing, squash, tennis, cooking, golf; *Clubs* Gleneagle Country; *Style—* Miss Margaret Marshall; Woodside, Gargunnock, Stirling FK8 3BP (☎ 0786 86633); c/o Harold Holt, 31 Sinclair Rd, London W14 0NS (☎ 01 603 4600, fax 01 603 0019, telex 22339 HUNTER)

MARSHALL, Mark Anthony; s of Prof T H Marshall (d 1981), of Cambridge, and Nadine, *née* Hambourg; *b* 8 Oct 1937; *Educ* Westminster, Trinity Coll Cambridge (BA); *m* 29 Aug 1970, Penelope Lesley, step da of George Seymour (d 1987), of Powick, Worcester; 2 da (Charlotte Dorothea b 1973, Frances Margaret b 1975); *Career* Dip Serv 1958-; counsellor: Tripoli 1979-80, Damascus 1980-83; ambassador Yemen Arab Republic 1987-; *Recreations* golf, fell walking; *Style—* Mark Marshall, Esq; c/o Foreign & Commonwealth Office, London SW1

MARSHALL, Lady; Meta; da of William Hawke, of Bugle, Cornwall; *m* 1926, Hon Mr Justice (Sir Archie Pellow) Marshall (d 1966); *Style—* Lady Marshall; Penlea, Penwinnick Rd, St Austell, Cornwall

MARSHALL, Michael Leicester John; s of Sir James Marshall, DL, JP (d 1977), and Rebecca Mary, *née* Gotley (d 1966); *b* 26 May 1924; *Educ* Eastbourne Coll, Coll of Estate Mgmnt; *m* 6 June 1959, Tessa Rosemary, da of charles Miles Skerett-Rogers (d 1972); 2 s (Julian b 24 April 1960, Thomas b 1 July 1964), 1 da (Antonia b 6 June 1961); *Career* Maj 5 Royal Gurkha Rifles (FF), active serv Arakan 1943-44, Kohima 1944 (wounded), Burma 1944-45, Capt 4 Bn Queens Regt TA 1947-50, ret; chartered surveyor: sr ptnr Chestertons, receivor Church Cmmrs for England, surveyor Royal Masonic Sch for Boys, hon surveyor Charterhouse; farmer; memb ct assts Corpn of Sons of the Clergy (former sr tres); memb Ct Worshipful Co Tylers and Bricklayers (master 1986-87); FRICS 1952; *Recreations* gardening, walking; *Clubs* Army and Navy, MCC; *Style—* Michael Marshall, Esq; East Brabourne House, Brabourne, Ashford, Kent TN25 5LR (☎ 030 381 2112)

MARSHALL, (Robert) Michael; MP (C) Arundel Feb 1974-; s of Robert Ernest Marshall and Margaret Mary (d 1983), of Hathersage, Derbyshire; *b* 21 June 1930,Sheffield; *Educ* Bradfield Coll, Harvard Univ (NBA), and Stanford Univ; *m* 1972, Caroline Victoria Oliphant, da of Alexander Oliphant Hutchison (d 1973), of Upper Largo, Fife; 2 step da; *Career* BBC cricket commentator 1954-69; Calcutta branch mangr United Steel (India) Ltd 1954-58 and md (Bombay) 1960-64; commercial dir Workington Iron & Steel Co Ltd 1964-67, md Head Wrightson Export Co Ltd 1967-69, mgmnt conslt Urwick Orr & Partners Ltd 1969-74; parly under sec of State for Industry 1979-81, parly advsr to Br Aerospace and Cable & Wireless 1981-; Hon DL New England Coll 1982; *Books* author/editor of 5 books incl biography of Jack Buchanan; *Recreations* cricket commentating, golf, theatre, ballet, writing and travel; *Clubs* Garrick, Lord's Taverners, MCC, Goodwood Golf; *Style—* Michael Marshall Esq, MP; Old Inn House, Slindon, Arundel, W Sussex; House of Commons, London SW1A 0AA (☎ 01 219 4046)

MARSHALL, Nigel Bernard Dickenson; s of Norman Dickenson Marshall (d 1958), of The Old Rectory, Lea, Gainsborough, and Gertrude Olga; *b* 9 April 1935; *Educ* Rugby, Queens' Coll Cambridge (MA, LLM); *Career* ptnr: Underwood and Co slrs London 1964-, Miller and Co slrs Cambridge 1969-88; *Recreations* gardening; *Clubs* United Oxford and Cambridge Univ, Cambridge Pitt, Oriental; *Style—* Nigel Marshall, Esq; The Old Rectory, Lea, Gainsborough, Lincs; 50 Rawlings Street, London SW3; 40 Welbeck Street, London W1

MARSHALL, Noel Hedley; CMG (1986); s of Dr Arthur Hedley Marshall, CBE, of Styvechale Coventry, and Margaret Louise, *née* Longhurst (d 1987); *b* 26 Nov 1934; *Educ* Leighton Park Sch, Lawrenceville Sch NJ USA, St John's Coll Cambridge; *Career* For (later Dip) Serv: third sec Br Embassy Prague 1959, FO 1961, second sec Br Embassy Moscow 1963, CRO 1965, first sec (tech asst) Br High Cmmn Karachi 1966 and Rawelpindi 1967, charge d'affaires Br Embassy Ulan Bater 1967, Rawalpindi 1968, FCO 1970, first sec (press) UK Representation to Euro Communities 1974, NATO Def Coll Rome 1977, cnsllr UK delegation conf on Disarmament Geneva 1978, head N American Dept FCO 1982, dip serv inspr 1985, min Br Embassy Moscow 1986-; *Recreations* offshore sailing, the theatre; *Clubs* Royal Ocean Racing; *Style—* Noel Marshall, Esq, CMG; c/o FCO, King Charles Street, London SW1A 2A4

MARSHALL, Sir Peter Harold Reginald; KCMG (1983, CMG 1974); s of Reginald Henry Marshall; *b* 30 July 1924; *Educ* Tonbridge, CCC Cambridge; *m* 1957, Patricia Rendell Stoddart (d 1981); 1 s, 1 da; *Career* diplomat; asst dir Treasury Centre for Admin Studies 1964-66, cnsllr UK Mission Geneva 1966-69, cnsllr and head of chancery Paris 1969-71, head of Financial Relations Dept FCO 1971-73, asst under-sec of state FCO 1973-75, UK rep to Economic and Social Cncl of UN 1975-79, ambassador and UK perm rep to Off of UN and other Int Orgns, Geneva 1979-83, dep cwlth sec-gen (Econ) 1983-; memb of the Bd of Govenors: English Speaking Union, Central Council of the Royal Commonwealth Soc; *Clubs* Travellers'; *Style—* Sir Peter Marshall, KCMG; Cwlth Secretariat, Marlborough House, Pall Mall, London SW1 (☎ 01 839 3411)

MARSHALL, Peter Izod; s of Charles Marshall (d 1987), of Buxton, Derbyshire, and Gwendoline Anne, *née* Parker; *b* 16 April 1927; *Educ* Buxton Coll; *m* 4 Aug 1955, Davina Mary, da of Ernest Hart (d 1980), of Grappen Hall, Cheshire; 1 s (David Bruce b 4 Feb 1960), 1 da (Helen Elizabeth (Mrs Le Houx) b 21 Feb 1957); *Career* commercial dir EMI Electronics Ltd 1962-67, dir of fin Norcros plc 1967-77, dir and dep chief exec The Plessey Co plc 1977-87, chm Ocean Tport and Trading plc 1987-; memb Jarrett Ctee on Br Univs; LRAM 1945, FCA 1955, CBIM 1986, FIOD 1986; *Recreations* music, swimming, golf; *Clubs* Les Ambassadeurs, Wentworth (Surrey); *Style—* Peter Marshall, Esq; Moyns, Christchurch Rd, Virginia Water, Surrey (☎ 09904 2118); 47 Russell Sq, London WC1B 4JP (☎ 01 636 6844, fax 01 636 0289, telex 291689)

MARSHALL, Sir Robert Braithwaite; KCB (1971, CB 1968), MBE (1945); s of Alexander Halford Marshall and Edith Mary, *née* Lockyer; *b* 10 Jan 1920; *Educ* Sherborne, CCC Cambridge; *m* 1945, Diana Elizabeth Westlake; 1 s, 3 da; *Career* served FO WW II; chm Nat Water Cncl 1978-82, chm Wateraid Tst, memb cncl Surrey Univ; 2 perm sec Dept of Environment 1973-78, indust sec DTI as 2 perm sec 1970-73 (dep sec 1966-70, under-sec 1964-66); served Ministries: Works, Aviation, Power, private sec to sec Cabinet Off 1950-53; chm Liberal Party's Trade & Industry Panel 1984-; *Style—* Sir Robert Marshall, KCB, MBE; Brooklands, Lower Bourne, Farnham, Surrey (☎ 025 125 2879)

MARSHALL, Roger Michael James; s of James Edward Frederick Marshall (d 1979), and Jeanne, *née* Warren; *b* 20 August 1948; *Educ* Truro Sch, LSE (BSc); *m* 4 May 1974, Margaret Elizabeth Marshall, da of John MacPherson, of The Manor House, Abbotskerswell, Devon; 2 da (Charlotte Emily b 1977, Anabelle Verity b 1978); *Career* articled to Price Waterhouse 1970, CA 1973, ptnr with Price Waterhouse 1981-; FCA; *Recreations* sailing, bridge, reading, skiing; *Style—* Roger Marshall, Esq; Price Waterhouse, 32 London Bridge St, London SE1 9SY

MARSHALL, Roy Edwin; s of John Archibald Marshall (d 1950), of Coverley Plantation Barbados, and Hilda Verne Green (d 1983); early settlers in Barbados; *b* 25 April 1930; *Educ* Lodge Sch St John's Barbados; *m* 1954, Shirley Marjorie, da of Lionel Butterworth (d 1938), of Poynton, Cheshire; 3 da (Shelley, Debra, Joanne); *Career* played first class cricket (Barbados v Trinidad) aged 15 years; toured: England 1950, Aust and NZ 1951-52 with the W Indies; played cricket for Hampshire 1953-72 (Capt 1966-70), scored 1000 in a season 18 times (6 times over 2000), scored more runs (35,725) than any non-qualified English cricketer; *Books* Test Outcast; *Recreations* cricket, golf; *Clubs* Cricketers (London), MCC, Hampshire CCC, Somerset CCC, Lords Taverners; *Style—* Roy Marshall, Esq; Westgate Inn, Taunton, Somerset TA1 EX (☎ 0823 84933)

MARSHALL, Sir (Oshley) Roy; CBE (1968); s of Fitz Roy Marshall and Corene Carmelita Marshall; *b* 21 Oct 1920; *Educ* Harrison Coll Barbados, Pembroke Coll Cambridge, Univ Coll London; *m* 1945, Eirwen Lloyd; 1 s, 3 da; *Career* vice-chllr Hull Univ 1979-85, head enquiry into immigration serv for Cmmn Racial Equality to 1981; called to the Bar 1947, prof law & hd law dept Sheffield Univ 1956-69 (visiting prof 1969-79), prof of Law & dean Law Faculty Univ of Ife Nigeria 1963-65, vice-chllr Univ of WI 1969-74; chm Cwlth Educn Liaison Ctee 1974-81 and Ctee Cwlth Legal Cooperation 1975, memb Police Complaints Bd 1977-81, vice-chm Cwlth Inst Governing Body 1980-81; chm: Cwlth Standing Ctee on Student Mobility 1982-, bd of govrs Hymers Coll 1985-; exec chm Cncl for Educn in the Cwlth 1985-, memb review ctee on the Cave Hill Campus of the Univ WI 1986, constitutional commn on the Turks and Caicos Islands 1986; kt 1974; *Clubs* Royal Cmlth Soc; *Style—* Sir Roy Marshall, CBE; Kirk House, Kirk Croft, Cottingham, North Humberside HU16 4AU (☎ 0482 847 413)

MARSHALL, Sally Christine; da of Maj John Trevor Marshall (d 1985), of Nottingham Broadstone, Dorset, and Marjorie Kathleen, *née* Cooke; *b* 19 Oct 1949; *Educ* Mountford House West Hallam Derbys, Clifton Hall Nottingham, Univ Coll of Wales Aberystwyth (BSc); *Career* investmt mangr Hill Samuel 1972-80; Henderson Admin Gp 1980-; dir Henderson Admin Ltd, dep md Henderson Pension Fund Mgmnt Ltd; Freedom of City of London; memb: Nat Assoc Pension Funds; *Recreations* golf, skiing, tennis, travel; *Clubs* Roehampton, Broadstone GC, Dorset; *Style—* Miss Sally Marshall; 4 Putney Common, London SW15 1HL; Henderson Pension Fund Management Ltd, 3 Finsbury Avenue, London EC2M 2PA (☎ 01 638 5757)

MARSHALL, Sally Rose; da of Thomas Barton Gerard (d 1988) of Newburgh Lancs and Clara Margery, *née* Salisbury (d 1985); *b* 2 Nov 1938; *Educ* Brentwood Sch Southport, Lady Margaret Hall Oxford (BA); *m* 27 Aug 1960, Geoffrey Wyndham Marshall, s of Wyndham Joseph Marshall of Reepham Norfolk; 2 s (Andrew Gerard b 7 Aug 1965, Julian Geoffrey b 18 July 1969), 1 da (Miranda Lucy b 2 Mar 1964); *Career* memb Norfolk CC (dep leader 1987-88, chm Libraries and Recreation Ctee); Con spokesman Assoc of Co Cncls Recreation Ctee, memb Library and Information Services Cncl; *Recreations* gardening, reading, antique restoration, local politics; *Style—* Mrs Sally Marshall; Salle Place, Salle, Reepham NR10 5S7 (☎ 0603 870638)

MARSHALL, Stuart Walter; s of Walter Clement Marshall, and Elsie Vera, *née* Hawkins; *b* 9 Sept 1935; *Educ* Beckenham and Penge GS; *m* 5 Aug 1961, Patricia Ann, da of Hugh Lawrence Bentley; 1 s (Adrian b 1967), 1 da (Anne b 1970); *Career* Coutts & Co 1952-: dep head branch 1981-86, head mgmnt serv div 1986-; cncl memb and hon tres Invalid Childrens Aid Nationwide (dir 1989), tstee WALK, govr Colfe's Sch; FCIB; *Recreations* fishing, shooting, skiing, gardening; *Style—* Stuart Marshall, Esq; Coutts & Co, 440 Strand, London WC2R 0QS (☎ 01 379 6262); Coutts & Co, New London Bridge House, 25 London Bridge St, London SE1 9SG ((☎ 01 357 7272)

MARSHALL, Thomas Elder; s of John Marshall and Theresea Welsh; *b* 16 Nov 1939; *Educ* Govan Sr Secdy Sch, Glasgow Univ (BSc, MBA), Strathclyde Univ (DMS); *m* 1963, Jessie Paton, da of John Muirhead Hamilton (d 1978); 3 da (Philippa b 1964, Alison b 1968, Judith b 1974); *Career* chartered engr, dir Haden Young Ltd, md Haden Robertson, gov and dir Scottish Engrg Tning Scheme Ltd, pres Electrical Contractors Assoc of Scot 1975-77, dir S W Farmer Gp plc, md Farmer Engrg Ltd 1985-86; md Didsbury Engrg Co Ltd 1986-87; *Recreations* riding, hill walking, vintage cars; *Clubs* Western; *Style—* Thomas Marshall, Esq; Duirinnis, The Loaning, Whitecraigs, Glasgow G46 6SE (☎ 041 639 5138); Bruntons (Musselburgh) Ltd, Inveresk Road, Musselburgh EH21 7UG (☎ 031 665 3888, telex 72212, fax 031 665 0486)

MARSHALL, Mrs A R; Valerie Margaret; da of Ernest Knagg; *b* 30 Mar 1945; *Educ* Brighton, Hove HS, Girton Cambridge, London Graduate Sch of Business

Studies; *m* 1972, Alan Roger Marshall; 1 s, 1 da; *Career* financial controller Industrial and Commercial Finance Corpn 1970-79, memb investment exec Scottish Development Agency 1979-, Monopolies and Mergers Cmmn 1977-, Scottish Design Cncl 1974-77; *Recreations* music, ballet, drama, golf; *Style*— Mrs A R Marshall; Valhalla, Garth Estate, by Fortingall, Perthshire; Kilmore, 16 Dalkeith Ave, Dumbreck Glasgow (☎ 041 427 0096)

MARSHALL, Wilfred Rufus; s of John Marshall (d 1939), of Ripley, Derbys, and Sarah, *née* Walters (d 1926); *b* 26 July 1912; *Educ* Ripley Cncl Sch; *m* 16 Sept 1936, Una Mary, da of Walter Crooks (d 1930), farmer, of Marehay, Derbys; 1 da (Valerie b 1937); *Career* RAF 1941-45 England, Scotland, Wales; dir: Hippodrome Cinema, Marshalls (Ironmongers), Marston Wetfish Suppliers; ret; ptnr (with w and da) in travel agency Safeway Services (later Safeway Travel Ltd) 1963-67; *Recreations* shooting, gardening, antique collecting, watch repairing, numismatics, local history; *Clubs* Jubilee; *Style*— Wilfred R Marshall, Esq; 17 Broadway, Ripley (☎ 0773 46655)

MARSHALL OF GORING, Baron (Life Peer UK 1985), of South Stoke, Co Oxfordshire; Sir Walter Charles Marshall; CBE (1973); s of late Frank Marshall, and Amy, da of Edgar Pearson, of Wales; *b* 5 Mar 1932; *Educ* Birmingham Univ; *m* 1955, Ann Vivienne, da of late Ernest Sheppard, of Cardiff; 1 s, (Hon Jonathan Charles Walter), 1 da (Hon Victoria Ann); *Career* AERE Harwell: scientific offr 1954-57, gp leader solid state theory 1959-60, head Theoretical Physics Univ 1960-66, dep dir 1966-68, dir 1968-1975; res physicist Univ of California 1957-58, and Harvard 1958-59; chm: Advsy Cncl Res and Devpt Fuel and Power 1974-77, Offshore Energy Technol Bd 1975-77, UKAEA 1981-82 (dep chm 1975-81, memb 1972-, dir Res Gp 1969-75), CEGB 1982-; chief scientist Dept of Energy 1974-1977; ed Oxford Int Series of Monographs on Physics 1966-; Maxwell Medal 1964, Glazebrook Medal 1975; Hon Dr Sci City Univ 1982, Hon DSc Salford, Foreign Assoc Nat Acad Engrg USA; fell Royal Swedish Acad Engrg Scis, FRS 1971, FBIM; kt 1982; *Style*— The Rt Hon Lord Marshall of Goring, CBE, FRS; Central Electricity Generating Board, Sudbury House, 15 Newgate Street, London EC1A 7AU

MARSHALL OF LEEDS, Baron (Life Peer UK 1980); Frank Shaw Marshall; s of Charles William Marshall (d 1959), of Wakefield; *b* 26 Sept 1915; *Educ* Wakefield, Downing Coll Cambridge (MA, LLM, Associate Fellow); *m* 2 April 1941, Mary (*see* Baroness Marshall of Leeds), da of Robert Barr (d 1961), of Shadwell House, Shadwell, Leeds; 2 da (Hon Angela Hermione, Hon Virginia Mary); *Career* served 1940-46 Capt RTR and War Off Staff Judge Advocate Generals Off; slr; a vice-chm Cons Pty 1979-85; special advsr to Govt Third London Airport; chm: Maplin Devpt Corpn 1973-74, Municipal Mutual Insur Ltd; vice-pres: Leeds & Holbeck Bldg Soc 1977-, Bldg Socs Assoc, Barr & Wallace Arnold Tst; chm Municipal Mutual Insur Gp of Cos; dir of Cos; vice-pres AA; FRSA; 1971; *Recreations* reading, working; *Style*— The Rt Hon the Lord Marshall of Leeds; Holtby, N Yorks; Ho of Lords

MARSHALL OF LEEDS, Baroness; Mary Marshall; *née* Barr; JP (City of Leeds 1964); da of Robert Barr (d 1961), of Shadwell House, Shadwell, Leeds, and Edith, *née* Midgeley (d 1964); *b* 11 Sept 1915; *Educ* Calder Girls' Sch Seascale Cumberland, Yorkshire Coll of Housecraft (Dip Domestic Sc); *m* 2 Aug 1941, Baron Marshall of Leeds (Life Peer), *qv*; 2 da (Hon Angela Hermione, Hon Virginia Mary); *Career* voluntary serv with Red Cross and YWCA; dir Oswalds Hotel Ltd 1955-; formerly dir: Yorkshire Ladies Hostels Ltd, Yorkshire Ladies Cncl of Educn; hon sec City of Leeds NSPCC for 12 years, now patron; patron Leeds Save the Children Fund; *Style*— The Rt Hon Lady Marshall of Leeds, JP; Holtby, York

MARSHALL OF RACHAN AND GLENHOVE, Henry (Harry) Bruce; DL (Tweeddale 1984); s of Maj James Rissik Marshall, TD, JP, DL, QC (d 1959), of Baddinsgill, W Linton, Peeblesshire, and Eileen Margaret, *née* Bruce (d 1976); *b* 19 Oct 1924; *Educ* Rugby, Trinity Coll Oxford, Edinburgh Univ (BSc); *m* 19 Sept 1951, Catriona Mary Mackenzie, da of Maj Alfred Badenoch, TD, of Edinburgh; 1 s (Gavin b 30 May 1955), 1 da (Elspeth (Mrs Fleming) b 24 May 1953); *Career* served in army 1945-48, 2 Lt Queen's Own Cameron Highlanders 1946, Lt 1947; memb Queen's Bodyguard for Scotland (Royal Co of Archers) 1958; avionic engr with Ferranti Ltd 1952-76; farmer/estate mangr 1971-; Elder of St Andrew's Church, W Linton; *Recreations* shooting, photography; *Clubs* Tweeddale Shooting; *Style*— Harry Marshall of Rachan and Glenhove, DL; Baddinsgill, West Linton, Tweeddale (☎ 0968 60683)

MARSHAM, Lady Anne Rhoda; o da of Lt-Col Hon Reginald Hastings Marsham, OBE (d 1922) (2 s of 4 Earl of Romney); raised to the rank of an Earl's da 1976; *b* 7 June 1909; *Career* served 1939-45 war as Section Offr, WAAF; Kenya Police Reserve 1952-60; *Style*— Lady Anne Marsham; c/o The Rt Hon the Earl of Romney, Wensum Farm, West Rudham, King's Lynn, Norfolk

MARSHAM, John Nelson; s of Capt Thomas Brabbam Marsham, OBE (d 1942), and Jane Wise, *née* Nelson (d 1979); *b* 20 Dec 1931; *Educ* Gordonstoun, Univ of Liverpool (LLB); *m* 14 May 1966, Anne Gillian Mary, da of Thomas Charles Caldwell (d 1975), of Eskdale, Cumbria; 1 s (Richard b 1968), 1 da (Sacha b 1967), 1 step s (Nicholas b 1963), 1 step da (Caroline b 1961); *Career* slr, sr ptnr Milburn & Co; *Recreations* shooting, fishing, stalking; *Style*— John Marsham, Esq; Mill Place, Irton, Holmrook, Cumbria; 26 Mertoun Place, Edinburgh; Rinnes, Grantown-on-Spey, Morayshire, Scotland; Milburn & Co, Lowther St, Whitehaven, Cumbria

MARSHAM, Julian Charles; JP; s of Col Peter Marsham, MBE (s of Hon Sydney Marsham, yst s of 4 Earl of Romney), and Hersey, da of Maj Hon Richard Coke (3 s of 2 Earl of Leicester, KG, JP, DL, by his 2 w, Hon Georgina Cavendish, da of 2 Baron Chesham); hp of kinsman, 7 Earl of Romney; *b* 28 Mar 1948; *Educ* Eton; *m* 1975, Catriona, da of Robert Christie Stewart CBE, TD (nephew of Sir Christopher Lighton, 8 Bt, MBE); 2 s (David b 1977, Michael b 1979), 1 da (Laura b 1984); *Career* land agent; farmer; *Recreations* shooting, fishing, silviculture, gardening; *Style*— Julian Marsham, Esq, JP; Gayton Hall, King's Lynn, Norfolk (☎ 055 386 259, estate off 055 386 292)

MARSHAM, Dr (Thomas) Nelson; CBE (1976, OBE 1964); s of Capt Thomas Brabban Marsham, OBE (d 1942), and Jane Wise, *née* Nelson; *b* 10 Nov 1923; *Educ* Merchant Taylors Sch Crosby, Univ of Liverpool (BSc, PhD); *m* 12 June 1958, Sheila Margaret, da of Michael Joseph Griffin (d 1962); 2 s (Phillip b 1961, James b 1967); *Career* radio offr Ocean Steamship Co 1941-46; Oliver Lodge res fell Liverpool Univ 1951-53, reactor mangr Calder Hall Nuclear Power Station 1955-64, dir tech ops and dep md reactor gp UKAEA 1965-77, md northern div UKAEA 1977-87, bd memb UKAEA 1979-87, non exec dir Br Nuclear Fuels plc 1979-; memb cncl Liverpool Univ 1980-85; FRS 1986, FEng 1986; *Recreations* sailing; *Clubs* East India; *Style*— Dr Nelson Marsham; Fairfield, Eskdale, Holmrook, Cumbria CA19 1UA (☎ 09403 252); BNFL plc, Risley Warrington, Cheshire

MARSLAND, Christopher John; s of Jack Ronald Marsland (d 1975), of Westerlands, Valley Prospect, Newark, Notts, and Victoria Irene, *née* Lees; *b* 18 Feb 1940; *Educ* Strathallan Sch Pertshire, Manchester Univ (BSc); *m* 1 May 1969, Carole, da of John Alexander Elliott (d 1981), of Bingham, Notts; 1 s (David b 1976), 2 da (Vikki b 1961, Helen b 1974); *Career* graduate trg scheme Wiggins Teape 1961-64, Br Shoe Corps Ltd 1965-88: work study engr factories div 1965-67, transferred to head off (head of mgmnt servs, salary admin); Warehouse: chief exec 1976, distribution dir 1977-84, retail ops dir 1985-86, md 1987-88; currently dir-: Sears plc, Br Shoe Corpn Ltd, BSC Footwear Supplies Ltd, Dolcis Ltd, Freeman Hardy & Willis Ltd, Lilley & Skinner Ltd, Saxone Shoe Co Ltd, Trueform Ltd, Zephyr Sports Ltd, Hoogenbosch Schoenen BV; sch govr Colrton Basset Sch; *Recreations* golf, shooting, equestrian sports; *Style*— Christopher Marsland, Esq; Tanglewood, Colston Bassett, Notts NG12 3FB (☎ 0949 468); British Shoe Corporation Ltd, Sunningdale Rd, Leicester LE3 1UR (☎ 0533 320 202, fax 0533 320 210, car tel 0836 277 373, telex 0533 34493)

MARSLAND, Prof David; s of Ernest Marsland, of Leavesden Green, Herts, and Fay, *née* Savoury; *b* 3 Feb 1939; *Educ* Watford GS, Christ's Coll Cambridge (BA, MA), LSE, Brunel Univ (PhD); *Career* dept of sociology Brunel Univ 1964-88: lectr, sr lectr, dir postgrad studies, prof assoc; prof social res West London Inst of Higher Educn 1989-; asst dir The Social Affairs Unit London 1981-; memb: social scis bd UNESCO 1983-86, social scis ctee CNAA 1987-, EC Social Res Assoc; formerly hon gen sec Br Sociological Assoc 1987-; BSA (1964), SRA (1985), MBIM (1987); *Books* Seeds of Bankruptcy: Sociological Bias Against Business and Freedom (1988), Cradle to Grave: Comparative Perspectives on the State of Welfare (1989), Changes in Education: Rescue and Reform (1989); *Recreations* reading and writing poetry, anti-communism; *Clubs* Arts; *Style*— Prof David Marsland; W London Inst, 300 St Margaret's Rd, Twickenham, Middx (☎ 01 891 0621)

MARSTON, Dr Geoffrey; s of Arthur Marston (d 1982), of Newark, Notts, and Mabel, *née* Binns; *b* 17 Mar 1938; *Educ* Magnus GS Notts, UCL (LLB, LLM, PhD); *Career* mgmnt trainee Assoc Br Maltsters Export Co Ltd 1960-62, project offr Australian public Serv Canberra 1962-67, sr lect in Law Australian Nat Univ Canberra 1967-70, attache de recherches Graduate Inst of Int Studies Geneva 1970-73, fell Sidney Sussex Coll and lectr in Law Cambridge Univ 1973-; *Books* The Marginal Seabed: United Kingdom Legal Practice (1981); *Recreations* mountain walking, beachcombing, photography, traditional jazz; *Clubs* Athenaeum; *Style*— Dr Geoffrey Marston; Sidney Sussex Coll, Cambridge CB2 3HU (☎ 0223 338800, fax 0223 338884)

MARSTON, James Leslie; s of John Kenneth Marston (d 1982), and Jeanie, *née* Cranmer (d 1984); *b* 30 Jan 1944; *Educ* Rothesay Acad I of Bute; *m* (m dis 1988); 1 s (Craig b 1976), 1 da (Natalie b 1979); *Career* tax mangr Roffe Swayne and Co 1969-73, sr ptnr McColl and Crow 1985- (ptnr 1974); chm Chartered Fin Gp plc 1987-; memb Inst Curative Hypnotherapists and involved charity work for disabled; racehorse owner; composer num published songs; FCA, FCCA, ATII, FIMBRA; *Recreations* music, sports, travel; *Style*— Leslie Marston, Esq; Tudor Court, Heatherlands Rd, Chilworth, Hants (☎ 0703 768140); 1-3 The Avenue, Southampton SO1 2SE (☎ 0703 335211, fax 0703 331205, car tel 0860 719773)

MARSTON, Hon Mrs; Vanessa Mary; *née* Cawley; da of 3 Baron Cawley; *b* 30 Dec 1951; *Educ* Downe House; *m* 1971, Dr John Anthony, s of Donald Marston, of the Br Embassy, Beirut; 4 da (Cicely b 1973, Emma b 1975, Camilla b 1977, Annabel b 1979); *Style*— The Hon Mrs Marston; Gorwell House, Barnstaple, N Devon (☎ 0271 75499)

MARTEL, Maj Charles Peter; s of Lt/Gen Giffard le Quesene Martel, KCB, KBE, DSO, MC, AMIMechE (d 1958), and Maud Martel *née* McKenzie (d 1982); of Huguenot decent Arms registered at Coll of Arms; *b* 6 June 1923; *Educ* Wellington, Sandhurst; *m* 19 Oct 1957, Susan Carole, da of J R Ropner, Esq, of The Limes, Dalton, N Yorks; 3 da (Carole b 1959, Virginia b 1964 (d 1971), Sarah b 1973), 1 s (Nicholas b 1961); *Career* regular army offr, Maj 1942-45: 5 Royal Inniskillen Dragoon Gds, wounded Europe 1944; memb Lloyds of London 1956-; memb Worshipful Co Gunmakers, Freeman City of London 1971; *Recreations* shooting, bridge; *Clubs* Pratt's, Turf, Beefsteak, Cavalry and Guards'; *Style*— Maj Charles Martel

MARTELL, Vice Adm Sir Hugh Colenso; KBE (1966, CBE 1957), CB (1963); s of Engr Capt Albert Arthur Green Martell, DSO (d 1951), and Susie, da of Williams Colenso; *b* 6 May 1912; *Educ* Edinburgh Acad, RNC Dartmouth; *m* 1, Marguerite Isabelle, da of Sir Dymoke White, 2 Bt; m 2, Margaret, da of Maj A R Glover (d 1979); *Career* joined RN 1926, serv WWII (despatches), Russian Convoys and Pacific, Capt 1952, Overall Operational Cdr Nuclear Tests in Montebellos NW Australia 1957, Rear-Adm 1962, Dir-Gen Naval Recruiting 1964-65, Admin and Reserves, Vice-Adm 1965, Chief Allied Staff NATO Forces Mediterranean 1965-67, ret; dir: Derritron Electronics Ltd, Reslosound Ltd, City and Military Personnel Conslts and Dirs Secs Ltd; chm Bury Manor Schs Tst Ltd; govr: Dorset House Sch, Manor House Sch; *Recreations* yachting; *Clubs* Royal Naval, RN Sailing Assoc; *Style*— Vice-Adm Sir Hugh Martell, KBE, CB

MARTEN, Francis William; CMG (1976), MC (1943); s of Vice Adm Sir Francis Arthur Marten, KBE, CB, CMG, CVO (d 1950), of Andoversford Glos, and Phyllis Raby, *née* Morgan (d 1972); *b* 8 Nov 1916; *Educ* Winchester, Christ Church Oxford; *m* 1, 1940, The Hon Avice Irene (d 1964), da of 9 Baron Vernon; 1 s (Michael), 1 da (Jennifer); m 2, 1967, Anne, da of Tan Chim EK, of Kuching, Sarawak; 1 s (David b 1971); *Career* WWII Lt-Col Rifle Bde 1939-46; Dip Serv 1946-69: HM Embassy Washington 1948-52, Teheran 1954-57, Bonn 1958-62, Leopoldville 1962-64, Imperial Def Coll 1965, dep high cmmr Eastern Malaysia 1965-67; (cnsllr of Embassy); *Style*— Francis Marten, Esq, CMG, MC; 113 Pepys Rd, London SE14 5SE (☎ 01 639 1060)

MARTEN, Lt Cdr George Gosselin; LVO (1985, MVO 1950), DSC (1942); s of Vice Adm Sir Francis Arthur Marten (d 1950), and Phyllis Raby, *née* Morgan; *b* 28 Dec 1918; *Educ* RNC, Dartmouth; *m* 25 Nov 1949, Hon Mary Anna, *née* Sturt, da of 3 Baron Alington (ka 1940), 1 s (Napier b 1952), 5 da (Victoria b 1950, Charlotte b 1952, Georgina b 1953, Annabel b 1954, Sophie b 1961); *Career* RN serv HMS Watchman 1938-41, HMS Penn 1942-43, in cmd HMS Wilton 1943-45, equerry to HM King George VI 1948-50; *Recreations* forestry, shooting; *Clubs* Turf; *Style*— Lt Cmdr George Marten, LVO, DSC; Crichel, Wimborne, Dorset

MARTEN, Hon Mrs (Mary Anna Sibell Elizabeth); OBE; da of 3 Baron Alington (d 1940); *m* 25 Nov 1949, Lt Cdr George Gosselin Marten, LVO, DSC, s of late Sir

Francis Arthur Marten, KBE, CB, CMG, CVO; 1 s, 5 da; tstee The Br Museum 1985-; *Style*— The Hon Mrs Marten, OBE; Crichel, Wimborne, Dorset

MARTIN, Alan Frederick Joseph Plunkett; s of Dr Hugh Thomas Plunkett Martin, of 30 Buckingham Mansions, Bath Rd, Bournemouth, and Sylvia Mary, *née* Gilbert; *b* 22 August 1951; *Educ* Realgymnasium Basel Switzerland, Univ of Basel; *m* 19 May 1979, Rita Maria, da of Walter Gasser, of Rorschach, St Gall, Switzerland; 3 da (Stephanie b 1980, Felicity b 1983, Dominique b 1986); *Career* Swiss Bank Corpn Basel 1975-77 and 1979-80 (NY 1981), Credit Commercial de France Paris 1978, SBCI Swiss Bank Corpn Investmt Banking Ltd London 1981- (exec dir 1986); *Recreations* family, music, gardening, skiing, photography; *Style*— Alan Martin, Esq; 36 Cumberland Drive, Esher, Surrey KT10 OBB (☎ 01 398 6215); Swiss Bank House, 1 High Timber St, London EC4V 3SB (☎ 01 329 0329, fx 01 329 8700, telex 887434)

MARTIN, Alan Gould; s of Arthur Herbert Martin (d 1962), of Hale, Cheshire, and Cecil Muriel (d 1980), da of John Gould, of Stafford; *b* 19 Jan 1920; *Educ* Monkton Combe Sch, Harvard Business Sch; *m* 21 Nov 1953, Barbara Goodier, da of John Goodier Haworth, of Bowdon; 2 s (John Goodier b 1954, Peter Michael b 1957); *Career* serv WWII RN 1940-46, navigator med destroyers Royal Hellenic Navy 1943; CA; dir Indust and Commercial Fin Corpn Ltd 1976-81; chm: Frank Horsell Gp plc 1980-85, Singleton Birch Ltd 1979-; dir: Nat and Provincial Bldg Soc 1970-87, W Yorks Indep Hosp plc 1980-, Robert Glew & Co Ltd 1981-, Rainford Venture Capital Ltd 1980-, Yorks Chemicals plc 1981- (chm 1984), Hillards plc 1982-87, Land Instruments Int Ltd 1982-, Boydell Brothers Ltd 1966-; govr St Aidans Sch Harrogate W Yorks; FCA 1947; Hellenic Distinguished Serv 1943; *Recreations* idleness; *Clubs* Leeds; *Style*— Alan Martin, Esq; Huby House, Strait Lane, Huby, Leeds LS17 0EA (☎ 0423 74254)

MARTIN, Col Alexander Robert Fyers; s of Robert Philipp Martin (d 1953), and Mary Stephanie Maule *née* Ffinch (d 1964); *b* 3 Nov 1914; *Educ* Aldenham Sch 1928-33, Clare Coll (MA), Cert of Prehis Archaeology; *m* 22 March 1941, Alison, da of Lt-Col Ralph Markland Bell (d 1928); 1 s (Robert b 1949), 2 da (Susan b 1943, Alexandra b 1945 d 1960); *Career* Col RA 1939-66; serv: UK, Egypt, W Europe; MA Br Embassy Bern 1958-61; Foreign Exchange Broker RP Martin & Co 1937-39; Def Sales Orgn 1967-75, Ret Offr Grade 1; dir Br Mfr and Res Co Grantham 1976-85; lectr (pt/t) in archaeology extramural dept London Univ 1976-85; *Recreations* archaeology, bridge, gardening; *Clubs* Army and Navy; *Style*— Col Alexander Martin; The Cherry Trees, Meadow Lane, Hartley Wintney, Hants RG27 8RF

MARTIN, Col (Robert) Andrew (St George); KC VO (1988), OBE (1959, MBE 1949), JP (1985); s of Maj William Francis Martin (ka 1915), and Violet Anne Philippa Wynter (d 1963), of The Poplars, Mountsorrel, Leicestershire; *b* 23 April 1914; *Educ* Eton, RMC Sandhurst, Staff Coll Camberley; *m* 1950, Margaret Grace, JP, da of John V Buchanan, MB, ChB (d 1966), and Waiata Godsal; 1 s (Robert); *Career* cmmn Oxford Bucks LI 1934-38, ADC to Govr-Gen of SA 1938-40, serv WWII, UK 1940-44, NW Europe (despatches) 1944-45, Malaya 1946-49, Cyprus 1957-59, BAOR 1951-55, mil sec to Govr-Gen Australia 1955-57, cmmnd 1 Green Jackets 1957-59, Bde Col Green Jackets Bde 1959-62, CRLS HQ Western Cmd 1962-65, Lord-Lt and Custos Rotulorum Leicestershire 1965-89; Order of Orange Nassau 1950 LLD (Hon) Leicester Univ 1984; hon D Tech Loughborough Univ 1988; KStJ 1966; landowner; *Recreations* hunting, shooting, gardening; *Clubs* Army & Navy, MCC; *Style*— Col Sir Andrew Martin, REVO, OBE; The Brand, Woodhouse Eaves, Loughborough, Leicestershire LE12 8SS (☎ 0509 890269)

MARTIN, Barrie Stuart Meredyth; s of James William Meredyth Martin of Mayfield, E Sussex and formerly of Shanghai and Hong Kong, and Joyce Stuart, *née* Bidwell; *b* 18 August 1941; *Educ* Shanghai Br Sch, St John's Beaumont, Trinity Coll Dublin (BA, LLB); *Career* articled clerk to Sir Charles Russell Bart and later ptnr Charles Russell and Co, asst slr Sprott and Sons; sr ptnr J M Rix and Kay slrs; memb: Law Soc; *Recreations* tennis, travel; *Clubs* The Sloane; *Style*— Barrie Martin, Esq; J M Rix and Kay, 84 High St, Heathfield, East Sussex TN21 8JG (☎ 04352 5211, fax 04352 6822); Postmill House, Argos Hill, Rotherfield, E Sussex TN6 3QH

MARTIN, (Rowland) Brownlow; s of Col Reginald Victor Martin (d 1973), of the Indian Med Serv, and Katharine, *née* Clifford (d 1963); *b* 30 May 1924; *Educ* Wellington; *m* 1948, Wendy; 1 s (Richard), 1 da (Melanie); *Career* chief exec Hosp Conslts & Specialists Assoc; FRSM; *Recreations* golf, racing; *Clubs* Berks GC, Ascot Race, Newbury Race, Windsor Race; *Style*— Brownlow Martin, Esq; Mares Nest, Cheapside, Ascot Berks (☎ 0990 22621); The Old Court House, London Rd, Ascot, Berks (☎ 0990 25052)

MARTIN, Cary John; s of John Martin, of 13 Woodlands Rd, Manchester M16 8WR, and Joan Molly Wilson, *née* Skinner; *b* 22 August 1956; *Educ* William Hulme's GS Manchester, Birmingham Univ (MA, BA), Christ's Coll Cambridge; *m* 23 Sept 1978, Ruth Lillian, da of Arthur Henry George Amy, of 17 Charnhill Drive, Bristol BS17 3JR; *Career* exec Mori 1979-85; md city mktg res and planning Dewe Rogerson 1988- (joined 1985); *Books* A Demotic Land Lease from Philadelphia (2 ed 1986); *Recreations* egyptology; *Style*— Cary Martin, Esq; 160 Finborough Rd, London SW10 9AH (☎ 01 373 4253); Dewe Rogerson, 3 London Wall Bldgs, London Wall, London EC2M 5SY (☎ 01 638 9571, fax 01 628 3444)

MARTIN, Charles Edmund; s of Flt Lt Charles Stuart Martin RAFVR (ka 1944), of Newcastle upon Tyne, and Sheila, *née* Richardson; *b* 19 Sept 1939; *Educ* Lancing, Selwyn Coll Cambridge (MA), Univ of Bristol (PGCE); *m* 6 Aug 1966, Emily Mary, da of Ernest Franklin Bozman, MC (d 1968), of Cambridge; 1 s (Joseph Ernest), 1 da (Charlotte Mary); *Career* voluntary serv overseas Sarawak 1958-59, asst master Leighton Park Sch Reading 1964-68, sixth form master and day housemaster Sevenoaks Sch Kent 1968-71, dep headmaster and hd of English Pocklington Sch York 1971-80; headmaster: King Edward VI Camp Hill Boys Sch Birmingham 1980-86, Bristol GS 1986-; HMC 1986, SHA 1980; *Recreations* walking, beekeeping, travel; *Clubs* E India, Public Schs; *Style*— Charles Martin, Esq; The Grammar Sch, Univ Rd, Bristol BS8 1SR (☎ 0272 736 006)

MARTIN, David; s of Edward Sydney Morris Martin, of Exeter, and Dorothy Mary, *née* Cooper; *b* 11 Feb 1952; *Educ* Worthing HS for Boys, St John's Coll Cambridge; *Career* ptnr Herbert Smith 1986-(tax slr 1979-, asst slr 1979-86); memb Religious Soc of Friends; *Recreations* reading, walking; *Style*— David Martin, Esq; 26 Pied Bull Court, Bury Place, London WC1A 2JR (☎ 01 831 6086); Herbert Smith, Watling House, 35 Cannon St, London EC4M 5SD (☎ 01 489 8000, fax 01 329 0426, telex 886633)

MARTIN, Prof David Alfred; s of Frederick Martin (d 1979), and Rhoda Miriam Martin (d 1981); *b* 30 June 1929; *Educ* Richmond and E Sheen GS, Westminster Coll Oxford (Dip Ed), LSE (BSc, PhD); *m* 1, 1953 (m dis 1957), Daphne Sylvia, *née* Treherne (d 1973); 1 s (Jonathan b 1956); m 2, 30 June 1962, Bernice, da of Frederick William Thompson (d 1956); 2 s (Izaak b 1965, Magnus b 1971), 1 da (Jessica b 1963); *Career* Nat Serv 1950-52; sch teaching 1952-59, lectr Sheffield Univ 1961-62, prof LSE 1971-89 (lectr 1962-67, reader 1967-71), Scurlock prof Southern Methodist Univ Dallas 1986-89; hon asst Guildford Cathedral 1983- (non-stipendiary priest 1984); pres Int Conf of the Sociology of Religion 1975-83, select preacher Cambridge Univ, fell Japanese Soc for the Promotion of Sci 1978-79, memb UK UNESCO ctee 1982-83, UK advsy ctee Encyclopaedia Britannica 1986-, chm Cncl for Academic Autonomy 1988-; memb London Soc for the Study of Religion 1973; *Books* Pacifism (1965), A Sociology of English Religion (1967), The Religious and the Secular (1971), A General Theory of Secularization (1978), The Breaking of the Image (1980); *Recreations* piano; *Style*— Prof David A Martin; Cripplegate Cottage, 174 St John's Rd, Woking, Surrey (☎ 04862 62134); LSE, Aldwych, London, WC2 (☎ 01 405 7686)

MARTIN, David John Pattison; MP (C) Portmouth South 1987-); s of John Besley Martin, CBE (d 1982), and Muriel, *née* Pattison; *b* 5 Feb 1945; *Educ* Kelly Coll Tavistock, Fitzwilliam Coll Cambridge (BA); *m* 8 Jan 1977, Basia Constance, da of Tadeusz Dowmvnt; 1 s (Henry b 1985), 4 da (Naomi b 1978, Melissa b and d 1980, Francesca 1981, Charis b 1983); *Career* barr Inner Temple, practised 1969-76; dir Martins Caravan Co and assoc co; govr Drummer Acad USA; *Recreations* music, golf; *Clubs* Hawks; *Style*— David Martin, Esq, MP

MARTIN, David Norman; s of Norman Henry Edward Martin, of Angmerins, Sussex, and Joyce Elizabeth Martin; *b* 27 August 1948; *Educ* Tulse Hill Sch London SW2; *Career* sales dir Shubette of London Gp 1971-78, owner and dir Whole Meal Vegetarian Cafe 1978-; *Recreations* golf, tennis; *Clubs* Purley Downs GC, Surrey Tennis and Country Club; *Style*— David Martin, Esq; 14 Oakfield Gdns, Dulwich Wood Ave, London SE19 1HF (☎ 01 670 0137); 1 Shrewsbury Rd, Streatham, London SW16 2AS (☎ 01 769 0137)

MARTIN, Prof Derek Humphery; s of Alec Gooch Martin (d 1986), of Eastbourne, and Winifred, *née* Humphery; *b* 18 May 1929; *Educ* Hitchin Boys GS, Eastbourne GS, Univ of Nottingham (BSc, PhD); *m* 7 July 1951, Joyce Sheila, da of William Samuel Leaper (d 1973), of Eastbourne; 1 s (Richard Jonathan b 1960), 1 da (Elizabeth Jane b 1962); *Career* prof of physics QMC London 1967- (lectr 1954-63, reader 1963-67); senator Univ of London 1980-87, hon sec Inst of physics 1984-; memb: ct Univ of Essex 1986-, Br Nat Ctee for Radioscience 1983-88, Br Nat Ctee for Physics 1987-, Royal Greenwich Observatory Estab Ctee 1977-80; ed Advances in Physics 1974-85; bd memb: Athlone Press 1973-83, IOP Pubns Ltd 1985-; Metrology Award of the Nat Physical Laboratory 1983; FInstP 1965, CPhys 1985;; *Books* Magnetism in Solids (1967), Spectroscopic Techniques (1967); *Clubs* Athenaeum; *Style*— Prof Derek Martin; Hermanus, Hillwood Grove, Brentwood, Essex, (☎ 0277 210546); Queen Mary College, Mile End Rd, London E14 NS

MARTIN, Douglas Whitwell; s of Rev Thomas Henry Martin (d 1955); *b* 17 Feb 1906; *Educ* Rossall, Lausanne Univ; *m* 1, 1931, Jessie Milroy (d 1965), da of Dr John Lawrie (d 1952); 3 s; m 2, 1967, Margaret Helen, da of Edwin James Simms (d 1964); *Career* Lloyd's underwriter 1950-69, joined Gill & Duffus Ltd 1929, (chm 1964-70), pres Gill & Duffus Gp plc 1973-85; *Recreations* reading, theatre; *Style*— Douglas Martin, Esq; 74 Fort George, St Peter Port, Guernsey, CI (☎ 0481 25 381)

MARTIN, Geoffrey Haward; CBE (1986); s of Ernest Leslie Martin (d 1967), of Colchester, and Mary Hilda *née* Haward (d 1987); *b* 27 Sept 1928; *Educ* Colchester Royal GS, Merton Coll Oxford (MA, DPhil), Univ of Manchester; *m* 12 Sept 1953, Janet Douglas, da of Douglas Hamer, MC (d 1981), of Sheffield; 3 s (Christopher b 1957, Patrick b 1963, Matthew b 1963), 1 da (Sophia b 1961); *Career* prof of history Univ of Leicester (formerly Univ Coll of Leicester) 1973-82 (lectr 1952-66, reader 1966-73), visiting prof Carleton Univ Ottawa 1958-59 and 1967-68, visiting res fell Merton Coll Oxford 1971, sr visiting fell Loughborough Univ of Technol 1987-, visiting prof of history univ of Toronto 1989-; chm: Br Records Assoc 1981, Cwlth Archivists Assoc 1984-88; Keeper of Public Records 1982-88; memb: FSA 1975, FRHistS 1958 (vice pres 1984-88), FRSA 1987; *Books* The Town: A Visual History (1961), The Royal Charters of Grantham (1963), Bibliography of British and Irish Municipal History (with Sylvia McIntyre 1972), Ipswich Recognizance Rolls (1973); *Recreations* fell-walking, gardening; *Clubs* Utd Oxford and Cambridge Univ, RCS; *Style*— Geoffrey Martin, Esq, CBE; Flat 27, Woodside House, Wimbledon, London SW19 7QN (☎ 01 946 2570)

MARTIN, (Thomas) Geoffrey; s of Thomas Martin (d 1973), Belfast, NI, and Sadie Adelaide, *née* Day; *b* 26 July 1940; *Educ* Newry GS, Queens Univ Belfast; *m* 6 July 1968, Gay Madeleine Annesley, da of Herbert Annesley Brownrigg, of Bognor Regis; 1 s (Thomas), 3 da (Blue Bell, Poppy, Gabriella); *Career* pres NUS 1966-68, dir Shelter 1972-73, dip staff Cwlth Secretarial 1973-79; hd: Euro Cmmn off NI 1979-85, Pres & Info Serv EC SE Asia 1985-87, External Relations Euro Cmmn Off London 1987-; *Recreations* running; *Clubs* Travellers'; *Style*— Geoffrey Martin, Esq; 64 Mortlake Rd, Kew, Richmond TW9 4AS (☎ 01 876 3714); 8 Storeys Gate, London SW1 4AS (☎ 01 222822)

MARTIN, Prof Geoffrey Thorndike; s of Albert Thorndike Martin (d 1947), and Lily, *née* Jackson (d 1964); *b* 28 May 1934; *Educ* Palmer's Sch, Grays Thurrock, Univ Coll London (BA), Corpus Christi Coll Cambridge, Christ's Coll Cambridge (MA, PhD); *Career* Univ Coll London: lectr in egyptology 1970-78, reader in egyptian archaeology 1978-87, prof of egyptology (Ad Hominem) 1987, Edwards prof of egyptology 1988; publications (selected): Egyptian Administrative and Private-Name Seals (1971), The Royal Tomb at El-Amarna (vol 1 1974, vol 2 forthcoming 1989), The Tomb of Hetepka (1979), The Sacred Animal Necropolis at North Saqqara (1981), Canopic Equipment in the Petrie Collection (with V Raisman, 1984), Scarabs, Cylinders, and other Ancient Egyptian Seals (1985), The Tomb Chapels of Paser and Raia (1985), Corpus of Reliefs of the New Kingdom (vol 1 1987), Excavations in the Royal Necropolis at El-Amarna (with A El-Khouly, 1987); Field Dir jt Egypt Exploration Soc and Leiden Museum exp in Egypt 1975-; FSA 1975, ctee memb Egypt Exploration Soc, Corresponding memb German Archaeological Inst 1982; *Recreations* travel, english history, book collecting; *Style*— Prof Geoffrey Martin; Department of Egyptology, University College London, Gower St, London WC1E 6BT (☎ 01 387 7050)

MARTIN, Glenn Philip; s of Walter Philip, and Eileen Denton, *née* Savage; *b* 11 Feb

1949; *Educ* Kings Coll Sch Wimbledon, Wadham Coll Oxford (BA); *m* 4 July 1970, Beryl, da of Albert Darby, of Sale; 3 s (Christopher b 1970, Alastair b 1979, Nicholas b 1984), 1 da (Sarah b 1973); *Career* assoc dir Swiss Bank Corpn 1988 (vice pres 1986); *Recreations* squash, tennis; *Clubs* City Swiss; *Style*— Glenn Martin, Esq; 14 Langham Dene, Kenley, Surrey CR2 5BY (☎ 01 668 9674); Swiss Bank Hse, 1 High Timber St, London EC4V 3SB (☎ 01 329 0329, fax 01 329 8700)

MARTIN, Harold Raymond (Harry); s of Lt Frederick Sidney Martin, DSM (d 1925), of Appledore, North Devon, and Blanche, *née* Hookway (d 1958); *b* 2 June 1920; *Educ* Bideford GS; *m* 4 Sept 1950, Pamela Mary, da of William Henry Baron; 1 s (Denys Raymond b 1954), 1 da (Susan Rosalind b 1951); *Career* WWII RA served: BEF France 1939-40, Western Desert 1940-41 (POW Italy 1941-43, Germany 1943-45); Nat Provincial Bank 1937-68; Nat Westminster Bank 1968-80; chief mangr Stock Office Servs, mangr Bishopsgate London; hon gen sec Nat Honey Shaw 1980-; Freeman City of London 1966, Liveryman Worshipful Co of Scriveners 1966; FCIB 1967; *Recreations* beekeeping, music, swimming; *Style*— Harry Martin, Esq; Gander Barn, Southfields Rd, Woldingham, Surrey (☎ 088 385 3152)

MARTIN, Hugh Hutton; s of Hugh Lumsden Martin (d 1968), and Ada Muriel Anne Martin; *b* 26 Nov 1940; *Educ* Merchiston; *m* 1964, Kay Roberta, da of Ramsay Kinnear Calder; 2 da; *Career* chm Martins Dundyvan Ltd; *Recreations* skiing, fishing, gastronomy; *Style*— Hugh Martin, Esq; Flat 3B Woodend, 19 Milverton Rd, Giffnock, Glasgow G46 7JN; Martins Dundyvan Ltd, Dundyvan Steel Works, Coatbridge, ML5 1EB (☎ 0236 33 601, telex 779606)

MARTIN, Ian Robert; s of William Otway Martin (d 1985), of Wallington, and Marion Weir, *née* Gillespie (d 1976); *b* 29 Dec 1935; *Educ* Wallington Co Sch, Christ Church Oxford (BA, MA); *m* 1 Aug 1964, Susan, da of Neville Joseph Mountfort, of Olton, Solihull; 3 s (Andrew, Roger, Alan), 1 da (Sally); *Career* Nat Serv RN 1954-61; worked on current affrs and feature programmes incl Face to Face BBC TV 1959-68, head of music and arts Thames TV 1988- (exec prodr documentaries 1968-70, ed This Week 1971, exec produc features 1972-75, controller features educn and religion 1976-85, head of documentaries 1986-87); exec producer many maj documentaries and specials incl: St Nicolas (1977), The Gospel According to St Mark (1979), Swan Lake (1980, Br fund-raising Telethon (1980), Rigoletto (1982), The Mikado (1987), Jessye Normans Christmas Symphony (1987), Martin Luther King - The Legacy (1988), In From the Cold? Richard Burton (1988), Twelfth Night (1988), Xerxes (1989) and The Midsummer Marriage (1989); public career involved local activities; govr Isleworth & Syon Sch, chm Hounslow Educn Advsy Ctee, memb Kensington Area Synod; BAFTA (former chm TV and Awards Ctees); *Books* From Workhouse to Welfare (1969); *Recreations* collecting puzzles and quotations; *Style*— Ian Martin, Esq; 83 Wood Lane, Isleworth, Middx TW7 5EG (☎ 01 560 4584); Thames TV, 306-316 Euston Rd, London NW1 (☎ 01 387 9494, fax 01 383 5089, telex 22816)

MARTIN, Janet Hazel; da of James Henry Wilkinson, of Dorchester, Dorset, and Florence Daisy, *née* Steer; *b* 8 Sept 1927; *Educ* Dorchester GS, S Dorset Tech Coll; *m* 15 Aug 1951, (Kenneth) Peter Martin, s of Leonard Henry Martin, of Steepleton Nr Dorchester; 1 s (Timothy b 4 June 1960), 1 da (Judith (Mrs Thomson) b 2 July 1957); *Career* pa NHS 1949-56, freelance interviewer various res insts 1967-86 residential socl worker (children with special needs) SW Hants Social Servs 1976-78, socl servs offr Test Valley Socl Servs 1978-86, psychosexual cnsllr (Aldermoor Clinic) NHS 1981-84, housing warden (elderly) Test Valley Socl Servs 1988- (residential care mangr 1986-87); memb: Wessex Psychotherapy Soc, Salisbury Arts Centre, Thomas Hardy Soc; lay memb press cncl 1973-78; *Recreations* books, buildings; *Style*— Mrs Janet Martin; Osborne House, West Wellow Hampshire, Linton House, Dorchester Dorset (☎ 0305 22771)

MARTIN, Lady; Jean MacGaradh; da of Thomas Hay Wilson (d 1957), of Edinburgh; *Educ* Edinburgh Univ (MA); *m* 1943, Sir David Christie Martin, CBE (d 1976); *Style*— Lady Martin; 3 Ct Drive, Stanmore, Middx HA7 4QH

MARTIN, (Patricia) Jean; *née* Smith; da of Thomas Gregory Smith, of Clifton, Bristol, and Amy Rose, *née* Tyley; *m* April 1963, Michael Graham Martin; *Career* md Audio Televisual Communications, fndr dir MJM Communications 1970-, her work is concerned with the skills of spoken communications, listening and advising on approximately 1000 business presentations each year; clients incl: Br Inst of Mgmnt, Ashbridge Mgmnt Coll, Br Tport Staff Coll, Nat West Bank, AERE Harwell; woked for multis in Paris, Brussels, Rome, Madrid, Copenhagen, Dublin; first conslt to offer trg to busines and professionals to "Meet The Media"; TV acclimatisations for Con ply Central off, Price WaterHouse, Northcliffe Newspaper Gp, Ciba Gigy, assoc memb of faculty Ashridge Mgmnt Coll 1983-85; LRAM, LGSM; *Recreations* gardening, cooking; *Style*— Mrs Jean Martin; Holmwood, 63 Downton Rd, Salisbury, Wilts SP2 8AT (☎ 0722 245 89)

MARTIN, Vice Adm Sir John Edward Ludgate; KCB (1972, CB 1968), DSC (1943); s of Surgeon Rear Adm W L Martin, OBE; *b* 10 May 1918; *Educ* RNC Dartmouth; *m* 1942, Rosemary Deck; 2 s, 2 da; *Career* serv WWII RN, Capt 1957, Cdr Br Forces Caribbean Area 1962-63, Rear Adm 1966, Flag Offr Middle E 1966-67 (despatches), Cdr Br Forces Gulf 1967-68, dir-gen Personnel Servs and Tning (Navy) 1968-70, Vice Adm 1970, Dep Supreme Allied Cdr Atlantic 1970-73, ret; Lt Govr and C-in-C of Guernsey 1974-80; pres Nautical Inst 1975-78; *Style*— Vice-Adm Sir John Martin, KCB, DSC; c/o Army and Navy Club, 36 Pall Mall, London SW1

MARTIN, (Leonard) John; VRD (1969); s of Leonard A Martin (d 1983), and Anne Elizabeth, *née* Scudamore (d 1975); *b* 20 April 1929; *Educ* Ardingly Coll; *m* 3 March 1956, Elisabeth Veronica, da of David Samuel Jones, MBE (d 1968); 1 s (Christopher John b 15 July 1958), 1 da (Rosemary Elisabeth (Mrs Scudamore) b 12 May 1960); *Career* Nat Serv Navy 1949-50, A Sub Lt RNVR, ret Lt Cdr 1975; actuary R Watson & Sons 1952-: qualified actuary 1954, ptnr 1957 sr ptnr 1983-; vice-pres Inst of Actuaries 1986-88; chm: Assoc Conslt Actuaries 1985-87, Occupational Pensious Jt Working Gp 1986-87, Consultative Gp of Actuaries in EEC 1988-; memb Occupational Pensions Bd 1988-; Liveryman: Guild of Air Pilots and Navigators, Worshipful Co of Actuaries; FIA 1954, FPMI 1958, FSS 1958; *Recreations* singing, sailing and flying; *Clubs* Naval; *Style*— John Martin, Esq; R Watson & Sons, Watson House, London Rd, Reigate, Surrey (☎ 07372 41 144, fax 07372 41 496, telex 946 070)

MARTIN, Sir John Miller; KCMG (1952), CB (1945), CVO (1943); s of Rev John Martin (d 1927), and Edith Godwin Martin (d 1945); *b* 15 Oct 1904; *Educ* Edinburgh Acad, Corpus Christi Coll Oxford (MA); *m* 1943, Rosalind Julia, da of Sir David Ross, KBE (d 1971); 1 s; *Career* entered Civil Serv 1927, (Dominions Off) seconded to Malayan Civil Serv 1931-34, sec of Palestine Royal Cmmn 1936, princ private sec to the Prime Minister 1941-45, asst under-sec Colonial Off 1945-56, dep under-sec of state Colonial Off 1956-65, Br high cmmr Malta 1965-67, ret; hon fell CCC Oxford; KStJ; *Style*— Sir John Martin, KCMG, CB, CVO; The Barn House, Watlington, Oxford OX9 5AA (☎ 049 161 2487)

MARTIN, Prof John Powell; s of Bernard Davis Martin (d 1986), and Grace Edith Martin (d 1976); *b* 22 Dec 1925; *Educ* Leighton Park Sch Reading, Univ of Reading (BA), LSE (Dip Soc Admin), Univ of London (PhD); *m* 1, 11 July 1951 (m dis 1981), Sheila Isabel, da of Stuart Feather (d 1985); 3 s (Andrew b 1953, Lawrence b 1955, Stuart b 1957); m 2, 16 Sept 1983, Joan Margaret, *née* Higgins; *Career* lectr LSE 1952-59, asst dir of res Inst of Criminology Cambridge 1960-66, fell King's Coll Cambridge 1964-67; Southampton Univ: prof of sociology and social admin 1967-87, prof of social policy 1987-; memb and vice-chm bd of visitors HM Prison Albany 1967-78; memb: IOW Health Authy 1974-, Hants Probation Ctee 1975-, Jellicoe Ctee on Bds of Visitors 1974-75; *Books* Social Aspects of Prescribing (1957), Offenders as Employees (1962), The Police: A Study in Manpower (with Gail Wilson, 1969), The Social Consequences of Conviction (with D Webster, 1971), Violence and the Family (ed, 1978), Hospitals in Trouble (1984), Licensed to Live (with J B Coker, 1985); *Recreations* sailing, DIY, photography; *Clubs* Lymington Town SC; *Style*— Prof John Martin; 4 Furzedown Rd, Southampton SO2 1PN (☎ 0703 552 795); Dept of Sociology and Social Policy, Univ of Southampton SO9 5NH (☎ 0703 595 000, fax 0703 593 939, telex 47661)

MARTIN, John Vandeleur; s of Col Graham Vandeleur Martin, MC, of Devizes, Wilts, and Margaret Helen, *née* Sherwood; *b* 17 Jan 1948; *Educ* Malvern, Pembroke Coll Cambridge (MA); *m* 7 Dec 1974, Stephanie Johnstone, da of Maj Michael Johnstone Smith, MC, of Bedford; 2 s (Timothy b 1979, Nicholas b 1985), 1 da (Josephine b 1983); *Career* called to the Bar Lincoln's Inn 1972, Northern circuit; Freeman City of London 1969, Liveryman Worshipful Co of Drapers 1973; *Recreations* opera, walking; *Style*— John Martin, Esq; 3 New Square, Lincoln's Inn, London WC2A 3RS (☎ 01 405 5296, fax 01 831 6803, telex 267699 EQUITY)

MARTIN, John William; s of John Joseph William Martin, and Doris May, *née* Bowden ; *b* 6 August 1935; *Educ* City of London Sch; *m* 26 March 1988, Murielle Fernande, da of Mr Davis; *Career* actuarial student Clerical Med and Gen Assus 1954-64, asst actuary Local Govt Offrs Insur Assoc 1964-65, dep investmt mangr central fin bd C of E 1965-70, investmt mangr Br Steel Pension Fund 1970-81, chm American Property Tst 1978-, gen mangr invesmts BP 1981-; tstee Walker Ground Southgate, Liveryman Worshipful Co Actuaries 1983; fell Inst Actuaries 1964; *Recreations* skiing, squash, tennis, opera ballet; *Style*— John Martin, Esq; 59 The Ridgeway, Cuffley, Herts (☎ 0707 872 492); Britannic House, Moor Lane, London EC2 (☎ 01 920 7388, fax 01 920 3736)

MARTIN, Jonathan Arthur; s of Arthur Martin (d 1977), of Gravesend, Kent, and Mabel Gladys, *née* Bishop (d 1969); *b* 18 June 1942; *Educ* Gravesend GS, St Edmund Hall Oxford (BA); *m* 4 June 1967, Joy Elizabeth, da of Cecil William Fulker, OBE (d 1970), of Chorleywood; 2 s (Stewart John Edmund b 1969, Andrew Robert Jonathan b 1972); *Career* BBC: gen trainee 1964-65, prodn asst Sportsview and Grandstand 1965-69, prodr Sportsnight 1969-74, ed Sportsnight and Match of the Day 1974-79; exec prodr: Wimbledon Tennis Coverage 1979-81, Grand Prix 1977-80, Ski Sunday 1978-80; managing ed Sport 1980-81, hd of Sport TV 1981-87, hd of Sport and Events Gp TV 1987-; *Recreations* skiing, watching sport, watching television, golf; *Style*— Jonathan Martin, Esq; Arkle, Valentine Way, Chalfont St Giles, Bucks HP8 4JB; BBC Television, Kensington House, Richmond Way, London W14 (☎ 01 743 1272)

MARTIN, Judy Gordon; da of Kenneth Robert Lockhart smith (d 1978), of Green Tye, Much Hadham, Herts, and Iris Opal Gordon, *née* Blake (d 1979); *b* 13 Nov 1928; *Educ* Bedford Sch, St James Secretarial Coll; *m* 24 June 1966, George Henry Martin, CBE, s of Henry Martin; 1 s (Giles b 9 Oct 1969), 1 da (Lucie b 9 Aug 1967); *Career* EMI Abbey Rd Studios 1948, PA to George Martin, head Parlophone Records 1955-65, sec to Oscar Preuss 1948-55, fndr memb Air Records 1965, ret to raise family 1967, co-fndr Air Studios Montserrat 1969; memb Hyde Park Christian Business and Professional Gp; *Recreations* gardening, reading, travel; *Clubs* Oriental; *Style*— Mrs George Martin

MARTIN, June Eileen; da of Edward William Martin (d 1983), and Vera Cecelia, *née* Hayes; *b* 13 June 1948; *Educ* Pontypridd Girls GS, Bangur Sch for Girls, Hatfield Polytech (BSc); *Career* manging consult Ernst & Whinney 1981-, business consult ICL 1972-81; *Recreations* small bore rifle shooting; *Style*— Miss June Martin; 1 Lambeth Palace Rd, London SE1 7EU (☎ 01 928 2000)

MARTIN, Prof Laurence Woodward; DL (Tyne and Wear 1987-); s of Leonard Martin (d 1983), and Florence Mary, *née* Woodward (d 1987); *b* 30 July 1928; *Educ* St Austell GS, Christ's Coll Cambridge (MA), Yale Univ (MA, PhD); *m* 18 Aug 1951, Betty, da of William Parnall (d 1958); 1 s (William Martin b 1962), 1 da (Jane Martin b 1959); *Career* Flying Offr RAF 1948-50; instr political sci Yale Univ 1955-56, asst prof of political sci MIT 1956-61, assoc prof of Euro diplomacy sch of advanced int studies Johns Hopkins Univ 1961-64, Woodrow Wilson prof on int politics Univ of Wales 1964-68 (dean faculty of social sci 1966-68), prof of war studies King's Coll London 1968-77, vice-chllr Univ of Newcastle upon Tyne 1978; dir Tyne Tees TV Ltd; *Books* The Anglo-American Tradition in Foreign Affairs (with Arnold Wolfers, 1956), Peace without Victory: Woodrow Wilson and British Liberalism (1958), Neutralism and Non-Alignment (1963), The Sea in Modern Strategy (1966), America and The World (jtly 1970), Arms and Strategy (1973), Retreat from Empire (jtly 1973), Strategic Thought in the Nuclear Age (ed 1979), The Two-Edged Sword: Armed Force in the Modern World (1982), Before The Day After (1985), The Changing Face of Nuclear Warfare (1987); *Style*— Prof Laurence Martin, DL; The Vice-Chancellor, Univ of Newcastle upon Tyne, Newcastle upon Tyne NE1 7RU (☎ 091 232 8511/091 222 6064, fax 091 222 6229, telex 53654 UNINEW G)

MARTIN, Prof Sir (John) Leslie; s of Robert Martin, of Manchester; *b* 17 August 1908; *Educ* Manchester Univ (MA, PhD); *m* 1935, Sadie, da of Dr Alfred Speight; 1 s, 1 da; *Career* practising architect; architect to LCC 1953-56, prof of architecture Cambridge Univ 1956, emeritus prof 1973-; Slade prof of fine arts Oxford 1965-66, visiting prof Yale 1973-74, Lethaby prof Royal Coll of Art 1981, emeritus fell Jesus Coll Cambridge 1976 (fell 1956, hon fell 1973); bldgs designed for Univs of Cambridge, Oxford, Leicester, Hull; RSAMD Glasgow; Gallery of Modern Art Gulbenkian Fndn, Lisbon, Royal Gold Medalist RIBA 1973; Hon LLD: Univ of Leicester, Hull,

Manchester; DUniv Essex; Cdr Order of Santiago da Espada, Portugal; RA 1986; FRIBA; kt 1957; *Clubs* Athenaeum; *Style*— Prof Sir Leslie Martin, RA; The Barns, Church St, Great Shelford, Cambridge CB2 5EL (☎ 0223 842399)

MARTIN, Lionel; s of Max Rosenthal, and Renée, *née* Marks; *b* 9 August 1950; *Educ* Quintin Sch; *m* 20 July 1975, Carole, da of Michael Packer; 3 da (Carly b 1978, Jojo b 1981, Lily b 1987); *Career* CA; ptnr Martin Greene Ravden; ACA 1973, FCA 1983, FCCA 1983; *Recreations* tennis, music (incl professional writing); *Clubs* The David Lloyd Slazenger Racquet; *Style*— Lionel Martin, Esq; 55 Loudoun Rd, St John's Wood, London, NW8 0DL (☎ 01 625 4545, fax 01 625 5265, car tel 0836 209 962, telex 21338 MARTIN G)

MARTIN, Lady; Margaret; da of Alfred Roberts; *m* 1930, Sir Charles Carnegie Martin, CBE (d 1969); *Style*— Lady Martin

MARTIN, Michael Charles; s of Charles Stanley Martin, (d 1980), and Muriel, *née* Mudd (d 1965); *b* 7 April 1933; *Educ* Malvern, Loughborough Univ (BSc); *m* 1, 2 May 1964 (m dis 1988), Katharine Valentine, da of Thomas Arthur Saul, of Skegness, Lincs; 1 s (Charles Thomas b 3 May 1967), 1 da (Arabella Katharine b 15 March 1966); m 2, 26 Sept 1988, Helen Gillard, *née* Coleman (d 1988); *Career* 2 Lt REME 1956-58, serv Germany; chm CS Martin Gp of Cos, dep chm Louis Newmark plc; former chm Leicester branch IOD and Inst of Prodn Engrs, memb Leicester C of C; govr Sports Aid Fndn E Midlands, pres Leics Lawn Tennis Assoc 1985-88, hon sec and tres Soc of Lawn Tennis Referees; Liveryman Worshipful Co of Makers of Playing Cards 1967, Master Worshipful Co of Framework Knitters 1988-89 (Liveryman 1962, Ct of Assts 1977); FInstD 1961, CEng 1968, MIProdE 1968, CBIM 1987; *Recreations* tennis, rugby referee, holiday golf, sailing; *Clubs* RAC, Army & Navy; *Style*— Michael Martin, Esq; The Paddocks, Hungarton, Leics LE7 9JY (☎ 053 750 230); CS Martin Hldgs Ltd, Martin House, Gloucester Crescent, Wigston, Leics LE8 2YL (☎ 0533 773399, fax 0533 787090, telex 34526)

MARTIN, Michael John; MP (Lab) Glasgow, Springburn 1979-; s of Michael and Mary Martin; *b* 3 July 1945; *Educ* St Patrick's Boys Sch Glasgow; *m* 1965, Mary McLay; 1 s, 1 da; *Career* Rolls Royce (Hillington) AUEW shop steward 1970-74, trade union organiser 1976-79; PPS to Rt Hon Denis Healey 1981-; *Style*— Michael Martin, Esq, MP; 144 Broomfield Rd, Balornock, Glasgow G21 3UE

MARTIN, Millicent; da of William Martin (d 1970), of Florida, and Violet, *née* Bedford (d 1946); *b* 8 June 1934; *Educ* Heath Park HS, Italia Conti Stage Sch; *m* 26 Sept 1977, Marc Alexander, s of Stanley Marteski; *Career* actress and singer; recent theatre work incl: 42nd Street New York (also Los Angeles and Las Vegas) 1981-85, Two Into One (Opposite Tony Randell) USA 1987, Follies Shaftesbury Theatre London 1988-89; tv incl Downtown Los Angeles 1986; *Recreations* cooking, swimming, dancing; *Style*— Miss Millicent Martin; Connecticut & NYC; PO Box 101, Redding Court, 06875, USA

MARTIN, Lady; Nina Margherita; da of Francesco Michele Amadini (decd); *m* 1938, as his 3 w, Sir Ernest Martin (d 1957); 1 s (Dick b 1949, m 1983); *Style*— Lady Martin; 1 Redcliffe Sq, South Kensington, London SW10 9LA (☎ 01 373 3857)

MARTIN, Hon Mrs (Penelope Christina); *née* Plowden; da of Baron Plowden (Life Peer); *b* 1941; *Educ* St Mary's Convent Ascot, New Hall Cambridge; *m* 1, 1965 (m dis 1975), Christopher Roper; m 2, 1981, Rees, s of Leslie Martin, of Te Awa Ave, Napier, NZ; 1 s (Henry b 1984); *Style*— The Hon Mrs Martin; 43 Lansdowne Gdns, London SW8 (☎ 01 720 5736)

MARTIN, Maj Gen Peter Lawrence de Carteret; CBE (1968, OBE 1964); s of late Col Charles de Carteret Martin, MD, CRD, IMS; *b* 15 Feb 1920; *Educ* Wellington, Sandhurst; *m* 1, 1949, Elizabeth Felicia, da of the late Col C M Keble, OBE; 1 s, 1 da; m 2, 1973, Valerie Elizabeth, nee Brown; 2 step s; *Career* DPS (Army) 1971-74, Col the 22 (Cheshire) Regt 1971-78, Col Cmdt Mil Provost Staff Corps 1972-74, chm Lady Grover's Hospital Fund for Offrs' Families 1975-85, (vice-pres 1985); nat exec ctee Forces Help Soc 1975-, gen ctee Ex-Servs Mental Welfare Soc 1977-; servs liaison offr Variety Club of GB 1976-86, head of admin Smith & Williamson 1976-86,; dir Utd Womens Homes Assoc 1981-; *Recreations* golf, tennis, walking, reading; *Clubs* Army & Navy; *Style*— Maj-Gen Peter Martin, CBE; 17 Station St, Lymington, Hants (☎ 0590 72620)

MARTIN, Peter Lewis; CBE (1980); s of George Lewis Martin (d 1938), of Leicester, and Madeleine Mary, *née* Kilby (d 1918); ancestors were parish clerks of Market Harborough, Leics ca 1600 until ca 1900; *b* 22 Sept 1918; *Educ* Kibworth Beauchamp Sch, Borough Poly, Leicester Coll of Art and Technol; *m* 1 June 1949, Elizabeth Grace, da of John David Melling (d 1955), of Parbold, Lancs; 2 da (Georgina b 1950, Ruth b 1952); *Career* RAF (engrg branch) 1940-46; Engr & Transport Staff Corps RE (TA), Maj 1977-83, now supernumary; consulting engr building servs; pres Inst of Heating & Ventilating Engrs 1970-71; chm: Heating & Ventilating Res Assoc 1967-68, Assoc of Consulting Engrs 1983-84; memb Engrg Cncl 1982-86; visiting prof Univ of Strathclyde 1974-85; Hon DSc Strathclyde 1985; memb: Worshipful Co of Plumbers (Master 1979-80), Worshipful Co of Fan Makers, Worshipful Co of Engineers; awarded gold (1976), silver (1956) and Bronze (1968) medals by Inst of Heating & Vetilating Engrs; C Eng, FIMechE, FCIBSE, MConsE; *Books* Heating and Air Conditioning of Buildings (co-author, 5th 1971, 6th 1979 and 7th 1989 edns); *Recreations* avoiding gardening; *Clubs* Lansdowne; *Style*— Peter Martin, Esq, CBE

MARTIN, (Roy) Peter; MBE (1970); s of Walter Martin (d 1959), and Annie Mabel, *née* Cook (d 1966); *b* 5 Jan 1931; *Educ* Highbury Co Sch, Birkbeck Coll London (BA, MA), Tübingen Univ; *m* 1, 31 March 1951 (m dis 1960), Marjorie Patricia Anne Peacock; m 2, March 1960 (m dis 1977), Joan Drumwright; 2 s (Adam b 1963, James b 1964); m 3, 11 April 1978, Catherine Mary Sydee; *Career* Nat Serv with RAF educn branch 1949-51; Br Cncl offr 1960-83; cultural attaché Br Embassy Budapest 1972-73; cultural cnsllr Br Embassy Tokyo 1979-83; freelance author 1983-; memb BAFTA, Crime Writers' Assoc, Mystery Writers of America, etc; *Books* Japanese Cooking (with Joan Martin 1970), (as James Melville) The Wages of Zen (1979), The Chrysanthemum Chain (1980), A Sort of Samurai (1981), The Ninth Netsuke (1982), Sayonara, Sweet Amaryllis (1983), Death of a Daimyo (1984), The Death Ceremony (1985), Go Gently Gaijin (1986), The Imperial Way (1986), Kimono For A Corpse (1987); *Recreations* music, books; *Clubs* Travellers', Detection; *Style*— Peter Martin, Esq, MBE; c/o Curtis Brown, 162-168 Regent St, London W1R 5TB

MARTIN, Richard Graham; s of Horace Frederick Martin MC (d 1974), and Phyllis Jeanette Graham Martin, *née* Macfie (d 1984); *b* 4 Oct 1932; *Educ* Sherbourne, St Thomas's Hosp, London Univ; *m* 1957, Elizabeth, da of Harold Savage, 2 s (Charles, Arthur), 1 da (Clare); *Career* vice-chm and chief exec Alled-Lyons plc (dir 1981); *Style*— Richard Martin, Esq; Allied-Lyons plc, Allied House, 156 St John St, London EC1 P1AR (☎ 01 253 9911)

MARTIN, Richard Lionel; TD (1965); s of Alfred John Martin (d 1948), and Ellen Mary, *née* Warren (d 1981); *b* 18 June 1932; *Educ* Churchers Coll Petersfield, Architectural Assoc Sch of Architecture London; *m* 13 Sept 1958, Gillian Mary, da of Lesley Vivian Taylor, of Weybridge, Surrey; 3 s (Nigel Peter b 1962, Richard John b 1964, David James b 1966); *Career* Nat Serv 1950-52, Royal Hampshire Regt: cmmnd 2 Lt 1951 served 1 BN, TA (V), promoted Lt 1952 serv 4 TA BN and 4/5 (TA) BN, promoted Capt 4/5 (TA) 1954; Capt 4/5 (TA) BN Cameronian Scottish Rifles 1964-67, ret 1967; London CC Architects dept 1957-63 (worked on Crystal Palace Sports Centre and Queen Elizabeth Concert Hall Haywood Gallery), Scott Brownrigg & Turner Architects and Planning Conslts 1963-, ptnr SBT Advsy Servs 1986-; Structural Steel Design Award 1972; Freeman City of London 1978, Liveryman Worshipful Co Arbitrators 1981; RIBA 1961, ARIAS 1964, FCIArb 1973, FFB 1976, MSCL 1985, MBIM 1987, MBAE 1988; *Recreations* classical music; *Clubs* Wig and Pen; *Style*— Richard Martin, Esq, TD; Colesons, South Hay, Binsted, Hants (☎ 04203 3237); SBT Advsy Servs Conslt Architects, 10-13 King St, London WC2E 8HZ (☎ 01 836 2091, fax 01 831 1231, telex 25897)

MARTIN, Roger John Adam; s of Geoffrey Richard Rex Martin, of The Green, Winchmore Hill, London (d 1985), and Hazel Martin (*née* Matthews); *b* 21 Jan 1941; *Educ* Westminister, Brasenose Coll Oxford, (BA); *m* m, 24 Aug 1972, Alison Ann Veronica, da of Air Vice-Marshal Robert Sharp, Washington DC USA (d 1956); 1 s (Adam b 1974); *Career* HM Dip Serv 1964-86 (resigned), serv Jakarta (1966-67), Saigon (1968-70), Geneva (1975-79); head of Middle E/N Africa Branch DTI (1981-83); depty high cmnr Harare (1983-86); Wells City Cnsllr 1987; chief exec Somerset Tst 1988-; *Books* Southern Africa: The Price of Apartheid (1988); *Recreations* climbing, sailing, lecturing, opera; *Clubs* Royal Cwlth Soc; *Style*— Mr Roger J A Martin; Coxley House, Coxley, Wells, Somerset (☎ 0749 72180)

MARTIN, Ronald Kerr; *Educ* (BSc, MSc); *Career* dir The Distillers Co 1982-, chm of the gp's Scotch Whisky Prodn Ctee July 1982-; chm of two subsidiaries of Distillers' Co: Scottish Grain Distillers July 1982-, Scottish Malt Distillers July 1982- (previously md); FIChemE; *Style*— Ronald Martin, Esq; The Distillers Co plc, 32-34 Melville St, Edinburgh EH3 7HD (☎ 031 225 7843)

MARTIN, Sir Sidney Launcelot; s of Sidney A Martin; *b* 27 Sept 1918; *Educ* Wolmers Boys' Sch Jamaica, Royal Coll of Sci, Imperial Coll London (MSc, DIC); *m* 1944, Olga Brett, *née* Dolphin; 3 s; *Career* material res lab Phillips Electrical Ltd 1942-63, Univ registrar 1963-64, princ and pro vice-chllr Cave Hill Campus Barbados 1964-83 (ret); Hon LLD (Univ of West Indies) 1984; ARIC 1940, FRIC 1949, FRSC, FIC 1981; kt 1979; *Style*— Sir Sidney Martin; c/o Univ of the West Indies, Cave Hill Campus, P O Box 64, Barbados (☎ 425 1310); 2 Balmoral Apts, Balmoral Gap, Hastings, Christchurch, Barbados (☎ 429 5288)

MARTIN, Stephen Alexander; s of James Alexander Martin of Bargor Co Dublin, NI, and Mamie, *née* Weir; *b* 13 April 1959; *Educ* Bangor GS, Univ of Ulster (BA); *m* 13 April 1987, Dorothy Esther Elizabeth, da of William Edwin Armstrong, of Belmont, Belfast; *Career* hockey player; Bronze Medallist World Champs Trophy 1984, Bronze Medallist Olympic Games 1984 (Los Angeles), Silver Medallist World Champs Trophy 1985, Gold Medallist Olympic Games 1988 (Seoul); 50 Caps GB 1983-88, 100 Caps Ireland 1980-88, player Ulster 1980-88; memb programme ctee NI Inst of Coaching 1985-88, memb Ulster Branch Cncl; *Recreations* hockey, golf; *Clubs* Holywood 87 Hockey, Donaghadee GC; *Style*— Stephen Martin, Esq; House of Sport, Upper Malone Rd, Belfast, BT9 5LA, (☎ 0232 381222)

MARTIN, Stephen Graham Balfour; s of Graham Hunter Martin (d 1985), and Ragna, *née* Balch-Barth; *b* 21 Oct 1939; *Educ* Tonbridge; *m* 27 Nov 1976, Elizabeth Mary, da of Dennis John Ward, of Chatteris; 1 s (Diccon Carl Henry b 1967), 1 da (Charlotte Louise Elizabeth b 1978); *Career* chm and md: Intermail Ltd, Martins Direct Mktg Ltd, Home Shopping Club Ltd; dir: Fineline Printing Ltd, Strategic Mktg Databases Ltd, Common Cause Ltd; FIWC, Dip DM; *Recreations* fishing, shooting, gardening, collecting watercolours & oils; *Clubs* In & Out, Flyfishers; *Style*— Stephen Martin, Esq; Manor Farm Chilton Foliat, Hungerford, Berks; Intermail Ltd, 10 Fleming Rd, Newbury, Berks (fax 0635 41678)

MARTIN, Lady; Thelma Idina; da of James Martin Stander; *m* 1961, as his 2 w, Sir Albert Victor Martin, CBE (d 1968); *Style*— Lady Martin; Little Dalby Hall, Melton Mowbray, Leics

MARTIN, Timothy Charles (Tim); s of Godfrey Martin (d 1975), of Findon, Sussex and Nancy Cordelia, *née* Orrom; *b* 17 May 1951; *Educ* Worthing HS, King,s Coll Cambridge (BA, MA); *m* 31 March 1984, Sarah, da of Arthur James Moffett, of Cooksey Green, Worcs; 2 s (Alexander Dods b 19 Aug 1985, Charles Murray b 15 Jan 1988); *Career* admitted slr 1977; Allen and Overy 1975-79, dir (corporate fin) Hill Samuel and Co 1986-87 (joined 1979); dir (Corp Fin) Barclays de Zoete Wedd Ltd 1988-; *Recreations* tennis, gardening, opera; *Clubs* Hurlingham, Lansdowne; *Style*— Tim Martin, Esq; Barclays de Zoete Wedd Ltd, Ebbgate House, Swan Lane, London EC4 (☎ 01 623 2323, fax 01 929 3846)

MARTIN, Trevor John Lloyd; s of William Gideon Martin (d 1973), of Hastings, Sussex, and Anna Jeanette, *née* Suters; *b* 21 Mar 1927; *Educ* Hastings GS, Chichester HS, King's Coll Cambridge (MA); *m* 12 Jan 1955, Anne Mary, da of Maj Robert Alured Denne (d 1969), of Villas-sur-Ollon, Switzerland; 2 s (William b 1966, Henry b 1967), 1 da (Marianne (Mrs Lee) b 1964); *Career* RAF educn branch, station educn offr RAF Stradishall 1948, RAF Mildenhall 1949 (Flying Offr), placed on reserve 1950; asst master Papplewick Sch Ascot 1951; Shellmex and BP Ltd: joined 1956, hd of retail planning 1967, regnl mangr BP Midland Regn 1968; BP Petroleum Co Ltd: automotive branch mangr 1972, retail divn mangr 1974, mktg coordinator 1975, mangr mktg servs and lubricants 1978, ret 1982; fndr Lindsell Chairs (a specialist antique business) 1982, fndr Edwardian Chairs Ltd and Late Victorian Chairs Ltd 1983, fndr Chair Restorations Ltd 1984, fndr Sedilia Victoriana 1985; visiting lectr UMIST 1980-81; ctee memb Chamber of Trade Coggeshall Essex, tres village hall fund Lindsell Essex, memb Royal Br Legion Coggeshall Branch; memb Cripplegate Ward Club; Freeman City of London 1974, Liveryman Worshipful Co of Carmen 1974; *Recreations* history, book collecting, rough gardening, carpentry; *Clubs* Utd Oxford & Cambridge, City Livery; *Style*— Trevor Martin, Esq; The Glebe House, Great Dunmow, Essex CM6 3QN (☎ 0371 84222); 11 Market Hill, Coggeshall, Essex CO6 1TS (☎ 0376

62766)

MARTIN, William Edward (Bill); s of Joseph Edward Martin (d 1987), of Upminster, Essex, and Pamela Maud, *née* Ruse; *b* 10 Mar 1951; *Educ* Beal Essex, Exeter Univ (BA), Univ of Wales (MSc); *m* 28 Aug 1976, Yvette Mary, da of James Geard McBrearty (d 1976); 1 s (Samuel b June 1978), 1 da (Anna b May 1980); *Career* economist DTI 1973-81, advsr central policy review staff Cabinet Off 1981-83, Phillips & Drew 1983-; advsr Treasy and Civil Serv Select Ctee 1986-; memb REconS; *Books* The Economics of the Profits Crisis (ed 1981); *Recreations* skiing; *Style—* Bill Martin, Esq; 80 Mount Crescent, Brentwood, Essex CM14 5DD (☎ 0277 262 047); UBS Phillips & Drew, Broadgate, London

MARTIN-BATES, James Patrick; JP (1961); s of Robert Martin-Bates, JP (d 1950); *b* 17 April 1912; *Educ* Glenalmond, Worcester Coll Oxford (MA); *m* 1939, Dorothy Clare, da of Prof James Miller (d 1962), of Kingston, Ontario, Canada; 1 s, 2 da; *Career* md PE Mgmnt Gp 1938-61, princ Admin Staff Coll 1961-72; dir: WS Atkins Gp 1970-86; dir: WS Atkins Ltd, Averys 1970-77, Charringtons Industl Hldgs 1972-77, Hutchinson 1958-78; chm Atkins Hldgs Ltd 1987-, Cncl Buckingham Univ 1977-87 (Hon Doctor); High Sheriff Bucks 1974-75; Burnham Medal, memb Br Inst of Mangmnt 1974 FCIS, CBIM; *Recreations* golf, fishing; *Clubs* Caledonian (London), Royal & Ancient St Andrews, Leander; *Style—* James Martin-Bates Esq, JP; Ivy Cottage, Fingest, nr Henley-on-Thames Oxon RG9 6QD (☎ 049 163 202)

MARTIN-BIRD, Col Sir Richard Dawnay; CBE (1971, OBE 1953), TD (1950), DL (Cheshire 1974); s of Richard Martin Bird and Mildred, *née* Yates; *b* 19 July 1910; *Educ* Charterhouse; *m* 1935, Katharine, da of Sir Arthur Selborne Jelf, CMG; 1 s (and 1 decd), 3 da; *Career* 8 Ardwick Bn, The Manchester Regt (TA) 1936-53, Lt-Col cmdg 1947-53, later Hon Col, Regtl Cllr The King's Regt 1967-, former ADC to HM The Queen, High Sheriff Greater Manchester 1976-77, chm TA&VR Assoc Lancs, Cheshire and IOM, later TA&VRA for New England and IOM 1968-75, chm and jt md Yates Brothers Wine Lodges Ltd Manchester, pres Wine and Spirit Assoc of GB 1978-79; DL Lancs 1964-74, kt 1975; *Style—* Col Sir Richard Martin-Bird, CBE, TD, DL; Stockinwood, Chelford, Cheshire SK11 9BE (☎ 0625 523)

MARTIN-JENKINS, Christopher Dennis Alexander; s of Lt-Col Dennis Frederick Martin-Jenkins, TD, of Cranleigh, Surrey, and Rosmary Clare, *née* Walker; *b* 20 Jan 1945; *Educ* Marlborough, Cambridge (BA, MA); *m* 1971, Judith Oswald, da of Charles Henry Telford Hayman (d 1952), of Brackley; 2 s (James b 1973, Robin b 1975), 1 da (Lucy b 1979); *Career* BBC sports broadcaster 1970-, cricket corr 1973-80 and 1984-, ed The Cricketer 1980- (dep ed 1967-70), played cricket for Surrey 2 XI and MCC; *Books* author of 12 books on cricket; *Recreations* cricket, golf, tennis; *Clubs* MCC; *Style—* Christopher Martin-Jenkins, Esq; Naldrett House, Bucks Green, W Sussex; BBC Broadcasting House; The Cricketer Ltd, 29 Cavendish, Redhill, Surrey

MARTIN-JENKINS, David Dennis; s of Dennis Frederick Martin-Jenkins, TD, of Maytree House, Woodcote, Guildford Rd, Cranleigh, Surrey, and Dr Rosemary Clare, *née* Walker; *b* 7 May 1941; *Educ* Kingsmead, Meols, St Bede's Eastbourne, Marlborough; *m* 24 June 1967, Anthea, da of Arthur Milton De Vinney (d 1983); *Career* dir: JW Cameron and Co Ltd 1972-82, Elerman Lines plc 1974-82, Tollemache and Cobbold Breweries Ltd 1976-82; chm: MN Offrs Pension Fund Investmt ctee 1976-82, Primesight Ltd 1984-, Fernhurst; dir: Nat Home Loans Corpn plc 1985-, Captial and Regnl Properties plc 1986-, County Inns plc 1986-, Select Country Hotels Ltd 1987-, Jackson's and Dist SLD, tres Lurgashall PCC; FCA 1965, FCT 1979; *Recreations* sport (Tranmere RoverS and Liverpool FC's), politics (SLD), hill walking (climbed Mount Mera (21000ft) Nepal 1986), the countryside; *Clubs* Lancashire CCC; *Style—* David Martin-Jenkins, Esq; Jobson's Cottage, Jobson's Lane, Haslemere, Surrey GU27 2BY (☎ 042 878 294)

MARTIN-JENKINS, Dennis Frederick; TD (1945); s of Frederick Martin Jenkins (d 1941), and Martha Magdalene, *née* Almeida; *b* 7 Jan 1911; *Educ* Marlborough; *m* 1937, Rosemary Clare, da of Dr Robert Alexander Walker, of Northants; 3 s (David, Christopher, Timothy); *Career* RA 1939-45, serv UK and Europe, Lt-Col; chm: Gen Cncl of Br Shipping for UK 1963, Ellerman Lines Ltd 1967-80 (md 1967-76), Int Chamber of Shipping 1971-77; pres Chamber of Shipping of UK 1965; memb: Mersey Docks and Harbour Bd, Port of London Authy, Nat Dock Labour Bd, Br Transport Docks Bd; prime warden worshipful Co of Shipwrights 1981; *Recreations* golf, gardening; *Clubs* Utd Oxford & Cambrdige Univ, Woking GC, Thurlestone GC; *Style—* Dennis Martin-Jenkins, Esq; Maytree Ho, Woodcote, Guildford Rd, Cranleigh, Surrey GU6 8NZ (☎ 0483 276278)

MARTIN-JENKINS, Timothy Dennis (Tim); s of Lt-Col Dennis Frederick Martin-Jenkins, TD, and Dr Rosemary Clare Martin-Jenkins; *b* 26 May 1947; *Educ* Marlborough, Cambridge Univ (MA), Harvard Univ (MBA); *Career* chm Ellerman Commercial Hldgs Ltd 1980-82, dir Ellerman Lines Ltd 1978-82, md Pacific Hldgs Inc; *Recreations* golf, skiing, tennis, music; *Clubs* Royal Hong Kong GC, Woking GC, Hawks, Hurlingham, Sheko, Hong Kong, Thurlestone GC, Chung Shan GC; *Style—* Tim Martin-Jenkins, Esq; 33 Horizon Drive, Chung Hom Kok, Hong Kong; Pacific Hldgs Inc, 3303 Bank of America Tower, Hong Kong

MARTIN-QUIRK, Howard Richard Newell; s of George Donald Martin, of Dorset, and Nelly Katie, *née* Newell, of Dorset; *b* 8 August 1937; *Educ* Lancing Coll Sussex, Christs Coll Cambridge (MA), UCL (BSc Arch, MSc); *m* 1, 4 Jan 1964, Sally Anne (d 1976), da of Ernest Davies, of London; m 2, 1 Oct 1976, Mary Teresa, da of Dudley C Quirk, JP; *Career* architect & architectural historian, author. sr tutor Kingston Poly Sch of Arch 1970-, ptnr Martin Quirk Assoc 1983-, chief oenologist Chiddingstone Vineyards Ltd 1984-; *Recreations* music, chess, squash rackets, gardening, wine; *Clubs* Architectural Assoc, Soc of Architectural Historians, Victorian Soc, Wagner Soc, EVA; *Style—* Howard R N Martin-Quirk, Esq; Sorrel, Vexour Farm, Chiddingstone, Edenbridge, Kent TN8 7BB (☎ 0892 870439); Kingstone Polytechnic 5496151, MQA 8780010/0892 870439

MARTIN-SMITH, Patrick (Geoffrey Brian); MC (1945); s of Capt Alfred Martin Martin-Smith, (of The Worcestershire Regiment, Helenic Order of the Redeemer for Serv in Greece WWI), (d 1930), and Dorothea Blanchard Muir, *née* Reeves (d 1970); maternal ggf Reuben Green, last clerk of vestry Kensington parish, before Royal Borough in 1889, vote of thanks for help and advice to City Corpn of Melbourne 1877); *b* 26 Sept 1917; *Educ* Downside, Clare Coll Cambridge (MA); *m* 12 April 1947, Phyllis (Dorothy), da of Menry Brown (d 1931); 2 s (Michael b 1948, Nicholas b 1950); *Career* diplomat; serv Army Capt, The Worcestershire Regt; 12 Commando and 30 Commando, Med and Italy 1939-47, transferred to SOE, parachute mission to NE Italy and Austria 1944, Allied Cmmn Austria 1945-47, HM Dip Serv 1947-70; Vienna Legation, 3 sec 1947-49; Dip Serv, Warsaw 2 sec 1951, Instanbul 2 sec 1954-56, F and CO, PUSD 1957-64, Leopoldville, Kinshasa 1 sec 1964-68, Tel Aviv, 1 sec 1968-70; ret; 1972 now researing SOE in Italy, advsr to BBC, on Italian series on SOE 1984; *Recreations* travel, historical research; *Clubs* Special Forces; *Style—* Patrick Martin-Smith, Esq, MC; 28 Vicars Close, Victoria Park, London E9 7HT (☎ 01 985 2225); Llauro 66300 Thuir, France (☎ 68 39 40 36)

MARTINDALE, Air Vice-Marshal Alan Rawes; CB (1984); s of the late Norman Martindale, and the late Edith, *née* Rawes; *b* 20 Jan 1930; *Educ* Kendal GS, Univ Coll Leicester (BA); *m* 1952, Eileen Alma Wrenn; 3 da; *Career* cmmnd RAF 1951, dep dir of Supply Mgmnt MOD Harrogate 1971-72 (dir 1974-75), cmd supply offr RAF Germany 1972-74, RCDS 1976, Air Cdre Supply and Movements RAF Support Cmd 1977, dep gen mangr NATO Multi-Role Combat Aircraft Mgmnt Agency 1978-81, dir of Supply Policy (RAF) MOD 1981-82, dir gen of Supply (RAF) 1982-84; dist gen mangr Hastings Health Authy 1985-; FBIM, FILOM, LHSM; *Recreations* gardening, squash, skiing; *Clubs* RAF; *Style—* Air Vice-Marshal Alan Martindale, CB; Taylors Cottage, Mountfield, Robertsbridge, East Sussex TN32 5JZ

MARTINEAU, David Nicholas Nettlefold; s of Frederick Alan Martineau, of Valley End House, Chobham, Surrey, and Vera Ruth, *née* Naylor; *b* 27 Mar 1941; *Educ* Eton, Trinity Coll Cambridge (MA, LLB); *m* 20 Jan 1968, Elizabeth Mary, da of Maurice James Carrick Allom, of Gibbons Place, Ightham, Kent; 1 s (Luke b 27 March 1970), 1 da (Alice b 8 June 1972); *Career* called to the Bar Inner Temple 1964, rec 1986 (asst rec 1982); *Recreations* skiing, water skiing, windsurfing, walking; *Clubs* Hawks, MCC; *Style—* David Martineau, Esq; 37 Bedford Gardens, London, W8 (☎ 01 727 7825); 2 Garden Ct, Temple, London, EC4Y 9BL (☎ 01 353 4741)

MARTINEAU, (Alan) Denis; s of Col Sir Wilfrid Martineau, MC, TD (d 1964), of 30 Rotton Park Rd, Edgbaston, Birmingham and Upper Coscombe, Temple Guiting, Nr Cheltenham, Glos, and Elvira Mary Seton, *née* Lee Strathy (d 1982); *b* 5 April 1920; *Educ* Rugby, Trinity Hall Cambridge (BA, MA); *m* 5 July 1952, Mollie, da of 2 Lt John Lewis Davies, MBE (d 1987), of St Brides Major, Glamorgan; 3 s (Jeremy b 1955, Peter b 1956, Charles b 1961); *Career* Army 1940-46, cmmnd Royal Warwickshire Regt 1941, served as Capt in ME, N Africa and Italy; slr 1950; ptnr Ryland Martineau & Co 1954-84, NP, dir TSB Gp plc (chm W Midlands Regnl Bd); memb Birmingham City Cncl 1961-, Lord Mayor 1986-87; dir: City of Birmingham Symphony Orchestra (chm 1968-74), Birmingham Repertory Theatre, Birmingham Botanical Gardens; chm: cncl of Order of St John W Midlands, Birmingham Civic Soc, Sir Wilfrid Martineau Sch; pres Birmingham Bach Soc, vice pres SENSE in the W Midlands, vice patron Birmingham County Royal Br Legion; memb: Law Soc 1952, Soc of Provincial Notaries 1965; OStJ 1988; *Recreations* music, Birmingham history, the country, watching sport; *Style—* Denis Martineau, Esq; 10 Vicarage Road, Edgbaston, Birmingham B1S 3ES (☎ 021 454 0479); Pike Cottage, Upper Coscombe, Temple Guiting, Glos

MARTINEAU, Jeremy John; s of Capt Denis Martineau, of Birmingham, and Mary Rena, *née* Davies; *b* 16 April 1955; *Educ* Rugby, Trinity Hall Cambridge (MA); *Career* slr 1981, asst slr Freshfields London 1981 (articled clerk 1979-81, ptnr Ryland Martineau Birmingham 1985-87 (asst slr 1981-84), ptnr Martineau Johnson Birmingham 1987-; sec Inst of Fiscal Studies Midlands Regn; tstee Feeney Tst; memb Law Soc 1981; *Recreations* various sports, photography, foreign travel, music; *Style—* Jeremy Martineau, Esq; 102 Gordon Rd, Harborne, Birmingham B17 9EY (☎ 021 426 4142); Martineau Johnson, St Philips House, St Philips Place, Birmingham B3 2PP (☎ 021 200 3300, fax 021 200 3330, telex 339793 RYLMAR G)

MARTINEAU, Rt Rev Robert Arnold Schürhoff; s of late Prof C E Martineau, MA, MCom, FCA; *b* 22 August 1913; *Educ* King Edward's Sch Birmingham, Trinity Hall Cambridge, Westcott House Cambridge; *m* 1941, Elinor Gertrude, da of late Rev Keinion Ap-Thomas; 1 s, 2 da; *Career* chaplain RAFVR 1941-46; vicar: Ovenden 1946-52, Allerton 1952-66; residentiary canon of Ely 1966-72, bishop of Huntingdon 1966-72, bishop of Blackburn 1972-81; *Style—* The Rt Rev Robert Martineau; Gwenallt, Park St, Denbigh, Clwyd (☎ 074 571 4089)

MARTINS d'ALMEIDA, Henriques Manoel; s of Valentim Martins d'Almeida (d 1969), and Melina Frances Greville Dodge Martins d'Almeida (d 1976); *b* 5 Sept 1918; *Educ* St Francis RC Sch, Rowan Rd Secdy Sch, City of London Coll; *m* 1, 31 Jan 1946, Kathleen Harper; 1 s (Paul Manoel b 1946); m 2, 7 Nov 1987, Sheila Gabrielle Henry; *Career* joined Portuguese Consular Serv 1933, appointed chllr 1949, vice consul 1957, consular offr i/c of Portuguese Consulate Gen London for various periods 1949-63, appointed consul for Portugaln Southampton 1964, dean of Southampton Consular Corps 1968-72, appointed Portuguese Govt MDAP Shipping agent London 1952, rep of Guild of Fruit and Hort Prods of S Miguel Azores 1949-52; ret 1983; *Recreations* philately, travel, history, bowls; *Clubs* Naval, Anglo-Portuguese Soc (London); *Style—* Henriques Martins d'Almeida, Esq; Walnut Tree Cottage, Cedars Lane, Capel St Mary, Ipswich, Suffolk IP9 2JA; Walnut Tree Cottage, Cedars Lane, Capel St Mary, Ipswich, Suffolk IP9 2JA (☎ 0473 311 056)

MARTON, Christopher; s of Henry Brooks Marton (d 1978), and Eileen, *née* Moon (d 1980); *b* 18 August 1939; *Educ* Eccles HS, Liverpool Tech Coll (Masters Cert of Competency); *m* 14 Jan 1969, Margaret Christine, Marton, da of Henry Clarence Broughton (d 1972); 2 s (Andrew Christopher b 1 June 1969, Robert Charles b 3 Oct 1971); *Career* apprentice MN 1956-60, MN Offr 1960-72; master: hydrographic survey ship 1972-73, offshore supply vessels 1973-74; marine surveyor and conslt 1974-; cncl memb: Naval Club London, PCC; Freeman: City of London 1981, Worshipful Co of Loriners 1982; *Recreations* cricket, shooting, squash, gardening; *Clubs* Lighthouse, Rugby, Lancs CCC; *Style—* Capt Christopher Marton; 10 Church Green, Milton Ernest, Bedford NK44 1RH; Noble Denton & Associates Ltd, Noble House, 131 Aldersgate St, London EC1A 4EB (☎ 01 606 4901, fax 01 606 5035, telex 885 802)

MARTONMERE, 1 Baron (UK 1964); (John) Roland Robinson; GBE (1973), KCMG (1966), PC (1962); s of Roland Walkden Robinson (decd), of Blackpool and Mary Collier, *née* Pritchard; *b* 22 Feb 1907; *Educ* Trinity Hall Cambridge (MA, LLB); *m* 1930, Maysie, da of Clarence Warren Gasque (decd); (1 s Richard decd), 1 da (Loretta); *Heir* gs, John Stephen Robinson; *Career* Flying Offr RAFVR 1941, Wing Cdr 1944; barr 1929-, MP (C) Widnes Div Lancashire 1931-35, Blackpool 1935-45, Blackpool (South) 1945-64; former pres Assoc of Health and Pleasure Resorts; chm: Cons Pty Cwlth Affrs Ctee 1954-56, Cwlth Parly Assoc 1961; govt and C-in-C Bermuda 1964-72; hon Freeman Town of St George and City of Hamilton Bermuda;

KStJ; kt 1954; *Clubs* Carleton, Royal Lytham St Annes GC, Royal Bermuda YC, Royal Yacht Sqdn (Cowes); *Style*— The Rt Hon The Lord Martonmere, GBE, KCMG, PC; El Mirador, Lyford Cay PO Box N 7776, Nassau, Bahamas (☎ 809 293 02222); Romay House, Tuckers Town, Bermuda

MARTYN, Charles Philip; s of James Godfrey Martyn (d 1970), of London, and Kathleen Doris, *née* Crawford; *b* 17 July 1948; *Educ* St Dunstans Coll London, Exeter Univ (LLB); *Career* slr: Coward Chance London 1972-77 (articled clerk 1970-72), Clifford Turner 1977-79; jt gen mangr Sumitomo Bank Ltd London 1988- (legal advsr 1979-84, sr mangr 1984-86, dep gen mangr 1986-88); tstee: N London Rudolf Steiner Sch, Waldorf Sch London; cncl memb Anthroposophical Soc GB; memb Law Soc; *Recreations* studying Rudolf Steiner's work, green politics, gardening, Bach, green economics; *Style*— Philip Martyn, Esq; The Sumitomo Bank Ltd, Temple Ct, 11 Queen Victoria St, London EC4N 4TA (☎ 01 236 7400, fax 01 236 0049)

MARTYN, (Charles) Roger Nicholas; s of Rev Charles William Martyn late of Aylsham, of Norfolk Clerk in Holy Orders, and Doris Lilian (Batcheller) (d 1956); *b* 10 Dec 1925; *Educ* Charterhouse; Merton Coll Oxford (MA); *m* 24 Sept 1960, Helen Ruth, da of Samuel Frank Everson, of Camberley, Surrey (d 1981); 1 s (Nicholas b 1963, Christopher b 1965); 1 da (Sarah b 1962); *Career* 60th Rifles, The Kings Royal Rifle Corps 1944-47; admitted to Roll of slrs 1952; ptnr Sherwood & Co, Parly Agent 1954-63; ptnr Lee, Bolton & Lee 1961-73; master of the Supreme Ct 1973-; *Recreations* sailing, walking, morology, book-binding; *Clubs* Thames Barge, Salcombe Yacht; *Style*— Master Roger Martyn; Royal Courts of Justice, Strand, London WC2

MARTYN-HEMPHILL, Hon Charles Andrew Martyn; s of 5 Baron Hemphill; *b* 8 Oct 1954; *Educ* Downside, Oxford; *m* 1985, Sarah J F, eld da of Richard Lumley, of Roundwood, Windlesham, Surrey; 2 da (Clarissa b 1986, Amelia b 1988); *Career* dir Morgan Grenfell Int Fund Mgmnt; *Recreations* sailing, skiing, shooting, hunting; *Style*— Hon Charles Martyn-Hemphill; 7 St Maur Rd, London SW6 4DR

MARTYN-HEMPHILL, Hon Mary Anne Martyn; da of 5 Baron Hemphill; *b* 29 Nov 1958; *Style*— The Hon Mary Anne Martyn-Hemphill

MARVIN, John Charman; s of Robert George Marvin (d 1979), and Vera Emily, *née* Charman; *b* 18 Mar 1933; *Educ* Christ's Hosp, King's Coll Cambridge (MA); *m* 29 March 1958, Wendy, da of Matthew Raeside (d 1976); 2 s (Timothy b 1964, Matthew b 1968), 1 da (Hilary b 1961); *Career* Nat Serv RNVR Lt 1954-56; Reserve Lt Cdr 1956-69; dir ICI Plastics Div 1956-83; md Hickson Int plc 1983-; *Recreations* sailing, windsurfing, tennis (real); *Style*— John C Marvin, Esq

MARWICK, Prof Arthur John Brereton; s of William Hutton Marwick, and Maeve Cluna, *née* Brereton; *b* 29 Feb 1936; *Educ* George Heriot's Sch Edinburgh, Edinburgh Univ (MA, DLitt), Balliol Coll Oxford (BLitt); unmarried; 1 da; *Career* asst lectr in history Univ of Aberdeen 1959-60, lectr in history Univ of Edinburgh 1960-69, dean and dir of studies in arts Open Univ 1978-84, visiting prof in history State Univ of NY at Buffalo 1966-67, visiting scholar Hoover Inst and visiting prof Stanford Univ 1984-85, directeur d'études invité l'Ecole des Hautes Etudes en Sciences Sociales Paris 1985; FRHistS; *Books* The Explosion of British (1963), Clifford Allen (1964), The Deluge (1965), Britain in the Century of Total War (1968), The Nature of History (third edn 1989), War and Social Change in the Twentieth Century (1974), The Home Front (1976), Women at War 1914-1918 (1977), Class: image and reality in Britain, France and USA since 1930 (1980), Illustrated Dictionary of British History (ed 1980), British Society since 1945 (1982), Britain in Our Century (1984), Class in the Twentieth Century (1986), Beauty in History: society politics and personal appearance c 1500 to the present (1988), Total War and Social Change (1988); *Clubs* Open Univ Football and Tennis; *Style*— Prof Arthur Marwick; 67 Fitzjohns Ave, Hampstead, London NW3 6PE

MARWICK, Sir Brian Allan; KBE (1963, CBE 1954, OBE 1946), CMG (1958); s of James Walter Marwick (d 1931), and Elizabeth Jane, *née* Flett (d 1957); *b* 18 June 1908; *Educ* Univ of SA (BA), Univ of Cape Town (MA), Corpus Christi Coll Cambridge; *m* 1934, Riva Lee (d 1988), da of Maj Harry Claud Cooper (d 1959); 2 da (Sally, Tessa); *Career* entered Colonial Serv 1925; first asst sec: Swaziland 1947-48, Basutoland 1949-52; dep resident cmmr and govt sec Swaziland 1952-55, admin sec high cmmr Basutoland Bechuanaland Protectorate Swaziland 1956, resident cmmr then HM cmmr Swaziland 1956-64; perm sec: Miny of Works and Town Planning Bahamas 1965-68, Miny of Educn and Culture Bahamas 1968-71; *Books* The Swazi-An ethnographic account of the natives of the Swaziland Protectorate (1940, new impression 1966); *Recreations* gardening; *Style*— Sir Brian Marwick, KBE, CMG; Sea Bank, Shore Rd, Castletown, Isle of Man (☎ 0624 823782)

MARYON DAVIS, Alan Roger; s of Cyril Edward Maryon Davis, of Osterley, Middx, and Hilda May, *née* Thompson; *b* 21 Jan 1943; *Educ* St Paul's Sch London, St John's Coll Cambridge, St Thomas's Hosp Med Sch, London Sch of Hygiene and Tropical Med (MSc); *m* 14 March 1981, (Glynis) Anne, da of Dr Philip Trefor Davies (d 1970) of Hartlepool; 2 da (Jessica b 1983, Elizabeth b 1985); *Career* med conslt, writer and broadcaster; clinical med 1969-74, community and preventive med 1974-, chief MO Health Educn Cncl 1984-87, hon sr lectr in community med St Mary's Hosp Med Sch 1985- 89, hon specialist in community med Paddington and N Kensington Health Authy 1985-88, conslt in public health med W Lambeth Health Authy 1988-, hon sr lectr in public health med Utd Med and Dental Schs Guy's and St Thomas's Hosps 1988-; BBC Radio 4 series: Action Makes the Heart Grow Stronger 1983, Back in 25 Minutes 1984, Not Another Diet Programme 1985, Cancercheck 1988; BBC TV series: Your Mind in Their Hands 1982, Save a Life 1986, Bodymatters 1985- 88; regular med columnist for Woman magazine; MRCP 1972, FFCM 1986; *Books* Family Health & Fitness (1981), Bodyfacts (1984), Diet 2000 (with J Thomas 1984), How to Save a Life (with J Rogers 1987), Pssst a Really Useful Guide to Alcohol (1989); *Recreations* relaxing in the dales, singing in the group Instant Sunshine; *Style*— Dr Alan Maryon Davis; 4 Sioella Rd, London SW4 6HX (☎ 01 720 5659); West Lambeth Health Authority, St Thomas's Hospital, London SE1 7EH (☎ 01 928 9292)

MASCHLER, Thomas Michael; s of Kurt Leo Maschler; *b* 16 August 1933; *Educ* Leighton Park; *m* 1970, Fay Goldie (the writer on restaurants Fay Maschler), da of Arthur Coventry (d 1969); 1 s (Benjamin Joseph b 1974), 2 da (Hannah Kate b 1970, Alice Mary b 1972); *Career* publisher; chm Jonathan Cape 1970- (editorial dir 1960, md 1966); prodn asst André Deutsch 1955, ed MacGibbon & Kee 1956-58, fiction ed Penguin Books 1958-60; *Recreations* tennis, skiing; *Style*— Thomas Maschler Esq; 15 Chalcot Gdns, London NW3 (☎ 01 586 3574)

MASEFIELD, Sir Peter Gordon; s of Dr (William) Gordon Masefield, CBE, JP, MRCS, LRCP, DPM, sometime Hon Gen Sec BMA, by his w Marian Ada, da of Edmund Lloyd-Owen, of New York. Sir Peter's gf was 2 cousin of John Masefield, Poet Laureate 1930-67; *b* 19 Mar 1914; *Educ* Westminster, Chillon Coll (Switzerland), Jesus Coll Cambridge; *m* 1936, Patricia Doreen, da of Percy Rooney; 3 s, 1 da; *Career* pres Croydon Airport Soc; dep chm Br Caledonian; chm London Tport 1980-82 (memb 1973-), Project Mgmnt Ltd 1972-; jt dep chm Caledonian Airways Gp 1978-; dir Worldwide Estates Ltd 1972-, Nationwide Bldg Soc 1973-; previously: pilot (license 1937-70), aircraft designer (with Fairey Aviation), aviation journalist (air corr Sunday Times), advsr to Lord Beaverbrook when Ld Privy Seal & Sec War Cabinet Ctee on Post War Civil Air Tport 1945-46; formerly md Bristol Aircraft Ltd, Beagle Aircraft Ltd; sometime chm Br Airports Authy; CEng, FRAeS, FCIT, CIMechE; kt 1972; *Style*— Sir Peter Masefield; Rosehill, Doods Way, Reigate, Surrey RH2 0JT (☎ 74 42396)

MASEFIELD, (John) Thorold; CMG (1986); s of Dr Geoffrey Bussell Masefield, and (Mildred) Joy Thorold, *née* Rogers; *b* 1 Oct 1939; *Educ* Dragon, Repton, St John's Coll Cambridge (MA); *m* 18 Aug 1962, Jennifer Mary, da of Rev Dr Hubert Carey Trowell, OBE; 2 s (Nigel Anthony b 26 March 1964, Roger Francis b 24 Dec 1970), 2 da (Sally Clare b 18 Dec 1966, Helen Rachel b and d Aug 1968); *Career* Dip Serv: joined Cwlth Relations Off 1962; private sec to Permanent Under Sec 1963-64, second sec Br High Cmmn Kuala Lumpur 1964-65, second sec Br Embassy Warsaw 1966-67, FCO 1967-69, first sec UK delgn to disarmament conf Geneva 1970-74, dep head policy planning staff FCO 1974-77, dep head far eastern dept FCO 1977-79, cnsllr and consul gen Br Embassy Islamabad 1979-82, head of personnel serv dept FCO 1982-85, head of far eastern dept FCO 1985-87; fell Center for Int Affairs Harvard Univ 1987-88, memb Civil Serv Selection Bd 1988-; *Recreations* fruit and vegetables; *Clubs* Royal Cwlth; *Style*— Thorold Masefield, Esq, CMG; c/o FCO, London SW1A 2AH

MASEFIELD, Hon Mrs; Hon Veronica Margery; da of 8 Baron Hawke (d 1939), and Francis Alice Wilmer; *b* 30 Jan 1915; *m* 1940, Jack Briscoe, s of George Henry Masefield; 1 da (Delphinia b 1947); *Style*— The Hon Mrs Masefield; Down Lodge, East Harting, Petersfield, Hants (☎ 073 085 291)

MASHAM OF ILTON, Baroness (Life Peer UK 1970); Susan Lilian Primrose Cunliffe-Lister (Countess of Swinton); da of Maj Sir Ronald Norman Sinclair, 8 Bt, and Reba Inglis, later Mrs R H Hildreth (d 1985); *b* 14 April 1935; *Educ* Heathfield Ascot, London Poly; *m* 8 Dec 1959, 2 Earl of Swinton, *qv* (works under title Lady Masham of Ilton); 1 s, 1 da (both adopted); *Career* sits as Independent peer in House of Lords; pres N Yorks Red Cross 1963, pres Yorks Assoc for Disabled; memb bd Visitors for Wetherby Borstal 1963, now Youth Custody Centre; pres Spinal Injuries Assoc, late memb Peterlee and Newton Aycliffe Corpn; vice-pres: Chartered Soc of Physiotherapy, Action for Dysphasic; patron of Disablement Income Group, Adults (DIA), tstee of Spinal Res Tst, memb Parly All Pty Disablement Gp Drug Misuse Ctee, and Penal Affairs Gp; memb Winston Churchill Tst; patron Yorks Faculty of GPs, memb Yorks RHA, vice-pres Hosp Saving Assoc; vice-pres Coll of Occupational Therapists; Gen Advsy Cncl of BBC; chm Home Office Ctee on Young People, Alcohol and Crime; chm Phoenix House (Drug Rehabilitation Centres); Hon MA (York and Open Univs), hon fell Royal Coll of GPs; *Recreations* swimming, breeding Highland ponies, gardening; *Style*— The Rt Hon the Lady Masham of Ilton; Dykes Hill House, Masham, Ripon, Yorks (☎ 0765 89241)

MASKALL, Michael Edwin; s of Leslie George Maskall (d 1968), and Alice Rose, *née* Hare (d 1984); *b* 26 Oct 1938; *Educ* Brentwood Public Sch; *m* (m dis 1987); 2 s (Andrew James b 6 March 1963, Jake Alexander b 17 April 1971), 2 da (Louise Claire b 6 March 1963, Michelle Amanda b 30 Sept 1965); *Career* CA 1961; ptnr i/c int tax and trade Price Waterhouse 1985 (ptnr 1976-); FCA 1971; *Books* International Taxation Management And Strategy (1985), European Trends In Taxation Towards 1992 (1988); *Recreations* skiing, wind surfing; *Clubs* Pickwick (Orsett, Essex); *Style*— Michael Maskall, Esq; Price Waterhouse, Southwark Towers, 32 London Bridge St, London SE1 9SY (☎ 01 407 8989, fax 01 378 0647, telex 884657/8)

MASKELL, Miles Gerald; s of Capt Gerald Nye Maskell, MC (d 1970), of Cape Town, SA, and Faith Gertrude, *née* Saunders; *b* 2 Oct 1936; *Educ* Diocesan Coll Cape Town, Le Rosey Rolle Switzerland, Magdalene Coll Cambridge; *Career* asst to chm John Harvey & Sons Ltd (Bristol) 1959-60, advertising sales rep Time Inc 1960-63, sales dir Domtar Ltd 1963-74, chm and princ shareholder greens Ltd 1974-87, jt md and shareholder Quorom Ventures Ltd 1988-; Liveryman Worshipful Co of Vintners; *Recreations* golf, bridge; *Clubs* White's, City of London, Berks GC; *Style*— Miles Maskell, Esq; Quorum Ventures Ltd, 257-259 Fulham Rd, London SW3 6HY (☎ 01 352 2422, fax 01 351 9607)

MASON, Hon Sir Anthony Frank; AC (1988), KBE (1972, CBE 1969); s of F M Mason; *b* 21 April 1925; *Educ* Sydney GS, Sydney Univ; *m* 1950, Patricia, da of Dr E N McQueen; 2 s; *Career* admitted Bar NSW 1951, QC 1964, Cwlth slr-gen 1964-69, vice-chm UN Cmmn on Int Trade Law 1968, judge Ct of Appeal Supreme Ct NSW 1969-72, justice High Ct of Aust 1972-87 (chief justice 1987); pro-chllr ANU 1972-75 (Hon LLD), Hon LLD Univ of Sydney 1988; *Style*— The Hon Sir Anthony Mason, KBE; Judges' Chambers, High Ct of Australia, PO Box E435, Queen Victoria Terrace, ACT 2600, Australia

MASON, David; s of George Edward and Florence Kate Mason, of Northborough, Peterborough; *b* 3 Nov 1944; *Educ* Deacon's GS Peterborough, RAC Cirencester (MRAC, NDA); *m* 1970, Shirley Ann, da of John James Adams (d 1962), of Grimsby; 2 s, 1 da; *Career* trials offr Rotherwell Plant Breeders 1968-72, cereal trials co-ordinator N American Plant Breeders 1973-75; dir Rothwell Plant Breeders 1975-79, md Mickerson RPB Ltd 1979-; *Recreations* gardening, family, shooting; *Clubs* Farmers'; *Style*— David Mason, Esq; Glebe House, Southdale, Caistor, Lincoln LN7 6LS; Nickerson RPB Ltd, JNRC, Rothwell, Caistor, Lincoln (☎ 0472 89 471, telex 52072)

MASON, Prof David Kean; CBE (1987); s of George Hunter Mason (d 1983), of Glasgow Rd, Paisley, and Margaret MacCulloch Kean (d 1975); *Educ* Paisley GS, Glasgow Acad, Univ of St Andrews (LDS, BDS), Univ of Glasgow (MB ChB, MD); *m* 3 June 10967, Judith Anne, da of John Campbell Armstrong (d 1979), of Belfast, N Ireland; 2 s (Miachael b 1971, Andrew b 1979), 1 da (Katie b 1974); *Career* hon conslt dental surgn Greater Glasgow Health Bd 1965-; prof oval med Univ of Glasgow 1967- (dean dental educn 1980-); *Recreations* golf, tennis, gardening, enjoying countryside pleasures; *Clubs* Royal and Ancient GC, St Andrews; *Style*— Prof David Mason, CBE; Greystones, Houston Rd, Kilmacolm, Renfrewshire, PA13 (☎ 050 587 2001); Glasgow Dental Hosp & Sch, 378 Sauchiehall St, Glasgow G2 3JZ (☎ 041 332 7020)

MASON, Derek; s of Sydney George, and Carmen, *née* Rees; *b* 3 August 1945; *Educ* Dyffryn GS, Oxford Sch of Architecture (Dip Arch), Open Univ 1978 (BA); *m* 15 April 1968, Sandra Eve, da of Capt R I Buchanan (d 1987); 2 da (Domneva b 1968, Jenna b 1980); *Career* chartered architect; ARIBA 1971, ACI Arb 1987; *Recreations* squash, tennis, architectural history; *Style*— Derek Mason, Esq; Le Hurel, La Rue du Maupertuis, St Mary, Jersey, CI; Mason Design Ptnrship, Broadcasting House, Rouge Bouillon, St Helier, Jersey, CI

MASON, Hon Mrs (Elizabeth); *née* Eden; da of 7 Baron Auckland (d 1955); *b* 1928; *Educ* Brondesbury; *m* 1954, Maj Frederic Edward Isdale (Robin) Mason; 2 s, 1 da; *Style*— The Hon Mrs Mason; Reed Hall, Holbrook, nr Ipswich, Suffolk (☎ 0473 328327)

MASON, Hon Elizabeth-Anne; da of 3 Baron Blackford (d 1977), and of Sarah, da of His Hon Judge Sir Shirley Worthington-Evans, Bt; *b* 15 Feb 1965; *Style*— The Hon Elizabeth-Anne Mason; 17 The Gateways, Sprimont Place, London SW3

MASON, Sir Frederick Cecil; KCVO (1968), CMG (1960); s of Ernest Mason (d 1966), and Sophia Charlotte, *née* Dodson (d 1953); *b* 15 May 1913; *Educ* City of London Sch, St Catharine's Coll Cambridge (BA); *m* 1941, Karen, da of Christian Rorholm (d 1968), of Denmark; 2 s, 1 da (and 2 da decd); *Career* entered Consular Serv 1935; serv: Antwerp, Paris, Belgian Congo, Faroes, Pamana, Chile, Oslo, FO, Bonn, Athens, Tehran; head econ rels dept FO 1960-64, under-sec Miny of Overseas Devpt and Cwlth Rels Off 1965-66, ambass Chile 1966-70, ambass to UN Geneva 1971-73, ret; dir New Ct Natural Resources 1973-83; UK memb Int Narcotics Control Bd 1974-77; chm Anglo-Chilean Soc in London 1979-83; *Recreations* ball games, walking, bird watching, painting, singing; *Clubs* Canning; *Style*— Sir Frederick Mason, KCVO, CMG; The Forge, Church St, Ropley, Hants SO24 0DS (☎ 096 277 2285)

MASON, George Verrinder; s of George Ashton Frederick Mason (d 1945), of Enfield, Middx, and Elsie Dorothy, *née* Verrinder; *b* 25 June 1930; *Educ* Ardingly Coll; *m* 15 Sept 1956, Josephine Elizabeth, da of Stanley Northcott, of Bishop's Lydeard, Somerset; 3 s ((George) Stephen b 1960, Richard Henry b 1964, James Robert b 1967), 1 da (Sally Elizabeth b 1958); *Career* Nat Serv 2 Lt RASC 1953-55; admitted slr 1953, ptnr Laytons 1960-68, sr ptnr Braby & Waller 1981-(ptnr 1968-81); pres Rickmansworth Hockey Club; memb Law Soc 1953; *Recreations* hockey, watching cricket, fishing; *Clubs* MCC; *Style*— George Mason, Esq; Juniper House, Harefield Rd, Rickmansworth, Herts WD3 1PB (☎ 0923 776 732); Braby & Waller, 82 St John St, London EC1M 4DP (☎ 01 250 1884, fax 01 250 1749, telex 889264)

MASON, Sir (Basil) John; CB (1973); s of John Robert Mason (d 1937); *b* 18 August 1923; *Educ* Fakenham GS, Univ Coll Nottingham (BSc, DSc); *m* 1948, Doreen Sheila Jones; 2 s (Barry b 1955, Nigel b 1962); *Career* serv WWII Flt Lt RAF; prof of cloud physics Imperial Coll London 1961-65; dir-gen Meteorological Off 1965-83; perm rep of the UK at the World Meteorological Orgn 1965-83 (memb exec ctee 1966-75 and 1977-83); tres and sr vice-pres The Royal Soc 1976-86; pro-chllr Surrey Univ 1980-85; memb advsy bd Res Cncls 1983-6; dir UK/Scandinavian Acid Rain Programme 1983-; pres: Br Assoc 1982-83, Univ Manchester Inst of Tech 1986-; chm Coordinating Ctee for Marine Sci and Technol 1987-; FRS; kt 1979; *Recreations* music, walking, foreign travel; *Style*— Sir John Mason, CB; 64 Christchurch Rd, East Sheen, London SW14 7AW (☎ 01 876 2557)

MASON, Sir John Charles Moir; KCMG (1980, CMG 1976); o s of Charles Moir Mason, CBE (d 1967), and Madeline Mason; *b* 13 May 1927; *Educ* Manchester GS, Peterhouse Cambridge (MA); *m* 1954, Margaret Newton, da of Noel David Vidgen (d 1971); 1 s, 1 da; *Career* Lt XX Lancashire Fusiliers 1946-48, Capt Royal Ulster Rifles Korea 1950-51; HM Foreign Serv 1952, third sec FO 1952-54, sec & private sec to Ambass Br Embassy Rome 1954-56, sec sec Warsaw 1956-59, second sec FO 1959-61, first sec (commerical Damascus 1961-65), first sec & asst head of dept FO 1965-68, dir Trade Dvpt and dep consul-gen New York 1968-71, head Euro Integration Dept FCO 1971-72, seconded as under-sec ECGD 1972-75, asst under-sec state (econ) FCO 1975-76, ambass to Israel 1976-80, Br high cmmr to Australia 1980-84; chm: Lloyds Bank NZA, Sydney 1985, Thorn EMI (Australia) 1985, VSEL (Australia) 1985, Spencer Stuart Bd of Advice, Sydney 1985, Prudential Corpn Australia 1987, Prudential Fin 1987, Prudential Funds Mgmnt 1987, Lloyds International 1987, Multicon 1987, North Shore Research Fndn 1987; dir: Wellcome (Australia) 1985, Fluor Daniel (Australia) 1985, Pirelli Australia 1987, Nat Bank of New Zealand 1985; *Clubs* Athenaeum, Union (Sydney), Melbourne; *Style*— Sir John Mason, KCMG; 147 Dover Rd, Dover Heights, NSW 2030, Australia

MASON, John Harold; s of Albert Leonard Mason, of Blackheath, and Agnes Jane, *née* Smith (d 1956); *b* 10 Sept 1932; *Educ* Westminster City Sch; *m* 25 July 1959, Monica, da of Thomas Stevenson (d 1949), of Ravenstone; 3 s (Felix b 1962, Guy b 1964, Toby b 1966), 1 da (Tina b 1960); *Career* RAOC 1951-53, cmmnd 1952, serv Germany and Belgium; The HongKong and Shangai Banking Corpn 1954-86, serv: London, HongKong, Cambodia, Vietnam, Japan, Philippines, India, Singapore, and Brunei 1954-76; mangr Thailand 1976-78, rep HongKong Bank Gp in Aust and gen mangr HongKong Fin Aust 1979-80, area mangr Brunei 1980-83, chief exec offr Japan 1984-86, ret; chm: Banks Assoc of Brunei 1980-83, personnel standing ctee (memb gen ctee) Inst of Foreign Bankers Japan; *Recreations* sailing, choral singing, walking; *Clubs* Oriental, Naval, Hong Kong Royal YC, Lym YC, RHK Jockey, RHK YC; *Style*— John Mason, Esq; Birchcroft, 29 Westfield Rd, Lymington, Hants SO41 9QB (☎ 0590 78084)

MASON, John Muir; MBE (1987); s of James William Mason, Sheriff Clerk, of Wigtown (d 1962), and Tomima Watt, *née* Muir (d 1972); *b* 21 Jan 1940; *Educ* Kirkwall GS, Orkney, Douglas Ewart High Sch Newton Stewart, Edinburgh Univ (BL); *m* 25 Jan 1967, Jessica Hilary Miller, da of John Groat (d 1981) of Stronsay, Orkney Islands; 1 s (James Muir Angel b 1969), 2 step s (Peter John Chalmers b 1960, Rognvald Inkster b 1963); *Career* slr; sr ptnr Waddell & Mackintosh Slrs, Troon; chm The Rev James Currie Memorial Tst, life govnr Imperial Cancer Res Fund; tstee Niel Gow Memorial Tst, md J D C Publicatiosn Ltd, dir of private cos, princ conductor and musical dir of The Strings of Scotland and The Scottish Fiddle Orchestra; *Recreations* music, history; *Style*— John Mason, Esq, MBE; 27 Victoria Dr, Troon, Ayrshire (☎ 0292 312796); 36 West Portland St, Troon, Ayrshire (☎ 0292 312222)

MASON, Keith Edward; s of Arthur Ernest Mason (d 1982), and Nellie Louise, *née* Hawkes; *b* 3 May 1943; *Educ* Westminster GS; *m* 11 Feb 1964 (m dis 1988) Jacqueline Claire, da of Robert W Mitcham; 3 s (Sean 9 March 1965, Nicholas b 11 Feb 1967, Stuart b 24 March 1974), 1 da (Jacqueline b 22 Aug 1968); *Career* asst mangr admin Bank of London and S America 1971-72, head of data processing Lloyds and Bolsa Int 1972-73; C Hoare & Co: head of data processing 1974-77, head of accounts 1977-83, mangr admin 1983-87, gen manr 1987-; *Recreations* rowing, reading, music; *Clubs* London Rowing, Stewards Enclosure Henley; *Style*— Keith Mason, Esq; 119 Kenilworth Ct, Lower Richmond Rd, Putney, London SW15 1WA (☎ 01 788 3434), C Hoare & Co, 37 Fleet St, London EC4P 4DQ (☎ 01 353 4522, fax 01 353 4521, telex 24622)

MASON, Prof (John) Kenyon French; CBE (1973); s of Air Cdre John Melbourne Mason, CBE, DSC, DFC (d 1955), and Alma Ada Mary, *née* French (d 1983); *b* 19 Dec 1919; *Educ* Downside, Cambridge (MA, MD), Univ of Edinburgh (LLD); *m* 14 Jan 1943, Elizabeth Hope, (d 1977), da of Trevor Latham, (d 1960) 2 s (Ian b 1944, Paul b 1947); *Career* RAF: Sqdn MO 1943-47, pathologist trg 1948, conslt in pathology and offr i/c dept of aviation and forensic pathology RAF Inst of Pathology 1955-73, ret Gp Capt 1973; appt regius chair forensic med Univ of Edinburgh 1973- ret 1985; hon fell Faculty of Law Univ of Edinburgh 1985-; King Haakon VII Freedom Medal (Norway) 1945, pres Br Assoc in Forensic Med 1982-84; FRCP; *Books* Forensic Medicine for Lawyers (2 ed 1983), Law and Medical Ethics (2 ed co-author 1987), Butterworths Medico-legal Encyclopaedia (co author 1987), Human Life and Medical Practice (1988); *Clubs* RAF; *Style*— Prof Kenyon Mason, CBE; 66 Craiglea Dr, Edinburgh EH10 5PF (☎ 031 447 2301); Faculty of Law, Old College, South Bridge, Edinburgh EH8 9YL (☎ 031 667 1011 ext 4295)

MASON, Hon Mrs; Hon (Kristina Elizabeth); da of Baroness Robson of Kiddington (Life Peeress 1974); *b* 1946; *m* 1967, Iain McLaren Mason; *Style*— The Hon Mrs Mason; The Dower Hse, Kiddington, Woodstock, Oxon

MASON, His Hon (George Frederick) Peter; QC (1963); s of George Samuel Mason (d 1966), of Keighley, and Florence May Mason (d 1965); *b* 11 Dec 1921; *Educ* Lancaster Royal GS, St Catharine's Coll Cambridge (BA, MA); *m* 1, 30 Dec 1950 (m dis 1977), Faith Maud, *née* Bacon; 2 s (Jonathan b 18 Nov 1952, Michael b 1 April 1962), 3 da (Pippa b 25 July 1951, Melodie b and d 1957, Alison b 17 Oct 1960); m 2, 6 March 1981, Sara Lilian, da of Sir Robert Ricketts, 7 Bt, of Forwood House, Minchinhampton, Glos; *Career* aWII cmmnd 78 Medium Regt RA (Duke of Lancaster's Own Yeomanry), Staff Capt RA 13 Corps ME and Italy; barr 1947, dep chm Agric Land Tbnl W Yorks and Lancs 1962, dep chm West Riding Qtr Sessions 1965; rec of York 1965; circuit judge 1970-87, sr judge Snaresbrook Crown Ct 1974-81, sr judge Inner London Crown Ct 1983-87: Freeman City of London 1977, Liveryman Worshipful Wax Chandlers Co 1981; FCIArb 1986, lay memb Cncl of Assoc of Futures Brokers and Dealers 1987; *Recreations* golf, cycling in foreign parts, music; *Clubs* Athenaeum, Hawks (Cambridge); *Style*— His Hon Peter Mason, QC; Lane Cottage, Amberley, Glos GL5 5AB (☎ 045 387 2412); 11 King's Bench Walk, Temple, London EC4 (☎ 01 353 3337, fax 01 583 2190)

MASON, Richard Graham; s of Arthur Ernest Mason (d 1988), and Catherine Mary, *née* Boakes (d 1964); *b* 21 June 1944; *Educ* Wilson's GS Camberwell London SE5; *m* 2 Sept 1967, Lynda Miriam Mary, da of Frederick William Tothill (d 1983); 1 s (Andrew Philip b 1970), 1 da (Karen Elizabeth b 1973); *Career* Bank of England: exchange control dept 1965-79, sec City EEC Ctee 1980-84, sec Capital Mkts ctee 1980-84, Sec City Taxation Ctee 1980-82; exec dir Br Invisible Exports Cncl 1984- (sec and tres 1982-84); tres Chertsey PCC 1969-82; memb Chertsey Jt Church Cncl 1980-87, Chertsey PCC 1987-89, Runnymede Deanery Synod 1989-; memb: CBI Export Promotions Ctee 1984-, London C of C Int Trade Ctee 1984-, Br Tourist Authy Devpt Ctee 1984-; ACIB 1966, MIEx 1987; *Books* various articles on invisible exports; *Recreations* walking, gardening; *Clubs* Overseas Bankers; *Style*— R G Mason, Esq; Betoncroft, 21A Abbey Rd, Chertsey, Surrey KT16 8AL (☎ 0932 564 773); Windsor House, 39 King St, London EC2V 8DQ (☎ 01 600 1198, fax 01 606 4248, telex 941 3342 BIEG)

MASON, The Ven Richard John; s of Vice Adm Frank Trowbridge Mason, KCB (d 1988), of 114 High St, Hurstpierpoint, W Sussex, and Dora Margaret, *née* Brand; *b* 26 April 1929; *Educ* Shrewsbury; *Career* clerk in Holy Orders, asst curate Bishop's Hatfield Herts 1958-64, domestic chaplain to the Bishop of London 1964-69, vicar of Riverhead Kent 1969-73; vicar of Edenbridge Kent 1973-83, archdeacon of Tonbridge 1977-; min of St Luke Sevenoaks 1983-; *Recreations* watching cricket; *Style*— The Ven Richard Mason; St Luke's House, 30 Eardley Rd, Sevenoaks, Kent TN13 1XT (☎ 0732 452462)

MASON, Roger James; s of Philip Talbot Mason (d 1965), of Solihull, and Monica Beryl, *née* Mangham (d 1986); *b* 12 July 1937; *Educ* Solihull Sch, Univ of Birmingham (LLB); *m* 26 Oct 1967, Merle Ann (NP), da of George William Hill, of Rugby; *Career* slr in private practice 1962-, notary public in private practice 1967-, cmmr for oaths 1968-; memb: W Midland Rent Assessment Ctee 1980-, W Midland Rent Tbnl 1980, W Midland Leasehold Valuation Tbnl 1981-; FCIArb 1975; memb Provincial Notaries Soc 1967; *Recreations* sailing, making home made jam, thinking; *Clubs* Vintage Motor Cycle, Morgan Three Wheeler; *Style*— Roger Mason, Esq; The Close, Beausale, Warwick CV35 7PD (☎ 0926 484424); Biddle, Mason & Co, Stowe House, 1688 High St, Knowle, Solihull, W Midlands B93 OLY (☎ 0564 776127)

MASON, Prof Sir Ronald; KCB (1980); s of David John Mason (d 1950) and Olwen, *née* James; *b* 22 July 1930; *Educ* Quakers Yard, Univ of Wales (BSc), London Univ (PhD, DSc); *m* 1, 1952, Pauline Pattinson; 1 s (decd), 3 da; m 2, 1979, Elizabeth Rosemary, da of Maj Theodore Walpole Grey-Edwards; *Career* prof of inorganic chemistry Sheffield Univ 1963-71, prof of chemistry Sussex Univ 1971-, pro vice-chllr Sussex Univ 1977-78 chief scientific advsr MOD 1977-83; Advsy Bd Res Cncls 1977-83; Sci Res Cncl 1971-73; many visiting professorships in USA, Canada, France, Israel, New Zealand, Australia; dep chm Hunting Engrg Ltd 1985-87 (chm 1987-88), visiting prof Int Rels Univ Coll of Wales 1985-, pres BHRA 1987-, dir Thom UK Hldgs 1987-; FRS; *Recreations* cooking, and stirring; *Clubs* Athenaeum; *Style*— Prof Sir Ronald Mason, KCB; Chestnuts Farm, Weedon HP22 4NH (☎ 0296 641353); BHRA Cranfield, Beds MK43 0AJ (☎ 0234 750422); 905 Nelson House, Dolphin Sq, London SW1; Univ of Sussex, Falmer, Brighton, East Sussex (☎ 0273 606755)

MASON, Stephen Maxwell; s of Harold Geoffrey Mason (d 1986), and Ursula, *née* Habermann; *b* 19 May 1949; *Educ* Bradford GS, Gonville and Caius Coll Cambridge (MA); *m* 26 March 1976, Judith Mary, da of Hebbert, of 2 Manley Rd, Ilkley; 2 da (Fiona b 1979, Nicola b 1985), 1 s (Alistair b 1981); *Career* slr; ptnr Mason Bond, Leeds, sec Bradford Law Centre Mgmnt Ctee, author of articles on package holiday law including Don't Shoot the Tour Operator (1983), Holiday Damages — the Gravy train Slows Down (1987); *Recreations* writing, travel by train; *Clubs* Law Soc; *Style—* Stephen Mason, Esq; Abbey House, Park Row, Leeds LS1 5NG (☎ 0532 424444, telex 556681, fax 0532 467542)

MASON, Sydney; s of Jack Mason (d 1936); *b* 30 Sept 1920; *m* 1945, Rosalind, da of Woolf Victor (d 1975); *Career* mangr Land Securities plc 1943-49, md Hammerson Property Investmt & Devpt Corpn plc 1949- (chm 1958-); Liveryman Worshipful Co of Masons; *Recreations* painting, in oils and acrylics; *Clubs* Naval, Royal Thames YC, City Livery; *Style—* Sydney Mason, Esq; 100 Park Lane, London W1 (☎ 01 629 9494)

MASON, Terence Harold; s of Harold Henry Mason, of Walsall, W Mids, and Winifred May, *née* Sadler; *b* 7 July 1941; *Educ* Queen Mary's GS Walsall; *m* 25 Sept 1971, Beryl, da of Albert Ernest Hughes, of Claverley, Shrops; *Career* articled clerk Herbert Pepper & Rudland Chartered Accountants, Walsall 1957-64, audit mangr Peat Marwick Mitchell CAs Birmingham 1964-66, gp fin dir Tarmac Plc Wolverhampton 1986- (other fin posts 1966-86); memb Ironbridge Gorge Museum Dept Tst; FCA 1964, RSA 1987; *Recreations* golf, theatre, arts; *Style—* Terence Mason, Esq; Stratton Ct, Long Common, Claverley, Shropshire (☎ 07466 577); Tarmac plc, Hilton Hall, Essington, Wolverhampton WV11 2BQ (☎ 0902 307 407, fax 0902 307 408, telex 338544)

MASON, Timothy Ian Godson; s of Ian Godson Mason, of Alverstoke Hants, and Muriel Marjorie Berkeley Mason, *née* Vaile; *b* 11 Mar 1945; *Educ* St Alban's Sch Washington DC USA, Bradfield Coll Berks, Christ Church Oxford (BA, MA); *m* 1975, Marilyn Ailsa, da of Frederic George Williams (d 1969), of Christchurch NZ; 1 s (Giles b 1982), 1 da (Grace b 1979); *Career* asst admin Oxford Playhouse 1966-67, asst to Peter Daubeny World Theatre Season London 1967-69; admin: Ballet Rambert 1970-75, Royal Exchange Theatre Manchester 1975-77; dir: Western Aust Arts Cncl 1977-80, Scottish Arts Cncl 1980-; *Recreations* arts, family; *Style—* Timothy Mason, Esq; 37 Park Rd, Edinburgh EH6 4LA; Scottish Arts Cncl, 19 Charlotte Sq, Edinburgh EH2 4DF (☎ 031 226 6051)

MASON, William Ernest; CB (1983); s of Ernest George Mason, and Agnes Margaret Mason, *née* Derry; *b* 12 Jan 1929; *Educ* Brockley GS, LSE (BSc); *m* 1959, Jean; 1 s, 1 da; *Career* Miny of Food 1949-54, MAFF 1954, princ 1963, asst sec 1970, under-sec 1975, Fisheries sec 1980, dep sec (Fisheries and Food) MAFF 1982-89; *Recreations* music, reading, gardening; *Clubs* Reform; *Style—* William Mason, Esq, CB; The Haven, Fairlie Gdns, London SE23 3TE (☎ 01 699 5821); Ministry of Agriculture, Fisheries and Food, Whitehall Place, London SW1 (☎ 01 233 5459)

MASON OF BARNSLEY, Baron (Life Peer UK 1987); Roy Mason; PC (1968); s of Joseph Mason; *b* 18 April 1924; *Educ* LSE; *m* 1945, Marjorie, da of Ernest Sowden; 2 da; *Career* former coal miner; MP (Lab) Barnsley 1953-83, Barnsley Central 1973-87; oppn spokesman Def and Post Off 1960-64; min of State BOT 1964-67; min Def Equipment 1967-68, postmaster-gen 1968, min Power 1968-69; pres BOT 1969-70; oppn spokesman Civil Aviation Shipping Tourism Films & Trade 1970-74; sec of state: Def 1974-76, NI 1976-79; oppn spokesman Agric Fish & Food 1979-; former NUM official; chm Yorks Gp Labour MPs (vice-chm 1980); *Style—* The Rt Hon Lord Mason of Barnsley, PC; 12 Victoria Ave, Barnsley, S Yorks

MASON-HORNBY, Anthony Feilden; s of Capt Paul Randle Feilden Mason (d 1944), of The Cedars, Sandhurst, Berks, and Joyce Madeline, *née* Wigan (d 1984); assumed additional name and arms of Hornby by Royal Licence 15 Sept 1987, under terms of will of late Edmund Geoffrey Stanley Hornby (d 1923); *b* 9 Mar 1931; *Educ* Eton, RAC Cirencester (MRAC, dip Estate Mgmnt); *m* 11 June 1960, Cecily Barbara, da of Lt-Col Henry Gordon Carter, MC, DL (d 1966), of Tan-y-Bryn, Bangor, N Wales; 2 s (Francis b 1961, Christopher b 1963), 1 da (Catherine b 1964); *Career* landowner 1966-; warden and co-founder of Ogwen Cottage Mountain Sch 1959-64; Br Mountaineering Cncl Guide 1961-64; fndr and dir The Westmorland Singers 1974; chm tstees St John's Hospice Lancaster 1980-; *Recreations* climbing, shooting, singing; *Clubs* Climbers', Swiss Alpine; *Style—* Anthony Mason-Hornby, Esq; Dalton Hall, Burton, Cumbria (☎ 0524 781228)

MASSEREENE AND FERRARD, 13 & 6 Viscount (I 1660 & 1797); John Clotworthy Talbot Foster Whyte-Melville Skeffington; DL (Co Antrim 1957); also Baron of Loughneagh (I 1660), Baron Oriel of Collon (I 1790), and Baron Oriel of Ferrard (UK 1821, which sits as); patron of one living; s of 12 (& 5) Viscount, DSO, JP, DL (d 1956, himself ggs of Harriet, w of 2 Viscount Ferrard, and Viscountess Massereene in her own right; Harriet's f was the 4 & last Earl of Massereene; the Viscountcy of Massereene (but not that of Ferrard) is the only Irish Peerage heritable by a female), and Jean Barbara Ainsworth, JP (d 1937), da of Sir John Stirling Ainsworth, MP ; *b* 23 Oct 1914; *Educ* Eton; *m* 15 March 1939, Annabelle Kathleen, er da of late Henry David Lewis, of Combwell Priory, Hawkhurst; 1 s, 1 da; *Heir* s, Hon John David Clotworthy Whyte-Melville Skeffington, *qv*; *Career* Lt Black Watch SR 1933-36 and 1939-49 WWII invalided; served invasion; small vessels pool RN 1944; sits as Cons in House of Lords; driver leading Br Car Le Mans Grand Prix 1937; gold staff offr Coronation of HM The Queen 1953; Cons whip Cons Peers Ctee (IUP) House of Lords 1958-65, jt chm 1965-70; Peers memb Inter-Parly Union Delgn to Spain 1960; former chm: London Scottish Clans Assoc & Victoria League for Kent; former pres Kent Hotels & Restaurants Assoc and other socs; MFH Ashford Valley Foxhounds 1953-54, vice-pres Animal Welfare Year 1976-77; memb Deer Ctee Br Field Sports Soc; company dir; promoted and ran 1st scheduled air serv Glasgow, Oban, Isle of Mull; memb parly delegation to Malawi 1976, an original pioneer in commercial development of Cape Canaveral USA; presented operetta Countess Maritza at Palace Theatre, London; former dir Aviation & Shipping Ltd; chm Sunset & Vine plc (TV); pres Monday Club 1981-; former chm Ferrard Hldgs Ltd; Freeman City of London, memb Worshipful Co of Shipwrights; Cross Cdr Order of Merit SMOM; *Books* The Lords (1973); *Recreations* sailing - (yacht 'Benmore Lady'); *Clubs* Royal Yacht Sqdn, Turf, Carlton, Pratt's, House of Lords YC (former cdre); *Style—* The Rt Hon the Viscount Massereene and Ferrard, DL; Chilham Castle, Canterbury, Kent (☎ 0227 730319); Knock, Isle of Mull, Argyll (☎ 06803 356)

MASSEY, Hon Mrs (Lavinia); *née* Bootle-Wilbraham; da of 6 Baron Skelmersdale (d 1973); *b* 1937; *m* 1969, Robert Brian Noel Massey; 2 s; *Style—* The Hon Mrs Massey; Waterstone House, Waterstone Close, Itchenor, nr Chichester, W Sussex

MASSEY, Roy Cyril; s of Cyril Charles Massey (d 1967), of Birmingham, and Beatrice May Massey (d 1986); *b* 9 May 1934; *Educ* Moseley GS Birmingham, Univ of Birmingham (BMus); *m* 22 Feb 1975, Ruth Carol Craddock, *née* Grove; *Career* organist: St Alban's Conybere St Birmingham 1953-60, St Augustine's Church Edgbaston Birmingham 1960-65, Croydon Parish Church 1965-68; warden Royal Sch of Church Music Addington Palace Croydon 1965-68, conductor Birmingham Bach Soc 1966-68, organist and master of the choristers Birmingham Cathedral 1968-74, dir of music King Edward's Sch Birmingham 1968-74, organist and master of the choristers Hereford Cathedral 1974-, conductor Three Choirs Festival and Hereford Choral Soc 1974-; memb cncl: CO, Royal Sch of Church Music; fell St Michael's Coll Tenbury 1979-88; chm: Hereford Concert Soc, Hereford Competitive Music Festival; FRSCM 1972; *Recreations* motoring, old buildings, book collecting; *Clubs* Cons (Hereford); *Style—* Roy Massey, Esq; 14 Coll Cloisters, Cathedral Close, Hereford HR1 2NG (☎ 0432 2720211); The Cobbles, Stretton Grandison, Hereford

MASSIMO OF ROCCASECCA DEI VOLSCI, Prince (Title of Papal and Italian Royal Decree 31 March 1932) Stefano Shaun Francesco Filippo Gabriel Charles James; Don Stefano, Prince of Roccasecca dei Volsci; s of Prince Vittorio Massimo and his 2 wife Dawn Addams, the film actress; *b* 10 Jan 1955,London,; *Educ* Collegio san Giuseppe de Merode Rome, Collegio alla Querce Florence; *m* 1973, Atalanta Edith, da of Maj Ivan Foxwell, *qv*, and Lady Edith Sybil, *née* Lambart, gda of 9 Earl of Cavan, KP, PC, DL; 3 s (Don Valerio b 1973, Don Cesare b 1977 Don Tancredi b 1986); *Heir* Don Valerio Massimo; *Career* photographer; *Clubs* Circolo degli Scacchi, (Rome); *Style—* Prince Stefano Massimo of Roccasecca Dei Volsci; c/o National Westminster Bank, Bloomsbury Way, London WC1A 2TS

MASSY, Hon David Hamon Somerset; s and h of 9 Baron Massy; *b* 4 Mar 1947; *Educ* St George's Coll Weybridge; *Career* serving with Merchant Navy; *Style—* The Hon David Massy

MASSY, Hon Graham Ingoldsby Somerset; s of 9 Baron Massy; *b* 1952; *Style—* The Hon Graham Massy

MASSY, 9 Baron (I 1776); Hugh Hamon John Somerset Massy; s of 8 Baron (d 1958); *b* 11 June 1921; *Educ* Clongowes Wood Coll, Clayesmore Sch; *m* 1943, Margaret Elizabeth, da of John Flower (decd); 4 s, 1 da; *Heir* s, Hon David Hamon Somerset Massy; *Career* serv 1940-45 War, Private RAOC; *Style—* The Rt Hon the Lord Massy; 88 Brooklands Rd, Cosby, Leicester

MASSY, Hon John Hugh Somerset; s of 9 Baron Massy; *b* 1950; *m* 1978, Andrea, da of Alan West of Leicester; *Style—* The Hon John Massy

MASSY, Hon Muriel Olive; da of 7 Baron Massy; *b* 1892; *Style—* The Hon Muriel Massy

MASSY, Hon Paul Robert; s of 9 Baron Massy; *b* 1953; *m* 1976, Anne Bridget, da of James McGowan, of Leicester; 1 s; *Style—* The Hon Paul Massy

MASSY, Hon Sheelagh Marie Louise; da of 9 Baron Massy; *b* 1958; *Style—* The Hon Sheelagh Massy

MASSY-BERESFORD, Michael James; s of Brig Tristram Hugh Massy-Beresford (d 1987), and Helen Lindsay, *née* Lawford (d 1979); *b* 10 April 1935; *Educ* Eton, Jesus Coll Cambridge (BA), RMCS (MSc); *Career* Oxford and Bucks LI 1955-59, Royal Green Jackets 1959-81; dir Miltrain Ltd 1981-; *Recreations* water sports, bicycling; *Style—* Michael Massy-Beresford, Esq; 11 Charleville Mansions, Charleville Road, London W14 9JB (☎ 01 385 1983)

MASSY-GREENE, Sir (John) Brian; AC; s of Sir Walter Massy-Greene (decd); *b* 20 April 1916; *Educ* SCEGS, Geelong GS Vic, Clare Coll Cambridge (MA); *m* 1942, Margaret Elizabeth, da of Dr Walter Sharp, OBE (decd); 2 s, 2 da; *Career* WWII 1939-45, NG AIF Lt 1942-45; joined Metal Mfrs Ltd 1939 (gen mangr 1953-62); chm: consolidated Gold Fields Aust Ltd 1966-76, The Bellambi Coal Co Ltd 1964-72, Goldsworthy Mining Co Ltd 1965-76, the Mt Lyell Mining & Rlwy Co Ltd 1969-76, Lawrenson Alumsac Hldgs Ltd 1964-73, Dalgety Aust Ltd 1964-73; dir: Pacific Dunlop Ltd 1968-86 (dep chm 1977-79, chm 1979-86), Cwlth Banking Corpn 1968- (dep chm 1976-85, chm 1985-88); dir and chm Hazelton Air Servs Hldgs Ltd 1984; dir Santos Ltd (chm 1985-); memb: exec ctee Aust Mining Ind Cncl 1967-76 (pres 1971), Mfr Indust Advsy Ctee CSIRO 1968-75, Aust Inst Mining and Metallurgy; FAIM; FIEA; kt 1972; *Recreations* farming, fishing, flying; *Clubs* Australian (Sydney); *Style—* Sir Brian Massy-Greene, AC; 1/7 Quambi Place, Edgecliff, NSW 2027, Australia

MASTERS, Mrs Sheila Valerie (Mrs Barry Noakes); da of Albert Frederick Masters, of ELtham, London, and Iris Sheila, *née* Ratcliffe; *b* 23 June 1949; *Educ* Eltham Hill GS, Univ of Bristol (LLB); *m* 3 Aug 1985, (Colin) Barry Noakes, s of Stuart Noakes, Brenchley; *Career* Peat Marwick McLintock: 1970-, ptnr 1983-, ptnr in charge Pub Sector Practice 1986-; seconded to HM Treasy as accounting/ commercial advsr 1979-81, seconded to Dept of Health as dir fin mgmnt on NHS Mgmnt Bd 1988; elected to London Soc of CA 1984, elected to Cncl ICEAW 1987, appointed to Ctee of Enquiry MAFF 1988; FCA, ATII; *Books* Tolley's Stamp Duties (1980); *Recreations* skiing, horse-racing, opera, early classical music; *Style—* Mrs Sheila Masters; Spyways, High St, Goudhurst, Kent TN17 1AL (☎ 0580 211 427); Peat Marwick McClintock, Blackfriars, London EC4V 3PD (☎ 01 236 8000, fax 01 248 6552)

MASUDA, Yosuke; s of Kazuo Masuda (d 1957), of Tokyo, and Miyoko, *née* Hameda (d 1983); *b* 27 April 1946; *Educ* Waseda Sch, Waseda Univ Tokyo (BSc), QMC London (LLB); *m* 16 Feb 1975, Yuriko, da of Yoshiaiki Ohnari, dir of Miny of Int Trade and Indust Tokyo; 1 s (Christopher Toshihiro b 1977), 2 da (Alison Nobuko b 1980, Margaret Takako b 1988); *Career* structural engr Kumagai Gumi Co Ltd 1969, asst project mangr Hong Kong Mass Transit Railway 1976-79, md Kumagai Gumi UK Ltd 1985, assoc dir Kumagai Co Ltd Tokyo 1988; called to the Bar Middle Temple 1984; memb: Japanese C of C UK, Anglo Japanese Assoc; fell QMC London; memb Japanese Inst of Civil Engrs; *Books* Pneumatic Caisson Design (1975); *Recreations* theatre, travel, classical music, fishing, riding; *Clubs* Reform; *Style—* Yosuke Masuda, Esq; The Lawn, 109 Camlet Way, Hadley Common, Herts (☎ 01 449 0272); 8 St James Sq, London SW1 (☎ 01 925 0066, fax 01 930 8004)

MATANLE, David John Link; s of Leslie William Matanle, of Crediton, Devon, and Dorothy Ellen, *née* Palfreman (d 1968); *b* 22 April 1933; *Educ* Queen Elizabeth's Sch Crediton Devon; *m* 14 Sept 1959, (Margaret) Jean, da of George Edward Clifford (d 1959), of Bristol; 2 da (Ann b 16 Dec 1963, Helen b 15 July 1965); *Career* Nat Serv RAF 1951-553; Purser Orient Line 1954-60, accountant P & O 1960-66, accountant and asst sec Gibbards Ltd 1966-68, co sec Braithwaites plc 1968-72, dir: John Perring ltd 1972-83, dir and co sec Cullens Stores plc 1983-88; dir: Manor Distribution Servs Ltd 1988-, Grangedown Ltd 1988-; sec: Bookham CC 1978-84, Bookham Sports Assoc 1979-84; govr Coll for the Distributive Trades 1981-83, chm educn ctee Nat Assoc of Furnishers 1981-83; Freeman City of London 1979, memb Worshipful Co of Furnituremakers 1979; FCIS 1966, MBIM 1973; *Recreations* sports, music, walking; *Style—* David Matanle, Esq; 43 Eastwick Pk Ave, Gt Bookham, Surrey (☎ 0372

54385); 36 The Pk, Gt Bookham, Surrey; Preston Farm, Lower Rd, Gt Bookham, Surrey (☎ 0372 57397)

MATES, Lt-Col Michael John; MP (C) E Hants 1983-; s of Claude Mates; *b* 9 June 1934; *Educ* Salisbury Cathedral Sch, Blundell's, King's Coll Cambridge; *m* 1, 1959 (m dis 1980), Mary Rosamund Paton; 2 s, 2 da; m 2, 1982, Rosellen, da of W T Bett, of West Wittering, W Sussex; *Career* army offr 1954-74 (Royal Ulster Rifles, Queen's Dragoon Gds RAC, Maj 1967, Lt-Col 1973); vice-chm Cons NI Ctee 1979-81 (Sec 1974-79), Cons Home Affrs Ctee 1979-; chm All Party Anglo-Irish Gp 1979-, memb Select Ctee Def 1979-, MP (C) Petersfield Oct 1974-1983; Liveryman Worshipful Co of Farriers' 1975 (Asst 1981, Renter Warden 1983, Middle Warden 1984, Upper Warden 1985); *Style*— Lt-Col Michael Mates, MP; House of Commons, London SW1A 0AA

MATHER, Sir (David) Carol (Macdonell); MC (1944); s of Loris Emerson Mather, CBE (d 1975) and Leila Gwendoline, *née* Morley; yr bro of Sir William Mather, *qv*; *b* 3 Jan 1919; *Educ* Harrow, Trinity Coll Cambridge; *m* 1951, Hon Philippa Selina Bewicke-Copley, da of 5 Baron Cromwell, (*see* Hon Lady Mather); 1 s (Nicholas), 3 da (Selina, Rose, Victoria); *Career* joined Welsh Gds 1940, served Commandos, SAS: WWII, Palestine 1946-48; GSO 1 MI Directorate WO 1957-61, Mil Sec to GOC-in-C E Cmd 1961-62, ret as Lt-Col 1962; CRD 1962-70, Parly candidate Leicester N W 1966, MP (C) Esher 1970-87, sec Cons Home Affrs Ctee 1974-, sec Cons Foreign Affrs Ctee 1972-, oppn whip 1975-79; ld cmmr of the Treasy 1979-81, vice-chamberlain of HM's Household 1981-83, comptroller 1983-86; dir Nat Employees Life Assurance; cncl memb: RGS, Severn Regnl Ctee Nat Tst; kt 1987; *Clubs* Brooks's; *Style*— Sir Carol Mather, MC; Oddington House, Moreton-in-Marsh, Glos

MATHER, Graham Christopher Spencer; eld s of Thomas Mather and Doreen Mather; *b* 23 Oct 1954; *Educ* Hutton GS, New Coll Oxford (MA); *m* 18 Sept 1981, Fiona Marion McMillan, da of Sir Ronald Bell, QC, MP (d 1982); 1 s (Oliver b 20 June 1987); *Career* slr Cameron Markby 1980 (conslt 1986-); IOD: asst to Dir-Gen 1980-83, head of Policy Unit 1983-86; Inst of Econ Affairs: dep dir 1987, gen dir 1987-; radio and tv broadcaster, contributor to The Times, various papers and jnls; memb: Westminster City Cncl 1982-86, cncl Small Business Res Tst, econ advsy ctee Cncl for Charitable Support, HM Treasury Working Party on Freeports 1983; contested (C) Blackburn 1983; *Clubs* Oxford and Cambridge; *Style*— Graham Mather, Esq; 2 Lord North St, London SW1P 3LB (☎ 01 799 3745, fax 01 799 2137)

MATHER, John Williamson; s of John Williamson Mather (d 1979), of Coatbridge, Scotland, and Janet Murdoch, *née* McIntyre; *b* 30 Sept 1929; *Educ* Coatbridge Secdy Sch, Glasgow Univ, Inst of Chartered Accountants of Scotland; *m* 1, 5 Dec 1954 (m dis), Jean; 1 da (Elizabeth b 8 Feb 1961); m 2, 4 Dec 1971, Mavis, da of William Henry Horne, of Burley Lane Farm, Ashe, Basingstoke, Hants; *Career* joined Portals Hldgs plc (fin controller 1966-69, md Portals Ltd 1969-72, md Portals Hldgs plc 1972-86, special projects dir 1987-); *Recreations* badminton, tennis, fell walking; *Style*— John W Mather, Esq; Burley Lane Farm, Ashe, Basingstoke, Hants RG25 3AG (☎ 0256 770267); Portals Holdings plc, Laverstoke Mill, Whitchurch, Hants (☎ 025 682 2360)

MATHER, Sir Kenneth; CBE (1956); s of Richard Wilson Mather (d 1966); *b* 22 June 1911; *Educ* Nantwich, Acton GS, Manchester Univ (BSc), London Univ (PhD, DSc); *m* 1937, Mona (d 1987), da of Harold Rhodes (d 1958); 1 s; *Career* lectr UCL 1934-38, head of genetics dept John Innes Inst 1938-48, prof of genetics Birmingham Univ 1948-65 (hon prof 1971-84, emeritus prof 1984); vice-chllr Southampton Univ 1965-71; Hon LLD Southampton Univ 1972; Hon DSc: Bath 1974, Manchester 1980, Wales 1980; FRS; kt 1979; *Clubs* Athenaeum; *Style*— Sir Kenneth Mather, CBE; The White House, 296 Bristol Rd, Edgbaston, Birmingham B5 7SN (☎ 021 472 2093)

MATHER, Hon Lady (Philippa Selina); *née* Bewicke-Copley; o da of 5 Baron Cromwell, DSO, MC (d 1966); *b* 5 Dec 1925; *m* 13 Jan 1951, Sir (David) Carol MacDonell Mather, MC, *qv*; 1 s, 3 da; *Style*— The Hon Lady Mather; Oddington House, Moreton-in-Marsh, Glos

MATHER, Sir William Loris; CVO (1986), OBE (1957), MC (1945), TD and 2 Clasps (1949), DL (Cheshire 1963); s of Loris Emerson Mather, CBE (d 1976), and Gwendoline Leila, *née* Morley (d 1976); elder bro of Sir Carol Mather, MC, *qv*; *b* 17 August 1913; *Educ* Oundle, Trinity Coll Cambridge (MA); *m* 1937, Eleanor, da of Prof R H George (d 1979), of Providence, Rhode Island; 2 s, 2 da; *Career* serv WWII, Middle E, Western Desert, Italy, Belgium, Holland and Germany; cmd Cheshire Yeo 1954-57, Dep Cdr 23 Armd Bde TA 1957-60, Col; chm: Mather & Platt Ltd 1960-78, CompAir Ltd 1978-83, Neolith Chemical Co Ltd 1983-, Advanced Mfrg Technol Centre 1985-; dir: Dist Bank, Nat Westminster Bank 1960-84 (chm Northern Bd), Br Steel Corpn (regnl dir) 1968-73, Manchester Ship Canal Co 1970-85, Wormald Int Ltd 1977-78; Imperial Continental Gas Assoc 1980-83; chm: NW Econ Planning Cncl 1968 -75, IOD 1979-82; pres: Manchester C of C and Indust 1964-66 (emeritus dir 1978-), Br Pump Makers Assoc 1968-79, Manchester Guardian Soc for Protection of Trade 1971-85, Gtr Manchester E Scouts 1972-, Br Mech Engrg Confedn 1974-79, Assoc of Colls of Higher and Further Educn 1975-76, Manchester Univ Inst of Sci and Technol 1976-85, Civic Tst for the NW 1980- (chm 1961-80), Econ League for the NW 1982-, Manchester YMCA 1982- (chm 1958-82); memb cncl Duchy of Lancaster 1977-85; High Sheriff Cheshire 1969-70, Vice Lord-Lieut Cheshire 1975-; hon fell Manchester Coll of Art and Design 1967, hon memb Town Planning Inst 1977; Hon DEng Liverpool 1980, Hon LLD Manchester 1983; CEng, FIMechE, hon fell Univ of Manchester Coll of Technol 1986; CBIM, FRSA; kt 1968; *Recreations* field sports, wintersports, golf; *Clubs* Naval & Military, Leander; *Style*— Sir William Mather, CVO, OBE, MC, TD, DL; Whirley Hall, Macclesfield, Cheshire SK10 4RN (☎ 0625 22077)

MATHER-JACKSON, Lady; (Evelyn) Mary; er da of Lt-Col Sir Henry Kenyon Stephenson, 1 Bt, DSO, of Hassop Hall, Bakewell; *m* 1923, Sir Anthony Mather-Jackson, 6 Bt, JP, DL (d 1983); 3 da; *Style*— Lady Mather-Jackson; Archway House, Kirklington, Newark, Notts (☎ Southwell (0636) 2070)

MATHERS, Baroness; Jessie Newton; da of George Graham, JP, of Peebles and Edinburgh (decd); *m* 1940, as his 2 w, 1 and last Baron Mathers, Kt, PC, DL (d 1965); *Style*— The Rt Hon Lady Mathers; 50 Craiglea Drive, Edinburgh 10 (☎ 031 4477 555)

MATHERS, Sir Robert William; s of W Mathers; *b* 2 August 1928; *Educ* CEGS Qld; *m* 1967, Betty, da of W Greasley; 3 da; *Career* cr Retailers Assoc Qld 1952, past pres Footwear Retailers Assoc Qld 1960-63, chm Manpower Devpt Ctee of Retailers Assoc Qld 1972, chm and md Mathers Enterprises Ltd 1973-88, chm Kinney Shoes (Aust) Ltd 1988-; dir: The Nat Mutual Life Assoc of Australasia Ltd, Kidston Gold Mines Ltd; memb Fin Advsy Ctee XII Cwlth Games Australia (1982) Fndn Ltd 1977, tstee World Wildlife Fund Australia 1981-87; memb: Cncl of Griffith Univ 1978-88, Australiana Fund 1980, tstee Queensland Art Gallery 1983-87, Queensland Cncl of the Australian Bicentennial Authy 1980-89, Brisbane Rotary Club; dep chm Nat Fin Ctee of The Australian Stockman's Hall of Fame & Outback Heritage Centre 1984-, cncllr of Enterprise Australia since 1983, dep chm of the ctee 1985 to bid for Brisbane Olympics 1992, Econ Devpt Steering Ctee Brisbane 1985, 1986; FAMI, FRMIA, FAMI; kt 1981 (for serv to the retail ind and the community); *Style*— Sir Robert Mathers; 1 Wybelenna St, Kenmore, Qld 4069, Australia

MATHESON, Andrew Malcolm Hugh; o s of Capt Alexander Francis Matheson, RN (d 1976), and Frances Mary, *née* Heywood-Lonsdale; *b* 30 June 1942; *Educ* Gordonstoun, RAC Cirencester; *m* 1972, Judith Helen Mackay, da of (Aldred) Ian Mackay Baldry; 3 s (Alexander b 1974, Hamish b 1976, Philip b 1979); *Career* Gren Gds 1962-66; Asst Chief Cmmr for Scotland (Scout Assoc); ARICS 1970; *Style*— Andrew Matheson, Esq; Brahan, Dingwall, Ross-shire

MATHESON, Duncan; *b* 10 June 1941; *Educ* Rugby, Trinity Coll Cambridge (MA, LLM); *Career* barr Inner Temple 1965, rec Crown Ct 1985, practising SE circuit; *Style*— Duncan Matheson, Esq; 1 Crown Office Row, Temple, London EC4Y 7HH (☎ 01 353 1801, fax 01 583 1700)

MATHESON, Maj Fergus John; yr s of Gen Sir Torquhil George Matheson, 5 Bt, KCB, CMG (d 1963), and Lady Elizabeth Keppel, da of 8 Earl of Albemarle; hp to Btcy of bro, Sir Torquhil Alexander Matheson of Matheson, 6 Bt; *b* 22 Feb 1927; *Educ* Eton; *m* 17 May 1952, Hon Jean Elizabeth Mary, *née* Willoughby *qv*, da of 11 Baron Middleton, KG, MC; 1 s (Maj Alexander Matheson, Coldstream Gds b 1954, m 1983, *see* Michael Oswald, LVO), 2 da (Elizabeth Angela Matilda b 1953, Fiona Jean Lucia b 1962); *Career* serv 1 and 3 Bns Coldstream Gds (Palestine, N Africa and Germany) 1945-64, Adjt Mons OCS 1952-55, RARO Coldstream Gds 1964-; one of HM Bodyguard of Hon Corps of Gentlemen at Arms 1979-; *Clubs* Army & Navy; *Style*— Maj Fergus Matheson; Hedenhan Old Rectory, Bungay, Norfolk (☎ 050 844 218)

MATHESON, Hamish Clive Duncan; s of Maj James Matheson, of 66 Ouse Lea, Clifton, York, and Elizabeth Crawford, *née* Donaldson; *b* 6 Oct 1953; *Educ* Archbishop Holgates York, Univ of Liverpool (BSc); *m* 29 Oct 1977, Patricia Ewid Mary Matheson; 3 s (Benjamin James, Andrew George, Daniel Crawford); *Career* social work Scotland 1974-75, copywriter Dorlands 1978, creative dir Wagner Advtg 1982-; memb Writers Guild; *Recreations* film, reading, swimming; *Style*— Hamish Matheson, Esq; Hazel Bank, Miwster Rd, Busbridge, Godalming; 6 Queens Rd, Upper Hale, Farham, Surrey; Hickley's Ct, Farham, Surrey (☎ 0252 737 040)

MATHESON, Hon Mrs; Jean Elizabeth Mary; JP (1976); da of 11 Baron Middleton, KG, MC (d 1970), and Angela Florence Alfreda (d 1978); *b* 26 Jan 1928; *m* 1952, Maj Fergus John Matheson, *qv*; 1 s, 2 da; *Clubs* Army & Navy; *Style*— The Hon Mrs Matheson, JP; Hedenham Old Rectory, Bungay, Norfolk (☎ 050 844 218)

MATHESON, Sir (James Adam) Louis; KBE (1976, MBE 1944), CMG (1972); s of William Matheson (d 1927), and Lily Edith Matheson (d 1951); *b* 11 Feb 1912; *Educ* Bootham Sch York Eng, Manchester Univ (BSc, MSc), Birmingham Univ (PhD); *m* 1937, Audrey Elizabeth, 3 s; *Career* Capt Home Guard Eng; prof Civil Engrg Melbourne Univ 1947-50, Beyer prof of engrg Manchester Univ 1951-59, vice-chllr Monash Univ 1960-76, chllr Papua New Guinea Univ of Technol 1973-75, chm Australian Sci and Technol Cncl 1975-76, chm Newport Review Panel 1977; Kernot Mem Medal 1970, P N Russell Mem Medal 1977; Hon FICE, Hon FIEAust, FTS, FEng, Hon DSc Hong Kong, Hon LLD Univ: Manchester, Monash, Melbourne; *Books* Hyperstatic Structures (Vol I 1959, Vol II 1960), Still Learning (1980); *Recreations* music, woodcraft; *Clubs* Melbourne; *Style*— Sir Louis Matheson, KBE, CMG; 26/166 West Toorak Rd, South Yarra, Vic 3141, Australia (☎ 03 266 4957/03 787 1931)

MATHESON OF MATHESON, Maj Sir Torquhil Alexander; 6 Bt (UK 1882), of Lochalsh, Co Ross, DL for Somerset; s of Gen Sir Torquhil George Matheson, 5 Bt, KCB, CMG (d 1963) and Lady Elizabeth Matheson, ARRC (d 1986), o da of 8th Earl of Albemarle, GCVO, CB, VD, TD; *b* 15 August 1925; *Educ* Eton; *m* 1954, Serena Mary Francesca, da of Lt-Col Sir (James) Michael Peto, 2 Bt; 2 da; *Heir* bro, Maj Fergus John Matheson; *Career* serv WWII with 5 Bn Coldstream Gds, (despatches Palestine 1945-48) Maj 1959, seconded KAR (Kenya) 1961-64, ret 1964; Wiltshire Regt (TA) 1965-67; farmer; one of HM Body Guard of the Hon Corps of Gentlemen at Arms 1977-; succeeded as Chief of Clan Matheson 1975; DL for Somerset 1987; *Clubs* Army & Navy, Leander; *Style*— Maj Sir Torquhil Matheson of Matheson, Bt, DL; Standerwick Ct, Frome, Somerset

MATHEW, John Charles; (QC 1977); s of Sir Theobald Mathew, KBE, MC, (d 1964), of 7 Cranley Mansions, London SW7, and Phyllis Helen, *née* Russell (d 1982); *b* 3 May 1927; *Educ* Beaumont Coll; *m* 6 Sept 1952, (Jennifer) Jane, da of Reginald Bousfield Lagden, OBE, MC (d 1944), of Calcutta; 2 da (Sally b 1955, Amanda b 1957); *Career* RN 1945-47; barr Lincoln's Inn 1949-, jr Prosecuting Counsel to the Crown 1959 (sr 1964-67); *Recreations* golf, tennis, cinema; *Clubs* Garrick; *Style*— John Mathew, Esq, QC; 47 Abingdon Villas, London W8 (☎ 01 937 7535, fax 01 353 0075, telex 8956431 ANTON G)

MATHEW, Olga; *née* HSH Princess Olga Romanoff; da of HH Prince Andrew of Russia (eld s of HIH The Grand Duke Alexander, 4 s of HIH The Grand Duke Mikhail, 4 s of Tsar Nicholas I of Russia) by his 2 w, Nadine, da of Lt-Col Herbert McDougall, of Belgravia; *b* 8 April 1950; *m* 1975, Thomas Mathew, 2 s of Francis Mathew, formerly with The Times; 2 s (Nicholas b 1976, Francis Alexander b 1978), 1 da (Alexandra b 1981); *Style*— HSH Princess Olga Romanoff, Mrs Thomas Mathew; Welford House, nr Rugby, Northants

MATHEW, Theobald David; s of Robert Mathew (d 1954), and Joan Alison, da of Sir George Young, Bt, MVO; *b* 7 April 1942; *Educ* Downside Abbey, Balliol Coll Oxford (MA); *Career* Green staff offr at Investiture of HRH Prince of Wales 1969, Rouge Dragon Pursuivant of Arms 1970, Windsor Herald of Arms 1978-; dep tres College of Arms; OStJ 1986; *Recreations* sailing, cricket, music, sketching; *Clubs* Athenaeum, MCC, Middlesex CCC, Royal Harwich Yacht; *Style*— Theobald Mathew, Esq; 76 Clifton Hill, London NW8 (☎ 01 624 8448)

MATHEWSON, George Ross; CBE; s of George Mathewson, of Craiglynn, 42 Fairies Rd, Perth, by his w Charlotte Gordon, *née* Ross; *b* 14 May 1940; *Educ* Perth Acad, St Andrews Univ (BSc, PhD), Canisius Coll Buffalo NY (MBA); *m* 1966, Sheila Alexandra Graham, da of Eon Bennett (d 1975), Bridge of Earn, Perth; 2 s; *Career* asst lectr St

Andrews Univ 1964-67; with Bell Aerospace (Buffalo, NY) in res and devpt and avionics engrg 1967-72, joined ICFC Edinburgh 1972, area mangr Aberdeen 1974, asst gen mangr and dir 1979; chief exec and memb Scottish Devpt Agency 1981-87; dir strategic planning and development, the Royal Bank of Scotland Gp plc 1987-; Hon LLD Dundee 1983; *Recreations* rugby, golf, business; *Clubs* New (Edinburgh); *Style*— George Mathewson, Esq, CBE; Larach-Beg, Corsee Rd, Banchory, Kincardineshire (☎ 033 02 3482); The Royal Bank of Scotland Gp plc, 42 St Andrew Square, Edinburgh EH2 2YE (☎ 031 556 8555)

MATHIAS, Julian Robert; s of Anthony Robert Mathias (d 1973), of London, and Cecily Mary Agnes, *née* Hughes; *b* 7 Sept 1943; *Educ* Downside, Univ Coll Oxford (MA); *Career* mangr Hill Samuel and Co Ltd 1964-71, ptnr Buckmaster and Moore 1971-81, dir Foreign and Colonial Mgmnt Ltd 1981-; *Recreations* wine tasting, bridge, golf, shooting; *Clubs* Boodle's, City of London, Berkshire GC; *Style*— Julian Mathias, Esq; Foreign and Colonial Managment Ltd, 1 Laurence Pountney Hill, London EC4R 0BA (☎ 01 623 4680, fax 01 626 4947, telex 886197, 8811745)

MATHIAS, Dr Peter; CBE (1984); s of John Samuel Mathias (d 1960), and Marion Helen, *née* Love; *b* 10 Jan 1928; *Educ* Colston's Hosp, Jesus Coll Cambridge (BA, MA), Harvard Univ; *m* 5 April 1958, (Elizabeth) Ann, da of Robert Blackmore (d 1979), of Bath; 2 s (Sam b 3 Mar 1959, Henry b 15 May 1961), 1 da (Sophie b 25 July 1964); *Career* Cambridge Univ: history lectr 1955-68, res fell Jesus Coll 1952-55, fell and dir history studies Queens' Coll 1955-68 (tutor 1957-68), sr proctor 1965-66; Chicele prof econ hist Oxford Univ 1969-87 (fell All Souls Coll); LittD (Oxon) 1985, DLitt (Cantab) 1987; The Master Downing Coll Cambridge 1987-; hon tres Econ Hist Soc 1967-88, curator Bodleian Library 1972-87, pres Int Econ Hist Assoc 1974-78 (hon pres 1978-), vice-pres Royal Historical Soc 1975-80, hon tres Br Acad 1979-, chm int advsy ctee Buckingham Univ 1979-84, chm advsy panel Hist Med Wellcome Tst 1980-88, memb advsy bd Res Cncls 1983-86, pres Business Archives Cncl 1984- (vice-pres 1980-84, chm 1967-72); visiting prof: Toronto Univ (1961), Delhi Univ (1967), California Univ Berkeley (1967), Pennsylvania Univ (1972), Virginia Univ (Gildersleeve prof) Columbia (1972), John Hopkins Univ (1979), Natal Univ (1980), Australian National Univ (1981), Geneva Univ (1986); memb syndic Fitzwilliam Musuem Cambridge 1987-; Hon Litt D (Buckingham Univ 1985), Hon D Litt (Birmingham Univ 1988); memb Econ Hist Soc 1951-, fell Royal Hist Soc 1972, FBA 1977;; *Books* The Brewing Industry in England 1700-1830(1959), English Trade Tokens(1962), Retailing Revolution(1967), The First Industrial Nation(1969, 1983), The Transformation of England(1979), Science and Society (ed and contrib, 1972); *Recreations* travel; *Clubs* Utd Oxford and Cambridge Univ; *Style*— Dr Peter Mathias, CBE; The Master's Lodge, Downing College, Cambridge CB2 1DQ (☎ 0223 334 868)

MATHIAS, Sir Richard Hughes; 2 Bt (UK 1917), of Vaendre Hall, St Mellons, Co Monmouth; s of Sir Richard Mathias, 1 Bt (d 1942); *b* 6 April 1905; *Educ* Eton, Balliol Oxford; *m* 1, 1937 (m dis 1960), Gladys Cecilia Turton, da of Edwin Hart, of New Hextalls, Bletchingley, Surrey; 2 da; m 2, 1960, Mrs Elizabeth Baird Murray (d 1972), da of Dr Miles of Hendrescythan, Glamorgan; m 3, 1973, Mrs Hilary Mary Vines (d 1975), da of William Howells, of Cardiff; *Heir* none; *Career* serv RAF 1940-46, staff appointment Air Miny 1942-46; memb London Stock Exchange; memb cncl: Royal Nat Mission to Deep Sea Fishermen 1953-54, Hurstpierpoint Coll 1965- (chm 1967-74); fell of Corpn of SS Mary and Nicolas (Woodard) Schs 1965-80; *Clubs* Reform; *Style*— Sir Richard Mathias, Bt; 8 Oakwood Ct, Abbotsbury Rd, London W14 8JU

MATHIAS, Prof William James; CBE (1985); s of James Hughes Mathias (d 1969), of Llwynbedw, Whitland, Dyfed, and Marian, *née* Evans (d 1980); *b* 1 Nov 1934; *Educ* Whitland GS, Univ Coll of Wales Aberystwyth (BMus), RAM Wales (DMus); *m* 17 Sept 1959, (Margaret) Yvonne, da of Mervyn Collins (d 1967); 1 da (Rhiannon b 10 Oct 1968); *Career* lectr in music Univ Coll N Wales Bangor 1959-68, sr lectr in music Univ of Edinburgh 1968-69, prof and head of music dept Univ Coll N Wales Bngor 1970-88; freelance composer and conductor 1988-; pres Incorporated Soc of Musicians 1988-89; vice pres: Br Arts Festivals Assoc 1988-, Royal Coll of Organsits 1985; artictic dir N Wales Music Festival 1972-; govr: Nat Museum of Wales 1973-78, Nat Youth Orchestra of GB 1985-; memb: Welsh Arts Cncl 1974-81 (chm music ctee 1982-88), music advsy ctee Br Cncl 1974-83, Br Section ISCM 1976-80, BBC Central Music Advsy Ctee 1979-86, Welsh advsy ctee Br Cncl 1979-, cncl Composers' Guild of GB; pubns incl: Piano Concerto No 2 1964, Piano Concerto No 3 1970, Harpsichord Concerto 1971, Harp Concerto No 2 1973, Clarinet Concerto 1976, Horn Concerto 1984, Organ Concerto 1984; orchestral compositions incl: Symphony No 1 1969, Festival Overture 1973, Celtic Dances 1974, Vistas 1977, Vivat Regina (for brass band) 1978, Requiescat 1979, Dance Variations 1979, Symphony No 2 (Summer Music, cmmnd by Royal Liverpool Philharmonic Soc) 1983, Ceremonial Fanfare (for two trumpets) 1983, Anniversary Dances (for centenary of Univ Coll Bangor) 1985, Carnival of Wales 1987; chamber compositions incl: String Quartet 1970, Capriccio for flute and piano 1971, Wind Quintet 1976, Concertino 1977, Zodiac Trio 1977, Clarinet Sonatina 1978; choral and vocal compositions incl: A Vision of Time and Eternity (for contralto and piano) 1974, Ceremony after a Fire Raid 1975, The Fields of Praise (for tenor and piano) 1977, A Royal Garland 1978, Shakespeare Songs 1980, Songs of William Blake (for mezzo-soprano and orchestra0 1980, Rex Gloriae (four Latin motets) 1981, The Echoing Green 1985, O Aula Nabilis (for opening of orangery at Westonbirt Sch by TRH Prince and Princess of Wales) 1985, Veni Sancte Spiritus (Hereford Three Choirs Festival) 1985, Gogoneddawg Arglwydd (for Nat Youth Choir of Wales) 1985; numerous organ compositions; anthems and church music incl: O Sing unto the Lord 1965, Make a Joyful Noise 1965, Missa Brevis 1974, Arise Shine 1978, Let the People Praise Thee O God (anthem composed for the wedding of the Prince and Princess of Wales) 1981, Missa Aedis Christi-in memoriam William Walton 1984, Salve Regina 1986, As Truly as God is our Father 1987; opera: The Servants (libretto by Iris Murdoch) 1980; Hon DMus Westminster Choir Coll Princeton USA 1987; LRAM 1958, FRAM 1965; *Clubs* Athenauem, Cardiff and Co; *Style*— Prof William Mathias, CBE; Y Graigwen, Cadnant Rd, Menai Bridge, Anglesey, Gwynedd LL59 5NG (☎ 0248 712 392)

MATHIESON, Ian Douglas; s of Robert James Mathieson (d 1958), of Harrow, and Violet Lilian, *née* Jones (d 1981); *b* 1 Oct 1942; *Educ* Harrow Weald GS, Coll of Estate Mgmnt Univ of London (BSc), UCL (DipTP); *m* 19 Aug 1967, Lesley, da of Jack Stanley Glass, of Pinner; 2 s (Mark James b 1973, John Robert b 1977); *Career* chartered surveyor in local govt and private practice until 1973, md Commercial Union Properties Ltd 1984- (property investmt mangr 1974-80, dir 1980-), dep md Commercial Union Asset Mgmnt Ltd 1987-; memb Wycombe Dist Health Authy 1983-, Freedom City of London 1986; ARICS 1967, FRICS 1985; *Clubs* RAC, Overseas League; *Style*— Ian Mathieson, Esq; Schomberg Ho, 80-82 Pall Mall, London SW1Y 5HF (☎ 01 283 7500, ext 3558, fax 01 283 7500)

MATHIESON, Jeffrey George; OBE (1988); s of Walter Douglas Mathieson, OBE, MC (d 1983), of Middleton Thatch, Freshwater, IOW, and Florence Winifred, *née* Burley (d 1988); *b* 17 Feb 1925; *Educ* Whitgift Sch Croydon; *m* 16 Sept 1961, Patricia (d 1988), da of Fredrick Murton Faers (d 1975); 2 da (Jacqueline b 31 May 1963, Ann b 12 Sept 1966); *Career* RAF 1943-47, Navigator/Wireless Operator (Air Crew); asst valuer Corpn of Birmingham 1952-54, asst estates offr Basildon Devpt Corpn 1954-59; Corpn of London: asst estates offr 1959-63, princ asst estates offr 1963-79, dep city surveyor 1979-; Freeman City of London 1970, Liveryman Worshipful Co of Chartered Surveyors 1982; FRICS 1976; *Recreations* golf, gardening, cooking; *Style*— Jeffrey Mathieson, Esq, OBE; 2 Sandown Close, Tunbridge Wells, Kent TN2 4RL (☎ 089282 2839); Corporation of London, PO Box 270, Guildhall, London EC2P 2EJ (☎ 01 260 1502, fax 01 260 1119)

MATHIESON, Kenneth Alasdair; s of Ronald Alexander Mathieson, of Salisbury Wilts, and Sheila Mary Browning, *née* Harris, of E Grafton, Marlborough, Wilts; *b* 22 Sept 1945; *Educ* King Alfred Sch Wantage, Bath Univ BSc (1971), followed by BArch (1974); *m* 13 June 1970 (m diss), Rosemary, da of Kenneth Faire, Swindon, Wilts; *Career* founded Mathieson Cox Assocs 1975, left 1984 to concentrate on own property devpts; formed West Hendred Properties 1983; RIBA; *Recreations* food, wine (have own wine bar), photography, travel; *Clubs* Mensa (Oxford branch); *Style*— Kenneth A Mathieson, Esq; 10 High St, Highworth, Wilts (☎ 0793 763025); Silver St, Bourton, Oxfordshire; Calle Alsabini 56, Figurettes, Ibiza, Spain; The Old Pumphouse, Cnwc Y Llo Rd, Builth Wells, Powys

MATHIESON, William Allan Cunningham; CB (1970), CMG (1955), MBE (1945); s of Rev William Miller Mathieson (d 1935), of Scotland, and Elizabeth Cunningham, *née* Reid (d 1957); *b* 22 Feb 1916; *Educ* Dundee HS, Edinburgh Univ (MA), King's Coll Cambridge; *m* 18 May 1946, Elizabeth Frances, da of Henry Marvell Carr, RA, RP (d 1970), of London; 2 s (Alexander b 1947, Rhoderick Henry b 1951); *Career* RA 1940-45, Maj Europe; Colonial Off 1939-45, asst sec 1949, cnsllr colonial affairs, Br Mission to the UN New York 1951-54; head E Africa Dept Colonial Off 1955-58, min of educn Labour and Lands Govt of Kenya 1958-60, under-sec Dept of Tech Co-Operation 1961-64, min of Overseas Dvpt 1964, dep sec 1968-75, sr conslt UN Devpt Prog New York 1976-81, memb exec bd UNESCO 1968-74, memb bd of tstees, Int Wheat and Maize Improvement Centre Mexico 1976-86, memb and chm bd of tstees Int Serv for Nat Agric Res The Hague 1979-84, memb Governing Cncl Int Centre of Insect Physiology and Ecology Nairobi 1983-; *Recreations* gardening, angling, photography, archaeology, travel; *Style*— William Mathieson, Esq; 13 Sydney House, Woodstock Rd, Bedford Park, London W4 1DP (☎ 01 994 1330)

MATSON, Malcolm John; s of Gp Capt Jack Norman Matson, of Hinton Wood, Bournemouth, and Winnie Ruth, *née* Parker; *b* 4 Oct 1943; *Educ* Strodes Sch, Trinity Coll of Music, Univ of Nottingham (BA), Harvard Univ USA (MBA); *m* 13 Sept 1969 (m dis 1988), Judith Helen Welby, da of Arthur Kenneth Colley (d 1986); 2 s (Thomas Daniel Blandford b 5 Feb 1975, Henry Samuel Quarrington b 21 Dec 1978), 1 da (Cecilia Elspeth Adean b 26 Feb 1980); *Career* J Walter Thompson 1966-69, Winston Churchill Fell 1969, mgmnt conslt 1972-84, non exec chm Silverbrands Ltd 1976-, gen comm mangr Westland Helicopters Ltd 1978-81, dir Assoc Helicopter Conslts 1983-, conslt MMG Patricof (venture capital) 1982-84, fndr and chm Nat Telecable Mgmnt Ltd 1984-; memb cncl PITCOM (Parly Inf Techno Ctee); Freeman City of London 1967, Liveryman Worshipful Co of: Coopers 1967, Glass Sellers 1988; FBIM 1982; *Recreations* music, motor cycling, thinking, walking; *Clubs* Lansdowne; *Style*— Malcolm Matson, Esq; Ramsam, Priestlands Lane, Sherborne, Dorset DT9 4EY (☎ 01 493 493 8388, fax 01 323 4890)

MATTHEW, Richard Anthony; s of Donald Matthew, of Bournemouth, and Agnes Freda, *née* Wood; *b* 29 July 1948; *Educ* Bournemouth Sch, Oxford Poly (BSc); *m* 11 June 1977, Jane Vera, da of Godfrey Richard George Judd, of Bournemouth; 1 s (Andrew b 1979), 2 da (Clare b 1982, Sally b 1984); *Career* slr; *Recreations* soccer, running; *Clubs* Lanz Sportz Centre, Burlington Sports; *Style*— Richard A Matthew, Esq; 34 Walsingham Dene, Littledown, Bournemouth; Matthew & Matthew, 187/189 Seabourne Rd, Southbourne, Bournemouth (☎ 0202 431943 fax 0202 420054)

MATTHEWMAN, His Hon Judge; Keith Matthewman; QC (1979); s of Lt Frank Matthewman (d 1976), and Elizabeth, *née* Lang (d 1985); *b* 8 Jan 1936; *Educ* Long Eaton GS, Univ Coll London (LLB); *m* 1962, Jane, da of Thomas Maxwell (d 1957); 1 s; *Career* barr Middle Temple 1960; commercial asst (int div) Rolls Royce Ltd 1961-62; practice at the Bar 1962-83 (Midland Circuit and later Midland-Oxford Circuit), rec Crown Ct 1979-83, circuit judge (Midland and Oxford) 1983-; memb Heanor UDC 1960-63; memb of the Ctee of The Cncl of Her Majesty's Circuit Judges 1984-89, memb Nottinghamshire probation ctee 1986-; *Recreations* gardening, reading; *Clubs* United Servs (Nottingham); *Style*— His Hon Judge Matthewman, QC; Nottingham Crown Ct, Nottingham

MATTHEWS, Dr Aubrey Royston; s of Douglas Royston Matthews and Phyllis Mary Matthews; *b* 14 Nov 1931; *Educ* Queen Elizabeth's Hosp Bristol, Bristol Univ; *m* 1960, Hazel, *née* Ellis; 3 children; *Career* Shell Int Petroleum Ltd: Venezuela 1958-62, Trinidad 1962-66, USA 1967-68, UK 1968-73, Netherlands 1973-74; dir Dr Colin Phipps & Ptnrs Ltd (Conslts) 1974-79, tech dir Clyde Petroleum plc 1979-; *Recreations* opera, cricket, theatre; *Clubs* Reform, MCC; *Style*— Dr Aubrey Matthews; Folly End, Cook's Folly Rd, Sneyd Park, Bristol (☎ 0272 683282); Clyde Petroleum plc, Coddington Ct, Coddington, Ledbury, Herefordshire HR8 1JL (☎ 053 186 811, telex 35320)

MATTHEWS, Col Denis Holman; s of Ben Matthews (d 1970), of Dorset, and Susan, *née* Holman; *b* 18 May 1922; *Educ* Downside, London Univ, London Hosp (MRCS, LRCP); *m* 4 April 1961, Ann Margaret, da of Capt Maurice Symington OBE (d 1975), of Oporto; 1 s (Mark b 1962), 2 da (Emma b 1963, Georgina (twin) b 1963); *Career* Capt Rifle Bde 1942-46, regular cmmn RHG (The Blues), Sugn Maj RMO RHG and Household Cavalry Regt 1957-65, Lt Col RAMC DADMS Southern Cmd 1965-67; ADMS: M East Cmd 1967, Home Cos Dist 1968; CO: 15 Fd Ambulance 1969-71, Catterick Mil Hosp 1971-74; Col ADMS London Dist and HQ Household Div 1974-77 ret 1977; Capt of Invalids Royal Hosp Chelsea 1985, confracter Abbey of St Gregory the Great Downside 1939; *Style*— Col Denis Matthews; Stud House, Pimperne, Nr

Blandford, Forum, Dorset (☎ 0258 453415)

MATTHEWS, Dr Geoffrey Vernon Townsend; OBE (1986); s of Geoffrey Tom Matthews (d 1943), of Northwood, Middx, and Muriel Ivy Matthews (d 1984); *b* 16 June 1923; *Educ* Bedford Sch, Christ's Coll Cambridge (MA, PhD); *m* 1, 6 July 1946 (m dis 4 May 1961), Josephine, da of Col Alured Charles Lowther O'Shea Bilderbeck, of Bexhill-on-Sea; 1 s (Vincent Anthony b 1951), 1 da (Rosalind Josephine b 1953); m 2, 2 Jan 1964 (m dis 3 Jan 1978), Janet, da of William Kear, of Sevenoaks; m3, 26 Jan 1980, Mary Elizabeth, da of William Evans, of Vancouver; 1 s (Alexander William Geoffrey b 1983), 1 da (Catriona Elizabeth b 1981); *Career* Flt Lt and Sci Offr RAFVR 1943-46, serv operational res sections (Bomber Cmd, SE Asia Cmd, Air Miny); dep dir and dir of res and conservation Wildfowl Tst Slimbridge 1955-88, special lectr Bristol Univ 1956-88, hon professorial fell Univ Coll Cardiff 1970-88, dir Int Waterfont Res Bureau 1969-88, author of numerous papers on bird migration/orientation and wetland and waterfowl conservation; vice pres Br Ornithologists Union 1972-74 (union medal 1980), pres Assoc for the Study of Animal Behaviour; memb advsy ctee on birds, Nature Conservancy Cncl, Anglo-Soviet Enviromental Protection Agreement; memb Severn Barrage ctee Dept of Energy 1978-81, chm enviromental advsy panel Severn Tidal Power Gp 1987-89, memb many other ctees; corr fell: American Ornithologists Union 1969, Swiss Soc for Bird Study 1975; FIBiol; Officier De Orde Van De Gouden Ark (Netherlands, 1987); *Books* Bird Navigation (1955, 2 ed 1968), also author of chapters in a number of multi-authored books; *Recreations* listening to music, collecting bird stamps, collecting fossils, DIY; *Clubs* Victory; *Style*— Dr Geoffrey Matthews, OBE; Uplands, 32 Tetbury St, Minchinhampton, Stroud, Glos GL6 9JH (☎ 0453 884 769)

MATTHEWS, Jeffery Edward; s of Henry Edward Matthews (d 1960), and Sybil Frances, *née* Cooke (d 1951); *b* 3 April 1928; *Educ* Alleyn's, Brixton Sch of Building (NDD); *m* 12 Sept 1953, (Sylvia Lilian) Christine, da of Cecil Herbert William Hoar (d 1974), 1 s (Rory b 1956), 1 da (Sarah Jane b 1958); *Career* graphic designer J Edward Sander 1949-52, pt/t tutor 1952-55, lettering and calligraphy assesor SIAD 1970-; designs for the PO: decimal 'To Pay' labels 1971, font of numerals for definitive 1968, definitives for Scotland Wales NI and IOM 1971, Royal Silver Wedding, 1972, 25th Anniversary of the Coronation 1978, London 1980, 80th Birthday of the Queen Mother 1980, Christmas 1980, Wedding of Prince Charles and Lady Diana Spencer 1981, Quincentenary of the College of Arms 1984, 60th Birthday of the Queen 1986, Wedding of Prince Andrew and Sarah Ferguson 1986, Order of the Thistle Tercentenary of Revival 1987; also: first day covers, postmarks, presentation packs, souvenir books, and posters; other work includes: title banner lettering and coat of arms Sunday Times 1968, cover design and lettering for official programme Royal Wedding 1981, The Royal Mint commemorative medal Order of the Thistle 1987, official heraldry and symbols HMSO, hand-drawn lettering COI, calligraphy, packaging, promotion and book binding designs, logotypes, brand images and hand-drawn lettering; for various firms incl: Unicover Corp USA, Harrison & Sons Ltd, Metal Box Co, DRG, Reader's Digest Assoc Ltd, Encyclopaedia Britannica Int Ltd, ICI, H R Higgins Ltd; work exhibited in A History of Bookplates in Britain and at V & A Museum 1979; Citizen & Goldsmith of London (Freedom by Patrimony) 1949; FCSD 1978, FRSA 1987, AIBD 1951; *Books* contributor to: Designers In Britain (1964, 1971), 45 Wood-Engravers (1982), Royal Mail Year Book (1984, 86, 87), ; *Recreations* furniture restoration, playing the guitar, gardening, DIY; *Style*— Jeffery Matthews, Esq; 46 Kings Hall Road, Beckenham, Kent BR3 1LS

MATTHEWS, (Edwin) Jimmy (James Thomas); TD; s of Lt Edwin Martin Matthews (ka 1917), and Emily Ethel, *née* Thomas (d 1965); *b* 2 May 1915; *Educ* Glenhow Prep Sch, Saltburn by the Sea, Sedbergh Yorks; *m* 20 Sept 1939; *Heir* Katherine Mary, da of Joseph Alfred Hirst (decd); 2 da (Julie b 1943, Prudence b 1945); *Career* WWII RA (TA) Maj serv UK, France, Belgium (Dunkirk) 1939-46; slr 1938, ptnr Chadwick Son & Nicholson 1946-50, area sec No 6 (W Midland) Legal Aid Ctee of Law Soc 1950-56, sec of Law Soc for Legal Aid and Contentious Business 1956-65, toured Legal Aid Offs in USA for Ford Fndn 1953, memb Cncl Br Acad of Forensic Scis 1965-68, special conslt to NPBI 1965-68, memb Lord Chllrs Advsy Ctee on Legal Aid 1972-77, chief Taxing Master of the Supreme Ct 1979-83 (master 1965-78); contrib to: Halsbury Laws of England, Atkins Ct Forms, Matthews and Oulton on Legal Aid Advice, The Supreme Ct Practice; lectr for College of Law and commercial organisations 1983-; *Recreations* flyfishing, gardening, theatre, french wine; *Style*— E J T Matthews, Esq, TD; 2 Downside Rd, Winchester SO22 5LU (☎ 0962 62478)

MATTHEWS, Prof John; s of John Frederick Matthews (d 1973), of Aylesbury, Bucks, and Catherine Edith, *née* Terry (d 1979); *b* 4 July 1930; *Educ* Royal Latin Sch Buckingham, Chartered Engr 1980, Chartered Physicist 1984; *m* 20 Feb 1982, Edna Agnes Luckhurst, da of Charles Ernest Stratton, of Southwark, London; 2 da (Jane Katherine b 1956, Shirley Rose (Mrs Calvert) b 1959); *Career* scientific offr GEC res laboratories 1951-59; Nat Inst of Agric Engrg 1959-84: head tractor and cultivation dept 1967-82, asst dir mktg 1982-84; dir AFRC Inst of Engrg Res 1984-; former pres Inst of Agric Engrs; FInstP, FIAgrE, FErgS, FRAgS, memb ASAE, CEng 1980, CPhys 1984; *Clubs* Lions Int; *Style*— Prof John Matthews; Church Cottage, Tilsworth, Leighton Buzzard, Beds LU7 9PN (☎ 0525 210204); AFRC Inst Engrg Res, Wrest Park, Silsoe, Beds (☎ 0525 60000, 0525 61436, fax 0525 60156, telex 825808 AFRCER G)

MATTHEWS, John Chester; s of Leonard Matthews, and Olive, *née* Chester; *b* 1 May 1920; *Educ* Chigwell Sch, Greshams Sch, Guy's Hosp London (MRCS, LRCP, LMSSA, LDS); *m* 27 Feb 1954 (m dis 1974), Ann Barbara, da of John Dudley Paine Hunt, of The Cottage, Knowsley Way, Hildenboroygh, Kent; 2 s (Richard Chester b 1957, Peter John Gunn b 1958), 1 da (Susan Ann b 1956); *Career* Guy's Hosp London: Medicine 1939-45, Dental Surgery 1950-53; sr med offr Princess Alice meml Hosp Eastbourne 1945, naval surgn MN 1945-50, asst dental surgn Chichester and Wimpole St London, Princ dental surgn, Bath, Som: 1954-75, Student of graphology 1982-; MRCS 1945; Freeman Worshipful Co of Apothecaries; FRCS soc of Apothecaries of London, LRCP 1945, LMSSA, RCA 1953, LDS 1953; *Recreations* Classical Music, Graphological Analysis, Laughing; *Clubs* Br Med Assoc, Br Inst of Graphology; *Style*— Dr John Matthews; Bell Cottage, 20 Bell St, Shaftesbury, Dorset (☎ 0747 51668)

MATTHEWS, John Waylett; s of Lt Percy Victor Matthews (d 1970), and Phyllis Edith, *née* Waylett; *b* 22 Sept 1944; *Educ* Forest Sch; *m* 27 May 1972, Lesley Marjorie, da of Alastair Herbert Menzies Halliday; 2 s (Jonathan b 1975, Edward b 1977), 1 da (Anna b 1981); *Career* Dixon, Wilson and Co 1962-69, N M Rothschild and Sons 1969-71, exec dir Co Natwest Ltd 1971-, non-exec dir Perry Gp plc 1979-, dep chm Beazer plc; FCA;; *Recreations* golf, squash, hockey, tennis, bridge; *Clubs* Crail GS, Chigwell GC; *Style*— John Matthews, Esq; 52 Ollards Grove, Loughon, Essex (☎ 01 508 9060); Co Natwest Ltd, Drapers Gdns, 12 Throgmorton Ave, London EC2P 2ES (☎ 01 826 8219, fax 01 638 6660, telex 882121)

MATTHEWS, (Horatio) Keith; CMG (1964), MBE (1946), JP (IOW 1975); s of Horatio Matthews (d 1970), and Ruth Fryer McCurry (d 1987); *b* 4 April 1917; *Educ* Epsom Coll, Gonville and Caius Coll Cambridge (BA); *m* 1940, Jean Andree, da of Maj Wm Batten (d 1934); 2 da (Julia, Clare); *Career* Indian Civil Serv Madras 1940-47; FO 1948, 1 sec Lisbon 1949, Bucharest 1951, FO 1953, Imperial Def Coll 1955, Political Off ME Forces Cyprus 1956, cnsllr 1958, UK High Cmmn Canberra 1959, political advsr GOC Berlin 1961, Corps of Insprs Dip Serv 1964, min Moscow 1966, high cmmnr Ghana 1968, under-sec gen UN NY 1971, sr directing staff Royal Coll of Def Studies 1973; ret 1974; *Clubs* Bembridge Sailing; *Style*— Keith Matthews, Esq, CMG, MBE, JP; Elm House, Bembridge, IOW PO35 5UA (☎ 0983 872327)

MATTHEWS, Maj-Gen Michael; CB (1984); s of William Matthews (d 1984), of Byways, Chagford, Devon, and Marjorie Hilda Matthews; *b* 22 April 1930; *Educ* Kings Coll Taunton, RMA Sandhurst; *m* 1955, Elspeth Rosemary, da of late Sir John Maclure, 3 Bt OBE; 2 s (Graeme, James), 2 da (Nichola, Julie); *Career* cmmnd RE 1951; dir Personal Servs (Army) 1980, Engr-in-Chief (Army) 1983, sec to TA Cncl 1986; Companion Inst of Civil Engrs, FBIM; *Clubs* Army & Navy, MCC; *Style*— Maj-Gen Michael Matthews, CB; c/o Lloyds Bank, Chagford, Newton Abbot, Devon

MATTHEWS, Michael Gough; s of late Cecil Gough Matthews, and Amelia Eleanor Mary Matthews; *b* 12 July 1931; *Educ* Chigwell Sch, RCM; *Career* pianist; RCM: dir jnr dept and prof of piano 1972-75, registrar 1975, vice-dir 1978-84, dir 1985-; dip of honour and prize Chopin Int Piano Competition 1955, Italian Govt scholarship 1956, Chopin fellowship Warsaw 1959; memb: governing ctee Royal Choral Soc, Nat Youth Orchestra, Royal Philharmonic Soc, mgmnt bd London Int String Quartet Competition; vice-pres: Royal College of Organists, Nat Youth Choir, Herbert Howells Soc, Hon FLCM 1976, hon RAM 1979; ARCO, ARCM, FRCM 1972, FRSAMD 1986, hon GSM, FRSA; *Recreations* gardening; *Clubs* Athenaeum; *Style*— Michael Gough Matthews, Esq; c/o RCM, Prince Consort Rd, London SW7 2BS

MATTHEWS, Neil Howard; s of Howard Matthews, and Gwyneth Thompson, *née* Davies; *b* 2 August 1948; *Educ* Duffryn G, Port Talbot Welsh Sch of Architecture, Cardiff; BSc, BArch; *m* 29 July 1972, Averil Susan, da of Flt-Offr RAF Ronald Abbott, of 132 Bolgoed Rd, Pontardulais, W Glam; 1 da (Lydia Dee Matthews b 1978), 1 s (Jack Timothy Rhys Matthews b 1986); *Career* architect/developer; pncpl Neil H Matthews Assoc, md ASA Project Mgmnt Ltd 1983; Jabbeam Ltd 1985, Mitre UNK Ltd 1985-; Holwell Property co 1986; Rhodethorn Dvpts Ltd, 8, Croftstone Ltd 1987; played for Bridgend, Glam Wanderers, Llanelli & Aberawn (rugby); 11/21 swimmer of the year BLDSA, selected GB team scheld, Holland, School championships (swimming), Wales 11/21 water polo team 1967, John Williams prizwinner WSA 1972; *Recreations* squash, swimming; *Style*— Neil Matthews, Esq; Frongelli House, Llanedi, Pontarducais SA4 1YR (☎ 0792 883251); 2 Station Rd, Pontarducais

MATTHEWS, Sir Peter Alec; Hon AO (1980); s of Maj Alec Matthews; *b* 21 Sept 1922; *Educ* Vancouver, Oundle; *m* 1946, Sheila Bunting; 4 s, 1 da; *Career* serv WWII, Maj RE; dir: Vickers Australia 1971-, Lloyds Bank 1974-, Br Electric Traction 1976-, Sun Alliance & London Insur 1979-, Lloyds and Scottish 1983-; chm: Lloyds Bank (Central London Regional Bd) 1978-, Pegler-Hattersley 1979 (dir 1977-), Engrg Industs Cncl 1980-, Vickers 1980-84 (md 1970-79); pres Engrg Employers' Fedn 1982-84; memb IOD; hon fell Univ Coll London 1982; FBIM, FRSA; kt 1975; *Style*— Sir Peter Matthews, AO; Ladycross House, Dormansland, Surrey RH7 6NP (☎ 034287 650)

MATTHEWS, Sir Peter Jack; CVO (1978), OBE (1974), QPM (1970), DL (Surrey 1981); s of Thomas Matthews; *b* 25 Dec 1917; *Educ* Blackridge Public Sch W Lothian; *m* 1944, Margaret, da of Cecil Levett; 1 s; *Career* chief constable Surrey 1968-82 (Suffolk 1967-68, E Suffolk 1965-67), with Met Police 1946-65 (seconded to Cyprus 1955, joined 1937), serv WWII as Flt Lt & pilot RAF; chm Home Off Standing Ctee on Police Dogs 1978-; Int pres: Int Police Assn 1966-70 (Br pres 1964-70); specialist advsr Def Select ctee House of Commons 1983-; ACPO rep of Interpol 1977-80; CBIM; kt 1981; *Clubs* RAF (Piccadilly, London); *Style*— Sir Peter Matthews, CVO, OBE, QPM, DL

MATTHEWS, Richard Bonnar; CBE (1971), QPM (1965); s of Charles Richard Matthews (d 1960), of Dudley House, Marine Parade, Worthing, and Beatrice Alexandra, *née* Bonnar (d 1975); *b* 18 Dec 1915; *Educ* Stowe; *m* 1 Jan 1943, Joan Emily, da of Basil Worsley (d 1978), of The Pound, Henstridge, Somerset; 2 da (Miranda b 22 Jan 1944, Rosemary b 23 Dec 1946); *Career* WW11 serv Lt RNVR 1939-45; Met Police 1936-; asst chief constable E Sussex 1954-56; chief constable: Cornwall and Isles of Scilly 1956-64, Warwickshire 1964-76; chm Traffic Ctee Assoc of Chief Police Offrs 1973-76, memb Williams Ctee on obscenity and Film censorship 1977-79, chm bds for Civil Serv cmmn 1979-85; *Recreations* fishing, skiing, gardening; *Clubs* Naval; *Style*— Richard Matthews, Esq, CBE, QPM; Smoke Acre, Great Bedwyn, Marlborough, Wiltshire SN8 3LP (☎ 0672 870 584)

MATTHEWS, Sir Stanley; CBE (1957); s of Jack Matthews; *b* 1 Jan 1915; *Educ* Wellington Sch Hanley; *m* 1, 1935 (m dis 1975), Elizabeth Hall, da of J Vallance; 1 s, 1 da; m 2, 1975, Mila (Gertrud Winterova); *Career* played association football with Stoke City FC 1931-47, Blackpool FC 1947-61 (FA Cup 1953), Stoke City FC 1961-65; gen mangr Port Vale FC 1965-68; played 88 times for England; kt 1965; *Clubs* Nat Sporting; *Style*— Sir Stanley Matthews, CBE; Idle House, Marsaxlokk, Malta (☎ 71068)

MATTHEWS, Baron (Life Peer UK 1980), of Southgate; Victor Collin Matthews; s of A Matthews; *b* 5 Dec 1919; *Educ* Highbury; *m* 1942, Joyce Geraldine, *née* Pilbeam; 1 s; *Career* serv WWII RNVR; chm and chief exec Express Newspapers Ltd 1977-85; gp md Trafalgar House Ltd 1968-77, dep chm 1973-85, gp chief exec 1977-83; chm: Cunard Steam-Ship Co Ltd 1971-83, Cunard Cruise Ships Ltd 1978-83, Cunard Line Ltd 1978-83, Fleet Publishing Int Hldgs Ltd 1978-81, Eastern Int Investmt Tst Ltd 1974-81, The Ritz Hotel (London) Ltd 1976-83; dir: Associated Container Transportation (Aust) Ltd 1972-82, Cunard Crusader World Travel Ltd 1974-85, Racecourse Hldgs Tst Ltd 1977-85, Associated Communications Corpn Ltd 1977-82, Goldquill Ltd 1979-83, Darchart Ltd 1980-83, Garmaine Ltd 1980-83; chm: Ellerman Lines 1983-85; Evening Standard Co Ltd 1980-85, Fleet

Hldgs plc 1982-85, Trafalgar House Devpt Hldgs 1970-83; Trafalgar House Constr Hldgs 1977-83; FCIOB, FRSA, CBIM FCIOB, FRSA, CBIM; *Clubs* MCC, RAC; *Style*— The Rt Hon the Lord Matthews; Waverley Farm, Mont Arthur, St Brelade, Jersey, CI

MATTHEWS-MAXWELL, Maj Christopher Ranulph George; TD (1979 and Clasp 1985); 26 Lord of Mounton and Lord of the Manor of Cophill; formerly patron of two livings; s of Lt-Col Arthur Charles Matthews-Maxwell, 25 Lord of Mounton (d 1958), and Georgina Muriel, *née* Reay (d 1953); *b* 28 June 1945; *Educ* King's Sch, Skerry's Coll, Newcastle Poly; *m* 1983, Bronwen Nicola Grendon, *née* Grendon-Jones (late Maj QARANC); *Career* cmmnd Royal Northumberland Fusiliers 1967, transferred to T&AVR 1970, Maj 1980, HAC 1981; chartered sec and farmer; owner of Mounton and Cophill Estates; Centre for Mgmnt in Agric, BIM Mgmnt Gp; govr RNLI; memb and serv ctee chm Norumberland Health and Family Practioner Ctees; Hospitaller Order of St John of Jerusalem 1983; Freeman City of London, Liveryman Worshipful Co of Meadmakers; FCIS, CDipAF, DipMM, MIPM, MBIM, FRSA; *Recreations* hunting, shooting, skiing, sailing, equestrian sports; *Clubs* Constitutional, Prince Albert Brussels; *Style*— Maj Christopher Matthews-Maxwell, TD; Royal Bank of Scotland, Grey St, Newcastle upon Tyne

MATTOCK, John Clive; s of Raymond Jack Mattock, of 10 Brownlands Rd, Sidmouth, E Devon, and Eva Winifred Zoë, *née* Ward; *b* 21 Jan 1944; *Educ* Dartford GS; *m* 1985, Susan, da of Richard Clulow, of 97 Upper Mealines, Harlow, Essex; 2 s (Anthony b 1986, Christopher b 1988);; *Career* stockbroker, md UTC Securities plc; dir: Stalwart Assur Gp plc 1986, Takare plc 1986; dep chm: UTC Gp plc 1985, Peak Tst Ltd 1988; FCA 1967; *Recreations* tennis, country pursuits; *Clubs* Bexley Lawn Tennis (vice-pres); *Style*— J C Mattock, Esq; Chippens Bank House, Hever, Kent; UTC Securities plc, 23 Finsbury Circus, London EC2 (☎ 01 628 7090)

MATUSCH, Antony Hugh; s of Frederick Hugh Matusch (d 1964); *b* 9 Oct 1940; *Educ* Stowe; *m* 1972, Helen Mary, *née* Blakesley; 2 s; *Career* chm and md F Bender Ltd 1964-; FCA; *Recreations* yachting; *Clubs* Royal Yacht Sqdn, MCC; *Style*— Antony Matusch, Esq; 23 Maunsel St, London SW1

MAUCHLINE, Lord; Michael Edward Abney-Hastings; assumed by deed poll 1946 surname of Abney-Hastings; s of Countess of Loudoun, *qv*, and (first husb) Capt Walter Strickland Lord; h to Earldom of mother; *b* 22 July 1942; *Educ* Ampleforth; *m* 1969, Noelene, da of W J McCormack; 2 s, (Hon Simon Abney-Hastings b 1974, Marcus William b 1981), 3 da (Hon Amanda Louise b 1969, Hon Lisa b 1971, Hon Rebecca (twin) b 1974); *Heir* s, Hon Simon Abney-Hastings b 1974; *Style*— Lord Mauchline; 74 Coreen St, Jerilderie, NSW 2716, Australia

MAUD, Hon Humphrey John Hamilton; CMG (1982); s of Baron Redcliffe-Maud (Life Peer); *b* 17 April 1934; *Educ* Eton, King's Coll Cambridge, Nuffield Coll Oxford; *m* 1963, Maria Eugenia Gazitua; 3 s; *Career* Nat Serv Coldstream Gds 1953-55; instr in Classics Univ of Minnesota 1958-59; joined FO 1959; served: Madrid 1961-63, Havana 1963-65, FCO 1966-67, seconded to Cabinet Off 1968-69, Paris 1970-74, at Nuffield Coll Oxford studying economics 1974-75, head Financial Rels FCO 1975-79, min Madrid 1979-82, ambass Luxembourg 1982-85, asst under-sec of state (int economic affairs and trade rels) FCO 1985-; *Recreations* music; *Clubs* Utd Oxford and Cambridge Univ; *Style*— The Hon Humphrey Maud, CMG

MAUDE, Hon Charles John Alan; s of Baron Maude of Stratford-upon-Avon (Life Peer); *b* 1951; *Educ* Abingdon, Corpus Christi Coll Cambridge; *Career* stage designer; *Style*— The Hon Charles Maude; Flat 2, 8 Maresfield Gdns, London NW3 (☎ 01 794 6955/ 3730)

MAUDE, Hon (Robert) Connan Wyndham Leslie; s and h of 8 Viscount Hawarden; *b* 23 May 1961; *Style*— The Hon Connan Maude

MAUDE, Hon Francis Anthony Aylmer; MP (C) N Warwickshire 1983-; s of Baron Maude of Stratford-upon-Avon (Life Peer) and Barbara Elizabeth, *née* Earnshaw; *b* 4 July 1953; *Educ* Abingdon Sch, Corpus Christi Coll Cambridge (BA); *m* 1984, Christina Jane, yr da of A Peter Hadfield, of Copthorne, Shrewsbury; 2 da (Julia Elizabeth Barbara b 26 Dec 1986, Cecily Mary Anne b 1988); *Career* barr in chambers of Sir Michael Havers, QC, MP; *Recreations* skiing, cricket, music, opera; *Style*— The Hon Francis Maude, MP; House of Commons, London SW1A 0AA

MAUDE, Hon Henry Cornwallis; yrs of 7 Viscount Hawarden (d 1958), and Marion, *née* Wright (d 1974); *b* 3 Mar 1928; *Educ* Marlborough, Worcester Coll Oxford (MA); *m* 8 Aug 1964, Elizabeth Georgina, o da of David McNaught Lockie, of Grasse, France; 2 s, 2 da; *Career* schoolmaster, farmer; *Recreations* swimming, reading, gardening; *Style*— The Hon Henry Maude; Wingham Well House, Wingham, Canterbury, Kent

MAUDE, Mrs John; Maureen Constance; e; da of Hon Arthur Ernest Guinness, 2 s of 1 Earl of Iveagh (d 1949); *b* 31 Jan 1907; *m* 1, 3 July 1930, 4 Marquess of Dufferin and Ava (ka 1945); 1 s (5 Marquess), 2 da; m 2, 14 Sept 1948 (m dis 1954), Maj (Harry Alexander) Desmond Buchanan, MC, *qv*; m 3, 20 Aug 1955, His Honour John Maude, QC (d 1986) *qv*; *Style*— Mrs John Maude; Great Maytham Hall, Rolvenden, Kent

MAUDE, Hon Thomas Patrick Cornwallis; s of 8 Viscount Hawarden; *b* 1 Oct 1964; *Style*— The Hon Thomas Maude

MAUDE OF STRATFORD-UPON-AVON, Baron (Life Peer UK 1983); Sir Angus Edmund Upton; TD, PC (1979); only child of Col Alan Maude, CMG, DSO, TD, by his w Dorothy, *née* Upton; *b* 8 Sept 1912; *Educ* Rugby, Oriel Coll Oxford; *m* 1946, Barbara Elizabeth Earnshaw, da of John Sutcliffe; 2 s, 2 da; *Career* serv WWII RASC; author and journalist; fin journalist: The Times 1933-34, Daily Mail 1935-39; MP (C) Ealing S 1950-57 (resigned pty whip in protest over withdrawal from Suez), MP (Ind Cons) 1957-58, fought Dorset by-election 1962, MP (C) Stratford-upon-Avon 1963-83; ed Sydney Morning Herald 1958-61; dir Cons Political Centre 1951-55, chm CRD 1975-79, dep chm Cons Pty 1975-79; *Style*— The Rt Hon the Lord Maude of Stratford-upon-Avon, TD, PC; Old Farm, South Newington, nr Banbury, Oxon (☎ 0295 720464)

MAUDE-ROXBY, John Henry; s of Wilfred Maude-Roxby, Capt Army, of Mount House, Burwash, Sussex (d 1954), and Dulcie Schnoeter (d 1961); *b* 4 Mar 1919; *Educ* Radley, Hertford Coll Oxford (BA); *m* 1, Joan (d 1963), da of Geofrey Foster of New Zealand (d 1952); 1 s (Richard 1947); m 2, 22 Oct 1966, Kathleen, da of Thomas Cuddy, of Lunesdale, Hulyhead, Anclesey (d 1953); *Career* formerly Col RA 1939-59; (despatches); chm and md Allied Suppliers Ltd 1959-73; dir Cavenham Ltd 1972-73, dep chm and md Morgan Edwards Ltd 1973-74; dir gen Inst of Grocery Distribution 1974-77; regnl trading mangr Mercia region Nat Tst 1979-84; *Recreations* writing, gardening; *Clubs* Army & Navy, Vincent's (Oxford); *Style*— John Maude-Roxby, Esq; Cameron Choat and Ptnrs, Dury House, 126-128 Cromwell Rd, London SW7 4ET (☎ 01 373 4537/8)

MAUDE-ROXBY, Richard Gay; s of John Henry Maude-Roxby; *b* 7 June 1947; *Educ* Dauntseys Sch; *m* 1971, Lynda Helena Marjorie, *née* Sanders; 1 c; *Career* dir: buying and mktg, Booker Food Servs, Produce Importers Alliance 1978-82; *Recreations* shooting, fishing; *Style*— Richard Maude-Roxby, Esq; Charmandean, Green Lane, Prestwood, Great Missenden, Bucks (☎ 024 06 2566)

MAUDSLAY, John Rennie; s of Maj Sir Rennie Maudslay, GCVO, KCB, MBE (d 1988), and Jane Ann, *née* McCarty; *b* 26 May 1953; *Educ* Eton; *m* 12 April 1986, Alexandra, da of Dr William Lothian, MB, ChB, of Shoreham, Kent: 1 da (Georgina b 1987); *Career* memb of Lloyd's 1979; ptnr Barder & Marsh 1988; Freeman of City of London, Liveryman of Worshipful Co of Mercers 1980; *Recreations* shooting, fishing; *Clubs* White's; *Style*— John Maudslay, Esq; 3 Orbel Street, London SW11 (☎ 01 228 7908); Barder & Marsh, Lumley House, 43-51 St Mary Axe, London EC3 (☎ 01 626 3910)

MAUGHAN, Air Vice-Marshal Charles Gilbert; CB (1976), CBE (1970), AFC (1960); s of Charles Alexander (d 1964), of London, and Magdalene Maria, *née* Tacke (d 1979); *b* 3 Mar 1923; *Educ* Sir George Monoux GS, Harrow Co Sch; *m* 14 June 1947, Pamela Joyce, da of late Cecil Wicks, of London; 1 s (David b 24 Nov 1953), 1 da (Susan b 12 July 1950); *Career* Fleet Air Arm (Swordfish, Albacore, Seafire) 1942-46, joined RAF 1949, CO 65 Sqdn (Hunter) 1958, Won Daily Mail Air Race London-Paris 1959, CO 9 Sqdn (Vulcan) 1964; Station Cdr: RAF Honnington (Victor) 1964, RAF Waddington (Vulcan) 1965; Gp Capt Opns HQ Bomber Cmd 1967, Air Attache Bonn 1970, AI Admin Strike Cmd 1974, Sr ASO Strike Cmd 1975, ret RAF 1978; gen sec Royal Br Legion 1978-83, inspr on panel of ind insprs DOE and Tport 1983-; tstee Katherine Lady Berkeley Sch; Chevalier Legion d'Honneur France 1960; *Recreations* walking, travel, theatre; *Style*— Air Vice-Marshal Charles Maughan, CB, CBE, AFC; Whitestones, Tresham, Wotton under Edge, Gloucs GL12 7RW (☎ 066 689 272)

MAUGHFLING, David John; s of Frank Rosewarne Maughfling, of Cornwall, and Alice Ann, *née* Hooper (d 1957); *b* 25 Sept 1938; *Educ* Truro Cathedral Sch; *m* 16 July 1968, Peggy Elizabeth Frances, da of Harold Hollis (d 1979), of Glos; 1 s (Edward b 1972), 1 da (Morwenna b 1970); *Career* ptnr Little & Co 1966-; assoc memb Inst of Chartered Accountants in England & Wales 1963 (fell 1973); *Recreations* jazz music, ceramics, genealogy; *Clubs* Cheltenham Graduates, Gloucester Lunch; *Style*— David J Maughfling, Esq; 181 Leckhampton Road, Cheltenham, Glos GL53 0AD (☎ 0242 516543); Little & Co, 45 Park Road, Gloucester GL1 1LP (☎ 0452 20920)

MAULEVERER, Peter Bruce; QC (1985); s of Maj Algernon Arthur Mauleverer, of Arncliffe, Springfield Rd, Poole, Dorset (d 1979), and Hazel Mary Mauleverer *née* Flowers (d 1983); *b* 22 Nov 1946; *Educ* Sherborne, Durham Univ (BA); *m* 7 Aug 1971, Sara, da of Dr Michael Hudson-Evans, of Yew Tree plc, St Maughans, Monmouth, Gwent; 2 s (Edward b 1972, Barnaby b 1974), 2 da (Harriet b 1977, Clementine b 1982); *Career* barr QC (1985), rec Crown Ct 1985; hon sec General Int Law Assoc 1986; *Recreations* sailing, skiing; *Style*— Peter B Mauleverer, QC; 4 Pump Ct, Temple EC4Y 7AN (☎ 01 353 2656, telex 8813250 REFLEX G, fax 01 583 2036)

MAUNDER, Prof Leonard; OBE (1977); s of Thomas George Maunder (d 1975), and Elizabeth Ann Maunder, *née* Long (d 1985); *b* 10 May 1927; *Educ* Bishop Gore GS Swansea, Univ Coll Swansea (BSc), Edinburgh Univ (PhD), MIT (ScD); *m* 1958, Moira Anne, da of Edwin George Hudson (d 1977); 1 s (David), 1 da (Joanna); *Career* instr and asst prof MIT 1950-54; Aeronautical Res Lab US Air Force 1954-56; lectr Univ of Edinburgh 1956-61; prof of mech engrg 1967- (prof of applied mechanics, 1961) dean of faculty of engrg Univ of Newcastle upon Tyne 1973-78; chm: SRC/DTI Working Pty for the Teaching Co Scheme 1981-, SRC Engrg Bd 1976-80, advsy cncl on R & D for fuel and power Dept of Energy 1981-; memb NRDC 1976-81 cncl Br Technol Gp 1981-; dep chm Newcastle Hosps Mgmnt Ctee 1971-73, memb Newcastle Dist Health Authy; pres: Int Fedn for the Theory of Machines & Mechanisms 1976-79; pres Engrg Br Assoc for the Advancement of Sci 1980; vice-pres Instn of Mech Engrs 1976-81; Christmas lectr Royal Instn 1983; memb Advsy Cncl on Sci Technol 1987-; *Books* Gyrodynamics and its Engineering Applications (with R N Arnold, 1961), Machines in Motion (1986), numerous papers in the fields of applied mechanics; *Style*— Prof Leonard Maunder, OBE; Stephenson Bldg, The Univ of Newcastle upon Tyne NE1 7RU (☎ 0632 2328511, telex 53654)

MAURICE, Clare Mary; *née* Rankin; da of Antony Colin Deans Rankin, of Peacock Cottage, Manton, Marlborough, Wiltshire, and Barbara Rankin, *née* Vernon; *b* 25 Feb 1954; *Educ* Sherborne Sch for Girls, Univ of Birmingham (LLB); *m* 20 Dec 1980, Ian James Maurice, s of Douglas Creyke Maurice (d 1968); 1 da (Anna b 10 Mar 1987); *Career* admitted slr 1978, ptnr Allen & Overy 1985 (articled 1976, asst slr 1978); *Recreations* theatre, travel; *Clubs* Reform; *Style*— Mrs Ian Maurice; 56 Sterndale Rd, London W14 0HU (☎ 01 603 0508); Allen & Overy, 9 Cheapside, London EC2V 6AD (☎ 01 248 9898, fax 01 236 2192)

MAURICE, Hon Mrs; Hon Pamela Mary Violet; JP (Wilts 1951); da of Baron Goddard, GCB (Life Peer, d 1971; Lord Chief Justice of Eng 1946-58), and Marie Linda (d 1928), da of Sir Felix Schuster, 1 Bt; *b* 28 Dec 1907; *Educ* St Paul's Girls' Sch; *m* 1934, James Burdett, MRCS, LRCP (d 1979), s of Col George Thelwall Kindersley Maurice, CMG, CBE (d 1950, late AMS); 1 s (Martin Thelwall Rayner b 1938), 1 da (Rosanagh Mary b 1935 (Mrs Simon Anthony Evans)); *Style*— The Hon Mrs Maurice; Batt's Farm, Wilton, Marlborough, Wilts SN8 3SS (☎ 0672 870287)

MAURICE, Dr Rita Joy; da of Albert Newton Maurice (d 1944), and Florence Annie, *née* Dean (d 1971); *b* 10 May 1929; *Educ* East Grinstead Co Sch, Univ Coll London (BSc, PhD); *Career* lectr in economic statistics Univ Coll London 1951-58; chief statistician Miny of Health and Central Statistical Off 1959-72; head of economics and statistics div, DTI; dir of statistics Home Off 1979-; memb cncl Royal Statistical Soc 1976-82; *Style*— Dr Rita Maurice; Home Office, Queen Annes Gate, London SW1 (☎ 01 213 5205)

MAVOR, Air Marshal Sir Leslie Deane; KCB (1970, CB 1964), AFC (1942), DL (N Yorks 1976); s of William David Mavor (d 1943); *b* 18 Jan 1916; *Educ* Aberdeen GS; *m* 1947, June Lilian, da of Lt-Col Cyril Henry Blackburn (decd); 4 s; *Career* joined RAF 1937, AOC 38 Gp 1964-66, Asst Chief of Air Staff (Policy) 1966-69, AOC-in-C RAF Tning Cmd 1969-72, ret 1973; princ Home Off Home Def Coll 1973-80; co-ordinator of Voluntary Effort in Civil Def 1981-84; FRAeS; *Recreations* shooting, fishing, golf, gliding; *Clubs* RAF, Yorkshire; *Style—* Air Marshal Sir Leslie Mavor, KCB, AFC, DL; Barlaston House, Alne, Yorks (☎ 034 73 412)

MAVOR, Michael Barclay; CVO (1983); s of William Ferrier Mavor, of 10 Greenriggs Ave, Melton Park, Newcastle-upon-Tyne, and Sheena Watson, *née* Barclay; *b* 29 Jan 1947; *Educ* Loretto, St John's Coll Cambridge (MA); *m* 20 Aug 1970, (Jane) Elizabeth, da of Albert Sucksmith (d 1956), of Lima, Peru; 1 s (Alexander b 31 Oct 1981), 1 da (Veronica b 5 Oct 1977); *Career* Woodrow Wilson Fell at Northwestern Univ Evanston Illinois USA 1969-72; asst master at Tonbridge 1972-78; course tutor for The Open Univ 1974-76; headmaster Gordonstoun 1979-; *Recreations* fishing, golf, painting, theatre ; *Clubs* Hawks'; *Style—* Michael Mavor, Esq, CVO; Gordonstoun Sch, Elgin, Moray IV30 2RF (☎ 0343 830445, fax 0343 830074)

MAW, John Nicholas; s of Clarence Frederick Maw (d 1967), and Helen, *née* Chambers (d 1950); *b* 5 Nov 1935; *Educ* Wennington Sch Wetherby Yorks, RAM; *Style—* John Maw, Esq; c/o Faber Music, 3 Queen Sq, London WC1N 3AU

MAWBY, Raymond Llewellyn; s of John Henry Mawby (d 1961), of Rugby; *b* 1922; *Educ* Long Lawford Co Sch; *m* 1944, Carrie S, da of late Ernest Aldwinckle, of Leicester; 1 da ; *Career* memb Electrical Trades Union, former pres and shop steward Rugby Branch; former memb Rugby Borough Cncl, MP (C) Totnes 1955-83, PPS to Postmaster-Gen 1956-60, asst PMG 1963-64; *Style—* Raymond Mawby, Esq; 29 Applegarth Ave, Newton Abbot, S Devon

MAWBY, Trevor John Charles; s of George Albert Mawby (d 1983), and Kathleen Ellen Mawby *née* Clegg; *b* 19 Feb 1949; *Educ* Eastfield HS, Bristol Poly; *m* 5 Sept 1970, Susan Patricia, da of Eric Tippins (d 1960); 2 s (James b 1977, Thomas b 1982); *Career* CA qualified 1971; chief exec Walter Lawrence plc 1985-; dep md Walter Lawrence plc 1984-85; chief exec Walter Lawrence Manufacturing Ltd 1984-85; gp fin dir Walter Lawrence plc 1980-84; present main dirships: chief exec Walter Lawrence plc; dir Walter Lawrence Properties Ltd; chm: Walter Lawrence Construction Ltd, Walter Lawrence Homes Ltd, Tricom Supplies Ltd, Rock Asphalte Ltd, Nat Flooring Co Ltd, Walter Lawrence Project Mgmnt Ltd; *Recreations* cinema, theatre, golf, squash; *Style—* Trevor Mawby, Esq; 18 Luard Rd, Cambridge CB2 2PJ (☎ 0223 210841); Lawrence House, Sun St, Sawbridgeworth, Herts CM21 9LX (☎ 0279 725 001, telex 817480, fax 0279 725004, car tel 0836 236646)

MAWDSLEY, Jack; s of Evan Mawdsley, of Stamford Lincs, and Ellen, *née* Whitaker; *b* 29 Nov 1938; *Educ* Bolton Sch Lancs, Longton HS Stoke-on-Trent, Royal Sch of Mines London Univ (BSc); *m* 29 July 1961, (Christine) Gillian, da of Alfred Maurice Smith, of Wolverhampton; 1 s (Tristan b 16 May 1966), 1 da (Larret b 20 Feb 1965); *Career* chartered engr, main bd dir Tarmac plc 1987 (regnl dir 1976, md 1985, chief exec 1986); non-exec dir: BR London Midland Bd 1987, Needwood Hldgs 1988; chm: Nat Jt Industl Cncl (Roadstone) 1981- 86, BACMI Indust Trade Assoc 1988-; vice-pres: Matlock Town FC 1976-86, Derbyshire Angling Club 1982-86; pres Matlock Cycling Club 1978-84; CE MIME 1963, FIMM 1965, FIQ 1985; *Recreations* game fishing, golf, opera, walking, bird watching; *Style—* Jack Mawdsley, Esq; Tarmac Quarry Prods Ltd, Millfields Rd, Ettingshall, Wolverhampton WV4 6JP (☎ 0902 353 522, fax 0902 353 980, car tel 0860 350 522, telex 339 825)

MAWER, Air-Cdre Allen Henry; DFC (1943); s of Sqdn-Ldr Gordon Mawer (d 1958), of Lewes, Sussex, and Emily Naomi, *née* Block (d 1983); *b* 16 Dec 1921; *Educ* Bancrofts Sch Essex; *m* 1, 29 March 1947, Pamela Mitchell (d 1982), da of David Thomas (d 1965), of Llanrwst N Wales; 1 s (Simon b 1948), 1 da (Gillian b 1953); m 2, 25 Nov 1982, Elizabeth Mary Stokes, *née* Abraham; *Career* WWII RAF: Flying trng 1940-41, operational flying 37 Sqdn 1941-42, flying intr 1942-43, operational flying 624 Special duties sqdn 1943-44, Air Miny Intelligence 1945-47; Transport Cmd RAF Flying duties 242 sqdn 1948-50, Visual Interservs Trg and Res Estab 1950-51, flying and staff duties RAF Transport Cmd 1951-55, RAF Staff Coll 1956, jt staff offr HQ M E Cyprus 1957-59, Jt Servs Staff Coll 1959-60, dir staff RAF Staff Coll 1960-62, Wing Cdr flying RAF Luqa Malta 1963-65, CO RAF Scampton 1965-68, Imperial Def Coll 1968, Gp Capt plans HQ Bomber Cmd 1969, Cmdt RAF Coll of Air Warfare 1969-71, Air Cdre plans HQ Strike Cmd 1971-73, Air Cdr Malta 1973-75; gen mangr Basildon New Town Devpt Corpn 1975-78, md London Docklands Devpt Orgn 1978-79, memb Lord Chllrs Panel of Independent Inspectors 1983-; vice-chm Mid Essex Health Authy 1982-88; pres Burnham on Crouch branch Royal Br Legion, memb Nat Exec Forces Help Soc and Lord Roberts Workshops; Croix de Guerre 1944; *Recreations* shooting, painting, golf; *Clubs* RAF, Royal Burnham YC; *Style—* Air-Cdre Allen Mawer, DFC; 68 High St, Burnham on Crouch, Essex CM0 8AA (☎ 0621 782 968)

MAWHINNEY, Brian Stanley; MP (C) Peterborough 1979-; s of Stanley Mawhinney; *b* 26 July 1940; *Educ* Royal Belfast Academical Instn, Queen's Univ Belfast (BSc), Univ of Michigan (MSc), London Univ (PhD); *m* 1965, Betty Louise Oja; 2 s, 1 da; *Career* asst prof radiation res Univ of Iowa 1968-70; sr lectr Royal Free Hosp Sch of Medicine 1970-; memb MRC 1980-83; contested (C) Stockton-on-Tees Oct 1974; PPS to min of State Treasury (Barney Hayhoe) 1982-; *Style—* Dr Brian Mawhinney, MP; House of Commons, London SW1A 0AA (☎ 01 219 6205)

MAWSON, David; JP (Norwich 1972), DL (Norfolk 1986); s of John William Mawson (d 1964), of Keri Keri NZ, and Evelyn Mary *née* Bond; *b* 30 May 1924; *Educ* Merchant Taylor's Sch Sandy Lodge, Wellington Coll NZ, Auckland Univ NZ, Kingston-upon-Thames Coll of Art; *m* 1951, Margaret Kathlyn, da of Charles Joseph Norton, FRIBA (d 1942), of Norwich, Norfolk; 1 s (Iain), 1 da (Diana); *Career* architect 1953- (to Norwich Cathedral 1977-), ptnr Feilden & Mawson 1956-; chm: Norfolk Soc (CPRE) 1971-76 (vice-pres 1976-), Br Assoc of Friends of Museums 1973-, Friends of Norwich Museums 1985-; fndr pres World Fedn of Friends of Museums 1975-81; pres: Norfolk Club 1986, Norfolk Assoc of Architects 1977-79 (memb 1952-); hon tres Heritage Co-ordination Gp 1980-86, memb Ctee of Nat Heritage 1973-, FSA, RIBA; *Recreations* yachting, photography; *Clubs* Norfolk (Norwich); *Style—* David Mawson, Esq, JP, DL; Gonville Hall, Wymondham, Norfolk NR18 9JG (☎ 0953 602166); Feilden & Mawson Architects, Ferry Rd, Norwich NR1 1SU (☎ 0603 629571, telex 975247 CHACOM G)

MAWSON, Desmond Leonard; s of Leonard Mawson (d 1947), and Amelia Mawson, *née* Husley (d 1985); *b* 26 Dec 1923; *Educ* Firth Park GS Sheffield, Rotheram Tech Coll; *m* 27 Dec 1944, Eva, da of Henry Boulton (d 1971); 1 da (Lynne b 1949); *Career* WWII navigator RAF (Flt Sgt); serv: Europe, Middle E, Burma, India 1942-46; chm and chief exec Ross, Catherall Gp plc 1987- (chm and md 1985-87, md 1968-85); memb IOD, MInstP; *Recreations* golf, walking; *Clubs* IOD; *Style—* Desmond L Mawson, Esq; Sherwood, Aughton Lane, Aston, Sheffield (☎ 0742 872201); Ross Catherall Gp plc, Forge Lane, Killamarsh, Sheffield (☎ 0742 488882, fax 0742 475999)

MAWSON, Dr Stuart Radcliffe; s of Alec Robert Mawson (d 1950), and Ena Sylvia Victoria, *née* Grossmith (d 1944); *b* 4 Mar 1918; *Educ* Canford, Trinity Coll Cambridge, St Thomas's Hosp (MA, MB, BChir), FRCS;; *m* 1948, June Irene, da of George Frederick Percival (d 1950); 2 s, 2 da; *Career* Capt RAMC 1943-46; hon consulting surgn in otolaryngology King's Coll Hosp London (conslt NHS 1951-79), pres section of otology, RSM 1974-75; FRCS; *Publications incl* Diseases of the Ear, Arnhem Doctor; *Recreations* sailing, golf; *Style—* Dr Stuart Mawson; Whinbeck, Knodishall, Saxmundham, Suffolk IP17 1UF

MAXEY, Peter Malcolm; CMG (1982); *b* 26 Dec 1930; *Educ* Bedford Sch, CCC Cambridge; *m* 1, 1955 (m dis 1978), Joyce Diane Marshall; 2 s, 2 da; m 2, 1978, Christine Irene Spooner; *Career* entered Foreign Serv 1953, seconded to Lazard Bros 1971-72, cnsllr CSCE Delgn Geneva 1973, head UN Dept FCO 1974-77, cnsllr Dublin 1977, loaned to Cabinet Off as under-sec 1978-81, ambass GDR 1981-84, ambass & dep perm rep to UN (New York) 1984-; *Style—* Peter Maxey Esq, CMG; UK Mission to UN, 845 Third Avenue, New York, NY 10022, USA; c/o Foreign and Cwlth Off, London SW1

MAXMIN, Dr (Hiram) James; s of Henry W Maxmin, of 527 Manor Rd, Elkins Park 17, Penna, USA, and Louise, *née* Strousse (d 1977); *b* 26 Sept 1942; *Educ* Cheltenham HS, Grinnell Coll Iowa (BA), Fitzwilliam Coll Cambridge, Kings Coll London (PhD); *m* 9 July 1968, Dr Jacqueline S Maxmin, da of L P Viden, 3 s (Peter b 29 Nov 1972, Jonathan b 7 June 1977, Ben b 21 April 1983), 1 da (Kate b 3 Feb 1971); *Career* trainee Unilever Ltd 1968-69, Lever Bros 1969-71, dir Unilever Orgn 1971-73, mktg dir Volvo Concessionaires UK 1975-78, jt chm and md Volvo UK 1978-83, dir Thorn EMI plc 1983-, chm and chief exec Thorn Home Electronics 1983-, pres Thorn EMI inc (USA) 1983-; lectr at business coll, fund raiser Fitzwilliam Coll Cambridge, involved in local educn initiatives; SMMT (offr), FIMI 1983, CBIM 1985; *Recreations* rugby, fishing, swimming; *Style—* Dr James Maxmin; 16A Alexander Sq, London SW3; 110 Marlborough St, Boston, Mass, 02116 (USA); Lake View Farm, Morang Cove Rd, Nobelboro, Damiscrotta, Maine (USA); Thorn Emi plc, 4 Tenterden St, Hanover Sq, London W1R 9AH (☎ 06284 75441, 617 367 0111, fax 06284 75356, 617 267 1407 (OGA)); Thorn-Emi Inc, 38 Newbury St, Boston, Mass 02116

MAXTON, John Alston; MP (Lab) Glasgow, Cathcart 1979-; s of John and Jenny Maxton; *b* 5 May 1936; *Educ* Lord Williams' GS Thames, Oxford Univ; *m* Christine Maxton; 3 s; *Career* joined Lab Pty 1970; oppn spokesman: health, local govt and housing in Scotland 1985-87, Scotland 1987-; memb: Scottish Select Ctee 1981-83, Public Accounts ctee 1983-84; *Style—* John Maxton, Esq, MP; House of Commons, London SW1

MAXTONE GRAHAM, James Anstruther (Jamie); s of Anthony James Oliphant Maxtone Graham (d 1971), of Cultoquhey, and Joyce Anstruther (d 1953) (author of Mrs Miniver); *b* 10 May 1924; *Educ* Eton, Gordonstoun; *m* 1, 1952 (m dis 1972), Diana Evelyn, da of Thomas Lowe Magregor (d 1953), of Edinburgh; 2 s (Robert Oliphant b 1955, Anthony James b 1958), 1 da (Mary Alma b 1953); m 2, 1972 (m dis 1976), Diana Irene, *née* Pilcher; *Career* Lt Scots Gds 1942-47; farmed in Perthshire until 1962; freelance writer 1962-78, (mainly sporting subjects for American magazines) 1962-78, running 39 Steps smallest restaurant in Britain 1976-80, world's biggest dealer in vintage fishing tackle 1979-; *Books* Eccentric Gamblers (1975), The Best of Hardy's Anglers' Guides (1982), To Catch a Fisherman (1984), Fishing Tackle of Yesterday: A Collector's Guide (1989); *Recreations* fly-fishing, bridge, cooking, travel, collection of vintage fishing tackle; *Style—* Jamie Maxtone Graham, Esq; Lyne Haugh, Lyne Station, Peebles, Scotland EH45 8NP (☎ 07214 304)

MAXTONE GRAHAM, Robert Mungo; s of Anthony James Oliphant Maxtone Graham (d 1971), of Cultoquhey, Crieff, Perthshire, and Joyce Anstruther d 1953 ('Jan Struther' author of 'Mrs Miniver'); the Maxtone of Cultoquhey line is traced back to 1410 (see Burke's L G, 1972, ed Vol III, pp 390-391); *b* 6 May 1931; *Educ* USA: Stowe, Trinity Coll Cambridge (MA), Edinburgh Univ; *m* 1962, Claudia Eva Elizabeth Page-Phillips, da of Frederick Tannert (d 1980), of 238a Southlands Rd, Bickley, Kent; 1 da (Ysenda b 1962), and 1 stepda (Livia b 1958); *Career* Nat Serv cmmnd Scots Gds 1949-51 serv Malaya; advocate of the Scots Bar 1957, legal assoc Royal Town Planning Inst, town planning conslt, fndr and proprietor Malthouse Arcade Hythe Kent; *Recreations* genealogy, book-collecting, photography; *Style—* Robert Maxtone Graham, Esq; 6 Moat Sole, Sandwich, Kent (☎ 0304 613270); 8 Atholl Crescent Lane, Edinburgh 3 (☎ 031 228 3338); 55 rue des Teinturies, Avignon, France (☎ 90865292)

MAXWELL, Lady Avena Margaret Clare; *née* Stanhope; da of 11 Earl of Harrington; *b* 29 Mar 1944; *m* 1969, Adrian J Maxwell, s of Maj James Maxwell, of Buckby; 2 da (Sacha b 1974, Kerry b 1978); *Style—* Lady Avena Maxwell; South Lodge, Carrick-on-Suir, Co Tipperary, Ireland

MAXWELL, (Wellwood George) Charles; s of Maj George Cavendish Maxwell, of Four Acre House, West Green, Hartley Wintney, Hants, and Margaret Elizabeth, *née* Bishop; *b* 27 June 1952; *Educ* Stowe; *m* 15 Sept 1977, Anne, da of Rear-Adm Bryan Cecil Durant, CB, DSO, DSC (d 1983); 1 s (George b 4 April 1981), 1 da (Eloise b 18 Nov 1983); *Career* dir: Finsbury Distillery Co 1981 (md 1986), JE Mather & Sons Ltd 1983; Freeman City of London 1974, memb Worshipful Co of Distillers 1974; *Recreations* shooting, motor racing, rough gardening, wine, music, stamp collecting; *Clubs* Cavalry Guards, BARC; *Style—* Charles Maxwell, Esq; Squirrels, Kennel Lane, Frensham, Surrey; Finsbury Distillery Co Ltd, 5-17 Moneland St, London EC1 (☎ 01 253 7646, fax 01 251 0263, telex 24357)

MAXWELL, Cdr (John) David; DL (Co Down 1988), RN; s of Capt Thomas K Maxwell RN (d 1972); *b* 21 June 1929; *m* 1954, Georgiana Angela, 27 Baroness de Ros (d 1983); 1 s (28 Baron de Ros, *qv*), 1 da (Hon Diana Maxwell, *qv*); m 2, 1984, Patricia Carolyn Coveney, *née* Ash; *Career* High Sheriff Co Down 1981; *Style—* Cdr David Maxwell, DL, RN; Old Ct, Strangford, Co Down, N Ireland

MAXWELL, Hon Diana Elizabeth; da of Cdr (John) David Maxwell, RN, *qv*, and 27 Baroness de Ros (d 1983); sister of 28 Baron de Ros, *qv*; *b* 6 June 1957; *Educ* Godstowe Sch High Wycombe, Hillcourt Sch Dunlaoghaire; *Style—* The Hon Diana Maxwell

MAXWELL, of Kirkconnell Francis Patrick; s of Robert William Maxwell-Witham (d 1961), and Bettina Margaret Grierson, *née* Melross, family enlarged Kirkconnell House in 1760 with first bricks used in Scotland; *b* 7 June 1954; *Educ* Downside; *m* 16 July 1983, Nicola Mary, da of Edward Henry Lovell, of 24 Hendrick Ave, London SW12; 2 da (Georgiana b 1985, Bettina b 1986); *Recreations* shooting, curling, choral singing, genealogy, history; *Style*— Francis Maxwell of Kirkconnell; Kirkconnell, New Abbey, Dumfries DG2 8HL (☎ 038 785 276)

MAXWELL, Hugh William George; s of Hugh Sinclair Maxwell, and Bridget Patricia Maxwell (d 1969); *b* 12 Feb 1943; *m* 19 Sept 1970, Florence Fay, da of Kenneth Pearce, OBE, of Dorset; 2 s (Benjamin b 1973, Daniel b 1975; *Career* CA; *Recreations* golf; *Clubs* Hankley Common Golf; *Style*— Hugh W G Maxwell, Esq; Aintree, Frensham, Surrey GU10 3AA; Maxwell & Co Chartered Accountants, Millbridge House, Frensham, Surrey GU10 3AB (☎ 025125 4545, fax 025125 2176; car phone 0860 362430)

MAXWELL, John Frederick Michael; s of late Lt Frederic Michael Maxwell (RIN), of Sidcup, Kent, and Mabel Doreen, *née* Turner; *b* 20 May 1943; *Educ* Dover Coll, New Coll Oxford (MA); *m* 1, 1964 (m dis 1986), Jennifer Mary; 1 s (Edward b 1967) 1 da (Alice b 1966); m 2, 1 Sept 1986, Jayne Elizabeth, da of George Douglas Hunter (d 1984), of Birmingham; *Career* barr Inner Temple 1965, Midland and Oxford circuit; acting stipendiary magistrate in Birmingham; chm: Samye Ling Tibeton Centre Eskdalemuir Dumfrieshire, W Midlands Buddhist Centre; *Recreations* yachting; *Clubs* Gravesend Sailing; *Style*— John Maxwell, Esq; Grey Walls, 1131 Warwick Rd, Solihull, W Mids B91 3HQ (☎ 021 705 2670); 4 Fountain Ct, Steelhouse Lane, Birmingham B4 6DR (☎ 021 236 3476)

MAXWELL, Sir Michael Eustace George; 9 Bt (Ns 1681), of Monreith; o s of Maj Eustace Maxwell (d 1971), and Dorothy Vivien (Dodo), *née* Bellville; suc u, Sir Aymer Maxwell, 8 Bt, 1987; *b* 28 August 1943; *Educ* Eton, London Univ; *Heir* unascertained; *Style*— Sir Michael Maxwell, Bt; Monreith House, Port William, Newton Stewart, Scotland DG8 9LB (☎ 098 87 248); 30 Yeldham Road, London W6 8JE (☎ 01 748 3208)

MAXWELL, Hon Lord; Peter Maxwell; s of Cdr Desmond Herries Maxwell, RN, of Munches, Dalbeattie, Kirkcudbrightshire; *b* 21 May 1919; *Educ* Wellington, Balliol Oxford, Edinburgh Univ; *m* 1941, Alison, da of James Readman; 1 s, 2 da (and 1 s decd); *Career* served WW II Capt A & SH & RA Normandy; advocate Scotland 1951, QC 1961, sheriff pncpl Dumfries & Galloway 1970-73, senator Coll Justice (Lord of Session) 1973-; chm Scottish Law Cmmn 1982-; *Style*— The Hon Lord Maxwell; 1c Oswald Rd, Edinburgh EH9 2HE

MAXWELL, Sir Robert Hugh; KBE (1961), OBE (1942); s of William Robert Maxwell; *b* 2 Jan 1906; *m* 1935, Mary Courtney Jewell; 2 s; *Career* Commander Order of George I of Greece, Order of Merit Syria; *Clubs* Athens; *Style*— Sir Robert Maxwell, KBE, OBE; Ct Hay, Charlton Adam, Somerton, Somerset (☎ 045 822 3269)

MAXWELL, (Ian) Robert; MC (1945); s of Michael and Ann Hoch; *b* 10 June 1923; *Educ* self-educated; *m* 1945, Elisabeth, *née* Meynard; 3 s (and 1 s decd), 4 da (1 da decd); *Career* serv WWII (MC); in German section FO (head of press section Berlin) 1945-47; publisher: Daily Mirror, Daily Record, Sunday Mail, Sunday Mirror, The People, Sporting Life 1984-; chm: Mirror Gp Newspapers Ltd, Robert Maxwell & Co Ltd 1948-; dir Computer Technol Ltd 1966-77, chm and chief Int Learning Systems Corpn Ltd 1968-69; dir: Hollis plc 1982, Central Television plc 1983-, Mirrorvision 1985-, Clyde Cablevision 1985-, Philip Hill Investmt Tst 1986-, Maxwell Media Paris 1987-, Gauthier-Villars (Publishers) Paris 1961-70; co-chm Scottish News Enterprises Ltd 1975-76; fndr, publisher and chm Pergamon Press Oxford, London and New York 1949-, chm Maxwell Communication Corp plc (formerly BPCC plc) 1981-; chm: Oxford Utd FC plc 1982, Derby Co FC plc 1987 chm SelecTV plc 1982-; dir: Reuters plc, Central Television plc 1983-; has endowed a fellowship in trade union mgmnt studies at Balliol Coll Oxford; MP (Lab) Buckingham 1964-70, fought Buckingham both 1974 elections, memb mgmnt ctee Oxford City Lab Pty; chm: Lab Nat Fund Raising Fndn 1960-69, Lab Working Pty on Sci, Govt and Indust 1963-64, Nat Aids Tst Fundraising Gp 1987-; memb Cncl of Europe (vice-chm Ctee on Sci and Technol) 1968; tres The Round House Tst (formerly Centre 42) 1965-83; Kennedy fell Harvard Univ 1971, hon memb Acad of Astronautics 1974, memb: Cncl of Newspaper Publishers Assoc 1984-, Club of Rome 1979- (exec dir Br Gp); Hon Dr Moscow State Univ 1983; co-produced: Mozart's Don Giovanni, Salzburg Festival 1954, Bolshoi Ballet 1957, Swan Lake 1968; Stara Plenina (first class) Bulgaria 1983, Order of the Polar Star (Offr first class) Sweden 1984; *Publications* The Economics of Nuclear Power (1965), Public Sector Purchasing (1968), Man Alive (jt author, 1968), Leaders of the World Series (gen ed, 1980-); *Recreations* chess, football; *Style*— Robert Maxwell, Esq, MC; Headington Hill Hall, Oxford OX3 0BW (☎ 0865 64881, telex 83177)

MAXWELL, Dr Robert James; JP (1971); s of Dr George Barton Maxwell, MC (d 1972), and Cathleen Maxwell, *née* Blackburn; *b* 26 June 1934; *Educ* Leighton Park Sch Reading, New Coll Oxford (BA, MA), Univ of Pennsylvania (MA), London Sch of Economics (PhD); *m* 1960, Jane, da of Geoffrey FitzGibbon, JP, of Dursley Gloucestershire; 3 s (Patrick, Benedict, Geoffrey), 2 da (Catherine, Favell); *Career* Lieut Cameronians (Scottish Rifles) 1952-54; asst mangr Union Corpn 1958-66, princ McKinsey and Co 1966-75, admin Special Tstees for St Thomas' Hosp London 1975-80, sec King Edward's Hosp Fund for London 1980-; dir: Leighton Park Sch Reading, Royal Inst of Pub Admin, Nat Inst of Social Work, London Sch of Hygiene and Tropical Medicine (chm of the ct); pres Euro Assoc of Programmes in Health Service Studies; *Recreations* walking, poetry; *Clubs* Brooks's; *Style*— Dr Robert Maxwell, JP; 98 Bluehouse Lane, Oxted, Surrey (☎ Oxted 3753); 14 Palace Ct, London W2 4HT (☎ 01 727 0581)

MAXWELL, Hon Simon Kenlis; s of Lt-Col Hon Somerset Arthur Maxwell, MP (d of wounds 1942); *b* 12 Dec 1933; *Educ* Eton; *m* 1964, Karol Anne, da of Maj-Gen G E Prior-Palmer, CB, DSO; 2 s, 1 da; *Style*— The Hon Simon Maxwell; The Dower House, Westcote, Kingham, Oxon

MAXWELL-HYSLOP, Robin - Robert John; MP (C) Tiverton Nov 1960-; s of Capt A H Maxwell-Hyslop, GC, RN (decd), and Mrs Maxwell-Hyslop (decd), of Prideaux House, Par, Cornwall; *b* 6 June 1931; *Educ* Stowe, Christ Church Oxford (MA); *m* 1968, Joanna Margaret, er da of Thomas McCosh (decd) and Mrs McCosh of Pitcon, Dalry, Ayrshire; 2 da; *Career* Capt TARO RA; Rolls-Royce 1954-1960; contested N Derby (C) 1959; chm: Br - Brazilian Parly Gp; Gp memb: Trade and Indust Select Ctee 1971, Standing Orders Ctee 1977-, Procedure Select Ctee 1978-; *Style*— Robin Maxwell-Hyslop, Esq, MP; 4 Tiverton Road, Silverton, Exeter, Devon

MAXWELL-LAWFORD, Nicholas Anthony; OBE 1986; s of Capt F Maxwell-Lawford MBE (k rail accident 1937), of Achimota Coll Accra, Gold Coast, and Ruth Claire, *née* Jerred; *b* 8 Nov 1935; *Educ* Stonyhurst Coll, GWEBI Coll of Agric, S Rhodesia (Dip AG), Harvard Business Sch; *m* 8 Sept 1962, Mary Susan, da of Richard Fauconburg Bellasis (d 1984) of Rioki, Kiambu, Kenya; 1 s (Richard b 1965), 3 da (Helena b 1967, Frances b 1970, Antonia b 1973); *Career* Nat Serv: Devonshire Regt 1955 and seconded KAR 1955-56, ADC & pte sec to HE The Govr of Nyasaland Sir Robert Armitage, KCMG, MBE, 1959-61; joined Barclays Bank Ltd: var apps 1961-69, local dir for branches local Head Off 1969-73, local dir Lombard St local Head Off 1973-75, asst gen mangr Barclays Bank Int 1976, res dir Barclays Bank SA, Paris 1977, regnl dir SW Regnl Off 1987-; dir: Barclays Bank SA, Fauconbury (Holdings) Ltd, Sisley SA Paris; Freeman City of London 1965, Liveryman Drapers Co 1968; Kt of Grace and Devotion Sov order of Malta 1977, City of Paris medal in Silver-Gilt 1986; *Style*— Nicholas Maxwell-Lawford, Esq; The Old Rectory, Buckerell, Honiton, Devon, EX14 OEJ

MAXWELL-SCOTT, Dame Jean Mary Monica; DCVO (1984), CVO (1969); da of Maj-Gen Sir Walter Maxwell-Scott, 1 and last Bt, CB, DSO, DL (d 1954), and Mairi, *née* MacDougall; *b* 8 June 1923; *Educ* Couvent des Oiseaux, Westgate-on-Sea; *Career* VAD Red Cross Nurse 1941-46; lady-in-waiting to HRH Princess Alice Duchess of Gloucester 1959-; *Clubs* New Cavendish; *Style*— Dame Jean Maxwell-Scott, DCVO, CVO; Abbotsford, Melrose, Roxburghshire TD6 9BQ

MAXWELL-SCOTT, Sir Michael Fergus Constable; 13 Bt (E 1642), of Haggerston, Northumberland; s of Rear-Adm Malcolm Joseph Raphael Constable Maxwell-Scott, DSO, RN (decd), gs of Lord Herries of Terregles, ggs of 3 Bt; suc kinsman, Sir Ralph Stanley de Marie Haggerston, 12 Bt 1972; *b* 23 July 1921; *Educ* Ampleforth, Trinity Coll Cambridge; *m* 1963, Deirdre Moira, da of Alexander McKechnie (decd); 2 s (Dominic, Matthew), 1 da (Annabel); *Heir* s, Dominic Maxwell-Scott; *Style*— Sir Michael Maxwell-Scott, Bt; 10 Evelyn Mansions, Carlisle Place, London SW1 (☎ 01 828 0333)

MAXWELL-SCOTT, Mrs Patricia Mary; OBE (1972); da of Maj-Gen Sir Walter Joseph Maxwell-Scott, 1 Bt, CBE, DSO (d 1954), of Abbotsford, Melrose, and Mairi, *née* Macdougall (d 1924); resumed her maiden name in the Court of Session Edinburgh 1953; *b* 11 Mar 1921; *Educ* Convent of Les Oiseaux Westgate-on-Sea Kent; *m* 8 Sept 1944 (separated), Sir (Harold Hugh) Christian Boulton, 4 Bt, *qv*; *Career* pres: Roxburgh branch BRCS, Border branch Save the Children Soc, Border branch Spartie Soc; hon Sheriff of Selkirk 1971-; *Recreations* reading, travelling; *Style*— Mrs Patricia Maxwell-Scott, OBE; Abbotsford, Melrose, Roxburghshire TD6 9BQ (☎ 0896 2043)

MAY, Anthony Tristram Kenneth; QC (1979); s of Dr Kenneth Sibley May (d 1985), and Joan Marguérite, *née* Oldaker (d 1985); *b* 9 Sept 1940; *Educ* Bradfield Coll, Worcester Coll Oxford (MA); *m* 4 May 1968, Stella Gay, da of Rupert George Pattisson (d 1976); 1 s (Richard b 1974), 2 da (Charmian b 1971, Lavinia b 1972); *Career* barr Inner Temple 1967, rec 1985, bencher Inner Temple 1985; chm Guildford Choral Soc; *Recreations* gardening, music, books; *Style*— Anthony T K May, Esq, QC; 10 Essex St, London WC2R 3AA (☎ 01 240 6981)

MAY, Prof Brian Albert; s of Albert Robert May (d 1986), and Eileen, *née* May; *b* 2 June 1936; *Educ* Faversham GS, Univ of Aston (BSc); *m* 2 Aug 1961, Brenda Ann, da of Norman Smith; 3 s (Christopher b 15 March 1964, Timothy b 1965, Jeremy b 1967); *Career* Nat Serv Craftsman REME Kenya and Malaya 1954-56; design engr Massey Ferguson 1962-63; Silsoe Coll: lectr and sr lectr 1963-72, head dept of agric engrg 1972-75, head of coll 1976; prof agric engrg Cranfield Inst of Technol 1975- (dean of faculty 1976-), head Cranfield Rural Inst 1987-; ed The Agricultural Engineer 1970-75; chm Br Agric Educn and Trg Servs 1984-86, pres Inst Agric Engrs 1984-86, dir Br agric Export Cncl 1985-88, memb Br Cncl Agric and Veterinary Advsy Ctee 1985-, bd dir Br Soc for Res in Agric Engrg; MIMechE, FIAgrE, FRAgs, MASAE, CEng; *Books* Power on the Land (1975); *Recreations* reading, photography, people; *Clubs* Farmers; *Style*— Prof Brian May; Fairfield, Greenway, Campton, Beds (☎ 0462 813451); Cranfield Rural Inst, Silsoe Campus, Silsoe, Beds (☎ 0525 61527, telex 265871 MONREF G EUM 300)

MAY, Brian William; s of Donald Richard Vincent May, and Phoebe Louise, *née* Flain; *Career* dir St James Press Ltd (holding co of A2 Motel Guides) 1977-89, fndr publisher A2 series which became the hotel directory with largest circulation in the world; fund raiser RSPB; *Recreations* climbing, tennis, sailing, ornithology; *Style*— Brian May, Esq; 39 Alleyn Rd, Dulwich, SE21 8AD (☎ 670 0221); 5, 11 Worship St, London EC2 (☎ 01 588 6631)

MAY, David Oliver; s of John Oliver May (d 1960), and Joan, *née* Harrison; *b* 1 Mar 1935; *Educ* Wellington, Southampton Univ; *m* March 1960, Baroness Catherine, da of Baron Van Den Branden De Reeth (d 1966); 2 s (Brian, Dominic), 1 da (Georgia); *Career* Nat Serv Sub Lt RN 1954-55; chm: Berthon Boat Co Ltd, Lymington Marina Ltd, Newmil Garage, Lymington Marine Garage, Nat Boat Shows 1986-88; tstee Br Marine Inds Fedn 1988; dir: Vi-Tal Hosp Prods Ltd, Imatronic Ltd, Transatlantic Capital Ltd; Liveryman Worshipful Co of Shipwrights; FRINA 1964; *Recreations* yacht racing, sailing, shooting; *Clubs* Royal Thames YC, Royal Ocean Racing, RN, Royal Lymington YC, Royal London YC, Island Sailing; *Style*— David May, Esq; The Shipyard, Lymington, Hants

MAY, Derwent James; s of Herbert Alfred May (d 1982), and Nellie Eliza, *née* Newton (d 1959); *b* 29 April 1930; *Educ* Strodes Sch Egham, Lincoln Coll Oxford (MA); *m* 22 Sept 1961, Yolanta Izabella, da of Tadeusz Sypniewski, of Lodz, Poland (d 1970); 1 s (Orlando James b 1968), 1 da (Miranda Izabella b 1970); *Career* theatre and film critic Continental Daily Mail Paris 1952-53, lectr English Univ of Indonesia 1955-58, sr lectr english lit Univs of Warsaw and Lodz Poland 1959-63, ldr writer TLS 1963-65, lit ed The Listener 1965-86, lit and arts ed The Sunday Telegraph 1986-, contrib of Nature Notes to The Times 1981-; memb Booker Prize Jury 1978, memb Hawthornden Prize ctee 1987-; *Books* The Professionals (1964), Dear Parson (1969), The Laughter in Djakarta (1973), A Revenger's Comedy (1979), Proust (1983), The Times Nature Diary (1983), Hannah Arendt (1986); *Books*; ed: Good Talk: An Anthology from BBC Radio (1968), Good Talk 2 (1969), The Music of What Happens: Poems from The Listener 1965-80 (1981); *Recreations* birdwatching, opera; *Clubs* Beefsteak; *Style*— Derwent May, Esq; 201 Albany St, London NW1 (☎ 01 387 0848); The Sunday Telegraph, 181 Marsh Wall, London E14 (☎ 01 538 7390)

MAY, Hon Jasper Bertram St John; s and h of 3 Baron May; *b* 24 Oct 1965; *Educ* Harrow; *Style*— The Hon Jasper May

MAY, Rt Hon Lord Justice; John Douglas; PC (1982); s of E A G May (d 1942), of Shanghai; *b* 28 June 1923; *Educ* Clifton, Balliol Coll Oxford (MA); *m* 1958, Mary, da of Sir Owen Morshead, GCVO, KCB, DSO, MC; 2 s, 1 da; *Career* served WW II Lt

(SpSc) RNVR; barr Inner Temple 1947, master of the Bench 1972, QC 1965, rec of Maidstone 1971, ldr SE Circuit 1971, high ct judge (Queen's Bench) 1972-82, presiding judge Midland & Oxford Circuit 1973-77, lord justice of appeal 1982-; memb Parole Bd 1977-80 (v-chm 1980), chm Inquiry into Prison Servs 1978-79; kt 1972; pres Clifton Coll 1987-; *Clubs* Vincents' (Oxford); *Style*— The Rt Hon Lord Justice May; Royal Cts of Justice, Strand, London WC2A 2LL (☎ 01 936 6186)

MAY, Sir Kenneth Spencer; CBE (1976); s of Norman Spencer May (decd), and Olive Martha Langsford (decd); *b* 10 Dec 1914; *Educ* Woodville HS; *m* 1943, Betty Clara Scott; 1 s (Brian), 1 da (Julie); *Career* served WW II AIF 1940-45, Mid East and New Guinea, Maj; chm: Mirror Newspapers Ltd 1969-80, Nationwide News Pty Ltd 1969-80; dir: News Ltd 1969-88, The News Corpn Ltd 1979-, Santos Ltd 1980-83, Independent Newspapers Ltd Wellington NZ 1971-84, Airlines of SA 1981-86; editorial staff The News 1930-, political writer 1946-56; asst mangr The News 1959-64, gen mangr 1964-69; *Recreations* golf, lawn bowls; *Style*— Sir Kenneth May, CBE; 26 Waterfall Terrace, Burnside, S Australia 5066

MAY, 3 Baron (UK 1935); Sir Michael St John May; 3 Bt (1931); s of 2 Baron (d 1950), by his 2 w Ethel; *b* 26 Sept 1931; *Educ* Wycliffe Coll, Magdalene Cambridge; *m* 1, 1958 (m dis 1963), Dorothea Catherine Ann, da of Charles McCarthy; m 2, 1963, Jillian Mary, da of Albert Edward Shipton; 1 s, 1 da (Hon Miranda b 17 Oct 1968); *Heir* s, Hon Jasper Bertram St John May b 24 Oct 1965; *Career* late Lt Royal Corps of Signals; *Style*— The Rt Hon the Lord May; Gautherns Farm, Sibford Gower, Oxfordshire (☎ 029 578 696)

MAY, Brig Peter Harry Mitchell; DSO (1945), OBE (1957, MC 1941); s of Dr George Ernest May (d 1956), of Herts, and Rachel Marguerite Mitchell (d 1971); *b* 19 Dec 1913; *Educ* Haileybury, RMC Sandhurst; *m* 22 Oct 1955, Elizabeth Anne, da of Lt Col George Montagu Parkin, MC (d 1974); *Career* cmmnd Durham LI 1933; joined 1 BN Catterick 1933, Shanghai (1937), Tientsin China (1938) Hong Kong 1938, Egypt 1939-40; Western Desert 1940-41, Syria 1942, ME Staffcoll Haifa 1942, HQ 8 Army 1942; Brig Maj 4 Para Bde 1942; 2 i/t 1 Bn LI 1942-43, Cdr 1 Bn 1943-44 serv Italy, AA & QMG 10 Din 1945 serv Italy, Cdr 1 Bn Durham LI 1945-46, RAD Staff Coll Bracknell 1946, GSO1 (Air) Airborne Div Palestine and UKDAWMG; Instr Army Staff Coll Camberley 1951, 10 Para Bn 1953, Cdr 1Bn Durham LI Canal Zone Egypt 1953-55; 16 Airborne Div (TA) London 1955-56; GSOI 56 Armd Div TA London; cdr 149 Infantry Bde (TA), dep col Durhsm LI 1977-80; co civil def offr Northumberland 1962-68; co pres St John Northumberland later Northumbria 1970-82; C St J 1982;; *Recreations* shooting; *Clubs* Army & Navy, Northern Counties (Newcastle); *Style*— Brig Peter H M May, DSO, OBE, MC; Hawkwell House, Stamfordham, Northumberland NE18 0QT (☎ 06 616 385)

MAY, Robert McCredie; s of Henry Wilkinson May, of Sydney, Australia; *b* 8 Jan 1936; *Educ* Sydney Boys' HS, Sydney Univ (BSc, PhD); *m* 1962, Judith, da of Jerome Feiner, of New York, USA; *Career* Gordon Mackey lectr in applied mathematics Harvard Univ 1959-61; prof: of physics Sydney Univ 1962-73, biology Princeton Univ 1973, zoology Princeton Univ 1975-; visiting prof Imperial Coll London 1975-; chm: Univ Res Bd, Princeton Univ 1977-87; memb Smithsonian Cncl 1985-88; FRS; *Recreations* tennis, bridge, running; *Clubs* Athenaeum; *Style*— Robert May Esq; 6 Leacroft, Sunningdale, Berks; 25 Scott Lane, Princeton, New Jersey 08540, USA

MAY, Roger; s of Fred May, ISM (d 1967), and Agnes Doreen, *née* Abrahams (d 1971); *b* 12 June 1931; *Educ* High Storrs GS Sheffield; *m* 1, 14 March 1953 (m dis 1973); 2 s (Paul b 1958, Jonathan b 1962); m 2, 1973, (Margaret) Yvonne; *Career* slr; former Justices' Clerk, Barry, Cowbridge, Penarth; dep High Ct and Co Ct registrar; memb Law Soc; *Recreations* photography, travel; *Style*— Roger May, Esq; Hillcrest, Quarhouse, Brimscombe, Stroud, Gloucestershire; Frome House, London Road, Stroud, Gloucestershire

MAY, Stephen Charles; s of Paul May, CBE, and Dorothy Ida, *née* Makower (d 1961); *b* 5 Sept 1937; *Educ* Berkhamsted Sch, Christ Church Oxford (MA); *m* 2 June 1977, Jeannette de Rothschild (d 1980), da of Frederick Ernest Bishop (d 1940); *Career* Nat Serv 2 Lt RA 1956-58; John Lewis Partnership: joined 1961-, md Edinburgh 1973-75, md Peter Jones 1975-1977, dep dir personnel 1977-78, dir personnel 1978-; *Recreations* skiing, tennis, travel; *Clubs* Vanderbilt; *Style*— Stephen May, Esq; The John Lewis Partnership, 4 Old Cavendish St, London W1A 1EX (☎ 01 637 3434, fax 01 637 3434 ext 6301, telex 27824 Jonel G)

MAY, Walter Anthony Holland; MC (1945); s of Bertram May (d 1959), of Falmouth, Cornwall, and Alice Kathleen, *née* Kent (d 1965); *b* 15 Dec 1919; *Educ* Shrewsbury, Loughborough Engrg Coll (Dip Eng), MIT Boston USA; *m* 10 Jan 1942, (Wendy) Mary, da of Eric G Attenborough (d 1969), of Letchmore Heath, Herts; 1 s (Michael Walter b 1950), 2 da (Rosemary Elizabeth b 1942, Veronica Kathleen b 1945); *Career* 2 Lt RE TA 1938, 54 div 249 Field Co RE 1939, Maj SME 1943-44, 14 Field Sqdn RD 1944-45, acting CRE Gds Armd Div 1945; George Kent Ltd: personnel mangr 1947-51, exec dir 1951-84, fin dir 1955-63, dep md 1963-71; md Int Div Brown Boveri Kent Plc 1971-81, dir BECENTA Ltd 1986; non-exec dir: ABB Kent (Holdings) Plc 1984-, Luton Int Airport Ltd 1988-; chm: BIMCAM 1966-67, Luton & Dist Employment Ctee 1961-76, Eastern Regnl Industl Savings Ctee 1968-78; pres Mid-Anglian Engrg Employers Assoc 1979-82, memb Policy Ctee Engrg Employers Fedn 1980-86, Mgmnt Bd Engrg Employers Fedn 1979 (ret 1989), memb Eastern Regnl Cncl CBI 1985-; involved in local politics over many years; FBIM, IOD; *Recreations* tennis, golf; *Style*— Walter May, Esq; Rose Farm, Whitwell, Herts (☎ 043 887 543); ABB Kent (Hldgs) Plc, Biscot Rd, Luton, Beds LU3 1AL (☎ 0582 31255, fax 0582 421 115, telex 825066 BBKENT G)

MAYALL, David William; s of Arthur William Mayall, of Derby, and Pamela, *née* Bryant; *b* 19 July 1957; *Educ* Repton, Univ of Cambridge (MA); *m* 22 June 1985, Wendy Madeleine, da of Peter Blaalck of Douglas, IOM; 1 s (James b 13 April 1988); *Career* called to the barr Grays Inn 1979; *Recreations* bridge, tennis, golf; *Style*— David Mayall, Esq; 5 Rookfield Close, London N10 (☎ 01 444 1683); 1 Verulam Bldgs, Grays Inn, London WC1R 5LQ (☎ 01 242 7646)

MAYALL, Sir (Alexander) Lees; KCVO (1972), CVO (1965, CMG 1964); s of Alexander Mayall (d 1943); *b* 14 Sept 1915; *Educ* Eton, Trinity Coll Oxford; *m* 1, 1940 (m dis 1947), Renee Eileen Burn; 1 da; m 2, 1947, Hon Mary Hermione, *qv*, da of 4 Baron Harlech, KG, GCMG, PC (d 1964); 1 s, 2 da; *Career* entered Dip Serv 1939; cnsllr: Tokyo 1958-61, Lisbon 1961-64, Addis Ababa 1964-65; HM vice-marshal of Dip Corps 1965-72, ambass Venezuela 1972-75, ret; *Style*— Sir Lees Mayall, KCVO, CVO, CMG; Sturford Mead, Warminster, Wilts (☎ 037 388 219)

MAYALL, Hon Lady; Mary Hermione; *née* Ormsby-Gore; da of 4 Baron Harlech KC, GCMG, PC (d 1964); *b* 1914; *m* 1, 1936 (m dis 1946), Capt Robin Francis Campbell, DSO, s of Rt Hon Sir Ronald Hugh Campbell, GCMG (decd); 2 s; m 2, 1947, Sir Alexander Lees Mayall, KCVO, CMG, *qv*; 1 s, 2 da; *Style*— The Hon Lady Mayall; Sturford Mead, Warminster, Wilts (☎ 037 388 219)

MAYBURY, Air Cdre Peter Lawrence; s of Lysander Montague Maybury (d 1971), of Portsmsouth, and Florence Edna, *née* Kaines; *b* 10 August 1928; *Educ* Sherborne, Cambridge Univ, Univ Coll Hosp (MA MBBChir); *m* 18 Sept 1954, Helen Lindsay Livingstone, da of Daniel Wills (d 1946), Res Comm Central Johore; 2 da (Nicola Helen b 1956, Karen Peta b 1958); *Career* medical practitioner qualified 1952; joined RAF medical branch 1954, Air Cdre served UK, RAF Germany, Libya, Cyprus; dep princ medical offr HQ RAF Germany 1967-70, Cmd health medical offr HQ Strike cmd 1975-78, dep dir health and research, MOD 1978-80 (dir 1980-82), ret 1982; RAF Central Medical Estab London: sr med offr, dep pres Central Medical Bd 1982-; FFCM, MFOM; *Recreations* gardening, walking, sailing; *Clubs* RAF; *Style*— Air Cdre Peter Maybury; Puddledock Garden, Clay Hall Lane, Acton, Sudbury, Suffolk (☎ 0787 77092); Central Medical Establishment, RAF Kelvin House, Cleveland Street, London (☎ 01 836 4651)

MAYER, Thomas (Tom); CBE (1985); s of Hans (d 1967), and Jeanette, *née* Gumperz (d 1956); *b* 17 Dec 1928; *Educ* Kings Sch Harrow, Regent Street Poly (BSc); *m* 1975, Jean Patricia, da of John Ernest Frederick Burrows, of 6 Boyne Rd, Dagenham; 1 s (Peter), 1 da (Helen); *Career* md Marconi Communications Systems Ltd 1969-81, chm and md Thorn EMI Electronics Ltd 1981-86, chief exec Thorn EMI Technol Gp 1986-; dir: Thorn EMI plc 1987-, Thorn EMI Electronics Ltd 1981-, Babcock Thorn 1986-, Soc of Br Aerospace Cos Ltd 1984-; memb Nat Electronics Cncl; FEng, FIEE, FRSA, FRTS; *Clubs* RAC, Whiteleaf Golf; *Style*— Tom Mayer Esq; 1590 AD, Burton Lane, Monks Risborough, Bucks HP17 9JF; Thorn EMI Technology, Sunbury House, 79 Staines Road West, Sunbury-on-Thames, Middx TW16 7AA

MAYER, William Edgar; s of John William Mayer, of Old Colwyn, nr Wales, and Adelaide Gertrude Mayer, *née* Saunders ; *b* 1 July 1910; *Educ* Epworth Coll N Wales; *m* 1, 1933, Margaret Elizabeth Cowell, da of Richard Greaves (d 1938), of Polperro, Cornwall; 1 s (Peter); m 2, 1945, Evelyn, da of Bertram Hayes (d 1966), of Chorley, Lancs; 1 s (Christopher b 1960), 1 da (Hilary b 1951); *Career* chartered architect; asst architect New Works Div (Min of Works 1945); artist: has given many exhibitions at various galleries, theatres, academys (UK) national winner of the 1000 TV Times Great Outdoors painting competition 1978; memb soc of Geneologists; RIBA; FRSA; *Recreations* genealogy, painting; *Clubs* Royal Soc of Arts, Adelphi (London); *Style*— William E Mayer, Esq; Stone Cottage, 145 Town Lane, Whittle-le-Woods, Chorley, Lancs PR6 8AG (☎ 02572 62068); The Studio, 145 Town Lane, Whittle-le-Woods, Chroley, Lancs PR6 8AG (☎ 02572 62068)

MAYHEW, Audrey Louise; da of George Ernest Mayhew (d 1969), of London, and Wilhelmina Louise, *née* Brandt (d 1977); *b* 20 Jan 1925; *Educ* North London Collegiate Sch, Girton Coll Univ of Cambridge (MA); *Career* actg headmistress (former dep headmistress) Lewes Girls' GS, dep headmistress Ealing Girls' GS, headmistress St Elphin's Sch Darley Dale Matlock Derbys; memb: AAM, AHM, Kent and E Sussex Girtonians Assoc; *Recreations* Greek and Roman Studies, music, oil painting, gardening, foreign travel; *Clubs* Country Gentlemen's Assoc; *Style*— Miss Audrey Mayhew; Haslemere, Mushroom Field, Kingston, Lewes, E Sussex BN7 3LE (☎ 0273 474 374)

MAYHEW, Lady Beryl Caroline Rees; da of Russell James Colman (Lord Lieut of Norfolk, 1929-44); *m* 1932, as his 2 w, Sir Basil Edgar Mayhew, KBE (d 1966); *Style*— Lady Mayhew; Ingles Ct Hotel, Folkstone, Kent CT20 2SN (☎ 0303 43593)

MAYHEW, Hon Christopher James; yr son of Baron Mayhew (Life Peer); *b* 1959; *Style*— Hon Christopher Mayhew; 34 Morden Road, London SW19 3BR

MAYHEW, Baron (Life Peer UK 1981); Christopher Paget Mayhew; s of Sir Basil Edgar Mayhew, KBE, and Dorothea, da of Stephen Paget and gda of Sir James Paget, 1 Bt, whereby His Lordship is 2 cous of the present (4) Bt, Sir Julian (Gentleman Usher to HM), and Paul Paget, the architect, also great nephew to a brace of Bishops (Francis, sometime Bp of Oxford, and Henry, sometime Bp of Chester); *b* 12 June 1915; *Educ* Haileybury, Ch Ch Oxford; *m* 1949, Cicely Elizabeth, da of George Ludlam; 2 s, 2 da; *Career* served Surrey Yeo RA WW II, Maj; MP (L) S Norfolk 1945-50, Woolwich E (subsequently Greenwich, Woolwich E) 1951-74 (when resigned from Labour Pty and joined Libs), MP (Lib) July-Oct 1974; stood (Lib) for Bath 1974 & 1979, min Def (RN) 1964-66, Lib Spokesman Def 1974-; stood (Lib) for Surrey as prospective MEP 1979, London SW Sept 1979; chm ME Int (Publishers), ANAF Fndn; *Books* Men Seeking God, Britain's Role Tomorrow, Party Games, Publish It Not, The Middle East Cover Up, Time to Explain; *Recreations* golf, music; *Clubs* National Liberal; *Style*— The Rt Hon the Lord Mayhew; 39 Wool Rd, SW20 (☎ 01 946 3460)

MAYHEW, Hon David Francis; er s of Baron Mayhew (Life Peer), *qv*; *b* 31 July 1951; *Educ* St Paul's, Ch Ch Oxford (BA PPE, BA Theol, MA); *m* 1979, Elizabeth Helen, da of Lt-Col Pusinelli, of Chinagarth, Thornton-le-Dale, N Yorks; 3 da; *Career* careers offr, area sec TOC H; *Recreations* windsurfing, golf, gardening, politics; *Style*— The Hon David Mayhew; The White House, Whickham View, Newcastle-upon-Tyne NE15 6SY (☎ 091 274 3757)

MAYHEW, Hon Judith Emily Ann; yr da of Baron Mayhew (Life Peer); *b* 1955; *Career* professional muscian; *Style*— The Hon Judith Mayhew; 3 Shelton Rd, Merton Park, London SW19

MAYHEW, Lionel Geoffrey; s of Geoffrey Dixon Mayhew (d 1963), of Speldhurst, Tunbridge Wells, Kent, and Bertha Irene, *née* Short (d 1929); *b* 5 Dec 1916; *Educ* Eton, Trinity Coll Oxford (MA); *m* 19 Oct 1939, Beatrice, da of Thomas Vowe Peake (d 1956), of The Grange, Rawnsley, Cannock, Staffs; 1 s (David Lionel b 20 May 1940), 3 da (Jane Barbara (Mrs Thomas) b 28 March 1943, Bridget Ann (Mrs Martin) b 2 Dec 1944, Rosamund Betty (Mrs Weaver) b 29 June 1949); *Career* RMC Sandhurst 1939-40, cmmnd Royal Leics Regt 1940, joined 2/5 (later 7) Bn, transferred Intelligence Corps 1943, served with SHAEF and in Air Miny (partly concerned with German Secret Weapons V1 & V2), WO (GSO 2) MI 14 Ch, demobbed Maj 1946; stockbroker; London Stock Exchange 1947-49; Liverpool Stock Exchange 1949: joined 1949, memb 1955, memb ctee 1963 (ctee chm 1971-74); memb SE Cncl 1975-78; sr ptnr Neilson Hornby Crickton & Co 1978-86, Neilson Milnes 1986-87, ret; chm City of Chester Cons Assoc 1960-65; Chester Grosvenor Nuffield Hosp: chm Fund raising ctee 1971-74, chm med advsy ctee 1974-81; Liveryman Worshipful Co of Gold and Silver Wyre Drawers 1949 (memb of Ct 1968, Master 1979); *Recreations* shooting, stalking, gardening; *Clubs* RAC, Racquet Club (Liverpool); *Style—* Lionel G Mayhew, Esq

MAYHEW, Hon Mrs (Margaret Louise); 3 da of Baron Brock (Life Peer; d 1980); *b* 8 May 1936; *Educ* Malvern Girls' Coll; *m* 1962 (m dis 1988), (John Alexander) Simon Cary Mayhew, eldest son of Maj John de Perigault Gurney Mayhew, S Staffs Regt; 2 da (Ella b 1963, Matilda b 1965); *Style—* The Hon Mrs Mayhew; c/o Wright, Webb Syrett, 10 Soho Square, London W1V 6EE

MAYHEW, Sir Patrick Barnabas Burke; PC (1986), QC (1972), MP (C) Tunbridge Wells Feb 1974-; s of (Alfred) Geoffrey (Horace) Mayhew, MC, and Sheila Margaret Burke Roche; *b* 11 Sept 1929; *Educ* Tonbridge Sch, Balliol Coll Oxford (MA); *m* 1963, Jean Elizabeth, 2 da of John Gurney, *qv*, of Walsingham Abbey, Norfolk; 4 s; *Career* served 4/7 Royal Dragoon Gds, Capt (Nat Serv and AER); barr Middle Temple 1955, bencher 1980; contested (C) Camberwell and Dulwich 1970, vice-chm Cons Home Affrs Ctee and memb exec 1922 Ctee 1976-79, parly under-sec Employment 1979-81, min state Home Off 1981-83, slr-general 1983-87; attorney-gen 1987-; kt 1983; *Clubs* Pratt's, Beefsteak, Garrick; *Style—* The Rt Hon Sir Patrick Mayhew, PC, QC, MP; House of Commons, London SW1A 0AA

MAYHEW-SANDERS, Sir John Reynolds; s of Jack Mayhew-Sanders (d 1982); *b* 25 Oct 1931; *Educ* Epsom Coll, RNC Dartmouth, Jesus Coll Cambridge; *m* 1958, Sylvia Mary, da of George S Colling (d 1959); 3 s, 1 da; *Career* chm John Brown & Co Ltd 1978-83 (chief exec 1975-83, dir 1972-83) and Overseas Project Bd 1980-83; non-exec dir: Rover Gp plc 1980-88, Dowty Gp plc 1982-86; memb: cncl of Engrg Employers' Fedn 1977-80, BOTB 1980-83, BBC Consultative Gp Industl & Business Affairs 1981-83; formerly with Mayhew-Sanders chartered accountants and with PE Consulting Gp Ltd; served with RN 1949-54, pres Br-Soviet C of C 1983-88; govr Sadler's Wells Fndn 1983-, a dir Sadler's Wells Tst and chm New Sadler's Wells Opera Co, chm Heidrick & Struggles 1985-87, chief exec Samuelson Gp plc 1987-88; FCA; kt 1982; *Recreations* fishing, shooting, music, gardening; *Style—* Sir John Mayhew-Sanders; Earlstone House, Burghclere, nr Newbury, Berkshire (☎ 063 527 288)

MAYNARD, (Henry) Charles Edward; s of Henry Maynard, of Coleshill, Bucks, and Diana Elizabeth, *née* Lee; *b* 10 Feb 1941; *Educ* Bryanston, Imperial Coll London (BSc); *m* 17 March 1984, Susan Marjorie, da of Edward George Hedges Barford; 1 da (Catherine Anna b 1 May 1986); *Career* ptnr Moores & Rowland CA's 1969 (ptnr i/c London Off 1979-85, vice chm Moores & Rowland Int 1987-); memb Worshipful co of Chartered Accountants in England and Wales; FCA 1962; *Recreations* golf, tennis, skiing, sailing, victorian watercolours; *Clubs* Hurlingham, Royal West Nofolk GC; *Style—* Charles Maynard, Esq; Moores & Rowland, Cliffords Inn, Fetter Lane, London EC4 1AS (☎ 01 831 2345, fax 01 831 6123)

MAYNARD, Edwin Francis George (Frank); s of Edwin Maynard, and Nancy Frances, *née* Tully; *b* 23 Feb 1921; *Educ* Westminster, Middle East Staff Coll; *m* 1, May 1945 (m dis 1962), Patricia Baker; 1 s (John Edwin b 1947), 1 da (Ann b 1948); m 2, Feb 1963, Anna Maria McGettrick; 2 s (Gareth b 1964, James b 1966); *Career* Royal Fusiliers 1939-40, cmmnd 4/8 Prince of Wales Own Punjab Regt, Capt 1941 Middle East & Burma HQ 17 Indian Div 43 45, Maj GSO II (I) 1945, Instr Intelligence Sch India 1946; BBC French Serv 1948, FO 1949, consul & oriental Sec Jedda 1950, 1st sec Benghazi 1952, FO 1954, commercial sec and supt consul Bogota 1956, 1st sec info Khartoum 1959, FO 1960 Baghdad 1962, fndr dir Dip Serv Language Centre 1966, cncllr 1967 Aden, cncllr commercial New Delhi 1968-72, commercial minister Buenos Aires 1972-76, Chargé d'Affaires 1974-75, deputy high cmmr Calcutta 1976-80; business conslt and dir; memb local Conservation Soc; *Recreations* shooting, fishing, languages, gardening; *Clubs* Brooks's, Circulo de Armas Buenos Aires, Bengal Club; *Style—* Frank Maynard, Esq; Littlebourne Ct, Littlebourne, Canterbury, Kent

MAYNARD, Frederick Gerard; s of Edwin Maynard, FRCS, MD (d 1951); *b* 9 Oct 1924; *Educ* Westminster; *m* 1956, Olivia Jane, da of Edward Percy Dorian Reed (d 1942); 2 da (Venetia Jane, Teresa Susan); *Career* served WW II, Capt SAS, France, Germany, South East Asia; chm Maynard, Reeve & Wallace Ltd 1961-80; Lloyd's underwriter; Croix de Guerre (France) 1944; *Clubs* City of London, Special Forces; *Style—* Frederick Maynard Esq; 43 Bury Walk, London SW3

MAYNARD, Prof Geoffrey Walter; s of Walter F Maynard, and Maisie, *née* Bristow; *b* 27 Oct 1921; *Educ* Univ of London, LSE (BSc), Univ of Wales (PhD); *m* 1949, Marie Lilian, *née* Wright; 2 da (Joanna b 1956, Victoria b 1961); *Career* taught at several univs in UK and USA; at various times conslt: FCO, World Bank, Harvard Univ Devpt Advsy Serv; held advsy posts to number of developing countries incl Argentina and Liberia; ed Bankers' Magazine 1968-72, dep chief econ advsr HM Treasy 1976-77 (under sec 1972-74), vice pres and dir of econs Europe and Middle East Chase Manhattan Bank 1977-86 (econ conslt 1974), econ conslt Investcorp Int Ltd 1986-; *Books* princ books incl: Economic Devpt and the Price Level (1961), A World of Inflation (jtly, 1976), The British Economy Under Mrs Thatcher 1979-87 (1988); *Recreations* walking; *Clubs* Reform; *Style—* Prof Geoffrey Maynard; Flat 219, Queens Quay, 58 Upper Thames St, London EC4

MAYNARD, (Vera) Joan; JP (Thirsk 1950), MP (Lab) Sheffield Brightside Oct 1974-; *b* 1921; *Career* memb Labour Party NEC 1970-, vice-chm 1981-82; chm Campaign Gp Labour MPs 1982-, memb of Select Ctee on Agric 1979-; sponsored by Agric Trade Gp TGWU; memb of NUAAW (now TGWU) since 1947; Yorks County sec and vice-pres 1966-72; former Parish, District and CC; *Style—* Miss Joan Maynard, JP, MP; House of Commons, SW1A 0AA

MAYNARD, John David; s of Albert William Henry Maynard (d 1968), of Surrey, and Ellen Hughes-Jones (d 1970); *b* 14 May 1931; *Educ* Whitgift Sch, Charing Cross Hosp London (Gold Medal Clinical Medicine and surgery, MB, BS); *m* 1, 13 Aug 1955, Patricia Katharine (dis 1971), da of C W F Gray (d 1985), of Sutton, Surrey; 2 s (Andrew b 1959, Nicholas b 1962), 2 da (Sarah b 1956, Julia b 1962); m 2, 23 June 1972, Gillian Mary, da of H F Loveless, FRICS, of Milford-on-Sea, Hampshire; 1 s (Timothy b 1976); *Career* Capt RAMC 1954; snr conslt surgeon Guy's Hosp London 1967-, curator Gordon Museum, Guy's Med Sch 1969-, teacher London Univ 1963-; chm The Salivary Gland Tumour Panel England 1970-, late Hunterian Prof RCS 1963; surgical tutor: RCS 1967-76, Guy's Hosp Med Sch 1967-76; snr examiner Surgery London Univ 1962-85; examiner surgery the Soc of Apothecaries 1962-70, lectr Anatomy The London Hosp 1958-59; Liveryman The Worshipful Soc of Apothecaries 1962; scientific fell the Zoological Soc 1956, FRSM 1958; fell: The Hunterian Soc 1985, Assoc of Surgeons 1967; FRCS; memb: Med Soc of London 1961-, The Chelsea Clinical Soc 1962-, The Br Med Assoc 1954-; author papers on diseases of salivary glands; *Books* Surgery (jt author 1974), Surgery of Salivary Glands in Surgical Mgmnt (1984, 1988), Contemporary Operative Surgery (1979); *Recreations* golf, mountaineering, photography; *Clubs* Carlton; *Style—* John D Maynard, Esq; 14 Blackheath Park, London SE3 9RP (☎ 01 852 6766); Mountsloe, Frogham, Fordingbridge, Hants SP6 2HP (☎ 04255 3009); Guy's Hosp, London SE1 9RT (☎ 01 407 7600 ext 3372); 92 Harley St, London W1N 1DF (☎ 01 935 4988)

MAYNARD, Air Chief Marshal Sir Nigel Martin; KCB (1973), CB 1971, CBE 1963, DFC 1942, AFC 1947); s of Air Vice-Marshal Forster Herbert Martin Maynard, CB, AFC (d 1976); *b* 28 August 1921; *Educ* Aldenham; *m* 1946, Daphne, da of Griffith Llewellyn (d 1972); 1 s, 1 da; *Career* served WW II RAF, Gp Capt 1958, ADC to HM The Queen 1961-65, Air Cdre 1965, Air Vice-Marshal 1968, Cmdt Staff Coll Bracknell 1968-70, Air Cdr Far East 1970-71, Dep C-in-C Strike Cmd 1972, C-in-C RAF Germany and Cdr 2 Allied Tactical Air Force 1973-76, Air Chief Marshal 1976, C-in-C Strike Cmd 1976-77, ret; *Recreations* travel; *Clubs* Naval and Military, RAF, MCC; *Style—* Air Chief Marshal Sir Nigel Martin, KCB, CB, CBE, DFC, AFC; Manor House, Piddington, Bicester, Oxon (☎ 0844 238270)

MAYNE, Prof David Quinn; s of Leslie Harper Mayne (d 1963), and Jane Theresa, *née* Quin; *b* 23 April 1930; *Educ* Christian Brothers Coll Boksburg SA, Univ of The Witwatersrand SA (BSc, MSc), Univ of London (PhD, DSc); *m* 16 Dec 1954, Josephine Mary, da of Joseph Karl Hess (d 1968); 3 da (Susan Francine (Mrs Leung) b 9 March 1956, Maire Anne b 16 July 1957, Ruth Catherine b 18 April 1959); *Career* lectr Univ of the Witwatersrand 1950-54 & 1957-59, R & D engr Br Thomson Houston Co; Rugby 1955-56, reader Imperial Coll London 1967-71 (lectr 1959-67), res fell Harvard 1971-, prof Imperial Coll 1971-(head electrical eng dept 1984-88);FIEE 1980, FIEEE 1981, FRS 1985, FEng 1987; *Books* Differential Dynamic Programming (1970); *Recreations* walking; *Style—* Prof David Mayne; 123 Elgin Crescent, London W11 2JH (☎ 01 229 1744); Dept Electrical Engineering, Imperial College, London SW7 2BT (☎ 01 589 5111 ext 5113)

MAYNE, James Edward Mosley; s of Rupert Eric Mosley Mayne; *b* 16 July 1944; *Educ* Wellington Coll, Pembroke Oxford; *m* 1970, Patricia Ann Mary, *née* Mayer; 1 s, 2 da; *Career* barr; chm: Habit Precision Engrg plc 1979-, Wymanor Investments Ltd 1976-, Flextech plc 1986-; *Recreations* shooting, fishing, skiing; *Clubs* United Oxford and Cambridge Univ, Boodles; *Style—* James Mayne Esq; The Manor House, Wycomb, Melton, Nowbray, Leics

MAYNE, Very Rev Michael Clement Otway; s of Michael Ashton Otway Mayne (d 1933), and Sylvia Clementina, *née* Lumley Ellis; *b* 10 Sept 1929; *Educ* Kings' Sch Canterbury, Corpus Christi Coll Cambridge (BA, MA); *m* 16 Oct 1965, Alison Geraldine, da of Henry Erskine McKie (d 1985); 1 s (Mark b 1968) 1 da (Sarah b 1966); *Career* Nat Serv, Pilot Offr RAF 1949-51; asst curate St John the Baptist Harpendon 1957-59, domestic chaplain to Bishop of Southwark 1959-65, vicar Norton Letchworth 1965-72, head religious progs BBC Radio 1972-79, vicar Great St Mary's (Univ Church) Cambridge 1979-86, dean of Westminster 1986-, dean Order of the Bath; chm Govrs Westminster Sch, memb cncl St Christophers Hospice; FSA 1987; *Books* Prayers for Pastoral Occasions (1982), Encounters (ed 1985), A Year Lost and Found (1987); *Recreations* theatre, reading novels and poetry, bird watching; *Style—* The Very Rev The Dean of Westminster; The Deanery, Deans Yard, Westminster Abbey, London SW1P 3PA (☎ 01 222 2953)

MAYNE, Dr Richard John; s of John William Mayne (d 1975), of London, and Kate Hilda Mayne, *née* Angus; *b* 2 April 1926; *Educ* St Paul's Sch London, Trinity Coll Cambridge (MA, PhD); *m* 1, 1954, Margaret Ellingworth Lyon; m 2, 1970, Jocelyn Mudie, da of William James Ferguson, of London; 2 da (Zoë, Alice); *Career* official of the Euro Communities 1956-63, dir Federal Tst 1971-73, head of UK Offs Commn of The Euro Communities 1973-79, co-ed Encounter 1985-; *Books* The Community of Europe, The Recovery of Europe, The Europeans, Postwar, Western Europe (ed), The Memoirs of Jean Monnet (trans); *Recreations* travel, fellwalking, sailing (Flying Falcon); *Clubs* Groucho, Les Misérables (Paris); *Style—* Dr Richard Mayne; Albany Cottage, 24 Park Village East, London NW1 7PZ (☎ 01 387 6654); Encounter, 44 Great Windmill Street, London W1V 7PA (☎ 01 434 3063)

MAYO, Hon Mrs; Hon Christine Mary; *née* Plumb; yr da of Lord Plumb (Life Peer), *qv*; *b* 1950; *m* 1973, Benjamin John Mayo; 3 da (Katherine Elizabeth b 1977, Sarah Louise b 1979, Stephanie Caroline b 1983); *Style—* The Hon Mrs Mayo; The Garth, Kirkby Lane, Great Broughton, N Yorks

MAYO, Lady; Gwen Alister Brookes; da of John MacInnes, of Naracoorte, S Australia; *m* 1958, as his 2 w, Hon Sir Herbert Mayo (d 1972); *Style—* Lady Mayo; 90 Northgate St, Unley Park, S Australia

MAYO, Col (Edward) John; OBE (1976); s of The Rev Thomas Edward Mayo, JP (d 1973), of Axminster Devon, and Constance Muriel, *née* Knibb; *b* 24 May 1931; *Educ* Kings Coll Taunton; *m* 1961, Jacqueline Margaret Anne, MBE, da of Brig Charles Douglas Armstrong, CBE, DSO, MC (d 1985); 1 s (Charles); *Career* cmmd RA 1951, served in Malta, N Africa, Malaya, W Germany; cmdt 17 Trg Regt and Depot RA 1972-75, Col Gen Staff HQ BAOR 1979-83, ret; dir gen Help the Aged 1983-, tstee: Helpage India 1985, Helpage Kenya 1985, Helpage Sri Lanka 1986; FRSA; *Recreations* gardening, fine arts, travel, swimming; *Clubs* Army & Navy, MCC, Special Forces; *Style—* Col John Mayo; Sehore House, Tekels Ave, Camberley, Surrey (☎ 0276 29653); Help the Aged, St James's Walk, Clerkenwell, London EC1 (☎ 01 253 0253)

MAYO, John William; s of Malcolm Guy Mayo (d 1968); *b* 8 Oct 1920; *Educ* St Paul's; *m* 1959, Susan Margaret; 3 s, 1 da; *Career* Capt RA (UK, Ceylon, India); ptnr Linklaters & Paines slrs (qualified 1947, joined firm 1947, ptnr 1952, snr ptnr 1980-85), S G Warburg & Co Ltd 1985-; Hon FRCGP 1979; *Recreations* bridge, golf; *Clubs* Royal Wimbledon GC, Hunstanton GC, Ealing FC (RU); *Style—* John Mayo, Esq; 38 Marryat Rd, Wimbledon, London SW19 5BD (☎ 01 946 1537); The Mill Cottage, Ringstead, Hunstanton, Norfolk (☎ 048 525 391); S G Warburg & Co Ltd, London EC2M 2PA (☎ 01 860 0950)

MAYO, Peter Dereck Buckpitt; s of Leonard George Mayo (decd Wellington, NZ, date unknown), and Margery Muriel, *née* Buckpitt (d 1986); *b* 2 Oct 1920; *Educ* Colfes GS, Kings Coll Dental Hosp, LDS, RCS, Eng; *m* 14 April 1945, Mary, da of John Macnamara (d 1950), of O'Connell St, Kilkee, Co Clare, Ireland (d 1940); 2 s(David b 1946, Christopher b 1959), 1 da (Felicity b 1951); *Career* surgn Lt (D) RNVR 1945-48, RNB Chatham, Royal Marines Deal HMS Hornet Gosport, HMS Excellent Whale

Island Portsmouth; W Suffolk Deniac Ctee, dental rep on W Suffolk Health Ctee, Opthalitic and Disciplinary Ctees, vice-chm Bd of Visitors HMP Highpoint 1986-, chm 1987; *Recreations* swimming, gardening, horse racing; *Style—* Peter Mayo, Esq; Maythorpe, Malting End, Wickhambrook, Newmarket, Suffolk (☎ 0440 820 313)

MAYO, Rear-Adm Robert William; CB (1965), CBE (1962); s of Frank Mayo (d 1934); *b* 9 Feb 1909; *Educ* Weymouth Coll, HMS Conway; *m* 1942, Sheila (d 1974), da of late John Colvill, JP; 1 s; m 2, 1980, Betty Basina, da of Albert Terry, of Gravesend; *Career* RNR 1925-37, Royal Mail Lines, Master Certificate 1936, joined RN 1937, Capt 1953, Rear-Adm 1964, naval dep Allied Forces N Europe 1964-66, ret 1966; Hon Sheriff Campbeltown 1971; *Recreations* gardening, sailing; *Clubs* Royal Scottish Automobile, Royal Naval Sailing Assoc; *Style—* Rear-Adm Robert Mayo, CB, CBE; Bellgrove, Campbeltown, Argyll (☎ 0586 52101); 8 Silverless St, Marlborough (☎ 0672 53951)

MAYO, 10 Earl of (I 1785); Terence Patrick Bourke; also Baron Naas (I 1776) and Viscount Mayo (I 1781); s of Hon Bryan Longley Bourke (d 1961), and nephew of 9 Earl (d 1962); *b* 26 August 1929; *Educ* St Aubyns Rottingdean, RN Coll Dartmouth; *m* 1952, Margaret Jane Robinson, da of Gerald Harrison, DL (d 1954); 3 s; *Heir* Lord Naas; *Career* Lt RN 1952, served Suez 1956; Solo Aerobatic Displays, Farnborough 1957; md Irish Marble Ltd Merlin Park Galway; memb Lib Pty 1963-65, stood for Dorset S as Lib candidate 1964; memb Gosport Borough Cncl 1961; *Clubs* Naval and County Galway; *Style—* The Rt Hon the Earl of Mayo; Doon House, Maam, Co Galway, Eire

MAYOR, Hugh Robert; QC (1986); s of George Mayor, Esq, of 9 Greyfriars Crescent, Fulwood, Preston, and Grace Mayor; *b* 12 Oct 1941; *Educ* Kirkham GS, St John Coll Oxford MA (Oxon), MA (Leicester); *m* 1970, Carolyn Ann, da of Gp Capt Dennis Raymond Stubbs RAF, DSO, DFC, OBE, of Pond Farm, Sutton, Norfolk (d 1973); 1 s (Nicholas Dennis Robert b 1973), 1 da (Sally Jane b 1975); *Career* barr, (Grays Inn 1968) Midland and Oxford Circuit, rec 1982; QC 1986; *Recreations* sailing, tennis; *Style—* Hugh R Mayor, Esq, QC; 33 Eastgate, Hallaton, Leics (☎ 085 889 200); 2 Dr Johnson's Buildings, Temple (☎ 01 353 5371)

MAYORCAS, Joseph David; s of M J Mayorcas (d 1986), of Barnes, London, and Lilian, *née* Valins; *b* 2 Dec 1937; *Educ* Latymer Upper; *m* 6 Oct 1973, Caroline Marguerite, da of Basil Rogers, of Kew, Surrey; 3 da (Claire and Miranda twins b 1974, Alice b 1980); *Career* dir for 30 years of Mayorcas Ltd (dealing in antique textiles and tapestries); *Recreations* opera, theatre, cinema, keeping fit; *Style—* Joseph David Mayorcas, Esq; 52 Grove Park Gardens, London W4 3RZ; 38 Jermyn Street, London SW17 6DN

MAYS, Colin Garth; CMG (1988); s of William Albert Mays (d 1982), and Sophia May Mays, *née* Pattinson (d 1972); *b* 16 June 1931; *Educ* Acklam Hall Sch, St John's Coll Oxford (BA); *m* 1956, Margaret Patricia, da of Philemon Robert Lloyd, and Gladys Irene Lloyd, *née* Myers, of Marske by Sea Cleveland; 1 s (Nicholas b 1964); *Career* HM Diplomatic Serv: FO 1955-56, Sofia 1956-58, Baghdad 1958-60; UK Delgn to the Conference of the 18 Nation Ctee on Disarmament Geneva 1960, Bonn 1960-65, FCO 1965-69, Prague 1969-72, FCO (head of Info Admin Dept 1974-) 1972-77; commercial cnsllr Bucharest 1977-80, seconded to PA Mgmnt Conslts Ltd 1980-81; overseas inspr Diplomatic Serv 1981-83, Br high cmmr Seychelles 1983-86; Br high cmmr The Bahamas 1986-; Liveryman Worshipful Co of Painter Stainers; *Recreations* sailing, travel; *Clubs* Travellers; *Style—* Colin Mays, Esq, CMG; c/o FCO, King Charles St, London SW1A 2AH

MAYS-SMITH, (Robert) Martin; s of Lt-Col Robert Shankland Mays-Smith, MBE (d 1980), of Randolphs, Iden, Rye, Sussex, and Brenda Mary Hilda, *née* Rickett; *b* 17 Nov 1930; *Educ* Eton, Trinity Coll Cambridge; *m* 22 June 1963, Jennifer Joan, da of Capt Eustace Makins (d 1968), of Wood Farm, Little Fransham, Dereham, Norfolk; 3 da (Kate b 6 March 1964, Henrietta b 17 Jan 1966, Arabella b 10 July 1970); *Career* Irish Guards 1949-51; Bank of England 1954-63, Barclays Bank 1863-69, (Local dir Oxford 1968-69); md: William Brandt & Sons & Co Ltd 1969-72, Nat & Grindlays Bank 1970-72; dir A L Sturge Holdings Ltd, Kleinwort Benson Ltd 1972- (banking dir 1972-84, head banking div 1984-87), Kleinwort Benson Gp plc 1988-, Rockfort Gp plc, Empire Stores (Bradford) plc, First Nat Fin Corpn; vice pres The London Life Assoc Ltd; memb: cncl Save the Children Fund, governing body of Ripon Coll; Liveryman Worshipful Co of Clothworkers; FCIB 1983; *Recreations* fishing, music specially opera; *Clubs* Leander; *Style—* Martin Mays-Smith, Esq; Beedon House, Beedon, Newbury, Berkshire RG16 8SW (☎ East Ilsley 233); Kleinwort Benson Ltd., 20 Fenchurch St, London EC3P 3DB (☎ 01 623 8000)

MEACHER, Michael Hugh; MP ((Lab) Oldham W 1970-); s of George Hubert Meacher (d 1969), of Berkhamsted, Herts; *b* 4 Nov 1939; *Educ* Berkhamsted Sch, New Coll Oxford; *m* 1, 1962 (m dis 1987), Molly Christine, da of William Reid, of Grayshott, Surrey; 2 s, 2 da; m 2, 1988, Lucianne, da of William Craven, of Gerrards Cross, Bucks; *Career* joined Lab Pty 1962, sec Danilo Dolci Tst 1964, lectr in social admin York Univ 1966-69 and LSE 1970; parly under-sec state: Dept of Indust 1974-75, DHSS 1975-76, Dept of Trade 1976-79; memb Treasy Select Ctee 1980-83, chm Select Ctee on Lloyd's Bill 1982, defeated Lab dep leadership election 1983, elected to shadow cabinet 1983, memb NEC Oct 1983-; front bench oppn spokesman: Health and Social Security 1983-87, Employment 1987-; author; *Books* Taken for a Ride (1972), Socialism with a Human Face (1982); *Style—* Michael Meacher, Esq, MP; 5 Cottenham Park Rd, London SW20

MEAD, Brian Leonard; s of Leonard William Mead, of 93 Meadway, Ilford, Essex, and Lillian Elizabeth, *née* Crick; *b* 12 Mar 1944; *Educ* Mayfield Boys Sch; *m* 18 Aug 1972, (m dis 1986), Faith Margaret, da of Harlod Scholes, of Manchester; 1 da (Elizabeth b 1983); *Career* slr; Jackson Pixley & Co ACs: articles 1962-67, admitted slr 1967, mangr 1968-70; sr mangr Mann Judd CAs 1971-73, assoc gp fin dir Green Shield Training Stamp Co Ltd 1973-78, gp fin dir Cray Electronics Holdings plc 1979-; cdre Little Ship Club London 1982-85; FCA 1967, MInstD 1980; *Recreations* sailing, yacht racing, cruising; *Clubs* Royal Southern, Little Ship, RYA; *Style—* Brian Mead, Esq; The Haven, 5 Sylvan Lane, Hamble, Southampton, Hampshire (☎ 0703 456 101); Cray Electronics Holdings Plc, Cray Manor, 12 Manor Ct, Fareham, Hampshire (☎ 0489 885 667, fax 0489 885 634, car phone 0836 772 386, telex 47375)

MEAD, Rev Colin Harvey; s of Lt-Col Roger Mead, OBE (d 1964), of the Middle East, and Marjorie McGlashan Kirk Mead, *née* Tait (d 1961); *b* 4 June 1926; *Educ* Bloxham Sch, Trinity Coll Oxford; *m* 4 April 1953, Constance Jean, da of Alfred John Harding KCMG, CBE (d 1953), of Barton-on-Sea; 1 da (Susan b 1954), 2 s (David b 1957, Kenneth b 1964); *Career* CA; ptnr Grant Thornton, ret; pres Southern Soc of CAs 1972-73; ordained non-stipendiary min C of E 1984, asst priest St Marks Talbot Village; govr: Wentworth Milton Mount Sch 1968- (chm 1987-), Bloxham Sch 1981-; played Hockey for: Oxford Univ 1943-44, Hampshire, Oxfordshire; FCA; *Recreations* tennis, swimming, bridge; *Clubs* Bournemouth Sports (life vice-pres), Rotary Bournemouth, Bournemouth 41; *Style—* Rev Colin Mead; Summerleaze, 59 Alyth Rd, Talbot Woods, Bournemouth, Dorset BH3 7HB (☎ 0202 763647)

MEAD, Janet Mabel; da of Frank William Mead (d 1983), and Peggy Gertrude Florence Lyne, *née* Martin; *b* 4 July 1942; *Educ* St Martin-in-the-Fields HS, Univs of Barcelona, Madrid and Grenoble (various language and translators diplomas, Dip CAM); *Career* personal mgmnt Petroleos Mexicanos Paris 1965-68, PRO for Ted Bates Advertising Agency Paris 1968-72, travelled extensively in S America 1972-73, corporate communications mangr HB Maynard Inc 1973-76, marketing services mangr Thomas Ness Ltd 1976-80, gen mangr Retailine Research Ltd 1980-82, md Assoc Research Ltd 1982; dir: Penarvon plc 1983, Retail Audits Ltd 1981; *Recreations* theatre, travel, running, painting, talking; *Clubs* Zonta Int London II (fndr memb); *Style—* Miss Janet Mead; Assoc Research Ltd, Banderway House, 158-162 Kilburn High Rd, London NW6 (☎ 01 328 3213)

MEAD, Richard Barwick; s of Thomas Gifford Mead, OBE, of 4 Wyndham Lea, W Chiltington, W Sussex, and Joyce Mary, *née* Barwick; *b* 18 August 1947; *Educ* Marlborough, Pembroke Coll Cambridge (MA); *m* 25 June 1971, Sheelagh Margaret, da of James Leslie Thom, of Holly Cottage, Stoke St Milborough, Ludlow, Shropshire; 2 s (Timothy b 1973, Rupert b 1977), 1 da (Nicola b 1975, d 1976); *Career* audit supervisor Arthur Young 1969-73 (ptnr and nat dir corporate finance 1985-), corporate fin exec Brandis Ltd 1973-75, dir and hd Corporate Fin Dept Anthony Gibbs & Sons Ltd 1975-83, dir corporate fin Credit Suisse First Boston Ltd 1983-85; FCA 1972; *Recreations* gardening, history, music, family; *Style—* Richard Mead, Esq; Shambles, Watts Cross, Hildenborough, Tonbridge, Kent TN11 9NB (☎ 0732 832 858); Arthur Young, Rolls House, 7 Rolls Bldgs, Fetter Lane, London EC4A 1NH (☎ 01 831 7130, fax 01 405 2147, telex 888604)

MEADE, Eric Cubitt; s of William Charles Abbott Meade (d 1970), and Vera Alicia Maria, *née* Cubitt (d 1981); *b* 12 April 1923; *Educ* Ratcliffe Coll Syston Leics; *m* 2 July 1960, Margaret Arnott, da of Archibald McCallum; 2 s (Vincent b 20 April 1961, Christopher b 5 April 1963), 1 da (Veronica b 11 Feb 1965); *Career* WWII Hampshire Regt 1942-46, served N Africa, Italy (cmmnd in field), Capt 1944 (POW 1944-45); CA 1947, sr ptnr Deloitte Haskins & Sells 1982-85 (employed 1949-58, ptnr 1958-85); chm: Parly Law Ctee 1974-76, Investigation Ctee 1976-77, Consultative Ctee of Accountancy Bodies Ethics Ctee 1977-83; memb Audit Cmmn 1986-, lay member Slrs Complaints Bureau 1985-; FCA (memb cncl 1969-79); *Recreations* tennis, bowls; *Clubs* Hurlingham; *Style—* Eric Meade, Esq; 56 Hurlingham Ct, Ranelagh Gdns, London SW6 3UP (☎ 01 736 5382)

MEADE, John Herbert; s of Adm the late Hon Sir Herbert Meade-Fetherstonhaugh, GCVO, CB, DSO (s of 4 Earl of Clanwilliam); hp to Earldom of Clanwilliam; *b* 27 Sept 1919; *Educ* RNC, Dartmouth; *m* 1956, Maxine, *née* Hayden Scott; 1 s (Patrick James Meade b 1960), 2 da; *Clubs* Turf; *Style—* John Meade, Esq; Blundells House, Tisbury, Wilts

MEADE, Lady Sophia Catherine Gathorne-Hardy; da of 4 Earl of Cranbrook, CBE; *b* 1936; *m* 1957, Simon Robert Jasper Meade; *Style—* Lady Sophia Meade

MEADE, Lady Sophia Hester; da of 6 Earl of Clanwilliam; *b* 14 Oct 1963; *Style—* Lady Sophia Meade

MEADE-KING, Richard Oliver; s of (William) Oliver Meade-King (d 1971), and Ellen Collins, *née* Sherlock; *b* 30 Jan 1926; *Educ* Radley, Jesus Coll Cambridge (BA); *m* 22 Dec 1951, Hilary Scott, da of Charles Woodhouse (d 1968); 1 s (Charles) 1 da (Tessa (Mrs Mackenzie)); *Career* Sub Lt Fleet Air Arm RNVR 1944-46; Binnie Deacon and Gourley Consulting Engrs 1949-58: asst rese engr Sillent Valley Water Tunnel Project, surveyor of potential hydro electric sites Nigeria, designer sewerage and surface water drainage Lusaka; English China Clays 1958-86 (ret), dir ECCI 1967-86; memb bd of ECC subsidiaries incl: chm ECC Carbonates, chm Fordiman Sales Ltd, dep chm Anglo American Clays Inc and Kaolin Australia, dir for ops of co's in Japan Brazil Portugal Spain France Italy; fndr chm Country Ventures Ltd (ret 1986); former memb Plymouth Cattwater Harbour Cmmrs, memb Fowey Harbour Cmmrs; *Style—* Richard Meade-King, Esq; Penellick, Par, Cornwall

MEADOWCROFT, Michael James; *b* 6 Mar 1942; *Educ* Unif of Bradford (MPhil); *m* 1, (m dis); 1 s, 1 da; m 2, 1987, Elizabeth Bee; *Career* chm Mersyside Regnl Young Lib Orgn 1961, local govt offr 1962-67, sec Yorks Lib Fedn 1967-70;memb Leeds City Cncl 1968-83, asst sec Joseph Rowntree Social Serv Tst 1970-78; gen sec Bradford Metropolitan Cncl for Voluntary Service 1978-83, chm Lib Party Assembly Ctee 1977-81; contested Leeds W (Lib) Feb and Oct 1974, MP Leeds W (Lib) 1983-87; *Books* Liberal Party Local Government Handbook (1974), Local Government Finance (1975), A Manifesto for Local Government (1975), The Bluffers Guide to Politics (1975), Liberal Values for a New Decade (1980), Social Democracy - Barrier or Bridge (1981), Liberalism and the Left (1982), Liberalism and the Right (1983); *Style—* Michael Meadowcroft, Esq; Waterloo Lodge, 72 Waterloo Lane, Bramley, Leeds LS13 2JF

MEADOWS, Dr John Christopher; s of Dr Swithin Pinder Meadows, and Doris Steward, *née* Noble; *b* 25 Mar 1940; *Educ* Westminster, Univ of Cambridge (BA, MB, BChir MD); *m* 9 Jul 1966, Patricia, da of John Appleton Pierce, of IOM; 2 s ; *Career* former conslt neurologist St George's Hosp, cnslt neurologist King Edward VII Hosp, hon neurologist Newspaper Press Fund; FRCP; *Recreations* gardening, walking, travelling, reading; *Style—* Dr John C Meadows; c/o 143 Harley Street, London W1N 1DJ (☎ 01 935 1802)

MEADOWS, William Robert; s of William de Warenne Meadows (d 1974), of Norfolk, and Marianne Alice Stokes (d 1930); *b* 10 August 1926; *Educ* Sherborne, Corpus Christi Coll Cambridge; *m* 8 Nov 1960, Alison Rosemary, da of Sir Austin Anderson (d 1973), of Surrey; 1 s (William b 1972), 2 da (Victoria b 1962, Marianne b 1963); *Career* Lt RM Commandos 1944-47, served Europe, Far East; glass engraver and lectr; memb Baltic Exchange 1951-68; Somerset CC: chm educn ctee 1981-83, chm 1983-85; chm: Somerset Co Cadet Ctee 1987-, Exmoor Nat Park Ctee 1987-; *Recreations* gardening, painting, fishing; *Style—* William R Meadows, Esq; The Old House, Milverton, Taunton, Somerset TA4 1LR

MEAGER, Hon Mrs; (Joan Beryl); da of 5 Baron Henley; *b* 1893; *m* 1914, Kildare Stucley Meager; 1 s, 1 da; *Style—* The Hon Mrs Meager; 117 Brighton Rd, Worthing,

Sussex

MEAKIN, Henry Paul John; s of Wing Cdr Henry John Walter Meakin, DFC, RAF (d 1989), of 9 Glanmore Rd, PO Chisipiti, Harare, Zimbabwe, and Elizabeth Wilma, *née* Fairbairns; *b* 2 Jan 1944; *Educ* Plumtree Sch Rhodesia; *m* 2 Jan 1971, Vicki Lynn, da of Maurice James Bullus, of Hilltop Hall, Pannal, Harrogate, N Yorks; 2 s (Oliver b 1975, Harry b 1980), 1 da (Katie b 1972); *Career* exec dir Pensord Press Ltd 1970-74; chm: Aspen Communications 1979-85 (md 1975-78), chm Aspen Communications plc 1985-; dir: Wiltshire Radio plc 1981-85, GWR Radio 1985-87; chm GWR gp plc 1988-; *Recreations* tennis, golf, music; *Style—* Henry Meakin, Esq; Aspen Communications plc, 18 Thomas St, Cirenchester, Gloucs GL7 2AX (☎ 0285 652176, fax 0285 656620, telex 43225)

MEALE, (Joseph) Alan; MP (Lab) Mansfield 1987-; s of Albert Henry Meale (d 1986), and Elizabeth, *née* Catchpole; both parents trade union shop stewards; *b* 31 July 1949; *Educ* Ruskin Coll Oxford; *m* 15 March 1983, Diana, da of Lt Cdr John Gillespy, RN (ret); *Career* nat employment devpt offr (Home Off funded) 1977-79, asst to Ray Buckton (gen sec ASLEF) 1979-83, parly and political advsr to Michael Meacher, MP 1983-87; *Books* author and ed various publications; *Recreations* reading; *Clubs* Mansfield Lab; *Style—* Alan Meale, Esq, MP; 4 Welbeck St, Mansfield, Notts; House of Commons, London SW1A 0AA

MEANEY, Sir Patrick Michael; s of Joseph Francis Meaney (d 1953), and Ethel Clara Meaney (d 1966); *b* 6 May 1925; *Educ* Wimbledon Coll, Northern Poly; *m* 1967, Mary June, da of Albert William Kearney (d 1986); 1 s (Adam b 1968); *Career* served HM Forces 1941-47; md Thomas Tilling plc 1973-83 (dir 1961-83), dir Cable & Wireless plc 1978-83, ICI plc 1981-, chm Rank Orgn 1983- (dir 1979-); dep chm Horserace Levy Board 1985-, dep chm Midland Bank plc 1985- (dir 1979-); dir MEPC plc 1986-; pres Inst of Mktg 1981-; memb: cncl London C of C 1977-82, Br N American Ctee 1979-, CBI 1980-, cncl Royal Society of Arts 1987-, Br Exec Serv Overseas 1987-, Stock Exchange Listed Cos Advsy Ctee 1987-, President's Ctee Advertising Assoc 1987-, advsy bd World Econ Forum 1979-; kt 1981; *Recreations* sport, music, education; *Clubs* Br Sportsmans, Harlequin FC; *Style—* Sir Patrick Meaney; Harefield House, Sandridge, Herts AL4 9EG; 6 Connaught Place, London W2 (☎ 01 629 7454, telex 263549)

MEARA, Dr Robert Harold; s of Robert Meara (d 1935), of Gwent, and Anne Davies (d 1958); *b* 8 Dec 1917; *Educ* Jones' Haberdashers Sch Pontypool, St Catharines Coll Cambridge (MA); *m* 18 Feb 1943, Mair, da of William Jones (d 1958), of Glamorgan; 1 s (Jolyon b 1956), 2 da (Jennifer b 1944, Imogen b 1955); *Career* dermatologist; emeritus conslt physician: Middlx Hosp London, St John's Hosp for Diseases of the Skin; former hon dermatologist to Br Army; *Recreations* music, walking, bridge, travel; *Clubs* Royal Soc of Medicine; *Style—* Dr Robert H Meara; 34 Channings, Kingsway, Hove, E Sussex (☎ 0273 733809); 132 Harley St, London W1N 1AH (☎ 01 935 3678)

MEARS, Rt Rev John Cledan; *see*: Bangor, Bishop of

MEARS, Roger Malcolm Loudon; s of Dr K P G Mears of Vancouver Island, Canada, and Dr Eleanor, *née* Loudon, of Sleaford, Lincs; *b* 15 Feb 1944; *Educ* City of London Sch, Corpus Christi Coll Cambridge (MA, DipArch);; *m* 4 Nov 1978, Joan Adams, da of William Archer Speers, of Brooklyn Heights, NY; 3 da (Emily b 1981, Rebecca b 1983, Jessica b 1986) ; *Career* architect with own practice and particular interest in historic bldgs; *Recreations* music, viola player, watermills and milling; *Style—* Roger Mears, Esq; 2 Compton Terr, London N1 2UN (☎ 01 359 8222)

MEATH, 14 Earl of (I 1627); Anthony Windham Normand Brabazon; also Baron Ardee (I 1616) and Baron Chaworth (UK 1831), in which title he sits in House of Lords; s of 13 Earl, CB, CBE (d 1949), by his w Lady Aileen Wyndham Quin (da of 4 Earl of Dunraven); *b* 3 Nov 1910; *Educ* Eton, RMC Sandhurst; *m* 30 July 1940, Elizabeth Mary, o da of Capt Geoffrey Vaux Salvin Bowlby, Royal House Gds (d 1915); 2 s, 2 da; *Heir* s, Lord Ardee; *Career* ADC to Gov Bengal 1936, Capt Gren Gds 1938, Maj 1941, ret 1946; *Style—* The Rt Hon the Earl of Meath; Killruddery, Bray, Co Wicklow, Ireland

MEATH, Bishop of (RC); Most Rev John McCormack; s of Peter McCormack, of Moynalty, Kells, Co Meath; *b* 25 Mar 1921; *Educ* St Finian's Coll Mullingar, Maynooth Coll, Lateran Univ; *Career* ordained 1946, bishop of Meath 1968-; *Style—* The Most Rev the Bishop of Meath; Bishop's House, Dublin Rd, Mullingar, Co Westmeath, Ireland (☎ 044 48841)

MEDAWAR, Nicholas Antoine Macbeth; s of late Antoine Nicholas Medawar, and Annie Innes Logietulloch, *née* Macbeth; *b* 25 April 1933; *Educ* Keswick Sch, Trinity Coll Dublin (BA, LLB);; *m* 1, 1962 (m dis 1977), Joyce Catherine, *née* Crosland-Boyle; 1 s (Anthony Crosland b 1962), 1 da (Zohara Dawn b 1966 (decd)); m 2, 1977, Caroline Mary, *née* Collins; *Career* Nat Serv 1957-59 Cyprus; barr Gray's Inn 1957, QC 1984, rec 1985; *Recreations* walking; *Style—* Nicholas Medawar, Esq; 4 Paper Buildings Temple London, EC4 7EX (☎ 01 583 0816, fax 01 353 4979)

MEDD, William Gordon; s of William Thomas Medd (d 1959); *b* 30 Dec 1920; *Educ* Scarborough HS, Univ of Liverpool; *m* 1943, Joan, *née* Fenwick; 1 s; *Career* biochemist, biscuit mfr, dir Assoc Biscuit Mfrs (ABM) 1967-82, O P Chocolate 1973, W & R Jacob (Dublin) 1976; reg cllr CBI 1975-81; *Recreations* golf; *Clubs* Scarborough NC; *Style—* William Medd, Esq; Highmoor Croft, Hutton Buscell, Yorks (☎ 0723 863486)

MEDDINGS, Hon Mrs (Susan); *née* Delfont; er da of Baron Delfont (Life Peer), *qv* ; *b* 10 April 1947; *Educ* Millfield; *m* 1982, Mark Derek Meddings (a film special effects technician), s of Derek Meddings; 1 s, 1 da; *Career* stills photographer (films and television); *Style—* The Hon Mrs Meddings; 34 Hamilton Gdns, St John's Wood, London NW8

MEDFORTH-MILLS, Dr (Leslie) Robin; s of Cyril Mills, and Nora, *née* Medforth; *b* 8 Dec 1942; *Educ* Univ of Durham (BA, PhD); *m* 24 Sept 1983, HRH Princess Helen of Roumania, *qv* 2 da of HM King Michael of Roumania, GCVO; 1 s (Nicholas Michael de Roumanie b 1 April 1985), 1 da (Elisabetta Karina de Roumainie b 4 Jan 1989); *Career* third world devpt conslt: Nigeria 1964-67, Sudan 1967-71, Ghana 1971, Sierra Leone 1972-74, Sudan (Int Lab Orgn) 1974-81, UN Fund for Population Activities 1981-87; sr res fell centre for overseas res and devpt Univ of Durham 1987-; conslt UN Children's Fund (UNICEF) Geneva 1987-; *Recreations* genealogy, antique silver, calligraphy; *Clubs* Athenaeum; *Style—* Dr Robin Medforth-Mills; Flass Hall, Esh Winning, Durham DH7 9QD; Centre for Overseas Res and Devpt, Univ of Durham, South Rd, Durham DH1 3LE (☎ 091 374 2495, fax 091 373 2466)

MEDHURST, Brian; O'LEARY Terence Daniel; s of Eric Gilbert Medhurst (d 1983), by his w Bertha May; *b* 18 Mar 1935; *Educ* Godalming GS, Trinity Coll Cambridge (MA); *m* 1960, Patricia Anne, da of Bernard Charles Beer (d 1982); 2 s, 1 da; *Career* The Prudential Assur Co Ltd: investmt mangr 1975-80, jt chief investmt mangr 1981-82, gen mangr 1982, chm Br Insur Assoc Investmt Protection Ctee until 1982, memb Cncl Inst of Actuaries 1982-87 (fell 1962-), md (int div) Prudential Assur Co Ltd; dir: Prudential Nominees Ltd 1981-, Prudential Staff Pensions Ltd 1984-, Prudential Corpn 1985-, St Helens Tst Ltd (chm) 1985, Prudential Corpn Canada 1985, Prudential Life of Ireland Ltd 1985-, Maricourt Ltd 1985-, Jackson Nat Life Insur Co 1986-, Brooke Hldgs Inc 1986; Brroke Life Insur Co 1986-, Chrissy Corpn 1986-, Prudential Corpn Aust 1988-, Emeric Insur Co 1988-, Prudential Hldg Srl 1988-; *Recreations* squash, golf, piano duets, tree felling; *Clubs* North Hants GC, Royal Aldershot Offrs'; *Style—* Brian Medhurst, Esq; Prudential Corpn, Central Cross, 1 Stephen St, London W1P 2AU (☎ 01 548 3500)

MEDLAND, David Arthur; s of James William Medland (d 1986), and Merle Ermyntrude, *née* Rotchell; *b* 23 Sept 1946; *Educ* St Paul's Sch Darjeeling India; *m* 20 Oct 1973 (m dis 1979), Patricia Ann, da of Timothy Wood (d 1971); 1 stepson (Christopher James b 25 Dec 1968); *Career* CA; Robson Rhodes 1965-: asst mangr 1973, mangr 1974, sr mangr 1976; ACA 1971, FCA 1979; *Books* The Unlisted Securities Market - A Review; *Recreations* pianist, theatre, sport; *Style—* David A Medland, Esq; Robson Rhodes, 186 City Rd, London EC1V 1NU (☎ 01 251 1644, fax 01 250 0801, telex 885734)

MEDLAND, Peter; s of Gerald Berthold Medland (d 1931), and Rowena, *née* Grant (d 1931); *b* 5 Dec 1927; *Educ* Taunton Sch; *m* 25 March 1962, Ann, da of Reginald Newman (d 1969); 1 s (Graham b 1968); *Career* MN 1942-53 (ret as Capt); various exec posts local govt 1955-85; dir and regnl mangr Wessex Hldgs 1987-; ABIM 1973, MIMunBM 1974; *Clubs* Naval, Lions; *Style—* Peter Medland, Esq; Spring Hill, Long St, Sherborne, Dorset (☎ 0935 816 819)

MEDLEY, (Edward) David Gilbert; s of Cecil Rhodes Medley, of 2 Westside, Allington, Salisbury, Wilts, and Edith Sarah, *née* Dear; *b* 18 May 1935; *Educ* Univ of Southampton (BSc), London Univ (BDS); *m* 30 Aug 1968, Elizabeth Beatrice, da of Alex Pennington, of Greenhill Cottage, Dimmocks Lane, Sarratt, Herts; 2 da (Jocelyn Sarah Rosalind b 1971, Sarah Elizabeth Jane b 1974); *Career* dental surgeon Gen Practice 1967-71; Winchester Area Health Authy 1971-; fndr memb and dir Dental Sci Advancement Fnd; chm Salisbury Med Soc 1985-86; memb Winchester: dist Jt Consultative Ctee, Dist Dental Advsy Ctee, Community Jt Advsy Ctee; accredited rep Br Dental Assoc; parish cnsllr Grateley Parish Cncl; MIBiol, CBiol, LDS, RCS; *Recreations* jazz, sailing, badminton; *Clubs* Concorde; *Style—* David Medley, Esq; The Rookery, Grateley, Andover, Hants (☎ 026 488 641)

MEDLEY, Peter; s of Tom Medley (d 1982), and Doris, *née* Smith (d 1957); *b* 22 August 1935; *Educ* Southcoates HS Hull, Hull Municipal Tech Coll; *m* 14 June 1958, Stella, da of Frederick Carnaby Robertson (d 1946); 1 s (Simon Andrew (Sam) b 21 Feb 1965), 1 da (Jennifer Kate b 27 Aug 1967); *Career* RE 1953-55; Caxton Press (W Africa) Ltd and McCorquodale and Co (W Africa) Ltd 1963-79 (md of both 1974-79), divnl dir books and magazines McCorquodale & Co Ltd 1980-86, chm Norton-Opax Book Printing Ltd 1986-; chm Waveney and Yare Housing Assoc 1984-, co fndr Nigeria Printers & Publishers Assoc 1976; memb: Inst of Printing, Inst Indust Mangrs; *Recreations* sailing, dinghy racing; *Style—* Peter Medley, Esq; The White House, The Causeway, Boxford, Suffolk (☎ 0787 210836); Norton-Opax Book Printing Ltd, 16 Mason Rd, Cowdray Centre, Colchester, Essex (☎ 0206 45582, fax 0206 572637)

MEDLEY, Ralph Cyril; DSO (1942), OBE (1945); s of Prof Dudley Julius Medley (d 1953), and Isobel Alice, *née* Gibbs (d 1942); *b* 2 Oct 1906; *Educ* Osborne, Dartmouth; *m* 16 June 1934, Letitia Ethel, da of Brig-Gen Harry Augustus Boyce, CMG, DSO (d 1953); 2 da (Shirley Vivian b 1935, Carolyn b 1938); *Career* Midshipman HMS Benbow 1924-26, Sub-Lt HMS Cornwall 1928-29; Lt 1933-36: HMS Sandwich, HMS Devonshire, HMS Crusader; RN Staff coll at Greenwich 1937, Lt-Cdr 1937; cmd 1938-39: HMS Stronghold, HMS Beagle; 1939-42: HMS Exeter, HMS Ajax (Battle of the River Plate) and other Cruisers; Cdr 1940; 1942-43: HMS Beagle (second time), HMS Burnham on Atlantic and Arctic convoy work; lent RCN for cmd C3 Atlantic Escort Gp 1943-44, Staff Offr under Adm Sir John Cunningham and Adm Willis at Caserta Italy and Malta 1944-46, Capt 1947, cmd HMS Cardigan Bay and 4 Frigate Fiotilla on China Station, dep dir Ops Div Admty 1950-52, Jt Servs Staff Coll 1952-54, COS to Adm Jaujard at NATO HQ Fortainbleau 1955-57, ret 1957; chm (later pres) Aylesbury Sea Cadet Corps; Hon Asst Worshipful Co of Saddlers (clerk 1960-70 and 1980); *Books* author of books on family history for privite circulation inc A Medley Omnibus (1987); *Recreations* genealogy; *Clubs* Genealogy; *Style—* Capt Ralph Medley; 1A Aynhoe Park, Banbury Oxon (☎ 0869 810641)

MEDLICOTT, Michael Geoffrey; s of late Maj Geoffrey Henry, of Hythe, Kent, and late Beryl Ann, *née* Burchell; *b* 2 June 1943; *Educ* Downside, Lincoln Coll Oxford (MA); *m* 8 Sept 1973, Diana Grace, da of Brian Fife Fallaw, of Gosforth, Northumberland; 1 s (Oliver), 3 da (Charlotte, Annabel, Flora); *Career* dir Europe P & O 1983-86 (gen mangr fleet 1975-80, gen mangr Europe 1980-83), md P & O Air Holidays 1980-86, dir P & O Travel 1980-84, md Swan hellenic 1983-86, chief exec Br Tourist Authy 1986; memb: cncl of mgmnt Passenger Shipping Assoc 1983-86, bd of mgmnt Heritage of London Tst 1986-, Br Travel Educn Tst 1986-, Tidy Britain Gp 1986; FRSA; *Recreations* philately, gardening, tennis; *Style—* Michael Medlicott, Esq; 7 Glebe Ave, Enfield, Middx EN2 8NZ (☎ 01 363 3189); Thames Tower, Black's Rd, London W6 (☎ 01 846 9000)

MEDLYCOTT, Sir Mervyn Tregonwell; 9 Bt (UK 1808), of Ven House, Somerset; s of late Thomas Anthony Hutchings Medlycott (d 1986, 2 s of Sir Hubert Medlycott, 7 Bt), of Edmondsham House, Dorset, and Cecilia Mary Eden, da of late Maj Cecil Harold Eden, of Cranborne, Dorset; s unc, Sir Christopher Medlycott, 8 Bt (d 1986); *b* 20 Feb 1947; *Educ* Milton Abbey; *Career* genealogist; fndr Somerset and Dorset Family History Soc 1975 (hon sec 1975-77, chm 1977-84, pres 1986-); memb: Assoc of Genealogists and Record Agents (AGRA), Historic Houses Assoc; *Style—* Sir Mervyn Medlycott, Bt; The Manor House, Sandford Orcas, Sherborne, Dorset (☎ 096 322 206)

MEDVEI, Dr (Victor) Cornelius; CBE (1965); s of Maurice William Cornelius Medvei (d 1941), and Frederica, *née* Ladany (d 1918); *b* 6 June 1905; *Educ* Prince Eszterhazy Gymnasium Vienna, Univ of Vienna, Med Coll of St Bartholomew's Hosp London; *m*

1946, Sheila Mary, da of John Morgan Wiggins (d 1969); 1 s, 2 da; *Career* conslt physician (princ med offr TMS) i/c of For Serv Med Serv 1958-70, conslt (examining) physician UN (London) Assoc, chief asst endocrine Dept St Bartholomew's Hosp London; pres: section of history of medicine RSM London 1986-87, Harveian Soc of London 1970, Osler (med) Club of London 1981-82; Chev de l'Ordre Nat du Mérite (France) 1980; MD, FRCP; *Books* The Mental and Physical Effects of Pain (1949), A History of Endocrinology (1982); *Recreations* reading, travel, study of history (especially medical history); *Clubs* Garrick, Royal Cwlth Soc; *Style*— Dr Cornelius Medvei, CBE; 38 Westmoreland Terrace, London SW1V 3HL (☎ 01 834 8282)

MEDWAY, Lord; John Jason Gathorne-Hardy; s and h of 5 Earl of Cranbrook; *b* 26 Oct 1968; *Style*— Lord Medway

MEE, Bertie; OBE (1983); s of Edwin Mee (d 1951), and Gertrude, *née* Wylde (d 1955); *b* 25 Dec 1918; *Educ* Highbury Sch Nottingham; *m* 26 March 1949, Doris, da of Jess Leonard Edwards (d 1960); 2 da (Beverley b 1959, Allyson b 1961); *Career* Sgt RAMC 1939-46, tutor Army Sch of Physiotherapy 1940-42; rehabilitation offr NHS 1947-60; Arsenal FC: physiotherapist 1960-66, mangr 1966-76 (UEFA Cup Winners 1970, Football League Championship and FA Cup Double 1971-); dir Watford FC 1977-, chm Milas Gp of Cos (health care); memb: Aspire Spinal Injury Charity, Olympic Fin Servs Charity; pres FA Remedial Med Soc, vice pres Football League Exec Staffs Assoc, memb cncl Inst Sports Med; Freeman: City of London, Worshipful Co of Fan Makers; MCSP 1942; *Recreations* reading, music, spectator-sports; *Clubs* City Livery Club, Bishopsgate Ward; *Style*— Bertie Mee, Esq, OBE; MCSP; 120 Friars Walk, Southgate, London N14 5LH (☎ 01 368 3607)

MEECH, Lady; Rachel Crease; da of Robert Anderson, of Wellington, NZ; *m* 1938, late Sir John Valentine Meech, KCVO; *Style*— Lady Meech; 205 Barhard St, Highland Park, Wellington, NZ

MEEHAN, (Tony) Anthony Edward; s of the late Edward Joseph Meehan, of 8 Highburgh Rd, Glasgow, and Mary, *née* Whelan; *b* 24 August 1943; *Educ* St George's Maida Vale London; *m* 24 Oct 1975, Linda Jane, da of John Alexander Portugal Stone,of Vancouver Is, BC; 1 s (Michael Anthony b 1980), 1 da (Clare Louise b 1982); *Career* md Tony Meehan and Assocs Ltd 1976-, chief exec and md TMA Communications 1985-, chm IPR Scottish Gp 1987- (vice chm 1985-87, chmn educn ctee 1984-87); *Clubs* Royal Overseas League, Scottish Society of Epictereens; *Style*— Tony Meehan, Esq; Mook House, Old Mogdock Rd, Strathblane, Stirlingshire (☎ 041 339 9305, telex 777582, fax 041 339 7165)

MEEK, Charles Innes; CMG (1961); s of Charles Kingsley Meek, DSc (d 1965), and Margery Helen Hopkins (d 1960); ggf Gen Sir Thomas Gordon was one of well-known twins with identical careers, the other Gen Sir John Gordon; *b* 27 June 1920; *Educ* Magdalen Coll Oxford (MA); *m* 1947, Nona, da of Charles Corry Hurford (d 1955); 2 s (Innes, Kingsley), 1 da (Sheena); *Career* 2 Lt A and SH 1940-41; Colonial Admin Serv Tanganyika 1941, head of The Civil Serv 1961, perm sec to PM, sec to The Cabinet, chief exec White Fish Authy 1962 (chm 1973), ret 1982; chm Nautilus Conslts 1986; *Recreations* travel, bridge, The Spectator crossword; *Clubs* Royal Overseas League; *Style*— Charles Meek Esq, CMG; 2 Hiham Green, Winchelsea, E Sussex TN36 4HB (☎ 0797 226640)

MEEK, Hedley Jack; s of Leonard Meek (d 1939), and Muriel Irene, *née* Woolridge; *b* 8 May 1925; *Educ* Purley Secdy Sch, Calne Secdy Sch Wilts; *m* 1948 (m dis 1972); 1 s (Andrew), 2 da (Anne, Elizabeth); *Career* chm and md Nevill Long Gp 1959- (sales mangr 1955-59); pres: Southall C of C 1971-72, Fibre Bldg Bd Fedn 1976-78; vice-pres Suspended Ceilings Assoc 1980-82 (dir 1982-83), dir Fibre Bldg Bd Orgn Ltd 1983-; rep of employers on Ealing and Hillingdon War Pensions Ctee 1982-84; deacon Gold Hill Baptist Church Chalfont St Peter 1969-71, pres St John Ambulance Cadet Div London (Prince of Wales's) Dist (Western Div 1986); FBIM, FInstD; *Recreations* horticulture, photography, music; *Clubs* IOD; *Style*— Hedley Meek, Esq; Little Bekkons, 10 Westfield Rd, Beaconsfield, Bucks HP9 1EG (☎ 0494 672 505); Nevill Long Gp, Hyde Wharf, Hayes Rd, Southall, Middx UB2 5NL (☎ 01 574 6151, fax 01 571 9739, telex 934602)

MEEK, Prof John Millar; CBE (1975); s of Alexander Meek (d 1972), of W Kirby, Wirral, and Edith, *née* Montgomery (d 1976); *b* 21 Dec 1912; *Educ* Monkton Combe Sch Bath, Univ of Liverpool (BEng, DEng), Univ of California Berkeley; *m* 18 July 1942, Marjorie, da of Bernard Ingleby (d 1957), of Sale, Cheshire; 2 da (Rosalind b 1945, Sara b 1947); *Career* res engr Met-Vickers Electrical Co Ltd Trafford Park 1934-38 and 1940-45, pres electrical engrg Univ of Liverpool 1946-78, prof IEE 1968-69; memb IBA 1969-74; Hon DSc Univ of Salford 1971; FIEE 1954, FInstP 1956; *Books* The Mechanism of the Electric Spark (1941), Electrical Breakdown of Gases (1953), High-Voltage Laboratory Technique (1953); *Recreations* golf, gardening, theatre; *Clubs* Royal Cwlth Soc; *Style*— Prof John Meek, CBE; 4 The Kirklands, W Kirby, Wirral (☎ 051 625 5850)

MEEK, Marshall; CBE (1989); s of Marshall Meek (d 1955), of Auchtermuchty Fife, and Grace Robertson, *née* Smith (d 1970); *b* 22 April 1925; *Educ* Bell Baxter HS Cupar Fife, Glasgow Univ (BSc); *m* 2 March 1957, Elfrida Marjorie, da of William George Cox (d 1946), of Purley, Surrey; 3 da (Hazel Valerie b 1960, Ursula Katherine b 1962, Angela Judith b 1966); *Career* chief naval architect Ocean Tport & Trading Ltd 1967-78 (joined 1953), head of ship technol Br Shipbuilders 1979-85, dep chm Br Maritime Tech 1985-86, visiting prof in naval arch: Strathclyde Univ 1972-83, UCL 1983-86; JP Liverpool 1977-78; past pres NE Coast Inst of Engrs & Shipbuilders 1984-86, vice pres RINA 1980-; memb: panel of nautical assessors DOT, tech ctee Lloyds Register of Shipping; chm Norumberland Branch Gideons Int 1988; hon RDI (RSA) 1986; FRINA, FIMarE, CEng, FRSA; *Books* contrib num Tech Papers to learned jnls; *Recreations* garden; *Clubs* Caledonian; *Style*— Marshall Meek, Esq, CBE; Redstacks, Tranwell Woods, Morpeth, Northumberland NE61 6AG; (☎ 0670 517 221)

MEERS, Dr John Laurence; s of Laurence Wilfred Victor Lord Meers, of 343 Victoria Avenue, Southend-on-Sea, Essex, and Elizabeth Audrey, *née* Hooker; *b* 4 Feb 1941; *Educ* Westcliff HS Essex, London Univ (BSc, PhD); *m* 1961 (m dis 1982), Pamela Mary, *née* Milsom; 1 s (Ian), 1 da (Jennifer); m 2, 1985, Catherine Felicity, da of Sqdn Ldr Nicholas John Crawford Pollock, OBE, of 44 The Ham, Westbury, Wilts; *Career* res and dvpt dir John and E Sturge Ltd 1978-87, tech dir Sturge Enzymes 1979 (md 1982-84); dir: Glumamates Ltd 1981-87, Sturge Chemicals Ltd 1981-87; memb biotechnology directorate Science and Engrg Res Cncl; chm Ryedale Constituency SDP 1981; memb: Fauna and Flora Preservation Soc, Rare Breeds Survival Tst; chief exec Enzymatix Ltd 1987-; *Recreations* preservation of rare breeds of farm-stock; *Clubs* Europe House, Fauna and Flora Pres Soc; *Style*— Dr John Meers; 9 Willow Walk, Cambridge CB1 1LA (☎ 0223 65393); Enzymatix Ltd, 59 Fulham High St, London SW6 C017 (☎ 01 731 6163)

MEGAHY, Thomas; MEP (Lab) SW Yorks 1979-; s of Samuel and Mary Megahy; *b* 16 July 1929; *Educ* Wishaw HS, Ruskin Coll Oxford, Coll of Educ (Tech) Huddersfield, London Univ (BSc Econ, Dip Econ and Pol Sci, Dip FE Leeds); *m* 1954, Jean, *née* Renshaw; 3 s; *Career* former railway worker and lectr; vice pres European Parliment; *Style*— Thomas Megahy, Esq, MEP; 6 Lady Heton Grove, Mirfield, West Yorks WF14 9DY

MEGARRY, Rt Hon Sir Robert Edgar; PC (1978); s of Robert Lindsay Megarry, OBE, LLB (d 1952), of Belfast and Croydon, Surrey, and Irene Marion, da of Maj-Gen Edgar Clark (d 1929); *b* 1 June 1910; *Educ* Lancing, Trinity Hall Cambridge (MA, LLD); *m* 1936, Iris, da of Elias Davies (d 1962), of Neath, Glamorgan; 3 da; *Career* slr 1935-41; Miny of Supply: princ 1940-44, asst sec 1944-46; barr Lincoln's Inn 1944; book review ed and asst ed Law Quarterly Review 1944-67; asst reader in equity Inns of Ct 1946-51 (reader 1951-67), memb Lord Chllr's Law Reform Ctee 1952-73, QC 1956, bencher Lincoln's Inn 1962 (and tres 1981); high ct judge 1967-85; visitor: Essex Univ 1983-, Clare Hall Cambridge 1984-88; vice-chllr High Ct Chancery Div 1976-81, vice-chllr Supreme Ct 1982-85; chm: Friends of Lancing Chapel 1969-, Cncl of Law Reporting 1972-87, Comparative Law Section of Br Inst of Int and Comparative Law 1977-, memb Advsy Cncl on Public Records 1980-85; pres Lancing Club 1974-; Hon LLD: Hull, Nottingham, London, The Law Soc of Upper Canada; FBA; kt 1967; *Books* The Rent Acts (1939), Miscellany-At-Law (1955), The Law of Real Property (with Prof H W R Wade, QC, 1957), Lawyer and Litigant in England (The Hamlyn Lectures, 1962), A Second Miscellany-At-Law (1973); *Recreations* heterogeneous; *Style*— The Rt Hon Sir Robert Megarry; 5 Stone Bldgs, Lincoln's Inn, London WC2A 3XT (☎ 01 242 8607); Institute of Advanced Legal Studies, Charles Clore House, 17 Russell Square, London WC1B 5DR (☎ 01 637 1731)

MEGAW, Rt Hon Sir John; CBE (1956), TD (1951), PC (1969); 2 s of Hon Mr Justice Megaw (d 1947), of Belfast; *b* 16 Sept 1909; *Educ* Royal Academical Inst Belfast, St John's Coll Cambridge, Harvard Law Sch; *m* 1938, Eleanor Grace Chapman; 1 s, 2 da; *Career* served WW II, Col RA; barr Gray's Inn 1934, QC (1953, NI 1954), rec Middlesbrough 1957-61, high ct judge (Queen's Bench) 1961-69, pres Restrictive Practices Ct 1962-68, lord justice of appeal 1969-80, chm Ctee of Inquiry into Civil Serv pay dispute 1981-82; last judge to pass death sentence (1964, later commuted to life imprisonment); Hon LLD Queen's Univ 1968; Hon Fell St John's Coll Cambridge Legion of Merit (US) 1946; kt 1961; *Style*— The Rt Hon Sir John Megaw, CBE, TD; 14 Upper Cheyne Row, London SW3

MEGSON, Raymond James; s of Roderick Kevin Megson, and Margaret Elizabeth, *née* Welsh; *b* 4 Sept 1945; *Educ* North Sydney HS, Douglas Ewart, Edinburgh Univ; *m* 11 Oct 1976, Kim Frances, da of Norman McCreddie; 3 s (Jason b 1977, Calum b 1983, Gregor b 1985), 1 da (Paula b 1978); *Career* slr (LLB, JP, SSC); pres The Faculty of Procurators of Midlothian; memb Edinburgh Sheriff Ct Standing Advsy Ctee; rugby: ex-centre for Edinburgh Wanderers, Scottish co-optimists, Edinburgh Dist, Scottish Int Panel Rugby Referee England v Japan 1986, Wales v England 1987; LLB, JP, SSC; *Recreations* jogging, golf, rugby, tennis; *Clubs* Edinburgh Wanderers, Mortonhall Golf, Mortonhall Tennis; *Style*— Raymond J Megson, Esq, JP; 22 Cluny Drive, Edinburgh (☎ 447 2343); Grindlay St Ct, Edinburgh (☎ 228 2501)

MEHIGAN, Patrick Joseph; s of Patrick Denis Mehigan (d 1965), of Dublin, and Johanna, *née* Scully (d 1971); *b* 1 August 1924; *Educ* Catholic Univ Sch Dublin, UCD (BEng); *m* 17 Sept 1957, Eithne, da of Comdt Daniel Vincent Horgan, of Lansdowne Hotel, Pembroke Rd, Dublin; 2 s (Declan, Brian), 3 da (Sinead, Caoileann, Caralosa); *Career* chm Nicholas O'Dwyer and Ptnrs consulting engrs 1970- (trainee engr 1945-47, asst engr 1948-54, sr engr 1956-57, ptnr and dir 1961-), res engr Waterville Water Supply Scheme 1947-48, sr res engr North Dublin Water Supply 1954-56, sr engr and section leader Howard Humphreys and Sons Consulting Engrs London 1957-61; hon sec Marist Boys club 1951-57 and 1961-87 (later Marist Boys Home for Homeless Boys), dir of Rehabilitation Inst 1975- (Irelands largest charity); dir Dublin and Central Properties Public Quoted Co 1975-80, memb exec ctee FIDIC 1976-81; FIEI 1957, FICE 1961, FIWEN 1962; *Recreations* golfing, sailing; *Clubs* Milltown GC, Royal Irish YC; *Style*— Patrick Mehigan, Esq; 6 de Vesci Terrace, Dun Laoghaire, Co Dublin (☎ 0001 801432); Nicholas O'Dwyer and Partners, Consulting Engrs, Carrick House, Dundrum Centre, Dublin 14 (☎ 0001 984499, fax 984957, telex 30350 NOD E1)

MEHROTRA, HE Prakash Chandra; s of F Gopalji Mehrotra and M Raj Dulari; *b* 26 Feb 1925; *Educ* Allahabad Univ; *m* 1978, Priti Mehrotra; 1 s, 4 da; *Career* govr Assam to 1984, Indian high cmmr to UK 1983-; *Style*— HE Mr Prakash Mehrota; Indian High Cmmn, Aldwych, London WC2

MEHTA, Pravin Shantilal; s of Shantilal B Mehta, of Bhavnagar, India, and Kanchan Mehta; *b* 23 Mar 1944; *Educ* Gujarat Univ India (BCom, BA, LLB, MLW); *m* 19 Oct 1968, Merunissa, da of Abdul Azis Lalani; 1 s (Meenaz b 2 Dec 1970); *Career* accounts mangr Assoc Servs Ltd 1965-68, chief accountant later co sec and chief dealer Commodity Analysis 1968-78; trading dir GNI Ltd 1978-: ACIS, MBIM; *Recreations* astrology; *Clubs* Durbar, Royal Overseas League; *Style*— Pravin Mehta, Esq; Glen House, 34D Oakleigh Park South, London N20 (☎ 01 446 3554); GNI Limited, Colechurch House, No 1 London Bridge Walk, London SE1 (☎ 01 407 2773/01 378 7171, fax 407 3848, car 0860 266936)

MEIKLE, Alan; CBE (1987); s of Malcolm Coubrough Meikle, MC & Bar, (d 1947), of Wick Grange, Pershore, Worcs, and Mary Alma, *née* Fletcher (d 1985); *b* 22 Mar 1928; *Educ* St Michael's Coll Tenbury Wells, Pangbourne Coll Berks, Birmingham Sch of Arch (Dip Arch); *m* 1, 30 Aug 1958, Marjorie Joan (d 1981), da of Arundel Spencer Clay (d 1982); 2 s (Stewart b 1959, Robert b 1960), 1 da (Grace b 1963); m 2, 22 Oct 1988, Barbara Joan Zienau, *née* Warland; *Career* midshipman RNR 1945-46; furniture designer Herts CC 1952-55, asst arch Notts CC 1955-71; co property offr Hereford & Worcs CC 1982-88 (co arch 1971-82); designer of sports centres, schools, libraries and other pub bldgs; advsr audit commn DES and NEDO, vice pres RIBA 1980-81 (memb cncl 1977-83), chm Assoc Heads of Co Property Depts 1986; RIBA 1953; *Recreations* sailing, sculpture, furniture design; *Style*— Alan Meikle, Esq, CBE; 22 Orchard Way, Leigh, Worcester, WR6 5LF (☎ 0386 32957)

MEINERTZHAGEN, Daniel; s of Louis Meinertzhagen, gs of Daniel Meinertzhagen, who settled in London from Bremen 1826; ancestor Johann von Meinertzhagen, Cllr of Cologne 1464-76, the Meinertzhagens stemming from a Hanseatic patrician family which sat regularly in the ruling cncls of the free imperial cities of Cologne (1402-1683) and Bremen (1696-1803) and which received hereditary honours in 1683 (nobility for all members following Cologne custom of according this to families whose heads held the Lord Mayorship), 1748 (Kt of HRE for Obercassel line), 1764 (Prussian recognition) and 1769 (Countship of HRE, now extinct); bro of Luke (d 1984) and Sir Peter, unc of Nicholas Meinertzhagen, *qqv*; *b* 2 Mar 1915; *Educ* Eton, New Coll Oxford; *m* 1940, Marguerite, da of A Leonard; 2 s; *Career* served WW II as Wing Cdr RAFVR; former chm Lazard Bros and Co Ltd merchant bankers; chm: Royal Insur Co 1974-, Alexanders Discount Co; dir: Costain Gp, Tozer Kemsley and Millbourn Hldgs, Brixton Estate; *Clubs* White's; *Style*— Daniel Meinertzhagen Esq; Bramshott Vale, Liphook, Hants (☎ 723243)

MEINERTZHAGEN, Nicholas Neil; only s of Luke Meinertzhagen (d 1984; late sr ptnr Cazenove and Co), and Sheila Cameron, da of late Neil Cameron Macnamara, CBE; nephew of Daniel and Sir Peter, *qv*; *b* 26 August 1943; *Educ* Eton, New Coll Oxford, Aix-en-Provence Univ; *m* 1, 1966 (m dis 1978), Erzsébet Sarolta, da of János von Kenyeres, Capt Royal Hungarian Hussars, and Countess Eva Toldalagi de Nagy Ertse (Erzsébet m 1979 Count Ferdinand von und zu Trauttmansdorff-Weinsberg of the mediatised princely house); 2 da; m 2, 1980, Princesse Anne de Polignac, *docteur-ès-sciences*, er da of Prince Edmond de Polignac (first cous of 7 Duc de Polignac and 2 cous of HSH Prince Rainier III of Monaco), and Ghislaine Brinquant, desc of 3 consec Generals Durand de Villers; 1 da; *Career* antiquarian bookseller; former memb London Stock Exchange assoc with Cazenove and Co 1969; *Clubs* St Johanns (Vienna); *Style*— Nicholas Meinertzhagen, Esq; 82 Ritherdon Rd, London SW17 8QG (☎ 01 672 2288); 22, rue de l'Elysée F-75008 Paris (☎ 01033 1 4265 52 62)

MEINERTZHAGEN, Sir Peter; CMG (1966); yst son of Louis Ernest Meinertzhagen (d 1941), and Gwynedd, da of Sir William Llewellyn, GCVO, PRA; yr bro of Daniel, *qv*, and Luke (d 1984), unc of Nicholas, *qv*; *b* 24 Mar 1920; *Educ* Eton; *m* 1949, Dido, da of (William) Jack Pretty, of Cranleigh, Surrey; 1 s (Simon b 1950), 1 da (Tana (Mrs Knyvett)); *Career* serv WWII Maj Europe and Far East (despatches); Croix de Guerre; gen mangr Cwlth Devpt Corpn 1973-85; appointed bd Booker Tate Ltd 1988; kt 1980; *Clubs* Muthaiga Country (Nairobi); *Style*— Sir Peter Meinertzhagen, CMG; Mead House, Ramsbury, Wilts SN8 2QP (☎ 0672 20715)

MEIR, John Thomas; JP (1976); s of John Thomas Meir (d 1939), of Burslem, Stoke-on-Trent, and Maria, *née* Hilton (d 1985); *b* 24 Feb 1935; *Educ* Watlands CS Sch (Dip: Econ, Eng); *m* 26 Dec 1955, Ivy, da of Edward Roberts (d 1965), of Newcastle, Staffs; 1 da (Lesley b 1961); *Career* RAMC 1953-56; relief signalman BR; co cnllr Staffs 1972-; memb: Ass of CCs 1981, Police Negotiating BD 1982-; dep ldr Newcastle-under- Lyme Borough Cncl 1972-, offr Boys Bde; *Recreations* football, cricket; *Style*— John T Meir, Esq, JP; 6 Silverton Close, Bradwell, Newcastle, Staffordshire, ST5 8LU (☎ 0782 660 947)

MEIRION-JONES, Prof Gwyn Idris; s of Maelgwyn Meirion-Jones, of Manchester, and Enid, *née* Roberts (d 1962); *b* 24 Dec 1933; *Educ* N Manchester GS, King's Coll London (BSc, MPhil, PhD); *m* 1 April 1961, Monica, da of George Havard, of Winchester (d 1961); *Career* Nat Serv RAF 1954-56; schoolmaster 1959-68, lectr in geography Kingston Coll of Technol 1968; City of London Poly (formerly Sir John Cass Coll): sr lectr in geography 1969, head of geography 1970-89, 1983-89, Leverhulme res fell 1985-87, Emeritus Prof 1989-; Br Assoc for the Advancement of Sci: memb cncl 1977-80, memb gen ctee 1977-83, anthropology section (sec 1973-78, rec 1978-83); author and conslt on historic bldgs; Ancient Monuments soc: cncl memb 1974-79 and 1983-, hon sec 1976-79, vice pres 1979, ed 1985-; memb Royal Cmmn on the Historical Monuments of England 1985-, pres Surrey Domestic Buildings Res Gp 1986-, ed Medieval Village Res Gp 1978-86; contrib papers to scientific, archaeological and ethnological jls; Hon corr memb Société Jersiaise 1980-; FSA 1981; *Books* La Maison Traditionnelle (1978), The Vernacular Architecture of Brittany (1982); *Recreations* food, wine, music, walking, swimming; *Clubs* Athenaeum; *Style*— Prof Gwyn Meirion-Jones, FSA; 11 Avondale Rd, Fleet, Hampshire GU13 9BH (☎ 0252 614 300)

MEISL, Charles George; s of Joseph Meisl (d 1958), of London, and Margaret, *née* Haller (d 1982); *b* 13 August 1917; *Educ* High Sch Prague Czechoslavakia, Athenee d'Ixelles Brussels; *m* 30 Oct 1959, Diana Jane, da of Thomas Stanley Lovell (d 1969); 3 s (Alan b 1955, Alexander b 1962, Guy b 1965), 1 da (Melissa b 1954); *Career* served WW II WO Czech Sqdn; dir Brit-Over (continental) Ltd 1958-60 (md 1962-84), fndr chm and md SEV (UK) Ltd 1962-84; racing and rally driver 1948-55, motoring journalist (UK, Germany, Austria), co-fndr and past chm Br Balloon and Airship Club, past pres Int Balloon Ctee, fell Inst of Motor Indust; govr Milton Keynes Coll of Further Educn; Liveryman Worshipful Co of Coachmakers; Czechoslovak War Cross and Medal for Valour; *Recreations* education, business, aviation and automotive history, ballooning; *Style*— Charles G Meisl, Esq; The Old Rectory, Middle Claydon, Buckingham MK18 2EU

MELBOURNE, Archbishop (RC) of 1974-; Most Rev Sir Thomas Francis Little; KBE (1977); s of Gerald Thompson Little (d 1972), and Kathleen, *née* McCormack (d 1967); *b* 30 Nov 1925; *Educ* Pontificial Urban Univ de Propaganda Fide Rome (D Sacred Theology); *Career* ordained priest 1950, sec Apostolic Delgn to Aust NZ and Oceania 1955-59, asst priest St Patrick's Cathedral Melbourne 1959-65, dean 1965-70, appointed regnl bishop (Northern and Western Areas) Archdiocese of Melbourne; *Style*— His Grace The Archbishop of Melbourne, KBE; St Patrick's Cathedral, Melbourne, Vic 3002, Australia (☎ 03 662 2332)

MELCHETT, 4 Baron (UK 1928); Sir Peter Robert Henry Mond; 4 Bt (UK 1910); s of 3 Baron Melchett (d 1973, gs of 1 Baron, better known as Sir Alfred Mond, first chm of ICI and min of Health 1921-22); *b* 24 Feb 1948; *Educ* Eton, Pembroke Coll Cambridge, Keele Univ Staffordshire; *Career* sits as Lab peer in House of Lords; at LSE and Addicition Res Unit 1973-74; a lord in waiting (govt whip) 1974-75, parly under-sec state DOI 1975-76, min state NI Off 1976-79; chm working pty on pop festivals 1975-76, Community Indust 1979-85, Greenpeace UK 1986-88; pres Ramblers' Assoc 1981-84; *Style*— The Rt Hon the Lord Melchett; The House of Lords, London SW1

MELDON, Hon Mrs; (Dorothy) Albreda; da of Gen Sir Robert C A Bewicke-Copley, KBE, CB (d 1923), and sis of 5 Baron Cromwell, DSO; *m* 1926, Lt-Col Philip Albert Meldon, DSO, RA, MA (d 1942); *Style*— The Hon Mrs Meldon; 7 Editha Mansions, Edith Grove, SW10

MELGUND, Viscount; Gilbert Timothy George Lariston Elliot-Murray-Kynynmound; s and h of 6 Earl of Minto, MBE; *b* 1 Dec 1953; *Educ* Eton (BSc Hons)); *m* 30 July 1983, Diana Barbara, da of Brian S L Trafford, of Tismans, Rudgwick, W Sussex; 3 s (Gilbert b 1984, Lorne b and d 1986, Michael b 1987); *Heir* s, Hon Gilbert Francis Elliot-Murray-Kynynmound b 15 Aug 1984; *Career* Lt Scots Gds 1972-76; memb Royal Co of Archers; ARICS; *Clubs* White's; *Style*— Viscount Melgund

MELIA, Dr Terence Patrick; s of John Melia (d 1975), and Kathleen, *née* Traynor (d 1984); *b* 17 Dec 1934; *Educ* Sir John Deanes GS Northwich, Leeds Univ (PhD); *m* 21 May 1976, Madeline, da of Arthur Carney (d 1975); 1 da (Alexandra b 1980); *Career* tech offr ICI Ltd 1961-64, lectr and sr lectr Salford Univ 1964-70, princ N Lindsey Coll of Technol 1970-74; HM Inspr of Schs 1974-: regnl staff inspr NW 1982-84, chief inspector higher educn 1985-; FRSC, CChem; *Recreations* golf, gardening; *Clubs* Berhamsted GC; *Style*— Dr Terence Melia; Dept of Education and Science, Elizabeth House, York Rd, London SE1 7PH (☎ 01 934 9842)

MELLANBY, Prof Kenneth; CBE (1953), OBE (1944); s of Emeritus Professor Alexander Lawson Mellanby (d 1951), of Bridge of Weir, Renfrewshire, and Anne Warren, *née* Maunder (d 1963); *b* 26 Mar 1908; *Educ* Barnard Castle Sch, Kings Coll Cambridge (BA, ScD), London Univ (PhD); *m* 1, 1933 (m dis 1948), Helen Neilson; 1 da (Jane b 13 July 1938); m 2, 15 April 1949, Jean Louie, da of Robert Copeland (d 1965), of Clitheroe, Lancs; 1 s (Alexander b 15 May 1950); *Career* WW11 Sqdn - Ldr CO Sheffield Univ Air Sqdn RAFVR 1939-43, Maj RAMC 1943 attached SACSEA Kandy serv: Assam, Burma; res worker London Sch of Hygiene and Tropical Med (Wandsworth fell) 1930-36, Sorby Fell Royal Soc 1937-45 (interrupted by WW11), reader med entomology London Univ 1945-47, fndr-princ Univ of Ibadan Nigeria 1947-53, head entomology dept Rottamsted Experimental Station 1955-62, fndr-dir Monts Wood Experimental Station 1961-74, ed Int Journal Enviromental Pollution 1974-88, currently enviromental conslt; hon prof Univs: Leicester, Cardiff, PCL; pres: Cambridge Cncl for the Protection of Rural England, Bedfordshire and Huntingdonshire Wildlife Tst; hon DSc Univs: Ibadan, Bradford, Leicester, Essex, Sheffield; pres Inst of Biology 1971; *Books* Seabies (1943), Human Guinea-pigs (1945), The Birth of Nigeria's University (1958), Pesticides and Pollution (1967), The Mole (1971), The Biology of Pollution (1972), Can Britain Feed Itself (1975), Talpa The Story of a Mole (childrens book 1976), Farming and Wildlife (1981), Waste Wildllife and the Countryside (1989); *Clubs* Atheneum; *Style*— Prof Kenneth Mellanby, CBE, OBE; 38 Warworth St, Cambridge CB1 1EG (☎ 0223 328 733)

MELLAR, Gordon Hollings; s of George Herbert Mellar (d 1962), and Gladys, *née* Hollings; *b* 15 Oct 1935; *Educ* High Storrs GS Sheffield, Trinity Coll Cambridge (MA); *m* 17 Aug 1963, Ann Mary, da of Herbert Bates (d 1961); 1 s (Toby b 21 March 1972), 1 da (Sadie b 8 June 1969); *Career* Nat Serv cmmn RAF (pilot trg) 1954-56, Flying Offr (pilot) No 616 S Yorks Sqdn RAUXAF 1956-57; dir Centrax Ltd 1977- (mechanical engr 1959-, dep md gas turbines div 1976-); marker and referee Newton Abbot Squash Club; memb: Mid Devon Road Club, Newton Abbot Photographic Club; FIMechE; *Recreations* squash, cycling, photography, golf; *Style*— Gordon Mellar, Esq; Centrax Ltd, Newton Abbot, Devon TQ12 4SQ (☎ 0626 53342, 0626 52251, fax 0626 52250, telex 42935 CENTRX G)

MELLING, John Kennedy; s of John Robert Melling (d 1948), of Westcliff-on-Sea, Essex, and Ivy Edith May, *née* Woolmer (d 1982); *b* 11 Jan 1927; *Educ* Thirsk Sch Westcliff, Westcliff HS for Boys; *Career* CA; dramatic and literary critic, lectr, author, broadcaster, playwright, historian; memb Ctee of Crime Writers' Assoc 1985-88, int life vice-pres American Fedn of Police,UK rep Criminal Investigators Assoc USA, awarded Knight Grand Cross Order of Michael the Archangel of the Nat Assoc of Police USA; govr Corpn of the Sons of the Clergy;memb Worshipful Co of Poulters 1980-81; FCA, FFB, FRSA, FTII, MCFA; *Books* Discovering Lost Theatres, Discovering London's Guild's and Liveries (fourth edn), Murder Done To Death, The Gilded Cage (play); *Recreations* reading, collecting theatre and crime ephemera; *Clubs* City Livery; *Style*— John Melling, Esq; 85 Chalkwell Ave, Westcliff-on-Sea, Essex SS0 8NL (☎ 0702 76012; tel address Drumbeat Southend-on-Sea; 9 Blenheim St, New Bond St, London W1Y 9LE (☎ 01 499 2519/7249; tel address Dilettante W1)

MELLINGER, Lucas Emmanuel Matthias; s of Dr Frederick Mellinger (d 1970) of Los Angeles, USA, and Eva, *née* Schlesinger (d 1959); *b* 9 July 1921; *Educ* Bunce Court Sch, Northern Poly (DipArch); *m* 27 Sept 1957 (m dis 1987), Janet Elizabeth, da of Sidney Kybert (d 1964); 1 s (Simon b 1964), 1 da (Karina b 1959); *Career* Corpl RE 1940-46; architect, planning conslt, design conslt; planning offr Notts Co Cncl 1948-50, chief tech and res asst Wells Wintemute Wells Coates 1950-53, private practice 1953-; former conslt to: Br Film Inst, Cinematograph Exhibitors Assoc, Film Prodn Assoc; architect of exhibitions, Trade Fairs, restaurants incl: Hatchetts (Piccadilly), The Sands (Bond St), Dukes (Duke St), Xenon Nightclub (Piccadilly); conslt to Housing Assocs and Charitable Tsts, Church Authorities, Leisure Indust; patentee of: Furniture Sets and Assemblies for Sedentary Work, Window Fitting; three times winner Institutions Int Design Award; FRIBA, FRTPI, FCSD; *Recreations* armchair philosophy, politics; *Clubs* Private; *Style*— Lucas E M Mellinger, Esq; 60 Richmond Hill Court, Richmond, Surrey TW10 6BE (☎ 01 940 8255); 4 Kew Green, Richmond, Surrey TW9 3BH (☎ 01 948 5437/8)

MELLIS, Capt RN David Barclay Nairne; DSC (1941); s of Rev David Barclay Mellis (d 1961), of 2 Belgrave Place, Edinburgh, and Margaret Blaikie, *née* MacKenzie (d 1970); *b* 13 June 1915; *Educ* RNC Dartmouth, RNC Greenwich; *m* 13 April 1940, Anne Patricia, da of Lt Col Walter Stuart Wingate-Gray, MC (d 1977); 1 s (Patrick b 1943), 2 da (Matilda b 1941, Charlotte b 1952); *Career* RN: Cadet 1929, Midshipman 1933, Sub Lt 1935, serv HMS: Malaya 1932, York 1934, Gallant 1936-37; Lt 1937, navigation specialist 1938, Persian Gulf and China HMS Bideford 1938-39; HMS: Malcolm, Worcester, Mackay (Portsmouth and Harwich), 1940-41, Manchester 1942, Rotherham (Eastern Fleet) 1942-43, staff of Cdre D Eastern Fleet 1943-45, Lt Cdr 1945, Staff HMS Dryad 1945-47, Fleet Navigation Offr Indies HMS Norfolk 1947-49, Lt HMS Dryad 1949-51, Cdr 1951 in cmd HMS Redpole 1951-52, Admty 1952-54, in cmd HMS St Kitt's 1954-55, 2 i/c and Exec Offr Centaur 1956-57, staff of CinC Med as Asst Capt of the Fleet 1957-58, Capt 1958, JSSC 1958, Br naval attache Athens 1959-61, in cmd HMS Puma Captain 7 Frigate Sqdn (S Atlantic and S America) 1961-63, in cmd HMS Dryad 1963-65, COS to CinC Med and as COMEDSOUEAST (Nato appt) 1965-67, Cdre 1965-67, ret 1967; comptroller Duart Castle Mull 1967-68, Admty Approved Master 1969-79; jt fndr: Royal Naval Pipers Soc 1951, Royal Naval Club Argyll 1969; tax cmmr Lorn & Mull, chm Mull branch (Cons) 1974-88; Cdre Western

Isles YC 1975-81, tstee Royal Highland YC; Elder church of Scotland; *Recreations* sailing, fly fishing, bridge, arguing; *Clubs* New (Edinburgh), Royal Scottish Pipen Soc; *Style—* Capt David Mellis, DSC, RN; High Water, Aros, Isle of Mull, Argyll PA72 6JG (☎ 068 03 370)

MELLISH, Baron (Life Peer 1985) of Bermondsey, Greater London; Robert Joseph Mellish; PC (1967); *b* 1913; *Educ* St Joseph's RC Sch Deptford; *m* 1938, Ann, da of George Warner, of Bermondsey; 5 s; *Career* Served WWII turn as Lance-Corpl then rose to Maj RE SE Asia; MP (L till July 1982 when resigned from Labour Party, continuing to sit as Ind Labour MP; resigned seat Nov 1982) Southwark, Bermondsey, 1974-; Oppn chief whip 1970-74, Parly sec Treasy and govt chief whip 1969-70 and 1974-76, min Public Bldg and Works 1967-69, jt parly sec Miny Housing 1964-67, pps to First Ld of Admlty then to Min Pensions then Min Supply 1951 and 1950-51, MP (L) Bermondsey Rotherhithe 1946-50, Bermondsey 1950-764; dep chm Docklands Urban Dvpt Corpn 1981-; left school at 14, worked as clerk in docks, joined TGWU 1929, organiser for dockers 1938-40; Papal Knight Order of St Gregory the Great 1959; *Style—* The Rt Hon Lord Mellish, PC; c/o House of Lords, London SW1

MELLON, James; CMG (1979); *b* 25 Jan 1929; *Educ* Glasgow Univ; *m* 1, 1956, Frances Murray (d 1976); 1 s, 3 da; m 2, 1979, Mrs Philippa Shuttleworth, *née* Hartley; *Career* Foreign Off 1963: commerical cnsllr E Berlin 1975-76, head of Trade Rels and Export Dept FCO 1976-78, high cmmr Ghana and ambass to Togo 1978-83, ambass to Denmark 1983-; *Style—* HE Mr James Mellon, CMG; Br Embassy, Kastelsvej, DK 2100, Copenhagen, Denmark; c/o Foreign and Cwlth Off, King Charles St, London SW1

MELLOR, Clare Ibbetson (Cim); s of Aubrey Rollo Ibbetson Mellor, CBE (d 1977), and Edith Madeline, *née* Anderson; *b* 4 Mar 1923; *Educ* Shrewsbury, Christ Church Oxford (MA), Harvard (Henry fell); *m* 12 Oct 1957, Elizabeth Dewar, da of Harry Montgomery Everard; 1 s (Nicholas b 1960), 2 da (Lucy b 1958, Sophie b 1963); *Career* WWII 1942-46, RAFVR Flt Lt; dir Metal Box plc 1977-83, Business in the Communtiy 1984-86; memb: Collyer ctee, mechanical and electrical requirements bd DTI; memb Worshipful Co of Tinplate Workers; FBIM, FRSA; *Recreations* innovation, golf; *Clubs* Leander, MCC, Huntercombe GC; *Style—* C I Mellor, Esq; Twilly Springs House, West Hendred, Wantage, Oxon OX12 8RW (☎ 0235 835 035)

MELLOR, David; OBE (1981); s of Colin Mellor (d 1970), and Ivy Mellor (d 1975); *b* 5 Oct 1930; *Educ* Sheffield Coll of Art, Royal Coll of Art (hon fell 1966), Br Sch at Rome; *m* 1966, Fiona, da of Col Gerald Heggart MacCarthy (d 1943); 1 s, 1 da; *Career* designer, manufacturer and retailer; conslt DoE 1963-70, chm design cncl ctee Inquiry into Standards of Design in Consumer Goods in Britain 1982-84; chm Crafts Cncl 1982-84; tstee V & A Museum 1983-88; *Style—* David Mellor, Esq, OBE; Broom Hall, Broomhall Rd, Sheffield S10 2DR; (☎ 0742 664124)

MELLOR, David John; QC (1987), MP (Cons Putney 1979-); s of Douglas H Mellor; *b* 12 Mar 1949; *Educ* Swanage GS, Christ's Coll Cambridge; *m* 1974, Judith Mary Hall; 2 s; *Career* chm Cambridge Univ Cons Assoc 1970; barr Inner Temple 1972, SE circuit; contested (C) W Bromwich E Oct 1974, PPS to Francis Pym as Ldr of House 1981, parly under sec state: Energy 1981-83, Home Off 1983-86; min of state: Home Off Sept 1986- June 1987, FCO June 1987- July 1988, Health July 1988; former special tstee Westminster Hosp, hon assoc Br Vet Assoc, memb Nat Youth Orchestra; FZS; *Style—* David Mellor, Esq, QC, MP; House of Commons, London SW1

MELLOR, David John; s of John Robert Mellor, of IOM, and Muriel, *née* Field; *b* 12 Oct 1940; *Educ* Plumtree Sch Southern Rhodesia (Zimbabwe), Kings Coll London (LLB); *m* 21 May 1966, (Carol) Mary, (barr), da of David Morris Clement, CBE, of 19 The Highway, Sutton, Surrey; 2 da (Freya Mary Asquith b 1968, Annabelle Elizabeth Asquith b 1972); *Career* barr Inner Temple 1964, on Deputy Circuit Judge List 1978-, rec Crown Ct 1986-; *Clubs* Norfolk; *Style—* David Mellor, Esq; The Old Hall, Mulbarton, Norwich (☎ 0508 70241); 10A Wensum St, Norwich NR3 1HR (☎ 0603 617351, fax 0603 653584)

MELLOR, Derrick; CBE (1984); s of William Mellor, and Alice, *née* Hirst; *b* 11 Jan 1927; *m* 4 Feb 1954, Kathleen, *née* Hodgson; 2 s (Simon David b 1959 Michael John b 1962), 1 da (Helen Lucy b 1960); *Career* Army 1945-49; BOT 1950-57; Trade Cmmn Serv 1958-64: Kuala Lumpur and Sydney; Dip Serv 1961-: Malaysia, Australia, Denmark, Venezuela; ambass Paraguay 1979-84, ret 1984, re-employed FCO 1984-; occasional lectr SOAS; *Recreations* golf, tennis; *Clubs* Royal Cwlth Travellers; *Style—* Derrick Mellor, Esq, CBE; Summerford Farm, Withyham, E Sussex (☎ 089 277 826); FCO, King Charles St, London SW1

MELLOR, Frank Edward; JP (Liverpool 1961), DL (Merseyside 1976); s of Robert Mellor (d 1928); *b* 27 Jan 1912; *Educ* Waterloo GS, Liverpool Poly; *m* 1963, Mavis, da of Gavin Black (d 1957); *Career* flying offr 1940-46; sr mktg exec Pharmaceutical and Fine Chemicals Indust, ret 1973; memb: Liverpool Regnl Hosp Bd 1969-73, Mental Health Review Tribunal 1967-82, Supplementary Benefits Tribunal 1976-82, Parole Bd HM Prison Liverpool 1967-69, Industl Tribunals 1976-82; chm St Helens and Knowsley Area Health Authy 1973-78; FRSA, FInstM; *Recreations* point to point and Nat Hunt racing, golf; *Style—* Frank Mellor Esq, JP, DL; Lapsley, Bleak Hill Rd, Windle, St Helens, Merseyside WA10 6DW (☎ 0744 21508)

MELLOR, Hugh Salusbury; s of Wing Cdr Harry Manners Mellor, MVO (ka 1940), and Diana Marion, *née* Wyld; *b* 16 Mar 1936; *Educ* Harrow, Christ Church Oxford (MA); *m* 6 Feb 1966, Sally, da of Flt Lt Clive Newton Wawn, DFC, RAAF, of 2a Moralla Rd, Kooyang, Victoria, Australia; 2 s (Nicholas Hugh b 29 May 1967, Andrew Harry Clive b 3 Jan 1970), 1 da (Sari b 14 July 1972); *Career* Nat Serv 2 Lt Coldstream Gds 1954-56; asst dir Morgan Grenfell & Co Ltd 1968 (joined 1960), exec Dalgety plc (formerly Dalgety Ltd) 1970 (bd memb 1968); dir: London bd Aust Mutual Provident Soc 1979-, Burmah Oil plc 1984, Bank of NZ (London) 1983-, Meghraj bank Ltd 1987-; FRSPB, fell Br Tst for Ornithology; *Recreations* ornithology, entomology; *Style—* Hugh Mellor, Esq; Blackland Fatrm, Stewkley, Leighton Buzzard, Beds; Fealar Lodge, Blairgowrie, Perthshire (☎ 0525 240 296); c/o Dalgety plc, 19 Hanover Square, London W1 9AD (☎ 01 499 7712, fax 01 493 0892, telex 23874)

MELLOR, Maj James Thomas Paulton; MC (1946), TD (1948), DL (Argyll 1964); s of Maj James Gerald Guy, MC (d 1950); *b* 15 Mar 1918; *Educ* Eton; *m* 1946, Eve, da of Lt Col Walter Thomas Forrest Holland, AFC (d 1976); 1 s, 1 da; *Career* served 1939-40 Argyll and Sutherland Highlanders, POW 1940-45 (Colditz 43-45); Maj TA 1946; with Walpamur Co (Darwen) 1946-58; landowner, farmer 1958-; *Recreations* shooting, fishing, curling, ski-bobbing; *Style—* Major James Mellor, MC, TD, DL; Barndromin Farm, Knipoch, by Oban, Argyll PA34 4QS (☎ 085 26 273)

MELLOR, John Francis; 3 Bt (UK 1924), of Culmhead, Somerset; s of Sir John Mellor, 2 Bt (d 1986); *b* 9 Mar 1925; *Educ* Eton; *m* 1948, Alix Marie, da of late Charles François Villaret; *Career* 1939-45 war with RASC and Intelligence Corps; accountant; *Style—* Sir John Mellor, Bt; Birchlea, Lone Oak, Redehall Rd, Smallfield, Horley, Surrey

MELLORS, Peter Howard; s of Bertram Mellors (d 1983), of Nottingham and Agnes, *née* Edginton (d 1977); *b* 30 Dec 1976; *Educ* The Kings Sch Peterborough, St John's Coll Cambridge (MA, LLM); *m* 27 June 1959, Jennifer Anne, da of Harold Thomas (d 1951); 2 s (Timothy b 1962, Nicholas b 1964), 1 da (Elisabeth b 1965); *Career* Inst Lt RN 1948-51; slr 1954, notary public; Registrar of Diocese of Southwell and Bishop's legal sec 1970-; vice-chm: Legal Advsy Cmmn C of E; chm: Ecclesiastical Law Assoc 1981-84; pres: Notts Law Soc 1983-84; *Recreations* ancient buildings, travel; *Style—* Peter Mellors, Esq; Burgage Green, Southwell, Notts NG25 0DN (☎ 0636 814705); 24 Friar Lane, Nottingham NG1 6DW (☎ 0602 470831, telex: 377958, fax: 0602 410105)

MELLOWS, Prof Anthony Roger Mellows; TD (1969); s of Laurence Beresford Mellows (d 1984), and Margery Phyllis, *née* Winch; *b* 30 July 1936; *Educ* King's Coll London (LLB, BD, LLM, PhD, LLD); *m* 1973, Elizabeth Angela, da of Ven Benjamin George Burton Fox, MC, TD (d 1978); *Career* slr, Alexanders 1962-, prof of the law of property London Univ 1974-, chm London Law Int Ltd 1973-, dep chm James Wilkes plc 1982-87, chm Dumenil Unit Tst Mgmnt Ltd 1983-; dir: Lord Rayleigh's Farms Inc 1980-, Strutt and Parker (Farms) Ltd 1985-; KStJ 1988; *Books* Taxation for Executors and Tstees (1967, 6 edn 1984), Taxation of Land Transactions (1973, 3 edn 1982), The Law of Succession (1970 4 edn 1983), The Modern Law of Tsts (jt 1966, 5 edn 1983); *Clubs* Athenaeum; *Style—* Prof Anthony Mellows, TD; 22 Devereux Ct, Temple Bar, London WC2R 3JJ; 203 Temple Chambers, Temple Avenue, London EC4Y 0EN (☎ 01 353 6221)

MELLY, (Alan) George Heywood; s of Francis Heywood and Edith Maud Melly; *b* 17 August 1926; *Educ* Stowe; *m* 1, 1955 (m dis 1962), Victoria Vaughan; 1 da; m 2, 1963, Diana Margaret Campion Dawson; 1 s, 1 step-da; *Career* AB RN 1944-57; asst in London Gallery 1948-50; professional jazz singer, music critic and film scriptwriter; with John Chilton's Feetwarmers 1974-; Critic of the Year, IPC Nat Press Awards 1970; pres Br Humanist Assoc 1972-74; *Books* incl: I Flook (1962), Owning Up (1965), Revolt into Style (1970), Flook by Trog (1970), Rum Bum and Concertina (1977), The Media Mob (with Barry Fantoni 1980), Tribe of One: Great Naive and Primitive Painters of the British Isles (1981), Mellymobile (1982), Scouse Mouse (1984); *Recreations* trout fishing, singing and listening to 1920s blues, collecting modern painting; *Clubs* Colony Room, Chelsea Arts; *Style—* George Melly, Esq; 33 St Lawrence Terrace, London W10 5SR

MELLY, (Charles) William; s of Flt-Lt Charles Patrick Melly, of Flat 3, Cranmere, 35 Station Rd, Budleigh Salterton, Devon, and Daphne Joyce, *née* Ferris; *b* 19 Feb 1947; *Educ* Warwick Sch; *m* 31 May 1980, Gail Elizabeth, da of Lancelot Reginald William Watkins; 2 s (Edward b 1982, William James b 1985); *Career* Smith Keen Cutler Ltd 1981-: ptnr 1981-86, dir 1986-87, md 1987-; memb Int Stock Exchange 1970; *Recreations* motor racing, snooker, horse racing; *Clubs* RAC; *Style—* William Melly, Esq; Everglade House, Penn La, Tanworth-in-Arden, Solihull, W Mids B94 5HH; Smith Keen Cutler Ltd, Exchange Bldgs, Stephenson Place, Birmingham B2 4NN (☎ 021 643 9977, fax 021 643 0345)

MELROSE, Prof Denis Graham; s of Thomas Robert Gray Melrose (d 1983), of WellS, Somerset, and Floray, *née* Collings (d 1985); *b* 20 June 1921; *Educ* Sedbergh, Univ Coll Oxford (MA, BM, BCh), Univ Coll Hosp London Univ; *m* 18 April 1945, Ann Meredith, *née* Warter; 2 s (Simon Graham Kempthorne b 15 May 1946, Angus John b 27 March 1950); *Career* Surgn Lt RNVR 1946-48; Nuffield travelling fell 1955, Fulbright travelling fell 1956, Heller fell and assoc in surgery Stanford Univ California 1957-58, lectr (later reader) Royal Postgrad Med Sch London 1952-68, prof of surgery Science Univ of London 1968- (now emeritus); conslt advsr, chief med offr and chief scientific offr DHSS, chm Concerted Action for Extracorporeal Respiration EEC, govr Euro and Int Socs of Artificial Organs; contrib numerous articles and chapters in books, particularly on heart surgery, heart/lung machines and med engineering; MRCP, FRCS; memb Cardiac Soc; *Recreations* sailing, skiing; *Clubs* RNSA; *Style—* Prof Denis Melrose; 62 Belvedere Court, Upper Richmond Road, London SW15 6HZ, (☎ 01 788 0116)

MELROSE, Margaret Elstob; *née* Jackson; DL (Cheshire 1987); da of Samuel Chantler Jackson (d 1978), of Prestbury, Cheshire, and Annie Young, *née* Arnot (d 1978); *b* 2 May 1928; *Educ* Howell's Sch, Denbigh, and Girton Coll, Camb (Drapers' Co Scholarship); *m* 19 June 1948 (m dis), Kenneth Ramsay Watson, s of late Albert Watson; assumed surname of Melrose by deed poll; 1 da (Joanne b 1953); *Career* vice-consul for the Lebanon for N England, Scotland and N Ireland 1963-67; memb Cheshire CC 1967- (chm 1984-85 and 1986-87); chm: Cheshire Rural Community Cncl 1988-, Manchester Airport Conslt Ctee 1986-, Tatton Park Mgmnt Ctee 1985-, NW Regnl Childrens' Planning Ctee 1977-81; memb: Macclesfield RDC 1968-74, Nether Alderley Parish Cncl (former chm) 1968-, Runcorn New Town Devpt Corpn 1975-81; Gen Cmmr for Taxes (Salford) 1985-; vice-pres: Cheshire Agric Soc 1985-, Ploughing and Hedgecutting Soc 1986-; pres Macclesfield Constituency Cons Assoc 1988, sec Cheshire CC Cons Gp 1983- (sec 1973-75, dep Whip 1975-77, chief Whip 1977-83); *Recreations* golf, sailing, horses, bridge, country life; *Clubs* Wilmslow Golf, Cheshire County; *Style—* Mrs Margaret Melrose, DL; Merryman's Cottage, Gt Warford, Alderley Edge, Cheshire SK9 7TP (☎ 0565 873115); work: County Hall, Chester CH1 1SG (☎ 0244 602424, telex 61347, DX no 19986, fax 0244 603800)

MELSOM, Andrew John; s of Maj John George Melsom, and Anne Sabine Rowbotham,*née* Pasley; *b* 1 Feb 1953; *Educ* Uppingham; *m* 2 Feb 1980, Melanie Clare, da of Maj Derek Hague, MC (d 1965); 2 s (Harry George b 8 Aug 1984, Jack Andrew b 25 Aug 1987, d 1988); *Career* with Foote Cone and Belding 1971, dir J Walter Thompson 1982-, founding ptnr BMP Business (Advertising) 1985, author/dir Best of the Fringe Theatrical Revue Duke of Yorks Theatre 1976, fund raiser for the Fndn for the Study of Infant Deaths; *Books* Are you there Moriarty (1979), Play it Again Moriarty (1980); *Recreations* tennis, film; *Style—* Andrew J Melsom, Esq; South Hse, Ham, Marlborough, Wilts, SN8 3RB (☎ 04884 389); 12 Bishops Bridge Road, London, W2 6AA (☎ 01 723 5713, fax 01 262 0564)

MELVILLE, Anthony Edwin; s of Sir Leslie Melville, KBE, of Deakin, Australia, and Mary Maud Melville; *b* 28 April 1929; *Educ* SCEGS Sydney, Univ of Sydney (BA),

Univ of Cambridge (MA); *m* 22 Dec 1964, Pauline Marianne Surtees, da of Maj Alan Fraser Simpson (d 1965); 2 da (Elizabeth, Alice); *Career* teacher Geelong GS 1950, sixth form master and housemaster Haileybury and ISC 1953-69, headmaster The Perse Sch Cambridge 1969-87, ret 1987; *Recreations* gardening, cooking, reading, travel; *Clubs* East India; *Style—* Anthony Melville, Esq; 4 Field Way, Cambridge (☎ 045 871)

MELVILLE, (Richard) David; s of Col Robert Kenneth Melville, of 12 Cope Place, London, and Joan Emerton, *née* Hawkins; *b* 22 April 1953; *Educ* Wellington Coll, Pembroke Coll Cambridge (MA); *m* 31 Oct 1981, Catharine Mary, da of His Hon William Granville Wingate, QC, *qv*, of Cox's Mill, Dallington, Heathfield, E Sussex; 1 s (Thomas Wingate b 29 Aug 1985), 1 da (Emma Rose b 21 July 1987); *Career* called to the Bar Inner Temple 1975; memb legal aid ctee Law Soc, ctee memb London Common Law Bar Assoc; *Recreations* sailing; *Clubs* Royal Corinthian YC, BAR YC, Utd Oxford and Cambridge; *Style—* David Melville, Esq; 2 Garden Ct, Temple, London EC4Y 9BL (☎ 01 353 4741, fax 01 353 3978)

MELVILLE, Sir Harry Work; KCB (1958); s of Thomas Melville (d 1973); *b* 27 April 1908; *Educ* George Heriot's Sch Edinburgh, Edinburgh Univ (DSc, PhD), Trinity Coll Cambridge (PhD); *m* 1942, Janet Marian Cameron; 2 da; *Career* sci advsr Miny of Supply 1940-43, superintendent Radar Res Station 1943-45; prof of chemistry Aberdeen Univ 1940-48, Birmingham Univ 1948-56; chief sci advsr for Civil Defence Midlands Regn 1952-56, sec to Privy Cncl for Scientific and Industl Res 1956-65, chm SRC 1965-67, princ Queen Mary Coll London 1967-76, memb Parly and Scientific Ctee 1971-75; FRS; *Style—* Sir Harry Melville, KCB; Norwood, Dodds Lane, Chalfont St Giles, Bucks (☎ 024 07 2222)

MELVILLE, James; *see*: MARTIN, (Roy) Peter; *Style—* Prof Michael Lappert; 18 St John St, Manchester (☎ 061 834 0843)

MELVILLE, Sir Leslie Galfreid; KBE (1957, CBE 1953); s of Richard Ernest Melville, of NSW; *b* 26 Mar 1902; *Educ* Sydney C of E GS, Sydney Univ; *m* 1925, Mary Maud, da of C A Scales; *Career* memb ctees on SA Finances 1927-30, prof of econs Adelaide Univ 1929-31, econ advsr Cwlth Bank 1931-49, memb advsy cncl Cwlth Bank 1945-51, chm UN Sub-Ctee on Employment and Economic Stability 1947-50, exec dir Int Monetary Fund and Int Bank for Reconstruction and Dvpt 1950-53, vice-chllr ANU Canberra 1953-60, memb Bd of Reserve Bank of Australia 1959-63 and 1965-74; *see Debrett's Handbook of Australia and New Zealand for further details*; *Style—* Sir Leslie Melville, KBE; 71 Stonehaven Crescent, Deakin, ACT 2600, Australia

MELVILLE, Michael Rowland; s of Sir Ronald Henry Melville, KCB, *qv* and Enid Dorcas Margaret, *née* Kenyon; *b* 18 August 1941; *Educ* Charterhouse, Magdalene Coll Cambridge (LLB), London Graduate Sch of Business Studies; *m* 24 Sept 1966, Gillian Edith, da of Archibald Somerville Miller (d 1977) of Castle Douglas, Kirkcudbrightshire; 1 s (Malcolm b 1975), 2 da (Virginia b 1970, Susannah b 1973); *Career* merchant bankers, dir J Henry Schroder Wagg and Co Ltd 1979-; *Recreations* fishing, stalking, gardening, shooting; *Style—* Michael Melville, Esq; Deep Well House, Great Chishill, nr Royston, Cambridgeshire (☎ 0763 838 433); 120 Cheapside, London EC2V 6DS (☎ 01 382 6000)

MELVILLE, 9 Viscount (UK 1802); Robert David Ross Dundas; also Baron Duneira (UK 1802); only s of Hon Robert Maldred St John Melville Dundas (ka 1940, yr s of 7 Viscount); suc uncle 1971; the 2 Viscount was First Lord of the Admty (1812-27 and 1828-30) and an enthusiast for Arctic exploration; Melville Sound is named after him; *b* 28 May 1937; *Educ* Cargilfield, Wellington; *m* 23 July 1982, Fiona Margaret, da of late Roger Kirkpatrick Stilgoe, of Derby House, Stogumber, Taunton; 2 s (Robert b 1984, James b 1986); *Heir* s, Hon Robert Henry Kirkpatrick Dundas b 23 April 1984; *Career* served in Scots Gds (Nat Serv), Reserve Capt Scots Gds; Lt Ayrshire Yeo (TA); ccncllr and dist cncllr Midlothian; pres Lasswade Civic Soc; *Recreations* shooting, fishing, golf, chess; *Clubs* Turf, Cavalry and Guards', Midlothian Cnty, House of Lords Motor, Bunnyrigg and Dist Ex-Serviceman's; *Style—* Capt Rt Hon the Viscount Melville; Solomon's Ct, Chalford, nr Stroud, Glos (☎ 0453 883351); 3 Roland Way, London SW7 (☎ 01 370 3553)

MELVILLE, Sir Ronald Henry; KCB (1964, CB 1952); s of Henry Edward Melville (d 1976), of Whitacre, Bengeo, Hertford; *b* 9 Mar 1912; *Educ* Charterhouse, Magdalene Coll Cambridge; *m* 1940, Enid Dorcas Margaret, da of late Harold Godfrey Kenyon, of Ware, Herts; 2 s (*see* Melville, Michael R) 1 da; *Career* entered Civil Serv 1934, asst under-sec of state Air Miny 1946-58, dep under-sec of state 1958-60, dep under-sec of state War Off 1960-63, second perm under-sec of state MOD 1963-66, perm sec Miny of Aviation 1966-71, attached Civil Serv Sept 1971-72, ret; dir Westland Aircraft 1974-82; chm: Nat Rifle Assoc 1972-84, jt shooting ctee for Gt Britain 1985-88; *Clubs* Brooks's; *Style—* Sir Ronald Melville, KCB; The Old Rose and Crown, Braughing, Ware, Herts

MELVILLE-ROSS, Timothy David; s of Lt-Cdr Antony Stuart Melville-Ross, RN (ret), of 3 Wallands Cres, Lewes, Sussex, and Anne Barclay Fane (*née* Gamble); *b* 3 Oct 1944; *Educ* Uppingham, Portsmouth Coll of Technol (Dip Business Studies); *m* 19 Aug 1967, Camilla Mary Harlackenden, da of Lt-Col Richard Harlackenden Cawardine Probert, of Bevills, Bures, Suffolk; 2 s (Rupert b 1971, James b 1972); 1 da (Emma b 1975); *Career* chief gen mangr Nationwide Building Soc 1985-87, chief exec Nationwide Anglia Building Soc 1987-; chm Phoenix Initiative, cncl memb Industl Soc and Policy Studies Inst; memb UK Advisory Bd of INSEAD; *Recreations* reading, bridge, walking, the countryside, family; *Style—* Timothy Melville-Ross, Esq; Little Bevills, Bures, Suffolk (☎ 0787 227424); Nationwide Anglia Building Soc, Chesterfield House, London WC1V 6PW

MELVIN, Peter Anthony Paul; s of Charles George Thomas Melvin (d 1959), and Elsie, *née* Paul (d 1983); *b* 19 Sept 1933; *Educ* St Marylebone GS, Poly Sch of Architecture (DipArch); *m* 23 April 1960, Muriel, da of Col James Cornelis Adriaan Faure (d 1984); 2 s (Jeremy Paul b 1964, Stephen James b 1967), 1 da (Joanna Claire b 1962); *Career* chm: Eastern Region of the RIBA 1974-76; memb Cncl RIBA 1977-83 and 1985-88, vice pres RIBA 1982-83 and 1985-87; visiting fell Natal Sch of Architecture 1983; FRIBA 1971, FRSA; *Recreations* music, walking, sketching, looking; *Clubs* Arts; *Style—* Peter Melvin, Esq; Woodlands, Beechwood Drive, Aldbury, Tring, Hertfordshire HP23 5SB (☎ 044 285 211); The Archway, 105 High St, Berkhamsted, Hertfordshire HP4 2DG (☎ 0442 862123/4/5)

MELZACK, Harold; s of Lewis Melzack (d 1938), and Celia, *née* Eisenstark (d 1987); *b* 6 Feb 1931; *Educ* Christ's Coll London, Coll of Estate Management; *m* 22 June 1954, June, da of Leonard Lesner, of London NW11; 2 da (Gillian b 1957, Susan b 1960); *Career* chartered surveyor, jt sr ptnr Smith Melzack and Co; former chm: Br Numismatic Trade Assoc; Freeman Worshipful Co of Chartered Surveyors; FCIArb; *Recreations* golf, numismatics, historic documents, bridge; *Clubs* Arts, Hartsbourne Golf and Country, Bushey; *Style—* Harold Melzack, Esq; Smith Melzack and Company, 17/18 Old Bond St, London W1X 3DA (☎ 01 493 1613, fax 01 493 5480)

MELZER, Arthur David; s of Albert Cecil Melzer (d 1982), of Brisbane, Australia, and Winifred Le Machond (d 1982); *b* 24 August 1932; *Educ* Brisbane Boys GS, Univ of Queensland (BSc, Dip Phys Ed); *m* 1957, Shirley Grace, da of William Tab Rooney, of Brisbane, Australia; 4 s; *Career* geologist; Premier Consolidated Oilfields plc 1982-, md Premier Oil Pacific Ltd 1986; *Recreations* walking, swimming, tennis, squash; *Clubs* Oriental, Tanglin, Broome Park Country; *Style—* David Melzer, Esq; 24 Thorndon Hall, Ingrave, Essex (☎ 0277 812046); Premier Consolidated Oilfields plc, 23 Lower Belgrave St, London SW1W 0HR (☎ 01 730 0752; telex 918121); Premier Oil Pacific Ltd, Representative Office, 541 Orchard Road, No 14-03 Liat Towers, Singapore 0923 (☎ 65 732 6644, telex R S 55017 POPLSE, fax 733 8290)

MENCIK DE MENSTEIN, Ferdinand Adalbert Jan; s of Dr Alexander Vladimir Menčik de Menstein (d 1973), and Eleonora Josefa Dolezal (d 1982); *b* 9 Feb 1916; *Educ* Charles Univ Prague; *m* 20 June 1942, Eva Maria, da of Dr Hugo Forster (d 1973); 2 s (Alexander Frederick b 1951, Richard Hugo b 1957), 2 da (Michaela Maria b 1944, Gabiela Maria b 1945); *Career* exec of Bata Shoe Organisation - (multinational) 1946-54, md of Batga, NZ Ltd 1954-59, chm and md Fabr de Calzado Peruano Lima 1970-73, dep chm The British Bata Shoe Co Ltd 1965-80, held numerous bd appointments in Europe incl pres Bata sa France; dir: Bata sa France, Bata BMV Nederland ret from exec position and presently memb of Bds, panels at the UN Industl Organization; Cdr of O of Merit France 1960; Chevalier of legion d'honneur France 1975; kt soverign O of Malta 1980; *Recreations* shooting, skiing; *Clubs* Club de la Chasse Paris; *Style—* Ferdinand A J Mencik de Menstein, Esq; 11 Boulevard Delessert, Paris 75016 (☎ 45204114; Mas Pissa Vinaigre, 83680 La Garde Freinet (☎ 94436063); Kinsky, 10 Waldegrave Gdns, Twickenham; Bata sa Europe, 38 Avenue de l'Opera 75083 (☎47424171, telex 211854)

MENDELSOHN, Martin; s of Arthur Mendelsohn (d 1961), and Rebecca, *née* Caplin (d 1975); *b* 6 Nov 1935; *Educ* Hackney Downs Sch; *m* 20 Sept 1959, Phyllis Linda, da of Abraham Sobell, of 2 Mariel House, Windermere Ave, Wembley, Middx; 2 s (Paul Arthur b 1962, David Edward b 1964); *Career* slr 1959, ptnr Adlers slrs 1961- (sr ptnr 1984-), legal conslt Br Franchise Assoc; UK rep Int Franchise Assoc, fndr chm int franchising ctee of sect on business law Int Bar Assoc; warden Kenton Synagogue 1976-78, supporter of Jewish Welfare Bd, hon slr to various charitable insts; Freeman City of London 1964, Liveryman Worshipful Co of Arbitrators; memb: The Law Soc, Int Bar Assoc, American Bar Assoc; *Books* author: Obtaining A Franchise (for DTI 1977), Comment Negocier une Franchise (jtly, 1983), The Guide to Franchising (19850, How to Evaluate a Franchise (1987), How to Franchise your Business (jtly 1987), International Franchising An Overview (ed 1984), The Journal of International Franchising and Distribution Law; contrib and lectr to pubns and audiences worldwide; *Recreations* cricket, philately; *Clubs* MCC; *Style—* Martin Mendelsohn, Esq; 22-26 Paul St, London, EC2A 4JH, (☎ 01 481 9100, fax 01 247 4701, car tel 0836 205353, telex 883831 ADLERS G)

MENDOZA, June Yvonne (Mrs Mackrell); da of John Morton, and Dot, *née* Mendoza; *Educ* Lauriston Girls Sch Melbourne, St Martins Sch of Art; *m* Keith Mackrell; 1 s (Ashley), 3 da (Elliet, Kim, Lee); *Career* portrait painter; portraits incl: HM The Queen, HRH The Prince of Wales, HRH The Princess of Wales, HM Queen Elizabeth The Queen Mother, The Princess Royal, Margaret Thatcher, Corajon Aquino; gp portraits incl: House of Commons in session, cncl Royal Coll of Surgns, Australian House of Representatives; continuing series of musicians incl: Yehudi Menuhin, Georg Solti, Joan Sutherland, Paul Tortelier; Hon DLitt Univ of Bath 1986; *Style—* Miss June Mendoza; 34 Inner Park Rd, London SW19 6DD

MENGERS, Johnny Pierre Nicolas; s of Kurt Victor Mengers (d 1977), and Erzsebet, *née* Schlomm (d 1978); *b* 1 April 1933; *Educ* Harrow, Lausanne Univ; *m* 1 (m dis), 23 July 1958, Margaret; m 2 (m dis), 20 June 1968, Joan; 2 s (Jason b 14 April 1970, Jake b 20 June 1972); m 3, 8 April 1980, Christine, da of Karl Sprung, of Vienna, Austria; 1 da (Tiffany b 2 May 1980); *Career* chm DAKS Simpson Gp plc 1983, (joined 1983 then mangr of Ladies Div export exec, mktg dir, asst md, jt md, md, dep chm); *Recreations* boxing, judo (black belt), sailing, antiques; *Clubs* Annabels, Marks, Harry's Bar, Royal Thames Yacht; *Style—* Johnny Mengers, Esq; 32 Pembroke Gardens Close, London W8 6HR (☎ 01 602 441); 32 Jerymn Street, London SW1Y 6HS (☎ 01 439 8781, telex 22466 DAKSIM G, fax 01 437 3633)

MENHENNET, Dr David; s of Thomas William Menhennet, of Redruth, Cornwall (d 1970), and Everill Waters, *née* Nettle; old Cornish Familes, both sides; *b* 4 Dec 1928; *Educ* Truro Sch Cornwall, Oriel Coll Oxford (BA), Queen's Coll Oxford (MA, DPhil); *m* 29 Dec 1954, Audrey, da of William Holmes (d 1958), of Accrington, Lancs; 2 s (Mark b 1956, Andrew b 1958); *Career* librarian of the House of Commons 1976- (dep librarian 1967-76, joined 1954); FRSA 1966; *publications* Parliament in Persective (with J Palmer, 1967), The Journal of the House of Commons: A Bibliographical and Historical Guide (1971), gen ed House of Commons Library Documents Series (1972); *Recreations* walking, gardening, visiting old churches; *Clubs* Athenaeum; *Style—* Dr David Menhennet; Librarian, House of Commons, London SW1A 0AA

MENIN, Rt Rev Malcolm James; *see*: Knaresborough, Bishop of

MENNIM, (Alexander) Michael; s of Percy Mennim (d 1965), of York, and Edith Margaret, *née* Allen (d 1985); *b* 2 Nov 1921; *Educ* Pocklington Sch, Leeds Sch of Architecture, London Univ (DipTP); *m* 4 Jan 1952, Eleanor Janet, da of James Simms-Wilson (d 1976) of Strensall, York; 1 s (Peter b 1955), 3 da (Elizabeth b 1953, Anne b 1958, Diana b 1960); *Career* Capt Indian Mountain Artillery 1946, served Burma; architect, sr ptnr private practice Ferrey and Mennim, princ works incl: Wolfson Coll Cambridge 1977, conservation of St Magnus Cathedral, Kirkwall, Orkneys 1984; lectr on conservation of historic buildings Inst of Advanced Architectural Studies Univ of York; conslt conservation architect; ARIBA 1952; hon fell Wolfson Coll, Univ of Cambridge; *Recreations* travel associated with the conservation of historic buildings; *Clubs* Yorkshire; *Style—* Michael Mennim, Esq; Croft Cottage, Sutton on the Forest, York Y06 1DP (☎ (0347) 810 345)

MENPES, Hon Mrs (Marjorie); 2 da of Baron Cooper of Stockton Heath (Life Peer; d 1988); *b* 1941; *m* 1, 1959 (m dis 1969), Neville Finch; 1 s (Paul Alexander b 1959), 2

da (Kerrie Anika b 1962, Heidi Erica b 1964); m 2, 1974 (m dis 1979), Robert Dennis Menpes; 1 s (Jamie Daniel b 1975); *Career* work at Thames Television; *Style—* The Hon Mrs Menpes; York Lodge, 56 York Road, Weybridge, Surrey KT13 9DX

MENSFORTH, Sir Eric; CBE (1945), DL (South Yorks 1971); s of Sir Holberry Mensforth, KCB, CBE (d 1951); *b* 17 May 1906; *Educ* Altrincham HS, Univ Coll Sch, King's Coll Cambridge; *m* 1934, Betty, JP, da of late Rev Picton W Francis; 3 da; *Career* dir and pres Westland Aircraft Ltd; dir: John Brown and Co Ltd, Boddy Industs Ltd; gen tres Br Assoc for Sci 1971-76; Vice Lord Lt S Yorks 1974-81; d master Co of Cutlers in Hallamshire 1965-66, kt 1962; *Clubs* Alpine, RAC; *Style—* Sir Eric Mensforth, CBE, DL; 42 Oakmead Green, Woodcote Side, Epsom, Surrey KT18 7JS (☎ 03727 42313)

MENSLEY, Michael James; s of John Keith Sayers Mensley, and Lilian May, *née* Pawley; *b* 17 Nov 1951; *Educ* Coalville GS; *m* 9 Dec 1972, Pauline Ann, da of Thomas Turner (d 1953); 2 s (Paul b 1982, Thomas b 1985); *Career* co-fndr and now jt md The Mensley Gp, dir The Leicester and Dist Knitting Indust Assoc Ltd; *Recreations* motor sport; *Style—* Michael Mensley, Esq; 10 Chatsworth Drive, Syston, Leicester (☎ 0533 694037); The Mensley Group, Melton Rd, Syston, Leicester (☎ 0533 605705, telex 341668, fax 0533 607308)

MENTER, Sir James Woodham; s of late Horace Menter and late Jane Anne, *née* Lackenby; *b* 22 August 1921; *Educ* Dover GS, Peterhouse Cambridge (MA, PhD, ScD); *m* 1947, Marjorie Jean, da of late Thomas Stodart Whyte-Smith, WS; 2 s, 1 da; *Career* tres and vice-pres Royal Soc 1972-76; princ Queen Mary Coll London Univ 1976-86; dir: Tube Investmts Res Laboratories 1961-68, Tube Investmts 1965-86, Br Petroleum Co 1976-87, Steetley Co 1981-85; FRS; kt 1973; *Style—* Sir James Menter; Carie, Kinloch Rannoch, by Pitlochry, Perthshire

MENTETH; *see*: Stuart-Menteth

MENUHIN, Hon Mrs (Brigid Gabriel); *née* Forbes-Sempill; da of late Lord Sempill (19 in line) by 2 w, Cecilia, *qv*; half-sis of Lady Sempill, *qv*; *b* 1945; *m* 1983, Jeremy Menuhin, yr s (by 2 m) of Sir Yehudi Menuhin, *qv*; *Style—* The Hon Mrs Menuhin

MENUHIN, Sir Yehudi; KBE (1965), OM (1987); s of Moshe Menuhin; *b* 22 April 1916,NY; *Educ* privately; *m* 1, 1938, Nola Ruby Nicholas, of Australia; 1 s (Krov), 1 da (Zamira Benthall); m 2, 1947, Diana Rosamond Gould; 2 s (Gerard, Jeremy, m Hon Brigid Gabriel, *qv*); *Career* violinist and conductor; début with San Francisco Orchestra aged 7; gave over 500 concerts during WW II; artistic dir Bath Festival for 10 years and fndr Bath Festival Orchestra; fndr: Yehudi Menuhin Sch Surrey 1963, Int Menuhin Music Acad Gstaad (venue of summer Festival since 1956), Live Music Now (a charitable orgn); pres Euro String Teachers' Assoc; former pres (served full-term of six years) Int Music Cncl of UNESCO, pres Musicians' Int Mutual Aid Fund; sr fell RCA, hon fell and pres Trinity Coll of Music; hon doctorates incl: Oxford Univ (1962), St Andrews Univ (1963), Queen's Univ Belfast (1965), London (1969), Cambridge Univ (1970), Ottawa (1975), Sorbonne (1976); awards and honours for WWII; humanism and music incl: Croix de Lorraine (Fr), Ordre de la Couronne and Ordre de Léopold (Belgium), Order of Merit (FDR), Nehru Peace Prize (for raising famine funds) India 1968; - medals of Cities of Paris, New York and Jerusalem, Cobbett Medal from Worshipful Co of Musicians, Gold and Mozart Medals from Royal Philharmonic Soc (1962 and 1965), Gold Medal from Canadian Music Cncl (1975), Albert Medal from Royal Soc of Arts 1981, Una Vita Nella Musica (Italy 1983); *Publications* incl: Menuhin Music Guides, Unfinished Journey (autobiography, awarded Peace Prize of German Book Fedn), Music of Man (also CBC TV series), Conversations with Menuhin (with Robin Daniels), The King, the Cat and the Fiddle (for children, with Christopher Hope), Life Class; *Clubs* Athenaeum, Garrick; *Style—* Sir Yehudi Menuhin, OM, KBE; c/o Anglo Swiss Artists' Mgmnt Ltd, 4 Primrose Mews, Sharpleshall Street, London NW1; off: ☎ 01 586 7711, telex 298787 Yehudi)

MENZIES, Lady; Agnes Cameron; da of John Smart; *m* 1935, Sir Laurence James Menzies (d 1983); 1 s, 1 da; *Style—* Lady Agnes Menzies; Timbers, Vincent Close, Esher, Surrey (☎ 0372 64257)

MENZIES, Ian Caithness; s of Sir Peter Thomson Menzies *qv*; *b* 11 Feb 1940; *Educ* Uppingham, Edinburgh Univ (MA), Inst of Chartered Accountants of Scotland; *m* 24 Sept 1966, Elizabeth Ann, da of James Murray, of 19 Thomson Rd, Currie Edinburgh; 2 s (Rory b 1969, Alexander b 1970); 1 da (Dinah b 1967); *Career* dir: J Henry Schroder Wagg and Co Ltd 1974-85, Head Wrightson Ltd 1974-77, Davy Corpn 1977-80, LCP (Hldgs) plc 1980-87; dir and gen mangr Gen Accident Fire and Life Assurance Corp plc 1985-; memb CBI Ind Pol Ctee 1980-; *Recreations* bridge, tennis, squash, gardening; *Clubs* Caledonian; *Style—* Ian Menzies, Esq; Pitheavlis, Perth, Scotland, (☎ Perth 21202, telex 76237, fax 0738 21614 or 01 606 1030)

MENZIES, Ian William; s of Adam Menzies (d 1946), of Muirhead, Glasgow, and Margaret McDermid Stewart Colvin (d 1961); *b* 30 Dec 1927; *Educ* Coatbridge Sch Strathclyde, Royal Tech Coll Glasgow (BSc), Univ of London (LLB); *m* 1, 1952, June Alice (d 1978), da of Joseph Mullard (d 1951), of Liverpool; 3 da (Margaret b 1952, Sheena b 1955, Alison b 1957); m 2, 1983, Dr Monica Patricia Hunter, da of Thomas Burrows, of Swansea; *Career* Nat Serv 2 Lt RAEC 1947-49, 2 Lt RE RAOR 1949-82; res engr Kuwait 1954-56, ptnr Menzies & Durkin Zambia 1956-59, res engr Ghana 1960-62, ptnr Charles Weiss & Ptnrs 1975-87, dir Charles Weiss Patnership Ltd 1987-; memb: cncl CIARB, Tonbridge Civic Soc; Freeman City of London, Liveryman, Worshipful Co Arbitrators; FICE, MIStructE, FCIARB, FRSA; *Recreations* armory, genealogy, cosmology; *Style—* Ian Menzies, Esq; Charles Weiss Partnership Ltd, Riverview House, Beavor Lane, Hammersmith, London, W6 9AR, (☎ 01 748 7843 fax 01 748 5704)

MENZIES, John Maxwell; s of John Francis Menzies (d 1940), and Cynthia Mary, *née* Graham (d 1988); *b* 13 Oct 1926; *Educ* Eton; *m* 4 June 1953, Patricia Elinor Trevor, yst da of Cdr Sir Hugh Trevor Dawson, 2 Bt, CBE (d 1976), and former w of Maj Raymond Alexander Carnegie, Scots Guards; 4 da (Miranda Jane (Mrs Jenkinson) b 1954, Sarah Jane (Mrs Rawlence) b 1955, Cynthia Emma (Mrs Harrison) b 1958, Katherine Patricia b 1960); *Career* cmmnd Grenadier Gds 1945-48; chm John Menzies plc 1952-; dir: Scottish American Mortgage Co 1959-63, Standard Life Assur Co 1960-63, Vidal Sassoon Inc 1969-80, Gordon and Gotch plc 1970-85, Ivory and Sime plc 1980-83, Atlantic Assets Tst 1973-88 (chm 1983-88), Independent Investmt Co plc 1973- (chm 1983-), Personal Assets Tst plc 1981-, Nimslo Int Ltd 1980-, Rocky Mountains Oil and Gas Ltd 1980-85, Bank of Scotland plc 1984-, Guardian Royal Exchange Assurance 1985-, Guardian Royal Exchange plc 1984-; tstee Newsvendors Benevolent Instn (pres 1968-74); memb Berwickshire CC 1954-57; memb Royal Co of Archers (Queen's Body Guard for Scotland); landowner (1950 acres); *Recreations* farming, shooting, reading, travel; *Clubs* Turf, Boodle's, New (Edinburgh); *Style—* John Menzies, Esq; Kames, Duns, Berwickshire (☎ 089 084 202); John Menzies plc, 108 Princes St, Edinburgh EH2 3AA (☎ 031 225 8555)

MENZIES, Dame Pattie Maie; GBE (1954); da of Senator J W Leckie; *b* 2 Mar 1899; *m* 1920, Rt Hon Sir Robert Menzies (former Prime Minister of Australia, d 1978); 1 s (and 1 decd), 1 da; *Career* GBE awarded 'in recogniton of years of incessant and unselfish performance of public duty'; *Style—* Dame Pattie Menzies, GBE; 7 Monaro Close, Kooyong, Vic 3144, Australia

MENZIES, Sir Peter Thomson; s of John Caithness Menzies (d 1918) and Helen, *née* Aikman; *b* 15 April 1912; *Educ* Musselburgh GS, Edinburgh Univ (MA); *m* 1938, Mary McPherson Alexander, da of late John Turner Menzies, and Agnes, *née* Anderson; 1 s, 1 da; *Career* joined ICI 1939, dir 1956-72, dep chm 1967-72; joined Imperial Metal Industs 1962, chm 1964-72; dir: Commercial Union Assur Co 1962-1982, Nat West Bank 1968-82; chm: Electricity Cncl 1972-77, London exec ctee Scottish Cncl (devpt and indust) 1977-82; gen tres and vice-pres Br Assoc for the Advancement of Sci 1981-86; kt 1972; *Clubs* Caledonian; *Style—* Sir Peter Menzies; Kit's Corner, Harmer Green, Welwyn, Herts (☎ 043 871 4386)

MENZIES, (Rowan) Robin; s of Capt George Cunningham Paton Menzies, DSO (d 1968), and Constance Rosabel, *née* Grice Hutchinson; *b* 30 Oct 1952; *Educ* Stowe, Trinity Coll Cambridge (BA); *Career* ptnr Baillie Gifford and Co investmt mangrs, dir Baillie Gifford Japan Tst plc and Baillie Gifford Technol plc; *Style—* Robin Menzies, Esq; 3 Glenfinlas St, Edinburgh EH3 6YY (☎ 031 225 2581, fax 031 220 1721, telex 72310 BGCO)

MENZIES-WILSON, Hon (Christian Victoria Gordon); da (by 1 m) of 2 Baron Catto; *b* 1955; *m* 1983, Charles Menzies-Wilson, er s of W N Menzies-Wilson, of Holland Park, London; 1 s (Richard Napier b 1988), 1 da (Cathryn Lucy b 1986); *Style—* The Hon Mrs Menzies-Wilson; Newport House, Newport Lane, Braishfield, nr Romsey, Hants SO51 OPL

MENZIES-WILSON, William Napier; CBE (1985); s of James Robert Menzies-Wilson (d 1977), of Fotheringhay Lodge, Nassington, nr Peterborough, and Jacobine Joanna Napier, *née* Williamson-Napier (d 1955); *b* 4 Dec 1926; *Educ* Winchester, New Coll Oxford (MA), Northwestern Univ Chicago ; *m* 25 July 1953, Mary Elizabeth Darnell, da of Ralph Juckes, MC (d 1982), of Fiddington Manor, nr Tewkesbury, Glos; 2 s (Charles Napier b 1957, James Ralph b 1959), 1 da (Gillian Elizabeth b 1960); *Career* Lt Rifle Bde 1945-47; chm Ocean Transport and Trading plc 1980-87; dir National Freight Consortium; chm Viking Resources Tst, Edinburgh Tankers plc, Help The Aged; *Recreations* gardening, shooting, golf; *Clubs* Brooks's, Hon Co of Edinburgh Golfers; *Style—* William Menzies-Wilson, Esq, CBE; Last House, Old, nr Northampton NN6 9RJ (☎ 0604 781 346)

MERCER, Rt Rev Eric Arthur John; s of Ambrose John Mercer (d 1975), of Deal, Kent; *b* 6 Dec 1917; *Educ* Dover GS, Kelham Theol Coll; *m* 1951, Rosemary Wilma, da of John William Denby (d 1963), of Barrow on Humber; 1 s, 1 da; *Career* served WW II, W Desert, Capt and Adj 14 Foresters 1943, Italian campaign 1944 (despatches), dep asst Adj and QMG 66 Inf Bde Palestine 1945, GSO HQ MEF 1945; ordained 1947, rector: St Thomas Stockport 1953-59, St Bridget with St Martin Chester 1959-65; Chester diocesan missioner 1959-65, bishop suffragan of Birkenhead (Dioc of Chester) 1965-73, bishop of Exeter 1973-85; chm C of E Men's Soc 1973-78; dep chm Church Cmmrs' Pastoral Ctee 1976-85, memb bd of govrs Church Cmmrs 1980-85; *Recreations* fly fishing; *Clubs* Army and Navy; *Style—* The Rt Rev Eric Mercer; c/o The Vigarage Hindon Salisbury SP3 6ER

MERCER, Dr (Robert) Gilles Graham; s of Leonard Mercer (d 1961), of Langholm, Dunfrieshire, and Florence Elizabeth, *née* Graham; *b* 30 May 1949; *Educ* Austin Friars Sch Carlisle, Churchill Coll Cambridge (MA), St Johns Coll Oxford (DPhil); *m* 2 March 1974, Caroline Mary, da of Alfred Harold Brougham (d 1983), of Tackley, Oxfordshire; 1 s (Edward b 1977); *Career* head of history Charterhouse 1974-76, asst princ MOD 1976-78, dir of studies and head of history Sherborne 1979-85, headmaster Stonyhurst Coll 1985-; FRSA 1983; *Books* The Teaching of Gasparino Barzizza (1979); *Recreations* travel, swimming, art, music, reading; *Clubs* Public Sch, E India; *Style—* Giles Mercer, Esq; St Philip's, Stonyhurst, Lancs BB6 9PT (☎ 025 486 220); Stonyhurst Coll, Stonyhurst, Lancs BB6 9PZ (☎ 025 486 345, fax 025 486 732, telex 635587 STONY G)

MERCER, John Charles Kenneth; s of Charles Wilfrid Mercer (d 1975), of Glanyraron Rd, Tycoch, Swansea, and Cecil Maud, *née* Lowther (d 1949); *b* 17 Sept 1917; *Educ* Ellesmere Coll (LLB); *m* 19 Aug 1944, Barbara Joan, da of Arnold Sydney Whitehead, CB, CBE (d 1966); 1 s (David), 1 da (Susan (Mrs Jones)); *Career* WWII Capt RA; slr 1946, rec 1975-82; memb: Royal Cmmn on Criminal Procedure 1978-81, SW Wales River Authy 1959-84; memb Law Soc; *Recreations* fishing, shooting, golf; *Clubs* Clyne GC, City & County, Swansea Amateur Anglers; *Style—* John Mercer, Esq; 334 Gower Rd, Killay, Swansea (☎ 0792 202 931); 147 St Helens Rd, Swansea (☎ 0792 650 000, fax 0792 458 212)

MERCER, (Andrew) Philip; s of Maj Laurence Walter Mercer (d 1951), of Huntingtower, Pertshire, and Josephine Madeline, *née* Moran; *b* 24 August 1937; *Educ* Stonyhurst, Edinburgh Univ (BArch); *m* 2 Oct 1965, Alexandra Margaret, da of Capt John Cyril Dawson, of Sussex; 2 da (Claudia Alexandra b 1977, Portia Andrea (twin); *Career* CA; princ of architectural practice 1969- (specialising in planning matters in Central London and historic buildings in Scotland); *Recreations* skiing, yachting, tennis, travelling; *Clubs* RIBA; *Style—* Philip Mercer, Esq; Hillslap Tower, Roxburghshire (☎ 089 686 276); 49 Hereford Road, London W2 5BB (☎ 01 221 5819 or 01 229 6621)

MERCER, Terence; s of Sydney Agnew Mercer (d 1971), of N Yorks, and Molly, *née* Lewis (d 1971); *b* 4 Sept 1931; *Educ* Ermysteds GS Skipton Yorks, Leeds Coll of Commerce; *m* 21 Nov 1959, Frances Karene, da of Col Francis Henry Jordan, DSO, MC (d 1975); 2 s (Nicholas Justin b 1962, Simon Jonathan Jordan de Suakville b 1965); *Career* cmmnd Army (2 yrs MELF) 1954, AER 1956-59; chm Tattersall Advertising Ltd Harrogate 1971; cncl memb: Ripon Cathedral Tst Appeal, Ripon Diocesan Synod 1970-73, Nat Tst Fountains Abbey Appeal 1984-85; hon publicity advsr: The Save the Children Fund, Yorks North Cons Euro Constituency Cncl 1981-83, IAM, ROSPA, Noise Abatement Soc; FZS, FRSA, MIPA, MIOD; *Recreations* field sports, charity work, sketching, politics; *Style—* Terence Mercer, Esq; Low Bridge House, Markington, Harrogate, North Yorkshire HG3 3PQ (☎ 0765 87393); Tattersall Advertising Ltd, Harrogate, North Yorkshire HG1 5LL (☎ 0423 504676, fax 0423

508092)

MERCER NAIRNE, Lord Robert Harold; s of 8 Marquess of Lansdowne, PC; *b* 1947; *Educ* Gordonstoun, Univ of Kent at Canterbury, Univ of Washington Graduate Sch of Business Admin; *m* 1972, Jane Elizabeth, da of Lt-Col Lord Douglas Gordon; 2 s, 1 da; *Style*— Lord Robert Mercer Nairne; The Old Manse, Kinclave, by Stanley, Perthshire; 10105 SE, 25th Bellevue, Washington 98004, USA

MERCHANT, Piers Rolf Garfield; s of Garfield Frederick Merchant, of Nottingham, by his w Audrey Mary Rolfe-Martin; descended from feudal Barons of Kendal via the Lancaster line; *b* 2 Jan 1951; *Educ* Nottingham HS, Durham Univ (MA); *m* 1977, Helen Joan, da of James Frederick Albert Burrluck, of Colchester; *Career* MP (C) Newcastle Central 1983-87; dir of Corporate Publicity Northern Engrg Industs plc; *Recreations* DIY, electronics, horology, genealogy; *Clubs* Senior Common Room of Univ Coll Durham; *Style*— Piers Merchant, Esq; 4 Bodmin Ct, Low Fell, Gateshead NE9 6UP (☎ 091 284 6436); 91 St Georges Drive, London SW1 (☎ 01 630 9294)

MEREDITH, David John; s of John Meredith (d 1980), of Stansted, and Edith Elizabeth Brown; *b* 30 Nov 1936; *Educ* Bishops Stortford Coll; *m* 10 June 1961, Deirdre Elizabeth, da of Ernest Richard Allen (d 1978), of Garstang; 2 s (Alun John b 1963, Simon David b 1966), 1 da (Bronwen Ann b 1962); *Career* md Crosville Motor Services Ltd 1976-; *Style*— David Meredith, Esq; Flint Close, Neston, South Wirral, Cheshire (☎ 051 336 2080); Crosville Motor Services Ltd Crane Wharf, Chester CH1 4SQ

MEREDITH, Richard Alban Creed; s of Rev Canon Ralph Creed Meredith (d 1970), Vicar of Windsor, and Sylvia, *née* Aynsley (d 1987); *b* 1 Feb 1935; *Educ* Stowe, Jesus Coll Cambridge; *m* 1968, Hazel Eveline Mercia Parry; 1 s, 1 da; *Career* asst master King's Sch Canterbury 1957-70, (house master 1962-70); headmaster: Giggleswick Sch 1970-78, Monkton Combe Sch 1978-; *Recreations* music, gardening, walking; *Clubs* E India; *Style*— Richard Meredith, Esq; Head Master's House, Shaft Rd, Monkton Combe, Bath BA2 7HH; (☎ 022 122 3278, off 3523)

MEREDITH HARDY, Simon Patrick; s of Patrick Talbot Meredith Hardy (d 1986), of Bembridge, IOW, and Anne, *née* Johnson; *b* 31 Oct 1943; *Educ* Eton; *m* 26 July 1969, Hon Joanna Mary Meredith Hardy, da of Rt Hon Lord Porritt, GCMG, GCVO, CBE; 2 s (Henry b 1975, George b 1978); *Career* cmmnd LG 1964, ADC to HE The Govr Gen of NZ 1967-68, left army 1969; stockbroker; dir County Natwest Ltd; memb Int Stock Exchange; *Style*— Simon P Meredith Hardy, Esq; County Natwest, 135 Bishopsgate, London EC2 (☎ 01 382 1000)

MEREDITH-HARDY, Hon Mrs (Joanna Mary); da of Baron Porritt, GCMG, GCVO, CBE (Life Peer and 1 Bt); *b* 19 July 1948; *m* 26 July 1969, Simon Patrick Meredith-Hardy; 2 s; *Style*— The Hon Mrs Meredith-Hardy; 23 Baronsmead Rd, London SW13

MEREDITH-HARDY, Michael Francis; s of late Howard Meredith Hardy; *b* 12 May 1923; *Educ* Eton, Pembroke Coll Cambridge; *m* 1955, Penelope Jane JP, da of late Hon Bartholomew Pleydell-Bouverie, s of 6 Earl of Radmoz and late Lady Doreen Pleydell-Bouverie, da of 6 Earl of Donoughmore; 4 s; *Career* 5 Royal Inniskilling Dragoon Gds 1942, Maj 1947-, Capt City of London Yeo TA Staff Offr London Armd Div TA 1948-55; barr 1951-76; chm: Nat Insur Appeal Tbnl DHSS 1967-, Nat Insur Appeal Trbnl Dept Employment 1967-, Appeal Bd Road Traffic Act 1972 Dept Environment 1969-, Examiner High Ct of Justice 1969-89; Immigration appeal adjudicator for Home Office 1980-; High Sheriff Hertford 1980; ptnr (W Australia) Plantagenet Wines; *Recreations* painting; *Style*— Michael Meredith-Hardy, Esq; Radwell Mill, Baldock, Herts (☎ 0462 730 242)

MEREDITH-HARDY, Richard; s of Maj Michael Francis Meredith Hardy, *qv*, of Radwell Mill, Baldock, Herts, and Penelope Jane, *née* Pleydell-Bouverie; *b* 23 August 1957; *Educ* Eton, Birmingham Poly; *m* 5 Dec 1987, Nicola Louise, da of Hugh Morgan Lindsay Smith, of Bank Farm, Brandon Creek, Downham Market, Norfolk; *Career* roperty developer, farmer, explorer; organiser of two safaris to Africa 1980 and 1981, Microlight Aircraft Pilot; achievements: world record distance holder 1985-, first flight from London to Capetown 1985-86, Steve Hunt Meml Trophy Winner 1986 and 1988, Br Nat Champion 1987 and 1988, Gold Colibri winner (highest award from Fédération Aeronautique Internationale) 1988, European Individual and Team Champion 1988-89; *Recreations* flying; *Clubs* BMAA, Royal Aero; *Style*— Richard Meredith-Hardy, Esq; Radwell Lodge, Baldock, Herts SG7 5ES (☎ 0462 834 776)

MERIVALE, John Herman; yr s of Philip Merivale, actor (d 1946), and Valentine Viola (Viva), *née* Birkett, actress (d 1934); step s of Dame Gladys Cooper (d 1971), and ggs of Rev Charles Merivale, DD, DCL (1808-93), Dean of Ely and author of The History of the Romans under the Empire; *b* 1 Dec 1917; *Educ* Rugby, New Coll Oxford; *m* 1, 5 May 1941 (m dis 1948), Jane Sterling (actress as Jan Sterling), da of William Allen Adriance (d 1953), of New York City, USA; m 2, 29 May 1986, Dinah Sheridan, actress, da of James Archer Sheridan, photographer (d 1958), and formerly w of (i) Jimmy Hanley, and (ii) Sir John Davis (*qv*); *Career* served 1939-45 War with RACF and RAF as Pilot 86 Sqdn (ret as Fying Offr); stage, screen and TV actor; trained Old Vic Sch, has appeared in many productions in London and New York City; *Recreations* reading, music; *Style*— John Merivale, Esq; 7a Berkeley Gdns, London W8 (☎ 01 727 8567)

MERIVALE-AUSTIN, Hon Mrs Alison Mary; 3 da of 2 Baron Rankeillour, GCIE, MC (d 1958), and Grizel, *née* Gilmour; *b* 21 Jan 1927; *m* 1, 29 Jan 1945 (m dis 1959), Maj Bruce Gardiner Merivale-Austin, The Black Watch, eldest s of William Merivale-Austin, of Waterford, Barbados; 2 da; m 2, 4 June 1960 (m annulled 1963), Maj Cyril Ernest Stearns, OBE, late KRRC (d 1968), 2 s of late Ernest Fuller Stearns, Teddington, Middx; *Style*— The Hon Mrs Alison Merivale-Austin

MERMAGEN, Air Commodore Herbert Waldemar (Tubby); CB (1960), CBE (1945, OBE 1941), AFC (1940); s of L W R Mermagen (d 1930), of Southsea, and Kate, *née* Fooks (d 1965); *b* 1 Feb 1912; *Educ* Brighton Coll; *m* 1937, Rosemary, da of Maj Mainwaring Williams (ka 1917); 2 s (Jeremy, Jonathan); *Career* joined RAF 1930, serv WWII Fighter Cmd UK, ME, France, Germany (SHAEF), AOC Br Air Cmd Berlin 1945-46, sr RAF Liaison Offr UK, Servs Liaison Staff Aust 1948-50, AOC RAF Ceylon 1955-57, Air Offr i/c Admin RAF Transport Cmd 1958-60, ret 1960; dir Sharps Pixley Ltd (Bullion Brokers) 1962-77; Cdr Legion of Merit USA 1946, Medal for Distinguished Servs USSR 1945, Chevalier Legion d'Honneur France 1951; *Recreations* golf; *Clubs* RAF; *Style*— Air Cdre H W Mermagen, CB, CBE, AFC; Allandale, Vicarage St, Painswick, Glos GL6 6XS; c/o Lloyds Bank, Montpellier Branch, Cheltenham GL50 1SH (☎ 0952 813217)

MERRETT, Richard James; s of Cecil Ernest Merrett (d 1972), of Seaton, Devon, and Jessie, *née* Lynes (d 1988); *b* 20 Feb 1935; *Educ* Charterhouse, Univ Coll Oxford (MA); *m* 29 May 1965, Rosemary Sarah (Sally), da of Cdr Ian Mike Milsted, RNVR (d 1978), of Bath; 1 s (James b 1973), 2 da (Emma b 1967, Rebecca b 1969); *Career* 2 Lt RA 1953-55, Lt TA 1955-58; called to the Bar Inner Temple 1959, presently head of chambers in Exeter, dep circuit judge/asst rec 1977-82; *Style*— Richard Merrett, Esq; Lark Rise, Kentisbeare, Cullompton, Devon EX15 2AD (☎ 08846 209); Barnfield Chambers, 15 Barnfield Rd, Exeter EX1 1RR (☎ 0392 74898, fax 0392 412368)

MERRIAM, Michael Kennedy; s of Sir Laurence Pierce Brooke Merriam, MC, JP, DL (d 1966), and Lady Marjory, *née* Kennedy (d 1988), da of 3 Marquess of Ailsa; *b* 16 April 1925; *Educ* Eton; *m* 14 June 1947, Anne Teresa, o da of late Lt-Col Philip Moss Elvery, DSO, MC; 1 s (Andrew William Kennedy b 1948), 1 da (Teresa Anne (Mrs Mark Woodhouse) b 1954); *Career* RNVR: ordinary seaman 1943, midshipman 1944, Sub-Lt 1944, Lt RNR 1965; Bx Plastics Ltd 1946-70 (dir 1963), America Square Assocs Ltd 1971-72, chm and md Bradford & Sons Ltd 1982-(md 1972-); *Recreations* country sports; *Clubs* Naval; *Style*— Michael Merriam, Esq; Stowell Ho, nr Sherborne, Dorset DT9 4PE; Bradford & Sons Ltd, 98 Hendford, Yeovil, Somerset BA20 2QR (☎ 0935 23 311, fax 0935 32 075)

MERRICKS, Walter Hugh; s of Dick Merricks, of Icklesham, Rye, E Sussex, and Phoebe, *née* Woffenden (d 1985); *b* 4 June 1945; *Educ* Bradfield Coll Berks, Trinity Coll, Oxford (MA); *m* 27 Nov 1982, Olivia, da of the late Dr Elio Montuschi; 1 s (William b 1983), 1 da (Susannah b 1986), 1 step s (Daniel b 1971); *Career* slr 1970, Hubbard Travelling Scholar 1971, dir Camden Community Law Centre 1972-76, lectr in law Brunel Univ 1976-81, legal affrs writer New Law Jl 1982-85, asst sec gen Law Soc 1985- (memb 1970-); memb: Royal Cmmn on Criminal Procedure 1978-81, Ctee on Fraud Trials 1984-86; *Style*— Walter Merricks, Esq; The Law Society, 113 Chancery Lane, London WC2A 1PL

MERRIDALE, Philip David; CBE (1988); s of Earnest David Merridale (d 1970), of St Albans, Herts, and Ruby Edith, *née* Paull (d 1965); *b* 2 May 1927; *Educ* St Albans Sch; *m* 10 Sept 1955, (Judith) Anne Bonynge, da of Earnest James Parry (d 1972), of Romsey, Hants; 1 s (David b 1956), 2 da (Catherine b 1959, Allison b 1962); *Career* RA 1945, Intelligence Corps 1946-48; commercial supervisor Marconi Instruments Ltd, antiques and fine arts dealer 1958-88; licenced lay reader Diocese of Winchester 1968-88, memb Hants CC 1973-78; chm: Ramsey and Stockbridge Dist Cncl 1968-67, Hants Educn Authy 1974-88, Nat Cncl of Local Educn Authys 1983, Educn Ctee of Assoc of CCs 1983-85; ldr Employers Panel for Teachers Pay Negotiations 1983-85, govr Portsmouth Poly 1974-88; FRSA 1985; *Recreations* walking in the countryside; *Style*— Philip Merridale, Esq, CBE; April Cottage, Pilton, Rutland LE15 9PA (☎ 0780 720092)

MERRILLS, Austin; OBE (1981); s of Austin Merrills; *b* 15 April 1928; *Educ* King Edward VII Sheffield, Sheffield Univ; *m* 1953, Daphne Olivia, *née* Coates; 1 s, 2 da; *Career* chm and chief exec Ireland Alloys (Hldgs) Ltd (Scotland); *Recreations* skiing, walking, rugby (spectator), gardening, paintings, food and wine; *Clubs* Caledonian; *Style*— Austin Merrills, Esq, OBE; Clyde Ho, Kirkfieldbank, Lanark (☎ 0555 3664; off: 0698 822461, telex 778977)

MERRIMAN, Hon Violet Grace; OBE (1948); da of 1 and last Baron Merriman, GCVO, OBE, PC (d 1962); *b* 1911; *Educ* Bedgebury Park and in France; *Career* joined ATS 1938, Ch Cdr 1943; *Style*— The Hon Violet Merriman; c/o Westminster Bank, 195 Earls Ct Rd, SW5

MERRISON, Lady; Maureen Michèle; *née* Barry; da of John Michael Barry (d 1944), and Winifred Alice, *née* Raymond; *b* 29 Oct 1938; *Educ* Royal Masonic Sch for Girls, Bedford Coll London Univ (BA hons); *m* 23 May 1970, as his 2 w, Sir Alexander (Alec) Walter Merrison, FRS (d 1989), s of Henry Walter Merrison (d 1965); 1 s (Benedict b 1974), 1 da (Andria b 1972); *Career* lectr in history Univ of Bristol 1964-; dir HTV Gp plc, Greater Bristol Tst, vice chm at Govrs Colston's Girls Sch, memb St John Ambulance Ctee; *Style*— Lady Merrison; The Manor, Hinton Blewett, Bristol BS18 5AN (☎ 0761 52259); The Dept of History, Univ of Bristol BS8 1TB; HTV Gp plc , The Television Centre, Culverhouse Cross, Cardiff CF5 6XJ (☎ 0272 303 030/ 0222 590 590, fax 0222 59613, telex 497703)

MERRITT, Prof John Edward; s of Leonard Merritt (d 1942), and Janet Merritt (d 1960); *b* 13 June 1926; *Educ* Gosforth Modern Sch, Univ of Durham (BA), Univ Coll London (Dip Educn); *m* 12 June 1948, Denise, da of John George Redvers Edmundson (d 1965); 2 s (Austen David, John Quentin); *Career* RAF 1944-45, Green Howard 1945, Sandhurst RMA 1945-46, Lt Border Regt 1946-48; educnl psychologist Lancs LEA 1957-59, sr educnl phychologist Hull LEA 1960-64, lectr Univ of Durham 1964-70, prof of teacher educn Open Univ; chm Fifth World Congress on Reading Vienna 1974, memb Nat Cmmn of Inquiry into Uses of English 1973-75, Int Merit Award Int Reading Assoc 1977, hon res fell Charlotte Mason Coll Ambleside; FRSA 1984-; *Books* Reading and the Curriculum (1971), The Reading Curriculum (1972), Reading: Today and Tomorrow (1972), What Shall We Teach? (1974); *Recreations* fell walking, climbing, running, theatre; *Clubs* Kendal Amateur Athletics; *Style*— Prof John Merritt; Wetherlam, Fisherbeck Park, Ambleside, Cumbria LA22 OAJ (☎ 05394 32259); Charlotte Mason Coll, Ambleside, Cumbria LA22 OAJ (☎ 05394 33066)

MERRIVALE, 3 Baron (UK 1925); Jack Henry Edmond Duke; s of 2 Baron, OBE (d 1951); *b* 27 Jan 1917; *Educ* Dulwich, Ecole des Sciences Politiques Paris; *m* 1, 30 Sept 1939 (m dis 1974), Colette, da of John Douglas Wise; 1 s, 1 da; m 2, 1975, Betty, widow of Paul Baron; *Heir* s, Hon Derek John Philip Duke; *Career* joined RAF 1940, Flt Lt 1944 (despatches); formerly chm Scotia Investmts Ltd, chm Anglo-Malagasy Soc; past pres Inst of Traffic Admin, pres Railway Devpt Assoc; chm Br Ctee for the Furthering of Rels with French-Speaking Africa; Chev Nat Order of Malagasy; FRSA 1964, Fndr Memb Club of Dakar 1974, Freedom City of London 1979; *Style*— The Rt Hon the Lord Merrivale; 16 Brompton Lodge, 9-11 Cromwell Rd, SW7 2JA (☎ 01 581 5678)

MERRY, Wing-Cdr Robert Thomas George; s of Cyril Arthur Merry (d 1964), and Clara Catherine, *née* Stollmeyer (d 1988); *b* 25 Oct 1937; *Educ* Rossall, St Bartholomew's Hosp Med Coll (MBBS); *m* 17 Aug 1963, Gillian Irene Kathleen, da of Francis Xavier Perkins (d 1944); 1 s (Charles b 1970), 2 da (Victoria b 1965, Alexandra b 1969); *Career* conslt neurologist, advsr in neurology to the RAF; MRCPsych, FRCP; *Recreations* gardening, rambling, golf; *Clubs* MCC, Royal Soc of Medicine; *Style*— Wing-Cdr Robert T G Merry; Myles House, Ashmead, Dursley, Gloucs

MERSEY, 4 Viscount (UK 1916); Richard Maurice Clive Bigham; also Master of

Nairne (*see below*), and Baron Mersey (UK 1910); s of 3 Viscount Mersey (d 1979), and Lady Katherine Evelyn Constance Petty-Fitzmaurice (since her f's death Lady Nairne in her own right), da of 6 Marquess of Lansdowne; ha to Lordship of Nairne; *b* 8 July 1934; *Educ* Eton, Balliol Coll Oxford; *m* 6 May 1961, Joanna Dorothy Corsica Grey, er da of John Arnaud Robin Grey Murray, CBE; 1 s (and 1 s decd); *Heir* s, Hon Edward John Hallam Bigham b 23 May 1966; *Career* served Irish Gds Germany and Egypt 1952-54, Lt; film dir and prodr (documentary); pres Soc of Industl Emergency Servs Offrs (SIESO) 1987; *Books* The Hills of Cork and Kerry (1987); *Recreations* mountaineering, music; *Style*— The Rt Hon the Viscount Mersey; 1 Rosmead Rd, London W11 (☎ 01 727 5057)

MERTHYR, Barony of; *see*: Lewis, Trevor

MERTON, John Ralph; MBE (1942); s of Sir Thomas Ralph Merton, KBE (d 1969), and Violet Margery, da of Lt-Col William Harcourt Sawyer; *b* 7 May 1913; *Educ* Eton, Balliol Coll Oxford; *m* 1938, Viola Penelope, da of Adolf von Bernd (d 1975); 3 da (1 decd); *Career* serv WWII; Air Photo Reconnaissance Res, Lt-Col 1944; portrait painter; Legion of Merit (USA); works incl triple portrait of H.R.H. The Princess of Wales, cmmd for The Principality of Wales (1988) and hanging in City Hall; *Recreations* music, making things, underwater photography; *Clubs* Garrick; *Style*— John Merton, Esq, MBE; Fourth Floor, 50 Cadogan Sq, London SW1; Pound House, Oare, Nr Marlborough, Wiltshire, SN8 4JA (☎ 0672 63539)

MERTON, (Robert) Ralph; s of Sir Thomas Ralph Merton, KBE, FRS (d 1969); *b* 26 April 1914; *Educ* Eton, Balliol Coll Oxford; *m* 1950, Esther Frances, da of Cdr John Leslie Whitehead Allison; 1 s, 1 da; *Career* served in 1939-45 War, Maj 1944; md Alginate Industs Ltd 1950-80; High Sheriff Berks 1964; *Recreations* shooting, country life; *Clubs* Garrick; *Style*— Ralph Merton, Esq; The Old Rectory, Burghfield, Berks (☎ 073 529 2206)

MERTON, Viscount; Simon John Horatio Nelson; only s, and h, of 9 Earl Nelson; *b* 21 Sept 1971; *Style*— Viscount Merton

MERTON, William Ralph; s of Sir Thomas Ralph Merton, KBE, FRS (d 1969), of Berks, and Violet Marjory Sawyer (d 1976); *b* 25 Nov 1917; *Educ* Eton, Balliol Coll Oxford (MA); *m* 1, 6 July 1950, Anthea Caroline, da of Henry F Lascelles (d 1936); 3 s (Michael b 1951, Rupert b 1953, Jeremy b 1961); m 2, 30 April 1977, Judy, da of Col Alexander John Buckley Rutherford, CVO, CBE (d 1979), of Henley-on-Thames; *Career* WWII Sci asst to Lord Cjerwe;; War Cabinet 1939-45, operational res unit HQ Coastal Cmd RAF 1941-43; barr Inner Temple; merhant banker; dir: Fulmer Res Inst 1946-80 (chm 1958-74), Erlangers Ltd 1950-60; chm Alginate Industs Ltd 1952-79, dir Robert Fleming and Co Ltd 1963-80; chm: Robert Fleming Hldgs Ltd 1974-80, Technol Investmts Tst Ltd, Sterling Tst Ltd, US and Gen Tst Corpn Ltd; *Recreations* gardening, woodworking, tennis; *Style*— William R Merton, Esq; Kingsbrook House, Headley, Newbury, Berkshire (☎ Headley 458)

MERZ, Johanna Dalbiac; da of Lt-Col Robert Francis Bridges, RAMC (d 1951), and Charlotte Lucy Chauncy, *née* Luard (d 1972); *b* 1 July 1930; *Educ* Westonbirt Sch, RCM; *m* 6 May 1954, Felix Wolfgang Merz, s of Victor Merz; 2 da (Felicity b 1954, Juliet b 1958); *Career* dir Johanna Merz Photography 1979-86; asst ed Alpine Journal; *Clubs* Alpine; *Style*— Mrs Johanna D Merz; 14 Whitefield Close, Putney SW15 3SS (☎ 01 789 9702)

MESSEL, (Linley) Thomas De Cusance; s of Col Linley Messel, TD (d 1971, er bro of both Oliver Messel, CBE (the portraitist and costume and set designer), and Anne (mother, by 1 husb, of 1 Earl of Snowdon) who later m 6 Earl of Rosse), and his 2 w, Elizabeth Désirée, da of Sir Arthur Downes and formerly w of Bernhart Stehelin; *b* 9 Jan 1951; *Educ* Milton Abbey; *m* 1981, Penelope Jane, da of Timothy Donald Barratt (d 1978), of Hazel Mount, Millom, Cumbria; 1 s (Harold b 1986); *Career* Lt Blues and Royals 1978-82; designer and furniture manufacturer, specialising in painted, gilded and lacquered furniture and objects of art; exhibitions: Abbot Hall Museum Kendal 1984, Cole and Son Mortimer St W1 1985; *Recreations* painting, gardening; *Clubs* Brooks's; *Style*— Thomas Messel, Esq; Bradley Court, Wotton-under-Edge, Gloucestershire (☎ 0453 843220, 842980)

MESSER, Cholmeley Joseph; s of Col Arthur Albert Messer, DSO, CBE, FRIBA (d 1934), of Woking, Surrey, and Lilian Hope, *née* Dowling; *b* 20 Mar 1929; *Educ* Wellington Coll; *m* 1956, Ann Mary, da of Eliot Kingsmill Power (d 1969), of Pirbright, Surrey; 2 da; *Career* 2 Lt, KRRC, ME; slr, ptnr Lawrance Messer and Co slrs 1957-67; dir Save and Prosper Gp Ltd 1968- (chm 1981-); chm: Code of Advertising Practice Ctee 1976-78, Unit Tst Assoc 1979-81; *Recreations* golf, gardening, armchair sport, history; *Clubs* City of London; *Style*— Cholmeley Messer, Esq; The Manor House, Normandy, Guildford, Surrey GU3 2AP (☎ 0483 810910); office: 1 Finsbury Avenue, London EC2M 2QY (☎ 01 588 1717)

MESSERVY, Sir (Roney) Godfrey Collumbell; s of Roney Forshaw Messervy,and Bertha Crosby, *née* Collumbell; *b* 17 Nov 1924; *Educ* Oundle, Cambridge Univ; *m* 1952, Susan Patricia Gertrude, da of Reginald Arthur Nunn, DSO, DSC, RNVR; 1 s, 2 da; *Career* served WWII RE; with Lucas subsid CAV 1949- (dir and gen mangr 1966), dir Joseph Lucas Ltd 1971-, Joseph Lucas (Industs) 1972-, Costain Gp 1978-; chm and chief exec Lucas Industs 1980- (md 1974-80, dep chm 1979-80); memb: C of C Cncl, Soc of Motor Mfrs and Traders Cncl, Engrg Industs Cncl; kt 1986; *Style*— Sir Godfrey Messervy; Lucas Industries Ltd, Great King St, Birmingham B19 2XF (☎ 021 554 5252)

MESSING, Jack Joseph; s of Hyman Messing (d 1963), of Newcastle Upon Tyne, and Hylda, *née* Cohen (d 1941); *b* 30 July 1923; *Educ* Royal GS Newcastle Upon Tyne, Kings Coll Univ of Durham, Sutherland Dental Sch (BDS), RCS (FDS); *m* 30 March 1949, Maureen, da of Prof Ralph Bass (d 1959), of Belfast, NI; 1 s (Allan M b 1955), 1 da (Julie Owen b 1952); *Career* hosp registrar and teacher Newcastle Upon Tyne Dental Hosp 1946-52, sr registrar operative dental surgery Dept Eastman Dental Hosp London 1952-54; Univ Coll Hosp London: teaching and res at Dental Sch 1954-83, postgrad tutor serving as chm of NW Thames Dental Post Grad Ctee, emeritus reader 1983, conslt operative Dental Surgery; teaching Malta Dental Sch (bi-ennial) visits; former memb Local Dental Ctee; pres: Br Endodontic Soc 1969-70, Middx and Herts branch Br Dental Assoc 1976-77, life memb Br Dental Assoc; *Books* Operative Dental Surgery (with G E Ray 2 edn 1982), Endodontics (with C J R Stock 1988); *Recreations* music, photography, golf, languages; *Style*— Jack Messing, Esq; 28 Dobree Ave, London NW10 2AE (☎01 459 1404)

MESTON, Diana, Baroness; Diana Mary Came; o da of late Capt Otto Sigismund Doll, FRIBA, of 16 Upper Cheyne Row, London SW3; *m* 12 July 1947, 2 Baron Meston (d 1984); 2 s; *Style*— The Rt Hon Diana, Lady Meston; Hurst House, Grange Rd, Cookham Rise, Berks

MESTON, 3 Baron (UK 1919); James; s of 2 Baron Meston (d 1984), and Diana, Baroness Meston, *qv*; *b* 10 Feb 1950; *Educ* Wellington, St Catharine's Coll Cambridge; *m* 1974, Jean Rebecca Anne, yr da of John Carder, of Stud Farm House, Chalvington, Sussex; 1 s (Thomas), 2 da (Laura b 1980, Elspeth b 1988); *Heir* s, Hon Thomas James Dougall Meston b 21 Oct 1977; *Career* barr Middle Temple 1973; *Clubs* Hawks; *Style*— The Rt Hon the Lord Meston; 16 Upper Cheyne Row, London SW3

MESTON, Hon William Dougall; yr s of 2 Baron Meston (d 1984), and Diana, Baroness Meston, *qv*; *b* 17 May 1953; *Educ* Wellington; *m* 1982, Elizabeth Mary Anne, yst da of Dr Peter Dawes, and Dr Joan Dawes (d 1983), of Cavendish Mansions, London, and Mijas, Spain; 2 s (Dougall b 1985, Felix b 1987); *Career* dir and fin conslt; *Clubs* Naval and Military; *Style*— The Hon William Meston; Maltings Cottage, Bentley, nr Ipswich, Suffolk 1P9 2LT

METCALF, John; s of John Metcalf (d 1967); *b* 31 Dec 1922; *Educ* Univ Coll Sch, Downing Coll Cambridge; *m* 1954, Shelagh, *née* Branagan; 1 s, 1 da; *Career* chm Dorland Advtg Ltd 1971-84, dep chm and jt md Hobson Bates & Ptnrs Ltd 1955-68; *Recreations* gardening, writing; *Clubs* Garrick, RAF; *Style*— John Metcalf, Esq; Brookland, Wisborough Green, W Sussex (☎ 0403 700325); A13 Albany, Piccadilly, London W1 (☎ 01 439 7600)

METCALF, Malcolm; MC (1944), DL (1979); s of Charles Almond Metcalf (d 1976); *b* 1 Dec 1917; *Educ* Merchant Taylors' Sch Crosby; *m* 1945, Charis, da of Edward Thomas (d 1959); 2 s; *Career* Capt Middle East and Italy; chartered sec; memb Surrey CC 1965-89, (ldr 1973-77, vice-chm 1977-78, chm 1978-81); memb Met Water Bd 1965-74 (vice-chm 1971-72); memb: Thames Conservancy 1970-74, Thames Water Authy 1973-78 and 1981-87, Assoc of CCs 1975-88; *Recreations* golf; *Clubs* MCC, Burhill GC; *Style*— Malcolm Metcalf, Esq, MC, DL; 1 The Lodge, Watts Rd, Thames Ditton, Surrey KT7 0DE (☎ 01 398 3057)

METCALFE, Lady Alexandra Naldera; CBE (1975); da of 1 and last Marquess Curzon of Kedleston (d 1925); *b* 1904; *m* 1925 (m dis 1955), Maj Edward Dudley Metcalfe, MVO, MC, IA (d 1957); 1 s, 2 da; *Career* CStJ, Order of Merit 1 Class of Italy, Order of Merit 4 Class Italian Republic, Cross of Merit 1 Class SMOM Malta; *Style*— Lady Alexandra Metcalfe, CBE; 65 Eaton Place, SW1

METCALFE, David Patrick; s of Maj Edward Dudley Metcalfe, MVO, MC (d 1957), and Lady Alexandra Metcalfe, *qv*; *b* 8 July 1927; *Educ* Eton; *m* 1, 1957 (m dis 1964), Alexandria Irene Boycun, Lady Korda (d 1966); 2 s, 1 da; m 2, 1968 (m dis 1973), Countess Anne Chauvigny de Blot; 1 s; m 3, 1979, Sally Cullen Howe, da of Edward Everett Cullen III, of Pennsylvania, USA; 2 step da; *Career* Lt Irish Gds Germany 1945-48; memb Lloyd's 1952; former dir: Stewart Smith Ltd Insur Brokers, Stewart Wrightson Ltd Insur Brokers, Wigham Poland Hldgs Ltd Insur Brokers; present dir: Sedgwick Intl Ltd Insur Brokers, Triton (Europe) Ltd; *Recreations* skiing, tennis, shooting, golf; *Clubs* White's, Buck's, Travellers' (Paris), The Brook (New York); *Style*— David Metcalfe, Esq; 15 Wilton St, London SW1 (☎ 01 235 1833); Sedgwick House, The Sedgwick Centre, London E1 8DX (☎ 01 377 3838)

METCALFE, George Ralph Anthony; s of Sir Ralph Ismay Metcalfe (d 1977), and Betty Penhorwood, *née* Pelling (d 1976); *b* 18 Mar 1936; *Educ* Lancing Coll, Durham Univ (BSc, BSc); *m* 11 Aug 1962, (Anne) Barbara, da of Anthony Watson, of Cumbria; 2 da (Elizabeth Anne (Mrs Smedley), Sarah Rosalind (Mrs Faulkner));; *Career* asst to md marine div Richardsons Westgarth 1954-63, head of planning Polaris project Vickers Armstrongs Engrs 1963-70, md Initial Servs (chm and dir var subs of BET and Initial Servs) 1970-78, md Bath & Portland Gp 1978-83, chm and chief exec UMECO Hldgs 1983-; memb: S Regnl Cncl CBI, Small Firms Cncl CBI, W of England branch IOD; vice chm Berks Business Gp; Freeman City of London, Liveryman Worshipful Co of Shipwrights; FRSA; *Recreations* sailing, music, gardening; *Clubs* Travellers; *Style*— George Metcalfe, Esq; The Close, Purton, Wilts SN5 9AE (☎ 0793 770 758)

METCALFE, Harold Arthur; William Henry Metcalfe (d 1930), of Wimbledon, and Marion Joan, *née* Taylor; *b* 2 Jan 1926; *Educ* Prince Henry's GS Yorkshire, Leeds Univ (Dlp Arch), RIBA; *m* 3 Jan 1954, Margaret Doreen, da of William Lawrence Rawling, of Menston, Yorks (d 1965); *Career* RAFVR 1943-44, Army RA (field) 1944-48 Lt; architect works incl: BUPA Hosp Pentwyn Cardiff, Hotels throughout the UK (incl Inn on the Avenue Cardiff), Leisure Complexes (incl Kiln Park Tenby 1987-88), Schls for Dyfed CC (Llandovery Co HS 1986, Whitland GS 1987-88), Houses (incl houses for Hammond Innes, and Peter Bowles); Prince of Wales award for Theatre Moridunum, Civic Tst and Civic Soc awards; Hon Testimonial Royal Humane Soc 1963; *Recreations* tennis, golf, swimming; *Style*— Harold A Metcalfe, Esq; The Saltings, Llangain, Carmarthen, Dyfed SA33 5AJ (☎ 0267 428); 32 Spilman Street, Carmarthen, Dyfed SA31 1LQ (☎ 0267 237427)

METCALFE, Air Cdre Joan; CB (1981), RRC (1976, ARRC 1965); da of Willie Metcalfe (d 1978), of Leeds, and Sarah Hannah, *née* Booth (d 1979); *b* 8 Jan 1923,; *Educ* West Leeds HS for Girls, Leeds Coll of Commerce, St James Hosp Leeds (SRN), Leeds Health Authy (SCM); *Career* joined PMRAFNS 1948, PMRAF Hosp Halton 1948 and 1951-52; RAF Hosps: Wroughton 1948-49, 1953-57 and 1970-71, Holton Hall 1959-62, Wegberg 1962-64, Ely 1964-67, Akrotiri 1959 and 1971-73; HQ Staff Support Cmd 1973-78, dir RAF Nursing Servs Air Force Dept MOD 1978-81; Flying Offr 1948, Flt Offr 1952, Sqdn Offr 1960, Wing Offr 1970, Gp Offr 1973, Air Cmdt 1978, Air Cdre 1980; *Recreations* varied; *Clubs* RAF; *Style*— Air Cdre Joan Metcalfe, CB, RRC; 10 Amport Close, Hardstock, Winchester, Hants SO22 6LP (☎ 0962 880260)

METCALFE, Stanley Gordon; s of Stanley Hudson Metcalfe, and Jane Metcalfe (d 1975); *b* 20 June 1932; *Educ* Leeds GS, Pembroke Coll Oxford (MA); *m* 1968, Sarah, da of John F A Harter; 2 da; *Career* dep chm Ranks Hovis McDougall plc 1987-; *Recreations* golf, cricket; *Clubs* MCC, I Zingari; *Style*— Stanley Metcalfe, Esq; The Oast House, Lower Froyle, Alton, Hants GU34 4LX (☎ 0420 22310); Ranks Hovis McDougall plc, RHM Centre, 67 Alma Rd, PO Box 178, Windsor, Berks SL4 3ST (☎ 075 35 57123)

METHERELL, Anthony William; s of William Frederick Metherell (d 1936), and Emily Russell, *née* Brockwell; *b* 28 May 1919; *Educ* Cheltenham, Pembroke Coll Cambridge; *Career* RA (field) 1936-46, cmmnd 2 Lt 1940, served in France 1940, Maj personnel selection branch WO 1944-46; underwriting memb LLoyds 1945, farmer 1951, chm Sanders & Co 1962, chm James Walker Goldsmith & Silversmith plc 1983, former dir of 20 other cos; memb BRCS (cert of hon 1973), memb Feathers Clubs Assoc; tstee Sussex Aids Tst; Freeman Worshipful Co of Wheelwrights 1946, Freeman Worshipful Co of Glovers 1950; *Clubs* Carlton, City Livery; *Style—* Anthony Metherell, Esq; Mullion House, 46 Sussex Sq, Brighton; 34 Falmouth House, Clarendon Place, London W2 2NT; 33 Brook St, London W1 1AJ (☎ 01 629 4752)

METHERELL, Ian Patrick; s of Clarence George Metherell and Ethel Muriel,, *née* Dyer; *b* 19 Sept 1943; *Educ* Bideford GS, Univ Southampton (BA); *m* 7 April 1968, Louise Whitefield, da of James Edward Westwood (d 1986); 2 s (Andrew b 1977, Nicholas b 1981); *Career* PR conslt; chief exec: MPR Leedex Gp Ltd 1987; tres PR Conslts Assoc 1987; non exec dir Mosaic Mgmnt Consulting Gp 1987; FIPR 1988; *Style—* Ian Metherell, Esq; West End House, Hills Place, London W1R 1AG (☎ 01 734 9681, fax 01 734 4913)

METHERELL, Hon Mrs (Rosamond Ann); raised to the rank of a Baron's da 1980; da of Rt Hon John Emerson Harding Harding-Davies (who was nominated a Life Peer 16 June 1979, but who d 4 July 1979 before the Peerage was cr), and Baroness Harding-Davies, *qv*; *b* 1946; *m* 1968, Charles Marten, s of Col Reginald Marten Metherell (d 1954); 2 s, 1 da; *Style—* The Hon Mrs Metherell; 59 Chiddingstone St, London SW6

METHLEY, Peter Charles; s of Charles Harry Methley, of Surrey, and Alice Elizabeth, *née* Stimpson (d 1984); *b* 2 April 1938; *Educ* Kings Coll Sch; *m* 15 July 1961, Marianne, *née* Evans; 1 s (Michael Peter b 1965), 2 da (Lisette b 1963, Annette b 1970); *Career* insur broker Lloyds, chm and chief exec H J Symons Gp of C os chief exec C E Heath plc 1986; chm: Leslie and Godwin Ltd 1979-85, Stewart and Wrightson Int Gp 1969-79; played hockey for Guildford and Surrey 1956-70; Freeman City of London; Freeman Worshipful Cos of: Insurers (fndr memb), Paviors; *Recreations* golf, tennis; *Clubs* Sunningdale GC, Royal and Ancient GC of St Andrews; *Style—* Peter Methley, Esq; Longreach, Links Road, Bramley, Surrey GU5 0AL (☎ 0483 893037); Symons House, 22 Alie Street, London E1 8DH (☎ 01 488 2131, fax 01 488 1080, telex 888483)

METHUEN, 6 Baron (UK 1838); Anthony John Methuen; s of 5 Baron Methuen (d 1975, himself s of Field Marshal Lord Methuen who cmd in S Africa during the Boer War and who was in his turn sixth in descent from the yr bro of the Ambass to Portugal who negotiated the treaty with that country which bears his name) and Grace, JP, da of Sir Richard Durning Holt, 1 Bt; *b* 26 Oct 1925; *Educ* Winchester, RAC Cirencester; *Heir* bro, Hon Robert Alexander Holt Methuen; *Career* Served Scots Gds and Royal Signals 1943-47; lands offr Air Min 1951-62; ARICS, QALAS 1954; *Clubs* Lansdowne; *Style—* The Rt Hon the Lord Methuen; Corsham Court, Corsham, Wilts SN13 0BZ (☎ 0249 712214)

METHUEN, Peter Humphrey; L......; s of Lt-Col Lionel Harry Methuen, OBE, MC (d 1956), of IOW, and Violet Trevor (d 1975); *b* 6 May 1919; *Educ* Wellington; *m* 12 April 1956, Dawn Mary Kathleen, da of Lt-Col Walter Grey North Hamilton Dalrymple (d 1970); 1 s (Piers b 1966); *Career* WWII Capt Queen's Royal Regt served Belgium, POW (despatches) 1939-46; with Lloyds of London 1938-39, employed in antique field UK and USA 1946-52, various directorships in furnishing (incl own co) 1952-86; elected cncl Royal Boro of Kensington and Chelsea 1967-: chm Planning Ctee 1968-72, chm Colville/Tavistock Regeneration Ctee 1972-77, ald and dep ldr 1970, Mayor 1977-78; Silver Jubilee Medal 1977; *Recreations* sailing; *Clubs* Royal Yacht Sqdn, Royal Thames YC, Pratts; *Style—* Peter H Methuen, Esq; Elliston, St Boswells, Roxburghshire (☎ 0835 22747); 6 Warwick Sq, London SW1

METHUEN, Hon Robert Alexander Holt; s of 5 Baron Methuen (d 1975), and hp of bro, 6 Baron; *b* 22 July 1931; *Educ* Shrewsbury, Trinity Cambridge; *m* 1958, Mary Catherine Jane, da of Ven Charles German Hooper, Archdeacon of Ipswich; 2 da; *Style—* The Hon Robert Methuen; Stoneycroft Farm, Kniveton, Ashbourne, Derbys

METHVEN, Lady; Karen Jane; da of Dr Walter Anderson Caldwell, by his w Jean Drummond Hislop; *b* 28 June 1945; *Educ* St Leonard's Fife, Edinburgh Univ (BSc); *m* 1977, Sir (Malcolm) John Methven (d 1980, dir-gen CBI 1976-80); *Career* business conslt and co dir; ICI Ltd 1968-81; dir: Recent Prodns Ltd 1983-, Walden Assocs Ltd 1985, Marine Logic Ltd 1986-, Sussex County Bldg Soc 1986-; pres Guild of Medical Secs 1982-; tstee: Soc for the Promotion of New Music 1982-, Univ of Southampton Devpt Tst; memb: cncl of Friends of ENO 1980-, fund raising ctee Order of St John 1981-, advsy cncl Social Affrs Unit 1981-, CNAA 1982, US-UK Educnl Cmmn 1983-87, chm Southampton Philharmonic Soc; *Recreations* opera, piano, music, theatre, sailing (yacht, 'Zemfira'), skiing, windsurfing; *Clubs* St James's (ctee memb), IOD, Reform, Royal Southern YC, Royal Gourock YC, Clyde Cruising, Royal Yachting Assoc, Ski Club of GB, Down Hill Only, Kandahar; *Style—* Lady Methven; 20 Bushwood Rd, Richmond, Surrey TW9 3BQ (☎ 01 940 4271)

MEXBOROUGH, 8 Earl of (I 1766); John Christopher George Savile; also Baron Pollington (I 1753) and Viscount Pollington (I 1766); s of 7 Earl (d 1980; himself gs of the 4 Earl who, as Lord Gaverstock, featured in a minor role in Disraeli's Coningsby, and who, for the last seven and a half months of his life, enjoyed the distinction of being the last living ex-member of the unreformed House of Commons); *b* 16 May 1931; *Educ* Eton, Worcester Coll Oxford; *m* 1, 1958, (m dis 1972), Lady Elisabeth Hariot Grimston, da of 6 Earl of Verulam; 1 s, 1 da; m 2, 1972, Catherine Joyce, da of James Kenneth Hope, CBE, DL, and formerly wife of Maj the Hon Nicholas Crespigny Laurence Vivian; 1 s (Hon James b 1976), 1 da (Lady Lucinda b 1973); *Heir* s, Viscount Pollington; *Career* late 2 Lt Grenadier Gds; *Clubs* All England Lawn Tennis; *Style—* The Rt Hon the Earl of Mexborough; Arden Hall, Hawnby, York (☎ 043 96 348); 13 Ovington Mews, London SW3 (☎ 01 589 3669)

MEXBOROUGH, Dowager Countess of; Josephine Bertha Emily; da of late Capt Andrew Mansel Talbot Fletcher; *m* 1930, John Raphael Wentworth Savile, 7 Earl of Mexborough (d 1980); 2 s, 1 da (decd); *Style—* The Rt Hon Dowager Countess of Mexborough; The Dower House, Arden Hall, Hawnby, York YO6 5LS (☎ (043 96) 213)

MEYER *see also*: de Meyer

MEYER, Sir Anthony John Charles; 3 Bt (UK 1910), of Shortgrove, Newport, Essex; MP (C) Clwyd North West 1983-; s of Sir Frank Meyer, 2 Bt, MP (d 1935), of Ayot House, Ayot St Lawrence, Herts, by his w Georgina (d 1962), *née* Seeley; *b* 27 Oct 1920; *Educ* Eton, New Coll Oxford; *m* 10 Oct 1941, Barbadee Violet, da of A Charles Knight, JP, FSA (d 1958), of Herne Place, Sunningdale; 1 s, 3 da; *Heir* s, (Anthony) Ashley Frank Meyer b 23 Aug 1944; *Career* Lt Scots Gds WWII; Foreign Serv 1947; first sec: Paris 1956, Moscow 1957; FO 1958-62; PPS to Rt Hon Maurice Macmillan as: chief sec Treasy 1970-72, sec state for Employment 1972-74; chm Franco-Br Parly Rels Ctee; MP (C): Eton and Slough 1964-66, Flint West 1970-1983; fndr and dir of Solon 1969, tstee Shakespeare Nat Memorl Theatre, vice-chm: Franco-Brit cncl, Cons European affrs ctee; Offr Légion d'Honneur (France); *Recreations* music, opera, travel, ski-ing, cooking; *Clubs* Beefsteak; *Style—* Sir Anthony Meyer, Bt, MP; 9 Cottage Place, Brompton Square, London SW3 (☎ 01 589 7416); House of Commons, London SW1A 0AA (☎ 01 219 4343)

MEYER, Ashley Paul; s of Harold Edward Leonard Meyer, of Eastbourne, and Margaret Irene, *née* Armstrong; *b* 27 Jan 1948; *Educ* Mill Hill, Clarks Business Sch (Business Studies Dip); *m* 28 Aug 1971, Linda Margaret, da of Ronald George Franklin, and Patricia Marie, *née* Fletcher; 1 s (Toby b 1974); *Career* gp chief exec and md Gillow Gp plc; dir: Proctors Ltd, Aurosa Ltd, Lenham Ltd, Macowards Ltd, Lablanc Ltd; *Recreations* golf, sailing; *Clubs* Royal Eastbourne GC, Newhaven Marina YC; *Style—* Ashley Meyer, Esq; Gillow plc, 145 Tottenham Court Road, London W1P 9LL (☎ 01 387 2833)

MEYER, Christopher John Rome; CMG (1988); s of Flt Lt Reginald Henry Rome Meyer (ka 1944), and Evelyn, *née* Campani (now Mrs Duncan Finlayson Macdonald); *b* 22 Feb 1944; *Educ* Lancing, Peterhouse Cambridge (MA), Sch of Advanced Int Studies Bologna; *m* 11 Dec 1976, Franscoise Elizabeth, da of Air Cdre Sir Archie Winskill, KCVO, CBE, DFC (and Bar), AE, of Anchors, Coastal Rd, East Preston, West Sussex; 2 s (James b 21 March 1978, William b 20 June 1984), 1 step s (Thomas (Hedges) b 28 Aug 1972); *Career* Dip Serv: third sec West and Central African dept FO 1966-7, trg russian language 1967-8, third (later second) sec Br Embassy Moscow 1968-70, second (later first) sec Madrid 1970-73; FCO: first sec E Euro and Soviet dept 1973-76, first sec planning staff 1976-78; first sec UK rep to Euro Community Brussels 1978-82, cnsllr head of chancery Moscow 1982-84, head news dept and chief FCO spokesman 1984-88; visiting fell Centre for Int Affrs Harvard Univ 1988-89; min (commercial) Washington 1989; *Recreations* squash, reading, music; *Style—* Christopher Meyer, Esq; King Charles St, London SW1A 2AH

MEYER, Rt Rev Conrad John Eustace; s of late William Eustace Meyer; *b* 31 Mar 1989; *Educ* Clifton, Pembroke Coll Cambridge, Westcott House; *m* 1960, Mary, da of late Alec John Wiltshire; *Career* Lt (S) RNVR and later chaplain RNVR; vicar Devoran Truro 1954-64; diocesan: youth chaplain 1956-60, sec for educn 1960-69; hon canon of Truro 1960-69, archdeacon of Bodmin 1969-79, examining chaplain to Bishop of Truro 1973-79, area bishop of Dorchester 1979-87, provost of Western Div of the Woodard Schs 1970-; chm of Appeal Ctee SPCK; *Recreations* civil def (Fell (HC) Inst of Civil Def), archaeology, swimming, walking; *Clubs* Royal Cwlth Soc; *Style—* The Rt Rev Conrad Meyer; Hawk's Cliff, 38 Praze Road, Newquay, Cornwall TR7 3AF (☎ 0637 873003)

MEYER, James Henry Paul; s of late Leo Henry Paul Meyer; *b* 5 Nov 1938; *Educ* Hilton Coll SA, Millfield; *m* 1964, Janet, *née* Baker; 3 c; *Career* chm and md Federated Land Ltd 1959-82; *Recreations* squash, showjumping, flying; *Clubs* RAC; *Style—* James Meyer, Esq; Keston Stud, Downs Lane, Leatherhead, Surrey (☎ 0306 5995)

MEYER, Michael Leverson; s of Percy Barrington Meyer (d 1955), of London, and Eleanor Rachel, *née* Benjamin (d 1929); *b* 11 June 1921; *Educ* Wellington, Christ Church Oxford (MA); 1 da (Nora b 1968); *Career* operational res section Bomber Cmd HQ 1942-45; lectr in eng lit Uppsala Univ Sweden 1947-50, visiting prof of drama Dartmouth Coll USA 1978 and Univ of Colorado 1986; memb: ed advsy bd Good Food Guide 1958-72; author; FRSL 1971, govr LAMDA 1962-; Gold Medal of the Swedish Acad (1964), Knight Cdr of the Order of the Polar Star first class Sweden 1977; *Books* Eight Oxford Poets (ed with Sidney Keyes, and contrib 1941), Collected Poems of Sidney Keyes (ed 1945), The Minos of Crete (ed by Sidney Keyes, 1948), The End of the Corridor (1951), The Ortolan (play, 1967), Henrik Ibsen: The Making of a Dramatist (1967), Henrik Ibsen: The Farewell to Poetry (1971), Henrik Ibsen: The Top of a Cold Mountain (1971, Whitbread Biography Prize), Lunatic and Lover (play, 1981), Summer Days (ed 1981), Ibsen on File (1985), Strindberg: a biography (1985), File on Strindberg (1986); translated: The Long Ships (by Frans G Bengtsson, 1954) Ibsen Brand 1960, The Lady from the Sea (1960), John Gabriel Borkman (1960), When We Dead Awaken (1960), The Master Builder (1960), Little Eyolf (1961), Ghosts (1962), The Wild Duck (1962), Hedda Gabler (1962); Peer Gynt (1963), An Enemy of the People (1960), The Pillars of Society (1963), The Pretenders (1964), A Doll's House (1965), Rosmersholm (1966), Emperor and Galilean (1986); Strindberg: The Father (1964), Miss Julie (1964), Creditors (1964), The Stronger (1964), Playing with Fire (1964), Erik the Fourteenth (1964), Storm (1964), The Ghost Sonata (1964), A Dream Play (1973), To Damascus (1975), Easter (1975), The Dance of Death (1975), The Virgin Bride (1975); *Recreations* real tennis, eating, sleeping; *Clubs* Garrick, Savile, MCC; *Style—* Michael Meyer, Esq; 4 Montagu Sq, London W1H 1RA

MEYER, Montague John; s of late John Mount Montague Meyer, CBE; *b* 18 Dec 1944; *Educ* Cranleigh; *m* 1972, Diana Ruth, da of William Edward Curtis Offer; 2 da; *Career* timber merchant; chief and md Montague L Meyer Ltd 1979-82, dep chm and md Meyer Int plc 1982-84, md MacMillan Bloedel Meyer Ltd 1979-84, dir MacMillan Bloedel Ltd Vancouver BC 1980-82; md MBM Forest Products Ltd 1984-; chm Compass Forest Products Ltd 1985-; *Recreations* sports, reading, charity works; *Clubs* MCC; *Style—* Montague Meyer, Esq; 24 Kensington Park Road, London W11 3BU (☎ 01 299 5303)

MEYER, Rollo John Oliver (Jack); OBE (1968); s of Rev Canon Horace Rollo Meyer (d 1958), and late Arabella Crosbie, *née* Ward; *b* 15 Mar 1905; *Educ* Haileybury, Pembroke Coll Cambridge (BA, MA); *m* 1 Aug 1931, Joyce Evelyn, da of Richard Sydney Symons (d 1954), of Bournemouth; 2 da (Jillian b 1932, d 1978, Jacqueline b 1934); *Career* WWII Flt Lt RAF 1939-45; Gill & Co cotton brokers Bombay 1926-29, private tutor to HH Thakore Satib of Kathiawar India 1929, headmaster Dhrangadra Palace Sch Kathiawar 1929-35, fndr and headmaster Millfield Sch 1935-70, headmaster Campion Sch Athens 1973-78, co-fndr and headmaster St Lawrence Coll Athens 1979-83, co-fndr and first rector Byron Coll Athens 1983-; chm of govrs Shute Sch Devon 1970 and 1972; previously active in a wide variety of sports esp at Cambridge Univ and in India; *Recreations* a little writing (mostly to the Press), a little specialist teaching, much tv; *Clubs* MCC (Veteran); *Style—* Jack Meyer, Esq, OBE; Milton Lane, Wells, Somerset (☎ 0749 72080)

MEYER, Ronald; s of Frederic Charles Meyer (d 1962), and Sarah Anne, *née* Jackson; *b* 17 Sept 1923; *Educ* Lawrence Sherrif GS Rugby, Rugby Tech Coll; *m* 24 Aug 1946, Dorothy, da of Stanley Charles Whiteman (d 1948), of Rugby; 3 s (Malcolm b 1949,

Christopher b 1953, Stephen b 1960); *Career* chartered elec engr; ptnr McAuslan & Ptnrs 1960-88, dir Parkman Gp conslting engrs 1988-, chm IEE (Mersey & N Wales Centre) 1980; memb: CEng, FIEE, MCIBSE, MConsE; *Recreations* gardening, model making, walking; *Style—* Ronald Meyer, Esq; Inglefield Cottage, Mill Rd, Higher Bebington, Wirral (☎ 051 608 7981); Parkman Tooth Davies Ltd, 25 Hamilton Square, Birkenhead, Wirral (☎ 051 647 7711, fax 051 666 2203)

MEYJES, Sir Richard Anthony; DL (Surrey 1983); s of Anthony Charles Dorian Meyjes; *b* 30 June 1918; *Educ* Univ Coll Sch Hampstead; *m* 1939, Margaret Doreen Morris; 3 s; *Career* served WWII; slr 1946; with Shell Petroleum Co London 1946-58, Manila Philippines 1958-64, London 1964-70, as mktg co-ordinator, dir and personnel co-ordinator 1972-76; head of business team Civil Serv 1970-72; dir: Coates Bros plc 1976-84 (chm 1977-84), Foseco Minsep 1976-, Portals Hldgs 1976-88; chm cncl Univ of Surrey 1980-85, vice pres Assoc of Optometrists 1988-; High Sheriff Surrey 1984-85; Master Worshipful Co of Spectacle Makers 1985-87; Hon DUniv Surrey 1988; CBIM, FRSA, FIOD; kt 1972; *Style—* Sir Richard Meyjes, DL; Long Hill House, The Sands, nr Farnham, Surrey GU10 1NQ (☎ 025 18 2601)

MEYNELL, Hon Mrs; Hon Alexandra Rachel Mary Catherine Angelica; *née* Lampson; da of 2 Baron Killearn; *b* 1947; *m* 1966, Nicholas Edward Hugo Meynell; 2 s; *Style—* The Hon Mrs Meynell; Ladysmith Farm, Hoar Cross, Burton-on-Trent, Staffs (☎ 028 375 306)

MEYNELL, Dame Alix Hester Marie (Lady Meynell); DBE (1949); da of late Surgn Cmdr L Kilroy, RN, and late Hester Kilroy; *b* 2 Feb 1903; *Educ* Malvern Girls' Coll, Somerville Coll Oxford; *m* 1946, Sir Francis Meynell, RDI (d 1975); *Career* joined Civil Serv Bd of Trade 1925, seconded Monopolies and Restrictive Practices Cmmn as sec 1949-53, under sec Bd of Trade 1946-55, resigned Civil Serv 1955; barr 1956; md Nonesuch Press Ltd 1976-; memb: SE Gas Bd 1956-69, Harlow New Town Corpn 1956-65, ctees of investigation for England, Scotland and GB under Agric Mktg Acts 1956-65, Monopolies Cmmn 1965-68; memb Cosford RDC; *Books* Public Servant, Private Woman;; *Style—* Dame Alix Meynell, DBE; The Grey House, Lavenham, Sudbury, Suffolk (☎ 0787 247526)

MEYNELL, Godfrey; MBE (1963); s of Capt Godfrey Meynell, VC, MC, QVO (ka 1935), and Sophia Patricia, *née* Lowis; Derbyshire landowners since 12th century; *b* 20 July 1934; *Educ* Eton, Magdalene Coll Cambridge (BA); *m* 11 June 1960, Honor Mary, da of Maj J H A Davis (d 1961); 1 s (Godfrey b 1964), 2 da (Diana Violet b 1962, Katharine Jill b 1966); *Career* HM Overseas Civil Serv, asst advsr W Aden Protectorate; Home Civil Serv 1968-, regnl controller (Housing) DOE E Midland Regnl Forestry Conservation 1984-; High Sheriff of Derbyshire 1982-83; *Recreations* forestry, conservation; *Style—* Godfrey Meynell, Esq, MBE; Meynell Langley, Derby DE6 4NT (☎ 033 124 207); c/o Dept of Environment, Cranbrook House, Nottingham

MEYNELL, Hon Mrs; Hon Elizabeth Margaret; *née* Gretton; yr da of 2 Baron Gretton, OBE; *b* 25 July 1945; *Educ* Downham Sch, Switzerland and Italy; *m* 1968, Christopher Mark, s of Canon Mark Meynell; 2 s (Mark John Henrik, Guy Francis); *Style—* The Hon Mrs Meynell; c/o Stapleford Park, Melton Mowbray, Leics (☎ 057 284 229)

MEYNELL, Hugh Bernard; s of Cuthbert Charles Meynell (d 1973), and Irene Mary, *née* Hickman; *b* 7 Jan 1931; *Educ* Ampleforth, Columbia Univ NY; *m* 23 June 1956, Paula Faine, da of Paul Ellis Gibbons (d 1972); 1 s (Edward James b 15 Dec 1959), 1 da (Rosemary Jane (Mrs Douglas) b 11 Oct 1957); *Career* Nat Serv 2 Lt RA 1949-51; chm Meynell Values Ltd Wolverhampton 1978-88, dir S Staffs Water Co 1982-, chm Dynafluid 1988-; pres Boys Bde Wolverhampton; Freeman: City of London 1985, Worshipful Co Plumbers 1985; MInstM 1976, memb Inst Sales Mgmnt 1979; *Recreations* shooting, cricket, tennis; *Clubs* MCC; *Style—* Hugh Meynell, Esq; Brockton Ct, nr Shifnal, Shropshire TF11 9LZ (☎ 095271 247); Dynafluid Ltd, Hortonwood 33, Telford TF1 4EX fax 0952 607738)

MEYNELL, Hugo Ivo; s of Lt-Col Hugo Francis Meynell, OBE (d 1974), and Doris Isabel, *née* Morrison; *b* 23 Nov 1931; *Educ* Stowe, RMA Sandhurst; *m* 1, 1961, Sarah Virginia, da of Gen Sir Richard McCreery GCB, KBE, DSO, MC (d 1967); 2 s (Luke Hugo b 1964, Alexander Michael b 1966), 1 da (Lucia Anna b 1968); m 2, 1984, Audrey Tennant, da of George Henderson (d 1968); *Career* joined 12 Royal Lancers (POW) 1952, Malaya 1952-54, Capt 1955, Suez Landing 1956 (despatches 1957), WO 1960-2; The Economist Newspaper 1963 (dep md 1973, dir 1978), md The Economist Pubns 1984-; memb cncl Buckingham Univ 1980;; *Recreations* country pursuits; *Clubs* Cavalry and Guards; *Style—* Hugo I Meynell, Esq; 38 Halsey St, London SW3 (☎ 01 589 5014); The Old Manor House, Whichford, Shipston on Stour, Warwickshire (☎ 060 884 293); The Economist Newspaper Ltd, 25 St James's St, London SW1A 1HG (☎ 01 839 7000, fax 01 839 2968, telex 24344)

MEYNELL, Laurence Walter; s of late Hubert Meynell, and late Agnes, *née* Sollom; *b* 9 August 1899; *Educ* St Edmund's Hall Ware; *m* 1, 1932, Shirley Ruth (d 1955), da of late Taylor Darbyshire; 1 da; m 2, Joan Belfrage (d 1986); *Career* WWI serv HAC 1917, 2 Lt RFA 1918; WWII: Sqdn Ldr RAF (despatches) 1939-45; author; literary ed Time and Tide 1958-60, past pres Johnson Soc; *Books* as Robert Eton incl: The Pattern, The Dividing Air, The Bus Leaves for the Village, Not in our Stars, Palace Pier, The Faithful Years, St Lynn's Advertiser, The Dragon at the Gate; as Laurence Meynell incl: Bluefeather, Paid in Full His Aunt Came Late, Too Clever by Half, Smokey Joe, District Nurse Carter, The End of the Long Hot Summer, A Little Matter of Arson, The Fatal Flaw, Sleep of the Unjust, Parasol in the Park, The Open Door, The Abiding Thing; as Stephen Tring (for children) incl: The Cave by the Sea, Penny Dreadful, Barry's Exciting Year, Penny Patient, Penny Dramatic, Penny in Italy, Penny Goodbye; *Recreations* cricket, tennis; *Clubs* Author's; *Style—* Laurence Meynell, Esq; 19 The Drive, Hove, Sussex

MEYRICK; *see*: Tapps-Gervis-Meyrick

MEYRICK, Sir David John Charlton; 4 Bt (UK 1880), of Bush, Pembrokeshire; s of Col Sir Thomas Frederick Meyrick, 3 Bt, TD, DL (d 1983), and his 1 w, Ivy Frances, *née* Pilkington (d 1947); *b* 2 Dec 1926; *Educ* Eton, Trinity Hall Cambridge (MA); *m* 29 Sept 1962, Penelope Anne, da of Cdr John Bertram Aubrey Marsden-Smedley, RN (d 1959); 3 s; *Heir* s, Timothy Thomas Charlton; *Career* chartered surveyor and land agent; *Recreations* riding, sailing; *Style—* Sir David Meyrick, Bt; Bush House, Gumfreston, Tenby, Dyfed SA70 8RA

MEYRICK, Dr Roger Llewellyn; JP(1971-); s of Thidal Francis Meyrick (d 1965), of Swansea, and Helen Viviene, *née* Jones (d 1979); *b* 31 Mar 1930; *Educ* Dulwich Coll, King's Coll London, King's Coll Hosp Univ of London (MB BS); *m* 6 March 1954, Barbara Treseder, da of Reginald George Coombs (d 1974), of Stroud, Gloucs; 1 s (Huw b 1 Jan 1966), 3 da (Olivia b 1 March 1955, Daryl b 28 April 1956, Clare b 16 Dec 1958); *Career* princ gen med practice Lewisham London 1954-, hosp practitioner dermatology Lewisham Hosp 1972-, facilitator in gen practice Lewisham and N Southwark 1988-; RCGP: chm of S London Faculty 1969-72, provost of S London Faculty 1977-80, pres W Kent Medicochirurgical Soc 1972-73; chm Magistrates Assoc SE London 1987-; Freeman City of London 1970, Liveryman Worshipful Soc of Apothecaries 1970; MRCS, LRCP, FRCGP, FRSM 1967, memb BMA 1954; *Books* Understanding Cancer (ed jtly 1977), Principles of Practice Management (contrib, 1984), Patient Health Education; *Recreations* local medical history, gardening; *Clubs* Royal Cwlth Soc; *Style—* Dr Roger Meyrick, JP; 37 Manor Way, Beckenham, Kent BR3 3LN (☎ 01 650 8207); 80 Torridon Rd, Catford, London SE6 1RB (☎ 01 698 5281)

MEYRICK, Timothy Thomas Charlton; s and h of Sir David Meyrick, 4 Bt; *b* 5 Nov 1963; *Educ* Eton, Bristol Univ; *Style—* Timothy Meyrick Esq; c/o Bush House, Gumfreston, Tenby, Dyfed

MEYSEY-THOMPSON, Sir (Humphrey) Simon; 4 Bt (UK 1874), of Kirby Hall, Yorkshire; s of Guy Herbert Meysey-Thompson (d 1961), and kinsman of Sir Algar de Clifford Charles Meysey-Thompson, 3 Bt (d 1967); *b* 31 Mar 1935; *Style—* Sir Simon Meysey-Thompson, Bt; 10 Church St, Woodbridge, Suffolk (☎ 039 43 2144)

MIALL, (Rowland) Leonard; OBE (1961); s of Rowland Miall (d 1955), of Lastingham, Yorks, and Sara Grace, *née* Dixon (d 1975); *b* 6 Nov 1914; *Educ* Bootham Sch York, Freiburg Univ, St John's Coll Cambridge; *m* 1, 18 Jan 1941, Lorna Barbara (d 1974), da of George Rackham (d 1974), of Bucks; 3 s (Roger b 1944, Tristram b 1947, St John b 1952), 1 da (Virginia b 1948); m 2, 10 Oct 1975, Sally Greenaway Bicknell, da of Gordon Leith (d 1965), of Johannesburg; *Career* pres Cambridge Union 1936, ed Cambridge Review 1936, lectured in USA 1937, sec Br-American Assoc 1937-39, joined BBC inaugurated talks broadcast to Europe 1939, German talks and features ed 1940-42, memb Br Political Warfare Mission to US 1942-44 (dir news San Francisco 1943, head NY off 1944), personal asst to Dep Dir-Gen Political Warfare Exec 1944, attached to psychological warfare div of SHAEF 1945; rejoined BBC special corr Czechoslovakia 1945, actg dip corr 1945, chief corr in US 1945-53; head of TV talks 1954, asst controller current affrs and talks, TV 1961, special asst to dir of TV planning start of BBC-2 1962, asst controller programme services TV 1963-66, BBC rep in USA 1966-71, controller, overseas and foreign relations BBC 1971-74; res historian 1975-84, inaugurated BBC lunchtime lectrs 1962; advsr ctee on broadcasting New Delhi 1965, fndr Cwlth Bdcasting Assoc 1975, dir Visnews Ltd 1976- (dep chm 1984-85 overseas dir BAFTA 1974-, memb cncl Royal TV Soc 1984-, Fell RTS 1985, FRSA, Certificate of Appreciation NYC 1970; ed Richard Dimbleby broadcaster 1966; contrib to DNB; *Recreations* travel, gardening; *Clubs* Garrick, Metropolitan (Washington DC), Union (Cambridge); *Style—* Leonard Miall, Esq, OBE; Maryfield Cottage, High St, Taplow Village, Maidenhead SL6 0EX (☎ 0628 60419); (☎ 0628 604195)

MICHAEL, Kathryn Jean; da of Charles Godfrey Nairn (d 1961), of Harley St, London W1, and Kaye, *née* Davey; *b* 20 Sept 1941; *Educ* Malvern Girls Coll, Marymount Coll Barcelona Spain; *m* 5 March 1976, (Louis Sydney) Michael Bill, OBE; *Career* Unilever Ltd 1967-69, BBDO Ltd 1969-71, Limas Ltd 1971-78, dir Ogilvy & Mather Ltd 1978-; memb Womens Advtg Club of London (pres 1977-78); MIPA 1976; *Recreations* friends and flowers; *Clubs* RAC; *Style—* Mrs Kathryn Michael; 53 Holland Park, London W11 3RS; Ogilvy & Mather Ltd, Brettenham House, Lancaster Place, London WC2 (☎ 01 836 2466)

MICHAEL, Simon Laurence; s of Anthony Denis Michael, of London, and Regina, *née* Milstone; *b* 4 Jan 1955; *Educ* Kings Coll London (LLB); *m* 7 Sept 1987, Elaine Laura, da of Cameron Hudson Duncan (d 1983); 1 s (Kay b 1988); *Career* called to the Bar Middle Temple 1978; *Books* The Usurper (jtly, 1988), The Cut Throat (1989); *Style—* Simon Michael, Esq; Francis Taylor Building, Temple, London EC4Y 7BY (☎ 01 353 9942, fax 01 353 9924)

MICHAELS, David; s of Alexander Michaels, of Stanmore, and Evelyn, *née* Susman; *b* 7 Nov 1943; *Educ* Christ's Coll Finchley, UCL (BSc), Kings Coll Chelsea; *m* 1970, Diane Lorraine, da of Alfred Radley; 1 s (Peter b 1979), 1 da (Lucy b 1975); *Career* GEC 1965, Chaco Survey 1967, Freemans 1968, Logica 1969, NM Rothschild & Sons 1971, chm The Guidehouse Gp plc 1980-, dir of numerous cos incl: The Hornby Gp plc, WH Wllen and Co plc, Alliance Property and Conslt plc (vice-chm), Lachmead Gp plc; chm Friends of Open Air Theatre Regent's Pk, dir New Shakespeare Co Ltd; cncl memb Nat Consumer Cncl; Freeman City of London, Liveryman Worshipful Co Glovers; DMS, FSS, FRSA; *Books* The Sufferings of the Cancer Patient (jtly, 1967), How to Buy a Company (contrib 1988); *Recreations* theatre, music, piano, clarinet; *Clubs* Groucho, City Livery; *Style—* David Michaels, Esq; Vestry House, Greyfriars Passage, Newgate St, London EC1A 7BA (☎ 01 606 6321)

MICHAELS, Robert Stewart John; s of Alexander Michaels, of Stanmore, and Evelyn, *née* Susman; *b* 20 Dec 1941; *Educ* Ravensfield Coll Orange Hill, St Martins Sch of Art; *m* 19 June 1966, Marilyn, da of Edward Lee; 2 s (Mark John Louis b 4 Oct 1972, Daniel David b 19 Sept 1977); *Career* chm and md Robert Michaels Hldgs Ltd 1974-; dir: Mardan Properties Ltd, John Crowther plc 1987, Robert Mark Ltd, Marongate Ltd; tstee Bryanston Tst, underwriting memb Lloyds; Freeman City of London 1979, life memb Guild of Freeman City of London; Liveryman Worshipful Cos: Horners, Farriers, Patternmakers; FInstD 1980; *Recreations* family, reading, tennis, skiing, cricket, racing cars; *Clubs* Annabels, Queens, RAC, Ferrari Owners; *Style—* Robert Michaels, Esq; Robert Michaels Holdings Ltd, 12 Great Portland St, London W1N 6JQ (☎ 01 580 1656, fax 01 706 4690)

MICHEL, Keith; s of Capt George Richard Michel, RAOC, of Thatchdale, Pennymead Drive, E Horsley, Surrey, and Winifred Eve Michel (d 1972); *b* 19 May 1948; *Educ* Bradfield, Fitzwilliam Coll Cambridge (MA), Law Coll Guildford; *m* 16 Dec 1972, Rosemary Suzannah, da of Stanley Joseph Simons, of Southgate, London; 1 s (Edward b 30 April 1980); *Career* slr; articled clerk Coward Chance (now Clifford Chance) 1971-73, asst slr Clyde & Co 1973-75, ptnr Holman Fenwick & William 1975- (former asst slr); Oxford Blue soccer (twice); memb: Grasshoppers CC, Old Bradfieldion FC; various articles in legal pubns 1986-88 incl: Lloyds List, Lloyds Maritime, Commercial Law Quarterley, Law Society's Gazette; memb Law Soc 1973; *Recreations* family life, football, cricket, wind surfing, history, archaeology, wildlife conservation; *Style—* Keith Michel, Esq; Marlow House, Lloyds Ave, London EC3N 3AL (☎ 01 488 2300, fax 01

481 0316, telex 8812247 HFW LON)

MICHELHAM, Marie-José;; *née* Dupas; *m* 1980, as his 2 w, 2 Baron Michelham (d 1984, when the title became extinct); *Style—* Rt Hon Lady Michelham

MICHELL, Maj (Allan Edwyn) Dennis; s of Cdr Roland Allen Creagh Michell (d 1986), and Catherine Margaret, *née* Bennett (d 1974); *b* 14 Nov 1917; *Educ* Canford, RMC Sandhurst; *m* 1, 31 March 1941, Pamela, da of late Francis Seabrooke, of Bucks; 1 da (Susan b 1942); m 2, 18 Dec 1948, Patricia Anne, da of Brig-Gen Rupert Farquhar Riley, CMG, DSO (d 1941), of Norfolk; 2 da (Linda b 1951, Juliet b 1956); *Career* cmmnd E Surrey Regt serv: BEF, Dunkirk, N Africa, Italy; KAR Mau-Mau Campaign Kenya 1952-60; *Recreations* shooting, painting, photography, sailing; *Clubs* Royal Lymington YC; *Style—* Maj Dennis Michell; Corner House, Nelson Place, Lymington, Hants SO41 9RY (☎ 0590 73459)

MICHELL, Francis Victor; CMG (1955); s of Pierre William Michell (d 1939); *b* 17 Jan 1908; *Educ* Barry Sch, Jesus Coll Oxford; *m* 1943, Betty Enid Tempest, da of William Tempest Olver, JP (d 1958); *Career* entered Foreign Off 1941, Br Embassy Rio de Janeiro 1941-46, Br Consulate-Gen Istanbul 1947-51, memb UK Cmmn-Gen Singapore 1951-53, FO Off 1953-65; *Clubs* Travellers'; *Style—* Francis Michell Esq, CMG; Nettlesworth Farm, Vines Cross, Heathfield, East Sussex (☎ 043 52 2695)

MICHELL, Cdr John Percy Pitt; LVO (1954), OBE (1958); s of Charles Percy Rodney Micheal (d 1943), of Yorks and Somerset, and Emily Constance Wybourne (d 1960); *b* 25 Feb 1914; *Educ* RNC Dartmouth and Greenwich; *m* 15 Aug 1938, Angela Margaret Shaw, da of Harry James Davis (d 1961), of Canada; 2 s (Rodney Drake Palmer b 1943, Simon Charles b 1951), 1 da (Miranda Margaret b 1940); *Career* RN 1927, WWII serv: Antarctic, Pacific, Indian Ocean, Red Sea, E Med, N Russian Convoys, Battle of Atlantic, Lt-Cdr, ret 1948 (invalided); Central African Cncl Rhodesia 1948-53, comptroller to Govr Gen Fedn of Rhodesian and Nyasaland (acting Cdr) 1953-57, official sec and comptroller to Govr Gen 1957-64; *Recreations* cricket, tennis, rugby, shooting; *Style—* Cdr John Michell, LVO, OBE; The Old Rectory, Clipston, nr Market Harborough LE16 9RW (☎ 085 886 275)

MICHELL, Keith Joseph; s of Joseph Michell (d 1957), and Alice Maude Alsat (d 1957); *b* 1 Dec 1926; *Educ* Warnertown Sch, Port Pirie HS, SA Sch of Arts and Crafts, Adelaide Teachers Coll, Adelaide Univ, Old Vic Theatre Sch; *m* 1957, Jeannette Laura, da of Frank Sterk (d 1985); 1 s (Paul b 1960), 1 da (Helena b 1961); *Career* artist and actor; memb original Young Vic Theatre Co; first appearance London And so to Bed 1951; leading actor Shakespeare Meml Theatre Co 1952-56: Twelfth Night (Orsino), Macbeth (Macduff), Henry IV (Hotspur), As you like it (Orlando), The Taming of the Shrew (Petruchio), Midsummer Nights Dream (Theseus); joined Old Vic 1956: Much Ado about Nothing (Benedick), Anthony & Cleopatra (Anthony), Two Gentlmen of Verona (Proteus); starred in musicals: Irma la Douce (Oscar/Nestor), Robert and Elizabeth (Robert), Man of La Mancha (Don Quixote), On the 20th Century (Oscar), La Cage Aux Folles (Georges); artistic dir Chichester Festival Theatre 1974-77; plays incl: The Chances (Don John), Kings Mare (Henry VIII), Hamlet (Hamlet), Dear Love (Robert), Abelard and Heloise (Abelard), Oedipus Tyrannus (Oedipus), Cyrano de Bergerac (Cyrano), Othello (Iago and Othello), Twelfth Night (dir), Murder in the Cathedral (Becket), The Apple Cart (Magnus), Pete McGynty and the Dream Time (Pete McGynty), On the Rocks (Sir Arthur), The Tempest (Prospero), Jane Eyre (Rochester), Portraits (Augustus John), Royal Baccarat Scandal (Gordon-Cumming); appearances in 8 Films; TV and video: many classical prodns: Pygmalion, Mayerling, Wuthering Heights, Ring Round the Moon, An Ideal Husband, Anthony and Cleopatra, Six Wives of Henry VIII, Capt Beaky and his Band, Pirates of Penzance (Maj-Gen), The Gondoliers, Ruddigore (Robin Oakapple); records: Ancient and Modern, At the Shows, Words Words Words, Capt Beaky and his Band; one man painting shows: Jamaica 1960, New York 1963, Portugal 1963, Don Quixote 1970, Hamlet 1972, Shakespeare Sonnets (Lithographs), Capt Beaky 1982; Best Musical Actor London Critics 1968, Show Business Personality 1971, Top Actor (SUN) 1971, Special Award Variety Club 1971, Best Actor Soc of Films and TV Arts 1970, Outstanding Actor Performance Emmy Award Nat Acad of TV Arts 1971, British Film Award 1973, Logie Award 1974; *Recreations* swimming, reading; *Style—* Keith J Michell, Esq; c/o Jean Diamond, London Management Ltd, 235 Regent St, London W1

MICHELMORE, Clifford Arthur; CBE (1969); s of (Albert) Herbert Michelmore (d 1921), of Cowes, IOW, and Ellen, *née* Alford (d 1947); *b* 11 Dec 1919; *Educ* Cowes HS, RAF Coll, Leicester Coll of Technol; *m* 4 March 1950, Jean, da of Guy Vivian Metcalfe (d 1962), of Reigate, Surrey; 1 s (Guy Alford b 1957), 1 da (Jenny Gwen b 1959); *Career* RAF 1935-47; Br Forces Network 1947; BBC 1950: Tonight, 24 Hrs, Holiday; Home on Sunday 1984-; md: RMEMI 1970-80, Michelmore Enterprises 1967-, CP Video 1987-; *Books* Businessmans Book of Golf (1981), Holidays in Britain (1986), Two-Way Story (with Jean Metcalfe, 1987); *Recreations* golf, sailing; *Clubs* Garrick, RAF, Walton Heath; *Style—* Clifford Michelmore, Esq, CBE; White House, Upper West St, Reigate RH2 9BU (☎ 0737 245014); Brookfield, Bembridge, IOW PO3 5XW (☎ 09837 2480)

MICHELMORE, Col James Franck Godwin; TD (1956, with two clasps), DL (Devon 1973-); s of Sir Godwin Michelmore, KBE, CB, DSO (d 1982) of Exeter, and Margaret Phoebe, *née* Newbolt (d 1965); family in S Devon from 1334 at least, documents from 1570; *b* 15 Feb 1924; *Educ* Rugby, Balliol Coll Oxford (BA, MA); *m* 19 Sept 1953, June Elizabeth, da of Bernard Shaw Harvey (d 1973) of Mylor, Cornwall; 2 s (Robert b 1957, William b 1959), 1 da ((Elizabeth) Kate b 1956); *Career* serv 6 Regt RHA 1943-46 (India 1945-46); Royal Devon Yeo RA (TA) 1947-66, CO 1962-66, Col SW Dist 1967-73, ADC (TA) to HM The Queen 1970-75; chm Devon TAVRA 1974-83; slr 1950, registrar Diocese of Exeter, legal sec Ct and Bishops 1963-; played hockey for Devon 1947-57 and W of England 1954; govr St Lukes Coll Exeter 1974-77; chm: Ecclesiastical Law Assoc 1978-81; *Recreations* fishing, walking, gardening; *Clubs* Army and Navy; *Style—* Col James Michelmore, TD; Westhay, Streatham Rise, Exeter EX4 4PE (☎ 0392 73525); 18 Cathedral Yard, Exeter (☎ 0392 36244)

MICHIE, Ian Stuart; s of James Kilgour Michie (d 1967), and Marjorie Crain Pfeiffer (d 1986); *b* 4 Jan 1929; *Educ* Marlborough, Harvard Business Sch Advanced Mgmnt Program; *m* 16 June 1966, Maria Teresa, da of Franklin August Reece (d 1968), of Massachusetts; *Career* investmt banker, dir Kleinwort Benson Ltd 1972-74, md Brandis Ltd 1974-75; *Recreations* shooting, fishing, stalking, golf, skiing; *Clubs* Cavalry and Guards, Huntercombe GC, The Seniors Golfing Soc, The Pigrims, The Greenjackets Golfing Soc; *Style—* Ian S Michie, Esq; 12 Cheyne Gardens, London SW3 5Q1 (☎ 01 351 9108); Fiduciary Trust (International) SA, 30 Old Burlington Street, London W1X 1LB (☎ 01 439 8946)

MICHIE, Hon Mrs (Janet Ray); *née* Bannerman; MP (Lib) Argyll and Bute 1987-; er da of Baron Bannerman of Kildonan, OBE (Life Peer; d 1969), and Ray, *née* Mundell ; *b* 4 Mar 1934; *Educ* Aberdeen HS for Girls, Lansdowne House Sch Edinburgh, Edinburgh Sch of Speech Therapy; *m* 1957, Lt-Col Iain Michie; 3 da; *Career* former speech therapist Argyll & Clyde Health Bd; MCST; *Style—* The Hon Mrs Michie, MP; Tigh an Eas, Glenmore Road, Oban, Argyll

MICHIE, William; MP (Lab) Sheffield, Heeley 1983-; s of Arthur Michie, and Violet Michie; *b* 24 Nov 1935; *Educ* Secdy Mod Sch; *m* 1987, Judith Ann; 2 s; *Career* shop steward, electrician; *Recreations* darts, soccer; *Clubs* WMC Affiliated; *Style—* William Michie, Esq, MP; House of Commons, London SW1

MICKLEM, Thomas Charles Weguelin; s of Maj Charles Micklem (d 1955), of Long Cross House, Chertsey, Surrey, and Diana Gertrude May, *née* Loyd (d 1963); *b* 4 Nov 1926; *Educ* Eton; *m* 15 June 1957, Marian Cicely, da of Lt-Col Sir Weston Cracroft-Amcotts (d 1975); 1 s (Jeremy b 1961), 2 da (Philippa b 1958, Sylvia b 1964); *Career* engr (ret), farmer 1957-77; memb Chichester DC 1973 (past ctee chm); *Recreations* things scientific and mechanical, fishing; *Clubs* Farmers'; *Style—* Thomas Micklem, Esq; Foxbridge Farm, Kirdford, Billingshurst, Sussex (☎ 0403 752287)

MICKLETHWAIT, Richard Miles; o s of Richard Gerald Micklethwait, TD (d 1976), of Ardsley House, Barnsley, Yorks, and Hon Ivy Mary, *née* Stapleton (d 1967), yr da of 10 Baron Beaumont; the Micklethwait family has been seated at Ardsley since the 17 century (*see* Burke's Landed Gentry, 18 edn, vol I, 1965); *b* 21 Nov 1934; *Educ* Ampleforth, Christ Church Oxford; *m* 26 Jan 1961, Jane Evelyn, eldest da of William Melville Codrington, CMG, MC (d 1963), of Preston Hall, Oakham, Rutland; 2 s (Richard John b 11 Aug 1962, William James b 13 July 1964); *Career* Capt Grenadier Gds 1954-64; High Sheriff of Rutland 1972; *Clubs* Turf, Pratt's; *Style—* Richard Micklethwait, Esq; Preston Hall, Oakham, Rutland, Leics LE15 9NJ (☎ 057 285 219)

MICKLETHWAIT, Sir Robert Gore; QC (1956); 2 s of St John Gore Micklethwait, KC, JP (d 1951), and Annie Elizabeth, *née* Aldrich-Blake (d 1948); 2 cousin once removed of Richard Miles Micklethwait, *qv*; *b* 7 Nov 1902; *Educ* Clifton, Trinity Coll Oxford (MA); *m* 25 July 1936, Philippa Jennette, 2 da of Sir Ronald Bosanquet, KC (d 1952), of Dingestow Court, Mon; 3 s (Anthony Robert b 1939, Peter Bernard b 1945, Brian Hugh b 1947), 1 da (Daphne Louisa b 1941); *Career* barr Middle Temple 1925, rec of Worcester 1946-59, bencher 1951; Staffs QS: dep chm 1056-59, reader 1964, dep tres 1970, tres 1971; chief nat insur cmmr 1966-75 (dep cmmr 1959-61, nat insur cmmr and industl injuries cmmr 1961-66); Hamlyn lectr 1976; Hon LLD Newcastle-upon-Tyne 1975; hon knight Hon Soc of Knights of the Round Table 1972; kt 1964; *Style—* Sir Robert Micklethwait, QC; 71 Harvest Rd, Englefield Green, Surrey TW20 0QR (☎ 0784 32521)

MICKLEWRIGHT, Dr (Frederick Henry) Amphlett; s of Frederick William Micklewright (d 1964), and Daisy, *née* Argent (d 1959); *b* 22 April 1908; *Educ* Dulwich, St Peters Hall (now St Peters Coll) Univ of Oxford (BA, MA), UCL (PhD); *m* 9 Aug 1943, Irene Isabel, da of William Burnett (d 1950); 1 da (Jane Clare Bernardette Amphlett (Mrs Rates); *Career* barr Middle Temple 1967; numerous antiquarian articles in Notes and Queries 1943-70; contrib legal and historical papers 1975-84: New Land J1, Law Guardian, Criminal Law Reviews, eclesiastical and theological 1935-80, Congregational Quarterly Hibbert J1, Population Studies; FRHistS 1943, FSAScot 1945; *Recreations* reading; *Style—* Amphlett Micklewright, Esq

MIDDLEMAS, Prof (Robert) Keith; s of Robert James Middlemas, of Northumberland, and Eleanor Mary, *née* Crane; *b* 26 May 1935; *Educ* Stowe, Pembroke Coll Cambridge (MA, DPhil, DLitt); *m* 30 Aug 1958, Susan Mary, da of Laurence Edward Paul Tremlett (d 1956); 1 s (Hugo b 1969), 3 da (Sophie b 1961, Lucy b 1964, Annabel b 1965); *Career* Mil Serv Kenya 1953-55; clerk in House of Commons 1958-67, acad serv Univ of Sussex 1967-; *Books* The Master Builders (1963), The Clydesiders (1965), Baldwin (with A J L Barnes 1969), Diplomacy of Illusion (1972), Whitehall Diary by Thomas Jones 3 vols (ed 1969-71), Engineering and Politics in Southern Africa (1975), Politics in Industrial Society (1978), Power and the Party: Changing Faces of Communism in Western Europe (1979), Industrial Unions and Government: Twenty-One Years of NEDC (1984), Power Competition and The State: vol I: Britain in Search of Balance 1940-61 (1986); *Recreations* world wide travel, landscape gardening, sailing; *Clubs* Flyfishers', North London Rifle; *Style—* Prof Keith Middlemas; West Burton House, West Burton, Pulborough, West Sussex (☎ 0798 831516); University of Sussex, Brighton, Sussex (☎ 0273 506755)

MIDDLEMAS, Robert James; TD (1946); s of Robert Middlemas (d 1959), of Bilton Hill, Alnmouth, Northumberland, and Catherine, *née* Simpson; *b* 22 April 1906; *Educ* Malvern, Pembroke Coll Cambridge (MA); *m* 16 May 1933, Eleanor Mary, da of Thomas Thornton Crane (d 1962), of Birkenhead; 1 s ((Robert) Keith b 1935); *Career* 7 Bn Royal Northumberland Fus TA 1928-46, Capt WWII serv France 1940 (POW); slr in private practice, ret 1974; pt-t clerk to justices: Glendale Ward, West Coquetdale Ward, North Coquetdale Ward 1953-72; pt-t gp sec, chief fin offr and supplies offr to Alnwick and Rothbury Hosp mgmnt ctee 1947-67 (NHS); memb Br Rifle Team to Canada 1931; *Recreations* rifle shooting, game shooting, fishing; *Clubs* Northern Constitutional (Newcastle-upon-Tyne), North London Rifle (Bisley); *Style—* Robert Middlemas, Esq, TD

MIDDLETON, Edward Bernard; s of Lt-Col Bernard Middleton (d 1987), and Bettie Mabel, *née* Knight; *b* 5 July 1948; *Educ* Aldenham; *m* 22 May 1971, Rosemary Spence, da of Maj Denis Frederick Spence Brown, TD, of The Close, Dorrington, Lincoln; 3 s (Nicholas b 1976, Simon b 1978, Hugo b 1982); *Career* sr Pannell Fitzpatrick & Co London 1971-73, mangr Panrell Bellhouse Nwangi & Co Nairobi 1973-75; ptnr Pannell Kerr Forster London 1979- (mangr 1975-79); seconded to DTI as dir/under-sec in the industl devpt unit; FCA 1972; *Recreations* sailing, photography, walking; *Style—* Edward Middleton, Esq; Barrans, Bury Green, Little Hadham, Ware, Herts (☎ 0279 586 84); Pannell Kerr Forster, New Garden House, 78 Hatton Garden, London EC1N 8JA (☎ 01 831 7383, fax 01 405 6736)

MIDDLETON, Sir George Proctor; KCVO (1962, CVO 1951, MVO 1941); s of late A Middleton; *b* 26 Jan 1905; *Educ* Forres Acad, Aberdeen Univ (MB ChB); *m* 1931, Margaret Wilson (d 1964), er da of late A Silver, of Aberdeen; 1 s, 1 da; *Career* med practitioner; surgn apothecary to HM Household Balmoral 1932-73; *Style—* Sir George Middleton, KCVO; Highland Home, Ballater, Aberdeen (☎ 0338 55478)

MIDDLETON, John; s of John Middleton (d 1932), of Newcastle-upon-Tyne, and Martha, *née* Moran; *b* 19 Mar 1932; *Educ* St Cuthberts GS Newcastle-upon-Tyne; *m* 1971, Lillian, da of Sydney Butcher (d 1973), of Newcastle-upon-Tyne; 1 s (John b 1974); *Career* Nat Serv REME, attached to Highland LI in Egypt; gen sec Tobacco Mechanics Assoc; *Recreations* fishing, camping and rambling, birdwatching; *Style—* John Middleton, Esq; 16 Clifton Terrace, Whitley Bay, Tyne and Wear, NE26 2JD (☎ 091 251 3254)

MIDDLETON, John Grant; s of Edward Francis Beresford Middleton, MBE, of Low Fell, and Veronica Mary, *née* Seed; *b* 8 Mar 1934; *Educ* Ushaw Coll Durham, Durham Univ (LLB); *m* 30 Sept 1961, Pamela, da of Canon David Jones (d 1942); 1 s (James b 1964), 2 da (Catherine b 1966, Jessica b 1974); *Career* Royal Northumberland Fus: 2 Lt 1956-58, Lt 1958-59; Capt Army Legal Serv 1959; admitted slr 1955; sr ptnr Stoneham Langton & Passmore 1986- (ptnr 1961-86); memb: Barnes and Sheen CAB, City of Westminster Law Soc, Law Soc 1956; *Recreations* Bach choir, chess, bridge, golf, motorcycling; *Clubs* Naval & Military; *Style—* Grant Middleton, Esq; 2 Kitson Rd, Barnes, London SW13 9HJ (☎ 01 748 5773); 8 Bolton St, London W1Y 8AU (☎ 499 8060, fax 629 4460, telex 21640 INTLAW G)

MIDDLETON, Lawrence Monck; s of late Lt Hugh Jeffery Middleton, RN (3 s of 7 Bt); *b* 23 Oct 1912; *Educ* Eton, Edinburgh Univ (BSc); *Career* h to Baronetcy of bro, Sir Stephen Hugh Middleton, 9 Bt; *Style—* Lawrence Middleton, Esq; Winterhayes, South Perrott, Beaminster, Dorset

MIDDLETON, 12 Baron (GB 1711); Sir (Digby) Michael Godfrey John Willoughby; 13 Bt (E 1677), MC (1945), DL (N Yorks); s of 11 Baron Middleton, KG (d 1970) ; *b* 1 May 1921; *Educ* Eton, Trinity Coll Cambridge; *m* 14 Oct 1947, Janet, JP (fndr chm Lloyd's External Names Assoc), da of Gen Sir James Handyside Marshall-Cornwall, KCB, CBE, DSO, MC; 3 s; *Heir* s, Hon Michael Charles James Willoughby; *Career* 2 Lt Coldstream Gds 1940, Temp Maj served in NW Europe 1944-45 (despatches and, Croix de Guerre); land agent 1951; JP E Riding Yorks 1958; ccncllr: E Riding 1964-74, N Yorks 1974-77; memb Yorks and Humberside Econ Planning Cncl 1968-79; pres: Yorks Agric Soc 1976, CLA 1981-83; Hon Col 2 Bn Yorks (TAVR) Volunteers 1976-; memb: Nature Conservancy Cncl 1986-, House of Lords select ctee on Euro Community; *Clubs* Boodle's; *Style—* The Rt Hon the Lord Middleton, MC, DL; Birdsall House, Birdsall, Malton, N Yorks YO17 9NR (☎ 094 46 202)

MIDDLETON, Michael Humfrey; CBE (1975); s of Humfrey Middleton (d 1976), and Lilian Irene, *née* Tillard (d 1939); *b* 1 Dec 1917; *Educ* King's Sch Canterbury; *m* 10 April 1954, Julie Margaret, da of Guy James Kay Harrison (d 1980), of Cark Manor, Cark-in-Cartmel, Cumbria; 1 s (Hugo b 1955), 2 da (Kate b 1958, Rose b 1961); *Career* dir Civic Tst 1969-86, sec gen UK Campaign for Euro Architectural Year 1972-76, sec Architectural Heritage Fund 1976-86, art critic The Spectator 1946-56, asst ed Picture Post 1948-52, ed House and Garden 1955-57; Pro Merito Medal of Cncl of Europe 1976; *Books* Group Practice in Design (1967), Man Made the Town (1987); *Recreations* travel, the arts; *Style—* Michael Middleton, Esq, CBE; 84 Sirdar Rd, London W11 4EG

MIDDLETON, Michael William; s of Cyril Herbert Charles Middleton, and Edna May, *née* Woods; *b* 3 Sept 1942; *Educ* Chesterton Sch Cambridge; *m* 1966, Elizabeth, da of Albert Allen (d 1942), of Bollington; 1 s (James Spencer b 1969), 1 da (Emma Louise b 1971); *Career* chm Ede & Ravenscroft Gp of Cos; dir: Cyril Middleton & Co Gp of Cos, Middleton Farms Ltd; *Recreations* shooting; *Clubs* East India; *Style—* Michael Middleton, Esq; 54 Storey's Way, Cambridge CB3 0DX

MIDDLETON, Sir Peter Edward; GCB (1984); *b* 2 April 1934; *Educ* Sheffield City GS, Univ of Sheffield (BA), Univ of Bristol; *m* Valerie Ann, *née* Lindup (d 1987); 1 s (Tom), 1 da (Emma); *Career* HM Treasy 1962: dep sec 1980-83, perm sec 1983-; visiting fell Nuffield Coll Oxford (MA); govr London Business Sch 1984, memb Council Manchester Business Sch, govr Ditchley Foundation 1985; *Clubs* Reform; *Style—* Sir Peter Middleton, GCB; HM Treasury, Parliament St, London SW1

MIDDLETON, Sir Stephen Hugh; 9 Bt (E 1662), of Belsay Castle, Northumberland; s of Lt Hugh Jeffery Middleton, RN (d 1914, s of 7 Bt); suc unc, Sir Charles Arthur Middleton, 8 Bt, 1942; *b* 20 June 1909; *Educ* Eton, Magdalene Coll Cambridge; *m* 21 May 1962, Mary E (d 1972), da of Richard Robinson (d 1933); *Heir* bro, Lawrence Monck Middleton; *Style—* Sir Stephen Middleton, Bt; Belsay Castle, Newcastle-upon-Tyne

MIDDLETON, Hon Vanessa Rachel; *née* Cornwallis; 2 da of 3 Baron Cornwallis, OBE, DL (by his 2 w); *b* 27 July 1958; *m* 1986, Jeremy Middleton, of Sydney, NSW; *Style—* The Hon Mrs Middleton; 104 Prince Albert Road, Mosman, NSW

MIDDLETON, William; s of Charles Ferdinand Paul Middleton (d 1946), and Linda, *née* De Angelis; *b* 26 Feb 1923; *Educ* London Univ, Rome Univ; *Career* slr; sr ptnr Middleton Potts London; dir: Monkedison (UK) Ltd 1968, Snia (UK) Ltd 1970, Eni Chem (UK) Ltd 1971, BCI Nominees Ltd 1982, Api Servs Ltd 1984; *Recreations* tennis, bridge; *Clubs* Hurlingham, City of London; *Style—* William Middleton, Esq; 68 Albert Hall Mansions, London SW7; Middleton Potts, 3 Cloth Street, London EC1 (☎ 01 600 2333, telex 928357, fax 01 600 0108)

MIDGLEY, (David) William; JP (North Tyneside); s of Norman Midgley, of Huddersfield, and Margaret, *née* Alderson (d 1986); *b* 1 Feb 1942; *Educ* Huddersfield Coll; *m* 1, 19 Dec 1964, Anne Christine (d 1976), da of Charles Foreman, of Huddersfield; 1 s (Edward William b 1967), 1 da (Rachel Sarah b 1969); m 2, 10 June 1977, Ada Margaret, da of John Banks; 1 da (Louise Isobel b 1980); *Career* chief exec Newcastle Building Soc 1986; chm: NBS Estates Ltd 1988, Strachans (Newcastle) Ltd 1989; dir NBS (fin servs) Ltd 1987; ctee memb: MIND, Newcastle Cncl for the Disabled; govr Ferversham Sch Newcastle; FCIOB; *Recreations* golf; *Clubs* Northern Constitutional; *Style—* William Midgley, Esq, JP; 17 Beaumont Drive, Whitley Bay, Tyne and Wear, NE25 9UT (☎ 091 2511807); Grainger Chambers, Hood St, Newcastle-Upon-Tyne (☎ 091 2326676, fax 091 2610015, car tel 0860 415847)

MIDLETON, 12 Viscount (I 1717); Alan Henry Brodrick; also Baron Brodrick of Midleton (I 1715) and Baron Brodrick of Peper Harow (GB 1796); the full designation of the Viscountcy is Midleton of Midleton; s of Alan Rupert Brodrick (d 1972), and Alice Elizabeth, *née* Roberts; suc uncle 11 Viscount 1988; *b* 4 August 1949; *Educ* St Edmund's Canterbury; *m* 1978, Julia Helen, da of Michael Pitt, of Lias Cottage, Compton Dundon, Somerton, Somerset; 2 s (Hon Ashley Rupert, Hon William Michael b 1982), 1 da (Hon Charlotte Helen b 1983); *Heir* s, Hon Ashley Rupert Brodrick b 25 Nov 1980; *Style—* The Rt Hon Viscount Midleton; Elder Cottage, Forest Road, Onehouse, Stowmarket, Suffolk

MIDLETON, Countess of; Irène Lilian; da of late Alfred Edward Creese (d 1943), of Ewell, Surrey, and Emilie, *née* Lees (d 1983); *b* 22 Sept 1917; *Educ* Holy Cross Convent Haywards Heath; *m* 1975, as his 3 w, 2 Earl of Midleton (d 1979 when the Earldom became extinct and the Viscountcy passed to a kinsman); *Career* actress (as Rène Ray), authoress, painter; 50 films incl The Passing of the Third Floor Back 1935, which made her a star, 35 plays incl An Inspector Calls (NY 1947); 8 TV plays incl The Adding Machine, radio incl Conversation Piece BBC 1987; Inter Arts Guild 1969; Palme d'Or des Beaux Arts Dip, mention speciale du Jury Section Peinture; *Books* Emma Conquest (1950), A Man Named Seraphin (1951), The Tree Surgeons (1958), Angel Assignment (1988); *Style—* The Rt Hon the Countess of Midleton; Martello Lodge, St Brelade's Bay, Jersey, Channel Islands (☎ 0534 41171)

MIDLETON, Dowager Viscountess; Sheila Campbell; da of late Charles Campbell MacLeod, of Cawthorpe House, Bourne, Lincs; *m* 12 Aug 1940, 11 Viscount Midleton (d 1988); *Style—* The Rt Hon Dowager Viscountess Midleton; Frogmore Cottage, 105 North Road, Bourne, Lincs

MIDWINTER, Stanley Walter; CB (1982); s of Lewis Henry Midwinter (d 1975), of London, and Beatrice Sophia, *née* Webb; *b* 8 Dec 1922; *Educ* Regent St Poly Sch, Sch of Architecture (dip); *m* 1954, Audrey Mary, da of Joseph Pepper (d 1950), of Cavan; 1 da (Victoria); *Career* WWII RE 1942-46, serv: N Africa, Italy, Greece; architect and planning conslt; planning offr London CC 1949-55, borough architect and planning offr Larne NI 1955-60, housing and planning inspr England and Wales 1960-76, dep chief planning inspr Depts of Environment and Tport 1976-78 (chief planning inspr 1978-84), assessor of Belvoir Coalfield Inquiry 1979; Town Planning Inst Examination Prize 1952, Thomas Adams Prize 1955, President's Prize 1958; memb: RIBA 1948, RTPI 1952; *Recreations* motor cruising (Reedling); *Style—* Stanley Midwinter, Esq, CB; 14 Collett Way, Frome, Somerset, BA11 2XR (☎ 0373 71060)

MIECZKOWSKI, Hon Mrs; (Caroline Sarah Aline); da of 2 Baron Grenfell, TD (d 1976), and his 1 w, Elizabeth Sarah Polk, da of Capt Hon Alfred Shaughnessy (ka 1916), 2 s of 1 Baron Shaughnessy (d 1923); *b* 28 July 1933; *m* 1965, Zbyszek Leon Mieczkowski, s of Stefan Mieczkowski de Zagroba (d 1956), of Dzierzanowo, Poland; 1 s (Stefan b 1967), 1 da (Helena b 1970); *Style—* The Hon Mrs Mieczkowski; Rose Cottage, Henley Park, Henley-on-Thames, Oxon RG9 6HY (☎ 0491 572819)

MIECZKOWSKI, Zbyszek Leon; s of late Stefan Mieczkowski de Zagroba (d 1956), of Dzierzanowo Poland; *b* 22 June 1922; *Educ* Zamoyski Gimn, Warsaw, Dlugosz Coll Poland; *m* 1965, Hon Caroline Sarah Aline, *qv*, da of 2 Baron Grenfell, TD (d 1976); *Career* WWII with Polish Forces 1939-45, France and Germany Campaign with Br Liberation Army, 1 Polish Armed Div; Industrialists: chm Polish Library Cncl 1978-81, patron Joseph Conrad Soc (UK); *Recreations* reading, hunting, tennis; *Clubs* Brooks's; *Style—* Zbyszek Mieczkowski, Esq; Rose Cottage, Henley Park, Henley-on-Thames, Oxon RG9 6HY (☎ 0491 572 819)

MIERS, Rear Adm Sir Anthony Cecil Capel; VC (1942), KBE (1959), CB (1958), DSO (1941, and bar 1942); s of Capt Douglas Nathaniel Carleton Capel Miers, Queen's Own Cameron Highlanders (ka France 1914), and Margaret Annie, *née* Christie (d 1961); *b* 11 Nov 1906; *Educ* Edinburgh Acad, Stubbington House, Wellington; *m* 1945, Patricia Mary, da of David McIntyre Millar (d 1942); 1 s (John), 1 da (Angela); *Career* joined RN 1924, Sub Lt submarines 1929, Lt 1930, cmd HM Submarine L54 1936-37, HMS Iron Duke 1937, Lt Cdr 1938, psc 1938; staff of Adm of Fleet Sir Charles Forbes in 1938-40: HMS Nelson, HMS Rodney, HMS Warspite (despatches 1940); cmd HM Submarine Torbay 1940-42, Cdr 1942, staff of Fleet Adm C W Nimitz (C-in-C US Pacific Fleet in Pearl Harbor) 1942-44, cdr 8 Submarine Flotilla Br Pacific Fleet 1944-45, cmd HMS Vernon 11 (Ramillies and Malaya) 1946, Capt 1946, jssc 1947; cmd: HMS Blackcap 1948-50, HMS Forth and 1 Submarine Flotilla in Med Fleet 1950-52; Capt RN Coll Greenwich 1952-54, cmd HMS Theseus 1955-56, Rear Adm 1956, Flag Offr Middle East 1956-59, ret 1959; dir Francis Sumner 1959-62, chm and md Buttons Ltd 1960-62, with Mills & Allen and London & Provincial Poster Gp 1962-71, (conslt 1971-83), dir for devpt co-ordination Nat Car Parks 1971-, chm Hudson's Offshore Ltd 1972-73; FIOD 1960; Burgess and Freeman of Burgh of Inverness 1955, Freeman City of London 1966, Upper Warden Worshipful Co of Tin Plate Workers 1983; chm RN Scholarship Fund 1968-73, nat pres Submarine Old Comrades Assoc 1967-81; hon kt hon Soc of kts of Round Table 1967; Offr US Legion of Merit 1946; *Recreations* swimming, table tennis; *Clubs* Army and Navy, Br Sportsman's, MCC, Hurlingham, London Scottish Football, RN 1765 and 1785, Hampshire Hogs Cricket, Anchorites (pres 1969); *Style—* Rear Adm Sir Anthony Miers, VC, KBE, CB, DSO; 8 Highdown Rd, Roehampton, London SW15 5BU (☎ 01 788 6863); Nat Car Parks Ltd, PO Box 4NH, 21 Bryanston St, Marble Arch, London W1A 4NH (☎ 01 499 7050)

MIERS, Sir (Henry) David Alastair Capel; KBE (1985), CMG (1979); s of Col R D M C Miers, DSO (d 1974); *b* 10 Jan 1937; *Educ* Winchester, Oxford Univ; *m* 1966, Imelda Maria Emilia, *née* Wouters; 2 s, 1 da; *Career* Dip Serv, head Middle E Dept FCO 1980-83 (private sec to min of state FO 1968, Paris 1972, cnsllr Tehran 1977-80), ambassador to Lebanon 1983-85; *Style—* Sir David Miers, KBE, CMG; c/o Foreign and Cwlth Off, King Charles St, London SW1A 2AH

MIKARDO, Ian; s of Morris Mikardo, of Portsmouth; *b* 9 July 1908; *Educ* Portsmouth; *m* 1932, Mary, da of Benjamin Rosetté, of London; 2 da; *Career* MP (Lab): Reading 1945-50, Reading South 1950-55, Reading 1955 1959, Poplar 1964-74, Tower Hamlets Bethnal Green and Bow 1974-83, Bow and Poplar 1983-87; chm select ctee on Nationalised Industs 1966-70, pres ASTMS 1968-73, chm Parly Lab Pty March-Nov 1974; vice-pres Socialist Int 1978-83 (hon pres 1983-); *Books* Centralised Control of Indust (1944), Frontiers in the Air (1946), Keep Left (jtly 1947), The Second Five Years (1948), The Problems of Nationalisation (1948), Keeping Left (jtly 1950), The Labour Case (1950), It's a Mug's Game (1951), Socialism or Slump (1959); Backbencher (1988); *Style—* Ian Mikardo, Esq,; 89 Grove Hall Court, London NW8 9NS

MILBANK, Sir Anthony Frederick; 5 Bt (UK 1882), of Well, Co York, and Hart, Co Durham; s of Sir Mark Vane Milbank, 4 Bt, KCVO, MC (d 1984), and Hon Verena Aileen, da of 11 Baron Farnham; *b* 16 August 1939; *Educ* Eton; *m* 1970, Belinda Beatrice, da of Brig Adrian Clements Gore, DSO, of Horton Priory, Sellinge, Ashford, Kent; 2 s, (Edward b 1973, Toby b 1977), 1 da (Alexina b 1971); *Heir* s, Edward Mark Somerset Milbank b 9 April 1973; *Career* farmer and landowner; former: dir M & G Securities, govr Royal Marsden Hosp; *Recreations* all sports: field, team, individual and winter; *Style*— Sir Anthony Milbank, Bt; Barningham Park, Richmond, N Yorks DL11 7DW (☎ (0833) 21202)

MILBANK, Denis William Powlett; TD (1944); yst s of Sir Frederick Richard Powlett Milbank, 3 Bt (d 1964), and (Harriet Anne) Dorothy, *née* Wilson (d 1970); *b* 6 July 1912; *Educ* Radley; *m* 5 July 1934, Doreen Frances, da of Sir Richard Pierce Butler, OBE (d 1955), of Ballintemple, Carlow, Ireland; 1 s (Mark Richard b 1937), 2 da (Penelope Ann b 1935, Susan Fiona b 1942); *Career* Maj RA (TA) 1938-46, WWII serv Middle E and Italy (despatches); with Walpamun Co 1928-48; farming in Kenya 1948-74, Safari tour ldr 1969-74, dist cmdt Kenya Police Res 1952-59; sec Yorks Regn Br Field Sports Soc 1974-77; *Recreations* shooting, safaris; *Clubs* Muthaiga Country (Nairobi); *Style*— D W P Milbank, Esq, TD; Southbrook, Galphay, Ripon, N Yorks

MILBANK, Hon Lady; Hon Verena Aileen; da of 11 Baron Farnham, DSO (d 1935); *b* 4 August 1907; *m* 1, 3 Feb 1934, Charles Lambart Crawley (d 1935); m 2, 12 Feb 1938, as his 2 w, Maj Sir Mark Vane Milbank, 4 Bt, KCVO, MC; *Style*— The Hon Lady Milbank; The Gate House, Barningham, Richmond, N Yorks

MILBORNE-SWINNERTON-PILKINGTON, Richard Arthur; s and h of Sir Thomas Henry Milborne-Swinnerton-Pilkington, 14 Bt; *b* 4 Sept 1964; *Educ* Eton, RAC Cirencester; *Career* insur broker Willis Faber; *Recreations* racing, shooting; *Style*— Richard Milborne-Swinnerton-Pilkington, Esq

MILBORNE-SWINNERTON-PILKINGTON, Sir Thomas Henry; 14 Bt (NS 1635); o s of Sir Arthur William Milborne-Swinnerton-Pilkington, 13 Bt (d 1952), and Elizabeth Mary, er da of late Col John Fenwick Harrison, JP, DL, of King's Walden Bury, Hitchin; *b* 10 Mar 1934; *Educ* Eton; *m* 1961, Susan, eld da of Norman Stewart Rushton Adamson, of Durban, S Africa; 1 s, 2 da (Sarah b 1962, Joanna b 1967); *Heir* s Richard Arthur Milborne-Swinnerton-Pilkington b 4 Sept 1964); *Career* chm: Charente Steamship Co Ltd 1977-, Thomas & James Harrison Ltd 1980-; *Clubs* White's; *Style*— Sir Thomas Milborne-Swinnerton-Pilkington, Bt; King's Walden Bury, Hitchin, Herts

MILBORROW, Ruan Leslie; s of Robert Leslie Milborrow (d 1986), of Grove Cottage, 31 Nutter Lane, Wanstead, London, and Elizabeth Edith, *née* Cook; *b* 11 July 1958; *Educ* Forest Sch Snaresbrook, RAC Cirencester (MRAC, Dip FM); *Career* sr art dir Yellowhammer Advtg Ltd 1989- (graduate trainee 1984); Freeman City of London 1984; *Books* The Riddle of Atrophic Rhinitis (1982), The Official Sloane Ranger Directory (contrib 1984);; *Recreations* restoring my MG, collecting modern first editions, polo, theatre; *Clubs* RAC, Cirencester Park Polo; *Style*— Ruan Milborrow, Esq; Grove Cottage, 31 Nutter Lane, Wanstead, London E11 2HZ (☎ 01 989 4002); Yellowhammer plc, 76 Oxford St, London W1A 1DT (☎ 01 436 5000, fax 01 436 4630, telex 8953837

MILBURN, Sir Anthony Rupert; 5 Bt (UK 1905), of Guyzance, Parish of Acklington, Northumberland; s of Maj Rupert Leonard Eversley Milburn (d 1974, yr s of 3 Bt), and Anne Mary, *née* Scott-Murray; suc unc, Sir John Milburn, 4 Bt (d 1985); *b* 17 April 1947; *Educ* Eton, RAC Cirencester (ARICS, MRAC); *m* 1977, Olivia Shirley, yst da of Capt Thomas Noel Catlow, CBE, RN, (ret), of Tunstall, Lancs; 2 s (Patrick b 1980, Jake b 1987), 1 da (Lucy b 1982); *Heir* s, Patrick Thomas Milburn b 4 Dec 1980; *Career* landowner; company dir; *Clubs* New (Edinburgh); *Style*— Sir Anthony Milburn, Bt; Guyzance Hall, Acklington, Morpeth, Northumberland (☎ 0665 711247)

MILBURN, Colin; s of Jack Milburn (d 1985), and Bertha Elizabeth, *née* Clarke; *b* 23 Oct 1941; *Educ* Stanley GS Co Durham; *Career* played cricket 9 times for England: highest score 193 v Pakistan Karachi 1969, highest first class score 243 for Western Aust v Queensland in Brisbane 1968, BBC radio presenter test matches and one-day finals, after dinner speaking and promotional work; *Recreations* watching all sports; *Clubs* MCC (hon life memb); *Style*— Colin Milburn, Esq; (☎ 0207 70760

MILBURN, Very Rev Robert Leslie Pollington; s of George Leslie Milburn (d 1961); *b* 28 July 1907; *Educ* Oundle, Sidney Sussex Coll Cambridge, New Coll Oxford; *m* 1944, Margery Kathleen Mary, *née* Harvie; 1 s (decd), 1 da; *Career* asst master Eton 1930-32, fell and chaplain Worcester Coll Oxford 1934-57 (domestic bursar 1936-47, estates bursar 1947-57, tutor, hon fell 1979), dean of Worcester 1957-68, master of the Temple 1968-80; FSA; *Books* Early Christian Interpretations of History (1954), Early Christian Art and Architecture; *Style*— The Very Rev Robert Milburn; 5 St Barnabas, Newland, Malvern, Worcs WR13 5AX (☎ 06845 561 044)

MILDMAY-WHITE, Hon Mrs (Helen Winifred); *née* Mildmay; ARRC (1942), JP (Devon 1952); assumed surname of Mildmay-White 1955; da of 1 Baron Mildmay of Flete (d 1947; eldest s of Henry Bingham Mildmay, JP, DL, by his w Georgiana Bulteel, maternal gda of 2 Earl Grey), Lord Mildmay of Flete was third in descent from Sir Henry Paulet St John (later St John-Mildmay), 3 Bt, and Jane, eldest da and co-heir of Carew Mildmay, which surname Sir Henry added to his own by Royal Licence (1790), Sir Henry was eighth in descent from William St John (1538-1609), whose half-bro, Nicholas St John, was ancestor of the Viscounts Bolingbroke, Jane, *née* Mildmay, was eighth in descent from William Mildmay, er bro of Rt Hon Sir Walter Mildmay, chllr of the Exchequer and tres to Queen Elizabeth I and fndr of Emmanuel Coll Cambridge; *b* 17 August 1907; *Educ* at home, Queen's Coll (Harley St); *m* 29 Sept 1945, Lt Cdr (Richard) John Bramble White, DL (d 1969), who assumed the name of Mildmay-White by Deed Poll 1958, s of Cdr (S) Richard Ernest White, RN (ret), of Bickington, Devon; 2 s, 1 da; *Career* WWII RN 1939-45 naval nurse VAD RN Hosp Plymouth; chm maternity ctee NHS Plymouth 1956; county pres Devon Girl Guides 1962-65; *Recreations* gardening, racing (steeplechasing; horses: Cromwell, Lochroe, Uncle Bing); *Style*— The Hon Mrs Mildmay-White, ARRC, JP; 82 Mothecombe, Holbeton, Plymouth, Devon PL8 1LB (☎ 075 530 224)

MILES, Adrian Spencer; s of Herbert Beal Miles (d 1952), of London, and Marjorie Phyllis, *née* Harris; *b* 16 Nov 1947; *Educ* Rutlish Sch, QMC London (LLB); *m* 28 June 1975, Hilary, da of William Nelson (d 1980); 1 s (Jonathan Francis b 20 May 1968), 2 da (Julie Clare b 11 Oct 1978, Anna Kirsty b 7 July 1980); *Career* admitted slr 1972, Boodle Hatfield 1972-74, Norton Rose 1974-76, ptnr Wilde Sapte 1976-; memb Law Soc; *Recreations* chess, tennis, music; *Style*— Adrian Miles, Esq; Queensbridge House, 60 Upper Thames St, London EC4V 3BD (☎ 01 236 3050, fax 01 236 9624, telex 887793)

MILES, Baron (Life Peer UK 1979), of Blackfriars in the City of London; Bernard James Miles; CBE (1953); s of Edwin James Miles, and Barbara, *née* Fletcher; *b* 27 Sept 1907; *Educ* Uxbridge Co Sch, Pembroke Coll Oxford, City Univ; *m* 1931, Josephine Wilson, da of Benjamin Hinchliffe; 1 s, 2 da (1 decd); *Career* actor; fndr with his w of the Mermaid Theatre, Puddle Dock, EC4 1959; author; hon fell Pembroke Coll Oxford 1969, Hon DLitt City Univ 1974; kt 1969; *Books* The British Theatre, God's Brainwave, Favourite Tales from Shakespeare; *Style*— The Rt Hon the Lord Miles, CBE; c/o The House of Lords, London SW1A 0PW

MILES, Brian; RD; s of Terence Clifford Miles (d 1945), and Muriel Irene, *née* Terry; *b* 23 Feb 1937; *Educ* Reeds Sch, HMS Conway Cadet Sch; *m* 10 Oct 1964, (Elizabeth) Anne, *née* Scott; 1 s (Martin b 30 Aug 1966), 2 da (Amanda b 29 May 1968, Sara b 10 April 1970); *Career* P & O Shipping Co: cadet 1954-57, deck offr 1958-64, master marine (FG) 1964; RNLI: inspr of Lifeboats 1964-73, staff appts 1974-81, dep dir 1982-87, dir 1988-; memb Parkstone Rotary Club, chm Dolphin Tst; MNI; Gold Medal Of Spanish Red Cross; *Recreations* country sports, walking, reading, music, theatre; *Style*— Brian Miles, Esq, RD; 8 Longfield Dr, West Parley, Wimborne, Dorset BH22 8TY (☎ 0202 571 739); RNLI West Quay Rd, Poole, Dorset BH15 1HZ (☎ 0202 671 133, telex 41328)

MILES, Hon Mrs (Christine Helena); *née* Weld-Forester; da of 7 Baron Forester (d 1977), and Marie Louise Priscilla, *née* Perrott; *b* 20 Mar 1932; *Educ* Lawnside Great Malvern; *m* 1, 31 July 1951 (m dis 1981), 7 Baron Bolton; 2 s, 1 da; m 2, 22 July 1985, Philip David Miles, s of Maj Walter Harold Miles (d 1982); *Style*— The Hon Mrs Miles; Hinton Hall, Lea Cross, nr Shrewsbury SY5 8JA (☎ 074 384 203)

MILES, Dillwyn; s of Joshua Miles (d 1932), of Newport, Pembrokeshire, and Anne Mariah, *née* Lewis (d 1946); *b* 25 May 1916; *Educ* Fishguard County Sch, UC of Wales Aberystwyth; *m* 2 Feb 1944, Joyce Eileen (d 1976), da of Lewis Craven Ord (d 1952), of Montreal and London; 1 s (Anthony b 1945), 1 da (Marilyn b 1946); *Career* ME (Army Capt) 1939-45, nat organiser Palestine House London 1945-48; community centres offr Wales 1948-54; dir: Pembrokeshire Community Cncl 1954-75, Dyfed Rural Cncl 1975-81; chm Nat Assoc of Local Cncls 1975-87 (vice-pres 1987-); The Herald Bard 1967-; memb: Pembrokeshire CC 1947-63, Cemaes RDC 1947-52, Haverfordwest Borough Cncl 1957-63, Pembrokeshire Coast Nat Park Ctee 1952-75, Prince of Wales Ctee 1971-80, Sports Cncl for Wales 1969-70, Nature Conservancy Cncl for Wales 1966-73, Soc for Promotion of Nature Reserves 1961-73; Mayor of Newport, Pembrokeshire 1950, 1966, 1967 and 1979 (Alderman 1951-); Mayor of Haverfordwest 1961, Sheriff 1963; Burgess of the Ancient Borough of Newport 1935, Burgess of the Borough of Haverfordwest 1974; FRGS 1945; *Books* The Royal National Eisteddfed of Wales (1978), A Pembrokeshire Anthology (1983), Portrait of Pembrokeshire (1984), Pembrokeshire Coast National Park (1987); *Recreations* walking, food, wine; *Clubs* Savile, Wig and Pen; *Style*— Dillwyn Miles, Esq; 9 St Anthony's Way, Haverfordwest, Pembrokeshire, Dyfed SA61 1EL (☎ 0437 5275)

MILES, John Seeley; s of Thoms Miles (d 1965), and Winifred, *née* Seeley (d 1981); *b* 11 Feb 1931; *Educ* Beckenham GS, Beckenham Art Sch; *m* 1955, Louise Rachel, da of George Rowland Wilson (d 1983); 1 s (Jonathan b 1964), 2 da (Catherine b 1958, Sophia b 1960); *Career* asst to Hans Schmoller Penguin Books 1955-58, formed Banks and Miles 1958 with Colin Banks; conslt: Zoological Soc, Regents Park and Whipsnade 1958-62, Expanded Metal Co 1960-83, Consumers Assoc 1964, Post Off 1972-83; Curwen Press 1970-73, Br Cncl 1968-83, E Midlands Arts Assoc 1974-79, Enschede en Zn, Netherlands 1980-, Br Telecom 1980, Br Airports Authy; design advsr Monotype Corpn 1985-; typographic advsr HMSO 1985-; chm Arbitration Ctee Assoc Typographique Int 1984-, govr Central Sch of Arts and Craft 1978-85; memb CGLI 1986; *Books* Design for Desktop Publishing (1987); *Recreations* gardening, painting; *Clubs* Arts, Double Crown; *Style*— John Miles, Esq; 24 Collins St, Blackheath, London SE3 0GU (☎ 01 318 4739); Banks & Miles, 1 Tranquil Vale, Blackheath, London SE3 0BU (☎ 01 318 1131)

MILES, Keith Charles; s of Leslie Maurice Miles, of Reading, Berks, and Doris Ellen Wyard Miles; *b* 28 Nov 1941; *Educ* Owens Sch; *m* 20 Dec 1969, Slava, da of Jože Blenkuš (d 1977); 1 s (Andrew Karel Scott b 1973), 1 da (Jane Helena Louise b 1977); *Career* CA; dir fin and ops Cable Authy 1985-88, dir of fin and admin Inst of Econ Affrs 1988-; Liveryman: Worshipful Co of Glass Sellers, Worshipful Co of CAs; *Recreations* skiing, reading, swimming; *Style*— Keith Miles, Esq; 19 Elmtree Green, Gt Missenden, Bucks HP16 9AF

MILES, Malcolm John; s of John Frederick Miles, MBE, of Kingston-upon-Thames, Surrey, and Phyllis Maud, *née* Umpelby; *b* 5 Mar 1945; *Educ* London Coll For Distributive Trades (Dip Bus Studies), Chicago Univ ; *m* 22 Nov 1969, Ann Therisa, da of Roy Augustine O'Dwyer, of Dorking, Surrey; 1 s (Alexander Malcolm (Bertie) b 1978); *Career* 225 water sports Binbeca Minorca 1971, account dir McCann Erickson London 1971-74, assoc dir Ted Bates London 1975-76; md McCann Erickson London 1985- (dep md 1984, dir account mgmnt 1982, bd dir 1980, assoc dir 1977); chm McCann Network UK and vice-chm McCann London 1988-; memb: tobacco ctee EAAA Brussels 1980-84, marketing ctee CBI 1986-88, cncl CBI 1987-; MCAM (1973), MAA (1969), MIPA (1980); *Recreations* shooting, gardening, family; *Clubs* RAC, ESU; *Style*— M J Miles, Esq; 36 Howland St, London, W1A 1AT (☎ 01 580 6690, fax 323 2883, car tel 0836 255 886 and 0860 511084, telex 28231)

MILES, Dame Margaret; DBE (1970); da of Rev E G Miles and Annie, *née* Jones; *b* 11 July 1911; *Educ* Ipswich High Sch, Bedford Coll Univ of London (BA); *Career* history teacher Westcliff High Sch 1935-39, Badminton Sch 1939-44; lectr Dept of Educn Univ of Bristol 1944-46; headmistress Pate's Grammar Sch Cheltenham 1946-52, headmistress Mayfield Sch Putney 1952-73; memb Schools Broadcasting Cncl 1958-68, Educ Advsy Cncl ITA 1962-67, Nat Advsy Cncl on Tning and Supply of Teachers 1962-65, BBC Gen Advsy Cncl 1964-73, campaign for Comprehensive Educn 1966 (chm 1972, pres 1979-), RSA Cncl 1972-77, Central Bureau for Educnl Visits and Exchanges 1978-82; chm Advsy ctee on Dvpt Educn ODM 1977-79; pres Br Assoc for Counselling 1980-; fell Bedford Coll 1983; Hon DCL Univ of Kent at Canterbury 1973; fell King's Coll, Lond 1985; *Books* And Gladly Teach (1965); Comprehensive Schooling, Problems and Perspectives (1968); *Recreations* opera, films, gardening, golf; *Clubs* Univ Women's, Aberdovey Golf; *Style*— Dame Margaret Miles, DBE; Tanycraig, Pennal, Machynlleth, Powys

MILES, Nicholas Charles James; s of Kenneth Norman Miles, of Whitegate Cottage, Crowborough, E Sussex, and Audrey Mary, *née* Rhodes; *b* 23 Oct 1958; *Educ* Tonbridge, Corpus Christi Coll Cambridge (BA); *Career* dir: BMP Business Ltd 1985-87, Lowe Bell Financial Ltd 1987-; performed in Death in the Aisles, Nightcap Cambridge Footlights Revues 1979; *Recreations* tennis, golf, revue; *Clubs* Annabel's, RAC, Bachelors; *Style*— Nicholas Miles, Esq; 4 Rorel Rd, London SW4; 4 Red Lion Court, London EC4 (☎ 01 353 9203, car 0836 293357)

MILES, (Richard) Oliver; CMG (1984); s of George Cockburn Miles (d 1980), and

Olive Catherine, *née* Clapham (d 1973); *b* 6 Mar 1936; *Educ* Ampleforth, Merton Coll Oxford; *m* 1968, Julia Lyndall, da of Prof Joseph Sidney Weiner (d 1982); 3 s (Joe b 1972, Tom b 1973, Hugh b 1977), 1 da (Lucy b 1979); *Career* ambassador: Libya 1984, Luxembourg 1985; N Ireland Off 1988-; *Clubs* Travellers; *Style—* Oliver Miles, Esq, CMG; c/o Stormont House, Belfast BT4 3ST; Foreign and Cwlth Off, King Charles St, London SW14 2AH

MILES, Sir Peter Tremayne; KCVO (1986); s of Lt-Col E W T Miles, MC (d 1943), Manor House, Kington Langley, Chippenham, Wilts, and Mary Albinia, *née* Gibbs (d 1979); *b* 26 June 1924; *Educ* Eton, RMA Sandhurst; *m* 25 July 1956, Philippa Helen, da of E M B (Jack) Tremlett (d 1977), of Noddings Farm, Chiddingfold, Surrey; 2 s (Napier b 1 Sept 1958, Patrick b 1 June 1960), 1 da (Davina b 8 Jan 1964); *Career* 1 Royal Dragoons 1944-49; J F Thomasson and co 1949-59, md Gerrard and Nat Discount Co Ltd 1964-80 (joined 1959), dir P Murray Jones Ltd 1966-75, dir Astley and Pearce Hldgs 1975-80 (chm 1978-80), keeper of the privy purse and tres to HM The Queen 1981-87, receiver gen to Duchy of Lancaster 1981-87, memb Prince of Wales' Cncl 1981-87, dir Br and Cwlth Hldgs 1988-; *Clubs* White's, Pratt's, Cavalry and guards, Swinley Forest Golf, City of London; *Style—* Sir Peter Miles, KCVO; Mill House, Southrop, Lechlade, Glos (☎ 036 785 287); B & C Hldgs plc, Kings House , 36-37 King St, London EC2V 8BE (☎ 01 600 3000, fax 01 600 0736)

MILES, Philip John; s and h of Sir William Napier Maurice Miles, 6 Bt; *b* 10 August 1953; *Style—* Philip Miles Esq

MILES, (Frank) Stephen; CMG (1964); s of Harry Miles (d 1929), and Mary Miles, *née* Brown (d 1965); *b* 7 Jan 1920; *Educ* John Watson's Sch Edinburgh, Daniel Stewart's Coll Edinburgh, St Andrews Univ (MA), Harvard Univ (MPA); *m* 1953, Margaret Joy, da of Godfrey Theaker (d 1974); 3 da (Ann, Judith, Susan); *Career* WWII Fleet Air Arm 1942-46, Lt (A) RNVR; Scottish Home Dept 1948; Dip Serv 1948-80: NZ 1949-52, E and W Pakistan 1954-57, Ghana 1959-62, Uganda 1962-63, Br dep high cmmr Tanzania 1963-65 (actg high cmmr 1963-64); actg high cmmr Ghana March-April 1966, consul-gen St Louis Missouri 1967-70, dep high cmmr Calcutta 1970-74; high cmmr: Zambia 1974-78 and Bangladesh 1978-79; dir of studies overseas servs unit Royal Inst of Public Admin 1980-83, dist cncllr Tandridge DC 1982-, chm Limpsfield Parish Cncl 1987-; *Recreations* cricket, tennis, golf; *Clubs* Royal Cwlth Soc, MCC, Tandridge GC; *Style—* Stephen Miles, Esq, CMG; Maytrees, 71 Park Rd, Limpsfield, Oxted, Surrey RH8 0AN (☎ 0883 713132)

MILES, William Miles; s of William Miles (d 1978), of 30 Highway Rd, Leics, and Gladys Violet, *née* Beaver, *qv*; *b* 26 Sept 1933; *Educ* Wyggeston Sch Leicester, Trinity Hall Cambridge (MA, LLM); *m* 1961, Jillian Anne, da of Robert Walker Wilson (d 1970), of 47 Roehampton Drive, Wigston Fields, Leicester; 3 s (William Robert b 1962, Jonathan Andrew b 1964, David James b 1965); *Career* asst slr Leicester and Doncaster County Boroughs 1960-65; sr asst slr Exeter 1965-66; asst Town Clerk Leicester 1966-69; dep Town Clerk Blackpool 1969-73; city legal advsr Newcastle-upon-Tyne 1973-74, chief exec Gateshead 1974-84; chief exec and clerk, clerk to Lieutenancy West Yorks CC 1984-86; dir Yorkshire Enterprise Ltd 1984-; *Recreations* bridge, athletics, mountain walking; *Style—* William Miles, Esq; 23 Moor Crescent, Gosforth, Newcastle-upon-Tyne NE3 4AP (☎ 091 2851 1996)

MILES, Sir William Napier Maurice; 6 Bt (UK 1859), of Leigh Ct, Somersetshire; s of Lt-Col Sir Charles William Miles, 5 Bt, OBE (d 1966); *b* 19 Oct 1913; *Educ* Stowe, Jesus Coll Cambridge; *m* 1946, Pamela Dillon; 1 s, 2 da; *Heir* s, Philip John Miles; *Career* chartered architect (retd); ARIBA, AA dipl; *Clubs* Royal Western Yacht; *Style—* Sir William Miles, Bt; Old Rectory House, Walton-in-Gordano, nr Clevedon, Avon (☎ 0272 873365)

MILFORD, John Tillman; s of Roy Douglas Milford MB, (d 1982), of Grianachan, Strathtay, Perthshire, and Jessie Rhind (d 1972); *b* 4 Feb 1946; *Educ* Hurstpierpoint, Exeter Univ (LLB); *m* 1975, Mary Alice, da of Edmund Anthony Spriggs, MD, FRCP, of River House, Wylam, Northumberland; 3 da (Alice b 1977, Sarah b 1979, Emily b 1981); *Career* barr Inner Temple 1969; practising Newcastle-upon-Tyne 1970-; Crown Court Rec 1985-; *Recreations* fishing, shooting, gardening; *Clubs* Northern Counties, (Newcastle-upon-Tyne); *Style—* John T Milford, Esq; Hill House, Haydon Bridge, Hexham, Northumberland; 12 Trinity Chare, Quayside, Newcastle-upon-Tyne (☎ 232 1927)

MILFORD, 2 Baron (UK 1939); Sir Wogan Philipps; 2 Bt (UK 1919); s of 1 Baron Milford (d 1962; 6 s of Rev Sir James Philipps, 12 Bt, by Hon Mary Best, sis of 5 Baron Wynford; also yst bro of 1 Viscount St Davids), and Ethel Speke, niece of the African explorer John Speke (discoverer of Lake Victoria and, with Sir Richard Burton, Lake Tanganyika); *b* 25 Feb 1902; *Educ* Eton, Magdalen Coll Oxford; *m* 1, 1928 (m dis 1944), the novelist Rosamond Lehmann; 1 s (and 1 da decd); m 2, 1944, as her 2 husb, Cristina (d 1953), former w of 15 Earl of Huntingdon and da of the Marchese Casati by his w, the Marchesa, subject of the celebrated portrait by Augustus John; m 3, 1954, Tamara, *née* Kravetz, widow of William Rust, sometime ed The Daily Worker; 1 s; *Heir* s, Hon Hugo Philipps; *Career* farmer, painter, trades unionist, former memb Henley and Cirencester RDCs, late Int Brigade; *Style—* The Rt Hon Lord Milford

MILFORD HAVEN, 4 Marquess of (UK 1917); George Ivar Louis Mountbatten; also Earl of Medina and Viscount Alderney (both UK 1917); s of 3 Marquess of Milford Haven, OBE, DSC (d 1970, himself gs of HSH Prince Louis of Battenberg, who relinquished, at the King's request, the style and title of Serene Highness and Prince of Battenberg, instead assuming the surname of Mountbatten by Royal Licence 1917); gn of late Earl Mountbatten of Burma and, through his paternal grandmother (Nada), ggggs of Emperor Nicholas I of Russia; *b* 6 June 1961; *Educ* Gordonstoun; *m* 8 March 1989, Sarah Georgina, er da of George Alfred Walker, *qv*; *Heir* bro, Lord Ivar Alexander Michael Mountbatten; *Career* with Chieftain Drilling (subsidiary of Exxon Corpn) 1982-; *Style—* The Most Hon the Marquess of Milford Haven; Moyns Park, Birdbrook, Essex

MILFORD HAVEN, Janet, Marchioness of Janet Mercedes Mountbatten; *née* Bryce; JP (Inner London 1979); o da of late Maj Francis Bryce, OBE, KRRC, and Gladys Jean, *née* Mosley; *b* 29 Sept 1937,Bermuda; *Educ* Trafalgar Sch for Girls Montreal Canada; *m* 17 Nov 1960, as his 2 w, 3 Marquess of Milford Haven, OBE, DSC (d 1970); 2 s (George, 4 Marquess of Milford Haven b 1960, Lord Ivar Mountbatten b 1963, *qqv*); *Style—* The Most Hon Janet, Marchioness of; Milford Haven, JP; Moyns Park, Birdbrook, Essex

MILHOFER, Anthony Charles; s of Manfred Milhofer (d 1984), of Chislehurst, Kent, and Veronica Catherine, *née* Glover (d 1983); *b* 25 May 1940; *Educ* Cranleigh; *m* 3 Sept 1966, Elizabeth, da of John Ragg (d 1985), of W Byfleet, Surrey; 3 s (Peter John b 1969, Martin Roger b 1972, Ian David b 1979); *Career* Abbey Nat Bldg Soc: joined 1959, branch mangr Staines 1963-64, asst estab offr 1965-66, dep mangr personnel and trg 1967-70, branch mangr Holborn 1971-73, regnl mangr SE Eng 1974-79, divnl mangr sales 1979-83, mangr Southern operations 1984, ret as head of R&D 1988; sales and mktg conslt fin servs industry, chm travel agency 1989; Freeman of City of London, Worshipful Co of Horners (1972); FCIS, FMIB 1974;; *Style—* Anthony Milhofer, Esq; Grove Farm, Grove, Leighton Buzzard, Bedfordshire LU7 0QU (☎ 0525 372 225)

MILKINA, Nina; da of Jacques Milkine, and Sophie; *b* 27 Jan 1919; *Educ* privately; *m* 1943, Alastair Robert Masson Sedgwick; 1 s (Alexander Paul b 1958), 1 da (Katrina b 1960); *Career* concert pianist (Hon RAM), noted for performances of Mozart's piano works; studied: Paris with Leon Conus of Moscow Conservatoire, composition with Sabaniev and Glazunov, in Eng with Harold Craxton, Tobias Matthay; first public performance with Lamoreux Orch in Paris, aged 11; BBC cmmn to broadcast all Mozart's piano sonatas; gave Mozart Bicentenary Recital Edinburgh Int Festival; recorded for: Westminster Record Co, Pye, ASV; first composition pub aged 11 by Boosey and Hawkes; adjudicator at major music competitions; *Recreations* chess, swimming; *Style—* Miss Nina Milkina; 20 Paradise Walk, London SW3 4JL (☎ 01 352 2501)

MILLAIS, Geoffroy Richard Everett; s and h of Sir Ralph Regnault Millais, 5 Bt; *b* 27 Dec 1941; *Educ* Marlborough; *Style—* Geoffroy Millais, Esq

MILLAIS, Sir Ralph Regnault; 5 Bt (UK 1885), of Palace Gate, Kensington, Co Middlesex and of St Ouen, Jersey; s of Sir Geoffroy William Millais, 4 Bt (d 1941); the 1 Bt was Sir John Everett Millais, the artist and pres RA; *b* 4 Mar 1905; *Educ* Marlborough, Trinity Cambridge; *m* 1, 4 Sept 1939 (m dis 1947), Felicity Caroline Mary Ward, da of Brig-Gen William Ward Warner, CMG (d 1950), and formerly w of Maj John Peyton Robinson, 8 Hussars; 1 s (Geoffroy), 1 da (Caroline); m 2, 22 Oct 1947 (m dis 1971), Irene Jessie (d 1985), er da of late Edward Albert Stone, of St Anne's Mont à l'Abbé, St Helier, Jersey, and formerly w of Stephen Eric Alley; m 3, 1975 Mrs Babette Sefton-Smith, da of Maj-Gen Harold Francis Salt, CB, CMG, DSO (d 1971); *Heir* s, Geoffroy Richard Everett Millais; *Career* joined RAFVR 1939, Sqdn Ldr 1940, Wing Cdr 1941, Belgium, Holland 1944-45, Air Min 1939-46; asst private sec to the Home Secretary 1926-27; business career 1927-39 and 1946-73 (ret 1973); *Recreations* restoration of vintage cars, fishing; *Style—* Sir Ralph Millais, Bt; Gate Cottage, Winchelsea, E Sussex TN36 4HL

MILLAN, Rt Hon Bruce; PC (1975); s of David Millan; *b* 5 Oct 1927; *Educ* Harris Acad Dundee; *m* 1953, Gwendoline May Fairey; 1 s, 1 da; *Career* MP (Lab): Glasgow Craigton 1959-83, Glasgow Govan 1983-88; parly under-sec def (RAF) 1964-66, Scotland 1966-70, min state Scottish Off 1974-76, sec state Scotland 1976-79; oppn front bench spokesman Scotland 1979-83, euro cmmr 1989-; *Style—* The Rt Hon Bruce Millan; 10 Beech Ave, Glasgow G41 (☎ 041 427 6483)

MILLAR; *see*: Hoyer Millar

MILLAR, Angus George; WS (1955); s of George William Russell Millar (d 1929), of Port Dickson, Malaya, and Audrey Margaret, *née* Watson (d 1954); *b* 1 July 1928; *Educ* Loretto, Jesus Coll Oxford (BA), Edinburgh Univ (LLB); *m* 25 April 1959, Julia Mary, da of Alan Reginald Cathcart (d 1967), of Kirkcudbright; 3 s (James b 1961, Charles b 1963, Roderick b 1967); *Career* Nat Serv 1950-52 Royal Signals, 2 Lt 1951, Lt 1952; trainee analyst and asst mangr Baillie Gifford and Co Investmt Mangrs Edinburgh 1955-61 (ptnr 1961-, sr ptnr 1984-); dir: Investors Capital Tst plc 1970-85, UK Provident Inst 1978-86; dep chm Assoc of Investmt Tst Cos 1980-82; memb: fin ctee of Nat Tst for Scot, ctee of Friends of Royal Hosp for Sick Children Edinburgh; patron Appeal for Prince's Scot Youth Business Tst; *Recreations* travel, hill walking, visiting art galleries, golf; *Clubs* New (Edinburgh), East India; *Style—* Angus G Millar, Esq, WS; Baillie Gifford and Co, 3 Glenfinlas St, Edinburgh, EH3 6YY (☎ 031 225 2581, fax 031 225 2358, telex 72310 BGCO G)

MILLAR, Anthony Bruce (Tony); s of James Desmond Millar (d 1965), and Josephine Georgina, *née* Brice; *b* 5 Oct 1941; *Educ* Haileybury, Imperial Serv Coll; *m* 3 July 1964, Judith Anne, da of Capt John Edward Jester (d 1984), of Drayton, Hants: 2 da (Cassilda Anne b 1966, Katrina Mary b 1967); *Career* asst to gp mgmnt accountant and gp tres Viyella Int Fedn Ltd 1964-67; Utd Tport overseas Ltd Nairobi 1967-70: chief accountant to subsidiary, gp internal auditor for E Africa, PA to chief agent; dep gp fin controller Utd Tport Overseas Ltd London 1970-72, conslt Fairfield property co 1975-77 (fin dir 1972-75), md Provinical Laundries Ltd 1974-81, dep chm Hawley Gp Ltd 1981, exec chm The Albert Fisher Gp plc 1982-; ACA 1964, FCA 1974, CBIM 1986; *Recreations* swimming, walking, bridge, racehorse owner; *Clubs* Mark's; *Style—* Tony Millar, Esq; The Albert Fisher Gp plc, Fisher House, 61 Thames St, Windsor, Berks SL4 1PQ (☎ 0753 857 111, fax 0753 850911, car ☎ 0860 519395, telex 849716)

MILLAR, (Thomas) Cecil; s of Thomas Nicholl Millar (d 1942), of Co Antrim, NI, and Mary Millar, *née* Hollinger (d 1985); *b* 7 Dec 1921; *Educ* Acad Ballymena, Trinity Coll Dublin (BA, MB); *m* 1944, Joan Maureen, da of Tom Fletcher (d 1936); 1 s (Graeme b 1966), 1 da (Jacqueline b 1959); *Career* general practitioner; past pres Rotary Club; pres: Horticultural Assoc, Civic Soc; BCH; BAO; MRCGR; *Recreations* football, rugby, tennis, badminton; *Clubs* Rotary; *Style—* Dr Cecil Millar; Trostan House, Dene Bank Road, Oswaldtwistle, Hyndburn, Lancs (☎ (0254) 32206); 17/19 Rhyddings Street, Oswaldtwistle, Hyndborn, Lancs (☎ (0254) 32206)

MILLAR, David Lindsay; OBE (1976); s of David McIntyre Millar (d 1942), of Ardler, Perthshire, and Gwendoline Mary Slade, *née* Forbes; *b* 21 July 1928; *Educ* Guildford GS, Perth WA; *m* 20 Sept 1957, Jacqueline, da of Col Charles Francis Rivett-Carnac (d 1958), of Oak Farm, Dickleborough, Norfolk; 3 s (Guy, Mark, Nicholas); *Career* chief mangr The Chartered Bank Hong Kong 1971-75; Standard Chartered Bank London: gen mangr 1976-79, sr gen mangr 1980-82, sr exec dir commercial banking ops 1983-87; chm The Exchange Banks Assoc Hong Kong 1971-73, memb Banking Advsy Ctee to the Hong Kong Govt 1971-75, dir Trade Devpt Cncl Hong Kong 1973-75, chm The Overseas Bankers Club London 1984-86; ACIB 1971 (memb 1947-71), FCIB 1975; *Recreations* tennis, golf, skiing, sailing, fishing; *Style—* David Millar, Esq, OBE; Bepton Lodge, Bepton, Midhurst, W Sussex GU29 OHX (☎ 073081 6130)

MILLAR, Dr (John Harold) Derek; MBE (Mil 1944), DL (Humberside 1981); s of

James Charles Millar (d 1947), and Elizabeth Ethel Cowie (d 1963); *b* 23 Jan 1914; *Educ* The Edinburgh Acad, Edinburgh Univ (MB, ChB, MD, MRCPEd); *m* 1947, Isobel Margaret, da of Dr John Jardine, CB, OBE, MD, FRCSEd, DPH, (d 1974), of Cobden Crescent, Edinburgh; 1 s, 1 da; *Career* RAMC 1939-45, medical specialist, with Br Land Army 1944-45, Maj N Africa 1941, POW Italy 1941-43, Hon Maj 1946, civilian MO Rapier Barracks, Kirton Lindsay 1978-84; conslt physician Grimsby Gen Hosp 1948-60, sr conslt and physician Scunthorpe Gp of Hosps 1948-79; hon conslt; FRCP; *Recreations* golf, fishing, gardening; *Clubs* Army and Navy; *Style—* Dr Derek Millar, MBE, DL; Garden Cottage, Low St, Winterton, Scunthorpe (☎ 0724 732371)

MILLAR, Ian Alastair Duncan; CBE (1978), MC (1945), JP (1952), DL (1960); s of late Sir James Duncan Millar; *b* 22 Nov 1914; *Educ* Gresham's Sch Holt, Cambridge Univ; *m* 1945, Louise Reid, da of W McCosh (d 1937); 2 s, 2 da; *Career* served Corps of Royal Engrs 1940-45, Maj; contested (L) parly elections Banff 1945, Kinross and W Perthshire 1949 and 1963; CCllr 1946-79 (Perthshire and Kinross) convener 1975-78; regional cllr and convenor Tayside 1974-78; memb N of Scotland Hydro Electric Bd 1956-70, dep chm 1970-72; dir Macdonald Fraser & Co 1961-, chm United Auctions (Scotland) Ltd 1967-74; chm Consultative Ctee on Freshwater Fisheries, Freshwater and Salmon Fisheries (Scotland) Act 1976 1981-; *Recreations* learning about and catching salmon, meeting people; *Clubs* Royal Perth Golfing Soc; *Style—* I A D Millar Esq, CBE, MC, JP, DL; Reynock, Remony, Aberfeldy, Perthshire (☎ 088 73 400)

MILLAR, Sir Oliver Nicholas; GCVO (1988, KCVO 1973, CVO 1963, MVO 1953); s of Gerald Arthur Millar, MC (d 1975); *b* 26 April 1923; *Educ* Rugby, Courtauld Inst of Art; *m* 1954, Delia Mary, da of Lt-Col Cuthbert Dawnay, MC (d 1964); 1 s, 3 da; *Career* FBA 1970; dir The Royal Collection 1987; surveyor of pictures to HM The Queen 1972-88 (asst surveyor 1947, dep surveyor 1949-72); surveyor emeritus 1988-; tstee Nat Portrait Gallery 1972-; memb Reviewing Ctee on Export of Works of Art 1975-87; tstee Nat Heritage Meml Fund 1988-; *Recreations* drawing, golf, gardening; *Clubs* Brooks's, MCC; *Style—* Sir Oliver Millar, GCVO; Yonder Lodge, Penn, Bucks (☎ 049 481 2124)

MILLAR, Peter Carmichael; OBE (1978); s of Rev Peter Carmichael Millar (d 1963), and Ailsa Ross Brown, *née* Campbell; *b* 19 Feb 1927; *Educ* Aberdeen GS, Glasgow Univ, St Andrews Univ (MA), Edinburgh Univ (LLB); *m* 1953, Kirsteen Lindsay, da of Col David Carnegie, CB, OBE, TD, DL (d 1961); 2 s (Neil b 1959, Alastair b 1959), 2 da (Anne b 1955, Alison b 1958); *Career* served RN 1944-47; WS 1954-, 1954 dep keeper of HM Signet 1983-; chm: Mental Welfare Cmmn for Scotland 1983-, Church of Scotland General Tstees 1973-85; ptnr: W & T P Manuel WS 1954-63, Aitken Kinnear & Co W S 1963-87, Aitken Nain WS 1987-; *Recreations* golf, hill walking; *Clubs* New (Edinburgh), Hon Co of Edinburgh Golfers, Bruntsfield Links Golfing Soc; *Style—* Peter C Millar, Esq, OBE; 25 Cramond Road North, Edinburgh EH4 (☎ 031 336 2069); 7 Abercromby Place, Edinburgh EH3 (☎ 031 556 6644, telex 728112, fax 031 556 6509)

MILLAR, (John) Richard; s of William Hugh Millar (d 1967), and Eileen Phyllis May Millar; *b* 16 Feb 1940; *Educ* Wellington; *m* 2 Dec 1978, Rosemary Margaret, da of Alfred Thomas Hanson, of 3 Riverside, Gargrave, N Yorks; *Career* slr 1963, ptnr Bischoff & Co 1968-; memb Law Soc 1963; Freeman City of London, Worshipful Co of Slrs; *Recreations* sailing, gardening; *Clubs* Offshore Yachts Class Owners Assoc, Little Ship; *Style—* Richard Millar, Esq; Epworth House, 25 City Rd, London EC1Y 1AA (☎ 01 628 4222, fax 01 638 3345)

MILLAR, Sir Ronald Graeme; s of Ronald Hugh Millar and Dorothy Ethel Dacre, *née* Hill; *b* 12 Nov 1919; *Educ* Charterhouse, King's Coll Cambridge; *Career* served WW II Sub-Lt RNVR; playwright and political writer; speech writer to PM 1975-; dep chm Haymarket Theatre 1977-; former actor with appearances in Mr Bolfry, The Sacred Flame, Murder on the Nile, Jenny Jones (own play), Zero House; screenwriter in London and Hollywood where films worked on inc: The Miniver Story, Scaramouche, Rose Marie, Betrayal; plays produced in London inc: Frieda, The Bride Comes Back, Robert and Elizabeth (book and lyrics), Number 10, Abelard and Heloise; adaptations for the theatre of works by C P Snow inc: The New Man, The Masters, The Case in Question, A Cost of Varnish; kt 1980; *Recreations* music; *Clubs* Brooks's, Dramatists'; *Style—* Sir Ronald Millar; 7 Sheffield Terrace, London W8 (☎ 01 727 8361)

MILLARD, Sir Guy Elwin; KCMG (1972), CMG (1957), CVO (1961); s of Col Baldwin Salter Millard, and Phyllis Mary Tetley; *b* 22 Jan 1917; *Educ* Charterhouse, Pembroke Coll Cambridge Univ; *m* 1, 1946 (m dis 1963), Anne, da of Gordon Mackenzie, of Toronto; 1 s, 1 da; m 2, 1964, Mary Judy, da of James Dugdale by his w Pamela (*see* Pamela, Countess of Aylesford); 2 s; *Career* served WW II RN; Foreign Serv 1939-76: min UK Delegation to NATO 1964-67, ambass Hungary 1967-69, min Washington 1970-71; ambass to: Sweden 1971-74, Italy 1974-76; chm Br-Italian Soc 1977-83; *Style—* Sir Guy Millard, KCMG, CVO; Fyfield Manor, Southrop, Glos (☎ 036785 234)

MILLARD, Richard Edward; CBE (1974); s of Frederick Stanley Millard (d 1970), of Epping, and Edith Mary, *née* Howarth (d 1970); *b* 15 April 1914; *Educ* St Paul's, Law Soc Sch of Law (LLB); *m* 2 April 1949, Rachel Anne, da of Lawrence John Cumberbatch Southern (d 1975), of Boldre, Hants; 1 s (Martin b 1950), 1 da (Fiona b 1953); *Career* slr; clerk: Bucks CC 1955-74, of the Peace 1955-71, Thames Valley Police Authy 1967-74, to Lieutenancy 1955-74; chm County Clerks Soc 1972-74; memb: Royal Cmmn Penal System 1964-66, advsy cncl on Penal System 1966-74, Cncl of Univ of Buckingham 1974-89 (vice-chm 1976-87); JP 1974; asst cmmr Local Govt Boundary Cmmn 1974-85; Hon DUniv Buckingham (1988); *Recreations* golf, gardening; *Clubs* Naval and Military; *Style—* Richard E Millard, Esq, CBE; Whitecliff, Whiteleaf, Aylesbury HP17 0LR (☎ 084 44 6170)

MILLBOURN, Lady; Ethel Marjorie; da of late Joseph E Sennett; *m* 1931, Sir (Philip) Eric Millbourn, CMG (d 1982), sometime chm Cncl Administration Malta Dockyard; 1 s, 1 da; *Style—* Lady Millbourn; Conkwell Grange, Limpley Stoke, Bath, Avon BA3 6HD (☎ Limpley Stoke 022 122 3102)

MILLEN, Brig Anthony Tristram Patrick; s of Maj Charles Reginald Millen, MC (d 1959), and Annie Mary, *née* Martin (d 1979); *b* 15 Dec 1928; *Educ* Mount St Mary's Coll, Staff Coll Camberley, Joint Servs Staff Coll; *m* 24 Nov 1954, Mary Alice Featherston, da of Maj Robin Quentin Featherston Johnston (ka 1941); 3 s (Robin b 1956, Nicholas b 1958, Patrick b 1964, d 1964), 2 da (Alice b 1961, Philippa b 1966); *Career* 5 Royal Inniskilling Dragoon Gds 1948, CO Royal Hong Kong Regt (The Volunteers) 1969-71, def advsr Br High Cmmn Ottawa 1980-83, ret 1983; chm Army Benevolent Fund (Thirsk area); *Recreations* sailing; *Style—* Brig Anthony Millen; The Manor House, Hutton Sessay, Thirsk, North Yorkshire YO7 3BA (☎ 0845 401 444)

MILLER, Alan John McCulloch; DSC (1941), VRD (1950); s of Louis McEwan Miller (d 1950), of Helensburgh, Dumbartonshire, and Mary, *née* McCulloch; *b* 21 April 1914; *Educ* Kelvinside Academy, Strathclyde Univ; *m* 1940, Kirsteen Ross, da of Col Frank George Orr, CBE (d 1945); 3 s (Michael, Graeme, Alan), 1 da (Susanne); *Career* commnd RNVR (Clyde Div) 1938; served RN 1939-45; chm and md: Bestobell Ltd 1951-73, William Simons & Co Ltd; 1956-60; chm: Miller Insulation Ltd, Low and Bonar plc 1977-82, BNES Southern Africa Ctee 1970; *Recreations* sailing, skiing, golf, shooting; *Clubs* Army and Navy, Royal Thames Yacht, Royal Cruising, Royal and Ancient (St Andrews), Sunningdale Golf; *Style—* Alan Miller, Esq, DSC, VRD; Granfers, Southdown, Chale, Isle of Wight P038 2LE (☎ (0983) 79486)

MILLER, Alfred Henry; s of Sydney Charles Miller (d 1939), of Eastbourne, and Clara, *née* Rapley (d 1939); *b* 10 May 1901; *Educ* Eastbourne GS; *m* 14 April 1928, Doris, da of Frederick Boys (d 1943), of Eastbourne; 1 s (Robin b 21 Oct 1935), 1 da (Gillian b 31 Aug 1930); *Career* sr ptnr Perkins Copeland & Co Eastbourne; actively involved with St John Ambulance Brigade 1940- (pres Eastbourne Ambulance Div); FCA 1928; OStJ 1968; *Style—* Alfred Miller, Esq; Meadowgate, 45 Park Ave, Willingdon, Eastbourne, E Sussex BN21 2XG (☎ 0323 503 291); Perkins, Copeland & Co, Chartered Accountants, 15 Gildredge Rd, Eastbourne, E Sussex BN21 4RA (☎ 0323 411 019)

MILLER, Ambrose Michael; s of Ambrose Miller of Beer, Devon, and Margaret Dorothy, *née* Dennett; *b* 15 April 1950; *Educ* Radley, Magdalene Coll Cambridge, King's Coll London (B Mus); *m* 4 April 1981, Celia Frances Sophia, da of Sir Desmond Arthur Pond (d 1986); *Career* mangr Royal Ballet Orch 1974-81, gen mangr Scottish Baroque Ensemble 1981-83, fndr and artistic dir Euro Community Chamber Orch 1983; dir Artslink Int Ltd 1986-; Freeman City of London, Liveryman Worshipful Co of Musicians; *Recreations* cooking, reading; *Style—* Ambrose Miller, Esq; Five Bells, Offwell, Honiton, Devon (☎ 0404 83 701); Rougnac, 16320 Villebois Lavalette, France; (☎ telex 9312100405 EC G)

MILLER, Hon Mrs (Ann Kathleen); da of 12 Baron Aylmer (d 1982), and Althea, Baroness Aylmer, *qv*; *b* 1941; *Educ* Mount Douglas HS, Victoria Coll; *m* 1972, Gregor Byron Miller, s of late John Brown Miller; 1 s, 2 step da; *Recreations* tennis, cycling, music; *Style—* The Hon Mrs Miller; 2765 Skilift Place, West Vancouver, BC, Canada

MILLER, Sir (Oswald) Bernard; s of Arthur Miller; *b* 25 Mar 1904; *Educ* Sloane Sch, Jesus Coll Oxford; *m* 1931, Jessica Marie Ffoulkes; 3 s; *Career* John Lewis Partnership: joined 1927, dir 1935, chm 1955-72; former memb: Monopolies Cmmn, Cncl for Industl Design, Econ Devpt Ctee for Distributive Trades (and chm Retail Distributors Assoc 1953); chm South Regnl RSA 1974-80 and memb cncl of RSA 1977-83; Univ of Southampton: chm cncl 1982-88, tres 1974, pro chllr 1983-, Hon LLD 1981; hon fell Jesus Coll Oxford 1968; kt 1967; *Books* Biography of Robert Harley, Earl of Oxford (1927); *Style—* Sir Bernard Miller; The Field House, Longstock, Stockbridge, Hants (☎ 0264 810627)

MILLER, Christian Mona; da of Sir Arthur Grant of Monymusk, 10 Bt (d 1931), and Evelyn Alice Lindsay, *née* Wood (d 1976); *b* 3 Dec 1920; *Educ* private; *m* 1, 14 Nov 1942 (m dis 1951), Michael Fife William Angas, Gren Guards, s of late Laurence Lee Bazley Angas, of New York; 2 da (Auburn b 1945, Cherill b 1947); m 2, 5 Jan 1953, John Gordon Ogston Miller, s of John Poynter Miller (d 1937); *Career* author, books inc: The Champagne Sandwich (1969), Daisy, Daisy (1981), A Childhood in Scotland (1981); *Recreations* trying to find some spare time in which to write; *Style—* Mrs Christian Miller; Old Stables, Newton, Newbury, Berkshire RG15 9AP (☎ 0635 40945)

MILLER, David James; s of James Samuel Miller, of Lymington, Hants, and Beryl Mary, *née* Jones; *b* 28 Feb 1952; *Educ* Stockport GS, Emmanuel Coll Cambridge (MA); *m* 17 Sept 1988, Sophie Kay Voss, da of Flemming Christian Rathsach, of Pindon Manor, Bucks; *Career* barr Middle Temple, legal advsr and unit tst business mangr Sun Alliance Insur Gp 1977-86, dep chief exec Life Assur & Unit Tst Regulatory Orgn 1986-89; *Recreations* travel, history of art; *Clubs* United Oxford and Cambridge; *Style—* David Miller, Esq; 37 Granville Sq, London WC1X 9PD (☎ 01 833 3963); Sun Alliance, Bartholomew Lane, London, EC2

MILLER, Lady Diana Mary; *née* Pelham; da of 5 Earl of Yarborough, MC, DL (d 1948), and Nancye, *née* Brocklehurst, niece of 1 and last Baron Ranksborough; co-heiress (with sis, Lady Wendy Lycett, *qv*) to Baronies of Fauconberg (E ante 24 June 1295) and Conyers (E 1509), through paternal grandmother; *b* 5 July 1920; *m* 1952, Robert Miller, s of Capt Gordon Molineux Miller (d 1952); 2 da (Marcia Anne b 1954, adopted by her aunt, Lady Wendy Lycett, *qv*, whose surname she assumed ; Beatrix Diana b 1955); *Career* SRN; *Style—* Lady Diana Miller

MILLER, Sir (Ian) Douglas; s of Dr Joseph John Miller (d 1902), and Annie Clare, *née* Doolan (d 1935); *b* 20 July 1900; *Educ* Xavier Coll Melbourne, Sydney Univ (MB, ChM, Hon MD); *m* 1939, Valerie Phyllis Laidley, da of John Laidley Mort, BE (d 1971); 3 s (John, David, Adrian), 2 da (Katharine, Christina); *Career* Lt-Col AIF Middle E; FRCS, FRACS, Hon LittD (Singapore), Hon MD (Sydney); surgn and neurosurgn St Vincent's Hosp Sydney 1929-60, lectr in anatomy Sydney Univ 1930-46, pres Royal Aust Coll Surgns 1957-59, chm Bd St Vincent's Private Hosp 1976-; FRCS, Hon FRCSE; kt 1961; *Books* A Surgeon's Story (1985), Earlier Days St Vincent's Hospital (1970); *Clubs* Australian Sydney; *Style—* Sir Douglas Miller; 170 Kurraba Rd, Neutral Bay, NSW, Derralea, Bingara 9692941; 149 Macquarie St, Sydney, NSW 2000, Australia (☎ 27 4405)

MILLER, Sir Douglas Sinclair; KCVO (1972), CBE (1956, OBE 1948); s of Albert Edward Miller (d 1954); *b* 30 July 1906; *Educ* Westminster, Merton Coll Oxford; *m* 1933, Valerie Madeleine Carter; 1 da; *Career* Colonial Serv 1930-61; sec King George's Jubilee Tst 1961-71; devpt advsr Duke of Edinburgh Award Scheme 1971-85; *Style—* Sir Douglas Miller, KCVO, CBE; The Lodge, 70 Grand Ave, Worthing, West Sussex (☎ 0903 501195)

MILLER, Lady; Elizabeth; da of C E Barberie; *m* 1957, Sir Roderick William Miller, CBE (d 1971); *Style—* Lady Millar; 9 Hillside Ave, Vaucluse, NSW 2030, Australia

MILLER, Lady; Ella Jane; da of John Stewart, of Edinburgh; *m* 1933, Sir James Miller, GBE, LLD (d 1977); *Style—* Lady Miller; Belmont, Ellersly Rd, Edinburgh EH12 6JA

MILLER, Harry; s of Sir Ernest Henry John Miller, 10 Bt (d 1960); h to Btcy of bro, Sir John Miller, 11 Bt; *b* 1927; *m* 1954, Gwynedd Margaret, da of R P Sherriff, of Paraparaumu, New Zealand; 1 s, 2 da; *Style—* Harry Miller, Esq; Komako, RD,

Ashhurst, New Zealand

MILLER, Hal - Hilary Duppa; MP (C) Bromsgrove 1983-; s of Lt Cdr John Duppa-Miller, GC, of Somerset West, SA, and Hon Barbara (d 1966), yr da of 1 Viscount Buckmaster; *b* 6 Mar 1929; *Educ* Eton, Merton Coll Oxford, London Univ; *m* 1, 1956, Fiona McDermid; 2 s, 2 da; m 2, 1976, Jacqueline Roe, yr da of T C W Roe, of Brighton and Lady Londesborough; 1 s, 1 da; *Career* colonial serv Hong Kong 1955-68; MP (C) Bromsgrove and Redditch 1974-83; PPS to: sec of state Defence 1979-81, chllr Duchy of Lancaster 1981 (resigned); pps to chm of Cons Party 1984, vice-chm Cons Party 1984-87; fell of Econ Devpt Inst of World Bank (Washington); *Style*— Hal Miller, Esq, MP; Moorcroft Farm, Sinton Green, Worcester WR2 6NW (☎ 0905 640309); House of Commons, London SW1 (☎ 01 219 4531)

MILLER, Hon Mrs (Honor Leslie); *née* Brooke; er da of Baron Brooke of Cumnor, PC, CH (Life Peer, d 1984), and Baroness Brooke of Ystradfellte, DBE (Life Peeress), *qv*; *b* 2 April 1941; *Educ* St Mary's Calne, Univ of Grenoble, St James's Secretarial Coll; *m* 6 Aug 1966, Dr (Thomas) Nigel Miller, er s of Nathaniel Allan Miller, FRCS; 3 s, 2 da; *Career* Nightingale Nurse: St Thomas's Hosp; personal asst to Rev P M Jenkins, Housemaster of The Hall Repton Sch; *Recreations* English watercolours, the 'cello, reading, decorative arts; *Style*— The Hon Mrs Miller; Laurel Hill, Repton, Derby

MILLER, Jack Michael; s of Col Harry Raymond (Pat) Miller, of 46 St Winifreds Road, Teddington, and Eileen Mary, *née* Whiteing; *b* 10 Jan 1946; *Educ* Cranleigh Sch; *m* 2 June 1972, Elizabeth Alison, da of Lt-Col Ronald Francis Boyd Campbell, of 30 Marine Drive, Torpoint; 1 da (Caroline b 29 Dec 1977); *Career* Gunner HAC; slr; articled Rider Heaton Meredith & Mills 1964-70; Midland Bank plc; Legal dept 1970-, dep sr legal advsr UK Banking 1988-; memb Bedford Parish Soc; Freeman of the City of London, Liveryman of the Worshipful Co of Haberdashers; *Recreations* cricket, sport generally, trivia; *Clubs* MCC, RAC, Tatty Bogle, Cricket Soc; *Style*— Jack Miller, Esq; 41 Fairfax Rd, London W4; 11 Old Jewry, London Ec2R 8AA (☎ 01 260 7381, fax 01 260 7393)

MILLER, James; CBE (1986); s of Sir James Miller, GBE (d 1977), of Belmont, Ellerlsly Rd, Edinburgh, and Ella Jane, *née* Stewart; *b* 1 Sept 1934; *Educ* Edinburgh Acad, Harrow Sch, Balliol Coll Oxford (MA); *m* 1, 27 July 1959, Kathleen (d 1966), da of James Dewar (d 1969), of Edinburgh; 1 s (James b 1962), 2 da (Susan b 1960, Gail b 1962); m 2, 11 Jan 1969, Iris, da of Thomas James Lloyd-Webb (d 1959), of Southampton; 1 da (Heather b 1970); *Career* RE 1956-58, cmmnd 2 Lt 1957; James Miller & Ptnrs (The Miller Gp Ltd 1986): joined 1958, dir 1960, chm and md 1970; chm Fedn of Civil Engrg Contractors 1985; pres Edinburgh C of C 1981-83, ct asst Merchant Co of Edinburgh 1982-85; chm: Scottish section Fedn of Civil Engrs 1981-83, Scottish branch chartered Inst of Arbitrators 1985-87; Freeman: City of London 1956, Worshipful Co of Horners 1956; FCIOB 1974, FCIArb 1976, CBIM 1983; *Recreations* shooting; *Clubs* City Livery; *Style*— James Miller, Esq, CBE; Belmont, Ellersly Rd, Edinburgh EH12 6JA (☎ 031 337 6595); The Miller Group Ltd, Miller House, 18 South Groathill Avenue, Edinburgh EH4 2LW (☎ 031 332 2585, fax 031 332 3426, telex 727551 MILCON G)

MILLER, James Lawson; s of David Wardrop Miller (d 1966), and Helen Frew Baxter (d 1952); *b* 26 Jan 1951; *Educ* The John Lyon Sch Harrow, St John's Coll Cambridge (MA); *m* 29 June 1957, Margaret Ann, da of Beverly Robinson (d 1984); 2 s (David b 1958, Jeremy b 1959), 1 da (Jane b 1962); *Career* chartered builder; construction co chief exec; chm and dir: J Lawson Holdings Ltd, J Lawson & Co Ltd, J Lawson Building Ltd, J Lawson Timber Products Ltd, Lawson Plant Hire Ltd, J Lawson Property Ltd 1965-; chm R Harding (Cookham) Ltd 1985-; pres The Builders Conference 1985; *Books* Computer Aided Estimating (1977); *Recreations* duplicate bridge, Church of England activities; *Clubs* Leander; *Style*— James L Miller, Esq; Nilgiris, Packhorse Road, Gerrards Cross, Bucks SL9 8UE; J Lawson & Co Ltd, 12 Greenock Road, London W3 8DR (☎ 01 992 4821)

MILLER, Lady; Jane Elizabeth Simson; da of Francis Elliott; *m* 1925, Lt-Col Sir James MacBride Miller, MC, TD (d 1977); *Style*— Lady Miller; Duneaton, West Bay Rd, North Berwick, East Lothian (☎ 0620 2756)

MILLER, Air Cdre John; CBE (1966), DFC (1945), AFC (1953); s of John William Miller, of Sprotborough, Yorks; *b* 3 Dec 1921; *Educ* Wath-upon-Dearne GS; *m* 1947, Joan Macgregor (decd); 1 s, 1 da; m 2, 1988, Philippa Anne, da of Maj I S Tailyour;; *Career* Air Cdre RAF (ret); dir: A J Gooding Gp 1982-, Flying Pictures Ltd, Naturestone Ltd, FCA; *Clubs* RAF; *Style*— Air Cdre John Miller, CBE, DFC, AFC; Orchard Close, Pitchcombe, nr Stroud, Glos (☎ 0452 813477)

MILLER, John Albert Peter; s of Albert Ernest Miller (d 1966), of Cornwall, and Irene Gertrude Ann, *née* Viellville; *b* 30 July 1931; *Educ* St Joseph's Coll Beulah Hill, Croydon Art Sch; *Career* Nat Serv Lt RASC 1949-51; painter; exhibitions incl: London, NY, Vancover; recent cmmns incl: Nat Tst and Lord St Levan 10 historical paintings of St Michael's Mount 1979, Dean and Chapter Truro Cathedral Cornubia-Land of Saints 1980 (unveiled by HRH Prince of Wales, portrait of Rt Worship Hon Robert Eliot 1988); sole agent David Messum Gallery 1981-, public collections: Victoria and Albert Museum, Cornwall CC, Avon CC; private collections: TRH Prince and Princess of Wales, TRH Prince and Princess Michael Kent, John Le Carre, Bryan Forbes, Jean Shrimpton, Robin Hanbury Tenison, Nanette Newman, Lady Violet Bonham-Carter; memb Newlyn Soc of Artists (former chm), art conslt Truro Diocesan Advsy ctee; FRSA 1964; *Books* Cooking With Vegetables (with late Marika Hanbury Tenison 1980), Leave Tomorrow Behind (1989); *Recreations* travel, gardens, books; *Style*— John Miller, Esq; Sancreed House, Sancreed, Penzance, Cornwall

MILLER, Sir John Holmes; 11 Bt (E 1705), of Chichester, Sussex; s of Sir Ernest Henry John Miller, 10 Bt (d 1960); *b* 1925; *m* 1950, Jocelyn Edwards; 2 da; *Heir* bro, Harry Holmes Miller; *Style*— Sir John Miller, Bt

MILLER, Air Vice-Marshal John Joseph; CB (1981); s of Frederick George Miller (d April 1985), and Freda Ruth, *née* Haskins (d March 1985); *b* 27 April 1928; *Educ* Portsmouth GS; *m* 10 Nov 1950, Adele Mary, da of Hubert Colleypriest (d 1957); 1 s (Michael b 1960), 2 da (Penelope b 1953, Robin Jennifer b 1958); *Career* RAF 1946-83; barr Gray's Inn 1958; dir Personnel Mgmnt (RAF); MoD 1975-78; ass chief Defence Staff (Personnel and Logistics) 1978-81; dir gen Personal Services (RAF) 1982-83; dir Inst of Personnel Mgmnt 1982-; *Recreations* theatre, music, book collecting; *Clubs* RAF; *Style*— Air Vice-Marshal John Miller, CB; 35 Huntsmans Meadow, Ascot, Berks (☎ 0990 20413); IPM House, Camp Road, Wimbledon SW19 4UN (☎ 01 946 9100, telex 947203 IPMWIM G)

MILLER, Lt-Col Sir John Mansel; GCVO 1987 (KCVO 1974, CVO 1966), DSO (1944), MC (1944); 3 s of Brig-Gen Alfred Douglas Miller, CBE, DSO, JP, DL (d 1933), and Ella Geraldine, *née* Fletcher (d 1935); *b* 4 Feb 1919; *Educ* Eton, RMA Sandhurst; *Career* 2 Lt Welsh Gds 1939, served WW II, ADC to Field Marshal Lord Wilson Washington DC 1945-47, cmd 1 Bn Welsh Gds 1958-61; Crown Equerry 1961-87; Extra Equerry to HM The Queen 1987-; pres: Coaching Club 1975-82, Hackney Horse Soc 1978-80, Nat Light Horse Breeding Soc 1981-82, Br Driving Soc 1982-, Royal Windsor Horse Show Club 1985-, Br Show Jumping Assoc 1989-; patron: Side-Saddle Assoc 1982-, Coloured Horse and Pony Soc 1988-; *Recreations* hunting, shooting, polo, driving; *Clubs* Pratt's, White's; *Style*— Lt-Col Sir John Miller, GCVO, DSO, MC; Shotover House, Wheatley, Oxford OX9 1QS (☎ 086 77 2450)

MILLER, John Tennant; TD (1959); s of William Tennant Miller (d 1968), of Ceylon and Sussex, and Dorothy Elizabeth, *née* White (d 1929); *b* 31 Jan 1923; *Educ* Trinity Coll Glenalmond, Glasgow Univ (BSc); *m* 28 Dec 1950, Wendy Moira, da of Rev Douglas Gordon McLean (d 1985), of East Lothian; 1 s (Ian b 1954), 2 da (Jane b 1951, Anne b 1957); *Career* WWII cmmnd RE 1941, 4 Parachute Sqdn RE 1942-45; 300 Parachute Sqdn RE TA 1950-59 (co 1957-59); Ramsay & Primron (consulting engrs) Glasgow and Edinburgh: jr engr 1951-54, sr engr 1954-63, ptnr 1963-88, ret 1988; vice-chm govrs St Margaret's Sch Newington 1985-87 (memb 1963-87), memb bd of govrs Clifton Hall Sch Newbridge 1985-; fndr memb Woodcutters Cricket Club Edinburgh 1964 (pres 1983-); FIEE 1967, ACE 1969, FRSA 1980; *Recreations* sailing, golf, gardening; *Style*— John Miller, Esq, TD; Sayohana, Links Rd, Longniddry, East Lothian (☎ 0875 52170)

MILLER, Dr Jonathan Wolfe; CBE (1983); s of Emanuel Miller, DPM, FRCP; *b* 21 July 1934; *Educ* St Paul's, St John's Coll Camb (MB, BCh 1959); *m* 1956, Helen Rachel Collet; 2 s, 1 da; *Career* television, theatre and opera director; former res fell History of Medicine UCL; presenter (BBC series) and author The Body in Question 1978; *Style*— Dr Jonathan Miller, CBE; 63 Gloucester Crescent, London NW1

MILLER, Maj Gen Joseph Esmond; MC (1943); s of Col John Francis Xavier Miller, OBE (d 1960), and Margaret, *née* Main (d 1943); *b* 22 Sept 1914; *Educ* St George's Coll Weybridge, Univ of London, St Bart's Hosp Med Coll; *m* 1946, Kathleen Veronica, da of Louis Lochée Bayne (d 1919); 1 s; *Career* cmmnd RAMC 1940, WWII served in N Africa, Sicily, Italy 1943, Holland and Germany 1944; field ambulance cdr 1950, sr med offr RMA Sandhurst 1954, Germany and Aden 1957-61, chief instr RAMC Field Training Centre 1961-65, CO Br Mil Hosp Hong Kong 1965-68; dep dir med servs: BAOR 1969-71, Scotland 1972, HQ UK Land Forces 1972-73; dir med servs UK Land Forces 1973-76, ret; QHS 1973-76; MRCS, LRCP, MFCM, MRCGP; CStJ; *Recreations* golf, gardening; *Style*— Maj-Gen Joseph Miller, MC; The Beechings, Folly CLose, Salisbury, Wilts SP2 8BU (☎ 0722 21423)

MILLER, Dr Kenneth Allan Glen; CBE (1988); s of Dr Allan Frederick Miller (d 1967), of Edinburgh, and Margaret Hutchinson, *née* Glen (d 1971); *b* 27 July 1926; *Educ* Upper Canada Coll Toronto, Trinity Hall Cambridge (BA, MA), Univ Coll of Wales Aberystwyth (PhD); *m* 24 April 1954, Dorothy Elaine, da of Dr Derek G Brown (d 1967), of W Kilbride; 3 s (Andrew b 1955, Ian b 1957, Allan b 1961); *Career* res asst to prof of physics Aberystwyth 1946-49; ICI: various posts on prodn & design Billingham 1949-59, seconded to Br Tport cmmn 1959-60, asst tech mangr heavy organic chemicals div 1960-63, engrg mangr 1963-65, engrg dir 1967-71, engrg advsr to main bd 1971-74; md: APV Ltd 1974-77, APV plc 1977-82; dir gen The Engrg Cncl 1982-88; memb: Ctee for Indust Technol 1972-76, Univ Grants Ctee 1981-83; chm steering ctee for Mfrg Advsy Serv 1977-81, cncl memb Careers Res Advsy Centre 1988-; FIMechE 1965, EEng 1981, CBIM 1985; *Recreations* gardening, photography; *Clubs* Leander; *Style*— Dr Kenneth Miller, CBE; 4 Montrose Gdns, Oxshott, Leatherhead, Surrey KT22 0UU (☎ 0372 842093)

MILLER, Dr Maurice Solomon; JP (Glasgow 1957); s of David Miller (d 1954), of Glasgow, and late Minnie Miller; *b* 16 August 1920; *Educ* Shawlands Acad Glasgow, Glasgow Univ (MB, BS); *m* 1944, Renée, da of Joseph Modlin (d 1956), of Glasgow; 2 s, 2 da; *Career* Fl Lt RAF (medical offr) UK and Italy 1945-47, memb Glasgow Corpn 1950-, baillie of Glasgow 1954-57, MP (Lab): Glasgow Kelvingrove 1964-74, East Kilbride 1974-87; pps to min state for Cwlth Affairs (George Thomas) 1967, asst govt whip 1968-69; *Books* Window on Russia (1956); *Recreations* oil and water colour painting, swimming; *Style*— Dr Maurice Miller, JP, MP; 82 Springkell Ave, Glasgow G41 4EH

MILLER, Michael; RD (1966), QC (1974); s of Lt-Cdr John Brian Peter Duppa-Miller, GC, of Somerset West, Cape Province, South Africa, and The Hon Barbara, *née* Buckmaster (d 1966); *b* 28 June 1933; *Educ* Westminster Sch, Ch Ch Oxford (BA, MA); *m* 18 Oct 1958, Mary Elizabeth, da of Donald Spiers Monteagle Barlow, of Harpenden, Herts; 2 s (George b 1962, Edward b 1970), 2 da (Charlotte b 1959, Alexandra b 1967); *Career* Ordinary Seaman RNVR 1950, Nat Serv 1955-57, cmmnd Sub-Lt RNVR 1956, Lt-Cdr RNR 1973; barr Lincoln's Inn 1958, practicing at Chancery Bar and Int Bar 1959-, bencher 1984, memb Bar Cncl 1988-, assoc memb Hong Kong Bar Assoc 1976-; memb Lab Pty (Kensington) 1964 (tres 1980-84); *Style*— Michael Miller, Esq, RD, QC; 8 Stone Bldgs, Lincolns Inn, London WC2 (☎ 01 242 5002, fax 01 831 8237, telex 268072)

MILLER, Michael Dawson; s of Cyril Gibson Risch Miller, CBE (d 1976), and Dorothy Alice, *née* North-Lewis; *b* 12 Mar 1928; *m* 17 July 1954, Gillian Margaret, da of Dr Eric Gordon-Fleming (d 1948); 3 da (Caroline b 1957, Clare b 1961, Jane b 1961); *Career* Parachute Regt Regulars 1946-48 (TA 1949), HAC 1957-63; articled clerk 1949, practising slr 1954-55, ptnr Thos R Miller & Son 1962- (ptnr Bermuda 1969-, exec 1955-62); dir: AB Indemnitas Stockholm 1983-, Thos Miller War Risks Servs 1985-; Liveryman: Worshipful Co of Shipwrights 1977, Worshipful Co of Solicitors 1986; memb: Law Soc 1954, London Maritime Arbitrators Assoc 1963; Silver Medal Hellenic Merchant Marine Greece 1983; *Recreations* offshore racing, cruising, opera, mountain walking, history, reaching remote places, ancient civilisations, targeting intellectuals; *Clubs* Royal Ocean Racing, Royal Bermuda Yacht, City, Hurlingham; *Style*— Michael Miller, Esq; 52 Scarsdale Villas, London W8 6PP, Dairy Cottage, Donhead, St Andrews, Wilts (☎ 01 937 9935); Thos R Miller & Son, Int House, 26 Creechurch Lane, London EC3A 5BA (☎ 01 283 4646, fax 01 283 5614, telex 885271)

MILLER, Michael George; s of Robert Miller; *b* 17 June 1925; *Educ* Torquay GS, Wales Univ; *m* 1, 1948, Elizabeth Jane (d 1971); 2 da; m 2, 1972, Sadie Lorna; *Career* chartered engr, dir in charge Racal-Decca Serv Ltd 1981-, dir Decca Radar Ltd 1965-

80, serv mangr BAC (GW Div) 1958-63, res offr REME 1944-58; *Recreations* golf; *Clubs* Directors'; *Style*— Michael Miller, Esq; 11 Lyne Place Manor, Bridge Lane, Virginia Water, Surrey (☎ 0932 65532)

MILLER, Michael George; s of George James Miller (d 1977), of Cirencester, and Edith Mary Miller (d 1960); *b* 19 Sept 1927; *Educ* Cirencester GS, RAC; *m* 1957, Elizabeth Mary, JP, da of William Bew Todd (d 1972), of Foston; 2 s, 2 da; *Career* dir Furness Travel Ltd 1973-77, sales mangr Stita Farm Tours 1977-; MRAC; *Recreations* squash, tennis, swimming, walking; *Style*— Michael Miller Esq; Orchard Cottage, Alstone, Tewkesbury, Glos GL20 8JD; Stita Farm Tours, 27 Cambray Place, Cheltenham GL50 1JN (☎ 0242 515712)

MILLER, Hon Mrs (Patricia); *née* Makins; da of 1 Baron Sherfield, GCB, GCMG; *b* 1946; *m* 1966, Michael Ordway Miller, s of Albert O Miller, of Carmel, California; *Style*— The Hon Mrs Miller; 3 Sunset way, Muir Beach, Calif, USA; 1655, Sequoia, Tahoe City, Calif, USA

MILLER, Lady (Beatrix) Patricia; *née* de la Poer Beresford; da of 6 Marquess of Waterford (d 1911); *b* 1902; *m* 1926, Lynden Roberts Miller (d 1973); 1 s, 1 da; *Style*— Lady Patricia Miller; Georgestown House, Kilmacthomas, Co Waterford

MILLER, Sir Peter North; s of Cyril Thomas Gibson Risch Miller, CBE (d 1976), and Dorothy Alice North Miller; *b* 28 Sept 1930; *Educ* Rugby, Lincoln Coll Oxford (MA), City Univ (DEc); *m* 1955, Katharine Mary; 2 s (Richard, Andrew), 1 da (Teresa); m 2, 1979, Boon Lian, *née* Leni; *Career* joined Thos R Miller & Son (Insur) 1953, ptnr 1959, sr ptnr and chm 1971-83; memb Ctee Lloyd's Insur Brokers' Assoc 1973-77, dep chm 1974-75, chm 1976-77; memb: Ctee on Invisible Exports 1975-77, memb Insur Brokers' Registration Cncl 1977-81, memb Ctee of Lloyd's 1977-80, 1982-; chm: Lloyd's 1984, 1985, 1986 and 1987, Br Ctee of Bureau Veritas 1980-; memb HM Commission of Lieutenancy for the City of London; kt 1988; *Recreations* all forms of sport (except cricket), particularly running, riding, tennis and sailing, wine, music, visiting old churches; *Clubs* Brook's, City, Vincent's, Thames Hare and Hounds; *Style*— Sir Peter Miller; Sarratt, Coombe End, Kingston-upon-Thames, Surrey KT2 7DQ; Lloyd's, Lime St, London EC3M 7HL

MILLER, Robert (Robin) Beatson; s of Taverner Barrington Miller, JP (d 1944), of Wadhurst, Sussex, and Catharine Mildred, *née* Beatson (d 1960); *b* 11 Nov 1915; *Educ* Radley, RCM, Royal Sch of Church Music, Hertford Coll Oxford (MA, BMus, ARCO), Yale Univ USA; *m* 1 Aug 1955, Pamela Tregoning, da of Sir Geoffrey Vickers, VC, of Goring-on-Thames; 1 s (Peter Burnell b 1958), 1 da (Anne Tregoning b 1956); *Career* Fl Lt RAFVR 1943-47 (intelligence with Bomber Cmd and and the SE Asia Cmd); organist and choirmaster Philadelphia USA (war serv) 1938-42, asst music master Tonbridge Sch 1947-48, dir of music Ardingly Coll Sussex 1948-53, dir of music Oundle Sch 1954-72; conductor Tunbridge Wells Choral Soc 1948-53, conductor Stamford Choral and Orchestral Soc 1954-64; Liveryman Worshipful Co of Grocers 1964; ISM, Music Masters Assoc (pres 1964, hon sec 1974-79); *Recreations* playing the double bass, gardening, making wine; *Style*— Robin Miller, Esq; Orchard House, 39 Benefield Rd, Oundle, Peterborough PE8 4EU

MILLER, Dr Robert Glendinning; s of Lt-Col Sinclair Miller DSO, MC, MA, BSc, MD, MRCP, DPH (d 1961), of Harrogate, and Norah Isabel (d 1954), da of Rt Hon Robert Graham Glendinning, MP; *b* 24 Dec 1918; *Educ* King James GS Knaresborough, Trinity Hall Cambridge (BA 1940, MB BChir 1942, MA 1944, MD 1962); *m* 19 April 1954, (Alice) Mary Curzon, da of George Molyneux, of Bolton, Lancs; 1 s (Christopher b 1955), 1 da (Elizabeth b 1957); *Career* cmmnd Lt RAMC (War Emergency cmmn) 1943, promoted to Capt 1944; cnslt physician with special interest in Geriatrics Bedford Gp of Hosps; Beds Dist Health Authority 1955-83; hon cnslt in Geriatric Medicine Bedford Gen Hosp 1983-, asst dep coroner Co of Bedford 1982; barr Gray's Inn 1972; pres Bedford Med Soc 1974-75; dep med dir Bedford Gp of Hosps 1966-68; memb N Beds Cncl for Voluntary Services 1970-; vice-pres Bedford and Dist Branch, Burma Star Assoc 1977-82, pres 1982-; *Recreations* gardening, walking, travel, reading; *Style*— Dr Robert Miller; Meadow View, Clapham, Bedford MK41 6EL (☎ 0234 52545)

MILLER, Robert Michael; s of Hugh Begg Miller (d 1979); *b* 4 April 1943; *Educ* Hamilton Acad; *m* 1972, Janis, *née* Fleming; 2 children; *Career* chartered accountant 1968, md The Blackie Publishing Gp 1978-; *Recreations* golf, reading; *Clubs* Caledonian; *Style*— Robert Miller, Esq; 2 Glenburn Rd, Hamilton, Lanarks

MILLER, Robin Anthony; s of William Ernest Alexander Miller, CBE, BEM (d 1970), of Plymouth, Devon, and Winifred Albreta, *née* Tavener; *b* 15 Sept 1937; *Educ* Devonport HS; Wadham Coll Oxford (MA); *m* 25 Aug 1962, Irene Joanna, da of Alistair James Kennedy, MRCVS (d 1977), of Thornhill, Dumfriesshire, Scotland; 2 s (Iain Douglas b 27 Nov 1969, Richard Scott b 23 Nov 1971), 1 da (Helen Cordella b 8 March 1976); *Career* barr Middle Temple 1960; recorder of the Crown Court 1978-; *Style*— Robin A Miller, Esq; St Michael's Lodge, 192 Devonport Rd, Plymouth PL1 5RD (☎ 0751 564943); 2 King's Bench Walk Temple London EC4

MILLER, Roger Geoffrey; s of Robert Ralph Miller; *b* 5 August 1952; *Educ* St Dunstan's Coll London, Trinity Coll Cambridge; *m* 1971, Diana Evelyn, da of late Brig Henry Latham; 3 children; *Career* mgmnt conslt; md RTZ Computer Servs Ltd 1978-; *Recreations* sailing; *Style*— Roger Miller, Esq; 18 Bramcote Rd, London SW15 (☎ 01 788 4309)

MILLER, Roger Simon; s of Rev George Handscomb Miller (d 1980), of Northfield House, Todber, Dorset, and Jean Eileen, *née* Smith (d 1979); *b* 16 Feb 1938; *Educ* Highfield Sch, Harrow, Trinity Coll Oxford (BA); *m* 1, 16 June 1962 (m dis 1976), Sara Elizabeth Battersby, da of Alfred Perceval Athins (ka in Malaya 1942), of Kuala Selangor; 2 da (Caroline b 1964, Anna b 1966); m 2, 27 Oct 1978 (m dis 1988), Roslyn Mary, da of Alfred John Atkinson, of Ryde, IOW; *Career* Nat Serv Lt 3 Greenjackets (The Rifle Bde); Imperial Group Ltd 1966-77, dir Pilgrim Pipe Co 1971-74, proprietor Appleby and McGrath 1977-82, dir Int Mgmt Selection 1980-84, schoolmaster Sunningdale Sch 1981-; party candidate (Lib): Horncastle Linc 1970 and 1974, Weston-super-Mare 1974; area commr St John Ambulance: Avon 1976-79, Wiltshire 1979-81; Freeman City of London, Liveryman Worshipful Co of Carpenters 1959; *Books* Influential Dates in British History (1988); *Recreations* cricket (forestry with Sussex, later Dorset County Clubs), horses (long distance riding and hunting); *Clubs* Nat Lib; *Style*— Roger Simon Miller, Esq; The Hill, Charters Road, Sunningdale, Berkshire (☎ 0990 291116); Sunningdale Sch, Berkshire (☎ 0990 20159)

MILLER, Ronald Kinsman; s of William Miller (d 1986), of Kelvedon, Essex, and Elsie May, *née* Kinsman (d 1956); *b* 12 Nov 1929; *Educ* Colchester Royal GS; *m* 1952, Doris Alice, da of Patrick Dew (d 1984), of Greenwich; 1 s (Timothy John b 1960); 1 da (Felicity Jane b 1958); *Career* Nat Serv RN 1948-50; barr Gray's Inn 1953, entered Inland Revenue Slr Off 1965, Law Offr Dept 1977-79, slr Inland Revenue 1986 (princ asst slr 1981); *Recreations* music, reading, gardening; *Clubs* Athenaeum; *Style*— Ronald K Miller, Esq; 4 Liskeard Close, Chislehurst, Kent BR7 6RT Somerset House, Strand, London WC2R 1LB (☎ 01 438 6645)

MILLER, Dr Roy Frank; s of Thomas Richard Miller (d 1978), and Margaret Ann, *née* Tattum; *b* 20 Sept 1935; *Educ* Wembley Co GS, Univ of Exeter (BSc), Univ of London (PhD); *m* 18 March 1962, Ruth Naomi, da of William Kenchington (d 1957); 1 s (Stephen b 1965); *Career* Royal Holloway Coll: lectr in physics 1960, sr lectr 1972-73, vice- princ 1978, prin 1981-85; vice-princ Royal Holloway and Bedford New Coll 1985-; res assoc Case Western Res Univ Cleveland Ohio 1968-; chm: Inst of Classical Studies and Canterbury Hall Univ of London; tstee and govr Strode's Coll Egham; FInstP 1978, FRSA 1983, CPhys 1986; *Recreations* music, climbing; *Clubs* Athenaeum; *Style*— Dr Roy Miller; Celyn, 3 Parsonage Rd, Englefield Green, Egham, Surrey; RHBNC, Egham, Surrey TW20 OEX (☎ 0784 34455, fax 0784 37520)

MILLER, Sir Stephen James Hamilton; KCVO (1979); s of Stephen Miller; *b* 19 July 1915; *Educ* Arbroath HS, Univ of Aberdeen (MD); *m* 1949, Heather Prudence Motion; 3 s; *Career* ophthalmic surgn: St George's Hosp 1951-80, Nat Hosp Queen Sq 1955-78, King Edward VII Hosp for Offrs; surgn Moorfields Eye Hosp 1954-80; surgn-oculist to: HM's Household 1965-74, HM The Queen 1974-80; hospitaller St John Opthalmic Hosp Jerusalem 1980-; chm and tstee The Frost Fndn; tstee Smith and Nephew Fndn, vice-chm Iris Fund, memb Cncl of the Guide Dogs for the Blind; Freeman City of London, Liveryman Worshipful Soc of Apothecaries; FRCS; KStJ 1978, GCStJ 19878; *Books* Clinical Ophthalmology (1987); *Recreations* golf, fishing, music; *Clubs* Caledonian, Muirfield, Woking Golf; *Style*— Sir Stephen Miller, KCVO; Sherma Cottage, Pond Rd, Woking, Surrey GU22 0JT (☎ 048 62 62287); 123 Harley St, London W1N 1HE (☎ 01 935 4488)

MILLER, Stewart Crichton; s of William Young Crichton Miller (d 1964), of Kirkcaldy, Fife, and Grace Margaret, *née* Finlay; *b* 2 July 1934; *Educ* Kirkcaldy HS Univ of Edinburgh (BSc); *m* 25 June 1960, Catherine Proudfoot, da of Alexander McCourtie (d 1957), 2 s (David b 1963, Gordon b 1965), 2 da (Sarah b 1970, Lucy b 1971); *Career* joined Rolls Royce 1954, held various appts in technology, design and devpt; chief engr RB211-535 1977-84, dir advanced engrg 1984-85; dir engrg and bd memb 1985-; memb various ctees MOD and DTI; FEng 1987, FRAeS 1986, FIMechE 1987; *Recreations* music, walking; *Style*— Stewart Miller, Esq; Rolls Royce plc, 65 Buckingham Gate, London SW1E 6AT (☎ 01 222 9020, telex 918 091)

MILLER, Timothy Peter Francis; s of Col John Francis Miller, of Camberley, Surrey, and Barbara Mary, *née* Cooke; *b* 9 Nov 1940; *Educ* Douai Sch, Magdalen Coll Oxford (MA); *m* 12 Nov 1965, Lisa, da of Glyn Beynon Davies (d 1979); 2 s (Charles b 1977, Alexander b 1983), 2 da (Lucasta b 1966, Cressida b 1968); *Career* md Framlington Gp plc 1983-88 (dir 1979-88), dir M & G Gp plc parly candidate (C) Hackney North and Stoke Newington 1979; tstee: Child Psychotherapy Tst;; *Recreations* opera, cycling, books, motor sport; *Clubs* Beefsteak, City of London, MCC; *Style*— Timothy Miller, Esq; 9 Bartholomew Villas, London NW5 2LJ (☎ 01 485 7294); M & G Group plc, Three Quays, Tower Hill, London EC 6BQ (☎ 01 626 4588)

MILLER JONES, Hon Mrs (Betty Ellen); da of 1 and last Baron Askwith, KCB, KC (d 1942), and late Baroness Askwith, CBE, *née* Peel; *b* 26 June 1909; *Educ* Lycée Français London; *m* 1950, Keith Miller Jones (d 1978); *Career* author; FRSL; *Style*— The Hon Mrs Miller Jones; 9/105 Onslow Sq, London SW7 (☎ 01 589 7126)

MILLER MUNDY, Andrew Godfrey; s of Maj Edward Peter Godfrey Miller Mundy, MC (d 1981), and Margaret Cecil Wallace, *née* Clarke (d 1985); *b* 21 Dec 1944; *Educ* Eton; *m* 20 April 1972, Bridget Anne Geraldine, da of Brig Michael David Lindsay Gordon-Watson, OBE, MC, of Cranborne, Dorset; 1 s (Rory b 1977), 1 da (Flora b 1974); *Career* 9/12 Royal Lancers 1963-66; *Recreations* shooting, fishing, hawking, painting, flirting; *Style*— Andrew G Miller Mundy, Esq; Flodaby, Isle of Harris, Western Isles (☎ 085 983 234)

MILLER MUNDY, Lady Bridget; *née* Elliot-Murray-Kynynmound; da of 5 Earl of Minto (d 1975); *b* 1921; *m* 1, 1944 (m dis 1954), Lt-Col James Averell Clark, Jr, DFC, USAF; 1 s; m 2, 1954 (m dis 1963), Maj Henry Lyon Garnett, CBE; m 3, 1966 (m dis 1970), Maj (Edward) Peter Godfrey Miller Mundy, MC (d 1981); *Style*— Lady Bridget Miller Mundy

MILLER OF GLENLEE, Sir (Frederick William) Macdonald; 7 Bt (GB 1788), of Glenlee, Kirkcudbrightshire; s of Sir Alastair George Lionel Joseph Miller of Glenlee, 6 Bt (d 1964), and his 1 w, Kathleen (d 1978), yr da of Stephen G Howard, CBE, JP, DL, MP Sudbury 1919-22; Sir Macdonald is descended from Sir William Miller of Glenlee, 2 Bt, who as a Lord of Session took the title Lord Glenlee and d 1846; Sir Thomas, 1 Bt (d 1789) was Lord Pres of the Ct of Session, with the courtesy title of Lord Barskimming; *b* 21 Mar 1920; *Educ* Tonbridge; *m* 2 Sept 1947, Marion Jane Audrey, o da of late Richard Spencer Pettit, of Sudbury, Suffolk; 1 s, 1 da; *Heir* s, Stephen William Macdonald Miller of Glenlee; *Career* served 1939-43: Beds and Herts Regt 1940, Black Watch 1941-42, RAC 1943; Cons agent for: Whitehaven Div of Cumberland 1947-50, Wembley North 1950-52, N Norfolk 1952-65, Lowestoft (renamed Waveney) 1965-82; Suffolk Cons Euro agent 1980-82, political conslt 1982-85; dep Traffic cmmr 1974-85; memb: Eastern Sea Fisheries Jt Ctee 1981-86 (chm 1981-83), Suffolk Family Practitioners Ctee 1982-; chm Suffolk CC 1988-89 (vice-chm 1986-88, chm educn ctee 1985-88, memb 1977-); *Recreations* gardening; *Style*— Sir Macdonald Miller of Glenlee, Bt; Ivy Grange Farm, Westhall, Halesworth, Suffolk (☎ 098 681 265)

MILLER OF GLENLEE, Dr Stephen William Macdonald; s and h of Sir Macdonald Miller of Glenlee, 7 Bt; *b* 20 June 1953; *Educ* Rugby, St Bartholomew's Hosp (MB, BS); *m* 1978, Mary Carolyn, o da of G B Owens, of Huddersfield; 1 s (James b 1981), 1 da (Katherine b 1983); *Career* LMSSA, FRCS; *Style*— Dr Stephen Miller of Glenlee; Fairview Cottage, New Road, Rumburgh, Suffolk

MILLES-LADE, Lady Diana; da of Hon Henry Augustus Milles-Lade, JP (d 1937), and sis of 4 Earl Sondes; *b* 1919; *Career* granted 1942, rank, title and precedence as an Earl's da which would have been hers had her father survived to succeed to the title; *Style*— Lady Diana Milles-Lade; 37 Lennox Gdns, SW1

MILLETT, Anthony Derek; s of Denis Millett (d 1965), of 45 Grosvenor Sq, London W1, and Adele, of 36 Curzon St; *b* 20 April 1936; *Educ* Harrow; *Career* chm and md

Millett Stores Ltd; dir: Black & Edgington Ltd, Gaiety Theatre; *Recreations* cricket, theatre, old films, Churchilliana; *Clubs* MCC, Butterflies, Harrow Wanderers, Gentlemen of Leicestershire, Middlesex County Cricket; *Style*— Anthony Millett, Esq; 62c Old Brompton Rd, London SW7 3LQ (☎ 01 584 4978); Black & Edgington Ltd, 53/54 Rathbone Place, London W1

MILLETT, The Hon Mr Justice; Hon Sir Peter Julian Millett; s of Denis Millett (d 1965), of London, and Adele Millett, *née* Weinberg; *b* 23 June 1932; *Educ* Harrow, Trinity Hall Cambridge (MA); *m* 1959, Ann Mireille, da of David Harris (d 1980), of London; 3 s (Richard, Andrew, Robert d 1965); *Career* standing jnr counsel to BOT and Dept of Trade and Indust 1967-73; Bencher Lincoln's Inn 1980, memb Insolvency Law Review Ctee 1977-82, High Ct Judge Chancery Div (1986), QC (1973), kt (1986); *Style*— The Hon Sir Peter Millett; 18 Portman Close, London W1H 9HJ (☎ 01 935 1152); Kewhurst Ave, Cooden, Sussex (☎ 04243 2970)

MILLETT, Robert David; VRD; s of Douglas Gladstone Millett (d 1980), of 23 St Lucia, West Parade, Bexhill-on-Sea, Sussex, and Mary Ann Elizabeth Coffer, *née* Manclarke; *b* 3 Jan 1930; *Educ* City of London Sch, Peterhouse Cambridge (MA, LLB); *m* 31 Aug 1957, Margaret (Peggy) Pettigrew Brownlie, da of William Smith (d 1970); *Career* Nat Serv RN 1949-50, RNVR then RNR London Div, ret cdr (supply branch) 1976; admitted slr 1956; Lewis and Dick: articled (London) 1953-56, asst slr (Ewell) 1956-59, ptnr (Surrey) 1960-, currently sr ptnr (Surrey and Sussex); pres Nat Chamber of Trade (bd memb and chm legislation and taxation ctee until 1987); former: pres Rotary Club of Ewell 1967-68, pres Mid Surrey Law Soc 1983, chm Ewell C of C, chm Surrey Cncl Nat Chamber of Trade, govr Glynn Sch Ewell; Freeman City of London, Liveryman Worshipful Co of Scriveners; memb: HAC, Law Soc; *Recreations* photography, stamp collecting, railways; *Clubs* RAC, Wardroom Mess HMS President; *Style*— Robert Millett, Esq, VRD; Craigmore, 35 Golfside, Cheam Surrey; (☎ 01 643 7761); 12a Wellswood Park, Wellswood, Torquay, South Devon; 443 Kingston Rd, Ewell, Epsom, Surrey (☎ 01 393 0055)

MILLIGAN, Air Cdre Frederick Moir; CBE (1977, OBE 1951), AFC (1942); s of Dr Wyndham Anstruther Milligan (d 1950), of London W1, and Eleanor Nystrom (d 1920); *b* 24 Sept 1915; *Educ* Sherborne, King's Coll London; *m* 2 June 1938, Mollie, da of Clifford Stanley Ickringill (d 1983), of Keighley, Yorks; 1 da (Ann b 1939); *Career* cmmnd RAF 1935, served Egypt 1935-40, flying inst UK and Canada 1940-42, CO 90 and 623 Sqdn Bomber Cmmnd (despatches) 1943-48, Far East RAF 1948-51, seconded Cabinet Off 1951-54, CO RAF Bassingbourn 1954-56, chief air plans Operation Grapple, Christmas Island 1956-57; IDC 1958, chief of staff and air attaché British Jt Services Mission (RAF Staff) Washington 1959-61; ADC Central Reconnaissance Estab 1961-64, ret 1964; sec: The Rayne Fndn, The Rayne Charitable Tst 1964-83; tstee The Rayne Fndn 1983-; *Recreations* travel; *Style*— Air Cdre Frederick Milligan, CBE, AFC; 11/2 Eglinton Crescent, Edinburgh EH12 5DD (☎ 031 225 5951)

MILLIGAN, George William Elliott; s of George Burn Milligan (d 1985), of Tullochard, Kingussie, and Kathleen Dorothea Milligan; *b* 2 April 1945; *Educ* Trinity Coll Glenalmond, Univ Coll Oxford (BA), Glasgow Univ (MEng), Cambridge Univ (PhD); *m* 18 July 1986, Baroness Barbara Wanda Borowska, da of Baron Tadeusz Borowski, and Countess Janina, step da of Herbert Charles Story, of Tunbridge Wells; 2 s (Robert George b 1968, Jan Charles b 1970);; *Career* chartered Civil Engnr, Lectr Oxford Univ and tutor and fellow of Magdalen Coll Oxford 1979-, author of tech papers on Soil Mechanics and co-author of books on Basic Soil Mechanics and Reinforced Soil;; *Recreations* golf, walking, fishing, music; *Style*— Dr George W E Milligan; 9 Lathbury Road, Oxford OX2 7AT (☎ 0865 58558, 0865 273137); Dept of Engineering Science, Parks Road, Oxford OX1 3PJ

MILLIGAN, Terence Alan (Spike); s of Capt Leo Alphonso Milligan MSM, RA (d 1969), and Florence Winifred, *née* Kettleband; 4 generations RA Indian Army including Indian Mutiny; *b* 16 April 1918; *Educ* Convent Jesus and Mary Poona, St Paul's Christian Brothers de la Salle Rangoon, SE London Poly; *m* 1, 1952, June Angela, da of Richard Marlowe; 1 s (Séan b 1954), 2 da (Laura b 1952, Silé b 1957); m 2, 1962, Patricia (d 1978), da of Capt William Ridgway; 1 da (Jane b 1966); m 3, 1983, Shelagh, da of Col Gordon Sinclair; *Career* WWII, RA, N Africa, Italy; factory worker, van boy, stockroom asst, asst, stationery salesman, semi-pro musician, radio script writer, solo comic, musical comedy trio; TV script writer, author, poet, illustrator, painter, composer; *Recreations* reading war histories, biographies, dining and wining, squash; *Clubs* Ronnie Scotts (life memb); *Style*— Spike Milligan, Esq; Carpenters Meadows, Dumbwoman's Lane, Udimore Rye, Sussex TN31 6AD; 9 Orme Court, Bayswater, London W2 (☎ 01 727 1544)

MILLIGAN, Wyndham Macbeth Moir; MBE (1945), TD (1947); s of Wyndham Anstruther Milligan, MD, FRCS (d 1950), and Helen Eleonore, *née* Nyström (d 1920); *b* 21 Dec 1907; *Educ* Sherborne, Gonville and Caius Coll Cambridge (MA); *m* 27 Dec 1941, Helen Penelope Eirene, da of John Demetrius Cassavetti (d 1960); 2 s (David Wyndham Anstruther b 1945, Iain Anstruther b 1950, Niall Fraser b 1956), 2 da (Fiona Katharine b 1944, Rosemary Jane b 1948); *Career* WW II served Scots Guards (Maj) in Europe 1939-45; asst master Eton Coll 1932-39, housemaster Eton 1946-54; Warden Radley Coll 1954-68; Princ of Wolsey Hall Oxford 1968-80; FRSA 1968; *Recreations* gardening, sketching, reading; *Style*— Wyndham M M Milligan, Esq, MBE, TD; Church Hill House, Stalbridge, by Sturminster Newton, Dorset DT10 2LR (☎ 0963 62815)

MILLING, Henry Miles; s of late Henry Robert Milling; *b* 30 Nov 1934; *Educ* Oundle, Imperial Coll London; *m* 1968, Ann Cartledge, née Bradbury; 2 da; *Career* marketing dir Fairey Engrg 1978-, head of sales and marketing NEI Int Combustion 1975-78, proposals mangr GEC Power Station Projects 1970-75; *Recreations* sailing, tennis, golf, skiing; *Style*— Henry Milling, Esq; Beech Tree House, Davenport Lane, Mobberley, Knutsford, Cheshire

MILLN, Hon Mrs (Susan Margaret); *née* Annesley; 2 da of 14 Viscount Valentia, MC, MRCS, LRCP (d 1983; he established his succession 1959 after title had become dormant in 1951 - had not been proved since 1844 when the 9 Viscount died), and Joan, Viscountess Valentia (d 1986); *b* 18 Feb 1931; *Educ* Byculla; *m* 1954, Peter Lindsay Milln, s of Alexander Lindsay Milln (d 1932); 1 s (Jeremy), 3 da (Teresa, Eleanor, Jesica); *Career* landowner; *Recreations* riding, sailing, (yacht 'Slip-Shod'), gardening; *Style*— The Hon Mrs Milln; Bosinver, St Austell, Cornwall (☎ 0726 72128)

MILLNER, Brian David; s of Edwin Millner (d 1932); *b* 7 Oct 1930; *Educ* Scarborough HS, Cambridge Univ (MA); *m* 1956, Adina Josephine, *née* Tonn; 1 s, 1 da; *Career* sundry Pilkington Gp Appointments 1954-73, marketing mangr Chance Pilkington 1973-79, dir 1979-80; dir: Chance (Optical) Ltd 1976-80; Chance Pilkington KK (Japan) 1977-80, Gp public affairs advsr Pilkington plc 1980-; *Recreations* motoring, gardening, reading, travel; *Style*— Brian Millner, Esq; 3 Church Walk, Tarleton, Lancs (☎ 0772 814811); Pilkington plc, Prescot Rd, St Helens, Merseyside WA10 3TT (☎ 0744 692313)

MILLNER, William Frank (Tim); s of William Millner (d 1982), and Una Mary, *née* Wallis; *b* 4 Jan 1932; *Educ* St Paul's, St Thomas's Hosp Med Sch (MB BS); *m* 1, 31 March 1959 (m dis 1984), Patricia Jane Elizabeth, *née* James; 2 s (Russell William James b 1960, Justin Christie James b 1962); m 2, 18 Feb 1984, Margaret-Ann (Maggie), da of James Robin Streather; 1 da (Lucinda Ann Streather b 1984); *Career* surgn Lt RN 1957-62, MO HMS Resolution Christmas Island Grapple Sqdn (nuclear testing) 1958-59, Families MO HMS Terror Singapore 1959-61; orthopaedic surgn and conslt N Herts Health Authy 1972-; memb NW Thames RHA 1978-86; FRCS, FRCSE; *Recreations* watching rugby; *Clubs* Royal Soc of Medicine, Old Pauline; *Style*— Tim Millner, Esq; Radwell Dene, Radwell, Baldock, Herts S97 5ES (☎ 0462 730478); 10 Harly St, London W1 (☎ 01 580 4280)

MILLS, Barbara Jean Lyon; QC (1986); da of John Lyon Warnock, and Nora Kitty Warnock; *b* 10 August 1940; *Educ* St Helen's Sch Northwood Middx, Lady Margaret Hall Oxford (MA); *m* 1962, John Angus Donald Mills, s of Kenneth McKenzie Mills; 1 s (Peter b 1971), 3 da (Sarah b 1962, Caroline b 1965, Lizzie b 1969); *Career* barr Middle Temple 1963; Recorder 1981-;; *Style*— Mrs Barbara J L Mills, QC; 3 Temple Gardens, Temple, London EC4 (☎ 01 353 3533)

MILLS, Maj Bernard Herbert Gordon; CBE (1989); s of James Gordon Coleman Mills (d 1959), and Ellen, *née* Goodson (d 1974); *b* 21 Feb 1932; *Educ* St John's Sch Leatherhead, RMA Sandhurst, Queens' Coll Cambridge (MA); *Career* enlisted RAC 1950; cmmnd Suffolk Regt 1952 served: Trieste, Germany, Cyprus; 22 SAS Regt 1955-57 Malaya, HQ 4 Div Germany 1959-60, 1 Royal Anglian Regt 1960-62 Berlin and UK, Muscat Regt Sultan of Oman's Armed Forces 1962-64, ret 1964; political advsr; Govt Kingdom of Yemen 1964-67, Govt Kingdom of Saudi Arabia 1967-69; field dir Nigeria Save the Children Fund 1969-70, del (later chief del) Int Union for Child Welfare in Nigeria East Pakistan and Bangladesh 1970-74, dir Duranton Ltd (Antony Gibbs Gp) 1975-79, Cambridge Univ (student); UN Relief and Works Agency: offr i/c Central Lebanon Area 1982-83, asst dir i/c operation South Lebanon 1983-85, dep dir Jordan 1985-86, dir ops Gaja and rep Egypt 1986-88; currently dir Bernard Mills Conslts Ltd; *Recreations* walking, conversation; *Clubs* Special Forces; *Style*— Maj Bernard Mills, CBE; 2 The Maltings, Walsham-le-Willows, Bury St Edmunds, Suffolk IP31 3BD (☎ 03598 8830); Flat 7, 71 Charlwood St, London SW1Y 4PG (☎ 01 630 7227)

MILLS, Hon Catherine Gray; da of 4 Baron Hillingdon; *b* 18 Sept 1963; *Style*— The Hon Catherine Mills

MILLS, Vice Adm Sir Charles Piercy; KCB (1968, CB 1964), CBE (1957), DSC (1953); s of Capt Thomas Piercy Mills (d 1944), of Woking, and Eleanor May Mills (d 1978); *b* 4 Oct 1914; *Educ* RNC Dartmouth; *m* 1944, Anne, da of Cecil Francis Cumberlege (d 1975); 2 da; *Career* joined RN 1928, served WW II (despatches), Korea 1950-52, Capt 1953, Suez Operations 1956, Rear Adm 1963, Vice Adm 1966, Flag Offr 2 i/c Far East Fleet 1966-67; C-in-C Plymouth 1967-69, Lt-Govr and C-in-C Guernsey 1969-74; KStJ 1969; *Recreations* golf, yachting; *Style*— Vice Adm Sir Charles Mills, KCB, CBE, DSC; Park Lodge, Aldeburgh, Suffolk (☎ 072 885 2115)

MILLS, Christopher David; s of Fred Mills, of 64 St Anthony Rd, Sheffield, and Grace Amy, *née* Milner (d 1976); *b* 15 April 1949; *Educ* Abbeydale Boys' GS, London Univ (LLB); *m* 24 Oct 1984, (Diane) Elizabeth, da of Eric Skuse; 1 da (Harriet Elisheba Christy); *Career* barr Inner Temple 1972, memb: RSPB, Sorby Nat History Soc; *Recreations* walking, birdwatching, badminton; *Style*— Christopher D Mills, Esq; Little Ranah Farm, Whams Rd, Sheffield, S30 5HJ: 19 Figtree Lane, Sheffield, S1 2DJ (☎ 0742 759 708, 01 738 380)

MILLS, 3 Viscount (UK 1962); Sir Christopher Philip Roger Mills; 3 Bt (UK 1953); also Baron Mills (UK 1957); o s of 2 Viscount Mills (d 1988); *b* 20 May 1956; *m* 29 March 1980, Lesley A, er da of Alan Bailey, of Lichfield, Staffs; *Style*— The Rt Hon Viscount Mills

MILLS, Colin James Edmund; s of James Oliver Mills (d 1986), of Holcot, Northamptonshire, and Ada *née* Cox; *b* 28 Nov 1937; *Educ* Northampton GS, Leicester Sch of Architecture (Dip Arch); *m* 2 Sept 1961, Eileen Patricia, da of Charles Frederick Swain (d 1926); 1 s (James b 1965), 3 da (Kathryn b 1967, Rosalind b 1969, Clare b 1982); *Career* chartered architect; ptnr, Morrison & Partners, dir Morrison Design Partnership 1977-86, princ Colin J E Mills 1986-; *Recreations* painting, ornithology, philately, reading; *Style*— Colin Mills, Esq; Chevindalo, 474 Duffield Rd, Allestree, Derby DE3 2DJ (☎ 0332 558805)

MILLS, Cdr Denis Woolnough; CBE (1988, OBE 1970), DSC (1943); s of Paymaster Lt Walter Thomas Mills, RNR (d 1955), of Chatham, and Gertrude Ethel, *née* Coomber (d 1978); *b* 31 July 1920; *Educ* Kings Sch Rochester; *m* 1, 1942 (m dis 1948), Deidre Murchie; 2 s (Michael, Nigel); m 2, 1948 (m dis 1960), Lucille Roberta Farnhill; 1 s (Paul), 1 da (Virginia); m 3, 19 Dec 1960, (Eileen) Mary, da of Cecil Surry of Portsmouth (d 1978); *Career* cadet RN HMS Erebus and Vindictive 1937-38, Midshipman HMS Revenge and Ramillies 1938-40, Sub Lt HMS Birmingham and submarine offrs trg class 1940, HM submarines Cachalot, H43, Clyde 1941-42 (Lt 1941), 1 Lt HM submarine Thunderbolt 1942-43, Cmd HM submarines Sea Wolf, Sea Devil, Surf, Auriga, Aeneas 1943-48, Underwater Detection Estab Portland 1949-50 (Lt Cdr 1949), HMS Theseus (Korea) 1950-51, CO HM submarine Telemachus 1951-52, ops offr 4 Sub Sqdn Sydney 1952-53, RN staff course, Greenwich 1953-54, ops offr, 1 Sub Sqdn Med 1954-56 (Cdr 1956), plans and intelligence offr staff of Flag Officer Submarines 1956-59, plans offr staff of C-in-C Eastern Atlantic Area 1959-61, exec offr HMS Ausonia 1961-63, Polaris Exec 1963-65, personnel offr staff of Flag Offr Submarines 1965-70; mgmnt and devpt Br Steel Corpn 1970-80; memb ctee Teeside branch IPM 1973-81 (hon sec 1973-76), co-fndr Assoc of Mgmnt Insts on Teeside 1973 (ctee 1973-81, hon tres 1973-76); hon tres Middlesbrough Cons Assoc (also hon sec 1983-88 and election agent 1983-89; FIPM (hon life), MBIM; *Recreations* golf; *Clubs* Naval; *Style*— Cdr Denis Mills, CBE, DSC, RN

MILLS, Edward David William; CBE (1959); s of late Edward Ernest Mills; *b* 19 Mar 1915; *Educ* Regent St Polytechnic Sch of Architecture; *m* 1939, Elsie May, da of late W Bryant; 1 s, 1 da; *Career* chartered architect and design conslt; sr ptnr Edward

D Mills and Ptnrs Architects; patron Society of Architectural Illustrators 1986-; chm Faculty of Architecture Br Sch at Rome; author, including books on architecture; Alfred Bossom Res fell of Royal Inst of Br Architects, Churchill Fell 1969; FRIBA, FSIA, FRSA; *Recreations* photography, writing, travel; *Style—* Edward Mills, Esq, CBE; Gate Hse Farm, Newchapel, Lingfield, Surrey RH7 6LF (☎ 0342 832 241; off: 01 437 8305/6)

MILLS, Sir Frank; KCVO (1983), CMG (1971); s of Joseph Francis Mills; *b* 1923; *Educ* King Edward VI Sch Nuneaton, Emmanuel Coll Cambridge; *m* 1953, Trilby Foster; 1 s, 2 da; *Career* diplomatic serv; high cmmr in Ghana 1975-78, dir of communications 1978-81, high cmmr in Bangladesh 1981-83; chm Camberwell Health Authy 1984-; chm Royal Cwlth Soc for the Blind 1985-; *Style—* Sir Frank Mills, KCVO, CMG; 14 Sherborne Road, Chichester, Sussex PO19 3AA

MILLS, Maj-Gen Giles Hallam; CB (1977), CVO (1984), OBE (1964); s of Col Sir John Digby Mills (d 1972), of Bisterne, Ringwood; *b* 1 April 1922; *Educ* Eton; *m* 1947, Emily Snowden Hallam, da of Capt William Hallam Tuck, of Maryland USA; 2 s, 1 da; *Career* 2 Lt KRRC 1941, served WW II in N Africa and Italy (despatches), 2 Green Jackets 1962, Lt-Col 1963, Col 1966, Brig 1967, Maj-Gen 1974, Dir of Manning 1974-77, ret; Maj and resident govr HM Tower of London and Keeper of the Jewel House 1979-84, ret; *Recreations* history, country activities; *Clubs* Army and Navy; *Style—* Maj-Gen Giles Mills, CB, CVO, OBE; Leeland Ho, Twyford, Winchester, Hants SO1 1NP (☎ 0962 713298)

MILLS, Lady; Hilda Grace Shirley; da of H Gavin Young; *m* 1940, as his 2 w, Maj-Gen Sir Arthur Mordaunt Mills, CB, DSO (d 1964); *Style—* Lady Mills; 29 Normans, Norman Rd, Winchester

MILLS, Iain Campbell; MP (C) Meriden 1979-; s of John Steel Mills and Margaret Leitch; *b* 21 April 1940; *Educ* Prince Edward Sch Salisbury, Rhodesia; *m* 1971, Gaynor Lynne Jeffries; *Career* Dunlop: Rhodesia 1961-64, UK 1964-79; sec to Cons Tport Ctee 1979-81; pps to: min state Indust 1981-82, sec state Employment 1982-85, Sec of State for Trade and Indust 1983-85, Chllr of the Duchy of Lancaster, chm Cons Party 1985-87; memb The Development Select Cttee 1987-; *Clubs* Carlton, House of Commons Yacht; *Style—* Iain Mills, Esq, MP; House of Commons, London SW1

MILLS, Hon Jessica Anne; da of 4 Baron Hillingdon; *b* 1 April 1957; *Style—* The Hon Jessica Mills

MILLS, Joan, Viscountess; Joan Dorothy Mills; da of James Shirreff, of London; *m* 6 Oct 1945, 2 Viscount Mills (d 1988); 1 s (3 Viscount, *qv*), 2 da (Felicity (Hon Mrs Pickford) b 1947, Phillipa (Hon Mrs Arthurton) b 1950); *Style—* The Rt Hon Joan, Viscountess Mills; Whitecroft, 24 Abbey Road, Knaresborough, N Yorks HG5 8HY (☎ 0423 866201)

MILLS, Sir John Lewis Ernest Watts; CBE (1960); *b* 22 Feb 1908; *Educ* Norwich; *m* 1941, Mary Hayley Bell, playwright; 1 s, 2 da; *Career* actor (won Academy Award Oscar 1971 as best supporting actor, for his part in Ryan's Daughter), producer, director; memb Cncl of RADA 1965-; chm of the Stars Organisation for Spastics for 3 yrs; pres Mountview Theatre Sch; kt 1976; *Books* Up in the Clouds, Gentlemen Please (autobiography); *Recreations* golf, painting; *Clubs* Garrick, St James's (chm); *Style—* Sir John Mills, CBE; c/o ICM, 388/396 Oxford St, London W1

MILLS, John Micklethwait; TD; s of Col Sir John Digby Mills, TD (d 1972), and Carola Marshall, *née* Tuck; *b* 29 Nov 1919; *Educ* Eton, Ch Ch Oxford (MA); *m* 2 Nov 1960, Mrs Prudence Mercy Emmeline Cooper-Key, da of Sir Ronald Wilfred Matthews (d 1959); 1 s (John b 1961); *Career* WWII 2 Lt Hampshire Regt 1939, 7 Commando Bardia and Crete, Warwicks Yeo M East and Italy, Capt 1943, Maj 1945; chm W Hants Water Co (dir 1948-), appointed by Miny of Agric Avon and Dorset River Bd 1959 (subseqently elected dep chm 1963); Wessex Water Authy 1974-: chm quality advsy panel 1974-83, chm regnl fishery ctee 1974-, pollution control ctee 1988-; JP 1948, High Sheriff Hants 1958, DL 1970, Verderer of the New Forest 1960-64, memb Ringwood RDC 1968-74, chm Ringwood bench 1979-84, pres Hampshire branch Country Landowners Assoc 1982-87 (chm 1967-70), fndr memb Timber Growers Orgn 1960 (chm Southern Region 1960-65); ARICS 1948; *Recreations* shooting, fishing; *Clubs* White's, MCC; *Style—* John Mills, Esq, TD; Bisterne Manor, nr Ringwood, Hampshire BH24 3BN (☎ 0425 474246); 69 Porchester Terr, London W2

MILLS, Maj John Rice Francis; s of Lt-Col Frank Mills, DSO (d 1945); *b* 18 Jan 1921; *Educ* Harrow; *m* 1968, Matilda, da of Lt Col William Warburton Hayes, JP, DL (d 1953);; *Career* Royal Welch Fusiliers 1941-42, Kings African Rifles 1942-47, game warden and Nat Park warden Uganda 1948-62, high sheriff Anglesey 1966; *Recreations* training and working labrador retrievers, fishing; *Style—* Major John Mills; Rhiwlas, Pentraeth, Anglesey, Gwynedd LL75 8YG (☎ 024 870 204)

MILLS, Leif Anthony; s of Victor William Mills (d 1967), and Bergliot, *née* Ström-Olsen; *b* 25 Mar 1936; *Educ* Kingston GS, Balliol Coll Oxford (BA); *m* 2 Aug 1958, Gillian Margaret, da of William Henry Smith (d 1966); 2 s (Adam, Nathaniel), 2 da (Susannah, Harriet); *Career* 2 Lt Royal Mil Polic e 1957-59; Nat Union of Bank Employees 1960-: res offr 1960-62, asst gen sec 1962-68, dep gen sec 1968-72, gen sec 1972-; parly candidate (Lab) contested: Salisbury gen election 1964, Salisbury by election 1968; TUC: memb Non Manual Workers Advsy Ctee 1967-72, memb Gen Cncl 1983-, chm Fin Servs Ctee 1983; memb: off of Manpower Econs Advsy Ctee on Equal Pay 1971, Ctee to Review the Functioning of Fin Insts (Wilson Ctee) 1977-80, Civil Serv Pay Res Unit Bd 1978-81, BBC Consultative Gp on Social Effects of TV 1978-80, Armed Forces Pay Review Body 1980-87, Monopolies and Mergers Cmmn 1982-, TUC ctees and int ctees of FIET; *Recreations* rowing, chess; *Clubs* Oxford and Cambridge, Weybridge Rowing; *Style—* Leif Mills, Esq; 31 Station Road, West Byfleet, Surrey (☎ 09323 42829); Sheffield House, 1b Amity Grove, Raynes Park, London SW20 OLG (☎ 01 946 9151, fax 01 879 3728)

MILLS, Lady; Mary Austen; da of Sydney Austen Smith; *m* 1926, Air Chief Marshal Sir George Holroyd Mills, GCB, DFC (d 1971); *Style—* Lady Mills; c/o Lloyds Bank, 6 Pall Mall, SW1

MILLS, Michael Victor Leighton; s and h of Sir Peter Frederick Leighton Mills, 3 Bt; *b* 30 August 1957; *Style—* Michael Mills Esq; 15 Paul Place, Paul Ave, Dayan Glen, 1460, Johannesburg, Transvaal, S Africa

MILLS, Neil McLay; s of Leslie Hugh Mills (d 1980) and Gwladys (d 1982); *b* 29 July 1923; *Educ* Epsom Coll, London Univ; *m* 1950, Rosamund Mary, da of Col A C W Kimpton, of Pythouse, Tisbury, Wilts; 2 s, 2 da; *Career* served WWII Lt RNVR (despatches 1944); Lloyd's Insur Broker; chm: Bland Welch & Co 1965-74, Bland Payne Hldgs 1974-79, Sedgwick Forbes Bland Payne 1979-80, Sedgwick Gp plc 1980-84; dir: Midland Bank Ltd 1974-79, Wadlowgrosvenor Int Ltd 1984-88, Citicorp Insur Gp Inc 1985, Polly Peck Int plc 1985-, AVI Ltd 1986-; cncl memb Oak Hill Theological Coll 1958-62, vice pres Insur Inst of London 1971-84, tstee and govr Lord Mayor Treloar Tst 1975-81; *Recreations* mowing; *Clubs* City of London, Pilgrims; *Style—* Neil McLay Mills, Esq; The Dower House, Upton Grey, nr Basingstoke, Hants (☎ 025 681 435); 15 Markham Sq, London SW3 (☎ 01 584 3995)

MILLS, Peter Francis; *b* 20 Sept 1945; *Educ* Liverpool Coll & Univ; 1 s, 1 da; *Career* chartered accountant, dir: Cow & Gate Ltd and Cow & Gate (Kenya) Ltd; *Recreations* golf, microprocessors; *Style—* Peter Mills, Esq; 1 The Chestertons, Bathampton, Bath BA2 6UJ

MILLS, Sir Peter McLay; *b* 22 Sept 1921; *Educ* Epsom, Wye Coll; *m* 1948, Joan Weatherley; 1 s, 1 da; *Career* farmer 1943-; MP (C): Torrington 1964-74, W Devon 1974-1983 Torridge and W Devon 1983-; parly sec Miny Ag Fish and Food 1972, parly under-sec NI 1972-74, chm Conservative Agric Ctee 1979-87; memb: Cwlth Parly Assoc Exec Ctee 1979-87 (dep chm UK Branch), Foreign Affrs Select Ctee 1980-82; kt 1982; *Style—* Sir Peter Mills,; 21 Vauxhall Walk, London SE11 (☎ 01 735 4004); Priestcombe, Crediton, Devon (☎ 036 34 418);

MILLS, Richard Michael; s of Richard Henry Mills (d 1979), of 11 Adelaide Rd, Surbiton, Surrey, and Catherine, *née* Keeley; *b* 26 June 1931; *m* 1, Feb 1960 (m dis 1967), Lynda, da of Charles Taylor; 1 da (Janey b 1960); m 2, 8 Aug 1983, Sheila Susan, da of James White (d 1986); 2 s (Matthew b 1986, Christopher b 1988); *Career* Nat Serv RAF 1949-51; theatrical producer and mangr; assistant stage mangr 1948; worked in every capacity, including acting and stage mgmnt, in the theatre; Bernard Delfont Ltd 1962-, dir 1967-, dep chm and chief exec 1970-, chm and chief exec 1979; md: Prince of Wales Theatre 1970-, Prince Edward Theatre 1978-; memb: Nat Theatre Bd 1976 (Finance and Gen Purposes Cttee 1976-), Drama Panel Arts Cncl 1976-77, English Tourist Bd 1982-85; over 100 shows workd on 1948-62 include: The Iceman Cometh, The Ginger Man, Sammy Davis Jnr, Maurice Chevalier, Our Man Crichton, The Night of the Iguana, The Killing of Sister George, Funny Girl, The Odd Couple, Martha Graham, Sweet Charity, Streetcar named Desire, Charley's Aunt, Paul Daniels, over 100 pantomimes and summer seasons; *Recreations* golf, poker; *Clubs* RAC, Wentworth Golf, Royal Mid-Surrey Golf; *Style—* Richard Mills, Esq; Bernard Delfont Ltd, Prince of Wales Theatre, Coventry St, London W1V 8AS (☎ 01 930 9901, fax 01 976 1336)

MILLS, Ronald James; JP (Middlesex); s of Samuel Walter Mills (d 1949), of 1 Warkworth Gdns, Isleworth, Middx, and Ellen Eliza Jane, *née* Urand (d 1967); *b* 8 Feb 1918; *Educ* Sir Walter St John's Sch, Battersea Poly, Inns of Court Sch of Law; *m* 1 Dec 1945, Olive May, da of John King (d 1957), of Wandsworth, London; 2 s (Richard John b 1954, Gordon James b 1957); *Career* RCS: joined 1939, cmmnd 1940, serv E Africa India Burma 1941-45; transferred to REME 1942, field serv Burma, staff duties HQ SE Asia Cmd, demobbed as Capt 1946; jr engr GPO (Radio Branch) 1937-39; barr Lincolns Inn 1954; HM Patent Off: asst examiner 1946-47, examiner 1947-50, asr examiner 1950-79, ret 1979; conslt patent controller Racal-Decca Ltd 1979-86; visiting lectr in law City of London Poly and other Colls of higher Educn 1970-; memb: Hounslow Health Amemities Assoc, Hounslow Brentford and Isleworth Cons Assoc, Hounslow Cons Club, Littleton Sailing Club Shepperton Middx; memb Bar Assoc for Commerce Fin and Industry; FIEE, FCI Arb; *Recreations* sailing, shooting, photography, motoring, ex serv & fraternal bodies; *Clubs* Civil Serv, Bar YC, Civil Serv Sailing; *Style—* Ronald Mills, Esq JP; 12 Naseby Close, The Grove, Isleworth, Middx TW7 4JQ (☎ 01 560 7406)

MILLS, Ronald Stephen; s of late Peter Mills, of Nottingham, and Daisy (d 1978); *b* 2 Mar 1947; *Educ* Glaisdale Sch; *m* 1969, Jean, da of Lenoard Marshall, of Nottingham; 2 da; *Career* CA 1968, dir William Lawrence & Co Ltd; *Recreations* running, church, gardening; *Style—* Ronald Mills Esq; 7 Cedar Tree Rd, Bestwood Lodge, Arnold, Nottingham; William Lawrence & Co Ltd, Colwick, Nottingham (☎ 0602 616484; telex 377973)

MILLS, Maj Stanton Jack Machell (John); s of Rev Canon Frank Rupert Mills (d 1954), former canon of Truro Cathedral and Proctor in Convocation, and Beatrice May Ives (d 1968); *b* 26 August 1917; *Educ* Monkton Combe Sch, St Peters Coll Oxford (MA); *m* 1940, Margaret Ingham (m dis), da of Louis Porritt (d 1936); m 2, 1948, Margaret Anne (d 1973), da of Lionel Connor (d 1959); m 3, 1974, Zoë, da of Henry Pether (d 1941); 4 s (Michael, David, Christopher, Simon), 1 da (Elizabeth); *Career* cmmnd Royal Lincolns 1938, seconded Indian Army 1942-45, 9 JAT Regt seconded Indian Para Regt 1944-45, Bde Maj Nowshera Bde 1944, Asst Cmdt Army Sch of Frontier Warfare 1943, seconded Para Regt 1946-48, 2 i/c trg and holding Bn 1948, staff appts GHQ MELF 1954-56, GSO 2 MOD 1956-58, ret 1958; headmaster St Edmunds Sch Suffolk 1958-75; memb IAPS 1959; *Recreations* golf, cricket watching (played hockey and cricket for the Army); *Clubs* MCC, Vincents (Oxford), Lord's Taverners, Frilford Heath GC; *Style—* Maj John Mills; Dean Manor Cottage, Dean, Oxford OX7 3LB (☎ 060 876 391)

MILLS, (William) Stratton; s of John Victor Stratton Mills, CBE (d 1964), of 92 Circular Rd, Belfast, and Margaret Florence, *née* Byford; *b* 1 July 1932; *Educ* Campbell Coll Belfast, Queen's Univ Belfast (LLB); *m* 7 Aug 1959, Merriel Eleanor Ria, da of Robert James Whitla (d 1981), of 4 Knockdarragh Park Belfast; 3 s (Jeremy Victor Stratton b 3 Aug 1966, Rupert James Stratton b 5 March 1968, Angus William Stratton b 23 Nov 1971); *Career* admitted slr NI 1958, ptnr Mills Selig & Bailie Belfast 1959-; MP (Unionist & Cons) Belfast North 1959-74 (ret), PPS to parly sec Miny of Tport 1961-64, chm Cons pty Broadleaf Ctee 1970-73; memb: Estimates Ctee 1964-70, exec ctee 1922 Ctee of Cons Pty 1967-70 and 1973, One Nation Gp 1972-73; chm Ulster Orchestra Soc Ltd 1980-; *Recreations* golf, gardening; *Clubs* Carlton, Reform (Belfast); *Style—* Stratton Mills, Esq; 20 Callender St, Belfast (☎ 0232 243 878, fax 0232 231 956)

MILLS, Hon Ursula Sybil; da of 3 Baron Hillingdon (d 1952); *b* 1918; *Style—* The Hon Ursula Mills

MILLS, William; s of William Frederick Mills (d 1963), of Blackheath, London, and Ada Maud, *née* East (d 1984); *b* 7 July 1938; *Educ* Sutton Valence; *m* 27 Feb 1965, Pamela Anne, da of Stanley Gilbert Dean; 1 s (James William b 11 July 1974), 2 da (Melissa Jane b 17 May 1970, Kate Emma b 24 Jan 1972); *Career* RE 1957-59; Prudential Assur: taxation mangr 1977-80, controller 1980-84, chief accountant 1984-85; Prudential Corpn gp chief accountant 1985-; Freeman City of London, memb Worshipful Co of Painters and Stainers; FCA 1973; *Recreations* opera, gardening;

Style— William Mills, Esq; Sunbury, Foxhole Lane, Matfield, Tonbridge, Kent (☎ 089 272 3464); Prudential Corporation, 142 Holborn Bars, London EC1N 2NH (☎ 01 936 0278)

MILLWARD, Dr Neil; s of Haydn Millward (d 1988), of Abergavenny, and Lilian Audrey, *née* Powley; *b* 14 Mar 1942; *Educ* Queen Elizabeth's Sch Crediton Devon, Univ of Bristol (BSc), Univ of Manchester (PhD); *m* 28 Oct 1972, Pamela Hilary Marion, da of Maj Gilbert Hanley Thorp (d 1984), of Coates, W Sussex; 2 s (Piers b 1975, Christian b 1977); *Career* engr GEC Ltd 1964-66, res fell Univ of Manchester 1966-68, visiting scholar Harvard Business Sch 1968-69, res fell Manchester Business Sch 1969-73, indust relations offr Pay Bd 1973-74, princ res offr Dept of Employment 1984; *Books* Workplace Industrial Relations in Britain (with WW Daniel 1983), British Work Industrial Relations 1980-1984 (with M Stevens 1986); *Recreations* sailing, crafts, music; *Style*— Dr Neil Millward; 53 Cloudesley Rd, London N1 OEL (☎ 01 278 3170); Dept of Employment, 11 Tothill St, London SW1P 9NF (☎ 01 273 4880)

MILLWATER, Dennis Curtis; s of William Milson Millwater, of Rogerstone, Gwent (d 1974), and Kathleen Irene Millwater (d 1969); *b* 31 Mar 1934; *Educ* Bassaleg GS Gwent, Univ of Bristol; *m* 5 Aug 1957, Marlene Beatrice, da of Kenneth Collins, of Cliffs End, Ramsgate; 3 s (Christopher b 26 April 1961, Grahame b 28 April 1963, Jonathan b 23 Aug 1967); 1 da (Sara b 20 July 1977); *Career* pensions supt Northern Assur Co Ltd 1957-68, pensions controller Commercial Union Gp 1968-69, dir De Falke Halsey Ltd 1969-71; gp dir: H Clarkson (Insur Holdgs) Ltd 1971-81, Clarkson Puckle Gp Ltd 1981-87, Bain Clarkson Ltd 1987; chief exec Bain Clarkson (Fin Servs) Ltd; gen cmmr of Taxes; memb: FPMI, ACII; *Recreations* golf, music, cycling; *Clubs* Royal St Georges Golf Sandwich; *Style*— Dennis Millwater, Esq; The Shieling, 32 Harkness Drive, Canterbury, Kent CT2 7RW (☎ 0227 463026); Bain Dawes House, 15 Minories, London EC3 (☎ 01 481 3232, fax 01 481 2324, car 883808)

MILLWOOD, Yvonne Ann; da of Louis Joseph (d 1958), of Cardiff, and Betty, *née* Cowen (d 1986); *b* 2 Feb 1933; *Educ* Cardiff HS for Girls; *m* 1964; *Career* snr advertising control offr independent broadcasting authy; formerly consumer and educn publicist and journalist; *Recreations* fell walking, music, theatre; *Style*— Yvonne A Millwood, Esq; Bridge Yard Cottage, Wighton, Wells Next The Sea, Norfolk; IBA, 70 Brompton Road, London SW3 (☎ 01 584 7011)

MILMAN, Sir Dermot Lionel Kennedy; 8 Bt (GB 1800), of Levaton-in-Woodland, Devonshire; s of Brig-Gen Sir Lionel Charles Patrick Milman, 7 Bt, CMG (d 1962), and Marjorie Aletta Clark-Kennedy (d 1980); Sir Francis Milman, 1 Bt, who d 1821, was physician to King George III from 1806 and pres Royal Coll of Physicians; *b* 24 Oct 1912; *Educ* Uppingham, CCC Cambridge (MA); *m* 1941, Muriel, da of late John Edward Scott Taylor, of King's Lynn; 1 da (Celina); *Heir* bro, Derek Milman; *Career* served WWII with RASC in France, UK, Burma, India (despatches), Maj; schmaster: Epsom Coll 1934-38, Fettes Coll 1938-39 and 1946; Br Cncl Serv overseas and home 1946-76; former vice-capt Beds County Cricket Club; *Recreations* played Rugby Int for England 1937-38 and cricket for Cambridge Univ; *Style*— Sir Dermot Milman, Bt; 7 Old Westhall Close, Warlingham, Surrey (☎ 088 32 4843); Nat West Bank, 42 The Green, Warlingham

MILMO, John Boyle; QC (1984); s of Dermod Hubert Francis Milmo, MB, ChB (d 1973), and Eileen Clare Milmo, *née* White; *b* 19 Jan 1943; *Educ* Downside Sch, Dublin Univ (MA, LLB); *Career* barr Lincoln's Inn 1966, recorder Crown Ct 1982-; *Clubs* Utd Services (Nottingham); *Style*— John Milmo, Esq, QC; 24 The Ropewalk, Nottingham NG1 5EF (☎ 472581)

MILNE, Alasdair David Gordon; s of Charles Milne, surgeon, by his w Edith; *b* 8 Oct 1930, in Cawnpore; *Educ* Winchester, New Coll Oxford; *m* 1954, Sheila Kirsten Graucob; 2 s, 1 da (Kirsty); *Career* served in Gordon Highlanders; joined BBC as gen trainee 1954, with BBC TV current affairs 1955-57, dep editor Tonight 1957-61, editor 1961-62, head Tonight Productions 1963-65; left BBC to become ptnr Jay Baverstock Milne & Co (freelance TV film producers) 1965-67 and ran This Week for Rediffusion TV; controller BBC Scotland 1968-72, dir programmes BBC TV 1973-77, md BBC TV 1977-82, dep dir-gen BBC 1980-82, dir-gen BBC 1982-87, Hon DUniv Stirling 1983, hon fell New Coll Oxford; *Style*— Alasdair Milne, Esq; 30, Holland Park Ave, London, W11 3QU

MILNE, David Alistair; s of Peter Barry Milne, of Edinburgh, and Una Mary, *née* Horton; *b* 29 August 1952; *Educ* Malvern, Pembroke Coll Oxford (MA); *m* 30 Aug 1975, Clare Eveline Agatha, da of Maj Peter Howard Crassweller, of Edinburgh; 1 s (Andrew b 11 March 1983), 1 da (Nicola b 26 July 1979); *Career* Nippon Credit Bank 1974-77, dir Guinness Mahon and Co Ltd 1977-87, dir hd of capital mkts Br and Cwlth Merchant Bank 1987-present; memb Inst of Bankers; *Recreations* tennis, bridge, theatre, ballet; *Clubs* Lansdowne, Riverside, Oversead Bankers; *Style*— David Milne, Esq; 35 York Ave, London SW14 7LQ; British & Commonwealth Merchant Bank, 66 Cannon St, London EC4N 6AE (☎ 01 248 0900, fax 01 248 0906, telex 884040)

MILNE, David Calder; QC (1987); s of Ernest Ferguson Milne, OBE, of Walton Heath, Surrey, and Helena Mary, *née* Harkness; *b* 22 Sept 1945; *Educ* Harrow, Oxford Univ (MA); *m* 26 May 1978, Rosemary Ann, da of Frederick Bond (d 1979); 1 da (Bryony b 1980); *Career* articled to Whinney Murray and Co (Accountants) 1966-69, qualified CA 1969; called to the Bar Lincolns Inn 1970, QC 1987; FCA (1974); *Recreations* natural history, music, golf, rugby football; *Clubs* Garrick, Hurlingham, Gnomes, Walton Heath Golf; *Style*— David Milne, Esq, QC; 14a Castlenau, Barnes, London SW13 9RU (☎ 01 748 6415); 4 Pump Ct, Temple, London EC4Y 7AN (☎ 01 583 9770, fax 01 353 6366, telex 886702 PUMPCO G)

MILNE, Maj-Gen Douglas Graeme; s of late George Milne and Mary, *née* Panton; *b* 19 May 1919; *Educ* Robert Gordon's Coll, Aberdeen Univ (MB, ChB); *m* 1944, Jean Millicent, *née* Gove; 1 da (Pamela Mary); *Career* cmmnd RAMC 1943, dir of Army Health and Res 1973-75, dep dir-gen Army Med Servs 1975-78, ret; QHS 1974-78; Col Cmdt RAMC 1979-83; FFCM, DPH; *Recreations* gardening, fishing; *Style*— Maj-Gen Douglas Milne; 17 Stonehill Rd, London SW14 8RR (☎ 01 878 2828)

MILNE, Hon George Alexander; s and h of 2 Baron Milne; *b* 1 April 1941; *Educ* Winchester; *Style*— The Hon George Milne; 188 Broom Rd, Teddington, Middx (☎ 01 977 9761)

MILNE, 2 Baron (UK 1933); George Douglass Milne; TD; s of Field Marshal 1 Baron Milne, GCB, GCMG, DSO (d 1948); *b* 10 Feb 1909; *Educ* Winchester, New Coll Oxford; *m* 2 April 1940, Cicely, 3 da of Ronald Leslie; 2 s, 1 da; *Heir* s, Hon George Alexander Milne; *Career* Maj (TA) 1940; WWII 1939-45, NWEF, MEF, POW; CA; ptnr Arthur Young McClelland Moores 1947-73, dep chm London & Northern Gp 1973-87; Master Worshipful Co of Grocers 1961-62 (sr memb 1984-); MICAS; *Style*— The Rt Hon the Lord Milne; 33 Lonsdale Rd, Barnes, London SW13 (☎ 01 748 6421)

MILNE, Hon Iain Charles Luis; s of 2 Baron Milne, and Cicely Abigaile Leslie; *b* 16 Sept 1949; *Educ* Oundle; *m* 15 Aug 1987, Berta (Ita), da of Enrique Urzua Guerrero, of San Felipe, Chile; *Career* Inst of Chartered Accnts in England and Wales, Assoc 1974, fell 1980, Freeman City of London 1971, Liveryman of Worshipful Co of Grocers 1985; *Clubs* Roy Mid Surrey Golf; *Style*— The Hon Iain Milne; c/o BAT Co Ltd, Westminster Ho, 7 Millbank SW1P 3JE

MILNE, Sir John Drummond; s of Frederick John Milne and Minnie Elizabeth; *b* 13 August 1924; *Educ* Stowe, Trinity Coll Cambridge, RMC Sandhurst; *m* 1948, Joan Akroyd; 2 s, 2 da; *Career* chm: Blue Circle Industs plc (cement gp), DRG plc, Royal Insur plc; dir var other cos; kt 1986; *Recreations* golf, shooting, skiing; *Clubs* Boodles, MCC, Berkshire Golf; *Style*— Sir John Milne; Blue Circle Industs plc, Portland House, Stag Place, London SW1E 5BJ (☎ 01 828 3456, telex 927757 BC LDN G)

MILNE, Prof Malcolm Davenport; s of Alexander Milne (d 1951), of Romiley, Cheshire, and Lilian, *née* Gee (d 1962); *b* 22 May 1915; *Educ* Stockport Sch, Univ of Manchester (BSc, MD ChB); *m* 17 June 1941, Mary, da of Matthias Thorpe (d 1935); 1 s (David Malcolm b 1950), 1 da (Janet Mary (Mrs Siegle) b 1946); *Career* WWII RAMC, Lt 1940, Capt 1941; active serv with 8 Army 1941-45: Egypt, Libya, Tripolitania, Tunisia (despatches), Italy, Austria; Actg and Temp Maj 1944-46; lectr in med: Univ of Manchester 1947-52, Univ of London 1952-61; prof of med Westminster Med Sch and Univ of London 1961-80; FRCP 1958, FRS 1978; *Recreations* pure mathematics, haute cuisine; *Clubs* Athenaeum; *Style*— Prof Malcolm Davenport; 19 Fieldway, Berkhamsted, Herts HP4 2NX (☎ 0442 864 704)

MILNE-WATSON, Andrew Michael; s and h of Sir Michael Milne-Watson, 3 Bt, CBE; *b* 10 Nov 1944; *Educ* Eton; *m* 1, 1970, Beverley Jane Gabrielle, er da of late Philip Cotton, of Majorca; 1 s (David b 1971), 1 da (Emma b 1974); m 2, 1983, Mrs Gisella Stafford, da of Hans Tisdall, of Cheyne Walk, London SW10; 1 s (Oliver b 1985); *Career* chm Minerva Publication Ltd 1982-; *Clubs* RAC; *Style*— Andrew Milne-Watson Esq; 22 Musgrave Cres, London SW6 4QE

MILNE-WATSON, Sir Michael; 3 Bt (UK 1937), of Ashley, Longbredy, Co Dorset, CBE (1953); yr s of Sir David Milne-Watson, 1 Bt, DL, sometime Chief of the Scottish Clans Assoc of London and md and Govr of the Gas Light & Coke Co (d 1945); suc bro, Sir Ronald Milne-Watson, 2 Bt, 1982; *b* 16 Feb 1910; *Educ* Eton, Balliol Coll Oxford; *m* 1940, Mary Lisette, da of late Harold Carleton Bagnall, of Auckland, NZ; 1 s; *Heir* s, Andrew Michael Milne-Watson, *qv*; *Career* Sub-Lt RNVR; joined Gas Light & Coke Co 1933, md 1945, govr 1946-49, chm N Thames Gas Bd 1949-64; Liveryman Grocers' Co 1947; dir Industl & Commercial Fin Corpn Ltd 1963-80, chm Richard Thomas & Baldwins Ltd 1964-67, dep chm Br Steel Corpn 1967-69; dir: Northern Assur Co Ltd 1960-65, Northern & Employers Assur Co Ltd 1961-68, Commercial Union Assur Co 1968-81; chm The William Press Gp of Cos 1969-74, pres Cncl of Reading Univ 1975-80, dir Fin Corpn for Indust Ltd 1974-80; govr Br Utd Provident Assoc Ltd 1975, chm 1976-81, pres Socy of Br Gas Indust 1970-71, pres Pipeline Indust Guild 1971-72, Govnr Nuffield Nursing Homes Tst, CBE 1953; kt 1969; *Recreations* fishing, walking; *Clubs* MCC, Leander, Atheneaum; *Style*— Sir Michael Milne-Watson, Bt, CBE; 39 Cadogan Place, London SW1X 9RX; Oakfield, Mortimer, Berks (☎ 073 529 2373)

MILNER, Andrew; s of Thomas Milner and Amy, *née* Buckenham; *b* 2 Feb 1951; *Educ* Guthlaxton GS, Hull Coll of Higher Educn; *m* 1978, Linda Catherine, da of David Fullam, of Driffield; 1 s, 2 da; *Career* chm and md Humber Fertilisers Ltd 1980-; senator Junior Chamber Int, pres Hull Inc C of C and Shipping 1988; *Recreations* gardening, jogging, Junior Chamber; *Clubs* Farmers'; *Style*— Andrew Milner, Esq; Dale Farm, Dale Road, Brantingham, Brough, North Humberside HU15 1QN (☎ 0482 666875) Winchester Chambers, Stoneferry, Hull (☎ 0482 20458, telex 592592 KHMAIL G (quote mail box HUMUS 144))

MILNER, Lady Charlene Mary Olivia; *née* French; da of 3 Earl of Ypres; *b* 17 May 1946; *m* 1965, Charles Mordaunt Milner, yr s of Sir George E M Milner, 9 Bt; 3 s; *Style*— Lady Charlene Milner; PO Box 41, Klatmuts, Cape, S Africa

MILNER, Hon Meredith Ann; da of 2 Baron Milner of Leeds; *b* 28 Sept 1956; *Style*— The Hon Meredith Milner; 34b Tomlins Grove, London E3 4NX

MILNER, Sir (George Edward) Mordaunt; 9 Bt (GB 1717), of Nun Appleton Hall, Yorkshire; s of Brig-Gen George Francis Milner, CMG, DSO (d 1921), and cousin of 8 Bt (d 1960); *b* 7 Feb 1911; *Educ* Oundle; *m* 1, 1935, Barbara (d 1951), da of H N Belsham, of Hunstanton, Norfolk; 2 s, 1 da; m 2, 1953, Katherine Hoey, of Dunfermline; *Heir* s, Timothy William Lycett Milner; *Career* serv in 1939-45 War with RA (Capt); stipendiary steward of the Jockey Club (SA) 1954-59, exec steward 1977-80, steward Cape Turf Club 1959-76; memb Cncl of Thoroughbred Breeders Assoc (SA) 1976-; author; *Books* Inspired Info, Vaulting Ambition, The Last Furlong, Notes on Thoroughbred Breeding, The Noble Horse; *Recreations* writing, racing; *Clubs* Rand; *Style*— Sir Mordaunt Milner, Bt; Natte Valleij, Klapmuts, Cape, S Africa (☎ 02211 5171); 40 Avenue Rd, Newlands Capetown, S Africa (☎ 021 66 4146); Mordaunt Milner Stud, Klapmuts (☎ 02211 5573)

MILNER, Hon Richard James; s and h of 2 Baron Milner of Leeds; *b* 16 May 1959; *m* 25 June 1988, Margaret, yst da of G F Voisin, of Jersey, CI; *Style*— The Hon Richard Milner

MILNER, Roy; *b* 20 May 1925; *Educ* Birmingham Univ (BSc); *m* 1951, Eileen Patricia; *Career* chm and md Kodak Ltd 1981-; Queen's Award for Export 1970, 1978, 1982; CBIM; *Style*— Roy Milner Esq; Kodak Ltd, Kodak Ho, Station Rd, Hemel Hempstead, Herts (☎ 0442 61122)

MILNER, Timothy William Lycett; s and h of Sir George Edward Mordaunt Milner, 9 Bt; *b* 11 Oct 1936; *Style*— Timothy Milner Esq

MILNER OF LEEDS, 2 Baron (UK 1951); Arthur James Michael Milner; AE (1952); s of 1 Baron Milner of Leeds, MC, PC (d 1967); *b* 12 Sept 1923; *Educ* Oundle, Trinity Hall Cambridge (MA); *m* 1951, Sheila Margaret, da of late Gerald Hartley, of North Hill Ct, Leeds; 1 s, 2 da; *Heir* s, Hon Richard James Milner; *Career* sits as Labour Peer in Ho of Lords; joined RAFVR 1942, served 1942-46, cmmnd 1943; served with RAuxAF 609 (W Riding) Sqdn 1947-52, Flight Lt; slr 1951; ptnr Milners, Curry & Gaskell (legal firm); oppn whip in Lords 1971-74; *Style*— The Rt Hon the Lord Milner of Leeds, AE; 2 The Inner Ct, Old Church St, London SW3 5BY (☎ 01 352 7588); Milners Curry & Gaskell, Columbia Ho, 69 Aldwych, London WC2B 4DU (☎ 01 242 1883)

MILNER WILLIAMS, Lt Col Charles William Michael; TD (1984); s of John William Milner Williams, OBE (d 1985), of Wimbledon, and Ernestine Violet (Nan), *née* Von Otto (d 1972); *b* 7 Oct 1944; *Educ* Prince of Wales Sch Nairobi Kenya (HMC); *m* 10 Sept 1966, Margaret Joyce, da of Jack Bowerman, of Luton, Beds; 1 da (Victoria b 1971); *Career* Platoon Cdrs Course HAC 1969-70, cmmnd RCT (V) 1974, Capt 1978, Maj CO 285 Movement Control Sqdn 1983, Lt Col S01 CCCC BRSC Liaison and Movements TA 1986, cmd and staff course TA 1985, Jt servs Movements Staff Course 1986; res dept FCO 1964-68, HM inspr of taxes Inland Revenue 1968-; govr: Rutlish Sch London Borough of Merton 1978-, Rickards Lodge HS 1978 (chm 1986-), dep chm Wimbledon Cons Assoc 1978-81, Hazelhurst (Wimbledon) Ltd; ACIS 1983; *Recreations* classical music (early), geneaology and heraldry, walking the dog; *Clubs* Naval and Military; *Style*— Lt Col Charles Milner Williams, TD; Alexandra House, Kingsway, London WC2

MILNER-BARRY, Sir (Philip) Stuart; KCVO (1975), CB (1962, OBE 1946); s of late Prof E L Milner-Barry; *b* 20 Sept 1906; *Educ* Cheltenham, Trinity Coll Cambridge; *m* 1947, Thelma Tennant, da of Charles Tennant Wells; 1 s, 2 da; *Career* stockbroker L Powell Sons & Co 1929-38, chess corespondent The Times 1938-45, temp civil servant FO 1940-55, princ HM Treasy 1945 (asst sec 1947, under-sec 1954), dir Estabs and Orgn Min of Health 1958-60; under-sec: HM Treasy 1966, Civil Serv Dept 1968-77; *Clubs* Brooks's; *Style*— Sir Stuart Milner-Barry, KCVO, CB, OBE; 12 Camden Rd, London SE3 (☎ 01 852 5808)

MILNER-GULLAND, (Laurence) Harry; s of James D Gulland (d 1956), of Sussex, and Margaret Edith, *née* Milner (d 1933); *b* 24 Mar 1908; *Educ* Haileybury, Peterhouse Cambridge (MA); *m* 1 Aug 1934, Ruth Rainsford Nancy, da of Sir Thomas Bavin, KCMG (d 1941); 2 s (Robert Rainsford b 1936, Nicholas James b 1940); *Career* headmaster of Cumnor House Sch, Danehill, Sussex 1938-75; *Books* School Story (Biddles, Guildford 1976), Dom Gérénus (transl from Eugène le Roy, 1986); *Recreations* calligraphy; *Clubs* MCC; *Style*— Harry Milner-Gulland, Esq; Pk Cottage, Danehill, Haywards heath, Sussex (☎ 0444 290778); Cumnor House, Danehill, Haywards Heath, Sussex (☎ 0444 290347)

MILNER-WILLIAMS, Margaret Joyce; *née* Bowerman; da of Jack Bowerman, of Luton, Beds, and Anne Lilian, *née* James; *b* 28 Dec 1941; *Educ* Burlington Sch London, Goldsmith Coll London (Cert Ed); *m* 10 Sept 1966, Charles William Michael Milner-Williams, s of John William Milner-Williams, OBE (d 1985), of Wimbledon, and Nairobi, Kenya; 1 da (Victoria Margaret Anne b 1971); *Career* asst mistress Hugh Christie Sch Tonbridge 1963-64, organiser Greater London Young Cons Central Off 1964-66, Cons Pty agent West Lewisham constituency 1966-67, princ Hazlehurst Sch Wimbledon 1970 (asst mistress 1967-70), chm Hazlehurst (Wimbledon) Ltd; chm Independent Schs Assoc Inc and memb jt cncl 1982-85; memb: Ctee of Independent Schs Info Serv 1985-, Isis Assoc Ctee 1988-, delegacy Goldsmiths' Coll 1976-82; Page scholar English Speaking Union 1988; *Recreations* music, reading, public speaking, travel; *Style*— Mrs Margaret Milner-Williams; 22 Waldemar Rd, Wimbledon, London SW19 7LJ; Parque Santiago, Playa de Las Americas, Tenerife, Canary Islands; Hazelhurst School, 17 The Downs, Wimbledon, London SW20 8HF (☎ 01 946 1704)

MILNES COATES, Sir Anthony Robert; 4 Bt (UK 1911), of Helperby Hall, Helperby, North Riding of Yorkshire; only s of Lt-Col Sir Robert Milnes-Coates, 3 Bt, DSO, JP (d 1982), and Lady Patricia Milnes-Coates, *qv*; *b* 8 Dec 1948; *Educ* Eton, St Thomas's Hosp (BSc, MB, BS); *m* 1978, Harriet Ann, yr da of Raymond Burton, of The Old Rectory, Slingsby, York; 2 da (Sara b 1981, Sophie b 1984); *Heir* Thomas b 1986; *Career* MRCP, MD; *Style*— Sir Anthony Milnes Coates, Bt; Hereford Cottage, 135 Gloucester Rd, London SW7; Helperby Hall, Helperby, York

MILNES-COATES, Lady (Ethel) Patricia; *née* Hare; er da of 4 Earl of Listowel (d 1931); *b* 29 Oct 1912; *m* 1, 1936, Lt-Col Charles Thomas Milnes Gaskell (k in flying accident while on active serv 1943); 3 s (James b 1937, Andrew b 1939, Tom b 1942); m 2, 1945, Lt-Col Sir Robert Edward James Clive Milnes-Coates, 3 Bt, DSO (d 1982); 1 s (Sir Anthony, 4 Bt, *qv*), 1 da (Mrs Peter Brodrick); *Style*— Lady Patricia Milnes-Coates; Moor Ho Farm, Helperby, York

MILROY, Rev Dominic Liston; OSB; s of Adam Milroy, by his w Clarita; *b* 18 April 1932; *Educ* Ampleforth, St Benet's Hall Oxford; *Career* headmaster Ampleforth 1980- (housemaster 1964-74, head modern languages 1963-74), prior Int Benedictine Coll of St Anselmo Rome 1974-79; *Style*— The Rev Dominic Milroy, OSB; Ampleforth College, York YO6 4ER (☎ 043 93 224)

MILSOM, Gerald Martin William; OBE (1987); s of Arthur Milsom (d 1983), of Dedham Vale Hotel, Dedham, Essex, and Dorothy Eileen, *née* Chambers; *b* 28 August 1930; *Educ* Epsom Coll 1944-49; *m* 1, 28 Sept 1957 (m dis), June Philippa, da of Luther HA Andler (d 1986); 2 s (David b 1958, Paul b 1964), 1 da (Nicola b 1960); m 2, 27 July 1978, Diana Joy, da of Frank Pinhey of Pond Farm, Gt Bromley, Colchester; *Career* Nat Serv Lt Army Catering Corps 1949-51; hotelier, purchased: Le Talbooth Restuarant 1952, Maison Talbooth 1970, The Pier at Harwich 1978, Dedham Vale Hotel 1981, The Pavilion on the Square Colchester 1988; Master Innholder 1979; fndr Pride of Britain Consortuim of Country House Hotels 1983, chm BHRCA bd mgmnt 1989- (vice chm 1987-89); memb Essex CC 1963-73 (Alderman 1971), chm East Anglia Tourist Bd 1971-82 (currently chm), govr Norwich City Coll (memb bd catering cncl); Freeman: City of London 1973, Worshipful Co of Distillers 1973; FHCIMA 1971, FInstD 1983; *Recreations* golf, walking; *Style*— Gerald Milsom, Esq, OBE; Wilderness Cottage, Dedham, Colchester, Essex CO7 6HP (☎ 0206 323 150); PO Box 96, Southbroom 4277, Natal, South Africa; Le Talbooth, Dedham, Colchester, Essex CO7 6HP (☎ 0206 323 150, fax 0206 322 752, telex 987083 LETALB G)

MILSOM, (Ernest) James; s of Ernest William Milsom, of Edgware, Middx, and Jane, *née* Somers (d 1979); *b* 2 April 1928; *Educ* St James' RC Secdy Sch Edgware, Middlesex Poly; *m* 23 Feb 1951, Anne Kathleen (Nancy), da of Harry Deadman (d 1945), of Edgware; 2 s (Michael James b 23 April 1955, Séan Francis b 8 Oct 1959), 1 da (Julia Anne b 15 April 1953); *Career* WWII RN 1939-45; conslt engr; ptnr: Henry Goddard & Ptnrs 1963-68, McAuslan & Ptnrs 1968-77; with own practise EJ Milson & Assoc 1977-; CEng, FIEE, FCILBSE, MConsE, KCSJ 1972; *Recreations* landscape & portrait painting, music, reading, marquetry; *Style*— James Milsom, Esq; EJ Milsom and Associates, Consltg Engineers - Building Services, 250A Kingsbury Rd, Kingsbury, London NW9 0BS (☎ 01 204 9024)

MILSOM, Prof Stroud Francis Charles (Toby); QC (1985); s of Harry Lincoln Milsom (d 1970), of Rock, Cornwall, and Isobel Vida, *née* Collins (d 1979); *b* 2 May 1923; *Educ* Charterhouse, Trinity Coll Cambridge (BA, MA), Univ of Pennsylvania Law Sch; *m* 11 Aug 1955, Irène, da of Witold Szereszewski (d 1940), of Wola Krysztoporska, Poland; *Career* Admty 1944-45; lectr and prize fell Trinity Coll Cambridge 1948-55, tutor and dean New Coll Oxford 1956-64, prof legal history London Univ 1964-76, prof law and fell St John's Coll Cambridge 1976-; visiting prof: New York Univ Law School 1958-70, Yale Law Sch 1968-; Harvard Law Sch and dept of history 1973, Colorado Law Sch 1977, Monash Law Sch 1981; Maitland Meml lectr Cambridge 1972, Ford's lectr in English history Oxford 1985-86, pres Selden Soc 1985-88 (literary dir 1964-80), memb Royal Cmmn on Historical Manuscripts 1975-, hon bencher of Lincoln's Inn 1970; hon LLD Glasgow 1981, hon LLD Chicago 1985; FBA 1967, memb American Philisophical Soc 1984; *Books* Novae Narrationes (intro, translation notes, Pollock & Maitland 1963), History of English Law (intro to reissue 1968), Historical Foundations of the Common Law (1968, second ed in 1981), The Legal Framework of English Feudalism (1976), Studies in the History of the Common Law (1985), Sources of English Legal History (with JH Baker, 1986); *Clubs* Athenaeum; *Style*— Prof SFC Milsom, QC; 113 Grantchester Meadows, Cambridge CB3 9JN (☎ 0223 354100); St John's Coll Cambridge CB2 1TP (☎ 0223 338600)

MILTON, Alan James; MBE (1983); s of John Phillips Milton (d 1968), and Alice Bowen, *née* Jones (d 1977); *b* 23 June 1935; *Educ* Emanuel Sch London; *m* 25 March 1972, Heather Valerie, da of Douglas Roy Salt, OBE, of 1 The Ridings, Leavenheath, Suffolk; 2 s (Jason James b 1973, Damian John b 1976); *Career* Nat Serv RAF 1953-55; trainee Glyn Mills and Co 1951-53; Standard Chartered Bank Gp: official Bank of Br W Africa Ltd 1955; mangr 1958-: Bank of W Africa Ltd, Standard Bank of W Africa Ltd, Standard Bank Nigeria Ltd; asst gen mangr mktg First Bank of Nigeria Ltd 1984, dep regnl mangr The Chartered Bank Bombay 1984 (mangr W India 1986), currently mangr ops First Bank of Nigeria Ltd London (mangr mktg 1987); formerly dir Standard Chartered Insur Brokers Lagos; former tstee: St Saviours Sch Educn Tst Lagos, Corona Schs Lagos, Breach Candy Hosp Tst Bombay; formerly pres UK Citizens Assoc W India; *Recreations* golf, philately, table tennis, walking, reading, boating, classical music; *Clubs* Royal Overseas League, Lagos YC, Ikoyi (Lagos), Willingdon (Bombay); *Style*— Alan Milton, Esq, MBE; 6 Neate House, Lupus St, London SW1V 3EG (☎ 01 821 7992); 24 Kings Walk, Shoreham-by-Sea, West Sussex BN43 5LG (☎ 0273 453931); First Bank of Nigeria Ltd, 29-30 Kings St, London EC2V 8EH (☎ 01 606 6411, fax 01 606 3134, telex 893013 FIRBAN)

MILTON, Frank William; s of Capt Cyril Frank, of Worthing, Sussex and Mabel Laura, *née* Neal; *b* 29 Nov 1949; *Educ* Hove Co GS, Univ Coll Oxford (BA); *m* 29 Sept 1973, Lesley Pamela, da of Capt Dennis Arthur Jack Adams, RE, of Glossop Derbys; 2 s (Andrew Paul Frank, Graham Alexander Neil); *Career* trainee Turner & Newall 1972-73, sales asst Shell Chemicals UK Ltd 1973-75, (sales rep 1975-78), planning mangr Shell Int Chemical Co Ltd 1978-80, ptnr Deloitte Haskins Sells Mgmnt Conslts 1984 (joined 1980); CDipAF, MInstM; *Recreations* hill walking, windsurfing, house renovation, running; *Style*— Frank Milton, Esq; Alligin, Norrels Drive, E Horsley, Surrey KT24 5DL (☎ 04865 3832); Hillgate House, 26 Old Bailey, London EC4M 7PL (☎ 01 248 3913, fax 01 236 2367)

MILTON-THOMPSON, Surgeon Vice Admiral Sir Godfrey James; KBE (1988); s of Rev James Milton-Thompson (d 1968), of Pool Hall, Menheniot, Cornwall, and May Le Mare, *née* Hoare (d 1982); *b* 25 April 1930; *Educ* Eastbourne Coll, Queens' Coll Cambridge (MA, MB, BChir), St Thomas's Hosp; *m* 1952, Noreen Helena Frances, da of Lieut Col Sir Desmond Fitzmaurice, of Boars Hill Oxford; 3 da (Helena, Richenda, Louisa); *Career* hon physician to HM The Queen 1982-; Medical Dir Gen (Naval) 1984-, Surgn Gen Defence Medical Services 1988; CStJ 1985, memb Chapter General Order of St John 1988-; FRCP, DCH; *Recreations* fishing, literature, collecting English paintings; *Clubs* Naval & Military; *Style*— Surgeon Vice Admiral Sir Godfrey Milton-Thompson, KBE; c/o Barclays Bank, 44 High St, Gosport, Hants

MILVERTON, 2 Baron (UK 1947); Rev Fraser Arthur Richard Richards; s of 1 Baron Milverton, GCMG (d 1978), and Noelle Benda, da of Charles Basil Whitehead, of Torquay; *b* 21 July 1930; *Educ* Ridley Coll, Ontario, Clifton Coll, Egerton Agricultural Coll Njoro Kenya, Bishop's Coll Cheshunt Herts; *m* 1957, Mary Dorothy, da of Leslie Aubrey Fly (d 1983; a composer of music, teacher and civil servant), of Bath; 2 da (Susan b 1962, Juliet b 1964); *Heir* bro, Hon Michael Hugh Richards; *Career* sits as Cons peer in Ho of Lords; Roy Signals 1949-50, Kenya Police 1952-53; deacon 1957; curate: St George's Beckenham Kent, St John Baptist Sevenoaks Kent, St Nicholas Great Bookham Surrey; vicar Okewood Hill with Forest Green Surrey, rector Christian Malford with Sutton Benger and Tytherton Kellaways (Wilts) 1967-, chaplain Wilts ACF to 1981; *Recreations* family, current affairs, reading, int rugby, cricket, tennis, swimming; *Style*— The Rev the Rt Hon the Lord Milverton; The Rectory, Christian Malford, Chippenham, Wilts (☎ 0249 720466)

MILVERTON, Noelle, Baroness; Noelle Benda; da of Charles Basil Whitehead of Torquay; *m* 1927, 1 Baron Milverton, GCMG (d 1978); *Style*— The Rt Hon Noelle, Lady Milverton; Flete, Ermington, nr Ivy Bridge, South Devon

MINCHIN, Peter David; s of Maj Cecil Reduers Minchin (d 1953), of Ryde, IOW, and Ena Mary, *née* Flux (d 1974); *b* 5 Mar 1932; *Educ* Ryde Sch, IOW, Allhallows Rousdon Devon; *m* 2 April 1960, Angela, da of Maj Henry Hugh Petley (d 1976), of Heathfield House, Old Heathfield, Sussex; 2 s (David b 25 Dec 1963, Jeremy b 3 Sept 1965), 1 da (Alexandra b 2 Aug 1968); *Career* RN 1950-57: Lt (Observer) Fleet Air Arm 1955, ret 1957; ptnr: Kitcat & Aitkin 1958-63, Pidgeon de Smitt (and predecessor firms) 1963-81; gen mangr Securities Gp of Kuwait 1982-85, ptnr/dir Scrimgeour Vickers Ltd 1985-86, md Lloyds Bank Stockbrokers Ltd 1986-, dir Lloyds Merchant Bank Ltd 1986-, chm Chambers & Remington Ltd 1988-, memb bd Securities Assoc 1988-, memb Stock Exchange 1963- (memb cncl 1976-82 and 1988-); *Recreations* tennis, bridge, reading; *Style*— Peter Minchin, Esq; 83 Defoe Ho, Barbican, London EC2Y 8DN (☎ 01 588 5748); 40/66 Queen Victoria St, London EC4P 4EL (☎ 01 248 2244, fax 01 236 1632)

MINCHINTON, (Emeritus) Prof Walter Edward; s of Walter Edward Minchinton (d 1928), of Brixton, London, and Annie Border Clark (d 1982); *b* 29 April 1921; *Educ* Queen Elizabeth's Hosp, Bristol; LSE, Univ of London (BSc); *m* 1945, Marjorie, da of Richard Sargood (d 1979); 2 s (Paul Richard b 1949, David Walter b 1958), 2 da (Anne Border b 1952, Susan Clare b 1954); *Career* 1942-45 RAOC, REME, Roy Signals, NW Europe; Univ Coll Swansea: asst lectr 1948-50, lectr 1950-58, sr lectr 1958-64; Univ of Exeter prof economic history 1964-86 (head of Dept 1964-83); fell Royal Historical Soc; *Books* incl: The British Tinplate Industry (1957), The Trade of Bristol in the C18 (1957), Politics and the Port of Bristol in C18 (1963), Industrial South Wales

1750-1914 (1969), Mercantilism, System or Expediency (1969), Wage Regulation in Pre-Industrial England (1972), American Material in the House of Lords Record Office (1983), A Guide to Industrial Archaeology Sites in Britain (1984), Devon's Industrial Past: a Guide (1986), Life to the City: an illustrated history of Exeter's water supply from the Romans to the present day (1987), Britain and the Northern Seas: some essays (1988); *Recreations* walking, music, industrial archaeology; *Style*— Prof Walter Minchinton; 53 Homefield Rd, Exeter EX1 2QX (☎ 0392 77602)

MINNITT, Hon Mrs (Primrose Keighley); *née* Balfour; da of 1 Baron Riverdale, GBE (d 1957); *b* 20 April 1913; *m* 1, 1933, Oliver Grahame Hall (who assumed by deed poll 1945 the christian name of Claude in lieu of Oliver and the surname of Muncaster in lieu of his patronymic who d 1974); 2 s; m 2, 1975, Robert John Minnitt, CMG, *qv*; *Clubs* Lansdowne; *Style*— The Hon Mrs Minnitt; Whitelocks, Sutton, nr Pulborough, Sussex (☎ 079 87 216)

MINNITT, Robert John; CMG (1955); s of late Charles Frederick Minnitt; *b* 2 April 1913; *Educ* Marlborough, Trinity Coll Cambridge (MA); *m* 1, 1943, Peggy Christine (d 1973), da of Eric William Sharp; 1 s, 2 da; m 2, 1975, Hon Primrose Keighley, *qv*, widow of Claude Muncaster (d 1974); *Career* entered Colonial Serv (Hong Kong) 1935, chief sec Western Pacific High Cmmn 1952, ret 1958; furniture designer and craftsman 1960; civil serv Cwlth Off 1966; ret 1969; *Recreations* furniture making; *Clubs* Lansdowne; *Style*— Robert Minnitt, Esq, CMG; Whitelocks, Sutton, nr Pulborough, Sussex (☎ 079 87 216)

MINNS, (Frederick) John; s of Percival John (d 1915), and Alice Gertrude, *née* Morris (d 1916); *b* 17 June 1910; *Educ* Oxford Municipal Secdy Sch; *m* 1935, Enid Lucy, da of George Ernest Payne (d 1976); 2 s (Michael b 1937, Howard b 1942), 1 da (Carolyn b 1948); *Career* WWII observer Royal Observer Corps 1939-45, offr i/c Oxford Bldg Rescue Squad 1939-45; building contractor; dir and fndr Frederick J Minns & Co Ltd 1934 (chm 1936-69), jt md Swift Trg Rifle Co Ltd & STAW 1940-46; chm: Minns Mfrg Co Ltd 1950-69, Cherwell Land Devpt Co Ltd 1954-, Oxford Plant Ltd 1955-79, Minox Structures Ltd 1965-85, Minns Oxford Ltd 1956-; cncllr: Oxford City cncl 1951-57, Abingdon RDC 1938-49; FCIOB; *Recreations* swimming, bridge, snooker, solar energy research and application; *Clubs* Clarendon (Oxford, pres 1956-57), Rotary (Oxford), Isis Probus; *Style*— John Minns, Esq; Solway, Badger Lane, Hinksey Hill, Oxford OX1 5BL (☎ 0865 735245); Minns Oxford Ltd, 7 West Way, Oxford

MINOGUE, Hon Sir John Patrick; s of J P Minogue; *b* 15 Sept 1909; *Educ* St Kevin's Coll Melbourne Univ; *m* 1938, Mary, da of T O'Farrell; *Career* barr 1939, QC Vic 1957, QC NSW 1958, Chief Justice Papua New Guinea 1970-74, Law Reform Cmmr Vic 1977-82 (ret), pres of the Graduate Union of Melbourne Univ 1982-, vice pres of the English Speaking Union (Vic Branch) 1982; kt 1976; *Style*— The Hon Sir John Minogue; Marengo Vale, Seymour, Vic 3660, Australia

MINOPRIO, (Frank) Charles; 2 s of late (Charles) Anthony Minoprio (whose gf, *née* Franz Carl Anton, was born at Frankfurt but became a naturalised UK citizen 1856, while Franz's gf, Vincenz Alois, was originally a native of Pavia, but adopted Frankfurt citizenship in 1788), of Campden Hill, Kensington; *b* 9 August 1939; *Educ* Harrow, Grenoble Univ; *m* Patricia Mary, er da of late Brian W Dixon, of Godstone; 1 s (George b 1969), 2 da (Victoria b 1966, Charlotte b 1972); *Career* served as Lt RA in Germany; wine merchant; Hatch Mansfield & Co, Ltd Haulfryn Est Co Ltd, master of wine; chm: Champagne Academy 1986; Master of the Worshipful Co of Distillers 1987; *Recreations* tennis, squash, gardening; *Style*— Charles Minoprio, Esq; The Manor House, Milton Ernest, Bedford (☎ 02302 2237) Hatch Mansfield & Co, Ltd, 19 Ryder St, St James's, London SW1

MINTER, Jonathan Charles; s of John Minter, CBE, of Essex, and Barbara Geraldine MacDonald, *née* Stanford; *b* 22 July 1949; *Educ* Repton, Birmingham Univ (BA); *m* 9 July 1983, Diana Claire, da of Austin Brown, of Sussex; 1 s (Benjamin b 1986), 1 da (Isabel b 1988); *Career* investmt banker; dir: Baring Int Investmt Ltd 1987-, Baring Int Investment Mgmnt Ltd 1988; *Recreations* shooting, sailing; *Clubs* Royal Ocean Racing; *Style*— Jonathan C Minter, Esq; Hill Farm House, Langham, nr Colchester, Essex CO4 5NX; Baring International Investment Ltd, 9 Bishopsgate, London EC2

MINTO, Bruce Watson; s of James Andrew Minto, of Craig-Knowe, of Biggar, and Christina Greenshields, *née* Watson; *b* 30 Oct 1957; *Educ* Biggar HS, Edinburgh Univ (LLB); *m* 27 Aug 1983, Christine Rosemary, da of Dr Richard Thomas Stanley Gunn, of Kingsborough, Glasgow; 2 s (Andrew Richard b 1986, £ Jonathan Bruce b 1988); *Career* legal asst Dundas & Wilson CS 1981-85 (law apprentice 1979-81), fndr ptnr Dickson Minto WS 1985-; Notary Public; *Recreations* golf, rugby, music; *Style*— Bruce Minto, Esq; 9 Braid Road, Edinburgh (☎ 031 447 4490); 11 Walker Street, Edinburgh (☎ 031 225 4455, fax 031 225 2712, 6/7 Gough Sq, London (☎ 01 353 4455, fax 01 353 0005)

MINTO, 6 Earl of (UK 1813); Gilbert Edward George Lariston Elliot-Murray-Kynynmound; 9 Bt (S 1700), MBE (Mil 1955), OBE (1986), JP (Roxburghshire 1961), DL (Roxburgh, Ettrick and Lauderdale 1983); also Baron Minto (GB 1797) and Viscount Melgund (UK 1813); s of 5 Earl of Minto (d 1975, s of 4 Earl, who was govr gen of Canada 1898-1904 and viceroy of India 1905-10), and Marion, OBE, da of George William Cook, of Montreal; *b* 19 June 1928; *Educ* Eton, RMA Sandhurst; *m* 1, 1952 (m dis 1965), Lady Caroline Child-Villiers, da of 9 Earl of Jersey; 1 s, 1 da; m 2, 1965, Mary Elizabeth (d 1983), da of late Peter Ballantine, of Gladstone, New Jersey, USA; *Heir* s, Viscount Melgund; *Career* 2 Lt Scots Gds 1948, served in Malaya 1949-51; ADC to: C-in-C Far East Land Force 1951, CIGS 1953-55, govr of Cyprus 1955, RARO 1956, ret Capt; Brig Queen's Bodyguard for Scotland (Royal Co of Archers); chm Scottish Cncl on Alcoholism 1973-, memb Borders Regnl Cncl 1974-80 and 1986-; dep traffic cmmr Scotland 1975-81; exec vice pres S Scotland C of C 1978-80 (pres 1980-82); dir Noel Penny Turbines Ltd; *Clubs* Puffin's; *Style*— The Rt Hon the Earl of Minto, OBE, JP, DL; Minto, Hawick, Roxburghshire (☎ 045 087 321)

MINTO, Graeme Sutherland; MBE (1984); s of Dr Kenneth Ross Minto (d 1981), and Mona Isobel, *née* Claxon; *b* 18 April 1943; *Educ* Oundle Sch, Christ's Coll Cambridge (MA); *m* 3 Sept, 1966, Mary Carolyn, da of John Priest; 1 s (Robert b 1975), 2 da (Lucy b 1968, Catherine b 1969); *Career* former chm Domino Printing Sciences plc (fndr 1978, md 1978-84; chm 1978-88), dir: Elmjet Ltd, Datapaq Ltd; memb Cambs Co Ctee; DMS, CBIM, MIMechE, MIEE, CEng; *Books* author/lecturer on numerous occasions on ink jet printing, growth of high tech businesses; *Recreations* skiing, golf, Rotarian; *Style*— Graeme Minto, Esq, MBE; 7 Long Rd, Cambridge CB2 2PP (☎ 0223 244296)

MINTON, Peter Kenneth; s of David James Minton, and Ada, *née* Martin (d 1974); *b* 4 Nov 1935; *Educ* Bromley Co GS; *m* 1, 1956 (m dis 1970) Pamela; 3 da (Lesley Anne b 1957, Jane b 1960, Catherine b 1963); m 2, Christine Jaqueline, *née* Lobb; 2 s (Alexander b 1980, Kenrick b 1982); *Career* electronics engr, technical journalist, industl and financial conslt, investmt analyst; memb: SLD, Henry Doubleday Res Assoc, Bucks and Oxfordshire Naturalists Tst; assoc memb Soc of Investmt Analyts; *Recreations* environmental conservation, long distance walking, organic gardening; *Clubs* National Liberal; *Style*— Peter Minton, Esq; Underwood Hardwick Rd, Whitchurch, Reacing (☎ 0735 72516); Sheppards, 1 London Bridge, London (☎ 01 378 7000)

MINTY, Norman; s of Norman Edward Ernest Minty (d 1934), of Oxford, and Gertrude May North (d 1958); *b* 10 Sept 1925; *Educ* Dragon Sch Oxford, St Edwards Sch Oxford, Edinburgh Univ; *m* 15 Sept 1956, Daphne Louise, da of Rev Basil Claude Gadsden (d 1958), of Witney on Wye, Herefordshire; 3 s (Christopher Edward b 1960, Jefery Norman b 1960, Richard Drury b 1962); *Career* Flt Lt 1943-46; snr ptnr Niell & Co Oxford, non exec dir Minty plc; life memb Oxford Lawn Tennis Club; Freeman City of London; FICA; *Recreations* gardening, tennis; *Clubs* RAF London, Clarendon Oxford, Grewin Oxford; *Style*— Norman Minty Esq; The Old House, Wheatley, Oxford; Cranbrook House, Summertown, Oxford (☎ Oxford 52925)

MIQUEL, Raymond Clive; CBE (1981); *b* 28 May 1931; *m* married with children; *Career* Arthur Bell & Sons: joined 1956, md 1968-85, chm 1973-85; chm Wellington Importers Ltd USA 1984-85, Gleneagles Hotels plc 1984-85, chm and chief exec Belhaven plc 1986-88; visiting prof business devpt Glasgow Univ, chm Scottish Sports Cncl, memb Sports Cncl, govr Sports Aid Fndn, memb Centl Cncl of Physical Recreation; CBIM; *Style*— Raymond Miquel, Esq, CBE; Whitedene, Caledonian Cres, Gleneagles, Perthshire (☎ 076 46 2642)

MIRZOEFF, Edward O; s of Eliachar Mirzoeff, of Edgware, Middx, and Penina, *née* Asherov; *b* 11 April 1936; *Educ* Hasmonean GS, Queen's Coll Oxford (BA, MA); *m* 4 June 1961, Judith, da of Harry Topper, of Finchley; 3 s (Nicholas b 1962, Daniel b 1965, Sacha b 1969); *Career* market researcher Socl Surveys (Gallup Poll) Ltd 1959-60, asst ed Shoppers' Guide Magazine 1962-63; BBC TV 1963-; prodr Choice 1964-66 series ed Bird's-Eye View 1969-72; prodr and dir of many documentaries incl: Metro-Land, A Passion for Churches, The Queen's Realm, The Front Garden, The Englishwoman and the Horse, Police - Harrow Road, The Regiment, Target Tirpitz, The Ritz; series prodr: Year of the French, In at the Deep End, Just Another Day, prodr The Richard Dimbleby Lecture for 10 years, exec prodr Documentary Features 1982, ed 40 Minutes 1985-; awards: BAFTA award for best documentary 1982, BAFTA award for best factual series 1986, BFI Commercial Film and TV award 1988, Samuelson Award Birmingham Festival 1988; memb BAFTA (cncl memb 1988-89); *Recreations* opera, theatre, cinema, country walks, books; *Style*— Edward Mirzoeff, Esq; BBC Televison, Kensington House, Richmond Way, London W14 0AX (☎ 01 743 1272, fax 01 749 8378, telex 265781)

MISCAMPBELL, Gillian Margaret Mary; *née* Gibbs; OBE (1982); da of Brig Francis William Gibb (d 1969), of Darkfaulds Cottage, Rosemount, Blairgowrie, Perthshire, and Agnes Winifred Gibb; *b* 31 Dec 1935; *Educ* St Leonards Sch; *m* 5 April 1958, Alexander Malcolm Miscampbell, s of Alexander Miscampbell (d 1965), of Carrick Cottage, Stanley Rd, Hoylake, Cheshire; 3 s (Andrew Ian Farquharson b 18 June 1959, Ian Alexander Francis b 27 Feb 1962, Alexander James b 19 Aug 1964); *Career* vice chm Nat Women's Advsy Ctee Cons Pty 1979-80, chm Ayles Cons Assoc 1975-78, memb Bucks CC 1977-(chm Educ Ctee 1985-), memb Cncl Buckingham Univ 1985-, memb Area Manpower Bd 1985-88, chm Aylesbury Vale Health Authy 1981-; *Style*— Mrs Alec Miscampbell, OBE; Colonsay, Quainton, Bucks (☎ 0296 75 318); Aylesbury Vale Health Authy, Ardenham Lane, Aylesbury, Bucks (☎ 0296 437 501)

MISCAMPBELL, Norman Alexander; MP (C) Blackpool North 1962-; QC 1974; s of Alexander Miscampbell (d 1965); *b* 20 Feb 1925; *Educ* St Edward's Sch, Trinity Coll Oxford; *m* 1961, Margaret, da of Berenger Kendall; 2 s, 2 da; *Career* barr Inner Temple 1952, contested (C) Newton (Lancs) 1955 and 1959, pps to Attorney-Gen 1972-74; *Style*— Norman Miscampbell Esq, MP; 7 Abbey Road, West Kirby, Cheshire

MISCHLER, Norman Martin; s of Martin Mischler (d 1965), of Brondesbury Park, London, and Sarah Martha, *née* Lambert (d 1959); *b* 9 Oct 1920; *Educ* St Paul's, St Catharine's Coll Cambridge (MA); *m* 30 April 1949, Helen Dora, da of Dr Alfred Sinclair (d on active serv 1944); 1 s (Stepehen Martin b 1951), 1 da (Kathryn Noel b 1953); *Career* Maj IA, serv India and Burma; dir: Burts & Harvey Ltd 1954-66, Burt Boulton & Haywood Ltd 1957-66, Baywood Chemicals 1957-66, PR Chemicals 1958-66; vice-chm Burt Boulton & Haywood 1963-66; dep md Hoechst UK Ltd 1966-75 (chm 1975-84); chm: Hoechst Ireland Ltd 1976-84, Harlow Chemical Co Ltd 1972-74, Kalle Infotec Ltd 1972-74; dir: Rochas Perfumes Ltd 1975-79, Berger Jenson & Nicholson Ltd 1975- (chm 1975-84); vice-chm German Chamber of Industry and Commerce 1977-84; cncl memb Chemical Industries Assoc 1975-84; Freeman City of London (Paviors' Co); Officer's Cross of Fed Order of Merit W Germany; *Recreations* golf, opera, fishing; *Clubs* Hawks, Cambridge; *Style*— Norman Mischler, Esq; Scott House, Bungay, Suffolk (☎ 0986 2767)

MISHCON, Hon Peter Arnold; s of Baron Mishcon (Life Peer); *b* 1946; *m* 1967, Penny Green; 1 s, 3 da; *Style*— The Hon Peter Mishcon

MISHCON, Hon Russell Orde; s of Baron Mishcon (Life Peer); *b* 1948; *m* 1975, Marcia Leigh; 1 s, 1 da; *Style*— The Hon Russell Mishcon

MISHCON, Baron (Life Peer UK 1978); Victor Mishcon; DL (Gter London); s of Rabbi Arnold Mishcon; *b* 14 August 1915; *Educ* City of London Sch; *m* 1; 2 s, 1 da; m 2, 1976, Joan, da of Bernard Monty; *Career* sits as Labour Peer in House of Lords; slr 1937, sr ptnr Victor Mishcon & Co; memb Nat Theatre Bd 1968-, S Bank Theatre Bd 1977-82; former chm LCC, and chm of various ctees; former memb: GLC (chm of its Gen Purposes Ctee), ILEA; former memb of Lambeth Borough Cncl, chm of its Finance Ctee; contested (Lab): NW Leeds 1950, Bath 1951, Gravesend 1955 and 1959; memb: chief oppn spokesman Home Affrs and spokesman Legal Affairs 1983-; vice-chm All Party Solictors Parly Gp; *Style*— The Rt Hon the Lord Mishcon, DL; 125 High Holborn, London WC1V 6QP (☎ 01 405 3711); House of Lords, London SW1A 0AA

MISIEWICZ, Dr George; *b* 28 Mar 1930; *Educ* Lord Weymouth's GS, London Univ (BSc, MB, BS); *m* Marjorie Alice; *Career* conslt physician and jt dir, dept of gastrenterology and nutrition, Central Middx Hosp London; memb external scientific staff MRC, pres Br Soc of Gastroenterology 1987-88; ed: Gut 1980-87, Euro Jl of Gastroenterology and Hepatology 1989; hon conslt: gastroenterologist RN, BA; FRCP

(London and Edinburgh); *Books* Diseases of the Gut and Pancreas (jt ed); *Recreations* music, paintings, reading, theatre, the country; *Style—* Dr George Misiewicz; 148 Harley Street, London W1N 1AH (☎ 01 935 1207); 18 The Avenue, Richmond, Surrey TRW9 2AJ (☎ 01 940 7807); Department of Gastroenterology & Nutrition, Central Middlesex Hospital, London NW10 7NS (☎ 01 961 4594)

MISKIN, George William Semark; JP, DL (1982); s of Cdr G S Miskin (d 1972), and Margaret Edith, *née* Facer (d 1974); *Educ* Haileybury & Imperial Serv Coll, Sch of Navigation Southampton; *m* 26 Aug 1959, Mary Hersey, da of William David Murdoch (d 1942); 1 s (Charles b 28 Sept 1960), 2 da (Suzanne b 25 Sept 1962, Jennifer b 19 June 1965); *Career* navigation offr P & OSN Co 1945-60; London Stock Exchange: joined 1960,memb 1962, ptnr 1972-86; non-exec dir: C & W Walker 1972-85, Possum; chm Frensham Fly Fishers; memb: Ct of Univ of Surrey, KGV Fund for Sailors, Dreadnought Seamans Soc; magistrate 1970, High Sheriff 1981-82; Honourable Co of Master Mariners: Liveryman 1968, Warden 1972, Master 1983-84; *Recreations* fishing, skiing, sailing, bibliophile, carpentry; *Clubs* Fly Fishers, Royal Southern; *Style—* George Miskin, Esq, JP, DL; Hankley Edge, Tilford, Surrey GU102DD (☎ 025 125 2122); Parrish Stockbrokers, 4 London Wallbuildings EC2M 5NX (☎ 01 628 9926, fax 01 588 2449, telex 883787)

MISKIN, His Hon Judge Sir James William; QC (1967); s of late Geoffrey Miskin, of Buxted, Sussex; *b* 11 Mar 1925; *Educ* Haileybury Coll, Brasenose Coll Oxford; *m* 1, 1951, Mollie Joan, da of Eric Milne; 2 s, 2 da; m 2, 1980, Sheila Joan Collett; *Career* barr Inner Temple 1951, recorder of Crown Ct 1972-75, recorder of London 1975-; kt 1983; *Style—* His Hon Judge Sir James Miskin, QC; Central Criminal Court, City of London, EC4M 7EH

MISKIN, Raymond John; s of Sidney George Miskin (d 1979), and Hilda, *née* Holdsworth (d 1976); *b* 4 July 1928; *Educ* Woking GS for Boys, Southall Technical Coll (HNC Mech); *m* 14 July 1951 (m dis 1981), Betty; 1 s (Gerald d 1971), 1 da (Karen b 1959); *Career* chartered engr, conslt; sec: Inst of Quality Assurance 1969-71, Inst of Production Engrs 1976-87; hon memb: Inst of Industl Engrs, Indian Inst of Production Engrs; memb: Soc of Manufacturing Engineers; FIMechE, FIProdE, MRAeS, FIQA, FRSA; *Recreations* golf; *Clubs* Athenaeum; *Style—* Raymond Miskin, Esq; c/o Lloyds Bank, Addlestone, Surrey GU16 5UU

MITCALFE, Capt John Stanley; OBE (1965), VRD (1964); s of (William) Stanley Mitcalfe, MC (A/Maj; d 1962), of Underwood, Riding Mill, Northumberland, and Mary Catherine Louise, *née* Burn (d 1964); *b* 27 Feb 1927; *Educ* Rugby, Brasenose Coll (MA); *m* 1, 30 July 1953 (m dis 1974), Ann, da of William Andrew McClelland, of Westering, Silecroft, Cumbria; 4 da (Mary b 6 March 1954, Susan b 30 Oct 1955, Caroline b 28 Sept 1957, Veronica b 19 Feb 1962); m 2, 30 March 1979, Carol Ann, da of late Frederick Bradley, of Carlisle, Cumberland; *Career* joined RNVR 1944, served in Minesweepers in Far Eastern theatre until 1948, HMS Calliope Tyne Div Headquarters, Cdr and Exec Offr 1962-63, CO and (A) Capt Tyne Div RNR 1966-70, RNR Aide-de-Camp to The Queen 1971, ret 1972; dir various family Cos Northumberland 1952-70; dist cmmnr Boy Scout Assoc (Hexham), county cmmr sea scouts (Northumberland); *Recreations* game fishing, grouse and pheasant shooting; *Style—* Capt J Stanley Mitcalfe, OBE, VRD; Bradley Ings, 5 Aireside Tce, Cononley, N Yorks BD20 8LY (☎ 0535 32414)

MITCHARD, Anthony Keith; s of Albert Ernest James Mitchard and Florence, *née* West; *b* 26 Dec 1934; *Educ* King Edward's Sch Bath; *m* 2 April 1956, Kathleen Margaret, da of Albert Henry Smith; 2 s (Michael David b 1963, John Robert b 1967), 3 da (Andrea Marie b 1958, Susan Elizabeth b 1959, Alison Judith b 1971); *Career* chief exec: Avon Rubber plc (dir 1974-); dep chm: Community Cncl for Wiltshire Tstee, Burnbake Trust; *Recreations* golf, cricket, reading; *Style—* Anthony Mitchard, Esq; Avon Rubber plc, Melksham, Wiltshire SN12 8AA (☎ 0225 703101, telex 44142, fax 0225 707880, car tel 0836 250459)

MITCHARD, Sherly Anne; da of Dennis Robert Wilkins Chappel, and Joan Gladys, *née* Woolcott; *b* 15 Feb 1953; *Educ* Weirfield Sch Taunton, Portsmouth Poly (BA); *m* 28 June 1980 (m dis 1985), Gerald Steven Paul Mitchard, of Cheltenham, Gloucestershire; *Career* auditor Peat McLintock 1975-79 (tax dept 1979-81), Arthur Anderson & Co 1981-84 (sr mangr 1983), ptnr Clark Whitehall 1987 (joined 1985); memb ICAEW 1978, ACA 1978; *Recreations* interior decoration, gardening, psychic studies; *Clubs* Network; *Style—* Ms Sherly Mitchard; 151 De Beauvoir Rd, London, N1 4DL (☎ 249 4835); Clark Whitehill 25 New Street Sq, London EC4 (☎ 353 1577)

MITCHELL, Andrew; MBE (1984); s of Mitchell Andrew (d 1959), of Scotland, and Catherine Mary Macrae; *b* 6 Nov 1925; *Educ* Fettes Coll Edinburgh; *m* 1955, Liv Ragnhild, da of Eilert Holst (d 1942), of Norway; 1 s (Andrew b 1969), 1 da (Katrina b 1965); *Career* Capt The Black Watch, ME 1944-46; dir: Thorn EMI Elstree Studios 1973-, Thorn EMI Screen Entertainment Ltd 1976-, Childrens Film and TV Fndn 1977-, Garrirights Ltd 1977-, Thorn EMI Films 1978-, Argonaut Films 1979-, Bowden Ltd (resigned 1981), EMI Wardour Street 1982-, Technicolor Ltd (resigned 1984); md Thorn EMI Elstree Film Studios 1986-; *Style—* Andrew Mitchell, Esq, MBE; 67 Wood St, Barnet, Herts EN5 4BT (☎ 01 449 6984); Thorn EMI Elstree Studios, Borehamwood, Herts WD6 1JG (☎ 01 953 1600, telex 922436 EFilms G)

MITCHELL, Andrew John Bower; MP (Cons) Gedling 1987; s of David Bower Mitchell, MP, *qv*, and Pamela Elaine, *née* Haward; great-gf Lord Mayor of London and Master of the Vintners Co; *b* 23 Mar 1956; *Educ* Rugby, Jesus Coll Camb (MA); *m* 27 July 1985, Sharon Denise, da of David Benedict Bennett; 1 da (Hannah Katherine b 1987); *Career* First Royal Tank Regt (SSLC) 1975; pres Cambridge Union 1978, chm Cambridge Univ Cons Assoc; contested (C) Sunderland S 1983 general election, appt pps Foreign & Cwlth Off to Hon William Waldergrove, MP; chm: The Coningsby Co 1983-84, Lazard Bros & Co Ltd 1979-87, financial conslt Elvino Co 1982, conslt Lazard Bros 1987; United Nations Military Medal; Liveryman Worshipful Co of Vintners; *Recreations* skiing, sailing, reading; *Clubs* Carlton and District Constitutional; *Style—* Andrew Mitchell, Esq, MP; 30 Gibson Square, Islington, London N1 (☎ 01 226 5519); Dovecote Farmhouse, Tithby, Nottinghamshire (☎ 0949 39587); House of Commons, London SW1 (☎ 01 219 4494)

MITCHELL, (John) Angus Macbeth; CB (1979), CVO (1961, MC 1946); s of John Fowler Mitchell, CIE (d 1984), of Bath, and Sheila Macbeth Mitchell, MBE; both parents were joint authors of Monumental Inscriptions in 8 Scottish counties; *b* 25 August 1924; *Educ* Marlborough, Brasenose Coll Oxford (BA); *m* 1948, Ann Katharine, da of Herbert Stansfield Williamson (d 1955), of Oxford; 2 s (Jonathan, Andrew), 2 da (Charlotte, Catherine); *Career* served WWII RAC, Capt NW Europe 1943-46; civil servant Scottish Off 1949-84, sec Scottish Educn Dept 1976-84; chm of Ct Univ of Stirling 1984-, memb Cmmn on Local Authy Accounts in Scotland 1985-, chm Scottish Action on Dementia 1985-, vice-convener Scottish Cncl of Voluntary Orgns 1986-, memb Historic Bldgs Cncl for Scotland 1988-; Hon LLD Dundee 1983; kt Order of Orange-Nassau (Netherlands) 1946; *Books* Procedures for the Reorganisation of Schools in England (1987); *Recreations* old Penguins, genealogy, maps; *Clubs* New (Edinburgh); *Style—* Angus Mitchell, Esq, CB, CVO, MC; 20 Regent Terr, Edinburgh EH7 5BS (☎ 031 556 7671)

MITCHELL, Austin Vernon; MP (Lab) Great Grimsby 1983-; s of Richard Mitchell; *b* 19 Sept 1934; *Educ* Woodbottom Cncl Sch, Bingley GS, Manchester Univ, Nuffield Coll Oxford (DPhil); *m* 1 (m dis), Patricia Jackson; 2 da (Kirri, Susan); m 2, Linda McDougall; 1 s (Jonathan), 1 da (Hannah); *Career* MP (Lab) Grimsby 1977-1983, oppn whip; former Univ lectr in history and politics, journalist with Yorks TV 1969-71 and 1973-77, presenter BBC Current Affrs 1972-73; pps to Mr Fraser Min of State for Prices and Consumer protection 1977-79, opposition whip, Treasy Lab Solidarity, Fell of the Indust and Parly Tst; *Books Incl:* Westminster Man: A Tribal Anthology of the Commons People (1982), The Case for Labour (1983), Whigs in Opposition 1815-30, Politics and People in New Zealand, Half Gallon Quarter Acre Pavlova, Can Labour Win Again, Yes Maggie there is an Alternative; *Recreations* photography, comtemplating exercise; *Style—* Austin Mitchell, Esq, MP; House of Commons, SW1 (☎ 01 219 4559); 1 Abbey Park Rd, Grimsby, S Humberside (☎ 0472 42145); 9 Brooksville Ave, Queen's Park London NW6 (☎ 01 219 4559)

MITCHELL, Dr Brian Redman; s of Irvin Mitchell (d 1969), of Marsh House, Oxenhope, Yorks, and Dora Eleanor, *née* Redman (d 1981); *b* 20 Sept 1929; *Educ* Malsis Sch, Sedbergh Sch, Univ of Aberdeen (MA), Peterhouse Coll Cambridge (PhD); *m* 1, 25 Aug 1952, Barbara, da of Douglas Gordon Hay (d 1946); m 2, 11 Sept 1968, Ann Leslie, da of David Leslie Birney (d 1942); 2 s (David b 1969, Peter b 1972); *Career* Flt-Lt RAF, ret 1958; res offr Cambridge Univ dept of applied econs 1958-67, univ lectr Cambridge and fell Trinity College 1967-; *Recreations* watching cricket and rugby football, gardening; *Clubs* MCC; *Style—* Dr Brian Mitchell; 20 High Street, Toft, Cambridge CB3 7RL (☎ 0223 262516); Trinity College, Cambridge (☎ 0223 338502)

MITCHELL, (Richard George) Bruce; s of George Fowler Mitchell (d 1953), of Rugby, and Marjorie Alice, *née* Barker (d 1986); *b* 2 Nov 1923; *Educ* Marlborough, Gonville & Caius Coll Cambridge; *m* 10 June 1950, Sheila, da of Francis Moorhouse Dean, MBE (d 1970); 1 s (Ian Moorhouse b 25 Feb 1957); *Career* mktg exec BXL Plastics Ltd 1963-73, mangr mkt devpt Br Industl Plastics Ltd 1973-80, fedn sec Glass and Glazing Fedn 1981-88; memb Parly Advsy Ctee for Tport Safety; Freeman City of London 1977, Liveryman Worshipful Co Horners 1977; fell Plastics and Rubber Inst 1967; *Books* Plastics in the Building Industry (1968), Glass Reinforced Plastics (jtly 1970), Developments in Plastics Technology (jtly 1982); *Recreations* freelance journalism, golf; *Style—* Bruce Mitchell, Esq; Danes Way House, 3 Danes Way, Oxshott, Leatherhead, Surrey KT22 OLU (☎ 0372 842851)

MITCHELL, Charles Herbert; DL (Staffordshire); *b* 18 Feb 1932; *Educ* Shrewsbury Sch, London Univ (BSc); *m* 21 Dec 1958, Mary Rose, *née* Shaw; 2 s (Jonathan b 1960, Julian b 1966), 1 da (Annabel b 1962); *Career* Nat Serv RE 1950-52, cmmnd UK and BAOR TA 1952-60, Capt RE; joined William Walker and Sons Ltd 1950; dir: Century Oils Gp plc, Amicoil Ltd, Anglo Pennsylvanian Oil Co Ltd, AP Oil (UK) Ltd, Braybrooke Bros (Waste Oils) Ltd, Braybrooke Chemical Services Ltd, Century Holdings (Nederland) BV, Century Oils Australia Pty Ltd, Century Oils Canada Inc, Century Oils (Europe) SA, Eclipsol Oil Co Ltd, Hein de Windt BV, Hein de Windt Europe BV, NGF 86 (Stoke-on-Trent Staffordshire) Ltd, PHA Smit Doetinchem BV, 7 Oils Limited, Specification Fuel Oils Ltd, Wood Mitchell & Co Ltd; apptd gen cmmnr Taxes 1977, fndr memb and dep chm of Management Ctee of Business Initiative (Enterprise Tst) 1981, cncl memb N Staffordshire Chamber of Commerce Industry 1981; chm: Industrial Ambass Programme, Local Employers Network, UK rep to European Cmmn for Regeneration 1977-80; pres of UK Delegation to European Union Independent Lubricant Manufacturers (UEIL) 1982- (European pres of UEIL 1982-83, 1984-85 and re-appted 1986-87); *Recreations* golf, tennis, squash, swimming, shooting, fishing, gardening, music; *Style—* Charles Mitchell, Esq, DL; c/o Century Oils Gp plc, New Century St, Hanley, Stoke-on-Trent ST1 5HU Staffs (☎ 0782 202521)

MITCHELL, Christopher Meredyth; s of Francis John Lindley Mitchell (d 1958), of Old Heathfield, Sussex, and Irene Springett, *née* Butt (d 1949); *b* 16 Nov 1925; *Educ* Rossall, Sidney Sussex Coll Cambridge (MA); *m* 13 Sept 1958, Hilary Margaret, da of John Howard Gaunt, of Manchester; 2 s (David b 1960, Steven b 1969), 1 da (Sarah b 1963); *Career* ptnr Kennedy & Donkin 1958, jt sr pntr Kennedy & Donkin 1976-86, dir Kennedy & Donkin Gp 1987-; chm: Assoc of Consulting Engrs 1977-78, Br Conslts Bureau 1988-89; pres Br section societé Des Ingénieurs et Scientifiques de France 1988-89; pres Woking Mind, chm Godalming-Joigny Friendship Assoc, memb governing body Guildford Coll of Technol; memb Woking UDC 1968-74, Woking Borough Cncl 1974-82, Mayor of Woking 1974-75; Freeman City of London, Liveryman Worshipful Co of Engrs 1988; FIEE; *Recreations* astronomy, ornithology, music, European languages; *Style—* Christopher Mitchell, Esq; Two Roods, 20 Warren Rd, Guildford, Surrey (☎ 0483 504407); Kennedy & Donkin Gp, Westbrook Mills, Godalming, Surrey (☎ 04868 25900, fax 04868 25136, telex 859373 KDHO G)

MITCHELL, Lt-Col Colin Campbell; s of Colin Mitchell, MC (d 1967), of Argyll Scotland, and Janet Bowie, *née* Gilmour (d 1978); granted arms by Lord Lyon from m of Colin Mitchell (b 1830) to Isabella Campbell (1834-94), of Minard, Argyll; *b* 17 Nov 1925; *Educ* Whitgift, Staff Coll Camberley; *m* 1956, Jean Hamilton Susan, da of Wing Cdr Stephen Phillips, MC (d 1969), of Taplow, Bucks; 2 s (Lorne, Angus), 1 da (Colina); *Career* Argyll and Sutherland Highlanders 1943-67, served Italy, Palestine, Korea, Cyprus, Kenya, Borneo, Aden; staff appts: ADC to GOC-in-C Scottish Command, MO4, War Office, 51 Highland Div; Bde Maj KAR, GSO1 to CDS (Earl Mountbatten); MP W Aberdeenshire (Cons) 1970-74; PPS to sec of state for Scotland 1972-73; Sardar Malakhan (1980); *Recreations* golf, shooting; *Clubs* Garrick, Puffins (Edinburgh); *Style—* Lt-Col Colin Mitchell; The Old Farmhouse, Hill Farm, Gressenhall, Dereham, Norfolk NR19 2NR (☎ 036 269 5305)

MITCHELL, Sir David Bower; MP (C) N W Hampshire 1983-; s of James Mitchell (d 1959), and Mona Elizabeth Blackett, *née* Bower (d 1956); gs of Sir Alfred L Bower and Dorcas M Bower, *née* Blackett (see Blacketts of Wylan-earlier Debretts); *b* 20 June 1928; *Educ* Aldenham; *m* 1954, Pamela Elaine, da of Dr Clifford Haward; 2 s

(Andrew, Graham), 1 da (Suki); *Career* former wine shipper and dir El Vino Co Ltd; memb St Pancras Cncl 1956-59, MP (C) Basingstoke 1964-1983, oppn whip 1965-67, PPS to Social Servs Sec 1970-74, chm Cons Smaller Business Ctee 1974-79; parly under-sec state: Indust 1979-81, NI 1981-83, Tport 1983-; min of state Tport 1986-; kt 1988; *Clubs* Carlton; *Style*— Sir David Mitchell, MP; Rosscourt Mews, Palace Street, London SW1 (☎ 01 828 7605); Berry Horn Cottage, Odiham, Hants (☎ 025 671 2161)

MITCHELL, David Ronald; s of Sir Frank Herbert Mitchell, KCVO, CBE (d 1951), of Forest House, Crowborough, Sussex, and Grace Penelope, *née* Maffey (d 1959); *b* 26 Sept 1919; *Educ* Eton, Royal Sch of Mines, Imperial Coll (ARSM, BSc); *m* 29 Aug 1953, Joyce Rosamund Amy (Joy), da of Sir Edgar Waterlow, BT (d 1953), of Winscombe House, Crowborough, Sussex; *Career* opencast mining in Leics Miny of Fuel and Power 1942-43, Amalgamated Tin Mines of Nigeria (part of London Tin Gp) 1943-45, temp with Pauling & Co (civil engrs) Orkney and Middx 1945-46, chm Anglo Oriental (Malaya) Ltd 1959-67 (joined 1947, dir 1953), chm (previously chief exec) London Tin Corpn 1972-76, dir Chartered Bank and Standard Chartered plc 1974-88; chm Henham Conservation Soc 1978-81; fell Inst of Mining and Metallurgy; *Recreations* music, gardening, previously golf; *Clubs* MCC, City of London; *Style*— David R Mitchell, Esq; Wood End Cottage, Henham, Bishop's Stortford, Herts CM22 6AZ (☎ 0279 850254)

MITCHELL, David William; CBE (1983); s of William Baxter Mitchell (d 1983), and Betty Steel, *née* Allan (d 1959); *b* 4 Jan 1933; *Educ* Merchiston Castle Sch Edinburgh; *m* 1965, Lynda Katherine Marion, da of Herbert John Laurie Guy (d 1975); 1 da (Louisa-Jayne b 1972); *Career* cmmnd (NS) Royal Scots Fus 1950; bd memb Western Regional Hosp 1965-72, pres Timber Trades Benevolent Soc of UK 1974, CBI Scottish Cncl 1979-85, dir Mallinson-Denny (Scotland) 1977-; pres: Scottish Timber Trade Assoc 1980-82, Scottish Cons and Unionist Assoc 1981-83; memb Scottish Cncl (Devpt and Indust) 1984-, bd memb Cumbernauld New Town 1985 chm 1987; *Recreations* fishing, shooting, golf; *Clubs* Western (Glasgow), Prestwick, Royal and Ancient of St Andrews; *Style*— David Mitchell, Esq, CBE; Dunmullen House, Blanefield, Stirlingshire G63 9AJ; Grangemouth Sawmills, Earls Rd, Grangemouth FK3 8XF (☎ 0324 483294)

MITCHELL, Air Cdre Sir (Arthur) Dennis; KBE (1977), CVO (1961, DFC 1944 and bar 1945, AFC 1943); s of late Col A Mitchell, DSO, RA; gggs of Col Hugh Henry Mitchell (who cmd 4 Bde at Battle of Waterloo and who was only Bde Cdr below the rank of Gen to be mentioned in Duke of Wellington's despatches) and Lady Harriet Somerset, da of 5 Duke of Beaufort; *b* 26 May 1918; *Educ* Nautical Coll Pangbourne, RAF Coll Cranwell; *m* 1949, Mireille Caroline, da of Comte Henri Cornet de Ways Ruart; 1 s (Michael); *Career* joined RAF 1936, served WW II, Dep Capt The Queen's Flight 1956-59, Capt 1962-64; ADC to HM The Queen 1958-62, extra equerry 1962-; md Aero Systems (SA); founder of Brussels Airways (SA), Aero Distributors (SA); *Recreations* golf; *Clubs* Naval and Military, RAF; *Style*— Air Cdre Sir Dennis Mitchell, KBE, CVO, DFC, AFC; 10 Chemin des Chasseurs, 1328 Ohain, Belgium (☎ 02 653 13 01, off: 02 653 00 33)

MITCHELL, Sir Derek Jack; KCB (1974), CB (1967, CVO 1966); s of Sidney Mitchell; *b* 5 Mar 1922; *Educ* St Paul's, Christ Church Oxford; *m* 1944, Miriam, da of E F Jackson; 1 s, 2 da; *Career* served WW II RAC; sr advsr Shearson Lehman Bros Int 1979-; dir: Bowater Industs plc 1979-, Bowater Incorporated 1984-, Standard Chartered plc 1979-; ind dir The Observer 1981-; memb: Nat Theatre Bd 1977-, Cncl UCL 1978-82, PLA 1979-82; 2 perm sec Treasury 1973-77, econ min, head UK Treasury and Supply Delgn, exec dir IMF and World Bank Washington 1969-72; formerly with Miny Agric and Fish and Dept Econ Affrs; former princ private sec to: chllr Exchequer (Reginald Maudling), and to PMs, Rt Hon Harold Wilson and Rt Hon Sir Alec Douglas-Home; joined Treasury 1947; *Clubs* Garrick; *Style*— Sir Derek Mitchell, KCB, CB, CVO; One Broadgate, London EC2M 7HA (☎ 01 260 2580, telex 899621)

MITCHELL, Lady; Elizabeth; da of late Charles Leigh Pemberton; *b* 12 Feb 1921; *Educ* Wimbledon HS, Francis Holland Sch, St Hilda's Coll Oxford, London Univ (LLB); *m* 1945, Sir George Irvine Mitchell, CB, QC (d 1978), 1 s, 1 da; *Career* barr Grays Inn, pt-t chm of Industl Tbnls (1977); Treasy Slrs Dept 1973-77; lectr South Bank Polytech 1973; work for Family Planning Assoc; Broke Advsy Centres; Pregnancy Advsy Service; JP 1966-83; *Style*— Lady Mitchell; 14 Rodway Rd, Roehampton, London SW15

MITCHELL, Dr (Robert) Gordon; s of Robert Stanley Mitchell (d 1948), of Levin N Is NZ and Rina Hinemoa, *née* Bagnall; *b* 29 Oct 1921; *Educ* Loughborough GS, Manchester Univ (LDS MB ChB), Royal Coll of Surgeons (FDS); *m* 12 May 1956, Elizabeth Burchell, da of Frank Stanley Edmonds (d 1936); 2 da (Susanne (Mrs Price) b 1957, Juliet (Mrs Burnham) b 1959); *Career* Capt RADC 1945-48; sr registrar oral surgery Eastman Dental Hosp London 1953-56, conslt surgn and dental supt Birmingham Dental Hosp 1957-87, conslt in oral surgery and oral medicine The Priory Hosp Birmingham Droitwich Pte Hosp 1988-; chm: Assoc of Dental Hosp UK 1969-72, Examiners Central Examing Bd for Dental Hygiene 1971-75; memb: standing Dental Advsy Ctee DOH 1972-81, Dental Advsy Ctee med Protection Soc 1981-86, exec ctee Birmingham Central Health Dist 1969-75, chm Divn of Dentists Birmingham Univ 1975-81; hon sr lectr Birmingham Univ; BMA, BDA, FBAOMS, Worcs Odontological Soc; *Recreations* cricket, ornithology, gardening; *Style*— Dr Gordon Mitchell; The Hill House, Stoke Rd, Wychbold, Droitwich, Worcs WR9 OBT (☎ 052 786 211); The Priory Hospital, Priory Rd, Edgbaston, Birmingham

MITCHELL, Harold Charles; CIE (1948); s of late Daniel Charles Mitchell (d 1947), of Bristol, and Helen Mitchell (d 1949); *b* 7 Mar 1896; *Educ* Fairfield Sch; *m* 1923, Edna Evadne (d 1982), da of Frederick Fleetwood Bion, CIE (d 1949, a former chief engr of irrigation United Provinces, India); 1 da (Valerie Ann); *Career* RNVR Bristol 1912-19, served WW I (Antwerp 1914), Indian Police 1920, central intelligence offr United Provinces and Ajmer 1937, dep inspr gen of Police HQ and railways 1946, ret 1949; pres Indian Police (UK) Assoc 1980-86; *Clubs* Naval; *Style*— Harold Mitchell, Esq, CIE; 41 Clarefield Ct, Sunningdale, Ascot, Berks SL5 0EA (☎ 0990 23962)

MITCHELL, James Alexander Hugh; s of late William Moncur Mitchell; *b* 20 July 1939; *Educ* Winchester, Trinity Cambridge; *m* 1962, Janice Page, *née* Davison; 3 s; *Career* chm Mitchell Beazley Ltd, senior vice-pres American Express Co Communications Division; *Recreations* fishing, shooting, gardening; *Clubs* Garrick; *Style*— James Mitchell, Esq; Teasel, Wilsford-cum-Lake, Nr Amesbury, Wilts

MITCHELL, John Anthony; s of Dennis George Mitchell (d 1978), and Jean Louise, *née* Tinker; *b* 27 Dec 1946; *Educ* King's Coll Taunton, Brasenose Coll Oxford (BA); *m* 24 Feb 1968 (separated), Philippa Lyndsey, da of Harry Richard Minchin, of the Isle of Wight; 2 s (Bendor b 1969, Adam b 1982), 2 da (Samantha Jane b 1968, Jasmin b 1985); *Career* dir Lloyds Merchant Bank Ltd, London, dep chm Lloyds International Ltd Sydney; *Recreations* sailing, golf, reading; *Clubs* Royal Solent Yacht, Royal Sydney Yacht Squadron; *Style*— John Mitchell, Esq; 58 Willeshall Road, London SW4; 40/66 Queen Victoria Street, London EC4 (☎ 01 248 2244)

MITCHELL, Dr John Matthew; CBE (1975); s of Clifford George Arthur Mitchell (d 1933), and Grace Maud, *née* Jamson (d 1976); *b* 22 Mar 1925; *Educ* Ilford Co HS, Worcester Coll Oxford, Queens' Coll Cambridge (MA), Vienna Univ (PhD); *m* 5 April 1952, Eva, da of Dr Friedrich V Rupprecht (d 1964); 3 s (Oliver James Clifford b 1952, Gregory Charles Matthew b 1954, Dominic John Frederick b 1965), 1 da (Clarissa Maria b 1956); *Career* WWII Naval Intelligence 1943-46; Br Cncl served: Austria, Egypt, Yugoslavia, E Pakistan, Fed Repub of Germany, Britain (controller educn sci and med div); ret asst dir gen Br Cncl; currently translator and conslt in int affrs; fell Wolfson Coll Cambridge 1972-73; FIL; *Books* International Cultural Relations (1986); *Recreations* golf, tennis, theatre, chess, bridge; *Clubs* National Liberal, Tandridge GC; *Style*— Dr John Mitchell, CBE; The Cottage, Pains Hill Corner, Limpsfield, Surrey RH8 0RB (☎ 0883 723 354)

MITCHELL, John Wallace; s of George Harold Mitchell (d 1974), of Hove, and Martha Maude, *née* Wallace (d 1986); *b* 31 May 1931; *Educ* Brighton, Hove and Sussex GS; *Career* telecommunications (radar) engr coast def SE Eng REME 1949-51; CA; Charter Knight & Co 1951-57, Remington Rand Univac Computers 1957-60, Rank Orgn (Mgmnt) Ltd 1960-63, Harold Whitehead & Ptnrs Mgmnt Conslts 1963-67, Thornton Baker Assocs 1967-77, Stoy Horwath Ltd 1977-82, Wallace Mitchell & Co 1982-89; contested local cncl elections 1989; memb: Brighton Hove and dist Scottish Assoc, Sussex Assoc Scottish Soc (fndr chm), Aldrington Scottish Dance Club, Brighton and Hove Motor Club; tres United Wards Club of City of London; former: chm Brighton Velo Club, sec Br League Racing Cyclists; Freeman City of London 1977, Liveryman Worshipful Co Chartered Accountants 1977 and Worshipful Co Carmen 1986; FCA 1957, FBCS 1958, FInst D 1962, FIMC 1965, FVRS 1972, FRS 1975, MIAM 1985, FSA (Scotland) 1988; *Books* Whetherly Books of Scottish Country Dance (Nos 1-22, 1967-88), A Course of Instruction in Scottish Dancing (1984, and 1988); *Recreations* teach Scottish dancing, motor sport, charitable work; *Clubs* Carlton, RAC, City Livery; *Style*— John Mitchell, Esq; Wallace Mitchell & Co, Whetherly House, 52 Shirley Drive, Hove, Sussex BN3 6UF (☎ 0273 553862)

MITCHELL, Jonathan Stuart; s of Rev Ronald Frank Mitchell, and Marjory Mabel, *née* Callaghan; *b* 29 Jan 1947; *Educ* Mill Hill Sch, Trinity Coll Dublin (BA, MA); 1 s (Christian Stuart b 21 Nov 1980), 1 da (Emily Katherina b 4 April 1982); *Career* barr Grays Inn, practising SE circuit 1974-; mktg div Couraulds Textiles 1969-72, PR John Laing 1972-73; memb: exec ctee SDP Southwark 1981-87, local govt candidate SDP Dulwich 1982, 1984, 1986, SLD 1988-89, Herne Hill Baptist Church; *Recreations* gardening, swimming, rowing; *Style*— Jonathan Mitchell, Esq; 35 Pickwick Rd, Dulwich, London SE21 7JN; 11 South Sq, Grays Inn, London WC1R 3EV (☎ 01 831 2311)

MITCHELL, Sheriff (James Lachlan) Martin; RD (1969); s of Lachlan Martin Victor Mitchell, OBE, MB (d 1956); *b* 13 June 1929; *Educ* Cargilfield, Sedbergh, Edinburgh Univ (MA, LLB); *Career* Cdr RNR (ret 1974); advocate 1957-74, standing jr counsel in Scotland to Admiralty Bd 1963-74; sheriff Lothians and Peebles 1974 (floating sheriff 1974-78), sheriff at Edinburgh 1978; *Recreations* fishing, photography, the gramophone; *Clubs* New (Edinburgh), Highland (Inverness); *Style*— Sheriff Martin Mitchell, RD; 3 Great Stuart St, Edinburgh EH3 6AP (☎ 031 225 3384); Sheriff's Chambers, Sheriff Ct, Lawnmarket, Edinburgh EH1 2NS (☎ 031 226 7181)

MITCHELL, Mary, Lady; Mary; *née* Pringle; da of late William Pringle, of Whytbank and Yair Selkirkshire; *m* 1947, Sir Harold Paton Mitchell, 1 and last Bt (d 1983); 1 da (Mary-Jean b 1951 m Peter Brian Green; 2 s); *Career* DStJ; *Recreations* travel, reading; *Style*— Mary, Lady Mitchell; Maison Silence, 3920, Zermatt, Valais, Switzerland; Prospect, Ocho Rias, Jamaica

MITCHELL, Nigel Campbell; s of Lt Cdr Malcolm Alexander Mitchell RN, of Perth, Scot, and Wilhelmina Winifred, *née* Thompson; *b* 10 July 1953; *Educ* St Edwards Oxford, LSE (LLB); *m* 25June 1988, Prudence Gaynor, da of Clement Rodney Spencer, of Edgbaston, Birmingham; *Career* barr Lincolns Inn 1978, in practised at 3 Paper Bldgs, Temple, 1978-; *Recreations* deep-sea fishing, scuba diving, golf; *Clubs* RAC; *Style*— Nigel Mitchell, Esq; 3 Paper Buildings, Temple, London EC4Y 7EU (☎ 01 583 8055, car 0836 206 765)

MITCHELL, Norman; s of Walter Arnold Driver (d 1961), of Sheffield, and Ellizabeth, *née* Slimm (d 1959); *b* 27 August 1918; *Educ* Carter Knowle Cncl Sch Sheffield, Nether Edge GS, Sheffield Univ, Guildhall Sch of Music & Drama (LGSM); *m* 31 Aug 1946, Pauline Margaret, da of William George Southcombe; 1 s (Christopher b 22 May 1948), 1 da (Jacqueline Margaret b 28 Jan 1955); *Career* serv WWII: Lance Corpl 10 FD Surgical Unit 1939-45 (Western Desert 1940-43, Italy 1943-45), Army Bureau of Current Affrs Play Unit 1945-47; actor; RSC Stratford-upon-Avon and tour of Aust 1948-50, BBC Drama Rep Co 1952 and 53; over 2000 tv transmissions incl: Vanity Fair, All Creatures Great and Small; over 100 films incl: Oliver, St Trinian's series, Carry On series; West End theatre incl: A View from the Bridge and The Visit for Peter Brook, Shadow of Heroes for Sir Peter Hall, The Clandestine Marriage for Sir Anthony Quayle; dir of charities: Royal Gen Theatrical Fund, Entertainments Charities Tst; cncllr Br Actors Equity Assoc 1983-88 (memb exec 1983-85 and 1985-87); memb: Cinema ITV Veterans, Monte Cassino Venerans; Africa Star (8th Army Clasp), Italy Star, VM; *Books* Amos Goes To War (1987); *Recreations* collecting books (fine editions); *Clubs* Savage, Green Room, Folio, BBC; *Style*— Norman Mitchell, Esq; Kingfisher Cottage, 2a Summer Gdns, East Molesey, Surrey KT8 9LT (☎ 01 398 4930); Eric L'Epine Smith & Carney Associaters, 10 Wyndham Place, London W1H 1AS (☎ 01 724 0739)

MITCHELL, The Very Rev Patrick Reynolds; s of Lt-Col Percy Reynolds Mitchell, DSO (d 1954), of Whitestaunton Manor, Chard Somerset, and Constance Margaret, *née* Kerby (d 1955); *b* 17 Mar 1930; *Educ* Eton, Merton Coll Oxford (MA), Wells Theological Coll; *m* 1, 1959, Mary Evelyn (d 1986), da of John Savile Phillips (d 1960); 3 s (Andrew Patrick b 1964, Julian Mark b 1968, Nicholas David b 1970), 1 da (Sarah Jane b 1962); m 2, 1988, Mrs Pamela Douglas- Pennant, da of late A G Le Marchant, of Wolford Lodge, Honiton, Devon; *Career* Nat Serv Welsh Gds 1948-49; curate St Mark's Mansfield 1954-57, priest vicar Wells Cathedral, chaplain Wells Theological Coll 1957-61, vicar St James' Milton Portsmouth 1961-67, vicar Frome Selwood Somerset 1967-73, dean of Wells 1973-; hon Freeman City of Wells 1986; res fell Merton Coll Oxford 1984; FSA; *Recreations* family, music, gardening; *Style—* The Very Rev Patrick Mitchell; The Dean's Lodging, The Liberty, Wells, Somerset (☎ 0749 72192); The Cathedral Offices, The West Cloister, Wells (☎ 0749 74483)

MITCHELL, Raymond; s of John Mitchell, of Helston, Cornwall, and Nora *née* Polglase; *b* 24 May 1933; *Educ* Probus Sch for Boys, South West Coll of Commerce Chartered Association of Certified Accountants (Dip in Mgmnt Accounting Business Studies); *m* 15 Feb 1958, Jean Patrica; 3 da (Sandra b 1960, Jennifer (Mrs Fishe b 1962, Lorraine b 1962); *Career* auditor Touche Ross & Co 1954-61, mgmnt appts BP 1961- 73, gp fin controller BBA Gp Ltd 1973-76, dir BBA Automatic Ltd 1976-82, fin dir BBA Gp plc 1982-87, chm Mitcor Servs Ltd 1988-; corp affairs Div BBA Gp plc 1987-88, JDipMA, memb ACCA cncl 1979-; *Recreations* golf, badminton; *Clubs* Sand Moor GC Leeds; *Style—* Raymond Mitchell, Esq; 2 Fern Chase, Bracken Pk, Leeds LS14 3JL (☎ 0532 893330);

MITCHELL, Robert; OBE (1984); s of Robert Mitchell, and Lizzie, *née* Snowdon; *b* 14 Dec 1913; *Educ* W Ham Secdy Sch, St John's Coll Cambridge (MA); *m* 31 Jan 1946, Reinholda (Ronnie) Thorretta Louise Clara, da of HREL Kettlitz (d 1959), of Bilthoven, Holland; 2 s (Robert b 1946, Hugh b 1948), 1 step s (Simon Ritsema Van Eck b 1938); *Career* Flt Lt RAF 1939-46, liaison offr Royal Dutch Meteorogical Serv 1945-46; md R Mitchell & Co (Eng) Ltd 1946-81 (chm 1958-81); Parly cand (C) W Ham S 1964 and 1966; memb: Wanstead and Woodford Cncl 1958-65 (dep mayor 1960-61), GLC 1964-86 (chm 1971-72), London and SE Regnl Cncl 1969-79, CBI ctee State Intervention in Private indust 1976-78, Smaller Firms Cncl 1977-79; chm nat jt negotiating ctee Local Authy Fire Bdes 1970-71; ctee memb Crystal Palace Nat Sports Centre 1965-88, chm Wanstead & Woodford Cons Assoc 1965-68 (vice pres 1968-), govr Chigwell Sch 1966-, chm Fire Bde and Ambulance 1967-71, chm Covent Garden Devpt Ctee 1972-73, chm Professional and Gen Servs Ctee 1977-79, verderer Epping Forest 1976-; rep: Cambridge Univ Swimming Club 1932-35 (Capt 1935), Eng and GB Waterpolo 1934-48 (incl 1936 & 1948 Olympic Games), Br Univs World Univ Games Swimming and Waterpolo 1933 & 1935, Rest of World v Champions Water Polo Univ Games 1935; Capt Plaistow Utd Swimming Club 1946-49 (pres 1955); Freeman: City of London 1971, Worshipful Co of Gardeners; Grand Offr Order of Orange-Nassau Holland 1972, Order of Rising Sun Japan 1971, Order of Star Afghanistan 1971; *Recreations* looking out of my window watching the seasons change in Epping Forest; *Clubs* Carlton, Hawks (Cambridge); *Style—* Robert Mitchell, Esq, OBE; Hatchwood House, Nursery Rd, Loughton, Essex IG10 4EF (☎ 01 508 9135); Little Brigg, Bessingham, Norwich, Norfolk

MITCHELL, Robin Paul; s of Frederick James Mitchell, of Enfield, Middx, and Maud Patricia, *née* Pawson; *b* 15 Feb 1955; *Educ* Latymer Sch; *m* Maria Ann, da of Sean Joseph Kealy, of Enfield, Middx; 2 s (John Paul b 26 April 1979, David Frederick b 2 Feb 1981), 1 da (Lucy Elizabeth b 9 April 1986); *Career* Charles Stanley & Co: unauthorised clerk 1973-75, authorised clerk 1975-81, sr dealer 1981-85, head dealing 1985-; memb: Int Stock Exchange Securities Assoc; *Recreations* football, cricket; *Clubs* Norseman FC, Old Edmontians; *Style—* Robin Mitchell, Esq; Charles Stanley & Co, Gdn House, 18 Finsbury Circus, London EC2M 7BL

MITCHELL, Hon Dame Roma Flinders; DBE (1982, CBE 1971), QC (1962); da of Harold Flinders Mitchell (d 1918), and Maude, *née* Wickham (d 1938); *b* 2 Oct 1913; *Educ* St Aloysius Coll, Adelaide Univ (LLB, DUniv); *Career* first woman QC in Australia 1962, first woman Supreme Ct judge in Australia 1965-83, vice-pres Law Cncl of Australia 1965, vice-pres Law Soc of SA 1965, chm Parole Bd of SA until 1981, chm Heritage Ctee of SA 1978-81, memb cncl Order of Australia 1979-, chllr Adelaide Univ, chm Winston Churchill Memorial Tst of Australia (former pres), chm Human Rights Cmmn of Australia 1981-86, nat pres Ryder Cheshire Fndn 1982-, memb bd of govrs S Aust Festival of Arts 1982-85; *Clubs* Queen Adelaide (SA), Lyceum (SA); *Style—* The Hon Dame Roma Mitchell, DBE, QC; 256 East Terrace, Adelaide, S Australia 5000 (☎ 08 223 5373)

MITCHELL, Sir (Seton) Steuart Crichton; KBE (1954), CB (1951, OBE 1941); s of Dr A Crichton Mitchell; *b* 9 Mar 1902; *Educ* Edinburgh Acad, RNC Osborne, RNC Dartmouth; *m* 1929, Elizabeth Duke; *Career* serv in WWI with RN, serv WWII in Admlty; chief engr Armament Design 1945-51, controller Royal Ordnance Factories 1951-56 and 1956-59, controller Guided Weapons and Electronics Miny of Aviation 1959-62; memb Br Tport Cmmn 1962, vice-chm Br Railways Bd 1963-64; chm: Machine Tool Indust EDC 1964-67, Shipbuilding Indust Trg Bd 1964-; memb: Central Trg Cncl 1965-, Nat Econ Devpt Ctee 1967-71; advsr (part-time) Miny of Technology 1965-67; US Legion of Merit; *Style—* Sir Steuart Mitchell, KBE, CB, OBE; 137 Swan Ct, Chelsea Manor St, London SW3 5RY (☎ 01 352 5571)

MITCHELL, Terence Leonard; s of Leonard Alfred James Mitchell, and Sarah Anne Mitchell; *b* 19 July 1934; *Educ* Worthing Boys HS, Univ of Auckland NZ (Dip Arch); *m* m 1, 1961 (m dis); 1 s, 2 da; m 2, 1989, Antonina Knight, da of late Constantine Popoff; *Career* violinist and music teacher until age 26, played under the batons of Sir Adrian Boult, Sir Malcolm Sargeant and John Hopkins; since qualifying in 1964 practised as architect; now chm Marquis Homes Ltd, dir Venture Inns of Br Ltd; notable works incl: award winning Cathedral Sq (Christchurch NZ) 1974, award winning Norman Kirk Courts (Christchurch NZ) 1978, holiday complex for Sudeley Castle 1985, The Hayes Retirement Village (Prestbury, Glos) 1987, The Allasdon Dene Hotel & Leisure Centre Lydney Glos; now specialising in the restoration of historic buildings; ARIBA, ANZIA;; *Recreations* English history and architecture, music, artist; *Style—* Terence Mitchell, Esq; 37 Hailes St, Winchcombe, Glos GL54 5HU (☎ 0242 603910); Marquis Homes Ltd, Marquis House, 2 North St, Wincombe, Glos GL54 5LH (☎ 0242 602243)

MITCHELL, William Vernon; s of Peter Mitchell (d 1976), and Ann Mitchell (d 1986); *b* 1 May 1923; *Educ* Dollar Acad, Liverpool Tech Coll; *m* 1944, Muriel Olive Cooke; 2 children; *Career* tech dir Lever Brothers Ltd to 1983; MRIC; *Recreations* golf; *Style—* William Mitchell, Esq; 15 Uplands Way, Sevenoaks, Kent (☎ 0732 456887)

MITCHELL ANDERSON, Hon Mrs (Cecilia Claribel); *née* Cavendish; da of 6 Baron Waterpark by his 1 w Isabel Jay, (Mrs Cavendish); *b* 11 June 1903; *m* 1933, James Mitchell Anderson, MD, ChB (d 1963); 2 da (Isabel, Annabel); *Style—* The Hon Mrs Mitchell Anderson; Courtenay Beach, Kingsway, Hove, Sussex BN3 2WF (☎ 0273 733622)

MITCHELL LAMBERT, Ian William; s of Ernest Joseph Lambert (d 1976), of Coventry, and Ivy Muriel, *née* Mitchell; *b* 3 Mar 1942; *Educ* Slough GS, King Henry VIII Sch Coventry, Univ of Wales (UC Swansea), Univ of Kent; *m* 21 Oct 1978, Mavis Crazencea, da of Agrippa Amado Rogers (d 1980), of SA; 1 s (Derek b 1969); *Career* theologian, author, industl relations consIt; lay pastor Weald Methodist Church; chm and md: Job Generation (Hldgs) Ltd, Job Generation Ltd; chm Job Generation Tning Tst; dir: IPSET, Centre for the Study of Early Christianity (UK off); chm Emeritus Professional Assoc of Teachers; memb: Industrial Tribunals; fell Coll of Preceptors; FBIM; *Clubs* Royal Cwlth; *Style—* Ian Mitchell Lambert, Esq; Tangnefedd, Windmill Road, Weald, Sevenoaks, Kent TN14 6PJ (☎ 0732 463460)

MITCHELL-INNES, Alistair Campbell; s of Peter Campbell Mitchell-Innes (d 1960); *b* 1 Mar 1934; *Educ* Charterhouse; *m* 1957, Penelope Ann, *née* Hill; 1 s, 2 da; *Career* Lt Queens Own Royal W Kent Parachute Regt 1953-54; dir Brooke Bond Gp plc 1979-85, vice-chm Walls Meat Co Ltd 1975-77, dir Macfisheries Ltd 1971-75, chief exec Nabisco Gp Ltd 1985-; *Recreations* golf, walking; *Clubs* Caledonian, MCC, Berks GC; *Style—* Alistair Mitchell-Innes, Esq; Langton Lodge, Sunningdale, Berks (☎ 0990 24993; off: 01 248 6422)

MITCHISON, Prof Hon (Nicholas) Avrion; s of Baron Mitchison, CBE, QC (Life Peer, d 1970); *b* 5 May 1928; *Educ* Leighton Park Sch, New Coll Oxford; *m* 1957, Lorna Margaret, da of Maj-Gen J S S Martin, CSI; 2 s, 3 da; *Career* prof of zoology and comparative anatomy UCL 1970-; *Style—* Prof the Hon Avrion Mitchison; 14 Belitha Villas, London N1

MITCHISON, Dr Hon Denis Anthony; CMG (1984); s of Baron Mitchison, CBE (Life Peer, d 1970); *b* 6 Sept 1919; *Educ* Abbotsholme Sch, Trinity Coll Cambridge, Univ Coll Hosp London; *m* 1940, Ruth Sylvia, da of Hubert Gill; 2 s, 2 da; *Career* prof of Bacteriology Royal Postgraduate Med Sch 1971-84, ret; dir Med Res Cncl Unit for Laboratory Studies of Tuberculosis 1956-84; *Style—* Dr the Hon Denis Mitchison, CMG; 14 Marlborough Rd, Richmond, Surrey (☎ 01 940 4751)

MITCHISON, Prof Hon (John) Murdoch; 2 s of Baron Mitchison, CBE, QC (Life Peer, d 1970), and Naomi Mitchison, the writer, *née* Haldane; *b* 11 June 1922; *Educ* Winchester, Trinity Coll Cambridge; *m* 21 June 1947, Rosalind Mary, da of late Edward Murray Wrong, of Toronto, Canada; 1 s, 3 da; *Career* prof of zoology Edinburgh Univ 1963-; memb Sci Bd SRC 1976-79; memb Royal Cmmn on Environmental Pollution 1974-79; author; FRS; *Style—* Prof the Hon Murdoch Mitchison; Great Yew, Ormiston, E Lothian (☎ 0875 340530, work 031 667 1081)

MITCHISON, Baroness; Naomi Margaret; *née* Haldane; CBE (Civil 1985); da of late John Scott Haldane, CH; *b* 1 Nov 1897; *Educ* Dragon; *m* 1916, Baron Mitchison, CBE, QC (Life Peer, d 1970); 3 s, 2 da; *Career* author; hon fell Wolfson Coll Oxford 1983, Hon DLitt Strathclyde Stirling Dundee 1983; *Style—* The Rt Hon the Lady Mitchison, CBE; Carradale Ho, Carradale, Campbeltown, Scotland

MITFORD, Hon Emma; da of 5 Baron Redesdale; *b* 1959; *Style—* The Hon Emma Mitford

MITFORD, Hon Georgina Clementine; 6 da of 5 Baron Redesdale; *b* 18 Sept 1968; *Style—* The Hon Georgina Mitford

MITFORD, Hon Georgina Kathryn Mercia; 3 da of 5 Baron Redesdale; *b* 1961; *Style—* The Hon Georgina Mitford

MITFORD, Hon Henrietta Jane; da of 5 Baron Redesdale; *b* 4 August 1965; *Style—* The Hon Henrietta Mitford

MITFORD, Jessica Lucy (Hon Mrs Treuhaft); da of 2 Baron Redesdale (d 1958); *b* 11 Sept 1917; *m* 1, Esmond Marcus David Romilly (d 1942); 1 da; m 2, 1943, Robert Edward Treuhaft; 1 s; *Career* author; *Books* Hons and Rebels, The American Way of Death, The Trial of Dr Spock, Kind and Usual Punishment, The American Prison Business, A Fine Old Conflict, The Making of a Muckraker; *Style—* Miss Jessica Mitford; 6411 Regent St, Oakland, Calif 94618, USA

MITFORD, Hon Tessa; da of 5 Baron Redesdale; *b* 1960; *Style—* The Hon Tessa Mitford

MITFORD, Hon Victoria-Louise; da of 5 Baron Redesdale; *b* 1962; *Educ* Haileybury; *Career* advtg exec Financial Times New York Off; *Recreations* travel, theatre, fashion design, writing; *Style—* The Hon Victoria-Louise Mitford

MITFORD-SLADE, Major Anthony Cecil Wyndham; s of Col Cecil Townley Mitford-Slade (d 1986), of Somerset, and Phyllis, *née* Buxton (d 1985); *b* 13 Mar 1932; *Educ* Eton, RMA Sandhurst; *m* 9 May 1959, Mary Dawn, da of Lt-Col Stanley Clive Rogers (d 1972) of Somerset; 3 s (Christopher b 1962, Richard b 1965, Timothy b 1976), 1 da (Rosemary b 1960); *Career* cmmnd Somerset LI (Prince Albert's) 1952, serv Malaya, W Germany, Berlin and Guyana Def Force (despatches 1955), ret 1983; self-employed farmer; *Recreations* shooting; *Clubs* Farmers; *Style—* Maj Anthony C W Mitford-Slade; Montys Court, Norton Fitzwarren, Taunton, Somerset (☎ 0823 432 255)

MITFORD-SLADE, Patrick Buxton; surname changed from Mitford to Mitford-Slade (d 1986), by deed poll of 1942; s of Col Cecil Townley Mitford-Slade (d 1986), by his w Phyllis (d 1985); *b* 7 Sept 1936; *Educ* Eton, RMA Sandhurst; *m* 1964, Anne Catharine, da of Maj Arthur Holbrow Stanton, MBE; 1 s, 2 da; *Career* Capt Royal Green Jackets 1954-69, memb Stock Exchange 1972, asst sec Panel on Takeovers and Mergers 1970-72, ptnr Cazenove & Co 1973-, jt dep chm Cncl Stock Exchange (memb 1976-) 1982-85, chm: City Telecommunications Ctee 1983-; Stock Exchange Projects Ctee 1984-86; Offs Assoc 1985-; md Cazenove Money Brokers 1986-; *Recreations* shooting, fishing, gardening, racing; *Clubs* City of London; *Style—* Patrick Mitford-Slade, Esq; Cazenove & Co, 12 Tokenhouse Yard, London EC2 (☎ 01 588 2828)

MITSON, (Sydney) Allen; s of Sydney Mitson, of Snaresbrook, London, and Catherine, *née* Gooding; *b* 24 May 1933; *Educ* Exeter Sch, Forest Sch (BA); *m* 1, 1959 (m dis 1971), Elizabeth Angela, da of R Garner (d 1966), of Buckhurst Hill, Essex; 2 s (Andrew b 1963, Michael b 1966); m 2, 1973, Valerie Angela, da of J Sherratt (d 1988), of Waltham Abbey, Essex; 1 step s (John b 1967); *Career* Nat Serv Royal Signals; sales promotion mangr Rotaflex 1960-65, formed Emess Lighting 1966 (formed into public Co 1980), md Emess Lighting (UK) Ltd 1980-; underwriting memb Lloyds 1977-; Freeman City of London 1983, Liveryman Worshipful Co of Gold and Silver Wyre Drawers 1983; *Recreations* walking, swimming; *Style—* Allen Mitson, Esq; Emess Lighting (UK) Ltd, 6 Anderson Rd, Woodford Green, Essex IG8 8ET (☎ 01 551 7191, fax 01 551 6509, telex 8954105)

MITSON, John Dane; s of Capt Leonard Mitson (d 1969), of Nottingham, and Edith, *née* Bradley (d 1973); *b* 28 Feb 1929; *Educ* Oakham Sch, Sidney Sussex Coll Cambridge (MA, LLM); *m* 31 May 1954, Rita, da of Neville Thomas Dowen (d 1964), of Leicester; 1 s (Matthew b 30 May 1964), 3 da (Johanna b 21 March 1959, Katharine b 15 May 1960, Emma b 24 Aug 1963); *Career* BQMS RA Singapore 1947-49; admitted slr 1956; legal sec to Bishop and registrar of diocese of St Edmondsbury and Ipswich 1975-; sr ptnr Birketts Ipswich; memb Law Soc; *Recreations* music, theatre, rugby; *Clubs* Ipswich & Suffolk; *Style*— John Mitson, Esq; Drift Cottage, The Drift, Dedham, Colchester CO7 6AH (☎ 0206 323116); 20/26 Museum St, Ipswich (☎ 0473 232300)

MITTON, Brian Frederick; s of Alfred Mitton (d 1984), and Kate, *née* Jackson; *b* 21 June 1931; *Educ* Carlisle GS, Carlisle Cathedral Choir Sch; *m* 4 Nov 1968, Wendy, da of Inspr John McNeil; 3 s (Bradley John Snowden b 1969, Glenn Frederick Barclay b 1971, Alexander David Clark b 1975); *Career* trainee refrigeration engr 1946-51; with Refrigeration (Mitton) Ltd 1954- (md 1971-); qualified coach in badminton, swimming and squash with Nat Assocns; *Recreations* badminton, squash, running, gardening; *Clubs* Brampton Badminton, Brampton Squash; *Style*— Brian F Mitton, Esq; Quarrybeck House, Brampton, Cumbria CA8 2EY (☎ 06977 2020); Refrigeration (Mitton) Ltd, Cecil Street, Carlisle, Cumbria CA1 1NT

MIZRAHI, Jeffrey Isaac Ezzat; s of Jacoub Mizrahi, of Camiore, Provincia Di Lucca, Italy, and Odette Mizrahi; *b* 2 Feb 1940; *Educ* Millfield, Durham Univ (BA); *m* 1, 1962 (m dis 1978), Joan Rudd; 1 s (James b 1976), 3 da (Jacqueline b 1965, Juliette b 1967, Jeanette b 1973); m 2, 26 Aug 1988, Florence, da of Mathew Kinsella ; *Career* econ conslt Economist Intelligence Unit 1965-67, dep chief economist Charter Consolidated 1967-75, chief economist James Capel 1975-78, vice pres Bank of America Int 1978-83, dir and chief economist SBC1, Savory Milln 1983-88, dir Swiss Bank Corpn portfolio mgmnt 1989-; ACII, memb Soc Business Economists; *Recreations* tennis, bridge, squash; *Style*— Jeffrey Mizrahi, Esq; Swiss Bank Corp, Norfolk House, 31 St James Square, London SW1 (☎ 01 606 4000, fax 01 321 0370, telex 927 244)

MLINARIC, David; *b* 12 Mar 1939; *m* 1969, (Katherine) Martha, da of Sir Robert Laycock (d 1968) and Lady Laycock, *qv*; 1 s, 2 da; *Career* interior designer; *Style*— David Mlinaric Esq; 61 Glebe Place, London SW3

MOAT, Frank Robert; s of Frank Robert Moat (d 1976), of Tynemouth, and Grace, *née* Hibbert; *b* 10 August 1948; *Educ* Giggleswick, The Coll of Law (LLB); *Career* called to the Bar Lincoln's Inn 1970, memb Western Circuit, in practise in London and on the Western Circuit, rep on the Bar Cncl Western Circuit 1989; memb wine ctee of the Western Circuit, fndr memb of ctee of Kensington and Chelsea Nat Tst Assoc; *Recreations* theatre, music, antiques, architecture; *Clubs* Garrick, Hampshire; *Style*— Frank Moat, Esq; 5 Prior Bolton St, Canonbury, London N1 2NX (☎ 01 226 8177); 36 Bilberry Ct, Staple Gardens, Winchester, Hants SO23 8SP (☎ 0962 68531); Francis Taylor Bldg, Temple, London EC4Y 7BY (☎ 01 353 2182, fax 01 583 1727)

MOATE, Roger Denis; MP (C) Faversham 1970-; s of late Harold Stanley Moate, of Chiswick, and Elizabeth Freestone; *b* 12 May 1938; *Educ* Latymer Upper Sch; *m* 1 (m dis), Hazel Joy, da of late F J Skinner, of Somerset; 1 s, 1 da; m 2, Auriol, da of late W B G Cran, of Huddersfield; *Career* dir Alexander Howden Insur Brokers Ltd, hon sec Br-American Parly Gp, chm: Lloyds Brokers, Frank Bradford & Co Ltd, Theatre Prodns plc; *Recreations* skiing, tennis; *Style*— Roger Moate Esq, MP; The Old Vicarage, Knatchbull Rd, London SE5

MOBBS, Sir (Gerald) Nigel; DL (Bucks 1985); s of Lt-Col Gerald Aubrey Mobbs (d 1976), of Gt Missenden, and Elizabeth, *née* Lanchester; *b* 22 Sept 1937; *Educ* Marlborough, Christ Church Oxford; *m* 14 Sept 1961, Hon (Pamela) Jane Marguerite Berry, *qv*, da of 2 Viscount Kemsley; 1 s (Christopher William b 1965), 2 da (Virginia Elizabeth b 1968, Penelope Helen b (twin) 1968); *Career* joined Slough Estates plc 1960, dir 1963, md 1971, chm and chief exec 1976-; dir: Barclays Bank plc 1979-, Woolworth Hldgs 1983-, Cookson Hldgs 1985-, Charterhouse Gp 1974-83 (chm 1977-83), Tishman Hldg Corp (USA) 1989-, Charterhouse Gp Int (USA) 1985-; chm Aims of Indust 1985-; pres Br Property Fedn 1974-81; vice-pres Assoc of Br C of C 1976- (chm 1974-76); High Sheriff of Bucks 1982-83; chm Cncl of Univ of Buckingham 1987-; memb Cncl Univ of Reading 1987-; chm Property Servs Agency Advsy Bd 1980-86; memb Cwlth War Graves Cmmn 1988-; chm Advsy Panel on Deregulation (DTI) 1988-; Upper Warden Worshipful Co of Spectacle Makers 1988-89; Hon DSc City Univ 1988, Hon Fell Coll of Estate Mgmnt; OStJ 1987; kt 1986; *Recreations* riding, hunting, skiing, golf; *Clubs* Toronto; *Style*— Sir Nigel Mobbs, DL; Widmer Lodge, Lacey Green, Aylesbury, Bucks HP17 0RJ (☎ 024 028 265); Slough Estates plc, 234 Bath Rd, Slough, Bucks SL1 4EE (☎ 0753 37171)

MOBBS, Hon Lady (Pamela Jane Margaret); *née* Berry; da of 2 Viscount Kemsley; *b* 27 May 1937; *m* 1961, Sir Gerald Nigel Mobbs; 1 s, 2 da; *Style*— The Hon Lady Mobbs; Widmer Lodge, Lacey Green, Aylesbury, Bucks HP17 0RJ (☎ 024 028 265)

MOBERLY, Sir John Campbell; KBE (1984), CMG (1976); 2 s of Sir Walter Hamilton Moberly, GBE, KCB, DSO (d 1973), and Gwendolen, *née* Gardner (d 1975); *b* 27 May 1925; *Educ* Winchester, Magdalen Coll Oxford (BA); *m* 18 April 1959, Patience, yst da of Sir Richard George Proby, 1 Bt, MC (d 1979), of Elton Hall Peterborough; 2 s (Richard b 1962, Nicholas b 1963), 1 da (Clare b 1967); *Career* serv WWII RN 1943-47 Lt RNVR (despatches); entered HM For (later Dip) Serv 1950; serv: London, Lebanon, Bahrain, Qatar, Greece, USA 1950-73; dir Middle E Centre for Arab Studies 1973-75, ambass to Jordan 1975-79, asst under sec FCO 1979-82, ambass to Iraq 1982-85, ret; *Style*— Sir John Moberly, KBE, CMG; 35 Pymers Mead, Croxted Rd, W Dulwich, London SE21 8NH (☎ 01 670 2680); The Cedars, Temple Sowerby, Penrith, Cumbria CA10 1RZ (☎ 07683 61437)

MOBERLY, Sir Patrick Hamilton; KCMG (1986, CMG 1978); yr s of George Hamilton Moberly, MC (d 1972), and Alice Violet, *née* Cooke-Hurle (d 1954); ggs of George Moberly, headmaster of Winchester and Bishop of Salisbury; *b* 2 August 1928; *Educ* Winchester, Trinity Coll Oxford; *m* 5 May 1955, Mary Frances, da of Capt Hugh de L Penfold (d 1979), of Guernsey, CI; 2 s (Andrew b 1960, James b 1962), 1 da (Jennifer b 1958); *Career* HM Dip Serv 1951-87, with postings in Iraq, Czechoslovakia, Senegal, London, Canada and Israel 1953-74, asst under-sec of state 1976-81, ambass: Israel 1981-84, SA 1984-87; *Recreations* tennis, opera,; *Clubs* Utd Oxford & Cambridge Univ; *Style*— Sir Patrick Moberly, KCMG; 38 Lingfield Rd, London SW19 4PZ

MOBERLY, William James Dorward; s of Brig James Vincent Charles Moberly, DSO, OBE (d 1982), and Brida Helen Mary, *née* Espeut (d 1980); *b* 4 Sept 1938; *Educ* Blundell's, Sidney Sussex Coll Cambridge (MA); *m* 17 Oct 1970, Angela, da of Thomas Eric Douglas Mason, of Broomhall, Oxshott, Surrey; 2 s (Nicholas James, Mark Thomas); *Career* CA, articled clerk Ball Baker Deed & Co 1960-63, asst Thomson McLintock & Co 1963-66; ptnr: Ball Baker Deed & Co 1966 (subsequently Ball Baker Carnaby Deed), Pannell Kerr Forster; dir Thousand and One Lamps Ltd; tres Friends of Cobham Cottage Hosp; Liveryman Worshipful Co of Curriers; *Books* Partnership Management; *Recreations* golf, gardening, bridge; *Clubs* St Georges Hill GC, Rye GC; *Style*— William Moberly, Esq; 125 Fairmile Lane, Cobham, Surrey; Pannell Kerr Forster, 36 Essex St, London WC2R 3AS (☎ 01 583 1188, fax 01 353 3552, telex 264123)

MOCATTA, Sir Alan Abraham; OBE (1944), QC (1951); s of Edward Mocatta and Flora Mocatta; *b* 1907; *Educ* Clifton, New Coll Oxford (MA); *m* 1930, Pamela Halford, JP; 4 s; *Career* serv WWII rising to Lt-Col Gen Staff (Army Cncl Secretariat) WO 1942-45; barr 1930, chm Treasy Ctee on Cheque Endorsement 1955-56, memb Restrictive Practices Ct 1961-81 (pres 1970), High Ct judge (Queen's Bench) 1961-81, tres Inner Temple 1982; chm Cncl Jews' Coll 1945-61, pres Bd of Elders Spanish and Portuguese Jews' Congregation (Bevis Marks) 1967-82 (vice pres 1961-67); kt 1961; *Books* Scrutton on Charter Parties (jt ed 14-19 edns), Rowlatt on Principal and Surety (ed 3 edn), Halsbury's Laws of England (conslt ed of 4 edn); *Style*— Sir Alan Mocatta, OBE, QC; 18 Hanover Ho, London NW8 7DX (☎ 01 722 2857)

MOFFAT, Sir John Smith; OBE (1944); s of Rev Malcolm Moffat; *b* 1905,April; *Educ* Grey HS Port Elizabeth S Africa, Glasgow Univ; *m* 1930, Margaret Prentice; 2 da; *Career* Colonial Serv 1927-51; ldr Rhodesian Lib Pty until disbanded 1962; MLC N Rhodesia 1951-64, memb Federal Parly Salibury 1954-62; farmer; kt 1955; *Style*— Sir John Moffat, OBE

MOFFAT, Dr Robin John Russell; s of A C Russell Moffat (d 1969), of London, and Gladys Leonora, *née* Taperell; *b* 18 Oct 1927; *Educ* Whitgift Sch Croydon, Guy's Hosp Med Sch, Univ of London (LRCP, MRCS, DRCOG, MRCGP); *m* 1, 8 Sept 1949 (m dis 1980), Audrey Heathcote, da of F B H Wride (d 1955), of Winchester; 2 s (Jeremy Guy b 7 Dec 1954, Timothy Julian b 3 Nov 1960), 1 da (Pamela Jane b 25 Aug 1951); m 2, 18 Nov 1980, Beryl Gwendoline Longmoor, *née* Wild; *Career* Nat Serv RN 1946-48, ORA (SBA branch) RN Hosp Haslar; house surg Guy's Hosp 1954-55, house physician Croydon Hosp 1957, resident obstetrician Mayday Hosp 1957-58, gen med practice Croydon 1958-88, met police surgn 1959-88, sr forensic med examiner1988-, MO Whitgift Fndn 1960-, chief MO TSB Bank 1978-; memb (ex-pres) Croydon Med Soc, fndr memb Croydon Medico-Legal Soc, chm Met Gp Assoc of Police Surgns GB; memb: MOs of Schs Assoc (ex-pres), Br Acad of Forensic Sciences, Cons Med Assoc; Liveryman Worshipful Co of Apothecaries; FRSM (hon sec section of clinical forensic med); *Recreations* racing, book collection; *Clubs* Carlton, Nat Sporting; *Style*— Dr Robin Moffat; 8 Arundel Terrace, Kemptown, Brighton, E Sussex BN2 1GA (☎ 0273 674 552); 10 Harley St, London WIN 1AA (☎ 01 580 4280, car phone 0860 228 407)

MOFFAT OF THAT ILK, Francis; MC (1946), JP (Dumfries 1953), DL (Dumfries 1957); Chief of the Name and Arms of Moffat, confirmed by Lord Lyon King of Arms 1983; up to this point the Moffats had been a 'heidless' family for about 420 years; s of Capt William Murdoch Moffat, JP (d 1948), of Craigbeck, Moffat, and Jean Guthrie Troup (d 1918); *b* 21 Mar 1915; *Educ* Shrewsbury, Trinity Coll Cambridge (BA); *m* 1946, Margaret Eva, da of William Chambers Carrington (d 1945), of Luton; 2 da (Jean b 1947, Margaret b 1950); *Career* ret landowner and farmer; serv King's Own Scottish Borderers 1940-45, NW Europe, Maj; convener Dumfries CC 1969-75 (vice-convener 1961-69); *Recreations* genealogy, reading, photography; *Style*— Maj Francis Moffat of that Ilk, MC, JP, DL; Redacres, Moffat, Dumfriesshire (☎ 0683 20045)

MOFFATT, Clive; s of Harold and Olive Moffatt; *b* 27 Dec 1948; *Educ* Thornes House Sch, LSE (BSc); *m* 1977, Kathleen Elizabeth, da of Robert Maguire; 1 s, 1 da; *Career* res economist to New Zealand Treasury 1972-75; conslt economist and writer Economist Intelligence Unit Ltd London 1975-76, chief sub-ed (fin unit and CEEFAX) BBC 1976-78, business ed Investors Chronicle 1978-79, corporate affrs conslt Guiness Peat Gp plc 1979-81; chief exec Blackrod Ltd (independent TV production subsidiary of Television South plc) 1981-; dir: Blackrod Interactive Servs Ltd, Lifestyle TV Ltd; chm BISFA Video and Television Gp; *Recreations* rugby, cricket, art, music; *Style*— Clive Moffatt, Esq; 53 Lavington Rd, London W13 (☎ 01 567 4716); Blackrod Ltd, Threeways Ho, 40-44 Clipstone St, London W1P 7EA (☎ 01 637 9376 and 580 6934, telex 269859)

MOFFATT, Hon Mrs (Ruth Lesley); *née* Jackson; da of Baron Jackson of Burnley (Life Peer, d 1970); *b* 22 May 1945; *Educ* Sutton HS, Univ of Wales Bangor (BSc), Aberdeen Univ (MSc); *m* 1970, David John Moffatt; 1 s, 1 da; *Career* Royal Soc Leverhulme scholar 1968-69, lectr Univ of Leeds 1969-70, pt-t tutor for Open Univ 1979-82; parish cncllr, memb WI cmtee for Community & Int Affairs; *Recreations* lacemaking, gardening, tennis, conservation; *Style*— The Hon Mrs Moffatt; 26 Townsend Lane, Upper Boddington, Daventry, Northants

MOFFATT, Dr William Henry; s of John Harry Moffatt, MPSI (d 1967), of Belfast, and Edith Margaret, *née* Reid (d 1961); *b* 11 April 1926; *Educ* Methodist Coll Belfast, Queen's Univ Belfast (MB, BCh); *m* 12 June 1959, Elsie Mary, da of Samuel Bullock, of Enniskillen, Co Fermanagh (decd); 1 s (John Samuel William b 1964), 1 da (Christine Mary b 1968); *Career* Capt RAMC Nat Serv Suez Canal Zone 1951-53; conslt physician in Geriatric Medicine Newtownabbey Hosp Gp 1965-, dir NI Hosp Advsy Serv 1984-; memb: tstees Leopardstown Park Hosp Tst, Dublin (disabled Irish ex-servicemen of WWs I&II), and War Pensions Ctee for NI, BAO, FRCPI; *Recreations* gardening, fishing, reading; *Style*— Dr William H Moffatt; 7 School Lane, Greenisland, Carrickfergus, NI BT38 8RF (☎ Belfast 863253); Greenisland Hosp, Shore Road, Newtownabbey, NI (☎ Belfast 865181)

MOGER, Christopher Richard Derwent; s of Richard Vernon Derwent Moger, of Dartmouth, S Devon, and Cecile Eva Rosales, *née* Power; *b* 28 July 1949; *Educ* Sherborne, Bristol Univ (LLB); *m* 27 July 1974, Victoria, da of Arthur George Cecil Trollope, of Overton, Hants; 3 s (Robin b 1979, Sholto b 1981, Dominic b 1985); *Career* called to the Barr Inner Temple 1972; *Recreations* fishing, tennis, chess; *Clubs* The Hurlingham; *Style*— Christopher Moger, Esq; 4 Pump Ct, Temple, London EC4Y 7AN (☎ 01 353 2656, fax 01 583 2036, telex 8813250 Reflex G)

MOGFORD, Stephen George; *b* 20 June 1914; *Educ* Exeter, London Univ (BA, BSc); *m* 1946; 1 s (Stephen); *Career* int banker, ret; dep chm Italian Int Bank Ledenhall St; ret vice-chm Barclays Bank Int, former dir Barclays Bank plc; *Recreations* gardening, music; *Clubs* Reform, Overseas Bankers; *Style*— Stephen G Mogford, Esq;

Warrington Place Farmhouse, Paddock Wood, Kent TN12 6HE

MOGG, Gen Sir John; GCB (1972, KCB 1966, CB 1964), CBE (1960), DSO (1944 and Bar 1944), DL (Oxford 1979); s of Capt H B Mogg, MC, by his w Alice, *née* Ballard; *b* 17 Feb 1913; *Educ* Malvern, RMC Sandhurst (Sword of Honour); *m* 1939, Cecilia Margaret, yr da of Rev John Molesworth (himself 5 in descent from 1 Viscount Molesworth); 3 s (Col Nigel (Royal Green Jackets) b 1940, m Tessa Wright, 2 s; Patrick b 1942; Rev Timothy, who has assumed the name Rawdon-Mogg, b 1945, m Rachel Eastman; 2 s, 1 da); *Career* serv Coldstream Gds 1935-37, Oxf & Bucks LI 1937, serv WWII (despatches), joined Durham LI & serv NW Europe 1944-45; instr Staff Coll 1948-50; Cdr 10 Para Bn 1950-52; chief instr Warminster Inf Sch 1952-54, GSO 1 IDC 1954-56, Cdr C'wlth Bde Gp Malaya 1958-60, War Off 1961-62, Cmdt RMA Sandhurst 1963-66; Cdr 1 Corps 1966-68, GOC-in-C S Cmmd 1968, Army Strategic Cmmd 1968-70; Adj-Gen 1970-73, Dep Supreme Allied Cdr Europe 1973-76; ADC Gen to HM 1971-74; pres Army Benevolent Fund 1980- (chm 1976); chm Operation Drake for Young Explorers 1978-; dir Lloyds Bank (S Midland Regional Bd) 1976-; Vice Lord-Lt Oxon 1979-; Meritorious Medal (Malaya); *Style*— Gen Sir John Mogg, GCB, CBE, DSO, DL; Church Close, Watlington, Oxon (☎ 049 161 2247)

MOGG, Reginald Arthur; s of Arthur Mogg (d 1975), and May Elizabeth, *née* Keen; *b* 24 August 1945; *m* 9 Sept 1972, Marilyn Susan, da of Joseph Ladds (d 1986); 1 s (Jonathan b 1975), 1 da (Teresa b 1973); *Career* fin dir: Maxwell Communication Corp plc since 1985; FCA; *Recreations* golf; *Style*— Reginald Mogg, Esq; 64 Alders Close, Wanstead, London E11 3RR; Maxwell Communication Corporation plc, PO Box 283, 33 Holborn, London EC1N 2NE (☎ 01 822 2128)

MOIR, Christine Ann Frances; da of Ronald William Moir, of Auckland, New Zealand, and Patricia Josephine, *née* Woods; *b* 11 August 1946; *Educ* St Mary's Coll Auckland NZ, Univ of Auckland (BA, MA); *Career* ed Property Investmt Review 1972-76, hd city desk and ed fund mangrs letter Financial Times 1976-82, fin ed Observer 1982-; *Books* The Acquisitive Streak (1986); *Recreations* reading, riding, the arts, travel; *Clubs* Reform; *Style*— Miss Christine Moir; c/o The Observer, Chelsea Bridge House, Queenstown Rd, London SW8 4NN (☎ 01 350 3496, fax 01 627 5570)

MOIR, Christopher Ernest; s and h of Sir Ernest Ian Royds Moir, 3 Bt; *b* 22 May 1955; *Educ* King's Coll Sch Wimbledon; *m* m, Vanessa Moir; 2 s (twins) (Oliver Royds and Alexander Victor b 1984), 1 da (Nina Louise b 1976); *Heir* Oliver Royds Moir; *Career* CA; *Style*— Christopher Moir Esq; 77 Dora Rd, Wimbledon, London SW19 7JT

MOIR, Sir Ernest Ian Royds; 3 Bt (UK 1916), of Whitehanger, Fernhurst, Co Sussex; s of Sir Arrol Moir, 2 Bt (d 1957); *b* 9 June 1925; *Educ* Rugby, Gonville and Caius Coll Cambridge; *m* 1954, Margaret Hanham, da of George Carter, of Huddersfield, Yorks; 3 s; *Heir* s, Christopher Ernest Moir; *Style*— Sir Ernest Moir, Bt; Three Gates, Coombe Lane West, Kingston upon Thames, Surrey KT2 7DE (☎ 01 942 7394)

MOLDEN, Nigel Charles; s of Percival Ernest Molden, of 60 York Rd, Headington, Oxford OX3 8NP, and Daisy Mary, *née* Currill; *b* 17 August 1948; *Educ* City of Oxford HS, Poly of Central London, Brunel Univ (BSc, MSc); *m* 14 Aug 1971, (Hilary) Julia, da of Frederick Withers Lichfield (d 1969); 3 s (Nicholas Stuart b 1974, Simon Charles b 1977, Alexander Giles b 1983); *Career* md The Magnum Music Gp Ltd 1985-; vice-chm Beaconsfield Town Cons Assoc; FInstM 1988, FInstD 1982, FBIM 1987; *Recreations* theatre, rugby football, motor sports; *Clubs* Royal Overseas League; *Style*— Nigel Molden, Esq; Ashcombe House, Deanswood Rd, Jordans, Beaconsfield, Bucks HP9 2UU (☎ 0494 678177); Stone Cottage, Cowl Lane, Winchcombe, Gloucs; Magnum House, High St, Lane End, Bucks HP14 3JG (☎ 0494 882858, fax 0494 882631, telex 837685 MAGNUM G)

MOLE, Arthur Charles; s of Sir Charles Johns Mole, KBE, MVO (d 1962), of Walton-on-Thames, and his 1 w, Annie, *née* Martin (d 1962); *b* 25 Feb 1926; *Educ* St George's Coll Weybridge, King's Coll London (BSc); *m* 1957, Hon Susan Mary, *qv*, da of Baron Hinton of Bankside, KCB (Life Peer; d 1983); 2 s; *Career* project design engr Atomic Power Constructions Ltd 1957-65, gen mangr Engrg Morganite Carbon Ltd 1965-72; dir: Morgan Electrical Carbon Ltd 1968-76; md MBM Technol 1976-86; dir Morganite Refractories 1982-86; dep chm Morgan ROCTEC Ltd 1986-; *Style*— Arthur Mole Esq; Polurrian, 2 Second Ave, Worthing, W Sussex BN14 9NX (☎ 0903 209122); 32 Devon Ct, Freshwater East, Pembroke (☎ 0646 672467)

MOLE, Lady; Marjorie; da of late Capt Frederick William Butt-Thompson; *m* 1962, as his 2 w, Sir Charles Johns Mole, KBE, MVO (d 1962); *Style*— Lady Mole; The Bucknalls, Westbourne, Emsworth, Hants

MOLE, Hon Mrs (Susan Mary); da of Baron Hinton of Bankside, KBE, OM (Life Peer, d 1983), and Lillian, *née* Boyer (d 1973); *b* 6 Feb 1932; *Educ* Wentworth Milton Mount; *m* 1957, Arthur Charles Mole, *qv*, s of Sir Charles John Mole, KBE, MVO (d 1962), of Walton-on-Thames; 2 s; *Career* state registered nurse; *Style*— The Hon Mrs Mole; Polurrian, Second Ave, Charmandean, Worthing, W Sussex BN14 9NX (☎ 0903 209122); 32 Devon Ct, Freshwater East, Pembroke (☎ 0646 672467)

MOLESWORTH, Allen Henry Neville; s of Col Roger Bevil Molesworth (d 1974); *b* 20 August 1931; *Educ* Wellington, Trinity Coll Cambridge; *m* 1970, Gail Cheng Kwai, da of Chan Lum Choon, of Singapore; *Career* Lt Queen's Own Hussars; CA, mgmnt conslt 1967-76, fin and admin controller Crown Agents 1976-84, chief accountant BT Properties 1984-; *Recreations* skiing, shooting, restoring antiques; *Style*— Allen Molesworth, Esq; c/o Lloyds Bank, 6 Pall Mall, London SW1

MOLESWORTH, Wing Cdr John Henry Nassau; DSO (1945), AFC (1943), DFC (1941); s of Maj John Davenport Newall Molesworth (d 1952), of Poynings Sussex, and Mary Norman (d 1958); *b* 24 Sept 1913; *Educ* Oakham Sch, Wye Agric Coll, London Univ; *m* 1 June 1946, Pamela Joan, da of Mr Guildford (d 1944), of Ramsgate; 1 s (Peter b 1956); *Career* war serv: Wing Cdr, GD pilot RAF 1939-45; (despatches 2); farmer Kenya 1930's; Mann Crossman & Paulin 1945-; ret Grand Metropolitan Hotels (brewing div) 1976; *Recreations* cricket, shooting; *Style*— Wing Cdr John H N Molesworth, DSO, AFC, DFC; Beehive Cottage, Eltisley, nr St Neots, Cambs PE19 4TH (☎ Croxton 642)

MOLESWORTH, 11 Viscount (I 1716); Richard Gosset Molesworth; also Baron Philipstown (I 1716); s of 10 Viscount (d 1961); 3 Viscount (Richard, d 1758), was ADC to Duke of Marlborough, whose life he saved at Battle of Ramillies by giving his horse to the unhorsed Duke (he later became C-in-C of HM Forces in Ireland); *b* 31 Oct 1907; *Educ* Lancing; *m* 1958, Anne Florence (d 1983), da of John Mark Freeman Cohen; 2 s; *Heir* s, Hon Robert Bysse Kelham Molesworth; *Career* serv WWII, RAF (Middle E Forces); former farmer; Freeman City of London 1978; *Style*— The Rt Hon the Viscount Molesworth; Garden Flat, 2 Bishopswood Rd, Highgate, London N6 (☎ 01 348 1366)

MOLESWORTH, Hon Robert Bysse Kelham; s and h of 11 Viscount Molesworth, by his w, Anne, *née* Cohen (d 1983); *b* 4 June 1959; *Educ* Cheltenham, Sussex Univ (BA); *Style*— The Hon Robert Molesworth; Garden Flat, 2 Bishopswood Rd, Highgate N6 4PR

MOLESWORTH, Hon William John Charles; yr s of 11 Viscount Molesworth, and Anne Florence, *née* Cohen (d 1983); *b* 20 Oct 1960; *Educ* Cheltenham, Trinity Coll Cambridge (BA), Bath Coll of Higher Educn (PGCE), LTCL; *Recreations* athletics, singing; *Clubs* 1; *Style*— The Hon William Molesworth; Garden Flat, 2 Bishopswood Rd, Highgate, London N6 4PR

MOLESWORTH-ST AUBYN, Lt-Col Sir (John) Arscott; 15 Bt (E 1689), MBE (1963), JP (Devon 1971), DL (Cornwall 1971); s of Sir John Molesworth-St Aubyn, 14 Bt, CBE (d 1985), and Celia Marjorie (d 1965), da of Lt-Col Valentine Vivian, CMG, DSO, MVO; *b* 15 Dec 1926; *Educ* Eton; *m* 2 May 1957, Iona Audrey Armatrude, da of Adm Sir Francis Loftus Tottenham, KCB, CBE (d 1966); 2 s, 1 da; *Heir* s, Capt William Molesworth-St Aubyn, RGJ, b 23 Nov 1958; *Career* serv KRRC and Royal Green Jackets (in Libya, Palestine, Malaya, Brunei, British Guiana and Borneo) 1945-69, Staff Coll 1959, Jt Servs Staff Coll 1964, Lt-Col 1967-69; high sheriff Cornwall 1975; chm West Local Land Drainage Ctee SW Water Authy 1974-; pres Wessex Regn Historic Houses Assoc 1984-86; vice-chm SW Regn Timber Growers UK 1978-; chm Cornwall Branch, memb Nat Cncl CLA; *Recreations* shooting, ornithology; *Clubs* Army and Navy; *Style*— Lt-Col Sir Arscott Molesworth-St Aubyn, Bt, MBE, JP, DL; Pencarrow, Bodmin, Cornwall; Tetcott Manor, Holsworthy, Devon (☎ 040 927 220)

MOLINEUX, Lt Cdr Peter Ranby; s of Frederick Alfred Molineux (d 1969), of Kent, and Kathleen Margaret, *née* Ranby (d 1975); *b* 28 April 1931; *Educ* RNC: Dartmouth and Greenwich; *m* 30 July 1955, Jane Gwenydd, da of Patrick Erskine Cruttwell, of Brompton Ralph, Somerset; 2 s (William b 1959, Patrick b 1966), 2 da (Petronella b 1957, Lucy b 1960); *Career* HM Submarines 1952-59, Capt HMS Monkton 1959-61, Lt Cdr 1961, naval instr RAF Coll Cranwell 1961-63, HMS Caesar, MHQ Pitreavie, HMS Bulwark, rét 1969; princ DHSS 1969; churchwarden: St John Baptist Wonersh 1976-77, All Saints Witley 1981-88; *Recreations* reading mil and naval history, walking with dogs; *Style*— Lt Cdr Peter Molineux; Vine Cottage, Witley, Surrey (☎ Wormley 2298); Alexander Fleming House, London SE1 (☎ 01 407 5522)

MOLL, John Graeme (Francis); s of Frederick Charles Moll, of 62 Silverdale Rd, Sheffield 11, Yorks, and Anita Lilian, *née* Francis;; *b* 15 August 1947; *Educ* Repton; *Career* sci and med photographer Royal Free Hosp London 1974- (radiographer 1969-73); chm Braintree and Bocking Civic Soc 1988, memb Anglian Water customer consultative ctee (S Grp) 1984-, Freeman City of London, Liveryman Worshipful Co of Apothecaries (1968), AIMBI (1986), ARPS (1986); *Recreations* chess, reading, community affairs, health economics, theatre, working; *Style*— Francis Moll, Esq; 10 Brook Close, Braintree, Essex (☎ 0376 25974); Dept of Histopathology, Royal Free Hospital, Pond Street, Hampstead, London NW3 (☎ 01 794 0500 extn 3544)

MOLLISON, (James) Pender Ross; s of John Dender Duff Mollison, and Mary Ross Thomson *née* Munro (both k in the Yokohama earthquake 1923); *b* 10 August 1916; *Educ* Merchiston Castle Sch Edinburgh; *m* 4 Jan 1944, Joan Patricia, da of Lt-Col Walter Latham Loring (ka Sept 1914); 2 da (Lavinia Duff Lawrie b 1951, Fiona Pender Gilmore b 1954); *Career* Capt Canadian Army, Staff Coll Camberley 1945; ret co dir Maclaine Watson & Co Ltd, Malcolm Maclaine Ltd; *Recreations* water colour painting, golf; *Clubs* Caledonian; *Style*— Pender Mollison, Esq; Little Bowlish, Shepton Mallet, Somerset (☎ 0749 4480)

MOLLOY, Michael John; s of John George Molloy, of Ealing, London W13, and Margaret Ellen, *née* West; *b* 22 Dec 1940; *Educ* Ealing Sch of Art; *m* 13 June 1964, Sandra June, da of Hubert Edwin Foley (d 1988), of Suffolk; 3 da (Jane b 1965, Catherine b 1966, Alexandra b 1968); *Career* ed: Mirror Magazine 1969-70, Daily Mirror 1975-85; ed in chief Mirror Gp Newspapers 1985, dir Mirror Gp Newspapers 1976; *Books* The Black Dwarf (1985), The Kid from Riga (1987), The Harlot of Jericho (1989); *Recreations* writing; *Clubs* Reform, Savile; *Style*— Michael Molloy, Esq; c/o Mirror Gp Newspapers, Holborn Circus, London EC1P 1DQ (☎ 01 354 0246)

MOLLOY, Michael William; s of William Molloy (d 1982), of Sydney, Aust, and Alice, *née* McMahon (d 1975); *b* 5 Jan 1940; *Educ* Public Sch Sydney Aust; *m* 10 Nov 1983, Adrienne Esther, da of Charles Dolesch, of Phoenix, Arizona, USA; *Career* camera operator: for Nick Roeg on Performance and Walkabout, for Stanley Kubrick on Clockwork Orange, Barry Lyndon; dir of photography: Mad Dog, Summerfield, The Shout, The Kidnapping of the President, Shock Treatment, Dead Easy, The Return of Captain Invincible, Reflections, The Hit, Bethune, (Director Phillip Borson starred Donald Sutherland on location in China), Scandal (dir Michael Caton-Jones starred John Hurt, Joanne Whalley); memb: Br Soc of Cinematographers; *Recreations* still photography, cooking, fishing; *Style*— Michael Molloy, Esq; 3 Glebe Place, London SW3 5LB;(☎ 01 351 6138); 100 Florence Terrace, Scotland Island, NSW 21O5, Australia (☎ 02 997 1282); CCA Personal Management, 4 Court Lodge, 48 Sloane Square, London SW1 48AT

MOLLOY, Sylvia Clark; da of James Lamb Leyden (d 1934), of S Shields, Co Durham, and Hannah Elisabeth Clark (d 1958); *b* 27 Mar 1914; *Educ* Westoe Secdy Sch S Shields, Univ of Durham (MA); *m* 16 Oct 1940, Patrick Reginald Hembrough Molloy, s of John Harper Molloy (d 1927); 2 s (Philip b 1943, Terence b 1946); *Career* art teacher St Asaph Co Sch N Wales 1936, resigned to go to Burma 1940; portrait painter: 2 high ct judges and bank dir Rangoon 1947, supreme ct judge S Africa 1948; professional artist 1948-63, pub collections incl: Miny of For Affrs, Bloemfontein Art Gallery, Port Elizabeth Art Gallery, City of Johannesburg Art Gallery; art teacher Stratton Sch Biggleswade Beds 1963; head of art dept: Mater Dei Sch Welwyn Gdn City Herts 1966-70, St Francis Coll Letchworth Herts 1970-73; runs own private sch 1973-; exhibitions: Mall Galleries London, one-man shows London and provinces, RA Summer Exhibition 1981, work featured in BBC Look East 1986; leading role in local art galleries (pres, critic and demonstrator), pres Business and Professional Women's Club SA 1961-62; fell Free Painters and Sculptors 1985, memb Nat Soc 1987; *Style*— Mrs Sylvia Molloy

MOLLOY, Baron (Life Peer 1981), of Ealing in Greater London William John; *b* 28 Oct 1918; *Educ* Elementary Sch Swansea, Univ of Wales and Univ Coll Swansea; *m* Eva Lewis, 1 da (Marion); *Career* serv Field Cos RE 1939-46; memb: TGWU 1936-46, Civil Service Union 1946-52; Co-op and USDAW 1952; parly advsr COHSE

1974-79; ed Civil Service Review 1947-52; ldr Fulham Borough Cncl 1952-62; MP (Lab) Ealing N 1964-79; former vice chm Parly Lab Pty Gp for Common Market and Euro Affairs; chm PLP Social Services Gp 1974; parly advsr London Trades Cncl Tport Ctee 1968-79; memb House of Commons Estimates Ctee 1968-70, pps to PMG and Min of Posts and Telecommunications Assemblies Cncl of Europe and WEU 1969-73; memb: Parly and Scientific Ctee 1982-, EC, CAABU; parly and scientific Assoc political conslt: Confedn of Health Servs Employees 1980-, Br Library Assoc 1984-; former Advsr to Arab League; pres Metropolitan Area Royal Br Legion 1984, hon pres London Univ Union and Debating Soc 1983-; (Court Reading Univ 1968, Exec Cncl RGS 1976); pres and tstee Health Visitors Assoc; hon assoc Br Vetinary Assocn; hon fell Univ Wales 1987; fellow World Assoc of Arts and Sciences; *Recreations* horse-riding, music, collecting dictionaries; *Style—* The Rt Hon Lord Molloy of Ealing, FRGS, FWAS; 2a Uneeda Drive, Greenford, MDX and House of Lords Westminster SW1 (☎ 01 578 7736)

MOLONY, Lady; Carmen Mary; da of late Frankland Dent; *m* 1936, Sir Joseph Thomas Molony KCVO, QC (d 1978); *Style—* Lady Molony; 4 Parkside Gdns, Wimbledon Common, SW19

MOLONY, (Sir) (Thomas) Desmond; 3 Bt (UK 1925), of the City of Dublin (but does not use title); s of Sir Hugh Francis Molony, 2 Bt (d 1976); *b* 13 Mar 1937; *Educ* Ampleforth, Trinity Coll Dublin; *m* 1962, Doris, da of late E W Foley, of Cork; 4 da; *Heir* unc, Sir Joseph Thomas Molony, KCVO, QC; *Style—* Desmond Molony Esq

MOLONY, Peter John; s of Sir Joseph Molony, KCVO, QC (d 1977), 2 s of 1 Bt, and Carmen Mary, *née* Dent; gs of Rt Hon Sir Thomas Molony, 1 Bt; hp to Btcy of kinsman Desmond Molony, 3 Bt (*qv*, who does not use title); *b* 17 August 1937; *Educ* Downside, Trinity Coll Cambridge (MA); *m* 1964, Elizabeth Mary, da of Henry Clevaux Chaytor, of Cambridge; 4 s (Sebastian b 1965, Benjamin b 1966, Benedict b 1972, Francis b 1975), 1 da (Jane b 1967); *Heir* er s Sebastian; *Career* CA; sr vice pres Sea Containers Inc 1968-73; dir: Post Off 1973-75, Scottish & Newcastle Breweries 1975-79, Rolls-Royce plc 1979-86; md Chaytor King Ltd 1986-, memb exec ctee Christian Assoc of Business Executives; FCA; *Recreations* music, gardening; *Clubs* Utd Oxford and Cambridge Univ; *Style—* Peter J Molony, Esq; Rock House, Great Elm, nr Frome, Somerset (☎ 0373 812332); 1 Eaton Place, London SW1X 8BN (☎ 01 235 2939)

MOLSON, Baron (Life Peer UK 1961); (Arthur) Hugh Elsdale Molson; PC (1956); s of late Maj John Elsdale Molson, MD, MP, of Goring Hall, Worthing; *b* 29 June 1903; *Educ* RNC: Osborne and Dartmouth, Lancing and New Colls Oxford; *m* 1949, Nancy, da of late W H Astington; *Career* serv 36 Searchlight Regt RA 1939-41; barr; MP (U) W R Yorks (Doncaster Div) 1931-35 and Derbyshire (High Peak Div) 1939-61, parly sec Min of Works 1951-53, jt parly sec Min of Tport and Civil Aviation 1953-57, Min of Works 1957-59; memb Monckton Cmmn on Rhodesia & Nyasaland 1960; chm of Cmmn of Privy Cnsllrs on Buganda-Bunyoro Dispute 1962; pres of the Town & Country Planning Assoc. 1963- chm Cncl for the Protection of Rural England 1968-71, pres 1971-80; *Clubs* Athenaeum; *Style—* The Rt Hon the Lord Molson, PC; 20 Marsham Court, Marsham Street, London SW1P 4JY (☎ 01 828 2008)

MOLYNEAUX, Rt Hon James Henry; PC (1983), MP (UU) Lagan Valley 1983-; s of William Molyneaux (d 1953), of Seacash, Killead, Co Antrim; *b* 27 August 1920; *Educ* Aldergrove Sch Co Antrim; *Career* RAF 1941-46, memb Antrim CC 1964-1973, vice-chm Eastern Special Care Hosp ctee 1966-73, chm Antrim branch of NI Assoc for Mental Health 1967-1970, MP (UU) Antrim South 1970-1983, vice pres UU Cncl 1974-, ldr UU Pty House of Commons 1974-, UU Pty 1979-; JP (1957-86 Co Antrim); *Style—* The Rt Hon James H Molyneaux, MP; Aldergrove, Crumlin, Co Antrim, NI (☎ 084 94 22545)

MONAGHAN, Neill Roderick; s of Reginald John Monaghan, of Preston Bowyer, Somerset, and Doreen Margaret, *née* Simpkin; *b* 2 April 1954; *Educ* Maret Sch Washington DC, Royal GS High Wycombe Bucks, Univ of Newcastle upon Tyne (LLB); *m* 11 June 1988, Emma, da of Fred Majdalany, MC (d 1967 Lancashire Fusilliers), of Little Saling, Essex; *Career* barr Lincoln's Inn 1979; ward chm Putney (C) Assoc 1984-85; *Recreations* tennis, music, motoring, travel, country pursuits; *Clubs* Chelsea Arts; *Style—* Neill Monaghan, Esq; 3 Temple Gardens, Temple, London EC4Y 9AU (☎ 01 583 1155, fax 01 353 5446)

MONBIOT, Raymond Geoffrey; MBE (1981); s of Maurice Ferdinand Monbiot (d 1976); *b* 1 Sept 1937; *Educ* Westminster, London Business Sch; *m* 1961, Rosalie Vivien Gresham, da R G Cooke, CBE, MP (d 1970); 3 children; *Career* J Lyons & Co Ltd 1956-78, md Associated Biscuits Ltd 1978-82; chm: Campbell's UK Ltd 1982-, Campbell's Soups Ltd 1983-; dir Unger Meats Ltd 1983-, pres Campbell's Frozen Foods Europe 1987-; chm: BIM Westminster Branch 1978-82, BIM Cncl 1981-84, Wessex Industl Cncl 1980-, chm Upper Thames Euro Constituency 1982-84; chm Oxon and Bucks Euro Constituency 1984-, pres S Oxon Cons Assoc 1980- (chm 1974-78); Duke of Edinburgh Award Industl project 1976-87; memb business liaison Ctee London Business Sch 1984-; *Books* How to Manage Your Boss (1980); *Recreations* writing, charity work, cooking; *Clubs* IOD, Leander; *Style—* Raymond Monbiot, Esq, MBE; Peppard Hse, Peppard Common, Henley-on-Thames, Oxon (☎ 049 17 424); Campbell's UK Ltd, Kennet Hse, 80 King's Rd, Reading, Berks RG1 3BS (☎ 0734 586326)

MONCK, 7 Viscount (I 1801); Charles Stanley Monck; also Baron Monck (I 1797) and Baron Monck (UK 1866; title in House of Lords); s of 6 Viscount Monck, OBE, JP, DL (d 1982, himself twelfth in descent from the yr bro of the ancestor of George Monck, who for his services in bringing about the Restoration in 1660 was cr Duke of Albemarle) by his 2 w; *b* 2 April 1953; *Educ* Eton; *Heir* bro, Hon George Stanley Monck; *Style—* The Rt Hon the Viscount Monck; Piglrims Farm, Overton, Hants RG25 3DS (☎ 0256 770352)

MONCK, Hon George Stanley; 2 s of 6 Viscount Monck, OBE, JP, DL (d 1982), and Brenda Mildred, *née* Adkins; hp to bro, 7 Viscount; *b* 12 April 1957; *Educ* Eton, Christ Church Oxford; *m* 24 May 1986, Camilla Elizabeth Valerie, 2 da of John Arthur Naylor (d 1983), of Basingstoke, Hants; *Career* mangr Beecham Pharmaceuticals; *Recreations* cricket, squash, real tennis, fishing, The Times Crossword; *Clubs* MCC, Royal Tennis Ct (Hampton Ct); *Style—* The Hon George Monck; Pilgrims' Farm, Overton, Basingstoke, Hants (☎ 0256 770352); Al Haya Medical Estabishment, PO Box 7633, RIYADH 11472, Saudi Arabia (☎ 464 2826)

MONCK, Hon James Stanley; 3 s of 6 Viscount Monck, OBE, JP, DL, and Mrs G M Palmer; *b* 5 July 1961; *Educ* Eton; *Style—* The Hon James Monck; Pilgrims Farm, Overton, Hants RG25 3DS (☎ 0256 770352)

MONCK, Hon Mrs (Margaret St Clair Sydney); *née* Thesiger; da of 1 Viscount Chelmsford, GCSI, GCMG, GCIE, GBE (d 1933); *b* 1911; *m* 1934, John Monck (who assumed surname of Monck in lieu of Goldman by deed poll), s of Maj Charles Sydney Goldman (d 1958); 2 s; *Style—* The Hon Mrs Monck; Aldern Bridge Hse, Newbury, Berks (☎ 0635 45566)

MONCK, Hon Mrs; Hon (Isolde) Sheila Tower; *née* Butler; da of 27 Baron Dunboyne (d 1945); *b* 1925; *m* 1949, Cdr Penryn Victor Monck, RNVR; 1 s, 2 da; *Style—* The Hon Mrs Monck; Yaverland Manor, Sandown, I O W

MONCKTON, Alan Stobart; DL (Staffs 1988); s of Maj R F P Monckton, TD, DL (d 1975); *b* 5 Sept 1934; *Educ* Eton; *m* 1961, Joanna Mary, *née* Bird; 2 s (Piers b 1962, Toby b 1970, and 1 s decd), 2 da (Davina b 1964, Sophie b 1967 (twin)); *Career* chartered surveyor, landowner, farmer, forester; dir Halifax Bldg Soc and various private cos; memb CLA (chm Staffs branch 1979-81), memb Timber Growers UK Cncl; High Sheriff of Staffs 1975-76; FRICS; *Recreations* bridge, shooting, philately; *Style—* Alan Monckton, Esq, DL; Horsebrook Hall, Brewood, Stafford ST19 9LP (☎ 0902 850239)

MONCKTON, Hon Anthony Leopold Colyer; yst s of 2 Viscount Monkton of Brenchley, CB, OBE, MC, DL; *b* 25 Sept 1960; *Educ* Harrow, Magdalene Coll Camb; *m* 1985, Philippa Susan, yr da of late Gervase Christopher Brinsmade Wingfield; 1 s (Edward Gervase Colyer b 1988); *Career* cmmnd 9/12 Royal Lancers 1982, Capt 1984; *Clubs* MCC, Cavalry and Guards'; *Style—* Capt The Hon Anthony Monckton; BFPO 33, W Germany

MONCKTON, Hon Christopher Walter; s and h of 2 Viscount Monckton of Brenchley, CB, OBE, MC, by his w Marianna Laetitia, da of Cdr Robert Tatton Bower, RN; *b* 14 Feb 1952; *Educ* Harrow, Churchill Coll Cambridge (MA), Univ Coll Cardiff (Dip Journalism); *Career* reporter Yorks Post 1974-75 (ldr writer 1975-77), press offr Cons Central Off 1977-78, ed the Universe 1979-81, managing ed Telegraph Sunday Magazine 1981-82, ldr writer The Standard 1982, asst ed Today 1986-; special advsr to PM's Policy Unit (Home Affs) 1982-; memb: Int MENSA Ltd 1975-, St John Ambulance Bd (Wetherby Div) 1976-77, Hon Soc of the Middle Temple 1979-; sec: Health Study Gp 1981-, Employment Study Gp 1982-; kt SMO Malta 1973, OStJ 1973; *Books* The Laker Story (co-author with Ivan Fallon, 1982); *Recreations* clocks and sundials, computers, cycling, fell-walking, inventions, motor-cycling, number theory, politics, public speaking, punting, recreational mathematics, sci fiction, Yorks; *Clubs* Beefsteak, Brooks's, Pratt's; *Style—* The Hon Christopher Monckton; 71 Albert Rd, Richmond, Surrey (☎ 01 940 6528); Runhams Farm, Harrietsham, Maidstone, Kent (☎ (0622 85) 313)

MONCKTON, Herbert Anthony; s of Francis Guy Monckton (d 1969), and Jessica Hamilton (d 1979); *b* 13 July 1923; *Educ* Malvern; *m* 1948, Peggy, da of Fred Bunting (d 1978); 2 da; *Career* Lt RM 1942-45; former brewer; historical res author; asst md: Flower & Sons Ltd Stratford-upon-Avon 1955-68, Whitbread E Pennines Ltd 1968-80; chm and md Publishing and Literary Servs Ltd Sheffield 1981-88; memb Inst of Brewing 1949-; *Books* A History of English Ale and Beer, A History of The English Public House, Story of The Brewer's Cooper, Story of British Beer, Story of The British Pub, Story Of The Publican Brewer; *Recreations* walking, bird-watching, historical research; *Style—* Herbert Monckton, Esq; 6 Whirlow Park Rd, Sheffield S11 9NP (☎ 0742 369668)

MONCKTON, Hon Jonathan Riversdale St Quintin; s (twin) of 2 Viscount Monckton of Brenchley, CB, OBE, MC; *b* 15 August 1955; *Educ* Ladycross, Worth; *Career* monk of the Order of St Benedict Worth Abbey; *Style—* The Hon Jonathan Monckton

MONCKTON, Hon (John) Philip; s and h of 12 Viscount Galway and Fiona Margaret Monckton, *née* Taylor; *b* 8 April 1952; *Educ* Univ of W Ontario (MA); *m* 1980, Deborah Kathleen, da of A Bruce Holmes, of Ottawa, Canada; *Career* vice pres Steepe & Co Sales Promotion Agency, memb Canadian Olympic Rowing Team 1974-84, Gold Medal Pan-Am Games 1975, Silver Medal Pan-Am Games 1984, Bronze Medal Olympic Games 1984, BC Premiers Award, Sport Canada Certificate of Excellence, Cara pres Award 1984; *Recreations* rowing, squash; *Clubs* Vancouver Rowing, Burnaby Lake Rowing; *Style—* The Hon J Philip Monckton; 43 Braemar Avenue, Toronto, Ontario, Canada M5P 2LI (☎ 416 482 3799); Suite 500, 120 Eglinton Avenue East, Toronto, Ontario, Canada M4P 1EZ (☎ 416 488 1999)

MONCKTON, Hon Mrs (Rachel Jean); da of The Rt Hon the Viscount Galway, CD of 583 Berkshire Drive, London, Ontario, Canada N67 353 and Fiona Margaret, *née* Taylor; Gen Robert Monckton, govr of New Brunswick and New York State; *b* 21 June 1957; *m* 1978, (m dis), Ronald John Pressey; 2 s (Michael b 1980, Christopher b 1981); *Style—* The Hon Rachel Pressey; 44 Byron Ave, London, Ont N6C 1C5, Canada

MONCKTON, Hon Rosamond Mary; only da of 2 Viscount Monckton of Brenchley, CB, OBE, MC; *b* 26 Oct 1953; *Educ* Ursuline Convent Tildonk Belgium; *Career* asst md Cartier London 1979, sales and exhibition mangr Tabbah Jewellers (Monte Carlo) 1980, promotions mangr Asprey 1982-85, md Tiffany London 1986-; Freeman Worshipful Co of Goldsmiths 1982; *Recreations* parties and champagne, dogs and voyages; *Style—* The Hon Rosamond Monckton; 29 Lavender Gardens, London SW11 1DJ

MONCKTON, Hon Timothy David Robert; 2 s of 2 Viscount Monckton of Brenchley, CB, OBE, MC; *b* 15 August 1955; *Educ* Harrow, RAC Cirencester; *m* 1984, Jennifer, 2 da of Brendan Carmody, of Sydney Australia; 2 s (Dominic b 1985, James Timothy b 1988); *Career* chm Albert Abela & Co Ltd 1985, Knight of honour and devotion Sovereign Order of Malta; *Style—* Hon Timothy Monckton; Flat 3, 19 Lavender Gdns, London SW11 1DN (☎ 01 350 0190)

MONCKTON, Hon (Rose) Wynsome; da of 11 Viscount Galway (d 1980); *b* 1937; *Career* occupational therapist; *Style—* The Hon Wynsome Monckton

MONCKTON OF BRENCHLEY, 2 Viscount (UK 1957); Maj-Gen Gilbert Walter Riversdale Monckton; CB (1966), OBE (1956, MC 1940, DL (Kent 1970)); s of 1 Viscount Monckton of Brenchley, GCVO, KCMG, PC, MC, QC (d 1965), by his w Mary, da of Sir Thomas Colyer-Fergusson, 3rd Bt; *b* 3 Nov 1915; *Educ* Harrow, Trinity Coll Cambridge (MA); *m* 1950, Marianna Laetitia, OStJ, Dame of Honour & Devotion (Sovereign Mil Order Malta), Pres St John's Ambulance Kent 1972-80, and High Sheriff Kent 1981-82, 3 da of Cdr Robert Tatton Bower, of Gatto-Murina Palace, Mdina, Malta, by his w Hon Henrietta, *née* Strickland, 4 da of 1 and last Baron

Strickland; 4 s, 1 da; *Heir* s, Hon Christopher Walter Monckton; *Career* serv WWII; dep dir Personnel Admin 1962, DPR War Office (Maj-Gen) 1963-65, CoS HQ BAOR 1965-67; dep chm Gulf Guarantee Tst; Liveryman Worshipful Co of Broderers 1962, (Master 1978), pres Kent Assoc of Boys Clubs 1965-78, Inst of Heraldic and Genealogical Studies 1965, Kent Archaeological Assoc 1968-75, Medway Productivity Assoc 1968-74, Maidstone and Dist Football League 1968, vice-chm Scout Assoc Kent 1968-74, pres Anglo-Belgian Union 1974-80, chm Cncl of the OStJ for Kent 1969-74; landowner and farmer (300 acres); Grand Offr Order of Leopold II (Belgium 1978), Cmdr Order of the Crown (Belgium) KStJ; - Bailiff Grand Cross Obedience Sov Mil Order Malta, Grand Cross Merit 1980; FSA; *Clubs* Brooks's, MCC, Cavalry & Guard's, Casino Maltese, Valetta Malta; *Style—* The Rt Hon the Viscount Monckton of Brenchley, CB, OBE, MC, DL; Runhams Farm, Runham Lane, Harrietsham, Maidstone, Kent (☎ 0627 850 313)

MONCREIFF, Hon Donald Graham Fitz-Herbert; 2 s of 4 Baron Moncreiff (d 1942), and Lucy Vida, *née* Anderson; *b* 1919; *Educ* Dollar Academy; *m* 17 Aug 1955, Catriona Sheila, da of James MacDonald, of Devonshaw House, Dollar, Kinross-shire; 1 s, 3 da; *Career* Lt Argyll and Sutherland Highlanders 1940; *Clubs* New (Edinburgh); *Style—* The Hon Donald Moncreiff; Machruin, Lawers, Perthshire

MONCREIFF, 5 Baron (UK 1874); Lt-Col Sir Harry Robert Wellwood Moncreiff; 15 Bt (NS 1626), of Moncreiff and 5 Bt (UK 1871), of Tulliebole; s of 4 Baron (d 1942); *b* 4 Feb 1915; *Educ* Fettes; *m* 1952, Enid Marion Watson (d 1985), da of late Maj H W Locke, of Belmont, Dollar, Clackmannan; 1 s; *Heir* s, Hon Rhoderick Harry Wellwood Moncreiff; *Career* 2 Lt RASC 1939, Maj 1943, ret 1958, Hon Lt-Col; *Style—* The Rt Hon the Lord Moncreiff; Tulliebole Castle, Fossoway, Kinross (☎ Fossoway 236)

MONCREIFF, Hon Rhoderick Harry Wellwood; s and h of 5 Baron Moncreiff; *b* 22 Mar 1954; *Educ* E of Scotland Coll of Agric (H N D); *m* 1982, Alison Elizabeth Anne, d da of late James Duncan Alastair Ross, of West Mayfield, Dollar, Clackmannanshire: 2 s (Harry James Wellwood b 12 Aug 1986, James Gavin Francis b 29 July 1988) ; *Heir* (Harry James Wellwood b 1986); *Style—* The Hon Rhoderick Moncreiff

MONCREIFF, Hon Robert Frederick Arthur; s of 4 Baron Moncreiff (d 1942) and Lucy Vida (d 1976), eld da of David Lechmere Anderson; *b* 25 Jan 1924; *Educ* Dollar Acad Scotland; *m* 1951, Aileen Margaret Marr, da of Robert Marr Meldrum (d 1976); 1 s (Richard b 1964), 1 da (Gillian b 1954); *Career* Warrant Offr RAF, Burma; hotelier, ret; *Clubs* Cons (Galashiels); *Style—* The Hon Robert Moncreiff; 33 Talisman Ave, Galashiels, Selkirks (☎ 0896 57533)

MONCREIFFE OF MONCREIFFE, (Katharine) Elisabeth; 24 Feudal Baroness of Moncreiffe; da of Cdr Sir Guy Moncreiffe of that Ilk, RN, 9 Bt, 22 Feudal Baron and sis of Capt Sir David Moncreiffe of that Ilk, MC, 10 Bt and 23 Feudal Baron; *b* 23 May 1920; *Educ* Private-London, Paris, Munich, Florence; *Heir* Hon Peregrine Moncreiffe, *qv*; *Career* serv WWII WRNS - special duties linguist; *Recreations* breeder and int chief judge of German Shepherd dogs; *Clubs* Cavalry and Guards', Kennel; *Style—* Miss Moncreiffe of Moncreiffe; Moncreiffe, Bridge of Earn, Perthshire

MONCREIFFE OF MONCREIFFE, Hon Peregrine David Euan Malcolm; Fiar of the Barony of Moncreiffe and Baron of Easter Moncreiffe (both Scottish territorial baronies); 2 s of late Countess of Erroll (d 1978), and Sir Iain Moncreiffe of that Ilk, 11 Bt (d 1985); *b* 16 Feb 1951; *Educ* Eton, Christ Church Oxford (MA); *m* 27 July 1988, Miranda Mary, da of Capt Mervyn Fox-Pitt, of Grange Scrymgeour, Cupar, Fife; *Career* Lt Atholl Highlanders; Slains Pursuivant 1970-78; investmt banker; Credit Suisse First Boston 1972-82; Lehman Bros Kuhn Loeb/Shearson Lehman 1982-86; E F Hutton & Co 1986-88; chm Scottish Ballet; memb Royal Co of Archers (Queen's Body Gd for Scotland); Freeman City of London, memb Worshipful Co of Fishmongers 1987; *Recreations* running, rowing, rustic pursuits, dance; *Clubs* Turf, White's, Pratt's, Beefsteak, Puffin's (Edinburgh), New (Edinburgh), Leander, Royal and Ancient GC (St Andrews), Brook (NY); *Style—* The Hon Peregrine Moncreiffe of Moncreiffe; Easter Moncreiffe, Perthshire PH2 8QA (☎ 0738 812338)

MONCREIFFE OF THAT ILK, Lady; Hermione Patricia; *née* Faulkner; o da of Lt-Col Walter Douglas Faulkner, MC (ka 1940), and Patricia Katharine (now Dowager Countess of Dundee); *b* 14 Jan 1937; *m* 1 May 1966, Sir Rupert Iain Kay Moncreiffe of that Ilk, 11 Bt (d 1985); 2 step s (Earl of Erroll, Hon Peregrine Moncreiffe of that Ilk, *qqv*), 1 step da (Lady Alexandra Hay, *qv*); *Style—* Lady Moncreiffe of that Ilk; 117 Ashley Gardens, London SW1 (☎ 01 828 8421)

MONCRIEFF *see also*: Scott Moncrieff

MONCRIEFF, Capt Charles St John Graham; s of Lt-Col Douglas Graham Moncrieff (d 1983), of Rhynd, Perth, and Henrietta Doreen Moncrieff St John (d 1987); *b* 11 Jan 1931; *Educ* Eton, RMA Sandhurst; *m* 15 June 1957, Joanna Dava, da of Maj Basil Arthur John Peto (d 1953); 1 s (Alexander b 1967), 3 da (Charlotte b 1959, Miranda b 1961, Rosanna b 1965); *Career* Capt Scots Gds 1951 (ret 1960); farmer; memb QBGS RCA; *Recreations* fishing; *Style—* Capt Charles Moncrieff; c/o Bank of Scotland, 110 St Vincent St, Glasgow

MONCRIEFF, Lady; Mary Katherine; da of late Ralph Wedmore; *b* 18 May 1908; *m* 1955, as his 2 w, Prof Sir Alan Aird Moncrieff, CBE, MD, FRCP, FRCOG (d 1971, former prof of child health at London Univ); *Style—* Lady Moncrieff; Waterford Cottage, Buckland Rd, Bampton, Oxon 0X8 2AA (☎ 0993 850359)

MOND, Gary Stephen; s of Ferdinand Mond, of London, and Frances, *née* Henry; *b* 11 May 1959; *Educ* Univ Coll Sch Hampstead London NW3, Trinity Coll Cambridge (MA); *Career* CA 1981-84, Guinness Mahon & Co Ltd 1984-86, assoc dir of corporate fin subsid of a merchant bank, dir public property devpt and construction co, md Bow Pubns Ltd 1987-88; chm Gtr London Cons 1985-86, asst tres Chelsea Cons Assoc 1986-88, Parly candidate (C) Hamilton Scotland 1987; competitive butterfly swimmer, nat under 14 champ 1972, GB Int and Olympic Trialist 1976, Cambridge blue, former World Record Holder furthest distance ever swam butterfly six and a quarter miles 1980, ACA 1985; *Recreations* swimming, theatre, chess; *Clubs* Coningsby; *Style—* Gary Mond, Esq; 56 Coleherne Ct, Old Brompton Rd, London SW5 0EF (☎ 01 244 7413); 62 Marsham Ct, Marsham St, London SW1P 4JX;

MOND, Hon Pandora Shelley; da of 3 Baron Melchett (d 1973); *b* 11 Sept 1959; *Style—* The Hon Pandora Mond

MONEY, Ernle David Drummond; s of Lt-Col E F D Money DSO (d 1970), of Cambridge, and Dorothy Blanche Sidney (d 1984), o da of David Anderson of Scotland; *b* 17 Feb 1931; *Educ* Marlborough, Oriel Coll Oxford (MA); *m* 1960, Lister, da of Lt-Col Dudley Lister, MC of Hurlingham; 1 s (Horry b 1963); 3 da (Sophie b 1961, Jolyan b 1964, Pandora b 1966); *Career* barr Lincoln's Inn 1958, memb gen Cncl of Bar 1962-66, MP (C) Ipswich 1970-74, oppn shadow min for the Arts 1974, co-opted memb GLC Arts Bd 1973-74, 1975-76; conslt various Art Galleries, Victorian pictures, Fine Arts corr, The Contemporary Review 1968-; pres Ipswich Town FC Supporters 1974-80; ctee memb various heritage organisations; *Books* The Nasmyth Family of Painters (with Peter Johnson 1975), Margaret Thatcher a biography (with Peter Johnson 1976); *Recreations* football, opera, pictures, antiques; *Clubs* Carlton; *Style—* E D D Money, Esq; 10 St John's Villas, London N19 (☎ 01 272 6815); 1 Gray's Inn Square, Grays Inn, London WC1 (☎ 01 405 8946)

MONEY, John Kyrle; s of Edward Douglas Money (d 1974), and Edith Lillian (d 1984); the Money family have been East India merchants since 1850; *b* 21 Mar 1927; *Educ* Stowe, Trinity Coll Cambridge; *m* 1957, Verena, da of Dr Heinrich Gottfried Mann, of Frankfurt; 2 da; (Patricia b 1958, Joanna b 1961); m 2, 1983, Sally Elizabeth, da of Michael Staples, of Tadworth, Surrey; 1 da (Kate b 1984), 1 s (Oliver b 1986); *Career* East India merchant and co dir 1951-79, chm Rubber Growers Assoc 1978, dir Peacock Estates Ltd; *Books* A Plantation Family (1979); *Clubs* Kandahar, Wentworth; *Style—* John K Money, Esq; 18 Pembroke Gdns Close, London W8 6HR (☎ 01 602 2211)

MONEY, Robert George; s of late Thomas George Money; *b* 18 Feb 1937; *Educ* Poly; *m* 1961, Joan May, 1 c; *Career* md Robert Money Fine Wines Ltd; *Recreations* music; *Clubs* Farmers'; *Style—* Robert Money, Esq; Conifers, Roselands Avenue, Mayfield, Sussex

MONEY-COUTTS, Lt-Col Hon Alexander Burdett; OBE (1946); s of 6 Baron Latymer (d 1949); *b* 1902; *Educ* Eton, New Coll Oxford; *m* 1930, Mary Elspeth, da of Sir Reginald Arthur Hobhouse, 5 Bt (d 1947); 1 s, 2 da (adopted); *Career* serv Royal Scots Fus; Lt-Col 1944; Master Worshipful Co of Tobacco Pipe Makers and Tobacco Blenders 1964; *Style—* Lt-Col the Hon Alexander Money-Coutts; Askett House, Askett, nr Aylesbury, HP17 9LT Bucks (☎ 084 44 5498)

MONEY-COUTTS, Hon Mrs (Penelope) Ann Clare; da of Thomas Addis Emmet (d 1934), and Baroness Emmet of Amberley (Life Peeress); *b* 1932; *m* 1951 (m dis 1965), Hon Hugo Nevill Money-Coutts; 2 s, 1 da; *Career* govr Cobham Hall, Kent 1962-86; EEC Brussels 1972-73, sec gen Euro Orgn for Res and Treatment of Cancer (EORTC) 1976-,; *Style—* The Hon Mrs Ann Money-Coutts; Flat 4, 43 Onslow Sq, London SW7 3LR (☎ 01 581 5191); EORTC Foundation, 132-135 Long Acre, London WC2E 9AH (☎ 01 379 3505)

MONEY-COUTTS, Hon Crispin James Alan Nevill; eldest s and h of 8 Baron Latymer, *qv*; *b* 8 Mar 1955; *Educ* Eton, Keble Coll Oxford; *m* 1978, Hon Lucy Rose Deedes, yst da of Baron Deedes (Life Peer); 1 s (Drummond William Thomas b 11 May 1986), 2 da (Sophia Patience b 1985, Evelyn Rose b 1988); *Style—* The Hon Crispin Money-Coutts; c/o Coutts & Co, 440 Strand, London WC2R 0QS

MONEY-COUTTS, David Burdett; s of Lt-Col the Hon Alexander Burdett Money-Coutts, OBE (2 s of 6 Baron Latymer), and Mary Elspeth, er da of Sir Reginald Arthur Hobhouse, 5 Bt; *b* 19 July 1931; *Educ* Eton, New Coll Oxford (MA); *m* 17 May 1958, (Helen) Penelope June Utten, da of Cdr Killingworth Richard Utten Todd, RIN; 1 s (Benjamin b 1961), 2 da (Harriet b 1959, Laura b 1965); *Career* served 1 Royal Dragoons 1950-51, Royal Glos Hussars (TA) 1951-67; joined Coutts & Co 1954, (dir 1958, md 1970-86, chm 1976-); dir: Nat Discount Co 1964-69, United States & General Tst Corpn 1964-73, Charities Investmt Mangrs 1964- (chm 1984-), Nat Westminster Bank 1976- (and SE Regn 1969-88, chm 1986-88); chm S Advsy Bd 1988-; Dun & Bradstreet 1973-87, Phoenix Assur 1978-85; Sun Alliance and London Insur 1984-, M & G Gp 1987; Gerrard & Nat 1969- (dep chm 1969-89); hon tres Nat Assoc of Almshouses 1960-; govr Middx Hosp 1962-74 and chm Med Sch 1974-88; memb: Cncl Univ Coll London 1987-, Health Educn Cncl 1973-76, Kensington, Chelsea and Westminster AHA(T) 1974-82, chm Old Etonian Tst 1976-, tstee Multiple Sclerosis Soc 1967-, memb Bloomsbury Health Authy 1982-(vice-chm 1982-88), tstee Mansfield Coll Oxford 1988-; *Clubs* Leander; *Style—* David Money-Coutts, Esq; Magpie House, Peppard Common, Henley-on-Thames, Oxon RG9 5JG; 440 Strand, London WC2R 0QS

MONIBA, HE Dr Harry Fumba; *Career* Liberian ambass to UK 1981-; *Style—* HE Dr Harry Fumba Moniba; The Liberian Embassy, 21 Princes Gate, London SW7 (☎ 01 589 9405/6/7; home: 01 942 7997)

MONIER-WILLIAMS, His Honour Judge; Evelyn Faithfull; s of Roy Thornton Monier-Williams, OBE (d 1967), and Gladys Maive; *b* 29 April 1920; *Educ* Charterhouse, Univ Coll Oxford (MA); *m* 1948, Maria-Angela (d 1983), da of Rudolf Georg Oswald (d 1939), of Oberhausen, Germany; 1 s (Christopher Roy), 1 da (Vivien Angela, *see* Hon Mrs Mark Piercy); *Career* serv RA Mediterranean and NW Europe as Capt; called to the Bar Inner Temple 1948, circuit judge 1972-, master of the bench Inner Temple, reader 1987, elected tres; *Style—* His Hon Judge Monier-Williams; Inner Temple, London EC4

MONINS, Ian Richard; s of Capt John Eaton Monins, JP (d 1939), of Kent, and Margaret Louise, *née* Carter (d 1982); one of the oldest Kentish families dating back to 11 century; *b* 13 April 1930; *Educ* Groton USA, Eton; *m* 2 April 1954, Patricia Lillian, da of Percival Read (d 1967), of Kent; 2 s (Symond b 1958, Stephen b 1961), 2 da (Gay b 1955, Daryl b 1956); *Career* farmer; Nat Serv Lt The Buffs 1950-52; farmer; md Gaychild Ltd 1954-69; chm St Louis Hldgs and subsidiaries 1974-; coinage advsr to Jersey States Treasy 1980-86; vice pres: Societe Jersiase 1981-83 and 1985-87; Jersey Heritage Tst 1986-87; FRNS; *Recreations* tennis, building follies, numismatics; *Style—* Ian R Monins, Esq; Homeland, St John, Jersey (☎ 0534 61618)

MONJACK, Philip; s of Jack Monjack of 53 Beauchamp Court, Marsh Lane, Stanmore, Middlesex and Tilly *née* Levene; *b* 4 Sept 1942; *Educ* The Grocers Co Sch; *m* 5 Sept 1965, Carol Daphne, da of Jack Kohn of 1 Kenlor Ct, Heather Walk, Edgware, Middx; 2 s (Richard b 1967, Jonathan b 1969), 1 da (Suzanne b 1973); *Career* CA 1965; sr ptnr Leonard Curtis & Co; ptnr: Leonard Curtis & Ptnrs, Philip Keith & Co; alternate dir Imry Property Hldgs plc 1983-86; FCA, Fell of Insolvency Practitioners Assoc; *Recreations* tennis, soccer; *Clubs* RAC; *Style—* Philip Monjack Esq, FCA; 30 Eastbourne Terrace, London W2 6LF (telex: 22784, fax: 01 723 6059)

MONK, Colin Arthur Hercules; s of James Joseph Monk and Katie *née* Ansell; *b* 8 April 1934; *Educ* Charterhouse; *m* 14 Sept 1962, Agnes Elizabeth; 1 s (James b 1968); *Career* merchant banker, tres and md Hill Samuel 1980, chief exec Daiwa Europe 1980-; *Recreations* golf, snooker, darts; *Clubs* The Crafty Cockney Darts, Plaistow; *Style—* Colin Monk, Esq; Coombe Heights, Fitzgeorge Avenue, New Malden, Surrey;

Daiwa Europe, City Tower, London WC2

MONK, Paul Nicholas; s of George Benbow Monk, of Godalming, Surrey, and Rosina Gwendoline, *née* Ross; *b* 3 Dec 1949; *Educ* Royal GS Guildford, Pembroke Coll Oxford (MA); *m* 14 Feb 1985, Roma Olivia Cannon, da of Hamilton Haigh; 2 da (Georgina, Lucinda); *Career* slr 1974; articled to Durrant Cooper & Hambling 1972-74, Allen & Overy 1975-(ptnr 1979); memb Worshipful Co Slrs; memb Law Soc 1972 ; *Recreations* sailing, cross-country skiing; *Clubs* Hurlingham, Royal Southern YC; *Style*— Paul Monk, Esq; 9 Cheapside, London EC2V 6AD (☎ 01 248 9898, fax 01 236 2192, telex 8812801)

MONK, Ronald Frank; s of Wing Cdr Ronald Cecil Howe Monk (d 1972), of Webridge, Surrey, and Madeline, *née* Booth-Haynes (d 1984); *b* 13 Sept 1944; *Educ* Charterhouse; *m* 6 Sept 1969 (m dis 1980), (Felicity) Jane, da of Dr David Arthur (d 1986), of Pyrford, Surrey; 2 s ((Ronald) William Howe b 10 July 1974, Charles David Hambly b 2 Feb 1976); *Career* accountant Finnie Ross Welch & Co 1962-68, merchant banker corporate fin SG Warburg & Co Ltd 1969-72, dir James Finlay plc 1972-79, chm James Finlay Bank Ltd (part of the Finlay Gp), dir and chm Setas Securities Ltd (investmt bankers) 1979-83; Falcon Resources plc (an oil Co): fndr, chm chief exec offr 1983-89; FCA 1969; *Recreations* swimming, sailing, foreign travel; *Clubs* Annabels; *Style*— Ronald Monk, Esq; 4 South Park Mews, Woolneigh St, London SW6 3AY (☎ 01 731 6437); 50 Stratton St, London SW1 (☎ 01 731 6437)

MONK, Ronald William (Ron); s of William George Monk (d 1979), of Guildford, Surrey, and Edith May, *née* Barnes (d 1985); *b* 8 Oct 1928; *Educ* Woking Co GS, Coll of Estate Mgmnt; *m* 7 July 1962, Jennifer (Jennie)Leach, da of Capt Warren Leach Smith (d 1977), of Milford, Surrey; 1 s (Alastair b 15 Jul 1968); *Career* Queen's Westminster's Rifles/Queen's Royal Rifles 1955-62; surveyor; sr ptnr Monk & Deere (chartered quantity surveyors) Croydon Surrey; RICS: memb gen cncl 1973-, memb professional practice ctee 1973- (vice chm), chm rules of conduct ctee 1983-88, chm Surrey branch 1972-73, memb official referees users ctee 1982-; construction indust arbitrator 1966-, independent surveyor; chm: Shalford Parish Cncl 1973-83, Surrey Co Assoc of Parish & Town Cncls 1975-78; Freeman: City of London 1979, Worshipful Co of Chartered Surveyors 1979; FRICS 1951, FCIArb 1968; *Recreations* walking, gardening, railways (including model railways); *Style*— R W Monk, Esq; Orchard House, 17 Denton Rd, Meads, Eastbourne, E. Sussex BN20 7SS (☎ 0323 26249); Monk & Deere, Chartered Quantity Surveyors, 107 High St, Croydon, Surrey CRO 1QG (☎ 01 688 5666)

MONK, (William) Roy; s of William Herries Monk (d 1963), and Ethel Jane Monk (d 1965); *b* 4 August 1925; *Educ* Bolton GS, Manchester Univ; *m* 25 March 1962, Deirdre Ruth, da of Percival Wilson (d 1983); 2 s (Calvin Anthony b 1964, Gareth Robin b 1965), 1 da (Candida Jane b 1962); *Career* trainee air crew RAF 1943-45; dir: Garnar Booth plc, Garbra Leather Co, Gryfe Tannery Ltd, Derrick Hosegood Gp Ltd, Odell Leather Industs Ltd, Phillips Rubber Co Ltd, Spencer Leather Co, Wilson & Tilt Ltd, Br Leather Confedn; pres E Lancs Sub Aqua Club; life memb Nat Tst; chm fund raising ctee Oakfield Home for Young Mentally Retarded Adults; M Inst Export 1950; *Recreations* sub aqua, archaeology, walking remote coastlines; *Clubs* RAC; *Style*— W Roy Monk, Esq; Manor Farm House, Easton Maudit, Wellingborough, Northants NN9 7NR; Odell Leather Industries, Odell, Bedford MK43 7BA

MONK, Rear Adm (Anthony John) Tony; CBE (1973); s of Capt Frank Leonard Monk, RD RNR (d 1941), and Mrs Barbara Ellerd-Styles, *née* Ashby; *b* 14 Nov 1923; *Educ* Whitgift Sch Croydon, RNC Dartmouth, RN Engrg Coll Devonport, The Coll of Aeronautics Cranfield (MSc), London Univ (BSc); *m* 14 April 1951, Elizabeth Ann, da of Oliver Samson (d 1952); 4 s (Michael b 1952, Peter b 1958, Andrew b 1961, Jonathan b 1967), 1 da (Anstace b 1954); *Career* naval offr 1941-78; Naval Liaison Offr N Ireland and Supt RN Aircraft Yard Belfast 1970-73; Port Adm, Rosyth 1974-76; Rear Adm Engrg, Naval Air Cmd 1976-78; dir gen: The Brick Devpt Assoc 1979-84; appeal orgnr The Royal Marsden Hosp 1984-87; *Recreations* swimming (ASA teacher); *Clubs* Stocks; *Style*— Rear Adm Tony Monk, CBE; 7 London Rd, Widley, Portsmouth PO7 5AT (☎ 0705 378121); 1 Cissbury, Windsor Rd, Ascot SL5 7LF (☎ 0990 20229)

MONK BRETTON, 3 Baron (UK 1884); John Charles Dodson; DL (E Sussex 1983); s of 2 Baron, CB, JP, DL (d 1933), by his w Ruth (herself da of Hon Charles Brand and gda of 1 Viscount Hampden and 23 Baron Dacre); *b* 17 July 1924; *Educ* Westminster, New Coll Oxford; *m* 1958, Zoé Diana, da of Ian Douglas Murray Scott (d 1974); 2 s; *Heir* s, Hon Christopher Mark Dodson; *Career* takes Cons whip in House of Lords; farmer; *Clubs* Brooks's; *Style*— The Rt Hon the Lord Monk Bretton, DL; Shelley's Folly, Cooksbridge, nr Lewes, E Sussex (☎ (0273) 231)

MONKSWELL, 5 Baron (UK 1885); Gerard Collier; s of William Adrian Larry Collier, MB (disclaimed Barony of Monkswell for life 1964; d 1984) and his 2 w, Helen, *née* Dunbar; *b* 28 Jan 1947; *Educ* George Heriot's Sch Edinburgh, Portsmouth Poly; *m* 1974, Ann Valerie, da of James Collins, of Liverpool; 2 s (James Adrian b 1977, Robert William Gerard b 1979); 1 da (Laura Jennifer b 1975); *Heir* s Hon James Adrian b 29 March 1977; *Career* mechanical engr; serv admin mangr MF Industl; formerly product quality engr Massey Ferguson Man Co Ltd; *Recreations* swimming, watching films, reading; *Style*— The Rt Hon the Lord Monkswell; 513 Barlow Moor Rd, Chorlton, Manchester M21 2AQ (☎ 061 881 3887); Gerard Collier MF Industrial, Barton Dock Rd, Stretford, Manchester M32 0YH (☎ 061 865 4400)

MONRO, Sir Hector Seymour Peter; AE (1953), JP (Dumfries 1963), DL (1973), MP (C) Dumfries 1964-; s of late Capt Alastair Monro, Cameron Highlanders (s of Brig-Gen Seymour Monro, CB, and Lady Ida, eldest da of 5 Earl of Lisburne), and Marion, child of Lt-Gen Sir John Ewart, KCB, JP; *b* 4 Oct 1922; *Educ* Canford, King's Coll Cambridge; *m* 1949, Elizabeth Anne, da of Maj Harry Welch, of the Sherwood Foresters, formerly of Longstone Hall, Derbyshire; 2 s; *Career* served WWII Flt-Lt RAF, RAuxAF 1946-53; Scottish Cons whip 1967-70, Lord cmmr Treasy 1970-71, parly under-sec Scottish Off 1971-74; oppn spokesman: Scottish Affrs 1974-75, Sport 1974-79; parly under-sec Environment 1979-81 (with special responsibility for sport); chm Dumfriesshire Unionist Assoc 1958-63; memb: Royal Co of Archers (Queen's Bodyguard for Scotland), Dumfries T&AFA 1959-67, NFU Scotland Area Exec Ctee; Hon Air Cdre 2622 (Highlands) RAuxAF Regt Sqdn 1982-; pres: Scottish Rugby Union 1976-77, Auto Cycle Union 1983-, Nat Small-Bore Rifle Assoc 1987-; memb Native Conservancy Cncl 1982-; kt 1981; *Recreations* country sports, vintage cars, flying, golf; *Clubs* RAF, RSAC, MCC; *Style*— Sir Hector Monro, AE, JP, DL, MP; Williamwood, Kirtlebridge, Dumfries (☎ 046 15 213)

MONRO, (Andrew) Hugh; s of Andrew Killey Monro, FRCS, of Rye, Sussex, and Diana Louise, *née* Rhys; *b* 2 Mar 1950; *Educ* Rugby, Pembroke Coll Cambridge (MA, PGCE); *m* 27 July 1974, Elizabeth Clare, da of Lyndon Rust, of Mayhill, Glos; 1 s (James b 1983), 1 da (Lucy b 1980); *Career* production mangr Metal Box Co 1972-73, teacher Haileybury 1974-79, (Noble & Greenough, Boston, Mass 1977-78), head of history and housemaster Loretto Sch 1980-86; headmaster Workshop Coll 1986-; govr Westbourne Sch Sheffield, memb cncl Local Hospice Movement; *Recreations* golf, American politics; *Clubs* Hawks; *Style*— Hugh Monro, Esq; Headmasters House, Workshop Coll, Workshop, Notts S80 3AP (☎ 0909 472 391)

MONRO, Hon Mrs Mary Katherine; *née* Lampson; da of 1 Baron Killearn, GCMG, CB, MVO, PC (d 1964), and Rachel Helen Mary (d 1930), yr da of late William Wilton Phipps; *b* 7 August 1915; *m* 1952, as his 2 w, Lt-Col Alexander George Falkiner (decd), s of Maj G Nowlan Monro, DL (d 1933); 1 s (adopted); *Career* a lady-in-waiting to HRH the late Princess Royal 1948-51; *Recreations* curling, travelling; *Style*— The Hon Mrs Monro; 15 Glencairn Crescent, Edinburgh EH12 5BT (☎ 031 337 9543)

MONSELL, 2nd Viscount (UK 1935); Lt-Col Henry Bolton Graham Eyres Monsell; s of 1st Viscount Monsell, GBE, PC (d 1969); *b* 21 Nov 1905; *Educ* Eton; *Heir* none; *Career* served in N Africa with Intelligence Corps (despatches) 1939-45; Medal of Freedom with Bronze Palm (USA); *Clubs* Travellers'; *Style*— The Rt Hon the Viscount Monsell; The Mill House, Dumbleton, Evesham, Worcs WR11 6TR

MONSLOW, Baroness Jean Baird; da of Rev Angus Macdonald; *m* 1960, as his 2 w, Baron Monslow (d 1966; Life Peer); *Style*— The Rt Hon the Lady Monslow; 4 Kirklea Circus, Glasgow 12

MONSON, Hon Andrew Anthony John; s of 11 Baron Monson; *b* 12 May 1959; *Educ* Eton and Merton Coll, Oxford (Eng Lit); *Career* barr, called to the Bar Middle Temple in 1983; *Recreations* books, theatre, bridge, boardgames, tennis, skiing; *Clubs* Lincolnshire; *Style*— The Hon Andrew Monson; 7A Melrose Gdns, London W6

MONSON, Hon Anthony John; s of 10 Baron Monson (d 1958); *b* 1944; *Educ* Malvern; *Style*— The Hon Anthony Monson; 35 Lynwood Grove, Orpington, Kent

MONSON, Maj Hon Jeremy David Alfonso John; 2 s of 10 Baron Monson (d 1958); *b* 29 Sept 1934; *Educ* Eton, RMA Sandhurst; *m* 4 Dec 1958, Patricia Mary, yst da of late Maj George Barker, MFH; 1 s, 1 da; *Career* 2 Lt Grenadier Gds 1954, served in Cyprus Emergency 1956-57, Capt 1959, Maj 1964, mil asst to Def Services Sec 1964-66, ret 1967; memb: CC Berks 1981-; Thames Valley Police Authy 1982-; SBStJ 1971; *Clubs* Cavalry and Guards', White's; *Style*— Major the Hon Jeremy Monson; Keepers Cottage, Scarletts Wood, Hare Hatch, Nr Reading, Berks RG10 9TL

MONSON, 11 Baron (GB 1728); Sir John Monson; 15 Bt (E 1611); s of 10 Baron Monson (d 1958), and Bettie Northrup, da of late Lt-Col E Alexander Powell of Connecticut, USA, (who m 2, 1962, Capt James Arnold Phillips d 1983); *b* 3 May 1932; *Educ* Eton, Trinity Coll Cambridge; *m* 1955, Emma, da of Anthony Devas (d 1958), and Mrs Rupert Shephard; 3 s; *Heir* s, Hon Nicholas John Monson; *Career* sits as Independent in House of Lords; pres Soc for Individual Freedom; *Style*— The Rt Hon the Lord Monson; The Manor House, South Carlton, nr Lincoln (☎ Lincoln 730263)

MONSON, Sir (William Bonnar) Leslie; KCMG (1965, CMG 1950), CB (1964); s of John William Monson, MBE (d 1929), and Selina Leslie Stewart (d 1958); *b* 28 May 1912; *Educ* Edinburgh Academy, Hertford Coll Oxford (BA); *m* 1948, Helen Isobel, da of Francis Roland Browne (d 1950); *Career* Dominions Office 1935-39, Colonial Office 1939-47, chief sec W African Cncl 147-51, asst under-sec state Colonial Office 1952-64, high cmmr Zambia 1964-66, dep under-sec state Commonwealth Office 1967-68, dep under-sec FCO 1968-72, ret; dir Overseas Relations St John Ambulance HQ 1975-81; KStJ 1975; *Clubs* United Oxford & Cambridge University; *Style*— Sir Leslie Monson, KCMG, CB; Golf House, Goffers Rd, Blackheath, London SE3 0UA (☎ 01 852 7257)

MONSON, Hon Nicholas John; s & h of 11 Baron Monson; *b* 19 Oct 1955; *Educ* Eton; *m* 1981, Hilary, only da of Kenneth Martin, of Nairobi; 1 s (Alexandra), 1 da (Isabella); *Career* PR and journalist; founder and ed The Magazine 1982-84; dir: Strategic Solutions (PR) 1985-87, Grenfell Communications Ltd (PR); md The Organiser Co (publishing); *Books* The Nouveaux Pauvres (1984); *Recreations* backgammon, chess, tennis; *Clubs* Buck's, The Lincolnshire, Annabel's; *Style*— The Hon Nicholas Monson; 24 Fentiman Rd, London SW8 1LS

MONSON, Hon Stephen Alexander John; s of 11th Baron Monson; *b* 5 Jan 1961; *Career* 20th Century Br Fine Art conslt (USA); USA rep for membs of Royal Soc of Portrait Painters; *Style*— The Hon Stephen Monson; 9 Bray House, Duke of York St, St James's, London SW1Y 6JX (☎ 01 930 5641, 0101 212 832 3630)

MONT, Joan Mary; da of Joseph Francis Stephen Grant (d 1931), of Leeds, and Kathleen, *née* Williamson; *b* 20 Mar 1930; *Educ* Brighton & Hove HS for Girls, RADA (Dip); *m* 6 Sept 1952, Neville, s of Flt Lt Cyril Mont, of 78 The Drive, Hove, E Sussex; 3 da (Sarah b 1957, Vanessa b 1963, Fiona b 1970); *Career* memb E Sussex CC: Moulsecoomb (Brighton) div 1975-81, chm educn fin and gen purposes sub-ctee 1977-79, chm sch sub-ctee 1979-81, chm educn ctee 1981-85, Rottingdean (Brighton) div 1981-, ldr of cc and chm of policy and resources ctee 1985; memb: ct and cncl Univ of Sussex 1981, cncl Brighton Poly 1981 (chm fin and gen purposes ctee 1981-85), exec cncl and educn ctee ACCs 1985, cncl Local Educn Authys 1988; govr: Brighton and Hove HS for Girls (GPDST) 1979, Hastings Coll of Art & Technol 1981, Eastbourne Coll of Art & Technol 1981; *Recreations* painting, dressmaking, and reading; *Style*— Mrs Joan Mont; Pelham House, St Andrew's Lane, Lewes, E Sussex (☎ 0273 481401)

MONTAGU, Hon Anthony Trevor Samuel; s of 3 Baron Swaythling, OBE; *b* 1931; *Educ* Eton; *m* 1962, Deirdre, da of Ronald Henry Senior, DSO, TD; 2 s, 1 da; *Career* chm and chief exec Abingworth plc; *Style*— The Hon Anthony Montagu; 78 Chelsea Park Gdns, London SW3 (☎ 01 352 1834)

MONTAGU, Hon David Charles Samuel; s and h of 3 Baron Swaythling, OBE; *b* 6 August 1928; *Educ* Eton, Trinity Coll Cambridge; *m* 1951, Christiane Françoise (Ninette), da of Edgar Dreyfus (d 1976); 1 s (Charles Edgar Samuel b 1954), 1 da (Nicole Mary b 1956) and 1 da decd; *Career* chm Samuel Montagu & Co Ltd 1970-73, chm and chief exec Orion Bank Ltd 1974-79; chm: Ailsa Investmt Tst plc 1981-87, exec chm Rothmans Int plc 1988-; dir: Daily Telegraph plc, Horeserace Totalisator Bd, J Rothschild Hldgs plc; *Recreations* shooting, racing, theatre; *Clubs* White's, Pratt's, Portland, Knickerbocker (New York), Union (Sydney); *Style*— The Hon David Montagu; 14 Craven Hill Mews, Devonshire Terrace, London W2 3DY (☎ 01 724 7860); Rothmans Int plc, 15 Hill St, London W1X 7FB (☎ 01 491 4366, telex 24764)

MONTAGU, John Edward Hollister; does not use courtesy title of Viscount Hinchingbrooke; s and h of Alexander Victor Edward Paulet Montagu (10 Earl of Sandwich, who disclaimed peerages for life 1964), and Rosemary Maud Peto; *b* 11 April 1943; *Educ* Eton, Trinity Coll Cambridge (MA); *m* 1 July 1968, (Susan) Caroline, o da of Canon Perceval Ecroyd Cobham Hayman; 2 s, 1 da; *Career* freelance journalist and conslt; info offr Christian Aid 1974-86, ed Save the Children Fund 1987-89; *Style*— John Montagu, Esq; 69 Albert Bridge Rd, London SW11 4QE (☎ 01 223 0997)

MONTAGU, Hon (George Charles) Robert; s of Victor Edward Paulet Montagu (disclaimed Earldom of Sandwich for life 1964); *b* 1949; *Educ* Eton; *m* 1970, Donna Marzia Brigante Colonna, da of Conte Brigante Colonna; 2 s, 2 da; *Style*— The Hon Robert Montagu; The Old Farmhouse, 44 Long Street, Cerne Abbas, Dorset (☎ 03003 281)

MONTAGU, (Alexander) Victor Edward Paulet; s of 10 Earl of Sandwich; suc f on his death in 1962 and disclaimed peerages for life 1964; 4 Earl sponsored Captain Cook's voyages and gave his name to the Sandwich Islands, as well as to the sandwich; *b* 22 May 1906; *Educ* Eton, Trinity Coll Cambridge; *m* 1, 27 July 1934 (m dis 1958), Rosemary Maud, o da of late Maj Ralph Harding Peto (gs of Sir Morton Peto, 1 Bt); 2 s, 4 da; m 2, 7 June 1962 (m annulled 1965), Lady Anne Cavendish, MBE (d 1981), da of 9 Duke of Devonshire, KG, PC (d 1938), and widow of Christopher Holland-Martin, MP; *Heir* to disclaimed peerages, s, John Edward Hollister Montagu; *Career* joined Northamptonshire Regt (TA) 1926, served in France 1940 and afterwards on gen staff Home Forces, private sec to Rt Hon Stanley Baldwin MP 1932-34; tres Junior Imperial League 1934-35, MP (C, but resigned party whip 1956 in protest at withdrawal from Suez and sat as an Ind C in 1957 only) S Dorset 1941-62; chm Tory Reform Ctee 1943-44; vice-chm Cons Foreign Affairs Ctee 1957-58; pres Anti-Common Market League 1962-64; chm Cons Trident Gp 1973-75; contested Lancs (Accrington Div) at gen election 1964; *Style*— Victor Montagu, Esq; Mapperton, Beaminster, Dorset DT8 3NR (☎ 0308 862441)

MONTAGU DOUGLAS SCOTT *see also*: Scott

MONTAGU DOUGLAS SCOTT, Lady Charlotte-Anne; da of 9 and 11 Duke of Buccleuch and Queensberry, KT, VRD, JP; *b* 9 Jan 1966; *Style*— Lady Charlotte-Anne Montagu Douglas Scott

MONTAGU DOUGLAS SCOTT, Lord Damian Torquil Francis Charles; 3 and yst s of 9 and 11 Duke of Buccleuch and Queensberry, KT, VRD, JP; *b* 1969; *Career* page of honour to HM The Queen; *Style*— Lord Damian Montagu Douglas Scott

MONTAGU DOUGLAS SCOTT, Lord George Francis John; s of 7 and 9 Duke of Buccleuch and Queensberry, KT, GCVO (d 1935), and Lady Margaret Bridgeman (da of 4 Earl of Bradford by his w, Lady Ida Lumley, da of 9 Earl of Scarbrough); *b* 8 July 1911; *Educ* Eton, Christ Church Oxford; *m* 1938, Molly (Mary Wina Mannin), da of Lt-Col Harry Bishop, of Harewood, Andover; 1 s, 2 da; *Career* farmer, co dir; Bt-Col TA Reserve ; memb Royal Co of Archers (Queen's Bodyguard for Scotland); *Recreations* racing, gardening; *Clubs* Cavalry; *Style*— Lord George Montagu Douglas Scott; 60 Glebe Place, SW3; The Old Almshouse, Weekley, Kettering, Northants

MONTAGU DOUGLAS SCOTT, Lord (William Henry) John; 2 s of 9 and 11 Duke of Buccleuch and Queensberry, KT, VRD, JP; *b* 6 August 1957; *Career* page of honour to HM Queen Elizabeth The Queen Mother; *Style*— Lord John Montagu Douglas Scott

MONTAGU DOUGLAS SCOTT, Lady William; Lady Rachel; *née* Douglas-Home; da of 13 Earl of Home, KT, TD (d 1951), and Lady Lilian Lambton (da of 4 Earl of Durham); is sis of Baron Home of the Hirsel, KT, PC; *b* 10 April 1910; *m* 1937, Lord William Walter Montagu Douglas Scott, MC, MP Roxburgh and Selkirk 1935-50 (d 1958), 2 s of 7 and 9 Duke of Buccleuch and Queensberry, KT, GCVO; 1 s, 4 da; *Style*— Lady William Montagu Douglas Scott; Beechwood, Melrose, Roxburghshire

MONTAGU DOUGLAS SCOTT, Lady; Valerie Margaret Steriker; *née* Finnis; da of late Cdr Steriker Finnis, RN; *b* 31 Oct 1924; *Educ* Downe House, Waterperry Hort Coll Oxford; *m* 1970, as his 2 w, Sir David John (Montagu Douglas) Scott, KCMG, OBE (d 1986); *Career* horticulture, photography; Victoria Medal of Honour (Hort) as Valerie Finnis; *Recreations* looking at pictures; *Style*— Lady Montagu Douglas Scott; The Dower House, Boughton House, Kettering, Northants NN14 1BJ (☎ 0536 82279)

MONTAGU DOUGLAS SCOTT, Lady Victoria Doris Rachel; *née* Haig; da of Field Marshal 1 Earl Haig (d 1928); *b* 1908; *m* 1929 (m dis 1951), Brig Andrew Montagu Douglas Scott, DSO, Irish Gds (d 1971); 1 s, 1 da; *Style*— Lady Victoria Scott; The Pavilion, Park Rd, Isleworth, Middx TW7 6BD

MONTAGU OF BEAULIEU, 3 Baron (UK 1885); Edward John Barrington Douglas-Scott-Montagu; s of 2 Baron, KCIE, CSI, VD, JP, DL, sometime MP New Forest (d 1929, gs of 5 Duke of Buccleuch and Queensberry, KG, KT), by his 2 w, Alice Pearl, *née* Crake (*see* Hon Mrs Edward Pleydell-Bouverie); *b* 20 Oct 1926; *Educ* Ridley Coll Ontario, Eton, New Coll Oxford; *m* 1, 1959 (m dis 1974), (Elizabeth) Belinda, o da of Capt Hon John de Bathe Crossley, JP (d 1935, yr bro of 2 Baron Somerleyton); 1 s, 1 da (Hon Mary Rachel b 1964); m 2, 1974, Fiona Margaret, da of R L D Herbert; 1 s (Hon Jonathan Deane b 1975); *Heir* s, Hon Ralph Douglas-Scott-Montagu b 13 March 1961; *Career* sits as Cons peer in House of Lords; proprietor of Beaulieu Abbey (originally a Cistercian fndn of 1204); served with Grenadier Gds 1945-48; fndr Montagu Motor Car Museum 1952 and Motor Cycle Museum 1956, opened Nat Motor Museum at Beaulieu 1972; fndr and ed Veteran and Vintage Magazine 1956-79; pres: Historic Houses Assoc 1973-78, Union of European Historic Houses 1978-81, Fédération Internationale des Voitures Anciennes 1980-83, Museums Assoc 1982-84, memb Devpt Cmmn 1980-84, Southern Tourist Bd, Assoc of Br Tport Museums; vice-pres Tport Tst; chm Historic Bldgs and Monuments Cmmn 1983-; pres English Vineyards Assoc; chllr Wine Guild of the UK; author and lectr; *Publications include* The Motoring Montagus (1959), Jaguar (1961), The Gordon Bennett Races (1963), Lost Causes of Motoring: Europe (Vol I and II, 1969 and 1971), Early Days on the Road (1976), Royalty on the Road (1980), Home James (1982), The British Motorist (1987), English Heritage (1987); *Recreations* shooting, water sports, sailing (yacht 'Cygnet of Beaulieu'); *Clubs* Bucks, RAC, House of Lords Yacht (Vice-Cdre), Beaulieu River Sailing (Cdre), Nelson Boat Owners' (Cdre), Veteran Car, and many international historic car clubs; *Style*— The Rt Hon the Lord Montagu of Beaulieu; Palace House, Beaulieu, Brockenhurst, Hants (☎ 0590 612345); Flat 11, Wyndham House, 24 Bryanston Sq, London W1 (☎ 01 262 2603)

MONTAGU-POLLOCK, Sir Giles Hampden; 5 Bt (UK 1872), of the Khyber Pass; s of Sir George Seymour Montagu-Pollock, 4 Bt (d 1985), and Karen-Sofie, da of Hans Ludvig Dedekam, of Oslo, Norway; *b* 19 Oct 1928; *Educ* Eton, de Havilland Technical Sch; *m* 1963, Caroline Veronica, da of Richard F Russell, of London; 1 s, 1 da (Sophie b 1969); *Heir* s, Guy b 1966; *Career* with Airspeed Ltd 1949-51, G P Eliot at Lloyd's 1951-52, de Havilland Engine Co Ltd 1952-56; advertising mangr: Bristol Aeroplane Co Ltd 1956-59, Bristol Siddeley Engines Ltd 1959-61; assoc dir J Walter Thompson Co Ltd 1961-69; dir: C Vernon & Sons Ltd 1969-71, Acumen Marketing Gp 1971-74, 119 Pall Mall Ltd 1972-78; mgmnt conslt in marketing 1974-, assoc of John Stork & Ptnrs Ltd 1980-88, Korn/Ferry Int Ltd 1988-; MInstM; *Recreations* water-skiing, skiing, photography; *Clubs* United Services', Inst of Directors; *Style*— Sir Giles Montagu-Pollock, Bt; The White House, 7 Washington Rd, London SW13 9BG (☎ 01 748 8491)

MONTAGU-POLLOCK, Guy Maximilian; s and h of Sir Giles Hampden, 5 Bt, and Caroline Veronica, da of Richard F Russell; *b* 1966; *Educ* Eton, Hatfield Polytechnic; *Style*— Guy Montagu-Pollock, Esq; c/o The White House, 7 Washington Road, Barnes, London SW13

MONTAGU-POLLOCK, Sir William Horace; KCMG (1957, CMG 1946); 3 s of Sir Montagu Montagu-Pollock, 3 Bt, by his w Margaret, *née* Bell, sis of late Countess of Glasgow (w of 8 Earl); Sir William's 1 cous, William Bell, m Belinda, da of Geoffrey Dawson, former ed The Times; *b* 12 July 1903; *Educ* Marlborough, Trinity Cambridge; *m* 1, 1933 (m dis 1945), Frances, da of Sir John Fischer Williams, CBE, KC; 1 s (Hubert), 1 da (Fidelity); m 2, 1948, Barbara, da of late Percy Jowett, CBE, FRCA, RWS (formerly w of Thomas Gaskell, by whom she had a da Josceline, who m David Dimbleby, the TV personality); 1 s (Matthew); *Career* Foreign Service to 1962; ambass to: Damascus 1952-53, Peru 1953-58, Switzerland 1958-60, Denmark 1960-62; *Style*— Sir William Montagu-Pollock, KCMG; Playa Blanca, Yaiza, Lanzarote, Canary Islands; 181 Coleherne Court, London SW5 0DU

MONTAGU-SMITH, Gp Capt Arthur; DL (Morayshire 1970); *b* 17 July 1915; *Educ* Whitgift Sch, RAF Staff Coll (psc); *m* 1942, Elizabeth Hood, da of late Thomas Hood Wilson Alexander, JP, FRCSE, of Lhanbryde, Moray (d 1941); 1 s, 1 da; *Career* joined RAF 1935, Adj 99 Sqdn 1938-39; served WW II (NW Europe, N Africa, Med) Fl-Cdr 264 Sqdn 1940 (Battle of Britain rosette), Fl-Cdr 221 Sqdn 1941 (despatches 1942), OC 248 Sqdn 1942-43, dep dir RAF Trg USA (Washington) 1944, OC 104 Wing France 1945; Hon ADC Govr NI 1948-49, Air Advsr New Delhi 1949-50, RAF rep COS Ctee UN New York 1951-53, HM Air Attaché Budapest 1958-60, ret 1961; memb Moray TAFA 1961-68, regnl exec Small Industs Cncl and Scottish Devpt Agency 1962-80; hon county rep Moray and Nairn RAF Benevolent Fund 1964-, dir Elgin and Lossiemouth Harbour Co 1966-, memb Elgin Dist Cncl 1967-75, former pres Victoria League Moray and Nairn, former chm Moray Assoc of Youth Clubs, chm Elgin and Lossiemouth branch of Scottish Soc for Prevention of Cruelty to Animals 1971-82; *Clubs* RAF; *Style*— Gp Capt Arthur Montagu-Smith, DL; Woodpark, Elgin, Moray IV30 3LF (☎ 034 384 2220)

MONTAGU-STUART-WORTLEY-MACKENZIE, Lady Rowena; da of 4 Earl of Wharncliffe (d 1987); *b* 14 June 1961; *Style*— Lady Rowena Montagu-Stuart-Wortley-Mackenzie

MONTAGUE, Adrian Alastair; s of Charles Edward Montague (d 1985), of Godden Green, Sevenoaks, Kent, and Olive, *née* Jones (d 1956); *b* 28 Feb 1948; *Educ* Mill Hill Sch, Trinity Hall Cambridge (MA); *m* 1, May 1970 (m dis 1982), Pamela Joyce; 1 s (Edward b 1977), 2 da (Emma b 1974, Olivia b 1980); m2, 8 Nov 1986, Penelope Jane Webb; 1 s (William b 1988); *Career* Linklaters & Paines: asst slr 1973-74, asst slr Paris 1974-77, asst slr London 1977-79, ptnr 1979-; non-exec dir: Munichre Investmt Hldgs 1988-, Munichre Equity Investmt Ltd 1988-; Int Bar Assoc section on business law ctee: vice chm 1982-86, chm 1987, sub-ctee chm 1988; firm rep to Maj Projects Assoc; memb Law Soc; *Style*— Adrian Montague, Esq; Pegsdon Barns, Pegsdon, Nr Hitchin, Herts SG5 3JY; Linklaters & Paines Barrington House 59-67 Gresham St, London EC2V 7JA (☎ 01 606 7080, fax 01 606 5113, telex 881334)

MONTAGUE, Hon Keith Norman; s and h of 2 Baron Amwell; *b* 1943; *Educ* Ealing GS, Nottingham Univ (BSc), CEng, MICE, MIHE, FGS; *m* 1970, Mary, da of Frank Palfreyman, of Potters Bar, Herts; 2 s; *Style*— The Hon Keith Montague

MONTAGUE, Michael Jacob; CBE (1970); s of late David Elias Montague and Ethel Montague; *b* 10 Mar 1932; *Educ* High Wycombe Boys' GS, Magdalen Coll Sch Oxford; *Career* chm: Yale and Valor plc (domestic appliance and security manufacturers) 1965- (md 1963), English Tourist Bd 1979-84; Nat Consumer Cncl 1984-87; *Recreations* walking, rowing; *Clubs* Oriental; *Style*— Michael Montague, Esq, CBE; Yale & Valor plc, Riverside House, Corney Rd, Chiswick, London W4 2SL (☎ 01 995 4104, fax 994 9569)

MONTAGUE, Hon Sheila Elizabeth; da of 2 Baron Amwell; *b* 1949; *Style*— The Hon Sheila Montague; 34 Halliford Rd, Sunbury-on-Thames, Middlesex

MONTAGUE BROWNE, Anthony Arthur Duncan; CBE (1965, OBE 1945), DFC (1945); s of Lt Col A D Montague Browne, DSO, OBE (d 1969), of Ross-on-Wye, and Violet Evelyn, *née* Downes (d 1969); *b* 8 May 1923; *Educ* Stowe, Magdalen Coll Oxford (Scholar), and abroad; *m* 1, 1950 (m dis 1970), Noel Evelyn Arnold-Wallinger; 1 da (Jane Evelyn b 1953); m 2, 1970, Shelagh Margery Macklin, da of late Col Hugh Mulligan, CMG, of Cheshire; *Career* serv WWII as pilot RAF, entered HM Diplomatic Serv 1946, FO 1946-49, Br Embassy Paris 1949-52, pte sec to Prime Minister (Sir Winston Churchill) 1952-55, seconded as pte sec to Sir Winston Churchill 1956-65, seconded to Roy Household 1965-67, resigned as cncllr 1967; md Gerrard & National plc 1967-83, dir: Columbia Pictures Prodn (UK) Ltd 1967-72, Int Life Insurance Ltd 1967-70, dep chm (and London rep) Guaranty Tst Bank (Bahamas) Ltd 1983-86; chm: Westward Travel Ltd 1984, Land Leisure plc 1987-88; dep chm Highland Participants plc 1987-, dir Security Pacific Tst (Bahamas) Ltd 1986-, and other cos; chm of cncl and tstee Winston Churchill Memorial Tst, vice pres Univs Fedn for Animal Welfare; hon LLD Westminster Coll Fulton USA (1988); *Recreations* wildlife, reading; *Clubs* Boodles's, Pratts; *Style*— Anthony Montague Browne, CBE, DFC; Hawkridge Cottages, Bucklebury, nr Reading, Berks RG7 6EG; Highland Partiafact plc, 46/47 Pall Mall, London SW1Y 5JG (☎ 01 408 1067, fax 01 493 8633)

MONTAGUE-JOHNSTONE, Roland Richard; s of Maj Roy Henry Montague-Johnstone, MBE, of 16 Leonard Ct, London W8, and Barbara Marjorie, *née* Warre; *b* 22 Jan 1941; *Educ* Eton; *m* 24 Feb 1968, Sara Outram Boileau, da of Lt-Col John Garway Outram Whitehead, MC (d 1983), of 10 Blackfriars St, Canterbury; 2 s (Andrew, William); *Career* KRRC served NI and Berlin 1958-62; ptnr Slaughter and May 1973- (articled clerk 1962-67, asst slr 1967-73); memb: Law Soc; *Recreations* reading, walking, gardening; *Clubs* Celer Et Audax, Royal Green Jackets, English

Speaking Union; *Style—* Roland Montague-Johnstone, Esq; 17 Airedale Ave, Chiswick, London W4; Poorton Hill, Powerstock, Dorset; 35 Basinghall Street, London EC2V 5DB (☎ 01 600 1200, fax 01 726 0038, telex 883486)

MONTEAGLE OF BRANDON, 6 Baron (UK 1839); Gerald Spring Rice; s of 5 Baron (d 1946), and Emilie de Kosenko (d 1981), da of late Mrs Edward Brooks of NY; *b* 5 July 1926; *Educ* Harrow; *m* 1949, Anne, da of Col Guy James Brownlow, DSO, DL (d 1960); 1 s, 3 da; *Heir* s, Hon Charles James Spring Rice; *Career* Capt Irish Gds, ret 1955; memb: London Stock Exchange 1957-76, Lloyd's 1978-, HM Bodyguard of Hon Corps of Gentlemen-at-Arms 1978-; *Clubs* Cavalry and Guards, Pratt's, Kildare St and University (Dublin); *Style—* The Rt Hon the Lord Monteagle of Brandon; 242A Fulham Rd, London SW10 (☎ 01 351 3455)

MONTEFIORE, Rt Rev Hugh William; s of late Charles Sebag-Montefiore, OBE (whose f, Arthur, was paternal gs of Sarah, sis of Sir Moses Montefiore, 1 and last Bt, and a philanthropist); *b* 12 May 1920; *Educ* Rugby, St John's Coll Oxford (MA, hon fell 1981), Cambridge (BD); *m* 1 Jan 1945, Elisabeth Mary Macdonald, da of late Rev William Paton, DD; 3 da; *Career* ordained priest 1950; former examining chaplain of Bishops of: Newcastle, Worcester, Coventry, Blackburn; dean and fell Gonville and Caius Coll Cambridge 1953-63, canon theologian of Coventry 1959-69, vicar Great St Mary's Cambridge 1963-70, hon canon of Ely Cath 1969-70, bishop suffragan of Kingston-upon-Thames 1970-78, bishop of Birmingham 1978-87; chm C of E Gen Synod's Board of Social Responsibility 1983-87; author; chm Transport 2000 1987-; Hon DD: Aberdeen 1976, Birmingham 1984; *Recreations* walking, water colour painting; *Clubs* Royal Cwlth Soc; *Style—* The Rt Rev Hugh Montefiore; 23 Bellevue Rd, Wandsworth Common, London SW17 7EB (☎ 01 672 669)

MONTEITH, Charles Montgomery; s of James Monteith (d 1965), and Marian Monteith (d 1974); *b* 9 Feb 1921; *Educ* Royal Belfast Academical Inst, Magdalen Coll Oxford (MA, BCL); *Career* served WW II Royal Inniskilling Fusiliers, India and Burma, Maj 1940-45; barrister Gray's Inn 1949; joined Faber & Faber 1953, dir 1954, vice-chm 1974-76, chm 1977-81; sr editorial conslt 1981-; fell All Souls Coll Oxford 1948- (sub-warden 1967-69); Hon DLitt: Ulster, Kent; *Clubs* Beefsteak, Garrick; *Style—* Charles Monteith, Esq; c/o Faber & Faber Ltd, 3 Queen Sq, London WC1 (☎ 01 278 6881)

MONTEITH, Lt-Col (Robert Charles) Michael; OBE (1984), MC (1943), TD (1945), JP (1957), DL (Lanarks 1959); s of Maj Joseph Basil Monteith, CBE, JP, DL (d 1960), and Dorothy, *née* Nicholson (d 1956); *b* 25 May 1914; *Educ* Ampleforth; *m* 19 July 1950, (Mira) Elizabeth, da of John Fanshawe (d 1944); 1 s (Robert b 17 Jan 1952); *Career* joined Lanarkshire Yeo 1933, served WWII with MELF, MEF and BAOR, Lt-Col 1945; qualified as chartered accountant Edinburgh 1939; contested (Univ) Hamilton Div 1950 and 1951; CC (1940-64 and 1967) Lanarkshire, Vice-Lt 1964; chm Lanark Dist Cncl 1974; part-time memb Mental Welfare Cmmn for Scotland 1962-83; memb East Kilbride Devpt Corpn 1972-76, memb Royal Co of Archers (Queen's Body Guard for Scotland); chm Clydesdale DC 1974-84; memb British Assoc SMOM 1956; OStJ 1974; landowner (1200 acres); *Recreations* field sports, curling; *Clubs* New (Edinburgh), Puffin's (Edinburgh); *Style—* Lt-Col Michael Monteith, OBE, MC, TD, JP, DL; Cranley, Cleghorn, Lanarks (☎ 0555 870 330)

MONTGOMERIE, Lord; Hugh Archibald William Montgomerie; s and h of 18 Earl of Eglinton and Winton; *b* 24 July 1966; *Style—* Lord Montgomerie

MONTGOMERIE, Lorna Burnett (Mrs John Anderson); da of (James) Fraser Montgomerie, of South View, 7A West Lennox Drive, Helensburgh, Dunbartonshire G84 9AB, and Jane Burnett Sangster (Jean), *née* McCulloch; *b* 23 Oct 1953; *Educ* St George's Sch of Montreal Canada, North London Collegiate Sch Edgware, Churchill Coll Cambridge (BA, MA), Coll of Law Lancaster Gate; *m* 8 July 1983, John Venner Anderson, s of Prof John Anderson MD, 14 Styles Way, Park Langley, Beckenham, Kent BR3 3AJ; *Career* slr Supreme Ct 1978, asst slr Biddle & Co 1978-80, Annotator Halsbury's Statutes 1981, ed Encyclopeaedia of Forms and Precedents (4 ed) 1981-85, R & D mangr Butterworth Law Publishers Ltd 1985-; articles written for: Dance 1986-87, The New Law Jnl 1987-88; memb: Ctee of Holborn Law Soc 1983-, London Legal Educn Ctee (as representing Holborn Law Soc) 1988-, Law Soc Panel monitoring articles in Holborn Area 1987-; memb Law Soc 1978-; *Recreations* reading, DIY, house renovation, sailing; *Clubs* Lansdowne; *Style—* Ms Lorna Montgomerie; Butterworth Law Publishers Ltd, 88 Kingsway, London WC2B 6AB (☎ 01 405 6900, fax 01 405 1332)

MONTGOMERIE, Hon Roger Hugh; DFC; s of 16 Earl of Eglinton (d 1945); *b* 1923; *Educ* Eton, New Coll Oxford; *Career* served in RAF 1943-46; *Style—* The Hon Roger Montgomerie, DFC; Lanehead, Dunscore, Dumfries

MONTGOMERIE, Major William Dunn; MBE (1919), JP (1942); s of John Cuminghame Montgomerie, JP (d 1933), and Jessie Helen Viola Montgomerie (d 1930); *b* 3 Jan 1892; *Educ* West of Scotland Agric Coll; *m* 14 March 1928, Janette Laird, da of William Taylor (d 1912); 2 s (William b 1929 (decd), Kenneth b 1933); *Career* mil serv 1914-19, 8 Bn Blackwatch France 1915-16, 2 Bn Blackwatch Mesopotania 1917-19; RPC 1939-46; *Style—* Major William Montgomerie, MBE, JP; Duckray, by Ayr, Ayrshire KA6 6LY (☎ 0292 570247)

MONTGOMERY, Hon Mrs; Bridget Ann; *née* Fisher; yr da (by 1 m) of 3 Baron Fisher; *b* 24 Dec 1956; *m* 1982, Bruce Stewart Irlam Montgomery, s of Dr S R Montgomery, of Haslemere, Surrey; 1 s (Patrick Christopherson Ross b 1987), 2 da (Caroline b 1984, Katherine b 1985); *Style—* The Hon Mrs Montgomery; c/o Kilverstone Hall, Thetford, Norfolk

MONTGOMERY, Clare Patricia; da of Dr Stephen Ross Montgomery, of Telegraph Cottage, Blackdown, Haslemere, Surrey, and Ann Margaret, *née* Barlow; *b* 29 April 1958; *Educ* Millfield, UCL (LLB); *Career* barr Gray's Inn 1980; memb British Ladies Fencing Team 1984-85 ; *Recreations* fencing; *Style—* Miss Clare Montgomery; 1B Bonny St, London NW1 9PE (☎ 01 482 4083); 3 Raymond Bldgs, Gray's Inn, London WC2 1RR

MONTGOMERY, David; CMG (1984), OBE (1972); s of late David Montgomery and Mary, *née* Walker Cunningham; *b* 29 July 1927; *m* 1955, Margaret Newman; 1 s, 1 da; *Career* RN 1945-48; FO 1949-52, Bucharest 1952-53, FO 1953-55, Bonn 1955-58, Düsseldorf 1958-61, Rangoon 1961-63, Ottawa 1963-64, Regina Saskatchewan 1964-65, FCO 1966-68, Bangkok 1968-72, Zagreb 1973-76, FCO 1976-79, British dep high cmmr to Barbados 1980-84 and (non-resident) to Antigua and Barbuda, Dominica, Grenada, St Kitts and Nevis, St Lucia, St Vincent and the Grenadines; ret 1984; FCO 1987-; *Style—* David Montgomery, Esq, CMG, OBE; 8 Ross Court, Putney Hill, London SW15 3NY

MONTGOMERY, Sir (Basil Henry) David; 9 Bt (UK 1801), of Stanhope, Peeblesshire, JP (Kinross-shire 1966), DL (Kinross 1960 and Perth 1975); s of Lt Col Henry Keith Purvis-Russell-Montgomery, OBE (d 1954), and nephew of 8 Bt (d 1964); *b* 20 Mar 1931; *Educ* Eton; *m* 1956, Delia, da of Adm Sir (John) Peter Lorne Reid, GCB, CVO; 2 s (1 decd), 4 da; *Heir* s, James David Keith Montgomery; *Career* Tayside Regnl Cncl 1974-79, vice pres Convention of Scottish Local Authorities (COSLA) 1978-79, Nature Conservancy Cncl 1974-79, chm Forestry Commission 1979-; Hon LLD Dundee 1977; *Style—* Sir David Montgomery, Bt, JP, DL ; Kinross House, Kinross

MONTGOMERY, David John; s of William John Montgomery, and Margaret Jean, *née* Flaherty; *b* 6 Nov 1948; *Educ* Bangor GS, Queen's Univ Belfast (BA); *m* 12 April 1971 (m dis 1987), Susan Frances Buchanan, da of James Francis Buchanan Russell, QC; *Career* asst chief sub ed Daily Mirror 1978-80 (sub ed 1973-78), chief sub ed The Sun 1980-82; asst ed: Sunday People 1982-84, News of the World 1985-87; ed and md Today 1987- (newspaper of Year 1988); dir: News Gp Newspapers 1986, Satellite TV plc 1986, News UK 1987-; *Style—* David Montgomery, Esq; News (UK) Ltd, Allen House, 70 Vauxhall Bridge Rd, London SW1V 2RP (☎ 01 630 6951, fax 01 821 0969)

MONTGOMERY, Sir (William) Fergus; MP (C) Altrincham and Sale Oct 1974-; s of William and Winifred Montgomery of Hebburn; *b* 25 Nov 1927; *Educ* Jarrow GS, Bede Coll Durham; *m* Joyce, da of George Riddle, of Jarrow; *Career* RN 1946-48; memb Hebburn Cncl 1950-58; Young Cons Orgn: nat v-chm 1954-57, nat chm 1957-58; contested (C) Consett (Durham) 1955; MP (C): Newcastle upon Tyne E 1959-64, Brierley Hill (Staffs) 1967-Feb 1974, Dudley West Feb 1974; PPS to: Sec of State for Educn and Science 1973-74, Ldr of the Oppn 1975-1976; kt 1985; *Style—* Sir Fergus Montgomery, MP; 181 Ashley Gdns, Emery Hill St, London SW1 (☎ 01 834 7905); 6 Groby Place, Altrincham, Cheshire (☎ 061 928 1983)

MONTGOMERY, Gp Capt George Rodgers; CBE (1946), DL (Norfolk 1979); s of John Montgomery (d 1956); *b* 1910; *Educ* Royal Acad Belfast; *m* 1, 1932, Margaret McHarry (d 1981), da of late William J Heslip; 2 s (Patrick, Michael); m 2, 1982, Margaret Stephanie, *née* Reynolds, wid of Colin Vanner Hedworth Foulkes; *Career* cmmnd RAF 1928, served Middle East and UK 1928-38, served WWII Gp Capt, air attaché and air advsr Tokyo 1948-49, Cmdt RAF Sch of Admin 1950-52, cmd RAF Hednesford 1953-54, dep dir Orgn (Estab) Air Miny and chm RAF W Euro Estab Ctee Germany 1955-57, ret 1958; organizing sec Friends of Norwich Cathedral 1959-62, sec Norfolk Naturalists Tst 1963-75 (hon vice pres 1976-), memb ct and hon appeal sec Univ of E Anglia; memb: Norfolk Naturalists Tst Cncl, Gt Bustard Tst Cncl 1972; hon vice pres Broads Soc 1983-; *Recreations* river cruising, gardening, nature conservation; *Clubs* RAF, Norfolk (Norwich); *Style—* Gp Capt George Montgomery, CBE, DL; 24 Cathedral Close, Norwich, Norfolk NR1 4DZ (☎ 0603 628024)

MONTGOMERY, Hon Henry David; s of 2 Viscount Montgomery of Alamein, CBE; *b* 2 April 1954; *Educ* Wellington, Seale Hague Argicultural Coll; *m* 1980, Caroline J, da of Richard Odey, of Hothan Hall, York; *Style—* The Hon Henry Montgomery; Bridge House, Combe, near Presteigne, Powys

MONTGOMERY, James David Keith; s and h of Sir (Basil Henry) David Montgomery, 9 Bt, and Delia, *née* Reid; *b* 13 June 1957; *Educ* Eton, Univ of Exeter; *m* 24 Sept 1983, Elizabeth Lynette, eldest da of Lyndon Evans, of Tyla Morris, Pentyrch, Glamorgan; 1 s (Edward Henry James b 1986), 1 da (Iona Rosanna b 1988); *Career* Capt Black Watch 1976-85; investmt advsr N M Rothschild 1985-; *Recreations* golf, cricket, sailing, photography; *Style—* James Montgomery, Esq; 70 Hillier Rd, London SW11 (☎ 01 228 5352); Five Arrows House, St Swithins Lane, London EC4N 8NR (☎ 01 634 2934)

MONTGOMERY, Dr Stephen Ross; s of Sir Frank Percival Montgomery (d 1972), of Belfast, and Joan, *née* Christopherson; *b* 15 Jan 1931; *Educ* Trinity Coll Glenalmond, Clare Coll Cambridge (MA), MIT (SM, ScD); *m* 15 June 1955, Ann, da of Stewart Irlam Barlow (d 1942), of Northumberland; 1 s (Bruce b 1956), 3 da (Clare b 1958, Joy b 1961, Jane b 1963); *Career* chartered mechanical engr; dir External Relations UCL, previously lectr and sr lectr in mechanical engineering UCL, mangr London Centre for Marine Technology; *Recreations* converting houses; *Style—* Dr Stephen R Montgomery; Telegraph Cottage, Blackdown, Haslemere, Surrey GU27 3BS (☎ 0428 54297); University College London, Gower Street, London WC1E 7JE (☎ 01 380 7202)

MONTGOMERY CAMPBELL, Hon Mrs (Mary); *née* Adderley; da of 6 Baron Norton (d 1961), and Elizabeth, Lady Norton, *née* Birkbeck (d 1952); *b* 8 Sept 1922; *m* 1950, Hugh Montgomery Campbell (d 1980), s of the Rt Rev and Rt Hon Bishop Henry Colville Montgomery Campbell, KCVO, MC, PC, DD (d 1970, formerly Lord Bishop of London); 1 s (Philip), 2 da (Elisabeth, Veronica); *Career* served WW II Third Offr WRNS; *Style—* The Hon Mrs Montgomery Campbell; 16 Ashworth Rd, London W9 (☎ 01 286 5781)

MONTGOMERY CUNINGHAME, Lady Barbara Susanne; MBE (1964); raised to rank of Baronet's widow 1948; 2 da of Lt-Col Hugh Annesley Gray-Cheape, DSO (d 1917), of Forfar, Co Angus, and Carsina Gordon Gray-Cheape (d 1952); *b* 2 Mar 1911; *m* 1934, Lt-Col Alexander William James Henry Montgomery Cuninghame, DSO, Royal Scots Fusiliers (ka Normandy 1944), eldest s of Col Sir Thomas Andrew Alexander Montgomery Cuninghame, 10 Bt, DSO (d 1945); *Style—* Barbara, Lady Montgomery Cuninghame, MBE; Yalford Kelly, Lifton, Devon PL16 0HQ

MONTGOMERY CUNINGHAME, Sir John Christopher Foggo; 12 Bt (NS 1672), of Corsehill, Ayrshire; s of 10 Bt, DSO, JP (d 1945) and bro of 11 Bt (d 1959); *b* 24 July 1935; *Educ* Fettes, Worcester Coll Oxford; *m* 9 Sept 1964, Laura Violet, 2 da of Sir Godfrey Nicholson, 1 Bt, *qv*; 3 da; *Heir* none; *Career* Nat Serv 2 Lt Rifle Bde; dir: Inertia Dynamics Corpn Arizona, Purolite Int Ltd, R A Lee plc; *Style—* Sir John Montgomery Cuninghame, Bt; The Old Rectory, Brightwalton, Newbury, Berks RG16 0BL

MONTGOMERY OF ALAMEIN, 2 Viscount (UK 1946); David Bernard Montgomery; CBE (1975); o s of 1 Viscount Montgomery of Alamein, KG, GCB, DSO (d 1976), and Elizabeth, *née* Hobart (d 1937); *b* 18 August 1928; *Educ* Winchester, Trinity Coll Cambridge; *m* 1, 27 Feb 1953 (m dis 1967), Mary Raymond, yr da of Sir Charles Connell (d 1973); 1 s, 1 da; m 2, 30 Jan 1970, Tessa, da of Lt-Gen Sir Frederick A M Browning, GCVO, KBE, CB, DSO (d 1965), and Lady Browning, DBE (Daphne du Maurier, the writer, d 1989), and former w of Maj Peter de Zulueta; *Heir* s, Hon Henry David Montgomery; *Career* sits as Cons peer in House of Lords; dir Yardley Int 1963-74, md Terimar Services Ltd (overseas trade consultancy) 1974-; memb editorial advsy bd Vision Interamericana 1974-; cllr Royal Borough of Kensington and Chelsea 1974-78; chm: Hispanic and Luso Brasilian Cncl Canning House 1978-1980 (pres 1987-), Antofagasta (Chile) and Bolivia Railway Co and subsids 1980-1982, Brazilian C of C GB 1980-1982; non-exec dir: Korn/Ferry Int 1977-, Northern Engrg Industs 1980-87; patron D-Day and Normandy Fellowship 1980-, Eight Army Veterans Assoc 1984-; pres: Restaurateurs Assoc of GB 1982-, Centre for International Briefing Farnham Castle 1983-, Anglo-Argentine Soc 1976-87, Redgrave Theatre Farnham 1978-; *Recreations* sailing; *Clubs* Garrick, Royal Fowey Yacht, Canning; *Style*— The Rt Hon Viscount Montgomery of Alamein, CBE; Isington Mill, Alton, Hampshire GU34 4PW (☎ 0420 23126, telex 858623 TELBUR)

MONTLAKE, Henry Joseph; s of Alfred and Hetty Montlake; *b* 22 August 1930; *Educ* Ludlow GS, London Univ (LLB); *m* 14 Sept 1952, Ruth, *née* Rochelle; 4 s (Jonathan b 18 Oct 1956, Andrew b 2 July 1958, Nicholas b 30 Dec 1959, Charles b 13 Jan 1962); *Career* cmmnd RASC 1954; slr 1952, cmmr for Oaths 1955; sr ptnr H Montlake & Co 1954-, dep registrar of Co Cts 1970-78, dep circuit judge and asst recorder 1978-83, recorder of the Crown Ct 1983-; pres: West Essex Law Soc 1977-78, Assoc of Jewish Golf Clubs and Socs 1983- (sec 1977-83); Capt Abridge GC 1965 (chm 1964); chm Ilford Round Table 1962-63; memb law Soc; *Recreations* golf, The Times crossword, people, travel; *Clubs* Wig and Pen, Dyrham Park GC, Abridge Golf and Country; *Style*— Henry Montlake, Esq; Chelston, 5 St Mary's Avenue, Wanstead, London E11 2NR (☎ 01 989 7228); 197 High Rd, Ilford, Essex IG1 1LX (☎ 01 553 1311, telex 262774, fax 01 553 3066)

MONTMORENCY; *see*: de Montmorency

MONTROSE, 7 Duke of (S 1707); Sir James Angus Graham; also Lord Graham (S 1445), Earl of Montrose (S 1505), Marquess of Montrose (S 1644, new charter granted 1706), Marquess of Graham and Buchanan, Earl of Kincardine, Viscount Dundaff, Lord Aberuthven, Mugdock and Fintrie (all S 1707), Earl Graham and Baron Graham (GB 1722); also Hereditary Sheriff of Dunbartonshire; s of 6 Duke, KT, CB, CVO, VD (d 1954), by his w Lady Mary Douglas-Hamilton (da of 12 Duke of Hamilton); collaterally descended from the Hon Sir William Graham, cr 1625 Bt of Braco, Co Perth (a Nova Scotia Btcy); *b* 2 May 1907; *Educ* Eton, Christ Church Oxford; *m* 1, 20 Oct 1930 (m dis 1950), Isobel Veronica, da of Lt-Col Thomas Byrne Sellar, CMG, DSO (d 1924); 1 s, 1 da; m 2, 17 April 1952, Susan Mary Jocelyn, widow of Michael Raleigh Gibbs, and da of Dr John Mervyn Semple; 2 s, 2 da; *Heir* s, Marquess of Graham, *qv*; *Career* Lt RNVR 1930, ret, rejoined 1939, Lt-Cdr RNVR; memb Federal Parliament of Rhodesia and Nyasaland 1958; min of agric Lands and natural resources S Rhodesia 1962-64, min of agric Rhodesia 1964-65, Rhodesia min of Defence and External Affairs 1965-68; *Style*— His Grace the Duke of Montrose; Dalgoram, PO Baynesfield, Natal, S Africa 3770 (☎ Thornville Junction 630); Auchmar, Drymen, Glasgow

MONTROSE, Kenneth; s of Harry Montrose (d 1955), of London, and Sophie, *née* Davis (d 1976); *b* 13 Jan 1928; *Educ* Glendale Coll Southend-on-Sea, Wesfield Modern Sch Hinckley Leics; *m* 12 March 1949, Mary (d 1984), da of William Joseph Moreton (d 1968), of Hinckley, Leics; 1 s (Michael b 27 Sept 1949), 1 da (Gillian Mary (Mrs Townsend) b 29 Nov 1953); *Career* enlisted RN 1945, serv air mechanic 1 class far East, demobbed 1947, seaman (sr position) Merchant Marines 1947-48; tech author Leyland Motors Gp 1950-54 (publicity mangr 1954-63), started own building and investment co 1963, chm Broadgate Printing gp 1963-; *Books* contributions to various tech manuals; *Recreations* pubs, walking, swimming; *Clubs* Wellington, Wig & Pen, Chestnuts, Tudor; *Style*— Kenneth Montrose, Esq; Broadgate Printing Group, Crondal Rd, Exmall, Coventry (☎ 0203 341713)

MONTWILL, Andrew Theodore; s of Theodore Montwill (d 1940), and Julia, *née* Wilkowska (d 1943); *b* 9 Nov 1921; *Educ* St Andrews Univ (MA); *m* 1948, Olive Mary Donaldson, da of William Donaldson Buchanan (d 1954), of Newport, Fife; 1 da (Helen); *Career* dir: Simons & Co Ltd, Harry M Beames & Co Ltd, UFS (Western) Ltd, United Fruit Shippers Ltd, William Hardy Caterers Ltd, William Hardy & Co (Newcastle) Ltd, William Hardy & Sons (Middlesbrough) Ltd (ret 1985); *Recreations* golf, bridge, dining out; *Clubs* Chestfield GC, Herne Bay & Whitstable Lions; *Style*— Andrew Montwill, Esq; Colliecraig, 16 Grasmere Road, Chestfield, nr Whitstable, Kent (☎ Chestfield 3271)

MONYPENNY, Edwin Richard; s of John Henry Gill Monypenny, FInstP, FIM (d 1949), of Sheffield, and Florence Annie, *née* Shepard (d 1977); *b* 25 Mar 1917; *Educ* King Edward VII Sch Sheffield, Sheffield Univ (MB, ChB); *m* 5 Nov 1945, Isabelle Guthrie (LRCP, MRCS, FFARCS), da of John Russell Little (d 1928), of Edinburgh; 1 s (Ian James b 1950), 1 da (Ann Elizabeth b 1947); *Career* Capt RAMC India 1947-48; conslt i/c Dept of Radiotherapy and Oncology N Staffordshire Royal Infirmary 1965-82, jr anatomy lectr Sheffield Univ 1947-48, Surgical Registrar appointments in Sheffield and London 1948-58, Radiotherapy and Oncology Registrar appointments in Sheffield, Belfast and the Royal Marsden Hosp London 1958-65, memb Faculty Bd for Radiotherapy and Oncology 1976-82, Royal Coll of Radiologists, vice-pres Royal Soc of Medicine 1980-82, pres Section of Oncology 1980-81, pres Section of Radiology 1981-82; conslt in medical educn cancer Relief Macmillan Educn Unit 1985-, memb Patient Care Ctee Nat Soc for Cancer Relief 1978-84, chm Cncl of Mgmnt 1982-87; now hon appeal dir St Giles Hospice Whittington Lichfield; FRCS, FFR, FRCR; *Recreations* gardening, house improvements, walking; *Clubs* Royal Society of Medicine; *Style*— Edwin R Monypenny, Esq; Wilkins Pleck, Whitmore, Newcastle-under-Lyme, Staffordshire ST5 5HN (☎ 0782 680351); Consluting Rooms, 11 King St, Newcastle-under-Lyme, Staffordshire ST5 3EH (☎ 0782 614174)

MOODIE, David Garrioch; s of late Peter Alexander Moodie; *b* 19 May 1926; *m* 1952, Mary Smith Hunter, *née* Williamson; 1 s, 1 da; *Career* CA, md Black & Edgington plc 1973-84, chm and md Andrew Mitchell Gp plc 1984-; MICAB; *Recreations* golf, skiing, sailing; *Clubs* Caledonian; *Style*— David Moodie, Esq; Barnbeth, Bridge of Weir, Renfrewshire (☎ 0505 612201); Andrew Mitchell Gp plc, 6 Gareloch Rd, Port Glasgow, Renfrewshire PA14 5XW (☎ 0475 44117)

MOODY, (William) Anthony; s of John Andrews Moody, of Malvern, and Olive Irene, *née* Elliott (d 1988); *b* 14 August 1926; *Educ* King's Sch Worcester; *m* 29 Jan 1951, Marjorie June, da of Thomas John Hayward (d 1980); 1 s (Michael b 1955), 1 da (Pamela (Mrs Curtis) b 1953); *Career* dir: Gascoigne Moody Assocs Ltd 1984-, GMA PR 1984-, GMA Exhibition Servs 1984-; MIPR; *Recreations* walking, gardening, caravanning; *Clubs* Birmingham Press; *Style*— Anthony Moody, Esq; 40 Rowley Bank, Stafford, Staffs ST17 9BA (☎ 0785 420 04); Gascoigne Moody Assocs Ltd, 100 Hagley Rd, Edgbaston, Birmingham B16 8LT (☎ 021 454 4044, fax 021 454 4939)

MOODY, Rev Aubrey Rowland; s of Capt Rowland Harry Mainwaring (ka 1914), and Sybil Marie Conway Bishop (d 1944); *b* 31 July 1911; *Educ* Eton, RMC Sandhurst; *Career* Coldstream Gds 1931-33, and 1941-46, N Africa and 3 Commando Sicily and Italy, hon attaché HM Embassy Athens 1938-40, personal SO to HM King George of Greece 1942-43; social work in Stepney 1946-47, co cncllr Essex 1949-52, first chm Bd of Visitors Hill Hall Prison Epping 1952; ordained 1955, asst curate Wanstead Parish Church 1955-57, vicar of Feering 1957; *Style*— Rev Aubrey Moody; Feering Vicarage, Colchester, Essex CO5 9NL (☎ 0376 70226)

MOODY, Philip Edward; s of Frederick Osborne Moody, and Hilda Laura, *née* Frost; *b* 28 July 1954; *Educ* Bentley GS Calne Wilts; *Career* CA; articled clerk Monahan & Co Chippenham 1972-82, fndr ptnr Solomon Hare Chippenham 1983-88, lead ptnr Solomon Hare Bristol 1989-; ACA 1980, ATII 1982; *Recreations* walking, photography, snooker, cricket; *Style*— Philip Moody, Esq; 118 Oxford Rd, Calne, Wilts SN11 8AH (☎ 0249 813 428); Solomon Hare, Oakfield Ho, Oakfield Grove, Clifton, Bristol BS8 2BN (☎ 0272 238 555/0272 237 000, fax 0272 238 666, car tel 0836 209 385)

MOODY STUART, Lady; Judith; da of late Leonard Isaac Henzell, OBE; *m* 1925, Sir Alexander Moody Stuart, OBE, MC (d 1971); *Style*— Lady Moody Stuart; c/o Mrs Groom, 16 Christopher Way, Emsworth, Hants PO10 7QZ (☎ 024 34 4246)

MOOLAN-FEROZE, Sir Rustam; s of Dr Jehangir Moolan-Feroze (d 1962), and Diana Lester; *b* 4 August 1920; *Educ* Sutton Valence, London Univ (MB, BS, MD); *m* 1947, Margaret, da of Harry Dowsett (d 1975); 3 s, 1 da; *Career* Surgn-Lt RNVR 1943-46, Atlantic and Far East; conslt obstetrician and gynaecologist Kings Coll Hosp London 1952-85; conslt obstetrician Queen Charlotte's Hosp London 1952-73; conslt gynaecologist Chelsea Hosp for Women 1952-73; first pres Euro Assocn of Gynaecologists and Obstetricians 1985-88; dean Inst of Obstetrics and Gynaecology London Univ 1954-67; pres Royal Coll of Obstetricians and Gynaecologists 1981-84; presently hon pres Euro Assoc of Gynacologists and Obstetritians; contributor to medical books 1981-84; kt 1983; FRCS; FRCOG; *Recreations* swimming, gardening; *Clubs* RAC; *Style*— Sir Rustam Feroze, MD; 21 Kenwood Drive, Beckenham, Kent BR3 2QX (☎ 01 650 2972); 127 Harley St, London W1N 1DJ (☎ 01 935 8157)

MOOLLAN, Sir Cassam Ismael; QC (Mauritius 1969); s of Ismael Mahomed Moollan (d 1972), and Fatimah, *née* Nazroo (d 1962); *b* 26 Feb 1927; *Educ* Royal Coll Port Louis, LSE, London Univ (LLB); *m* 1954, Rassool Bibie Adam, da of Adam Sulliman Moollan (d 1964); 1 s (Oomar), 2 da (Aisha, Naseem); *Career* barr Lincoln's Inn; private practice Mauritius 1951-55, dist magistrate 1955-58, crown counsel 1958-64, sr crown counsel 1964-69, solicitor-gen 1966-70, puisne judge Supreme Court Mauritius 1970-78, sr puisne judge 1978, chief justice Mauritius 1982-88; actg govr-gen on several occasions between 1984-88; Chevalier de la Legion d'Honneur France 1986; kt 1982; *Recreations* tennis, bridge, Indian classical and semi-classical music; *Clubs* Port Louis Gymkhana; *Style*— Sir Cassam Moollan, QC; 22 Hitchcock Ave, Quatre Bornes, Mauritius (☎ 546949); 43 Sir William Newton St, Port Louis, Mauritius (☎ 20794; 083881)

MOON; *see*: Graham Moon

MOON, Gertrude, Lady; Mary Gertrude; da of late Herbert E Waggoner, of Bowen, Illinois, USA; *m* 1954, as his 2 w, Sir Richard Moon, 3 Bt (d 1961); *Style*— Gertrude, Lady Moon

MOON, Sir Peter James Scott; KCVO (1979, CMG 1979); *b* 1 April 1928; *m* 1955, Lucile Worms; 3 da; *Career* high commissioner Singapore 1982-84, Tanzania 1978-82, ambass Madagascar 1978- (non-resident), counsellor Cairo 1975-78, also seconded to NATO Brussels, served in New York, Colombo, Cape Town Pretoria (with CRO), formerly with Home Office; *Style*— HE Sir Peter Moon, KCVO, CMG; British Embassy, PO Box Safat 2, Kuwait; c/o Foreign and Commonwealth Office, London SW1

MOON, Sir Roger; 6 Bt (UK 1887), of Copsewood Grange, Warwickshire; s of Jasper Moon (d 1975, gs of 1 Bt); s bro, Sir Edward Moon, 5 Bt 1989; *b* 17 Nov 1914; *Educ* Sedbergh; *m* 16 Dec 1950, Meg, da of late Col Arthur Mainwaring Maxwell, DSO, MC; 3 da (Sarah Corinna b 1951, Gillian Adele (Mrs Johnston) b 1954, Patricia Isolda (Mrs Hogg) b 1955); *Heir* bro, Humphrey Moon b 1920; *Recreations* golf, shooting; *Style*— Sir Roger Moon, Bt; Mill House, Ruyton-xi-Towns, Shropshire (☎ 0939 260354)

MOONEY, Denis; s of Denis Mooney (d 1966), of Greenock, and Catherine McIlroy; *b* 27 August 1951; *Educ* St Columbas Sch Greenock, Moray House Edinburgh (DYCS); *m* Sheila, da of Jack Casey (d 1967), of Manchester; 1 s (Jack b 1987), 1 da (Fiona b 1984); *Career* Intermediate Treatment Offr Lothian Regnl Cncl 1975-80, Intermediate Treatment Unit mangr Sefton Borough Cncl 1980-83, res Granada TV 1983-86, sr prodr Scottish TV 1986-, present: memb ACTT; *Recreations* golf, watching football; *Clubs* Heraghtys; *Style*— Denis Mooney, Esq; 12a Leslie Rd, Glasgow G41 4PY (☎ 041 423 7862); Scottish Television, Glasgow (☎ 041 332 9999, fax 041 332 9999 ext 4618)

MOORE, Alan Edward; CBE (1980); s of Charles Edward Moore (d 1985), of Hemel Hempstead, Herts, and Ethel *née* Middleton; *b* 5 June 1936; *Educ* Berkhamstead Sch; *m* 2 Sept 1961, Margaret Patricia *née* Beckley; 1 s (Andrew b 9 June 1968), 1 da (Kathryn Moore b 9 May 1963); *Career* RAF; with Glyn Mills 7 Co 1953, dep dir Williams & Glyns Bank 1971-, dir gen Bahrain Monetary Agency Bahrain 1974-79, tres Lloyds Bank Int 1981- (dir M East and Africa Div 1980-), dir of treasy Lloyds Bank 1985-, dir of Corporate Banking and Treasy Lloyds Bank plc 1988- AIB 1958, ACIS 1963, FACT 1985; *Recreations* photography, industrial architecture, model railways, steam trains; *Style*— Alan Moore, Esq, CBE; Lloyds Bank Plc, 71 Lombard Street, London, EC3P 3BS (☎ 01 626 1500, fax 01 626 6041, telex 888301)

MOORE, Anthony (Tony); s of Percy George Moore, of Leicester and Doris Irene, *née* Mackey; *b* 29 June 1944; *Educ* Mitcham Co GS, St Edmund Hall Oxford (MA); *m* 22 July 1967, Kathryn Muriel (Kate), da of Edward Henry Garfoot, of Leicester; *Career* media mangr Frank Gayton Advertising Ltd 1966-74, dir Meares Langley Moore Ltd 1974-; Bishop Street Methodist Church; MIPA 1971; *Recreations* walking, reading, theatre, squash; *Style*— Tony Moore, Esq; 46 Holmfield Rd, Leicester LE2 ISA (☎ 0533 706 707); Bosworth House, Southgates, Leicester LE1 5RR (☎ 0533 538 611, fax 0533 515 544)

MOORE, Hon Mrs; Hon Astraea Joan Denholm; da of Baron Barnetson (d 1981), and Joan Fairley, *née* Davidson; *b* 24 Sept 1941; *Educ* St Serf's Sch Edinburgh; *m*

1963, John Robert Dawson Moore, s of John Dawson Moore (d 1985); 1 s (Andrew b 1964), 2 da (Jacqueline b 1966, Charlotte b 1972); *Recreations* tennis, swimming, yoga; *Style—* The Hon Mrs Moore; Nether Soonhope House, Peebles, Scotland EH45 8BJ (☎ 0721 20756)

MOORE, Hon Benjamin Garrett Henderson; s and h of Viscount Moore; *b* 21 Mar 1983; *Style—* The Hon Benjamin Moore

MOORE, Charles Hilary; s of Richard Gillachrist Moore, of Brussels, and Ann Hilary, *née* Miles; *b* 13 Oct 1956; *Educ* Eton, Trinity Coll Cambridge (BA); *m* 1981, Caroline Mary, da of Ralph Lambert Baxter, of Brasted Chart, Kent; *Career* editorial staff Daily Telegraph 1979, ldr writer Daily Telegraph 1981-83, asst ed and political columnist The Spectator 1983-84, ed The Spectator 1984-; *Clubs* Beefsteak; *Style—* Charles Moore, Esq; 60 Ripplevale Grove, London N1; The Spectator, 56 Doughty St, London WC1 (☎ 01 405 1706)

MOORE, Air Vice-Marshal Charles Stuart; CB (1962), OBE (1945); s of Ernest A Moore (d 1950), and Eva Beryl, *née* Druce (d 1919); *b* 27 Feb 1910; *Educ* Sutton Valence Sch, RAF Coll Cranwell; *m* 1, 1937, Anne (d 1957), da of late Alfred Rogers; m 2, 1961, Jean Mary, da of late J C Wilson; 1 da (Katrina b 1967); *Career* served 1930-39 in UK and Middle East and 1939-45 in Egypt, Sudan and UK, Gp Capt 1947, dep dir Plans Air Miny 1947-49, attended National War Coll Washington DC and appointed to Air Univ Alabama USA 1949-53, AOC No 66 (Scottish) Gp 1953-55, Air Cdre 1954, Dir of Intelligence Air Miny 1955-58, AOA NEAF 1958-62, Acting Air Vice-Marshal 1960, ret 1962; first sec (temp) Foreign Service serving in Tehran 1962-69; *Recreations* travelling, photography, music; *Clubs* Royal Air Force; *Style—* Air Vice-Marshal Charles Moore CB, OBE; Ferndene, The Avenue, Crowthorne, Berkshire (☎ 0344 772300)

MOORE, Christopher M; o s of Sir Harry Moore, CBE, *qv*; *b* 1 Dec 1944; *Educ* Winchester, Pembroke Coll Cambridge (MA 1966); *m* 2 Sept 1972, Charlotte C, da of J Glessing, of Montague, Hankham, E Sussex; 3 s (Tercel R, Wiluf M, Frederick C); *Career* banker, merchant dir Jardine Fleming and Co Ltd 1973-76, dir Robert Fleming and co Ltd 1977-, dir Robert Fleming Hldgs 1988-; FCA; *Recreations* hunting, flying, tennis, music, books; *Clubs* White's, Pratt's, Leander; *Style—* Christopher Moore, Esq; Thornborough Grounds, Bourton, Buckingham (☎ 0280 81 2170); 25 Copthall Avenue, London EC2R 7OR (☎ 01 638 5858, fax 01 638 9110, telex 297451)

MOORE, Lady; Daphne; da of late William John Benson, CBE; *m* 1921, Sir Henry Monck-Mason Moore, GCMG (d 1964); *Career* CStJ; *Style—* Lady Moore; 409 Grosvenor Sq, Rondebosch, Cape Province, S Africa

MOORE, Lt-Col Darrell John Robert; DL (Cambs 1972); s of William John Moore (d 1939); *b* 19 May 1908; *Educ* Bedford Sch, Sandhurst; *m* 1947, Hilda Irene, da of Edmund Bland Hammond, OBE, MC (d 1971); 1 s, 2 da; *Career* served WW II, cmd 1 Bn Gurkhas 1945-47; farmer; chm Anglo-American Civil Liaison Ctee Alconbury 1967-73; High Sheriff Huntingdon and Peterborough 1970-71; *Recreations* golf, gundogs; *Clubs* Army and Navy; *Style—* Lt-Col Darrell Moore, DL; 22 De Vere Close, Hemingford Grey, Huntingdon, Cambs (☎ 0480 65775)

MOORE, Debbie; 1 da (Lara b 1973); *Career* former fashion model; fndr chm md and fashion designer Pineapple Dance Studios (which joined unlisted securities market 5 Nov 1982) 1979-, 3 Pineapple centres opened in London, 1 in NY, licensing of Pineapple name on range of footwear and hosiery; Pineapple Fashion Stores at all centres sell fashion collections; Business Woman of Year 1984; *Books* Pineapple Dance Book (1983, paperback 1985), When A Woman Means Business (1989); *Style—* Ms Debbie Moore; Pineapple Group Ltd, 60 Paddington St, London W1M 3RR (☎ 01 487 3444)

MOORE, Denis Aubrey; *b* 9 Oct 1924; *Educ* Salesian Coll Farnborough Hants; *m* 14 June 1948, Ellen Craswell Smith; 1 s (Michael John b 31 July 1949), 3 da (Christine Anne b 8 Feb 1952, Susan Margaret b 25 June 1957, Frances Alexandra b 23 July 1967); *Career* Fleet Air Arm 1942-46; fndr Formica Manufacturing Co 1956-58, md Formica Ltd, md Formica Int LTd 1963 (chm 1970); De La Rue Co: joined 1946, dir 1965, memb exec ctee 1970, dir industl ops 1972, dep chief exec 1977-87; FIOD; *Recreations* golf; *Clubs* East India, MCC, St Georges Hill Weybridge; *Style—* Denis Moore, Esq; 10 Weybridge Park, Weybridge, Surrey KT13 8SQ (☎ 0932 842 585); The De La Rue Co plc, 3/5 Burlington Gdns, London W1A 1DL (☎ 01 734 8020)

MOORE, Dudley Stuart John; s of John Moore (d 1971), of Dagenham, Essex, and Ada Frances, *née* Hughes (d 1981); *b* 19 April 1935; *Educ* London Guildhall Sch (Music), Co HS Dagenham, Magdalen Coll Oxford (BA, BMus, Organ Scholar); *m* 1, 1966, Suzy Kendall; m 2, 1975, (m dis), Tuesday Weld; 1 s (Patrick b 1976); *Career* entered TV 1959; appearances include: Beyond the Fringe; also: Sunday Night at the London Palladium, Love Story, Royal Command Performance, Wayne and Shuster, Eamonn Andrews Show, Music Int, Late Night Line Up, Not Only But Also (2 series), Billy Cotton Band Show, Juke Box Jury, Now, Ready Steady Go, The Whole Scene Going, Prince of Wales Show, 5 o'clock Club, Top of the Pops, Bruce Forsyth Show, Dusty Springfield Show, Cilla Black; films include: The Wrong Box, 30 is a Dangerous Age Cynthia, Alice in Wonderland, Those Daring Young Men in Their Jaunty Jalopies, Bedazzled, The Bed Sitting Room, Hound of the Baskervilles, Foul Play, 10, Wholly Moses, Arthur, Six Weeks, Lovesick Romantic Comedy, Unfaithfully Yours, Best Defence, Micki and Maude, Santa Claus - the Movie, Like Father Like Son, Arthur 2, On the Rocks, albums: Beyond The Fringe and All That Jazz, The Other Side of Dudley Moore, Derek and Clive-Live, Derek and Clive-Ad Derek Nauseam, and Clive-Come Again, 30 Is a Dangerous Age Cynthia, Bedazzled, Dudley Moore Trio-Down Under, Dudley Moore and Cleo Laine - Smilin' Through, The Music of Dudley Moore - Double Album; *Clubs* St James's, Annabel's, Harry's Bar, Tramp; *Style—* Dudley Moore Esq; 73 Market St, Venice, California 90291 USA (☎ 213 396 5937)

MOORE, Sir Edward Stanton; 2 Bt (UK 1923), of Colchester, Essex, OBE (1970); s of Maj Edward Cecil Horatio Moore (ka 1917), and Kathleen Mary, *née* Oliver; gs of 1 Bt (d 1923); *b* 28 Dec 1910; *Educ* Mill Hill, Cambridge; *m* 6 Nov 1946, Margaret, er da of late T J Scott-Cotterell, Chipstead Valley, Surrey; *Career* served in RAF 1940-46, Wing Cdr; vice pres British Chamber of Commerce Belgium and Luxembourg 1963-64, pres British C of C Spain 1969-72, dir European British Cs of C 1970-72; md BEA Spain and Western Mediterranean, 1965-72; dir Gibraltar Airways; *Recreations* walking, gardening, ornithology; *Clubs* Chichester Yacht,; *Style—* Sir Edward Moore, Bt, OBE; Church House, Sidlesham, W Sussex PO20 7RE (☎ 024 356 369)

MOORE, Edwin Hardwick; s of Edwin Eastwood Moore (d 1951), of Mulroy House, Sutton Coldfield, and Edith Mary Moore (d 1961); *b* 6 Oct 1910; *Educ* Repton, Christ's Coll Cambridge (MA); *m* 1938, Phyllis Mary, da of Edmund Poole Underwood, of Chalfont St Giles (2 Lt Royal Fus, ka 1916); 2 da; *Career* chm and md Alfred Adams and Co West Bromwich 1937-80; memb: Warwickshire CC 1959-74 (alderman 1967-74), Severn River Authority 1965-74; High Sheriff West Midland Co 1975-76; chm Adpac Ltd Droitwich 1980-83; landowner (560 acres); *Recreations* farming, shooting, fishing; *Clubs* Birmingham; *Style—* Edwin Moore, Esq; Ashfurlong Hall, Sutton Coldfield, Warwickshire B75 6JL (☎ 021 308 0007)

MOORE, Gordon Charles; s of Dr John Edward Moore (d 1959), of Westerlea, Keswick, Cumbria, and Jessie Hamilton Moore, *née* Pears (d 1973); *b* 23 July 1928; *Educ* Uppingham, St Catharine's Coll Cambridge (MA, LLM); *m* 1956, Ursula, da of John Rawle (d 1971), of 23 Paganel Rd, Minehead, Somerset; 1 s (Andrew b 1964), 2 da (Davone b 1958, Lindsey b 1961); *Career* slr; town clerk Bradford Co Borough Cncl 1968-73, chief exec Bradford Met Dist Cncl 1973-86; Hon DLitt (Bradford); *Recreations* music, railways, walking; *Style—* Gordon C Moore, Esq; 22 Fern Hill Rd, Shipley, W Yorks BD18 4SL (☎ 0274 585606)

MOORE, Rt Rev Harry Wylie; *see*: Cyprus and The Gulf, Bishop of

MOORE, Viscount; Henry Dermot Ponsonby Moore; s and h of 11 Earl of Drogheda, KG, KBE; *b* 14 Jan 1937; *Educ* Eton, Trinity Coll Cambridge (BA); *m* 1, 15 May 1968 (m dis 1972), Eliza, da of Stacy Barcroft Lloyd, Jr, of Philadelphia; m 2, 1978, Alexandra, da of Sir Nicholas Henderson, GCMG; 2 s (Benjamin Garrett Henderson b 1983, Garrett Alexander b 1986), 1 da (Marina Alice b 1988); *Heir* s, Hon Benjamin Moore; *Career* Lt Life Gds 1957; photographer (professional name Derry Moore); *Books* The Dream Come True, Great Houses of Los Angeles (with Brendan Gill 1980), Royal Gardens (with George Plumptre 1982), Stately Homes of Britain (with Sybilla Jane Flower 1982), Washington, Houses of the Capital (with Henry Mitchell 1982), The English Room (with Michael Pick 1984), The Englishwoman's House (with Alvilde Lees-Milne 1984), The Englishman's Room (with Alvilde Lees-Milne), 1986; *Clubs* Garrick, Brooks's; *Style—* Viscount Moore; 40 Ledbury Rd, London W11

MOORE, Sir Harry - Henry Roderick (Harry); CBE (1971); er s of Roderick Edward Moore (d 1946); *b* 19 August 1915; *Educ* Malvern, Pembroke Coll Cambridge; *m* 1944, Beatrice Margaret, da of Maj J W Seigne (d 1955); 1 s, 1 da; *Career* WWII 1939-46 Lt-Col served: N Africa, Italy, N Europe; CA 1939, dir Hill Samuel Gp 1949-79; chm: Associated Engrg 1955-75, Staveley Industs 1970-79, Molins plc 1978-85; chm: Bd of Govrs The London Hosp 1960-74, N E Thames Regnl Health Authy 1974-84; High Sheriff Bucks 1966; kt 1978; *Recreations* shooting, racing; *Clubs* White's, Pratt's, Leander, Rand (Johannesburg); *Style—* Sir Harry Moore, CBE; Huntingate Farm, Thornborough, nr Buckingham, Bucks MK18 2DE (☎ 0280 812241); 70 Chesterfield House, Chesterfield Gdns, London W1Y 5TD (☎ 01 491 0666)

MOORE, Prof (William) James; s of William James Reginald Moore (d 1965), and Alice, *née* Lewis (d 1972); *b* 16 August 1932; *Educ* King Edwards GS Aston Birmingham, Univ of Birmingham (BSc, BDS, PhD, MB, ChB, DSc); *m* 4 Feb 1960, Mary Eileen, da of Edwin Mills (d 1983), of Black Notley, Essex; 1 s (Richard James b 29 Nov 1961), 1 da (Sarah Louise b 3 Oct 1964); *Career* Sqdn Ldr short serv cmmn RAF 1960; lectr in anatomy Univ of Birmingham 1966-68, prof of anatomy Univ of Leeds 1976-88 (sr lectr in anatomy 1970-76); memb: N Yorks Area Health Authy 1982-83; memb Anatomical Soc GB and Ireland 1966, fell Br Assoc of Clinical Anatomists 1980; *Books* Growth of the Facial Skeleton in the Hominoidea (with Prof C L B Lavelle 1974), The Mammalian Skull (1981), Anatomy for Dental Students (1983); *Recreations* gardening; *Clubs* RAF; *Style—* Prof James Moore; The Old Post Office, Talaton, Devon EX5 2RL (☎ 0404 822 803)

MOORE, Hon Mrs; Hon Janie St George; *née* Caulfeild; yr da of 11 Viscount Charlemont (d 1971), and Lydia Clara, *née* Kingston; *b* 9 April 1921; *m* 27 June 1942, David Dominic Moore, BSc, MIE (Aust); 2 da (Colleen, Louise); *Style—* Hon Mrs Moore; 30 Maxwell St, Turramurra, Sydney, NSW, Australia

MOORE, Maj-Gen Sir (John) Jeremy; KCB (1982, CB 1982), OBE (Mil 1973), MC (1952) and Bar (1962); s of Lt-Col Charles Percival Moore, MC (d 1959), and (Alice Hylda) Mary, *née* Bibby; *b* 5 July 1928; *Educ* Cheltenham; *m* 1966, Veryan Julia Margaret Acworth; 1 s (Andrew b 1971), 2 da (Helen b 1967, Sarah b 1969); *Career* joined RM 1947, CO 42 Commando RM 1972-73, Cmdt RM Sch of Music 1973-75, Royal Coll Defence Studies 1976, Cdr 3 Commando Bde RM 1977-79, Maj-Gen Commando Forces RM 1979-82, Cdr Land Forces Falkland Islands during campaign of 1982, on staff CDS 1982, ret 1983; dir gen Food and Drink Fedn 1984-85, defence conslt 1985-; memb cncl Cheltenham Coll, govr Knighton House Sch; *Recreations* music, painting, sailing, hillwalking; *Style—* Maj-Gen Sir Jeremy Moore, KCB, OBE, MC; c/o Cox's and King's Branch, Lloyds Bank Ltd, 6 Pall Mall, London SW1

MOORE, Joan; da of Duncan Mackay (d 1936), and Martha, *née* Gentle, (d 1967); *b* 29 Nov 1918; *Educ* Perse Sch for Girls Cambridge; *m* 7 Jan 1965, Charles James Robotham, s of Charles Moore (d 1938); *Career* ptnr D Mackay Ironmongers & Engrs' Suppliers Cambridge, dir and co sec Donald Mackay Engrg Cambridge Ltd; memb Br Red Cross Soc Cambridge branch, branch ctee memb and organiser Ely Centre; *Recreations* music; *Style—* Mrs Joan Moore; 8 Barton Rd, Ely CB7 4DE (☎ 0353 663 258); 85 East Rd, Cambridge CB1 1BY (☎ 0353 63 132)

MOORE, Brig Jock Arthur Hume; CBE (1966, OBE 1945); s of Herbert Durie Moore, DSO, MBE (d 1964), of Lee-on-Solent, Hants, and Vera Critchley, *née* Salmonson (d 1970); *b* 6 Feb 1913; *Educ* Tonbridge; *m* 23 Aug 1938, Frances (Fan) Robinson, da of Col Thomas Melville Dill, OBE (d 1945), of Bermuda; 2 s (Ian Melville b 22 April 1940, Tom Durie b 21 Dec 1945), 1 da (Joanna Ruth b 7 May 1952); *Career* Lt RAOC 1936, Capt and Adj 5AA Workshop 1938, dep asst dir 6 armd Div (Lt-Col 1942-43), Staff Coll 1944, Dep Cdr REME 7 Base Workship Egypt 1945-46, asst dir REME HQ ME 1946-48, Asst QMG HQ Western Cmd 1954-56, asst dir REME WO 1956-58, Cd and dep dir 1 Br Corps BAOR 1958-60, dir REME Far East Land Forces 1960-62, Inspr Corps of REME 1963-66, dir REME BAOR 1966-68, ret 1968; appeals sec Charity House of St Barnabus 1974-89; FIMechE, CEng; *Recreations* skiing, sailing, travel, reading; *Style—* Brig Jock Moore, CBE; Moorings, 101 Coll Ride, Bagshot, Surrey GU19 5EF (☎ 0276 72472)

MOORE, Colonel John; TD (1969), DL (1985); s of Joseph Leslie Moore (d 1982), of Newton Aycliffe, Co Durham, and Kathleen Irene (d 1985); *b* 5 August 1932; *Educ* Stockton GS; *m* 23 June 1956, Sheila Margaret, da of Andrew Morton (d 1960), of Newton, Aycliffe; 2 da (Margaret b 1958, Alison b 1961); *Career* Nat Serv cmmnd RE 1955, TA 1956-87: Adj Engr Regt 1967-69, OC 120 Field Sqdn 1969-73, CO III Engr

Regt 1977-81, Dep Cdr 1982-87; chief asst co surveyor Linsey CC 1969-73, dep dir Tech Servs Humberside CC 1973-78 (dir 1978-88) dep chief exec Humberside CC 1988-; chm Humberside Scout Cncl, pres Kilham Branch Royal Br Legion; FICE 1958; *Recreations* golf, caravanning; *Style*— Col John Moore, TD, DL; The Shieling, West End, Kilham, Driffield, Humberside YO25 0RR (☎ 026 282 254); Humberside County Council, County Hall, Beverley, Humberside HU17 9BA (☎ 0482 867 131, fax 0482 867 335)

MOORE, Hon Sir John Cochrane; s of Ernest W Moore (d 1930); *b* 5 Nov 1915; *Educ* N Sydney Boy's HS, Sydney Univ (BA, LLB); *m* 1946, Julia Fay, o da of Brig Geoffrey Drake-Brockman, MC, of Perth, W Australia; 2 s, 2 da; *Career* AIF 1940, RO Hon Capt 1945; admitted Bar NSW 1940, Dept of External Affairs 1945, second sec Aust Mission to UN 1946-47, barr 1947-59, pres Aust Conciliation and Arbitration Cmmn 1973- (dep pres 1959-72, acting pres 1972-73); kt 1976; *Style*— Hon Sir John Moore; 10 The Grange, McAuley Place, Waitara, NSW 2077, Australia

MOORE, Rt Hon John Edward Michael; PC (1986), MP (C) Croydon Centl Feb 1974-; s of Edward O Moore; *b* 26 Nov 1937; *Educ* Licensed Victuallers' Sch Slough, LSE (BSc); *m* 1962, Sheila Sarah Tillotson; 2 s, 1 da; *Career* Nat Serv Royal Sussex Regt Korea 1955-57; chm Cons Assoc 1958-59, pres Students' Union 1959-60, memb Ct of Govrs 1977-; worked in banking and stockbroking and took part in Democratic politics in Chicago 1960-65; chm Dean Witter Int Ltd 1975-79 (dir 1968-79), Lloyd's underwriter 1978-; vice-chm Cons Pty 1975-79, parly under-sec Energy 1979-83, (min state) econ sec Treasy June-Oct 1983, fin sec Treasy, responsibilities incl taxation (appointed after promotion of Nicholas Ridley to sec state Tport) 1983-86; sec state for: Tport 1986-87, Health and Social Security 1987-88, Social Security 1988-; *Recreations* sport; *Clubs* RAC; *Style*— The Rt Hon John Moore, MP; House of Commons, London SW1

MOORE, Capt, Prof John Evelyn; s of Maj William John Moore (d 1958), of Melbourne and Cambridge, and Evelyn Elizabeth, *née* Hooper (d 1935); *b* 1 Nov 1921; *Educ* Sherborne, RN Staff Coll; *m* 8 Jan 1945 (m dis 1967), Joan, da of Capt Frank Pardoe (d 1962), of S Africa; 1 s (Peter b 8 Jan 1958), 2 da (Lavinia b 19 Jan 1947, Fay b 4 Sept 1950); m 2, Barbara, *née* Kerry; *Career* RN: special entry cadet 1939; serv HM Ships (1939-45): Rodney, Impulsive, Nigeria, Challenger; HM Subs: Truant, Rover, Trident, Vigorous, Tradwind 1946-49; in cmd HM Totem 1949-50, RN Staff Coll 1950-51, Staff 2 S/M Sqdn 1951-52, serv HM Ships Dainty and Diamond 1952-54; in cmd: HM Sub Alaric 1954-55, HM Subs Tactician and Telemachus 1955-57; Cdr NATO SO Plans NE Med 1957, Admty (Plans Div) 1960-63, Cdr Sub HMS Dolphin 1963-65, in cmd 7 Submarine Sqdn Singapore 1965-67, Capt COS Naval Home Cmd 1967-69, Def Intelligence Staff i/c Soviet Naval Intelligence 1969-72, ret 1972; ed Jane's Fighting Ships 1972-87; prof int relations Aberdeen Univ; FRGS 1942; *Books* Seapower and Politics, The Soviet Navy Today, Submarine Development, Warships of Royal Navy, Warships of Soviet Navy, Submarine Warfare Today and Tomorrow (jtly); *Recreations* gardening, swimming, archaelolgy; *Clubs* Naval, Anchorites; *Style*— Capt John Moore, RN; Elmhurst, Rickney, Hailsham, E Sussex BN27 1SF (☎ 0323 765862/ 763294)

MOORE, Sir John Michael; KCVO (1983), CB (1974), DSC (1944); s of Algernon William Moore (d 1970), and Amy Elizabeth, *née* Jeffreys (d 1940); *b* 2 April 1921; *Educ* Whitgift Middle Sch Croydon, Selwyn Coll Cambridge; *m* 1, 1947 (m dis 1963), Kathleen, da of Capt C C Pawley (d 1982); 1 s, 1 da; m 2 1963 (m dis 1985), Margaret, da of J Ward (d 1935); *Career* Lt RNVR 1940-46, with Miny of Transport and DOE 1946-72, dep sec (personnel mgmnt) CSD 1972-78, second Crown Estate cmmr 1978-83; Humane Soc Bronze Medal 1942; *Recreations* sailing, mountain walking; *Style*— Sir John Moore, KCVO, CB, DSC; High Spinney, Old Coach Rd, Wrotham, Kent TN15 7NR (☎ 0732 822340)

MOORE, (Harold) Jonathan; s of Harold Moore, of Cambs, and Edna Rose, *née* Jewson (d 1985); *b* 26 Feb 1947; *Educ* The Leys Sch Cambridge; *m* 3 da (Lucy Anna Elizabeth b 1974, Charlotte Jane b 1976, Susannah Amy b 1980); *Career* fndr and sr ptnr Moore Young & Co CAs, ret 1987, md Wheelpower Ltd (electro-mechanical and mfrg co), inventor/designer with designs registered in 7 countries, dir Orchard Estates Property Devpt, fin conslt; fndr memb March Port Appreciatio Soc; FCA 1972, FCCA 1978; *Recreations* golf, sailing, tennis, skiing; *Clubs* Royal W Norfolk GC, March and County; *Style*— Jonathan Moore, Esq; Addison House, Addison Rd, Wimblington, Cambs PE15 0QT (☎ 0354 741124); Wheelpower Ltd, West Winch, Kings Lynn, Norfolk (☎ 0553 840261, fax 0354 54846, car ☎ 0836 216032)

MOORE, (Georgina) Mary; *née* Galbraith; da of Prof Vivian Hunter Galbraith (d 1976), of Oxford Univ, and Georgina Rosalie, *née* Cole-Baker (d 1982); *b* 8 April 1930; *Educ* The Mount Sch York, Lady Margaret Hall Oxford (MA); *m* 1963, Antony Ross, s of William Arthur Moore (d 1962); 1 s (Arthur James b 1967); *Career* HM Diplomatic Service 1951-63; princ St Hilda's Coll Oxford 1980-; *Books* (under the pseudonym Helena Osborne): novels: The Arcadian Affair (1969), Pay-Day (1972), White Poppy (1977), The Joker (1979); plays: The Trial of Madame Fahmy (Granada TV 1980), An Early Lunch (BBC Radio 4 1981), An Arranged Marriage (BBC Radio 4 1982); *Clubs* University Women's; *Style*— Mrs Mary Moore; Touchbridge, Boarstall, nr Aylesbury, Bucks HP18 9UJ (☎ 0844 238247); office: St Hilda's Coll, Oxford (☎ 0865 276884)

MOORE, Mike; s of Jack Francis Moore, BEM, of Epsom, Surrey and Joan Florence, *née* Walker; *b* 6 Jan 1969; *Educ* Bideford Sch of Art and Design, Reading Sch of Art and Design; *Career* photographer: Thomson Regional Newspapers 1976-79, London Evening Standard 1980-85, The Today Newspaper 1986-; Midland Bank press awards commendation 1977 and 1978, World Press Photo Fndn Gold medal 1978, Br Press Awards commendation 1981, Ilford Press Awards commendation 1984, Royal Photographer of the Year 1987, Press Photographer of the Year 1987; *Recreations* tennis, watersports; *Clubs* Ferrari Owners; *Style*— Mike Moore, Esq; 3 Evelyn Terrace, Richmond, Surrey, (☎ 01 940 1097); Today Newspaper Picture Desk, 70 Vauxhall Bridge Rd, London SW1 (☎ 01 630 1300), car (☎ 0836 242018)

MOORE, Nigel Sandford Johnson; s of Raymond Johnson Moore (d 1977), and Lucy Mary, *née* Kirby; *b* 12 April 1944; *Educ* Radley Coll; *m* 16 Aug 1969, Elizabeth Ann, da of Joseph Henry Bowker (d 1986); 1 s (Peter b 9 Jan 1983), 2 da (Louise b 20 Feb 1974, Rachel b 1 Mar 1977); *Career* Buckley Hall Devin & Co 1962-68; CA Ernst and Whinney: Sydney Aust 1969-71, ptnr (UK) 1973-, human resources 1973-81, practice devpt dept 1983-86, managing ptnr London Office 1986-88, euro liaison and devpt 1988-; FCA 1977; *Recreations* theatre, golf, tennis; *Clubs* City of London, IOD, The Pilgrims, Wildernesse; *Style*— Nigel Moore, Esq; Vinesgate, Chart Lane, Brasted Chart, Westerham, Kent TN16 1LR (☎ 0959 64510); Becket House, 1 Lambeth Palace Rd, London SE1 7EU (☎ 01 928 2000, fax 01 928 1345, telex 885234)

MOORE, (Sir) Norman Winfrid; 3 Bt (UK 1919), of Hancox, Whatlington, Sussex (but does not use title); s of Sir Alan Hilary Moore, 2 Bt, MB (d 1959); *b* 24 Feb 1923; *Educ* Eton, Trinity Cambridge; *m* 14 July 1950, Janet, o da of Paul Singer; 1 s, 2 da; *Heir* s, Peter Alan Cutlack Moore; *Career* Lt RA, served 1942-45 War; principal scientific offr Nature Conservancy 1958-, sr principal scientific offr 1965-83, ret; visiting prof Wye Coll London Univ 1979-83; *Style*— Norman Moore, Esq; The Farm House, Swavesey, Cambs

MOORE, Dr Patrick Cald Well; CBE (1968); s of Capt Charles Caldwell Moore MC (d 1947), and Gertrude Lilian, *née* White (d 1981); *b* 4 Mar 1923; *Educ* privately educated; *Career* war service RAF, Flt-Lieut; astronomer; author of over 80 books; *Recreations* cricket, chess, tennis, music; *Clubs* CCC, Lord's Taverners, Sussex; *Style*— Dr Patrick Moore, CBE; Farthings, West St, Selsey, Sussex (☎ Selsey 603668)

MOORE, Peter; s of Benjamin Moore (d 1936), of Beverley, N Humberside, and Gladys May, *née* Forrest (d 1960); *b* 29 Mar 1929; *Educ* Marist Coll Hull, Gordonstoun, HMS Conway (N Wales); *m* Sept 1952, Betty Jean Stanley, da of James Stanley (d 1953), of Riversdale Road, Hull; 1 s (Karl b 1954), 1 da (Susan Jane b 1956); *Career* md: Peter Moore (Hull) Ltd 1964-, Harry Oxtoby and Co Ltd 1961; *Recreations* theatre; *Style*— Peter Moore, Esq; The Hill, Woodgates Lane, North Ferrby, N Humberside (☎ 633592); 45 Newland Avenue, Hull (☎ 42366)

MOORE, Peter Alan Cutlack; s and h of (Sir) Norman Winfrid Moore, 3 Bt (does not use title); *b* 21 Sept 1951; *Educ* Eton, Trinity Coll Cambridge, St John's Coll Oxford; *Career* DPhil (Oxon), BP; *Style*— Peter Moore, Esq; 52 Gloucester Ave, Primrose Hill, London NW1 8JD

MOORE, Very Rev Peter Clement; s of Rev George Guy Moore (d 1967), and Vera Helen, *née* Mylrea (d 1947); *b* 4 June 1924; *Educ* Cheltenham Coll, Ch Ch Oxford (MA, DPhil); *m* 29 June 1965, Mary Claire, da of Malcolm Duror, of Appin Argyll; 1 s (Twysden b 1970), 1 da (Damaris b 1966); *Career* dean of St Albans Cathedral 1973-, minor canon of Canterbury Cathedral 1947-49, curate of Bladon W Woodstock 1949-51, chaplain New Coll Oxford 1949-51, vicar of Alfrick with Lulsey 1952-53, Hurd librarian to Bishop of Worcester 1953-62, vicar of Pershore with Pinvin and Wick 1963-67, canon residentiary of Ely Cathedral 1967-73; memb: Archbishops Liturgical Cmmn 1968-77, Gen Synod 1978-85 and Governing Body SPCK; sr warden and asst Worshipful Company of Glaziers and Painters of Glass; tstee Historical Churches Preservation Tst; select preacher Oxford Univ 1986-87; OStJ; *Books* Tomorrow is too late (1970), Man Woman and Priesthood (1978), Crown in Glory (1982), Bishops: but what kind? (1982), In Vitro Veritas (contributor 1985), Synod of Westminster (1986); *Recreations* gardening, bookbinding, fly fishing; *Clubs* United Oxford and Cambridge; *Style*— The Very Rev the Dean of St Albans; The Deanery, St Albans, Herts (☎ 0727 52120); Thruxton House, Thuxton, Hertford (☎ 098121 376)

MOORE, Peter David; s of Frederick Cecil Moore, and Joan Lambert *née* Wickham; *b* 5 June 1945; *Educ* King George V GS Southport Lancs; *m* 28 April 1973, Susan Janet, da of Duncan Ferguson Ure; 1 s (Stephen David b 5 May 1978), 1 da (Philippa Jane b 1 Jan 1976); *Career* CA: Arthur Andersen 1969-71, Money Dealer Bankers tst co 1971-72, co sec Martin Bierbaum GP Plc (formerly R P Martin Plc) 1972-79, fin dir Martin Bierbaum gp Plc 1979-; FCA 1969; *Recreations* sporting; *Clubs* Richmond RFC, Dorking RFC; *Style*— Peter Moore, Esq; c/o Martin Bierbaum Gp Plc, 4 Deans Ct, London, EC4V 5AA

MOORE, Prof Peter Gerald; TD (1963); s of Leonard Jiggens Moore, of Wimbledon, and Ruby Silvester, *née* Wilburn (d 1979); *b* 5 April 1928; *Educ* Kings Coll Sch Wimbledon, UCL (BSc, PhD), Princeton Univ USA; *m* 27 Sept 1958, Sonja Enevoldson, da of William Ivor Thomas of Cooden (d 1973); 2 s (Richard b 1973, Charles b 1967), 1 da (Penelope (Mrs Lawrenson) b 1960); *Career* 2 Lt 3 Regt RHA 1949-51, 2 Lt (later Lt, later Capt) 290 Field Regt (City of London) RA TA 1951-61, Capt (later Maj) 254 Field Regt RA TA 1961-65; lectr Univ Coll London 1951-56, asst econ advsr NCB 1956-59, head statistical servs Reed Paper Gp 1959-65; London Business Sch: prof statistics 1965-72, dep princ 1972-84, princ 1984-; pt/t: ptnr Duncan C Fraser 1974-77, dir Copeman Paterson Ltd 1984-; membs: Drs and Dentists Renumeration Body 1971-, Ctee on 1971 Census Security 1971-73, UGC 1978-84 (vice chm 1980-83); conslt Wilron Ctee on fin insts 1977-80, memb cncl Univ of Sci and Technol Hong Kong 1986-; Liveryman Tallow Chandlers Co (memb ct 1987-); Hon DSc Heriot Watt Univ 1985, Fellow: UCL 1988, Royal Statistical Soc 1952-(pres 1989-), Inst of Actuaries 1956-(pres 1984-8); *Books* Anatomy of Decisions (1976), Reason By Numbers (1980), The Business of Risk (1983); *Recreations* golf, walking, travelling; *Clubs* Athenaeum, Knole Park GC; *Style*— Professor Peter Moore, TD; 3 Chartway, The Vine, Sevenoaks, Kent TN13 3RU (☎ 0732 451 936); London Business Sch, Sussex Place, Regent's Park, London NW1 4SA (☎ 01 262 5050, fax 01 724 7875, car tel 0836 709 004, telex 27461)

MOORE, Brig Peter Neil Martin; DSO (1942, and bars 1944 and 1952), MC (1941); s of Arthur Montague Moore (d 1966), of 3a Holnest Park House, Sherborne, Dorset, and Amy Dorothy, *née* Peacock (d 1967); *b* 13 July 1911; *Educ* Clifton, RMA Woolwich, Trinity Hall Cambridge (BA); *m* 29 Aug 1953, (Enid) Rosemary, da of Col Herbert Bland Stokes, CBE (d 1962), of South Wraxall Lodge, Bradford-on-Avon, Wilts; 3 s (Michael b 1955 (decd), Martin b 1960, Robert b 1969), 3 da (Lucinda b 1956, Anne b 1957, Melanie b 1959); *Career* cmmnd 1931, Royal Bombay Sappers and Miners 1935-40; N Africa: Staff Capt 7 Indian Inf Bde 1940, 2 i/c 4 Field Sqdn RE 1941, OC 1 (later 3) Field Sqdn RE 1942, GSO1 instr Middle East Staff Coll 1943, GSO1 Br Liaison Offr with Jugoslav partisans 1943-45, cmd RE 6 Airborne Div Palestine 1946, GSO1 WO 1947, CO 35 Engr Regt 1949, cdr RE 1 Inf Div 1950, cdr 28 Field Engr Regt Cwlth Div Korea 1951, GSO1 instr Jt Servs Staff Coll 1953, cdr 28 Cwlth Inf Bde Malaya 1955, Brig GS weapons WO 1959, Dep Cmdt Sch of Land/Air Warfare 1962, ret 1963; princ MAFF 1963-76, courses res offr Coll of Estate Mgmnt 1976-87; chm local parish cncl; Partisan Gold Star 1970; *Recreations* fly fishing, military history; *Clubs* Naval and Military, Special Forces, Ocean Racing; *Style*— Brig Peter Moore, DSO, MC; Hastings Hill House, Churchill, Oxford OX7 6NA (☎ 060 871 778)

MOORE, (John) Royston; CBE (1983); s of Henry Roland Moore (d 1944), and Jane Elizabeth, *née* Wood (d 1958); *b* 2 May 1921; *Educ* Manchester Central GS, Manchester Univ (BSc); *m* 28 March 1947, Dorothy Mackay, da of Charles Roe Hick (d 1960); 2 s (Stephen Charles Royston b 1953, Andrew John Royston b 1957); *Career* princ Bradford Tech Coll (Later Bradford Coll of Further and Higher Educn) 1959-80 (ret); cncllr Baildon UDC 1965-70 (leader 1968); W Riding CC 1970-73, W Yorkshire CC 1973-86 (leader 1978-81, opposition leader 1981-86); chm Cons Nat Advsy Ctee on Educn 1967-70; advsr Overseas Dvpt Dept on Further Educn, E Africa 1963-69, San Salvador 1969-73; memb cncl City and Guilds of London Inst 1978- (chm Ctee for work overseas 1973-87); chm Bradford Health Authority 1982-; memb cncl Nat Assoc of Health Authorities; dir: Yorkshire Enterprise Ltd (formerly W Yorkshire Enterprise Bd Ltd) 1983-, White Rose Enterprise Ltd; White Rose Investment Ltd, N Yorkshire Dvpt Ltd, and other cos; Hon MA Bradford, FRCS, C Chem; *Recreations* cricket, bridge; *Style—* J Royston Moore, Esq, CBE; Bicknor, 33 Station Road, Baildon, Shipley; W Yorkshire BO17 6HS (☎ 1274 581777)

MOORE, Hon Mrs; Hon (Constance) Sheila; 2 da of 11 Baron Digby, KG (d 1964); *b* 20 Sept 1921; *m* 27 Nov 1945, Charles Arthur Moore, eldest s of late Charles Arthur Moore, of Greenwich, Connecticut, USA; *Career* in ATS 1939-40, with British Security Co-Ordination 1943-45; *Style—* The Hon Mrs Moore; Bearforest House, Mallow, Co Cork (☎ 022 21568) 5310; Chemin de Vie, Atlanta, Georgia 30342 USA (☎ 404 256 9222)

MOORE, Terence (Terry); s of Arthur Doncaster Moore, and Dorothy Irene Gladys, *née* Godwin; *b* 24 Dec 1931; *Educ* Strand Sch Univ of London (BSc); *m* 17 Sept 1955, Tessa Catherine, da of Ernest Walter Wynne; 2 s (Simon Jeremy b 1961, Adam Gavin B 1965), 1 da (Anna Louise b 1968); *Career* Nat Serv Army; mktg fin econs Shell Int 1948-64, economist Locana Corpn 1964-65; Conoco: economist, mangr econs planning, gen mangr and dir 1965-74, dep md mktg ops 1974-79, md supply and trading 1979-86, gp md/chief exec offr 1986-; pres Oil Industs Club 1988-89; ACII, AICS, FRSA; *Recreations* jogging, badminton, reading, music; *Style—* Terry Moore, Esq; 4 Oaklands Rd, Groombridge, nr Tunbridge Wells, Kent TN3 9SB (☎ 0892 864 568); Conoco Ltd, Park House, 116 Park St, London W1Y 4NN (☎ 01 408 6759, fax 01 408 6989, telex 915211)

MOORE, Trevor Anthony; s of Ronald Frederick Moore (d 1957), and Jean Daphne, *née* Wallis; *b* 3 Feb 1957; *Educ* Christ's Hosp, St Catharine's Coll Cambridge (MA); *Career* articled clerk Dawson & Co 1979-81, admitted slr 1981, Freshfields 1981- (ptnr 1987-); memb Worshipful Co of Slsr; memb Law Soc; *Recreations* long distance running, squash, french/France; *Style—* Trevor Moore, Esq; 273 Ivydale Rd, London SE15 3DZ; Grindall House, 25 Newgate St, London EC1A 7LH (☎ 01 606 6677, fax 01 639 6022)

MOORE, Sir William Roger Clotworthy; 3 Bt (UK 1932), of Moore Lodge, Co Antrim; TD (1963); s of Sir William Samson Moore, 2 Bt (d 1978), and Ethel Coburn Gordon (d 1973); *b* 17 May 1927; *Educ* Marlborough Coll, RMC Sandhurst; *m* 17 May 1954, Gillian, da of John Brown, of Lisburn, Co Antrim; 1 s, 1 da; *Heir* s, Richard William Moore; *Career* Lt Royal Inniskilling Fusiliers 1945, Maj North Irish Horse 1958; high sheriff Co Antrim 1964; dir numerous cos; chm bd of visitors HM Prisons Castledillon Co Armagh 1971-72; BBC broadcaster, public speaker; *Recreations* shooting, country pursuits, travel; *Clubs* Boodle's, Army and Navy; *Style—* Sir William Moore, Bt, TD; c/o Boodles, 28 St James's St, London SW1

MOORE OF WOLVERCOTE, Baron (Life Peer UK 1986); Philip Brian Cecil; GCB (1985, KCB 1980, CB 1973), GCVO (1983, KCVO 1976), CMG (1966), QSO (1986), PC (1977); s of late Cecil Moore, ICS; *b* 6 April 1921; *Educ* Dragon Sch Oxford, Cheltenham, BNC Oxford; *m* 1945, Joan Ursula Greenop; 2 da; *Career* served WW II RAF Bomber Cmd, and POW; pps to First Lord of the Admty 1957-58 (asst private sec 1950-51); dep high cmmr Singapore 1963-65 (dep UK cmmr 1961-63); chief of PR MOD 1965-66; private sec to HM The Queen and keeper of the Queen's Archives 1977-86 (dep private sec 1972-77, asst private sec 1966-72); hon fell Brasenose Coll Oxford 1981; *Clubs* Athenaeum, MCC; *Style—* The Rt Hon Lord Moore of Wolvercote, GCB, GCVO, CMG, QSO; Hampton Court Palace, Surrey KT8 9AU (☎ 01 943 4695)

MOORE-BICK, Martin James; QC (1986); s of John Ninian Moore-Bick, and Kathleen Margaret, *née* Beall; *b* 6 Dec 1946; *Educ* Skinners Sch Tunbridge Wells, Christ's Coll Cambridge (MA); *m* 3 Aug 1974, Tessa Penelope, da of George Michael Gee; 2 s (Christopher b 1980, Matthew b 1983), 2 da (Catherine b 1977, Elizabeth b 1977); *Career* barr Inner Temple 1969; *Recreations* music, literature, gardening; *Style—* Martin Moore-Bick, Esq, QC; Litle Bines, Witherenden Hill, Burwash, Etchingham, E Sussex (☎ 0435 883 284); 3 Essex Ct, Temple, London EC4 (☎ 01 583 9294, fax 01 583 1341, telex 893468 SXCORT G)

MOOREHEAD, (Hon) Kerena Ann; *née* Mond; does not use style of Hon; er da of 3 Baron Melchett (d 1973); *b* 17 May 1951; *Educ* Univ of E Anglia; *m* 1980, Richard Moorehead; 1 da (Lucy, b 1981); *Style—* Mrs Richard Moorehead; 58 Mallinson Rd, London SW11 1BP

MOORES, Cecil; s of John William Moores, and Louisa *née* Fethney; *b* 10 August 1902; *Educ* Higher Elementary Sch; *m* 11 June 1930, Doris May Moores; 2 s (Nigel b 25 Jan 1936 (d 1977), David b 15 March 1946), 1 da (Patricia (Mrs Martin) b 23 Aug 1931); *Career* Littlewoods Pools Orgn: dir then md 1924-77, chm 1977-79, pres 1979-; *Recreations* golf, cricket, shooting, football, music, fishing; *Clubs* Formby GC, Formby CC; *Style—* Cecil Moores, Esq; Littlewoods Pools, Walton Hall Avenue, Liverpool L67 1AA (☎ 051 526 3677)

MOORES, Sir John; CBE (1972); s of John William Moores; *b* 25 Jan 1896; *Educ* Higher Elementary Sch; *m* 1923, Ruby Knowles; 2 s (*see* Peter Moores), 2 da (er da Betty m 2 Baron Grantchester, *qv*); *Career* fndr of the Littlewoods Orgn 1924: Littlewoods Pools 1924, Littlewoods Mail Order Services 1932, Littlewoods Stores 1936; kt 1980; *Style—* Sir John Moores, CBE; c/o The Littlewoods Organisation, JM Centre, Old Hall St, Liverpool L70 1AB (☎ 051 235 2222)

MOORES, Peter; s of Sir John Moores, CBE, *qv*, and the late Ruby Moores; *b* 9 April 1932; *Educ* Ch Ch Oxford; *m* 1960 (m dis), Luciana, da of Salvatore Pinto, Naples; 2 children; *Career* dir (chm 1977-80) The Littlewoods Orgn 1965-; dir Singer and Friedlander 1972-; Trustee Tate Gallery 1978-85; Govr BBC 1981-83; Fndr of The Peter Moores Fndn 1964, hon MA Christchurch, Gold Medal of the Italian Republic 1974, hon memb RNCM; *Recreations* windsurfing, shooting, opera; *Style—* Peter Moores, Esq; Parbold Hall, Wigan, Lancashire

MOORFOOT, Frederick James; CBE (1981); s of Jesse Moorfoot (d 1957); *b* 10 Sept 1916; *Educ* Scunthorpe GS, Pembroke Coll Cambridge (MA); *m* 1939, Cynthia Patricia, *née* Read; 2 s, 1 da; *Career* chm Kodak Ltd 1979-81 (dir and manufacturing mangr 1968-71, chm and md 1971-79); chm: Ectona Fibres Ltd 1971-85, Royal Philharmonic Assoc (fund raising body) 1981-85; FRPS (tres 1982-); FInstD, CBIM, FRSA; *Recreations* golf, bridge, music, theatre, photography; *Style—* Frederick J Moorfoot, Esq, CBE; 7 Lower Plantation, Sarratt Lane, Loudwater, Rickmansworth, Herts WD3 4PQ (☎ 0923 771291)

MOORHEAD, Michael Dennis; s of Patrick Moorhead, of Verwood, Ringwood Hants, and Pamela Eric Beckett, *née* Roper; *b* 13 June 1946; *Educ* Kings Coll Sch, Manchester Univ (BSc); *m* 10 March 1984, Janette, da of Roger Taylor of Meriden, Coventry; 1 s (Giles b 1984), 1 da (Chloe b 1986); *Career* cmmd RAF Engr Branch, Flt-Lt, 1964-78; res fell Birmingham Univ 1978; dir: Neptune Radar 1983, Neptune Conslts 1986; *Recreations* swimming, skiing, travel; *Clubs* RAF; *Style—* Michael Moorhead, Esq; Neptune Radar Ltd (☎ 0452 730479)

MOORHEAD, Peter Gerald; s of George Aloysius Moorhead (d 1965), and Miriam, *née* Mostyn; *b* 16 Dec 1937; *Educ* Ampleforth, Christ Church Oxford, Manchester Univ; *m* 1 Feb 1961, Astrid Josephine, da of John Joseph Muraszkas-Marshall (d 1986); 1 s (Dominic b 27 Nov 1962), 2 da (Julie (Mrs Clouth) b 10 Dec 1961, Susan b 5 April 1965); *Career* Pilot Offr: RAF (Nat Serv) 1956-58, RAFVR 1958-62; md Frank Young & Co Ltd 1965-83; dir: Tonge Dyeing Co Ltd 1965-83, Tonge Dyeing Co (Hldgs) Ltd 1968-83; md: Tonge and Young Ltd 1983-, Hall Green & Co Ltd 1963-87; life memb Oxford Union Soc, Ampleforth Soc, Catholic Union; FIOD, memb Textile Inst; *Recreations* watching sport, gardening, photography; *Clubs* Pathfinder; *Style—* Peter Moorhead, Esq; Greystones, 7 Highgate Rd, Altrincham, Cheshire WA14 4QZ, (☎ 061 928 8357); Tonge and Young Ltd, Waterside Works, Blackley New Rd, Manchester M9 3ER, (☎ 061 740 1867 car phone 0860 811344)

MOORHOUSE, Adrian David; MBE (1987); s of Clifford Moorhouse, of Bingley, W Yorks, and Kathleen, *née* Thompson; *b* 24 May 1964; *Educ* Bradford GS; *Career* breaststroke swimmer, Olympic Games 1988 Gold Medallist 100m (fourth place 1984); Cwlth Games: 1982 Gold 100m (Silver 4x100m medley relay, Bronze 200m), 1986 Gold 200m (Silver 100m, Silver 4x100m medley relay); Euro Championships: 1983 Gold 200m (Silver 100m), 1985 Gold 100m, 1987 Gold 100m (Bronze 200m); holder: world record 100m breaststroke short course, Euro and Cwlth record 100m breaststroke long course; min's nominee W Yorks and Humberside Sports Cncl; memb MENSA 1988; *Recreations* music, films, literature; *Style—* Adrian Moorhouse, Esq; Cottingley Bar, Bingley, West Yorkshire (☎ 0274 562624)

MOORHOUSE, Lady Diana Merial; *née* Coke; da of Hon Arthur George Coke (ka 1915, 2 s of 3 Earl of Leicester) and sis of 6 Earl; raised to the rank of an Earl's da 1977; *b* 7 Nov 1907; *m* 30 July 1930 (m dis 1938), Trevor Moorhouse (d 1975), o s of late Maj S Moorhouse; 1 da (1 s decd); *Style—* Lady Diana Moorhouse; 1 Stoke Green Cottages, Stoke Poges, Slough, Bucks

MOORHOUSE, Geoffrey; s of William Heald (d 1971), and Gladys, *née* Hoyle, now Mrs Moorhouse; *b* 29 Nov 1931; *Educ* Bury GS; *m* 1, 15 May 1956 (m dis 1975), Janet Marion, da of Alec Murray (d 1978), of Christchurch NZ; 2 s (Andrew b 1962, Michael b 1966), 2 da (Brigid b 1965, d 1981, Jane b 1961); *Career* coder RN 1950-52; journalist 1952-70 (chief features writer Manchester Guardian 1963-70), author; FRGS 1972, FRSL 1982; *Books* The Other England (1964), Against All Reason (1969), Calcutta (1971), The Missionaries (1973), The Fearful Voice (1974), The Diplomats (1977), The Boat and The Town (1979), The Best-Loved Game (1979, Cricket Soc Award), India Britannica (1983), Lord's (1983), To the Frontier (1984, Thomas Cook Award), Imperial City (1988), At the George (1989); *Recreations* listening to music, hill walking, looking at buildings, watching cricket and rugby league; *Clubs* Lancashire CCC; *Style—* Park House, Gayle, Nr Hawes, North Yorks DL8 3RT (☎ 096 97 456)

MOORHOUSE, (Cecil) James (Olaf); MEP (EDG) London S and Surrey E 1984-, (London S 1979-84); s of late Capt Sidney Moorhouse; *b* 1 Jan 1924; *Educ* St Paul's Sch, King's Coll Univ of London (BSc), Imperial Coll Univ of London (DIC); *m* 1958, Elizabeth, da of late Dr Charles Huxtable; 1 s (Olaf), 1 da (Phoebe); *Career* project engr BOAC 1948-53, tech advsr Shell Int Petroleum Co and Shell Operating Cos 1953-72; environmental conservation advsr Shell UK Ltd 1972-73, Gp Environmental Affairs advsr RTZ 1973-80, conslt Rio-Tinto Zinc Corpn 1981-84; Euro Democratic spokesman on Europe's External Econ Rels, memb ctee EFTA Parliamentarians 1984-86 Tport spokesman 1987-; parly rapporteur: trade and econ rels between Euro community and Japan, on trade and econ rels between the EC and the countries of the Pacific Basin and on the economic significance of Antarctica; *Clubs* RAC; *Style—* James Moorhouse Esq, MEP; Jordan Cottage, 18 Orbel Street SW11 3NZ (☎ 01 228 8080); 14 Buckingham Palace Road, London SW1W 0QP

MOORIN, Raymond Leslie; s of Joseph Wilson Moorin (d 1957), and Edith, *née* Waterston (d 1985); *b* 1 Mar 1939; *Educ* Emanuel Sch, Wandsworth Tech Coll, Borough Poly; *m* 14 Aug 1965, (Victoria) Wendy, da of Edwin McCloed Miller, of Merseyside; 3 s (Robert b 1966, Patrick b 1969, Matthew b 1971); *Career* bldg servs engr Slough Borough Cncl 1964-70, mechanical and electrical engr Dept Educn & Sci 1970-72, assoc HL Dawson & Assocs 1972-73, sr ptnr Multi Bldg Servs Design Ptnrship 1973-; sr Steward Wesley Church High Wycombe; C Eng, M Inst E 1968, MIMechE 1969, M Inst R 1972, FCIBSE 1975, M Cons E 1976, FRSA 1988; *Recreations* golf, squash, tennis; *Clubs* Burnham Beeches GC; *Style—* Raymond Moorin, Esq; Lyndale, 21 Coates Lane, High Wycombe, Bucks HP13 5EY (☎ 0494 33147); MBS House, 150 West Wycombe Rd, High Wycombe, Bucks HP12 3AE (☎ 0494 441251/3, fax 0494 32465, car tel 0836 205514)

MOORMAN, Raymond Anthony Gilbert; s of Raymond Moorman (d 1980) and Norah Isabel *née* Gilbert; *b* 9 May 1937; *Educ* Blundell's Sch, Cambridge Univ (MA); *m* 12 Jan 1963, Jane Ethne, da of Stanley Alkman (d 1975); 3 da (Sarah b 14 May 1964, Rebecca b 10 Aug 1966, Lucinda b 5 June 1969); *Career* Nat Serv PO RAF 1955-57; trainee & mangr Union Corp 1960-69; md Capital & Counties plc 1985- (dir 1971, joined 1969); *Recreations* real tennis, golf; *Clubs* Queen's Royal Tennis Court, Tiverton Golf; *Style—* Raymond Moorman, Esq; Capital & Counties Plc, 40 Broadway, London, SW1

MOOTHAM, Dolf C; s of Sir Orby Mootham, and Maria Augusta Elisabeth *née* Niemöller (d 1973); *b* 2 August 1933; *Educ* Bryanston Sch, Trinity Coll, Cambridge (BA); *Career* dir: TSB Gp plc 1987-, Hill Samuel Bank Ltd 1967-; *Clubs* Brooks's; *Style—* Dolf Mootham, Esq; 25 Milk St, London EC2V 8LU (☎ 01 606 7070)

MOOTHAM, Sir Orby Howell; ED (1942); s of Delmé George Mootham, (d 1954); *b* 17 Feb 1901; *Educ* Leinster House Sch Putney, London Univ (MSc); *m* 1, 1931, Maria Augusta Elisabeth (d 1973), da of Wilhelm Niemöller, of Cassel, Germany; 1 s, 1 da; m 2, 1977, Beatrix Douglas, da of Nigel Douglas Connell, of Taranaki, New

Zealand, and widow of Basil Robert Ward (d 1976); *Career* barr Inner Temple 1925, hon bencher 1958, chief judicial offr Br Mil Admin Burma 1943-45; judge: Rangoon High Ct 1945-46, Allahabad High Ct 1946-55; chief justice Allahabad India 1955-61, dep chm Essex QS 1964-71, Surrey QS 1970-71, rec of the Crown Ct 1972; kt 1962; *Books* Burmese Buddhist Law (1939), The East India Company's Sadar Cts 1801-1834 (1983); *Clubs* Athenaeum; *Style*— Sir Orby Mootham, ED; 25 Claremont Rd, Teddington, Middx TW11 8DH (☎ 01 977 1665)

MORAHAN, Christopher Thomas; s of Thomas Hugo Morahan (d 1969), and Nancy Charlotte, *née* Baker (d 1977); *b* 9 July 1929; *Educ* Highgate, Old Vic Theatre Sch; *m* 1, 1954, Joan, *née* Murray (d 1973); m 2, 1974, Anna (acting name Anna Carteret), da of Col Peter Wilkinson, of Pulborough, W Sussex; 2 s (Ben, Andrew), 3 da (Lucy, Rebecca, Harriet); *Career* Nat Serv RA 1947-49, 2 Lt; TV theatre and film dir: dir Greenpoint films Granada Film prodns; head plays BBC TV 1972-76; tv prodns incl: Talking to a Stranger 1966, The Gorge, The Jewel in the Crown 1984, In the Secret State 1985, After Pilkington 1987 (Prix Italia 1987), Troubles 1988, The Heat of The Day 1989; cinema: Clockwise 1986; assoc Nat Theatre 1977-88; theatre prodns incl: This Story of Yours, Flint, State of Revolution (NT), Man and Superman (NT), Wild Honey (NT), Melon, Major Barbara; Theatre Awards: Olivier, Plays and Players Drama, London Standard (for Wildhoney), SFTA Best Play Dir 1969, BAFTA Best Series Dir 1985, Desmond Davis Award for Outstanding Creative Achievement in TV 1985, Peabody Award 1985, Broadcasting Press Guild Award 1984, Primetime Emmy Award 1985; *Recreations* photography, birdwatching; *Style*— Christopher Morahan, Esq; c/o Michael Whitehall Ltd, 125 Gloucester Rd, London SW7 4TE (☎ 01 244 8466)

MORAN, Graham Dennis; s of Dennis John Moran (d 1986), and Janet Pearl, *née* Challinor; *b* 11 July 1945; *Educ* Donnington Wood Sch, Sir John Hunt Comprehensive Sch; *m* 19 June 1965, Patricia Elizabeth, da of Hugh Thomas Stepney (d 1967), of Westminster; 1 s (Philip b 1967), 1 da (Jacqueline b 1965); *Career* 1 Bn Welsh Gds 1962-87, Colour Sgt, served Germany, Ireland, Cyprus Kenya, Canada, The Falklands; admin (for Nat Tst) Anglesey Abbey 1987-; *Recreations* gardening, game shooting; *Style*— Graham Moran, Esq; The Cottage, Anglesey Abbey, Lode, Cambridge CB5 9EJ (☎ 0223 811 200)

MORAN, Dr John Denton; RD (1977); s of Paul Francis Moran, of Marine Gate, Brighton, and Mary, *née* Denton; *b* 3 Nov 1940; *Educ* Downside Sch; Univ of London: Guys Hosp (LDS, RCS), St Georges Hosp (MB, BS); *m* 16 June 1973, Jane, da of Gen Sir Malcolm Cartwright-Taylor, KCB (d 1969); 1 s (Paul b 29 Jan 1976), 2 da (Iona b 16 Sept 1973, Louise b 18 March 1975) ; *Career* RNR: Surgn Sub Lt (D) 1962, Surgn Lt (D) 1964, Surgn Lt Cdr (D) 1969, dental offr HMS Centaur RN 1965, med and dental offr White City and Jamaica Rd RMR, resigned 1979; dental house surgn St Bartholomews Hosp 1964, med house surgn ENT dept St George Hosp Tooting 1970, med house physician Christchurch and Boscombe Hosps Bournemouth 1971, GP Brandon Manitoba Canada 1972, private dental practice Harley St 1973-; MO: Margaret Pyke Centre 1974, Marie Stopes 1978-, Menopause Clinic 1979-; Cert FPA, Dip Psycho-Sexual Counselling; Freeman City of London 1979, Liveryman Worshipful Co Barber Surgns 1980; BMA, FRSM, Assoc Memb of Zoological Soc LN; FDI; *Recreations* golf, shooting, skiing, walking, bridge; *Clubs* RAC, Royal Ashdown, Sloop; *Style*— Dr John Moran, RD; Belvedere Farm, Cinder Hill Lane, Horsted Keynes, W Sussex (☎ 825 790246); 92 Harley St, London W12 (☎ 01 935 2182)

MORAN, 2 Baron (UK 1943); (Richard) John McMoran Wilson; KCMG (1981, CMG 1970); s of 1 Baron, MC (d 1977), formerly Dr (then Sir) Charles McMoran Wilson, and Dorothy, *née* Dufton (d 1983); *b* 22 Sept 1924; *Educ* Eton, King's Coll Cambridge; *m* 29 Dec 1948, Shirley Rowntree, eldest da of late George James Harris, MC, of Bossall Hall, York; 2 s, 1 da; *Heir* s, Hon James Wilson; *Career* served WWII RNVR; entered Foreign Service 1945; ambass: Chad 1970-73, Hungary 1973-76, Portugal 1976-81; high cmmr Canada 1981-84; sits as cross-bencher in House of Lords; vice chm: Atlantic Salmon Tst, All-Party conservation Gp of Both Houses of Parliament; pres Welsh Salmon and Trout Anglers Assoc; memb Regnl Fisheries Advsy Ctee, Welsh Water Authy; Grand Cross Order of the Infante Portugal 1978; *Books* CBI: A Life of Sir Henry Campbell-Bannerman (Whitbread award for biography 1973); Fairfax (1985); *Recreations* fishing, fly-tying, bird watching; *Clubs* Beefsteak, Flyfishers' (pres 1987-88); *Style*— The Rt Hon Lord Moran, KCMG; c/o House of Lords, Westminster, London SW1

MORAN, Peter Myles; s of Myles Moran (d 1957); *b* 3 August 1936; *Educ* St Edward's Coll, Liverpool Univ (LLB); *m* 1963, Miriam Rosemary, *née* Macey; 2 da; *Career* slr; dir: Fred Parkes Hldgs Ltd, Weelsby Estates; part-time chm Social Security Appeal Tribunals; *Recreations* tennis, squash, golf; *Clubs* Carlton; *Style*— Peter Moran, Esq; Langton House, Horncastle, Lincs (☎ 065 82 2296); office: Chattertons, Solicitors, 5 South St, Horncastle, Lincs LN9 6DS (☎ 065 82 2456/7011, telex 56286)

MORAY, Countess of; Barbara; da of John Archibald Murray, of Fifth Av, N Y; *b* 1903; *m* 21 June 1924, 18 Earl of Moray (d 1943); 3 da; *Style*— The Rt Hon Barbara, Countess of Moray; 174 Ebury St, London SW1

MORAY, 20 Earl of (S 1562); Douglas John Moray Stuart; JP (Perthshire 1968); also Lord Abernethy and Strathearn (S 1562), Lord Doune (S 1581), Lord St Colme (S 1611), and Baron Stuart of Castle Stuart (GB 1796); s of 19 Earl of Moray (d 1974; himself 11 in descent from 1 Earl, an illegitimate s of James V of Scotland, Regent of Scotland from 1567 until his murder in 1570 by Hamilton of Bothwellhaugh), and Mabel Helen Maud (May) (d 1968), only child of late Benjamin 'Matabele' Wilson, of Battlefields, S Rhodesia; *b* 13 Feb 1928; *Educ* Trinity Cambridge (BA), Hilton Coll Natal; *m* 27 Jan 1964, Lady Malvina Dorothea Murray, er da of 7 Earl of Mansfield (d 1971); 1 s, 1 da (*see* Lady Louisa Stuart); *Heir* s, Lord Doune; *Career* FRICS; *Clubs* New (Edinburgh); *Style*— The Rt Hon the Earl of Moray, JP; Darnaway Castle, Forres, Moray (Forres 0309 72101); Doune Park, Doune, Perthshire (☎ 0786 841333)

MORAY ROSS AND CAITHNESS, Bishop of 1970-, Rt Rev George Minshull Sessford; s of Charles Walter Sessford (d 1951), of Aintree, Lancs, and Eliza Annie, *née* Minshull; *b* 7 Nov 1928; *Educ* Oulton HS, Liverpool Collegiate Sch, St Andrews Univ (MA); *m* 1, 25 June 1952, Norah (d 1984), da of David Hughes (d 1951), of Aintree; 3 da (Christine Mary (Mrs Parker) b 23 Oct 1953, Aileen Margaret (Mrs McHardy) b 14 Nov 1956, Clare Louise (Mrs Coutts) b 3 Nov 1958); m 2, 8 Aug 1987, Joan Gwendoline Myra, wid of late Rev Charles Wilfred Black; *Career* RASC, 8 Br Inf Bde 1947-49; curate St Mary's Cath Glasgow 1953-58, chaplain Anglican Students Glasgow Univ 1955-58, parish priest Holy Name Cumbernauld 1958-66, rector Forres 1966-70; *Recreations* sailing; *Style*— The Rt Rev the Bishop of Moray Ross and Caithness; Spynie House, 96 Fairfield Rd, Inverness IV3 5LL (☎ 0463 231059)

MORDANT, Sally Rachel; da of Capt Henry Collins (d 1948), and Eileen Marjorie Rachel, *née* Davis (d 1971); *b* 25 May 1930; *m* 12 Apr 1957, Richard Alfred Colman Mordant, s of the late Philip Mordant; 2 s (Simon b 1959, Jonathan b 1961); *Career* freelance journalist and PR cnslt; md SRM Consultancy Services Ltd; MIPR 1979; *Recreations* entertaining, theatre, literature; *Style*— Mrs Sally Mordant; Apartment 11, 23 Hyde Park Square, London W2 2NN (☎ 01 935 6878)

MORDAUNT, Gerald Charles; s of Eustace John (d 1988), and Anne Francis, *née* Gilmour (d 1978); *b* 16 July 1939; *Educ* Wellington Coll; *m* Sept 1965 (m dis 1981), Carol, da of Brig R M Villiers DSO (d 1972), of Scotland; 2 s (James b 1968, Christopher b 1970), 2 da (Tanya b 1974, Harriet b 1980); *Career* chm Alex Anders Laing and Cruickshank 1987- (joined Laing and Cruickshank 1959, head of equities 1986); memb Stock Exchange; *Recreations* tennis, shooting, wine; *Style*— Gerald C Mordaunt, Esq; Hovells Farm, Coggeshall, Colchester, Essex (☎ 0206 61700); Alexanders, Laing and Cruickshank, Piercy Hse, 7 Copthall Ave, London, EC2R 7BE (☎ 01 588 2800, fax 01 588 5819, telex 888 397)

MORDAUNT, Sir Richard Nigel Charles; 14 Bt (E 1611), of Massingham, Parva, Norfolk; s of Lt-Col Sir Nigel John Mordaunt, 13 Bt, MBE (d 1979); *b* 12 May 1940; *Educ* Wellington; *m* 1964, Myriam Atchia; 1 s, 1 da (Michele b 1965); *Heir* s, Kim John Mordaunt b 1966; *Style*— Sir Richard Mordaunt, Bt; 12 Ebor Rd, Palm Beach, New South Wales, Australia

MORDAUNT-SMITH, Hon Mrs (Kathleen Marcia); *née* Browne; da of 3 Baron Oranmore and Browne, KP, PC (d 1927); *b* 17 Jan 1903; *m* 24 June 1926, Maj Cotterell Boughton Mordaunt-Smith (d 1956), yst s of Mordaunt Kirwan Mordaunt-Smith, of Milton Bank, Laugharne, Carmarthenshire; 1 s, 1 da; *Style*— The Hon Mrs Mordaunt-Smith; 73 Onslow Square, SW7

MORE NISBETT, Patrea Evelyn; da of David Agar MacDonald (d 1967), of Dorset, and Elisabeth May, *née* Ferguson; *b* 2 Mar 1944; *Educ* Cranborne Chase, Sorbonne Univ, House of Citizenship Bucks; *m* 2 March 1968, George Alan More Nisbett, s of Surgn-Cdr John Graham More Nisbett, of E Lothian; 3 s (William David Hamilton b 1979, Alexander Talbot John b 1982, Charles Neilson George b 1984); *Career* contrib incl: Scottish Ed Harpers and Queen Magazine, Sloane Ranger Handbook; occasional writer Observer/Scotsman, Scottish Correspondent The Good Schools Guide, advsr to Travel Industry/pr; *Style*— Mrs Patrea Evelyn More Nisbett; 43 Godfrey St, London SW3 (☎ 01 352 3259, car tel 0836 703412); The Drum, Gilmerton, Edinburgh EH17 8RX (☎ 031 664 7215)

MORE-MOLYNEUX, Maj James Robert; OBE (1983), DL; s of Brig-Gen Francis More-Molyneux Longbourne, CMG, DSO, and Gwendoline, da of Rear Adm Sir Robert More-Molyneux, GCB; *b* 17 June 1920; *Educ* Eton, Cambridge Univ; *m* 1948, Susan, da of Capt Frederick Bellinger; 1 s (Michael George); *Career* served WWII, Italy; landowner; chm: Loseley Park Farms and Loseley Dairy Products Ltd; Vice Lord-Lt of Surrey 1982-; *Clubs* Farmers'; *Style*— Maj James More-Molyneux, OBE, DL; Loseley Park, Guildford, Surrey GU3 1HS (☎ 0483 66090) Estate office (☎ 571881)

MORELAND, Robert John; s of Samuel John Moreland, MC, TD, of 3 The Firs, Heathville Road, Gloucester, and Norah Molly, *née* Haines (d 1980); *b* 21 August 1941; *Educ* Glasgow Acad, Dean Close Sch Cheltenham, Nottingham Univ (BA), Warwick Univ; *Career* civil servant Canada 1966-72; mgmnt conslt Touche Ross & Co 1974-; MEP (EDG) Staffs 1979-84, memb Economic and Social Ctee of European Community (since Sept 1986); *Recreations* swimming, golf, watching cricket; *Clubs* Carlton, RAC; *Style*— Robert Moreland, Esq; 3 The Firs, Heathville Rd, Gloucester GL1 3EW (☎ 0452 22612); 7 Vauxhall Walk, London SE11 5JT (☎ 01 582 2613); Rue Ravenstein 2, 1000 Brussels, Belgium (☎ 010 32 2 519 9011)

MORETON, Lady Alison Jeannette; da of 6 Earl of Ducie; *b* 9 Mar 1954; *Educ* Westwings Sch Glos; *Style*— Lady Alison Moreton

MORETON, Anthony John; s of William Herbert Moreton (d 1969), of Cardiff, and Margaret Clara, *née* Jenkins (d 1978); *b* 8 July 1930; *Educ* Penarth County Sch, Cardiff Tech Coll, Ruskin Coll Oxford, Exeter Coll Oxford (MA); *m* 27 May 1967, Ena, da of Thomas Kendall (d 1955), of Merthyr Tydfil; *Career* Nat Serv cmmnd Flying Offr RAF 1954-56; ldr writer and sub ed Western Mail 1956-58, features sub ed New Chronicle 1958-60, Daily Telegraph 1960-63, welsh correspondent Financial Times 1987- (regnl affrs ed 1963-87); cncllr: London Borough Wandsworth 1962-68 (chm libraries ctee), London Borough Lambeth 1965-68 (chm fin and gen purposes ctee); tres Holy Trinity Clapham 1962-74, chm Lambeth Arts and Recreations Assoc 1966-72, church warden St Gwynno's Vaynor Merthyr Tydfil 1985-; Freeman Worshipful Co Glovers 1985; *Recreations* golf, gardening, walking; *Clubs* Cardiff County, Aberdare GC; *Style*— Anthony Moreton, Esq; Pandy Farm, Merthyr Tydfil CF47 8PA (☎ 0685 723003)

MORETON, Lord; David Leslie Moreton; s and h of 6 Earl of Ducie; *b* 20 Sept 1951; *Educ* Cheltenham Coll, Wye Agric Coll (B Sc Agric); *m* 1975, Helen, da of M L Duchesne, of Brussels; *Style*— Lord Moreton; Talbots End Farm, Cromhall, Glos

MORETON, Hon Douglas Howard; s of 6 Earl of Ducie; *b* 21 Oct 1958; *Educ* Stouts Hill Glos; *Style*— Hon Douglas Moreton

MORETON, Sir John Oscar; KCMG (1977, CMG 1966), KCVO (1976), MC (1944); s of Rev Charles Oscar Moreton, of Chipping Norton, Oxon; *b* 28 Dec 1917; *Educ* St Edward's Sch Oxford, Trinity Coll Oxford; *m* 1945, Margaret Katherine, da of Sir John Claud Fortescue Fryer, KBE (d 1948); 3 da; *Career* served WWII RA, Maj 1945; asst master Uppingham 1946-48; entered Colonial Off 1948, Kenya 1953-55, private sec to sec of state 1955-59, CRO 1960, Nigeria 1961-64, IDC 1965, asst under-sec Cwlth Off 1965-69, ambass Vietnam 1969-71, high cmmr Malta 1972-74, dep perm rep (status of ambass) UK Mission to UN 1974-75, min Br Embassy Washington 1975-77; dir Wates Fndn 1978-87; Gentleman Usher of the Blue Rod Order of St Michael and St George 1979-; *Clubs* Army and Navy; *Style*— Sir John Moreton, KCMG, KCVO, MC; Woodside House, Woodside Rd, Cobham, Surrey KT11 2QR

MORETON, (Cecil) Peter; s of Cecil Roland Moreton, of 27 Castle St, Wellingborough, Northants NN8 1LW, and Jessie Maud Moreton, of Northants; *b* 25 July 1927; *Educ* Wellingborough Sch, London Univ, Coll of Estate Mgmnt; *m* 6 April 1953, Eileen, da of Walter Harry Frost (d 1962), of 71 Polwell Lane, Barton Seagrave,

Kettering, Northants; 1 s (Nicolas b 1961), 1 da (Penny b 1958); *Career* articled clerk W & H Peacock Bedford 1944-52, asst H P Barnsley Hereford 1952-53, asst Stimpson Lock & Vince Watford 1953-59, regnl surveyor Northampton Town & Co Bldg Soc 1959-70, chief surveyor Anglia Bldg Soc 1977-87 (dep chief surveyor 1970-77), regular appearances on nat & local TV and radio as spokesman on housing & valuation matters, regular writer in UK & Int magazines, free-lance weekly broadcaster for BBC 1982-, conslt surveyor to RICS Insur Servs London, regular lectr on surveying matters; pres Round Table Watford and Northampton (past chm, sec, pres), past chm RICS branches Beds, Herts, Leics, Northants (sec), past pres Nene Valley Rotary Club (sec), dist vice-chm Rotary Dist 107, past appeals organiser OPWA; past chm: ARC Ctee Deaf Appeal, Northants 47 Surveyors, CBSI Branch, 41 Club; chm Happy Feet Appeal, past memb surveyors panel to the BSA 1977-87, memb RICS Residential Valuation & Survey Ctee; FRICS 1965, FCBSI 1985, FSVA 1988, Paul Harris Fell Rotary Int 1985; *Recreations* sport, golf, cricket, gardening, music; *Clubs* Rotary; *Style*— Peter Moreton, Esq; 86 Church Way, Weston Favell, Northampton NN3 3BY (☎ 0604 406 371); RICS Insur Servs Ltd, Plantation House, 31-35 Fenchurch St, London (☎ 01 481 1445)

MORETON, Hon Robert Matthew; s of 6 Earl Ducie; *b* 8 Mar 1964; *m* 9 July 1988, Heather, da of Colin Lynton-Jenkins, of Alveston, Avon; *Style*— The Hon Robert Moreton

MORGAN; *see*: Hughes-Morgan

MORGAN, Alan William; s of Alfred Charles Morgan, ISO, of Stoke Bishop, Bristol, and Eliza Dora, *née* Sproul-Cran; *b* 4 Oct 1951; *Educ* Clifton, Trinity Coll Oxford (MA), Harvard Business Sch (MBA); *m* 17 Oct 1981, Janet Cullis, da of Rainier Campbell Connolly, of London; 2 s (Campbell b 1983, Edward b 1986), 1 da (Georgina b 1988); *Career* called to the Bar 1974, joined Brands 1974-76, Harvard Business Sch 1976-78, princ McKinsey & Co 1978-; *Recreations* horse racing, theatre, books, walking; *Clubs* RAC, Oxford and Cambridge; *Style*— Alan Morgan, Esq; 74 St James's St, London SW1 (☎ 01 839 8040)

MORGAN, Andrew Vladimir Rhydwen; s of His Hon Judge Peter Hopkin Morgan, of Chippenha, Wilts, and Josephine Mouncey, *née* Travers; *b* 20 Oct 1942; *Educ* Abermad Sch Aberystwyth, Harrow, RADA; *m* 21 Jan 1967, Jacqueline, da of Dennis Webb, of Knaresborough, Yorks; 1 s (Nicholas Simon Hopkin b 9 June 1968), 1 da (Zoe Olivia Lucy b 28 Dec 1972); *Career* freelance film and TV dir; work incl: Swallows and Amazons for Ever, White Peak Farm, Knights of God, Hard Cases, Dr Who; Freeman City of London 1965, Liveryman Worshipful Co Fishmongers 1965; *Recreations* inland waterways; *Style*— Andrew Morgan, Esq; 28 Wyndham St, London W1H 1DD (☎ 01 723 4507)

MORGAN, Bill (John) William Harold; s of John Henry Morgan (d 1973), and Florence Ada, *née* Dorricott; *b* 13 Dec 1927; *Educ* Wednesbury Boys HS, Birmingham Univ (BSc Eng); *m* 1952, Barbara, da of Wilfred Harrison; 2 da (Elaine, Jane); *Career* RAF 1949-51, Flag Offr; Winner of Royal Society's SG Brown award and medal 1968, for an outstanding contribution to the promotional development of mechanical inventions, various sr management roles in English Electric Co 1951-69; dir: GEC plc 1973-83, Hill Samuel & Co 1983-, Simon Engrg plc 1983-; dep chm Petbow Hldgs 1983-, chm AMEC plc 1984- (dir 1983); FEng 1973, FIMechE, CBIM; *Style*— J W A Morgan Esq; Mullion, Whitmore Heath, Nerwcastle-under Lyme, Staffs (☎ 0782 680 462); AMEC plc, Sandiway House, Northwich, Cheshire (☎ 0606 883 885)

MORGAN, Ven Chandos Clifford Hastings Mansel; CB (1974); s of Arden Henry William Llewelyn Morgan (d 1940), of Anglesey, and Elinor Clifford, *née* Hughes (d 1948); direct descendants of the Morgans of Biddlesden Park, Bucks and Hughes of Kinmel Hall nr St Asaph N Wales; *b* 12 August 1920; *Educ* Stowe, Jesus Coll Cambridge (MA); *m* 1946, Dorothy Mary (d 1963), da of John Latham Oliver, of Fordcombe, Tunbridge Wells; 1 s (Arden); *Career* clerk in Holy Orders, ordained Holy Trinity Tunbridge Wells 1944; chaplain RN 1951-75, chaplain of the fleet and archdeacon of RN 1972-75; chaplain Dean Close Sch Cheltenham 1976-83, rector St Margarets Lothbury 1983-, chaplain to the Lord Mayor of London 1988-89; *Recreations* riding, gardening; *Clubs* National; *Style*— The Ven Chandos Morgan, CB; Westwood Farmhouse, Lydford-on-Fosse, Somerton, Somerset (☎ 096 324 301); St Margaret Church, Lothbury, City of London EC2R 7HH (☎ 01 606 8330)

MORGAN, Christopher; s of Geoffrey Morgan, of Ashtead, Surrey, and Bertha Florence, *née* Jaffe (d 1948); *b* 6 Oct 1937; *Educ* Oundle, St Johns Coll Cambridge (MA), Heidelberg Univ; *m* 18 Sept 1971, Pamela Rosamund, da of John Kellock Laurence, of Ham Common, Richmond, Surrey; 1 s (James Edward b 1977), 2 da (Juliette Rachel b 1973, Claudia Lucy b 1974); *Career* articled Deloitte Haskins & Sells 1959 (ptnr 1973-); ACA 1962, FCA 1972; *Books* A Brief Guide to the Sandilands Report (1975), The Securities Association's Capital Adequacy Requirements (1988), Auditing Investment Business (1989); *Recreations* music, mountain walking, astronomy; *Clubs* Riverside; *Style*— Christopher Morgan, Esq; Barnes, London SW13; Minchinhampton, Gloucestershire; Deloitte Haskins & Sells, PO Box 207, 128 Queen Victoria Street, London SW13 0EE

MORGAN, David Llewellyn; s of David Bernard Morgan, JP (d 1955), of Cardiff, and Eleanor Mary, *née* Walker; *b* 5 Oct 1932; *Educ* Charterhouse, Trinity Coll Cambridge (MA); *Career* slr 1959; asst slr: Richards Butler 1959-63 (ptnr 1965-), Herbert Smith 1963-65; non-exec dir Deymel Investmts Ltd 1966- (chm 1977-); Liveryman Worshipful Co of Clockmakers 1963, Liveryman City of London Solicitors Co; memb: Law Soc 1959, City of London Law Soc (co law sub-ctee); *Recreations* DIY in house and garden; *Clubs* United Oxford and Cambridge, Traveller's, Cardiff and County; *Style*— D L Morgan, Esq; Flat 15, 52 Pont St, London SW1X 0AE (☎ 01 589 3538); 15 St Botolph St, London EC3A 7EG (☎ 01 247 6555, fax 01 247 5091, telex 949494 RBLAW G)

MORGAN, David Reginald; s of late Reginald Morgan; *b* 28 Jan 1945; *Educ* Monkton Combe Sch; *m* 1968, Annabella, da of late Dr Thomas Owen Mason; 2 children; *Career* dir Avon Tin Printers Ltd 1974-83, md 1983-; Avon Tin Inc (USA) 1979-, chm ATP Management Ltd; hon tres Metal Packaging Mfrs Assoc of GB 1985 (cncl memb); Liveryman Tinplate alias Wire Workers Co; *Recreations* shooting, photography, reading; *Style*— David Morgan, Esq; Rock Cottage, Quarry Rd, Frenchay, Bristol (☎ 0272 566853)

MORGAN, Col David Richard; OBE (1971), TD (1963, DL Merseyside 1976); s of Samuel Morgan (d 1966), and Elizabeth, *née* Roberts (d 1956); *b* 27 August 1921; *Educ* Neath, St Luke's Coll Univ of Exeter (Dip PhysEd); *m* 1955, Sarah Gaynor, da of David Charles Roberts (d 1968), of Liverpool; 2 s (Huw, John), 1 da (Siân); *Career* served Palestine and Cyprus, Lt-Col; CO Univ of Liverpool OTC 1963-72; Hon Col Merseyside ACF; chm: ACF Sports & PA Ctee NW England; Army Benevolent Fund Merseyside Appeal; schoolmaster (ret); memb: Cncl The King's Regt, Mil Educn Ctee Liverpool Univ; High Sheriff of Merseyside 1989-90; *Recreations* rugger, music, tree husbandry; *Clubs* Waterloo, Artists; *Style*— Col David Morgan, OBE, TD, DL; 28 Hastings Rd, Birkdale, Southport, Merseyside PR3 2LW (☎ 0704 64298)

MORGAN, David Treharne; TD (1983); s of Maj Hugh Treharne Morgan, OBE, TD, of Alchornes, Lordswell Lane, Crowborough, Sussex, and Betty Gladys Boys, *née* Schreiber; *b* 21 Oct 1941; *Educ* Dragon Sch, Winchester, Innsbruck Univ; *m* 7 July 1973, Heather, da of William Thomson (d 1953), of Steilston House, Dumfries; 1 da (Claire b 2 Aug 1979); *Career* TA; joined HAC 1964, cmmnd 2 Lt 1975, transferred RCT 1977, Lt movement control offr 1977, Capt 2 i/c 282 MC Sqdn 1979, Maj Cmdg 281 MC Sqdn 1984, Lt Col Liaison offr to MOD (Netherlands) 1988; slr 1970, ptnr R A Roberts 1973-83, Wright Son & Pepper 1987-; chm N Norfolk Railway plc 1973-, dir W Somerset Railway plc 1982-; chm: Tport Tst, Assoc of Railway Preservation Socs Ltd; tres Int Trauma Fndn; Freeman City of London 1982, Liveryman Worshipful Co of Glaziers; memb Law Soc 1970, fell IOD; *Recreations* skiing, preserved railways; *Clubs* Norfolk; *Style*— David Morgan, Esq; 7 Cheyne Place, London SW3 4HH (☎ 01 352 6077); Wright Son & Pepper, 9 Grays Inn Square, London WC1R 5JF (☎ 01 242 5473, fax 01 831 7454, telex 27871)

MORGAN, David William; s of Capt William Thomas Morgan, of 11 The Cloisters, Parkway, Welwyn Garden City, and Amy Elizabeth, *née* Hurren; *b* 21 Oct 1943; *Educ* Enfield GS, St Catharine's Coll Cambridge (MA); *m* 14 July 1984, Janis Irene, da of Richard Tyler, of Stevenage, Herts; 2 s (Christopher William, James David), 1 step da (Tara Jane Lawrence); *Career* gp dir Hunting Gate GP Ltd 1971-, slr in private practice Morgans; govr Hitchin Girls Sch, dir Hitchin Town FC, vice chm N Herts Cons Assoc; memb Law Soc, RICS; *Recreations* tennis, travel, skiing, soccer; *Style*— David Morgan, Esq; Beech House, London Road, St Ippollitts, nr Hitchin, Herts (☎ 0462 54608)

MORGAN, Derek William Charles; s of Thomas Brinley Morgan (d 1978), of Heath, and Brenda Vanessa, *née* Megraw; *b* 28 Nov 1934; *Educ* Neath GS, Nottingham Univ (BA); *m* 17 Aug 1963, Anne Yvette, da of Evan Morgan Davies (d 1977), Bridgend; 2 da (Siân, Louise); *Career* Nat Serv RE 1956-58; mangr Littlewoods Ltd 1958-61, plant mangr Ilford Ltd 1961-67, dir PA Consltg Gp 1967-; non-exec dir: Morganite Electrical Carbon Ltd 1982, Corgi Toys ltd 1987-, BK Thomas & ptnrs 1988-; Neath Devpt ptnrship 1981-88, memb Welsh Health Common Servs Authy 1982-, Mid Glamorgan Health Authy 1987-, Wales regnl cncl CBI 1987-, Birmingham chamber of Indust and Commerce 1987-, Welsh Health Manpower Steering Gp 1986-; dir Business Action Team (Birmingham) Ltd 1988-, Exec Second Mgmnt Ltd 1984-; chm: Ogwr ptnrship Tst 1988-, Artificial Limb and Appliance Serv Ctee for Wales 1988-; govr Univ Coll Swansea 1982-; High Sheriff of Mid Glamorgan 1988-89; Freeman City of London 1986, Liveryman Worshipful Co of Tin plate (wire) Workers 1986; FIMC 1976, FBIM 1979; *Recreations* walking, wine, reading, cricket; *Clubs* Cardiff and Co (Cardiff); *Style*— Derek Morgan, Esq; Erw Graig, Merthyr Mawr

MORGAN, Douglas Charles; s of Herbert Morgan (d 1918), and Elsie Morgan (d 1969); *b* 22 Sept 1918; *m* 11 May 1941, Jean Eileen, da of William Marjoram (d 1974); 2 s (Michael David Charles b 1949, Gerald Dennis b 1950); *Career* TA 1938, Br and Indian Army 1939-46; builders merchant, memb Lloyds; cncl memb: City of London Livery Club, United Wards Club of the City of London; memb: Guild of Freemen, Freeman of England, Lime St Coleman St Ward Clubs, Royal Soc of St George; ctee memb: Farringdon Ward Clubs, Inst of Dirs City of London Branch; Liveryman: Worshipful Co of Builders Merchants 1979, Worshipful Co of Loriners 1985; FInstBM 1969, FInstOD 1973, FInstOR 1980; *Style*— Douglas Morgan, Esq; Alde Cottage, Baker St, Orsett, Essex (☎ 0375 891 498); Kentford, Leiston Rd, Aldeburgh, Suffolk; D C Morgan Co Ltd, 36 Lodge Lane, Grays, Essex (☎ 0375 373 815, fax 0375 390 280)

MORGAN, (David) Dudley; s of Thomas Dudley Morgan; *b* 23 Oct 1914; *Educ* Swansea GS, Jesus Coll Cambridge (MA, LLB); *m* 1948, Margaret Helene, da of late David MacNaughton Duncan; 2 da; *Career* served WWII, RAF in Intelligence Corps UK 1940-42, Legal Br India 1942-46, Wing Cdr 1945; admitted slr 1939; sr ptnr Theodore Goddard & Co Slrs 1974-80, ret; formerly dir: Crown House plc, Pritchard Services Gp plc and additional cos; Lloyd's underwriter; *Clubs* Carlton; *Style*— Dudley Morgan, Esq; St Leonard's House, St Leonard's Rd, Nazeing, Waltham Abbey, Essex (☎ Nazeing 099 289 2124)

MORGAN, Lady; Eirene Marjorie; da of Very Rev Canon L M Hay-Dinwoody (d 1962) and Marjorie (d 1920), da of John Hay of Leith; *b* 25 August 1899; *m* 1, 1920, Capt Cecil Allen, RN (d 1960); 2 da (and 1 da decd) *see* 7 Baron Newborough; m 2, 1962, as his 2 w, Adm Sir (Llewellyn) Vaughan Morgan, KBE, CB, MVO, DSC (d 1969); *Style*— Lady Morgan; Webbs Green Cottage, Soberton, Hants SO3 1PY (☎ 048 97 477)

MORGAN, Hon Eleri; da of Baron Elystan-Morgan (Life Baron); *b* 1960; *Style*— Hon Eleri Morgan

MORGAN, Lady Ena Muriel; *née* Evans; late Edward Franklin Evans; *m* 1930, Sir Clifford Naunton Morgan (d 1986); *Style*— Lady Morgan; Rolfe's Farm, Inkpen, Berks

MORGAN, Eric Albert George; s of late Albert E Morgan; *b* 24 May 1928; *Educ* Ilford County HS, St Catherine's Coll Oxford (MA); *m* 1952, Mary, *née* Evans; 2 da; *Career* md British-American Cosmetics 1970-84; chm: Yardley & Co 1970-84, Lentheric 1970-84, Germaine Monteil Cosmetiques Corpn (USA) 1970-84; hon citizen Georgia (USA) 1976; Master Worshipful Co of Marketers 1988; govr Kingston Poly; MIEx, FInstM, FRSA; *Recreations* management education, writing, TV; *Clubs* RAC; *Style*— Eric Morgan, Esq; Sas-sa-Quin, 8 Princes Drive, Oxshott, Surrey (☎ 0372 84 2875)

MORGAN, Sir Ernest Dunstan; KBE (1971, OBE 1951, MBE 1940), JP (Sierra Leone 1952); s of Thomas William Morgan; *b* 17 Nov 1896; *Educ* Zion Day Sch, Methodist Boys' HS; *m* 1, 1918, Elizabeth Mary Agnes Collier; 1 da; m 2, 1972, Monica Davies; 1 s, 3 da; *Career* druggist 1917; memb Freetown City Cncl 1938-44; chm: Blind Welfare Soc 1946-52, Public Service Cmmn 1948-52; memb Fourah Bay Coll Cncl 1950-54; MHR Sierra Leone 1956-61; *Recreations* tennis; *Style*— Sir Ernest Morgan, KBE, JP; 15 Syke St, Freetown, Sierra Leone (☎ Freetown 23155 and 22366)

MORGAN, Hon Mrs; Hon Fionn Frances Bride; *née* O'Neill; da of 3 Baron O'Neill (d 1944); *b* 9 Mar 1936; *Educ* Heathfield, St Anne's Coll Oxford; *m* 26 July 1961 (m dis 1976), John Albert Leigh Morgan, CMG, *qv*; 1 s, 2 da; *Style*— The Hon Mrs Fionn Morgan; 182 Ebury St, London SW1W 8VP (☎ 01 730 1140)

MORGAN, Col Frank Stanley; CBE (1940), ERD (1947), JP (Glamorganshire 1951), DL (1946); s of Frank Arthur Morgan; *b* 10 Jan 1893; *Educ* Marlborough, Christ Church Oxford; *m* 1, 1918, Gladys Joan (d 1953), da of Lt-Col Henry Murray Ashley Warde, CBE, DL; m 2, 1956, Lt-Col Minnie Helen Morgan, MBE, TD, DL, *qv*; *Career* serv 1914-18 War with Pembroke Yeo and Imperial Camel Corps, 1939-45 War with RCS, Col 1940, Brig 1943-44, ret (Col) 1945; *Recreations* country pursuits, travel; *Style*— Col Frank Morgan, CBE, ERD, JP, DL; Herbert's Lodge, Bishopston, Swansea, W Glamorgan SA3 3DW (☎ 044 128 4222)

MORGAN, (William) Geraint (Oliver); s of Morgan Morgan (d 1950), of Wond Farm, Newport Poynell, Bucks, and Elizabeth, *née* Oliver (d 1980); *b* 2 Nov 1920; *Educ* Aberystwyth, Cambridge (BA), London Univ (LLB); *m* 7 Sept 1957, Jill Sheila McGlashan, da of John Archibald Maxwell (d 1952), of 8 Westcliffe Rd, Southport, Merseyside; 2 s (Owen b 11 June 1964, Llewelyn b 25 June 1968), 2 da (Frances (Mrs Parry) b 2 July 1959, Bronwen (Mrs Campbell) b 8 Nov 1962); *Career* WWII RM, demob with hon rank of Maj 1946; barr Gray's Inn 1947, QC 1971, rec Crown Ct 1972, memb Payne Ctee on Recovery of Judgement Debts 1965-59; Parly candidate (Cons) Merioneth 1951 and Hayton 1955; MP (Cons) Denbigh 1959, 1964, 1966, 1974, 1979; resigned Cons Pty 1983 and now supports Welsh Nat Pty (Plaid Cymru), chm Welsh Party Pty 1966-67; memb: Investiture ctee of HRH The prince of Wales 1969-69, Gorsedd of Royal Nat Eisteddford of Wales 1969; FCIArb; *Recreations* reading; *Style*— Gerairt Morgan, Esq; 13 Owen Road, Prescot, Merseyside L35 0PJ (☎ 051 236 9402)

MORGAN, (William) Geraint Oliver; QC (1971), MP (C) Denbigh 1959-; *b* 13 August 1914; *Educ* Univ Coll Wales Aberystwyth, Trin Hall Cambridge; *m* J Maxwell; 2 s, 2 da; *Career* served WW II Royal Marines, reaching rank of Maj; barr Gray's Inn 1947, rec Crown Ct 1972-; fought Merioneth 1951, Huyton 1955; memb Ct Univ of Wales; *Style*— Geraint Morgan Esq, QC, MP

MORGAN, Howard James; s of Thomas James Morgan, of Sutton Coldfield, and Olive Victoria, *née* Oldnaugh; *b* 21 April 1949; *Educ* Fairfax HS Sutton Coldfield, Univ of Newcastle Upon Tyne (MA); *m* 27 Aug 1977, Susan Ann, da of Alexander Sandilands; 1 s (Alexander James b 26 May 1985); *Career* artist; many private cmmns and work in the Nat Portrait Gallery; exhibitions incl: Anthony Mauld 1983, Claridges 1985, Richmond Gallery 1987 and 1988, Agnew 1985 and 1988, Cadogan Contemporary 1987 and 1989; memb Royal Soc of Portrait Painters 1986; *Recreations* riding, 1938 Citroën, books; *Clubs* Chelsea Arts; *Style*— Howard Morgan, Esq; 12 Rectory Grove, Clapham Old Town, London SW4 (☎ 01 720 7460); 401 Wandsworth Rd, Battersea, London SW8 (☎ 01 720 1181)

MORGAN, James Rees; s of Dr Richard Glyn Morgan MC, (d 1972), of Newport Gwent, and Nancy *née* Griffiths (d 1984); *b* 14 August 1936; *Educ* Mill Hill Sch, Magdalene Coll Cambridge (MA), Birmingham Univ (MSc); *m* 15 Nov 1960, Jane, da of David Murray MacFarlane (d 1988), of Newport Gwent; 1 s (Charles James Glyn b 1962), 1 da (Amelia Kate b 1963); *Career* Nat Serv RAF 1954-56, RO 1955 (qualified 1956), PO Royal AAF, 614 Sqds 1956; Massey Ferguson 1959-62, gp planning engr Automotive Products 1963-64, Mgmnt Consult Arthur Young & Co 1964-66, (1973-), operational res scientist Inst for Operational Res 1966-73, dir Mgmnt Consultancy 1978 (ptnr 1981); memb Stratford on Avon RDC 1969-74, Stratford DC 1973-76; C Eng, MI Prod E 1967; *Recreations* gardening, skiing, watching rugby football, theatre; *Clubs* RA, Birmingham; *Style*— James Morgan, Esq; Arthur Young, Rolls House, 7 Rolls Buildings, New Fetter Lane, London, EC4A 1NH, (☎ 01 831 7130)

MORGAN, John (David) Howard; s of John Herbert Morgan, of Johannesburg, S Africa, and Enid Joan, *née* Coke-Smith (d 1979); *b* 4 Oct 1938; *Educ* Frensham Heights Sch, Kings Coll Cambridge (MA), Roy Sch of Mines Imp Coll (MSc, DIC); *m* 24 Oct 1967, Barbara Mary, da of Alan Hanna (d 1947), of Durban S Africa; 3 s (Matthew b 1970, Oliver b 1973, Jasper b 1973); *Career* mech engr 1960-75, stockbroker/mining analyst; dir Shearson Lehman Hutton Securities 1988-; Freedom of the State of Montana USA (1987) MIMM 1977, CEng, Stock Exchange London 1978; *Recreations* tennis, gardening, skiing; *Clubs* Hurlingham; *Style*— David Morgan, Esq; 1 Campden Grove, London W8 4JG (☎ 01 937 2050); 1 Broadgate London EC2M 7HA (☎ 01 260 2716)

MORGAN, John Albert Leigh; CMG (1982); s of John Edward Rowland Morgan and Ivy Ann Ashton; *b* 21 June 1929; *Educ* LSE (BSc), Univ of Korea (Hon DSc); *m* 1, 1961 (m dis 1975), Hon Fionn Frances Bride *qv*, da of 3 Baron O'Neill (d 1944); 1 s, 2 da; m 2, 1976, Angela Mary Eleanor, da of Patrick Warre Rathbone; 1 s, 1 da; *Career* served Army 1947-49, cmmnd 1948; entered Foreign Service 1951, served in Moscow (twice), Peking and Rio de Janeiro, head Far Eastern Dept FCO 1970-72, head Cultural Relations Dept FCO 1972-80; ambass: Korea 1980-83, Poland 1983-86, Mexico 1986-; hon fell LSE; Hon LLD Mexican Inst of Int Law, Hon DSc Univ of Korea; FRAS; *Clubs* Travellers'; *Style*— John Morgan, Esq, CMG; c/o Foreign and Commonwealth Office, London SW1

MORGAN, John Christopher; s of Ieuan Gwyn Jones Morgan, of Winchester, and Gwen, *née* Littlechild; *b* 31 Dec 1955; *Educ* Peter Symonds Winchester, Univ of Reading (BSc); *m* 1 Sept 1984, Rosalind Jane, da of John Kendrew; 2 s (James b 1986, Charles b 1988); *Career* chm: Morgan Lovell plc 1977-, Overbury & Sons Ltd 1985-; ISVA; *Recreations* sailing, reading; *Clubs* RAC; *Style*— John Morgan, Esq; 52 Poland St, London W1 (☎ 01 434 4192)

MORGAN, (Ivor) John; s of Capt Alfred Morgan (d 1961), of London, and Dorothy, *née* Barnet; *b* 25 April 1931; *Educ* Taunton Sch Somerset; *m* 9 June 1955, Shirley, da of Henry Morrison Bullen (d 1987), of Staindrop, Co Durham; 2 da (Penelope b 1957, Jane b 1960); *Career* Lt RA 1953-56; Higgs & Hill plc 1948-60; md: Builders Amalgamated Ltd 1960-66, Higgs & Hill Property Hldgs 1966-74; pres dir gen Golf St Cyprien SA 1975-79, sr ptnr John Morgan Assoc 1979-; fndr memb Mary Rose Tst; vice chm govrs Wispers Sch Haslemere 1970-75; Diplome de Prestige De Tourisme France 1977; Freeman City of London 1955, Liveryman Paviors Company 1974; FCIOB, MCInstM; *Recreations* fly-fishing, sailing, vintage sports cars; *Clubs* Fly Fishers, Piscatorial Soc, Royal Artillery YC, Vintage Sports Car; *Style*— John Morgan, Esq; George House, Petworth, Sussex (☎ 0798 42312); Le PetitMas, Golf St Cyprien, St Cyprien, France; 32 Queen Annes Gate, London SW1

MORGAN, John William Harold (Bill); s of John Henry Morgan (d 1973), and Florence Ada, *née* Dorricott; *b* 13 Dec 1927; *Educ* Wednesbury Boys HS, Birmingham Univ (BSc); *m* 1952, Barbara, da of Wilfred Harrison; 2 da (Elaine, Jane); *Career* served RAF 1949-51 Flying Offr; various sr mgmnt roles in English Electric Co 1951-69, md English Electric-AEI Machines Gp (following merger with GEC) 1969-73; asst md and mainboard dir: GEC plc 1973-83, Hill Samuel & Co 1983-, Simon Engrg plc 1983-88; dep chm Petbow Hldgs plc 1983-86; chm AMEC plc 1984-88 (dir 1983), dir AMEC plc 1988-; Winner of Royal Society SG Brown Award and Medal 1968 an outstanding contrib to the promotion and dvpt of mechanical inventions; memb cncl Fellowship of Engrs 1987-; FEng, FIMechE, MIEE, FRSA; *Style*— J W H Morgan Esq; Mullion, Whitmore Heath, Newcastle-under Lyme, Staffs (☎ 0782 680462); AMEC plc, Sandiway House, Northwich, Cheshire (☎ 0606 883885)

MORGAN, Kenneth; OBE (1978); s of Albert Edward Morgan (d 1975), of Downend, Bristol, and Lily Maud, *née* Stafford; *b* 3 Nov 1928; *Educ* Stockport GS; *m* 1950, Margaret Cynthia, da of Roland Ellis Wilson (d 1981), of Stockport; 3 da (Helen, Sarah, Jane); *Career* Lt RAOC 1946-49 (Egypt and Palestine); journalist: Stockport Express, Kemsley Newspapers 1944-, Exchange Telegraph Co 1956-62; Central London sec NUJ 1962-66; nat organiser NUJ 1966-70; gen sec NUJ 1970-77; memb exec ctee Nat Fedn of Professional Workers 1970-77; Press Cncl: consultative memb 1970-77, jt sec 1977-78, dep dir and conciliator 1978-79, dir 1980-; memb Jt Standing Ctee Nat Newspaper Indust 1976-77; Assoc Int Press Inst 1980; tstee Reuters 1984; dir: Journalists in Europe Ltd, Reuters Founders Share Co; FRSA; *Recreations* theatre, history, inland waterways; *Style*— Kenneth Morgan Esq, OBE; 151 Overhill Rd, Dulwich, London SE22 (☎ 01 693 6585); 1 Salisbury Square, London EC4 (☎ 01 353 1248)

MORGAN, Kenneth; s of Edward John Morgan (d 1981), of 19 Long Drive, East Acton, London, and Kate, *née* Reed; *b* 8 July 1946; *Educ* St Clement Danes GS; *m* 28 June 1969, Jean Margaret, da of Edward Albert Woods, of 36 Singleton Rd, Dagenham, Essex; 4 da (Sarah b and d 1972, Alexandra Jane b 1973, Joanna Louise b 1976 (d 1978), Elizabeth Susan b 1979); *Career* CA, 1968; jr ptnr Summers Morgan & Co 1970 (sr ptnr 1977); FCA; *Recreations* ldr of St Andrew's Church Chorleywood youth gp; *Style*— Kenneth Morgan, Esq; Old Berkeley, Homefield Rd, Chorleywood, Herts WD3 5QJ (☎ 09278 4459); Summers Morgan & Co, 1st Floor, Sheraton House, Lower Rd, Chorleywood, Herts WD3 5LH (☎ 09278 4212, telex 29573 SMCO G, fax 09278 4056)

MORGAN, Prof Kenneth Owen; s of David James Morgan (d 1978), of Aberystwyth, and Margaret *née* Owen; *b* 16 May 1934; *Educ* Univ Coll Sch, Oriel Coll Oxford (BA, MA, DPhil, DLitt); *m* 4 Jan 1973, Jane, da of Gunther Keeler (d 1949), of W Germany; 1 s (David b 4 July 1974), 1 da (Katherine Louise b 22 Sept 1978); *Career* lectr history Univ Coll Swansea 1958-66 (sr lectr 1965-66), visiting fell American Cncl of Learned Socs Columbia Univ NY 1962-63, fell and praelector modern history and politics The Queen's Coll Oxford 1966-89, lectr Univ of Oxford 1967-89, princ Univ Coll of Wales Aberystwyth 1989-; BBC political commentator, radio and tv 1964-79; ed Welsh History Review 1965-; memb: Bd Celtic studies 1972-, Welsh Political Archive 1985-, cncl Nat Library of Wales 1989-; hon fell Univ Coll of Swansea 1985; FRHistS 1964, FBA 1983; *Books* contrib: David Lloyd George: Welsh Radical as World Statesman (second edn 1964), Freedom or Sacrilege? (1966), Keir Hardie (1968), Lloyd George: Family Letters 1885-1936 (1973), Lloyd George (1974), Keir Hardie: Radical and Socialist (1975), Consensus and Disunity: the Lloyd George Coalition Government 1918-1922 (1979), Wales in British Politics 1868-1922 (third edn 1980), Portrait of a Progressive: the Political Career of Christopher, Viscount Addison (1980), Rebirth of a Nation: Wales 1880-1980 (1981), David Lloyd George 1863-1945 (1981), The Age of Lloyd George (1983), Welsh Society and Nationhood: Historical Essays (1984), the Oxford Illustrated History of Britain (1984), Labour People: Leaders and Lieutenants - Hardie to Kinnock (1987), The Oxford History of Britain (1988), The Red Dragon and the Red Flag: the cases of James Griffiths and Aneurin Bevan (1989); *Recreations* sport, music, travel (especially France and Italy), architecture; *Style*— Prof Kenneth Morgan; Plas Penglais, Aberystwyth, Dyfed SY23 3DF (☎ 0970 623 583); Univ Coll of Wales, Old College, King Street, Aberystwyth, Dyfed SY23 2AX (☎ 0970 617 192, fax 0970 611 446)

MORGAN, Kenneth S; s of Edward Henry Morgan and Florence May, *née* Wheeler; *b* 6 August 1925; *Educ* Battersea, Dartford GS; *m* 2 Nov 1952, Patricia Eva, da of Joseph Hunt, of Kingsway, Derby; 1 s (Richard b 1962), 1 da Lindsay b 1956); *Career* ed official report (Hansard) House of Commons; pres Cwlth Hansard Editors Assoc; *Books* The Falklands Campaign (digest of Parly debates); *Recreations* military history; *Style*— Kenneth S Morgan, Esq; 3 Highfield Road, Bexleyheath, Kent (☎ 0322 525333); House of Commons (☎ 01 219 3388)

MORGAN, (Frank) Leslie; CBE (1988, MBE 1973); s of Edward Arthur Morgan Llanfair-Caereinion, of Powys (d 1959), and Beatrice, *née* Jones (d 1930); *b* 7 Nov 1926; *Educ* Llanfair GS, Univ Coll of Wales (BA); *m* 16 June 1962, Victoria Stoker, da of Harold Jeffery (d 1972), of Wollaston, Worcs; 1 s (Christopher b 1969), 2 da (Amanda b 1964, Penelope b 1966); *Career* Capt RAOC 1945-48 (res 1950-59); chm: Morgan Bros (Mid Wales) Ltd 1959-, Mid Wales Devpt 1981-; memb: Welsh Cncl 1970-79, Welsh Devpt Agency 1981-, Welsh Tourist Bd 1982-, Br Tourist Authy Devpt Ctee 1982-; dir: Abbey Nat Bldg Soc (Welsh Bd) 1981-, Devpt Corpn Wales 1981-83; chm and pres Montgomeryshire Cos Assoc 1964-81, pres Montgomeryshire Agric Soc 1986; *Recreations* reading, travel, jogging, swimming, cycling; *Style*— Leslie Morgan, Esq, CBE; Wentworth House, Llangyniew, Welshpool, Powys, UK (☎ 0938 810462)

MORGAN, Lt-Col Minnie Helen; MBE (1944), TD (1948), DL (W Glamorgan 1974); da of late Maj Charles Pine, OBE; *b* 26 July 1906; *Educ* Braunston House Newport IOW; *m* 1956, Col Frank Stanley Morgan, CBE, ERD, JP, DL, *qv*; *Career* TA and Reg Army Offr ATS/WRAC 1939-56 (ret); div cmmr W Glamorgan Girl Guides 1956-66; *Recreations* country pursuits, travel; *Style*— Lt-Col M H Morgan, MBE, TD, DL; Herbert's Lodge, Bishopston, Swansea, W Glamorgan (☎ 044128 422 22)

MORGAN, Hon Owain; s of Baron Elystan-Morgan (Life Peer); *b* 1962; *Style*— Hon Owain Morgan; c/o Rt Hon Lord Elystan-Morgan, Careg Afon, Dolau, Bow Street, Dyfed

MORGAN, Rear Adm Sir Patrick John; KCVO (1970), CB (1967), DSC (1942); o s of Vice Adm Sir Charles Eric Morgan, KCB, DSO (d 1951), and Winifred Eva, *née* James; *b* 26 Jan 1917; *Educ* RNC Dartmouth; *m* 1944, Mary Hermione, da of Col Neil

Fraser-Tytler, DSO, MC, TD, DL (d 1937); 3 s, 1 da; *Career* served WWII (despatches), Capt 1956, naval attaché Ankara 1957-59, asst chief of staff Northwood 1961-62, CO Commando Ship HMS Bulwark 1963-64, Rear Adm 1965, Flag Offr Royal Yachts 1965-70, ret; extra equerry to HM The Queen 1965; *Style*— Rear Adm Sir Patrick Morgan, KCVO, CB, DSC; Swallow Barn, Well Rd, Crondall, Farnham, Surrey GU10 5PW (☎ 0252 850107)

MORGAN, Richard Francis; s of David Francis Morgan, OBE (d 1961), of Latches, Oxshott, Surrey, and Helen Joyce, *née* Stallard (d 1971); *b* 29 August 1929; *Educ* Charterhouse, Kings Coll Cambrige (MA), Univ of London (LLB); *m* 3 Sept 1966, Sarah Pereerine, da of Cdr Edward Owen (d 1943), of Petersfield Hants; 2 s (Jonathan b 1967, Daniel b 1968); *Career* 2 Lt RASC 1948-50; fin dir: Central Wagon 1969-72, RHP Gp plc 1972-81, Laporte Industs plc 1981-84, BICC plc 1985-; fell Scottish CA's 1953-; *Recreations* mountaineering; *Style*— Richard Morgan, Esq; 11 Malbrook Rd, London SW15 (☎ 01 788 6251); BICC plc, Devonshire House, Mayfair Place, London W1X 5FH (☎ 01 629 6472)

MORGAN, Richard Martin; JP (Glos); s of His Hon Judge H Trevor Morgan, QC, DL (d 1976), of Swansea, W Glamorgan, and Leslie Martin, *née* Phillips (d 1982); *b* 25 June 1940; *Educ* Sherborne Sch, Univ of Cambridge (MA, Dip, Ed), York Univ; *m* 20 July 1968, Margaret Kathryn, step da of The Rt Rev Bishop Launcelot Fleming KCVO; 3 da (Pippa b 1969, Victoria b 1971, Rachel b 1975); *Career* asst master Radley Coll 1963 (housemaster 1969), headmaster Cheltenham Coll 1978-; pres Cheltenham Muscular Dystrophy Gp, JP Gloucs; *Recreations* watercolours, walking, rackets; *Clubs* Free Foresters, Jesters; *Style*— Richard Morgan, Esq, JP; College House, Thirlestaine Rd, Cheltenham, Glos GL53 7AA (☎ 0242 527 709)

MORGAN, Roger Hugh Vaughan Charles; o s of Charles Langbridge Morgan, FRSL, membre de l'Institut de France (d 1958), and Hilda Campbell Vaughan, FRSL (d 1985); bro of Marchioness of Anglesey, DBE, *qv*; *b* 8 July 1926; *Educ* Phillips Acad Andover Mass, Eton, BNC Oxford (MA); *m* 1, 15 Sept 1951 (m dis 1965), (Catherine Lucie) Harriet, da of Gordon Waterfield, of Hythe Kent; 1 s (James b 1955), 1 da (Lucie b 1959), and 1 s decd (Piers b 1952); m 2, 26 Feb 1965, Susan, da of Hugo Vogel (d 1966), of Milwaukee, USA; 1 s (Tobias b 1968); *Career* Gren Guards 1944-47 (Capt); House of Commons Library 1951-63; House of Lords Library 1963-, Librarian, House of Lords 1977-; *Recreations* photography, printing; *Clubs* Garrick, Beefsteak; *Style*— Roger Morgan, Esq; 30 St Peter's Square, London W6 9UH; Cliff Cottage, Laugharne, Dyfed

MORGAN, Tom; CBE (1982); s of Thomas Morgan; *b* 24 Feb 1914; *m* 1940, Mary Montgomery, da of Stephen McLauchlan; 2 s; *Career* former regional dir Unigate Ltd; Lord-Lieut for City of Edinburgh and Lord Provost of City of Edinburgh 1980-84; *Style*— Tom Morgan, Esq, CBE; 400 Lanark Rd, Edinburgh EH13 0LX (☎ 031 441 3245)

MORGAN, Prof Walter Thomas James; CBE (1959); s of Walter Morgan (d 1917), and Annie Morgan (d 1961); *b* 5 Oct 1900; *Educ* Raines Fndn, Univ of London (PhD, DSc), ETH Zurich Switzerland (Dr Sctech); *Career* Beit Meml Med res fell 1927-28, first asst and biochemist serum Dept Lister Inst 1928-37, Rockfeller res fell ETH Zurich 1936; Lister Inst: reader 1938-57, prof of biochemistry 1951-68 (now prof emeritus), dep dir 1952-68, dir 1972-75; Winner: Conway Evans Prize 1964, Karl Landsteiner Award USA 1967, Royal Medal Royal Soc 1968, Paul Ehrlich Prize Germany 1968; Hon MD Freiburg Univ 1964, Hon DSc Michigan Univ USA 1969; FRS 1949, FRCP 1982; *Clubs* Athenaeum; *Style*— Prof Walter Morgan, CBE; 57 Woodbury Drive, Sutton, Surrey SM2 5RA (☎ 01 642 2319); Clinical Research Center, Northwick Park Hospital, Harrow, Middx (☎ 01 864 5311)

MORGAN-GILES, Rear Adm Sir Morgan Charles; DSO (1944), OBE (1943, MBE 1942), GM (1942), DL (Hants 1983); s of F C Morgan-Giles, OBE (Naval Architect, d 1964), of Teignmouth, Devon, and Ivy Carus-Wilson (d 1936); *b* 19 June 1914; *Educ* Clifton; *m* 1, 11 May 1946, Pamela (d 1966), da of Philip Bushell, of Sydney, Australia; 2 s (Philip b 1949, Rodney (m Sarah, da of Sir Hereward Wake, Bt, *qv*) b 1955), 4 da (Penelope (m Nigel Cartwright) b 1947, Melita (m Victor Lampson, s of late Lord Killearn) b 1951, Camilla (m John, er s of Sir Eric Drake, CBE, DL, *qv*) b 1953, d 1988), Alexandra (m Maj Edward Bolitho) b 1958); *Career* Cadet RN 1932, China Station 1933-35, HMS Echo 1936, torpedo specialist 1938; WWII: Atlantic convoys, Norway, Med, West Desert and Tobruk Garrison 1942, attached RAF 1942, sr naval offr visiting (Dalmatia) and liaison with Commandos and Marshal Tito's partisan Forces 1943-44, RN Staff Coll 1945, Force W In Bangkok and Far East, HMS Norfolk 1946; Trieste 1948-49, i/c HMS Chieftain 1950-51, Admty 1953-54, Capt chief of intelligence staff Far East 1953-54, Capt (D) Dartmouth Trg Sqdn 1957-58, Capt HMS Vernon 1959-60, i/c HMS Belfast Far East Station 1961-62, Rear Adm Pres RN Coll Greenwich 1962, ret 1964; vice chm Cons Def Ctee 1965-75, chm HMS Belfast Tst 1971-78, vice pres RNLI 1985- (memb mgmnt ctee 1981-); MP (Cons) Winchester 1964-79; Princ Warden Worshipful Co of Shipwrights 1987-88 (memb 1965-); Partisan Star Yugoslavia 1953; kt 1985; *Recreations* sailing (yacht 'Melita'), country pursuits; *Clubs* Royal Yacht Squadron, Carlton, Australian (Sydney); *Style*— Rear Adm Sir Morgan Morgan-Giles, DSO, OBE, GM, DL; Frenchmoor Farm, West Tytherley, Salisbury SP5 1NU (☎ 0794 41045)

MORGAN-GRENVILLE, Gerard Wyndham; s of Maj Hon Robert William Morgan-Grenville, gv, and Elizabeth Hope *née* Bine Renshaw (d 1968); *b* 26 Mar 1931; *Educ* Eton; *m* 1, 27 April 1955 (m dis 1981), Virginia Anne, da of Major Peto, MP; 2 s (Hugo b 5 Aug 1958, George b 4 June 1964), 1 da (Laura b 1 Jan 1961); m 2, 1984, Fern, *née* Roberts; *Career* Nat Serv Rifle Bde 1951-53, ADC to Gen Festing (Chief of Staff SHAPE) 1952-53; dir: Dexam Int Ltd (fndr), Dexam Int Hldgs Ltd, Industl Agencies Ltd, Goodwood Metalcraft Ltd, Charterbarge Ltd, Charterbarge Sarl (France), Quarry Trading Co, Great Scottish and Western Railway Ltd; chm Soc for Environmental Improvement, vice pres Abercombie and Kent Inc, chm and fndr Nat Centre for Alternative Technol; cmmr Countryside Cmmn 1983-85, memb Countryside Cmmn for Wales 1983-84; *Books* Cruising the Sahara, Barging into France, Barging into Burgundy, Barging into Southern France, Nuclear Power - What it means to you; *Recreations* walking, exploring, sand-yachting; *Clubs* St James'; *Style*— Gerard Morgan-Grenville, Esq; Le Manoir De L'Eglise, Sully 14400 Bayeux, France (☎ 010 3331 2147 12, fax 010 333 121 5734)

MORGAN-JONES, Digby; s of Stanley Alfred Morgan Jones (d 1984), of Beach Lodge, Lane End, Bembridge, IoW, and Eileen Mary Morgan-Jones (d 1973); *b* 14 April 1931; *Educ* Merchant Taylors'; *m* 27 June 1959, Jean, da of Charles Paterson (d 1969), of Hove, Sussex; 2 s (Kevin b 8 Nov 1961, Paul b 2 May 1967), 1 da (Fiona b 30 Dec 1964); *Career* nat serv RAF 1955-71; CA 1954-, RCA in Practice Wenham Crane (ptnr 1962-); former pres Soc of Association Executives, previously dir: Samuel Royston Dvpts Ltd, Travel Ideas Ltd; dir: Clean Air Soc; dir: The Federation of Piling Specialists, chm Assoc of Industrial Filter and Separator Manufactors; exec sec Nat Association Title Distributers; Sec Federation of Drum Reconditioners; FCA; *Recreations* sport, youth work (crusaders and scouts); *Clubs* Canning; *Style*— Digby Morgan-Jones, Esq; Meadowsteep, Berry Lane, Chorleywood, Herts WD3 5EY (☎ 09278 2123); 20/21 Tooks Court, London EC4A 1LA (☎ 01 831 7581)

MORGAN-OWEN, John Gethin; CB (1984), MBE (1945), QC (1981); s of Maj-Gen Llewellyn Isaac Gethin Morgan-Owen, CB, CMB, CBE, DSO (d 1960), of Alton, Hants, and Ethel Berry, *née* Walford (d 1950); family descends from Sir John Owen, Royalist Sgt-Maj-Gen in N Wales during Civil War; *b* 22 August 1914; *Educ* Shrewsbury, Trinity Coll Oxford (BA); *m* 1950, Mary, da of Capt Frederick James Rimington, MBE, (d 1941); 2 s (Gethin, Huw), 1 da (Margaret); *Career* served WWII, 2 Lt Supplementary Res S Wales Borderers 1939, N Norway 1940, D Day landing 1944, 2 Bn S Wales Borderers 1939-44, DAA & QMG 146 Inf Bde 1944-45; barr Inner Temple, Wales & Chester circuit, practised at Cardiff, dep judge advocate 1952, dep judge advocate gen Germany 1953-56, vice judge advocate gen 1972-74, judge advocate gen of the Forces 1979-84, jt chm disciplinary appeals ctee ICAEW 1985-87, asst judge advocate gen 1986; *Recreations* beagling, inland waterways, travel; *Clubs* Army and Navy; *Style*— John Morgan-Owen, Esq, CB, MBE, QC; St Nicholas House, Kingsley Bordon, Hants GU35 9NW

MORGAN-OWEN, John Maddox; DL (Derby 1986); s of Lt-Col Morgan Maddox Morgan-Owen, DSO, TD, JP (d 1950), of Willington Hall, Derbys, and Doris Marjorie, *née* Turner (d 1957); *b* 26 June 1931; *Educ* Shrewsbury; *m* 4 Oct 1958, Elsa Courtenay (Jill), da of Cdr Ronald Arthur Orlando Bridgeman, RD, RNR (d 1962), of Rockliffe Hall, Flintshire; 1 s (Timothy Maddox b 1961); *Career* Derbyshire Yeo 1949-52, 24 Regt of Foot S Wales Borderers 1952-55; insurance conslt; gen cmmr of Income Tax 1972-, chm E Mids Museum Serv 1988-; memb: Derbyshire CC 1967- (dep ldr Cons gp 1977-), S Derbyshire Dist Cncl 1973-79, COSIRA Derbyshire ctee 1972-88; vice chm Derbyshire Historic Bldgs Tst 1984-; *Recreations* shooting, music; *Clubs* MCC; *Style*— John Morgan-Owen, Esq, DL; Pennfield House, Melbourne, Derby DE1 1EQ (☎ 0332 862774)

MORGAN-WITTS, Maxwell; s of George Frederick Vincent Lionel Morgan-Witts (d 1944); *b* 27 Sept 1931; *Educ* Mount Royal Coll Calgary, Acad of TV and Film Arts Toronto; *m* 1958, Pauline Ann Lynette, da of Alan Lawson (d 1982); 1 s, 1 da; *Career* CBC TV actor/presenter 1952; radio prodr/writer India, Ceylon, Aust and Canada 1953-55; Granada TV exec prodr 1956-64; BBC TV documentary film series exec-ed 1964-72; author, indep prodr of films and corporate videos 1972-; *Books* (written with a co-author) incl: The San Francisco Earthquake, Voyage of the Damned, The Day Guernica Died, Ruin From The Air, The Day The Bubble Burst, Pontiff, The Year of Armageddon; *Recreations* sailing, swimming, skiing, theatre, travel; *Clubs* Hurlingham Racquet Club; *Style*— Maxwell Morgan-Witts, Esq; 3 Place du Lac, Le Village, Les Hauts de Vaugrenier, 06270 Villeneuve-Loubet, France; 26 Woodsford Sq, London W14 8DP

MORIARTY, QC (1974) Gerald Evelyn; s of Lt Col Gerald Rwash Moriarty (d 1981), and Eileen, *née* Maloney (d 1978); *b* 23 August 1928; *Educ* Downside, St John's Coll Oxford (MA); *m* 17 June 1961, Judith Mary, da of Hon William Robert Atkin (d 1984); 4 s (Michael b 25 Aug 1962, Matthew b 12 Aug 1963, Thomas b 20 Jan 1966, John b 12 Jan 1973); *Career* call to Bar Lincoln's Inn 1951, rec 1976, chm exam in public Bedfordshire Structure Plan 1978, bencher 1983, memb gen cncl Bar 1986-; *Recreations* golf, reading; *Clubs* Reform; *Style*— Gerald Moriarty, Esq, QC; 3 Stone Buildings, Lincoln's Inn, London WC2A 3XL (☎ 01 430 2318); 2 Mitre Court Buildings, Temple, London EC4Y 7BX (☎ 01 583 1380)

MORIARTY, Brig Joan Olivia Elsie; CB (1979), RRC (1977); da of Lt-Col Oliver Nash Moriarty, DSO (d 1974), of Pyleigh, Lydeard St Lawrence, Taunton, Somerset, and Georgina Elsie, *née* Moore (d 1974); *b* 11 May 1923; *Educ* Royal Sch Bath, St Thomas's Hosp (nurse trg), Queen Charlotte's Hosp Hammersmith (midwifery trg); *Career* joined QAIMNS (later QARANC) res 1947, reg cmmn 1948; served: UK, Gibraltar, Singapore, Malaya, Cyprus, BAOR; Maj 1960, Lt-Col 1971, Col 1973, matron Mil Hosp Catterick 1973-76, cmdt QARANC Trg Centre Aldershot 1976, Brig 1976, matron-in-chief and dir of Army Nursing Servs 1976-80, ret 1981; govr Royal Sch Bath 1978-88, tstee QARANC, tstee Queen Mary's Roehampton Hosp Tst; OStJ 1977; *Recreations* country pursuits, travel; *Clubs* Naval and Military; *Style*— Brig Joan Moriarty, CB, RRC

MORIARTY, Michael John Patrick; s of Alexander Hugo Moriarty; *b* 22 Nov 1942; *Educ* St Stephen's, Welling, Kent; *m* 1965, Pearl Joy; 1 s, 2 da; *Career* memb Stock Exchange 1977; dir: Shaw & Marvin Ltd 1978-80, Zootopia 1979-83; *Recreations* gardening; *Style*— Michael Moriarty Esq; Woodside, Foxendown Lane, Meopham, Kent (☎ 0474 812232)

MORISON, Hugh; s of Archibald Ian Morison, of 19 Old Rectory Gardens, Felpham, Sussex, and Enid Rose, *née* Mawer; *b* 22 Nov 1943; *Educ* Chichester HS for Boys, St Catherine's Coll Oxford; (MA); *m* 1971, Marion, da of Fred Aubrey Smithers, of 84 Yarborough Crescent, Lincoln; 2 da (Emma b 1972, Lucy b 1975); *Career* civil servant Scottish Off 1966-; under sec Scottish Home and Health Dept 1984-; *Recreations* hill walking, cycling, literature, archeology; *Clubs* Royal Commonwealth Soc; *Style*— Hugh Morison, Esq; Scottish Office, St Andrew's House, Edinburgh EH1 3DE (☎ 031 556 8400)

MORISON, John Lowson; s of John Miller Morison (d 1982), of Mavisbank, Guildtown, Perth, and Janet Muriel, *née* Jackson; *b* 6 May 1945; *Educ* Cargilfield, Edinburgh, Rugby, Univ of Edinburgh; *m* 22 May 1970, Gillian Anne, da of (John) Kirke Craig (d 1984), of Rock Cottage, Clachan Seil, by Oban Argyll; 3 s ((John) Courtenay b 1971, Barclay Jackson b 1972, Barnaby Lowson b 1977), 1 da (Nicola Helen b 1976); *Career* farmer£Australia and NZ 1965-67, former dist cncllr, dir Royal Highland and Agric Soc Scotland, memb exec bd Nat Sheep Assoc; *Recreations* shooting, skiing, tennis, sailing; *Clubs* Royal Perth Golfing Soc, Clyde Corinthian Sailing; *Style*— John Morison, Esq; Newmiln, Guildtown, Perth PH2 6AE (☎ 0738 51132)

MORISON, Hon Lord; (Alastair) Malcolm Morison; QC (1965); s of Sir Ronald Morison, QC (d 1975), of Iden Sussex, and Frances Isabelle Salvesen; *b* 12 Feb 1931;

Educ Winchester; *m* 1, (m dis 1975), Lindsay Oatts, 1957; 1 s (Simon), 1 da (Joanna) m 2, 1979, Birgitte Hendil; *Career* senator Coll of Justice in Scotland 1985; *Recreations* fishing, golf; *Clubs* New (Edinburgh); *Style*— The Hon Lord Morison, QC; 6 Carlton Terr, Edinburgh (☎ 031 556 6766); Parliament House, Edinburgh

MORISON, Thomas Richard Atkin; QC (1979); s of late Harold Thomas Brash Morison, of Ensor Mews, London, and Hon Nancy Morison, *née* Atkin (d 1978); gs of Lord Atkin (Baron Atkin of Aberdovey) and Lord Morison; *b* 15 Jan 1939; *Educ* Winchester, Oxford Univ (MA); *m* 1963, Judith Rachel Walton, da of Rev R J W Morris, OBE, of Shaftesbury; 1 s (Ben b 1969), 1 da (Lucy b 1967); *Recreations* reading, walking, dogs; *Clubs* Oriental; *Style*— Thomas Morison, Esq, QC; Fountain Ct, Temple, London EC4 9DH (☎ 01 353 7356, telex 8813408 FONLEG G)

MORLAND, Charles F H; s of Sir Oscar Morland, GBE, KCMG (d 1980), and Alice, *née* Lindley; *b* 4 Sept 1939; *Educ* Ampleforth, Kings Coll Cambridge (MA); *m* 19 Sept 1964, Victoria, da of Lt-Col R B Longe, of Suffolk; 2 s (Nicholas b 1967, Henry b 1969); *Career* md Riggs AP Bank Ltd; *Recreations* opera, travel; *Style*— Charles F H Morland, Esq; Marston Hill Farm, Greatworth, Banbury, Oxfordshire (☎ 029576 639)

MORLAND, Martin Robert; CMG (1985); s of Sir Oscar Morland, GBE, KCMG (d 1980), and Alice, da of Rt Hon Sir F O Lindley, GCMG, PC; *b* 23 Sept 1933; *m* 1964, Jennifer Avril Mary Hanbury-Tracy; 2 s, 1 da; *Career* Nat Serv Grenadier Gds 1954-56; HM Dip Serv: Br Embassy Rangoon 1957-60, News Dept FO 1961, UK Delgn Geneva 1965-67, private sec to Lord Chalfont 1967-68, Euro integration dept FCO 1965-73, cnsllr Rome 1973-77, seconded to Cabinet Off as head of EEC Referendum Unit 1975, head of maritime aviation and enviroment dept FCO 1977-79, cnsllr and head of Chancery Washington 1979-82, seconded to Hardcastle & Co Ltd 1982-84, under-sec Cabinet Off 1984-86, ambass to Burma 1986-; *Clubs* Garrick; *Style*— Martin R Morland, Esq, CMG; c/o FCO, London SW1

MORLAND, Miles Quintin; s of Cdr Henry Morland, RN, and Vivienne Yzabel Suzanne Nicholson Walters, *née* Hogg; *b* 18 Dec 1943; *Educ* Radley, Lincoln Coll Oxford; *m* 10 March 1972, Guislaine, da of Guy Vincent Chastenet de la Maisoneuve; 2 da (Catherine Natasha b 29 Aug 1973, Georgia Susanna b 18 Dec 1976); *Career* md The First Boston Corpn 1983-; *Recreations* foreign weekends; *Clubs* Travellers (Paris); *Style*— Miles Morland, Esq; 6 Hereford Sq, London SW7; United Kingdom House, 2A Great Titchfield St, London W1

MORLEY, Cecil Denis; CBE (1967); s of late Cornelius Cecil Morley; *b* 1911; *Educ* Clifton, Trinity Coll Cambridge; *m* 1936, Lily Florence, da of Edward Albert Younge; 1 s; *Career* served in 1939-45 War as Maj RA (TA); slr 1935; sec to Cncl of Stock Exchange London 1949-65, sec-gen 1965-71; *Recreations* gardening, travel; *Style*— Denis Morley, Esq, CBE; Bearsward, Coastal Rd, Kingston Gorse, W Sussex BN16 1SJ (☎ 0903 782837)

MORLEY, Lady; Hedy Katharina; da of late Prof Julius von Landesberger-Antburg, of Vienna; *m* 1939, Sir Alexander Francis Morley, KCMG, CBE (d 1971); *Style*— Lady Morley; 47 Campden Hill Sq, W8

MORLEY, 6 Earl of (UK 1815); Lt-Col John St Aubyn (Parker); JP (Plymouth 1972); Viscount Boringdon (UK 1815), Baron Boringdon (GB 1784); s of Hon John Holford Parker (d 1955); suc unc, 5 Earl, 1962; *b* 29 May 1923; *Educ* Eton; *m* 1955, Johanna Katherine, da of Sir John Molesworth-St Aubyn, 14 Bt, CBE; 1 s, 1 da; *Heir* s, Viscount Boringdon; *Career* 2 Lt KRRC 1942, transferred to Royal Fus 1947; served: NW Europe 1944-45, Palestine and Egypt 1945-48, Korea 1952-53 and Middle East 1953-55 and 1956; Staff Coll Camberley 1957, cmd 1 Bn Royal Fus 1965-67, Lt-Col, ret 1970; pres: Plymouth Inc Chamber of Trade and Commerce 1970-, W Country Tourist Bd 1971-, Fedn of C of C and Traders Assocs of Co of Cornwall 1972-79; chm Farm Indust Ltd Truro 1970-86; regnl dir Devon and Cornwall Regnl Bd Lloyds Bank 1971; dir: Lloyds Bank Ltd 1974-78, Lloyds Bank UK Mgmnt Ltd 1978-85; chm Plymouth Sound Ltd 1974-; govr: Seale-Hayne Agric Coll 1973, Plymouth Poly 1975-82 (chm 1977-82); memb Devon and Cornwall Regnl Ctee of Nat Tst 1969-84; Devon: DL 1973, Vice Lord-Lt 1978-82, Lord-Lt 1982-; KStJ; pres: Cncl of Order of St John for Devon 1979, Devon Co FA; Hon Col: Devon ACF 1978-87, 4 Bn Devonshire and Dorset Regt 1987-; *Style*— The Rt Hon the Earl of Morley, JP; Pound House, Buckland Monachorum, Yelverton, S Devon PL20 7LJ (☎ 0822 853162)

MORLEY, Michael Harlow Fenton; s of Very Rev Dean Fenton Morley, of Bath, and Marjorie Rosa, *née* Robinson; *b* 18 June 1940; *Educ* Radley, Cambridge Univ (MA), Univ of Harvard (MBA); *m* 1963, Delia Elizabeth, da of Charles J Robertson, of Combe Hay Manor, Bath (d 1983); 1 s (Oliver b 1971), 2 da (Candida b 1965, Octavia b 1968); *Career* Samuel Montagu & Co 1968-72, chm London & Western Tst Ltd 1972-74, chief exec C Tennant Sons & Co Ltd 1974-81, md Charterhouse Gp plc 1981-84, chm Paragon Gp Ltd 1984-89, chief exec and dep chm Portals Hldgs plc 1988-; Monteverdi Tst 1985-; dir (non exec) Globe Investmt Tst plc 1989-, Close Brothers Gp plc 1985-; *Recreations* tennis, shooting, skiing, piano and organ; *Clubs* Brooks's, Leander; *Style*— Michael Morley, Esq; The Manor House, Priston, Bath BA2 9EH; 12 Kensington Place, London W8 7PT

MORLEY, Dr (William) Neil; RD (1969, clasp 1979); s of Eric Morley, JP (d 1964), of 22 North Park Rd, Bradford, West Yorks, and Barbara, *née* Mitchell (d 1986); *b* 16 Feb 1930; *Educ* Merchiston Castle Sch Edinburgh, Edinburgh Univ (MB ChB); *m* 13 March 1958, Patricia, da of Walter McDonald; 3 s (David b 1963, Alistair b 1964, Christopher b 1966), 1 da (Carolyn b 1961); *Career* Surgn Lt HMS Falcon 1955-57, served Malta, Surgn Lt Cdr RNR 1959-84; conslt dermatologist Gtr Glasgow Health Bd 1963-, civil conslt to RN in Scotland 1979-; memb med appeal tbnl DHSS 1979; memb Incorp of Barbers of Glasgow 1975, FRCP Edinburgh, FRCP Glasgow 1975, FRSM; *Books* Colour Atlas of Paediatric Dermatology; *Recreations* golf, fishing; *Clubs* Glasgow GC; *Style*— Dr Neil Morley, RD; Parkhall, Balfron, Glasgow G63 OLQ (☎ 0360 40124)

MORLEY, Norman (Eyre); DSC (and 3 bars); s of Nathaniel Eyre Morley the artist (d 1898), and Annie Elizabeth, *née* Howell (d 1939); *b* 6 Jan 1899; *Educ* Battersea GS, Post Graduate Course Architect, Northern Polytechnic, UCL; *m* 26 April 1930, Audrey Lillian, da of Seymour Tuely (d 1946); 1 s (James Eyre b 1938), 1 da (Pamela Audrey b 1931); *Career* WWI joined Harrison's Rennie Line as Cadet 1915, Temp Midshipman RNR HMS Excellent 1916, HMS Iron Duke 1917, coastal motor boats 1917-19; took part in Zeebrugge operation and awarded DSC for attack on Kurundstadt Harbour; served London Div RNVR 1921-33; WWII rejoined RNVR (Lieut) HMS Hebe (took part in Dunkirk operation) 1939-41, HMS Eastbourne (Lt Cdr) in cmd mine sweeping N Sea (despatches) 1941-42, cmd HMS Mutine (bar to DSC for duties at Salerno) 1942-44, CDR HMS Rhyl (second bar to DSC for work in S France landings and third bar for mine sweeping Gulf of Patras) 1944, cmd HMS Acute 1945; architect in private practice before joining architect's dept of Courage (Brewers) Ltd in 1930 becoming chief architect to Courage Gp; ret 1964; donated medals to RN Museum Portsmouth; *Recreations* painting, sailing, pig breeding, calf rearing; *Style*— Norman Morley, Esq, DSC

MORLEY, Peter John; s of Edward Joseph Morley, and Edith Ella, *née* Westerside; *b* 9 August 1955; *Educ* Thorpe House, Hutton; *m* 29 June 1985, Amanda Julie Jane, da of Edward Ashton St John Salt; 1 s (Edward James Peter b 21 Nov 1988); *Career* account exec Eagle Alexander 1977-81, account dir Travel Press Serv 1981-83, dir SGL Communications plc Gp 1983-, md SGL Property Ltd 1983-; MIPR, PRCA; *Recreations* shooting, most sport, boys trips; *Clubs* RAC, Annabels, Scribes; *Style*— Peter Morley, Esq; SGL, Kingsgate House, 536 Kings Rd, London SW10 0UH (☎ 01 351 2377)

MORLEY, Sheridan Robert; s of Robert Morley and Joan, *née* Buckmaster; *b* 5 Dec 1941; *Educ* Sizewell Hall Suffolk, Merton Coll Oxford (MA); *m* 1965, Margaret Gudejko; 1 s, 2 da; *Career* newscaster, reporter and scriptwriter ITN 1964-67, interviewer Late Night Line Up BBC 2 1967-71, presenter Film Night BBC 2 1972, dep features ed The Times 1973-75, drama critic and arts ed Punch 1975-89, London Drama Critic Int Herald Tribune 1979-; regular presenter: Kaleidoscope BBC Radio 4, Meridian BBC World Service; frequent radio and tv broadcasts on the performing arts; memb Drama Panel Br Cncl 1982-, narrator: Side by Side by Sondheim 1981-82, Noël and Gertie (Coward anthology) 1983-86; *Books* A Talent to Amuse: the life of Noël Coward (1969), Review Copies (1975), Oscar Wilde (1976), Sybil Thorndike (1977), Marlene Dietrich (1977), Gladys Cooper (1979), Noël Coward and his Friends (1979), The Stephen Sondheim Songbook (1979), Gertrude Lawrence (1981), The Noël Coward Diaries (1982), Tales from the Hollywood Raj (1983), Shooting Stars (1983), The Theatregoers' Quiz Book (1983), Katherine Hepburn (1984), editor of theatre annuals and film and theatre studies including Punch at the Theatre (1980), The Other Side of The Moon (the biography of David Niven) and Spread A Little Happiness (1987), Elizabeth Taylor (1988), Out in the Midday Sun (1988), Odd Man Out: The Life of James Mason (1989); contributions to The Times, Evening Standard, Radio Times, Mail on Sunday, Sunday Telegraph, Playbill (NY), High Life and The Australian; *Recreations* talking, swimming, eating, narrating Side by Side by Sondheim and Noël and Gertie; *Clubs* Garrick; *Style*— Sheridan Morley, Esq; Prince of Wales Theatre offices, Coventry St, London W1 (☎ 01 930 6677, fax 01 930 0091)

MORLEY-JOEL, Lionel; s of Samuel Joel (d 1970), of Finchley, and Hannah, *née* Parker (d 1979); great nephew of Solly Joel the colourful character who became a diamond magnate in S Africa; *b* 2 Jan 1922; *Educ* Finchley HS, later business studies at an Acad in Brussels; *m* 1, 25 Feb 1943, Joyce Margaret, da of Frederick Charles Grierson (d 1961); 1 da (Wendy b 1947); m 2, 30 Aug 1986, Maria Christina, da of Charles Lett Lynch (d 1986); *Career* fndr Newbourne Publishing Gp 1946 (md and chm 1946-84), md Classic Publications 1954-84, dir Recorder Press 1952-84, md City and Rural Properties 1985-87, currently dir Magnat Advertising and conslt in advertising and marketing to Newbourne Gp (now a subsidiary of Ladbroke plc); *Recreations* golf, amateur radio, horology; *Style*— Lionel Morley-Joel, Esq; Whitespar, Queen Hoo Lane, Rewin, Herts AL6 0LT (☎ 043 879 201, business 01 388 3171)

MORNINGTON, Earl of; Arthur Gerald Wellesley; s and h of Marquess of Douro, and HRH Princess Antonia von Preussen; gs of 8 Duke of Wellington; *b* 31 Jan 1978; *Style*— Earl of Mornington

MORO, Hon Mrs (Anne Margaret Theodosia); da of 5 Baron Huntingfield, KCMG (d 1969); *b* 1918; *m* 1940 (m dis 1984), Peter Moro; 3 da; *Style*— The Hon Mrs Moro

MORONY, Gen Sir Thomas Lovett; KCB (1981), OBE (1969); s of Thomas Henry Morony, CSI, CIE (d 1962); sometime inspr-gen of Police Centl Provinces, of India, and Berar), and Evelyn Myra (d 1984), eld da of Rt Rev Ernest Lovett, CBE, sometime Bp of Salisbury; *b* 23 Sept 1926; *Educ* Eton; *m* 22 April 1961, Elizabeth, da of G W N Clark (d 1955), of Upperlands, Co Derry; 2 s (Thomas George Michael b 1962, Matthew Lovett b 1964); *Career* cmmnd RA 1947, served Palestine, N Africa, Germany, Hong Kong, E Africa and Belgium, Bde Maj King's African Rifles 1958-61, GSO 2 DS Staff Coll Camberley 1963-64, GSO 2 DS Royal Mil Staff Coll of Science 1964-65, GSO 1 HQ Northern Army Gp (NATO) 1965-67, cmd 22 Air Def Regt RA 1967-69, cmd 1 Artillery Bde 1970-73, dep cmdt Staff Coll Camberley 1973-75, dir RA 1975-78, Cmdt RMCS 1978-80, VCGS 1980-83, UK mil rep to HQ NATO 1983-86; Col cmdt: RA 1978-, RHA 1983-; Master Gunner St James's Park 1983-88; ADC Gen to HM The Queen 1984-86; chm govrs Sherborne Sch; pres CCF Assoc; vice-pres Royal Patriotic Fund; *Recreations* music, country pursuits; *Clubs* Army and Navy; *Style*— Gen Sir Thomas Morony, KCB, OBE; c/o Bank of Scotland, 8 Morningside Rd, Edinburgh EH10 4DD

MORPETH, Sir Douglas Spottiswoode; TD; s of Robert Spottiswoode Morpeth (d 1979), and Louisa Rankine, *née* Dobson; *b* 6 June 1924; *Educ* George Watson's Coll Edinburgh, Edinburgh Univ (BCom); *m* 1951, Anne Rutherford, da of Ian Cardean Bell, OBE, MC (d 1966); 2 s, 2 da; *Career* Lt-Col cmdg 1 Regt HAC (RHA) 1964-66, former sr ptnr Touche Ross & Co, chm Clerical Medical & Gen Life Assurance Soc, first chm tstees Br Telecom Staff Superannuation Scheme 1982-, dep chm Brixton Estate plc, chm British Borneo Petroleum Syndicate; dir: Allied Irish Bank, Pergamon AGB; dep chm Leslie Langton Hldgs Ltd; vice-pres HAC 1986-88, Master Worshipful Co of Chartered Accountants 1977, hon tres Royal Coll of Music 1984-; FCA, FRCM; kt 1981; *Recreations* golf, tennis, gardening; *Clubs* Athenaeum, RAC, City Livery; *Style*— Sir Douglas Morpeth, TD; Summerden House, Shamley Green, nr Guildford, Surrey GU5 0UD (☎ 0483 892689); Clerical Medical Investment Gp, 15 St James's Sq, London SW1Y 4LQ (☎ 01 930 5474, fax 01 321 1846)

MORPETH, Viscount; George William Beaumont Howard; Master of Ruthven; s and h of 12 Earl of Carlisle, MC; *b* 15 Feb 1949; *Educ* Eton, Balliol Coll Oxford; *Heir* Master of Ruthven; *Career* joined 9/12 Royal Lancers 1967, Lt 1970, Capt 1974, Maj (Prince of Wales, Royal Armoured Corps) 1981-87, Parly candidate (Lib) Easington Co Durham 1987; *Clubs* Beefsteak,; *Style*— Maj Viscount Morpeth; 8 Mill Terrace, Easington Village, County Durham (☎ 0915 272946)

MORPURGO DAVIES, Prof Anna Elbina Laura Margherita; da of Augusto Morpurgo (d 1939), and Maria, *née* Castelnuovo, of Rome; *b* 21 June 1937; *Educ* Liceo-Ginnasio Giulio Cesare Rome, Univ of Rome (MA); *m* 8 Sept 1962 (m dis 1978), John Kenyon Davies, s of Harold Davies; *Career* assistente in classical philology Univ of Rome 1959-61, jr fell Center for Hellenic Studies Washington DC 1961-62, univ lectr in classical philology Oxford Univ 1964-71, fell St Hilda's Coll Oxford 1966-71, prof of comparative philology Univ of Oxford 1971-, fell Somerville Coll Oxford 1971-; visiting prof: Univ of Pennsylvania 1971, Yale Univ 1977; Collitz prof Linguistic Soc of America 1975, Semple lectr Univ of Cincinnati 1983, TBL Webster prof Stanford Univ 1988; hon fell St Hilda's Coll Oxford 1971; Hon DLitt St Andrews Univ 1981; FBA 1985, FSA 1974, foreign hon memb American Acad of Arts & Sciences 1986, corresponding memb Oesterreichische Akademie der Wissenschaften (Wien) 1988; *Books* Mycenaeae Graecitatis Lexicon (1963), Linear B A 1984 Survey (ed with Y Duhoux, 1985); numerous articles in Br and foreign periodicals; *Style—* Prof Anna Morpurgo Davies; Somerville College, Oxford OX2 6HD (☎ 270 600)

MORRELL, Lady; Audrey Louise; da of Louis Alston, of Port of Spain, Trinidad; *m* 1924, Capt Sir Arthur Routley Hutson Morrell, KBE (d 1968); 2 s (Robert David, John Alston); *Style—* Lady Morrell; Thamesfield House, Wargrave Road, Henley-on-Thames, Oxon

MORRELL, Frances Maine; *née* Galleway; da of Frank and Beatrice Galleway; *b* 28 Dec 1937; *Educ* Queen Anne Sch York; *m* 1964, Brian Morrell; 1 da; *Career* leader ILEA 1983-87; memb GLC Islington S and Finsbury 1981-86; former policy advsr to: Sec of State for Indust, Sec of State for Energy ;1974-79; memb Sadler's Wells bd of dirs; *Books* From the Elect of Bristol a study of consultants grievances, A Ten Year Industrial Strategy for Britain (with Benn and Cripps) A Planned Energy Policy for Britain (with Benn and Cripps), Manifesto: A radical strategy for Britains future (with others); *Style—* Mrs Frances Morrell; c/o County Hall, London SE1 7PB

MORRELL, John; s of John Morrell (d 1938), of Sunderland, and Dorothy Ann, *née* Thompson; *Educ* Beds Collegiate Sunderland; *m* 27 Dec 1947, Nora, da of John Edward Bates (d 1960), of Ripley, Derbys; 1 s (Nicholas John b 9 July 1952), 1 da (Patricia Margaret b 28 July 1957); *Career* WWII RAF 1940-46, radar mechanic Lancaster Sqdn radar teacher Cranwell; CA; ptnr W J James & Co Brecon S Wales 1952-; former pres Brecon Chamber of Trade, tres Brecon Rotary Club, fndr and former Capt Penoyre GC; FCA 1951; *Recreations* golf, sports; *Clubs* Cradoc GC; *Style—* John Morrell, Esq; Brendon, 1 Sunnybank, Brecon, Powys LD3 7RW (☎ 0874 2576); Bishop House, 10 Wheat St, Brecon, Powys LD3 7DG (☎ 0874 2381, fax 0874 2427)

MORRELL, Leslie James; OBE (1986), JP (1962); s of James Morrell, DL, and Eileen, *née* Browne; *b* 26 Dec 1931; *Educ* Portora Royal Sch Enniskillen, Queen's Univ Belfast (BA agric); *m* 1958, Anne, da of Robert W Wallace, OBE (d 1973), of Belfast; 2 s (Richard, Jonathan), 1 da (Clare); *Career* Londonderry CC 1968-73, NI Assembly 1973-75, Miny of Agric NI Exec 1973-74, fndr chm James Butcher Housing Assoc Ltd 1976 (sec 1982-); chm: Virus Tested Seed Potato Growers' Assoc 1978-88, NI Water Cncl 1982, NI Agric Advsy Ctee of BBC 1986-, Gen Advsy Ctee of BBC 1980-86; fndr memb: NI Fedn Housing Assoc (chm 1978-80), NI Inst of Agric Science 1960-; memb: Coleraine Borough Cncl 1973-77, Royal Ulster Agric Soc; landowner; *Style—* Leslie J Morrell, Esq, OBE, JP; Dunboe House, Castlerock, Coleraine, BT51 4UB (☎ 0265 848352)

MORRELL, Peter Richard; s of Frank Richard Morrell (d 1974), of Whitehill House, Dane End, Hertfordshire, and Florence Ethel, *née* Gleave; *b* 25 May 1944; *Educ* Westminster, Univ Coll Oxford (MA); *m* 6 June 1970, (Helen) Mary Vint, da of Capt William Norman Collins, of Peterborough; 2 da (Helen b 1971, Harriet b 1976); *Career* slr 1970 barr 1974, asst recr 1986-; chm Nassington and Yarwell Cons Assoc, pres Nassington and Yarwell Garden Soc; govr Harrogate Ladies' Coll, Parly candidate Ilkeston Derbys 1974; *Recreations* fishing, stalking, photography, writing; *Style—* Peter Morrell, Esq; 2 Crown Office Row, Temple, London EC4Y 7HJ (☎ 01 353 1365, fax 01 353 4591)

MORRIS *see also*: Temple-Morris

MORRIS, Air Marshal Sir (Arnold) Alec; KBE (1981), CB (1979); s of Harry Morris; *b* 11 Mar 1926; *Educ* King Edward VI Sch E Retford, King's Coll London, Southampton Univ; *m* 1946, Moyna Patricia, da of Norman Boyle; 1 s (Piers), 1 da (Susan (twin)); *Career* RAF 1945, RCDS 1974, dir Signals 1975-76, dir gen Strategic Electronic Systems MOD 1976-79; AO Engrg HQ Strike Cmd 1979, ch engr RAF 1981-83, ret; exec British Aerospace 1984-; pres Soc Electronic and Radio Technicians 1975-80; *Style—* Air Marshal Sir Alec Morris, KBE, CB; 6 Liverpool Rd, Kingston-upon-Thames, Surrey

MORRIS, Rt Hon Alfred; PC (1979), QSO (1989), MP (Lab & Co-op) Manchester Wythenshawe 1964-; s of George Henry Morris, and Jessie, *née* Murphy; *b* 23 Mar 1928; *Educ* Ruskin Coll Oxford, St Catherine's Coll Oxford; *m* 1950, Irene Jones; 2 s, 2 da; *Career* former schoolmaster; contested (Lab & Co-op) Liverpool Garston 1951; PPS to: Min Ag Fish and Food 1964-67, lord pres of cncl and ldr of House of Commons 1968-70; memb Gen Advsy Cncl BBC 1968-74 and 1983-; chm PLP Food and Agric Gp 1971-74 (vice-chm 1970-71), Britain's first Min for the Disabled 1974-79; chm World Planning Gp appointed to draft "charter for the 1980s" for disabled people world wide 1979-80; oppn front bench spokesman: social services 1979-81 (and 1970-74), and on the disabled 1981-; chm: Co-op Parly Gp 1982-, Anzac Gp of MPs and Peers 1982-; jt tres British-American Parly Gp 1983-; piloted Chronically Sick and Disabled Persons Act 1970 through Parl as a private memb, also the Food and Drugs (Milk) Act 1970 and the Police Act 1972; first recipient of Field Marshal Lord Harding Award for distinguished service to the disabled 1971; Louis Braille Memorial Award for outstanding services to the blind 1972; Tstee of Crisis at Christmas and Earl Snowdon's Fund for Handicapped Students; chm Managing Tstees of Parly Contributory Pension Scheme and of House of Commons Members' Fund; chm Parly and Sci Ctee 1989-; hon assoc Br Vetinary Assoc 1982; *Books* Human Relations in Industry 1960, VAT: A Tax on the Consumer 1970, and numerous publications on the problems and needs of disabled people; *Recreations* gardening, tennis, snooker and chess; *Style—* The Rt Hon Alfred Morris, QSO, MP; House of Commons, London SW1A 0AA; 20 Hitherwood Drive, London SE19 1XB

MORRIS, Alfred Cosier; s of Stanley Bernard Morris (d 1970), of Anlaby, E Yorks, and Jennie, *née* Fletcher; *b* 12 Nov 1941; *Educ* Hymers Coll Hull, Univ of Lancaster (MA); *m* 26 Sept 1970, Annette, da of Eamonn Donovan, Cork, Ireland; 1 da (Jessica b 24 April 1980); *Career* articled clerk Oliver Mackrill 1958-63, co sec fin controller and dir various cos 1963-71, sr Leverhulme res fell in univ planning and orgn Univ of Sussex 1971-74, visiting lectr in fin mgmnt Univ of Warwick 1973, gp mgmnt accountant Arthur Guiness Ltd 1974-76, mgmnt conslt Deloitte Haskins & Sells 1976-77, fin advsr subsids of Arthur Guiness 1977-80, acting dir South Bank Poly 1985-86 (dep dir 1980-85), advsr House of Commons select ctee educn Sci and arts 1980-83; dir Bristol Poly 1986-, tstee Bristol Cathedral; fell Humberside Coll; FCA 1963, FSS, FRSA; *Books* Resources and Higher Education (jt ed and contrib, 1982); *Recreations* windsurfing, sailing; *Clubs* Athenaeum; *Style—* Alfred Morris, Esq; Park Ct, Sodbury Common, Old Sodbury, Avon BS17 6PX (☎ 0454 319900); Bristol Poly, Coldharbour Lane, Frenchay, Bristol BS16 1QY (☎ 0272 656 261, fax 0272 583 758)

MORRIS, Lady (Victoria) Audrey Beatrice; da of late Charles John Alton Chetwynd, Viscount Ingestre, MVO (d 1915) and sis of 21 Earl of Shrewsbury and Waterford (d 1980); raised to the rank of an Earl's da 1921; *b* 1910; *m* 1, 1932 (m dis 1936), 6 Baron Sheffield (d 1972); m 2, 1945, His Honour Judge Gwyn Morris, QC; *Style—* Lady Audrey Morris; Penylan Hall, Llechryd, Cardiganshire

MORRIS, (Albert) Bert; *b* 21 Oct 1934; *Educ* Skerrys Coll Liverpool, Massachusetts Inst of Technol; *m* 14 Dec 1987, Patricia, *née* Lane; 1 s (Jonathan), 1 da (Ailsa); *Career* Nat West Bank plc: head of money transmission 1979-83, gen mangr mgmnt servs (former dep gen mangr 1983-85) 1985-88, chief exec support servs 1989; dir: Nat West Bank plc 1989, Westments Ltd 1985, Eftpos UK Ltd 1987, APACS (admin) Ltd; chm BACS Ltd, former chm Off Banking Ombudsman Bd 1985-87; FCIB; *Recreations* golf, politics; *Style—* Bert Morris, Esq; 41 Lothbury, London EC2P 2BP (☎ 01 726 1717, fax 726 1743)

MORRIS, Prof Brian Robert; s of Capt William Robert Morris, MN (d 1964), of Cardiff, and Ellen Elizabeth, *née* Shelley; *b* 4 Dec 1930; *Educ* Cardiff HS, Worcester Coll Oxford (MA, DPhil); *m* 18 Aug 1955, Sandra Mary da of Percival Samuel James (d 1967); 1 s (Christopher Justin Robert b 1959), 1 da (Lindsay Alison Mary (Mrs Boxall) b 1957); *Career* Nat Serv Welch Regt 1949-51; fell Shakespeare Inst Univ of Birmingham 1956-58, lectr Univ of Reading 1960-65 (asst lectr 1958-60), lectr and sr lectr Univ of York 1957-71 (lectr 1965-67), prof of english literature Univ of Sheffield 1971-80, princ St David's Univ Coll Lampeter 1980-; chm: literature panel Yorks Arts Assoc 1973-77, UGC/NAB working pty on Librarianship and Info Sci 1986-87, Museums and Galleries Cmmn 1985- (memb 1975-); vice pres: Cncl for Nat Parks 1985-, Museums Assoc 1985-, Welsh advsy ctee Br Cncl 1983-, Anthony Panizzi Fndn 1987-; memb: Archbishops' Cncl on Evangelism 1971-75, cncl Poetry Soc 1980-, Nat Library of Wales 1981-, Br Library Bd 1980-, Welsh Arts Cncl 1983-86 (memb literature ctee 1978-86); tstee: Nat Portrait Gallery 1977-, Nat Heritage Meml Fund 1980; gen ed: New Mermaid Dramatists 1964-, New Arden Shakespeare 1974-82;; *Books* The Poems on John Cleveland (with Eleanor Withington, 1967), John Cleveland: a Bibliography of his poems (1967), New Mermaid Critical Commentaries 1 to 3 (1969-72), Mary Quant's London (1973), Ritual Murder (ed 1980); edited plays: Ford's The Broken Heart (1965), 'Tis Pity She's A Whore (1968), Tourneur's The Atheist's Tragedy (with Roma Gill, 1976), Shakespeare's The Taming of the Shrew (1981): Poetry: Tide Race (1976), Stones in the Brook (1978), Dear Tokens (1987); *Recreations* music, mountains, museums; *Clubs* Athenaeum, Beefsteak; *Style—* Prof Brian Morris; Bryn, North Rd, Lampeter, Dyfed SA48 7HZ (☎ 0570 422 335); Saint David's Univ Coll, Lampeter, Dyfed SA48 7ED (☎ 0570 422 351, fax 0570 423 423)

MORRIS, Hon Mrs; Carolie Madge Warrand; *née* de Montmorency; da of 7 Viscount Mountmorres (d 1951), and Katherine Sofia Clay, *née* Warrand (d 1971); *b* 29 August 1920; *Educ* Brentwood Sch Southport, Chelsea Coll of Physical Educn (DipPhysEd), W London Sch of Physiotherapy (MCSP); *m* 1947, Douglas Osmond Morris, s of Walter Osmond Morris (d 1944); 1 s (Andrew ka Falkland Islands 1982), 1 da (Diana); *Career* served 1940-45, WAAF Section Offr; physiotherapist; superintendent Poole Gen Hosp 1965-81, now in private practice; *Style—* The Hon Mrs Morris; Danebury Hill, 15 Greenwood Ave, Lilliput, Poole, Dorset (☎ (0202) 707688)

MORRIS, Hon Caroline Harriet; da of 2 Baron Morris of Kenwood; *b* 23 April 1961; *Style—* The Hon Caroline Morris

MORRIS, Hon Charles Christopher; s of Baron Morris of Grasmere, KCMG (Life Peer); *b* 24 May 1929; *Educ* Keswick Sch, Balliol Coll Oxford; *m* 1951, Cynthia Prudence, da of Sir Alan Parsons, KCIE (d 1964); 2 s, 2 da; *Career* asst youth employment offr Newcastle upon Tyne 1952-54, teacher Wilsthorpe County Secdy and Melton Mowbray Modern Boys' Schs 1955-63 asst then head of Liberal Studies Mid Herts Coll of Further Ed 1963-67, vice-princ Sutton Coldfield Coll 1967-; *Style—* The Hon Charles Morris; 170 Station Rd, Wylde Green, Sutton Coldfield, Warwickshire (☎ 021 354 7821)

MORRIS, Rt Hon Charles Richard; PC (1978), MP (Lab) Manchester Openshaw Dec 1963-; s of George Morris; *b* 14 Dec 1926; *Educ* Brookdale Park Sch Manchester; *m* 1950, Pauline, da of Albert Dunn, of Manchester; 2 da; *Career* served RE 1945-48; oppn front bench spokesman and shadow dep leader of the House 1981-; min of state: CSD 1974-79, Environment March-Oct 1974; PPS to Harold Wilson when Leader Oppn 1970-74, dep chief whip 1969-70, vice-chamberlain HM Household 1967-69, asst govt whip 1966-67, PPS to Postmaster Gen 1964; fought Cheadle 1959, pres Clayton Labour Party 1950-52, sec NW Gp Labour MPs 1979-; memb Manchester Corpn 1954-64 (chm Tport Ctee 1959-62, dep chm Establishment Ctee 1963-64), memb Post Office Workers Union (on NEC 1959-63); *Style—* The Rt Hon Charles Morris, MP; 24 Buxton Rd West, Disley, Stockport, Cheshire (☎ 066 32 2450)

MORRIS, David Edward Alban; s of Clifford Morris (d 1981), and Florence Irene, *née* Thomas; *b* 24 August 1935; *Educ* Shrewsbury, Univ Coll Oxford (MA); *m* 23 Sept 1972, Moira Louise, da of Dr Alfred William Callaghan; 2 s (William b 11 Sept 1974, Richard b 16 June 1977); *Career* CA, ptnr Peat Marwick McLintock 1974-; cncl memb: Mgmnt Consultancies Assoc, Br Conslts Bureau, Templeton Coll Oxford; FCA; *Clubs* Hurlingham; *Style—* David Morris, Esq; 3 Spencer Hill, London SW19 4PA; Peat Marwick McLintock, 1 Puddle Dock, Blackfriars, London EC4V 3PD (☎ 01 236 8000)

MORRIS, David Elwyn; s of Rev S M Morris (d 1958), and K W Morris, *née* Irish (d 1952); *b* 22 May 1920; *Educ* Mill Hill Sch, Brasenose Coll Oxford (MA); *m* 1, 1947, Joyce Hellyer (d 1977); 1 s (Barry b 1951), 1 da (Ann b 1949); m 2, Gwendolen Wood (d 1988), wid of Dr J K Pearce; *Career* Capt Br Army India 1944-46; Friends Ambulance Unit in China 1942-44; barr 1949-54, slr 1955-76, registrar of princ Registry of Family Div of High Ct Justice 1976-; *Publications* China Changed My Mind (1948), The End of Marriage (1971), Pilgrim Through This Barren Land (1974); *Recreations* reading; *Style—* David E Morris, Esq; 8 Rodney House, Pembridge Crescent, London W11 3DY (☎ 01 727 7975)

MORRIS, David Glyndwr; s of Owen Glyndwr Morris, of Coventry, and Doreen Iris

Morris; *b* 12 August 1941; *Educ* King Henry VIII Sch Coventry, Lanchester Coll Coventry; *m* 1966, Susan Joan, da of Edwin Taylor (d 1972); 2 da (Shelley b 1969, Justine b 1972); *Career* chm and md: Criterion Insurance Co Ltd, Criterion Life Assurance Ltd, Criterion Financial Services Ltd 1984-; ind md Criterion Hldgs Ltd; *Recreations* golf, shooting, travel; *Clubs* IOD, Bramshaw GC; *Style—* David Morris, Esq; Criterion Assurance Gp, Swan Court, Swan Street, Petersfield, Hants (☎ Petersfield 63218)

MORRIS, David Scott; s of John Hilary Morris, of Bow, Brickhill, Bucks, and Frances Deans, *née* Cooper; *b* 20 Dec 1940; *Educ* Westmont Sch IOW, Royal Liberty GS Essex; *m* 23 Oct 1965, Jennifer Lois, da of Alan George Skinner (d 1986), of Pymble, Sydney, Australia; 1 da (Catriona Lucy b 1967); *Career* admitted slr 1965; HM Coroner for Huntingdon 1987; pres: Milton Keynes and Dist Law Soc 1985-86, Beds Law Soc 1987-88; dir of several private cos; memb: Law Soc, IOD; *Recreations* travel, gardening, cycling, walking; *Clubs* Carlton; *Style—* David S Morris, Esq; The Old Vicarage, Granborough, Bucks (☎ 029667 217); 64-70 St Loyes, Bedford (☎ 0234 50444, telex 825263, fax 0234 219635)

MORRIS, Dr Desmond John; s of Capt Harry Howe Morris (d 1942), and Dorothy Marjorie Fuller, *née* Hunt; *b* 24 Jan 1928; *Educ* Dauntsey's Sch Wiltshire, Birmingham Univ (BSc), Oxford Univ (DPhil); *m* 1952, Ramona Joy, da of Windsor Baulch, of Marlborough Wiltshire; 1 s (Jason b 1968); *Career* zoological res worker Oxford Univ 1954-56, head of Granada TV and Film Unit at Zoological Soc of London 1956-59, curator of mammals at Zoological Soc of London 1959-67, dir Inst of Contemporary Arts 1967-68, res fell Wolfson Coll Oxford 1973-81; tv series: Zootime (weekly 1956-67), Life (fortnightly 1965-67), The Human Race (1982), The Animals Roadshow 1987-89; one man (paintings) shows: London Gallery 1950, Ashmolean Museum Oxford 1952, Stooshnoff Fine Art London 1974, Quadrangle Gallery Oxford 1976, Lasson Gallery London 1976, Pub Art Gallery Swindon 1977, Galerie d'Eendt Amsterdam 1978, Mayor Gallery London 1987, Shippee Gallery New York 1988, Keats Gallery Knokke 1988; *Books* The Reproductive Behaviour of the Ten-spined Stickleback (1958), The Story of Congo (1958), Curious Creatures (1961), The Biology of Art (1962), Apes and Monkeys (1964), The Big Cats (1965), The Mammals, a Guide to the Living Species (1965), Men and Snakes (with Ramona Morris (1965), Men and Apes (with Ramona Morris 1966), Men and Pandas (with Ramona Morris 1966), Zootime (1966), Primate Ethology (editor 1967), The Naked Ape (1967), The Human Zoo (1969), Patterns of Reproductive Behaviour (1970), Intimate Behaviour (1971), Manwatching, a Field-guide to Human Behaviour (1977), Gestures, their Origins and Distribution (co-author 1979), Animal Days (autobiography 1979), The Soccer Tribe (1981), Inrock (fiction 1983), The Book of Ages (1983), The Art of Ancient Cyprus (1985), Bodywatching, a Field-guide to the Human Species (1985), The Illustrated Naked Ape (1986), Catwatching (1986), Dogwatching (1986), The Secret Surrealist (1987), Catlore (1987), The Animals Roadshow (1988), Horsewatching (1988); *Recreations* painting, archaeology; *Style—* Dr Desmond Morris; c/o Jonathan Cape, 32 Bedford Sq, London WC1B 3EL

MORRIS, Air Marshal Sir Douglas Griffith; KCB (1962, CB 1954), CBE (1945), DSO (1945), DFC (1941); s of David Griffith Morris (d 1947), of S Africa; *b* 3 Dec 1908; *Educ* St John's Coll Johannesburg; *m* 1936, Audrey Beryl, da of Percy Heard (d 1967); 1 s, 1 da; *Career* joined RAF 1930, served WWII, ADC to HM King George VI 1949-52, ADC to HM The Queen 1952, COS 2 Allied Tactical Air Force HQ Germany 1955-57, Asst Chief of Air Staff (Air Defence) Air Miny 1957-60, COS HQ Allied Air Forces Central Europe 1960-62, AOC-in-C RAF Fighter Cmd 1962-66, ret; memb St Dunstan's Cncl 1968-85; *Recreations* gardening, golf, skiing; *Clubs* RAF, Rye GC (Capt 1975); *Style—* Air Marshal Sir Douglas Morris, KCB, CBE, DSO, DFC; Friar's Cote, Northiam, Rye, E Sussex (☎ 079 74 3270)

MORRIS, Hon Edward Patrick; s of 2 Baron Morris (d 1975), and Jean Beatrice, who m 2, Baron Salmon *qv*; gs of 1 Baron Morris (d 1935, last PM of Newfoundland 1909-18 and memb of War Cabinet 1916-18); *b* 9 Dec 1937; *Educ* Downside; *m* 1963, Mary Beryl, da of Lt-Col D H G Thrush, of Canterbury; 1 s, 1 da; *Career* co dir (Export) Barrow Hepburn 1973-75, export mangr Portex Ltd Hythe Kent 1976-83, sales dir Concord Laboratories Ltd Folkestone 1983-; *Recreations* golf, veteran car (1930 Rolls Royce); *Style—* The Hon Edward Morris; Hornsdown Cottage, Elham, Canterbury, Kent (☎ 030 384 575); Concord Laboratories Ltd, Park Farm Rd, Folkestone, Kent (☎ 0303 43531, telex 966598)

MORRIS, Hon Mrs; Hon (Elizabeth); *née* Hill; 2 da of Baron Hill of Luton, PC, MD (Life Peer); *b* 21 Mar 1935; *m* 6 June 1964, David Maxwell Morris, eld s of Maxwell Morris, of 12 Cleveland Row, St James's, London SW1; 2 s, 1 da; *Style—* The Hon Mrs Morris; 9 St Leonards Rd, Exeter

MORRIS, Ernest John (Johnny); OBE (1984); s of Ernest Edward Morris (d 1951), and Fanny Collorick (d 1933); *b* 20 June 1916; *m* 1951, Sybil Eileen, da of Charles Minett (d 1951); *Career* broadcaster (radio) Johnny's Jaunts, Around the World in 25 Years; (TV) The Hot Chestnut Man, Animal Magic (ran for 21 yrs); concert performances include several one-man operas (words by Johnny Morris, music by David Haslam, Douglas Coombes and Sidney Sager); *Recreations* singing, gardening, watching wildlife; *Style—* Johnny Morris, Esq, OBE; Hopgrass Barn, Bath Road, Hungerford, Berks RG17 0SL

MORRIS, Lady; Ghislaine Margaret; *née* Trammell; *m* 1959, Sir Willie Morris, KCMG (d 1982), sometime Ambass Cairo; 3 s; *Style—* Lady Morris; 26 Bickerton Road, Headington, Oxford OX3 7LS

MORRIS, Ingrid Mary; da of R W Morris and Mrs Morris, *née* Bundy; *b* 10 Oct 1945; *Educ* Nat Cathedral Sch for Girls Washington DC, Herts and Essex HS Bishops Stortford, Architectural Assoc Sch of Architecture (AA Dip, RIBA, SADG); *m* 1 s (Vasiles b 1981); *Career* architect; estab Bone and Morris private practice with Jeanne Bone 1976 (formerly with McNab and Jamieson 1968-69, Prano and Rogers 1972-74); former memb Co of Women in Architecture 1974-76; visiting lectr: Royal Univ of Malta 1974-77, Univ of Queensland 1982; hon librarian and memb of cncl Architectural Assoc Sch of Architecture 1985-87, RIBA rep on ARCUK Educn Ctee 1987-, RIBA assessor RIBA Housing Awards Northern Region; *Recreations* swimming, skiing, painting; *Clubs* Arts; *Style—* Miss Ingrid Morris; 33 Ovington Sq, London SW3 1LJ (☎ 01 589 8535); Bone and Morris, 6 Stanhope Mews West, London SW7 5RB (☎ 01 835 1172, fax 01 244 8722)

MORRIS, Jack Anthony; s of Samuel Cyril Morris, of London, and Golda, *née* Berkovitch, of London; *b* 23 June 1956; *Educ* Christ's Coll GS; *m* 1 Nov 1983, Susan Anne, da of Harry Lee, of London; 1 s (Robert Edward b 27 May 1987), 1 da (Emily Kate b 14 May 1985); *Career* dep chm City Indust Ltd 1980-, The Business Design Centre London 1985-; FID 1988; *Recreations* running, 1930s & 1940s popular music, cinema history, music hall, vaudeville, variety; *Style—* Jack Morris, Esq; Business Design Centre, Upper St, Islington Green, London N1 0QH (☎ 01 359 3535, fax 01 226 0590, telex 264488-Aggie)

MORRIS, James Nathaniel; s of Arthur Russel Morris (d 1977), and Mildred Maud Langley, *née* Rogers; *b* 6 Nov 1942; *Educ* Wycliffe Coll Glos, Univ of Birmingham (BSc); *m* 1965, Barbara, da of Henry Herbert Goldstaub; 2 s, 2 da; *Career* md Electrothermal Engrg Ltd 1976-; CEng, MIChemE; *Recreations* squash, music; *Style—* James Morris, Esq; 18 Snakes Lane, Woodford Green, Essex IG8 0BS (☎ 01 504 2365); Electrothermal Engineering Ltd, 419 Sutton Rd, Southend-on-Sea, Essex SS2 5PH (☎ 0702 612211; telex 995387)

MORRIS, James Peter; s of Frank Morris MBE, JP (d 1978), of Kexbrough, Yorks, and Ann Mary Collindridge (d 1968); *b* 17 Sept 1926; *Educ* Holgate GS Barnsley, Univ of Manchester (BA, Teaching Dip); Later Dip CAM; *m* 1, 1953 (m dis), Peggy; m 2, 1974, Margaret, da of Alan Law (d 1987), of Puisley; *Career* served RAF based UK 1945-48; res dept Labour Party 1952-59; Govt Info Servs: HM Treasury and other depts 1960-73 (chief info offr 1968-73); dir info GLC 1973-77; sec-gen Nat Cold Storage Fedn 1978-; *Recreations* cricket, painting, politics, theatre, voluntary activity in community; *Clubs* MCC, Reform; *Style—* J P Morris, Esq; 88 Ridgmount Gdns, London WC1E 7AY (☎ 01 637 2141); Tavistock House North, Tavistock Square, London WC1H 9HZ

MORRIS, James Richard Samuel; CBE (1986); s of James John Morris (d 1976), and Kathleen Mary, *née* McNaughton (d 1976); *b* 20 Nov 1925; *Educ* Ardingly Sch, Birmingham Univ (BSc Chem Eng); *m* 1958, Marion Reid, da of Dr James Sinclair; 2 s (Simon b 1960, Andrew b 1962), 2 da (Jane b 1963, Katherine b 1965); *Career* Courtaulds Ltd 1950-80, dir British Nuclear Fuels Ltd 1971-85, visiting prof of chem engrg Univ of Strathclyde 1979-87, chm and md Brown and Root (UK) Ltd 1980-, chm of cncl and pro-chllr Loughborough Univ 1982-, industl advsr Barclays Bank 1980-85; *Recreations* gardening, farming, skiing, shooting; *Clubs* Athenaeum; *Style—* J R S Morris, Esq, CBE; Breadsall Manor, Breadsall Village, Derby (☎ 0332 83168); Brown & Root (UK) Ltd, 125 High St, Colliers Wood, London SW19 2JR (☎ 01 534 0172)

MORRIS, (Catharine) Jan; *b* 2 Oct 1926; *Educ* Oxford Univ (MA); *Career* author; *Books* Venice (1960), Spain (1964), Oxford (1965), The Pax Britannica Trilogy (1973-78), Conundrum (1974), The Matter of Wales (1984), Last Letters from Hav (1985), Among the Cities (1985), Manhattan '45 (1987), Hong Kong (1988), 5 books of collected travel essays, ed The Oxford Book of Oxford (1978); *Style—* Ms Jan Morris; Trefan Morys, Llanystumdwy, Gwynedd, Cymru (☎ 0766 522222)

MORRIS, Rt Hon John; PC (1970), QC (1973), MP (Lab) Aberavon 1959-; s of D W Morris, of Talybont, Cardiganshire; *b* 1931,Nov; *Educ* Ardwyn (Aberystwyth), Univ Coll of Wales Aberystwyth, Gonville and Caius Cambridge, Acad of Int Law The Hague; *m* 1959, Margaret, da of Edward Lewis, OBE, JP, of Llandysul; 3 da; *Career* served Royal Welch Fusiliers and Welch Regt; oppn spokesman Legal Affrs 1979-81, sec state Wales 1974-79, Min Defence (Equipment) 1968-70, jt parly sec Tport 1966-68, parly sec Miny Power 1964-66; memb UK Delgn Consultative Assembly Cncl of Europe and WEU 1963-64, N Atlantic Assembly 1970-74; barr Gray's Inn 1954, legal advsr Farmers' Union of Wales, rec SE circuit 1982-; Hon LLD Wales 1983, memb shadow cabinet and spokesman legal affrs Nov 1983-; *Style—* The Rt Hon John Morris, QC, MP; House of Commons, SW1

MORRIS, Hon John Martin; s (twin) of 3 Baron Killanin, MBE, TD; *b* 4 April 1951; *Educ* Ampleforth, St Conleth's Coll Dublin; *m* 1972, Thelma, da of Mrs Mansfield, of Monkstown, co Dublin; 2 s (Roderic, Michael); *Career* photographer; *Recreations* falconry, fishing; *Style—* The Hon John Morris; 5 Rus-in-Urbe, Lower Glenageary Rd, Dun Laoghaire, co Dublin

MORRIS, John Stanley; s of Sydney Morris, of Sonning-on-Thames, Berks, and Betty Joan, *née* Talbot; *b* 14 April 1939; *Educ* Uppingham; *m* 6 Oct 1962, Diane Mary Druce, da of Leonard William Chopping, of Henley-on-Thames, Oxon; 3 s (William b 27 Nov 63, Simon b 8 May 1966, Ashley b 11 Jan 1969); *Career* qualified CA 1962; ptnr: Fryer Sutton Morris & Co 1962-69, Fryer Whitehill & Co 1969-77; fin dir Lubrication Engrg Gp 1977-81 (conslt 1982-); fndr tres Reading Valley Round Table; memb Worshipful Co of Feltmakers; FCA 1969; *Recreations* golf; *Clubs* Calcot Park GC (Capt 1974), Phyllis Court (Henley); *Style—* John Morris, Esq; Rowan House, Greenwood Rd, Reading RG3 4JG (☎ 0734 427578, fax 0734 451113)

MORRIS, Hon Jonathan David; s and h of 2 Baron Morris of Kenwood; *b* 5 August 1968; *Style—* The Hon Jonathan Morris

MORRIS, Judith Anne; da of Harold Morris (d 1986), of London, and Eve, *née* Sutton; *b* 23 August 1948; *Educ* Buckingham Gate Sch, Camden HS for Girls, City Univ London (BSc, MSc); *Career* sr sessional optometrist contact lens dept Moorfields Eye Hosp London 1971-, sr lectr Inst of Optometry London 1983-; pres Br Contact Lens Assoc 1983-84 (ed jl of Br Contact Lens Assoc 1984-89), vice pres Br Coll of Optometrists 1987- (cncl memb and examiner 1980-); memb Lambeth Southwark and Lewisham Family Practitioners Ctee 1988-; Freeman City of London 1972, fell Worshipful Co of Spectacle Makers 1971; fell Br Coll of Optometrists 1971; *Recreations* theatre, ballet, bridge; *Style—* Miss Judith Morris; 9 Cosway St, London NW1 (☎ 01 724 1176); The Institute of Optometry, 56 Newington Causeway SE1 (☎ 01 407 4183)

MORRIS, Keith Norton; s of Capt Alfred Lawrence Morris (d 1984), and Marywyn, *née* Norton; *b* 3 July 1950; *Educ* Bishop Veseys GS; *m* 6 Sept 1972, Valerie, *née* Coombes; 1 s (Timothy), 2 da (Charlotte, Abigail); *Career* articled clerk Binder Hamlyn 1968-74, gp accountant Deblen Fin Ltd 1974-75, fin dir Forthminster Hldgs Ltd 1975-84, md W H Wilkins Ltd 1984-, fin controller Aqua Gp 1987; FCA, FIOD, MBIM; *Recreations* gardening, DIY, travel; *Style—* Keith Morris, Esq; 'Windyridge', Charlemont Rd, Walsall W Mids WS5 3NQ (☎ 0922 646982, 021 541 1601, telex 337370, fax 021 552 3748)

MORRIS, Hon Linda Jane; da of 2 Baron Morris of Kenwood; *b* 28 April 1965; *Style—* The Hon Linda Morris

MORRIS, Lady; Mair Eluned; *née* Williams; *m* 1940, Sir Gwilym Morris, CBE, QPM, DL, CStJ (d 1982), sometime Ch Constable S Wales Constabulary; 1 s, 1 da; *Career* a state registered nurse; CStJ; *Style—* Lady Morris; Erw Deg, 39 Llantrisant Rd, Llandaff, Cardiff (☎ 0222 551877)

MORRIS, Mary, Baroness; Mary; da of late Rev Alexander Reginald Langhorne; *m* 2 Baron Morris (d 1975); *Style*— The Rt Hon Mary, Lady Morris; The Old Farmhouse, Lower Denford, Hungerford, Berks RG17 0UN

MORRIS, Max; *b* 15 August 1913; *Educ* Hutcheson's Glasgow, Kilburn GS London, UCL (BA), Inst of Educn London, London Sch of Economics; *m* 1961, Margaret; *Career* Capt RASC 1944; headmaster Willesden HS 1967-78, cnsllr Harringay Borough Cncl 1984-6, pres Nat Union of Teachers 1973-74; *Books* The People's Schools (1939), From Cobbett to the Chartists (1948), Your Children's Future (1955), An A-Z of Trade Unionism & Industrial Relations (with Jack Jones, 1982 and 1986), co-ed Thirteen Wasted Years (1987); *Recreations* walking, swimming; *Style*— Max Morris, Esq; 44 Coolhurst Rd, London N8

MORRIS, 3 Baron (UK 1918); Michael David Morris; s of er twin s of 2 Baron Morris (d 1975); *b* 9 Dec 1937; *Educ* Downside; *m* 1, 1959 (m dis 1962), Denise Eleanor, da of Morley Richards; m 2, 1962 (m dis 1969), Jennifer, da of Tristram Gilbert; 2 da; m 3, 1980, Juliet Susan, twin da of Anthony Buckingham; 2 s, 1 da (Hon Lucy Juliet b 18 June 1981); *Heir* s, Hon Thomas Morris; *Career* sits as Conservative in House of Lords; FICA; *Style*— The Rt Hon Lord Morris; 8 Carlos Place, London W1 (☎ 01 499 2807)

MORRIS, Hon Michael Francis Leo; known as 'Mouse'; s (twin with John) of 3 Baron Killanin, MBE, TD; *b* 4 April 1951; *Educ* Ampleforth, St Conleth's Coll Dublin; *m* (Shanny) Shanney Clark; 2 s (James, Christopher); *Career* former steeple chase jockey, race horse trainer; *Recreations* fox hunting; *Clubs* Turf; *Style*— The Hon Michael Morris; Everards Grange, Fethard, Co Tipperary, Ireland (☎ 052 31474)

MORRIS, Michael Wolfgang Laurence; MP (C) Northampton 1974-; s of Cyril Laurence Morris; *b* 25 Nov 1936; *Educ* Bedford Sch, St Catharine's Coll Cambridge (MA); *m* 1960, Ann Phyllis, da of Percy Appleby (d 1973); 2 s (Julian b 1961, Jocelyn b 1972), 1 da (Susannah b 1965); *Career* served Nat Serv, pilot offr RAF and NATO Wings; dir Benton & Bowles (advertising agency) 1971-81, fndr AM Int Pub Affrs Consits 1976-; contested (C) Islington N 1966, PPS to NI Min of State 1979-81, memb of Pub Accounts Ctee 1979-; chm: Br-Sri Lanka Parly Gp, Br Singapore Parly Gp; Br Malaysia Gp: Cncl of Europe and Western Euro Union 1983-, Mr Speaker's Panel 1984-; govr Bedford Sch 1982-; vice-chm Br-Indonesia Gp; tres: Br-Thailand Gp, Br Asian Gp; sec Br-Burma Gp; *Recreations* field sports, cricket, golf (capt Parly Golf Soc), shooting, tennis, heritage, forestry, budgerigars; *Clubs* Carlton, George Row (Northampton), John O'Gaunt GC; *Style*— Michael Morris, Esq, MP; Caesar's Camp, Sandy, Beds (☎ 0767 80388)

MORRIS, Hon Michaela Mary; da of 3 Baron Morris; *b* 1965; *Style*— The Hon Michaela Morris

MORRIS, Prof Norman Frederick; s of Frederick William Morris (d 1974), of Luton, Beds, and Evelyn, *née* Biggs (d 1971); *b* 26 Feb 1920; *Educ* Dunstable Sch, St Mary's Hosp Med Sch Univ of London (MB BS); *m* 2 June 1944, Lucia Xenia (Lucy), da of Dr Benjamin Rivlin (d 1964), of Stratford, London; 2 s (David, Nicholas), 2 da (Jacqueline, Vanessa); *Career* Sqdn Ldr RAFVR (medical section) 1946-48; res surgical offr East Ham Meml Hosp 1945-46 (dep res 1944-45), sr registrar dept obstetrics & gynaecology Royal Postgrad Med Inst 1950-53, sr lectr dept obstetrics & gynaecology Royal Postgrad Med Inst 1956-58, prof obstetrics and gynaecology Charing Cross Hosp Med Sch 1958-85, med dir IVF Unit Cromwell Hosp 1985-; dean faculty of med Univ of London 1971-76 (dep vice chllr 1976-80), dep chm NW Thames Health Authy 1976-80; fndr and pres Int Soc of Psychosomatic Obstetrics and Gynaecology 1972-; chm Br Soc of Psychosomatic Obstetrics and Gynaecology and Andrology 1988-; hon memb: societas Gynaecologa et Obstetrica Italica 1979, Australian Soc of Psychosomatic Obstetrics and Gynaecology 1981; FRSM, FRCOG; *Books* Sterilisation of Men and Women (1976), The Baby Book (1953); *Recreations* travelling, music, reading; *Clubs* Athenaeum; *Style*— Prof Norman Morris; 16 Provost Rd, London NW3 4ST; Cromwell Hosp, Cromwell Rd, SW5 (☎ 01 722 4244)

MORRIS, Lady; Olive Irene; da of William Davies, of Swansea; *m* 4 June 1938, Sir Herbert Edward Morris, 7 Bt (d 1947); 29 Belle Vue Rd, West Cross, Swansea

MORRIS, Paul Christopher Early; s of Christopher John Morris, of Kensington, London W8, and Alice Ruth, *née* Early; *b* 21 Sept 1950; *Educ* Westminster Abbey Choir Sch, Westminster, UCNW Bangor (BA); *Career* organist & choirmaster Christ Church Llanfairfechan N Wales 1970-73; admitted slr 1978, ptnr Winckworth & Pemberton 1981- (asst slr 1978-81); asst registrar Diocese of Southwark, hon sec The Avenues Youth Project N Kensington; Freeman City of London 1984, Liveryman Worshipful Co of Wheelwrights 1984, Freeman Worshipful Co Weavers 1988; *Recreations* music; *Clubs* Oriental; *Style*— Paul Morris, Esq; 35 Great Peter St, Westminster SW1P 3LR (☎ 01 222 7811, fax 01 222 1614)

MORRIS, Paul William; s of William Henry Morris (d 1987), of Bexhill-on-Sea, and the late Norah, *née* Abbott; *b* 20 May 1942; *Educ* Downsmeade Sch Eastbourne; *m* 30 Jan 1965, Carole, da of William Joseph Cornelius Owden, of Tunbridge Wells; 2 s (Nicholas b 1967, Dominic b 1972), 2 da (Karen b 1969, Elizabeth b 1979); *Career* articled HS Humphrey and Co Eastbourne, CA 1966; sr tax ptnr BDO Binder Hamlyn 1988- (joined 1972); Freeman City of London, Liveryman Painter Stainers Co; FCA 1966; *Recreations* cricket, tennis, walking, painting, art, theatre; *Style*— Paul Morris, Esq; BDO Binder Hamlyn, 8 St Bride St, London EC4A 4DA (☎ 01 353 3020, fax 01 583 0031, telex 24276)

MORRIS, Quentin Mathew; s of John Eric Morris (d 1942); *b* 28 Mar 1930; *Educ* St Clement Danes Sch, LSE (BSc); *m* 1951, Eva; 1 s, 1 da; *Career* Inland Revenue 1952-64, British Petroleum Co 1964-85 (dir gp fin 1977-85); dir: Globe Investment Tst 1984-, Granada Gp 1981-, Johnson Matthey plc 1984-, Haden Gp 1985-87, Channel Tunnel Gp 1985-86, Waterford Glass Gp 1984-, Waterford-Wedgwood Hldgs 1986-, UGC (Unipart Gp) 1987-, Kilsallaghan Hldgs 1988-, Med Sickness Annuity & Life Assur Soc 1989-; chm BSB Working Gp which constructed the successful bid for the UK Satellite broadcasting franchise 1986; advsr to PO on Sale of Girobank 1988-89; govr LSE 1982-; special tstee Middx Hosp 1980-; cncl memb Middx Hosp Med Sch 1982-88; tstee Whitechapel Art Gallery 1983-88, and chm devpt tst Whitechapel Art Gallery 1983-87; *Recreations* skiing, shooting, squash, modern art, walking in cities; *Clubs* Reform, City of London, MCC; *Style*— Quentin Morris, Esq; Globe Investment Tst plc, Globe House, Temple Place, London WC2R 3HP (☎ 01 836 7766, fax 01 240 5599)

MORRIS, Hon (George) Redmond Fitzpatrick; s and h of 3 Baron Killanin, MBE, TD; *b* 24 Jan 1947; *Educ* Gonzaga Coll Dublin, Ampleforth, Trinity Coll Dublin; *m* 1972, Pauline, da of Geoffrey Horton, of The Lawns, Cabinteely, Co Dublin; 1 s (Luke), 1 da (Olivia); *Career* film prodr; *Style*— The Hon Redmond Morris; 4 The Vineyard, Richmond, Surrey

MORRIS, Sir Robert Byng; 10 Bt (UK 1806), of Clasemont, Glamorganshire; s of late Percy Byng Morris, himself gs of Sir John Morris, 2 Bt (whose wife was Hon Lucy Juliana Byng, 7 and yst da of 5 Viscount Torrington); suc second cousin, Sir Cedric Morris, 9 Bt, 1982; *b* 25 Feb 1913; *m* 1947, Christine Kathleen, da of Archibald Field, of Toddington, Glos; 1 s (Andrew Jamieson), 3 da (Geraldine b 1948, Gillian b 1959, Roberta b 1965); *Heir* s, Allan Lindsay Morris, b 27 Nov 1961, m 1986, Cheronne, eld da of Dale Whitford, of Par, Cornwall; *Style*— Sir Robert Morris, Bt; RR2 Norton Creek Rd, St Chrysostome, Québec, Canada

MORRIS, Robert Leslie; s of Lt-Col John Douglas Leslie Morris, OBE, of 1 Grove Rd, Melton Constable, Norfolk NR24 2DE, and Doris Mabel, *née* Young; *b* 16 Sept 1939; *Educ* Felsted; *m* 10 Aug 1963, Maureen Iris, da of Edward Arthur Day; 1 s (David Leslie b 1967), 1 da (Lynda Leslie b 1965); *Career* CA 1963, articled clerk Grant Thornton (formerly Thornton Baker), asst accountant Williams Harvey Ltd 1965-67, chief accountant A King & Sons Ltd 1967-70; Glaciator Ltd 1970-74, co sec Cresswell & Williamson Ltd 1974-83; self-employed CA 1983-88, ptnr Harris Kafton 1988-; memb: Fakenham and dist light operatic soc, Fakenham and dist angling club; FCA 1963, ATII 1963; *Recreations* sea & freshwater angling, backstage local operatic soc; *Clubs* Fakenham Angling, Fakenham Operatic; *Style*— Robert Morris, Esq; Old White Horse, Briningham, Melton Constable, Norfolk NR24 2PY (☎ 0263 860 514); 1 Royal Oak Chambers, Fakenham, Norfolk NR21 9DY (☎ 0328 51306)

MORRIS, Robert Vernon; s of Harold Vernon Morris (d 1986), of 82 Lichfield Ave, Hereford, and Dorothy Agnes, *née* Foulkes; *b* 27 May 1932; *Educ* St Mary's Coll Bitterne Park Southampton, LSE (LLB); *m* 19 Sept 1959, Patricia Margaret, da of Thomas Norman Trevor (d 1968), of 66 Laynes Rd, Glos; 3 s (Nicholas b 1960, Timothy b 1963, James b 1965), 1 d (Sally b 1970); *Career* Nat Serv 1956-58 Intelligence Corps GCHQ Cheltenham; slr Supreme Ct 1957, sr ptnr Rowberry Morris Glos (offs also at Bristol, Hereford, Tewkesbury); pres Glos Rotary Club 1981-82, chm Glos Civic Tst 1983-, sec Glos Historic Bldgs 1980-; chm: Glos Legal Assoc 1985-88, Glos Social Security Appeal Tbnl 1984, cdr St John Ambulance Glos 1988-; memb Law Soc 1957; OStJ 1986; *Recreations* jogging; *Clubs* St John House, LSE Soc; *Style*— Robert Morris, Esq; The Hill House, Hartpury, Glos GL19 3DB (☎ 0452 70 235); Morroway Ho, Station Rd, Glos GL1 1DW (☎ 0452 301 903, fax 0452 411 115)

MORRIS, Roger John Bowring; s of Timothy George Bowring Morris, of Shrewsbury, and Mabel, *née* Baxter; *b* 13 June 1946; *Educ* Liverpool Coll, Peterhouse Cambridge (MA, LLM); *m* 6 July 1985, Ann, da of George Morris Whittle, of Brentwood, Essex; 1 s (Edward b 1986); *Career* slr 1970, atricled clerk and asst St Helens CBC 1968-72, asst town clerk 1973-74 (assoc town clerk 1973-74), dir of admin Grimsby BC 1974-81; town clerk and chief exec: City of Durham 1981-86, Northampton BC 1986-; Freeman (joiner) City of Durham 1986; memb Law Soc 1970, Soc Local Authy Chief exec (hon slr); *Books* Parliament and The Public Libraries (1977), Solicitors and Local Authorities (1982, Supplement 1986); *Recreations* family, writing, tennis, hill walking, skiing; *Clubs* Northampton Rotary; *Style*— Roger Morris, Esq; Highway House, 95 High Street, Weston Favell, Northampton NN3 3JX (☎ 0604 405922); Northampton Borough Council, 61 Derngate, Northampton NN1 1UY (☎ 0604 29033)

MORRIS, Rear Adm Roger Oliver; s of Dr Oliver Nixon Morris (d 1983), of Plymouth, and Sybil Helga (Mollie), *née* Hudson (d 1973); *b* 1 Sept 1932; *Educ* Mount House Sch Tavistock, RNC Dartmouth; *Career* Cmd HM Ships: Medusa 1964-65, Beagle 1968-70, Fawn 1972, Hecla 1975-78, Hydra 1970-71 and 1979-80; Royal Coll of Defence Studies 1978; dir of hydrographic plans and surveys in Hydrographic Dept Taunton 1980-82 (asst hydrographer 1982-84), hydrographer of the Nav 1985-; FRCIS, FRGS; *Recreations* heraldry, opera, ornithology; *Clubs* Royal Cwlth Soc; *Style*— Rear Adm R O Morris; Hydrographic Dept, Ministry of Defence, Taunton, Somerset TA1 2DN (☎ 0823 337900)

MORRIS, Rosalind Anita; da of Dennis Bernard Robin (d 1987), and Susan, *née* Kaye; *b* 20 Jan 1950; *Educ* St Paul's Girls' Sch; *m* 23 March 1972 (m dis 1978), Ronald Michael; *Career* sr buyer Marks and Spencer Fashion Gp; former chm: Women in Business, Joint Israel Appeal (JIA); memb Network; *Recreations* theatre, art, interior design, tennis, needlework; *Style*— Mrs Rosalind Morris; Marks and Spencer plc, Michael House, 57 Baker Street, London, WI (☎ 01 935 4422)

MORRIS, Timothy Denis; DL (W Midlands 1975); s of Denis Edward Morris, OBE, of 123 Clare Park, Crondall, nr Farnham, Surrey, and Angela Mary Skey, *née* Moore; *b* 14 Feb 1935; *Educ* Tonbridge, Pembroke Coll Cambridge (MA); *m* 12 Sept 1959, Caroline, da of Edward Victor Wynn (d 1983), of Chipping Campden, Glos; 1 s (Andrew b 23 April 1962), 1 da (Juliet b 30 July 1964); *Career* Nat Serv Sub Lt RNVR 1953-55; newspaper exec; dir: The Birmingham Post and Mail Ltd 1967- (chm 1982-), Cambridge Newspapers Ltd 1970-77, BPM Holdings Ltd 1977-, Press Assoc Ltd 1980-87 (chm 1985-86), Burton Daily Mail Ltd 1983-, South Hamps Newspapers Ltd 1985- (chm 1985-86), Yattendon Investmt Tst Ltd 1985-, Reuters Founder Share Co Ltd 1987-, Midland Newspapers Ltd 1988-; chm Packet Newspapers Ltd 1986-; county cmmr Warwickshire Scouts 1974-77; pres W Midlands Newspaper Soc 1975-76; chm Birmingham Civic Soc 1979-83; dir Birmingham Hippodrome Theatre Tst 1980-; pres Newspaper Soc 1984-85; *Recreations* golf, philately; *Clubs* Naval; *Style*— Timothy Morris, Esq, DL; The Birmingham Post & Mail Ltd, PO Box 18, 28 Colmore Circus, Queensway, Birmingham B4 6AX (☎ 021 236 3366, fax 021 236 9638, car ☎ 0860 632485)

MORRIS, Rev William James; JP (Glasgow 1971); o s of William John Morris, and Eliza Cecilia Cameron Johnson; *b* 22 August 1925; *Educ* Cardiff HS, Univ of Wales (BA, BD), Edinburgh Univ (PhD); *m* 1952, Jean Daveena Ogilvy, MBE, o da of Rev David Porter Howie, of Kilmarnock, Ayrshire; 1 s; *Career* ordained 1951; min: St David's Buckhaven 1953-57, Peterhead Old Parish 1957-67; chaplain HM Prison Peterhead 1963-67; memb Convocation of Univ of Strathclyde, chm cncl Soc of Friends of Glasgow Cathedral, min of Glasgow Cathedral 1967-; chaplain to: HM The Queen in Scotland 1969-, the Lord High Cmmr to Gen Assembly of Church of Scotland 1975-76; memb: IBA Scotland 1979-84, bd of govrs Jordanhill Coll of Educn 1983-; hon pres City of Glasgow Soc of Social Serv; hon memb: Rotary Clubs of Dennistonn and Glasgow, Royal Scottish Automobile Club, RNVR Club; chaplain Strathclyde Police; Sub-ChStJ; Hon LLD Strathclyde 1974, Hon DD Glasgow 1979, Hon FRCPS Glasgow;

Books A Walk Through Glasgow Cathedral (1986); *Recreations* being a paternalistic do-gooder, gardening, sunbathing in SW France; *Clubs* New (Edinburgh); *Style*— Rev William Morris, JP; 94 St Andrews Drive, Glasgow (☎ 041 427 2757)

MORRIS JONES, Hon Mrs; Hon (Jane Elizabeth Stirling); *née* Howard; da (by 1 m) of 4 Baron Strathcona and Mount Royal; *b* 23 Jan 1955; *Educ* Sherborne Sch for Girls, Somerville Coll Oxford; *m* 17 Oct 1987, Nigel Morris Jones, o s of M H Morris Jones, of Tarvin, Cheshire; *Style*— The Hon Mrs Morris Jones; 143 Portland Rd, London W11 4LR (☎ 01 243 8252)

MORRIS OF BALGONIE & EDDERGOLL, The Yr Stuart Gordon Cathal; s of Raymond Stanley Morris of Balgonie & Eddergoll, and Margaret Newton Morris, *née* Stuart; *b* 17 April 1965; *Educ* Bell-Baxter HS, Elmwood Coll; *Career* historian, armorist, author; tstee Balgonie Heritage Tst; liveryman Worshipful Co of Meadmakers 1982; fndr memb of Heraldry Soc of Scotland; FSA (Scot) 1983, Assoc RSA 1986; *Recreations* archery, heraldry, genealogy, mead making, historical researching; *Style*— The Younger of Balgonie & Eddergoll; Balgonie Castle, by Markinch, Fife KY7 6HQ (☎ 0592 750119)

MORRIS OF GRASMERE, Baron (Life Peer UK 1967); Sir Charles Richard Morris; KCMG (1963); s of M C Morris (d 1954); *b* 25 Jan 1898; *Educ* Tonbridge Sch, Trinity Coll Oxford; *m* 1923, Mary, da of Prof de Selincourt; 1 s, 1 da; *Career* Lt RGA 1916-19, served war 1939-43; fell and tutor Balliol Coll Oxford 1921-43, vice-chllr Univ of Leeds 1948-63; chm Council for Trg of Health Visitors and Council for Trg in Social Work 1963-71; pro-chllr of Bradford Univ 1966-72; chm Local Govt Trg Bd 1968-75; kt 1953; *Clubs* Athenaeum; *Style*— The Rt Hon the Lord Morris of Grasmere, KCMG; Ladywood, White Moss, Ambleside, Cumbria (☎ 286)

MORRIS OF KENWOOD, 2 Baron (UK 1950); Philip Geoffrey Morris; JP (Inner London 1967); s of 1 Baron (d 1954); *b* 18 June 1928; *Educ* Loughborough Coll Sch, Loughborough Coll; *m* 1958, Hon Ruth Joan Gertrude Rahle, da of Baron Janner (Life Peer); 1 s, 3 da; *Heir* s, Hon Jonathan David Morris; *Career* served 1946-49 with RAF, rejoined 1951-55, flying offr 1953; *Style*— The Rt Hon Lord Morris of Kenwood, JP; Lawn Cottage, Orchard Rise, Kingston, Surrey KT2 7EY (☎ 01 942 6321)

MORRIS OF KENWOOD, Baroness; Hon Ruth Joan Gertrude Rahle; da of Baron Janner (Life Peer); *b* 1932; *m* 1958, 2 Baron Morris of Kenwood; *Career* slr 1956, memb GAC of IBA, exec memb WOYL; govr Broadwood Hall Sch; patron New Working Woman; *Style*— The Rt Hon the Lady Morris of Kenwood; Lawn Cottage, Orchard Rise, Kingston upon Thames, Surrey

MORRIS-EYTON, Lt-Col Robert Charles Gilfrid; TD, DL (Salop 1973); s of Robert Edward Morris-Eyton (d 1936), of Newport, Shropshire, and Violet Mary (d 1972), da of Sir William Lewthwaite, Bt; *b* 8 May 1921; *Educ* Bilton Grange, Shrewsbury Sch, Trinity Coll Cambridge (BA); *m* 1956, Jean Jocelyn, da of Maj-Gen E G Miles, CB, DSO, MC (d 1977), and Lady Marcia Miles, da of 7 Earl of Roden; 1 s (Robert Anthony), 1 da (Katherine); *Career* 2 Lt to Lt 75 Shropshire Yeo Med Regt RA (Mid East and Italy) 1942-45, Lt to Lt-Col Shropshire Yeo (TA) 1947-67; memb Salop CC 1965-81 (chm 1974-77); bd memb Telford Devpt Corpn 1968-75; chm West Mercia Police Authy 1978-79; pres Wrekin div Cons Assoc 1978-80; High Sheriff 1980-81, Vice Lord Lieut of Shropshire 1987; farmer and landowner (600 acres); *Recreations* shooting; *Clubs* Farmers; *Style*— Lt-Col R C G Morris-Eyton, TD, DL; Calvington, Newport, Shropshire (☎ 095 279 316)

MORRIS-JONES, Lady; Leila Augusta Paget; da of Samuel Manning Crosby, and wid of J Ilidge Marsland; *m* 1931, Sir (John) Henry Morris-Jones, MC, DL (d 1972); *Style*— Lady Morris-Jones; c/o Maj F P U Phillips, The Orchard, Linney, Ludlow, Salop

MORRIS-MARSHAM, Jack Richard; s of Richard Henry Anstruther Morris-Mansham (d 1975), of Spilfeathers, Ingatestone, Essex, and Iris Rose Sophia Blackburn, *née* Larking; (refer Peerage and Barontage, E of Romney); *b* 27 Nov 1936; *Educ* Eton; *m* 1, 7 Sept 1963 (m dis 1978), Agnes Margaret (Molly), da of Maj-Gen Walter Rutherfoord Goodman, CB, DSO, MC (d 1976), of Little Bealings Holt, Woodbridge, Suffolk; 2 s (James Jonathan b 1964, Dominic Rutherfoord b 1967), 1 da (Tiffany Jane b 1969); m 2, 30 Jun 1978, Ann Christine (d 1980), da of Howard Sargent Backhouse of Storrington, Sussex; m 3, 28 May 1983, Serena Sybil, da of Gp Capt Geoffrey K Fairclough of Ashfield Ct, Ballybriffas, Co Leix, Eire; *Career* Lt Cdr RNR 1954-73; mktg dir BMW Concessionaries 1970-74, vice chm The Colt Car Co Ltd 1982- (md 1981-82, mktg dir 1974-81); *Recreations* bridge, shooting, snorkelling, gardening; *Clubs* Naval; *Style*— Jack Morris-Marsham, Esq; Brookside, Ewen, Cirencester, Glos GL7 6BU (☎ 0285 770 555); The Colt Car Co Ltd, Watermoor, Cirencester, Glos GL7 1EF (☎ 0285 65 5777, telex 43452, fax 658026, car tel 0836 251780)

MORRISH, Christopher George; s of Harold Gabriel Morrish (d 1953), of Surrey, and The Hon Helen Mary Chubb (d 1969); *b* 8 August 1910; *Educ* Clifton Coll Bristol, Pembroke Coll Cambridge (MA); *m* 12 Jan 1937 (m dis 1950), Emily Beryl, da of Clarence Coward (d 1941); 1 s (Michael b 1947), 1 da (Christine b 1944); m 2, 15 June 1957, Lily Ivy, da of Sidney Hayward (d 1958); 1 s (Paul b 1959); *Career* HM Forestry Cmmn Cambridge 1937, dist estates offr 1946-50, conservancy land agent, area mangr The Stars and Stripes USAF Lakenheath 1950-67, mangr General Refridgeration Thetford 1967-77, ret 1977; *Recreations* gardening; *Style*— Christopher G Morrish, Esq; Langhurst, Green Lane, Thetford, Norfolk IP24 2EX (☎ 0842 2358)

MORRISH, Mr John Edwin (Jack); s of Henry Edwin Morrish, of Shanklin, IOW, and Ada Minnie, *née* Tapping; *b* 23 Sept 1915; *Educ* Univ Coll Sch Hampstead, Northampton Poly; *m* 1 Oct 1937 (m dis 1943), Nora *née* Lake, 1 da (Anna b 1938) m 2, 12 Aug 1944 (m dis 1977), Violet, da of Daniel Saunders; 1 s (Victor b 1947); m 3, 17 July 1985, Betty Lupton, da of John Wear, of Heckmondwicke, W Yorks: 1 da (Elizabeth b 1952); *Career* PO engr 1932-48 and 1945-54, coalminer 1943-45, asst sec CS Union 1954 -72, gen sec Customs & Excise Gp 1972-76, asst gen sec CS Soc 1974- 76, various vol orgns 1977-81, census offr 1981, dep ldr and co cnllr Northants (chm educn ctee 1981-85); memb: Assoc of CCs and Educn Ctee 1981-85, advsy ctee for Supply and Educn of Teachers 1981-84, Burnham Ctee 1981-86, chm govrs Nene Coll, borough cncllr Hounslow (vice chm educn ctee) 1986-89, bd memb Nat Fedn for Educn Res; *Books* The Future of Forestry (1971); *Recreations* thinking, pursuit of justice, music, theatre; *Clubs* Civil Serv; *Style*— Jack Morrish, Esq; The Old Bakehouse, 1 Church St, Broughton, Kettering, Northants NN14 1LK (☎ 0536 790 914)

MORRISH, John Sutherland Cavers; s of Capt Leo Grafton Morrish; *b* 4 Nov 1946; *Educ* George Watson's Coll, Edinburgh Univ; *m* 1977, Elspeth Joan, da of Robert Leslie Findlay; 2 ch; *Career* fin dir GEC Medical Equipment Ltd 1976-81, fin and investment mangr, small business div of Scottish Devpt Agency 1981-; *Recreations* golf; *Style*— John Morrish, Esq; c/o Scottish Development Agency, 17 Cockspur Street, London SW1

MORRISH, Peter Sydney; s of Sydney Victor Morrish (d 1969), of Hove, Sussex, and Elizabeth McLaren, *née* Dewar (d 1969); *b* 30 Dec 1924; *Educ* Sutton Valence, Emmanuel Coll Cambridge (MA); *m* 18 Sept 1954, June Seymour, da of Lancelot Stephen Richard Monckton (d 1979), of Bearsted, Kent; 1 s (Lancelot Peter b 19 Oct 1956), 1 da (Annabel June b 24 Feb 1959); *Career* Sub Lt RNVR 1942-46, Channel, Far East Coastal Forces and attached Fleet Air Arm; land agent and chartered surveyor; ptnr Burrows Clements Winch & Sons 1952-55; chm: Castlemaine Farms Ltd 1955-, Wealden Hops Ltd 1986-; vice-chm Nat Hop Assoc; vice-chm governing body Sutton Valence Sch, tstee Utd Westminster Schs, chm Management Ctee Mascalls Youth Wing, memb ctee Friends of Kent Churches; Freeman City of London 1964; memb: Worshipful Co of Broderers 1964, Worshipful Co of Fruiterers 1975; ARICS 1946; *Recreations* skiing, golf, environment; *Clubs* Farmers', Royal St George's GC, Rye GC; *Style*— Peter S Morrish, Esq; Castlemaine, Horsmonden, Tonbridge, Kent (☎ 089 272 2213); Castlemaine Farms Ltd, Horsmonden, Tonbridge, Kent TN12 8HG; Wealden Hops Ltd, Nettlestead Oast, Paddock Wood, Kent (☎ 089 283 6061)

MORRISH, Hon Mrs (Rosalind Beatrice); *née* Wade; yr da of Baron Wade, DL (Life Peer, d 1988); *b* 11 Dec 1937; *m* 21 Oct 1961, Richard David Morrish, s of late Eric John Morrish, of Leeds; 2 s (Jonathan b 1964, Thomas b 1966), 1 da (Judith b 1969); *Style*— The Hon Mrs Morrish; 34 St Margaret's Rd, Horsforth, Leeds

MORRISON, Hon Alasdair Andrew Orr; s of 1 Viscount Dunrossil, GCMG, MC, PC, QC (d 1961); *b* 25 Mar 1929; *Educ* Fettes, Balliol Coll Oxford, Chicago Univ; *m* 1958, Frances Mary, da of late Wilfrid Rippon Snow, of Adelaide, S Australia; 1 s, 2 da; *Career* chm Orchid Ctee RHS; *Style*— The Hon Alasdair Morrison; Maisemore Park, nr Gloucester, Glos (☎ 0452 21747); work: Shell International Petroleum Co Ltd (☎ 01 934 2288)

MORRISON, Hon Alasdair Godfrey; s of 2 Viscount Dunrossil; *b* 4 April 1962; *m* 19 Sept 1987, Tania, o da of J A Redman, of Minehead, Somerset; *Style*— The Hon Alasdair Morrison; 90 St Stephen's Ave, London W12

MORRISON, Alastair McLeod; MC (1944); s of Brig Hugh McLeod Morrison, MC (d 1984); *b* 2 Mar 1924; *Educ* ISC; *m* 1957, Diana Elizabeth, da of late Col Forester Metcalfe Griffith-Griffin, MC; 1 s, 2 da; *Career* served 4/7 Royal Dragoon Gds, NW Europe and Palestine, Capt, ret 1952; dir Howard Machinery Ltd (overseas md France 1953-57, USA 1957-60) 1970-84, chm J Mann & Son Ltd 1973 (md 1970-73), dir AO Smith Harvestore Inc USA 1979-84; patron Tree Cncl; *Recreations* field sports; *Clubs* Cavalry and Guards; *Style*— Alastair Morrison, Esq, MC; Leigh Hill, Savernake, nr Marlborough, Wilts SN8 3BH (☎ 0672 810230)

MORRISON, His Hon Judge Alexander John Henderson; s of Dr Alexander Morrison (d 1980), and Jean Walker Murdoch (d 1961); *b* 16 Nov 1927; *Educ* Derby Sch, Emmanuel Coll Cambridge (MA, LLB); *m* 1978, Hon Philippa Ann *qv*, da of 1 Baron Hives (d 1965); *Career* barr Gray's Inn 1951, dep chm Derbyshire QS 1964-71, Crown Ct rec 1971-80; regnl chm of Industl Tbnls 1971-80; pres Mental Health Review Tribunals 1983; circuit judge 1980-; *Recreations* golf (pres Derbyshire Union of Golf Clubs 1979-81); *Style*— His Hon Judge Morrison; 17 Eastwood Drive, Littleover, Derby (☎ 0332 45376)

MORRISON, Hon Andrew William Reginald; eld s and h of 2 Viscount Dunrossil, of Government House, Bermuda, by his 1 w, Mavis, da of A Llewellyn Spencer-Payne; *b* 15 Dec 1953; *Educ* Eton, Univ Coll Oxford; *m* 2 da; *Career* merchant banker; Chicago off Kleinwort Benson (N America) Corpn 1981-; *Recreations* poetry, tennis, squash, cricket (when in England); *Clubs* Racquet (Chicago), Withington Cricket; *Style*— The Hon Andrew Morrison; 1550 N Laxe Shore Drive, Chicago, Illinois 60610, USA (☎ 312 440 1861); 90 St Stephen's Ave, London W12 8JD; Kleinwort Benson (North America) Corpn, Three First National Plaza, Suite 2315, Chicago, Illinois 60602, USA (☎ 312 236 0253)

MORRISON, Hon Sir Charles Andrew; MP (C) Wilts (Devizes Div) 1964-; 2 s of 1 Baron Margadale, TD, JP, *qv*; bro of The Hon James, The Hon Peter (MP) and of Hon Dame Mary Anne Morrison *qqv*; gs of 2 Viscount Hambleden; *b* 25 June 1932; *Educ* Eton; *m* 1, 28 Oct 1954, Hon (Antoinette) Sara Frances Sibell, da of 2 Viscount Long; 1 s, 1 da; m 2, 1984, Rosalind Elizabeth, da of late Hon Richard Edward Lygon (d 1970), and formerly w of Gerald John Ward; *Career* 2 Lt Life Gds 1951-52, Capt Royal Wilts Yeo 1952-66; chm: The Game Conservancy, 1987-, Br Tst for Conservation Volunteers 1972-78 (pres 1978-82); pres Nat Anglers Cncl; prime warden Fishmongers Co 1986-87; memb cncl Salmon & Trout Assoc; vice chm 1922 Ctee 1974-83 chm Nat Ctee for Electoral Reform 1985-; kt 1988; *Recreations* shooting, gardening, fishing; *Clubs* White's, Pratt's; *Style*— The Hon Sir Charles Morrison, MP; House of Commons, London SW1 (☎ 01 219 5012/4008); Brook House, Luckington, nr Chippenham, Wilts (☎ 0666 840371)

MORRISON, Hon Mrs (Charlotte Anne); *née* Monckton; o da of 9 Viscount Galway (d 1971), and Lady Teresa Agnew, *née* Fox-Stangways, da of 7 Earl of Ilchester; *b* 16 April 1955; *m* 24 Sept 1983 (m dis 1987), Guy Martin James Morrison, s of Martin James Faber Morrison; 1 s (Simon b 1984); *Style*— The Hon Mrs Morrison; The Manor House, Abbotsbury, Dorset DT3 4JJ (☎ 0305 871408); Bishopfield House, Bawtry, Doncaster, Yorks (☎ 0777 818224); 83 Onslow Gardens, London SW7

MORRISON, David Du Bois; s of John Macfarlane Morrison (d 1978), and Eleanor Buell, *née* Morris; *b* 3 April 1952; *Educ* George Watson's Coll Edinburgh, St Andrews Univ (BSc); *m* 25 June 1977, Julia Katherine, da of Tony Richard Hillier Godden CB, of Edinburgh; 3 s (James, Alexander, Charles); *Career* ptnr Wood Mackenzie and Co 1983 (joined 1976), dir Co Natwest Wood Mackenzie and Co Ltd (after merging with Natwest Investmt Bank); MInstPet; memb: Stock Exchange, Soc of Investment Analysts; *Recreations* music, painting, photography, running, squash; *Clubs* New (Edinburgh); *Style*— David Morrison, Esq; Beehive Cottage, Aston, Herts; County Natwest Wood Mackenzie & Co, Drapers Gardens, Throgmorton Avenue, London EC2P (☎ 01 382 1000)

MORRISON, 2 Baron (UK 1945); Dennis Glossop Morrison; s of 1 Baron, PC (d 1953); *b* 21 June 1914; *Educ* Tottenham County Sch; *m* 1, 1940 (m dis 1958), Florence, da of Augustus Hennes, of Tottenham; m 2, 1959, (m dis 1975), Joan, da of Willam Meech, of Acton; *Heir* none; *Career* formerly with Metal Box Co; Ld-Lt's rep for Tottenham 1955-, vice pres Acton C of C until 1987; *Style*— The Rt Hon the Lord Morrison; 7 Ullswater Avenue, Felixstowe, Suffolk (☎ 039 42 77405)

MORRISON, Derrick John Richard; JP; s of John Cyril (d 1972), and Violet Constance Osborne (d 1988); *b* 4 August 1922; *Educ* Eastcote Boys' Sch, Trent Park Coll of Educn, London Univ (LCP, Dip Ed); *m* 18 Aug 1951, Patricia Margaret, da of Claude Tilly (d 1966); *Career* RAF Med Branch 1941-47; headmaster West Hill Sch Leatherhead 1960-87, chm Woking Juvenile Ct 1970-87, memb Surrey Magistrates Soc; *Recreations* sailing, golf, gardening; *Clubs* Rotary Int; *Style*— Derrick J R Morrison, Esq, JP; Cherrywood, Brentmoor Rd, West End, Woking, Surrey GU24 9NF

MORRISON, Cdr Edwin Allen; OBE (1983), DL (Hampshire); s of John Wheatley Morrison (d 1945), of Snows Oreen House, Shotley Bridge, Co Durham, and Kathleen, *née* King (d 1953); *b* 13 May 1905; *Educ* Royal Naval Coll: Osborne, Dartmouth; *m* 16 Dec 1931, Valerie Patricia Anne, da of Col Harold Charles Wortham, CMG, DSO; 1 s (Euan b 1941), 3 da (Elspeth b 1936, Fenella b 1943, Malvina b 1946); *Career* served HMS: Thunderer 1922-23, RNEC Keyham 1923-27, Iron Duke 1927, Effingham 1927-29, Fisgard 1930-32, Curacoa 1932-33, RNEC 1933-35, Hero 1936-37, Nelson 1937-40, Daedalus 1940-41, Charybdis 1941-42, Spartan 1942-44, Landrail 1944-45, Merganser 1945-46, President 1946-48, Condor 1948-49, Resource 1949; mangr family shipping and property interests; memb Chapter Gen OStJ; formerly: cdr St Johns Ambulance, memb hosp mgmnt, chm diocesan finance; Citizen and Pattenmaker of London 1950; KStJ 1944; *Recreations* sailing; *Clubs* Army & Navy, RYS, Royal Ocean Racing, Royal Lymington YC; *Style*— Cdr Edwin Morrison, OBE, DL; The Bury House, Odiham, nr Basingstoke, Hampshire RG25 1LZ (☎ 0256 702 103)

MORRISON, Frances Margaret (Fran); da of Lt-Cdr William Morrison, RNVR, of Cove, Scotland, and Hilary Mary, *née* Wootton; *Educ* Queen's Park Sch Glasgow, St Andrews Univ (MA); *m* 22 Sept 1984 (m dis), Trevor Deaves, s of Alan Deaves, of Cranleigh, Surrey; 2 s (Adam b 1984, Dominic b 1986); *Career* broadcaster and media conslt, news and current affrs reporter/presenter BBC Radio and TV, sole female memb presenting team of BBC TV's Newsnight at its launch 1979; reporter/presenter BBC TV: Nationwide 1981-83, 60 Minutes 1983-84; reporter BBC TV Watchdog 1984-85, reporter various documentary progs BBC TV 1978-86, presenter various arts and music progs BBC TV 1978-, media conslt 1986-, freelance journalist 1978-; *Recreations* travel, theatre, visual arts; *Clubs* Network; *Style*— Ms Fran Morrison; c/o Jon Roseman Assocs, 103 Charing Cross Rd, London W1 (☎ 01 439 8245)

MORRISON, Hon Mrs (Helena Geneva); *née* Garner; o da of Baron Garner, GCMG (d 1983; Life Peer); *b* 28 Jan 1947; *Educ* Bishop Strachan Sch, Toronto, Canada; Tortington Park; *m* 1981, Iain Morrison; *Style*— The Hon Mrs Morrison; 33 North Street, Marcham, Abingdon, Oxon

MORRISON, Maj Hon James Ian; TD (1963), DL (Wilts 1977); s and h of 1 Baron Margadale, *qv*; eld bro of The Hon Charles and The Hon Peter Morrison (MPs), and of The Hon Dame Mary Anne Morrison, *qqv*, and Margaret Ester Lucy, *née* Smith da of 3 Viscount Hambleden (d 1980), ggs of James Morrison who purchased much of the property at present owned; *b* 17 July 1930; *Educ* Eton, RAC Cirencester; *m* 1952, Clare, da of Anthony Lister Barclay, of Broad Oak End, Hertford; 2 s (Alastair, Hugh), 1 da (Fiona) (*see* Viscount Hon Hugh Trenchard); *Career* 2 Lt Life Gds 1949-50, Maj Royal Wilts Yeo; farmer and co dir; Wilts ccnclr 1955 and 1973-77, alderman 1969, High Sheriff 1971; chm W Wilts (Westbury) Cons Assoc 1967-71 (pres 1972-84); chm: Tattersall's Ctee 1969-80, Wilts CLA 1978-81; Hon Col A (Royal Wilts Yeo) Sqdn Royal Yeo RAC TA 1982-89, (Royal Wilts Yeo) Sqdn Royal Wessex Yeo 1982-89, Royal Wessex Yeo RAC TA 1984-89; memb: Queen's Body Guard for Scotland, Royal Company of Archers; landowner; *Recreations* racing, field sports; *Clubs* White's, Jockey; *Style*— Maj the Hon James Morrison, TD, DL; Hawking Down, Hindon, Salisbury, Wilts (☎ 074 789 234); Estate Office, Fonthill Bishop, Salisbury, SP3 5SH (☎ 074 789 246); Islay Estate Office, Bridgend, Islay, Argyll PA44 7PB (☎ 049 681 221)

MORRISON, John; s of Thomas Patrick Morrison, and Marie, *née* Boylan; *b* 6 Mar 1949; *Educ* St Edward's Coll Liverpool, St Catherine's Coll Oxford (BA); *m* 29 Feb 1980, Judith, da of Ronald Lee, of Bury, Lancashire; 1 s (Nicholas), 1 da (Joanna); *Career* news trainee BBC 1971, scriptwriter ITN 1973, prog ed Channel 4 News 1982, features ed The Independent 1986, ed Newsnight BBC 1987-; *Style*— John Morrison, Esq; 7065 Television Centre, London W12

MORRISON, Rev John Anthony; s of Maj Leslie Claude Morrison (d 1967), of Hastings, Sussex, and Mary Sharland, da of Sir Frank Newson-Smith, 1 Bt (d 1971); *b* 11 Mar 1938; *Educ* Haileybury, Jesus Coll Cambridge (BA, MA), Lincoln Coll Oxford (MA), Chichester Theol Coll, Seminaire de la Mission de France Pontigny; *m* 20 July 1968, Angela, da of Maj Jonathan Eric Bush (d 1978), of Leatherhead; 2 s (Dominic b 19 June 1970, Nicholas b 11 May 1974), 1 da (Philippa b 26 March 1972); *Career* ordained deacon 1964, priest 1965 Birmingham; curate: St Peter Birmingham 1964-68, St Michael-at-the-North Gate Oxford 1968-74; chaplain Lincoln Coll Oxford 1968-74, vicar Basildon Berks 1974-82, rural dean Bradfield 1978-82, vicar Aylesbury Bucks 1982-, rural dean Aylesbury 1985-, examining chaplain to Bishop of Oxford 1973-, proctor in convocation and memb Gen Synod 1980-; memb: Oxford Diocesan Synod 1973-, Bishop's Cncl 1976-82 and 1985-; chaplain: Mayor of Aylesbury, Aylesbury Br Legion; Freeman City of London 1961, Liveryman Worshipful Co of Spectaclemakers 1962; *Recreations* rowing, gardening; *Clubs* Leander, Vincent's; *Style*— The Rev John Morrison; The Vicarage, Parson's Fee, Aylesbury, Bucks HP20 2QZ (☎ 0296 24276)

MORRISON, Hon Mrs; (Louisa Mary Constance); da of 14 Baron Napier and (5) Ettrick; *b* 5 Feb 1961; *m* 25 July 1987, Capt Alexander F Morrison, er son of Peter Morrison; *Style*— The Hon Mrs Morrison; Forest Lodge, Great Park, Windsor

MORRISON, Hon (Dame) Mary Anne; DCVO (1982, CVO 1970); does not use style of Dame; da of 1 Baron Margadale, sis of the Hon James, the Hon Sir Charles and the Rt Hon Peter Morrison *qv*; *b* 17 May 1937; *Educ* Heathfield Sch Ascot, abroad; *Career* woman of the bedchamber to HM The Queen 1960-; *Style*— The Hon Mary Morrison, DCVO; Islay Estate Office, Bridgend, Islay, Argyll (☎ 049 681 221); Fonthill Hse, Tisbury, Wilts SP3 5SA (☎ 0747 870202)

MORRISON, Rev Hon Nial Ranald; s of 1 Viscount Dunrossil, GCMG, MC, PC, QC (d 1961), and Catharine Allison, *née* Swan (d 1983); *b* 27 July 1932; *Educ* Fettes Coll, Jesus Coll Oxford (MA); *m* 1959, Sheila Mary, da of late Alexander Forbes, of Gloucester; 3 s, 2 da; *Career* ordained 1956, asst curate St Catharine's Gloucester 1956-58, Stroud Parish Church 1959-62, vicar of Randwick Stroud 1962-; minor canon Gloucester Cathedral 1979-86, C of E chaplain Standish Hosp 1982-; *Recreations* music, cycling, botany; *Style*— The Rev the Hon Nial Morrison; The Vicarage, Randwick, Stroud, Glos (☎ 045 36 4727)

MORRISON, Rt Hon Peter Hugh; MP (C) Chester 1974-; 3 s of 1 Baron Margadale, *qv*; bro of The Hon James, Sir Charles (MP), and The Hon Dame Mary Anne Morrison, *qqv*; *b* 2 June 1944; *Educ* Eton, Keble Oxford; *Career* formerly PA to Peter Walker; investment mangr, ind businessman; oppn whip 1976-79, lord cmmr Treasy 1979-81, under-sec of state Employment 1981-83; min of state: Employment 1983-85, Trade and Indust 1985-1986; dep chm Conservative Party 1986-, min of state Energy 1987-; chm one Nation Forum and Cons Collegiate Forum; *Clubs* White's, Pratt's; *Style*— The Rt Hon Peter Morrison, MP; 81 Cambridge St, London SW1; Eallabus, Bridgend, Islay, Argyll; Stable House, Puddington, Wirral, Cheshire

MORRISON, Hon Mrs (Philippa Ann); *née* Hives; da of 1 Baron Hives, CH, MBE (d 1965); *b* 1928; *m* 1980, His Hon Judge Morrison, *qv*; *Style*— The Hon Mrs Morrison; 17 Eastwood Drive, Littleover, Derby (☎ 0332 45376)

MORRISON, Hon Ranald John; s of 2 Viscount Dunrossil, Govr of Bermuda, and Mavis Viscountess Dunrossil, *née* Dawn Spencer-Payne; *b* 19 Dec 1956; *Educ* Summerfields, Westminster, Univ Coll London (BSc); *m* 1979, Henrietta Frances, da of late J H Wilson, of Addison Road, London (d 1969); 1 s (Richard b 1983), 2 da (Allison b 1984, Rebecca b 1987); *Career* proprietor Garage Door Co est 1982; *Recreations* cricket; *Clubs* Withington CC, Old Westminster CC; *Style*— The Hon Ranald Morrison; 37 Brigstocke Rd, St Pauls, Bristol; 5 Glenfrome Road, St Werburghs, Bristol, Avon (☎ 0272 554594)

MORRISON, Lady; Rosemary; *m* 1, E H U de Groot (decd); 2 da; m 2, 1959, Sir Nicholas Morrison, KCB, sometime perm under sec Scottish Office and chm Local Govt Boundary Cmmn for Eng (d 1981); *Style*— Lady Morrison; Gosse Ford, Clare, Suffolk CO10 8PX (☎ 0787 277200)

MORRISON, Hon Mrs; Hon (Antoinette) Sara Frances Sibell; *née* Long; da of 2 Viscount Long (ka 1944), and of Laura, Duchess of Marlborough, *qv*; *b* 9 August 1934; *Educ* England, France; *m* 1954 (m dis 1985), Hon Charles Andrew Morrison; 1 s, 1 da; *Career* exec dir: Gen Electric Co 1975-, Abbey Nat Building Soc 1979-; non-exec dir The Fourth Channel Television Co 1980-85, Imperial Gp 1981-; chm Nat Cncl Soc Serv 1977-, (vice-chm 1970-77); former memb: Nat Consumer Cncl, The Volunteer Centre; chm Nat Cncl for Voluntary Organisations until 1981; *Style*— The Hon Mrs Morrison; 16 Groom Place, London SW1X 7BA; Wyndham's Farm, Wedhampton, Devizes, Wilts SN10 3QE

MORRISON, Lady Sophia Louise Sydney; *née* Cavendish; yst da of 11 Duke of Devonshire, MC, PC, *qv*; *b* 18 Mar 1957; *m* 1, 1979 (m dis 1987), Anthony William Lindsay Murphy, er s of Christopher Murphy, of 17 Napier Ave, SW6; m 2, 19 July 1988, Alastair Morrison, eld s of the Hon James Morrison, *qv*; *Books* The Duchess of Devonshire's Ball (1984), The Mitford Family Album (1985); *Recreations* hunting, racing, tropical gardens; *Style*— Lady Sophia Morrison; The Quadrangle, Tisbury, Wilts (☎ 0747 870709)

MORRISON, (James) Stewart; s of Stewart Kirkwood Morrison (d 1933), of Chelsea, and Felice, *née* Showell (d 1989); *b* 12 Oct 1926; *Educ* Merchant Taylors, Wadham Coll Oxford (MA); *m* 27 Sept 1958, Dr Jane Bomford, da of Dr Edgar Davey; 1 s (Charles b 1964), 1 da (Catherine b 1972); *Career* dir Clarnico Ltd 1953-70, md Associated Deliveries Ltd 1970-85 (dep chm 1986), dep appeals dir Assoc for Spina Bifida and Hydrocephalus (ASBAH) 1986-; pres Jr C of C London 1966-67, memb cncl London C of C and Indust 1969-80; Confectioners Benevolent Fund: pres 1982, chm 1987-88, tstee 1988-; Freeman City of London 1967; MBIM 1951, memb Lloyds 1985; *Recreations* travel, reading, gardening ; *Style*— Stewart Morrison, Esq; Washwell House, Painswick, nr Stroud, Glos GL6 6SJ (☎ 0452 813556; 26 Ormonde Gate, Chelsea, London SW3 4EX (☎ 01 352 7152); ASBAH, 22 Upper Woburn Place, London WC1H OEP (☎ 01 388 1382)

MORRISON, William McKenzie Meek; s of William Morrison (d 1968), and Helen McGregor McKenzie (d 1977); *b* 6 Sept 1925; *Educ* Charles Adams GS Wem Salop, Birmingham Tech Coll; *m* 1, 1950, Margaret Millicent Hinton (d 1978); 2 s; m 2, 1980, Irmgard Anne Adelheid, da of late William Karl Köhrner of W Germany; 1 step s; *Career* dir: Turner MFG Co Ltd 1955-79, Hydraulics & Pneumatics Ltd 1957-78; tech dir Spicer Drivetrain Gp-Dana Ltd 1979-83; former chm Midlands branch Inst of Marine Engrs; awarded Crompton-Lanchester Medal (Inst of Mech Engrs) 1974; CEng, FIMarE, FIProdE, FIMechE, memb Soc of Automotive Engrs (USA); *Recreations* oil painting, motoring; *Style*— William Morrison, Esq; 57 Seagar St, Sandwell, W Bromwich, W Midlands (☎ 021 525 1142); W M Morrison & Associates, Consulting Engineers, Bridge House, 57 Seagar St, Sandwell, W Bromwich, W Midlands (☎ 021 525 1142)

MORRISON OF LAMBETH, Baroness; Edith; da of late John Meadowcroft; *m* 1955, as his 2 w, Baron Morrison of Lambeth, PC (Life Peer) (d 1965); *Career* dir FCI Ltd and BNEIS; *Style*— The Rt Hon Lady Morrison of Lambeth

MORRISON-BELL, Sir William Hollin Dayrell; 4 Bt (UK 1905); s of Capt Sir Charles Reginald Francis Morrison-Bell, 3 Bt (d 1967), and Prudence Caroline, *née* Davies; *b* 21 June 1956; *Educ* Eton, St Edmund Hall Oxford; *m* 6 Oct 1984, Cynthia Hélène Marie, yr da of Teddy White, of 41 Iverna Gardens, London, W8; 1 s; *Heir* s, Thomas Charles Edward Morrison-Bell b 13 Feb 1985; *Style*— Sir William Morrison-Bell, Bt; 106 Bishops Rd, London SW6 (☎ 01 736 4940)

MORRISON-LOW, Sir James Richard; 3 Bt (UK 1908), of Kilmaron, Co Fife, DL (Fife 1978); s of Sir Walter John Morrison-Low, 2 Bt, JP (d 1955; assumed by deed poll the additional surname of Morrison 1924), and Dorothy Ruth, *née* de Quincey (d 1946); Sir James Low, 1 Bt, was Lord Provost of Dundee 1893-96; *b* 3 August 1925; *Educ* Harrow, Merchiston, Faraday House (Dip); *m* 1953, Ann Rawson, da of Air Cdre Robert Gordon, CB, CMG, DSO (d 1954); 1 s, 3 da (Alison, Jean, Susan); *Heir* s, Richard Walter Morrison-Low, *qv*; *Career* serv 1943-47, Royal Corps of Signals, Capt; CEng, MIEE, FInstD 1982; electrical engineer Osborne & Hunter Ltd Glasgow 1952, dir 1956; trustee TSB: Cupar 1958-78, Fife Area Bd TSB 1978-82; chm Scottish Traction Engine Soc 1961-63; dir Nat Inspection Cncl for Electrical Installation Contracting 1982-, pres Electrical Contractors Assoc of Scotland 1982-84; memb: technical ctee Assoc Internationale des Entreprises d'Equipment Electrique 1981-, wiring regulations ctee Inst of Electrical Engrs 1982-; chm Fife Area Scout Cncl 1966-84; Hon Pipe Maj of Royal Scottish Pipers' Soc 1981-83; landowner (1000 acres);

Recreations piping, shooting, fishing, steam rollers & traction engines; *Clubs* New (Edinburgh); *Style—* Sir James Morrison-Low, Bt, DL; Kilmaron Castle, nr Cupar, Fife KY15 4NE (☎ Cupar (0334) 52248); Osborne & Hunter Ltd, 42-46 North Frederick St, Glasgow (☎ 041 552 2147)

MORRISON-LOW, Richard Walker; s and h of Sir James Richard Morrison-Low, 3 Bt; *b* 4 August 1959; *Style—* Richard Walker Morrison-Low Esq

MORRISON-LOW, Dowager Lady; (Henrietta) Wilhelmina Mary; da of Maj Robert Walter Purvis (d 1956) and Henrietta Walton, *née* Gilmour (d 1962), of Gilmerton House, nr St Andrews, Fife; *b* 25 Mar 1914; *Educ* Queens Gate Sch London; *m* 1948, as his 2 w, Sir Walter John Morrison-Low, 2 Bt (d 1955); *Style—* Dowager Lady Morrison-Low; Kingsbarns House, 6 The Square, Kingsbarns, nr St Andrews, Fife KY16 8SS (☎ 033 488 245)

MORRISON-SCOTT, Sir Terence Charles Stuart; DSC (1944), DL (W Sussex 1982); o s of Robert Charles Stuart Morrison Morrison-Scott, DSO (d 1940); *b* 24 Oct 1908; *Educ* Eton, Ch Ch Oxford, Royal Coll of Science; *m* 1935, Rita, 4 da of late E J Layton; *Career* served WWII, RN; dir: Br Museum (Natural History) 1960-68 (scientific staff 1936-) Sci Museum 1956-60; memb Properties Ctee Nat Trust 1968-83, chm Nature Conservation Panel 1970-81, Architectural Panel 1973-82; kt 1965; *Clubs* Athenaeum, Brooks's; *Style—* Sir Terence Morrison-Scott, DSC, DL; Upperfold House, Fernhurst, Haslemere, Surrey (☎ 0428 53046)

MORRISS, Nicholas Anson; s of Kenneth Cherry Morriss, MBE, of Haslemere, Surrey, and Diana Mary, *née* Gunning; *b* 17 Sept 1950; *Educ* Radley, York Univ (BA); *m* 29 June 1974, Suzette Anne, da of Richard Tilney, of Orford, Suffolk; 1 s (Alexander b 11 Feb 1984), 1 da (Fenella b 27 June b 1987); *Career* CA; Price Waterhouse: London 1972-76, Cape Town 1976-78, mangr London 1978-79; asst dir Barclay de Zoete Wedd (formerly Barclays Merchant Bank) 1979-86, ptnr corp fin Deloitte Haskins & Sells 1986-, dir Deloitte Corp Fin 1986-; FCA 1975; ; *Recreations* squash, golf, skiing, tennis; *Style—* Nicholas Morriss, Esq; 3 Akehurst St, Roehampton, London SW15 5DR (☎ 01 788 8590); Deloitte Haskins & Sells, Hillgate House, 26 Old Bailey, London EC4M 7PL (☎ 01 248 3913, fax 01 236 2367)

MORRISSEY, Lady Joanna Agnes; *née* Townshend; da of 7 Marquess Townshend; *b* 1943; *m* 1, 1962, Jeremy George Courtenay Bradford (m dis 1968); 1 s; m 2, 1978, James Barry Morrissey; *Style—* Lady Joanna Morrissey

MORRISSEY, Michael Peter; s of Peter Anthony Morrissey, of Langshott Wood, Surrey, and Sheila Margaret, *née* Berrett (d 1984); *b* 15 August 1959; *Educ* Worth Sch Sussex; *m* 30 May 1987, Sally-Anne, da of Derek Harris, of Weybridge, Surrey; *Career* enlisted 1977, RMA Sandhurst 1978; Irish Guards: cmmnd 2 Lt 1978, Lt 1980, Capt 1983, Maj 1988; serv: Cyprus, Kenya, NI, Belize, Canada, Germany; currently co cdr Bn Irish Gds; *Recreations* shooting, riding, rugby, cricket; *Clubs* Cavalry and Guards; *Style—* Michael Morrissey, Esq; 38 Tonsley Hill, London SW18

MORROW, Sir Ian Thomas; s of Thomas George Morrow (d 1973), and Jamesina, *née* Hunter (d 1919); ggs of Tom Morris who was Open Golf Champion and gn of Young Tom Morris who was also Open Golf Champion; *b* 8 June 1912; *Educ* Dollar Acad; *m* 1, 1940 (m dis 1967), Elizabeth Mary Thackeray (decd); 1 s, 1 da; m 2, 1967, Sylvia Jane, da of Arthur Taylor; 1 da; *Career* jt sr ptnr Robson Morrow & Co 1942-51, md Brush Gp 1953-58, dep chm and md UK Optical & Industl Hldgs 1958-86 (chm 1979-86), chm Kenwood Mfrg Co 1961-68, chm Assoc Fire Alarms 1965-72, dep chm Siebe Gorman Hldgs 1970-82, dir Hambro's 1972-; chm: MAI plc 1974, Laird Gp 1975-87 (dep chm 1973-75), Strong and Fisher (Hldgs) plc 1981-, Additional Underwriting Agencies (No 3) Ltd 1985-, Int Harvester Co of GB Ltd 1974-85; dep chm: Rolls Royce Ltd 1970-71, Rolls Royce (1971) Ltd 1971-73, CMD 1971-72; memb Press Cncl 1974-80; CA, FCMA, JDipMA, FBIM; kt 1973; *Recreations* reading, music, golf, skiing; *Clubs* Nat Lib, RAC, Royal and Ancient (St Andrews); *Style—* Sir Ian Morrow; 2 Albert Terrace Mews, London NW1 7TA (☎ 01 722 7110); work: 41 Bishopsgate, London EC2P 2AA (☎ 01 588 4662)

MORROW, Capt John Geoffrey Basil; CVO (1957), DSC (1945); s of Canon G Clare Morrow (d 1953), and Winifred Mary, *née* Bazin (d 1957); *b* 8 Jan 1916; *Educ* Summerfields Oxford, RNC Dartmouth, Greenwich; *m* 23 June 1940, (Dorothy April) Bettine, da of Norman Frederick Hugh Mather, MCS, (d 1963); 2 s (Anthony b 1944, James b 1948), 2 da (Angela b 1941, Mary b 1946); *Career* cmmnd RN 1937, serv WWII Atlantic and Med; cmd HMS Wakeful 1953, HMS Harrier 1957, HMS Ausonia 1960; naval attaché Copenhagen 1955, Cdre COS to C-in-C Plymouth 1963, ret 1966 as Capt; Cdr Order of Dannebrog 1957; *Recreations* country pursuits, painting; *Style—* Capt John Morrow; 11 Westerleigh, 35 West Cliff Rd, Bournemouth BH4 8AZ (☎ 0202 763833)

MORSE, Capt David Henry; CBE (Mil); s of Rear Adm Harold Edward Morse, DSO, of Dorset (d 1975), and Helen Aileen, *née* Currie (d 1970); *b* 28 Jan 1932; *Educ* RNC Dartmouth; *m* 27 July 1957, Jill Salwey, da of Gerald William Leigh Holland (d 1971), of Switzerland; *Career* RN 1945-84, served in Korean War, Suez 1956, Kuwait 1961, Hong Kong riots 1967, withdrawal from Aden 1967; cmdg offr HMS Crofton 1961-63, promoted Cdr 1967, CO HMS Lowescroft 1970-71, Staff Offr Ops to Flag Offr 1 Flotilla 1974-75, promoted Capt 1975, operational requiremnets staff Central Staff MOD 1976-79, Capt HMS Intrepid 1979-80, dir RN Staff Coll 1981-82, Capt RN Presentation Team 1980-81, Cdre Clyde and Capt HMS Neptune 1982-84, ret from active list RN 1985; farmer and charity conslt 1985-;; *Recreations* golf, tennis; *Style—* David H Morse, CBE; Kings House, Powerstock, Dorset DT6 3TG (☎ 030 885 361)

MORSE, Hon Mrs; Hon (Jennifer); da of Baron Delfont (Life Peer); *b* 1949; *m* 1974, Andrew Morse; *Style—* The Hon Mrs Morse; c/o Rt Hon Lord Delfont, c/o 7 Soho St, Soho Sq, London W1V 5FA

MORSE, Sir (Christopher) Jeremy; KCMG (1975); s of late Francis John Morse and Kinbarra, *née* Armfield-Marrow; *b* 10 Dec 1928; *Educ* Winchester, New Coll Oxford; *m* 1955, Belinda Marianne, da of Lt-Col R B Y Mills; 3 s, 1 da; *Career* Lt KRRC 1948-49; exec dir Bank of England 1965-72, chm Lloyds Bank 1977- (dep chm 1975-77); non-exec dir ICI 1981-; chm: Ctee of London Clearing Bankers 1980-82, Deputies Ctee of Twenty IMF 1972-74; pres: Br Bankers Assoc 1984-, Euro Banking Fedn 1988-; memb: Cncl of Lloyds 1987-, NEDC 1977-81; former chm City Arts Tst; FIDE judge for Chess Compositions 1975-; Warden Winchester 1987-; chllr Bristol Univ 1988-; *Recreations* poetry, problems and puzzles, coarse gardening, golf; *Clubs* Athenaeum; *Style—* Sir Jeremy Morse, KCMG; 102a Drayton Gdns, London SW10 (☎ 01 370 2265)

MORSE, Rodney Johns; s of James Morse (d 1986), and Elsie, *née* Cripps; *b* 26 Jan 1944; *m* 25 May 1968, (Maureen) Ann Morse, da of John Kenny Woodward, of Leighton Buzzard, Beds; 1 da (Carrie Alisa b 25 Aug 1971); *Career* underwriter Lloyds 1986-, dir Wellington Underwriting Agencies Ltd 1986-; ACII; *Style—* Rodney Morse, Esq; Linwood, Sevenoaks Rd, Ightham, Sevenoaks, Kent (☎ 0732 882537); 120 Fenchurch St, London EC3M 5BA (☎ 01 929 2811, fax 01 220 7234, telex 268892 WELTN G)

MORSHEAD, Lady; Myrtle Catherine Hay; da of William Woodside Grazyer (d 1932), of Melbourne, Australia and Annie Grant-Woodside Hay (d 1959); *b* 13 Jan 1898; *Educ* Melbourne C of E Girls GS; *m* 1921, Lt-Gen Sir Leslie James Morshead, KCB, KBE, CMG, DSO, ED (d 1959), s of William Morshead; 1 da (Elizabeth); *Career* formerly vice-pres of Ladies Assoc of Dr Barnardo's Homes in Aust, memb NSW Cncl of Dr Barnardo's Homes, patron Sydney Hosp Graduate Nurses Assoc and Sydney Nurses Memorial Club, memb ctees Day Nursery and Dist Nursing Assocs; *Clubs* Royal Sydney GC, Queen's (Sydney); *Style—* Lady Morshead; 9 St Marks Rd, Darling Point, Sydney, NSW, Australia 2027

MORSON, Dr Basil Clifford; CBE (1987), VRD (1970); s of Albert Clifford Morson, OBE (d 1975), of London, and Adela Frances Maud Phené (d 1982); *b* 13 Nov 1921; *Educ* Beaumont Coll, Wadham Coll Oxford, Middx Hosp Med Sch; *m* 1, (m annulled 1982), Pamela, *née* Gilbert; m 2, 9 Feb 1983, Sylvia, MBE, da of Hugh Frederick Dutton (d 1972), of Yorks; 1 s (Christopher Alan), 2 da (Caroline Mary, Clare Elizabeth (Mrs Morris)); *Career* ordinary seaman RN 1942, Sub Lt RNVR 1943, Surgn Lt 1953, ret as Surgn Cdr RNR 1980; conslt pathologist: St Marks Hosp London 1956-86, RN (emeritius civilian conslt in pathology); tres RCPath 1983-88 (vice-pres 1978-81); memb Worshipful Co of Barbers; FRCS, FRCP, FRCPath; *Books* Textbook of Gastrointestinal Pathology (1972, 1979), Pathology of the Alimentary Tract (1987), Atlas of Gastrointestinal Pathology (1988); *Recreations* gardening, ornithology; *Style—* Dr Basil Morson, CBE, VRD; 52 Gordon Place, London W8 4JF (☎ 01 937 7101)

MORTIMER, David John; s of Eric Richardson Mortimer (d 1976), and Doris Mabel, *née* Somes; *b* 3 May 1938; *Educ* King's Sch Canterbury, St John's Coll Oxford (MA); *m* 1965, Sheila Gail, *née* Ross; 2 s (Mark, Gavin); *Career* publisher; dir: Longman Gp Ltd 1972-85, Int Language Centres Ltd 1983-85, Macmillan Educn Ltd 1985-88; chief exec off business trg; chm Macmillan Intek Ltd 1985-; *Recreations* music, sport, walking, reading; *Clubs* MCC; *Style—* David Mortimer, Esq; Calidcote, High St, Lindfield, W Sussex (☎ 04447 3115)

MORTIMER, James Edward; *b* 12 Jan 1921; *Educ* Ruskin Coll Oxford, LSE; married; 2 s, 1 da; *Career* former apprentice fitter RN Shipyards Portsmouth, TUC Econ Dept 1946-48, offr Draughtmen's and Allied Technicians Assoc 1948-68, chm ACAS 1974-81, gen sec Labour Pty 1982-85; chm: Econ Devpt Ctee Chemical Indust 1973-74, Econ Devpt Ctee Mech & Electrical Engrg Construction 1974-82; memb: Nat Bd for Prices and Incomes 1968-71, Wilberforce Inquiry into Power Dispute 1970, Armed Forces Pay Review Body 1971-74, bd London Tport 1971-74; former memb CBI Employment Affrs Ctee; dir: London Co-op Soc 1968-71, Yorks TV 1981-82; visiting fell Henley Admin Staff Coll 1976-82, sr visiting fell Bradford Univ 1977-82, visiting prof industl rels Imperial Coll London 1979-82; Hon DLitt Bradford 1982; *Style—* James Mortimer, Esq; 31 Charleston St, London SE17 1RL

MORTIMER, John Clifford; CBE (1986), QC; s of Clifford Mortimer, and Kathleen May, *née* Smith; *b* 21 April 1923; *Educ* Harrow, Brasenose Coll Oxford; *m* 1, 1949, Penelope Ruth *née* Fletcher; 1 s, 1 da; m 2, Penelope *née* Gollop; 1 da; *Career* barr, playwrite and author; called to the Bar 1948, master of the Bench, Inner Temple 1975; full length plays inc: The Wrong Side of the Park (1960), Cat Among The Pigeons (1969), A Voyage round My Father (1970, filmed 1982), I Claudius (adpted from Robert Graves) 1972, The Bells of Hell (1977); film scripts inc: John Mary (1970), Brideshead Revisited (TV 1981), Edwin (TV 1984); novels inc: Charade (1947), Three Winters (1956), Rumpole of the Bailey (1978; BAFTA writer of the year award), Rumpole's Return (1980); autobiography; Clinging to the Wreckage (1982); pres Berks, Books & Oxon Naturalists Tst 1984, memb Nat Theatre Bd 1968-; Italic Prize 1958, Hon DLitt Susquehanna Univ (1985), Hon LLD Exeter (1986), Hon DLitt St Andrews (1987);; *Recreations* working, gardening, opera; *Clubs* Garrick; *Style—* John C Mortimer, QC

MORTIMER, Katharine Mary Hope; da of Robert Cecil Mortimer, DD, Bishop of Exeter 1949-73 (d 1976), and Mary Hope, *née* Walker; *b* 28 May 1946; *Educ* St Mary and St Anne Abbots Bromley, Somerville Coll Oxford (BA, BPhil); *m* 7 July 1973 (m dis 1986), John Noel, s of Rev John Malcolm Nicholson (d 1982); 1 s (Andrew Robert b 1982); *Career* dir: N M Rothschild & Sons Ltd 1985- (non exec 1988-), N M Rothschild Asset Mgmnt (Hldgs) 1987- (non exec 1988-), Securities and Investmts Bd, policy dir 1985-87, Nat Bus Co 1979-, chief exec Walker Books Ltd 1988-; govr Imperial Coll of Sci & Technol June 1987-; cncl memb ESRC July 1984-86, memb governing body Inst of Devpt Studies Sussex June 1983-, non exec dir Centre for Economic Policy Res June 1986; memb: BBC General Advsy Cncl October 1987-, Royal Cmmn for the Exhibition of 1851, 1987-; *Style—* Miss Katharine Mortimer; 73 Ravenscourt Rd, London W6 0UJ; Walker Books Ltd, 87 Vauxhall Walk, London SE11 5HJ (☎ 01 793 0909)

MORTIMER, Penelope Ruth; da of Rev Arthur Forbes Gerard Fletcher (d 1959), and Caroline Amy, *née* Maggs (d 1973); *b* 19 Sept 1918; *Educ* Croydon HS, New Sch Streatham, Blencathra Rhyl, Garden Sch Lane End, St Elphin's Sch for Daughters of the Clergy, Univ Coll London; *m* 1, 1937, (m dis 1949), Charles Francis Dimont; 4 da (Madelon, Caroline, Julia, Deborah); m 2, 1949, (m dis 1972), John Clifford Mortimer, QC; 1 s (Jeremy), 1 da (Sally); *Career* writer; *Books* Johanna (as Penelope Dimont 1947), A Villa in Summer (1954), The Bright Prison (1956), With Love & Lizards (with John Mortimer 1957), Daddy's Gone A-Hunting (1958), Saturday Lunch with The Brownings (1960), The Pumpkin Eater (1962), My Friend Says It's Bulletproof (1967), The Home (1971), Long Distance (1974), About Time (autobiog 1979), The Handyman (1983), Queen Elizabeth: A Life of the Queen Mother (1986); *Style—* Penelope Mortimer; The Old Post Office, Chastleton, Moreton-in-Marsh, Glos GL56 0AS (☎ 060 874 242)

MORTIMER, Maj Ralph Edward Bates; s of Sir Ralph Elphinstone Mortimer, OBE, JP (d 1955), and Violet Stokes (d 1973); *b* 7 Sept 1908; *Educ* Harrow; *m* 20 April 1935, Pamela Astley, da of late Basil Eden Maxsted, of Essex; 1 da (Patricia Jane (Mrs Maltby b 1937); *Career* regular army offr; Maj Royal Northumberland Fus Maj, serv Palestine, Egypt, Western Desert inc Torbruk Siege Sudan, Ailo with Rhodesian Air Force later with 52 mountain Divn in Holland and Germany; *Recreations* hunting, shooting, cricket, tennis, squash, fishing; *Clubs* Naval & Military; *Style—* Maj Ralph E B Mortimer; Rookery Farm, Dedham, nr Colchester, Essex (☎ 0206 323138)

MORTON, (Robert) Alastair Newton; s of late Harry Newton Morton, and late Elizabeth Martino; *b* 11 Jan 1938; *Educ* St John's Coll, Witwatersrand Univ (BA), Worcester Coll Oxford (MA); MIT; *m* 1964, Sara Bridget Stephens; 1 s, 1 da; *Career* Anglo American Corp of SA (mining) 1959-63; Int Fin Corpn (Washington) 1964-67; Industl Reorgn Corpn 1967-70; exec dir 117 Gp (investmt tsts) 1970-72, chm Draymont Securities 1972-76, md BNOC 1976-80; Guinness Peat Gp (chief exec 1982-87; chmn 1987-); co-chm, Eurotunnel Gp 1987-; *Clubs* Kehenor Sailing, Univer (New York); *Style—* Alastair Morton, Esq; Guinness Peat Group plc, 32 St Mary at Hill, London EC3P 3AJ (☎ 01 623 6222); Eurotunnel, Portland House, Stag Place, London SW1E 5BT

MORTON, Hon Mrs (Alicia Dorothy); *née* Maffey; yr da of 2 Baron Rugby; *b* 14 Jan 1960; *m* 1981, Richard M, 2 s of John Morton, of Draycote, Rugby; *Style—* The Hon Mrs Morton; The Flat, Manor Farm, Draycote, Rugby, Warwicks

MORTON, Hon Alistair Charles Ralph; s of Baron Morton of Shuna (Life Peer); *b* 1958; *Educ* Royal High Sch Edinburgh, Glasgow U (MA); *m* 1983, Jacqueline Anne, da of William Brown, of Edinburgh; *Style—* Hon Alistair Morton

MORTON, Adm Sir Anthony Storrs; GBE (1982), KCB (1978); s of Dr Harold Morton, of Bridlington; *b* 6 Nov 1923; *Educ* St Anselm's Bakewell, Loretto; *Career* joined RN 1941, Cdr 1956, Capt 1964, Sr Naval Offr NI 1968-70, Rear-Adm 1971, naval memb Sr DSD RCDS 1971-72, ACDS (Policy) 1973, Vice-Adm 1975, flag offr First Flotilla 1975-77, Vice CDS 1977-78, vice-chief Naval Staff 1978-80, UK mil rep NATO 1980-83, ret RN 1984; King of Arms of Order of British Empire 1983-, Rear Adm of UK 1988-; *Recreations* sailing, fishing, shooting; *Clubs* RYS, RCC, ICC; *Style—* Adm Sir Anthony Morton, GBE, KCB; Flat 6, Amhurst, 90 St Cross Rd, Winchester, Hants SO23 9PX (☎ 0962 56393)

MORTON, Rev Arthur; CVO (1979), OBE (1961); s of Arthur Morton; *b* 29 June 1915; *Educ* Imperial Service Coll Windsor, Jesus Coll Cambridge, Wycliffe Hall Oxford; *m* 1940, Medora Gertrude Harrison; 2 da; *Career* clerk in Holy Orders; dir NSPCC 1954-79; *Recreations* gardening, reading; *Style—* Rev Arthur Morton, CVO, OBE; 25 Cottes Way, Hillhead, Fareham, Hants (☎ 0329 3511)

MORTON, Sir Brian; s of Alfred Oscar Morton (d 1954); *b* 24 Jan 1912; *Educ* Campbell Coll Belfast, Coll of Estate Mgmnt London; *m* 1937, Hilda Evelyn Elsie, da of John Hillis (d 1950); 1 s (and 1 s decd); *Career* chartered surveyor and estate agent 1936-64; memb Craigavon Devpt Cmmn 1967-69; chm: Londonderry Devpt Cmmn 1969-73, Harland & Wolff (shipbuilders) 1975-80; Hon DSc Univ of Ulster; FRICS; kt 1973; *Recreations* golf, gardening, sailing, landscape painting; *Clubs* Royal Co Down GC, Malone GC; *Style—* Sir Brian Morton; Rolly Island, Comber, Co Down, NI BT23 6EL

MORTON, Air Cdre Crichton Charles; CBE (1946); s of Charles Crichton Morton (d 1953); *b* 26 July 1912; *Educ* King William's Coll IOM, RAF Coll Cranwell; *m* 1956, Diana Yvonne, da of late Maj-Gen R C Priest, CB, RMS, and widow of Gp Capt N D Gilbart-Smith, RAF; *Career* joined RAF 1930, serv WWII, Air Cdre 1959, inspr Radio Serv 1955-58, chief signals offr HQ SHAPE 1958-60, chm Br Jt Communications Electronics Bd 1960-62, cmd electronics offr HQ Bomber Cmd 1962-66, ret; *Recreations* voluntary work; *Style—* Air Cdre Crichton Morton, CBE; 102 Torre Tramontana, Apartado De Correos 50, 17250 Playa De Aro, Gerona, Spain (☎ 972 817871)

MORTON, (William) Douglas; s of William Douglas (d 1973) of Doncaster and Emma Elizabeth *née* Jowitt; *b* 11 June 1924; *Educ* Doncaster GS, St John's Coll Cambridge; *m* 16 April 1949, Beryl, da of Alfred George Tucker (d 1969) of Doncaster; 2 s (Nicholas Michael b 1954, Christopher David b 1957); *Career* md: GEC AEI Engrg Ltd Manchester 1967-68, GEC Power Engrg Ltd 1968-70, GEC Telecommunications Ltd Coventry 1970-82; dir: Telephone Mfrs of SA (Pty) Ltd 1970-82, Gen Electricity Co plc London 1973-83; gp md Aurora plc Sheffield 1983-; pres Tema Telecommunications Engrg and Mfrg Assoc 1979-80; *Recreations* gardening, contract bridge; *Style—* Douglas Morton, Esq; Woodside, Nesfield Off Hackney Lane, Barlow, Sheffield S18 5TB (☎ 0742 890531); Aurora plc, Aurora House, 61 Manchester Road, Sheffield S10 5DY (☎ 0742 686922, fax: 681340)

MORTON, Hon Douglas William; s of Baron Morton of Shuna (Life Peer); *b* 1963; *Educ* Broughton HS, Edinburgh; *Style—* Hon Douglas Morton

MORTON, Lady; Hilda Sherwood; JP; da of Robert John Calver, SSC, of Edinburgh; *m* 1927, as his 2 w, Sir George Morton, KBE, QC (d 1953); MA, BSc, LRAM; *Style—* Lady Morton, JP; 37 Moray Pla, Edinburgh, EH3 6BT

MORTON, 21 Earl of (S 1458); John Charles Sholto Douglas; DL (West Lothian 1982); also Lord Aberdour (no actual cr, but designation of the eld s & h, incorporated with the Earldom in a charter of 1638, where the Earls of Morton are described as *domini Abirdour*); s of Hon Charles William Sholto Douglas (d 1960, 2 s of 19 Earl of Morton); suc cous, 20 Earl 1976; *b* 19 Mar 1927; *m* 1949, Mary Sheila, da of late Rev Canon John Stanley Gibbs, MC, of Didmarton House, Badminton, Glos; 2 s, 1 da; *Heir* s, Lord Aberdour, *qv*; *Career* md Dalmahoy Country Club, Scottish dir Bristol & W Building Soc, ptnr Dalmahoy Farms, chm Edinburgh Polo Club; *Clubs* Edinburgh Polo, Dalmahoy Country; *Style—* The Rt Hon the Earl of Morton, DL; Dalmahoy, Kirknewton, Midlothian

MORTON, Hon Kenneth John; s of Baron Morton of Shuna (Life Baron); *b* 1960; *Educ* Broughton HS, Edinburgh, Edinburgh Univ (BSc); *m* 1984, Isobel Ann, da of John MaLean Cowan, of Greenock; *Style—* Hon Kenneth Morton

MORTON, Reginald John; s of Maj John Henry Morton (d 1987), of Manchester, and Alice Blanche Gladys, *née* Chappelier; *b* 17 Sept 1951; *Educ* Manchester GS, Birmingham Univ (LLB); *m* 6 Oct 1979, Jennifer Mary, da of Reginald Carr, of Small Dole, W Sussex; 2 s (Jonathan b 1985, Thomas b 1988); *Career* slr Clifford Chance (formerly Clifford-Turner) 1975-85, ptnr Titmuss Sainer & Webb 1987- (joined 1985) memb: Law Soc 1975; *Recreations* snooker, golf; *Clubs* Duffers Snooker; *Style—* Reginald Morton, Esq; 2 Serjeants Inn, London EC4 (☎ 01 583 5353, fax 01 353 3683, car tel 08367 45939, telex 23823 ADVICE G)

MORTON, Robert Edward; s of Charles Morton, and Yvonne, *née* Galea; *b* 20 May 1956; *Educ* Canford Sch Wimborne Dorset, Oriel Coll Oxford (BA); *m* 12 Dec 1981; 2 da (Caroline b 13 Aug 1983, Georgina b 21 Jan 1985); *Career* res analyst: Simon & Coates 1978-83, de Zoete & Bevan 1983-86 (ptnr 1986-); dir Barclays de Zoete Wedd 1986 - (head conglomerates and overseas traders res teams); memb Stock Exchange; *Recreations* squash, gardening, music; *Clubs* Gresham, Royal Thames YC; *Style—* Robert Morton, Esq; Barclays, de Zoete, Wedd, Ebbgate House, 2 Swan Lane, London EC4R 3TS (☎ 01 623 2323)

MORTON EVANS, Kenneth; OBE (1943), TD (1945) (and 2 bars); Capt Henry Morton Glyn Evans, OBE, JP, of Llangennech Park, Carmarthenshire (d 1928), (o s of David Evans, JP, DL (d 1909), who acquired Llangennech ca 1880), and Hilda Dalrymple (d 1973), da of William Henry Delano, CE, of Barkston Gdns, SW; *b* 19 Nov 1909; *Educ* Charterhouse New Coll Oxford (BA, BSc); *m* 1, 1 June 1939 (m dis), Ginette Hewitt; 1 s (Michael b 1942), 1 da (Angela b 1944); m 2, 12 June 1964, Georgina, da of Capt Ughtred Shuttleworth, formerly of Petersfield, Hants, and wid of Leonard Clough-Taylor; *Career* landowner 1928-50; serv WWII as Lt-Col Signals Intelligence; Govt Official 1946-64; chief UK AEA Security 1953-57; *Recreations* skiing, amateur radio transmission, gardening; *Style—* Kenneth Morton Evans, Esq, OBE, TD; Pond End House, Blackmoor, Liss, Hants GU33 6BU (☎ 04203 2105)

MORTON JACK, His Hon Judge David; s of Col William Andrew Morton Jack OBE (d 1950), of Lemonfield Co, Galway, and Margery Elizabeth Happell (d 1978); o heir of the O'Flaherties of Lemonfield where he still owns what remains of the O'Flahertie estate; *b* 5 Nov 1936; *Educ* Stow; Trinity Coll, Oxford (MA); barr Lincoln's Inn; *m* 1972, Elvira Rosemary, da of Francis Gallo Rentoul, of 1 Chara Place, W4; 4 s (Edward b 1975, Richard b 1977, Henry b 1979, George b 1981); *Career* 2 Lt Royal Irish Fusiliers 1955-57 (LT AER 1957-60); barr SE Circuit 1962-86; rec Crown Ct 1979-86; CJ 1986-; *Recreations* fishing, shooting, reading, music; *Style—* His Hon Judge David Morton Jack; 1 Harcourt Buildings, Temple EC4Y 9DA (☎ 086 733 223)

MORTON LEE, Cdr John; OBE (1973); s of Lt Cdr Henry Morton Lee (d 1983), of Chichester, W Sussex, and Gladys Mildred, *née* Smith; *b* 18 Jan 1930; *Educ* RN Coll Dartmouth; *m* 23 April 1957, Patricia Lee, da of late George Garnet Pendray, of Lourenco Marques; 2 s (Michael b 30 Nov 1958, Peter b 13 Jan 1964); *Career* Midshipman HMS Anson and HMS Vengeance 1948-49, Sub Lt Greenwich 1949, HMS Sluys 1950, HMS Unicorn 1951, Lt i/c HMSDML 3514 1951-53, language trg 1954, HMS Undaunted 1954-55, i/c HMS Chelsham 1956, i/c HMS Upton 1957-58, HMS Ganges 1958-60, Lt Cdr HMS Leopard 1961-62, RN Staff Coll Greenwich 1963, i/c HMS Pellew 1964-65, Cdr SO Ops to FO2 Far East Fleet 1965-66, i/c HMS St George 1967-68, i/c HMS Eskimo 1969-70, Staff Planning Offr to Comnavsouth 1970-73, Naval Asst to Dir PR 1973-75, Naval Attaché Spain 1976-79, memb Admty Interview Bd 1979-81, Project Offr NATO Frigate for 90's 1981-84, ret 1984; Fine art dealer 1984-; exhibitor at antique fairs across the country; memb SE Hants C of C; memb: CGA, London and Provincial Antique Dealers Assoc, Br Maritime League, Nat Tst, Trout and Salmon Fishing Assoc; *Recreations* golf, fishing; *Clubs* Naval, Royal Navy Club of 1765 and 1785, Hayling GC; *Style—* Cdr John Morton Lee, OBE; Cedar House, Bacon Lane, Hayling Island, Hants PO11 0DN (☎ 0705 464 444)

MORTON OF SHUNA, Baron (Life Peer UK 1985) Hugh Drennan Baird; QC; s of Rev Thomas Ralph Morton, DD (d 1977), and Janet Maclay MacGregor, da of Hugh Baird, of Glasgow; *b* 10 April 1930; *Educ* Glasgow Acad, Glasgow Univ (BL); *m* 1956, Muriel, da of Charles Miller, of Edinburgh; 3 s (Alistair, Kenneth, Douglas); *Career* admitted Faculty of Advocates 1965, advocate depute 1967-71 and 1974-79; memb Criminal Injuries Compensation Bd 1979-88; Senator of the Coll of Justice in Scotland 1988; *Style—* Rt Hon Lord Morton of Shuna; 25 Royal Circus, Edinburgh EH3 6TL

MOSCOW, Dr David; s of Emanuel Moscow (d 1981), and Rachel, *née* Davidovitch; *b* 3 May 1937; *Educ* Paramiter's GS London, Univ of London (BSc), Univ of Leicester, Univ of Leeds (PhD); *m* 1 1960 (m dis 1972), Jennifer Dianne, da of William Thomas Redgate (d 1986); 4 da (Sarah b 1964, Emma b 1968, Susan b 1967, Linda b 1969); m 2 1975, Patricia Ann, da of Frank Edward Gostling, OBE, of Oxshott, Surrey; *Career* personnel offr BAC 1960-63, lectr Leeds Univ 1963-67; res assoc Netherlands Inst for Preventive Med 1967-70, chm Sheppard Moscow and Assoc Ltd 1970-84 (jt md 1984-86), conslt to cos such as ICI, Shell and nat orgns NHS and Bank of Eng; FID (1977); FBIM 1983, FIMC 1986; *Recreations* golf, sculpture; *Style—* Dr David Moscow; Cross Keys House, Cross Keys, Sevenoaks, Kent (☎ 0732 457411)

MOSDELL, (Lionel) Patrick; s of William George Mosdell (d 1938), of Mortimer, Berks, and Sarah Ellen, *née* Gardiner (d 1962); *b* 29 August 1912; *Educ* Abingdon Sch, St Edmund Hall Oxford (BA); *m* 3 Aug 1945, (Muriel) Jean, da of John Oscar Sillem (d 1958), of Hove, East Sussex; 1 s (John b 1949), 1 da (Susan b 1946); *Career* serv WWII: Gunner Sussex Yeo RA 1939, cmmnd RB 1941, serv Libyan Arab Force, Force 133 Capt, No 1 Special Force, serv: Egypt, Cyrenaica, Eritrea, Abyssinia, Italy; demob 1945; slr 1938; barr Gray's Inn 1952, sr resident magistrate Northern Rhodesia 1956 (registrar Lands and Deeds 1946, resident magistrate 1950); High Ct judge: Tanganyika 1960-64, Kenya 1966-72; asst slr Law Soc 1964-66; pt/t chm: Surrey and Sussex Rent Assessment Panel 1972-82, S London regnl Nat Insur local tbnl 1974-84, Immigration Appeal Tbnl 1975-84, Pensions Appeal Tbnls 1976-86; SSAFA (V) 1988; *Recreations* cycling; *Clubs* Special Forces, Royal Cwlth Soc; *Style—* Patrick Mosdell, Esq; 10 Orpen Rd, Hove, East Sussex BN3 6NJ

MOSELEY, Sir George Walker; KCB (1982, CB 1978); s of William Moseley, MBE, and Bella Moseley; *b* 7 Feb 1925; *Educ* Glasgow HS, St Bees Sch Cumberland, Wadham Coll Oxford (MA); *m* 1950, Anne Mercer; 1 s, 1 da; *Career* serv RAF and RAF Levies Iraq 1943-48; Miny Housing and Local Govt: asst private sec to min 1951-52, private sec to parly sec 1952-54, princ private sec to min 1963-65, asst sec 1965-70, under-sec 1970-76; dep sec DOE 1976-78, dep sec CSD 1978-80, 2 perm sec DOE 1980-81, second perm sec DOE 1981-85; cmmr Historic Bldgs and Monuments Cmmn 1986-; chm: Br Cement Assoc 1987-; Tstee Civic Tst 1987-;; *Style—* Sir George Moseley, KCB; 4 Ormond Ave, Hampton, Middx

MOSELEY, His Hon Judge (Thomas) Hywel; s of Rev Luther Moseley, of Porthceiro, Llanbadarn Fawr, Aberystwyth SY23 3HW, and Megan Eiluned, *née* Howells (d 1977); *b* 27 Sept 1936; *Educ* Caterham Sch Surrey, Queens' Coll Cambridge (MA, LLM); *m* 25 June 1960, Monique Germaine Thérèse, da of Edmond Gaston Drufin (d 1977); 3 da (Catrin b 1961, Eirian (twin) b 1961, Gwenda b 1969); *Career* barr Gray's Inn and Wales and Chester Circuit 1964, rec 1981, circuit judge 1989, prof of law Univ Coll of Wales Aberystwyth 1970-83; QC 1985; *Recreations* beekeeping; *Style—* His Hon Judge Hywel Moseley, QC; Nantceiro, Llanbadarn Fawr, Aberystwyth, Dyfed SY23 3HW (☎ 0970 62 3532); 23 Old Bldgs, Lincoln's Inn, London WC2 (☎ 01 405 1701)

MOSER, Sir Claus Adolf; KCB (1973), CBE (1965); s of Dr Ernest Moser and Lotte Moser; *b* 24 Nov 1922,Berlin,; *Educ* Frensham Heights Sch, LSE; *m* 1949, Mary

Oxlin; 1 s, 2 da; *Career* LSE: asst lectr 1946-49, lectr 1949-55, reader 1955-61, prof social statistics 1961-70, visiting prof 1970-75; statistical advsr Ctee Higher Educn 1961-64, dir Central Statistical Off and head of Govt Statistical Serv 1967-78, visiting fellow Nuffield Coll Oxford 1972-80, pres Royal Statistical Soc 1978-80; memb: governing body RAM 1967-79, BBC Music Advsy Ctee 1971-; chm bd of dirs Royal Opera House Covent Gdn 1974-87, vice-chm N M Rothschild & Sons 1978-84 (now dir); dir: Economist Intelligence Unit 1979-83, The Economist 1979-, Equity and Law Life Assur Soc 1980-87, Octopus Publishing Gp 1982-88; warden Wadham Coll Oxford 1984-; tstee Pilgrims Tst 1982-, tstee Br Museum 1988-, London Philharmonic Orch 1988-; pres elect Br Assoc for the Advancement of Sci 1988-; FBA 1969; Hon FRAM, hon fell LSE, Hon DSc Southampton; Hon DSc: Leeds, City Univ, Sussex; Hon DUniv: Keele, Surrey, York; Hon DTech Brunel; Cdr de l'Ordre National du Mérite (France); *Style—* Sir Claus Moser, KCB, CBE; 3 Regent's Park Terrace, London NW1 7EE (☎ 01 458 1619); N M Rothschild and Sons Ltd, New Court, St Swithin's Lane, London EC4P 4DU (☎ 01 280 5000); Wadham College, Oxford

MOSER, Robin Allan Shedden; s of Allan Hugh Shedden Moser (d 1970), of Betchworth, Surrey, and Mary Dorothy Chatfeild-Clarke *née* Shanks; *b* 3 June 1947; *Educ* Radley; *m* 17 Feb 1983, Sally, da of Walter Douglas Knowles (d 1985), of Beckenham, Kent; 3 s (Robert David Shedden b 1975, Patrick Allan Shedden b 1978, Edward Alexander Shedden b 1983); *Career* CA; banker; dir CL-Alexanders Laing & Cruickshank Hldgs Ltd 1986; md and chief exec CL-Alexanders Discount plc 1984; dir and CL-Alexanders Laing & Cruickshank Gilts Ltd 1985; chm Gillett Investmts Ltd 1983; FCA; *Recreations* golf, sailing; *Clubs* Saffron Wadlden Golf, Hertford Co Yacht; *Style—* Robin Moser, Esq; Mill End, Clavering, Saffron Walden, Essex (☎ 0799 550 360); CL-Alexanders Discount plc, 65 Cornhill, London EC3V 3PP (☎ 01 6265467)

MOSES, Geoffrey Haydn; s of Canon Haydn Moses (d 1983), of Llanelu Vicarage, Dyfed, and Beryl Mary, *née* Lloyd); *b* 24 Sept 1952; *Educ* Ystalyfera GS, Emmanuel Coll Cambridge (BA), King's Coll London (PGCE); *m* 24 July 1981, Anne Elizabeth, da of Harry Mason; *Career* opera singer; debuts: WNO Barber of Seville (pncpl singer 1978-82), Royal Opera House Covent Garden Tales of Hoffman 1981, Glyndebourne Touring Opera Don Giovanni 1982, Kent Opera Don Giovanni 1983, Opera North Madam Butterfly 1983, Glynebourne Festival Opera Arabella 1983 Scottish Opera Barber of Seville 1984, Belgian Opera Simon Boccanegra 1983, Hamburg State Opera Barber of Seville 1984, Netherlands Opera Salomé 1988; concerts and recitals at : Gothenberg, Frankfurt Alte Oper, Royal Festival Hall, Royal Albert Hall; *Recreations* walking, swimming, reading, wine; *Style—* Geoffrey Moses, Esq; 12 Ferrers Rd, Lewes, E Sussex (☎ 0273 473 088) Harrison/ Parrot Ltd, 16 Penzance Pl, London W11 4PA (☎ 01 229 9166, fax 01 221 5042, telex 892 791 Birds G)

MOSES, Very Rev Dr John Henry; s of Henry William Moses (d 1975), of London, and Ada Elizabeth Moses; *b* 12 Jan 1938; *Educ* Ealing GS, Nottingham Univ, Trinity Hall & Dept of Educn Cambridge, Lincoln Theol Coll (Gladstone Meml Prize, BA, PhD); *m* 25 July 1964, Susan Elizabeth, da of James Wainwright (d 1980), of London; 1 s (Richard), 2 da (Rachel, Catherine); *Career* asst curate St Andrew's Bedford 1964-70, rector Coventry East Team Minstry 1970-77, examining chaplain to Bishop of Coventry 1972-77, rural dean Coventry East 1973-77, archdeacon of Southend 1977-82, provost of Chelmsford 1982-; memb Gen Synod 1985-, church cmmr 1988-; visiting fell Wolfson Coll Cambridge 1987; *Clubs* Athenaeum; *Style—* The Very Rev the Provost of Chelmsford; The Provost's House, 3 Harlings Grove, Waterloo La, Chelmsford, Essex CM1 1YQ (☎ 0245 354 318); The Cathedral Office, Guy Harlings, New St, Chelmsford, Essex CM1 1NG (☎ 0245 263 660)

MOSES, Kenneth (Ken); CBE (1988); s of Thomas Moses, of Adelaide, S Australia, and Mary, *née* Holland; *b* 29 Nov 1931; *Educ* Cowley GS St Helens Lancs, Wigan and Dist Mining Coll (HND); *m* 1949, Mary, da of William Price (d 1958), of St Helens, Lancs; 1 s (Philip b 1952), 2 da (Linda b 1949, Carol b 1962); *Career* mining engr; area dir North Derbys Br Coal 1981-85, tech dir Br Coal 1985; memb Corpn Br Coal 1986; FEng, Fell Inst of Mining Engrs, MPhil Nottingham 1988; *Recreations* reading, gardening, walking; *Style—* Ken Moses, Esq, CBE; Oaktrees, 6 Heath Ave, Mansfield NG18 3EU (☎ 0623 653843); British Coal, Eastwood Hall, Eastwood, Notts (☎ 0773 531313)

MOSHINSKY, Elijah; s of Abraham Moshinsky, and Eva, *née* Krasavitsky; *b* 8 Jan 1946; *Educ* Camberwell, Melbourne Univ (BA), Oxford Univ (D Phil); *m* 5 June 1970, Ruth, da of Oscar Dyttman, of Melbourne, Aust; 2 s (Benjamin b 6 Dec 1980, Jonathan b 5 May 1983); *Career* assoc prodr Royal Opera House 1988- (princ guest prodr 1975-88); prods at Royal Opera House Peter Grimes 1974, Lohengrin 1979, The Rakes Progress 1980, Macbeth 1981, Samson and Delilah 1981, Handel's Samson 1985 Otello 1986, Die Entführung aus dem Serail 1987; for ENO: Le Grand Macabre 1980, The Mastersingers of Nuremberg 1984; for BBC TV: All's Well that Ends Well 1980, A Midsummer Nights Dream 1981, Cymbeline 1982, Coriolanus 1983, Love's Labours Last 1984, Ghost's 1986; *Recreations* reading, music; *Clubs* Garrick; *Style—* Elijah Moshinsky, Esq; 28 Kidbrooke Grove, London SE3 (☎ 01 858 4179)

MOSIMANN, Anton; s of Otto Albert Mosimann, and Olga, *née* Von Burg (d 1966) ; *b* 23 Feb 1947; *m* 13 April 1973, Kathrin, da of Jakob Roth; 2 s (philipp Anton b 1975, Mark Andreas b 1977); *Career* apprentice Hotel Baeren Twann Switzerland 1962-64, commis entremetier Palace Hotel Villars 1964-65, chef tournant and sous chef Queen Elizabeth Hotel Montreal 1966-69, 1 chef tournant Palace Hotel St Moritz 1969-70, exec chef Swiss Pavilion Expo 70 Osaka Japan 1970, sous chef Kulm Hotel St Moritz winter seasons 1972-73 and 1873-74 (chef restaurateur 1971-72), commis patissier Palace Hotel Gstzad 1974-75; dir of cuisine Dorchester Hotel London 1986- (maitre chef des cuisines 1975) and chef patron Masimann's London 1988-; winner numerous Gold Medals and awards world wide; Frequent TV and radio appearances; *Books* Cuisine a la Carte (1981), The Street Seafood Book (1985), Cuisine Naturelle (1985), Anton Masimann's Fish Cuisine (1988); *Recreations* jogging, squash, vintage, bars, collecting antique cookery books; *Style—* Anton Mosimann, Esq; 46 Abingdon Villas, Kensington W8 (☎ 01 937 4383); Mosimann's, 116 West Kalkin St, Belgrave Square, London SW1X 8JL (☎ 01 235 9625, fax 01 245 6354)

MOSLEY, Hon Clare; da of 3 Baron Ravensdale, MC, by his 1 w; *b* 1959; *Educ* Bedales Sch; *Style—* The Hon Clare Mosley; 130 Elgin Ave, London W11

MOSLEY, Hon Lady; Hon Diana; *née* Freeman-Mitford; da of 2 Baron Redesdale, JP (d 1958); one of the Mitford sisters; *b* 17 June 1910; *m* 1, 1929 (m dis 1934), Hon Bryan Walter Guinness (afterwards 2 Baron Moyne, *qv*); 2 s (Jonathan, Desmond Guinness, *qqv*); m 2, 1936, as his 2 w, Sir Oswald Ernald Mosley, 6 Bt (d 1980); 2 s (Alexander, Max); *Publications* A Life of Contrasts (memoirs), The Duchess of Windsor, Loved Ones (memoirs), The Writings of Rebecca West; *Style—* The Hon Lady Mosley; 1 Rue des Lacs, 91400, Orsay, France (☎ 010 331 60104211)

MOSLEY, Hon Ivo Adam Rex; 2 s of 3 Baron Ravensdale, MC, by his 1 w; *Educ* Bryanston Sch, New Coll Oxford; *m* 1977, Xanthe Jennifer Grenville, da of Sir Michael Bernard Grenville Oppenheimer, 3 Bt; 3 s (Nathaniel b 1982, Felix b 1985, another b 1988); *Style—* The Hon Ivo Mosley; 11 Lawrence St, London SW3

MOSLEY, Max Rufus; 4 s (but only 2 by his 2 w, Diana, *see* Hon Lady Mosley) of Sir Oswald Mosley, 6 Bt; half-bro of Hon Jonathan Guinness, *qv*; *b* 13 April 1940; *Educ* Christ Church Oxford; *m* 1960, Jean Marjorie, er da of James Taylor; 2 s (Alexander b 1970, Patrick b 1972); *Career* sec Oxford Union Soc 1960, called to Bar Gray's Inn 1964, fndr dir March Cars Ltd, legal advsr to Formula One Constructors Assoc; pres of the Mfrs Cmmn of the Fedn Internationale du Sport Automobile; *Recreations* wine, skiing, walking; *Style—* Max Mosley, Esq; 4 Brompton Sq, London SW3 2AA

MOSLEY, Hon Michael; granted 1967 the title rank and precedence of a Baroness's son, which would have been his had his mother survived to succeed to Barony of Ravensdale; s of Sir Oswald Ernald Mosley, 6 Bt (d 1980), by his 1 w Lady Cynthia Curzon (da of 1 and last Marquess Curzon of Kedleston); n of Baroness Ravensdale (d 1966); *b* 1932; *Educ* Eton, LSE; *Style—* The Hon Michael Mosley; Durham Cottage, Christchurch St, Chelsea, London SW3 (☎ 01 352 5409)

MOSLEY, Nicholas; *see*: 3 Baron Ravensdale

MOSLEY, Hon Robert; 3 s of 3 Baron Ravensdale, MC, by his 1 w; *b* 1955; *Educ* Bedales; *m* 1980, Victoria McBain; 1 s (Gregory b 1981), 1 da (Vija b 1984); *Style—* The Hon Robert Mosley; Ballagawme Farm, Kirkmichael, IOM

MOSLEY, Hon Shaun Nicholas; s and h of 3 Baron Ravensdale, MC; *b* 5 August 1949; *Educ* Bryanston Sch, Hertford Coll Oxford; *m* 1978, Theresa Clifford; 1 s (Daniel b 1982); *Style—* The Hon Shaun Mosley; c/o 9 Church Row, Hampstead, NW3 (☎ 01 435 8222)

MOSLEY, Simon James; yr s of John Arthur Noel Mosley (3 s of Sir Oswald Mosley, 5 Bt, and his 1 w, Katharine, da of Capt Justinian Edwards-Heathcote), and his 1 w, Caroline Edith Sutton, *née* Timmis; *b* 8 April 1927; *Educ* Eton, Christ Church Oxford; *m* 15 Dec 1957, Maria, o da of Iraklis Zeris (d 1980); 1 s (George b 1959), 1 da (Claire b 1964); *Career* slr 1956-, pres Holborn Law Soc 1967-68, memb Cncl Law Soc 1969-81; govr The Coll of Law 1973-; chm: Trinity Int Hldgs plc Gp 1985-, Octavian Gp Ltd 1984-; *Clubs* Cavalry and Guard's; *Style—* Simon Mosley, Esq; 23 Little Boltons, London SW10

MOSS, Anthony David; s of David Samuel Moss (d 1970), of Eltham Coll London SE9, and Phyllis Holland, *née* Newton (d 1973); *b* 24 Jan 1932; *Educ* Cranbrook, Jesus Coll Cambridge (MA); *m* 25 Aug 1956, Jennifer Ann, JP, da of Prof William Hume-Rothery, OBE (d 1968), of Oxford; 1 s (Nicholas Hume) 2 da (Philippa Jane (Dr Madgwick), Charlotte Katharine (Mrs Nobbs)); *Career* cmmnd Nat Serv 1951-52 (serv Libya); Metal Box Co Ltd 1956-64, slr 1968, ptnr Hyde Mahon Bridges (formerly Hyde Mahon & Pascall) 1969-; hon tres Cmmrs of Ely Place 1976-; memb: Lord Mayor and Sheriffs Ctee 1987, Livery Ctee Corpn of London; donation govr Christs Hosp; Freeman City of London 1969, Liveryman and memb Ct of Worshipful Co of Ironmongers (Master 1987-88); memb Law Soc, The Georgian Gp; *Recreations* historic buildings, walking; *Clubs* City Livery; *Style—* Anthony Moss, Esq; The Bury Farm, Chesham, Bucks HP5 2JU (☎ 0494 775878); Hyde Mahon Bridges (Solicitors) 33 Ely Place, London EC1N 6TS (☎ 01 405 9455, fax 01 831 6649, telex 25210)

MOSS, David Anscombe; s of Edwin John Moss, and Catherine Moss; *b* 27 Dec 1927; *m* 14 July 1951, Joan (d 1969), da of David Lee; 1 s (Vincent David b 1958), 1 da (Carolyn Fleur b 1960); *Career* retd political agent W Herts Constituency Lab Pty (formerly Hemel Hempstead); former: book keeper, asst to civil engr, tport mangr; ldr Lab Gp Herts Co Cncl, chm Policy and resources ctee; memb cncl: Hemel Hempstead Rural dist Cncl 1962-67, Kings Langley Parish Cncl 1962-67, Herts Co Cncl 1973-77, 1981-; govr Dacroum Coll of Further Educn (former Sch govr), vice-chm Dacorum Educn advsy ctee (former chm), vice-chm Dacorum Youth and Community ctee; *Recreations* reading, walking; *Style—* David Moss, Esq; 19 Priory Gardens, Berkhamsted (☎ 0442 873 512)

MOSS, Dr Edward Herbert St George; s of Sir George Sinclair Moss, KBE, of N Devon (d 1959), and Lady Gladys Lucy Moss, *née* Moore (d 1971); *b* 18 May 1918; *Educ* Marlborough, Pembroke Coll Cambridge (BA, MA), Univ of Surrey (PhD); *m* 2 June 1948, Shirley Evelyn, da of Alfred Seymour Baskett (d 1960), of Bournemouth; 2 s (Anthony b 1949, Andrew b 1955), 1 da (Nicola b 1951); *Career* diplomat, civil servant, writer; army serv W Desert, Intelligence Off 50Div, Lt-Col and instr Mil Govt Sdtaff Centre; Foreign (Dip) Serv entered 1945, serv in: Tokyo, Belgrade (1 sec, hd of Chancery 1951), Detroit, London, asst sec (hd of DS3 DS8) MOD 1960, Dep Educn and Sci, under sec Univ Grants Ctee 197, ret 1978; *Books* Fire from a Flint - Daily Readings with William Law (ed 1986); Seeing Man Whole - A New Model for Psychology 1989; *Recreations* gardening, writing; *Style—* Dr Edward H Moss; Prospects, 29 Guildown Ave, Guildford, Surrey GU2 5HA; (☎ 0483 66984)

MOSS, John Ringer; CB (1972); 2 s of late James Moss, of Fressingfield, Suffolk, and Louisa, *née* Ringer; *b* 15 Feb 1920; *Educ* Manchester GS, Brasenose Coll Oxford (MA); *m* 1946, Edith Bland, da of George Wheeler, of Liverpool; 2 s (Michael, Martin), 1 da (Charlotte); *Career* Army 1940-46 Capt RE served India, Burma, Malaya; Civil Serv Miny of Agric 1947-70, (princ private sec 1959-60, dep sec 1970-80); advsr to cos in Assoc Br Foods Gp 1980-; chm cncl Royal Veterinary Coll 1983-; *Style—* John Moss, Esq, CB; 16 Upper Hollis, Gt Missenden, Bucks

MOSS, Malcolm Douglas; MP (C) Cambs NE 1987; s of Norman Moss (d 1976), and Annie, *née* Gay; *b* 6 Mar 1943; *Educ* Audenshaw GS, St John's Coll Cambridge (MA, Cert Ed); *m* 28 Dec 1965, Vivien Lorraine, da of Albert Peake (d 1964); 2 da (Alison Claire b 1969, Sarah Nicole b 1972); *Career* asst master Blundell's Tiverton Devon 1966-68 (head dept 1968-70), insur conslt Barwick Asoocs 1971-72 (gen mangr 1972-74), co-fndr and dir Mandrake (Insur and Fin Brokers) Ltd 1974- (chm 1986-, changed name to Mandrake Assocs Ltd 1988); dir : Mandrake (Insur Servs) Ltd 1976-81 (resgned), Mandrake Collinge Ltd 1977-, Mandrake (Insur Advsy Serv) Ltd 1978, Mandrake (Fin Mgmnt) Ltd 1985-87 (resigned); chm Mandrake Gp plc 1986-; dir Fens Business Enterprises Tst Ltd 1983-, chm: Fens Business Enterprise Tst Ltd 1983-87 (resigned); *Recreations* amateur dramatics, tennis, skiing; *Clubs* Oxford and Cambridge, Lords and Commons Tennis and Ski; *Style—* Malcolm Moss, Esq, MP; Boston House, South Brink, Wisbech, Cambs PE14 0RT (☎ 0945 65997); 88 St

George's Sq, London SW1 (☎ 01 821 0269); House of Commons (☎ 01 219 6933, secretary 01 219 4037); Business address: 6 North Brink, Wisbech, Cambs PE13 1JR (☎ 0945 65177)

MOSS, Martin Grenville; CGE (1975); s of Horace Grenville Moss (d 1975), and Gladys Ethel, *née* Wootton (d 1981); *b* 17 July 1923; *Educ* Lancing; *m* 2 Feb 1953, Jane Hope, *née* Bown; 2 s (Matthew b 4 June 1955, Hugo b 24 Feb 1962), 1 da (Louisa b 25 Oct 1958); *Career* WWII: trainee pilot RAF 1942-43, pilot coastal cmd 1943-44, actg Sqdn Ldr 1945-46; sr welfare offr Iraq and Persia 1945-46; md: Woodlands nightsbridge 1953-66, Debenham and Freebody 1964-66, Simpson Piccadilly 1966-73 and 1980-85; chm and chief exec offr May Dept Stores Int USA 1974-80, dir Nat Tst Enterprises 1985-88; dep chm Design Cncl 1971-75 (memb 1964-75); memb: cncl RCA 1953-58, cncl RSA 1977- (chm 1983-85), Royal Fine Art Commn 1982-84; Order of the Lion of Finland 1970; *Recreations* gardening, painting, classic cars; *Clubs* RAF; *Style—* Martin Moss, Esq, CBE; Parsonage Farm, Bentworth, Alton, Hants GU34 5RB;

MOSS, Lady; Monica; *née* Meriton-Reed; *m* 1919, Sir Eric de Vere Moss, CIE, formerly ICS (d 1981); 1 s, 3 da; *Style—* Lady Moss; Bracken Lodge, Brookside Close, Runcton, Chichester, W Sussex (☎ 784521)

MOSS, Montague George; s of Harry Neville Moss (d 1982), and Ida Sophia, *née* Woolf (d 1971); *b* 21 April 1924; *Educ* Harrow, New Coll Oxford; *m* 28 Sept 1955, Jane, da of David Levi, MS, FRCS, of 23 Ranulf Road, London NW2; 2 s (Andrew b 7 Feb 1958, David b 15 Sept 1959), 1 da (Joanna b 15 Aug 1956); *Career* served in army 1943-47, cmmnd KRRC 1944, demob as Capt; dir Moss Bros Ltd: dir 1953-, chm 1981-87, pres 1987-; pres Fedn of Merchant Tailors of Gt Br 1965-66 and 1985-86; pres Tailor's Benevolent Inst 1980-; Freeman City of London 1948, memb Worshipful Co of Carmen 1949; FRSA; *Recreations* public speaking, music; *Clubs* Jesters, MCC, Old Harrovian Eton Fives; *Style—* Montague Moss, Esq; 4 Melina Place, London NW8 9SA (☎ 01 286 0114); Moss Bros, 131 New Bond St, London W1 (☎ 01 629 4723)

MOSS, Hon Mrs (Susannah Elizabeth); *née* Yerburgh; o da of 2 Baron Alvingham, CBE, *qv*; *b* 1953; *m* 1979, Edward I J G Moss; 2 da (Alice Elinor b 1983e, Victoria Elizabeth b 1986); *Style—* Hon Mrs Moss; 24 Rusham Rd, London SW12 8TH

MOSS, Timothy Campbell; s of William Denniss Moss, and Phyllis May *née* Charnock (d 1971); *b* 31 Jan 1937; *Educ* Wintringham GS; *m* 13 Sept 1969, Sheila Elizabeth, da of Samuel Dunwoody (d 1983); 2 da (Claire b 1971, Rachel b 1973); *Career* Nat Serv RAEC 1959-61, sgt; articled clerk Forrester Boyd & Co 1953-58, Coopers & Lybrand 1961- (ptnr 1974-); ICEAW, FCA 1959; *Recreations* golf, bridge; *Clubs* Croham Hurst GC; *Style—* Timothy Moss, Esq; Coopers & Lybrand, Plumtree Ct, London EC4A 4HT (☎ 01 822 4567 fax 01 822 4681)

MOSS, Dr Trevor Simpson; s of William Moss (d 1937), of Highfield, Willslock, Uttoxeter, and Florence Elizabeth, *née* Simpson (d 1954); *b* 28 Jan 1921; *Educ* Alleyne's GS Uttoxeter, Downing Coll Cambridge (BA, MA, Phd, ScD); *m* 6 March 1948, Audrey, da of Ernest Nelson (d 1948), of Holly St, Durham City; *Career* WWII various hon cmmns as Fl Lt RAF 1943-45: N Africa 1943, invasion of Normandy and S France 1944, Denmark 1945; res scientist (radar) TRE 1941-53, (res scientist 1953-68) head radio and navigation dept RAE 1968-78 , dep dir RSRE 1978-81; exec ed: Infrared Physics 1961-, Progress in Quantum Electronics 1978-; Max Born prize Br and German Physical Socs 1975, Dennis Gabor award Int Soc of Optical Engrs 1988; AIMEE 1949, FInstP 1968, CPHYS 1987; *Books* Photconductivity (1952), Optical Properties of Semiconductors (1959), Semiconductor Optoelectronics (1973), Handbook on Semiconductors (4 vols 1980-82), over 100 papers published in int jls; *Style—* Dr Trevor Moss; Acathon, Shelsley Meadow, Colwall, Malvern, Worcs (☎ 0684 40079)

MOSS, Victor Peter Cannings; s of Frederick James Reynolds Moss (d 1979), of Marlborough, Wilts, and Olive May Moss *née* Cannings (d 1987); *b* 12 Mar 1921; *Educ* Marlborough GS, Worcester Trg Coll; *m* Dec 1949, Joan, da of Samuel Holland (d 1978), of Kidderminster, Worcs; 1 da (Melanie b 1950), 1 s (Peter b 1963); *Career* author; teaching various schools and colls 1950-70; full time writer, broadcaster, lectr 1970-; more than 50 books published: mainly educnl; broadcasts: mainly world serv, numerous radio and TV programmes mainly literary; memb Soc of Authors (ctee memb of Educational writers gp); *Publications* educnl books: over 50 on History, English, Sociology, Commerce, Statistics, series of 9 for Chinese Schools in Hong Kong; other pub: Encounters with the past (hypnotic regression pub UK, USA, France, Holland, Australia), Ghosts over Britain; *Recreations* opera, travel, wine, work; *Style—* Victor Moss, Esq; Brook Cottage, Ripe Lewes, Sussex BN8 6AR (☎ 032 183 216)

MOSSÉ, Peter Sylvaih; s of Leon Mossé (d 1980), of Monaco, and Leonie, *née* King; *b* 25 Jan 1925; *Educ* Shrewsbury, Sandhurst; *m* 6 Sept 1947; *Heir* Sheila, da of C M D Belton, of Shrewsbury (d 1971); 2 da (Jennifer b 1949, Carol b 1952); *Career* chm; Capt 14/20 King's Hussars serv Italy; chm P S Mossé & Ptnrs Ltd, Lloyds Brokers; *Recreations* skiing, golf; *Clubs* Cavalry and Guards; *Style—* Peter Mossé, Esq; The Orchard, Bishops Caundle, Sherborne, Dorset (☎ 01 488 4303)

MOSSÉ, Peter Sylvain; s of Leon Moosé (d 1980), of Monaco, and Leonie, *née* King; *b* 25 Jan 1925; *Educ* Shrewsbury, Sandhurst; *m* 6 Sept 1967, (Evelyn) Sheila, da of Carl Moritz Dunsford Belton; 2 da (Jennifer (Mrs Pettman) b 1 June 1969, Carol (Mrs Grant) b 22 Dec 1952); *Career* Capt 14/25 King's Hussars 1943-54; dir C T Bowring & Muir Beddal Lloyds Brokers 1964, chm P S Mossé & Ptnrs Ltd 1968-; govr Sandroyd Prep Sch; memb LIBA; *Recreations* golf, skiing, woodwork; *Clubs* Cavalry and Guard's; *Style—* Peter Mossé, Esq; P S Mossé & Ptnrs Ltd, 41 Crutched Friars, London EC3N 2NT (☎ 01 488 4303)

MOSSE, Richard Hugh; s of Rev Charles Herbert Mosse (d 1970), and Beatrice Elizabeth, *née* Watson (d 1981); *b* 30 May 1924; *Educ* Radley; *m* 29 May 1954, Barbara Mary, da of Lt-Col Harold Montague Towlson (d 1970); 3 da (Kate b 1961, Caroline (Mrs Matthews) b 1965, Elizabeth b 1966); *Career* Capt Welsh Guards, France and Germany 1944-45, Palestine 1946-48; admitted slr 1957, NP 1976; pres Chichester and District Law Soc 1978-79, clerk to gen cmmr of taxes Chichester and Bognor Regis 1988-; sr ptnr Rapers Solicitors; sec to Board of Chichester Festival Theatre 1966-, pres Aldwick branch Royal Br Legion 1971, life govr Imperial Cancer Res Fund 1987, chm Fishbourne PCC 1987-; memb Law Soc 1957; *Books* Capital Transfer Tax (1975); author num articles on Capital Taxation; *Recreations* golf, fell walking; *Clubs* RAC; *Style—* Richard Mosse, Esq; 3 The Old Stables, Grassmere Close, Felpham Village, Bognor Regis, W Sussex (☎ 0243 788155); Rapers, 55 West St, Chichester, W Sussex (☎ 0243 788155, fax 0243 775290)

MOSSELMANS, Carel Maurits; TD; s of Adriaan Willem Mosselmans (d 1956), of The Hague, Holland, and Nancy Henriette van der Wyck (d 1963); *b* 9 Mar 1929; *Educ* Stowe, Trinity Coll Cambridge (MA); *m* 4 Jan 1962, Hon Prudence Fiona, da of Baron McCorquodale of Newton, KCO, PC (d 1971); 2 s (Michael b 1962, Julian b 1964); *Career* insur broker; chm Sumitomo Marine & Fire Insur Co (Europe) Ltd 1981-; Sedgewick Lloyds Underwriting Agents Ltd 1975-89, Sedgewick Gp plc 1984-89; non-exec dir: Coutts & Co (1981-); *Recreations* shooting, fishing, golf; *Clubs* White's, Cavalry & Guard's; *Style—* Carel M Mosselmans, Esq, TD; 15 Chelsea Sq, London SW3 (☎ 01 352 0621); Sedgwick Gp plc, Sedgwick House, The Sedgwick Centre, London E1 8DX (☎ 01 377 3456)

MOSSELMANS, Hon Mrs (Prudence Fiona); da of 1 and last Baron McCorquodale of Newton (d 1971), and Winifred Sophia Doris Clark (d 1960); *b* 27 June 1936; *m* 1962, Carel Maurits Mosselmans, TD, *qv*; 2 s; *Style—* The Hon Mrs Mosselmans; Seameads, Sandwich Bay, Kent (☎ 030 461 3558); 15 Chelsea Square, London SW3 (☎ 01 352 0621)

MOSSMAN, Frances Anne; da of Francis Joseph McGarry, of Southampton, Hants, and Kathleen, *née* Gralton; *b* 6 Jan 1949; *Educ* La Sante Union Convert HS Southampton, Winchester Sch of Art, Trent Poly (Dip Fashion and Textiles); *m* 7 July 1978, Andrew Vernon Mossman, s of John Vernon Mossman, of Putney, London, and Diss, Norfolk; 1 s (Tomás b 28 April 1988); *Career* design dir Sabre Int Textiles 1978-84; Next plc: merchandise dir (menswear) 1985-86, product dir (all clothing) 1986-87, ed dir Next Directory 1987; assessor: RCA, CNAA Kingston Poly; reading, walking in the country; *Style—* Mrs Frances Mossman; 79A Warrington Crescent, London W9 1EH (☎ 01 289 2337); Home Farm, Little Everdon, Northants (☎ 032 736 233); Next plc Desford Rd, Enderby, Leicester (☎ 0533 866 411)

MOSSOP, Lady; Jean Maud Bennett; MBE (1945); da of A B Paton and wid of Lt Cdr William Alexander Elliot, RN; *m* 1950 as his 2 w, Sir Allan George Mossop (d 1965); *Career* serv WWII, 1 Offr, WRNS; *Style—* Lady Mossop, MBE; Evergreen, Evergreen Ave, Newlands, 7700 S Africa

MOSTYN, Lady; Cristina Beatrice Maria; o da of Marchese Pier-Paolo Vladimiro Orengo, of Casa Orengo, La Mortola, Italy; *m* 23 June 1963, Sir Jeremy John Anthony Mostyn, 14 Bt (d 1988); 1 s (Sir William, 15 Bt, *qv*), 2 da (Casimira Anita Maria b 3 Dec 1964, Rachel Joanna Maria b 26 Aug 1967); *Style—* Lady Mostyn; The Coach House, Lower Heyford, Oxon

MOSTYN, Gen Sir (Joseph) David Frederick; KCB (1984), CBE (1974, MBE 1962); s of J P Mostyn (d 1929), and J D S Keenan, *née* Moss; *b* 28 Nov 1928; *Educ* Downside, RMA Sandhurst; *m* 1952, Diana Patricia, da of Col Sheridan, MC (d 1950), of Kylemore, Fleet, Hants; 4 s (Philip, Mark, Rupert, Matthew), 2 da (Celia, Kate); *Career* cmmnd Oxford and Bucks LI 1948, Candaian Staff Coll 1958, instr Staff Coll Camberley 1963-66, MOD 1967-68, cmd 2 Royal Green Jackets 1969-71, Cmdt Offs Wing War Min 1971-72, cmd 8 Inf Bde 1972-74, dep dir Army Trg 1974-75, RCDS 1976, BGS Rhine Army 1977, dir Personal Servs 1978-80, GOC Berlin 1980-83, mil sec 1983-86, Adj-Gen 1986-88; Col Cmdt: Light Div 1983-86, Army Legal Corps 1983-88, ADC (Gen) 1986-89; landowner (165 acres); ADC (General); *Recreations* all field sports; *Clubs* Army and Navy; *Style—* Gen Sir David Mostyn, KCB, CBE; c/o Lloyds Bank, 54 Broad St, Lyme Regis, Dorset

MOSTYN, Hon Llewellyn Roger Lloyd; s and h of 5 Baron Mostyn, MC, by his 1 w Yvonne (*see* Maj Sir William Wrixon-Becher, Bt, MC); *b* 26 Sept 1948; *Educ* Eton, The Inns of Ct Sch of Law; *m* 1974, Denise Suzanne, da of Roger Duvanel, an artist, of France; 1 s (Gregory b 1984), 1 da (Alexandra b 1975); *Career* late Capt Army Legal Servs; barr Middle Temple 1973 (practising Criminal Bar), teacher at Bromley Coll of Technol; *Recreations* literature, history, classical music, tennis, sport, rugger; *Clubs* White's; *Style—* The Hon Llewellyn Mostyn; 9 Sloane Ave, London SW3 (☎ 01 589 2288); 185 Temple champions, Temple Ave, London E19, 353/3507/8

MOSTYN, 5 Baron (UK 1831); Capt Sir Roger Edward Lloyd Lloyd-Mostyn; 6 Bt (GB 1778), MC (1942); s of 4 Baron (d 1965); *b* 17 April 1920; *Educ* Eton, RMC Sandhurst; *m* 1, 1943, Yvonne Margaret, da of A Stuart Johnson, of Henshall Hall, Congleton, Cheshire; 1 s, 1 da; m 2, Mrs Sheila Edmondson Shaw, DL (Clwyd 1982), da of Maj Reginald Fairweather; *Heir* s, Hon Llewellyn Roger Lloyd Lloyd-Mostyn; *Career* 2 Lt 9 Lancers 1939 (despatches 1940), temp Maj 1945; *Style—* The Rt Hon the Lord Mostyn, MC; Mostyn Hall, Mostyn, Clwyd, N Wales (☎ Mostyn 222)

MOSTYN, Sir William Basil John; 15 Bt (E 1670), of Talacre, Flintshire; o s of Sir Jeremy John Anthony Mostyn, 14 Bt (d 1988), and Cristina Beatrice Maria, o da of Marchese Pier-Paolo Vladimiro Orengo; snr male rep of Tudor Trevor, Lord of Hereford (10 cent); *b* 15 Oct 1975; *Heir* unc, Trevor Alexander Richard Mostyn b 23 May 1946; *Style—* Sir William Mostyn, Bt; The Manor House, Lower Heyford, Oxon

MOSTYN-OWEN, Elizabeth; da of Lt-Col Roger Arthur Mostyn-Owen, DSO (d 1947), of Oswestry, Shropshire, and Margaret Eva, *née* Dewhurst (D 1976); *b* 10 July 1926; *Educ* St Mary's Sch Wantage, Univ of London (BA); *m* 9 July 1947 (m dis 1960), Harold Warren Freeman-Attwood, s of Maj Gen H A Freeman-Attwood, DSO, OBE, MC (d 1963); 1 s (Julian David Warren Freeman-Attwood b 1953), 1 da (Rosamond Margaret Freeman-Atwood b 1951); *Career* freelance art historian/lectr/journalist, memb exec ctee Int Assoc of Art Critics, London correspondent for Il Giornale dell'Arte; *Style—* Mrs Elizabeth Mostyn-Owen; 38 Ladbroke Square, London W11 3ND (☎ 01 727 3491)

MOTHERWELL, Bishop of (RC) 1983-; Rt Rev Joseph Devine; s of Joseph Devine, of Nazareth House, Glasgow, and Christina, *née* Murphy (d 1981); *b* 7 August 1937; *Educ* Blairs Coll Aberdeen, St Peter's Coll Dumbarton Pontificial Scots Coll Rome, Gregorian Univ Rome (PLD); *Career* personal sec to Archbishop of Glasgow 1964-66, lectr in philosophy St Peter's Coll Dumbarton 1966-74, chaplain Glasgow Univ 1974-77, auxiliary bishop Glasgow 1977-83; Papal Bene Merenti 1962; *Recreations* reading, music, soccer; *Style—* The Rt Rev the Bishop of Motherwell; Bishop's House, 17 Viewpark Rd, Motherwell ML1 3ER, (☎ 63715); Diocesan Centre, Coursington Rd, Motherwell, (☎ 69114/5)

MOTION, Andrew; s of Lt Col A R Motion, of Braintree Essex, and C G Motion (d 1982); *b* 26 Oct 1952; *Educ* Radley, Univ Coll Oxford; *m* 1985, Jan, da of C M Dalley, of Maldon, Essex; 2 s (Andrew Jesse, b 1986, Lucas Edward b 19 May 1988), 1 da (Sidonie Gillian Elizabeth (twin) b 19 May 1988); *Career* poetry ed Chatto of Windows; prizes incl: Avon Observer Prize 1982, John Llewelyn Rhys Prize 1984, Somerset Maugham Award 1987, Dylan Thomas Prize 1988; *Books* Dangerous Play, Poems

1974-84, The Lamberts, Natural Causes; *Style*— Andrew Motion, Esq; Chatto & Windus, 30 Bedford Square, London WC1

MOTION, Hon Mrs (Penelope Mary); da of 2 Viscount Harcourt, KCMG, OBE (d 1979); *b* 1933; *m* 1954, Capt Anthony David Motion; 1 s; *Style*— The Hon Mrs Motion; Buckland, Irishtown, via Northam, Western Australia (☎ 096 221130)

MOTL, Hon Mrs; Hon Marion Ann; *née* Molloy; da of Baron Molloy (Life Peer), by his 1 w, Eva Mary (d 1980); *b* 3 June 1947; *Educ* Holland Park Comprehensive Sch, Charing Cross Hosp Sch of Nursing (SRN, SCM); *m* 1974, Laurence George, s of Charles Leopold Motl; 2 da (Julia, Ann); *Career* staff nurse Charing Cross Hosp 1970, staff mid-wife and sister Central Middx Hosp 1973; *Style*— The Hon Mrs Motl; 6225 Idylwood Lane, Edina, Minneapolis 55436, USA

MOTT, Dr David Hugh; s and h of Sir John Harmar Mott, 3 Bt; *b* 1 May 1952; *Educ* Shrewsbury, Sussex Univ (BSc), Birkbeck Coll London (MSc), QMC London (PhD); *m* 1980, Amanda Jane, da of Lt Cdr D W P Fryer, RN, of Fleet, Hants; 2 s (Matthew b 1982, Jonathan b 1984); *Career* princ conslt Software Scis Farnborough; memb BCS; *Style*— Dr David Mott

MOTT, John Charles Spencer; *b* 18 Dec 1926; *Educ* Brixton Sch of Building, Battersea Poly, Rutherford Coll of Technol, Newcastle upon Tyne; *m* 1953, Patricia Mary; 2 s; *Career* serv Lt RM 1943-46; chm and chief exec French Kier Hldgs plc 1974-86; (dir 1963-); chm May Gurney Hldgs Ltd (construction gp) 1986-; FEHG, FICE, FIStructE, CBIM; *Recreations* golf, chm May Gurney Hldgs Ltd (construction group) 1986-; *Clubs* Danish; *Style*— John Mott, Esq; 91 Long Rd, Cambridge (☎ 0223 841320)

MOTT, Sir John Harmar; 3 Bt (UK 1930), of Ditchling, Co Sussex; s of Sir Adrian Spear Mott, 2 Bt (d 1964), and Mary Katherine, *née* Stanton (d 1972); *b* 21 July 1922; *Educ* Dragon, Radley, New Coll Oxford (MA, BM, BCh), Middx Hosp; *m* 1950, Elizabeth, da of Hugh Carson, FRCS (d 1981); 1 s, 2 da (David) (Jennifer, Alison); *Heir* s, David Hugh Mott; *Career* serv 1939-45 with RAF, Flying Offr 1943-46, Far East; MRCGP; qualified as med practitioner 1951; regnl med offr DHSS 1969-84, ret; pt/t med referee; vice-chm Kingsley branch Eddisbury Cons Assoc 1988, memb Mid-Ches Pitt Club 1988; *Recreations* photography, classical archaeology and history; *Style*— Sir John Mott, Bt; Staniford, Brookside, Kingsley, Cheshire WA6 8BG (☎ 0928 88123)

MOTT, Capt John William; LVO (1956); s of Maj Sydney Albert Mott (d 1924), and Grizle, *née* Cuninghame; *b* 5 Mar 1917; *Educ* RN Dartmouth and Keyham; *m* 1, 22 Oct 1946, Theophila, da of John Littleton of Torpoint, Cornwall; 2 da; m 2, 5 Dec 1963, Ann, da of Arthur Slater of Sheffield; *Career* naval offr HMS Exeterin S Atlantic 1938-40, HMS Malaya in Med 1940-42, HMS Jamaca 1942-43, Pilot Fleet Air Arm 1943, Staff HMS Thunderer 1945, Admty 1950, HMY Britannia 1952-56, IDC 1964, NA Belgrade 1965-67; CO RN Air Station Arbroath 1967-69; Nat Tst for Scotland rep for SW Scotland at Culzean Castle 1969-82; *Recreations* water colour painting, hill walking; *Style*— Capt John Mott, LVO; Little Craigfin, Maybole, Ayr KA19 9LR (☎ 06 554 424)

MOTT, His Hon Judge Michael Duncan; s of Francis John Mott (d 1979), and Gwendolen, *née* Mayhew; *b* 8 Dec 1940; *Educ* Rugby, Gonville and Caius Coll Cambridge (MA); *m* 19 Dec 1970, Phyllis Ann, da of V James Gavin, of Dubuque, Iowa, USA; 2 s (Timothy b 1972, Jonathan b 1975); *Career* called to the Bar Inner Temple 1963, chambers Birmingham 1964-69, res magistrate Kenya 1969-71, Midland and Oxford circuit 1972-85, dep circuit judge 1976-80, rec 1980-85, circuit judge 1985-; parish cncllr 1982-86, parish organist 1984-; memb Hon Soc of Inner Temple; *Recreations* music, travel, skiing, tennis; *Clubs* Cambridge Union, Union & County (Worcs); *Style*— His Hon Judge Mott; c/o Circuit Administrator, Midland & Oxford Circuit, 2 Newton St, Birmingham B4 7LU

MOTT, Sir Nevill Francis; s of Charles Francis Mott (d 1967); *b* 30 Sept 1905; *Educ* Clifton, St John's Coll Cambridge (MA); *m* 1930, Ruth Eleanor, da of Gerald Horder (d 1939); 2 da; *Career* Melville Wills prof of theoretical physics Bristol Univ 1933-48, Henry Overton prof Bristol Univ 1948-53, Cavendish prof of physics Cambridge Univ 1953-71; Nobel Prize for Physics 1977; FRS; kt 1962; *Clubs* Athenaeum; *Style*— Sir Nevill Mott; 63 Mount Pleasant, Aspley Guise, Milton Keynes MK17 8JX (☎ 0908 583257); The Cavendish Laboratory, Madingley Rd, Cambridge CB3 0HE

MOTT, Philip Charles; s of Charles Kynaston Mott (d 1981), of Taunton, Somerset, and Elsa, *née* Smith; *b* 20 April 1948; *Educ* King's Coll Taunton, Worcester Coll Oxford (BA, MA); *m* 19 Nov 1977, Penelope Ann, da of Edward Gaffery; 2 da (Sarah b 1981, Catherine b 1983); *Career* called to Bar Inner Temple 1970, practicing Western Circuit 1970-, rec of the Crown Ct 1987-; *Recreations* the countryside, sailing; *Clubs* Hampshire (Winchester), Exeter and County (Exeter); *Style*— Philip C Mott, Esq; Lamb Building, Temple, London EC4Y 7AS (☎ 01 353 6381, fax 01 583 1786)

MOTT-RADCLYFFE, Sir Charles Edward; DL (Norfolk 1976); assumed additional surname of Mott 1927; s of Lt-Col Charles Edward Radclyffe, DSO, and Theresa Caroline, only child of John Stanley Mott, of Barningham Hall, Norfolk; *b* 25 Dec 1911; *Educ* Eton, Balliol Coll Oxford; *m* 1, 1940, Diana (d 1955), da of Lt-Col William Gibbs, CVO, JP (d 1963); 3 da; m 2, 1956, Stella Constance, da of Lionel GS Harrisson (d 1953), of Caynham Cottage, Ludlow; *Career* serv Capt Rifle Bde in Greece, Syria, and Italy, (RARO); hon attaché HM Diplomatic Corps Athens 1936, Rome 1936-38; MP (C) Windsor Berks 1942-70; chm Cons Pty Foreign Affrs Ctee 1951-59; memb: Historic Buildings Cncl for Eng 1962-70, Plowden Ctee on Overseas Representational Servs 1962-63; pres CLA Norfolk branch 1973-87; high sheriff Norfolk 1974-75; pres Norfolk CCC 1973-74 (chm 1975-89); Cdr of Order of Phoenix (Greece); kt 1957; *Recreations* cricket, shooting; *Clubs* Bucks, Turf, MCC,; *Style*— Sir Charles Mott-Radclyffe, DL; Barningham Hall, Matlaske, Norfolk (☎ 026 377 250)

MOTTERSHEAD, Frank William; CB (1957); s of Thomas Hastings Mottershead (d 1969), and Adeline Mottershead (d 1930); *b* 7 Sept 1911; *Educ* King Edwards Sch Birmingham, Cambridge Univ (BA, MA); *Career* princ private sec to First Lord of the Admty 1944-46; dep sec: MOD 1958-65, DHSS 1965-71; *Clubs* Utd Oxford and Cambridge Univ; *Style*— Frank Mottershead, CB; Old Warden, Gravel Lane, Chipping, Campden, Glos GL55 6HS

MOTTISTONE, 4 Baron (UK 1933); David Peter Seely; CBE (1984); 4 s of 1 Baron Mottistone, CB, CMG, DSO, TD, PC (d 1947; himself 4 s of Sir Charles Seely, 1 Bt), by his 2 w, Hon Evelyn Izmé Murray, JP, da of 10 Lord and 1 Viscount Elibank and widow of George Nicholson (s of Sir Charles Nicholson, 1 Bt) - by whom she was mother of Sir John Nicholson, 2 Bt ; Lord Mottistone succeeded his half-bro, 3 Baron, 1966; *b* 16 Dec 1920, (HRH The Duke of Windsor stood sponsor); *Educ* RN Coll Dartmouth; *m* 1944, Anthea Christine, da of Victor McMullan, of Co Down; 2 s, 3 da (1 decd); *Heir* s, Hon Peter John Philip Seely; *Career* sits as Cons in House of Lords; Cdr RN 1955, Capt RN 1960 (D) 24 Escort Sqdn 1963-65; ret at own request 1967; dir personnel trg Radio Rentals Ltd 1967-69, dir Distributive Indust Trg Bd 1969-75; dir Cake & Biscuit Alliance 1975-81, parly advsr Biscuit, Cake, Chocolate & Confectionary Alliance 1981- (export sec 1981-83); dep Lt IOW 1981; Lord Lt IOW 1986-; FIEE, FIPM, FBIM; *Clubs* Royal Yacht Sqdn, Royal Cruising, Royal Naval Sailing Assoc, Island Sailing, Royal Cwealth Soc; *Style*— The Rt Hon the Lord Mottistone, CBE; Old Parsonage, Mottistone, IOW PO30 4EE (☎ 0983 740264)

MOTTLEY, Peter Henry; s of Edward George Mottley (d 1969), and Elizabeth Louisa, *née* Watt; *b* 29 Jan 1987; *Educ* Edmonton Co GS, Univ of Sheffield (BA); *m* 1964 (m dis 1982), Diana Margaret, da of Leslie Fisher Griffiths (d 1970); 1 da (Jocelyn b 1967); *Career* creative conslt/writer, professional actor 1960-62, creative dir Nicklin Advtg 1978-81; plays: The Last Will and Testament of Popsy Petal (1984), After Agincourt (1986); *Books* The Sex Bar (1972); *Recreations* theatre, supporting W Ham Utd, music, cooking; *Style*— Peter Mottley, Esq; 9 Aston Close, Pangbourne, Berks (☎ 07357 2826)

MOTTRAM, Maj-Gen John Frederick; CB (1982), MVO (1976), OBE (1969); s of F W Mottram (d 1972), and Margaret (d 1984); *b* 9 June 1930; *m* 1956, Jennifer, da of M J Thomas (d 1971); 1 s, 1 da; *Career* RM 1948; jt warfare attaché BR Embassy Washington 1974-77, Col Gen Staff Dept of Cmdt Gen RM and ADC to HM The Queen 1978-80, Maj-Gen Trg and Reserve Forces RM 1980-83, dir-gen Fertiliser Manufacturers Assoc 1983-86; chief exec, Gen cncl of Bar 1987-; *Recreations* fishing; *Clubs* Army & Navy; *Style*— Maj-Gen John Mottram, CB, MVO, OBE; c/o Army and Navy Club, Pall Mall, London SW1

MOTTRAM, Richard Clive; s of John Mottram, of Chislehurst, Kent, and Florence Bertha, *née* Yates; *b* 23 April 1946; *Educ* King Edward VI Camp Hill Sch for Boys Birmingham, Univ of Keele (BA); *m* 24 July 1971, Dr Fiona Margaret, da of Keith David Erskine (d 1974); 3 s (Keith b 1974, David b 1981, Thomas b 1985), 1 da (Ruth b 1977); *Career* Home CS, assigned MOD 1968, Cabinet Off 1975-77, private sec to Perm Under Sec of State 1979-81, private sec to Sec of State for Def 1982-86, asst under sec MOD 1986-; *Recreations* theatre, cimema, tennis; *Style*— Richard Mottram, Esq; c/o MOD, Whitehall, London SW1 (☎ 01 218 9000)

MOUBRAY-JANKOWSKI, Anthony; s of Josef Orzel-Jankowski VM (d 1967), of Aberdour, Fife, and Barbara, *née* Moubray (d 1964); *b* 2 Oct 1946; *Educ* King's Sch Canterbury; *m* 13 Oct 1969, Danielle Marian, da of Leslie Green; 1 s (Arran b 1970) 2 da (Selena b 1972, Barbara b 1979); *Career* CA; Lee Evans Ptnrship, RIBA: chm Canterbury Chapter, sec Architects in Agriculture and the countryside; conslt: King's Sch Canterbury, Strutt and Parker; ARIBA; *Recreations* music, theatre, skiing, swimming, social work; *Style*— Anthony Moubray-Jankowski, Esq; Kenfield House, Petham, Canterbury (☎ 022 770 721); 9 Lower Grosvenor Place, London SW1 (☎ 01 630 7981, fax 01 630 6152)

MOUGHTON, Barry John; s of victor John Moughton, (d 1940), and Doris Emma, *née* Bosworth; *b* 28 May 1932; *Educ* Merchant Taylor's, Brasenose Coll Oxford (MA), McGill Univ Montreal (MCL); *m* 13 Sept 1958, Elizabeth Anne, da of Harold Edwin Parr, of Ferring, Worthing, Sussex; 1 s (Jonathan), 2 da (Katharine (Mrs Nisbet), Julia); *Career* Nat Serv 2 Lt RA 1950-51; admitted slr 1958, ptnr Turner Kenneth Brown 1963- (formerly Turner Peacock, prev EF Turner and Sons); chm: Churches of Dorking Housing Assoc 1965-, Surrey Fedn Housing Assoc 1974-81; vice-chm Leith Hill Music Festival 1979-85, pres Rotary Club London 1984-85, fndn chm Rotary Dist 113 1977-78; chm Dorking Urban Dist cncl 1967-68 (cncllr 1962-68), JP 1967-70; Freeman City of London 1984, memb Worshipful Slrs Co 1985; memb Law Soc 1959; *Recreations* choral singing; *Style*— Barry Moughton, Esq; 100 Fetter Lane, London EC4A 1DD (☎ 01 242 6006, fax 01 242 3003)

MOULD, Air Cdre John Edwin Michael; CBE (1964); s of Clifford Mould (d 1938); *b* 12 Nov 1914; *Educ* Farnham GS; *m* 1945, Molly, da of Richard Bateman; 1 s, 1 da; *Career* Artists' Rifles 1937-38, RAF Equipment Branch 1939, serv WWII, Middle E Centre for Arab Studies 1944-45, dir staff RAF Staff Coll 1951-53, Air Cdre 1965, dir of Equipment 2 (RAF) MOD 1965-67, Dep COS (Logistics and Admin) HQ 2 ATAF 1967-69, ret 1970; Ocean Accident and Guarantee Corpn 1932-38; vice-pres Surrey Wildlife Tst 1977-; *Clubs* Royal Cwealth Soc, RAF; *Style*— Air Cdre John Mould, CBE; Limes, Middle Ave, Farnham, Surrey (☎ 0252 715418)

MOULE, Cncllr Brian; s of Richard Moule (d 1952), and Amy Moule, *née* Westwood; *b* 7 April 1932; *Educ* Coventry St Sch, St George's and Sladen; *m* 1956, Phyllis Ruth; 1 s (Steven b 1969), 1 da (Wendy b 1968); *Career* Wyre Forest DC 1980-, Mayor of Kidderminster 1982 and 1986, gen sec Power Loom Carpet Weavers' & Textile Workers' Union 1982-, gen sec Nat Affiliation of Carpet Trade Unions; memb NEDO, TUC jt Textile Ctee, Health and Safety Exec, Br Standards Inst for Wool Textile, govr of Kidderminster Coll of Further Educn; *Style*— Cncllr Brian Moule Esq; 17 Batham Rd, Kidderminster (☎ 0562 4608); Carpet Weavers' Hall, Callows Lane, Kidderminster (☎ 0562 3192)

MOULTON; *see*: Fletcher-Moulton

MOULTON, Dr Alexander Eric; CBE (1976); s of John Coney Moulton, and Beryl Latimer, *née* Greene; *b* 9 April 1920; *Educ* Marlborough, Kings Coll Cambridge (MA); *Career* innovating engr, inventor of the Moulton Bicycle, and Hydrolastic and Hydras Car suspension and Moulton Coach etc; fndr: Moulton Devlt Ltd 1957, Noulton Bicycles 1962; chm ctee on engrg design Educn Design Cncl 1975-76 (Moulton Report); awards incl: Design Centre Award 1964, Gold Medal Triennale Milan 1964, Bid late Memb Plaque for encouragement to Cycling 1964, Queens Award to Indust 1967, Design Medal Soc of Industl Artists and Designers 1976, James Clayton Prize, Crompton-Lanchester Medal, Thomas Hawksley Gold Medal; Royal Designer for Indust (Master of Faculty 1981-83); hon do ctorate Royal Coll of Art 1967, hon DSc Univ of Bath 1971; I Mech E 1979, REng 1980 (vice-pres 1988); *Publications* numerous on engrg and educn; *Recreations* cycling, canoeing, shooting; *Clubs* Brook's; *Style*— Dr Alexander Moulton, CBE; The Hall, Bradford-on-Avon, Wilts BA15 1AH (☎ 02216 5895, fax 02216 4742, telex 44356 MOULTN G)

MOULTON, Maj-Gen James Louis; CB (1956), DSO (1944), OBE (1950); s of Capt John Davis Moulton, RN (d 1922), and Beatrice Nutter, *née* Cox; *b* 3 June 1906; *Educ* Queen Elizabeth's GS Barnet, Sutton Valence; *m* 1937, Barbara Aline, da of John

Melvill Coode (d 1949), of Hooe, Plymouth; 1 s (Robert), 1 da (Caroline); *Career* RM 1924, Pilot in Fleet Air Arm 1930-35, Staff Coll Camberley 1938-39; serv: France, Belgium (Dunkirk), Madagascar, NW Europe (DSO, dsspatches 1945); cmd 48 Commando 1944-45, 4 Commando Bde 1945, Commando Sch 1947-49, 3 Commando Bde 1952-54, Maj-Gen RM Portsmouth 1954-57, Chief of Amphibious Warfare 1957-61, ret; *Books* The Norwegian Campaign of 1940 (1960), Haste to the Battle (1963), Defence in a Changing World (1964), The Royal Marines (1972, enlarged edition 1981), Battle for Antwerp (1978), numerous articles on defence and military history; *Recreations* hill walking; *Style—* Maj Gen J L Moulton, CB, DSO, OBE; Fairmile, Woodham Rd, Woking, Surrey GU21 4DN (☎ 048 62 5174)

MOULTON, Jonathan Paul (Jon); s of Douglas Cecil Moulton, of Stoke-on-Trent, and Elsie Turner Moulton (d 1984); *b* 15 Oct 1950; *Educ* Hanley HS, Univ of Lancaster (BA); *m* 13 Aug 1973, Pauline Marie, da of Stanley Dunn, of Stoke-on-Trent; 1 s (Spencer Jonathan b 1980), 1 da (Rebecca Clare b 1978); *Career* mangr Coopers & Lybrand 1972-80; Citicorp Venture Capital 1980-85: dir NY 1980-81, gen mangr London 1981-85, managing ptnr Schroder Ventures 1985-; non-exec dir: Hornby Hobbies Plc 1981-, Halls Homes & Gdns Plc 1982-, Parker Pen Ltd 1986-, Haden MacLellan Hldgs Plc 1987-, Interconnection Systems Ltd 1987-, FCA 1983, FBIM; ; *Recreations* chess, fishing; *Style—* Jon Moulton, Esq; Arbury, Knockholt, Kent TN14 7NE (☎ 0959 33472); Schroder Ventures, 20 Southampton St, London WC2E 7QG (☎ 01 379 5010, fax 01 240 5072)

MOULTON, Hon Mrs Hugh; Marie Josephine; da of late Sebastian Bergaentzle; *m* 1937, as his 2 w, Hon Hugh Fletcher Moulton, MC (d 1962); *Style—* The Hon Mrs Hugh Moulton; 16 Argyll Rd, London W8

MOULTON, Hon Sylvia May Fletcher; CBE (1960, OBE 1942), JP; da of Baron Moulton (Life Peer; d 1921); *b* 1902; *Educ* Girton Coll Cambridge (BA); *Career* barr Middle Temple 1929, former regnl admin for Women's Voluntary Servs for Civil Def; *Style—* Hon Sylvia Moulton, CBE, JP; Court House, Barcombe, Sussex

MOULTRIE, John Farbon (Jack); CBE (1980); s of John Felix Hawksford Moultrie (d 1961), and Elsie May, *née* Wass; *b* 26 June 1914; *Educ* Loxford Secdy Modern Ilford, Coll of Estate Mgmnt; *m* 2 Sept 1939, Irene Hazel (d 1982) da of Thomas James Cast (d 1945) 3 da (Margaret b 1942, Vivian b 1944, Katherine b 1946); *Career* Capt HG 1940-44; chartered surveyor; articled 1930, sr ptnr 1956-86; cncllr Dagenham Borough Cncl 1950-60, Hornchurch UDC 1960- 65; London Borough Cncl of Havering 1965-86: cncllr 1965-86, ldr 1968-71, 1974-77, 1979-82 and 1982-84, ldr of oppn 1971-74, Mayor 1977-78; chm: Rush Green Hosp League of Friends (fndr and pres), Oldchurch Hosp Scanner Appeal, gen Cnmm of Taxes (Barking), LAMIT; pres: Upminster Cons Assoc, Rotary Club Dagenham 1963-63; served on LBA and AMA; JP 1954-86 (chm Barking Bench NE London); Liveryman Worshipful Co of Bakers 1964; Freeman: City of London 1964, London Borough of Havering 1986; FRICS; *Recreations* bowls, gardening, local politics; *Clubs* Carlton; *Style—* Jack Moultrie, Esq, CBE; 11 The Woodfines, Hornchurch, Essex RM11 3HR (☎ 04024 42244); 1 High Road, Chadwell Heath, Romford, Essex RM6 6PX (☎ 01 590 1219)

MOUND, Dr Laurence Alfred; s of John Henry Mound, and Laura May, *née* Cape; *b* 22 April 1934; *Educ* Warwick Sch, Univ of London (BSc, DSc); *m* 1, 27 Aug (m dis 1985), Jean Agnes, da of Andrew Solari, of Lincoln; 1 s (Nicholas b 1960), 2 da (Sarah Anne b 1965, Helen Catherine b 1967); m 2, 22 June 1987, Sheila Helen, da of Maurice Frank Halsey, of Hythe; *Career* entomologist; Federal Dept of Agric Res Nigeria 1959-61, Empire Cotton Growing Corpn Sudan 1961-64, keeper of entomolgy Br Museum Natural History 1981-(sr princ sci offr 1964-75, dep keeper of entomology 1975-81), conslt dir Cwlth Inst of Entomology 1980-; FLS, FRES; *Recreations* looking at insects; *Style—* Dr Laurence Mound; British Museum (Natural History), Cromwell Rd, London SW7 5BD (☎ 01 938 9474)

MOUNSEY, Joseph Backhouse; s of Colin Anthony Mounsey, of Clover House, Kingston Hill, Surrey, and Helen, *née* Roake; *b* 27 Mar 1949; *Educ* Leighton Park Sch Reading, New Coll Oxford (MA); *m* 18 Nov 1978, Elizabeth Anne, da of Peter William Burton (d 1970); 1 da (Elizabeth Helen b 1979); *Career* vice pres: Int Investmts, The Manufacturers Life Insur Co 1980-86; md: The Manufacturers Life Insur Co (UK) Ltd 1983-, Manulife Management Ltd 1983; vice pres and gen mngr UK The Manufacturers Life Insur Co 1986-, chm Western Trust & Savings Hldgs Ltd 1987; dir: ManuLife (Singapore) Pte Ltd, ManuLife Holdings (HK) Ltd, Manulife Menorah Ltd, Western Trust & Savings Ltd; *Clubs* Reform; *Style—* Joseph Mounsey, Esq; 'Wharfedale', 8 Densley Close, Welwyn Garden City, Herts AL8 7JX (☎ 0707 324032); Manulife House, St George's Way, Stevenage, Herts SG1 1HP (☎ 0438 356101)

MOUNSEY, Michael Fryer; s of George Fryer Mounsey (d 1961), and Elizabeth Alberta, *née* McMurray (d 1966); *b* 12 Sept 1915; *Educ* Leighton Park Sch Reading, King's Coll Cambridge (MA 1940); *m* 11 May 1945, Ola Blanche, da of David Bone Nightingale Jack (d 1958); 1 da (Tessa b 13 Aug 1952); *Career* served with Friends Ambulance Unit in WWII 1939-44 in Finland, Norway, Egypt and Greece (POW 1941-44); local dir Barclays Bank Nottingham 1956-79; dir Barclays Bank (UK) Ltd 1971-79; Winter War Remembrance Medal (Finland) 1940; *Recreations* gardening, tennis; *Style—* Michael Mounsey, Esq; Bassingfield House, 198 Tollerton Lane, Tollerton, Notts NG12 4FW (☎ 06077 2603)

MOUNSEY, Simon Charles Finch; s of Charles Francis Ewart Mounsey (d 1964), and Mrs Audrey Trollope; *b* 25 August 1937; *Educ* Stowe; *m* 1963, Susan, da of Lt-Col George Edwin Noel Everett; 3 da; *Career* served 2 Lt Cyprus 1956-57; md Hays Business Services Ltd 1982-; *Recreations* golf; *Clubs* Piltdown Golf; *Style—* Simon Mounsey Esq; Barnes House, Piltdown, Uckfield, East Sussex TN22 3XN (☎ 082 572 2144); Hays Business Services Ltd, Datasafe House, 22 Vine Lane, SE1 (☎ 01 403 2033, telex 894859)

MOUNSEY-HEYSHAM, Giles Herchard; s of Maj Richard Herchard Gubbins Mounsey-Heysham (d 1960), of Castletown, Rockcliffe, Carlisle, and Mrs Isobel Margaret Rowcliffe; *b* 15 August 1948; *Educ* Gordonstoun, Royal Agric Coll Cirencester; *m* 24 April 1982, Penelope Auriol, da of William Anthony Twiston-Davies (see Debrett's Peerage and Baronetage, Archdale, Bt); 3 s (Toby b 23 Jan 1984, Benjamin b 3 Mar 1986, Rory b 2 Feb 1989); *Career* chartered surveyor; Smiths Gore 1970-72, Cluttons 1973-(ptnr 1976); FRICS 1982 (memb 1972); *Recreations* music, skiing, walking, travelling, shooting; *Clubs* Boodles (dep chm); *Style—* Giles Mounsey-Heysham, Esq; Castletown, Rockcliffe, Carlisle CA6 4BN (☎ 0228 74 792); Cluttons, Castletown, Rockcliffe, Carlisle (☎ 0228 74 792, fax 0228 74 464)

MOUNT, Air Cdre Christopher John; CBE (1956), DSO (1943, DFC 1940, DL (Royal County of Berkshire 1984)); s of Capt Francis Mount (d 1915), and Gladys Mary, *née* Llewelyn (d 1968); *b* 14 Dec 1913; *Educ* Eton, Trinity Coll Oxford; *m* 1947, Audrey Mabel, da of Lt-Col Marshal Falconer Clarke, DSO (d 1953), of Glasbury-on-Wye, Hereford; 2 s (David Richard, Antony Francis); *Career* Air Cdre RAF served in UK Middle East and Europe; slr, ptnr C R Thomas & Son Slr Maidenhead 1970-78 and conslt 1978-83 (when firm was dissolved); conslt Wrights Slrs Maidenhead; *Recreations* gardening; *Style—* Air Cdre Christopher John Mount, CBE, DSO, DFC, DL; Garden House, Bagshot Rd, Ascot, Berks (☎ 0990 22225)

MOUNT, (William Robert) Ferdinand; s of late Robert Francis Mount (2 s of Sir William Mount, 1 Bt, CBE) and Lady Julia Pakenham, da of 6 Earl of Longford; hp of unc, Sir William Mount, 2 Bt; *b* 2 July 1939; *Educ* Eton, Vienna Univ, Ch Ch Oxford; *m* 1968, Julia Margaret, twin da of Archibald Julian Lucas; 2 s (and 1 s decd), 1 da; *Career* former CRD desk offr (home affrs and health and social security); former chief ldr writer Daily Mail, columnist The Standard 1980-82, political correspondent The Spectator to 1982; head PM's Policy Unit 1982-83, literary editor The Spectator 1984-; *Books* The Theatre of Politics (1972), The Man Who Rode Ampersand (1975), The Clique (1978), The Subversive Family (1982); *Style—* Ferdinand Mount Esq; 17 Ripplevale Grove, London N1 (☎ 01 607 5398)

MOUNT, Paul Morrow; s of Ernest Edward Mount, and Elsie Gertrude, *née* Morrow; *b* 8 June 1922; *Educ* Newton Abbot GS, Paignton Sch of Art, RCA; *m* 1, 1947 (m dis), Jeanne Rosemary Martin; 1 s (Martin b 1950), 1 da (Margaret b 1956); m 2, 11 Oct 1978, June Sylvia, da of Lt Col William George Hilary Miles, RM; *Career* served WWII with Friends' Ambulance Unit, attached to 13 EME Bn Med 2 EME Div Blindee (Free French); initiated and ran Art dept, Yaba Nigeria 1955-61, freelance sculptor 1962, sculptor commns inc: Br Steel Corpn, Fibreglass Ltd St Helens, York House Bristol, CRS and Leo supermarkets, Swiss Embassy Tafawa Balewa Sq, Chase Manhattan Bank Lagos, Bauchi Meml, Nigeria, cabinet offices Accra; ARCA (1948), RWA, Penwith Soc; *Recreations* music; *Style—* Paul Mount, Esq; Nancherrow Studio, St Just, Penzance, Cornwall TR19 7LA (☎ 0736 788 552)

MOUNT, Lt-Col Sir William Malcolm; 2 Bt (UK 1921), of Wasing Place, Reading, Berks, ED (1942), DL (Berks 1946); s of Sir William Arthur Mount, 1 Bt, CBE, MP, JP, DL (d 1930); *b* 28 Dec 1904; *Educ* Eton, New Coll Oxford; *m* 1929, Elizabeth Nance, JP, da of Owen John Llewellyn; 3 da; *Heir* n, (William Robert) Ferdinand Mount; *Career* Lt 99 Bucks and Berks Yeo, Field Bde RA (TA) 1926, Capt 1937, Maj 1938, transfd Reconnaissance Corps 1941, Lt Col; jt master S Berks Foxhounds 1935-39; memb CC Berks 1938 (vice-chm CC 1960); High Sheriff 1947, Vice-Lt 1960-75; *Clubs* Farmers'; *Style—* Lt-Col Sir William Mount, Bt, ED, DL; Wasing Place, Aldermaston, Berks RG7 4NG (☎ 0734 713398)

MOUNT CHARLES, Earl of; Henry Vivian Pierpoint Conyngham; s and h of 7th Marquess Conyngham by his 1 w, Eileen; *b* 23 May 1951; *Educ* Harrow, Harvard Univ; *m* 1, 1971 (m dis 1985), Juliet Ann, da of Robert R B Kitson, of Churchtown, Morval, Cornwall; 1 s, 1 da (Lady Henrietta Tamara Juliet b 1976); m 2, 1985, Lady Iona C Grimston, yr da of late 6 Earl of Verulam; *Heir* s, Viscount Slane; *Career* Irish Rep Sothebys 1976-78; consultant Sothebys 1978-84; chm: Slane Castle Ltd, Slane Castle Productions; tstee Irish Youth Foundation; dir Grapevine Arts Centre, Dublin; landowner (1450 acres); *Clubs* Kildare St & Univ, Dublin (Dublin); *Style—* Earl of Mount Charles; Beauparc House, Beauparc, Navan, Co Meath

MOUNT CHARLES, Countess Iona Charlotte; da of 6 Earl of Verulam (d 1973), of Gorhambury, St Albans, Herts, and Marjorie Ray, *née* Duncan; *b* 25 Oct 1953; *m* 1985, Henry Vivian Pierpoint, s of Marquess Conyngham; *Style—* Lady Iona Grimston; c/o Rt Hon Dowager Countess of Verulam, Pre Mill House, Redbourn Rd, St Albans, Herts

MOUNT EDGCUMBE, 8 Earl of (GB 1789); Robert Charles Edgcumbe; also Viscount Mount Edgcumbe and Valletort (GB 1781) and Baron Edgcumbe of Mount Edgcumbe (GB 1742); yr s of George Aubrey Valletort Edgcumbe (d 1977, bro of 7 Earl, who d 1982) and his 1 w, Meta, da of late Charles Robert Lhoyer, of Nancy, France; descended from Sir Richard Edgcombe (d 1489), a supporter of Henry Tudor, Earl of Richmond (later Henry VII), who was knighted on the field of Bosworth, and later became a PC and comptroller of the Household; *b* 1 June 1939; *m* 1960, Joan, da of Ernest Wall, of Otorohanga; 5 da; *Heir* half-bro, Piers Edgcumbe, *qv*; *Career* farmer; ex mangr Lands and Survey Dept NZ; landowner (2200 acres); *Style—* The Rt Hon The Earl of Mount Edgcumbe; Empacombe House, Mount Edgcumbe, Cornwall PL1 0HZ

MOUNTAIN, Sir Denis Mortimer; 3 Bt (UK 1922), of Oare Manor, Co Somerset, and Brendon, Co Devon; s of Lt-Col Sir Brian Edward Stanley Mountain, 2 Bt (d 1977), and Doris Elsie, Lady Mountain, *qv*; *b* 2 June 1929; *Educ* Eton; *m* 18 Feb 1958, (Hélène) Fleur Mary, da of John William Kirwan-Taylor, of Switzerland; 2 s (Edward, William), 1 da (Georgina); *Heir* s, Edward Brian Stanford Mountain; *Career* Lt Royal Horse Guards; chm and md Eagle Star Insur Co Ltd 1974-85 (dir 1959), pres Eagle Star Hldgs plc 1985-; dir: Philip Hill Investmt Tst plc 1967-86, Rank Orgn plc 1968-, Bank of Nova Scotia (Canada) 1978-, Allied London Properties plc 1986-; *Recreations* fishing, shooting; *Clubs* Nat Sporting, Blues and Royals; *Style—* Sir Denis Mountain, Bt; 12 Queens Elm Sq, Old Church St, London SW3 6EB (☎ 01 352 4331); Shawford Park, Shawford, nr Winchester, Hants (☎ 0962 712289); Eagle Star Holdings plc, 60 St Mary Axe, London EC3A 8BA (☎ 01 929 1111)

MOUNTAIN, Doris Lady; Doris Elsie; eld da of late Eric Charles Edward Lamb; *m* 8 June 1926, Sir Brian Edward Stanley Mountain, 2 Bt (d 1977); 2 s, 1 da; *Style—* Doris Lady Mountain; 75 Eaton Sq, SW1

MOUNTAIN, Edward Brian Stanford; s and h of Sir Denis Mortimer Mountain, 3 Bt; *b* 19 Mar 1961; *m* 24 Oct 1987, Charlotte Sarah Jesson, da His Hon Judge Henry Pownall, QC, of 57 Ringmer Ave, London SW6; *Career* Army Officer, Second in Command the Blues and Royals Mounted Squadron (Capt) Household Cavalry Regiment; *Recreations* shooting, fishing, skiing; *Clubs* Cavalry and Guards Club; *Style—* Edward Mountain Esq

MOUNTAIN, John Letten; s of Lt Col Harold Mountain (d 1946), of Nunsfield, Grimsby, and Dorothy Somerville, *née* Letten (d 1987); *b* 31 Dec 1913; *Educ* Malvern, Cambridge Univ (MA); *m* 10 Nov 1942, Dawn, da of Chauncy Robert Dashwood Strettell (d 1948), of Claygate, Surrey; 1 s (Charles b 1948), 2 da (Vanessa (Mrs Walduck) b 1947, Juliet (Mrs Donald) b 1952); *Career* Lt 5 Lincolns TA RE 1938, Capt AA RA till 1946; slr and NP 1938, sr ptnr Bates and Mountain 1946-, clerk to Co

Justices (pt/t) 1946-64, clerk to Cmmrs of Inland Revenue 1946-88; Lloyd Underwriter 1971-, chm Grimsby & Cleethorpes Church Extension Soc (ret), govr St James choir Sch (ret); memb Law Soc; *Recreations* travel, shooting, tennis; *Style—* John Mountain, Esq; Little Grimsby Hall, Louth, Lincolnshire LN11 0UU (☎ 0507 602 757); Casa de Arriba, La Novia, Mijas, Malaga (☎ 010 3452 485 385); 37 Bethlehem St, Grimsby, S Humberside DN31 1JJ (☎ 0472 357 291, fax 0472 241 118)

MOUNTAIN, Nicholas Brian Edward; yr s of Sir Brian Edward Stanley Mountain, 2 Bt (d 1977), and Doris Elsie, *née* Lamb; *b* 15 Feb 1936; *Educ* Eton, St Catharine's Coll Camb (BA); *m* 30 July 1965, Penelope, yr da of late Maurice Holberton Shearme, of Brompton Square, London SW3; 1 s (Henry b 1967), 1 da (Nathalie b 1970); *Career* Lt Royal Horse Guards 1954-56; joined Eagle Star Insurance Co Ltd 1959, gen mangr responsible for UK business 1974, exec dir responsible for UK business 1984, exec dir responsible for investment and property 1987; *Recreations* shooting, fishing, skiing; *Style—* Nicholas Mountain, Esq; 17 Hollywood Road, London SW10 9HT; 60 St Mary Axe, London EC3A 8JQ (☎ 01 929 1111, fax 01 626 1266, telex 914962)

MOUNTBATTEN, Lord Ivar Alexander Michael; s of 3 Marquess of Milford Haven, OBE, DSC (d 1970); hp of bro, 4 Marquess; *b* 9 Mar 1963; *Educ* Gordonstoun Sch Scotland, Middlebury Coll Vermont USA; *Style—* Lord Ivar Mountbatten; Moyns Park, Birdbrook, Essex

MOUNTBATTEN OF BURMA, Countess (UK 1947); Patricia Edwina Victoria Knatchbull; CD (1976), JP (Kent 1971), DL (Kent 1973); also Viscountess Mountbatten of Burma (UK 1946), Baroness Romsey (UK 1947); da of Adm of the Fleet 1 Earl Mountbatten of Burma, KG, GCB, OM, GCSI, GCIE, GCVO, DSO, PC (assas 1979) and Hon Edwina Ashley, CI, GBE, DCVO (d 1960, da of 1 and last Baron Mount Temple, himself gs of 7 Earl of Shaftesbury, the philanthropist); Edwina's mother was Maud, da of Sir Ernest Cassel, the banker and friend of Edward VII; sister of Lady Pamela Hicks, *qv*; *b* 14 Feb 1924; *Educ* Malta, England, NYC; *m* 26 Oct 1946, 7 Baron Brabourne, *qv*; 4 s (and 1 s k 1979, with his gf), 2 da; *Heir* s, Lord Romsey, *qv*; *Career* served 1943-46 WRNS; Col-in-Chief Princess Patricia's Canadian Light Inf 1974; vice Lord Lieut Kent 1984; DStJ 1981; vice-pres: BRCS; dep vice-chm NSPCC; chm Sir Ernest Cassel Educnl Tst; pres WESPNEU; SOS Children's Villages; Shaftesbury Homes and Arethusa; vice-pres: SSAFA, FPA, Nat Childbirth Tst, Royal Life Saving Soc, Shaftesbury Soc Royal Coll of Nursing, Nat Soc for Cancer Relief, Royal Nat Coll for the Blind; patron of Commando Assoc; VAD (RN) Assoc; HMS Kelly Reunion Assoc; vice patron Burma Star Assoc; vice-pres of various assocs, cncls and soc, patron of various assocs and tsts; *Style—* The Rt Hon the Countess Mountbatten of Burma, CD, JP, DL; New House, Mersham, Ashford, Kent (☎ 0233 623466); 39 Montpelie Walk, London SW7 1JH (☎ 01 589 8829)

MOUNTEVANS, 3 Baron (UK 1945); (Edward Patrick) Broke Andvord Evans; s of 2 Baron Mountevans (d 1974); *b* 1 Feb 1943; *Educ* Rugby, Trinity Coll Oxford; *m* 1974, Johanna, da of Antonius Keyzer, of The Hague; *Heir* bro, Hon Jeffrey de Corban Richard Evans; *Career* Lt ret 74 MC regt RCT, AER 1966; joined management of Consolidated Gold Fields Ltd 1966; joined British Tourist Authority 1972, mangr Sweden and Finland 1973, mangr Promotion Services 1976, asst marketing mangr 1982-; *Recreations* reading, travel; *Style—* The Rt Hon the Lord Mountevans; c/o The House of Lords, London SW1

MOUNTEVANS, Deirdre, Baroness; Deirdre Grace; da of John O'Connell, of Buxton House, Co Cork; *m* 1940, 2 Baron Mountevans (d 1974); *Style—* The Rt Hon Deirdre Lady Mountevans; 2 Durwood House, Kensington Court, London W8

MOUNTFIELD, Peter; s of Alexander Stuart Mountfield (d 1984), of Lanthwaite, Hightown, Liverpool, and Agnes Elizabeth Mountfield *née* Gurney (d 1987); *b* 2 April 1935; *Educ* Merchant Taylor's Sch, Crosby, Trinity Coll Cambridge (BA), Harvard Univ; *m* 1958, Evelyn Margaret, da of Walter Frederick Smithies (d 1963), of Liverpool; 3 s (Andrew b 1962, Benjamin b 1964, Christopher b 1968); *Career* civil servant, HM Treasy 1958- (under sec 1977-); *Recreations* walking, reading, looking at buildings; *Style—* Peter Mountfield, Esq; HM Treasury, Parliament St, London SW1A 2RG

MOUNTFORD, Margaret Rose; *née* Gamble; da of James Ross Gamble, of Bangor, NI, and Kathleen Margaret, *née* Stevenson; *b* 24 Nov 1951; *Educ* Strathearn Sch Belfast, Girton Coll Cambridge (MA); *Career* admitted slr 1976, ptnr Herbert Smith 1983-; Liveryman Worshipful Co of Solicitors; memb Law Soc; *Recreations* travel, opera, wine; *Clubs* Cwil; *Style—* Ms Margaret Mountford; Watling House, 35 Cannon St, London EC4 (☎ 01 489 8000, fax 01 329 0426)

MOUNTFORD, Roger Philip; s of Stanley W A Mountford, of Leatherhead, Surrey (d 1984), and Evelyn Mary Richardson (d 1979); *b* 5 June 1948; *Educ* Kingston GS, LSE (BSc), Stanford Graduate Sch of Business (Sloan Fell, MS); *m* 24 July 1981, Jane Rosemary, da of The Rev Canon Eric Edwin Stanton, hon Canon of Canterbury (d 1984); 2 da (Laura Jane b 1983, Annabel Louise b 1985); *Career* merchant banker; md Hambro Pacific Ltd 1983, dir Hambros Bank Ltd 1984; *Recreations* riding, theatre, musical; *Clubs* Carlton, Hong Kong, Royal Hong Kong Jockey; *Style—* Roger Mountford, Esq; 2110 Connaught Centre, 1 Connaught Place, Central, Hong Kong (telex 83012 HMBRO HX, fax 5-201932)

MOUNTFORT, Guy Reginald; OBE (1970); s of Arnold George Mountfort (d 1943), and Alice Edith, *née* Hughes (d 1959); *b* 4 Dec 1905; *Educ* GS; *m* 1931, Joan Hartley, da of Ernest Pink (d 1949), of Broadstone, Dorset; 2 da (Penelope Joy b 1934, Carol Gillian b 1938); *Career* Army serv 1939-46: 12 Regt HAC and British Army Staff Washington DC, Lt Col N Africa, Italy, Burma, Pacific; md Ogilvy & Mather Ltd London 1966; dir Ogilvy & Mather Int Inc (New York) 1964-66; pres Br Ornithologists' Union 1970-75; (Union Medal 1967); ldr of expdns to study wildlife in Spain, Bulgaria, Hungary, Jordan, Pakistan, Bangladesh, Nepal, India and The Gambia in all of which protected wildlife reserves were created; author of numerous books on the conservation of wildlife and on ornithology; fndr memb of World Wildlife Fund 1961; (Gold Medal 1976, memb of Hon 1986); Medal of Société D'Acclimatation 1936; FZS (Scientific fell, Stamford Raffles prize 1986) Cdr of the Netherlands Order of the Golden Ark 1980; *Recreations* travel, gardening, ornithology; *Style—* Guy Mountfort, Esq; Hurst Oak, Lyndhurst, Hants SO43 7DN

MOUNTGARRET, 17 Viscount (I 1550); Richard Henry Piers; also Baron Mountgarret (UK 1911, which sits as in House of Lords); s of 16 Viscount Mountgarret (d 1966); hp to Earldoms of Ossory and Ormonde, also to Chief Butlership of Ireland; *b* 8 Nov 1936; *Educ* Eton, Sandhurst; *m* 1, 1960 (m dis 1969), Gillian, da of Cyril Buckley, of Chelsea; 2 s, 1 da; m 2, 1970, Mrs Jennifer Fattorini, da of Capt D Wills, of Wrington, Somerset; m 3, 1983, Mrs Angela Ruth Waddington, da of Thomas Porter, of Tadcaster; *Heir* s, Hon Piers James Richard Butler; *Career* formerly Capt Irish Gds; pres Yorkshire County Cricket Club 1984-; *Recreations* shooting, stalking, cricket; *Clubs* White's, Pratt's; *Style—* The Rt Hon the Viscount Mountgarret; Stainley House, South Stainley, Harrogate, Yorks (☎ 0423 770087); 15 Queensgate Place, SW7 (☎ 01 584 6998)

MOURGUE, Harold George; s of Alfred George Mourgue (d 1973), and Maria May, *née* Hunter (d 1969); *b* 7 Sept 1927; *Educ* (interrupted by war) Colfes GS, Ilfracombe GS (evacuee); *m* 1948, Joan Elsa Stella, da of John William Simms (d 1975); 1 s (Anthony John b 1949), 1 da (Jacqueline Susan b 1952); *Career* RN 1945-47; CA 1953, Harker Holloway & Co CAs 1948-53, mgmnt accountant and mangr 1953-60 Unilever, fin controller (dir and gen mangr) Ultra Radio & TV Ltd 1961-62, chief accountant Thorn Electrical Inds 1962-68, co sec Thorn EMI plc 1967-72 (fin dir 1970-85, vice-chm 1983-87); non-exec dir: Turner & Newall plc 1983-, Rolls Royce plc 1985-, Thames Television plc, NM Rothschild Asset Mgmnt Hldgs Ltd; chm Thorn EMI Pension Fund, memb Industrial Devpt Advsy Bd 1985-; *Recreations* literature, music, gardening, antiques; *Style—* Harold Mourgue, Esq; Myton, 8 Baslow Rd, Eastbourne, E Sussex (☎ 0323 33198)

MOUTAFIAN, Princess Helena; MBE (1976); da of Prince Alexei Gagarin (d 1938), and Countess Ana Phillipovitz (d 1944); *b* 2 May 1930; *m* 14 Jan 1955, Artin Moutafian, s of Nikogos Moutafian (d Armenia 1914); 2 s (Nicholas b 6 Nov 1958, Mark b 21 Dec 1960); *Career* dir Moutafian Commodities Ltd; dep pres St John Ambulance Bde London (Prince of Wales's) Dist, hon vice-pres Women's Cncl, patron Kingston and Dist Charity, life patron NSPCC; patron Nat Assoc for Health, Br Cncl Univ for Peace; involved in projects for uniting world religions; CStJ 1982, Croix de Chevalier Ordre de la Courtoisie Française 1976, Etoile Civique, Grande Medaille de Vermeil de la Ville de Paris 1977, Freedom of the City of Paris 1977; awarded silver medal of Grollo d'Ore for her paintings in Venice; *Recreations* painting, writing; *Clubs* English Speaking Union; *Style—* Princess Helena Moutafian, MBE; 12 Greenway Gardens, Hampstead, London NW3 7DH

MOVERLEY, Rt Rev Gerald; *see*: Hallam, Bishop of

MOWAT, Magnus Charles; s of John FM Mowat, MBE (d 1988), of Lake House, Ellesmere, Shropshire and Elizabeth Rebecca, *née* Murray (d 1977); *b* 5 April 1940; *Educ* Haileybury; *m* 27 April 1968, Mary Lynette St Lo, da of Alan D Stoddart, of Crowcombe, Taunton, Somerset; 3 s (Charles b 15 April 1969, Alexander b 27 June 1970, Hugh b 7 June 1973); *Career* CA; Peat Marwick & Co 1959-67, Hill Samuel & Co Ltd 1968-70, ptnr Illingworth & Henriques Stockbrokers 1970-84, dir Barclays de Zoete Wedd Ltd 1984-89; chm: Manchester YMCA, Booths Charities Manchester; memb govrs Packwood Haugh Sch Shrewsbury; FCA 1964; *Recreations* shooting, gardening, music; *Clubs* St James (Manchester); *Style—* Magnus Mowat, Esq; New Park House, Whitegate, Northwich, Cheshire (☎ 0606 882 084); Capron Cottage, Triscombe, Taunton, Somerset; Barclays de Zoete Wedd Ltd, 50 Fountain St, Manchester (☎ 061 832 7222, fax 061 833 9374, car tel 0836 519 329)

MOWBRAY, Dowager Lady; Diana Margaret; da of late Sir Robert Heywood Hughes, 12 Bt; *m* 1927, Sir George Robert Mowbray, 5 Bt, KBE (d 1969); *Style—* Dowager Lady Mowbray; Starvehill House, Mortimer, Berks

MOWBRAY, Sir John Robert; 6 Bt (UK 1880), of Warennes Wood, Berkshire, JP (W Suffolk 1972); s of Sir George Robert Mowbray, 5 Bt, KBE (d 1969); *b* 1 Mar 1932; *Educ* Eton, New Coll Oxford; *m* 1957, Lavinia Mary, da of Lt-Col Francis Edgar Hugonin, OBE; 3 da; *Heir* none; *Style—* Sir John Mowbray, Bt, JP; Hunt's Park, Great Thurlow, Haverhill, Suffolk (☎ Thurlow 232)

MOWBRAY, SEGRAVE AND STOURTON, 26, 27 and 23 Baron (E 1283, 1295 and 1448 respectively); Charles Edward Stourton; CBE (1982); s of 25 Baron Mowbray, (26) Segrave and (22) Stourton, MC, JP (d 1965; himself gs of 23, 24 and 20 Baron, who had inherited the Barony of Stourton from his f, and had abeyance of Baronies of Mowbray and Segrave terminated in his favour 1878) and of Sheila, da of Hon Edward W K Gully, CB (d 1931; 2 s of 1 Viscount Selby); *b* 11 Mar 1923; *Educ* Ampleforth, Ch Ch Oxford; *m* 1952, Hon Jane Faith de Yarburgh-Bateson, da of 5 Baron Deramore (d 1964), by his w Nina Macpherson-Grant; 2 s; *Heir* s, Hon Edward William Stephen Stourton; *Career* sits as Conservative in House of Lords; Lt Gren Gds 1943; memb of Lloyd's 1952; dir Securicor (Southern) Ltd 1965-66, Securicor (Scotland) 1966-70; Cons whip in House of Lords and front bench spokesman 1967-70 and 1974-78; lord in waiting 1970-74 and 1979-80; dep chief oppn whip House of Lords 1978-79; chllr of the Primrose League 1974-79; hon pres Safety Glazing Assoc 1975-78; Kt of Honour and Devotion SMO Malta; *Style—* The Rt Hon the Lord Mowbray, Segrave and Stourton, CBE; Marcus, by Forfar, Angus (☎ Finavon 219); 23 Warwick Sq, SW1

MOWBRAY, SEGRAVE AND STOURTON, Baroness; Hon Jane Faith; *née* de Yarburgh-Bateson; da of late 5 Baron Deramore; *b* 1933; *m* 1952, 26 Baron Mowbray, Segrave and Stourton, *qv*; *Style—* The Rt Hon the Lady Mowbray, Segrave and Stourton; 23 Warwick Sq, London SW1; Marcus, By Forfar, Angus

MOWER, Brian Leonard; s of Samuel William (d 1975), and Nellie Elizabeth Rachel (d 1976); *b* 24 August 1934; *Educ* Hemel Hempstead GS; *m* 1 Oct 1960, Margaret Ann, da of Cecil Roland Wildman; 1 s (John b 1964); 1 da (Kerry b 1961); *Career* RAF 1954-56; exec Service Advertising Co 1956-66; CS: sr info offr HM Treasy 1966-69, princ info offr, Centl Statistical Off 1969-78, dep head of info HM Treasy 1978/80, head info Dept of Employment 1980-82, dep press sec PM 1982, dir info Home Off 1982; *Recreations* bridge, walking, reading; *Style—* Brian Mower, Esq; 34 Wrensfield, Hemel Hempstead, Herts HP1 1RP (☎ 0442 52277); Home Office, Queen Anne's Gate, London SW1 (☎ 01 213 3616)

MOWER, Roger Leonard; s of Maj Leonard Charles Mower (d 1983), of Manchester, and Beatrice, *née* Monahan; *b* 19 April 1951; *Educ* Bolton Sch Lancs; *m* 25 March 1972, Pauline Carole, da of Geoffrey Holland Barlow, of Audlem, Cheshire; 2 s (James b 1979, Paul b 1981); *Career* dir Clarke Construction Ltd 1979-84, md Mears Contractors Ltd 1985-86, chief exec Multi Construction (UK) Ltd 1987-; *Style—* Roger Mower, Esq; Pitt Cottage, The Mount, Highclere, Newbury, Berks; Multi Construction (UK) Ltd, Roberts House, 59 Durnsford Rd, Wimbledon, London SW19 8HX (☎ 01 947 1299)

MOWLL, Christopher Martyn; s of Christopher Kilvinton Mowll (d 1940), and Doris Ellen, *née* Hutchinson (d 1986); *b* 14 August 1932; *Educ* Epsom Coll, Gonville and Caius Coll Cambridge (MA); *m* 4 Oct 1958, Margaret Francis, da of John Maclelland

Laird (d 1988); 4 s (Gordon Howard Martyn b 1959, Ian Robert Mowll b 1961, David Christoher Mowll b 1961, Richard Laird Mowll b 1965); *Career* admitted slr 1956; slr to Clothworkers Co; memb: Cncl of the Nat Library for the Blind 1964-79, Cncl Metropolitan Soc for the Blind 1964- (tres 1965-79, vice chm 1971-79, chm 1979-), memb exec cncl RNIB 1982-, Br-Australia Bicentennial Ctee 1984-88; Freeman of the City of London 1979, Liveryman of the Worshipful Co of Clothworkers 1979 (clerk and sec to Clothworkers Fndn 1978-); memb Law Soc 1956-; *Style—* Christopher Mowll, Esq; Clothworkers' Hall, Dunster Ct, Mincing Lane, London EC3R 7AH (☎ 01 623 7041)

MOXOM, John Matthew Cameron; s of Reginald John Moxom (d 1988), of 97 Queens Rd, Hertford, Herts, and Jeannie Bryce, *née* Mitchell (d 1986); *b* 6 April 1945; *Educ* Pilgrims' Sch Winchester, Winchester Coll, Queens' Coll Cambridge (BA, MA); *Career* barr 1968, pupillage 1968-69, in practice 1969-88; litigation dept Steed and Steed slrs 1988-; chm St Christophers Fellowship 1982- (vice chm 1979-82, member 1970-); memb Belchamp St Paul Parish Cncl 1988-; Freedom City of London, Liveryman Worshipful Co Goldsmiths; *Books* Kemp and Kemp on the Quantam of Damages (asst ed 1975-); *Recreations* walking, gardening, cinema, theatre; *Style—* John Moxom, Esq; Pannells, Belchamp St Paul, nr Sudbury, Suffolk CO10 7BS (☎ 0787 277410); Steed and Steed Slrs, 6 Gainsborough St, Sudbury, Suffolk CO10 6ET (☎ 0787 73387, fax 0787 880287)

MOXON, Rev Michael Anthony; s of Rev Canon Charles Moxon (Canon Residentiary and Precentor of Salisbury Cathedral, d 1985), of Hungerford Chantry, The Close, Salisbury, Wilts, and Phyllis Mary, *née* Carter; *b* 23 Jan 1942; *Educ* Merchant Taylor's Sch, Durham Univ, London Univ, Salisbury Theol Coll (BD); *m* 9 Jan 1969, Sarah Jane, da of Francis Kynaston Needham Cresswell (d 1982), of Littlehampton; 2 s (twins, Nicholas and Benjamin b 21 Nov 1969), 1 da (Emma-Jane b 1 Aug 1971); *Career* ordained: deacon 1970, priest 1971; asst priest Lowestoft Gp Ministry 1970-74, minor canon St Paul's Cathedral 1974-81 (jr cardinal 1974-78, sr cardinal 1978-79), warden Coll of Minor Canons 1979-81, sacrist St Paul's Cathedral 1977-81, vicar Tewkesbury with Walton Cardiff 1981-, proctor in convocation (memb Gen Synod) 1985-, chaplain to HM the Queen 1986-; memb Cncl for the Care of Churches; *Recreations* reading, music, cricket; *Style—* The Rev Michael Moxon; The Abbey House, Tewkesbury, Glos GL20 5SR (☎ 0684 293333)

MOXON, Prof (Edward) Richard; s of Gerald Richard Moxon, CBE (d 1980), and Margaret, *née* Forster Mohun; *b* 16 July 1941; *Educ* Shrewsbury Sch, St Johns Coll Cambridge (BA, MA, BChir); *m* 20 Oct 1973, Marianne, da of Prof George Graham; 2 s (Christopher Alan b 1978, Timothy Stewart b 1987); *Career* sr house offr Hosp for Sick Children 1969, res fell Childrens Hosp Med Centre Boston USA 1971-74 (ast resident pediatric 1970), asst prof pediatrics John Hopkins Hosp Baltimore USA 1974-78 (assoc prof and eudowood chief of pediatric infections diseases 1978-84), prof of paediatrics Oxford Unvi 1984-; *Recreations* sport, music, lit; *Style—* Prof Richard Moxon; 17 Moreton Rd, Oxford OX2 7AX; Dept Paediatrics, John Radcliffe Hosp, Headington OX3 9DU

MOY, Peter Charles Duffield; s of Eric Thomas Moy (d 1980), and Andrea Katherine Stillingfleet, *née* Duffield (d 1966); *b* 18 July 1927; *Educ* Charterhouse; *m* 12 March 1967, Judith Webb, da of Eric Arthur Cashmore, (d 1972), of Sandiway, Cheshire; 1 da (Lucy Andrea b 1969); *Career* HM Grenadier Gds and Essex Regt 1945-48; mechanical and solar engrg design and devpt; grantee of several British and foreign letters patent; *Recreations* gardening, golf; *Style—* Peter C D Moy, Esq; Highfield Lodge, North Creake, Fakenham, Norfolk (☎ 0328 738108)

MOYLAN, His Honour Judge (John) David FitzGerald; s of Sir John FitzGerald Moylan, CB, CBE (d 1967), of Haywards Heath and Bury W Sussex, and Ysolda Mary Nesta Moylan, *née* FitzGerald (d 1966); *b* 8 Oct 1915; *Educ* Charterhouse (sr scholar), Ch Ch Oxford (Holford exhibitioner); *m* 1946, Jean Mary Valerie, da of Frederick Cormack Marno-Edwards (d 1981), of Clare, Suffolk; 1 s (Andrew), 2 da (Susan, Anne); *Career* served WW II 1939-46 in RM, Maj; formerly judge of County Ct 1967-72, circuit judge 1972-; *Style—* His Honour Judge David Moylan; Ufford Hall, Fressingfield, Diss, Norfolk

MOYLE, Rt Hon Roland Dunstan; PC (1978); s of Baron Moyle, CBE, JP, sometime MP Stourbridge & PPS to Clement Attlee (Life Peer d 1974), and his 1 w, Elizabeth; *b* 12 Mar 1928; *Educ* Bexleyheath and Llanidloes County Sch Powys, Univ Coll of Wales (Aberystwyth), Trinity Hall Cambridge; *m* 1956, Shelagh Patricia Hogan; 1 s, 1 da; *Career* served Royal Welch Fusiliers 1949-51; called to the Bar Gray's Inn; served various industrial relations posts in Wales Gas Bd, Gas Cncl, Electricity Cncl; MP (Lab): Lewisham N 1966-74, Lewisham East 1974-83; pps to: chief sec Treasury 1966-69, Home sec 1969-70; oppn spokesman: Army 1971, Higher Education and Science 1972-74; parly sec Miny Agric Fish and Food 1974; Min: NI 1974-76, State Health 1976-79; front bench oppn spokesman: Health 1979-81, Foreign and Cwlth Affrs 1981-83, Defence and Disarmament 1983-; dep chm Polcie Complaints Authy 1985-; former memb Race Relations and Immigration Select Ctee, vice-chm PLP Def Gp, sec and exec cncl memb British American Parly Gp 1968-83; *Style—* The Rt Hon Roland Moyle; 19 Montpelier Row, Blackheath, London SE3 0RL

MOYNE, 2 Baron (UK 1932); Bryan Walter Guinness; s of Rt Hon 1 Baron Moyne, DSO, TD, PC (assass Cairo 1944, as min resident in M East; né Hon Walter Guinness, 3 s of 1 Earl of Iveagh, KP, GCVO), and Lady Evelyn Erskine (d 1939; da of 14 Earl of Buchan); *b* 27 Oct 1905; *Educ* Eton, Christ Church Oxford; *m* 1, 1929 (m dis 1934), Hon Diana Freeman Mitford, da of 2 Baron Redesdale; 2 s; m 2, 1936, Elisabeth, da of Thomas Nelson (ka 1917), of Edinburgh and Achnacloich; 3 s (and 1 s decd), 5 da; *Heir* s, Hon Jonathan Guinness; *Career* late Maj M East, France; barr; vice-chm Arthur Guinness Son & Co 1949-79; tstee Iveagh and Guinness Housing Charitable Tsts; poet, novelist, playwright; FRSL; memb Irish Acad of Letters; *Books* writes as Bryan Guinness; *Novels include* Singing Out of Tune (1933), Landscape with Figures (1934), A Week by the Sea (1936), A Fugue of Cinderellas (1956), The Giant's Eye (1964), The Girl with the Flower (1966), Helenic Flirtation; memoirs: Dairy (sic) not kept (1975); Potpourri from the Thirties (1982); Personal Patchwork (1987); *Poetry*: Under the Eyelid, The Clock, Collected Poems (1956); *Plays*: The Fragrant Concubine (1938), A Riverside Charade (1954); *Recreations* hurdle rod splitting, travel, gardening; *Clubs* Athenaeum, Carlton, University and Kildare Street (Dublin); *Style—* Lord Bryan Moyne; Knockmaroon House, Castleknock, Co Dublin, Ireland; Biddesden House, Andover, Hants (☎ 0264 790237)

MOYNIHAN, 3 Baron (UK 1929); Sir Antony Patrick Andrew Cairnes Berkeley Moynihan; 3 Bt (UK 1922); s of 2 Baron Moynihan, sometime Chm Exec Ctee Liberal Pty (d 1965), by his 1 w Ierne; *b* 2 Feb 1936; *Educ* Stowe; *m* 1, 1955 (m dis 1958), Ann, da of Reginald Herbert; m 2, 1958 (m dis 1967), Shirin Berry; 1 da; m 3, 1968 (m dis 1979), Luthgarda Maria, da of Alfonzo Fernandez; 3 da (Hon Antonita Maria Carmen b 31 March 1969, Hon Aurora Luzon Maria Dolores b 1971, Hon Kathleen Maynila Helen Imogen Juliet b 1974); m 4, 1981, Editha Edvarda, da of late Maj-Gen Edvardo Ruben, Philippine Army; 1 s (Hon Andrew Berkeley); *Heir* s, Hon Andrew Berkeley Moynihan b at Manila, Philippines 7 March 1989; *Career* dog breeder; *Style—* The Rt Hon the Lord Moynihan

MOYNIHAN, Hon Colin Berkeley; MP (C) Lewisham East 1983-; s of 2 Baron Moynihan, OBE, TD (d 1965), and June Elizabeth, *née* Hopkins; *b* 13 Sept 1955; *Educ* Monmouth Sch, Univ Coll Oxford (MA); *Career* pres Oxford Union Soc 1976; personal asst to chm Tate & Lyle Ltd 1978-80, mangr Tate & Lyle Agribusiness 1980-82; chief exec Ridgways Tea and Coffee Merchants 1980-83; political asst to Foreign Sec 1983, PPS to Rt Hon Kenneth Clarke as Min of Health and PMG 1986-87, Parly under sec of state DOE and min for Sport 1987-; memb: Bow Gp 1978 (chm Bow Gp Industry Ctee 1985-87), Paddington Cons mgmnt ctee 1980-81; sec: Foreign and Cwlth Affairs Ctee 1985, Major Spectator Sports Ctee CCPR 1979-87, CCPR Enquiry into Sponsorship of Sport 1982-83; memb Sports Cncl 1982-85, steward British Boxing Bd of Control 1979-87; tstee: Oxford Univ Boat Club 1980-83, Sports Aid Tst 1983-87; govr Sports Aid Fndn (London and SE) 1980-82, chm All Party Gp on Afghanistan 1984, vice chm Cons Backbenchers Sports Ctee; Freeman City of London 1978, Liveryman Worshipful Co of Haberdashers; Oxford Double Blue rowing and boxing 1976 and 1977, Olympic Silver Medal rowing 1980; Int Rowing Fedn: World Gold Medal lightweight rowing 1978, World Silver Medal rowing 1981; *Recreations* reading the Economist, collecting Nonsuch books, music, sport; *Clubs* Brooks's, Royal Commonwealth Soc, Vincent's (Oxford); *Style—* The Hon Colin Moynihan, MP; Flat 42, Buckingham Court,78 Buckingham Gate, London SW1; House of Commons, London SW1

MOYNIHAN, Ierne, Baroness; Ierne Helen; *née* Candy; da of Cairnes Candy (d 1949), of Mt Barker, W Australia; *b* 1910; *Educ* Private; *m* 1931, (m dis 1952), 2 Baron Moynihan (d 1965); 1 s, 2 da; *Clubs* Hurlingham, Queen's, Zoological Soc (life fell); *Style—* Ierne, Lady Moynihan; 56 Holland Park Av, London W11 3QY (☎ 01 727 7986)

MOYNIHAN, Hon Miranda Dorne Irene; da of 3 Baron Moynihan; *b* 1959; *Style—* The Hon Miranda Moynihan

MOYNIHAN, Sir Noël Henry; s of Dr Edward B Moynihan (d 1956); *b* 24 Dec 1916; *Educ* Ratcliffe, Downing Coll Cambridge (MA, MB, BChir); *m* 1941, Margaret Mary (d 1989), da of William Lovelace (d 1938), barr at law, and sometime sec of Brooks's Club and Turf Club; 2 s, 2 da; *Career* served WW II pilot RAF (despatches 2); family doctor 1954-; co-fndr Medical Cncl on Alcoholism 1963 (memb cncl 1963-87, vice pres 1972-87); pres: Harveian Soc of London 1967 (memb of cncl 1963-68 and 1978-81), Chelsea Clinic Soc 1978 (memb of cncl 1969-78); sec Medical Soc of London 1981-82 (memb cncl 1980-85), memb bd Royal Med Benevolent Fund 1973-77; pres Downing Coll Cambridge Assoc 1985-86, chm Save the Children Fund 1977-82 (vice-chm 1972-77); freeman City of London 1959; Kt SMO Malta 1958 (Offr of Merit 1964, Cdr of Merit 1979), Kt St Gregory 1966; CStJ; assoc fell Downing Coll Cambridge; MRCS, LRCP, FRCGP; kt 1979; *Books* The Light in the West (1956), Rock Art of the Sahara (1979); *Recreations* Save the Children Fund, studying rock art of the Sahara; *Clubs* Carlton, MCC, Hawks (Cambridge), Achilles; *Style—* Sir Noël Moynihan; 25-27 Sloane Court West, London SW3 4TD (☎ 01 730 1828); Herstmonceux Place, Flowers Green, East Sussex (☎ (032383) 2017)

MOYOLA, Baron (Life Peer UK 1971); James Dawson Chichester-Clark; PC (NI 1966), DL (Co Derry 1954); s of Capt James L C Chichester-Clark, DSO and bar (d 1933), and Mrs C E Brackenbury, of Moyola Park, Castle Dawson, Co Derry, N Ireland; bro of Sir Robin Chichester-Clark, *qv*; *b* 12 Feb 1923; *Educ* Eton; *m* 1959, Moyra Maud, widow of Capt T Haughton & da of Brig Arthur de Burgh Morris, CBE, DSO; 1 step s, 2 da; *Career* sits as Cons Peer in House of Lords; memb N Ireland Parliament 1960, chief whip 1963-67, ldr of the House and chief whip 1966-67, min of Agric 1967-69; prime minister NI 1969-71; *Recreations* shooting, fishing, gardening; *Style—* The Rt Hon the Lord Moyola, PC, DL; Moyola Park, Castledawson, Co Derry, N Ireland

MTAŴALI, His Excellence Bernard Brenn; s of Ernest Michael Mtaŵali (d 1971), and Rose Mtaŵali Mkandaŵire (d 1957); *b* 18 Oct 1935; *Educ* Livingstona Secondary Sch and Blantyre Secondary Sch, Allahabad Univ, BSc Agric Cambridge Univ, UK DIP, Agric; *m* 23 Dec 1966, Ruth; 4 s (Ernest Chimwemwe b 1967, Ronald b 1970, Lutamyo b 1974, Bernard Chawanangwa b 1977); 1 da (Sangwani b 1971); *Career* Malawi Govt Serv dist agric offr 1962, princ sec Ministry of Agric & Natural Resources 1974-78, gen mangr General Farming Co Ltd Aug 1978-83, exec sec Tobacco Exp Assoc of Malaw 1984-86, Malawi high cmmr in Canada 1986, Malawi high cmmr GB 1987; *Recreations* walking, football, gardening; *Clubs* Country, Limbe, Malawi, The Royal Over-Seas League, Travellers'; *Style—* His Excellence Bernard Mtaŵali; 70 Winnington Rd, Hampstead, London N2 0TX UK (☎ 01 458 5727); 33 Grosvenor Street, London W1H 0DE UK (☎ 01 491 4172, telex 263308)

MUCH, (Alan) Fraser; s of Capt Frank Llewellyn Much, MC (ka 1918), and Jessie Mary, *née* Riddell (d 1971); *b* 14 Mar 1910; *Educ* Kings Coll Taunton; *m* 27 July 1940, Helen Isabella, da of Robert Gordon Barker (d 1967); 1 s (Ian b 1944), 3 da (Anne b 1941, Catherine b 1948, Rosalind b 1952); *Career* served WWII London Scottish and RAOC (Col), memb Barlow Mission to USA re tropical warfare 1939-45; accountant Asbury Riddell & Co 1929-36; ICI: tres dept 1936-39, packaging and materials handling advsr 1946-65; gp mgmnt servs controller T & N plc; served on numerous tech ctees of BSI and ISOC 1946-65; FCA, fndr memb Inst of Materials Mgmnt, fndr memb Inst of Packaging (chm 1961-62, vice pres); *Recreations* rubber bridge, active in local affairs; *Style—* Fraser Much, Esq; The Green, Dunster, W Somerset TA24 6SD (☎ 0643 821 238)

MUDDIMAN, (Colin) Trevor; s of Arthur Edgar Lânwer Muddiman (d 1961); *b* 4 June 1929; *Educ* Wellington Coll; *m* 1962, Stella Kathleen; *Career* farmer; memb Eastern Electricity Bd 1973-78 and 1980-89; chm Eastern Electricity Consultative Cncl 1973-78; chm Farmers' Club Charitable Tst; memb Lloyds; Freeman Worshipful Co of Farmers 1960 (Memb of Ct 1975, Master 1985); *Clubs* Farmers' (chm and pres 1981), Royal London Yacht; *Style—* Trevor Muddiman, Esq; Gade House, Little Gaddesden,

Berkhamsted, Herts HP4 1QT

MUDGE, Hon Mrs (Maureen Ann); da of Baron Wigg, PC (Life Peer); *b* 1934; *m* 1964, Alfred John Mudge; *Style*— The Hon Mrs Mudge; 1580 Mississauga Valley Blvd, Mississauga, Ont, Canada

MUELLER, Dame Anne Elisabeth; DCB (1988), CB (1980); da of Herbert Constantin Mueller (d 1952), and Phoebe Anne, *née* Beevers (d 1973); *b* 15 Oct 1930; *Educ* Wakefield Girls High Sch, Somerville Coll Oxford (MA); *m* 1958 (m dis 1978), James Hugh Robertson, s of Sir James Robertson, GCMG GCVO (d 1983); *Career* dep sec Dept of Trade and Indust 1977-84, dir Euro Investmt Bank 1978-84; second perm sec: Cabinet Off (head of mgmnt and personnel off) 1984-87, HM Treasy 1987-; *Clubs* United Oxford & Cambridge University; *Style*— Dame Anne Mueller, DCB, CB; c/o HM Treasury, Parliament Street, London SW1P 3AG (☎ 01 270 3000)

MUFF, Hon Peter Raymond; s of 2 Baron Calverley (d 1971); *b* 12 August 1953; *Educ* Grange Boys' Sch Bradford; *Career* asst engineer (control and instrumentation) Central Electricity Generating Bd; TEng, MIEleciE; *Recreations* squash, electronics, domestic cat shows; *Clubs* Abyssinian Cat; *Style*— The Hon Peter Muff; Oakhurst Farm, 377 Shadwell Lane, Leeds LS17 8AH

MUIR, Andrew Peter; s of Leslie Malcolm Muir, of Weaverham, Cheshire, and Audrey Britland, *née* Hill; *b* 25 Dec 1955; *Educ* Bromsgrove Sch, Lanchester Poly (HND); *m* 6 May 1978, Bernie Ann, da of Charles George Overton, of Bromsgrove, Worcs; 2 s (Christopher Stuart b 1985, Gordon James b 1986); *Career* dir: Nationwide Refrigeration supplies Ltd 1984-87, Cory Coffee Ltd 1986-87, (gp systems) Suter plc Distribution Gp 1985-87; md Suter Systems Ltd 1987-, dep chm Compass Software Ltd 1987-; AMBCS 1985; *Recreations* swiming, shooting, motor cycling; *Style*— Andrew Muir, Esq; Chisbury Lane House, Chisbury, Marlborough, Wilts SN8 3JA; La Jouverie, Coulouvray Boisbenatre, 50670 St Pois, Normande, France (☎ 0672 870187); Suter Systems Ltd, Turnfields Ct, Turnfields, Thatcham, Newbury, Berks RG13 4PT (☎ 0635 67070, fax 0635 60208, car tel 0836 247683)

MUIR, (Charles) Augustus Carlow; s of Rev Walter Muir (d 1947), and Elizabeth, *née* Carlow (d 1942); *b* 15 Nov 1892; *Educ* George Heriot's Edinburgh, Edinburgh Univ (MA); *m* 11 Nov 1916, Jean Murray Dow (d 1972), da of late William Walker; m 2, 27 Oct 1975, Mair Gibby, da of Rev Benjamin Davies (d 1963); *Career* enlisted 1914, cmmnd KOSB, serv France and Gallipoli, staff appts until 1918; author; The Third Warning (1925), and seventeen other novels, The History of the Fife Coal Company (1953), and twelve other industrial and mercantile histories, other pubns incl: Candlelight in Avalon: a Spiritual Pilgrimage (1954), The Very Rev Dr John White, CH: A Biography (1958), The First of Foot: The History of The Royal Scots The Royal Regiment (1961), The Vintner of Nazareth: a Study of Palestine in the early days of Christ (1972), A Victorian Shipowner: A Portrait of Sir Charles Cayzer, Baronet of Gartmore (with Mair Davies 1978), The Saintsbury Memorial Volume (1945), A Last Vintage: Essays by George Saintsbury (1950), How to Choose and Enjoy Wine (1953); *Clubs* Savage, Saintsbury, Royal Scots Edinburgh; *Style*— Augustus Muir, Esq; 26 Bentfield Rd, Stansted Mountfitchet, Essex CM24 8HW (☎ 0279 812289)

MUIR, Elizabeth Jean; da of Capt Kenneth Edward Muir, MBE, of Bridgend, S Wales, and Elsie, *née* Harris; *b* 20 August 1947; *Educ* Cowbridge Girls HS, Homerton Coll Cambridge, Cardiff Coll of Educn (Dip Ed); *Career* mktg conslt; maths and physics teacher Cardiff Secdy Sch 1967-73, creative exec Parke-Davis Pharmaceuticals 1973-76, prod gp mangr Warner Lambert Animal Health, sales and mktg controller Memory Lane Cakes (Dalgety Spillers Co) 1978-82, fndr and md The Alternative Mktg Dept Ltd 1982-; specialist mktg in Greece (veterinary prods and professional servs); first woman memb Welsh Regnl Cncl CBI 1985-; memb: Syllabus Advsy Gp BTEC courses Pontypridd Tech, Br Hellenic C of C; bd memb: Welsh Water Authy 1986-, Health Promotion Authy for Wales 1987-, Secdy Housing Assoc for Wales 1988-; MInstM, MInstSM; *Recreations* dinner parties with friends, motor racing, knitting, travel in Greece; *Style*— Miss Elizabeth Muir; Sunningdale House, 13 Tydraw Rd, Roath Pk, Cardiff CF2 5UA (☎ 0222 499214, fax 0222 372798)

MUIR, Frank; CBE (1980); s of charles James Muir, and Margaret, *née* Harding; *b* 5 Feb 1920; *Educ* Chatham House Ramsgate, Leyton County HS; *m* 16 July 1949, Polly, *née* McIrvine; 1 s (Jamie), 1 da (Sally); *Career* served RAF 1940-46; writer and broadcaster with Denis Norden 1947-64, collaborated for 17 yrs writing comedy scripts, resident in TV and radio panel games, asst head of BBC Light Entertainment Gp 1964-67, head of entertainment London Weekend TV 1968-69, resumed TV Series Call My Bluff 1970; Hon LLD St Andrews 1978, Hon DLitt Kent 1982; *Books Incl:* The Frank Muir Book: An Irreverent Companion to Social History, A Book at Bathtime, What-a-Mess children's stories; *Recreations* working; *Clubs* Garrick; *Style*— Frank Muir Esq, CBE; Anners, Thorpe, Egham, Surrey (☎ 0932 562759); A Torra, Monticello, Corsica

MUIR, Dr (Isabella) Helen Mary; CBE (1981); da of George Basil Fairlie Muir, ICS (d 1959), and Gwladys Helen Muir (d 1969); *b* 20 August 1920; *Educ* Down House, Somerville Coll Oxford (MA, DPhil); *Career* research fellow Sir William Dunn Sch of Pathology, Oxford Univ 1947-48, scientific staff Nat Inst for Medical Research Biochemistry Div (London) 1948-54; Empire Rheumatism research fellow St Mary's Hosp Medical Unit 1954-58, Pearl research fellow and hon lectr St Mary's Hosp Med Sch 1959-66, head Biochemistry Div Kennedy Inst of Rheumatology 1966-; trustee Wellcome Tst 1982-; hon prof Charing Cross Hospital Medical Sch; FRS 1977; Hon DSc: Edinburgh 1982, Strathclyde 1983; Bunim Medal of American Arthritis Assoc 1978, Neil Hamilton Fairley Medal of the Royal College of Physicians for an outstanding contribution to medicine 1981, Ciba Medal of the Biochemical Society 1981; *Recreations* gardening, equestrian sports, natural history; *Style*— Dr Helen Muir, CBE, FRS; Kennedy Institute of Rheumatology, 6 Bute Gardens, Hammersmith, London W6 7DW (☎ 01 748 9966)

MUIR, Jean Elizabeth (Mrs Leuckert); CBE (1984); da of Cyril Muir, and Phyllis, *née* Coy; *Educ* Dame Harper Sch Bedford; *m* 1955, Harry Leuckert; *Career* fashion designer; dress of the year award Br Fashion Writers Gp 1964, fndr Jean Muir Ltd 1966; Jean Muir Exhibition: Lotherton Hall Leeds, Birmingham, Belfast, Bath, Stoke on Trent; memb bd for design BTEC; Awards: Ambassador Award for Achievement 1965, Maison Blanche Rex Int Fashion Award New Orleans (1967, 1968, 1974), Hommage de la mode award Fedn Francaise du Prêt á Porter Feminin, Br Fashion Cncl Award for Servs to Industry 1985, chartered Soc of Designers Medal for Outstanding achievement 1987, Textile Inst Medal 1987, Aust Govt Bicentennial Award presented by T R H Prince and Princess of Wales at Sydney Opera House 1988; tstee V and A 1983, memb Design Cncl 1983-88, memb bd of mgmnt British Knitting and Clothing Export Cncl 1989; Hon Citizen of New Orleans, Hon Doctor RCA 1981, Hon DLit Newcastle 1985, Hon Dlit Ulster 1987; FRSA, RDI, FCSD; *Style*— Ms Jean Muir, CBE; 59/61 Farringdon Rd, London EC1M 3HD (☎ 01 831 0691, fax 01 831 0826, telex 25883 JEMUIR G)

MUIR, Sir John (Harling); 3 Bt (UK 1892), of Deanston, Perthshire, TD, DL (Perthshire 1966); s of James Finlay Muir (d 1948), and nephew of 2 Bt (d 1951); *b* 7 Nov 1910; *Educ* Stowe; *m* 1936, Elizabeth Mary, da of late Frederick James Dundas; 5 s, 2 da; *Heir* s, Richard James Kay Muir; *Career* served WWII 1939-45; dir: James Finlay & Co Ltd Glasgow 1946-80, Grindlay's Hldgs Ltd, Royal Insur Co Ltd, Scottish United Investors Ltd; memb Queen's Body Gd for Scotland (Royal Co of Archers); memb: Fourth Dist Salmon Fishery Bd, Forth River Purification Bd; *Recreations* shooting, fishing, gardening; *Clubs* Oriental; *Style*— Sir John Muir, Bt, TD, DL; Bankhead, Blair Drummond, Perthshire (☎ 0786 841207)

MUIR, Sir Laurence Macdonald; VRD; s of Andrew Muir; *b* 3 Mar 1925; *Educ* Yallourn State Sch, Scotch Coll, Melbourne Univ (LLB); *m* 1948, Ruth Richardson; 2 s, 2 da; *Career* RN 1942-66; barr and slr Supreme Ct Victoria 1950; formerly sr ptnr Potter Ptnrs; sharebroker (ret 1980); dir: Australia and NZ Banking Gp Ltd, AGI Int Ltd, memb Parliament House Construction Authy, FSIA, FAIM, kt 1981; *see Debrett's Handbook of Australia and New Zealand for further details*; *Style*— Sir Laurence Muir, VRD; Meadow End, Kyla Park, Tuross Head, NSW 2537

MUIR, Lady Linda Mary; *née* Cole; da of 6 Earl of Enniskillen, MBE; *b* 1944; *m* 1975, as his 2 w, Richard James Kay Muir, *qv*; 2 da; *Style*— Lady Linda Muir; Park House, Blair Drummond, by Stirling, Perthshire

MUIR, Richard James Kay; s and h of Sir John Muir, 3 Bt, TD; *b* 25 May 1939; *m* 1, 1965 (m dis 1974), Susan Elizabeth Gardner; 2 da; m 2, 1975, Lady Linda Mary Cole, da of 6 Earl of Enniskillen; 2 da; *Style*— Richard Muir Esq; Park House, Blair Drummond, by Stirling, Perthshire

MUIR, Lady Rosemary Mildred; *née* Spencer-Churchill; da of 10 Duke of Marlborough (d 1972), and Hon Alexandra Mary Cadogan (d 1961); *b* 24 July 1929; *m* 1953, Charles Robert Muir (d 1972), s of Roland Huntly Muir (d 1975); 2 s (Alexander, Simon), 1 da (Mary); *Career* a maid of honour to HM The Queen at the Coronation 1953; *Clubs* Sunnydale Golf, Berkshire Golf; *Style*— Lady Rosemary Muir; Orange Hill House, Binfield, Berks (☎ 0344 483485)

MUIR MACKENZIE, Sir Alexander Alwyne Brinton; 7 Bt (UK 1805), of Delvine, Perthshire; s of Sir Robert Henry Muir Mackenzie, 6 Bt (d 1970), and Charmian Cecil de Vere, *née* Brinton (d 1962); *b* 8 Dec 1955; *Educ* Eton, Trinity Coll Cambridge; *m* 1984, Susan Carolyn, da of John David Henzel Hayter, 1 s (b 17 Feb 1989), 1 da (Georgina Mary b 1987); *Heir* s, b 17 Feb 1989; *Style*— Sir Alexander Muir Mackenzie, Bt; Buckshaw House, Holwell, nr Sherborne, Dorset DT9 5LD

MUIR MACKENZIE, Lady; Mary Teresa; er da of late Dr James Mathews and widow of John Geoffrey Turner, of Farnham, Surrey; *m* 25 July 1963, as his 2 w, Capt Sir Robert Henry Muir Mackenzie, 6 Bt (d 1970); *Style*— Lady Muir Mackenzie; Flat A, 62 Pont St, London SW1

MUIR WOOD, Sir Alan Marshall; s of Edward Wood; *b* 8 August 1921; *Educ* Abbotsholme Sch, Peterhouse Cambridge; *m* 1943, Winifred Lanagan; 3 s; *Career* served WW II, engr offr RN; sr ptnr Sir William Halcrow & Ptnrs 1979-84 (ptnr 1964-84, formerly asst then sr engr, now conslt); dir Halcrow Fox & Assocs 1977-84, Orange Fish Consultants; former asst engr BR (Southern Regn) and research asst Docks & Inland Waterways Exec; first (and hon life) pres Int Tunnelling Assoc Channel Tunnel; fell Imperial Coll 1980; hon fell: Peterhouse 1982, Portsmouth Poly 1984; Hon LlD Dundee 1985; Hon DSc City Univ 1978; Hon DSc Southampton Univ 1986 recipient of Telford Medal 1976; FEng, FICE (pres 1977-78), FRS; kt 1981; *Books* Coastal Hydraulics (1969, 2 ed with C A Fleming 1981); *Clubs* Athenaeum; *Style*— Sir Alan Muir Wood; Franklands, Bere Court Rd, Pangbourne, Berks (☎ 073 57 2833)

MUIR-SIMPSON, Richard Mannington; s of Denzil Lorimer Muir-Simpson, OStJ, TD (d 1976), and Bridget Katherine Grant, *née* Sayers; *b* 24 April 1946; *Educ* Loretto Sch, Univ of Sheffield (LLB); *m* 8 Oct 1976, Patricia Guthrie, da of Guthrie Baxter Wilson, of Angus; 2 s (Andrew b 1978, Simon b 1980); *Career* investmt mangr Invory & Sime plc; dir inc: Lyle Finance Int Ltd 1976-81, Log Services Ltd 1978-81, Genton Barns (Scotland) Ltd 1981-82, Wavebreaker Marine Ltd 1981-82, Gaeltec Ltd 1981-87, Omega Electric Ltd 1983-85, Stepp Electronics Ltd 1983-87; deacon The Incorporation of Wrights in Glasgow 1982-82, pres The Grand Antiquity Soc of Glasgow 1983-84, memb The Trades House of Glasgow 1981-84, MICAS; *Recreations* tennis, skiing, gardening, politics, music; *Clubs* RSAC, Edinburgh Sports; *Style*— Richard M Muir-Simpson, Esq; Redmarley, Kippen, Stirlingshire FK8 3HS (☎ 0786 87351); Ivory & Sime plc, 1 Charlotte Square, Edinburgh EH2 4DZ (☎ 031 225 1357, telex 727242, fax 031 225 2375)

MUIRHEAD, Capt (James) Alan; MBE (1971), JP (1968); s of Brig James Ingram Muirhead, CIE, MC (d 1964), of Moffat, Dumfriesshire, and Dorothy Alaine Denholm, *née* Fraser (d 1978); *b* 18 Nov 1924; *Educ* Sherborne Dorset, Bishop Cotton Sch's Bangalore and Simla; *m* 24 July 1948, Mary, da of Lt-Col Joseph Charles Annear, TD (d 1958), of Falmouth; 1 s (James David Charles b 1949), 1 da (Julia Anne b 1953); *Career* Capt RE; served India, Malaya, Java 1942-49; perm cmmn 1946; ret 1949; dir: J C Annear & Co Ltd 1953-73, J H Bennetts Ltd 1978-88 (chm 1983-88); ccnclr Cornwall 1988-; *Recreations* sailing, gardening; *Clubs* Royal Cornwall Yacht; *Style*— Capt Alan Muirhead, MBE, JP; Sparnon, Budock, Falmouth, Cornwall TR11 5DJ (☎ 0325 72560);

MUIRHEAD, Alastair William (Sandy); s of William Calliope Muirhead, OBE (d 1983), and Joan Andrade, *née* Sutherland; *b* 12 Sept 1953; *Educ* Tonbridge Sch Kent, St John's Coll Oxford (BA); *m* 19 April 1980, Linda Anne, da of Robert Johnson, s of Wakefield; 2 da (Joanna b 19 Feb 1983, Nicola b 12 March 1985); *Career* Price Waterhouse 1976-80, Saudi Int Bank 1980-84, dir Charterhouse Bank Ltd 1987- (joined 1984); Hon MA Oxon; ACA; *Recreations* fly fishing, gardening, hill walking; *Style*— Alastair Muirhead, Esq; Charterhouse Bank Ltd, 1 Paternoster Row, St Pauls, London EC4M 7DH (☎ 01 248 4000, 01 248 6522)

MUIRHEAD, Sir David Francis; KCMG (1976), CMG (1964, CVO 1957); s of late David Muirhead; *b* 30 Dec 1918; *Educ* Cranbrook Sch; *m* 1942, Hon Elspeth, *née* Hope-Morley, *qv*; 2 s, 1 da; *Career* served WWII; entered Foreign Office 1947 (cnsllr FO 1960-64, under-sec 1966-67); ambass: Peru 1967-70, Portugal 1970-74, Belgium

1974-78; Grand Cross Military Order of Christ (Portugal) 1973, Grand Cross Order of Distinguished Service (Peru) 1985; *Clubs* Travellers'; *Style—* Sir David Muirhead, KCMG, CVO; 16 Pitt St, London W8 (☎ 01 937 2443)

MUIRHEAD, Hon Lady (Elspeth Rachel Marianne Winifred Hope); yr da of 2 Baron Hollenden, JP (d 1977), by his w Hon Mary Gardner (d 1982), da of 1 Baron Burghclere; *b* 1917; *m* 1942, Sir David Francis Muirhead, KCMG, CVO, *qv*; 2 s, 1 da; *Style—* The Hon Lady Muirhead; 16 Pitt St, London W8 (☎ 01 937 2443)

MUIRHEAD, William Mortimer; s of Denis Butler Muirhead; *b* 11 July 1947; *Educ* The Armidale Sch NSW, St Dunstans Coll SE6; *m* Jeanne Elizabeth, nee Meins; 2 s; *Career* dir: Saatchi & Saatchi Garland-Compton, Saatchi & Saatchi Compton 1980-; *Recreations* rugby, tennis, squash, ski-ing; *Clubs* RAC, Zanzibar, Mortons; *Style—* William Muirhead Esq; 'Ightham', Merlewood Drive, Chislehurst, Kent; 'Tramontana', Encounter Bay, Victor Harbour, S Australia

MUIRSHIEL, Viscount (UK 1964); John Scott Maclay; KT (1973), CH (1962), CMG (1944), PC (1952), JP (Renfrewshire 1968), DL (Renfrewshire 1981); 5 s of 1 Baron Maclay (d 1951); *b* 26 Oct 1905; *Educ* Winchester, Trinity Cambridge; *m* 1930, Betty L'Estrange (d 1974), da of Maj Delaval Astley, CB, JP, DL (d 1951, g nephew of 16 Baron Hastings); *Heir* none; *Career* Capt 57 Searchlight Regt RA TA, seconded to Min of War Transport 1940; memb British Shipping Mission to USA 1941, head of mission 1944; MP (Lib Nat) Montrose district of Burghs 1940-50, MP (Nat Lib & C) Renfrewshire (Western div) 1950-64; parly sec to min of Production 1945, min Transport and Civil Aviation 1951-52, min state Colonial Affairs 1956-57, sec state Scotland 1957-62; chm Jt Exchequer Bd for N Ireland 1965-73; former dir: Maclay & Macintyre Ltd, Clydesdale Bank, National Provincial Bank, P & O Steamship Co Ltd; tstee National Galleries of Scotland 1966-76; chm Scottish Civic Trust 1967-; chm tstees Burrell Collection; Lord-Lt of Renfrewshire 1967-80; Hon LLD Edinburgh 1963, Strathclyde 1966, Glasgow 1970; *Clubs* Boodle's, Western (Glasgow), Royal Yacht Sqdn; *Style—* The Rt Hon The Viscount Muirshiel, KT, CH, CMG, PC, JP, DL; Knapps Wood, Kilmacolm, Renfrewshire PA13 4NQ (☎ 050 587 2770)

MUKHERJEE, Tara Kumar; s of Sushil Chandra Mukherjee (d 1976), of Calcutta, Indian, and Sova Moyee, *née* Banerjee; *b* 20 Dec 1923; *Educ* Scottish Church Collegiate Sch Calcutta India, Calcutta Univ; *m* 15 May 1951, Betty Patricia, da of David Derby (d 1982), of Leicester; 1 s (Karl b 1956), 1 da (Jasmin b 1952); *Career* shop mangr Bata Shoe Co Ltd India 1941-44, buyer Brevitt Shoes Leicester 1951-56, sundries buyer Br Shoe Corpn 1956-66, prodn admin Priestley Footwear Ltd Great Harwood 1966-68, head store mangr Br Shoe Corpn 1968-70, branch mangr Save and Prosper Gp 1978-84 (dist mangr 1970-78), area mangr Guardian Royal Exchange 1985-88, md Owl Fin Servs Ltd 1988; pres: Confedn of Indian Orgns UK 1975-, Indian Film Soc Leicester; memb: Br Euro Movement, cncl of mgmnt Coronary Prevention Gp 1985-; tstee: Haymarket Theatre Leicester, Asian Community Resources Tst London; played for Bihar Ranji Cricket trophy 1941; FLIA; *Recreations* first class cricket; *Clubs* Leic CC, Indian National (Leicester); *Style—* Tara Mukherjee, Esq; Tallah, 1 Park Ave, Hutton, Brentwood, Essex CM13 2QR (☎ 0277 215438); 8 Celina Close, Bletchley MK2 3LT (☎ 0277 263207, 0908 78832)

MULCAHY, Geoffrey John; s of late Maurice Frederick Mulcahy; *b* 7 Feb 1942; *Educ* King's Sch Worcester, Manchester Univ, Harvard Univ; *m* 1964, Valerie Elizabeth, *née* Ison; 1 s, 1 da; *Career* finance dir British Sugar Corporation Ltd 1977-82, gp chief exec Kingfisher plc; *Recreations* squash, sailing; *Clubs* Lansdowne; *Style—* Geoffrey Mulcahy, Esq; 75 Alleyn Rd, Dulwich, London SE21 8AD

MULCAHY, Russell Ian; s of Edward Joseph Mulcahy (d 1988), and Joan, *née* Sydney; *b* 23 June 1953; *Educ* Corrimal HS NSW Australia; *Career* film ed channel 7 Sydney Aust, winner Sydney Film Fest with 2 short films 1976 and 77, moved to England 1978; filmed numerous pop videos and video albums 1980- incl: Derek and Clive Get the Horn (for Peter Cook and Dudley Moore), Duran Duran The Video Album, The Tubes Completion Backwards Principle, Elton John The Fox; feature films incl: Razorback 1985, Arena An Absurd Notion (with Duran Duran) 1985, Highlander 1986; awards incl: BAFTA Special Craft Award 1982, American Videos Award best dir 1982, Int Film and TV Festival silver and bronze awards 1983, two Grammy Awards best long and short videos 1983, D & AD Awards best director and best music video 1983, Br Phonographic Indust Award video of the year 1984, three American video Awards 1984, Golden Rose of Montreux best story-line (music section) 1986; memb Directors Guild of America; *Recreations* scuba diving, writing, cinema, theatre; *Clubs* White Elephant, Browns; *Style—* Russell Mulcahy, Esq; 22 Golden Sq, London W1 (☎ 01 439 9527, fax 01 437 0022 car tel 0860 327 186, telex 295 493 MGMM UK G)

MULCHINOCK, Michael Cyril George; s of Cyril Edward Mulchinock (d 1977), and Alethea Mary, *née* Bone (d 1988); gs of William Pembroke Mulchinock, the poet who wrote 'The Rose of Tralee'; *b* 5 June 1929; *Educ* Monkton Combe, Royal W of England Acad Sch of Architecture; *m* 5 Feb 1955 (m dis 1987), (Doreen) Elizabeth , da of Gordon Bunce (d 1967); 1 s (Simon b 9 March 1963), 2 da (Sarah b 5 April 1959, Emily b 23 May 1967); *Career* asst staff architect Gallaher Ltd 1958-63; princ in private practice 1963-65; ptnr Elsworth Sykes Ptnrship 1965-86 (dir 1986-); dir: Elsworth Sykes Property Servs 1986-, Elsworth Sykes Northern 1988-, ESP Planning 1988-, Folio Personnel 1988-; memb Architects Benevolent Soc Exec 1985- (memb cncl and chm Winter Charity Ball ctee 1981-85); chm: Knockholt (Kent) Amenity Soc 1970-77, Judd Street Ress Assoc (London WC1) 1985-86; FRIBA, memb SPAB; *Recreations* writing, community interests; *Clubs* Reform; *Style—* Michael C G Mulchinock, Esq; 2 Sandwich Street, London WC1 H9PL (☎ 01 388 3558); Elsworth Sykes Partnership, 287 Regent Street, London W1R 8BX (☎ 01 409 2662, fax 01 493 3128, telex 298749)

MULDOON, Rt Hon Sir Robert David; GCMG (1983), CH (1977), PC (1976), MP; s of James Henry Muldoon, and Mamie R Muldoon; *b* 25 Sept 1921; *Educ* Mt Albert GS; *m* 1951, Thea Dale, *née* Flyger; 1 s, 2 da; *Career* CA; pres NZ Inst of Cost Accountants 1956; MP Tamaki 1960-; parly under-sec to Min of Fin 1963-66, min of Tourism 1967, min of Finance 1967-72, dep PM 1972, dep ldr Nat Pty and dep ldr of the oppn 1972-74, ldr of the opposition 1974-75, chm Bd of Govrs IMF and World Bank 1979-80, chm Ministerial Cncl OECD 1982, Prime Minister New Zealand and min of Fin 1975-84; FCANZ, CMANZ, FCIS, FCMA; *Books* The Rise and Fall of a Young Turk (1974), Muldoon (1977), My Way (1981), The New Zealand Economy, A Personal View (1985), No 38 (1986); *Clubs* Professional (NZ); *Style—* The Rt Hon Sir Robert Muldoon, GCMG, CH, MP; 7 Homewood Place, Birkenhead, Auckland 10, New Zealand

MULGRAVE, Earl of; Constantine Edmund Walter Phipps; s and h of 4 Marquess of Normanby, KG, CBE; *b* 24 Feb 1954; *Educ* Eton, Worcester Coll Oxford; *Career* writer , company directer; *Publications* (as Constantine Phipps) Careful with the Sharks (1985); *Clubs* Travellers; *Style—* Earl of Mulgrave; Mulgrave Castle, Whitby, N Yorks

MULHALLEN, Lady Katherine Lillian; *née* Edgcumbe; 2 da of 6 Earl of Mount Edgcumbe, TD (d 1965), and Lillian Agnes, *née* Arkwright (d 1964); *b* 1 May 1910; *m* 1, 1 Aug 1936 (m dis 1957), Gp-Capt Francis Campbell de la Poer Beresford-Peirse, s of Rev Pieb Richard Windham de la Poer Beresford-Peirse; 1 s (decd), 2 da; m 2, Cdr R Gabbett Mulhallen, CBE, RN; *Style—* Lady Katherine Mulhallen

MULHOLLAND, Brian Henry; only s and h, of Sir Michael Henry Mulholland, 2 Bt, by his 2 w, Elizabeth; *b* 25 Sept 1950; *Educ* Eton; *m* 1976, Mary Joana, yst da of Maj Robert J F Whistler, of Achaeon, Camberley, Surrey; 2 s (Andrew b 1981, William b 1986), 1 da (Tara b 1980); *Career* co dir; brands mangr Matthew Clark Gp plc with responsibility for Irish Distillers 1982-85; dir Lanyon Devpts Ltd 1985-; *Recreations* fishing, gardening; *Clubs* MCC; *Style—* Brian Mulholland, Esq; The House by the Green, Worplesdon Hill, nr Woking, Surrey GU22 0QY (☎ 04867 2481)

MULHOLLAND, Martin Edward Harcourt; s of Hon John Mulholland, MC, (d 1948, yst s of 2 Baron Dunleath), and Hon Olivia Vernon, DCVO, *née* Harcourt (d 1984), 2 da of 1 Viscount Harcourt; *b* 23 Feb 1927; *Educ* Eton; *m* 24 Feb 1953, (Lilian) Diana Tyndal, da of Maj John Lucas, MC (d 1968); 3 s (John b 1953, Simon b 1955, Giles b 1959); *Career* Lt Irish Gds 1945-48, Palestine 1947-48; High Sheriff of Co Antrim 1961; Liveryman Pipemakers' and Tobacco Blenders' Co 1986; with Gallaher Ltd 1948-86 (gen mangr Public Affairs 1979-86), chm and md Public Affairs Advice 1986-; *Recreations* shooting, fishing, politics; *Style—* Martin Mulholland, Esq; North Hall, E Chiltington, Lewes, Sussex BN7 3QS (☎ 0273 890251); Public Affairs Advice Ltd, North Hall, E Chiltington, Lewes, Sussex BN7 3QS (☎ 0273 890821)

MULHOLLAND, Maj Sir Michael Henry; 2 Bt (UK 1945), of Ballyscullion Park, Co Derry; s of Rt Hon Sir Henry Mulholland, 1 Bt (d 1971), of Ballyscullion Park, Bellaghy, N I; hp to Barony of Dunleath; *b* 15 Oct 1915; *Educ* Eton, Pembroke Coll Cambridge; *m* 1, 1942 (m dis 1949), Rosemary, da of late Maj David Ker, OBE; m 2, 1949, Elizabeth, da of Laurence Hyde; 1 s; *Heir* s, Brian Henry Mulholland; *Career* 2 Lt Oxford and Bucks LI 1936, served WWII 1939-45, Maj 1946; *Style—* Maj Sir Michael Mulholland, Bt; Storbrooke, Massey Ave, Belfast (☎ 0232 63394)

MULJI, Hon Mrs; Hon Rosaleen Elisabeth; *née* Guinness; da of 2 Baron Moyne; *b* 1937; *Educ* St Anne's Coll Oxford (MA); *m* 1965, Sudhir Mulji; 2 s, 2 da; *Style—* The Hon Mrs Mulji; 150 Malcha Marg, New Delhi, 110021

MULKERN, John; CBE (1987), JP (Surrey 1988); s of Thomas Mulkern (d 1973), of Stretford, Manchester, and Annie Proctor, *née* Tennant (d 1984); *b* 15 Jan 1931; *Educ* Stretford GS, Harvard Business Sch; *m* 5 June 1954, May Egerton, da of Arthur Peters (d 1987), of Leatherhead, Surrey; 1 s (Neil b 1959), 3 da (Susan b 1957, Gaynor b 1962, Rosalind b 1967); *Career* Minys of Supply and Aviation (final post princ) 1949-65; Br Airports Authy 1965-87: head of fin, dep dir admin and personnel, dep gen mangr Heathrow, dir Gatwick, md and bd memb 1977-87, chm Br Airports Int Ltd 1978-82; int aviation conslt 1987-, chm Manchester Handling Ltd 1988-; pres: Western Euro Airports Assoc 1981-83, Int Civil Airports Assoc (Europe) 1986-87; chm Airports Assocs Coordinating Cncl 1982, bd memb Airport Operators Cncl Int 1978-81; Ordre Du Zaire 1975 (Chevalier Zaire Nouveau Civil), Malaysian Distinguished Order of Chivalry Class Five 1974, Cavalheiro Order of Rio Branco Class Five Brazil 1976, Chevalier de L'Ordre National Du Mérite France 1976; FCIT 1973 (memb cncl 1979-82), CBIM 1981, FInstD 1982; *Recreations* travel, music, theatre; *Style—* John Mulkern, Esq, CBE, JP; Dorwyn, 23 St Mary's Rd, Leatherhead, Surrey KT22 8HB (☎ 0372 372 378)

MULLALY, Terence Frederick Stanley; s of Col Brian Reginald Mullaly (d 1965), and Eileen Dorothy Stanley (d 1973); gf Maj Gen Sir Herbert Mullaly, KCMG, CB, CSI, Cdr East Coast Defences during 1914-18 war; *b* 14 Nov 1927; *Educ* in India, England, Japan and Canada, Downing Coll Cambridge (BA, MA); *m* 1949, Elizabeth Helen, da of Frank Burkitt, of Bournemouth; *Career* art historian and art critic The Daily Telegraph 1958-86; pres Br section of the Int Assoc of Arts Critics 1967-73, vice-chm Br Art Medal Soc 1982-87 (pres 1988-); memb: cncl of the Attingham Summer Sch Tst 1985-, cncl of the Derby Porcelain Int Soc 1985-88, advsy ctee of the Cracow Art Festival 1974, Palermo Art Festival 1976; artistic advsr of Grand Tours 1975-, dir of Special Tours 1986, UK del to the Conference on Security and Co-op in Europe (CSCE) Cultural Forum Budapest 1985, Premio Pietro Torta Per il restauro di Venezia 1983, FSA, FRNS, FRSA; Commendatore Ordine Al Merito della Repubblica Italiana 1974; l'Ordre du Mérite Culturel Poland 1974; OM Poland (Silver Medal) 1977, SM Ordine Constantiniano di S Giorgio 1982; *Books* Ruskin a Verona (1966), catalogue of the exhibition Disegni veronesi del Cinquecento (1971), contrib Cinquant Anni di Pittura veronese 1580-1630 (1974), ed and contrib to catalogue of the exhibition Modern Hungarian Medals (1984), Caterina Cornaro, Queen of Cyprus (1989), author of articles in numerous learned jls and magazines; *Style—* Terence Mullaly Esq; Waterside House, Lower St, Pulborough, W Sussex RH20 2BH (☎ 07982 2104)

MULLAN, Lt Cdr Charles Heron; CBE (1979), VRD (1949, DL Co Down 1974); s of Frederick Heron Mullan, DL (d 1972), of Cairn Hill, Newry, and Minnie, *née* Broackes (d 1948); *b* 17 Feb 1912; *Educ* Castle Park Dalkey, Rossall, Clare Coll Cambridge (BA, MA); *m* 6 Sept 1940, Marcella Elizabeth Sharpe, da of James Alexander McCullagh (d 1954), of Ballycastle, Co Antrim; 1 s (Christopher Desmond Heron b 5 Sept 1947); *Career* joined RNVR 1936, Lt 1940, Lt Cdr 1948, served 1939-45 with RN: Channel, N Sea, N Atlantic; slr 1948; MP (U U) Imperial Parliament Co Down 1946-50; memb Ulster Unionist Cncl 1946-60; resident magistrate N Ireland 1960-82, stipendiary magistrate Belfast 1964-79; King Haakon VII War Decoration (Norway) 1944; *Recreations* ornithology, walking; *Style—* Lt Cdr Charles Mullan, CBE, VRD, DL; Casanbarra, Carrickmore Road, Ballycastle, Co Antrim BT54 6QS, Northern Ireland (☎ 02657 62323)

MULLENS, Maj-Gen Anthony Richard Guy; s of Brig Guy John de Wette Mullens, OBE (d 1981), and Gwendoline Joan, *née* Maclean; *b* 10 May 1936; *Educ* Eton, RMA Sandhurst; *m* 31 Oct 1964, Dawn Elizabeth Hermione, da of Lt-Col John Walter Pease (d 1983); *Career* cmmnd 4/7 Royal Dragoon Guards 1956, ADC to COMD 1 Br Corps 1958-60, Adj 1963, Staff Coll Camberley 1967-68, MOD 1968-70, regtl duty 1970-72, Brigade Maj 1972, dir staff Staff Coll 1973-76, CO 4/7 Royal Dragoon Guards 1976-80, Cdr 7 Armd Brigade 1980-82, MOD 1982- 85, GoC 1 Armd Div 1985, MOD 1987; Dp

Chief of Defence Staff (Systems) 1989-; Liveryman Worshipful Co of Armourers and Brasiers 1974, Coachmakers & Coach Harness Makers 1977 Niedersachsen Verdienst Kreuz (Am Bande 1982, First Class 1987); *Recreations* travel, riding, skiing; *Clubs* Cavalry and Guards; Hurlingham; *Style—* Maj-Gen Anthony Mullens; c/o Lloyds Bank, Guards & Cavalry Section, 6 Pall Mall, London SW1; Ministry of Defence, Whitehall

MULLENS, Peter Arthur Glanville; OBE (1985); s of George Glanville Mullens (d 1969), and Mabel Lavinia; *b* 16 Mar 1925; *Educ* Llandovery Coll, Sidney Sussex Coll Cambridge; *m* 5 Apr 1952, Edwina Mary, da of Dr Rufus John Isaac (d 1978); 1 s (William b 1953), 2 da (Fiona b 1956, Lynette b 1961); *Career* RAF 1943-47, cmmnd Air Bomber 1944, Accountant Offr 1945-47 (serv Hong Kong, Shanghai), Fl-Lt; CA ptnr Mullen & Robinson 1953; memb Port Talbot Incorp C of C; memb Welsh Industl Devpt Advsy Bd, tres Univ Coll of Swansea; FCA 1951; *Recreations* reading, walking, riding; *Style—* Peter Mullens, Esq, OBE; Archways, 2 Stratford Drive, Porthcawl, Mid Glamorgan, CF36 3LG (☎ 0656 771 639); Mullens & Robinson, 18 Station Road, West Glamorgan SA13 1B4 (☎ 0639 885 203)

MULLER, Charles Alister; s of Charles James Muller (d 1936), and Edith Daphne Keswick *née* Swinscow (d 1942); *b* 16 May 1925; *Educ* Worth Preparatory Sch; Downside Coll; *m* 1950, Mary Nelson, da of Major Everard Nelson Exton MC (d 1980); 1 s (Paul b 1951); 3 da (Catherine b 1954, Sophie Bell (m) b 1963, Carlotta b 1966); *Career* 1952 mgmnt trainee Bain Claukion Gp (subsid Inchcap plc) at Lloyds; international insurance broker (non marine) Lloyds & London Mkts 1942-85; first insurance participant the International Cmmn on Large Dam 1967 and subsequently; introduced Environmental Impairment Liability (pollution insurance) worldwide 1974; ret, part-time conslt 1985; FRGS, FRSA; life memb Arctic Inst of N America; memb: Lloyds Unerwriting, Underground Space Assoc; registered insurance broker; *Publications* An Introduction to the Insurance of Construction Projects (1966), Comprehensive Insurance for Dams, its Scope and Feasibility (1970 with E M de Saventhem), Proposals for the Channel Tunnel Insurance (1971 with E M de Saventhem), Earth-Sheltered Housing Insurance - its Coverages and Costs (with E M de Saventham and R A Taylor), Regulating Hazardous Wastes Insuring Pollution Liability (1981), Risk and Insurance (1981), Insuring Innovation (1981, with E M de Saventhem and R M Aickin); *Clubs* City University, Canning; *Style—* Charles A Muller, Esq

MULLER, Franz Joseph; QC (1978); s of Wilhelm Muller (d 1982), and Anne Maria Muller, *née* Ravens; *b* 19 Nov 1938; *Educ* Mount St Mary's Coll, Univ of Sheffield (LLB); *m* 1985, Helena, da of Mieczyslaw Bartosz; 1 s (Julian b 1986); *Career* graduate apprentice Utd Steel Cos 1960-61, commercial assoc Workington Iron & Steel Co Ltd 1961-63; barr 1964, recorder Crown Ct 1977, non exec dir: Richards of Sheffield Hldgs plc 1969-77, Satinsteel Ltd 1970-77, Rodgers Wostenholm Ltd 1975-77; memb SRC Univ Coll Durham 1981, govr Mount St Mary's Coll 1984-86; *Recreations* fell walking, listening to music, skiing; *Style—* Franz Muller, Esq, QC; Sheffield (☎ 669187); Witherslack, Cumbria (☎ 492); 11 Kings Bench Walk, Temple, London EC4 (☎ 01 353 3337)

MULLETT, (Aidan) Anthony; QPM (1982); s of Bartholomew Joseph Mullett (d 1976), and Mary Kate, *née* Sheehan (d 1980); *b* 24 May 1933; *Educ* Moat Boys Sch Leicester; *m* 7 Sept 1957, Monica Elizabeth, da of Paul Gerald Coney (d 1968); 1 s (Philip b 1963), 1 da (Beverley b 1958); *Career* RAF 1950-56; Leicester City Police 1957, Leicestershire and Rutland Constabulary 1966, asst Chief Constable West Mercia Constabulary 1975, dep Chief Constable Dyfed Powys Police 1982, Chief Constable West Mercia Constabulary 1985; chm Hereford and Worcester Outward Bound Assoc, pres Shropshire Outward Bound Assoc, memb Hereford Worcester and Shropshire St John Ambulance Cncl, vice pres Hereford and Worcester Co Scout Cncl; *Recreations* golf; *Clubs* Worcester Golf and Social, Evesham GC; *Style—* Anthony Mullett, Esq, QPM; West Mercia Constabulary, Police Headquarters, Hindlip Hall, Worcester WR3 8SP (☎ 0905 723 000, fax 0905 54 226)

MULLEY, Hon Deirdre; da of Baron Mulley (Life Baron); *b* 1951; *Style—* The Hon Deirdre Mulley

MULLEY, Baron (Life Peer UK 1984), of Manor Park in the City of Sheffield; Rt Hon Frederick William Mulley; PC (1964); s of late William Mulley; *b* 3 July 1918; *Educ* Bath Place C of E Sch, Warwick Sch, Christ Church Oxford; *m* 1948, Joan Doreen, da of Alexander Morris Phillips, of London; 2 da; *Career* served WWII, Worcs Regt (POW Germany 1940-45); fell St Catharine's Coll Cambridge 1948-50, barr Inner Temple 1954; MP (Lab) Sheffield Park 1950-83, pps to min of works 1951, dep sec state Defence and min of Def for Army 1964-65, min Aviation 1965-67, jt min state Foreign and Cwlth Office 1967-69, min Disarmament 1967-69, min Tport 1969-70 and 1974-75, sec state Educn and Science 1975-76, sec state Def 1976-79, pres Assembly of WEU 1980-83; memb Nat Exec Ctee Lab Pty 1957-58, 1960-64 and 1965-80, chm Lab Pty 1974-75, a vice-pres Peace Through NATO 1985-; dep chm Sheffield Devpt Corpn 1988-; *Style—* The Rt Hon the Lord Mulley, PC; 3 Denny Crescent, London SE11 4UY

MULLIGAN, Andrew Armstrong; s of Col Hugh Waddell Mulligan, CMG, MD, DSc (d 1982), and Beatrix Aimee Armstrong; Mulligans settled in Co Down Ulster in 1610, prominent landowners, in professions and Presbytarian Church; *b* 4 Feb 1936; *Educ* Gresham Sch Norfolk, Magdalene Coll Cambridge (rugby blue, MA); *m* 1964, Pia Ursula, da of Eiler Theodore Schiuler; 4 da (Fionn, Maia, Joachim, Kate); *Career* pres: Mulligan Communications Inc, Service de Television Mitgrational; former dir (min and cnsllr) delgn of cmmn of Euro Communities Washington DC, sec gen EEC Cmmn Brussels, former prodr and reporter BBC Panorama and ITN, for corr Observer Paris, memb Irish Wanderers Ulster, capt Irish Rugby Team 1960, memb: Br Lions Aust and NZ 1959, Barbarians Canada 1957 and SA 1958; *Recreations* tennis, skiing, landscape painting, yacht ('Wildgoose'); *Clubs* Kildare Univ (Dublin), Hawks (Cambridge); *Style—* Andrew Mulligan Esq; 1855 Shepherd St, Washington DC 20011, USA

MULLIGAN, Reginald Graham; s of Frederick George Mulligan, of Marbella, Spain, and Gladys Mulligan; *b* 4 Dec 1944; *Educ* Ottershaw Sch, Coll of Air Trg Hamble; *m* 10 Nov 1974, Linda Mary, da of Lenord Wood; 2 s (Maxwell Thomas b 6 Dec 1976, Daniel Graham b 24 April 1979); *Career* pilot: BEA 1965-66, BOAC 1966-78; chm Fairflight 1978-; *Recreations* golf; *Clubs* Royal MD Surrey GC; *Style—* Reginald Mulligan, Esq; Fairflight Ltd, Biggin Hill Airport, nr Westerham, Kent TN16 3B (☎ 0959 74651, fax 0959 71929)

MULLIN, Prof John William; s of Frederick Mullin (d 1972), of Queen's Ferry, Chester, and Kathleen Nellie, *née* Oppy (d 1988); *b* 22 August 1925; *Educ* Hawarden Co Sch, Univ Coll Cardiff (BSc, DSc), UCL (PhD); *m* 22 Aug 1952, Averil Margaret, da of William Davies (d 1971), of Cwmgwili, Camarthen; 1 s (Jonathan b 1957), 1 da (Susan b 1960); *Career* RAF 1945-48; UCL 1956-: lectr chemical engrg 1956-61, reader 1961-69, prof 1969-85, Ramsay meml prof and head of dept 1985-, dean of engrg 1975-77 and 1980-85, vice provost 1980-86; memb ct of govrs Univ Coll Cardiff 1982-, vice chm cncl sch of pharmacy 1988 (memb 1983-); winner of Moulton medal Inst of Chem Engrs 1970; Freeman City of London 1984, memb Worshipful Co of Engrs 1984; fell: Univ Coll Cardiff 1981, UCL 1981; FRSC (1958), FIChemE 1959, FEng 1983; *Books* Crystallization (2 edn 1972), Industrial Crystallization (ed 1976); *Recreations* gardening; *Clubs* Athenaeum; *Style—* Prof John Mullin; 4 Milton Rd, Ickenham, Uxbridge, Middx UB10 8NQ; Dept of Chemical Engrg, UCL, Torrington Place, London WC1E 7JE (☎ 01 387 7050)

MULLIN, Peter; s of Thomas Mullin, of Ashbourne, Derbyshire, and Margaret, *née* Bull (d 1953); *b* 28 Mar 1989; *Educ* Lewes GS, Durham Univ (BA), Makerere Coll Univ of East Afric (Dip Ed); *m* 7 Jan 1984, (Pamela) Susan, da of Arthur Earnest Dunbar Lott, of Highcliffe, Dorset; *Career* fin conslt; formerly schoolmaster and faculty head Adeyfield Sch Hemel Hempstead 1976-86, educ offr Uganda 1967-73 and Kenya 1973-76; *Books* The Tropical World (Edward Arnold 1985); *Recreations* bridge, Lions International, amateur dramatics; *Clubs* St Mellion (Cornwall); *Style—* Peter Mullin, Esq; Middle Dimson Farmhouse, Gunnislake, Cornwall PL18 9NX (☎ 0822 832342)

MULLINER, Stephen Nigel; s of Dr Gerald Norman Mulliner, of Osmington, Weymouth, Dorset, and Kathleen Wilma, *née* Ritchie; *b* 4 Sept 1953; *Educ* Downside, Emmanuel Coll Cambridge (MA, LLB); *m* 18 Aug 1979, Sarah Lucinda, da of Lt-Col John Arthur Speirs, of Coombe Bissett, Salisbury, Wiltshire; 2 s (Andrew b 1983, Jonathan b 1985), 1 da (Lucy b 1983); *Career* assoc dir SBCI Swiss Bank Corpn Investmt Banking Ltd 1987-89, gen mangr Tokai Int Ltd 1989-, non exec chm James Smith & Sons (Norwood) plc 1989- (non exec dir 1988-); Br Open Croquet Champion 1988, President's Cup Winner 1981, 1983, 1986 and 1987, Men's Champion, 1985 and 1986, World Invitation Singles Champion 1986, 1987 and 1988, Br Open Doubles Champion 1980, 1981, 1984, 1986 and 1988; vice chm The Croquet Assoc 1988-; *Books* The World of Croquet (1987), Play The Game - Croquet (1989); *Recreations* croquet, golf, bell ringing, running, computing; *Clubs* Roehampton; *Style—* Stephen Mulliner, Esq; Witherden, Weydown Rd, Haslemere, Surrey GU27 1DT; Tokai Int Ltd, Mercury Hse, Triton Ct, 14 Finsbury Sq, London EC2 (☎ 01 638 6030)

MULLINS, Alan; s of Philip Mullins, of Herts, and Betty Mullins (d 1981); *b* 29 July 1987; *Educ* Newton House Prep Sch, Christ's Coll Finchley, LSE; *m* 15 Feb 1974, Elizabeth Anne, da of Eric Victor Aylott, of Herts; 2 da (Elizabeth Anne b 1954, Geraldine b 1957); *Career* dir: Baco Aluminium Supply Co Ltd 1963-69, Skymetals Ltd 1979-; *Recreations* 3 day eventing, squash, skiing; *Style—* Alan Mullins, Esq; Beech House, Benington, Herts (☎ 043885 529); Skymetals Ltd, 13 North Orbital Road, Estate, St Albans (☎ 0727 35221, telex 299344, fax 0727 57838)

MULLINS, Edwin Brandt; s of Claud William Mullins (d 1968), and Elizabeth Gwendolen Mullins, *née* Brandt; *b* 14 Sept 1933; *Educ* Midhurst GS, Merton Coll Oxford (BA, MA); *m* 1, 1960, Gillian (d 1982); 1 s (Jason), 2 da (Frances, Selina); m 2, 1984, Anne; *Career* author, tv and radio scriptwriter; TV series incl: 100 Great Paintings, The Great Art Collection, A Love Affair with Nature, Masterworks, Paradise on Earth; *Books* Alfred Wallis (1967), Braque (1968), The Pilgrimage to Santiago (1974), Sirens (1983), The Painted Witch (1985), The Golden Bird (1987), The Lands of the The Sea (1988); *Recreations* art galleries, reading, walking, natural history, watching cricket; *Style—* Edwin Mullins, Esq; 7 Lower Common South, London SW15 1BP

MULLINS, Dr Leonard; CMG (1976); s of Robert Mullins (d 1964) and Eugenie Alice Dyson (d 1960); *b* 21 May 1918; *Educ* Eltham Coll, UCL (BSc, PhD, DSc); *m* 1943, Freda Elaine, *née* Churchouse, da of Frederick Churchouse (d 1945); 2 da (Margaret, Janet); *Career* physicist; dir of res Malaysian Rubber Producers' Res Assoc 1062-83, pres Plastics and Rubber Inst 1981-83; Cdr Malaysian Order of Chivalry JMN (Hon) 1975; CPhys, FPRI, FInstP; *Style—* Dr Leonard Mullins, CMG; 32 Sherrardspark Rd, Welwyn Garden City, Herts (☎ 0707 323 633)

MULLINS, (Sarah Virginia); *née* Samuel; o da of 4 Viscount Bearsted, MC, TD, *qv*; *b* 1947; *m* 1, 1969 (m dis), Duncan John Lloyd Fitzwilliams, yr s of late Charles Collinsplatt Fitzwilliams, TD, JP, DL, of Cilgwyn, Newcastle Emlyn, S Wales; m 2, 1980, Brian Mullins; *Heir* Hon Mrs; *Style—* The Hon Mrs Mullins; c/o The Rt Hon Viscount Bearsted, MC, TD, Farley Hall, Farley Hill, nr Reading, Berks RG7 1UL

MUMFORD, Lady Mary Katharine; *née* Fitzalan Howard; CVO (1982), LVO (1974); da of 16 Duke of Norfolk, KG, GCVO, GBE, TD, PC (d 1975); hp to Lordship of Herries of Terregles; *b* 14 August 1940; *m* 1986, GP Capt Anthony Mumford, CVO, OBE; *Career* lady-in-waiting to HRH Princess Alexandra, the Hon Mrs Angus Ogilvy, GCVO 1964-; *Style—* Lady Mary Mumford, CVO, LVO; 50 Lennox Gardens, London SW1X 0DJ; North Stoke Cottage, North Stoke Arundel, W Sussex

MUMFORD, Rt Rev Peter; *see*: Truro, Bishop of

MUMFORD, William Frederick; CB (1989); s of Frederick Charles Mumford (d 1968), and Hester Leonora, *née* Hunter (d 1973); *b* 1930; *Educ* St Albans Sch, Lincoln Coll Oxford (MA); *m* 1958, Elizabeth Marion, da of Nowell Hall (d 1977); 3 s (Richard b 1963, Timothy b 1965, Simon b 1968), 1 da (Lucy b 1970); *Heir* 1958, Elizabeth Marion, da of Hall Nowell (d 1977); 3 s (Richard b 1963, Timothy b 1965, Simon b 1968), 1 da (Lucy b 1970); *Career* Nat Serv: RA 1949-50; Home Civil Serv (Air Miny) 1953-: asst princ 1953-58, princ 1958-60, first sec UK deleg to NATO (Paris) 1960-65, princ 1965-67, asst sec 1967-73, def secretarial MoD, dep head UK deleg to MBFR Exploratory talks (Vienna) 1973, princ private sec to Sec of State for Def 1973-75, under sec Machinery of Govt Div, CS Dept 1975-76; asst sec-gen for Def Planning and Policy, NATO (Brussels) 1976-80, asst under-sec of state, MoD 1980-; Nat Serv: RA 1949-50; Home Civil Serv (Air Ministry) 1953; assist princ 1953-8, princ 1958-60; first sec UK deleg to NATO (Paris) 1960-65, princ 1965-67; assist sec 1967-63; defence secretarial MoD; dep head UK deleg to MBFR Exploratary talks (Vienna) 1973; princ private sec to Sec of State for Defence 1973-75; under-sec Machinery of Govt Div, Civil Service Dept 1975-76; assist sec-gen for Defence Planning and Policy, NATO (Brussels) 1976-80; assist under-sec of State, MoD 1980-; *Recreations* book collecting, music; *Style—* William Mumford, Esq, CB; c/o Barclays Bank, 366 Strand, London WC2R 0JQ

MUMMERY *see also*: Lockhart-Mummery

MUMMERY, John Frank; s of Frank Stanley Mummery, of Bridge, Kent, and Ruth, *née* Coleman ; *b* 5 Oct 1938; *Educ* Oakleigh Ho, Dover Co GS Pembroke Coll Oxford (MA, BCL); *m* 11 Mar 1967, Elizabeth Anne Lamond, da of Dr Glyn Lackie (d 1985), of Edinburgh; 1 s (David b 1974), 1 da (Joanna b 1968); *Career* Nat Serv Border Regt RAEC 1957-59; called to the Bar Gray's Inn 1964, bencher 1985, rec (1989); Atkinscholar, jt ed Copinger and Skone James on Copyright (12th ed 1980); jr cnsl trey Chancery 1981-, cnsl attorney gen in charity matters 1977-81, memb Legal Advsy Cmmn of General Synod of Church of England (1988-); *Recreations* long walks with family, friends and alone; *Style—* John Mummery, Esq; 5 Cannonbury Grove, London N1 2HP (☎ 01 226 4140), 5 New Square, Lincolns Inn, London WC2A 3RJ (☎ 01 404 0404)

MUNDAM, Eric Alec; s of John Munday (d 1978), of London E17, and Katherine Munday, *née* Jessup (d 1982); *b* 7 Oct 1927; *Educ* Sir George Monoux GS (FCA); *m* 17 Dec 1950, Margaret Elizabeth, da of Ernest Wilson, of London E17; 2 s (Jonathan b 1959, Jeremy b 1962); *Career* war serice; HO Naval Air Mechanic 1946-48; CA; Plessey Co 1957-83, Rosenthal China Ltd 1955-57; cncllr Heath Park Ward London Branch, chm Planning Ctee; dep Mayor 1984, Mayor 1985; *Recreations* bringing up grandson; *Clubs* Romford Conservative; *Style—* Eric A Mundam, Esq; 25 Pettits Lane, Romford, Essex (☎ 0708 20575)

MUNDAY, Norman Sidney; s of Sidney Ernest Munday of Chingford E4, and Phyllis May, *née* Morris (d 1979); *b* 8 July 1935; *Educ* Sir George Monoux GS (AIWSc); *m* 22 Nov 1958, Pauline Lily Elizabeth, da of George Charles Butler (d 1973) of Walthamstow E17; 1 s (Adam b 1963), 1 da (Amanda b 1959); *Career* chm Tower Timber Gp Ltd 1975-, hon chm Timber Res & Devpt Assoc 1986-88; court of assistants Guild of Freemen City of London; chm: Linex Nederland B.V., Turm Timber Agencies Ltd, Gormans Timber & Builders Merchants Ltd, Munply Distributors Ltd, Indo Turm Ltd; memb: Inst of Directors, Assoc Inst of Wood Science (AIWSc), The Greater London Council 1967-73; *Recreations* golf, travel; *Clubs* West Essex Golf (captain 1984), City Livery; *Style—* Norman Munday, Esq; 'Birkdale', Bury Road, Sewardstone Bury, London E4 7QL; Tower Timber Group Ltd, 77-79 Station Road, Chingford, London E4 7BU (☎ 01 524 5285, telex 896 864, car tel 0836 229527)

MUNDAY, Peter James; s of Frederick Lewis James Munday (d 1987), of Esher, Surrey, and Lily Charlotte Rebecca, *née* Fowler; *b* 31 Oct 1938; *m* 1 (m dis 1984), Inger Kristina Fageresjo; 1 da (Lisa Kristina b 1975); m 2, 22 Dec 1984, Linda (Lin) Ann, da of Leslie Breckon, of 102 Wenalt Rd, Cardiff; 1 da (Emma Sophie b 1986); *Career* Nat Serv RCS 1957-59; admitted slr 1968, sr ptnr Mundays 1976- (ptnr 1968-); Notary Public 1975; chm & tstee the Princess Alice Hospice Esher, tstee Esher War Meml Property Fund, Friend of St Georges Church; Freeman City of London, Liveryman Worshipful Co Bakers; memb: Law Soc 1968, Notaries Soc 1975; *Recreations* hockey, squash, cricket; *Clubs* MCC; *Style—* Peter Munday, Esq; Pinewood Lodge, Warren Lane, Oxshott, Surrey (☎ 0372 67272); The Bellbourne, 103 High St, Esher, Surrey (☎ 0372 67272, fax 0372 63782, telex 897742)

MUNDAY, Raymond Geoffrey Todd; s of John Dale Munday (d 1925), of Lancs, and Florence Adelaide, *née* Worthington (d 1980); *b* 15 Mar 1922; *Educ* King George V Sch Southport (BSc), RCS London; *m* 14 Sept 1946, Angela Catherine, da of Horace Clive Burdett (d 1964); 1 s (David b 1947), 2 da (Catherine b 1954, Rosemary b 1958); *Career* aerospace engr Bristol Aeroplane Co 1949; FRAeS 1966; chartered engr 1968; dir Br Aerospace Electronic and Space Systems (Bristol) 1978 (dir and gen mangr space and communications div (Stevenage) 1981, ret 1984), chm UK Industl Space Ctee 1982-84, euro engr 1988, currently conslt and UK rep arianspace; ARCS; *Clubs* Naval; *Style—* Raymond G T Munday, Esq; 53 High St, Ashwell, Herts SG7 5NP (☎ 046274 2760)

MUNDY, Lady Bridget; *née* Elliot-Murray-Kynynmound; da of 5 Earl of Minto (d 1975); *b* 1921; *m* 1, 1944, Lt-Col James Averell Clark, Jr, DFC, USAF; 1 s (Christopher); m 2, 1954 (m dis 1963), Maj Henry Claude Lyon Garnett, CBE; m 3, 1966 (m dis 1970), Maj (Edward) Peter Godfrey Miller Mundy, MC; *Style—* Lady Bridget Mundy

MUNFORD, Dr William Arthur; MBE (1946); s of Ernest Charles Munford (d 1948), of London, and Florence Margaret, *née* Dinneen (d 1959); *b* 27 April 1911; *Educ* Hornsey Co Sch, LSE (BSc, PhD); *m* 25 Aug 1934, Hazel Despard, da of Frank Arthur Wilmer (d 1956), of London; 2 s (Michael b 1935, Jeremy b 1940), 1 da (Alison b 1945); *Career* borough librarian Dover 1934-45, food exec offr and emergency feeding organiser Dover 1939-45, city librarian Cambridge 1945-53, dir gen and librarian Nat Library for the Blind 1954-82 (librarian emeritus 1982-); FLA 1933, hon FLA 1977; *Books* Books for Basic Stock (1939), Penny Rate (1951), William Ewart MP (1960), Edward Edwards (1963), Louis Stanley Jast (with W G Fry 1966), James Duff Brown (1968), A History of the Library Association 1877-1977 (1976), The Incomparable Mac Sir JYW Macalister (with S Godbolt 1983), Who Was Who in British Librarianship 1800-1985 (1987); *Recreations* reading, writing, cycling, rough gardening, serendipity; *Clubs* Nat Liberal; *Style—* Dr William Munford, MBE; 11 Manor Ct, Pinehurst, Grange Rd, Cambridge CB3 9BE (☎ 0223 62962)

MUNIR, (Ashley) Edward; s of The Hon Sir Mehmed Munir, CBE (d 1957), and Vessime, *née* Ziai (d 1979); *b* 14 Feb 1934; *Educ* Brentwood, St John's Coll, Cambridge MA (Cantab); *m* 6 June 1960, Sureyya, da of Shukri Dormen, of Istanbul, Turkey; 1 s (Simon b 24 Oct 1964); *Career* barr Gray's Inn 1956, Crown counsel 1960-64, legal asst Govt Legal Serv 1964, under sec MAFF 1982 (asst slr 1975); *Publications* Perinatal Rights 1983; *Books publications* Perinatal Rights (1983); *Recreations* walking, playing the double-bass, listening to music; *Clubs* United Oxford and Cambridge Univ; *Style—* Edward Munir, Esq; 55 White Hall, London SW1 (☎ 01 270 8369)

MUNN, Sir James; OBE (1976); s of Douglas Herbert Hamilton Munn (d 1973), and Margaret Graham Munn, *née* Dunn (d 1965); *b* 27 July 1920; *Educ* Stirling HS, Glasgow Univ (MA); *m* 1946, Muriel Jean Millar, da of Norman MacLeod Moles (d 1964); 1 da (Elizabeth); *Career* Indian Civil Service 1941-48, dep sec Supply Dept Govt of Bihar; teaching 1948-83; rector: Rutherglen Academy 1966-70, Cathkin HS 1970-83; chm: Consultative Ctee on the Curriculum 1980-87, Manpower Services Ctee for Scotland 1984-88, Manpower Services Cmmn 1987-88, Officier d' Académie (1967); *Style—* Sir James Munn, OBE; 4 Kincath Ave, High Burnside, Glasgow G73 4RP (☎ 041 634 5634);

MUNN, Rear Adm William James; CB (1962), DSO (1941, OBE 1946); s of late Lt-Col R G Munn, CMG; *b* 15 July 1911; *Educ* Britannia RNC Dartmouth; *m* 1940, Susan Astle, da of late St J V H Sperling, of Teviot Bank, Hawick, Roxburghshire; 2 s; *Career* served 1939-45 War, Capt 1951, CO RNC Dartmouth 1956-58, cmdg HMS Gambia 1958, Rear-Adm 1960, COS C-in-C Home Fleet 1961, ret 1963; sec St John Cncl for Suffolk 1973-81; *Recreations* golf; *Clubs* Royal Worlington GC; *Style—* Rear Adm William Munn, CB, DSO, OBE; Beechbrook House, Dalham, Newmarket, Suffolk CB8 8TH (☎ 063 879 425)

MUNRO; *see*: Gun-Munroe

MUNRO, Alan Gordon; CMG (1984); s of Sir Gordon Munro, KCMG, MC (d 1967), and Lilian Muriel Beit (d 1976); *b* 17 August 1935; *Educ* Wellington Coll, Clare Coll Cambridge (MA); *m* 1962, Rosemary Grania Bacon, da of CDR N A Bacon; 2 s (twins), 2 da; *Career* HM Diplomatic Service, consul gen Rio de Janerio 1974-77, FCO head of East African Dept 1977-78, head of Middle East Dept 1979, head of Personnel Operations Dept 1979-81, dir of Defence Sales, Middle East 1981-83; HM ambass Algiers 1984-87, dep under sec of state FCO 1987-; *Recreations* conservation, history; *Clubs* Travellers; *Style—* HE Mr Alan Munro, CMG; c/o Foreign and Commonwealth Office, King Charles St, London SW1 2AH

MUNRO, Dame Alison; DBE (1985), CBE (1964); da of John Donald (d 1927), of Cape Town, SA, and Helen Barrow Wilson (d 1927); *b* 12 Feb 1914; *Educ* Girls HS Wynberg SA, St Paul's Girls Sch London, St Hilda's Coll Oxford (MA); *m* 3 Sept 1939, Alan Lamont Munro (da 1941), s of Prof J W Munro, CBE (d 1968), of Sunningdale, Berks; 1 s (Alan b 1941); *Career* miny of Aircraft Prodn 1942-45, princ Miny of Civil Aviation 1945, asst sec Miny of Tport and Civil Aviation 1949, under sec Miny of Aviation 1958, high mistress St Paul's Girls Sch 1964-74, chm Merton Sutton and Wandsworth AHA 1974-82, chm Chichester Health Authy 1982-88; memb: bd Br Euro Airways 1966-73, Br Library 1973-79, Br Tourist Authy 1973-81; chm: Central T'port Consultative Ctee 1980-85, DHSS Maternity Servs Advsy Ctee 1980-85, Code Monitoring Ctee on Baby Milk 1985-; *Recreations* tennis, scottish county dancing, sailing; *Clubs* Royal Cwlth Soc; *Style—* Dame Alison Munro, DBE, CBE; Harbour Way, Ellanore Lane, W Wittering, W Sussex PO20 8AN (☎ 0243 513274)

MUNRO, Hon Mrs (Diana Mary); *née* Colville; da of 2 Baron Clydesmuir, KT, CB, MBE, TD; *b* 1947; *m* 1973, Christopher I C Munro; 1 s, 1 da; *Career* temp lady in waiting to HRH The Duchess of Gloucester 1980-; *Style—* The Hon Mrs Munro; 26 Pembroke Square, W8 6PB

MUNRO, Dowling Donald; MD, FRCP; s of John Munro (d 1980), of Great Missenden, Bucks, and Etta Mansfield Munro, *née* Cottrell; *b* 29 May 1931; *Educ* Merchant Taylors Sch Crosby, London Univ, Royal Free Hosp Sch of Medicine; *m* 1, 7 Sept 1962, Pamela Grace (d 1977); 2 da (Fiona b 1964, Janet b 1966); m 2, 22 Mar 1980, Isobella Sinclair, da of William Thomas Wales (d 1971) of Abergavenny, Monmouth; *Career* Capt RAMC Cyprus; conslt Dermatologist: St Bartholomews Hosp London, and Harley Street 1968, Royal Masonic Hosp; civilian conslt dermatologist Royal Navy 1981, United States Public health res fell in Dermatology, Western Reserve Univ Cleveland Ohio 1964; *Books* publication in medical journals including British Journal of Dermatology, editor "Steroids and the Skin" Blackwell (1976); *Recreations* apiaculture, horticulture, ornithology; *Clubs* Royal Society of Medicine; *Style—* Dr Dowling D Munro, MD, FRCP; Old Ley, Burtons Lane, Chalfont St Giles, Bucks HP8 4BQ (☎ 024 04 2189); 99 Harley Street, London W1N 1DF; St Bartholomews Hospital, London EC1

MUNRO, Hon Mrs (Elizabeth Mary); *née* Bannerman; yr da of Baron Bannerman of Kildonan, OBE (Life Peer, who d 19690); *b* 8 Sept 1938; *m* 1, 1960 (m dis 1971), Daniel Shade Munro; m 2, 1972 (m dis 1980), Ian Buchanan Anderson; *Style—* Hon Mrs Munro; The Braes, Uplawmoor, Renfrewshire, Scotland

MUNRO, Hugh Murray; s of Hugh Munro, of Aberdeen, and Alice Wilson, *née* Murray (d 1985); *b* 30 Dec 1946; *Educ* Aberdeen GS, Strathclyde Univ (BA), Glasgow Univ (MSc); *m* 9 Aug 1974, Valerie Morag Munro, da of Stuart Ingram (d 1984), of Glasgow; 1 s (Craig), 1 da (Lorna); *Career* ptnr Arthur Anderson and Co Glasgow 1981-87 (joined 1968), managing ptnr Arthur Young Aberdeen 1987-; MICAS; *Recreations* skiing, gardening; *Clubs* Aberdeen Petroleum, FP Club, Aberdeen Rotary; *Style—* Hugh Munro, Esq; The White House, 285 N Deeside Rd, Milltimber, Aberdeen (☎ 0224 732165); Ardoch Lodge, Braes of Taymouta, Kenmore, Perthshire (☎ 08873 204); Arthur Young, 50 Huntly St, Aberdeen (☎ 0224 640033, fax 0224 630753, telex 739458)

MUNRO, Ian Arthur Hoyle; s of Gordon Alexander Munro (d 1984), of Bradford, Yorks, and Muriel Rebecca, *née* Hoyle (d 1938); *b* 5 Nov 1923; *Educ* Huddersfield Coll, Royal Lancaster GS, Paston Sch North Walsham, Royal Liberty Sch Romford, Univ of London Guy's Hosp Med Sch (MB, BS); *m* 4 Aug 1948, Dr Olive Isabel, da of Ernest John Jackson (d 1946); 3 s (Andrew b 1950, Robert b 1960, John b 1965), 2 da (Jane b 1952, Deborah b 1956); *Career* RAMC 1947-50, radiologist Br Mil Hosp Klagenfurt BTA; editorial staff The Lancet 1951- (ed 1976-88); FRCP 1984; *Recreations* cricket, crosswords; *Clubs* Athenaeum, Yorks CCC; *Style—* Ian Munro, Esq; Oakwood, Bayley's Hill, Sevenoaks, Kent TN14 6HS (☎ 0732 454993)

MUNRO, Sir Ian Talbot; 15 Bt (NS 1634), of Foulis-Obsdale, Ross-shire; s of Robert Hector Munro and first cousin once removed of Sir Arthur Herman Munro, 14 Bt (d 1972); *b* 18 Dec 1929; *Educ* Bradfield Sch Berks; *Heir* unc, Malcolm Munro; *Career* marine consultant; *Style—* Sir Ian Munro, Bt; 38 Clarence Gate Gdns, London NW1

MUNRO, John Bennet Lorimer; CB (1959), CMG (1953); s of Rev James Lorimer Munro, OBE (d 1963), and Annie Irving, *née* Stenhouse (d 1948); *b* 20 May 1905; *Educ* The Edinburgh Academy, Edinburgh Univ, Oxford Univ (MA); *m* 2, 1965, Margaret, da of John Deacey, of Blackfort House Foxford C Mayo; 3 s from first m (Bruce, John, Alan); *Career* Indian Civil Service 1928-39; Treasy, Miny of Supply, Bd of Trade; idc FO Export Credits 1939-65; *Style—* John Munro Esq, CB, CMG; 77 Shirley Drive, Hove, Sussex BN3 6UE

MUNRO, Malcolm; s of Charles Munro, FAA, FLAA (d 1959); h to Btcy of n Sir Ian Talbot Munro, 15 Bt; *b* 24 Feb 1901; *m* 1931, Constance, da of late William Carter; 1 da; *Style—* Malcolm Munro, Esq; Whitegates, Rock, Wadebridge, Cornwall (☎ 020 886 3360)

MUNRO, (David) Michael; s of Charles Rowcliffe Munro, and Moira Rennie, *née* Ainslie; *b* 3 Nov 1944; *Educ* Trinity Coll Glenalmond; *m* 22 Sept 1973, Jeanine (Tina) Beverley, da of Lt-Col James Linsday-Stewart, of Cuesta De Reina, Jesus Pobre, Pro Alicante, Spain; 3 da (Alexandra b 1977, Antonia b 1982, Annabel b 1987); *Career* CA 1968; analyst Kleinwort Benson 1968-70, ptnr Chiene & Tait CA 1970-83, jt md Quayle Munro Ltd 1983; dir Shanks & McEwan Gp plc, The Life Assoc of Scotland

Ltd; *Recreations* fishing, shooting; *Clubs* New (Edinburgh); *Style*— Michael Munro, Esq; Cockairnie Ho, Aberdour, Fife KY3 0RZ (☎ 0383 860 363); 42 Charlotte Sq, Edinburgh EH2 4HQ (☎ 031 226 4421, fax 031 225 3391, telex 72244)

MUNRO, Robert Malcolm; s of late Malcolm William Munro, of Chelmsford, and Sheila Mary Munro, *née* Lamont (d Jan 1975); *b* 16 May 1937; *Educ* Trinity, Mid-Essex Tech Coll, Manchester Business Sch; *m* 2 March 1961, Irene Mavis, da of William David Percy, of Chelmsford; 2 s (Nigel Robert b 1964, Philip Spencer b 1966); *Career* dir Nordic Bank Ltd 1980-83), md Williams & Clyns Leasing Co Ltd, exec dir The Union Discount Co of London plc (1972-80); *Recreations* tennis, golf, music, theatre; *Style*— Robert Munro, Esq; 39 Cornhill, London EC3 (☎ 01 623 1020)

MUNRO OF FOULIS, Capt Patrick; TD; assumed by decree of Lyon Court 1937 the surname and arms of Munro of Foulis and recognised as Chief of Clan Munro, in succession to his gf, Sir Hector Munro of Foulis, 11 Bt (d 1935); s of Lt-Col Cecil Hugh Orby Gascoigne, DSO (d 1929) and Eva Marion Munro (d 1976), eldest da of Sir Hector Munro of Foulis, 11 Bt; *b* 1912; *Educ* Imperial Serv Coll, RMC; *m* 1946, Eleanor Mary, da of Capt the Hon William French (3 s of 4 Lord De Freyne (d 1974), and Victoria Louise, *née* Bellasis, *qv*; 3 s, 1 da; *Heir* Hector Munro, Younger of Foulis; *Career* serv WWII: (POW), Capt Seaforth Highlanders; DL Ross and Cromarty (Vice-Lt 1969), Hon Sheriff 1973; *Clubs* Puffin's (Edinburgh), MCC; *Style*— Capt Patrick Munro of Foulis; Foulis Castle, Evanton, Ross-shire

MUNRO OF LINDERTIS, Sir Alasdair Thomas Ian; 6 Bt (UK 1825), of Lindertis, Angus; s of Sir (Thomas) Torquil Alphonso Munro of Lindertis, 5 Bt, JP (d 1985) and his 1 w, Beatrice Maude (d 1974), da of Robert Sanderson Whitaker, of Villa Sofia, Palermo; *b* 6 July 1927; *Educ* Landon Sch USA, Georgetown Univ Washington, Pennsylvania Univ, IMEDE Lausanne Switzerland; *m* 1954, Marguerite Lillian, da of late Franklin R Loy, of Dayton, Ohio, USA; 1 s, 1 da (Karen Fiona b 1956); m 2, 1980, Robert David MacMichael, Jr; *Heir* s, Keith Gordon Munro b 1959; *Style*— Sir Alasdair Munro of Lindertis, Bt; River Ridge, Box 34E, Waitsfield, Vermont 05673, USA; Ruthven Mill, Meigle, Perthshire

MUNRO-FERGUSON OF RAITH AND NOVAR, Arthur Brocklehurst Luttrell; assumed name Munro-Ferguson and recognised by the Lord Lyon in the designation 'Munro-Ferguson of Raith and Novar' 1951; s of Ralph Paganel Luttrell (d 1978), and Alice, *née* Brocklehurst (d 1958); his father's mother was sis of 1 and last Viscount Novar of Raith (d 1934); *b* 10 Nov 1921; *Educ* Stowe, Trinity Coll Cambridge (BA), Edinburgh Univ, Aberdeen Univ (BSc); *m* 1, 1952 (m dis 1980), Jane Euphemia Beatrice, da of Lewis Reynolds (d 1940), of Natal; 2 s, 2 da; m 2, Mary Griselda, da of William Robertson (d 1935), and formerly w of John Chubb; *Career* served WWII in Far East, Royal Corps of Signals, Capt; chm Scottish Woodland Owners and Timber Growers 1977-80; chm: Highland Deephaven Ltd, Moray Firth Salmon Fisheries Co Ltd; *Clubs* Army and Navy, New (Edinburgh); *Style*— Arthur Munro-Ferguson of Raith and Novar; Novar, Evanton, Ross-shire IV16 9XL (☎ 0349 830284); Novar Estates Office, Evanton IV16 9XL (☎ 0349 830208)

MUNROW, Roger Davis; s of William Davis Munrow, CBE (d 1986), former chief inspector of Audit Ministry of Housing & Local Government, and Constance Caroline *née* Moorcroft (d 1977); *b* 20 Mar 1929; *Educ* Bryanston, Oriel Coll Oxford (MA); *m* 5 Oct 1957, Marie Jane, da of Jack Edward Beresford (d 1982); 3 da (Julia b 1958, Virgina b 1962, Kate b 1965); *Career* chief master The Supreme Court (Chamery Division) 1986 (master 1985-86), formerly under-sec (legal) Treasury slrs Dept 1981-86; admitted as a slr 1956; entered Treasury slr Dept 1959; *Recreations* swimming; *Style*— Roger Munrow, Esq; Royal Court of Justice, Strand WC2

MUNSON, Alma Russell; s of Russell Oliver Munson, of Emdon, Straight Rd, Boxted, Colchester, Essex, and Gladys Mary, *née* Clarke; *b* 15 May 1934; *Educ* NE Essex Tech Coll, Colchester (ACA); *Career* Nat serv 1952; articled clerk Evans Peirson and Co 1956-62, accountant in charge and audit mangr Deloitte Haskins and Sells 1962-71, Guardian Royal Exchange: compliance offr 1985-88 (internal audit mangr 1971-85), chief accountant Guardian Assurance plc 1988-; memb indust membs ctee Inst of Chartered Accountants; memb london Bd of Princes Youth Business Tst; Freeman City of London 1980, Liveryman Worshipful Co of Chartered Accountants 1980; FCA 1962, FIIA 1986; *Recreations* opera, music, theatre; *Style*— Alma Munson, Esq; 8 Devonshire Mews West, London W1; 98 Mile End Rd, Colchester, Essex (☎ 01 486 7023); Guardian Royal Exchange, Royal Exchange, London EC3V 3LS (☎ 01 283 7101, telex 883232)

MUNSTER, Countess of; (Dorothy) Alexa; da of Lt-Col E B Maxwell, OBE, MC (d 1973); *b* 22 Dec 1924; *Educ* St Leonard's Sch, Edinburgh Univ (MusBac); *m* 1979, as his 3 w, Viscount Fitz-Clarence, now 7 Earl of Munster, *qv*; *Career* pianist, harpsichordist and organist; coach and repetiteur for BBC Radio and TV, ITV and LWT 1952-78; korrepetitorin Zürich Opera House 1965-66; lectr in harpsichord, piano and Baroque workshop Royal Scottish Academy of Music and Drama 1978-84; organist and choirmaster: Neilston Parish Church 1982-83, St John's Church Paisley 1983-4, St John's UR Church Northwood 1984-87/Guildford UR Church 1987, Ifield Parish Church 1988- lectr and coach at Institutes of Adult Education and freelance pianist and harpsichordist 1984-; LRAM, ARCO; *Recreations* fishing, skiing; *Style*— The Rt Hon the Countess of Munster; 78 Busey Hall Rd, Bushey, Herts WD2 2EQ

MUNSTER, 7 Earl of (UK 1831); Anthony Charles Fitz-Clarence; also Viscount FitzClarence and Baron Tewkesbury (both UK 1831); s of 6 Earl of Munster (d 1983), and his 1 w, Monica Sheila Grayson, da of Lt-Col Sir Mulleneux Grayson, KBE, 1 Bt (she d 1958, having obtained a divorce 1930); gggs of King William IV by Mrs Jordan, the actress and singer who had ten children by him; *b* 21 Mar 1926; *Educ* St Edward's Sch Oxford; *m* 1, 1949 (m dis 1966), Louise Marguerite Diana, da of Louis Delvigne of Liege, Belgium; 2 da; m 2, 1966 (m dis 1979), Mrs Pamela Margaret Hyde, da of Arthur Spooner; 1 da; m 3, 1979, Alexa, *qv*; *Heir* none; *Career* served RN 1942-46; graphic designer 1950-57, Daily Mirror Newspapers 1957-66, IPC Newspaper Div (SUN) 1966-69, freelance 1971-79), stained glass conservator for the Burrell Museum 1979-83, conservator with the Chapel (stained glass) Studio 1983-; FRSA 1987; *Style*— The Rt Hon the Earl of Munster; Mulberry Cottage, Park Farm, Haxted Rd, Lingfield, Surrey RH7 6DE

MUNSTER, Vivian, Countess of; Vivian; *née* Schofield; da of late Benjamin Schofield, JP, of Greenroyde, Rochdale, Lancs, step da of late Judge A J Chotzuer (MP Upton); *Educ* Roedean and Paris; *m* 1939, as his 2 w, 6 Earl of Munster (d 1983); *Heir* Antony Charles, 7 Earl of Munster (b 1926); *Recreations* swimming, walking, bridge; *Clubs* Hurlingham; *Style*— The Rt Hon Vivian, Countess of Munster; 1 Arundel Court, Jubilee Place, London SW3 3TJ

MURAKAMI, Takashi; *b* 28 Mar 1937; *Educ* Keio Univ Tokyo (BA), Univ of California Berkeley (MBA); *m* 26 June 1965, Masako; 1 s (Gen b 1971), 2 da (Junko b 1966, Akiko b 1968); *Career* Nikko Securities Co Ltd 1960-86, md Nikko Capital Management UK Ltd 1987-; *Recreations* golf, baseball; *Style*— Takashi Murakami, Esq; Nikko Capital Management Ltd, 17 Godliman St, London EC4V 5BD (☎ 01 248 0592, fax 01 236 1531, telex 885879 NICAM G)

MURANKA, Tony; s of Albert Muranka, of 62 Oakleigh Avenue, Clayton, Bradford, West Yorkshire, and Freda Joyce, *née* Fieldhouse; *b* 21 May 1952; *Educ* Grange GS, Bradford Coll of Art (Dip Art); *Career* dir and head of art Deighton & Mullen Ltd 1987-; Designers and Art Directors Association silver award 1978, 1984, 1987; Awards: Campaign Press (silver) 1986, Campaign Poster (silver) 1981, Creative Circle Honours (golds) 1984, 1985 (2), 1986 (2), 1987, 1988 (2), 1989, British Television (silver) 1985; *Recreations* Enduro competitor, sleeping; *Style*— Tony Muranka, Esq; 23 Clarence Rd, Kew, Richmond, Surrey TW9 3NL (☎ 01 948 7443); Deighton & Mullen Ltd, 41 Great Pulteney St, London W1R 3DE (☎ 01 434 0040, fax: 01 439 1590)

MURDEN, Michael John; s of Jack Murden (d 1985) and Leslie *née* Price; *b* 2 Dec 1943; *Educ* Bolton Sch, Univ of Newcastle Upon Tyne (BSc); *m* 25 July 1973, Mary Angela, da of Felix Sullivan (d 1984) of Jarrow; 3 s (Philip Daniel b 22 Aug 1975, Christopher James b 10 Feb 1978, Simon Charles b 12 Nov 1979); *Career* prodn mangr: Vickers Ltd 1967-69 (student apprentice 1962-66), Swan Hunter Shipbuilders Ltd 1969-72; md Cammell Laird Shipbldg Ltd 1984-88 (devpt mangr 1973-74, shipbldg gen mangr 1974-76, prodn dir 1976-82, dep md 1982-84); md Northumbrian Water 1989-, non exec dir Vickers Shipbldg & Engrg 1985; dir: Merseyside C of C, (dep chm) Wirral C of C, Cavendish Enterprises Ltd, In Business Ltd; memb NW cncl CBI, govr Wirral Met Coll, chm Wirral Phoenix Initiative; C Eng, MRINA; *Recreations* music, sailing, swimming; *Style*— Michael Murden, Esq; 1 Ryecroft Road, Heswall, Merseyside, L60 1XB (☎ 051 342 8224); Northumbrian Water, Northumbrian House, Regent Centre, Gosforth, Newcastle Upon Tyne NE3 3PX (☎ 091 284 3151)

MURDOCH, Lady; Barbara Marshall; da of late James Cameron; *m* 1962, as his 2 w, Prof Sir Walter Murdoch, KCMG, CBE (d 1970); *Style*— Lady Murdoch; Blithedale, S Perth, W Australia

MURDOCH, Dame Elisabeth Joy; DBE (1963), CBE (1961); da of Rupert Greene and Marie, *née* de Lancey Forth; *b* 1909; *m* 1928, Sir Keith Arthur Murdoch (d 1952, chm and md The Herald and Weekly Times, dir and fndr Aust Newsprint Mills Pty Ltd, dir-gen of Information for C'wlth of Australia); 1 s, 3 da; *Career* pres Royal Children's Hosp Melbourne 1954-65, tstee Nat Gallery Vic 1968-76; Hon LLD Melbourne 1982; *Style*— Dame Elisabeth Murdoch, DBE, CBE; Cruden Farm, Langwarrin, Vic 3910, Australia

MURDOCH, Gordon Stuart; s of Ian William Murdoch (d 1978), and Margaret Henderson McLaren, *née* Scott (d 1974); *b* 7 June 1947; *Educ* Falkirk HS, Sidney Sussex Coll Cambridge (MA, LLB); *m* 27 Dec 1976, Sally Kay, da of Henry Cummings, of Ludlow, Shropshire; 2 s (Thomas b 1979, Alexander b 1982); *Career* barr Inner Temple 1970; *Style*— Gordon Murdoch, Esq; 4 Paper Bldgs, Temple, London EC4Y 7EX (☎ 01 583 0816, fax 01 353 4979)

MURDOCH, Dame Iris; DBE (1987), CBE (1976); da of Wills John Hughes Murdoch, and Irene Alice Richardson; *b* 1919; *Educ* Froebel Educnl Inst London, Badminton Sch Bristol, Somerville Coll Oxford (hon fell 1977); *m* 1956, Prof John Oliver Bayley, Warton Prof of English Lit and fell St Catherine's Coll Oxford; *Career* lectr Royal Coll of Art 1964-67: fell and tutor St Anne's Coll Oxford 1948-63, hon fell 1963-; Hon DLitt Oxon 1987; philosopher; author; *Books* Sartre, Romantic Rationalist (1953), Under the Net (1954), The Flight from the Enchanter (1955), The Sandcastle (1957), The Bell (1958), A Severed Head (1961, play 1963), An Unofficial Rose (1962), The Unicorn (1963), The Italian Girl (1964, play 1967), The Red and the Green (1965), The Time of the Angels (1966), The Nice and The Good (1968), Bruno's Dream (1969), A Fairly Honourable Defeat (1970), The Sovereignty of Good (1970), An Accidental Man (1971), The Black Prince (1973, James Tait Black Memorial Prize), A Word Child (1975), Henry and Cato (1976), The Fire and the Sun (1977), The Sea, the Sea (1978, Booker Prize 1978), Nuns and Soldiers (1980); *Plays* The Servants and the Snow (1970), The Three Arrows (1972), Art and Eros (1980); *Poems* A Year of Birds (1978), The Philospher's Pupil (1983), The Good Apprentice (1985), Acastos (1985), The Book and the Brotherhood (1987); *Style*— Dame Iris Murdoch, DBE

MURDOCH, Richard Bernard; s of Bernard Murdoch (d 1933), of Tunbridge Wells, and Amy Florence, *née* Scott (d 1956); mother's f Archdeacon A T Scott; *b* 6 April 1907; *Educ* Charterhouse, Pembroke Coll Cambridge; *m* 1932, Peggy Robinson, da of William Rawlings; 1 s (Timothy), 2 da (Belinda, Jane); *Career* Sqdn Ldr RAF; actor and radio, TV; *Recreations* golf; *Clubs* RAC, Walton Heath GC, Stage Golfing Soc; *Style*— Richard Murdoch, Esq; 2 Priory Close, Harrow Rd West, Dorking, Surrey RH4 3BG (☎ Dorking 886596)

MURDOCH, Robert Clive; s of Lt-Col Clive Murdoch, DSO (d 1944), and Janet Homewood, *née* Motion (d 1963); *b* 7 Mar 1922; *Educ* Wellington Coll; *m* 1, 1951 (m dis 1976), Mary Anne, da of late Capt A K MacEwan; 3 da (Miranda Jane b 1954, Serena Janet b 1957, Camilla Anne b 1958); m 2, Susan Mary, da of late Erick Graham Mattingley; *Career* WWII Capt Grenadier Gds, served N Africa, Italy 1942-46; farmer 1947-; dir Hops Mktg Bd 1955-82, Checkers and Checkers Growers Ltd 1957- (sometime vice-chm); *Recreations* farming, all country pursuits; *Clubs* Farmers; *Style*— Robert C Murdoch, Esq; Wester Hill, Linton, Maidstone, Kent ME17 4BT (☎ 0622 7452277); Murdoch & Allfrey Ltd, Clockhouse, Linton, Maidstone, Kent (☎ 0622 743173)

MURDOCH, Robert Henry; MBE (1944); s of George Murdoch (d 1969), of Denburn, Newport on Tay, Fife, and Emma Elizabeth, *née* Shewring (d 1984); *b* 3 July 1914; *Educ* Univ Coll Sch; *m* 28 June 1940, Jill, da of James Malcolm Kinkaid (d 1954), of Monkseaton, Northumberland; 1 s (David b 1942), 2 da (Janet b 1944, Susan b 1948); *Career* 2 Lt RE (SR) 1938, Capt RE BEF 1939-40, Maj HQ Southern Cmd 1941, Lt-Col AQMG (M) 21 Army Gp HQ 1944; traffic apprentice LNER 1932; NCB: tport mangr Scottish div 1947, mktg mangr Lothians area 1960, commercial mangr Scottish regn 1967, mktg dir Scotland 1973-78; memb: Tport Users Consultative Ctee Scotland 1948-54, Clean Air Cncl Scotland 1973-78; chm: branch area ctee Scotland BIM 1972-74 (chm Edinburgh and Borders branch 1969-72), Mgmnt Assoc SE Scotland 1976; pres Rotary Club Edinburgh 1978-79, govr dist 102 Rotary Int 1985-86; FBIM;

Recreations golf, gardening; *Style*— Robert Murdoch, Esq, MBE; 3 Westerdunes Ct, North Berwick, East Lothian (☎ 0620 3331)

MURDOCH, (Keith) Rupert; AC (1984); only s of Sir Keith Murdoch, sometime chm & md The Herald & Weekly Times Ltd, *Melbourne Herald*, *Sun-News Pictorial*, *Weekly Times* (d 1952) by his w Dame Elisabeth Murdoch, DBE (herself da of Rupert Greene by his w Marie, *née* de Lancey Forth), president of the Royal Children's Hospital Melbourne; *b* 11 Mar 1931; *Educ* Geelong GS, Worcester Coll Oxford (MA); *m* 1, 1956 (m dis); 1 da (Pru); m 2, 1967, Anna Maria, da of J Torv, of Scotland; 2 s (Lachlan, James), 1 da (Elisabeth); *Career* hon fellow Worcester Coll Oxford 1982-; publisher; gp chief exec News Ltd Australia; chm and chief exec News International (UK), chm and pres News America Publishing Inc, publisher and editor New York Post, jt chm Ansett Transport Industries 1982- (jt ch exec and md 1979-82); dir: William Collins 1981-, United Telecasters Sydney; UK newspapers owned include The Sun and The Times; proprietor Sun-Times (Chicago) 1983-; co-owner with Robert Stigwood of R & R Film Productions Sydney; *Style*— Rupert Murdoch Esq, AC; 2 Holt St, Sydney, NSW 2000, Australia; Cavan, Yass, NSW, Australia; c/o New York Post, 210 South Street, New York City, NY 10002, USA; 30 Bouverie St, London EC4

MURDOCK, Christopher; s of Dr Charles Rutherford Murdock MD (d 1968), and Eirene Noland Murdock; *b* 15 August 1946; *Educ* Brackenber House Belfast, Portora Royal Sch Enniskillen; *m* 31 Jan 1970, Dorothy Rosemary Richardson; 2 s ((Chrisopher) Jeremy b 1973, Antony John b 1975), 1 da (Rosemary Sarah) Alexandra b 1980); *Career* joined NHS 1965, asst dist admin offr Armagh and Dungannon dist 1974-75, dist personnel offr S Belfast Dist 1975-76, asst dist admin offr E Belfast and Castlereagh Dist 1976-84; gp admin Purdysburn Unit of Mgmnt 1984-; *Recreations* photography, supporting children's equestrian interests, currently hon tres of E Down Foxhounds; *Style*— Christopher Murdock, Esq; Eastern Health and Social Services Board, c/o Purdysburn Hospital, Saintfield Road, Belfast BT8 8BH (☎ 0232 401333)

MURERWA, Dr Herbert Muchemwa; s of Gamanya Murerwa, of Chinyika Sch, Goromonzi, Zimbabwe; *b* 31 May 1941; *Educ* Mutare Teachers Coll, George Williams Coll Illinois (BA), Harvard Univ (Ed M, Ed D); *m* 23 Aug 1969, Ruth Chipo, da of Rev Elijah Dhliwayo; 1 s (Simbarashe b 1982), 4 da (Mudiwa b 1969, Gamu b 1971, Tapiwa b 1975, Danai b 1980); *Career* programme dir Zimbabwe YMCA 1964-69, coll lectr Salem Coll Mass USA 1973-75, econ affrs offr UN 1979-80, permanent sec Zimbabwe Govt 1980-84, Zimbabwe high cmmr to the UK 1984-; *Recreations* reading, tennis, jogging; *Clubs* Travellers'; *Style*— HE Dr Herbert Murerwa; 26 Denewood Rd, London N6 (☎ 01 836 7755); Zimbabwe House, 429 Strand, London WC2 0SA (☎ 01 836 7755)

MURISON, Robert Fraser; OBE (1978), QPM (1971), DL (Fife 1975); s of William Murison (d 1937); *b* 15 Feb 1919; *Educ* Dunfermline HS, Glasgow Univ; *m* 1948, Isobel Stirrat, *née* Tennent; 2 da; *Career* serv WWII Black Watch and 8 Gurkha Rifles 1942-46, Capt India and Sumatra; police offr Lanarkshire Constabulary 1937-42 and 1946-63, dep cmdt Scottish Police Coll 1963-65; chief constable Fife 1965-84; N Zone Home Def Police Cdr Designate 1974-84; *Recreations* gardening, amateur radio; *Style*— Robert F Murison, Esq, OBE, QPM, DL; 2 Abbots Walk, Kirkcaldy, Fife KY2 5NL (☎ 0592 262436)

MURLEY, Sir Reginald Sydney; KBE (1979), TD (1948); s of Sydney Herbert Murley (d 1968), of New York, and Beatrice Maud, *née* Baylis (d 1951); *b* 2 July 1916; *Educ* Dulwich, St Bartholomew's Hosp, Univ of London; *m* 1 Feb 1947, Daphne, da of Ralph Eddowes Garrod (d 1964); 3 s (David Peter b 1949, Gavin Michael b 1951, Anthony Jonathan b 1957), 3 da (Susan Elizabeth Butler (step da) b 1942, Jennifer Jane b 1948, Hilary Daphne b 1953); *Career* RAMC, WWII, Field Units, Surgn to No.1 and 2 Maxillofacial Surgical Units; No.53 Field Surgical Unit, Maj 1939-45, TA Middle E, E Africa, Italy, NW Europe; anatomy demonstrator 1946; surgical chief asst St Bartholomews 1946-54; conslt surgeon St Albans Hosp 1947-80; Royal Northern Hosp 1952-80; Mackenzie Mackinnon Res fell RCP and RCS & Cattlin, Res fell 1950-51; pres: RCS 1977-80, Hunterian Soc 1970, Hunterian Orator 1978, Med Soc London 1982, Harveian Soc 1983, John Charnley Tst 1983-; hon fell: RACS, RCS in Ireland 1980-, Coll of Surgeons SA; hon memb: Italian Surgical Soc 1979, Hon FDS, RCS Eng 1981, Polish Surgical Soc 1983, Br Assoc of Plastic Surgns 1983-, Br Assoc of Clinical Anatomists 1983-, Reding Pathological Soc 1985-; vice-pres Int Soc of Surgery 1985-86, Hunterian Prof RCS 1950; orator 1981 & Bradshaw lectr 1981, Syme Orator, RACS 1979, pres Fellowship for Freedom in Med 1972-86, cncl Freedom Assoc 1982-, Patron Jagiellonian Tst, cncl of Health Unit of Instit Economic Affairs; cncl Social Affairs Unit; Patron of Youth and Family concern 1984; *publications*: med and surgical papers on Thyroid, Breast, Vascular, and Salivary Diseases; contributions to surgical textsbooks; papers on medical economics, and surgery; MRCS, FRCS 1946, LRCP; *Recreations* reading, history & economics, gardening, music; *Clubs* Royal Automobile; *Style*— Sir Reginald Murley, KBE, TD; Cubden Hill House, 63 Cobden Hill, Radlett, Herts WD7 7JN; Consulting Suite, Wellington Hospital, Wellington Place NW8 9LE

MURPHY, Brian Arthur; s of Arthur Albert Murphy (d 1982), and Constance Margaret, *née* Young; *b* 3 May 1951; *Educ* Emanuel Sch London, Keble Coll Oxford (BA); *m* 30 April 1977, Jane, da of John Champion Stevenson, of Atherstone, Warkwicks; 1 s (Giles b 10 March 1980), 1 da (Leila b 14 June 1982); *Career* slr, dep head legal servs Allied Lyons plc 1982; chm Danesborough Branch of Milton Keynes Cons Assoc; Freeman City of London, Liveryman Worshipful Co of Founders; memb Law Soc 1976; *Clubs* Ski Club of GB; *Style*— Brian Murphy, Esq; The Old Rectory, Little Brickhill, Bucks MK17 9NA (☎ 01 253 9911, fax 01 251 8041)

MURPHY, Christopher Philip Yorke; s of Philip John Murphy, and Dorothy Betty Murphy; *b* 20 April 1947; *Educ* Devonport HS, Queen's Coll Oxford (MA); *m* 1969, Sandra Gillian, da of William John Ashton; *Career* former associate dir D'Arcy MacManus & Masius; pres Oxford Univ Cons Assoc 1967; held number of Cons Party Offs 1968-72; parish cncllr Windlesham Surrey 1972-76; contested (C) Bethnal Green and Bow Feb and Oct 1974, MP (C) Welwyn Hatfield 1979-87; memb select ctee on Statutory Instruments 1980- (its representative on Cwlth Delegated Legislation Ctee 1980-87); vice-chm: Cons Parly Urban and New Town Affairs Ctee 1980-, Cons Parly Arts and Heritage Ctee 1981-86; UK delegate to Cncl of Europe/WEU 1983-; vice-pres: C of E Artistic Heritage Cmmn 1984-87, C of E Youth and Drugs Cmmn 1986-; memb Nat Ctee for 900 Anniv of Domesday Book 1986; hon associate Cncl of Europe; life memb Cwlth Parly Assoc; freeman City of London; hon Citizen of Cork; writer, lectr and conslt; Hon Sec La Sociétè Serequioise; FRSA; *Recreations* arts, heritage, travel, conservation, politics, walking, horticulture; *Clubs* Oxford Union, La Sociétè Guermesiaise; *Style*— Hon Christopher Murphy; Rondellerie Cottage, Sark, CI

MURPHY, Gerald James; JP; s of James Murphy (d 1956), and Agnes Murphy, *née* Youles; *b* 28 June 1989; *Educ* Finchley GS, The Architectural Association Sch of Architecture (AADipl); *Career* fndr ptnr architectural practice Gerald Murphy & Ptnrs 1962; after amalgamation sr ptnr Gerald Murphy Burles Newton & Ptnrs; works of note inc: Brentwood Cathedral, New Docklands Church, conversion Wembley Stadium for Pope's visit; memb: Borough of Haringey Dist Health Authy 1981-; cons parly candidate 1973-78, chm London N Euro Constituency Cncl 1978-84, former int pres Serra Int, vice-chm Issues Ctee of the Catholic Union of GB; Freeman City of London; KCSG, kt Cdr with Star of the Religious Order of the Holy Sepulchre of Jerusalem; ARIBA, ACIArb; *Recreations* filming, painting; *Style*— Gerald J Murphy, JP; 8 Highgate High St, London N6 5JL (☎ 01 341 1277); 4 Highgate High St, London N6 5JL (☎ 01 341 1307, fax 01 341 0851)

MURPHY, Harry Maughan; s of Harry Murphy (d 1961), of Grimsby, Lincolnshire, and Mary Ellen, *née* Donald (d 1959); *b* 7 June 1924; *Educ* Humberstone Fndn Sch Clee Lincs, Durham Univ, Cambridge Univ, London Univ (BSc); *m* 1, 20 Jan 1947 (m dis), Margaret Jean, da of James Edward Simpson (d 1949), of Middleton, Lancs; m 2 Minnie, *née* Fisher; 1 s (Harry Edward b 1962), 1 da (Charlotte Emma b 1964); *Career* RAF 1942-47, Pilot 1943, Russian interpreter 1946; with The APV Co (Eastern Euro Sales) 1950-56; Colonial Serv: lab offr employment and trg offr Dept of Lab and Mines N Rhodesia Govt 1956-66; lectr Grimsby Coll of Technol 1966-68, cmmr of lab Gilbert and Ellice Islands 1968-73, dep dir of lab industl relations offr Gibraltar Govt 1973-83, industl relations conslt; chm Gibraltar Clay Pigeon Shooting Assoc, cncllr Crawley Sussex 1955, memb legislative assembley and exec cncl Gilbert and Ellice Islands Colony; *Recreations* shooting; *Clubs* Grimsby Cons, Gibraltar Clay Pigeon Shooting, Casino Calpe Gibraltar; *Style*— Harry Murphy, Esq; 9 Prince of Wales Battery, Gibraltar (☎ Gibraltar 71812); P O Box 726, Gibraltar

MURPHY, Rev John Gervase (Gerry) Maurice Walker; LVO (1987); s of Capt William Stafford Murphy, MC (d 1951), of Bangor NI, and Yvonne Iris Murphy, *née* Wilson (d 1971); *b* 20 August 1926; *Educ* Methodist Coll Belfast, Dublin Univ (BA, MA); *m* 1957, Joy Hilda Miriam, da of Canon T L Livermore, MA, of Heacham; 5 da (Maryan, Desiree, Nicola, Geraldine, Felicity); *Career* Royal Army Chaplains Dept 1955-77; Sr Chaplain: Br Cwlth Bde 1964-67, RMA Sandhurst 1971-73; Asst Chaplain Germany: BAOR 1973-75, SEAT Dist 1975-77, bishop's chaplain to Holiday Makers Norwich Diocese, rural dean: Blofield 1978-79, Heacham and Rising 1985-; rector of Sandringham Gp of Parishes and domestic chaplain to HM The Queen 1979-; canon Norwich 1987-; *Clubs* London Irish RFC, Public Sch Wanderers RFC; *Style*— The Rev J G M W Murphy, LVO; Rectory, Sandringham, Norfolk PE35 6EH

MURPHY, Sir Leslie Frederick; s of Frederick Charles Murphy; *b* 17 Nov 1915; *Educ* Southall GS, Birkbeck Coll London; *m* 1940, Marjorie Iris Cowell; 1 s, 1 da; *Career* chm: NEB 1977-79 (dep-chm 1975-77); dir: chm Petroleum Economics 1980-88; Unigate 1968-75, Schroders 1979- (dep chm 1973-75), Simon Engrg 1980-85; memb NEDC 1977-79; bd memb Church Army 1964-, chm Church Army Housing 1973-82; kt 1978; *Recreations* golf, music; *Clubs* Oriental; *Style*— Sir Leslie Murphy; Hedgerley, Barton Common Rd, Barton-on-Sea, Hants; Petroleum Economics Ltd, 17-19 Barter St, London WC1A 2AQ (☎ 01 404 0221, telex 22573 PETECS G)

MURPHY, Michael; s of Francis Murphy, and Dorothy Byrne Kerry; *b* 12 Feb 1954; *Educ* Lourdes Secdy Sch, Glasgow, Napier Coll Edinburgh; *m* 29 May 1982, Carolynne Dawn, da of Derrick Thomas Evans; 1 s (Michael Stuart b 1984), 1 da (Kimberly Jane b 1987); *Career* md PR Conslts Scotland Ltd, dir The Art of Mktg Ltd; *Recreations* curling, reading; *Style*— Michael Murphy, Esq; Broom Lodge, Lochwinnoch Rd, Kilmacolm, Renfrewshire PA13 4HA; 9 Lynedoch Crescent, Glasgow G3 6EQ (☎ 041 333 0557, fax 041 332 7990, car phone 0836 700984)

MURPHY, Michael Joseph; s of Joseph Murphy (d 1972), and Delia Hurst (d 1964); *b* 10 Dec 1919; *Educ* Christian Brothers Coll Dun Laoghaire; *m* 1941, Joan (d 1980), da of William Stanley Huggard (d 1952); 2 s, 4 da; *Career* co dir; pres Golfing Union of Ireland 1963-65, chm Council of Nat Golf Unions 1969; dir Ulster Bank Ltd 1969; *Recreations* reading, golf administration; *Clubs* United Servs, Dublin, Royal & Ancient GC; *Style*— Michael Murphy, Esq; Hilltop, Ballina, Co Mayo, Eire (☎ 096 21754); work: Lord Edward St, Ballina, Co Mayo, Eire (☎ 096 21344)

MURPHY, Patrick James; CMG (1985); s of James Vincent Murphy (d 1946), and Cicely Mary Murphy, *née* Crowley; *b* 11 Mar 1931; *Educ* Cranbrook, Gonville and Caius Coll Cambridge (BA); *m* 1, 10 Oct 1959, Barbara; 2 s (Michael b 1962, John b 1964); m 2, 26 June 1974, Jutta; 1 s (Nicholas b 1977); *Career* RAF 1950-52, Pilot Offr Fighter Control Branch, Royal Aux AF 1950-52, Flt Lt on reserve 1952-55; memb Oxford & Cambridge Far Eastern Expedition 1955-56; asst producer BBC General Overseas Serv 1956-57; entered FO (late FCO) 1957, serv FO 1957, Frankfurt 1950, Berlin 1959, FO 1962, second sec (commercial) and consul PHNOM PENH 1966-69; consul Düsseldorf 1969-71; consul Hamburg 1971-74; FCO 1974-77; first sec Vienna 1977-81; cnsllr FCO 1981-87, ret HM Dip Serv 1987; sr advsr Sultanate of Oman 1987-; *Recreations* travel, wine, boating, skiing; *Clubs* RAF; *Style*— Patrick Murphy, CMG; POB 5272, Ruwi, Sultanate of Oman (☎ 600800); c/o R.3 Section, Lloyds Bank, 6 Pall Mall, London SW1

MURPHY, Paul Peter; MP (Lab) Torfaen 1987; s of Ronald Murphy, and Marjorie Murphy (d 1984); *b* 25 Nov 1948; *Educ* St Francis RC Sch Abersychin, W Monmouth Sch Pontypool, Oriel Coll Oxford (MA); *Career* memb Torfaen Borough Cncl 1973-87; lectr in history & politics, Ebbw Vale Coll of Further Educn 1971-87; *Recreations* music; *Style*— Paul Murphy, Esq; House of Commons, Westminster, London SW1A 0AA

MURPHY, Stuart John; s of John William Murphy, OBE (d 1978), of 25 Fowler's Hill, Salisbury, Wilts, and Kathleen Beryl, *née* Lait; *b* 7 Feb 1933; *Educ* City of London Sch, Poly of Central London (DipArch, Dip Town Planning); *m* 1 Dec 1966, Jane Elizabeth, da of George Tinkler (d 1963), of London; 1 s (Giles b 1969), 1 da (Sara b 1972); *Career* London Div RNVR 1950-63, Nat Serv 1958-59, Sub Lt RNR 1959, serv 1 Lt Vernon Sqdn; ret 1963; architects dept London CC 1956-63, sr architect Llewellyn Davies & Weeks 1963-65, gp architect City of Westminster Dept Architecture and Planning 1965-68, controller of architecture (borough architect) London borough Harrow 1971-76 (dep borough architect and planner 1968-71), city architect and planning offr Corpn of City of London 1979-86 (dep city architect and planning offr 1976-79), princ and architect town-planning and urban design conslt in own private practice 1987-; memb cncl RIBA, former pres Cities of London & Westminster Soc Architects 1984-86, chm pub sector gp 1987-89; sr vice-pres Soc Chief Architects of Local Authy Architects (ed yearbook 1987-89), memb various socs involved with civic amenity and urban design; parish clerk St Lawrence Jewry Next Guildhall Church 1978-; Freeman City of London 1954, Liveryman Worshipful Co Merchant Taylors 1968, memb Worshipful Co Parish Clerks 1978, fndr memb Worshipful Co Chartered Architects (chm organising ctee 1984-85, Liveryman and memb Ct Assts); FRIBA 1970, FRTPI 1973, FRSA 1977, FBIM 1978; *Books* Debretts Great Cities of the World (contrib 1987); *Recreations* theatre and music hall history, gardening; *Clubs* Players Theatre; *Style—* Stuart Murphy, Esq; Hillier House, 509 Upper Richmond Rd, London SW14 7EE (☎ 01 878 3227, fax 01 878 7153, telex 9413819 HILHOUG)

MURPHY-O'CONNOR, Rt Rev Cormac; *see*: Arundel and Brighton, Bishop of

MURRAY, Angus Fraser; CBE (1972); s of John Murray, DL (d 1952), of Dornoch, and Margaret Forsyth, *née* Grant (d 1982); *b* 11 Feb 1909; *Educ* Dornoch Acad, Glasgow Univ; *m* 28 June 1941, Eileen Nancy Colomb, da of Maj Charles Hyacinth O'Rorke (d 1954); 2 s (John, Patrick), 2 da (Helen, Pauline); *Career* sec and investmt mangr Prudential Assur Co Ltd 1965-71, dir: Prudential Assur Co Ltd 1972-78, Prudential Corpn plc 1978-83, Rugby Portland Cement Co plc 1972-85, Mercantile Investmt Tst Co Ltd 1972-82; KStJ 1973; FIA; *Recreations* skiing, walking, planting trees; *Clubs* Caledonian; *Style—* Angus Murray, Esq, CBE; Tir-Nan-Og, Highclere, Newbury, Berks (☎ 0635 253822); Balloan House, Dornoch, Sutherland (☎ 0862 810282)

MURRAY, Sir (John) Antony Jerningham; CBE (1980); s of Capt John Challenger Murray (d 1939), of Oaksey Manor, Malmesbury, Wilts, and Cecilia Annette, *née* Jerningham; *b* 21 Jan 1921; *Educ* Eton, New Coll Oxford; *m* 23 July 1943, Hon Winifred Mary Hardinge, da of 2 Baron Hardinge of Penshurst, GCB, GCVO, MC, PC (d 1960); 1 s ((George) Alexander John b 8 Dec 1947); *Career* 2 Lt Gren Guards 1941, Capt 1945, Maj 1946, ret; dir Christmas Island Phosphate Co Ltd 1947-51; dep chm W India Ctee 1961-63 (chm 1963-65, vice-pres 1966-); hon advsr to govt of Barbados in UK 1961-; pres N Cerney Cricket Club; tstee Sir Frank Worrell UK Meml Fund; kt 1987; *Recreations* salmon fishing; *Clubs* Boodle's, White's, RAC; *Style—* Sir Antony Murray, CBE; Woodmancote Manor Cottage, Cirencester, Glos GL7 7ED (☎ 028583 226); c/o Barbados High Commission, 1 Great Russell Street, London WC1 (☎ 01 631 3391)

MURRAY, Athol Hollins; s of Richard Hollins Murray, ACA (d 1957; invented reflective road studs (Cats' Eyes)), of Dinmore Manor, Herefs, and Elsie Gwendoline, *née* Knee (d 1959); *b* 27 Jan 1922; *Educ* Shrewsbury; *m* 16 Aug 1947, Sheila, da of Herman Edward Hulme, MBE (d 1964), of Bowdon, Cheshire and Beaumaris, Anglesey; 2 s (Andrew b 1954, Charles b 1958), 2 da (Katherine b 1962, Elizabeth b 1965); *Career* RAF 1941-46, Air Sea Rescue and Marine Craft Serv; incorporated valuer; ptnr Stuart Murray & Co Manchester and Branches 1949-78, md The Hollins Murray Gp Ltd 1978-; chm: Northern Realty Co Ltd, Barrowmore Village Settlement nr Chester 1979-; FSVA 1968 (pres 1972-73), ASA 1974; *Recreations* golf, philately; *Clubs* Hale and Ringway GC, Royal Philatelic Soc (London and Cape Town); *Style—* Athol Murray, Esq; Erlesdene Garden Cottage, Green Walk, Bowdon, Altrincham, Cheshire WA14 2SL (☎ 061 941 6006); The Hollins Murray Group Ltd, Hollins House, Cottesmore Gardens, Hale Barns, Altrincham, Cheshire WA15 8TS (☎ 061 904 9412)

MURRAY, Dr Athol Laverick; s of George Murray (d 1949), of Tynemouth, Northumberland, and Margery, *née* Laverick (d 1974); *Educ* Lancaster Royas GS, Jesus Coll Cambridge (BA, MA), Univ of Edinburgh (LLB, PhD); *m* 11 Oct 1958, (Irene) Joyce, da of George Kilpatrick Cairns (d 1953), of Edinburgh; 1 s (Ewan Geoge b 1968), 1 da (Helen Cairns b 1966); *Career* res asst FO 1954; Scottish Record Off: asst keeper 1954-83, dep keeper 1983-84, keeper 1985-; author of articles on Scottish history in various jnls; chm of cncl Scottish Record Soc 1981-, chm Conf of Medieval Scottish Historical Res 1986-89; FRHistS 1971, FSA Scot 1982; *Books* The Royal Grammar School Lancaster (1951), Sebright School Wolverley (1953), The Lag Charters (1957); *Recreations* walking, reading; *Clubs* Royal Cwlth Soc; *Style—* Dr Athol Murray; 33 Inverleith Gardens, Edinburgh EH3 5PR (☎ 031 552 4465); Scottish Record Off, HM Gen Register House, Edinburgh EH1 3YY (☎ 031 556 6585)

MURRAY, Rear-Adm Sir Brian Stewart; KCMG (1982), AO (1978); s of A S Murray (decd); *b* 26 Dec 1921; *Educ* Hampton HS, RNC Dartmouth; *m* 1, 1954, Elizabeth (d 1962); 1 s, 2 da; m 2, 1973, Janette (CStJ 1982), da of J J Paris; *Career* Rear-Adm (RAN 1939), CO HMAS Sydney 1970-71, Hon ADC HM The Queen 1971-72, Naval Off i/c Vic 1974-75, dep chief of Naval Staff to 1978, govr of Vic 1982-; grape grower, winemaker and owner of vineyard Doonkuna; KStJ 1982; *Style—* HE Rear-Adm Sir Brian Murray, KCMG, AO; c/o Government House, Melbourne, Australia

MURRAY, Hon Catherine Anne; da of Baron Murray of Gravesend (Life Peer) (d 1980); *b* 1964; *Educ* Emmanuel Coll Cambridge; *Style—* The Hon Catherine Murray

MURRAY, Maj Charles Graham; MBE (1945), JP (1962), DL (1975) S Yorks; s of Charles Graham Murray (d 1946); *b* 28 Jan 1920; *Educ* St Cyprian's Sch Eastbourne, Stowe; *m* 1949, Susan Madeleine, da of William Raymond Stephenson Bennet Grange Sheffield; 3 da; *Career* Capt RA 1940-46, Maj RA (TA) 1947-52; md Tempered Spring Co Sheffield 1948-82; Master Cutler 1974-75; *Recreations* walking, gardening; *Clubs* Sheffield; *Style—* Maj Graham Murray, MBE, JP, DL; 3 Belgrave Drive, Sheffield S10 3LQ (☎ 0742 30 2123)

MURRAY, Colin Keith; s of Brig George Murray, CBE, DSO, MC (d 1983), and Elizabeth Agnes, *née* Wheeler (d 1982); *b* 18 June 1932; *Educ* Wellington; *m* 1 Feb 1964, Precelly Elizabeth Caroline, da of Col David Gwyn Davies-Scourfield MC, of Eversley Cross House, Eversley Cross, Hants; 1 s (William b 1970), 2 da (Sophia b 1965, Harriet b 1966); *Career* Seaforth Highlanders 1950, 2 Lt seconded 1 Bn Kings African Rifles 1951, Capt 11 Bn Seaforth Highlanders (TA) 1952-64; reinsur broker CT Bowring & Co Ltd 1953-63; R J Kiln & Co Ltd: dep underwriter and dir 1963-74, active underwriter non-marine syndicates 1974-84, chm 1985; Lloyds: memb of cncl 1989- (1983-86), jr dep chm 1989-; Freeman Worshipful Co of Insurers; *Recreations* music, bridge, gardening, country sports; *Clubs* The City; *Style—* Colin Murray, Esq; The Long House, Hurstbourne Priors, nr Whitchurch, Hampshire (☎ 0256 892 606); R J Kiln & Co Ltd, 117 Fenchurch St, London EC3M 5AL (☎ 01 481 9601, fax 01 488 1848, telex 8955661)

MURRAY, (John) David Hedley Murray; s of John Hedley (d 1963) Phyllis Adelaide Neilson, *née* Freeman (d 1954); *b* 5 Feb 1921; *Educ* St Bees, Coll of Estate Mgmnt; *m* 20 April 1948, Rosamund Ann, da of Lt-Cdr Douglas Algernon Dawson, RNVR (ka 1944); 2 da (Julia b 1950, Carol b 1953); *Career* Capt 15 Punjab Regt IA, serv 5th Bn NE frontier; land agent; late md T Murray Ltd; FRICS; *Recreations* shooting, fishing; *Style—* John Murray, Esq; Foresters Hall, Middleton Tyas, Richmond, N Yorks (☎ 032577 722)

MURRAY, Hon David Paul; s of Baron Murray of Epping Forest (Life Peer), and Lady Murray, *née* Heather Woolf; *b* 8 April 1960; *Educ* Buckhurst Hill Co HS; *m* 1984, Moria Denise, da of Patrick Joseph Roche of Milltown, Dublin; 1 da (Elizabeth b 1985), 1 s (Joseph b 1987); *Career* govt serv; *Clubs* RAF; *Style—* Flt Lt The Hon David Murray; RAF Wittering, Peterborough, Cambs PE8 6BP (☎ 0780 783235)

MURRAY, Derek; s of Alexander Murray (d 1968), and Eva, *née* Grey (d 1987); *b* 12 Mar 1926; *Educ* Kelvin Grove Sch Gateshead, Wakefield Tech Coll; *m* 29 July 1958, Doreen, da of Ernest Jackson (d 1941); 1 s (Jonathan b 1967), 1 da (Caroline b 1970); *Career* sub-ed: Shields Gazette 1950-54, Newcastle Evening Chronicle 1954-60, London Evening Standard 1960-61; ITN: writer 1961-63, chief sub-ed 1963-70, programme ed 1970-78, asst ed 1978-81, chief asst ed 1981-83, dep ed 1983-87, ret; *Recreations* singing, golf; *Clubs* Letchworth GC, Rugby; *Style—* Derek Murray, Esq; 12 Aubreys, Manor Park, Letchworth, Herts (☎ 0462 677473)

MURRAY, Hon Mrs Diana Lucy; da of Baron Home of the Hirsel, KT, PC, (Life Peer); *b* 1940; *m* 1936 (m dis 1976), James Archibald Wolfe Murray; *Style—* The Hon Mrs Diana Murray

MURRAY, Hon Mrs (Dinah Karen Crawshay); da of Baron Greenwood of Rossendale, PC, (Life Peer); *b* 1946; *m* 1970, David Murray; 3 s (Bruno, Leo, Fergus); *Style—* The Hon Mrs Murray; 62 Belsize Park, London NW3

MURRAY, The Hon Mr Justice; Sir Donald Bruce; s of Charles Benjamin Murray (d 1977), and Agnes Mary, *née* Patterson (d 1955); *b* 24 Jan 1923; *Educ* Belfast Royal Acad, Queen's Univ Belfast (LLB), Trinity Coll Dublin (BA); *m* 21 Aug 1953, Rhoda Margaret, da of Thomas Parke (d 1973); 2 s (Adrian Timothy Lawrence b 30 Oct 1954, Paul Ralph Stephen b 27 April 1961), 1 da (Rosalind Louise b 9 May 1958); *Career* called to the Bar Grays Inn 1945, asst party draftsman to NI Govt 1945-51, asst lectr faculty of law Queen's Univ Belfast 1951-53, called to the Bar NI 1953, QC NI 1964, high ct Judge Chancery divn NI 1975; govr Belfast Royal Acad, memb bd Cathedral of St Anne Belfast, chm bd SLS Legal Publns NI; memb Hon Soc of Inn of Ct NI (Bencher 1971), memb Hon soc of Grays Inn (Hon Bencher 1987); *Recreations* playing the piano, dx-ing, snooker; *Clubs* Royal Belfast GC; *Style—* The Hon Mr Justice Murray; Royal Courts Of Justice, Chichester St, Belfast, N Ireland (☎ 0232 235 111)

MURRAY, Sir Donald Frederick; KCVO (1983), CMG (1973); s of Archibald Thomas Murray (d 1960), and Freda May, *née* Byfield (d 1964); *b* 14 June 1924; *Educ* Colfes GS, Kings Sch Canterbury, Worcester Coll Oxford; *m* 17 Dec 1949, Marjorie, da of Charles Culverwell (d 1977); 3 s (Ian b 1951, Neil b 1958, Alexander b 1960), 1 da (Gillian b 1953); *Career* RM (41 Commando) 1943-46; For Serv: entered FO 1948, third sec Warsaw 1948, FO 1951, second sec Vienna 1953, first sec political off ME Forces 1956, FO 1957, first sec commerce Stockholm 1958, first sec and head of chancery Saigon 1962, FO 1964, cnsllr 1965, head of SE Asia dept 1966, cnsllr Tehran 1969, RCDS 1973, HM ambass Tripoli 1974, asst undersec of state FCO 1977, HM ambass Stockholm 1980, ret 1984; assessor chm Civil Serv Selection Bd 1984-86, dir Goodlass Wall & Co Ltd 1985-, tstee World Resource Fndn 1986-, chm Kent Co SSAFA 1985-, Channel Tunnel complaints cmmr 1987-; competed Oxford vs Cambridge cross country 1942, athletics 1943, small-bore shooting 1947; Grand Cross Order of North Star Sweden 1983; *Style—* Sir Donald Murray, KCVO, CMG; Oxney House, Wittersham, Kent TN30 7ED

MURRAY, Douglas James; s of James Charles Murray (d 1938), of Croydon, Surrey, and Emily Agnes, *née* Ludgate (d 1957); *b* 26 Feb 1914; *Educ* Whitgift Sch; *m* 4 Nov 1939, Joan Margaret, da of James Frederick Lintott (d 1962), of Croydon, Surrey; 2 da (Elizabeth Ann b 1942, Susan Margaret b 1949); *Career* banker; joined TA 1932, serv WWII India and Burma (Maj); chm Barclays Bank London Mangrs Club 1965; AIB; *Recreations* golf, photography; *Clubs* Royal Eastbourne GC; *Style—* Douglas Murray, Esq; 7 Wells Close, Eastbourne BN20 7TX (☎ 0323 639237)

MURRAY, Ewan Skinner; OBE (1984); s of Alexander Murray (d 1959), of Glasgow, and Sophia, *née* Smith (d 1984); *b* 18 Sept 1931; *Educ* Hyndland Sr Secdy Sch Glasgow; *Career* Nat Serv RAF Tenga, Singapore 1950-51; insur official Iron Trades Insur Gp 1960-; memb Garscube Harriers 1947-(hon sec 1952-62), memb ctee Scottish Cross Country Union 1956-(hon gen sec 1963-71, pres 1972, life vice-pres 1979-), ctee memb Scottish Amateur Athletic Assoc 1960-(hon tres 1970-71, hon gen sec 1971-83, life vice pres 1981-); Br Olympic Assoc: athletics admin offr Moscow 1980, cncl memb 1984-, dir 1987-; Cwlth Games Cncl for Scotland: cncl memb 1973-83, athletics team mangr Brisbane 1982, vice chm 1983-87, chm 1987-; Br Amateur Athletic Bd: cncl memb 1972-84, selection ctee memb 1972-84, team admin offr 1978-80, chm 1984-, hon life vice-pres 1987-; cncl memb Euro Athletic Assoc 1987-; OStJ 1987, FSA Scotland; *Recreations* athletics; *Style—* Ewan Murray, Esq, OBE; 25 Bearsden Rd, Glasgow G13 1YL (☎ 041 959 4436); Iron Trades Insur Gp, 105 West George St, Glasgow G2 1QN (☎ 041 204 0441, fax 041 221 8928)

MURRAY, Hon Geoffrey Charles; 2 s of 11 Earl of Dunmore; *b* 1949; *m* 1974, Margaret Irene, da of H Bulloch, of Blackwall, Tasmania; *Style—* The Hon Geoffrey Murray; 73 Pomona Rd, Riverside, Tasmania

MURRAY, Gen Sir Horatius; GCB (1962), CB (1945, KBE 1956, DSO 1943); s of late Charles Murray; *b* 18 April 1903; *Educ* Peter Symond's Sch Winchester, RMC Sandhurst; *m* 1953, Beatrice MacDermott (d 1983), da of Frederick Cuthbert; *Career* 2 Lt The Cameronians 1923, Camerons 1935, serv WWII: N Africa, Sicily, Italy, France GOC 6 Armoured Div 1944-45, dir Personnel Services WO 1946-47, Cdr 1 Div 1947-50, Cdr Northumbrian Dist 1951-53, Cdr Cwlth Div Korea 1953-54, GOC-in-C Scottish Cmd and govr Edinburgh Castle 1955-58, C-in-C Allied Forces N Europe 1958-61, ret; Col The Cameronians (Scottish Rifles) 1958-64; Cdr Legion of Merit (USA) 1945; Kt Cdr Order of the Sword (Sweden) 1961; *Style—* Gen Sir Horatius Murray, GCB, CB, KBE, DSO; c/o Vicarage Gate Nursing Home, Vicarage Gate, Kensington, London W8

MURRAY, (James) Iain; s of James Ian Murray (d 1977), and Jean Parker, *née*

McLeod Baxter (d 1984); *b* 12 Nov 1932; *Educ* Rugby, Corpus Christi Coll Cambridge (BA, MA); *m* 21 Mar 1969, Ursula Jane, da of Eric Sayle, MD (d 1985); 1 s (Alexander b 9 Nov 1972), 2 da (Katherine b 13 July 1970, Fiona b 10 Aug 1979); *Career* Nat Serv 1951 Sgt RCS; articled clerk Freshfields 1956-59, slr 1959, Robert Fleming & Co, 1960-62 (seconded for 9 mths on Wall St to G H Walker Investmt Bankers), slr Linklaters and Paines 1963- (ptnr 1967); Law Ctee: City of London Slrs Co 1967-77, Law Soc 1968-78, CBI 1987; lectred on various legal topics at home and abroad; memb of the Incorporation of Maltmen in Glasgow 1954, Liveryman of the City of London Slrs Co, memb Law Soc 1959; *Recreations* walking; *Clubs* The City of London, Travellers, New (Edinburgh); *Style*— Iain Murray, Esq; Linklaters and Paines, Barrington House, 59-67 Gresham St, London EC2V 7JA (☎ 01 606 7080, fax 01 606 5133, telex 884349/888167)

MURRAY, Sir James; KCMG (1978, CMG 1966); s of James Hamilton Murray (d 1938), of King's Cross, Isle of Arran, by his w Hester Macneill Buie; *b* 3 August 1919; *Educ* Bellahouston Acad, Glasgow Univ; *m* 1982, Mrs Jill Charmian Chapuisat, *née* Gordon-Hall; 2 step da; *Career* serv WWII RA India, Burma, Malaya, Scotland rising to GSO 2 WO; with FO (later FCO) 1947-79: ambass & perm rep to UN at Geneva 1978-79, dep perm rep (in New York) 1974-78 with rank of Ambass 1976-, asst under-sec FCO 1973-74, consul-gen San Francisco 1970-73, head Far East Dept FO 1967-70, cnsllr Djakarta 1967-67, dep head UK Delegn to EEC 1963-65, ambass to Rwanda & Burundi 1962-63; Hanson Industs New York 1983-; *Clubs* River (New York), Brooks's, Beefsteak, Pratt's; *Style*— Sir James Murray, KCMG; 220 Columbia Heights, Brooklyn Heights, New York, NY 11201, USA

MURRAY, James Patrick; CMG (1958); s of Brig-Gen Edward Rushworth Blakiston Murray (d 1942), and Hilda Dorothea Paul (d 1942); *b* 10 Oct 1906; *Educ* St Edward's Sch Oxford, Christ Church Oxford (MA); *m* 1934, Margaret Ruth, da of Rev Alfred Edward Buchanan (d 1950); 3 s; *Career* sr provincial cmmr N Rhodesia 1955-61, cmmr for N Rhodesia in UK 1961-64 (became Zambia 1964); ret; *Style*— James Murray, Esq, CMG; Trewen, Shaftesbury Rd, Woking, Surrey GU22 7DU (☎ 048 62 61988)

MURRAY, Jennifer Susan (Jenni); da of Alvin Bailey, of Barnsley, Yorks, and Winifred, *née* Jones; *b* 12 May 1950; *Educ* Barnsley Girls HS, Univ of Hull (BA); *m* 1, (m dis) Brian Murray; ptnr David Forgham-Bailey; 2 s (Edward Louis b 1983, Charles Edgar b 1987); *Career* prodr/presenter BBC Radio Bristol 1973-76, presenter reporter BBC TV South 1977-82; presenter "Newsnight", BBC TV Lime Grove 1983-85, "Today" BBC Radio 4 1986-87; presenter "Womans Hour" BBC Radio 4 1987-; documentary films for TV inc: The Duchy of Cornwall, Everyman, Stand by Your Man, Breaking the Chain; *Recreations* horses, books, swimming, the children; *Clubs* Metropolitan (West End & Battersea); *Style*— Ms Jenni Murray; Womans Hour, BBC, Broadcasting House, London (☎ 01 580 4468)

MURRAY, Hon Mrs (Jill); *née* Constantine; o da of Baron Constantine of Stanmore, CBE (Life Peer), *qv*; *b* 1938,R[; *m* 1965, - Murray; *Style*— The Hon Mrs Murray; 46 Linksway, Northwood, Middx

MURRAY, Hon Mrs; Hon Jill Diane; *née* Constantine; da of Baron Constantine of Stanmore, CBE; *b* 21 Dec 1938; *m* 1965, Geoffrey Murray; 1 s (Guy), 1 da (Tracy); *Style*— The Hon Mrs Murray

MURRAY, John Grey; CBE (1975, MBE 1945); s of Thomas Robinson Grey and Dorothy, da of Sir John Murray, KCVO, JP, DL, himself gs of John Murray, the friend and publisher of Byron; added the surname Murray by Deed Poll 1930; *Educ* Eton, Magdalen Coll Oxford; *m* 1939, Diana, da of Col Bernard James and Hon Angela Kay-Shuttleworth, da of 1 Baron Shuttleworth; 2 s (John b 1941, m Virginia Lascelles; Hallam b 1950), 2 da (Joanna b 1940, m 4 Viscount Mersey, *qv*; Mrs Nigel (Freydis Marianne) Campbell); *Career* late Maj RA, serv WWII; publisher; sr dir John Murray (Publishers) 1968-, asst ed Quarterly Review, co-ed Cornhill Magazine; *Recreations* Byron, archives, music; *Clubs* Brooks's, Pratt's, Beefsteak; *Style*— John Murray Esq, CBE; 50 Albemarle Street, London W1

MURRAY, Kenneth Alexander George; CB (1977); s of late George Dickie, and Isobella Murray; *b* 17 June 1916; *Educ* Skene St and Central Schs Aberdeen, Aberdeen Univ (MA, BEd); *m* 1942, Elizabeth Ward, da of late Arthur Simpson; 1 da (Alison); *Career* dir Civil Serv Selection Bd and Civil Serv cmmr 1964-77; special advsr to the Home Off on Police Serv, Prison Serv, and Fire Serv Selection 1977-; dir Home Off Unit 1977-80; selection advsr to Church of Scotland and C of E; formerly selection advsr: Govt of Nigeria, Govt of Pakistan, Govt of India; fell Brit Psychological Soc; *Recreations* reading, theatre, bridge, cricket; *Clubs* MCC, Royal Cwlth Soc; *Style*— Kenneth Murray, Esq, CB; 15 Melvinshaw, Leatherhead, Surrey (☎ 0372 372995)

MURRAY, Martin Charles; s of Brian Murray, Crosby, and Muriel Gertrude, *née* Spense; *b* 13 April 1955; *Educ* Merchant Taylors', Emmanuel Coll Cambridge (MA, LLB), Harvard Univ (LLM); *Career* admitted slr Supreme Ct 1981, Clifford-Turner 1979-83, S&W Berisford plc 1983-86, Hanson plc 1986-; memb Law Soc; *Recreations* hedonism; *Style*— Martin Murray, Esq; 45 Mexfield Rd, Putney, London SW15 2RG (☎ 01 874 5063); Hanson Plc, 1 Grosvenor Place, London SW1X 7JH (☎ 01 245 1245, fax 01 245 9939)

MURRAY, Lady; Mauricette; da of Count Bernhard Kuenburg, of Vienna; *m* 1935, Sir (Francis) Ralph Hay Murray, KCMG, CB (d 1983; ambass to Greece 1962-67, govr BBC 1967-73); 3 s, 1 da; *Style*— Lady Murray; 35 Vicarge Street, Woburn Sands, Milton Keynes, Bucks MK17 8RE (☎ (0908) 583 546)

MURRAY, Cdr (Douglas) Neil (Toler); s of Thomas Prain Douglas Murray, MBE (d 1986), of Angus, and Sybil Enid Murray, *née* Toler; *b* 4 July 1932; *Educ* Stowe, RN as Naval Cadet; *m* 4 April 1959, Avril Jocelyn, da of John Wardrop-Moore, of London SW1 (d 1977); 1 s (Samuel Patrick b 1975), 1 da (Cicely Catherine b 1970); *Career* RN 1950-75, Lt 1954; Lt Cdr 1962; in cmd: HMS Brinkley (minesweeper) 1960-61, HMS Exmouth (frigate) 1965-66, HMS Tenby (frigate) 1970-72; mainly served in home waters and Med; marine supt and conslt for N Sea Offshore Oil Indust 1975-85, master (seagoing) with PNG Shipping Corpn 1979-80; md Aberdeen Shipbuilders (res and dvpt) Ltd 1986-; chm Montrose Marine Ltd 1987-; Cdr 1969 (ret 1975); *Clubs* Royal Northern, Univ Aberdeen; *Style*— Cdr Neil Murray; Cleish Hills, Kinross (☎ 05775 205)

MURRAY, Nicholas Julyan Edward; s of Sir Ralph Hay Murray, KCMG, CB (d 1986), of Whaddon Hall Mews, Whaddon, Bucks, and Muaricette, *née* Countess Kuenburg; *b* 7 Mar 1939; *Educ* Bedford Sch, English Sch Cairo, Univ of St Andrews (MA); *m* 14 July 1973, Caroline Anne, da of Capt A McClintock, of Glenbower, Coolbawn, Nenagh, Co Tipperary, Ireland; 1 da (Anstice Aileen Thérèse b 22 Jan 1981); *Career* SH Benson Ltd 1962-71 (dir 1968), dir Ogilvy Benson & Mather Ltd 1971-72, md Murray Parry & Ptnrs 1972-81, dir Woodyer Hutson Chapman 1981-86, md Conzept Int Mgmnt Business Devpt Consits 1986-; memb and professional advsr Bd of Trade (missions Tokyo 1968, San Francisco 1969); chm Friends of the Vale of Aylesbury 1987, (memb ctee 1975-, vice-chm 1985); FInstD; *Books* Chronicle of the Villages of the Vale of Aylesbury (1986); *Recreations* sailing; *Clubs* Sussex YC, Lough Derg YC; *Style*— Nicholas Murray, Esq; The Old Vicarage, Aston Abbotts, Aylesbury, Bucks HP22 4NB (☎ 0296 681 617); 38 Perrers Rd, London W6; Conzept Int, Riverview House, Beavor Lane, London W 6 (☎ 01 748 7874)

MURRAY, Rev (Hugh) Peter William; s of Sir Hugh Murray, CIE, CBE (d 1941), of Lyndhurst, and Dorothy Christine, *née* Mather (d 1968); *b* 17 Sept 1913; *Educ* Winchester Coll, New Coll Oxford (MA); *m* 6 Feb 1941, Marion Olive, da of Albert Augustine Neatby, of Somerset; 1 s (Hugh b 1957), 1 da (Anne b 1953); *Career* Colonial Admin Serv Course Oxford 1936-37 and Nigeria 1937-53, snr Dist Offr, Supervisor Overseas Services Courses, Oxford Univ 1953-59 (ret 1959); Diocesan Reader 1959, chm Fairfore Deanery House of Laity and memb Diocesan Bds & Ctee Glos 1960-75; Holy Orders, deacon and priest 1975, asst curate Coln St Aldwyns, Hatherop & Quenington 1975-81, ret (with permission to officiate) 1981; *Recreations* shooting, fishing (until disabled); *Style*— The Rev Peter Murray; Millfield, Coln St Aldwyns, Cirencester, Glos GL7 5AN (☎ 028 575 372)

MURRAY, Roger Garth; s of John Sefton (d 1961) of London SE25, and Irene Constance *née* Leatherdale; *b* 24 April 1930; *Educ* St Martins Sch of Art London; *m* m 1, 24 Oct 1955 (m dis), Ann, da of Norman Garrett; 1 da (Lyndis b 1957); m 2 (m dis), Jean Margaret, *née* Ayre; 1 da (Ailsa b 1965); m 3, (m dis), Margaret, *née* Bates; 1 da (Claire b 1971); *Career* Nat Serv Army 1948, stg; chm: Steve Bowden Wilson Ltd 1985, McCann Erikson Ltd, 1985-; memb bd of govs, Ocean Youth Club, Br Sail Trg Org; MIPA (1965); *Recreations* sailing, hot air ballooning, painting; *Style*— Roger Murray, Esq; McCann Erickson Ltd, Bonis Hall, Prestbury, Cheshire, (☎ 0625 828274, car tel 0836 606374)

MURRAY, Rt Hon Lord; Ronald King Murray; PC (1974); s of James King Murray, MIEE; *b* 15 June 1922; *Educ* George Watson's Coll Edinburgh, Edinburgh Univ, Jesus Coll Oxford; *m* 1950, Sheila Winifred Gamlin; 1 s, 1 da; *Career* serv WWII REME India and SEAC; called to Scottish Bar 1953, standing jr counsel to BOT in Scotland 1961-64, QC Scotland 1967, sr advocate dep 1967-70 (advocate-depute 1964-67), Ld Advocate 1974-79, Ld of Session 1979-; MP (Lab) Leith 1970-79; *Recreations* sailing; *Style*— The Rt Hon Lord Murray; 31 Boswall Rd, Edinburgh EH5 3RP (☎ 031 552 5602)

MURRAY, Dr Ronald Ormiston; MBE (1945); s of John Murray (d 1921), of Glasgow, and Elizabeth Ormiston, *née* MacGibbon (d 1922); *b* 14 Nov 1912; *Educ* Glasgow Acad, Loretto, St John Coll Cambridge, St Thomas's Hosp London (MB, BChir, MA, MD); *m* 1, 20 July 1940, Catherine Joan Suzette (d 1980), da of Sir Henry John Gauvain (d 1945); 1 s (Nigel b 1944), 2 da (Clare b 1948, Virginia b 1950); m 2, 1981, Jane, *née* Tierney, wid of Dr J G Mathewson; *Career* WWII cmmnd Lt RAMC TA 1939, attached 2 Bn London Scottish, Maj OC 3 Field Dressing Station 1943-45, Lt-Col CO 130 Field Ambulance 1945-46; assoc prof of radiology American Univ Hosp Beirut Lebanon 1954-56, conslt radiologist Royal Nat Orthopaedic Hosp and Inst of Orthopaedics London 1956-77; Robert Jones lecture RCS 1973, Baker travelling prof Australasia 1974, Caldwell lectr American Roengten Ray Soc 1975, Skinner lectr RCR 1979; memb: Cambridge Univ Swimming Team 1933-34, Br Univs Swimming Team 1934; played rugby for: Cambridge Univ XV 1934-35, Scotland XV 1935; Hon FACR 1968, FRACR 1979, FFR RCSI 1981; *Books* Radiology of Skeletal Disorders (with H G Jacobson and D J Stoker, 3 edn 1989), Orthopaedic Diagnosis (with H A Sissons and H B S Kemp, 1984), contrib to Sutton's Textbook of Radiology and Imaging (3 edn 1987); *Recreations* golf, bridge; *Clubs* Utd Oxford and Cambridge Univ, Berks and RYF GC, Hawks (Cambridge); *Style*— Dr Ronald Murray, MBE; Little Court, The Bury, Odiham, Hants RG25 1LY (☎ 0256 702 982)

MURRAY, Dame (Alice) Rosemary; DBE (1977), JP (Cambridge 1953), DL (Cambs 1982); da of Adm Arthur John Layard Murray, CB, DSO, OBE (d 1959), and Ellen Maxwell, *née* Spooner; *b* 28 July 1913; *Educ* LMH Oxford (MA, DPhil, hon fell); *Career* serv WRNS WWII; memb: Wages Cncl 1968-, cncl Girls' Public Sch Day Tst 1969-, Armed Forces Pay Review Body 1973-83; dir Midland Bank 1978-84; ind dir The Observer 1981-; former lectr in chemistry Girton Coll Cambridge (also Sheffield Univ and Royal Holloway Coll London); former pres Nat Assoc Adult Educn; former pres New Hall Cambridge, former vice-chllr Cambridge Univ; hon fell New Hall Robinson Coll Cambridge; Hon DSc: New Univ Ulster, Leeds, Pennsylvania, Wellesley; Hon DCL Oxon; Hon DL Univ S California; Hon LLD Sheffield; *Style*— Dame Rosemary Murray, DBE, JP, DL; 9 Grange Court, Cambridge CB3 9BD

MURRAY, Rowland William; s and h of Sir Rowland William Patrick Murray, 14 Bt; *b* 22 Sept 1947; *m* 1970, Nancy Diane, da of George C Newberry, of Orlando, Fla; 2 s (Ryan b 1974, Rowland b 1979); *Style*— Rowland Murray, Esq

MURRAY, Sir Rowland William Patrick; 14 Bt (NS 1630), of Dunerne, Fifeshire; s of Rowland William Murray (d 1946), and nephew of 13 Bt, DSO (d 1958); *b* 26 Oct 1910; *Educ* Univ of Georgia; *m* 1944, Josephine Margaret, da of Edward D Murphy; 4 s, 2 da; *Heir* s, Rowland William Murray; *Career* enlisted US Army 1942, 2 Lt 1943, serv with 84 Div 335 Inf Regt, ret Capt 1946; *Style*— Sir Rowland Murray, Bt; 239 Kenlock Pla, NE, Atlanta, Georgia 30305, USA

MURRAY, Ruby, Lady; Ruby; da of S Hearn, of Helmdon, Northants; *m* 1938, as his 2 w, Lt-Col Sir Edward Robert Murray, 13 Bt, DSO (d 1958); *Style*— Ruby, Lady Murray

MURRAY, Hon Mrs (Sally Ann Hale); *née* Willis; da of Baron Willis (Life Peer); *b* 8 Jan 1951; *Educ* Chislehurst & Sidcup Girls' GS, Crownwoods Sch; *m* 1974, Robin James, s of James Patrick Murray, of Bexley; 1 s (James b 1980); *Career* Civil Serv 1974-77, advice worker (Citizens Advice Bureau) 1977-80; *Recreations* cooking, embroidery, needlework; *Style*— The Hon Mrs Murray; 24 Thirlmere Rise, Bromley, Kent (☎ 01 464 9135)

MURRAY, Hon Stephen William; s of Baron Murray of Epping Forest (Life Peer); *b* 1959; *Style*— The Hon Stephen Murray; c/o 29 The Crescent, Laughton, Essex

MURRAY, Hon Timothy John; s of Baron Murray of Gravesend (Life Peer, d 1980); *b* 1966; *Style*— The Hon Timothy Murray

MURRAY, Hon Mrs - Hon Virginia; da of Baron Bowden (Life Peer); *b* 3 April 1943; *Educ* E Anglian Girls' Sch, Reading Univ, Manchester Univ; *m* 1967, David Ian

Murray; *Career* sch teacher; *Style*— The Hon Mrs Murray; 61 Woburn Drive, Hale, Cheshire

MURRAY, Hon Lady (Winifred Mary); *née* Hardinge; da of 2 Baron Hardinge of Penshurst, GCB, GCVO, MC, PC (d 1960), and Helen Mary, *née* Cecil (d 1979); f Private Sec to HMS King George V, Edward VIII and George VI, gf Viceroy of India; *b* 2 May 1923; *Educ* private; *m* 23 July 1943, Maj Sir (John) Antony Jerningham Murray, CBE, *qv*; 1 s; *Career* artist; exhibited: Artist Int, Grosvenor Gallery, Upper St Gallery, Clarendon Gallery; *Style*— The Hon Lady Murray; Woodmancote Manor Cottage, Cirencester, Glos GL7 7ED (☎ 028583 226)

MURRAY OF BLACKBARONY, Lady; Diane Margaret; da of Robert Campbell Bray, of Buenos Aires Argentina, and Enriqueta Carolina, *née* Edye; *b* 3 April 1949; *m* 1980, Nigel Andrew Digby, s of Sir Alan John Digby Murray of Blackbarony (d 1978); *Recreations* tennis, rowing, painting (oils), piano, music; *Clubs* Venado Tuerto Polo and Athletic, Tigre Boat; *Style*— Lady Murray of Blackbarony; CC 115, (2624) Arias, Provincia de Cordoba, Argentina

MURRAY OF BLACKBARONY, Sir Nigel Andrew Digby; 15 Bt (NS 1628), of Blackbarony, Peeblesshire; s of Sir Alan John Digby Murray of Blackbarony, 14 Bt (d 1978), and Mabel Elisabeth, *née* Schiete; *b* 15 August 1944; *Educ* St Paul's Sch Argentina, Salesian Agric Tech Sch, RAC Cirencester; *m* 1980, Diana Margaret, da of Robert Campbell Bray; 1 s (Alexander b 1981), 1 da (Rachel b 1982); *Heir* s, Alexander Nigel Robert Murray; *Career* farms own land (crops, dairy, bees); private pilot's licence from Midland Sch of Flying at Castle Donnington; landowner (1180 acres); *Recreations* tennis, golf, rowing, camping, mountain walking, fishing, skiing; *Clubs* Venado Tuerto Polo & Athletic, Tigre Boat; *Style*— Sir Nigel Murray of Blackbarony, Bt; Establecimiento Tinamú, CC 115, 2624 Arias, Provincia de Córdoba, Argentina (☎ (0462 60) 473)

MURRAY OF EPPING FOREST, Baron (Life Peer UK 1985); Lionel; OBE (1966), PC (1976); *b* 2 August 1922; *Educ* Wellington GS Salop, London Univ, NCLC, New Coll Oxford; *m* 1945, Heather Woolf; 2 s, 2 da; *Career* gen sec TUC 1973-84 (joined 1947, head econ dept 1954-69, asst gen sec 1969-73); memb NEDC 1973-; memb Anglo-German Fndn for Study of Industl Soc Bd Tstees 1977-; hon fell: Sheffield City Poly, New Coll Oxford; Hon DSc: Aston, Salford; Hon LLD St Andrews; *Style*— The Rt Hon the Lord Murray of Epping Forest, OBE, PC; 29 The Crescent, Laughton, Essex

MURRAY OF GRAVESEND, Baroness; Margaret Anne; *née* Wakeford; JP (1971); da of Frederick Charles Wakeford, of Crayford; *b* 6 Dec 1928; *m* 1960, Baron Murray of Gravesend (Life Peer) (d 1980); 1 s, 1 da; *Career* mangr Gravesend Churches Housing Assoc; memb: Dartford and Gravesend Dist Health Authy 1982-, Lambeth Cncl 1958-65; *Style*— The Rt Hon Lady Murray of Gravesend, JP; 13 Parrock Rd, Gravesend, Kent (☎ 0474 365958)

MURRAY OF NEWHAVEN, Baron (Life Peer UK 1964); Sir Keith Anderson Hope Murray; KCB (1963); s of Lord Murray, CMG, PC, a Scottish Lord of Session (d 1936), and Annie Florence, *née* Nicolson (d 1968); *b* 28 July 1903; *Educ* Edinburgh Acad, Edinburgh Univ (BSc), Cornell Univ NY (PhD), Oriel Coll Oxford (BLitt, MA); *Career* serv WWII, Fl-Lt RAF 1941-42; Agric Econ Res Inst 1929-39, Miny of Food 1939-40; seconded from RAF as dir of food and agric Middle E Supply Centre 1942-45; late JP Oxford; formerly dir Bristol Aircraft and Metal Box Co; res offr Oxford Univ 1932-39, fell Lincoln Coll Oxford 1937 (bursar 1937-53, rector 1944-53); chm Univ Grants Ctee 1953-63; dir Leverhulme Tst 1964-72; chllr Southampton Univ 1964-74; visitor Loughborough Univ 1968-78; hon fell: Oriel and Lincoln Colls Oxford, Downing Coll Cambridge, Birkbeck Coll London; Hon LLD: W Aust, Bristol, Cambridge, Hull, Edinburgh, Southampton, Liverpool, Leicester, California, London, Strathclyde; Hon DCL Oxford; Hon DLitt Keele; Hon DUniv: Stirling, Essex; kt 1955; *Clubs* United Oxford and Cambridge University; *Style*— The Rt Hon the Lord Murray of Newhaven, KCB; 224 Ashley Gardens, London SW1P 1PA (☎ 01 828 4113)

MURRAY OF OCHTERTYRE, Sir Patrick Ian Keith; 12 Bt (NS 1673), of Ochtertyre, Perthshire; s of Sir William Patrick Keith Murray of Ochtertyre, 11 Bt (d 1977) and Susan Elizabeth Hudson, *née* Jones; *b* 25 Mar 1965; *Educ* Christ Coll Brecon Powys, London Acad of Music & Dramatic Art; *Heir* kinsman, Maj Peter Keith-Murray; *Style*— Sir Patrick Murray of Ochtertyre, Bt; Sheep House, Hay-On-Wye, Hereford

MURRAY-AYNSLEY, Lady; Annemaria Eleanor; da of late Judge Emil Curth (d 1940), of Trebnitz, Silesia, and Gertrude Curth (1942); *b* 24 Feb 1904; *Educ* Real Gymnasium Hirschberg, Vienna Univ, Heidelberg (MD); *m* 1, 1934, Dr Erich Goldberg (d 1942); m 2, 1952 as his 2 w, Sir Charles Murray Murray-Aynsley (d 1967); *Career* md Heidelberg and Pisa, specialist in children's diseases; former dist surgeon St John Ambulance Bde Singapore, hon conslt Singapore Anti-TB Assoc; prisoner Sumatra 1942-45; memb; BMA, German Paediatric Assoc; *Recreations* music, reading; *Clubs* Utd Oxford and Cambridge Univ, Women's Corona; *Style*— Lady Murray-Aynsley; 5 Piazza Conti, Florence 50132, Italy (☎ Florence 582404)

MURRAY-LEACH, ROGER; s of Robert Murray-Leach, of Newport, Shropshire (d 1949), and Mary Barbara, *née* Caisley (d 1986); *b* 25 June 1943; *Educ* Aldenham, Architectural Assoc Sch; *m* 1 June 1968 (m dis), Sandra Elizabeth, da of John Tallent, of Herefordshire; 1 s (Robert b 17 Feb 1978), 1 da (Tamsin b 13 April 1972), 1 s adopted (Jon James (JJ) b 20 April 1974); *Career* prodn designer; films incl: Local Hero 1983, Defence of the Realm 1986, A Fish Called Wanda 1988; Freeman: Worshipful Co of Haberdashers 1970, City of London 1969; *Recreations* riding, skiing; *Style*— Roger Murray-Leach, Esq; 108 Kings Rd, Windsor, Berks SL4 2AP (☎ 0753 863 087, car tel 0860 353 763)

MURRELL, David Brian; s of William Percy John Murrell (d 1988), of Minehead, Somerset, and Muriel Mary Elizabeth, *née* Stevens (d 1988); *b* 7 Feb 1946; *Educ* Taunton Sch; *m* 29 Nov 1969, Sheila Mary, da of Lt Alured Francis Fairlie-Clarke (d 1984), of Norton Fitzwarren, Somerset; 1 s (Alan Murrell b 1970), 2 da (Deborah b 1972, Julia b 1974); *Career* qualified as CA with Amherst and Shapland of Minehead 1967; joined Peat Marwick McLintock 1968: ptnr 1981, hd of media and entertainment indust practice 1984, reporting accountant on offer for sale prospectuses issued by Chrysalis 1985 and Virgin 1986, delisting of Virgain 1988; accounting tax and consulting servs provided to: The Observer, Today, Virgin, Polygram, LWT, Cable Authy, Saatchi and Saatchi, Rank Orgn, RCA/Columbia, Working Title Films, Initial Pictures, London Films, IPPA, Cinema and TV Benevolent Fund, Pink Floyd and Amnesty Pop Tours; Joint sponsor: Br Cinema Advtg Awards, Br Tv Advtg Awards, Campaign Press Awards, Cinema 1989, Critics Circle Film Awards, Br Morie Weekends; fin advsr Comic Relief 1989, fin tutor Nat Film and TV Sch, barker Variety Club; ACA 1968, FCA 1978; *Books* Numerous Articles on Fin and Tax in Leading Media & Entertainment Indust Trade Magazines; *Recreations* golf, photography; *Clubs* West Hill GC, Old Tautonians London Golfing Soc (former capt); *Style*— David Murrell, Esq; Peat Marwick McLintock, 1 Puddle Dock, Blackfriars, London EC4V 3PD, (☎ 01 236 8000, fax 01 248 6552)

MURRIE, Sir William Stuart; GCB (1963, CB 1946), KBE (1951); s of Thomas Murrie (d 1907); *b* 19 Dec 1903; *Educ* Harris Academy Dundee, Edinburgh Univ, Balliol Coll Oxford; *m* 1932, Eleanor Boswell (d 1966); *Career* sec Scottish Educn Dept 1952-57, sec Scottish Home Dept 1957-59, perm under-sec state Scottish Off 1959-64; *Clubs* Reform, New (Edinburgh); *Style*— Sir William Murrie, GCB, KBE; 7 Cumin Place, Edinburgh, Scotland EH9 2JX (☎ 031 667 2612)

MURRISH, Peter; s of John James Murrish (d 1962), of Cornwall, and Rita Alice, *née* Mennear (d 1989); *b* 20 April 1929; *Educ* Penzance Co GS; *m* 19 Feb 1951, Margaret Ethel, da of Maj Wilson James Stedman (d 1957), of Cornwall; 1 s (Stephen Peter b 1955), 2 da (Deborah Roxanne b 1953, Suzanne Jacqueline b 1961); *Career* charity admin, PR and fund-raising conslt; PR and devpt offr Northern Arts Assoc 1968-69, capital appeals The Spastics Soc 1971-76; dir: Parsons Lewis Davies & Ptnrs Ltd 1970-72, John F Rich Co Ltd 1976-79; md Franks Murrish (Appeals) Ltd 1979-82, chm Cornwall Animal Welfare Tst 1984-, dir Isles of Scilly Environmental Tst 1985-, chm Cinnamon Trust 1986-; memb Hertfords CC 1964-67; *Recreations* walking, reading, socialising; *Clubs* Scillonian; *Style*— Peter Murrish, Esq; Hugh House, St Mary's, Isles of Scilly TR21 0LS (☎ 0720 22156); Wingletang, Academy Terrace, St Ives, Cornwall TR26 1HJ (☎ 0736 796515); Hamewith, The Parade, St Mary's, Isles of Scilly TR21 0LP (☎ 0720 22153)

MURSELL, Sir Peter; MBE (1941), DL (W Sussex 1962); s of T A Mursell, of Kettering; *b* 20 Jan 1913; *Educ* Bedales, Downing Coll Cambridge; *m* 1938, Cicely, da of M F North, of Weybridge; 2 s, 2 da; *Career* serv WWII as Sr Cdr ATA; former memb: Ctee Mgmt in Local Govt, Royal Cmmn on Local Govt in England, Water Space Amenity Cmmn, Inland Waterways Amenity Advsy Cncl; chm W Sussex CC 1962-67 and 1969-74 (memb 1947-74), vice Lord-Lt W Sussex 1974-; dir London Shop Property Tst 1980-; kt 1969; *Clubs* Farmers'; *Style*— Sir Peter Mursell, MBE, DL, HM Vice Lord-Lt for W Sussex; Dounhurst Farm, Wisborough Green, Billingshurst, W Sussex RH14 0AB (☎ 040 377 501)

MURTA, Prof Kenneth Hall; s of John Henry Murta (d 1976), of Sunderland, Co Durham, and Florence, *née* Hall (d 1977); *b* 24 Sept 1929; *Educ* Bede GS, Univ of Durham (Dip Arch, BArch); *m* 1 April 1955, Joan, da of Joseph Wilson; 2 s (Andrew John b 1956, Eden Wilson b 1966) 2 da (Catherine Anne b 1958, Patricia Zaria b 1960); *Career* Nat Serv RAF 1947-49; Newcastle City architect, SW Milburn & Ptnrs (Sunderland) 1954-56 (princ architect 1956-59); Sr lectr Amahdu Bello Univ (Zaria Nigeria) 1959-62; Univ of Sheffield: lectr, sr lectr 1962-74, prof 1975, dean faculty of architectural studies 1974-77 and 1984-88; significant designs incl: American Cathedral Kaduna North Nigeria, All Saints Diocese of Sheffield, St Laurence Diocese of Derby; memb bd Arch Ed, ARCUK, chm Yorks regn RIBA 1985; ARIBA 1954, FRIBA 1968, FRSA 1981; *Recreations* cricket, soccer, travel, church visiting; *Style*— Prof Kenneth Murta; Underedge, Back Lane, Hathersge, Derbyshire; University of Sheffield, Sheffield, (☎ 0433 50833)

MURTON, Hon (Henry) Peter John Connell; s of Baron Murton of Lindisfarne (Life Peer); *b* 1941; *m* 1962 (m dis 1972), Louisa, da of late Maj Percy Montague Nevile, of Skelbrooke Park, Yorks; *Style*— The Hon Peter Murton; 49 Carlisle Mansions, Carlise Place, London SW1P 1HY

MURTON OF LINDISFARNE, Baron (Life Peer UK 1979); (Henry) Oscar Murton; OBE (1946), TD (1947, clasp 1951), PC (1976), JP (Poole 1963); s of Edgar Murton, of Hexham, Northumberland; *b* 8 May 1914; *Educ* Uppingham; *m* 1, 1939, Constance (d 1977), da of Fergus O'L Connell, of Co Durham; 1 s, 1 da (d 1986); m 2, 1979, Pauline, da of Thomas Keenan, of Johannesburg; *Career* serv Royal Northumberland Fus (TA) 1934-39, Staff Coll Camberley 1939, Lt-Col Gen Staff 1942-46; md Dept Stores NE England 1949-57; MP (C) Poole 1964-79, asst govt whip 1971-72, lord cmmr Treasy 1972-73, dep chm Ways and Means 1973-76 (chm and dep speaker 1976-79), dep chm of Ctees House of Lords 1981-, dep speaker 1983-; *Recreations* sailing, painting, reading history; *Style*— The Rt Hon the Lord Murton of Lindisfarne, OBE, TD, PC; 49 Carlisle Mansions, Carlisle Place, London SW1P 1HY (☎ 01 834 8226)

MUSGRAVE, Christopher John Shane; s and h of Sir Richard James Musgrave, 7 Bt; *b* 23 Oct 1959; *Style*— Christopher Musgrave Esq

MUSGRAVE, Sir Christopher Patrick Charles; 15 Bt (E 1611), of Hartley Castle, Westmorland; s of Sir Charles Musgrave, 14 Bt (d 1970); *b* 14 April 1949; *m* 1978, Megan, da of Walter Inman: 2 da (Helena b 1981, Antonia b 1987); *Heir* bro, Julian Nigel Chardin Musgrave; *Recreations* sailing; *Style*— Sir Christopher Musgrave, Bt; c/o Royal Bank of Scotland plc, Silver St, Kingston upon Hull, E Yorks HU16 5PJ

MUSGRAVE, Julian Nigel Chardin; s of Sir Charles Musgrave, 14 Bt (d 1970); h to Btcy of bro, Sir Christopher Patrick Charles Musgrave, 15 Bt; *b* 8 Dec 1951; *Educ* S Wymondham Coll, QMC London (BSc); *m* 1975 Glshanbanu Buddrudin; 2 da (Anar b 1980, Ruth b 1983); *Career* md Games World Ltd; dir Orkfest Ltd; mktg conslt; MInstM; *Recreations* creative bookkeeping; *Style*— Julian Musgrave, Esq

MUSGRAVE, Sir Richard James; 7 Bt (I 1782), of Tourin, Waterford; s of Sir Christopher Norman Musgrave, 6 Bt, OBE (d 1956); *b* 10 Feb 1922; *Educ* Stowe; *m* 1958, Maria, da of late Col M Cambanis, of Athens; 2 s, 4 da; *Heir* s, Christopher John Shane Musgrave; *Career* 2 Lt 1940, serv 1940-45 India, Middle E, Capt Poona Horse, 17 Queen Victoria's Own Cavalry; *Recreations* shooting, bridge; *Clubs* Kildare Street (Dublin); *Style*— Sir Richard Musgrave, Bt; Riverstown, Tara, Co Meath, Eire (☎ 041 25121); Syros, Greece

MUSGRAVE, Hon Mrs (Rosemary Jane); *née* Watkinson; da of 1 Viscount Watkinson, CH, PC; *b* 1947; *m* 1976, Barrie Musgrave, 1 s; *Style*— The Hon Mrs Musgrave

MUSGRAVE, Thea (Mrs Mark); da of James P Musgrave (d 1972), of Edinburgh, and Joan, *née* Hacking; *b* 27 May 1928; *Educ* Moreton Hall Oswestry, Edinburgh Univ (BMus), Private Study in Paris with Nadia Boulanger; *m* 2 Oct 1971, Peter Mark, s of Irving Mark (d 1987), of Sarasota, Florida; *Career* composer; orchestral works incl: Concerto for Clarinet and Orchestra 1968 (cmmd Royal Philharmonic Society) 1968,

Memento Vitae 1969, Viola Concerto (cmmd BBC) 1973, Peripeteia (cmmnd RPO) 1981, The Seasons 1988 (cmmnd Academy of st Martin's in the Fields); chamber and instrumental works incl: Chamber Concerto No 1 1962, Chamber Concerto No 2 1966, Chamber Concerto No 3 1966, Space Play (cmmnd Serge Koussevitsky Music Fndn) 1974, Pierrot 1985; vocal and choral music incl: Rorate Coeli 1974, An Occurrence at Owl Creek Bridge cmmnd BBC 1981, For the Time Being: Advent 1986; operas incl: The Voice of Ariadne cmmnd Royal Opera House 1973, Mary, Queen of Scots cmmnd Scottish Opera 1977, A Christmas Carol cmmnd Virginia Opera Assoc 1979, Harriet, The Woman Called Moses cmmnd jtly Royal Opera House and Virginia Opera Assoc 1984; Beauty and the Beast (ballet) 1968; increasingly active as conductor of own work; performances at festivals: Edinburgh, Warsaw, Aldeburgh, Cheltenham, Zagreb, Florence Maggio Musicale, Venice Biennale; numerous broadcastings and recordings; distinguished prof Queen's Coll City Univ New York; memb: Centl Music Advsy Panel BBC, Music Panel Arts Cncl GB, exec ctee Composers' Guild GB, ctee Award for Cwlth fund of New York; hon fell New Hall Cambridge 1973; hon doctorates: Cncl Nat Academic Awards 1976, Smith coll USA 1979, Old Dominion Univ Norfolk, Virginia 1980; *Style—* Miss Thea Musgrave; c/o Novello & Co L & S, 8 Lowes James St, London WIR 4DN

MUSGROVE, Harold John; s of Harold John Musgrove (d 1984), and Francis, *née* Clements (d 1983); *b* 19 Nov 1930; *Educ* King Edward GS Birmingham, Birmingham Tech Coll; *m* 1959, Jacquelin; 2 s (Michael b 1963, James b 1972), 2 da (Sarah b 1969, Laura b 1970); *Career* cmmnd RAF 1945, navigator; chm and chief exec Austin Rover Gp Ltd 1982- (apprentice 1945, sr mgmnt positions within Truck and Bus Gp 1963, chm and md Austin Morris Ltd 1980-, chm Light Medium Cars Gp 1981-); vice-pres Motor Mfrs and Traders 1986-; Midlander of the Year award 1980, Instn of Prodn Engrs Int award 1981, The Soc of Engrs Churchill Medal 1982; *Style—* Harold Musgrove Esq; Austin Rover Gp Ltd, Fletchamstead Highway, Canley, Coventry CV7 9GS (☎ (0203) 75511, telex 31567)

MUSHIN, Alan Spencer; s of Dr Louis Mushin (d 1984); *b* 31 Jan 1938; *Educ* Haberdashers' Aske's Sch London, London Hosp Med Coll (MB BS); *m* 27 Feb 1972, Joan Carolyn, da of Dr Simon Behrman, of Harley St, London; 1 s (James b 1976), 1 da (Rosalind b 1974); *Career* conslt: ophthalmic surgn Moorfield Eye Hosp London, London Hosp, Queen Elizabeth Hosp for children; memb: Opthalmogical Soc of the UK, Br Paediatric Assoc, BMA, FRSM, FRCS; *Books* papers on paediatric opthalmology; *Recreations* photography, philately, gardening; *Clubs* Savage; *Style—* Alan S Mushin, Esq; 935 Finchley Rd, London NW11 7PE (☎ 01 455 7212); 82 Harley Street, London W1N 1AE (☎ 01 580 3116); The Dower House, Oxney, St Margarets-at-Cliffe, Kent

MUSKER, Hon Lady (Audrey Elizabeth); *née* Paget; da of 1 and last Baron Queenborough (d 1949); *b* 1922; *m* 1, Jan 1945, Cmdt Christian Martell, DFC, French Air Force (d Aug 1945); m 2, 1946 (m dis 1956), Ronan Nelson; 1 s, 2 da; m 3, 1956 (m dis 1974) Lt-Cdr Claud Peter Harcourt Lucy, RN; m 4, 1982, Sir John Musker, *qv*; *Recreations* flying, skiing, scuba diving, sailing, tapistry; *Style—* Hon Lady Musker; 4 Cliveden Place, London SW1; Shadwell Park, Thetford, Norfolk (☎ 0842 3257)

MUSKER, Sir John; s of Capt Harold Taylor Musker, JP (d 1946), of Snarehill Hall, Thetford, and Margaret Gray, *née* McMonies (d 1952); *b* 25 Jan 1906; *Educ* privately, St John's Coll Cambridge; *m* 1, 6 June 1932 (m dis 1955), late Elizabeth Susan Eva, yr da of Capt Henrik Loeffler, of 51 Grosvenor Sq, W1; 2 da; m 2, 14 Sept 1955, Rosemary Honor (d 1980), da of Maj-Gen Merton Beckwith-Smith, DSO, MC, and formerly w of John Llewellyn Pugh; m 3, 1982, Hon Audrey Elizabeth, *née* Paget *qv*, da of 1 and last Baron Queenborough (d 1949); *Career* serv WWII, Lt RNVR; banker; chm: Cater Brightwen & Co (bankers) 1938-, Cater Ryder & Co 1960-71 (dir 1960-79); hon tres London Municipal Soc 1936-46; memb LCC City of London 1944-49; kt 1952; *Clubs* White's; *Style—* Sir John Musker; 4 Cliveden Place SW1; Shadwell Park, Thetford, Norfolk (☎ 0842 753257)

MUSKER, Lady Rose Diana; *née* Lambton; da of Anthony Lambton (6 Earl of Durham, peerages disclaimed 1970); *b* 1952; *m* 1979, Herbert Oliver Fitzroy Musker; *Style—* Lady Rose Musker

MUSSELL, Hon Mrs (Margaret Jean); *née* Shaw; da of 2 Baron Craigmyle (d 1944); *b* 20 Feb 1915; *m* 1949, (Laurence) Shirl Mussell (d 1956); 3 da (1 adopted); *Style—* The Hon Mrs Mussell; Dyke Croft, Ravenglass, Cumbria CA18 1RN

MUSSON, Hon Lady; Elspeth Lorraine; *née* Bailey; granted title rank and precedence of a Baron's da which would have been hers had her f survived to succeed to the title of Baron Glanusk 1948; da of Hon Herbert Crawshay Bailey, JP (d 1936; 4 s of 1 Baron Glanusk) and Hon Mrs Bailey (d 1948); sis of 4 Baron; *b* 1915; *m* 1939, Gen Sir Geoffrey Randolph Dixon Musson, GCB, CBE, DSO *qv*; 1 s, 1 da (decd); *Style—* The Hon Lady Musson; Barn Cottage, Hurstbourne Tarrant, Andover, Hants SP11 0BD (T Hurstbourne Tarrant 026 476 354)

MUSSON, Gen Sir Geoffrey Randolph Dixon; GCB (1970), CBE (1945), DSO (1944); s of Robert Dixon Musson (d 1957); *b* 9 June 1910; *Educ* Shrewsbury, Trinity Hall Cambridge; *m* 1939, Hon Elspeth Lorraine, *qv*; 1 s, 1 da (decd); *Career* 2 Lt KSLI 1930, Brig 1944, cmd Cwlth Forces in Korea 1954-55, Maj-Gen 1958, Maj-Gen cmd 7 Armd Div 1958 and 5 Div 1958-59, COS MELF 1959-62, Col KSLI 1963-68, Lt-Gen GOC in Northern Cmd 1964-67, Adj Gen MOD 1967-70, Gen 1968, Col LI 1968-72, vice-chm Nat Savings Ctee, chm HM Forces Savings Ctee 1970-78, vice-pres Royal Patriotic Fund Corpn 1974-83; pres Victory (Servs) Club 1970-80; *Clubs* Army and Navy; *Style—* Gen Sir Geoffrey Musson, GCB,CBE, DSO; Barn Cottage, Hurstbourne Tarrant, Andover, Hants SP11 0BD (T 026 476 354)

MUSSON, John Nicholas Whitaker; s of Dr J P T Musson, OBE (d 1968), and Gwendoline, *née* Whitaker (d 1981); *b* 2 Oct 1927; *Educ* Clifton, Brasenose Coll Oxford (MA); *m* 12 Sept 1953, Ann, da of A S Priest (d 1983), of Santa Barbara, California; 1 s (Richard b 1965), 3 da (Caroline b 1955, Clare (Mrs Bourne) b 1960, Kate b 1962); *Career* Lt Welsh Guards, The Lancs Fusiliers in Austria 1945-48; dist offr N Nigeria HM Colonial Admin Serv 1951-59, staff dept BP London 1959-61, asst master and housemaster Canford Sch Dorset 1961-72, warden Glenalmond Coll (formerly Trinity Coll Glenalmond) 1972-87; chm Scottish div HMC 1981-83, currently Scottish sec Independent Schs Careers Orgn; *Clubs* New (Edinburgh); *Style—* John Musson, Esq; 47 Spylaw Road, Edinburgh EH10 5BP (☎ 031 337 0089)

MUSSON, Peter John; s of Eric Thomas Musson, of W Yorks, and Mary Veronica, *née* Daly (d 1987); *b* 29 Mar 1947; *Educ* Health GS; *m* 20 Dec 1975, Anne Marie, da of Bruce Hamilton Woods (d 1961); 2 s (Michael b 1982, George b 1988), 1 da (Katharine b 1977); *Career* mgmnt conslt (corporate) 1974; dir: Manchester C of C & Indust 1981-82, Cardiokinetics Ltd 1983; FCA 1968; *Style—* Peter J Musson, Esq; Sunnybank, 85 North Road, Glossop, Derbyshire SK13 9DX (☎ 04574 67022)

MUSSON, Samuel Dixon; CB (1963), MBE (1943); s of Robert D Musson; *b* 1 April 1908; *Educ* Shrewsbury, Trinity Hall Cambridge; *m* 1949, Joan Isabella, da of Col Delme Davies-Evans; *Career* barr 1930, princ asst slr Min of Health 1958-63, chief registrar Friendly Socs and Industl Assur Cmmn 1963-72; *Recreations* country pursuits, farming, gardening, racing; *Clubs* Savile; *Style—* Samuel Musson, Esq, CB, MBE; The Beehive, Fairview Rd, Headley, Bordon, Hants (☎ 0428 713183)

MUSTILL, Hon Mr Justice; Hon Sir Michael John; s of Clement William Mustill; *b* 10 May 1931; *Educ* Oundle, St John's Coll Cambridge; *m* 1960 (m dis 1983), Beryl Reid Davies; *Career* barr Gray's Inn 1955, QC 1968, rec Crown Ct 1972-78, judge High Ct of Justice (Queen's Bench Div) 1978-; chm Civil Serv Appeal Tbnl 1971-78; kt 1978; *Style—* The Hon Mr Justice Mustill; 8 Prior Bolton St, London N1

MUSTO, (Franklyn) Keith; s of Frank Lawson Musto, and May Musto (d 1945); *b* 12 Jan 1936; *m* 31 Oct 1959, Gillian, Reginald Walter Marrison, of Essex; 1 s (Nigel b 1965), 1 da (Joanne b 1969); *Career* dir Musto Ltd 1966-; won: Heron Nat Championship 1955, Albercore Nat Championship 1960, Hornet Nat Championship 1961, FD Br Nat Championship 1962, 1963 and 1964; second in the FD Worlds 1963; won silver medal at Tokyo Olympics and Euro FD Championship 1964; formed Co Musto & Hyde Sails 1965; won Tempest Euro Championship 1967; formed Musto & Hyde Accessories 1971; serv in Japan as Nat Sailing Coach to Japanese Olympic squad 1973; co began devpt of three-layer clothing system 1980; Dutch Yacht "Flyer" won the Whitbread Round The World Race (crew wearing Musto inner, middle and outler layer clothing) 1982; co won Silk Cut Design Award 1985; co expanded into second factory and doubled the size of its production facility 1986; co winner Br Design Award 1987; *Recreations* sailing; *Clubs* Thorpe Bay Yacht, Royal Yachting Assoc; *Style—* Keith Musto, Esq; Hunts Farm, Heath Rd, Ramsden Heath, Billericay, Essex; Musto Ltd, 1 Armstrong Rd, Benfleet, Essex (☎ 0268 759466, fax 0268 795541, telex 995466)

MUSTOE, Anne; *née* Revill; *b* 24 May 1933; *Educ* Girton Coll Cambridge (MA); *m* 1960, Nelson Edwin, QC (d 1976); *Career* admin asst Guest Keen & Nettlefolds Ltd 1956-60, head of economics and classics and careers advsr Francis Holland Sch London 1965-69, independent tour operator 1969-72, dep headmistress Cobham Hall Kent 1975-78, headmistress St Felix Sch Southwold 1978-87, pres Girls' Schs Assoc 1984-85, chm ISIS 1986-87, mgmnt conslt CORAT (Christian Organisations Res and Advsy Tst) 1988-; JP (Suffolk) 1981-85; *Recreations* cycling, music; *Style—* Mrs Anne Mustoe; c/o PCA Finance, 90 Gloucester Mews, West London W2 6DY (☎ 01 402 9082)

MYATT, Alan Arthur; s of Capt Percy Edward Myatt, MC (d 1950), of 104 Blakesley Rd, Stechford, Birmingham, and Alice Maud, *née* Brown (d 1968); *b* 9 Mar 1923; *Educ* Solihull Sch; *m* 6 Nov 1947, Marjorie, da of Arthur John Barker (d 1953), of Noctorum Highwood, Uttoxeter; 1 s (Richard b 2 Nov 1952), 1 da (Diana (Mrs Tait) b 4 June 1949); *Career* 153 Field Regt Leicestershire RA 1942-45; RHS Waters & Ptnrs 1945-49 Tarmac Ltd 1949-51, Wellington VDC 1951-58, memb Chelmsford Boro & Rd joint Sewerage Ctee 1958-63; ptnr: Willcox Raikes & Marshall (joined 1963) 1969-73, Mander Raikes & Marshall 1973-88; FICE 1949-, M ConsE 1969, FIWEM; *Recreations* golf, bridge, travel; *Clubs* Fulford Heath GC, Sutton Coldfield GC; *Style—* Alan Myatt, Esq; 9 Forest Lawns, 124 Streetly Lane, Sutton Coldfield, W Midlands (☎ 021 353 0532)

MYDDELTON, Prof David Roderic; s of Dr Geoffrey Cheadle Myddelton, of Glutieres-sur-Ollon, Switzerland, and Jacqueline Esther, *née* Nathan; *b* 11 April 1940; *Educ* Eton, Harvard Business Sch (MBA); *m* 28 April 1986, Hatherly Anne D'Abo; 1 step s (Charles b 1975), 1 step da (Louise b 1974); *Career* CA 1961; lectr: fin and accounting Cranfield 1965-69, accounting London Business Sch 1969-72; Cranfield: prof fin and accounting 1972-, acting head sch mgmnt 1985-86; ACIS 1966, FCA 1971; *Books* The Power to Destroy (1969), Financial Decisions (1983), On A Cloth Untrue (1984), The Economy And Business Decisions (1984), Accounting And Decision Making (1984), Essential Management Accounting (1987), The Meaning of Company Accounts (1988); *Recreations* crossword puzzles, jigsaw puzzles; *Style—* Prof David Myddelton; 112 Randolph Ave, London W9 1PQ (☎ 01 286 0880); Cranfield Sch of Mgmnt, Cranfield, Bedford MK43 OAL (☎ 0234 751 122)

MYDDELTON, Lady Mary (Margaret) Elizabeth; *née* Mercer Nairne; da of late Maj Lord Charles George Francis Mercer-Nairne, MVO (2 s of 5 Marquess of Landsdowne) and sis of 8 Marquess; *b* 1910; *Educ* Private; *m* 1931, Lt-Col Ririd Myddelton, LVO, JP, DL (d 1988); 2 s 1 da; *Recreations* painting, fishing, gardening; *Style—* Lady Margaret Myddelton; Chirk Castle, Chirk, Clwyd LL14 5AF

MYDDELTON, Hon Mrs (Sarah Cecily); *née* Allsopp; da of 5 Baron Hindlip; *b* 1944; *m* 1967, Hugh Robert Myddleton, s of Lt-Col Ririd Myddleton, LVO, JP, DL (d 1988), and Lady Mary Myddleton (sis of 8 Marquess of Lansdowne, PC); *Style—* The Hon Mrs Myddelton; 139 Holland Park Ave, WII

MYERS, Bernard Ian; s of Edward Nathan Myers (d 1986), and Isabel Violet, *née* Viner; *b* 2 April 1944; *Educ* Hendon Co GS, LSE (BEcon); *m* 17 Sept 1967, Sandra Hannah, da of Samuel Barc (d 1980); 1 s (Andrew b 1972), 2 da (Lara b 1969, Lyndsey b 1974); *Career* accountant 1962-72, merchant banker 1972-, md (gp fin and overseas) N M Rothschild & Sons Ltd 1988- (dir 19760); dir many assoc cos inc: Shield Tst Ltd 1976-, Smith New Ct plc 1985-, Spiremore Ltd 1986-, N M R Int NV 1983, Rothschild Inc 1984-, Arrow Capital Ltd 1987-; FCA; *Recreations* opera, tennis, theatre; *Style—* Bernard I Myers, Esq; 44 Gordon Ave, Stanmore, Middx HA7 3QH; N M Rothschild & Sons Ltd, New Ct, St Swithin's Lane, London EC4P 4DU (☎ 01 280 5000, fax 01 929 1643)

MYERS, Brig Edmund Charles Wolf (Eddie); CBE (1944), DSO (1943); s of Dr C S Myers, CBE (d 1946), of Winsford, nr Minehead, Somerset, and Edith, *née* Seligman (d 1965); *b* 12 Oct 1906; *Educ* Haileybury, RMA Woolwich, Cambridge Univ (BA), Sch of Mil Engrg; *m* 12 Oct 1943, Louisa Mary Hay (Lutie), da of Aldred Bickham Sweet-Escott (d 1945), of W Somerset; 1 da (Thalia b 1945); *Career* cmmnd RE 1926, Subaltern Fd Co Aldershot 1929-35, Capt (later Maj) Egypt 1935-40, ME Staff Coll Haifa 1940, OC Fd Sqdn W Desert N Africa 1940-41, Lt-Col insts ME Staff Coll 1941 and combined Trg Centre Egypt 1942, Col (later Brig) cmd SOE mil mission to Greek Resistance 1942-43, liason offr SOE HQ London and SHAEF 1944, cmd 1 Airborne Div RE (incl Arnhem and Norway) 1944-45, Col asst dir intelligence HQ

SACSEA 1945-46, sr mil rep Jt Intelligence Bureau MOD 1946-49, Lt-Col cmd 32 Assault Engr Regt UK 1949-50, Col GS TA Directorate WO 1950-51, Cdr 1 Br Cwlth Div RE Korea 1951-52, dir staff RAF Staff Coll 1952-54, Brig chief engr Br Tps in Egypt 1955-56, dep dir personnel admin WO 1956-59, ret 1959; chief civil engr Cleveland Bridge & Engrg Co 1959-65, construction mangr Power Gas Corpn Davy Int 1965-68; regnl sec BFSS 1968-70, chm local Royal Br Legion Benevolent Ctee 1973-83; MICE 1960, memb Inst RE 1926; Dutch Bronze Lion 1944, USA Order of Merit 1952, Norwegian Liberty Medal 1945; *Books* Greek Entanglement (1955, second edn 1985); *Recreations* gardening, formerly riding and flying; *Clubs* Army & Navy, Special Forces; *Style*— Brig Eddie Myers, CBE, DSO; Wheatsheaf House, Broadwell, Moreton-in-Marsh, Glos GL56 OTY (☎ 0451 30183)

MYERS, Lady; Elsie; *m* 1917, Sir James Eckersley Myers, OBE (d 1958); *Style*— Lady Myers; 28 Victoria Park, Colwyn Bay, Denbighshire

MYERS, Gordon Elliot; CMG (1979); s of William Lionel Myers (d 1984), and Yvonne, *née* Alexander (d 1938); *b* 4 July 1929; *Educ* Kilburn GS, Univ Coll Oxford (MA); *m* 23 April 1963, Wendy Jane, da of Charles Thomas Lambert (d 1971), of London; 2 s (Andrew James b 1964, Malcolm John b 1965), 1 da (Lucinda Joy Lambert b 1968); *Career* currently under sec, Arable Crops Pigs & Poultry at Min of Agric Fisheries & Foods; formerly Min Agric at Off of UK Permanent Representative to Euro Communities (1975-79); *Recreations* music, theatre, gardening, tennis; *Clubs* Utd Oxford and Cambridge; *Style*— Gordon Myers, Esq, CMG; Woodlands, Nugents Park, Hatch End, Middx HA5 4RA; Ministry of Agriculture Fisheries & Food, 10 Whitehall Place, London SW1A 2AA

MYERS, John David; s of Frank Myers (d 1949), and Monica, *née* Paden (d 1973); *b* 30 Oct 1937; *Educ* Marist Coll Hull, St Marys Coll Strawberry Hill Middx, Loughborough Coll of Physical Educn, Hull Univ; *m* 17 April 1974, Anne McGeough, wid, da of Michael Purcell (d 1985); 1 s (Ian James b 1972); *Career* school master 1958-64, barr Gray's Inn 1968, Hull practise 1969-82, chm Indust Tbnls 1982-; *Recreations* music, wine, golf, bridge, cooking; *Clubs* Hull GC; *Style*— John Myers, Esq; Strand House, 75 Beverley Rd, Hull (☎ 0482 204 33)

MYERS, Prof Norman; s of John Myers (d 1963), of Higher Lees Farm, Whitehall, nr Slaidburn, Yorks, and Gladys, *née* Haworth; *b* 24 August 1934; *Educ* Clitheroe Royal GS, Keble Coll Oxford (MA), Univ of California, Berkeley (PhD); *m* 11 Dec 1965, Dorothy Mary, da of Frank Halliman (d 1966), of Nairobi, Kenya; 2 da (Malindi b 3 Oct 1970, Mara b 13 Aug 1973); *Career* Nat Serv RA 1952-53 (invalided out); dist off Oversea Admin Kenya 1958-60, teacher Delamere Boys Sch Nairobi 1961-64, professional wild-life photographer and TV film-maker E Africa 1965-68, conslt in environment and devpt 1972-; res and projects in over 80 countries incl assignments for: The World Bank, UN Agencies, Nat Acads of US, OECD, EEC, World Cmmn Environment and Devpt; chm and visiting prof int environment, Univ of Utrecht Netherlands, Regents lectr Univ of California, adjunct prof Univ of Michegan, res assoc Oxford Forestry Inst and Int Devpt Centre Oxford Univ; sr fell World Wildlife Fund US, sr assoc Int Union for Conservation of Nature an Natural Res Geneva; visiting fell: World Res Inst Washington DC, East-West Center Honolulu; Gold Medal and Order of Golden Ark World Wildlife Fund Int, Gold Medal of New York Zoological Soc, Global 500 Roll of Honour UN Environment Programme, special acievement award Int Environment Protection Sierra Club US, distinguished achievement award Soc for Conservation Biology; memb: World Acad Arts and Sci 1988, Int Platform Assoc; *Books* The Long African Day (1972), The Sinking Ark (1979), Conversion of Tropical Moist Forests (1980), A Wealth of Wild Species (1983), The Primary Source: Tropical Forests and Our Future (1984), The Gaia Atlas of Planet Management (1986); *Recreations* marathon running, photography, mountaineering; *Clubs* Achilles; *Style*— Prof Norman Myers; Upper Meadow, Old Road, Headington, Oxford OX3 8SZ (☎ 0865 750387, telex 83147 VIAOR G attn Myers)

MYERS, Sir Philip Alan; OBE (1977), QPM (1972), DL (Clwyd 1983); *b* 7 Feb 1931; *m* 1951, Hazel; 2 s; *Career* Shrops Constabulary 1950-67, W Mercia Police 1967-68, dep chief constable Gwynedd Constabulary 1968-70, chief constable N Wales Police 1970-81, one of HM's Insprs of Constabulary 1982-; Kt 1985; *Style*— Sir Philip Myers, OBE, QPM, DL

MYERS, Rosemary Sylvia Dagmar; da of Dr George Norman Myers (d 1981), of Harrogate, and Florence Karen, *née* Danielsen (d 1979); *b* 31 May 1938; *Educ* Perse Girls Sch Cambridge, Harrogate Sch of Art, Cambridge Sch of Art (NDD); *m* 21 May 1962 (m dis 1968), Peter Goodliffe; 1 s (Jonathan Michael b 14 Feb 1963), 1 da (Judith Tamzin b 19 June 1965); *Career* artist; freelance illustrator 1962-73 for: The Times, The Economist, Wine Magazine; transferred to print-making 1973, acquired own press 1977 (well known for unusual use of lino and wood in printing); works exhibited in: Open Br Print Bristol, New English Art Club Mall Gallery, Soc of Wood Engravers, Royal W of Eng Acad, Royal Soc of Painters, Etchers and Engravers; print prize awards 1978 and 79; pres Cambridge Drawing Soc 1989-, ctee Friends of Arts Theatre Cambridge; *Books* has written and illustrated numerous articles on dolls' houses, currently featured in Int Dolls' House News; *Style*— Ms Rosemary Myers; 2 Babraham Rd, Cambridge (☎ 0223 247370)

MYERS, Prof Sir Rupert Horace; KBE (1981, CBE 1976); s of H Myers; *Educ* Melbourne HS, Melbourne Univ (BSc, MSc, PhD); *m* 1944 Io Edwina King; 1 s, 3 da; *Career* vice-chllr and princ Univ of New South Wales 1969-81, fndn prof of metallurgy 1969-81, emeritus prof 1980-; chm Aust govt ctee of inquiry into Technological Change in Aust 1979-80; dir: Energy Resources of Aust Ltd 1981-, CSR Ltd 1981-, IBM Aust Ltd 1987-; chm: Technoproduct Hldgs Ltd 1985-, Mega Resources Ltd 1987-, NSW State Pollution Control Cmmn 1971-; pres Aust Acad of Technological Sciences and Engrg 1989-(vice pres 1984-88); Hon LLD Strathclyde 1973, Hon DSc Wollongong 1976, Hon DEng Newcastle (Aust), Hon DLitt New South Wales; FTS; *see Debrett's Handbook of Australia and New Zealand for further details*; *Clubs* Australian; *Style*— Prof Sir Rupert Myers, KBE; 135 Neerim Rd, Castlecove, NSW 2069, Australia

MYERS, Stephen David; s of Leon Daniel Myers, of London, and Matilda, *née* Cohen (d 1968); *b* 15 Sept 1942; *Educ* Quintin Sch, Uni of Durham (BSc); *m* 28 Jan 1965, Marion Elaine, da of Geoffrey Michael Myers, of London; 1 s (Joel b 1970), 1 da (Nicola b 1966, d 1985); *Career* conslt civil engr; assoc J D & D M Watson 1972-79 (Milan and Athens) ptnr Watson Hawksley Gp 1979-; invitation lectr Water Pollution Control and Enviromental Mgmnt: City of Beijing PRC, Univ of Turin, Univ of Harloin, Univ of Newcastle; conslt Asian Devpt Bank Manila 1985, gp mission ldr to Turkey Br Water Inds 1987; FICE 1968, FIWEM 1970, FHKIE 1981; *Recreations* photography, trekking, bridge; *Clubs* Royal Hong Kong

MYERSCOUGH-JONES, (Arthur) David; s of Frederick Cecil Sidney Jones, of 2 Lansdown Mansions, Lansdown Rd, Bath, and Lilian Dorothy Jones; *b* 15 Sept 1934; *Educ* Bickertn House Sch Southport, Southport Sch of Art, Centrg Sch of Art (DA); *m* 21 Feb 1963, (Ursula Theodora Joy) Pelo, da of Charles Graham Cumpston (d 1968), of Barton Hall, Pooley Bridge, Cumbria; 1 s (Richard b 23 June 1969), 3 da (Frances b 23 Feb 1966, Ellen b 21 July 1971, Madeleine b 15 Sep 1974); *Career* theatre designer; Citizens Theatre Glasgow 1958-60, resident designer Mermaid Theatre London 1961-65; tv designer Owen Wingrace (world premiere) 1971, The Flying Dutchman (Royal TV Soc Award) 1976, Therese Raquin (BAFTA Design Award) D & AD Gold Silver Award) 1983, Cosi Fan Tutte and The Theban Plays (ACE Nomination for Art Direction Los Angeles) 1988 and 1989; FCSD 1985; *Recreations* music, opera and painting; *Style*— David Myerscough-Jones, Esq; 6 The Vineyards, Bath, Avon BA1 5NA (☎ 0225 319 479); Room 400, Design Department, BBC Televison Centre, Wood Lane, London W12 7RJ (☎ 01 576 7403)

MYERSON, His Hon Judge Arthur Levey; QC (1974); s of Barnett Myerson, of Leeds, and Eda Jane Myerson, *née* Lewene; *b* 25 July 1928; *Educ* Blackpool GS, Queens' Coll Cambridge (BA, LLB), Open Univ (BA); *m* 1960, Elaine Shirley, da of Sam Harris (d 1953), of Leeds; 2 s (Simon, Nicholas); *Career* RAF 1946-48 AC1; barr 1952, circuit judge 1978, cncl of circuit judges 1985-; *Recreations* reading, walking, sailing; *Clubs* Royal Cwlth, Moor Allerton GC; *Style*— Judge Arthur Myerson, QC

MYHILL, Stephen Richard; s of Frederick James Myhill, and Sybil Eileen Myhill (d 1976); *b* 17 June 1945; *Educ* Hatfield Sch; *m* 1, 24 Sept 1966 (m dis 1980), Anne Beatrice, da of Eric William Hyatt, of Birch Green, Hertford; 2 s (Carl b 23 July 1968, Douglas b 12 Nov 1970); m 2, 26 Jan 1985, Susan Ann, da of Peter Cresswell, of Kensington; 2 da (Kirsty b 29 Oct 1985, Sophie b 18 Aug 1987); *Career* securities offr Midland Bank 1962-71, business devpt exec Access Credit Card 1972-79, gen mangr Diners Club Saudi Arabia 1979-80, dir of mktg Citibank (UK) 1981-87, dir personal banking Girobank 1987-; ACIB 1967, memb Mktg Soc 1988; *Recreations* golf, tennis, travel, DIY; *Style*— Stephen Myhill, Esq; 10 Milk St, London EC2 (☎ 01 600 6020)

MYLES, David Fairlie; CBE (1988); s of Robert Cownie Myles (d 1973), of Dalbog, Edzell, Brechin, Scotland, and Mary Ann Sidey, *née* Fairlie (d 1963); *b* 30 May 1925; *Educ* Brechin HS; *m* 9 Feb 1951, Janet Isabella, da of David Gall, of Glenskenno, Montrose; 2 s (Robert Gall, Peter David), 2 da (Catherine MacDonald (Mrs Booth), Lorna Isobel (Mrs Sinclair)); *Career* RM 1943-46; tenant hill farmer 1958-, dir Kincardineshire Auction Mart Ltd 1963-81; memb: Tport Users Consultative Ctee Scotland 1973-79, Meat Promotion Exec MLC 1975-79, N of Scotland Hydro-Electric Bd 1985-89, Dairy Produce Quota Tbnl for Scotland 1985-; gov appointee Potato Mktg Bd 1988-; MP (Cons) Banff 1979-83, Cons candidate Orkney and Shetland election 1983, dist cncllr Angus 1984-; NFU Scotland: exec chm Angus area, memb cncl 1970-79, convenor orgn and publicity ctee 1976-79; pres N Angus and Mearns Cons Pty 1974-78 (chm 1971-74), memb Angus Tourist Bd 1984-; *Recreations* curling, traditional scots fiddle music; *Clubs* Brechin Rotary, London Farmers; *Style*— David Myles, Esq, CBE; The Gorse, Dunlappie Rd, Ezell, Angus DD9 7UB (☎ 035 64 207); Dalbog, Edzell, Brechin, Angus DD9 7UU (☎ 035 64 265)

MYLNE, Nigel James; QC (1984); s of Maj Harold James Mylne, 10 Royal Hussars (d 1942), and Dorothy Evelyn Hogg, *née* Safford (d 1985); *b* 11 June 1939; *Educ* Eton; *m* 1, 4 April 1967 (m dis 1978), Julie Felicity Selena, da of Cdr Christopher Phillpotts, RN (d 1982); 2 s (Jonathan b 1970, Dominic b 1972), 2 da (Jessica b 1969); m 2, 18 Jan 1980, Mrs Judy Camilla Wilson, da of Maj Francis Gawain Hamilton Monteith (d 1975); 1 s (James b 1981); *Career* 2 Lt 10 Royal Hussars (nat serv); barr Middle Temple 1963; Rec Crown Ct 1983-; Liveryman Worshipful Co of Haberdashers; *Recreations* beekeeping; *Clubs* White's, Garrick, Pratt's; *Style*— Nigel Mylne, Esq, QC; 67 Thurleigh Road, London SW12 8TZ (☎ 01 673 2200); 2 Harcourt Bldgs, Temple, London EC4 (☎ 01 353 2112)

MYNORS, David Rickards Baskerville; OBE (1985); s of Rev Aubrey Baskerville Mynors (d 1937), and Margery Musgrave, *née* Harvey (d 1974); *b* 16 Sept 1915; *Educ* Eton, New Coll Oxford (MA); *m* 6 July 1938, Mary Laurence, da of Charles Leslie Garton (d 1940), of Oxon; 5 s (Robert b 1939, Peter b 1941, Edward b 1947, James b 1949, Charles b 1952), 1 da (Eleanor b 1950); *Career* Maj Scots Gds serv Middle E and Italy 1939-45, (despatches, US Bronze Star); Courtaulds 1937-67 (dir 1955); dir: Nat Provident Inst 1957-87 (dep chm 1968-87), Imperial Tobacco 1967-71, RFD Gp 1972-86 (chm 1974-83), Berisfords Gp 1976-87 (chm 1980-87), HP Bulmer 1974-83; rowed for Oxford 1935; memb: Ct of Assts Weavers Co 1955- (upper bailiff 1968-69), Oxfordshire Health Authy 1974-85 (vice-chm 1979-85); *Clubs* Cavalry and Guards', Leander; *Style*— David Mynors, Esq, OBE; Quarry House, Shellingford, Faringdon, Oxon SN7 7QA (☎ 03677 508)

MYNORS, Sir Humphrey Charles Baskerville; 1 Bt (UK 1964) of Treago, Co Hereford; s of Rev Aubrey Baskerville Mynors (d 1937), of Langley Burrell, Wilts, and Margery Musgrave, *née* Harvey, sis of Sir Ernest Harvey, 1 Bt; yr bro of Sir Roger Mynors, *qv*; *b* 28 July 1903; *Educ* Marlborough, Corpus Christ Coll Cambridge; *m* 1939, Lydia Marian, da of Prof Sir Ellis H Minns; 1 s, 4 da; *Heir* s, Richard Baskerville Mynors; *Career* joined Bank of England 1933, sec 1939, dir 1949, dep govr 1954-64; chm Fin Corpn for Indust Ltd 1964-74; former dir: Gen Electric Co, Imperial Gp, Legal & General Assur, Pilkington Bros and H P Bulmer; *Style*— Sir Humphrey Mynors, Bt; Treago, St Weonards, Hereford (☎ 098 18 208)

MYNORS, Richard Baskerville; s and h of Sir Humphrey Charles Baskerville Mynors, 1 Bt; *b* 5 May 1947; *Educ* Marlborough, Corpus Christi Coll Cambridge; *m* 1970, Fiona Bridget, da of Rt Rev George Edmund Reindorp; 3 da (Alexandra b 1975, Frances b 1978, Victoria b 1983); *Career* schoolmaster and asst dir of music King's Sch Macclesfield 1970-73; dir of music: Wolverhampton G S 1973-81, Merchant Taylors' 1981-88, Belmont Abbey Sch Hereford 1988-; *Recreations* gardening, DIY, organ building; *Style*— Richard Mynors, Esq; The Furnace Farmhouse, St Weonards, Hereford HR2 8NZ (☎ 09818 494); Belmont Abbey School, Hereford HR2 9RZ (☎ 0432 277 362)

MYNORS, Sir Roger (Aubrey Baskerville); s of Rev Aubrey Baskerville Mynors (d 1937), Rector of Langley Burrell, Wilts, and Margery Musgrave, *née* Harvey, sis of Sir Ernest Harvey, 1 Bt; er bro of Sir Humphrey Mynors, 1 Bt, *qv*; *b* 28 July 1903; *Educ* Eton, Balliol Coll Oxford; *m* 1945, Lavinia Sybil, da of Very Rev Cyril Argentine Alington (d 1955); dean of Durham and sometime headmaster of Eton; *Career* princ HM Treasy 1940-44; prof of latin: Cambridge 1944-53, Oxford 1953-70; fell Balliol Coll

Oxford 1926-44; FBA; kt 1963; *Style—* Sir Roger Mynors; Treago, St Weonards, Hereford HR2 8QB (☎ 098 18 208)

MYRDDIN-EVANS, George Watkin; s of Sir Guildhaume Myrddin-Evans, KCMG, CB (d 1964), formerly of Chester Place, Regents Park; *b* 26 Mar 1924; *Educ* Rugby, Christ Church Oxford (MA in law); *m* 1966, Anna Katharine, 2 da of John Fowell Buxton, TD, of Morley Hall, Ware, sometime High Sheriff of Herts (ggn of Sir Edward Buxton, 2nd Bt), by his w Katharine (yst da of Sir Nicholas Bacon, 13 Bt); 1 s (David Guildhaume, b 14 April 1967); *Career* serv in France 1944, Capt Coldstream Gds 1945; memb Lloyd's 1951-, chm Gardner Mountain & Capel-Cure Agencies 1973-84, Oxford Rugby Football and Athletics versus Cambridge; Cons memb St Pancras Borough Cncl 1953-56 & 1959-62, dep mayor 1961; *Recreations* shooting, fishing, real tennis; *Clubs* White's, Pratt's, City of London, Cardiff & Co; *Style—* George Myrddin-Evans, Esq; Church House, Llandefalle, Brecon, Powys (☎ 087 485 210); 10 Campana Rd SW6 4AU (☎ 01 731 3281)

N

NAAS, Lord; Charles Diarmuidh John Bourke; s and h of 10 Earl of Mayo; *b* 11 June 1953; *Educ* St Aubyn's Rottingdean, Portora Roy Sch Enniskillen, Queen's Univ Belfast, Bolton St Coll of Technol Dublin; *m* 1975, Marie Antoinette Cronnelly; 1 da (Hon Corinne Mary Jane b 1975); *Style*— Lord Naas; Doon House, Maam, Co Galway, Eire

NABARRO, David Joseph Nunes; s of Eric John Nunes Nabarro, JP, of 11 The Marlowes, London NW8, and Cecily, *née* Ornstein; *b* 5 July 1948; *Educ* Clifton Coll Bristol, Univ of Newcastle upon Tyne; *m* 26 March 1976 (m dis 1985), Victoria Marsland, da of John Lloyd Owen (d 1966), of Cheadle, Cheshire; 2 s (Leo b 4 Feb 1980, Alexei b 19 Oct 1982); *Career* trainee Joseph Sebag and Co 1969-72, ptnr Laurie Mibank and Co 1972-85, exec dir Prudential Bache Capital Funding (Equities) Ltd 1986-; dir: MAID Systems Ltd 1986, Paisley Hyer Gp plc 1987, Giltvote plc 1988, Savoy & Strand Gp, Penguin Gp Hotel plc; Freeman City of London; memb Int Stock Exchange, AMSIA; *Recreations* skiing, garden design; *Clubs* City of London; *Style*— David Nabarro, Esq; Broadlands, 27 Broadlands Rd, London N6 4AE (☎ 01 341 3221); Prudential-Bache Capital Funding (Equities) Ltd, 9 Devonshire Sq, London EC2M 4HP (☎ 01 220 7252, fax 01 929 0493, car 0860 511125)

NABARRO, Eric John Nunes; JP (1972); s of Joseph Nunes Nabarro (d 1948), and Rosetta Nabarro (d 1972); *b* 5 April 1917; *Educ* Clifton; *m* 1947, Cecily, da of Henry Orenstein (d 1937); 1 s, 1 da; *Career* Capt RA, Iceland, N Africa, Italy; sr ptnr Eric Nabarro & Co 1960-82; tres Bd of Deputies of Br Jews 1973-79, pres Spanish, Portuguese Jewish Congregation 1984-88 (vice pres 1982-84); tstee Ravenswood Fndn 1985-, vice pres Victoria Community Centre 1963-; FCA; *Recreations* travel, golf, jogging; *Clubs* MCC, RAC; *Style*— Eric Nabarro Esq, JP; 11 The Marlowes, London NW8 6NB (☎ 01 586 1240)

NABARRO, Prof Frank Reginald Nunes; MBE (1946); s of Stanley Nunes Nabarro (d 1958); *b* 7 Mar 1916; *Educ* Nottingham HS, Univ of Oxford (MA, BSc), Univ of Birmingham (DSc); *m* 1948, Margaret Constance, da of James Dalziel (d 1954); 3 s, 2 da; *Career* Univ of Witwatersrand Johannesburg S Africa: prof of physics 1953-84, dean faculty of science 1968-70, dep vice-chllr 1978-80, hon res professional fellow 1985-; hon DSc: Witwatersrand 1987, Natal 1988, Cape Town 1988; FRS, hon FRSSAF;; *Books* Theory of Crystal Dislocations (1967, 1987); *Recreations* gardening; *Style*— Prof Frank Nabarro, MBE; 32 Cookham Rd, Auckland Park, Johannesburg 2092, S Africa (☎ 726 7745)

NABARRO, Sir John David Nunes; s of Dr David Nunes Nabarro (d 1958); *b* 21 Dec 1915; *Educ* Oundle, UCL (MD); *m* 1948, Joan Margaret, da of William Gladstone Cockrell (d 1946); 2 s, 2 da; *Career* actg Lt-Col RAMC TA; physician; emeritus conslt physician Middx Hosp, hon conslt physician Royal Prince Alfred Hosp Sydney; dir: Cobbold Laboratories, Middx Hosp Med Sch; fell UCL, chm Jt Conslts Ctee 1979-84; kt 1982; *Recreations* gardening; *Style*— Sir John Nabarro; 33 Woodside Ave, London N12 8AT (☎ 01 445 7925); 121 Harley St, London W1N 1DH (☎ 01 935 7200)

NAESMYTH OF POSSO, Maj (Richard) William; s of Rev George Cresswell Naesmyth Naesmyth of Posso (d 1983), and Christobel Sara, *née* Slatter, 16th Naesmyth of Posso (Peeblesshire) since Charter in 1554; Sir James Naesmyth of Posso (d 1720) was cr a Nova Scotia Baronet 1706 (ext 1928); *b* 19 Dec 1938; *Educ* Haileybury; *m* 22 March 1980, Xenia Anglea Mary, da of Very Rev Rudolph Henderson-Howat (d 1957), Dean of Brechin; 1 s (Alexander Cresswell Benedict b 3 April 1983), 1 da (Georgina Charlotte Xenia b 30 April 1981); *Career* cmmnd RA 1959, served in Germany thrice during 1960s, attached Zambia Artillery 1965-67, Trucial Oman Scouts/Union Def Force 1970-74; *Recreations* genealogy, heraldry; *Style*— Maj Richard Naesmyth of Posso, Esq; 90 Airfield Rd, Marham, Kings Lynn PE33 9PA; RHQ RA, Government House, Woolwich SE18 6XR (☎ 01 854 2252, ext 3710)

NAGDA, Kanti; s of Vershi Bhoja Nagda of India; *b* 1 May 1946; *Educ* City HS Kampala Uganda, Coll of Further Educn Chippenham, E African Univ Uganda; *m* 1972, Bhagwati, *née* Desai; 2 children; *Career* accountant, Hollander Hyams Ltd 1972-82; pres Anglo-Indian Circle 1973-, sec gen Confedn of Indian Orgns (UK) 1975-, hon ed conslt Int Asian Guide and Who's Who 1975-, asst ed Oshwah News 1975-83; mangr Community Centre 1982-, pres Greenfords Lions Club 1988-89; *Recreations* cricket, photography; *Style*— Kanti Nagda, Esq; 170 Tolcarne Drive, Pinner, Middx HA5 2DR (☎ 01 863 9089)

NAGGAR, Guy Anthony; s of Albert Naggar, of Italy, and Marjorie, *née* Smouha; *b* 14 Oct 1940; *Educ* Ecole Centrale des Arts et Manufactures Paris; *m* 6 Dec 1964, Hon Marion, da of Baron Samuel of Wych Cross (Life Baron, d 1987); 2 s (Albert b 15 July 1967, Jonathan b 24 Jan 1971), 1 da (Diane b 11 May 1969); *Career* dir: Banque Financiere de la Cite Geneva 1970-88, Charterhouse Gp Ltd 1980-81; chm Dawnay Day & Co Ltd 1981-; *Style*— Guy Naggar, Esq; 15 Grosvenor Gdns, London SW1W 0BD (☎ 01 840 8060)

NAGGAR, Hon Mrs (Marion); *née* Samuel; da of Baron Samuel of Wych Cross (Life Peer); *b* 1944; *m* 1964, Guy Antony Naggar; 2 s, 1 da; *Style*— The Hon Mrs Naggar; 61 Avenue Rd, London NW8

NAHUM, Peter John; s of Denis Ephraim Nahum, of Columbia, and Allison Faith, *née* Cooke; *b* 19 Jan 1947; *Educ* Sherborne; *m* 29 Aug 1987, Renate Angelika, da of Herr Ewald Meiser, of Germany; *Career* dir Peter Wilson's Sotheby's 1966-84; regular contrib as painting expert Antiques Roadshow 1980- (discovered the lost Richard Dadd painting 1986, subsequently sold to Br Museum); *Books* Prices of Victorian Painting Drawings and Watercolours (1976), Monograms of Victorian and Edwardian Artists (1976); *Recreations* gardening, sailing, photography, theatre, travel, walking; *Clubs* Reform; *Style*— Peter Nahum, Esq; 12 Islington Park St, London N1 1PU (☎ 01 607 3232); 5 Ryder St, London SW1Y 6PY (☎ 01 930 6059 car 0836 299335)

NAIDU, Gajen Kumar; s of Rao Bahadur Sirdar K P Naidu, and Shrimati Rangubai Naidu; f was due for a knighthood but India's Independence in 1947 prevented it; *b* 3 Jan 1933; *Educ* Agra Univ India (LLB, MA); *m* 30 Jan 1962, Perveez Naidu, da of late Cowas Hormuz; 2 s (Vinay b 1963, Vijay b 1966); *Career* chm Copeland Gp of Co's 1982-87; student thesis on 'Kalbelia" (Indian snake-charmers) was highly acclaimed & became a standard reference; FBIM; *Recreations* shooting, golf, photography, travel; *Style*— Gajen K Naidu, Esq; work: (telex 295141 TXLINK G REF MBX 016994962)

NAILOR, Prof Peter; s of Leslie Nailor (d 1960), of Wokingham, Berks, and Lily Matilda, *née* Jones (d 1961); *b* 16 Dec 1928; *Educ* Mercers' Sch, Wadham Coll Oxford (BA, MA); *Career* Home Civil Serv: Admty 1952, MOD 1964, asst sec 1967; prof of politics Univ of Lancaster 1969-76, visiting prof Carleton Univ Ottawa 1976-77, visiting res fell ANU Canberra 1977, prof of history RNC Greenwich 1977 (dean and academic princ 1982-84 and 1986-88) visiting lectr City Univ 1977-88, visiting prof Univ of Poona 1983, provost Gresham Coll 1988; external examiner 1970-88: King's Coll London, LSE, Aberdeen Univ, Lancaster Univ, Manchester Univ, Reading Univ, Salford Univ, Southampton Univ, N Staffs Univ; univ res thesis examiner: Aberdeen, Dundee, E Anglia, Edinburgh, Exeter, Keele, Lancaster, London, Manchester, Oxford, Salford, Southampton, Wales, York, ANU; chm Br Int Studies Assoc 1988-90, memb Academic Advsy Cncl 1978-88 (chm 1984-86), cncl memb Royal Inst of Int Affairs 1984- (chm res ctee 1986-); memb: FCO Advsy Panel on Arms Control and Disarmament 1975-88, MOD Advsy Panel on Historical Records 1979-88, ed bd The JL of Arms Control and Disarmament 1980-, Political Sci and Int Rels Ctee of the Socl Sci Res Cncl 1975-79 (chm 1979-81), Postgraduate Trg Bd Socl Sci Res Cncl 1979-81; regnl lectr HO Regnl Sci Advsy Orgn 1979-88; Liveryman Worshipful Co of Mercers 1972; *Books* The Nassau Connection (1988); author of numerous books and articles on def topics; *Recreations* gardening, cooking; *Style*— Prof Peter Nailor; c/o Gresham College, Mercers' Hall, Ironmonger Lane, London EC2V 8HE

NAIPAUL, Vidiadhar Surajprasad; *b* 1932; *Educ* Univ Coll Oxford (BA); *m* 1955, Patricia Ann Hale; *Career* author; Hon DLitt Cambridge 1983, Hon DLitt London 1988; *Books* The Mystic Masseur (winner of John Llewelyn Rhys Memorial Prize, 1958), A House for Mr Biswas (1961), In A Free State (winner of Booker Prize, 1971), A Bend in the River (1979), The Return of Eva Perón (1980), Among the Believers (1981), The Enigma of Arrival 1987, A Turn in the South (1989); *Style*— V S Naipaul, Esq; c/o Aitken & Stone, Literary Agents, 29 Fernshaw Rd, London SW10 0TG

NAIRAC, Lady Jane Fortune Margaret; *née* Ogilvy; da of 13 Earl of Airlie, DL; *b* 24 June 1955; *m* 1980, François Nairac, son of Paul Nairac, of Vacoas, Mauritius; 2 da (Jessica Doune b 1985, Annabel Lydia b 1988); *Style*— Lady Jane Nairac; 57 Westover Rd, London SW18 2RF

NAIRN, Andrew; s of Capt Andrew Nairn, MC (d 1971), of Glasgow, and Margaret Cornfoot, *née* Turner (d 1972); *b* 31 July 1944; *Educ* Strathallan Sch; *m* 1, 25 April 1970 (m dis 1983), Susan Anne, da of Richard Alphonse Napier; 1 s (Jonathan Richard b 1981), 1 da (Penelope Margaret b 1976); m 2, 1983, Glynis Vivienne, *née* Sweet; 1 step s (Barnaby Craggs b 1971), 1 step da (Charlotte Craggs b 1974); *Career* trainee CA Thomson Jackson Gourlay and Taylor 1962-67, Hodgson Impey and predecessor firms 1967- (ptnr 1970-); dep chm Dulwich Cons Assoc 1978; MICAS; *Recreations* fly fishing, golf; *Clubs* Vagabonds; *Style*— Andrew Nairn, Esq; 52 Redhill Wood, New Ash Green, Kent DA3 8QP (☎ 0474 873 724); Hodgson Impey, 20-26 Cursitor St, London EC4A 1HY (☎ 01 405 2088, fax 01 831 2206)

NAIRN, Sir Michael; 4 Bt (UK 1904), of Rankeilour, Collessie, and Dysart House, Dysart, Fifeshire; s of Sir (Michael) George Nairn, 3 Bt, TD (d 1984), and Helen Louise, *née* Bruce; *b* 1 July 1938; *Educ* Eton, INSEAD; *m* 1, 1972, Diana Gordon (d 1982), eldest da of F Leonard Bligh, of Pejar Park, Woodhouselee, NSW, Australia; 2 s (Michael Andrew b 1973, Alexander Gordon b 1975), 1 da (Emma Helen Beatrice b 1980); m 2, 1986, Sally Jane Hastings; *Heir* s, Michael Andrew b 1973; *Style*— Sir Michael Nairn, Bt; Pitcarmick, Bridge of Cally, Blairgowrie, Perthshire PH10 7NW

NAIRNE, Lady (12 holder of S Lordship cr 1681); Lady Katherine Evelyn Constance Bigham; *née* Petty-Fitzmaurice; da of 6 Marquess of Lansdowne, DSO, MVO (d 1936), and Elizabeth, da of Sir Edward Hope, KCB (ggs of 2 Earl of Hopetoun); suc bro, 7 Marquess (ka 1944), in the Lordship of Nairne; *b* 22 June 1912; *m* 1933, 3 Viscount Mersey (d 1979); 3 s (incl 4 Viscount); *Heir* s, 4 Viscount Mersey; *Style*— The Rt Hon the Dowager Viscountess Mersey; Bignor Park, Pulborough, Sussex

NAIRNE, Rt Hon Sir Patrick Dalmahoy; GCB (1981, KCB 1975, CB 1971), MC (1943), PC (1982); s of Lt-Col Charles Silvester Nairne (d 1966), of Plover Hill, Compton, Winchester; *b* 15 August 1921; *Educ* Radley, Univ of Oxford (MA); *m* 1948, Penelope Chauncy, er da of Lt-Col Robert Francis Bridges, RAMC, by his w Charlotte, da of Edward Luard (seventh in descent from Abraham Luard, who settled in England 1685 as a result of the Revocation of the Edict of Nantes); 3 s (Alexander b 1953, James b 1960, Andrew (twin) b 1960), 3 da (Katharine b 1949, Fiona b 1951, Margaret b 1961); *Career* formerly with Admlty (joined 1947); perm sec DHSS 1975-81, second perm sec Cabinet Off 1973-75, dep under-sec MOD 1970-73 (asst under-sec logistics 1967-70, private sec to Def Sec 1965-67); master St Catherine's Coll Oxford 1981-88 (hon fell 1988), chllr Univ of Essex 1983-; tstee: Nat Maritime Museum 1981, Joseph Rowntree Meml Tst; vice-pres Soc of Italic Handwriting 1987, dep-chm W Midlands bd Central Ind TV, pres Seamen's Hosp Soc; FRSA; Hon LLD: Leicester 1980, St Andrew's 1984; Hon DU Essex 1983; *Recreations* water-colour painting; *Clubs* United Oxford and Cambridge Universities; *Style—* The Rt Hon Sir Patrick Nairne, GCB, MC; Yew Tree, Chilson, nr Charlbury, Oxford

NAISH, Capt Arthur John Brabant; CBE (1963); s of Capt the Rev Francis Clement Prideaux Naish, MBE (d 1961) and Irene Stainforth Brabant Naish (d 1969); *b* 21 Dec 1911; *Educ* St Edward's Sch Oxford, Sidney Sussex Coll Cambridge (MA); *m* 1943, Margaret Naish, MBE, da of Stanley Charles Waddington (d 1975); 2 s (Antony, Dominic), 2 da (Vanessa, Victoria); *Career* served with RN 1940-67, N Atlantic Convoys as Sub-Lt to Lt 1940-41, Cdr 1945, Capt 1953; teacher 1934-37, Civil Serv 1967-77; *Recreations* sailing; *Clubs* Cambridge Univ Cruising; *Style—* Capt Arthur Naish, CBE, RN; St Christopher's, Ditteridge, Box, Corsham, Wilts (☎ 0225 742 414)

NAISH, John Alexander; s of William Henry Naish (d 1987), and Elizabeth Lyon, *née* Pirie; *b* 12 April 1948; *Educ* Queen Elizabeth's Hosp Bristol, Dr Challoner's GS Amersham, City of London Coll (BA); *m* 18 Sept 1982, Bonnie Kam Pik, da of Pham Tak, of Hong Kong; 1 s (William b 3 April 1987); *Career* dir Hill Samuel Bank Ltd 1985; FCIB 1983; *Recreations* golf, astronomy; *Style—* John Naish, Esq; 405 Homat Sharon, 9-3 Minami Azabu 4-Chome, Minato Ku, Tokyo (☎ 010 813 446 8952); Hill Samuel Bank Ltd, 6th Floor Shoyu Kaikan Bldg 3-3-1 Kasumigaseki, Tokyo (☎ 010 813 501 6491, fax 010 813 597 0471, telex 02223044 J)

NAKHLA, Nassef Latif; s of Latif Nakhla (d 1941), and Lily Elias (d 1977); *b* 12 July 1930; *Educ* English Sch Cairo, Battersea Poly (BSc Eng); *m* 6 Nov 1953, Joan, da of Anthony Sidonio (d 1944); 1 s (Karim b 1959), 1 da (Dina b 1957); *Career* dir: Lennard Devpts Ltd 1966-71 (chm and md 1971-87), Poly-Lina Ltd; *Recreations* squash, swimming, music, socialising; *Clubs* RAC; *Style—* Nassef L Nakhla, Esq; Poly-Lina Ltd, Millmarsh Lane, Brimsdown, Enfield, Middx EN3 7PU (☎ 01 804 8141, telex 266032, fax 01 805 0059)

NALDER, Hon Sir Crawford David; s of H A Nalder; *b* 14 Feb 1910; *Educ* State Sch Wagin, Wesley Coll Perth; *m* 1, 1934, Olive M (d 1973); 1 s, 2 da; m 2, 1974, Brenda Wade (d 1988); *Career* MLA WA (Country Pty): for Wagin 1947-50, for Katanning 1950-74; min: for War Serv Land Settlement 1959-66, for Agric 1959-71, for Electricity 1962-71; ldr Country Pty 1962-73, dep premier WA 1962-71; farmer; kt 1974; *Style—* The Hon Sir Crawford Nalder; Unit 4, 7 Dale Place, Booragoon, W Aust 6154

NALL, Sir Michael Joseph; 2 Bt (UK 1954), of Hoveringham, Co Nottingham, DL (Notts 1970); s of Col Sir Joseph Nall, 1 Bt, DSO, TD, DL (d 1958); *b* 6 Oct 1921; *Educ* Wellington; *m* 1951, Angela Loveday Hanbury, da of Air Chief Marshal Sir Alex Coryton, KCB, KBE, MVO, DFC; 2 s; *Heir* s, Edward William Joseph Nall; *Career* joined RN 1939, serv 1939-45, 1949 psc, Lt Cdr 1950, ret 1961; gen mangr Guide Dogs for the Blind Assoc 1961-64, High Sheriff Notts 1971, pres Nottingham Chamber of Commerce & Industry 1972-74; banker, ret; chm Southwell Diocesan Pastoral Ctee 1968-86, memb: Nottinghamshire Scout Assoc 1968-88, Robin Hood Charity Tst 1974-88; *Recreations* field sports; *Clubs* United Service, Nottingham; *Style—* Sir Michael Nall, Bt, DL; Hoveringham Hall, Nottingham NG14 7JR (☎ 0602 663634)

NALL-CAIN, Hon David Lawrence Robert; JP (Cheshire 1964); 2 s of 2 Baron Brocket (d 1967), and Angela Beatrix, *née* Pennyman, of Ormsby Hall, N Yorks; *b* 1 Sept 1930; *Educ* Eton, Magdalene Coll Cambridge (MA); *m* 1958, Lady Katherine Elizabeth Palmer, yr da of Maj Visc Wolmer (ka 1942; eldest s of 3rd Earl of Selborne, whom he predeceased); granted the rank of an Earl's da 1985; 1 s (James b 1961), 2 da (Caroline b 1959, Annabel b 1963); *Career* 2 Lt 12 Royal Lancers 1949, also Derbys Yeo; chartered surveyor, dir Tetley Walker 1960-65; chm Hertfords Soc 1967-69, govr St Patricks Hosp Dublin 1973-77; FRICS; *Recreations* fishing, shooting, stalking; *Clubs* Cavalry and Guards'; *Style—* The Hon David Nall-Cain, JP; Ballacleator, St Judes, IOM (☎ Kirk Andreas 0624 880 753)

NALL-CAIN, Hon David Michael Anthony; s of Hon Ronald Charles Manus Nall-Cain (d 1961), and gs of 2 Baron Brocket (d 1967); raised to the rank of a Baron's son 1969; *b* 1955; *Educ* Harrow; *Style—* The Hon David Nall-Cain

NALL-CAIN, Lady Katherine Elizabeth; *née* Palmer; da of Viscount Wolmer (s of 3 Earl of Selborne, ka 1942), and Priscilla (*see Baron Newton*); granted the rank of an Earl's da 1985; *b* 24 July 1938; *m* 1958, Hon David Lawrence Robert Nall-Cain, *qv*; 1 s, 2 da; *Style—* Lady Katherine Nall-Cain; Ballacleator, St Judes, IOM

NALL-CAIN, Hon Richard Christopher Philip; s of Hon Ronald Charles Manus Nall-Cain (d 1961), and Elizabeth Mary Trotter, *née* Stallard; gs of 2 Baron Brocket (d 1967); raised to the rank of a Baron's s 1969; *b* 5 April 1953; *Educ* Eton; *m* 9 Dec 1978, Juliet Paula Vivian, da of J E V Forester, of Villa Mont Gras d'Eau, St Brelade, Jersey, CI; 1 s (Sam Richard Christopher b 8 June, d 16 Aug 1987), 2 da (Rebecca Elizabeth Emily b 11 July 1981, Claire Antonia Louise b 1 Nov 1982); *Career* RMAS 1971, Lt Royal Green Jackets 1972-78; served: Belize, Gibraltar, Cyprus, UK; Hawker Siddeley Dynamics Engrg Ltd 1979-84: successively asst mktg mangr, admin mangr, engrg admin mangr; dir Edeco Hldgs Ltd 1984 (gp planning dir 1985, chief exec 1986); pres Welwyn Garden City branch Royal Br Legion; FBIM 1988, FInstD 1979, MInstP 1984, AFA 1988; *Recreations* photography, shooting, cricket, DIY; *Clubs* MCC, Henley Royal Regatta, National Rifle Assoc; *Style—* The Hon Richard Nall-Cain; Manor House, Ayot Little Green, Welwyn, Herts AL6 9BA (☎ 0707 334047); Edeco Holdings Ltd, 24 Haymarket, London SW1Y 4DG (☎ 01 930 8711, fax 01 930 0305)

NANCE, His Hon Judge Francis James; JP (Lancs 1963); s of Herbert James Nance of S Africa (d 1922); *b* 5 Sept 1915; *Educ* St Francis Xavier's Coll Liverpool, Univ of Liverpool; *m* 1943, Margaret Gertrude, nee Roe; 2 s; *Career* Capt Royal Signals NW Europe (despatches 1945) 1940-45; barr 1936, dep chm Lancs QS 1963-66, cmmr Liverpool and Manchester Crown Cts 1966-71, county ct judge 1966-, circuit judge 1972-; *Recreations* chess, travel; *Clubs* Athenaeum (Liverpool); *Style—* His Hon Judge Nance; c/o Queen Elizabeth II Law Courts, Liverpool, Merseyside

NANCROFT, 3 Baron (UK 1987); Sir Benjamin Lloyd Stormont; 3 Bt (UK 1982); s of 2 Baron Mancroft, KBE, TD (d 1987); *b* 16 May 1957; *Educ* Eton; *Heir* none; *Style—* The Rt Hon the Lord Mancroft; 33 York Mansions, Prince of Wales Drive, London SW11

NANDY, Hon Mrs (Ann Luise); *née* Byers; da of Baron Byers, OBE, PC, DL (Life Baron, d 1984), and Baroness Byers, *qv*; *b* 30 April 1946; *Educ* Sherborne, Univ of York (BA), Univ of Bradford (MA); *m* 1972, Dipak Nandy; 2 da (Francesca b 1977, Lisa b 1979); *Career* library clerk House of Commons Library 1968-71, asst ed Where magazine 1971-73, head family servs dept London Cncl of Socl Serv 1973-77, res student Univ of Bradford 1977-82, res with Granada TV 1982-84, prodr with Granada TV 1984-; *Style—* The Hon Mrs Nandy; c/o Hunters Hill, Blindley Heath, Lingfield, Surrey

NANKIVELL, Owen; s of John Hamilton Nankivell (d 1967), and Sarah Ann *née* Mares (d 1975); *b* 6 April 1927; *Educ* Torquay GS, Univ of Manchester (BA, MA); *m* 1956, Mary Burman, da of Hubert Earnshaw (d 1966); *Career* statistician; Colonial Off 1952-56, Central Statistical Off 1956-65, chief statistician Dept of Econ Affrs 1965-68, under-sec HM Treasy 1968-72, asst dir centl statistical off Cabinet Off 1972-79, chief economist Lucas Industs plc 1979-82, econ conslt and dir The Hinksey Centre 1982-; *Books* All Good Gifts, A Christian View of Affluence (1979); *Recreations* singing, travel, practising Christian; *Style—* Owen Nankivell, Esq; 12 Whittington Rd, Worcester WR5 2JU (☎ 0905 352948)

NAPIER, Barbara Langmuir; OBE (1975); da of James Langmuir Napier (d 1932), and Siblie Agnes, *née* Mowat (d 1932); family tree established back to 1695; ggn of Robert Napier of W Shandon (1791-1876), noted shipbuilder and co-fndr of Cunards (with Sam Cunard); *b* 21 Feb 1914; *Educ* Hillhead HS Glasgow, Univ of Glasgow (MA); *Career* organising sec Redlands Hosp Glasgow 1937-41, warden Queen Margaret Hall Univ of Glasgow 1941-44, gen advsr to women students 1942-64, sr tutor to women students 1964-74, ret 1974; JP 1955-80; memb exec ctee Nat Advsy Centre on Careers for Women 1963-68 and 1972-77, govr Notre Dame Coll of Educn Glasgow 1959-64, hon govr Westbourne Sch Glasgow 1981- (govr 1951-77, chm 1969-77); ind memb of three wages cncls (GB), dep chm of one, fndr memb (later pres and hon memb) Assoc of Principals Wardens and Advsrs to Univ Women Students 1942-77, holder of Winifred Cullis Lecture Fellowship of Br-American Assoc 1950, pres Standing Conf of Women's Orgns of Glasgow 1955-57, memb Scottish Ctee Ind Television Authy 1957-64; *Recreations* books, radio (and some TV), cats, dogs; *Clubs* College (Glasgow); *Style—* Miss Barbara Napier, OBE; 67 Brisbane St, Largs, Ayrshire KA30 8QP (☎ 0475 675495)

NAPIER, Hon Mrs Neville; (Helen) Catherine; *née* Sanderson; *m* 1967, as his 2 wife, Cdr the Hon Neville Archibald John Watson Ettrick Napier, RN (d 1970); *Style—* The Hon Mrs Neville Napier; Kippilaw, St Boswells, Roxburghshire (☎ 0835 22742)

NAPIER, Donald George; s of George Alker Napier (d 1934), and Ida Fernis, *née* Banning (d 1963); *b* 7 Nov 1914; *Educ* Tideswell GS Derbys; *m* 1, 12 June 1945, Isabel Norah (d 1982), da of George Alfred Close (d 1939); 2 da (Hilaré b 1946, Gillian b 1949); m 2, 21 Aug 1984, Jill Claire, da of Alexander Bentham (d 1979); *Career* chm and md W H Bramall & Co Ltd 1938-84; dir: Robert Riley (Hldgs) Ltd 1963-77, Excelsior Industl Hldgs Ltd 1984-86; *Recreations* gardening, walking; *Style—* Donald Napier, Esq; Hill Grove, Dymock, Gloucs GL18 2AR (☎ 053 185 495)

NAPIER, Master of; Hon Francis David Charles Napier; s and h of 14 Lord Napier and (5) Ettrick; *b* 3 Nov 1962; *Educ* Stanbridge Earls Sch; *Career* Lloyds; *Style—* The Master of Napier; Forest Lodge, Great Park, Windsor

NAPIER, Isabel, Lady Isabel Muriel; *née* Surtees; da of Maj Henry Siward Balliol Surtees, JP, DL (d 1955), of Redworth Hall, Co Durham; *m* 1931, Sir Joseph William Lennox Napier, 4 Bt, OBE (d 1986); 2 s (Robert, John); *Style—* Lady Isabel Napier; 17 Cheyne Gdns, Chelsea, London SW3 (☎ 01 352 4968)

NAPIER, Dr John Archibald Lennox; s and h of Sir William Archibald Napier of Merchistoun, 13 Bt; descended from John Napier inventor of logarithms; *b* 6 Dec 1946; *Educ* St Stithians, Witwatersrand Univ Johannesburg (MSc, PhD); *m* 9 Dec 1969, Erica Susan, da of late Kurt Kingsfield, of Johannesburg; 1 s (Hugh b 1977), 1 da (Natalie b 1973); *Career* res engr; *Clubs* Johannesburg Country; *Style—* Dr John Napier; Merchistoun, PO Box 65177, Benmore 2010, Transvaal, S Africa (☎ 011 783 2611)

NAPIER, Maj-Gen Lennox Alexander Hawkins; CB (1983), OBE (1970), MC (1957), DL (1984); s of Maj Charles McNaughton Napier; *b* 28 June 1928; *Educ* Radley, RMA Sandhurst; *m* 1959, Jennifer Wilson; 1 s, 2 da; *Career* cmmnd S Wales Borderers 1948, cmd 1 Bn S Wales Borderers and 1 Bn Royal Regt of Wales 1967-70, instr JSSC 1970-72, MOD 1972-74, Bde Cdr Berlin Inf Bde 1974-76, Div Brig Prince of Wales's Div 1976-80, GOC Wales 1980-83, ret; Col Cmdt Prince of Wales's Div 1980-83, Col Royal Regt of Wales (24/41 Foot) 1983-; inspr Public Inquiries 1983-, chm Central Tport Consultative Ctee 1985-; OstJ (1969); *Books* Armed Services Careers Year Book 1987-88; *Recreations* riding, shooting; *Clubs* Landsdowne; *Style—* Maj-Gen Lennox Napier, CB, OBE, MC, DL; c/o Barclays Bank, 17/18 Agincourt Sq, Monmouth, Gwent

NAPIER, Hon (Hugh) Lenox; 4 s of 13 Baron Napier and (4) Ettrick, TD (d 1954), and (Violet) Muir, er da of Sir Percy Wilson Newson, 1 and last Bt (d 1950); *b* 18 July 1943; *Educ* privately; *Style—* The Hon Lenox Napier; Glenfarg House, Dron, Perthshire (☎ 073 885 233)

NAPIER, Hon (Charles) Malcolm; s of 13 Baron Napier and 4 Ettrick, TD (d 1954); *b* 1933; *Educ* Canford; *m* 1969, Lady Mariota Cecilia Murray, *qv*; 3 da (Eloise, Maryel, Cecilia); *Career* formerly Lt 1 Royal Dragoons, served 1952-53; fndr-memb cncl Anglo-Rhodesian Soc, memb of Queen's Body Gd for Scotland (Royal Co of Archers); *Clubs* Cavalry, Pratt's, Turf, City & Civil Service (Cape Town); *Style—* The Hon Malcolm Napier; Bardmony House, Alyth, Perthshire (☎ 082 83 2645); 1 Newton Spicer Drive, Highlands, Harare, Zimbabwe

NAPIER, Lady Mariota (Cecilia); *née* Murray; da of 7 Earl of Mansfield and Mansfield (d 1971); *b* 1945; *m* 1969, Hon (Charles) Malcolm Napier, *qv*; *Style—* Lady Mariota Napier; Bardmony House, Alyth, Perthshire (☎ 082 83 2645); Hanover Place, 314 Rhodes Ave, Salisbury, Zimbabwe

NAPIER, Hon Michael Elibank; s of Brig Lord Robert John Napier (d 1987), 5 Baron Napier of Magdala, OBE, of 8 Mortonhall Rd, Edinburgh, and Lady Elizabeth Marian Napier, *née* Hunt; *b* 25 April 1953; *Educ* Trinity Coll Glenalmond, St Johns Coll Cambridge (MA), Univ of Newcastle (PhD); *Career* univ lectr, Univ of Nottingham 1984-; *Recreations* real tennis, orienteering, music; *Style—* The Hon Michael Napier; 3 Elswick Drive, Beeston, Nottingham NG9 1NQ (☎ 0602 252095); Dept of Civil Engineering, University Park, Nottingham NG7 2RD (☎ 0602 484848 ext 3663)

NAPIER, (Trevylyan) Miles Wentworth; s of Cdr Trevylyan Michael Napier, DSC, RN (d 1940), of Stokehill Wood, Buckland, S Devon, and Priscilla, *née* Hayter (da of Sir William Goodenough Hayter, KBE, KCMG); *b* 12 Oct 1934; *Educ* Wellington, Millfield; *m* 20 April 1971, Mary Philomena Ann, da of Edward Bourke, of

Rathfarnham, Co Dublin; 1 s (Lennox b 20 May 1975); *Career* Rifle Bde and 60 Rifles 1952-54, Offr Cadet Leics and Derys Yeo 1967-68; handicapper to Jockey Club and Nat Hunt Ctee 1964-67, conslt to Bloodstock and Racing Data (Prestell) 1981-; memb: Racing Press 1973-, Br Sporting Art Tst, Friends of Pavilion Opera; author; *Books* Thoroughbred Pedigrees Simplified (1973), Breeding a Racehorse (1975), Blood Will Tell (1978), The Racing Men of TV (1979), Keylocks Dams or Winners of all Flat races in Great Britain and Ireland (co-compiler 1967-68 and 1979-84); *Recreations* riding, sporting art, history, opera; *Style*— Miles Napier, Esq; Banbury House, Gt Easton, Market Harborough, Leicestershire (☎ 0536 770 449)

NAPIER, Sir Oliver John; s of James Joseph Napier (d 1975), of Belfast, and Sarah Frances Napier, *née* Bready; *b* 11 July 1935; *Educ* St Malachys Coll Belfast, Queens Univ Belfast (LLB); *m* 1961, Kathleen Brigid (d 1974), of Belfast; 3 s (James, John, Kevin), 5 da (Brigid, Veronica, Nuala, Emma, Mary-Jo); *Career* slr, memb Bd of Examiners Law Soc of NI 1964-68, min of Law Reform NI Exec 1973-74; memb: Belfast City Cncl 1977-, NI Assembly 1973-74 and 1982-, NI Constitutional Convention 1975-76; ldr Alliance Pty of N Ireland 1973-84, chm Standing Advsy Cmmn on Human Rights 1988-; kt 1985; *Recreations* gardening; *Clubs* Northern Law; *Style*— Sir Oliver Napier; Glenlyon, Victoria Rd, Holywood, Co Down, NI (☎ 5986); Napier & Sons Slrs, 1/9 Castle Arcade, High St, Belfast (☎ 244602)

NAPIER, Sir Robin Surtees; 5 Bt (UK 1867), of Merrion Sq, Dublin; assumed forenames of Robin Surtees in lieu of those of Robert Aubone Siward; s of Sir Joseph William Lennox Napier, 4 Bt, OBE (d 1986), by his w, Isabel Muriel, *née* Surtees; *b* 5 Mar 1932; *Educ* Eton; *m* 1971, Jennifer Beryl, da of late Herbert Warwick Daw, of Flint Walls, Henley-on-Thames; 1 s; *Heir* s, Charles Joseph b 1973; *Career* 2 Lt Coldstream Gds 1950-51; dir Charterhouse Japhet plc (Merchant Bankers) 1967-83, chm Standard Fireworks plc 1980-86; dir: Brickhouse Dudley plc 1981-86, Marlar Int 1983-, Dane & Co Ltd 1987-, Test and Itchen Fishing Assoc 1981-88; UK rep for Rothschild Bank AG 1983-; *Recreations* shooting, fishing, gardening; *Clubs* City of London, Flyfishers', Union (Sydney); *Style*— Sir Robin Napier, Bt; Upper Chilland House, Martyr Worthy, Winchester, Hants SO21 1EB (☎ 096278 307); New Court, St Swithin's Lane, London EC4P 4DU (☎ 01 280 5000)

NAPIER, Brig Vivian John Lennox; MC (1919), DL (Brecknock 1958); 3 s of Maj Sir William Lennox Napier, 3 Bt (ka 1915); *b* 13 July 1898; *Educ* Uppingham, RMC Sandhurst; *m* 1958, Marion Avis, da of Lt-Col Sir John Lloyd, MC; *Career* Brig E Africa, dist cmmr Kenya, vice-lt Brecknock 1964-74; OStJ; *Recreations* fishing; *Style*— Brig Vivian Napier, MC, DL; Ty Nant, Groesffordd, Brecon, Powys

NAPIER AND ETTRICK, 14 Lord (Napier S 1627) and 5 Baron (Ettrick UK 1872); Sir Francis Nigel Napier; 11 Bt (Nova Scotia 1666), of Thirlestane, CVO (1985, LVO 1980), DL (Selkirk 1974, Ettrick and Lauderdale 1975); s of 13 Lord Napier and Ettrick, TD, JP, DL (d 1954, eleventh in descent from first Lord, himself s of John Napier of Merchistoun, the inventor of logarithms); the Napiers of Merchistoun are co-heirs general of the ancient Celtic Earls of Lennox; *b* 5 Dec 1930; *Educ* Eton, RMA Sandhurst; *m* 1958, Delia Mary, da of Archibald D B Pearson, of Upper Sattenham, Milford, Surrey; 2 s (Master of Napier b 1962, Hon Nicholas b 1971, *qv*), 2 da (Hon Louisa (Hon Mrs Morrison) b 1961, Hon Georgina b 1969); *Heir* s, Master of Napier; *Career* Maj Scots Gds (R of O), Malaya 1950-51 (invalided); Adjt 1 Bn Scots Gds 1955-57; equerry to HRH the late Duke of Gloucester 1958-60 (ret 1960), sits as Ind Peer in House in Lords, in the City 1960-62, dep ceremonial and protocol sec Cwlth Rels Off 1962-68; Cons whip House of Lords 1970-71, comptroller and equerry to HRH The Princess Margaret, Countess of Snowden 1973- (private sec, comptroller and equerry 1974-); pres St John Ambulance Assoc and Bde London 1975-83; memb Royal Co of Archers (Queen's Body Gd for Scotland 1953-), on behalf of The Queen handed over the Instruments of Independence to Tuvalu (Ellice Islands) 1989; CStJ 1988 (OStJ 1982); Liveryman Worshipful Co of Grocers 1963; *Clubs* White's, Pratt's, Royal Caledonian Hunt; *Style*— Major the Lord Napier and Ettrick, CVO, DL; Forest Lodge, The Great Park, Windsor (☎ 0753 861262); Thirlestane, Ettrick, Selkirkshire; Nottingham Cottage, Kensington Palace, London W8 4PU

NAPIER AND ETTRICK, Dowager Baroness; (Violet) Muir; da of Sir Percy Wilson Newson, 1 and last Bt (d 1950), and Helena (d 1967), da of late Col Denham Franklin, RAMC; *b* 26 August 1909; *Educ* Heathfield Ascot; *m* 1928, 13 Baron Napier and (4) Ettrick, TD (d 1954); 4 s (1 decd); *Career* nat pres YWCA of Scotland 1961-82; *Style*— The Rt Hon Dowager The Lady Napier and Ettrick; Glenfarg House, Dron, Perthshire PH2 9PT (☎ 073 885 708)

NAPIER OF MAGDALA, 6 Baron (UK 1868), in Abyssinia and of Caryngton, Co Chester Robert Alan Napier; er s of 5 Baron Napier of Magdala, OBE (d 1987), and Elizabeth Marian, *née* Hunt; *b* 6 Sept 1940; *Educ* Winchester, St John's Coll Cambridge (BA); *m* 4 Jan 1964, Frances Clare, er da of late Alan Frank Skinner; OBE, of Monks Close, Woolpit, Suffolk; 1 s (Hon James Robert), 1 da (Hon Frances Catherine b 2 July 1964); *Heir* s, Hon James Robert Napier b 29 Jan 1966; *Recreations* sailing, music; *Clubs* Leander; *Style*— The Rt Hon Lord Napier of Magdala; 21 King St, Chester CH1 2AH (☎ 0244 316095)

NAPIER OF MERCHISTOUN, Sir William Archibald; 13 Bt (NS 1627), of Merchistoun; s of Sir Robert Archibald Napier, 12 Bt (d 1965), and his 1 w Violet, *née* Payne; *b* 19 July 1915; *Educ* Stowe; *m* 1942, Kathleen Mabel, da of late Reginald Henry Greaves, of Tafelberg, Cape, S Africa; 1 s; *Heir* s, John Archibald Lennox Napier, *qv*; *Career* served 1939-45 War as Capt S African Engrs in Middle East; consulting engr; *Clubs* Johannesburg Country, Rand; *Style*— Sir William Napier of Merchistoun, Bt; Merchiston Croft, PO Box 65177, Benmore, Transvaal 2010, S Africa (☎ Johannesburg 7832651); PO Box 65177, Benmore, Transvaal, 2010, S Africa

NAPLEY, Sir David; s of Joseph Napley; *b* 25 July 1915; *Educ* Burlington Coll; *m* 1940, Leah Rose, da of Thomas Saturley; 2 da; *Career* served WWII Queen's Royal (W Surrey) Regt and Indian Army; contested (C) Rowley Regis and Tipton 1951, Gloucester 1955; slr, sr ptnr Kingsley Napley, pres Law Soc 1976-77 (memb cncl 1962-86, vice pres 1975-76); memb: ed bd Criminal Law Review 1967-, Home Office Law Revision Ctee 1971-; dir Br Academy of Forensic Sciences 1974- (chm 1960-74, pres exec cncl 1967), chm examining bd ISVA 1981-84, pres West Ham Boys' Club 1981- (tstee 1979-), memb Cncl Imperial Soc Kts Bachelor 1981-; kt 1977; *Latest book* Not Without Prejudice (1982); *Style*— Sir David Napley; 107-115, Long Acre, London WC2E 9PT (☎ 01 240 2411, telex 28756)

NAPOLITAN, Leonard; CB (1970); s of Domenic Napolitan (d 1971), and Rose G, *née* Heales (d 1977); *b* 9 April 1919; *Educ* Highbury Co Sch, LSE (MSc); *m* 1945, Dorothy, da of Harry H Laycock (d 1958); 2 da; *Career* asst agric economist Univ of Bristol 1947-48, MAFF 1948-1977, (ret as under sec and dir of econs and stats); FRSA; *Style*— Leonard Napolitan, Esq, CB; 4 Rectory Gdns, Church Stretton, Shrops (☎ 0694 722 303)

NAPPER, Capt Derek William; CBE (1973, MBE 1946); s of William Ernest Napper (d 1974); *b* 28 August 1922; *Educ* RNC Dartmouth, RNC Greenwich; *m* 1945, Isobel, da of John Cowie, OBE; 4 s; *Career* Capt RN (Cdre) 1936-73 (despatches 1942), COS to Cdr Far East Fleet, dir Def Operational Plans MOD, ret 1973; gen mangr admin W of Eng Ship Owners Mutual Insur Assoc 1973-79; dir: of customer trg Racal Electronics 1980-82, Corporate Servs Interexec (London) 1983-85; memb ctee of Not Forgotten Assoc; *Recreations* painting, swimming; *Clubs* Army and Navy; *Style*— Capt Derek Napper, CBE, RN; Thorn, Melton, Woodbridge, Suffolk (☎ 039 43 2448)

NAPPER, John Pelham; s of John Mortimer Napper (artist, d 1951), and Dorothy Charlotte, *née* Hill (d 1976); *b* 17 Sept 1916; *Educ* Frensham Heights, private tutors, Royal Acad Schs of Art; *m* 1, 8 June 1935 (m dis 1945), Hedvig Sophie Armour; m 2, 20 Nov 1945, Pauline, da of Paul Victor Davidson, DSO (Lt-Col Royal Warwicks Regt, d 1946); *Career* served WWII, cmmnd RA 1941, War Artist to Ceylon Cmd 1943, seconded to RNVR 1944, demobbed 1946; painter; teacher life painting St Martin's Sch of Art 1949-57, visiting prof Fine Arts Univ of Southern Illinois Carbondale USA 1968-69, lived and worked in France 1957-68; One Man Exhibitions: The Leicester Galleries London 1949 1961 and 1962,The Adams Gallery London 1957 and 1959, The Walker Art Gallery Liverpool (Retrospective) 1959, La Maison de la Pensée Francaise Paris 1960, Galerie Lahumière Paris 1963 and 1965, Galerie Hervé Paris 1965, Larcada Gallery NY 1967 1970 1972 1975 and 1977, Browse & Darby Ltd London 1978 and 1980, Oldham Art Gallery (Retrospective) 1984, Thos Agnew and Sons Ltd London 1986, Albemarle Gallery London 1988; Prizes: Medaille d'Argent Salon des Artistes Francaises (Paris) 1947, Int Exhibition of Fine Arts (Moscow) 1957, The Critics Prize (awarded by the Int Assoc of Art Critics) 1961; AAUP 1968; *Style*— John Napper, Esq; c/o Albemarle Gallery, 18 Albemarle St, London W1X 3HA (☎ 01 355 1880)

NAQVI, (Syed Zakir Husain) Haider; s of Syed Ather Husain Naqvi (d 1954), and Saghir Fatima, *née* Rizvi; *b* 14 Oct 1949; *Educ* Karachi Univ (BCom, MA); *m* 18 March 1977, Marja-Liisa, da of Paavo Ilmari Nyssönen, of Sorsakoski, Finland; 2 da (Chantal Samreen b 1980, Sabrina Yasmeen b 1986); *Career* CA; internal auditor Philip Industs (UK) Ltd 1975-77, gp fin controller London Export Corpn (Hldgs) Ltd 1977-78, ptnr Haider Naqvi & Co CAs 1978-; FCA 1973; Assoc Inst of Chartered Secs & Admins 1974; *Recreations* squash, keeping fit, snooker, chess; *Style*— Haider Naqvi, Esq; 75 Lake View, Canons Drive, Edgware, Middx HA8 7SA (☎ 01 958 3196); 225 Hale Lane, Edgware, Middx HA8 9QF (☎ 01 958 8015, fax 01 958 8535, telex GECOMS-G 8951182)

NARES, Anthony James; s of John George Alastair MacKintyre Nares, RN (ka 1942), of Villa Pavillon, Monte Carlo, Monaco, and Marguerite Emily Louise Buchanan-Dunlop, *née* McFarlane; *b* 17 Feb 1942; *Educ* Charterhouse; *m* 19 July 1975, Thomasin Sarah, da of (Alfred) Ronald Dashwood Gilbey, CBE (d 1978), of Dorset; 1 s (George b 10 Aug 1982); *Career* Royal Horse Gds (The Blues) 1964-68; md: Lippincott & Margulies 1969-78, Centaur Communications 1978-; launched: Marketing Week 1978, Creative Review 1981, Money Marketing 1984, Design Week 1985, New Accountant 1988; *Recreations* skiing, shooting; *Clubs* Turf; *Style*— Anthony Nares, Esq; 8 Bloomfield Terr, London SW1W 8PG (☎ 01 439 4222); Ellingham Farm, Ringwood, Hants; 50 Poland St, London W1 (☎ 01 494 0300, car tel 0836 226298)

NASH, David Harwood; s of Victor Nash, of Welwyn, Herts, and Anne, *née* Richardson; *Educ* St Albans Sch; *m* 20 June 1960, Susan Margaret, da of John Charlesworth Haldane; 1 s (James Harwood), 2 da (Charlotte Harwood, Annabel Haldane); *Career* ptnr: Binder Hamlyn 1966-76, Nash and Co 1977-82, Finlay Robertson 1982-86, Robertson Nash 1986-87, Pannell Kerr Forster 1987-; dir DSC Hldgs plc 1984-, memb Lloyds; memb Brompton Soc; FCA; *Recreations* skiing, sailing, tennis; *Clubs* MCC; *Style*— David Nash, Esq; 10 Pelham St, London SW7 2N6 (☎ 01 225 0702); 78 Hatton Gdn, London EC1 (☎ 01 831 7393)

NASH, (Denis Frederic) Ellison; OBE (1982), AE (1944); s of late Frederic Arthur Nash; *b* 10 Feb 1913; *Educ* Dulwich, St Bartholomew's Hosp Med Coll London; *m* 1938, Joan Mary, *née* Andrew; 2 s, 2 da; *Career* consulting surgn St Bartholomew's Hosp, formerly dean of Medical Coll Univ of London; FRCS; *Recreations* gardening, photography, work with disabled; *Clubs* Guild of Freemen, City of London; *Style*— D F Ellison Nash, Esq, OBE, AE; 28 Hawthorne Rd, Bickley, Kent (☎ 01 467 1142)

NASH, Eric Charles; s of Charles Nash (d 1984), and Ellen, *née* Fowkes (d 1981); *b* 6 Mar 1927; *Educ* Carshalton Sch; *m* 15 March 1952, Jean, da of James Murray Miller (d 1963); 2 s (Ian b 18 March 1953, Andrew b 24 Dec 1955); *Career* Army 1944-48; Distillers Co Ltd 1948-58, non marine mangr W E Found & Co Ltd 1958-76; account exec: Alexander Howden & Co Ltd 1976-87, How F Devitt & Sons Ltd 1987; pres Southern Co Athletic Assoc, dir AAA; Freeman City of London, memb Worshipful Co of Bakers 1982; MBIM; *Recreations* athletics; *Style*— Eric Nash, Esq; 12 Margaret Rd, Bexley, Kent DA5 1DU (☎ 01 303 4573); Howson F Devitt & Sons Ltd, 100 Whitechapel Rd, London (☎ 01 247 8888, fax 01 377 0022, telex 886129)

NASH, James Gardiner; MBE; s of Col William Nash, CBE, TD (d 1981) and Eileen, *née* Kirkcaldie (d 1985); *b* 30 July 1934; *Educ* Stowe; *m* 15 Aug 1965 (m dis 1984), Sally Anne Randall; 2 s (Thomas b 1967 Matthew b 1969); *Career* Nat Serv 1953-55, 2 Lt 12 Royal Lancers in Malaya, Leics and Derby Yeo 1955-59; political offr Aden Protectorate 1959-65 (Colonial Off), FO London and Bahrain 1965-67; chartered surveyor: City of London 1969-88, Egypt 1974-77; walked Venice to Addis Ababa 1956-57, rode a horse Istanbul to Jerusalem 1988; govr Alexandria Schs Tst, sec Ward of Cheap Club 1984-88; OStJ 1978; Freeman City of London 1982, memb Worshipful Co of Broderers Co 1982; FRICS 1977-89; *Recreations* cooking, gardening, Middle East, writing poor verse; *Clubs* Cavalry & Guards; *Style*— James Gardiner Nash, Esq, MBE; 72 Buttesland St, London N1 6BY (☎ 01 253 0638)

NASH, John Alfred Stoddard; s of Lewis John Alfred Maurice Nash, of New Cottage, High Rd, Chipstead, Surrey, and Josephine Karen, *née* Stoddard (d 1962); *b* 22 Mar 1949; *Educ* Milton Abbey Sch, Corpus Christi Coll Oxford (MA); *m* 6 Aug 1963, Caroline Jennifer, da of Geoffrey Hamilton Paul (d 1985) of Kirton Lodge, Ipswich, Suffolk; 1 s (Charles b 1985), 1 da (Josephine b 1984); *Career* asst dir Lazard Brother and Co Ltd 1975-83, md Advent Ltd 1986 (joined 1983), chm Br Venture capital

Assocn 1988-89; *Recreations* golf, tennis, skiing; *Clubs* Turf; *Style*— John Nash, Esq; Advent Ltd, 25 Buckingham Gate, London SW1E 6LD (☎ 01 630 9811)

NASH, John Edward; s of Joseph Ronald Nash (d 1977); *b* 25 June 1925; *Educ* Sydney Univ (BEc), Balliol Coll Oxford (BPhil); *m* 1947, Ralda Everard Tyndall, *née* Herring; 2 s (Antony James, Jeremy Robert), 2 da (Regina Jane, Camilla Kate); *Career* dir: Samuel Montagu & Co Ltd 1956-73, monetary affrs EEC Cmmn 1973-77, Reckitt & Colman Ltd 1966-73 and 1977-87, SG Warburg & Co Ltd London 1977-87, chm: Mercury Money Mkt Tst 1978-86, SG Warburg Bank AG Zurich 1977-87 (memb advsy bd 1987-); hon tres and memb bd of tstees World Wide Fund for Nature 1985-; *Recreations* golf, skiing, horse racing, music; *Clubs* Turf, Buck's, MCC; *Style*— John Nash, Esq; Chalet Gstelli, CH-3781 Gsteig-bei-Gstaad, Switzerland (☎ Gstaad 51162)

NASH, Norman Charles Russell; s of Robert Russell Nash (d 1966), of Ballymoney, NI, and Evan Alice Nash, *née* Phillips (d 1976); *b* 15 Sept 1928; *Educ* Uppingham; *m* 2 April 1956, Mary Elizabeth, da of Lt-Col J R H Greeves, TD, JP (d 1988), of Altona, Strandtown, Belfast, N I; 1 s (Patrick b 1958), 2 da (Cressida b 1960, Polly b 1963); *Career* CA: articled to Macnaird Mason Evans and Co London 1947 (qualified 1951), ptnr Burke Covington and Nash London 1952, fndr and sr ptnr Nash Broad 1973-, fndr and int sec GMN Int 1977- fndr and dir Unity Security Balloting Services Ltd 1987; vice pres Rosslyn Park FC 1959- (hon tres 1957-59), ctee memb Hurlingham club 1960-76 (chm fin ctee 1970-75), hon tres Assoc of Hon Stewards Wimbledon Lawn Tennis Championships 1975-, cncl memb St Margarets Church Putney 1960-86 (churchwarden 1982-86); chm cassette library of recorded books Calibre Ltd 1983-, memb ctee London Soc of Chamber Music 1984-, cncl memb and memb gen purposes ctee Royal Sch of Church Music 1985-; ACA 1952, FCA 1957; *Recreations* skiing, gliding, music, canal boats; *Clubs* MCC, City of London; *Style*— Norman Nash, Esq; Flat 5J, Portman Mansions, Chiltern St, London W1H 1PU (☎ 01 935 5570); The Red House, Burdrop, Sibford Gower, Banbury, Oxon OX15 5RQ (☎ 029 578 275); Nash Broad Chartered Accountants, 42 Upper Berkeley St, London W1H 8AB (☎ 01 723 7293, fax 01 724 3488, telex 23722)

NASH, Paul Frank Anthony; s of Frank Nash, of 25 Romberg Rd, Tooting, London, and Hilda, *née* Chorley (d 1969); *b* 18 Nov 1946; *Educ* Salesian Coll Battersea; *m* 27 Feb 1971, Jill Antonia, da of Jack Mallett, of 24 Burnt Wood Grove, Wandsworth Common, London; 1 s (Henry b 1980), 2 da (Victoria b 1973, Charlotte b 1974); *Career* md RP Martin plc 1987 (dir 1977); memb For Exchange and Currency Deposit Brokers Assoc 1987; *Recreations* golf, cricket, gardening; *Clubs* MCC; *Style*— Paul Nash, Esq; RP Martin plc, 4 Deans Ct, London EC4V 5RA (☎ 01 600 8691, fax 01 236 3537)

NASH, Philip; s of John Hollett Nash (d 1975), of Bushey, Herts, and Edith Grace, *née* Knee (d 1987); *b* 14 Mar 1930; *Educ* Watford GS; *m* 27 June 1953, Barbara Elizabeth, da of George Bangs, of Bushey, Herts; 1 s (Simon John b 1959); *Career* Nat Serv RAF 1949-50; HM Customs and Excise 1950-: on loan Civil Serv Coll 1970-75, asst sec and head mgmnt servs 1978-81, asst sec customs directorate 1981-86, cmmr and dir customs 1986-; *Style*— Philip Nash, Esq; HM Customs and Excise, Dorset House, Stamford St, London SE1 (☎ 01 928 0533)

NASH, Raymond Cecil; MBE (1945); s of George Percy Nash (d 1950), of 4 Holmes Grove, Henleaze, Bristol, and Rosina Louise, *née* Wilkins (d 1916); *b* 13 Jan 1914; *Educ* St Brendans Coll Clifton Bristol; *m* 24 June 1939, Betty Denise, da of Gilbert Frank Bulphin (d 1953), of 50 Harcourt Rd, Redland, Bristol; 1 s (Michael b 1943), 1 da (Hazel b 1941); *Career* Princess Louise's Kensington Regt TA 1939, WWII, cmmnd Glos Regt 1940, 2 Bn the Glos Regt 1940 (ADI 1942) (served Normandy D Day Landings); idc 1937, WH Grigg & Perkins CAs of Bristol 1948 (later Grigg Nash & Co Accountants of Minehead (sr ptnr 1963-, ret 1988); sec Minehead and Dist Chamber of Trade 1947-72, formerly chm Minehead Publicity Assoc, cdre Minehead Sailing Club, Worshipful Master Exmoor Lodge of Freemasons; dep prov grand master prov Grand Lodge of mark Master Masons of Somerset 1986-89; former ctee memb: Taunton & Dist Youth Employment Ctee, SW Dist Soc of CAs: FCA 1937; *Recreations* sailing, golf, freemasons; *Style*— Raymond Nash, Esq; Carmel, 4 Warden Rd, Minehead, Somerset TA24 5DS (☎ 0643 2869)

NASH, Thomas Arthur Manly; CMG (1959), OBE (1944); s of Col Llewellin Thomas Nash, CMG (d 1928), and Editha Gertrude *née* Sloggett (d 1947); *b* 18 June 1905; *Educ* Wellington, Univ of London (BSc, PhD, DSc); *m* 1930, Marjorie Wenda, da of Walter Alexander Wayte (d 1950); 1 s (decd); *Career* Colonial Serv 1927-59; entomologist; tstee res; Tanganyaika 1927-32, Nigerian Sleeping Sickness Serv 1933-47; dir: W African Inst for Trypanosomiasis Res 1954-59, Tsetse Res Laboratory Bristol Univ Langford 1962-71; *Books* Africa's Bane: The Tsetse Fly (1969), A Zoo Without Bars (1984); *Recreations* gardening; *Style*— Dr Thomas Nash, Esq, CMG, OBE; Spring Head Farm, Upper Langford, nr Bristol BS18 7DN (☎ 0934 852 321)

NASH, Thomas Philip; s of Peter H Nash, and (Constance) Phyllis, *née* Wright; *b* 21 August 1946; *Educ* Ipswich Sch, Oxford Poly (Dip Arch); *m* 17 June 1972, Catherine Mary, da of Dr E W C Buckell; 3 s (Edward b 1979, Robert b 1982, Henry (twin) b 1982), 1 da (decd); *Career* architect, own practice, specialising church works; memb RIBA; *Recreations* sailing, reading, painting; *Clubs* Norfolk; *Style*— Thomas Nash, Esq; 22 West Parade, Norwich NR2 3PW (☎ 0603 627802)

NASH, The Ven Trevor Gifford; s of Frederick Walter Gifford Nash (d 1963), of Bedford, and Elsie Violet Louise Nash, JP, *née* Martin (d 1984); *b* 3 May 1930; *Educ* Haileybury, Clare Coll Cambridge (MA), Cuddesdon Coll Oxford; *m* 28 Oct 1957, Wanda Elizabeth, da of Sir Leslie Brian Freeston, KCMG, OBE (d 1958), of Kent; 4 da (Lois b 1958, Penelope b 1960, Phoebe b 1964, Joanna b 1968); *Career* Nat Serv Greece 1948-50; ordained 1955, chaplain TA 1956-61; curate: Cheshunt, Kingston upon Thames 1955-61; priest-in-charge Stevenage 1961-63, vicar of Leagrave Luton 1963-67, sr chaplain St George's Hosp London 1967-73, vicar St Lawrence and St Swithin Winchester 1973-82, priest-in-charge Holy Trinity Winchester 1977-82, rural dean of Winchester 1977-82, Bishop's advsr for Miny of Healing 1973-, archdeacon of Basingstoke 1982-, memb of Gen Synod 1983-; dir of Luton Samaritans 1966-67; *Recreations* music, sport, reading, clay modelling; *Style*— The Ven the Archdeacon of Basingstoke; 3 Crossborough Hill, Basingstoke, Hants (☎ 0256 28572)

NASTA, Krishna (Kris); s of Kanayalal Nasta (d 1967), and Winifred Mary, *née* Milnthorpe; *b* 28 August 1943; *Educ* Eltham Coll, Univ of Salford (BSc); *m* 5 July 1969, Ann Beatrice, da of William Frederick Clifton; 1 s (Matthew b 27 Sep 1975), 1 da (Alison b 17 June 1972); *Career* GEC 1967-69, Reyrolle-Parsons 1969-70, ITT Business Systems 1970-71, home sales exec Plessey Of Systems 1976-79 (mktg exec 1971-75), gen mangr European Telecommunications Teradyne Ltd 1980-89, vice pres Teradyne Inc 1989; *Recreations* bridge, music, reading, raquet sports; *Style*— Kris Nasta, Esq; 7 Hilgay Close, Guildford, Surrey (☎ 0483 66569); Teradyne Ltd, The Western Centre, Bracknell, Berks (☎ 0344 426899, fax 0344 481355, telex 049713)

NATERPARK, 7 Baron (I 1729); Sir Frederick Caryll Philip Cavendish; 8 Bt (GB 1755); s of Brig-Gen Frederick Cavendish, bro of 6 Baron and 6 in descent from William Cavendish, love child of 3 Duke of Devonshire; suc unc 1948; *b* 6 Oct 1926; *Educ* Eton; *m* 1951, Danièle, da of Roger Guirche, of Paris; 1 s, 2 da; *Heir* s, Hon Roderick Cavendish; *Career* served Gren Gds, Kenya Police Reserve; sales dir CSE Aviation Ltd 1962-; dep chm and md CSE Int 1984; *Clubs* Cavalry and Guards'; *Style*— The Rt Hon Lord Waterpark; 2/74 Elm Park Rd, London SW3 (☎ 01 351 3663); Park House, Bletchingdon, Oxford (☎ (0869) 50238)

NATHAN, Clemens Neumann; s of Kurt Arthur Nathan (d 1958), of London, and Dr Else Nathan, *née* Kanin; *b* 24 August 1933; *Educ* Berkhampsted Sch, Scottish Coll of Textiles, Univ of Leeds; *m* 4 June 1963, (Barbara) Rachel, da of Geoffrey H Whitehill (d 1971), of London; 1 s (Richard Abraham b 15 Oct 1965), 2 da (Jennifer Ruth b 13 May 1964, Elizabeth Rebecca b 18 Oct 1970); *Career* chm Cunart Co Ltd 1958-, conslt textile technologist on bd of various textile orgns, govt advsr; pres: Anglo Jewish Assoc, CCJO (UN NGO); presidential advsr Alliance Israelite Universelle; govr: Distributive Trades Coll, Shenkar Coll Israel; tstee Biochem Inst Israel, vice pres Textile Inst; Textile Inst Medal (for servs to textile indust and Inst) 1987; Freeman Worshipful Co of Glovers; CText, FTI, FRAI; Cavaliere Al Merito Della Republica Italiana, Israel Econ Cncl Medal; *Books* Marketing, Textiles; *Recreations* swimming, mountaineering, art, history, music; *Clubs* Athenaeum; *Style*— Clemens Nathan, Esq; 2 Ellerdale Close, London NW3; 231 Oxford St, London W1 (☎ 01 437 1355, fax 01 439 6721, telex 25362)

NATHAN, Derek Maurice; s of Joseph Albert (d 1973), and Grace Julia, *née* Abrahams; ggf fndr of Glaxo, gggf fndr of Shell; *b* 24 Sept 1929; *Educ* Oundle, Univ of London; *m* 15 Dec 1954, Mary Catherine, da of Louis Lavine (d 1940); 1 s (Timothy b 1957), 1 da (Sara b 1956); *Career* md: Dual Devpts Ltd Printbrokers 1967-, Douglas A Lyons & Assocs Ltd Sound Reproduction Factors 1973-; *Recreations* philately, golf; *Clubs* Royal Philatelic Soc London, British West Indies Study Circle, Wimbledon Park GC, Ramblers Golfing Soc (convenor); *Style*— Derek M Nathan, Esq; 52 Morrish Rd, London SW2 4EG (☎ 01 674 9585, fax 01 6721 6908)

NATHAN, Hon Jennifer Ruth; da of 2 Baron Nathan; *b* 4 June 1952; *Style*— The Hon Jennifer Nathan; Collyers Farm, Lickfold, Petworth, Sussex

NATHAN, QC Kandiah Shanmuga; s of Sanmugam Kandiah Nathan, and Sundram, *née* Murugesu; *b* 24 May 1930; *Educ* Methodist Boy's Sch Kuala Lumpur, Japanese Sch Malaya, Anglo Chinese Sch Malaya, Univ of London (LLB); *m* 1966, Elizabeth Mary Woodwark; 2 s, 1 da; *Career* teacher Singapore 1950-52, lab offr Malaya 1952-57, asst personnel offr City Cncl Singapore 1957-59, barr Lincoln's Inn 1963, industl rels advsr Malayan Mining Employers Assoc 1963-64, memb Indust Tbnl Malaya 1964, advocate and slr Malaysia and Singapore 1964-69, immigrations cnsllr UK Immigrant's Advice Serv 1970-72; *Recreations* golf, gardening; *Clubs* Royal Cwlth Soc, Cwlth Golf Soc, Royal Selangor, Royal Selangor GC; *Style*— K S Nathan, Esq, QC

NATHAN, Peter Geoffrey; s of Maj Cyril H Nathan (d 1977), of Prestwick, Chiddingfold, Surrey, and Violet, *née* Simon (d 1974); *b* 27 July 1929; *Educ* Charterhouse, Oriel Coll Oxford (MA), Univ of Paris (Dip in Etudes de Civilisation Française); *m* 14 May 1970, Caroline Monica, da of Lt Cdr Anthony C Mullen, RINVR; 2 s (Hugo b 1975, Anthony b 1981), 2 da (Arabella b 1972, Venetia b 1973); *Career* writer RN 1948-49; Herbert Oppenheimer Nathan & Vandyk 1954-88 (admitted slr 1958, ptnr 1959-88), conslt Boodle Hatfield 1988; chm London Playing Fields Soc 1984-, memb cncl of the Br Heart Fndn, tstee Oriel Coll Devpt Tst, chm Butterflies CC, hon memb Geographical Assoc; chm Chiddingfold branch of Farnham Cons Assoc 1965-70, memb Community Health Cncl for Kensington, Chelsea and Westminster representing Royal borough of Kensington and Chelsea 1974-78; Master Worshipful Co of Gold and Silver Wyre Drawers; *Recreations* cricket, tennis, riding, reading, opera; *Clubs* MCC, Vincent's, Oriental, City Livery, City Univ; *Style*— Peter Nathan, Esq; 59 Rowan Rd, London W6 7DT; 43 Brook St, London W1Y 2BL (☎ 01 629 7411, fax 01 629 2621, telex 261414)

NATHAN, Philip Charles; s of Denis William Nathan, of S Woodham, Perrers, Essex, and Grace Pauline, *née* Brennan; *b* 11 May 1951; *Educ* Alexandra Park Sch; *Career* stockbroker; head of dealing Charles Stanley & Co Ltd; dist offr Lions Int E Anglia (formerly pres Rayleigh Essex); memb: Int Stock Exchange, Securities Assoc; *Style*— Philip Nathan, Esq; Charles Stanley & Co Ltd, Garden House, 18 Finsbury Circus, London EC2M 7BL (☎ 01 638 5717, fax 01 638 8836, car tel 0836 251559, telex 8952218)

NATHAN, 2 Baron (UK 1940); Capt Roger Carol Michael Nathan; s of 1 Baron, PC (d 1963); bro of Hon Lady Waley-Cohen; *b* 5 Dec 1922; *Educ* Stowe, New Coll Oxford; *m* 1950, Philippa, da of Maj Joseph Bernard Solomon, MC, of Sutton End, Pulborough, Sussex; 1 s, 2 da; *Heir* s, Hon Rupert Harry Bernard Nathan; *Career* served WWII, Capt 17/21 Lancers (despatches, wounded twice); slr; sr ptnr Herbert Oppenheimer Nathan & Vandyk until 1986, conslt Denton Hall Burgin and Warrens, assoc memb Bar Assoc of City of New York and New York County Lawyers Assoc; pres Jewish Welfare Bd 1967-71, hon pres Central Br Fund for Jewish Relief and Rehabilitation 1971-77 (chm 1975-77), vice-pres RSA 1977- (chm 1975-77); vice-chm Cancer Res Campaign 1987- (chm exec ctee 1970-75, tres 1979-87); memb: Royal Cmmn on Environmental Pollution 1979-, House of Lords select ctee on Euro Communities 1983-88; chm: House of Lords select ctee on Murder and Life Imprisonment 1988-, Environment sub-ctee 1983-87; pres: UK Environmental Law Assoc 1987-; Nat Soc for Clean Air 1987-; Master Worshipful Co of Gardeners' 1963; Hon LLD Sussex; FSA, FRSA, FRGS; *Clubs* Athenaeum, Cavalry and Guards; *Style*— The Rt Hon the Lord Nathan; 20 Copthall Ave, London EC2 (☎ 01 628 9611); Collyers Farm, Lickfold, Petworth, W Sussex (☎ 079 85 284)

NATHAN, Hon Rupert Harry Bernard; s and h of 2 Baron Nathan; *b* 26 May 1957; *Educ* Univ of Durham (BA); *Career* Marine Surveyor; *Recreations* motorcycles, travel, house renovation, boxing (to watch *not* participate!); *Style*— The Hon Rupert Nathan

NATHANSON, Hon Mrs (Victoria Elizabeth Anne); *née* Thorneycroft; da of Baron Thorneycroft, CH, PC, by his 2 w, Carla, da of Conte Malagola-Cappi, of Ravenna, and formerly w of Conte Giorgio Roberti; *b* 25 June 1951; *Educ* St Mary's Convent Ascot; *m* 1975, Richard H Nathanson; 2 s (Daniel b 1978, Alexander b 1980), 1 da

(Susannah b 1985); *Style—* The Hon Mrs Nathanson; 25 Enmore Rd, London SW15 (☎ 01 788 2718)

NAUGHTON, Philip Anthony; QC (1988); s of Francis Naughton, of Littlehampton, Sussex, and Madeleine, *née* Wales; *b* 18 May 1943; *Educ* Wimbledon Coll, Univ of Nottingham (LLB); *m* 6 July 1968, Barbara Jane, da of Prof F E Bruce, of Esher, Surrey; 2 s (Sebastian b 18 March 1974, Felix b 24 April 1978), 1 da (Charlotte b 8 Sept 1972); *Career* in indust 1964-71, barr Gray's Inn 1971; *Recreations* walking, fishing, sailing, theatre, music; *Clubs* Hampshire; *Style—* Philip Naughton, Esq, QC; 3 Serjeants Inn, London EC4Y 1BQ (☎ 01 353 5537, fax 01 353 0425, telex 264093 SERJIN G)

NAYLOR, Lt-Col Donald Russell; MBE (1945); s of John Alfred Naylor (d 1937), of Glenshee Lodge, Trinity Rd, Wandsworth Common, London SW18, and Ellen Louise, *née* Russell (k by enemy action 1940, at The Thatch, Petersham, Richmond); *b* 22 Feb 1916; *Educ* Emanuel Sch, ICL (BSc); *m* 19 Aug 1939, Olive Lucy, da of Charles William Johns (d 1965); 2 s (John b 1943, Philip b 1953), 1 da (Judith b 1940); *Career* Sapper RE 1939, cmmnd 2 Lt RAOC (Mech Eng) 1941, Capt OME RAOC 1 Army 1942, Capt EME 16 Base W/Shops REME N Africa 1943, Maj DADME AFHQ Italy 1944-45, Lt-Col ADME AFHQ 1946 (hospitalised with poliomielitis contracted in Italy); Lt-Col 1948; chm Rosser & Russell Ltd 1976-78 (dir 1948-78); chm and dir; TES Ltd 1978-81, H & V Welfare Ltd 1973-86, CCH Ltd & Welfare Hldgs Ltd 1973-86; pres Heating & Ventilating Contractors Assoc UK 1972-73, chm Coombe Roads Assoc Ltd 1980-86; Freeman City of London, Liveryman Worshipful Co of Fanmakers 1976; CEng, MIMechE, ACGI, FCIBSE, FInstD, FRSA; *Recreations* boat building, motor cruising, shooting, bric-a-brac; *Style—* Lt-Col Donald Naylor, MBE; 15 Kingsdown, 115A Ridgway, Wimbledon, London SW19 4RL (☎ 01 947 6385)

NAYLOR, Prof Ernest; s of Joseph Naylor (d 1961), and Evelyn Keeton (d 1981); *b* 19 May 1931; *Educ* Swanwick Hall, Univ of Sheffield (BSc), Univ of Liverpool (PhD, DSc); *m* 7 Sept 1956, (Carol) Gillian, da of Harold Denovan Bruce (d 1970); 2 da (Elizabeth, Helen); *Career* cmmnd RAF educn branch 1954-56; reader in zoology Univ Coll Swansea 1968 (asst lectr 1956, lectr 1959, sr lectr 1963), prof of marine biology Univ of Liverpool 1971-82, dir Port Erin Marine Laboratory IOM 1971-82; Univ Coll of N Wales: Lloyd Roberts prof of zoology 1982-88; head of sch of animal biology 1983-88, Lloyd Roberts prof of marine zoology sch of ocean sci 1988-; cncl memb NERC 1976-82, specialist advsr to House of Lords select ctee on marine sci and technol 1985, memb coordinating ctee on marine sci and technol 1988; FIBiol 1972; *Books* British Marine Isopods (1972), Cyclical Phenomena in Marine Plants and Animals (jt ed with R G Hartnoll, 1979); *Recreations* gardening; *Style—* Prof Ernest Naylor; School of Ocean Sciences, University College of North Wales, Marine Science Laboratories, Menai Bridge, Anglesey, Gwynedd (☎ 0248 351151, fax 0248 716367)

NAYLOR, (Charles) John; s of Arthur Edgar Naylor, MBE, and Elizabeth Mary Naylor; *b* 17 August 1943; *Educ* Royal GS Newcastle upon Tyne, Haberdasher's Aske's, Clare Coll Cambridge (MA); *m* 1968, Margery; 2 s; *Career* jr and sr exec posts in indust 1965-75, dir YMCA Nat Centre Lakeside Cumbria 1975-80, dep nat sec Nat Cncl of YMCA's 1980-82, nat sec Nat Cncl of YMCA's 1982-, vice-chm Nat Cncl for Vol Youth Servs 1985-88, (memb nat advsy cncl); *Recreations* running, the outdoors particularly mountains, theatre, church, growing family; *Style—* John Naylor, Esq; Nat Cncl of YMCA's, 640 Forest Rd, London E17 3DZ (☎ 01 520 5599)

NAYLOR, Prof Malcolm Neville; RD (1967); s of Roland B Neville, MBE (d 1969) of Walsall, Staffs, and Mabel Louisa, *née* Neville (d 1976); *b* 30 Jan 1926; *Educ* Queen Mary's Sch Walsall, Univ of Glasgow, Univ of Birmingham (BSc, BDS), Univ of London (PhD); *m* 10 Jan 1956, (Doreen) Mary, da of Horace E Jackson, CBE (d 1966), of Gerrard Cross, Bucks; 1 s (Andrew b 1960); *Career* RNVR 1943-77: Seaman Offr 1943-47 served HMS Suffok, dentist 1954-77, ret as Surgn Capt (D) and sr dental surgn; civil conslt dental surgn RN 1969-, jr hosp appts Birmingham and Dundee 1954-59; Guys Hosp: res fell dental sch 1959-62, sr lectr in preventive dentistry dental sch 1962-66, reader Univ of London 1966-70, hon conslt 1966-, prof of preventive dentistry 1970-, head of dept of periodontology and preventive dentistry 1980; Univ of London: memb sea cadet sport cncl 1975-, chm cncl Mil Educn Ctees of Univs of UK 1982-, dep chm bd of studies in dentistry 1986; memb Sea Cadet Assoc Cncl 1976, vice chm Bacons Sch 1978, chm of govrs St Saviours and St Olaves Sch 1987-; govr: Whitelands Coll, Roehampton Inst for Higher Educn; lay reader C of E 1974-; Queen's hon dental surgn 1976; Hon Col Univ of London OTC 1979; Hon Liveryman Worshipful Co of Bakers 1981, Freeman City of London 1981; BDA 1955, IADR 1959, RSM 1959; *Recreations* sailing (cruising off-shore), home and family; *Clubs* Royal Solent YC, RN Sailing Assoc; *Style—* Prof Malcolm Naylor, RD; Carrick Lodge, Roehampton, London SW15 5BN (☎ 788 5045); Guy's Hospital, London SE1 SRT (☎ 01 407 7600 ext 2866, fax 01 407 3913)

NAYLOR, (William) Maurice; CBE (1973); Thomas Naylor (d 1956), of Stockport, and Agnes, *née* Porter (d 1974); *b* 20 Dec 1920; *Educ* St Joseph's Coll Market Drayton, Univ of Manchester (BA); *m* 1948, Maureen, da of John Walsh (d 1959), of Marple, Cheshire; 1 s (Michael b 1951), 2 da (Anne b 1949, Elizabeth b 1956); *Career* dir Nat Assoc of Health Authys in England and Wales 1981-83, regnl admin Trent Regnl Health Authy 1973-81, sec Sheffield Rgnl Hosp Bd 1963-81, past pres Inst of Health Servs Mgmnt; MBA Univ of Sheffield; FHSM; *Style—* Maurice Naylor, Esq, CBE; 8 Middlefield Croft, Dore, Sheffield S17 3AS

NAYLOR, (Thomas) Peter; DL; s of Thomas Humphrey Naylor (d 1966), of Ashton, Chester, and Quenelda Anne, *née* Williamson (d 1942); *b* 5 Dec 1923; *Educ* Eton; *m* 22 June 1946, Patricia Elisabeth, da of Maurice Illingworth (d 1965), of Far Sawrey; 1 s (Adam b 1954); *Career* Pilot, served Coastal Cmd 1944-45, RAFVR 1942-46; chm Demerara Co (Hldgs) Ltd Liverpool 1968-69 (dir 1954--59, md 1960-69), non-exec dir Prov Gp plc 1970- (formerly Prov Insur Co Ltd); memb: N Lonsdale Rural DC 1970-74, Cumbria CC 1974-85 (chm 1976-80); chm: cncl Inc Liverpool Sch Tropical Medicine 1969-73, tstees Lake Dist Art Gallery and Museum Tst 1983-; jt hon rep Nat Art Collections Fund Cumbria 1984-88; ACA 1950, FCA 1955; *Recreations* field sports; *Clubs* Boodle's, RAF; *Style—* Peter Naylor, Esq, DL; The Clock Hse, Far Sawrey, Ambleside, Cumbria LA22 0LJ (☎ 09662 3528)

NAYLOR-LEYLAND, Lady Isabella; da of Antony Lambton (formerly 6 Earl of Durham); *b* 17 May 1958; *m* 1980, Sir Philip Vyvian Naylor-Leyland, 4 Bt, *qv*; *Style—* Lady Isabella Naylor-Leyland

NAYLOR-LEYLAND, Jameina, Lady; Jameina Flora; *née* Reid; da of James Freeman Reid; *m* 1980, as his 3 w, Sir Vivyan Edward Naylor-Leyland, 3 Bt, who d 1987; 2 da (Virginia b 16 April 1983, Jessica Pamela b 27 March 1987); *Style—* Jameina, Lady Naylor-Leyland; Le Neuf Chemin, St Saviour's, Guernsey, CI

NAYLOR-LEYLAND, Sir Philip Vyvian; 4 Bt (UK 1895), of Hyde Park House, Albert Gate, London; s of the late Sir Vivyan Edward Naylor-Leyland, 3 Bt (d 1987), and Elisabeth-Anne Marie Gabrielle, da of late Viscount Fitzalon of Derwent; *b* 9 August 1953; *Educ* Eton, Sandhurst, New York Univ, RAC Cirencester; *m* 1980, Lady Isabella, 5 and yst da of Antony C F Lambton, *qv* (6 Earl of Durham, who disclaimed his peerage 1970); 1 s (Thomas Philip b 1982), 1 da (Violet Mary b 1983); *Heir* Thomas Philip; *Career* Lt, LG (ret); *Recreations* hunting, coursing, shooting; *Clubs* Whites; *Style—* Sir Philip Naylor-Leyland, Bt; Nantclwyd Hall, Ruthin, N Wales; The Ferry House, Milton Park, Peterborough, Cambs

NEAGLE, Hon Mrs (Lena Margaret); eld da of 2 Viscount Hall; *b* 31 Oct 1950; *Educ* Godstowe Sch, Wycombe Abbey and Univ of St Andrew's; *m* 1985, Frederick Neagle, eld s of late William Neagle; *Style—* Hon Mrs Neagle; Belgrave Cottage, Upper Belgrave St, London SW1

NEAL, Sir Eric James; s of James Charles Neal (d 1971), and May Neal (d 1981); *b* 3 June 1924; *Educ* Adelaide Sch of Mines; *m* 1950, Thelma Joan, da of Richard Edwin Bowden; 2 s; *Career* dir: Boral Ltd 1972- (chief exec 1973-, md 1982), Wormald Int Ltd 1978-, The Aust Inst of Petroleum Oil Co of Aust 1982; memb Def Review Ctee 1981-82; kt 1982; *Style—* Sir Eric Neal; 93 Pentecost Ave, St Ives, NSW 2075, Australia

NEAL, Frederick Albert; s of Frederick William George (d 1971), and Fanny Elizabeth (d 1979); *b* 22 Dec 1932; *Educ* Cambridge, London Univ (BA); *m* 1958, Gloria Maria, da of Alfred Moirano, of London; *Career* Govt Service, economic cnsllr Br High Cmmn Ottawa 1975-80, Dept of Trade & Indust 1980-83, UK permanent rep to Int Civil Aviation Orgn 1983-; *Recreations* golf; *Clubs* Naval & Military, Roy Overseas League, South Herts GC, Roy Montreal GC; *Style—* Frederick Neal Esq; Suite 928, 1000 Sherbrooke St West, Montreal, Canada H3A 3GH

NEAL, Harry Morton; s of Godfrey French Neal (d 1985), and Janet Bryce Morton (d 1960); *b* 21 Nov 1931; *Educ* Uppingham, Univ of London (BSc), City and Guilds Coll (FCGI); *m* 1954, Cecilia Elizabeth, da of Col Mervyn Crawford, DSO (d 1977); 1 s (Michael b 1956), 3 da (Camilla b 1960, Janet b 1961, Alexandra b 1967); *Career* Flying Offr RAF 1953; md Harry Neal Ltd (bldg and civil engrg contractors) 1963-86 (chm 1985); chm: City and Guilds of London Inst 1979-, Connaught Hotel Ltd 1980-; dir Savoy Hotel 1982-; memb: Lloyd's, Technician Educn Cncl 1982-83, Business and Technician Educn Cncl 1983-, bd of govrs Willesden Tech Coll 1983-86, Ct of City Univ 1982-, mgmnt ctee Courtauld Inst of Art 1983-; pres Gtr London NW Co Scout Cncl 1983-; Liveryman Worshipful Co of Carpenters Chev de Tastevin 1981; FIC, FCIOB, FRSA; *Recreations* gardening, shooting; *Style—* Harry Neal, Esq; Great Sarratt Hall, Sarratt, nr Rickmansworth, Herts WD3 4PD

NEAL, Capt John Harry; s of Harry Neal (d 1983), and Gladys Eva, *née* Gasser (d 1987); *b* 22 Oct 1928; *Educ* Latymer Upper Sch, King Edward VII Nautical Sch, Sir John Cass Coll; *m* 6 June 1954, (Ruby Lily) Jane, da of Richard Henry Craswell (d 1971); 1 s (Andrew b 29 April 1959), 2 da (Sarah b 23 June 1962, Rebecca b 30 July 1964); *Career* Navigating Offr: Anglo Saxon Petroleum Co (formerly Cadet) 1946-52, Royal Fleet Aux Serv 1952-57, Cable and Wireless plc (later Capt and mangr marine and survey) 1957-83; assoc Submarine Cable Conslts Ltd 1984-; steward and guide Romsey Abbey; memb: Romsey Amateur Operatic and Dramatic Soc, Romsey Horse and Cattle Show, ctee Southampton Master Mariners Club; memb: RIN 1952, RINA 1956; Liveryman Hon Co of Master Mariners 1974 (memb 1968); Freeman City of London 1974; *Recreations* fishing and gardening; *Clubs* Southampton Master Mariners; *Style—* Capt John Neal; 32 Harrage, Romsey, Hants

NEAL, Sir Leonard Francis; CBE (1971); s of Arthur Henry Neal (d 1939), and Emma Mary Neal (d 1947); *b* 27 August 1913; *Educ* LSE, Trinity Coll Cambridge (MA); *m* 1939, Mary Lillian Puttock; 1 s (Geoffrey), 1 da (Susan); *Career* industl rels conslt; memb Br Railways Bd 1967-71; chm: Cmmn on Industl Rels 1971-74, MAT Tport Int Gp 1974-83; non exec dir Pilkington Bros 1976-83; chm: Employment Conditions Abroad Ltd 1976-84, Trade Union Reform Ctee, Centre for Policy Studies 1978-86; sometimes visiting prof of industl rels Univ of Manchester, broadcaster and lectr; kt 1974; *Books* Managers Guide to Industrial Relations; *Recreations* gardening, reading; *Style—* Sir Leonard Neal, CBE; Brightling, E Sussex

NEAL, Michael Harry Walker; s of Harry Morton Neal, of Herts, and Cecilia Elizabeth, *née* Crawford; *b* 9 July 1956; *Educ* Eton, Univ of St Andrews (MA), Bartlett Sch of Architecture (UCL, MSc); *m* 4 July 1987, Sophia Mary, da of Sir Geoffrey Christopher John Palmer, Bt; 1 s (Harry Neal b 1988); L.....; *Career* md Harry Neal Ltd 1987, memb Lloyds 1984; Freeman City of London 1977; Liveryman: Worshipful Co of Carpenters 1977, Worshipful Co of Loriners 1989; *Recreations* fishing; *Clubs* The Royal Perth Golfing Soc; *Style—* Michael Neal, Esq; c/o Harry Neal Ltd, Kingsbury Rd, London NW9 8XA

NEAL, Richard Clive; s of Philip Neal, of Hong Kong, and Dorothy Alice, *née* Watson (d 1967); *b* 19 Mar 1939; *Educ* Wellesbourne House Sch; *m* 9 May 1964, Barbara Maureen, da of David Price (d 1983), of Dudley; *Career* md: Supra Chemicals and Paints Ltd 1965 (chm 1972), Supra Gp plc 1972 (chm 1983); exec dir Evode Gp plc 1987; *Recreations* golf; *Clubs* Stourbridge GC, Ferrari Owners; *Style—* Richard Neal, Esq; Green Ridges, Ounty John Lane, Pedmore, Stourbridge, W Midlands DY8 2RG; Supra Group Ltd, Hainge Rd, Tividale, Warley, W Midlands (☎ 021 557 9361, telex 336238, fax 021 557 6884)

NEALE, Sir Alan Derrett; KCB (1972, CB 1968), MBE (1945); s of W A Neale (d 1941); *b* 24 Oct 1918; *Educ* Highgate, St John's Coll Oxford; *m* 1956, Joan Frost; 1 s; *Career* WWII served with Intelligence Corps; entered Bd of Trade 1946, asst sec 1958, under-sec 1963, second sec 1967-68, third sec HM Treasy 1968-71, second perm sec 1971, perm sec MAFF 1973-78; memb Monopolies and Mergers Cmmn 1981-86, (dep chm 1982-86), dep chm Assoc of Futures Brokers and Dealers 1987-; *Clubs* Reform; *Style—* Sir Alan Neale, KCB, MBE; 95 Swains Lane, Highgate Village, London N6 6PJ (☎ 01 340 5236)

NEALE, Frank Leslie George; s of Hugh Neale, and Mona, *née* Clarkson; *b* 25 August 1950; *Educ* King Henry VIII Sch Coventry, St John's Coll Cambridge (MA), Manchester Business Sch (MBA); *m* 16 June 1976, Helen, da of Ronald Carter; 3 s (Michael James b 29 May 1979, Jeremy John Simon b 20 Jan 1985, Rory William b 1 Jan 1989); *Career* econ intelligence unit 1973-77, PA Mgmnt Conslts 1977-83, Citicorp Venture Capital 1983-88, ptnr Phildrew Ventures; cncl memb Br Venture Capital

Assoc; MIMC; *Recreations* memb Watford FC Supporters Club; *Style*— Frank Neale, Esq; 143 Cassiobury Dr, Watford, Herts WD1 3AH (☎ 0923 31 282); Triton Ct, 14 Finsbury Sq, London EC2 1PD (☎ 01 628 6366, fax 01 638 6217)

NEALE, Gerrard Anthony; MP (C) North Cornwall 1979-; s of Charles Woodhouse Neale (d 1985), of Painswick, Gloucs, and Phyllis Muriel, *née* Harrison; *b* 25 June 1941; *Educ* Bedford Sch; *m* 29 Dec 1965, Deirdre Elizabeth, da of late Charles Howard McCann (Lt Cdr RN), of Cornwall; 1 s (Alexander Charles b 7 June 1973), 2 da (Belinda Clare b 23 July 1967, Tania Katharine b 7 Jan 1970); *Career* slr 1966; ptnr Heald Nickinson Slrs, dir Telephone Rentals plc 1979-; Parly candidate (C) N Cornwall 1974, pps to George Younger, MP (Sec of State for Defence) 1987-; *Recreations* sailing; *Style*— Gerrard Neale, Esq, MP; House of Commons, Westminster, London SW1A 0AA (☎ 01 219 3610)

NEALE, Michael Cooper; CB (1987); s of Frank Neale (d 1966), of Findon, Sussex and Nottingham, and Edith Kathleen, *née* Penney; *b* 2 Dec 1929; *Educ* W Bridgford GS Nottingham, QMC London (BSc, MSc); *m* 13 Oct 1956, Thelma, da of Charles Weare (d 1971) of Worthing, Sussex; 1 s (Nicholas b 1961), 2 da (Judith b 1959, Elizabeth b 1962); *Career* Engr Offr RAF 1953-56 served Aden; Scientific Civil Serv 1956-87, dep dir (R&D) Nat Gas Turbine Estab 1973-80, dir gen engines MOD 1980-87; sec Royal Cmmn for the Exhibition 1851; Royal Aeronautical Soc Silver Medallist 1987; *Recreations* following cricket, railway history; *Style*— Michael Neale, Esq, CB; 108 Wargrave Rd, Twyford, Reading, Berks RG10 9PJ (☎ 0734 341759); Royal Commission for the Exhibition of 1851, Sherfield Building, Imperial College of Science Technol and Medicine, London SW7 2AZ

NEALE, Timothy Peter Graham; s of Maj Archibald Graham Neale, TD, of St Anthonys, Burwash, E Sussex, and Ann Urling, *née* Clark; *b* 15 Dec 1939; *Educ* Radley; *m* 18 April 1970, Elizabeth Francis, da of William Frank George Harvey (d 1988); 2 da (Elizabeth b 1972, Jennifer b 1974); *Career* CA; ptnr: Hope Agar 1967-68, Kidsons 1988-; tres Sidlow Bridge PCC 1967-87, govr Micklefield Sch Reigate 1980-, capt Reigate Hockey Club 1972-76, chm Reigate Redhill and Dist Railway Users Assoc 1987-; ACA 1963, FCA 1972; *Recreations* gardening, watching sport; *Clubs* RAC, MCC; *Style*— Timothy Neale, Esq; 20 Raglan Rd, Reigate, Surrey RH2 0DP (☎ 0737 243580); Russell Sq House, 10-12 Russell Sq, London WC1B 5AE (☎ 01 436 3636, fax 01 436 6603, telex 263901)

NEAMAN, Prof Yfrah; OBE (1983); *b* 13 Feb 1923; *Educ* Birkbeck Coll London, Premier Prix Conservatoire National Supérieur de Musique Paris; studies with Carl Flesch, Jacques Thibaud & Max Rostal; *m* 16 March 1953, Gillian Mary, da of Maurice E Shaw (d 1977), of London; 1 s (Samuel Lister b 1964), 1 da (Rachel Cecilia b 1965); *Career* GSM: prof of violin, head of strings dept 1962-78, head of dept of advanced solo studies 1974-; recital concerts with orchestras, radio and TV appearances, public master classes in Europe, N and S America, China, Japan, Korea, Africa and Asia; artistic dir Carl Flesch Int Violin Competition (London), artistic conslt Portsmouth Int String Quartet Competition, artistic advsr Wells Cathedral Sch England; recordings made for: Argo, Lyrita, and Yugoton records; ed several works by various composers; Liveryman Worshipful Co of Musicians; *Style*— Prof Yfrah Neaman, OBE; 11 Chadwell St, London EC1R 1XD (☎ 01 837 4455); Guildhall Sch of Music & Drama, Barbican, London EC2Y 8DT (☎ 01 628 2571)

NEAME, Basil Desmond; CBE (1970); s of Sir Thomas Neame (d 1972), of Preston Lea, Faversham, Kent, and Gwendolyn Mary, *née* Thompson, CBE (d 1972); *b* 14 Oct 1921; *Educ* Cheltenham; *m* 3 April 1948, Stella, da of Lt-Col William Edward Roe (d 1956), of Valence Dene, Godmersham, nr Canterbury, Kent; 2 s (Andrew b 1951, Charles b 1957), 2 da (Patricia (Mrs Cuomo) b 1949, Bridget (Mrs Schillereff) b 1954); *Career* Signalman Royal Signals 1941, cmmnd 2 Lt Cadet RE 1942, Fo Co attached Madras Sappers & Miners 1942, Lt 405 Ind Fo Co, Capt 1944, Maj 1945, demob 1946; farmer Kent, chm East Kent Packers Ltd 1973-80 (dir 1970-), local dir Royal Insur Co 1955-87; Nat Farmers Union: chm Kent 1956-58, memb Nat Cncl 1956 and 1960-66, memb Agric Apprenticeship Ctee Kent (chm 1953-61, chm Nat Cncl 1960-67); chm Agric Trg Bd 1966-70; govr: Wye Coll 1971-87, E Malling Res Station 1960-87 (tstee 1985); *Recreations* bird watching; *Clubs* Farmers; *Style*— Basil Neame, Esq, CBE; Macknade Manor, Faversham, Kent ME13 8XF (☎ 0795 532 070); Macknade, Faversham, Kent ME13 8XF (☎ 0795 532 216)

NEAME, Robert Harry Beale; s of Jasper Beale Neame (d 1961), and Violet Evelyn, *née* Cobb (d 1976); The Neame family have been resident in E Kent and can be traced back 500 years; *b* 25 Feb 1934; *Educ* Harrow; *m* 1, 1961, Sally Elizabeth, *née* Corben; 1 s (Jonathan), 2 da (Charlotte, Sarah); m 2, 1974, Yvonne Mary, *née* Mackenzie; 1 da (Moray); *Career* cmmnd 17/21 Lancers 1953-55 (army racquets champion 1954); chm Shepherd Neame Ltd 1971- (joined 1956, dir 1957, mktg dir 1961), former dir and chm Faversham Laundry Co, chm SE Eng Tourist Bd 1979-, regnl dir Nat Westminster Bank plc 1982-; dir: Kent Econ Devpt Bd 1984-, Folkestone Racecourse 1984-; local dir Royal Insur (UK) Ltd 1971-; memb Faversham CC 1965-, ldr Kent CC 1982-84, chm Int Union of Local Authys 1986-; memb Assoc of Brewing; *Recreations* shooting, riding, cricket, golf, squash, rackets; *Clubs* MCC, I Zingari, Butterflies, Escorts, Jesters, Band of Brothers, Press, Roy St George's, Free Foresters; *Style*— Robert Neame, Esq; Dane Court Farmhouse, Kits Hill, Selling, Faversham, Kent (☎ 030381 284); c/o Shepherd Neame Ltd, 17 Court St, Faversham, Kent (☎ 079 5822206)

NEARN, Graham Bradshaw; s of Henry John Nearn (d 1986), and Eva Charlotte, *née* Sayers; *b* 29 Sept 1933; *Educ* Purley Count GS, City of London Coll; *m* 5 March 1966, (Margaret) Jane, da of Dr John Stewart Norwell (d 1984); 2 s (Robert Bradshaw b 24 April 1967, Simon John 27 March 1969), 2 da (Eliza Alexandra Jane b 2 Nov 1972, Janina Charlotte 5 May 1977); *Career* md (former dir 1959-70) Caterham Cars Ltd (manufacturer Caterham super 7 Sports car, *née* Lotus Super 7) 1970-, dir Dist Fin Ltd 1970-72, chm London Property Conversions Ltd 1972-89; chm Specialist Car Manufacturers Gp Soc of Motor Manufacturers and Traders; *Books* The Caterham & Lotus Sevens (1986); *Recreations* golf, sailing, motor sport; *Clubs* Edenbridge GC, Whitstable YC, Ashton Martin Owners, Lotus 7; *Style*— Graham Nearn, Esq; Winburne, Ashurst, Kent TN3 9TB; 34 Island Wall, Whitstable, Kent (☎ 089 274 341); Caterham Cars Ltd, Seven House, Townend, Caterham, Surrey CR3 5UG (☎ 0883 46 666, fax 0883 49 086, car tel 0836 595 763)

NEARS, Colin Gray; s of William Charles Nears (d 1974), of Ipswich, and Winifred Mildred *née* Gray (d 1983); *b* 19 Mar 1933; *Educ* Ipswich Sch, King's Coll Cambridge (MA); *Career* freelance tv dir; prodr music and arts BBC TV 1967-87, memb cncl and chm advsy panel on dance Arts Cncl of GB 1982-; author and dir of programmes (on literature, the Visual Arts, music and dance) Review 1971-72, BAFTA Award for Best Specialised Programme 1973; Prix Italia Music Prize 1982; *Recreations* reading, gardening, painting, swimming; *Style*— Colin Nears, Esq; 16 Ashchurch Terr, London W12 9SL (☎ 01 749 3615)

NEARY, Jack Edward; s of Albert Edward Neary (d 1963), and Grace, *née* Lewin (d 1974); *b* 1 April 1922; *Educ* Sir Anthony Brown's Sch Brentwood Essex, Coll Estate Mgmnt (Dip RICS); *m* 6 Aug 1949, (Margaret) Katherine Ferguson, da of Ferrers Augustus Collyer Munns (d 1975); 1 s (Robert b 1950), 1 da (Sara b 1954); *Career* cmmnd RA, served 25 Indian Mountain Regt and 7 Indian Div Burma Campaign Kohima to Rangoon; chartered quantity surveyor; sr ptnr Banks Wood & Ptnrs; RICS: memb ctee Central London branch 1964-72 (hon sec 1964-69, chm 1971-72), memb continental gp ctee 1971-75 and 1980, memb int ctee 1971-77 and 1980-84, memb gen cncl 1972-73 and 1982-84; rep on Br Standards Inst 1981-; Quantity Surveyors' Div: memb div cncl 1968-77, memb div exec ctee 1972-77, chm int affrs ctee 1972-77, memb branch ctee 1970-72, rep gen practice div cncl 1971-73, rep bldg surveyors' div cncl 1973-74; Queen's Sheriff City of London 1985-86; former pres: Bishopsgate Ward Club, City Livery Club; pres Aldgate Ward Club, United Wards Club; past master Tower Ward Club; hon tres Save the Children Fund Brentwood; OStJ 1986; Freeman: Worshipful Co Shipwrights 1947 (Prime Warden 1984-85), City of London 1952; Freeman and Liveryman Worshipful Co Chartered Surveyors 1977, Master Worshipful Co of Constructors 1988-89; ARICS 1951, FRICS 1956; *Recreations* motor sport; *Clubs* City Livery, IOD, Wings NY; *Style*— Jack Neary, Esq; Honeywood, Glanthams Close, Shenfield, Essex (☎ 0277 223598); Flat 1, 8 York Bldgs, London WC2N 6JN; Banks, Wood & Partners, 6 Kinghorn St, London EC1A 7BP (☎ 01 600 0260, fax 01 606 3350, car 0836 603 652, telex 995568 BANQUO G)

NEARY, Martin Gerard James; s of Leonard Walter Neary, of 25 Manor House, Marylebone Rd, London, and Jeanne Marguerite, *née* Thébault; *b* 28 Mar 1940; *Educ* City of London Sch, Chapel Royal Choir, Gonville and Caius Coll Cambridge (MA); *m* 22 April 1967, Penelope Jane, da of Sir Brian Warren, of London, and Dame Josephine Barnes, DBE, *qv* London; 1 s (Thomas b 1974), 2 (Nicola b 1969, Alice b 1972); *Career* prof of organ Trinity Coll London 1963-72, organist and master of music St Margaret's Westminster 1965-71; conductor: Twickenham Musical Soc 1966-72, St Margaret's Westminster Singers 1967-71, Waynflete Singers 1972-87; organist and master of the music Winchester Cathedral 1972-87, organist and master of the choristers Westminster Abbey 1988-; dir Southern Cathedrals Festival 1972, 1975, 1978, 1981, 1984 and 1987; many organ recitals and broadcasts in UK, Europe and America, has conducted premières of music by many Br composers, numerous recordings incl Lloyd Webber Requiem (golden disc); pres: Cathedral Organists' Assoc 1985-88, Royal Coll Organists 1988-; hon citizen Texas 1971; Hon FTCL 1969, Hon RAM 1988; FRCO; *Books* Early French Organ Music (ed 2 vols 1975); *Recreations* watching cricket; *Clubs* Athenaeum; *Style*— Martin Neary, Esq; 2 Little Cloister, Westminster Abbey, London SW1P 3PL (☎ 01 222 6923); Chapter Office, 20 Deans Yard, London SW1P 3PA (☎ 01 222 5152)

NEATE, Alfred; JP (Herts); s of William Neate (d 1945); *b* 29 Jan 1909; *Educ* Sutton Valence, Oriel Coll Oxford; *m* 1933, Olga Margaret, *née* Spall; 1 s, 1 da; *Career* memb Willesden Borough Cncl 1932-39, regnl controller (NW) Miny of Aircraft Prodn 1942-45, Miny of Supply 1946-51, dir-gen of machine tools, Miny of Supply 195l, dir Wickman Ltd and subsidiaries 1953-58; gen tax cmmr; Master Worshipful Co of Makers of Playing Cards 1980-81; *Recreations* rowing and gardening; *Clubs* Carlton, Naval and Military, Oriental, Rand (Johannesburg); *Style*— Alfred Neate, Esq, JP; 18 Copper Beech Close, Boxmoor, Hemel Hempstead, Herts HP3 0DG (☎ 0442 52882)

NEATE, Francis Webb; s of Francis Webb Neate (d 1982), of 1 Holmesdale Road, Kew, Richmond, Surrey, and Fiona L M, *née* O'Brien; *b* 13 May 1940; *Educ* St Wilfrid's Sch Seaford Sussex, St Paul's, Brasenose Coll Oxford Univ (BA), Univ of Chicago Law Sch (JD); *m* 25 Aug 1962, Patricia Ann, da of Anthony Vincent Hugh Mulligan (d 1982), of 6 Daylesford Ave, Putney, London; 2 S (Vincent b 1968, Patrick b 1970), 2 da (Polly b 1966, Emily b 1973); *Career* Slaughter and May: articled clerk 1964-66, asst slr 1966-71, ptnr 1972-; memb: Law Soc, City of London Slrs Co, Int Bar Assoc; *Recreations* cricket, reading, family; *Clubs* MCC, Berkshire CCC, Richmond CC, Falkland CC; *Style*— Francis Neate, Esq; 2 Daylesford Ave, Putney, London SW15 5QR (☎ 01 876 1902); Slaughter and May, 35 Basinghall St, London EC2V 5DB (☎ 01 600 1200)

NEAVE, Maj Sir Arundell Thomas Clifton; 6 Bt (GB 1795), of Dagnam Park, Essex, JP (Anglesey 1950); s of Sir Thomas Lewis Hughes Neave, 5 Bt (d 1940); *b* 31 May 1916; *Educ* Eton; *m* 1946, Richenda Alice Ione, da of Sir Robert Joshua Paul, 5 Bt (d 1955); 2 s, 2 da; *Heir* s, Paul Arundell Neave; *Career* served 1939-45 (Dunkirk), Maj Welsh Gds 1945, ret 1947; *Clubs* Carlton, Pratt's; *Style*— Maj Sir Arundell Neave, Bt, JP; Greatham Moor, Liss, Hants

NEAVE, Julius Arthur Sheffield; CBE (1978, MBE 1944), JP (Brentwood), DL (Essex 1983); s of late Col Richard Neave, and Helen Mary Elizabeth, *née* Miller; *b* 17 July 1919; *Educ* Sherborne; *m* 1951, Helen Margery, da of the late Col P M Acton-Adams, DSO; 3 da; *Career* served in 13/18 Royal Hussars; gen mangr Mercantile & Gen Reinsurance Co Ltd 1966- (joined 1938, md 1980-82), dir Prudential Corpn plc; first chm Reinsurance Offices Assoc, received Founders Award Gold Medal of Int Seminars 1977; pres: Insurance Inst London 1976-77, Geneva Assoc 1983-86, Chartered Insurance Inst 1983-84; Master Worshipful Co of Insurers' 1984; High Sheriff of Essex 1987-88; *Recreations* golf, shooting, fishing, tennis, needlework; *Clubs* Cavalry & Guards; *Style*— Julius Neave, Esq, CBE, JP, DL; Mill Green Park, Ingatestone, Essex CM4 0JB (☎ 0277 353 036)

NEAVE, Paul Arundell; s and h of Sir Arundell Thomas Clifton Neave, 6 Bt; *b* 13 Dec 1948; *Educ* Eton; *m* 1976, Coralie Jane Louise, da of Sir Robert George Caldwell Kinahan, ERD; 2 s; *Career* stockbroker; *Recreations* photography; *Style*— Paul Neave Esq; 7 Franconia Rd, London SW4 (☎ 01 622 0491)

NEAVE, Hon Richard Patrick Sheffield; s of Baroness Airey of Abingdon (Life Peeress), and of Airey Middleton Sheffield Neave, DSO, OBE, MC, TD, MP (assas 1979); *b* 1947; *Educ* Eton, City of London Poly; *m* 1980, Elizabeth Mary Catherine, da of Cuthbert Edward Riddell, of Hermeston Hall, Worksop, Notts; 2 s; *Career* company sec Baltic Int Freight Futures Exchange Ltd; *Style*— The Hon Richard Neave; 16 Maze Rd, Kew, Richmond, Surrey

NEAVE, Hon William Robert Sheffield; yr s of Baroness Airey of Abingdon (Life Peeress), and Airey Middleton Sheffield Neave, DSO, OBE, MC, TD, MP (assass

1979); *b* 13 August 1953; *Educ* Eton; *m* 19 May 1986, Joanna Mary Stuart, 2 da of James Stuart Paton, of The Old Vicarage, Gt Hockham, Norfolk; 1 s (Richard Digby Stuart b 21 May 1987); *Career* exec dir Willis Faber and Dumas Ltd; *Recreations* photography books; *Style*— The Hon William Neave; 20 Kirkstall Rd, London SW2 4HF

NEC, Bronislaw; OBE (1978); s of Emil Netz (d 1958), and Helena, *née* Kaminska; *b* 4 Nov 1924; *Educ* early educn in Germany and Poland, Glasgow (CDA), Newton Abbot (Dipfm); *m* 30 April 1949, Jessie Anderson Banks, da of Archibald Small (d 1971); 1 s (Anthony b 1957), 1 da (Helen b 1949); *Career* agronomist; HMOCS served Malawi: livestock offr 1955-68, princ animal husbandry offr 1969-71, chief agric offr 1971-75, dir of planning Miny of Agric 1975-78; agric advsr to EEC delgn in Tanzania and Ghana 1978-87; *Recreations* golf, game shooting, game fishing; *Clubs* Country Gentlemen's Assoc; *Style*— Bronislaw Nec, Esq, OBE; Summerfield, E Boldre, nr Brockenhurst, Hants SO42 7WU (☎ 059 065 618)

NEEDHAM, Hon Christopher David; s of 5 Earl of Kilmorey (d 1977); *b* 30 July 1948; *Educ* Milton Abbey; *m* 1974, Marina, eld da of Rodi Malvezzi, of Milan, Italy; 1 s (Francis b 22 June 1982), 1 da (Armyne b 31 Oct 1978); *Style*— The Hon Christopher Needham; 63 Foro Buonaparte, Milan, Italy

NEEDHAM, Hon Mrs Peter; Janet Beatrice Winifred; da of late Capt George Taylor Ramsden, MP; *m* 1951, Hon (Arthur Edward) Peter Needham (d 1979, raised to the rank of an Earl's s 1962), s of late Maj Hon Francis Edward Needham, MVO (2 s of 3 Earl of Kilmorey); 2 s, 1 da; *Style*— The Hon Mrs Peter Needham; The Old Manor House, Helmsley, York

NEEDHAM, Hon (Patrick) Jonathan; s of 5 Earl of Kilmorey; *b* 30 July 1951; *m* 1979, Jane, da of Geoffrey Hinbest, of Bristol; *Career* restaurateur; *Style*— The Hon Jonathan Needham; Flat 26, Marlborough Buildings, Bath, Avon

NEEDHAM, Peter Southwood; s of William Needham, of Hobart, Tasmania; *b* 9 Jan 1924; *Educ* Hobart HS; *m* 1, 1945, Anne Louise; 2 da (Elizabeth Anne, (Mrs McCormick), Rosemary Jane, (Mrs Buckle); m 2, 1971, Susan Augusta, da of Philip H Band, of Westhampton Beach, NY; 3 step children; *Career* business conslt, dir Gardiner-Hill Needham Exec Mgmnt Ltd; *Clubs* Hurlingham, RAF; *Style*— Peter Needham, Esq; c/o GHN, 16 Hanover Sq, London W1R 9AJ

NEEDHAM, Phillip; s of Ephraim Needham, of Dunstable, and Mabel Jessie, *née* Foskett; *b* 21 April 1940; *Educ* Ashton GS Dunstable, Univ of Birmingham (BSc), Imp Coll (MSc, DIC); *m* 24 March 1962, Patricia Ann, da of Henry Farr, of Leighton Buzzard; 2 s (Paul b 1963, David b 1964), 2 da (Jennifer b 1967, Claire b 1974); *Career* agric devpt and advsy servs MAFF: head of soil sci 1982-85, sr agric scientist 1985-87, dep dir R & D 1987-88, dir farm and countryside serv and commercial dir 1988; *Style*— Phillip Needham, Esq; MAFF, Nobel House, 17 Smith Sq, London SW1P 3HX (☎ 01 238 5776)

NEEDHAM, Richard Francis; MP (C) N Wilts 1983-; 6 Earl of Kilmorey (I 1822), also Hereditary Abbot of the Exempt Jurisdiction of Newry and Mourne, Viscount Kilmorey (I 1625) and Viscount Newry and Morne (I 1822), but does not use titles; s of 5 Earl of Kilmorey (d 1977), and Helen, da of Sir Lionel Faudel-Phillips, 3 and last Bt; *b* 29 Jan 1942; *Educ* Eton; *m* 1965, Sigrid Juliane, da of late Ernst Thiessen, and Mrs John Gairdner; 2 s (Viscount Newry and Morne b 1966, Hon Andrew b 1969), 1 da (Lady Christina b 1977); *Heir* s, Viscount Newry and Morne; *Career* memb of Lloyds; formerly: cncllr Somerset, chm RGM Print Hldgs Ltd; govr Br Inst of Florence 1983-85, fndr memb Anglo-Japanese 2000 Gp; personal asst to Rt Hon James Prior, MP, oppn spokesman on Employment 1974-79, MP (C) Chippenham 1979-1983, sec Cons Employment Ctee 1979-81 (vice-chm 1981-83), memb Public Accounts Ctee 1982-83, PPS to Rt Hon James Prior Sec of State for NI 1983-84, PPS to Rt Hon Patrick Jenkins Sec of State for Environment 1984-85; min of Health and min of Environment for NI 1985-; *Publications* The Honourable Member (1983); *Clubs* Pratts; *Style*— Richard Needham, Esq, MP; House of Commons, London SW1

NEEDHAM, Sheila June; da of Steven Ellis Needham (d 1981), and Grace Kathleen, *née* Tarrant; *b* 22 June 1937; *Educ* Sutton HS; *Career* held several secretarial positions in London and USA 1955-71; dir of Scribe-Ex Ltd 1965-74, fndr and md Needham Printers Ltd 1974-; pres: NE Dist London Printing Assoc 1981, Farringdon Ward Club 1984-85; memb: Inst of Printing 1985, Br Assoc of Women Entrepreneurs; Freeman City of London, Liveryman Worshipful Co of Stationers and Newspaper Makers; FBIM; *Recreations* travel, theatre, walking, gardening; *Clubs* City Livery, IOD, Network, City Women's Network; *Style*— Miss Sheila J Needham; Needham Printers Ltd, Titchfield Ho, 69-85 Tabernacle St, London EC2A 4BA (☎ 01 250 3338)

NEESON, David Ivor; s of (Horace) Ivor Charles Neeson, of Belchamp, St Paul, Essex, and Jean Gibson, *née* Wade; *b* 19 Oct 1946; *Educ* Beal GS Ilford Essex; *m* 28 Dec 1972, Christine Pearl, da of Frank Hunt (d 1980), of Romford, Essex; 1 s (Rory), 1 da (Eloisa); *Career* investmt asst corpn of Lloyds 1965-67, stockbroker and ptnr Bisgood Bishop and Co 1967-76, vice pres Merrill Lynch Int 1976-82; Morgan Stanley Int: joined 1982, vice pres 1984, exec dir 1985, md 1986-; memb UK equity ctee London Stock Exchange; *Recreations* golf, tennis, shooting, hiking; *Clubs* Wildernesse GC (Seal); *Style*— David Neeson, Esq; Morgan Stanley International, Kingsley House, 1A Wimpole St, London W1 (☎ 01 709 3898)

NEGRETTI, (Paul) Antony; s of Paul Ernest Negretti (d 1953), of Lane House, Lodsworth, and Marjorie, *née* Layton (d 1964); *b* 26 April 1912; *Educ* Oundle, Lausanne Univ; *m* 1943, Audrey Elsie Townsend, da of Sir Grey Humberston d'Estoteville Skipwith, Bt (d 1950), of Upper Link House, St Mary Bourne, Hants; 1 s, 1 da; *Career* Maj The Black Watch (RHR); served: France, Gibraltar, N Africa, Sicily, Italy, and Germany; chm: Negretti & Zambra, 1954-71; Mayor of Westminster 1963-64, pres Royal Tennis Court 1973-87, vice-pres Tennis and Rackets Assoc 1981; *Recreations* formerly playing, now writing about tennis, cricket, golf, rugby, football, ice hockey, lawn tennis, skiing; *Clubs* Brooks's, MCC; *Style*— Antony Negretti, Esq; 6 Conway House, Ormonde Gate, London SW3 (☎ 01 352 7882); Thornborough Manor, Buckingham (☎ 0280 812270)

NEGRETTI, Antony Simon Timothy; s of Paul Antony Negretti, *qv*; *b* 2 Dec 1945; *Educ* Eton; *Career* bill broker and banker, dir: Page & Gwyther Holdings Ltd, Page & Gwyther Ltd, Page & Gwyther Investments Ltd; *Recreations* tennis, golf, skiing, shooting; *Clubs* Boodle's; *Style*— Antony Negretti Esq; 15 Roland Way, London SW7 (☎ 01 370 1887)

NEGUS, Norma Florence (Mrs David Turner-Samuels); *née* Miss Norma Shellabear; da of George David Shellabear and Kate Laura, *née* Calvert; *b* 31 July 1932; *Educ* Malvern Girls Coll; *m* 1, 1956 (m dis 1960), Richard Negus; m 2, 1976, David Jessel Turner-Samuels, QC; *Career* fashion promotion in UK Canada and USA 1950-61, merchandise ed Harper's Bazaar 1962-63, asst promotion mangr Vogue and House and Garden 1963-65, unit mangr Trends merchandising and fashion promotion unit 1965-67, export mktg mangr Glenoit UK 1967-68; called to the Bar Gray's Inn 1970; Met stipendiary magistrate 1984-, asst rec 1985-; *Recreations* writing, swimming, travel; *Style*— Miss Norma Negus; New Court, Temple, London EC4Y 9BE (☎ 01 353 7613); Cherry Tree Cottage, Petworth Rd, nr Haslemere, Surrey GU27 3BG (☎ 0428 51970)

NEGUS, Richard Charles; s of Bertie Arthur Charles Negus (d 1967), of Quendon, Essex, and Kate, *née* Brassington (d 1947); *b* 29 August 1927; *Educ* Battersea GS, Camberwell Sch of Arts & Crafts; *m* 20 Sept 1949, Pamela Denise; 2 s (Dominic Charles b 1952, Toby Wheatcroft b 1953), 1 da (Kate Georgina b 1955); *Career* conslt designer; staff Fest of Br 1948-51; fndr ptnr: Negus Sharland 1951, Negus & Negus 1970-87; private practice 1987-; conslt to: Cotton Bd 1960-67, BNEC 1969-75, Pakistan Airlines 1975-80, Rank Organisation 1979-82, City of Westminster 1973-75, Lloyds Bank 1972-75, Vickers plc & Rolls Royce plc 1980-82, SDP 1981-87, N Dairies 1985-87, Royal Armouries 1984-87, Nat Maritime Museum 1984-86, Science Museum 1987-, John Lewis, English Heritage 1983-, Royal Parks & Palace DOE; memb: Designers & Art Dirs Assoc, Post Office Stamps Advsy Ctee; FRSA (past), memb Design Cncl; assessor schs of Art: Birmingham, Bradford, Norwich; memb Ct of RCA; former govr schs of Art: Camberwell, Chelsea; lectr various Colls of Art; memb: CNAA, BTEC; memb Tylers & Bricklayers Co; FCSOC (former pres), FSTO, FRSA; *Books* Designing for Export, Airline Liveries; contrib to: The Designer, Design Magazine, Graphics, Gebrauchgraphick, Architectural Review, Architect's Journal, Rolls Royce Magazine; *Recreations* the countryside, yachting; *Style*— Richard Negus, Esq; 44 Canonbury Park South, London N1; Little Gravenhurst, Stairbridge Lane, Bolney, W Sussex (☎ 01 226 2381)

NEIDPATH, Lord; James Donald Charteris; full title Lord Douglas of Neidpath, Lyne and Munard; s and h of 12 Earl of Wemyss and (8 of) March, KT, JP, *qv*; *b* 22 June 1948; *Educ* Eton, Univ Coll Oxford, St Antony's Oxford, RAC Cirencester (BA, DPhil, Dip in Rural Estate Mgmnt); *m* 1983 (m dis 1988), Catherine Ingrid, da of Hon Jonathan Bryan Guinness, *qv*, of Osbaston Hall, Nuneaton, Warwicks; 1 s, 1 da (b 1987); *Heir* s, Hon Francis Richard Charteris, b 15 Sept 1984; *Career* page of honour to HM Queen Elizabeth The Queen Mother 1962-64, memb Royal Co of Archers (Queen's Body Guard for Scotland); land agent, ARICS; *Books* The Singapore Naval Base and the Defence of Britain's Eastern Empire 1919-41 (1981); historial reviews in The Spectator, Literary Review and Field; *Recreations* history; *Clubs* Brooks's, Pratt's, Puffin's, Ognisko Polskie; *Style*— Lord Neidpath; Stanway, Cheltenham, Glos (☎ 038673 469)

NEIL, Andrew Ferguson; s of Maj James Neil (d 1987), and Mary, *née* Ferguson; *b* 21 May 1949; *Educ* Paisley GS, Glasgow Univ (MA); *Career* political advsr to sec state Environment (Rt Hon Peter Walker) 1971-73, UK ed The Economist 1982-83 (joined staff 1973), ed The Sunday Times 1983-, exec chm Sky TV 1988-; *Books* The Cable Revolution (1982); *Recreations* skiing, dining out in London, New York and Aspen, Colorado; *Clubs* RAC, Tramp; *Style*— Andrew Neil, Esq; The Sunday Times, 1 Pennington Street, London E1 (☎ 01 782 5640, fax 01 782 5420)

NEIL, John Knox; s of William Neil, and Anna, *née* Holland; *b* 23 April 1922; *m* 10 April 1972, Jeanie Elizabeth, da of John Dunlop; 1 s (Robert Bruce Dunlop b 11 Nov 1973), 1 adopted s (Philip John b 8 Feb 1969), 1 adopted da (Susan Margaret b 16 Feb 1965); *Career* md and co sec Doorfit Prods Ltd 1980- (jt md 1958-80); *Recreations* squash; *Clubs* Stourbridge; *Style*— John Neil, Esq; Doorfit Products Ltd, Icknield House, Heaton St, Birmingham B18 5BA (☎ 021 554 9291, fax 021 554 3859)

NEILD, Dr Paul Graham; s of Edward Neild, of Blackpool, Lancs, and Mona Neild; *b* 18 Feb 1946; *Educ* Merchant Taylors' Sch Crosby, Liverpool Univ (BA), Manchester Univ (MA), Wellington Univ New Zealand (PhD); *m* 10 Feb 1968, Shian Helena, da of Llewelyn Thomas (d 1983), of Liverpool; 3 s (Simon b 1975, Adrian b 1975, Mark b 1978); *Career* Phillips and Drew 1971 (jr ptnr 1975, managing ptnr 1977, dir 1985-88), business conslt 1988; special econ advsr: House of Commons select ctee on the Treasy and Civil Serv 1979-85, Domestic Equity Markets ctee Stock Exchange 1987-88; memb Stock Exchange; *Recreations* horse racing; *Style*— Dr Paul Neild; The Hermitage, Rideaway, Hemingford Abbots, Cambs

NEILL, Alistair; s of Alexander Neill, MBE, (d 1969), of Edinburgh; *b* 18 Nov 1932; *Educ* George Watson's Coll, Edinburgh Univ (MA), Wisconsin Univ (MS); *m* Mary Margaret; 1 s, 2 da; *Career* Instr Lt RN 1968-70; actuary; gen mangr Scot Widows Fund; vice pres Faculty of Actuaries; FFA, FIA; *Books* Life Contingencies; *Recreations* golf, curling, squash rackets; *Style*— Alistair Neill, Esq; Scottish Widows Fund & Life Assurance Society, PO Box 902, 15 Dalkeith Road, Edinburgh, EH16 5BU

NEILL, Rt Hon Lord Justice; Rt Hon Sir Brian Thomas; PC (1985); s of Sir Thomas Neill, JP (d 1937); bro of (Francis) Patrick Neill, *qv*, and Lady (Annie Strachan) Neill (d 1985); *b* 2 August 1923; *Educ* Highgate, CCC Oxford (MA); *m* 1956, Sally Margaret Backus; 3 s; *Career* served WWII Rifle Bde; barr Inner Temple 1949, QC 1968, rec of the Crown Ct 1972-78, judge of the High Ct (Queen's Bench Div) 1978-84, lord justice of appeal 1985-; chm ctee on Rhodesia Travel Restrictions 1973-78; Master Worshipful Co of Turners 1980-81; kt 1978; *Style*— The Rt Hon Lord Justice Neill, PC; c/o Royal Courts of Justice, Strand, London WC2

NEILL, George Edwin; s of Capt Edwin Maekin Neill, MC (d 1977), and Violet Gertrude, *née* Schunck (d 1986); *b* 9 Jan 1929; *Educ* Shrewsbury; *m* 17 March 1951, (Kathleen) June, da of James Arthur Dawes (d 1968); 2 s (Christopher Edwin b 23 July 1953, Peter Mark b 18 Nov 1954); *Career* 2 Lt 4/7 Royal Dragoon Gds 1947, served in Tripoli 1948-49; dir Elson & Neill Ltd 1951-; organiser for local British horse trials; *Recreations* sailing, skiing, riding, tennis; *Clubs* Cruising Assoc; *Style*— George E Neill, Esq; Elson & Neill Ltd, 34 Knutsford Road, Alderley Edge, Cheshire (☎ 0625 585411, fax 0625 586230, telex 668601)

NEILL, Gordon Webster McCash; DSO; *b* 1919, ; *Educ* Edinburgh Acad; *m* 1950, Margaret Mary, *née* Lamb; 1 s (John Victor), 1 da (Fiona Margaret); *Career* WWII RAF 1939-46; legal apprentice 1937-39, ptnr Neill & Gibb 1947, amalgamated business to form Neil & Mackintosh SSC 1967 (princ), Notary Public 1947, Hon Sheriff; chm Dundee area bd Br Law Insur Co Ltd, former chm Scottish Gliding Assoc; chm Arbroath C of C 1980-83; FIOD 1958; memb: Soc of Slrs and Procurators in Angus (pres 1977-80), Soc of Slrs in Supreme Cts of Scotland, Law Soc of Scotland, Scottish

Law Agents' Soc; *Clubs* Rotary (Arbroath, former pres); *Style*— Sheriff Gordon Neill, DSO; Craigard, Viewfield Road, Arbroath; 93 High Street, Arbroath, Angus, Scotland

NEILL, Rt Hon Sir Ivan; PC (NI 1950); *b* 1 July 1906; *Educ* Ravenscroft Nat Sch, Shaftesbury House Tutorial Coll Belfast, Queen's Univ Belfast (BSc); *m* 1928, Margaret Helena Allen; *Career* WWII Maj RE; memb NI Parliament 1949-73; min of: Lab and Nat Insur 1950-62, Home Affrs 1952, Educn 1962-64, Fin and ldr of House of Commons 1964; resigned from govt 1965, min of Devpt 1968-69, speaker House of Commons 1969-73; FRGS; kt 1973; *Style*— The Rt Hon Sir Ivan Neill; Greenlaw, Ballywilliam, Donaghadee, Co Down, N Ireland

NEILL, Very Rev Ivan Delacherois; CB (1963), OBE (1958); s of Robert Richard Neill (d 1951), and Bessie Montrose, *née* Purdon (d 1950); *b* 10 July 1912; *Educ* St Dunstans Coll, Jesus Coll Cambridge (MA); *m* 1938, Enid Eyre Godson, da of Roderick George Bartholomew (d 1969), of The Orchards, Outwood, Surrey; 1 s (Robert), 1 da (Patricia); *Career* ordained 1936, Chaplain's Dept Reg Army 1939-66, BEF 1939-40, Orkneys 1941-42, Sandhurst 1942, sr chaplain N Aldershot 1943, sr chaplain 43 Wessex Div BLA/BWEF 1943-45 (despatches), dep asst chaplain gen 1 Br Corps 1945-46, sr chaplain Gds Depot 1946-50, DACG Canal N Egypt 1950-53; DACG Catterick 1953-54; warden Chaplain's Depot Bagshot 1954-57; SCF SHAPE Paris 1958; ACG Middle East 1958-60; chaplain gen 1960-66; QHC 1962; chaplain to HM Queen 1962-66; provost of Sheffield 1966-74 (non emeritus); govr Monkton Sch 1964-82 (chm 1971-82), pres C of E Fndn at St Paul and St Mary Cheltenham 1978-88; Knight Offr Order of Orange Nassau with swords 1946; *Recreations* continuing Christian ministry, off-shore boating; *Clubs* National; *Style*— The Very Rev Ivan Neill, CB, OBE; Greathed Manor, Lingfield, Surrey RH7 6PA; Churchtown, Broadway, Co Wexford (☎ 01 353 5331221)

NEILL, Lt-Col James Hugh; CBE (1969), TD (1950), JP (S Yorks 1985); s of Col Sir Frederick Neill, CBE, DSO, TD (d 1967); *b* 29 Mar 1921; *Educ* Rugby; *m* 1, 1943, Jane Margaret (d 1980), *née* Shuttleworth; 2 da (and 1 decd); m 2, 1982, Catherine Anne Maria, *née* O'Leary; 1 s; *Career* WWII Lt-Col served: Norway, India, Burma, Germany; chm James Neill Hldgs Ltd 1963-; Master Cutler of Hallamshire 1958-59; High Sheriff Hallamshire 1971-72, Lord Lt S Yorks 1985- (DL 1974); pres Sheffield C of C 1984-85; *Recreations* golf, racing, horse trials, shooting; *Clubs* Royal and Ancient GC, Hon Co of Edinburgh Golfers, Lindrick (Sheffield), E India, Sports; *Style*— Lt-Col Hugh Neill, CBE, TD; Barn Cottage, Lindrick Common, nr Worksop, Notts S81 8BA (☎ 0909 562806)

NEILL, John Mitchell; s of Justin Bernard Neill, and Johanna Elisabeth, *née* Bastiaans; *b* 21 July 1947; *Educ* George Heriott Sch Edinburgh, Univ of Strathclyde (BA, MBA); *m* 24 May 1975, Jaqueline Anne, da of Phillip Brown (d 1985); 2 s (Richard John b 19 July 1979, Alexander James b 4 Nov 1982); *Career* mktg mangr Europe AC Delco 1972-73 (planning mangr 1969-71), sales and mktg dir Br Leyland Parts & KD Div 1976 (merchandising mangr 1974-75), md Leyland Car Parts Div 1977-78, md BL Components 1979-80, md Unipart Gp 1981-82, gp md Unipart Gp Ltd 1983-86, gp chief exec Unipart Gp of Cos 1987-; memb pres ctee Business in the Community; FInstM; *Recreations* tennis, skiing; *Style*— John Neill, Esq; UGC Ltd, Unipart House, Cowley, Oxford OX4 2PE (☎ 0865 778966, fax 0865 118067, telex 83331)

NEILL, John Whitley; s of Lt-Col Frederick Henry Neill (d 1985), of Farnham, Surrey, and Elizabeth, *née* Whitley (d 1986); *b* 15 May 1934; *Educ* Rugby; *m* 6 Nov 1971, Cecilia Anne, da of Air Vice-Marshal Neill Charles Ogilvie-Forbes, OBE, of Marlow, Bucks; 1 s (John James Whitley b 16 July 1972); *Career* Nat Serv 1958-60, sr under offr Officer Cadet Sch, 2 Lt RA 22 Field Regt; articled CA Whinney Smith and Whinney 1952-57, mgmnt trainee Greenall Whitley and Co (Brewers) 1960-65; dir: Greenall Whitley and Co Warrington 1965-70, Mackie and Co Ltd (newspaper propietors) 1962-75; accountant Artgate Ltd 1975-86 (dir 1979-86), dir Joca Properties Ltd (investmt property co) 1970-, dir Tyerheath Ltd (property devpt co) 1987-; hockey player for GB at Olympic Games in 1960, 1964 and 1968 (Capt); hockey selector for England 1986-; Devon Hockey Selector, sec Local Property Holders Assoc; former tax cmmr Warrington and Exeter; FCA; *Recreations* hockey, tennis, squash, gardening; *Clubs* Naval; *Style*— John Neill, Esq; 5 Baring Cres, Exeter EX1 1TL

NEILL, Sir (Francis) Patrick; QC (1966); s of Sir Thomas Neill, JP (d 1937); bro of Hon Brian (Thomas) Neill, *qv*; *b* 8 August 1926; *Educ* Highgate Sch, Magdalen Coll Oxford; *m* 1954, Caroline Susan, da of Sir Piers Debenham, 2 Bt (d 1964); 4 s, 2 da; *Career* served Rifle Bde 1944-47; fell All Souls Oxford 1950-77 (warden 1977-); barr Gray's Inn 1951, rec of Crown Ct 1975-78, judge of Cts of Appeal of Jersey and Guernsey 1977-; chm Press Cncl 1978-83, first chm Cncl for Securities Industry 1978-85; vice-chllr Oxford Univ 1985-; kt 1983; *Style*— Sir Patrick Neill, QC; All Souls College, Oxford

NEILL, Robert James MacGillivray; s of John MacGillivray Neill, of Ilford, Essex, and Elsie May, *née* Chaston; *b* 24 June 1952; *Educ* Abbs Cross Sch Horchurch, LSE (LLB); *Career* barr Middle Temple 1975; dir: NE Thames Business Advsy Centre 1984-, Energy Concern Ltd 1986-; memb: Havering London Borough Cncl 1974- (chief whip), GLC for Romford (C) 1985-86; first ldr London Fire & Civil Defence Authy 1985-87, oppn spokesman fire and public protection ctee Assoc of Met Authorities; Parly candidate (C) Dagenham 1983 and 1987; *Books* author of various articles on civil defence,lLegal affrs, Etc; *Recreations* sailing, travel, opera; *Clubs* Athenaeum, Carlton, Bar YC; *Style*— Robert Neill, Esq; 3 Hare Ct, Temple, London, EC4Y 7BJ, (☎ 01 353 7561, fax 01 353 7741)

NEILSON, Maj Nigel Fraser; MC; s of Lt-Col William Neilson, DSO (d 1960), of Hawkes Bay, NZ, and Maud Frances Alice, *née* Anson (d 1967); *b* 12 Dec 1919; *Educ* Wellington House Westgate-on-Sea, Hereworth NZ, Christ's Coll NZ, RADA; *m* 22 Oct 1949, Pamela Catherine Georgina, da of Capt Samuel Marshal Philpot Sheppard (d 1945), of Well Cottage, Coulsden, Surrey; 1 s (Peter Nigel b 1958), 1 da (Susan Catherine Hiraani b 1952); *Career* cmmnd Staffs Yeo, served 1 Cavalry Div Palestine, transferred to Trans-Jordanian Frontier Force Cavalry Regt (took part in the last cavalry charge in history against French Spahis), returned Staffs Yeo (tanks) El Alamein Western Desert, GSO3 7 Armd Div, Anzio landing Italy, Allied force HQ Algiers, psc, joined SAS HQ, transferred 2 Liaison French SAS served Holland and France, served COS Bergen Norway, returned to theatre 1946, played and sang in many shows and concerts in London and USA, had own BBC programme Beginners Please, 2 i/c PR dept J Walter Thomson, left to become personal consIt to A S Onassis (introduced by Sir Winston Churchill), opened own int PR Co representing major int cos: London, NZ, Malaysia, Singapore, US; helped produce HRH Prince Charles's first int Broadcast, represented Queen's Silver Jubilee Appeal, memb cncl of Drake Fellowship, former pres and memb ctee NZ Soc, currently independent int PR consIt; Legion D'Honneur, Croix de Guerres Avec Palm; *Recreations* shooting; *Clubs* Buck's, Annabel's, Wig and Pen, Special Forces; *Style*— Maj Nigel Neilson, MC; Bank of New Zealand, BNZ House, 91 Gresham St, PO 402, London EC2V 7BL; Neilson Assocs, 81 Lower Grosvenor Place, London SW1W 0EN

NEIVENS, Peter; OBE (1982), QPM (1974); s of Charles Neivens (d 1953), and Matilda Rose Neivens, *née* Costello (d 1977); *b* 4 June 1922; *Educ* Sir John Cass Tech Sch Aldgate; *m* 1948, Margaret Dorothy; 1 s; *Career* 9 years Merchant Navy, 2 offr British Tankers 1938-47; 24 years Metropolitan Police (rank of dep asst cmmr, dir of information); dir Trident (special responsibility for compliance) 1981-; 1939-45 Star, Atlantic Star, Burma Star, Victory Medal 1939, Police Long Service Medal and Good Conduct Medal 1969; *Recreations* cricket, birdwatching, walking; *Clubs* Clermont; *Style*— Peter Neivens, Esq, OBE, QPM; 25 Third Ave, Walton-on-the-Naze, Essex (☎ Frinton 3521); Trident House, 29 Farm St, London W1X 8AA

NELDER, Prof John Ashworth; s of Reginald Charles Nelder (d 1979), and Edith May Ashworth Briggs (d 1954); *b* 8 Oct 1924; *Educ* Blundell's, Sidney Sussex Coll Cambridge, Birmingham Univ (DSc); *m* 13 Jan 1954, Mary, da of Reginald Hawkes (d 1969); 1 s (Jan b 1956), 1 da (Rosalind b 1958); *Career* WWII RAF 1943-46; head of statistics dept: Nat Vegetable Res Station 1950-68, Rothamsted Experimental Station 1968-84; visiting prof Imperial Coll London 1972-; pres: Int Biometric Soc 1978-79, Royal Statistical Soc 1985-86; Hon DSc Université Paul Sabatier Toulouse 1981; FRS 1981, Fell Int Statistical Inst; *Books* Generalized Linear Models (with P McCullagh); *Recreations* music (especially piano-playing), natural history; *Style*— Prof John Nelder; Cumberland Cottage, Crown St, Redbourn, St Albans AL3 7JX (☎ 058 285 2907); Imperial College, Mathematics Dept, 180 Queen's Gate, London SW7 2BZ (☎ 01 589 5111 ext 5839)

NELIGAN, Timothy Patrick Moore; s of Moore Dermot Neligan (d 1977), of Worthing, and Margaret Joan, *née* Cockell (d 1975); *b* 16 June 1934; *Educ* Tonbridge; *m* 30 Nov 1957, Felicity Caroline, da of Norman Rycroft, of Thornton Hough, Cheshire; 2 s (Patrick b 1963, Timothy b 1963), 2 da (Henrietta b 1958, Kate b 1959); *Career* pupil Capt H Ryan Price racehorse trainer 1953-55, exec agric div ICI 1955-57, brewer and mangr Arthur Guinness (Park Royal) Ltd 1957-73, dir Goodwood Racecourse Ltd 1973-77, md United Racecourses Ltd 1977-; pres no 621 cadet div St John Ambulance, vice-chm Epsom & Walton Downs Conservators, memb SE Eng Tourist Bd; Freeman City of London 1980, Liveryman Worshipful Co Farriers (Middle Warden 1988-89); MInstM 1977; *Books* The Epsom Derby (with Roger Mortimer, 1984); *Recreations* fishing, travel; *Style*— Timothy Neligan, Esq; Toll House, Sandown Park, Esher, Surrey KT10 9AJ (☎ 0372 67839); Sandown Park Racecourse, Esher, Surrey KT10 9AJ (☎ 0372 64348, 726311, fax 0372 65205)

NELLIST, David John; MP (Lab) Coventry South-East 1983-; *b* 1952,July; *Style*— David Nellist Esq, MP; House of Commons, London SW1A 0AA

NELLIST, Robert Henry Harger (Bob); s of John Harger Nellist (d 1966), of Rickmansworth, Herts, and Mary Ellen, *née* Eyles; *b* 25 August 1937; *Educ* St Edwards Sch Oxford, Trinity Coll Oxford (MA); *m* 31 Aug 1963, Audrey May, da of Harry John (Bill) Aubon (d 1982), of Harrow, Middx; 2 s (Andrew John b 29 July 1964, James Harry b 5 Feb 1969), 2 da (Annabel Kate b 28 June 1966, Louisa Mary (twin) b 5 Feb 1969); *Career* Nat Serv RM 1956-58, cmmnd Temp 2 Lt, troop offr 45 Commando Cyprus and Malta; CA; mangr Binder Hamlyn 1961-66, mgmnt consIt McKinsey & Co Inc 1966-69, divnl md (later gp fin dir) Hestair plc 1971-77, dir accounting Rolls-Royce plc 1977-79, dep fin dir The Plessey Co plc 1979-84, gp fin dir Thorn EMI plc 1984-; memb 100 Gp CA; memb: fraternity of friends St Albans Abbey, hon guide St Albans Cathedral; FCA 1964, MIMC 1970, JDipMA 1981, CBIM 1985 ; *Recreations* reading, hi-fi, music, trying to be fit not fat, personal computing; *Clubs* Vincents; *Style*— Bob Nellist, Esq; Spooner's, 28 Park Lane, St Albans, Herts AL2 2JB (☎ 0727 72319); Thorn EMI plc 4 Tenterden St, Hanover Sq, London W1A 2AY (☎ 01 355 4848, fax 01 355 4494, car tel 0836 600 977, telex 264855 THORN G)

NELSON, Lt-Col Andrew Sclanders; TD, JP (Kirkcudbrightshire 1966), DL (Wigtown 1982); s of R F W R Nelson, of Bothwell, Lanarks; *b* 1915; *Educ* Glenalmond; *m* 1940, Diana Dorothy Nicholson, of Eyamdale House, Eyamdale, Derbys; 1 s, 2 da; *Career* WWII (despatches twice), ret as Lt-Col; JP Lanarks 1952, DL Lanarks 1960; AMIMechE; *Style*— Lt-Col Andrew Nelson, TD, JP, DL; Auchinleck Lodge, Minnigaff, Newton Stewart, Wigtownshire DG8 7AA (☎ 0671 2851)

NELSON, (Richard) Anthony; MP (C) Chichester Oct 1974-; s of Gp Capt R Gordon Nelson; *b* 11 June 1948; *Educ* Harrow, Christ's Coll Cambridge (MA); *m* 1974, Caroline Victoria, da of B A Butler; 1 s (Carlton b 1981), 1 da (Charlotte-Anne b 1979); *Career* contested (C) E Leeds Feb 1974, memb of select ctee on Sci and Tech 1975-79; PPS: Min for Housing and Construction 1979-83, Min for Armed Forces 1983-; dir Chichester Festival Theatre 1962-; FRSA; *Recreations* music, rugby, football; *Style*— Anthony Nelson, Esq, MP; House of Commons, London SW1

NELSON, Campbell Louis; s of George Francis Nelson (d 1913), and Kate Nelson, *née* Wilson (d 1977); *b* 14 Dec 1910; *Educ* Seaford Coll, King's Coll London; *m* 1939, Pauline Frances, *née* Blundell (d 1978); 1 s, 1 da; *Career* Lt KRRC (Motor Bns) 1941-44; CA; ptnr Limebeer & Co, 1935-74 (sr ptnr 1951-74); dir and chm Great Northern London Cemetry Co 1945; md Apex (Trinidad) Oilfields Ltd 1954-60, dir Noyapara Tea Co Ltd 1964-79; chm: British-Borneo Petroleum Syndicate plc 1957-85 (exec dir 1948-85), Ultramar plc 1971-80 (md 1960-80, dir 1947-), Scottish Offshore Investors plc 1975-85, Gellatly Hankey & Co Ltd 1976-81 (dir 1970-81); memb: cncl Maritime Trust 1979-, cncl Indonesian Assoc 1980-; patron St James and St Vedast Schs 1980-; dir Harrisons (Clyde) Ltd 1981-; FCA 1933; *Recreations* golf, bridge; *Clubs* City of London, Royal & Ancient GC, Sunningdale GC Golf; *Style*— Campbell Nelson Esq; 2 Chelsea House, 26 Lowndes St, London SW1 (☎ 01 235 8260); Queenshill, Ridgemount Rd, Sunningdale, Berks (☎ 0990 20088)

NELSON, Cathleen, Lady; (Annie) Cathleen (Elizabeth); da of Lt-Col Loftus Bryan, DL; *m* 1923, as his 2 w, Sir James Hope Nelson, 2 Bt (d 1960); *Style*— Cathleen, Lady Nelson

NELSON, David George Hargraves; OBE (1984); s of Sir Amos Nelson (d 1947), of Gledstone Hall, Skipton-in-Craven, Yorks, and Harriet, *née* Hargraves; *b* 13 June 1933;

Educ Harrow, Christ Church Oxford (MA); *m* 27 Feb 1965, Arniorel Brandreth, da of Brig Basil Hildebrand Ryves-Hopkins (d 1959); 1 s (James b 1971), 2 da (Lucinda b 1966, Victoria b 1968); *Career* Nat Serv Kings Dragoon Gds 1951-53; dir: Amos Nelson 1958-, James Nelson 1959-63, David Nelson 1968-, Skipton Building Soc 1970-74; chm: Skipton Cons Assoc 1970-77, Skipton and Ripon Cons Assoc 1983-88; memb cncl Order of St John N Yorks; *Recreations* shooting; *Clubs* Lansdowne; *Style—* David Nelson, Esq, OBE; Old Gledstone, Nr Skipton, N Yorks BD23 3JR; Les Vouguets, 26160 Pont-de-Barret, France

NELSON, Edward Holgate; s of James Nelson (d 1957), and Elsie, *née* Holgate (d 1960); *b* 26 Jan 1934; *Educ* Stowe; *m* 30 April 1957, Jean Elizabeth, da of Leonard Brown, of Heights House, Salterforth, Lancashire; 3 s (Mark b 1959, Simon b 1963, Matthew b 1968), 1 da (Sarah b 1966); *Career* Nat Serv RASC 1952-54; dir: E Gomme Ltd 1978-86, Hartley Nelson & Co 1978-, Clover Mill Ltd 1978, G Plan Ltd 1986-, Gomme Hldgs Ltd 1986, Polytex Hldgs Ltd 1987-, Silas Poker Ltd 1987-; pres N Lancs Furniture Manufacturers 1978-81; Freeman City of London 1987, Liveryman Worshipful Co of Furniture Makers 1987; *Recreations* travel in France, French Wines; *Clubs* Sloane; *Style—* Edward Nelson, Esq; Wynstone, Colne, Lancashire BB8 9QW (☎ 0282 863 423); G Plan Ltd, Clover Mill, Nelson, Lancashire BB8 9OHT (☎ 0282 67 755, fax 0282 601 124, car tel 0836 587 154)

NELSON, Edward Spencer; s of Amos Christopher Nelson (d 1974), and Mary, *née* Spencer; *b* 10 Sept 1907; *Educ* Canford; *m* 21 Nov 1969, Sanda Elizabeth, da of John H Powell, of Corner Cottage, Coates, nr Cirencester, Glos; 1 s (Amos John b 10 April 1978), 1 da (Daisy Sophia Elizabeth b 13 June 1980); *Career* cmmnd 2 Lt 12 Royal Lancers 1953, Lt Yorks Hussars 1955, Capt Duke of Lancaster's Own Yeo 1956, resigned cmmn 1966; mangr in family firm James Nelson Textiles 1955-62, mgmnt Coutaulds 1962-64, professional racing driver 1964-68 (Springbok Champion 1967-68), sr mgmnt Mirror Gp Newspapers 1968-79, dir Fleet Deliveries Ltd 1979-87, exec Pergamon Hldgs 1987-; dir Br Racing Drivers Club 1972-; bobsleighed for GB World Champs 1965 and 1966; Freeman City of London 1982, Liveryman Worshipful Co of Weavers 1982; memb Bruderschaft St Christoph Austria; *Recreations* motor racing, shooting, skiing, motorcycling; *Clubs* Cavalry and Guards, City Livery; *Style—* Edward S Nelson, Esq; 104 Tachbrook Street, Pimlico, London SW1; Pergamon Holdings Ltd, 33 Holborn Circus, London EC1 (☎ 01 822 2216)

NELSON, Hon Lady (Elizabeth Ann Bevil); *née* Cary; da of 14 Visc Falkland; *b* 1927; *m* 1945, Sir William Vernon Hope Nelson, 3 Bt, OBE; *Style—* The Hon Lady Nelson; c/o Barclays Bank, Market St, Crewkerne, Somerset

NELSON, Dr Elizabeth Hawkins; da of Harry Dadmun Nelson (d 1965), of Summit, New Jersey, and Grecthen, *née* Hawkins (d 1984); *b* 27 Jan 1931; *Educ* Hanover HS Hanover New Hampshire USA, Middlebury Coll Vermont USA (BA), Inst of Psychiatry Univ of London (PhD); *m* 1, 1960 (m dis 1972), Ivan Piercy; 2 s (Christopher b 5 March 1963, Nicholas b 3 Aug 1965), 1 da (Catherine b 15 Sept 1961); m 2, 26 July 1975, Claude Jacob Esterson, s of Elias Esterson; *Career* res psychologist Mars Ltd 1953-55, mkt res exec Benton and Bowles Ltd 1955-57, dir and md res unit Benton and Bowles Ltd 1957-64, fndr dir and chm Taylor Nelson Gp 1965-; memb family practitioners ctee Open Univ 1986-; Freeman Worshipful Co of Marketors; fell and cncl memb Royal Soc of Arts, Assoc Memb BPsS (chartered psychologist), pres elect World Assoc of Public Opinion Res; *Recreations* bridge, choral singing, opera; *Style—* Dr Elizabeth Nelson; 57 Home Park Rd, Wimbledon, London SW19 (☎ 01 946 2317); Taylor Nelson Group Ltd, Taylor Nelson House, 44-46 Upper High St, Epsom, Surrey KT17 4QS (☎ 03727 29688, fax 03727 44100, car tel 0860 223690)

NELSON, Hon Henry Roy George; s and h of 2 Baron Nelson of Stafford; *b* 26 Oct 1943; *Educ* Ampleforth, King's Coll Cambridge (MA); *m* 8 June 1968, Dorothy, yr da of Leslie Caley, of Tibthorpe Manor, Driffield, E Yorks; 1 s (Alistair b 1973), 1 da (Sarah Jane b 1981); *Career* joined RHP Bearings 1970; gen mangr: transmission bearings 1973-78, automotive bearings 1978-81: mfrg dir industl bearings 1981-83; md: Hopkinsons Ltd 1983-85, industl div Pegler-Hattersl plc 1985-86; gp md GSPK Ltd 1986-; memb Govt Ctee of Enquiry into Engrg Profession 1978-80; FIMechE, MIEE, CEng; *Style—* The Hon Henry Nelson; Ackworth Grove, Pontefract Rd, High Ackworth, Nr Pontefract, Yorks WF7 7EE (☎ 0977 704742)

NELSON, Ian Digby; s of Theodore Nelson Nelson (d 1959), of Cleevelands, Cheltenham Glos, and Hannah Willis (d 1966); *b* 9 June 1926; *Educ* Edward VI GS Morpeth, London Univ and Loughborough Univ (BSc Eng, DLC);; *m* 12 Aug 1949, Eileen Nellie, da of Frederick James Caldwell (d 1965), of Outwoods Drive Loughborough; 3 s (Richard b 1950, John b 19532, Andrew b 1955); *Career* Lt Royal Engrs 1945-48; dir: Engrg Rolls-Royce Motors (dir resources and special projects 1976-81, gen works mangr 1971-76, personnel and admin 1967-71), Plan Invest Gp plc 1984; pres of Engrg Employers Assoc Cheshire Mersyside (N Wales and S Lancs 1978-79); dep chm NW Liaison ctee of Understanding Br Indust project 1977-82; MIMechE, CEng; *Recreations* gardening, caravanning; *Style—* Ian Nelson, Esq; 128 Main Rd, Wybunbury, Nantwich, Cheshire CW5 7LR (☎ (0270) 841200)

NELSON, Hon James Jonathan; s of 2 Baron Nelson of Stafford; *b* 17 June 1947; *Educ* Ampleforth, McGill Univ Canada (BCom); *m* 18 Nov 1977, Lucilla Mary, da of Roger Gopsill Brown, of Albrighton, Shropshire; 3 da (Camilla Amy b 1982, Lara Kitty b 1986, Eloise Violet b 1988); *Career* commercial banking offr Morgan Tst Co of New York 1969-73, dir Foreign & Colonial Mgmnt Ltd 1974-, md Foreign & Colonial Ventures Ltd 1985-; Freeman of City of London 1986; *Recreations* golf, tennis, skiing, shooting, fishing; *Clubs* Queen's, Hurlingham, New Zealand; *Style—* The Hon James Nelson; 61 Fentiman Road, London SW8; 1 Laurence Pountney Hill, London EC4R OBA (☎ 01 623 4680, fax 01 626 4947, telex 886197)

NELSON, Jamie Charles Vernon Hope; s and h of Sir William Vernon Hope Nelson, 3 Bt, OBE; *b* 23 Oct 1949; *m* 25 June 1983, Maralyn Pyatt Hedge; 1 s (Liam Chester b 1982); *Career* forester, teacher; *Style—* Jamie Nelson, Esq; 39 Montacute Road, Tintinhull, Yeovil, Somerset BA22 8QD

NELSON, Lady (Margaret) Jane; *née* FitzRoy; er da of William Henry Alfred FitzRoy, Viscount Ipswich (ka 1918), and sis of 9 Duke of Grafton (d 1936); raised to rank and precedence of a Duke's da 1931; *b* 1916; *m* 1936, Maj-Gen Sir (Eustace) John Blois Nelson, KCVO, CB, DSO, OBE, MC, *qv*; 2 da; *Style—* Lady Jane Nelson; Tigh Bhaan, Appin, Argyll, Scotland (☎ 063 173)

NELSON, Hon Mrs (Joanna); *née* Quinton; da of Baron Quinton (Life Peer), and Marcelle, *née* Wegier; *b* 1955; *m* 1, 1974 (m dis 1981), Francis Joseph Fitzherbert-Brockholes; m 2, 1981, Jonathan Nelson, of New York, NY, USA; children; *Style—* The Hon Mrs Nelson

NELSON, Maj-Gen Sir (Eustace) John Blois; KCVO (1965, MVO 1953), CB (1964), DSO (1944), OBE (1948), MC (1943); s of Roland Hugh Nelson (d 1940), and Hylda Blois, da of Sir John Blois, Bt (d 1955); *b* 15 June 1912; *Educ* Eton, Trinity Coll Cambridge (MA); *m* 1936, Lady (Margaret) Jane, *qv*; 2 da (yr da Juliet m 1960 Sir Montague Cholmeley, Bt, *qv*); *Career* cmmnd Grenadier Gds 1933, served WWII (wounded 3 times, despatches), cmd 3 Bn Grenadier Gds 1944-45 serv Italy, 1 Gds Parachute Bn 1946-48 serv Palstine, 1 Bn Grenadier Gds 1951-53 serv N Africa, IDC 1958, Brig cmdg 4 Gds Bde Gp 1959-61, GOC London Dist and Maj-Gen cmdg Household Bde 1962-65, GOC Berlin (Br Sector) 1966-68, ret; chm Christian Youth Challenge Tst; pres Trident Project; Silver Star (USA) 1944; *Recreations* sailing, fishing; *Style—* Maj-Gen Sir John Nelson, KCVO, CB, DSO, OBE, MC; Tigh Bhaan, Appin, Argyll, Scotland (☎ 063 173252)

NELSON, Hon Mrs John; Kathleen Mary; *née* Burr; *m* 1941, Capt Hon John Marie Joseph Horatio Nelson (d 1970); 2 s, 1 da; *Style—* The Hon Mrs John Nelson; Dunbar Cottage, Potten End, Berkhamsted, Herts

NELSON, Michael Edward; s of Thomas Alfred Nelson (d 1977); *b* 30 April 1929; *Educ* Latymer Upper Sch, Magdalen Coll Oxford; *m* 1960, Helga Johanna, da of Pieter Den Ouden (d 1942); 2 s (Patrick, Paul), 1 da (Shivaun); *Career* journalist; jt mangr Reuters Econ Servs 1960-62 (mangr 1962-75), asst gen mangr Reuters Ltd 1967-73, (jt dep md and gen mangr 1976-81), dep md and gen mangr 1981-; chm Visnews Ltd 1985-; *Clubs* Garrick; *Style—* Michael Nelson, Esq; Reuters Limited, 85 Fleet St, London EC4P 4AJ (☎ 01 250 1122)

NELSON, Paul Maurice; s of Aubrey Nelson, of Putney, London, and Myrtle, *née* Herman; *b* 22 August 1956; *Educ* Latymer Upper Sch, Christ Church Coll Cambridge (BA, MA); *m* 1 May 1983, Dora Jennifer, da of Max Lawson; *Career* slr 1981; Linklaters & Paines: articled clerk 1979-81, asst slr 1981-87, ptnr 1987-; memb Law Soc 1981; *Recreations* reading, art, cinema; *Style—* Paul Nelson, Esq; Barrington House, 59-67 Gresham St, London EVC2 (☎ 01 606 7080)

NELSON, 9 Earl (UK 1805); Peter John Horatio Nelson; also Baron Nelson of the Nile & of Hilborough (UK 1801) and Viscount Merton of Trafalgar & of Merton (UK 1805); s of Capt Hon John Nelson, RA (5 s of 5 Earl and yr bro of 6, 7 and 8 Earls); Lord Nelson (suc uncle, 8 Earl, Sept 1981) is fifth in descent from the 2 Earl; The 2 Earl's mother Susannah was sister to the 1 Earl and his yr bro, the celebrated naval hero; Horatio Nelson's Barony of Nelson (GB) and Viscountcy of Nelson (UK) were extinguished with him, but his Barony of Nelson of the Nile & of Hilborough have descended to the present Peer along with his er bro's Earldom and Viscountcy (the two last titles being created, like the aforesaid Barony, with special remainder to ensure the survival of dignities honouring one of Britain's greatest sons); The Admiral's Dukedom of Bronté, however, passed, through the marriage of the 1 Earl's da Charlotte with the 2 Baron Bridport, to the Viscounts Bridport, *qv*; *b* 9 Oct 1941; *Educ* St Joseph's Coll Ipswich, Nat Inst of Agric Lincs; *m* 1969, Maureen Diana, da of Edward Patrick Quinn, of Kilkenny; 1 s (and 1 s, Peter Francis Horatio, b and d 1970), 1 da (Lady Deborah b 1974); *Heir* s, Viscount Merton, *qv*; *Career* main bd dir of Business Planning and Devpt Inc; pres: Royal Naval Commando Assoc, Nelson Soc; vice-pres Jubilee Sailing Tst; memb cncl Friends of Nat Maritime Museum; hon life memb: Royal Naval Assoc, Royal Naval Museum; pres Int Fingerprint Soc; *Clubs* St James's; *Style—* The Rt Hon the Earl Nelson; House of Lords, London SW1A 0PW

NELSON, Air Marshal Sir (Sidney) Richard Carlyle; KCB (1963, CB 1962), OBE (1949); s of M O Nelson, of Smithville, Ontario, Canada, and Jane Amelia, *née* Cartwright (d 1970); *b* 14 Nov 1907; *Educ* Univ of Alberta Canada (MD), graduate RAF Staff Coll; *m* 1939, Christina Elizabeth, da of R S Powell, of London; 2 s (Richard, Peter); *Career* joined RAF 1935, served WWII, Gp Capt 1953, Air Cdre 1957, PMO Tech Trg Cmd 1957-59, Air Vice-Marshal 1959, PMO Bomber Cmd 1959-62, QHP 1961-67, Air Marshal 1962, dir-gen RAF Med Servs 1962-67, ret; dir of res and med servs Aspro-Nicholas 1967-72; *Recreations* fishing, golf; *Clubs* Royal Lymington YC, RAF; *Style—* Air Marshal Sir Richard Nelson, KCB OBE; Caffyn's Copse, Shappen Hill Lane, Burley, Ringwood, Hants BH24 4EP (☎ 042 53 3308)

NELSON, Richard William; s of Cyril Aubrey Nelson (d 1971), and Gillian Mary, *née* Nelson; *b* 14 June 1950; *Educ* Nottingham HS, Bristol Univ (LLB); *m* 29 April 1978, Elizabeth Mary, da of Percy Graham Cope, of Burton Joyce, Nottingham; 1 s (William Henry b 1987); *Career* slr; J & A Bright Richards & Flewitt 1977-80, ptnr Freeth Cartwright & Sketchley 1980-83, sr ptnr Nelson Johnson & Hastings 1983-, chm Stanmarsh Ltd, dir Denmoors Ltd; vice chm and cncl memb Nottingham Hospice, ctee memb Old Nottinghamians Soc, former capt Old Notts CC;; *Clubs* sport, rugby union, cricket, fishing, cinema, the arts; *Style—* Richard Nelson, Esq; 165 Harrow Rd, Wollaton Park, Nottingham (☎ 0602 287 140); Scarborough House, 30-32 Bridlesmith Gate, Nottingham (☎ 0602 586 262, fax 0602 584 702)

NELSON, Robert Franklyn; QC (1985); s of Clarence William Nelson, of North Rigton, Harrogate, Yorks, and Lucie Margaret, *née* Kirkby; *b* 19 Sept 1942; *Educ* Repton, St Johns Coll Cambridge (BA, MA); *m* 14 Sept 1968, Anne-Marie Sabina, da of Francis William George Hall, of Bellingham House, Hook Green Lane, Wilmington, Kent; 2 s (Joshua b 1970, Bartholomew b 1973); *Career* barr Middle Temple 1965; Harmsworth Entrance Exhibition 1963; rec 1986-; *Recreations* opera, cricket, golf; *Style—* Robert Nelson, Esq, QC; Honey Cottage, Fairseat, Nr Wrotham, Kent (☎ 0732 822263); 1 Paper Buildings, Temple, London EC4

NELSON, Vincent Leonard; s of Simeon Augustus Nelson, of Mandeville, Jamaica, and Leah Rebecca, *née* Wright; *b* 12 Jan 1958; *Educ* Fairfax Sch Yorks, Univ of Birmingham (LLB); *m* 17 Sept 198, Ina Frances Nelson, da of John Frances Easton, of The Old Hall, Barley, Herts; *Career* called to the Bar Inner Temple 1980, legal advsr Thames TV Int 1982-83, Channel 4 1983-84, head of business affrs HTV 1984-89; memb Hon Soc Inner Temple; *Recreations* collector of modern British paintings 1900-58; *Style—* Vincent Nelson, Esq; 6 Fawnbrake Ave, London SE24 OBY (☎ 01 274 3424); 2/2A Drayson Mews, Kensington, London W8 4LY (☎ 01 376 2755)

NELSON, Maj Sir William Vernon Hope; 3 Bt (UK 1912), of Acton Park, Acton, of Denbigh, OBE (Mil 1952); s of William Hope Nelson (d 1953), and nephew of 2 Bt (d 1960); *b* 25 May 1914; *Educ* Beaumont, RMA Sandhurst; *m* 21 Nov 1945, Hon Elizabeth Ann Bevil Cary, da of 14 Viscount Falkland (d 1984); 3 s, 3 da; *Heir* s, Jamie Charles Vernon Hope Nelson; *Career* 2 Lt 8 Hussars 1934, Palestine 1936-39 (despatches, medal with clasp), Korea 1950-51; *Style—* Maj Sir William Nelson, Bt,

OBE; c/o National Westminster Bank, Market St, Crewkerne, Somerset

NELSON, Winifred, Countess; Winifred Mary; da of G Bevan, of Swansea; *m* 1945, 8 Earl Nelson (d 1981); 1 da (Lady Sarah Roberts, *qv*); *Style—* The Rt Hon Winifred, Countess Nelson; 9 Pwlldu Rd, Bishopston, Swansea SA3 3HA (☎ 044 128 2682)

NELSON OF STAFFORD, 2 Baron (UK 1960); Sir Henry George Nelson; 2 Bt (UK 1955); s of 1 Baron Nelson of Stafford (d 1962), sometime chm English Electric Co; *b* 2 Jan 1917; *Educ* Oundle, King's Coll Cambridge (MA); *m* 1940, Pamela Roy, da of Ernest Roy Bird, MP (d 1933); 2 s, 2 da; *Heir* s, Hon Henry Roy George Nelson; *Career* chllr Aston Univ Birmingham 1966-79, lord high steward Borough of Stafford 1966-71, dir English Electric Co Ltd 1943 (dep md 1949, md 1956, chm 1962-66), chm The Gen Electric Co plc 1966-83 (dir 1987); jt dep chm Br Aircraft Corpn 1960-77, chm Royal Worcester plc 1978-83; dir: Bank of England 1961-87, Int Nickel Co of Canada 1964-88, Enserch Corp USA 1984-89, London Bd of Advice Nat Bank of Australasia 1950-81; pres: Soc of Br Aircraft Constructors 1961-62, Beama 1966-67, Orgalime 1968-80, Inst of Electrical Engrs 1970-71; chm: Def Industries Cncl 1971-77, Br Nat Ctee World Energy Conf 1971-74; pres Sino-Br Trade Cncl 1973-83; memb House of Lords Select Ctee Science and Technol; Freeman City of London; prime warden Worshipful Co of Goldsmiths 1983-84; Benjamin Franklin Medal RSA 1959; FEng, FICE, Hon FIMechE, Hon FIEE, FRAeS; *Clubs* Carlton; *Style—* The Rt Hon the Lord Nelson of Stafford; Wincote Farm, Eccleshall, Stafford; 244 Cranmer Court, Whiteheads Grove, London SW3

NELSON-ROBERT, Lady Sarah Josephine Mary; *née* Nelson; da of 8 Earl Nelson (d 1981); *b* 7 Jan 1947; *m* 1978, Dr John Clive Roberts; *Style—* Lady Sarah Nelson-Robert; Oak End, Chalfont Park, Gerrards Cross, Bucks (☎ 0753 882880)

NELSON-SMITH, David Austin; s of Adrian Nelson-Smith (d 1978); *b* 6 April 1936; *Educ* Brighton Coll, CCC Cambridge; *m* 1965, Joyce Yvonne, *née* Naef; 1 s (Mark b 1966), 1 da (Nicola b 1968); *Career* chm and md Tradax England Ltd 1978-83, dir Cargill UK Ltd 1983-; pres Grain and Feedstuffs Trade Assoc 1985-; pres Comité du Commerce des Cereales et des Aliments du Bétail de la CEE 1987-; *Style—* David Nelson-Smith Esq; Cargill UK Ltd, 3 Shortlands, London W6 8RT

NELTHORPE, Lt-Col Roger Sutton; MBE (1945), TD (1949, and 3 clasps), JP (1947), DL (1950); s of late Col Oliver Sutton Nelthorpe; *b* 5 Mar 1918; *Educ* Eton, RAC Cirencester; *Career* Lt-Col 1959 with TA, landowner and farmer; *Recreations* shooting, forestry, agric; *Style—* Lt-Col Roger Nelthorpe, MBE, TD, JP, DL; Scawby Hall, Scawby Brigg, S Humberside, DN20 9LX (☎ Brigg 54205); Estate Office, Scawby, Brigg, S Humberside DN20 9AE (☎ Brigg 54272)

NEPEAN, Lt-Col Sir Evan Yorke; 6 Bt (UK 1802), of Bothenhampton, Dorsetshire; s of Maj Sir Charles Evan Molyneux Yorke Nepean, 5 Bt (d 1953); *b* 23 Nov 1909; *Educ* Winchester, Downing Cambridge; *m* 1940, (Georgiana) Cicely, da of late Maj N E G Willoughby; 3 da; *Heir* none; *Career* served 1932-57 with Royal Corps of Signals, UK, India, Middle East and BAOR, Lt-Col 1943, ret 1957; MA (Cantab), MIEE, CEng; *Recreations* sailing; *Clubs* Royal Lymington YC; *Style—* Lt-Col Sir Evan Nepean, Bt; Goldens, Teffont, Salisbury, Wilts (☎ Teffont 275)

NESBITT, Garry; s of Harry Nesbitt (d 1968), and May Nesbitt; *b* 6 Dec 1942; *Educ* Aida Foster Stage Sch; *m* 28 Aug 1971, Penny, da of E S A Baker; 2 s (Tristan b 1974, Julian b 1989), 2 da (Tania b 1978, Carola b 1981); *Career* fndr Our Price Music Retail Chain 1971 (chm and md), business floated publicly 1984, and acquired by WH Smith 1986 (for £46m with 140 stores), currently dep chm Our Price Music (with 290 stores, the largest specialist retailer of music in the UK); *Recreations* keeping fit, tennis, water skiing, fine wine collecting; *Style—* Garry Nesbitt, Esq

NESBITT, John Sheridan; s of Leslie Haughton Nesbitt (d 1954), and Charlotte Sims (d 1984); *b* 8 Nov 1929; *Educ* William Hulme's GS Manchester, Manchester Univ (LLB); *m* 15 Nov 1958, Elizabeth Anne, da of Arthur Cecil Harker; 3 s (Colin b 1959, Michael b 1961, David b 1963); *Career* barr Grays Inn 1954; publisher Schofield & Sims Ltd Educnl Publishers (dir 1955, md 1974-81, chm 1981-); *Recreations* angling (flyfishing); *Clubs* Kilnsey Angling; *Style—* John Nesbitt, Esq; The Old Hall, Kettlewell, Skipton, North Yorkshire (☎ 075 676 294); Schofield & Sims Ltd, Dogley Mill, Fenay Bridge, Huddersfield, W Yorkshire

NESBITT, Hon Mrs (Patricia Catherine); da of 2 Baron Bethell (d 1965); *b* 20 May 1933; *Educ* St Mary's Convent Ascot; *m* 1956, Michael William Nesbitt, DFC, s of Philip Nesbitt (d 1955); 1 s, 2 da; *Style—* The Hon Mrs Nesbitt; Rotherwood, Fittleworth, Pulborough, Sussex (☎ 079 882 396)

NESS, Lady Brigid Katharine Rachel; *née* Guinness; da of 2 Earl of Iveagh, KG, CB, CMG (d 1967), and Gwendoline, *née* Onslow (d 1966); *b* 20 July 1920; *m* 1, 1945, HRH Prince Frederick von Preussen (d 1966); 3 s, 2 da; m 2, 1967, Maj Anthony Patrick Ness, s of Capt Gordon Stuart Ness, of Braco Castle, Perthshire (ka 1914); *Career* farmer; *Style—* Lady Brigid Ness; Patmore Hall, Albury, Ware, Herts SG11 2JU

NESS, Air Marshal Sir Charles Ernest; KCB (1980, CB 1978), CBE (1967, OBE 1959); s of Charles Wright Ness (d 1934); *b* 4 April 1924; *Educ* George Heriot's Sch, Edinburgh Univ; *m* 1951, Audrey Parker; 1 s; *Career* joined RAF 1943, flying and staff appts with Bomber Cmd and USAF; Station Cdr Steamer Pt Aden 1965-67, Air Cdr Gibralter 1971-73, dir of Orgn and Admin Plans RAF 1974-75, Cdr S Maritime Air Region 1975-76, dir gen Personnel Mgmnt (RAF) MOD 1976-80, air memb for Personnel 1980-83; mil advsr to ICL 1983-; chm: Air League 1987-; chm: govrs Duke of Kent Sch, RAF Benevolent Fund Educnl Tst 1987-; *Style—* Air Marshal Sir Charles Ness, KCB, CBE; Perseverance Cottage, Wentworth, Nr Ely, Cambs

NETCOTT, Cecil Henry; OBE (1970); s of Henry Netcott (d 1936), of Stapleton, Bristol, and Beatrice, *née* Stoneham (d 1962); *b* 8 May 1913; *Educ* Bristol GS, London Univ (LLB); *m* 1, 20 June 1942 (m dis), Winifred Gladys, da of Henry James Shepston (d 1936); 1 da (Rosamond Beatrice b 1954); m 2, 2 Aug 1977, Doreen Peggy, da of Richard Tether, of Gloucester; *Career* slr 1936-82; clerk to Justices (pt-t) Long Ashton Somerset 1949, hon sec Somerset Justices Clerks Soc 1953-82, nat pres Justices Clerks Soc 1967-68, pres Bristol Law Soc 1961-62, chm Local Appeals Tbnl 1963-83, asst registrar County Cts and asst dist registrar of High Ct of Justice Bristol 1969-70; clerk to Justices: Weston Super Mare 1972-82, Axbridge and Burnham-on-Sea 1972-74 ret 1982; *Recreations* music, choral conducting, walking; *Style—* Cecil H Netcott, Esq, OBE; Addington House, The Village, Burrington, nr Bristol, Avon (☎ 0761 62292)

NETHERTHORPE, Baroness; Belinda; o da of late Frederick Hedley Nicholson, of Friars Gate, Firbeck, Worksop, Notts; *m* 1960, 2 Baron Netherthorpe (d 1982); 2 s, 2 da; *Style—* The Rt Hon the Lady Netherthorpe; Boothby Hall, Boothby Pagnell, Grantham, Lincs (☎ 047685 374)

NETHERTHORPE, 3 Baron (UK 1959); James Frederick Turner; s of 2 Baron Netherthorpe (d 1982); *b* 7 Jan 1964; *Educ* Harrow; *Heir* yr bro, Hon Patrick Andrew Turner b 4 June 1971; *Style—* The Rt Hon Lord Netherthorpe; Boothby Hall, Boothby Pagnell, Grantham, Lincs (☎ 047685 374)

NETHERTHORPE, Margaret, Baroness; Margaret Lucy; *née* Mattock; da of James Arthur Mattock, of Sheffield; *b* 13 July 1916; *Educ* Hunmanby Hall, Scarborough; *m* 3 Oct 1935, 1 Baron Netherthorpe (d 1980); 4 s; *Recreations* gardening, travel; *Style—* The Rt Hon Margaret Lady Netherthorpe; The Garden House, Monken Hadley, Hertfordshire EN5 5QF

NETHERTON, Derek Nigel Donald; s of John Gordon Netherton, of London and Beryl Agnes, *née* Freeman; *b* 4 Jan 1945; *Educ* Charterhouse, Kings Coll Cambridge (MA); *m* 8 May 1976, Pamela Jane, da of Col W Rollo Corkill, of Banstead, Surrey; 4 s (Charles b 1981, George b 1984, Patrick b 1987, David (twin) b 1987); *Career* dir Schroder Wagg 1981-; FIA; *Style—* Derek N D Netherton, Esq; c/o J Henry Schroder Wagg & Co Ltd, 120 Cheapside, London EC2V 6DS (☎ 01 382 6000)

NETHERWOOD, John; s of Willie Netherwood, of Huddersfield, and Florence, *née* Girling; *b* 5 Nov 1944; *Educ* Rawthorpe Sch Huddersfield; *m* 19 Feb 1967, Anita Margaret, da of Raymond Jessop (d 1987); 2 da (Jane Alison b 1969, Joanne Helen b 1970); *Career* chm: United Forktrucks Ltd 1975-, B V (UK) Ltd 1972-; exec dir Allied Partnership Gp plc 1985-; *Recreations* flying, sailing; *Style—* John Netherwood, Esq; Briarwood, Parker Lane, Mirfield, West Yorkshire (☎ 0924 496094); United Forktrucks Limited, Huddersfield Road, Mirfield (☎ 0924 496831, telex 556676, fax 0924 497912

NEUBERGER, Prof Albert; s of Max Neuberger (d 1931), of Hassfurt, Bavaria, and Bertha, *née* Hiller (d 1973); *b* 15 April 1908; *Educ* Gymnasium Würzburg, Univ of Würzburg (MD), Univ of London (PhD); *m* 1943, Lillian Ida, da of Edmond Dreyfus; 4 s (David Edmond b 19 Jan 1948, James Max b 4 Nov 1949, Anthony John b 30 Nov 1951, Michael Samuel b 2 Nov 1953), 1 da (Janet b 27 Aug 1957, d 1985); *Career* advsr (Brig) med directorate GHQ Delhi 1945; Beit Meml res fell 1936-40, res biochemistry dep Cambridge 1939-42, memb scientific staff MRC 1943, head biochemistry dept Nat Inst for Med Res 1950-55, chair of chemical pathology St Mary's Hosp Med Sch 1955-73, princ Wright Fleming Inst of Microbiology 1958-62; chm: Jt ARC/MRC Ctee on Food and Mutrition Res 1971-73, governing body Lister Inst of Preventive Med 1971-88, Inter-Research Cncl Ctee on Pollution Research 1975-78; hon pres Br Nutrition Fndn 1982-86; memb: MRC 1962-66, Cncl of Scientific Policy 1968-69, Agric Res Cncl 1969-79, Independent Ctee on Smoking and Health 1973-83, scientific advsy ctee Rank Prize Funds 1982-86; Hon LLD Aberdeen 1967, Hon PhD Jerusalem 1968, Hon DSc Hull 1981; FRS 1951, FRIC 1957, FRCP 1966, foreign hon memb American Acad of Arts and Scis 1972; Kaplun Prize Israel 1973; *Clubs* Athenaeum; *Style—* Prof Albert Neuberger; 37 Eton Ct, Eton Ave, London NW3 3HJ (☎ 01 586 5470); Dept of Biochemistry, Charing Cross & Westminster Medical Sch, St Dunstan's Rd, London W6 8RP (☎ 01 741 4032, 01 846 7031)

NEUBERT, Michael Jon; MP (C) Romford 1983-; s of Frederick Neubert; *b* 3 Sept 1933; *Educ* Queen Elizabeth's Sch Barnet, Bromley GS, RCM Downing Coll Cambridge; *m* 1959, Sally Felicity Bilger; 1 s; *Career* industl and travel conslt, Parly candidate (C): Hammersmith N 1966, Romford 1970; ldr Bromley Cncl 1967-70, Mayor 1972-73; chm Bromley Cons Assoc 1968-69, MP (C) Romford Havering Feb 1974-83; PPS to: Min Social Security and Disabled 1980, Mins State NI Off 1981, Min State Employment 1981-82, Lord Cockfield as Trade Sec 1982-83; asst govt whip 1983-86, govt whip and Lord Cmmr of the Treasy 1986-88; under sec of state for the Armed Forces 1988-; *Books* Running your own Society (1967); *Recreations* music, theatre, cinema, literature, script, writing, countryside; *Clubs* Romford Cons and Constitutional; *Style—* Michael Neubert, Esq, MP; House of Commons, London SW1A 0AA

NEUFELD, Charles Walter; s of Carl Neufeld, of Graz, Styria; *b* 7 July 1924; *Educ* Austrian Gymnasium, Newbury GS, Reading Univ; *m* 1947, Dolores René, da of Luke Marcus François (d 1964), of Durban; 4 children; *Career* chm Newfeld Gp: Newfeld Ltd, C W Neufeld Ltd, Bendy Toys Ltd, Conallcrete Products, Ovation Ltd, Guthrie Bendy Ltd, Bendy Int; *Recreations* sport, music; *Style—* Charles Neufeld, Esq; 54 Hans Place, London SW1; Upper Ribsden, Windlesham, Surrey

NEUMANN, Jan; CBE (1984); s of Frantisek Neumann (d 1940); *b* 26 June 1924; *Educ* Friends' Sch Gt Ayton, London Univ (BSc); *m* 1947, Barbara Joyce, da of Ernest Gove (d 1938); 2 s; *Career* Flt Sgt RAF, Flt Engr Coastal Cmd; chartered engr; dir: Yard Ltd 1969-, Yarrow & Co Ltd 1978-87; memb bd S of Scotland Electricity Bd 1986-; FEng; *Recreations* swimming, bowling; *Style—* Jan Neumann, Esq, CBE; 38 Norwood Park, Bearsden, Glasgow (☎ 041 942 5371); Yard Ltd, Charing Cross Tower, Glasgow G2 4PP (☎ 041 204 2737)

NEVILE, Christopher William Kenneth; s of Kenneth Nevile (d 1960), of Swinderby, Lincoln, and Elizabeth Mary, *née* Brown; *b* 27 April 1957; *Educ* St Hugh's Wood Hall SPA, Rugby, Exeter Univ (LLB); *Career* stockbroker; assoc dir Scrimgeour Vickers until 1987, dir Adams & Nevile Ltd 1987-; *Recreations* shooting, fishing, golf, cricket, squash; *Clubs* Cannons; *Style—* Christopher W K Nevile, Esq; 53 Hambalt Road, London SW4 (☎ 01 675 2628); Adams & Nevile Ltd, Warnford Court, Throgmorton Street, London EC2N 2BD (☎ 01 638 0321)

NEVILL, Lady Beatrix Mary; da of Lord Lambton; *b* 1949; *m* 1982, Guy Nevill, *qv*; *Style—* Lady Beatrix Nevill; The Garden House, Eridge Park, Tunbridge Wells, Kent; 25 Musgrave Rd, New King's Rd, London SW6

NEVILL, Lady Rupert; Lady (Anne) Camilla Eveline; *née* Wallop; da of 9 Earl of Portsmouth (d 1984); *b* 12 July 1925; *Educ* Longstone Hall; *m* 1944, Lord Rupert Nevill, CVO, JP, DL (d 1982), yr s of 4 Marquess of Abergavenny, sometime private sec to HRH The Duke of Edinburgh ; 2 s (Guy b 1945, page of honour to HM 1958-61; Christopher b 1955), 2 da (Angela b 1948; Henrietta b 1964); *Career* served with WREN in London; chm Regnl Arts Assoc for Kent, Surrey and Sussex; pres E Sussex and W Kent branch of NSPCC; dir Southern Television, tstee Charities Aid Fndn, memb reviewing ctee on Export of Works of Art 1982-; tstee Glyndebourne Arts Tst; *Style—* Lady Rupert Nevill; 35 Upper Addison Gardens, London W14 (☎ 01 603 4919/603 4957); Old House Farm, Glynde, Lewes, Sussex (☎ 0273 813706)

NEVILL, Maj-Gen Cosmo Alexander Richard; CB (1958), CBE (1954), DSO (1944); s of Maj Charles Nevill, DSO, OBE (d 1940), of Eccleston, Leamington Spa, and ggs of Charles Nevill, of Nevill Holt, Leics who married Lady Georgina Bingham sis of F M 3 Earl of Lucan; *b* 14 July 1907; *Educ* Harrow, Sandhurst; *m* 1934, Grania, da of Maj Guy Goodliffe, MC, of Birdstown, Co Donegal, and gda of Col Sir Frederick Shaw 5 Bt of Bushy Park, Co Dublin; 1 s (Capt Richard Nevill, m 1961 Caroline, da of Adm Sir Guy Grantham, GCB, CBE, DSO), 1 da (Charmian, m 1965 Capt David Gwynne-James); *Career* 2 Lt Royal Fusiliers 1927; served WWII on staff in India and cmd 2 Bn Devonshire Regt D-Day Normandy 1944; on Mil Staff Ctee, UN New York 1946-48; cmd 1 Bn Royal Fus 1950-51, cmdt Sch of Inf 1954-56, GOC 2 Inf Div 1956-58, Maj-Gen 1957, ret 1960; Col Royal Fusiliers (City of London Regt) 1959-63; memb W Suffolk CC 1962-67; hon lay canon St Edmundsbury Cathedral 1979-85; *Recreations* painting; *Clubs* Army and Navy; *Style—* Maj-Gen Cosmo Nevill, CB, CBE, DSO; Holt, Edwardstone, Boxford, Suffolk CO6 5PJ (☎ 0787 210428)

NEVILL, Guy Rupert Gerard; er s of Lord Rupert Nevill, CVO, JP, DL (d 1982), by his w Lady Anne, *née* Wallop, da of 9 Earl of Portsmouth; hp to unc, 5 Marquess of Abergavenny; *b* 29 Mar 1945; *Educ* Eton; *m* 1982, Lady Beatrix Lambton, da of Lord Lambton; *Career* page of honour to HM 1958-61; *Style—* Guy Nevill Esq; The Garden House, Eridge Park, Tunbridge Wells, Kent; 10c Bramerton St, London SW3; 25 Musgrave Rd, New King's Rd, London SW6

NEVILL, John Robert Ralph Austin; s of Frederick Reginald Nevill (d 1949), of Rosecroft, Newbury, Berks, and Jeanne, *née* Fageol (d 1975); *b* 15 Feb 1928; *Educ* Ampleforth; *m* 30 July 1955, Ann Margaret Mary, da of Archibald Corble (d 1944), of Cookham, Berks; 4 s (Dominic b 1957, Ralph b 1959, Christopher b 1962, Anthony b 1966), 2 da (Cecilia b 1956, Caroline b 1960); *Career* Lt DCLI 1947-48; dir: Nevill Developments 1956-, The Nevill Gallery; former: dir Family Housing Assoc Folkestone Area, chm and vice-pres Canterbury and E Kent branch English Speaking Union, chm and pres SE region English Speaking Union; Knight of Honour and Devotion Br Assoc Sovereign Mil Order of Malta 1975; Freeman City of London, Liveryman Worshipful Co of Gardeners; memb Hon Soc of Gray's Inn 1951; *Recreations* travelling, fishing, photography; *Clubs* Carlton, The English Speaking Union; *Style—* John Nevill, Esq; 5 Tite St, London SW3 4JU; 8 Radnr Cliff, Folkestone, Kent CT20 2JN (☎ 01352 7368/0303 48403); Nevill Gallery, 43 St Peter's St, Canterbury, Kent CT1 2BG (☎ 0227 65291)

NEVILL, Capt (Cosmas Guy) Richard; s of Maj-Gen C A R Nevill, CB, CBE, DSO, *qv*, of Holt, Boxford, Colchester, Essex, and Grania, *née* Goodliffe; *b* 12 July 1937; *Educ* Summer Fields Sch Oxford, Harrow, RMA Sandhurst; *m* 8 April 1961, Caroline Jane, da of Adm Sir Guy Grantham, GCB, CBE, DSO, *qv*, of Tandem House, Nayland, Colchester, Essex; 2 s (Giles b 12 Oct 1963, Alexander b 11 Nov 1965), 1 da (Serena b 30 Oct 1967); *Career* cmmnd 1 Bn Royal Fus (City of London Regt) 1957; serv 1957-64: Bahrain, Kenya, Malta, N Africa, Germany; Capt 1962, ret 1964; investmt mangr Nevill Hldgs Jersey 1964, chm Birdstown Estate Co Donegal 1964-80; dir: Londonderry Properties 1974-89, Tandem Tweeds Colchester 1974-88; investmt mangr Joyce Ltd Kenya 1979-88, asst mangr Cavendish Furniture Co Ltd Suffolk 1986-87; *Recreations* sport, travel, fishing, shooting, philately, music; *Clubs* Army & Navy, MCC, I Zingari, Free Foresters, Tennis & Rackets Assoc, Hampton Court Royal Tennis; *Style—* Capt Richard Nevill; Woodlands, Great Horkesley, Colchester, Essex (☎ 0206 271 226)

NEVILL, Lady Rose; 3 and yst da of 5 Marquess of Abergavenny; *b* 15 July 1950; *Style—* Lady Rose Nevill; c/o Lt. Col Most Hon Marquess of Aberqavenny, KG, OBE, Eridge Park, Tunbridge Wells, Kent, TN3 9JT

NEVILLE, Dr Adam Matthew; TD (1963); *b* 5 Feb 1923; *Educ* QMC (BSc), Univ of London (MSc, PhD, DSc), Univ of Leeds (DSc); *m* 29 March 1952, Mary Hallam, *née* Cousins; 1 s (Adam Andrew b 11 May 1955), 1 da (Elizabeth Louise b 5 Feb 1955); *Career* War Serv RA Middle East and Italy, Maj RETA; academic engr 1950-, prof of civil engrg Univ of Leeds 1968-78, princ and vice chllr Univ of Dundee 1978-87; pres The Concrete Soc 1974-75, chm ctee of Princs of Scottish Univs 1984-86, pres cncl of Europe Ctee on univs 1984-86; Freeman: City of London 1977, Worshipful Co of Fan Makers 1978; memb Bonnetmaker Craft of Dundee 1979; Hon LLD St Andrews 1987, hon memb American Concrete Inst 1986; OStJ 1983; FICE, FIStruct, FCIArb, FRSE, FEng; *Books* Properties of Concrete (1963), Basic Statistical Methods (with J B Kennedy, 1964), Creep of Concrete: plain, reinforced and prestressed (1970), Structural Analysis: a unified classical and matrix appraoch (with A Ghali, 1977), Hardened Concrete: physical and mechanical aspects (1971), High Alumina Cement Concrete (1975), Creep of Plain and Structural Concrete, (with W H Digler and J J Brooks, 1983), Concrete Technology (with J J Brooks, 1987); *Recreations* skiing, travel; *Clubs* Athenaeum, New (Edinburgh), Traveller's Century (Los Angeles); *Style—* Dr Adam Neville, TD; 24 Gun Wharf, 130 Wapping High St, London E1 9NH (☎ 01 265 1087, fax 01 265 1087)

NEVILLE, Prof Bernard Richard; s of R G Neville (d 1941); *b* 24 Sept 1934; *Educ* St Martin's Sch of Art, RCA; *Career* lectr: Shoreditch Coll 1954-56, Central Sch Art and Design 1957-60, St Martin's Sch of Art and RCA 1959-74; freelance illustrator 1956-60 (incl Good Housekeeping, Womans' Journal, Vogue, Harpurs Bazaar), freelance journalist 1956-60 (incl Vogue, Sketch), designer (later design dir) Liberty Prints 1961-71, advsy panel Nat Dip Design 1964-66, art critic Vogue 1965-66, govr Croydon Coll Art 1966-67, designer and design dir Ten Late Holland 1969-71, design conslt dress fabrics Cantoni 1971-84, prof textile design RCA 1984 (fell 1985); commissions and collections incl: Cotton Board Manchester 1950, Liberty prints 1961-71, Verve 1960, Gravate, Islamic 1963, Jazz 1964, Tango 1966, Renaissance 1967, Chameleon 1969, Cantori Casa 1977, Int Wool Secretariat 1975-77, English Country House Collection for Sekers Int 1981-82, Romanex de Boussac France 1982-87; designed costumes for: films (Genevieve 1953, Next to No Time 1955, The Admiral Crichton 1957), musicals (Marigold 1958), opera (Cosi fan tutte Glyndebairne 1962); memb Victorian Soc and Chelsea Soc; FRSA 1966-77, FSIAO 1970-87, FCSD 1987; *Recreations* admiring well built buildings, passionate conservationist and environmentalist, tree worshipper; *Style—* Prof Bernard Neville; Royal College of Art, Kensington Gore, London SW7 (☎ 01 584 5020)

NEVILLE, Air Cdre Christopher Roger Gartside; CBE (1972, OBE 1967), DL (Devon 1987); s of Gp Capt RHG Neville, OBE, MC; *b* 10 Sept 1924; *Educ* Malvern, Brasenose Coll Oxford; *m* 1958, Shelagh Maureen, da of late Lt-Col H H Mulholland; 2 s, 1 da; *Career* Air Cdre RAF 1975, Fighter Units ME, NATO (Europe), UK, cmdg RAF Coningsby 1970-72, princ SO to dep Saceur 1972-74, dir RAF Cmd control and ADP 1975-79; Oxford blue athletics, former capt and chm RAF and Combined Servs athletics; FBIM; *Recreations* golf; *Clubs* RAF; *Style—* Air Cdre Christopher Neville, CBE, DL; Orchard Lea, Wiggaton, Ottery St Mary, Devon (☎ 040 481 2497)

NEVILLE, Donald George; s of Lionel George Neville (d 1963), of Bexhill, and Letitia Helen, *née* Puddicombe (d 1987); *b* 31 Dec 1929; *Educ* Merchant Taylors', London (LLB), Sch of Law; *m* 18 April 1953, Daphne Elizabeth, da of Ernest Hall (d 1967), of Pinner, Middx; 2 s (Richard b 1955, Stuart b 1957), 2 da (Virginia b 1962, Miranda b 1964); *Career* Nat Serv 1952-54, 2 Lt RAPC (later Capt/Paymaster) 5 Queen's Royal Regt TA 1957-63; sr ptnr Cardales McLeish slrs London and Surrey 1974-86; dir various cos; dep chm Dominion Int Gp plc 1975-88; chm SE Region Historic Houses Assoc 1979-81; owner various historic houses open to public incl: Detillens, Limpsfield, Castle Mill Dorking, and Haxted Mill Edenbridge *Publications* Medal Ribbons and Orders of Imperial Germany and Austria (1974), Medal Ribbons of the World (1977), History of the Early Orders of Knighthood and Chivalry (1979); *Recreations* gardening, antiques and study and collection of orders of chivalry; *Clubs* IOD, Thames Rowing; *Style—* Donald Neville, Esq; Detillens, Limpsfield, Surrey (☎ 0883 713342); The Bell, 57 West Street, Dorking, Surrey (☎ 0306 887979)

NEVILLE, His Hon Judge (Eric) Graham; *b* 12 Nov 1933; *Educ* Kelly Coll Tavistock, Sidney Sussex Coll Cambridge; *m* 20 August 1966, Jacqueline Catherine; *Career* RAF Gen Duty Flying Offr 1952-54; rec Crown Ct 1975, circuit judge 1980-; *Recreations* yachting; *Clubs* Royal Western Yacht, Royal Fowey Yacht; *Style—* His Hon Judge Graham Neville; Exeter Crown Court, The Castle, Exeter

NEVILLE, Prof (Alexander) Munro; s of Alexander Munro Neville (d 1983), of 48 Cailes Rd, Troon, Ayrshire, and Georgina Stewart, *née* Gerrard; *b* 24 Mar 1935; *Educ* Univ of Glasgow (MB ChB, PhD, MD), Harvard Univ Boston, Univ of London (DSc), RCP; *m* 5 Sept 1961, Anne Margaaret Stroyan, da of Dr Hugh Black, (d 1975), of 2 Alton Road, Paisley; 1 s (Munro b 26 Nov 1964), 1 da (Judeth b 25 Nov 1963); *Career* sr lectr pathology Univ of Glasgow 1967-70, MRC res fell Inst of Cancer Res London 1970-73, prof pathology Univ of London 1973-85, dir Ludwig Inst for Cancer Res Zurich 1985- (dir London 1975-85); MRCPath 1969, FRCPath 1979; *Recreations* golf, gardening, history; *Clubs* Banstead Downs; *Style—* Prof Munro Neville; 42 Eagle St, London WC1R 4AP; Feldblumenstr 125, 8134 Adliswil, Switzerland (☎ 01 495 9005); Ludwig Institute for Cancer Research, Stadelhoferstr 22, 8001 Zurich Switzerland (☎ 01 251 5377 (Ch), fax 01 251 5438 (CH)

NEVILLE, Sir Richard Lionel John Baines; 3 Bt (UK, 1927), of Sloley, Norfolk; s of Sir Reginald James Neville, 1 Bt (d 1950); suc half-bro, Sir (James) Edmund Henderson Neville, 2 Bt, MC, 1982; *b* 15 July 1921; *Educ* Eton, Trinity Coll Cambridge; *Heir* none; *Career* served Burma 1943-45 as Capt Oxford and Bucks and W African Frontier Force; *Style—* Sir Richard Neville, Bt; Sloley Hall, Norwich

NEVILLE, Hon Robin Henry Charles; DL (Essex 1980); s and h of 9 Baron Braybrooke; *b* 29 Jan 1932; *Educ* Eton, Magdalene Coll Cambridge (MA), RAC Cirencester; *m* 1, 1955 (m dis 1974), Robin Helen Brockhoff; 4 da (Amanda b 1962, Caroline b 1968, Victoria and Arabella (twins) b 1970), and 1 da decd (Henrietta); m 2, 1974, Linda, da of Arthur Norman, of Robblyns, Saffron Walden; 3 da (Sara Lucy b 1975, Emma Charlotte b 1979, Lucinda Octavia b 1984); *Career* farmer and landowner; cmmnd Rifle Bde 1951, served with 3 Bn King's African Rifles in Kenya and Malaya 1951-52; RDC cncllr 1959-69, CC for Stansted 1969-72; memb: cncl of CLA 1965-83, Agric Land Tbnl Eastern Area 1975-; chm: Price Tst 1983-, Rural Devpt Cmmn for Essex 1984-; dir Essex and Suffolk Insur Co until taken over by Guardian Royal Exchange; *Recreations* flying, railways, motorcycling; *Clubs* Boodle's; *Style—* The Hon Robin Neville, DL; Abbey House, Audley End, Saffron Walden, Essex CB11 4JB (☎ 0799 22484, office 22354)

NEVILLE-JONES, (Lilian) Pauline; CMG (1987); da of Roland Neville-Jones, RAMC (ka 1941), and Cecilia Emily Millicent Winn, *née* Rath; step f Dr John Michael Winn; *b* 2 Nov 1939; *Educ* Leeds Girls' HS; Lady Margaret Hall Oxford (BA); *Career* Dip Serv; joined FCO 1963; third sec Salisbury Rhodesia 1964-65, third sec (later second sec) Singapore 1965-68, FCO 1968-71 (dealing with Med), first sec Washington 1971-75, dep chef de cabinet (later chef de cabinet to Christopher Tugendhat) Cmmn of Euro Communities Brussels 1977-82, sabbatical Royal Inst of Int Affrs London and Institut Francais des Relations Internationales Paris 1982-83, head policy planning staff FCO 1983-87, min (economic) Bonn Embassy 1987- (and min 1988-); *Recreations* cooking, gardening, antiques; *Style—* Miss Pauline Neville-Jones; c/o Royal Bank of Scotland, Westminster Branch, 21-23 Victoria St, London SW1A 0HA; British Embassy, Friedrich Ebert Allee 77, 5300 Bonn I, W Germany

NEVIN, Eric; s of William Albert Nevin, and Mabel, *née* Griffiths (d 1974); *b* 12 July 1931; *Educ* St Mary's Coll Crosby, HMS Conway Sch, Liverpool Tech Coll, Sch of Navigation, Liverpool Coll of Commerce, City of London Coll; *m* 1958, Jean (d 1984), da of late John Gardner, of Liverpool; 1 s (Michael), 1 da (Cheryl); *Career* served at sea with Alfred Holt & Co 1948-58, gained Master's Foreign-going Certificate 1957, asst dist sec MNAOA Liverpool 1959 (nat sec 1961, asst gen sec 1971, gen sec 1974-); dir: Merchant Navy Offrs Pension Fund Tstees Ltd, Merchant Navy Offrs Pensions Investmts Ltd, Ensign Tst plc, Merchant Navy Investmts Mgmnt Ltd, Oceanair Servs Ltd, Conway Cadet Sch Tst Ltd, Merchant Navy Welfare Bd Ltd; memb: Thames Water Authy, Jt Ctee for Nat Awards in Nautical Science, cncl for Nat Acad Awards Marine Studies Subject Bd, Ship and Marine Technol Requirements Bd (and its successor Marine Technol Ctee), Nat Econ Depts Ctee for the Movement of Exports, King George's Fund for Sailors, Merchant Seamen's War Meml Soc, Marine Soc, Conway Tst, Nat Maritime Bd, Merchant Navy Welfare Bd, Merchant Navy Officers' Pension Fund; govr: HM Conway Merchant Navy Sch, London Nautical Sch, Merchant Navy Coll (vice-chm), City of London Poly; *Style—* Eric Nevin, Esq; Oceanair House, 750 High Road, Leytonstone, London E11 3BB (☎ 01 989 6677, telex 892648 NUMAST G)

NEVIN, His Hon Judge; Thomas Richard Nevin; TD (1949 and Bar), JP (1965); s of late Thomas Nevin, JP, of Mirfield, Yorks; *b* 9 Dec 1916; *Educ* Bilton Grange, Shrewsbury Sch, Leeds Univ (LLB); *m* 1955, Brenda Micaela, da of Dr B C Andrade-Thompson, MC; 1 s (and 1 decd); *Career* Lt-Col RA, London Bombardment, India and Burma; barr NE Circuit for 19 years, asst rec of Leeds 1961-64, rec of Doncaster 1964-67, dep chm Yorks W Riding QS 1965-71 (E Riding 1968-71), chm Northern Agric Land Tbnl 1963-67 (dep chm 1961-63), a circuit judge and Crown Ct liaison judge (formerly judge of County Cts) 1967-84, a dep High Court judge 1974-84; Freeman City of London; *Recreations* numismatics and our past; *Style—* His Hon Judge Nevin, TD, JP; c/o 11 King's Bench Walk, Temple, EC4 (☎ 01 236 3337)

NEW, Anthony Sherwood Brooks; s of Valentine Gill New (d 1963), and Grace Fanny, *née* Baines (d 1981); *b* 14 August 1924; *Educ* Highgate Sch, Northern Poly Sch of Architecture (Dip Arch); *m* 11 April 1970, (Ann) Elizabeth, da of Bernard Harding Pegge (d 1972), of Elsted, Sussex; 1 s (Nicholas b 1976), 1 da (Susannah b 1972); *Career* Nat Serv leading radio mechanic RN 1945-47; architect; private practice, Derby Cathedral 1970-, numerous churches in London; OStJ; Freeman City of London 1976; FRIBA 1952, MIStructE 1954, FSA 1971; *Books* Observer's Book of Postage Stamps (1967), Observer's Book of Cathedrals (1972), A Guide to the Cathedrals of Britain (1980), P S A Guide to Historic Buildings (London) (1983), A Guide to the Abbeys of England & Wales (1985), New Observer's Book of Stamp Collecting (1986), A Guide to the Abbeys of Scotland (1988); *Recreations* travel, photography, drawing; *Style*— Anthony New, Esq; Architect's Office, Priory Church of St Bartholomew The Great, W Smithfield, London EC1A 7JQ (☎ 01 600 8512)

NEW, Dudley Holt; s of Joseph New (d 1937), of Worthing, and Bessie, *née* Holt (d 1953); *b* 17 Nov 1907; *Educ* Dauntseys Sch, Imperial Coll London (BSc Eng, DIC), ; *m* 9 April 1936, Doris Edith, da of Frederick George Berry (d 1955), of Bideford; 2 s (David b 1937, Kenneth b 1940); *Career* joined RE supplementary reserve 1932, garrison engr Sheerness 1939-41, CO 39 (Fortress) CO RE Freetown 1941-42, DCRE Freetown 1942-43, transferred to army reserve 1942, garrison engr Truro 1943, Adj and ACRE 102 CRE 1943-44, CO 207 Works Section RE Antwerp 1944-45, Engr and Tport Staff Corps RE TA 1962, Lt-Col RE TA; apprentice fitter GWR Works Swindon 1923-28, designer The Trussed Concrete Steel Co Ltd 1935-39; chief engr: Holland & Hannen and Cubitts Ltd 1945-52, Nuclear Civil Constructors 1952-62; ptnr G Maunsell and Ptnrs 1962-73 (conslt 1973-), author of various papers on engrg matters; cncllr London Borough of Lewisham 1947-54, former chm of govrs SE London Coll; former govr: Sedgehill Comprehensive Sch, Malory Comprehensive Sch; Liveryman Worshipful Co of Engrs; FICE 1934, FIMechE 1947, FIStructE 1938, MConsE 1963, FCIArb 1975, CEng, FCGI; *Recreations* reading, gardening; *Clubs* RAC; *Style*— Dudley New, Esq; Ennerdale, 54A Allerford Rd, Catford, London SE6 3DF (☎ 01 697 2728); G Maunsell and Ptnrs, Yeoman House, 63 Croydon Rd, London SE20 7TP (☎ 01 778 6060, telex 946171)

NEW, HE Laurence Anthony Wallis; CB (1986), CBE (1980); s of Lt-Col Stanley William New, MBE (d 1956), of Grayshott House, Grayshott, Hants, and Constance Mary, *née* Marhsall (d 1973); *b* 25 Feb 1932; *Educ* King William's Coll Isle of Man, RMA Sandhurst; *m* 11 Aug 1956, Anna Doreen, da of Gp Capt Conrad Edward Howe Verity, OBE (d 1984), of Farthings, Earleydene, Ascot, Berks; 2 s (Richard b 1961, Robert b 1969), 2 da (Amanda b 1958, Deborah Ann b 1966); *Career* cmmnd RTR 1952; served in Hong Kong, Germany, Malaya and Borneo, CO 4 RTR 1971-73, Bde Maj 1971, Def and Mil attaché Tel Aviv 1974-77; Col GS MOD 1977-79; Brig GS MOD 1981-82, ACGS (Op Regs) 1983-84, ACDS (Land Systems) MOD 1985; Lt Govr of the Isle of Man 1985-; Freeman City of London, Liveryman Glass Sellers' Co 1985; FBIM 1979; CBIM 1986; KStJ 1985; *Recreations* water colour painting, cello, family tennis, walking; *Clubs* Army and Navy; *Style*— HE Maj-Gen Laurence New, CB, CBE; Government House, Isle of Man

NEWALL, Alexander Severin; *b* 15 Nov 1913; *Career* chm and md Alexander Newall Gp of Co's; co-fndr and pres Br Aerophilatelic Fedn; *Style*— Alexander Newall, Esq; 81 Redington Rd, Hampstead NW3 7RR (☎ 01 794 2644); 338 City Rd, London EC1V 2PX (☎ 01 837 0192, fax 01 837 9642, telex 263672 ETALON)

NEWALL, Christopher Stirling; s of Peter Stirling Newall, of Great Hinton, Wilts, and Rosemary, *née* Marriage; *b* 8 April 1951; *Educ* The Downs Sch, Abbotsholme Sch, Courtauld Inst of Art Univ of London (BA); *m* 10 Oct 1985, Jenifer Hylda, da of Sir Derek Ryan, 3 Bt; 1 s (Alfred Stirling b 8 Feb 1987); *Career* writer and art historian; *Books* Victorian Watercolours (1987), George Price Boyce (catalogue Tate Gallery exhibition, 1987), The Engravings after Burne-Jones (intro to catalogue, 1987); *Style*— Christopher Newall, Esq; 10 Barnsbury Sq, London N1 1JL (☎ 01 607 4360)

NEWALL, Hon David William Norton; s of 2 Baron Newall; *b* 2 July 1963; *Educ* Eton, Sandhurst; *Career* estate agent; co dir; *Clubs* Winchester House, RAC; *Style*— The Hon David Newall; 30 Ashbury Rd, London SW11

NEWALL, 2 Baron (UK 1946); Francis Storer Eaton Newall; s of Marshal of the RAF 1 Baron Newall, GCB, OM, GCMG, CBE, AM (d 1963, Chief of Air Staff during Battle of Britain); *b* 23 June 1930; *Educ* Eton, Sandhurst; *m* 1956, Pamela, da of Hugh Rowcliffe, TD, of Pinkney Park, Malmesbury (d 1978), by his 1 w, Margaret (da of Sir Henry Farrington, 6 Bt); 2 s, 1 da; *Heir* s, Hon Richard Newall; *Career* takes Cons whip in Lords; Capt 11 Hussars, served Germany, Malaya, Singapore, NI; adj Royal Glos Hussars; conslt and company dir; Cons whip and oppn front bench spokesman Lords 1976-79; fndr memb House of Lords All Pty Def Study Gp; delegate Western Euro Union and Cncl of Europe 1983-; responsible for Farriers Registration Acts and Betting and Gaming amendment (Greyhound Racing) Acts; led Parly visits to Cyprus, Oman, Bahrain, Qatar, Morocco; chm Br Greyhound Racing Bd; *Recreations* shooting, travel; *Clubs* Cavalry & Guards; *Style*— The Rt Hon the Lord Newall; Wotton Underwood, Aylesbury, Bucks (☎ Brill 0844 238376); 18 Lennox Gdns, London SW1 (☎ 01 589 9370)

NEWALL, Paul Henry; TD (1967), DL (Greater London 1977); s of Leopold Newall (d 1956), and Frances Evelyn, *née* Bean (d 1981); *b* 17 Sept 1934; *Educ* Harrow, Magdalene Coll Cambridge (MA); *m* 1 March 1969, Penelope Moyra, da of Sir Julian Ridsdale, CBE, MP, *qv*; 2 s (Rupert b 1971, James b 1973); *Career* Nat Serv 1953-55: cmmnd Royal Fusiliers, serv Egypt and Sudan; TA 1955-70: Maj 1961, cmd City of London Co 5 Bn RRF 1967-70; chm City of London TA & VRA 1986-; ptnr Loeb Rhoades & Co 1971-77; overseas dir: Shearson Loeb Rhoades (UK) 1979-81, Shearson American Express (UK) 1981-84; dir Shearson Lehman Int Ltd 1985-, exec dir Shearson Lehman Hutton Securities 1988-; vice-pres City of London sector Br Red Cross, govr Mencap City Fndn, patron Samaritans Nat Appeal, churchwarden St Stephen's Walbrook; JP City of London, visiting magistrate HM Tower of London, HM Lt City of London 1975-; elected Ct of Common Cncl 1980, alderman (Walbrook Ward) City of London 1981-; memb: Ct Worshipful Co of Bakers (second warden), Ct Guild of Freeman of City of London; Liveryman Worshipful Co of Gold and Silver Wyre Drawers; *Recreations* fencing, fly fishing, water skiing, tennis, trees; *Clubs* City Livery, Walbrook Ward (pres), United Wards, MCC; *Style*— Paul Newall, Esq, TD, DL; One Broadgate, London EC2

NEWALL, Hon Richard Hugh Eaton; s and h of 2 Baron Newall; *b* 19 Feb 1961; *Style*— The Hon Richard Newall

NEWBIGGING, David Kennedy; OBE (1982); s of David Locke Newbigging, OBE, MC (d 1948) and Lucy Margaret Newbigging (d 1970); *b* 19 Jan 1934; *Educ* Oundle; *m* 1968, Carolyn Susan, da of Geoffrey Band (d 1974); 1 s, 2 da; *Career* 2 Lt Nat Serv; Jardine Matheson & Co Ltd: joined 1954 (dir 1967, md 1970, chm and sr md 1975-83); chm and md Hong Kong Land 1975-83; chm: Hongkong & Kowloon Wharf & Godown Co Ltd 1970-80, Hongkong Electric Holdings Ltd 1982-83 (dir 1975-83), Jardine Fleming & Co Ltd 1975-83; dir: Hongkong & Shanghai Banking Corpn Ltd 1975-83, Hongkong Telephone Co Ltd 1975-83, Rennies Consolidated Holdings Ltd 1975-83; memb: Legislative Cncl Hong Kong 1978-82, Exec Cncl Hong Kong 1980-84, Int Cncl Morgan Guaranty Tst Co of New York 1977-; *Recreations* most outdoor sports; *Clubs* Hurlingham, Turf, The Royal Hongkong Jockey; *Style*— David Newbigging Esq, OBE; 35 Mt Kellett Rd, The Peak, Hong Kong (☎ 5-96334); Jardine, Matheson & Co Ltd, 48/F Connaught Centre, Hong Kong (☎ 5-8438388)

NEWBOLD, Sir Charles Demorée; KBE (1970), CMG (1957), QC (Jamaica 1947); s of Charles Elches Newbold (d 1962), of Port-of-Spain, Trinidad, and Laura May (d 1962); *b* 11 June 1909; *Educ* Lodge Sch Barbados, Keble Coll Oxford (BA); *m* 1936, Ruth, da of Arthur Louis Vaughan (d 1960), of Port-of-Spain; 2 da; *Career* barr Gray's Inn 1931; joined Colonial Legal Servs, magistrate Trinidad 1937, legal draftsman Jamaica 1941-43, slr-gen Jamaica 1943-48, legal sec E Africa High Cmmn 1948-61; memb E Africa Cent Legislative Assembly 1948-61; Justice of Appeal E Africa Ct of Appeal 1961-65 (vice pres 1965-66, pres 1966-70) Grand Cordon Star of Africa (Liberia); chm Ctee of Supply 1948-61, cmmr for Revision of East Africa High Cmmn Laws 1951, jt ed Trinidad Law Reports 1928-33, ed East African Tax Laws Reports 1948-61; kt 1966; *Recreations* cricket, tennis; *Style*— Sir Charles Newbold, KBE, CMG, QC; 7 St Mary's Garden, Chichester, West Sussex (☎ 0243 532431)

NEWBOROUGH, 7 Baron (I 1776); Lord Robert Charles Michael Vaughan Wynn; 9 Bt (GB 1742), DSC (1942); s of 6 Baron Newborough, OBE, JP, DL (d 1965); *b* 24 April 1917; *Educ* Oundle; *m* 1, 1945 (m dis 1971), Rosamund, da of Maj Robert Barbour, of Bolesworth Castle, Tattenhall, Cheshire; 1 s, 2 da; m 2, 1971, Jennifer, yst da of late Capt Cecil Allen, RN, and Lady (Eirene) Morgan, *qv*; *Heir* s, Hon Robert Wynn; *Career* served 2 Lt 9 Lancers, 5 Inniskilling Dragoon Gds and Lt 16/5 Lancers 1935-39, invalided 1940, took part in Dunkirk evacuation as civilian, RNVR Cmmn, cmd MTB 74 St Nazaire raid 1942 (despatches and DSC) wounded, (POW Colditz, escaped); farmer; High Sheriff Merioneth 1963; *Recreations* fishing, yachting; *Clubs* Naval & Military, Goat and Bembridge Sailing; *Style*— The Rt Hon the Lord Newborough, DSC; Rûg, Corwen, Clwyd, N Wales (☎ 0490 2510; Estate Office: 2153)

NEWBOUND, Maurice Ernest; s of Ernest Henry Newbound (d 1959), and Violet Lily, *née* Roberts (d 1969); *b* 13 April 1925; *m* 1, 22 March 1945 (m dis 1973), Ivy Christine, da of Charles Young; 1 s (David b 1952); m 2, 12 April 1975, Shirley Jean Nena, da of Arthur Ratcliffe; *Career* RAF 1943-45; md and chm: Westbourne Int Hldgs Ltd 1957-83, Westbourne Gp Pty Ltd 1969-73, G S Estates Ltd 1974-; dir Swan House Special Events Ltd 1988-; md Painting & Decorating Promotions Ltd 1988-; launched: Br first shopfitting magazine 1954, several pubns & exhibitions at home and abroad & retained as conslt on several; ctee memb Somerset Rural Devpt Commn 1981-; chm: Somerset Centre Inst of Dir 1979-81, Holistic Health Contact Gp 1984-, advsy cncl for UK Natural Health Week 1988; pres: Natural Health Network 1982-, advsy cncl of IDD 1965-; memb: Parly Gp for Alternative & Complementary Med, Br Export GP 1958-64; FMInstM 1977; *Recreations* swimming, gardening; *Clubs* Victory; *Style*— Maurice Newbound, Esq; Chardstock House, Chard, Somerset TA20 2TL (☎ 04606 3229); Chardstock House, Chard, Somerset TA20 2TL (fax 04606 3809)

NEWBURGH, 12 Earl of (S 1660); Filippo Giambattista Camillo Francesco Aldo Maris Rospigliosi; also Viscount Kynnaird and Lord Levingston (S 1660), Prince Rospigliosi (HRE & Papal, 1668 & 1854 respectively, bestowed by Emperor Leopold I & Pope Pio Nono, also respectively), 14 Prince of Castiglione (by the Sicilian cr of 1602, and a further cr of the kingdom of Italy occurred 1897), 11 Duke of Zagarolo (Papal title of 1668), Marquis of Giuliana (Sicily 1543, It 1897), Count of Chiusa (Sic 1535, It 1897), Baron di Valcorrente e della Miraglia (Sic 1780, It 1897), Lord (Signore) of Aidone, Burgio, Contessa, and Trappeto (1854), conscribed Roman noble (1854), and Patrician of Venice (1667), Genoa (1786) and Pistoia; s of 11 Earl of Newburgh (d 1986), and Donna Giulia, da of Don Guido Carlo de Duchi Visconti di Modrone, Count of Lonate Pozzolo; *b* 4 July 1942; *m* 1972, Baronessa Donna Luisa, da of Count Annibale Caccia Dominoni; 1 da (Princess Benedetta Francesca Maria b 1974); *Heir* da, Mistress of Newburgh, b 4 June 1974; *Style*— Prince Rospigliosi; Piazza St Ambrogio 16, 20123 Milan, Italy

NEWBURY, Hon Mrs (Julia Elizabeth Heather); *née* Hamilton; da of 13 Lord Belhaven and Stenton; *b* 1956; *m* 1975, Richard Newbury; *Style*— The Hon Mrs Newbury

NEWBURY, (George) Malcolm; JP (1979); s of George Theodore Newbury, of Droitwich, Worcs, and Kathleen Mary, *née* Partridge; *b* 14 Feb 1936; *Educ* King Edwards Sch Birmingham, St John's Coll Cambridge (MA); *m* 29 July 1960, Lone, da of Arne Petersen-Hinrichsen, of Copenhagen, Denmark; 1 s (Nicholas George Arne b 1972), 2 da (Pollyanna b 1962, Amanda b 1965); *Career* farmer; chm Lincs Ctee Royal Jubilee & Prince's Tsts 1985; *Recreations* gardening, tree planting, hare coursing, sport, travel; *Style*— Malcolm Newbury, Esq, JP; Birthorpe Manor, Sleaford, Lincolnshire NA34 0EX

NEWBY, Hon Mrs (Ailsa Ballantyne); da of Baron Thomson of Monifieth (Life Peer); *b* 1956; *m* 1978, Richard Newby; 1 s (Mark b 1985); *Style*— The Hon Mrs Newby

NEWBY, Frank; OBE (1986), JP (Horsham); s of Alexander Gilbert Leslie (d 1963), of Harrogate, and Dorothy, *née* Broadbank (d 1984); *b* 29 May 1927; *Educ* Wallington GS Harrogate, Univ of Loughborough (DLC), Univ of Manchester (MEd), Univ of Southampton (PhD); *m* 10 Sept 1949, Margaret Jean, da of Frank Thomsett (d 1966), of Croydon; 2 da (Lindsey Margaret Davies b 1953, Amanda Ruth Distin b 1959); *Career* Sgt RAFVR 1944-48; head lower sch Hazlewick Sch 1955-61; headmaster: Eastwood Sch Keighley 1962-67, Forest Community Sch Horsham 1967-; co pres W Sussex teachers assoc NUT 1978-79 and 1988-89; dep chm Horsham bench (chm domestic panel); memb St Marys Parish Church, former pres Horsham Rotary Club, chm Horsham Temp Accommodation Charitable Tst; Freeman: City of London 1979, Worshipful Co of Misicians 1984; FCollP 1983, FBIM 1986; *Recreations* music, reading, sailing; *Style*— Dr Frank Newby, OBE; 44 Heron Way, Horsham, West

Sussex RH13 6DL (☎ 0403 62920); Forest Community School, Comptons Lane, Horsham, W Sussex RH12 5NW (☎ 0403 61086/7/8)

NEWBY, (Percy) Howard; CBE (1972); s of Percy Newby (d 1961), of Wendover, Bucks, and Isobel Clutsam, *née* Bryant (d 1980); *b* 25 June 1918; *Educ* Hanley Castle GS Worcester, St Paul's Coll Cheltenham; *m* 12 July 1945, Joan, da of Harry Charles Thompson (d 1965), of Wendover, Bucks; 2 da (Sarah (Mrs Schenk) b 1947, Katharine b 1963); *Career* RAMC 1939-42; lectr Cairo Univ 1942-46; BBC Radio 3 (formerly the Third Programme) 1958-78: controller 1958-71, dir of programmes 1971-75, md 1971-78; chm English Stage Co 1978-85; Atlantic Award for Literature 1946, Somerset Maugham Prize 1948, Yorkshire Post Fiction Award 1968, Booker Prize 1969; memb Soc of Authors 1947; *Books* A Journey to the Interior (1945), The Picnic of Sakkara (1955), Something to Answer For (1968), Saladin in his Time (1983); *Style*— Howard Newby, Esq, CBE; Garsington Ho, Garsington, Oxford OX9 9AB (☎ 086 736 420)

NEWBY, John; s of Harry Newby, of Garforth, Leeds, and Ann Newby; *b* 17 Dec 1939; *Educ* St Annes Sch Leeds, City HS Leeds; *m* 28 Sept 1963, Margaret Ann, da of Andy Wilson, of Scarborough; 2 da (Helen b 31 Aug 1966, Carmel b 28 July 1968); *Career* dir: Wiggins Plant Ltd 1983, Wiggin Gee Homes Ltd 1988-; Wiggin Gee Property Ltd 1988-, md: Wiggins Contruction Ltd 1985- (dir 1982), Gee Walker & Slater Ltd 1986, Headcrown Construction 1986-; gp md Wiggins Gee Gp 1988-; *Recreations* golf, philately, gardening; *Clubs* London Rugby, Chelsea, Ballard GC; *Style*— John Newby, Esq; 57 Hart Rd, Thundersley, S Benfleet, Essex (☎ 0268 792 591)

NEWCASTLE, 10 Bishop of (1882) 1981-; Rt Rev Andrew Alexander Kenny Graham; patron of the Archdeaconries of Northumberland and Lindisfarne, four residentiary Canonries, the Hon Canonries, and seventy-five livings; the see of Newcastle was founded in May 1882; s of Andrew Harrison Graham (d 1954), and Magdalene Graham (d 1955); *b* 7 August 1929; *Educ* Tonbridge, St John's Coll Oxford; *Career* warden Lincoln Theol Coll 1970-77, bishop suffragan of Bedford 1977-81, chm: advsy cncl for Church's Ministry 1983-87, Doctrine Cmmn 1987-; *Recreations* hill walking; *Clubs* Utd Oxford and Cambridge; *Style*— The Rt Rev the Lord Bishop of Newcastle; Bishop's House, 29 Moor Road South, Gosforth, Newcastle-upon-Tyne NE3 1PA (☎ 091 2852220)

NEWCASTLE, Diana, Duchess of; Lady Diana; *née* Montagu Stuart Wortley; da of 3 Earl of Wharncliffe, of Wortley Hall, Sheffield (d 1953), and Elfrida Wentworth Fitzwilliam (d 1980); *b* 2 June 1920; *m* 1946 (m dis 1959), 9 Duke of Newcastle, OBE (d 1988); 2 da; *Career* served WWII Mechanised Tport Corps; *Recreations* living; *Style*— Diana, Duchess of Newcastle; Cortington Manor, Warminster, Wilts

NEWCASTLE, Duchess of; Sally Anne Wemyss Hope; er da of Brig John Henry Anstice, DSO, of Kyrenia, Cyprus, and Sydney, *née* Williamson; *m* 1 (m dis), Fikret Jemal; m 2, 23 Oct 1959, as his 3 w, 9 Duke of Newcastle, OBE (d 1988); 5 Quay Hill, Lymington, Hants

NEWCOMBE, John Fernley; s of Arthur Fernley Newcombe (d 1978), of Worksop, Notts, and Norah Kathleen Newcombe; *b* 12 May 1928; *Educ* King Edward VI Sch Rotford, Trinity Coll Cambridge, Bart's London (MA, MB, MChir); *m* 4 July 1953, Barbara Joan, da of Charles Arnold Brittain (d 1979), of 110 Furniss Avenue, Dore, Sheffield; 1 s (Guy Charles Fernley b 1962), 1 da (Alyson Clare b 1960); *Career* consult surgn Central Middx Hosp London 1965- (sub dean Med Sch 1970-76); pres Med Soc of London 1986-87; FRCS (memb Ct of Examiners); *Recreations* golf, sailing, painting; *Style*— John Newcombe, Esq; 36 Sandy Lodge Rd, Rickmansworth, Herts WD3 1LJ (☎ 09274 22370); 88 Harley St, London W1N 1AE (☎ 01 631 4033)

NEWCOMBE, Timothy Richard; TD (1985); s of D J Newcombe, of Tolkwith, York, and Elizabeth Edith Esme, *née* Thorncey-Taylor; *b* 28 Nov 1947; *Educ* Pocklington Sch East Yorks; *m* 31 July 1988, Margaret, da of Eamonn Callaghan, of Leeds; *Career* Royal Green Jackets 1961-62; volunteers: 1 Bn 1972-83, 3 Bn 1983-87; Res List 1987-; called to the Bar Inner Temple 1972; *Recreations* fishing, shooting; *Clubs* Sloane; *Style*— Timothy Newcombe, Esq; St Pauls House, 23 Park Square South, Leeds LS1 2ND (☎ 0532 455 866, fax 0536 455 807)

NEWCOMBE, William Francis Lister; CBE (1976, OBE 1955, MBE 1946), TD (1950); s of William Arthur Newcombe (d 1930), of Sussex, and Marjorie Beatrice, *née* Greaves (d 1977); *b* 8 Dec 1912; *Educ* Haileybury Coll Hertford; *m* 15 Sept 1934, Eileen Marjorie, da of Percy Joseph Hood (d 1937), of IOW; 2 da (Josephine b 1935, Veronica b 1936); *Career* 2 Lt RA (TA) 1938, Capt 1940, ADGB 1939-42, War Office 1942-45; gen sec Army Cadet Force Assoc 1946-77, sec CCF Assoc 1952-77; hon sec Haileybury Soc 1957-80 (pres 1981-82), life govr Haileybury & ISC 1958- (cncl memb 1961-81); ed Haileybury Register 1984; *Recreations* reading, gardening; *Clubs* East India, Devonshire, Sports, Public Schs, MCC; *Style*— William F L Newcombe, Esq, CBE, TD; Trout End, Wendens Ambo, Saffron Walden, Essex CB11 4JY (☎ 0799 40267)

NEWELL, Prof Kenneth Wyatt; s of Herbert William Newell (d 1965), and Mary Irene, *née* Hare (d 1980); *b* 7 Nov 1925; *Educ* Wanganui Collegiate Sch NZ, Otago Univ NZ (MB ChB), London Univ (DPH), Tulane Univ USA (MD); *m* 1 (m dis 1958), Winifred Elizabeth, *née* Liddel; 3 s (Michael b 1949, Richard b 1950, James 1953); m 2, Catherine Margaret, *née* Clark (d 1976); 1 s (Peter b 1962); m 3, 22 Jan 1977, Priscilla Jane, da of Wing Cdr Arthur Ronald Watts, OBE; *Career* epidemiologist Epidemiological Res Laboratory London 1954-56, lectr Queens Univ Belfast 1956-58, epidemiologist WHO Indonesia 1958-60, William Hamilton Watkins prof of epidemiology Tulane USA 1960-67; dir: div res epidemiology and communications sci WHO Geneva 1967-72, div strengthening health servs WHO Geneva 1972-77; prof of community health Wellington Clinical Sch Univ Otago 1977-83, Middlemas Hunt prof of tropical health Liverpool Sch of Tropical Med 1983; FFCM 1985, MCCM (NZ) 1980, FRSTMM 1984; *Recreations* gardening, fishing; *Style*— Prof Kenneth Wyatt; Five Oaks, Street Hey Lane, Willaston, South Wirral (☎ 051 327 4057); Dept International Community Health, Liverpool School Tropical Medicine, Pembroke Place, Liverpool L3 5QA (☎ 051 708 9393)

NEWENS, Arthur Stanley; MEP (London Centl) 1984-; s of Arthur Ernest Newens (d 1977), of Loughton, Essex, and Celia Jenny, *née* Furssedonn (d 1966); *b* 4 Feb 1930; *Educ* Buckhurst Hill Co HS, UCL (BA); *m* 1, 1954, Ann (d 1962)), da of John Barlow Sherratt (d 1966), of Stoke-on-Trent; 2 da; m 2, 1966, Sandra Christina, da of John Arthur McMullen Frith, of Chingford; 1 s, 2 da; *Career* miner (coalface worker) 1952-56, teacher 1956-64 and 1970-74; MP: (Lab) Epping 1964-70, Harlow (Lab and Co-op) 1974-83; chm Liberation (formerly Movement for Colonial Freedom) 1967-; former memb centl exec ctee of Co-op Union and of exec ctee of Co-op Pty, pres London Co-operative Soc 1977-81 (dir 1971-77); chm: PLP Foreign Affrs Ctee 1982-83, Tribune Gp of Lab MPs 1982-83; organising sec Harlow Cncl for Vol Serv 1983-84; chm Br Labour Gp in EP 1985-87; author of several books, pamphlets on politics and local history; *Recreations* family, reading, hist res, gardening; *Style*— Arthur Newens, Esq, MEP; The Leys, 18 Park Hill, Harlow, Essex (☎ 0279 20108)

NEWENS, Peter Gordon; s of John Newens, and Mabel Gordon Newens; *b* 8 Mar 1902; *Educ* Richmond Co Sch; *m* 8 Oct 1946, Edith Joan, da of Harold Shotton, of Shrewsbury; 1 s (Peter John b 31 July 1948); *Career* WWII serv: E Surrey Regt, transferred Army Physical Trg Corps Argyle md Southern Regt; proprieter The Maids of Honour Shop Kew (family business 1853); *Recreations* horse driving, riding, flying; *Clubs* Hackney Driving, Fairoaks Flying, Veteran Car; *Style*— Peter Newens, Esq

NEWEY, His Hon Judge John Henry Richard; US Bronze Star (1944); s of Lt-Col Thomas Henry Newey, ED (d 1983), and Irene Kathleen Mary (d 1989); *b* 20 Oct 1923; *Educ* Ellesmere Coll Shropshire, Queens Coll Cambridge (MA, LLM); *m* 31 July 1953, Mollie Patricia, da of Herbert Chalk (d 1982); 3 s (Robert b 1956, Guy b 1959, Michael b 1963), 2 da (Jane b 1962, Annabel b 1966); *Career* served Capt, Centl India Horse, Indian Army 1942-47 in India, Middle East, Italy and Greece; barr Middle Temple 1948, bencher Middle Temple 1977, prosecuting counsel to PO SE circuit 1963-64, standing counsel to PO at Common Law 1964-70, personal injuries jr to Treasy 1968-70, QC 1970-, dep chm Kent Quarter Sessions 1970-71, Recorder 1972-80, a Judge of Official Referees Ct in London 1980-, Commissary Gen of City and Diocese of Canterbury 1971-, Parly boundary cmmnr for Eng 1980-88; *Recreations* excursions, history; *Style*— His Hon Judge Newey, QC; St David's, 68 The Drive, Sevenoaks, Kent TN13 3AF (☎ 0732 454597); Royal Courts of Justice, Strand, WC2A 2LL)

NEWEY, Sidney Brian; s of Sydney Frank Newey, of Burton upon Trent, and Edith Mary, *née* Moore; *b* 8 Jan 1937; *Educ* Burton upon Trent GS, Worcester Coll Oxford (MA); *m* 16 Dec 1967, Margaret Mary, da of Rev Canon David Stevens, of Belton in Rutland, Leics; 1 s (Edmund); *Career* joined BR: mgmnt trainee 1960, stationmaster Southall 1965-70, freight planning mangr W Region 1970-78, div mangr Birmingham 1978- 80, dep gen mangr London Midland Region 1980-85, gen mangr W Region 1985-87, dir prov BR HQ 1987; MCIT; *Recreations* fell walking, reading, music, carpentry, village and church affairs; *Style*— Sidney Newey, Esq; Chestnut Cottage, The Green South, Warborough, Oxon OX9 8DN (☎ 086 732 8322); British Rail Headquarters, 24 Eversholt St, London NW1 1DZ (☎ 01 922 4123)

NEWILL, Dr Robert George Douglass; s of Robert Daniel Newill (d 1955), of Wellington, Shropshire, and Gladys Victoria, *née* Beckett (d 1978); *b* 5 Dec 1921; *Educ* Shrewsbury, St Bart's Hosp and London Univ (MD); *m* 25 March 1950, Patricia Margaret, da of Humphrey Charles Bradshaw-Bowles (d 1958), of Baslow, Derbyshire; 2 da (Heather b 1956, Angela b 1958); *Career* Capt RAC 1941-46; reproductive endocrinologist, UCH London (ret 1985); *Books* author 'Infertile Marriage' and res papers on infertility subjects; *Recreations* yachting, ornithology, choral singing; *Clubs* Aldeburgh Yacht, Little Ship (London); *Style*— Robert Newill, Esq; Fern Court, Park Road, Aldeburgh, Suffolk IP15 5ET (☎ Aldeburgh 3109)

NEWIS, Kenneth; CB (1967), CVO (1970, MVO 1958); s of Herbert Thomas Newis (d 1943), of Manchester, and Gladys, *née* Lindop (d 1961); *b* 9 Nov 1916; *Educ* St John's Coll Cambridge (MA); *m* 1943, Kathleen, da of John Barrow (d 1977), of Davenport, Cheshire; 2 da (Gillian, Margaret); *Career* civil servant, sec Scottish Devpt Dept (Scottish Off) 1973-76, ret 1976; chm Queen's Hall (Edinburgh) Ltd; vice-chm: MHA Housing Assoc Ltd, Cockburn Assoc (Civic Tst Edinburgh); *Recreations* music; *Clubs* New (Edinburgh); *Style*— Kenneth Newis, Esq, CB, CVO,MVO; 11 Abbotsford Park, Edinburgh EH10 5DZ (☎ 031 447 4138)

NEWLAND, Prof David Edward; s of Robert William Newland (d 1979), of Knebworth, Herts, and Marion Amelia, *née* Dearman; *b* 8 May 1936; *Educ* Alleyne's Sch Stevenage, Selwyn Coll Cambridge (BA, MA), MIT (ScD); *m* 18 July 1959, Patricia Frances, da of Philip Mayne, of Marton, N Yorkshire; 2 s (Andrew David William b 1961, Richard David Philip b 1963); *Career* English Electric Co London 1957-61, instr and asst prof MIT 1961-64, lectr (later sr lectr) Imperial Coll London 1964-67, prof of mechanical engrg Sheffield Univ 1967-76, prof of engrg (1975) Cambridge Univ 1976-, fell Selwyn Coll Cambridge 1976; memb Royal Cmmn on Environmental Pollution 1984-, cncl memb Fellowship of Engrg 1985-88; govr St Paul's Schs 1978-, churchwarden Ickleton 1979-87; FEng, FIMechE, FIEE; *Books* An Introduction to Random Vibrations and Spectral Analysis (second edn 1984), Mechanical Vibration Analysis and Computation (1989); *Clubs* Athenaeum; *Style*— Prof David Newland; Cambridge University Engineering Department, Trumpington St, Cambridge CB2 1PZ (☎ 0223 332670, fax 0223 359153, telex 81239)

NEWLANDS OF LAURISTON, William Alexander; s of Frank Newlands, Balnamuir, Ballinluig, Perthshire (d 1971), and Annie Shand-Henderson (d 1986); the family is descended from Jasper Newlands of that Ilk (in record 1469) of the barony of Newlands in the Sheriffdom of Kincardine; Laird of Lauriston (Castle founded 1243), St Cyrus, Kincardineshire; granted the undifferenced arms of Newlands by Warrant of the Lord Lyon, King of Arms, 1987; *b* 5 Nov 1934; *Educ* Dollar Acad, Robert Gordon's Coll Aberdeen; *m* 1, 1960, Kathleen Cook (m dis 1976); 1 s (Hamish Newlands of Lauriston ygr b 1965); 2 da (Fiona b 1960, Riona b 1962); m 2, 1985, Dorothy, da of the late John Walker, of Montrose; *Career* Far East Air Force 1953-55, Game Conservancy, Int Union for Conservation of Nature (Morges, Switzerland); (as Willy Newlands), travel ed, Daily Mail 1982-; (Travel Writer of the Year 1983-84 and 1987-88), author of numerous articles and books on game management, wildlife, travel, inc Where to Go 1988; *Recreations* breeding gamecocks, shooting pheasants; *Clubs* Caledonian; *Style*— William Newlands of Lauriston; Rose Cottage, 16 Stanhope Mews South, London SW7 (☎ 01 373 7140); Lauriston Castle, St Cyrus, Kincardineshire (☎ 0674 854 88); Daily Mail, London EC4Y 0JA (☎ 01 353 6000)

NEWMAN, Hon Lady (Ann Rosemary Hope); raised to the rank of a Baron's da; da of Capt Hon Claude Hope Hope-Morley (d 1968), and sis of 3 Baron Hollenden; *b* 10 August 1916; *m* 1946, Sir Ralph Alured Newman, 5 Bt (d 1968); *Style*— The Hon Lady Newman; Blackpool House, Dartmouth, S Devon

NEWMAN, Archibald Richard (Archie); s of Arthur Percy Newman (d 1948), of London, and Ada Ethel Toms (d 1977); *b* 10 April 1931; *Educ* Latymer's GS, London Univ; *m* 5 July 1958, Rita Margaret, da of Eugene William Beushaw (d 1986), of London; 1 s (Nigel Richard Ellery b 1970), 1 da (Josephine Margaret b 1967); *Career*

Nat Serv 1949-51, No 2 Higher Educn Centre Aldershot; press and pubns dept London Tport Exec 1952-57, res asst Br Tport Advertising 1957-59, dep head of press R (Eastern Regn) 1954-61; pres offr : Assoc TV 1961-63, The Electricity Cncl 1963-65; press and info offr GLC 1965-66, dir of public affairs and sponsorship The Royal Philiharmonic Orchestra 1966-85; chm and md Tiger Promotions and Prodns Ltd 1985-, propr Archie Newman Communications 1985-; chm: Edmonton Youth Cncl 1946-48, St Bartholomew-The-Great 850th Anniversary Dance and Music Galas 1887; memb Govt Arts and Heritage Advsy Ctee 1986-; memb: RIPA 1955-65, IPR 1958-70, Royal Soc of Musicians; hon life memb Royal Philharmonic Orch; *Books* Beecham Stories (with Harold Atkins, 1978); *Recreations* visual arts, walking, gardening, photography, travel; *Clubs* Royal Overseas, Wig and Pen; *Style—* Archie Newman, Esq; Greystoke, 101 Aldsworth Ave, Goring-by-Sea, Worthing, West Sussex BN12 4UT (☎ 0903 44 625); Quebec Court, Suite 57, 21 Seymour St, Marble Arch, London W1H 5AD (☎ 01 262 3951, fax 01 706 2184)

NEWMAN, Hon (Corinne Deborah); da of Baron Lloyd of Hampstead (Life Peer); *b* 23 July 1951; *Educ* City of London Sch for Girls, Camberwell Sch for Arts & Crafts; *Style—* The Hon Mrs Newman; 12, 600 Military Road, Mosman, Sydney, NSW 2088, Australia

NEWMAN, His Hon Judge Cyril Wilfred Francis; QC (1982); s of Wilfred James Newman (d 1970), and Cecilia Beatrice Lily Newman (d 1977); *b* 2 July 1937; *Educ* Sacred Heart Coll Droitwich, Lewes Co GS, Merton Coll Oxford (MA); *m* 1966, Winifred, da of Theodore de Kok, of Zürich, Switzerland; 2 s, 1 da; *Career* pres Oxford Univ Law Soc 1959, OU Middle Temple Soc 1959; barr 1960; asst cmmr Parly Boundary Cmmr for Eng 1976, rec SE circuit 1982-, memb Criminal Injuries Compensation Bd 1985-86; circuit judge SE circuit 1986-; *Recreations* sailing, country sports, skiing, swimming, opera and church music; *Clubs* Bar Yacht (hon tres 1973-88, rear cdre 1985); *Style—* His Hon Judge Cyril Newman, QC; Orlestone Grange, Orlestone, Nr Ashford, Kent TN26 2EB (☎ 023 373 2306)

NEWMAN, Sir Francis Hugh Cecil; 4 Bt (UK 1912), of Cecil Lodge, Newmarket, Cambridge;; s of Sir Gerard Robert Henry Sigismund Newman, 3 Bt (d 1987); *b* 12 June 1963; *Educ* Eton, Univ of Pennsylvania USA; *Career* N M Rothschild Asset Mgmnt Ltd, Harry Neal Ltd; *Recreations* shooting, rowing; *Clubs* Eton Vikings; *Style—* Sir Francis Newman, Bt; Burloes, Royston, Herts (☎ 0763 42150); 40 Cadogan Place, London SW1 (☎ 01 235 3331)

NEWMAN, Sir Geoffrey Robert; 6 Bt (UK 1836), of Mamhead, Devonshire; s of Sir Ralph Alured Newman, 5 Bt (d 1968), and Hon Ann Rosemary Hope Newman, *née* Hope-Morley; *b* 2 June 1947; *Educ* Heatherdown, Kelly Coll; *m* 1980, Mary Elizabeth, da of Col Martin St John Valentine Gibbs, CB, DSO, TD; 1 s (Robert b 1985), 2 da (Frances b 1983, Elsie b 1987); *Heir* s, b 4 Oct 1985; *Career* 1 Bn Grenadier Gds 1967-70, Lt T&AVR until 1979; *Style—* Sir Geoffrey Newman, Bt; Blackpool House, Dartmouth, S Devon

NEWMAN, George Michael; QC (1981); s of Wilfred James Newman (d 1970), of Seaford, Sussex, and Celia Beatrice Lily, *née* Browne (d 1977); *b* 4 July 1941; *Educ* Lewes Co GS, St Catharine's Coll Cambridge; *m* 1966, Hilary Alice Gibbs, da of late Robert Gibbs Chandler, of Battle Sussex; 2 s (Benedict b 1968, Matthew b 1970), 1 da (Clarissa b 1971); *Career* barr, rec 1985; *Recreations* tennis, skiing, sailing, walking; *Style—* George Newman, Esq, QC; 1 Crown Office Row, Temple, London EC4 (☎ 01 583 9292, telex 8953152)

NEWMAN, Graham Reginald; s of A H G Newman (d 1948), and Ethel, *née* Wadey (d 1979); *b* 26 July 1924; *Educ* Canford, Hertford Coll Oxford; *m* 26 July 1952, Joycelyn Helen; *Career* RCS India and Far East 1941-46, ret Capt; chm: Tatham Bromage (Hldgs) Ltd and gp of cos 1953-; elected to Baltic Exchange 1947, chm Baltic 1977-79, pres Baltic Charitable Soc 1982-84; memb ctee of mgmnt RNLI and sub-ctees; Renter Warden Ct of Assts Shipwrights' Co; *Recreations* sailing; *Style—* Graham Newman, Esq, FICS; 2 Makepeace Ave, Highgate, London N6 6EJ (☎ 01 340 6452)

NEWMAN, Hon Mrs; Hon Jean Sybil; *née* Loch; da of 2 Baron Loch, CB, CMG, MVO, DSO (d 1942); *b* 1908; *m* 1930, Guy Arthur Newman, s of late Sir Sigmund Neumann, 1 Bt; 3 da; *Style—* The Hon Mrs Newman; Stanners Hill Manor, Chobham, Surrey

NEWMAN, John Francis; s of Sir Cecil Gustavus Newman, 2 Bt (d 1955), and Joan, CBE (d 1969), da of Canon Hon Robert Grimston (s of 2 Earl of Verulam); *b* 25 Jan 1930; *Educ* Eton, Sandhurst; *m* 1963, Caroline, da of Lt-Col Angus Rose, of Perthshire (d 1981); 1 s, 2 da; *Career* formerly Lt RHG; chm Rom River Co; dir: Blick plc, Hoogovens UK Ltd and other cos; *Recreations* shooting, farming, golf; *Clubs* White's, Pratt's, MCC; *Style—* John Newman Esq; 28 St Luke's St, SW3 (☎ 01 352 7808); Compton Park, Compton Chamberlayne, Salisbury, Wilts (☎ 072 270 294)

NEWMAN, John Victor; s of Jack Newman (d 1980), and Florence Celia, *née* de Fraine; *b* 23 Jan 1943; *Educ* Whitgift Sch; *m* 19 April 1969, Pamela Jane, da of Lionel Charles Thomas Box (d 1981), of Coulsdon; 5 s (James Alexander b 26 April 1972, Robin Anthony Mark b 25 April 1974, d 10 July 1974, Jeremy Edward b 6 Aug 1975, Christopher Jon b 15 July 1978, Anthony Jonathan b 15 Dec 1986); *Career* CA 1968; ptnr Spain Bros Newman & Co CAs 1971-74, dir of Co of Veteran Motorists Ltd 1971; Guild of Experienced Motorists: chief exec 1984, chm 1987; tres PCC 1980-86, tres Parish Centre 1987-; registered insur broker 1979; FCA 1978, FInstIC 1979; *Clubs* Gravetye Manor Country, Sloane; *Style—* John Newman, Esq; Woodside, Bonfire Lane, Horsted Keynes, Haywards Heath, W Sussex RH17 7AG (☎ 0825 790582); GEM 1 East Grinstead House, E Grinstead, W Sussex RH19 1UF (☎ 0342 324444, car 0860 321987)

NEWMAN, John Watson; s of Frederick John Newman, of Cobham, and Joan G Newman; *b* 24 Nov 1945; *Educ* Woodbridge Sch; *m* 11 Oct 1969, Lesley Jean, da of Jack Barber, of 5 Lincoln Ct, Weybridge, Surrey; 1 s (Richard b 1979), 2 da (Amanda b 1974, Sarah b 1975); *Career* CA/industrialist; acquisition mangr Hanson Tst plc 1969-77; dir: Tyzack Turner plc, Newship Go Ltd, Ben Turner & Son Ltd, Ben Turner Industl Ltd, Clarke & Spears Gp Ltd, G J Durafencing Ltd, Guestport Ltd, James Gibbons Mfrg Ltd, Mepstar Finance Ltd, Newship Ltd, Newship Distribution Ltd, Newship Hldgs Ltd, Newship Industs Ltd, Newship Investments plc, Newship Mfrg Ltd, Newship Products Ltd, Newship Properties Ltd, V W Gp Ltd, Wilfield Ltd; FCA; *Recreations* tennis; *Style—* John Newman, Esq; Longridge, South Rd, St George's Hill, Weybridge, Surrey; Fernside Place, 1979 Queen's Rd, Weybridge, Surrey

NEWMAN, Karl Max; CB (1979); s of Dr Karl Neumann (d 1978), and Alice *née* Gruenebaum; *b* 26 Mar 1919; *Educ* Ottershaw Coll, Ch Ch Oxford (MA); *m* 1952, Annette Muriel, da of Ronald Cross Sheen (d 1973); 1 s, 1 da; *Career* Army 1940-42; barr 1946-49; under-sec Lord Chllr's Off 1972-82 (legal asst 1949-56, sr legal asst 1956-62), legal advsr Euro Unit Cabinet Off 1972-82, counsel to Chm of Ctees House of Lords 1982-87; *Recreations* travelling, philately, visiting picture galleries; *Clubs* Utd Oxford and Cambridge Univ; *Style—* Karl Newman Esq, CB; 17 Marryat Rd, Wimbledon, London SW19 (☎ 01 946 3430)

NEWMAN, Sir Kenneth Leslie; GBE (1987), QPM (1982); s of John William Newman and Florence Newman; *b* 1926,Aug; *Educ* London Univ; *m* 1949, Eileen Lilian; 1 s, 1 da; *Career* WWII RAF; Palestine Police 1946-48, Met Police 1948-73, cdr New Scotland Yard 1972, chief constable RUC 1976-79 (sr dep chief constable 1973), cmdt Bramshill Police Coll and HM inspr Constabulary 1980-82, Met Police cmmr 1982-87; vice pres Def Manufacturers Assoc, tstee Police Fndn, non-exec dir various cos; visiting prof law Bristol Univ; CBIM, KStJ; kt 1978; *Style—* Sir Kenneth Newman, GBE, QPM; c/o New Scotland Yard, Broadway, London SW1

NEWMAN, Michael Francis; s of Oliver Frank Newman, of Winchmore Hill, London N21, and Beatirce Elizabeth, *née* Watts; *b* 21 June 1915; *Educ* St Ignatius Coll, UCW Aberystwyth (BSC), Hatfield Poly (MSC); *m* Maura, da of James Slattery; 1 s (Matthew Paul Francis b 27 Jan 1981), 2 da (Jennifer Elizabeth b 22 Nov 1978, Angela Marie b 18 Oct 1980); *Career* programmer GEC 1968, communications programmer IPC 1970 (worked on Munich Olympics Scoreboard System 1972), sr programmer ITT 1973; joined Stock Exchange: sr programmer 1975, mangr special systems gp 1981, head info tech 1983, project mangr SEAQ 1984, dir mkts tech 1987, dir servs mktg 1988; occasional memb Stock Exchange Chess Third Team; MBCS 1975; *Recreations* golf, soccer, chess; *Clubs* Bishop Stortford Golf; *Style—* Michael Newman, Esq; The International Stock Exchange, London EC2 (☎ 01 588 2355 ext 28148)

NEWMAN, Michael Henry; s of Henry Ernest Newman, of E Croydon, Surrey, and Rhoda May, *née* Symonds (d 1986); *b* 19 Oct 1945; *Educ* Whitgift Sch; *m* 15 Jan 1977, Jennifer Mary, da of Matthew McCargo Roger (d 1977), of Glasgow; *Career* CA 1968; chief exec Britannia Arrow Holdings plc 1979-86 (dir from 1977), dep chm Employers Life Assur Co Ltd 1983-86, dir Singer & Friedlanders 1984-86; with Incaval SA Geneva; *Recreations* travel, gardening; *Style—* Michael Newman, Esq; 37 Wool Road, Wimbledon, London SW20 0HN (☎ 01 947 9756); 3 Rue Pierre Fatio, Geneva 1204 (☎ 22 36 8282, fax: 22 86 5286)

NEWMAN, Nanette (Mrs Bryan Forbes); da of Sidney Newman, and Ruby Newman; *b* 29 May 1939; *Educ* Sternhold Coll London, Italia Conti Stage Sch, RADA; *m* 1958, Bryan Forbes, *qv* ; 2 da (one of whom Sarah, m Sir John Leon, 4 Bt, *qv*); *Career* actress, writer; films incl: The L-Shaped Room 1962, The Wrong Arm of the Law 1962, Seance on a Wet Afternoon 1963, The Wrong Box 1965, The Whisperers 1966, Deadfall 1967, The Madwoman of Chaillot 1968, The Raging Moon 1971 (variety club best film actress award), The Stepford Wives 1974, International Velvet 1978 (Evening News best film actress award); tv appearances incl: Call my Bluff, What's My Line, The Fun Food (Factory Crown Series), London Scene, Stay with me till Morning, Jessie (title-role), Let There be Love; books incl: God Bless Love (1972), Lots of Love (1973), Vote for Love (1976), The Root Children (1978), The Pig Who Never Was (1979), The Dayloners Coffee Table Book (1982), The Cat Lovers Coffee Table Book (1983), My Granny was a Frightful Bore (1983), A Cat and Mouse Love Story (1984), Pigalow (1985), Small Beginnings (1987); *Recreations* needlepoint; *Style—* Miss Nanette Newman; Bryan Forbes Ltd, Seven Pines, Wentworth, Surrey

NEWMAN, Peter John; s of Peter Laurence Newman; *b* 5 July 1938; *Educ* St John's Johannesburg, St John's Coll Cambridge; *m* 1963, Patricia Anne, *née* Wright; 3 s; *Career* Davy Corpn cos 1960-: gen mangr Loewy Robertson Engrg Co 1979- (Queen's Award for Export 1980), md Davy McKee (Sheffield) 1984-87, chief exec metals 1988; pres Dorset C of C 1983, cncl memb Sheffield C of C, chm bd of govrs Sheffield City Poly, memb of bd Sheffield Devpt Corpn; *Recreations* sailing, gardening; *Style—* Peter Newman, Esq; White Edge, Froggatt Edge, Calver, nr Sheffield (☎ 0433 30314)

NEWMAN, Philip Harker; CBE (1976), DSO (1940), MC (1942); s of John Harker Newman (d 1942), of Ingatestone, Essex, and Violet Grace, *née* Williams (d 1960); *b* 22 June 1911; *Educ* Cranleigh, Middx Hosp Med Sch, London Univ; *m* 7 Oct 1943, (Elizabeth) Anne, *née* Basset; 2 s (Richard b 1944, Anthony (Tony) b 1946), 1 da (Penelope (Penny) b 1948); *Career* RAMC 1939-45; Lt 1939, Maj 1939, Lt-Col 1945; conslt orthopaedic surgn Middx Hosp and King Edward VII Hosp for Offrs 1946-76, conslt surgn Royal Nat Orthopaedic Hosp and Inst of Orthopaedics 1946-76; former pres Br Orthopaedic Assoc; chm med bd St John Ambulance 1977-82, cncl of mgmnt Jl of Bone and Joint Surgery; FRCS; memb: BMA, RSM; hon fell SA Coll of Surgns; *Books* Safer Than A Known Way - An Escape Story of World War II (1983); *Recreations* golf; *Clubs* Aldeburgh Golf (Capt 1986); *Style—* Philip Newman, Esq; Foxearth, Saxmundham Rd, Aldeburgh, Suffolk (☎ 072 885 3373)

NEWMAN, Richard Claude; s of Sir Ralph Alured Newman, 5 Bt (d 1968); *b* 2 May 1951; *Style—* Richard Newman, Esq ; Blackpool House, Dartmouth, S Devon

NEWMAN, Ronald William; s of William James Newman (d 1945), and Louisa Ellen, *née* Taylor (d 1974); *b* 6 April 1921; *Educ* Wandsworth Sch; *m* 1943, Victoria, da of James Walter Brady (d 1965); 3 da (Jane, Frances, Clare); *Career* Flt Lt RAFVR 1940-46; sr exec offr Miny of Agric 1946-58, statistical orgn advsr Centl Bureau of Statistics Jerusalem 1958, O&M advsr to Lesotho, Botswana and Swaziland 1959-62, chief exec offr Miny of Agric 1962-65, first sec HM Diplomatic Serv 1965-75, cnsllr (econ) Khartoum 1975-76, HM consul-gen Casablanca 1976-77; *Recreations* flying, farming, squash, swimming; *Clubs* Civil Serv; *Style—* Ronald Newman Esq; 20 Cranley Close, Guildford, Surrey (☎ 0483 576728); 707 Tafelberg, Esselen St, Hillbrow, Johannesburg, S A (☎ 11 642 0776); Pioneer Farm, Warwick, New York, USA (☎ 914 986 3479)

NEWMAN, The Lady Selina (Mary); *née* Abney-Hastings; da of Countess of Loudon; *b* 1946; *m* 1967, William E Newman; 1 s (Christopher James Loudon b 1972), 1 da (Selina Anne b 1968); *Style—* Lady Selina Newman

NEWMAN, William Frederick; s of Lt William Daniel Newman, of 1 Hannover Ct, Ebury St, Old Portsmouth, and Peggy Annie Georgina, *née* Hill; *b* 9 May 1943; *Educ* Arts Educnl Tst (Art and Drama); *m* 1, 4 Sept 1966 (m dis), Margaret Rosica, da of Basil Clark Fred Vinter, of London; 2 s (William Alexander b 1981, Matthew Lawrence b 1985), 2 da (Caron Tracy b 1967, Amanda Jane b 1970); m 2, Sally Elizabeth, da of Samuel George Packham; *Career* architectural conslt; Eric Cumine 1961-64, Ian Fraser Turner Lansdown Holt Architects 1964-74, currently princ of Architects and bldg

Surveyors; *Style—* William Newman, Esq; 6 Holmesdale Rd, Teddington, Middx (☎ 01 977 1196); 19 Bloomsbury Sq, London WC1A 2NS (☎ 01 637 3688, fax 01 637 3680, car ☎ 0860 798 379)

NEWNES, Rowland; s of Robert Watkin Newnes (d 1920), of Wrexham, and Emily, *née* Morris (d 1946); *b* 19 Oct 1914; *Educ* Grove Park GS Wrexham; *m* 24 Aug 1946, Mary, da of William Lloyd Evans (d 1975), of Chatham, 2 s (Philip Maurice b 1953, Daid Julian b 1958), 1 da (Diana Mary b 1948); *Career* Flt Lt RAF Britain and N Africa; slr; dep town: clerk Wrexham 1939-46, Chatham 1946-48, (town clerk Chatham 1948-61); sec Kent Borough and Urban Dist Assoc 1951-66, slr Medway Water Bd 1955-61, town clerk Gillingham 1961-66, princ asst co clerk Kent CC 1966-70, dir of social servs, Co of Kent and Co Borough of Canterbury 1971-74, chm Kent Area Rent Assessment Panel and SE regnl Rent Assessment Panel 1977-86; *Recreations* golf, walking, gardening; *Style—* Rowland Newnes, Esq; Red Marley, 248 Maidstone Road, Chatham, Kent ME4 6JN (☎ (0634) 43016)

NEWNS, Sir (Alfred) Foley (Francis Polden); KCMG (1963, CMG 1957), CVO (1961); s of Rev Alfred Newns (d 1930); *b* 30 Jan 1909; *Educ* Christs' Hosp, St Catharine's Coll Cambridge; *m* 1, 1936, Emma Jean (d 1984), da of Ambrose Bateman (d 1950); 1 s, 1 da; m 2, 9 April 1988, Mrs Beryl Wattles; *Career* colonial admin serv Nigeria 1932, sec to Cncl of Ministers 1951-54, sec to Govr-Gen and Cncl of Ministers 1955-59, dep govr Sierra Leone 1960, actg govr 1960, advsr to Govt 1961-63, sec to Cabinet Govt of Bahamas 1964-71; FRSA; *Recreations* nature study, music, art, African affairs; *Style—* Sir Foley Newns, KCMG, CVO; 47 Barrow Rd, Cambridge CB2 ZAR (☎ 0223 356903)

NEWNS, George Henry; s of George Newns (d 1916); *b* 27 July 1908; *Educ* Whitgift Sch, King's Coll London, KCH Med Sch (MD); *m* 1936, Eileen Deirdre, da of late Lawrence Kenny; 1 s, 1 da; *Career* chm Leukaemia Res Fund 1962-, civilian paediatric conslt to Admty 1962-74, hon conslt in Paediatrics to the Army 1966-74, dean Inst of Child Health London Univ 1949-73 (dean emeritus 1974-), conslt paediatrician-physician Hosp for Sick Children Gt Ormond St 1946-73, hon consulting physician 1974-; FRCP; *Recreations* walking, reading, music; *Style—* George Newns Esq; 12 Milborne Grove, London SW10 (☎ 01 373 2011)

NEWPORT, Viscount; Alexander Michael Orlando Bridgeman; s and h of 7 Earl of Bradford; *b* 6 Sept 1980; *Style—* Viscount Newport

NEWPORT, Helen Mary; da of George Alan Newport (d 1984), and Jeanne Mary Cross; *b* 28 Feb 1944; *Educ* Bicester GS, Oxford Coll of Technol; *m* ; 1 da (Emma b 1986); *Career* ski teacher Verbier Ski Sch; restaurant mangr 1974-79; md Helen Newport & Co Ltd (representing Allied Dunbar plc 1966-79); fin mgmnt conslt 1979-; speaker on fin planning nat and int; *Books* wrote regularly as 'Our Girl in the Alps' for Ski Magazine; *Recreations* travel, skiing, racing, eventing; *Clubs* Uine & Craven Hunt, Sloane, Ski of GB, Lia (achievement forum), Millon Dollar Round Table, Network; *Style—* Miss Helen Newport; Choctaw Cottage, 5 Stroud Green, Newbury RG14 7JAA (☎ Newbury 41649); Helen Newport & Co Ltd, c/o Allied Dunbar plc, 14/14A The Broadway, Newbury RG13 1BA (☎ 0635 36660, fax 0635 421402)

NEWRY AND MORNE, Viscount; Robert Francis John; s and h of Richard Needham, 6 Earl of Kilmorey (who does not use the title); *b* 30 May 1966; *Educ* Eton, Lady Margaret Hall Oxford; *Style—* Viscount Newry and Morne

NEWSAM, Peter Anthony; s of William Oswald Newsam (d 1974), of Maidenhead; *b* 2 Nov 1928; *Educ* Clifton, Queens' Coll Oxford; *m* 1953, Elizabeth Joy Greg; 4 s, 1 da; *Career* former civil servant BOT (asst princ); schoolmaster 1956-63, asst educn offr Yorks N Riding 1963-66, asst dir of educn Cumberland 1966-70, dep educn offr Yorks W Riding 1970-72, dep educn offr ILEA 1972-76 (educn offr 1977-82); chm Cmmn for Racial Equality 1982-; visiting fellow Nuffield Coll Oxford 1982-83; kt 1987; *Style—* Sir Peter Newsam; Commission for Racial Equality, Elliot House, Allington St, SW1 (☎ 01 828 7022);1 Park Lodge, Blackheath Park, London SE3

NEWSOM, George Harold; QC (1956); s of Rev George Ernest Newsom (d 1934), and Alethea Mary, *née* Awdry (d 1961); *b* 29 Dec 1909; *Educ* Marlborough, Merton Coll Oxford (MA); *m* 11 May 1939, Margaret Amy, da of Lucien Arthur Allen, OBE, of London; 2 s (George Lucien b 10 June 1948, William Arthur Charles b 24 Sept 1951), 1 da (Elizabeth Margaret Alethea (Mrs Thompson) b 6 Feb 1942); *Career* served WWII as princ in Trading with the Enemy Dept Treasy and Bd of Trade; barr Lincoln's Inn 1934 (bencher 1962, tres 1980); dep chm Wiltshire QS 1964-71; chllr: Diocese of St Albans 1958-, Bath and Wells 1971-, London 1971-; author (with late C H S Preston); memb The Faculty Jurisdiction of The Church of England 1988; *Publications* Restrictive Covenants affecting Freehold Land; *Recreations* golf, tennis, walking; *Clubs* Athenaeum; *Style—* George Newsom, Esq, QC; The Old Vicarage, Bishop's Cannings, Devizes, Wilts SN10 2LA (☎ 0380 86 660)

NEWSOME, Dr David Hay; s of Capt Charles Todd Newsome, OBE (d 1970), of Kenilworth, Warwickshire, and Elsie Mary, *née* Hay (d 1960); *b* 15 June 1929; *Educ* Rossall, Emmanuel Coll Cambridge (MA, LittD); *m* 12 April 1955, Joan Florence, da of Lt-Col Leslie Hamilton Trist, DSO, MC (d 1970), of Coldwaltham, Sussex; 4 da (Clare b 1956, Janet b 1958, Louise b 1960, Cordelia b 1961); *Career* Nat Serv 1948-50, Capt RAEC (substantive Lt); asst master Wellington Coll 1954-59; fell Emmanuel Coll Cambridge 1959-70 (sr tutor 1965-70), univ Lectr in ecclesiastical history Cambridge 1961-70; headmaster Christ's Hospital Horsham 1970-79, master of Wellington Coll 1980-89; memb governing bodies: Westcott House Cambridge 1960-65, Ardingly Coll 1965-69, Eastbourne Coll 1965-69, Epsom Coll 1965-69; FRHistS 1970, FRSL 1980; *Books* A History of Wellington College 1859-1959 (1959), Godliness and Good Learning (1961), The Parting of Friends (1966), Two Classes of Men (1974), On the Edge of Paradise: A C Benson the Diarist (1980 Whitbread prize for biog of the year), Edwardian Excursions (1981); *Recreations* fell-walking, music; *Clubs* Public Schools, MCC; *Style—* Dr David Newsome; The Master's Lodge, Wellington College, Crowthorne, Berks (☎ 0344 772353); The Retreat, Thornthwaite, Keswick, Cumbria (☎ 059 682 372)

NEWSON-SMITH, Sir John Kenneth; 2 Bt (UK 1944), of Totteridge, Co Hertford, DL (City of London); s of Sir Frank Newson-Smith, 1 Bt (d 1971); *b* 9 Jan 1911; *Educ* Dover Coll, Jesus Coll Cambridge; *m* 1, 1945, Vera Margaret (m dis 1971), da of late Dr Wilfred Greenhouse Allt, CVO, CBE; 1 s, 2 da; m 2, 1972, Anne, da of Harold Burns (d 1987); m 3, 1988, Sarah Lucretia Wimberley Ramsay; *Heir* s, Peter Frank Graham Newson-Smith; *Career* joined HAC 1933, RN 1939, Lt RNVR 1941; memb: Ct of Common Cncl 1945 (dep 1961-), HM Cmmn of Lieutenancy for City of London (HM Lt 1947); chm London United Investmts Ltd 1968-71 (dep chm 1971-); *Clubs* City Livery and Naval; *Style—* Sir John Newson-Smith, Bt, DL; 39 Godfrey St, London SW3 (☎ 01 352 0722)

NEWSON-SMITH, Peter Frank Graham; s and h of Sir John Kenneth Newson-Smith, and Vera Margaret Greenhouse Allt; gf Lord Mayor of London (paternal), gf Dr Greenhouse Allt, CVO, CBE, princ of Trinity Coll of Music London (maternal); *b* 8 May 1947; *Educ* Dover Coll, Trinity Coll of Music; *m* 1974, Mary-Ann, da of Cyril C Collins and w of Anthony Owens; 1 s (Oliver), 1 da (Emma); *Heir* Oliver Nicholas Peter Newson-Smith; *Career* dir of music Clayesmore Preparatory Sch; Freeman City of London 1969; liveryman Worshipful Co of Musicians 1971; *Recreations* gardening, sailing; *Style—* Peter Newson-Smith Esq; Lovells Court, Burton Street, Marnhull, Sturminster Newton, Dorset DT10 1JJ; Clayesmore Preparatory School, Iwerne Minster, Blandford Forum, Dorset DT11 8PH

NEWTON, Lady (Alice Mary); da of late Henry Barber, of Surbiton and widow of Glyn Rosser; *m* 1968, as his 2 w, Sir Edgar Henry Newton, 2 Bt (d 1971); *Style—* Alice, Lady Newton; 14 Castle Hill View, Sidford, Sidmouth, Devon

NEWTON, Antony Harold; OBE (1972), MP (C) Braintree Feb 1974-; s of Harold Newton, of Dovercourt, Harwich; *b* 29 August 1937; *Educ* sssends' Sch Saffron Walden, Trinity Coll Oxford; *m* 1, 1962 (m dis 1986), Janet Dianne, er da of Phillip Huxley, of Sidcup; 2 da; m 2, 1986, Mrs Patricia Gilthorpe; *Career* parly under-sec DHSS 1982, min for the Disabled DHSS 1983-84; min for Social Security and the Disabled (DHSS) 1984-86, min for Health (DHSS) 1986-; asst govt whip 1979-81 (govt whip 1981-82); vice-chm Fedn of Univ Cons & Unionist Assocs, asst dir CRD 1970-74 (head econ section 1965-70), previously sec & res sec Bow Gp, fought Sheffield Brightside 1970; economist; *Clubs* St Stephen's; *Style—* Antony Newton, Esq, OBE, MP; House of Commons, SW1

NEWTON, Air Vice-Marshal Barry Hamilton; CB (1988), OBE (1975); s of Bernard Hamilton Newton, FCA (d 1932), of Southgate, Middx, and Dorothy Mary Newton, *née* Thomas (d 1979); *b* 1 April 1932; *Educ* Highgate, RAF Coll Cranwell; *m* 1959, Lavinia, da of Col John James Aitken, CMG, DSO, OBE (d 1947), of Taunton, Somerset; 1 s (Charles), 1 da (Melanie); *Career* cmmnd RAF 1953, Personal Staff Offr to Cdr Second Allied Tactical Air Force and CINC RAF Germany 1967, OC Ops Wing RAF Cottesmore 1969, asst dir Def Policy 1978, Cabinet Off 1979-81, Air Cdre Flying Trg HQ RAF Support Cmd 1982, sr dir Staff (Air) RCDS 1984, Cmdt Jt Serv Def Coll Greenwich 1986, ADC to HM The Queen 1983, Gp Capt 1976, Air Cdre 1982, AVM 1984; *Recreations* shooting, music, reading; *Clubs* RAF; *Style—* Air Vice-Marshal Barry Newton, CB, OBE; c/o Nat Westminster Bank plc, 48 Blue Boar Row, Salisbury, Wilts SP1 1DF

NEWTON, Christopher David; JP (1974 (Inner London), TD 1971); s of James George Newton (d 1979), and Ethel Jane, *née* Davies (d 1987); *b* 2 Jan 1938; *Educ* John Fisher Sch, Surrey; *m* 12 Sept 1970, Jennifer Mary, da of Maj David Turville Constable Maxwell, TD (d 1985), of Bosworth Hall, Husbands Bosworth, Leics; 1 s (James Nicholas Turville b 1971), 1 da (Lucinda Rosalinde Mary b 1975); *Career* served Welsh Guards 1955-58, Westminster Dragoons (TA) 1959-72, Capt, ret; dir and chm: John Newton & Co Ltd, John Newton (Developments) Ltd, Newtonite Ltd, Marketing Services (London) Ltd 1978-; Freeman City of London 1985-, Livery Ctee Memb Fanmakers Co 1986-, underwriting memb of Lloyds 1988-; *Recreations* hunting (Beaufort Hunt), cross-country skiing; *Clubs* Cavalry and Guards; *Style—* Christopher Newton, Esq; Rumsey House, Calne, Wilts SN11 9LT (☎ 0249 816283); 160 Piccadilly, London W1V 0BX (☎ 01 409 0414, fax 629 2279, telex 8813153)

NEWTON, Christopher John; s of Henry Newton (d 1975), of Leicester and London, and Florence Alice, *née* Wilton (d 1978); *b* 24 June 1936; *Educ* Market Bosworth GS, Royal Ballet Sch Sadler's Wells; *Career* joined Royal Ballet Co Corps de Ballet 1954-1970 (soloist 1958-70), joined Faculty of US Int Univ San Diego Cal to teach dance notation and repertoire 1970-73; Royal Ballet: re-joined as dance notator and repetiteur 1973-80, ballet master 1980-88, artistic co-ordinator 1988; has re-produced ballets of Frederick Ashton, Antony Tudor, Rudolph Nureyev and Roland Petit between 1970 and 1988 for American Ballet Theatre, Joffrey Ballet, SF Ballet, Paris Opera Ballet and Deutsch Oper Ballet of Berlin, also staged own Production of Swan Lake - Act III for Pensylvania Ballet; re-produced and staged Frederick Ashton's 3 act Ballet Ondine from incomplete film records 1988, (created in 1958 and last performed in 1966); MRAD, AIChor; *Recreations* textile crafts; *Style—* Christopher Newton, Esq; Royal Ballet Company, Royal Opera House, Covent Garden, London WC2E 7QA (☎ 01 240 1200, telex 27988)

NEWTON, Derek Henry; s of Sidney Wellington Newton (d 1976), of Worthing, Sussex, and Sylvia May Newton, *née* West (d 1959); *b* 14 Mar 1933; *Educ* Emanuel Sch; *m* 1957, Judith Ann, da of Rowland Hart (d 1973); 2 da (Katherine, Amanda); *Career* insurance broker; chm C E Heath plc 1983-87 (ret); dir: Glaxo Insur (Bermuda) Ltd 1980-, Glaxo Tstees Ltd 1980-, Forecast Trading Ltd 1984-, Farley Health Products Pensions Ltd 1985-, Glaxo Animal Health Pensions Ltd 1985-, Clarges Pharmaceuticals Ttees Ltd 1985-; govr BUPA Med Res & Dvpt Ltd 1981-; *Recreations* cricket, golf; *Clubs* Surrey County Cricket (chm 1980-); *Style—* Derek Newton, Esq; Pantiles, Meadway, Oxshott, Surrey (☎ 037284 2273)

NEWTON, George Peter Howgill; s and h of Sir Harry Michael Rex Newton, 3 Bt; *b* 26 Mar 1962; *Educ* BA; *m* 30 Jan 1988; Jane L, twin da of John Rymer; *Career* parish assist; memb Girdlers' Livery Co; *Style—* George Newton, Esq

NEWTON, Sir (Leslie) Gordon; s of John Newton; *b* 1907; *Educ* Blundell's Sch, Sidney Sussex Coll Cambridge; *m* 1935, Peggy Ellen Warren; 1 s (decd); *Career* ed The Financial Times 1950-72 (dir 1967-72); chm LBC 1974-77; dir: Trust House Forte 1973-80, Mills & Allen (Int); kt 1966; *Style—* Sir Gordon Newton; 51 Thames House, Phyllis Ct Dr, Henley-on-Thames, Oxon RG9 2NA

NEWTON, Joanna Dawson (Mrs Richard Oulton); *née* Newton; da of Guy Geoffrey Frederick Newton (d 1969), and Rosemary Enid, *née* Stowers; *b* 28 May 1921; *Educ* Headington Sch Oxford, Banbury Art Sch, Bryam Shaw Sch of Art; *m* 14 Sept 1985, Richard Arthur Courtenay Oulton, s of Harry Charles Neil Maxwell Oulton, MC (d 1981); *Career* painter; exhibitions incl: Whitechapel Gall 1982, Nat Portrait Gall (Imperial Tobacco Portrait Award) 1983, Vanessa Devereux Gall 1984, Royal Acad (summer exhibition) 1985, The Mall Galleries (Nat Art exhibition) 1986, National Portrait Gall (Imperial Tobacco Portrait award) 1986, Royal Acad (summer exhibitons 1988); *Recreations* tennis, films, art galleries; *Clubs* Chelsea Arts; *Style—* Ms Joanna Newton; 14 Chesilton Rd, London SW6 (☎ 01 731 5581)

NEWTON, Rev Dr John Anthony; s of Charles Victor Newton (d 1963), and

Kathleen, *née* Marchant; *b* 28 Sept 1930; *Educ* Boston GS, Univ Coll Hull (BA), Inst of Historical Res Univ of London (PhD), Fitzwilliam Coll Cambridge (MA); *m* 28 Dec 1963, Rachel, da of Maurice Horne Giddings (d 1968), of Louth, Lincs; 4 s (Mark b 5 Nov 1964, Christopher b 27 Sept 1966, David b 31 Dec 1970, William b 24 March 1976); *Career* Chaplain Kent Coll Canterbury 1955, asst tutor Richmond Coll 1958, min Louth Lincs 1961; tutor in church history: Didsbury Coll Bristol 1965, St Paul's Coll Limuru Kenya 1972; princ Wesley Coll Bristol 1973, supt W London Mission, pres Methodist Conf 1981-82, chm Liverpool Dist of Methodist Church 1986, free church moderator for Merseyside and jt pres Merseyside Churches Ecumenical Assembly 1987, chm Merseyside Cncl of Voluntary Serv, tstee Liverpool Industl Mission Ecumenical Ctee, hon memb Merseyside C of C and Indust; Hon DLitt Hull 1982; *Books* Susanna Wesley and the Puritan Tradition in Methodism (1969), The Palestine Problem (1971), Search for a Saint: Edward King (1977), Marcus Ward (1984); *Recreations* walking, gardening, reading, book collecting; *Clubs* Athenaeum (Liverpool); *Style*— Rev Dr John Newton; 49 Queen's Drive, Mossley Hill, Liverpool L18 2DT (☎ 051 722 1219)

NEWTON, John Garnar; s and h of Sir Kenneth Garnar Newton, 3 Bt, OBE, TD; *b* 10 July 1945; *Educ* Reed's Sch Cobham; *m* 27 May 1972, Jacynth Anne Kay, *née* Miller; 3 s (Timothy Garnar b 1973, Alistair Blair (twin) b 1973, Andrew Robert b 1975); *Style*— John Newton Esq

NEWTON, Sir Kenneth Garnar; 3 Bt (UK 1924), of Beckenham, Kent; OBE (1969, MBE 1944), TD; s of Sir Edgar Henry Newton, 2 Bt (d 1971); *b* 4 June 1918; *Educ* Wellington; *m* 1, 1944, Margaret Isabel (d 1979), da of Rev Dr George Blair, of Dundee; 2 s; m 2, 1980, Pamela, wid of F T K Wilson; *Heir* s, John Garnar Newton; *Career* served 1939-45, Lt-Col 1944; gen cmmr for Income Tax 1961-; md Garnar Booth plc 1961-, (chm 1972); pres Br Leather Fedn 1968-69, Int Cncl of Tanners 1972-78; Master: Leathersellers' Co 1977-78, Feltmakers' Co 1983-84; chm govrs Colfe's Sch 1982-; *Style*— Sir Kenneth Newton, Bt, OBE, TD; Wildways, High Broom Lane, Crowborough, Sussex;

NEWTON, Sir (Harry) Michael Rex; 3 Bt (UK 1900), of The Wood, Sydenham Hill, Lewisham, Kent and Kottingham House, Burton-on-Trent, Co Stafford; s of Sir Harry Kottingham Newton, 2 Bt, OBE (d 1951); *b* 7 Feb 1923; *Educ* Eastbourne Coll; *m* 1958, Pauline Jane, da of Richard John Frederick Howgill, CBE, of Branscombe, Sullington Warren, Storrington, Sussex; 1 s, 3 (adopted) da; *Heir* s, George Peter Howgill Newton; *Career* served 1941-46 with KRRC; dir Thomas Parsons & Sons Ltd; memb Girdlers' Co; Freeman City of London; *Clubs* Bath, Roy Ocean Racing; *Style*— Sir Michael Newton, Bt; Weycroft Hall, nr Axminster, Devon (☎ 3232)

NEWTON, 4 Baron (UK 1892); Peter Richard Legh; JP (Hants 1951); s of 3 Baron (d 1960); *b* 6 April 1915; *Educ* Eton, Ch Ch Oxford; *m* 1948, Priscilla (who had m, 1936, Capt Viscount Wolmer, s and h of 3 Earl of Selborne and who was k accidentally while on active serv 1942; 2 s, 1 da), da of Capt John Egerton-Warburton (d 1915) and Hon Mrs Waters (d 1968, herself da of 2 Baron Newton); 2 s; *Heir* s, Hon Richard Thomas Legh; *Career* 2 Lt Grenadier Gds 1937, Capt 1941, Maj 1945; MP (C) Hampshire (Petersfield) 1951-60; asst govt whip 1953-55, a lord cmmr of the Treasy 1955-57, vice-chamberlain HM Household 1957-59, (tres 1959-60); jt parly sec Min of Health 1962-64, min of state Dept of Educn and Science 1964; CC Hants 1949-52 and 1954-55; *Clubs* Carlton; *Style*— The Rt Hon the Lord Newton, JP; Vernon Hill House, Bishop's Waltham, Hants (☎ 2301)

NEWTON, (John) Simon; s of John David Newton, and Mary, *née* Bevan; *b* 22 August 1945; *Educ* The Birkenhead Sch, UCL (LLB); *m* 4 July 1970, Katharine Margaret Headlay, da of Sir Terence Garvey (d 1986); 1 s (Thomas b 1975), 1 da (Alexander b 1973); *Career* called to the Bar Middle Temple 1970; chm Salmon & Trout Assoc (Liverpool and Merseyside branch); *Recreations* golf, fishing; *Clubs* Royal Liverpool Golf; *Style*— Simon Newton, Esq; Refuge Assurance House, Derby Square, Liverpool L2 1TS (☎ 051 709 4222)

NEWTON, Stella Mary; OBE (1976); da of Henry James Pearce (d 1944), of Manchester, and Georgiana Wilkie Maria, *née* Hoby (d 1964); *b* 17 April 1901; *Educ* Froebel Educnl Inst London, Withington Girls Sch Manchester; *m* 6 Jan 1934, Eric Newton, CBE, formerly Oppenheimer, s of Lehmann Oppenheimer (d 1917), of Manchester; *Career* stage designer; designed costumes for the first prodns of T S Eliot's The Rock, Murder in the Cathedral, The Family Reunion, as well as many other plays; studied the dress of the Italian Renaissance; advsr to Art Historians of the Nat Gallery on the dating of paintings by Costume 1952-62; inaugurated dept for study of the History of Dress at London Univ's Courtauld Inst of Art 1965, only full-time, post-graduate, two-year course on the subject, ret 1974 to become author and free-lance lectr; six lecture tours in Univs in the USA; FRSA; *Books* Hyacinth Pink (a book for children 1958), Health, Art and Reason, Dress reformers of the 19th century (1974), Renaissance Theatre Costume (1975), Fashion in the Age of the Black Prince (1980), The Dress of the Venetians 1495-1525 (1988); *Style*— Mrs Stella Newton, OBE

NEWTON, Hon Mrs - Hon Ursula Helen Rank; da of 1 and last Baron Rank (d 1972); *b* 1919; *m* 1952, Robert Lancelot Newton (d 1969); 1 s, 2 da; *Style*— The Hon Mrs Newton; Church Farm, Saltby, Melton, Mowbray, Leics

NEWTON DUNN, Col (ret) Thomas Robert; MC (1945); s of Dr Thomas William Newton Dunn (d 1966), of Salisbury, and Frances Lucy, *née* Owen (d 1972); *b* 6 Dec 1915; *Educ* Charterhouse, Gonville and Caius Cambridge (BA); *m* 1, 1939, Justine (d 1983), da of Maj-Gen Justic Crossland Tilly, DSO, MC (d 1941); 1 s (Charles b 1945), 1 da (Sally b 1943); m 2, 9 Oct 1985, Nancy, wid of Col John F Weston Simons; *Career* from TA into RTC, 2 Lt 1936 Dewar Tank Mission USA 1940, Army Staff Washington 1942, WO 1942, Staff Coll Camberley 1943, served 11 RTR Europe, instr Indian Def Serv, Lt-Col Staff Coll Wellington 1954, chief instr Mons Offr Cadet Sch 1956-58, GSO 1 SHAPE 1958-60, mil advsr to Br High Cmmn India 1960-63, Col AAG WO 1963-66, mil advsr to Br High Cmmn Uganda 1966-68, NATO Def Coll Rome 1968, NATO HQ Naples 1968-69, Col AAG MOD 1969-71, ret 1971; re-employed as ret offr with Royal Corps of Transport 1972-78, Offr Legion of Merit US 1947; *Recreations* photography, travel, gardening; *Clubs* Army and Navy; *Style*— Col Thomas Newton Dunn, MC; Yew Tree House, Old Orchard, Odiham, Basingstoke RG25 1AR (☎ 025 671 2666)

NEWTON DUNN, William Francis (Bill); MEP (EDG Lincs 1979- and for Gibraltar); s of Lt-Col Owen F Newton Dunn, OBE, and Barbara Mary, *née* Brooke; *b* 3 Oct 1941; *Educ* Marlborough, Gonville and Caius Cambridge (MA), Insead Business Sch Fontainebleau (MBA); *m* 17 Oct 1970, Anna Terez, da of Michel Arki; 1 s (Thomas b 1973), 1 da (Daisy b 1976); *Career* Freeman Worshipful Co of Haberdashers; *Books* 'Greater in Europe' (1986); *Style*— Bill Newton Dunn Esq, MEP; 10 Church Lane, Navenby, Lincoln LN5 0EG (☎ 0522 810812)

NEY, Kevin Philip; s of John Martin Ney (d 1938), of Crosby, and Frances Sheils (d 1977); *b* 31 Mar 1922; *Educ* St Mary's Coll, Crosby; *Career* served RNVR 1941-46, Lt 1944 (despatches 1944) in N Atlantic, Sicily, Salerno, Normandy and Pacific Fleet; CA 1946; ptnr: Robert J Ward & Co 1948-71, Tansley Witt & Co 1971-79, Arthur Andersen & Co 1979-81; dir: Burns, Oates & Washbourne 1955-71, John Wainwright & Co (chm) 1962-, Brasseys Publishers 1977-79, and Britannia Arrow Hldgs plc (dep chm) 1977-; chm Nat Employers Life Assurance Co 1983-; hon tres The Catholic Union of GB 1973-; FCA; *Recreations* gardening, chess, photography, graphology; *Clubs* Naval and Military, Bath and County; *Style*— Kevin P Ney, Esq, FCA; 150 Cliffords Inn, Fetter Lane, London EC4; Coley House, East Harptree, Bristol BS18 6AW

NIALL, Sir Horace Lionel Richard; CBE (1957, MBE 1943); s of Alfred George Niall (d 1929), and Jane Phyllis Niall (d 1967); *b* 14 Oct 1904; *Educ* Mudgee HS, Sydney Univ; *m* 1965, Una Lesley, da of Gubert William Leslie Fane de Salis; 1 da; *Career* Maj AIF, New Guinea WWII; public servant PNG Admin 1927-64 (ret with rank of dist cmmr), MLA PNG 1951-64, PNG del to UN Trusteeship Cncl 1963, MHA PNG 1964-69, speaker PNG 1964-69; kt 1974; *Style*— Sir Horace Niall, CBE; 9 Commodore, 50 Palm Beach Rd, Palm Beach, NSW 2108, Australia (☎ 919 5462)

NIBLETT, Keith Ivor; s of Ivor Niblett (d 1982), of Middlewich, Cheshire, and Jean Olive, *née* Evans (now Mrs Wales); *b* 8 June 1947; *Educ* Chester and Lowestoft GS, Univ of Bath (BA), Norwich Coll (DMS); *m* 1, Feb 1966 (m dis 1967), Julie Martin; m 2, 4 Aug 1967, Jayne Lizabeth, da of Arthur James Hague, of Gunton, nr Lowestoft; 3 s (Stephen Robert b 3 May 1968, John Keith James b 28 March 1973, Marcus Simon William b 7 May 1975), 1 da (Lisa Jayne b 25 May 1967); *Career* mangr Thetford and Walton Times 1972-74, gp mangr Norwich Mercury Series of Newspapers 1975-78, viewdata mangr Prestel Viewdata Systems 1978-79, sr exec Eastern Co's Newspapers Gp Ltd 1979, gen mangr Adprint Magazine Publishers 1986-88; visiting sr lectr business studies Norwich Coll 1981-, sr tutor Boulton and Paul Gp and Br Electric Traction; chm Norwich Round Table No 1 1984, nat cncllr Round Table 1985-87, chm Norfolk Area Round Table 1987-88, former mktg advsr Norfolk and Norwich Triennial Festival, former exec Eastern Region Br Inst Mgmnt, former publicity sec S Norfolk Cons Assoc; LRAM 1965, MInstM 1977, MBIM 1979, DMS 1979; *Books* Viewdata in Action (1978); *Recreations* squash, music; *Clubs* East Anglian Lawn Tennis and Squash Raquets (Norwich), Adelaide (Norwich); *Style*— Keith Niblett, Esq; Hillside House, Hillside Rd, West Bungay, Suffolk NR35 1PJ (☎ 0986 3690); Boulton and Paul Gp Ltd, Pottergate Centre, 83-85 Pottergate, Norwich NR2 1DZ (☎ 0603 615 817, fax 0603 626 972, telex 97326 GOPAUL G)

NIBLOCK, (Henry) Pat; OBE (1972); s of Joseph Niblock (d 1932), of Belfast, and Isabel, *née* Bradford (d 1928); *b* 25 Nov 1911; *Educ* Elementary and Business Tr Sch Belfast; *m* 14 May 1940, Barbara Mary, da of Capt Wilshire Davies, OBE (d 1948), of Reading; 2 s (Michael b 21 Feb 41, Timothy b 13 Oct 1942); *Career* Diplomat Serv; vice consul: Bremen 1947-50, Bordeaux 1950; commercial attaché Copenhagen 1951-52; consul: Frankfurt am Main 1953-57, (chargé d'affaires) Monrovia 1957-58, Houston 1959-62; chargé d'affaires Port au Prince 1962-63, first sec and consul Brussels 1964, consul (commercial) Cape Town 1965-68, consul-gen Strasbourg 1968-72; memb Past Rotarians Club Eastbourne; *Recreations* bowls, walking; *Clubs* Civil Serv; *Style*— Pat Niblock, Esq; 10 Clifton House, 2 Park Ave, Eastbourne, E Sussex BN22 9QN (☎ 0323 505 695)

NICCOL, Dame Sister Mary Leo (Kathleen); DBE (1973, MBE 1963); da of Henry Malcolm Niccol (d 1930), and Agnes Teresa, *née* Cannell; *b* 3 April 1895; *Educ* Auckland Teachers' Coll, Auckland Univ, Trinity Coll London (LTCL); *Career* memb of the Congregation of the Sisters of Mercy Auckland, dir St Mary's Sch of Music, music teacher, teacher of Kiri Te Kanawa, DBE, *qv*; *Recreations* reading, listening to music; *Style*— Dame Sister Mary Leo Niccol, DBE; St Mary's Convent, New St, Ponsonby, Auckland 1, New Zealand (767 575 and 763 534); PO Box 47025, Ponsonby, Auckland 1, New Zealand

NICE, Geoffrey; s of William Charles Nice, and Mahala Anne, *née* Tarryer (d 1982); *b* 21 Oct 1945; *Educ* St Dunstans Coll Catford, Keble Coll Oxford; *m* 1974, Philippa, da of Kemlo Abbot Cronin Gross, OBE, ERD; 3 da (Amelia b 1975, Taffa b 1976, Mahalah b 1980); *Career* barr, rec of Crown Ct 1987-; Parly candidate Dover SDP/Lib Alliance) 1983 and 1987; *Recreations* music, tennis, skiing; *Style*— Geoffrey Nice, Esq; Manor Farm, Adisham, Canterbury (☎ 0304 840156); Farrars Building, Temple, London EC4 (☎ 01 583 9241)

NICHOL, David Brett; s of Philip George Nichol (d 1974), of Gullane, E Lothian, and Kathleen, *née* Brett; *b* 20 April 1945; *Educ* Sedbergh; *m* 22 July 1977, Judith Mary, da of Godfrey Arthur Parker (d 1966), of Godalming, Surrey; 4 da (Alexandra b 1979, Tessa b 1981, Leonie b 1982, Flora b 1986); *Career* chartered accountant; Deloitte & Co 1962-68, County Bank London 1968-70, Martin Corpn Australia 1970-71, WI Carr Hong Kong 1971-72, dir Ivory & Sime plc 1972-; tstee Royal Botanic Gdns Edinburgh 1986; FCA; *Recreations* shooting, skiing, golf; *Clubs* New RA, Hon Co of Edinburgh Golfers; *Style*— David B Nichol, Esq; Rossie, Forgandenny, Perthshire PH2 9EH; Ivory & Sime plc, One Charlotte Square, Edinburgh, EH2 4DZ (☎ 031 225 1357, fax 031 225 2375, telex 727242 IVORYS G)

NICHOL, Duncan Kirkbride; OBE (1988); s of James, and Mabel (d 1984); *b* 30 May 1941; *Educ* Bradford GS, St Andrews Univ (MA); *m* 18 March 1972, Elizabeth Elliot Mitchell, da of Herbert Wilkinson (d 1967), of Blackpool; 1 s (Andrew b 1973), 1 da (Rachael b 1977); *Career* acting gp sec and hosp sec Manchester Royal Infirmary 1969-73, dep gp sec and acting gp sec Univ Hosp Mgmnt Ctee of S Manchester 1973-74, dist admin S Manchester Dist 1974-77, area admin Salford DHA 1977-81, regnl gen mangr Marsey RHA 1984-89 (regnl admins 1981-84), chief exec offr NHS Mgmnt Bd 1989-; memb Central Health Servs Cncl 1980-81, pres IMSM 1984-85 (memb cncl 1976-), chm Kings Fund Educn Ctee 1987-, CBIM 1988, AMA 1967; *Recreations* golf, walking; *Style*— Duncan Nichol, Esq, CBE; 1 Pipers Close, Heswell, Wirral, Merseyside L60 9LJ, (☎ 051 342 2699); Richmond House, 79 Whitehall, London SW1 2NS, (☎ 01 210 5160, fax 01 210 5409)

NICHOL, Dr William Dorrien; s of John Buchanan Nichol (d 1947), of Dunedin, New Zealand, and Annie Elizabeth, *née* Cavanagh (d 1939); *b* 12 Dec 1914; *Educ* Otago

Boys' HS, Otago Univ Med Sch (MB ChB (NZ)); *m* 24 May 1952, Joan Pauline, da of Ralph Palmer Taylor (d 1962), of Edinburgh; 2 s (Robert Moray b 1956, John Alastair b 1957), 1 da (Helen Catriona b 1953); *Career* NZ Med Corps 1943-6 CMF Capt; conslt radiologist St Bartholomews Hosp London 1951-80, dir X-ray dept St Bartholomew's Hosp 1971-80, asst and clinical fell Massachusetts Gen Hosp in Radiology Harvard Coll 1952-3; FFR, FRCR; *Recreations* golf, electronics, woodwork; *Style*— Dr William Nichol; Chasewood House, Chasewood Avenue, Enfield, Middlesex (☎ 01 363 9444); 121 Harley Street, London W1 (☎ 01 935 2235)

NICHOLAS, (John) Barry Moylan; s of Archibald John Nicholas (d 1978), and Rose Elizabeth, *née* Moylan (d 1947); *b* 6 July 1919; *Educ* Downside, Brasenose Coll Oxford (MA); *m* 9 July 1948, Hildegart Elizabeth, da of Prof Hans Cloos (d 1935), of Bonn; 1 s (Peter b 1955), 1 da (Frances b 1950); *Career* RCS 1939-45, Maj 1943; barr Inner Temple 1950; Oxford Univ: fell Brasenose Coll 1947-78, tutor 1947-72, All Souls reader in roman law 1949-71, prof of comparative law 1971-78, memb Hebdomadal cncl 1975-83, princ Brasenose Coll 1978-89; hon: bencher Inner Temple 1984, Dr Paris V 1987; *Books* Introduction to Roman Law (1962), Jolowicz and Nicholas Historical Introduction to Roman Law (3 ed 1972), French Law of Contract (1982); *Clubs* Utd Oxford & Cambridge; *Style*— Barry Nicholas, Esq; 18A Charlbury Rd, Oxford OX2 6UU (☎ 0865 58512); Brasenose Coll, Oxford OX1 4AJ (☎ 0865 277 830)

NICHOLAS, David; CBE (1982); *b* 25 Jan 1930; *Educ* Neath GS, Univ Coll of Wales Aberystwyth (BA); *m* 1952, Juliet Powell Davies; 1 s (James), 1 da (Helen); *Career* Natl Serv Army 1951-53; journalist: Wakefield Express, Yorkshire Post, Daily Telegraph, Observer; joined ITN 1960, dep ed 1963, ed & chief exec 1977-; dir Worldwide TV News (WTN); *Recreations* sailing, walking, riding; *Clubs* Reform; *Style*— David Nicholas, Esq, CBE; c/o Independent Television News, ITN Ho, 48 Wells St, London W1P 4DE

NICHOLAS, Sir Harry (Herbert Richard); OBE (1949); s of Richard Henry Nicholas; *b* 13 Mar 1905; *Educ* Elementary Sch Bristol, evening classes, correspondence courses; *m* 1932, Rosina Grace Brown; *Career* asst-gen sec Tport and Gen Workers' Union 1956-68 (actg gen sec 1964-66); TUC Gen Cncl 1964-67, memb nat exec ctee Labour Party 1956-64 and 1967-68, tres Labour Party 1960-64, gen sec Labour Party 1968-72; kt 1970; *Style*— Sir Harry Nicholas, OBE; 33 Madeira Rd, Streatham, London SW16 2DG (☎ 01 769 7989)

NICHOLAS, Prof Herbert George; s of Rev William Daniel Nicholas, of Treharris, and Mary Elizabeth Nicholas; *b* 8 June 1911; *Educ* Mill Hill, New Coll Oxford (BA, MA), Yale Univ; *Career* American div MOI 1941-45, first sec Br Embassy Washington 1945-60, fell and tutor Exeter Coll Oxford 1944-51 (lectr 1938-44); lectr modern history and politics Oxford 1948-56, faculty fell Nuffield Coll Oxford 1948-58, fell New Coll Oxford 1951-80 (hon fell 1980-), Nuffield reader in comparative study of insts 1956-68, Rhodes prof of american history and instns 1969-78; chm Br Assoc for American Studies 1960-62; Hon Doctorate Univ of Pittsburgh 1968; FBA 1969 (vi pres 1975-76); *Books* The American Union (1948), The British General Election of 1950 (1951), To the Hustings (1956), The United Nations as a Political Institution (1952, 2 ed 1975), Britain and the United States (1963), The Nature of American Politics (1980), Washington Despatches 1941-45 (ed 1981); *Recreations* gardening, listening to music; *Clubs* Athenaeum; *Style*— Prof HG Nicholas; New Coll, Oxford OX1 3BN (☎ 0865 248 451)

NICHOLAS, James Donald; s of Capt Donald Louis Nicholas (d 1973), and Evaone Chavasse; one of mother's father's twin brothers, Noel Godfrey Chavasse won VC and Bar 1914-18 War; *b* 1 April 1951; *Educ* Bradfield, Royal Agric Coll Cirencester; *m* 20 May 1975, Rachael Jane, da of Cecil Gifford, of Cheltenham, Gloucs; 1 step s (Rupert b 1969), 2 step da (Katherine b 1965, Abigail b 1973); *Career* dir: Nicksons Animal Feeds Ltd 1985-, District Estates and assoc cos 1985; ptnr S Wales Fishery Michaelchurch-on-Arrow 1978-; memb Salmon and Trout Assoc-; *Recreations* fly fishing for trout and salmon, stalking, shooting, travel, gastronomy; *Clubs* Boodles, Flyfishers; *Style*— James Nicholas, Esq; Welsh Court, Yatton, Ross-on-Wye,Herfordshire (☎ 053 184 294, car tel 0836 622 058)

NICHOLAS, (Angela) Jane Udale; da of Bernard Alexander Royle Shore, CBE (d 1985), and Olive Livett, *née* Udale (d 1981); father a leading viola player, teacher and writer; *b* 14 June 1929; *Educ* Ballet Rambert Sch, Arts Educn Tst, Sadler's Wells Sch; *m* 1964, William Alan, s of Percy Edgar Nicholas (d 1960); *Career* ballet dancer, fndr memb Sadler's Wells Theatre Ballet 1946-50, memb Sadler's Wells Ballet at Covent Garden 1950-52; freelance dancer, singer, actress 1952-60; drama offr Br Cncl 1961-70, music offr and dance offr Arts Cncl 1970, dir Dance and Mime 1979- (asst dir 1975-79); *Recreations* collecting antique china; *Style*— Mrs Jane Nicholas; 21 Stamford Brook Rd, London W6 0XJ (☎ 01 741 3035); Arts Cncl, 105 Piccadilly, London W1V 0AU (☎ 01 629 9495)

NICHOLAS, Mark Charles Jefford; s of Peter Jefford (d 1969), and Anne Evelyn Nicholas; mothers acting name was Anne Loxley; *b* 29 Sept 1957; *Educ* Bradfield; *Career* Capt Hampshire CCC; capt: Eng 'B' Sri Lanka tour 1986, Eng counties XI Zimbabwe 1985; *Books* 100 yrs at Soton - a centenary of Hampshire Cricket at Southampton, 'Macko'; *Recreations* theatre, squash, golf, music; *Clubs* Berkshire Golf; *Style*— Mark Nicholas, Esq; c/o Hampshire CCC, Northlands Rd, Southampton SO9

NICHOLAS, Trevor Ian; s of Harold Lionel Nicholas, of 15 Riverview Gardens, Twickenham, Middx, and Gwendoline Doris, *née* Blyth; *b* 14 Sept 1936; *Educ* Hampton GS, Harvard Business Sch; *m* 17 Oct 1959, Ruth, da of Gottlieb Joswig (d 1954); 2 da (Kim b 1 April 1961, Katja b 12 Sept 1963); *Career* Barclays Bank plc 1974-: mangr business advsy serv 1974-75, gen mangr asst 1977, asst gen mangr software devpt 1978-79, div gen mangr Barclaycard 1980-82, div gen mangr mgmnt servs 1982-84, gen mangr resources 1985-87, dir info systems and resources 1988-; pres Barclays Hort Soc; memb: Nat Tst, RSPB, Woodland Tst, Ramblers Assoc RHS, English Heritage, RVC Animal Care Tst, Wildfowl Tst, Historic Houses Assoc, Royal Forestry Soc; FCIB; *Recreations* music, reading, photography, natural history, eisteddford, conservation; *Style*— Trevor Nicholas, Esq; 16 Oakwood, Berkhamsted HP4 3NQ (☎ 0442 866 921); Director Information Systems & Resources, Barclays Bank plc, Head Office, 54 Lombard Street, London EC3P 3AH (☎ 01 626 1567, fax 01 929 0394, telex 887 591 and 886 111)

NICHOLETTS, Lady; Nora Beswick; da of Francis Butt, MB; *m* 1956, Air Marshal Sir Gilbert Edward Nicholetts, KBE, CB, AFC and bar (d 1983, pioneer of flying boats); *Style*— Lady Nicholetts; Stoborough Croft, Wareham, Dorset

NICHOLL, His Hon Judge Anthony John David; s of Brig David William Dillwyn Nicholl (d 1972), and Mrs D W D Nicholl (d 1975); *b* 3 May 1935; *Educ* Eton, Pembroke Coll Oxford; *m* 1961, Hermione Mary, da of William Harcourt Palmer Landon (d 1978); 1 s (William b 19 May 1962), 2 da (Charlotte b 30 Oct 1963, Lucy b 4 June 1967); *Career* barr Lincoln's Inn 1958, in practice London 1958-61 and Birmingham 1961-88; head of chambers 1976-87, rec Crown Ct 1978-88, chm Fountain Ct Chambers Birmingham 1984-88, circuit judge MO circuit 1988-; memb Birmingham Medico-Legal Soc; *Recreations* history, walking, gardening, riding; *Style*— His Hon Judge Anthony Nicholl; 2 Fountain Court, Steelhouse Lane, Birmingham B4 6DR (021 236 3882)

NICHOLL, Henry Rice; s of Maj Basil Rice Nicholl (ka 1916); *b* 28 April 1909; *Educ* Winchester, RMC Sandhurst; *m* 1936, Marjorie Joicey, da of Robert Dickinson, of Styford Hall, Stocksfield (d 1927); 2 s (Charles m Fiona Trotter, Edward m Elizabeth Innes), 1 da (*see* St John, Edmund Oliver); *Career* served in WWII in N Africa and Italy; cmmnd Rifle Bde 1929, cmd 7 Bn Rifle Bde 1946, ret 1948; High Sheriff Northumberland 1969, MFH Haydon 1959-67; *Style*— Lt-Col Henry Nicholl; High Lipwood, Haydon Bridge, Hexham, Northumberland NE47 6EB (☎ 043 484 205)

NICHOLLS; *see*: Harmar-Nicholls

NICHOLLS, Brian; s of Ralph Nicholls, of Crieff, Scotland, and Kathleen, *née* Bulled (d 1966); *b* 21 Sept 1928; *Educ* Haberdashers' Aske's, Regent St Poly (BSc), Harvard Business Sch; *m* 1961, Mary Elizabeth, da of Alexander Harley, of Milnathort, Scotland; 1 s (Simon b 1964), 2 da (Jane b 1966, Anne b 1968); *Career* dir: CJB Projects Ltd 1972-75, CJB Pipelines Ltd 1974-75, CJB - Mohandessi Iran (dep chm) 1975; John Brown Engrg 1978-, JBE Inc (USA) 1982-; vice pres John Brown Power Ltd 1987-; industl advsr Dept of Trade 1975-78; cncl memb: Br Chemical Engrg Contractors Assoc 1973-75, Br Overseas Trade Bd 1978; exec ctee memb Scottish Cncl Devpt and Indust 1984-; *Recreations* hill walking, sailing, music, writing; *Clubs* Royal Northern and Clyde Yacht; *Style*— Brian Nicholls, Esq; Croy, Shandon, by Helensburgh, Dunbartonshire G84 8NN Scotland

NICHOLLS, Dr Christine Stephanie; da of Christopher James Metcalfe (d 1986), of Mombasa, Kenya, and Olive, *née* Kennedy (d 1982); *b* 23 Jan 1943; *Educ* Kenya HS, Lady Margaret Hall Oxford (BA, MA), St Antony's Coll Oxford (DPhil); *m* 12 March 1966, Anthony James, s of Ernest Alfred Nicholls (d 1981), of Carshalton, Surrey; 1 s (Alexander b 1970), 2 da (Caroline b 1972, Isabel b 1974); *Career* Henry Charles Chapman res fell Inst of Cwlth Studies London Univ 1968-69, freelance writer BBC 1970-74; sec Wolvercote Local History Soc; *Books* The Swahili Coast (1971), Cataract (with Philip Awdry 1985), Dictionary of National Biography (jt ed 1971); *Recreations* reading novels; *Style*— Dr Christine Nicholls; 27 Davenant Rd, Oxford OX2 8BU (☎ 0865 511 320); Dictionary of National Biography, Clarendon Building, Bodleian Library, Broad St, Oxford OX1 3BG (☎ 0865 277 232/277 236)

NICHOLLS, Clive Victor; QC (1982); s of Alfred Charles Victor Nicholls, and Lilian Mary, *née* May; *b* 29 August 1932; *Educ* Brighton Coll, Trinity Coll Dublin (MA, LLB), Sidney Sussex Coll Cambridge (BA, LLM); *m* 23 July 1960, Alison Virginia, da of late Leonard Arthur Oliver; 3 s (Jeremy Oliver b 1962, James Colin Oliver b 1967, John Patrick Oliver b 1969), 3 da (Jacqueline Alison b 1963, Judie Victoria b 1965, Jill Caroline b 1965); *Career* barr Gray's Inn 1957; rec of Crown Court 1984-; chm Tstees of Bob Champion Cancer Tst; patron Multiple Birth Assoc; *Recreations* sailing, fly-fishing; *Style*— Clive V Nicholls, Esq, QC; 3 Raymond Buildings, Gray's Inn, London WC2 1RR (☎ 01 831 3833, fax 01 831 4989)

NICHOLLS, Colin Alfred Arthur; QC (1981); s of Alfred Charles Victor Nicholls (d 1987), and Lilian Mary, *née* May; *b* 29 August 1932; *Educ* Brighton Coll, Dublin Univ (MA, LLB); *m* 23 Oct 1976, Clarissa Allison Spenlove, da of Clive Dixon (d 1976); 2 s (Benjamin Clive b 30 Aug 1977, Jonathan Charles b 6 Jan 1979); *Career* barr Gray's Inn 1957, rec of Crown Ct 1983-; memb cncl Cwlth Lawyers' Assoc; patron Multiple Births Fndn; *Recreations* painting (exhibitor RHA); *Style*— Colin Nicholls, Esq, QC; 3 Raymond Buildings, Gray's Inn, London WC2 1RR (☎ 01 831 3833, fax 01 831 4989), car ☎ 0836 717 941

NICHOLLS, David Alan; CMG (1984); s of Thomas Edward Nicholls (d 1971), and Beatrice Winifred Nicholls; *Educ* Cheshunt GS, St John's Coll Cambridge (BA); *m* 1955, Margaret; 2 da (Amanda, Camilla); *Career* entered Home Civil Serv 1954; asst sec MOD 1969-75, Cabinet Office 1975-77, under-sec MOD 1977-80, asst sec-gen NATO 1980-84, dep under sec MOD 1984-; chm Soc for Italic Handwriting; *Recreations* sketching, printmaking; *Style*— David Nicholls, Esq, CMG; c/o Midland Bank, Church Street, Stretton, Shropshire

NICHOLLS, Lady; Dominie; da of Peter Vlasto (d 1941), of The Woodlands, Fulwood Park, Liverpool, and Aziza Pallis; the Vlasto family settled in the (then) Genoese Island of Chios after the fall of Constantinople in 1453 and fled to England and France after the massacres there in 1823; *b* 30 Dec 1911; *Educ* Priors Field; *m* 1935, Sir John Walter Nicholls, GCMG, OBE (d 1970), s of William Nicholls, of Kenwood, Radlett, Herts; 1 s (John Peter Benedict), 2 da (Julia Anne, Caroline Dominie); *Career* the w of a British diplomat for thirty-five years, minister's w in Moscow (1949-51), ambassador's w in Israel, Yugoslavia, Belgium and S Africa; *Recreations* gardening, walking; *Style*— Lady Nicholls; The Burgh House, London Rd, Saffron Walden, Essex CB11 4ED (☎ 0799 23486)

NICHOLLS, Rt Hon Lord Justice; Sir Donald James Nicholls; PC (1986); *b* 1933; *Career* barr 1958, QC 1974, High Court judge; lord justice of appeal; kt 1983; *Style*— The Rt Hon Lord Justice Nicholls; Royal Courts of Justice, Strand, London WC2A 2LL

NICHOLLS, Air Marshal Sir John Moreton; KCB (1978), CBE (1970), DFC (1953), AFC (1965); s of Alfred Nicholls and Elsie, *née* French; *b* 5 July 1926; *Educ* Liverpool Collegiate, St Edmund Hall Oxford, RAF Coll; *m* 1, 1945, Enid Jean Marjorie Rose (d 1975); 2 da; m 2, 1977, Shelagh Joyce Hall, *née* Strong; *Career* RAF, Vice-Chief of Air Staff 1979-80; *Style*— Air Marshal Sir John Nicholls, KCB, CBE, DFC, AFC; Dove Barn, Old Coast Road, Ormesby St Margaret, Norfolk NR29 3QH

NICHOLLS, Nigel Hamilton; CBE (1982); s of Bernard Cecil Hamilton Nicholls, of Dorking, Surrey (d 1969), and Enid Kathleen Nicholls (*née* Ewynne); *b* 19 Feb 1938; *Educ* King's Sch, Canterbury, St Johns Oxford (BA, MA); *m* 14 Oct 1967, Isobel Judith, da of Rev Canon Maurice Dean Verwood, of Dorset; 2 s (Jonathan b 1969, Christopher b 1972); *Career* asst princ Admty 1962, MOD 1964, asst private sec MOD for RN 1965-66 (princ 1966), directing staff RCDS 1971-73, asst private sec to Sec of State for Defence 1974-75, (asst sec 1974); def cnsllr UK Delgn to MBFR Talks Vienna 1977-80 (dep head of delgn 1978-80), asst under sec of state 1984, under sec Cabinet Office 1986; *Recreations* choral singing, genealogy, mountain walking; *Clubs* Utd Oxford and Cambridge Univ; Cabinet Office, 70 Whitehall, London SW1A 2AS

NICHOLLS, Patrick Charles Martyn; MP (C) Teignbridge 1983-; s of Douglas Charles Martyn Nicholls (d 1950), and Margaret Josephine Nicholls (d 1982); *b* 14 Nov 1948; *Educ* St Peter's Harefield, Redrice Coll; *m* 1976, Bridget Elizabeth Fergus, da of Edward Alan Owens, of Otterton, Devon; 1 s, 2 da; *Career* slr 1974; jt sec Legal Ctee 1983-, co-opted memb Soc of Con Lawyers 1983-; vice chm exec ctee Soc of Cons Lawyers; memb: standing ctee on Police and Criminal Evidence Bill, standing ctee on Video Recordings Bill; PPS to Rt Hon J S Gummer, min of state MAFF July 1986-May87, parly under sec of state Dept of Employment 1987-; *Recreations* skiing, opera, theatre and historical research; *Style—* Patrick Nicholls, Esq, MP; Glebe House, Farringdon, Nr Exeter, Devon; House of Commons, London SW1A 0AA (☎ 01 219 4095)

NICHOLLS, Philip; CB (1976); s of William Herbert Nicholls (d 1960); *b* 30 August 1914; *Educ* Malvern, Pembroke Coll Cambridge; *m* 1955, Sue, *née* Shipton; 2 s (Mark William, Paul Conolly); *Career* Maj 8 Bn Worcestershire Regt HQ E Africa Cmd (mil asst to GOC-in-C), Allied Cmmn for Austria, FO (German section) 1940-48, asst master Malvern Coll 1936 (sr classical master 1939, resigned 1947), HM tresy 1949-70, a forestry cmmr (Fin and Admin) 1970-75, memb of cncl Malvern Coll 1960- (vice-chm 1963-88); *Style—* Philip Nicholls Esq, CB; Barnard's Green House, Malvern, Worcestershire (☎ 0684 574446)

NICHOLLS, Sue; *see*: Harmar-Nicholls, Hon Susan

NICHOLLS, Rt Rev Vernon Sampson; s of Ernest C Nicholls (d 1957), of Truro, Cornwall, and Ellen Nicholls (d 1970); *b* 3 Sept 1917; *Educ* Truro Sch, Durham Univ, Clifton Theol Coll Bristol; *m* 1943, Phyllis, da of Edwin Potter (d 1965), of Stratford-on-Avon; 1 s, 1 da; *Career* chaplain to the Forces 1944-46, vicar of Meopham 1946-56, rural dean of Cobham 1954-56, vicar and rural dean of Walsall 1956-67, archdeacon of Birmingham 1967-74, bishop of Sodor and Man 1974-83; memb of the Tynwald 1974-83; hon asst bishop of Coventry 1983-; JP (IOM) 1974-83; *Recreations* gardening, meeting people; *Clubs* Royal Cwlth Soc; *Style—* The Rt Rev Vernon Nicholls; Thie My Chree, 4 Winston Close, Hathaway Park, Shottery, Stratford-on-Avon CV37 9ER (☎ 0789 294478)

NICHOLLS, Hon Mrs (Virginia Jean Furse Maud); da of Baron Redcliffe-Maud, GCB, CBE (Life Peer; d 1982); *b* 1943; *m* 1970, Roger Frank Nicholls; *Style—* The Hon Mrs Nicholls; Ennore, Kenwyn Rd, Truro, Cornwall

NICHOLS, Andrew Charles; s of Dudley Nichols (d 1965), of Kent, and Winifred Gertrude, *née* Burrows (d 1982); *b* 23 April 1949; *Educ* Cranbrook, Bristol Univ (BA, BArch), Univ of Pennsylvania (MLA); *m* 15 Sept 1978, Evelyn Margaret, da of Stewart Gould; 1 s (Christopher b 1984), 1 da (Louisa Madeleine b 1988); *Career* architect and landscape planner in practice as Hutton Nichols Partnership 1979-, lectr Univ of Bristol 1977-79, dir Hawthorn Farm 1984-87; RIBA 1974, ALI 1978; *Style—* Andrew C Nichols, Esq; Pond House, Northend, Henley-on-Thames, Oxon RG9 6LG (☎ 0491 63354, fax 0491 63 228)

NICHOLS, Rev Barry Edward; s of Albert Owen Nichols (d 1986), and Gwendoline Cicely, *née* Rumbold (d 1981); *b* 23 Jan 1940; *Educ* Epsom Coll, Southwark Ordination Course; *m* 28 Feb 1970, Anne, da of Frederick Albert Hastings, BEM, of 19 Dulverton Court, Adelaide Rd, Surbiton, Surrey; 1 s (Stephen b 1977), 2 da (Sarah b 1972, Rebecca b 1977); *Career* joined Arthur Young 1957 (ptnr 1970-, firm managing ptnr 1983-85); ordained priest C of E 1970, hon curate St Andrews and St Marks Surbiton Surrey 1969-; FCA ; *Recreations* gardening, reading, swimming; *Clubs* Northern Counties; *Style—* The Rev Barry Nichols; 32 Corkran Rd, Surbiton, Surrey KT6 6PN (☎ 01 390 3032); Arthur Young, Rolls House, 7 Rolls Building, Fetter Lane, London EC4A 1NH (☎ 01 831 7130, fax 01 405 2147, telex 888604)

NICHOLS, Sir Edward Henry; TD; s of Henry James Nichols; *b* 27 Sept 1911; *Educ* Queen Elizabeth GS Mansfield, Selwyn Coll Cambridge (BA, LLB); *m* 1941, Gwendoline Hetty Elgar; 1 s; *Career* served WWII RA (TA), Hon Lt-Col; slr 1936, town clerk and clerk of peace Derby 1949-53, town clerk of London 1953-74; Hon DLitt City Univ; kt 1972; *Clubs* City Livery; *Style—* Sir Edward Nichols, TD; 35A The Avenue, Claygate, Surrey KT10 0RX (☎ 0372 65102)

NICHOLS, (Peter) John; s of Peter Nichols, of 3 Newington Ct, Bowdon, Cheshire, and Edith Nan, *née* Rhodes; *b* 24 Dec 1949; *Educ* Shrewsbury, Leicester Univ (BSc); *m* 15 Sep 1973, Elaine Mary, da of William H W Chadwick, of 38 Hillington Rd, Sale, Ches; 2 s (James b 1979, Matthew b 1982), 1 da (Katharine b 1986); *Career* J N Nichols (Vimto) plc 1970- (dir 1978-86, md 1986-); *Recreations* golf, sailing, skiing; *Clubs* Ringway Golf; *Style—* John Nichols, Esq; Southwood, Hargate Drive, Hale, Cheshire; J N Nichols (Vimto) plc, Ledson Road, Wythenshawe, Manchester M23 9NL (☎ 061 998 8801, fax 061 998 9446, car tel 0836 744326, telex 667482)

NICHOLS, Kenneth Gordon; s of Harry Archibald Nichols (d 1976), and Christina McKenzie Young (d 1973); *b* 4 Jan 1925; *Educ* Uppingham, Downing Coll Cambridge; *m* 18 Dec 1946, Dorothy Karalena, da of Robert Simpson Friends (d 1932), 2 s (Stephen b 1951 (decd 1970), Harry b 1953), 1 da (Caroline b 1956); *Career* served WWII Flt Lt RAF, fighter pilot Middle East 1943-46; former chm Belfast Linen Gp for; dir: Restwell Belfast Linen Warehouse Cop Ltd, Wholesale Textile Co Cambridge Ltd, DM & KG Nichols Ltd; pres City of London Linen Trades Assoc 1977; *Recreations* golf; *Clubs* RAF (London), Gog Magog Golf, Cambridge, Woburn Golf and Country, Cannes Golf (France); *Style—* Kenneth Nichols, Esq; Trinity House Hills Rd, Cambridge CB2 2BE (☎ 247784); Belfast Linen Group, Coldhams Rd, Cambridge (☎ 0223 411311)

NICHOLS, Peter Richard; s of Richard George (d 1965), of Bristol, and Violet Annie Ladysmith Poole; *b* 31 July 1927; *Educ* Bristol GS, Bristol Old Vic Theatre Sch; *m* 1960, Thelma, da of George Reginald Reed, of Bristol; 1 s (Daniel), 3 da (Abigail d 1971, Louise, Catherine); *Career* author and playwright; screen and stage plays: The Gorge (TV), A Day in the Death of Joe Egg (stage), Forget-me-not Lane (stage), Privates on Parade (stage and screen), Passion Play (stage), Poppy (stage musical); FRSL; *Books* Feeling You're Behind (autobiography, 1984); *Recreations* planning to overthrow the existing political structure, playing the vibraphone; *Style—* Peter Nichols, Esq; Old Rectory, Hopesay, Nr Craven Arms, Shropshire; Agent: Margaret Ramsay Ltd, 14 Goodwin's Ct, WC2 (☎ 01 240 0691)

NICHOLS, Robin Anthony; s of Thomas George Nichols (d 1981), of Eastcote, Middx, and Irene Joan Buck; gs of George Nichols, OBE (despatches thrice, d 1935); *b* 28 April 1944; *Educ* Pinner Co GS, City of London Coll for Chartered Bldg Soc Exams; *m* 5 March 1967, Paula Theresa, da of Joseph Severen Spiegelhalter (d 1983), of Wembley, Middx); 1 s (Grant Anthony b 1970), 1 da (Sarah Kate b 1973); *Career* dir and chief exec Greenwich Bldg Soc 1981-; dir Bldg Soc Ombudsman Co Ltd 1987; memb: cncl of Bldg Soc Assoc 1983, and for Bldg Soc Ombudsman (1987); govr Blackheath HS 1987-; FCBSI; *Recreations* sport, music, theatre, MENSA; *Style—* Robin Nichols, Esq; 15 Highfield Drive, Shortlands, Bromley, Kent BR2 0RX (☎ 01 460 3369); 279 Greenwich High Rd, London SE10 8NL (☎ 01 858 8212)

NICHOLS, Rt Rev Mgr Vincent Gerard; s of Henry Joseph Nichols, and Mary Nichols, *née* Russell; *b* 8 Nov 1945; *Educ* St Mary's Coll Crosby, Gregorian Univ Rome (STL, PhL), Manchester Univ (MA), Loyola Univ Chicago (MEd); *Career* chaplain St John Rigby VI Form Coll Wigan 1972-77, priest in the inner city of Liverpool 1978-81, dir of Upholland Northern Inst Lancs (with responsibility for the in-service training of clergy and for adult Christian educn 1981-84); advsr Cardinal Hume and Archbishop Worlock at the Int Synods of Bishops 1980, 1983 and 1987, gen sec Bishops' Conf of England and Wales 1984-; *Style—* Rt Rev Mgr Vincent Nichols; Bishops' Conference Secretariat, 39 Eccleston Sq, London SW1V 1PD (☎ 01 630 8220)

NICHOLSON, Andrew Broadfoot; s of John Nicholson, of Kidsdale, Whithorn, Newton-Stewart, and Helen, *née* Macfie; *b* 20 June 1933; *Educ* Sedbergh, Aberdeen Univ (BSc); *m* 11 April 1973, Joanna Mary, da of Noel Bechely-Crundall (d 1968), of Membury House, Ramsbury, Wilts; 2 s (Rupert, Charles); *Career* Nat Serv 1956-57; cmmnd KOSB; chm Bell Lawrie Ltd 1986-; memb Stock Exchange 1962-; *Recreations* shooting, fishing, skiing; *Clubs* Caledonian; *Style—* Andrew Nicholson, Esq; The Old Manse, Bedrule, Denholm, Hawick; Erskine House, 68 Queen St, Edinburgh (☎ 031 225 2566)

NICHOLSON, Air Cdre Angus Archibald Norman; CBE (1961), AE (1945); s of Maj Norman Nicholson (d 1949), of Hoylake, and Alice Frances, da of Rt Hon Sir Archibald Salvidge, PC, KBE, leader of Liverpool City Cncl 1909-28 (d 1969); *b* 8 Mar 1919; *Educ* Eton, King's Coll Cambridge; *m* 1943, Joan Mary, da of Ernest Beaumont; 1 s, 1 da; *Career* flying duties, Bomber Cmd and Middle East 1939-45, Directing Staff Staff Coll 1948-51, Bomber Cmd 1954-58, Staff of Chief of Def Staff 1958-61, CO RAF Northolt 1962-63, dir Def Plans (Air) MOD 1966-68, def advsr to British High Cmmn in Canada and head British Def Liaison Staff Ottawa 1968-70, ret 1970; dep sec-gen Cncl of European and Japanese Nat Shipowners' Assocs (CENSA) 1971-80 (ret); MBIM, FBIM; *Recreations* sailing, golf, tennis, music; *Clubs* Army & Navy, Leander, Royal Lymington Yacht; *Style—* Air Cdre Angus Nicholson, CBE, AE

NICHOLSON, Hon Mrs (Ariadne Maria); *née* Balfour; da of 4 Baron Kinross, OBE, TD; *b* 31 Jan 1939; *m* 1961, Richard, s of late Robert Nicholson, and Mrs Kenneth Seth-Smith (stepmother of Viscountess Buckmaster); 3 s, 1 da; *Style—* The Hon Mrs Nicholson; Ochiltree Cottage, Linlithgow, W Lothian

NICHOLSON, Sir Bryan Hubert; s of Reginald Hubert Nicholson (d 1977); *b* 6 June 1932; *Educ* Palmers Sch Grays, Oriel Coll Oxford; *m* 1956, Mary Elizabeth, da of Albert Cyril Harrison; 2 children; *Career* Nat Serv Lt; chm Rank Xerox (UK) Ltd 1980-84 (dir 1972-80); dir: Rank Xerox Ltd 1977-87, Sperry Rand Ltd 1969-72, Sperry Rand (Aust) Pty Ltd 1966-69, Evode Gp plc 1981-84, Baker Perkings Hldgs plc 1982-84; chm Manpower Services Commission 1984-87; chm Post Off 1987-, CNAA 1988-, Nationalised Industs Chms Gp 1988-; memb NEDC 1985; kt 1987; *Recreations* tennis, bridge; *Clubs* Utd Oxford and Cambridge Univ; *Style—* Sir Bryan Nicholson; Point Piper, Lilley Drive, Kingswood, Surrey KT20 6JA

NICHOLSON, Charles Christian; s and h of Sir John Norris Nicholson, 2 Bt, KBE, CIE; *b* 15 Dec 1941; *Educ* Ampleforth, Magdalen Oxford; *m* 1975, Martha Rodman, da of Stuart Warren Don, and wid of Niall Hamilton Anstruther-Gough-Calthorpe; *Style—* Charles Nicholson, Esq; Turners Green Farm, Elvetham, Hants

NICHOLSON, Clive Anthony Holme; s of Dennis Thomas Holme Nicholson, MBE, of Barnet, Herts, and Eileen Blanche, *née* Fitkin; *b* 24 Feb 1947; *Educ* Merchant Taylors'; *m* 12 Dec 1970, Patricia Mary, da of Ernest Johnson (d 1979), of Lancaster; 3 da (Amanda b 5 Dec 1972, Zoe b 27 May 1975, Gemma b 8 Aug 1981); *Career* CA; Deloitte & Co, Lusaka, Zambia 1970-72; Saffery Champness (formerly Safferys) 1972- (ptnr 1975-); Liveryman Merchant Taylors' Co 1974; FCA 1979, FHKSA 1985; *Style—* Clive A H Nicholson, Esq; La Hougue, La Hougue Road, Vale, Guernsey, CI (☎ 0481 47560); PO Box 141, La Tonnelle House, Les Banques, St Sampson, Guernsey, CI (☎ 0481 21374; fax, 0481 22046; telex, 4191487 Rysaf G)

NICHOLSON, Hon Sir David Eric; s of J A Nicholson; *b* 26 May 1904; *m* 1934, Cecile (d 1987), da of M E Smith; 2 s, 2 da; *Career* dir; MLA Qld 1950-72, speaker of Legislative Assembly 1960-72; kt 1972; *Style—* The Hon Sir David Nicholson; Villa 37, Peninsula Gdns, 65 Miller St, Kipper Ring, Qld: 4020 Aust

NICHOLSON, David John; MP (C) Taunton 1987-; s of John Francis Nicholson, of Cliff Cottage, Moelfre, Anglesey, N Wales, and Lucy, *née* Warburton Battrum;; *b* 17 August 1944; *Educ* Queen Elizabeth GS Blackburn, Christ Church Oxford (MA); *m* 23 May 1981, Frances Mary, da of Brig T E H Helby (d 1984), of Avon House, Aveton Gifford, nr Kingsbridge, S Devon; 1 s (Julian b 1984), 1 da (Eleanor b 1986); *Career* head of political section Cons Res Dept 1974-82, dir Home Affairs Assoc of Br C of C 1982-86 (dep dir gen 1986-87), sec Cons backbench Social Security ctee; *Books* The Leo Amery Diaries (Vol I 1980), The Empire at Bay (Vol II 1988); *Recreations* travel, gardening, music, the country; *Clubs* Reform, Taunton Cons, Wellington Cons; *Style—* David J Nicholson, Esq, MP; Allshire, nr Brushford, Somerset EX16 9JG; House of Commons, (☎ 01 219 3000)

NICHOLSON, Dennis Thomas Holme; MBE (1946); s of Thomas Holme Nicholson, OBE (d 1954), and Ethel Lilian, *née* Turner (d 1956); *b* 6 May 1921; *Educ* Merchant Taylors'; *m* 22 Sept 1945, Eileen Blanche, da of S A Fitkin; 2 s (Clive Anthony Holme b 1947, Paul Thomas Holme b 1957), 1 da (Wendy Barbara Holme b 1950); *Career* served WWII in HAC and Border Regt; CA 1949-, ptnr Saffery Champness 1950-81, ret 1986; dir: Berry Star Quest plc, GT Japan Investmt Tst plc; Freeman City of London, Master Worshipful Co of Merchant Taylors 1983; FCA; Cross of Knight of the Royal Order of the Phoenix (with swords) 1946; FCA; *Recreations* sport, gardening, charitable activities; *Clubs* MCC, Totteridge Cricket, Special Forces, Barnet RFC; *Style—* Dennis Nicholson, Esq, MBE; Gilts, 62 Hadley Highstone, Barnet, Herts EN5 4PU (☎ 01 449 9664)

NICHOLSON, Hon Mrs (Diana Mary); *née* Seely; da of 4 Baron Mottistone, and Anthea Christine, da of Victor McMullan of N I; *b* 30 July 1954; *Educ* The Queens Sch

Chester; *m* 1977, Edward Anthony Spours Nicholson, s of Anthony John Nicholson; 1 s (Alexander James Edward b 8 Oct 1988); *Career* Fodor Guidebooks NY 1978-79, Simon & Shuster Inc NY 1979-80, ed Marmac Publishing Co Atlanta USA 1980-83, mangr Dark Blues Mgmnt Ltd 1983-86; freelance writer 1986-; *Recreations* sailing, skiing; *Clubs* Island Sailing; *Style*— The Hon Mrs Nicholson; Plaza de Maria Guerrero 1, El Viso, 28002 Madrid, Spain

NICHOLSON, Edward Rupert; s of Alfred Edward Nicholson (d 1950), and Elise, *née* Dobson (d 1949); *b* 17 Sept 1909; *Educ* Whitgift Sch; *m* 18 June 1935, Mary Peggy (d 1983), da of Richard Elley (d 1936); 1 s (Anthony Richard b 1939), 1 da (Brenda Mary (Mrs Wright) b 1943); *Career* ptnr Peat Marwick (Mitchell) McLintock 1949 (joined 1933), liquidator Davies Investmts Ltd Wimbledon 1967, receiver Rolls Royce Ltd 1971, liquidator Court Line Ltd 1974; chm tech advsy ctee Inst of CA in England & Wales 1969-70; govr Whitgift Fndn 1976- (chm 1978-), chm Croydon Business Venture Ltd 1983-, memb PO Review Ctee 1976; Liveryman Worshipful Co of Horners 1964 (Master 1984); FCA 1932; *Recreations* golf, gardening; *Clubs* Caledonian, Walton Heath; *Style*— Rupert Nicholson, Esq; Grey Wings, The Warren, Ashtead, Surrey KT21 2SL (☎ 03 22 72655)

NICHOLSON, Emma Harriet; MP (C) Torridge and W Devon 1987-; da of Sir Godfrey Nicholson, 1 Bt, *qv*; *b* 16 Oct 1941; *Educ* St Mary's Sch Wantage, RAM; *m* 9 May 1987, Michael Harris Caine, s of Sir Sydney Caine, KCMG, *qv*; *Career* ICL computer programmer, programming instr, systems analyst 1963-66, computer conslt John Tyzack & Ptnrs 1967-69, McLintock, Mann & Whinney Murray 1969-73, computer and gen mgmnt conslt; dir of fundraising Save the Children Fund 1977-85 (joined 1974), vice chm CP 1983-87; dep chm: The Duke of Edinburgh's Award 30th Anniversary Tribute 1986, Int Project 1987; chm: The Friends of The Duke of Edinburgh's Award Scheme 1988-, Suzy Lamplugh Educn Project 1988-; patron CRUSAID; pres: Hatherleigh dist branch Save The Children Fund, Plymouth and West Devon Cassette, Talking Newspaper; memb bd Howard League, Fellow Elect, Indust and Parl Tst; *Recreations* church music, walking; *Clubs* The Reform; *Style*— Emma Nicholson MP; c/o The House of Commons, London SW1A 0AA

NICHOLSON, Rev Prof Ernest Wilson; s of Ernest Tedford Nicholson (d 1977), Veronica Muriel, *née* Wilson (d 1963); *b* 26 Sept 1938; *Educ* Portadown Coll, Trinity Coll Dublin (BA, MA), Glasgow Univ (PhD), Cambridge Univ (BD, DD), Oxford Univ (DD by incorporation); *m* 5 April 1962, (Annie) Hazel Josephine, da of Samuel John Jackson; 1 s (Peter), 3 da (Rosalind, Kathryn, Jane); *Career* lectr in hebrew and semitic languages Trinity Coll Dublin 1962-67, univ lectr in divinity Cambridge Univ 1967-79, fell Wolson Coll 1967-69, fell and chaplain Pembroke Coll 1969-79 (dean 1973-79), Oriel prof of the Interpretation of Holy Scripture Univ of Oxford 1979- (fell); FBA 1987; *Recreations* music, walking; *Style*— The Rev Prof Ernest Nicholson; 19 Five Mile Drive, Oxford OX2 8HT (☎ 0685 58759); Oriel College, Oxford OX1 4EW (☎ 0865 276 583)

NICHOLSON, Lady; Evelyn Odell; da of late Capt R G Westropp (late RA), of Egypt and Camberley, and late Mary Helena Westropp; *b* 7 August 1904; *m* 1926, Gen Sir Cameron Gordon Graham Nicholson, GCB, KBE, DSO, MC (d 1979); 1 s, 2 da; *Style*— Lady Nicholson; Greyhayes, St Breward, Bodmin, Cornwall PL30 4LP

NICHOLSON, George Howard Joseph; er s of Roydon Joseph Nicholson, of Amberley, W Sussex, and Evelyn Sophia Carlton, *née* Reader; *b* 4 April 1936; *Educ* Wellington; *m* 13 Aug 1974, Adele Janet, er da of (George) Richard Barbour, of Bolesworth Castle, Tattenhall, Chester; 2 s (Joseph William b 1975, Oliver Christian b 1977); *Career* Nat Serv 2/Lt King's Dragoon Gds 1954, Lt Inns of Ct Regt (TA) 1956, British Colombia Regt (Canadian Militia) 1957-60; cub reporter Vancouver Sun 1956, advtg exec Erwin Wasey Ruthrauf and Ryan 1959, appeals organiser shelter 1967, campaign dir Craigmyle and Co 1972, appeal sec Br Olympic Assoc 1978-; former borough cncllr RBK and C, parly candidate (C) Bermondsey and Rotherhithe 1970; Liveryman Leathersellers Co (Warden 1986-87); *Recreations* field sports; *Clubs* Brooks's; *Style*— George Nicholson, Esq; 16 Chelsea Embankment, London SW3 4LA (☎ 01 352 9202); Coomb Dale Lodge, Bickerton, Malpas Cheshire; British Olympic Association, 1 Wandsworth Plain, London SW18 1EH (☎ 01 874 8978, fax 01 871 9104, telex 932312 BOA G)

NICHOLSON, Sir Godfrey; 1 Bt (UK 1958), of Winterbourne, Royal Co of Berks; s of Richard Francis Nicholson (d 1940), of Woodcott, Hants, and Helen Violet Portal (d 1927); *b* 9 Dec 1901; *Educ* Winchester, Ch Ch Oxford; *m* 1936, Lady Katharine Constance, *née* Lindsay (d 1972), da of 27 Earl of Crawford and 10 Balcarres (d 1940); 4 da (*see* Richard Luce, Sir John Montgomery Cunninghame, Michael Caine); *Heir* none; *Career* served with Royal Fus and Commandos 1939-42; MP (C): Morpeth 1931-35, Farnham Div Surrey 1937-66; distiller; FSA; *Clubs* Pratt's, Athenaeum; *Style*— Sir Godfrey Nicholson, Bt; Bussock Hill House, Newbury, Berks (☎ 0635 248260)

NICHOLSON, (Charles) Gordon (Brown); QC (1982); s of William Addison Nicholson, OBE, of Edinburgh (d 1987), and Jean Brown (d 1967); *b* 11 Sept 1935; *Educ* George Watson's Coll Edinburgh, Edinburgh Univ (MA, LLB); *m* 1963, Hazel Mary, da of Robert Riddle Nixon (d 1976); 2 s (David, Robin); *Career* barr Scotland 1961, advocate depute 1968-70; Sheriff of: Dumfries and Galloway at Dumfries 1970-76, Lothian and Borders at Edinburgh 1976-82; cmmr Scotish Law Cmmn 1982-; *Books* The Law and Practice of Sentencing in Scotland 1981 (supplement 1985); *Recreations* music; *Clubs* New (Edinburgh); *Style*— Sheriff Gordon Nicholson, QC; 1A Abbotsford Park, Edinburgh EH10 5DX (☎ 031 447 4300); Scottish Law Cmmn, 140 Causewayside, Edinburgh (☎ 031 668 2131)

NICHOLSON, Graham Beattie; s of John Arthur Nicholson (d 1975), and Ena Patricia; *b* 22 Feb 1949; *Educ* Bloxham Sch, Trinity Hall Cambridge; *m* 30 Oct 1982, Pamela Soel Luang; 1 da (Vanessa b 1978); *Career* slr Freshfields: NY off 1979-80, ptnr 1980, Singapore off 1980-83, manging ptnr co dept 1986-; memb City of London Slrs co 1983; memb Law Soc; *Recreations* music, sailing, racquet sports; *Style*— Graham Nicholson, Esq; Grindall House, 25 Newgate St, London, EC1, (☎ 01 606 6677)

NICHOLSON, Lady; Jean; da of late Alexander Landles; *m* 1927, Sir Harold Stanley Nicholson, 14 Bt (d 1961 when the title became dormant); *Style*— Lady Nicholson; Brough Lodge, Fetlar, Shetland, Grimista, Shetland

NICHOLSON, Col John Aubrey Hastings; MC (1944), TD (1955 and 2 bars), DL (1974); s of Cyril Aubrey Nicholson (d 1974); *b* 27 Mar 1920; *Educ* Uppingham, Queens' Coll Cambridge; *m* 1946, Dawn Eanswythe Lillian, *née* Leighton; 1 s, 3 da; *Career* served WWII, NW Europe, Col; stockbroker; ret; *Recreations* shooting, fishing, sailing, golf; *Clubs* Hawks (Cambridge), Sheffield, Sicklehome Golf; *Style*— Col John Nicholson, MC, TD; Quinton, Saltergate, Bamford in the Peak, Sheffield S30 2BE (☎ Hope Valley 0433 51429)

NICHOLSON, Sir John Norris; 2 Bt (UK 1912), of Harrington Gdns, Royal Borough of Kensington, KBE (1971), CIE (1946); s of Capt George Crosfield Norris Nicholson, (ka 1916), s of 1 Bt, and Hon Evelyn Izme, JP (who m 2 1917, as his 2 w, 1 Baron Mottistone, CB, CMG, DSO), da of 10 Baron and 1 Viscount Elibank and gs of Sir Charles Norris Nicholson, 1 Bt (d 1918); *b* 19 Feb 1911; *Educ* Winchester, Trinity Coll Cambridge; *m* 1938, (Vittoria) Vivien, da of Percy Trewhella, of Villa St Andrea, Taormina, Sicily; 2 s, 2 da; *Heir* s, Charles Christian Nicholson; *Career* Lt 4 Bn Cheshire Regt 1939, Capt 1940, min of Shipping 1941, rep of min of War Tport in Delhi; formerly chm Ocean Steamship Co Ltd, Martin's Bank Ltd; dir: Barclays Bank, Royal Insurance Co; pres Chamber of Shipping 1970; JP and Vice-Ld Lt Isle of Wight 1974-80; Keeper of the Rolls Isle of Wight 1974-86; Ld-Lt 1980-86; *Clubs* Royal Yacht Sqdn (Cdre 1980-86); *Style*— Sir John Nicholson, Bt, KBE, CIE, HM Lord-Lieut of the Isle of Wight; Mottistone Manor, Isle of Wight (☎ 0983 740322)

NICHOLSON, (John) Leonard; s of Percy Merwyn Nicholson (d 1938), and (Jane) Winifred, *née* Morris (d 1965); *b* 18 Feb 1916; *Educ* Stowe, Inst Actuaries, LSE (BSc, MSc); *Career* Inst Statistics Oxford Univ 1940-47, Miny of Home Security 1943-44, statistician 1947-52, chief statistician 1952-68 Central Statistical Off Simon res fell Manchester Univ 1962-63, chief econ advsr DHSS 1968-76, prof quantitative econs Brunel Univ 1972-74, sr res fell Policy Studies Inst 1976-81, fell Rockafella Fndn 1984; fell Royal Statistical Soc 1940-; memb: Int Assoc Res Income and Wealth 1952-, Int Inst Public Finance 1969-; *Books* L.....; *Publications* Variations in Working Class Family Expenditure (1949), The Interim Index of Industrial Production (1949), Redistribution of Income in the UK (1965), Poverty Inequality and Class Structure (contrib ed D E Wedderburn, 1974), The Personal Distribution of Incomes (contrib ed A B Atkinson, 1976), Public Economics and Human Resources (contrib V Halberstadt and A J Culyer 1977), Human Resources Employment and Development vol 2: Concepts, Measurement and Long Run Perspective (ed P Streeten and H Maier 1983), Social Security Research (DHSS 1977), Definition and Measurement of Poverty (DHSS 1979), numerous articles in economic and statistical jls; *Recreations* enjoyment of music, painting, real tennis; *Clubs* MCC, Queens Arts Theatre; *Style*— Leonard Nicholson, Esq; 53 Frognal, London NW3 6YA (☎ 01 435 8015)

NICHOLSON, (Edward) Max; CB (1948), CVO (1971); s of Edward Prichard Nicholson (d 1945), of Hangersley, Ringwood, Hants, and Constance Caroline, *née* Oldmeadow (d 1945); *b* 12 July 1904; *Educ* Sedbergh, Hertford Coll Oxford; *m* 1, 6 Aug 1932 (m dis 1964), Eleanor Mary Lloyd, da of George Edward Crawford, of Putney, London; 2 s (Piers b 1934, Thomas Gavin b 1938); m 2, 1965, Marie Antoinette Mauerhofer; 1 s (David Ian b 1965); *Career* controller of lit Miny Info 1939 resigned Oct 1939, head econ & inter allied branch Miny Shipping, head allocation of tonnage div and miny rep on Anglo-US combined shipping adjustment bd Miny War Transp 1941-45, chm Anglo-Sov Shipping Ctee 1941-45, attended Quebec, Yalta and Potsdam Confs, head off of Lord Pres of the Cncl 1945-52, chm Official ctee Festival of Br 1951; memb: advsy cncl on Scientific Policy 1948-64, Cwlth Scientific Ctee; dir gen Nature Conservancy 1952-65; chm: Environmental Ctee of London Celebrations for Queen's Jubilee, London Looks Forward Conf 1977; chm Land Use Consits 1965-; asst ed The Week-end Review London 1930-33, gen sec Pol and Econ Planning (PEP) 1933-39, chm Br Tst for Ornithology 1947-49 (first hon sec 1933-39), tstee The Observer 1952-65, chm ctee to organise World Wildlife Fund 1961; memb special ctee of Int Cncl of Scientific Unions for Int Biological Prog (convener conservation section 1963-74), pres RSPB 1980-85; scientific fell Zoological Soc, hon FRIBA; hon memb: Br Ecological Soc, fell American Ornithologists Union, Royal Town Planning Inst; Europa Preis fur Landespflege 1972; FSA, FRGS, MBOU; Commandeur (Netherlands) Order of the Golden Ark 1973; *Books* Birds in England (1926), How Birds Live (1927), Birds and Men (1951), and other books on ornithology, most lately as an ed of the 7-vol Oxford Birds of the Western Palearctic (1977-), Other books include The System (1967), The Environmental Revolution (1970), The New Environmental Age (1987); *Clubs* Athenaeum; *Style*— Max Nicholson, Esq, CB, CVO; 13 Upper Cheyne Row, London SW3; Land Use Consultants, 43 Chalton St, London NW1 (☎ 01 383 5784, fax 01 383 4798)

NICHOLSON, Pamela Mary Reina; *née* de Pommard; da of Boris Nicoloff de Pommard (d 1980), of Paris, and Aime, *née* Salomon; *b* 11 Sept 1937; *Educ* Northlands Buenos Aires Argentina, Roedean Brighton Sussex, La Chatelainie St Blaise Neuchatel Switzerland; *m* 10 May 1958, William John Nicholson, s of William Douglas Marshall Nicholson, JP (d 1986); 2 s ((William) Guy Marshall b 8 Jan 1961, Tom Marshall b 8 June 1985), 1 da (Deborah Mae Marshall (Mrs Bigley) b 15 May 1962); *Career* mktg and sales dir William Nicholson & Son Ltd Leeds 1970-85 (dir 1962-85), ptnr Art Study Tours 1978-, dir Country Travels Ltd 1987-; memb: Nat Bee Keepers Assoc, regnl Br Heart Fndn 1968-73, regnl Royal Br Legion 1968-, Womens Inst; Nat Assoc Decorative and Fine Art Socs: hon sec and chm Harrogate gp, memb nat exec cncl, fndr chm and vice-pres Nidd Valley branch; *Recreations* photography, skiing, apiculture, painting, writing; *Style*— Mrs William Nicholson; South Hill, Whixley, York YO5 8AR (☎ 0423 330533)

NICHOLSON, Paul Douglas; DL (Co Durham 1980); eld s of Frank Douglas Nicholson, TD, DL (d 1984), and Pauline, yr da of Maj Sir Thomas Lawson-Tancred, 9 Bt; *b* 7 Mar 1938; *Educ* Harrow, Clare Coll Cambridge; *m* 1970, Sarah, 4 and yst da of Sir Edmund Bacon, 13 and 14 Bt, KG, KBE, TD (d 1982), of Raveningham Hall, Norfolk; 1 da; *Career* Lt Coldstream Guards; chm Vaux Gp plc 1976-; chm: northern region CBI 1977-79, northern bd Nat Enterprise Bd 1979-84, Northern Investors Ltd 1984, Tyne & Wear Urban Devpt Corpn 1987-; High Sheriff of Co Durham 1980-81; *Recreations* shooting, deerstalking, flying; *Clubs* Boodle's, Northern Counties; *Style*— Paul Nicholson Esq, DL; Quarry Hill, Brancepeth, Durham, DH7 8DW (☎ 091 3780275); Vaux Group plc, The Brewery, Sunderland, Tyne and Wear SR1 3AN (☎ 091 5676277)

NICHOLSON, Sir Robin Buchanan; s of Carroll and Nancy Nicholson; *b* 12 August 1934; *Educ* Oundle, St Catharine's Coll Cambridge (PhD); *m* 1958, Elizabeth Mary (d 1988), da of Sir Sydney Caffyn; 1 s, 2 da; *Career* md Inco Europe 1976-81 (dir 1975-81); chief sci advsr Cabinet Off 1981-85, metallurgist (prof metallurgy Manchester Univ 1966); dir Pilkington Bros plc 1986-; non exec dir: Rolls Royce plc 1986-, BP plc

1987-; memb SRC 1978-81; FEng, FRS, FIM, MInstP; kt 1985; *Clubs* MCC; *Style*— Sir Robin Nicholson; Whittington House, 8 Fisherwick Rd, Whittington, nr Lichfield, Staffs WS14 9LH (☎ 0543 432081)

NICKERSON, Robert Joseph; s of Sir Joseph Nickerson, of Lincoln, and Marjorie Allen, *née* Reynolds; *b* 28 Mar 1939; *Educ* Wintringham GS, Royal Agric Coll; *m* 6 July 1964, Prudence Ann, da of William Johnson (d 1976), of Grimsby, S Humberside; 1 s (Edward b 1966), 2 da (Mary-Anne b 1968, Victoria b 1975); *Career* dir: Robert Nickerson & Son 1957-, RJN Marine Ltd 1977-, R J Nickerson Ltd 1976-, South Reston Pigs Ltd 1972-, South Reston Pigs (Ombersley) Ltd 1972-, Robert Nickerson Farms 1980-, Flonico Ltd 1979-86, Lincs Co Peas 1983-86, Midwold Pea Growers 1973-84, Cotswold Pig Devpt Co 1972-80; yacht designer/builder and ocean racing skipper; successes in two-handed races in yachts to own design and build incl: Round Br Race first in class 1982, Azores and Back first monohull 1983, Vilamoura and Back first monohull 1983, Azores and Back first overall 1987; established record for monohulls from Falmouth to the Azores, completing the 1200 mile trip in under 6 days; *Recreations* sailing, shooting; *Clubs* Royal Ocean Racing, Royal Thames Yacht, Ocean Cruising, Cruising Assoc, Grimsby and Cleethorpes Yacht; *Style*— Robert J Nickerson, Esq; The Elms, Market Rasen, Lincolnshire LN8 3JW (☎ 0673 842 524, work 0673 842 870)

NICKLIN, Keith Richard; s of James Edward Nicklin (d 1979), of London, and May Marjorie; *b* 12 Dec 1935; *m* 12 Aug 1983, Judith Louise, da of Leslie Eric Whiting (d 1983); 2 da (Amy b 1983, Sophie b 1986); *Career* chm & chief exec: Nicklin Group Holdings Ltd; chm: Nicklin Advertising Ltd, John Bowler Associates Ltd; *Recreations* horse racing, fishing; *Clubs* Les Ambassadeurs; *Style*— Keith Nicklin, Esq; Benifold, Headley Down, Hampshire; Northway House, Bracknell, Berks (☎ 0344 51061, fax: 0344 55131, car ☎ 0836 240859)

NICKOLL, Eric William (Bill); s of Albert William Nickoll (d 1980), of Poole, Dorset, and Winifred Elizabeth, *née* Phillpot; *b* 25 April 1939; *Educ* Orange Hill GS; *m* 1, 1964 (m dis 1980), Dorothy Margaret, da of John Walley Holme, of Chorley, Lancs; 1 da (Rebecca b 1971); m 2, 1982, Margaret Rita, da of Phillip Reginald Dodge, of Hanwell, London; 1 s (Matthew b 1983); *Career* serv mangr NCR 1962-72; md: Gen Comp Sys Ltd 1972-84, Bell Tech Servs Ltd 1984-86; chm Intersect Ltd 1986-, md Kalamazoo plc 1987-89, pres Kalamazoo Inc 1988-; FBIM 1981, FIOD 1984; *Recreations* gardening, horology, woodworking, business; *Style*— Bill Nickoll, Esq; Manor Lodge, 12 Golden Manor, London W7 (☎ 01 567 7459); Kalamazoo plc, Northfield, Birmingham B31 2RW (☎ 021 411 2345, fax 021 475 7566, car tel 0836 660 633, telex 336700)

NICKOLLS, Malcolm Charles; s of Capt Charles Nickolls, RE (ret) (d 1985), and Lillian Rose, *née* Taylor; *b* 20 Mar 1944; *Educ* Rickmansworth GS, Brighton Coll of Art (Dip Arch), Thames Poly (Dip Landscape Arch); *m* 26 Aug 1967, Mary Delia Margaret, da of Ronald Edward Groves, CBE; 2 da (Joanna Helen b 1973, Deborah Sally b 1976); *Career* architect and landscape architect; private practice under style of NKD Architects 1975-; chm Professional Purposes 1982-, hon off ARCUK 1982-; princ building J Paul Getty Jnr Conservation Centre; publishing Electronic Art Studio, Photography and Computer Graphics; MRIBA 1970-; memb Landscape Inst 1977; MCIA 1976; memb cncl ARCUK 1979; *Recreations* cycling, computers, technology, science, invention; *Clubs* MENSA; *Style*— Malcolm Nickolls, Esq; Bishops Meadow, Weedon, Buckinghamshire (☎ 0296 641666); Friars House, Rickfords Hill, Aylesbury, Buckinghamshire (☎ 0296 88122, fax: 0296 436330, telecom gold 81:TWH129, one to one 16420001)

NICKSON, Sir David Wigley; KBE (1987), CBE (1981, DL Stirling and Falkirk 1982); Dr of Stirling Univ; s of Geoffrey Wigley Nickson (d 1983), and Janet Mary, *née* Dobie; *b* 27 Nov 1929; *Educ* Eton, RMA Sandhurst; *m* 18 Oct 1952, (Helen) Louise, da of late Lt-Col Louis Latrobe Cockcraft, DSO, MVO; 3 da (Felicity (Mrs James Lewis) b 3 Nov 1955, Lucy (Mrs Melfort Campbell) b 8 July 1959, Rosemary (Mrs George Petronanos) b 11 Feb 1963); *Career* vice-chm and gp md William Collins plc 1976-83; chm CBI Scotland 1979-81 (pres 1986-88), Scottish & Newcastle Breweries 1983- (dep chm 1982), Countryside Cmmn for Scotland 1983-85, Top Salary Review Body 1989, Scottish Devpt Agency 1989-, Atlantic Salesman Tst; dir: Gen Accident Fire & Life Assur Corpn plc, Clydesdale Bank plc 1981-88, Radio Clyde Ltd 1981-85, Edinburgh Investmt Tst plc; memb: Queen's Body Gd for Scotland (Royal Co of Archers), Scottish Ind Devpt Advsy Bd 1974-79, Scottish Econ Cncl 1979-, NEDC 1985-88; chm Atlantic Salmon Tst 1988-;; *Recreations* fishing, shooting, stalking, birdwatching, countryside; *Clubs* Boodle's, Flyfishers', MCC, Western (Glasgow); *Style*— Sir David Nickson, KBE, CBE, DL; Renagour House, Aberfoyle, Stirling FK8 3TF (☎ 08772 275); Scottish Development Agency, 120 Bothwell Street, Glasgow

NICKSON, Edward Anthony (Tony); DL (Lancashire 1982); s of Sydney Nickson (d 1945), and Elizabeth, *née* Bailey (d 1972); *b* 14 Dec 1918; *Educ* Shrewsbury; *m* 27 April 1946, Gammie, da of Alexander Gammie (d 1970), of Aberdeen; 2 da (Avril b 1949, Gill b 1952); *Career* CA 1949; hon tres Royal Lytham St Annes Golf 1963-86 (Capt 1968, and Centenary Year 1986); author; pres Lancashire Union of Golf Clubs 1983-84, chm English Golf Union Northern Gp of Counties 1986-; High Sheriff Lancs 1980-81; FCA; *Books* The Lytham Century (ed and publisher 1985); *Recreations* golf; *Clubs* Royal Lytham & St Annes Golf, Royal and Ancient Golf; *Style*— Tony Nickson, Esq, DL; 12 Regent Avenue, Lytham-St-Annes, Lancs FY8 4AB

NICKSON, Jack; s of Clifford Nickson (d 1965), of London W1, and Violet Lily, *née* Keen (d 1970); *b* 31 Jan 1926; *Educ* Malden Coll, London Univ (MB BS); *m* 1, 1954, (m dis) Betty Helena, da of William Kift (d 1941); 1 s (Martin Christopher b 1959), 1 da (Jacqueline b 1963); m 2, 14 July 1979, Elly Ingegärd, da of Ivar Jansson (d 1979), of Sweden; 1 s (Steven Erik b 1982), 1 da (Annika Christine b 1980); *Career* physician, princ gen practice 1958-86 (ret), currently orthopaedic physician conslt; dir Jaywood Properties Ltd 1964-87; *Recreations* ornithology, gardening, travel, pastel painting, inventing; *Style*— Dr Jack Nickson; Warren Down, Peasemore, Newbury, Berks (☎ 0635 248331); The Surgery, High St, Chieveley, Newbury (☎ 0635 248251)

NICKSON, John Howard; TD (1945); s of Howard Groves Davies Nickson (d 1953), and Nellie Nickson, *née* Leadbeater (d 1964); *b* 17 Nov 1912; *Educ* Mill Hill; *m* 1 Jan 1944, Pamela Kay, da of Maj Timothy Herbert Curtis (d 1966); 2 s (Simon John Curtis b 1945, Jeremy David Bedford b 1947), 1 da (Cecelia Anne b 1952); *Career* veteran Co HAC 1938- (joined B Battery 1932) served WWII cmmnd RA, TA 1938, Maj 1942, ret 1945; chm A Younger Ltd 1953-86 (dir 1934-); memb Worshipful Co of Furniture Makers (Master 1976-77); *Recreations* hunting, racing, gardening; *Clubs* East India, IOD; *Style*— John Nickson, Esq, TD; South Well, Marnhull, Dorset DT10 1NJ (☎ 0258 820294)

NICOL, Angus Sebastian Torquil Eyers; s of Henry James Nicol (d 1977), and Phyllis Mary, *née* Eyers; *b* 11 April 1933; *Educ* RNC Dartmouth; *m* 20 April 1968, Eleanor Denise, da of Lt Cdr William Lefevre Brodrick, RN (ka 1943); 2 da (Catharine Sophia b 1968, Augusta Devorgilla Margaret b 1972); *Career* RN (ret as Sub-Lt 1956), served HMS Euryalus, HM MMS 1630, HMS Brocklesby, and HMS Coquette; literary ed Connell & Co 1956-61; Bar Middle Temple 1963, recorder 1982-; founder memb and first vice-chm The Monday Club 1961; dir The Highland Soc of London 1981 (sec 1982), sr steward The Argyllshire Gathering 1983; conductor London Gaelic Choir 1985; tstee of URRAS Clann Mhic Neacail 1987-; publications: some poems and short stories (in Gaelic); *Recreations* shooting, fishing, sailing, music, Gaelic literature; *Clubs* Flyfishers'; *Style*— Angus Nicol, Esq; 5 Paper Buildings, Temple, London EC4Y 7HB (☎ 01 353 8494)

NICOL, Davidson Sylvester Hector; CMG (1964); s of Jonathan Josibiah Nicol (d 1952), and Winifred Clarissa Willoughby (d 1978); *b* 14 Sept 1924; *Educ* CMS Sch, Kaduna & Port Harcourt Nigeria, Prince of Wales Sch Sierra Leone, Cambridge Univ, London Univ; *m* 1950, Marjorie (m dis), da of Arthur Johnston (d 1958); 3 s (Charles, Olu, Syl), 2 da (Aina, Ayo); *Career* fell and supervisor in Nat Sciences and Medicine Christs Coll Cambridge 1957-59 (hon fell 1972), princ Fourah Bay Coll Sierra Leone 1960-68, first vice-chllr Univ of Sierra Leone 1966-68, permanent rep and ambass for Sierra Leone to UN 1969-71 (memb security cncl 1970-71, pres 1970, chm Ctee of 24-decolonisation, memb econ and social cncl 1969-70), high cmmr for Sierra Leone in London 1971-72, ambass to Norway, Sweden and Denmark 1971-72; dir: Central Bank of Sierra Leone, Consolidated African Selection Tst Ltd (London), Davesme Corpn; memb Cwlth PM's Conf London 1965 and 1969, Singapore 1971; pres World Fedn of UN Assoc 1983-, under sec-gen of the UN, exec dir UN Inst for Trg and Res (UNITAR) 1972-82, hon sr fell UNITAR 1983, vice pres Royal African Soc; Hon DSc: Newcastle upon Tyne, Kalamazoo Michigan, Laurentian Ontario; Hon DLitt, Davis and Elkins Coll, Hon LLD Leeds, Tuskegee Alabama, Hon LHD Barat Illinois, Independence Medal Sierra Leone 1961, Gd Cdr: Order of Rokel Sierra Leone 1974, Star of Africa Liberia 1974, International Peace Gold Medal (Indian Fedn UNAs) 1986; memb Royal Cwlth Soc; *Publications* Africa, A Subjective View (1964), contributions to: Malnutrition in African Mothers and Children (1954), HRH the Duke of Edinburgh's Study Conference (vol 2 1958), The Mechanism of Action of Insulin (1960), The Structure of Human Insulin (1960), New and Modern Roles for Commonwealth and Empire (1976); editor: Paths to Peace, Essays on the UN Security Council and its Presidency (1981), Regionalism and the New International Economic Order (1981), The United Nations Security Council: towards greater effectiveness (1981), Creative Women (1982), also contributed to Journal of Tropical Medicine, Biochemistry Journal, Nature, Journal of Royal African Soc, Times, Guardian, New Statesman, Encounter, West Africa; Journal Modern African Studies; *Recreations* rowing, travel, creative writing; *Clubs* Utd Oxford & Cambridge, Royal Cwlth Soc; *Style*— Dr Davidson Nicol, CMG; 140 Thornton Rd, Cambridge CB3 0ND, Cambs; Christ's Coll, Cambridge CB2 3BU

NICOL, Baroness (Life Peer, UK 1982), of Newnham, in Co of Cambridge; (Olive Mary) Wendy Nicol; JP (1972); da of James Rowe-Hunter (d 1962), and Harriet Hannah (d 1932); *b* 21 Mar 1923; *Educ* Cahir Sch Eire; *m* 1947, Dr Alexander Douglas Ian Nicol, s of Alexander Nicol (d 1962); 2 s, 1 da; *Career* Civil Serv 1943-48; memb: Cambs City Cncl 1972-82, Supplementary Benefits Tbnl 1976-78, Careers Serv Consultative Panel 1978-81; oppn dep chief whip 1987-; spokesman on natural environment; public serv in many and varied areas; *Recreations* reading, walking; *Style*— The Rt Hon the Lady Nicol, JP; 39 Grantchester Rd, Newnham, Cambridge CB3 9ED (☎ 0223 323 733)

NICOLL, Prof Donald MacGillivray; s of Rev George Manson Nicol (d 1957), and Mary Patterson, *née* MacGillivray; *b* 4 Feb 1912; *Educ* King Edward VII Sch Sheffield, St Paul's London, Pembroke Coll Cambridge (MA, PhD), Br Sch of Archaeology Athens; *m* 15 July 1950, Joan Mary, da of Lt-Col Sir Walter Campbell, KCIE (d 1974); 3 s (Christopher, Stephen, Theodore); *Career* Friends' Ambulance Unit 1942-46; lectr in classics Univ Coll Dublin 1952-64, visiting fell Dumbarton Oaks Washington DC 1964-65, visiting prof Byzantine history Univ of Edinburgh 1966-70, Indiana Univ 1965-66, sr lectr and reader in Byzantine history, Koraes prof of modern Greek prof and Byzantine history language and literature King's Coll London 1970-88, asst princ and vice-princ King's Coll London 1977-81, prof emeritus Univ of London 1988-; FBA, MRIA, FRHistS, FKC; *Books* The Despotate of Epiros 1204-1267 (1957), Meteora - The Rock Monasteries of Thessaly (second edn 1975), The Byzantine Family of Kantakouzenos (1968), The Last Centuries of Byzantium 1261-1453 (1972), Byzantium - its ecclesiastical history and relations with the western world (1972), Church and Society in the Last Centuries of Byzantium (1979), The End of the Byzantine Empire (1979), The Despotate of Epiros 1267-1479 - A Contribution to the History of Greece in the Middle Ages (1984), Studies in Late Byzantine History and Prosopography (1986), Byzantium and Venice - A Study in Diplomatic and Cultural Relations (1988); *Recreations* book-binding; *Clubs* Athenaeum; *Style*— Prof Donald Nicol; 16 Courtyards, Little Shelford, Cambridge CB2 5ER (☎ 0223 843 406); from 1 July Director, The Gennadius Library, American Sch of Classical Studies, Souedias 54, Athens, Greece

NICOLL, William; CMG (1974); s of Ralph Nicoll (d 1947), of Dundee, and Christina Mowbray, *née* Melville (d 1959); *b* 28 June 1927; *Educ* Morgan Acad Dundee, Univ of St Andrews (MA), Univ of Dundee (LLD); *m* 1954, Helen Morison, da of William Morison Martin M.M. (d 1970), of Pitlochry; 2 da (Sheila, Barbara); *Career* dep UK perm rep to the EEC 1977-82, dir gen Cncl of Euro Communities 1982-; *Books* contributor to Government and Industry, edited by W Rogers (1986); *Clubs* Royal Cwlth Soc; *Style*— William Nicoll Esq, CMG; 170 Rue de la Loi, Brussells 1048, (☎ 02 234 6246)

NICOLLE, (Robert Arthur Bethune) Bobby; s of Arthur Villeneuve Nicolle (d 1970) of St Peter's House, Jersey and Alice Margarite *née* Cobbold (d 1980); *b* 24 Sept 1934; *Educ* Eton, Trinity Coll Cambridge (MA); *m* 21 Jan 1963, Anne Carolyn, da of Sir Anthony Kershaw, MC MP of West Barn, Didmarton, Badminton, Glos; 2 s (Darcy b 1965, Harry b 1971), 1 da (Fiona b 1967); *Career* Lt Grenadier Gds active serv Cyrpus 1957-58; joined Kleinwort Sons & Co 1958, merchant bankers; dir: Kleinwort Benson 1973, Kleinwort Grieveson Investmt Mgmnt 1986, Kleinwort Overseas

Investmt Tst plc 1986, Signet Fund (Bermuda) 1972; chm Colonial Mutual Life Insur of Aust 1987; special tstee St Thomas' Hosp 1981, tres Iris Fund 1973; *Recreations* skiing, shooting, fox hunting; *Clubs* Buck's; *Style*— Bobby Nicolle, Esq; 45 Gloucester St, London SW1; The Tithe Barn, Didmarton, Badminton GL9 1DT; Kleinwort Benson Ltd, 20 Fenchurch Street, London EC3 (☎ 01 623 8000)

NICOLLE, Geoffrey Reginald; s of Reginald Francis Nicolle (d 1961), of Caerleon, Gwent, and Hilda Alice, *née* Shepherd (d 1965); *b* 5 June 1934; *Educ* Caerleon Endowed Sch, W Monmouth GS, Univ Coll Wales Aberystwyth (BA); *m* 28 March 1959, Sonia Aileen, da of Harry Joseph Bain (d 1960), of Hockley, Essex; 1 s (Philip David b 1963), 1 da (Mary Olwen (Mrs McSparron) b 1962); *Career* headmaster Rosemarket Voluntary Sch (Pembrokeshire) 1965-; holder of the nat collection of primula (garden and border auriculas) for Nat Cncl for the Conservation of Plants and Gardens, pres Dyfed Co Div NUT; *Books* Rosemarket: A Village Beyond Wales (1982); *Recreations* gardening, plant breeding, garden plant conservation, local history; *Style*— Geoffrey Nicolle, Esq; Rising Sun Cottage, Nolton Haven, Haverfordwest, Pembs, Dyfed (☎ 0437 710 542); Rosemarket Voluntary Sch, Rosemarket, Milford Haven, Pembs, Dyfed (☎ 0646 600 620)

NICOLSON, Sir David Lancaster; s of Murdoch Charles Tupper Nicolson (d 1940), of Amherst, Nova Scotia; *b* 20 Sept 1922; *Educ* Haileybury, Imperial Coll London (BSc); *m* 1945, Joan Eileen, da of Maj W H Griffiths, RA (d 1973); 1 s, 2 da; *Career* WWII serv Royal Corps Naval Constructors at sea and Europe (despatches Normandy 1944); chm: Northern telecom plc 1987, BTR plc 1969-84, BA 1971-75, prodn mangr Bucyrus Erie Co Milwaukee 1950-52; mangr (later dir) Prodn Engrg Ltd 1953-62, chm P-E Consulting Gp 1963-68, Rothmans Int 1975-84, VSEL 1986-87, Farmer Stedall plc 1982-87, Bulk Tport Ltd 1984-, LASMO plc 1983-, Ciba-Geigy plc (UK) 1978-, Confedn Life Insur Co 1981-88, Todd Shipyards Corp 1976-, Britannia Arrow Hldgs plc 1987, STC plc 1987, European Movement 1985-, Union Gp plc 1987; dir: GKN plc 1984-, Northern Telecom Ltd (Con) 1987, Dawnay Day Int Ltd 1988-; European advsr NY Stock Exchange 1985; Pro Chllr Surrey Univ 1987; MEP London Central 1979-84; memb: cncl CBI 1972, IOD 1971-76, BIM 1964-69, Inst Prod Engrs 1966-88, City and Guilds of London Inst 1968-76, SRC Engrg Bd 1969-71, Brit Shipbuilding Mission to India 1957, Cncl Templeton Coll 1982-; pres Assoc for Brit C of C Commerce 1983-86; chm: Mgmnt Conslts Assoc 1964, America European Community Assoc 1981-; govr Imperial Coll London Univ 1966-77 (hon fell 1971), Cranleigh Sch 1979-; lectures and broadcasts on mgmnt subjects in USA and UK; FEng 1977; Fellow Imperial Coll 1971; FBIM; FRSA; kt 1975; *Books* contribs to tech jls; *Recreations* sailing, collecting antiques; *Clubs* Brooks, Royal Thames YC; *Style*— Sir David Nicolson; Howicks, Dunsfold, Surrey (☎ 048 649 296)

NICOLSON, Hon Mrs (Katharine Ingrid Mary Isabel); *née* Ramsay of Mar; da and heiress of Lady Saltoun, *qv*, by her husb Capt Alexander Ramsay of Mar, Grenadier Gds; assumed surname and arms of Fraser by Warrant of Lord Lyon Kings of Arms 1973; through her f's mother (late Lady Patricia Ramsay, da of HRH The Duke of Connaught, 3 s of Queen Victoria), Mrs Nicolson is 3 cous of HM The Queen; *b* 11 Oct 1957; *m* 3 May 1980, Capt Mark Malise Nicolson, Irish Gds, o s of Malise Nicolson, MC, *qv*, of Frog Hall, Tilston, Malpas, Cheshire; 2 da (Louise Alexandra Patricia b 2 Sept 1984, Juliet Victoria Katharine b 3 March 1988); *Style*— The Hon Mrs Nicolson; 41 Napier Ave, London SW6 3PS

NICOLSON, Malise Allen; MC; s of Sir Kenneth Nicolson, MC (d 1964), of Norton Bavant Manor, Warminster; *b* 31 Oct 1921; *Educ* Eton; *m* 1946, Vivien, da of Arthur Ridley, CBE (d 1974), of Hexham; 1 s (Mark, m 1980, Hon Katherine, eldest da of Capt Alexander Ramsay, of Mar o Lady Saltoun, 2 da (Mrs (Dinah) Henry Verey, Mrs (Emma) Nicholas Higgin); *Career* serv WWII Maj Burma; chm Booker Line 1968-83, Coe Metcalf Shipping 1977-83; dir Booker McConnell 1968-83, Mersey Docks & Harbours 1974-80; pres Gen Cncl of Br Shipping 1982-83; *Recreations* racing, farming; *Clubs* Cavalry and Guards; *Style*— Malise Nicolson, Esq, MC; Frog Hall, Tilston, Malpas, Cheshire (☎ 082 98 320)

NICOLSON, Nigel; MBE (1945); s of Hon Sir Harold Nicolson, KCVO, CMG, sometime MP Leics W (d 1968, the biographer, critic and broadcaster, 3 s of 1 Baron Carnock), and Hon 'Vita' (Victoria) Sackville-West, CH, JP (also a writer, author of The Edwardians), only child of 3 Baron Sackville; bro of late Benedict Nicolson, the art historian; hp to 1 cousin, 4 Baron Carnock; *b* 19 Jan 1917; *Educ* Eton, Balliol Coll Oxford; *m* 1953, Philippa, da of Sir Eustace Tennyson d'Eyncourt, 2 Bt; 1 s (Adam b 1957, m 1982 Olivia Fane), 2 da (Juliet, b 9 June 1954 and m 1977 James Macmillan Scott (2 da, Clementina b 1981, Flora b 1985); Rebecca b 1963); *Career* dir Weidenfeld and Nicolson 1946-; MP (C) Bournemouth and Christchurch 1952-59; FRSL; author; *Books Incl:* Lord of the Isles (1969), Great Houses of Britain (1965), Harold Nicolson; Diaries and Letters 1930-39 (1966), 1939-45 (1967), 1945-62 (1968; editor of 3 vols), Portrait of a Marriage (1973), Alex (Field Marshal Alexander of Tunis) (1973), Letters of Virginia Woolf (editor 6 vols 1975-1980), Mary Curzon (1977, Whitbread Prize) ; *Recreations* archaeology; *Clubs* Beefsteak; *Style*— Nigel Nicolson, Esq, MBE; Sissinghurst Castle, Cranbrook, Kent (☎ 0580 714239)

NICOLSON OF TARANSAY, (Aeofric Lachlan) Bryan; s of Seymour Nicolson (d 1985), and Margaret Isabella, *née* Baillie; *b* 7 Oct 1913; *Educ* New Silksworth HS, Ruskin Coll, Coll of Piping Glasgow, Dr Kenneth MacKay's Sch of Piping Laggan Newtonmore; *Career* advsr to Bumble Bee Boutique; fndr and Armiger Principal The Most Hon Co of Armigers; genealogist and compiler of histories of the Clan Nicolson and its heraldry; *Recreations* fishing, golf, music, gardening; *Style*— A L B Nicolson of Taransay; 49 Avebury Drive, Washington Village, District 9, Tyne-Wear NE38 7BY (☎ 416 4429)

NIDDRIE, Robert Charles (Bob); s of Robert Hutchin Niddrie (d 1975), of Morestead, Winchester, and Gladys Ellen, *née* Vaudin; *b* 29 Jan 1935; *Educ* Brockenhurst GS; *m* 11 Sept 1965, Maureen Joy, da of Leonard Willis (d 1976), of Morestead, Winchester; 1 s (Alastair b 13 Sept 1967), 2 da (Alison b 15 Dec 1969, Rachel b 30 Dec 1971); *Career* RMR 1951-59 and 1962-72, (Capt) Nat Serv RM and 2 Lt Queen's Own Nigeria Regt 1959-61; ptnr: Whittaker Bailey & Co 1963-75 (amalgamated with Price Waterhouse), Price Waterhouse 1975- (sr ptnr i/c Southampton Off); Round Table: chm Southampton 1971-72, chm Area 1 1973-74 IOD Hants branch: fndr chm 1980-86, memb ctee 1980-89, memb cncl 1980-86; memb: Rotary Club Southampton, 41 Club Southampton, bd mgmnt Western Orchestral Soc; tstee TVS Telethon Tst; FCA 1958, ATII 1964 Independence Medal Nigeria 1960, Congo Medal UN 1961; *Recreations* gardening, books, travel, music, theatre, fine food, wine; *Clubs* Royal Southern Yacht, Royal Southampton Yacht; *Style*— Bob Niddrie, Esq; Morestead Ho, Morestead, Winchester, Hants SO21 1LZ (☎ 096 274 397); Price Waterhouser, The Quay, 30 Channel Way, Ocean Village, Southampton SO1 1XS (☎ 0703 330 077, fax 0703 223 473, telex 477 260)

NIELD, Sir Basil Edward; CBE (1956, MBE (Mil) 1945), DL (Ches 1962); s of Charles Edwin Nield, of Upton Grange, Upton-by-Chester (d 1941), and Mrs F E L Nield, *née* Whalley (d 1931); *b* 7 May 1903; *Educ* Harrow, Magdalen Coll Oxford (MA); *Career* Lt-Col, serv M East and Western Europe (despatches); barr 1925, KC 1945; MP (C) Chester 1940-56; rec Salford 1948-56, chllr Diocese of Liverpool 1948-56, rec Manchester 1956-60, judge of the High Ct 1960-78; kt 1957; *Books* Farewell to the Assizes (1972); *Recreations* travel; *Clubs* Carlton; *Style*— Sir Basil Nield, CBE, DL; Osborne House, Isle of Wight PO32 6JY (☎ 0983 200 056)

NIELD, Sir William Alan; GCMG (1972), KCB (1968, CB 1966); s of William Herbert Nield, of Stockport; *b* 21 Sept 1913; *Educ* Stockport GS, St Edmund Hall Oxford; *m* 1937, Gwyneth Marion Davies; 2 s, 2 da; *Career* RAF and RCAF WWII (despatches), Wing Cdr; joined Civil Serv 1946, under-sec MAFF 1959-64, dep under-sec Dept of Economic Affrs 1965-66, a dep sec of the Cabinet 1966-68, perm under-sec of state Dept of Economic Affrs 1968-69, perm sec Cabinet Off 1969-72, perm sec NI Off 1972-73; dep chm Rolls Royce (1971) Ltd 1973-76; pres St Edmund Hall Assoc 1981-83; *Clubs* Farmers; *Style*— Sir William Nield, GCMG, KCB; South Nevay, Stubbs Wood, Chesham Bois, Bucks (☎ Amersham 3869)

NIETER, Lady Pamela; *née* Paulet; raised to rank and precedence of a Marquess's da 1970; da of Maj Charles Standish Paulet (d 1953; gs of late Rev Lord Charles Paulet, 2 s of 13 Marquess of Winchester), and Jane Lilian Cunningham, *née* Fosbery (d 1972); *b* 23 Nov 1909; *Educ* privately in England and Switzerland; *m* 1976, Hans Martin Nieter-O'Leary, s of Dr Edward Nieter (d 1935), of Berlin; *Career* film production manager; *Style*— Lady Pamela Nieter; 10 Upper Road, Higher Denham, Uxbridge UB9 5EJ

NIGHTINGALE, Sir Charles Manners Gamaliel; 17 Bt (E 1628), of Newport Pond, Essex; s of Sir Charles Athelstan Nightingale, 16 Bt (d 1977); *b* 21 Feb 1947; *Educ* St Paul's; *Heir* 2 cous, Edward Lacy George Nightingale; *Career* higher exec offr DHSS 1977-; *Style*— Sir Charles Nightingale, Bt; 14 Frensham Court, 27 Highbury New Park, N5

NIGHTINGALE, Edward Humphrey; CMG (1955); s of Rev Edward Charles Nightingale (d 1938); *b* 19 August 1904; *Educ* Rugby, Emmanuel Coll Cambridge (MA); *m* 1944, Evelyn Mary, da of Mervyn Swire Ray (d 1981); 3 s, 1 da; *Career* Sudan Political Serv 1926-54, dep civil sec Sudan Govt 1951-52, govr Equatoria Province Sudan 1952-54; farmer Kenya 1954-; Order of The Nile (fourth class 1940); *Recreations* polo, photography, carpentry, apiculture; *Clubs* Muthaiga (Nairobi), Rift Valley Sports (Nakuru); *Style*— Edward Nightingale, Esq, CMG; Nunjoro Farm, PO Box 100, Naivasha, Kenya (☎ Karati (Naivasha) 2 Y 1)

NIGHTINGALE, Edward Lacy George; s of late Manners Percy Nightingale, MRCS, LRCP; hp of 2 cous Sir Charles Manners Gamaliel Nightingale, 17 Bt; *b* 11 May 1938; *Educ* Exeter Sch; *Career* easter Mariner 1966, left Merchant Navy 1974; sub-postmaster Lynmouth; memb Devon CC 1981-85; vice-chm Exmoor Nat Park Ctee 1982-85; memb N Devon DC 1987-; *Recreations* all types of sport; *Style*— Edward Nightingale, Esq; Kneesworth, Lynton, N Devon EX35 6HQ (☎ 0598 52204)

NIGHTINGALE, Hon Mrs (Evelyn Florence Margaret Winifred); *née* Gardner; da of Baron Burghclere (d 1921); *b* 1903; *m* 1, 1928 (m dis 1930), Evelyn Arthur St John Waugh; m 2 1930 (m dis 1936), John Edward Nourse Heygate (later 4 Bt and who d 1976); m 3, 1937 Ronald Nightingale (d 1977); 1 s (Benedict), 1 da (Virginia); *Style*— The Hon Mrs Nightingale; 12 Church St, Ticehurst, Sussex TN5 7AH

NIGHTINGALE, Sir John Cyprian; CBE (1970), BEM (1941), QPM (1965), DL (Essex 1975); s of Herbert Paul Nightingale (d 1965), of Sydenham, London; *b* 16 Sept 1913; *Educ* Cardinal Vaughan Sch, Univ Coll London; *m* 1947, Patricia Mary, da of Dr Norman Maclaren, of West Kilbride, Ayrshire; *Career* serv RNVR 1943-45; joined Metropolitan Police 1935; asst chief constable Essex 1958-62, chief constable 1962, chief constable of Essex and Southend-on-Sea 1969-75, chief constable Essex 1975-78; chm Police Cncl 1976-78; memb Parole Bd 1978-82; kt 1975; *Style*— Sir John Nightingale, CBE, BEM, QPM, DL; Great Whitman's Farm, Purleigh, Essex

NIGHTINGALE, Lady; Nadine; da of late (Charles) Arthur Diggens; *m* 1932, Sir Charles Athelstan Nightingale, 16 Bt (d 1977); 1 s, 2 da; *Style*— Lady Nightingale; 12 Jacob's Pool, Okehampton, Devon

NIGHTINGALE, William Howard; s of William Hunt Nightingale (d 1965), and Annie Stephens-Spinks, of Bolton; *b* 30 Nov 1943; *Educ* Bolton Sch 1955-61; *m* 16 Sept 1967, Pamela Mary, da of Robert Noel Forster, of "Ardwyn", Lostock, Bolton; 2 s (Michael b 1969, Andrew b 1970), 2 da (Emma b 1972, Katherine b 1972); *Career* slr; *Recreations* golf; *Clubs* Bolton Golf; *Style*— William Nightingale, Esq; Old Hall Farm, Old Kiln Lane, Bolton BL1 7PZ; 87 Market Street, Westhoughton BL5 3AA

NIGHTINGALE OF CROMARTY, Michael David; OBE (1960); Baron of Cromarty (feudal); lord of the manor of Wormshill and a lord of the level of Romney Marsh; s of Victor Russell John Nightingale, of Wormshill, Kent (d 1951) and Bathsheba, *née* Buhay (d 1942); *b* 6 Dec 1927; *Educ* Winchester, Wye Coll, Magdalen Coll Oxford (BSc, BLitt); *m* 1956, Hilary Marion Olwen, da of John Eric Jones, of Swansea; 2 s (John, Alexander), 3 da (Emma, Rebecca, Rachel); *Career* Esquire Bedell Univ of London 1953-; dep steward Royal Manor of Wye 1954-, sec Museums Assoc and ed Museums Journal 1954-60, investmt advsr London Univ 1954-66, dir Charterhouse Japhet 1965-70; chm: Chillington Corpn 1986-, Anglo-Indonesian Corpn 1971-, Anglo-Eastern Plantations plc 1985-; Churches Ctee of Kent Archaeological Soc 1973-, North Downs Soc 1983-; bd memb Cwlth Devpt Corpn 1985-; memb: Gen Synod C of E 1979-85 (panel of chm 1984-85), Kent CC 1973-77, Maidstone Borough Cncl 1973- (ldr 1976-77, Mayor 1984-85), Ct of Assistants, Rochester Bridge 1985-; Freeman City of London; FSA; *Recreations* antiquarian, music; *Clubs* Athenaeum; *Style*— Michael Nightingale of Cromarty, OBE; Cromarty House, Ross and Cromarty (☎ 038 17 265); Wormshill Ct, Sittingbourne, Kent (☎ 062 784 235)

NIGHTINGALE OF CROMARTY, Younger, John Bartholomew Wakelyn; er s and h of Michael David Nightingale of Cromarty, OBE, *qv*; *b* 7 Sept 1960; *Educ* Winchester, Magdalen Coll Oxford (MA, DPhil); *Career* Harmsworth sr res scholar Merton Coll Oxford 1984-86; fell Magdalen Coll Oxford 1986-; tstee: Cromarty Harbour, Cromarty Arts Tst; author of articles on medieval history; *Recreations* woodland management, restoration of old buildings; Cromarty House, Ross and

Cromarty IV11 8XS (☎ 03817 265); 21 Dartmouth Row, Greenwich, London SE10 8AW

NIMMO, Derek Robert; s of Harry Nimmo (d 1959), and Marjorie Sudbury, *née* Hardy (d 1988); *b* 19 Sept 1932; *Educ* Quarry Sch Liverpool; *m* 9 April 1955, Patricia Sybil Anne, da of Alfred John Brown (d 1955), of Santiago, Chile; 2 s (Timothy St John b 1956, Piers James Alexander b 1967), 1 da (Amanda Kate Victoria b 1959, m 1983 Hon Nicholas Howard, *qv*); *Career* actor, author, producer; first appearance Bolton Hippodrome as Ensign Blades in Quality Street 1952; stage appearances incl: Waltz of The Toreadors Criterion 1957, Duel of Angels Apollo 1958, The Amorous Prawn Savill 1959, See How They Run Vauderville 1964, Charlie Girl Adelphi 1965-71 and overseas 1975, Why Not Stay for Breakfast? Apollo 1973 and overseas 1975, See How They Run, A Friend Indeed Shaftesbury 1984; television series incl: All Gas and Gaiters, Oh Brother, Oh Father, Sorry I'm Single, The Bed Sit Girl, My Honourable Mrs, The World of Wooster, Blandings Castle, Life Begins at Forty, Third Time Lucky, Hell's Bells, If It's Saturday it must be Nimmo, Just a Nimmo; films incl: Casino Royale, The Amorous Prawn The Bargee, Joey Boy, A Talent for Loving, The Liquidator, Tamahine, One of our Dinosaurs is Missing; radio: Just a Minute 1967; produced and appeared in numerous prodns which toured world-wide for Intercontinental Entertainment; *Books* Derek Nimmo's Drinking Companion (1979), Shaken & Stirred (1984), Oh Come All Ye Faithful! (1986), Not In Front Of The Servants (1987), Up Mount Everest Without A Paddle (1988); *Recreations* sailing, travel, horse racing; *Clubs* Garrick, Athenaeum (Liverpool), Lords Taveners; *Style—* Derek Nimmo, Esq; c/o Barry Burnett, Suite 42, Grafton House, 2 Golden Sq, London

NIMMO, Lady; Dorothy Wordsworth; da of Walter Gillies; *m* 1922, Sir Robert Nimmo (d 1979); *Style—* Lady Nimmo; 8 Anderson Drive, Perth

NIMMO SMITH, William Austin; QC (1982); s of Dr Robert Herman Nimmo Smith, and Ann Nimmo Smith, *née* Wood; *b* 6 Nov 1942; *Educ* Eton Coll; Balliol Coll, Oxford (BA), Edinburgh Univ (LLB); *m* 1968, Dr Jennifer, da of Rev David Main; 1 da (Harriet b 1972), 1 s (Alexander b 1974); *Career* advocate admitted to Faculty of Advocates 1969; standing jnr counsel to Dept of Employment 1977-82; QC 1982; advocate deputey 1983-86; chm Medical Appeal Tribunals 1986-, Pt/t memb Scottish Law cmmn 1988-; *Recreations* hill walking, music; *Clubs* New Club, Edinburgh; *Style—* William A Nimmo Smith, Esq, QC; 29 Ann St, Edinburgh EH4 1PL (☎ 031 332 0204); Advocates Library, Parliament House, Edinburgh EH1 1RF (☎ 031 226 5071)

NIND, Philip Frederick; OBE (1979), TD (1946); s of William Walker Nind, CIE (d 1964), of Oxford, and Lilian Marie Feodore, *née* Scott (d 1968); *b* 2 Jan 1918; *Educ* Blundell's, Balliol Coll Oxford (MA); *m* 8 Aug 1944, Fay Allardice, da of Capt John Roland Forbes Errington (d 1945); 2 da (Nicola b 1945, Charlotte b 1949); *Career* WWII 1939-46 Royal Fusiliers, SOE Greece and Albania 1943-44, Mil Govt Berlin 1945-46, ret Maj; Shell Gp of Cos 1939-68: Venezuela, Cyprus, Lebanon, Jordon, London; dir Fndn for Mgmnt Educn 1968-83, sec Cncl of Indust for Mgmnt Educn 1969-83; vice-pres Euro Fndn for Mgmnt Devpt Brussels 1978-83; served on various ctees of: CBI, CNAA, UGC, NEDO; memb exec ctee Royal Acad of Dancing 1970-88, chm Abinger Common Cons Assoc 1977-79; hon fell London Business Sch; CBIM 1968-83, FRSA 1983; Chevalier Order of Cedars of Lebanon 1959, Grand Cross Orders of St Mark and Holy Sepulchre Greek Orthodox Church 1959; *Books* A Firm Foundation (1985); *Clubs* Special Forces; *Style—* Philip Nind, Esq, OBE, TD

NISBET, Prof Robin George Murdoch; s of Robert George Nisbet (d 1955), of Glasgow, and Agnes Thomson, *née* Husband (d 1973); *b* 21 May 1925; *Educ* Glasgow Acad, Glasgow Univ (MA), Balliol Coll Oxford (MA); *m* 16 April 1969, (Evelyn Pamela) Anne, da of Dr John Alfred Wood (d 1953); *Career* tutor in classics Corpus Christi Coll Oxford 1952-70, prof of latin Univ of Oxford 1970; FBA 1967; commentary on Cicero in Pisonem (1961), commentary on Horace: Odes I (1970), Odes II (1978); *Style—* Prof Robin Nisbet; 80 Abingdon Rd, Cumnor, Oxford OX2 9QW (☎ 0865 862 482); Corpus Christi Coll, Oxford (☎ 0865 276 757)

NISBET-SMITH, Dugal; s of David and Margaret Nisbet-Smith, of Invercargill, NZ; *b* 6 Mar 1935; *Educ* Southland Boys' HS NZ; *m* 1959, Dr Ann Patricia, da of John Taylor, of Gt Harwood, Lancs; 1 s, 2 da; *Career* Scottish Daily Record and Sunday Mail: devpt mangr 1969-71, prodn dir 1971-73, md 1974-78; dir Mirror Gp Newspapers 1976-78; dir/gen mangr Times Newspapers Ltd 1978-80, md Times Newspapers 1980-81; int publishing advsr to HH The Aga Khan 1981-83; dir The Newspaper Soc 1983-; *Recreations* travel, sculpture, painting; *Clubs* RAC; *Style—* Dugal Nisbet-Smith, Esq; 19 Highgate Close, Hampstead Lane, London N6

NISSEN, George Maitland; CBE (1987); s of Col Peter Norman Nissen (d 1930), and Lauretta, *née* Maitland (d 1954); *b* 29 Mar 1930; *Educ* Eton, Trinity Coll Cambridge; *m* 1956, Jane Edmunds, *née* Bird; 2 s, 2 da; *Career* KRRC 2/Lt, Royal Greenjackets TA Capt; memb Stock Exchange 1956; dir Securities Assoc, Cncl of Stock Exchange 1973-86; dep chm of the Stock Exchange 1978-81; sr ptnr Pember & Boyle 1982-86; dir Morgan Grenfell Gp 1985-87; *Recreations* music, railways, walking; *Style—* George Nissen, Esq, CBE; Swan House, Chiswick Mall, London W4 (☎ 01 994 8203); Morgan Grenfell Group plc, 23 Great Winchester Street, London EC2P 2AX (☎ 01 588 4545, telex 8953511)

NISSEN, Karl Iversen; s of Christian Nissen, of Milton NZ (d 1939), and Caroline, *née* Hollick (d 1932); *b* 4 April 1906; *Educ* Otago Boys HS Dunedin NZ, Otago Univ (BSc, MB, ChB, MD); *m* 15 June 1935, (Mary Margaret) Honor, da of Charles Henry Schofield, (d 1970), of Bridlington, Yorks; 1 s (John Christian Doughty b 1941), 1 da (Margreta b 1938); *Career* WWII Surgn Lt Cdr RNVR 1943-45; surgn Royal Nat Orthopaedic Hosp London 1946-71; orthopaedic surgn: Harrow Hosp 1946-71, Peace Meml Hosp Watford 1948-71; chm Friends of Holwelld Sch; FRCS 1937; *Recreations* for travel; *Clubs* Naval; *Style—* Karl Nissen, Esq; Prospect House, The Ave, Sherborne, Dorset DT9 3AJ (☎ 0935 81 35 39)

NIVELLES, Patrick Lawrence; s of Louis Henri Nivelles, of France, and Katherine Mary, *née* McLaughlin (d 1958); *b* 1 April 1946; *Educ* Worth Abbey Sussex, Univ of East Anglia (BA Hons), Univ of Warwick (MSc); *m* 25 Jan 1969, Marie-Andree, da of John Cyril Smith, of Warwickshire; 1 s (Guy b 1974), 1 da (Faye b 1976); *Career* merchant banker, previously with First Nat Bank of Boston, GKN plc; currently gen mangr Bank Hispano Ltd; *Recreations* shooting, travel; *Clubs* East India, Cowdray Park Polo; *Style—* Patrick L Nivelles, Esq; Brookhurst Grange, Holmbury Hill, Ewhurst, Surrey; 15 Austin Friars, London EC2N 2DJ (☎ 01 628 4499)

NIVEN, Sir (Cecil) Rex; CMG (1954), MC (1918); s of late Rev Dr George Cecil Niven and Jeanne Niven, of Torquay, Devon; *b* 20 Nov 1898; *Educ* Blundell's Sch Tiverton, Balliol Coll Oxford (MA); *m* 1, 1925, Dorothy Marshall (d 1977), da of David Marshall Mason, formerly MP Coventry and E Edinburgh (d 1956); 1 da (and 1 da decd); m 2, 1980, Pamela Mary Catterall, da of George Catterall Leach (d 1937), of Sibton Park Kent; *Career* 2 Lt RFA 1918-19, Corpl Lagos Def Force 1939-42; admin offr (and finally sr resident Nigeria) 1921-54, speaker N Nigeria Assembly 1953-60, special cmmr N Nigeria 1960-62; dep sec Southwark Diocesan Off 1962-70; memb: cncl RSA, Paddington Hospital's Mgmnt Ctee 1962-72, cncl Imp Soc of Knights Bachelor 1966-, Gen Synod of C of E 1975-80; patron Deal Protection Soc; fndr chm NE Kent Br Oxford Soc 1986; FRGS 1919, life memb BRCS 1983; kt 1960; *Books* author of 13 books of Africa incl A Nigerian Kaleidoscope (1983); *Clubs* Royal Over Seas League; *Style—* Sir Rex Niven, CMG, MC; 12 Archery Sq, Walmer, Kent CT14 7HP (☎ 0304 361863)

NIVISON, Hon John; s of 3 Baron Glendyne; *b* 18 August 1960; *Style—* The Hon John Nivison

NIX, Prof John Sydney; s of John William Nix (d 1968), of SE London, and Eleanor Elizabeth, *née* Stears (d 1978); *b* 27 July 1927; *Educ* Brockley Co Sch, Univ Coll of the South-West (BSc), Cambridge (MA); *m* 7 Oct 1950, Mavis Marian, da of George Cooper, of Teignmouth; 1 s (Robert David John b 10 Jan 1955), 2 da (Alison Mary b 23 July 1952, Jennifer Ann b 7 May 1959); *Career* Instr Lt RN 1948-51; sr res offr Farm Econs Branch Cambridge Univ 1957-61 (1951-61); Wye Coll London: farm mgmnt liaison offr and lectr 1961-70, sr tutor 1970-72, sr lectr 1972-75, head Farm Business Unit 1974-, reader 1975-82, prof of farm business mgmnt (personal chair) 1982-; fndr memb Farm Mgmnt Assoc 1965, prog advsr Southern TV 1966-81; chm: ed ctee Farm Management (CMA) 1971, bd of Farm Mgmnt (BIM) 1979-81; Nat Award for Outstanding and Contrib to Advancement of Mgmnt in Agric Indust BIM 1982, author of numerous articles for jls, memb many nat study gps and advsy ctees; CBIM 1983, FRSA 1984, FRAgS 1985; *Books* Farm Planning and Control (with C S Barnard, 1979), Farm Mechanisation For Profit (with W Butterworth, 1983), Land and Estate Management (1987), Farm Management Pocketbook (1988); *Recreations* theatre, cinema, travel, rugby, cricket; *Clubs* Farmers; *Style—* Prof John Nix; Keynton, Cherry Garden La, Wye, Ashford, Kent TN25 5AR (☎ 0233 812 274); Wye Coll, Wye, Ashford, Kent TN25 5AH (☎ 0233 812 401, fax 0233 813 320, telex 96118)

NIXON, Alan Borthwick; s of John Borthwick (d 1952), and Elsie Mary Nixon, *née* Woodcock; *b* 13 July 1921; *Educ* Royal GS Newcastle-on-Tyne, St Edwards Sch Oxford, Newcastle Coll (BSC); *m* 1 May 1945, Kathleen Mary, da of George Horrell (d 1968); 1 s (Nigel John Borthwick b 1948), 1 da (Angela Mary b 1950); *Career* civil engr; serv WWII (Lt-Col) Middle E; chm and md Purdie Lumsden & Co Ltd 1942-80; former chm: Fedn of Civil Engrg Contractors, N Counties Construction Safety Gp, Civil Engrg Gp Trg Assoc; FICE, FICB; Fell Inst of Nuclear Energy; *Recreations* golf, art; *Clubs* Exeter City, County; *Style—* Alan Nixon, Esq; Downhams Cottage, Woodbury, Salterton, Exeter, Devon EX5 1PQ (☎ 0395 32464)

NIXON, Anthony Michael; s of (Hector) Michael Nixon, of Eng, and Joan Dorothy, *née* Whitaker; *b* 24 June 1957; *Educ* Canford Sch Wimborne Dorset, Trinity Coll Cambridge (MA); *m* Sheila Frances, da of Hugh Richardson, of Eng; *Career* barr 1979, asst legal advsr Overseas Containers Ltd 1983-85, commercial lawyer Amesham Int plc 1985-87, dir of legal res S J Berwin & Co 1987-88, conslt Hewitt Assocs 1988-; reader/writer St Albans Talking Newspaper, Freeman: City of London, Worshipful Co of Glass Sellers; ACIArb 1982, BACFI 1982; *Recreations* music, walking, painting, birdwatching; *Style—* Anthony Nixon, Esq; Hewitt Associates, Romeland House, Romeland Hill, St Albans, Herts AL3 4EZ (☎ 0727 66233, fax 0727 30122)

NIXON, Maj Cecil Dominic Henry Joseph; MC; s of late Maj Sir Christopher William Nixon DSO, 2 Bt, and hp of bro Rev Sir Kenneth Michael John Basil Nixon, SJ, 4 Bt; *b* 5 Feb 1920; *Educ* Beaumont Coll; *m* 1953, Brenda, da of late Samuel Lycett Lewis and wid of Maj M F McWhor; 3 s, 2 da; *Heir* Simon Michael Christopher; *Career* Maj, Royal Ulster Rifles, bursar The Med Coll; chm: The Devon Sheltered Homes Tst of St Bartholomew's Hospital; *Recreations* ornithology, rugby, cricket, gardening; *Style—* Maj Cecil Nixon, MC; 9 Larpent Ave, SW15

NIXON, Sir Edwin Ronald; CBE (1974) DL (Hampshire 1986); s of William Archdale Nixon, and Ethel, *née* Corrigan; *b* 21 June 1925; *Educ* Alderman Newton's Sch Leicester, Selwyn Coll Cambridge (MA); *m* 1952, Joan Lilian, *née* Hill; 1 s, 1 da; *Career* chm IBM Utd Kingdom Hldgs Ltd 1979- (chm and chief exec 1979-85, chief exec 1965-85), dir Nat Westminster Bank plc 1975- (dep-chm 1987-), dir Amersham Int plc 1987-, (chm 1988-) dir Royal Insur plc; kt 1984; *Recreations* tennis, sailing, golf; *Clubs* Athenaeum; *Style—* Sir Edwin Nixon, CBE, DL; Starkes Heath, Rogate, nr Petersfield, Hants GU31 5EJ (☎ 073 080 504); National Westminster Bank plc, 41 Lothbury, London EC2P 2BP (☎ 01 726 1000)

NIXON, (Philip) Graham; s of Horace Stanley Nixon of Greenacre, Rugby Road, Burbage, Leicestershire, and Dorothy Mary, *née* Collidge; *b* 12 June 1942; *Educ* Hinckley GS, Leicester Coll of Art; *m* 3 July 1965, Maureen, da of Edward Wilford, of Sunways, Doctors Fields, Earl Shilton, Leics; 2 s (Mark b 1967 (decd), Paul b 1969); *Career* chm: Ferry Pickering Group plc; dir: Ferry Pickering Sales Ltd, Ferry Pickering Boxes Ltd, Ferry Pickering Publishing Ltd, Ferry Pickering Plastics Ltd, Ferry Pickering Mouldings Ltd, Ferry Pickering Toolmakers Ltd; *Recreations* shooting and sports in general; *Style—* Graham Nixon, Esq; The Old Rectory, Rectory Lane, Nailstone, Nuneaton CU13 0QQ; Ferry Pickering Group plc, PO Box 6, Coventry Road, Hinckley, Leicestershire (☎ 0455 38171)

NIXON, Lady; Joan Lucille Mary; da of Robert Felix Mervyn Brown of Rangoon, Burma; *m* 1949, Maj Sir Christopher John Louis Joseph Nixon, 3 Bt, MC, (d 1978); 3 da (Anne (Mrs J A Miller) b 1954, Mary (Mrs Nixon-Lechaire) b 1957, Sally b 1961); *Style—* Lady Nixon; c/o Lloyds Bank, St George's Road, Wimbledon, London SW19

NIXON, Rev Sir Kenneth Michael John Basil; 4 Bt (UK 1906), of Roebuck Grove, Milltown, Co Dublin and Merrion Sq, City of Dublin, SJ; s of late Sir Christopher William Nixon, 2 Bt, DSO, and bro of 3 Bt (d 1978); *b* 22 Feb 1919; *Educ* Beaumont Coll, Heythrop Coll Oxon; *Heir* bro, Maj Cecil Dominic Henry Joseph Nixon, MC; *Career* RC priest; ordained 1952; teaching memb of the Jesuit Community at St George's Coll Salisbury 1954-; *Style—* Rev Sir Kenneth Nixon, Bt, SJ; St George's Coll, PB 7727, Causeway, Zimbabwe (☎ Salisbury 24650)

NIXON, Neville John; JP (1980); s of John Henry Nixon (d 1980), of Cheadle Hulme, Cheshire, and Catherine Ada, *née* Birchall; *b* 26 July 1934; *Educ* Stockport GS; *m* 16 Sept 1961, (Alice) Margaret, da of James Ernest Lugton, FRPS (d 1956), of Cheadle

Hulme; 1 da (Shirley Margaret (Mrs Palk) b 1964); *Career* RAF 1956-58; ptnr John H Nixon & Co (CAs) 1958-; dir: Blackfriars Vintners Ltd 1978-80, Gaythorn Fin Co Ltd 1983-, Nixon & Ptnrs Ltd 1988-; life govr Imp Cancer Res Fund; CA 1956, ATII 1963; *Recreations* genealogy, walking, gardening; *Style—* Neville J Nixon, Esq, JP; John H Nixon & Co, Chartered Accountants, Athena House, 35 Greek Street, Stockport, Cheshire SK3 8BA (☎ 061 477 8787)

NIXON, Patrick Michael; OBE (1984); s of John Moylett Gerard Nixon, of Chilmark, Wilts, and Hilary Mary, *née* Paterson (d 1956); *b* 1 August 1944; *Educ* Downside, Magdalene Coll Cambridge (MA); *m* 26 Aug 1968, Elizabeth Rose, da of Edward Carlton, of Southampton; 4 s (Simon b 1970, Paul b 1971, Christopher b 1975, Damian b 1978); *Career* Dip Serv 1965, Middle E Centre for Arab Studies Lebanon 1966-68, third (later sec) sec Br Embassy Cairo 1968-70, second sec (commercial) Br Embassy Lima 1970-73, first sec FCO 1973-77, first sec and head of Chancery Br Embassy Tripoli 1977-80, dir Br Info Servs NY 1980-83, asst (later head) Nr E and N Africa dept FCO 1983-87, HM Ambass to State of Quatar and Doha 1987-; offr Brazil order of the Southern Cross 1976; *Style—* Patrick Nixon, Esq, OBE; c/o FCO, King Charles St, London SW1

NOAD, Sir Kenneth Beeson; s of James Beeson Noad (d 1939); *b* 25 Mar 1900; *Educ* Maitland HS, Sydney Univ; *m* 1935, Eileen Mary, da of William Ryan; *Career* consulting physician; former pres RACP, dir Northcott Neurological Centre 1958, pres Med Legal Soc of NSW 1964-68, pres Aust Post-Graduate Fedn of Med 1966, vice-pres Aust Academy of Forensic Sci; kt 1970; *Style—* Sir Kenneth Noad; BMA House, 135 Macquarie St, Sydney, NSW 2000, Australia

NOAKES, George; *see*: Wales, Archbishop of

NOAKES, Philip Reuben; OBE (1962); s of Charles William Noakes (d 1939), and Elizabeth Farey, *née* Timpson (d 1956); *b* 12 August 1915; *Educ* Wycliffe Coll, Queens' Coll Cambridge (BA, MA); *m* 20 Jan 1940, Moragh Jean MRCS, LRCP, da of William Arnott Dickson, MD, MRCP, FRCS; 2 s (Jonathan Arnott b 1944, Anthony Robin b 1947); *Career* Capt-Adj 2 Fife and Forfar Yeo 1940-46 (despatches); chief info offr; Colonial Off 1948-67; HM Dip Serv: info cnsllr Ottawa 1967-72, consul gen Seattle 1973-75; *Recreations* fishing, shooting, bird watching, gardening; *Clubs* Royal Overseas League; *Style—* Philip Noakes, Esq; Little St Mary's, St Mary's Lane, Uplyme, Lyme Regis, Dorset DT7 3XH (☎ 0297 33371)

NOAKES, Vivien; da of Marcus Langley, FRAcS (d 1977), and Helen *née* Oldfield Box (d 1983); *b* 19 Feb 1937; *m* 9 July 1960, Michael, s of Basil Noakes (d 1969); 1 da (Anya b 1961), 2 s (Jonathan b 15 May 1963, Benedict b 9 Feb 1965); *Career* writer; guest curator of the Maj Exhibition, Edward Lear at the Royal Acad of Arts and Nat Academy of Design, NY 1985; *Books* Edward Lear: The Life of a Wanderer (1968, 2nd edn 1979, 3rd edn 1985), Edward Lear 1912-1888 (1985), Selected Letters of Edward Lear (1988); *Recreations* friends, reading, cooking; *Clubs* Arts; *Style—* Vivien Nokes; 146 Hamilton Terrace, London NW8 9UX (☎ 01 328 6754)

NOBLE, Adrian Keith; s of William John Noble (d 1987), of Chichester Sussex, and Violet Ena, *née* Wells; *b* 19 July 1950; *Educ* Chichester HS, Univ of Bristol (BA), Drama Centre London; *Career* assoc dir: Bristol Old Vic Co 1976-80, RSC Co 1981-; guest dir Manchester Roy Exchange Theatre Co; *Style—* Adrian Noble, Esq; c/o Barbican Theatre, London EC2Y 8BQ (☎ 01 628 3351)

NOBLE, Lady; Barbara Janet Margaret; da of Brig Kenneth Joseph Gabbett, Indian Army (d 1948), and Gladys Mary Gell (d 1981); *b* 1917; *Educ* St Helen's Blackheath; *m* 1938, Cdr Rt Hon Sir Allan Herbert Percy Noble, KCMG, DSO, DSC, PC, DL (d 1982), sometime memb of Lloyd's, chm Tollemache & Cobbold Breweries, min of state Foreign Affrs, s of late Adm Sir Percy Noble, GBE, KCB, CVO; *Recreations* racing; *Style—* Lady Noble

NOBLE, Barrie Paul; s of Major Frederic Arthur Noble, (d 1978), of Witney, Oxon, and Henrietta, *née* Evans; *b* 17 Oct 1938; *Educ* Hele's Sch Exeter, New Coll Oxford (BA), Univ of Dakar Senegal; *m* 17 July 1965, Alexandra (Sandra) Helene, da of Robert Frederick Truman Giddings, of Cap Del Prat Gran, Encamp, Andorra; 1 s (Timothy b 1966); *Career* memb HM Dip Serv; FO 1962, third later second sec Br Embassy Leopoldville (Kinshasa) 1965; second sec (comm) Br Dep High Cmmr Kaduna 1967; first sec FCO 1969; Br Embassy Warsaw 1972; FCO 1975; cnsllr UK Mission to the UN, Geneva 1980; cnsllr FCO Oct 1984-; *Recreations* skiing, bridge, ancient cars, grass cutting; *Clubs* RAF, Ski Club of Great Britain, Rolls Royce Enthusiasts; *Style—* Barrie Noble, Esq; c/o Foreign & Commonwealth Office, London SW1 (☎ 01 270 0796)

NOBLE, Sheriff David; JP (1970); s of Donald Noble (d 1942), and Helen Kirk Lynn Noble, *née* Melville (d 1971); *b* 11 Feb 1923; *Educ* Inverness Royal Acad, Edinburgh Univ (MA, LLB); *m* 1947, Marjorie Scott, da of James Scott Smith (d 1971), of Bramhall Cheshire; 2 s (Andrew, David), 1 da (Jill); *Career* war serv RAF Bomber Cmd Europe 1942-46, Flt-Lt; writer to the signet Edinburgh 1949-83; sheriff at Oban, Campbeltown and Fort William 1983-; *Recreations* sailing (Jennie G); *Style—* Sheriff David Noble, JP; Woodhouselee, North Connel, Oban, Argyll PA37 1QZ (☎ Connel 678)

NOBLE, David Brunel; s and h of Sir Marc Brunel Noble, 5 Bt; *b* 25 Dec 1961; *m* 26 Sept 1987, Virginia Ann, yr da of late Roderick Wetherall, of Platt Oast, St Mary's Platt, Kent; *Style—* David Noble Esq

NOBLE, Prof Denis; s of George Noble (Flt-Lt RFC, d 1957), and Ethel, *née* Rutherford; *b* 16 Nov 1936; *Educ* Emanuel Sch London, UCL (BSc, PhD); *m* Jan 1965, Susan Jennifer, da of Fl-Lt Leslie H Barfield; 1 da (Penelope Jean b 27 Aug 1967), 1 adopted s (Julian Aidan b 29 Aug 1970); *Career* asst lectr physiology UCL 1961-64, tutorial fell Balliol Coll Oxford 1963-84, praefectus of Holywell Manor 1971-89, Burdon Sanderson prof cardiovascular physiology Univ of Oxford 1984, fndr dir Oxsoft Ltd 1984-; The Physiological Soc: hon sec 1974-80, for sec 1986-; memb founding gp Save Br Sci, numerous appearances on radio and tv, writer of various articles in nat press; fell UCL 1986, Hon MRCP 1988; FRS 1979; Correspondant Etranger de l'Académie Royale de Médecine de Belgique; *Books* The Initiation of the Heart Beat (1975), Electric Current Flow in Excitable Cells (1975); *Recreations* foreign languages, guitar; *Style—* Prof Denis Noble; Univ Laboratory of Physiology, Parks Road, Oxford OX1 3PT (☎ 0865 272528, fax 0865 272 469)

NOBLE, Eric; s of Ernest Charles Noble (d 1935), of Manchester, and Lorrie, *née* Whitney (d 1952); *b* 21 Dec 1911; *Educ* St Philip's Hulme Manchester, St Mary's Rd Central Sch Newton Heath Manchester; *Career* served with rank up to captain with Intelligence Corps and Royal Indian Army Supply Corps (tank transporters); pioneer memb of Blood Transfusion Serv when blood passed directly from donor to patient; Manchester Scout Gang Show memb took part in all 78 shows for HM Forces from Sept 1939 until disbanded due to call-up demands; produced 'Great Oaks', Ralph Reader's Cavalcade of Scouting in Manchester; asst to ch admin off Pan Pacific Jamboree 1949; dist cmmr Gorton Manchester; FCA; *Recreations* swimming, cycle touring; *Style—* Eric Noble, Esq; 46 Northen Grove, West Didsbury, Manchester M20 8NW (☎ 061 445 3402); 309 Kentish Town Rd, London NW5 2JT (☎ 01 482 2029)

NOBLE, Sir (Thomas Alexander) Fraser; MBE (1947); s of Simon Noble, of Cromdale, Morayshire (d 1926); *b* 29 April 1918; *Educ* Nairn Academy, Aberdeen Univ; *m* 1945, Barbara Anne Mabel, da of John Sinclair, of Nairn; 1 s, 1 da; *Career* mil serv 1939-40; entered Indian Civil Serv 1940, serv NWFP 1941-47; lectr in political economy Aberdeen Univ 1948-57, sec Carnegie Trust for Scottish Univs 1957-62, vice-chllr Univ of Leicester 1962-76, memb and chm various Govt Advsy Ctees, chm Advsy Cncl on Probation and After Care 1965-70, chm UK Ctee of V-Chllrs and Princs 1970-72, vice-chllr and princ Aberdeen Univs 1976-81; Hon LLD: Aberdeen 1968, Leicester 1976, Glasgow 1981, Washington Coll 1981; kt 1971; *Recreations* golf; *Clubs* Royal Northern and Univ (Aberdeen); *Style—* Sir Fraser Noble, MBE; Hedgerley, Victoria St, Nairn (☎ 53151)

NOBLE, (Charles Henry Scott) Harry; s of Charles Scott Noble (d 1983), and Betty Balfour Noble, *née* Corsar; *b* 5 Jan 1947; *Educ* Fettes Coll, Edinburgh U (LLB); *Career* chartered accountant; Thomson McLintock and Co 1968-74; asst dir Kleinwort, Benson Ltd 1982- (joined 1974); *Recreations* skiing; *Style—* Harry Noble Esq; 7 Amner Road, London SW11 (☎ 01 223 5755); c/o Kleinwort Benson Ltd, 20 Fenchurch St, EC3 (☎ 01 623 8000)

NOBLE, Sir Iain Andrew; 3 Bt (UK 1923), OBE, of Ardkinglas and Eilean Iarmain; er s of Sir Andrew Napier Noble, 2 Bt, KCMG (d 1987), and Sigrid, *née* Michelet; *b* 8 Sept 1935; *Educ* Eton, Univ Coll Oxford (MA); *Heir* bro, Timothy Peter Noble, *qv*; *Career* Nat Serv 1954-56, 2 Lt Intelligence Corps 1956-59, 2 Lt 8 Argyll & Sutherland Highlanders (TA); dir: Lennox Oil Co plc 1980-85, Noble & Co Ltd 1980-, Adam & Co plc 1983-, Darnaway Venture Capital plc 1984-, New Scotland Insur Gp plc 1986-, and other cos; memb Scottish Cncl (devpt and indust) Edinburgh 1964-69, jt fndr and md Noble Grossart Ltd (Merchant Bankers) Edinburgh 1969-72, proprietor of Fearann Eilean Iarmain estate in Skye 1972-; co-fndr and chm Seaforth Maritime Ltd Aberdeen (offshore oil servs) 1972-77; fndr Lennox Oil Co plc Edinburgh 1980-86; co-fndr and chm Noble & Co Ltd of Edinburgh Issuing House Edinburgh 1980-; dep chm Traverse Theatre Co 1966-69; memb Edinburgh Univ Court 1971-73; tstee: Nat Museums of Scotland 1985-, Sabhal Mor Ostaig (Gaelic Business Coll, co fndr) 1973-85; memb The Securities Assoc 1988; Scotsman of the Year (Knights Templer Award) 1982, chm Scottish-Australian Bicentenial Cairn Ctee 1987-88; *Clubs* New (Edinburgh); *Style—* Sir Iain Noble; An Lamraig, Eilean Iarmain, An t-Eilean Sgitheanach IV43 8QR; offices: An Oifig, Eilean Iarmain, Ise of Skye IV43 8QR (☎ 047 13 266, telex 75252 IARMAIN G, fax 047 13 260); 5 Darnaway St, Edinburgh EH3 6DW (☎ 031 225 9677)

NOBLE, Lady; Irene Susan; OBE (1970), JP; da of J D Taylor, of Wimbledon; *m* 1935, Col Sir Arthur Noble, KBE, CB, DSO, TD, DL (d 1982), sometime Ch Instr Sch of Inf; 3 s, 2 da; *Style—* Lady Noble; Marchings, Chigwell, Essex IG7 6DQ

NOBLE, James (Douglas Campbell); s of Capt Frederick Burnaby Noble, RN (d 1946), and Elsie Mackintosh, *née* Mackintosh (d 1962); *b* 20 April 1921; *Educ* Bradfield Coll, Canford Sch; *m* 1, 25 Aug 1956, Patricia Jean, da of Harold Strange Taylor-Young, FRCS; 1 s (Robert b 1965), 3 da (Sarah b 1957, Charlotte b 1960, Diana b 1961); m 2, 15 April 1978, Teresa Jane, da of Lt-Col Douglas Forster, DSO (d 1983) - 11th Hussars (Prince Albert's Own); *Career* Mil Service; The Royal Sussex Regt 1940, cmmnd The Argyll & Sutherland Highlanders 1940, 2 Battalion A & S H Singapore 1941, POW Thailand 1942-45, ret 1946; Investmt Dept Kleinwort Sons & Co 1946-52, memb The Stock Exchange London 1953-82, ptnr Fielding Newson & Smith & Co 1953-62, finance dir H M Tennent Ltd 1958-73, investment advsr to King George V's Pension Fund for Actors and Actresses (1911) 1960-82, ptnr Colegrave & Co The Stock Exchange London 1962-73, chm H M Tennent Ltd 1973-77, ptnr Kitcat & Aitken the Stock Exchange London 1973-81; tstee The Royal Ballet Benevolent Fnd 1978-84, memb Investment Ctee Peterhouse Cambridge 1983-85, tstee Cambridge Health Authy Tst Fnd 1986-; appointed: official speaker for The Far East POWs Assoc (E Anglia) 1984-, lectr to 22 Special Air Services Regt Courses Stirling Lines Hereford 1985-, official speaker for the Burma Star Herts Cambs and Essex Borders Branch ; *Recreations* walking, reading, writing, correspondence, conversation, travel, preaching, lecturing; *Clubs* The City of London, The Free Foresters, The Arabs CC; *Style—* James Noble, Esq; 25 Portugal Place, Cambridge (☎ 0223 312277)

NOBLE, John Bernard; s of John Leslie Noble (d 1974), of Rushden, Northants (b of Larry Noble, former actor), and Annie, *née* Mowbray; ggu was Matthew Noble (1817-76), sculptor: statue of Queen Victoria at Bombay 1872; *b* 26 Nov 1923; *Educ* Tech Coll, Yorks; *m* 19 Nov 1946, Valerie Alma, da of John Looch (d 1943), of Oudtshoorn, CP, S Africa; 1 s (Richard b 1954), 1 da (Anne b 1948); *Career* Pilot, Tr Cmd RAF 1942-45, Area Flying Control, Aden RAF 1945-46 (King's Commendation of Valuable Servs in the Air 1946), Flt-Lt; qualified as ophthalmic optician 1948; FBOA; *Recreations* painting, film making; *Style—* John Noble, Esq; 7 Kimbolton Rd, Higham Ferrers, Rushden, Northants (☎ 55312); J B Noble, Optician, Church St, Rushden, Northants; Kempston, Bedford

NOBLE, Sir Marc Brunel; 5 Bt (UK 1902), of Ardmore and Ardardan Noble, Cardross, Co Dumbarton; s of Sir Humphrey Brunel Noble, 4 Bt, MBE, MC (d 1968, whose mother Celia Brunel James, was gda of Isambard Kingdom Brunel, the celebrated Victorian engineer), of Walwick Hall, Hexham, Northumberland, and Celia, *née* Weigall (d 1982); *b* 8 Jan 1927; *Educ* Eton; *m* 27 Jan 1956, Jennifer Lorna, yr da of late John Mein-Austin, of Flint Hill, W Haddon, Rugby, Northants; 2 s, 1 da (and 1 da decd); *Heir* s, David Brunel Noble; *Career* Maj (ret) King's Dragoon Gds (cmmnd 1947), transfd 1 Royal Dragoons 1958; Cwlth cmmr Scout Assoc 1972-, chm Ctee of Cncl Scout Assoc 1979-80; co pres Kent Scout Cncl, govr Sibton Park Sch; High Sheriff of Kent 1985-86; *Recreations* shooting, travel; *Clubs* Cavalry and Guards; *Style—* Maj Sir Marc Noble, Bt; Deerleap House, Knockholt, Sevenoaks, Kent TN14 7NP (☎ 0959 33222)

NOBLE, Hon Mrs Mary Myfanwy; da of 1 Baron Davies (d 1944); *b* 1923; *m* 1958 (m dis 1979), Hugh McAskill Noble; 3 s; *Career* formerly in Women's Royal Canadian Naval Serv; CStJ; *Style—* The Hon Mrs Mary Noble; 17 Dick Place, Edinburgh

NOBLE, Peter Saxton Fitzjames; CBE (1977); 2 s of Sir Humphrey Noble, 4 Bt, MBE, MC (d 1968), of Walwick Hall, Humshaugh, Hexham, Northumberland, former High Sheriff of Northumberland (d 1968), and Celia Stewart Weigall (d 1982); bro of Sir Marc Noble, 5 Bt, and descendant of Sir Andrew Noble, 1 Bt, famous physicist and expert on explosives; *b* 22 May 1929; *Educ* Eton, Magdalene Coll Cambridge; *m* 1, 1954 (m dis 1966), Elizabeth Emmeline, da of Launcelot William Gregory Eccles, CMG, MC; 1 s (Simon Peter Saxton Fanshaw b 1958); m 2, 1966 (m dis 1980), Helena Margaret, da of Thomas Essery Rose-Richards and formerly w of David Anthony Harries; 1 s (James Essery Brunel b 1968); m 3, 1980, Penelope Margaret, da of late Leslie Landeau; *Career* int wine conslt; former chm: UK Wine and Spirit Assoc, Wine Devpt Bd; président d'honneur EEC Wine and Spirit Gp; dir: Int Wine & Spirit Competition Ltd, The Grape Connection Ltd; *Style—* Peter Noble Esq, CBE; Flax Cottage, 17 Ham Common, Richmond, Surrey TW10 7JB (☎ 01 940 7576)

NOBLE, Robert Milne; s of John Noble (ka 1940), and Mary Bella *née* Milne; a fishing family from a remote NE Scotland village; *b* 2 Dec 1931; *Educ* Maiduff High Sch Scotland; *m* 11 Sept 1954, 1 s (Robert b 1963), 2 da (Janet b 1957, Helen b 1961); *Career* dep chmn: Moss Communications plc; chm: Golf Illustrated Ltd, CBA Promotions Ltd; FCCA; ACIS; *Recreations* golf, walking; *Clubs* RAC, Leander, Huntercombe Golf; *Style—* Robert Noble, Esq; Hart House, Sonning on Thames, Berks

NOBLE, Lady; Sigrid; *née* Michelet; 2 da of Johan Michelet, Norwegian Diplomatic Service; *m* 16 Oct 1934, Sir Andrew Napier Noble, 2 Bt, KCMG (d 1987); 2 s, 1 da; *Style—* Lady Noble; 11 Cedar House, Marloes Road, London W8 (☎ 01 937 7952)

NOBLE, Timothy Peter; yr s of Sir Andrew Napier Noble, 2 Bt, KCMG (d 1987); hp of bro Sir Iain Andrew Noble, 3 Bt; *b* 21 Dec 1943; *Educ* Eton, Univ Coll Oxford (MA); *m* 1976, Elizabeth Mary, da of late Alexander Wallace Aitken: 2 s (Lorne Andrew Wallace b 1980, Andrew Iain Brunnel b 1984), 1 da (Sasha Heidi Elizabeth b 1978); *Career* barr Gray's Inn 1969; INSEAD, Fontainebleau (MBA) 1970; exec dir: Lyle Shipping plc Glasgow 1976-84, Noble & Co Ltd Edinburgh 1984-; *Clubs* New (Edinburgh); *Style—* Timothy Noble, Esq; Ardnahane, Barnton Avenue, Edinburgh 4

NOBLE, William; CBE (1973); s of Arthur Noble (d 1936), of Belfast and Elizabeth Jane Noble, OBE (d 1978); *b* 5 Jan 1909; *Educ* Royal Belfast Academical Inst, Queens Univ Belfast (LLB); *m* 1938, Henrietta Maude, da of Capt William Kernahan (d 1950), of Belfast; 3 s; *Career* controller estate duty office Miny of Fin N Ireland 1960-73; chm Ulster Soc for Promoting the Educn of the Deaf Dumb and Blind 1977- ; *Recreations* golf, painting; *Clubs* Royal Belfast GC; *Style—* William Noble, Esq, CBE; Ongar, Jordanstown Rd, Newtownabbey, N Ireland (☎ 0232 863 121)

NOCK, Sir Norman Lindfield; s of Thomas Nock; *Educ* SCEGS; *m* 1927, Ethel Evelina Bradford, da of E H Stafvater; 1 s; *Career* chm Nock & Kirby Ltd 1925-79, Lord Mayor Sydney 1938-39 (memb City Cncl 1934-43), pres Adult Deaf and Dumb Soc of NSW 1948-69; kt 1939; *Style—* Sir Norman Nock; Box 4250, GPO Sydney, NSW 2001, Australia

NOEL, Col Archibald Charles William; MC (1940); s of the Hon Charles Hubert Francis Noel OBE, (d 1947), and Jane Francis Regina Mary, *née* Douglas Dick (d 1964); *b* 5 Jan 1914; *Educ* The Oratory Sch, RMC Sandhurst; *m* 30 Aug 1945, Bridget Mary (d 1976), da of Brig WA Fetherstonhaugh CB,CBE SDSO (d 19470; 2 s (Charles b 1948, Edward b 1958), m 2, 22 Dec 1977, Andrée Marie, Pierre Duchen, of Bayonne France;; *Career* Welsh Guards 1934, France 1939-45, (POW), Staff Coll 1946, cmd 1 Bn Welsh guards 1952-56, Mil Sec HQ Eastern cmd 1957-58, SHAPE 1960-62, Mil Attache SA 1962-66;; *Clubs* Cavalry and Guards; *Style—* Col ACW Noel, MC

NOEL, Lady Celestria Magdalen Mary; da of 5 Earl of Gainsborough; *b* 27 Jan 1954; *Educ* St Mary's Convent Ascot, St Hilda's Coll Oxford; *Style—* Lady Celestria Noel; 8 Peel St, London W8

NOEL, Maj Douglas Robert George; s of Maj The Hon Charles Noel (d 1948), and The Hon Mrs Charles Mary Noel Douglas, *née* Dick (d 1964); *b* 16 April 1924; *Educ* Oratory Sch; *m* June 1949, Eleanor Susan Jane, da of Brig G Younghusband (d 1970), of Breconshire; 2 s (James b 1950, William b 1953), 1 da (Caroline b 1956); *Career* offr; Coldstream Guards 1942-79; *Style—* Maj Douglas R G Noel; 25 Broomhouse Rd, London SW6 3QU (☎ 01 736 5492)

NOEL, Hon Edward Andrew; The Honourable; s of 5 Earl of Gainsborough and Mary, da of Hon John Joseph Stourton, TD; *b* 22 Oct 1960; *Educ* Farleigh House Sch Basingstoke, Ampleforth, Uni de L'Institute Britannique (Paris); *Career* businessman; landowner (160 acres); *Recreations* travelling, scuba-diving, shooting, music; *Clubs* Boodles, St James's, Bembridge Sailing; *Style—* The Hon Edward Noel; Flat 4, 14 Edith Grove, London SW10 0NW (☎ 01-352 0023/4)

NOEL, Hon Gerard Edward Joseph; s of 5 Earl of Gainsborough; *b* 23 Jan 1955; *Educ* Ampleforth, London Univ; *m* 1985, Charlotte, yr (twin) da of Sir William Stratford Dugdale, 2 Bt, CBE, MC; *Style—* The Hon Gerard Noel; The Manor House, Withington, nr Cheltenham, Glos

NOEL, Hon Gerard Eyre Wriothesley; s of 4 Earl of Gainsborough, OBE (d 1927); *b* 1926; *Educ* Georgetown USA, Exeter Coll Oxford; *m* 1958, Adele Julie Patricia, da of Maj Vivian Nicholas Bonville Were (decd); 2 s, 1 da; *Career* barr Inner Temple 1952; author (works incl books on Harold Wilson, Barry Goldwater and Princess Alice, Queen Victoria's Forgotten Daughter); publisher & journalist, former dir Herder Book Co, dir Search Press 1972-; asst ed *Catholic Herald* 1968-71 (ed 1971-76, editorial dir 1976-81, ed-in-chief 1981-); contested (L) Argyll 1959; memb exec Ctee Cncl of Christians and Jews 1974-; Liveryman Worshipful Co of Stationers and Newspapermakers; Freeman City of London; *Books* Paul VI, The Path from Rome, Goldwater, Harold Wilson, Princess Alice, The Great Lock-Out of 1926, Ena, Spain's English Queen; *Clubs* Garrick, Beefsteak; *Style—* The Hon Gerard Noel; Chipping Campden, Glos

NOEL, Capt Gerard John Hamlyn; s of Maj Edward Francis Hamlyn Noel, MRCVS (d 1953), and Doris Marie Noel, *née* Verrieres (d 1983); *b* 8 Dec 1930; *Educ* Wellington Mil Coll of Sci; *m* 7 Sept 1963, Gillian Ralphia, da of Walter Terence Barrand Head (d 1983); 1 s (Richard Noel b 1965), 1 da (Victoria Noel b 1969); *Career* Royal Engrs, serv BAOR 1951-52; Far E 1958-61; attached Army Air Corps as Pilot, BAOR 1961-67; ret 1967; fruit farming; *Recreations* shooting, skiing, tennis; *Clubs* Ski Club of GB; *Style—* Capt Gerard J H Noel; Squirrels Hall, Stratford St Mary, by Colchester, Essex (☎ 0206 298276); Squirrels Hall, Fruit Farm, Stratford St Mary, by Colchester, Essex (☎ 0206 298276)

NOEL, Rear Admiral (Gambier) John Byng; CB; s of Gambier Baptist Edward Noel and Beatrice Eva Francis (d 1967); see Gainsborough & Torrington; *b* 16 July 1914; *Educ* Hill House St Leonards-on-Sea, RNC Dartmouth; *m* 4 March 1936, Joan, da of Percy Herbert Stevens (d 1943); 4 da (Caroline b 1936, Penelope b 1939, Virginia b 1943, Vanessa b 1943); *Career* 1939-45 HMS Aurora and HMS Norfolk (despatches twice), Capt 1959, Far E, Rear Adm (UK) 1967-69; *Recreations* gardening; *Clubs* Anglo-Belgian; *Style—* Rear Adm John Noel, CB; Woodpeckers, Church Lane, Haslemere, Surrey GU27 2BJ

NOEL, Hon Thomas; s of 5 Earl of Gainsborough; *b* 9 Mar 1958; *Educ* Ampleforth, RAC Cirencester; *Style—* The Hon Thomas Noel; Flat 10, 38 Redcliffe Rd, London SW10

NOEL-BAKER, Hon Francis Edward; s of late Baron Noel-Baker, PC (Life Peer UK 1977, d 1982), and Irene (d 1956); *b* 7 Jan 1920; *Educ* Westminster, Gordonstoun, King's Coll Cambridge (1st cl Hons Exhibition); *m* 1957, Barbara Christina, yr da of late Engineer Josef Sonander (d 1936), of Norrköping, Sweden; 4 s, 1 da; *Career* joined Royal Tank Regt 1940, transferred Intelligence Corps 1941 (despatches), Capt 1942; MP (Lab): Brentford and Chiswick 1945-50, Swindon 1955-69, resigned from Lab Pty 1969 and joined SDP 1981, left and joined Cons Pty 1984; chm: Br Greek Parly Gp 1958-69, PLP Overs eas Dvpt Ctee 1964-68, UN Parly Ctee 1966-69; pres Euro Cncl for the Village and Small Town (ECOVAST), hon pres Union of Forest Owners of Greece 1968-; govr Campion Sch Athens 1974-78; dir: North Euboean Enterprises Ltd 1973-, Fini Fisheries Cyprus 1976-; memb Ecology Party 1978-, Soil Assoc 1979-; joined Cons Pty 1984; *Books* Greece the Whole Story (1945), Spanish Summary (1946), The Spy Web (1954), The Land & People of Greece (1957), Looking at Greece (1968), My Cyprus File (1986), Book Eight (1987); *Recreations* gardening, writing; *Clubs* Special Forces (London), Athens Club, Travellers (London); *Style—* The Hon Francis Noel-Baker; Greece (☎ 0227 41204, telex 214716 ELBR GR); office: 27 Bryanston Square, London W1 (☎ 01 723 9405, telex 917506)

NOEL-BUXTON, 3 Baron (UK 1930); Martin Connal; s of 2 Baron Noel-Buxton (d 1980), by his 1 w, Nancy, *née* Connal; *b* 8 Dec 1940; *Educ* Bryanston, Balliol Coll Oxford; *m* 1, 1964 (m dis 1968), Miranda Mary, da of H A Chisenhale-Marsh, of Gaynes Park, Epping, Essex; m 2, 1972 (m dis 1982), Sarah Margaret Surridge (she m, 1982, Peter E W Adam), da of Neil Charles Wolseley Barrett TD, of Twickenham Rd, Teddington; 1 s, 1 da (Hon Lucy b 1977); m 3, 18 Dec 1986, Mrs Abigail Marie Granger, da of Eric Philip Richard Clent; *Heir* s, Hon Charles Connal Noel-Buxton b 17 April 1975; *Career* slr 1966; *Style—* The Rt Hon the Lord Noel-Buxton; House of Lords, London SW1A 0PW

NOEL-BUXTON, Hon Michael Barnett Noel; s of 1 Baron Noel-Buxton, PC (d 1948); *b* 1920; *Educ* Harrow, Balliol Coll Oxford; *Career* serv RA 1940-46, with Colonial Civil Serv (Gold Coast) 1947-59; *Clubs* Flyfishers'; *Style—* The Hon Michael Noel-Buxton; Stretchney, Diptford, Totnes, Devon (☎ 054 882 342)

NOEL-PATON, Hon (Frederick) Ranald; s of Baron Ferrier (Life Peer), *qv*; *b* 7 Nov 1938; *Educ* Rugby, Haverford Coll Pennsylvania, McGill Univ Montreal (BA); *m* 1973, Patricia, da of late Gen Sir William Gurdon Stirling, GCB, CBE, DSO; 4 da; *Career* Br Utd Airways Ltd 1965-70, Br Caledonian Airways Ltd 1970-86, gen mangr West Africa 1975-79, Far E 1980-86; dir Caledonian Far E Airways 1984-86; Gp md John Menzies plc; dir: Pacific Assets Tst plc, Gen Accident Fire & Life Assur Corpn plc, The Royal Bank of Scotland plc; *Recreations* gardening, golf, fishing, ornithology, the arts; *Clubs* New (Edinburgh), Hong Kong, Shek O Country; *Style—* The Hon Ranald Noel-Paton; Easter Dunbarnie, Bridge of Earn, Perth PH2 9ED (☎ 073881 2395)

NOEST, Peter J; *b* 12 June 1948; *Educ* St George's Coll, Weybridge, The RAC Cirencester; *m* Lisabeth Penelope Moody; l s (Timothy Peter b 1974), 1 da (Lisa Jane b 1976); *Career* chartered surveyor (land agency/general practise); Knight Frank & Rutley: ptnr Amsterdam 1972-77, ptnr London 1977-81, full equity ptnr 1981, resigned 1983; Hampton & Sons: conslt, sr commercial ptnr 1984; dir of devpt Lambert Smith Hampton plc; Hdlgs; FRICS; *Books* contributor to Office Development, Estates Gazette (1985); *Recreations* hunting, tennis, farming, conservation, forestry, travel, wine; *Clubs* Turf, Oriental, Landsdowne; *Style—* Peter Noest, Esq; Little Park, Wootton Bassett, Wilts SN4 7QW (☎ 0793 852348

NOLAN, David John; s of David Nolan, of Liverpool, and Constance Cordelia, *née* O'Donaghue; *b* 8 May 1949; *Educ* St Edwards Coll Liverpool, Royal Manchester Coll of Music; *m* 7 Jan 1977, Lyn Marie, da of Henry Steven Broughton, of Vermont, USA; 1 s (Jonathan David b 1978); *Career* princ violin LSO 1974-76, ldr London Philharmonic Orchestra 1976-, frequent soloist with Br's maj orchs and conductors, and a large concerto repertoire ranging from Bach to Berg; ARMCM; *Recreations* jogging, rose gardening; *Style—* David Nolan, Esq; Blythewood, West Rd, St Georges Hill, Weybridge, Surrey KT13 0LY (☎ 0932 844449)

NOLAN, Hon Mr Justice; Hon Sir Michael Patrick Nolan; yr s of James Thomas Nolan and Jane, *née* Walsh; *b* 10 Sept 1928; *Educ* Ampleforth, Wadham Coll Oxford; *m* 1953, Margaret, yr da of Alfred Noyes, CBE, the poet, by his w Mary, da of Capt Jasper Graham Mayne, CBE, of Gidleigh Park, Chagford, Devon, by his w Cecily; 1 s, 4 da; *Career* serv RA 1947-49 and TA 1949-55; High Court Judge (Queen's Bench) 1982-; presiding judge Western Circuit 1985-88; rec Crown Ct 1975-82, QC 1968, QC (NI) 1974, barr NI 1974, barr Middle Temple 1953, memb Bar Cncl 1973-74, memb Senate Inns of Ct and Bar 1974-81, tres 1977-79; memb Sandilands Ctee Inflation Accounting 1973-75; memb governing body Convent of Sacred Heart Woldingham 1973-82, govr Combe Bank Sch 1974-82; kt 1982; *Style—* The Hon Mr Justice Nolan; Royal Courts of Justice, Strand, London WC2A 2LL

NOLAN, Sir Sidney Robert; OM (1983), CBE (1963); s of late S Nolan; *b* 22 April 1917; *Educ* Melbourne State & Tech Schs; *m* 1948, Cynthia Hansen (d 1976); 1 da; *Career* Hon LLD ANU, Hon DLitt London, DLitt (hon causa) Sydney, hon fell York Univ; artist; winner of numerous art awards; represented in: Tate Gallery London, Museum of Modern Art NY, all state national art galleries in Australia; exhibited in Brussels, London, New Delhi, New York, Pittsburgh, Venice; kt 1981; *Style—* Sir Sidney Nolan, OM, CBE; c/o Marlborough Fine Art Ltd, 6 Albermarle Street, London W1

NOON, Anthony John; s of John Michael Noon (d 1967), of Lane End, Rose Hill Park West, Sutton, Surrey, and Amelia Lucy, *née* Newman (d 1958); *b* 20 Dec 1932; *Educ* Boys HS Sutton, Epsom Coll (LLB); *m* 30 March 1964, Cecilia Mary, da of William Cecil Graham, of Epsom, Surrey; 2 da (Jennifer Caroline b 1965, Jacqueline Anne b 1975); *Career* RAF Pilot Officer 1956; slr 1955, asst slr Wanstead and Woodford

Borough Cncl 1958-60, slr Babcock & Wilcox Ltd 1963-71, dir legal and contract Servs The Plessey Co plc 1976-, (dep legal advsr 1963-71, legal advsr 1971-76); memb Law Soc 1955; *Recreations* reading, walking, windsurfing; *Style*— Anthony Noon, Esq; 15 Aldeburgh Place, Woodford Gn, Essex I68 OPT (☎ 01 504 2047); The Plessey Company plc, Vicarage Lane, Ilford, Essex IG1 4AQ (☎ 01 553 8055, fax 01 553 8372, telex 897971)

NOONE, Dr Paul; s of Michael John Noone, OBE (d 1982), of Darlington, and Florence Miriam, *née* Knox (d 1988); *b* 4 Mar 1939; *Educ* Christ Church Oxford (BA), Oxford Univ and Middx Hosp Med Sch (BM, CLB, MA); *m* 1, 1962 (m dis 1981), (Pamela) Ahilya Nehaul, da of Dr Balbir Balgreen Nehaul, OBE, of Leeds; 2 s (Michael b 7 Sept 1963, Thomas b 8 Jan 1971); m 2, 29 July 1982, Mailia Rudrani Tambimultu, da of Dr James Tambinulta, of Sri Lanka; 1 step s (Amrik b 23 Jan 1973), 3 step da (Kamani b 28 Sept 1969, Amirthi b 29 Aug 1970, Dheemati b 8 Nov 1976); *Career* sr registrar in microbiology 1969-70, lectr in bateriology sch of pathology Middx Hosp Med Sch 1971-72, conslt med microbiologist 1972-; chm NHS Conslts Assoc 1978-88, memb ASTHS delgn to TUC Annual Congress 1971-72; lectured extensively throughout the world on various aspects of antibiotics and infection; contrib over 90 articles to med jls; MRCPath 1971, FRCPath 1983; *Books* A Clinciian's Guide to Antimicrobial Therapy (second edn 1980); *Recreations* spending time with family & friends; *Style*— Dr Paul Noone; 39 wykeham Hill, Wembley, Middx HA9 9RY (☎ 01 908 3392); Royal Free Hosp, Pond St, Hampstead, London NW3 2QG (☎ 01 794 0500)

NORBURY, 6 Earl of (I 1827); Noel Terence Graham-Toler; also Baron Norwood (I 1797), Baron Norbury (I 1800), and Viscount Glandine (I 1827); s of 5 Earl (d 1955); *b* 1 Jan 1939; *m* 1965, Anne, da of late Francis Mathew; 1 s, 1 da (Lady Patricia Margaret b 1970); *Heir* s, Viscount Glandine; *Clubs* RAC; *Style*— The Rt Hon the Earl of Norbury; c/o Stock Exchange, EC2

NORBURY, Lt-Col Peter; s of Robert Norbury (d 1963), of Jersey, and Edith Fortuna Victoria, *née* Lansell (d 1981); *b* 21 Feb 1924; *Educ* Melbourne GS Victoria, St Lawrence Coll Ramsgate Oundle, Truro Cathedral Sch; *m* 2 Jan 1948, Barbara Joy, da of Griffith Bowen Morgan (d 1955), of Maidstone; 2 s (Mark b 1949, David b 1953), 1 da (Sally b 1950); *Career* enlisted 1942, cmmnd RE 1943, OC 4 Dog Platoon NW Europe 1944-45; chief trainer War Dogs Trg Sch 1946-49, Singapore Plant Sqdn 1950-52, GHQ Far E Land Forces 1953-54, Staff Coll Camberley 1955, Field Sqdn BAOR 1960-62, Jt Servs Staff Coll 1962, HQ 1 (BR) Corps BAOR 1963-65, staff of exercise LOGTRAIN Thailand (SEATO) 1965, 2 i/c Div Engrs 1965-66, Cmdg Depot Regt RE 1967-69, Br Advsr Sudanese Staff Sch Omdurman 1969-70, staff of C-in-C's Ctee 1970-73, ret 1973; Housing & Planning Inspr Planning Inspectorate DOE 1973 (Sr Inspr 1976-); Liveryman Worshipful Co of Arbitrators 1988, Freeman City of London; ACIArb, MBIM; *Recreations* model engrg, general workshop practice; *Clubs* Naval; *Style*— Lt-Col Peter Norbury; Apple Tree House, Gussage All Saints, Wimborne, Dorset BH21 5ET (☎ 0258 840552)

NORCLIFFE, Thomas Anthony Firth; s of Thomas Stainthorpe Norcliffe, of The Ave, Liphook, Hampshire, and Doris Margaret, *née* Firth; *b* 21 Jan 1939; *Educ* Felsted Sch, Royal Free Hosp Med Sch, Royal Dental Hosp, Univ of the Pacific Dental Sch (BDS, LDS, RCS); *m* 1 April 1966, Susan Howard, da of Michael Howard Rawlings (d 1943); 1 s (Thomas b 1977), 2 da (Sarah b 1967, Belinda b 1970); *Career* dental surgn Harley St London 1963-, sr ptnr Norcliffe Invest Jacobs & Ward; Freeman City of London 1978, Liveryman Worshipful Co of Curriers 1978; memb: BDA, FDI; fell: Int Coll of Dentists (1984), Piere Fauchard Acad (1987); *Recreations* english watercolours, music, golf, fishing, tennis; *Clubs* RSM; *Style*— Anthony Norcliffe, Esq; 6 Green St, London W1 (☎ 01 629 0043); The Old Farmhouse, Hazeley Bottom, Hampshire; 90 Harley St, London W1 (☎ 01 935 2240/01 935 2249)

NORCROSS, Eric; s of William Edwards Norcross (d 1959), and Ruth Norcross, *née* Haworth (d 1957); *b* 17 August 1932; *Educ* Queen Elizabeth's GS Blackburn, Univ Manchester, (BSc); *m* 23 July 1958, Megan Veronica, da of John North (d 1963), of Middlestown, Yorks; 1 da (Fiona Heather b 1959); *Career* works mgmnt Mullard Ltd 1954-69; asst sec Dept of Employment 1969-76; dir Advisory Conciliation and Arbitration Service (ACAS) 1976-; *Recreations* home life; *Clubs* Civil Serv; *Style*— Eric Norcross, Esq; Ponderosa, Barncroft Rd, Berkhamsted, Herts HP4 3NL (☎ 044 27 2408); ACAS, 11-12 St James's Sq, London SW1 (☎ 01 210 3720)

NORCROSS, Lawrence John Charles; OBE (1986); s of Frederick Marshall Norcross (d 1934), and Florence Kate, *née* Hedges (d 1979); *b* 14 April 1927; *Educ* Moor Lane Sch Chessington Surrey, Ruskin Coll Oxford, Leeeds Univ (BA); *m* 17 Aug 1958, (Janet) Margaret, da of John William Wallace; 3 s (Matthew b 25 May 1959, Alastair b 22 Sept 1960, Daniel b 14 April 1969), 1 da (Joanna b 27 Aug 1962); *Career* serv RN 1942-49 (E Indies Fleet 1944-45 HMS Nigeria); asst master: Singlegate Sch 1957-61, Abbey Wood Sch 1961-63; housemaster Battersea County Sch 1963-74, headmaster Highbury Grove Sch 1975-87 (dep head 1974-75); exec ctee memb Nat Cncl for Educational Standards 1977- (tstee 1982-); memb: education study gp Centre for Policy Studies 1980-, Univ Entrance and Schools Examination Cncl London Univ 1979-84; tstee Educ Res Tst 1985-; memb Headmasters' Conference 1985-87; *Books* The ILEA; A Case for Reform (with F Naylor, 1981), The ILEA After the Abolition of the GLC (with F Naylor and J McIntosh, 1985), contributor to The Wayward Curriculum (1986); *Recreations* watching cricket, wining and dining, listening to music, solving crosswords; *Clubs* Surrey CCC; *Style*— Lawrence Norcross, Esq, OBE; 3 St Nicholas Mansions, 6-8 Trinity Crescent, London SW17 7AF (☎ 01 767 4299); Crockwell Cottage, Crockwell Street, Long Compton, Shipston-on-Stour, Warwickshire

NORDEN, Denis; CBE (1980); s of George Norden (d 1977), and Jenny Norden (d 1979); *b* 6 Feb 1922; *Educ* City of London Sch; *m* 1943, Avril Rosen; 1 s (Nicolas), 1 da (Maggie); *Career* writer and broadcaster, co-author (with Frank Muir) radio series Take it From Here, tv series Whacko has appeared for 2 decades in radio series My Word!, radio and tv series My Music; written and appeared in tv series Looks Familiar 1973-, also various outbreaks of It'll be Alright on the Night; *Books* My Word (series with Frank Muir), Coming To You Live (with Sybil Harper and Norma Gilbert); *Recreations* loitering; *Clubs* Odeon Saturday Morning; *Style*— Denis Norden Esq, CBE; c/o April Young, 2 Lowndes Street, London SW1X 9ET (☎ 01 259 6458)

NORDEN, Desmond Spencer; s of Percy Spencer Norden (d 1977), and Letitia, *née* Elliott (d 1977); *b* 10 April 1925; *Educ* SE Essex Tech Coll; *m* 14 June 1947, Sheila Mary, da of William Alfred Shrub (d 1974); 1 s (Robert Spencer b 1948), 1 da (Linda Margaret b 1950); *Career* enlisted RE 1945, transferred E Surrey Regt, cmmnd 1946, demob Lt 1947; works accountant Mackay Industl Equipment Ltd 1958 (works accountant 1948), co sec Mechanical Handling Equipment Co Ltd, accountant Mackay Industl Equipment Ltd 1962-65, chm and md Fry Pollard Ltd 1984 (accountant 1966, md 1970); life vice-pres Worcester Park Athletic Club (joined 1951, tres 1963-78, chm 1978-84); Freeman City of London 1983, memb Worshipful Co of Builders Merchants 1984; *Recreations* golf, cricket; *Clubs* Surbiton GC, Worcester Park Athetic; *Style*— Desmond Norden, Esq; 15 Gilhams Ave, Banstead, Surrey SM7 1QL (☎ 01 393 5139); Fry & Pollard Ltd, 30 Engate St, London SE13 7HA (☎ 01 852 1092, fax 01 318 0236)

NORELL, Dr Jack; s of Henry Norell (d 1981), and Malka Norell (d 1987); *b* 3 Mar 1927; *Educ* Guy's Hosp Med Sch; *m* 1948 (m dis 1971), Brenda, *née* Honeywell; 1 s (Paul David Michael); *Career* RAF 1945-48; GP 1956-; dean of studies RCGP 1974-81, med exec offr JCP IGP, ed 'The Practitioner' 1982-83, cncl memb RCGP 1984-; pres: Balint Soc of GB 1984-87, section gen practice RSH 1989-, Int Balint Fedn 1989-; MB, BS, FRCGP; *Books* 6 Minutes for the Patient (1971), Training for General Practice (1981), What Sort of Doctor (1985), While I'm Here Doctor (1987), Aids & The General Practitioner (1988); *Recreations* walking, driving, teaching, music; *Clubs* Medical Soc of London, Hunterian Soc; *Style*— Dr Jack Norell; 50 Nottingham Terrace, York Gate, Regents Park, London NW11 (☎ 01 607 4611); 58 Roman Way, London N7 8XF (☎ 01 486 2979)

NORFOLK, Jeremy Paul; s of David Ernest Norfolk, and Olive, *née* Bellerby; *b* 7 Mar 1948; *Educ* The King's Sch Canterbury, Aberdeen Univ (MA); *m* 20 July 1972, Rosemary Frances, da of George Austen Raffan (d 1980); 1 s (Guy b 15 July 1974), 1 da (Claire b 3 Nov 1976); *Career* Citibank NA 1975-83; md Adam & Co plc 1988- (joined 1983); *Recreations* golf, tennis, music; *Style*— Jeremy Norfolk, Esq; 8 Henderland Rd, Edinburgh (☎ 031 337 2640); Adam & Co plc, 22 Charlotte Sq, Edinburgh (☎ 031 225 8484, fax 031 225 5136, telex 72182)

NORFOLK, Lavinia, Duchess of; Lavinia Mary; *née* Strutt; CBE (1971); da of 3 Baron Belper (d 1956), and Eva, Countess of Rosebery, DBE, *qv*; *b* 22 Mar 1916; *m* 1937, 16 Duke of Norfolk, KG, GCVO, GBE, TD, PC (d 1975); 4 da (Lady Herries, Lady Mary Mumford, Lady Sarah Clutton, Countess of Ancram, *qqv*); *Career* a bearer of the Queen's Canopy at Coronation of King George VI; Lord Lt of W Sussex 1975-; *Style*— Her Grace Lavinia, Duchess of Norfolk; Arundel Park, Sussex (☎ 0903 882104)

NORFOLK, Leslie William; CBE (1973, OBE 1944), TD (1946); s of Robert Norfolk (d 1954), of Nottingham, and Edith Florence, *née* Preston (d 1948); *b* 8 April 1911; *Educ* Southwell Minster GS, Univ Coll Nottingham (BSc); *m* 21 July 1944, Anne Isabel Etta Waller (Nancy), da of Sir Hugh Wesley Allen Watson (d 1952), of London; 2 s (Wiliam b 13 April 1945, James b 22 March 1947), 1 da (Jane b 5 Jan 1949); *Career* serv WWII: cmmnd 2 Lt 5 Bn The Sherwood Foresters (TA) 1931, 1 War Staff Course Staff Coll Camberley 1939, transferred to RE, BEF 1940, Lt-Col Staff RE Gilraltar 1941, Staff Offr RE HQ Northern Cmd 1944; Col 1 CE Works Z Res 1951; asst and subsequently ptnr E G Phillips Son & Norfolk (Conslt Engrs) Nottingham 1933; ICI: construction mangr dyestuffs div 1945, resident engr Kingston Onario Canada 1954, asst chief engr metals div 1955, engrg mangr Severnside Works 1957, engrg dir Duperial SAIC Buenos Aires 1959, personnel & servs dir HOC div 1964; chief-exec Royal Dockyards MOD (Navy) 1969, engrg conslt Bath 1972; memb ctee: mgmt Bath Indust Heritage Centre 1974, Bath & Co Club 1969 (later chm); MIEE 1938, MIMechE 1949, MICE 1943; *Recreations* home workshop, indust archaeology, gardening; *Style*— Leslie Norfolk, Esq, CBE, TD; Beechwoods, Beechwood Rd, Combe Down, Bath BA2 5JS (☎ 0225 832104)

NORFOLK, 17 Duke of (Premier E Dukedom 1483 with precedence 1397); Miles Francis Fitzalan Howard; KG (1983), GCVO (1986), CB (1966), CBE (1960), MC (1944), DL (W Sussex 1977); also Earl of Arundel (E 1139 if the claim by tenure, which was admitted by the Crown in 1433, is recognised; otherwise 1292; either way, the Premier E Earldom), Baron Beaumont (E 1309), Baron Maltravers (E 1330), Earl of Surrey (E 1483), Baron FitzAlan, Baron Clun, Baron Oswaldestre (all E 1627), Earl of Norfolk (E 1644), and Baron Howard of Glossop (UK 1869); Earl Marshal and Hereditary Marshal of England (1672) and Chief Butler of England; s of 3 Baron Howard of Glossop, MBE (d 1972) and Baroness Beaumont, OBE (d 1971); suc 2 cous once removed (16 Duke) 1975; *b* 21 July 1915; *Educ* Ampleforth, Christ Church Oxford (MA, hon student 1983); *m* 1949, Anne Mary Teresa jt chm Help The Hospices, da of Wing Cdr Gerald Constable-Maxwell, MC, DFC, AFC, through whom she enjoys the same degree of kinship with the 16 Duke as her husb; 2 s, 3 da; *Heir* s, Earl of Arundel; *Career* sits as Cons in House of Lords; serv WWII France, N Africa, Sicily, Italy (despatches, MC) and NW Europe; head of Br Mil Mission to Russian Forces in Germany 1957-59, cmd 70 Bde KAR 1961-63, GOC 1 Div 1963-65; dir: Mgmnt and Support Intelligence MOD 1965-66, Serv Intelligence MOD 1966-67, ret Maj-Gen Grenadier Gds; chm Arundel Castle Tstees Ltd, pres Building Socs Assoc 1982-86; hon fell St Edmund's House Cambridge 1983; kt SMO Malta; hon Bencher Inner Temple 1984-; *Style*— Maj-Gen His Grace The Duke of Norfolk, KG, GCVO, CB, CBE, MC, DL; Carlton Towers, Goole, Humberside (☎ 0405 860 243); Bacres House, Hambleden, Henley-on-Thames, Oxon (☎ 0491 571 350) ; Arundel Castle, Sussex (☎ 0903 882173)

NORLAND, Otto Realf; s of Realph I O Norland (d 1963), and Aasta, *née* Saether (d 1968); *b* 24 Feb 1930; *Educ* Norwegian Univ Coll of Econ and Business Admin Bergen Norway, Inst of Bankers London; *m* 1955, Gerd Ellen, da of Alfred Andenaes (d 1971); 1 s (Realph), 2 da (Karen, Eva); *Career* dir: Alcoa of Great Britain 1968-84 (chm: 1978-84), Aluminium Fedn 1979-84 (vice-pres 1981, pres 1982); London rep Deutsche Schiffahrtsbank AG 1984-, Hambros Bank Ltd 1953-84 (md 1964-79), chm Otto Norland Ltd, FCIB; *Recreations* salmon fishing, skiing, polar exploration; *Clubs* Norwegian, London, Norske Selskab Oslo; *Style*— Otto Norland, Esq; Grocers' Hall, Princes St, London EC2R 8AQ (☎ 01 726 8726, telex 889205)

NORMAN, Rear Adm Anthony Mansfeldt; CB (1989); s of Cecil Mansfeldt Norman (d 1963), and Jean Seymour, *née* Vale (d 1963); *b* 16 Dec 1934; *Educ* RNC Dartmouth; *m* 26 March 19621, Judith, da of Raymond Pye (d 1984); 1 s (Christopher Mansfeldt b 31 Oct 1964), 1 da (Caroline Louise b 26 Dec 1962); *Career* RN; various appts at sea and ashore 1948-65, exchange with USN Sandiego California 1965-67, staff ops offr 2 Frigate Sqdn 1967-69, staff ops offr Flag Offr Aircraft Carriers 1969-72, Admty Underwater Estab 1972-73, Nautical Def Coll 1974, CO HMS Mohawk 1975,

CO HMS Argonaut 1976, Fleet anti-submarine warfare offr 1976-78, CO HMS Broadsward 1978-81, dep dir Naval Plans 1981-83, Capt 2 Frigate Sqdn and CO HMS Broadward 1983-85, Capt Sch of Maritime Ops 1985-86, dir gen Naval Personnel Servs 1986-89; *Recreations* tennis, squash, hill walking, bridge, music appreciation; *Clubs* Army and Navy, Anchorites, Veteran of Great Britain LFC; *Style—* Rear-Adm Anthony Norman, CB; c/o National Provincial Bank, 208 Piccadilly, London W1A 2DG

NORMAN, Hon Mrs Barbara Jacqueline; *née* Boot; JP; da of 2 and last Baron Trent, KBE (d 1956), and Margaret Joyce Pyman (1975); *b* 26 Sept 1915; *m* 1934 (m dis 1973), Maj Willoughby Rollo Norman, 2 s of Maj Rt Hon Sir Henry Norman, 1 Bt (d 1939); 1 s, 2 da; *Style—* The Hon Mrs Barbara Norman, JP; Wilton Lodge, Lovell Rd, Winkfield, Berks

NORMAN, Barry Leslie; s of Leslie Norman (film prod (Mandy, The Cruel Sea) and dir (Dunkirk, The Long and the Short and the Tall)), and Elizabeth *née* Crafford; *b* 21 August 1933; *Educ* Highgate; *m* 1957, Mary Diana, da of Arthur Narracott (decd); 2 da (Samantha, Alexandra); *Career* writer and broadcaster; dir Nat Film Fin Corp 1980-85; writer and presenter Film 1987 (BBC TV), Talking Pictures (BBC TV 1988; presenter at various times: To-day, Going Places, Breakaway, The Chip Shop (all BBC Radio 4); Winner Richard Dimbleby Award BAFTA 1980; *Recreations* cricket; *Clubs* Groucho, BAFTA, Lords Taverners; *Style—* Barry Norman, Esq; c/o Curtis Brown, 162-168 Regent St, London W1

NORMAN, Bruce Anthony John; s of Arthur Stewart Norman (d 1965), and Lillian Gertrude, *née* Robinson-Longland; *b* 2 Nov 1936; *Educ* Northampton GS, Univ of Nottingham (BA), Univ of Manchester; *m* 6 Aug 1960, Psyche Patricia, da of Darrel Catling, of Travellers Rest, Church St, Hatfield, Herts; 1 s (Casper Giles Patrick b 16 March 1968), 1 da (Rebecca Tamsin b 10 June 1966); *Career* writer, producer, dir; with CBS and KPFA USA 1964-65, joined TV in England 1966; credits inc: Coronation Street (scripts) 1968, Cities at War (scripts) 1969; Dickens 1970; films written produced and directed for BBC tv incl: Pretty Maid 1970, Case of the Midwife Toad 1971, The Code Breakers 1971, The Rat Man 1972, The Birth of Television (BBC's 40th anniversary documentary), Tigris the Voyage of Thor Heyerdahl 1978, The Crime of Captain Colthurst 1980; exec prodr: Living Legends, Six English Towns, The Raising of the Mary Rose, Doomsday 1986, Footsteps 1987, Discoveries Underwater 1988; series ed: Horizon 1974-76, Chronicle 1976-84 and 1989-, Timewatch 1982-85; head of history and archaeology unit BBC tv 1976-; BAFTA award for Horizon, Writer's Guild of GB award for Cities at War and Microbes and Men, Prix Futura silver medal Berlin for The Writing on the Wall; Freedom City of Vallejo, Cal USA 1964; memb BAFTA, Royal Television Soc; *Books* Secret Warfare (1974), The Inventing of America (1976), The Birth of Television (1977), Footsteps (1987); *Style—* B A J Norman, Esq; BBC TV, Elstree, Herts (☎ 01 207 8520)

NORMAN, David Mark; s of Lt-Col, Mark Richard Norman, CBE of Garden House, Moor Place, Much Hadham, Herts, and Helen, *née* Bryan; *b* 30 Jan 1941; *Educ* Eton, McGill Univ (BA), Harvard Business Sch (MBA); *m* 9 July 1966, Diana Anne Norman, da of John Vincent Sheffield, CBE, of New Barn House, Laverstoke, Whitchurch, Hampshire; 1 s (Jonathan b 1972), 3 da (Anna b 1967, Isabella b 1971, Davina b 1981); *Career* Nocros Ltd 1967-77 (dir of ops and main bd dir 1975-77), chief exec Nocros Printing & Packaging 1971-75, md Russell Reynolds Assoc Inc 1978-82 (exec dir 1977-78); chm: Norman Resources Ltd 1982-83, Norman Broadbent Int Ltd 1983-, Charles Barker Plc 1987-; govr Royal Ballet Sch, chm Tennis and Rackets Assoc, memb Royal Opera House Ballet Bd; *Recreations* golf, tennis, rackets, classical music, opera, ballet; *Clubs* Boodle's, All England Lawn Tennis & Croquet, Queens, RAC; *Style—* David Norman, Esq; Burkham House, Alton, Hants GU34 5RS (☎ 025 683 211); 30 Farringdon Street, London EC4A 4EA (☎ 01 634 1000, fax 01 489 9330, car tel 0836 505465, telex 883588)

NORMAN, Hon Mrs; Doreen Albinia de Burgh; *née* Gibbs; da of 1 Baron Wraxhall (d 1931); *b* 1913; *m* 1937, Charles Bathurst Norman; 1 s, 1 da; *Style—* The Hon Mrs Norman; Villa Villetri, Vallée des Vaux, Jersey

NORMAN, (Aleida) Elisabeth Mabel May; da of Willem Roosegaarde Bisschop (d 1944), of 35 York Ter, London, and May *née* Cowan (d 1964); *b* 25 Sept 1921; *Educ* Queen's Coll London, Somerville Coll, Oxford (MA, BM, BCh); *m* 11 March 1950, Archibald Percy Norman, s of George Percy Norman (d 1940), of Eastbourne; 5 s (Duncan b 7 Aug 1952, Archie b 1 May 1954, Thomas b 3 Nov 1955, Sandy b Feb 1957, Donald b 13 March 1960); *Career* jr hosp appts at: Radcliffe Infirmary Oxford 1946, Queen Elizabeth Hosp for Children London 1947, Hosp for Sick Children Great-Ormond St 1947-48; chm of friends of Royal Earslwood 1967-82, of bd of govrs Royal Earlswood and Tadworth Ct Hosp Schs 1976-81; memb E Surrey Community Health Cncl 1975-79, vice-chm Mid Surrey Community Health Cncl 1979-82, memb Mid Surrey Dist Health Authy 1982-; memb and vice-chm Surrey MENCAP 1975- (memb nat cncl 1981-87), vice chm MENCAP 1987-;; *Style—* Mrs Elisabeth Norman; White Lodge, Heather Cl, Kingswood, Surrey KT20 6NY (☎ 0737 832626)

NORMAN, Geoffrey; JP (Inner London 1982); s of William Frederick Trafalgar Norman (d 1972), and Vera May Norman, *née* Goodfellow; *b* 25 Mar 1935; *Educ* Harrow Co Sch, Brasenose Coll Oxford (MA); *m* 1958, Dorothy Frances (d 1978), da of Donald Thomas Henry King of Devon; 2 s (Neil, Mark), 2 da (Helen, Clare); *Career* slr 1959, clerk to the Justices North Hertfordshire 1966-77, sec Magistrates' Assoc 1978-86; memb Legal Aid Duty Slr Ctee 1983-85, asst sec of Cmmnr 1986-; Freeman City of London (Curriers' Co); *Recreations* painting, badminton; *Style—* Geoffrey Norman, Esq, JP; Easter Cottage, Gosmore, Hitchin, Herts

NORMAN, Vice-Adm Sir (Horace) Geoffrey; KCVO (1963), CB (1949), CBE (1942); s of W H Norman (d 1945); *b* 25 May 1896; *Educ* Trent Coll, RNC Keyham, Cambridge Univ; *m* 1923, Norah Frances, da of late Brig-Gen S Geoghegan, CB, of Bournemouth; 1 s, 1 da; *Career* joined RN 1914, serv HMS Queen Elizabeth 1914-16, which he commanded in 1943; Capt 1938, Rear Adm 1947, Chief of Staff to C-in-C Mediterranean Station 1948-50, Admty 1950, Vice-Adm 1951 (ret); sec Nat Playing Fields Assoc 1953-63; *Style—* Vice-Adm Sir Geoffrey Norman, KCVO, CB, CBE; Chantry Cottage, Wickham, Fareham, Hants (☎ Wickham 832248)

NORMAN, Jessye; da of Silas Norman and Janie King; *b* 15 Sept 1945; *Educ* Howard Univ Washington DC (BM), Peabody Conservatory Univ of Michigan (MMus); *Career* operatic debut Deutsche Opera Berlin 1969, La Scala Milan 1972, Roy Opera House Covent Garden 1972, NY Metropolitan Opera 1982; American debut Hollywood Bowl 1972, Lincoln Centre NYC 1973; tours incl: N and S America, Europe, Middle E, Australia, Israel; many int festivals incl: Aix-en-Provence, Aldeburgh, Berlin, Edinburgh, Flanders, Helsinki, Lucerne, Salzburg, Tangle wood, Spoleto, Hollywood, Ravinia; Hon DMus: Howard 1982, Univ of the Sewanee 1984, Boston Conservatory 1984; Musician of the Year Musical America 1982, prizes include: Grand Prix du Disque (Acad du Disque Francais) 1975, 1976, 1977, 1982, 1984; Grand Prix de Disque (Acad Charles Cros) 1983; Deutscher Schallplatteboreus 1975, 1982; Cigale d'Or Aix-en-Provence Festival 1977, IRCAM record award 1982, commandeur de l'Ordre des Arts et des Lettres France 1984; DMus Univ of Michigan 1987; Grammy Award 1984; *Style—* Miss Jessye Norman; c/o Shaw Concerts Incorporated, 1995 Broadway, New York, NY 100023 USA

NORMAN, (Herbert) John La French; s of Herbert La French Norman, of 26 Park Farm Close, London, and Hilda Caroline, *née* West; *b* 15 Jan 1932; *Educ* King Edward VI Sch Norwich, Imperial Coll London Univ (BSc); *m* 11 Aug 1956, Jill Frances, da of Bernard Thomas Sharp (d 1953); 1 s (Bernard b 1965), 2 da (Elizabeth b 1961, Sarah b 1962); *Career* Wm Hill & Son and Norman & Beard Ltd (organ builders by appt to HM The Queen): dir 1960-70, md 1970-74; responsible for work on organs in cathedrals inc: Gloucester, Norwich, Lichfield, Chelmsford, Brisbane; other work incl organs in: Bath Abbey, Southwell Minster, concert hall of Royal Coll of Organists; organ conslt 1974- at: Lancing Coll, Harrow Sch, Mill Hill Sch, Sherborne Abbey, Pershore Abbey; memb: organs advsy ctee Cncl for Care of Churches 1987-, organs sub-ctee London Diocesan Advsy Ctee 1975-; churchwarden Holy Trinity Lyonsdown New Barnet 1986-, memb Synod Diocese of St Albans 1980-86; Freeman City of London, Liveryman Worshipful Co of Musicians 1972; ARCS, FIMIT, fell Inc Soc Organ Builders; *Books* The Organ Today (1966, revised edn 1980), The Organs of Britain (1984), ed Musical Instument Technology 1969-, ed The Organbuilder 1983-; *Recreations* writing about organs, listening to music; *Style—* John Norman, Esq; 15 Baxendale, London N20 OEG (☎ 01 445 0801); IBM United Kingdom, 103 Wigmore Street, London W1H OAB (☎ 01 935 6600)

NORMAN, Keith John; s of Wilson Norman (d 1974), of Wigston Magna, Leicestershire, and Ivy May Langham (d 1985); *b* 8 July 1931; *Educ* Kibworth GS; *m* 25 March 1954, Barbara Lucy, da of Oswald Tomlin Johnson (d 1968), of Wigston Magna, Leicestershire; 1 s (Christopher Keith b 1959), 1 da (Claire Lucy b 1955); *Career* RAF, LAC 1949-51; fin dir: William Cotton Ltd, John Jones Loughborough Ltd, George Woodcock & Sons Ltd Scotland 1969-74; chm and chief exec Ladies Pride Gp of Cos 1987-; (gp fin dir and sec 1974-84, dep chm and jt md 1984-87); chm and jt md Leslie Wise Gp plc 1987-; *Recreations* rotary international, sailing; *Style—* Keith J Norman, Esq; The Farm, Newgate End, Wigston Magna, Leicestershire; 346 St Saviours Road, Leicester (☎ Leics 730071)

NORMAN, Kenneth Roy; s of Clement Norman (d 1978), and Peggy, *née* Nichols (d 1980); *b* 21 July 1925; *Educ* Taunton Sch Somerset, Downing Coll Cambridge (BA, MA); *m* 12 August 1953, Pamela Norman, da of George Raymont; 1 s (Timothy), 1 da (Felicity); *Career* WWII Lt RA serv Br and Indian Armies; fell and tutor Downing Coll Cambridge 1952-64, reader indian studies Univ of Cambridge 1978- (lectr 1955-78); FBA 1985, for memb Roy Danish Acad 1983; *Books* Elders Verses I (1969), Elders Verses II (1971), Pali Literature (1983), The Group of Discourses (1984); *Recreations* walking and reading; *Style—* Roy Norman, Esq; 6 Huttles Green, Shepreth, Royston, Herts SG8 6PR (☎ 0763 60541); Faculty of Oriental Studies, University of Cambridge, Sidgwick Avenue, Cambridge CB3 9DA (☎ 0223 335133)

NORMAN, Sir Mark Annesley; 3 Bt (UK 1915), of Honeyhanger, Parish of Shottermill, Co Surrey; s of Sir Nigel Norman, 2 Bt, CBE (d 1943), and Lady Perkins, (d 1986); *b* 8 Feb 1927; *Educ* Winchester, RMC; *m* 1953, Joanna, da of Lt-Col Ian Kilgour and Aura (ggda of Gen Sir George Walker, 1 Bt, GCB, KCTS); 2 s (Nigel James b 5 Feb 1956, Antony Rory b 9 Sept 1963), 1 da (Lucinda Fay b 7 Dec 1965); *Heir* s, Nigel Norman; *Career* late Lt Coldstream Gds and Flying Offr 601 (Co of London) Sqdn RAuxAF; High Sheriff Oxfordshire 1983/84, Air Cdre RAuxAF 1983, Hon Air Cdre 4624 (Co of Oxford) Movements Sqdn RAuxAF 1984-; dep Lt Oxfordshire 1985-; chm St Luke's Oxford 1986-88; patron and churchwarden St Peter's Church Wilcote; *Recreations* gardening, shooting, workshop; *Clubs* White's, Pratt's, RAF, MCC; *Style—* Sir Mark Norman, Bt; Wilcote Manor, Charlbury, Oxon (☎ 099 386 357)

NORMAN, Nigel James; s and h of Sir Mark Norman, 3 Bt; *b* 5 Feb 1956; *m* 1985, Joanna, *née* Naylor-Leyland; *Career* army; now with Grenfell Gp; *Style—* Nigel Norman, Esq; 49 Nevern Sq, London SW5; 49 Shelgate Rd, London SW11

NORMAN, Peter Alfred; s of Capt Lionel Norman, MC (ka 1916 Scots Gds), of London, and Violet May, *née* Bevan (d 1956); *b* 15 Nov 1907; *Educ* Eton, King's Coll Cambridge (MA); *m* 6 April 1939, Patricia Mary, da of Maj William Edward Wilders (d 1940), of Duffcarrick, Ardmore, Co Waterford, Ireland; 2 s (Kerry Lionel Patrick b 3 Jan 1941, d 28 Aug 1962, Shane Henry b 12 Sept 1946); *Career* RASC: gazetted 2 Lt 1940, landed Aandalsnes Norway 1940 (despatches), returned to UK 1940, Capt seconded to W African Frontier Force serv Sierra Leone, Nigeria, India, Burmah; demobbed 1946; trainee Barclays Bank (DC & O) Ltd 1929-31, trainee and export sales Ford Motor Co Ltd (Trafford Park and Dagenham) 1931-40, sales mangr Henry Ford & Son Ltd Cork Ireland, devpt mangr Mercantile Credit Co of Ireland Ltd 1959-63, ptnr O'Donnell & Fitzgerald (stockbrokers) 1964, firm merged to become Bloxham Toole O'Donnell 1981; dir Standard Chartered Bank (Ireland) Ltd; chm Aldbourne Civic Soc; *Recreations* shooting; *Clubs* Kildare St and Univ Club, Dublin; *Style—* Peter A Norman, Esq; Barn Cottage, South St, Aldbourne, Wilts SN8 2DW (☎ 0672 40357)

NORMAN, Baroness; Priscilla; CBE (1963), JP (Co of London 1944); da of late Maj Robert Reyntiens by his w Lady Alice Bertie (da of 7 Earl of Abingdon); *b* 1899; *m* 1, 1921 (m dis 1929), Col Alexander Koch de Gooreynd (who assumed surname of Worsthorne by deed poll 1923); 2 s (*see* Simon Towneley and Peregrine Worsthorne); m 2, 1933, 1 and last Baron Norman, DSO, PC (d 1950); *Career* vice-pres RCN; vice-chm Women's Voluntary Serv for Civil Def 1938-41; author; *Books* In the Way of Understanding (1982); *Style—* The Rt Hon the Lady Norman, CBE, JP; 67 Holland Park, London W11 3SG (☎ 01 229 6483)

NORMAN, Dr Remington Harvard; s of Wing Cdr Roland Frank Holdway (d 1957), of London, and Prof Muriel Harvard Sim, *née* Johnson; *b* 3 Dec 1944; *Educ* Harrow, Hertford Coll Oxford (MA, DPhil), Inst of Masters of Wine (MW); *m* 1 (m dis 1980), Camilla, *née* Cordwell; 1 s (James Fortesque b 1980), 1 da (Glenda Camilla b 1979); m 2, 23 Sept 1984, Geraldine Marie Claire Norman; *Career* fndr md and chm Collete Cellar Ltd London, dir and jt champagne degulas Epernay 1981-, chm and md Caldwell's Wine Consutancy 1979-89; *Recreations* qualified ski instr, opera (esp

Wagner), organ music; *Clubs* Garrick, MCC; *Style*— Dr Remington Norman

NORMAN, Sir Richard Oswald Chandler; KBE (1987); s of Oswald George Norman (d 1941), of London, and Violet Maud, *née* Chandler (d 1981); *b* 27 April 1932; *Educ* St Paul's, Balliol Coll Oxford; *m* 30 Dec 1982, Jennifer Margaret, da of William James Tope, of London; *Career* fell and tutor Merton Coll Oxford and univ lectr in chemistry 1958-65; prof of chemistry Univ of York 1965-83; chief scientific advsr: MOD 1983-, Dept of Energy 1988-; rector Exeter Coll Oxford 1987-; *Books* Principles of Organic Synthesis (1968), Modern Organic Chemistry (1972); *Recreations* gardening, music, watching cricket; *Clubs* Utd Oxford and Cambridge Univ; *Style*— Sir Richard Norman, KBE; The Rector's Lodging, Exeter College, Oxford OX1 3DP (☎ 0865 279 644)

NORMAN, Sir Robert Wentworth; s of William Henry Norman (d 1937), of Sydney, NSW, Australia, and Minnie Esther, *née* Brown (d 1939); *b* 10 April 1912; *Educ* Sydney GS; *m* 1942, Grace Amelia, da of Sidney Percy Hebden (d 1935); 1 s (William), 1 da (Sally); *Career* Capt AIF Middle E and Pacific WWII; co dir; former chief gen mangr and dir Bank of NSW and other public cos; Order of the Rising Sun (Japan) 1982; kt 1970; *Recreations* reading, bowls, gardening; *Clubs* Union (Sydney), Royal Sydney Golf; *Style*— Sir Robert Norman; 432 Edgecliff Rd, Edgecliff, NSW 2027, Australia (☎ 32 1900)

NORMAN, Ronald; OBE (1986); s of Leonard William Norman (d 1970), of Hendon, London, and Elsie Louise, *née* Cooke (d 1978); *b* 29 April 1937; *Educ* Dulwich Coll, King's Coll London (BSc); *m* 1, 15 July 1961 (m dis 1973), Jennifer Mary, da of Edward Lionel Mansfield (d 1984), of Troutbeck, Cumbria; 2 s (Guy b 1962, Richard b 1964), 1 da (Sally-Ann b 1968); m 2, Joyce, *née* Lyon, of Hartlepool; *Career* RE 1955-57, 2 Lt Germany; civil engr John Laing Construction 1960-62, res fell Civil Engrg Res Assoc 1962-64, mgmnt conslt Urwick Orr and Ptnrs 1964-66, md CM Yuill Hartlepool Developers 1966-76 (chm and md 1976-85), chm R Norman Durham Developers 1985-; bd memb English Industl Estates 1983-, chm Teeside Devpt Corpn 1987-; MICE; *Recreations* walking, photography, book-collecting; *Style*— Ronald Norman, Esq, OBE; Hart-on-the-Hill, Dalton Piercy, Hartlepool, Cleveland TS27 3HY; 3E Mountjoy Research Centre, Durham DH1 3UR (☎ 091 3846120, fax 091 384 2962)

NORMAN, Dr the Hon Stella Maria; da of Baron Zuckerman, OM, KCB, FRS (Life Peer), and Baroness Zuckerman (Lady Joan Rufus Isaacs, da of 2 Marquess of Reading); *b* 1947; *Educ* Cranborne Chase Sch, E Anglia Univ, London Univ; *m* 1977, Dr Andrew R Norman; 1 s, 1 da; *Style*— Dr the Hon Stella Norman; Waterfield Sudbourne, Woodbridge, Suffolk

NORMAN, Rev Canon William Beadon; er s of Maj-Gen Charles Wake Norman, CBE, DL (d 1974), of West Farleigh Hall, Maidstone, Kent, and Nora, *née* Beadon; descended from James Norman (d 1787), of Bromley Common, Kent (*see* Burke's Landed Gentry, 18 edn, vol I, 1965); *b* 14 Feb 1926; *Educ* Eton, Trinity Coll Cambridge (BA 1949, MA 1955), Ridley Hall Cambridge; *m* 8 Oct 1952, Beryl, er da of John George Embleton Welch (d 1963), of Wolverhampton, Staffs, and later of Harrisberg, Pennsylvania, USA; 3 s (Stephen b 1954, James b 1959, Paul b 1961), 4 da (Henrietta b 1956, Julia (Mrs Dickens) b (twin) 1956, Sarah (Mrs Whitehouse) b (twin) 1961, Charity b 1964); *Career* serv RAC 1944-46, cmmnd 9 Lancers 1946, (war substantive) Lt 1946-47; barr Lincoln's Inn 1950; ordained deacon 1952, priest 1953; curate of St John, Beckenham 1952-54; CMS Missionary, Tutor and Acting Principal, Buwalasi Theological Coll Uganda 1955-65; vicar of Alne with Aldwark, diocese of York 1965-74; vicar of Blackheath, diocese of Birmingham 1974-79; team rector, Kings Norton, diocese of Birmingham 1979-; rural dean of Warley 1974-79, and of Kings Norton 1982-87; Hon Canon of Mbale, Uganda 1963-65, and of Birmingham 1978-; warden of Diocesan Readers' Bd 1984-; *Recreations* reading, walking; The Rectory, Kings Norton, Birmingham B30 3EX (☎ 021 458 7522)

NORMAN, Willoughby Rollo; s of Rt Hon Sir Henry Norman, 1 Bt (d 1939), by his 2 w, Hon Florence Priscilla McLaren, CBE (d 1964), yr da of 1 Baron Aberconway; half-unc to Sir Mark Norman, 3 Bt; *b* 12 Oct 1909; *Educ* Eton, Magdalen Coll Oxford; *m* 1, 1934 (m dis 1973), Hon Barbara Jacqueline Boot, da of 2 Baron Trent (d 1956); 1 s (Jeremy), 2 da (Sarah, Roselle); m 2, 1973, Anna Caroline, da of Capt William Greville Worthington (d 1942), and former w of Oliver Patrick Miller Haskard; *Career* Maj Grenadier Gds 1939-45, chm The Boots Co Ltd 1961-72 (vice-chm 1954-61), dir English China Clays (v-chm 1968-81), dir Nat Westminster Bank 1963-79 (chm Eastern Region until 1979), dir Sheepbridge Engrg Ltd 1961-79, dir Guardian Royal Exchange Assur until 1979; High Sheriff of Leicestershire 1960; *Recreations* shooting, deer stalking, gardening; *Clubs* White's, Pratt's; *Style*— Willoughby Norman Esq; The Grange, South Harting, Petersfield, Hants (☎ Harting 216); 28 Ranelagh House, Elystan Place, SW3 (☎ 01 584 9410)

NORMANBY, Marchioness of; Hon Grania Maeve Rosaura; *née* Guinness; o da of 1 Baron Moyne, DSO, TD, PC (assas in Cairo 1944), and Lady Evelyn Erskine (d 1939), da of 14 Earl of Buchan; *b* 14 April 1920; *m* 10 Feb 1951, 4 Marquess of Normanby; 2 s, 5 da; *Career* formerly Section Offr, WAAF; pro chllr Univ of Dublin 1985; JP North Yorks 1971-83; Hon LLD Dublin; *Style*— The Most Hon the Marchioness of Normanby; Lythe Hall, nr Whitby, N Yorks; Argyll House, 211 King's Rd, SW3 (☎ 01 352 5154)

NORMANBY, 4 Marquess of (UK 1838); Oswald Constantine John Phipps; KG (1985), CBE (1974), JP (NR Yorks 1937), DL (1960); Baron Mulgrave (I 1767), Baron Mulgrave (GB 1794), Earl of Mulgrave and Viscount Normanby (UK 1812); s of Rev 3 Marquess of Normanby (d 1932); *b* 29 July 1912; *Educ* Eton, Ch Ch Oxford; *m* 10 Feb 1951, Hon Grania Maeve Rosaura Guinness, JP, da of 1 Baron Moyne, DSO, PC (assass 1944); 2 s, 5 da; *Heir* s, Earl of Mulgrave; *Career* serv WWII, Lt 5 Bn The Green Howards (wounded, prisoner, repatriated); pps to Sec of State for Dominion Affrs 1944-45, to Lord Pres of the Cncl 1945; a lord in waiting to HM The King 1945; Cncl of St John for North Yorks (formerly NR of Yorks): chm 1948-77, pres 1977-87; chm King's Coll Hosp 1948-74; Lord-Lt NR Yorks 1965-74, N Yorks 1974-87; pres: TA&VR Assoc for N England 1971-74, TA&VRA N Yorks and Humberside 1980-83; Hon Col Cmdt Green Howards 1970-82, Dep Hon Col 2 Bn Yorks Volunteers 1971-72; vice-pres RNLI 1984- (ctee memb 1972-84); pres Nat Library for the Blind 1977-88 (chm 1946-77), vice-pres St Dunstan's 1980- (cncl memb 1944-80); Art-Collections Fund 1981-86; High Steward York Minster 1980-88; KStJ; Hon DCL Durham 1963, Hon DCL York 1985; fell King's Coll Hosp Med Sch; *Style*— The Most Hon the Marquess of Normanby, KG, CBE; Lythe Hall, nr Whitby, N Yorks (☎ 0947 83233); Argyll House, 211 King's Rd, SW3 (☎ 01 352 5154)

NORMAND, Hon Mrs William; Ann Elizabeth; da of James Cumming (d 1974), of Biggar, Lanarkshire; *b* 12 Jan 1923; *Educ* Downe House; *m* 1945, Hon William Normand (d 1967, s of Baron Normand, Life Peer and Lord of Appeal who d 1962); 1 s, 1 da (*see* Macdonald Lockhart, Angus H); *Style*— The Hon Mrs William Normand; 15 Ravelston Heights, Edinburgh EH4 3LX (☎ 031 332 2308)

NORMAND, Richard John; MC, TD (and bar); s of Capt Patrick Hill Normand, DSO (d 1943), of Wiltshire, and Matilda Marion Marsh (d 1921); *b* 28 Jan 1912; *Educ* Fettes, Univ of Edinburgh (MA, LLB); *m* 10 Aug 1942, Audrey Mary, da of Joseph Harry Green (d 1956), of E London; 3 da (Nicola b 1948, Bridgid b 1951, Tessa b 1953); *Career* Maj 7/9 Royal Scots serv: Home Forces 1939-40 and 1942-44, France 1940, W Africa 1940-42, Holland and Germany 1944-45; Staff Coll Camberley 1943-44; Writer to the Signet; *Recreations* shooting, golf, bridge; *Clubs* New (Edinburgh), Royal & Ancient GC (St Andrews), Hon Co of Edinburgh Golfers (Muirfield) Gullane GC; *Style*— Richard J Normand, MC, TD; Seamews Whim Rd, Gullane, E Lothian, Scotland (☎ 0620 842106)

NORMANTON, 6 Earl of (I 1806); Shaun James Christian Wellbore Ellis Agar; also Baron Mendip (GB 1794), Baron Somerton (I 1795 & UK 1873, which sits as), and Viscount Somerton (I 1800); s of 5 Earl of Normanton (d 1967), and his 2 w, Lady Fiona Pratt, da of 4 Marquess Camden; *b* 21 August 1945; *Educ* Eton; *m* 29 April 1970, Victoria Susan, da of Jack Beard, of Ringwood, Hants; 1 s, 2 da (Lady Portia b 1976, Lady Marisa b 1979); *Heir* s, Viscount Somerton b 1982; *Career* Capt Blues & Royals to 1972; farmer (owns 7,000 acres in Hants); *Recreations* shooting, skiing; *Clubs* White's, Royal Yacht Sqdn; *Style*— The Rt Hon the Earl of Normanton; Somerley, Ringwood, Hants (☎ 0425 473253; office: 0425 473621)

NORMANTON, Sir Tom; TD, MEP (EDG) Cheshire E 1979-; s of late Tom O Normanton; *b* 12 Mar 1917; *Educ* Manchester GS, Manchester Univ (BA); *m* 1942, Annabel Bettine, da of late Dr Fred Yates; 2 s, 1 da; *Career* war serv 1939-46 (Europe and N Africa despatches), Maj; contested (C) Rochdale 1959 and 1964, MP (C) Cheadle 1970-87; AMBIM, vice-chm Manchester branch IOD 1969-71, pres: Br Textile Employers Assoc 1970-71, Int Fedn of Cotton and Allied Textiles Industs 1976-78; dir: Industl Trg Servs Ltd 1972-, N Regnl Bd Commercial Union Assur Ltd 1974-86, Manchester C of C 1970-; UK memb European Parliament Strasbourg 1973-1979, oppn energy spokesman 1975-79; chm Euro All Pty Gp Friends with Israel; memb Supervisory Bd of Euro Inst for Security 1986-; kt 1987; *Clubs* Beefsteak, RYS, St James's (Manchester); *Style*— Sir Tom Normanton, TD, MEP; Bollin Ct, Macclesfield Rd, Wilmslow, Cheshire (☎ 0625 524930); Nelson House, Nelson Place, Lymington, Hants (☎ 0590 75095)

NORREYS, Lord; Henry Mark Willoughby Bertie; s and h of 14 Earl of (Lindsey) and 9 (Abingdon); *b* 6 June 1958; *Educ* Eton, Edinburgh Univ; *Heir* bro, Hon Alexander Michael Richard Bertie; *Clubs* Puffin's (Edinburgh); *Style*— Lord Norreys of Rycote; Gilmilnscroft, Sorn, Mauchline, Ayrshire KA5 6ND

NORRIE, 2 Baron (UK 1957); George Willoughby Moke; s of 1 Baron Norrie, GCMG, GCVO, CB, DSO, MC (d 1977), and Jocelyn Helen (d 1938), da of Richard Henry Gosling, of Hawthorn Hill; *b* 27 April 1936; *Educ* Eton, RMA Sandhurst; *m* 1964, Celia Marguerite, JP, da of Major John Pelham Mann, MC, of New York, USA; 1 s, 2 da (Hon Clare b 1966, Hon Julia b 1968); *Heir* s, Mark Willoughby John Norrie b 31 March 1972; *Career* cmmnd 11 Hussars (PAO) 1956, ADC to C in C M East Cnd 1960-61, GSO3 (int) 4 Gds Bde 1967-69, ret 1970; dir: Fairfield Nurseries (Hermitage) Ltd 1976-89, Int Garden Centre (Br Gp) Ltd 1984-86, Hilliers (Fairfield) Ltd 1989; pres: Royal Br Legion (Newbury) 1972- Br Tst for Conservation Volunteers 1989-; dir Conservation Practice Ltd 1988; House of Lords Euro Communities Ctee (Environment) 1988; *Clubs* MCC, Cavalry; *Style*— The Rt Hon the Lord Norrie; East Gate House, Craven Hill, Hamstead Marshall, Newbury, Berks RG15 0JD (☎ 0488 57026, work 0635 200442)

NORRIE, Hon Guy Bainbridge; s of 1 Baron Norrie, GCMG, GCVO, CB, DSO, MC (d 1977), and his 2 w, Patricia Merryweather, da of late Emerson Muschamp Bainbridge, MP; *b* 3 May 1940; *Educ* Eton; *m* 1968, Sarah Georgina, o da of Maj George Rudolph Hanbury Fielding, DSO of Val d'Ogoz, Château d'Oex Vaud Switzerland; 2 s (Andrew b 1970, James b 1973); *Career* Lt-Col (ret) Royal Hussars, GSO3 HQ 1 Br Corps 1966-67, RN Staff Coll 1972, GSO2 MOD Directorate of Army Trg 1973-74, GSO1 Directing Staff, Staff Coll Camberley 1977-78; Lloyd's underwriting agent; dir Willis Faber & Dumas (Agencies) Ltd 1980-83; dir: Beaumont Underwriting Agencies Ltd 1981-85, Wellington Underwriting Agencies Ltd 1986-; *Recreations* fishing, shooting, skiing; *Clubs* City of London, Cavalry and Guards'; *Style*— The Hon Guy Norrie; Old Church Farm, Broughton, nr Stockbridge, Hants SO20 8AA; Wellington Underwriting Agencies Ltd, 120 Fenchurch St, London EC3M 5BA, (☎ 01 929 2811)

NORRIE, Patricia, Baroness; Patricia Merryweather; *née* Bainbridge; DStJ; da of Emerson Bainbridge, MP (d 1911), of Auchnashellach, Ross-shire, by his 2 wife Norah Mossom, *née* Merryweather; *b* 8 Dec 1906; *Educ* St James West Malvern; *m* 1938, as his 2 w, 1 Baron Norrie, GCMG, GCVO, CB, DSO (d 1977); 1 s, 2 da; *Style*— The Rt Hon Patricia, Lady Norrie; The Old Vicarage, Leckhampstead, Newbury, Berks (☎ 048 82 282)

NORRINGTON, Ian Arthur; s of Charles Arthur Norrington (Capt RA), of Peterborough, Victoria, Aust, and Georgina Marina, *née* Beardmore (d 1974); *b* 1 Oct 1936; *Educ* Downside; *m* 21 Sept 1968, Brigitte Maria, *née* Albrecht; 1 s (Christopher Charles b 1972), 1 da (Antonia Jane b 1974); *Career* Midshipman RNVR 1955-57, Lt RNR 1957-64; De Beers Consolidated Mines Ltd (The Diamond Trading Co Ltd) 1957-71: mangr Govt Diamond Off Kenewa Sierra Leone W Africa 1964-67, mangr Br Congo Diamond Distributors Ltd Kinshasa Zaire 1967-70; ptnr W I Carr Sons and Co 1971-79, dir Ian Norrington (Jewellery) Ltd, ptnr Grieveson Grant and Co 1979-86, dir Kleinwort Benson Securities Ltd 1986-88; Liveryman Worshipful Co of Goldsmiths; memb Int Stock Exchange 1974; *Recreations* shooting, fishing, tennis, jewellery; *Style*— Ian Norrington, Esq; Kleinwort Benson Securities Ltd, 20 Fenchurch St, London EC3 (☎ 01 623 8000)

NORRINGTON, Roger Arthur Carver; OBE (1980); s of late Sir Arthur Norrington, and Edith Joyce, *née* Carver; *b* 16 Mar 1934; *Educ* Dragon, Westminster, Clare Coll Cambridge (BA); *m* 1, 1964 (m dis 1982), Susan Elizabeth McLean, *née* May, 1 s, 1 da; m2, 1986, Karalyn Mary, *née* Lawrence; *Career* conductor music dir Shütz Choir of London 1962-, freelance singer RCM 1962-72, princ conductor Kent Opera 1966-84; débuts: Br 1962, BBC radio 1964, TV 1967, Germany Austria Denmark and Finland 1966, Portugal 1970, Italy 1971, France and Belgium 1972, USA 1974, Holland 1975,

Switzerland 1976; musical dir London Classical players 1978-, co-dir Early Opera Project 1984-, princ conductor Bournemouth Sinfonietta 1985-89, chief guest conductor Jerusalem Symphony Orch 1986-88, co dir Historic Arts 1986, guest conductor for many Br and Foreign Orchs appearing at: Covent Garden, The Coliseum, The Proms, NY, Boston, San Francisco, Paris, Vienna and elsewhere; regular broadcasts at home and abroad, numerous recordings, occasional contrib to various musical jls; Cavaliere Order al Merita della Repubilica Italiana 1981; *Style*— Roger Norrington, Esq, OBE

NORRIS; *see*: Foxley-Norris

NORRIS, Dame Ada May; DBE (1976, OBE 1954), CMG (1969); da of Allan Herbert Bickford (d 1911), and Alice Hannah, *née* Baggs; *b* 28 July 1901; *Educ* Melbourne HS, Melbourne Univ (MA); *m* 1929, Hon Sir John Gerald Norris, *qv*; 2 da (Rosemary Anne Balmford, Elizabeth Jane); *Career* teacher 1925-29, pres Austral Advsy Cncl for Physically Handicapped 1955-57, Aust rep UN Cmmn on Status of Women 1961-63, exec ctee Australian Cncl of Women 1966-79, pres Aust Nat Cncl of Women 1967-70, chm Nat Ctee for Int Women's Year 1974-76, chm Nat Status of Women Ctee 1976-80, UN Peace Medal 1975; *see Debrett's Handbook of Australia and New Zealand for further details*; *Style*— Dame Ada Norris DBE, CMG; 10 Winifred Cres, Toorak, Victoria, Australia (☎ 241 5166)

NORRIS, Alan John; s of Jesse Oliver Norris (d 1980), of Newport, Gwent, and Queenie Iris Norris; *b* 7 June 1942; *Educ* St Julians Newport Gwent, Newport and Monmouthshire Coll of Advanced Technol (HNC, Dip); *m* 1, 31 July 1965 (m dis 1969), Jane Margot Inkin, da of F Vernon Dixon; m 2, 14 June 1975, Penelope Catherine, da of Lt-Col (William) Edwin Daniel (d 1974), of Leigh, Surrey; 1 s (Oliver William Edwin b 28 June 1982); *Career* graduate trainee to O & M offr Alcan 1960-66, princ opm offr Osram (GEC) 1966-67, latterly systems and programming mangr United Glan (formerly sr systems analyst, computer ops mangr) 1967-76, London branch mangr Computer People 1976-79, chm and chief exec computastaff Gp 1979-; chm Fecon Ltd; chm computing sec FRES; MInstM 1968; *Recreations* skiing, swimming, golf, travel, wine meteorology; *Clubs* RAC; *Style*— Alan Norris, Esq; Lovelands Mead, Lovelands Lane, Kingswood, Tadworth, Surrey KT20 6XG (☎ 0737 248151); Gatton Place, St Matthews Rd, Redhill, Surrey RH1 1TA (☎ 0737 774100, fax 0737 772949, telex 894364)

NORRIS, Sir Alfred Henry; KBE (1960, OBE 1950, MBE 1938); s of late Alfred James Norris, of Hornchurch, Essex; *b* 27 April 1894; *Educ* Cranbrook Sch; *m* 1, 1925, Betty Davidson (decd); m 2, 1936, Winifred Gladys, da of late Archibald Henry Butler; 3 s; *Career* serv WWI with King's Own Royal (Lancaster) Regt; ret CA and co dir; FCA; *Style*— Sir Alfred Norris, KBE; 11 Abbey Close, Elmbridge, Cranleigh, Surrey

NORRIS, Vice-Adm Sir Charles Fred Wivell; KBE (1956), CB (1952), DSO (1944); s of Charles Harry Norris (d 1958); *b* 16 Dec 1900; *Educ* RNC Osborne and Dartmouth, Cambridge Univ; *m* 1924, Violet (d 1987), da of Harry Cremer, JP (d 1925); 1 s; *Career* joined RN 1913, serv WWI in HMS Malaya, serv WWII HMS Sheffield and HMS Bellona (despatches twice), Capt 1941, Rear Adm 1950, dir Naval Trg and dep chief of Naval Personnel 1950-52, Flag Offr Flotillas Med 1953-54, C-in-C E Indies Station 1954-56 (ret); dir Br Productivity Cncl 1957-65; *Style*— Vice-Adm Sir Charles Norris, KBE, CB, DSO; Clouds, 56 Shepherds Way, Liphook, Hants GU30 7HH

NORRIS, David Owen; s of Albert Norris, of Long Buckby, Northants, and Margaret Amy, *née* Owen; *b* 16 June 1953; *Educ* Daventry GS, Royal Acad of Music, Keble Coll Oxford (BA, MA); *m* 23 Oct 1985, Fiona, da of Alan Clarke, of Aldringham, Suffolk; 1 s (Barnaby William b 1987); *Career* prof RAM 1978-, dir Petworth Festival 1986-, presenter Radio 3 "The Works" 1989-, prom debut as pianist 1987; staff union sec RAM 1984-87, govr Herbert Shiner Sch Petworth, ctee memb Park Lane sp 1985-; FRAM; *Recreations* naval and detective fiction; *Clubs* Nat Lib; *Style*— David Owen Norris, Esq; Magog Lodge, Brinksole, Petworth, W Sussex (☎ 0798 426 02); 60 Old Oak Lane, London NW10 6UB (☎ 01 961 4830)

NORRIS, Sir Eric George; KCMG (1969, CMG 1963); s of Henry Frederick Norris, of Bengeo, Hertford (d 1944); *b* 14 Mar 1918; *Educ* Hertford GS, St Catharine's Coll Cambridge; *m* 1941, Pamela, da of Cyril Crane, of Southsea, Hants; 3 da; *Career* Maj Royal Corps of Signals 1940-46; joined Dominions Off 1946, Br Embassy Dublin 1948-50, UK High Cmmn Pakistan 1952-55, UK High Cmmn Delhi 1956-57, dep high cmmr Bombay 1957-60, IDC 1961, dep Br high cmmr Calcutta 1962-65, Cwlth Off 1965-68, Br high cmmr Kenya 1968-72, dep under-sec of State FCO 1972-73, Br high cmmr Malaysia 1974-77 (ret); dir Gray Mackenzie Ltd, London Sumatra Plantations Ltd; chm Royal Cwlth Soc 1980-84, dep chm Inchcape and Co 1981-86 (dir 1977-); *Clubs* E India; *Style*— Sir Eric Norris, KCMG; Homestead, Great Amwell, Herts (☎ Ware 870739); Inchcape plc, 40 St Mary Axe, London EC3A 9EU (☎ 01 283 4680)

NORRIS, John; s of Arthur Henry Norris (d 1986), of Bishopsthorpe, York, and Elsie Eleanor, *née* Robinson (d 1958); *b* 12 Sept 1929; *Educ* Marlborough, Gonville and Caius Coll Cambridge (BA); *m* 7 July 1956, Elizabeth Ann, da of Col Francis Edward Buller Girling, OBE, MC (d 1949), of Fleet, Hants; 1 s (Peter John b 1961), 2 da (Jane Elizabeth b 1960, Rachel Mary b 1964); *Career* Nat Serv; ptnr Thomson McLintock & Co 1966-87, ptnr Peat Marwick McLintock 1987-; chm Teeside Soc of CAs 1970-71, memb review body to consider the govt and admin of Durham Univ 1971-73, cncl memb St John's Coll Durham; FCA 1960; *Recreations* fell walking, reading, DIY, gardening; *Clubs* Northern Counties; *Style*— John Norris, Esq; 47 Moor Cres, Gosforth, Newcastle upon Tyne NE3 4AQ (☎ 091 285 3591); Peat Marwick McLintock, Maybrook House, 27 Graingerst St, Newcastle upon Tyne NE1 5JT (☎ 091 232 8815, fax 091 232 8615, 091 232 3391)

NORRIS, Hon Sir John Gerald; ED (1945); s of John Alexander Norris (d 1962), and Mary Ellen, *née* Heffernan (d 1964); *b* 12 June 1903; *Educ* Camberwell State Sch, Melbourne HS, Melbourne Univ (LLM, Hon LLD); *m* 1929, Dame Ada, DBE, CMG *qv*; 2 da; *Career* serv AMF and AIF, Lt-Col Australia and New Guinea 1939-45; barr Vic 1925, memb Ctee of Counsel 1934-39 and 1952-55 (hon sec 1939-50), lectr commercial law Melbourne Univ 1932-52, KC 1950, actg co ct judge 1950-51, judge of Vic co ct 1955-72, pres Medico-Legal Soc of Vic 1958-59, memb cncl Melbourne Univ 1965-81, actg judge Supreme Ct 1969-72, Supreme Ct judge 1973-75, Royal cmmr WA 1975-76, conducted inquiries for Victorian Govt 1978-81; kt 1982; *Clubs* Australian (Melbourne), RACV; *Style*— The Hon Sir John Norris, ED; 10 Winifred Crescent, Toorak, Vic 3142, Australia (☎ 241 5166)

NORRIS, Steven John; s of John Francis Birkett Norris, of Nottingham, and Eileen Winifred, *née* Walsh; *b* 24 May 1945; *Educ* Liverpool Inst HS, Worcester Coll Oxford (MA); *m* 23 Aug 1969, Peta Veronica, da of Rear Adm Peter Cecil-Gibson, CB; 2 s (Anthony Hugh b 4 Sept 1974, Edward George Steven b 26 Dec 1985); *Career* MP (C) Oxford E 1983-87; Epping Forest 1988-; chm: Motor Distribution Co, The Crime concern Tst Ltd, The Grant Maintained Schs Tst Ltd; vice-chm W Berks Dist Health Auth 1982-85; 1977-85; memb Berks CC 1977-85, govr: Mary Hare GS for the Deaf, memb Select Ctee on Social Services 1985; Freeman City of London, Liveryman Worshipful Co of Coachmakers' and Coachharness Makers; *Recreations* reading; *Clubs* Carlton; *Style*— Steven Norris, Esq; Crt Farm House, Wylye, Warminster, Wilts BA12 0RF (☎ 09856 394)

NORRIS, Sydney George; s of George Samuel Norris (d 1980), of Liverpool, and Agnes Rosa, *née* George; *b* 22 August 1937; *Educ* Liverpool Inst HS for Boys, Univ Coll Oxford (MA), Cambridge Univ (Dip in Criminology), Univ of California (MCrim); *m* 1965, Brigid Molyneux, da of Geoffrey Molyneux Fitzgibbon, of Wotton under Edge; 2 s (Simon b 1969, Daniel b 1971), 1 da (Sarah b 1967); *Career* 2 Lt Intelligence Corps 1956-58; Harkness fell 1968-70, princ Home Off 1967-74 (asst princ 1963-67), sec Advsy Cncl on Penal System 1970-73, princ private sec Home Off 1973-74; asst sec: Prison Dept 1974-79; Treasy 1979-81, princ estab and fin offr NI Off 1983-85, dir operational policy Prison Serv 1985-88, asst under sec Police Home Off 1988-; *Recreations* running, fell walking, gardening; *Style*— Sydney G Norris, Esq; Home Office, London SW1

NORRIS, William John; s of John Phillips Norris, QGM, of Salisbury, Wilts and Joan Hattersley, *née* Barnes; *b* 3 Oct 1951; *Educ* Sherborne, New Coll Oxford (MA); *m* 3 Oct 1987, Lesley Jacqueline, da of Douglas Osborne of Hythe, Kent; 1 da (Charlotte Louise b 15 Oct 1988); *Career* called to the Bar 1974; amateur jockey; *Books* The Collected Letters of C W Catte (ed); *Recreations* racing, sailing, cricket; *Clubs* Royal Cruising, Lobsters; *Style*— William Norris, Esq; Lobster Cottage, Lower Daggons, Fordingbridge, Hants (☎ 07254 375); Farrars Building, Temple, London EC4 (☎ 01 583 9241)

NORRIS, William Vernon Wentworth; s of William Henry Norris, of 9 Dunnally Park, Shepperton-on-Thames Midds, and Eileen Louise *née* Willmott; *b* 11 May 1937; *Educ* Bedford Sch; *m* 1, 10 Oct 1960 (m dis 1982), Penelope Anne, da of Herbert James Dimmock (d 1987), of Brookwood, Surrey; 1 s (Richard b 1965), 1 da (Sally b 1962); m 2, 5 May 1982, Catherine, da of Bernard James Knowles; 1 da (Katie b 1982); *Career* slr 1959, lectr Gibson & Weldon 1959-61, Allen & Overy 1961-(ptnr 1964); chm Law Soc Revenue Law ctee, gov Christs Hosp, memb Addington Soc; memb Law Soc 1959; *Recreations* poetry; *Style*— William Norris, Esq; 9 Cheapside, London, EC2V 6AD, (☎ 01 248 9898, fax 01 236 2192, telex 8812801)

NORTH, Barony of (E 1554);; abeyant 1941; *see* Hon Mrs Bowlby and Hon Mrs North-Beauchamp

NORTH, Hon Mrs (Carolyn); da of 2 Baron Banbury of Southam; *b* 1947; *m* 1977, Christopher (Kim) J A North (d 1988); *Style*— The Hon Mrs North

NORTH, Hon Charles Evelyn; s of 8 Earl of Guilford (d 1949); *b* 1918; *Educ* Eton, London Univ; *m* 1, 1942, Maureen O'Callaghan (m dis 1957), da of Maj F C B Baldwin; 1 s, 1 da; m 2, 1959, Joan Aston, da of Maj F B Booker (d 1954), of Edenmore House Raheny, Co Dublin; *Career* Pilot Offr RAFVR 1940, Flt-Lt 1942, on staff Air Miny and Miny of Aircraft Prodn; dir J M W North and Co Ltd London; professional engr with Dept of the Environment; ret 1983; *Style*— The Hon Charles E North; Park End House, Eythorne, Dover, Kent (☎ 0304 830368)

NORTH, Geoffrey; MBE (1976), JP (1978); s of William Henry North (d 1971), and Florence, *née* Parr (d 1930); *b* 26 July 1924; *Educ* Hillhouse Central Sch Huddersfield; *m* 21 Dec 1946, Yvonne Elizabeth, da of John Richard Barrett (d 1971); 1 s (Antony b 3 Nov 1947), 2 da (Laraine b 26 May 1951, Julie b 31 Jan 1956); *Career* cmmnd Pilot Offr 1945 and Flying Offr 1946 RAF 1943-46; md Avon Rubber Co Ltd Bridgend 1974-82, chm and md Avonride Ltd 1982-; memb (former pres) Rotary Club Bridgend, former chm Bridgend YMCA; FIIM; *Recreations* rugby, union football; *Style*— Geoffrey North, Esq, MBE, JP; 12 Fitzhamon Rd, Porthcawl, Mid-Glam CF36 3JA (☎ 0656 716 194); Avonride Ltd, Spelter, Site, Caerau Maesteg, Mid Glam (☎ 0656 739 111, fax 0656 737 677, car tel 0836 765 399, telex 498660)

NORTH, Maj Geoffrey Edward Ford; MC (1943), JP (South Molton 1970), DL (Devon 1982); s of S T Ford North (d 1963), of Comeragh Ct, Hook Heath, Surrey, and Margaret Wilmot, *née* Booth (d 1978); *b* 21 Jan 1917; *Educ* Winchester, New Coll Oxford; *m* 9 March 1950, Hon Margaret Isolda de Grey, 2 da of Lt-Col 8 Baron Walsingham, DSO, OBE, DL (d 1965), of Merton Park, Thetford, Norfolk; 1 s (David John Ford b 1959), 3 da (Amanda Ford (Lady Weldon) b 1951, Joanna (Hon Mrs K I M Fraser) b 1953, Belinda Jane b 1955); *Career* WWII serv 10 Royal Hussars, Adj 1942, Sqdn Ldr GSO I (Equitation) Eighth Army HQ 1945, 2 i/c 10 Royal Hussars 1945 (despatches twice, C in C Commendation for Gallantry 1942); barr 1939; chm: City Offices Co Ltd 1978-83 (dir 1951-78), Greycoat Gp 1981-83; British rep World Hereford Conf 1976 and 1980, chm South Molton Bench 1981-87; memb: Devon county ctee CLA 1958-88, cncl Devon County Agric Assoc 1962-88 (pres 1978); pres: Hereford Cattle Breeders 1978, Devon County Show 1978; *Recreations* fishing, shooting, skiing, bicycling; *Style*— Maj Geoffrey North, MC, JP, DL; Holmingham, Bampton, Devon (☎ 0398 31259); La Farigouletter, Le Rey d'Agneou, 83550 Vidauban, Var, France (☎ 94 73 03 42)

NORTH, Jeremy William Francis; s and h of Sir (William) Jonathan Frederick North, 2 Bt; *b* 5 May 1960; *Educ* Marlborough; *Style*— Jeremy North Esq; Frogmore, Weston-under-Penyard, Herefordshire

NORTH, Sir (William) Jonathan Frederick; 2 Bt (UK 1920), of Southwell, Co Nottingham; s of late Hon John Montagu William North (s of 8 Earl of Guilford), and his 1 w, Muriel Norton Hicking; suc (under special remainder) his maternal gf, Sir William Norton Hicking, 1 Bt, 1947; *b* 6 Feb 1931; *Educ* Marlborough; *m* 1956, Sara Virginia, da of late Air Chief Marshal Sir Donald Hardman, GBE, KCB, DFC (*see* Hardman, Lady); 1 s, 2 da; *Heir* s, Jeremy William Francis North; *Style*— Sir Jonathan North, Bt; Frogmore, Weston-under-Penyard, Herefordshire HR9 5TQ

NORTH, Hon Mrs; Hon Margaret Isolda; *née* de Grey; 2 da of 8 Baron Walsingham, DSO, OBE (d 1965); *b* 14 August 1926; *m* 9 March 1950, Maj Geoffrey Edward Ford North, MC, s of Stephen Thomas Ford North, of Ashdale, Woking, Surrey; 1 s, 3 da; *Career* serv WWII WRNS 1943-46; *Recreations* bicycling; *Style*— The Hon Mrs North; Holmingham Farm, Bampton, Tiverton, Devon

NORTH, Dr Peter Machin; CBE; s of Geoffrey Machin North (d 1974), and Freda

Brunt, *née* Smith; *b* 30 August 1936; *Educ* Oakham Sch, Keble Coll Oxford; *m* 1960, Stephanie Mary, eldest da of Thomas L Chadwick (d 1963); 2 s (Nicholas Machin b 1964, James William Thomas b 1971), 1 da (Jane Amanda b 1962); *Career* Lt Royal Leicestershire Regt Cyprus 1955-56, teaching asst Northwestern Univ Sch of Law Chicago 1960-61, lectr Univ Coll of Wales Aberystwyth 1961-63, Nottingham 1963-65, tutor in law Keble Coll Oxford 1965-76, (fell 1965-84, hon fell 1984), hon fell Univ Coll of N Wales, hon bencher Inner Temple; law cmmr for Eng and Wales 1976-84; princ Jesus Coll Oxford 1984-; chm Road Traffic Law Review 1985-88; *Recreations* locking; *Clubs* Utd Oxford and Cambridge Univ; *Style*— Dr Peter North, CBE; Jesus College, Oxford OX1 3DW (☎ 0865 279701)

NORTH, Lord; Piers Edward Brownlow; s and h of 9 Earl of Guilford, DL; *b* 9 Mar 1971; *Style*— Lord North; Waldershare Park, Dover, Kent

NORTH, Hon Mrs; Hon Rosemary Victoria; *née* Orde-Powlett; da of 7 Baron Bolton and his 1 w, Hon Christine Helena, *née* Weld Forester (*see* Hon Mrs Miles); *b* 1952; *m* 1974, John Richard Bentley North; 1 s, 1 da; *Style*— The Hon Mrs North; RMB 590, Boddington, W Australia 6390

NORTH, Lady; Thelma Grace; *née* Dawson; *m* 1924, Rt Hon Sir Alfred North, KBE, PC, sometime Chm NZ Press Cncl and Pres NZ Ct of Appeal (d 1981); 2 s, 1 da; *Style*— Lady North; 28 Mahoe Av, Remuera, Auckland, New Zealand

NORTH, Sir Thomas Lindsay; s of late J North; *b* 11 Dec 1919; *Educ* Rutherglen; *m* 1944, Kathleen, da of L B Jefferis; 2 da; *Career* G J Coles & Co Ltd: joined 1938, NSW state mangr and assoc dir 1960, supermarket dir 1963, dir and gen mangr 1968-73, md 1975-80, chm 1980-; dir various subsidiary companies; kt 1982; *Style*— Sir Thomas North; 31 Power St, Toorak, Vic 3142, Australia

NORTH-BEAUCHAMP, Hon Mrs; Hon Susan Silence; *née* North; da of late Hon Dudley William John North, MC, and sis of 13 Baron North (d 1941); *b* 19 Jan 1920; *m* 1944, Frederick Guy Beauchamp, MD, MRCS; 3 da; co-heiress to Barony; *Career* assumed by deed poll 1943 the additional surname of Beauchamp; *Style*— The Hon Mrs North-Beauchamp; 19 Beaumont St, London WI

NORTHAMPTON, Archdeacon of; *see*: Marsh, Ven Bazil Roland

NORTHAMPTON, 7 Marquess of (UK 1812); Spencer Douglas David Compton; DL (Northants 1979); also Earl of Northampton (UK 1618), Earl Compton, and Baron Wilmington (both UK 1812); patron of 9 livings; s of 6 Marquess of Northampton, DSO (d 1978), and his 2 w, Virginia, yst da of David Rimington Heaton, DSO, of Brookfield, Crownhill, S Devon; *b* 2 April 1946; *Educ* Eton; *m* 1, 13 June 1967 (m dis 1973), Henriette Luisa Maria, o da of late Baron Adolph William Carel Bentinck, sometime Netherlands ambass to France; 1 s, 1 da; m 2, 1974 (m dis 1977), Annette Marie, da of Charles Anthony Russell Smallwood; m 3, 1977 (m dis 1983), Rosemary Ashley Morritt, o da of P G M Hancock, of Truro, and formerly w of Hon Charles Dawson-Damer (bro of 7 Earl of Portarlington); 1 da; m 4, 1985, Hannelore Ellen, da of late Hermann Erhardt of Landsberg-am-Lech, and formerly w of Hon Michael Pearson, *qv*; 1 da; *Heir* s, Earl Compton; *Career* landowner and proprietor of Castle Ashby (constructed 1574, with an Inigo Jones frontage of 1635) and Compton Wynyates (built 1480-1520); *Clubs* Turf; *Style*— The Most Hon the Marquess of Northampton, DL; Compton Wynyates, Tysoe, Warwick (☎ (029 588) 229); Castle Ashby, Northampton (☎ Yardley Hastings (060 129) 234)

NORTHARD, John Henry; OSt J, CBE (1987, OBE 1979); s of William Henry Northard (d 1979) and Nellie, *née* Ingham; *b* 23 Dec 1926; *Educ* St Bedes GS Bradford Yorks, Barnsley Mining & Tech Coll; *m* 11 Oct 1953, Marian Josephine, da of George Frederick Lay (d 1938); 2 s (Richard b 1953, Martin b 1955), 2 da (Barbara b 1957, Victoria b 1970); *Career* colliery mangr Yorks 1955-57, gr mang Leics Collieries 1963-65 (colliery mangr 1957-63), dep chief mining engr Staffs Collieries 1965-70: NCB: area dir N Derbys area 1973-81 (area dep dir (mining) 1970-73), area dir Western Area 1981-85, opns dir 1985; dep chm Br Coal Corpn 1988 (memb bd 1986); pres Inst Mining Engrs 1982, vice-pres Coal Trades Benevolent Assoc (nat chm 1986), 1 vice-chm organising ctee World Mining Congress; OStJ; CEng, FEng, FIMinE, CBIM, FRSA; *Style*— Mr John Northard, Esq, CBE; British Coal Corpn, Hobart House, Grosvenor Place, London SW1X 7AE (☎ 01 235 2020, fax 01 235 2020 ext 34010)

NORTHBOURNE, 5 Baron (UK 1884); Sir Christopher George Walter James; 6 Bt (GB 1791); only s of 4 Baron Northbourne (d 1982), of Northbourne Court, Kent, and Katharine Louise (d 1980), yr da of late George Nickerson, of Boston, Mass, and his w Ellen (d 1950), who m as her 2 husb Rear-Adm Hon Sir Horace Hood, KCB, MVO, DSO (ka Jutland 1916), and was through him mother of 6 and 7 Viscounts Hood; *b* 18 Feb 1926; *Educ* Eton, Magdalen Coll Oxford (MA); *m* 1959, Marie-Sygne, da of Henri Claudel and gda of Paul Claudel, the poet and diplomat; 3 s, 1 da; *Heir* eldest s, Hon Charles James; *Career* co dir sits as Ind in House of Lords; FRICS; *Clubs* Brooks's, Farmers', Tarratine Yacht; *Style*— The Rt Hon the Lord Northbourne; Coldharbour, Northbourne, Kent (☎ 0304 611277); 11 Eaton Place, SW1 (☎ 01 235 6790); Evistones, Otterburn, Northumberland; office: Betteshanger Farms Ltd and Kent Salads Ltd, Betteshanger, Deal, Kent (☎ 0304 366947)

NORTHBROOK, 5 Baron (UK 1886); Sir Francis John Baring; 7 Bt (GB 1793), JP (Hants 1954), DL (1972); s of 4 Baron (d 1947); *b* 31 May 1915; *Educ* Winchester, Trin Oxford; *m* 1951, Rowena Margaret, da of Brig-Gen Sir William Henry Manning, GCMG, KBE, CB (d 1932); 1 s, 3 da; *Heir* s, Hon Francis Thomas Baring; *Career* chm Winchester Dist Health Authy 1981; *Style*— The Rt Hon the Lord Northbrook, JP, DL; East Stratton House, East Stratton, Winchester, Hants (☎ Micheldever 469)

NORTHCOTE, Lady Catherine Cecilia Mary; da of 3 Earl of Iddesleigh (d 1970); *b* 1931; *Educ* Univ Coll London; *Career* lectr, sr lectr and head of history Maria Assumpta Coll of Educn 1964-79; later EFL teacher Hishôten Coll Usaka Japan; *Books* People of the Past Series (OUP), Nurse in the Crimea (1966), A 12th Century Benedictine Nun (1967), A Docker goes on Strike (1968), Radio Script (BBC School History); *Style*— Lady Catherine Northcote; c/o Pynes, Exeter, Devon EX5 5EF

NORTHCOTE, Donald Henry; s of Frederick Northcote (d 1983); *b* 27 Dec 1921; *Educ* George Monoux GS, London Univ, Cambridge (BSc, MA, PhD, ScD, FRS); *m* 1948, Eva Marjorie, nee Mayo; 2 da; *Career* prof plant biochem Cambridge 1972-, master Sidney Sussex Coll Cambridge 1976-; *Recreations* sailing (yacht 'Sprite'); *Clubs* Utd Oxford and Cambridge; *Style*— Donald Northcote, Esq; The Masters Lodge, Sidney Sussex Coll, Cambridge (☎ 0223 355860)

NORTHCOTE, Hon Edward Frederic; TD (1975); s of 3 Earl of Iddesleigh (d 1970); *b* 29 July 1934; *Educ* Downside, Trinity Coll Oxford (MA); *m* 1963 (m dis 1980), Vivien Sheena, da of Col Robert John Augustine Hornby, OBE, of Banbury, Oxon; 2 s, 1 da; *Career* serv Oxford Univ OTC 1953-55; Maj Intelligence Corps, serv Cyprus 1957; chartered cost and mgmnt accountant; princ offr HM Treasy 1969-71; *Style*— The Hon Edward Northcote, TD; c/o Lloyds Bank, 16 St James's St, London SW1

NORTHCOTE, Hon Mrs; Hon Mary Betty; *née* Cunliffe; da of 1 Baron Cunliffe (d 1920); *b* 1898; *m* 1921, Lt-Col Otho Stuart Irwin Northcote (d 1966); 1 da; *Style*— The Hon Mrs Northcote; 7 Bolus Ave, Kenilworth, Cape Province, SA

NORTHCOTE, His Hon Judge; Peter Colston; s of William George Northcote (d 1936), and Edith Mary, *née* Watkins (d 1943); *b* 23 Oct 1920; *Educ* Ellesmere Coll, Bristol Univ; *m* 1947, Patricia Elizabeth, da of James Roger Bickley (d 1983); 2 s (Robin, Michael); *Career* WWII Maj Rajput Regt Far E 1939-46; barr Inner Temple 1948, circuit judge 1973-, chm Nat Inst Tbnl, W Midland Rent Tbnl, AG Land Tbnl; *Recreations* travel, music, winter sports; *Clubs* Army and Navy; *Style*— His Hon Judge Northcote; Wroxeter Grange, Shrewsbury, Salop (☎ 074 375 279)

NORTHCOTE, (Cecil Henry) Stafford; OBE (1982); 2 s of Capt (Hon Maj) Cecil Stafford Northcote (Rifle Brigade) (d 1912), and Ida, o da of Capt Joseph Boulderson; Cecil was gs of the Rev Stafford Northcote, the latter being 3 s of Sir Stafford Northcote, 7th Bt, and yr bro of 1st Earl of Iddesleigh; *b* 8 June 1912, (posthumously); *Educ* Douai Sch, Queen's Coll Oxford (MA); *m* 28 Dec 1936, Winifreda Iola Marguerite (Freda), da of Frederick Williams (d 1913); 2 s (Amyas Henry b 25 Nov 1937, Hugh b 22 Nov 1938), 1 da (Julia b 17 July 1941); *Career* RAEC 1941-42; headmaster St Bedes Bishton Hall Prep Sch 1936-78; memb: euro cncl Stafford and Salop Div, Colwich Parish Cncl 1949- (chm 1955-58), Staffordshire CC 1958-81; former memb Stafford RDC, Mid-Staffordshire Cons Assoc rep on Staffordshire E Euro Constituency Cncl; fndr govr Newman Coll Birmingham 1970-; chm: Colwich & Little Haywood branch Cons Assoc 1948-88, Stafford and Stone Cons Assoc 1972-81 (pres 1982-85); pres Mid-Staffordshire Cons & Unionist Assoc 1985-88; former govr various local educn estabs; memb Ct Keele Univ; High Sheriff of Staffordshire 1981-82; OStJ 1984; Knight of the Sovereign and Mil Order of Malta (Honour and Devotion) 1957, KSG 1977; *Recreations* walking, gardening (assisting), cricket (watching); *Clubs* Staffordshire Country; *Style*— Stafford Northcote, Esq, OBE; Bishton Hall, Wolseley Bridge, Staffs (☎ 0889 881277)

NORTHCOTE-GREEN, Roger James; MC (1944), TD (1950) and clasp (1952), JP (1960); s late of Rev Edward Joseph Northcote-Green, and late Mary Louise Catt; *b* 25 July 1912; *Educ* St Edwards Sch, Queen's Coll Oxford (MA); *m* 1947, Joan Edith Lillian, da of Ernest Arthur Greswell; 3 s (David, Christopher, Simon), 1 da (Rosamund); *Career* war serv with Oxford and Bucks LI Burma, Brig Maj 53 Ind Inf Bde Malaya, PSC Quetta 1944-45; asst and housemaster St Edward's 1936-39 and 1946-52, headmaster Worksop Coll 1952-70; rugby football Oxford Univ Richmond, Capt Oxfordshire; OUR FC Rep RU Ctee 1947-52; memb: Cryptics Free Foresters Golf; *Recreations* gardening; *Clubs* E India; *Style*— Roger Northcote-Green, Esq, MC, TD, JP; Manor Cottage, Woolston, Williton, Somerset (☎ 0984 32445)

NORTHCOTT, Montague Walter Desmond; s of Cdr W C Northcott, JP, DL, RNR, (d 1965) of 9 Ranulf Rd, London NW2, and Irene Violet, *née* Lay (d 1972); *b* 25 April 1931; *Educ* Harrow; *m* 24 Aug 1966, Annie Margaret; 1 s (Richard Walter Montague b 1967), 1 da (Joanna Rosemary Marion b 1969); *Career* Cunard Steamship Co 1952-67, Hogg Robinson Travel 1968-, underwriting member of Lloyds, memb Inst of Travel & Tourism; Master Worshipful Co of Haberdashers' 1985, Upper Warden Worshipful Co of Painters' Stainers' 1988, Liveryman Worshipful Co of Loriners'; tstee Northcott Fndn, govr Haberdashers' Aske's Schs 1972-82, Jones GS Fndn 1985-88, chm St Andrews Church Restoration Appeal; FRSA; *Recreations* tennis, golf, swimming, gardening; *Clubs* RAC, City Livery; *Style*— Montague Northcott, Esq; The Old Rectory, Little Berkhamsted, Hertfordshire SG13 8LP

NORTHCOTT, Simon John; s of Maj Guy Denis Stanley Northcott, of Basingstoke, Hants, and Sylvia Mary Rait Kerr; *b* 22 June 1954; *Educ* Wellington Coll, Nottingham Univ (BSc), Cranfield Sch of Management (MBA); *m* 18 Aug 1979, Susan Caroline Elizabeth, da of Neville Poyser, of Rio de Janeiro, Brazil; *Career* md Petrocon Drilling Tools plc 1984-86; dir and gen man Victaulic Industl Polymers 1987-; *Recreations* skiing, golf, shooting, sailing; *Style*— Simon J Northcott, Esq; 8 Barnwell, nr Oundle, Northants PE8 5PM (☎ 0832 73145); St Peters Road, Huntingdon, Cambs PE18 7DJ (☎ 0480 52121, telex 32221, fax 0480 50430)

NORTHESK, Betty, Countess of; Elizabeth; da of late Anthony A Vlasto; *m* 1929, 11 Earl of Northesk (d 1963); 1 da (adopted); *Style*— The Rt Hon Betty, Countess of Northesk; Glenley Farmhouse, Glenogil, by Forfar, Angus, Scotland DD8 3SY (☎ Fern 216)

NORTHESK, 13 Earl of (S 1647); Robert Andrew Carnegie; also Lord Rosehill and Inglismaldie (S precedence 1639); s of 12 Earl of Northesk (d 1975) and Dorothy, da of Col Sir William Campion, KCMG, DSO, DL, himself s of Col William Campion, CB, VD, JP, DL, and Hon Gertrude Brand, da of 1 Viscount Hampden and 23 Baron Dacre, GCB, PC; the 1 Earl of Northesk was yr bro of 1 Earl of Southesk; *b* 24 June 1926; *Educ* Pangbourne, Tabor Naval Acad Mass USA; *m* 1949, Jean, yr da of Capt John MacRae, of Argyll, and Lady Phyllis Hervey (da of 4 Marquess of Bristol; 1 s (David b 1954), 2 da (Karen b 1951, Mary b 1953), (and 1 s decd); *Heir* s, Lord Rosehill; *Career* serv RN 1942-45; landowner and farmer; memb Br Racing Drivers Club 1957-; dir Int Fedn Charolais Cattle, Cncl Br Charolais Cattle Soc 1972-; chm Midhurst RDC 1972-74; dir Chandler Hargreaves Whittall (IOM) 1979-, IOM Bank 1980-, Buchan Sch (IOM) 1980-; dir NEL Britannia Int Assurance 1984; *Recreations* gardening, shooting, motor racing, silversmithing; *Style*— The Rt Hon Earl of Northesk; Springwaters, Ballamodha, IOM (☎ 0624 823291)

NORTHFIELD, Baron (Life Peer UK 1975); (William) Donald Chapman; s of W H Chapman of Barnsley, Yorks; *b* 25 Nov 1923; *Educ* Barnsley GS, Emmanuel Coll Cambridge; *Career* sits as Lab peer in House of Lords; formerly memb Cambridge Borough Cncl, gen sec Fabian Soc 1949-53, MP (Lab) Birmingham (Northfield) 1951-70; res fell Nuffield Coll Oxford 1971-73, visiting fell Centre for Contemporary European studies Univ of Sussex 1973; chm: HM Devpt Cmmrs 1974, Telford New Town Devpt Corpn 1975, Consortium Devpts Ltd 1985, co dir; economist, writer; *Style*— The Rt Hon the Lord Northfield; 21 Denny St, London SE11 4UX

NORTHLAND, Viscount; Edward John Knox; er s and h of 7 Earl of Ranfurly, *qv*; *b* 21 May 1957; *Style*— Viscount Northland; c/o Maltings Chase, Nayland, Colchester, Essex

NORTHUMBERLAND, Archdeacon of; *see*: Thomas, Ven William Jordison

NORTHUMBERLAND, Duchess of; Elizabeth Diana; er da of 8 Duke of Buccleuch, KT, GCVO, TD, PC; *m* 12 June 1946, 10 Duke of Northumberland, KG, GCVO, TD, PC, JP (d 1988); 3 s, 3 da (and 1 da decd); *Career* served WW II 1942-45 as 3 Offr WRNS; *Style—* Her Grace the Duchess of Northumberland; Alnwick Castle, Northumberland NE66 1NQ; Syon House, Brentford, Middlesex; Clive Lodge, Albury, Surrey

NORTHUMBERLAND, 11 Duke of (GB 1776); Henry Alan Walter Richard Percy; 14 Bt (E 1660); also Baron Percy (GB 1723), Earl of Northumberland and Baron Warkworth (GB 1749), Earl Percy (GB 1776), Earl of Beverly (GB 1790), and Lord Lovaine, Baron of Alnwick (GB 1784); eldest s of 10 Duke of Northumberland, KG, GCVO, TD, PC, JP (d 1988); *b* 1 July 1953; *Educ* Eton, Ch Ch Oxford; *Heir* br, Lord Ralph Percy, *qv*; *Career* landowner; Pres Alnwick and Dist Ctee for the Disabled 1981-; *Recreations* tennis, shooting, National Film Institute; *Clubs* Turf, Queen's; *Style—* His Grace the Duke of Northumberland; Alnwick Castle, Alnwick, Northumberland (☎ 0665 2456); Syon House, Brentford, Middlesex (☎ 01 560 2353); Clive Lodge, Albury Park, Guildford, Surrey (☎ 048 641 2695)

NORTON, Hon Adam Gregory; yr s of 2 Baron Rathcreedan, TD; *b* 2 April 1952; *Educ* Wellington Coll, Lincoln Coll Oxford; *m* 1980, Hilary Shelton, da of Edmond Ryan, of Anchorage, Kentucky, USA; 2 da (Emily Beatrice Norton b 25 July 1984, Georgina Christine Ryan b 4 June 1988); *Clubs* Savile; *Style—* The Hon Adam Norton; 60 Marmora Rd, East Dulwich, London SE22

NORTON, Hon Christopher John; s and h of 2 Baron Rathcreedan, TD; *b* 3 June 1949; *Educ* Wellington, RAC Cirencester; *m* 1978, Lavinia Anne Ross, da of Alan George Ross Ormiston, of Coln Orchard, Arlington, Bibury, Glos; 2 da (Jessica Charlotte b 13 Nov 1983, Serena Clare b 12 Aug 1987); *Career* pedigree livestock auctioneer; *Recreations* horse racing, gardening; *Clubs* Turf; *Style—* The Hon Christopher Norton; Waterton Farm House, Ampney Crucis, Cirencester, Gloucestershire (☎ 0285 4282)

NORTON, Sir Clifford John; KCMG (1946, CMG 1933), CVO (1937); s of late Rev George Norton; *b* 17 July 1891; *Educ* Rugby, Queen's Coll Oxford (MA); *m* 1927, Noel Evelyn (d 1972), da of late Sir Walter Charleton Hughes, CIE (d 1922); *Career* served WWI with Suffolk Regt in Gallipoli and Palestine; political offr Damascus 1919; entered Dip Serv 1921, private sec to permanent under-sec of state for Foreign Affairs 1930-37, cnsllr Br Embassy Warsaw 1937-39, FO 1939-42, envoy to Berne 1942-46, ambassador to Greece 1946-51, hon citizen of Athens 1951, UK del (alternate) to UN Gen Assembly NY 1952 and 1953, former pres Anglo-Swiss Soc; hon fell Queen's Coll Oxford 1963; *Style—* Sir Clifford Norton, KCMG, CVO; 21a Carlyle Sq, London SW3 (☎ 01 352 9125)

NORTON, Cyril Arthur John; CBE (1980); s of John Henry Norton (d 1939), of Hayes, Kent, and Louisa Alice, *née* Block (d 1970); *b* 13 Oct 1916; *Educ* Haberdashers' Aske's Hatcham Sch; *m* 8 Dec 1945, Jacqueline Yvonne Monica, da of Frank Richmond-Coggan, MA (d 1958), of Hayes, Kent; 1 s (Anthony b 1951, d 1980), 1 step s (Peter (Thompson) b 1944, d 1968); *Career* WWII cmmnd Queen's Royal Regt 1940, Maj 1943, serv NW Europe 1944-45; cons Agent; E Woolwich 1948-50, Battersea 1950-56, cons Central Office Agent Counties 1955-61, sec Gtr London Planning Ctee 1961-63, chief Central Office Agent Gtr London Area 1963-73; dir The Russell Ptnrship Ltd (publishing and parly affairs advsrs) 1974-; chm political ctee Junior Carlton Club 1975-77 (vice chm 1973-75); Freeman: City of London 1937, Worshipful Co of Shipwrights 1937; Polonia Restituta (offr), awarded by Polish Govt in exile 1971; *Recreations* theatre, travel, watching cricket; *Clubs* Carlton, Army and Navy, MCC; *Style—* Cyril Norton, Esq, CBE; Flat 2, 7 Third Ave, Hove, Sussex BN3 2PB (☎ 0273 739823); The Russell Ptnrship Ltd, 16 Gt Coll St, London SW1P 3RX (☎ 01 222 2096, fax 01 222 8550)

NORTON, Hon Elizabeth Ann; da of 2 Baron Rathcreedan; *b* 1954; *Educ* Benenden; *Career* gen Mangr Supertravel Ltd 1987; *Recreations* skiing, food and drink; *Style—* The Hon Elizabeth Ann Norton; 35 Lancaster Road, London W11 1QJ

NORTON, Hon Francis John Hilary; s of 7 Baron Grantley, MC; *b* 28 Sept 1960; *Style—* The Hon Francis Norton; 12 Amberley Ct, Overton Rd, London SW9 7HL

NORTON, Col (Ian) Geoffrey; JP (1973-), TD (1963), DL (S Yorks 1979-); s of Cyril Needham Norton, MBE (d 1979), of 18 Slayleigh Lane, Sheffield, and Winifred Mary, *née* Creswick (d 1973); *b* 8 June 1931; *Educ* Stowe; *m* 4 April 1961, Eileen, da of Ernest Hughes, of 5 Normancroft Court, Sheffield; *Career* Nat Serv 1949-51, cmmnd RASC 1950, TA 1951-76, Hallamshire Bn York and Lancaster Regt 1951-67, Yorks Volunteers 1967-72, cmd 1 Bn Yorks Volunteers 1970-72, Dep Cdr (TAVR) NE Dist 1973-76, Regtl Col Yorkshire Volunteers, ADC to HM the Queen 1973-78; chm John Norton and Son (Sheffield) Ltd 1976- (md 1965-76), chm Chartan Aldred Ltd (formerly Shirley Aldred and Co Ltd) 1976- (dir 1959-76); chm: Yorks and Humberside TAVR Assoc 1985-, Friends of Sheffield Childrens Hosp 1979-85, St Georges Chapel Sheffield Cathedral 1982-; FInstD; *Recreations* pottering in the garden, music, reading; *Clubs* Army and Navy; *Style—* Col Geoffrey Norton, JP, TD, DL; 22 Cortworth Road, Sheffield S11 9LP (☎ 0742 366304); Chartan-Aldred Ltd, Oakwood Works, Sandy Lane, Worksop, Notts S80 3EY (☎ 0909 476861, fax 0909 500632)

NORTON, James Henry Llewelyn; s of Adam Henry Williams Petre Norton, and Margaret Vera Vittery, *née* Stephens; *b* 16 Feb 1948; *Educ* Eton; *Career* Morgan Grenfell Gp plc; dir: Morgan Grenfell Guernsey Ltd (chm), Morgan Grenfell Ltd, Morgan Grenfell Jersey Ltd ; *Recreations* architecture, skiing; *Clubs* Turf, Annabels; *Style—* James Norton, Esq; Colerne Manor, Chippenham, Wilts SN14 8AY; c/o Morgan Grenfell & Co Ltd, 23 Gt Winchester St, London EC2 (telex 8953511 MGLDN G, fax 01 588 5598)

NORTON, James William; CBE (1965); s of William Francis Duesbury Norton (d 1949); *b* 22 Feb 1918; *Educ* Marlborough, Dresden, Nottingham Univ; *m* 1952, Mary Helen, da of late William Reeves of Arkansas USA; *Career* Capt WW II; Dunlop Rubber Co Ltd 1937, resident rep in Iran 1948-65, local rep in Iran Fedn of Br Industs (now CBI) 1961-65, dir and jt md F Longdon & Co Ltd 1969-78; *Recreations* gardening, golf, tennis, travel, cars; *Clubs* E India Devonshire, Royal Soc of St George, Turf (Cairo), Imperial Iranian Sports (Teheran); *Style—* James Norton Esq, CBE; Random House, Hob Hill, Hazelwood, Derbys (☎ 0332 840822)

NORTON, 7 Baron (UK 1878) John Arden Adderley; OBE (1964); s of 6 Baron (d 1961); *b* 24 Nov 1915; *Educ* Radley, Magdalen Coll Oxford; *m* 1946, Betty Margaret, JP, da of late James McKee Hannah, of Domaine de Fontvieille, Aix-en-Provence; 2 s; *Heir* s, Hon James Nigel Arden Adderley; *Career* Lt RE 1940, served 1940-45, Maj 1944; Oxford Univ Greenland Expdn 1938, asst master Oundle Sch 1938-39; *Style—* The Rt Hon the Lord Norton, OBE; Fillongley Hall, Coventry, W Midlands (☎ 0676 40303)

NORTON, Hon Michael Adrian; s of 1 Baron Rathcreedan (d 1930); *b* 6 August 1907; *Educ* Wellington, Trinity Coll Cambridge (BA); *Recreations* foreign travel; *Clubs* Reform; *Style—* The Hon Michael Norton; 6 Carisbrooke Ct, 63/69 Weymouth St, London W1N 3LD (☎ 01 386 4756)

NORTON, Lady (Olive Penelope); MBE (1968); da of Col Arthur Mordaunt Murray, CB, MVO (gggs of 3 Duke of Atholl; d 1920) and his 2 w, Mabel, *née* Nicholson (d 1964); *b* 28 Jan 1908; *Educ* Royal School for Officers' Daughters Bath; *m* 1, 1928 (m dis 1942), Charles Russell Wood; 1 s (Peter b 1930); m 2, 1948, Sir (Walter) Charles Norton, MBE, MC (d 1974); *Career* many charity commitments; *Clubs* Hurlingham; *Style—* Lady Norton, MBE; 23 Hans Place, London SW1

NORTON, Richard Glover; s of Ven Hugh Ross Norton (d 1969; chaplain Bde of Gds 1938-44, asst chaplain gen 1944-45, archdeacon of Sudbury 1945-58), and Jessie Muriel, *née* Glover (d 1965); *b* 1 Nov 1925; *Educ* Denstone Coll; *m* 1953, Philippa Margaret, da of Capt William Laurence Thompson Fisher (d 1968), of Billockby Hall, Norfolk; 2 s (Richard b 1959, George b 1962); *Career* Gren Gds 1943-47 Capt (Germany 1945-47); slr: ptnr Slaughter & May 1957-86; dir The Law Debenture Corp plc 1986-; *Recreations* land management, golf; *Clubs* Cavalry and Guards; MCC; *Style—* Richard Norton, Esq; Burnham Wood, Welwyn, Hertfordshire AL6 0ES (☎ 043 879 254); The Law Debenture Corp plc, Princes House, 95 Gresham St, London EC2V 7LY (☎ 01 606 5451, telex 888347)

NORTON, Hon Richard William Brinsley; s of 7 Baron Grantley, MC, and Lady Deirdre Elisabeth Freda Hare, da of 5 Earl of Listowel; *b* 30 Jan 1956; *Educ* Ampleforth, New Coll Oxford (MA, pres Union); *Career* merchant banker; Conservative Research Dept 1977-81, cllr Royal Borough of Kensington and Chelsea 1982-86, Conservative candidate for Wentworth in 1983 general election; Kt SMO Malta, OStJ; *Recreations* Bridge; *Clubs* White's, Pratt's; *Style—* The Hon Richard Norton; 8 Halsey St, London SW3

NORTON, Tom; TD (1966), JP (1961), DL (1962); s of Tom Norton, JP (d 1955), of Llandrindod Wells; *b* 15 April 1920; *Educ* Hanley Castle, Birmingham Univ; *m* 1948, Pauline Fane, da of late A L F Evans, DIG Indian Police; 3 s, 1 da; *Career* joined TA (RA) 1939, served in WWII (despatches 1946), demobilised as Hon Capt 1946, cmmnd TA (REME) 1947; chm The Automobile Palace (Hldgs) Ltd (dir 1947-); High Sheriff Radnorshire 1966; *Recreations* gardening, old cycles; *Style—* Tom Norton, Esq, TD, JP, DL; Sargodha, Brookfields, Cefnllys Lane, Llandrindod Wells, Powys (☎ 0597 2079)

NORTON-GRIFFITHS, Sir John; 3 Bt (UK 1922), of Wonham, Betchworth, Co Surrey; s of Sir Peter Norton-Griffiths, 2 Bt (d 1983), and Kathryn, *née* Schrafft (d 1980); *b* 4 Oct 1938; *Educ* Eton; *m* 1964, Marilyn Margaret, da of Norman Grimley of Liverpool; *Heir* bro, Dr Michael Norton-Griffiths; *Career* Sub-Lt RN; chartered accountant, pres Main Street Computers Inc 1980-; FCA; *Style—* Sir John Norton-Griffiths, 3 Bt; 17 Royal Drive, Bricktown, NJ 08723, USA

NORTON-GRIFFITHS, Dr Michael; yr s of Sir Peter Norton-Griffiths, 2 Bt (d 1983); hp of bro, Sir John Norton-Griffiths, 3 Bt; *b* 11 Jan 1941; *Educ* Eton, Keble Coll Oxford (BA, DPhil); *m* 9 Jan 1965, Ann, o da of late Gp Capt Blair Alexander Fraser, RAF, of Bath (whose mother was Joan, da of Blair Cochrane, OBE, JP, ggs of 9 Earl of Dundonald); 1 s (Alastair b 1976); *Career* dir Serengeti Ecological Monitoring Programme Tanzania 1969-73; independent environmental conslt Kenya 1974-76; man dir EcoSystems Ltd, environmental conslts Kenya 1977-87; Sahel Programme Coordinator, Int Union for the Conservation of Nature and Natural Resources (IUCN), East African regnl office Kenya 1987-88, co ordinator Pan African environment monitoring network UN Environment Prog (UNEP) Nairobi 1989-, conslt in environmental surveys and impact assessments to CIDA, DLCOEA, EDF, FAO, GTZ, IBRD, IFAD, ILCA, Netherlands Technical Assistance, NORAD, SIDA, IUCN, UNESCO, UNEP, USAID 1974-87; *Books* Serengeti: dynamics of an ecosystem (1978); *Recreations* flying, balooning, deep sea fishing, snakes; *Clubs* Muthaiga Country; *Style—* Dr Michael Norton-Griffiths; Box 21791, Nairobi, Kenya

NORTON-SEALEY, John Evan; s of Clarence Norton-Sealey (d 1980), of Clevedon, Avon, and Amy Gwendoline, *née* Hodges (d 1965); *b* 19 Sept 1939; *Educ* St Nicholas Public Sch Clevedon Avon, St Davids Sch (now Millfield) Congresbury Somerset; *Career* sales mangr G E Taylor & Sons Bristol 1956, dir Rexmore (Taylor) Bristol 1984, div dir West England Rexmore Wholesale Ltd 1986, dir Covefold Ltd 1987; involved with Crimewatch for many years under chief constable Donald Smith Avon and Somerset; life memb NATD, aux memb Nat Assoc Teachers of Movement and Dancing GB; hon memb Nat Geographic Soc Washington DC 1975; *Recreations* travelling extensively USA, USSR, Poland and central America; *Clubs* Cadbury Ct Country (Yatton Bristol); *Style—* John Norton-Sealey, Esq; 37 Cecil Ave, Bristol BS5 7SE; G E Taylor & Sons (RSW) Ltd, Wapping Wharf, Cumberland Rd, Bristol BS1 6UP (☎ 0272 291 616, fax 0272 250 616)

NORWICH, Dean of; *see*: Burbridge, Very Rev (John) Paul

NORWICH, 2 Viscount (UK 1952); John Julius Cooper; s of 1 Viscount Norwich, GCMG, DSO, PC (Duff Cooper), sec of State for War 1935-37, First Lord of Admiralty 1937-38, min of Info 1940-41, and ambass to France 1944-47, and Lady Diana Cooper, *née* Manners (d 1986); *b* 15 Sept 1929; *Educ* Upper Canada Coll Toronto, Eton, Strasbourg Univ, New Coll Oxford; *m* 1952 (m dis 1985), Anne Frances May, da of Hon Sir Bede Clifford, GCMG, CB, MVO (yst s of 10 Baron Clifford of Chudleigh), and Alice, *née* Gundry, of Cleveland Ohio; 1 s, 1 da; *Heir* s, Hon Jason Cooper; *Career* author, broadcaster (as 'John Julius Norwich'); with FO 1952-64; chm Venice in Peril Fund, memb Exec Ctee Nat Tst 1969-; maker of some thirty programmes (historical or art-historical) for television; FRSL, FRGS; Ordine al Merito della Repubblica Italiana; *Books* two-volume history of Norman Sicily: The Normans in the South, The Kingdom in the Sun; two-volume history of Venice: The Rise to Empire, The Greatness and the Fall; Mount Athos, Sahara, The Architecture of Southern England, Christmas Crackers, Fifty Years of Glyndebourne; *Recreations* Venice, commonplace books; *Clubs* Garrick, Beefsteak; *Style—* The Rt Hon the Viscount Norwich; 24 Blomfield Rd, London W9 1AD (☎ 01 286 5050)

NORWICH, 70 Bishop of (cr 1091), 1985-; Rt Rev Peter John Nott; s of Cecil Frederick Wilder Nott (d 1956), and Rosina Mabel, *née* Bailey; *b* 30 Dec 1933; *Educ* Bristol GS, Dulwich Coll, RMA Sandhurst, Fitzwilliam Coll Cambridge (MA), Westcott

House Cambridge; *m* 1961, Elizabeth May, da of Herman Philip Maingot (d 1942); 1 s (Andrew), 3 da (Joanna, Victoria, Lucy); *Career* Regular Army 1951-55, Lt RA; deacon 1961, priest 1962; curate of Harpenden 1961-64, chaplain and fell Fitzwilliam Coll Cambridge 1964-69, chaplain New Hall Cambridge 1966-69, rector of Beaconsfield 1969-77, bishop of Taunton 1977-85; *Recreations* gardening, music, sketching, sport; *Clubs* Royal Cwlth Soc, Norfolk (Norwich); *Style*— The Rt Rev the Bishop of Norwich; The Bishop's House, Norwich NR3 1SB (☎ 0603 629001)

NORWOOD, David Barry; s of Denis Norwood MA (Oxon), JP (d 1969), of East Beach, Lytham, Lancashire, and Eileen Hewitt, *née* Williams; *b* 16 Dec 1926; *Educ* Manchester GS, St John's Coll, Cambridge (MA 1951); *m* 2 Sept 1972, Sylvia, da of George Nathaniel Waight (d 1947), of The Mill House, Chilton Foliat, Hungerford, Berkshire; 1 step s (David Hunt b 1949), 1 step da (Sarah (Mrs Mackay) b 1952); *Career* schoolmaster (ret 1987); RAF (Education Branch) 1949-53, Flt-Lt; Bradfield Coll, Berkshire 1953-87: housemaster 1963-82, second master 1983-87 (oc ccf 1960-66); memb Governing Body of: Edgeborough Sch Farnham Surrey (chm 1986-87), St Andrew's Sch Pangbourne, Berkshire, Lucton Pierrepont Educational Tst, Leominster, Herefords; *Recreations* classical music, crosswords, the countryside (hockey 1945-65); *Style*— David Norwood, Esq; 10 Karen Court, Dilwyn, Hereford HR4 8HU (☎ 0544 318672)

NORWOOD, Sqdn Ldr Gerard Thomas; s of William Norwood (d 1961), of Northamptonshire, and Florence Lofts (d 1968); *b* 8 Jan 1922; *Educ* Laxton Sch, Oundle; *m* 1, 4 Sept 1943 (m dis 1975), Margaret Veronica, da of Bernard McKenna (d 1965), of Lancs; 3 da (Sylvia b 1946, Pauline b 1952, Christine b 1952 (twin)); m 2, 12 April 1975, Susan Dorothy, da of Major Edmund Roy Nurse, MC (d 1969), of Huntingdonshire; *Career* RAF Offr 1941-77, aircrew Bomber Cmd 1943-45, Rhodesian Air Trg Gp 1946-50, Radar Res and Devpt Flying 1950-54, tport cmd 1954-57, lectr in electronics 1957-60, Air Miny 1960-64, RAF Wyton, Recce Force 1964-67, MOD 1967-70, HQ Trg Cmd 1970-77 (ret); full memb Inst of Br Carriage and Automobile Manufacturers, chm RSPCA Hunts and March Branch Ctee, ctee memb of Cncl for the Protection of Rural England Huntingdon Branch, pres Old Laxtonian Club 1987-88; *Recreations* restoration of medieval timbered bldgs and vintage cars; *Clubs* RAF, Piccadilly; *Style*— Sqdn Ldr Gerard Norwood; Weavers, Wennington, Huntingdon, Cambs (☎ 048 73 435)

NOSS, John Bramble; s of John Noss (d 1956), of Portsmouth, and Vera Ethel, *née* Mattingly; *b* 20 Dec 1935; *Educ* Portsmouth GS; *m* 6 July 1957, Shirley May, da of Harry Cyril Andrews (d 1986), of Portsmouth; 2 s (Steven John b 1961, Robin Philip b 1966), 1 da (Kim Caroline Graham b 1959); *Career* RAF 1955-57; Dip Serv: Br Embassy Beirut 1957-59, Br Embassy Copenhagen 1960-63, FO 1964, Russian language trg 1964-65, third (later second) commercial sec Br Embassy Moscow 1965-68, second commercial sec Br Embassy Santiago 1968-70, FCO 1970-73, first sec econ Br Embassy Pretoria 1974-77, first sec commercial Br Embassy Moscow 1977-78, FCO 1978-81, consul inward investmt Br Consulate-Gen NY 1981-85, Br high cmmr honiara Solomon Islands 1986-88, cnsllr commercial and economic Br Embassy Helsinki 1988-; *Recreations* reading, photography, jogging, golf; *Style*— John Noss, Esq; c/o Foreign and Commonwealth Office, King Charles St, London SW1A 2AH; British Embassy, Uudenmaankatu 16-20, 00120 Helsinki, Finland (☎ 010 358 064 7922, fax 010 358 0611 747, telex 121122 A/B UKHKI SF)

NOSSAL, Sir Gustav Joseph Victor; CBE (1970); s of Rudolf Immanuel Nossal (d 1962), and Irene Maria Nossal; *b* 4 June 1931; *Educ* Sydney Univ (MB, BS), Melbourne Univ (PhD); *m* 1955, Lyn Beatrix, da of Mark Ernest Dunnicliff; 2 s, 2 da;; *Career* res fell Walter and Eliza Hall Inst of Med Res 1957-59, asst prof Stanford Univ Sch of Med California USA 1959-61, dep dir (Immunology) Walter and Eliza Hall Inst of Med Res 1961-65 (dir 1965-); kt 1977; *Style*— Sir Gustav Nossal, CBE; 46 Fellows St, Kew, Vic 3101, Australia (☎ 861 8256)

NOTT, Brig Donald Harley; DSO (1941), OBE (1954), MC (1939) and bar (1942), DL (Worcs 1963); s of late John Harley Nott; *b* 27 April 1908; *Educ* Marlborough, Sandhurst; *m* 1 1933, Eve, *née* Harben (m dis); 1 da; m 2 1947, Elfriede Eugenie, da of Maj Eugen August von Kahler, Imperial Austrian Army; 1 s, 1 da; *Career* serv 1939-45 Palestine, Mid E, Ethiopia; psc Canada, NATO Defence Coll Paris; asst Civil Defence offr Worcs 1959-69; Col The Worcestershire Regt 1961-67; Haile Selassie Mil Medal; OStJ; *Recreations* archery, fishing, shooting, painting; *Style*— Brig Donald Nott, DSO, OBE, MC, DL; Four Seasons, Battenhall Ave, Worcester (☎ 0905 354402)

NOTT, Rt Hon Sir John William Frederic; KCB (1983), PC (1979); s of Richard W K Nott, and Phyllis, *née* Francis; *b* 1 Feb 1932; *Educ* Bradfield, Trinity Coll Cambridge; *m* 1959, Miloska Sekol; 2 s, 1 da; *Career* serv 2 Gurkha Rifles 1952-56, barr 1959, gen mangr S G Warburg 1960-66; MP (C) Cornwall St Ives 1966-83, min of state Treasy 1972-74, oppn spokesman for Trade 1976-79, Treasy and Econ Affrs 1975-76, trade sec 1979-81, def sec 1981-83; exec dir Lazard Bros 1983- (chm 1985), dep chm Royal Insur plc 1986; *Style*— The Rt Hon Sir John Nott, KCB; 21 Moorfields, London EC2 (☎ 01 588 2721)

NOTT, Rt Rev Peter John; *see* Norwich, Bishop of

NOTTAGE, Raymond Frederick Tritton; CMG 1964; s of Frederick, and Frances Nottage; *b* 1 August 1916; *Educ* Hackney Downs Sec Sch; *m* 1941, Joyce Evelyn, da of Sidney Philpot; 3 da; *Career* dep chm Assoc of Lloyd's Members 1985-; civil servant, PO HQ 1936-47, Ctee on Trg in Pub Admin for o'seas countries 1961-63; vice-pres Int Inst of Admin Sciences 1962-68, memb Governing Body Inst of Dvpt Studies Univ of Sussex 1966-76; *Books* Sources of Local Revenue (with S H H Hildersley 1968), Financing Public Sector Pensions (1975), Pensions - a Plan for the Future (with Gerald Rhodes 1986); *Style*— Raymond Nottage, Esq; Lloyd's, Lime St, London EC3 7DQ (☎ 01 283 4026)

NOTTINGHAM, Bishop of (RC) 1974-; Rt Rev James Joseph McGuinness; s of Micheal McGuinness, and Margaret, *née* McLean; *b* 7 Oct 1925; *Educ* St Colum's Coll Derry, St Patrick's Coll Carlow, Oscott Coll Birmingham; *Career* ordained 1950, curate St Mary's Derby 1950-53, sec to Bishop Ellis 1953-56, parish priest Corpus Christi Parish Clifton Nottingham 1956-72, vicar gen Nottingham Diocese 1969, coadjutor Bishop of Nottingham and titular Bishop of St German 1972-74; *Recreations* gardening; *Style*— The Rt Rev the Bishop of Nottingham; Bishop's House, 27 Cavendish Rd East, The Park, Nottingham NG7 1BB (☎ 0602 474 786, fax 0602 475 235)

NOULTON, John David; s of John Noulton, 44 Littleton St, London SW18, and Kathleen, *née* Sheehan; *b* 5 Jan 1939; *Educ* Clapham Coll; *m* 7 Oct 1961, Anne Elizabeth, da of Edward Byrne (d 1985); 3 s (Mark John b 1963, Stephen Anthony b 1965, Simon Anthony b 1966), 1 da (Jane Antonia b 1968); *Career* asst princ Dept of Tport 1970-72, princ DOE 1972-76, private sec to Min of State Rt Hon Denis Howell, MP 1976-78, Sec Property Servs Agency 1976-81, under sec Dept of Tport 1985 (asst sec 1981-85); dir Br Channel Tunnel Bo plc 1982-89, chm Channel Tunnel Intergovernmental Cmmn 1989; dir Marine and Ports 1989-; Friend of Richmond Park, memb Kingston Soc; MCIT 1986; *Recreations* walking, boating, writing, music; *Style*— John Noulton, Esq; 12 Ladderstile Ride, Kingston Hill, Coombe, Surrey KT2 7LP (☎ 01 541 0734); Dept of Transport, Sunley House, 90-93 High Holborn, London WC1V 6LP (☎ 01 405 6911)

NOURSE, Christopher Stuart; s of Rev John Nourse, of Hythe, Kent, and Helen Jane Macdonald, *née* Allison; *b* 13 August 1946; *Educ* Hurstpierpoint Coll Sussex, Edinburgh Univ (LLB); *Career* legal exec Life Offices Assoc 1970-72; various managerial positions: Royal Opera House, English Opera Gp, Sadler's Wells Royal Ballet 1972-80; gen mangr and admin Sadler's Wells Royal Ballet 1980-, mgmnt Royal Opera House 1988-; memb Hon Soc of Middle Temple; *Recreations* opera, ballet, music, paintings and prints, animals, walking and the country-side; *Style*— Christopher Nourse, Esq; Royal Opera House, Covent Garden, London WC2E 9DD (☎ 01 240 1200); Sadler's Wells Theatre, Rosebery Avenue, London EC1R 4TN (☎ 01 278 8383)

NOURSE, Hon Mr Justice; Hon Sir Martin Charles; s of late Henry Edward Nourse, MD, MRCP, of Cambridge, and Ethel Millicent, da of Rt Hon Sir Charles Henry Sargent, Lord Justice of Appeal (*see* Sir Edmund Sargent); *b* 3 April 1932; *Educ* Winchester, Corpus Christi Coll Cambridge; *m* 1972, Lavinia, da of Cdr David Malim; 1 s, 1 da; *Career* 2 Lt (Nat Service) Rifle Bde 1951-52, London Rifle Bde Rangers (TA) 1952-55, Lt 1953; barr Lincoln's Inn 1956, memb Gen Cncl of the Bar 1964-68, jr counsel to Bd of Trade in Chancery Matters 1967-70, QC 1970, attorney-gen Duchy of Lancaster 1976-80, judge of the Courts of Appeal of Jersey and Guernsey 1977-80, judge of the High Court of Justice Chancery Division 1980-; kt 1980; *Style*— The Hon Mr Justice Nourse; North End House, Grantchester, Cambride CB3 9NQ; 1 Stone Bldgs, Lincoln's Inn, London WC2; Royal Courts of Justice, Strand, London WC2

NOWELL, Peter Jack; s of Roger Nowell, of Reading, and Suzanne Elisabeth Nowell; *b* 13 Oct 1948; *Educ* Reading Sch, LSE (MSc); *m* 1 May 1976, Wendy Margaret, da of Raymond Bonfield (d 1986); 2 da (Lucy b 1977, Emma b 1980); *Career* equity fnd mangr Prudential Assur Co Ltd 1971-81, fixed income dir Prudential Portfolio Mangrs 1982-87, chief exec Prudential Corporate Pensions 1988-; FIA 1974; *Recreations* skiing, squash; *Style*— Peter Nowell, Esq; Prudential Corporate Pensions, Abbey Gardens, Reading, Berks RG11 3AH (☎ 0734 578 857, fax 0734 578 613)

NUGEE, Edward George; TD (1964); s of Brig George Travers Nugee, CBE, DSO, MC (d 1977), and Violet Mary Brooks, *née* Richards, of Jacaranda Cottage, Binfield Heath, Henley-on-Thames, Oxon; *b* 9 August 1928; *Educ* Brambletye Sch, Radley, Worcester Coll Oxford (BA, MA), Eldon Law Scholarship 1953; *m* 1 Dec 1955, Rachel Elizabeth Nugee, JP, *qv*da of Lt-Col John Moritz Makower, MBE, MC, of Hampstead Farmhouse, Binfield Heath, Henley-on-Thames, Oxon; 4 s (John b 1956, Christopher b 1959, Andrew b 1961, Richard b 1963); *Career* Nat Serv RA 1947-49 (office of COS Far East Land Forces, Singapore 1948-49), TA serv Intelligence Corps 100 APIU 1950-64, ret Capt 1964; barr Inner Temple 1955, ad eundem Lincoln's Inn 1968, Legal Aid Lawyer Lewisham CAB 1954-72; memb: CAB advsy ctee Family Welfare Assoc 1969-72, ctee Greater London CAB 1972-74, mgmnt ctee Forest Hill Advice Centre 1972-76, memb Cncl Legal Educn 1967- (chm bd of studies 1976-82), jr counsel to Land Cmmn 1967-71, counsel for litigation under Commons' Registration Act (1965) 1968-77, advsy ctee on legal educn 1971-, memb Inst of Conveyancers 1971 (pres 1986-87); conveyancing cncl 1972-77 to: Treasy, WO, MAFF, Forestry Cmmn, MOD, DOE; Lord Chllrs Law Reforms Ctee 1973-, conveyancing cncl of the Ct 1976-77; chm Ctee of Inquiry into Mgmnt of Privately Owned Blocks of Flats 1984-85; chm govrs Brambletye Sch 1972-77, memb cncl Radley Coll 1975-, churchwarden Hampstead Parish Church 1979-83; *Books* Nathan on the Charities Act 1960 (jt author 1962), Halsbury's Laws of England (4th edn, Real Property, jt ed, 1982); *Recreations* travel, history, church and family life; *Style*— Edward Nugee, Esq, TD; 10 Heath Hurst Rd, Hampstead, London NW3 2RX (☎ 01 435 9204); 3 New Sq, Lincoln's Inn, London WC2A 3RS (☎ 01 405 5296, fax 01 831 6803, telex 267 699)

NUGEE, Rachel Elizabeth; JP (Inner London Thames 1971, dep: chm 1985-); da of Lt Col John Moritz Makower, MBE, MC, of Hampstead Farmhouse, Binfield Heath, Henley-on-Thames, Oxon, and Adelaide Gertrude Leonaura, *née* Franklin (d 1984); *b* 15 August 1926; *Educ* Roedean, Lady Margaret Hall, Oxford (MA), Reading Univ (Dip Social Studies); *m* 1 Dec 1955, Edward George Nugee, s of Brig George Travers Nugee, CBE, DSO, MC (d 1977); 4 s (John b 9 Nov 1956, Christopher b 23 Jan 1959, Andrew b 1 Oct 1961, Richard b 3 June 1963); *Career* (voluntary serv) vice-chm Centl Pubns Ctee of the Mother's Union 1970-74, pres Mother's Union London Diocese 1974-76, Central (Int) Pres of the MU 1977-82, vice-chm Central Social Concern Ctee of MU 1983-85, rep for MU on Womans Nat Cmmn 1983-88, chm Bookshop Ctee of MU 1989-, memb: Royal Free Hosp (Hampsted Gen Hosp), House Ctee and Patients Servs Ctee 1961-72; memb London Diocesan Bd for Social Responsibility 1984-85 and 1987-, chm Edmonton area SR Policy Ctee 1987-, tstee Marriage Res Fund 1984-; *Recreations* active support of church and family life; reading (especially history), visiting friends; *Style*— Mrs Rachel Nugee, JP; 10 Heath Hurst Road, Hampstead, London NW3 2RX (☎ 01 435 9204)

NUGENT, Christopher George Ridley; s and h of Sir Robin George Colborne Nugent, 5 Bt; *b* 5 Oct 1949; *Educ* Eton, Univ of E Anglia; *Style*— Christopher Nugent, Esq

NUGENT, Lady; Cynthia Maud; da of late Capt Frederick William Ramsden; *m* 1917, Rt Hon Sir Roland Thomas Nugent, 1 Bt (d 1962, when title became extinct); *Style*— Lady Nugent; Quinton Castle, Portaferry, Co Down

NUGENT, Lady Elizabeth Maria; *née* Guinness; JP (Berks 1981); da of Maj Arthur Onslow Edward Guinness, Viscount Elveden and sis of 3 Earl of Iveagh; raised to the rank of an Earl's da 1969; *b* 31 Oct 1939; *Educ* Priorsfield Godalming Surrey; *m* 1960, David Hugh Lavallin Nugent, s of Sir Hugh Nugent, 6 Bt; 3 s, 1 da; *Recreations* racing; *Style*— Lady Elizabeth Nugent, JP; Chaddleworth House, Chaddleworth, Newbury; Ross Castle, Mount Nugent, Co Cavan

NUGENT, Sir John Edwin Lavallin; 7 Bt (I 1795), of Ballinlough, Westmeath; JP (Berks 1962); a Count of the Holy Roman Empire; er s of Sir Hugh Charles Nugent, 6 Bt (d 1983), and Margaret, Lady Nugent, *qv*; *b* 16 Mar 1933; *Educ* Eton; *m* 1959,

Penelope Anne, er da of Brig Richard Nigel Hanbury, CBE, TD, DL (d 1972); 1 s, 1 da (Grania Clare b 1969); *Heir* s, Nicholas Myles John b 17 Feb 1967; *Career* Lt Irish Gds; md Lambourn Holdings Ltd (gp consisting of garage, coachbuilding and horse transport companies); high sheriff Berkshire 1981; *Recreations* gardening, shooting, fishing; *Clubs* Kildare and University (Dublin); *Style—* Sir John Nugent Bt, JP; Limes Farm, Upper Lambourn, Newbury, Berks RG16 7RG (☎ 0488 71369, 0488 71011)

NUGENT, John Michael; s of James Patrick Nugent, of 16 Sandford Rd, Sale, Cheshire, and Beatrice May, *née* Peart; *b* 26 Jan 1942; *Educ* Stretford GS, Manchester Univ (BA (Econ) Hons); *m* 1967, Kay, da of Thomas Thompson, of Barton Moss, Manchester; *Career* WCB Containers Ltd: sales dir 1971-72, md 1972-79, chm 1979-82; dir White Child & Beney Ltd 1973-80; md White Child & Beney Gp Ltd 1980-82, chm 1982-: The Stamford Gp Ltd, Opto Int Ltd, Opto Int Inc, Mailbox Int Ltd, Mailbox Mouldings Ltd, Micropol Ltd; *Recreations* golf, cricket, supporting Manchester United, travel; *Clubs* Mellor and Townscliffe Golf; *Style—* John M Nugent, Esq; 38 Fernwood, Marple Bridge, Cheshire SX6 5BE (☎ 061 449 8567); Bayley St, Staly Bridge, Cheshire (☎ 061 330 6511)

NUGENT, Maisie, Lady; Maisie Esther; da of late Jesse Arthur Bigsby; *m* 1921, Capt Sir (George) Guy Bulwer Nugent, 4 Bt (d 1970); *Style—* Maisie, Lady Nugent; Bannerdown House, Batheaston, Bath

NUGENT, Margaret, Lady; Margaret Mary Lavallin; da of late Rev Herbert Lavallin Puxley, of The White House, Chaddleworth, Newbury, Berks; *b* 22 Jan 1911; *Educ* The Vine Hants; *m* 28 Sept 1931, Sir Hugh Charles Nugent, 6 Bt (d 1983); 2 s; *Style—* Margaret, Lady Nugent; Cronk Ghennie House, Bowring Road, Ramsey, Isle of Man (☎ 0624 812887)

NUGENT, Wing-Cdr Neil Algernon David; s of Maj Lionel Hugh Nugent (d 1970), and Coral Valentine, *née* Goudie; *b* 6 Nov 1926; *Educ* (DMS); *m* 27 April 1957, Diana Clare Nugent, da of Wing-Cdr Reginald George Burnett, MBE, of Emsworth, Hants; 2 s (Christopher, David), 3 da (Clare, Gail, Lindsay); *Career* RAF navigator RCAF Winnipeg 1954, 52 Sqdn Changi 1955, exchange duties 426 and 437 sqdns RCAF Trenton 1960, Specialist Navigation RAF Coll of Air Warfare Manby 1964, Flight Cdr 511 Sqdn 1967, Sqdn-Cdr 53 Sqdn 1970; so to: inspr of air transport servs 1973, C in C's Ctee (home) 1973; co emergency planning offr Surrey 1983- (dep offr 1979-83); played hockey for Kent and S Eng 1950 and 1951, represented GB at the Olympic Games 1952 (bronze medal), capt Hindhead GC 1988; *Recreations* golf, gardening, caravanning; *Style—* Wg-Cdr Neil Nugent; Cherry Tree, Linkside South, Hindhead, Surrey GU26 6NX (☎ 042 873 4230); County Hall, 6 Penrhyn Rd, Kingston-upon-Thames, (☎ 01 541 9160, fax 01 541 9005, telex 263312)

NUGENT, Hon Patrick Mark Leonard; 2 s of 13 Earl of Westmeath; *b* 6 April 1966; *Educ* Douai; *Style—* The Hon Patrick Nugent

NUGENT, Sir Peter Walter James; 5 Bt (UK 1831), of Donore, Westmeath; s of Sir Walter Richard Nugent, 4 Bt (d 1955); *b* 26 July 1920; *Educ* Downside; *m* 1947, Anne Judith, da of Maj Robert Smyth, of Gaybrook, Mullingar, Co Westmeath; 2 s, 2 da; *Heir* s, Walter Richard Middleton Nugent; *Career* 2 Lt Hampshire Regt 1941, and with 10 Baluch Regt in India, Maj 1945; Tattersalls Irish agent; dir Tattersalls Newmarket and Tattersalls (Ireland); *Style—* Sir Peter Nugent, Bt; Blackhall Stud, Clane, Co Kildare (☎ 045 68263)

NUGENT, Sir Robin George Colborne; 5 Bt (UK 1806), of Waddesdon, Berkshire; s of Sir George Guy Bulwer Nugent, 4 Bt (d 1970), of Bannerdown House, Bath; *b* 11 July 1925; *Educ* Eton, RWA Sch of Architecture; *m* 1947, Ursula Mary, da of Lt-Gen Sir Herbert Cooke, KCB, KBE, CSI, DSO (d 1936); 2 s, 1 da; *Heir* s, Christopher George Ridley Nugent; *Career* Lt Gren Gds 1944-48; ARIBA; *Clubs* Cavalry and Guards; *Style—* Sir Robin Nugent, Bt; Bannerdown House, Batheaston, Bath, Avon (☎ 0225 858481)

NUGENT, Baroness; Rosalie; da of late Brig-Gen Hon Charles Strathavon Heathcote-Drummond-Willoughby, CB, CMG, 2 s of 1 Earl of Ancaster by his w, Lady Evelyn Gordon (2 da of 10 Marquess of Huntly); Brig-Gen Hon Charles Heathcote-Drummond-Willoughby m Lady Muriel Erskine, da of 14 Earl of Buchan; *m* 1935, 1 and last Baron Nugent (d 1973); *Career* is in remainder to Barony of Willoughby de Eresby; *Style—* The Rt Hon Lady Nugent; 40 Bramerton St, London SW3 (☎ 01 352 8861)

NUGENT, Sean Charles Weston; does not use title of Lord Delvin; s and h of 13 Earl of Westmeath; *b* 16 Feb 1965; *Educ* Ampleforth; *Style—* The Hon Sean Nugent

NUGENT, Walter Richard Middleton; s and heir of Sir Peter Walter James Nugent, 5 Bt; *b* 15 Nov 1947; *Style—* Walter Nugent, Esq; Flat Yamate-Cho, Naka-Ku, Yokahama, Japan

NUGENT OF GUILDFORD, Baron (Life Peer UK 1966); Sir (George) Richard Hodges Nugent; 1 Bt (UK 1960), PC (1962), JP (Surrey 1941); yr s of Col George Roubiliac Hodges Nugent, OBE, RA (d 1935), of Churt, Surrey, and Violet Stella, *née* Sheppard (d 1966); *b* 6 June 1907; *Educ* Imperial Service Coll, RMA Woolwich; *m* 29 July 1937, Ruth, da of late Hugh Granville Stafford, of Tilford, Surrey; *Career* CC 1942, county alderman Surrey 1951-52; MP (C) Guildford 1950-66; parly sec: Miny of Agric Fisheries and Food 1951-57, Miny of Transport 1957-59; sits as Cons in Lords, dep speaker House of Lords; chm: Thames Conservancy 1960-74, Select Ctee for Nationalised Industries 1961-64, Standing Conference on London and SE Regional Planning 1962-81, Nat Water Cncl 1973-78; past pres Assoc of River Authorities 1965-74; memb Diocesan Synod 1970-; pres Royal Soc for Prevention of Accidents 1985; chm Mount Alvernia Hosp Guildford 1987-; hon freeman Borough of Guildford; DUniv (Surrey); FRSA, Hon FIPHE; pres Univ of Surrey Soc; *Clubs* RAC; *Style—* The Rt Hon the Lord Nugent of Guildford, PC, JP; Blacknest Cottage, Dunsfold, nr Godalming, Surrey GU8 4PE (☎ 048 649 210)

NUNAN, Manus; QC (1962); s of Manus Timothy Nunan, (d 1979) ; *b* 26 Mar 1926; *Educ* St Mary's Coll Dublin, Trinity Coll Dublin; *m* 1, 1960 (m dis), Anne Monique, da of Jean Fradin (d 1978); 1 s (Manus b 1972), 1 da (Nathalie b 1961); m 2, 1987, Valerie, *née* Robinson; *Career* barr King's Inns 1950, barr Gray's Inn 1956; Colonial Legal Servs 1953-64: crown counsel Nigeria 1953-62, slr-gen Northern Nigeria 1962-64, min of Govt and memb Exec Cncl of Northern Nigeria 1962; rec Crown Ct 1978-84; *Clubs* Kildare St and Univ (Dublin); *Style—* Manus Nunan, Esq, QC; La Calmeraie, Route de l'aude, 09110 Ax les Thermes, France

NUNBURNHOLME, 4 Baron (UK 1906); Ben Charles Wilson; s of 3 Baron Nunburnholme (d 1974), and Lady Mary Thynne (da of 5 Marquess of Bath); *b* 16 July 1928; *Educ* Eton; *m* 1958 (m dis), Ines Dolores, da of Gerard Walravens; 4 da; *Heir* bro, Hon Charles Thomas Wilson; *Career* Capt RHG 1953, Maj 1962, resigned 1969; *Style—* The Rt Hon the Lord Nunburnholme

NUNN, Antony Stuart; s of C Stuart Nunn (d 1974); *b* 24 May 1927; *Educ* Haileybury; *m* 1956, Pamela May, da of late William Hall, MBE; 2 da; *Career* Marine underwriter, chm (dep chm 1980-81) Inst of London Underwriters 1982, dir Malvern Insurance Co Ltd 1978-, dir Kyoei Marine & Fire Insurance Co (UK) Ltd 1971-, dir Sirius Insurance Co (UK) Ltd 1978-, dep underwriter Lloyd's Syndicate, memb Lloyds 1970-71; *Recreations* golf, cricket, hockey; *Clubs* MCC, Sloane; *Style—* Antony Nunn, Esq; Shirlands, 158 Old Woking Rd, Pyrford, Surrey

NUNN, Dr John Francis; s of Francis Nunn (d 1929), of Colwyn Bay, and Lilian, *née* Davies (d 1980); *b* 7 Nov 1925; *Educ* Wrekin Coll, Birmingham Univ (MB, ChB, PhD, MD); *m* 24 Sept 1949, Sheila Ernestine, da of Ernest Carl Doubleday (d 1952); 1 s (Geoffrey Francis b 1951), 2 da (Carolyn b 1954, Shelley b 1954 (twin)); *Career* Nat Serv Colonial Med Serv Malaya 1949-53; Leverhulme res fell RCS 1957-64, prof of anaesthesia Univ of Leeds 1964-68, head of div of anaesthesia Clinical Res Centre MRC 1968-, dean of faculty of anaesthetists RCS 1979-82, pres section of anaesthetists RSM 1984-85; Hon fell: FFARACS, FFARCSI; FFARCS 1955, FRCS 1983, memb RSM; *Books* Applied Respiratory Physiology (third edn 1987), General Anaesthesia, (ed, fifth edn 1989); *Recreations* Egyptology, skiing, modal engineering; *Style—* Dr John Nunn; 3 Russell Rd, Moor Park, Northwood, Middx HA6 2LJ; 17 Queen's Rd, Swanage, Dorset; Division of Anaesthesia, Clinical Research Centre, Harrow, Middx HA1 3UJ (☎ 01 864 5311)

NUNN, Rear Adm John Richard Danford; CB (1980); s of Surg Capt Gerald Nunn, OBE, RN (d 1967), and Edith Florence, *née* Brown; *b* 12 April 1925; *Educ* Epsom Coll, RN Engineering Coll (BSc), RN Coll Greenwich (MSc), Downing Coll Cambridge (MPhil); *m* 1951, Katharine Mary, da of Leonard Paris (d 1970); 3 da; *Career* RN, served: Home Fleet and British Pacific Fleet 1945 (HMS Devonshire, HMS Vengeance 1947), Korean and Malaysian Emergency 1950 (HMS Amethyst), Mediterranean 1957 (HMS Tiger), Home Fleet and Far East 1967 (HMS Glamorgan); Sea Dart Chief Engr 1968-70, Cabinet Office 1970-73, NATO Defence Coll 1974-75, SACLANT 1975-78, Port Admiral Rosyth 1978-80, Fell commoner Downing Coll 1980, editor The Naval Review 1980-83; bursar and official Fell Exeter Coll Oxford 1981-88; *Recreations* sailing (yacht 'Solenteer'), tennis, gliding, travel; *Clubs* Naval, Royal Naval Sailing Assoc; *Style—* Rear Adm John Nunn, CB; Warner's Cottage, Keepers Hill, Corhampton, Hants SO3 1LL (☎ 0489 877287); 2 Sadler Walk, St Ebbe's, Oxford OX1 1DP (☎ 0865 244681)

NUNN, Peter George; s of Ernest Nunn (d 1983), of Ferndown, Dorset, and Greta, *née* Houlton; *b* 21 April 1946; *Educ* The County GS Wath-upon-Dearne S Yorks; *m* 10 Sept 1977, Joan Margaret, da of Lawrence Smith (d 1961), of Pinner, Middx; *Career* barr Lincoln's Inn; dir: Hogg Robinson Fin Services Ltd, Paul Davies Hair Studios Ltd; FPMI; *Recreations* golf, horse racing, good food and wine, English 18 century procelain, English setters; *Clubs* Moor Park Golf; *Style—* Peter Nunn, Esq; East House, Moss Lane, Pinner, Middx (☎ 01 866 8185); Hogg Robinson Financial Services Ltd, 42/46 Greyfriars Road, Reading (☎ 0734 583683)

NUNN, Trevor Robert; CBE (1978); s of Robert Alexander Nunn, and Dorothy May, *née* Piper; *b* 14 Jan 1940; *Educ* Northgate GS Ipswich, Downing Coll Cambridge (BA), Newcastle-upon-Tyne Univ (MA); *m* 1969 (m dis 1986), Janet Suzman; 1 s (Joshua b 1980); m 2 1986 Sharon Lee Hill; 1 da (Laurie b 1986); *Career* producer Belgrade Theatre Coventry, assoc dir Royal Shakespeare Co (chief exec and artistic dir 1968-78, chief exec and jt artistic dir 1978-86); dir: Cats World-wide 1981, Starlight Express London 1984, Lady Jane (film) 1984, Les Miserables London and worldwide (1985), Chess London (1986) and NY; *Style—* Trevor Nunn, Esq, CBE; Homevale Ltd, 28/29 Southampton St, London WC2 7JA (☎ 01 240 5435, fax: 01 240 1945)

NUNNELEY, Charles Kenneth Roylance; s of Robin Michael Charles Nunneley, of Edgefield, Norfolk, and Patricia Mary, *née* Roylance, of Pluckley, Kent; *b* 3 April 1936; *Educ* Eton; *m* 1961, Catherine Elizabeth Armstrong, da of Sir Denys Burton Buckley, of 105 Onslow Sq, London SW7; 1 s (Luke b 1963), 3 da (Alice b 1964, Clare b 1967, Frances b 1969); *Career* 2 Lt Scots Gds, served chiefly BAOR; chartered accountant (qualified 1961); merchant banker; dep chm Robert Fleming Holdings 1986- (dir 1968) and dir of various Fleming Gp Cos; memb Court of Assts Worshipful Co of Grocers 1975- (master 1982-83), dep chm Clerical Medical and Gen Life Assurance Soc 1978- (dir 1974), dir: Monks Investment Trust 1977-, Macmillan Ltd 1982-, Investment Management Regulatory Organisation 1986-; govr Oundle Schs 1975-, Reed's Sch 1983-; *Recreations* squash, shooting, photography, tennis; *Clubs* Hurlingham; *Style—* C K R Nunneley, Esq; 19 Rosaville Road, London SW6 7BN (☎ 01 381 6683); Fyfield House, Pewsey, Wilts SN9 5JS (☎ (0672) 62588); office: 25 Copthall Avenue, London EC2R 7DR (☎ 01 638 5858)

NUREYEV, Rudolf; s of Hamet Nureev and Farida Nureeva; *b* 17 Mar 1938; *Educ* UFA, Vaganova Sch attached to Kirov Ballet Leningrad; *Career* ballet dancer, choreographer, leading dancer Kirov Ballet 1958-61, defected at Le Bourget airport 1961, joined de Cuevas Grand Ballet 1961, debut in London in gala organized by Fonteyn 1961, debut with Roy Ballet London in Giselle 1962, since has appeared regularly with all leading ballet companies of the world, his repertoire ranging from classic to modern ballets; choreographic prodns include: La Bayadere (1963), Swan Lake, Raymouda (1964), Tancredi, Sleeping Beauty, Don Quixote (1966), Nutcracker (1967), Romeo and Juliet (1977), Manfred (1979), The Tempest (1982), Washington Square (1985); films: An Evening with the Royal Ballet (1963), Romeo and Juliet, Swan Lake, Le Jeune Homme et la Mort (1966), I am a Dancer (1982), Exposed (1983); artistic dir Paris Opera Ballet 1983-; *Recreations* music; *Style—* Rudolf Nureyev, Esq; Théâtre National de l'Opéra de Paris, 8 Rue Scribe, 75009 Paris; c/o S A Gorlinsky Ltd, 33 Dover St, London W1X 4NJ

NURSAW, James; CB (1983), QC (1988); s of William George Nursaw, and Lilian May, *née* Howell; *b* 18 Oct 1932; *Educ* Bancroft's Sch, Christ's Coll Cambridge (MA, LLB); *m* 29 Aug 1959, Eira, da of E W Caryl-Thomas, MD (d 1968); 2 da (Margaret (Mrs Huw Hallybone), Catherine); *Career* Nat Serv Flying Offr RAF; barr Middle Temple 1955, sr res offr Cambridge Univ dept of criminal science 1958, joined Home Off 1959, legal sec Law Offs Dept 1980-83, legal advsr Home Off and NI Off 1983-88, HM procurator gen and treasy slr 1988-; Liveryman Worshipful Co of Loriners; *Clubs* United Oxford and Cambridge University, MCC; *Style—* James Nursaw, Esq, CB, QC; Queen Anne's Chambers, Broadway, London SW1H 9JS

NURSE, Bramwell William Henry; s of Brig William Henry Nurse (d 1976), and

Minnie Florence, *née* Whitmill (d 1983); *b* 19 May 1921; *Educ* St Dunstan's Coll Catford London; *m* 9 July 1949, Beatrice Annie, da of Brig William Frederick Curl (d 1973); 1 s (Gordon Bramwell b 1950), 1 da (Joy Beatrice (Mrs Humphries) b 1953); *Career* CA, gp md Howes Gp, hon tres Motor Agents Assoc 1981-86, former chm Peugeot/Talbot Dealer Assoc; chm: Morlwy Nurseries Ltd (Wicklewood), Plaxtol Bakery Ltd, SA Wood (confectioners) Ltd; FCA, FIOD; *Recreations* music, yachting; *Style—* Bramwell Nurse, Esq; 2 Yare Valley Drive, Cringleford, Norwich NR4 7SD (☎ 0603 52159)

NUTLEY, Ronald Frank; s of Walter Francis Nutley (d 1987), of Tonbridge, Kent, and Lucy, *née* Vincent (d 1962); *b* 17 April 1932; *Educ* Sussex Road Sch, Tonbridge, London Coll of Printing; *m* 22 June 1957, Patricia, da of Charles James Percy Waghorn (d 1988), of 2 Priory St, Tonbridge, Kent; 1 da (Jennifer Jane b 1963); *Career* signaller 1 Bn Queen's Own Royal West Kent served Malaya 1950-52; BR engr, gen mgmnt Brown Knight & Truscott Ltd 1955-80 (works and personnel dir 1972-80), md David Evans & Co, dir Sekers Int plc 1982, chief exec Sekers Silks Ltd 1986; dir: Richard Allan Scarves, FBIM, MIOP, FInstD; *Recreations* reading, art and design, jogging, swimming, tennis, community service; *Clubs* Tonbridge Lions, IOD, RAC; *Style—* Ronald Nutley, Esq; Aalsmeer, 13 Higham Lane, Tonbridge, Kent TN10 4JB (☎ 0732 351 017); David Evans & Co, Bourne Rd, Crayford, Kent DA1 4BP (☎ 0322 57 521, fax: 0322 50 476)

NUTMAN, Dr Phillip Sadler; s of William John Nutman (d 1919), and Elizabeth Hester, *née* Hughes (d 1954); *b* 10 Oct 1914; *Educ* Teignmouth GS, Univ of Exeter, Imperial Coll, London Univ (BSc, DIC, PhD); *m* 3 Feb 1940, Mary Meta, da of Leslie Stanbury (d 1977); 2 s (Robert Frances b 1945, Allen Philip b 1955), 1 da (Hester Mary b 1951); *Career* agric res scientist (ret); Rothamsted Experimental Station 1939-79 (head dept soil microbiology 1957-79), Sr Res fell CSIRO Canberra Aust 1953-56, Hannaford res fell Waite Inst Adelaide 1980; Huxley Research Medallist; numerous res pubns in plant physiology, genetics and microbiology, currently ed Research Studies Press and Journal of Tropical Agriculture; ARCSc, FRS, MIBiol; *Recreations* music (piano and organ), carpentry, gardening; *Style—* Dr Phillip Nutman; Great Hackworthy Cottage, Tedburn St Mary, Exeter, EX6 6DW (☎ 0647 61 364)

NUTT, John Allister; s of Henry Nutt (d 1976), and Frances Plowright; *b* 13 July 1933; *Educ* Worksop Coll; *m* 2, 1976, Jean Rosemary, da of Sir Arnold Hodson, KCMG (d 1942); 2 da, 2 step da; *Career* chm: SPP plc 1972-, Braithwaite Gp plc 1987-, Booker McConnell Engineering 1981-, dir Booker McConnell plc 1983-84; chm British Pumps Manufacturers Assoc 1978-81; memb Nat Econ Dvpt Office Pumps and Valves Sector Working Party 1976-81; FCA; *Clubs* Royal Commonwealth; *Style—* John Nutt, Esq; Filbert House, East Ilsley, Newbury, Berks RG16 0LG; office: Theale Cross, Reading, RG3 1JD (☎ 0734 425555, telex 848189)

NUTTALL, Beris Muriel; DL (Stafford 1974); da of Fred Nuttall (d 1975), of Holme View, 50 Delph Lane, Netherton, Huddersfield, and Dorothy, *née* France (d 1980); *b* 8 July 1924; *Educ* Holme Valley GS Huddersfield, Avery Hill Coll London (teachers certificate of London Univ with distinction); *Career* school teacher, dep head Longton HS Stoke-on-Trent 1968-84, on management Leonard Cheshire Home Sandbach 1970-; chm Staffs Branch Animal Health Trust; FRSA, MCCEd; *Recreations* philately, collecting commemorative ware, owner 1911 Swift Car 2 seater tourer; *Clubs* Veteran Car of GB, Lady Memb Yorkshire County Cricket Club, Shepley (Yorks) Croquet Club; *Style—* Miss Beris M Nuttall, DL; 14 Little-Field, Trent Vale, Stoke-on-Trent ST4 5LR (☎ 0782 46162); Holme View, 50 Delph Lane, Netherton, Huddersfield (☎ 0484 665301)

NUTTALL, Rev Derek; s of Charles William Nuttall (d 1956), of Codnor Park, Derbyshire, and Doris (d 1976); *b* 23 Sept 1937; *Educ* Somercotes Secdy Derbyshire, Overdale Theol Coll, Selly Oak Birmingham; *m* 24 July 1965, Margaret Hathaway, da of Rev Principal Arthur Lawson Brown (d 1984); 2 s (David b 2 May 1969, Andrew b 12 May 1971), 1 da (Alison b 30 March 1967); *Career* semi-skilled Industl Work 1953-60, office clerk 1960-61, Theol Coll 1961-65, Ministry in Falkirk 1965-67, ordained 1967, Ministry and Community Work in Aberfan 1967-74, nat organiser CRUSE Bereavement Care 1974-78 (dir 1978-); vice chm Centl Scotland Branch The Samaritans; gen sec: Community Assoc, Church and Community Ctees; memb: Exec of Int Fedn of Widow/Widower Organisations 1980-, Weybridge United Reformed Church, Royal Soc of Medicine; *Recreations* golf, reading, music; *Style—* The Rev Derek Nuttall; 51 Spinney Hill, Addlestone, Weybridge, Surrey (☎ 0932 846897); Cruse House, 126 Sheen Road, Richmond, Surrey TW9 1UR (☎ 01 940 4818)

NUTTALL, Harry; s and h of Sir Nicholas Keith Lillington Nuttall, 3 Bt; *b* 2 Jan 1963; *Style—* Harry Nuttall Esq

NUTTALL, Sir Nicholas Keith Lillington; 3 Bt (UK 1922), of Chasefield, Parish of Bowdon, Co Chester; s of Lt-Col Sir (Edmund) Keith Nuttall, 2 Bt (d on active service 1941); *b* 21 Sept 1933; *Educ* Eton, RMA Sandhurst; *m* 1, 1960 (m dis 1971), Rosemary Caroline, da of Christopher York, DL, sometime MP for Ripon (whose mother was Violet, er da of Rt Hon Sir Frederick Milner, 7 Bt, and whose paternal ggf's mother was Lady Mary Lascelles, yst da of 1 Earl of Harewood), of Long Marston Manor, Long Marston; 1 s, 1 da; m 2, 1971, Julia Jill, da of Thomas Williamson; m 3, 1975 (m dis 1983), Miranda Elizabeth Louise, former w of late Peter Sellers, CBE, the actor, and da of Richard Quarry by his former w Diana, who m, 1951, 2 Baron Mancroft; 3 da (Gytha Miranda b 1975, Amber Louise b 1976, Olympia Jubilee b 1977); m 4, 1983, Eugenie Marie Alicia, eldest da of William Thomas McWeeney; 1 s (Alexander b 1985); *Heir* s, Harry Nuttall; *Career* Maj RHG, ret 1968; *Clubs* White's; *Style—* Sir Nicholas Nuttall, Bt; PO Box N7776, Nassau, Bahamas (☎ 809 32 67938)

NUTTALL, Peter Scott; s of Dr John Ramsbottom Nuttall (d 1986), of Pool-in-Wharfedale, Yorks, and Alice, *née* Bradford; *b* 25 June 1934; *Educ* Oakham Sch, Worcester Coll Oxford (MA Law); *m* 1, Sept 1959, Sylvia, da of Harold Barker, of Bilbrough, York; 1 s (Mark b 1962), 1 da (Katie b 1961); m 2, Sept 1983, Sheila Mary, da of Edwin Wilson, of Grimsby, Lincs; *Career* sr ptnr Kitcat & Aitken 1982-86 (md 1986-), chm RBC Kitcat Ltd 1986-; *Recreations* walking, cricket; *Style—* Peter Nuttall, Esq; Old Beams, Whitchurch, Aylesbury, Bucks (☎ 0296 641167); 71 Queen Victoria Street, London EC4V 4DE (☎ 01 489 1966, telex 888297, fax 329 6150)

NUTTALL, Richard Wardleworth; s of Henry Clarence Wardleworth Nuttall, FRCS (d 1972); *b* 20 Oct 1927; *Educ* Marlborough, St John's Coll Cambridge (MA), Univ of Geneva (MBA); *m* 1953, Veryll Bambury, da of William Sever (d 1972); 1 s (David), 3 da (Fiona, Veronica, Heather); *Career* financial conslt, former company dir; former dir: RTZ Sales Ltd, RTZ Services Ltd, Alreco Ltd, RTZ Metals Ltd (dep md), RTZ Metals Stockholding Ltd (md), Devon Boats Ltd (chm and md), Haven Associates Ltd; *Recreations* sailing, athletics; *Style—* Richard Nuttall, Esq; 6 Parsonage Lane, Silverton, Exeter EX5 4JB, Devon (☎ 0392 860-861)

NUTTALL, (Benjamin William) Stuart; JP (Chesterfield); s of William Nuttall (d 1972), and Eleanor, *née* Broomhead; *b* 14 Jan 1933; *Educ* Lady Manners GS Bakewell, Leicester Coll of Advanced Technol, Chesterfield Coll of Technol; *m* 19 Feb 1955, Eileen Margaret, da of Francis Joseph Eady (d 1977); 2 da (Jacqueline (Mrs Thornhill) b 24 April 1958, Caroline (Mrs Ludlam) b 8 Oct 1959) ; *Career* Nat Serv RAF 1951-53; mgmnt trainee to prodn mangr heavy tube div Tube Investmts Ltd 1953-66, prodn mangr Cable Div Aerialite Ltd 1966-68, plant mangr Corby Tube Works 1968-70, dep md USI Engrg 1970-72, md The Clay Cross Co 1972-; currently: chm and chief exec Biwater Mfg Div, coporate dir Biwater Ltd; dir: Chesterfield and N Derbys C of C, Br Cast Iron Res Assoc; nat chm Br Foundry Assoc, vice pres Chesterfield and Dist Bowls Assoc; pres: Clay Cross div St John's Ambulance Bde, Biwater Pipes and Casting sports clubs; memb Worshipful Co of Founders, Freedom City of London 1988; CEng 1977, FIProdE 1960, FIBF 1977, FIQ 1982, FIIM 1979, FInstD 1985; *Recreations* motor sport, horse breeding, various sporting activities; *Clubs* Aston Martin Owners; *Style—* Stuart Nuttall, Esq, JP; The Spinney, Ashover Rd, Woolley Moor, Derbys DE5 6FF (☎ 0246 590 266); Biwater Pipes & Castings Ltd, Clay Cross, Chesterfield, Derbys S45 9NG (☎ 0246 250 740, fax 0246 250 741, car tel 0860 622 329, telex 54301)

NUTTER, Thomas Albert; s of Christopher Nutter (d 1983), and Dorothy Lucy, *née* Banister; *b* 17 April 1943; *Educ* Camrose Sch Edgware, Willesden Technical Coll; *Career* clothes designer, made-to-measure tailor, menswear retailer; opened own shop in Savile Row 1969, clients included: the Beatles (three of whom wore his suits in the Abbey Road album cover), Mick and Bianca Jagger, Eric Clapton; designer Lincroft Kilgour Gp 1977, launched first major ready-to-wear collection for Austin Reed shops 1978, designer for Daido Worsted Mills (and the Milliontex Corpn) 1980, went solo again with shop in Savile Row 1982, customers today include (apart from those already named): Lord Montagu of Beaulieu, Elton John, Peter Bowles, M Saatchi, Lord Ralph Kerr; *Style—* Thomas Nutter, Esq; Flat 3, 26-27 Conduit St, London W1; 19 Savile Row, London W1X 2EB (☎ 01 734 0831)

NUTTGENS, Patrick John; CBE (1982); s of Joseph Edward Nuttgens (d 1982), and Kathleen Mary, *née* Clarke (d 1937); *b* 2 Mar 1930; *Educ* Ratcliffe Coll Leicester, Edinburgh Univ (MA, PhD), Edinburgh Coll of Art (DipArch); *m* 21 Aug 1954, Bridget Ann, da of Dr Alexander Guthrie Badenoch (d 1964), of Edinburgh; 5 s (Nicholas, James, Giles, Alexander, Tom) 3 da (Lucy, Susan, Peggy); *Career* lectr Edinburgh Univ 1957-62, prof York Univ 1968-70 (reader 1962-68), dir Leeds Poly 1970-86; chm York Georgian Soc 1970- (sec 1962-70); Royal Cmmn on Historical Monuments for Scot, Royal Fine Art Cmmn 1983-, DUniv York Univ 1985, DUniv Open Univ 1985, DLitt Sheffield Univ 1985; ARIBA, FRSA, ARIAS; *Books* Landscape of Ideas (1972), York the Continuing City (1974), Story of Architecture (1983), Understanding Modern Architecture (1988) ; *Recreations* reading, writing, drawing; *Clubs* Yorkshire; *Style—* Patrick J Nuttgens, Esq, CBE; Roselea Cottage, Terrington, York, YO6 4PP (☎ 065 384 408); University of York, The Kings Manor, York

NUTTING, Rt Hon Sir (Harold) Anthony; 3 Bt (UK 1902), of St Helens, Booterstown, Co Dublin, PC (1954); s of Lt-Col Sir Harold Stansmore Nutting, 2 Bt (d 1972); *b* 11 Jan 1920; *Educ* Eton, Trinity Coll Cambridge; *m* 1, 1941 (m dis 1959), Gillian Leonora, da of Edward Joliffe Strutt (3 s of Hon Edward Strutt, CH, 5 s of 2 Baron Rayleigh); 2 s (John, *qv*, David b 1944), 1 da (Zara Nina, b 1947, m 1966 Martin Stephenson); m 2, 1961, Anne Gunning, da of Arnold Barthrop Parker, of Cuckfield, Sussex; *Heir* s, John Grenfell Nutting; *Career* served in Leicestershire Yeo 1939-40, served in HM Foreign Service in France, Spain and Italy 1940-45; MP (C) Leics 1945-56, jt parly under-sec state for Foreign Affairs 1951-54, min state 1954-56, ldr UK Delegation to UN Assembly and to UN Disarmament Cmmn 1954-56; resigned 1956; chm: Young Conservative Movement 1946, Cons Nat Union 1950, Cons NEC 1951; special writer New York Herald Tribune 1957-59; author; *Books* Lawrence of Arabia (1961), The Arabs (1964), Gordon of Khartoum (1966), No End of a Lesson (1967), Scramble for Africa (1968), Nasser (1972); *Style—* The Rt Hon Sir Anthony Nutting, Bt; 2 Douro Place, London W8; Achentoul, Kinbrace, Sutherland

NUTTING, David Anthony; DL (Essex 1988); yr s of Rt Hon Sir (Harold) Anthony Nutting, 3 Bt, *qv*; *b* 13 Sept 1944; *Educ* Eton, Trinity Coll Cambridge (MA); *m* 25 April 1974, Tessa Anne, o da of Sir Nigel John Mordaunt, 13 Bt, MBE (d 1979); 3 da (Belinda b 18 Aug 1975, Serena b 24 Nov 1977, Alexandra b 27 Dec 1978); *Career* chm: Strutt & Parker (Farms) Ltd 1987-, Select Sires Ltd 1982-; dir: Lord Rayleigh's Dairies Ltd 1970, Bridge Farm Dairies Ltd 1987-; chm: Essex Agric Soc, Br Cattle Breeders Club 1978-79; memb advsy bd Inst of Animal Physiology 1983-86; memb Freeman Worshipful Co of Farmers 1975; *Recreations* fishing, shooting, racing; *Style—* David Nutting, Esq, DL; Whitelands, Hatfield Peverel, Chelmsford, Essex (☎ 0245 380372)

NUTTING, Prof Jack; s of Edgar Nutting (d 1973), Mirfield, W Yorkshire, and Ethel, *née* France (d 1985); *b* 8 June 1924; *Educ* Univ of Leeds (BSc, PhD), Univ of Cambridge (MA, ScD); *m* 4 Sept 1950, Thelma, da of Thomas Kippax (d 1967), of Morecambe; 1 s (Peter Robert b 1961), 2 da (Alison Rosemary (Mrs Murray) b 1953, Jean Ruth (Mrs Tyson) b 1957); *Career* lectr dept of metallurgy Univ of Cambridge 1954-60 (demonstrator 1949-54), prof of Metallurgy and hd of dept Univ of Leeds 1960-; former pres: Instn of Metallurgists, The Metals Soc, Hist Metallurgy Soc; pres Richard Thorpe Soc Mirfield HS; Awards: Beilby Medal and Prize 1964, Hatfield Medal and Prize 1967, Platinum Medal 1988; Hon SDc Acad Mining and Metallurgy Krakow Poland 1969, Hon DSc Univ of Moratuwa Sri Lanka; FIM 1960, FEng 1981; *Books* The Microstructure of Metals (1965); *Recreations* walking, photography, cooking, gardening; *Style—* Prof Jack Nutting; 57 Weetwood Lane, Leeds LS16 5NP, West Yorkshire (☎ 0532 751400); School of Materials, Division of Metallurgy, University of Leeds, Leeds LS2 9JT, West Yorkshire (☎ 0532 332349, fax 0532 422531, telex UNILDSG 556473)

NUTTING, John Grenfell; s and h of Rt Hon Sir (Harold) Anthony Nutting, 3 Bt, *qv*; *b* 28 August 1942; *Educ* Eton, McGill Univ Canada (BA); *m* 1973, Diane, da of Capt Duncan Kirk, and widow of 2 Earl Beatty; 1 s, 1 da, 1 step s, 1 step da; *Career* barr Middle Temple 1968, sr treasury counsel 1988- (jr treasy counsel 1981, first jr treasy counsel 1987-88), rec of the Crown Court 1986-; memb Bar Cncl 1976-80 and 1986-

87, chm Young Bar 1978-79; *Clubs* White's; *Style*— John Nutting, Esq; 3 Raymond Buildings, Gray's Inn, London WC2; Chicheley Hall, Newport Pagnell, Bucks MK16 9JJ

NUTTING, Peter Robert; JP (Inner London 1978); s of Capt Arthur Ronald Stansmore Nutting, OBE, MC (d 1964), of N Breache Manor, Ewhurst, and Patricia Elizabeth, *née* Jameson; *b* 22 Oct 1935; *Educ* Cheam, Eton; *m* 1965, Cecilia Hester Marie-Louise, da of Cosmo Rea Russell, of Parapet House, Lenham, Kent; 2 s, 1 da; *Career* Lt Irish Gds, Suez Canal 1955-56; stockbroker, ptnr W I Carr & Sons Co 1963-67, (last) chm E & J Burke Ltd 1965-68 (gf, Sir John Nutting, 1 Bt, was first chm); dir James Wilkes plc, chm Travel and General Insur Co plc; dir of other public and private cos; memb Lloyd's; landowner (350 acres); *Recreations* shooting, tennis, golf, sailing; *Clubs* Royal Yacht Squadron, Boodle's, Pratt's; *Style*— Peter Nutting, Esq, JP; North Breache Manor, Ewhurst, Surrey (☎ 0483 277328); 103 More Close, St Pauls Court, London W14 (☎ 01 846 9734)

NYAKYI, Anthony Balthazar; *b* 8 June 1936; *Educ* Makerere Coll, Univ of E Africa (BA); *m* 1969, Margaret Nyakyi; 2 s, 2 da; *Career* Tanzanian high commissioner to UK 1981-; *Style*— His Excellency Mr Anthony Balthazar Nyakyi; High Commission for the United Republic of Tanzania, 43 Hertford St, London W1 (☎ 01 499 8951/4)

NYE, Prof John Frederick; s of Hadyn Percival Nye, MC (d 1977), of Hove and Old Marston, and Jessie Mary, *née* Hague (d 1950); *b* 26 Feb 1923; *Educ* Stowe, King's Coll Cambridge (MA, PhD); *m* 28 Dec 1953, Georgiana, da of Walter Ernest Wiebenston, of Bellingham, Washington, USA; 1 s (Stephen b 1960), 2 da (Hilary b 1957, Carolyn b 1963); *Career* univ demonstrator dept of mineralogy Cambridge Univ 1949-51, memb tech staff Bell Telephone Labs N Jersey USA 1952-53; Bristol Univ: lectr 1953-65, reader 1965-69, prof 1969-85, Melville Wills prof of Physics 1985-88, emeritus prof 1988-; pres: Int Glaciological Soc 1966-69, Int Cmmn of Snow and Ice 1971-75; Antarctic Serv Medal USA 1974; FRS, 1976, foreign memb Royal Swedish Acad of Sci; *Books* Physical Properties of Crystals (second edn, 1985); *Recreations* gardening; *Style*— Prof John Nye; 45 Canynge Rd, Bristol BS8 3LH (☎ 0272 733769); H H Wills Physics Laboratory, Tyndall Ave, Bristol BS8 1TL (☎ 0272 303030)

NYE, Robert Thomas; s of Oswald William Nye, of Southend-on-Sea, Essex, and Frances Dorothy, *née* Weller; *b* 15 Mar 1939; *Educ* Southend HS; *m* 1, 1959 (m dis 1967), Judith Pratt; 3 s (Jack, Taliesin, Malory); m 2, 1968, Aileen, da of Robert Campbell (d 1972), of Whang House, Beith, Ayrshire; 1 da (Rebecca), 1 step s (Owen), 1 step da (Sharon); *Career* poet, novelist and critic; reviewer of new fiction The Guardian 1966-, poetry ed The Scotsman 1967-, poetry critic The Times 1971-; Eric Gregory Award 1963, Guardian Fiction Prize 1976, Hawthornden Prize 1977; *Publications* poems: Juvenilia 1 (1961), Juvenilia 2 (1963), Darker Ends (1969), Division on a Ground (1979); novels: Doubtfire (1967), Falstaff (1976), Merlin (1978), Faust (1980), The Voyage of the Destiny (1982); short stories: Tales I Told My Mother (1969), The Facts of Life and Other Fictions (1983); editions: A Choice of Sir Walter Ralegh's Verse (1972), William Barnes of Dorset; A Selection of his Poems (1973), A Choice of Swinburne's Verse (1973), The Faber Book of Sonnets (1976), PEN New Poetry (1986); *Recreations* gambling; *Style*— Robert Nye, Esq; c/o Barclays Bank, 3 Cross Buildings, Newtown, Powys, Wales SY16 2AJ

O

O'BRIEN, Barry John; s of John O'Brien, and Patricia, *née* Barry; *b* 27 Oct 1952; *Educ* St Illtyd's Coll Cardiff, UCL (LLB); *m* 29 Sept 1984, Susan Margaret; 1 da (Joanna Elizabeth); *Career* slr Slaughter and May 1978-83 (articled clerk 1976-78), ptnr Freshfields 1986- (slr 1983-86); Liveryman Worshipful Co Slrs; memb Law Soc; *Recreations* sport; *Style*— Barry J O'Brien, Esq; 29 Devonia Rd, Islington, London N1 (☎ 01 359 4587); 25 Newgate St, London EC1 (☎ 01 606 6677, fax 248 3487/8/9)

O'BRIEN, Dermod Patrick; QC (1983); s of Lt Dermod Donatus O'Brien (d 1939), and Helen Doreen Lesley Scott, *née* Scott O'Connor (d 1971); for family history see History of the O'Briens by Hon Donough O'Brien 1949, O'Brien of Thomond by Ivar O'Brien 1986; *b* 23 Nov 1939,; *Educ* Ampleforth, St Catherine's Coll Oxford (MA); *m* 1974, Zoë Susan, da of Roderick Edward Norris, of Sussex; 2 s (Edward b 1977, Timothy b 1980); *Career* barr Inner Temple 1962, rec of the Crown Ct (Western Circuit) 1978; landowner; *Recreations* fishing, shooting, skiing; *Style*— Dermod P O'Brien, Esq, QC; Little Daux Farm, Billingshurst, West Sussex RH14 9DB (☎ 040 831 4800); 2 Temple Gardens, Temple, London EC4Y 9AY (☎ 01 583 6041)

O'BRIEN, Sir Frederick William Fitzgerald; KB (1984), QC (1960); s of Dr Charles Henry Fitzgerald O'Brien, of 7 Brandon Street, Edinburgh (d 1968), and Helen Jane MacDonald (d 1962); *b* 19 July 1917; *Educ* Royal HS, Univ of Edinburgh (MA, LLB); *m* 1950, Audrey Muriel, da of Joseph Lloyd Owen, of 2131 Niagara Street, Windsor, Ontario; 2 s (David b 1954, Neil b 1957), 1 da (Susan b 1952); *Career* admitted Faculty of Advocates 1947, cmmr Mental Welfare Cmmn of Scotland 1962-65, home advocate depute 1964-65; sheriff princ of Caithness, Sutherland, Orkney and Shetland 1965-75, interim sheriff princ of Aberdeen, Kincardine and Banff 1969-71, sheriff princ of N Strathclyde 1975-78, sheriff princ of Lothian and Borders 1978-, sheriff of Chancery in Scotland 1978-, interim sheriff princ of S Strathclyde 1981; chm: Sheriff Ct Rules Cncl 1975-81, Northern Lighhouse Bd 1983-84 and 1985-87; kt 1984; *Recreations* music, golf; *Clubs* New (Edinburgh), Scottish Arts, Bruntsfield Golf; *Style*— Sir Frederick O'Brien KB, QC; 22 Arboretum Road, Edinburgh EH2 5PN (☎ 031 552 1923); Sheriff Court House, Lawnmarket, Edinburgh (☎ 031 226 7181)

O'BRIEN, Hon Mrs Henry - Edith Lawrie; widow of T M Steele; *m* 1964, as his 2 w, Capt the Hon Henry Barnaby O'Brien (d 1969); *Style*— The Hon Mrs Henry O'Brien; 3 Ibris Place, N Berwick, E Lothian

O'BRIEN, James Patrick; yr s of late John David O'Brien; hp of bro, Sir Timothy O'Brien, 7 Bt, *qv*; *b* 22 Dec 1964; *Style*— James O'Brien Esq

O'BRIEN, Hon Mrs Fionn; Josephine Reine; da of Joseph Eugene Bembaron (d 1953), of The Old House, Westcott, Surrey; *m* 1939, Hon Fionn Myles Maryons O'Brien (d 1977), s of 15 Baron Inchiquin; 1 s (18 Baron), 1 da; *Recreations* portrait painting; *Style*— The Hon Mrs Fionn O'Brien; 1 Dault Rd, London SW18 2NH

O'BRIEN, Most Rev Keith Michael Patrick; *see*: St Andrews and Edinburgh, Archbishop of (RC)

O'BRIEN, Michael Anthony; s of Dr Donal O'Brien, and Patricia Mary, *née* Dowdall; *b* 7 Sept 1950; *Educ* The Oratory Sch Reading, Trinity Coll Dublin (BA); *m* 7 Sept 1971, Robin Patricia Antonia, da of Roger Greene, (d 1954), of Wellington Quay, Dublin; 4 da (Louise b 1974, Pippa b 1976, Tara b 1977, Alice b 1987); *Career* CA; chm and chief exec: Bannertill Ltd, KDM Leasing Ltd, Leisure Projects Int Ltd, Loupiptar Investmts Ltd, Mineral and Energy Resources Corp Ltd, Mineral and Energy (UK) Ltd; asst dir C T Bowring & Co (Lloyd's Insur Brokers) 1975-78, gp fin controller Mining Investmt Corpn Ltd 1978-79, chief exec Anglo Int Mining Corpn Ltd 1979-82; FCA; *Recreations* horses, ponies, swimming, tennis; *Clubs* Br Show Pony Soc, S of England Agric Soc; *Style*— Michael O'Brien, Esq; 57 High St, Tunbridge Wells, Kent TN1 1XU (☎ 0892 511866, fax 0892 48440, car phone 0860 372637)

O'BRIEN, (Charles) Michael; s of Richard Alfred O'Brien, CBE (d 1970), of Beckenham, Kent, later of Queensland, Aust, and Nora, *née* McKay (1964); *b* 17 Jan 1919; *Educ* Westminster, Christ Church Oxford (MA); *m* 4 Nov 1950, Joyce, da of Rupert Henry Prebble (d 1958), of Beckenham, Kent; 2 s (Philip b 1952, Christopher b 1954); *Career* WWII, cmmnd 2 Lt RA 1940, Capt RA (Burma), demob 1946; actuary : asst actuary Equitable Life Assur Soc 1951, gen mangr and actuary Royal Nat Pension Fund for Nurses 1955-84, dir M & G Assur Gp 1984, chm Federated Pension Servs 1983-; govr Westminster Sch 1972-; FIA 1949 (hon sec 1961-63, pres 1976-78), FPMI; *Recreations* walking, gundog training,; *Style*— Michael O'Brien, Esq; The Boundary, Goodley Stock, Crockham Hill, Edenbridge, Kent TN8 6TA (☎ 0732 866 349)

O'BRIEN, Hon Michael John; s of Baron O'Brien of Lothbury, GBE, PC (Life Peer); *b* 1933; *Educ* Marlborough; *m* 1964, Marion Sarah, da of late Walter Graham Blackie; 2 s (James 1967, Charles 1972), 1 da (Sarah b 1969); *Career* memb of London Stock Exchange; *Recreations* fishing, shooting, stalking; *Clubs* Boodles; *Style*— The Hon Michael O'Brien; The Lodge, Thursley, nr Godalming, Surrey GU8 6QF (☎ 0252 702235)

O'BRIEN, Maj Murrough Richard; s of Lt-Col Hon Murrough O'Brien, DSO, MVO (2 s of 14 Baron Inchiquin); hp to 18 Baron Inchiquin; *b* 25 May 1910; *Educ* Eton, Balliol Coll Oxford (MA); *m* 1, 1942 (m dis 1951), Irene Clarice (d 1977, formerly w of (1) 10 Marquess of Queensberry, (2) Sir James Dunn, 1 Bt, da of H W Richards, of Regent's Park); m 2, 1952, Joan, da of Charles Pierre Jenkinson, and wid of Capt Woolf Barnato; 1 s (Conor b 1952, m 1982, Vivian, da of Col Adrian Rouse), 1 da (Mrs Jorge de Paiva Raposo b 1956); *Career* served WW II Irish Gds; *Clubs* White's; *Style*— Maj Murrough O'Brien; Primrose Hill, West Drive, Sunningdale, Berks; 34 Connaught Sq, London W2 (☎ 01 262 5954)

O'BRIEN, Oswald; MP (Lab) for Darlington 1983-; s of Thomas O'Brien, and Elizabeth O'Brien; *b* 6 April 1928; *Educ* St Mary's GS Darlington, Fircroft Coll Birmingham, Univ of Durham (BA); *m* 1950, Freda Rosina Pascoe; 1 s; *Career* RN 1945-48; Tutor WEA 1963-64, staff tutor Univ of Durham 1964-78, sr industl rels offr Cmmn on Industl Rels 1970-1972 (secondment), dir of studies and vice-princ Co-Op Coll 1978-83; Dept Employment second ACAS arbitrator in shipbuilding 1968-78, chm Soc of Industl Tutors 1978-82, former pres, sec and tres Darlington Lab Pty (and sec), former memb Darlington County Borough and Dist Cncls, co-opted memb Durham Co Educn Ctee; FBIM; *Books* Going Comprehensive (jtly 1970); *Recreations* singing, dancing, reading, conversation; *Style*— Oswald O'Brien, Esq, MP; House of Commons, London SW1

O'BRIEN, Sir Richard; DSO (1944), MC (and bar 1942, 1944); s of Dr Charles O'Brien and Marjorie Maude O'Brien; *b* 15 Feb 1920; *Educ* Oundle, Clare Cambridge; *m* 1951, Elizabeth M D Craig; 2 s, 3 da; *Career* served WWII in N Africa, ME, Italy, Greece with Sherwood Foresters and Leicester Regt, PA to C-in-C Army Gp 1945-46; Richard Sutcliffe Ltd, (rose to position of prodn dir 1948, left 1958); dir and gen mangr Head Wrightson Mineral Engr 1958-61, dir indust rels BMC 1961-66, indust manpower advsr DEA 1966-68; memb: Cncl Indust Soc 1962-85, Policy Studies Inst 1978- (chm cncl 1984-); dir manpower and exec dir Delta Metal 1972-76 (joined 1968), chm Manpower Services Cmmn 1976-82, memb NEDC 1977-82, former chm CBI Employment Policy Ctee, chm Crown Appts Cmmn 1979-, chm Engr Indust Trg Bd 1982-85; JP Wakefield 1955-61; Hon DSc Aston, Hon DLitt Warwick 1983; Hon LLD: Bath 1981, Liverpool 1981, Birmingham 1982; DCL (Lambeth) 1987, hon DL (CNAA) 1988, hon fell Sheffield Poly, memb cncl Birmingham Univ; kt 1980; *Style*— Sir Richard O'Brien, DSO, MC; 24 Argyll Rd, London W8 (☎ 01 937 8944)

O'BRIEN, Timothy Brian; s of Brian Palliser Tighe O'Brien (d 1966), and Elinor Laura, *née* Mackenzie; *b* 8 Mar 1929; *Educ* Wellington, Corpus Christi Cambridge (MA), Henry Fell Yale Univ; *Career* designer: BBC Design Dept 1954, Assoc Rediffusion 1955-56; head of design ABC TV 1956-66, theatrical designer and chm Soc of Br Theatre Designers in partnership with Tazeena Firth (est 1961), most recent prodn Otello Royal Opera House 1987; Gold Metal for set design Prague Quadriemale 1975; *Recreations* sailing (co owner Bathsheba Everdene); *Style*— Timothy O'Brien, Esq; 33 Lansdowne Gdns, London SW8 2EQ (☎ 01 622 5384)

O'BRIEN, (Michael) Vincent; s of Daniel Patrick O'Brien (d 1943); *b* 9 April 1917; *Educ* Mungret Jesuit Coll Limerick; *m* 1951, Jacqueline, *née* Wittenoom; 2 s (David, Charles), 3 da (Elizabeth McClory, Susan Magnier, Jane Myerscough); *Career* racehorse trainer, began training 1944 Co Cork, moved to Co Tipperary 1951, won all major English and Irish steeplechases (3 consecutive Grand Nationals, Champion Hurdles and 4 Gold Cups); since 1959 has concentrated on flat racing; trained winners of 16 English classics (incl 6 Derbys) and 27 Irish classics (incl 6 Irish Derbys), French Derby, 3 Prix de l'Arc de Triomphe and Washington Int; trainer of Nijinsky, first triple crown winner since 1935; Hon LLD Nat Univ 1983; *Recreations* golf, fishing; *Style*— Vincent O'Brien, Esq; Ballydoyle House, Cashel, Co Tipperary, Ireland (☎ 062 61222, telex 70714, fax 062 61677)

O'BRIEN, William; MP (Lab) Normanton 1983-; *Educ* Univ of Leeds; *m* Jean; 3 da; *Career* coalminer Wakefield DC 1945-83; memb: of Finance and Gen Purposes Ctee 1973-83 (former dep ldr and chm), NUM 1945- (local branch official 1956-83), Public Accounts Ctee 1983, Energy Select Ctee 1986; JP Wakefield 1979; *Recreations* reading; *Style*— William O'Brien, Esq, JP, MP; House of Commons, London SW1

O'BRIEN, Adm Sir William Donough; KCB (1969, CB 1966), DSC (1942); s of Maj William Donough O'Brien (d 1916); *b* 13 Nov 1916; *Educ* RNC Dartmouth; *m* 1943, Rita, da of Lt-Col Albert Micallef ISO, of Malta; 1 s, 2 da; *Career* joined RN 1930, served WWII, Flag Offr Aircraft Carriers 1966-67, Cdr Far East Fleet 1967-69, C-in-C Western Fleet 1970-71, ret; chm: King George's Fund for Sailors 1974-86, Kennet and Avon Canal Tst 1974-; pres Assoc of RN Offrs 1974- (Rear-Adm 1979-84, Vice Adm 1984-86); *Clubs* Army and Navy; *Style*— Adm Sir William O'Brien, KCB, DSC; The Black Barn, Steeple Ashton, Trowbridge, Wilts BA14 6EU (☎ 0380 870496)

O'BRIEN OF LOTHBURY, Baron (Life Peer UK 1973); Leslie Kenneth O'Brien; GBE (1967), PC (1970), FRCM (1979); e s of Charles John Grimes O'Brien; *b* 8 Feb 1908; *Educ* Wandsworth Sch; *m* 1, 1932, Isabelle (d 1987), da of Francis Pickett, MBE; 1 s (Hon Michael b 1933); m 2, 6 Jan 1989, Mrs Marjorie Taylor, da of Albert Cecil Ball; *Career* ind peer in House of Lords; Private Artists Rifles 1928-32, Bank of England 1927-73: chief cashier 1955-62, govr 1966-73; pres Br Bankers Assoc 1973-80, vice chm Banque Belge 1981-88, dir Belgian & Gen Investmts 1981-88; advsr: J P Morgan & Co 1973-79, Morgan Grenfell 1974-87; *Recreations* music, theatre, tennis; *Clubs* Athenaeum, Boodle's, Garrick, Grillions, MCC, AELTC; *Style*— The Rt Hon the Lord O'Brien of Lothbury; 3 Peter Ave, Oxted, Surrey (☎ 0883 712535)

O'BROIN, Breandan; s of Michael O'Broin (d 1962) of Dublin, and Kathleen O'Broin (d 1975); *b* 21 Jan 1946; *Educ* Colaiste Mhuire Dublin, Coll of Commerce Dublin; *m* 3 April 1970, Miriam Frances, da of Frank Murray (d 1985), of Edinburgh; 2 s (Hugh b 1972, Timothy b 1976), 2 da (Kate b 1971, Judith b 1974); *Career* copywriter: Arks 1964-68, Young Advertising 1968-70; creative dir CDP Assocs 1970-; ICAD 1966, MIAPI 1968; *Recreations* cricket, badminton, walking; *Clubs* Merrion CC; *Style*— Breandan O'Broin, Esq; 2 Sandycove Ave West, Sandycove, Co Dublin (☎ 0001 808267); CDP Associates, 46 Wellington Rd, Dublin 4 (☎ 0001 689627, fax 0001 681341, telex 30334)

O'CATHAIN, Detta; OBE (1983); da of Caoimhghin O'Cathain (d 1986), of Dublin, and Margaret, *née* Prior (d 1977); *b* 3 Feb 1938; *Educ* Laurel Hill Limerick Ireland, Univ Coll Dublin (BA); *m* 4 June 1968, William Ernest John Bishop, s of William Bishop, of Bristol (d 1968); *Career* md milk markt, Milk Markt Bd; dir: Midland Bank plc 1984, Tesco plc 1985, Sears plc 1987, Bd memb of Book Tst; cncl memb of the Industl Soc, memb of exec bd of the Nat Dairy Cncl; *Recreations* reading, walking, keep-fit, theatre, music; *Style—* Detta O'Cathain; The Old Malthouse, Queen St, Arundel, W Sussex (☎ 0903 883775); 19 Fairwater House, Twickenham Rd, Teddington, Middx (☎ 01 977 9495); Milk Marketing Board, Thames Ditton, Surrey (☎ 01 398 4101, car tel 0836 283438)

O'COCK, Brig Michael James Palmer; CBE (1974), MC (1945); s of Wilfred Palmer O'Cock (d 1947), of London, and Margaret Eleanor, *née* Gregson (d 1972); *b* 19 June 1919; *Educ* Harrow, Trinity Coll Cambridge (BA); *m* 1, 1943, Elizabeth Jane (d 1970), da of late Col W D'Arcy Hall, MC; 2 da (Susan, Caroline); m 2, 1975, Helen Jane Sibbald, da of Capt Henry Mangles Denham, CMG, RN; *Career* 2 Lt Irish Gds 1940, served NW Europe 1944-45, Lt-Col cmd Irish Gds 1964-66, def attaché Bonn 1968-70, COS London Dist 1972-74; *Recreations* shooting, skiing, fishing; *Clubs* Cavalry and Guards, MCC; *Style—* Brig Michael O'Cock, CBE, MC; Church Farm, Kington Langley, Chippenham, Wilts SN15 5NN (☎ 024 975 264)

O'CONNELL, Bernard John; s of William O'Connell, and Dorothy, *née* Veale; *b* 22 Nov 1942; *Educ* St Brendans Coll, Univ of Sheffield; *m* 12 Feb 1966, Mary Jacqueline, da of Capt Norman Clark (d 1959); 1 s (James b 1967), 1 da (Anna b 1971); *Career* consumer res mangr Cadburys 1967-69, markt mangr Imperial Tobacco 1969-72, chm and md Markt Solns 1973-78, md Noble Whelan O'Connell 1978-84, chm The O'Connell Partnership 1984-; markt awards: Silver 1975, Gold 1975 and 1977, Grand Prix 1977; *Recreations* golf, skiing, guitar; *Clubs* Raffles, Morton, Ski Club of GB, Chesham Crackerpullers Downhill Racing; *Style—* Bernard O'Connell, Esq; Woodland Ct, Long Park, Chesham Bois, Amersham, Bucks (☎ 02403 3338)); 10 Wrights Lane, London W8 6TA (☎ 01 937 2575, fax 01 937 7534)

O'CONNELL, Judith Anne; *née* Shennan; da of (Robert) Gordon Shennan (d 1982), and Gladys, *née* Coomber; *b* 11 June 1944; *Educ* Gardeners Rd Sydney Australia; *m* 1, 1962 (m dis 1971), Maurice Charles O'Connell; m 2, 1972 (m dis 1976), Alasdair Sutherland; *Career* advertising copywriter Sydney Aust 1958-62, photographic fashion model Sydney, Paris, London 1962-73, modelled spring collections Pierre Cardin Paris 1967, PR Janice Wainwright London 1974-75, set up London off and shops Mulberry (Design) Ltd 1976-83, fndr O'Connell Trievnor Agencies (Br and Euro fashion and mktg 1983-), freelance columnist trade and consumer magazines; memb exhibitors ctee Br Fashion Cncl; *Recreations* writing, reading, photography, cats, rock and roll, tennis; *Clubs* Groucho; *Style—* Mrs Judith O'Connell; 306 London Hse, 26-40 Kensington High St, London W8 4PF (☎ 01 938 2646, fax 01 938 2647, telex 23152 REF 1436)

O'CONNELL, Maurice James Donagh MacCarthy; s and h of Sir Morgan Donal Conail O'Connell, 6 Bt *qv*; *b* 10 June 1958; *Style—* Maurice O'Connell Esq; 41 Lowndes St, London SW1

O'CONNELL, Sir Morgan Donal Conail; 6 Bt (UK 1869), of Lakeview, Killarney, Co Kerry, and of Ballybeggan, Tralee, Co Kerry; s of Capt Sir Maurice James Arthur O'Connell, 5 Bt, MC (d 1949); *b* 29 Jan 1923; *Educ* Abbey Sch Fort Augustus Inverness-shire; *m* 1953, Elizabeth, da of late Maj John MacCarthy O'Leary, of Coomlegane, Millstreet, Co Cork; 2 s (Maurice *qv*, John b 1960), 4 da (Frances b 1954, Susan b 1956, Katherine b 1964, Claire b 1969); *Heir* s, Maurice James Donagh MacCarthy O'Connell; *Career* served 1943-46 with RCS; *Style—* Sir Morgan O'Connell, Bt; Lakeview House, Killarney, Co Kerry, Ireland (☎ 31845)

O'CONNOR, Surgn Rear Adm Anthony; LVO (1966); s of Armel John O'Connor (d 1949), of Ludlow Shrops, and Lucy Violet, *née* Bullock-Webster (d 1946); *b* 8 Nov 1917; *Educ* Ludlow GS, Kings Coll London Univ, Westminster Hosp London (MB, BS); *m* 1946, Catherine Jane Hayes, da of Surgn Capt John Marcus Hayes (d 1966); 3 da (Susan, Judy, Patricia); *Career* joined RN as MO (RNVR) 1942, cmmn 1946, MO HM Yacht Britannia 1965-66, HM The Queen's hon physician 1969-75, dep med dir Gen (Naval) 1972, Surgn Rear Adm 1975, ret; dir Red Cross Blood Transfusion Serv W Aust 1975-84; CStJ 1972; *Recreations* gardening; *Style—* Dr Anthony O'Connor, LVO; Pump House, Wolverton, nr Basingstoke, Hants RG26 5RT (☎ 0635 298451)

O'CONNOR, Air Vice-Marshal Patrick Joseph Gerard; CB (1975), OBE (1943); s of Charles Edward O'Connor (d 1942), of Boston House, Straffan, Co Kildare, Ireland, and Mary Josephine, *née* Doyle (d 1960); *b* 21 August 1914; *Educ* Mount St Joseph Coll Roscrea Co Tipperary, Nat Univ of Ireland; *m* 16 July 1946, Elsie Elizabeth, da of David Craven (d 1945), of Leeds, Yorks; 1 s (Charles b 1951), 3 da (Mary b 1947, d 1977, Anna b 1948, Geraldine b 1950); *Career* RAF med branch 1940-77, Air Vice-Marshal, conslt advsr neurology and psychiatry RAF, hon physician to HM The Queen; conslt neurology and psychiatry: CAA 1977-, Br Airways 1977, Harley St 1977-; memb: RSM 1950, Int Acad Aviation Med, ABN; FRC Psych, FRCP; *Books* Int Civil Aviation Organization Manual, Standards for Neurology and Psychiatry (1970); *Recreations* gardening; *Clubs* RAF; *Style—* Air Vice-Marshall Patrick O'Connor, CB, OBE; St Benedicts, Bacombe Lane, Wendover, Bucks HP22 6EQ (☎ 0296 623 329); 108 Harley St, London W1 (☎ 01 935 8033)

O'CONNOR, Rt Hon Lord Justice; Rt Hon Sir Patrick McCarthy O'Connor; PC (1980); s of William Patrick O'Connor; *b* 28 Dec 1914; *Educ* Downside, Merton Coll Oxford (Hon Fell 1987); *m* 1938, Mary Garland (d 1984), da of William Griffin, KC, of Vancouver; 2 s, 2 da; *Career* barr Inner Temple 1940, jr counsel to PO 1954-60, QC 1960, rec Southend 1961-66 (Kings Lynn 1959-61), high ct judge (Queen's Bench) 1966-80, lord justice of Appeal 1980-; dep chm IOW QS 1957-71, vice-chm Parole Bd 1974-75, govr Guy's Hosp 1956-60; kt 1966; *Style—* The Rt Hon Lord Justice O'Connor; 210 Rivermead Ct, London SW6 3SG (☎ 01 731 3563); Royal Courts of Justice, Strand, London WC2

O'CONNOR, Hon Mr Justice; Rory; s of James Edward O'Connor (d 1956); *b* 26 Nov 1925; *Educ* Blackrock Coll, Univ Coll Dublin; *m* 1963, Elizabeth, *née* Dew; 1 s (Rory Brendan b 1967), 2 da (Fiona b 1964, Siobhan b 1981); *Career* called to the barr King's Inns 1949, resident magistrate Kenya 1956, magistrate Hong Kong 1962, dist judge 1970, Supreme Ct Judge Hong Kong 1977-; memb of The Judicial Services Commn 1987; *Recreations* travel, reading; *Clubs* Royal Hong Kong Jockey, Utd Services Recreation (Hong Kong); *Style—* The Hon Mr Justice O'Connor; Flat 7E, Barnton Court, 9 Canton Rd, Kowloon, Hong Kong (☎ 3 7227315)

O'CONNOR-FENTON, Maj Alan; TD; s of Rev Charles Edward O'Connor-Fenton (d 1923), and Edith, *née* Marples (d 1950); *b* 27 Feb 1905; *Educ* Lancing Coll, Univ of Sheffield; *m* 20 June 1936, Ruth Frances, da of George Wilkinson (d 1950), of Sheffield; 1 s (Timothy b 1939), 1 da (Jane b 1948); *Career* cmmnd RA TA 1928, WWII served N Africa, Italy, Germany 1939-45; tool manufacturer Sheffield; Freeman Cutlers Co of Hallamshire 1952, chm Sheffield Royal Teaching Hosp 1953, memb bd of govrs Sheffield Utd Hosps 1953; tax cmmr W Riding Yorks 1962, ret 1977; *Recreations* fishing, sailing, water colour painting; *Style—* Maj Alan O'Connor-Fenton, TD; Bower Gdns, Salisbury, Wilts SP1 2RL (☎ 0722 22040)

O'CONOR CAMERON, Desmond Roderic; s and h of Denis Armar O'Conor, The O'Conor Don, and Elizabeth, *née* Harris (now Mrs James Cameron); *b* 22 Sept 1938; *Educ* Sherborne; *m* 23 May 1964, Virginia Anne, da of late Sir Michael Sanigear Williams, KCMG; 1 s (Philip Hugh b 17 Feb 1967), 2 da (Emma Joy (Mrs Mark Leveson-Gower) b 17 April 1965, Denise Sarah b 8 Dec 1970); *Career* RNVR (HMS President) 1959-60; Bank of London and Montreal Ltd Guatemala and Honduras 1960-64, J Henry Schroder Wagg & Co Ltd London 1969-70, dir Schroders Int Ltd Rio de Janeiro 1977-78, Kleinwort Benson Ltd London 1979- (dir 1980-); dir: Kleinwort Benson Australia Ltd Sydney, Kleinwort Benson (Hong Kong) Ltd Hong Kong, Kleinwort Benson (Singapore) Ltd Singapore; dir Latin American Trade Advisory Gp (LATAG) (Bd of Trade sponsored organisation); chm Soldiers and Sailors Home Eastbourne; *Recreations* tennis, skiing, sailing; *Style—* Desmond O'Conor Cameron, Esq; Horsegrove House, Kleinwort Benson Ltd, 20 Fenchurch St, London EC3 (☎ 01 623 8000)

O'CONOR DON, The; Denis Armar O'Conor; O Conchubhair Dun; s of Charles O'Conor Don (27 in descent from Conor, Concovar or Conchobhar, King of Connaught in tenth century and from whom the family name derives), and Evelyn, yst da of Adm the Hon Armar Lowry-Corry, himself 2 s of 3 Earl of Belmore; the present O'Conor Don's forbear 23 generations back was Turlough Mor O'Conor (d 1163), High King over all Ireland; suc his 2 cous (a Jesuit priest) Nov 1981; *b* 1912; *Educ* Downside; *m* 1, 1937 (m dis 1943), Elizabeth, da of Rev Stanley Punshon Marris; 1 s; m 2, 1943, Rosemary June, da of Capt James Piers O'Connell-Hewett; 2 s (Kieran Denis b 1958, Rory Dominic b 1963); *Heir* s, Desmond Roderic Cameron O'Conor (b 1938, m 1964 Virginia, eldest da of Sir Michael Williams, KCMG, *qv*; 1 s Philip b 1967, 2 da Emma b 1965, Denise b 1971); *Career* former Lt Lincolnshire Regt; KCLJ, KMLJ; *Recreations* hound breeding and showing, beagling; *Style—* The O'Conor Don; Ashbourne, Corrig Rd, Dun Laoghaire, Co Dublin, Eire (☎ 0001 80 24 22)

O'DELL, Denis Herbert; s of Edmund James O'Dell (d 1973), of 123 Coventry Rd, Bedford, and Gertrude Emma, *née* Witney; *b* 18 Dec 1919; *Educ* Bedford Modern Sch; *m* 22 April 1950, Elizabeth Mary, da of Stanley Richard Evans (d 1960), of 12 Biddenham Turn, Bedford; 1 s (William Richard b 1951), 1 da (Judith Mary b 1952); *Career* RAF 1940-46, Flying Offr, served Malta 1941-43, trg cmd S Rhodesia, flying instr 1943-45; proprietor O'Dell's Garage 1946-52, md O'Dells Garage Ltd 1952-73, dir Sheerwater Motors Ltd 1973-74, md Sheerwater Motors Ltd 1974-; dir: Ben housing Assoc Ltd 1982-87, Ben Motor and Allied Trades Benevolent Fnd 1987-; chm Ben Welfare Ctee 1986-; TEng, FIMI; *Recreations* natural history, walking, Lynwood Ben Club, trade politics; *Clubs* RAF, RSPB, RHS, FMI, WWF, Woodland Tst, CGA; *Style—* Denis O'Dell, Esq; End Cottage, Elmscott, Hartland Devon EX39 6EX (☎ 023 74 620); Sheerwater Motors Ltd, Sheerwater, Woking, Surrey GU21 5JZ (☎ 048 62 61517)

O'DONNELL, Dr Michael; s of Dr James Michael O'Donnell (d 1957), and Nora, *née* O'Sullivan (d 1976); *b* 20 Oct 1928; *Educ* Stonyhurst, Trinity Hall Cambridge, St Thomas's Hosp; *m* 1952, Catherine, da of Frank Dorrington Ward (d 1972); 1 s (James), 2 da (Frances, Lucy); *Career* family doctor 1953-64; ed World Medicine 1966-81, contrib to Stop the Week BBC 1977-, chm My Word BBC 1983-, written and presented tv documentaries in USA and UK incl: O'Donnell Investigates BBC 1985, 1986 and 1988, Medical Express BBC 1983, Plague of Hearts BBC 1983, Inside Medicine BBC 1973, A Part of Life YTV 1977, Is Your Brain Really Necessary YTV 1978; presenter Relative Values 1987-; memb Gen Med Cncl 1971-, ed World Medicine 1966-81; *Books* The Devil's Prison (1982), An Insider's Guide to the Games Doctors Play (1986); The Long Walk Home (1988), How to Suceed in Business without Sacrificing Your Health (1988); contrib: The Times, The Guardian, Daily Mail, International Management, British Medical Journal; *Recreations* walking, golf, music; *Clubs* Garrick; *Style—* Dr Michael O'Donnell; Handon Cottage, Markwick Lane, Loxhill Godalming, Surrey GU8 4BD (☎ 048 632 295)

O'DONOGHUE, His Hon Judge Michael; s of Dr James O'Donoghue, MB (d 1948), of Boundary St, Liverpool, and Vera Maude, *née* Cox (d 1981); *b* 10 June 1929; *Educ* Rhyl County Sch, Univ of Liverpool (LLB); *Career* served RAF 1951-53, Flying Offr; HM circuit judge; *Recreations* music, sailing (yacht Equity III), photography, painting; *Clubs* Athenaeum (Liverpool), Roy Welsh YC; *Style—* His Hon Judge Michael O'Donoghue

O'DONOGHUE OF THE GLENS, The; Geoffrey Vincent Paul O'Donoghue; *b* 1937; *m* Frances Kelly; *Heir* s, Conor, b 1964; *Style—* The O'Donoghue of the Glens; Glas Choill, Screggan, Tullamore, Co Offaly; The Glens, Flesk, Co Kerry

O'DONOVAN, The O'Donovan Morgan Gerald (Daniel); s of Brig The O'Donovan, MC (Morgan (John) Winthrop, d 1969) of Hollybrook House, Skibbereen, Co Cork, and Cornelia, *née* Bagnell (d 1974); officially recognised Chief of the Name of one of the most ancient families of Ireland, traceable from Gaelic times; *b* 4 May 1931; *Educ* Stowe, Trinity Coll Cambridge (MA); *m* 19 Sept 1959, Frances Jane, da of Field Marshal Sir Gerald Walter Robert Templer, KG, GCB, GCMG, KBE, DSO (d 1979); 1 s (Morgan (Teige) Gerald b 1961), 2 da (Katharine Jane b 1962, Cecilia (Mary) Cornelia b 1966); *Heir* s, Morgan (Teige) Gerald O'Donovan; *Career* farmer; J & P Coats Ltd Glasgow 1954-63, mgmnt appts in Cuba, Colombia, Singapore, Australia, Revertex Ltd London 1963-70, Wates & Co Ltd Dublin 1970-77 (md 1972-77); memb Gen Synod of Church of Ireland, govr Midleton Coll Co Cork; *Recreations* shooting, fishing, bird watching, vintage cars; *Clubs* Kildare Street and University Dublin; *Style—* The O'Donovan; Hollybrook House, Skibbereen, Co Cork Ireland (☎ 028 21245)

O'DONOVAN, Timothy Charles Melville; s of John Conan Marshall Thornton O'Donovan (d 1964), of London, and Enid Muriel, *née* Liddell (d 1958); *b* 10 Feb 1932; *Educ* Marlborough; *m* 19 Sept 1958, Veronica Alacoque, da of Leslie White (d 1981), of Hawkley, Hants; 2 s (Michael b 1962, Richard b 1966); *Career* Nat Serv with Life Gds 1950-52; chm Eckersley Hicks & Co Ltd Lloyd's Brokers 1979-84, dir public affrs

Bain Clarkson 1987-, dir Common Cause Ltd 1964-; steward St George's Chapel Windsor Castle 1978- (dep vice-capt 1983-), tstee Br Monarchy Museum Tst 1979-, chm A Princess for Wales Exhibition 1981, tstee The Environment Fndn 1985-, chm Pollution Abatement Technol Award Scheme 1983-87, chm Better Environment Awards for Industry 1987-; memb The Queen's Birthday Ctee 1986, organised EIIR A Celebration 1986 and Sixty Years a Queen 1987 exhibitions Windsor Castle; FRSA 1984; *Books* Above The Law? (1959), Annual Survey of Royal Family Duties since 1979 in The Times, The Daily Telegraph and Illustrated London News; *Recreations* watching cricket, collecting royal memorabilia, reading the Court Circular; *Clubs* MCC; *Style*— Tim O'Donovan, Esq; Mariners, The Avenue, Datchet, nr Windsor, Berks SL3 9DH; 15 Minories, London EC3N 1NJ (☎ 01 481 3232, fax 01 480 6137, telex 8813411)

O'DRISCOLL, John P; s of Prof M Kieran O'Driscoll, of Dublin, Ireland, and Robina, *née* Hanley; *b* 24 June 1950; *Educ* Clongowes Wood Coll, Trinity Coll Dublin (BA), Wharton Univ of Penn (MBA); *m* 23 June 1977, Catherine Elizabeth, da of Henri Pierre Fortier (d 1977); 1 s (Shane Brice b 20 May 1982), 1 da (Ciara Violaine b 9 Sept 1979); *Career* md Mellon Securities Ltd 1988-, gen mangr Mellon Bank (London branch) 1989-; *Recreations* riding, squash; *Style*— John O'Driscoll, Esq; 6 Devonshire Sq, London EC2M 4LB (☎ 01 626 9828)

O'DWYER, Thomas Rankin; s of Bryan Keating O'Dwyer (d 1982), and Patricia Rang O'Dwyer; *b* 30 April 1954; *Educ* George Washington HS Alexandria Virginia USA, Parsons Sch of Design NY USA (BA), St Martins Sch of Art; *Career* fashion conslt Nigel French Enterprises Ltd 1971-79; fashion ed: Men's Wear Magazine 1980-86, Fashion Weekly 1986-88, Sunday Mirror and Magazine 1988-; freelance work incl: Marie Claire, The Guardian (men's fashion corr 1984-88), DR, Living, Daily Express, Daily Mirror, Clothes Show Magazine, Unique, Ritz, Blitz; TV appearances incl: Night Network, South of Watford, Six O'Clock Show; radio appearances incl: Loose Ends, (first all male) Woman's Hour; chm seminar on men's fashion at ICA; judge: Woman Magazine Designer of the Year competition, Courtelle Design Awards; memb NUJ; *Recreations* reading, gossip, cooking, writing (witty) poetry, watching films, observing fashion (trend spotting), picturesque Eastend pubs, eating at Joe Allans; *Style*— Thom O'Dwyer, Esq; 38 The Cloisters, 145 Commercial St, London E1 6BU (☎ 01 377 6201); Sunday Mirror Magazine, Orbit House, 1 New Fetter Lane, London E1 (☎ 01 353 0246 ext 6647, fax 01 583 2800)

O'FERRALL, Lady Elizabeth (Cecilia); *née* Hare; da of 4 Earl of Listowel (d 1931); *b* 1914; *m* 1, 1936, Maj Viscount Elveden, RA (TA) (d 1945), s of 2 Earl of Iveagh; m 2, 1947, Edward Rory More O'Ferrall; *Style*— Lady Elizabeth O'Ferrall; The Old Rectory, Elveden, Suffolk; Gloucester Lodge, Regent's Park, London NW1

O'GRADY, The; Lt-Col Gerald Vigors de Courcy O'Grady; MC (1945); s of late Lt-Col Standish de Courcy O'Grady, CMG, DSO; *b* 5 Sept 1912; *Educ* Arnold House, Wellington, RMA; *m* 1, 1941, Pamela Violet (m dis 1961), da of Lt-Col T A Thornton, CVO, DL, of Brockhall, Northampton; 1 s, 1 da; m 2, 1961, Mollie, da of Robert Mclean, of Gibson Island, Maryland, USA; 2 da; *Career* joined RA 1932, Lt 1935, ADC to C-in-C India 1939, Maj 1940, instr RMA Sandhurst 1947, ret 1947; chm Limerick Show Soc 1975-78; chm: Irish Friesian Breeders Club, Irish Grassland Assoc, Limerick Hunt 1974-82; *Style*— The O'Grady of Kilballyowen, MC; Kilballyowen, Bruff, Co Limerick, Ireland (☎ 061 82213)

O'GRADY, Hon Mrs (Joan Eleanor); *née* Ramsbotham; da of late 1 Viscount Soulbury, GCMG, GCVO, OBE, MC; *b* 1917; *m* 1950, Maj Robert Hardress Standish O'Grady, MC, Irish Gds; 1 s, 2 da; *Style*— The Hon Mrs O'Grady; Midford Place, Midford, Bath, Avon

O'HAGAN, Antony (Tony) Richard; TD (1976, 1 clasp 1982, 2 clasp 1988); s of Capt Desmond O'Hagan, CMG, of Kianjibbi, Kiambu, Kenya, and Pamela Jane, *née* Symes-Thompson; *b* 3 Oct 1942; *Educ* Wellington; *m* 6 Dec 1975, Caroline Jessica, da of Walter Herbert Franklin (d 1987), of Clements Farm, Gt Rissington, Glos; 1 s (Richard Franklin b 19 Oct 1979), 1 da (Clare Pamela b 6 Sept 1976); *Career* HAC: non cmmnd serv 1962-67, 2 Lt 1967, Capt 1975, Maj 1982, TA Watch keeper 3 Armd Div HQRA 1984-; mangr Coopers & Lybrand 1972-73, gp accountant Hays Wharf Gp 1973-76, fin accountant Freemans Mail Order 1977-82, fin dir St Martins Property Corp Ltd 1986- (chief accountant 1982-85); memb fin and mgmnt ctees Hightown Housing Assoc Ltd, tres HAC 1987-; Freeman City of London 1979, Liveryman Worshipful Co of Fanmakers 1980 (chm Livery ctee 1989); FCA (1978); *Recreations* tennis, swimming, skiing, fishing, gardening; *Clubs* Army & Navy; *Style*— Tony O'Hagan, Esq, TD; 8 Anglefield Rd, Berkhamstead, Herts HP43JA (☎ 0442 875 682); St Martins Property Corp Ltd, Adelaide House, London Bridge EC4R 9DT (☎ 01 626 3411)

O'HAGAN, 4 Baron (UK 1870); Charles Towneley Strachey; MEP (EDG) Devon 1979-; s of Hon Thomas Strachey (d 1955), who assumed surname Strachey *vice* Towneley-O'Hagan 1938 and added forename Towneley; he was s of 3 Baron O'Hagan (d 1961) by his 1 w, Hon Frances Strachey (da of 1 Baron Strachie); *b* 6 Sept 1945; *Educ* Eton, New Coll Oxford; *m* 1, 1967 (m dis 1984), HSH Princess Tamara, former w of Lt Cdr Thomas Smith-Dorrien-Smith, of Tresco Abbey, Isles of Scilly, and er da of HSH Prince Michael Imeretinsky (of the Princely family of Bagration, sometime rulers of an independent Georgia), RAFVR, of Menton; 1 da (Hon Nino b 1968); m 2, 1985, Mrs Mary Claire Parsons, only da of Rev Leslie Roose-Francis, of Trencoth, Blisland, Bodmin, Cornwall; 1 da (Hon Antonia b 1986); *Heir* bro, Hon Richard Strachey; *Career* page of honour to HM 1959-62; ind memb Euro Parl 1973-75, jr oppn whip Lds 1977-79, sits as Cons in House of Lords; *Clubs* Newton Abbot Constitutional, Pratt's, TVRF; *Style*— The Rt Hon the Lord O'Hagan, MEP; Rashleigh Barton, Wembworthy, Chulmleigh, N Devon

O'HALLORAN, Sir Charles Ernest; s of Charles O'Halloran; *b* 26 May 1924; *Educ* Conway St Central Sch Birkenhead; *m* 1943, Annie Rowan; 1 s, 2 da; *Career* served WWII RN; provost Ayr 1964-67 (memb Ayr Cncl 1953, Freeman of Burgh 1975); stood (Lab) for Ayr Burghs Gen Election 1966, convener Strathclyde Regnl Cncl 1978-82, chm Irvine New Town Devpt Corpn 1982-85, memb Local Authys Accounts Cmmn for Scotland 1983-85; kt 1981; *Style*— Sir Charles O'Halloran; 40 Savoy Park, Ayr

O'HALLORAN, Michael Joseph; s of Martin O'Halloran (d 1968); *b* 20 August 1928; *Educ* Clohanes Nat Sch (Eire); *m* 1956, Stella Beatrice, da of James McDonald (d 1934); 1 s decd, 3 da (Diane b 1961, Bernadette d 1963, Mary b 1966); *Career* MP (Lab, NUR sponsored until 1981, SDP until 1983, Lab Ind 1983) Islington N 1969-83; former railway worker and building works mangr, returned to building indust 1983; *Recreations* rugby football, soccer football; *Clubs* Challoner; *Style*— Michael O'Halloran, Esq; 149 Cheam Rd, Cheam, Surrey SM1 4BR

O'HARA, James Patrick; s of William O'Hara (d 1978), and Breeda O'Hara; *b* 8 Mar 1935; *Educ* Christian Bros Sch Ballinroe Mayo, Harvard; *m* 21 April 1965, Patricia Marion, da of John Whyte (d 1985); 2 s (Patrick b 12 Feb 1966, Connor b 23 Feb 1971); *Career* Bank of Ireland: joined 1952, mangr Cork area off 1969, sr rep N America 1971, asst gen mangr Cork, gen mangr ops Dublin 1983, gen mangr branch banking London 1988, exec dir Bank of Ireland Gp Hldgs Britain Ltd, non exec dir Home Mortages Ltd; non exec dir Br Credit Tst; memb Inst of Bankers in Ireland; *Recreations* golf, tennis, fishing; *Clubs* Castle GC Dublin, Greystones Tennis; *Style*— James O'Hara, Esq; Bank of Ireland, 36 Queen St, London EC4A 1BN (☎ 01 329 4500, fax 01 489 1313, telex 8812635)

O'HIGGINS, Prof Paul; s of Richard Leo O'Higgins, MC (d 1973), of Rochester House, Uxbridge, Middx, and Elizabeth, *née* Deane (d 1984); *b* 5 Oct 1927; *Educ* St Columba's Coll Rathfarnham Co Dublin, Trinity Coll Dublin (MA, LLD), Clare Coll Cambridge (MA, PhD, LLD); *m* May 1951, Rachel Elizabeth, da of Prof Alan Dudley Bush, of Radlett, Herts; 1 s (Niall b 29 May 1961), 3 da (Maeve b 16 Feb 1953, Siobhan b 21 Sept 1956, Niav b 23 April 1964); *Career* Cambridge Univ: fell Christ's Coll 1959-, univ lectr 1965-79, reader in labour law 1979-84; lectr in labour law Cncl of Legal Educn/Inns of Ct Sch of Law 1976-84, regius prof of laws Trinity Coll Dublin 1984-87, prof of law King's Coll London 1987-; memb Office of Manpower economics advsy ctee on Equal Pay 1970-72; chm Cambridge branch: Assoc of Univ Teachers 1971-75, Nat Cncl for Civil Liberties 1970-78; memb staff side panel Civil Serv Arbitration Tbnl 1972-84, memb bureau Euro Inst of Social Security 1970-, tstee Cambridge Union Soc 1973-84, vice pres Inst of Safety and Public Protection 1973-, vice pres Haldane Soc 1981-, govr Br Inst of Human Rights 1988-, vice pres Inst Employment Rights 1989-; author; Joseph L Andrews Bibliographical Award of the American Assoc of Law Liberties 1987; MRIA 1986; *Books* Bibliography of Periodical Literature relating to Irish Law (1966, supplements 1975 and 1983), Public Employee Trade Unionism in the UK: The Legal Framework (with Ann Arbor, 1971), Censorship in Britain (1972), A Bibliography of British & Irish Labour Law (1975), Workers' Rights (1976), Employment Law (4 edn 1981), Labour Law in Great Britain and Ireland to 1978 (1981), Discrimination in Employment in Northern Ireland (1984), A Bibliography of Irish Trials and other Legal Proceedings (1986), A Bibliography of the Literature on British & Irish Social Security Law (1986); *Recreations* travel, talk, wine; *Clubs* Royal Dublin Soc; *Style*— Prof Paul O'Higgins; Christ's Coll Cambridge CB2 3BU (☎ 0223 334900)

O'KEEFFE, (Peter) Laurence; CMG (1983), CVO (1974); s of Richard O'Keeffe (d 1982), and Alice Gertrude Chase; *b* 9 July 1931; *Educ* De la Salle Coll Toronto Canada, St Francis Xavier's Coll Liverpool, Univ of Oxford (BA); *m* 1954, Suzanne Marie, da of Francis Jousse, of Versailles France; 3 da (Catherine, Isabel, Juliet); *Career* HM ambass Dakar Senegal (also accredited to Mali, Mauretania, Guinea, Geneva, Bissau, Cape Verde Islands); resident chm Civil Serv Selection Bd (Dip Serv); *Books* as Laurence Halley: Simultaneous Equations (1975), Abiding City (1986), Ancient Affections (1985); *Recreations* photography; *Clubs* Utd Oxford & Cambridge Univ, Dutch Treat (NY); *Style*— Laurence O'Keeffe, Esq, CMG, CVO; Wyle Cottage, Gt Wishford, Salisbury, Wilts (☎ 0722 790 393); Civil Services Commission, Kirkland House, 22 Whitehall, London SW1 (☎ 01 210 6691)

O'KELLY, Elizabeth; MBE (1959); da of Alfred Percival O'Kelly, (d 1940), and Nina Marguerite, *née* Stevens (d 1947); *b* 19 May 1915; *Educ* Withington Girls Sch, Royal Manchester Coll of Music (ARMCM); *Career* 2 Offr WRNS 1941-46; princ community devpt offr Cameroons 1950-62, advsr Govt of Sarawak on Woman's Insts 1962-65, actg dir Asian Christian Serv Vietnam 1967-69, gen sec Assoc Country Women of the World 1969-72; contrib numerous articles and conference papers on Third World Problems; memb ACWW, Int Womans Trib Centre NY, E Sussex Fedn of WI, Pestalozzi Int Children's Village Tst, Intermediate Tech Devpt GP; Order of the Star of Sarawak 1964; *Books* Aid and Self Help (1973), Rural Woman, their integration in Development Programmes (1978), Water and Sanitation for all (1982), Simple Technologies for Rural woman in Bangladesh (1977), Processing and Storage of Food grains for rural families (1979); *Recreations* music, gardening, walking; *Style*— Miss Elizabeth O'Kelly, MBE; Flat 2, Downash House, Rosemary Lane, Flimwell, E Sussex TN5 7PS (☎ 058 587 569)

O'KELLY, Surgn Rear Adm Francis Joseph; OBE (1965); s of Francis John O'Kelly (d 1960), of Drumkeeran Co Leitrim, and Elizabeth Mary, *née* Rogan (d 1965); *b* 24 Dec 1921; *Educ* St Patrick's Coll Cavan, Univ Coll Dublin (MB); *m* 1954, Winifred Mary Teresa, da of John Joseph Henry (d 1970), of Dalkey Co Dublin; 4 children (Maeve, Eithne, Francis, Ailish); *Career* RM Commandos in Middle and Far East 1948-52, HM Ships Unicorn, St Bride's Bay and Centaur, RN Air Station Brawdy, RN Barracks Chatham 1952-63, Naval MO of health appts in Far East and UK 1963-72, dep dir of Health and Res 1972-74, SMO Gibraltar 1974-77, QHP 1976-80; Surgn Rear Adm: Ships & Estabs 1977-78, Naval Hosp 1978-80, ret 1980; occupational health conslt Hong Kong Govt 1980-86, ret; CStJ 1980; *Recreations* reading, travel; *Style*— Dr Francis O'Kelly, OBE; Breffni, 38 Seamead, Stubbington, Fareham, Hants PO14 2NG (☎ 0329 662212)

O'KELLY, Hon Mrs (Mary Gail); *née* Mitchell-Thomson; da of 3 Baron Selsdon; *b* 1939; *m* 1963, Patrick John O'Kelly, MB, BCH; 3 s; *Style*— The Hon Mrs O'Kelly

O'LEARY, Catherine Elizabeth (Mrs Martyn Bennett); da of the late Cornelius Raphael O'Leary, and late Hannah Elizabeth Dennehy, *née* Neville ; *b* 14 August 1957; *Educ* Hollies Convent GS, Univ of Liverpool (LLB); *m* 6 Sept 1980, (John) Martyn Bennett, s of Dr John Garner Bennett, JP, of Crosby, Liverpool; 2 s (Henry b 1985, Edwin b 1987); *Career* called to the Bar Grays Inn 1979, pupil Lincolns Inn 1979-80, practising on Wales and Chester circuit 1980-; memb: Family Law Bar Assoc, Wales and Chester Fees and Legal Aid Ctee, Unity Theatre Liverpool; *Recreations* drama, cooking, riding, children; *Style*— Miss Catherine O' Leary; Stanthorne House, Burton Lane, Duddon, nr Tarporley, Cheshire CW6 0EP (☎ 082 924 303); 40 King St, Chester (☎ 0244 323 886)

O'LEARY, (Edmund) Eamon; s of James O'Leary (d 1961), and Margaret Mary, *née* Cullinane; *b* 14 Mar 1933; *Educ* St Kierans Coll Kilkenny, University Coll Cork (BSc); *m* 9 June 1958, da of Dennis Coffee (d 1955); 2 s (Michele Ann b 26 Nov 1960, Clodagh Denise b 10 March 1964); *Career* res engr Water CC 1954-58, asst engr

Rendell Palmer Tritton 1958-59, ptnr Veryard & Walsh & Ptnrs 1959-61, sr ptnr Veryard & Ptnrs 1971- (ptnr 1961-71); pres: S Wales branch Inst Vicil Engrs 1978, Concrete Soc Wales 1970 and 1976; memb exec ctee Tenovus,capt Radyr GC 1977; hon res fell Univ of Wales Cardiff; FICE, FInstrucE, MIHT, FRSA, MConsE; *Recreations* golf; *Clubs* Royal Porthcawl GC; *Style*— Eamon O'Leary, Esq; 39 Heol Don, Whitchurch, Cardiff CF4 2AS (☎ 0222 626516); Veryard & Partners, Crwys House, Crwys Rd, Cardiff CF2 4NB (☎ 0222 222664, fax 0222 28420)

O'LEARY, Maj John Charles; s of Francis Aloysious O'Leary (d 1970), and Helen Mary Agnes O'Leary (d 1938); *b* 23 August 1927; *Educ* Laxton; *m* 18 Oct 1952, Barbara, da of Dr Sydney Wray (d 1958); 2 s (Simon b 1954, Anthony b 1957), 1 da (Catherine (Mrs Walsh) b 1953); *Career* enlisted Army 1945, RMA Sandhurst 1947-48, cmmnd RA 1948, Regtl Serv 1948-58, Staff Coll 1959, Staff Regtl Serv 1960-77, ret Maj 1977; memb ctee W Surrey Hydon Hill Cheshire Home 1977-; Liveryman: Worshipful Co of Barbers 1981, Worshipful Soc of Apothecaries 1987 (Clerk 1977); MBIM 1977; *Recreations* walking, gardening, birdwatching; *Clubs* HAC; *Style*— Maj Charles O'Leary; Brackens Edge, 21 Kingswood Firs, Grayshott, nr Hindhead, Surrey GU26 6ET; Society of Apothecaries, Apothecaries Hall, Black Friars Lane, London EC4V 6EJ (☎ 01 236 1180)

O'LEARY, Terence Daniel; CMG (1982); s of Daniel O'Leary (d 1948), and Mary E, *née* Duggan (d 1979); *b* 18 August 1928; *Educ* Dulwich Coll, St John's Cambridge (MA); *m* 1960, Janet Douglas, da of Dr Hugh Berney (d 1978), of Masterton, NZ; 2 s (John, Daniel (twins)), 1 da (Helen); *Career* served Queen's Royal Regt, Capt RARO; HM Dip Serv 1953-78; serv ed: NZ, India, Tanganyika, Australia, Cabinet Off, S Africa, NZ; sr civil dir Nat Def Coll 1978-81, Br High Cmmr Sierra Leone 1981-84 (NZ and Samoa 1984-87), Govr of Pitcairn 1984-87; chm Petworth Preservation 1989-; *Clubs* Travellers, Wellington (NZ); *Style*— T D O'Leary, Esq, CMG; The Old Rectory, Petworth, W Sussex

O'LOGHLEN, Sir Colman Michael; 6 Bt (UK 1838), of Drumconora, Ennis; s of Henry Ross O'Loghlen (d 1944), and n of 5 Bt (d 1951); *b* 6 April 1916; *Educ* Xavier Coll Melbourne, Melbourne Univ (LLB); *m* 1939, Margaret, da of Francis O'Halloran of Melbourne; 6 s, 2 da; *Heir* s, Michael O'Loghlen; *Career* served 1942-45 with AIF New Guinea, Capt 1945; stipendiary magistrate Lae New Guinea, former actg judge of Supreme Ct of Territory of Papua and New Guinea; *Style*— Sir Colman O'Loghlen, Bt; 98 Williamsons Rd, Doncaster, Vic 3108, Australia

O'LOGHLEN, Michael; s and h of Sir Colman O'Loghlen, 6 Bt, LLB; *b* 21 May 1925; *Style*— Michael O'Loghlen Esq

O'MAHONY, Jeremiah Francis; s of Philip Joseph O'Mahony (d 1979), and Maria, *née* Kavanagh; *b* 23 Dec 1946; *Educ* Challoner Sch Finchley, Finchley GS; *m* 27 Jan 1973, Mary Josephine, da of Christopher James Blaney (d 1975); 4 s (Oliver James b 1976, Ronan b 1977, Ruadhri b 1980, Theodore b 1983), 1 da (Cressida b 1987); *Career* gp fin dir Ladbroke Group plc 1986-; FCA; *Recreations* running, swimming, tennis, reading, family; *Style*— Jeremiah O'Mahony, Esq; Ladbroke Gp plc, 87 Wimpole St, London W1

O'MALLEY, Donald Albert; s of Peter O'Malley, and Florence Rose O'Malley, *née* Evans; *b* 3 Feb 1931; *Educ* St Mary's Harry Cheshire; *m* 1954, Brenda Eileen, da of Jesse Wall (d 1984); 1 s (Simon), 1 da (Kim); *Career* carpet weaver; pres Power Loom Carpet Weavers' & Textile Workers' Union; *Style*— Donald O'Malley, Esq; 46 Castle Rd, Cookley, nr Kidderminster, Worcs (☎ 0562 850637); Gilt Edge Carpets, Mill St, Kidderminster, Worcs (☎ 0562 3434)

O'MALLEY, Stephen Keppel; *b* 21 July 1940; *Educ* Ampleforth, Waltham Coll Oxford; *m* 1963, Frances Mary, da of James Ryan; 4 s, 2 da; *Career* barr Inner Temple 1962, rec 1978-; wine tres of the Western circuit 1986-; co-fndr Bar European Gp 1977; *Books* The Manual of European Practice (1988), O'Malley & Layton Manual of European Practice (with Alexander Layton)

O'MORCHOE, The; David Nial Creagh O'Morchoe; CB (1979), MBE (1966); formerly of Oulartleigh and Monamolin; s of Col Nial Creagh O'Morchoe (The O'Morchoe), d 1970, when suc by his s David as Chieftain; *b* 17 May 1928; *Educ* St Columba's Coll Dublin, RMA Sandhurst; *m* 1955, Margaret (*Style* Madam O'Morchoe), da of Frank Brewitt, of Cork; 2 s (Dermot b 1956, Kevin b 1958), 1 da (Maureen b 1964); *Career* served Royal Irish Fus from 1948 in M East, Med, NW Europe, Kenya, Oman; late Cdr of Sultan of Oman's Land Forces; *Recreations* sailing, sheep farming; *Clubs* Friendly Brothers, Irish Cruising; *Style*— The O'Morchoe, CB, MBE; c/o Ulster Bank, Cork, Eire

O'NEIL, Hon Sir Desmond Henry; *b* 27 Sept 1920; *m* 1944, Nancy, da of R H Culver; 2 da; *Career* Capt Aust Signal Corps AIF 1940-46; MLA WA (Lib) for Canning 1959-62 and for East Melville 1962-80, govt whip 1962-65, min for Housing and Lab WA 1965-71, dep oppn ldr 1972-73; min for: Works and Water Supplies and Housing 1974-75, Works and Water Supplies and the NW 1975-77, Police and Traffic and Regnl Admin and the NW 1977-80, ret; chm: WA Greyhound Racing Assoc, WA Lotteries Cmmn; kt 1980; *Style*— The Hon Sir Desmond O'Neil; 42 Godwin Ave, South Como, W Australia 6152

O'NEIL, (James) Roger; s of James William O'Neil (d 1980), and Claire Williams O'Neil (d 1981); *b* 22 Feb 1938; *Educ* Laurel Hill Acad USA, Univ of Notre Dame (BSc), Cornwell Univ (MBA); *m* 30 Oct 1976, Joan, da of Mark Mathewson, of California, USA; 1 s (Mark Daniel b 1983), 1 da (Claire Kathyrn b 1980); *Career* Mobil Oil Corpn 1961-; formerly chm: Mobil Oil Cyprus Ltd, Mobil SE Asia, Mobil Oil Italiana SPA; chm and chief exec Mobil Oil Co Ltd 1987-; vice pres UK Petroleum Indust Assoc, memb of Cncl Inst of Petroleum, memb president's Cncl Asia Soc NY; FRSA 1988, FInstPet 1988; *Recreations* tennis, skiing, music, archaelogy; *Clubs* RAC, Hurlingham; *Style*— Roger O'Neil, Esq; 6 Kingston Hse North, Princes Gate, London SW7 (☎ 01 584 1987); Mobil Oil Co Ltd, 54-60 Victoria St, London SW1E 6QB (☎ 01 828 9777, fax 01 828 9777 ext 2432, telex 8812411 MOBIL G)

O'NEILL, Denis Basil; s of Gilbert Joseph Lane O'Neill (d 1961), of Putney, London, and Winifred Mary, *née* Erkine-White (d 1980); *b* 23 July 1922; *Educ* Douai Sch, Imperial Coll London (BSc, ACGI); *m* 27 Feb 1954, Jacqueline Mary, da of Guy Holman Tatum (d 1968), of Kensington, London; 2 s (Duncan b 1957, Robin b 1960), 1 da (Susan (Mrs Paul Austen) b 1955); *Career* WW11 Maj RE DAQMG HQ Central Cmd India 1942-47; consulting engr (vibration and noise) 1949-, chm Hawkes & Co Savile Row 1969-71; MICE 1963; *Recreations* music, theatre, travel, video photography, grandchildren; *Style*— Denis O'Neill, Esq; 2 Halsey St, London SW3

O'NEILL, Dennis James; s of Dr William Patrick O'Neill (d 1986), of Adelaide House, Pontarddulais, S Wales, and Eva Ann, *née* Rees; *b* 25 Feb 1948; *Educ* Gowerton GS, studied singing privately with Frederick Cox in London and Campogalliani (Mantova) Ricci in Rome; *m* 1, 4 April 1970 (m dis 1987), Margaret Ruth da of Rev Edward Collins, of Old Harlow, Essex; 1 s (Sean b 22 Dec 1979), 1 da (Clare b 21 July 1977); m 2, 11 Jan 1988, Ellen, da of Hans Einar Folkestad, of Tybakken, Norway; *Career* tenor and broadcaster; operatic debut: Royal Opera House Covent Garden 1979 (thereafter annually), Metropolitan Opera NYC 1986 (thereafter annually), Vienna State Opera 1981, Hamburg State Opera 1981, San Francisco 1984, Chicago Lyric 1985, Paris Opera 1986; many recordings; presenter 'Dennis O'Neill' BBC 2; pres Friends of WNO, fndr Dennis O'Neill Bursary; *Recreations* cookery, photography; *Style*— Dennis O'Neill, Esq; c/o Ingpen & Williams, 14 Kensington Ct, London W8 (☎ 01 937 5158/9, fax 0222 340660)

O'NEILL, Hon Grania Elizabeth; yst da of 2 Baron Rathcavan; *b* 5 Dec 1963; *Style*— The Hon Grania O'Neill

O'NEILL, Hon Hugh Torrens; o s and h of 2 Baron Rathcavan (by his 1 w); *b* 14 June 1939; *Educ* Eton; *m* 1983, Sylvie Marie-Thérèse, da of Georges Wichard, of Provence, France, and formerly w of Hilary Chittenden; 1 s (François b 1984); *Career* Capt Irish Gds; journalist: Irish Times, Observer, Financial Times; dir: Lamont Hldgs plc, Ulster Fin Ltd, The Old Bushmills Distillery Co Ltd; chm: St Quentin Ltd, NI Airports Ltd, NI Tourist Bd, FRX Int Ltd; *Recreations* food, travel; *Clubs* Beefsteak, Garrick; *Style*— The Hon Hugh O'Neill; 14 Thurloe Place, London SW7 2RZ (☎ 01 581 3511); Cleggan Lodge, Broughshane, Ballymena, Co Antrim (☎ 0266 84209)

O'NEILL, Martin John; MP (Lab) Clackmannan 1983-; s of John O'Neill; *b* 6 Jan 1945; *Educ* Trinity Acad Edinburgh, Heriot Watt Univ, Moray House Educn Coll Edinburgh; *m* 1973, Elaine Samuel; 2 s; *Career* former insur clerk, asst examiner Scottish Estate Duty Off, secondary schoolmaster, tutor Open Univ; MP (Lab) Stirlingshire E and Clackmannan 1979-1983, memb select ctee Scottish Affrs 1979-88, oppn front bench spokesman on: Scottish Affrs 1981-84, Def and Disarmourment 1984-88; princ spokesman June 1988-; *Style*— Martin O'Neill, Esq, MP; House of Commons, London SW1A 0AA (☎ 01 219 4548); constitutency office: 56 Mar St, Alloa FK10 1HR (☎ 0259 721536)

O'NEILL, Hon Moira Louisa; 3 da of 2 Baron Rathcavan; *b* 14 April 1961; *Style*— The Hon Moira O'Neill

O'NEILL, Hon Patrick Arthur Ingham; o s of Baron O'Neill of the Maine (Life Peer); *b* 18 Jan 1945; *Educ* Eton; *m* 1, 1975 (m dis 1984), Anne, da of Douglas Lillecrapp, of Adelaide, S Australia; 2 da (Sophie b 1976, Elizabeth Mary b 1981); m 2, 1984, Stella Mary, da of Sir Alexander Downer, KBE (d 1981), of Martinsell, Williamstown, S Australia; *Career* Lt QRI Hussars; reporter ABC TV, prodr Channel 10 Current Affairs; cllr: Nat Tst of S Australia 1982-84, Nat Tst of Australia NSW 1976-77; *Recreations* travel, conversation, music; *Style*— The Hon Patrick O'Neill

O'NEILL, 4 Baron (UK 1868); Raymond Arthur Clanaboy O'Neill; TD (1970), DL (Co Antrim 1967); s of 3 Baron O'Neill (ka Italy 1944); the O'Neills stem from the oldest traceable family in Europe; *b* 1 Sept 1933; *Educ* Eton, RAC Cirencester; *m* 1963, Georgina Mary, da of Lord George Montagu-Douglas-Scott (3 s of 7 Duke of Buccleuch), of The Alms House, Weekley, Kettering, Northants; 3 s (Hon Shane b 1965, Hon Tyrone b 1966, Hon Rory b 1968); *Heir* s, Hon Shane O'Neill; *Career* Lt-Col RARO, served with 11 Hussars Prince Albert's Own, also NI Horse (TA); chm: Ulster Countryside Ctee 1972-76, Royal Ulster Agric Soc Fin Ctee 1975-83 (pres 1984-86); memb: NI Tourist Bd 1973-80 (chm 1975-80), NI Nat Tst Ctee 1980- (chm 1981-); tstee Ulster Folk and Tport Museum 1969- (vice-chm 1987-); Hon Col NI Horse (TA) 1986-; *Recreations* railways, vintage motoring, gardening; *Clubs* Turf, Ulster Reform; *Style*— The Rt Hon the Lord O'Neill, TD, DL; Shanes Castle, Antrim, NI BT41 4NE (☎ 08494 63264); Conigre House, Calne, Wilts (☎ 0249 812354)

O'NEILL, Richard; s of Ashworth Richard O'Neill (d 1984), of Blucher, Newcastle upon Tyne, and Mabel Annie, *née* Page (d 1972); *b* 11 May 1926; *Educ* Lemington GS; *m* 18 March 1950, Eileen, da of Frederick Hudson Forster (d 1971), of Scotswood, Newcastle upon Tyne; 3 s (Terence Carey b 1951, Richard Carey b 1952, Shaun Carey b 1959); *Career* MN 1944-46; accountant NCB 1947-65, chief accountant Reed Int 1966-72, dir and gen mangr Roadpack Ltd (Newcastle) 1972-; ACMA 1959, FBIM 1972; *Recreations* gardening, golf; *Style*— Richard O'Neill, Esq; 40 Chapel House Rd, West Denton, Newcastle upon Tyne (☎ 091 2677564); Field Packaging, Station Rd, Killingworth, Newcastle upon Tyne NE12 ORH (☎ 091 216 0303, telex 53404 NFIELD G)

O'NEILL, Robert James (Robin); CMG (1978); s of Robert Francis O'Neill (d 1978), of Chelmsford, Essex, and Dorothy May, *née* Golding (d 1983); *b* 17 June 1932; *Educ* King Edward VI Sch Chelmsford, Trinity Coll Cambridge (MA); *m* 1958, Helen Mary, Da of Horace Wells Juniper; 1 s (Mark), 2 da (Celia, Miranda); *Career* HM Dip Serv (formerly HM For Serv) 1955, served Ankara 1957-60, Dakar 1961-63, Bonn 1968-72, dep govr Gibraltar 1978-81, under-sec Cabinet Off 1981-84, asst under-sec of State For and Cwlth Off 1984-86, ambass to Austria and concurrently head of UK delgn to negotiations on mutual reduction of forces and armaments and associated measures in Centl Europe 1986-89, ambass to Belgium 1989-; *Recreations* hill walking; *Clubs* Travellers'; *Style*— Robin O'Neill, Esq, CMG; c/o FCO, King Charles St, London SW1A 2AH

O'NEILL, Hon Shane Sebastian Clanaboy; s and h of 4 Baron O'Neill, TD, DL; *b* 25 July 1965; *Educ* Eton, RAC Cirencester; *Style*— The Hon Shane O'Neill

O'NEILL, Hon Mrs Nial; Virginia Lois; *née* Legge; da of John Douglas Legge, MC, former Capt Coldstream Gds (s of Lt-Col Hon Edward Legge, sometime asst serjeant-at-arms House of Commons and 3 s of 4 Earl of Dartmouth); *b* 5 May 1922; *m* 21 June 1966, Hon Nial O'Neill (d 1980), 3 and yst s of 1 Baron Rathcavan, PC; *Style*— The Hon Mrs Nial O'Neill; Crowfield House, Crowfield, Ipswich, Suffolk IP6 9TP

O'NEILL OF THE MAINE, Baron (Life Peer UK 1970); Hon Terence Marne O'Neill; PC (NI 1956), DL (Co Antrim 1948); s of Capt Hon Arthur O'Neill, of Shanes Castle, Co Antrim; bro of 3 Baron O'Neill and uncle of 4 Baron, *qv*; *b* 10 Sept 1914; *Educ* Eton; *m* 4 Feb 1944, Katharine Jean, da of William Ingham Whitaker, DL, of Pylewell Park, Lymington, by his w Hon Hilda Guilhermina, DGStJ, da of 6 Viscount Melville; 1 s, 1 da; *Career* former Capt Irish Gds; MP (U) NI Parl Bannside 1946-70; min: Home Affrs 1956, Fin 1956; PM of NI 1963-69; dir Phoenix Assur 1969-, dir Warburg Int Hldgs 1970-73; High Sheriff Co Antrim 1953; *Books* Ulster at the Cross Roads (autobiography of Terence O'Neill, PM of N Ireland 1963-69); *Clubs* Brooks's;

Style— The Rt Hon the Lord O'Neill of the Maine, PC, DL; Lisle Ct, Lymington, Hants

O'NIANS, Henry Melmoth (Hal); s of Percy Henry O'Nians (d 1957), of Tonbridge, Kent, and Agnes Aithnah, *née* Scott (d 1975); *b* 8 May 1923; *Educ* Tonbridge, Trinity Coll Oxford (BA); *m* 5 Oct 1951, Esmé Winifred, da of Arthur Cecil Howells (d 1978), of Abersychan, Mon; 3 da (Rachel (Mrs Hahn) b 1953, Judith (Mrs Stewart) b 1955, Helen b 1958); *Career* WWII RAC 1942-47; 2 Lt 141 RAC (The Buffs) 1944, Lt 1944, liaison offr HQ 31 Tank Bde 1944 (Normandy, France and Germany), 1 RTR 1945, Staff Lt Royal Mil Police Germany 1945-47; Bute Street Gallery 1956-60, 6 Ryder Street Gallery 1960-84, King Street Galleries St James's 1985-; memb Br Show Jumping Assoc; Freeman: City of London 1988, Worshipful Co of Poulters; *Recreations* swimming, art exhibitions; *Clubs* Army and Navy; *Style—* H M O'Nians, Esq; 66 Upper Berkeley St, London W! (☎ 01 724 3799); King Street Galleries, 17 King St, St James's, London SW1Y 6QV (☎ 01 930 9392/3993)

O'REGAN, (Bartholomew) Martin; s of Timothy O'Regan, RN (d 1965), of Stanmore, Middx, and Ellen, *née* Murphy (d 1981); *b* 2 Oct 1933; *Educ* Salvatorian Coll Harrow Weald, Univ of London (BSc); *m* 1, 1961 (m dis 1982), Romaulde Sabine, da of Richard Schulz; 1 s (Marc b 1962); m 2, 16 Nov 1984, Ann Patricia Lovell, da of James William Gamble Jones (d 1983), of Dublin; 1 step s (Paul Lovell b 1960), 1 step da (Sarah Lovell b 1964); *Career* Nat Serv 1959-61, cmmnd 1960, on staff 2 Div BAOR winter warfare ski-trg camp 1960-61, TA HAC 1955-59 and 1961-63, Lt (R) 1963; CA; Coopers & Lybrand 1955-63, Anglo-American Corp Africa 1963-66, dir Davies & Newman Hldgs Ltd and Dan-Air Servs Ltd 1966-78, fndr dir and chief exec Air Europe Ltd 1978-82; int aviation conslt (based Monaco) 1982-; chm: CA Students Soc of London 1958-59, SE London Accountants Gp 1980-81; memb Cncl Br Civil Aviation Standing Conf 1980-82; Freeman City of London 1977, Liveryman Worshipful Co of CAs 1977; ICA 1959, ICIA 1983, CIMA 1966; *Recreations* golf, swimming, aviation and travel; *Clubs* RAC and HAC; *Style—* Martin O'Regan, Esq; c/o Coutts & Co, 440 Strand, London WC2

O'REILLY, Francis Joseph; s of Lt-Col Charles Joseph O'Reilly, DSO, MC, (d 1952), of Naas, Co Kildare, and Dorothy Mary Martin (d 1978); *b* 15 Nov 1922; *Educ* Ampleforth, Trinity Coll Dublin (BA, BAI, LLD); *m* 1950, Teresa Mary, da of Capt John Williams, MC (d 1965), of Co Offaly, Ireland; 3 s (Charles, Peter, Paul), 7 da (Mary, Jane, Olivia, Margaret, Rose, Louise, Julie); *Career* Lt RE 1943-46, 7 Indian Divnl Engrs SE Asia Cmd 1945-46; chm: John Power & Son Ltd 1955-66, Irish Distillers Gp plc 1966-83, Player & Wills (Ireland) Ltd 1964-81, TI Irish Raleigh 1971-80, Ulster Bank Ltd 1982-; dir: Ulster Bank Ltd 1961-74 (dep chm 1974-82), Nat Westminster Bank plc 1982-, Irish Distillers Gp plc 1983-88; pres: Royal Dublin Soc 1986- (chm exec ctee 1980-86), Equestrian Fedn of Ireland 1964-79, Mktg Inst of Ireland 1983-85, Inst of Bankers in Ireland 1985-86; chllr Univ of Dublin (Trinity Coll) 1985- (pro-chllr 1983-85); Irish rep Fedn Equestre Internationale 1964-79; memb and tstee: Turf Club 1967-, Irish Nat Hunt Steeplechase Ctee 1967-; chm Kildare Hunt Club; *Recreations* foxhunting, racing, gardening, reading; *Clubs* Kildare Street & Univ (Dublin), Turf (Ireland); *Style—* Francis O'Reilly, Esq; The Glebe, Rathmore, Naas, Co Kildare, Ireland (☎ 45 62136); Ulster Bank Ltd, 33 College Green, Dublin 2, Ireland (☎ 01 777623, telex 93638)

O'RORKE, Timothy Mawdesley; s of Michael Sylvester O'Rorke, CBE; *b* 10 July 1929; *Educ* Haileybury, ISC, Queens' Coll Cambridge; *m* 1964, Anne Patricia, da of Brig Theodore Edward Dudley Kelly, CBE; 1 s, 2 da; *Career* CA with Imperial Continental Gas Assoc 1956 (sec 1969, fin dir 1972, md 1979-85); chm St Marylebone Housing Assoc 1986-; *Recreations* tennis, gardening, skiing; *Style—* Timothy O'Rorke, Esq; Denstone, Wadhurst, Sussex

O'SHAUGHNESSY, Hon Mrs (Maud Elizabeth); *née* Grosvenor; da of late 4 Baron Ebury, DSO, MC; *b* 1909; *m* 1, 1931 (m dis 1942), 2 Viscount Harcourt (d 1978); 3 da; m 2, 1942, late Lt-Col Edward O'Shaughnessy; 2 da (twins); *Style—* The Hon Mrs O'Shaughnessy; The Cottage, Buckland, Irishtown, via Northam 6401, W Aust

O'SHEA, David Michael; s of Francis Edward O'Shea (d 1954); *b* 27 Jan 1927; *Educ* St Ignatius Coll London, King's Coll London (LLB); *m* 1953, Sheila Winifred, da of late Reginald Charles Polking Lorne; 2 s; *Career* slr 1952; joined Met Police slr's dept 1956, slr Met Police 1982-87 (dep slr 1976-82), ret 1987; *Style—* David O'Shea, Esq; c/o New Scotland Yard, London SW1

O'SULLEVAN, Peter John; OBE (1977); s of late Col John Joseph O'Sullevan, DSO; *b* 3 Mar 1918; *Educ* Hawtreys, Charterhouse, Coll Alpin Switzerland; *m* 1951, Patricia, da of late Frank Duckworth of Manitoba Canada; *Career* commentator BBC TV 1946-incl: Australia, S Africa, Italy, USA; racing corr Daily Express 1950-86; *Recreations* racehorses, travel, reading, art, food and wine; *Style—* Peter O'Sullevan, Esq, OBE; 37 Cranmer Ct, Sloane Ave, London SW3 (☎ 01 584 2781)

O'SULLIVAN, Bernard Anthony; s of Michael Brendan O'Sullivan (d 1966), and Monica, *née* Thompson; *b* 23 Nov 1948; *Educ* St Benedict's Ealing, St Catharine's Coll Cambridge (MA); *Career* called to the Bar Inner Temple 1971; *Recreations* travel; *Style—* Bernard O'Sullivan, Esq; 27 Bonnington Sq, London SW8 1TF (☎ 01 820 0208); 2 Harcourt Bldgs, Temple, London EC4Y 9DB (☎ 01 583 9020)

O'SULLIVAN, Rev Mgr James; CBE (1973); s of Richard O'Sullivan (d 1957), and Ellen, *née* Ahern (d 1959); *b* 2 August 1917; *Educ* St Finnbarr's Coll Cork, All Hallows Coll Dublin; *Career* cmmnd Royal Army Chaplains Dept 1942, chaplain 49 Div Normandy 1944, sr chaplain (RC) Malaya 1952-54, chaplain Irish Gds 1954-56, princ chaplain MOD 1968-73, officiating chaplain to RAMC and QA Trg Centres 1973-; *Style—* The Rev Mgr O'Sullivan, CBE; Osgil, Vicarage Lane, Ropley, Alresford, Hants

O'SULLIVAN, (Carrol Austin) John (Naish); CB (1973); s of Dr Carrol Naish O'Sullivan (d 1929); *b* 24 Jan 1915; *Educ* Mayfield Coll, Univ of London; *m* 1939, Lillian Mary, *née* Molineux; 1 s, 1 da; *Career* admitted slr 1936, asst public tstee 1966-71, public tstee 1971-75; *Recreations* crosswords, and the hobby of the moment; *Style—* John O'Sullivan, Esq, CB; 13 Orchid Place, S Woodham Ferrers, Chelmsford, CM3 5LQ (☎ 0245 321530)

O'SULLIVAN, John Conor; s of James Vincent O'Sullivan (d 1976), of Harley St, London, and Maura O'Connor; *b* 25 Sept 1932; *Educ* Ampleforth, Oriel Coll Oxford (MA), Westminster Hosp Med Sch (BM, BCh); *m* 26 April 1958, Maureen, da of Douglas Charles Mitchell (d 1977), of Wembley; 1 s (Hugh b 1966), 3 da (Marika b 1959, Claire b 1960, Catherine b 1962); *Career* Nat Serv RAMC 1960-62, dep asst dir Med Serv HQ London dist, T/Maj 1961; conslt obstetrician and gynaecologist Central Middx Hosp 1974-86, conslt in gynaecological oncology Hammersmith Hosp 1976-84, sr lectr Royal Postgraduate Sch Inst Obstetrics and Gynaecology 1984-; Freeman City of London 1955, Liveryman Worshipful of Apothecaries; FRCS 1967, FRCOG 1983; *Recreations* golf, skiing; *Clubs* Royal Wimbledon GC; *Style—* John O'Sullivan, Esq; 96 Arthur Rd, Wimbledon, London SW19 7DT (☎ 01 946 6242); 114 Harley St, London W1 (☎ 01 580 6966)

O'SULLIVAN, Hon Mrs (Lesley Priscilla); *née* Ross; er da of Baron Ross of Newport (Life Peer), *qv*; *b* 2 Nov 1950; *m* Finian O'Sullivan; 44 Station Road, Netley, Southampton

O'TOOLE, Peter; s of Patrick Joseph O'Toole; *b* 1932; *Educ* RADA; *m* Sian Phillips (m dis); 2 da; *Career* actor; with Bristol Old Vic Co 1955-58; artistic dir Royal Alexander Theatre Co 1978; *Clubs* Garrick; *Style—* Peter O'Toole Esq; cøo Veerline Ltd, 54 Baker St, London W1M 1DJ (☎ 01 486 5888)

OAKELEY, Anne-Marie, Lady; Anne-Marie; *née* Dennis; da of Etienne Pierre Felix Dennis (d 1922), a cotton merchant of Le Havre, Seine Maritime, France, and Annabella Agnes Wilson; *m* 1, late Terence McKenna; 1 da (Virginia McKenna, actress *qv*, m Bill Travers); m 2, Jack Drummond Rudd (m dis); m 3, 1957, as his 3 w, Sir Charles Richard Andrew Oakeley, 6 Bt (d 1959); *Career* professional pianist; composes music under the name of Anne de Nys; *Style—* Anne-Marie, Lady Oakeley; 31 Residence de la Garoupe, Boulevard de la Garoupe, 06600 Cap d'Antibes, France (☎ 93 6138 63)

OAKELEY, Dr Henry Francis; s of Rowland Henry Oakeley, of Gower Bank, Littleworth, Chipping Campden, Glos, and Diana Margaret, *née* Hayward; *b* 22 July 1941; *Educ* Clifton, St Thomas' Hosp Med Sch, London Univ (MB BS); *m* 20 Jan 1968 (m dis 1988), Penelope Susan, da of Dr Wilfred Barlow; 2 s (Matthew Thomas b 15 Dec 1968, Edward James b 29 March 1970), 1 da (Rachel Mary b 15 Jan 1973); *Career* house offr and sr house offr 1965-69: St Thomas' Hosp, Nat Hosp Queen Sq, Frenchay Hosp; registrar 1970-72: St Thomas' Hosp Maudsley Hosp, St Georges Hosp; sr registrar Maudsley Hosp 1972-73, conslt psychiatrist St Thomas' Hosp 1973-; awarded AM/RHS for: Lycaste Locusta (Penny) 1978 and Lycaste Ciliata (St Thomas') 1989; former sec historical section RSM, former chm Lambeth Caring Houses Tst, chm psychiatrists ctee St Thomas' Hosp, memb Orchid Soc of Great Br; Freeman: Worshipful Co of Apothecaries 1974, City of London 1980; MRCP 1969, MRCPsych 1972; *Books* Psychiatric Emergencies in Metabolic Diseases (contrib 1980), Richard Oakeley Royalist and Country Gentleman 1580-1653 (1989); *Recreations* orchids, gardening, badminton, history of medicine, genealogy; *Clubs* Wimbledon Squash & Badminton; *Style—* Dr Henry Oakeley; St Thomas' Hosp, London SE1 7EH (☎ 01 928 9292)

OAKELEY, Sir John Digby Atholl; 8 Bt (GB 1790), of Shrewsbury; s of Sir Atholl Oakeley, 7 Bt, (d 1987); *b* 27 Nov 1932; *Educ* private tutor; *m* 1,1958, Maureen Frances, da of John Cox (d 1965), of Hamble Hants; 1 s (Robert), 1 da (Marina) and his 2 w, Patricia Mabel Mary, *née* Birtchell; *Heir* s, Robert John Atholl Oakeley b 13 Aug 1963; *Career* md Freedom Yachts Int Ltd; competed in Nat, Euro and World Championships in numerous sailing craft incl 12 metre, rep GB in Olympics (sailing); author; *Books* Winning, Downwind Sailing, Sailing Manual; *Recreations* sailing (yacht Freedom Flight); *Clubs* Royal Southern YC, Cruising Assoc; *Style—* Sir John Oakeley; 10 Bursledon Heights, Long Lane, Bursledon, Hants (☎ 042 121 3497); Freedom Yachts International Ltd, Portsmouth Rd, Lowford, nr Southampton, Hants (☎ 042 121 5197, telex 477575)

OAKES, Sir Christopher; 3 Bt (UK 1939), of Nassau, Bahama Islands; s of Sir Sydney Oakes, 2 Bt (d 1966); *b* 10 July 1949; *Educ* Bredon Tewkesbury, Georgia Military Acad USA; *m* 1978, Julie Dawn, da of Donovan Cowan, of Canada; 1 s, 1 da; *Heir* s, Victor Oakes b 7 March 1983; *Style—* Sir Christopher Oakes, Bt; PO Box SS 5529, Nassau, Bahamas

OAKES, Rt Hon Gordon James; PC (1979), MP (Lab) Halton 1983-; s of James Oakes (d 1957), of Widnes, and Florence, *née* Hewitt (d 1949); *b* 22 June 1931; *Educ* Wade Deacon Sch Widnes, Univ of Liverpool (BA); *m* 11 Sept 1952, Esther, da of Joseph O'Neill (d 1976), of Widnes; 3 s (Howard b 1956, Timothy b 1960, Julian b 1963); *Career* slr 1956; Mayor Widnes 1964-65 (memb borough cncl 1952-), chm Widnes Lab Pty 1953-58; contested (Lab): Bebington 1959, Manchester Moss Side (by-election) 1961; MP (Lab): Bolton W 1964-70, Widnes 1971-1983; parly under-sec: Environment 1974-76, Energy 1976; min state DES 1976-79, oppn front bench spokesman Environment 1970-74 (incl local govt) and 1979-; memb: Br delgn NATO Parliamentarians 1967-70, Race Relations Select Ctee 1969-70, NW Regnl Exec Lab Pty, Cwlth Parly Assoc Exec Ctee 1979-; vice-pres: Inst of Public Health Insprs, ACC 1983-, Bldg Soc Assoc 1984-; *Recreations* caravanning, travel; *Style—* The Rt Hon Gordon Oakes, MP; House of Commons, London SW1A 0AA (☎ 01 219 4139)

OAKES, Harry Philip; s of late Sir Harry Oakes, 1 Bt and hp of n, Sir Christopher Oakes, 3 Bt; *b* 30 August 1932; *m* 1958, Christiane, da of Rudolf Botsch, of Hamburg, Germany; 3 s, 1 da; *Style—* Harry Oakes, Esq; P O Box N222, Nassau, Bahamas

OAKES, James Scudamore; s of George Clifton Oakes (d 1933), of Njoro River Farm, Njoro, Kenya, and May Elizabeth, *née* Scudamore (d 1970); descendent of Lt-Col O H Oakes of Nowton Court, Bury St Edmunds; see Burke's Landed Gentry 18 Edn Vol II; *b* 13 July 1927,Nakuru, Kenya; *Educ* Wellington, Trinity Coll Oxford (MA); *m* 17 March 1956, Gillian Walsham, da of Lt-Col Henry Richard Hopking, (Suffolk Regt, d 1965), of Monks Vineyard, Nowton, Bury St Edmunds, Suffolk; 1 s (Christopher b 1957), 2 da (Victoria b 1960, Caroline b 1961); *Career* Nat Serv Fleet Air Arm RN 1945-48, Col Engr and Tport Staff Corps RE (TA) 1985-; joined asst engr Kennedy and Donkin 1952-57, gp and res engr Hunterston Nuclear Power Station Ayreshire 1957-64, res engr Cockenzie Power Station 1964-68 (ptnr 1965-86, gp conslt 1987-); FIMechE, FIEE, MAce; *Recreations* shooting, fishing, tennis; *Style—* James Oakes, Esq; Hoppery Hill, Headley, Hants GU35 8TB (☎ 0428 712583); Westbrook Mills, Godalming, Surrey (☎ 04868 25900, telex 859373 KDHOG, fax 04868 25136)

OAKES, Stephen Rodney; s of Brian Ernest Oakes; *b* 24 Oct 1948; *Educ* Alcester GS; *m* 1969, (m dis 1983), Rina Margaret, *née* Lovett; 1 s (Mark Alan b 1976), 1 da (Lyndsay Marie b 1973); *Career* fin accountant, co sec, fin dir, md; *Recreations* golf, DIY, chess; *Style—* Stephen Oakes, Esq; To-will-o's, Snitterfield Road, Bearley, Stratford upon Avon, (☎ 0789 762601)

OAKES, William Lyness; OBE (1987); s of William Lyness Oakes (d 1964), and Hilda Mary *née* Hardy (d 1970); *b* 20 Feb 1919; *Educ* Bedford Sch, Guy's Hosp (LDS, RCS); *m* 1, 1 Oct 1942, Joan Anne (d 1972), da of the late Maj T L Squires, OBE; 1 s

(Robert b 1948), 2 da (Wendy b 1944, Susan b 1950); m 2, 2 Feb 1974, Helen Patricia, da of Howard Green, of Bussage, Stroud, Glos; *Career* dental surgn RN 1942-46; in private practice 1946-81; hon dental surgn: Glocester Infirmary 1947-48, Horton Rd Hosp 1947-48; chm Glos Local Dental Ctee 1968-80, former memb SW Region Dental Advsy ctee, chm Glos Family Practitioner Ctee 1977-(memb 1974-), memb Glos CC 1981-, chm Glos Tourist Jt Ctee 1986-, exec memb Heart of Eng Tourist Bd 1981-(chm devpt ctee 1986-); *Recreations* gardening, music, meeting people; *Style—* William Oakes, Esq, OBE; Birds Frith Farm, Far Oakbridge, Stroud, Glos, GL6 7PB (☎ 028576 482); Oakes House, 53-59 London Rd, Gloucester GL1 3HE

OAKFORD, Colin Richard; s of Percy D Oakford (d 1963), and Constance Mary G Oakford, *née* Newman; paternal connections with construction of GWR tunnel at Box Wiltshire; *b* 9 August 1944; *Educ* Hardyes Sch Dorchester, Birmingham Sch of Arch (dip arch); *Career* sr architect Stockbuild Ltd 1967-71, private practice 1971; dir design bld co 1986; BIRM, ARIBA; *Recreations* watching rugby, squash, walking, architecture; *Clubs* Old Hardyeans, Dorchester; *Style—* Colin Oakford, Esq; 34 Maiden St, Weymouth; Le Vaujoint, Chielle 37190 Azay Le Rideau

OAKLEY, Andrew; s of Donald William Oakley, of Birmingham, and Minnie Andrews; *b* 4 Mar 1940; *Educ* King Edward VI GS Birmingham, Univ of Birmingham (B Comm); *m* 24 Nov 1978, Patricia May, da of Thomas O'Connell; *Career* Ernst and Whinney: joined Birmingham 1965, London 1970-, ptnr 1971-85, ptnr with nat responsibility for high tech 1985-88, practice devpt ptnr 1988-; ICEAW: memb Auditing Practises Ctee, memb of cncl 1986-, chm of info tech gp; ACA (1965), BCS (1968), FCA (1970), FBCS (1970); *Recreations* travel, gastronomy, occasional golf and chess; *Style—* Andrew Oakley, Esq; Ernst & Whinney, Becket House, 1 Lambeth Palace Rd, London SE1 7EU (☎ 01 928 2000 ext 3372, fax 01 928 1345, telex 885234)

OAKLEY, Christopher John; s of Ronald Oakley (d 1963), of Tunbridge Wells, Kent, and Joyce Barbara Oakley, *née* Tolhurst; *b* 11 Nov 1941; *Educ* The Skinners Sch Tunbridge Wells Kent; *m* 1962, (m dis 1986) Linda Margarets Viney, da of William John Edward Viney, of Tunbridge Wells, Kent; *Career* ed: Liverpool Echo 1983-, Lancashire Evening Post 1981-83; dep ed Yorkshire Post 1976-81; dir: Lancashire Evening Post Ltd 1982-83, Liverpool Daily Post and Echo Ltd 1983-; *Style—* Christopher Oakley, Esq; 54 Merrilocks Rd, Blundellsands, Liverpool L23 6UW (☎ 051 924 6927); Liverpool Daily Post and Echo Ltd, Old Hall St, Liverpool

OAKLEY, Geoffrey Michael Whittall; s of Harold Whittall Oakley, of St Martins, Guernsey, and Hazel Louise, *née* Peters; *b* 22 April 1953; *Educ* Oundle; *m* 3 April 1987, Joanna Helen, da of Fred Morgan Hodges, of Harborne, Birmingham; 1 s (Nicholas Frederick James b 1989), 1 da (Georgina Louise b 1987); *Career* ptnr Margetts & Addenbrooke 1977-86; dir: (non-exec) Aero Needles Gp plc 1976-84, (non-exec) Margetts Fin Servs Ltd 1985, Nat Investmt Gp plc 1986; memb: Stock Exchange 1976, Int Stock Exchange 1976; *Recreations* theatre, local history, antiques; *Style—* Geoffrey Oakley, Esq; St Mary's Close, 10 St Mary's Rd, Harborne, Birmingham B17 OHA (☎ 021 427 7150); Margetts & Addenbrooke, York House, 38 Great Charles St, Birmingham B3 3JU (☎ 021 200 2002)

OAKLEY, Lt Cdr George Eric; s of George William Oakley (d 1938), and Gertrude Louisa, *née* Baker (d 1943); *b* 10 Oct 1916; *Educ* Haberdasher's Askes', Hampstead Sch; *m* 19 June 1943, Dr Margaret Dorothy, da of Rev Lionel Dudley-Brown (d 1966), of Stone Rectory, Nr Dartford; 1 s (Michael Dudley b 1944), 1 da (Cecilia Diana b 1948); *Career* RN Staff Supply Offr to Flag Offr, 2 i/c Far East Station, Staff Planning Offr admin and Staff Offr logistics to Flag Offr, Scotland and COMNORLANT ret 1962; regnl sec The Open Univ W Midlands, bursar Bingley Coll of Educn 1967, admin offr W Mids Exam Bd 1970, organiser W Mids Open Univ (ret 1981); active fund raiser; *Recreations* golf, tennis, fishing, gardening; *Style—* Lt Cdr G E Oakley, RN; Otheridge Pool Cottage, Clifton-upon-Teme, Worcs

OAKLEY, Harold Whittall; s of William Edwin Oakley (d 1939), and Emma Florence Whittall (d 1954); *b* 4 Oct 1906; *Educ* Bishop Vesey's Sch, Sutton Coldfield; *m* 27 April 1946, Hazel Louise Peters; 1 s (Geoffrey), 1 da (Christine); *Career* Maj Cmdg 21 Army Gp RAOC NW Europe 1941-45; memb Stock Exchange 1938-81, sr ptnr Margetts and Addenbrooke 1950-77, vice-chm Glynwed Int plc 1967-73; govr Sir John Moore Sch Fndn 1970-87 (vice-chm 1986-87), hon tres Atherstone Hunt 1972-78, life govr RNLI; *Recreations* hunting, reading, music; *Clubs* Atherstone; *Style—* Harold Oakley, Esq; La Cloture, Coin Colin, St Martins, Guernsey CI (☎ Guernsey 35118)

OAKLEY, John Davidson; CBE (1980), DFC (1944); s of Richard Oakley and Nancy Mary Oakley; *b* 15 June 1921; *m* 1943, Georgina Mary, da of George Curzon Hare; 2 s; *Career* Sqdn Ldr RAF; formerly with Ford Motor Co, then Standard Triumph (Liverpool) Ltd; md: Copeland & Jenkins Ltd 1963-71, R Woolf & Co Ltd 1964-67; gp md L Sterne & Co 1967-69; chm: General Electric & Mechanical Systems Ltd 1970-73, Berwick Timpo Ltd 1970-82, Edgar Allen Balfour Ltd 1974-79, Australian Br Trade Assoc 1977-81; former dir: Blairs Ltd, Eagle & Globe Steel Ltd NSW, Nexos Office Systems Ltd; chm Grosvenor Devpt Capital Ltd 1981-, chm Berwick Timpo Toys to May 1982, chm Robert Jenkins Holdings Ltd 1983-, dep chm Gardners Transformers Ltd 1983-; dir: Beau Brummel Ltd 1972-84, Isis Industl Servs plc 1982-, Ionian Securities 1978-; memb Br Overseas Trade Advsy Cncl 1977-; chm Grosvenor Technol Fund 1985; memb Essex Cnty Cncl 1982-85; FRSA, FBIM, MIBCAM, FInstPS; *Recreations* golf, walking, tennis, bridge, politics; *Clubs* Reform, RAF, Bishop's Stortford Golf; *Style—* John Oakley Esq, CBE, DFC; 25 Manor Links, Bishop's Stortford, Herts CM23 5RA (☎ 0275 507552)

OAKLEY, Michael Dudley; s of Lt Cdr George Eric Oakley RN, of Clifton on Teme Worcester, and Dr Margaret Dudley, *née* Brown; *b* 5 Nov 1944; *Educ* Oundle Sch, Coll of Law; *m* 7 Oct 1967, Jennifer Catherine, da of Richard Percy Lazenby (d Nov 1987), of Oak Cottage Bulmer, York; 2 da (Catherine S b 2 Nov 1969, Victoria J b 6 Nov 1971), 1 s (William T D b 3 Oct 1973); *Career* slr; ptnr Denison Till; HM coroner N Yorks 1979-; lay memb Gen Synod C of E representing diocese of York 1980-; memb: Cncl of Archbishop of York, Working Party on Ordination of Women to the Priesthood, Cathedral Statutes Cmmn, various legislative revision ctees, panel of chm of Gen Synod; notary public 1985-; *Recreations* tennis, swimming, fishing, shooting; *Clubs* Yorkshire, East India; *Style—* Michael Oakley, Esq; Rose Cottage, Oswaldkirk, York YO6 5XT (☎ 04393 339); 4 Old Malton Gate, Malton, N Yorks YO17 0EQ (☎ 0653 600070, fax 0653 600049, car tel 0836 605902)

OAKLEY, Dr Nigel Wingate; s of Dr Wilfrid George Oakley, of London, and Hermione Violet Oakley; *b* 6 Dec 1933; *Educ* Rugby Sch, Kings Coll Cambridge (MA, MD); *m* 20 Oct 1962, Nicole Paule, da of Albert Mertz (d 1975); 1 da (Francesca b 1963); *Career* conslt Physician, St George's Hosp London, hon sr lectr St George's Hosp Med Sch, conslt Physician St Luke's Hosp for the Clergy; previously dep dir Metabolic Unit St Mary's Hosp London and Nuffield Fell in Med Univ of Pittsburgh; first reserve Br Olympic Rifle Team 1956, world individual Small-Bore Rifle Champion (50m), world Rifle Championships Moscow 1958, memb Br Int Small Bore Rifle Teams 1952-58; *Recreations* music, rifle shooting, DIY; *Clubs* RSM; *Style—* Dr Nigel W Oakley; The Homestead, London SW13 9HL (☎ 01 741 3311); 84 Harley Street, London W1N 1AE (☎ 01 580 9771)

OAKLEY, (Horace) Roy; CBE (1977); s of Horace William Oakley (d 1977), of Luton, and Beatrice Ann, *née* Parker (d 1973); *b* 26 Dec 1920; *Educ* Ashton GS Dunstable, UCL (BSc, MSc); *m* 1 Sept 1949, Evelyn Elsie, da of Joseph Albert Mariner, JP (d 1970); 1 s (Richard b 1956), 3 da (Elizabeth b 1953, Susan b 1957, Katherine b 1961); *Career* WWII cmmnd RE and served NW Europe (despatches) 1943-46, TAVR served Engr and Tport Staff Corps (Maj 1970, Col 1981, ret 1985); lectr UCL 1948-52 sr ptnr JD DM Watson (now Watson Hawksley) 1969-85 (ptnr from 1952); memb cncl: ICE 1969-75, UCL 1977-87; bd memb Br Standards Inst 1982-88, vice pres Construction Indust Res & Inf Assoc 1986- (chm 1982-86), pres Inst of Water Pollution Control 1983-84; FICE 1960, FIWEN 1970, FEng 1984 (memb cncl 1987); *Recreations* sport, walking, gardening, painting; *Style—* Roy Oakley, Esq, CBE; 53 The Park, St Albans, Herts AL1 4RX (☎ 0727 55 928); Terriers House, Amersham Rd, High Wycombe, Bucks (☎ 0494 26 240)

OAKLEY, Stephen Edward; s of Stanley Edward Oakley, of 246 Willow Rd, Enfield, Middlesex, and Maureen Rose Oakley, *née* Carr; *b* 19 June 1952; *Educ* Ambrose Fleming Tech GS, Enfield, Middlesex; *m* 1975, Patricia Anne, da of Francis John Hyde, of 4 Saxon Rd, Wheathampstead, Hertfordshire; 1 s (Marc Stephen Edward b 1986), 1 da (Laura Jane b 1981); *Career* Price Waterhouse Co 1969-79, chief and fin offr Mitsubishi Electric (UK) Ltd 1979-84, dir United Merchants plc 1984-88, gp fin dir Macarthy plc 1988-; FCA, ATII; *Recreations* soccer; *Style—* Stephen E Oakley; 31 Earlings Rd, Harpenden, Hertfordshire AL5 2AW (☎ 0582 761 200); MaCarthy plc, Delta House, 33 Hockcliffe St, Leighton Buzzard Bedfordshire (☎ 0525 850 470, fax 0525 382 381, care tel 0836 535 066)

OAKSEY, 2 Baron (UK 1947), and 4 Baron Trevethin (UK 1921); John Geoffrey Tristram Lawrence; OBE, JP; known as Lord Oaksey; s of 3 and 1 Baron Trevethin and Oaksey, DSO, TD (d 1971); *see* also Gp Capt Hugh S L Dundas; *b* 21 Mar 1929; *Educ* Eton, New Coll Oxford, Yale Law Sch; *m* 1, 1959 (m dis 1987), Victoria Mary, da of Maj John Dennistoun, MBE (d 1980); 1 s (Hon Patrick), 1 da (Hon Sara Victoria b 1961); m 2, 7 March 1988, Mrs Rachel Crocker; *Heir* s, Hon Patrick John Tristram Lawrence b 29 June 1960; *Career* P/O RAFVR and Lt 9 Lancers; racing corr to: Daily Telegraph (as 'Marlborough') 1957-, Sunday Telegraph 1961-88, Horse and Hound (as 'Audax') 1959-88; columnist Racing Post 1988-; commentator for ITV on Racing (World of Sport) 1969-, Channel Four; pres: Amateur Boxing Assoc, York Univ Turf Club; dir HTV; *Recreations* riding, skiing; *Clubs* Brooks's; *Style—* The Rt Hon the Lord Oaksey, OBE, JP; Hill Farm, Oaksey, Malmesbury, Wilts (☎ 066 67 303)

OAKSHOTT, Hon Sir Anthony Hendrie; 2 Bt (UK 1959), of Bebington, Co Palatine of Chester; s of Baron (and 1 Bt) Oakshott, MBE (Life Peer, d 1975); *b* 10 Oct 1929; *Educ* Rugby; *m* 1965 (m dis 1981), Valerie, formerly w of (1) Donald Ross and (2) Michael de Pret-Roose, and da of Jack Vlasto, of Hurst, Berks; *Heir* bro, Hon Michael Oakshott; *Clubs* White's; *Style—* The Hon Sir Anthony Oakshott, Bt; 42 Eaton Sq, London SW1 (☎ 01 235 2107); Beckley House, Bledington, Oxfordshire (☎ 06087 527)

OAKSHOTT, Hon Michael Arthur John; s of Baron Oakshott (Life Peer) and 1 Bt (d 1975); hp to Baronetcy of bro, Hon Sir Anthony Oakshott, 2 Bt; *b* 12 April 1932; *Educ* Rugby; *m* 1, 27 April 1957, Christina Rose Methuen (d 1985), da of late Thomas Banks, of Solai, Kenya; 3 s (Thomas Hendrie b 1959, Charles Michael b 1961, Angus Withington b 1965); m 2, April 1988, Helen Clare Jones, da of late Edward Ravell, of Woodhall Spa, Lincs; *Style—* The Hon Michael Oakshott; Isletower, Holywood, Dumfries DG2 0RW (☎ 0387 720596, fax 0387 721234)

OATES, Christine Tate; da of Herbert Johnson Oates (d 1963), of 6 The Parade, Truro, Cornwall, and Louisa Elizabeth, *née* Tate (d 1953); *b* 13 Jan 1913; *Educ* Bradford Girls' GS, Bradford Regnl Coll of Art, Royal Coll of Art (ARCA, ATD); *Career* art teacher: Ely HS 1939-43, Lancaster Girls' GS 1943-45, Truro HS 1945-70; painter and graphic artist 1970-; books illustrated incl: Especially Holly, Pydar Street and the High Cross Area (1974, second edn 1981), Princes Street and the Quay Area (1976), Boscawen Street Area (1978, second edn 1988), Lemon Street and its Neighbourhood (1983), River Street and its Neighbourhood (1985), From Moresk Road to Malpas (1988); major retrospective exhibition of paintings Royal Inst of Cornwall Art Gallery 1988; assoc: Penwith Soc of Artists St Ives, Newlyn Soc of Artists; memb: Truro Art Soc, Royal Inst of Cornwall, Truro Civic Soc, Nat Tst, Truro Old Cornwall Soc, Cornwall Bldgs Preservation Tst, Friends of the Earth, World Wildlife Fund, Truro HS Old Girls' Assoc, Nat Art Collections Fund, Cornwall Arts Centre Tst, Truro Bldgs Res GP, Newlyn Orion Galleries; hon life memb Nat Soc for Educn in Art and Design 1970-; FIAL 1959, The Truro City Trail (with illustrations by the author, 1984); *Recreations* gardening, conservation; *Clubs* Osarca, Saga; *Style—* Miss Christine Tate Oates; 6 The Parade, Truro, Cornwall TR1 1QE (☎ 0872 724 17)

OATES, Rev Canon John; s of John Oates (d 1964), of Yorkshire, and Ethel, *née* McCann (d 1959); *b* 14 May 1930; *Educ* Queen Elizabeth Sch Wakefield, Soc of the Sacred Mission Kelham; *m* 16 Jan 1962, Sylvia Mary, da of Herbert Charles Harris (d 1977), of Rickmansworth, Herts; 3 s (Jeremy b 20 Aug 1963, Alistair b 19 May 1968, Jonathan b 28 Dec 1969), 1 da (Rebecca b 6 Feb 1966); *Career* curate Eton Coll Mission Hackney Wick 1957-60, devpt offr C of E Youth Cncl and memb staff Bd of Educn 1960-64, devpt sec C of E Cncl for Cwlth Settlement 1964-65 (gen sec 1965-70), sec C of E Ctee on Migration and Int Affairs 1969-71, vicar Richmond Surrey 1970-84, rural dean Richmond and Barnes 1979-84, rector St Bride's Fleet St 1984-; commissary: of Archbishop of Perth W Aust and Bishop of N W Aust 1968-75, to Archibishop of Jerusalem 1969-75, to Bishop of Bunbury 1969-; hon canon Bunbury 1969-; chaplain: Press Club, Inst of Journalists, Inst of PR, Publicity Club of London; pres Richmond and Barnes Mental Health Assoc 1972-74; Freeman City of London, Chaplain Worshipful Co of Marketers; *Recreations* walking, travel, squash, broadcasting; *Clubs* Athenaeum, London Press, Wig and Pen; *Style*— The Rev Canon John Oates; St Bride's Rectory, Fleet St, London EC4Y 8AU (☎ 01 583 0239, 01 353 1301)

OATES, Sir Thomas; CMG (1962), OBE (1958), MBE (1946); er s of Thomas Oates, of Wadebridge, Cornwall; *b* 5 Nov 1917; *Educ* Callington GS Cornwall, Trinity Coll Cambridge (MA); *Career* Admty Scientific Staff 1940-46, temp Lt RNVR; entered Colonial Admin Serv 1948, seconded to HM Treasy 1953, fin sec Br Honduras 1955, Aden 1959-63, dep high cmmr Aden and Protectorate of S Arabia 1963-67, perm sec Gibraltar 1968-69, dep govr Gibraltar 1969-71, govr and C-in-C St Helena 1971-76; kt 1972; *Recreations* photography; *Clubs* East India, Royal Cwlth Soc; *Style*— Sir Thomas Oates, CMG, OBE; Tristan, Trevone, Padstow, Cornwall

OATLEY, Sir Charles William; OBE (1956); s of William Oatley (d 1944); *b* 14 Feb 1904; *Educ* Bedford Modern Sch, St John's Coll Cambridge (MA); *m* 1930, (Dorothy) Enid, *née*, West; 2 s; *Career* lectr and reader engrg dept Cambridge Univ 1945-60 (prof of electrical engrg 1960-71, emeritus prof 1971-), fell Trinity Coll Cambridge 1945-; FRS (Royal Medal 1969, Mullard Award 1973), FEng, FIEE, FIEEE; Foreign Assoc, Nat Acad of Engrg USA 1979; kt 1974; *Clubs* Athenaeum; *Style*— Sir Charles Oatley, OBE; 16 Porson Rd, Cambridge CB2 2EU (☎ 0223 356194)

OATLEY, Clive; s of James William Oatley OBE, of Burcote, Inglewood Park, St Lawrence, Isle of Wight, and Christina Margaret Oatley, *née* Webb; *b* 3 April 1938; *Educ* St Paul's, St Catharine's Coll Cambridge (MA); *m* 1, 1963; 1 s (Maxwell James); m 2, 1980, Brooke Randolph, da of Hon Joseph Simpson Farland, former US ambass to Panama, Pakistan and Iran, Virginia USA; 1 s (Maxwell b 1976), 1 da (Virginia b 1977); *Career* Lt 5 Royal Inniskilling Dragoon Gds 1956-58; chm: Bridge Oil Gp of Cos, Belgravia Int Trading SA; *Recreations* golf, tennis; *Clubs* Hawks, Royal Wimbledon Golf, RAC, Monaco Yacht; *Style*— Clive Oatley, Esq; Offices: Bridge Oil Ltd, 140 Brompton Road, SW3; Belgravia Int Ltd, 29 Chesham Place, SW1 (☎ 01 235 9555)

OATTS, Lt-Col Lewis Balfour; DSO (1945); s of John Henry Oatts (d 1929), and Florence Eleanor Brydges Jones (d 1919); *b* 6 April 1902; *Educ* Bedford Sch, RMC Sandhurst; *m* 20 Jan 1934, Marcia Cherry, da of William Morris (d 1945); 2 s (James b 1939, Michael b 1948), 1 da (Lindsay b 1935); *Career* army offrs cmmnd HLI 1922, cmd Chin Levies, Burma Campaign 1942-45, raised and cmd Chin Rifles 1945-47, cmd 71 Primary Trg Centre 1947-49; elected King's Bodyguard for Scotland (Royal Co of Archers) 1951; *Books* Proud Heritage (history of HLI, 4 vols), History of the Carabiniers, Emperor's Chambermaids (history 14/20 Kings' Hussars), Famous Regiments, The Jungle in Arms; *Recreations* hunting, shooting; *Style*— Lt-Col Lewis B Oatts, DSO; Temple House Bungalow, Arbury, Nuneaton, Warwickshire (☎ 0203 347478)

OBOLENSKY, Prof Sir Dimitri; s of Prince Dimitri Obolensky (d 1964), of Antibes, France, and Mary, *née* Countess Shuvalov; descended from Rurik, the Scandinavian fndr of the Russian state in 862, whose dynasty ruled Russia until 1598; *b* 1 April 1918; *Educ* Lycée Pasteur (Paris), Trinity Coll Cambridge (MA, PhD), Oxford (DLitt); *m* 1947, Elisabeth Lopukhin; *Career* univ lectr in Slavonic studies Cambridge 1946-48, student and fell of Christ Church 1950-85, prof of Russian and Balkan history Oxford 1961-85 (reader Russian and Balkan medieval history 1949-61); visiting prof in many foreign univs; vice-pres British Acad 1983-85; Hon Dr Sorbonne 1980; Hon DLitt Birmingham; fell Trinity Coll Cambridge 1942-48; FBA, FSA, FRHistSoc; kt 1984; *Clubs* Athenaeum; *Style*— Prof Sir Dimitri Obolensky; 29 Belsyre Court, Woodstock Road, Oxford OX2 6HU (☎ 0865 56496)

OBOLENSKY, Prince Nikolai; s of Prince Michael Obolensky, of Madrid, Spain, and Princess Anne Obolensky, *née* Helbronner (d 1980); descends from Rurik who conquered Russia in 870s; *b* 7 June 1956; *Educ* Harrow, RMA Sandhurst, Durham Univ (BA), IMDOE Lausanne (MBA); *m* 1987, Charlotte Isabella Sharpe; *Career* Major 17/21 Lancers 1986- (cmmnd 1978, Lt 1978, Capt 1981), ret 1988; *Recreations* mountaineering, flying, athletics; *Clubs* Cavalry & Guards, Landsdowne; *Style*— Prince Nikolai Obolensky; 28 Cameron Rd, Chesham, Bucks HP5 3BS (☎ 0494 773155)

OBORNE, Brig John Douglas; s of Lt Col T D Oborne, DSO (d 1985), and Elsie Cottrill, *née* Booth; *b* 28 Feb 1928; *Educ* Wellington Coll, Sandhurst RMC; *m* 9 Oct 1954, Margaret Elizabeth, da of Cdr A R P Brown (d 1973); 3 s (Peter Alan b 1957, Nicholas David b 1961, James Richard b 1963); *Career* Br Army cmmnd into 4/7 Royal Dragoon Gds 1948; Staff Coll Camberley 1961, Jt Servs Staff Coll 1968, Br Liason Offr US Army Armor Centre Fort Knox 1969-71, chief instr Junior Div Staff Coll 1971-73, cdr Br Army Trg Team in Sudan 1973-75, def advsr Br High Cmmn India 1977-80, vice pres Regular Cmmns Bd 1980-82; ADC to The Queen 1980-82; Def Attaché Br Embassy Dublin 1984-; *Recreations* walking, golf, travel; *Clubs* Cavalry and Guards, Kildare Street, Univ of Dublin; *Style*— Brig John D Oborne; Br Embassy, 33 Merrion Road, Dublin 4, Republic of Ireland (☎ 695211)

OCKENDEN, Brig Robert Vaughan (Rob); CBE (1982, OBE 1977); s of William Ockenden (d 1983), of Chigwell, Essex, and Norah Vaughan, *née* Paterson (d 1981); *b* 14 April 1933; *Educ* Chigwell Sch, RMA; *m* 13 April 1963, Patricia Alice Walker Taylor, da of Robert Cauwood (d 1987), of Wheal Vor, Cornwall; 1 s (Paul b 1967), 1 da (Jessica b 1969); *Career* cmmnd 2 RTR 1953, Col Staff Offr to QMG 1979-82, Col Staff Offr to SACEUR 1983-85, dir Def Operational Requirements 1985-88; chief exec NRA 1988-; FBIM 1988; *Recreations* the countryside, bird watching, gardening, motoring; *Clubs* Army & Navy; *Style*— Brig Rob Ockenden, CBE; Glovers Cottage, Faversham Rd, Lenham, Kent; National Rifle Assoc, Bisley Camp, Brookwood, Woking, Surrey (☎ 04867 2213, fax 0483 797 285)

ODAM, Joseph; s of Frank Moore Odam (d 1953), and Edna Jessie Maud Miller (d 1967); *b* 8 Dec 1925; *Educ* King's Sch Peterborough, Bedford Sch, Worcester Coll Oxford (Short Mil Course); *m* 21 April 1956, Jane Margaret, da of Harold Howart (d 1956), of Curwen Woods, Burton in Kendal, Westmoreland; 2 da (Stella Jane b 1957, Josephine Ann Lucinda b 1963); *Career* Capt 1 Royal Tank Regt 1944-51, Army of Occupation, Germany, BOAR, instr RAC Centre 1949-51; dir: Sydney C Banks plc 1966-, Joseph Odam Ltd, CF Howson Ltd 1975-, Peterborough Evening Telegraph 1967-; memb Lloyds 1977; dep pres East of England Agricultural Soc 1980- (chm 1969-72, hon life vice-pres 1976-), memb exec ctee NFU Peterborough; JP 1969 (chm Peterborough bench 1985-); Liveryman of the City of London, memb Worshipful Co of Farmers 1980; Jubilee Medal (1977); shrieve of the County of Cambridgeshire 1989-; *Recreations* tennis, skiing, rugby union, hockey; *Clubs* Farmers; *Style*— Joseph Odam, Esq; Haynes Farm, Thorney Rd, Eye, Peterborough, Cambs PE6 7UA (☎ 0733 222456); Joseph Odam Ltd, Eye Mill, Eye, Peterborough (☎ 0733 222253, telex 32334)

ODDIE, Christopher Peter; s of Alfred Birtwistle Oddie, of N Lancs, and Elsie Mary, *née* Bateman; *b* 26 Sept 1948; *Educ* King Edward VII Sch Lytham Lancs; *m* 12 June 1971, Gail, da of Maj Horace George Ablett; 2 s (Simon Christopher b 19 Sept 1975, Matthew David b 1 July 1979); *Career* CA 1978; articled clerk T & H P Bee Preston 1967-72, ptnr: Tyson Westall CAs Lancs 1973-76, Grant Thornton CAs (formerly Thornton Baker) 1976-86; sr ptnr Lonsdale and Ptnrs CAs Lancaster and branches 1986-; tres Lancaster Cons Assoc, sec Lancaster Rotary Club; FICA; *Recreations* sailing; *Clubs* Royal Windermere YC; *Style*— Christopher Oddie, Esq; 10 Forgewood Drive, Halton, Lancaster, Lancs (☎ 0524 811 486); Lonsdale & Ptnrs, Priory Close, St Marys Gate, Lancaster LA1 1XB (☎ 0524 628 01, fax 0524 377 64)

ODDY, (William) Andrew; s of William Tingle Oddy (d 1985), and Hilda Florence, *née* Dalby; *b* 6 Jan 1942; *Educ* Bradford Gs, New Coll Oxford (BA, BSc, MA); *m* 4 Aug 1965, Patricia Anne, da of Albert Edward Whitaker, of Upton-upon-Severn, Worcs; 1 s (Guy b 1968), 1 da (Frances b 1970); *Career* British Museum: scientific offr 1966-69, sr scientific offr 1969-75, princ scientific offr 1975-81, hd of conservation 1981-85, keeper of conservation 1985-; author of over 150 papers, articles, notes and reviews in learned jls, ed/jt ed of the proceedings of 8 conferences; memb several learned socs and numerous ctees connected with the conservation of museum objects; Worshipful Co of Goldsmiths 1986, City of London 1986, FSA 1973; *Books* Romanesque Metalwork: Copper Alloys and their Decoration (with Susan La Niece and Neil Startford 1986); *Recreations* travel; *Style*— Andrew Oddy, Esq; 6 Ashlyns Rd, Berkhamsted, Hertforshire HP4 3BN; Dept of Conservation, The British Museum, London WC1b 3DG (☎ 01 323 8223, fax 01 323 8480, telex 94013362 BMUS G)

ODELL, Sir Stanley John; s of George Frederick Odell, and Florence May, *née* Roberts, (d 1972) ; *b* 20 Nov 1929; *Educ* Bedford Mod Sch; *m* 4 Dec 1952, (Eileen) Grace, da of Reginald Edward Percival Stuart; 4 da (Sally Strong b 1954, Carol 'Parry b 1956, Julie Warner b 1958, Susan Dawn b 1961); *Career* former chm Mid Bedfordshire Cons Assoc and Cons E Provincial Area, chm Nat Union of Cons and Unionist Assocs, chm Anglo - American ctee RAF Chicksands, chm Restoration ctee All Saints church Campton; kt 1986; *Recreations* politics, shooting; *Clubs* Farmers; *Style*— Sir Stanley Odell; Woodhall Farm, Campton, Shefford, Beds SG17 5PB (☎ 0462 813 230)

ODGERS, Graeme David William; s of William Arthur Odgers (d 1950), and Elizabeth Minty Odgers, *née* Rennie (d 1987); *b* 10 Mar 1934; *Educ* St John's Coll Johannesburg, Gonville & Caius Cambridge, Harvard Business Sch (MBA); *m* 1957, Diana Patricia Berge; 1 s (John), 2 da (Mary, Juliet) and 1 da decd; *Career* dir Keith Shipton & Co Ltd 1965-72, chm Odgers & Co (Mgmnt Consits) 1970-74, C T Bowring (Insur) Hldgs Ltd 1972-74, dir indust devpt unit Dept of Ind 1974-77, assoc dir (fin) GEC 1977-78, gp md Tarmac plc 1983-86 (gp fin dir 1979-83), Br Telecom plc: pt/t bd memb 1983-86, UK govt dir 1984-86, dep chm and chief fin offr 1986-87, gp md 1987; non exec dir Dalgety 1987-; *Recreations* tennis, golf; *Clubs* City of London; *Style*— Graeme Odgers, Esq; Brome House, High St, W Malling, Kent ME19 6NE

ODGERS, Paul Randell; CB (1970), MBE (1945), TD (1949); s of Dr Paul Norman Blake Odgers (d 1958), of Oxford, and Mabel Annie, *née* Higgins; *b* 31 July 1915; *Educ* Rugby, New Coll Oxford (MA); *m* 21 April 1944, Diana, da of Rupert Edward Francis Fawkes, CBE (d 1967), of Lechlade, Gloucestershire; 1 s (Robin (Dr Odgers) b 1948), 1 da (Caroline (Mrs Compston) b 1946); *Career* 2 Lt Oxford & Bucks LI 1939-40, Staff Capt 184 Inf Bde 1940-41, Staff Coll Camberley 1941, Staff Capt and Bde Maj Centl Inf Bde Malta 1941-42, DAAG HQ Malta Cmd 1942-43, GS02 HQ 8 Army 1943-44, GS02 Tactical HQ 21 Army Gp 1944-45; entered Bd of Educn 1937; Miny of Educn: princ 1945-48, asst sec 1948-56; asst sec Cabinet Off 1956-58, under sec Miny of Educn 1958-67, off of first Sec of State 1967-68, off of Sec of State for Soc Servs 1968-70, Cabinet Off 1970-71, dep sec DES 1971-75; memb: cncl Girl's Public Day Sch Tst 1976-, ctee GBGSA; govr St Marys C of E First Sch Haddenham, vice-pres Soc for Promotion of Roman Studies, ctee memb Haddenham Village Soc; *Clubs* United Oxford and Cambridge; *Style*— Paul Odgers, Esq, CB, MBE, TD; Stone Walls, Aston Rd, Haddenham, Bucks HP17 8AF (☎ 0844 291 830)

ODGERS, Richard Michael Douglas; DFC (1944); s of Dr Paul Norman Balke Odgers (d 1962), and Mable Annie, *née* Higgins; *b* 11 Jan 1920; *Educ* Rugby, New Coll, Oxford (MA); *m* 16 July 1949, Miriam Cholerton, da of Horace Charles Sydney Tyler; 1 s (James b 1954), 2 da (Charlotte b 1951, Clare b 1953); *Career* Capt 651 Sqdn Air OP RA Italy 1940-46; export mangr APV Co Ltd 1947-57, gen mangr Rank Orgn 1957-64, chm Curtis Brown Ltd (Literary Agents); *Recreations* sailing, skiing, music; *Clubs* Garrick, Royal Lymington YC; *Style*— Richard Odgers, Esq, DFC; The Coach House, Leeson, Langton Matravers, Swanage, Dorset BH19 3EU (☎ 0929 422636)

ODLING, Christopher Arthur; s of Harold Robert Odling (d 1975), of Esher, Surrey, and Myrtle Agnes, *née* Huband (d 1976); *b* 1 Dec 1929; *Educ* Radley, St Mary's Hosp London, Exeter Coll Oxford; *m* 6 Dec 1963, Patricia Blayney, da of Lt Col B G B Mitchell, DSC, DL, RM (d 1983), of Wiston; 1 s (Richard b 1970), 2 da (Philippa b 1964, Claire b 1966); *Career* Nat Serv Royal Warwicks Regt 1949-50; banker, Hong Kong and Shanghai Corp 1952, admin Br Bank of The M East in Oman 1981, fin mangr Gabbitas Thring Educ Tst 1982-83, admin mangr Centre for Int Briefing 1984-85; govr Sir Thomas Picton Sch Haverfordwest; asst dist cmmr Pembroke Scout Assoc (memb 1955); memb Governing Body of Church in Wales; MBIM 1977; *Recreations* scouting, walking; *Clubs* Royal Hong Kong Jockey; *Style*— Christopher A Odling, Esq; Manor House, Wiston, Haverfordwest, Dyfed SA62 4PN (☎ Clarbeston 258)

ODLING, Maj-Gen William; CB (1963), OBE (1950), MC (1942); s of Maj William Alfred Odling (d 1944), and Mary Bennett Odling, *née* Case (d 1963); *b* 8 June 1909; *Educ* Temple Grove Prep Sch, Wellington, RMA Woolwich; *m* 10 Feb 1939, Margaret, da of Soanes Gardner (d 1932); 1 s (Antony Anselm b 1942), 2 da (Mary Anne b 1940, Elizabeth Jane b 1944); *Career* cmmnd RA 1929, service mainly in India until 1938, Capt 1938, Adj & TA 1939, CRA Medagascar Force 1942, GSOI RA COSSAC 1943, NW Europe Campaign (despatches) 1944, GSO 1 W O 1945, Maj 1946, GSOI (Trg) GHQMELF 1948, AQMGMELF 1950, Lt-Col 1951, AAG Col W O 1953, Coll 1953, CRA E Anglian Div 1957, Brig 1957, Brig AQ HQ E Cmd 1959, Maj-Gen i/c Admin GHQ FELF 1961-62, Maj-Gen 1961, COS GHQ FELF 1962-64, nat govr ESU (pres E Counties Regn); fndr chm Roman River Conservation Zone, memb Bishops Cncl & Fin Ctee Diocese of Chelmsford, chm Friends of Essex Churches, tres and later vice chm RADD; many and varied sporting achievements inc: winner John Crisp (Int) Novice Cup for Skiing, runner up Kadir Cup (India) 1935, hon sec (Master) Muttra Tent Club (winner Muttra Cup), first chm Colchester Garrison Beagles 1957, Cdre Atlanta (Yacht) Owners Assoc 1974- (pres hon sec), sailed all countries to Finland; *Recreations* gardening, building, conservation and local admin; *Clubs* Army and Navy; *Style*— Maj-Gen William Odling; Gun House, Fingringhoe, Colchester CO5 7AL (☎ 020 635320)

ODLING-SMEE, John Charles; s of Rev Charles William Odling-Smee, of Brearton, N Yorks, and Katharine Hamilton, *née* Aitchison; *b* 13 April 1943; *Educ* Durham Sch, St John's Coll Cambridge (BA); *Career* res offr Inst of Econs and Statistics Oxford Univ 1968-71 and 1972-73, (asst res offr 1965-66, fell in Econs Oriel Coll Oxford 1966-70), econ res offr Govt of Ghana 1971-72, sr res offr Centre for Urban Econs LSE 1973-75, econ advsr Central Policy Review Staff 1975-77, sr econs advsr HM Treasy 1977-80, sr economist IMF 1981-82, under-sec (econs) HM Treasy 1982-; *Books* British Economic Growth 1855-1973 (with RCO Matthews and CH Feinstein, 1982); articles in learned jls; *Style*— John Odling-Smee, Esq; 107 Clapham Manor St, London SW4 6DR (☎ 01 720 5167); HM Treasury, Parliament St, London SW1P 3AG (☎ 01 270 4439)

ODLING-SMEE, Peter Guy; s of Lt-Col Alfred John Odlng-Smee, OBE (d 1987), of Newton Ferrers, nr Plymouth, Devon, and Dorothy Nancy, *née* Bowles (d 1982); *b* 30 June 1938; *Educ* Charterhouse, Britannia RNC Dartmouth; *m* 12 July 1968, Marianne, da of Grosser Helge Fischer (d 1972), of Korsor, Denmark; 2 s (Christopher b 19 Oct 1970, Michael Kristian b 22 Nov 1973); *Career* RN; Sub Lt 1959, trg HMS Victorious and minesweepers, joined RN surveying Serv 1960, specialised in hydrographic surveying worldwide i/c RN Antarctic Survey Pty 1967-68, offr responsible for initiating Radio Navigational Warnings 1970, sr inst RN Sch of Hydrographic Surveying HMS Drake Plymouth, ret Lt Cdr 1976; sr surveyor Kelvin Hughes Ltd (worked Saudi Arabia, Indonesia, Libya) 1976-79, princ Odling-Smee Oberman Assoc 1979-, sr lectr in marine sci Plymouth Poly 1982-; UK rep Advsy Bd on Standards of Competence for Hydrographic Surveyors, memb Hydrographic Surveyor's Ctee RICS; FRICS; *Recreations* horse riding, foxhunting, skiing, sailing; *Clubs* Royal Western YC; *Style*— Peter Odling-Smee, Esq; Hanger Farm, Cornwood, Nr Ivybridge, Devon PL21 9HP (☎ 075 537 370); Department of Marine Science & Technology, Institute of Marine Studies, Plymouth Polytechnic, Drake Circus, Plymouth (☎ 0752 221 312 ext 5557, 4673, fax 0752 222 792, telex 45423 PP LRC G)

OEHLERS, Maj-Gen Gordon Richard; CB (1987); s of Dr Roderick Clarke Oehlers (d 1950), and Hazel Ethne Oehlers; *b* 19 April 1933; *Educ* St Andrews Sch, Singapore; *m* 27 Oct 1956, Rosie; 1 s (Michael b 1963), 1 da (Elizabeth b 1966); *Career* cmmnd RCS 1958, UK and ME 1958-64, Adj 4 Div Signals Regt 1964-66, CO 7 Signal Regt 1973-76, cdr 1 Br Corps RCS 1977-79, dir Ops Requirements 4 Army 1979-84; asst CDS (cmd, control, communications and info system) 1984-87; dir of Security and Investigation Br Telecom 1987-; FIEE, MIERE, CEng; *Recreations* lawn tennis, golf, bridge; *Style*— Maj-Gen Gordon Oehlers, CB; c/o National Westminster Bank plc, Petersfield, Hants

OESER, Francis Oscar Drury; s of Prof Oscar Oeser (d 1983), of Aust, and Dr Mary Drury Clarke (d 1976); *b* 19 May 1936; *Educ* Scotch Coll (Melbourne), Univ of Melbourne (BA Arch, Dip TRP); *m* 1 Feb 1963, Ann Charina, da of Keith Forge (d 1982) of Aust; 2 s (Marc Drury b 1969, Kim Francis b 1973), 1 da (Mia Elisabeth b 1971); *Career* archiectural and planning photographer, flautist, teacher, writer, performer; private practice: Sydney 1963-66, London 1976-; p/t tutor Univ of NSW (1964-66), NE London Poly (1976-80); author report 'Persian Tiling Practice' (1967); judge Britain-in-Bloom Competition 1976-; RIBA, MRTPI, FRAIA; *Books* Black Notes (1983), Seasons End (1984), Africa Sung (1987), Exhibition: The Way to Santiago (1988); *Recreations* skiing, sailing, cycling, history & literature, music, theatre; *Style*— Francis Oeser, Esq; 21 Dartmouth Park Ave, London NW5 1JL (☎ 01 267 6344); 122 Dartmouth Park Hill, London N19 5HT (☎ 01 263 9317)

OF MAR; *see*: Mar

OFFORD, Prof Robin Ewart; s of Frank Etchelles Offord, of Wissett, Suffolk, and Eileen Elisabeth, *née* Plunkett; *b* 28 June 1940; *Educ* Owen's Sch, Peterhouse Cambridge (MA, PhD); *m* 3 July 1963, Valerie Edna, da of Ronald Wheatley (d 1971); 1 s (Alan b 1964), 2 da (Jane b 1967, Alice b 1973); *Career* fell Univ Coll Oxford 1968-73, (Univ lectr in Molecular Biophysics 1972-80), fell and tutor in biochemistry Christ Church Oxford 1973-80, prof and dir Département de Biochimie Médicale Université de Genéve 1980-, ed Biochemical Journal 1972-79; memb: local ctees of Christian Aid 1970-80, various ctees and bds of the UK Med Res Cncl and UK Miny of Health, Comité Scientifique de la Fondation Jeantet de Médecine 1985-88; *Books* A Guidebook to Biochemistry (with MD Yudkin, 1971), Comprehensible Biochemistry (with MD Yudkin 1973), Biochemistry (1975, Spanish translation 1976), Semisynthetic Peptides and Proteins (with C di Bello, 1977), Simple Macromolecules (1979), Macromolecular Complexes (1979), Semisynthetic Proteins (1980); *Recreations* comparative linguistics, scuba diving, windsurfing, cross-country, skiing; *Style*— Prof Robin Offord; Collex-Bossy, Switzerland; Church Hanborough, Oxon; Département de Biochimie Médicale, Centre Médical Universitaire, 1211 Genéve 4 Suisse (☎ Geneva 22 90 15, fax Geneva 47 33 34, telex 421330 CMU CH)

OGDEN, Eric; MP (elected as Labour but resigned from party 1981 after failure to be reselected as constituency candidate, and joined SDP Oct 1981) Liverpool West Derby 1964-; s of Robert Ogden (d 1959); *b* 23 August 1923; *Educ* Queen Elizabeth's GS Middleton, Wigan Tech Coll; *m* 1, 1 s (David Norman); m 2, 1964, Marjorie, nee Smith; 2 s (Mark Robert b 1966, Martin Branston b 1967), 2 step-da (Christine Davies, Deborah Birtwes); *Career* Br Dutch and US Mercantile Marines 1942-46, coal miner, memb and sponsored by NUM; *Recreations* gardening, motoring, surviving; *Clubs* Europe House, Gillmoss & Dovecot; *Style*— Eric Ogden, Esq, MP; House of Commons, Westminster, London SW1 (☎ 01 219 5201)

OGDEN, Frank Collinge; CBE (1956); s of Paul Ogden (d 1932); *b* 30 Mar 1907; *Educ* Manchester GS, King's Coll Cambridge (MA); *m* 1944, Margaret, da of Fred Greenwood; 1 s, 3 da (1 da decd); *Career* Maj Gen Staff Intelligence; HM Dip Serv (ret); vice-consul: Cairo, Alexandria, Baghdad, Damascus 1930-41, general HQ Cairo 1941-42, Tabriz 1942; 1 sec: Bogotá 1944 (chargé d'affaires 1945), Shiraz 1947, Seattle 1949; consul-gen: Seattle 1952, Basra 1953, Gothenburg 1955; cnsllr Libya 1958, chargé d'affaires 1958-59, cnsllr and consul-gen HM Embassy Buenos Aires 1960-65; *Recreations* motoring, weeding the garden and washing-up; *Clubs* RAC, Civil Service; *Style*— Frank Ogden, Esq, CBE; Yellow Sands, 2 Thorney Drive, Selsey, Chichester, W Sussex PO20 9AQ (☎ 0243 602163)

OGDEN, Sir (Edward) Michael; QC (1968); s of Edward Cannon Ogden (d 1933), of Hove, Sussex, and Daisy, *née* Paris; *b* 9 April 1926; *Educ* Downside, Jesus Coll Cambridge (MA); *m* 21 Dec 1951, Joan Kathleen, da of Pius Charles Brodrick, of Bolton; 2 s (Edward, Henry), 2 da (Celia (Comtesse de Borchgrave d'Altena), Lucy); *Career* Royal Gloucs Hussars, 16/5 Queen's Royal Lancers 1944-47, Capt Inns of Ct Regt TA 1950-56, Capt; called to the Bar Lincoln's Inn 1950-, bencher 1977; memb cncl: Union Internationale Des Avocats 1962-83, Legal Educn 1969-74, Int Bar Assoc 1983-87; chm Criminal Injuries Compensation Bd 1975-89 (memb 1968-), assessor of compensation for persons wrongly imprisoned or charged 1977-, rec Hastings 1971, rec Crown Ct 1972-, tres Bar Cncl 1972-75, ldr SE circuit 1975-78; kt 1989; *Style*— Sir Michael Ogden, QC; 2 Crown Office Row, Temple, London EC4Y 7HJ (☎ 01 353 9337, fax 01 583 0589, telex 8954005 TWOCOR G)

OGDEN, Dr Peter James; s of James Platt Ogden, and Frances Ogden; *b* 26 May 1947; *Educ* Univ of Durham (BSc,PhD), Harvard Business Sch (MBA); *m* 22 Aug 1970, Catherine Rose, da of Harold Blincoe; 2 s (Cameron b 9 Oct 1977, Edward b 18 Aug 1981), 1 da (Tiffany b 1 Oct 1975); *Career* exec dir Merrill Lynch Int Bank Ltd 1976-81; md: Merrill Lynch White Weld Capital Markets Gp 1976-81, Morgan Stanley & Co 1981-87 (advsy dir 1987-), chm Computacenter Ltd 1987-; *Style*— Dr Peter Ogden; Computacenter Ltd, 91/92 Blackfriars Rd, London SE1 8HW

OGDEN, Shirley Georgina (Gina); da of Dr the Hon W S Maclay, CBE (d 1964), of Millwaters, Newbury, Berkshire, and 40 Kensington Sq, London W8, and Dorothy Maclay, *née* Lennox; *b* 4 July 1933; *Educ* Westonbirt Sch Glos, St Martin's Sch of Art London; *m* 25 June 1955 (m dis 1974), (Robert) David Ogden; 3 s (Robert Nicholas b 16 May 1958, Joseph Jeremy (twin) b 1958, Benjamin Patrick b 15 Nov 1966), 1 da (Emma Maclay 25 March 1961); *Career* memb Lloyds; elected Northamptonshire CC 1967 (re-elected 1970, 1973, 1977, 1981 and 1985), vice chm socl servs 1977-81, served on area and dist health authy 1977-85, chm educn ctee 1985-; chm: Daventry Constituency, Cons Assoc Nene Coll; dist and div cmmr for Girl Guides, also advsr Northamptonshire and the Midlands,; *Recreations* painting, tennis, bridge, gardening; *Style*— Mrs Gina Ogden; Cedar House, Hellidon, Daventry, Northamptonshire NN11 6LG (☎ 093 23 61919)

OGILVIE, Sir Alec Drummond; s of Sir George Drummond Ogilvie, KCIE, CSI (d 1966); *b* 17 May 1913; *Educ* Cheltenham Coll; *m* 1945, Lesley Constance Woollan; 2 s; *Career* served WW II Gurkha Rifles IA (POW); chm: Andrew Yule & Co Calcutta 1962-65 (md 1956), Powell Duffryn 1969-78 (dep chm 1967-69); dir: Westinghouse Brake & Signal Co Ltd 1966-79, Lindustries 1973-79, J Lyons & Co 1977-78; cncl memb: King Edward VII's Hosp for Offrs 1967- (vice pres 1979-), Cheltenham Coll 1973-85; kt 1965; *Recreations* gardening, walking; *Clubs* Oriental, MCC; *Style*— Sir Alec Ogilvie; Townlands, High St, Lindfield, West Sussex RH16 2HT (☎ 044 47 3953)

OGILVIE, Philip John; s of Maj Jasper John Ogilvie, MBE (d 1974), of Cricket St Thomas, Somerset, and Rosemary Margaret De Courcy Hughes, *née* Thurlow; *b* 12 Nov 1948; *Educ* Farleigh House, Ampleforth; *m* 9 Oct 1981, Loreto, da of Col Eduardo Vega de Seoane y Barroso, of Madrid; 2 s (Ian Alexander b 14 May 1985, William Jasper Charles b 1 April 1988); *Career* CA, articled Binder Hamlyn & Co 1966-70, ptnr Binder Dijker Otte & Co Madrid 1974-82, Barclays Bank Madrid & UK 1982-89, currently fin dir Fincasol Gp Salisbury and Sotogrande; pres Br C of C Spain 1985-86, hon sec Cncl Br Chambers of Commerce in Europe 1986-, memb Somerset & W Dorset Euro-Cncl (Cons pty 1986-88; FCA 1971; Knight of the Order of Malta; *Recreations* fishing, skiing; *Clubs* Army and Navy; *Style*— Philip Ogilvie, Esq; Kingston House, Higher Kingston, Dorchester DT2 8QE; Sotogrande, 11310 CAD1Z, Spain; Fincasol, 4 Bridge St, Salisbury SP1 2LX (☎ 010 3456 792811, fax 010 3456 792401, telex (Spain) 78192 FISO E)

OGILVIE THOMPSON, Julian; s of Hon N Ogilvie Thompson (chief justice SA to 1974), of Cape Province; *b* 27 Jan 1934; *Educ* Diocesan Coll Rondebosch Cape, Worcester Coll Oxford (Rhodes Scholar); *m* 1956, Hon Tessa Brand (*see* Hon Mrs O T); 2 s (Christopher William b 1958, Anthony Thomas b 1964), 2 da (Rachel Amanda b 1960, Leila Katharine b 1965), all four of whom are in remainder to the Barony of Dacre; *Career* dep chm Anglo American Corpn SA, chm De Beers Consolidated Mines, chm Minerals & Resources Corpn and Anglo American Gold Investmt Tst, vice-chm First National Bank of SA, dir: Charter Consolidated plc, Consolidated Gold Fields plc; *Recreations* shooting, fishing, golf; *Clubs* White's, Rand (Joburg), Kimberley, Brook (NY); *Style*— Julian Ogilvie Thompson, Esq; Froome, Froome St, Athol Ext 3, Johannesburg, S Africa (☎ 011 884 3925, office 011 638 2157)

OGILVIE THOMPSON, Hon Mrs (Tessa Mary); *née* Brand; da of late 4 Viscount Hampden and sis of Baroness Dacre, *qv*; *b* 21 April 1934; *m* 24 July 1956, Julian Ogilvie Thompson, *qv*; 2 s, 2 da; *Style*— The Hon Mrs Ogilvie Thompson; Froome, Froome St, Athol Extension, Johannesburg, S Africa (☎ 011 884 3925)

OGILVY, Hon Sir Angus James Bruce; KCVO (1989); s of 12 (de facto 9) Earl of Airlie, KT, GCVO, MC (d 1968); *b* 14 Sept 1928; *Educ* Eton, Trinity Coll Oxford (MA); *m* 1963, HRH Princess Alexandra of Kent; (*see* Royal Family section); 1 s (1 s dec'd), 1 da; *Career* Scots Gds 1946-48; memb HM Body Gd for Scotland (the Royal Co of Archers); pres: The Imperial Cancer Res Fund 1964-, Youth Clubs UK (formerly Nat Assoc of Youth Clubs) 1969- (chm 1964-69), the Carr-Gomme Soc 1983-, chm Cncl of the Prince's Youth Business Tst 1986-, patron Arthritus Care (formerly The Br Rheumatism and Arthritis Soc) 1978- (chm 1963-69, pres 1969-78); patron The Scottish Wildlife Tst 1974- (pres 1969-74), vice pres The Friends of the Elderley & Gentlefolk's Help 1969- (chm 1963-69, tres 1952-63), vice patron The Nat Children's Homes 1986-; tstee: The Leeds Castle Fndn 1975-, The Great Britain-Sasakawa Fndn 1985-; memb: Governing Cncl of Business in the Community 1984-, Governing Cncl of The Soc for the Promotion of Christian Knowledge 1984-; dir various public cos; *Recreations* architecture, music, reading; *Clubs* White's; *Style*— The Hon Angus Ogilvy; Thatched House Lodge, Richmond Park, Surrey (☎ 01 546 8833)

OGILVY, Hon Bruce Patrick; s of 13 Earl of Airlie, DL; hp of bro, Lord Ogilvy; *b* 7 April 1959; *Style*— The Hon Bruce Ogilvy

OGILVY, Lady Caroline; *née* Child-Villiers; da of 9 Earl of Jersey; *b* 1934; *m* 1, 1952 (m dis 1965), Viscount Melgund, MBE (now 6 Earl of Minto); 1 s, 1 da; m 2, 1969 (m dis 1972), the Hon John Douglas Stuart, s of 1 Viscount Stuart of Findhorn, CH,

MVO, MC (d 1971); m 3, 1980, Hon James Donald Diarmid Ogilvy, s of 12 Earl of Airlie; *Style*— Lady Caroline Ogilvy; Sedgebrook Manor, nr Grantham, Linc

OGILVY, Lord; David John Ogilvy; s and h of 13 Earl of Airlie; *b* 9 Mar 1958; *m* 1981, Hon Geraldine, *qv*; *Career* page of honour to HM The Queen 1971-; *Style*— Lord Ogilvy; Wellbank, Cortachy, Kirriemuir, Angus, Scotland

OGILVY, Sir David John Wilfrid; 13 Bt (NS 1626), of Inverquharity, Forfarshire, JP (E Lothian 1957), DL (1971); s of Gilbert Francis Molyneux Ogilvy, JP (4 s of Sir Reginald Ogilvy, 10 Bt, JP, DL, and Hon Olivia, da of 9 Lord Kinnaird, KT), and Marjory Katharine (d 1961), da of Charles Clive and Lady Katharine Feilding, da of 7 Earl of Denbigh; suc unc, Sir Herbert Ogilvy, 12 Bt, 1956; *b* 3 Feb 1914; *Educ* Eton, Trinity Coll Oxford (MA); *m* 31 Dec 1966, Penelope Mary Ursula, o da of Arthur Lafone Frank Hills, of White Court, Tonbridge, and Moira Emelina, eldest da of Henry Seymour Guinness, of the extensive brewing and banking family; 1 s; *Heir* s, Francis Gilbert Arthur Ogilvy b 22 April 1969, ed Edinburgh Acad, Glenalmond; *Career* served WW II RNVR, unexploded bomb disposal and miscellaneous weapon devpt in Britain and Sri Lanka; farmer and landowner; *Recreations* forestry; *Style*— Sir David Ogilvy, Bt, JP, DL; Winton Cottage, Pencaitland, East Lothian EH34 5AT (☎ 0875 340222)

OGILVY, Lady Elizabeth Clementine; *née* Ogilvy; da of 13 Earl of Airlie, DL; *b* 4 June 1965; *Style*— Lady Elizabeth Ogilvy

OGILVY, Lady; Hon Geraldine Theodora Mary Gabriel; *née* Harmsworth; da of 3 Viscount Rothermere; *b* 25 July 1957; *m* 1981, Lord Ogilvy, *qv*; *Style*— Lady Ogilvy; Wellbank, Cortachy, Kirriemuir, Angus

OGILVY, Hon James Donald Diarmid; s of 12 Earl of Airlie, KT, GCVO, MC, and Lady Alexandra Coke, da of 3 Earl of Leicester; *b* 28 June 1934; *Educ* Eton; *m* 1, 1959, (Magda) June, da of Robert Ducas, of N Y, by his 1 w, Magdalen, da of Maj Herbert Stourton, OBE (gs of 19 Baron Stourton, DL), and Hon Frances, only da of 4 Viscount Southwell; 2 s (Shamus Diarmid Ducas b 1966, Diarmid James Ducas 1970), 2 da (Laura Jane b 1960, Emma Louise b 1962); m 2, 1980, Lady Caroline, *née* Child-Villiers, da of 9 Earl of Jersey and former w of (1) Viscount Melgund, MBE (now 6 Earl of Minto), and (2) Hon John Stuart (s of 1 Viscount Stuart of Findhorn); *Career* Lt Scots Gds 1952-54; page of honour to King George VI 1947-51; ptnr Rowe & Pitman, chm Rowan Investmt Mangrs 1959-86, chm Mercury Rowan Mullens, dir Mercury Asset Mangmnt plc 1986-88, chief exec Foreign & Colonial Mangmnt Ltd 1988-; govr Queen Charlotte's and Chelsea Hosps 1966-76; chm Inst of Obstetrics and Gynaecology 1983-86; memb Royal Co of Archers (Queen's Bodyguard for Scotland); *Clubs* White's; *Style*— The Hon James Ogilvy; Sedgebrook Manor, Sedgebrook, Grantham, Lincs (☎ 0949 42337); 51 Eaton Sq, London SW1 (☎ 01 235 7595); Foreign & Colonial Management Ltd, 1 Laurence Pountney Hill, London EC4R OBA (☎ 01 623 4680)

OGILVY, James Robert Bruce; o son of Hon Sir Angus Ogilvy, KCVO, and HRH Princess Alexandra, GCVO, o da of HRH 1 Duke of Kent; *b* 29 Feb 1964; *Educ* Eton; *m* 30 July 1988, Julia Caroline (b 28 Oct 1964), eldest da of Charles Frederick Melville Rawlinson, *qv*

OGILVY, Hon Patrick Alexander; s of 13 Earl of Airlie, DL; *b* 24 Mar 1971; *Style*— The Hon Patrick Ogilvy

OGILVY-WEDDERBURN, Maj Sir Andrew John Alexander; 7 Bt (UK 1803), of Balindean, Perthshire; descended from Sir Alexander Wedderburn, 4 Bt (S 1704), of Blackness, who served as a volunteer at the Battle of Culloden (1746) where he was taken prisoner and executed, and his estate forfeited. His descendants continued to assume the title until Sir David (7 Bt, but for the attainder) was cr Bt in the present UK creation, with special remainder to the heirs male of the 4 Bt of the original creation; s of Cdr Sir (John) Peter Ogilvy-Wedderburn, 6 Bt (d 1977), and Elizabeth Katherine, Lady Ogilvy-Wedderburn, *qv*; *b* 4 August 1952; *Educ* Gordonstoun; *m* 1984, Gillian Meade, da of Richard Boyle Adderley, MBE, of Shepherds Hill, Pickering, N Yorks; 2 s (Peter Robert Alexander, Geordie Richard Andrew (twins) b 1987), 1 da (Katherine b 1985); *Heir* s, Peter Robert Alexander Ogilvy-Wedderburn; *Career* Maj Black Watch (Royal Highland Regt); memb Br Bobsleigh Team 1974-80, British Olympic Team (Bobsleigh) 1976 Innsbruck (1980 Lake Placid), Br 2 Man Bobsleigh Champion 1976-77 and 1978-79; *Recreations* bobsleighing, skiing, shooting; *Style*— Maj Sir Andrew Ogilvy-Wedderburn, Bt; Silvie, Alyth, Perthshire (☎ 082 83 2362)

OGLESBY, Peter Rogerson; CB (1982); s of Leonard William Oglesby (d 1978), and Jessie Oglesby, *née* Rogerson (d 1980); *b* 15 July 1922; *Educ* Woodhouse Grove Sch Yorks; *m* 1947, Doreen Hilda, da of Douglas James Hudson (d 1963); 3 da (Susan b 1952, Jane b 1955, Mary b 1957); *Career* civil servant; princ private sec: Douglas Houghton 1964-66, Michael Stewart 1966-68, Richard Crosman 1968; Cabinet Off 1968-70: sec of occupational pension bd 1973-74, under-sec and head of social security fin div 1975-79, dep-sec social security policy 1979-82; dir Regency Fin Gp plc 1983-; *Recreations* gardening; *Style*— Peter Oglesby, Esq, CB; 41 Draycot Rd, Wanstead, London E11 2NX

OGMORE, Constance, Baroness Alice Alexandra Constance; da of late Alderman Walter Robert Wills, Lord Mayor of Cardiff 1945-46, and Ada Mary, *née* Johns; *m* 1930, 1 Baron Ogmore, TD, PC (d 1976); 2 s 1 da; *Style*— The Rt Hon Constance, Lady Ogmore; 48 Cheyne Court, Royal Hospital Rd, SW3 (☎ 01 352 6131)

OGMORE, 2 Baron (UK 1950); Gwilym Rees Rees-Williams; s of 1 Baron Ogmore (d 1976), and Constance Alexandra, *née* Wills; *b* 5 May 1931; *Educ* Mill Hill; *m* 1967, Gillian, da of Maurice Slack, of Hindley, Lancs; 2 da (Christine b 1968, Jennet b 1970); *Heir* bro, Hon Morgan Rees-Williams; *Recreations* watching rugby, walking; *Style*— The Rt Hon Lord Ogmore; 4 Foster Rd, London W4 4NY (☎ 01 995 0775)

OGNALL, Hon Mr Justice; Sir Harry Henry; QC (1973); s of Leo Ognall, and Cecila Ognall; *b* 9 Jan 1934; *Educ* Leeds GS, Lincoln Coll Oxford (MA), Univ of Virginia (LLM); *m* 1; 2 s, 1 da; m 2, 1977, Elizabeth Young; 2 step s; *Career* called to Bar Gray's Inn 1958, bencher 1983, joined NE Circuit, rec 1972-86; judge of the High Ct 1986-, memb Criminal Injuries Compensation Bd 1976, arbitrator Motor Insurers' Bureau Agreement 1979-85, memb Senate of Inns of Ct 1980-83 (memb planning ctee and professional conduct ctee), memb criminal ctee Judicial Studies Bd 1986-89; kt 1986; *Recreations* golf, travel, music; *Style*— The Hon Mr Justice Ognall; Royal Courts of Justice, Strand, London WC2A 2LL

OGORKIEWICZ, Prof Richard Marian; s of Col Marian Anthony Ogorkiewicz (d 1962), of Poland, and Waldyna, *née* Pryfer (d 1986); *b* 2 May 1926; *Educ* SRW Sch Warsaw, Lycée de C Norwid Paris, George Heriot's Sch Edinburgh, Imperial Coll London (BSc, MSc); *Career* devpt engr: Ford Motor Co 1952-55, Humber Ltd 1955-57; lectr mech engrg Imperial Coll London 1957-58, conslt to various cos involved with armoured fighting vehicles 1972-, consulting ed Int Defense Review Geneva 1988-, visiting prof RMCS; memb 1964-: various sci advsy ctees, Miny of Aviation, Miny of Technol, MOD; pres Soc of Friends of the Tank Museum Dorset 1987-; FIMechE 1970; *Books* Armour (1960), Design and Development of Fighting Vehicles (1968), Armoured Forces (1970); *Recreations* gardening, walking; *Style*— Prof Richard Ogorkiewicz; 18 Temple Sheen, East Sheen, London SW14 7RP (☎ 01 876 5149)

OGSTON, Prof Derek; s of Frederick John Ogston (d 1981), of Aberdeen, and Ellen Mary, *née* Duncan; *b* 31 May 1932; *Educ* Kings Coll Sch Wimbledon, Univ of Aberdeen (MA, MB, ChB, PhD, MD, DSc); *m* 19 July 1963, (Cecilia) Marie, da of William Charles Clark (d 1975), of Aberdeen; 1 s (Keith b 1969), 1 da (Catriona b 1971, Nicola b 1973); *Career* Univ of Aberdeen: regius prof 1977-83, prof of med 1983-, dean faculty of med 1984-87, vice princ 1987-; FRCPE 1973, FRCP 1977, FRSE 1982, FIBiol 1987; *Books* Physiology of Hemostasis (1983), Antifibrinolytic Drugs (1984), Venous Thrombosis: Causation and Prediction (1987); *Recreations* travel; *Style*— Prof Derek Ogston; 64 Rubislaw Den South, Aberdeen, Grampian (☎ 0224 316 587); Dept of Medicine, Polwarth Building, Foresterhill, Aberdeen, Grampian (☎ 0224 681 818, ext 53016)

OGUS, Hugh Joseph; s of Louis Ogus (d 1951), of London, and Anne, *née* Goldstein (d 1986); *b* 23 Jan 1934; *Educ* Central Fndn Sch London, Queen Mary Coll London (BA); *m* 14 Aug 1960, Mavis, da of Michael Mendel (d 1971), of London; 1 s (Simon b 1964), 1 da (Deborah b 1967); *Career* various jr mgmnt posts Philips Electrical Ltd 1957-67, (commercial dir Salamandre Metalworks Ltd 1968-73, chm and md Poselco Ltd 1984-(md 1973-84); cncl memb Light Indust Fedn 1977-(pres 1982-83), chm of fin Mary Hare GS for the Deaf 1980-(vice chm of govrs 1984-), vice chm of govrs London Sch of Foreign Trade 1982-87, cncl memb Chartered Inst of Building Servs Engrs 1986-89, chm of govrs Mill Hill Oral Sch for Deaf Children 1987-(tres 1977-87); hon vice pres (former chm) 4 Hendon Scouts and Guides, pres Hendon North Liberal Assoc 1984-87 (chm 1981-84); Freeman City of London 1983, Liveryman Worshipful Co of Lightmongers (Ct asst), Assoc CIBSE 1977, FInstD 1983; *Recreations* music, travel, swimming, growing vegetables; *Style*— Hugh J Ogus, Esq; 2 Haslemere Ave, London NW4 2PX (☎ 01 202 7092); Poselco Ltd, Walmgate Rd, Perivale, Middx UB6 7LX (☎ 01 998 1431, fax 01 997 3350, telex 917972 POLITE G)

OHLENSCHLAGER, Brig Richard Norman; MBE (1963); s of Cdr Norman Albert Gustav Ohlenschlager, DSO, RN (d 1937), of Fareham, Hants, and Ima Millicent Jones; *b* 22 April 1925; *Educ* Radley Coll; *m* 15 April 1948, Ann Felicity Mary, da of Lt Col Arthur Cyril Whitcombe, MBE, RA (d 1979), of Seaview, IOW; 1 s (Guy b 1952), 2 da (Carol b 1950, Susan b 1954); *Career* Army Offr 1943-78; cmdt Royal Sch of Artillery Larkhill Wilts 1976-78; chm Ohlenschlager Bros Ltd 1969-81; civil servant; JP; *Recreations* sailing, skiing, gardening; *Clubs* Royal Yacht Sqdn, Seaview Yacht, Army and Navy; *Style*— Brig Richard N Ohlenschlager, MBE; Goodworth Cottage, Goodworth Clatford, Hampshire SP11 7QX (☎ 0264 52511); HQ United Kingdom Land Forces, Wilton, Salisbury, Wiltshire SP2 0AG (☎ 0722 336222)

OHLSON, Sir Brian Eric Christopher; 3 Bt (UK 1920), of Scarborough, North Riding of Co of Yorkshire; s of Sir Eric (James) Ohlson, 2 Bt (d 1983) and Lady Ohlson, *qv*; *b* 27 July 1936; *Educ* Harrow, RMA Sandhurst; *Heir* bro, Peter Michael Ohlson; *Career* cmmnd Coldstream Gds 1956, Capt, ret 1961; money broker; *Recreations* racing, cricket, theatre, bridge; *Clubs* Naval and Military, Hurlingham, MCC, Cavalry and Guards'; *Style*— Sir Brian Ohlson, Bt; 1 Courtfield Gdns, London SW5

OHLSON, Lady; Marjorie Joan; 2 da of late Charles Henry Roosmale-Cocq, of Dorking, Surrey; *m* 8 May 1935, Sir Eric James Ohlson, 2 Bt (d 1983); 2 s (*see* Sir Brian Ohlson, 3 Bt), 1 da; *Style*— Lady Ohlson

OHLSON, Peter Michael; s of Sir Eric Ohlson, 2 Bt (d 1983); hp of bro Sir Brian Ohlson, 3 Bt; *b* 18 May 1939; *Educ* Harrow, Trinity Coll Cambridge (BA); *m* 18 Oct 1968, Sarah, o da of Maj-Gen Thomas Brodie, CB, CBE, DSO; 2 da; *Career* ptnr Tyzack & Partners; *Style*— Peter Ohlson, Esq; 33 The Avenue, Kew, Surrey; Express Dairy Co Ltd, Victoria Rd, South Ruislip, Middx (☎ 01 845 2345)

OKELL, Robert; s of George Okell (d 1958), and Evelyn Christian, *née* Ramsbotham (d 1963); *b* 23 Nov 1923; *Educ* Charterhouse; *Career* Army serv 1942-47, Capt RA slr 1950, actg master Ross Harriers 1975-88; (hon sec 1950-85), vice pres Hereford Div Cons Assoc; *Recreations* hunting; *Style*— Robert Okell, Esq; Fern Bank, Ross-on-Wye, Hereford

OKEOVER; *see*: Walker-Okeover

OLAGBEGI II, Oba Alaiyeluwa, The Olowo of Owo; Sir Olateru; s of Oba Alaiyeluwa, Olagbegi I, Olowo of Owo; succeeded 1941; *b* 1910; *Educ* Owo Govt Sch; married with children; *Career* treasury clerk in Owo Native Administration 1935-41; kt 1960; *Style*— Oba Alaiyeluwa, Olagbegi II, The Olowo of Owo; P O Box 1, Afin Oba Olowo, Owo, Western Provinces of Nigeria (☎ Owo 1)

OLDENBURG, HH Duke Friedrich August Nikolaus Udo Peter Philipp of; elder s of HH Duke Peter of Oldenburg (2 s of HRH Nikolaus, Hereditary Grand Duke of Oldenburg, descended from Egilmar I, Count of Aldenburg, who was living in 1108. Hereditary Grand Duke Nikolaus m HSH Princess Helene of Waldeck and Pyrmont, whose paternal grandmother was HSH Princess Helene of Nassau. Princess Helene of Nassau's paternal gf's mother was Princess Caroline of Orange, whose mother was Princess Anne (Princess Royal), eldest da of King George II of Great Britain), by his w HSH Princess Gertrud, 2 da of HSH Udo, 6 Prince zu Löwenstein-Wertheim-Freudenberg; *b* 26 Sept 1952; *m* 1982, Belinda, da of Maj (Alison) Digby Tatham Warter, DSO, of Nanyuki, Kenya, by his w Jane, *née* Boyd (mother was Lady Mary Egerton, o da of 5 Earl of Wilton); 2 da (Anastasia b 10 Oct 1982, Alice b 15 April 1986); *Career* farmer; *Style*— His Highness Duke Friedrich August of Oldenburg; Anstey Hall, Anstey, Buntingford, Herts SG9 0BY

OLDFIELD, Hon Mrs; Hon (Alexandra Frances Margaret); *née* Davidson; el da of 2 Viscount Davidson; *b* 13 April 1957; *m* 1982, Richard John (b 1955), s of late Christopher Charles Bayley Oldfield (himself eighteenth in descent from Sir Alanus de Aldefeld, fndr and endower of the chapel at Aldefeld, who d 1281), and Mrs B R P Brooks, of London W6; 1 s (Christopher b 1986), 1 da (Leonora b 1985); *Style*— The Hon Mrs Oldfield

OLDFIELD, Lady (Mary) Elisabeth; *née* Murray; yr da of late 8 Earl of Dunmore, VC, DSO, MVO; *b* 28 Nov 1913; *m* 29 April 1937, Major Peter Carlton Oldfield,

OBE, Warwicks Yeo, yst s of Carlton Olfield, of Moor Hill, Harwood, Yorkshire; 1 da; *Style—* Lady Elisabeth Oldfield; Ham Cottage, Sydmonton, Newbury, Berks

OLDFIELD, Brig John Briton; OBE (1980), DL (Hants 1973); s of William Aitken Oldfield, JP (d 1966), of Sandsend, N Yorks, and Violet Ethelind, *née* Rickell (d 1951); *b* 28 April 1918; *Educ* Repton, RMC Sandhurst; *m* 25 March 1949, Pamela Carrol, da of Maj Robert Geoffrey Ward (d 1971), of Southampton; 1 s (Jonathan b 1954), 1 da (Amanda (Mrs O'Sullivan) b 1956); *Career* cmmnd The Green Howards 1938, served Palestine 1938-39, France and Western Desert (despatches 1945), Malaya 1951-52 (despatches 1953), dep sec Int Standing Gp NATO Washington DC 1957-59, CO 1 Bn The Green Howards 1960-62, staff NATO Defence Coll Paris (Col) 1962-64, Cdr TA Bde 1965-67, Dep Cdr Aldershot Dist 1967-69, ret 1969, Col The Green Howards 1975-82, Hon Col 2 Bn The Wessex Regt 1980-83, sec E Wessex TAVR Assoc 1970-82; *Books* The Green Howards in Malaya (1953); *Recreations* field sports, painting; *Clubs* Army and Navy; *Style—* Brig John Oldfield, OBE, DL; Paddock Cottage, Bramshaw, Lyndhurst, Hants SO43 7JN (☎ 0794 390 233)

OLDFIELD, Lady Kathleen Constance Blanche; *née* Balfour; yst da of 2 Earl of Balfour (d 1945); *b* 1912; *Educ* Newnham Coll Cambridge (MA); *m* 23 Aug 1933, Richard Charles Oldfield (d 1972), s of Sir Francis du Pre Oldfield; 2 da; *Recreations* gardening; *Clubs* Salisbury Centre, Edinburgh; *Style—* Lady Kathleen Oldfield; Woodhall Cottage, Pencaitland, East Lothian

OLDHAM, Alan John; s of John Albert Oldham (d 1952), of Hyde, Ches, and Hilda Pennington Oldham, *née* Beech (d 1981); *b* 6 Mar 1926; *Educ* Wrekin Coll, Clare Coll Cambridge (MA); *m* 29 June 1963, Jane Louise England, da of Norman Percival Fish (d 1972) of Som; 2 s (John b 1964, Paul b 1968), 1 da (Melanie b 1966); *Career* actuary; asst gen mangr Equity & Law Life Assur Soc plc 1973-86, consltg actuary Shucksmith & Co, gen cmmr Income Tax High Wycombe Dist 1979-, chm High Wycombe Div S Bucks & E Berks C of C 1984-85; memb cncl & hon tres Croquet Assoc; FIA; *Recreations* croquet, philately; *Style—* Alan Oldham, Esq; Terriers Green, Terriers, High Wycombe, Bucks HP13 5AJ (☎ 0494 26527); Lincoln House, Nutley Lane, Reigate, Surrey RH2 9HP (☎ 0737 222011)

OLDHAM, Christopher David Fitzjohn; s of Cdr Frederick William Fitzjohn Oldham, OBE (d 1984), of Gosfield Hall, Halstead, Essex, and Trereza Jessie, *née* Hawes; *b* 22 May 1934; *Educ* Harrow; *m* 21 Aug 1975, Susan Hilary, da of Hugh Arthur Fitzgerald Finch (d 1975), 10 Broadwater Down, Tonbridge Wells, Kent; 1 s (William H 1976); *Career* Nat Serv RN 1952-54; admitted slr 1960, sr ptnr Vizards London; church warden, former dep chm Lansdowne Club, stewardship advsr Southwark Diocese; memb Law Soc; *Recreations* gardening, stalking, railway modelling, historical reading; *Clubs* Lansdowne; *Style—* Christopher Oldham, Esq; 6 Parkfields, Putney, London SW15 6NH (☎ 01 789 5765); Vizards, 42/43 Bedford Row, London WC1R 4LL (☎ 01 405 6302, fax 01 405 6248, telex 261045)

OLDHAM, Sheila Dorothy; da of John Cunliffe Jackson (d 1965), of E Beach, Lytham St Annes, Lancs, and Dorothy May, *née* Fenton (d 1979); paternal gf William Jackson ARCS, fndr Ceramic Soc, jt inventor of Thermoscope; *b* 25 May 1928; *Educ* Howell's Denbigh, Liverpool Sch of Architecture; *m* 3 Aug 1948, Frederick Howard (d 1979), s of Harold Oldham (d 1976), of Rawtenstall, Lancs; 3 s (David Howard b 1949, Michael Jonathan b 1951, Charles Nicholas b 1957); *Career* cncllr (C) Haslingden Borough 1968, Rossendale (C) 1974, mayor Rossendale 1979-80, JP 1970; fndr, chm: Friends of Rossendale Hosp 1971-78, Rossendale Br Heart Fndn 1980-; tstee Richard Whitaker Charitable Tst; memb NW Regnl Health Authy 1982-86; chm Ctee for Employment of Disabled People E Lancs 1983-; memb: Lancashire Area Manpower Bd 1986-, DHSS Appeals Tbnl 1979-; pres: Helmshore Old People's Welfare; Rossendale Amateur Operative Soc, Rossendale Ladies' Choir; *Recreations* gardening; *Style—* Sheila Oldham; Stable House, Helmshore, Rossendale, Lancs (☎ 220819)

OLDMAN, Paul Anthony; s of Dennis Russel Oldman, (d 1977), and Dorothy Pamela, *née* Bradnum; *b* 22 Dec 1952; *Educ* Great Yarmouth GS, Univ of Manchester (LLB); *Career* ptnr Lovell White Durrant slrs (formerly Lovell White & King) 1987- (joined 1980), memb Law Soc; Freeman Worshipful Co of Slrs; *Recreations* reading novels, swimming, theatre, travel; *Style—* Paul Oldman, Esq; 19 Petherton Rd, London N5; 73 Cheapside, London EC2V 6ER (☎ 01 236 0066, fax 01 236 0084)

OLDROYD, James Colin; JP (1974); s of Joseph Chamberlain Oldroyd (d 1975), of Dewsbury, Yorks, and Lydia Helen, *née*, Lyons (d 1984); *b* 28 May 1935; *Educ* St Peter's Sch York, King's Coll Cambridge (MA); *m* 4 March 1961, Susan Norah, da of Edward Denville Hill (d 1988), of Cheadle; 2 s (Paul b 1961, Graham b 1961); *Career* 2 Lt RA 1957, Capt RA (TA) 1963; md Graham Motor Gp plc 1984-, dir Swan Nat Motors Ltd 1988-; CBIM 1986; *Style—* James Oldroyd, Esq; Roxburgh, Legh Road, Knutsford, Cheshire WA16 8NR (☎ 0565 3027); 1 Canute Square, Knutsford, Cheshire WA16 6BQ (☎ 0565 53117, fax 0565 55104)

OLDWORTH, Richard Anthony; s of Anthony Gilbert Frederick Oldworth, of Blackdown, Sussex, and Patricia, *née* Thompson; *b* 5 June 1957; *Educ* Radley, City of London Poly; *Career* CA; Peat Marwick Mitchell 1976-80, corporate finance exec County Bank 1980-83, head of Corporate Finance Bisgood Bishop & Co 1983-84, md Binns Cornwall 1984-; memb ACA 1980; *Recreations* flying, motorsport; *Clubs* City of London, Royal Solent YC; *Style—* Richard Oldworth, Esq; 22 Abercrombie St, London SW11 (☎ 01 228 1138); 36 St Andrew's Hill, London EC4 (☎ 01 489 1441, fax 01 489 1436, car tel 0836 700 309)

OLIPHANT, Capt (Laurence) Hugh; CBE (1977), DSC (1945); s of Rear Adm L R Oliphant, CBE (d 1951), of Miller's Hill, Thornton Le Dale, Yorks, and Hon Daphne Adelaide, *née* Willoughby; *b* 4 April 1922; *Educ* Nautical Coll Pangbourne; *m* 7 Feb 1953, Meriel, da of Arthur Hudson Fynn (d 1962), of The Barn, Helston, Cornwall; 2 da (Annabel b 1955, d 1980, Virginia (twin)); *Career* cadet RN 1940, volunteered for submarines 1942, 1 Cmnd HMS Tiptoe 1949, Cdr 1959, dir of staff Staff Coll 1965, Capt 1968, cmnd 1 Submarine Sqdn 1973, ret 1977; fundraising to establish Submarine Museum Gosport 1978-79, actg asst gen sec Missions to Seaman 1986-87 (dir Southern regn 1980-86); sec Lynchmere PCC 1987; *Recreations* travel, gardening ; *Style—* Capt Hugh Oliphant, CBE, DSC, RN; Forest Mead, Lynchmere, Haslemere, Surrey GU27 3NE (☎ 0428 727 021)

OLIPHANT OF CONDIE, Lt Cdr Ralph Henry Hood Laurence; s of Capt Henry Gerard Laurence Oliphant, DSO, MVO (d 1955), of Condie & Newton, and Ruth Barry (d 1967); *b* 3 August 1915; *Educ* Radley; *m* 1, 13 Sept 1941, Barbara Mary (d 1979), da of Rev Preb Herbert Mackworth Drake; 3 da (Susannah Mary b 1943, Charlotte b 1946, Barabara Louise b 1952, d 1969); m 2, 27 Nov 1980, Mary Diana Ryde, da of Denis George Mackail, (d 1971); *Career* PO RAF 1935, RN 1938; served WWII 1939-45 Fleet Air Arm Salerno & Normandy; cmd 886 Sqdn on: HMS Eagle, HMS Illustrations, HMS Formidable, HMS Attacker; Croix de Guerre (despatches); *Recreations* fishing, cricket; *Clubs* Naval & Military, MCC; *Style—* Lt Cdr Ralph Oliphant of Condie; National Westminster Bank, 352 Kings Rd, London SW3 5UX

OLIVER, Hon David Keightley Rideal; QC (1986); o s of Baron Oliver of Aylmerton (Life Peer), *qv*, and Mary Chichester, *née* Rideal (d 1985); *b* 4 June 1949, ; *Educ* Westminster, Trinity Hall Cambridge (BA), Université Libre de Bruxelles (Lic Special en droit Européen); *m* 1, 5 April 1972 (m dis 1987), Maria Luisa, da of Juan Mirasierras, of Avenida Reina, Madrid, Spain; 2 s (Daniel b 1974, Thomas b 1976); m 2, 20 Feb 1988, Judith Britannia Caroline, da of David Henry John Griffiths Powell; *Career* barr 1972; standing counsel to dir gen of Fair Trading 1980-86; *Recreations* gardening, bird watching, shooting; *Style—* The Hon David Oliver, QC; 13 Old Square, Lincoln's Inn, London WC2A 3UA (☎ 01 404 4800)

OLIVER, Dr Dennis Stanley; KSG (1980), CBE (1981); s of James Thomas (d 1961), and Lilian Mabel Bunn (d 1976); *b* 19 Sept 1926; *Educ* Deacon's Sch Peterborough, Birmingham Univ (Bsc, MSc, PhD); *m* 1, 1952 (m dis 1984), Enid Jessie; m 2, 1987, Elizabeth; *Career* res fell dept physics Univ of Bristol 1949-52, UKAEA head of Metallurgy Dounreay 1952-63, chief R&D offr Richard Thomas & Baldwin Ltd 1963-68, gp dir R & D Pilkingtons plc 1968-77 (exec dir 1977-86), admin L'Ecole Superieure du Verre, Charleroi, govr Euro Ind Res Man Assoc 1975-82 (pres 1977-81), pres Sci and Tech Ed Merseyside 1978-81 (patron 1981-), memb ct & cncl Cranfield Inst of Technol 1976-88 (visiting prof 1984-88); govr: Liverpool Inst of Higher Educn 1977-85, Christ's & Notre Dame Coll Liverpool 1977-87, Royal Nat Coll for Blind 1981-85; founding dir and dep chm cmmn of St Helens Tst 1978-86; dir: Anglo American Venture Fund Ltd 1980-84, Nat R&D Corp 1981-, Nat Enterprise Bd 1981-; founding dir and chm Industl Experience Projects Ltd 1981-86, Monotype Corp Ltd 1985-; founding tstee, Anfield Tst 1983-88; Liveryman: Worshipful Co of Spectaclemakers 1983- (asst 1985-88), Worshipful Co of Engineers 1985; memb advsy Cncl on Sci and Technol 1986-, visiting prof Mass Inst of Technol 1986-; mgmnt conslt 1986-; KSG, FEng 1981, FIM, FInstP, FBIM; *Recreations* music, poetry, cooking; *Clubs* IOD, City Livery; *Style—* Dr Dennis Oliver, KSG, CBE; Castell Bach, Bodfari, Denbigh, Clwyd LL16 4HT (☎ 074575 354)

OLIVER, Edward Morgan; s of Raife Morgan Oliver (d 1963), of Little Hall, Liston, Long Malford, Suffolk, and Nancy Evelyn, *née* Cutler (d 1985); *b* 22 April 1942; *Educ* Felsted Sch Essex; *m* 7 Aug 1965, (Carol) Louise, da of Edgar Cecil Watts (d 1975), of The Grove, Ditchingham, Bungay, Suffolk; 1 s (Raife Morgan b 1967), 1 da (Lynn Bridget b 1970); *Career* CA; ptnr: Peters Elworthy & Moore 1967-70, Shipley Blackburn 1970-; sec King Georges Pension Fund for Actors and Actresses 1971-; memb Herts CC 1972-80 (chm highways ctee 1977-80), Cons candidate NE Derbys 1979; Freeman City of London, Liveryman Worshipful Co of Vintners 1966; FCA 1965; *Recreations* field sports, amateur dramatics, gardening; *Style—* Edward Oliver, Esq; Maple Cottage, Arkesdon Rd, Clavering, nr Saffron Waldon, Essex; 14-16 Regent St, London SW1Y 4PS (☎ 01 839 4311)

OLIVER, Sir (Frederick) Ernest; CBE (1955), TD (1942, DL Leicester 1950); s of Sir Frederick Oliver (d 1939); *b* 31 Oct 1900; *Educ* Rugby; *m* 1928, Mary Margaret (d 1978), da of Herbert Simpson (d 1931); 1 s (decd), 2 da; *Career* served WW II RA (UK and Burma); memb Leicester Cncl 1933-74, lord mayor Leicester 1950-51, chm George Oliver (Footwear) 1950-73; pres: Leicester Cons Assoc 1952-66, Multiple Shoe Retailers' Assoc 1964-65; hon Freeman City of Leicester 1971; kt 1962; *Recreations* shooting; *Clubs* Leicestershire; *Style—* Sir Ernest Oliver, CBE, TD, DL

OLIVER, Ian David; s of Col Claude Danolds Oliver, OBE, TD, DL (d 1987), and Vera Scott *née* Grieve (d 1987); great-grandfather George Oliver founded Footwear Retail Company now George Oliver Footwear plc with 500 branches throughout UK; *b* 16 Nov 1934; *Educ* Uppingham Sch; *m* 10 Nov 1972, Jane, da of Royden Swinfen (d 1984); 2 s (Louis b 1962, Edward b 1981), 1 da (Katie b 1976); *Career* chm: G. Oliver Footware plc, pres: Multiple Shoe Retailers Assoc 1984-86 (chm 1981-84), Footwear Disstributors Fedn 1985-87; *Recreations* family, gardening; *Style—* Ian Oliver, Esq; Haddon Dale, West End, West Haddon, Northants (☎ 078 887 214); G. Oliver (Footwear) plc, Grove Way, Narborough, Leicester (☎ 0533 894444, telex 341270 OLIvER G, fax 892921)

OLIVER, Brig James Alexander; CBE (1965), MBE (1939, DSO 1942, and bar 1943, TD, DL); s of Adam Oliver (d 1944), of Arbroath, Angus; *b* 19 Mar 1906; *Educ* Trinity Coll Glenalmond; *m* 1932, Margaret Whytock, da of Thomas Scott, of Arbroath; *Career* 2 Lt The Black Watch (TA) 1926; Lt-Col 1942, Brig 1943; served WW II N Africa, Sicily and NW Europe (despatches), cmd: 7 Black Watch 1942-43, 152 Inf Bde (Highland Div) 1943, 154 Inf Bde 1944-45; ADC to HM The Queen 1953-63, Vice-Lt County of Angus 1967-82; chm: Angus & Dundee TA Assoc 1945-59, chm Earl Haig Fund (Scotland) 1972-73 (vice pres 1973), Hon Col 6/7 Black Watch 1960-67, Hon Col 51 Highland Volunteers 1960-70; slr ptnr Thornton Oliver WS (Arbroath); Hon LLD Dundee 1967; *Clubs* Naval and Military; *Style—* Brig James Oliver, CBE, MBE, DSO, TD, DL; West Newton, Arbroath, Angus DD11 5RQ (☎ 0241 72579)

OLIVER, The Venerable John; s of Walter Keith Oliver (d 1977), of Danehill, Sussex, and Ivy, *née* Nightingale (d 1981); *b* 14 April 1935; *Educ* Westminster (Queen's Scholar), Gonville and Caius Coll Cambridge (BA, MA, MLitt); *m* 16 Sept 1961, Meriel, da of Sir Alan Moore, Bt (d 1959), of Battle, Sussex; 2 s (Thomas b 1964, Henry b 1968), 1 da (Mary b 1971); *Career* curate Hilborough Gp of Parishes Norfolk 1964-68, chaplain and asst mstr Eton Coll 1968-72; Team Rect: Sth Molton Grp 1973-82 (Rur Dean 1974-80), Central Exeter 1982-85; Archdn of Sherborne Canon of Salisbury and P-in-C W Stafford 1985-; *Recreations* railways, music, architecture, walking; *Style—* The Venerable John Oliver; The Rectory, West Stafford, Dorchester, Dorset DT2 8AB (☎ 0305 64637)

OLIVER, Col the Rev Kenneth Cyril; CBE (1959), (OBE 1949, TD 1947); s of Capt Cyril Francis Harrison Oliver (ka 1916), and Margaret Grant, *née* White; *b* 13 June 1908; *Educ* Christ's Hosp, St Edmund Hall Oxford (BA, MA), Westcott House Cambridge; *m* 1, 31 Dec 1934, late Margaret Elizabeth, da of Robert William Crabtree, JP; 1 s (Robert Grant b 23 March 1938); m 2, 2 Feb 1963, Anne Mary Hargreave-Mawson, JP, da of late James Eastick; *Career* Chaplain HAC 1938; Sr Chaplain: 10 Armd Div 1942, 46 Inf Div 1944; Asst Chaplain Gen Paiforce 1945, Warden RAChD Centre Bagshot Park 1949, ACG Egypt 1952, ACG Household Bde 1953, ACG FARELF 1956; princ West Down Tutors 1962, chaplain Ford Open Prison

1967, vicar St Mary's Climping Sussex 1973, chaplain Queen Alexandra's Home for Disabled Ex-Servicemen 1980; Queen's Hon Chaplain 1958; cmmr Boy Scouts' Assoc, chm Children's Soc, govr Christ's Hosp; *Books* Chaplain at War (1986); *Recreations* rugby, cricket, tennis, squash; *Clubs* Army and Navy, MCC; *Style*— Col The Rev Kenneth Oliver, CBE, OBE, TD; Manor Cottage, Bury, Pulborough, W Sussex RH20 1PB (☎ 0798 831 404)

OLIVER, Prof Michael Francis; CBE (1985); s of Capt Wilfrid Francis Lenn Oliver, MC (d 1940); *b* 3 July 1925; *Educ* Marlborough, Edinburgh Univ (MD); *m* 1, 1948 (m dis 1979), Margaret Yool, da of Maj James Yool Abbey, DSO, MC (d 1932); 2 s (and 1 s decd), 1 da; m 2, 1985, Helen Louise, da of Cyril Cockrell; *Career* Duke of Edinburgh prof of cardiology Univ of Edinburgh 1979-; pres Br Cardiac Soc 1981-85, pres RCPE(d) 1985-88; chm: BBC Med Advsy Gp Scotland 1975-80, personal prof of cardiology 1976-79; UK rep Advsy Panel for Cardiovascular Diseases WHO 1972-, chm DOT Advsy Panel on Cardiovascular Diseases 1983-, examiner Cambridge and Edinburgh; hon MD Karolinska 1980, hon MD Bologna 1985; FRCP, FFCM, hon FACC, RCPE 1986-, FRSE 1987; *Books* 5 books on metabolic, clinical and epidemologic aspects of heart disease; *Recreations* all things Italian; *Clubs* Athenaeum, New (Edinburgh); *Style*— Prof Michael Oliver; Barley Mill Hse, Pencaitland, East Lothian (☎ 0875 340433); 28 Chalcot Rd, London NW1; Cardiovascular Research Unit, University of Edinburgh (☎ 031 667 1011)

OLIVER, (James) Michael Yorrick; s of Sqdn-Ldr George Leonard Jack Oliver, RAF (d 1984), of Ca'n Brotat, Pollensa, Mallorca, Balearics, Spain and Patricia Rosamund, *née* Douglas; *b* 13 July 1940; *Educ* Brunswick Sch, Wellington; *m* 22 June 1963, Sally Elizabeth Honor da of George Gerhard Exner, of Upcote, Drove Rd, Chilbolton, nr Stockbridge, Hants; 2 da (Sophia Tugela Rosamund b 14 Oct 1969, Justine Unthandi Electra b 29 Dec 1971); *Career* stockbroker; memb London Common Cncl 1980, alderman of Bishopsgate 1987; dep chm St John Ambulance City of London Appeal Ctee, govt Bishopsgate Fndn; *Recreations* archaeology, travel, fives, windsurfing; *Clubs* City Livery; *Style*— Michael Oliver, Esq; Kitcat & Aitken, Level 6 RBC Centre, 71 Queen Victoria St, London EC4V 4DE (☎ 01 489 1966, fax 01 329 6150, telex 888297)

OLIVER, Dr Ronald Martin; CB (1989); s of Cuthbert Hanson Oliver (d 1972), of Strawberry Hill, and Cecilia *née* O'Dockery (d 1981); *b* 28 May 1929; *Educ* Kings Coll Sch Wimbledon, Kings Coll London, St George's Hosp London (MB, BS, MD, DCh, DIH, DPH); *m* 2 March 1957, Susanna (Sue) Treves, da of Dr Alfred Delatour Blackwell, of Taunton; 3 s (Richard b 1958, James b 1960, Philip b 1966), 1 da (Sarah b 1971); *Career* Surgn Lt RNVR 1953-55, Surgn Lt Cdr 1959; jr hosp appts St George's Hosp 1952-56, trainee asst GP 1956-57, asst county mo Surrey CC 1957-59; mo: London Tport Exec 1959-62, Treasy Med Serv 1962-64; physician Br Embassy Moscow 1964-66, mo later sr mo CS Med Advsy Serv 1966-74, sr mo later sr princ mo DHSS, dep chief MO Dept at Health 1984-; memb BMA, FRSM, MRCS, LRCP, MRCP, MFCM, MFOM; *Recreations* golf, gardening, sailing; *Style*— Dr Ronald Oliver, CB; Greenhill House, Beech Ave, Effingham, Surrey KT24 5PH (☎ 0372 52887); Dept of Health, Richmond House, 79 Whitehall, London SW1A 2ND (☎ 01 210 5593)

OLIVER, Hon Mrs; Sarah Chichester; o da of Baron Oliver of Aylmerton (Life Peer), *qv*; has resumed her maiden name; *m* 1974 (m dis 1983), James Robert Goldsack; 2 da (Katy Louise b 1980, Rebecca b 1983); *Style*— Hon Mrs Sarah OLiver

OLIVER, Stephen John Lindsay; QC; s of Phillip Daniel Oliver (d 1979; Capt RN Carlton), and Audrey Mary Raylor; *b* 14 Nov 1938; *Educ* Rugby Sch 1952-56, Oriel Coll Oxford 1959-62 (MA) Jurisprudence; *m* 1967, Ann Dawn, da of Gordon Taylor, of Gerrards Cross; 1 s (Adam b 1970), 2 da (Rebecca b 1969, Rosemary b 1972); *Career* RNVR (sumbariner) 1958-59; barr; assis parly commr, asst rec; chm Blackheat Concert Halls 1986; *Recreations* music, sailing; *Clubs* Groucho; *Style*— Steophen J L Oliver, QC; 14 Eliot Place, Blackheat SE3 (☎ 01 583 9770); 4 Pump Court, Temple EC4Y 7AN

OLIVER OF AYLMERTON, Baron (Life Peer UK 1986), of Aylmerton, Co Norfolk; Peter Raymond Oliver; PC (1980); s of David Thomas Oliver (d 1947), and Alice Maud, da of George Kirby; *b* 7 Mar 1921; *Educ* The Leys Sch Cambridge, Trinity Hall Cambridge (hon fellow 1980); *m* 1, 1945, Mary Chichester (d 1985), da of Sir Eric Keightley Rideal, MBE, FRS; 1 s, 1 da; m 2, 1987, Wendy Anne, widow of Ivon Lloyd Lewis Jones; *Career* barr Lincoln's Inn 1948; QC 1965; High Court Judge (Chancery) 1974-80; Lord Justice of Appeal 1980-86; memb Restrictive Practices Ct 1976-80; chm Review Body on High Ct Chancery Div 1979-81; memb Supreme Court Rule Ctee 1982-85; Lord of Appeal in Ordinary 1986; kt 1974; *Style*— The Rt Hon Lord Oliver of Aylmerton; The Canadas, Aylmerton, Norfolk

OLIVER-BELLASIS, Hugh Richard; s of Lt-Col John Oliver-Bellasis, DSO, JP, DL (d 1979), and Anne Mary, *née* Bates; *b* 11 April 1945; *Educ* Winchester, RMA Sandhurst; *m* 7 Aug 1971, Daphne Phoebe, da of Arthur Christopher Parsons, of Hatchwood House Odiham; 2 da (Joanna b 8 April 1975, Nicola b 12 June 1978); *Career* 2 Lt Royal Fusiliers City of London Regt 1964, Welsh Guards 1970, Maj 1977 (ret); dir Manydown Co 1964, farmer 1980-, chm Hants Farm Devpts 1985-; vice chm Parish Cncl 1980-, memb Rural Devpt Strat Steering Gp 1987-, memb Miny of Agric SE Regnl Panel 1988, Hants Co Exec NFU 1989; chm The Cereals and Gamebirds Res Project 1983, Br Deer Soc 1988, cncl memb RASE, memb The Game Conservy Tst, memb ctee FACE (UK); Freeman City of London 1967, Liveryman Worshipful Co of Merchant Taylors' 1971; *Recreations* field sports, wine, food, motor racing; *Clubs* Army and Navy, Boodles, Farmers, MCC; *Style*— Hugh Oliver-Bellasis, Esq; Wootton House, Wootton St Lawrence, Basingstoke, Hants RG23 8PE; The Manydown Co, Worting Wood Farm, Basingstoke, Hants RG23 8PA (☎ 0256 464292, fax 0256 782270)

OLIVEY, Alan Keith; s of Hugh Norman Olivey (d 1980), of Upper Norwood, London, and Kathleen, *née* Mills; *b* 14 Oct 1947; *Educ* Heath Clark GS Croydon; *m* 11 Sept 1971, Janet Mary, da of Raymond Edgar Crewes Hutton, of Beckenham, Kent; 1 s (Richard b 1981), 1 da (Louise b 1977); *Career* CA: Sydenham Snowden Nicholson & Co 1964-71, Ernst & Whinney 1971- (partner from 1980); FCA 1970, ATII 1970; *Recreations* badminton, gardening, philately, photography; *Style*— Alan Olivey, Esq; 75 Elwill Way, Beckenham, Kent BR3 2RY (☎ 01 658 1519); Becket House, 1 Lambeth Palace Road, London SE1 7EU (☎ 01 928 2000, fax 01 928 1345, telex 885234 ERNSLO G)

OLIVIER, Brig Charles Harold Arthur; CBE (1959); s of Capt Robert Harold Olivier (ka 1914), and Beatrice Dorothea, *née* Malden (d 1968); *b* 29 August 1912; *Educ* Wellington, RMA Woolwich; *m* 1, 24 June 1937, Lois Mary (d 1959), da of late J E James; 1 s (Robert b 5 March 1950), 2 da (Carol b 9 Dec 1940, Katherine b 21 Sept 1942); m 2, 17 Sept 1960, Evelyn Elizabeth, 2 da of Sir (Charles) Norman Lockhart Stronge, 8 Bt, PC, MC (assassinated 1981); *Career* Brig 1960; chm (Col) Planning Staff SHAPE 1956-58, COS (Brig) NI Commd 1958-60, Brig-Author War Off 1962-63, Brig RA Eastern Cmd 1963-65, ADC to HM The Queen 1964-67, Brig RA and COS Western Commd 1966-67; dep cmdt, asst chief constable Police Coll Bramshill 1968-71, cnclr Test Valley Borough Cncl 1973-83, Winchester Diocesan Synod 1976-88; govr Cricklade Tertiary Coll 1977-; vice-chm Mid Hamps Tourism Panel 1978-; *Recreations* travel, cricket, astronomy; *Clubs* Army and Navy, MCC; *Style*— Brig Charles Olivier, CBE; Rosemary Cottage, The Green, Amport, Andover, Hants SP11 8BA (☎ 026 477 2602)

OLIVIER, Dr Henry; CMG (1954); s of Jakobus Olivier (decd); *b* 25 Jan 1914; *Educ* Umtali HS, Univ Cape town (MScEng), Univ Coll London (PhD) Witwatersrand; *m* 1, 1940, Lorna Renee Collier (d 1978); m 2, 1979, Johanna Cecilia van der Merwe; 1 s (decd), 1 da (Lynne); *Career* chief rep Sir Alex Gibb & Ptnrs Persia 1945-48, on loan to US Consult Engrs on Iran's Seven Year Plan 1949, chief engr Owen Falls Scheme Sir Alex Gibb & Ptnrs 1950-54, ptnr Sir Alex Gibb & Ptnrs (Africa) 1954-55 (resident dir and chief engr Gibb, Coyne, Sogei), i/c civil engrg works Kariba Hydro-Electric Scheme 1955-60, conslt Sir Alex Gibb & Ptnrs (mainly on Indus Basin Project W Pakistan) 1960-69, ptnr Gibb Hawkins Olivier & Ptnrs (construction engrs on water control structures of Orange River Project S Africa) 1962-69, chm LTA Ltd 1969-73; major projects constructed: Cabora Bassa Hydro-Electric project Mocambique, Orange Fish Tunnel S Africa; sr ptnr Henry Olivier and Assoc 1973, conceptual design of major water and power projects for Southern Africa territories of Lesotho, Swaziland and Transkei, pres S African Instn of Civil Engrs 1979, memb Exec Ctee SABRITA (S Africa Britain Trade Assoc) 1970-87; Hon DSc: Cape Town, Rhodesia (Zimbabwe); *Books* Irrigation and Water Resources Engineering (1972) Damit (1975), Great Dams in Southern Africa (1977); *Clubs* Country (Johannesburg), Country Jeffreys Bay; *Style*— Dr Henry Olivier, CMG; 14 Tulip Ave, Jeffreys Bay, 6330 RSA (☎ 04231 31621)

OLIVIER, Hon Julie Kate; da of Baron Olivier (Life Peer); *b* 1966; *Educ* Bedales; *Style*— The Hon Julie Olivier

OLIVIER, Baron (Life Peer UK 1970); Laurence Kerr Olivier; OM (1981); s of Rev Gerard Kerr Olivier, of Dorking, Surrey; *b* 22 May 1907; *Educ* St Edward's Sch Oxford; *m* 1, 1930 (m dis 1940), Jill Esmond; 1 s; m 2, 1940 (m dis 1961), Vivien Leigh (d 1967), da of Ernest Hartley (d 1959); m 3, 1961, Joan Plowright, CBE; 1 s, 2 da; *Career* actor, producer, stage and film dir; first stage appearance in special boys' performance as Katharine in the Taming of the Shrew at Shakespeare Festival Theatre Stratford-on-Avon 1922, with Birmingham Repertory Co 1926-28, played Capt Stanhope in Journey's End 1928, American début 1929 in Murder on the Second Floor, Victor Prynne in Private Lives London 1930 and New York 1931, Richard Kurt in Biography 1934, Bothwell in Queen of Scots 1934, Peter Hammond in Ringmaster 1935 (under his own mgmnt), alternated Romeo and Mercutio with John Gielgud in Romeo and Juliet 1935; Old Vic 1937-38: Hamlet (also performed at Elsinore, Denmark), Sir Toby Belch in Twelfth Night, Henry V, Macbeth, Iago in Othello, Coriolanus; under his own mgmnt produced and played Romeo in Romeo and Juliet with Vivien Leigh, New York 1939; Lieut (A) RNVR until released from Fleet Air Arm 1944 to co-direct the Old Vic Theatre Co 1944-49 (with John Burrell and Ralph Richardson); Old Vic 1944-45: Button Moulder in Peer Gynt, Sergius Saranoff in Arms and the Man, Richard III, Astrov in Uncle Vanya; Old Vic 1945-46: Hotspur and Justice Shallow in Henry IV, Oedipus Rex, Mr Puff in The Critic; Old Vic 1947: King Lear (also dir); Australian and NZ tour with Old Vic 1948; Old Vic 1949: Sir Peter Teazle in The School for Scandal, the Chorus in Antigone; dir A Streetcar Named Desired (starring Vivien Leigh) 1949; manager St James' Theatre 1950-51: Duke of Altair in Venus Observed (also dir), Antony in Antony and Cleopatra, Caesar in Caesar and Cleopatra (US 1951-52); The Sleeping Prince 1953; Straford-on-Avon 1955: Malvolio in Twelfth Night, Titus Andronicus, Macbeth; Archie Rice in The Entertainer 1957, Coriolanus 1959; dir: Chichester Festival Theatre 1962-63, National Theatre 1963-74; NT roles include: Othello 1964, Edgar in The Dance of Death, Shylock in Merchant of Venice 1970, James Tyrone in Long Day's Journey Into Night 1971, The Party 1974 (final stage appearance); Films include: Fire Over England, Wuthering Heights, Rebecca, Pride and Prejudice, Lady Hamilton; produced, directed and starred in: Henry V, Hamlet (Oscar 1949), Richard III (1956), The Prince and the Showgirl (1957), Sleuth (1972); Hon DLitt: Oxon 1957, London 1968; Hon Oscar 1979; *Books* Confessions of an Actor (1982), On Acting (1986); *Recreations* tennis, swimming, gardening; *Style*— The Rt Hon the Lord Olivier, OM; 33/34 Chancery Lane, London WC2

OLIVIER, Hon Richard; s of Baron Olivier (Life Peer); *b* 1961; *Educ* Univ of California; *m* 28 June 1987, Shelly, *née* Dupuis; *Style*— The Hon Richard Olivier

OLIVIER, Hon Tamsin; da of Baron Olivier (Life Peer); *b* 1963; *Educ* Bedales; *Style*— The Hon Tamsin Olivier

OLIVIER, Hon (Simon) Tarquin; s of Baron Olivier (Life Peer); *b* 1936; *m* 1965, Riddelle, da of Patrick Boyce Riddell Gibson; 1 da; *Clubs* Garrick; *Style*— The Hon Tarquin Olivier

OLIZAR, Michael George; s of Bohdan Olizar (d 1985), Lt Polish Forces, and Isabella, *née* Will; Col Adam Olizar served in King Jan Sobieski's army at relief of Vienna 1683; *b* 20 Jan 1947; *Educ* Salesian Coll Battersea, Centl London Poly (MSc); *m* 23 Sept 1978, Sarah Jane, da of Alistair Sawrey-Cookson (d 1973); 1 s (Douglas b 1985), 3 da (Helena b 1979, Isabel b 1981, Clare b 1983); *Career* transportation planner; winner of Christmas Day race (Peter Pan cup) in the Serpentine 1981; memb cncl and exec ctee of the Polish Inst and Sikorski Museum in London; AMIEE, MCIT; *Recreations* swimming, hill-walking; *Clubs* Serpentine Swimming, Hurlingham, Long Distance Walkers' Assoc; *Style*— Michael Olizar, Esq; 18 Hazlewell Rd, London SW15 (☎ 01 788 3115)

OLLARD, John Deacon; s of Alfred Ernest Ollard, and Violet Grace, *née* Taylor; *b* 1 Jan 1947; *Educ* Strand Sch London, LSE (BSc); *m* 20 March 1971 (m dis 1988), Pauline Jenniffer, da of Ernest John Simmonds (d 1985); 1 s (Mark Deacon b 17 June 1974); *Career* CA; Touche Ross & Co 1969-73, gp chief accountant industries Ltd 1973-77, gen mangr and chief exec engineered materials div Engelhard Corp; fndr memb Local Employers Network Surrey; memb MENSA, FCA (1972), JDipMA

(1979); *Recreations* sport of all kinds, particularly cricket; *Style*— John Ollard, Esq; 69 Pine Walk, Carshalton Beeches, Surrey SM5 4HA (☎ 01 642 2209); Engelhard Ltd, Davis Rd, Chessington, Surrey (☎ 01 397 5292)

OLLERENSHAW, Dame Kathleen Mary; DBE (1971), DL (1987); da of Charles Timpson, JP (d 1967), and Mary Elizabeth, *née* Stops (d 1954); *b* 1 Oct 1912,Manchester; *Educ* Ladybarn House Sch Manchester, St Leonards Sch, Somerville Coll Oxford (MA, DPhil); *m* 1939, Col Robert Ollerenshaw, ERD, TD, JP, DL (d 1986): 1 s, 1 da (decd); *Career* chm: Assoc of Governing Bodies of Girls Public Schs 1963-69, Ct of Royal Northern Coll of Music 1968-86 (companion 1978), educn ctee assoc Municipal Corpn 1968-71; memb: central advsy cncl on Educn in England 1960-63, CNAA 1964-74, SSRC 1971-75, Layfield Ctee of Enquiry into Local Govt Fin 1974-76; memb Manchester CC 1956-80: alderman 1970-74 (hon alderman 1980-), Lord Mayor 1975-76, dep Lord Mayor 1976-77, ldr Cons opposition 1977-79; vice pres Br Assoc for Commercial and Industl Educn (memb delgn to USSR 1963), memb educn ctee City & Guilds London Inst 1960-73 (hon fell 1980); pres; Inst of Mathematics and its Applications 1978 (fell 1964-, memb cncl 1972-, hon fell 1986-), Manchester Statistical Soc 1981-83 (memb 1950-, pres 1983-85); vice pres UMIST 1977-86 (hon fell 1987); dep pro-chllr Lancaster Univ 1978-, pro-chllr Salford Univ 1983-; dir Manchester Independent Radio Ltd 1972-83; hon memb: Manchester Technol Assoc 1976- (pres 1981); Manchester Literary and Philosophical Soc 1981-; hon Col Manchester and Salford Univs OTC 1977-81; DStJ 1983 (CStJ 1978, chm Cncl OStJ Greater Manchester, memb Chapter General OStJ 1978-); Mancunian of the year Jr C of C 1977; Freeman City of Manchester 1984; Hon Fell Somerville Coll Oxford 1978, Hon DSc Salford 1975, Hon LLD Manchester 1976, Hon DSc CNAA 1976; FIMA, FCP, FCGI; *Books* Education of Girls (1958), The Girls' School (1967), Returning to Teaching (1974), The Lord Mayor's Party (1976), First Citizen (1977); numerous res papers in mathematics jnls; *Clubs* English-Speaking Union; *Style*— Dame Kathleen Ollerenshaw, DBE, DL; 2 Pine Rd, Didsbury, Manchester M20 0UY (☎ 061 445 2948)

OLLEY, Martin Burgess; s of Robert William Olley (d 1969), of Sheringham, Norfolk, and Dorothy Lillian Alexander, *née* Burgess (d 1941); *b* 11 August 1932; *Educ* Gresham's Sch Holt Norfolk, Coll of Estate Mgmnt London; *m* 1, (m dis 1971), Averil Rosemary Phyllis, *née* Cann; 2 s (Clive Matthew Burgess b 1961, Edward Martin Burgess b 1967), 1 da (Lucy Ann Burgess b 1963); m 2, 14 June 1980, Moira Bernadette, da of Joseph Kelly (d 1968); *Career* RAF 1950-52; Norwich Union 1950-73 (London Estates mangr 1973-80, Norwich estates mangr 1980-82, chief estates mangr 1983-; memb gen cncl Br Property Fedn, former pres Norwich Wanderers CC; Freeman City of London 1974, Liveryman The Woolmen's Co 1978; FRICS; *Recreations* golf, boating, squash, tennis, walking; *Clubs* RAC, Pall Mall, Norfolk Broads YC; *Style*— Martin Olley, Esq; 1 Marston Lane, Eaton, Norwich, Norfolk NR4 6LZ (☎ 0606 56495); 55 Netheravon Rd, Chiswick, London W1 (☎ 01 994 5985); Norwich Union Insurance Gp, PO Box 4, Surrey St, Norwich, Norfolk NR1 3NG (☎ 0603 682256, fax 0603 683950, telex 97388)

OLLIFF, Dr Donald Edwin; s of William Olliff (d 1975), of Bath, and Elsie May, *née* Stinchcombe (d 1972); *b* 24 Nov 1919; *Educ* King Edward Sch Bath, Bristol Univ (MB ChB); *m* 4 April 1953, Jennifer Mary, d of Lt-Col Richard Comeley, MC (d 1955), of Bibury, Gloucestershire; 2 s (Simon b 1955, Hugh b 1957); *Career* served 4 & 5 Parachute Bdes as temp Lt-Col 1943-47; med practitioner, SRO Bristol Royal Infirmary 1949-51, physician Bristol Univ 1951-53, GP Chipping Campden 1953-, (tstee Sir Baptist Hick's Almshouses, chm Govrs Champden Sch, pres Glos BMA 1977); memb: medical Min Advsy Ctee, Soc for the Protection of Ancient Buildings, Bristol Medico-Chirurgical Soc, Antiquarian Horological Soc; writer of medical papers; Liveryman SA, Freeman City of London; FRSM; *Recreations* rowing, parachuting, gardening, archaeology; *Clubs* Army and Navy, St James; *Style*— Dr Donald Olliff; Grevels House, Chipping, Campden, Glos (☎ 0386 840296)

OLNEY, Robert C; s of Herbert M Olney, of USA; *b* 19 August 1926; *Educ* Cornell Univ (BA); *m* 1948, Wanda, *née* Gasch (d 1988); 3 children; *Career* non exec chm and md 3M UK plc-1979-88, vice pres and gen mangr Nat Adv Co Chicago 1976- (div dir 1973, mktg dir 1969, gen sales mangr 1959); currently: dir Yale and Valor plc, chm Yale and Nutone Inc Cincinatti; Companion BIM, MInstD; vice-pres Sports Aid Fndn; *Recreations* golf, skiing; *Clubs* Burhill Golf, Hinsdale Golf, RAC; *Style*— Robert C Olney, Esq; Tudor Hall, 10 Farmleigh Grove, Burwood Park, Walton on Thames, Surrey KT12 5BU

OLOWO OF OWO; *see*: Olagbegi II

OLSEN, Gary Kenneth (formerly Grant); s of Kenneth George Grant (d 1968), and Patricia, *née* Haste (d 1966); *b* 3 Nov 1957; *Educ* Archbishop Tenison GS; *Career* actor: plays incl: Metamorphosis 1986, Up On The Roof 1987, Serious Money 1987-88; TV incl: The Bill 1984, Prospects 1985; *Recreations* golf, snooker; *Clubs* Addington Court GC, Kings Cross Snooker; *Style*— Gary Olsen, Esq; C/O Lou Coulson, 37 Berwick St, London W11 (☎ 01 734 9633)

OLSEN, Roy; s of John Sigmund Olsen (d 1971), and Florence Mary Olsen, *née* Ashworth; *b* 20 April 1945; *Educ* St Margaret's Anfield Liverpool, Art HS Liverpool, Coll of Bldg (Liverpool); *m* 22 July 1972, Francesca Carey, da of Capt William Sidney Hall, MC of Wales; 2 s (Luke Joen b 1975, Alexander Hall b 1976); *Career* architect, princ private practice The Olsen Harrison (ptnrship); dir: Bontddu Properties Ltd, Link Property Servs Ltd; architectural awards Snowdonia Nat Park, Stone Fedn; RIBA; *Recreations* golf; *Clubs* Royal St David's GC; *Style*— Roy Olsen, Esq; Trem Yr Eglwys, Dolgellau, Gwynedd, Wales (☎ 0341 423071); Arran Buildings, Dolgellau, Gwynedd, Wales (☎ 0341 422932, fax 0341 422044)

OLSEN, (James) Wilfred; s of August Mavritz Olsen (d 1957), of East Sheen, London, and Ellen, *née* Lyche (d 1959); *b* 6 Feb 1920; *Educ* Kings Coll Wimbledon; *m* 28 Feb 1953, Georgina Francės; 2 s (Roger, Jeremy); *Career* RNVR: Lt Special Branch 1940-46, naval intelligence div Admty 1940-45, staff offr (intelligence) Kristiansand S Norway; sec: D & W Gibbs Ltd (Unilever) 1948-51, Hudson & Knight Ltd (Unilever) 1951-55, chief accountant Associated Newspapers; chm PO advsy ctee Bromley, former chm Bromley and Dist Consumers Gp, local referee CAs Benevolent Assoc, memb Knights of StGeorge; Liveryman Worshipful Co of CAs 1980; FCA 1947, ACIS 1948; Christian X Freedom Medal (Denmark) 1945; *Recreations* bridge, consumerish caravanning; *Clubs* Royal Overseas League; *Style*— Wilfred Olsen, Esq; Correnden, 4 Waldegrave Rd, Bromley, Kent BR1 2JP (☎ 01 467 5218)

OLSZOWSKI, Stefan; s of Tadeusz Olszowski, of Sevenoaks, Kent, and Zofia, *née* Zembrzuska; *b* 25 Jan 1936; *Educ* The Oratory Sch Woodcote Nr Reading; *m* 17 Sept 1960, Patricia Margaret, da of John B Coates (d 1987); 2 s (Mark b 1962, Gregory b 1968), 2 da (Catharine b 1961, Susan b 1963); *Career* dep chm Coates Bros plc 1980, chm Bracefine Hldgs Ltd 1976, dir JS Hamilton Hldgs Ltd 1986; *Recreations* sailing, shooting, travel; *Clubs* Itchenor Sailing; *Style*— Stefan Olszowski, Esq; East Hoe Manor, Hambledon, Nr Portsmouth, Hants PO7 6SZ; Meon House, Petersfield, Hants GU32 3JN (☎ 0730 64674)

OLVER, Sir Stephen John Linley; KBE (1975), MBE (1947, CMG 1965); s of late Rev S E L Olver; *b* 16 June 1916; *Educ* Stowe; *m* 1953, Maria, da of Gino Morena, of Gubbio, Italy; 1 s; *Career* served Indian Political Service 1944-47, Br Diplomatic Service Karachi 1947-50, FO 1950-53, Berlin 1953-56, Bangkok 1956-58, FO 1958-61, cnsllr Washington 1961-64, FO 1965-66, The Hague 1967-69; high cmmr: Sierra Leone 1969-72, Cyprus 1973-75; *Clubs* MCC; *Style*— Sir Stephen Olver, KBE, MBE, CMG; 7 Seymour Sq, Brighton BN2 1DP

OLYMPITIS, Emmanuel John; s of John Emmanuel Olympitis, and Argyro, *née* Theodorou; *b* 19 Dec 1948; *Educ* King's Sch Canterbury, Univ Coll London (LLB); *m* 26 Oct 1979 (m dis 1983), Jan Golding, da of Arnold Golding (d 1946), of NY, USA; 1 s (John Emmanuel b 1981); *Career* dir Bankers Tst Int Ltd 1976-80, vice-pres Bankers Tst Co NY 1976- 80, pres Centaur Resources Inc NY 1980-84, ptnr America Acquisitions Co NY 1981-85, Whittington Int plc (part of Aitken Hume Gp) 1986-, chief exec and dir Aitken Hume Int plc 1988; dir: Aitken Hume Ltd 1988, Sentinel Life plc 1988, Nat Securities & Res Corpn NY 1988; *Books* By Victories Undone (1988); *Recreations* writing, tennis, sailing; *Clubs* Turf, Newport Reading Room Rhode Island USA; *Style*— Emmanuel Olympitis, Esq; 45 Eaton Sq, London SW1 (☎ 01 235 9005); Kalymnos, Dodecanese Islands, Greece; Aitken Hume Int plc, 30 City Rd, London EC1Y 2AY (☎ 01 638 6011, fax 01 623 4008, telex 8811791 HUME G)

OMAN, Dr Julia Trevelyan; CBE (1986), RDI (1977); da of Charles Chichele Oman (d 1982), and Joan, *née* Trevelyan; *b* 11 July 1930; *Educ* RCA; *m* 1971, Sir Roy Colin Strong, *qv*; *Career* designer; BBC TV 1955-67 (incl Alice in Wonderland 1966); theatre: Brief Lives 1967 and 1974, Contry Dance 1967, Forty Years On 1968, The Merchant of Venice 1970, Othello 1971, The Importance of Being Earnest (Vienna) 1976, Hay Fever and the Wild Duck (London) 1980, The Shoemaker's Holiday (National Theatre) 1981, Die Csardosfürstin (Kassel) 1982, Mr and Mrs Nobody (Garrick London) 1986, A Man for all Seasons (Chichester and Savoy) 1987, The Best of Friends (Apollo) 1988; ballet: Enigma Variations (Royal Ballet London) (1968), Sospiri (Ashton Pas-de-Deux) 1980, Swan Lake (Boston Ballet) 1981, Nutcracker (Royal Ballet) 1984; opera: Eugene Onegin (Covent Garden) 1971, Un Ballo in Maschera (Hamburg) 1973, La Boheme (Covent Garden 1974), A Month in the Country (Royal Ballet London) 1976, Die Fledermaus (Covent Garden) 1977, Le Papillon (Ashton Pas-de-Deux) 1977, Otello (Stockholm) 1983, Arabella (Glyndebourne) 1984, The Consul (Connecticut Grand Opera) 1985; TV: Hay Fever (Denmark) 1978, Separate Tables (HTV and HBO) 1982; films incl: The Charge of the Light Brigade (art dir) 1967, Julius Caesar (prodn designer) 1969, Straw Dogs (design conslt) 1971; exhibitions: Samuel Pepys (Nat Portrait Gallery) 1970, Mme Taussaud's Hall of Historical Tableaux; FCSD Designer of the Year 1967, NCTA best art dir award 1983; photographic contrib Architectural Review and vogue; Hon DLitt Bristol Univ 1987; *Books* Elizabeth R (with Roy Strong, 1971), Mary Queen of Scots (1972), The English Year (1982); *Style*— Dr Julia Oman, CBE (Lady Strong); Oman Productions Ltd, The Laskett, Much Birch, Hereford HR2 8HZ

ONIANS, Richard Anderson; s of Frank Arnold Onians (d 1986), of Thetford, Norfolk, and Marie Elise, *née* Anderson (d 1957); *b* 21 April 1940; *Educ* Thetford GS, Stanford Exec Program; *m* 29 July 1961, Marianne Dorothy, da of Archibald Laidlaw (d 1978); 1 s (Henry b 1965), 1 da (Sarah b 1961); *Career* various positions (latterly vice pres electronics and venture capital) Monsanto Co 1959-84, chief exec Baring Bros Hambrecht and Quist Ltd 1984-, dir Baring Bros & Co Ltd; dir Anglia 2000; FRSA 1986; *Recreations* books, history, visual arts; *Clubs* Savile, Fifty Four; *Style*— Richard Onians, Esq; 140 Park Lane, London W1Y 3AA (☎ 01 408 0555, fax 01 493 5153)

ONIONS, Ronald Edward Derek; OBE (1984); s of Benjamin Edward Onions (d 1970), and Elizabeth Amelia, *née* Lewin (d 1973); *b* 27 August 1929; *Educ* Edmonton County GS; *m* 1951, Doris Margaret, da of Reginald Monro Moody; 2 d (Sarah, Louise); *Career* journalist; newspaper journalist 1950-58; Southern TV news ed 1958-60, reporter, producer and newscaster BBC news and current affairs 1960-67, BBC news Prodr NY and co-ordinator for EBU 1967-72, head of news Capital Radio 1973-74, ed IRN 1974-77, ed dir LBC/IRN 1977-83, managing ed Special Projects Visnews 1983-; *Recreations* ski-ing, bird watching; *Style*— Ronald Onions, Esq, OBE; 53 Portsmouth Road, Surbiton, Surrey (☎ 01 390 0654); 41 Oaklands Avenue, Saltdean, Sussex (☎ 0273 34077); Visnews, 10 Cumberland Ave, London NW10 7EH (☎ 01 965 7733, telex 22678)

ONSLOW, Cranley Gordon Douglas; MP (C) Woking 1964-; s of Francis Robert Douglas Onslow (d 1938); *b* 8 June 1926; *Educ* Harrow, Oriel Coll Oxford, Geneva U; *m* 1955, Lady June Ann, *qv*; 1 s, 3 da; *Career* serv RAC 1944-48 and Co of London Yeo (TA) 1948-52; Foreign Off 1951-60 (serv Burma), exec memb 1922 Ctee 1968-72, 1981-82 and 1983-, chm 1984, chm Cons Aviation Ctee 1970-72 and 1979-82, parly under-sec (Aerospace and Shipping) DTI 1972-74; oppn spokesman: Health and Social Security 1974-75, Def 1975-76; memb UK Delegation Cncl Europe and WEU 1977-81, chm select ctee on Def 1981-82, min of State FCO 1982-83; has represented the House of Commons at cricket, bridge, fishing and rifle shooting; dir: Argyll Gp, Rediffusion plc; *Style*— Cranley Onslow Esq, MP; Highbuilding, Fernhurst, W Sussex (☎ 0428 53404)

ONSLOW, Sir John Roger Wilmot; 8 Bt (GB 1797), of Althain, Lancashire; s of Sir Richard Wilmot Onslow, 7 Bt, TD (d 1963); *b* 21 July 1932; *Educ* Cheltenham; *m* 1, 1955 (m dis 1973), Catherine Zoia, da of Henry Atherton Greenway, of The Manor, Compton Abdale, nr Cheltenham; 1 s, 1 da; m 2, 1976, Susan Fay, da of E M Hughes, of Frankson, Vic, Aust; *Heir* s, Richard Onslow; *Style*— Sir John Onslow, Bt; c/o Barclays Bank Ltd, Fowey, Cornwall

ONSLOW, Lady June Ann; *née* Hay; da of 14 Earl of Kinnoull (d 1938), by his 2 w, Mary; *b* 1932; *m* 1955, Cranley Gordon Douglas Onslow, MP; 1 s, 3 da; *Career* tstee Leonard Cheshire Fndn 1974-; *Style*— Lady June Onslow; Highbuilding, Fernhurst, Sussex (☎ 0428 53404)

ONSLOW, 7 Earl of (UK 1801); Sir Michael William Coplestone Dillon Onslow; 11 Bt (E 1674, of 2 cr, with precedency 1660); also Baron Onslow (GB

1716), Baron Cranley (GB 1776), and Viscount Cranley (UK 1801); high steward of Guildford; s of 6 Earl, KBE, MC, TD (d 1971), and Pamela, Countess of Onslow, *qv*; bro-in-law of Auberon Waugh, *qv*; *b* 28 Feb 1938; *Educ* Eton, Sorbonne; *m* 1964, Robin, o da of Maj Robert Lee Bullard III, of Atlanta, Ga (Lady Onslow's mother subsequently m Lord Aberconway as his 2 w); 1 s, 2 da (Lady Arabella b 1970, Lady Charlotte b 1977); *Heir* s, Viscount Cranley, *qv*; *Career* sits as Conservative in House of Lords; Lloyd's underwriter, dir Yorkdale/Continental Assurance Co Ltd; farmer (800 acres in Surrey), dir of garden centre at Clandon 1982-; served Life Gds M East; govr: Univ Coll Buckingham, Royal GS Guildford; *Style—* The Rt Hon the Earl of Onslow; Temple Court, Clandon Park, Guildford, Surrey (☎ 0483 222754)

ONSLOW, Jo, Countess of - (Nina); MBE (1953); da of Thomas Sturdee; *m* 1962, 6 Earl of Onslow, KBE, MC, TD (d 1971); *Style—* The Rt Hon Jo, Countess of Onslow, MBE; Sturdee's, Freeland, Oxford

ONSLOW, Pamela, Countess of - Hon Pamela Louisa Ellinor; JP (Guildford 1952); da of 19 Viscount Dillon, CMG, DSO (d 1946); *b* 1915; *m* 1936 (m dis 1962), 6 Earl of Onslow, KBE, MC (d 1971); 1 s, 1 da; *Style—* Pamela, Countess of Onslow, JP; 12 Callcott St, W8

ONSLOW, Richard Paul Atherton; s and h of Sir John Roger Wilmot Onslow, 8 Bt; *b* 16 Sept 1958; *Style—* Richard Onslow Esq

OPENSHAW, Hon Mrs; Hon Julia; da of Baron Cross of Chelsea (Life Peer); *b* 1953; *m* 1973, Barney Walker; 1 s (Woolf b 1976), 1 da (Joanna b 1978); m 2, 1987; *Style—* The Hon Mrs Openshaw; c/o Rt Hon Lord Cross of Chelsea, PC, The Bridge House, Leintwardine, Craven Arms, Shropshire

OPENSHAW, (Charles) Peter (Lawford); s of His Hon Judge William Harrison Openshaw (d 1981), of Park Ho, Broughton, Preston, Lancs, and Elisabeth Joyce Emily, *née* Lawford; *b* 21 Dec 1947; *Educ* Harrow, St Catharine's Coll Cambridge (MA); *m* 15 Dec 1979, Caroline Jane, da of Vincent Seymour Swift, of Brookhouse, Lancs; 1 s (Henry b 1986), 1 da (Alexandra b 1984); *Career* called to the Bar 1970, practised on Northern Circuit, junior 1973, asst recorder 1984, recorder 1988; *Recreations* general country pursuits; *Clubs* United Oxford and Cambridge Univ; *Style—* Peter Openshaw, Esq; 2 Old Bank St, Manchester (☎ 061 832 3792)

OPIE, Roger Gilbert; CBE (1976); s of Frank Gilbert Opie (d 1969), of Adelaide, S Aust, and Fanny Irene Grace Opie (d 1969); *b* 23 Feb 1927; *Educ* Prince Alfred Coll S Aust, Univ of Adelaide (BA, MA), Oxford Univ (BA, BPhil); *m* 10 Sept 1955, Norma Mary, da of Norman Canter (d 1979), of Highgate, N London; 2 s (Christopher Francis b 1956, Julian Gilbert b 1958), 1 da (Mary Jane Tregoning b 1962); *Career* asst lectr in econ and statistics Univ of Adelaide 1949-51, asst lectr and lectr in econs LSE 1954-61, econ advsr HM Treasury 1958-60, fell New Coll Oxford 1961-; asst dir: HM Treasury Centre for Admin Studies 1964, planning div Dept of Economic Affrs 1964-66, econ advsr to chm NBPI 1967-70, memb Monopolies and Mergers Cmmn 1968-81, Price Cmmn 1977-80; city cncllr Oxford 1972-74, dist cncllr Oxford 1974-76; *Recreations* sailing; *Style—* Roger Opie, Esq, CBE; New College, Oxford OX1 3BN (☎ 0865 248451)

OPPEN, Richard John Stuart; s of Arthur Harrie Oppen (d 1976), and Muriel Evelyn, *née* Dent (d 1984); *b* 29 Jan 1937; *Educ* Dulwich Coll PS, City of London Sch; *m* 1 June 1963, Wendy, da of Leslie William Day Suffield (d 1979); 1 s (James b 11 July 1969), 1 da (Lucy b 27 Jan 1972); *Career* Nat Serv 3 Carabiniers (3DG) 1955-57; dir Galbraiths Ltd 1984-88; md Berge & CIA (UK) Ltd 1989-; Freeman City of London (1980), Liveryman Worshipful Co of Shipwrights (1982); *Recreations* country pursuits; *Clubs* Naval & Military; *Style—* Richard Oppen, Esq; 1 Clarendon Way, Chislehurst, Kent (☎ 0689 25253); 46 Albermarle St, London W1 (☎ 01 499 3186, fax 01 495 4808, telex 261675)

OPPENHEIM, (Tan Sri) Sir Alexander; OBE (1955); s of Rev Harris Jacob Oppenheim (d 1944); *b* 4 Feb 1903; *Educ* Manchester GS, Balliol Coll Oxford; *m* 1930 (m dis 1977), Beatrice Templer Nesbit; 2 s, 1 da; *Career* tutor in mathematics Oxford Univ 1924-27, lect in mathematics Edinburgh Univ 1930-31; prof of mathematics: Raffles Coll 1931-48, Univ of Malaya 1949-50 (dean of Faculty of Arts 1949-51 and 1954); vice-chllr Univ of Malaya 1957-65 (acting vice-chllr 1955), ret 1965; visiting prof: Reading Univ 1965-68, Univ of Ghana 1968-73, Univ of Benin Nigeria 1973-77; kt 1961; *Style—* Sir Alexander Oppenheim, OBE; Matson House, Remenham, Henley-on-Thames, Oxon RG9 3HB (☎ 049 12 2049)

OPPENHEIM, Lady Bridget Sarah; *née* Sinclair; da (by 2 m) of late 19 Earl of Caithness; *b* 1947; *Educ* Butterstone House, Perthshire, Runton Hill, Norfolk; *m* 1976, Nicholas Anthony Oppenheim, s of Sir Duncan Oppenheim; 1 s, 2 da; *Style—* Lady Bridget Oppenheim; 61 Park Rd, Chiswick, London W4

OPPENHEIM, Sir Duncan Morris; s of late Watkin Oppenheim, TD, of St Helens, Lancs; *b* 6 August 1904; *Educ* Repton; *m* 1, 1932, Joyce Mary Mitcheson (d 1933); m 2, 1936, Susan May (d 1964), da of Brig-Gen Ernest Macnaghten, CMG, DSO (d 1948); 1 s, 1 da; *Career* slr 1929; asst slr with Linklaters & Paines 1929-34; slr British American Tobacco Co 1934: dir 1943, chm 1953-66, pres 1966-72, advsr 1972-74; dep chm Cwlth Devpt Fin Co 1968-74; dir: Lloyds Bank 1956-74, Equity & Law Life Assur Soc 1966-75; chm: RCA 1956-72, Design Cncl (formerly Cncl of Industl Design) 1960-72, Br Nat Ctee of Int C of C 1963-64, court of govrs Admin Staff Coll Henley 1963-71, Royal Inst of Int Affrs 1966-71, Tobacco Securities Tst 1969-74, chm Overseas Devpt Ctee of CBI 1970-74, V&A Associates 1976-81 (memb advsy cncl V&A 1967-80); dep chm Crafts Cncl (formerly Crafts Advsy Ctee) 1971-83; govr Repton Sch 1959-79; Hon FSIA 1972; Hon Dr and Hon Fell RCA; Bicentenary Medal RSA 1969; kt 1960; *Clubs* Athenaeum, Royal Yacht Sqdn; *Style—* Sir Duncan Oppenheim; 43 Edwardes Sq, Kensington, London W8 (☎ 01 603 7431)

OPPENHEIM, Martin John Marcus; s of Henry John Oppenheim of Maidenhead and Beryl *née* Harpham; *b* 25 May 1950; *Educ* Cheadle Hulme Sch, King Edward VII Lytham; *m* 1, 2 Nov 1971, Dawn, da of Stanley Wells of Maidenhead; 3 s (Marcus b 1976, Karl b 1979, Maximillian b 1981), 1 da (Alexis b 1981); m 2, 6 Sept 1986, Krystyna, da of Stanislaw Banasiak of Southend on Sea; *Career* chartered accountant 1973; *Recreations* yachting, bridge; *Style—* Martin Oppenheim, Esq; 6 Porter Street, London W1M 1HZ (☎ 01 935 2372, fax: 01 486 0640, car ☎ 0836 213174)

OPPENHEIM, (James) Nicholas; *b* 15 June 1947; *Educ* Edinburgh Acad, Columbia Univ; *Career* dir: Kellock Tst plc 1976-86, Sterling Credit Gp plc 1980-82, Argyle Tst plc 1982-, The Smaller Cos Int Tst plc 1982-, Dewey Warren Hldgs plc 1983-, Bear Brand plc 1986-, Whitegate Leisure 1987-, Tranwood plc 1988; *Style—* Nicholas Oppenheim, Esq; Whitegate Leisure plc, 39 King St, London EC2Y 2DQ (☎ 01 623 9021, fax 01 606 3025, telex 8813392)

OPPENHEIM, Hon Phillip Anthony Charles Lawrence; MP (C) Amber Valley 1983-; o s of Henry M Oppenheim (d 1980), and Baroness Oppenheim-Barnes, PC (Life Peer), *qv*; *b* 20 Mar 1956; *Educ* Harrow, Oriel Coll Oxford (MA); *Career* dir What to Buy plc (own Co founded 1978); publishing offices in London and New York; rugby player for Amber Valley RUFC; landowner (270 acres); *Publications* three books on new technology; *Recreations* rugby, travel, reading, tennis, skiing; *Clubs* Leabrooks Miners Welfare, Annabels; *Style—* The Hon Phillip Oppenheim, MP

OPPENHEIM-BARNES, Baroness (Life Peer UK 1989), of Gloucester in the Co of Gloucester; Sally Oppenheim-Barnes; PC (1979); da of late Mark and Jeanette Viner, of Sheffield; *b* 26 July 1930; *Educ* Sheffield HS, Lowther Coll N Wales; *m* 1, 1949, Henry M Oppenheim (d 1980); 1 s (Hon Philip Anthony Charles Lawrence, *qv*), 2 da; m 2, 1984, John Barnes; *Career* MP (Cons) Gloucester 1970-87 when her s Philip, *qv*, was elected MP 1983, it was the first time that both a mother and son sat in the same Parl; formerly social worker with ILEA; chm Cons Parly prices and consumer protection ctee 1973-74 (vice-chm 1971-73), front bench opposition spokesman (seat in Shadow Cabinet) prices and consumer protection 1974-79, min state (consumer affrs) Dept of Trade 1979-82, chm ctee of enquiry into pedestrian safety at public road level crossings 1982-; non-exec dir Boots Co Main Bd 1982-; memb House of Commons ctee of privileges, pres Br Red Cross Soc Glos Dist; chm Nat Consumer Cncl 1987; Nat Waterway Museum Tst; *Recreations* tennis, bridge; *Clubs* Glos Cons Assoc, Vanderbitt Racquets; *Style—* The Rt Hon Lady Oppenheim-Barnes, PC; Quietways, The Highlands, Painswick, Gloucestershire

OPPENHEIMER, Harry Frederick; s of Sir Ernest Oppenheimer (d 1957), fndr chm & dir Anglo American Corpn of S Africa, sometime MP for Kimberley in Union of S Africa parliament, by his 1 w, Mary Lina (d 1934), da of Joseph Pollak; *b* 28 Oct 1908; *Educ* Charterhouse, Ch Ch Oxford; *m* 1943, Bridget, da of Foster McCall; 1 s (Nicholas b 1946), 1 da (Mary); *Career* served WW II 4 South African Armd Car Regt; MP (S African Parl) Kimberley City 1948-58; former chm: Anglo-American Corpn of S Africa (ret 1982), De Beers Consolidated Mines (ret 1984); Metals and Resources Corpn (ret 1985); chllr Univ of Cape Town; Hon DEcon Univ of Natal, Hon DLaws Rhodes Univ, Witwatersrand Univ, Leeds Univ, Hon D Litt Univ of Cape Town; *Style—* Harry Oppenheimer, Esq; Brenthurst, Parktown, Johannesburg, South Africa; PO Box 61631, Marshalltown, 2017 Johannesburg, South Africa (☎ 833 7912)

OPPENHEIMER, Michael Anthony; s of Felix Oppenheimer (d 1962), of Highgate, and Ingeborg Hanna Oppenheimer; *b* 22 Sept 1946; *Educ* Westminster, LSE (LLB); *m* 14 April 1973, Nicola Anne, da of Basil Vincent Brotherton (d 1961), of Pinner; 1 s (James b 1980), 1 da (Rebecca b 1978); *Career* called to the barr Middle Temple 1970 (Blackstone Exhibitioner), memb SE Circuit, asst recorder 1985, recorder 1989; memb Common Law and Commercial Bar Assoc, Family Law Bar Assoc; *Recreations* cinema, theatre, books, performing and listening to music; *Style—* Michael Oppenheimer, Esq; 58 Airedale Avenue, London W4 2NN (☎ 01 994 5090); 5 Raymond Buildings, Gray's Inn, London WC1R 5BP (☎ 01 831 0720, fax 01 831 0626)

OPPENHEIMER, Sir Michael Bernard Grenville; 3rd Bt (UK 1921), of Stoke Poges, Co Bucks; s of Sir Michael Oppenheimer, 2nd Bt (d 1933 after a flying accident), by his w Caroline (da of Sir Robert Harvey, 2nd & last Bt, and sis of Diana, Lady Balfour of Inchrye (divorced w of 1st Baron); m 2, Caroline, as his 2 w, Sir Ernest Oppenheimer, f by his 1 w of Harry Oppenheimer); *b* 27 May 1924; *Educ* Charterhouse, Christ Church Oxford (BLitt, MA); *m* 1947, (Laetitia) Helen BPhil, MA, er da of Sir Hugh Munro-Lucas-Tooth, 1 Bt; 3 da (Henrietta (Mrs Adam Scott) b 1954, m 1978, Matilda (Mrs Neil King) b 1956, m 1978, Xanthe b 1958, m 1977 Hon Ivo Mosley, *qv*); *Heir* none; *Career* served WW II, Middle East and Italy, SA Artillery, Lt; university lecturer in politics: Lincoln Coll Oxford 1955-68, Magdalen Coll Oxford 1966-68; *Clubs* Kimberley (S Africa), Victoria (Jersey); *Style—* Sir Michael Oppenheimer, Bt; L'Aiguillon, Grouville, Jersey, CI

OPPENHEIMER, Sir Philip Jack; s of Otto Oppenheimer, and Beatrice, *née* Rose; *b* 29 Oct 1911; *Educ* Harrow, Jesus Coll Cambridge (BA); *m* 1935, Pamela Fenn, da of Carl Ludwig Stirling, CBE, QC; 1 s, 1 da; *Career* served WW II RA, cmmnd Berkshire Yeomanry 1940, combined ops Special Service 1942, Lt-Col Italy and M East; chm The Diamond Trading Co (Pty) Ltd, dep chm Charter Consolidated to 1982; dir: De Beers Consolidated Mines, Anglo American Corpn of South Africa Ltd; Bronze Cross of Holland 1943, Cdr Ordre de Leopold 1977; kt 1970; *Recreations* horse racing and breeding, golf; *Clubs* Jockey, White's, Portland; *Style—* Sir Philip Oppenheimer

OPPERMAN, Hon Sir Hubert Ferdinand; OBE (1952); s of A Opperman (decd); *b* 29 May 1904; *Educ* Armadale State Sch; *m* 1928, Mavys Paterson, da of Harold Craig; 1 s, 1 da (decd); *Career* former champion cyclist, holder of numerous world cycling records; MHR for Corio Vic 1949-67, chief govt whip 1955-60; min for: Shipping and Transport 1960-63, Immigration 1963-67; Aust high cmmr in Malta 1967-72; Medals of City of Paris 1971, Brest 1971, Verona 1972, Médaille Mérite French Cycling Fedn 1978; OStJ 1974; kt 1968; *see Debrett's Handbook of Australia and New Zealand for further details*; *Style—* The Hon Sir Hubert Opperman, OBE; 6A-12 Marine Parade, St Kilda, Vic 3182, Australia

ORAM, Baron (Life Peer UK 1975), of Brighton, in the Co of E Sussex Albert Edward Oram; s of Henry Oram (d 1963), and Ada Edith Oram; *b* 13 August 1913; *Educ* Burgess Hill Elementary Sch, Brighton GS, London Sch of Economics; *m* 1956, (Frances) Joan, da of Charles Barber, of Lewes, Sussex; 2 s (Hon Mark b 1967, Hon Robin b 1968); *Career* served 1942-45 War; sits as Labour peer in House of Lords; research offr Co-operative Party 1946-55; MP (Lab and Co-op) East Ham (South) 1955-74; parly sec Miny Overseas Devpt 1964-69; a lord-in-waiting to HM The Queen (govt whip) 1976-78, Lords rep on Shadow Cabinet 1983-87; chm Co-Operative Development Agency 1978-81; *Books* Changes in China (with Nora Stettner); *Style—* The Rt Hon the Lord Oram; 19 Ridgeside Ave, Patcham, Brighton, E Sussex BN1 8WD (☎ 0273 505333)

ORAM, Rt Rev Kenneth Cyril; s of Alfred Charles Oram (d 1962), of London, and Sophie Oram (d 1944); *b* 3 Mar 1919; *Educ* Selhurst GS, Kings Coll London (BA, AKC), Lincoln Theol Coll; *m* 4 Sept 1943, Kathleen Mary, da of William Gregory Malcolm (d 1949), of London; 2 s (Andrew b 1945, Stephen b 1949), 1 da (Ruth b 1947); *Career* ordained: deacon 1942, priest 1943; asst curate: Cranbrook Kent 1942-45, St Mildred Addiscombe Croydon 1945-46, Upington and Prieska SA 1946-48; rector: Prieska 1949-51, Mafeking 1952-59, archdeacon of Bechuanaland and diocesan dir of Educn 1953-59; dean: Kimberley 1960-64, Grahamston 1964-74; bishop

Grahamston SA 1974-87 (dean of province 1983-87), asst bishop Lichfield 1987; *Recreations* music, walking; *Style—* The Rt Rev Kenneth Oram; 10 Sandringham Road, Stafford ST17 OAA (☎ 0785 53974)

ORAM, Dr Samuel; s of Samuel Henry Nathan Oram (d 1956), and Ada, *née* Dennis (d 1966); *b* 11 July 1913; *Educ* King's Coll London, King's Coll Hosp London (MB, BS, MD Gold Medal); *m* 20 Jan 1940, Ivy Rose, da of Raffaele Amato (d 1961); 2 da (Helen Ivy (Mrs Bellringer) b 1942, Christine Rose (Mrs Oram-Rayson) b 1947); *Career* WWII Lt Col RAMC Europe, W Africa, India and Andaman Islands; conslt physician in private practice 1947-; Kings Coll Hosp: conslt physician 1947-78, dir cardiac dept 1959-78, sr physician 1969-78; conslt cardiologist Croydon Gp of Hospt 1948-69, chief med offr Sun Life of Canada Life Assur Co 1952-83, med advsr Rio Tinto Zinc Corpn Ltd 1970-85; examiner in medicine: Univ of London, Royal Coll of Physicians, Soc of Apothecaries; assessor of MD Thesis Univ of Cambridge, censor Royal Coll of Physicians 1972-74, consulting cardiologist King's Health Dist (Teaching) 1980, emeritus lectr in medicine King's Coll Med Sch 1980; hon sec and tres Br Cardiac Soc 1951-56, pres Soc of Cardiological Technicians 1969-72; author of over 100 published papers; MRCS, LRCP, MRCP, FRCP; *Books* Clinical Heart Disease (2 edn 1981) ; *Recreations* golf, French; *Clubs* Athenaeum; *Style—* Dr Samuel Oram; 133 Cedar Drive, Parklands, Chichester, W Sussex PO19 3EL (☎ 0243 785521); 73 Harley St, London W1N 1DE (☎ 01 935 9942)

ORANGE, Brian Peter Harvey; s of Richard Brian Orange (d 1963), Mary Alice Kekewich, *née* Harvey (d 1979); *b* 4 Mar 1946; *Educ* Winchester Coll, Univ of Birmingham (BSc); *m* 23 May 1970, Anne Denise, da of The Hon Denis Gomer Berry (d 1983), of Brockenhurst Park; 3 s (Michael b 1973, Simon b 1974, Jonathan b 1976); *Career* md Orange Chemicals Ltd Winchester 1976-; cdr St John Ambulance Bde Hampshire 1985-; Cons Assoc; CstJ 1987; *Recreations* collecting bookmatches; *Clubs* Hampshire, Bembridge Sailing; *Style—* Brian P H Orange, Esq; Fromans House, Kings, Somborne, Hants (☎ 0794 388 235); Orange Chemicals Ltd, 34 St Thomas Street, Winchester, Hampshire (☎ 0962 842525)

ORANGE, Charles William; s of Richard Brian Orange (d 1963), of Oxshott, Surrey, and Mary Alice Kekewich, *née* Harvey (d 1979); *b* 23 June 1942; *Educ* Winchester; *m* 14 July 1973, Jane, da of (George) Peter Humphreys-Davies, CBE (d 1986), of Bucks Green, Sussex; 3 s (Richard b 1975, Hugh b 1978, George b 1980); *Career* asst mangr Peat Marwick Mitchell & Co 1968-71, gp fin controller UBM Gp plc 1973-82; fin dir: AAH Hldgs plc 1982-84, Assoc Br Ports 1985-, Assoc Br Ports Hldgs plc 1987-; former: ctee memb West of Eng Soc of Chartered Accountants, chm Sch PTA; FCA; *Recreations* tennis, opera, sheep; *Style—* Charles Orange, Esq; Hascombe, Godalming, Surrey GU8 4JA; Associated British Ports Holdings plc, 150 Holborn, London EC1N 2LR (☎ 01 430 1177, fax 01 430 1384, telex 23913)

ORANMORE AND BROWNE, 4 Baron (I 1836); Dominick Geoffrey Edward Browne; also (sits as) 2 Baron Mereworth (UK 1926); s of 3 Baron, KP, PC (d 1927), by his w Lady Olwen Ponsonby, herself da of 8 Earl of Bessborough, KP; *b* 21 Oct 1901; *Educ* Eton, Ch Ch Oxford; *m* 1, 1925, Mildred Helen (m dis 1936 and who d 1980 having m as her 2 husb Hon Hew Dalrymple, 2 s of 12 Earl of Stair), da of Hon Thomas Egerton (d 1953, 3 s of 3 Earl of Ellesmere and unc of 6 Duke of Sutherland) by Thomas's w Lady Bertha, *née* Anson, da of 3 Earl of Lichfield; 2 s, 1 da (and 2 da decd); m 2, 1936, Oonagh (m dis 1950), da of Hon Arthur Ernest Guinness (d 1949), gda of 1 Earl of Iveagh and sis of Maureen Marchioness of Dufferin and Ava; 1 s (and 2 s decd); m 3, 1950, the actress Sally Gray (otherwise Constance Vera, da of Charles Stevens); *Heir* s, Hon Dominick Geoffrey Thomas Browne; *Style—* The Rt Hon the Lord Oranmore and Browne; 52 Eaton Place, London SW1

ORCHARD, Jurat John James Morel; s of James William Orchard (d 1960), and Dorothy, *née* Harwood; *b* 4 June 1924; *Educ* UK and Ireland; *m* 24 Dec 1949, Maureen; 3 s (Martin b 1952, Nicholas b 1957, Jeremy b 1963); *Career* served Air Crew RAF 1942-47; with Midland Bank Ltd 1940-82; dir: Bank of Ireland (Jersey) Ltd 1983-, Aberdeen Mortgage Placement Co (CI) Ltd 1984-, Planet Financial and Legal Services Ltd 1984-; chm Bank of Ireland Tst Co (Jersey) Ltd 1984- (dir 1983); jurat of The Royal Ct 1986-; AIB; ctee memb Men of the Trees (Jersey); *Recreations* sailing; *Clubs* Royal Channel Islands Yacht (cdre); United; *Style—* Jurat John Orchard; La Vielle Maison, St Peter Jersey, CI

ORCHARD, Hon Mrs (Modwena Louise); da of 6 Baron Hatherton (d 1973), by his 2 w, Mary, Baroness Hatherton, *qv*; *b* 1947; *Educ* St Catherine's (Bude), Châtelard (Switzerland), Lonsdale (Norwich); *m* 1, 1968 (m dis 1974), Edward Willison; 2 da (Trecia b 1969, Rachel b 1971); m 2, 1978, Peter Fleming Orchard, s of Capt Frederick Henry Orchard (d 1958); 1 child; *Style—* The Hon Mrs Orchard; Copper Beeches, 9A Hartland Rd, Epping, Essex (☎ Epping 75601)

ORCHARD, Peter Francis; CBE (1982); s of Edward Henslowe Orchard (d 1958); *b* 25 Mar 1927; *Educ* Downside, Magdalene Coll Cambridge; *m* 1955, Helen, da of Sir Joseph Sheridan (d 1964); 2 s (Rupert b 1957, Timothy b 1963), 2 da (Marianne b 1959, Josephine b 1964); *Career* Capt 60th Rifles 1944-48; The De La Rue Co plc 1950- (chief exec 1977-87, chm 1987-), md Thomas De La Rue Int 1962-70, dir Delta plc 1981-; memb: Ct of Assts, Drapers' Co (master 1982); Hon Col 71 Yeomanry Signal Regt 1984-88; *Recreations* gardening, swimming, building, cricket; *Clubs* Travellers', MCC; *Style—* Peter Orchard, Esq, CBE; Willow Cottage, Little Hallingbury, Bishop's Stortford, Herts (☎ 0279 54101); The De La Rue Company plc, 5 Burlington Gardens, London W1A 1DL (☎ 01 734 8020)

ORCHARD, Dr Robin Theodore; s of George William Orchard, of Bexley Heath, Kent, and Christobel Edith Orchard; *b* 4 Oct 1940; *Educ* Chislehurst and Sidcup GS, Charing Cross Hosp Med Sch Univ of London (MB, BS); *m* 5 June 1965, Ann Seymour, da of Dr Thomas Seymour Jones (d 1986), of Wimborne, Dorset; 2 s (Timothy, Christopher), 2 da (Kathryn, Elizabeth); *Career* sr registrar Charing Cross Hosp WC2 and W6 1970-74, sr lectr in medicine Royal Dental Hosp 1976-82, post graduate clinical tutor St Helier Hosp 1978-86; conslt physician 1974-: St Helier Hosp Carshalton, Sutton Hosp, St Anthony's Hosp N Cheam; hon sr lectr St Georges Hosp Med Sch 1982-, Univ of London examiner in medicine and dental surgery 1982-; churchwarden St John's Selidon, Sy 1982-; Univ memb Croydon D H A 1987-; FRCP 1982, MRCS; *Recreations* cricket; *Style—* Dr Robin Orchard; Bowlers End, 67 Croham Rd, S Croydon, Surrey CR2 7HF (☎ 01 680 0253); St Helier Hosp, Wrythe Lane, Carshalton (☎ 01 644 4343)

ORCHARD-LISLE, Aubrey Edwin; CBE (1973); s of Edwin Orchard-Lisle (d 1934); *b* 12 Mar 1908; *Educ* W Buckland Sch N Devon, Coll of Estate Mgmnt; *m* 1934, Phyllis Muriel (d 1981), da of Arthur Henry Viall (d 1921); 1 s, 1 da; *Career* chartered surveyor, conslt ptnr Healey & Baker (former sr ptnr), govr Guy's Hosp 1953-74 (vice-chm bd 1963-74), govr Guy's Hosp Med Sch 1964-84, chm Special Tstees Guy's Hosp 1974-84 (special tstee 1974), property conslt NCB Superannuation Schemes 1953-; memb: Lambeth, Southwark, Lewisham AHA (Teaching) 1974-79, bd Gen Practice Fin Corpn 1966-80, Nat Bus Co 1971-83 (pt/t), Nat Bus Property Ctee 1971-83; dir Nat Bus Properties Ltd 1983-88; memb advsy panel: Nat Bus Pension Schemes, BEST (Estates) Ltd 1974-86; chm Advsy Panel for Instnl Fin in New Towns 1969-80; FRICS; *Recreations* work, gardening; *Clubs* Bucks, St Stephen's, Naval & Military, MCC; *Style—* Aubrey Orchard-Lisle, Esq, CBE; 30 Mount Row, Grosvenor Sq, London W1Y 5DA (☎ 01 499 6470); White Walls Quarry, Wood Rd, Marlow, Bucks (☎ 062 842573); Healey & Baker, 29 St George St, London W1 (☎ 01 629 9292)

ORCHARD-LISLE, Geoffrey; s of Edwin Orchard-Lisle (d 1934), and Lucy Ellen Orchard-Lisle *née* Lock; *b* 11 June 1910; *Educ* W Buckland Sch, Devon; *m* 16 Oct 1944, Rhona, da of George Comrie Nickels (d 1953); 2 s (John David b 1945, Simon Comrie b 1949); *Career* WWII Maj RA (anti-aircraft) England; jt md J Avery & Co (Est 1834) and (subsid) cos; (md 1953-70), pres Nat Assoc of Window Blind Manufacturers; *Recreations* cricket; golf; *Clubs* East Hert Golf, MCC, London Devonians CC, Soughgate CC, (represented CC Conference 1934, captained West End CC Business Assoc 1933); *Style—* Geoffrey Orchard-Lisle, Esq; Old Gaylors, Westmill, Buntingford, Herts SG9 9LB (☎ Royston 71530)

ORCHARD-LISLE, Mervyn Christopher; s of Ulric Lock Orchard-Lisle (d 1955), and Thelma Julie Spelman, *née* Burdett; *b* 6 June 1946; *Educ* Marlborough, Univ of Newcastle-upon-Tyne (BA, BArch); *m* 24 March 1979, Angela Jane, da of Edmund Louis Saunders, of Henham, Essex; 1 s (Alexander b 1985), 1 da (Lucy b 1983); *Career* chartered architect in private practice 1973-, sr ptnr Gotelee Orchard-Lisle; RIBA 1973; *Recreations* watercolours, books, motor cars, family life; *Style—* Mervyn Orchard-Lisle, Esq; Shepherd's Cottage, Heath End, East Woodhay, Newbury, Berks (☎ 0635 254282); c/o Gotelee Orchard-Lisle, 6 Cromwell Place, Northbrook St, Newbury, Berks (☎ 0635 36600, fax 0635 35053, telex, 848507)

ORCHARD-LISLE, Mervyn George; MBE (1946); s of late Edwin Orchard-Lisle, of Wembley, Middx, and late Lucy Ellen, *née* Lock; *b* 10 Oct 1912; *Educ* West Buckland Sch Devon, Coll of Estate Mgmnt; *m* 1, 5 June 1937, Phyllis Eileen Yvonne (d 1976), da of David Jones, of Wembley Middx; 1 s (David b 3 Aug 1938); m 2, 9 Dec 1977, Judith Ann, *née* Harrington; *Career* Maj RM Served RM Div, Combined Ops Landing Craft, 4 Commando Bde 1940-45, Admiralty 1945-46; sr ptnr Healey & Baker 1974-76 (joined firm 1930, ptnr 1947-76, ret 1976); pres: Herts Golf Union 1964-67, Hertfordshire Co Professional Golfers 1959-63, the GC Stewards Assoc of GB 1955-65; memb: Ctee of Mgmnt Inst of Urology 1959-66, bd of govrs St Paul's, St Phillip's and St Peter's Hosps 1957-64; FRICS; *Recreations* cricket, golf, travel, racing; *Clubs* Carlton, Turf, MCC; *Style—* Mervyn Orchard-Lisle, Esq, MBE; Les Vergers, Route De Fuont De Purgue, Tourrettes-sur-loup, 06140, Vence, France (☎ 93 59 34 92, fax 93 59 38 39)

ORCHARD-LISLE, Paul David; CBE (1988), TD (1971, DL 1986); s of Mervyn George Orchard-Lisle, MBE, of Les Vergers, Tourrettes sur Loup, Vence, France, and Phyllis Yvonne, *née* Jones (d 1975); *b* 3 August 1938; *Educ* Marlborough, Trinity Hall Cambridge (MA); *Career* chartered surveyor, sr ptnr Healey & Baker 1988; pres RICS 1985-6; Brig (TA) UKLF 1985; govr: Harrow Sch 1987, West Buckland Sch 1985; memb Cncl of Reading Univ; FRICS, FRSA; *Recreations* golf, squash; *Clubs* Athenaeum; *Style—* Paul Orchard-Lisle, Esq, CBE, TD, DL; Bedford House, Bidwell, Bedfordshire LU5 6JP (☎ 0582 867317); Healey & Baker, 29 St George Street, Hanover Square, London W1A 3BG (☎ 01 629 9292)

ORDE; *see*: Campbell-Orde

ORDE, L...... David John; JP (Northumberland 1965); s of Charles William Orde, KCMG (d 1980), and Frances Fortune, *née* Davidson (d 1949); *b* 25 August 1917; *Educ* Eton, Christ Church Oxford (BA, MA); *m* 1, 14 April 1942 (m dis 1947), Olivia Frances, da of late Richard Evelyn Beauchamp Meade-King; m 2, 10 June 1950, Audrey Elizabeth, da of Alfred Douglas Boot (d 1936); 1 s (Michael b 1957), 3 da (Lucinda (Mrs Bennett) b 1951, Rosemary (Mrs Oliphant) b 1953, Daphne (Mrs Farquharson) b 1956); *Career* WWII Capt RA 1939-46; chartered surveyor and land agent; JP Northumberland 1965-87, High Sheriff Northumberland 1970; FLAS 1954, FRICS; *Recreations* walking, shooting; *Style—* David Orde, Esq, JP; 14 Thorp Ave, Morpeth, Northumberland NE61 1JS (☎ 0670 514 435)

ORDE, His Hon Judge Denis Alan; s of John Orde, CBE, of Littlehoughton Hall, Northumberland, and Charlotte (d 1975); *b* 28 August 1932; *Educ* Oxford Univ (MA); *m* 1961, Jennifer Jane, da of Dr John Longworth (d 1982), of Mill Hill, Masham, Yorks; 2 da; *Career* served Army 1950-52, cmmnd 2 Lt 1951; RA (TA) 1952-64; barr Inner Temple 1956, recorder 1972-79, circuit judge 1979-; *Recreations* cricket, listening to music, biography, oil paintings of 19th Century; *Clubs* Carlton, Northern Counties; *Style—* His Hon Judge Orde; Chollerton Grange, Chollerton, nr Hexham, Northumberland; 11 King's Bench Walk, Temple, London EC4

ORDE-POWLETT, Hon (Patrick) Christopher; s of late 6 Baron Bolton; *b* 1931; *Educ* Eton, Jesus Coll Cambridge (MA); *m* 1962, Elizabeth Jane, da of A S Kent, of Worlington, Bury St Edmunds; 2 da; *Career* forestry adviser; conslt Allied Dunbar Financial Management; ARICS; *Style—* The Hon Christopher Orde-Powlett; Little Bordeaux, Little Chesterford, Saffron Walden, Essex CB10 1UA (☎ home: 0799 30410; office: 0223 323811)

ORDE-POWLETT, Hon Harry Algar Nigel; s and h of 7 Baron Bolton by his 1 w, Hon Christine Weld-Forester (now Hon Mrs Miles), da of 7 Baron Forester; *b* 14 Feb 1954; *Educ* Eton; *m* 1977, Philippa, da of Maj Peter Tapply; 3 s (Thomas Peter Algar b 16 July 1979, William Benjamin b 1981, Nicholas Mark b 1985); *Style—* The Hon Harry Orde-Powlett; The Corner House, Wensley, Leyburn, N Yorks

ORDE-POWLETT, Hon Michael Brooke; yr s of 7 Baron Bolton and his 1 w, Hon Christine Helena, *née* Weld-Forester (now Hon Mrs Miles), da of 7 Baron Forester; *b* 21 April 1959; *Educ* Gordonstoun; *m* 17 Jan 1985, Kate Mary, da of George William Laing, of Newsham, N Yorks; 1 s (James Michael b 21 May 1987), 1 da (Emma Katherine b 29 Nov 1988); *Career* farmer, landowner (420 acres); *Recreations* water skiing, skiing, motor cycling; *Style—* The Hon Michael Orde-Powlett; Howe Hills Farm, Leyburn, N Yorks (☎ Wensleydale 23746)

ORFORD, Richard Christopher Lewis; s of Christopher Wilson Orford (d 1978), late of Seer Green, Bucks, and Elizabeth Alice *née* Sharpe, f in law was an eminent E N T surgeon at St Bartholemews Hosp; *b* 13 Jan 1940; *Educ* Uppingham, Nat Inst of Dry Cleaning Silver Spring America; *m* 5 July 1969, Joan Emilia, da of Frederick Cecil Wray Capps (d 1970), of 16 Kent Terr, London NW1; 1 s (William b 1970), 1 da (Emily b 1972); *Career* launderer and dry cleaner; chm and md: Blue Dragon Hillingdon Ltd, Blue Dragon Beacon's Field Ltd, Blue Dragon Dry Cleaners Ltd; dir: of Assoc of Br Launderers & Cleaners Ltd 1979, Assoc of Br Laundry Cleaning and Rental Servs Ltd 1984-88, Liveryman of Worshipful Co of Launderers; *Recreations* sailing, skiing; *Clubs* Royal Southampton YC, Down Hill Onley (skiing); *Style*— Richard Orford, Esq; Hutchins End, Knotty Green, Beaconsfield, Bucks HP9 1XL (☎ 0494 674642); Blue Dragon Hillingdon Ltd, Whiteleys Parade, Wybridge Rd, Hillingdon, Middx UB10 0NZ (☎ 0895 36571)

ORGAN, (Harold) Bryan; s of Harold Victor, and Helen Dorothy Organ; *b* 31 August 1935; *Educ* Loughborough Coll of Art, Royal Academy Schs London; *m* Sandra Mary Mills; *Career* artist; lectr in drawing and painting Loughborough 1959-65; one-man exhibitions: Leicester, London, New York, Baukunst Cologne, Turin; represented: Kunsthalle, Darmstadt, Mostra Mercatao d'Arte Contemporanea Florence, 3rd Int Exhibitions of Drawing Germany, Sao Paulo Museum of Art Brazil; works in private and public collections in England, France, Germany, Italy, Switzerland, USA, Canada, Brazil; portraits include: Sir Michael Tippett, David Hicks, Mary Quant, Princess Margaret, Elton John, Harold Macmillan, The Prince of Wales, The Princess of Wales, Lord Denning, James Callaghan, The Duke of Edinburgh 1983; Hon MA Loughborough, Hon DLitt Univ of Leicester; *Style*— Bryan Organ, Esq; The Stables, Marston Trussell, nr Market Harbourough, Leics; c/o Redfern Gallery, 20 Cork St, London W1

ORKNEY, 8 Earl of (S 1696); Cecil O'Bryen Fitz-Maurice; also Viscount Kirkwall and Lord Dechmont (both S 1696); s of late Douglas Frederick Harold Fitz-Maurice (himself gs of Cdr Hon Frederick Fitz-Maurice, who was in turn 3 s of 5 Earl); suc kinsman, 7 Earl, 1951; *b* 3 July 1919; *m* 1953, Rose Katherine Durk, da of late J W D Silley; *Heir* kinsman, Oliver Peter St John; *Career* sits as Conservative peer in House of Lords; joined RASC 1939, served 1939-45 (N Africa, Italy, France, Germany and Holland) and 1950-51 (Korea); *Style*— The Rt Hon Earl of Orkney; 4 Summerland, Princes Rd, Ferndown, Dorset (☎ 893178)

ORLEBAR, Capt Christopher John Dugmore; s of Col John H R Orlebar, OBE, of St Helens, IOW, and Louise, *née* Crowe; *b* 4 Feb 1945; *Educ* Rugby, Southampton Univ, Coll of Air Trg Hamble; *m* 5 Feb 1972, Nicola Dorothy Mary, da of Dr Leslie Ford (d 1987), of Sheringham, Norfolk; 1 s (Edward b 1977), 1 da (Caroline b 1979); *Career* Cadet Pilot Southampton Univ Air Sqdn 1964-66, trainee pilot Coll of Air Trg Hamble 1967-69, First Offr and Navigator VC10 (awarded basic Instrs Trg Course), CAA Course Stansted for examiner/instr 1973, Sr First Offr Concorde 1976-86, appt examiner/instr to Concorde Fleet, chartered 2 Concordes for celebration of 50 anniversary of Schneider Trophy 1981; organised BBC documentary on Concorde in QED series 1983, writer and presenter BBC TV series Jet Trail 1984, published The Concorde Story to celebrate tenth anniversary of Concorde ops with BA and Air France; Capt Boeing 737 with BA 1986-; Freeman City of London 1975, Liveryman Worshipful Co of Air Pilots and Air Navigators; MRAeS 1984;; *Books* The Concorde Story (1986); *Recreations* family, Photography, music, sailing, canoeing, tennis, gardening; *Clubs* Royal Aeronautical Soc, Air League; *Style*— Capt Christopher Orlebar; Holt Cottage, Fairoak Lane, Oxshott, Surrey KT22 0TW, (☎ 0372 842100); British Airways, London (Gatwick) Airport

ORLEBAR, Richard Michael; s of Capt Richard Astry Bourne Orlebar (d 1980), of Hinwick House, Northants, and Barbara, da of Capt Frederick Charles Pilcher (d 1953); *b* 25 Oct 1938; *Educ* Stowe; *m* 1963, Barbara Anne, yst da of Francis Edward Gardner (d 1975), of Glebe Farm, Cranford, Kettering; 1 s (Richard Charles Edward b 1965); *Career* Royal Norfolk Regt 1957-60; dir of various private cos; landowner and proprietor of Hinwick House; *Recreations* shooting, skiing, swimming; *Style*— Richard Orlebar, Esq; Hinwick House, Nr Wellingborough, Northants (☎ Rushden 0933 53624)

ORLIK, Simon George; s of Herbet Orlik (d 1980), of Coombe, Granville Rd, St Georges Hill, Weybridge, Surrey, and Joan Primrose, *née* Gliksten; *b* 24 July 1946; *Educ* Charterhouse; *m* 24 July 1971, Jeanette Ann, da of Michael Lynch-Watson, of Worcester Pk, Surrey; 1 s (Elliott b 1974); *Career* dir: L Orlick Ltd 1972-, Roy Tallent Ltd 1972-, Mansells Ltd 1972-, Chapman Graham Mills Ltd 1981-87; memb cncl Tobacco Trade Benevolent Assoc, Tres Brentwood Veterans Hockey Club; Liveryman (memb ct) Worshipful Co of Tobacco Pipe Makers and Tobacco Blenders 1972; MInstD, FICAEW 1969; *Recreations* hockey, squash, tennis, music, travel, golf; *Style*— Simon Orlik, Esq; Orchard Cottage, Birch Lane, Stock Ingatestowe, Essex CM4 9NA

ORMAN, Dr Stanley; s of Jack Orman (d 1974), and Ettie, *née* Steiner (d 1984); *b* 6 Feb 1935; *Educ* Hackney Downs GS, Kings Coll London (BSc, PhD); *m* 1960, Helen, da of Joseph Hourman (d 1982); 1 s (David b 1961), 2 da (Ann b 1963, Lynn b 1969); *Career* Fullbright scholar; post doctoral res Brandeis Univ Waltham Mass USA, res in materials sci 1961-74; chief weapon system engr Chevaline 1981-82, min and cncllr Br Embassy Washington 1982-84; under-sec MOD 1984-, dir gen Strategic Def Initiative Participation Off 1986- (dep dir Awre Aldermaston 1984-86); Jelf Medalist Kings Coll 1957; published over 40 original papers in scientific journals; Capt London Univ Athletic Club 1957; *Recreations* sport, reading, designing bow ties; *Style*— Dr Stanley Orman; 311 The Meadway, Reading, Berks RG3 4NS (☎ 0734 424880); MOD, Northumberland House, Northumberland Ave, WC2N 5BP

ORME, Rt Hon Stan(ley); PC (1974), MP (Lab) Salford E 1983-; s of Sherwood Orme; *b* 5 April 1923; *Educ* part-time technical sch, Nat Cncl Labour Colls & WEA; *m* 1951, Irene Mary, da of Vernon Fletcher Harris; *Career* served RAF as Warrant Offr Air-Bomber Navigator (Bomber Command) 1942-47 in Europe & M East; fought (Lab) Stockport S 1959, MP (Lab) Salford W 1964-1983; min state: NI 1974-76, DHSS 1976, Social Security 1976-77; Social Security Min (with seat in Cabinet) 1977-79; ch oppn spokesman and memb shadow cabinet: Industry Dec 1980-Nov 1983, Energy Nov 1983-; memb AUEW; Hon DSc Univ of Salford 1985; *Recreations* walking, reading American literature, music (jazz & opera), supporting Manchester United; *Clubs* Lancs Country Cricket; *Style*— The Rt Hon Stanley Orme, PC, MP; 8 Northwood Grove, Sale, Cheshire M33 3AW (☎ 061 973 5341)

ORME-SMITH, Hon Mrs (Teresa Caroline); *née* Shaw; da of Baron Kilbrandon, PC (Life Peer); *b* 1940; *m* 1969, Christopher Orme-Smith; 1 s (Andrew b 1974), 2 da (Philippa b 1969, Nicola b 1971); *Style*— The Hon Mrs Orme-Smith; PO Rongai, Kenya

ORMEROD, Alec William; s of William Ormerod (d 1958), and Susan Ormerod (d 1972); *b* 19 July 1932; *Educ* Nelson, Christ's Coll Cambridge (MA, LLM); *m* 23 Oct 1976, Patricia Mary, da of George Frederick Large, of Alsager, Cheshire; *Career* Nat Serv Army 1956-58; admitted slr 1956, local govt 1958-63, sr ptnr Boyle & Ormerod Aylesbury 1963-88, met magistrate 1988-; cncllr Aylesbury Borough Cncl; Freeman City of London 1973; *Recreations* fine art, travel; *Clubs* Naval and Military; *Style*— Alec Ormerod, Esq; Camberwell Green Court, London SE5 (☎ 01 703 0909)

ORMEROD, Brig Denis Leonard; CBE (1976), MBE (1950); s of Harold Eric Ormerod, CBE (d 1959), and Kathleen Mary, *née* Bourke (d 1957); *b* 17 Feb 1922; *Educ* Downside; *m* 7 Oct 1950, Frances Mary Shewell, da of Brig Charles Edward Francis Turner, CBE, DSO, of Wadhurst, E Sussex; 2 s (Giles b 1957, Jonathan b 1962), 6 da (Jennifer b 1951, Julia b 1953, Teresa b 1959, Jessica b 1960, Clare b 1964, Katherine b 1968); *Career* Brig; cmmnd 1941 2 KEO Gurkhas (Indian Army), served in India, Italy, Greece 1941-47, transferred to RIF 1947, served in Palestine, Egypt 1947-48, Malaya 1948-50 (seconded to 1/2 Gurkhas), (despatches 1949), MBE 1950, Regt Serv RIF N Ireland, BAOR, Berlin, Tripoli 1950-60, RN Staff Coll 1960-61, Staff Sch of Inf 1961-63, CO 1 Bn RIF 1965-67 (BAOR, UK, Swaziland, Bechuanaland, Aden), asst Mil Sec Southern Cmd, Army Strategic Cmd 1967-69, Col GS MOD 1969-71, Cmd Ulster Defence Regt (11 Bns) 1971-73 (despatches 1973), Brig Inf 1 (BR) Corps 1973-76, sec NW England and IOM TA and VR Assoc 1976-87, DL Merseyside 1983-87; *Recreations* country pursuits, horses, music, gardening; *Clubs* Rhinefield Polo; *Style*— Brig Denis Ormerod, CBE, MBE; Kirkbank House, High Halden, Kent TN26 2JD (☎ 023 385 249)

ORMEROD, Dr Walter Edward; s of Prof Henry Ardenne Ormerod (d 1964), and Mildred Robina, *née* Caton (d 1984); *b* 22 Feb 1920; *Educ* Winchester, Queens Coll Oxford (MA, DSc, DM); *m* 7 Jan 1950, Elizabeth Noel, da of Thomas Henry Gilborn Stamper, MC (d 1980); 3 s (Henry b 1951, d 1987, William b 1952, Thomas b 1961), 5 da (Anne b 1953, d 1978, Sarah b 1954, Eleanor b 1955, d 1971, Philippa b 1958, Edith Mary b 1959); *Career* staff memb Nat Inst for Med Res 1949-51, lectr applied pharmacology St Mary's Hosp Med Sch 1951-54, sr lectr (reader and emeritus reader) London Sch of Hygiene & Tropical Medicine 1954-85 (sr res fell 1988-); *Publications* On the Pathology and Treatment of African Sleeping Sickness; on economic development and "aid" as major causes of ecological degradation and poverty in the tropics; *Style*— Dr Walter Ormerod; The Old Rectory, Padworth, Reading RG7 4JD; Dept of Electron Microscopy, London School of Hygiene & Tropical Medicine, Keppel Street, London WC1E 7HT (☎ 01 636 8636)

ORMISTON, James Alexander; MBE (1986), TD (1970); s of Sydney Alexander Ormiston (d 1972), of Wetheral, Cumberland, and Ada Joan *née* Johnston (d 1988); *b* 26 Sept 1928; *Educ* Carlisle GS; *m* 7 June 1952, Maureen Daphne, da of William Christopher Strong (d 1951); 2 da (Melanie Daphne b 1955, Victoria Marguerite b 1958); *Career* cmmnd Loyal Regt 1947, RWAFF 1947-49, S Lancs and Parachute Regts 1949-51, Bde Adj Lancs Bde 1951-53, Adj Army Sch of Physical Trg 1953-56; Border Regt TA 1956-74, unposted list MOD 1975-88 (Actg Lt-Col 1983-84); Grainger & Percy Bldg Soc 1960, exec Midleton Bldg Soc 1969, asst gen mangr Colne Bldg Soc 1978, asst regnl mangr Britannia Bldg Soc 1983-; chief cmdt Gtr Manchester Police Special Constabulary, vice pres Coldstream Gds Assoc Manchester, asst co dir St John's Ambulance Assoc Lancs 1980-83, chm NW Gp Bldg Socs Inst 1983-85, asst orgn sec Modern Pentathlon Assoc of GB 1953-56; memb ctee: SSAFA Cumberland 1962-69, Army Benevolent Fund Manchester 1971-78; tstee regtl chapel Carlisle Cathedral; CBSI 1970, MBIM 1976; *Recreations* inland waterways, reading, fishing, home and family; *Clubs* Army, Police; *Style*— James A Ormiston, Esq, MBE, TD; c/o Britannia Bldg Soc, Newton House, Leed, Staffs (☎ 0538 399 399)

ORMOND, Richard Louis; s of Conrad Eric Ormond, of Old Rectory, Cleggan, Co Galway, Eire (d 1979), and Dorothea Charlotte (d 1987), da of Sir Alexander Gibbons, 7 Bt, gn of painter, John Singer Sargent (Paternal); *b* 16 Jan 1939; *Educ* Marlborough Coll, Brown Univ USA, Christ Church Oxford (MA); *m* 10 May 1963, Leonée Jasper; 2 s (Augustus b 1972, Marcus b 1974); *Career* dir Nat Maritime Museum 1986, head of picture dept 1983-86 (asst keeper 1965-75, dep dir 1975-83) Nat Portrait Gallery; author of 'J S Sargent' (1970), Catalogue of Early Victorian Portraits in The Nat Portrait Gallery (1973), 'Lord Leighton' (co-author with Leonée Ormond 1975), 'Sir Edwin Landseer' (1982), 'Master of the Sea' (1986), 'F X Winterhalter and The Courts of Europe' (1987); *Recreations* cycling, walking, theatre; *Clubs* Garrick; *Style*— Richard Ormond, Esq; 8 Holly Terrace, London N6 6LX (☎ 01 340 4648); National Maritime Museum, London SE10 9NF (☎ 01 858 4422)

ORMONDE, 7 Marquess of (I 1825); James Hubert Theobald Charles Butler; MBE (1921); also Earl of Ormonde (I 1328), Earl of Ossory (I 1527), Viscount Thurles (I 1536), Baron Ormonde (UK 1821), and 31 Hereditary Chief Butler of Ireland (1177); s of Rev Lord James Butler (d 1929, 4 s of 2 Marquess, KP) and Annabella (d 1943) o da Rev Cosmo Reid Gordon; 12th Earl cr Duke of Ormonde 1661 as reward for fidelity to the crown, 2nd Duke was attainted 1715 for supporting the Stuarts; suc 1 cous, 6 Marquess, 1971; *b* 19 April 1899; *Educ* Haileybury, Sandhurst; *m* 1, 1935, Nan (d 1973), da of Garth Gilpin, of USA; 2 da (Lady Ann Soukup b 1940, Lady Cynthia Robb b 1946); m 2, 1976, Elizabeth (d 1980), da of Charles Rarden, of USA; *Heir* to Marquessate, Viscountcy and Barony none, to Earldoms of Ormonde and Ossory and Hereditary Chief Butlership: 17 Viscount Mountgarret (descends from 8 Earl of Ormonde); *Career* served WW I, late Lt KRRC; US businessman, ret; *Clubs* Naval and Military; *Style*— The Most Hon the Marquess of Ormonde MBE; 10 North Washington, Apartment 120, Hinsdale, Illinois 60521, USA

ORMROD, Hon Mrs (Barbara Helen); *née* FitzRoy; 4 da of Capt 2 Viscount Daventry, RN (d 1986); descent from Henry FitzRoy 1 Duke of Grafton 2 illegitimate s of King Charles II and Barbara Villiers, Duchess of Cleveland; *b* 19 Dec 1928; *m* 18 April 1952, Col Peter Charles Ormrod, MC, JP, DL *qv*; 2 da (Mrs Julian Holloway b 1958, Alice b 1964); *Recreations* sailing, gun dog trg; *Style*— The Hon Mrs Ormrod; Pen-y-Lan, Ruabon, Wrexham, Clwyd (☎ 0978 823336)

ORMROD, Major James Jardine; s of Maj Maurice Sarsfield Ormrod, DSO (d 1968), of Wrexham, and Eva Margareta, *née* Bell-Irvine (decd); *b* 3 Nov 1932; *Educ* Wellington, RMA Sandhurst; *m* 21 Sept 1961, Joanna Mary, da of Maj Gen C R Price, CB, CBE (d 1987), of Ogbourne St George; 1 s (Henry b 1965), 2 da (Jane b 1963,

Susan b 1969); *Career* joined Army 1950; cmmnd 2 Lt Queens Bays 1952; served BAOR Jordan, Libya, Aden; ret 1968 major; farmer 1968-; hon sec Sir W W Wynn's Hunt 1971-82; *Recreations* foxhunting, polo, golf; *Style—* Maj James Ormrod; Pickhill Old Hall, Marchwiel, Wrexham, Clwyd

ORMROD, Col Peter Charles; MC, JP (1958, DL 1972); s of Maj James Ormrod (d 1945), of Pen-y-lan, Ruabon, Wrexham, and Winifred Selina, *née* Bulkeley (d 1974); *b* 31 August 1922; *Educ* Harrow, RMC Sandhurst; *m* April 1952, Helen, da of Capt the Viscount Daventry, RN; 2 da (Jane Caroline (Mrs Holloway) b Jan 1969, Alice Amelia b Dec 1974); *Career* Capt 3 Bn Scots Gds 1941-47, NW Europe 1944-45; Maj 8 KR Irish Hussars 1947-55, Korea 1950-51; 4 Bn Royal Welsh Fusiliers TA 1957-64, Hon Col 3 Bn Royal Welsh Fusiliers 1984- dir: John Hughes (contractors) Ltd 1956-60, Flintshire Woodlands Ltd 1960-74, indept forestry conslt 1974-; dir: Abbey Nat Bldg Soc, Wrexham and Denbighshire Water Co; High Sheriff of Clwyd 1962, JP 1958, DL (Clwyd 1972); memb: Home Grown Timber Advsy Ctee, regnl advsy ctee Forestry Cmmn, Welsh Fisheries Advisory Ctee; AMICE, MICFor; *Recreations* shooting, sailing, photography; *Style—* Col Peter Ormrod, MC, JP, DL; Pen-Y-Lan, Ruabon, Wrexham, Clwyd LL14 6HS (☎ 0978 823336); Pen-Y-Lan Estate Office, Ruabon, Wrexham (☎ 0978 823336)

ORMROD, Rt Hon Sir Roger Fray Greenwood; PC (1974); s of Oliver Ormrod; *b* 20 Oct 1911; *Educ* Shrewsbury, Queen's Coll Oxford; *m* 1938, Anne Lush; *Career* serv RAMC WWII; pres Res Def Soc 1982-; QC 1958; Ld Justice Appeal 1974-82, when ret, High Ct judge (Family Div) 1961-74, barr Inner Temple 1936; hon fell Queen's Coll Oxford 1966, BM, BCh (Oxon), hon fell Manchester Poly, Hon FRCPsych, Hon LLD Leicester; chm: London Marriage Guidance Cncl, Notting Hill Housing Tst, Ctee Mgmnt Inst of Psdychiatry; Br Med Postgrad Fedn; visitor Royal Postgrad Med Sch 1975-, former hon prof Legal Ethics Birmingham Univ; FRCP; kt 1961; *Style—* The Rt Hon Sir Roger Ormrod; 4 Aubrey Rd, W8 (☎ 01 727 7876)

ORMSBY-GORE, Hon Alice Magdalen Sarah; da of 5 Baron Harlech, PC, KCMG (d 1985) by 1 w Sylvia (D 1967) da of Hugh Lloyd Thomas CMB, CVO, and Hon Gwendoline sis 5 Baron Bellow; *b* 22 April 1952; *Style—* The Hon Alice Ormsby-Gore; Paris, France; c/o Rainey Race Course Road, Oswestry, Salop

ORMSBY-GORE, Hon John Julian; s of 2 survg s of 4 Baron Harlech, KG, GCMG, PC (d 1964) and Lady Beatrice Harlech DCVO el da 4 Marquess of Salisbury; *b* 12 April 1925; *Educ* Eton, New Coll Oxford; *Career* Capt Coldstream Gds 1944; *Style—* The Hon John Ormsby-Gore; 14 Ladbroke Rd, London W11

ORNSBY, John Sidney; s of Leslie Sidney Ornsby, of Roca Marina, Palma de Mallorca, Spain, and Evelyn, *née* Buckland (d 1978); *b* 3 Oct 1936; *Educ* Bancroft's Sch Woodford Green Essex, QMC London (BSc) ; *m* 18 July 1959, Heather Doreen, da of Eric Stephen Padmore, of 21 Meryln, Devonshire Place, Eastbourne, E Sussex; 1 da (Suzanne Doreen b 1963); *Career* graduate engr Mobil Oil Co 1958-60; Ready Mixed Concrete Gp: joined 1960, dir UK Ltd and subsidary cos 1971-; dir Hall Ham River Ltd 1968-71, vice-pres Inst of Quarrying 1981- (chm 1979-81), chm Sand & Gravel Assoc of GB Ltd 1988-, appt to Verney Ctee on Aggregates 1973-77; FIQ 1978, CEng 1983, MIMechE 1983; *Recreations* bridge, gardening; *Clubs* St George's Hill, Claremont Park GC; *Style—* John Ornsby, Esq; Northfield House, Northfield Place, Weybridge, Surrey KT13 0RF (☎ 0932 847856); RMC House, 53/55 High St, Feltham, Middx (☎ 01 890 1313, fax 01 751 0006, telex 935547)

ORPEN, Capt Arthur Frederick St George; OBE, DSC (1943); s of Charles St George Orpen (d 1939), of Lisheens, Carrickmines, Co Dublin, and Cherrie Mary, *née* Darley (d 1950); Nephew of Sir William Orpen KBE, RA; *b* 19 Mar 1903; *Educ* Castle Park Sch Dalkey Co Dublin, RN Colls Osborne, Dartmouth and Greenwich; *m* 7 April 1940, Dorothy, wid of Cmdr A S H Morris, RN, da of Maj Marmaduke Johnathan Alderson (d 1925), of Tickhill, Yorks; *Career* cmd HM Submarine H50 1932, first Lt HM Yacht Victoria and Albert 1936-37, cmd HMS Gannet, sr naval offr Upper Yangtse, 1938-40, cmd HMS Wanderer and Hesperus, escort cdr Western Approaches 1940-42, cmd HMS Dido 1947-48; *Recreations* golf; *Clubs* Liphook GC; *Style—* Arthur Orpen, OBE, DSC

ORPEN-SMELLIE, Lt-Col Herbert John (Larry); OBE (1980); s of Maj William Archibald Smellie (ka 1940), and Elizabeth Staples Smellie, *née* Irwin, MBE; *b* 18 Jan 1930; *Educ* Wellington, RMA Sandhurst, Staff Coll Quetta; *m* 6 March 1954, Jean Rackley, da of Abram Rackley Watson, MBE (d 1987); 1 s (Giles b 1959), 1 da (Jane b 1963); *Career* cmmnd Essex Regt 1949 (joined 1948), Lt 1951, Temp Capt and instr Small Arms Lans Sch of Inf 1952-54, Capt 1955, Parachute Regt 1958 (Temp Maj 1958-59 and 1960-62), adj 1 Para 1958-59, Staff Coll 1961, Maj 1962, GSO 2 instr Fed of Malaya Armed Forces 1964-66, GSO 2 Ops HQ ME 1967, GSO 2 coord DG Weapons MOD 1968-70, 2 i/c 3 Para 1970-72, GSO 2 Staff Duties HQ NE Dist 1973-74, DAAG Mobilisation MOD 1974-76, chief instr Small Arms Lans Sch of Inf 1977-80, Lt-Col 1977, Special List 1980, ret 1984; RO III regtl sec 3 Royal Anglian Regt 1984-85, RO II G3 Trg HQ E Dist 1985-88, Lt HSF 1985, Maj OC 5 (HSF) Co 10 Para 1985-; rifle shooting, various GB Teams 1952-88 (Capt Canada 1975, Bisley 1980, NZ & Aust 1984), Capt Army Eight 1968-82; Awards: Queen's Silver Medal Bisley 1965 (Prince of Wales Prize 1988), Govr's Shield Hong Kong 1955 and 1956, Nova Scotia Grand Assoc Canada 1960 (Ontario 1975, Govr-Gen's 1 Stars 1956, 1960 and 1975); cncl memb Nat Rifle Assoc 1974-; pres: Essex County Rifle Assoc, SE Essex Branch Parachute Regt Assoc; memb RBL, govr local sch; MBIM 1973-86, MInstAM 1976-86; *Recreations* rifle shooting; *Style—* Lt-Col Larry Orpen-Smellie, OBE

ORR, Rt Hon Sir Alan Stewart; OBE (Mil 1944), PC (1971); s of William Orr (d 1948), and Doris, *née* Kemsley (d 1913); *b* 21 Feb 1911; *Educ* Fettes, Edinburgh Univ (MA), Balliol Oxford (LLB); *m* 1933, Mariana Frances Lilian (d 1986), da of Capt J C Lang, KOSB (ka Gallipoli 1915); 4 s; *Career* serv WWII RAF, Wing Cdr (despatches); barr Mid Temple 1936, pt/t law lectr UC London 1948-50, jr cnsl to Cmmrs Inland Revenue 1957-63, rec Windsor 1958-65, QC 1963, dep chm Oxford QS 1964-71, rec Oxford 1965, High Ct judge (Probate Divorce and Admty) 1965-71, presiding judge NE circuit 1970-71, lord justice of Appeal 1971-80; kt 1965; *Recreations* golf; *Clubs* Utd Oxford and Cambridge Univ; *Style—* The Rt Hon Sir Alan Orr, OBE; The Steps, Ratley, Banbury, Oxon OX15-6DT (☎ Edgehill (029587) 704)

ORR, Arthur Sidney Porter; VRD (1964, and bar 1974), DL (Co Down 1988); s of Sidney Orr (d 1980), of Old Holywood Road, Belfast, and Winifred Margurite, *née* McCurry (d 1974); *b* 18 Nov 1928; *Educ* Brackenber House Sch Belfast, St Columba's Coll Rathfarnham Co Dublin; *m* 17 March 1956, Evelyn Jane Ferguson, da of Derrick Harris (d 1932), of Malone Park, Belfast; 1 s (Timothy b 30 Sept 1962), 2 da (Dilys b 16 Sept 1957, Judith b 27 April 1959); *Career* Ordinary Seaman RNVR 1948, Midshipman 1949, Sub Lt 1950, Lt 1952; transferred RNR 1956, Lt Cdr 1960, CO HMS Kilmorey 1960-61, Cdr 1966, Capt 1968, CO HMS Caroline (Ulster Div RNR) 1969-72; ADC to HE The Govr of NI The Lord Wakehurst 1958-60, ADC to HM The Queen 1972; chm and md: McCaw Stevenson & Orr Ltd 1972 (works dir 1956), McCaw Stevenson & Orr (Printers) Ltd 1980, McCaw Steven & Orr plc 1984, OBH Plastics; dep chm bd of govrs NI War Meml Building, ctee memb Belfast Chamber of Commerce and Shipping, hon tres Eldon LOL VII, memb: Belfast Master Mariners Assoc, Lighthouse Advsy Ctee St Mary Axe; memb Royal Inst of Navigation; *Recreations* sailing, gardening; *Clubs* Royal North of Ireland Yacht, Irish Cruising, Cruising Assoc; *Style—* Arthur Orr, Esq, VRD, DL; Evergreen, Old Holywood Rd, Belfast BT4 2HJ (☎ 0232 63601); McCaw Stevenson & Orr plc, 162 Castlereagh Rd, Belfast BT5 5FW (☎ 0232 452 428)

ORR, Sir David Alexander; MC and bar (1945); s of Canon Adrian William Fielder Orr (1964), of Dublin and Grace, *née* Robinson (d 1967); *b* 10 May 1922; *Educ* Dublin HS, Trinity Coll Dublin (BA, LLB); *m* 1949, Phoebe Rosaleen, da of Harold Percival Davis (d 1980, late Indian Forest Service), of Dublin; 3 da (Bridget, Catherine, Paula); *Career* serv WWII RE; chm Unilever 1974-82, vice-chm Unilever NV 1974-82 (joined Unilever 1948, dir 1967-82), chm Leverhulme Trust; chm Armed Forces Pay Review Bd 1982-84, exec chm Inchcape 1983-86; non-exec dir Rio Tinto Zinc, Shell Tport, CIBA-Geigy UK, Bank of Ireland; pres Liverpool Sch of Tropical Medicine 1982-, chm Br Cncl 1985-; The Shakespeare Globe Tst 1985- Hon LLD Dublin, DUniv Surrey; Cdr Order of Orange Nassau 1979; FRSA; kt 1977; *Recreations* travel, golf, watching rugby; *Style—* Sir David Orr, MC; Home Farm House, Shackleford, Godalming, Surrey GU8 6AH (☎ Guildford 810350); 81 Lyall Mews West, London SW1 (☎ 01 235 7970), Inchcape plc, St James's House, 23 King St, London SW1Y 6QY

ORR, Sir John Henry; OBE (1972), QPM (1977); *b* 13 June 1918; *Educ* George Heriot's Sch Edinburgh; *m* 1942, Isobel Campbell; 1 s, 1 da; *Career* WWII flying RAF; chief constable Lothian and Borders Police 1975-83 (Dundee 1960-68, Lothian and Beebles 1968-75__; dir Scottish bd Nationwide Building Soc; OSTJ Jubilee Medal, FBIM; kt 1979 ; *Style—* Sir John Orr, OBE, QPM; 12 Lanark Rd West, Currie, Midlothian EH14 5ET

ORR, Robin - Robert Kemsley; CBE (1972); s of Robert Workman Orr (d 1942), and Florence Mary, *née* Kemsley (d 1943); *b* 2 June 1909; *Educ* Loretto Sch, RCM, Pembroke Coll Cambridge (MA, MusD); *m* 1, 1937 (m dis 1979), Margaret Ellen, da of late A C Mace; 1 s, 2 da; m 2, 1979, Doris Ruth, da of late Leo Meyer-Bechtler of Zürich; *Career* serv RAFVR 1941-45, Flt-Lt; composer, organist St John's Cambridge 1938-51, lectr Cambridge 1947-56; prof RCM 1950-56; prof of music: Glasgow Univ 1956-65, Cambridge Univ 1965-76 (emeritus 1976-); chm Scottish Opera 1962-76, dir Welsh Nat Opera 1977-83; fell St John's Coll Cambridge 1948-56 and 1965-76 (hon fell 1987-); FRCM, FRSAMD, Hon RAM; Hon DMus Glasgow, Hon LLD Dundee; *Compositions incl* Oedipus at Colonus (Cambridge 1950), Rhapsody for string orch (English Chamber Orch 1967), Symphony in One Movement (Edinburgh Festival 1965), Symphony No 2 (Edinburgh Festival 1975), Symphony No 3 (Llandaff Festival 1978); *Operas* Full Circle (1 act - 30 performances on TV and radio 1968-69), Hermiston (3 acts - Edinburgh Festival 1975), On The Razzle (3 acts - RSAMD commn and premiere Glasgow 1988); *Recreations* gardening, mountain walks; *Style—* Robin Orr, Esq, CBE; 16 Cranmer Rd, Cambridge (☎ 0223 352858)

ORR, Dr Robin Gooch; s of Daniel Orr (d 1959), of St Leonards-on-Sea, E Sussex, and Elizabeth, *née* Gooch (d 1933); *b* 23 Jan 1924; *Educ* Caterham Sch Surrey, Guy's Hosp Med Sch London Univ, London Sch of Hygiene and Tropical Med London Univ (MB BS); *m* 11 Sept 1951, (Muriel) Joy Morley, da of Capt William Harvey Stones (d 1940), of Harrogate, Yorks; 1 s (Jeremy b 1963, d 1975); *Career* Capt REME 1945-47; house appts Guys Hosp London 1953-55, asst indust med offr Boots Pure Drug Co 1956-59, indust med offr AERE Harwell 1959-71 and Beecham Pharmaceuticals 1971-74, chief occupational med offr Beecham Pharmaceuticals 1974-89; memb St Pauls Church Dorking; Freeman: City of London 1978, Worshipful Co of Apothecaries 1978; memb Soc of Occupational Med 1986, MFOM (RCP) 1979; *Recreations* golf, bridge, tennis; *Style—* Dr Robin Orr; 9 Pointers Hill, Westcott, Dorking, Surrey RH4 3PF (☎ 0306 888 596)

ORR EWING, Archibald Donald; s and h of Sir Ronald Orr Ewing, 5 Bt; *b* 20 Dec 1938; *Educ* Gordonstoun, Trinity Coll Dublin (BA); *m* 1, 1965 (m dis 1972), Venetia, da of Maj Richard Turner; m 2, 1972, Nicola, da of Reginald Black, of Brook House, Fovant, nr Salisbury, Wiltshire, and Eloise, *née* Innes-Ker, niece of 8 Duke of Roxburghe; 1 s (Alastair b 1982); *Career* landowner; memb Royal Co of Archers (Queen's Body Guard for Scotland); *Recreations* shooting, fishing, stalking, opera, theatre; *Clubs* New (Edinburgh), Pratt's; *Style—* Archibald Orr Ewing, Esq; 13 Warriston Cres, Edinburgh EH3 5LA (☎ 031 556 9319)

ORR EWING, Maj Edward Stuart; DL (Wigtownshire 1970); s of Capt David Orr Ewing, DSO, DL (d 1964, s of Charles Orr Ewing, MP Ayr 5 s of Sir Archibald Orr Ewing, 1 Bt), 2nd Mary da of late Benjamin Noaks of Nylstroom SA; *b* 28 Sept 1931; *Educ* Sherborne; *m* 1958 (m dis 1981), Fiona Anne Bowman, da of Anthony Hobart Farquhar, of Hastingwood House (see Burkes Landed Gentry 1965); 1 s (Alastair b 1964) 2 da (June b 1961, Victoria b 1962); m 2, 1981, Diana Mary, da of William Smith Waters, OBE, of Greenfoot, Dalston, Cumbria; *Career* serv The Black Watch 1950-69, Maj; landowner and farmer 1969-; *Recreations* country pursuits; *Clubs* New (Edinburgh); *Style—* Maj Edward Orr Ewing, DL; Dunskey, Portpatrick, Wigtownshire (☎ 077 681 211)

ORR EWING, Maj Sir Ronald Archibald; 5 Bt (UK 1886), JP (Perth 1956), DL (1963); s of Brig-Gen Sir Norman Archibald Orr Ewing, 4 Bt, CB, DSO (d 1960), and Laura Louisa, *née* Robarts (d 1968); *b* 14 May 1912; *Educ* Eton, RMC Sandhurst; *m* 6 April 1938, Marion Hester, da of late Col Sir Donald Walter Cameron of Lochiel, KT, CMG, and Lady Hermione Graham, da of 5 Duke of Montrose, KT; 2 s (Archibald *qv*, Jamie b 9 Jan 1948), 2 da (Janet (Mrs John Wallace) b 9 Nov 1940, Fiona (Mrs Adrian Drewe) b 3 March 1946); *Heir* s Archibald Donald Orr Ewing; *Career* Scots Guards 1932-53, ret as Maj; serv WWII, Middle E (POW 1942-45); memb Queen's Body Guard for Scotland (Royal Co of Archers); Grand Master Mason of Scotland 1965-69; *Recreations* travel, forestry; *Clubs* New (Edinburgh); *Style—* Maj Sir Ronald Orr Ewing, Bt, JP, DL; Cardross, Kippen, Stirling FK8 3JY (☎ 08775 220)

ORR-EWING, Hon (Ian) Colin; s of Baron Orr-Ewing, OBE (Life Peer); *b* 1942; *Educ* Harrow, Trinity Coll Oxford (BA); *m* 1, 1973, Deirdre, da of Lance Japhet; 1 s,

1 da; 2, 1986, Fleur, da of late Dr Gavin Knight; 1 da (Cordelia b 1988); *Career* dir: KCA Int Ltd, Berkeley Exploration & Producation Ltd, Glasgow Drilling & Equipment Inc, Simcol Investments, The Howey Foundation; ACCA; *Style—* The Hon Colin Orr-Ewing; Yew Tree House, Hungerford Newtown, Berks

ORR-EWING, Hamish; s of Capt Hugh Eric Douglas Orr-Ewing (gs of James Ewing, yr bro of Sir Archibald Orr Ewing, 1 Bt, JP, DL, MP) and 2 w Esme sis Sir Kenneth Stewart 1 Bt; Hamish is 3 cous of Baron Orr-Ewing, *qv*; *b* 17 August 1924; *Educ* Heatherdown, Eton; *m* 1 1948 (m dis 1954), Morar Margaret, sis of the TV journalist Ludovic Kennedy, *qv*, and da of late Capt Edward Kennedy, RN (ggs of Hon Robert Kennedy and 3 s of 11 Earl of Cassillis); 1 s (Roderick b 1951) (1 da decd); m 2 1954, Ann Mary Teresa, da of late Frederick Terry; *Career* Capt Black Watch 1942-47; chm Rank Xerox Ltd 1980-; dir Tricentrol Ltd 1975-; *Recreations* mechanics, country life, the Roman Empire; *Style—* Hamish Orr-Ewing Esq; 51 Clifton Hill, NW8 (☎ 01 624 5702); Fox Mill, Purton, Nr Swindon, Wilts (☎ 0793 770496)

ORR-EWING, Baron (Life Peer UK 1971); Sir (Charles) Ian Orr-Ewing; 1 Bt (UK 1963), OBE (Mil 1945); s of Archibald Ian Orr-Ewing (d 1942); and Gertrude Bertha, *née* Runge; *b* 10 Feb 1912; *Educ* Harrow, Trinity Coll Oxford; *m* 1939, Joan Helen Veronica, da of William Gordon McMinnies (d 1982), of Stoke Orchard, nr Cheltenham; 4 s (Hon Simon *qv*, Hon Malcolm *qv*, Hon Colin *qv*, Hon Robert *qv*); *Heir* to Btcy only, s, Hon (Alistair) Simon Orr-Ewing; *Career* sits as (C) peer in House of Lords; serv WWII RAF, Wing Cdr 1941, radar branch, serv N Africa 1943, chief radar offr Gen Eisenhower's staff 1945; graduate apprentice EMI 1934-37, employed BBC (TV) 1937-39 and dir outside broadcasts 1946-49; MP (C) Hendon N 1950-70; PPS to min of Lab 1951-55, parly under-sec Air Miny 1957-59, parly and financial sec to Admiralty 1959, civil lord of the Admiralty 1959-63; a vice-chm Cons 1922 Ctee 1966-70; vice-chm Assoc of Cons Peers 1978-86; chm Ultra Electric Hldgs 1965-79; chm Clayton Dewandre Ltd; dir: Carl Byoir plc 1977-86, MK Hldgs 1977-83, Dowty 1978-82; chm Metrication Bd 1972-77, pres: Harrow Wanderers 1983-, Harrow Assoc 1986-; vice-pres Lords and Commons Cricket 1988-; *Recreations* tennis, cricket, skiing; *Clubs* Boodle's, MCC, Vincent's (Oxford), All England LTC (Wimbledon); *Style—* The Rt Hon Lord Orr-Ewing, OBE; Flat 2, 9 Cheyne Gardens, London SW3 (☎ 01 730 3728)

ORR-EWING, Hon Malcolm Archie; s of Baron Orr-Ewing, OBE (Life Peer) *qv*; *b* 1946; *Educ* Harrow, Munich; *m* 1973, Clare Mary, da of Brig George Robert Flood, MC; 2 da (Harriet b 1975, Charlotte b 1978); *Style—* The Hon Malcolm Orr-Ewing; The Priory, Syresham, nr Brackley, Northants NN13 5HH

ORR-EWING, Hon Robert James; yst s of Baron Orr-Ewing, OBE (Life Peer) *qv*; *b* 1953; *Educ* Harrow; *m* 1982, Susannah Bodley Scott, da of Mark Bodley Scott, of Uppfield, Sonning on Thames; 2 s (William b 1985, Jack b 1987); *Career* barr Inner Temple 1976; proprietor Property Letting Co 1982-; *Style—* The Hon Robert Orr-Ewing; 2 Billing St, London SW10; 110-112 King's Rd, London SW3 (☎ 01 581 8025)

ORR-EWING, Hon (Alistair) Simon; s of Baron Orr-Ewing, OBE (Life Peer and 1 Bt); *qv*; ha to baronetcy; *b* 10 June 1940; *Educ* Harrow, Trinity Coll Oxford (BA); *m* 1968, Victoria, da of Keith Cameron (d 1981), of Fifield House, Oxon; 2 s (Archie b 1969, James b 1971), 1 da (Georgiana b 1974); *Career* chartered surveyor; cllr Royal Borough of Kensington and Chelsea 1982-, chm Town Planning Ctee 1986-88; Lloyds Underwriter 1986-; FRICS; *Recreations* skiing, tennis, shooting; *Clubs* MCC, Boodle's, IOD; *Style—* The Hon Simon Orr-Ewing; 29 St James Gardens, London W11 4RF (☎ 01 602 4513); office: Simcol Investments Ltd, 46 St James's Place (☎ 01 493 9586, telex 261802)

ORSON, Rasin Ward; CBE (1985); s of Rasin Nelson Orson, and Blanche, *née* Hyre; *b* 16 April 1927; *Educ* Stratford GS; LSE (BSc); *m* 1, 1950, Marie Goodenough; 2 s; m 2, 1979, Lesley Jean Vallance; *Career* memb The Electricity Cncl 1976-88; dir Chloride Silent Power Ltd 1974-88; COMPIEE; *Style—* Rasin Orson, Esq, CBE; The Old Garden, Dunorlan Park Tunbridge Wells TN2 3QA (☎ 0892 24027)

ORTON, David Wallace; s of Wallace Orton (d 1970), and Elsie, *née* Woods (d 1960); *b* 16 Mar 1923; *Educ* Lindisfarne Coll; *m* 1950, Pearl Bremner; *Career* film prod; dir D Orton Films Ltd; pres Guild of Film Prodn Execs 1985-86 (vice-pres 1987-); memb various ctees of the Br Film and TV Producers' Assoc; *Recreations* reading, gardening, country interests; *Clubs* St James's; *Style—* David Orton, Esq; The Red House, 3 King St, Potton, Beds SG19 2QT (☎ 0767 260272); Pinewood Studios, Iver, Bucks (☎ 0753 651 700)

ORTON, Michael Francis; s of Harry Orton (d 1957), and Mary Elizabeth,*née* Turner (d 1982); *b* 3 Oct 1931; *Educ* Co Tech Coll Wednesbury Staffs; *m* 23 July 1955, Angela Diane, da of Herbert Brown (d 1956); 2 da (Diana Mary, Tina Elizabeth); *Career* Nat Serv RMP 1952-54; sr ptnr LG Mouchel & Ptnrs (consulting engrs), dir Mouchel Assocs Ltd, ptnr LG Mouchel & Ptnrs Asia, dir Mouchel Asia Ltd; FIStructE, MIMechE, FRSA, memb Inst of Engrs; *Recreations* sailing; *Clubs* Papercourt SC; *Style—* Michael Orton, Esq; 18 Vincent Rd, Stoke D'Abernon, Cobham, Surrey (☎ 09326 3640); L G Mouchel & Partner, Consulting Engineers, West Hall, Parvis Rd, W Byfleet, Weybridge, Surrey (☎ 09323 41155, fax 09323 40673, telex 261309 MOUCHL G)

OSBORN, Fuller Mansfield; CBE (1972), DL (1975); s of Fuller Mansfield Osborn; *b* 1915; *Educ* Grocers' Co Sch Hackney Downs; *m* 1949, Mary Armstrong, da of William James Auld; *Career* WWII Maj RA SEAC; md Northern Rock Building Soc 1949-78 (chm 1982-87); chm: Cncl of Building Socs Assoc 1969-71, northern region advsy ctee of Land Cmmn, NE Regn and Newcastle/Tyne, Abbeyfield Northern Rock Housing Tst; pres Chartered Building Socs Inst 1984-85, Euro Fedn of Building Socs 1979-82; dep chm Washington New Town Corpn 1973-88, Ct and Cncl Newcastle upon Tyne Univ, Northern Econ Planning Cncl 1969-78; High Sheriff Tyne and Wear 1974-75; *Recreations* golf, beagling, cricket; *Clubs* Northern Counties (Newcastle upon Tyne); *Style—* Fuller Osborn Esq, CBE, DL; Arundel, 9 Furzefield Rd, Gosforth, Newcastle upon Tyne NE3 4EA (☎ 091 285 7703; office: 091 285 7191)

OSBORN, Harold Ernest; CBE (1963); s of Albert George Osborn (d 1956); *b* 25 Dec 1909; *Educ* Finchley Co Sch, LSE; *m* 1949, Gerda Ilse, da of Curt Treitel, of Berlin; *Career* CA 1933; London Passenger Tport bd 1936, on formation of Br Tport Cmmn appointed dir of accounts 1948 (fin controller 1962); comptroller: Tport Hldg Co 1963-73, Nat Freight Corpn 1969.72; vice-chm Exec Nat Freight Corp 1972-74, pension fund advsr to NFC 1974-78; *Clubs* Savile; *Style—* Harold Osborn Esq, CBE; 6 Park Ave, London NW11 7SJ (☎ 01 455 2566)

OSBORN, Sir John Holbrook; MP (Nat Lib and U) Sheffield, Hallam Div 1959-64, (C) 1964-; s of Samuel Eric Osborn and Aileen Decima, da of Col Sir Arthur Holbrook, KBE, MP; *b* 14 Dec 1922; *Educ* Rugby, Trinity Hall Cambridge (MA), Nat Foundry Coll; *m* 1, 1952 (m dis), Molly Suzanne, *née* Marten; 2 da (Sallie, Rachel); m 2, 1976, Joan Mary MacDermot, *née* Wilkinson (d 1989); *Career* Royal Corps of Signals 1943-47, serv W Africa Capt; RA TA 1948, Maj 1955; joined Samuel Osborn & Co Ltd 1947 (co founded by ggf Samuel Osborn): asst works mangr, prodn controller, cost controller in foundry and engrg subsid, dir Samuel Osborn and subsids 1951-79, gen mangr new precision castings co 1954-59; MP (Nat Lib and u) Sheffield, Hallam Div 1959-64, (C) 1964-87; PPS to Sec of State for Cwlth Relns and Colonies (Duncan-Sandys) 1963-64, MEP 1975-79; Freeman former searcher Cutlers' Co, Hallamshire, memb Sheffield C of C; former memb: Assoc of Br C of C, CBI (Yorks and Humberside) Inst of Dirs; jt hon sec 1922 Ctee 1968-87, memb exec Nat Union of Cons Pty 1970-87; vice-chm Cons Energy Ctee 1979-81, chm Cons Tport Ctee and All-Pty Road Study Gp 1970-74 life, former memb All-Pty Parly and Scientific Ctee 1960-87, memb Select Ctee on Sci and Technol 1970-73, sr (C) memb Select Ctee for Educn, Science and the Arts; memb Cncl Br Branch Inter-Parly; - Union 1968-75, former chm Anglo-Swiss Parly Gp and Br Soviet Parly Gp; chm All Pty Channel Tunnel; Gp 1984-87 life memb, formerly chm Parly Gp for Energy Studies 1985-87; kt 1983; - Union 1968-75, chm Anglo-Swiss Parly Gp and Br Soviet Parly Gp; chm All Party Channel Tunnel; Gp 1984; chm Parly Gp for Energy Studies 1985; kt 1983; *Publications* Change or Decay; *Recreations* golf, tennis, photography, gardening, skiing; *Style—* Sir John Osborn; Folds Head Close, Calver, Sheffield S30 1XJ; Flat 13, 102 Rochester Row, London SW1 (☎ office 01 219 4189)

OSBORN, Neil Frank; s of George James Osborn, of Hemel Hempstead, and Georgina Rose, *née* Nash; *b* 24 Oct 1949; *Educ* St Albans Sch, Worcester Coll Oxford (MA); *m* 15 April 1975, Holly Louise, da of Lt-Col George Francis Smith, of McLean, Virginia, USA; *Career* reporter The Daily Progress, Charlottesville VA USA 1972-74, freelance reporter, Lloyds List and Liverpool Daily Post 1975-77, sr ed Instn Investor NY 1978-83, US ed Euromoney NY 1983-85, ed Euromoney London 1985-; dir: Euromoney Pubns plc 1988-, Euromoney Inc 1985-; *Style—* Neil Osborn, Esq; Flat 4, 16 Wetherby Gardens, London SW5 OJP; Euromoney Publications plc, Whitefriars House, 6 Carmelite Street, London EC4Y OBN (☎ 353 6033, fax 353 7667, telex 928726 EUROMO G)

OSBORN, Sir Richard Henry Danvers; 9 Bt (E 1662), of Chicksands, Bedfordshire; s of Sir Danvers Lionel Rouse Osborn, 8 Bt (d 1983), and Constance Violette, *née* Rooke (d 1988); *b* 12 August 1958; *Educ* Eton; *Heir* kinsman, William Danvers Osborn, *qv*; *Career* Christie's 1978-83, ind fine paintings conslt; *Recreations* real tennis, shooting, racing; *Clubs* Turf, MCC; *Style—* Sir Richard Osborn, Bt; The Dower House, Moor Park, Farnham, Surrey GV10 1QX (☎ 02518 2658); 25 Queens Gardens, London W2 3BD (☎ 01 706 3525/3526); car telephone, 0860 367442

OSBORN, William Danvers; s of late Danvers Osborn and late Inez, da of Henry Smith, of Victoria BC; hp of kinsman Sir Richard Osborn, 9 Bt; assumed name William Danvers in lieu of Christian names George Schomberg 1936; 1 Bt received Baronetcy in recognition of all the family had suffered in the cause of Charles I 1662, 3 Bt altered spelling of family name from Osborne to avoid confusion with the family of the Duke of Leeds, He was Govr of NY and d there 1753; *b* 1909; *m* 1939, Jean Burns, da of R B Hutchinson, of Vancouver, BC; 1 da (Cheryl Elizabeth b 1945); *Style—* William Osborn Esq; 2676 Seaview Rd, Victoria, BC, Canada

OSBORNE, Anthony Robert; s of Robert Bertram Osborne, of Dorset, and Olive May Osborne, *née* Russell; *b* 20 Oct 1944; *Educ* Bristol Univ (LLB); *m* 8 May 1971, Anna, da of Kenneth Charles Smith, of Dorset; 2 s (James b 1975, Thomas b 1980), 1 da (Kate b 1974); *Career* slr, memb Clarke Willmott & Clarke; *Recreations* field sports; *Style—* Anthony Robert, Esq; Tilworth House, Tilworth, Axminster, Devon (☎ 02977 200); 50-54 Fore St, Chard, Somerset (☎ 04606 2777, telex 46269, fax 0460 677450)

OSBORNE, Sir Basil; CBE (1962); s of late Alderman W W Osborne, MBE; *b* 19 April 1907; *Educ* Metropolitan Business Coll; *m* 1934, Esma, da of late T Green; 1 s; *Career* Lord Mayor of Hobart, Tasmania 1959-70; Alderman 1952-76; chm Metropolitan Tport Tst 1971-78; business administrator, pres Asia Pacific Life Saving Cncl 1984-; OStJ; kt 1967; *see Debrett's Handbook of Australia and New Zealand for further details*; *Style—* Sir Basil Osborne, CBE; 6 Myella Drive, Chigwell, Tasmania 7011, Australia

OSBORNE, Charles Thomas; s of Vincent Lloyd Osborne; *b* 24 Nov 1927; *Educ* Brisbane State HS; *m* 1970 (m dis 1975), Marie Korbelarova; *Career* author; literature dir Arts Cncl of GB 1971-86; chief theatre critic Daily Telegraph 1987-; *Books Incl:* The Complete Operas of Verdi (1969), W H Auden: the life of a poet (1979), Dictionary of the Opera (1983), Giving It Away: memoirs (1986), The Complete Operas of Richard Strauss (1988); *Recreations* travel; *Style—* Charles Osborne, Esq; 125 St George's Road, London SE1 6HY (☎ 01 928 1534)

OSBORNE, David Francis; s of William Henry Osborne (d 1969), of Surrey, and Beatrice Irene, *née* Hinge; *b* 24 Oct 1937; *Educ* Dulwich, Jesus Coll Oxford (MA); *m* 25 March 1964 (m dis 1977), Sheila, da of John Charles Grattan Atkins; 1 s (Martin b 1965), 2 da (Katharine b 1967, Juliet b 1968); *Career* Unilever Ltd 1960-66; PA Int Mgmnt Conslts 1966-82; Hill Samuel & Co Ltd 1982-87; dir Electra Investmt Tst plc 1987-; MBIM, MICMA, MIMC; *Recreations* cricket, squash, ballet, reading, languages, bridge; *Clubs* MCC; *Style—* David Osborne, Esq; Vine Cottage, 48 High St, Wargrave, Reading, Berks RG10 8BY (☎ 073 522 4176), Electra Investment Trust plc, 65 Kingsway, London WC2B 6QT (☎ 01 831 6464, fax 01 404 5388, telex 265525 ELECG G), car ☎ 0836 223855

OSBORNE, HE Dr Denis Gordon; s of Alfred Gordon Osborne, of Woodburn Common, Bucks, and Frances Agnes Osborne; *b* 17 Sept 1932; *Educ* Dr Challoner's GS Amersham Bucks, Univ of Durham (BSc, PhD); *m* 16 May 1970, Christine Susannah, da of Percy Rae Shepherd (d 1987); 2 da (Ruth b 1971, Sally b 1973); *Career* lectr in physics: Univ of Durham 1957, Fourah Bay Coll Freetown SA 1958, Univ of Ghana 1958-63 (sr lectr 1963-64); dean of sci Univ of Dar Es Salaam 1968-70 (reader in physics 1964-66, prof of physics 1966-71), conslt World Bank Malaysia 1971 (Ethiopia 1972), res fell in physics UCL 1971-72; ODA London: princ UN 1972-75, princ ME 1975-77, sci and technol 1977-80, asst sec natural resources 1980-84, asst sec Eastern and Western Africa 1984-87; High Cmmr in Malawi 1987-; reader: St Barnabus Church Dulwich, St Peter's Church Lilongwe; govr Dulwich Coll; CPhys, FInstP 1966; *Books* Way Out: Some Parables of Science and Faith (1977), papers on geophysics, technol, educn and development; *Recreations* reading, writing, attempts at windsurfing; *Clubs* Royal Cwlth Soc; *Style—* HE Dr Denis Osborne; c/o FCO, King Charles St, London SW1A 2AH

OSBORNE, Hugh Daniel; s of Francis Mardon Osborne (d 1964), of Chagford, Devon, and Winifred Mary, *née* Bartlet; *b* 12 August 1927; *Educ* Harrow; *m* 12 July 1954, Geraldine Mary, da of Richard George Spring (d 1957), of Wexford, Ireland; 2 s (Charles Hugh b 13 June 1957, Henry Richard b 5 Feb 1961), 1 da (Clare Madeline b 13 April 1959); *Career* RM 1945-47; The Law Debenture Corpn plc: tst mangr 1963, dir 1967, md 1976-88, non exec dir 1988-; chm Assoc of Corp Tstees 1979-82; *Recreations* walking, fishing; *Clubs* City of London; *Style—* Hugh Osborne, Esq; 27 Montserrat Rd, Putney, London SW15 2LD; Ivy Cove, Chivelstone, Devon, (☎ 01 789 9498); The Law Debenture Corporation, Princes House, 85 Gresham St, EC2V 7LY, (☎ 01 606 5451, fax 01 606 0643, telex 888347)

OSBORNE, John James; s of Thomas Godfrey Osborne and Nellie Beatrice *née* Grove; *b* 12 Dec 1929; *Educ* Belmont Coll Devon; *m* 1, 1951 (m dis 1957), Pamela Elizabeth Lane; m 2, 1957 (m dis 1963), Mary Ure (d 1975); m 3, 1963 (m dis 1968), Penelope Gilliatt; m 4, 1968 (m dis 1977), Jill Bennett *qv*; m 5, 1978, Helen Dawson; *Career* dramatist and actor, First stage appearance, No Room at the Inn (Sheffield 1948); plays filmed: Look Back in Anger 1958, The Entertainer 1959 and 1975, Inadmissible Evidence 1965, Luther 1971; Films: Tom Jones (Oscar for best screenplay 1964); dir of Woodfall Films; *Books* Plays incl: Look Back in Anger 1957, The Entertainer 1957, Epitaph for George Dillon (with A Creighton), The World of Paul Stickey 1959, Luther 1960, A Subject of Scandal and Concern 1960, Plays for England 1963, A Bond Honoured 1966, The Hotel in Amsterdam 1967, Hedda Gabler (Adapt) 1970, West of Suez 1971, A Place Calling Itself Rome 1972, A Better Class of Person 1981; Hon Dr RCA 1970; *Clubs* Garrick; *Style—* John Osborne, Esq; c/o Fraser & Dunlop, 91 Regent St, London W1

OSBORNE, Col John Lander; CBE (1969, MBE 1943), TD (1947), DL (W Midlands 1975); s of Frank John Osborne, MC (d 1959), of Solihull, W Midlands, and Ida Marie, *née* Lander (d 1972); *b* 30 June 1917; *Educ* Solihull Sch, Villiars (Switzerland), Birmingham Sch of Architecture; *m* 1, 1942, Kate Honour (d 1980), da of Col Duncan Cameron, of Glasgow and Rawlpindi (d 1929); 1 da; m 2, 1981, Phyllis Mary Tipper, da of Harold Dyas James, of Little Aston, W Midlands (d 1964) ; *Career* WWII Lt-Col BEF Belgium and France 1939-40; serv 1942-46: N Africa, Middle E, Sicily, Italy; rejoined TA 1947, regt cdr RE 1950-57, chief engr W Mids Dist 1958-66, Hon Col 48 Div Engrs 1957-66, ADC to HM The Queen 1968-72; ptnr The John Osborne Partnership Chartered Architects 1947-82, conslt 1982-87; pres Birmingham and Five Counties Architectural Assoc 1962-64; chm W Midlands Regn RIBA 1970-72; *Recreations* sailing (yacht 'Wetherley'), skiing, golf, horticulture; *Clubs* Army & Navy, Royal Thames Yacht, Birmingham, Little Aston Golf; *Style—* Col John Osborne, CBE, TD, DL; Maidenwell, Broad Campden, Chipping Campden, Glos GL55 6UR (☎ 0386 840772)

OSBORNE, Kenneth Hilton; QC (Scot); s of Kenneth Osborne and Evelyn Alic, *née* Hilton; *b* 9 July 1937; *Educ* Larchfield Sch Helensburgh; Merchiston Castle Sch Edinburgh, Edinburgh Univ; *m* 1964, Clare Ann Louise Lewis; 1 s, 1 da; *Career* admitted to Faculty of Advocates in Scotland, 1962; QC (Scot) 1976; chm: Disciplinary Ctee, Potato Mktg Bd 1975-; chm Supreme Ct Legal Aid Ctee 1979-81; advocate-depute 1982-84; legal memb (pt/t) Lands Tbnl for Scotland 1985-87; *Clubs* New (Edinburgh); *Style—* Kenneth Osborne Esq, QC; 42 India St, Edinburgh EH3 6HB (☎ 031 225 3094) Primrose Cottage, Bridgend of Lintrathen, by Kirriemuir, Angus DD8 5JH (Lintrathen (057 56) 316)

OSBORNE, Sir Peter George; 17 Bt (I 1629); s of Lt-Col Sir George Francis Osborne, 16 Bt, MC (d 1960), and Mary, Lady Osborne, (d 1987) *née* Horn; Richard Osborne cr 1 Bt of Ireland 1629, and supported Parliament against the crown; 2, 7, 8, 9 and 11 Bt's were MPs (8 Bt, PC); *b* 29 June 1943; *Educ* Wellington, Christ Church Oxford; *m* 1968, Felicity, da of late Grantley Loxton-Peacock; 4 s (George b 1971, Benedict b 1973, Adam b 1976, Theo b 1985); *Heir* s, George Oliver Osborne b 23 May 1971; *Career* chm and md Osborne & Little plc; *Style—* Sir Peter Osborne, Bt; 36 Porchester Terrace, London W2; Vinnicke, Highdere, Nr Newbury, Berks

OSBORNE, Hon Mrs (Rosemary Alys Audrey); *née* Graves; da of 6 Baron Graves (d 1937), and Mary Isabel Ada, *née* Parker (d 1962); *b* 10 June 1910; *m* 1938, Maj Herbert Edward Osborne, MC (d 1951); *Recreations* riding; *Style—* The Hon Mrs Osborne; 35 Primrose Gdns, London NW3 4UL (☎ 01 586 2248)

OSBORNE, Trevor; s of Alfred Osborne, of Teddington, Middx, and Annie, *née* Edmonson (d 1986); *b* 7 July 1943; *Educ* Sunbury GS; *m* 26 July 1969, Pamela Ann, da of William Stephenson; 1 s (John b 1977), 1 da (Sarah b 1972); *Career* fndr and chm Speyhawk plc 1977-; cncl memb Br Property Fedn and Assoc of City Property Owners; memb Royal Opera House Devpt Bd; BPF visiting fell Reading Univ land mgmnt course; ldr Wokingham Dist Cncl 1980-82; pres Windsor Community Arts Centre; memb Worshipful Co of Chartered Surveyors; FRICS; *Recreations* travel, theatre, tennis; *Clubs* Arts, Carlton; *Style—* Trevor Osborne, Esq; Pinewood House, Nine Mile Ride, Wokingham, Berks; Flat 3, 113 Mount St, London W1; Speyhawk plc, 1 James St, London W1M 5HY (☎ 01 499 6060, fax 01 495 1413)

OSERS, Ewald; s of Paul Osers, (d 1923), of Prague, and Fini, *née* Anders (d 1942); *b* 13 May 1917; *Educ* Schools in Prague, Czechoslovakia, Prague Univ, Univ of London (BA); *m* 3 June 1941, Mary, da of Arthur Harman (d 1959); 1 s (Richard b 1951), 1 da (Ann Margaret b 1947); *Career* translator/writer; BBC 1939-77, chm Translators' Assoc 1971, 1980-81, 1983-84; chm Translators' Guild 1975-79; vice-pres Int Fed of Translators 1977-81, 1984-87; Schlegel-Tieck Prize 1971, CB Nathhorst Prize 1977, Josef Dobrovsky Medal 1980, Gold Pin of Honour of the German Translators' Assoc, Silver Pegasus of the Bulgarian Writers Union 1983, FRSL 1984, Dilia Medal Czechoslovakia 1986, European Poetry Translation Prize 1987, Vitezslav Nezval Medal of the Czech Literary Fndn 1987, P-F Caillé Medal 1987; translated over 90 books, 24 of them poetry; *Books* Wish You Were Here (1976) (Poems); *Recreations* music, skiing; *Style—* Ewald Osers, Esq; 33 Reades Lane, Sonning Common, Reading RG4 9LL (☎ 0734 723196)

OSIFELO, Sir Frederick (Aubarua); MBE (1972); s of Paul Iromea (d 1980), and Joy Ngangale (d.1975); *b* 15 Oct 1928; *Educ* Torquay Tech Coll (Dip Public and Social Admin); *m* 1949, Margaret Tanai da of Gogo (d 1941); 3 s (Samuel, Fredrick b 1965, Edward b 1969), 3 da (Catherine, Flory, Elizabeth); *Career* speaker of Legve Assembly Solomon Islands 1974-78; chm Public Serv Cmmn 1975-; Police and Prison Serv Commn since 1977; memb Judicial and Legal Service Commn 1977-; office orderly 1945-49; clerk 1950-66; 1st class magistrate 1967; admin offr: class B 1967, class A 1972; dist cmmr E Solomons 1972; sr sec 1973; cmmr of Lands and Surveys 1974; chm ctee of Prerogative of Mercy 1979-; chm on Constitutional Ctee 1975; chm ad hoc ctee on Solomon Islands Honours and Awards 1979; pres Amateur Sports Assoc 1975; Lay Canon 1977; kt 1977; *Style—* Sir Frederick Osifelo, MBE; PO Box 548, Honiara, Solomon Islands (☎ office 108 231111)

OSMAN, David Antony; s of Colin Alfred Earnest Osman, of 14 Fairgreen, Cockfosters, Barnet, Herts, and Grace Florence, *née* White; *b* 13 April 1953; *Educ* Minchenden GS, Nottingham Univ (BA); *m* 4 Sept 1986, Helen, da of Randall Jones-Pugh, of St Brides View, Roch, Dyfed; 2 da (Caroline b 15 Nov 1984, Nicola b 23 Jan 1987); *Career* dir RP Publishing Co Ltd 1975-78 (non-exec dir 1978 - dir RP Typesetters Co Ltd 1980-), UK economist Joseph/Carr Sebag & Co 1978-82, UK/int economist Laing & Cruickshank 1982-84, int economist James Capel & Co 1984-; fndr memb Enfield SDP 1981-87, SDP/Lib Alliance Pty candidate for Upminster 1983, vice-chm (fndr memb and sec) City SDP 1984-88, fndr memb Enfield SLD 1988; sec City Democratic Forum 1988-; memb Soc of Business Economists; *Recreations* chess, cycling, football, golf, snooker; *Clubs* Old Minchendenians Football Club; *Style—* David Osman, Esq; 10 Old Park Ridings, Winchmore Hill, London N21 2EU (☎ 01 360 4343); James Capel & Co, 6 Bevis Marks, London EC3A 7JQ (☎ 01 621 0011, fax 01 621 0496, telex 888866)

OSMOND, Sir Douglas; OBE (1958), QPM (1962), CBE (1968); *b* 27 June 1914; *Educ* London Univ (BSc); *Career* chief constable Shrops 1946-62, Hamps 1962-77; memb Roy Cmmn on Criminal Procedure 1978-81; pres Assoc of Chief Police Offrs 1967-69; chm Police Cncl for UK 1972 and 1974; bd of govrs Police Coll 1968-72; memb Inter-Depmtl Ctee on Death Certification and Coroners 1964-71; OStJ 1971; kt 1971; *Style—* Sir Douglas Osmond, CBE, QPM, DL; Woodbine Cottage, Ovington, Alresford, Hants SO24 0RF (☎ Alresford 3729)

OSMOND, John Gregory; s of John Gregory Osmond (d 1935), and Olive Eliza, *née* Williams (now Mrs Bryant); *b* 30 Sept 1925; *Educ* Taunton Sch; *m* 5 Jan 1951, Jean, da of Sqdn Ldr Henry Royston Vivian Harper; 2 s (Will b 1954, David b 1957), 1 da (Felicity b 1968); *Career* mil serv Coldstream Gds 1944-45, 9th Gurkha Regt (Lt) 1945-47; slr, former sr ptnr Alms & Young Taunton; former chm local Legal Aid Ctee, former chm and area chm Round Table', vice pres-tstee and former capt Taunton and Pickeridge Golf Club; *Recreations* golf, gardening; *Clubs* Taunton & Pickeridge Golf; *Style—* John Osmond, Esq; Edgecombe, Mill Lane, Corfe, Taunton, Somerset (☎ 0823 42 789); Alms & Young, 1 Church Square, Taunton (☎ 0828 337151)

OSMOND, Michael William Massy; CB (1977); s of Brig WRF Osmond, CBE (d 1952); *b* 20 Nov 1918; *Educ* Winchester, Christ Church Oxford; *m* 1943, Jill Stephenie, nee Ramsden; 1 s, 1 da; *Career* 2 Lt Coldstream Guards 1939-40; barr 1941, asst princ Miny of Prodn 1941-43, housemaster HM Borstal Usk 1943-45, legal asst Miny of Nat Insur 1946 (sr legal asst 1948), asst slr Miny of Pensions and Nat Insur 1958, princ asst slr DHSS 1969; legal advsr 1974-78: to DHSS, to Off of Population Censuses and Surveys and to Gen Register Off 1974-78; *Recreations* music, hunting; *Clubs* Utd Oxford and Cambridge Univ; *Style—* Michael Osmond Esq, CB; Waylands, Long Newnton, Nr Tetbury, Glos GL8 8RN (☎ 0666 53308)

OSMOND, Lady; Olivia Sybil; *née* Wells; da of Ernest Edward Wells, JP, (d 1948), of Kegworth, Leics, and Olivia Maud, *née* Orton (d 1956); *Educ* St Elphins Sch Darley Dale, Newnham Coll Cambridge (MA, MSc); *m* 5 Feb 1942, Sir Paul Osmond, CB, *qv*, 2 s (Oliver b 1944, Andrew b 1949); *Career* economist and statistician Nat Inst of Econ and Social Res 1938-39, Miny of Econ Warfare 1939-41, FO 1942-44, Int Fedn of Agric Prodrs 1951-60, econ advsr Miny of Health 1967; memb bd of govrs Bethlem Royal and Maudsley Hosp 1968-82 (vice-chm 1980-82), govr St Elphins Sch 1967-, assoc Newnham Coll 1977-; memb: European Union of Women (Br Section) Exec 1961-86, Cambridge Soc Cncl 1980- (chm exec ctee 1988-), Independent Schs Careers Orgn Cncl 1986-; *Recreations* gardening, travel, theatre; *Clubs* Utd Oxford and Cambridge Univ; *Style—* Lady Osmond, JP; 20 Beckenham Grove, Shortlands, Bromley, Kent BR2 0JU (☎ 01 460 2026)

OSMOND, Sir (Stanley) Paul; CB (1966); s of late Stanley C Osmond (d 1966) of Bristol; *b* 13 May 1917; *Educ* Bristol GS, Jesus Coll Oxford; *m* 1942, Olivia Sybil, JP, *qv*, da of late Ernest E Wells, JP; 2 s; *Career* WWII Glos Regt and staff 1940-46; Home Civil Serv 1939-75, sec to the Church Commrs 1975-80; kt 1980; *Clubs* Athenaeum; *Style—* Sir Paul Osmond, CB; 20 Beckenham Grove, Bromley, Kent BR2 0JU (☎ 01 460 2026)

OSMOTHERLY, Edward Benjamin Crofton; s of Crofton Robert Osmotherly, of London, and Elsie May, *née* Sargent (d 1967); *b* 1 August 1942; *Educ* East Ham GS, Fitzwilliam Coll Cambridge (MA); *m* 6 June 1970, Valerie Ann, da of L R Mustill, CBE, (d 1984); 1 s (John Nicholas b 1975), 1 da (Clare b 1972); *Career* asst princ Miny Housing and Local Govt 1963-68 (pte sec to parly sec and Min of State 1966-68), princ DOE 1968-76, asst sec DOE and Tport 1976-82; dep sec Dept of Tport 1989- (under sec 1982-88); Harness Fell Brookings Inst USA and Exec Fell Univ of California (Berkeley) 1972-73, sec ctee on Ry Fin 1982;; *Recreations* squash, reading; *Style—* Edward Osmotherly, Esq; Dept of Transport, 2 Marsham St, London SW1

OSTROM, Neil Ian Eric; s of Erik Hugo Magnus Ostrom (d 1981), and Florence Louise, *née* Mees (d 1971); *b* 26 July 1923; *Educ* Bedford Sch, Cambridge Univ, London Univ (BA); *m* 23 May 1953, Fay, da of William Henry Ceney (d 1982); 2 s (Mark, Toby), 1 da (Tessa); *Career* RAFVR 1942-47: trg as Air Observer 1942-43, Bomber Cmd 1944, Pathfinder Force Navigator 1944, (POW 1944-45); dir E V Hawtin Ltd 1958-68, dir Glynn Manson Orgn Ltd 1973, chm Stewart Nairn Gp plc 1974-82; chm designate Central London Branch BIM 1989-; FInst D 1984, FBIM 1984; *Recreations* languages, travel, writing, water sports, astronomy, music, investments; *Style—* Neil Ostrom, Esq; Priestfield, Watts Lane, Chislehurst, Kent BR7 5PS (☎ 467 1989)

OSWALD, Lady Angela Mary Rose; *née* Cecil; 3 da of 6 Marquess of Exeter, KCMG (d 1981), and yst da by his 1 w, Lady Mary, *née* Montagu Douglas Scott da of 7 Duke of Buccleuch; *b* 21 May 1938; *m* 1958, (William Richard) Michael Oswald, CVO, *qv*; 1 s (William Alexander Michael b 1962), 1 da (Mrs Alexander Fergus Matheson *qv*); *Career* Extra Woman of the Bedchamber to HM Queen Elizabeth, The Queen Mother 1981-83; Woman of the Bedchamber 1983-; *Style—* Lady Angela Oswald; Flitcham Hall, King's Lynn, Norfolk PE31 6BY (☎ 0485 600319); Apt 8a, Hampton Court Palace, E Molesey, Surrey (☎ 01 977 5673)

OSWALD, Adm Sir (John) Julian Robertson; GCB (1989, KCB 1987); s of Capt George Hamilton Oswald, RN (d 1971), of Newmore, Invergordon, and Margaret Elliot, *née* Robertson (d 1947); *b* 11 August 1933; *Educ* Beaudesert Park Sch, Britannia RNC Dartmouth, Royal Coll of Def Studies London; *m* 25 Jan 1958, Veronica Therese Dorette, da of Eric James Thompson, OBE (d 1975); 2 s (Timothy b 1958, Christopher b 1960), 3 da (Elisabeth b 1963, Victoria b 1967, Samantha b 1970); *Career* Cadet 1947-51, Midshipman RN 1952-53 (HM Ships Vanguard and Verulam), Sub Lt 1953-55 (HMS Theseus), Lt 1955-63 (HM Ships Newfoundland, Jewel, Excellent (gunnery specialist course), Victorious and Yarnton), Lt Cdr 1963-68 (HM Ships Excellent, Naiad, MOD (Naval Plans)), Cdr 1969-73 (HMS Bacchante, MOD (Defence Policy Staff)), Capt 1974-82 (MOD (asst dir Def Policy), Royal Coll of Def Studies, HMS Newcastle, RN Presentation Team BRNC Dartmouth), Rear Adm 1982-86 (Asst Chief of Def Staff (Programmes), Asst Ch of Defence Staff (Policy and Nuclear)), Vice-Adm 1986-87 (Flag Offr Third Flotilla and Cdr ASW Striking Force), Adm 1987- (C-in-C Fleet, Allied C-in-C Channel, C-in-C Eastern Atlantic), First Sea Lord and Ch of Naval Staff 1989-; *Recreations* gliding, tennis, fishing, family, stamps; *Clubs* Mensa; *Style—* Adm Sir J J Robertson Oswald; c/o Naval Secretary, Old Admiralty Building, Whitehall, London SW1 (☎ 01 218 9000)

OSWALD, Maj-Gen Marshall St John; CB (1965), CBE (1961), DSO (1945), MC (1943); s of William Whitehead Oswald; *b* 13 Sept 1911; *Educ* Rugby, RMA Woolwich; *m* 1, 1938, Mary Georgina Baker (d 1970); 1 s, 2 da; m 2, 1974, Barbara, widow of G A Rickards; *Career* cmmnd RA 1931; serv RHA and Field Artillery UK and India 1931-39; serv WWII (despatches, MC, DSO); DMI: WO, 1962-64, Min of Defence (Army) 1964-65; ret 1966; *Clubs* Army and Navy; *Style—* Maj-Gen Marshall Oswald, CB, CBE, DSO, MC; Eastfield House, Longparish, nr Andover, Hants (☎ 026 472 228)

OSWALD, (William Richard) Michael; CVO (1988, LVO 1979); s of Lt-Col William Alexander Hugh Oswald, ERD (d 1974), of Little Orchard, St George's Hill, Weybridge, Surrey, and Rosie- Marie, *née* Leahy (d 1985); *b* 21 April 1934; *Educ* Eton, King's Coll Cambridge (MA); *m* 21 April 1958, Lady Angela Mary Rose Cecil, *qv*, da of 6 Marquess of Exeter, KCMG (d 1981); 1 s (William Alexander Michael b 1962), 1 da (Katherine Davina Mary (Mrs Alexander Matheson) b 1959); *Career* 2 Lt 1 Bn King's Own Royal Regt 1953, BAOR and Korea, Lt 8 Bn Royal Fusiliers (TA) 1955, Capt 1958-61; memb cncl of The Thoroughbred Breeders Assoc 1964-; mangr Lordship and Egerton Studs Newmarket 1962-69; mangr The Royal Studs 1970-; *Recreations* shooting, painting; *Clubs* White's; *Style—* Michael Oswald, Esq, CVO; Flitcham Hall, King's Lynn, Norfolk PE31 6BY (☎ 0485 600319); Apt 8A Hampton Court Palace, E Molesey, Surrey (☎ 01 977 5673); The Royal Studs, Sandringham, Norfolk (☎ 0485 40588, telex 817043 RYLSTD G)

OSWALD, Dr Neville Christopher; TD (1946); s of Late Col Christopher Percy Oswald, CMG; *b* 1 August 1910; *Educ* Clifton, Queens' Coll Cambridge; *m* 1 1941, Patricia Rosemary Joyce Cooke (d 1947); 1 s, 1 da; m 2 1948, Marjorie Mary Sinclair; 1 da; *Career* formerly Col and Hon Col late RAMC; formerly conslt physician: St Bart's Hosp, Brompton Hosp, King Edward V11 Hosp for Offrs London King Edward V11's Hosp Midhurst; ret 1975; DL (Greater London) 1973-78; hon physician HM The Queen 1956-58; MD, FRCP; *Style—* Dr Neville Oswald, TD; The Old Rectory, Thurlestone, South Devon TQ7 3NJ (☎ 0548 560 555)

OSWALD, Col (Oswald) Robert Williamson; DSO (1944); s of Brig-Gen Oswald Charles Williamson Oswald, CB, CMG (d 1938), and Margaret Malcolm, *née* Carson (d 1968); *b* 2 Feb 1917; *Educ* Chillon Coll Switzerland, RMA Woolwich, RMCS Shrivenham; *m* 6 Oct 1945, Eileen Norah, da of Charles Frederick Andrew (d 1934), of Knightwood, Wick, Hants; 1 s (Jocelyn b 1949: m 1981, Caroline Biggs); 1 da (Sarah b 1947: m 1973, Dr John A Gibson, MD, FRCP); *Career* cmmnd RA 1937, serv WWII; Eritrea, Syria, W Desert, and Italy; CO 50 Medium/50 Missile Regt RA; dir Mil Studies at Royal Mil Coll of Sci (ret 1972),; first admin for Inst for Fiscal Studies (IFS) 1972-74; *Recreations* skiing, climbing, golf; *Style—* Col O R W Oswald, DSO; The Cottage, Brocton Gate, Brocton, Stafford ST17 0SS (☎ 0785 662638)

OTTAWAY, Richard Geoffrey James; MP (Cons Nottingham N 1983-87); s of Prof Christopher Wyndham Ottaway (d 1977), and Grace; *b* 24 May 1945; *Educ* Backwell Secdy Modern Sch, Bristol Univ (LLB); *m* 1982, Nicola Evelyn, da of John Kisch, CMG; *Career* Lt RN, Lt Cdr RNR; PPS to Baroness Young and Tim Renton, MP Min of State FCO, slr, head of legal servs Europe and Far E Coastal Corpn 1988; *Books* co author: Road to Reform, Thoughts for a Third Term (1987); *Recreations* yachting; *Clubs* Royal Corinthian Yacht, Island Sailing; *Style—* Richard Ottaway Esq; The Studio, 20 Church St, London W4 2PH

OTTER, Robert George (Robin); s of Francis Lewis Otter, MC (d 1946), of Ottershaw, Surrey and Helen *née* Stephens (d 1988); *b* 25 Feb 1926; *Educ* Marlborough, Univ Coll Oxford (BA, MA); *m* 16 Dec 1958, Elisabeth Ann, da of Eric Reginald St Aubrey Davies, MBE (d 1986); 2 s (Robert b 1960, David b 1966), 1 da (Lisette b 1968); *Career* RNVR 1944-47 cmmnd 1945 serv Far E 1945-46; dist offr/cmmr Kenya Colony Colonial Admin Serv 1951-62, slr and ptnr Moore, Brown & Dixon Tewkesbury 1963-; Parly liaison offr of Law Soc; lay chm Tewkesbury Deanery Synod, memb Gloucester Diocesan Synod and Bishops Cncl, govr Alderman Knight and Abbey Schs Tewkesbury, cncl memb Rotary Club and Civic Soc Tewkesbury; govr Three Counties Agric Soc, parly candidate 1966, 1970 and 1974, Euro parly candidate 1979; memb: Law Soc, Glos & Wilts Law Soc; *Books* contrib to A Modern Introduction to Law (ed Paul Denham, 1987); *Recreations* breeder of Gloucester cattle; *Clubs* Royal Cwlth Soc, Mombasa Club (Kenya), Oxford Union; *Style—* Robin Otter, Esq; 69/70 High St, Tewkesbury, Glos GL20 5LE (☎ 0684 292341, fax 0684 295147)

OTTER, Air Vice-Marshal Victor Charles; CBE (1967); s of Robert Otter; *b* 9 Feb 1914; *Educ* Weymouth GS; *m* 1943, Iris Louise Dykes; *Career* air offr engrg Air Support Command RAF 1966-69; ret; *Clubs* RAF; *Style—* Air Vice-Marshal Victor Otter, CBE; Harpenden, 21 Keats Ave, Littleover, Derby (☎ 0332 512 048)

OTTLEY, David Charles; s of Walter Jerimiah Ottley, and Jean Edna, *née* Jarman; *b* 5 August 1955; *Educ* Gable Hall Sch, Borough Road Coll; *m* 4 April 1987, Sara louise, da of Frank Noel Barrett, of Hillhouse, 54 London Rd, Buxton, Derbys; *Career* rep GB 36 occasions javelin; main achievements: 6 times AAAs Champion, World Student Games Silver Medal 1977, UK Closed Champian 1978-82, Olympic Silver Medal 1984, memb of Euro select team at Canberra World Cup 1985, Cwlth Gold Medal 1986; pres Telford Gateway Club (for the mentally handicapped), sec Telford Track Appeal; ILAM 1988; *Clubs* Telford Athletic; *Style—* David Ottley, Esq; Marlo, 8 Station Rd, Admaston, Telford, Shropshire, TF5 0AL (☎ 0952 57885); Telford Development Corporation, Priorslee Hall, Telford, Shrops (☎ 0952 613 131 ext 418)

OTTLEY, Lionel Edward Bruce; s of Capt Richard Bruce Hamilton Ottley, OBE (d 1948), of Sussex, and Claudia Violet Snagge (d 1984); *b* 5 August 1924; *Educ* Eton, Magdalene Coll Cambridge (BA); *m* 22 Feb 1952, Anne Jessica, da of Cdr Walter James Melrose, (d 1988), of Peebleshire; 2s (Richard b 1957, Charles b 1971), 1 da (Victoria b 1954); *Career* serv WWII Sub Lt RNVR 1942-46, Home Waters & Pacific; Br Metal Corpn 1949-64 (asst sec, overseas mangr, jt-asst mangr Gen Trading Div) Imperial Life Assur Co of Canada 1965-86 (special projects mangr); dir Wiltons (St James's) Ltd 1962-87, ret; *Recreations* fishing, shooting, sailing; *Clubs* London Flotilla; *Style—* Lionel E B Ottley, Esq; Tichborne Park Cottage, Tichborne, Alresford, Hants SO24 0ND

OTTO-JONES, John Alcwyn; s of Col Thomas Otto-Jones, CBE, TD, DL (d 1953), of Bredwardine, Hereford, and Kathleen Mary, *née* Hale (d 1979); *b* 7 Feb 1930; *Educ* Christ Coll Brecon, Cardiff Univ (BA), Wadham Coll Oxford (MA); *m* 1 Oct 1960, Bridget Mary, da of Ernest Jackson, of South Glamorgan; 1 s (Justin b 1963), 1 da (Candida b 1965); *Career* cmmnd RAEC 1950; slr and notary public; Under Sheriff of Glamorgan 1985; *Recreations* vintage cars, reading; *Clubs* Cardiff and County; *Style—* John Otto-Jones, Esq; The Court, St Nicholas, South Glamorgan (☎ 0446 760255); 29 Park Place, Cardiff (☎ 0222 225591)

OTTON, Sir Geoffrey (John); KCB (1980), (CB 1978); s of late John Alfred Otton; *b* 10 June 1927; *Educ* Christ's Hosp, St John's Coll, Cambridge (MA); *m* 1952, Hazel Lomas, *née* White; 1 s, 1 da; *Career* second permanent sec DHSS 1979- (under-sec 1971-75, dep sec 1975-79); chief advr to Supplementary Benefits Cmmn 1976-; *Style—* Sir Geoffrey Otton, KCB; 72 Cumberland Rd, Bromley, Kent (☎ 01 460 9610)

OTTON, Hon Mr Justice; Hon Sir Philip (Howard) Otton; s of late H A Otton; *b* 28 May 1933; *Educ* Bablake Sch Coventry, Birmingham Univ (LLB); *m* 1965, Helen Margaret, da of late P W Bates; 2 s, 1 da; *Career* barr Gray's Inn 1955, dep chm Beds QS 1970-72, jr counsel to the Treasy (Personal Injuries) 1970-75, rec Crown Ct 1972-83, QC 1975, govr Nat Heart and Chest Hosps 1979-84, master Bench Gray's Inn 1983-, High Ct judge 1983-; presiding judge Midland and Oxford circuit 1986-88; kt 1983; *Recreations* theatre, opera, travel; *Clubs* Garrick, Pillgrims, Roehampton; *Style—* The Hon Mr Justice Otton; Royal Courts of Justice, Strand, London WC2A 2LL

OTWAY, Mark McRae; s of Henry Arthur McRae Otway, of Surrey, and Ann, *née* Ingman; *b* 4 Oct 1948; *Educ* Dulwich, Churchill Coll Cambridge (MA); *m* 10 July 1973, Amanda Mary, da of Roland Stafford; 2 s (Miles Daniel b 1983, Paul David b 1985); *Career* ptnr (now head Advanced Systems Gp) Andersen Consulting 1982- (mangr 1975, joined 1970); FILDM 1983; *Recreations* sailing, music, theatre, squash; *Clubs* Utd Oxford & Cambridge Univ; *Style—* Mark Otway, Esq; 22 Albany Park Road, Kingston-on-Thames, Surrey KT2 5SW (☎ 01 546 8116); 2 Arundel Street, London WC2R 3LT (☎ 01 438 3835, car tel 0860 200743)

OUBRIDGE, Victor William; s of William Arthur Oubridge, JP, of Coventry (d 1942); *b* 1 April 1913; *Educ* Oundle, Jesus Coll Cambridge (BA); *m* 1937, Ruth Louise, da of Thomas Carpenter (d 1956); 1 s, 1 da; *Career* chm and md Br Piston Ring Co Ltd 1941-66, dir Assoc Engrg Ltd 1947-67; memb: Coventry Cathedral Reconstruction Ctee 1956-63, cncl CBI 1956-67, cncl BIM 1962-67, cncl Engrg Employers' Fedn 1963-65, mgmnt ctee S Warwicks Hosp Gp 1971-74, Warwicks Area Health Authy 1973-82; pres Coventry N Cons Assoc 1956-65, Coventry and Dist Engrg Employers' Assoc 1963-65; High Sheriff of Warwicks 1966-67; visiting prof of business admin Aston Univ 1969-73; CEng, FIMechE, FIProdE, FBIM; *Recreations* fishing, gardening, local history; *Style—* Victor Oubridge Esq; 21 Wasperton, Warwick (☎ 0926 624240)

OUCAN, 7 Earl of (I 1795); Sir Richard John Bingham; 13 Bt (S 1634); also Baron Lucan (I 1776) and Baron Bingham (UK 1934); patron of one living; s of 6 Earl, MC (d 1964, himself ggs of the Crimean War General who gave the order for the Charge of the Light Brigade) by his w Kaitlin, paternal gda of 1 Earl of Dartrey; *b* 18 Dec 1934; *Educ* Eton; *m* 1963, Veronica Mary, da of Maj Charles Moorhouse Duncan, MC (decd); 1 s, 2 da (Lady Frances b 30 June 1964, Lady Camilla b 24 Oct 1970); *Heir* s, Lord Bingham; *Career* Lt Coldstream Gds; *Style—* The Rt Hon the Earl of Lucan; address unknown

OUGH, Dr Richard Norman; s of Rev Conrad Jocelyn Ough (d 1977), and Alice Louisa, *née* Crofts; *b* 25 Jan 1946; *Educ* Stamford Sch, St Mary's Hosp Med Sch Univ of London (MB BS), City Univ London (MA, Dip Law); *m* 1, 1976 (m dis 1982), Shelley Jean Henshaw; 1 s (Geoffrey b 1977), 1 da (Elizabeth b 1978); m 2, 1984 (m dis 1988), Rona Mary Louise Hallam; *Career* med practioner Canada 1974-83; barr 1985, MRCS, LRCP, fell RSH; memb Hon Soc of Inner Temple, memb Hon Soc of Gray's Inn;; *Books* The Mareva Injunction and Anton Piller Order (1987); *Recreations* music, theatre; *Style—* Dr Richard Ough; 4 Paper Bldgs, Temple EC4Y 7EX (☎ 01 583 7765, fax 01 353 4674); Park Court Chambers, 40 Park Cross St, Leeds LS1 2QH (☎ 0532 433 277, fax 0532 421 285)

OUGHTRED, Peter B; JP; s of Col John Alwyn Oughtred MC (d 1958), and Phyllis Brown, *née* Jackson (d 1981); *b* 6 April 1921; *Educ* Leys Sch; *m* 1950, Lorna Agnes, da of John McLaren (d 1955); 3 s (Christopher, Angus, Nicholas), 1 da (Louise); *Career* WWII Capt E Yorks Regt UK and overseas 1940-47; chm and jt md W M Jackson & Son plc, chm Crystal of Hull Ltd, dir Beverley Race Co Ltd; farmer & landowner; JP, High Sheriff of Humberside 1987-88; FBIM, FID, FIOD; *Recreations* shooting, fishing, racing; *Clubs* Flyfishers; *Style—* Peter B Oughtred, Esq, JP; Raby Lodge, 26 Cave Rd, Brough, N Humberside HU15 1HL (☎ 0482 667381); Wodencroft Lodge, Cotherstone, Barnard Castle, Co Durham (☎ 083350 239); William Jackson & Son plc, 40 Derringham St, Hull HU3 1EW (☎ 0482 224131)

OULTON, Sir (Antony) Derek (Maxwell); KCB (1984, CB 1979), QC (1985); s of late Charles Cameron Courtenay Oulton; *b* 14 Oct 1927; *Educ* St Edward's Sch Oxford, King's Coll Cambridge (MA, PhD); *m* 1955, Margaret Geraldine, da of late Lt-Col G S Oxley, MC; 1 s, 3 da; *Career* barr Gray's Inn 1952; dep sec Lord Chancellor's Off 1976-82, perm sec 1982-; dep clerk of the Crown in Chancery 1977-82, clerk of the Crown in Chancery 1982-; *Style—* Sir Derek Oulton, KCB, QC; c/o Barclays Bank plc, 7 Town St, Thaxted, Dunmow, Essex CM6 2LD

OULTON, John Desmond Calverley; s of John Goerge Oulton (d 1952), of Clontarf Castle, Dublin; *b* 1921; *Educ* St Columba's Coll, Dublin Univ; *m* 1958, Moyra Ann, da of Col J H Graham-Hunter, RAMC; 2 s, 1 da; *Career* cmmnd London Irish Rifles 1940, invalided (ill-health); co dir; *Clubs* Royal Overseas; *Style—* John Oulton, Esq; 4

Colbourne Rd, Hove, E Sussex BN3 5DB (☎ 0273 779 556); Muxna, Kenmare, Co Kerry, Ireland

OULTON, Air Vice-Marshal Wilfrid Ewart; CB (1958), CBE (1953), DSO (1943), DFC (1943); s of Llewellin Oulton; *b* 27 July 1911; *Educ* Univ Coll Cardiff, RAF Cranwell; *m* 1935, Sarah, da of Rev E Davies; 3 s; *Career* cmmnd RAF 1931; dir Joint Anti-Submarine Sch 1946-48; Jt Servs Staff Coll 1948-50; air attaché: Buenos Aires, Montevideo, Asuncion 1950-53; idc 1954; dir of Operations Air Miny 1954-56; cmd Jt Task Force 'Grapple' for first Br megaton weapon tests in the Pacific 1956-58; SASO RAF Coastal Cmd 1958-60, ret as Air Vice-Marshal; chm Medsales Exec Ltd; fell Univ Coll Cardiff; CEng, FRIN, FIERE, FInstD; *Books* Christmas Island Cracker (1987); *Recreations* squash, music, sailing; *Clubs* RAF, Royal Lymington Yacht; *Style*— Air Vice-Marshal Wilfrid Oulton, CB, CBE, DSO, DFC; Farthings, Hollywood Lane, Lymington, Hants (☎ 0590 73498)

OUTHWAITE, Richard Henry Moffitt; s of Richard Moffitt Outhwaite (d 1971), and Barbara, *née* Hainsselin; *b* 1 Nov 1905; *Educ* Ashville Coll Harrogate; *m* 1, 3 May 1958 (m dis 1979), Lilian Irma, da of Paul Walter Heinemann (d 1977); 2 s (Paul, Alan) 4 da (Fiona, Susan, Katherine, Sophie); m 2, 2 Sep 1983, Ann Margaret, da of Donald Walter Mellor, CBE, of The Red House, West Hanningfield, Essex; *Career* dir: R J Merrett Syndicates ltd 1969-74, RHM Outhwaite Syndicates 1974-; Freeman: Worshipful Co of Shipwrights, Worshipful Co of Insurers; *Recreations* music, golf, field sports; *Style*— Richard Outhwaite, Esq; 85 Gracechurch St, London EC3 (☎ 01 623 1481)

OUTRAM, Sir Alan James; 5 Bt (UK 1858); s of late James Ian Outram (gs of 2 Bt) and Evelyn Mary, *née* Littlehales; suc gt uncl, Sir Francis Davidson Outram, 4 Bt, OBE, 1945; Lt-Gen Sir James Outram, GCB, KBE, received Baronetcy 1858 for service in Persia and India; *b* 15 May 1937; *Educ* Marlborough, St Edmund Hall Oxford; *m* 1976, Victoria Jean, da of late George Dickson Paton; 1 s, 1 da (Alison b 1977); *Heir* s Douglas Benjamin James Outram b 15 March 1979; *Career* Hon Lt-Col TA & VR; housemaster Druries Harrow Sch 1979- (formerly asst master); *Recreations* bridge, golf, tennis, cycling; *Style*— Sir Alan Outram, Bt; Harrow School, Harrow-on-the-Hill, Middlesex

OUTRIM, Hon Mrs (Olive Fenna); *née* Brockway; da of Baron Brockway (Life Peer), and his 1 w, Lilla, *née* Harvey-Smith; *b* 1924; *m* 1944, Cecil Outrim; children; *Style*— The Hon Mrs Outrim

OUTTEN, Alan Gilbert; s of Mark (Bertie) Outten (d 1986), and Mabel Letitia, *née* Griffiths; *b* 12 Jan 1933; *Educ* Drayton Manor GS, London Univ (LLB); *m* 28 May 1960, Margaret Therese, da of R James Joseph Hearty, of Newry, Co Down (d 1955); 4 s (Andrew b 1961, Brian b 1963, Alan b 1966, Christopher b 1973), 2 da (Catherine b 1965, Gemma b 1979); *Career* actuary; dir Forward Tst Gp Ltd and Subsidiary Co's; dep chm Motability Finance Ltd; chm Equipment Leasing Assoc; *Recreations* tennis, theatre, music; *Style*— Alan Outten, Esq; 16 Cleveland Rd, West Ealing, London W13 (☎ 01 997 6517); The Barn, Alfriston, East Sussex (☎ 0323 870020); Crown House, 145 City Rd, London EC1V 1JY (telex 8952620, facs 01 251 0064)

OVENDEN, Graham Stuart; s of Henry Ovenden (d 1986), of Winchester, and Gwendoline Dorothy, *née* Hill (d 1988); *b* 11 Feb 1943; *Educ* Itchen GS, Southampton Coll of Art, Royal Coll of Music (ARCM), Royal Coll of Art (MA); *m* 1 Mar 1969, Ann Dinah, da of George Walter Gilmore (d 1963), of Upper Winchendon, Bucks; 1 s (Edmunde Dante b 1973), 1 da (Emily Alice b 1976); *Career* artist, photgrapher and poet; numerous exhibitions incl the Tate Gallery and Royal Acad, one man shows in most major western countries; fndr memb The Brotherhood of Ruralists; *Books* Victorian Children (with Robert Melville, 1971), Pre-Raphaelite Photography (1972), Hill and Adamson Photographs (1973), Alphonse Mucha (1974), Clementina Lady Hawarden (1974), A Victorian Family Album (with Lord David Cecil, 1975), Satirical Poems and Others (1983), The Marble Mirror (poetry, 1984); *Style*— Graham Ovenden, Esq; Barley Splatt, Warleggan, Cornwall

OVENS, Maj-Gen Patrick John; OBE (1968), MC (1951); s of late Edward Alec Ovens; *b* 4 Nov 1922; *Educ* King's Sch, Bruton; *m* 1952, Margaret Mary White; 1 s, 2 da; *Career* cmmnd Royal Marines 1941; C-in-C Fleet Staff 1968-69; Cdr 3 Commando Bde 1970-72; RCDS 1973; COS to Cmdt Gen RM, MOD 1974-76; Cmdt Jt Warfare Establishment 1976-79; *Style*— Major-General Patrick Ovens, OBE, MC; Virginia House, Netherhampton, Salisbury, Wilts SP2 8PU (☎ Salisbury 0722 743113)

OVERALL, Sir John (Wallace); CBE (1962), MC and bar; s of Wallace Overall (d 1922), and Ethel Lavinia, *née* Davis (d 1957); *b* 15 July 1913; *Educ* Sydney Tech Coll; *m* 1943, Margaret Joan, da of late Cyril William Goodman, CBE (d 1979); 4 s (Andrew, Timothy, Michael, Jonathon); *Career* active service AIE in Africa and Mid East, engrg offr Infantry 1940-46, cmdg offr First Aust Parachute; ch architect with govr of Aust 1953-57; cmmr: Nat Capital Devpt Cmmn 1958-72, Nat Capital Dvpt Planning Ctee 1958-72 (and chm), Cities Cmmn 1972-73 (and chm); advsr to sec-gen on estab of UN Environment Conf 1975, UN in establishing provisional Ctee on Housing Aid in under-developed countries 1974, Tanzanian govt on behalf of the UN on design, devpt and construction of Dodoma as the Nat Capital of Tanzania 1974; memb: Aust Acad of Science and Industry Forum 1971-75, Parl House Construction Authority 1979; dir: CSR Co (Sydney) 1973-85, Lend Lease Devpt Corpn (Sydney) 1975-83, Alliance Hldgs 1975-83 (chm 1980-83), Gen Property Tst 1976-83; princ John Overall and Ptnrs 1973-83; pres and chm Aust Inst of Urban Studies 1970-71; L/FRAIA, L/FAPI; Gold Medal RAIA 1982. hon fell American Inst of Architecture; kt 1968; *see Debrett's Handbook of Australia and New Zealand for further details*; *Publications* Observations on Redevelopment of the Western Side of Sydney Cove Rocks Area to Grosvenor St (1967), papers to ANZAAS Conf and sundry professional journals; *Recreations* tennis, golf; *Clubs* Cwlth (Canberra), Royal Sydney Golf; *Style*— Sir John Overall, CBE, MC*; 3A Vancouver St, Red Hill, ACT 2603, Australia (☎ 9526 46)

OVEREND, Prof (William) George; s of Harold George Overend (d 1986), of Shrewsbury, and Hilda, *née* Parry (d 1974); *b* 16 Nov 1921; *Educ* Priory Sch Shrewsbury, Univ of Birmingham (BSc, PhD, DSc); *m* 12 July 1949, Gina Olava, da of Horace Bertie Cadman (d 1980), of Birmingham, Warwicks; 2 s (George Edmund (Ted) b 1958, Desmond Anthony b 1963), 1 da (Sheila Hilda b 1961); *Career* assoc prof Pennsylvania State Coll 1951-52; Univ of London: reader in organic chemistry 1955-57, prof of chemistry 1957-87, emeritus prof and Leverhulme emeritus fell 1987-; Birkbeck Coll London: head of dept of chemistry 1957-79, vice master 1974-78, master 1979-87; senator Univ of London 1978-87; memb Br Pharmacopoeia Cmmn 1962-80, memb Home Off Poisons Bd 1966-, vice pres Perkin Div Royal Soc of Chemistry 1976-78, chm cncl of govrs S Bank Poly 1980-; memb cncl Royal Soc of Chemistry 1972-78; Lampitt Medallist Soc of Chemical Indust 1965; hon fell Coll of Preceptor (hon FCP) 1986, hon fell Birkbeck Coll 1987, Hon DUniv Open Univ 1988; FRSC, FBIM, FRSA; *Books* The Use of Tracer Elements in Biology (1951), Programmes in Organic Chemistry I-VIII (ed, 1966-73); *Recreations* gardening; *Clubs* Athenaeum, RAC; *Style*— Prof George Overend; The Retreat, Nightingales Lane, Chalfont St Giles, Bucks HP8 4SR (☎ 02 404 3996); Department of Chemistry, Birkbeck Coll (Univ of London, Malet St, London WC1E 7HX (☎ 01 580 6622)

OVERTON, Sir Hugh Thomas Arnold; KCMG (1983, CMG 1975); s of late Sir Arnold Overton, KCB, KCMG, MC, and Bronwen Cecilie Vincent; *b* 2 April 1923; *Educ* Dragon Sch Oxford, Winchester, Clare Coll Cambridge; *m* 1948, Claire-Marie, da of Jean Binet (d 1961, Swiss composer); 1 s, 2 da; *Career* served RCS (France and Germany) 1943-45; Dip Serv 1947, served in Eastern Europe, Near East, Germany, N America; head of N America dept FCO 1971-74, consul gen Düsseldorf 1974-75, min (econ) Bonn 1975-80, consul gen NY and dir gen Br trade Devpt in USA 1980-83, ret; memb: cncl Dr Barnardo's 1985 (exec/fin ctee 1988), (and tstee) Bell Educnl Tst, Taverner Concerts Tst; *Clubs* RAC, Royal Inst of Int Affairs; *Style*— Sir Hugh Overton, KCMG; 30 North End House, Fitzjames Ave, London W14 0RS (☎ 01 603 6795)

OVEY, Richard; o s of Richard Henry Ovey, JP (d 1947), of Hernes, and Elizabeth Henderson, *née* Danforth (d 1974); descended from Thomas Ovey (d 1635), of Watlington, Oxfordshire; gs of Lt-Col Richard Lockhart Ovey, DSO, TD, JP, DL (d 1946), who acquired Hernes (*see* Burke's Landed Gentry, 18 edn, vol II, 1969); *b* 26 July 1939; *Educ* Eton, North of Scotland Coll of Agric; *m* 17 July 1965, Gillian Mary, o da of Cecil James Smith (d 1984), of Church Cottage, Rotherfield Greys, nr Henley-on-Thames, Oxon; 2 s (Richard (Dick) b 1967, Andrew b 1971), 1 da (Clare b 1969); *Career* landowner; chm Rotherfield Greys Parish Cncl; past pres and ctee memb H & DAA; past vice-chm SOCUA; *Recreations* shooting, fishing, sailing; Hernes, Henley-on-Thames, Oxon (☎ 0491 573245)

OWEN, Alan Charles; s of Thomas Charles Owen, and Florence Edith, *née* Blake; *b* 7 Mar 1939; *Educ* Elliot Central Sch Southfields London; *m* 11 Oct 1974 (m dis), Janet Ann, da of William David Butcher; 1 s (Ian Charles), 1 da (Larraine Carol); *Career* mangr Gilbert Eliott and Co Stockbrokers 1970 (ptnr 1977), memb Stock Exchange 1976, div dir Girozentrale Gilbert Eliott 1987-; memb Int Stock Exchange; *Recreations* keen squash player; *Style*— Alan Owen, Esq; Girozentrale Gilbert Eliott, 381 Salisbury House, London Wall London EC2M 5SB (☎ 01 628 6782, fax 01 628 3500, telex 888886)

OWEN, Alun Davies; s of Sidney Owen (d 1977), of Liverpool, and Ruth, *née* Davies (d 1950); *b* 24 Nov 1925; *Educ* Oulton HS Liverpool, Cardigan County Sch Dyfed Wales; *m* 12 Dec 1942, (Theodora) Mary, da of Dr Stephen O'Keefe (d 1942), of Dublin; 2 s (Teifion, Gareth Robert); *Career* coal miner(Bevin Boy) 1943; playwright and actor; author of plays for stage and tv incl: The Rough and Ready Lot 1961, Progress to the Park 1962, The Rose Affair 1962, A Hard Days Night 1964, Dare to be a Daniel 1965, George's Room 1971, Norma 1971; awards incl: Screenwriters and Prodrs Guild script of the year 1960, Screenwriters Guild Award best play 1961, Daily Mirror Award best play 1961, Golden Star Award best playwright 1967, Oscar nomination A Hard Day's Night 1964, Emmy Award The Male of the Species 1969, BAMFFE Award Canada best play 1985; memb Writers Guild of GB; *Recreations* reading, swimming; *Clubs* Chelsea Arts; *Style*— Alun Owen, Esq; c/o Julienn Friedmann, Blake Friedmann Literary Agency, 37-41 Gower St, London WC1E 6HH (☎ 01 631 4331)

OWEN, Hon Mrs (Ardyne Mary); da of 2 Viscount Knollys, GCMG, MBE, DFC (d 1966); *b* 1929; *m* 1958, Ronald James Owen; *Style*— The Hon Mrs Owen; Paradise Wood, Upper Hartfield, Sussex

OWEN, His Hon Judge Aron; *b* 16 Feb 1919; *Educ* Tredegar Co GS, Univ of Wales (BA, PhD); *m* 1946, Rose, JP, da of Solomon Alexander Fishman, Freeman City of London (d 1936); 1 s, 2 da; *Career* barr Inner Temple 1948; circuit judge 1980-; Freeman City of London; *Recreations* travel, gardening; *Style*— His Hon Judge Aron Owen; 44 Brampton Grove, Hendon, London NW4 4AQ (☎ 01 202 8151)

OWEN, (Alfred) David; s of Sir Alfred Owen, CBE (d 1975), and Lady Owen (Eileen Kathleen Genevieve); *b* 26 Sept 1936; *Educ* Brocksford Hall, Oundle, Emmanuel Coll Cambridge; *m* 1966, Ethne Margaret, da of Frank H Sowman, of Solihull; 2 s, 1 da; *Career* Lt RASC, Nat Serv; chm Rubery Owen Gp; tstee Community Projects Fndn 1978-; memb Br Overseas Trade Bd 1979-83, pres Birmingham C of C 1980-91; vice pres SMMT 1987-88, Pres Comite de Liaison de la Construction d'Equipments et de Pieces d'Automobiles 1988- (CLEPA); Hon Doctor of Science Aston Univ July 1988; *Recreations* industl archaeology, ornithology, walking, photography, music; *Clubs* National, RAC; *Style*— David Owen Esq; Mill Dam House, Mill Lane, Aldridge, Walsall, WS9 0NB (☎ 021 353 1221); Rubery Owen Holdings Ltd, PO Box 10, Darlaston, Wednesbury, W Midlands

OWEN, Rt Hon David Anthony Llewellyn; PC (1976), MP (Lab to 1981, SDP thereafter) Plymouth Devonport 1974-; s of Dr John William Morris Owen; *b* 2 July 1938; *Educ* Bradfield Coll, Sidney Sussex Coll Cambridge (hon fell 1977), St Thomas's Hosp (BA, MB, BChir, MA); *m* 1968, Deborah Schabert (Deborah Owen, literary agent); 2 s, 1 da; *Career* St Thomas's Hosp: house appts 1962-64, neurological and psychiatric registrar 1964-66, res fell med unit 1966-68; contested (Lab) Torrington 1964; pps to MOD (Admin) 1967, parly under-sec of state for Def for RN 1968-70, resigned over EEC 1972; MP (Lab) Plymouth Sutton 1966-74; parly under-sec of state DHSS 1974, min of state DHSS 1974-76 & FCO 1976-77, sec of state for For and Cwlth Affairs 1977-79; opposition spokesman on energy 1979-81; fndr memb SDP 1981, chm SDP Parly Ctee, SDP Spokesman with general responsibilities, later SDP spokesman For Affrs; memb SDP Working Party on Econ Policy 1981-; dep leader SDP MPs Oct 1982-, SDP spokesman for and def matters Nov 1982-, elected SDP Leader following resignation of Rt Hon Roy Jenkins after election (June) 1983-; *Style*— The Rt Hon David Owen, MP; 78 Narrow St, Limehouse, E14 (☎ 01 987 5441); Castlehayes, Plympton, Plymouth, Devon (☎ Plymouth 0752 336130); House of Commons, SW1 (☎ 01 219 4203)

OWEN, (Francis) David Lloyd; TD (1967); s of Robert Charles Lloyd Owen, of Glanmorfa, Dolgellau, Meirionnydd, and Jane Ellen, *née* Francis; *b* 24 Oct 1933; *Educ* Wrekin Coll; *m* 28 Oct 1965, Jennifer Nan, da of Richard Eric Knowles Rowlands, of

The Grange, Mickle Trafford, Chester; 2 da (Charis Jane b 7 May 1971, Anna Clare b 2 June 1974); *Career* Nat Serv 1952-54, cmmnd 22 Cheshire Regt 1953, TA 1954-67, Maj 1963; slr 1961-66, barr Gray's Inn 1967, practicing Northern Circuit, actg stipendiary magistrate 1981, dep circuit judge and asst rec 1977-88, rec 1988; *Recreations* country pursuits, sailing, geneology; *Clubs* Grosvenor (Chester); *Style*— David Owen, Esq, TD; The Pool House, Tarvin, Chester (☎ 0829 40300); Ty'n-Y-Parc, Sarn, Pwllheli, Gwynedd; Refuge Assurance House, Derby Sq, Liverpool (☎ 051 709 4222, fax 051 708 6311); Goldsmith Bldg, Temple, London EC4 (☎ 01 353 7881, fax 01 353 5319)

OWEN, Hon Mrs (Eiddwen Sara); *née* Philipps; yst da (by 1 m) of 2 Viscount St Davids, *qv*; *b* 28 June 1948; *m* 1986, Clive Geoffrey Owen; *Style*— The Hon Eiddwen Philipps; 4 Quarry Road, Kenilworth, Warwickshire CV8 1AE

OWEN, Eirwen Mary; CBE (1973); da of Richard John Owen (d 1951); *b* 24 Nov 1914; *Educ* Univ of Wales Aberystwyth; *Career* dep regnl cmmr for Wales 1939-45, head of overseas dept WVS 1944-56; memb cncl for Univ Coll of S Wales and Mon 1946-52, Royal Cmmn on the Press 1947-50; dir Admin Zoological Soc of London 1957 ; *Style*— Miss Eirwen Owen, CBE; 4 Hope Cote Lodge, Church Rd, Combe Down, Bath BA2 5JJ

OWEN, Frank Edwin Garthwaite; OBE, TD (1946); s of William Henry Owen (d 1948), of Highbury New Park, London, and Ethel Hettie, *née* Morris (d 1979); *b* 25 Sept 1909; *Educ* Owen's Sch London EC1 (fndn scholar), Univ Coll London (BA), LSE, Nat Inst of Industl Psychology; *m* 23 March 1940, Joan Mildred, da of Rev Edward Wightman Henry (d 1967), of Taxal Rectory, Chester; *Career* res and lecturing Univ Coll London; investigative conslt for Nat Inst of Industl Psychology; Industl exec; TA Inns of Ct Regt, cmmnd 118 Field Regt; attached Quatrième Régiment d'Artillerie; Malaya, Battery Capt; Japanese POW 1942-45 (Disability Medal); fndr and first princ Westham Adult Residential Coll 1947-77; memb cncl Assoc of Agric 1969-70; lecture tours Scandinavia 1948 and 1950; Smith-Mundt Fellowship USA and Fulbright Fell Chicago Univ 1953-54; visiting conslt Residential Coll projects: Philadelphia 1954, Kentucky 1961; Chevalier de la Légion d'Honneur 1959; *Recreations* riding, horse-breeding, hunting, theatre; *Style*— Frank Owen, Esq, OBE, TD; Georgian Wing, Williamscot House, Nr Banbury, Oxon OX17 1AE (☎ 029 575 8113)

OWEN, Lt-Col Garth Henry; TD; s of Henry Owen (d 1964); *b* 4 May 1924; *Educ* Rugeley GS; *m* 1948, Madeleine, *née* Day; *Career* served WW II RN 1941-46; RAFVR 1948-53; 639th Heavy Field Regt RA (TA) 1953-57; 125th (Staffordshire) Engr Regt (TA) 1957-67; Hon Col 125th (Staffordshire) Field Support Sqdn, RE (V) and The 143rd Plant Sqdn RE (V) T & AVR; DL (1967) Staffs; *Style*— Lt-Col Garth Owen, TD, DL; Carioca Cottage, Brackenridge, Fair Oak, Slitting Mill, Rugeley Staffs (☎ Rugeley 2875)

OWEN, Geoffrey Dorsett; s of Capt Geoffrey Dorsett Owen RN (d 1980), and Dorothy Rosamond France-Hayhurst (d 1956); *b* 28 May 1927; *Educ* St Albans Sch, Washington DC USA (Harvard Award), MC Gill Univ Montreal Canada, (External) London Univ; *m* 16 Jan 1965, Pamela Lane, da of William Trevor Morgan (d 1977), of Garlands, Gillham Wood Rd, Cooden, Sussex; 4 da (Rachel Mary b 1965, Rowena Clare b 1967 (decd), Alison Jane b 1968, Ruth Rosamond b 1971); *Career* assist architect W Wylton Todd ARIBA 1957, exhibited at Wessex Artists Exhibition 1960; princ (solo practice) flats, housing, sch bldgs, community centres 1956-87; *Recreations* metaphysics, painting, gardening, swimming, walking; *Style*— Geoffrey Owen, Esq; Riverwood, Droxford Rd, Wickham, Fareham, Hants PO17 5AY (☎ 0329 833102)

OWEN, Gerald Victor; QC (1969); s of Samuel Owen (d 1972), and Ziporah Owen (d 1974); *b* 29 Nov 1922; *Educ* Kilburn GS, St Catharine's Coll Cambridge (MA), Queen Mary Coll London Science Scholarship; Univ of London (LLB); *m* 21 March 1946, Phyllis; 1 s (Michael b 15 Oct 1948), 1 da (Juliet b 26 Dec 1952); *Career* barr Gray's Inn 1949, ad eundem Inner Temple 1969; QC 1969; dep circuit judge 1971; rec of Crown Ct 1979-; chm: Dairy Produce Quota Tribunal 1984-85, Med Appeal Tribunal 1984-; FRStatS; *Recreations* music; *Style*— Gerald Owen, Esq, QC; 3 Paper Buildings, Temple, London, EC4Y 7EU (☎ 01 353 1182)

OWEN, Harold; s of Owen William Owen, slr (d 1939); *b* 7 July 1909; *Educ* Rossall Sch; *m* 1934, Doris Melhuish, da of William Melhuish Thomas (d 1918); 3 da; *Career* served 1939-45 with RA, Maj; admitted slr 1932, ret; memb Liverpool Stock Exchange 1948-72; high sheriff Anglesey 1957; *Style*— Harold Owen Esq; Llynon Hall, Llanddeusant, Holyhead, Gwynedd LL65 4DS (☎ 040 788 203)

OWEN, Maj-Gen Harry; CB (1972); s of John Lewis Owen (d 1941), of Bangor, and Susan Kelly (d 1916); *b* 17 July 1911; *Educ* Univ Coll Bangor (BA); *m* 1952, Maureen, da of Leonard Livingstone Summers, of IOW; 1 s (Julian), 1 da (Elspeth); *Career* Maj-Gen West Indies, West Africa, Middle East, Far East, Germany; slr; dir Army Legal Service 1969-71; chm Med Appeal Tribunal 1972-84; *Recreations* swimming, philosophy; *Style*— Maj-Gen Harry Owen, CB; 40 North Park, Gerrards, Bucks SL9 8JP (☎ 0753 886777)

OWEN, Sir Hugh (Bernard Pilkington); 5 Bt (UK 1813); s of Sir John Arthur Owen, 4 Bt (d 1973), and Lucy, *née* Pilkington (d 1985); *b* 28 Mar 1915; *Educ* Chillon Coll Switzerland; *Heir* bro, John William Owen; *Style*— Sir Hugh Owen, Bt; 63 Dudsbury Rd, Ferndown, Dorset

OWEN, The Hon and Rt Worshipful Sir John Arthur Dalziel; QC (1970); s of Robert John Owen (d 1940), and Olive Barlow, *née* Hall-Wright; *b* 22 Nov 1925; *Educ* Solihull Sch, Brasenose Coll Oxford (MA, BCL); *m* 26 July 1952, Valerie, da of William Ethell (d 1988), of Solihull; 1 s (James Alexander Dalziel b 1 June 1966), 1 da (Melissa Clare (Hon Mrs Michael-John Knatchbull) b 12 Nov 1960); *Career* cmmnd 2 King Edward's Own Gurkha Rifles 1944; barr Gray's Inn 1951; dep chm Warwickshire QS 1967-71; rec of Crown Ct 1972-84; memb Senate of Inns of Ct and Bar 1977-80; dep ldr Midland and Oxford Circuit 1979-84; Dean of the Arches and Auditor of Chancery Ct York 1980-; Circuit judge at Old Bailey 1984-86; High Court Judge 1986-; chm W Midlands Area Mental Health Review Tribunal 1972-80; kt 1986; *Clubs* Garrick; *Style*— The Hon and Rt Worshipful Mr Justice John Owen; Royal Courts of Justice, Strand, London WC2A 2LL; 1 Verulam Buildings, Gray's Inn, London WC1R 5LQ (☎ 01 242 7722)

OWEN, Col John Edward; CBE (1989); s of John Joseph Owen (d 1948), of Abercwmboi and Mary May *née* McSweeney (d 1973); *b* 21 August 1928; *Educ* Aberdare County Sch 1939-43, Woolwich Poly 1945-48 (C Eng); *m* 8 Aug 1951, Jean Wardle, da of Eric Pendlebury, of Buxton, Derbyshire; 1 s (Stephen b 1952), 2 da (Jenny b 1954, Kate b 1963); *Career* cmmnd Reme 1950, OC 6 Infantry Workshop 1964-66, Lt Col 1966, Reme Sch of Artillery 1966-69, cdr Reme First Div BAOR 1969-71, Col HQ Deme 1971-72, ret 1972; dep chief engr Met Police 1972-76, (dir mgmnt 1976, chief engr 1976-86, dep receiver 1986-); dist cmmnr scouts 1967-69; memb RAC Tech ctee; FIEE 1972, FIERE 1972, FMS 1976, FBIM 1974, C DIP AF 1976; *Recreations* gardening, grand child; *Clubs* RAC; *Style*— Col John Owen, CBE; Metropolitan Police Office, New Scotland Yard, London, SW1H OBG (☎ 01 230 2491)

OWEN, John Halliwell; OBE (1975); s of Arthur Llewellyn Owen, OBE (d 1976), of Bebington, Wirral, and Doris Spencer, *née* Halliwell; *b* 16 June 1935; *Educ* Sedbergh, Queen's College Oxford (MA); *m* 1, 14 Dec 1963 (m dis 1971), Jacqueline Simone, da of James Ambrose, of Coin, Spain; 1 s (Adrian b 1967), 1 da (Carina b 1964); m 2, 15 Jan 1972, Dianne Elizabeth, da William George Lowry (d 1974), of St Stephens, Canterbury; 1 da (Catherine b 1972); *Career* Nat Serv 2 Lt RA 1954-56; Overseas Civil Serv Tanganyika Govt 1960-65: dist offr prov admin 1960-62, dist cmmr 1962-63, dist magistrate regnl local cts offr 1963-65; FO 1966-: second sec Dar-Es-Salaam 1968-70, FCO 1970-73, first sec Dhaka 1973-75, FCO 1975-76, first sec Accra 1976-80, FCO 1980-82, cnsllr Pretoria 1982-86, cnsllr FCO 1986-; *Recreations* wildlife, travel, gardening; *Clubs* Dar-Es-Salaam YC; *Style*— John H Owen, Esq; Foreign & Commonwealth Office, London SW1

OWEN, Maj-Gen John Ivor Headon; OBE (1963); s of Maj William Headon Owen, MC (d 1954), and Norita Alexandrina, *née* Morgan (d 1970); *b* 22 Oct 1922; *Educ* St Edmund's Sch Canterbury; *m* 1948, Margaret Jean, da of Edwin Hayes (d 1931); 3 da; *Career* 1942 Royal Marines, commando Far East 1943-46, constable Metropolitan Police 1946-47, rejoined Royal Marines, regimental serv to 1955, Staff Coll Camberley 1956, Brigade Maj, MOD (Admiralty) 1962-64, JSSC 1966-67; CO 45 Commando 1967-69; RCDS 1971, Maj-Gen Commando Forces RM Plymouth 1972-73, Maj-Gen 1972; UK partnership sec to KMG Thomson McLintock & Co 1974-87, Rep Col Cmdt RM 1985-86; tres Clergy Orphan Corp, memb Ctee of Sons of Clergy Corp; chm ctee Bowles outdoor pursuits centre; *Books* Brassey's Infantry Weapons of the World, and others; ed Current Military Literature; *Recreations* woodworking, gardening; *Clubs* Army and Navy; *Style*— Maj-Gen John Owen, OBE; Pollards Down, Rushlake Green, Heathfield, E Sussex TN21 9QX (☎ 0435 830664)

OWEN, John Wyn; s of Idwal Wyn Owen (d 1984), of Bangor, and Myfi, *née* Hughes; *b* 15 May 1942; *Educ* Friars Sch Bangor, St John's Coll Cambridge (BA, MA), Kings Fund Hosp Admin Staff Coll (ASHM); *m* 1 April 1967, Elizabeth Ann, da of William MacFarlane (d 1980), of Bangor; 1 s (Dafydd b 1974), 1 da (Sian b 1971); *Career* hosp sec Glantawe HMC Swansea 1967-70, staff trg offr Welsh Hosp Bd Cardiff 1968-70, divnl admin Univ Hosp of Wales HMC Cardiff 1970-72, asst clerk St Thomas' Hosp London 1972-74, admin St Thomas' Health Dist 1974-79; exec dir Utd Med Enterprises London 1979-85; dir: Allied Med Gp London 1979-85, Br Nursing Cooperations London 1979-85, Allied Med Gp Healthcare Canada 1982-85, Allied Shanning London 1983-85; Kings Fund Hosp Admin Staff Coll (AHSM); chm Welsh Health Common Servs Authy 1985-, dir Welsh NHS 1985-; tstee: Florence Nightingale Museum Tst, Mgmnt Advsy Serv; organist Utd Free Church Cowbridge 1985; *Recreations* organ playing, opera, travel; *Clubs* Athenaeum; *Style*— John Wyn Owen, Esq; Welsh Office, Cathays Park, Cardiff CF1 3NR (☎ 0222 823695)

OWEN, John Wynne; MBE (1979); s of Thomas David Owen (d 1977), of Pontardulais, S Wales, and Mair Eluned, *née* Richards (d 1988); *b* 25 April 1939; *Educ* Gowerton GS; *m* 1, 14 July 1962, Thelma Margaret (d 1987), da of Arthur James Gunton (d 1984), of Yarmouth, Isle of Wight; 1 s (David b 1970), 2 da (Sandra b 1963, Karen b 1969), 1 step da (Fiona Roberts b 1977); m 2, 19 March 1988, Carol, da of John Edmunds, of Wootton, IOW; *Career* HM For Serv 1956-58, Nat Serv RS 1958-60, cmmnd 2 Lt 1959; HM For Serv (later Dip Serv) in Indonesia 1960-61, Vietnam 1961-62, Paris 1962-63, El Salvador 1963-67, resigned between 1967 and 1970, returned to FO 1970-73, third and later second sec Br Embassy Tehran 1973-77, vice consul and later consul (commercial) Br Consulate Gen Sao Paulo Brazil 1978-80, first sec and consul Br Embassy Peking 1980-82, first sec FO 1983-85, special unpaid league 1985-; chm and md Gunham Plastics Ltd 1985 (dir since 1967), chm Channel Distribition Ltd 1986, chm and md Gunham Distribution Ltd 1986, Gunham Hldgs Ltd 1987, chm Br Laminated Plastics Fabricators Assoc 1987; dir: HS Bassett Ltd 1988, Manwood Properties Ltd 1988; chm RET Osborne Ltd 1988; Freeman City of London, Liveryman Worshipful Co of Loriners; FInstD 1980, FBIM 1985; *Recreations* swimming, tennis, walking; *Clubs* RAC, City Livery; *Style*— John Owen, Esq, MBE; 159 Ashley Gardens, Thirleby Rd, Westminster, London SW1P 1HW (☎ 01 834 3760); Gunham Hldgs Ltd, 40 Rivington St, London EC2A 3LX (☎ 01 739 7470, fax 01 739 9983, car tel 0836 288 409)

OWEN, Joslyn Grey; CBE (1979); s of William Owen, MBE (1973), and Nell, *née* Evans (d 1960); *b* 23 August 1928; *Educ* Cardiff HS, Worcester Coll Oxford (MA); *m* 24 June 1961, Mary Patricia, da of William Brooks (d 1969), of Rustington; 3 s (Mark William b 1963, Stephen Grey b 1966, Matthew James b 1968); *Career* RAF 1946-48; classics master and housemaster King's Sch Canterbury 1953-58; asst educn offr: Croydon 1958-62, Somerset 1962-66; chief educn offr Devon 1972- (dep chief educn offr 1968-72); sec The Schs Cncl for Curriculum & Examinations 1966-68; memb: cncl Exeter Univ, mgmnt ctee Atlantic Coll, St Luke's Fndn Tstees; govr Dartington Coll of the Arts; hon fell Plymouth Poly 1978; FRSA 1972, FCP 1974; *Books* Management of Curriculum Development (1973); *Recreations* reading, music; *Clubs* Reform; *Style*— Joslyn Owen, Esq, CBE; 4 The Quadrant, Exeter, Devon EX2 4LE (☎ 0392 743 26); Devon County Council, County Hall, Topsham Rd, Exeter, Devon EX2 4QG

OWEN, Prof Paul Robert; CBE (1974), FRS (1971); s of Joseph Owen; *b* 24 Jan 1920; *Educ* Queen Mary Coll, London Univ (BSc, MSc Manchester Dès S Aix-Marseille); *m* 1958, Margaret Ann, da of Herbert Baron; 2 s, 2 da; *Career* Zaharoff prof of aviation London Univ, at Imperial Coll of Science and Technol 1963-85; FEng, FRAeS, FCGI; Visiting Prof Univ Colorado, Boulder, USA 1986-87; Sr Research Fellow, Imperial Coll 1985-; *Style*— Professor Paul Owen, CBE, FRS; Flat 1, Stanley Lodge, 25 Stanley Crescent, London, W11 2NA (☎ 01 229 5111)

OWEN, Philip Anthony; s of Alec Owen (d 1959), of Hornsea, East Yorks, and Katherine Mary, *née* Pink; *b* 25 August 1944; *Educ* Pitmans Coll Hull, Queens' Coll Cambridge; *m* 5 Sept 1984, Deborah Anne, da of Arthur Harry Lewin, of Auckland NZ; 1 s (Simon b 1988), 1 da (Julia b 1987); *Career* slr; ptnr Allen & Overy 1982- (joined 1973); Liveryman Worshipful Co Slrs; memb Law Soc 1968; *Recreations* ocean racing, golf, skiing; *Clubs* Royal Yorkshire YC, Royal Wimbledon GC; *Style*— Philip Owen, Esq; 9 Cheapside, London EC2V 6AD (☎ 01 248 9898, fax 01 236 2192, telex

8812801)

OWEN, Philip Loscombe Wintringham; TD (1950), QC (1963), JP (Montgomeryshire 1959, Cheshire 1961); s of Rt Hon Sir Wintringham Stable, MC (d 1977), of Plas Llwyn Owen, Llanbrynmair, Powys, and Lucy Haden Stable (d 1976); assumed surname of Owen by deed poll, 1942; *b* 10 Jan 1920; *Educ* Winchester, Christ Church Oxford (MA); *m* 1949, Elizabeth Jane, da of Lewis Trelawny Widdicombe (d 1953); 3 s, 2 da; *Career* served WWII Royal Welch Fus, Maj TARO; received into RC Church 1943; barr Middle Temple 1949, bencher 1969; memb Gen Cncl of Bar of Eng and Wales 1971-77; a dep chm of QS: Montgomeryshire 1959-71, Cheshire 1961-71; rec: Merthyr Tydfil 1971, Crown Ct 1972-85; ldr Wales and Chester circuit 1975-77, legal assessor to: Gen Med Cncl 1970-, Gen Dental Cncl 1970-, RICS 1970-; Parly candidate (C) Montgomeryshire 1945, vice pres Montgomeryshire Cons and Unionist Assoc, former pres Montgomeryshire Soc, dir Swansea City AFC Ltd 1975-86; *Recreations* shooting, fishing, forestry, music, association football; *Style—* Philip Owen, Esq, TD, QC, JP; Plas Llwyn Owen, Llanbrynmair, Powys SY19 7BE (☎ 06503 542); 1 Brick Court, Temple, London EC4Y 9BY (☎ 01 583 0777)

OWEN, Robert Michael; QC (1988); s of Gwynne Llewellyn Owen (d 1986) of Fowey, Cornwall and Phoebe Constance Owen; *b* 19 Sept 1944; *Educ* Durham Sch Exeter Univ (LLB); *m* 9 Aug 1969, Sara Josephine, da of Sir Algernon Rumbold, KCMG, of Shortwoods, West Clandon, Surrey; 2 s (Thomas b 10 Nov 1973, Huw b 4 Jan 1976); *Career* called to the Bar 1968, rec 1987-; *Clubs* MCC, Royal Fowey Yacht; *Style—* Robert Owen, Esq, QC; 1 Crown Office Row, Temple, London EC4 (☎ 01 353 1801)

OWEN, Rowland Hubert; CMG (1948); s of William Rowland Owen (d 1924); *b* 3 June 1903; *Educ* Royal Sch Armagh, Trinity Coll Dublin (BA, LLB); *m* 1 1930, Kathleen Margaret Evaleen, *née* Scott (d 1965); m 2 1966, Shelagh Myrle, da of Kenneth Nicholson (d 1924); *Career* civil servant, IDC 1934; sr Br trade cmmr in India 1945-52, comptroller gen Export Credits Guarantee Dept 1953-58, dep controller HMSO 1959-64; organist and choirmaster Holy Trinity Bramley; pres Surrey Organists Assoc 1976, sec 1976-83; *Style—* Rowland Owen Esq, CMG; Oak Tree Cottage, Holdfast Lane, Haslemere, Surrey GU27 2EU (☎ Haslemere 0428 3748)

OWEN, Roy Howard; s of Ernest Henry Owen (d 1944), of Selwyn, Queens Drive, Liverpool, and Gladys May Owen, *née* Edwards (d 1966); *b* 22 June 1926; *Educ* Liverpool Inst, HS, Liverpool Univ (BArch, MCD); *m* 18 June 1968, Frances Maire, da of Joseph Patrick McNamara (d 1945), of Westcroft, Town Row, Liverpool; 1 s (David b 1976), 1 da (Sarah b 1972); *Career* chartered architect and town planning consIt; pres Liverpool Architectural Soc 1988-89; chm: W Derby Wastelands Charity 1980-, Liverpool Regnl Jt Cons Ctee for Bldg 1978-79; RIBA; MRTPI; *Recreations* opera, golf, association football, cricket; *Clubs* Liverpool Sportsmans Assoc, West Derby GC, English Golf Union; *Style—* Roy Owen, Esq; Studley, Vyner Road South, Oxton, Birkenhead L43 7PN (☎ 051 652 2898); 619/621 India Buildings, Water Street, Liverpool L2 0RA (☎ 051 236 0353)

OWEN, Samuel Griffith; CBE (1977); s of late Rev Evan Lewis Owen; *b* 3 Sept 1925; *Educ* Dame Allen's Sch, Durham Univ (MD); *m* 1954, Ruth, da of late Merle W Tate; 2 s, 2 da; *Career* instr in medicine Univ of Pennsylvania 1953-56, hon consIt physician Royal Victoria Infirmary Newcastle upon Tyne 1960-68; clinical sub-dean of Med Sch, Univ of Newcastle upon Tyne 1960-68; examiner in medicine Liverpool Univ 1966-68; 2 sec MRC 1968-82; memb: scientific co-ordinating ctee Arthritis and Rheumatism Cncl 1978-82, NW Thames RHA 1978-82; govr Queen Charlotte's Hosp for Women 1979-82; FRCP, memb Royal Soc of Med; *Style—* Dr S G Owen, CBE; 60 Bath Rd, Chiswick, London W4 (☎ 01 995 3228)

OWEN, Sheila Yorks; da of Capt William Owen (d 1950) (S African Mounted Rifles), of Hassocks, Sussex, and Ethel Lucy Yorks Owen, *née* Weedon (d 1974); *b* 13 Mar 1912; *Educ* Berkehamsted GS for girls, Queen Anne's Sch Caversham, Freiburgim Breisgau, Lycée Françaire, Geneva Univ, Mrs Foster's Sec Trg Coll; *Career* sec/translator Unilever Ltd London and Paris 1932-68, sec to: Mr V Cavendish (Duke of Portland) 1947-68, Ctee of Br Industl Interests in Germany 1950-68; hon sec Cons Assoc Bransh: Hernhill, Kent 1968-70, Dolgellau 1985-87, Meironnydd Nant Conwy 1986-87; FIL, (languages Dutch, Norwegian, Polish, Welsh, French, German); *Recreations* mountain walking, gardening; *Clubs* Royal OverSeas League, Monday; *Style—* Miss Sheila Owen; Clawdd Dawi, Aberarth, Aberaeron, Dyfed SA46 0JX (☎ 0545 571 008)

OWEN, Thomas Arfon; s of Hywel Peris Owen, of Tumble; *b* 7 June 1933; *Educ* Ystalyfera GS, Magdalen Coll Oxford; *m* 1955, Mary Joyce, da of Tom Ellis Phillips, of Ystalyfera (d 1972); 3 s, 1 da; *Career* dir Welsh Arts Cncl 1984-; registrar Univ Coll of Wales Aberystwyth 1967-84; memb Consumer Ctee for GB 1975-; High Sheriff of Dyfed 1976-77; memb: Health Authy S Glam 1984-87 (vice chm 1986-87); memb: cncl UWIST 1987-88, cncl Univ of Wales Coll at Cardiff 1988-, cncl Nat Library of Wales 1987-; *Recreations* reading, crosswords, public service; *Style—* Thomas Owen, Esq; Argoed, 6 Bronwydd Close, Cardiff CF2 5RA (☎ 0222 481738)

OWEN, Trevor Bryan; CBE (1987); s of Leonard Owen, CIE (d 1965), of Gerrards Cross, and Dilys, *née* Davies Bryan; *b* 3 April 1928; *Educ* Rugby, Trinity Coll Oxford (MA); *m* 1955, Gaie, da of Cyril Dashwood Houston (d 1975), of Newark, Notts; 1 s (Jonathan b 1958), 1 da (Jane b 1956); *Career* dir paints, agric and plastics divns ICI 1955-78; md Remploy Ltd 1978-88; chm: Bethlem and Maudsley Special Health Authy 1988-, PHAB 1988-; memb: govt of N Ireland Higher Educn Review Gp 1979-81, nat Advsy cncl on the Employment of Disabled People 1978-88, CNAA 1973-79, cncl CBI 1982-88, cncl Ind Soc 1967-88, cncl Inst of Manpower Studies 1975-87; chm bd of govnrs, Nat Inst for Social Work 1985-; *Books* Making Organisations Work (1978), The Manager and Industrial Relations (1979); *Style—* Trevor B Owen, CBE; 8 Rochester Terr, London NW1 9JN (☎ 01 485 9265); Remploy Ltd, 415 Edgware Rd, London NW2 6LR

OWEN, Tudor Wyn; s of Abel Rhys Owen (d 1974), of Aberdare, Glamorgan, and Mair, *née* Jenkins; *b* 16 May 1951; *Educ* Aberdare GS, King's Coll London (LLB); *Career* barr Gray's Inn 1974, practising S Eastern Circuit; memb: ctee of Criminal Bar Assoc 1987, Gen Cncl of the Bar 1988-, Bar Professional Conduct Ctee 1989-; memb Hon soc Gray's Inn; *Recreations* shooting, skiing, flying WWII fighter aircraft; *Clubs* Royal Aero; *Style—* Tudor Owen, Esq; 4 Paper Bldgs, Temple, London EC4Y 7EX (☎ 01 583 7765)

OWEN-JONES, David Roderic; s of John Eryl Owen-Jones, CBE, JP, DL, of RhiwDafnau, FFordd Menai, Caernarfon, Gwynedd, and Mabel Clara, *née* McIlvride; *b* 16 Mar 1949; *Educ* Llandovery Coll Dyfed, UCL (LLB, LLM); *Career* called to Bar Inner Temple 1972, Eastern circuit; parly candidate: (Lib) Carmarthen Div Feb and Oct 1974, (Lib Alliance) Rugby and Kenilworth 1983 and 1987; vice chm Assoc Lib Lawyers 1986-88, memb Lord Chancellors Advsy Ctee on the Appointments of JPs for Inner London; govr Int Students Tst 1981-84 (tstee 1981-); FRSA 1984; *Books* The Prosecutional Process in England and Wales (jtly); *Recreations* theatre, historical biography; *Clubs* Nat Lib (chm 1988-), Reform; *Style—* David Owen-Jones, Esq; 17 Albert Bridge Rd, London SW11 (01 622 1280); 3 Temple Gdns, Temple, London EC4y 9AU (☎ 01 583 0010)

OWEN-JONES, (John) Eryl; CBE (1969), JP (1974), DL (Caerns 1971, Gwynedd 1974); s of John Owen-Jones (d 1962), FTSC, Colwyn Bay; *b* 19 Jan 1912; *Educ* Portmadoc GS, Univ Coll of Wales Aberystwyth (LLB); Gonville and Caius Coll Cambridge (MA); *m* 1944, Mabel Clara, da of Grant McIlvride of Bombay (d 1920); 1 s (David), 1 da (Ann); *Career* Sqdn Ldr RAFVR 1945; admitted slr 1938, asst slr Chester Corpn 1939, legal staff offr Judge Advocate General's Dept Med; dep clerk; *Style—* Eryl Owen-Jones Esq, CBE, JP, DL; Rhiw Dafnau, Caernarfon, Gwynedd LL55 1LF (☎ 0286 67 3370)

OWEN-SMITH, Dr Brian David; s of Cyril Robert Smith, OBE, and Margaret Jane, *née* Hughes; *b* 29 May 1938; *Educ* Dulwich, Queens Coll Cambridge (MA, MB BChir), Guy's Hosp London (LRCP, MRCS, DPhys, Med); *m* 24 Sept 1966, Rose Magdalen, da of Lord Ponsonby of Shulbrede (d 1976); 1 s (Timothy Clive b 25 April 1968), 1 da (Emma Elizabeth Jane b 22 Aug 1971); *Career* Lilly fell in clinical pharmacology Indiana Univ USA 1970, sr registrar rheumatic diseases Royal Nat Hosp Bath 1972, chm Medmark Int 1988; currently: conslt in rheumatics and rehabilitation St Richard's Hosp Chichester W Sussex, med dir younger disabled unit Donald Wilson House, consIt sports injuries BUPA Hosp Havant; memb Chichester Soc; Freeman: City of London, Worshipful Co of Apothecaries; FRCP; *Recreations* squash, tennis, sailing; *Clubs* IOD; *Style—* Dr Brian Owen-Smith; 48 Westgate, Chichester B19 3EU (☎ 0243 786 688); 30b Southgate, Chichester, W Sussex PO19 1DP (☎ 0243 532 523, fax 0243 532 614)

OWENS, Bernard Charles; s of Charles Albert Owens, and Sheila, *née* O'Higgins (d 1985); *b* 20 Mar 1928; *Educ* Solihull Sch, LSE; *m* 1954, Barbara Madeline, da of Thomas Murphy (d 1971); 2 s (Michael b 1955, Peter b 1960); 4 da (Jacqueline b 1955, Jennifer b 1957, Teresa b 1961, Susan b 1963); *Career* chm: Unochrome Int Ltd (now Unochrome Ind plc) 1964-79 (and Van der Horst worldwide and 70 other assoc cos); md: Stanley Bros Ltd 1961-67; dir: Hobbs Savill & Bradford Ltd 1957-62, Trinidad Sugar Estates Ltd 1965-67, Cornish Brewery Co Ltd 1987-, Br Jewellery and Giftware Fedn Ltd 1987-; memb: Monopolies and Mergers Cmmn 1981-, Cncl Zoological Soc of London 1987- (fell 1980-), Order of Malta 1979-, of Lloyd's 1978-, HAC 1984-; life govr RNKI 1984-; parly candidate (C) Small Heath Birmingham 1959 and 1961; cncllr Solihull UK and Borough C 1954-64 (chm finance 1957-64); Lord of the Manor of Southwood; FRSA, FRGS; *Clubs* Carlton, City Livery, MCC, Wig & Pen, City Livery Yacht, Stroud RFC; *Style—* Bernard Owens, Esq; The Vatch House, Stroud, Gloucestershire GL6 7JY (☎ 04536 3402)

OWENS, Charles Arthur; LVO (1976); s of William Henry Owens (d 1969), of Birmingham, and Doris Owens, *née* Chew (d 1972); *b* 18 Feb 1922; *Educ* Holly Lodge HS; *m* 19 May 1947, Betty Goddard, da of Walter Wigglesworth (d 1966), of Doncaster; 1 s (Robert Charles b 26 March 1952), 1 da (Susan Elizabeth (Mrs Connelly) b 20 May 1949); *Career* RAF Halton 1938-40, Flt Lt Pilot 1942-46; DNL (Norwegian Airlines) 1946, BEA 1949, mangr Comet Flight 1958 (later flt ops dir), bd of mgmnt BEA/BA 1977, aviation conslt 1977; Guild of Air Pilots and Air Navigators 1946, Freeman City of London (Master 1975), Liveryman City of London; FCIT 1970, FRAeS 1976, MBAC 1979, FBIM 1980; *Books* Flight Operations (1982); *Recreations* travelling, swimming; *Clubs* RAF; *Style—* Charles Owens, Esq, LVO; 1 Chetwynd, 170 Canford Cliffs Rd, Poole, Dorset BH13 7ES (☎ 0202 700 997)

OWENS, Frank Arthur Robert; CBE (1971); s of Arthur Oakes Owens; *b* 31 Dec 1912; *Educ* Hereford Cathedral Sch; *m* 1, 1936, Ruby Lilian Long; 2 s; m 2, Olwen Evans, 1 s, 1 da; *Career* WWII RAF 1940-46 (despatches); ed Birmingham Evening Mail 1956-74; dir Birmingham Post & Mail Ltd 1964-75; memb: Def Press and Broadcasting Ctee 1965-74, West Midlands Econ Planning Cncl 1975-78, Press Cncl 1976-79, Lord Franks' Departmental Ctee on Official Secrets Act of 1911; pres Guild of British Newspaper Eds 1974-75; vice pres Newspapers Mutual Insur Soc 1972-85; hon Knight of Int Mark Twain Soc; *Style—* Frank Owens Esq, CBE; 31 The Dreel, Edgbaston, Birmingham B15 3NS (☎ 021 455 0209)

OWENS, John Ridland; s of Dr Ridland Owens (d 1968), of Lymington, and Elsie Owens; *b* 21 May 1932; *Educ* Merchant Taylors', St Johns Coll Oxford (MA); *m* 1, 1958 (m dis 1981), Susan Lilian, da of Cdr GR Pilcher, RN, of Yelverton; 2 s (David Ridland b 23 Feb 1962, James Graham b 27 Sept 1966), 1 da (Elizabeth Clare b 1 July 1960); m 2, 27 Sept 1985, Cynthia Rose, da of Sir Archibald Forbes, GBE, of Portman Sq, London W1; 1 s (Thomas Alasdair Ridland); *Career* Nat Serv 2 Lt RA served Germany 1951-52, Lt TA 1954, Gunner HAC 1957-61; section mangr ICI Ltd 1955-67, Md Cape Asbestos Fibres Ltd 1967-72, dir gen Dairy Trade Fedn 1973-83 (vice pres Assocn Industrie Laltaire de la Marche' Commun, dir Nat Dairy Cncl, memb Food and Drink Indust Cncl); dep dir CBI 1983-; memb: exec ctee PRONED, indust ctee RSA, Assocn of Businees Sponsorship of the Arts Cncl, advsy bd RA City and Guilds Inst Cncl, City Univ Ct; Freeman City of London, Liveryman Merchant Taylors (member ct); FRSA; *Recreations* painting, music, walking; *Clubs* Reform; *Style—* John Ridland, Esq; 40 Blenheim Terr, London, NW8 0EG; CBI Centre Point, 103 New Oxford St, London WC1A 1DU (☎ 01 379 7400)

OWENS, (John) Robin; s of Col Theobald David Cogswell Owen MC (d 1984), of Chichester, Hampshire and Irene, *née* Hamilton (d 1949); *b* 26 May 1939; *Educ* Wellington, Welbeck Coll, RMA Coll, Emmanuel Coll Cambridge (MA), RMA Sandhurst; *m* 1963, Margaret Ann, da of Harry Arthur Overton (d 1979), of Norfolk; 1 s (Nicholas b 1966), 1 da (Philippa b 1969); *Career* Second in command of the Hong Kong Fortress Sqdn, 1964-67, Projects Off of the 1st Bn Royal Engr, 1976-68, Retd with Rank of Capt, 1968; FCA, 1972; chm of Airbase Int Fin 1972-78, dir of Midland Montagu Leasing Ltd 1978-80, dir of the Forward Tst Gp 1980-84, dir of Gaty Lease Fin Ltd 1984-85, md of Park Place Fin 1985-86 and of Medens Tst 1986-; FCA; *Recreations* tennis, sailing; *Clubs* The United Oxford & Cambridge University Club; *Style—* Robin Owens, Esq; Park Cottage, Teston, Maidstone, Kent (☎ 0622 812208); Medens House, Station Way, Crawley, Sussex (☎ 0293 518877), Fax 0293 514514)

OWTRAM, Col (Henry) Cary; OBE (1970), TD (1946), DL (Lancs 1967); s of Lt-Col Herbert Hawkesworth Owtram, OBE, JP (d 1952), of Newland Hall, Nr Lancaster, and Ethel, *née* Fair (d 1920); *b* 8 Sept 1899; *Educ* shrewsbury; *m* 2 Aug 1922, Dorothy, da of Lt Col Charles James Daniel, CBE, DSO; 1 s (Charles) Robert Cary b 4 Oct 1930), 2 da (Ethel) Patricia b 19 June 1923, Dorothy Jean b 2 Nov 1925); *Career* WWI serv 2 Lt RM Artillery France 1918; capp 88 FD RA 1920-30; WWII: serv Maj 137 FD RA 1939, Lt-Col 1942 (despatches 1941/2), Malaya (POW 1942-45); Lt-Col 337 HAA RA 1947-50, hon col 288 AA RA 1960-68, total serv of 50 years; md cotton spinning companies 1930-72, chm various ctees cotton indust; pres: Lunesdales Farmers Trading Soc 1953-74, Preston Farmers Ltd 1974-84; Royal Lancs Agric Soc 1953-: memb cncl 1958-74, chm 1974-80, hon vice-pres 1987-; JP Lancashire 1953-73, High Sheriff Lancashire 1965; *Recreations* shooting, fishing, gardening; *Clubs* St James' (Manchester); *Style*— Col Cary Owtram, OBE, TD, DL; Newland Hall, Nr Lancaster, Lancs (☎ 0524 751 207)

OWTRAM , Godfrey Herbert; s of Col Herbert Hawkesworth Owtram, TD, OBE (d 1952), of Newland Hall, nr Lancaster, and Ethel Owtram, *née* Fair (d 1921); *b* 13 Feb 1907; *Educ* Shrewsbury, Brasenose Coll Oxford; *m* 1, 3 June 1930, Joan, da of Capt Oswald Gardner (ka 1916); 2 da (Susan Caroline b 1936, Christine Angela b 1938); m 2, 5 Oct 1946, Margaret Elizabeth, da of Ven Archdeacon Hamerton (d 1971); 1 s (Julian Godfrey Hermon b 1948); *Career* served WWII special duties; chm/fin dir many public Cos incl: Horrockses Crewdson & Co Ltd 1937-40, Petrochemicals Ltd (now Shell Chemicals) 1952-56, E H Bentall Gp 1957-65, Lewis & Peat Chemicals 1965-77; *Recreations* shooting, fishing, golf, bridge; *Clubs* Boodles; *Style*— Godfrey H Owtram, Esq; Oak Lodge, Matfield, nr Tonbridge (☎ 089 272 2106); Davers Stretton & Co Ltd, Petteridge (☎ 089 272 2710)

OXBURY, Harold Frederick; CMG (1961); s of Fredric Thomas Oxbury (d 1964); *b* 11 Nov 1903; *Educ* King Edward VI Sch Norwich, Trinity Coll Cambridge (MA); *m* 1, 1928, Violet Bennets (d 1954); 1 s, 1 da; m 2, 1954, Helen Shipley (d 1975), da of Amos Perry; *Career* Indian Civil Serv 1928-47, dir Colonies Dept 1947, Br Cncl: controller Finance 1956, asst dir-gen 1959, dep dir-gen 1964-66; *Books* Great Britons: 20th Century Lives (1985), Dictionary of National Biography (contrib), Concise Dictionary of National Biography (princ ed); *Style*— Harold Oxbury Esq, CMG; 122B Woodstock Rd, Oxford OX2 7NF

OXFORD, Kenneth Gordon; CBE (1981), QPM (1976), DL (Co of Merseyside 1988-); s of Ernest George Oxford, and late Gladys Violet, *née* Seaman; *b* 25 June 1924; *Educ* Caldecot Sch, Lambeth; *m* 1954, Muriel, *née* Panton; *Career* served RAF 1942-47, Bomber Cmd, SEAC; served Metropolitan Police 1947-69 (constable to detective chief supt); asst chief constable (crime) Northumbria Constabulary 1969-74; chief constable Merseyside Police 1976- (dep chief constable 1974-76); memb Forensic Science Soc 1970; Medico-Legal Soc 1975; chm: crime ctee Assoc of Chief Police Offrs of Eng, Wales and NI 1979-, jt standing ctee on Police use of Firearms 1979-, Assoc of Chief Police Offrs sub-ctee on Terrorism and Allied Matters 1982-; repe ICPO (Interpol) 1983; pres: NW Police Benevolent Fund 1978-, Assoc Chief Police Offrs of England, Wales and NI 1982-83; chm Merseyside Rgnl Ctee of Princes Tst 1978-82; pres Merseyside Branch BIM 1983- (chm 1978-82); CBIM; co dir Merseyside branch St John Ambulance Assoc 1976-; Freeman City of London 1983; FRSA; OStJ 1977; kt 1988; *Publications* articles and papers on crime and kindred matters; *Recreations* shooting, cricket, music, books, roses; *Clubs* Royal Cwlth Soc, Surrey Co Cricket, Liverpool Co Cricket, Liverpool St. Helens Rugby Football; *Style*— Sir Kenneth Oxford, CBE, QPM, DL; Chief Constable's Office, PO Box 59, Liverpool L69 1JD (☎ 051 709 6010)

OXFORD, 41 Bishop of (1542) 1987-; Rt Rev Richard Douglas Harries; patron of over 116 livings and the Archdeaconries of Oxford, Buckingham and Berks; the Bishopric was originally endowed with lands of dissolved monasteries by Henry VIII, but in Elizabeth I's reign many of these were removed from it; s of Brig William Douglas Jameson Harries, CBE, and Greta Miriam, da of A Barthurst Brown, MB, LRCP; *b* 2 June 1936; *Educ* Wellington Coll, RMA Sandhurst, Selwyn Coll Cambridge (MA), Cuddesdon Coll Oxford; *m* 1963, Josephine Bottomley, MA, MB, BChir, DCH; 1 s, 1 da; *Career* Lt RCS 1955-58; curate Hampstead Parish Church 1963-69, chaplain Westfield Coll 1966-69, lectr Wells Theological Coll 1969-72, warden Wells, Salisbury and Wells Theological Coll 1971-72, vicar All Saints' Fulham 1972-81, dean King's Coll London 1981-; FKC; *Books* Prayers of Hope (1975), Turning to Prayer (1978), Prayers of Grief and Glory (1979), Being a Christian (1981), Should Christians Support Guerrillas? (1982), The Authority of Divine Love (1983), Praying Round the Clock (1983), Seasons of the Spirit (1984), Prayer and the Pursuit of Happiness (1985), Morning has Broken (1985), Christianity and War in a Nuclear Age (1986), CS Lewis: The Man and his God (1987), The One Genius (1987), Christ has Risen (1988); contributor: What Hope in an Armed World (and ed 1982), Reinhold Niebuhr and the issues of our Time (and ed 1986), Stewards and the Mysteries of God (1975), Unholy Warfare (1983), The Cross and the Bomb (1985), Julian, Woman of our Time (1985), The Reality of God (1986); *Recreations* theatre, literature, sport; *Style*— The Rt Rev the Bishop of Oxford; Diocesan Church House, North Hinksey, Oxford OX2 0NB (☎ 0865 244566 ext 39)

OXFORD, Samuel; *Career* chm and ch exec Magnet & Southerns Ltd; chm and jt md Southerns-Evans plc; chm Magnet & Southerns Trustees Ltd; regnl dir (NW regnl bd) Lloyds Bank 1982-; *Style*— Samuel Oxford Esq; Magnet & Southerns plc, Sasco House, Mill Lane, Widnes, Cheshire WA8 0UJ (☎ 051 424 5500; telex 627166)

OXFORD AND ASQUITH, 2 Earl of (UK 1925); Julian Edward George; KCMG (1964, CMG 1961); also Viscount Asquith (UK 1925); s of Raymond Asquith (ka the Somme 1916) and gs of the Lib PM, Rt Hon Sir Herbert Asquith, KG, 1 Earl (d 1928), and Katharine Frances Horner (d 1976), da of Sir John Horner KCVO (d 1927); *b* 22 April 1916; *Educ* Ampleforth, Balliol Oxford (MA); *m* 28 Aug 1947, Anne Mary Celestine, CStJ, da of late Sir Michael Palairet, KCMG; 2 s, 3 da; *Heir* s, Viscount Asquith, *qv*; *Career* 2 Lt RE 1940; sits as Independent in House of Lords; asst dist cmmr Palestine Admin 1942-48, dep chief sec Br Admin Tripolitania 1949, dir of the Interior Tripolitanian Govt 1951, advsr to PM of Libya 1952, admin sec Zanzibar 1955, admin St Lucia 1958-61, govr and C-in-C Seychelles 1962-67, and cmmr Br Indian Ocean Territory 1965-67, constitutional cmmr Cayman Islands 1971, constitutional cmmr Turks and Caicos Islands 1973-74; KStJ; *Style*— The Rt Hon the Earl of Oxford and Asquith, KCMG; The Manor House, Mells, Frome, Somerset (☎ 0373 812324)

OXFUIRD, 13 Viscount of (S 1651); Sir George Hubbard; 13 Bt (NS 1627); also Lord Makgill of Cousland (S 1697); claim to Viscountcy admitted by Ctee for Privileges, House of Lords 1977; s of Sqdn Ldr Richard James Robert Haldane Makgill (d 1948, yr s of 11 Bt) and Elizabeth Lyman, *née* Hubbard (d 1981); s uncle 1986; *b* 7 Jan 1934; *Educ* Wanganui Collegiate Sch NZ; *m* 1, 1967 (m dis 1977), Alison Campbell, da of late Neils Max Jensen, of Randers, Denmark; 3 s; m 2, 1980, Valerie Cunitia Mary, da of Major Charles Anthony Steward, of The Platt, Crondall, nr Farnham, Surrey; 1 s; *Heir* s, Ian Arthur Alexander (Master of Oxfuird) b 14 Oct 1969; *Career* export area mangr Lansing Ltd 1979-; *Recreations* shooting, gardening, cricket, fishing; *Clubs* Caledonian; *Style*— The Rt Hon the Viscount of Oxfuird; Hill House, St Mary Bourne, Andover, Hants

OXFUIRD, Maureen, Viscountess of Maureen; *née* Magan; yr da of Lt-Col Arthur Tilson Shaen Magan, CMG (d 1965), and Kathleen Jane, *née* Biddulph (d 1969); *b* 11 Nov 1914; *m* 1, 9 Sept 1939 (m dis 1949), Lt-Col John Herbert Gillington, OBE, MC (d 1970); 1 s; m 2, 6 Oct 1955, as his 2 wife 12 Viscount of Oxfuird (d 1986); *Style*— The Rt Hon Maureen, Viscountess of Oxfuird; 2 Hillside, Heath Rd, Newmarket, Suffolk CB8 8AY (☎ 0638 666726)

OXLADE, Zena Elsie; CBE (1984); da of James Oxlade (d 1983), and Beatrice May Oxlade, *née* Oliver (d 1962); *b* 26 April 1929; *Educ* Latymer GS, Univ of London; *Career* SRN and registered nurse tutor; memb Gen Nursing Cncl for England and Wales 1975-83 (chm 1977-83); area nursing offr Suffolk 1978-, regnl nursing offr East Anglia 1981-; memb UK Cncl for Nurses Midwives and Health Visitors 1983-; *Recreations* motoring, reading, handicrafts; *Clubs* Soroptomist Int; *Style*— Miss Zena Oxlade, CBE; 5 Morgan Court, Claydon, Ipswich, Suffolk IP6 0AN (☎ 0473 831895); East Anglian Regional Health Authority, Union Lane, Chesterton, Cambs CB4 1RF (☎ 0223 61212)

OXLEY; *see*: Rice-Oxley

OXLEY, Humphrey Leslie Malcolm; CMG (1966), OBE (1956); s of William Henry Francis Oxley, (d 1960), and Cecilia, *née* Malcolm (d 1945); *b* 9 Oct 1909; *Educ* Epsom Coll; *m* 1945, Frances Olga, da of George Frederick Anstruther Bowden (d 1949); twin s (David, Peter); *Career* slr 1933; jr legal asst India Off 1933; cmmr for Oaths 1934; asst slr 1944; Cwlth Rels Off 1947, asst legal advsr CRO 1961; Dip Serv 1966, dep legal advsr 1967-69, legal advsr to HM's Cmmr and Magis Anguilla 1971-72; *Style*— Humphrey Oxley Esq, CMG, OBE; Sandpipers, Crooked Lane, Birdham, Chichester, W Sussex (☎ 0243 512682)

OXLEY, Peter John Reginald; s of Lt-Col Richard George Reginald Oxley (d 1969), and Jean Elspeth, *née* Anderson; *b* 2 Mar 1934; *Educ* Cheam, Eton, Magdalene Coll Cambridge (BA); *m* 3 Feb 1959, Vanla Joy, da of Capt Clive Denison Arbuthnot, RN, (d 1965); 2 s (Stephen b 1959, Timothy b 1962), 1 da (Rachel b 1966); *Career* dir: Skye Ceramics Ltd 1967-88, Witham Vale Contractors Ltd 1968-, Surdaw Press Ltd 1983-; treas Somerton & Frome Constituency Cons Assoc 1986-89; *Recreations* fishing, shooting, golf; *Style*— Peter Oxley, Esq; Queen Camel House, Nr Yeovil, Somerset (☎ 0935 850269)

OXMANTOWN, Viscount; (Lawrence) Patrick Parsons; s and h of 7 Earl of Rosse; *b* 31 Mar 1969; *Style*— Viscount Oxmantown

OXSPRING, Herbert; *Career* chm Kenning Motor Gp 1982-; *Style*— Herbert Oxspring Esq; c/o Kenning Motor Group Ltd, Manor Offices, Old Rd, Chesterfield, Derbys (☎ 0246 77241)

OXTOBY, David Jowett Greaves; s of John Henry Oxtoby (d 1972), of Horsforth, Yorks, and Ann Jowett, *née* Greaves (d 1978); *b* 23 Jan 1938; *Educ* Horsforth Cncl Sch, Bradford Coll of Art, RA Sch Piccadilly; *Career* artist, best known for visual interpretations of pop music, 44 one man shows, numerous exhibits in gp exhibitions; works in public collections incl: Br Museum, LA County Museum, Museum of Modern Art NY, Minneapolis Inst of Art, Tate Gallery, Victoria & Albert Museum; lectr numerous colls incl RA, visiting prof painting Mineapolis Inst of Art 1964-65, ret teaching 1972; *Books* painting reprod in: Oxtoby's Rockers (D Dandison 1978), V & A Museum Calendar (1985), Once Upon a Christmas (D Sandison 1986); *Recreations* cycling; *Style*— David Oxtoby, Esq; c/o David Sandison, 96 Brunswick, Park Rd, London N11 1JJ (☎ 01 368 3683)

ÖZBEK, (Ibrahim Mehmet) Rifat; s of Abdulazim Mehmet Ismet Özbet, of Istanbul, and Melike, *née* Pekis; *b* 8 Nov 1953; *Educ* Isik Lisesi Istanbul, St Martin's Sch of Art (BA); *Career* fashion designer Waiter Albini for Trell Milan 1977-79, Monsoon Co 1979-84, presented first collection 1984; Br Fashion Cncl Designer of the Year 1988; *Style*— Rifat Özbek, Esq; 18 Haunch of Venison Yard, London W1Y 1AF (☎ 01 491 7033, fax 01 629 1586)

P

PACE, Franco Giustino; s of Edmondo Pace (d 1959); *b* 28 Sept 1927; *Educ* Bologna Univ (doctorate in industl engrg), Milan Univ (post grad specialisation in chemistry); *m* 1955, Maria Vittoria, da of Dr Ing Salvatore Picchetti, of Italy; 1 s (Valerio); *Career* dir: Montedison UK Ltd 1973-, Polyamide Intermediates Ltd 1974-83, Farmitalia Carlo Erba Ltd 1978-; chm: Montefibre UK Ltd 1974-, Acna UK Ltd 1976-, Cedar Service UK Ltd 1982-, Internike Ltd 1984-, Selm Int Ltd 1986; vice-pres Italian Chamber of Commerce for Great Britain 1981-; Cavaliere Ufficiale Al Merito Della Repubblica Italiana 1980; *Clubs* Hurlingham; *Style*— Franco Pace, Esq; 10 Kensington Court Gdns, London W8 5QE (☎ 01 937 7143); Montedison UK Ltd, 7 Lygon Place, Ebury St, London SW1W 0JR (☎ 01 730 3405, telex 918743)

PACK, (Emeritus) Prof Donald Cecil; CBE (1978, OBE 1969); s of John Cecil Pack (d 1976), of Higham Ferrers, and Minnie (d 1955); *b* 14 April 1920; *Educ* Wellingborough Sch, New Coll Oxford (MA), St Andrews (DSc); *m* 1947, Constance Mary, da of Harry Cosier Gillam (d 1968), of Oxford; 2 s, 1 da; *Career* Univ of Strathclyde Glasgow: prof of Mathematics 1953-82 (hon prof 1982-85), vice-principal 1968-72; chm Scottish Certificate Educn Exam Bd 1969-77, chm Ctee of Inquiry into Truancy and Indiscipline in Scottish Schs 1974-77 (Pack Report 1977); memb: various Govt Scientific Ctees 1952-84, cncl Royal Soc of Edinburgh 1960-63, Gen Teaching Cncl for Scotland 1966-73, British Nat Ctee for Theoretical and Applied Mechanics 1973-78, cncl Gesellschaft für Angewandte Mathematik und Mechanik 1977-83, Scottish Arts Cncl 1980-85, European Music Year UK Ctee (chm Scottish Sub-Ctee); hon tres Inst of Mathematics and its Applications 1964-72; fndr-chm National Youth Orchestra of Scotland 1978-, govr Hamilton Coll of Education 1977-81; FIMA, FEIS, FRSE; *Recreations* golf, gardening, playing the violin; *Style*— Professor Donald Pack, CBE; 18 Buchanan Drive, Bearsden, Glasgow G61 2EW (☎ 041 942 5764)

PACKARD, Lt-Gen Sir (Charles) Douglas; KBE (1957, CBE 1945, OBE 1942), CB (1949), DSO (1943); s of Capt C Packard, MC, of Copdock, Suffolk; *b* 17 May 1903; *Educ* Winchester, RMA Woolwich; *m* 1937, Marion Cargill Thomson (d 1981), da of Dr James Lochhead, of Edinburgh; 1 s, 2 da; m 2, 1982, Mrs Patricia Miles-Sharp; *Career* 2 Lt RA 1923, WW II M East and Italy, dep chief Staff 15 Army Gp 1944-45, temp Maj-Gen and chief Staff Allied Cmmn Austria 1945-46; dir Mil Intelligence War Office 1948-49, chief of Staff GHQ MELF 1951-53, VQMG War Office 1953-56, mil advsr to W African Govts 1956-58, Lt-Gen 1957, GOC-in-C NI 1958-61; *Recreations* sailing, bird watching; *Clubs* RCC; *Style*— Lt-Gen Sir Douglas Packard, KBE, CB, DSO; Park Side, Lower Ufford, Woodbridge, Suffolk IP13 6DL (☎ 0394 460418)

PACKARD, Brig (Joseph) John; s of Maj Joseph Thomas Packard, OBE (d 1955), of Kings Lynn, and Rachel, *née* Powell (d 1944); *b* 14 May 1910; *Educ* Leiston GS, RMC Sandhurst; *m* 8 June 1942, (Mary) Faith, da of Capt Gerard Harrison; 4 s (Peter John b 9 April 1943, Mark Anthony Clive b 21 March 1947, Timothy Paul b 18 Jan 1952, Simon David b 27 June 1955), 1 da (Mary Anne Faith (Mrs Gray) b 16 March 1949); *Career* cmmnd E Yorks Regt 1932, active serv 1932-36 (India, Lucknow, Dinapore, NW Frontier), Adj depot E Yorks Regt at Beverley 1937-38, WO Intelligence 1938-39, GSO 3 (Intelligence) GHQ Br Expeditionary force in France 1939-40, Staff Coll Camberley 1940, cmdt Tactical Sch Iceland 1940-42, CO Hallamshire Bn York and Lancaster Regt 1942-43, serv Assam and Burma 1943-45, GSO1 (Inf) Delhi 1945-46, regtl and staff appts Austria and Germany 1947-51, memb Templar Ctee for army reorganisation 1951, serv 1 Bn Welch Regt Korea 1951-52, head mission to french forces in Germany 1952-56, mil attaché Vienna 1956-60, head mission to Soviet forces in Germany 1960-61; head info servs Fisons Ltd 1961-64; chm: Cripplegate Fndn 1985-86, Welch House Homes for the Elderly 1976-87, St Margaret's House Bethnal Green 1980-85; tstee City Parochial Fndn 1983-89, memb Blyth RDC 1964-71, chm Port and City of London Health and Social Servs 1978-80, Common Councilman City of London; Freeman City of London 1972, Liveryman Worshipful Co of Wax Chandlers 1974; *Books* The Fields and Field Names of Easton Suffolk (1971), Church and Churchyard Inscriptions of All Saints Easton Suffolk (1972), The Packards (1987); *Recreations* bowls, local history, genealogy; *Clubs* Naval and Military, Guildhall; *Style*— Brig John Packard; 143 Thomas More House, Barbican, London EC2Y 8BU (☎ 01 628 6904)

PACKARD, Richard Bruce Selig; s of John Jacob Packard, and Priscilla Lilian, *née* Joseph; *b* 20 Feb 1947; *Educ* Harrow, Middlesex Hospital Medical Sch (MD, DO); *m* 1, 21 March 1974 (m dis 1986), Veronica Susan; 2 s (Rupert b 1978, Hugo b 1980), 1 da (Elvira b 1984); m 2, 24 April 1987, Fiona Catherine; *Career* specialist training in ophthalmology; resident Moorfields Eye Hosp High Holborn 1975-78; sr registrar Charing Cross Hosps Fulham 1975-78; conslt ophthalmic surgn East Berkshire Health Authority from 1982; FRCS; *Books* Cataract and Lens Implant Surgery (1985); *Recreations* fly fishing, music; *Clubs* Garrick, MCC, American Academy of Ophthalmology; *Style*— Richard Packard, Esq; 128 Harley Street, London W1N 1AH

PACKER, Kerry Francis Bullmore; AC (1983); s of late Sir Douglas Frank Hewson Packer, KBE (d 1974), and Gretel Joyce, *née* Bullmore (d 1960); *b* 17 Dec 1937; *Educ* Cranbrook Sch Sydney NSW, Geelong C of E GS Vic; *m* 1963, Roslyn Redman, da of late Dr F H Weedon; 1 s, 1 da; *Career* exec Aust Consolidated Press and Conpress Ltd 1955; chm: Consolidated Press Holdings Ltd 1974-, Publishing and Broadcasting Ltd 1974-; chm Australian Consolidated Press Ltd Pty 1974-; *Recreations* golf, tennis, cricket, shooting, polo; *Clubs* Royal Sydney GC, Australian GC, Elanora County, Tattersall's, Athenaeum (Melbourne); *Style*— Kerry Packer, Esq; 54 Park St, Sydney, NSW 2000, Australia (☎ 02 20666, telex AA20514)

PACKER, Richard John; s of George Charles Packer (d 1979), and Dorothy May Packer; *b* 18 August 1944; *Educ* City of London Sch, Manchester Univ (BSc, MSc); *m* 1, Alison Mary, *née* Sellwood; 2 s (James b 1969, George b 1971), 1 da (Rachel b 1973); m 2, Lucy Jeanne, da of Edmund Neville-Rolfe, of Tisbury, Wilts; 2 s (Thomas b 1981, William b 1984); *Career* jnd MAFF 1967; asst princ: 1 sec Office of UK Representative to EC 1973-76; princ private sec Minister 1976-78; asst sec 1979; under sec 1985; dir ABM chemicals 1985-86; under sec MAFF 1987; *Recreations* many sporting and intellectual interests; *Style*— Richard J Packer, Esq; Room 104, Whitehall Place East, London SW1A 2HH (☎ 01 270 8059)

PACKER, William John; s of Harold George Edward Rex Packer (d 1967), of Windsor, and Evelyn Mary Packer, *née* Wornham (d 1983); *b* 19 August 1940; *Educ* Windsor GS, Wimbledon and Brighton Colls of Art; *m* 1965, Ursula Mary Clare, da of Thomas John Rosewarne Winn, of Sutton, Surrey; 3 da (Charlotte b 1968, Claudia b 1973, Katherine b 1976); *Career* art critic Financial Times 1974-; painter; responsible for several exhibitions including Arts Cncls 1 touring Br Art Show 1979-80; served on juries of many open exhibitions incl: John Moore's Liverpool Exhibition 1982, John Player Portrait Award 1983-87; teacher 1964-67, part-time 1967-77, external examiner 1979-87; memb: Fine Art Bd of Cncl for Nat Academic Awards 1976-83, Purchasing and Advsy Ctee to Govt Art Collection 1977-84, Crafts Cncl 1980-87; *Books* The Art of Vogue Covers (1980), Fashion Drawing in Vogue (1983), Henry Moore, A Pictorial Biography (1985); *Recreations* hockey, cricket, bookshops, riding; *Clubs* Brooks's, Chelsea Arts; *Style*— William Packer, Esq; 39 Elms Rd, Clapham, London SW4 9EP (☎ 01 622 1108)

PACKETT, Charles Michael; s of Sydney Duncan Packett, of Bradford, and Margaret Kathleen, *née* Smith; *b* 19 August 1955; *Educ* Ashville Coll Harrogate N Yorks; *m* 15 Aug 1981, Jayne Louise, da of Alan Childerstone Benson, of Baildon, Shipley; 2 da (Claire Louise b 21 Dec 1983, Sara Jayne b 2 Aug 1986); *Career* dir Sydney Packett & Sons Ltd (joined 1973, later assoc dir); memb insur advsy panel Bradford C of C; ACII, ABIIBA; *Recreations* fishing, shooting, golfing, walking, gardening, reading; *Clubs* Shipley GC, Shipley Cons, Fly Fishers (Hawksworth), Scotton Angling; *Style*— Charles Packett, Esq; 9 Firbeck, Harden, Bingley, W Yorks (☎ 0535 275 232); Sydney Packett & Sons Ltd, Lloyds Bank Chambers, Hustlergate, Bradford BD1 1PA (☎ 0274 308 755)

PACKETT, (Charles) Neville; MBE (1974), JP (1964); s of Sydney Packett, JP (d 1980), and Alice Maude Packett (d 1972); *b* 25 Feb 1922; *Educ* Bradford GS, Queen Elizabeth GS Kirkby Lonsdale Cumbria, Ashville Coll Harrogate Yorks; *m* 1969, Audrey Winifred. da of Frank Vincent Clough (d 1975); *Career* Royal Army Ordnance Corps WWII (Middle E and N Africa); md Sydney Packett & Sons 1975- (dir 1942-75); pres Insurance Inst of Bradford 1959-60, hon vice-pres The Utd Commercial Travellers' Assoc 1976- (nat pres 1975-76), govr Ashville Coll Harrogate 1970- (chm House Ctee 1977-), Master Worshipful Co of Woolmen 1979-80 (Liveryman 1959-); Upper Warden Worshipful Co of Tin Plate Workers 1985-86, (Liveryman 1957-); pres The Bradford Club 1985-86; Hon Adm Texas Navy USA 1978; co cmdr S and W Yorks St John Ambulance Bde 1982-; Grand Cross Order of St Agatha, Repub of San Marino 1980, Tonga Royal Medal of Merit in silver 1976, Kt Order of St Lazarus of Jerusalem 1972; KStJ 1985, FRSA, FRGS, ACII; *Publications* The County Lieutenancy in the UK, Republic of San Marino, Tongatapu Island (Kingdom of Tonga), the Republic of Nauru, the firm of Sydney Packett & Sons Ltd, The Texas Navy - A Brief History (1983); *Recreations* travel, amateur cine, heraldry, writing; *Clubs* City Livery (London), Nat Lib, Bradford; *Style*— Neville Packett, Esq, MBE, JP; Flat 20, Wells Court, Wells Promenade, Ilkley, W Yorks LS29 9LG (☎ Ilkley 601398); Lloyds Bank Chambers, Hustlergate, Bradford, W Yorks BD1 1PA (☎ Bradford 308755)

PACKMAN, Martin John; s of Ivan Desmond Packman, of Addington, Surrey, and Joan Emily, *née* Cook (d 1982); *b* 29 April 1949; *Educ* Simon Langton GS Canterbury, Welwyn Garden City GS, Univ of Lancaster (MA); *m* 17 Dec 1978, Lyn, da of James Green, of Holt, Norfolk; 1 s (Myles b 1980), 1 da (Charlotte b 1984) ; *Career* dir Baring Bros & Co Ltd 1987- (banking & capital mkts gp UK); ctee memb: Du Maurier Soc, Heath Mount Sch; FCA 1973; *Books* UK Companies Operating Overseas - Tax and Financing Strategies (jtly 1981); *Recreations* riding, tennis, skiing; *Style*— Martin Packman, Esq; 131 Handside Lane, Welwyn Garden City, Herts (☎ 0707 322442); Baring Bros & Co Ltd, 8 Bishopsgate, London EC2 (☎ 01 283 8833, fax 01 283 2633, telex 883622)

PADFIELD, Michael George Braddock; s of Stephen Padfield (d 1978), of Lambourne Hall, Abridge, Essex, and Brenda, *née* Sewell (d 1979); *b* 30 Dec 1922; *Educ* Loughton Sch for Boys; *m* 1, (m dis); 1 s (Matthew b 1958), 3 da (Clare b 1956, Charlotte b 1960, Abigail b 1963); m 2, Kathleen, *née* Dilks; *Career* farmer on own account: Stondon Hall Ongar Essex 1944-45, Wimbish Hall, Saffron Walden, Essex 1945-; chm Saffron Walden NFU 1965 and 1987-88, memb Cambs NFU exec ctee 1962-; Freeman City of London, Liveryman Worshipful Co of Farmers; *Recreations* shooting, hunting, skiing, tennis; *Clubs* Farmers, Whitehall Ct, Wig & Pen; *Style*— Michael Padfield, Esq; Wimbish Hall, Saffron Walden, Essex (☎ 079 987 202)

PADFIELD, Richard Aubrey; CBE (1979); s of Austin Bird Padfield (d 1961), and Lucy Anna Maude Padfield, *née* Borem (d 1970); *b* 25 Dec 1920; *Educ* Loughton Sch Essex, Chelmer Inst (BA); *m* 9 Oct 1948, Doreen, da of Thomas King Wignall (d 1955); 2 s (Christopher John b 1949, Timothy Richard b 1955), 2 da (Gillian Elizabeth Jane b 1951, Deborah Joy Lucy b 1957); *Career* HM Dip Serv (ret); princ estab offr FCO 1971-78; *Recreations* music, cricket, woodworking, charities; *Clubs* Royal Cwlth

Soc; *Style—* Richard Padfield, Esq, CBE; Bury Farm, Upshire, Waltham, Abbey, Essex EN9 3ST (☎ 0992 711 662)

PADMORE, Elaine Marguirite; da of Alfred Padmore (d 1971), and Florence, *née* Stockman; *b* 3 Feb 1947; *Educ* Newland HS Hull, Arnold Girls Sch Blackpool, Birmingham Univ (MA, BMus), Guildhall Sch of Music London; *Career* musician, singer, writer and broadcaster; ed music dept OUP 1970-71, lectr in opera Royal Acad of Music 1972-, radio prodr music dept BBC 1971-76, chief prodr opera BBC Radio 1976-82, announcer BBC Radio 3 1982-, artistic dir Wexford Festival Opera (Ireland) 1982-; Hon ARAH Royal Acad of Music 1984-; *Books* Wagner (Great Composers series), New Grove Dictionary of Music and Musicians; *Recreations* gardening, cats; *Style—* Miss Elaine Padmore; 11 Lancaster Ave, Hadley Wood, Herts EN4 0EP (☎ 01 449 5369)

PADMORE, Rosalind; *née* Culhane; LVO (1938), OBE (1949); yst da of late F W S Culhane, MRCS, LRCP, of Hastings, Sussex; *m* 1964, as his 2 wife, Sir Thomas Padmore, *qv*; *Career* asst private sec: to Mr Chamberlain 1934, to Sir John Simon 1937, Sir Kingsley Wood 1940; treasury welfare advsr 1943-64; *Style—* Lady Padmore, LVO, OBE; 39 Cholmeley Cres, London N6 5EX (☎ 01 340 6587)

PADMORE, Sir Thomas; GCB (1965, KCB 1953, CB 1947); s of Thomas William Padmore; *b* 23 April 1909; *Educ* Central Sch Sheffield, Queens' Coll Cambridge (MA); *m* 1, 1934, Alice (d 1963), da of Robert Alcock; 2 da (1 s decd); m 2, 1964, Rosalind Culhane, *qv*; *Career* PPS to Chancellor of Exchequer 1943-45, second sec HM Treasury 1952-62, perm sec Miny of Transport 1962-68; dir Metropolitan Cammell Ltd 1969-80, Laird Group Ltd 1970-79; chm Handel Opera Soc 1963-, hon tres Inst of Cancer Research 1973-82; FCIT; *Clubs* Reform; *Style—* Sir Thomas Padmore, GCB; 39 Cholmeley Crescent, Highgate, London N6 (☎ 01 340 6587)

PADOVAN, John Mario Faskally; s of Dr Umberto Mario Padovan (d 1966); *b* 7 May 1938; *Educ* St George's Coll Weybridge, King's Coll London (LLB), Keble Oxford (BCL); *m* 1963, Sally Kay; 3 s; *Career* CA 1963; County Bank Ltd: ch exec 1976-83, dep chm 1982, chm 1984; exec dep chm Hambros Bank Ltd 1984-86; dir: Tesco plc 1982-, MS Instruments plc 1985-; dir and head of corporate fin Barclays de Zoete Wedd Hldgs Ltd 1986-; *Style—* John Padovan, Esq; White House, Church Rd, Milford, Surrey (☎ 048 68 57 28)

PAGAN, Lady Marjorie; *née* Hoskins; late Sir Cecil Harold Hoskins; *m* 1948, Brig Sir John Ernest Pagan, CMG, MBE, ED (d 1986); 1 s, 2 da; *Style—* Lady Pagan; Kennerton Green, Mittagong, NSW 2575, Australia

PAGE, Sir Alex(ander) Warren; MBE (1943); s of Sydney E Page; *b* 1 July 1914; *Educ* Tonbridge, Clare Coll Cambridge; *m* 1940 (m dis) Anne Lewis Hickman; 2 s, 1 da; m 2, 1981, Mrs Andrea Mary Wharton; *Career* serv WWII REME rising to rank of Lt-Col; chief exec Metal Box Ltd 1970-77 and chm 1970-79 (joined 1936, md 1966), chm: Paine & Co 1981-87, Electrolux 1978-82, GT Pension Servs Ltd 1982-85; dir: J Lyons Co Ltd 1977-78, C Shippam 1979-85; memb Food Sci and Technol Bd 1973-; govr Colfe's Sch Lewisham 1977-; pres British Food Manufacturing Industs Res Assoc 1978-84; former memb IBA; chm PFC Int Portfolio Fund; FIMechE, CBIM; kt 1977; *Style—* Sir Alex Page, MBE; 2 Montagu Sq, W1 (☎ 01 935 9894); Merton Place, Dunsfold, Godalming, Surrey (☎ 048 649 211)

PAGE, Surgn-Col (John Patrick) Anthony; s of Dr Alfred Patrick Menzies Page, JP (d 1979), and Olive Frances Page (d 1964); *b* 9 June 1937; *Educ* Bedford Sch, Gonville and Caius Coll Cambridge (MA, MB, BChir); *m* 1, 4 Oct 1963 (m dis 1981), Carolyn Jane, da of Joseph Clement Deeks, MBE, of Sunningdale, Berks; 2 s (Timothy b 1963, Alexander b 1965), 2 da (Joanna b 1968, Louise b 1972); m 2, 16 Dec 1981, Alison Leila da of Maj Denis Thomas Keiller Don (d 1983); 1 s (Edward b 1986), 1 da (Victoria b 1983); *Career* cmmnd RAMC 1963, transferred to Household Cavalry RHG 1967 serv as Regtl MO to RHG Blues and Royals (on formation 1969) and to Household Cavalry Regt (Mounted), resigned 1974; GP Odiham Hamps 1974-78, rejoined as Regtl MO Blues and Royals Household Cavalry Regt and LG 1978-; UN Medal (Cyprus) 1965; *Recreations* hunting, fishing, gardening, family matters; *Clubs* The Cavalry and Guards, MCC; *Style—* Surgn-Col Anthony Page

PAGE, Bruce; s of Roger Page and Amy Beatrice Page; *b* 1 Dec 1936; *Educ* Melbourne HS and Melbourne Univ; *m* 1, 1964 (m dis 1969), Anne Gillison; m 2, 1969, Anne Louise, da of Frank G Darnborough; 1 s, 1 da; *Career* journalist with The Herald Melbourne 1956-60, Evening Standard 1960-62, Daily Herald 1962-64, Sunday Times 1964-76, Daily Express 1977, editor The New Statesman 1978-82 then technical dir 1982-; software developer; md Executive Producers Ltd 1983-; *Style—* Bruce Page, Esq; 35 Duncan Terrace, N1 8AL (☎ 01 359 1000); Executive Producers Ltd, 56/58 Clerkenwell Road, London EC1M 5PX (☎ 01 608 1451)

PAGE, Lady Cecilia Norah; *née* Stopford; da of 7 Earl of Courtown, OBE (d 1956), and Cicely Mary, OBE, JP (d 1973), yr da of late John Arden Birch; *b* 1917; *m* 1947, Cdr Thomas Philip Frederick Urquhart Page, RN, s of Sir Leo Francis Page; 1 s, 2 da; *Career* junior commander ATS 1939-45; *Style—* Lady Cecilia Page; Toller House, Toller Porcorum, Dorchester, Dorset

PAGE, Maj-Gen Charles Edward; CB (1974), MBE (1944), DL (1986); s of late Sir (Charles) Max Page, KBE, CB, DSO; *b* 23 August 1920; *Educ* Marlborough, Trinity Coll Cambridge, London Univ (BSc); *m* 1948, Elizabeth Marion, da of late Sir William Smith Crawford, KBE; 2 s, 1 da; *Career* Cdr Corps Royal Signals 1 (BR) Corps 1966-68, sec NATO Mil Ctee Brussels 1968-70, dep chief Defence (A) MOD 1971-74, ret 1974; Col Cmdt Royal Corps of Signals 1974-80; Hon Col Women's Transport Service (FANY); *Recreations* shooting, fishing, golf; *Clubs* Army & Navy, Royal and Ancient (St Andrews); *Style—* Major-General Charles Page, CB, MBE, DL; Church Farm House, Old Bosham, Chichester, W Sussex PO18 8HL (☎ Chichester (0243) 573191)

PAGE, (Christopher John) Chris; s of Albert Harold Page (d 1987), and Doris May, *née* Clarke; *b* 28 May 1947; *Educ* Eton House Sch, South Bank Poly (Dip Arch); *m* 7 July 1979, Janice Anne, da of Andrew John Sharman, of Wickford, Essex; 1 s (Richard b 1981), 1 da (Jacqueline b 1984); *Career* architect/program mngr; md: Atlanta Program Mngmnt Ltd 1986-, Atlanta Interiors 1987-; ptnr Chris Page Assocs; *Recreations* sailing, sketching, pre-history in UK; *Clubs* Eton House Old Boys; *Style—* Chris Page, Esq; 35 Challacombe, Thorpe Bay, Essex SS1 3TY (☎ 0702 585710); 45 Curlew St, London SE1 2ND (☎ 01 407 3307)

PAGE, David Norman; s of Bernard Page, of Edinburgh, and Catherine Page, *née* Adam; *b* 4 Sept 1957; *Educ* Bearsden Acad Strathclyde, Strathclyde Univ (dept of arch and building science) (BSc, BArch); *m* 14 Dec 1982, Fiona Sinclair, da of Archibald Sinclair, of Helensburgh; *Career* architect in private practice 1981-, lectr Strathclyde Univ, dept of arch and building sci 1982-; *Style—* David N Page, Esq; Roseangle, 49A William St, Helensburgh (☎ 0436 6781); 20A Royal Crescent, Glasgow (☎ 041 333 0786)

PAGE, Hon Mrs (Emma Rachel); *née* Lubbock; da of 3 Baron Avebury; *b* 16 April 1952; *Educ* Oxford Univ (BA); *m* 1977, Michael Charles Page, s of Maj-Gen Charles E Page, CB, MBE; 2 da (Sophie b 1982, Natasha b 1984); *Career* ptnr: Price Waterhouse; FCA, ATII; *Style—* The Hon Mrs Page; Lepe House, Exbury, Southampton, Hants

PAGE, Ewan Stafford; s of late Joseph William Page; *b* 17 August 1928; *Educ* Wyggeston GS Leicester, Christ's Coll Cambridge (MA, PhD, Raleigh Prize 1952), London Univ (BSc); *m* 1955, Sheila Margaret Smith; 3 s, 1 da; *Career* Instr RAF Tech Coll 1949-51, lectr in statistics Durham Colls 1954-57, dir Durham Univ Computing Lab 1957-63, Newcastle Univ Computing Lab 1963-78, visiting prof Univ of N Carolina 1962-63; prof of computing and data processing Univ of Newcastle upon Tyne 1965-78, pro-vice chancellor 1972-78 (acting vice-chancellor 1976-77); vice-chancellor Univ of Reading 1979-; *Style—* Dr E S Page; University of Reading, Whiteknights, Reading, Berks (☎ Reading 875123)

PAGE, Sir Frederick William; CBE (1961); s of late Richard and Ellen Sarah Page; *b* 20 Feb 1917; *Educ* Rutlish Sch Merton, St Catharine's Coll Cambridge (MA); *m* 1940, Kathleen Edith de Courcy; 3 s, 1 da; *Career* chief engr English Electric Aviation 1950, chief exec (Aircraft) 1959; dir Panavia Aircraft GmbH Germany 1969-83, chm 1977-79; chm BAC Ltd 1977; jt chm Sepecat (France) 1966-73, chm and chief exec Aircraft Gp of British Aerospace 1977-83; British Gold Medal Aeronautics 1962, RAeS Gold Medal 1974, Hon FRAeS 1980; FRS, FEng, Hon Fell UMIST 1970, Hon DSc Cranfield 1979; kt 1979; *Clubs* United Oxford and Cambridge University; *Style—* Sir Frederick Page, CBE, FRS, FEng; Renvyle, 60 Waverley Lane, Farnham, Surrey GU9 8BN (☎ Farnham 714999)

PAGE, Lady; Hilda Agatha (Dixon); *m* 1934, Rt Hon Sir (Rodney) Graham Page, MBE, PC, MP (C) for Crosby (d 1981); 1 s, 1 da; *Style—* Lady Page; 21 Cholmeley Lodge, Cholmeley Park, London N6 5EN (☎ 01 340 3579)

PAGE, (Charles) James; CBE (1978), QPM (1971); s of Charles Page; *b* 31 May 1925; *Educ* Sloane GS, Chelsea; *m* 1, 1947, Margaret Dobson; 2 s; m 2, 1971, Shirley Marina Woodward; *Career* HM Inspector of Constabulary, 1977-; vice-pres Police Athletic Assoc 1977; FBIM; CStJ 1974; Officer of Legion d'Honneur 1976; *Clubs* City Livery; *Style—* James Page, Esq, CBE, QPM; Government Buildings, Ovangle Rd, Lancaster

PAGE, Sir (Arthur) John; s of Sir Arthur Page, QC (d 1959); *b* 16 Sept 1919; *Educ* Harrow, Magdalene Coll Cambridge; *m* 1950, Anne, da of Charles Micklem, DSO, JP, DL (d 1957); 4 s; *Career* contested (C) Eton and Slough, Gen Election 1959, MP (C) Harrow 1960-87, sec Cons Parly Labour Affairs Ctee 1960-61 (vice-chm 1964-69, chm 1970-74), memb Br Delegn to Cncl of Europe and WEU 1972-87; pres: Independent Schools Assoc 1971-83, Waren Companies Assoc; chm Cncl for Ind Educn 1974; elected substitute pres (Int) Inter-Parly Union 1983; kt 1984; *Style—* Sir John Page; Hitcham Lodge, Taplow, Bucks (☎ Burnham 5056)

PAGE, John Brangwyn; s of late Sidney John Page, CB, MC; *b* 23 August 1923; *Educ* Highgate (Foundation Scholar), King's Coll Cambridge; *m* 1948, Gloria Vail; 1 s, 1 da; *Career* RAF 1942-46; Cambridge 1946-48; first dep chief cashier Bank of England 1968, chief cashier 1970-80, exec dir 1980-82; chm Agricultural Mortgage Corpn 1982-85; dir: Standard Chartered plc 1982-, Nationwide Anglia Building Soc 1982-; FIB, CBIM; *Style—* John Page, Esq; c/o Standard Chartered plc, 38 Bishopsgate, London EC2N 4DE

PAGE, Maj-Gen John Humphrey; CB (1977), OBE (1967), MC (1952); s of Capt W J Page, JP (d 1961), of Devizes, and Alice Mary Page (d 1981); *b* 5 Mar 1923; *Educ* Stonyhurst; *m* 1956, Angela Mary, da of Bernard Bunting (d 1962); 3 s, 1 da; *Career* cmmnd RE 1942; Asst Cmdt RMA Sandhurst 1971-74, dir of Personal Services (Army) Miny of Defence 1974-78, ret; dir London Law Trust 1979-, vice-chm Soldiers' Sailors' and Airmen's Families' Assoc 1983-7; chm Bd of Governers, St Mary's Sch, Shaftesbury; govr Stonyhurst Coll; Chm, tstees, Home Start cnsltncy; *Style—* Maj-Gen John Page, CB, OBE, MC; Jessamme Cottage, Long Sutton, Langport, Somerset TA10 9JP

PAGE, Sir John Joseph Joffre; OBE (1959); s of William Joseph Page (d 1935) and Frances Page (d 1977); *b* 7 Jan 1915; *Educ* Emanuel Sch; *m* 1939, Cynthia Maynard, da of Lionel Maynard Swan, CBE (d 1969); 2 s; *Career* RAF 1933-38 and 1939-46 (despatches 1943), Gp Capt; Iraq Petroleum Gp of Cos: 1938-39 and 1946-70, gen mangr 1955-58, chief rep 1961-70; Mersey Docks and Harbour Co: chm 1972-77 and 1980-84, ch exec 1975-77; dep chm Br Ports Assoc 1974-77; chm: Nat Ports Cncl 1977-80, Chester Health Authy 1981-82, NW RHA 1982-; FCIT; kt 1979; *Recreations* music, fishing; *Clubs* Oriental, RAF, MCC; *Style—* Sir John Page, OBE; Springhill, Hill Rd North, Helsby, Cheshire (☎ 092 82 2994); North-Western Regional Health Authority, Gateway House, Piccadilly South, Manchester M60 7LP

PAGE, Lady Katharine Rose Celestine; *née* Asquith; da of 2 Earl of Oxford and Asquith, KCMG; *b* 16 Oct 1949; *Educ* Mayfield Convent Sussex, King's Coll London; *m* 1, 1970 (m annulled 1984), Adam Nicholas Ridley (now Sir Adam Ridley) *qv*; m 2, 1985, (John) Nathaniel Micklem Page, 2 s of Sir (Arthur) John Page; *Career* art dealer; *Style—* Lady Katharine Page; Foreign and Commonwealth Office, King Charles Street, London SW1

PAGE, Michael Brian; s of James Gourlay Page, of Chester-le-Street, Co Durham, and Mary Jane, *née* McTeague; *b* 14 April 1937; *Educ* Chester-le-Street GS, Co Durham, Univ of Aston Birmingham (BSc Eng); *m* 1961, Jennifer Grace Elizabeth, da of Joseph Victor Wetton (d 1966); 3 da (Joanna b 1966, Kathryn b 1968, Sally b 1971); *Career* sales dir Brush Electrical Machines Ltd 1977-84; chm Hawker Siddeley Power Engrg Inc (USA) 1984, dir Hawker Siddeley Electric Ltd 1986-, md Hawker Siddeley Power Engrg Ltd & assoc companies 1984-; CEng, FIEE, FIMechE, FBIM, FInstD; *Recreations* golf, chess; *Clubs* Rothley Park Golf; *Style—* Michael Page, Esq; Blue Haze, 90 Station Rd, Cropston, Leicestershire LE7 7HE (☎ 0533 362527); Cliff Works, Burton on the Wolds, Loughborough LE12 5TT (☎ 0509 880541, fax 0509 881210, telex 341068)

PAGE, Richard Lewis; MP (C) Hertfordshire South West 1979-; s of Victor Charles Page (d 1968), and Kathleen Page; *b* 22 Feb 1941; *Educ* Hurstpierpoint Coll, Luton Tech Coll; *m* 3 Oct 1964, Madeleine Ann, da of Geoffrey Ronald Brown; 1 s (Mark Lewis b 29 March 1968), 1 da (Tracey Louise b 25 April 1970); *Career* dir of family co

1964-; cncllr Banstead UDC 1969-72; MP (C) Workington 1976-79; PPS to Sec of State for Trade and then ldr of the House 1982-87; nat tres Leukemia Research Fund; Freeman City of London, Liveryman Worshipful Co of Pattenmakers 1979; *Recreations* riding, shooting; *Style*— Richard Page, Esq, MP; House of Commons, London SW1

PAGE, Simon Richard; s of Eric Rowland Page (d 1985), and Vera (*née* Fenton); *b* 7 Mar 1934; *Educ* Lancing, LLB (External), Slr (Hons); *m* 1, 1963 (m dis 1977); 3 s, 1 da; m 2, 1984; *Career* 2 Lt RA 1958-59; slr 1959-75, pres W Surrey Law Soc 1972-73; dist registrar High Court of Justice, registrar Guildford, Epsom and Reigate Co Courts, recorder Crown Court from 1980, pres assoc of County Court and District Registrars 1983-84; *Recreations* squash lawn tennis, cricket, bridge; *Clubs* County (Guildford); *Style*— Simon R Page, Esq; c/o The Law Courts, Guildford

PAGE, Thomas Frederick Philip Urquhart; s of Sir Leo Page (d 1951), of Newton House, Farningdon, Berkshire, and Edith Violet, *née* Loder-Symonds (d 1973), of Hinton Manor, Berkshire; *b* 7 June 1918; *Educ* RNC Dartmouth, RNC Greenwich (psc, jssc); *m* 3 May 1947, Lady Cecilia Norah Stopford, da of 7 Earl of Courtown OBE, DL (d 1957), of Marlfield, Gorey, Co Wexford, Eire; 1 s (Nicholas b 1948), 2 da (Victoria b 1951, Juliet b 1955); *Career* serv 1939-41 in HMS Hereward 1941-45 POW; cdr HMS Loch Fada 1950-52 (ret 1958); dir Allied Suppliers Ltd 1968; chm Liptons (Ireland) Ltd 1971 (ret 1973); life memb The Indust Soc; *Recreations* gardening, painting; *Clubs* Army and Navy, MCC; *Style*— Commander Thomas Page, RN; Toller House Toller Porcorum Dorchester Dorset (☎ Maiden Newton 20461)

PAGE CROFT, Hugo Douglas; s of Richard Arthur Fitzroy Page Croft, of The Round House, Ware, Herts, and F A Rogerson; *b* 23 May 1944; *Educ* Shrewsbury; *m* 1969, Dawn, da of William Pryde (d 1980); 3 s, 1 da; *Career* brewer; memb Home Grown Cereals Authority 1978-84, md Moray Firth Maltings Ltd 1980-86; chm: Angus Barley Co Ltd, Moray Barley Co Ltd; md William Younger & Co Ltd 1986-; *Clubs* Pilgrim; *Style*— Hugo Page Croft, Esq; Murlingden, Brechin, Angus (☎ 03562 2371); Moray Firth Maltings Ltd, Longman Rd, Inverness

PAGE WOOD, Lady; Evelyn Hazel Rosemary; da of late Capt George Ernest Bellville; assumed by deed poll 1956 the additional surname of Page; *m* 1947, Sir David John Hatherley Page Wood, 7 Bt (d 1955); *Style*— Lady Page Wood; The Old Cottage, Wolverton, Basingstoke, Hants

PAGE WOOD, Matthew Page; s of Sir John Stuart Page Wood, 6 Bt (d 1955), and hp of nephew, Sir Anthony Page Wood, 8 Bt; assumed by deed poll 1955 the additional surname of Page before his patronymic; *b* 13 August 1924; *Educ* Radley Coll; *m* 1947, Betsann, da of Lt-Col Francis Christesson Darby Tothill; 2 da (Belinda Jane b 1952 (m 1, Richard John Crowder, m 2, Charles Hoste; 1 s), Miranda Elizabeth b 1962); *Career* Capt Coldstream Gds, ret 1948; New York Stock Exchange; memb: London Stock Exchange 1949-60, CDN Investmt Banker 1960-79; chm Hammersmith Cons Assoc 1963-74 (pres 1974-83); *Recreations* golf, fishing; *Clubs* Brooks's, City of London, MCC; *Style*— Matthew Page Wood, Esq; 31 Halsey St, SW3 (☎ 01 584 6008)

PAGE-TURNER, Noel Frederick Augustus; s of Frederick Ambrose Wilford Page-Turner (d 1936); ggs of Rev Dr Frederick Henry Marvell Blaydes, noted classical scholar; direct descendant of Andrew Marvell the Puritan poet and gggs of Sir Edward George Thomas Page-Turner 5th Bart. of Ambrosden, Oxfordshire; *b* 6 May 1934; *Educ* privately, RAC Cirencester; *m* 1960, Christine Mary, yst da of late R F Tetley, one of the brewing family of Boston Spa Yorkshire, 2 s (Edward b 1961, Gregory b 1964), 1 d (Cassandra b 1966); *Career* cmd Royal Devon Yeomanry Sqdn, Maj 1974-78, second in Cmd Royal Wesex Yeomanry 1978-83; gen commt Income Tax (Axminster div) 1984; landowner and farmer; *Recreations* shooting, heraldry, genealogy, the arts; *Style*— Noel Page-Turner, Esq; Woodhayes, Honiton, Devon EX14 0TP (☎ (0404) 2011)

PAGE-WOOD, Sir Anthony John; 8 Bt (UK 1837), of Hatherley House, Gloucestershire; s of Sir David John Hatherley Page Wood, 7 Bt (d 1955); *b* 6 Feb 1951; *Educ* Harrow; *Heir* unc, Matthew Page b 13 Aug 1924; *Career* dir Société Générale Strauss Turnbull (London) 1982-; *Style*— Sir Anthony Page-Wood, Bt; 22 Godfrey St, London SW3

PAGET, Clarence Arthur Edward; s of Hugh Arthur Paget (d 1924), and Catherine Honoria de Capell Brooke (d 1943); *b* 15 July 1909; *Educ* Eton, Hertford Coll Oxford (BA); *m* 24 Jan 1942, Cynthia Mary, *née* Hutchings (d 1972); 1 s, 3 da; *Career* serv WWII RA and Intelligence Corps 1940-45; book publisher; dir and chief ed Pan Books 1957-74; former dir David & Charles Inc (USA); *Recreations* walking; *Clubs* Utd Oxford and Cambridge Univ; *Style*— Clarence Paget, Esq; Green Farm House, Diss, Norfolk (☎ 0279 9741 303); 50 Stanbury Ct, 99 Haverstock Hill, London NW3 4RK (☎ 01 722 1720)

PAGET, Hon Mrs (Enid Louise); da of 1 and last Baron Queenborough (d 1949); *b* 1923; *m* 1947 (m dis) Count (Roland) de la Poype; 1 da; resumed the surname Paget; *Style*— The Hon Mrs Paget

PAGET, Henry James; s and h of Sir Julian Tolver Paget, 4 Bt; *b* 2 Feb 1959; *Educ* Radley Coll; *Career* Coldstream Guards; md Aachen Holdings Ltd; *Recreations* fishing, shooting and property renovation; *Clubs* RAC, Norfolk; *Style*— Henry Paget, Esq; 3, Bell Road, Norwich, Norfolk NR3 4PA (☎ Norwich 403087)

PAGET, Sir John Starr; 3 Bt (UK 1886), of Cranmore Hall, Co Somerset; s of Sir Richard Arthur Surtees Paget, 2 Bt (d 1955), and Lady Muriel Evelyn Finch-Hatton, CBE (d 1938); *b* 24 Nov 1914; *Educ* Oundle, Chateau D'Oex, Trinity Coll Cambridge (MA); *m* 1944, Nancy Mary Parish, JP, da of late Lt-Col Francis Woodbine Parish, DSO, MC, 60 Rifles; 2 s, 5 da; *Heir* s, Richard Herbert Paget, b 2 Feb 1957; *Career* dir: Napier & Sons 1959-61, Glacier Metal Gp 1963-65, Thermal Syndicate Ltd Wallsend 1939-83 (chm 1973-80); Hilger & Watts 1965-68, Rank Precision Industries Ltd 1968-70; chm Somerset Fruit Machinery Ltd 1986-, sr ptnr Haygrass Cider Orchards; Silver Medal Inst of Production Engrs 1950; Hon DTech Brunel: CEng, FIMechE; *Recreations* cooking, music; *Clubs* Athenaeum; *Style*— Sir John Paget, Bt; Haygrass House, Taunton, Somerset TA3 7B (☎ Taunton 331779)

PAGET, Lt-Col Sir Julian Tolver; 4 Bt (UK 1871), of Harewood Place, Middlesex, CVO (1984); s of Gen Sir Bernard Paget, GCB, DSO, MC (d 1961), and nephew of Sir James Francis Paget, 3 Bt (d 1972); *b* 11 July 1921; *Educ* Radley, Christ Church Oxford; *m* 1954, Diana Frances, da of late F S H Farmer; 1 s, 1 da; *Heir* s, Henry James Paget; *Career* joined Coldstream Gds 1940, served NW Europe 1944-45, ret as Lt-Col 1968; gentleman usher to HM The Queen 1971-; author; *Books* Counter-Insurgency Campaigning (1967), Last Past Aden 1964-67 (1969), The Story of the Guards (1976), The Pageantry of Britain (1979), The Yeomen of the Guard (1985); *Clubs* Cavalry and Guards, Pratt's, Flyfishers'; *Style*— Lt-Col Sir Julian Paget, Bt, CVO; 4 Trevor St, London SW7 (☎ 01 584 3524)

PAGET, Lady Mary Patricia Beatrice Rose; 3 da of 6 Marquess of Anglesey, GCVO; *b* 19 Jan 1918; *Style*— Lady Mary Paget

PAGET, Richard Herbert; s and h of Sir John Starr Paget, 3 Bt; *b* 17 Feb 1957; *Educ* Eton; *m* 1985 Richenda Rachel Collins da of Preb. John Collins; *Career* Office Automation Sales at Nixdorf Computer; *Recreations* tennis, cricket, parachuting; *Clubs* Naval and Military; *Style*— Richard Paget, Esq; Haygrass House, Taunton, Somerset; 20 Marloes Rd, London W8 (☎ 01 373 9760);

PAGET, Lord Rupert Edward Llewelyn; 2 s of 7 Marquess of Anglesey, DL; *b* 21 July 1957; *Educ* Dragon Sch, Westminster; *m* 21 Aug 1982, Louise Victoria Youngman; *Career* farmer; *Style*— Lord Rupert Paget

PAGET OF NORTHAMPTON, Baron (Life Peer UK 1974); Reginald Thomas Guy Des Voeux Paget; QC (KC 1947); s of late Maj Thomas Guy Frederick Paget, of Sulby Hall, Northants, by his w Emma Bettine, through whom Lord Paget of Northampton is gggs of Sir Charles Des Voeux, 1 Bt; *b* 2 Sept 1908; *Educ* Eton, Trinity Coll Cambridge; *m* 1931, Sybil Helen, da of late Sills Clifford Gibons, widow of Sir John Bridger Shiffner, 6 Bt and formerly wife of Sir Victor Basil John Seely, 4 Bt; *Career* Lt RNVR 1940-43 (invalided); sits as Labour peer in House of Lords; barr Gray's Inn and Inner Temple 1934; contested Northampton 1935; MP (Lab) Northanmpton, 1945-Feb 1974; hon sec UK Council of European Movement 1954; master Pytchley Hounds 1958-71; memb House of Lords Bridge Team in match against Commons 1982; *Books* Manstein - Campaigns and Trial (jointly 1951), Hanged - and Innocent? (1958), The Human Journey (1979); *Style*— The Rt Hon the Lord Paget of Northampton, QC; 9 Grosvenor Cottages, London SW1 (☎ 01 730 4034)

PAGET-TOMLINSON, Edward William; s of Edward Edmundson Paget-Tomlinson (d 1953), of Ulverston, Cumbria, and Alison, *née* Wordie (d 1958); *b* 17 Mar 1932; *Educ* Sherborne, Trinity Hall Cambridge (MA); *m* 20 March 1968, Pamela Lesley, da of Leslie Stuart Williams (d 1978), of Ulverston, Cumbria; 1 s (John Edward b 1976), 1 da (Lucy Elizabeth b 1980); *Career* keeper of shipping Liverpool Museum 1956-69, sr keeper and conslt Hull Town Docks (Maritine) Museum 1975-78;; *Books* Complete Book of Canal and River Navigation (1978), Montreux Oberland Bernois Railway (1985); *Recreations* drawing, walking; *Style*— Edward William Paget-Tomlinson, Esq; Easton House, Easton Wells, Somerset BA5 1EF (☎ Wells 870227)

PAICE, James Edward Thornton; MP (C), SE Cambridgeshire 1987-; s of Edward Percival Paice, of Trust Farm, Ennington, Suffolk, and Winifred Mary Paice *née* Thornton; *b* 24 April 1949; *Educ* Farmlingham Coll Suffolk, Writtle Agric Coll (NDA); *m* 6 Jan 1973, Ava Barbara, da of Robert Stewart Patterson, of Church Farm, Earl Soham, Suffolk; 2 s (Gordon b 1976, James b 1977); *Career* gen mangr/exec dir Framlingham Mgmnt and Training Services Ltd 1985-87; non exec dir 1987-; *Recreations* windsurfing, shooting; *Style*— James Paice, Esq, MP; House of Commons, London SW1 (☎ 01 219 4101)

PAICE, Robert Tasker; s of Charles Tasker Paice, (d 1960), of Hythe, Kent, and Joan Kathleen, *née* Commin (d 1981); *b* 2 July 1921; *Educ* Marlborough Magdalene Coll Cambridge (MA), Grenoble France; *m* 8 Oct 1955, Rosemary Alison, da of Richard Arthur Foster (d 1987), of St Martins, Guernsey, CI; 2 s (William b 1959, Edward b 1962), 1 da (Catherine (Mrs Finney), b 1957); *Career* cmmnd RNVR 1941, serv HMS Liverpool, HMS Newfoundland, HMS Vengeance and HMS Indefatigible, demobbed Lt Cdr 1946; Union Bank of Scotland 1947-49, md Ryders Discount Co Ltd 1960-81, dep chm Cater Allen Holdings plc, ret 1985; involved with Royal Br Legion; FIB; *Recreations* tennis, sailing, walking, painting; *Clubs* Royal Thames YC, City of London, Royal Ocean Racing, Naval; *Style*— Robert Paice, Esq; Andredsbourne, Mayfield, E Sussex TN20 6UN (☎ 0435 873119); c/o Cater Allen Ltd, 1 King William St, London EC4 7AU (☎ 01 623 2070)

PAIGE, Elaine; da of Eric Bickerstaff, of London; *Career* actress 1968-; films: Oliver, Whatever Happened to What's His Name; tv: Love Story, The Lady Killers, Phyllis Dixey, View of Harry Clarke, Unexplained Laughter; created role of Eva Peron in Evita London stage 1978, Show Business Personality of the Year Variety Club of GB Award 1978, Best Actress in a Musical SWET Award 1978, created role of Grizabella in Cats 1981, created role of Florence in Chess 1986; albums: Stages (triple platinum) 1983, Cinema (gold) 1984, Chess album 1985, I Know Him So Well duet with Barbara Dickson (No 1 Hit Single) 1985, Love Hurts (platinum) 1985, Christmas 1986, Recording Artiste of the Year Variety Club of GB Award 1986, Memories compilation album (platinum) 1987, The Queen Album 1988 (8th consecutive gold album); UK concert tours 1985 and 87, Head of the Year Award! 1987; *Recreations* skiing, antiques; *Style*— Miss Elaine Paige; EP Records Ltd, 196 Shaftesbury Ave, London WC2H 8JL (☎ 01 240 5617)

PAIGE, Rear-Adm Richard Collings; CB (1967); s of Herbert Collings Paige; *b* 4 Oct 1911; *Educ* Blundell's Sch Tiverton, RNEC Keyham; *m* 1937, Sheila Brambles Ward, da of late Dr Ernest Ward; 2 s; *Career* joined Navy 1929, Capt 1957, CO RNEC 1960-62, Cdre Supt HM Naval Base Singapore 1963-65, Adm Supt HM Dockyard Portsmouth 1966-68, Rear-Adm 1965; *Style*— Rear-Adm Richard Paige, CB

PAIGE, Victor Grellier; CBE (1978); s of Victor Paige; *b* 5 June 1925; *Educ* East Ham GS, Nottingham Univ; *m* 1948, Kathleen Winifred, da of Arthur Harris; 1 s, 1 da; *Career* dep chm Nat Freight Corpn 1977-82, memb Manpower Servs Cmmn 1974-80; chm: Port of London Authy 1980, Regnl Advsy Cncl for Further Educn E Mids 1967; Freeman City of London, Cdr Order of Orange Nassau The Netherlands; CIPM, FCIT, FBIM; *Style*— Victor Paige, Esq, CBE; Queen's Wood, Frithsden, Berkenhamsted, Herts

PAILTHORPE, Richard David Bruce; Dr David Bruce Leonard, of W Sussex, and Rene Joyce Jefferies; *b* 8 Dec 1952; *Educ* Wellington Sch Somerset, Univ of Reading (BSc); *m* 1 May 1976, Jane Carleton, da of Sir Richard Holderness, of W Sussex; 1 s (Nicholas b 1980), 1 da (Victoria b 1983; *Career* museum admin Weald and Downland Open Air Museum W Sussex; *Books* Goodwood Country in Old Photographs (1987); *Recreations* cricket, soccer, rugger, photography, local history, fly fishing; *Style*— Richard Pailthorpe, Esq; Spring Cottage, East Dean, nr Chichester, W Sussex (☎ (24363 702); Weald and Downland, Open Air Museum, Singleton, nr Chichester, W Sussex (☎ 024363 348)

PAIN, Barry Newton; CBE (1979), QPM (1976); s of Godfrey William Pain; *b* 25 Feb 1931; *Educ* Waverley GS Birmingham; *m* 1952, Marguerite Agnes King; 1 s, 1 da; *Career* constable Birmingham City Police 1951, dir Home Off Detective Training Sch

1965-67; supt 1967, dep divnl cdr Birmingham 1967, Staff offr HM Inspr of Constabulary Birmingham 1967, asst chief constable Staffs Constabulary (in charge of Crime and Public Order, Traffic and Communications, and Administration and Training), chief constable of Kent 1974-82, vice-pres Assoc of Chief Police Offrs 1980-81, pres 1981-82, Cmdt Police Staff Coll and HM Insprs of Constabulary for England and Wales 1982-87, attached to Turkish Police Force to advise on reorganization and training (ret); *Style*— Barry Pain, Esq, CBE, QPM

PAIN, Beville Wheeler; s of Douglas Wheeler Pain (d 1951), of Bignell Park, Bicester, Oxon, and Marguerita, *née* Reinhard (d 1980); *b* 27 April 1918; *Educ* Lancing Coll, Trinity Coll Cambridge Univ (MA); *m* 1949, Patience, da of Col J Maitland-Addison, RA (d 1954); *Career* Lt-Col Burma 1944-45, asst mil attaché British Embassy Paris 1947-50; dir Charter Consolidated 1967, Anglo-American Corpn of S Africa 1976, chm European Mining Cos Gp 1975-80, pres Mining Assoc UK 1977; *Recreations* shooting, travel; *Clubs* Boodle's, Travellers' (Paris), Inanda (Johannesburg); *Style*— Beville Pain, Esq; 1A Upper Cheyne Row, London SW3 (☎ 01 352 7251); Preston House, Firle, nr Lewes, Sussex (☎ Glynde 245)

PAIN, Hon Mr Justice - Hon Sir Peter (Richard); s of Arthur Richard Pain; *b* 6 Sept 1913; *Educ* Westminster, Christ Church Oxford; *m* 1941, Barbara Florence Maude Riggs; 2 s; *Career* barr Lincoln's Inn 1936, bencher 1972; QC 1965; a judge of the High Court of Justice Queen's Bench Div 1975-; chm Race Relations Bd Conciliation Ctee for Greater London 1968-71, South Metropolitan Conciliation Ctee 1971-73, memb Parole Bd 1978-80, pres Holiday Fellowship 1977-83; kt 1975; *Style*— The Hon Mr Justice Pain; Loen, St Catherine's Rd, Frimley, Surrey

PAIN, Richard Henry; s of Henry Francis Pain (d 1973), of Halfway House Farm, South Weald, Brentwood, Essex, and Hannah May, *née* Guttridge (d 1986); *b* 7 Sept 1929; *Educ* Brentwood Sch, Felsted Sch; *m* 3 Oct 1959, Ruth Constance, da of William Frederick Murrell (d 1969), of Brentwood, Essex; 2 s (Matthew Henry b 1960, Cosmo William b 1965), 1 da (Charlotte Mary (Mrs Taylor) b 1962); *Career* actuary Atlas Assur Co 1948-52; stockbroker: Rowe Swann & Co 1952-54, Grieveson Grant & Co 1954-62; Capel Cure Myers 1962-85, ptnr until 1985, ANZ Merchant Bank 1985-, dep chm Walthamstow Bldg Soc 1986 (dir 1978), fndr memb Soc Investmt Analysts; chm ctee: FT Actuaries All Share Index 1972-, FT Actuaries World Index 1985-; seconded to Talisman ctee stock exchange 1970-71, memb gilt edged maskets ctee Stock Exchange 1988; govr St Felix Sch Southwold 1985, chm Anglo Euro Comprehensive Sch Ingatestone 1988 (govr 1973-); contrib to various investmt and fin publications and to journal soc of investmt Analysts; Freeman City of London 1984, Liveryman Worshipful Co of Actuaries 1984; *Recreations* walking, beagling, collecting modern British paintings; *Style*— Richard Pain, Esq; c/o ANZ McCaughan Ltd, 65 Holborn Viaduct, London EC1 (☎ 01 236 5101)

PAIN, Lt-Gen Sir (Horace) Rollo (Squarey); KCB (1975, CB 1974), MC (1945); s of late Horace Davy Pain; *b* 11 May 1921; *m* 1950, Denys Sophia, *née* Chaine-Nickson; 1 s, 2 da; *Career* ret; late 4/7 Royal Dragoon Gds; head Br Def Staff, Washington 1975-78, ret; Col Comdt Mil Provost Staff Corps 1974-83, Col 4/7 Royal Dragoon Gds 1979-83; *Recreations* repairing the village church; *Clubs* Cavalry and Guards'; *Style*— Lt-Gen Sir Rollo Pain, KCB, MC; Eddlethorpe Hall, Malton, N Yorks (☎ Burythorpe 218)

PAINE, Dr Christopher Hammon; s of Maj John Hammon Paine (d 1987), of Chapel House, Gt Coxwell, Faringdon, Oxon, and The Hon Mrs J Shedden, MBE, *née* Vestey;; *b* 28 August 1935; *Educ* Eton, Merton Coll Oxford (MA, MSc, DM); *m* 3 Nov 1959, Susan, da of D Martin, of Bridgwater; 2 s (Edward b 1960 ,Simon b 1964), 2 da (Lucy b 1962, Alice b 1968); *Career* conslt in radiotherapy and oncology 1974-; dir Clinical Studies, Univ of Oxford 1980-84, gen mangr Oxfordshire Health Authy 1984-88; FRCP, FRCR; *Recreations* smallholding, country pursuits; *Clubs* Farmers; *Style*— Dr Christopher Paine, Esq; Dame Alice Farm, Watlington, Oxfordshire OX9 5EP (☎ 049161 2255); Dept of Radiotherapy, Churchill Hospital, Headington, Oxford OX3 7LJ (☎ 0865 64841, fax 0865 69223)

PAINE, Graham Ernest Harley; s of Harley Joseph Paine, of Greywood, Coombe Hill Rd, Kingston on Thames, Surrey, and Ninette, *née* Sutch; *b* 2 Sept 1954; *Educ* Dulwich Coll, Univ of Bristol (LLB); *Career* slr; ptnr Wilde Sapt 1984- (articled clerk 1978-80, asst slr 1980-84); memb London Young Slrs Gp; memb Law Soc; *Recreations* golf, skiing, theatre, tennis; *Style*— Graham Paine, Esq; Wilde Sapte, Queensbridge House, 60 Upper Thames St, London EC4 (☎ 01 236 3050, fax 236 9624, telex 887793)

PAINE, Jonathan; s of Cecil Finch Paine, and Freda Helen, *née* Weedon; *b* 3 Oct 1952; *Educ* Rugby, Merton Coll Oxford (BA); *m* 30 June 1979, Julie, da of Ronald Jork Barnes; *Career* J Henry Schroder Wagg & Co Ltd 1975-82; dir: Enskilda Securities 1982-87, corporate fin Swiss Bank Corpn Investment Banking Ltd 1988-; *Style*— Jonathan Paine, Esq; 1 High Timber St, London EC4 (☎ 329 0329)

PAINE, Peter Stanley; CBE (1980), DFC (1944); s of Arthur Bertram Paine; *b* 19 June 1921; *Educ* King's Sch, Canterbury; *m* 1942, Sheila Mary, da of late Frederick Wigglesworth; 2 s, 2 da; *Career* served 1940-46; Flt-Lt 2 Gp RAF; Punch Publishing Office, 1948-52, sales promotion manager Newnes Pearson 1948-52, Odhams Press 1948-52, sales dir and dir of Tyne Tees Television 1958-67, Sales dir and dir of Yorks Television 1967; md, Tyne Tees Television, dir Trident Television; memb Cncl of Independent Television Cos Assoc; *Style*— Peter Paine, Esq, DFC; Briarfield, Ashwood rd, Woking, Surrey (T 048 62 73183)

PAINES, Anthony John Cooper; s of Henry Wilfred Paines, KHG, MPS (d 1973), of Northwood, Middx, and Mary Agnes Paines, *née* Cooper; *b* 17 Nov 1925; *Educ* Mount St Mary's Coll, Lincoln Coll Oxford (MA); *m* 26 April 1952, Anne, da of Charles Philip Billot Holmdale, (former memb of the States of Jersey (d 1981), of St Martin, Jersey, CI; 2 s (Nicholas b 1955, Justin b 1963), 2 da (Caroline b 1957, Cathryn b 1959); *Career* RN 1944-47; admitted slr 1952, ptnr Allen & Overy 1958-88; memb Slrs Disciplinary Tribunal 1974-; JP 1967-77; *Books* Product Liability in Europe (contrib 1974), Merger Control in The EEC (1988); *Recreations* travel, boating, fishing, reading; *Style*— Anthony J C Paines, Esq; 28 Battersea Bride Rd, London, SW11 (☎ 01 585 1375); La Chaumiere, St Martin, Jersey, CI (☎ 0534 62441, fax 0534 65156); Allen & Overy, 9 Cheapside, London, EC2V 6AD (☎ 01 248 9898, fax 01 236 2192, telex 8812801)

PAINTER, Brig John Lannoy Arnaud; s of Brig Gordon Whistler Arnaud Painter, DSO (d 1960), and Kathleen Hay Lannoy, *née* Tweedie (d 1986); *b* 3 Jan 1925; *Educ* Lancing, Staff Coll Camberley, RNC Greenwich; *m* 4 Feb 1956, (Janet) Lois, da of Arnold Stanley Munro (d 1986); 2 s (Anthony Munro Arnaud b 24 Sept 1957, Angus Robin Arnaud b 29 May 1966), 1 da (Lindsay Caroline b 3 Sept 1959); *Career* serv KRRC and RA 1943-76, Korea, Malaya (with SAS), Palestine, Cyprus, W Africa (with RWAFF); Brig CRA 2 Div 70/71, DDRA 72/75; sr master Cundall Manor Sch 1976-88; *Recreations* walking, skiing, riding; *Style*— Brig John L A Painter; Abbayville, Upper Dunsforth, Great Ouseburn, Yorkshire YO5 9RU (☎ 0423 322842)

PAINTER, Dr Michael John; s of James Frederick Painter, of Bredbury, Cheshire, and Lettice Gillian, *née* Payne; *b* 24 Oct 1948; *Educ* Strode's Sch Egham Surrey, St Mary's Hosp Med Sch Univ of London (MB BS), Univ of Manchester (MSc); *m* 26 May 1973, Gillian Elizabeth, da of David Alexander Burgess (d 1973); *Career* conslt public health med, med offr environmental health Manchester City Cncl, port med offr Manchester Airport, memb bd Public Health Lab Serv 1985-, jt author papers on haemophilia and meningitis; Freeman City of London 1982, Liveryman Worshipful Co of Coopers 1982; memb: BMA 1973, Faculty Community Medicine 1985; *Recreations* photography, model railways, cycling; *Style*— Dr Michael Painter; 108 Wythenshawe Rd, Northenden, Manchester M23 OPA (☎ 061 998 9688); PO Box 362, Town Hall, Manchester M60 2JB (☎ 061 234 4867, fax 061 236 5909)

PAINTER, Michael William; s of William Bentley Painter (d 1984), of Coventry, and Maria, *née* Eggleton (d 1982); *b* 2 Mar 1938; *Educ* Bablake Sch Coventry; *m* 1, 23 Sept 1963, Jillian Margeret (d 1985), da of Harold Lane (d 1976); 1 s (Steven Michael b 1966), 2 da (Sarah b 1968, Rebecca b 1973), m 2, 26 Sept 1987, Susan Anne, da of Frederick Morley, of Swindon; 2 step da (Michelle b 1981, Rosanne b 1983); *Career* Nat Serv RAF 1958-60; dir Hogg Robinson UK Ltd 1973-85, dir Bowring UK Ltd 1985-, chief exec Bowring London Ltd 1985-; FCII, FBIIBA, FBIM; *Recreations* walking; *Clubs* RAC; *Style*— Michael Painter, Esq; Bowring London Ltd, The Bowring Building, Tower Place, London EC3 (☎ 01 283 3100, fax 01 929 2705, telex 882191)

PAIRMAN, Lynda Annette; *née* Miles; da of William John Edward Miles, of Edinburgh, and Sarah, *née* Carr; *b* 11 Feb 1958; *Educ* The Mary Erskine Sch Edinburgh, Univ of Edinburgh (LLB); *m* 20 Aug 1977, Gordon Alexander Pairman, s of Alexander George Pairman, of Glasgow; *Career* W & J Burness WS 1978-83 (ptnr 1984-), Herbert Smith & Co 1983-84; memb: Law Soc of Scotland, Soc of Writers to HM Signet; *Clubs* Caledonian; *Style*— Mrs Lynda Pairman; 16 Hope St, Charlotte Sq, Edinburgh (☎ 031 226 2561, fax 031 225 3949, car tel 0836 714 873, telex 727491)

PAISLEY, Rev Ian Richard Kyle; MP (DUP) North Antrim 1974-, MEP (Democratic Unionist Pty) NI 1979-; s of late Rev J Kyle Paisley; *b* 6 April 1926; *Educ* Ballymena Model Sch, Ballymena Tech HS, S Wales Bible Coll, Reformed Presbyterian Theol Coll Belfast; *m* 1956, Eileen Emily Cassells; 2 s, 3 da; *Career* ordained 1946; MP (Prot U) N Antrim 1970-74; minister Martyrs Memorial Free Presbyterian Church Belfast 1946-; memb: Int Cultural Soc of Korea; FRGS; *Books* History of 59 Revival, Christian Foundations (1960 repreinted 1985), Exposition of Epistle to Romans (1968 repr 1985), Massacre of St Bartholomew 1972, Ulster the Facts 1981, No Pope Here 1982, Paisley's Pocket Preacher 1987, Be Sure - 7 rules for public speaking 1987; *Style*— The Rev Ian Paisley, MP, MEP; House of Commons, London SW1; The Parsonage, 17 Cyprus Ave, Belfast BT5 5NT

PAISLEY, Capt Keith; s of David Paisley (d 1922), and Emily May, *née* Pattinson (d 1945); *b* 2 Mar 1916; *Educ* Dulwich, London Univ, Wye Coll (Dip Hort); *m* 2 June 1945, Elizabeth Pamela, da of Sidney Wilson-Kitchen (d 1970) of Kent; 2 s (Graeme b 1947, Duncan b 1948); *Career* Lt: TARO 1945-50, HG 1952-56; cmmn general list T&AVR Army Cadet Force 1958-72 (ret as hon Capt 1972); chartered biologist, vice-princ Kent Inst 1946-58, sr lectr Hadlow Coll of Agric 1958-76, scientific dir Soil Clinic 1976-86, scientific advsr Home Def, Home Off 1979-; Kent CC 1979-86, Powys CC 1986-; MIBiol, FRSA; *Recreations* photography, hill walking, nature conservation; *Clubs* Farmers'; *Style*— Capt Keith Paisley; Faircroft, Battle, Brecon, Powys (☎ Brecon 3783)

PAKENHAM, Hon Michael Aidan; 3 s of 7 Earl of Longford, KG, PC; *b* 3 Nov 1943; *Educ* Ampleforth, Trinity Coll Cambridge, Rice Univ Texas; *m* 1980, Meta (Mimi) Landreth, da of William Conway Doak, of Maryland, USA; 2 da (Alexandra b 1981, Clio b 1985); *Career* HM Dip Serv: cnsllr (External Affairs) UK Representation to European Communities, Brussels; *Recreations* tennis, golf, reading, bridge; *Clubs* MCC; *Style*— The Hon Michael Pakenham; FCO, King Charles St, London SW1A 2AH

PAKENHAM, Hon Patrick Maurice; s of 7 Earl of Longford, KG, PC; *b* 1937; *Educ* Ampleforth, Magdalen Coll Oxford; *m* 1968, Mary Elizabeth, da of Maj H A J Plummer, of Winchester; 3 s; *Career* barr Inner Temple 1962; *Style*— The Hon Patrick Pakenham; Little Meadow, London Rd, Sunningdale, Berks

PAKENHAM, Hon Mrs (Susan Elizabeth Moon); *née* Lever; da of 3 Viscount Leverhulme, TD; *b* 1938; *m* 1957 (m dis 1973) (Hercules) Michael Roland Pakenham; 1 s, 1 da (both adopted); *Style*— The Hon Mrs Pakenhamn; Oaklands, Lr Common Rd, W Wellow, Romsey, Hants

PAKENHAM, Thomas Frank Dermot; s and h of 7 Earl of Longford, KG, PC, but does not use courtesy title; *b* 14 August 1933; *Educ* Ampleforth, Magdalen Coll Oxford; *m* 1964, Valerie Susan, da of Maj Ronald Guthrie McNair Scott; 2 s, 2 da; *Style*— Thomas Pakenham Esq; Tullynally, Castelpollard, Co Westmeath (☎ 044 61159)

PAKENHAM-WALSH, John; CB (1986); s of Rev Wilfrid Pakenham-Walsh (d 1974), and Guendolen Maud, *née* Elliott; *b* 7 August 1928; *Educ* Bradfield Coll, Univ Coll Oxford (MA); *m* 29 Sept 1951, Deryn Margaret, da of Gp Capt Reginald Edgar Gilbert Fulljames, MC (d 1985); 1 s (John b 25 Nov 1961), 4 da (Carolyn 23 May 1953, Elizabeth b 19 Jan 1956, Sarah b 25 May 1965, Andrea b 7 Sept 1968) ; *Career* called to the Bar Lincoln's Inn 1951; Crown Counsel Hong Kong 1953-57, parly counsel Fedn of Nigeria 1958-61; joined Legal Advsrs Branch Home Office 1980-87, under sec (legal) Home Office 1980-81, standing counsel to Gen Synod of the Church of England 1988-; *Clubs* United Oxford and Cambridge Univ; *Style*— John Pakenham-Walsh, Esq, CB; Crinken House, Pathfields Close, Haselmere, Surrey, GU27 2BL (☎ 0428 2033); 36 Whitehall, London, SW1 (☎ 01 210 6612)

PAKINGTON, Hon Anne; da of 5 Baron Hampton, OBE (d 1974), Grace Dykes, *née* Spicer (d 1959); *b* 15 Oct 1919; *Educ* Somerville Coll Oxford (MA); *Style*— The Hon Anne Pakington; 5 King Charles Ct, Bath Rd, Worcester WR5 3EJ (☎ 0905 359 431)

PAKINGTON, Hon Auriol Mary Grace; da of 5 Baron Hampton, OBE (d 1974) and Grace Dykes (d 1959), 3 da of Rt Hon Sir Albert Spicer, 1 Bt, PC; *b* 8 Dec 1922; *Style*— The Hon Auriol Pakington; 68 Malvern Rd, Worcester WR2 4LQ

PAKINGTON, Hon Catharine Mary Grace; da of 6 Baron Hampton; *b* 25 Mar 1960; *Educ* Worcester GS for Girls, Worcester Tech Coll, Bristol Univ (BSc, PGCE); *Career* Christ-centred educn; *Style*— The Hon Catharine Pakington

PAKINGTON, Hon John Humphrey Arnott; s and h of 6 Baron Hampton; *b* 24 Dec 1964; *Educ* Dyson Perrins C of E HS, Shrewsbury Sch; Exeter Coll of Art and Design (BA); *Style*— The Hon John Pakington

PAKINGTON, Hon Sarah Jane Auriol; da of 6 Baron Hampton; *b* 25 Nov 1961; *Educ* Ellerslie Sch Malvern, Worcester Tech Coll, Bedford Coll London Univ (BA); *Style*— The Hon Sarah Pakington

PALAMOUNTAIN, Edgar William Irwin; s of William Bennett Palamountain (d 1958); *b* 24 Dec 1917; *Educ* Charterhouse, St John's Coll Oxford; *m* 1948, Eleanor Mary Aylward, da of Maj-Gen Sir Richard Lewis, KCMG; 1 s, 2 da; *Career* serv WWII, Army 1941-47 (despatches); RHA and Staff Capt 1943, Maj 1945, Acting Lt-Col 1946; Allied Cmmn for Austria 1945-47; md M & G Group 1968-77, chm 1977-79; chm: Unit Trust Assoc 1977-79, Wider Share Ownership Council 1969-; chm Council Univ of Buckingham 1979-; dir Esmee Fairbairn Charitable Trust, 1980-; FRSA 1984, DUniv Buckingham 1985; *Clubs* Boodle's, City of London, MCC; *Style*— Edgar Palamountain, Esq; Duns Tew Manor, Oxford (☎ Steeple Aston 40332); 35 Chelsea Towers, London SW3 (☎ 01 352 0789)

PALIN, Maj Hugh Mair; MBE (1943), TD (1960); s of Vero Calveley Palin (d 1937), and Margaret Janet, *née* Mair (d 1952); *b* 31 May 1912; *Educ* Brighton Coll; *m* 1, 10 Sept 1938 (m dis 1960), Enid Margery Maud, da of late Capt Thomas Free, MN; 1 s (Michael John b 1944), 1 da (Rosemary Grace b 1950); m 2, 28 Jan 1962, Peggy Ailsa Thelma, *née* Bailey; 1 s (Jonathan Hugh b 1963); *Career* Westminster Dragoons TA 1938-39, cmmnd 2 Lt RTR 1940, Capt 1941, Staff Coll Camberley 1942, Major N Africa 1942-43, served with 33 Armd Bde Normandy and NW Europe 1944-45, demob 1945; Warwicks Yeo TA 1948-53; dir Br Cycle and Motorcycle Mfrs Union 1953-67, dir Norton Villiers Triumph Ltd 1967, purchasing dir Skoda (GB) Ltd 1976-80; non exec dir: RAC 1979-88 (chm motorcycle ctee 1972-88), Auto Cycle Union 1979-; pres: Br Motorcyclists Fedn 1976, Bureau Permanent International des Constructeurs de Motorcycles 1977, Motor Cycle Assoc of GB; advsr to bd Norton Gp plc 1987-88, chm of cncl Nat Motor Museum Beaulieu; Freeman Stratford-on-Avon (as CO Stratford Sqdn Warwicks Yeo); Fell Motor Indust; *Clubs* RAC, Cavalry and Guards; *Style*— Maj Hugh Palin, MBE, TD; Bay View, Freshwater East, Pembroke, Dyfed (☎ 0646 672 629)

PALING, Her Hon Judge Helen Elizabeth (Mrs W J S Kershaw); da of A Dale Paling; *b* 25 April 1933; *Educ* Prince Henry's GS Otley, LSE (LLB); *m* 1961, William John Stanley Kershaw, PhD; 1 s, 3 da; *Career* barrister Lincoln's Inn 1955, recorder of the Crown Court 1972-85; Circuit judge 1985-; *Style*— Her Hon Judge Kershaw

PALING, Robert Roy; s of Reginald Roy Paling (d 1978), and Margery Emily, *née* Lyford; *b* 10 June 1940; *Educ* Shrivenham Sch, Faringdon Sch, The Coll Swindon; *m* 20 Feb 1965, Judith Dow, da of Reginald Albert Sheppard (d 1985); 1 da (Portia b 1968); *Career* sr conveyancing exec Lemon & Co Slrs Swindon 1980, conslt Dow Sheppard Relocation 1981, compiled Mortgage Guide for CBI Employee Relocation Cncl 1988; Sr Jt Master Shrivenham Beagles, memb Old Berks Hunt, Assoc of Masters of Harriers and Beagles 1970; memb Soc Lincensed Conveyancers 1987, Assoc Inst of Legal Execs 1965; *Recreations* hunting, cross country riding, shooting; *Clubs* RMCS Shrivenham; *Style*— Robert Paling, Esq; Orchard House, High St, Shrivenham, Swindon SN6 8AW (☎ 0793 782214); Lemon & Co, 34 Regent Circus, Swindon SN1 1PY (☎ 0793 27141, fax 0793 782328, car tel 0860 221 808)

PALLETT, Norman Ivor; s of Walter Albert Stanley Pallett (d 1949), of Hastings, and Helen Rebecca, *née* Shearman (d 1977); *b* 22 April 1929; *Educ* Alleyns Sch Dulwich; *m* 20 Sep 1952, Margaret Evelyn, da of Marcus Edward Turk, of Hastings; 1 s (Robert Nigel b 1954); *Career* CH Dobbie conslt engrs 1951- (ptnr 1970-84, managing ptnr 1984-); work incl: coastal engrg, public health, highways, railways; FICE, MIHT, MConsSE, FBIM; *Recreations* archaeology, railways, the Arab world; *Clubs* St Stephen's Constitutional; *Style*— Norman Pallett, Esq; Dobbie & Partners, Consulting Structural and Civil Engineers, 17 Lansdowne Rd, Croydon CR9 3UN (☎ 01 686 8212, fax 01 681 2499, telex 917220)

PALLEY, Dr Claire Dorothea Taylor; da of Arthur Aubrey Swait, Durban; *b* 17 Feb 1931; *m* 1952 (m dis 1985), Ahrn Palley; 5 s; *Career* princ St Anne's Coll Oxford 1984-; *Books* The Constitutional History and Law of S Rhodesia (1966), contrib num articles in learned jnls; *Style*— Prof Claire Palley; St Anne's College, Oxford

PALLEY, Eall Marcon (Marc); s of Dr Ahrn Palley, of Zimbabwe, and Dr Claire Dorothea Taylor, *née* Swait, qv; *b* 2 May 1954; *Educ* Clifton, St John's Coll Oxford (BA); *m* 28 July 1979, Sabina Mary, da of Maj-Gen F W E Fursdon, qv; 3 s (Charles b 9 Dec 1982, Frederick b 6 June 1985, Harry b 15 May 1988); *Career* slr Allen & Overy 1978-85, ptnr Berwin Leighton 1985-

PALLI, Lady Hermione; *see*: della Grazia, Duchessa

PALLISER, Rt Hon Sir (Arthur) Michael; GCMG (1977, KCMG 1973, CMG 1966), PC (1983); s of Adm Sir Arthur Palliser, KCB, DSC, of South Kensington (d 1956), and Margaret Eva, Lady Palliser; *b* 9 April 1922; *Educ* Wellington, Merton Coll Oxford (MA, hon fell 1986); *m* 1948, Marie Marguerite, da of Paul-Henri Spaak (d 1972), sometime PM of Belgium and sec-gen NATO; 3 s; *Career* late Capt Coldstream Gds; entered FO 1947, private sec to PM 1966, minister Paris 1969, ambass and head to UK Delegn to EEC Brussels 1971, ambass and UK perm rep to EEC 1973-75, perm under-sec and head of Dip Serv FCO 1975-82; appointed PM's special advsr during Falklands Crisis 1982, assoc fellow Sept 1982 Harvard Univ Center for Int Affrs; dep chm Midland Bank plc 1987-; non-exec dir Samuel Montagu & Co Ltd 1983-, (chm 1984-); non-exec dir: Booker McConnell 1983-, Ibec Inc (now Arbor Acres Farm Inc), (agribusiness assoc of Booker McConnell based in Connecticut) 1983-, BAT Industs 1983-, Eagle Star Hldgs 1983-, Shell Transport and Trading 1983-, United Biscuits (Hldgs) 1983-; chm Cncl Int Inst for Strategic Studies 1983-; memb Cncl Royal Inst of Int Affairs 1982-; pres British Section Int Social Servs 1982-; memb Security Cmmn 1983-; Chev Order of Orange Nassau 1944, Chev Légion d'Honneur 1957; *Recreations* travel, theatre; *Clubs* Buck's; *Style*— Rt Hon Sir Michael Palliser, GCMG; c/o Midland Bank plc, Poultry, London EC2P 2BX (☎ 01 260 8000)

PALLISTER, Dr (Richard) Alan; OBE (1946); s of Matthew John Pallister (d 1913), and Edith, *née* Tomlinson (d 1948); *b* 9 Sept 1903; *Educ* Rutherford Coll Newcastle-upon-Tyne, Durham Univ (MD); *m* 11 Aug 1927, Muriel, da of William Hogg (d 1947); 1 s (Michael b 1930); *Career* colonial med serv (Malaya) 1927-58, med dir Cwlth & Int Med Advsy Bureau 1958-68; *Style*— Dr Alan Pallister; Hanburys, Shootersway, Berkhamsted, Herts HP4 3NG (☎ 04427 3916)

PALLISTER, Anthony Gilbert Fitzjames; s of Rev J Pallister (d 1949), of Gt Dunham, and Elizabeth Mary, *née* Feast; *b* 11 Feb 1915; *Educ* King Alfreds Sch Wantage, Brighton Tech Coll; *m* 22 Aug 1942, Barbara Millecent, da of Adm George Bowes Hutton (d 1948), of Belton House, Rutland; 1 s (Julian Guy b 6 Dec 1943), 1 da (Jacqueline Ann (Mrs Robinson) b 14 Jan 1949); *Career* RASC 1940, cmmnd 2 Lt posted 11 Armd Div 1942, Capt 1943, Staff Capt HQ L of C 21 Army Gp 1944, Staff Capt HQ 21 Army Gp 1944, Maj DADST 1944, head of ST5 21 Army Gp 1945; asst D Winton Thorpe Consulting Engrs 1936-37, commercial asst Electric Power Co Shrops Worcs and Staffs 1937, educn and trg mangr Midlands Electricity Bd; sec Birmingham Outward Bd Assoc 1951-61, memb VSO Ctee Worcs 1970-, ILO expert Malaysia 1960 and 1971, pt/t advsr UPDEA W Africa 1974-76, memb governing bodies of Birmingham Poly and Worcs Coll of Higher Educn; County Magistrate Worcs 1963-80, chm of magristrates and memb Magistrates cts ctee, vice-chm and memb Hereford and Worcester Probation Ctee 1963-80; fndr chm: Midlands ctee for Trg of Probation Staff, Community Serv Ctee Hereford and Worcs; FIPM (chm Birmingham branch); *Recreations* tennis, hockey, golf; *Clubs* Union & County (Worcs); *Style*— Anthony Pallister, Esq; The Grove House, Sytchampton, Stourport on Severn, Worcs (☎ 0905 620371)

PALLOT, (Arthur) Keith; CB (1981), CMG (1966); s of Harold Pallot, of La Tourelle, Jersey (d 1937), and Janet Maud, *née* Perchard (d 1977); *b* 25 Sept 1918; *Educ* Newton Coll, RN cadet in training ship 1937; *m* 1945, Marjorie, da of J T Smith, of Rugby (d 1975); 2 da (Susan, Judith); *Career* joined RN 1936, ret as Lt-Cdr 1947; dir of Fin and Estab and asst sec Commonwealth War Graves Cmmn 1956-75, dir of Admin 1956-75, dir-gen 1975-82; *Recreations* golf, bridge; *Style*— Keith Pallot, Esq, CB, CMG; Northways, Stubbles Lane, Cookham Dean, Berks (☎ Marlow 062 84 6529)

PALMAR, Sir Derek James; s of Lt-Col Frederick James Palmar (d 1978), and Hylda, *née* Smith; *b* 25 July 1919; *Educ* Dover Coll; *m* 1946, Edith, da of William Brewster (d 1948); 1 s, 1 da; *Career* serv RA and Staff 1941-46, psc, Lt-Col 1945; Peat Marwick Mitchell & Co 1937-57; advsr Dept of Econ Affairs 1965-67, memb Br Railways Bd 1969-72, chm BR Southern Regnl Advsy Bd 1972-79, pres Bass plc 1987- (chm 1976-87, dir 1970-76, chief exec 1976-84); chm Rush & Tompkins Gp Ltd 1974-; chm Yorks TV 1982-, Boythorpe 1986-, Zoological Soc of London Development Tst 1986-, Leeds Univ Fndn 1986-, Nat Econ Devpt Ctee for Food and Drink Packaging Equipment 1986-; dir: Hill Samuel Gp 1957-70, Grindlays Bank plc 1973-85, Grindlays Hldgs plc 1979-85, Howard Machinery plc 1967-85, Drayton Consolidated Tst plc 1982-, Consolidated Venture Tst plc; City Merchants (Hldgs) Ltd 1985-; tstee: Civic Tst, memb Ct Brewers' Co, Freeman City of London; vice-pres The Brewers' Soc 1982- (chm 1980-82, vice-chm 1978-80); FCA, CBIM; kt 1986; *Recreations* shooting, gardening; *Clubs* Boodle's; *Style*— Sir Derek Palmar; 30 Portland Place, London W1 (☎ 01 637 5499)

PALMER *see also*: Prior-Palmer

PALMER, David Erroll Prior; s of Brig Sir Otho Prior-Palmer DSO, and Mrs Sheila Mary Peers, *née* Weller-Poley; *b* 20 Feb 1941; *Educ* Eton, Christ Church Oxford (MA); *m* 1974, Elizabeth Helen, da of Tom Young, of Chichester; 2 s (James b 1975, Alexander b 1977), 1 da (Marina b 1978); *Career* gen mangr and main bd dir Financial Times (features 1964-67, NY corr 1967-70, mgmnt ed 1970-72, news ed 1972-77, Frankfurt Project 1977-79, foreign ed 1979-80, dep ed 1981-83), chm St Clements Press; first Br finisher (third in class) 1976 Observer Transatlantic Race; *Books* The Atlantic Challenge (1977); *Recreations* sailing (National Swallow 'Archon'); *Clubs* Itchenor Sailing, Oxford and Cambridge Sailing; *Style*— David Palmer Esq; 45 Lancaster Ave, London SE27 9EL (☎ 01 670 0585); Dairy Cottage, W Broyle, Chichester (☎ (0243) 789552); Bracken Ho, 10 Cannon St, EC4P 4BY (☎ 01 248 8000)

PALMER, Andrew Enstace; CMG (1987), CVO (1981); s of Lt-Col Rodney H Palmer MC (d 1987), and Frances Pauline Ainsworth *née* Gordon-Duff; gf and other ancestors, chm of Huntley & Palmer's Biscuits, Reading; *b* 30 Sept 1937; *Educ* Winchester, Pembroke Coll Cambridge (MA); *m* 28 July 1962, Davina Cecil, da of Sir Roderick Barclay, GCVO, KCMG, of Great White End, Latimer, Bucks; 2 s (Rodney b 1963, Michael b 1977), 1 da (Juliet b 1965); *Career* 2 Lt The Rifle Bde 1956-58 (Nat Serv), HM Foreign Serv, later Dip Serv; American Dept, FO 1962-63; comm sec La Paz 1963-65; second sec Ottawa 1965-67; Treasy Centre for Admin Studies 1967-68; Central Dept, FO, later Southern Euro Dept, FCO 1968-72; first sec (press and information), Paris 1972-76; asst head of def dept FCO 1976-77; Royal Coll of Def Studies 1978 Course; cnsllr, head of Chancery and Col Gen, Oslo 1979- Oct 1982; head of Falkland Islands Dept 1982-85; HM Ambass to Cuba July 1986-, FCA Nov 1982- July 1985; fell Harvard Center for Int Affairs 1985-86; *Recreations* photography, fishing, following most sports; *Clubs* Brooks's, MCC, Vanderbilt Tennis; *Style*— Andrew Palmer, CMG, CVO; c/o Foreign & Commonwealth Office, London SW1A 2AH

PALMER, Lady Anne Sophia; *née* Walpole; da of 5 and last Earl of Orford (d 1931; fifth in descent from bro of Sir Robert Walpole, the 1 PM & 1 Earl of Orford of 1 cr, and 1 cous four times removed of the litterateur Horace Walpole, 4 and last Earl of Orford of the 1 cr); *b* 11 Dec 1919; *m* 1939, Col Eric Palmer, CBE, TD, DL (d 1980); 2 s; horticulturist, awarded Victoria Medal of Honour the highest award conferred by RHS; *Style*— Lady Anne Palmer; Rosemoor, Great Torrington, Devon

PALMER, Anthony Wheeler; QC (1979); s of late Philip Palmer; *b* 30 Dec 1936; *Educ* Wrekin Coll Salop; *m* Jacqueline, da of Reginald Fortnum, of Taunton; 1 s, 2 da; *Career* barr Gray's Inn 1962, rec Crown Ct 1980-; *Style*— Anthony Palmer, Esq, QC; 17 Warwick Ave, Coventry CV5 6DJ (☎ 0203 75340)

PALMER, Arthur Montague Frank; s of Frank Palmer (d 1965), of Northam, Devon, and Emily Palmer (d 1966); *b* 4 August 1912; *Educ* Ashford GS, Brunel Tech Coll (now Brunel Univ); *m* 1939, Dr Marion Ethel Frances Woollaston, da of Frank Woollaston, of Chiswick; 2 da; *Career* chartered engr and chartered fuel technologist; MP (Lab) Wimbledon 1945-50, MP (Lab and Co-Op): Cleveland Oct 1952-Sept 1959, Bristol Central 1964-74, Bristol N E 1974-83, did not contest Gen Election 1983; front bench oppn spokesman on energy 1957-59, chm Co-op Parly Gp 1970, vice-chm select ctee on Energy 1979-, chm select ctee Science and Technol 1966-70 and 1974-79, chm Parly and Scientific Ctee 1965-68; memb Brentford & Chiswick Cncl 1937-45, ed

Electrical Power Engrs 1945-72, chm Red Rose Gp 1982-83 (gp of Lab MPs formed to change party policy commitment to take UK out of EEC), vice chm Lab Movement in Europe 1983-; Defence Medal, Queen's Coronation Medal; CEng, FIEE, FInstE; *Books* Future of Electricity Supply (1944), Modern Norway (1949), Law and the Power Engineer (1961), Nuclear Power— the reason why (1983), Energy Policy in the Community (1985); *Recreations* walking, gardening, conversation; *Clubs* Athenaeum; *Style*— Arthur Palmer, Esq; Manton Thatch, Manton, Marlborough, Wilts SN8 4HR (☎ 0672 53313)

PALMER, Bernard Harold Michael; s of late Christopher Harold Palmer; *b* 8 Sept 1929; *Educ* St Edmund's Sch Hindhead, Eton, King's Coll Cambridge (BA, MA); *m* 1954, Jane Margaret, da of late E L Skinner; 1 s, 1 da; *Career* ed of the Church Times 1968-; *Recreations* cycling, penmanship; *Clubs* Royal Cwlth Soc; *Style*— Bernard Palmer, Esq; 143 Bradbourne Vale Rd, Sevenoaks, Kent (☎ 0732 453327)

PALMER, Hon Lady (Catherine Elizabeth); *née* Tennant; da of late 2 Baron Glenconner by his 2 w; *b* 10 Nov 1947; *m* 1976, Sir Mark Palmer, 5 Bt; 1 da; *Style*— The Hon Lady Palmer; Mill Hill Farm, Sherborne, Northleach, Glos (☎ Windrush 395); 15 Bramerton St, London SW3

PALMER, Charles Alan Salier; CBE (1969), DSO (1945); s of late Sir (Charles) Eric Palmer; *b* 23 Oct 1913; *Educ* Harrow, Exeter Coll Oxford; *m* 1939, Auriol Mary, da of late Brig-Gen Cyril R Harbord, CB, CMG, DSO; *Career* vice-chm Assoc Biscuit Mfrs Ltd 1963 (chm 1969-72); pres Reading Cons Assoc 1946-86; *Style*— Charles Palmer, Esq, CBE, DSO; Forest Edge, Farley Hill, Reading, Berks (☎ 0734 760223)

PALMER, Charles Lionel; s of Capt Lionel Hugo Palmer (d 1914; 6 s of 1 Bt), and hp of kinsman, Sir Mark Palmer, 5 Bt; *b* 7 Feb 1909; *Educ* Cheltenham, Trent Coll; *m* 1937, Karoline, da of late Maj Carl Gach, of Vienna; 2 da; *Career* formerly Capt Royal Canadian Army Serv Corps; *Style*— Charles Palmer Esq; 52 Patika Ave, Weston, Ontario, Canada

PALMER, Charles Stuart William; OBE (1973); s of Charles Edward Palmer, and Emma Byrne; *b* 15 April 1930; *Educ* Drayton Manor Co Sch; *Career* chm Br Olympic Assoc 1983- (vice-chm 1977-83); represented GB in judo 1949-59, studied judo in Japan 1951-55, 1 Dan 1948, 4 Dan 1955, 8 Dan 1980; pres Int Judo Fedn 1965-79 (hon life pres 1979-), sec-gen Gen Assoc of Int Sports Fedns 1975-84, pres Br Judo Assoc 1977 (chm 1962-85); govr Sports Aid Fndn 1979-; Gold Medal Euro Judo Union 1982; memb cncl of Royal Albert Hall; Key of City of Taipei 1974, Key of City of Seoul 1981; *Recreations* judo, ski-ing, music, languages; *Style*— Charles Palmer, Esq, OBE; 4 Hollywood Road, London SW10 9HY (☎ 01 352 6238)

PALMER, Charles William; s of Charles James Strachan Palmer (d 1961), of Estate Factor, Inverlochy, Castle Estate, Fort William, and Ida Patricia, *née* Miskimmin; *b* 17 Dec 1945; *Educ* Lochaber HS, Inverness Royal Acad, Univ of Edinburgh (UB); *m* 20 Dec 1969, Rosemary, da of Lt-Col Henry Walter Holt (d 1976), of Grantley Rd, Boscombe, Hants; 1 s (Richard James b 1971), 2 da (Lavinia Jayne b 1973, Emily Sarah b 1974); *Career* ptnr Allan McDougall & Co, slr Supreme Ct Edinburgh 1975; sheriff N Strathclyde at Dunoon and Dumbarton Sheriff cts 1986; memb Law Soc of Scotland; *Recreations* hill walking, music, photography; *Style*— Charles Palmer, Esq; 6 Great Stuart St, Edinburgh; Balliemore Cottage, Strachur SRG 7CC (☎ 031 225 4962); Dumbarton Sheriff Ct (☎ 0389 63266); Dunoon Sheriff Ct (☎ 0369 4166)

PALMER, Clifford Frederick; s of Charles Norman Palmer (d 1975), and Nora, *née* Drury; *b* 7 Sept 1948; *Educ* Henley-in-Arden HS; *m* 1, 1 June 1974 (m dis 1984), Janet Mary, da of Frank Wilson, of Kettering, Northants; m 2, 22 Sept 1984, Jill Mary, da of Maurice James Steward (d 1980) of Dennington, Suffolk; 4 da (Charlotte b 1984, Victoria b 1985, Kathryn b 1987, Sarah b 1987); *Career* Nat Farmers Union Mutual Insur Soc Stratford-upon-Avon 1965-69, SA Meacock & Co at Lloyds 1969-79, dir Clifford Palmer Underwritng Agencies Ltd at Lloyds 1979- (exec dir 1980); exec dir: Ashley Palmer Hldgs 1984, Martin Ashley Underwriting Agencies Ltd 1984, Ashley Palmer & Hathaway Ltd 1987; FCII; *Clubs* City of London; *Style*— Clifford Palmer, Esq; Croft Point, Links Rd, Bramley, Guildford, Surrey; The Corn Exchange, 52-57 Mark Lane, London EC3R 7NE (☎ 01 488 0103, fax 01 481 4995)

PALMER, David Vereker; s of Brig Julian William Palmer (d 1977), and Lena Elizabeth, *née* Vereker (d 1941); *b* 9 Dec 1926; *Educ* Stowe; *m* 10 June 1950, Mildred (Millie), da of Edward Asbury O'Neal (d 1977), of Alabama, USA; 3 da (Melanie (Mrs Montague-Evans) b 29 June 1951, Alice (Mrs Parsons) b 12 May 1959, Katherine b 21 Feb 1962); *Career* Capt Life Gds 1944-49, served in Europe and Middle East; with Edward Lumley & Sons 1949-59 (mangr NY off 1953-59); joined Willis Faber & Dumas Ltd 1959: dir 1961, ptnr 1965, dep chm 1972, chief exec 1978, chm 1982, ret 1988; chm Br Insur and Investmt Brokers Assoc 1987-89, pres Insur Inst of London 1985-86; cmmr Royal Hosp Chelsea 1980-88; Freeman City of London 1980, memb Worshipful Co of Insurers (Master 1982); ACII 1950, memb Lloyd's 1953; *Recreations* farming, shooting; *Clubs* City of London, Cavalry and Guards'; *Style*— David Palmer Esq; Burrow Farm, Hambleden, nr Henley-on-Thames, Oxon RG9 6LT (☎ 0491 571256); 18 Whaddon House, William Mews, London SW1X 9HG (☎ 01 235 7900); Ten Trinity Square, London EC3P 9AX (☎ 01 488 8111, fax 01 488 8223, telex 882141)

PALMER, Hon Mrs (Dorothy Cecily Sybil); *née* Loder; da of 1 Baron Wakehurst, and Lady Louise Beauclerk, da of 10 Duke of St Albans; *b* 1896; *m* 1922, Hon Lewis Palmer (d 1971), yst s of 2 Earl of Selborne, KG, GCMG, PC, by Lady Maud Cecil, da of 3 Marquess of Salisbury (the Cons PM); 1 s, 1 da; *Style*— The Hon Mrs Palmer; St Michel, Rue à l'Or, St Saviours, Guernsey, CI

PALMER, Felicity Joan; *b* 6 April 1944; *Educ* Erith GS, Guildhall Sch of Music and Drama (AGSM, FGSM), Hochschule für Musik Munich; *Career* mezzo-soprano; Kathleen Ferrier Meml Prize 1970; major appearances at concerts in: Britain, America, Belgium, France, Germany, Italy, Spain, Poland, Czechoslovakie, Russia; operatic appearances: London and throughout England, Paris, Bordeaux, Houston, USA, Bern, Zürich, Frankfurt, Hanover, Vienna; recordings with maj rec cos incl recital records and two Victorian ballad records; *Style*— Miss Felicity Palmer; 27 Fielding Rd, London W4 1HP

PALMER, Sir Geoffrey Christopher John; 12 Bt (E 1660); s of Lt-Col Sir Geoffrey Frederick Neill Palmer, 11 Bt (d 1951); *b* 30 June 1936; *Educ* Eton; *m* 1957, Clarissa Mary, da of Stephen Villiers-Smith; 4 da; *Heir* bro, Jeremy Charles Palmer; *Career* is a patron of two livings; *Style*— Sir Geoffrey Palmer, Bt; Carlton Curlieu Hall, Leicestershire (☎ 053 759 2656)

PALMER, Cdr Geoffrey Inderwick; s of John Henry Palmer (d 1954), of Rustington, Sussex, and Louisa, *née* Inderwick (d 1964); *b* 2 Jan 1913; *Educ* St Paul's; *m* 3 April 1943, Diana Millicent (d 1985), da of Arthur Cecil Fitzroy Plantagenet Somerset (d 1955), of Castle Goring, Worthing; 3 da (Juliet Elizabeth b 1945, Anthea Somerset b 1947, Catherine Annabella Inderwick b 1952); *Career* joined RN 1930; various sea and shore appts incl: Br mil mission to USSR 1941-43, sec to Adm Sir Geoffrey Miles 1949-57; ret as cdr 1961; underwriting memb Lloyds, former farmer, currently a picture dealer; *Recreations* shooting, the arts; *Clubs* MCC; *Style*— Commander Geoffrey Palmer; The Treasurer's House, Martock, Somerset (☎ 0935 823 288)

PALMER, Gerald Marley; s of Percy William Ernest Palmer (d 1932), of Bulawayo, S Rhodesia, and Esther, *née* Marley (d 1974); *b* 20 Jan 1911; *Educ* Milton HS S Rhodesia, London Univ (BSc); *m* 6 May 1939, Diana Fleetwood, da of Cornelius Percy Varley (d 1936), of Enfield; 1 da (Celia Fleetwood); *Career* Corpl Home Gd; apprenticeship Scammell Lorries Ltd 1927-38, Morris Motors Ltd 1938-42, Jowett Cars Ltd (designed Jowett Javelin car) 1942-49, tech dir Morris Motors 1949-55, asst chief engr Vauxhall Motors Ltd 1955-72, dir F J Payne (Mfrg) Ltd (designing equipment for disabled people) 1972-88; pres and chm Local Cons Assoc; CEng, FIMechE; *Recreations* sailing, vintage car racing; *Style*— Gerald Palmer, Esq; Orchard House, 4 Tree Lane, Iffley, Oxford (☎ 0865 779222)

PALMER, Col the Hon Sir Gordon William Nottage; KCVO (1989), OBE (1957, MBE 1944), TD (1950), JP (Berks 1956); s of 2 Baron Palmer (d 1950), and Marguerite (d 1959), da of William McKinley Osborne, of Boston, USA; hp of bro, 3 Baron Palmer, OBE; *b* 18 July 1918; *Educ* Eton, Christ Church Oxford (MA); *m* 6 May 1950, Lorna Eveline Hope, da of Maj Charles William Hugh Bailie (d 1978), of Manderston, Duns, Berwickshire; 2 s (Adrian b 1951, Mark b 1954); *Career* serv WWII, Berks Yeo 1939-41, Staff Capt RA, HQ 61 Div 1941, DAQMG Malta 1942, GSO2 ops GHQ Middle East 1943-44, Lt-Col instr Staff Coll Camberley, GSO2 HQ Div 1944-45; dir of cos and pt-t soldier; cmd Berks Yeo 1954-56, Hon Col Royal Yeo 1972-75, Hon Col 2 Bn The Wessex Regt 1983-85; chm Cake and Biscuit Alliance 1957-59, md Huntley & Palmers Ltd 1959-69, chm Assoc Biscuit Mfrs (renamed Huntley Palmer Foods) 1978-83, vice-chm Morlands Brewery 1983-; dir S Midlands Regional Bd Lloyds Bank plc 1976-; memb: cncl RCM 1955 (chm 1974-87), cncl Reading Univ 1954-75 (tres 1955-59, pres 1972-75), Br Nat Export Cncl 1966-69; warden Bradfield Coll 1984-; High Sheriff Berks 1965; DL Berks 1960, Vice-Lord Lt 1976, Lord-Lt 1978-; American Bronze Star 1944; FRCM 1965, FRAM 1983; Hon LLD Reading 1975; KStJ 1978; *Recreations* music, shooting, gardening; *Clubs* Cavalry and Guards'; *Style*— The Hon Gordon Palmer, OBE, TD, JP; Harris House, Mortimer, Berkshire RG7 3NT (☎ 0734 332317); Edrom Newton, Duns, Berwickshire TD11 3PU (☎ 089081 292)

PALMER, Hon Henry William; s of Viscount Wolmer (s of 3 Earl of Selborne (ka 1942), and Priscilla (*see Baron Newton*), and bro of 4 Earl); *b* 12 July 1941; *Educ* Eton, Christ Church Oxford (MA); *m* 1968, Minette, da of Sir Patrick William Donner, of Hurstbourne Park, Whitchurch, Hants; 3 s, 1 da; *Career* Ford Motor Co 1963-66, Assoc Industl Consits 1966-68, md The Centre for Interfirm Comparison 1985- (joined 1968, dep dir 1975); *Style*— The Hon Henry Palmer; Burhunt Farm, Selborne, Alton, Hants GU34 3LP (☎ 042050 209)

PALMER, Jeremy Charles; s of Lt-Col Sir Geoffrey Frederick Neill Palmer, 11 Bt (d 1951), and hp of bro, Sir Geoffrey Palmer, 12 Bt; *b* 16 May 1939; *Educ* Eton, Tours Univ; *m* 24 July 1968, Antonia, da of late Astley Dutton; 2 s; *Career* dir Laytons Wine Co; *Recreations* shooting, tennis; *Clubs* Queen's, Pratts; *Style*— Jeremy Palmer Esq; Lewesdon House, Stoke Abbott, Beaminster, Dorset; Laytons, 20 Midland Rd, London NW1 (☎ 01 388 5081)

PALMER, Sir John Chance; DL (1984 Devon); s of Ernest Clephan Palmer (d 1954), and Claudine Pattie Sapey; *b* 21 Mar 1920; *Educ* St Paul's, St Edmund Hall Oxford (MA); *m* 1945, Mary Winifred, da of Arthur Sidney Ellyatt, OBE (d 1973); 4 s; *Career* WWII RNVR 1939-46, serv Atlantic and Med; slr 1948; conslt Bevan Ashford (Tiverton, Exeter, Credition, Bristol and Swindon); memb cncl of Law Soc of England and Wales 1963 (pres 1978-79); govr Coll of Law 1965; pres: Devon and Exeter Law Soc 1972, S Western Law Soc 1973; chm: govrs Blundells Sch, cncl Exeter Univ, memb: Criminal Injuries Compensation bd 1981-, SW Region Mental Health Tbnl 1983-; Hon LLD Exeter 1980; kt 1979; *Style*— Sir John Palmer, DL; Hensleigh, Tiverton, Devon EX16 5NJ (☎ 0884 252959); Sunnycote, Riverside, Shaldon, Devon (☎ 0626 87 2350); 95 Cliffords Inn, Fetter Lane EC4 (☎ 01 831 7053)

PALMER, Sir John Edward Somerset; 8 Bt (GB 1791); s of Sir John Palmer, 7 Bt, DL (d 1963); *b* 27 Oct 1926; *Educ* Canford, Pembroke Coll Cambridge, Durham Univ; *m* 1956, Dione Catharine, da of Charles Duncan Skinner; 1 s, 1 da; *Heir* s, Robert John Hudson Palmer; *Career* Lt RA serv India; Colonial Agric Serv N Nigeria 1952-61; sr exec R A Lister & Co Ltd Dursley Glos 1962-63, min Overseas Devpt 1964-68, ind conslt 1969-79, dir Atkins Land and Water Mgmnt 1979-87; *Recreations* sailing, fishing, shooting; *Style*— Sir John Palmer, Bt; Gayton House, Gayton, Northampton (☎ 0604 858336)

PALMER, Dr Keith Francis; s of Frank Palmer (d 1987), of Cardiff, and Gwenda Evelyn, *née* Merrick; *b* 26 July 1947; *Educ* Howardian HS Cardiff, Birmingham Univ (BSc, PhD), Cambridge Univ (DDE); *m* 10 Aug 1974, Penelope Ann, *née* McDonagh; 4 da (Alexandra b 1977, Georgia b 1979, Katherine b 1981, Megan b 1982); *Career* NATO post-doctoral res fell Lamont Geophysical Observatory NY 1971-73, first asst sec fin Miny Papua New Guinea 1974-78, dir corp fin N M Rothschild & Sons Ltd 1984-; FGS 1987, memb RIIA 1984; *Recreations* geology, gemmology, music; *Clubs* IOD; *Style*— Dr Keith Palmer; New Court, St Swithins La, London, EC$ (☎ 01 280 5000)

PALMER, Lady Laura; *née* Elliot-Murray-Kynynmound; da of 6 Earl of Minto, MBE; *b* 11 Mar 1956; *m* 23 Feb 1984, John Reginald David Palmer, yr s of William Alexander Palmer, of Phillips Hall, Newbury, Berks; 2 s; *Style*— Lady Laura Palmer

PALMER, Leslie Robert; CBE (1964); s of Robert Palmer; *b* 21 August 1910; *Educ* Battersea GS, London Univ; *m* 1937, Mary Crick; 2 s, 1 da; *Career* hon tres and chm fin and admin dept Utd Reformed Church 1973-80; dir-gen defence accounts MOD 1969-72; *Style*— Leslie Palmer, Esq, CBE; 3 Trossachs Drive, Bath BA2 6RP (☎ 0225 61981)

PALMER, Sir (Charles) Mark; 5 Bt (UK 1886); s of Sir Anthony Frederick Mark Palmer, 4 Bt (ka 1941), and Lady (Henriette Alice) Abel Smith, *qv*; *b* 21 Nov 1941,(posthumous); *Educ* Eton; *m* 1976, Hon Catherine Elizabeth Tennant, da of Baron Glenconner; 1 da; *Heir* kinsman, Charles Lionel Palmer; *Career* was a page of honour to HM 1956-59; *Style—* Sir Mark Palmer, Bt; Mill Hill Farm, Sherborne, Northleach, Glos (☎ Windrush 395)

PALMER, Maj-Gen Sir (Joseph) Michael; KCVO; s of late Lt-Col William Robert Palmer, DSO; *b* 17 Oct 1928; *Educ* Wellington, Sandhurst; *m* 1953, Jillean Monica Sherston; 2 s, 1 da; *Career* Def Servs Sec 1982-85; dir Royal Armoured Corps 1978-81, ACS Allied Forces Central Europe 1976-78; Col 14/20 King's Hussars 1981-, Hon Col Duke of Lancasters Own Yeo 1988-; dir Alexander Laing and Cruickshank Mgmnt Servs; chm Copley Marshall & Co; Liveryman Worshipful Co of Salters; FBIM; *Recreations* riding, shooting, music, reading; *Clubs* Cavalry and Guards; *Style—* Maj-Gen Sir Michael Palmer, KCVO; Talbothays Lodge, West Stafford, nr Dorchester, Dorset DT2 8AL

PALMER, Monroe Edward; OBE (1981); s of William Polikoff, of Westcliff, Essex, and Sybil, *née* Gladstein (d 1980); *b* 30 Nov 1938; *Educ* Orange Hill GS; *m* 21 Jan 1962, Susette Sandra, da of Jack Hall, of London; 2 s (John b 1963, Andrew b 1965), 1 da (Fiona b 1981); *Career* sr ptnr Palmer Marshall; cncllr London Borough of Barnet (ldr SLD), tres Lib Pty 1977-83; FCA; *Recreations* politics, riding, fishing, reading; *Clubs* Nat Lib; *Style—* Monroe Palmer; 31 The Vale, London NW11 8SE (☎ 01 455 5140); 5 North End Rd, London NW11 7RJ (☎ 01 458 9281, fax 01 458 9381)

PALMER, Hon Mrs; Hon Patricia Margaret; *née* Feather; da of Baron Feather (Life Peer, d 1976), and Baroness Feather, *qv*; *b* 1934; *Educ* Green Sch Isleworth, French Inst London; *m* 1957, Stanley Lawrence Palmer; 1 s (James b 1966), 1 da (Gillian b 1962); *Recreations* music, travel; *Clubs* Harpenden Tangent; *Style—* The Hon Mrs Palmer; 24 Wheathampstead Rd, Harpenden, Herts

PALMER, Lt-Gen Sir (Charles) Patrick (Ralph); OBE (1974), CBE (1982), KBE (1987); s of Charles Dudley Palmer (d 1965), and Catherine Anne Hughes-Buller (d 1981); *b* 29 April 1933; *Educ* Marlborough, RMA Sandhurst, Staff Coll Camberley, Royal Coll of Def Studies; *m* 1, 19 Dec 1960, Sonia (d 1965), da of Hardy Wigglesworth (d 1944; 1 s (Neil Patrick b 1962); m 2, 3 Sept 1966, Joanna, da of Col Peter Stanhope Baines (d 1975); 2 da (Iona Catherine b 1967, Alison Joanna b 1969); *Career* cmmnd Argyll & Sutherland Highlanders 1953; served 1 Bn: Br Guiana, Berlin, Suez Operation, Cyprus, Borneo, Singapore, Aden; reformed & cmd First Bn A & SH 1972-74; chief of staff Hong Kong 1974-76; cdr 7 Armoured Bde 1977-78; cdr Br Mil & Advsy Trg Team Zimbabwe 1980-82; GOC NE Dist & Cdr 2 Inf Div 1982-84; Cmdt Staff Coll 1984-86; Mil Sec 1986-; Col A&SH 1982-; *Recreations* travel, outdoor interests; *Clubs* Army and Navy; *Style—* Lt-Gen Sir Patrick Palmer, OBE, CBE, KBE; c/o Royal Bank of Scotland, Drummond Street, Comrie, Perthshire, Scotland; Ministry of Defence, Whitehall, London

PALMER, Maj-Gen Philip Francis; CB (1957), OBE (1945); s of Lt-Col Francis James Palmer (d 1950); *b* 8 August 1903; *Educ* Trinity Coll Dublin, Durham Univ (BCh); *Career* Lt RAMC 1926, serv WWII 1939-45, Brig 1955, DMS MELF (Temp Maj-Gen) 1955-56, DDMS Northern Command, ret 1960; QHS 1956-60; Col Cmdt RAMC 1963-68; *Style—* Maj-Gen Philip Palmer, CB, OBE; c/o Holt Branch, Royal Bank of Scotland, Whitehall, London SW1

PALMER, Philip Stuart; s of Archdale Stuart Palmer (d 1932), of 18 Stanford Ave, Brighton, and Martha Phebe, *née* Ashdown (d 1939); *b* 2 July 1906; *Educ* Cheltenham, Brighton Tech Coll; *m* 10 July 1931, Sybil Madeline Conway (d 1973), da of the late Reginald Henry Cox, of 49 Tivoli Cres, Brighton; 2 s (Christopher b 1935, Philip b 1939); *Career* Ceylon Engrs CO railway workshop gp, Capt 1942, Maj 1942 (demob); pupil Brighton Locomotive Works 1925-28, asst to works mangr Southern Railway; Ceylon Govt Railway: asst mech engr 1931-38, dep mech engr 1938-47, actg chief mech engr 1945-46; Freeman Fox & Ptnrs: mech engr London 1948-68, sr railway engr 1969-71; City & Guilds of London Inst: memb of cncl 1958-76, jt hon sec 1969-75; Soc of Sussex Downsmen: cncl memb 1962-70, 1980-88, hon gen sec 1984-88; Freeman City of London 1927, Liveryman Worshipful Co of Mercers' 1927; CEng, FIMechE 1948; *Style—* Philip Palmer, Esq; 46 Berriedale Ave, Hove, East Sussex BN3 4JJ (☎ 0273 725 850)

PALMER, Hon Ralph Matthew; s and h of Baroness Lucas of Crudwell, and Lady Dingwall (in her own right), and Maj Hon Robert Jocelyn Palmer, MC; *b* 7 June 1951; *Educ* Eton, Balliol Coll Oxford; *m* 1978, Clarissa Marie, da of George Vivian Lockett, TD, of Stratford Hills, Stratford St Mary, Colchester; 1 s (b 1987), 1 da (Hannah Rachel Elise b 1984); *Style—* The Hon Ralph Palmer

PALMER, 3 Baron (UK 1933); Sir Raymond Cecil Palmer; 3 Bt (UK 1916), OBE (1968); s of 2 Baron Palmer (d 1950, gs of Samuel Palmer, a fndr of Huntley & Palmers, the purveyors of biscuits); *b* 24 June 1916; *Educ* Harrow, Univ Coll Oxford; *m* 1941, Victoria Ellen, da of late Capt Joseph Arthur Ronald Weston-Stevens, of Woolley Cottage, The Thicket, Maidenhead; 2 da (and 1 da decd); *Heir* bro, Col Hon Gordon William Nottage Palmer; *Career* Lt Gren Gds 1940-43; dir Assoc Biscuit Mfrs Ltd until 1980; chm: Huntley & Palmers Ltd 1969-80, Huntley Boorne & Stevens Ltd Reading 1956-80 (dep chm 1948); pres Berks CC; memb Southern Electricity Bd 1965-77; *Recreations* music; *Clubs* Cavalry and Guards'; *Style—* The Rt Hon the Lord Palmer, OBE; Farley Hill House, Farley Hill, Reading, Berkshire (☎ 0734 732260); Higher Moor, North Hill, Minehead, Somerset (☎ 0643 2360)

PALMER, Richard John; JP (1961); s of Reginald Howard Reed Palmer (d 1970); *b* 5 Nov 1926; *Educ* Eton; *m* 1951, Sarah Faith Georgina, da of 1 Viscount Churchill, GCVO (d 1934); 3 s, 1 da; *Career* dir Assoc Biscuit Mfrs, High Sheriff of Berks 1979-80; *Recreations* shooting, fishing; *Clubs* White's; *Style—* Richard Palmer Esq, JP; Queen Annes Mead, Swallowfield, Berks (☎ 0734 883264)

PALMER, His Hon Judge Robert Henry Stephen; s of Henry Alleyn Palmer (d 1965), and Maud Palmer, *née* Obbard (d 1973); *b* 13 Nov 1927; *Educ* Charterhouse, Univ Coll Oxford (MA); *m* 1955, Geraldine Elizabeth Anne, da of George Evan Evens (d 1950); 1 s (George), 2 da (Nicola, Katharine); *Career* barr 1950; dep chm Berks QS 1970; rec Crown Ct 1972-78, circuit judge 1978-, resident judge Acton Crown Ct; pres Mental Health Review Tbnl; *Recreations* self-sufficiency; *Style—* His Hon Judge Palmer; 44 Staveley Rd, Chiswick W4 3ES (☎ 01 994 3394)

PALMER, Maj Hon Robert Jocelyn; MC, JP (Hants), DL (1982); s of late 3 Earl of Selborne by 1 w, Hon Grace, da of 1 Viscount Ridley, and Hon Mary Marjoribanks, da of 1 Baron Tweedmouth; *b* 1919; *Educ* Winchester, Balliol Coll Oxford; *m* 1950, Baroness Lucas of Crudwell (in her own right), *qv*; 2 s, 1 da; *Career* late Maj Coldstream Gds, Italy (despatches) 1939-45; *Style—* Major The Hon Robert Palmer, MC, JP, DL; The Old House, Wonston, Winchester, Hants

PALMER, Robert John Hudson; s and h of Sir John Edward Somerset Palmer, 8 Bt, and Dione Catherine Palmer, *née* Skinner, of Gayton, Northampton; *b* 20 Dec 1960; *Educ* St Edward's Sch Oxford, Grey Coll Durham Univ (BA), Cambridge Univ (BA); *Career* chartered surveyor; *Recreations* rowing, yachting, skiing; *Clubs* Lansdowne; *Style—* Robert Palmer, Esq; Gayton House, Gayton, Northampton NN7 3EZ; 44 Brook Street, London W1Y 1YB (☎ 01 408 1161)

PALMER, Roger James Hume Dorney; s of Lt-Col Philip Dayrell Stewart Palmer (d 1979), of Dorney Ct, Bucks, and Aileen Frances, *née* Cook (d 1983); *b* 21 Mar 1947; *Educ* Eton, Gonville and Caius Coll Cambridge (BA); *m* 30 June 1979, Teresa (Tsa) Mary, da of Maj-Gen Reginald Henry Whitworth, CB, CBE, *qv*; 2 da (Susannah b 28 June 1984, Lara b 28 April 1986); *Career* ptnr Grieveson Grant & Co 1980-86; dir: Kleinwort Benson Ltd 1986-, Kleinwort Benson Securities 1986-; memb: London Stock Exchange 1980, Lloyds 1987; fndr: Palmer Milburn Beagles 1971, Berks & Bucks Draghounds 1974; tres Cambridge Sheep Soc; *Recreations* wolves, beagling, draghunting, wildlife photography; *Clubs* Groucho; *Style—* Roger Palmer, Esq; Kleinwort Benson, 20 Fenchurch St, London EC3

PALMER, Hon Mrs (Sarah Faith Georgina); *née* Spencer; da of 1 Viscount Churchill, GCVO (d 1934); *b* 5 June 1931; *m* 17 Dec 1951, Richard John Palmer, JP, yr s of Reginald Howard Reed Palmer, MC, of Hurst Grove, nr Reading, Berks; 3 s, 1 da; *Career* memb Berks CC 1981; *Style—* The Hon Mrs Palmer; Queen Anne's Mead, Swallowfield, Berks

PALMER, Sidney John; CB (1972), OBE (1953); s of Sidney Palmer (d 1919); *b* 29 Nov 1913; *Educ* Royal Dockyard Sch, RNC Greenwich; *m* 1941, Mavis Beatrice Blennerhassett, da of Jeremiah Hallett, of Plymouth; 4 s; *Career* chief constructor: Sydney 1945, Hong Kong 1946; prof of naval architecture RNC 1952-57, dep dir-gen Ships MOD 1968-73 (dir ship prodn 1966-67, head Royal Corps of Naval Construdors 1968-74); memb: Cncl RINA 1960, mgmnt ctee RNLI 1975; Liveryman & Worshipful Co of Shipwrights 1968; *Style—* Sidney Palmer Esq, CB, OBE; Bloomfield Ave, Bath, Avon (☎ 0225 312592)

PALMER, Hon Timothy John; s of Baroness Lucas, of Crudwell, and Dingwall; *b* 10 April 1953; *Educ* Eton, Balliol Oxford; *m* 1984, (Adèle Cristina) Sophia, 4 da of Lt-Col Hon Henry Anthony Camillo Howard, CMG (d 1977); 1 s (Henry Jocelyn b 2 Jan 1987), 2 da (Nan Cristina b 9 Sept 1985, Isabella Spring b 8 Feb 1989); *Style—* The Hon Timothy Palmer; West Woodyates Manor Farm, Salisbury, Wilts (☎ 07255 321)

PALMER, Maj-Gen Tony Brian; CB (1984); s of Sidney Bernard Palmer, and Ann, *née*Watkins; *b* 5 Nov 1930; *Educ* Luton Techn Coll, Gen Motors Inst of Techn (USA); *m* 1953, Hazel Doris Robinson; 2 s; *Career* cmmnd REME 1954, held various cmd and staff appts 1954-74, head of tech intelligence (Army) 1974-76, dir Orgn and Trg 1977-79, cdr Arborfield Garrison 1979-82, Col Cmdt REME 1985-, dir gen of electrical and mech engrg (Army) 1983-86 (conslt 1986); *Recreations* gardening, history, bird watching; *Clubs* Army and Navy; *Style—* Maj-Gen T B Palmer, CB; c/o Barclays Bank, 6 Market Place, Newbury, Berks

PALMER, William Alexander; CBE (1983); s of Reginald Howard Reed Palmer, MC, DL (d 1970), of Hurst Grove, nr Reading, Berks, and Lena Florence Palmer, *née* Cobham (d 1981); *b* 21 June 1925; *Educ* Eton; *m* 1949, Cherry Ann, da of late Arthur Gibbs (d 1945), of Sheffield Terr, London; 2 s, 2 da; *Career* serv Gren Gds 1943-47, Capt, serv NW Europe and Palestine; dir Huntley & Palmers Ltd 1951 (chm 1980-83), dir Huntley & Palmers Foods plc 1971-83, chm Huntley Broone & Stevens Ltd until 1983; pres: Flour Milling and Baking Res Assoc 1971-84, Royal Warrant Holders Assoc 1976-77; chm Cake & Biscuit Alliance 1980-83; High Sheriff of Berks 1974-75; tres Reading Univ 1982-; govr: Malvern Girls' Coll 1965-, King Edward's Sch Whitley; Berkshire ccncllr Lambourne Valley; *Recreations* shooting, tennis, gardening; *Clubs* Cavalry and Guards'; *Style—* William Palmer, Esq, CBE; Bussock Wood, Snelsmore Common, nr Newbury, Berks RG16 9BT (☎ 0635 248203); Latheronwheel House, Caithness (☎ 05934 206)

PALMER, William John; CBE (1973); s of William Palmer (d 1942), of Suffolk House, Cheltenham, and Mary Louisa, *née* Dibb (d 1962); *b* 25 April 1909; *Educ* Pate's GS Cheltenham, Christ's Coll Cambridge (MA) ; *m* 1, 29 July 1935, Zenaida (d 1944), da of Nicolai Maropoulo (d 1916), of Yalta, Russia; m 2, 10 Nov 1949, Vanda Ianthe Millicent, da of William Matthew Cowton (d 1970), of Brisbane, Queensland; 1 s (Nigel Arthur William b 1950), 2 da (Caroline Louise b 1951, Deborah Anne b 1954); *Career* barr Gray's Inn; joined ICS 1932, ret 1949; joined Colonial Legal Serv as magistrate Nigeria 1950 (judge 1958), judge of HM Chief Ct for the Persian Gulf 1967-72, memb Ct of Appeal for Anguilla 1973-80; *Recreations* walking, reading; *Clubs* East India; *Style—* William Palmer, Esq, CBE; Guys Farm, Icomb, Cheltenham, Glos GL54 1JD (☎ 0451 30219)

PAMPLIN, Terence Michael; s of Leslie Cecil Pamplin, and Edith Mary, *née* Hayes; *b* 30 May 1941; *Educ* Middx Poly, Hatfield Mgmnt Sch (Ba), LRAM, LTCL); *m* 15 March 1969, Elizabeth Ann, da of Richard Webb; 2 da (Iona b 1971, Kim b 1971); *Career* dir Arnold Dolmetsch Ltd 1973-77; head dept of music technol London Coll of Furniture 1983- (joined 1977); dir Early Musical Investmt Makers Assoc (past pres), fndr Nonsuch Guitar Soc (past chm); memb: Waverley BC, City & Guilds of London Inst, FIMIT (past pres), MIOA, MBIM; *Recreations* playing viol consorts and baroque trio sonatas, hill walking; *Clubs* City Livery, Musician Livery; *Style—* Terence M Pamplin, Esq; Little Critchmere, Manor Crescent, Haslemere, Surrey GO27 1PB (☎ 0428 51158); Dept of Music Technology, London Coll of Furniture, 41 Commercial Rd, London E1 1LA (☎ 01 247 1953)

PANAYIDES, HE Tasos Christou; s of Christos Panayides, and Efrosini Papageorghiou; *b* 9 April 1934; *Educ* Paphos gymnasium, teacher trg Coll Univ of London (Dip Ed), Univ of Indiana USA (MA, Dip Pub Admin); *m* 1969, Pandora, da of Georghios Constantinides, of Dramas No 8, Nicosia; 2 s (Alexandros b 1971, George b 1972), 1 da (Froso-Elena b 1976); *Career* teacher 1954-59; first sec to Pres 1960-68, dir Pres's Off 1969, ambass of Cyprus to: Fed Rep of Germany, Switzerland, Austria and Atomic Energy Organization, Vienna 1969-78; high cmmr of Cyprus in UK (ambass to Sweden, Norway, Denmark and Iceland) 1979-; chm: Cwlth Fndn Grants Ctee 1986-87, Cwlth Fund for Tech Co-operation 1986-8; hon fell Ealing Coll Higher Ed; Freeman City of London 1984; Grand Cross with a Star of Sash of the Fed Rep of Germany 1978, Grand Cross in Gold with Star and Sash of the Rep of Austria 1979, Golden Cross of the Archdiocese of Thyateira and Gt Britain, Grand Cross in Gold of the Patriarchate of Antioch; *Recreations* reading, history, swimming; *Style—* HE Tasos C Panayides; 5 Cheyne Walk, London SW3 (☎ 01 351 3989); Cyprus High Commission, 93 Park Street, London W1Y 4ET (☎ 01 499 2810, telex 263 343, fax

491 0691)

PANCKRIDGE, Surgn Vice-Adm Sir (William) Robert (Silvester); KBE (1962), CB (1960); s of W P Panckridge, OBE, MB, MRCS, LRCP; *b* 11 Sept 1901; *Educ* Tonbridge, Middx Hosp; *m* 1932, Edith Muriel (d 1983), da of Sir John Crosbie, of St John, Newfoundland; 1 da; *Career* PMO RN Coll Dartmouth 1948, med offr-in-charge RN Hosp Hong Kong 1952, RN Hosp Chatham 1958, Surgn Capt 1952, Surgn Rear-Adm 1958, Surgn Vice-Adm 1960, QHP 1958-63, med dir-gen of the Navy 1960-63; CStJ 1958; FRSM; *Style*— Surgn Vice-Adm Sir Robert Panckridge, KBE, CB; Waterfall Lodge, Oughterard, Co Galway, Eire (☎ 010 353 9182168)

PANDEY, HE Ishwari Raj; Hon GCVO (1986); s of Hemraj Panditgue (d 1953), Royal Preceptor (Raj Guru), of Kathmandu, Nepal, and Khaga Kumari, *née* Rgmi; ggggf resumed position of Royal Preceptor after helping the royal family to safety after the Kot episode, early 18th cent; *b* 15 August 1934; *Educ* Patna Univ India (BA), Bombay Univ India (MA), Pittsburgh Univ (MPIA); *m* 3 March 1953, Gita, da of Maj-Gen Chet Shumsher Jung Bahadur Rana (d 1948); 3 s (Bidhan, Bigyan, Siddhant), 2 da (Kabita, Amita); *Career* under-sec Govt of Nepal 1959-64 (dir undersec 1964-68), undersec Min of Foreign Affrs 1968-72, dep head of mission Royal Nepalese Embassy London 1968-72, and NY 1972-74, first sec Nepalese Mission to UN 1972 and 1975, head of mission Teheran 1974-79, jt sec Min Foreign Affrs, Kathmandu 1979-80, Min Nepalese Embassy New Delhi 1980-83, Nepalese Ambass London 1983- (also accredited to Denmark, Finland, Norway, Iceland and Sweden); decorated with Prasiddha Probala Gorakha-Dakshina Nepal, Vikhyat Trishakti Patta, Long Service Medal, King of Bhutan Coronation Medal; *Books* Economic Impact of Tourist Industry (1965); *Recreations* reading, travel; *Clubs* Hurlingham, Travellers'; *Style*— HE The Nepalese Ambassador; 12A Kensington Palace Gardens, London W8 4QU (☎ 01 229 4536)

PANK, Maj-Gen (John) David Graham; s of Edward Graham Pank (d 1982), of Deddington, Oxon, and Margaret Sheelah, *née* Snowball; *b* 2 May 1935; *Educ* Uppingham; *m* 27 July 1963, Julia Letitia, da of Col Michael Black Matheson, OBE, of Hurstbourne Tarrant, Andover; 2 s (William b 1965, Edward b 1970) 1 da (Victoria b 1964); *Career* cmmnd KSLI 1958, GSO3 ops HQ 99 Gurkha Bde 1965-66, Bde Maj HQ 24 Bde 1969-71, GSO1 Staff Coll 1973-74, CO 3 Bn LI 1974-76, asst dir def policy MOD 1977-79, Cdr LF 1983-85, dir gen personal servs (Army) 1985-88, appointed Col LI 1987, dir of inf 1988; pres: Army Cricket 1987, Combined Servs Cricket 1988; *Recreations* fishing, cricket, racing; *Clubs* Army and Navy IZ, Free Foresters, Mount (pres), Mounted Inf (chm); *Style*— Maj-Gen David Pank; c/o Royal Bank of Scotland, Holts Branch, Whitehall, London, SW1A 2EB

PANK, Edward Charles; s of Charles Clifford Pank (d 1974), of Norwich, and Marjorie Eira, *née* Bringloe, (d 1988); *b* 5 June 1945; *Educ* Framlingham Coll, Trinity Hall Cambridge (MA), St Thomas's Hosp London Univ (MB BS); *m* 17 Sept 1983, (Judith) Clare, da of Anthony Pethick Sommerville, of Frampton-on-Severn; *Career* slr 1969; dir Slater Walker Ltd 1970-76, co slr and sec Exco Int plc 1987-; memb Soc of Apothecaries 1986; MRCS, LRCP; *Style*— Edward Pank, Esq; Exco Int plc, 80 Cannon Street, London EC4N 6LS

PANK, Philip Durrell; s of Col P E D Pank, RAMC (d 1964), and Anne Roscoe Pank, *née* Thornely; *b* 3 Nov 1933; *Educ* Wellington Coll Berks, Architectural Assoc (Dip Arch); *m* 30 March 1962, Patricia Ann, da of Maj Ralph Maxwell Middleton, Black Watch (d 1967), of Harare, Zimbabwe; 2 s (William b 1965, Philip b 1970), 2 da (Sarah b 1963, Anna b 1970); *Career* Nat Serv, Northumberland Fus 1959-60; architect and painter in private practice 1965-; work incl: nurseries for Save the Children Fund, private houses for Harvey Unna (Highgate) and Harold Cooper (Hampstead Village), thermal power station for NEKA Iran 1977, Sari apartments complex Iran 1977, Banchi Technol Univ Nigeria 1981 (winner of limited competition), Mastmaker Ct workshops and offs for Pirin Ltd (Isle of Dogs) 1987, shopping complex Barnstaple High Street for Bullsmoor 1987; *Recreations* drawing, nature, travel; *Style*— Philip D Pank, Esq; 15 Torriano Cottages, London NW5 2TA (☎ 01 267 1199); Pan Goss Associates, 116 Grafton Road, London NW5 4BA (☎ 01 482 0400, telex 922 488 REFGOS)

PANKHURST, Air Vice-Marshal Leonard Thomas; CB (1955), CBE (1944); s of late Thomas William Pankhurst; *b* 26 August 1902; *Educ* Hampton GS; *m* 1939, Ruth, da of late Alexander Phillips; 1 s, 2 da; *Career* joined RAF 1925, WWII 1939-45 (despatches), Gp Capt, 1942, Air Cdre 1947, Actg Air Vice-Marshal 1954, dir-gen of personnel (I) Air Miny, 1954-57, ret; *Style*— Air Vice-Marshal Leonard Pankhurst, CB, CBE; Earl's Eye House, 8 Sandy Lane, Chester CH3 5UL (☎ 0244 20993)

PANNELL, Donald Roy; s of Harold Thomas Pannell (d 1973), of Southernlea, Totteridge, London, and Gladys Louisa, *née* Price (d 1980); *b* 14 Jan 1926; *Educ* Highgate Sch, Hertford Coll Oxford; *m* 11 June 1949, Eileen Eunice, da of John Herbert Haynes (d 1969), of Ravenscroft Pk, Barnet, Herts; 1 da (Jacqueline b 31 Aug 1951); *Career* RAC 1944-47; dir A Pannell Ltd Gp of Cos 1954-, chm Pannell (Properties) Ltd 1973 (dir 1960); fndr memb Nat Assoc of Waste Disposal Contractors (chm E Anglia region 1975-85, life memb 1985), memb Nat Assoc of Warehouse Keepers (memb Nat Cncl); Freeman City of London 1967, Liveryman Worshipful Co of Makers of Playing Cards 1967; MCIT, MILDM, MIOD; *Recreations* golf; *Clubs* South Herts GC; *Style*— Donald Pannell, Esq; 42 Lyonsdown Ave, New Barnet, Herts EN5 1DX (☎ 01 440 1568); A Pannell Ltd, 779/781 Finchley Rd, London NW11 8DN (☎ 01 458 9458, fax 01 458 7344)

PANNELL, Gordon Dennis; s of Harold Thomas Pannell (d 1972), and Gladys Louisa, *née* Price (d 1980); *b* 12 Nov 1930; *Educ* Highgate; *m* 28 July 1956, Stella Rose, Frederick Morris Roberts (d 1973); 2 s (Duncan b 1957, Malcolm b 1959), 1 da (Helen b 1963); *Career* Nat Serv REME; co dir (tport); chm 1972 Pannell Gp of Cos 1972 (dir 1951); fndr (past capt) Rd Haulage Assoc; memb Inst Tport, life memb IOD, Grand Lodge offr; *Recreations* golf, freemasonry; *Clubs* South Herts Golf; *Style*— Gordon D Pannell, Esq; Meadow View, The Pastures, Totteridge, London N20 8AN (☎ 01 445 7580); A Pannell Ltd, 779/781 Finchley Rd, London NW11 8DN (☎ 01 458 9458)

PANNETT, Juliet Kathleen; da of Charles Somers (d 1958), and May Relph, *née* Brice (d 1960); *b* 15 July 1911; *Educ* Harvington Coll Ealing, Wistons Sch Brighton, Brighton Coll of Art; *m* 4 Oct 1938, Maj Maurice Richard Dalton Pannett, s of Richard Dalton Pannett (d 1948), of London; 1 s (Denis b 7 Sept 1939), 1 da (Liz b 31 May 1947); *Career* special artist to the Illustrated London News 1957-64; portrait painter; artist: The Times, Daily Telegraph, Radio Times, one man exhibitions: Royal Festival Hall 1957 and 1958, Quantas Gallery 1959, NY 1960, Cleveland Ohio 1960, Cooling Gallery Bond St 1961, Coventry Cathedral Festival 1962, Gloucester Three Choirs Festival 1962, Brighton Corpn Gallery 1967, Arun Art Centre 1967 (1969, 1972, 1985, 1988), Fine Art Gallery London 1969, Mignon Gallery 1970; exhibitor: Royal Acad, Royal Soc of Portrait Painters, Royal Inst of Painters in Watercolours; Permanent collections: Nat Portrait Gallery, Brighton Art Gallery, Hove Art Gallery, Oxford, Cambridge, Maudsley Hosp, Army Physical Trg Sch Aldershot, Painters Hall Edinburgh Univ; portraits cmmnd for: RN, HM The Queen (of HRH Prince Andrew and, HRH Prince Edward), HRH Princess Marina, Lavinia Duchess of Norfolk, 10 PMs, 3 Lord Chief Justices; Freeman: City of London 1960, Worshipful Co of Painter Stainers 1960; FRSA 1960; *Recreations* watercolours, landscape, painting surgical operations; *Style*— Mrs Juliet Pannett; Pound House, Roundstone Lane, Angmering Village, Littlehampton, W Sussex BN16 4AL (☎ 0903 784446)

PANNONE, Rodger John; s of Cyril John Alfred Pannone (d 1982), and Violet Maud, *née* Weekes (d 1987); *b* 20 April 1943; *Educ* St Brendan's Coll Bristol, Manchester Coll of Law, London Coll of Law; *m* 13 Aug 1966, Patricia Jane, da of William Todd; 2 s (Mark b 24 Oct 1969, Richard b 7 Oct 1971), 1 da (Elizabeth b 19 July 1979); *Career* admitted slr 1969; slr Pannone Blackburn (Britain's first disaster practice); plaintiff's lawyer on: Blackburn train crash 1986, Manchester Aircraft disaster 1985, Zeebrugge disaster 1987; chm law and procedure ctee of the Law Soc; memb: Lord Chllr's Advsy Ctee on Civil Justice 1985-88, cncl Law Soc for England and Wales 1978-; past memb Supreme Ct Rule Ctee; dir Employment Relations Assocs Ltd; *Recreations* fell walking, wine and food; *Clubs* St James's (Manchester), Northern Lawn Tennis; *Style*— Rodger Pannone, Esq; 5 Darley Avenue, West Didsbsury, Manchester (☎ 061 445 4342); Pannone Blackburn, Solicitors, 123 Deansgate, Manchester M3 2BU (☎ 061 832 3000, fax 061 834 2067)

PANTCHEFF, Theodore Xenophon Henry; CMG (1977); s of Sophocles Xenophon Pantcheff (d 1949), of Buckhurst Hill, Essex, and Elliot Jessie, *née* Ramsbotham (d 1955); *b* 29 Dec 1920; *Educ* Merchant Taylors', Gonville and Caius Cambridge (MA); *m* 1954, Patricia Mary, *née* Tully; 2 s; *Career* Maj HM Forces Europe 1941-47; control commr for Germany 1948-51; Dip Serv 1951-77; vice-consul Munich 1954-56; first sec: Lagos 1958-60, Leopoldville 1961-63, cnsllr: seconded MOD 1969-71, FCO 1971-77, ret; Jurat of the Court of Alderney 1979; *Books* Alderney Fortress Island (1981), The Emsland Executioner (1987); *Clubs* Carlton, Société Guernsiaise (Guernsey), Alderney Society (Alderney); *Style*— Theodore Pantcheff, Esq, CMG; Butes Cottage, Alderney, Channel Islands (☎ 048 182 3169)

PANTON, Dr Francis Harry; MBE (1948); s of George Emerson Panton; *b* 25 May 1923; *Educ* City Sch Lincoln, Univ Coll, Nottingham Univ; *m* 1952, Audrey Mary, *née* Lane; 2 s; *Career* asst chief scientific advsr (Nuclear) MOD 1969-76, dir of Propellants, Explosives and Rocket Motor Estab Waltham Abbey, Westcott head of rocket motor exec MOD 1976-80, dir Royal Armament R & D Estab Fort Halstead 1980-84; conslt (Cabinet Off, Br Telecom, MOD) 1985-; *Clubs* Reform; *Style*— Dr Francis Panton, MBE; Cantis House, 1 St Peter's Lane, Canterbury, Kent (☎ 0227 452902)

PANUFNIK, Dr Andrzej; s of Tomasz Panufnik (d 1951), of Warsaw, Poland, and Matylda, *née* Thonnes (d 1945); *b* 24 Sept 1914; *Educ* Warsaw State Conservatoire, Vienna State Aca of Music (under Felix Weingartner); *m* 27 Nov 1963, Camilla Ruth, da of Cdr Richard Frederick Jessel, DSO, DSC, OBE, RN, (d 1988), of Bearsted Kent; 1 s (Jeremy b 1969), 1 da (Roxanna b 1968); *Career* composer and conductor; debut as conductor with Warsaw Philharmonic Orch 1936, conductor Cracow Philharmonic Orch 1945-46; musical dir: Polish State Film Prodns 1945-46, Warsaw Philharmonic Orch 1946-47; guest appearances with leading Euro orchs incl: Berlin Philharmonic, London Philharmonic, l'Orchestre Nationale Paris; settled in England 1954, musical dir City of Birmingham Symphony Orch 1957-59, numerous guest appearances with int and London orchs; compositions incl: 10 Symphonies, 3 Cantatas, 3 concertos, orchestral and chamber works; cmmns incl: Yehudi Menuhin Violin Concerto 1972, LSO 75 Anniversary Concerto Festivo 1979 and Concertino 1980, Boston Symphony Orch centenary Sinfonia Votiva 1981, Koussevitsky Fndn Arbor Cosmica 1983, Royal Philharmonic Soc Symphony No 9 1987, Chicago Symphony Orch centenary Symphony No 10 1988; hon RAM 1984, Doctorate London Univ Polish section 1985; memb: Guild of GB, Assoc of Br Composers PRS; *Books* Composing Myself (autobiog 1987); *Recreations* all arts, travelling; *Clubs* Garrick; *Style*— Dr Andrzej Panufnik; Riverside House, Riverside, Twickenham TW1 3DJ (☎ 01 892 1470);

PAO, Sir Yue-Kong; CBE (1976), JP; s of Sui-Loong Pao, JP (d 1982); hon chm World-Wide Shipping Gp, former owner of paper mill in China, moved to Hong Kong to start import-export business 1948); *b* 10 Nov 1918,Chekiang, China,; *Educ* Shanghai China; *m* 1940, Sue-Ing Haung; 4 da; *Career* chm: World-Wide Shipping Gp, The Hong Kong and Kowloon Wharf & Godown Co Ltd, Eastern Asia Navigation Co Ltd, World Int (Hldgs) Ltd, World Maritime Ltd, World Shipping and Investmt Co Ltd, Wheelock Marden Gp, Hong Kong Dragon Airline Ltd; dir Hang Seng Bank Ltd; conslt The Hong Kong and Shanghai Banking Corpn; advsr Industl Bank of Japan Ltd Tokyo; memb: Int Advsy ctee Chase Manhattan Bank NY, Asia/Pacific Advsy cncl American Telephone and Telegraph Int, Pacific Advsy cncl of the Utd Technologies Corpn; JP Hong Kong 1971; kt 1978; *Style*— Sir Yue-Kong Pao, CBE, JP; World-Wide Shipping Agency Ltd, Wheelock House, 6-7 Floors, 20 Pedder St, Hong Kong (☎ 5-8423888)

PAOLOZZI, Prof Sir Eduardo Luigi; CBE (1968); s of Rudolpho Antonio Paolozzi (d 1940), and late Carmella, *née* Rossi; *b* 7 Mar 1924; *Educ* Edinburgh Sch of Art, Slade Sch of Art; *m* 1951, Freda Madge, da of Ernest George Elliott (d 1959); 3 da; *Career* sculptor; tutor in ceramics RCA 1968-, lectr St Martin's Sch of Art 1955-56; Prof of: ceramics Fachhochschule Cologne 1977-81, sculpture Akademie der Bildenden Kunste Munich 1981-; maj works incl: fountain for Festival of Britain 1951, sculpture playground for Sir Terence Conran at Wallingford, cast aluminium doors for Hunterian Gallery at Glasgow Univ, cast iron sculpture Piscator at Euston Sq, mosaics for Tottenham Court Rd underground station, fountain for Garden Exhibition W Berlin 1985, and set design for film Herschel and the music of the Stars 1985; Br Critics Prize 1953, David E Bright Award 1960, Purchase Prize Solomon Guggenheim Museum 1967, Norma and William Copley Fndn Award 1967, First Prize Sculpture Carnegie Int Exhibition 1967, Saltire Soc Award 1975 and 1981, First Prize Rhinegarten Competition Cologne 1980, Grand Prix d'Honneur Int Print Biennale Yugoslavia 1983; Hon DLitt Glasgow 1980, Hon Dr RCA 1979; ARA, RA; kt 1989; *Clubs* Athenaeum; *Style*— Prof Eduardo Paolozzi, CBE; 107 Dovehouse St, London SW3; Akademie der Bildenden Kunste, Akadmiestrasse 2, 8000 Munchen 4, West

Germany

PAPADAKIS, Dr Andreas Constantine; s of Constantine Pavlou Papadakis, of Nicosia, Cyprus, and Natalia Christou (d 1978); *b* 17 June 1938; *Educ* Faraday House (DFH), Imperial Coll London (DIC), Brunel Univ (PhD); *Career* publisher: Acad Edns London 1968-, Architectural Design 1975-; ed: Architectural Design 1977-, Art and Design 1985-; *Recreations* boating ('Thistle'); *Clubs* Chelsea Arts, IOD; *Style*— Dr Andreas C Papadakis; 7 Holland St, London W8 4NA (☎ 01 937 6996); 42 Leinster Gardens, London W2 3AN (☎ 01 402 2141, telex 896928)

PAPADOPOULOS, Achilles Symeon; CMG (1980), LVO (1972), MBE (1954); s of Symeon Papadopoulos (d 1971); *b* 16 August 1923; *Educ* The English Sch Nicosia Cyprus; *m* 1954, Joyce Martin, *née* Stark; 1 s, 2 da; *Career* Dip Serv; HM ambass: El Salvador 1977-79, Mozambique 1979-80, Br high cmmr to Bahamas 1981-83; *Style*— Achilles Papadopoulos, Esq, CMG, LVO, MBE; 14 Mill Close, Great Bookham, Surrey KT23 3JX

PAPPIN, David Frederick; TD (1968); s of Eric Reginald Pappin (d 1979), of Eastbourne, and Evelyn Hope, *née* Pickering; *b* 13 Mar 1935; *Educ* Melville Coll, Edinburgh Univ (MA); *m* 1, 1958 (m dis 1977), Mary Elizabeth (now Mrs M E Towsey) da of George Trevor Norman Prideaux (d 1986), of Petersfield; 2 da (Amanda Ruth (Mrs Borthwick) b 1964, Brenda Claire b 1970); m 2, 30 Oct 1979, Maureen Grace da of Malcolm Henry Harper (d 1979); *Career* Nat Serv REME 1953-55 (cmmnd 1954); TA REME 1955-73 (Capt 1961); trainee actuary Liverpool & London & Globe Insur Co Ltd 1952-53 and 1958-61, res dept D A Bevan Simpson 1961-64; investment mangr: Minerals Separation Ltd 1964-66, Charterhouse Japhet Ltd 1966-67, Banque Belge Ltd 1967-70; ptnr: J & A Scrimgeour 1970-79, De Zoete & Bevan 1979-86; dir Barclays de Zoete Wedd (Gilts) Ltd 1986-88; dir Streets Communications Ltd 1988-; past chm Cobham Conservation Gp, pres Stoke d'Abernon CC; memb: FFA 1963, ASIA 1961; *Recreations* golf, barbershop singing; *Clubs* Gresham (past chm), MCC; *Style*— David Pappin, Esq, TD; West Dean, 58 Fairmile Lane, Cobham, Surrey KT11 2DE (☎ 0932 63535); 18 Red Lion Court, London EC4A 3HT (☎ 011 353 1090, fax 01 583 0661, telex 21827)

PAPPIN, Flt Lt Veryan Guy Henry; s of John Henry Pappin, of Mistletoe Cottage, 3 New Exeter St, Chudleigh, Devon, and Priscilla Cecil, *née* Pilditch; *b* 19 May 1958; *Educ* Dover Coll, Kelly Coll Tavistock, Luke's Coll Exeter Univ 1977-80 (BEd); *Career* joined RAF 1980, RAF Coll Cranwell 1981 flying offr physical educn branch; station physical educn offr: RAF Kinloss 1981-82, RAF Coll Cranwell 1982-84, parachute instr Trng Sch RAF Brize Norton 1984-86, RAF Wattisham 1986-; hockey: 37 caps Scotland 1981-; GB 1982-: Bronze Medalist Los Angeles Olympics 1984, Gold Medalist Seoul Olympics 1988; *Recreations* squash, hockey, outdoor activities; *Style*— Flt Lt Veryan Pappin; Officers Mess, RAF Wattisham, Ipswich, Suffolk, IP7 7RA

PAPWORTH, Frank; s of James Papworth (d 1977), and Eva Papworth, *née* Heap (d 1980); *b* 11 Jan 1926; *Educ* Bacup Central Sch; *m* 1950, Alice, da of John Andrew Almond (d 1955), of Rochdale, Lancs; 3 s (Paul, David, Andrew); *Career* dep chm and chief exec Biddle Hldgs plc 1983-, chm FH Biddle Ltd 1984, chm Mumford Bailey & Preston Ltd 1984-, chm and md Bennie Lifts Ltd; hon gen sec The Berean Publishing Tst, hon sec The Berean Forward Movement; tstee Chapel of the Opened Book; FCIS, FBIM, ASCA; *Style*— Frank Papworth, Esq; Shalom, 6 Manor Drive, Baston, Peterborough PE6 9PQ (☎ 077 86 328); Bennie Lifts Ltd, Queens Walk, Peterborough

PARAVICINI, Dennis Stewart; OBE (1977); s of John Paravicini, JP (d 1961), and Winifred Marian, *née* Stewart-Brown (d 1964); *b* 1 Oct 1930; *Educ* Stowe, Caius Coll Cambridge (MA); *m* 1963, Sally Vivienne, da of Cdr H L Hayes, OBE, RN; 1 s (James b 1976), 2 da (Georgina b 1964, Olivia (d 1974); *Career* Nat Serv Cmmn 5 Royal Inniskilling Dragoon Gds; joined Thomas De La Rue & Co Ltd 1953, md Thomas De la Rue Brasil SA 1960-63; vice-chm Anglo-Swiss Soc 1975-, tstee N Hampshire Med Tst 1978-, co sec the De La Rue Co plc 1980-85, chm Security Express 1980-85; tres Br Security Indust's Assoc 1980-85, CBI London Regnl cncllr 1980-86; chm N Hampshire Cons Assoc 1973-76, md Royal Mint Servs 1985-; *Recreations* travelling, sailing; *Clubs* Utd Oxford & Cambridge; *Style*— Dennis Paravicini, Esq, OBE; Street Ho, Bramley, Nr Basingstoke, Hants (☎ 0256 881283); Thomas De La Rue & Co Ltd, Basing View, Basingstoke, Hants (☎ 0256 29122)

PARBO, Sir Arvi (Hillar); s of Aado Parbo (d 1980), and Hilda Parbo; *b* 10 Feb 1926; *Educ* Clausthal Mining Acad Germany, Adelaide Univ; *m* 1953, Saima Soots; 2 s, 1 da; *Career* mining engr and co dir; chm and md Western Mining Corpn Hldgs Ltd 1974-, chm Alcoa of Australia Ltd 1978-, dir Aluminum Co of America, dir Chase AMP Ltd, memb int advsy ctee Chase Manhattan Bank; Cdr Cross of Order of Merit FDR 1979; kt 1978; *Style*— Sir Arvi Parbo; Longwood, 737 Highbury Rd, Vermont South, Vic 3133, Australia (☎ 232 8264)

PARDOE, Hon Mrs (Anna Josephine Bridget); da of 2 Baron Darling; *b* 1946; *m* 1971, Anthony Robert Pardoe; 1 s, 1 da; *Style*— The Hon Mrs Pardoe; Sharow Cottage, Sharow, Ripon, N Yorks

PARDOE, Prof Geoffrey Keith Charles; OBE (1988); s of James Charles Pardoe (d 1954), and Ada Violet, *née* Pert (d 1981); *b* 2 Nov 1928; *Educ* Wanstead Co HS, Loughborough Coll (DLC), London Univ (BSc), Loughborough Univ (PhD); *m* 20 June 1953, (Dorothy) Patricia; 1 s (Ian Edward Charles b 1964), 1 da (Jane Patricia b 1967); *Career* RAFVR 1946-58, Pilot Offr 1949; chief aerodynamicist: armaments div Armstrong Whitworth 1949-51, air weapons div De Havilland Props Ltd 1951-56; project mangr Blue Streak De Havilland Props Ltd 1956-60, chief engr weapons and space res Hawker Siddeley Dynamics 1960-63, chief project engr space div Hawker Siddeley Dynamics Ltd 1963-70, exec dir Br Space Devpt Co Ltd 1960-71, sales exec space Hawker Siddeley Dynamics Ltd 1971-73, dir Evosat SA Switzerland 1971-82, chm and md Gen Technol Systems Ltd 1973-; memb Aeronautical Res Cncl 1971-80, pres RAeS 1984/85, memb Def Advsy Bd 1984-, chm Watt Ctee on Energy 1985-; FBIS 1958, FRAeS 1968, FRSA 1976, FInstD 1985, FEng 1988; *Books* Challenge of Space (1964), Project Apollo: The Way to the Moon (1969), The Future for Space Technology (1984); *Recreations* flying, skiing, windsurfing, photography, badminton; *Clubs* RAF, IOD; *Style*— Dr Geoffrey Pardoe, OBE; 23 Stewart Rd, Harpenden, Herts, AL5 4DE (☎ 0582 460 719); General Technology Systems Ltd, Brunel Science Park, Kingston La, Uxbridge, Middx, UB8 3PQ (☎ 0895 56767, fax 0895 32078, telex 295607 GENTEC G)

PARDOE, John Wentworth; s of Cuthbert B Pardoe; *b* 27 July 1934; *Educ* Sherborne, Corpus Christi Coll Cambridge; *m* 1958, Joyce R Peerman; 2 s, 1 da; *Career* jt md Sight and Sound Educn Ltd 1979-; sr res fell Policy Studies Inst 1979-; presenter Look Here London Weekend TV 1979-81; *Style*— John Pardoe, Esq; Chy-an-Porth, Trevone, Padstow, Cornwall

PARDOE, Rex Aldous George; s of George Ernest Pardoe (d 1970), and Gladys Lily, *née* Waring (d 1946); *b* 21 Nov 1928; *Educ* SW Essex Tech HS; *m* 19 June 1948, Lyn Kathleen; 1 s (Russell Aldous 17 June 1963), 4 da (Cheryl Loraine b 18 Dec 1950, Janis Elaine b 5 Jan 1952, Karen Susan b 2 May 1953, Brigitte Louise b 8 July 1959); *Career* Nat Serv RN 1946-48; London and Essex Guardian Newspapers (Argus Press) 1978: ed, managing ed, md; chm Whitfield Sch Devpt Tst; pres: Rotary Club, Round Table; *Books* Battle of London (1972), 70 Glorious Years (1965); *Recreations* tennis, bridge; *Clubs* Whitehall, Loughton; *Style*— Rex Pardoe, Esq; 40 Keynchan Ave, Woodford Green, Essex (☎ 01 504 4394); News Centre, Fulbourne Rd, Walthamstow, London E17 4EW (☎ 01 531 4141)

PARDY, Bruce James; s of William Dryden Cribb Pardy (d 1979), and Mavis Irene Denize (d 1984); *b* 25 Nov 1939; *Educ* St Peter's Sch Cambridge NZ, Christ's Coll Christchurch NZ, Otago Univ NZ (MB, BMedSc, ChM); *m* 26 April 1980, Kathleen Margaret, da of Leslie George Henry Townsend Robertson; 1 s (Robert James Dryden b 1985), 1 da (Caroline Anne b 1983); *Career* conslt vascular and gen surgn Newham Gen Hosp and St Andrew's Hosp London, hon conslt surgn The Italian Hosp London, late sr registrar in surgery St Mary's Hosp London; memb: Vascular Soc of GB & Ireland, Surgical Res Soc; Assoc of Surgns UK and Ireland, RSM; med advsr The Raynaud's Assoc; FRACS, FRCS; *Recreations* sailing, camping, refurbishing; *Clubs* RSM; *Style*— Bruce Pardy, Esq; 49 Abingdon Villas, Kensington, London W8 6XA; 144 Harley Street, London W1N 1AH (☎ 01 935 0023)

PAREKH, Prof Bhikhu Chhotalal; s of Chhotalal Ranchhoddas Parekh, of Washington DC, USA, and Gajaraben; *b* 4 Jan 1935; *Educ* HDS HS India, Univ Bombay (BA, MA), Univ of London (PhD); *m* 14 April 1959, Pramila Parekh, da of Kanaiyalal Keshavlal Dalal, of Baroda, India; 2 s (Raj b 1960, Nitin b 1964), 1 da (Anant b 1967); *Career* lectr: Univ of Baroda 1957-59, Univ of Glasgow 1963-64; prof Univ of Hull 1982- (lectr, sr lectr, reader 1964-82), vice chllr Univ of Baroda 1981-84; visiting prof: Univ of Br Columbia 1967-68, Concordia Univ Montreal 1974-75, McGill Univ Montreal 1976-77; active in local Cncl for Racial Equality, dep chm Cmmn for Racial Equality 1985-; tstee Runnymeda Tst 1986-, Policy Studies Inst 1986-; *Books* Hannah Arendt (1981), Karl Marx's Theory of Ideology (1982), Contemporary Political Thinkers (1982), Gandhi's Political Philosophy (1988); *Recreations* reading, music; *Style*— Prof Bhikhu Parekh; 211 Victoria Ave, Hull HU5 3EF (☎ 0482 45530); Dept of Politics, Univ of Hull, Hull HU5 3E5 (☎ 0482 487752)

PARES, Michael; s of Andrew Pares, CBE, of Northwood, Middx, and Joan Pares; *b* 2 Dec 1943; *Educ* Uppingham, Edinburgh Univ (BSc); *m* 21 Sept 1968, Jennifer Pauline, da of H E White, of Arkley; 2 da (Catriona b 19 May 1971, Julie b 11 June 1973); *Career* Lt 131 Para Regt RE TA 1963-65; CA Arthur Young, McClellard Moores London 1968, mgmnt appts BOC gp Cos 1969-75, dir Bond & White Ltd (currenlty md); patron Muswell Hill & Highgate Br Legion; bursar Worshipful Co of Builders Merchants (Liveryman 1978, memb Ct 1988); MInstBM; *Style*— Michael Pares, Esq; Bond & White Ltd, 40 Muswell Hill Rd, Highgate N6 5UN

PARFECT, Maj John Herbert; MBE (1957); s of George Frederick Parfect (d 1970), and Hedwig, *née* Jordi (d 1948); *b* 9 April 1924; *Educ* Brentwood Sch, Manchester Univ, Columbia Univ NY; *m* 14 Aug 1948, (Mercia) Heather, da of Brig John Lawrence Maxwell, CBE, MC (d 1972), 1 s (Jeremy John b 1964), 4 da (Penelope b 1951, Wendy b 1952, Jane b 1954, Louise b 1958); *Career* WWII cmmnd RE serv Sicily and Italy 1943; serv: Bengal Sappers and Miners India 1945-47, Gurkha Engrs Malaya 1948-50, 6 Armd Div Engrs BAOR 1951-53, Staff Coll Camberley 1954, GSO2 Northern Cmd York 1955-57, OC 40 Field Sqdn Cyprus 1957-58, ret 1958; personnel mangr ICI 1958-81, self employed fin planning conslt Allied Dunbar 1981-; N Yorks CC 1977-, chm N Yorks Police Authy 1985; FIPM; *Recreations* beagling, military history, investments; *Clubs* Yorkshire; *Style*— Maj John Parfect, MBE; Colville Hall, Coxwold, York YO6 4AA (☎ 03476 305)

PARFITT, Judy Catherine Clare; da of Laurence Hamilton Parfitt (d 1973), and Catherine Coulton; *Educ* Notre Dame Convent, RADA; *m* 25 Aug 1963, Anthony Francis Steedman, s of Baron Anthony Ward; 1 s (David Lawrence b 29 Sept 1964); *Career* actress; theatre incl: DH Lawrence trilogy at Royal Court, Annie in A Hotel in Amsterdam 1968, Queen Mary in Vivat! Vivat! Regina! Picadilly Theatre 1970, Cleopatra at Young Vic, Duchess of Malfi at Royal Court, Ranyevskya in The Cherry Orchard at Riverside Studio's 1978, Eleanor in Passion Play at Wyndham's 1980; Films incl: Gertrude in Hamlet 1969, Madam Sarti in Galileo 1974, Getting it Right, Daimond Skulls, Maurice 1986; TV incl: Billette, The Edwardians 1973, Shoulder to Shoulder, Malice Aforethought 1979, Pride and Prejudice, Death of a Princess, Secret Orchards, Jewel in the Crown 1984 (BAFTA Best Actress nomination), The Charmer 1987; *Recreations* needlepoint, gardening, antiques, talking; *Style*— Miss Judy Parfitt; 7 High Park Road, Kew, Richmond, Surrey

PARGETER, Ronald Albert; s of Albert Henry Pargeter (d 1963); *b* 3 Oct 1919; *Educ* Archbishop Tenison's GS; *m* 1, 1943, Edna Margaret; 1 s (Simon), 1 da (Julia); m 2, 1978, Iva Patricia, *née* Stones; 2 da (Lindsay, Deborah); *Career* RAF 1939-45; dir Dalgety Chem Ltd 1978-80, dep chm K & K Greeff Chem Ltd 1976-84, pres Fed Euro Commerce Chimique 1980-82, chm BCDTA 1973-75 (pres 1986-); dir: Chemrite Int (Pty) Ltd 1979-, Br Tar Products plc 1982-, Sutcliffe Speakman plc 1986-; chm Rapadex Ltd 1980-; memb: exec cncl Br Importers Confedn 1981-84, cncl IOD (Sussex branch 1983-); Freeman City of London; *Recreations* golf, cricket, travelling; *Clubs* St Stephen's, RAF, Inst of Dirs, Cricketers; *Style*— Ronald Pargeter, Esq; Mill Hill, Mill Lane, Rodmell, East Sussex BN7 3HS (☎ 0273 472912)

PARGITER, Hon Donald; s of Baron Pargiter, CBE (Life Peer); *b* 1921; *m* 1947; *Style*— The Hon Donald Pargiter; 68 Tonbridge Rd, Maidstone, Kent

PARGITER, Hon Russell Ashby; s of Baron Pargiter, CBE (Life Peer, d 1982); *b* 5 May 1924; *Educ* Southall GS, St Thomas's Hosp Med Sch (MB, BS, DPM); *m* 1954, Elizabeth Edwina, da of Dr John George Jamieson Coghill; 2 s (Simon, Timothy b 1964), 1 da (Frances June); *Career* sr hon psychiatrist Royal Hobart Hosp 1959; pres Nat Marriage Guidance Cncl 1968-74, sr lecturer in psychiatry Tasmania Univ 1972-81, censor Royal Australian and NZ Coll of Psychiatrists 1975-83 (pres 1973-74), memb Family Law Cncl 1975-81, pres Med Protection Soc of Tasmania 1980-, vice pres Med Protection Soc London 1981-; FRCPhys, fell Royal Aust and NZ Coll of Psychiatrists; *Recreations* cruising under sail (yacht "Sulatu"), bush walking; *Clubs*

Derwent Sailing Sqdn; *Style—* The Hon Russell Pargiter; 42 Grays Rd, Ferntree, Tasmania 7054, (☎ 002 391231); 173 Macquarie Street, Hobart, Tasmania 7000 (☎ 002 237867)

PARHAM, Adm Sir Frederick Robertson; GBE (1959, CBE 1949), KCB (1955, CB 1951), DSO (1944); s of Frederick James Parham (d 1906), of Bath Somerset, and Jessie Esther Brooks, *née* Robertson (d 1961); *b* 9 Jan 1901; *Educ* RNC Osborne and Dartmouth; *m* 1, 1926, Kathleen Dobree (d 1973), da of Eugene Edward Carey, Guernsey; 1 s; m 2, 1978, Mrs Joan Saunders, *née* Charig; *Career* Cdr 1934, Rear-Adm 1949, Vice-Adm 1952, Adm 1956; a Lord Cmmr of the Admty, Fourth Sea Lord and Chief of Supplies and Tport 1954-55, C-in-C The Nore 1955-58, ret 1959; former vice-chm Br Waterways Bd; *Style—* Adm Sir Frederick Parham, GBE, KCB, DSO; The Coach House, Church Rd, West Lavington, Midhurst, W Sussex GU29 OEH (☎ 073 081 3183)

PARHAM, John Carey; s of Adm Sir Frederick Robertson Parham, GBE, KCB, DSO, *qv*, and Kathleen Dobree, *née* Carey; *b* 13 June 1928; *Educ* Rugby, Madgalen Coll Oxford; *m* 20 May 1959, Christian Mary, da of Cuthbert Fitzherbert (d 1986), of Berks; 1 s (Philip b 1960) 4 da (Katherine b 1962, Magdalen b 1964, Barbara b 1968, Henrietta (twin) b 1968); *Career* Nat Serv 1947-49, 2 Lt Mercers Troop 5 RHA; local dir: Barclays Bank Windsor, Barclays Bank London Western; exec chm Close Registrars Ltd 1988-; ACIB; *Recreations* swimming, gardening; *Clubs* Travellers'; *Style—* John Parham, Esq; Ladymead, South Ascot, Berkshire SL5 9HD (☎ 0990 20087); Close Registrars Ltd, Arthur House, 803 High Road, Leyton, London E10 7RA (☎ 01 556 5211, fax 01 539 2357, telex 8814274)

PARIKH, Bharat Amritlal; s of Amritlal Vithaldas Parikh, of Calcutta, and Padmalaxmi Amritlal, *née* Mehta; *b* 4 Oct 1946; *Educ* Univ of Calcutta (BCom), Univ of London (BSc); *m* 14 Feb 1972, Anuradha, da of Debesh Chandra Das, formerly permanent sec to Govt of India; *Career* dir Castle Keep Hotels Ltd; distrib Belgian handmade chocolates Parikh Daskalides; FCA; *Recreations* snooker, cricket; *Style—* Bharat A Parikh, Esq; 179 Coombe Lane, West Wimbledon, London SW20 0RG (☎ 947 4644); 17 Tottenham Court Road, London W1 (☎ 580 9633, 631-3810)

PARIS, Cecil Gerard Alexander; TD (1945); s of Lt Col Alexander Lloyd Paris (d 1968), of Bournemouth, and Geraldine Paris, *née* Brooke (d 1974); *b* 20 August 1911; *Educ* The King's Sch Canterbury; *m* 11 Sept 1937, Winifred Anna Blanche, da of Thomas Richardson, OBE (d 1969), of Northumberland; 2 s (James b 1945, Thomas b 1947), 1 da (Winifred b 1940); *Career* joined TA March 1939, cmmnd Hants Heavy Regt RA 1939, serv UK and BLA Eur 1944-45 (awarded Czech MC after serv with Czech Ind Armd Bde Gp), demob as Maj 1945; slr 1935-86, ptnr Paris Smith & Randall Southampton 1965-81; hon sec Hants Law Soc; player Hants CCC 1933-48 (Capt 1938, chm selection ctee 1952-67, club chm 1967-68, pres 1983-), govr Kings Sch Canterbury 1979-84, chm Wessex Body Scan Appeal 1983-; memb ctee MCC 1961-83 (chm of registration ctee and genral purposes ctee, pres 1975-76, tstee 1983-84, hon life vice-pres 1985-), chm ctee responsible for organising and running first (Prudential) World Cup Int Cricket Conf 1975; inaugural chm TCCB 1968-75; played for Hants RFU 1934-46 (capped 1935 when Hants won County Championship); pres and hon sec Hants Law Soc 1961; *Recreations* fly-fishing, cricket admin; *Clubs* MCC, Lord's Taverners, Free Foresters, Hampshire Hogs, Trojans, Forty; *Style—* Cecil G A Paris, TD; Lynsted, Southdown Road, Shawford, Winchester, Hants SO21 2BY (☎ 0962 712152)

PARIS, Gerrard Darell; s of Brig D K Paris, MC, OBE (d 1964), and Evelyn Maud (Cherry) Mills (d 1976); *b* 17 April 1930; *Educ* Wellington Coll Berks; *m* 4 May 1963, Zoë Ashworth, da of Edwin Ashworth Grigg (d 1951); 1 s (Geoffrey b 1959), 3 da (Robin b 1961, Judy b 1964, Bridget b 1967; *Career* RN 1954-56 (RN Res 1950-54, Lt exec branch 1956-62; Peat Marwick Mitchell & Co London 1948-64; Tarmac plc group: chief accountant 1964-67, fin controller 1967-70, fin dir 1970-79; exec dir Barclays de Zoete Wedd Ltd 1979-; FICA; *Recreations* gardening, walking, the sea, cooking; *Clubs* Naval London; *Style—* Gerard D Paris, Esq; The Old Rectory, Beckbury, Shifnal, Shropshire TF11 9DQ (☎ 095 287 238); BZWQ Ltd, Phoenix House, 1/3 Newhall Street, Birmingham B3 3NH (☎ 021 236 8563)

PARISH *see also*: Woodbine Parish

PARISH, Hon Mrs (Elizabeth Campbell); *née* Boot; da of 2 and last Baron Trent (d 1956); *b* 1927; *m* 1947, Maj Michael Woodbine Parish, MC, Notts Yeo; 1 s, 3 da; *Career* dir: Exploration Co plc, El Oro Mining & Exploration Co, General Explorations Ltd; *Style—* The Hon Mrs Parish; Walcot Hall, Lydbury North, Salop

PARISH, Maj Michael Woodbine; MC, DSM; s of Clement Woodbine Parish (d 1966), of Sussex, and Elsie Mary, *née* Bonham-Christie (d 1931); *b* 6 July 1916; *Educ* Eton; *m* 1, 1941 (m dis 1946), Ninette Sgourdeos; m 2, 1947, Hon Elizabeth Campbell Boot, da of 2 Baron Trent of Nottingham (d 1956); 1 s (Clement Robin b 1950), 3 da (Suzanne b 1948, Caroline b 1953, Emma b 1957); *Career* WWII Maj Sherwood Rangers Yeo (despatches twice, POW 1943), repatriated 1944, invalided out of army 1944; chm and md: The Exploration Co, El Oro Mining & Exploration Co; dir Bisichi Tin Co; *Recreations* work, walking, swimming; *Clubs* Beefsteak, Brookes's East India and Sports, Cavalry and Guards'; *Style—* Maj Michael Parish, MC, DSM; Walcot Hall, Lydbury North, Shropshire; 41 Cheval Place, London SW7 (☎ 01 581 2782)

PARISH, Hon Mrs (Monica Esmé Ebba); *née* Suenson-Taylor; da of 1 Baron Grantchester, OBE; *b* 17 Jan 1926; *Educ* Queen's Coll London, Newnham Coll Cambridge; *m* 1951 (m dis 1965), Graeme Spotswood Parish; 1 s (Andrew, k in an accident 1973), 1 da (Alexandra Francesca Spotswood (Mrs Nicholas Burnell) b 1953); *Style—* The Hon Mrs Monica Parish; 71 Prince's House, Kensington Park Rd, London W11

PARISH, Robert James; CMG (1980), OBE (1975); s of L R Parish; *b* 7 May 1916; *Educ* Melbourne C of E GS; *m* 1939, Nannette I, da of E L Lewis; 2 s, 1 da; *Career* chm Australian Cricket Bd 1975- (memb 1957-), mangr Macmillan Bloedel Pty Ltd Melbourne 1969-; *Style—* Robert Parish, Esq, CMG, OBE; 1 Lawrenny Ct, Toorak, Vic 3142, Australia

PARK, Andrew Edward Wilson; QC (1978); s of late Dennis Edward Park; *b* 27 Jan 1939; *Educ* Leeds GS, Univ Coll Oxford; *m* 1962, Ann Margaret Woodhead; 2 s (and 1 s decd), 1 da; *Career* barr Lincoln's Inn 1964, practice at Revenue Bar 1965-; *Style—* Andrew Park, Esq, QC; Blandford Cottage, Weston Green Rd, Thames, Surrey KT7 OHX (☎ 01 398 5349)

PARK, Hon Mrs (Christine Joanna); *née* Coleman; da of Baron Cohen of Brighton (Life Peer, d 1966); *b* 6 May 1942; *Educ* Rosedean, Univ of London (BA), Univ of Sussex (MA); *m* 1965, David Maxwell Park; 1 da (Nira b 1967); *Career* writer and ed; *Books* Joining The Grown Ups (1986), Close Company (ed jtly); *Style—* The Hon Mrs Park; 29 Downshire Hill, London NW3 1NT

PARK, Daphne Margaret Sybil Désirée; CMG (1971), OBE (1960); da of John Alexander Park (d 1952), and Doreen Gwynneth Park (d 1982); *b* 1 Sept 1921; *Educ* Rosa Bassett Sch, Somerville Coll Oxford, Newnham Coll Cambridge; *Career* WTS (FANY) 1943-47 (Allied Cmmn for Austria 1946-48); FO 1948; second sec Moscow 1954, first sec Leopoldville 1959, consul-gen Hanoi 1969-70, FCO 1973-79; princ Somerville Oxford 1980-; govr BBC 1982-87, memb Br Library Bd; chm Legal Aid Advsy Ctee to Lord Chllr, pro vice-chllr Univ of Oxford; *Recreations* good talk, politics and difficult places; *Clubs* Naval & Military, Royal Cwlth Soc, Special Forces, Oxford and Cambridge; *Style—* Miss Daphne Park, CMG, OBE; Somerville College, Oxford OX2 6HD (☎ 0865 515880)

PARK, George Maclean; s of James McKenzie Park; *b* 27 Sept 1914; *Educ* Onslow Drive Sch Glasgow, Coventry Tech Coll; *m* 1941, Joyce, da of Robert Holt Stead; 1 da; *Career* MP (Lab) Coventry NE 1974-87; PPS to: Dr J Gilbert (Min for Tport) 1975-76, E Varley (Sec of State for Indust) 1976-79; chm W Midland Gp Lab MPs; memb Public Accounts Ctee 1981-, jt chm All-Pty Motor Indust Gp 1979-87; JP (Coventry 1961-84); *Style—* George Park, Esq; 170 Binley Rd, Coventry CV3 1HG (☎ 0203 458589)

PARK, (James) Graham; s of James Park, OBE, JP (d 1959), of Salford, and Joan Clay, *née* Sharp (d 1987); *b* 27 April 1941; *Educ* Malvern, Manchester Univ (LLB); *m* 26 June 1969, Donald, s of Dr Charles Sydney Douglas Don (d 1973), of Manchester; 1 s (James b 1973); *Career* slr in ptnrship; Parly candidate (C) 1974 and 1979, chm Altrincham Sale Constituency 1983-87, dep tres Cons Party NW 1987-; Duchy of Lancaster, memb of Ct of Salford Univ 1987-; *Recreations* running, walking, lying down; *Style—* Graham Park, Esq; Little Garth, Alan Drive, Hale, Altrincham, Cheshire (☎ 061 980 7781); HLT Berry & Co, 25 South King Street, Manchester M2 6BB (☎ 061 834 0548)

PARK, Sir Hugh (Eames); s of late William Robert Park; *b* 24 April 1910; *Educ* Blundell's, Sidney Sussex Coll Cambridge; *m* 1938, Beryl Josephine, da of late Joseph Coombe; 3 da; *Career* barr Middle Temple 1936, QC 1960, bencher 1965, presiding judge Western circuit 1970-75, judge of the High Ct of Justice, Queen's Bench Div 1973-85 (Family Div 1965-73); hon fell Sidney Sussex Cambridge 1968; kt 1965; *Style—* Sir Hugh Park; 34 Ordnance Hill, St John's Wood, NW8 (☎ 01 586 0417); Gorran Haven, Cornwall (☎ 0726 842333)

PARK, Ian Grahame; JP; s of William Park (d 1982), and Christina Wilson, *née* Scott; *b* 15 May 1935; *Educ* Lancaster Royal GS, Queens' Cambridge; *m* 1965, Anne, da of Edward Turner (d 1979); 1 s (Adam); *Career* Nat Serv cmmnd Manchester Regt 1954-56; md Northcliffe Newspapers Gp 1982-, dir Assoc Newspapers Hldgs 1983-, md and ed-in-chief Liverpool Daily Post and Echo 1972-82, asst literary ed Sunday Times 1960-63; dir: Reuters 1978-82, Press Assoc 1978-83 (chm 1978-79 and 1979-80); pres Newspaper Soc 1980-81; *Clubs* Reform; *Style—* Ian Park Esq, JP; 6 Cheyne Row, London SW3; 35 John Street, WC1 (☎ 01 242 7070)

PARK, Ian Michael Scott; CBE (1982); s of Ian Macpherson Park (d 1960), of Aberdeen, and Winifred Margaret, *née* Scott; *b* 7 April 1938; *Educ* Aberdeen GS, Aberdeen Univ (MA, LLB); *m* 1964, Elizabeth Mary Lamberton, da of Alexander Marshall Struthers, OBE (d 1964), of Edinburgh; 2 s (Sandy b 1965, William b 1972); *Career* slr, ptnr Paull & Williamsons Advocates Aberdeen 1964-; memb Soc of Advocates Aberdeen 1962-; memb of Cncl Law Soc of Scotland 1974-84 (vice pres 1979-80, pres 1980-81), memb of Criminal Injuries Compensation Bd 1983-; chm Aberdeen Citizens Advice Bureau, frequent broadcaster on legal topics; *Recreations* golf, gardening, travel; *Clubs* New (Edinburgh); *Style—* Michael Park, CBE; Beechwood, 46 Rubislaw Den, South Aberdeen AB2 6AX (☎ 0224 313799); Investment House, 6 Union Row, Aberdeen (☎ 0224 631414)

PARK, Hon Mrs (Joanna MacAlister); er da of Baron Baker, OBE (Life Peer, d 1985); *b* 1933; *m* 1962, Prof David Michael Ritchie Park; 1 s, 1 da; *Career* former JP for Warwicks; *Style—* The Hon Mrs Park, JP; 15 Rothesay Place, Edinburgh

PARK, Richard Francis Hanbury; s of Jonathan Cyril Park, OBE (d 1979), and Frances Hanbury, *née* Dodds (d 1984); *b* 29 Mar 1933; *Educ* Winchester, Trinity Coll Cambridge (MA, LLM); *m* 3 July 1959, Patricia Zillah, da of Norman Louis Forrest (d 1988); of Barlaston, Stoke-on-Trent; 2 da (Caroline b 1963, Elizabeth b 1965); *Career* 1 Royal Dragoons 1951-53, Lanarkshire Yeo TA 1953-58; admitted slr 1959; sr ptnr Steavensons Plant & Park Darlington 1986- (ptnr 1959-86); clerk to Gen Cmmrs of Income Tax: Darlington, Bishop Auckland, Northallerton, Barnard Castle; chm Social Security Appeals Tbnl 1984-, pres Notaries Soc 1987-89; memb: Law Soc 1959, Slrs Benevolent Assoc; *Recreations* golf, tennis, walking, photography, music, pottery, gardening; *Style—* Richard Park, Esq; The Old Rectory, Hurworth, Darlington, Co Durham (☎ 0325 720 321); 12 Houndgate, Darlington (☎ 0325 466 794, fax 0325 55321)

PARK, William Dennis; s of Edward Park (d 1954) of Cockermouth, Cumbria, and Fanny Moyra Walker (d 1986); *b* 28 May 1934; *Educ* St Bees Cumbria; *m* 1 Jan 1959, Valerie Margaret, da of Wallace Rutherford Bayne, MD (d 1956), of Barrow-in-Furness, Cumbria; 1 s (Adam b 9 July 1961), 1 da (Clair b 9 Jan 1963); *Career* Nat Serv RAOC, RASC 1955-57 (army legal aid 1956-57); slr 1955, ptnr Morrison & Manters Swindon 1961-66, sr litigation ptnr Links Cates & Paines London 1971-; former pres London Slrs Litigators Assoc, cncl memb London Int Tst, memb ctee Br Inst of Int & Comparative Law; pres: Millon & Broughton Agric Soc 1989, Loweswater & Brackenthwaite Agric Soc; memb: Herdwick Sheep Breeder Assoc, Bleu du Maine Breeders Soc, Friends of the Lake Dist Nat Tst, English Heritage; subscribes: Melbecks Foxhounds, Ennerdale Eskdale Foxhounds, Black Combe Beagles; Lord of the Manor of Whicham and WhitBecks Cumbria; memb City of London Slrs Co; memb: Law Soc 1955, CIArb 1980; *Books* Hire Purchase and Credit Sales (1958), Collection of Debts (1962), Discovery of Documents (1966), Documentary Evidence (1985); *Recreations* farming, living in West Cumbria, hunting, shooting, fishing,; *Style—* William Park, Esq; Linklaters & Paines, Barrington House, 59-67 Gresham St, London, EC2, (☎ 01 606 7080)

PARKER *see also*: Dodds-Parker

PARKER, Sir (William) Alan; 4 Bt (UK 1844); s of Sir William Lorenzo Parker, 3 Bt, OBE (d 1971); *b* 20 Mar 1916; *Educ* Eton, New Coll Oxford; *m* 1946, Sheelagh Mary, da of late Dr Sinclair Stevenson; 1 s, 1 da; *Heir* s, William Peter Brian Parker;

Career WWII 1939-45, Capt RE, Middle E 1941-45; *Style*— Sir Alan Parker, Bt; Apricot Hall, Sutton-cum-Beckingham, Lincoln LN5 ORE (☎ 063 684 322)

PARKER, Allen Mainwaring; s of Eric Parker (d 1954), of Feathercombe, Hambledown, Surrey, and Ruth Margaret, *née* Messel (d 1933); *b* 23 Feb 1915; *Educ* Eton, Trinity Coll Oxford (MA); *m* 24 Mar 1945, Suzanne Beechey, da of Cdr Beechey Louis Rogers (d 1953), of Woodfield Cottage, Luston, Herefordshire; 1 s (James), 2 da (Suzanne, Tessa); *Career* WWII Maj KOYLI; sr classics master King's Coll Auckland NZ 1938-39, dir of extramural studies Univ of Birmingham 1955-82, vice chm Univ Cncl for Adult and Continuing Educn 1976-82; advsy memb Countryside Advsy Panel Hereford and Worcester CC; *Books* University Adult Education in the Later Twentieth Century (Report of the Convenor of a Working Party of the Universities Council for Adult Education 1970), University Studies for Adults (ed with Prof SG Raybould, 1972); *Recreations* gardening; *Style*— Allen Parker, Esq; The Wadhouse, Heightington, Bewdley, Worcs (☎ 02993 2477)

PARKER, Anthony; OBE (1972); s of Albert Sydney Parker; *b* 3 Oct 1929; *Educ* Sutton GS; *m* 1955, Jean Betty Mary, *née* Ede; 1 da; *Career* banker Bank of England 1949-73, dir foreign exchange dept Bank of Uganda 1965-66, controller foreign exchange Bermuda 1968-71, md Bermuda Monetary Authty 1969-71, dir W England Tst Ltd 1976-81, dir Globe Fin Servs Ltd 1981-; *Recreations* walking, music, reading, writing; *Style*— Anthony Parker, Esq; Beckwood, Dolphin Close, Haslemere, Surrey (☎ 0428 2973)

PARKER, Maj Anthony John; s of John Vernham Parker (d 1980), of 21 Golf Links Rd, Broadstone Dorset, and Freda Oakley, *née* Twitchett (d 1988); *b* 24 Nov 1923; *Educ* Whitgift Sch; *m* 13 Sept 1952, (Elsie) Patricia, da of Lt-Col Clifford Llewellyn Wilson, OBE, MC (d 1974) of Newbrook, Upper Golf Links Road, Broadstone, Dorset; 3 s (Jeremy (Capt RM) b 1954, Guy b 1955, Timothy b 1962), 1 da (Diana (Mrs Mills) b 1959); *Career* probationary 2 Lt RM 1942, Lt 1943, Home Fleet (HM Ships: Berwick, Anson, Kent) 1943, Med Fleet (HMS Birmingham) 1944, E Indies Fleet (HMS Nigeria) 1944-46, instr commando trg (qualified weapon trg offr and mil parachutist) 1946-49, 40 Commando RM (Malta, Hong Kong, Malaya) 1949-51, Capt 1951, staff offr amphibious trg (qualified landing craft offr) 1952-54, instr NCO's trg 1954-57, RAF Staff Coll 1957, instr Jt Sch Nuclear Def 1958-60, staff offr Depot RM 1960-62, 42 commando RM (Singapore, Brunei, Sarawak) 1962-64, staff offr amphibious trg 1964-67, Maj 1967, staff offr HQ Far East Cmd 1967-70, chief landing craft offr RM 1970-73, ret 1973; chief fishery offr S Sea Fisheries Dist 1974-88, pres S Sea Fisheries Dist Fishermen's Cncl; memb: RN Soc Rugby Referees, Dorset & Wilts Soc Rugby Referees, exec ctee Dorset Marine Ctee, mgmnt ctee Brownsea Island Nature Reserve, ctee Lytchett Matrovers Cons Assoc; vice-pres Poole Town Regatta, hon pirate Poole; memb: Lytchett Matravers Parish Cncl, Lytchett Matravers PCC; *Recreations* rugby football (referee assessor); *Clubs* Army and Navy; *Style*— Maj Anthony Parker; Alder Rise, Lytchett Matravers, Dorset (☎ 0202 622427)

PARKER, Anthony Key;- s of Frank James Parker (d 1943), and Edith Emma, *née* Gannaway (d 1974); *b* 7 April 1925; *Educ* Stamford Sch, Trinity Coll Cambridge (MA); *m* 1, 19 Feb 1955, Joanna Margaret (d 1975), da of Capt Vernon Edmund Lloyd, MC, RAMC (d 1973); 2 s (Andrew b 1958, Philip b 1960), 1 da (Elisabeth b 1963); m 2, 15 Dec 1980, Alison Margaret Bagnall, *née* Kynoch; *Career* Midshipman (Sp) RNVR HMS Collingwood 1945-46, Sub Lt (Sp) RNVR HMS Gabbard 1946, HMS St James 1946-47, HMS Aisne 1947; tech offr Zinc Devpt Assoc 1949-52, sr asst publicity dept Mond Nickel Co 1953-55, ed Butterworth & Co 1955-57, asst sec to the Syndics of CUP 1957-85; elder Church of Scotland, memb Scripture Union Ctee for Dumfries & Galloway; *Books* The Fenland (with Denis Pye, 1976); *Recreations* sailing, walking; *Clubs* Solway YC; *Style*— Anthony Parker, Esq; Drumathol, Southwick, Dumfries DG2 8AP (☎ 038 778 629)

PARKER, Cameron Holdsworth; s of George Cameron Parker, of Uplands, Monifieth, Angus (d 1968), and Mary Stevenson, *née* Houstin (d 1985); *b* 14 April 1932; *Educ* Morrison's Acad Crieff, Glasgow Univ (BSc); *m* 1, 20 July 1957, Elizabeth Margaret (d 1985), da of Andrew Sydney Grey Thomson(d 1957), of Dundee; 3 s (David b 1958, Michael b 1960, John b 1964); m 2, 23 May 1986, Marlyne, da of William Honeyman (d 1966), of Glasgow; *Career* bd memb Br Shipbuilders 1977-80 and 1981-83; chm and chief exec Scott Lithgow Ltd 1980-83, dir John G Kincaid & Co Ltd 1963 (md 1967, chm 1976-80), chm Campbeltown Shipyard Ltd, dir Drumdrishaig Shipping & Fishing Co Ltd, chm J Fleming Eng Ltd, chm Glasgow Iron & Steel Co Ltd, dir Glasgow Iron & Stell (Brick) Ltd, chm A Halliday (Greenock) Ltd, chm Inverclyde Pluming Serv Ltd, chm A Kenneth & Sons Ltd, chm Lancatch Ltd, chm Lithgow Electronics Ltd, dir Lithgows Pty Ltd, chm Malakoff E & E Ltd, chm Malakoff & Wm Moore Ltd, chm McKinlay & Blair Ltd, dir Motherwell Brick Co Ltd, chm Prosper Engineering Ltd, dir Argyll Salmon Ltd, md Lithgows Ltd 1984-; *Recreations* golf; *Clubs* Caledonian; *Style*— Cameron Parker, Esq; (☎ 050 587 3197); Lithgows Ltd, Netherton, Langbank, Renfrewshire PA14 6YG (☎ 0475 54 692)

PARKER, Charles George Archibald; JP (London W Central 1978); s of Capt C E Parker, MC (d 1962), of Ewelme, Oxfordshire, and Hilda M, *née* Starkey (d 1979); *b* 30 Jan 1924; *Educ* Eton, New Coll Oxford (MA); *m* 3 Nov 1958, Shirley, da of Col Frank Follett Holt, TD (d 1978), of Corryborough, Tomatin, Inverness-shire; 1 da (Davina (Mrs John Walter)); *Career* Capt Rifle Bde 1942-46, serv France (POW Germany); The Times Newspaper 1949-56, Charringtons 1956-61, BMA Pubns 1961-76, chm Ct and Judicial Publishing Co Ltd 1976-; chm: Cncl for Oxfordshire Order of St John, Tower Hill Improvement Tst; pres Assoc of Learned and Professional Soc Publishers, vice pres Nettlebed branch Royal Br Legion; High Sheriff of Oxfordshire 1989-90; Liveryman Worshipful Co of Stationers 1965; FRSA, FRGS; *Recreations* shooting, fishing, tennis; *Clubs* Beefsteak, Whites; *Style*— Charles Parker, Esq, JP; The White House, Nuffield, Oxon RG9 5SR

PARKER, Christopher John McKellen; s of Alfred Derek McKellen Parker, of Beltinge, Herne Bay, Kent, and Muriel Joyce, *née* Hargreaves; *b* 25 July 1945; *Educ* Dulwich, LSE (BSc); *m* 27 Dec 1969, Alison Eere, da of Robin Gordon Miller, of Shepherdswel, Dover, Kent; 3 s (Thomas D M Parker b 1972, Jonathan R E Parker b 1974, Samuel G Parker b 1980); *Career* dir Arbuthnot Latham & Co Ltd 1978-82, dir Caird Cp plc (formerly A Caird & Sons plc) 1982- (chm 1982-87); ACA 1969, FICA 1979; *Style*— Christopher Parker, Esq; Dennes House, Waltham, Canterbury, Kent CJ4 58D (☎ 022 770 389); 163 Andrewes House, Barbican, London EC2Y 8BA (☎ 01 638 5009); 33 Sexforde St, London EC1R 0HA (☎ 01 250 3003, fax 01 250 3001, car tel 8036 229 162)

PARKER, Christopher William Oxley; JP (Essex 1952), DL (Essex 1972); s of Lt-Col John Oxley Parker (d 1979); *b* 28 May 1920; *Educ* Eton, Trinity Coll Oxford; *m* 1947, Jocelyn Frances Adeline, da of Col C G Arkwright, MC (d 1980); 1 s, 2 da; *Career* WWII 1939-45, 147 Field Regt Essex Yeo RA 1939-42; dir: Barclays Bank Chelmsford Local Bd 1950-81, Strutt & Parker (Farms) Ltd, Lord Rayleighs Farms Inc, Lavenham Fen Farms Ltd; High Sheriff Essex 1961; *Recreations* shooting, golf; *Clubs* Boodle's, MCC; *Style*— Christopher Parker, Esq, JP, DL; Faulkbourne Hall, Witham, Essex (☎ 0376 513385)

PARKER, Dr David; s of Hubert Eric Robert Parker, 15 Holland Rd, Maidstone, Kent and Eileen Rose, *née* Goodson; *b* 28 May 1940; *Educ* Maidstone GS for Boys, Univ of Nottingham (BA), Univ of Sheffield (PhD); *m* 24 Sept 1966, Elinor Sheila Halling, da of Joseph Patrick Anthony Cheek, of 17 Church Hill, Combwich, nr Bridgewater, Somerset; 1 s (Daniel b 1969), 1 da (Clare b 1972); *Career* lectr: Univ of Sheffield 1966-68, Univ of Malaya 1968-74 (assoc prof 1974-75), curator The Dickens House Museum 1978-; Freedom of Independance Missouri USA 1983; memb Int Cncl of Museums 1978; *Recreations* cooking, guitar playing; *Clubs* Dickens Fellowship; *Style*— Dr David Parker; The Dickens House Museum, 48 Doughty Street, London, WC1N 2LF, (☎ 04 405 2127)

PARKER, Hon David; s of 8 Earl of Macclesfield; *b* 1945; *m* 1968, Lynne Valerie, da of George William Butler; 1 s, 2 da; *Style*— The Hon David Parker

PARKER, Rear Adm Douglas Granger; CB (1971), DSO (1945), DSC (1945), AFC (1952); s of R K Parker; *b* 21 Nov 1919; *Educ* W Hartlepool Tech Coll; *m* 1953, Margaret Susan, da of late Col W Cooper; 1 s, 1 da; *Career* joined RN 1940, Capt 1959, Rear Adm 1969, asst chief of naval staff (ops and air) 1969-71, ret; *Style*— Rear Adm Douglas Parker, CB, DSO, DSC, AFC; High Meadow, Walhampton, Lymington, Hants (☎ 0590 3259)

PARKER, Sir Douglas William Leigh; OBE (1954); s of W Parker; *b* 12 July 1900; *Educ* Sydney Univ (ChM), Liverpool Univ (MB); *m* 1933, Hilary, da of S Secretan; 2 s, 1 da; *Career* formerly dir of orthopaedic services Tasmanian Govt Health Dept, ret 1966; FRCS Ed, FRACS, OStJ; kt 1966; *Style*— Sir Douglas Parker, OBE; 30 Fisher Ave, Lower Sandy Bay, Hobart, Tasmania, Australia

PARKER, Eric Wilson; s of Wilson Parker (d 1983), and Edith Gladys, *née* Wellings; *b* 8 June 1933; *Educ* The Priory GS for Boys Shrewsbury; *m* 12 Nov 1955, Marlene Teresa, da of Michael Neale (d 1941); 2 s (Ian, Charles), 2 da (Karen, Sally); *Career* Sgt Pay Corps Cyprus 1956-58 (Nat Serv); articled clerk with Wheeler, Whittingham & Kent 1950-55; with Taylor Woodrow 1958-64; joined Trafalgar House plc 1965, fin/admin dir 1969, dep md 1973, gp md 1977, gp chief exec 1983, dep chm 1988; Trafalgar House Gp Co directorships incl: Cunard Crusader World Travel Ltd, Cunard Resorts Ltd, The Cunard Steam-Ship Co plc, Eastern Int Investmt Tot plc, Scott Lithgow Ltd, Trafalgar Ho Construction Hldgs Ltd, Trafalgar House Investmt Mgmnt Ltd, Trafalgar House plc; past directorships: Cleveland Redpath Engrg Hldgs Ltd, Cunard Line Ltd, Evening Standard Co Ltd, John Brown plc, New Ideal Hldgs plc, RGC Offshore plc, The Ritz Hotel (London) Ltd, Trollope and Colls Hldgs Ltd; non Trafalgar directorships: Cunard Gp Pensions Tstees Ltd, Metal Box plc, Touche Remnant Hldgs Ltd, Trafalgar House Tstees Ltd; FCA 1967 (ACA 1956), FRSA, CBIM; *Recreations* sports, horseracing, golf, wines; *Clubs* RAC, Tyrrell's Wood Golf (Leatherhead), MCC; *Style*— Eric Parker, Esq; Nower Hayes, The Drive, Tyrrell's Wood, nr Leatherhead, Surrey KT22 8QW; 54 Ovington Street, London SW3; The Old Barns, South Pool, nr Kingsbridge, S Devon; Trafalgar House plc, 1 Berkeley Street, London W1A 1BY (☎ 01 499 9020, fax 01 493 5484)

PARKER, (James) Geoffrey; s of Ian Sutherland Parker (d 1973), of Leicester, and Kathleen Lilian, *née* Cave (d 1976); *b* 27 Mar 1933; *Educ* Alderman Newton's Sch Leicester, Christ's Coll Cambridge (BA), Wadham Coll Oxford (CertEd); *m* 22 Sept 1956, Ruth, da of Edward Major, of Leicester; 2 da (Georgina b 1959, Katherine b 1960); *Career* RA 1954-56, Lance Bombardier 1955, 2 Lt 1955, Actg Capt 1956; asst master Bedford Modern Sch 1957-66, head history dept Tonbridge Sch Kent 1966-75, head master Queen Elizabeth GS Wakefield 1975-85, high master Manchester GS 1985-; memb: various HMC ctees, Advsy Cncl for Church's Miny; govr various schs and educnl bodies; QMC Conf 1975-; *Recreations* sailing, coarse gardening; *Clubs* East India, Devonshire, Sports and Public Schs; *Style*— Geoffrey Parker, Esq; The Manchester GS, Manchester N13 0XT

PARKER, Geoffrey John; CBE (1984); s of Stanley John Parker (d 1983), of London, and Alice Ellen (1984); *b* 20 Mar 1937; *Educ* Hendon Co GS; *m* 25 Nov 1957, Hazel Mary, da of Lawrence Edward; 2 s (Simon, Andrew), 2 da (Joanne, Amanda); *Career* Nat Serv RAF 1955-57; commercial dir Townend Car Ferries Ltd Dover (commercial dir) 1962-74, md Atlantic Steam Navigation Co Ltd 1974-86, chm and md Port of Felixstow 1976-87, dir Euro Ferries plc 1981 (chm 1986-87), chief exec Highland Participants plc 1987-; dir Nat Bus Co 1979-86; FCIT 1982, FITA 1986; *Recreations* golf, opera; *Clubs* Ipswich Golf; *Style*— Geoffrey Parker, Esq, CBE; 101 Valley Rd, Ipswich, Suffolk (☎ 0473 216 003); 77 Alder Lodge, Stevenage Rd, London SW6 (☎ 01 385 5434); Highland Participants plc, 46 Paul Mall, London SW1 (☎ 01 408 1948, fax 01 930 7807, car tel 0836 244 453, telex 263884 HICO G)

PARKER, Iain George McKim; s of Ernest Parker, of Harrogate (d 1971); *b* 29 Dec 1937; *Educ* Ashville Coll Harrogate, Emmanuel Coll Cambridge; *m* 1964, Judith Sian; 1 s, 1 da; *Career* Lt IPWO Nat Serv; chm: Otter Controls Ltd, Montogomery Thermostats Ltd, St Davids Assemblies Ltd, Tarka Controls Ltd; dir Otter Controls (NZ) Ltd 1967; *Recreations* mountain walking, photography, orchids; *Clubs* Utd Oxford and Cambridge; *Style*— Iain Parker, Esq; Cherry Trees, Combs, Chapel En Le Frith, Via Stockport, SK12 6UP (☎ office 0298 71177)

PARKER, James Mavin (Jim); s of James Robertson parker, and Margaret, *née* Mavin; *b* 18 Dec 1934; *Educ* Guildhall Sch of Music and Drama; *m* 1, 1 da (Louise b 1964); m 2, 2 Aug 1969, Pauline Ann, da of John George, of Reading; 2 da (Claire b 1974, Amy b 1976); *Career* Musician 4/7 Dragoon Gds; composer and conductor, joined Barrow Poets 1963; composed music for: Banana Blush (John Betjeman), Captain Beaky (Jeremy Lloyd); *printed music* Follow the Star (Wally K Daly), *childrens musicals* English Towns (tom Stanier, for flute and piano), A Londoner in New York (Suite for brass), *film and TV music* Mapp and Lucra, Wynne and Pekovsky, Good Behaviour, The Making of Modern London, The Blot; Hon GSM 1985; GSM (Silvermedal) 1959, LRAM 1959; *Recreations* tennis, 20 century art, literature; *Style*— Jim Parker, Esq; 19 Laurel Road, London SW13 OEE (☎ 01 876 8571)

PARKER, James Roland Walter; CMG (1978), OBE (1968); s of late Alexander Roland Parker, ISM; *b* 20 Dec 1919; *m* 1941, Deirdre Mary Ward; *Career* HM Diplomatic Serv (ret); formerly govnr and cdr-in-chief Falkland Islands and Dependencies, high cmmr Br Antarctic Territory 1976-1980; *Style—* James Parker Esq, CMG, OBE; Crockers Hill, Yarlington, Wincanton, Somerset BA9 8DJ (☎ 0963 40402)

PARKER, (Diana) Jean; *née* Morley; da of Capt Lewis William Reeve Morley (d 1988), of Grantham, Lincolnshire, and Amy, *née* Southwood (d 1973); *b* 7 June 1932; *Educ* Kesteven & Grantham Girls' Sch, Birmingham Univ (BComm); *m* 26 June 1959, Dudley Frost Parker (d 1971), s of Frederick Parker (d 1960), of Rugby; 1 s (Andrew b 1965), 1 da (Alison b 1960); *Career* dir: Vacu-Lug Traction Tyres Ltd 1957-, Langham Industs Ltd 1980-, Central Independent TV plc 1982-; memb bd E Midlands Electricity 1983-, memb Eastern advsy bd Nat West Bank plc 1985-, dir Br Steel (Indust) Ltd 1986-; CBI: memb cncl 1985-89, memb pres ctee 1985-89, chm smaller firms ctee 1986-88; chm: Lincolnshire Jt Devpt Ctee 1983-, N Lincolnshire Health Authy 1987-; former chm: Age Concern Grantham, Grantham C of C; former memb East Midlands Econ Planning Cncl, sec Friends of St Wulfram's Church; FBIM 1986; *Recreations* church architecture, reading fiction; *Style—* Mrs Jean Parker; Vacu-Lug Traction Tyres Ltd, Gonerby Hill Foot, Grantham, Lincolnshire (☎ 0476 62424, fax 0476 62736, car tel 0836 693 389)

PARKER, Hon Jocelyn George Dudley; s of 7 Earl of Macclesfield (d 1975); *b* 1920; *m* 1948, Daphne, da of late Maj G Cecil Whitaker, of Britwell House, Watlington, Oxon; 1 s, 1 da; *Career* European War 1939-45 as Lt RNVR; *Style—* The Hon Jocelyn Parker; Pyrton Field Farm, Watlington, Oxon

PARKER, John; CBE (1965); s of H A M Parker, schoolmaster; *b* 15 July 1906; *Educ* Marlborough, St John's Coll Oxford; *m* 1943, Zena Mimardiere; 1 s (Michael); *Career* MP (Lab) Romford 1935-45, Dagenham 1945-83, pres Fabian Soc 1980-; govr LSE 1949-81; father of the House of Commons 1979-83; hon sec Webb Tstees; memb: Historic Buildings Cncl 1974-84, Cncl Nat Tst 1969-81; tst memb History of Parliament 1978-; sr fell LSE; Yugoslav Red Star 1975; *Books* Father of the House: Fifty Years in Politics (1982); *Recreations* architecture, gardening; *Style—* John Parker Esq, CBE; 4 Essex Court, Temple, London EC4 (☎ 01 353 8521)

PARKER, Sir John (Edward); s of late Matthew Parker; *b* 28 Sept 1904; *Educ* Wesley Coll Melbourne, Queen's Coll Melbourne Univ; *m* 1932, Winifred Mary Becher; 2 s, 1 da; *Career* dep dir of Works Public Works Dept Perth WA 1953-62, dir of Engrg PWD Perth WA 1962-69, chm State Electricity Cmmn of WA 1969-74; kt 1975; *see Debrett's Handbook of Australia and New Zealand for further details*; *Style—* Sir John Parker; 11 Hopetoun St, South Perth, WA 6151, Australia (☎ Perth 67 1272)

PARKER, (Anthony) John; s of John Edward Parker (d 1977), of Nantwich, Cheshire, and Winnie May, *née* Bebbington; *b* 2 Oct 1942; *Educ* Nantwich Acton GS; *m* 21 June 1969, (Mary) Elizabeth, da of Frederick Langley, of Audlem, Cheshire; 2 s (Simon b 1972, Stephen b 1974), 1 da (Ann-Marie b 1978); *Career* quantity surveyor Brown & Richmond 1959-65, sr quantity surveyor Allott & Lomax 1965-71, dir Sika Contracts Ltd 1974-86 (sr mangr 1971-74), jt md (following mgmnt buy out) Sika Contracts 1986-; fndr memb and first chm Tech Ctee of Concrete Repair Assoc 1988-, memb working pty of The Concrete Soc (on repairs to reinforced concrete structures) 1988-; ARICS 1968, FInstD 1975; *Recreations* music, piano playing; *Clubs* IOD; *Style—* John Parker, Esq; Churton, Chester; Sika Contracts Ltd, Cuppin St, Chester, Cheshire CH1 2BN (☎ 0244 312 553)

PARKER, John Gordon; s of Henry Gordon Parker, CBE (d 1980), of Gooderstone, Norfolk, and Alice Rose, *née* Bennett (d 1974); *b* 20 May 1929; *Educ* Eton, Christ Church Oxford (BA), Mons Offr Cadet Sch; *m* 12 April 1958, Veronica Harriet, da of Blackburn of Roshven; 2 s (Hugo b 29 Sept 1963, d 1988, Edmund b 16 Nov 1972), 3 da (Sophie b 9 Feb 1959, Camilla b 9 March 1965, Lucinda b 27 Dec 1967); *Career* Nat Serv cmmnd 4/7 RDG 1948, Capt (AER) 1955; barr Inner Temple 1953, in practice 1953-59; dir Felixstowe Tank Devpt Ltd 1963-75, dir Favor Parker Ltd and subsides 1963-; govr Thetford GS, vice pres Hawk Tst (former chm); *Books* author of various articles in ornithological journals; *Recreations* shooting, bird watching; *Clubs* Cavalry and Guards'; *Style—* John Parker, Esq; Clavering House, Oxborough, Norfolk (☎ 036 621 781); Favor Parker Ltd, Stoke Ferry, King's Lynn, Norfolk (☎ 0366 500 911)

PARKER, Dr John Richard; s of Richard Robert Parker (d 1987), and Elsie Winifred, *née* Curtis; *b* 5 Nov 1933; *Educ* SE London Tech Coll, Regent St Poly (Dip Arch), UCL (Dip TP), Central London Poly (PhD); *m* 1959, Valerie Barbara Mary, da of Edward James Troupe Duguid (d 1952); 1 s (Jonathan b 1965), 1 da (Joanna b 1968); *Career* Nat Serv 2 Lt RE serv Canal Zone, Cyprus 1952-54, TA (Lt) 1954-64; with pte architects and commercial firms 1954-59, job architect LCC 1961-64, gp leader (spl projects) London Boro of Lambeth 1964-70, head central area team GLC 1970-86; fndr and md Greater London Conslts 1986-; originator many modern practices on dvpt at pub tport interchanges 1967-87, project mangr Piccadilly Circus reconstruction 1972-86, planning cnslt Ethiopian Govt on Addis Ababa 1986; Winston Churchill Fell 1967, RIBA Pearce Edwards Res Award 1969, Br Cncl Anglo-Soviet Travel Award 1988; ARIBA, FRTPI, FRSA ; *Publications* author of num pubns on urban design environmental planning, and pedestrians inc: Castles in the Air (1971), London's Canal (1976), Piccadilly Circus (1980), High-level Debate (1984), Improving Town Centres (1985), Safe Cities I (1986 and 1987); *Recreations* tennis, golf, drawing, painting, photography, astronomy, reading; *Clubs* Royal Cwlth; *Style—* Dr John Parker, Esq; 4 The Heights, Foxgrove Road, Beckenham, Kent BR3 2BY (☎ 01 658 6076); Greater London Consultants, Southbank House, Black Prince Road, London SE1 7SJ (☎ 01 735 8171, 01 582 5497/9279, fax 01 587 1320, telex 295555)

PARKER, (Thomas) John; s of Robert Parker (d 1957), and Margaret Elizabeth, *née* Bell; *b* 8 April 1942; *Educ* Belfast Coll of Technol; *m* July 1967, Emma Elizabeth, da of Alexander Blair, of Ballymena, N Ireland; 1 s (Graham b 31 July 1970), 1 da (Fiona b 1 June 1972); *Career* shipbuilder and engr; md Austin & Pickersgill (Shipbuilders) Sunderland 1974-78, bd memb for shipbuilding Br Shipbuilders Corpn 1978-80 (dep chief exec 1980), chm and chief exec Harland & Wolff Belfast 1983; memb: Indust Devpt Bd NI 1983-87, Br Coal Corpn 1986-; Hon DSc Queen's Univ of Belfast 1985, Hon ScD Trinity Coll Dublin 1986, FEng 1982, FRINA 1978, FIMarE 1979; *Recreations* sailing, reading, music, family pursuits; *Style—* John Parker Esq; Harland & Wolff plc, Queen's Island, Belfast BT3 9DU (☎ 0232 458456, telex 74396, fax 0232 458515)

PARKER, Vice-Adm Sir (Wilfred) John; KBE (1969, OBE 1953), CB (1965), DSC (1943); s of Henry Edmond Parker (d 1962), and Ida Mary Parker (d 1955); *b* 12 Oct 1915; *Educ* RNC Dartmouth, RNC Greenwich; *m* 1943, Marjorie Stuart, da of Alfred Nagle Jones (d 1961), of Halifax, Nova Scotia, Canada; 2 da; *Career* Capt RNC Dartmouth 1961-63, flag offr Medway and Adm Supt HM Dockyard Chatham 1966-69, ret 1969; *Clubs* Royal Navy; *Style—* Vice Adm Sir John Parker, KBE, CB, DSC; Flint Cottage, East Harting, Petersfield, Hants GU31 5LT (☎ 073 085 427)

PARKER, Jonathan Frederic; QC (1979); s of Sir (Walter) Edmund Parker (d 1981), and Elizabeth Mary, *née* Butterfield (d 1984); *b* 8 Dec 1937; *Educ* Winchester, Magdalene Coll Cambridge (MA); *m* 1967, Maria-Belen, da of Thomas Ferrier Burns OBE, of 14 Ashley Gardens, London SW1; 3 s (James b 1968, Oliver b 1969, Peter b 1971), 1 da (Clare b 1972); *Career* barr Inner Temple 1962; *Recreations* painting, sailing; *Clubs* Garrick; *Style—* Jonathan Parker Esq, QC; The Grange, Radwinter, Saffron Walden, Essex CB10 2TF (☎ 079987 375); 11 Old Sq, Lincoln's Inn, London WC2A 3TS (☎ 01 430 0341)

PARKER, Sir Karl Theodore; CBE (1954); s of late Robert William Parker, FRCS; *b* 1895; *Educ* Bedford, Paris, Zurich (MA, PhD); *m* Audrey (d 1976), da of Henry Ashworth James; 2 da; *Career* keeper of Ashmolean Museum Oxford Univ, ret 1962; tstee Nat Gallery 1962-69; hon fell Oriel Coll Oxford 1962; FBA; kt 1960; *Style—* Sir Karl Parker, CBE; 4 Saffrons Court, Compton Place Rd, Eastbourne

PARKER, Kenneth Alfred Lamport; CB (1959); s of A E A Parker and Ada Mary Parker; *b* 1 April 1912; *Educ* Tottenham GS, St John's Coll Cambridge; *m* 1938, Freda, OBE (1975), da of Ernest R W Silcock; 1 s, 1 da; *Career* Home Off 1934-67 (asst under-sec of state 1955-67), receiver for the Metropolitan Police Dist 1967-74; *Recreations* cellar, garden, library; *Clubs* Utd Oxford and Cambridge; *Style—* Kenneth Parker, Esq, CB; 18 Lichfield Rd, Kew, Surrey (☎ 01 940 4595)

PARKER, Lynne Eleanor; da of Ronald Samuel Parker and Audrey Eleanor, *née* Tyler; *b* 30 June 1956; *Educ* Ashford Co GS Middx, London Coll of Fashion; *Career* public relations conslt in own business Parker Lightman Public Relations 1983-; creator of Britain's Healthiest Couple Nat Competition; memb: Inst of Public Relations, Nat Union of Journalists, Network, Women in Enterprise; *Clubs* Groucho; *Style—* Ms Lynne Parker; 55 Wavendon Ave, London W4 4NT (☎ 01 474 3679); Parker Lightman, 36 Marshall St, London W1V 1LL

PARKER, Dame Marjorie Alice Collett; DBE (1977); da of W Shoppee, of Ballarat, Vic; *Educ* Ballarat State Sch; *m* 1926, Max Parker; 1 s; *Career* welfare worker Tasmania; dep-chm Australian Nat Cncl of Women, 1960-64, life-memb, 1974-, former vice-pres UN Assoc Launceston and former broadcaster/dir 7EX Radio Launceston; *Style—* Dame Marjorie Parker, DBE; Apsley, 5 Croydon Grove, Cypress St, Launceston, Tasmania 7250, Australia

PARKER, Cdr (John) Michael (Avison); CVO (1957, MVO 1953); s of late Capt C A Parker, CBE; *b* 23 June 1920; *Educ* Xavier Coll, Melbourne, Aus; *m* 1, 1943 (m dis 1958), Eileen Margaret Anne, nee Allan; 1 s, 1 da; m 2, 1962 (m dis), Carol (d 1977), da of Sir Ivo Thomson, 2 Bt; 1 s, 1 da; m 3, 1976, Mrs Jean Ramsay; *Career* RN (ret); chm: Mann's Tport, In-Situ Mining Conslts, Treglor Pty Ltd; dir Leo Burnett-Australia; *Style—* Cdr Michael Parker, CVO; Santosa, 33 Albany Rd, Toorak, Vic 3142

PARKER, His Honour Judge - Michael Clynes; s of Herbert Parker; *b* 2 Nov 1924; *Educ* City of London Sch, Pembroke Coll Cambridge; *m* 1950, Molly Leila Franklin; 1 s, 2 da; *Career* barr Gray's Inn 1949, QC 1979, a rec Crown Ct 1972-78, a Circuit judge 1978-; contested (L) S Kensington 1951; *Style—* His Honour Judge Parker; 17 Courtnell St, W2 (☎ 01 229 5249)

PARKER, Michael Joseph Bennett; s of Henry Gordon Parker, CBE, MM, TEM (d 1980), of Norfolk, and Alice Rose Parker, *née* Bennett (d 1975); *b* 22 June 1931; *Educ* Eton, Magdalene Coll Cambridge (BA Agric); *m* 1960, Tania Henrietta, da of Peter Frank Tiarks, of Beaminster; 2 s (Stephen b 1960, Benjamin b 1962), 1 da (Naomi b 1964); *Career* dir: Favour Parker Feeds (1963) and Farms (1965) Ltd, Avergene Ltd 1976, Br Chicken Ltd, Br Poultry Export Co Ltd 1985, Suffolk Sovereign Hldgs Ltd 1983 and various subsidiary Suffolk Sovereign Cos Ltd 1983-, Rowyell Roasters Ltd 1983, Sovereign Chicken Gp Ltd 1983, Aerotech Africa Ltd 1984, Pollohold Ltd 1963, Br Poultry Fedn Ltd 1984; memb UKAEA; *Recreations* country sports, windsurfing, lying in the sun; *Style—* Michael Parker, Esq; Gooderstone Manor, King's Lynn, Norfolk PE33 9SE (☎ 500911, telex 81135 FPFEED G)

PARKER, Hon Nigel Geoffrey; yst s of Hon John Holford Parker (d 1955) and bro of 6 Earl of Morley, qv; *b* 18 Nov 1931; *Educ* Eton, Trinity Coll Cambridge (BA); *m* 23 April 1965, Georgina Jane, eld da of Sir Thomas Gordon Devitt, 2 Bt; 1 s (Edward b 1967), 1 da (Theresa b 1966); *Career* late Grenadier Gds 1950-52; with Shell Petroleum Co Ltd; *Style—* The Hon Nigel Parker; Combe Lane Farm, Wormley, Godalming, Surrey

PARKER, Sir Peter; LVO (1985, MVO 1957); s of late Tom Parker and Dorothy Mackinlay Parker; *b* 30 August 1924; *Educ* Bedford Sch, London Univ, Lincoln Coll Oxford, Cornell and Harvard Univs; *m* 1951, Gillian, da of Sir Ernest Rowe-Dutton, KCMG, CB (d 1965); 3 s, 1 da; *Career* Maj Intelligence Corps 1943-47; fought Bedford as Labour candidate 1951; chm Br Rail Bd 1976-83, memb Br Airways Bd 1971-81; chm: Rockware Gp 1983- (dep chm 1981, chm 1971-76, dir 1976-83), Parkdale Hldgs plc 1988-, court of govrs LSE 1988-, Gp 4 Total Security Ltd 1988-, Whitehead Rice Ltd 1988-, Horace Holman Gp Ltd 1988-, Art Advertisers Ltd 1989-, The Japan Festival 1991 1987-; vice-chm Friends of the Earth Tst Ltd 1988, Tstees of HRH The Duke of Edinburgh's Cwlth Study Conference (UK Fund); dir: Renold Gp, H Clarkson & Co (Hldgs) 1976- (chm 1975-76), The United Kingdom - Japan 2000 Gp; dep chm Ct London Univ 1970-; CStJ 1982; hon fell Nuffield Coll Oxford and Westfield Coll Oxford; formerly with Booker McConnell, dir Booker Bros McConnell 1960-70; memb: Cncl BIM, Fndn Automation & Human Dvpt 1971-, NEDC 1980-; Hon LLD Bath 1983, Hon Dr The Open Univ; kt 1978; *Style—* Sir Peter Parker, LVO; 5 Chandos Street, London W1M 9DG (☎ 01 637 0369)

PARKER, Viscount; Richard Timothy George Mansfield Parker; s and h of 8 Earl of Macclesfield; *b* 31 May 1943; *Educ* Stowe, Worcester Coll Oxford; *m* 1, 1967 (m dis), Tatiana Cleone, da of Maj Craig Wheaton-Smith; 3 da (Hon Tanya b 1971, Hon Katharine b 1973, Hon Marian b (twin) 1973); m 2, 1986, Mrs Sandra Hope Mead; *Style—* Viscount Parker; Portobello Farm, Shirburn, Watlington, Oxon

PARKER, Sir Richard William; 12 Bt (E 1681), of Melford Hall, Suffolk; *see*: Hyde Parker, Sir Richard William

PARKER, Robert John; s of Eric Robert Parker (d 1984), and Joan Marjorie Parker; *b*

22 Feb 1952; *Educ* Whitgift Sch, St John's Coll Cambridge (MA); *m* 28 Aug 1982, Claudia Jane, da of Col Alexander Akerman; 1 s (Felix Alexander b 12 Feb 1987); *Career* asst dir NM Rothschild & Sons Ltd 1976-82; dir Credit Suisse First Boston 1982-; Freeman City of London, Liveryman Worshipful Co of Farriers; *Style—* Robert Parker, Esq; Credit Suisse First Boston, UK House, 2A Great Titchfield Street, London W1

PARKER, Robert Stewart; s of Robert Arnold Parker, and Edna, *née* Baines; *b* 13 Jan 1949; *Educ* Brentwood Sch, Trinity Coll Oxford (BA, MA); *Career* called to the Bar 1975, ad Eundem Lincoln's Inn 1977, Off of the Pty Cncl 1980, Dep Pty Cncl 1987, Law cmmn 1985-87; Freeman City of London 1984, Liveryman Worshipful Co of Wheelwrights 1984; MBIM 1984; *Books* Cases and Statutes on General Principles of English Law (with C R Newton,a 1980); *Recreations* the livery, cricket, bridge, books, music, computing; *Clubs* Athenaeum, City Livery; *Style—* Robert Parker, Esq; Office of the Parliamentary Counsel, 36 Whitehall, SW1A 2AY

PARKER, Hon Robin Michael; s of late Hon John Holford Parker and bro of 6 Earl of Morley; *b* 1925; *Educ* Eton; *Career* Col KRCC; Palestine 1946-48 (despatches) cmdg 2 Bn R Green Jackets 1967-69; final rank Brigadier; ret 1980; raised to the rank of an Earl's son 1963; *Style—* The Hon Robin Parker; Saltram, Plympton, Devon

PARKER, Rt Hon Lord Justice; Rt Hon Sir Roger Jocelyn Parker; PC (1983); s of Capt Hon T T Parker, DSC, RN (d 1975), and Marie Louise Leonie, *née* Kleinwort (d 1949); *b* 25 Feb 1923; *Educ* Eton, King's Coll Cambridge; *m* 1948, Ann Elizabeth Frederika, *née* White; 1 s, 3 da; *Career* serv Rifle Brigade 1942-47; barr Lincoln's Inn 1948, QC 1961, bencher 1969, High Ct judge (Queen's Bench) 1977-83, judge of the Cts of Appeal Jersey & Guernsey 1974-83, lord justice of appeal 1983; kt 1977; *Style—* The Rt Hon Lord Justice Parker; The Old Rectory, Widford, nr Ware, Herts (☎ Much Hadham (027 984) 2593)

PARKER, Ronald William; CBE (1959), JP (City and Co of Edinburgh); s of late Ernest Edward Parker, MBE, and Margaret, *née* Henderson; *b* 21 August 1909; *Educ* Royal HS Edinburgh; *m* 1937, Phyllis Mary, *née* Sherren; 2 s; *Career* CA 1933; chm Scottish Region (Scottish Div) NCB 1955-68, chm Scottish Gas Region (formerly Scottish Gas Bd) 1968-74; *Clubs* The New Edinburgh; *Style—* Ronald Parker Esq, CBE, JP; Claremont, 3 South Lauder Rd, Edinburgh EH9 2LL (☎ 031 667 7666)

PARKER, Timothy James; s of Malcolm Topsfield Parker (d 1978); *b* 28 Oct 1942; *Educ* London Coll of Printing, Bath Univ; *m* 1970, (m dis 1980), Patricia May, da of John Percy Robert Smith, of Dartmouth; 2 da; *Career* Chief Exec Booth Indust PLC, TJP Mgmnt dir: Forrest Recruitment Ltd; *Recreations* tennis, skiing, sailing, theatre; *Clubs* Royal Automobile, St James's, Manchester Tennis & Raquet; *Style—* Timothy Parker Esq; 2 Glenfield, Highgate Rd, Altrincham, Cheshire WA14 4QZ (☎ 061 928 6363)

PARKER, Lady Venetia Katherine; da of 6 Earl of Morley; *b* 1960; *Style—* Lady Venetia Parker; Pound House, Yelverton, Devon

PARKER, William Joseph; s of Roger Noel, and Olive Alice, *née* Deane; *b* 8 August 1946; *Educ* Wychwood Bournemouth, Trent Coll Long Eaton; *m* 16 Aug 1969, Hurst, da of Robert Stuart, of Grand Cayman, BWI; 1 s (Andrew b 1971), 1 da (Clare b 1973); *Career* dir numerous cos incl: W & J Parker Ltd, Leicester Slaughtering Co Ltd, Harrison & King Ltd, Marney Firms Ltd, Parker Farms Ltd, Agricaid Ltd; *Recreations* boating; *Style—* William J Parker, Esq; 26 Knighton Grange Road, Leicester LE2 2LE (☎ 0533 703758); W & J Parker Ltd, Cattle Market, Leicester LE2 7LU (☎ 0533 548484, fax 558579, car phone 0860 522726

PARKER, William Peter Brian; s & h of Sir (William) Alan Parker, 4th Bt; *b* 30 Nov 1950; *Educ* Eton; *m* 1976, Patricia Ann, da of R Filtness; 1 s (John b 1980), 1 da (Lucy b 1977); *Career* ACA; *Style—* William Parker Esq; Cedar House, Vicarage Lane, N Muskham, Newark, Notts

PARKER OF WADDINGTON, Baroness - Loryn; da of Oscar Tilton Bowser, of Kentucky, USA; *m* 1924, the Hon Sir Herbert Lister Parker, PC, later Baron Parker of Waddington (Life Peer 1958) (d 1972); *Style—* The Rt Hon the Lady Parker of Waddington; 20 Dunraven st, W1

PARKER-JERVIS, Roger; DL (Bucks 1982); s of George Parker-Jervis (himself gs of Hon Edward Parker-Jervis, 2 s of 2 Viscount St Vincent), and Ruth, da of Charles Farmer; *b* 11 Sept 1931; *Educ* Eton, Magdalene Coll Cambridge; *m* 1958, his 2 cous once removed Diana, eldest da of Capt Robert St Vincent Parker-Jervis (himself ggs of Hon Edward P-J, *see above*); 2 s (Edward Swynfen b 1959, Guy b 1960), 1 da (Lucy Alice b 1966); *Career* land agent; cmmn Nat Serv The Rifle Bde; ADC to govr of Tasmania 1954-56, memb Bucks Co Cncl 1967-, chm Bucks CC 1981-85, pres Timber Growers Orgn 1981-83, High Sheriff Bucks 1973; *Style—* Roger Parker-Jervis Esq, DL; Pond House, Great Hampden, nr Great Missenden, Bucks HP16 9RJ (☎ 024 028 531)

PARKES, Sir Alan Sterling; CBE (1956); s of E T Parkes, of Purley; *b* 1900; *Educ* Willaston Sch, Christ's Coll Cambridge (BA, ScD), Manchester Univ (PhD), Univ Coll London (DSc); *m* 1933, Ruth, da of Edward Deanesly, FRCS; 1 s, 2 da; *Career* chm Galton Foundation 1969-85; hon memb: Soc for Endocrinology, Soc for Study of Fertility, Soc for Cryobiology, Biosocial Soc, American Fertility Soc; fell Christ's Coll Cambridge 1961-69, hon fell 1970; fell UCL, FRS; kt 1968; *Style—* Sir Alan Parkes, CBE; 1 The Bramleys, Shepreth, Royston, Herts SG8 6PY

PARKES, Sir Basil Arthur; OBE (1966), JP; s of late Sir Fred Parkes; *b* 20 Feb 1907; *Educ* Boston GS Lincs; *m* 1933, May Lewis McNeill (d 1988); 2 s, 1 da; *Career* formerly with family trawler owning co; pres N Br Maritime Gp Ltd (formerly Utd Towing Ltd) 1960-; Offr de l'Ordre National de Mérite (France), hon brother Trinity House Kington upon Hull, vice-pres Br Tugowners Assoc; memb: Worshipful Co of Fishmongers, Worshipful Co of Poulters; Ordre de la Couronne; kt 1971; *Style—* Sir Basil Parkes, OBE, JP; Loghan-y-Yuiy, The Garey, Lezayre, nr Ramsey, Isle of Man

PARKES, Cyril; s of Joseph Thomas Parkes (d 1947), of Bell End, Rowley Regis, and Annie Sophia, *née* Bedford (d 1949); *b* 16 August 1904; *m* 30 May 1935, Agnes Elizabeth (Betty), da of William Watkins (d 1965) of Cradley Heath, Staffs; 2 s (Jonathon Michael Cyril b 1937, David Dulane b 1939); *Career* elec engr AEI (now EEC) 1919, engr with Wm Morris (later Lord Nuffield) 1924, hotel mangr 1929, butler to Lady Rose Wyborn; proprietor decorators merchant building business (expanded into chain of paint and wallpaper shops and paint mfr 1933-75; former memb: Staffordshire CC, Rowley Regis BC; fndr memb: Sons of Rest Mens Fellowship, Cradley Heath Speedway and Greyhound Stadium, Cradleigh Physically Handicapped Club; pres Cradley Heath FC; Rotarian for many years still active in many charitable projects; *Style—* C Parkes, Esq; Clent Hall, Clent, nr Stourbridge, W Midlands DY9 9PJ (☎ 0562 882 320)

PARKES, Daniel William; s of John William Parkes (d 1940), of 76 Laurel Grove, Penge, London, and May Emily, *née* Chesterman (d 1964); *b* 12 Dec 1919; *Educ* Northampton Poly; *m* 16 April 1971, Grace Iris, da of Fredrick Harold Simmons (d 1914); *Career* RAFVR 1939-45, propietor A & H Rowley Parkes & Co 1971- (journeyman 1945-47, ptnr 1947-71); instr Northampton Poly 1952-57, fndr memb Antiquarian Horological Soc 1952; Freeman City of London, Liveryman Worshipful Co Clockmakers 1976 (Freeman 1969 by gift); FRSA 1982; *Books* Early English Clocks (1982); *Recreations* singing in the choir, sailing; *Style—* Daniel Parkes, Esq; 95 Beaulie Ave, Sydenham, London SE26 6PW; 17 Briset St, Clerkenwell, London EC1M 5NR (☎ 01 253 3110)

PARKES, Sir Edward Walter; s of Walter Parkes; *b* 19 May 1926; *Educ* King Edward's Birmingham, St John's Coll Cambridge; *m* 1950, Margaret, JP (govr BBC, chm London Diocesan Bd of Educn, memb Schs Examination Cncl), da of John Parr; 1 s, 1 da; *Career* head engrg dept Leicester Univ 1960-65, prof mechanics Cambridge 1965-74, vice-chllr City Univ 1974-78; memb: advsy bd for res cncls 1974-83, Univ and Poly Grants Ctee Hong Kong 1974-; chm University Grants Ctee 1978-83; chm advsy panel to sec of state for Environment on issues relating to Black Country limestone 1983-; vice-chllr Univ of Leeds 1983-; ScD, FEng; kt 1982; *Clubs* Athenaeum; *Style—* Sir Edward Parkes; University of Leeds, Leeds LS2 9JT (☎ 431751)

PARKES, Francis Patrick; s of Alfred Herbert Parkes (d 1978); *b* 26 Mar 1932; *Educ* Bryanston, Aiglon Coll Switzerland; *m* June, da of James Alfred Coltas (d 1976); 1 s, 1 da; *Career* md Don Int (formerly Small and Parkes Ltd) 1965-70, dir Cape Industs 1970-82, mgmnt conslt 1982-; *Recreations* travel, gardening; *Style—* Francis Parkes Esq; Cherry Trees, Cane End, nr Reading, Berks (☎ Kidmore End 723416)

PARKES, John Hubert; CB (1984); s of Frank Hubert Parkes; *b* 1 Oct 1930; *Educ* George Dixon Sch Birmingham, Magdalen Coll Oxford; *m* 1956, Elsie Griffiths Henderson; 2 s; *Career* permanent sec Dept of Education N Ireland 1979-; *Style—* John Parkes, Esq, CB; c/o Dept of Education, Rathgael House, Balloo Rd, Bangor, Co Down, NI

PARKES, Norman James; CBE (1976, OBE 1960); s of Ernest William Parkes, CMG (d 1941), and his 1 w, Susannah Ellen, *née* Hall; *b* 29 July 1912; *Educ* Victorian State Schs; *m* 1937, Maida Cleave, da of James Nicholas Silk; 2 s; *Career* clerk of the Australian House of Representatives 1971-76, ret; *Recreations* Bowls; *Clubs* Canberra Press, Canberra Bowling; *Style—* Norman Parkes, Esq, CBE; 3/3 Nuyts St, Red Hill, Canberra, ACT 2603, Australia

PARKIN, Ian Michael; s of George Harold Parkin, of Lincett Ct, Lincett Ave, W Worthing, W Sussex, and Ethel Mary, *née* Fullerton; *b* 15 Oct 1946; *Educ* Dorking Co GS, Open Univ (BA); *m* 30 April 1977, Patricia Helen, da of Maj Frederick James Fowles, MC (d 1982); 2 s (Andrew b 1978, Richard b 1984), 1 da (Jennifer b 1981); *Career* CA; sr ptnr Pannell Kerr Forseter CI, ptnr Pannell Kerr Forster, Gibraltar; vice-pres Praxis Panorama A G Zürich, Switzerland; FCA; *Recreations* golf, reading, sailing; *Style—* Ian Parkin, Esq; Le Petit Jardin, La Rue a la Pendue, Millais, St Ouen, Jersey (☎ 0534 83218); Pannell Kerr Forseter, Trinity House, Bath St, St Helier, Jersey, CI

PARKIN, John Mackintosh; s of Thomas Parkin and Emily; *b* 18 June 1920; *Educ* Nottingham HS, Emmanuel Coll Cambridge (MA); *m* Biancamaria Giuganino; 2 da; *Career* serv RA WWII, Capt; asst under-sec state MOD 1974-80, asst sec Lord Chancellor's Dept 1981-82, admin Royal Courts of Justice 1982-85; *Style—* John Parkin, Esq; 35 Little Bornes, London SE21 8SD

PARKIN, Leonard; s of Leonard Parkin (d 1952), and Helena, *née* Wood (d 1975); *b* 2 June 1929; *Educ* Hemsworth GS Yorks; *m* 4 June 1955, Barbara Anne, da of Donald Rowley (d 1971), of York; 1 s (Jeremy b 1957); *Career* journalist and broadcaster; reporter and feature writer Yorks Observer and Telegraph and Argus Bradford 1951-54, reporter and sub-ed Yorks Evening News 1954-65; BBC reporter and foreign corr: Canada 1960, USA 1963-65; reporter Panorama and Twenty Four Hours 1965-67; IN 1967-87: reporter (later foreign corr and newcaster) News at Ten, News at 5.45, News at One; anchorman special ITN programmes, election specials; presenter corporate video programmes, dir Hyvision Ltd 1988; chm Welwyn Soc, fndr memb Welwyn Film Record Soc, pres Herts Fly Dressers' Guild, former pres The Lytton Players Stevenage; *Books* contributer to sporting magazines, The Field; *Recreations* cricket, trout fishing, shooting; *Clubs* MCC, The Lord's Taverners; *Style—* Leonard Parkin, Esq; The Moorings, Welwyn, Herts AL6 9EL; Hallgarth, Pickering, N Yorks YO18 7AW

PARKINS, Brian James Michael; JP; s of Ronald Anthony Parkins (d 1979), of Ilford, Essex, and Adelaide Florence, Percival; *b* 1 Nov 1938; *Educ* St Ignatius Coll London, King's Coll Hosp and Univ of London (BDS), Inst of Dental Surgery and RCS (LDS, FDS,), Northwestern Univ Chicago (MS); *m* 20 Oct 1966 (m dis 1980), Jill Elizabeth, da of James Dawson (d 1982), of Lytham St Annes; 1 s (Richard Mark b 1 March 1971), 1 da (Alison) Jane b 14 Nov 1967); m 2 19 May 1988, Mary Saunders, *née* Burton; *Career* conslt dental surgn; sr clinical lectr Inst of Dental Surgery 1969-81, private practice 1970-, recognised teacher of the Univ of London 1972, conslt in restorative dentistry UCL and Middx Hosp Sch of Dent 1982; pres Br Soc for Restorative Dentistry 1987-88 (cncl memb 1982-84); sec: ADSL and ADSE; examiner: Vol Bds, RCS for LDS Final Pe III and MGDS; hon memb ADA Pierre Fouchard Acad; FRSM, FICD, FACD; *Recreations* music; *Clubs* Lansdowne; *Style—* Brian Parkins, Esq, JP; 57 Portland Place, London W1N 3AH (☎ 01 580 7146)

PARKINSON, Rt Hon Cecil Edward; PC (1981), MP (C) Hertsmere 1983-; s of Sidney Parkinson, of Carnforth, Lancs; *b* 1 Sept 1931; *Educ* Royal Lancaster GS, Emmanuel Coll Cambridge; *m* 1957, Ann Mary, da of F A Jarvis, of Harpenden; 3 da (Mary, Emma, Joanna); *Career* joined West, Wake, Price & Co 1956, ptnr 1961-71; formerly with Metal Box Co, founded Parkinson Hart Securities Ltd 1967; chm Hemel Hempstead Cons Assoc 1966-69, chm Herts 100 Club 1968-69, contested (C) Northampton 1970, MP (C): Enfield W Nov 1970-74, Herts S 1974-1983; sec Cons Parly Fin Ctee 1971-72, PPS to Michael Heseltine as Min for Aerospace and Shipping (DTI) 1972-74, asst govt whip 1974, oppn whip 1974-76, oppn spokesman Trade 1976-79, min of state Dept of Trade 1979-81, chm Cons Pty and Paymaster-General 1981-83, chllr Duchy of Lancaster 1982-83, sec of state Trade and Indust June 1983-Oct 1983 (resigned); Sec of State for Energy 1987-, govr: Aldenham Sch, Royal

Lancaster GS; *Style*— The Rt Hon Cecil Parkinson, MP; The Old Vicarage, Northaw, Potters Bar, Herts

PARKINSON, Prof Cyril Northcote; s of William Edward Parkinson, ARCA, principal York Sch of Art, and Rose Emily Mary, *née* Curnow; *b* 30 July 1909; *Educ* St Peter's Sch York, Emmanuel Coll Cambridge (BA), King's Coll London (PhD); *m* 1, 1943 (m dis 1950) Ethelwyn Edith, da of Francis Graves, editor Windsor Express; 1 s (Christopher b 1945), 1 da (Alison b 1943); m 2, 1952, (Elizabeth) Ann (d 1983), da of Lt-Col Fry, MC, RA; 2 s (Charles b 1955, Jonathan b 1961), 1 da (Antonia b 1958); m 3, 1 June 1985, Iris Hilda (Ingrid), da of Norman Victor Waters (d 1971); *Career* 2 Lt TA Reserve 1932, Lt 22 London Regt (The Queen's) 1933, Capt Blundell's Sch Tiverton OTC, Capt 166 OCTU 1940, Maj Gen Staff 1943, demob 1944, Hon Lt-Col Alabama Militia; author, historian and journalist; seigneur of Anneville, Mauxmarquis and Beavoir; sr history master Blundell's Sch Tiverton, master RNC Dartmouth 1938 and 1944-46; lectr Univ of Liverpool 1947-50; Raffles prof of history Univ of Singapore 1950-58; prof emeritus Troy State Univ Alabama USA 1970-; chm Leviathan House (Publishers) 1972-; Fell of Emmanuel Coll Cambridge, Hon LLD, DLitt, Hon Dr of Business Organisation; FRHistS; *Books* numerous books and novels and contributions to Encyclopaedia Britannica, Economist, Guardian, Punch, Saturday Evening Post and other journals; *Recreations* printing, travel; *Clubs* Army and Navy, Royal Channel Islands Yacht; *Style*— Professor C Northcote Parkinson; 36 Harkness Drive, Canterbury, Kent CT2 7RW (☎ 0227 452742)

PARKINSON, Dr David Hardress; s of E R H Parkinson; *b* 9 Mar 1918; *Educ* Gravesend Co GS, Wadham Coll Oxford (MA, DPhil); *m* 1, 1944, Muriel Gwendoline Patricia (d 1971), da of Capt P W Newenham; 2 s; m 2, 1974 (m dis 1978) Daphne Margaret Scott-Gall; *Career* RA 1939-45, Maj; Royal Radar Estab: supt Low Temperature and Magnetics Div Malvern 1956-63, head Physics Gp 1963-68, head Physics and Electronics Dept and dep dir 1968-72; hon prof Birmingham Univ 1966-73; dir-gen Estabs Resources and Programmes MOD 1973-77; CPhys FInstP; *Recreations* silver-smithing; *Clubs* Royal Commonwealth Soc; *Style*— Dr David Parkinson; South Bank, 47 Abbey Rd, Great Malvern, Worcs WR14 3HH (☎ Malvern 5423)

PARKINSON, Desmond Frederick; CMG (1975); s of Lt-Col Percy Willoughby Parkinson (d 1941); *b* 26 Oct 1920; *Educ* Winchester, RMC Sandhurst; *m* 1, 1947 (m dis 1957), Ann Deborah Durnford; 2 s, 1 da; m 2, 1970, Heather Marguerite, da of Brig Ivor Douglas-Brown, OBE; 1 da; m 3, 1977, Patricia Jean Campbell Taylor; *Career* HM Dip Serv; serv: Rangoon, Jakarta, FO, Rabat, Lagos, FO, Singapore, Delhi, FCO 1967-78, ret; *Recreations* golf, gardening; *Clubs* Huntercombe Golf; *Style*— Desmond Parkinson, Esq, CMG; Woodrow, Silchester, nr Reading, Berks (☎ Reading 700257)

PARKINSON, Lady Elizabeth Mary; *née* Murray; da of 10 Earl of Dunmore (d 1981), and Patricia Mary, *née* Coles, now Mrs Geoffrey Fitze; *b* 1951; *m* 1973, John Michael Parkinson; 1 s, 2 da; *Style*— Lady Elizabeth Parkinson; RD Tasman Highway, Cambridge, Hobart, Tasmania 7170, Australia

PARKINSON, Ewart West; s of Thomas Edward Parkinson (d 1958), of 48 Belgrave Ave, Leicester, and Lilian Esther West, *née* Hammond (d 1966); *b* 9 July 1926; *Educ* Wyggeston Sch Leicester, Coll of Tech Leicester, London Univ (BSc, DPA); *m* 21 Aug 1948, Patricia Joan, da of Capt William John Lawson Wood (d 1985), of 30 Eastfield Rd, Leicester; 2 s (Mark b 1951, Michael b 1955), 1 da (Veronica b 1959); *Career* princ engr Bristol 1949-50, chief asst Dover 1954-57, dep Borough Engr 1957-60, dep city Surveyor Plymouth 1960-64, City Planning Offr Cardiff 1964-74, dir of Environment S Glam 1974-85; dvpt advsr and co dir 1985-; specialised rebuilding and regeneration war damaged cities; chm and fndr Star Leisure & Recreation Ist, Wales Sport Centre for the Disabled Tst; managing tstee Norwegian Ch Preservation Tst, vice-pres Wales Cncl for the Disabled; chm facilities ctee Sports Cncl for Wales 1966-78, fdr and 1 chm Co Planning Offrs Soc for Wales; hon life memb Int Fedn of Housing & Planning (The Hague), Nat Housing & Town Planning Cncl diamon jubilee silver medal; OStJ; FICE, FRTPI (pres 1975-76); *Books* publications: num papers presented worldwide; *Recreations* working, being with friends and family; *Style*— Ewart Parkinson, Esq; 42 South Rise, Cardiff (☎ 0222 756 394); W S Atkins & Ptnrs, Longcross Court, Cardiff (☎ 0222 485 159, fax 0222 485 138)

PARKINSON, Graham Edward; s of Norman Edward Parkinson (d 1984), of Cliffwood Avenue, Birstall, Leicestershire, and Phyllis Parkinson, (*née* Jaquiss); *b* 13 Oct 1937; *Educ* Loughborough GS; *m* 1963, Dinah Mary, da of Walter Bevan Pyper (d 1969), of Julian Court, Julian Way, Harrow on the Hill, Middx; 1 s (Nicholas b 1967), 1 da (Georgina b 1973); *Career* ptnr slrs Darlington & Parkinson 1969-82; Metropolitan Stipendory Magistrate 1982; *Recreations* music, theatre, reading; *Style*— Graham E Parkinson, Esq; Highbury Corner, Magistrates Court, Holloway Rd N7 (☎ 01 607 6757)

PARKINSON, (Thomas) Harry; CBE (1972), DL (Warwicks 1970); s of G R J Parkinson; *b* 25 June 1907; *Educ* Bromsgrove, Birmingham Univ; *m* 1936, Catherine Joan, da of C J Douglas-Osborn; 2 s, 1 da; *Career* admitted slr 1930; RAF 1939-45; Birmingham town clerk 1960-72, clerk of the Peace 1970-72; Hon DSc Aston 1972; *Style*— Harry Parkinson Esq, CBE, DL; Stuart House, Middlefield Lane, Hagley, Worcs (☎ Hagley 882422)

PARKINSON, Dr James Christopher; TD (1962), MBE (1963); s of Charles Myers Parkinson MPS(d 1949), of Blackburn, Lancs, and Sarah Louisa, *née* Aspinall (d 1958); *b* 15 August 1920; *Educ* Queen Elizabeth's GS Blackburn, Univ Coll Nottingham (BPharm), Sch of Pharmacy, London Univ (PhD); *m* 11 April 1950, Gwyneth Margot (Bunty), B Pharm, da of Rev John Raymond Harrison (d 1973); 3 s (Andrew John b 1952, David Charles b 1954, Robert James b 1956); *Career* cmmnd Lancs Fusiliers 1943, LT parachute regt 1944, Capt Camp Cmdt 2 Parachute Bde 1945, Capt GSO 3 6 Airborne Div 1946, Adj 4 Parachute Fd Amb TA 1948, GSO 3 Air 16 Airborne Div TA 1952, Maj GSO 2 Air 44 Indep Para Gp TA 1958, Ret 1963;lectr Sch of pharmacy London Univ 1948-54, head Sch of Pharmacy Brighton Tech Coll 1954-64, dep sec Pharm Soc GB 1964-67, princ Brighton Tech Coll 1967-70, dep dit Brighton Poly 1970-83; memb: Res Degrees Ctee and Bds of Study Cncl for Nat Acad Awards 1965-75, Hustpie-point PCC, Deanery Synod (past chm), Chichester Diocesan Synod (past lay chm), Mid-Downs DHA 1984-87, Gen Synod CE 1970-85; memb: Fell Royal Pharm Soc GB 1948-; *Recreations* gardening, walking; *Style*— Dr James Parkinson, TD, MBE; Ravensmere, 92 Wickham Hill, Hurstpierpoint, W Sussex BN6 9NR (☎ 0273 833369)

PARKINSON, (Robert) Michael; s of Robert Scott Parkinson, of Lancaster, and Rhoda, *née* Chirnside (d 1964); *b* 9 August 1944; *Educ* Wrekin Coll, Coll of Estate Mgmnt London Univ (BSc); *m* 26 Oct 1968, Elizabeth Ann, da of Michael Moore, of Lancaster; 2 s (Duncan b 27 Nov 1969, Andrew b 4 Sept 1971); *Career* ptnr Ingham & York (chartered surveyors, land agents, auctioneers and valuers) 1971-, dir Marsden Building Soc 1984-; memb (formerly sec and chm) Lancs Cheshire & Isle of Man Branch Land Agency and Argicultural Div of RICS;; *Recreations* mountaineering, country pursuits; *Clubs* Fell and Rock Climbing; Rotary (Clitheroe), Clitheroe Ex-Tablers (41); Frics 1976;; *Style*— Michael Parkinson, Esq; Twiston Mill House, Twiston, Clitheroe, Lancs BB7 4DE (☎ 020 05 481); Ingham & Yorke, Littlemoor, Clitheroe, Lancs BB7 1HG (☎ 0200 23 655)

PARKINSON, Sir Nicholas Fancourt; s of late Rev C T Parkinson and Dorothy Fancourt, *née* Mitchell (d 1978); *b* 5 Dec 1925; *Educ* Tudor House Moss Vale NSW, King's Sch Parramatta, Sydney Univ (BA), London Univ; *m* 1952, Roslyn Sheena, da of late A D Campbell; 2 da; *Career* RAAF 1943-46; Aust diplomat 1951-82, sec Dept of Foreign Affairs Canberra 1977-79 (dep sec 1974-76), Australian ambass to the USA 1976-77 and 1979-82; dir Sears World Trade (Aust) Pty Ltd 1982-86; kt 1980; *see Debrett's Handbook of Australia and New Zealand for further details*; *Style*— Sir Nicholas Parkinson; 62 Collings St, Pearce, ACT 2607, Australia (☎ 861004)

PARKINSON, Norman; CBE (1980); *b* 21 April 1913; *Educ* Westminster; *m* 1945, Wenda, *née* Rogerson (d 1987, model and biographer of Toussaint L'Ouverture); 1 s (Simon); *Career* photographer; *Style*— Norman Parkinson Esq, CBE; Tobago, W Indies

PARKINSON, Ronald Dennis; s of the late Albert Edward Parkinson and the late Jennie Caroline Clara, *née* Meagher; *b* 27 April 1945; *Educ* St Dunstan's Coll, Clare Coll Cambridge (MA); *Career* res asst V & A 1972-74, asst keeper, Tate Gallery 1974-78; asst keeper V & A 1978-; co-ed Richard Redgrave (1988); *Recreations* reading, shopping; *Clubs* Algonquin; *Style*— Ronald Parkinson, Esq; Victoria And Albert Museum, London SW7 2RL (☎ 938 8474)

PARKS, (Robert) Ralph; *Educ* Columbia Univ NY (MBA), Rice Univ Houston (BA); *m* Gwendoline E (Wendy); 1 s (Gavin b 1979), 1 da (Cecily b 1976); *Career* 1 Lt US Army Field Artillery, serv Korea; Merill Lynch 1970-80 (md 1980), ptnr Goldman Sachs & Co NY 1986-88 (vice pres 1981-86), md Goldman Sachs Int Ltd 1988-; *Style*— Ralph Parks, Esq; Goldman Sachs International Limited, 8/10 New Fetter Lane, London EC4A 1DB (☎ 01 489 5832, fax 01 489 5432, telex 887902 GOSAC)

PARKYN, Brian Stewart; s of Leslie Parkyn (d 1985), of Whetstone, London N20, and Gwen, *née* Scott (d 1976); *b* 28 April 1923; *Educ* King Edward VI GS Chelmsford; *m* 17 March 1951, Janet Anne, da of Charles Stormer (d 1971), of Eastbourne, Sussex; 1 s (Nicholas b 1954), 1 da (Jenifer b 1957); *Career* dir: Scott Bader Co Ltd 1953-83 (joined 1947), Trylon Ltd 1944-56, Halmatic Ltd 1979-87; princ Assoc Engrg Business Mgmnt Sch 1976-80, gen mangr trg Br Caledonian Airways Ltd 1981-88; cncl memb Cranfield Inst of Technol 1970-, RSA 1976-82 (hon tres 1977-82), chm Reinforced Plastics Gp of Br Plastics Fedn 1959-63; memb of ct: Bradford Univ 1972-75, RCA 1974-80; MP for Bedford 1966-70, memb Select Ctee Sci and Technol 1966-70, chm Carbon Fibre Sub Ctee 1969; FPRI 1969, FRSA 1964; *Books* Polyester Handbook (1953), Unsaturated Polyesters (1967), Glass Reinforced Plastics (ed 1970), Democracy Accountability and Participation in Industry (1979); *Style*— Brian Parkyn, Esq; 9 Clarendon Sq, Leamington Spa, Warwicks CV32 5QJ (☎ 0926 330 066)

PARLETT, Michael Harold James; s of Lyall Mervyn Malzard Parlett, of Belle Hougue, Cote du Nord, Trinity, Jersey CI, and Catherine, *née* McDougall Gray ; *b* 16 Nov 1940; *Educ* Winchester, Millfield, St Andrews Univ (BSc); *m* 2 Sept 1967, Elizabeth Ann, da of Dr Frederick Roy Gusterson; 2 da (Lucinda b 1969, Clare b 1971); *Career* Shell Int Petroleum 1961-68, shel Sekiyv 1968-73, investmt mangr Stewart Fund Mangrs 1973-74, exec dir Murray Johnstone Ltd 1974-83, vice-pres and dir Kemper Murray Johnstone Int Ltd 1983-; *Recreations* skiing, hill-walking; *Clubs* Western Club Glasgow; *Style*— Michael Parlett, Esq; Glebe House, Manse Rd, Linlithgow (☎ 0506 844247); 11 West Nile St, Glasgow (☎ 041 226 3131, fax 041 248 5420)

PARMOOR, 4 Baron (UK 1914); (Frederick Alfred) Milo Cripps; s of 3 Baron Parmoor, DSO, TD, DL (d 1977), and of Violet Mary Geraldine (d 1983), da of Sir William Nelson, 1 Bt; *b* 18 June 1929; *Educ* Ampleforth, Corpus Christi Coll Oxford; *Heir* cous, (Matthew) Anthony Leonard Cripps, *qv*; *Style*— The Rt Hon the Lord Parmoor; Dairy Cottage, Duck Street, Sutton Veny, Wilts

PARNELL, Alexandra; da of Capt Cyril Henry Parnell, (d 1985), of Dorking, Surrey, and Heather, *née* Beasley; *b* 3 May 1952; *Educ* Purley Co GS for girls; *m* 20 April 1974, (m dis 1982), Geoffrey Willis; *Career* asst sec to The Hon David Astor ed The Observer 1970-72, sec to Betty Reyburn, features ed Woman's Journal 1972-73, fashion asst Woman's Journal 1973-75, asst fashion ed Country Life 1975-78, fashion ed Woman's Journal 1978-, TV Broadcasting and radio; memb Inst of Journalists; *Recreations* cats, horses, foreign travel; *Clubs* Zanzibar; *Style*— Ms Alexandra Parnell; King's Reach Tower, London SE1 (☎ 01 261 6064, fax 01 261 6062, telex 915748 MAGDNG)

PARNELL, Hon Elizabeth Dagny; da of 8 Baron Congleton; *b* 1960; *Style*— The Hon Mrs Parnell

PARNELL, Hon John Patrick Christian; s and h of 8 Baron Congleton, *qv*; *b* 17 Mar 1959; *m* 1985, Marjorie-Anne, o da of John Hobdell, of The Ridings, Cobham, Surrey; 1 s (Christopher); *Style*— The Hon John Parnell

PARNELL, Hon Mary Clare; da of 8 Baron Congleton; *b* 1965; *Style*— The Hon Mary Parnell

PARNELL, Hon Thomas David Howard; s of 8 Baron Congleton; *b* 1963; *Style*— The Hon Thomas Parnell

PARNWELL, Peter Wilfred; s of Wilfred Horace Parnwell (d 1947), and Ella Edith, *née* Abbott (d 1965); *b* 24 May 1925; *Educ* Merchant Taylors'; *m* 1, 1947, Edna Buchanan; m 2, 1951, Evelyn Taylor; m 3, 1956, Gillian Pickrell; 2 s (Martin b 1956, Adrian b 1961); m 4, 1977, Anne Horsfall; *Career* WWII A & SH served Normandy and NW Europe (wounded); African traveller and safari operator, guide to Legion Etrangere, discovered Tibesti rock paintings, dir several trading cos; memb Legion of Frontiersmen; Freeman City of London; *Books* Puritan and Patriot - the life of Robert Balke; *Recreations* tennis, archaeology, cartophily; *Style*— Peter Parnwell, Esq

PARR, Hon Mrs (Caroline Mary); *née* Renton; da of Baron Renton, KBE, TD, PC, QC, DL; *b* 22 Nov 1948; *m* 1, 1970 (m dis 1974), Peter Dodds Parker; m 2, 1977, Robin Parr; has 1 child by each marriage; *Style*— The Hon Mrs Parr; Port Mary

House, Dundrennan, Kirkcudbright (☎ (05575) 654)

PARR, (Thomas) Donald; CBE (1986); s of Thomas Parr (d 1975), of Bramhall, Cheshire, and Elizabeth Parr; *b* 3 Sept 1930; *Educ* Burnage GS; *m* 1954, Gwendoline Mary, da of Frank Lawton Chaplin, of Cheadle, Cheshire (d 1969); 2 s, 1 da; *Career* chm William Baird plc 1981- (textile and industrial gp), regional dir Lloyds Bank, non exec dir Dunhill Hldgs plc; *Recreations* sailing (yacht 'Quailo'); *Clubs* Royal Yacht Sqdn, Royal Ocean Racing; *Style*— Donald Parr, Esq, CBE; Homestead, Homestead Rd, Disley, Stockport, Cheshire SK12 2JP; Broadstone House, Broadstone Rd, Reddish, Stockport, Cheshire SK5 7DL (☎ 061 442 8118); William Baird plc, 79 Mount St, W1Y 5HJ (☎ 01 409 1785, telex 886376)

PARRACK, Lt Cdr Paul Adrian; s of Stanley Herbert Parrack, of Petworth, W Sussex, and Emma Edith, *née* Gibb; *b* 10 Mar 1940; *Educ* Hove Co GS, Open Univ (BA); *m* 2 Feb 1963, Susan Margaret, da of Gordon Lay, of Horsham, W Sussex; 3 da (Skeeter b 1963, Keely b 1967, Eloise b 1977); *Career* naval airman RN 1958; served as a photographer in: HMS Victorious, HMS Simbang, HMS Protector; cmmnd Sub Lt (X) (aviation) 1970, asst flight deck offr HMS Eagle 1972-73, photo offr HMS Ark Royal 1975-76, exchange duty with US Navy (USN Photo Center Washington DC 1977-79); Photo Offr: staff of Capt submarine sea training 1979-81, staff of Flag Offr submarines 1981-83; 1 Lt HMS Cochrane 1983, offr cmdg Jt Servs Sch of Photography 1985-86; FBIPP 1986; *Recreations* sailing, photography, walking; *Style*— Lt Cdr Paul Parrack; 38 Denvilles Close, Havant, Hampshire (☎ 0705 471 350); Directorate General Aircraft (Navy), St Georges Ct, New Oxford St, London (☎ 01 632 3651)

PARRIS, Matthew Francis; s of Leslie Francis Parris; *b* 7 August 1949; *Educ* Waterford Sch Swaziland, Clare Coll Cambridge, Yale Univ USA; *Career* FO 1974-76; Cons research dept 1976-79, presenter Weekend World LWT 1986; MP (C) West Derbyshire 1979-86; *Recreations* running, travelling, reading; *Style*— Matthew Parris Esq; 41 Bramfield Rd, SW11 6RA

PARRITT, Clive Anthony; s of Allan Edward Parritt, MBE, and Peta, *née* Lloyd; *b* 11 April 1943; *Educ* private; *m* 1, 28 Sept 1968 (m dis 1984), Valerie Joyce, da of Jesse Sears, of Reigate, Surrey; 2 s (James b 1977, Daniel b 1980); m 2, 5 Oct 1985, Deborah, da of Kenneth Jones, of Tenby, Wales; 1 s (Matthew b 1987); *Career* CA; ptnr 1973-82: Fuller Jenks Beecroft, Mann Judd, Touche Ross & Co; managing ptnr 1987-: Howard Tilly & Co (ptnr 1982-), Baker Tilly (ptnr 1982-); memb Nat Assoc of CA Students Soc 1965-67 (chm London branch 1965-66); chm London Soc of CAs 1982-83 (tres 1980-82), chm Redhill and Reigate Round Table 1976-77, tres Br Theatre Assoc 1984-87, memb advsy panel to enterprise and deregulation unit DTI 1986-88; FCA 1966 (cncl memb 1983-); *Recreations* theatre, entertaining, gardening; *Style*— Clive Parritt, Esq; 50 Northchurch Road, London N1 4EJ (☎ 01 254 8562); Baker Tilly, Commonwealth House, 1 New Oxford Street, London WC1A 1PF (☎ 01 404 5541, fax 01 405 2836, telex 21594)

PARROT, Hon Mrs (Deirdre Barbara Elland); *née* Lumley-Savile; da of late 2 Baron Savile, KCVO (who assumed by Royal licence surname Savile after that of Lumley) by 2 w, Esmé, *née* Wolton; *b* 1928; *m* 1948, Col Kent Kane Parrot, US Air Force (ret); 2 s, 1 da; *Style*— The Hon Mrs Parrot; 5506 Grove St, Chevy Chase, Maryland, USA (☎ 301 656 3114)

PARROTT, Lady (Ellen Julie); da of Hermann Matzow, of Trondjem, Norway; *m* 1935, Sir Cecil (Cuthbert) Parrott, KCMG, OBE (d 1984); 2 s; *Style*— Lady Parrott

PARRY *see also*: Jones-Parry

PARRY, Alan; s of George Henry Edgar James Parry (d 1984), of Upper Gatton Park, Reigate, Surrey, and Jessica, *née* Cooke; *b* 30 Oct 1927; *Educ* Reedham Sch; *m* 17 April 1954, Shirley Ann, da of Esmonde Plunkett Yeoman (d 1962), of Tadworth, Surrey; 1 s (Simon), 1 da (Alannah); *Career* RN 1946-48; dir Sedgwick Gp 1960-81; chm: Carter Brito E Cunha Ltd 1982-87, Johnson & Higgins Ltd 1987-; dep chm Lloyd's 1987-88; dir The Reedham Childrens Tst; Freeman City of London, Liveryman Worshipful Company of Insurers 1981; FBIBA; *Recreations* fly fishing, farming, drama; *Clubs* Naval and Military; *Style*— Alan Parry, Esq; Upper Gatton Park, Reigate, Surrey, RH2 0TZ (☎ 07374 5388)

PARRY, Hon Mrs (Amanda Gwyneth Rosemary); *née* Borwick; yst da of 4 Baron Borwick, MC, *qv*; *b* 24 Jan 1965; *m* 16 May 1987, Brian Wynn Parry, eldest s of P Owen Parry, of Llandderfel, Gwynedd; *Style*— The Hon Mrs Parry ; Is Coed, Chapel Row, Llandderfel, Bala, Gwynedd, N Wales

PARRY, Hon Mrs Anna Josephine; *née* Banbury; da of 2 Baron Banbury of Southam, DL (d 1981); *b* 1950; *m* 1970, Michael Parry (m dis 1981); *Style*— The Hon Mrs Anna Parry; 26 Gowan Av, SW6

PARRY, Hon Catherine Anne; da of Baron Parry (Life Peer); *b* 1955; *Style*— The Hon Catherine Parry

PARRY, Emyr Owen; s of Ebenezer Owen Parry; *b* 26 May 1933; *Educ* Caernarfon GS, Univ Coll of Wales, Aberystwyth; *m* 1959, Enid Griffiths; 1 s, 1 da; *Career* admitted slr 1957, dep circuit judge 1975, rec Crown Ct 1979-; chm Nat Insur Appeals Tbnl Holyhead area 1969-, slr memb Lord Chllr's Co Ct Rule Ctee 1975; *Style*— Emyr Parry, Esq

PARRY, Erika Anne Blackmore; da of Brig Hugh Vivian Combe, DSO, MC (d 1972), ADC to HM King George VI 1943-52 and to HM The Queen 1952-53, and Phyllis Marjorie (Jill), *née* Durrant (d 1977); *Educ* Tortington Park Arundel Sussex; *m* Croose Parry; 2 da (Marie-Line, Rozelle); *Career* designer, creative design and prodn devpt conslt and author; created and designed 'Wild Tudor' tableware and giftware ranges in English Bone China for Aynsley China Ltd; designer of 250 different items for major internat cos items incl: china, enamel boxes, kitchenware, wall coverings, textiles, stationery, wrought iron entrance gates, silverware; MCSD, MBEDA; *Recreations* studying wildlife; *Style*— Mrs Erika Parry; Rushbrooke, Wonersh, Surrey GU5 0QS (☎ 0483 892303)

PARRY, Baron (Life Peer UK 1975), of Neyland, Dyfed; Gordon Samuel David Parry; s of Rev Thomas Lewis Parry, Baptist minister (d 1965), and Anne Parry (d 1958); *b* 30 Nov 1925; *Educ* Neyland Bd Sch, Pembroke Co Intermediate Sch, Trinity Coll Carmarthen, Inst of Educn, Liverpool Univ; *m* 1948, Glenys Catherine, da of Jack Leslie Incledon; 1 da (Catherine Anne); *Career* sits as Labour peer in House of Lords; teacher/journalist; house master and librarian Co Secondary Sch Haverfordwest 1952-68, warden Pembrokeshire Teachers' Centre 1968-78; chm Wales Tourist Bd 1978-83, memb Br Tourist Authy 1978-83, pres Br Inst of Cleaning Sci, chm British Cleaning Cncl, former chm Tidy Britain cncl chm Britain in Bloom, chm Milford Docks Co, dir Guidehouse; hon fell James Cook Univ Queensland Australia; fell: Tourism Soc, Br Inst of Cleaning Sci, Hotel and Catering and Industl Mgmnt Assoc; FRSA; *Recreations* watching rugby football; *Clubs* Neyland RFC, Neyland Yacht; *Style*— The Rt Hon Lord Parry; Willowmead, 52 Port Lion, Llangwm, Haverfordwest, Pembrokeshire, Dyfed, SA62 4JT (☎ 0646 600667); 2 Neyland Terrace, Neyland, Dyfed (☎ 0646 600 362); House of Lords, London SW1 The Milford Docks Company, The Docks, Milford Haven, Pembrokeshire, Dyfed (☎ 06462 2271)

PARRY, Sir (Frank) Hugh Nigel; CBE (1954); s of Charles Frank Parry; *b* 26 August 1911; *Educ* Cheltenham, Balliol Coll Oxford; *m* 1945, Ann Maureen, da of Henry Philip Forshaw; 2 da; *Career* entered Colonial Admin Serv 1939, Fedn of Rhodesia and Nyasaland 1953-63, Miny of Overseas Devpt 1965, actg head Middle East Devpt Div 1969-71, ret 1971; kt 1963; *Style*— Sir Hugh Parry, CBE; c/o Grindlays Bank, 13 St James's Sq, London SW1

PARRY, John Charles Frederick; s of Brig Richard Frederick Parry, MC, of Mersham, Kent, and Elspeth Stewart, *née* Wilson; *b* 3 June 1918; *Educ* Sherborne; *Career* dir: ANCO Commodities Ltd 1977-80, Conti Commondity Servs 1980-84; md Capcom Fin Servs Ltd 1984-; *Books* Options (1982); *Recreations* cricket, shooting, dining; *Clubs* Turf; *Style*— John Parry, Esq; Capcom Financial Services, 9-13 St Andrew St, London EC4 (☎ 01 583 0088, fax 01 528 7129, telex 945055)

PARRY, John Richard; s of David Parry (d 1957), of Thetford, Norfolk, and Alma Harriet, *née* Fuller; *b* 3 May 1934; *Educ* The GS Thetford, Fitzwilliam Coll Cambridge (MA); *m* 9 Sept 1961, Mary, da of William Dorrington, of Pinner, Middx; 1 s (Simon David William b 1964), 1 da (Anne-Louise b 1968); *Career* Nat Serv Bombadier RA 1952-54 (Suez Canal Zone); Commercial Union Properties Ltd: dir 1971, md 1978; Hammerson Property Investment and Devpt Corpn plc: dir 1984, dep md 1985, jt md 1986, md 1988; memb: Telford Devopt Corpn 1980-82 (dep chm 1982-86), property advsy gp DOE 1980-, cncl Br Property Fedn 1986-; magistrate Gore div Middx Petty Sessions 1980-84, memb parish cncl St Matthews Catholic Church Northwood; Freeman: City of London, Worshipful Co of Chartered Surveyors 1985; FRICS 1962; Coll of Estate Mgmnt Reading: memb The Charter Soc 1987, hon fell 1988; *Recreations* keeping fit, eating out, opera and ballet; *Clubs* Arts; *Style*— John Parry, Esq; 100 Park Lane, London W1Y 4AR (☎ 01 629 9494, fax 01 629 0498, car tel 0836 739 549, telex 261837)

PARRY, Margaret Joan; da of W J Tamplin, of Llantrisant, Glamorgan; *b* 27 Nov 1919; *Educ* Howell's Sch Llandaff Cardiff, Univ of Wales (BA); *m* 1946, Raymond Howard Parry; 2 s, 1 da; *Career* headmistress Heathfield Sch Ascot 1973-82; patron Univ of Birmingham; *Style*— Mrs Raymond Parry; Carreg Gwaun, 23A Murray Ct, Ascot, Berks SL5 9BP (☎ 0990 26299)

PARRY, Robert; MP (Lab) Liverpool, Riverside 1983-; s of Robert Parry; *b* 8 Jan 1933; *Educ* Bishop Goss RC Sch Liverpool; *m* 1956, Marie, *née* Hesdon; *Career* MP (Lab): Liverpool Exchange 1970-74, Liverpool Scotland Exchange 1974-1983; memb Campaign Gp Labour MPs 1982-, chm Merseyside Gp of Labour MPs 1976-; *Style*— Robert Parry Esq, MP; House of Commons, SW1A OAA

PARRY, Victor Thomas Henry; s of Thomas Parry (d 1957), of Newport, Gwent, and Daisy, *née* Nott (d 1964); *b* 20 Nov 1927; *Educ* Newport (St Julians) HS, St Edmund Hall Oxford (BA, MA), UCL; *m* 16 May 1959, Mavis, da of Charles Russull (d 1958), of London; 2 s (Richard b 1959, Matthew b 1962), 1 da (Katharine b 1968); *Career* with Manchester Public Libraries 1950-56, Colonial and Cwlth Relations Off Library 1956-60; librarian: The Nature Conservancy 1960-64, Br Museum (natural history) 1964-74, chief librarian and archivist Royal Botanic Gdns Kew 1974-78, librarian SOAS London 1978-83, dir Central Library Servs and Goldsmiths librarian Univ of London 1983-; sr examiner The Library Assoc 1959-68; chm: Circle of State Librarians 1966-68, London Gp UCR Library Assoc 1972-76, Govt Libraries Gp 1977-78; ed Soc for Bibliography of Natural History 1975-78; FLA 1959, FRSA 1984; *Books* Conservation of Threatened Plants (ed 1976); *Recreations* reading, ball games, railways; *Clubs* RSA; *Style*— Victor Parry, Esq; 69 Redway Dr, Twickenham TW2 7NN (☎ 01 894 0742); University Library, Senate House, Univ of London, Malet St, London WC1E 7HU (☎ 014 636 4514)

PARRY EVANS, Mary Alethea (Lady Hallinan); da of Dr Evan Parry Evans, MD, JP; *b* 31 Oct 1929; *Educ* Malvern Girls' Coll, Somerville Coll Oxford (BCL, MA); *m* 1955, Sir (Adrian) Lincoln Hallinan, *qv*; 2 s, 2 da; *Career* barr Inner Temple 1953, Wales and Chester circuit, a rec of the Crown Ct 1978-; *Style*— Lady Hallinan; chambers: 33 Park Place, Cardiff (☎ 0222 33313)

PARRY-CROOKE, David John; s of Maj Charles Philip Parry-Crooke (d 1978), of Friston, Suffolk, and Winifred Rosa, *née* Wales (d 1976, *see* Burkes Landed Gentry 18 Ed Vol III 1972, Kelly's Handbook the Titled, Landed and Official Classes, Victoria County History of Hampshire (Crooke), Middlesex (Crooke), Suffolk (Parry-Crooke)); *b* 3 Mar 1923; *Educ* Radley, Univ Coll Oxford; *m* 1, 22 Jan 1948, Griselda Mary Powell, da of Rev Canon Norman Powell Wiliams (d 1942), of Christ Church Oxford; 1 s (John Paul b 1953), 2 da (Charlotte Mary b 1950, Georgiana Mary b 1956); m 2, 1 Nov 1979, Elizabeth Dorothea, da of Dr William Crampton Gore, RHA (d 1945), of Enniskillen Co Fermanagh; *Career* WWII 19 King George V's Own Lancers IA 1942-46; Capt: India, Burma, Malaya; sometime rubber planter Malaya, farmer and travel conslt, landowner; voluntary work: The Samaritans, London, Suffolk Cons Pty; Master Workshipful Co of Tylers and Bricklayers 1976-77; *Recreations* model railways, photography, shooting, travel; *Clubs* MCC, Army and Navy; *Style*— David Parry-Crooke, Esq; 5 Dixwell Rd, Folkestone, Kent (☎ 0303 55 690)

PARRY-EVANS, Air Marshal Sir David; KCB (1985), CBE (1978); s of Gp Capt John Parry-Evans (d 1978), and Dorothy Parry-Evans; *b* 19 July 1935; *Educ* Berkhamsted; *m* 1960, Anne, da of Charles Reynolds (d 1966), and Gertrude Reynolds; 2 s; *Career* RAF 1956-: OC 214 Sqdn 1974-75, OC RAF Marham 1975-77, Air Cdre until 1981, dir Def Policy MOD 1979-81, Cmdt RAF Staff Coll Bracknell 1981-82, Air Vice-Marshal 1982, AOC No 1 and 38 Gps 1982-85, CIC RAF Germany, Cdr 2 Allied Tactical Air Force 1985-87, dep chief Defence Staff 1987-; *Recreations* rugby; *Clubs* RAF; *Style*— Air Marshal Sir David Parry-Evans, KCB, CBE; Air House, Royal Air Force, Rheindahlen, BFPO 40 (☎ 02161 47 4027)

PARSLOE, John; s of (Charles) Guy Parsloe (d 1985), and (Mary) Zirphie (Munro), *née* Faiers; *b* 14 Oct 1939; *Educ* Bradfield, Queen's Coll Oxford (MA); *m* 6 Oct 1973, (Helen) Margaret, da of Dr (Daniel) Arnold Rolfe (d 1985); 2 s (Thomas b 1974, William b 1979), 1 da (Alice b 1976); *Career* slr 1971; dir Mercury Asset Mgmnt Hldgs Ltd 1987; memb Law Soc 1971; *Style*— John Parsloe, Esq; 33 King William St, London EC4R 9AS (☎ 01 280 2800)

PARSLOW, Robert Edwin; s of William James Parslow (d 1948), of Northwood, Middx, and Winifred Ada, *née* Coles (d 1937); *b* 19 June 1929; *Educ* Harrow, Peterhouse Cambridge (MA); *m* 21 Jan 1956, Shirley Gordon, da of Dr Eric Gordon Fleming (d 1948), of St Johns Wood London NW8; 2 s (John b 23 March 1959, Roger b 27 Dec 1961); *Career* admitted slr 1955, sr ptnr Hyde Mahon Bridges 1983-; memb Law Soc; *Recreations* foreign travel; *Style*— Robert Parslow, Esq; 42 Granville Rd, Limpsfield, Oxted, Surrey RH8 ODA (☎ 0883 712 493); 33 Ely Place London EC1N 6TS (☎ 01 405 9455, fax 01 831 7721, telex 25210)

PARSONS, (Thomas) Alan; CB (1984); s of late Arthur and Laura Parsons; *b* 25 Nov 1924; *Educ* Clifton, Bristol Univ (LLB); *m* 1, 1947, Valerie Vambeck; 1 s; m 2, 1957, Muriel Lewis; 2 s; *Career* served WWII RM 1943-46; barr Middle Temple 1950, legal asst Miny of Nat Insur 1950, sr legal asst Miny of Pensions and Nat Insur 1955; DHSS: asst slr 1968, princ asst slr 1977-, chief adjudication offr 1984-86; *Style*— Alan Parsons Esq, CB; 11 Northiam St, Pennethorne Place, London E9 7HF

PARSONS, Hon Mrs Anne Constance; *née* Manningham-Buller; da of 1 Viscount Dilhorne, PC, and Lady Mary Lilian Lindsay, da of 27 Earl of Crawford and Balcarres, KT; *b* 13 August 1951; *Educ* Benenden; *m* 1982, John Chistopher Parsons, assist treas to HM The Queen 1985, s of Arthur Christopher Parsons, of Hatchwood House, Odiham, by his w Veronica, da of Maj-Gen Sir Guy de Courcy Glover, KBE, CB, DSO, MC, 2 s, 1 da (b 1988); *Style*— The Hon Mrs Parsons; 19 Melrose Gardens, London W6 7RN

PARSONS, Sir Anthony Derrick; GCMG (1981, KCMG 1975, CMG 1969), LVO (1965), MC (1945); s of late Col H A J Parsons, MC; *b* 9 Sept 1922; *Educ* King's Sch Canterbury, Balliol Coll Oxford; *m* 1948, Sheila Emily, da of Geoffrey Baird, of Goodnestone, Kent; 2 s, 2 da; *Career* HM Forces 1940: asst mil attaché Baghdad 1952-54; HM Dip Serv: FO 1954-55, Ankara 1955-59, Amman 1959-60, Cairo 1960-61, FO 1961-64, Khartoum 1964-65, political agent Bahrain 1965-69, cnsllr UK Mission to UN NY 1969-71, under-sec FCO 1971-74, ambassador Iran 1974-79, UK perm rep UN 1979-82; memb bd British Cncl 1982-86, PM's personal foreign affairs advsr 1983-; lectr and res fell Univ of Exeter 1984-87; Order of the Two Niles Sudan 1965; *Books* The Pride and The Fall (1984), They Say The Lion (1986); *Clubs* MCC, Overseas League; *Style*— Sir Anthony Parsons, GCMG, LVO, MC; Highgrove, Ashburton, S Devon

PARSONS, Geoffrey Penwill; OBE (1977); s of Francis Hedley Parsons; *b* 15 June 1929; *Educ* Canterbury HS Sydney, State Conservatorium of Music (with Winifred Burston) Sydney; *Career* concert accompanist; int recital series Geoffrey Parsons and friends, opening season of Barbican Centre 1983, twenty-fifth concert tour of Australia (with Dame Janet Baker); hon RAM 1975, hon GSM 1983, FRCM 1987; *Style*— Geoffrey Parsons, Esq, OBE; 176 Iverson Rd, London NW6 2HL (☎ 01 624 0957)

PARSONS, John Christopher; s of Arthur Christopher Parsons, of Hatchwood House, Odiham, Hants, and Veronica Rosetta de Courcy, *née* Glover; *b* 21 May 1946; *Educ* Harrow, Trinity Coll Cambridge (BA); *m* 20 Feb 1982, Hon Anne Constance Manningham-Buller, da of Viscount Dilhorne, PC; 2 s (Michael b 1983, David b 1985), 1 da (Lilah b 1988); *Career* CA; Dowty Gp Ltd 1968-72, Peat Marwick Mitchell & Co 1972-85; asst tres to HM The Queen 1985, dep keeper of the Privy Purse and dep tres to HM The Queen 1988; FCA, MIMC; *Clubs* Brooks's; *Style*— John Parsons, Esq; 19 Melrose Gdns, London W6 7RN (☎ 01 602 3035); Zion Cottage, Penton Mewsey, Andover, Hants SP11 0RQ ; Buckingham Palace, London SW1A 1AA (☎ 01 930 4832)

PARSONS, John William; CBE (1988); s of Frederick John Parsons (d 1988), of Wareham, Dorset and Dorothy Ellen, *née* Toop; *b* 24 July 1936; *Educ* Poole GS, Porthcurno Engrg Coll; *m* 1; 1958 (m dis 1979); 1 s (Christopher), 1 da (Yasmin); m 2, 1981, Sally-Anne, da of Robert St Vincent Parker-Jervis (d 1972); 1 s (Timothy); *Career* Actg Capt Royal Corps of Signals; Cable and Wireless 1960-78: head of business (Caribbean) 1966-72, md Euro cos 1972-78; md ITR Int Time Ltd 1979-82; chm and chief exec Time and Data Systems Int Ltd 1982-; memb Br Overseas Trade Bd 1985-, CBI Smaller Firms Cncl; chm Talbot Associates Ltd; dir: Mixsecure Ltd, Princes Youth Business Tst; pres Dorset Chamber of Commerce and Ind; cncllr: Purbeck DC, Corfe Castle pc; vice-chm of govrs Poole GS; CEng, FIEE, FInstD, FBIM, MIEE (USA); *Clubs* IOD, Exiles, RAC; *Style*— John Parsons, Esq, CBE; Townsend House, Corfe Castle, Wareham, Dorset BH20 5EG (☎ 0929 480265); Time and Data Systems International Ltd, Crestworth House, Sterte Ave, Poole, Dorset BH15 2AL (☎ 0202 666222, telex 417218 (TDSICO), fax 0202 679730)

PARSONS, Kenneth Charles; CMG (1970), OBE (1962); s of late W S Parsons, of Cardigan; *b* 9 Jan 1921; *Educ* Haverfordwest GS, Exeter Coll Oxford; *m* 1977, Mary Woolhouse; *Career* WWII oxon and Bucks LI 1941-46; joined Dip Serv 1949; serv: Moscow, Tokyo, Rangoon, Athens, FCO 1972-77; HQ Br Forces Hong Kong 1976-79 (with equivalent mil rank of Maj-Gen); *Style*— Kenneth Parsons Esq, CMG, OBE; 2 Ashfield Cottage, Rectory Rd, Crickhowell, Powys NP8 1DW (☎ 0873 810332)

PARSONS, Hon (Desmond Oliver) Martin; 2 s of 6 Earl of Rosse, KBE, and Anne, Countess of Rosse, *qv*; *b* 23 Dec 1938; *Educ* Eton, Aiglon Coll Switzerland; *m* 1965, Aline Edwina, da of Dr George Alexander Macdonald, of Rugby, and Marguerite Louise Edwina Macdonald; 2 s (Rupert Alexander Michael b 3 Sept 1966, Desmond Edward Richard b 30 October 1968); *Style*— The Hon Martin Parsons; Womersley Park, Doncaster

PARSONS, Sir (John) Michael; s of late Rt Rev Richard Godfrey Parsons, DD, Bishop of Hereford (d 1948), and Dorothy Gales Streeter (d 1956); *b* 29 Oct 1915; *Educ* Rossall, Univ Coll Oxford; *m* 1, 1946 (m dis 1964), Hilda Mary Frewen; 1 s, 2 da; m 2, 1964, Caroline Inagh Margaret, da of Col Laton Frewen, DSO (d 1976), of Ross-on-Wye; *Career* Maj IA 1939-46 (POW Singapore); dir Inchcape & Co Ltd: dir 1971-81, sr md 1976-81, dep chm and chief exec 1979-81; chm and dir Assam Investmts 1976-81, dir Cwlth Devpt Fin Co Ltd 1973-80; chm Cncl of Royal Cwlth Soc 1976-81, dep chm Utd World Colls 1982-86; kt 1970; *Recreations* golf; *Clubs* Oriental; *Style*— Sir Michael Parsons; Tall Trees, Warren Hill Lane, Aldeburgh, Suffolk IP15 5QB (☎ 072 885 2917)

PARSONS, Sir Richard Edmund Clement Fownes; KCMG (1982, CMG 1977); s of Dr Richard A Parsons (d 1960), of Kirkbeck House, Coniston, Cumbria (d 1960), and Mrs Richard Parsons (d 1977); *b* 14 Mar 1928; *Educ* Bembridge Sch, Brasenose Coll Oxford (BA); *m* 1960, Jenifer Jane (d 1981), da of Charles Reginald Mathews; 3 s; *Career* Nat Serv 1949-51; Dip Serv; joined FO 1951; formerly serv: Buenos Aires, Ankara, Washington, Vientiane; former cnsllr Lagos, head personnel ops dept 1972-76; ambassador: Hungary 1976-79, Spain 1980-84, Sweden 1984-; *Clubs* Travellers'; *Style*— Sir Richard Parsons, KCMG; British Embassy, Skarpögatan 6-8, 11527 Stockholm, Sweden; c/o Foreign and Commonwealth Office, King Charles St, SW1

PARSONS, Robert Frederick James; OBE (1985); s of Robert Frederick James Parsons (d 1957), of Camberley, and Grace Maude, *née* Hancock; *b* 19 August 1953; *Educ* Kingswood Sch Bath, Downing Coll Cambridge (MA); *Career* admitted slr 1961, ptnr Beachcroft & Co 1965- (now Beachcroft Stanleys), dir Property Owners Building Soc 1984-86; chm Fedn of Cons and Unionist Assoc 1957-58, pres Surrey West Euro Constituency Cons Cncl 1984-87, Parly candidate (Cons) Holborn and St Pancras South Feb and Oct 1974; memb Frimley and Camberley UDC 1962-71 and 1972-74 (ldr: 1965-67, 1969-71, 1972-74; chm 1967-69), memb Surrey CC 1970-77; memb: Standing Conf on London and SE Regnl Planning 1974-77, SE Regnl Econ Planning Cncl 1975-78, Surrey Family Practitioner Ctee 1986; pres: Surrey Heath (formerly Camberley) Scout Cncl 1969-, Camberley and Dist Horticultural Soc 1985-; chm: Camberley Soc 1967-70 (vice pres 1985-), St Tarcisusis RC Parish Pastoral Cncl 1971-, Woking Deanery RC Pastoral Cncl 1978-80 and 1987-, govrs Collingwood Sch Camberley 1979-, govrs St Tarcisusis RC Middle Sch 1983-; Freeman Worshipful Co of Slrs 1987; memb Law Soc 1961; *Recreations* travel, music, reading; *Clubs* Athenaeum, Travellers, St Stephens Constitutional; *Style*— Robert Parsons, Esq, OBE; Levington, 104 London Rd, Camberley, Surrey GU15 3TJ (☎ 0276 23491); Beachcroft Stanleys, 100 Fetter Lane, London EC4A 1BN (☎ 01 242 1011, fax 01 430 1532, telex 264607 BEALAW G)

PARSONS, Prof Roger; s of Robert Harry Ashby Parsons (d 1966), and Ethel, *née* Fenton (d 1973); *b* 31 Oct 1926; *Educ* King Alfred Sch Strathcona, HS Edmonton Alberta, Imperial Coll London (BSc, PhD, DIC), Univ of Bristol (DSc); *m* 8 June 1953, Ruby Millicent, da of Malcolm Turner (d 1971); 3 s (Gavin Christopher b 1954, Colin Mark b 1959, Magnus Frank b 1961), 1 da (Celia Janet b 1957); *Career* Deedes fell Univ of St Andrews 1951-54, lectr Univ of Bristol 1954-63 (reader in electrochemistry 1963-79), dir Laboratoire d'Electrochimie Interfaciale du CRNS Meudon France 1977-84, prof of chemistry Univ of Southampton 1985-, ed in chief Journal of Electroanalytical Chemistry 1963-; FRS 1980, ARCS 1946; Palladium Medal (UK) 1979, Brund Breyer Medal Australia 1980, Paul Pascal Prize France 1983, Galvani Medal Italy 1986; *Books* Electrochemical Constants (1959), Interfacial Electrochemistry (1972), Electrochemistry in Research and Development (1985), Standard Potentials in Aqueous Solution (1985); *Recreations* listening to music, going to the opera; *Style*— Prof Roger Parsons; 16 Thornhill Road, Bassett, Southampton SO1 7AT; Merrick, Moniaive, Thornhill, Dumfriesshire DG3 4EJ (☎ 0703 790143); Department of Chemistry, University of Southampton, Southampton SO9 5NH (☎ 0703 559122 ext 593711, fax 0703 593781, telex 47661 SOTONU G)

PARSONS-SMITH, Dr Basil Gerald; OBE (1945); s of Basil Thomas Parsons-Smith (d 1954), and Marguerite Ida, *née* Burnett; *b* 19 Nov 1911; *Educ* Harrow, Trinity Coll Cambridge (MA, MD), St Georges Hosp London; *m* 3 June 1939, Aurea Mary, da of William Stewart Johnston (d 1942), of Wood Hall, Sunningdale; 2 s (James b 1946, Nicholas b 1949), 1 da (Elizabeth Anne Jacobs b 1940); *Career* blood transfusion offr EMS HQ 1939, RAF Coastal Cmd 1941, med specialist to No 3 and No 5 RAF Hosps Middle East, cmd No 24 MFH Tripoli (despatches twice); neurologist Charing Cross Hosp London 1950-77, examiner in med RCP London; appeared in BBC TV film *Hospital 1922*; neurologist: Med Appeal Tbnl 1966-83, Vacine Damaged Tbnl London 1979-83; Liveryman Worshipful Co of Apothecaries; FRSM; *Recreations* horses and shetland pony stud; *Clubs* Cambridge Univ, Pitt (life memb); *Style*— Dr Gerald Parsons-Smith, OBE; Roughets House, Blechingley, Surrey RH1 4QX (☎ 0883 43929)

PART, Sir Antony Alexander; GCB (1974, KCB 1966, CB 1959), MBE (1943); s of late Alexander Francis Part; *b* 28 June 1916; *Educ* Harrow, Trinity Coll Cambridge; *m* 1940, Isabella Bennett; *Career* dep sec Miny of Education 1960-63 (under sec 1954-60); perm sec: MPBW 1965-68, BOT 1968-70, DTI 1970-74, DOI 1974-76; chm Orion Insur Co 1976-87; dir: Debenhams 1976-80, EMI 1976-80, Life Assoc of Scotland 1976-87, Lucas Industries 1976-87, Metal Box 1976-86, Savoy Hotel Gp 1976-87; chm: Ctee on North Sea Oil Taxation 1981, govt panel Direct Broadcasting by Satellite 1982; CBIM 1979; Hon DTech Brunel 1966; Hon DSc: Aston 1974, Cranfield 1976; hon fell LSE 1984; *Style*— Sir Antony Part, GCB, MBE; Flat 5, 71 Elm Park Gdns, London SW10 9QE (☎ 01 352 2950)

PARTINGTON, Alan; s of Arthur Partington, of Oakenclough, Oldham, and Annie, *née* Farrar (d 1977); *b* 23 Sept 1930; *Educ* Hulmegs Oldham; *m* 12 Sept 1953, Marian, da of Fred Smith (d 1964); 1 s (Ian Farrar b 1958), 1 da (Janet Mary Jarvis b 1954); *Career* Nat Serv RAF 1954-56; articled clerk Wm Wrigley & Son 1948-54, sr asst H L & H L Holden 1956-60, ptnr F Howarth & Co 1960-78, sr ptnr Alan Partington & Co 1978-; Lancastrian Bldg Soc (formerly Middleton Bldg Soc): dir 1969-, chm of dirs 1978-; chm govrs Bluecoat Sch Oldham 1981-87 (govr 1974-87), dep chm tstees Henshaw Tst 1978- (tstee 1976); FCA 1958; *Recreations* crown green bowls, wine, theatre; *Style*— Alan Partington, Esq; Wood Mount, 2 Woodland Park, Royton, Oldham OL2 5UY (☎ 061 624 0734); Alan Partington & Co, Sterling House, 501 Middleton Rd, Chadderton, Oldham OL9 9LA (☎ 061 652 8212)

PARTINGTON, Christopher John; s of George Partington (d 1977), of Merrington Old Hall, Bomere Heath, nr Shrewsbury, and Audrey Jean, *née* Bolton; father's maternal gf John Henry Davies, founded Manchester United FC; *b* 19 May 1953; *Educ* Ellesmere; *Career* angling historian conslt in antique fishing tackle, fndr Britain's Angling Heritage Tst; memb numerous angling socs; *Recreations* fishing, shooting, rowing, canoeing, country skiing, sailing, swimming, music, reading, writing; *Clubs* Salop; *Style*— Christopher Partington, Esq; The Vintage Fishing Tackle Shop, 103 Longden Coleham, Shrewsbury, Shropshire SY3 7DX (☎ 0743 69373)

PARTINGTON, (William) Rodney; s of Willie Partington (d 1986), of Polstead, Suffolk, and Sarah Alice, *née* Dickinson (d 1974); *b* 17 Jan 1944; *Educ* Derby Sch Bury Lancs, Bolton Tech Coll; *m* 30 July 1966, Glenda Ann, da of Joseph Daintree, of Sale, Ches; 1 da (Lisa b 24 April 1972); *Career* trainee Halifax Bldg Soc 1961-69, branch mangr Skipton Bldg Soc 1969-76, md Colchester Bldg Soc 1984-87 (gen mangr 1979, sec 1976); gen mangr and local dir Cheltenham & Glos Bldg Soc (incl Colchester Bldg Soc) 1987-88; Chartered Bldg Soc Inst: chm NW Gp 1974-75, chm E Anglian Gp 1980-81; memb Forum Colchester Rotary Club 1977-, dir Colchester Oaks Hosp 1987-; FCIS (1966), FBIM (1980); *Recreations* angling; *Style*— Rodney Partington, Esq; Stratford House, Polstead, Suffolk, (☎ 0206 262850)

PARTRIDGE, Hon Mrs Caroline Elizabeth Maud; *née* Cust; da of 6 Baron Brownlow; *b* 1928; *m* 1954 (m dis), John Arthur Partridge; 2 s, 1 da; *Style*— The Hon Mrs Caroline Partridge; 68 Scarsdale Villas, London W8 6PP

PARTRIDGE, Derek William; CMG (1987); s of Ernest Partridge (d 1984), of Wembley, Middx, and Ethel Elizabeth, *née* Buckingham (d 1985); *b* 15 May 1931; *Educ* Preston Manor County GS Wembley; *Career* RAF 1949-51; Dip Serv: FO 1951-54, Oslo 1954-6, Jedda 1956, Khartoum 1957-60, Sofia 1960-62, Manila 1962-d65, Djakarta 1965-67, FCO 1967-72, Brisbane 1972-74, Colombo 1974-77, FCO 1977-86 (head of migration and visa dept 1981-83, head nat and treaty dept 1983-86), Br high cmmr Freetown Sierra Leone 1986-; *Style*— Derek W Partridge, Esq, CMG; c/o National Westminster Bank plc, 1 St James's Square, London SW1Y 4JX; c/o FCO, King Charles St, London Sw1A 2AH

PARTRIDGE, Frances Catherine; da of William Cecil Marshall (d 1921), of 28 Bedford Sq, London WC1, and Margaret Anna, *née* Lloyd (d 1941); *b* 15 Mar 1900; *Educ* Bedales Sch, Newnham Coll Cambridge (BA); *m* 2 March 1933, Maj Reginald Sherring Partridge, MC (d 1960); 1 s (Lytton Burgo b 1935, d 1963); *Career* antiquarian bookseller 1922-28; edited Greville diaries with husband 1928-38 (8 vols), translator of French and Spanish works; FRSL; *Books* A Pacifist's War (1978), Memories (1981), Julia (1983), Everything To Lose (1985), Friends in Focus (1987); *Recreations* travel, music, reading, botany; *Clubs* Int PEN; *Style*— Mrs Frances Partridge; 16 West Halkin St, London SW1 (☎ 01 235 6998)

PARTRIDGE, Frank; s of John Partridge, of N Uist, Western Isles, and Flora Partridge; *b* 16 August 1953; *Educ* Abbey Sch Fort Augustus Inverness-shire, Edinburgh Univ (BA), Univ Coll Cardiff (Dip in Journalism); *Career* BBC: presenter Newsbeat Radio One 1982-88, sports corr 1988-; *Recreations* squash, swimming, cricket playing, watching and collecting; *Clubs* Lansdowne; *Style*— Frank Partridge, Esq; Room 3080, BBC, Broadcasting House, London W1A 1AA (☎ 01 927 4213)

PARTRIDGE, Ian Harold; s of Harold William (d 1972), and Eugenia Emily, *née* Stinson; *b* 12 June 1938; *Educ* Clifton, New Coll Oxford, RCM, Guild Sch of Music (LGSM); *m* 4 July 1959, Ann Pauline, da of William Maskell Glover (d 1965), of Bexhill, Sussex; 2 s (Daniel b 1964, Jonathan b 1967); *Career* concert singer and recitalist with wide repertoire from early baroque to new works, opera debut at Covent Gdn as Iopas in Les Troyens 1969, title role Britten's St Nicholas Thames TV (Prix Italia, 1977), regular appearances at London's concert halls with maj orchestras and conductors and at internat festivals throughout the world, frequent broadcaster on BBC Radio 3; many recordings incl: Schubert Die Schöne Müllerin, Winterreise Schumann Dichterliebe, Vaughan Williams On Wenlock Edge, Warlock The Curlew, Britten Winter Words; over 200 performances worldwide of An Evening with Queen Victoria (with Prunella Scales), master classes on Lieder, English Song and Early Music at Aldeburgh, Dartington, Trondheim, Vancouver etc; *Recreations* theatre, bridge, horse racing; *Style*— Ian Partridge, Esq; 127 Pepys Rd, Wimbledon, London SW20 8NP (☎ 01 946 7140)

PARTRIDGE, John Arthur; s of Claude Partridge (d 1958), of 18 Brompton Square, London SW7, and Iris Florence, *née* Franks (d 1982); *b* 6 July 1929; *Educ* Elstree Sch, Harrow; *m* 1, 1954 (m dis), Hon Caroline Elizabeth Maud Cust, da of 6 Baron Brownlow, of Belton House, Lincs (d 1978); 2 s (Frank David Peregrine b 14 Sept 1955, Claude Edward b 29 Aug 1962), 1 da (Sophia Josephine b 21 May 1959); m 2, Rosemary Fitzgibbon, da of Maj Robert Tyrell (d 1975), of Top House, Exton; *Career* ADC to Govr of S Aust Gen Lord Norric 1952-53; chm and md Partridge Fine Art Ltd 1958-, chm Fine Art and Antique Export Ctee 1979-; *Recreations* hunting, fishing, shooting, gardening; *Clubs* Brooks; *Style*— John Partridge, Esq; Prebendal House, Empingham, Rutland, Leicestershire (☎ 078 086 234); 144/146 New Bond St, London W1Y 0LY (☎ 01 629 0834)

PARTRIDGE, Michael John Anthony; CB (1983); s of Dr John Henry Partridge (d 1956), and Ethel Partridge; *b* 29 Sept 1935; *Educ* Merchant Taylors', St John's Coll Oxford (MA); *m* 1968, Joan Elizabeth, da of Trevor Grattan Hughes (d 1953); 2 s, 1 da; *Career* civil servant; dep sec DHSS 1981-83, dep sec Home Office with responsibility for police dept 1983-; *Recreations* skiing, reading, DIY; *Clubs* Utd Oxford and Cambridge; *Style*— Michael Partridge Esq, CB; Alexander Fleming House, Elephant and Castle, London SE1 (☎ 01 407 5522, ext 6905); 27 High View, Pinner, Middx HA5 3NZ

PARTRIDGE, Neil Russell; s of Wilfred Lincoln (d 1978), and Elizabeth Mary, *née* Dudley (d 1974); *b* 10 Feb 1954; *Educ* Dame Allan's Sch Newcastle-Upon-Tyne, Newcastle Univ (BA); *m* 1980, Sheila Anne, da of Gordon Kerr Henderson, of North Yorks; 1 s (William Lincoln b 1981), 1 da (Rebecca Anne b 1976); *Career* fin dir Vibroplant plc 1986; ACA; *Style*— Neil Partridge, Esq; Cranford, Lands Lane, Knaresborough, North Yorks

PARTRIDGE, Richard (Linnell); s of Dr Victor Stanley Partridge (d 1933), and Florence Gertrude Partridge, *née* Vandermin (d 1959); *b* 8 June 1919; *Educ* Westminster, Kings Coll Hosp London Univ (BDS, LDS RCS Eng); *m* 18 Dec 1942, Joan Partridge, OBE, da of Sydney Lefridge (d 1961); 3 s (Barrie b 1954, Roy b 1957, Clive b 1960); *Career* dental surgn (ret); *Recreations* tennis; *Style*— Richard Partridge, Esq; Roughwood, Felden Lane, Hemel Hempstead, Herts HP3 0BB (☎ (0442) 51924)

PARTRIDGE, Simon Harry Wood; OBE (1983); s of Rt Rev Frank Partridge (d 1941), of Bishopswood, Fareham, Hants, and Elizabeth Maud, *née* Barton (d 1965); *b* 17 August 1919; *Educ* Uppingham, Trinity Coll Univ of Oxford (MA); *m* 26 May 1951, Barbara Dagmar, da of Anton Emil Schou Bech (d 1981), of Copenhagen, Denmark; 2 s (Andrew b 17 March 1954, Jonathan b 8 Jan 1956); *Career* 57 HTR RAC 1939-40; chm and md: Butterworth Law Publishers Ltd 1974-76, Butterworth & Co (UK) Ltd 1976-82; dir Lloyd's of London Press Ltd 1982-; memb editorial bd Statutes in Force 1984; Liveryman Worshipful Co of Merchant Taylors 1952; *Recreations* golf, chess; *Clubs* Garrick; *Style*— Simon Partridge, Esq, OBE; High Rede, Kilndown, Cranbrook, Kent TN17 2RT (☎ 0892 890413)

PASCO, Richard Edward; CBE (1977); s of Cecil George Pasco (d 1982), and Phyllis Irene, *née* Widdison; *b* 18 July 1926; *Educ* King's Coll Sch Wimbledon, Central Sch of Speech and Drama; *m* 1 (m dis), Greta, *née* Watson; 1 s; m 2, 1967, Barbara, *née* Leigh-Hunt; *Career* Army Serv 1944-48; actor; many leading roles RSC, London, film, radio, TV; assoc artist RSC, Nat Theatre player; *Recreations* music, gardening, reading; *Clubs* Garrick; *Style*— Richard Pasco, Esq, CBE; c/o Michael Whitehall Ltd, 125 Gloucester Rd, London SW7 4TE

PASCO, Rowanne; da of John Pasco, and Ann, *née* MacKeonis; *b* 7 Oct 1938; *Educ* Ursuline Convent HS, Open Univ (MA); *Career* travel rep Horizon Holidays 1961-66, various radio and tv commercials whilst res in Hollywood California 1964-66; BBC 1976-79: reporter radio news, TV ed staff newpaper Ariel, prodr religious programmes radio; ed catholic newspaper The Universe 1979-87, first religious ed TV-AM 1987-; *Books* Faith Alive (ed jtly, 1988); *Style*— Ms Rowanne Pasco; TV-AM, Hawley Crescent, London NW1 8EF (☎ 01 267 4300)

PASCOE, Alan Peter; MBE; s of Ernest George Frank Pascoe, of Portsmouth, and Joan Rosina Pascoe; *b* 11 Oct 1947; *Educ* Portsmouth Southern GS, Borough Rd Coll, Univ of London (BEd); *m* 15 Aug 1970, Della Patricia, da of Douglas Charles Albert James; 1 s (Daniel James b 1984), 1 da (Lucy Joanna b 1980); *Career* int athlete 1967-78; rep GB in: 110m hurdles, 400m hurdles, 200m hurdles, 4x100 and 4x400m relay; GB team capt 1971 and 1972, Euro indoor champion 1969, Bronze Medallist 110m hurdles Euro Champs Athens 1969, Olympic Silver Medallist 4x400m relay 1972, Cwlth Games and Euro Champion record set in both events 1974, ranked No 1 in World 1975, Euro Cup winner 1973 and 1975, Cwlth Silver Medallist 4x400m 1974, Euro Gold Medallist 4x400m relay 1974, Cwlth Bronze Medallist 400m hurdles 1978; represented: Europe in World Cup, Cwlth v USA and USSR; memb: BBC Advsy Cncl 1975-79, Sports Cncl 1974-80; chm Alan Pascoe Assoc 1976-, dir WCRS Gp 1986-; *Recreations* theatre; *Style*— Alan Pascoe, MBE; 141-143 Drury Lane, London WC2B 5TB

PASCOE, Dr Michael William; s of Canon W J T Pascoe (d 1974), and Daisy, *née* Farlow; *b* 16 June 1930; *Educ* St John's Sch Leatherhead, Selwyn Coll Cambridge (BA, PhD); *m* 1, 24 March 1957 (m dis 1974), Janet, da of John Clark (d 1962), of Naphill, Bucks; 3 da (Katherine Jane (Mrs Burrows) b 1957, Joanna Mary b 1959, Madeline Bridget b 1961); m 2, 23 Dec 1974, Brenda Hale, *née* Reed; 1 da (Josephine Lucy b 1980); *Career* med physicist Mt Vernon Hosp 1955-57, textile scientist Br Nylon Spinners Ltd 1957-60, surface coating scientist ICI Paints 1960-67, lectr in material science Brunel Univ 1967-76; The Br Museum: principal scientific offr 1976-79, keeper of conservation and technical services 1979-81; conslt and advsr: Royal Acad of Arts, Science Museum, Mary Rose Tst, Public Record Off, Cncl for the Care of Churches; visiting prof ICCROM Rome (conservation centre); numerous publications on friction, textiles, engineering, conservation; former memb Historic Wrecks Ctee, former govr Camberwell Sch of Art and Crafts, tutor Open Univ 1973-84; FRSA 1969, MInstP 1958-83; *Recreations* painting and drawing, travel, museums; *Style*— Dr Michael Pascoe; 15 Parkfield Rd, Ickenham, Uxbridge UB10 8LN (☎ 0895 674 723); Science Dept, Camberwell Sch of Art & Crafts, Peckham Rd, London SE5 8UF (☎ 01 703 0987, fax 01 703 3689)

PASFIELD, Jonathan; s of John Alexander Pasfield, OBE (d 1973), and Mary Alys Flower Patten (d 1983); *b* 10 Sept 1940; *Educ* Lancing Coll, Trinity Coll Cambridge (MA), INSEAD Fontainebleau (MBA); *m* 2 Jan 1965, Jacqueline, da of Robert Alec Linford (d 1943); 2 s (James b 1965, Thomas b 1974), 2 da (Katharine b 1967, Lucy b 1972); *Career* dir Clifford's Diaries plc 1982-86; conslt in Food Industry; parish cncllr Shipley, Sussex; *Recreations* vintage lagondas, landscape gardening; *Style*— Jonathan Pasfield, Esq; Courtlands Farm, Brooks Green, Horsham, Sussex (☎ 0403 87 393)

PASKETT, Graham; s of George Paskett, of Amphion Radford Semele, Leamington Spa, Warwicks, and Joan, *née* McCubbin (d 1980); *b* 15 June 1946; *Educ* Blackdown Sch; *m* 15 June 1968, Jennifer Diana, da of Douglas Hamilton Sidders, of Breinton House, Hereford; 1 s (James Andrew Fergus b 1975), 1 da (Emma Jane Alice b 1970); *Career* chm: Paskett Public Relations Ltd 1976-, Onecolt Ltd 1981-; *Recreations* field sports particularly salmon fishing; *Style*— Graham Paskett, Esq; Roycroft Lodge, Uttoxeter, Staffordshire ST14 7PQ; Paskett Public Relations, 51 Friar Gate, Derby DE1 1DF (☎ 0332 372196, fax 0332 291035)

PASLEY, Sir (John) Malcolm Sabine; 5 Bt (GB 1794), of Craig, Dumfriesshire; s of Sir Rodney Marshall Sabine Pasley, 4 Bt (d 1982), and Aldyth (d 1983), da of Maj Lancelot Hamber; *b* 5 April 1926; *Educ* Sherborne, Trinity Coll Oxford (MA); *m* 1965, Virginia Killigrew, da of Peter Lothian Killigrew Wait, of Kew, Surrey; 2 s; *Heir* s, Robert Pasley; *Career* fellow Magdalen College Oxford; *Style*— Sir Malcolm Pasley, Bt; 25 Lathbury Rd, Oxford

PASLEY, Robet Killigrew Sabine; er s, and h of Sir Malcolm Pasley, 5 Bt; *b* 23 Oct 1965; *Style*— Robert Pasley, Esq; 25 Lathbury Rd, Oxford

PASMORE, (Edwin John) Victor; CH (1982), CBE (1959); s of Edwin Stephen Pasmore, MD, MRCP (d 1926), and Gertrude Eva, *née* Screech (d 1974); *b* 3 Dec 1908; *Educ* Harrow; *m* 3 June 1940, Wendy, da of Capt John Lloyd Blood (d 1956), of The Old Rectory, White Colne, nr Colchester, Essex; 1 s (John b 1941), 1 da (Mary b 1943); *Career* artist; visiting teacher LCC Camberwell Sch of Art 1945-49, Central Sch of Arts and Crafts 1949-53; master of painting Durham Univ 1954-61; conslt urban and architectural designer SW Area Peterlee New Town 1955-77; memb: London Artists Assoc 1932-34, The London Gp 1935-52, Euston Road Gp 1937-40; tstee Tate Gallery 1963-66; Retrospective exhibitions: Venice Biennale 1960, Musee des Arts Decoratifs Paris 1961, Stedelijle Copenhagen 1962, Kestner-Gesellschaft Hanover 1962, Kunsthalle Berne 1963, Tate Gallery 1965, Sao Paolo Biennale 1965, Cartwright Hall Bradford 1980, Royal Acad London 1980, Yale Center of British Art USA 1988; current exhibitions: London, NY, Rome, Milan, Zurich, Lubjlana, Messina, Oslo, Osaka, Tokyo, Delhi, Toronto; works represented in pub museums in: GB, Canada, Australia, NZ, Holland, Italy, France, Austria, Portugal, Switzerland, S America and the USA; Carnegie Prize, Pittsburgh Int USA 1964; Grand Prix d' Honneur, Graphics Biennale, Lubjlana 1977; Wollaston Award, Royal Acad 1984; hon degrees: Univ of Newcastle 1967, Univ of Surrey 1969, Univ of Warwick 1985, RCA 1969; *Books* Monograph and Catalogue Raisonné 1926-79 (1980), Burning Waters (poem with visual images, 1988); *Publications* Monographs and Catalogue Raisonée (1980); *Recreations* country walking, animals, natural philosophy; *Clubs* Arts; *Style*— Victor Pasmore, Esq, CH, CBE, RA; 12 St Germans Place, Blackheath, London SE3; Dar Gamri, Gudja, Malta; Marlborough Fine Art Ltd 6 Albemarle Street, London W1X 3HF (☎ 01 629 5161); Marlborough Gallery Inc, 40 West 57th Street, New York, NY 10018, USA

PASSEY, Michael Leighton Struth; s of Prof Richard Douglas Passey (d 1971), and Agnes Pattullo Passey *née* Struth (d 1976); *b* 22 Dec 1937; *Educ* Rugby, Trinity Coll Cambridge; *Career* slr 1964-67, lectr: Faculty of Law, Univ of Leeds 1967-; *Recreations* walking, investment; *Style*— Michael Passey, Esq; Faculty of Law, The Univ of Leeds (☎ 0532 431751)

PASSMORE, Gordon Seymour; s of Lt-Col Frank Frederick Seymour Passmore MBE (1975), of Pursers, Bramdean, Hants, and Claire Eileen, *née* Treacher (d 1984)

PASSMORE, John Francis Wolfe; s of Leonard Wolfe Passmore (d 1944), and Winifred, *née* Sladden (d 1981); *b* 9 Oct 1921; *Educ* Cranleigh; *m* 14 May 1949, Pamela Madeline, da of Otto Dunkels (d 1955); 3 s (Nicholas John Wolfe b 1950, Jeremy Cedric b 1952, David William b 1955); *Career* serv RE 1940-46, cmmnd 1941; sr ptnr Thomson Snell and Passmore (Slrs) 1979-86; *Recreations* gardening, photography; *Clubs* Naval and Military, Piccadilly; *Style*— John Passmore, Esq; Maynards, Groombridge, Tunbridge Wells TN3 9PR (☎ 0892 864335); 3 Lonsdale Gardens, Tunbridge Wells TN1 1NX (☎ 0892 510000, telex 95194, fax 0892 49884)

PASSMORE, Michael Bramwell; s of Brian Alfred Passmore (d 1985), of The Dog and Duck, W Wittering, Sussex, and Eileen Barbara, *née* Church; *b* 18 Sept 1928; *Educ* Bryanston Sch; *m* 14 Sept 1957, Anne Gillian, da of Joseph Hurrell Pillman, CBE (d 1968), of Ballards Corner, Limpsfield, Surrey; 2 s (Christopher b 1959, Stephen b 1960), 1 da (Stella b 1962); *Career* dir Albaster Passmore and Sons Ltd 1955-, chm Passmore Int 1981; *Recreations* sailing, walking; *Clubs* Royal Naval Sailing Assoc, Little Ship; *Style*— Michael Passmore, Esq; Scraces, Rectory Lane, Barming, nr Maidstone, Kent ME16 9NE (☎ 0622 26237); Passmore International, Tovil, Maidstone, Kent ME15 6XA

PASTERFIELD, Rt Rev Philip John; s of Bertie James Pasterfield (d 1955), of West Lavington Vicarage, and Lilian Bishop, *née* Flinn (d 1957); *b* 14 Jan 1920; *Educ* Denstone Coll Staffs, Trinity Hall Cambridge (MA), Cuddesdon Theol Coll; *m* 29 July 1948, (Eleanor) Maureen, da of William John Symons (d 1974), of Castlewood, Cheswardine, Salop; 3 s (Stephen b 1949, Andrew b 1951, Mark b 1955), 1 da (Verity b 1959); *Career* cmmnd Somerset LI 1940, India Cmd 1941, NW Frontier 1942, Arakan, Burma, Capt 1943-44, Adj, Maj 1945; curate Streatham London 1951-54, vicar W Lavington and chaplain King Edward VII Hosp Midhurst Sussex 1954-60, vicar Oxton Birkenhead 1960-68, chaplain TA 1961-68, rural dean Birkenhead 1966-68, canon residentiary St Albans Cathedral 1968-74, rural dean St Albans 1972-74, bishop suffragan Crediton 1974-84, asst bishop Diocese of Exeter 1984-; chm Cncl for Christian Care 1976-84, patron Hospicare Exeter 1980-84; *Recreations* ornithology, cricket, rugger, music; *Style*— The Rt Rev Philip Pasterfield; Wasley House, Harberton, nr Totnes, Devon TQ9 7SW (☎ 0803 865093)

PASTINEN, HE The Ambass of Finland Ilkka Olavi; Hon KCMG (1972); s of Martti Mikael Pastinen (d 1968), and Ilmi Saga, *née* Karlström (d 1963); *b* 17 Mar 1928; *Educ* Abo Akademi Finland (MpolSc), Inst d'Etudes Politiques Paris France, Inst Int des Sciences et Recherches Diplomatiques Paris France; *m* 23 July 1950, Eeva Marja, da of Otto Viitanen (d 1958), Inspr General of Schs and Knight White Rose of Finland; 2 da (Kristiina b 1955, Johanna b 1956); *Career* Dip Serv 1952-: Stockholm 1955-57, perm mission to Un 1957-60, Peking 1962-64, London 1966-69, ambass and dep rep of Finland to UN 1969-71, special rep of Sec Gen of UN to ctee of disarmament 1971-75, ambass and perm rep of Finland to UN 1977-83, ambass to Ct of St James 1983-; Cdr First Class of the Order of the White Rose of Finland 1986;; *Recreations* golf, music, bridge; *Clubs* Athenaeum, Travellers', Swinley Forest Golf; *Style*— HE The Ambass Ilkka Olavi; 14 Kensington Palace Gardens, London W8 (☎ 01 221 4433); Embassy of Finland, 38 Chesham Place, London SW1 (☎ 01 235 9531, fax 01 235 3680, telex 24786 Finamb G)

PASTON-BEDINGFELD; see Bedingfeld

PATCHETT, Terry; MP (Lab) Barnsley E 1983-; s of Wilfred and Kathleen Patchett; *Educ* Sheffield Univ; *m* 1961, Glenys Veal; 1 s, 2 da; *Style*— Terry Patchett Esq, MP; 71 Upperwood Rd, Darfield, nr Barnsley, S Yorks

PATEMAN, Rev Donald Herbert; s of Herbert (d 1967), of Leicester, and May, *née* Carter (d 1963); *b* 22 Feb 1915; *Educ* Wyggeston Sch Leicester, London Coll of Divinity (ALCD); *Career* RAF 1940-45; ordained (dio London) 1948, vicar of St Mark Dalston 1956-; *Style*— Rev Donald H Pateman; St Mark's Vicarage, Sandringham Rd, London E8 2LL (☎ 01 254 4741)

PATEMAN, Jack Edward; CBE (1970); s of William Edward Pateman; *b* 29 Nov 1921; *Educ* Gt Yarmouth GS; *m* 1949, Cicely Hope Turner; 1 s, 1 da; *Career* dir GEC Computers Ltd 1971-, chm 1978-; md Marconi Avionics Ltd 1971-, dir: Canadian Marconi Co 1971-, Elliott Bros (London) Ltd 1979-; *Style*— Jack Pateman Esq, CBE; Spindles, Ivy Hatch, Sevenoaks, Kent

PATER, John Edward; CB (1953); s of Edward Rhodes Pater (d 1942), and Lilian Oswald (d 1979); *b* 15 Mar 1911; *Educ* King Edward VI Sch Retford, Queens' Coll Cambridge (MA, PhD); *m* 1938, Margaret Anderson, da of Montague Cornwell Furtado (d 1950, former dep chief inspr of Taxes); 2 s, 1 da; *Career* civil servant: under-sec Miny of Health and DHSS 1947-73 (ret); govr Kingswood Sch 1973-85; *Publications* The Making of the National Health Service (1981); *Style*— John Pater Esq, CB; 1(b) Croham Mount, South Croydon CR2 0BR (☎ 01 651 1601)

PATERNÒ CASTELLO DI CÁRCACI, Duke (Duca) Don Gaetano Maria Giuseppe; 12 Duke of Cárcaci, 10 Baron of Placa and Baiana; s of Don Francesco Maria Domenico Paternò Castello, 11 Duke of Cárcaci, 9 Baron of Placa and Baiana; descendant of feudal family from Sicily and of Giovanni Paternò 1398; cr Dukes of Cárcaci in 1648 by King Philip IV; confirmed by Imperial Decree in Vienna in 1725 by Emperor Charles VI and recognised by Italian Govt 1903 and 1906; *b* 13 Sept 1923; *Educ* Docteur ès Sciences Politiques; *m* 1, 12 July 1960, Marie Regina (d 1973), 2 da of Sir Eugen Millington-Drake, KCMG (d 1972), and Lady Effie Mackay (d 1984), 4 da of 1 Earl of Inchcape; 1 s, 1 da; m 2, 1976, Brenda Mary, da of Dr A W Stafford; *Heir* s, Duke Don Alexander Paternò Castello di Cárcaci; *Career* Bailli Constantinian Order of St George of Naples; *Style*— HE The Duke of Cárcaci; 25 Holland Park Gardens, London W14

PATERSON *see also*: Jardine Paterson

PATERSON, Alison Bianca; da of Peter Noel Vesey Newsome, Bem, of Vancouver BC, and Valerie Janet Boogerman, *née* Phipps; *b* 12 Oct 1955; *Educ* Peak Sch Hong KOng, Wispers Sch Haslemere Surrey, Univ Coll London (BSc, Dip Arch), RIBA professional practice exam; *m* 15 Sept 1984, Richard O'Donnell Paterson, s of Brian O'Donnell Paterson (d 1977); *Career* urban devpt mangr Wimpey Homes (George Wimpey plc) London 1984-86, project dir Regalian Properies plc 1986-, dir of subsiduary Co's 1986- (Regalian Homes Ltd , Regalian Urban Renewal, Regalian Devpts Ltd; memb ARCUK 1983, memb RIBA; *Recreations* bridge, tennis; *Clubs* Hurlingham, RAC; *Style*— Mrs Alison Paterson; Napier Ave, Hurlingham, London SW6; Regalian Properites plc, 44 Grosvenor Hill, London SW1X 9JE (☎ 01 493 9613)

PATERSON, Anthony John; s of John McLennan Paterson (d 1978), and Isobel Margaret, *née* Reichwald; *b* 16 May 1951; *Educ* Winchester, Worcester Coll Oxford (LLB); *Career* slr; special constable 1976-79; candidate (Lib) for Finchley 1979, candidate (C) for Brent S 1987; memb cncl World Wildlife Fund; press offr cons Bow Gp 1983-84, parly liaison offr 1984-85, res sec 1985-87, author of 3 Bow Gp papers; memb Cons Pty's Agric and Countryside Forum 1985-; *Recreations* politics, reading, languages; *Style*— Anthony J Paterson, Esq; c/o Bates Wells & Braithwaite, 20 Old Bailey EC4 (☎ 2369081)

PATERSON, Dame Betty Fraser Ross; DBE (1981, CBE 1973), JP (1950), DL (Herts 1980); da of Robert Ross Russell (d 1934), and Elsie Marian Fraser (d 1918); *b* 14 Mar 1916; *Educ* Harrogate Coll, Western Infirmary Glasgow (MCSP); *m* 1940, Ian Douglas Paterson, s of George Stanley Vaughan Paterson (d 1935); 1 s (Ross), 1 da (Rosemary); *Career* memb: Chartered Soc of Physiotherapy 1938, Herts CC 1952-74, (chm 1969-73, alderman 1959-74), Cmmn for the New Towns 1961-74, (dep chm 1970-74), St Bartholomew's Hosp Govrs 1961-73, NE Met Regnl Hosp Bd 1960-73; chm: NW Thames Regnl Health Authy 1973-84, nat staff ctee Nurses and Midwives 1974-84; pres Herts Assoc of Local Cncls 1978, vice pres Herts Magistrates Assoc 1987, vice pres Herts Community Cncl 1987; *Recreations* music, cooking, foreign travel; *Style*— Dame Betty Paterson, DBE, JP, DL; 52 Free Trade Wharf, The Highway, London E1 9ES (☎ 01 791 0367)

PATERSON, Sir Dennis Craig; s of Lt-Col Gilbert Charles Paterson (d 1962); *b* 14 Oct 1930; *Educ* Collegiate Sch of St Peter's Adelaide, Adelaide Univ; *m* 1955, Mary Mansell, da of Frederick Mansell Hardy; 1 s (Thomas), 3 da (Mrs Julian Bickersteth, Mrs Mark Goedecke, Mrs David Murton); *Career* Capt Australian Citizens Mil Force; dir and chief orthopaedic surgn Adelaide Children's Hosp 1970-; consltt orthopaedic surgn: Royal Adelaide Hosp Adelaide 1964-, Queen Victoria Hosp 1968-, Regency Park Centre for Physically Handicapped Children Adelaide 1976-; pres Crippled Children's Association of S Australia 1970-84, Sociéte Internationale de Chirureve Orthopédique ed de Travmtologie (Sicot) 1987-; Queen's Silver Jubilee Medal 1977; FRCS, FRACS, MD (Adel); kt 1976; *Recreations* golf, tennis, gardening; *Clubs* Adelaide, Royal Adelaide Golf, Kooyong Golf; *Style*— Sir Dennis Paterson; 31 Myall Ave, Kensington Gdns, Adelaide, SA 5068, Australia (☎ 08 332 3364)

PATERSON, Hon Mrs; Hon Fiona; *née* Sharples; da (by 1 m) of Baroness Sharples, *qv*; *b* 1949; *m* 1981, Alexander Paterson; *Style*— The Hon Mrs Paterson

PATERSON, His Honour Judge; Frank David; s of David Paterson, of Liverpool (d 1956); *b* 10 July 1918; *Educ* Quarry Bank HS Liverpool, Liverpool Univ (LLB); *m* 1953, Barbara Mary, da of Oswald Ward Gillow (d 1949), of Formby, Lancs; 1 s, 2 da; *Career* barr Gray's Inn 1941, asst dep coroner Liverpool 1960-68, chm Min of Pensions and Nat Insur Tbnl Liverpool 1957-68, Mental Health Review Tbnl for SW Lancs and Cheshire 1963-68, Circuit judge (formerly County Court judge) 1968-; *Clubs* Athenaeum (Liverpool); *Style*— His Honour Judge Paterson; Vailima, 2 West Lane, Formby, Liverpool L37 7BA (☎ Formby 74345)

PATERSON, Sir George Mutlow; OBE (1946), QC (Sierra Leone 1950); s of Dr George William Paterson (d 1954), of Grenada, WI, and late Olivia Hannah, *née* Mutlow-Williams; *b* 3 Dec 1906; *Educ* Grenada Boys' Sch, St John's Coll Cambridge (MA, LLM); *m* 1935, Audrey Anita, da of late Maj C C B Morris, CBE, MC; 1 s, 2 da; *Career* Colonial Admin Serv Northern Nigeria 1929, barr Inner Temple 1933, magistrate Nigeria 1936, crown counsel Tanganyika 1937, War Serv King's African Rifles (wounded 1940, Lt-Col); slr-gen Tanganyika 1946-49, attorney-gen Sierra Leone 1949-54, Ghana 1954-57, chief justice N Rhodesia 1957-61, ret 1961; chm Industl Tbnls SW region of Eng 1965-79; kt 1959; *Recreations* reading; *Clubs* Bath and County (Bath); *Style*— Sir George Paterson, OBE, QC; St George's, Westbury, Sherborne, Dorset DT9 3RA

PATERSON, Graham Julian; s of Peter James Paterson, and Beryl, *née* Johnson; *b* 7 June 1955; *Educ* Dulwich, Magdalen Coll Oxford (BA); *Career* journalist Daily Telegraph 1977-86; ed 7 days section Sunday Telegraph 1988- (assoc ed 1987-88, home ed 1986-87); *Clubs* Travellers'; *Style*— Graham Paterson, Esq

PATERSON, Lt-Col Howard Cecil; TD (two clasps); s of Henry John Paterson, (d 1969), of Romanno Bridge, Peeblesshire, and Margaret Isobel, *née* Eunson (d 1983); *b* 16 Mar 1920; *Educ* Daniel Stewart's Coll Edinburgh, Edinburgh Coll of Art; *m* 21 July 1945, Isabelle Mary, da of Frederick Augustus Edward Upton (d 1960), of 28 College Rd, Southampton; 1 s (Colin Howard b 7 Aug 1948); *Career* Lt-Col RA (TA) (ret 1970), serv Europe; Ind Tourism Consl since 1981 (sr ptnr in Tourism Advsy Servs); sr dir Scottish Tourist Bd 1966-81; dept dir Scottish Co Indust Devpt Tst 1951-66; assist personnel mangr Jute Industs Ltd 1949-51; chm: Taste of Scotland Scheme 1976-86, Scottish Int Gathering Tst 1982-; vice-chm: Scottish Aircraft Collection Tst 1982-, John Buchan Soc; memb: Br Horse Soc Scottish Ctee, Scottish Treking & Riding Assoc Cncl, Edinburgh Area Ctee of Scottish Lowland Territorial and Volunteer Reserve Assoc, Scottish Landowners Fedn, Scottish Recreational Land Assoc, Rural Forum; author of Tourism in Scotland (1969), and Flavour of Edinburgh (with Catherine Brown) (1986); FSA Scot; *Recreations* fishing, shooting, drawing and painting, writing, wild life study, food; *Clubs* Caledonian, 32 Abercromby Place, Edinburgh; *Style*— Lt-Col Howard Paterson, TD; Dovewood, W Linton, Peebesshire EH46 7DS (☎ 0968 60346)

PATERSON, Sqdn Ldr Ian Veitch; CBE (1969), JP (Hamilton), DL (Lanarkshire, 1963); s of Andrew Wilson Paterson; *b* 17 August 1911; *Educ* Lanark GS, Glasgow Univ; *m* 1940, Anne Weir, da of Thomas Brown; 2 s, 1 da; *Career* dep chm Local Govt Boundary Commission 1974-; *Style*— Sqdn Ldr Ian Paterson, CBE; 35 Stewarton Drive, Cambuslang, Glasgow

PATERSON, James Rupert; s of Maj R E Paterson, MC, of Seaforth Highlanders, late of Palazzo Bonlini, Venice, Italy (d 1964), and Josephine Mary, *née* Bartlett (d 1986); *b* 7 August 1932; *Educ* St Augustine's Abbey Sch Ramsgate, The Nautical Coll Pangbourne, RMA Sandhurst; *m* 18 Aug 1956, Kay, da of Patrick Dinneen, of Rathmore, Co Kerry; 2 s (Dominic b 1961, Sean b 1963), 2 da (Sara b 1958, Helen b 1959); *Career* cmmnd RA 1953, serv Hong Kong, Cambridge (attached to faculty of slavonic languages), Paris, Singapore, Berlin (twice); HM Dipl Serv 1970-: FCO 1970-71, first sec Islamabad 1972-75; dep high cmmr Trinidad and Tobago 1975-78, FCO 1979-81, ambass Ulan Bator 1982-84, consul-gen Istanbul 1985-88, consul-gen Geneva 1988-; *Recreations* reading, writing, golf; *Style*— James Paterson, Esq; c/o FCO, (Geneva) King Charles St, London SW1 2AH

PATERSON, James Veitch; s of John Robert Paterson; *b* 16 April 1928; *Educ* Peebles HS, Edinburgh Acad, Lincoln Coll Oxford, Edinburgh Univ; *m* 1956, Ailie, da of Lt Cdr Sir (George) Ian Clark Hutchison; 1 s, 1 da; *Career* admitted to Faculty of

Advocates 1953; Sheriff of the Lothian and Borders (formerly Roxburgh, Berwick and Selkirk) at Jedburgh, Selkirk and Duns 1963-; *Style*— James Paterson, Esq; Sunnyside, Melrose, Roxburghshire (☎ Melrose 2502)

PATERSON, John Lamb; s of John L Paterson (d 1965), of Sydney, Australia, and Ina, *née* Grace (d 1959); *b* 17 July 1931; *Educ* Royal HA Edinburgh, Edinburgh Coll of Art (DA); *Career* Edinburgh Coll of Art: lectr dept of architecture 1963-70, dir first year studies 1970-72, head sch of design and crafts 1972-82, princ 1984-; architect and designer: Landmark Visitor Centre Carrbridge 1968-70, Grange Arts Centre Oldham 1972-76, Theatre Museum Covent Gdn London 1977-87, Conslt Property Servs Agency; Exhibitions: Parade Diaghilev Celebration Edinburgh 1979, Spotlight 50 anniversary Royal Ballet 1981, V & A 1982, 2087 (touring) 1986-88; Royal Scottish Acad Gold Medal for Architecture 1976; dep chm Friends of Edinburgh Int Festival, memb cncl Edinburgh Int Festival; ARIBA 1957, FRIAS 1977, FRSA 1985; *Books* IONA (1987); *Recreations* swimming, hill walking; *Clubs* New (Edinburgh); *Style*— John Paterson, Esq; Edinburgh Coll of Art, Lauriston Place, Edinburgh, EH3 9DF, (☎031 229 9311, fax 031 229 0089, cartel 086 064 1217)

PATERSON, John Mower Alexander; OBE (1985), JP, DL (Bucks 1982); s of Leslie Martin Paterson (d 1969), and Olive Harriette, *née* Mower (d 1980); *b* 9 Nov 1920; *Educ* Oundle, Queens' Coll Cambridge (MA); *m* 1944, Daisy Miriam Ballanger, da of Cdr Hugh Haddow Darroch Marshall, RNR (d 1958), of 18 Castle Hill, Dover; 1 s (Martin), 2 da (Rosemary, Lisa); *Career* Lt RE 1941-46; Cincinnati Milling Machines (Birmingham) 1946-48 dir and works mangr The Bifurcated and Tubular Rivet Co, Aylesbury 1948-60 (chm and md 1960-69), chm and md Bifurcated Engrg Ltd 1969-73, chm Bifurcated Engrg plc (now BETEC plc) 1974-85 (dir 1974-88), gen commr of Taxes Aylesbury Div 1959-, memb governing body Aylesbury Coll of Further Educn 1961- (chm 1977-88), Gd Cncl CBI 1971-84, Southern Regnl Cncl CBI 1971-85 (chm 1974-76), mgmnt ctee of Waddesdon Manor 1980-; Cncl of Order of St John in Bucks 1980- (chm 1981-); Pres Aylesbury Div Cons and Unionist Assoc 1984-85, dir Rickmansworth Water Co 1984- (chm 1988-); High Sheriff of Bucks 1978, Vice Lord Lt of Bucks 1984-; OStJ 1985, CStJ 1985; *Recreations* sailing (yacht "Gallivanter"), veteran cars, gardening; *Clubs* Royal Ocean Racing, Royal Yacht Squadron (Cowes), Royal Lymington Yacht; *Style*— John Paterson, Esq, JP, DL; Park Hill, Potter Row, Great Missenden, Bucks HP16 9LT (☎ 024 06 2995)

PATERSON, Very Rev John Munn Kirk; s of George Kirk Paterson, and Sarah Ferguson, *née* Wilson; *b* 8 Oct 1922; *Educ* Hillhead HS Glasgow, Edinburgh Univ (MA, BD); *m* 1946, Geraldine Lilian Parker; 2 s, 1 da; *Career* serv RAF WWII; former min St Paul's Milngavie, moderator of General Assembly of Church of Scotland 1984-85; Hon DD Aberdeen 1986; *Style*— The Very Rev John Paterson; 58 Orchard Drive, Edinburgh EH4 2DZ

PATERSON, (Isabel) Margaret; da of August Waldemar Reichwald (d 1929), and Isabel Nancy, *née* Bell (d 1955); *b* 20 Oct 1917; *Educ* Benenden, Inst of Household Mgmnt (Distinction), Cookery Demonstrating, City and Guilds Cookery Teaching (Dip); *m* 14 Dec 1949, John McLennan Paterson (d 1978), s of late Alexander Paterson; 2 s (Anthony John Paterson b 1951, Nigel Paterson b 1952); *Career* cookery author: The Craft of Cooking (1978), 'Masterclass' (chapter 1982), 1001 Ways to be a Good Cook (1986); *Recreations* travel, bridge, gardening, needlework; *Style*— Mrs Margaret Paterson

PATERSON, Martin James Mower; s of Mr John Mower Alexander Paterson, of Park Hill, Great Missenden Bucks, and Miriam Ballinger Paterson; *b* 14 Mar 1951; *Educ* Oundle, Univ of Birmingham (BSc), Cranfield Inst of Tech (MBA and Dip Inst of Mktg); *m* 9 July 1977, Anne Vivien, da of Vivien Errol, DSC; 2 s (David Mower Errol, Andrew James); *Career* Metal Box 1973-81: graduate tnee 1973-74, devpt technician 1974-76, Mtrg mangr 1975-78, works mangr (Thailand) 1978-81; Betec plc 1981- 84; dir and gen mangr Black and Luff Ltd 1981-82, divnl trg dir 1982-84; Cranfield Inst of Tech 1984-85, TI Gp plc 1985-86, special assignments exec Aeroquip Ltd (md Seals Div 1986-88), md STS Ltd 1988-; MI Prod E, MIM; *Recreations* sailing; *Clubs* Royal Lymingson Yacht, RORC; *Style*— Martin Paterson, Esq; Crossways House, Cowbridge, South Glamorgan, Wales CF7 7LJ (☎ 04463 3171); STS Ltd, Malvern Dr, Ty-Glas, Industrial Estate, Cardiff CF4 5WW (☎ 0222 753 221, fax 0222 755 174, telex 495 255)

PATERSON, Maurice Dinsmore; s of Maurice Sidney Paterson (d 1977), of Glasgow, and Agnes Dinsmore, *née* Joss; *b* 28 August 1941; *Educ* Glasgow HS; *m* 3 Oct 1967, Avril Grant, da of John Gordon Barclay (d 1984), of Glasgow; 2 s (Michael b 1970, Colin b 1974); *Career* joined Scottish Amicable 1959: asst sec 1968, gen mangr sales and mktg 1978, dir 1985; chm Glasgow Life and Pensions Gp 1972-73, pres Insur and Actuarial Soc of Glasgow 1987-88; FFA 1967; *Recreations* golf, badminton; *Clubs* Caledonian, Pollok Golf, Western Gailes Golf; *Style*— Maurice Paterson, Esq; 8 Merrylee Rd, Glasgow, G43 2SH (☎ 041 637 2690); Scottish Amicable Life Assurance Society, 150 St Vincent St, Glasgow G2 5NQ (☎ 041 248 2323)

PATERSON, (James Edmund) Neil; s of James D Paterson, and Nichola K, *née* Kerr; *b* 31 Dec 1915; *Educ* Banff Acad, Edinburgh Univ (MA); *m* 6 July 1939, Rosabelle, da of David MacKenzie; 2 s (Kerr b 1944, John b 1946), 1 da (Lindsay b 1940); *Career* Lt RNVR (Mine Sweepers) 1940-45; author and screenwriter; conslt Films of Scotland (memb 1954-76, dir 1976-79); govr: BFI 1958-60, Pitlochry Festival Theatre 1966-76, Nat Film Sch 1970-80; chm literature ctee Scottish Arts cncl 1967-76, dir Grampian TV 1960-86; memb: planning ctee Nat Film Sch 1969, Arts Cncl of GB 1974-76; Atlantic Award in Literature 1946, American Acad Award 1959; *Books* The China Run (1948), Behold Thy Daughter (1950), And Delilah (1951) Man on the Tight-Rope (1953), The Kidnappers (1957), Stories and Screenplays; *Style*— Neil Paterson, Esq; St Ronans, Crieff, Perthshire (☎ 0764 2615)

PATERSON, Noel Kennedy; CIE (1947), OBE (1943); s of Rev David Paterson, of Edinburgh, and Susannah Simpson Kennedy; *b* 25 Dec 1905; *Educ* George Heriot's Sch, Edinburgh Univ, St John's Coll Cambridge; *m* 1, 1934, Margaret Winifred Schreiber (d 1981); 2 s, 2 da; m 2, 1983, Joyce Margaret Burnard; *Career* ICS 1929, chief cmmr Andaman and Nicobar Islands 1944-47, UK trade cmmr Dublin, projects offr UK Freedom from Hunger Campaign 1961-75; *Style*— Noel Paterson Esq, CIE, OBE; Chestnut Cottage, Gabriels Farm, Park Lane, Twyford, Hants (☎ Twyford 713116)

PATERSON, Robert Andrew (Robin); o s of John Leggat Paterson (d 1983), of Beith, Ayrshire, and Winifred Purdon, *née* Ballantyne (d 1983); *b* 27 Oct 1936; *Educ* Strathallan Sch; *m* 27 July 1963, Diane Margaret, o da of Malcolm George Lillingston (ka 1941; see Burke's Landed Gentry, 18 edn, vol I, 1965), and Mary Lyons, yst da of Sir William McLintock, 1 Bt, GBE, CVO; 1 s (Jamie John Lillingston Paterson b 6 Aug 1967), 1 da (Joanna Mary Lillingston-Paterson b 16 May 1965); *Career* CA; ptnr Grieveson Grant & Co 1970-86, dir Kleinwort Benson Securities Ltd 1986-88, chm Paterson Printing Ltd 1988-, memb stock exchange; *Recreations* golf, skiing, gardening; *Clubs* New (Edinburgh); *Style*— Robert Paterson, Esq; Lees Ct, Matfield, Tonbridge, Kent TN12 7JU (☎ 089 272 2892); Paterson Printing Ltd, 21 Chapman Way, Tunbridge Wells, Kent TN2 3EF (☎ 0892 511212)

PATERSON-BROWN, Dr June; da of Wing-Cdr Thomas Clark Garden (d 1978), of South Esk Lodge, Temple, Gorebridge, Midlothian, and Jean Martha Garden BEM, *née* Mallace (d 1976); *b* 8 Feb 1932; *Educ* Esdaile Coll Edinburgh, Edinburgh Univ Med Sch (MB, ChB); *m* 29 March 1957, Peter Neville Paterson-Brown s of Keith Paterson- Brown (d 1981), of 17 Blackfolrd Rd, Edinburgh; 3 s (Simon b 1958, Timothy b 1960, William b 1965), 1 da (Sara b 1959); *Career* med offr Family Planning and Well Woman Clinics Hawick 1960-85, non- exec dir Border TV plc 1979-; former memb Roxburghshire Co Educn Ctee; chm: Roxburghshire Co Youth Ctee, Roxburgh Dist Duke of Edinburgh Award Ctee; co cmmr Roxburghshire and Peeblesshire Girl Guides Assocs 1977-82, chief cmmr UK and Cwlth Girl Guides 1985- vice chm and tstee Princes Tst 1980-, tstee MacRoberts Tsts 1987-, Queen's Silver Jubilee Medal 1977; *Recreations* skiing, golf, tennis, music, reading, fishing; *Clubs* Lansdowne; *Style*— Dr June Paterson-Brown; Norwood, Hawick, Roxburghshire TD9 7HP (☎ 0450 72352, fax 0450 77521)

PATIENT, Matthew Lemay; s of Cyril Mortimer Patient (d 1981), and Joan Mary Christine Grace Lemay; *b* 16 Mar 1939; *Educ* Brighton Coll; *m* 10 June 1967, Susan Elizabeth (Sue), da of Geoffrey Ernest Soar; 1 s (Jonathan b 1 Feb 1971), 2 da (Joanna Elizabeth b 1 April 1969 Alexandra Louise b 23 Nov 1973); *Career* CA, ptnr nat auditing 1966, and accounting tech ptnr 1981- Deloitte Haskins & Sells 1981-; dir: Professional Asset Indemnity Ltd, Padua Ltd, Global Insur Co Ltd; memb co affrs ctee IOD 1974-; ICAEW: memb parly and law ctee 1974-81, memb cncl 1984-88; CCAB: memb accounting standards ctee 1981-86 memb auditing practices ctee 1981-88 (chm 1986-88); ind memb Retail Trades (non-food) Wages Cncl 1982-, nominated memb cncl Lloyd's of London 1989; govr and vice-pres Brighton Coll, govr St Andrews Sch Woking; ACA 1963, FCA 1973, ATII; *Books* Accounting Provisions of The Companies Act 1985 (1985), Licensed Dealers Rules & Regulations 1983 (1983), various professional articles; *Clubs* Gresham, RAC; *Style*— Matthew Patient, Esq; 128 Queen Victoria St, London EC4P 4JX (☎ 01 248 3913, fax 01 248 3623, telex 894941)

PATON, Sir (Thomas) Angus Lyall; CMG (1960); s of Thomas Lyall Paton (d 1962), of Valley House, St John, Jersey, CI, and Janet, *née* Gibb (d 1959); *b* 10 May 1905; *Educ* Cheltenham, Univ Coll London (BSc, fell 1962); *m* 7 June 1933, (Eleanor) Joan Medora (d 1964), da of Maj George Arthur Delmé-Murray, DSO (d 1944); 2 s (Alan b 1942, John b 1952), 2 da (Janet b 1934, Anne b 1937); *Career* sr ptnr Sir Alexander Gibb & Ptnrs 1955-57, sr conslt 1977-84; pres Inst of Civil Engrs 1970-71, vice-pres Royal Soc 1977-78, fell Imperial Coll London 1978; Hon DSc: London 1978, Bristol 1981; Hon FICE 1975, FIStructE, FRSA, Foreign Assoc Nat Acad of Engrg (USA) 1979; kt 1973; *Books* Power From Water, co-author (1960); *Recreations* gardening, DIY; *Style*— Sir Angus Paton, CMG; L'Epervier, Route Orange, St Brelade, Jersey, CI (☎ 0534 45619)

PATON, David Romer; s of John David Paton, JP (d 1982), of Grandhome, Aberdeen AB2 8AR, and Fenella Mary, *née* Crombie (d 1949); *b* 5 Mar 1935; *Educ* Gordonstown, Keble Coll Oxford; *m* 2 July 1975, Juliette Burnet, da of Capt Christopher Arthur Burney (d 1980), of 35 Edwardes Square, London W8; 2 s (William b 1976, Matthew b 1979); *Career* chartered surveyor: John Sale & ptns 1964-67, to Marquis of Bristol 1967-72, Donaldsons 1972-75, Walker Son & Packman 1975-79, Leslie Lintott & Assocs 1979-; former chm: Royal Northern and Univ Club, Gordon Cons Assoc; chm: Aberdeen Civic Soc, North East Scotland Preservation Tst, pres Aberdeen C of C; dir: Aberdeen Maritme Museum Appeal Co Ltd, Aberdeen Salmon Co Ltd, Assoc of Br C of C; cncl memb Assoc of Scottish Dist Salmon Fishery Bds, memb Aberdeen Harbour Bd, ctee memb Architectural Heritage Soc of Scotland; sec of State appointee: NE River Purification Bd, HM Salmon Advsy Ctee, cncllr Thingoe Rural Dist Cncl 1970-74; Burgess of Guild City of Aberdeen 1983; FRICS, FRVA; *Recreations* conservation, fishing, bridge; *Clubs* Royal Northern and Univ; *Style*— David Paton, Esq; Grandhome, Aberdeen AB2 8AR (☎ 0224 722 202); Waverley Place, Aberdeen AB1 1XH (☎ 0224 624 400)

PATON, Maj-Gen Douglas Stuart; CBE (1983); s of Stuart Paton and Helen Kathleen, *née* Hooke (d 1953); *b* 3 Mar 1926; *Educ* Sherborne, Bristol Univ (MB, CHB, FFCM); *m* 1957, Jennifer Joan, da of Maj Edward Loxley Land (d 1968), of Losely, Lower Rd, Great Bookham, Surrey; 2 da; *Career* cmmnd RAMC 1952, CO CMH Aldershot 1973-76, RCDS 1977, DDMS HQ 1 (BR) Corps 1978-80, DDGAMS MOD 1981-83, cdr med servs BAOR in the rank of Maj-Gen 1983-86; chm BAMC Assoc 1988, govr Moorfields Eye Hosp 1988-, QHP 1981-86, CStJ 1986; *Recreations* skiing, opera, gardening, travel; *Style*— Maj-Gen Douglas Paton, CBE; Brampton, Springfield Rd, Camberley, Surrey GU15 1AB

PATON, (Alexander) Frank; s of Alec Paton, of Cheshire, and Gillian, *née* Carey; *b* 14 May 1929; *Educ* Oundle, Pembroke Coll Cambridge; *m* 10 Sept 1959, Dawn, *née* Wood; 2 s, 3 da; *Career* farmer and landowner; pres Int Farm Mgmnt Assoc, memb Cncl European Movement; fndr Somerset SDP; *Recreations* gardening, travel, wine; *Clubs* Farmers', 75; *Style*— Frank Paton, Esq; Sandcombe House, Enmore, Bridgwater, Somerset TA5 2ED (☎ 027 867 384)

PATON, Hon Mrs; Hon Rachel Audrey; *née* Eden; da of 9 Baron Auckland and Dorothy Margaret, JP, yr da of Henry Joseph Manser, of Beechwood, Friday St, Eastbourne, Sussex; *b* 9 June 1959; *m* 20 June 1981, Bramwell Paton, s of John Paton, of Maidenhead; 2 s (Alexander b 1983, Joe b 1986), 1 da (Charlotte Jane b 19-); *Style*— The Hon Mrs Paton; 22 Penwortham Road, Streatham London SW16 6RE

PATON, Prof Sir William Drummond Macdonald; CBE (1968); s of Rev William Paton, D D (d 1943), of St Albans, Herts, and Grace Mackenzie, *née* Macdonald (d 1967); *b* 5 May 1917; *Educ* Repton, New Coll Oxford (BA), UCH London (BM, BCh, MA, DM); *m* 22 Aug 1942, Phoebe Margaret, da of late Thomas Rooke, of Shinfield, nr Reading; *Career* house physician UCH 1942, pathologist Midhurst Sanatorium 1943-44, staff Nat Inst for Med Res MRC 1944-52; prof pharmacology: RCS 1954-59, Oxford Univ 1959-84; hon dir Wellcome Inst for History of Med 1983-87; serv for various orgns incl: MRC, Royal Soc, Res Def Soc, Physiological Soc, Pharmacological

Soc, Br Toxicological Soc; del Clarendon Press 1967-72; tstee: Rhodes Tst 1968-87, Wellcome Tst 1978-87; chm ctee on suppression of doping Jt Racing Bd 1970-71, advsr HO on intoximeter breathtesting 1984-85, memb Advsy Cncl for Sci and Technol 1970; JP 1956; Freeman City of London 1976, memb Soc of Apothecaries 1976; Hon DSc: London 1985, Edinburgh 1987; Hon DUniv Surrey 1986; FRS 1956, FRCP 1969, FRSA 1973, hon FFARCS 1975, hon FRSM 1982; kt 1979; *Books* Pharmacological Principles and Practice (1968), Man and Mouse (1984); *Recreations* music, old books, geology; *Clubs* Athenaeum; *Style*— Prof Sir William Paton, CBE; 13 Staverton Rd, Oxford OX2 6XH (☎ 0865 58355)

PATON-PHILIP, Philip; VRD (1957); s of Dr Wilfrid Paton-Philip, MC, MA, MB, DPH, DMRE, FCCP (USA) (d 1956), of Cambridge, and Mary Isobel, *née* Simpson (d 1985); *b* 12 Sept 1922; *Educ* St John's Coll Cambridge (MA, MB BChir, MChir, MRCS), LRCP (London); *m* 1, 1959 (m dis 1970), Julia, da of Stephen Vaux (d 1985), of Birchington, Kent; 1 s (Charles Philip b 1960); m 2, 1978, Christina, da of Dr Carl Henri Bernhardson, of Stockholm, Sweden; 2 s (Richard b 1980, James b 1982); *Career* Lt Cmdr RN and RNVR 1947-52, surgn in charge RN Surgical Chest Unit; conslting urological surgn: St Helier Hosp, Epsom Hosp, St George's Hosp; conslting surgeon specialising in kidney surgery and urology: St Bartholomew's Hosp, St Thomas's Hosp, Denver Med Coll Colorado USA; FRCS; *Recreations* riding, showjumping, skiing, sailing, carriage driving; *Clubs* Garrick, Savage, BHS, BSJA, British Driving Society, Royal Naval Medical; *Style*— Philip Paton-Philip, Esq, VRD; The Ship, Hurst Drive, Walton-on-the-Hill, Tadworth, Surrey; 149 Harley St, London W1 (☎ 01 935 4444)

PATON-SMITH, Carolin Mary; da of Alexander Ludovic Grant, TD, DL, JP (d 1986), of Marbury Hall, Whitchurch, Shrops, and Elizabeth Langley, *née* Buxton; *b* 24 Feb 1947; *Educ* Heathfield, Univ of Florence; *m* 19 Aug 1967, William Richard Paton-Smith, s of Norman William Paton-Smith, of Clevelands, Felsted, Nr Dunmow, Essex; 2 s (Ben b 21 July 1968, Harry b 9 Aug 1972); *Career* farmer/landowner; *Recreations* hunting; *Style*— Mrs Carolin Paton-Smith; Marbury Hall, Whitchurch, Shrops SY13 4LP (☎ 0948 3731)

PATON-WILLIAMS, Geoffrey Gordon; s of Rev Francis Paton-Williams (d 1974), Canon of Manchester, and Bertha Perrings (d 1985); *b* 17 June 1922; *Educ* Marlborough, Oriel Coll Oxford (MA); *m* 14 April 1951, Anne Vivian (d 1982), da of Lt-Col Arthur Nelson Forman (d 1962); 3 s (Jeremy Charles Geoffrey b 1954, Simon Francis b 1958, Arthur Michael Jonathan b 1961), 1 da (Charlotte Anne b 1952); *Career* WWII Rifle Bde 1941-46, Capt 8 Bn Normandy and the Baltic, Capt GSHQ BAOR; dir 1970-80: ICI Petrochemicals Div, ICI Petroleum Ltd, ICI Gastern Europe; md Enterprise (UK) Ltd 1980-81, ret; memb Ripon Diocesan Bd of Finance, jt chm Wensley Deanery Synod; *Recreations* tennis, golf, painting, woodwork; *Clubs* Naval & Military, MCC, Lans CC; *Style*— Geoffrey Paton-Williams, Esq; Hawkstone, Little Crakehall, Bedale, N Yorks DL8 1JH (☎ 0677 22639)

PATRICK, (Katherine) Emily (Mrs Michael Perry); da of William Pitt Patrick, of Ladwood Farm, Acrise, Folkestone, Kent, and Rosemary Marther, *née* Pulvertaft; *b* 4 Oct 1959; *Educ* Folkestone GS, Architectural Assoc, Cambridge Univ (MA); *m* 16 Oct 1986, Michael Luke Perry, s of David Edward Perry, of 20 Benslow Rise, Hitchin, Herts; 1 da (Beatrice Lillian b 8 Sept 1987); *Career* exhibited at: King St Gallery, Wraxall Gallery, Sarah Long's, Maire Gallery, Mall Galleries, Lefevre Gallery; one man shows at Agnew's 1986 and 1989; painted HRH The Princess of Wales for Royal Hants Regt 1987; first winner of Royal Soc of Portrait Painters' Caroll Prize 1988; *Recreations* walking; *Style*— Miss Emily Patrick; 2 St John's Park, London SE3 7TG

PATRICK, Graham McIntosh; CMG (1968), CVO (1981), DSC (1943); *b* 17 Oct 1921; *Educ* Dundee HS, St Andrews Univ; *m* 1945, Barbara Worboys; 2 s; *Career* Miny of Works 1946; DOE 1971: dir Scottish Servs, PSA 1975-81, ret; *Clubs* New (Edinburgh); *Style*— Graham Patrick, Esq, CMG, CVO, DSC; c/o Bank of Scotland, 57 Haymarket, London SW1

PATRICK, Harley Maxwell; s of Lt-Col Alfred Noel Patrick (d 1987), and Elisa Joyce Hyslop, *née* Maxwell; *b* 20 Jan 1929; *Educ* Trinity Coll Glenalmond, Corpus Christi Coll Cambridge (MA); *m* 19 Oct 1961, Caroline Heather, da of Cdr Louis Francis Cowell (d 1957); 3 da (Sophie b 1963, Elisa b 1965, Camilla b 1969); *Career* serv KOSB 1947-49; acting Capt and ADC to HE the Acting Govr of Cyprus 1969; dep gen mangr The Mercantile and Gen Reinsur Co 1976-82, chm of Reinsur Offs Assoc 1978-80, gen mangr of Tokio Reinsur Co Ltd 1982-; memb of Ct of Assts of Worshipful Co of Insurers; *Recreations* gardening, shooting; *Clubs* Lansdowne; *Style*— Harley M Patrick, Esq; Sattenham House, Rake Lane, Milford, Godalming, Surrey GU8 5AB (☎ 04868 21889); Tokio Reinsurance Co Ltd, 120 Fenchurch St, London EC3M 5BA (☎ 01 623 4343, telex 893569)

PATRICK, Margaret Kathleen; OBE (1976); da of late Roy Patrick and Rose Laura Patrick; *b* 5 June 1923; *Educ* Godolphin and Latymer Girls' Sch, Guy's Hosp Sch of Physiotherapy, Open Univ (BA); *Career* dist supt physiotherapist: Central, Birmingham Health Authy (Teaching) (formerly United Birmingham Hosps Mgmnt Ctee) 1951-80; former memb Birmingham AHA; vice-chm Bromsgrove and Redditch Health Authy 1982-; Hon Fell Chartered Soc of Physiotherapy 1988; *Style*— Miss Margaret Patrick, OBE; Cobbler's Cottage, Holy Cross Green, Clent, W Mids DY9 OHG

PATRICK, Peter Laurence; s of Anthony Frederick Herbert Patrick, of St Peters, Broadstairs, Kent, and Joyce Stanley, *née* Sowerby; *b* 11 July 1946; *Educ* Alleyne's Sch Stevenage, Univ Coll Durham (BA); *m* 22 April 1972, Teresa Mary, JP, da of William Roland Mills, MBE, of Billericay, Essex; 1 s (Edward William b 4 Nov 1973), 1 da (Frances Elizabeth b 10 July 1975); *Career* CA 1972; Price Waterhouse & Co: Newcastle 1967-70, London 1970-73, Paris 1973-76; computer audit mangr Howard Tilly & Co 1976-78, head of inspection Hambros Bank Ltd 1978-86, co sec Hambros plc and Hambros Bank Ltd 1986-; cncllr billericay East on Basildon DC 1984- (dep ldr Cons gp of cncllrs); tres Billericay Cons Assoc 1983-86, chm Towngate Theatre Co Basildon Essex, tstee Adventure Unlimited (Chelmsford Diocese Youth Charity), govr Quilters Sch Billericay, memb choir St Mary Magdalene Gt Burstead Essex; memb Inst of Bankers, assoc memb Br Computer Soc; *Recreations* singing, gardening, politics, history, architecture; *Style*— Peter Patrick, Esq; 6 Highland Grove, Billericay, Essex (☎ 0277 651137); Hambros Bank Ltd, 41 Tower Hill, London EC3N 4HA (☎ 01 480 5000)

PATTEN, Brian; *b* 7 Feb 1946; *Career* lectr Univ of Californa (San Diego) 1985; poet and author; poems: Little Johnny's Confessions (1967), Penguin Modern Poets (1967), Notes to the Hurrying Man (1969), The Irrelevant Song (1971) The Unreliable Nightingale (1973), Vanishing Trick (1976), The Shabby Angel (1978), Grave Gossip (1979), Love Poems (1981), Clares Countryside (1982), New Volume (1983), Storm Damage (1988); novels: Mr Moon's Last Case (1975); plays: The Pig and the Junk (1975), The Mouth Trap (with Roger McGough, 1982), Blind Love (1983); for younger readers: The Elephant and the Flower (1969), Jumping Mouse (1971), Emma's Doll (1976), The Sly Cormorant and the Fish (1977), Gansters Ghosts and Dragonflies (1981), Gargling with Jelly (1985), Jimmy Tag-along (1988); *Clubs* Chelsea Arts; *Style*— Brian Patten, Esq; c/o Unwin Hyman, 15-17 Broadwick St, London W1

PATTEN, Christopher Francis (Chris); MP (C) Bath, 1979-; s of late Francis Joseph Patten; *b* 12 May 1944; *Educ* St Benedict's Ealing, Balliol Coll Oxford; *m* 1971, Mary Lavender St Leger Thornton; 3 da; *Career* CRD 1966-70, dir 1974-79; worked in Cabinet Off 1970-72, Home Off 1972, pa to chm Cons Party 1972-74; pps to: Norman St John-Stevas as Chllr Duchy of Lancaster and Leader House of Commons 1979-81, Patrick Jenkin Sec of State for Soc Servs 1981; jt vice-chm Cons Fin Ctee Nov 1981-83, under-sec State NI Office 1983-85; minister of state DES 1985-86, min of state Foreign and Cwlth offr, min for Overseas Devpt 1986-; *Recreations* reading, learning Spanish, tennis; *Clubs* Beefsteak; *Style*— Chris Patten, Esq, MP; 47 Morpeth Mansions, Morpeth Terrace, SW1 (☎ 01 828 3082); Cromwell's Rest, 207 Conkwell, nr Winsley, Wilts (☎ 022 122 3378)

PATTEN, John Haggitt Charles; MP (C) Oxford West and Abingdon 1983-; s of Jack Patten and Maria Olga, *née* Sikora; *b* 17 July 1945; *Educ* Wimbledon Coll, Sidney Sussex Coll Cambridge (MA, PhD); *m* 1978, Louise Alexandra Virginia, da of late John Rowe; 1 da (Mary-Claire b 10 June 1986); *Career* fell Hertford Coll Oxford 1972- (univ lectr 1969-79); author and writer; MP (C) Oxford 1979-83, pps to Leon Brittan and Timothy Raison, min of State Home Off 1980-81; parly under-sec of state: NI Sept 1981-83, Health and Social Security 1983-85; min of state: Housing Urban Affrs and Construction 1985-87, Home Off 1987-; *Books* The Conservative Opportunity (with Lord Blake); The Penguin Guide to the Landscape of England and Wales (with Paul Coones), and three other books; *Recreations* talking to wife; *Clubs* Beefsteak; *Style*— John Patten, Esq, MP; House of Commons, London SW1A 0AA (☎ 01 219 4556)

PATTEN, Prof Tom; CBE (1981); s of William Patten (d 1954), of Midlem, Selkirkshire, and Isabella, *née* Hall (d 1986); *b* 1 Jan 1926; *Educ* Leith Acad, Univ of Edinburgh (BSc, PhD); *m* 29 March 1950, Jacqueline McLachlan; 1 s (Colin), 2 da (Diane, Gail); *Career* Capt REME 1946-48, served Palestine and Greece; chartered mechanical engr; prof and head dept of mechanical engrg Heriot-Watt Univ 1967-82, dir Inst of Offshore Engrg 1972-79, actg princ Heriot-Watt Univ 1980-81; princ dir: Pict Petroleum plc 1981, Melville St Investmts plc 1983, Sealand Industs plc 1987-; Hon D Eng Heriot-Watt Univ; FEng, FIMechE, FRSE; *Recreations* music, squash; *Clubs* New (Edinburgh), Caledonian; *Style*— Prof Tom Patten, CBE; 146/4 Whitehouse Loan, Edinburgh EH9 2AN (☎ 031 447 0769)

PATTERSON; *see*: Stewart-Patterson

PATTERSON, Maj-Gen Arthur Gordon; CB (1969), DSO (1964), OBE (1961), MC (1945); s of late Arthur Abbey Patterson, ICS; *b* 24 July 1917; *Educ* Tonbridge, RMC Sandhurst; *m* 1949, Jean Mary Grant; 2 s, 1 da; *Career* dir of Army Trg 1969-72, ret; *Style*— Maj-Gen Arthur Patterson, CB, DSO, OBE, MC; Burnt House, Benenden, Cranbrook, Kent

PATTERSON, (George) Benjamin; MEP (EDG Kent West 1979-); s of Prof Eric James Patterson (d 1972), of Stonehedge, Alphington Cross, Exeter, Devon (d 1972), and Dr Ethel, *née* Simkins; *b* 21 April 1939; *Educ* Westminster, Trinity Coll Cambridge (MA), LSE; *m* 5 Dec 1970, Felicity Barbara Anne, da of Gordon W Raybould, of Little Combe Bank, Sundridge, Sevenoaks, Kent; 1 s (Alexander b 6 Dec 1974), 1 da (Olivia b 15 April 1977); *Career* tutor Swinton Coll Masham Yorks 1961-65, ed CPC Monthly Report 1965-73, dep head Euro Parl London Off 1973-79, dir Wiltenbridge Ltd 1980-; Euro democratic gp spokesman on economic monetaqry and industl policy in the Euro Parl 1984-; cncllr London Borough of Hammersmith 1968-71; *Books* The Character of Conservatism (1973); *Clubs* IOD, Bow Group; *Style*— Ben Patterson, Esq, MEP; Elm Hill House, Hawkhurst, Kent TN18 4XU (☎ 0580 753260)

PATTERSON, Rt Rev Cecil John; CMG (1958), CBE (1954); *b* 9 Jan 1908; *Educ* St Paul's, St Catharine's Coll Cambridge (hon fell 1963), Bishop's Coll Cheshunt; *Career* archbishop of W Africa 1961-69, rep for the Archbishops of Canterbury and York for Community Relations 1970-72, hon asst bishop Diocese of London 1970-76; *Style*— The Right Rev Cecil Patterson, CMG, CBE; 6 High Park Rd, Kew, Surrey TW9 4BH (☎ 01 876 1697)

PATTERSON, Hon Mrs; Hon Fiona Elizabeth Cameron; *née* Corbett; da of 2 Baron Rowallan, KT, KBE, MC, TD (d 1977), and Gwyn Mervyn, *née* Grimond (d 1971); *b* 14 Nov 1942; *Educ* Southover Manor Sussex; *m* 1, 1966 (m dis 1972), as his 1 w, David Cecil, yr twin s of Hon Henry Cecil (bro of 3 Baron Amherst of Hackney); 2 s (Rupert b 1967, Benjamin b 1968); m 2, 1974, W G Patterson; 1 s (Joseph b 1981); *Style*— The Hon Mrs Patterson; Kisby's Farm, Ecchinswell, Newbury, Berks RG15 8TS; 43 Holland Villas Road, London W14

PATTERSON, George Sheldon; OBE (1960); s of John Robert Patterson, KBE, CMG (d 1976), of Penrith, Cumbria, and Esther Margaret, *née* Sheldon; *b* 25 July 1920; *Educ* RGS Newcastle-upon-Tyne, New Coll Oxford; *m* 17 April 1948, Anne Marie Stansfield, da of Dr Stanley Worthington (d 1958), of Leeds; 2 da (Linda b 1949, Diana b 1956); *Career* RA, ADC to Lt-Gen A E Percival; Malayan Civil Serv, ret 1960; dir P A Mgmnt Conslts ret 1980; *Recreations* golf; *Style*— George Patterson, Esq, OBE; Rye Hill, Lodge Hill Road, Farnham, Surrey

PATTERSON, John Allan; s of Dr William Gilchrist Patterson (d 1956), of Newcastle-upon-Tyne, and Mary Murray, *née* Eggie; *b* 10 Oct 1931; *Educ* Epsom Coll, King's Coll, Univ of Durham, Clare Coll Cambridge (BA); *m* 1956, Anne Marie, da of Folke Urban Lasson (d 1947), of Halmstad, Sweden; 1 s (Thomas b 1962), 2 da (Caroline b 1958, Christina b 1963); *Career* HM Dip Serv 1954-65 (Bangkok 1957-61, Rome 1961-4); HM Treasy 1965-81 (on loan to Cabinet Off 1974-78); dir Savings, head of Dept for Nat Savings 1986- (dep dir 1981-86); *Recreations* church, gardening, walking, languages; *Style*— John A Patterson, Esq; Department for National Savings, Charles House, 375 Kensington High St, London W14 8SD (☎ 01 605 9462)

PATTERSON, Dr Mark Jonathan David Damian Lister; s of Alfred Paterson (d 1972), and Frederica Georgina Mary Hammersley, *née* Lister Nicholson; *b* 2 Mar 1934; *Educ* private (MB, BS); *m* 25 Oct 1958, Jane Teresa Mary Scott, da of David Dominic Scott Stokes, of 5 Cochrane St, London NW8; 1 s (Damian b 1967), 2 da (Rebecca b 1972, Victoria b 1977); *Career* with NHS, Univ of London and MRC 1959-

67, conslt NHS and sr lectr Univ of London 1967-84; parly candidate (Cons) Ealing N 1974, memb GLC 1969-73 and 1977-81; memb Worshipful Co of Apothecaries 1965; MRCS, LRCP, MRCP; *Recreations* historic restoration of ancient buildings; *Style—* Dr Mark Patterson; Wolverton Manor, Shorwell, Newport, Isle of Wight PO30 3JS (☎ 0983 740604)

PATTERSON, Neil Michael; s of Robin Shanks Patterson (d 1964), and Nancy Mearns, *née* Milne; *b* 22 Mar 1951; *Educ* Trinity Coll Glen almond, Watford Art Sch; *m* 23 July 1983, Doris Karen, da of Ceferino William Boll, of Saguier, Province of Santa Fe, Argentina; *Career* sr writer Saatchi & Saatchi 1973; river columnist: Trout & Salmon 1976-78, Trout Fisherman 1982; creative dir: TBWA 1983-85, Young & Rubicam 1985-; *Recreations* fly fishing, guitar, cooking; *Clubs* Fly Fishers, DA & D; *Style—* Neil Patterson, Esq; Rose Cottage, 59 Bute Gdns, London W6 7DX (☎ 01 603 6931); Wilderness Lodge, Elcot Turn, Bath Rd, Kintbury, Berks; Young & Rubicam, Gtr London House, Hampstead Rd, London NW1 7QP (☎ 01 387 9366, fax 01 380 6570)

PATTERSON, Paul Leslie; s of Leslie Patterson, of Exeter, and Lilian, *née* Braund; *b* 15 June 1947; *Educ* RAM; *m* 12 Dec 1981, Hazel Rosemary, da of Dr Alexander Wilson, of Winchester; 1 s (Alastair b 1986), 1 da (Philippa b 1983); *Career* head composition RAM 1985- (prof composition 1972-), dir twentieth century music Univ of Warwick 1976-81, guest prof Yale Univ 1989; composer of large-scale choral music incl: Mass of the Sea, Stabat Mater, Te Deum, Requiem, Voices of Sleep; other compositions incl: orchestral music, chamber music, organ music, film and tv music; performances world-wide by leading musicians; featured composer at festivals incl: LLandaff 1985, Greenwich 1985, PLG 1987, Cheltenham 1988, Three Choirs 1988, Patterson South Bank 1988; composer in residence: Eng Sinfonia Nottingham 1969-70, SE Arts Canterbury 1981-83; cmmns incl: BBC, RPO, Polish Chamber Orch, Kings Singers, Eng Chamber Orch, London Sinfonietta; memb Arts Cncl Recordings Ctee; ARAM 1978, FRAM 1982, memb SPNM; Medal of Hon of Miny of Culture Poland 1987; *Recreations* sailing; *Style—* Paul Patterson, Esq; 31 Cromwell Ave, Highgate, London N6 5HN (☎ 01 348 3711)

PATTERSON, Hon Mrs; Hon Sandra Debonnaire; *née* Monson; da of 10 Baron Monson (d 1958); *b* 1937; *m* 1958 (m dis 1971), Maj William Garry Patterson; 1 s, 3 da; *Style—* The Hon Mrs Patterson; 23 Lamont Rd, London SW10

PATTIE, Sir Geoffrey Edwin; PC (1987), MP (C) Chertsey and Walton Feb 1974-; s of Alfred Edwin Pattie; *b* 17 Jan 1936; *Educ* Durham Sch, St Catharine's Coll Cambridge; *m* 1960, Tuëma Caroline, *née* Eyre-Maunsell; 1 s (and 1 da decd); *Career* served TA Queen Victoria's Rifles, later Queen's Royal Rifles then 4 Royal Green Jackets (Capt); barr 1964, contested (C) Barking 1966 and 1970; former memb GLC (Lambeth) and chm ILEA Fin Ctee; vice-chm: All-Pty Ctee on Mental Health 1977-79, Cons Parly Def Ctee 1978-79; parly under-sec of state: Def and RAF 1979-81, Procurement MOD 1981-83; min of state: MOD (Def Procurement) 1983-84, Indust and Info Technol 1984-87; kt 1987; *Clubs* Royal Green Jackets; *Style—* The Rt Hon Sir Geoffrey Pattie, MP; House of Commons, London SW1A 0AA (☎ 01 219 4055)

PATTINSON, Major Derek Armstrong; OBE (1985), JP (1956); s of Maj J W Pattinson (d 1931), and Isobel, *née* Armstrong (d 1951); *b* 8 August 1918; *Educ* Cockermouth; *m* 4 Sept 1952, Eileen Veronica, da of John Harrison (d 1986), of Penrith, Cumbria; 2 s (Nigel John b 1956, David Derek b 1960), 1 da (Julia b 1954); *Career* Gunner 1939, Maj 1946 served Far East; land agent to Earl of Lonsdale 1951-86; dir Tallantire Properties Ltd (chm 1987); FRICS, Dip Forestry; *Recreations* hunting, shooting, fishing; *Style—* Maj Derek A Pattinson, OBE, JP; Corrie, Watermillock, Penrith, Cumbria CA11 OJH (☎ 08536 582); Scott-Harden Estate Office, Lowther, Penrith, Cumbria (☎ 09312 392)

PATTINSON, (William) Derek; s of Thomas William Pattinson (d 1970), and Elizabeth, *née* Burgess (d 1986); *b* 31 Mar 1930; *Educ* Whitehaven GS, Queen's Coll Oxford (BA, MA); *Career* Civil Serv 1952-70: Inland Revenue Dept 1952-62 and 1965-68, HM Treasy 1962-65 and 1968-70, asst sec 1961; assoc sec-gen General Synod 1970-72, sec-gen of the General Synod of the Church of England 1972-; memb: Parish Clerks' Co (Master 1986-87), Woomers' Co; *Clubs* Savile; *Style—* Derek Pattinson, Esq; 4 Strutton Ct, Great Peter St, London SW1 (☎ 01 222 6307); Church House, Deans Yard, London SW1 (☎ 01 222 9011)

PATTINSON, Mark; 2 s of Geoffrey Pearson Pattinson, of Colchester, Essex, and Mary Agnes Borthwick Greig; *b* 13 May 1930; *Educ* Rugby, Trinity Coll Cambridge (MA); *m* 22 June 1963, Gillian Katharine, da of Sir William Mather, of Cheshire; 1 s (John b 1965), 3 da (Fiona b 1964, Diana b 1969, Rebecca b 1972); *Career* 5 Royal Inniskilling Gds 1951, 2 Lt 1952-56, 41 Capt RTR TA; dir: Manchester Liners Ltd 1970-80, Kishorn Shellfish Ltd 1988-; pres Marine Tport Int 1978-85, chm Kinlock Damph Ltd 1985-; FCA; *Recreations* skiing, tennis, stalking, fishing; *Clubs* Ski Club of GB; *Style—* Mark Pattinson, Esq; Couldoran Kishorn, Strathcarron, Rossshire IV54 (☎ 05203 227)

PATTINSON, Dr (John) Norman; s of John Allinson Pattinson (d 1935), of Windermere, and Muriel, *née* Hinde; *b* 13 April 1945; *Educ* Sedbergh, Emmanuel Coll Cambridge (BA, MB, BChir); *m* 15 June 1940, Catherine Ennis, da of Ernest Haighton (d 1963), of Colne, Lancs; 1 s (John Ernest b 1953), 2 da (Catherine Louise b 1941, Sarah Mildred b 1946, d 1975); *Career* MO RAF 1940-41, S of England, Egypt and N Africa 1941-44, S of England 1945-46, Actg Sqdn Ldr; radiologist (conslt): London Chest Hosp 1954-80, Middx Hosp London 1956-80; hon radiologist King VII Hosp for Offrs 1954-81, civil conslt radiology to RAF 1966-80; hon sec Faculty of Radiologists 1964-69 (vice pres 1970-72); DMRD 1947, FFR 1953, MRCP 1967; various publications on radiology; *Recreations* philately, milataria; *Style—* Dr Norman Pattinson; 37A Redington Rd, London NW3 7QY (☎ 01 794 2163, 01 580 1772); 64 Harley St, London W1

PATTISON, Prof Bruce; s of Matthew Pattison (d 1935), and Catherine, *née* Bruce (d 1949); *b* 13 Nov 1908; *Educ* Gateshead GS, Armstrong Coll Newcastle upon Tyne (BA, MA), Fitzwilliam Coll Cambridge (PhD); *m* 10 Aug 1937, Dorothy (d 1979), da of Ernest Graham; *Career* teacher: Henry Mellish Sch Nottingham 1933-35, Hymer's Coll Hull 1935-36; lectr in english UCL 1936-48, prof of educn Univ of London Inst of Educn 1948-76; *Books* Music and Poetry of the English Rennaissance (second edn 1970), Special Relations (1984); *Recreations* music, chess; *Clubs* Athenaeum, Nat Lib; *Style—* Prof Bruce Pattison

PATTISON, Dr David Arnold; s of David Pattison (d 1957), and Christina Russell Bone (d 1988); *b* 9 Feb 1941; *Educ* Kilmarnock Acad, Univ of Glasgow (BSc, PhD); *m* 1967, Anne, da of William Wilson (d 1974); 2 s (David b 1972, Graeme b 1974), 1 da (Isla b 1975); *Career* lectr Univ of Strathclyde 1967-70; dir Tourism Highlands and Islands Devpt Bd 1970-81, chief exec Scottish Tourist Bd 1981-85; dir leisure and tourism consulting Arthur Young 1985-; *Recreations* watching soccer and rugby, reading, gardening; *Clubs* Scottish Nat Orchestra (memb bd dir); *Style—* Dr David Pattison; 7 Cramond Glebe Gardens, Edinburgh EH4 6NZ; Arthur Young, 17 Abercromby Place, Edinburgh EH3 6LT

PATTISSON, John Harmer; s of Frederick Edward Pattisson (d 1946), of Meyricks Bidborough, Tumbridge Wells and Louise Mary, *née* Dalton (d 1973); *b* 24 April 1931; *Educ* Radley, Trinity Coll Oxford (MA); *m* 29 March 1958 (m dis 1975), Julia Jane, da of Maj Percy Montagu Nevile (d 1957), of Skelbrooke Park, Yorks and Yerdley House, Long Compton, Warwicks; 2 s (Edward b 1960, William b 1963); *Career* Nat Serv 2 Lt Oxford & Bucks LI 1950-52, Capt TA 1952-63; Dawnay Day Gp 1955- (dir 1964-, md 1969-80), exec dir Hanson Tst Ltd (formerly Wiles Gp Ltd) 1960-74; dir; Target Tst Gp Ltd 1973-81, J Rothschild & Co Ltd 1980-81, Hanson plc 1981-, New Ct Property Fund Mangrs Ltd 1984-, Wassall plc 1988-; memb cncl Radley Coll 1965-, vice - chm govrs City Technol Coll Kingshurst 1988-; *Clubs* Boodles, City Of London; *Style—* John Pattisson, Esq; 1C Elm Place, London SW7 3QH (☎ 01 370 4652); Hanson plc, 1 Grosvenor Place, London SW1X 7JH (☎ 01 245 1245, fax 01 823 1018, car telephone 0836 224 626, telex 917698)

PATTISSON, Patrick Henry; s of R D M Pattisson, of Chapel House, Selborne, Hants, and P Pattisson, *née* Wise; *b* 21 Dec 1932; *Educ* Rugby, St George's Hosp Med Sch (MB, BS); *m* 11 May 1957, Elizabeth Mary, da of Dr W G M Mackay (d 1977); 3 s (Douglas b 1958, John b 1962, Alexander b 1965), 1 da (Rosemary b 1960); *Career* Surgn Lt RN 1959-62; conslt surgn: gen and vascular surgery W Middx Univ Hosp, RFU, Royal Masonic Hosp; hon sr lectr Charing Cross Hosp and Westminster Med Sch; former chm S Middx Div BMA; FRCS (Eng), FRCS (Ed); *Recreations* rugby, skiing; *Style—* Patrick Pattisson, Esq; Chesterfield House, 32 Broad Lane, Hampton TW12 3AZ; 152 Harley Street, London W1 (☎ 01 935 1858)

PATTON, Doctor (John) Terence; RD (1970); s of Francis Patton, JP, KSG (d 1983), and Winefride, *née* Myhan (d 1977); *b* 18 May 1926; *Educ* St Francis Xavier's Coll Liverpool, Univ of Liverpool; *m* 16 April 1966, Belinda Richmond, da of Edwin Latham Black, of Hendre Uchaf, Abergele, N Wales; 1 s (James Terence (Sam) b 1967), 2 da (Philippa Mary b 1968, Rachel Belinda b 1971); *Career* RNVR and RNR 1952-78 ret Surgn Capt; conslt Radiologist Manchester Royal Infirmary 1965-, civil conslt radiology to RN 1982-, examiner in fellowship RCR 1974-78; examiner in radiology: Univ of Baghdad 1976, Univ of Aberdeen 1982-85, Malaysia 1986-, Edinburgh 1988-; hon FRCP (Ed) 1984; MRCS, LRCP, memb Br Inst Radiology 1962, FRCR 1963, FRCP 1984; *Books* Diagnostic Radiology (contrib and ed, 1986), Multiple Myeloma and other Paraprotienaemiar (contrib); *Recreations* sailing, music; *Clubs* Naval; *Style—* Terence Patton, Esq, RD; Dept of Radiology, Manchester Royal Infirmary, Oxford Rd, Manchester M13 (☎ 061 276 4311)

PATTULLO, (David) Bruce; s of Colin Arthur Pattullo; *b* 2 Jan 1938; *Educ* Rugby, Hertford Coll Oxford; *m* 1962, Fiona Jane Nicholson; 3 s, 1 da; *Career* tres and chief exec Bank of Scotland 1979-, dep tres 1978-79; dir: Standard Life Assur Co 1985-, British Linen Bank Ltd 1977-, Bank of Wales plc 1986-, Melville Street Investmts plc 1987-; *Clubs* New (Edinburgh), Caledonian; *Style—* Bruce Pattullo, Esq; 6 Cammo Rd, Edinburgh EH4 8EB (☎ 031 339 6012)

PAUK, Gyorgy; s of Imre Pauk, (d 1944), and Magda Pauk; *b* 26 Oct 1936; *Educ* Franz Liszt Music Acad Budapest; *m* 19 July 1959, Susan, *née* Mautner; 1 s (Thomas b 19 April 1962), 1 da (Catherine b 13 June 1966); *Career* violinist; as the youngest pupil of the Franz Liszt Music Acad toured numerous countries incl Hungary and Eastern Europe; first prize winner: The Paganini Competition, Marguerite Long/ Jacques Thibauld Competition, Munich Sonata Competition; London orchestral and recital debuts 1961; currently performs with maj orchestras of the world under such conductors as: Piere Boulez, Sir Colin Davies, Antal Dorati, Kondrashin, Lorin Maazel, Rozhdestvensky, Rattle, Previn, Tennstedt, Haitink, Sir George Solti; American debut with the Chicago Symphony Orch leading to subsequent return visits playing with: Cleveland Philadelphia, Los Angeles Philharmonic, Boston Symphony Orch; festival appearances incl: Aspen, Ravinia, Hollywood Bowl, Saratoga; many prizewinning recirdubgs incl works by Bartok, Schubert, Mozart, Brahms; hon memb Guidhall Sch, prof of music 1980 RAM; *Style—* Gyorgy Pauk, Esq; c/o IBBS and Tillett Ltd, 18/13 Pindock Mews, London W9 2PY (☎ 286 7526, telex 23330 IBBSEN G)

PAUL, Air Cdre (Gerard John) Christopher; CB (1956), DFC (1944); s of Edmund William Paul (d 1949), and Florence Rose, *née* Meyrick (d 1948); *b* 31 Oct 1907; *Educ* Cheltenham Coll, St John's Coll Cambridge (MA); *m* 1937, Rosemary (d 1975), da of Rear Adm Henry Gerald Elliot Lane, CB (d 1951); 2 s (Simon, Timothy), 1 da (Azalea); m 2, 1987, Mollie Denise, da of Joseph Samuels, MM (d 1954); *Career* Air Force Offrs Res 1927, RAF 1929, Fleet Air Arm 1931-36, 1939-45 War in England and N W Europe, cmd 98 Sqdn RAF during and prior to Normandy landings, Cmdt Central Flying Sch 1954-56, Air Cdre 1954, ret 1958; sec-gen Air League 1958-71, pres Popular Flying Assoc 1969-78; Belgian Croix de Guerre with Palme (1944), Czech War Cross (1945); FRAeS; *Recreations* dogs, garden; *Clubs* RAF; *Style—* Air Commodore Christopher Paul, CB, DFC; Wearne House, Old Alresford, Hants SO24 9DH

PAUL, Dr David Manuel; s of Kenneth Paul (d 1960), and Rachel, *née* Favell (d 1965); *b* 8 June 1927; *Educ* Selhurst GS Croydon, St Bartholomew's Hosp Med Coll, London Hosp Med Coll, DRCOD, DA, DMJ; *m* 14 Feb 1948, Gladys Audrey, da of William Garton, of The Wallhatch Hotel, Forest Row, Sussex; 2 da (Judith Audrey (Mrs Stevens) b 25 Nov 1948, Alison Jane (Mrs Putman) b 4 July 1950); *Career* GP,Duncan & Prns 1955-57; Purley War Meml Hosp: clinical asst anaesthetist 1956-68, clinical asst obstetrician 1958-68; clinical asst anaesthetist Croyden GP of Hosps 1956-68, devl surgn Met Police 1956-68; coroner: City of London 1966-, northern dist London 1968-; dept of forensic medicine Guys Hosp: hon lectr, hon conslt in clinical forensic medicine and ct practice 1966-; hon conslt in clinical forensic medicine Surry Constabulary 1967, pres Br Acad of Forensic Sciences 1987-88 (chm Med Section 1987-88 and exec cncl 1979-); Freeman City of London 1966, Freeman Worshipful Co of Apothecaries 1966; chm Warlingham and Dist Horse Club 1964-68; MRCS. LRCP, RSM 1988, BAFS 1964, memb Assoc of Police Surgs 1956, memb Medico Legal Soc 1964, memb Forensic Sci Soc 1964; *Recreations* travel, photography, equitation, fishing; *Style*— Dr David Paul; Cobhambury Farm, Edenbridge, Kent TN8 5PN (☎ 0732 863 280); Coroners Court, Milton Court, Moor Lane, London EC2 7BL (☎ 01 260 1598)

PAUL, Geoffrey David; s of Reuben Goldstein; *b* 26 Mar 1929; *Educ* Liverpool, Kendal, Dublin; *m* 1, 1952 (m dis 1972), Joy Stirling; 1 da; m 2, 1974, Rachel Mann; 1 s; *Career* ed Jewish Chronicle 1977-; *Books* Living in Jerusalem; *Style*— Geoffrey Paul, Esq; 25 Furnival St, London EC4A 1JT (☎ 01 405 9252)

PAUL, George William; s of William Stuart Hamilton Paul (d 1984), of Freston Lodge, Ipswich, and Diana Violet Anne, *née* Martin; *b* 25 Feb 1940; *Educ* Harrow, Wye Coll London Univ (BSc); *m* 1963, Mary Annette, da of Col Frank Mitchell, DSO, MC (d 1985); 2 s (Stuart, Oliver), 1 da (Bridget); *Career* chm Pauls plc 1985-; chief exec Harrisons and Crosfield plc 1987- (dir 1985-); master Essex and Suffolk Foxhounds 1978-85; ptnr in William Paul and Sons Farming (2,200 acres); *Recreations* farming, hunting, shooting, fishing; *Clubs* Boodle's, Farmers'; *Style*— George Paul, Esq; Harrisons & Crosfield plc, 1-4 Great Tower Street, London EC3R 4AB (☎ 01 626 4333, telex 885636)

PAUL, Sir John Warburton; GCMG (1965, KCMG 1962), OBE (1959), MC (1940); s of Walter George Paul; *b* 29 Mar 1916; *Educ* Weymouth Coll Dorset, Selwyn Coll Cambridge; *m* 1946, Kathleen Audrey, da of Dr A D Weeden, of Weymouth; 3 da; *Career* barr Inner Temple 1947; govr and C-in-C The Gambia 1962-65 (govr-gen 1965-66), British Honduras 1966-72, Bahamas 1972-73; govr-gen The Bahamas July-Oct 1973, Lt-govr Isle of Man 1974-80; dir Overseas Rels St John Ambulance 1981-, chm St Christopher's Motorists' Security Assoc 1980-; hon fell Selwyn Coll Cambridge; KStJ 1962; *Clubs* Athenaeum, MCC, Hawks (Cambridge); *Style*— Sir John Paul, GCMG, OBE, MC; Sherrens Mead, Sherfield-on-Loddon, Hampshire

PAUL, Julian Braithwaite; s of Michael Braithwaite Paul, MD, of Orchard Ho, Newchurch, Burton-on-Trent, Staffs, and Patricia Elisabeth Ann, *née* Mumm; *b* 18 May 1945; *Educ* Wrekin Coll Shrops, St John's Coll Oxford (BA, MA); *m* 3 Nov 1973, Diana, da of Ernest Trevor Davies (d 1981), of Epsom, Surrey; 1 s (Rupert b 1981), 2 da (Arabella b 1975, Henrietta b 1978); *Career* Arthur Andersen & Co CAs 1966-71, Citibank NA 1971-74, dep md Banco Hispano Americano Ltd 1974-87, sr banking dir Guinness Mahon & Co Ltd 1987-, memb exec ctee Guinness Mahon Hldgs plc; chm of govrs Valence Sch Westerham Kent, vice chm of govrs Sundridge and Brasted C of E Primary Sch; pres: Sundridge and Brasted Horticultural Soc, Brasted Cons Assoc; cllr Kent County Cncl 1985-; FCA 1979 ; *Recreations* politics, travel; *Clubs* Carlton, Coningsby, Bow Gp; *Style*— Julian Paul, Esq; The Mount Ho, Brasted, Westerham, Kent (☎ 0959 636 17); Guinness Mahon & Co Ltd, 32 St Mary at Hill, London EC3P 3AJ (☎ 01 623 9333, fax 01 283 4811, telex 884035)

PAUL, Noel Strange; CBE (1978); s of late S Evan Paul; *b* 1914; *Educ* Kingston GS; *m* 1950, Mary, da of Philip J Bone; *Career* dir The Press Council 1976-79; *Style*— Noel Paul, Esq, CBE; Plummers Farmhouse, Fordham, Colchester, Essex

PAUL, Robert Cameron (Robin); s of Dr Francis William Paul (d 1964), of Ealing, and Maureen Kirkpatrick, *née* Cameron; *b* 7 July 1935; *Educ* Rugby, Corpus Christi Coll Cambridge (BA, MA); *m* 1 May 1965, Diana Kathleen, da of Sir Arthur Bruce, KBE, MC, of Beaconsfield, Bucks; 2 da (Caroline b 1966, Juliet b 1968); *Career* Nat Serv 2 Lt RE (BAOR) 1953-55; ICI gen chemicals div 1959: works mangr Castner-Keller Works 1971, central personnel dept Millbank 1974, dir ICI Fibres 1976, dep chm ICI mond div 1979; non exec dir Mersey Docks & Harbour Co 1985-88, dep chm and md Albright & Wilson Ltd 1986-; tstee Duke of Edinburgh Cwlth Study Conference Fund, chm CBI Enviroment Ctee; C Eng, FRSA 1983, FIChemE 1984, CBIM 1987; *Recreations* music, golf; *Clubs* Oriental; *Style*— R C Paul, Esq; Albright & Wilson Ltd, 1 Knightsbridge Green, London SW1X 7QD (☎ 01 589 6393, fax 01 225 0839, telex 916225 ALBRIW G)

PAUL, Swraj; s of Payare Paul (d 1944), and Mongwati, *née* Lal; *b* 18 Feb 1931; *Educ* Punjab Univ (BSc), Mass Inst of Technol (BSc, MSc 1952); *m* 1 Dec 1956, Aruna; 3 s (Ambar b 20 Dec 1957, Akash b 20 Dec 1957 (twin), Angad b 6 June 1970), 2 da (Anjli b 12 Nov 1959, Ambika b 1964, d (1968); *Career* dir family-owned Apeejay-Surrendra Gp in India 1952-66; came to England 1966 and established Natural Gas Tubes Ltd; chm: Caparo Gp Ltd 1978-, Caparo Industs plc 1980-, United Merchant Bar plc 1984-, Barton Tubes Ltd Canada 1984-, Bull Moose Tube Co USA 1988-; Hon PhD American Coll of Switzerland 1986; Order of Padma Bhushan (India) 1983; *Books* Indira Gandhi (1985); *Clubs* MCC, RAC; India: Royal Calcutta Turf, Royal Calcutta Golf, Cricket of India (Bombay); *Style*— Swraj Paul, Esq; Caparo House, 103 Baker Street, London W1M 1FD (☎ 01 486 1417, fax 01 935 3242, telex 8811343)

PAULET, Lord Timothy Guy; raised to rank of Marquess's son 1970; s of George Paulet and bro of 18 Marquess of Winchester; *b* 1944; *m* 1973, Gilian Margaret (Jill), da of Capt Thomas Preacher (d 1969); 2 s (Timothy b 1975, Michael b 1976); *Style*— Lord Timothy Paulet

PAULSON, Godfrey Martin Ellis; CB (1966), CMG (1959), OBE (1945); s of Lt-Col Peter Z Paulson, OBE, (d 1932), and Mary Gertrude (d 1977), da of Dr W H Ellis, of Shipley Hall, Bradford; *b* 6 July 1908; *Educ* Westminster, Peterhouse Cambridge (BA, MA); *m* 26 Aug 1936, Patricia Emma, da of late Sir Hugh Murray, KCIE, CBE (d 1941), of Bramble Hill Lodge, nr Lyndhurst, Hants; 1 s (Peter Ellis b 1938), 1 da (Carol Anne (Mrs Bovill) b 1942); *Career* served 1939-45 Manchester Regt and on Gen Staff in Africa (Free French Forces), UK and NW Europe; Lt-Col 1945, Control Cmmn for Germany 1945, for Austria 1947-48; asst dist cmmr Colonial Serv Gold Coast 1930-32; admitted slr 1936; joined Foreign Serv 1946 (Venice, Stockholm, Far East, Singapore, Beirut, Rome, Nice and FO), ret 1970; memb: Br Section Franco-British Cncl 1976-88, exec ctee Franco-British Soc 1977-87; Order of St Charles (Monaco) 1981; *Recreations* military history, travelling; *Clubs* United Oxford and Cambridge University, Garrick, Special Forces, MCC; *Style*— Godfrey Paulson, Esq, CB, CMG, OBE; Yew Tree Cottage, Church Street, Hampstead Norreys, nr Newbury, Berks RG16 0DT (☎ 0635 201572)

PAULSON-ELLIS, Jeremy David; s of Christian William Geoffrey Paulson-Ellis (d 1982), and Vivien Joan Paulson-Ellis (d 1966); *b* 21 Sept 1943; *Educ* Sherborne; *m* 27 April 1973, Jennifer Jill, da of Harry Milne (d 1958); 2 s (Nicholas b 1976, Matthew b 1984), 1 da (Vivien b 1974); *Career* Citicorp Scrimgeour Vickers Int Ltd (formerly Vickers da Costa & Co): joined 1964, ptnr 1970, dir 1974, chm 1985-88; chm Genesis Investmt Ltd; memb investmt advsy cncl: Korea Int Tst 1982-87, Seoul Int Tst (and chm) 1985-87, Thailand Fund 1986-; ind memb Heathrow Airport Consultative Ctee 1984-88; AMSIA; *Recreations* tennis, travel; *Style*— Jeremy Paulson-Ellis, Esq; Broomlands, Langton Green, Tunbridge Wells, Kent TN3 0RA (☎ 0892 863 555); Genesis Investment Management Ltd, Bowater Ho West, 68 Knightsbridge, London SW1X 7LT (☎ 01 581 9866, fax 01 823 7098, car tel 0860 534 116)

PAULUSZ, Jan Gilbert; s of Jan Hendrik Olivier Paulusz, of Tanglewood, Westbury, Wiltshire, and Edith, *née* Gilbert; *b* 18 Nov 1929; *Educ* The Leys; *m* 18 April 1973, Luigia Maria, da of Luigi Attanasio; *Career* Nat Serv 2 Lt 1 Bn S Lancashire Regt 1951-53, Lt TA 1953-60 (Capt 1955); barr Lincoln's Inn 1957, rec of the Crown Ct 1980-; *Recreations* photography, mountain walking; *Style*— Jan Paulusz, Esq; 50 Royston Gardens, Redbridge, Ilford, Essex, 1G1 3SY (☎ 01 554 9078); 10 Kings Bench Walk, Temple, London EC4Y 7EB (☎ 01 353 7742)

PAUNCEFORT-DUNCOMBE, David Philip Henry; s and h of Sir Philip Digby Pauncefort-Duncombe, 4 Bt; *b* 21 May 1956; *Educ* Gordonstoun, RAC Cirencester; *m* 2 May 1987, Sarah Ann, er da of late Reginald T G Battrum; *Career* farmer; *Style*— David Pauncefort-Duncombe, Esq

PAUNCEFORT-DUNCOMBE, Sir Philip Digby; 4 Bt (UK 1859), of Great Brickhill, Buckinghamshire, DL (Bucks 1971); s of Maj Sir Everard Philip Digby Pauncefort-Duncombe, 3 Bt, DSO (d 1971); *b* 18 May 1927; *Educ* Stowe; *m* 4 April 1951, Rachel Moyra, yr da of Maj Henry Gerald Aylmer, gggs of 2 Baron Aylmer; 1 s, 2 da; *Heir* s, David Philip Henry Pauncefort-Duncombe; *Career* 2 Lt Gren Gds 1946, Hon Maj (ret 1960), Reg Army Reserve, Co Cmdt Bucks ACF 1967-70, memb HM Body Guard of Hon Corps of Gentlemen-at-Arms; High Sheriff of Buckinghamshire 1987-88; KASG; OStJ 1986; *Style*— Sir Philip Pauncefort-Duncombe, Bt, DL; Great Brickhill Manor, Milton Keynes, Bucks (☎ 052 526 205)

PAVEY, Martin Christopher; s of Archibald Lindsay Pavey, MC (d 1977), of Sherborne, Dorset, and Margaret Alice, *née* Salisbury; *b* 2 Dec 1940; *Educ* Magdalen Coll Sch Oxford, UCL (BA), Univ of Cambridge (PGCE), Univ of Nottingham (MA); *m* 9 April 1969, Louise Margaret, da of Dr Joseph Charles Henry Bird (d 1985), of Cambridge; 2 s (Nicholas b 1972, Robert b 1974); *Career* headmaster: Fairham Sch Nottingham 1976-81, Cranbrook Sch Kent 1981- 88, Latymer Upper Sch London 1988; memb: SHA, HMC; *Clubs* East India; *Style*— Martin Pavey, Esq; Latymer Upper Sch, London W6 (☎ 01 741 1851)

PAVITT, Laurence Anstice; MP (Lab and Co-op) Brent South, 1974-; s of George Anstice Pavitt; *b* 1 Feb 1914; *Educ* Elementary and Central Sch West Ham; *m* 1937, Rosina, *née* Walton; 1 s, 1 da; *Career* MP (Lab and Co-op) Willesden West Oct 1959-74, asst govt whip 1974-76, pps to Foreign Sec 1964-67; memb: Cncl of Europe 1979-83, MRC 1968-72; vice-pres Royal Coll of Nursing; *Style*— Laurence Pavitt, Esq, MP; House of Commons, SW1 (☎ 01 219 5225)

PAWLE, Lady Mary Clementine; da of 5 Marquess Camden (d 1983), and 1 w, Marjorie, Countess of Brecknock, DBE, *qv*; *b* 5 August 1921; *m* 1, 1940, Fl-Lt the Hon (Herbert) Oswald Berry (d 1952); m 2, 1953, (Shafto) Gerald Strachan Pawle; *Career* pres St John Ambulance Bde Cornwall, hon life pres St Ives Cons and Unionist Assoc; *Clubs* Army and Navy; *Style*— Lady Mary Pawle; Trehiven House, Madron, Penzance, Cornwall TR20 8SR (☎ 0736 64158)

PAWLEY, Margaret Grozier; da of James John William Herbertson, MVO, OBE (d 1974), of Folkestone, and Lilian Annie Charlotte Herbertson, *née* Rawlinson Wood (d 1985); *b* 22 Mar 1922; *Educ* Stratford House Sch Bickley, St Anne's Coll Oxford (MA), St Hugh's Coll Oxford; *m* 11 Jan 1958, Ven Bernard Clinton Pawley (d 1981), formerly Archdeacon of Canterbury, s of Lt Cdr Sylvester George Pawley, RN (d 1975), of Southwold; 1 s (Matthew James b 1962), 1 da (Felicity Ann b 1961); *Career* Lt Special Op Exec FANY Corps 1943-46, Middle East and Italy; tutor Open Univ 1975-84; *Books* Rome and Canterbury Through Four Centuries (with B C Pawley, 1974), Donald Coggan, Servant of Christ (1987), One Light for One World (The Sermons of Archbishop Runcie) (1988); *Recreations* reading, foreign travel; *Style*— Mrs Bernard Pawley; 3 North Court Oast, Old Wives' Lees, Canterbury, Kent (☎ 0227 730818)

PAWLYN, Doyran Allen (David); s of Clifford Peter Pawlyn, of Oxshott, Surrey, and Betty Winifred Mina, *née* Jones; *b* 11 April 1949; *Educ* Aldenham, Queen Elizabeth Coll London (BSc); *m* 24 Sept 1977, Celia Elizabeth, da of Antony Faraday Sandeman, of Winchelsea, East Sussex; 3 da (Katherine b 1980, Charlotte b 1982, Henrietta b 1987); *Career* ptnr Clark Whitehill CA's 1975; FCA 1973; *Recreations* photography, wine; *Style*— Doyran Pawlyn, Esq; 30 Lower Green Rd, Esher, Surrey.

PAWSEY, James Francis (Jim); MP (Cons Rugby and Kenilworth 1983-); s of Capt William John Pawsey (d 1941), of 24 Moseley Avenue, Coventry, and Mary Victoria, *née* Mumford (d 1958); *b* 21 August 1933; *Educ* Coventry Tech Sch, Coventry Tech Coll; *m* 1956, Cynthia Margaret, da of Arthur James Francis, of Earlsdon Ave, Coventry; 6 s (Mark, Michael, Gregory, Clive (twin), Philip, Adrian (twin)); *Career* MP (Cons Rugby 1979-83), memb Select Ctee of the Parly Cmmn for Admin, sec Anglo Portuguese Gp; tres Br Bangladesh Parly Gp 1984-; memb: Rugby RDC 1964-73, Rugby Borough Cncl 1973-75, Warwickshire CC 1974-79; pps: Dept of Educn and Sci 1982-83, DHSS 1983-84, NI Off 1984-86; exec Int Parly Union; chm Cons Backbench Educn Ctee; *Books* The Tringo Phenomenon; *Recreations* gardening; *Clubs* Carlton; *Style*— Jim Pawsey, Esq, MP; Shilton House, Shilton, Warwicks (☎ 0203 612922); Rugby and Kenilworth Cons Assoc, Albert Buildings, Albert St, Rugby (☎ 0788) 69556); House of Commons, London SW1A 0AA (☎ 01 219 5127)

PAWSON, Kenneth Vernon Frank; s of Capt Arnold Gilderdale Pawson (d 1937), and Freda Eunice Pawson; *b* 24 Sept 1923; *Educ* Rugby, Trinity Hall Cambridge; *m* 1950, Nicolette Vivian, da of Mervyn Thoresby (d 1965); 1 s, 2 da; *Career* Capt RB BAOR 1942-47; barr Gray's Inn 1949; md Joseph Hobson & Son Ltd (Brewers) 1954-74, chm and md Gale Lister & Co Ltd 1975-, exec dir Mount Charlotte Investmts plc 1974-; *Recreations* shooting, fishing, farming, old cars; *Style*— Kenneth Pawson, Esq; Haggas Hall, Weeton, nr Leeds, Yorkshire (☎ 0423 743200); 59 St Dunstans Rd, London W6; 2 The Calls, Leeds 2 (☎ 0532 439111, telex 557934)

PAXMAN, Jeremy Dickson; s of Arthur Keith Paxman, of Selby, Yorkshire, and Joan McKay, *née* Dickson, of Bramhope, Yorkshire; *b* 11 May 1950; *Educ* Malvern Coll, St Catharine's Coll Cambridge; *Career* reporter: BBC NI 1974-77, Tonight 1977-79, Panorama 1979-84; presenter Evening News 1985-86, presenter/interviewer Breakfast Time , numerous contributions to newspapers and magazines; Royal TV Soc Award 1984; *Books* A Higher Form of Killing (jtly, 1982), Through the Volcanoes (1985); *Recreations* fly fishing, mountains, day dreams; *Style*— Jeremy Paxman, Esq; c/o David Higham Assc, 5-8 Lower John St, London W1R 4HA

PAXMAN, Philip John; s of Edward Philip Paxman, JP (d 1949), and Dora Emily, *née*

Bowen (d 1985); *b* 24 Oct 1941; *Educ* Oundle, St Johns Coll Cambridge (MA, Vet MB); *m* 13 Dec 1968, Mary Elizabeth, da of A E Witherow (d 1988); 2 s (Jeremy Edward b 1972, James Philip b 1977); *Career* lectr RVC 1966-69, fndr and chief exec Volac Ltd 1970-87, fndr chief exec and chm Animal Biotechnol Cambridge Ltd 1985-, chm Championship Foods Ltd; dir: Scottish Beef Devpts Ltd, ARS Devpt Ltd, Cria Ovina de Malpica SA (Spain); winner RAS Technol prize 1985; tstee Cambridge Univ Vet School Tst, memb advsy gp AFRC Inst of Animal Physiology and Genetics Res; Freeman City of London, Liveryman Worshipful Co of Farriers; MRCVS; *Recreations* fishing; *Clubs* Farmers; *Style—* Philip Paxman, Esq; South Farm, Shingay Cum Wendy, Royston, Herts SG8 0HR (☎ 0223 207581); Animal Research Station, Univ of Cambridge, 307 Huntingdon Rd, Cambridge CB3 0JQ (☎ 0223 277222, fax 277605, car tel 0836 762299, telex 94013403)

PAXMAN, Hon Mrs; Hon Rosetta Anne; *née* O'Neill; 2 da of 2 Baron Rathcavan (but eldest by his 2 w); *b* 14 Sept 1954; *m* 1977, Capt John Michael Anthony Paxman, Coldstream Gds; 1 s (Truscote Phelim b 1985); 2 da (Musidora b 1980, Zena b 1982); *Style—* The Hon Mrs Paxman

PAYKEL, Prof Eugene Stern; s of Joshua Paykel (d 1962), and Eva, *née* Stern; *b* 9 Sept 1934; *Educ* Auckland GS NZ, Univ of Otago (MB, ChB, MD), Univ of Cambridge (MD), Univ of London (DPM); *m* 7 July 1969, Margaret, da of John Melrose (d 1966); 2 s (Nicholas b 1971, Jonathan b 1973); *Career* registrar (later sr registrar) Maudsley Hosp 1962-65, asst prof psychiatry and co-dir (later dir) Depression Res Unit Yale Univ 1966-71, prof of psychiatry St George's Hosp Med Sch Univ of London 1977-85 (conslt and sr lectr 1971-75, reader 1975-77), prof of psychiatry Univ of Cambridge and fell Gonville and Caius Coll 1985-; chief scientist advsr mental illness res liaison gp DHSS 1984-88, memb neuro sciences bd MRC 1981-85, hon sec Jt Ctee on Higher Psychiatric Trg 1988-, ed Jl of Affective Disorders 1979-; former examiner: Edinburgh Univ, Nottingham Univ, Manchester Univ, London Univ; RC Psych 1984-88: examiner, chm Social and Community psychiatry section, cncl memb, memb exec ctee, memb public policy ctee, memb res ctee; pres Br Assoc for Psychopharmacology 1982-84 (hon sec 1979-82); tstee Mental Health Fndn 1988- (Fndn's Fund Prize for Res in Psychiatry 1978); second prize Anna Monika Stiftung 1985; Maudsley lectr RCPsych 1988; MRCPEd 1960, MRCP 1961, MRCPsych 1971, FRCP 1977, FRCPEd 1978; *Books* The Depressed Woman (1971), Psychopharmacolgy of Affective Disorders (1979), Monoamine Oxidase Inhibitors: the state of the art (1981), Handbook of Affective Disorders (1982), Community Psychiatric Nursing for Neurotic Patients (1983); *Recreations* opera, music, theatre; *Clubs* Athenaeum; *Style—* Prof Eugene Paykel; Department of Psychiatry, Univ of Cambridge, Addenbrooke's Hosp, Hills Rd, Cambridge CB2 2QQ (☎ 0223 336961, fax 0223 242474)

PAYNE, Alan Jeffrey; CMG (1988); s of Sydney Ellis Payne (d 1967), of Enfield, Middx, and Lydia Ethel, *née* Sweetman (d 1980); *b* 11 May 1933; *Educ* Enfield GS, Queens' Coll Cambridge; *m* 6 June 1959, Emily Letitia, da of Frank Hodgkinson Freeman (d 1985); 3 s (Richard Andrew b 1960, David Jeffrey b 1963, Jeremy Martin b 1966); *Career* Nat Serv RN 1955-57; EMI Ltd 1957-62, NATO Secretariat Pais 1962-64; Dip Serv 1964-: first sec Kuala Lumpur 1967-70, asst head SW Pacific dept FCO 1970-72, head commercial dept Br Embassy Budapest 1972-75, dep head mission on promotion to cnsllr 1975-79, head Mexico and Caribbean dept FCO 1979-82, consul general Lyons 1982-87, Br high cmmr 1987-; FIL 1962; *Recreations* theatre, music, restoring old cars; *Style—* Alan Payne, Esq, CMG; c/o Foreign and Cwlth Office, Downing St, London

PAYNE, Christopher Frederick; CBE (1987), QPM (1975), DL (Cleveland 1983); s of Cdr Gerald Frederick Payne, OBE, BEM, QPM (d 1979), of Wallington, Surrey, and Amy Florence Elizabeth, *née* Parker; *b* 15 Feb 1930; *Educ* Christ's Coll Finchley, Hendon Tech Coll; *m* 4 Oct 1952, Barbara Janet, da of Herbert Charles Saxby (d 1944), of Hampstead Way, Hampstead; 1 s (Roger b 1961), 3 da (Gillian b 1954, Adrianne b 1956, Valerie b 1965); *Career* Nat Serv Intelligence Corps 1948-50; Met Police: joined 1950, chief inspector Ops Branch 1963, supt and chief supt Hammersmith 1965-68, sr command course 1965, HO R and D Branch 1968-70, chief supt D Dist 1970-71, cdr X Dist 1971-74, cdr Airport Dist 1974-76; chief constable of Cleveland Constabulary 1976-; dep chm Met Police Friendly Soc 1971-76, police advsr to ACC Social Servs Ctee 1979-, co dir St John Ambulance Cleveland 1978-85, chm St John Cncl Cleveland 1986-, vice chm Royal Jubilee and Prince's Tsts Ctee for Durham and Cleveland 1984-, vice pres Cleveland Youth Assoc 1983-, chm Cleveland Mental Health Support Gp 1981-86; CStJ 1985; Freeman of City of London 1987; CBIM 1988; *Recreations* painting, philately, gardening; *Clubs* Royal Cwlth Soc; *Style—* C F Payne, Esq, CBE, QPM, DL, Chief Constable of Cleveland; Cleveland Constabulary, P.O. Box 70, Police HQ, Ladgate Lane, Middlesbrough, Cleveland TS8 9EH (☎ 0642 326 326, fax 0642 326 326 ext 1311, telex 58516)

PAYNE, Lady Cynthia Lettice Margaret; *née* Bernard; da of late Lt-Col Ronald Percy Hamilton Bernard, ggs of 2 Earl Bandon; sis of 5 Earl Bandon, GBE, CVO, DSO (d 1979, when title became extinct); raised to the rank of an Earl's da 1925; *b* 1905; *m* 1, 1925 (m dis 1936), Lt-Col Francis Christian Darby Tothill, RB; 1 da; m 2, 1947, Air Cdre Lionel Guy Stanhope Payne, CBE, MC, AFC (d 1965); *Style—* Lady Cynthia Payne; 7 Thurloe Sq, London SW7

PAYNE, David John Allen; s of late Harry Payne, and late Edith Mary, *née* Kirby; *b* 29 July 1928; *Educ* Canterbury, Farnham, Brighton Coll of Art, Royal Acad Schs (NDD); *m* 11 Aug 1951, Iris Jean, da of late James Freeman; 1 s (Mark Allen b 21 April 1961), 1 da (Mary Anne b 30 Dec 1958); *Career* oil and watercolour artist, former sr lectr Bedford Coll of HE; exhibited: Ash Barn Gallery Petersfield 1978-80, Bedford Sch 1973-76, The Gallery Wellingborough 1983-85, Ellingham Mill 1979-82, sponsored exhibition at Sotheby's 1981, Portal Gallery 1986, RA 1976 and 78-87, New Ashgate Gallery Farnham 1987; work in permanent collections incl Beds CC Educn Loan Serv; work reproduced/reviewed: ITV Folio 1982, BBC RA review 1983, BBC Academy Illustrated 1983-84; painter of triptychs many sold at RA; *Style—* David Payne, Esq

PAYNE, Geoffrey John Nicholas; s of John Laurence Payne (d 1961), and Dorothy Gwendoline, *née* Attenborough; *b* 4 Jan 1945; *Educ* Eton, Trinity Coll Cambridge (BA); *m* 6 Jan 1986, Linda Jane, da of Donald Wallace Adamson, of Bristol; 2 s (Ralph John Anthony b 1986, Oliver Nicholas Pearsall b 1988); *Career* fin asst Royal Opera House 1968-70, subsidy offr Arts Cncl GB 1970-76, fin controller WNO 1976-82, gen admin Opera North 1982-; *Style—* Nicholas Payne, Esq; Opera North, Grand Theatre, 46 New Briggate, Leeds LS1 6NU (☎ 0532 439 999, fax 0532 435 745, telex 265871)

PAYNE, Maj-Gen George Lefevre; CB (1966), CBE (1963); s of Dr Ernest Lefevre Payne (d 1955), of Brunswick House, Kew, and Helena Payne (d 1957); *b* 23 June 1911; *Educ* The King's Sch Canterbury, RMC Sandhurst; *m* 1938, Betty Maud (d 1982), da of Surgn Capt H A Kellond-Knight, RN; 3 s; *Career* Army Offr; dir Ordnance Services MOD 1964-68, previously served RAOC UK, France (Col Cmdt 1968-72, Cdr Stores Orgn 1963-64, ret 1968; *Recreations* shooting, fishing; *Clubs* Royal Cwlth Soc, Army and Navy; *Style—* Major-General George Payne, CB, CBE; c/o Army and Navy Club, 36-39 Pall Mall, London SW1

PAYNE, Harold Lloyd; OBE (1972); s of Horace Frederick Payne (d 1956), of Blackheath, and Dora Kate, *née* Lloyd (d 1972); *b* 16 Oct 1920; *Educ* City of London Sch; *m* 12 June 1942, Mary Mildred, da of William George Hill (d 1951), of Blackheath; 1 da (Lorna b 1949); *Career* TA HAC 1939, II Regt RHA 1939, cmmnd 137 FD Regt RA 1941 (Japanese POW 1942-45); dir firm of Lloyds insur brokers 1937-80, memb Lloyds 1949-88, forest owner 1974-; tstee: Far East Fund, Queen Mary's Hosp Tst; pres Nat Fedn of Far Eastern POW Assocs; memb: bd govrs Westminster Hosp Gp 1970-74, central advsy ctee War Pensions, Kent West War Pensions Ctee, Br Membs Cncl World Veterans Fedn; vice chm Cncl Br Serv Ex-Serv Orgns; Freeman City of London 1951, Liveryman Worshipful Co of Carmen 1952; *Recreations* rugby, gardening; *Clubs* City Livery, Guild of Freemen; *Style—* Harold L Payne, Esq, OBE; Long View, 18 Whybourne Crest, Tunbridge Wells, Kent TN2 5BS (☎ 0892 27024); Foresters, Girnwood, Hawick, Roxburghshire, Scotland TD9 7PN (☎ 045088 203)

PAYNE, James Gladstone; s of Ralph Arthur Payne (d 1945), of NZ, and Mary Phillot, *née* Gladstone (d 1986); *Educ* Kings PS Auckland NZ, Wanganui Collegiate Sch NZ; *m* 24 July 1954, Margaret, da of Ronald Arthur Vestey (d 1988), of Thurlow Hall, Haverhill, Suffolk; 1 s (Micheal b 1959), 2 d (Nichola (Mrs McArthur) b 1955, Philippa Shirley (Mrs Beavan) b 1963); *Career* Nat Serv 1951-53 cmmnd 17/21 Lancers; md Assoc Container Transportation (Aust) Ltd 1969-73 (joined Blue StarLine 1953); dep chm 1974-79: Blue Star Line, Lamport and Holt Line, Booth Line; salmon farmer 1980-;chm Cncl of Euro and Japanese Shipowners Assoc 1977-79; *Recreations* swimming, sailing, stalking, scuba diving; *Clubs* Cavalry; *Style—* James Payne, Esq; Rickling Hall, Saffron Walden, Essex CB11 3YJ (☎ 079 988 342); Ardvar, Drumbeg-by-Lairg, Sutherland IV27 4NJ (☎ 057 13 244, fax 079 988 522, 057 132 02)

PAYNE, Hon Mrs; Hon Joan; *née* Spring Rice; o da of 5 Baron Monteagle of Brandon (d 1946), and Emilie de Kosenko;; *b* 16 August 1928; *m* 15 May 1953, Michael Shears Payne, MC, o surv s of Rawdon Shears Payne; 1 s, 1 da; *Style—* The Hon Mrs Payne; Scotlands Farm, Cockpole Green, Nr Wargrave, Berks RG10 8QP

PAYNE, Keith; VC (1969); s of Henry Thomas Payne; *b* 30 August 1933; *Educ* State Sch Ingham N Qld; *m* 1954, Florence Catherine Payne, *née* Plaw; 5 s; *Career* Aust Army Trg Team Vietnam 1969 (Warrant Offr), WO instr RMC Duntroon ACT 1970-72, 42 Bn Royal Qld Regt, Mackay 1973-75, Capt Oman Army 1975-76; *Style—* Keith Payne Esq, VC; St Bees Ave, Bucasia, via Mackay, Queensland, 4741, Australia (☎ 079 546125)

PAYNE, Keith Howard; s of Sydney William John Payne, and Jean Emily, *née* Blower (d 1966); *b* 16 July 1937; *Educ* Shooters Hill GS; *m* 1, Dec 1972 (m dis); m 2, 23 Nov 1984, Tania Jeannette, da of Frank John Trevisani; 1 da (Francesca Jean b 13 April 1987); *Career* Nat Serv personal staff Dep Supreme Allied Cdr in Europe SHAPE Paris 1955-57; fin journalist The Times 1958-68 (first banking 1965-68); Charles Barter City 1968-: dir 1970-74, asst md 1974-76, md 1976-80, dep chief exec and vice chm 1980-84, dep chm (restructed co) 1984-, dir Charles Barter PR 1988-; memb domestic promotion ctee Br Invisible Exports Cncl; Freedom Nova Scotia Province (following journalistic visit with The Times) 1965; MInstPR; *Recreations* swimming, walking, theatre; *Style—* Keith Payne, Esq; Charles Barker Group, 30 Farringdon St, London EC4A 4EA (☎ 01 634 1310, fax 248 3582)

PAYNE, Leonard Sidney; CBE (1983); s of Leonard Sydney Payne (d 1968), and Lilian May Leggatt (d 1967); *b* 16 Dec 1925; *Educ* Woodhouse GS; *m* 1944, Marjorie, da of Frederick Vincent; 2 s; *Career* md Mgmnt Diagnostics Ltd 1987-, distribution dir J Sainsbury plc 1974-86, vice-chm Nat Freight Corpn 1969-74, md Br Road Servs Ltd 1966-69; FCCA, CBIM, FCIT, MBCS, FIRTE; *Style—* Leonard Payne, Esq, CBE; Flat 4N, Maple Lodge, Lythe Hill Park, Haslemere, Surrey GU27 3TE

PAYNE, Lady; Maureen Ruth; da of William Charles Walsh; *m* 1951, as his 2 w, Sir Robert Frederick Payne (fndr memb British Acad of Forensic Sciences; d 1985), s of late Frederick Charles Payne; 1 s (1 step s and 1 step da); *Style—* Lady Payne; Longview, 26 Swanland Hill, North Ferriby, N Humberside HU14 3JJ (☎ (0482) 631533)

PAYNE, Michael Anthony; s of Albert John Payne, and Beryl Kathleen Cavey, *née* Slater; *b* 2 Sept 1939; *Educ* Stowe, City of Westminster Coll 1964-68; *m* 1965, Elizabeth Harvieston, da of Alan Brown, of Scotland; 1 s (Toby b 1970), 1 da (Sophie b 1968); *Career* Nat Serv 2 Lt Royal Regt of Artillery 1960-62; TA: gunner HAC, Capt 254 FD Regt RA; co sec: Hill Samuel and Co (Jersey) Ltd 1978-88, Hill Samuel Investmt Servs Gp (Jersey) Ltd 1984-; dir: Hill Samuel (CI) Tst Co Ltd 1979-, Hill Samuel Fund and Mangrs (Jersey) Ltd 1982-; fell Chartered Assoc of Certified Accountants; *Recreations* historical reading, glass engraving; *Clubs* Honorable Artillery Company, United (Jersey); *Style—* Michael Payne, Esq; 3 Ashley Close, Bagatelle Rd, St Saviour, Jersey, CI; 7 Bond St, St Helier, Jersey C1 (☎ 0535 419 2167, fax 0534 79018)

PAYNE, Michael William; s of Albert Leonard Payne, MM, RFC (d 1955), of Orpington, Kent, and Grace Maud, *née* Lyon (d 1974); *b* 18 April 1927; *Educ* Dulwich; *m* 2 June 1951, Angela Margaret Westmacott, da of Hugh Sherwood Leary (d 1955); 2 s (Thomas b 1976, William b 1978), 2 da (Susan b 1952, Sally b 1955); *Career* Sgt RAF 1945-48; trainee underwriter 1948-50, dep underwriter 1950-57, gen mangr 1957-68, sr ptnr Michael Payne & Ptnrs 1967-, active underwriter Sir William Garthwaite & Others 1969-71, active underwriter Michael Payne & Others 1973-; exec chm: Janson Payne Mgmnt Ltd 1986-, Michael Payne Syndicates Pty Ltd 1987-, chm Michael Payne Agencies Ltd 1989-, dir Janson Green Hldgs Ltd 1986-; memb Lloyds Law Reform Ctee 1968- (jt chm 1973-84), vice pres Insur of London; Freeman City of London 1979, memb Worshipful Co of Insurers 1980; *Books* Modern Requirements in Liability Insurance (1968); *Recreations* golf, opera, music; *Clubs* City of London; *Style—* Michael Payne, Esq; Wroughton, 47 Sundridge Ave, Bromley, Kent (☎ 01 460 4924); Shene Cottage, Vicarage St, Colyton, Devon (☎ 0297 52621); 85 Gracechurch St, London EC3V 0BH (☎ 01 623 6423, fax 01 283 4531, telex

8813816)

PAYNE, Sir Norman John; CBE (1976, OBE 1956, MBE 1944); s of late Frederick Payne, of Folkestone; *b* 9 Oct 1921; *Educ* John Lyon Sch Harrow, City and Guilds Coll London; *m* 1946 (sep), Pamela Vivien, *née* Wallis; 4 s, 1 da; *Career* Capt RE (despatches twice), served India and Burma; ptnr Sir Frederick Snow & Ptnrs 1955 (joined 1949); chm Br Airports Authy 1977- (chief exec 1972-77); Hon D Tech Loughborough Univ; FENG, FCGI, FICE, FCIT, FIHT, CIMB, Companion RACS 1987; kt 1985; *Recreations* amateur photography; *Clubs* Reform, RAC; *Style—* Sir Norman Payne, CBE; BAA plc, Corporate Office, 130 Wilton Rd, London SW1V 1LQ

PAYNE, Raef John Godfrey; s of Lt-Col Lancelot Hugo Humphrey Payne (d 1955), of Pentre Uchaf Hall, and Gwendolyn Marguerite, *née* Philpot (d 1981); *b* 17 August 1929; *Educ* Eton, Trinity Coll Cambridge; *Career* master-in-coll Eton 1957-65 (asst master 1952), asst master Kilquanity House Kirkcudbrightshire 1966, housemaster Eton 1967-84; *Recreations* retirement; *Style—* Raef Payne, Esq; Pentre Uchaf Hall, Maesbrook, Oswestry, Shropshire (☎ 0691 830 483)

PAYNE, Richard; s of Capt Matt Payne (d 1937), and Ellen Rosina, *née* Burdett (d 1989); *b* 26 June 1935; *Educ* Lancing, De Havilland Aeronautical Sch; *m* 30 Nov 1957, Ann Helen, da of Cyril Philip de Muschamp Porritt (d 1976); 2 s ((Peter) Matt, (Alexander) Richard de Muschamp), 1 da ((Helen) Annabel); *Career* supplies engr De Havilland's 1958-60, design and project engr Norris Bros (consulting engrs) 1961-62, tech mangr Kluber GmbH 1963-65, consulting engr 1966-68, fndr Thurne Engrg Co Ltd 1969 (md 1969-85, chm 1970-), md Edward Hines (engrs) Ltd 1970-89, md and chm Bronpole Gp 1975-; fndr: Thurne GmbH Germany 1985, Thurne Corpn 1985; chm Estuary Engrg 1989 (bought out by Thurne Engrg Co 1975); Queens Award for Technol 1988; MIMechE; *Recreations* sailing, skiing, gardening, reading; *Clubs* Norfolk; *Style—* Richard Payne, Esq; Bale Hall, Bale, Norfolk NR21 9DA (☎ 032 877 467); Bronpole Ltd & Thurne Engrg Co Ltd, Delta Close, Norwich (☎ 0603 41071, 0603 624281, fax 0603 487767, car 241878)

PAYNE, Richard William Newth; s of Stuart Dean Payne (d 1954), of Surrey, and Kathleen Amelia, *née* Newth (d 1981); *b* 14 Dec 1930; *Educ* Tonbridge, Univ of Bristol (BA); *m* 30 May 1964, Ann, da of David Windover Millard, of Surrey; 2 s (William b 1965, Timothy b 1967), 1 da (Annabel b 1971), 1 step s (Andrew Payne b 1956), 1 step da (Sarah b 1959); *Career* CA; ptnr W H Payne & Co 1955- (sr ptnr 1974-); dir: Marlowe Investmts (Kent) Ltd 1962-, Millard Estates Ltd 1980-; *Recreations* golf, gardening, bridge; *Clubs* MCC; *Style—* Richard Payne, Esq; Broadway, 11 Landscape Road, Warlingham, Surrey CR3 9JB; 5 Los Almendros, Moraira, Teulada, Alicante, Espana; Sandringham House, 199 Southwark, Bridge Road, London SE1 0HA

PAYNE, Lt-Col Robert Arnold; JP (1963); s of Robert William Tom Payne (d 1974), and Esther Victoria *née* Elliott (d 1967); *b* 1 Sept 1919; *Educ* Finchley HS, Finchley County GS; *m* 20 May 1950, Audrey Mary Jean, da of David Bradford, of 13 Russell Close, Little Chalfont, Bucks; 2 da (Jean Elizabeth b 6 July 1952, Patricia Mary (twin)); *Career* WWII Duke of Cornwall's LI 1939-40, cmmnd Bedfs Herts Regt 1940, Inf Signals Instr 1940, Orkney & Shetland Def Force 1941-42, Instn 160 Sp Gp OCTU 1942-43, 2 Bn Essex Regt 1944-45, Q staff 49 Inf Div HQ 1945-46; RARO 1949-, Herts ACF 1953-61; Dep Co Reader Cmdt 1958-61; memb: ACF Nat Trg Ctee 1961-63, advsy panel ACF Duke of Edinburgh's Award 1963-87; hon First Aid trg advsr Army and Combined Cadet Forces 1961-87; sr sec and accountancy asst Br Iron and Steel Corpn 1948-52, (gp sec and dir subsid cos Int Aeradio Ltd, sec and fin conslt 1952-77, and 1977-84); memb Middx branch Magistrates Assoc exec ctee 1977-83 (chm 1984-87); St John Ambulance 1936-: dep cmmr London (Prince of Wales's) Dist 1969-78; KStJ 1975; Cdr Co of Buckinghamshire 1978-; branch chm Royal Br Legion 1985-; Freeman City of London 1974, Liveryman Worshipful Co of Scriveners 1978; FCIS 1952, FBIM 1970, FFA 1977; Cross of Merit Sovereign Military Order of Malta 1971; *Recreations* St John Ambulance, stamp collecting; *Style—* Lt-Col R A Payne, JP; 72 Amersham Road, Little Chalfont, Amersham, Bucks HP6 6SL, (☎ 024 04 4900)

PAYNE, Robert Gardiner; s of Dr Robert Orlando Payne, and Frances Elisabeth, *née* Jackson (d 1987); *b* 12 July 1933; *Educ* Lady Barn House Sch Withington, Packwood Haugh Shrewsbury, Clifton, Trinity Hall Cambridge (MA); *m* 10 April 1963, Diana Catalina, da of Rupert Henry Marchington, of Wilton Crescent, Alderley Edge, Cheshire; 1 s (Philip Robert b 1968), 2 da (Frances Patricia b 1967, Emily Diana b 1972); *Career* Nat Serv 2 Lt RA 1952-54; slr 1961; ptnr: Skelton and Co (Manchester) 1963-66, March Pearson and Skelton 1966-; chm: Family Welfare Assoc of Manchester, Lady Barn House Sch; dep chm David Lewis Centre for Epilepsy; memb Law Soc; *Recreations* tennis, skiing, walking; *Clubs* St James' (Manchester); *Style—* Robert Payne, Esq; The Coach House, Brook Lane, Alderley Edge Cheshire SK9 7QJ (☎ 0625 583156); 41 Spring Gardens Manchester M2 2BB (☎ 061 832 7290, fax 061 832 2655, telex 669689)

PAYNE, Roger Jeremy; JP; s of Gordon Edgar Payne, OBE, JP (d 1988), and Dorothy Esther Payne; *b* 14 Dec 1937; *Educ* Wycliffe Coll Stonehouse Glos, Birmingham Sch of Architecture (DipArch); *m* 22 Aug 1964, Mary Nanette, da of William Henry Davis (d 1984); 1 s (Mark b 1969), 1 da (Sarah b 1972); *Career* sr ptnr Preece Payne Ptnrship; dir: Abbeybridge Property Gp Ltd, Claremont Rd Investmt Co Ltd, W Country Motor Hotel Servs, Preece Payne Conslt (Gibraltar); RIBA; *Recreations* theatre, power boating; *Clubs* Royal Yachting Assoc; *Style—* Roger Payne, Esq, OBE, JP; Little Gransmoor, Sussex Gardens, Hucclecote, Gloucester GL3 3ST; 39 Garbinell, Punta Montgo, L'Escala, Gerona, Spain; Bearland House, Longsmith St, Gloucester GL1 1HJ (☎ 24471, fax 410800)

PAYNE-GALLWEY, Sir Philip; 6 Bt (UK 1812); s of Lt-Col Lowry Philip Payne-Gallwey, OBE, MC, ggs of 1 Bt; suc kinsman, Sir Reginald Frankland-Payne-Gallwey, 5 Bt, 1964; assumed by Royal Licence 1966 the additional surname of Frankland before that of Payne and Gallwey; *b* 15 Mar 1935; *Educ* Eton; *Career* late Lt 11 Hussars; dir British Bloodstock Agency Ltd; *Style—* Sir Philip Payne-Gallwey, Bt; The Little House, Boxford, Newbury, Berks (☎ 048 838 315); The British Bloodstock Agency Ltd, 16/17 Pall Mall, London SW17 5LU (☎ 01 839 3393, telex 27403)

PAYNTER, Cecil de Camborne Pendarves; s of late Col E Pendarves Paynter, TD, of Fernchase Manor, Ashurst Park, Fordcombe, Kent, and Cicely Marion, *née* Hadow; *b* 17 July 1930; *Educ* Wellington, RMA Sandhurst; *m* 29 July 1961, Fiona Marion Naismith; 2 s (Michael John Pendarves b 1963, Andrew Francis de Camborne b 1965); *Career* Capt 3 Kings Own Hussars, Airborne Trg Offr N Somerset Yeo; regnl mangr Rank Hovis McDougal, md Magnet Signs and Joinery, chm of a vending machine and wholesale co; dir: Wine Standard's Bd, Bd of Tstees Wine and Spirits Educn Tst, Ct of Vintners' Co; memb cncl S England Agric Show and Soc, gp chm Royal Br Legion W Kent; *Recreations* country pursuits, golf, growing vines; *Clubs* Army and Navy; *Style—* Cecil de Camborne Paynter, Esq; Rookery Cottage, Hever, nr Edenbridge, Kent (☎ 034 286 350)

PAYNTER, Prof John Frederick; OBE (1985); s of Frederick Albert Paynter (d 1968), and Rose Alice, *née* Garbutt (d 1963); *b* 17 July 1931; *Educ* Emanuel Sch London, Trinity Coll of Music London, Univ of York (DPhil); *m* 25 July 1956, Elizabeth, da of Matthew George Hill; 1 da (Catherine Elizabeth b 12 Aug 1957); *Career* teacher primary and secdy schs 1954-62, lectr in music City of Liverpool Coll of Educn 1962-65, princ lectr in music Bishop Otter Coll Chichester 1965-69; Dept of Music Univ of York: lectr 1969, sr lectr 1974-82, prof 1982, head of dept 1983; dir Schs Cncl Project Music in the Secdy Sch Curriculum; int lectures in music educn, books translated into numerous languages; compositions incl: Landscapes (1972), The Windhover (1972), Galaxies for orchestra (1977), String Quartet (1981), The Inviolable Voice (1982), Piano Sonata (1987); Hon GSM Guildhall Sch of Music London; FRSA 1987; *Books* Sound and Silence (1970), Hear and Now (1972), The Dance and the Drum (1974), Music in the Secondary School Curriculum (1982); *Style—* Prof John Paynter, OBE; Dept of Music, Univ of York, Heslington, York YO1 5DD (☎ 0904 432 444)

PAYNTER, Air Cdre Noel Stephen; CB (1946), DL (Bucks 1963); s of Canon Francis Samuel Paynter (d 1954), and Helen Isabel (d 1953); descends from William Camborne, *alias* Paynter, of Deverell, Cornwall (arms granted 1569); *b* 26 Dec 1898; *Educ* Haileybury, RMC Sandhurst; *m* 1925, Barbara Grace, da of Frederick Hans Haagensen, artist (d 1950); 1 s, 1 da; *Career* Chief Intelligence Offr: RAF Middle East 1939-42, RAF Bomber Command 1942-45, Directorate of Intelligence Air Miny 1946; High Sheriff Bucks 1965; *Style—* Air Commodore N S Paynter, CB, DL; Lawn House, Edgcott, nr Aylesbury, Bucks (☎ Grendon Underwood 238)

PAYTON, Roger Louis; s of Leonard Joseph Payton (d 1984), and Vera Mary, *née* Crepin; *b* 18 Oct 1930; *Educ* Caterham Sch London (LLB); *m* 10 May 1958, Geraldine Eyre, da of Wilfrid Farley (d 1974); 1 s (Christopher b 1961), 1 da (Jane b 1959); *Career* admitted slr 1958; dir: Baring Bros & Co Ltd 1969-84, Richardsons Westgarth plc 1971- (chm 1988-), Gt Portland Estates plc, Davies & Newman Hldgs plc, Morland & Co plc, River Clyde Hldgs plc 1985-, Roskel plc; chm Waycom Hldgs Ltd 1987-; Master Worshipful Co of Gardeners 1981-82; FRSA, FInstD; *Recreations* gardening, tennis; *Clubs* Savile; *Style—* Roger L Payton, Esq; Little Bedwell, Essendon, Hatfield, Herts AL9 6JA (☎ 0707 42623); 145 Leadenhall St, London EC3V 4QT (☎ 01 283 8833, telex 883622/3, fax 01 283 2633)

PAYTON, Stanley Walden; CMG (1965); s of Archibald Walden Payton (d 1934), and Ethel Payton (d 1966); *b* 29 May 1921; *Educ* Monoux Sch, Royal Navy; *m* 1941, Joan, da of Thomas Henry Starmer (d 1983); 1 s, 1 da; *Career* Lt RNVR, served Fleet Air Arm 1940-46; Bank of England 1946-80 (chief of Overseas Dept 1975-80); first govr Bank of Jamaica 1960-64; *Recreations* golf, photography, music; *Clubs* Naval; *Style—* Stanley Payton, Esq, CMG; Pollards Park House, Chalfont St Giles, Bucks

PAYTON, Rev Wilfred Ernest Granville; CB (1965); s of Wilfred Richard Daniel Payton; *b* 27 Dec 1913; *Educ* Nottingham HS, Emmanuel Coll Cambridge, Ridley Hall Cambridge (MA); *m* 1946, Nita Mary Barber; 1 s, 1 da; *Career* ordained 1938, curate of Heanor 1938-41, chaplain RAF 1941-69, chaplain-in-chief, archdeacon, prebendary and canon of St Boltolph, Lincoln Cathedral 1965-69, vicar of Abingdon 1969-79, rural dean of Abingdon 1976-79, hon chaplain to HM The Queen 1965-69; *Style—* The Rev Wilfred Payton, CB; Westwood, Nailsworth, Gloucester GL6 0AW (☎ 045 383 4340)

PEACE, David Brian; MBE (1977); s of Herbert W F Peace (d 1951), of Sheffield, and Mabel, *née* Hammond (d 1915); *b* 13 Mar 1915; *Educ* Mill Hill Sch, Univ of Sheffield; *m* 2 Sept 1939, Jean Margaret, da of Rev McEwan Lawson, of Mill Hill; 2 da (Rachel (Mrs Davies) b 1942, Juliet (Mrs C R Johnson) b 1946); *Career* WWII Sqdn Ldr Airfield Construction Serv RAF 1942-46; town planner: Staffs CC 1948-61, dep co planning offr and head of environmental planning Cambs CC 1961-80; glass engraver; 10 one man shows since 1956; work in 10 public collections incl: V & A, Fitzwilliam & Kettles Yard Cambridge, Brierley Hill Nat Museum of Glass, Corning Museum USA, Keatley Tst collection; windows, screens, and doors in many churches incl: St Nicholas Liverpool, St Albans Cathedral, Westminster Abbey; memb: Cncl for Br Archaeology 1965-85, Ely Diocesan Advsy Ctee 1963-; Master Art Workers Guild 1973, Liveryman Worshipful Co of Glaziers 1977, pres Guild of Glass Engravers 1980-86; ARIBA 1938, FRTPI 1948 (memb cncl 1961-62 and 1972-73), FSA 1975; *Books* Glass engraving: Lettering and Design (1985), Historic Buildings Maps and Guides: Peak District (1954), North Wales (1958), A Guide to Historic Buildings Law (1965), various publications on historic conservation and work of Eric Gill; *Recreations* townscape, heraldry; *Clubs* Arts; *Style—* David Peace, Esq, MBE; Abbots End, Hemingford Abbots, Huntingdon, Cambs PE18 9AA, (☎ 0480 62472)

PEACEY, Col John Capel (Charles); s of Rev Capel Coope Peacey (d 1954), Rector of All Saints, Carleton Rode, Norfolk, and Marjorie Joyce, *née* Bradshaw (d 1986); *b* 11 Dec 1928; *Educ* Marlborough, Bournemouth Municipal Coll (Dip Mech Eng); *m* 17 July 1954, Dr Jean Menzies, da of Arnold Edwin Thirlby; 2 da (Susan (Mrs Graves), Diana (Mrs Taine)); *Career* cmmnd RE 1949, garrison engr Malaya 1950-52, tech trg offr Chatham 1953-56, troop cdr Nienburg Germany 1958-58, WOSB testing offr Barton Stacey Hants 1958-59, engrg course Chatham 1959-61, sr instr design Chatham 1961-65 , OC engr base workshops Singapore 1965-67, asst CRE 62 works Barton Stacey Hants 1967-69, Staff Offr II Mil Engrg Experimental Estab Christchurch Hants 1969-71, Staff Offr I logistics petroleum AFSOUTH Naples Italy 1971-73, chief instr Electrical and Mechanical Sch RSME Chatham 1973-75, CRE specialist team RE acting as consulting engrs for Govt of Malta 1975-77, cdr RE team Br mil mission to Saudi Nat Gd Riyadh Saudi Arabia 1978-80, chief infrastructure programmes and SACEURS rep on NATO infrastructure ctee 1980-83; dep sec ACE (asst sec from 1954); Freeman City of London, Liveryman Worshipful Co of Engrs 1986; FICE, FIMechE; *Recreations* golf; *Style—* Col Charles Peacey; 11 Prospect Row, Brompton, Gillingham, Kent ME7 5AL (☎ 0634 43123); 46 Riverside Ct, Nine Elms La, London SW8 5BY (☎ 01 627 2818); Association of Consulting Engineers, Alliance House, 12 Caxton St, London SW1H 0QL (☎ 01 222 6557, fax 01 222 0750)

PEACH, Denis Alan; s of Richard Peach (d 1979), of Worthing, and Alice Ellen, *née* Fraser (d 1982); *b* 10 Jan 1928; *Educ* Selhurst GS; *m* 1957, Audrey Hazel, da of Allan Chamberlain (d 1970); *Career* Home Off 1946-82 (asst under-sec state 1974-82); chief charity cmmr 1982-; *Recreations* painting, gardening; *Clubs* Reform; *Style—* Denis

Peach, Esq; 36 The Vale, Coulsdon, Surrey CR3 2AW (☎ 01 660 6752; office: 01 214 6069)

PEACH, Leonard Harry; s of Harry Peach (d 1985), of Walsall, Staffs, and Beatrice Lilian, *née* Tuck (d 1978), of Walsall, Staffs; *b* 17 Dec 1932; *Educ* Queen Mary's GS Walsall, Pembroke Coll Oxford (MA), LSE (Dip Personnel Mgmnt); *m* 15 March 1958, Doreen Lilian, da of John Roland Barker (d 1979), of West Molesey, Surrey; 2 s (Mark Philip b 1964, David John b 1967); *Career* Nat Serv 1951-53, 2 Lt 1 Bn S Lancs Regt 1952; Capt TA S Bn 5 Staffs Regt 1953-65; res asst to Randolph S Churchill 1956, various personnel mgmnt appts 1956-71, dir of personnel IBM (UK) Ltd 1971-72, gp dir personnel IBM (Europe, Africa, Middle East) 1972-75, dir of personnel and corporate affrs IBM (UK) Ltd 1975-85, seconded to DHSS as dir of personnel NHS Mgmnt Bd 1985-86, chief exec NHS Mgmnt Bd 1986-89, dir of personnel IBM (UK) Ltd 1989; dir IBM: UK Rentals 1971-76, UK Hldgs 1976-85 and 1989-, Pensions Tst 1976-85 and 1989-; chm NHS Trg Authy 1986-; memb: NHS Supervisory Bd 1986-89, Data Protection Tbnl 1985-; pres IPM 1983-85, chm IPM Servs Ltd, vice chm PCL; govr Portsmouth GS; FRSA 1979, CIPM 1983, CIBM 1988; *Recreations* opera, theatre, cricket, gardening; *Style*— Leonard Peach, Esq; Crossacres, Meadow Rd, Wentworth, Virginia Water, Surrey GU25 4NH (☎ 099 04 2258); IBM Ltd, P O Box 41, North Harbour, Portsmouth, Hants PO6 3AU (☎ 0705 321 212, telex 86741 IBM FOR G) 86741 (IBM PQR G)

PEACH, (Alfred) Nowell Hamilton; s of Alec Hamilton Peach (d 1961), of Clifton, Bristol, and Madeline Lucy Pugh White (d 1963); desc from John Peach (d 1670), Lord of the Manor, of Hollington, Derbys; *b* 30 June 1913; *Educ* Clifton, Bristol Univ Medical Sch (MB, ChB, FRCS); *m* 10 Sept 1949, Pauline Patricia Esther, da of Edward John Ward, of Pagham, W Sussex; 1 s (Michael b 1952), 4 da (Caroline b 1950, Judith b 1954, Elizabeth b 1956, Patricia b 1960); *Career* Fl-Lt (VR) Med Serv RAF 1939-46, M in D Malaya (Japanese POW), Java 1942-45; RSO Surgical Professorial Unit Bristol Royal Infirmary 1946, GP and surgn Horsham Hosp 1954-78, assoc surgical registrar Guys Hosp 1952-54; photographic works in: Br Birds Journal 1963-80, Birds of the World 1970; prints Nat Collection of Nature Conservancy Cncl 1968; FRCS; *Recreations* badminton (Glos Co colours 1936), bird photography; *Clubs* Zoological Photographic (former pres); *Style*— Nowell Peach, Esq; 124 Brighton Rd, Horsham, W Sussex RH13 6EY (☎ 62573)

PEACOCK, Prof Sir Alan Turner; DSC (1945); s of Prof Alexander David Peacock (d 1976), and Clara Mary, *née* Turner (d 1983); *b* 26 June 1922; *Educ* Dundee HS, Univ of St Andrews (MA); *m* 23 Feb 1944, Margaret Martha, da of Henry John Astell Burt (d 1960); 2 s (David Michael b 1945, Richard Alan b 1947); 1 da (Helen Mary (Mrs Charlton) b 1950); *Career* Lt RNVR 1943-45; prof of econs: Univ of Edinburgh 1956-62, Univ of York 1962-77, Univ of Buckingham 1978-84 (princ vice chllr 1980-84); chief econ advsr and dep sec DTI 1973-76, chm Ctee on Financing BBC 1985-86; res prof public fin Heriot-Watt Univ; chm Scottish Arts Cncl, exec dir David Hume Inst Edinburgh, managing tstee Inst of Econ Affrs 1987-, memb panel of econ advsrs Sec of State for Scotland 1987-; Hon D: Stirling 1974, Zurich 1984, Buckingham 1986; FBA 1979; kt 1987; *Books* numerous books and publications in professional journals mainly on economics topics and occasionally on music; *Recreations* trying to write serious music, wine spotting, jogging; *Clubs* Reform, Naval; *Style*— Prof Sir Alan Peacock, DSC; 8 Gilmour Rd, Edinburgh EH16 5NF (☎ 031 667 0544); David Hume Institute, 12 Hope St, Edinburgh EH2 4DD (☎ 031 225 6298)

PEACOCK, Hon Andrew Sharp; MHR (Lib) for Kooyong Vic 1966; s of Andrew Sharp Peacock (d 1962), of Brighton, Vic, and Iris Emily Peacock (d 1976); *b* 13 Feb 1939; *Educ* Scotch Coll Melbourne, Melbourne Univ (LLB); *m* 1963 (m dis 1977), Susan (she m 2, Robert Sangser, m 3, Francis Renouf), da of Hon Sir John Rossiter, KBE; 3 da (Caroline b 1964, Ann b 1965, Jane b 1966); *Career* Capt Army Res; barr and slr; pres Vic Lib Party 1965-66, min for Army 1969-72, min Assisting PM 1969-71, min Assisting Tres 1971-72, min for External Territories 1972, shadow min for Foreign Affrs 1973-75, min for Environment 1975, min for Foreign Affrs 1975-80, min for Industl Rels 1980-81; resigned from Cabinet 1981 but returned as min for Indust and Commerce Oct 1982-March 1983; ldr of the Oppn Fed Govt of Australia 1983-; shadow min for Foreign Affrs 1985-87; dep ldr of the Oppn and Shadow Tres 1987-; *Recreations* surfing, theatre, reading, horse racing; *Clubs* Melbourne; *Style*— The Hon Andrew Peacock, MP; 48 Berry Street, East Melbourne, 3002, Australia; House of Representatives, Canberra, ACT 2600, Australia (☎ 062 72 1211)

PEACOCK, Annette; da of Miles Coleman (d 1969), and Frieda, *née* Morell; *b* 8 Jan 1941; *Educ* El Cajon HS, LACC, Mill Brook, Julliard Sch of Music; *m* 1, 1960 (m dis 1967) Gary Peacock; 1 da (Solo b 5 Aug 1966); m 2, 31 Aug 1983, Jeremy Belshaw, s of Prof DGR Belshaw; 1 da (Avalon b 15 Oct 1983); *Career* originator of Free-Form Songform and Philosetry and voice plus band through prototype synthesizers, electronic arranger, prodr, record company proprietor; works incl LPs: Revenge 1969, Improvisie 1971, Dual Unity 1972, I'm The One 1972, X Dreams 1978, The Perfect Release 1979, Sky-Skating 1982, Been in the Streets Too Long 1983, I Have No Feelings 1986, Abstract-Contact 1988; performances incl: Wired For Sound Philharmonic Hall, Lincoln Center NYC 1970, Montrieux Jazz festival 1972, holographic actress in show with Salvador Dali on Broadway NYC 1973; MCPS, PRS;; *Style*— Ms Annette Peacock; Ironic Records, PO Box 58, Wokingham, Berks RG11 7HN (☎ 0344 772061, fax 0734 774520, telex 848210 infosG)

PEACOCK, Elizabeth Joan; MP (C) Batley and Spen 1983-; da of late John William Gates, and Dorothy Gates; *b* 4 Sept 1937; *m* 1963, Brian David, s of David Peacock, of East Marton, Skipton, N Yorks; 2 s; *Career* memb select ctee on Employment 1983-87, vice-chm Back Bench Party Orgn Ctee 1984-86, memb exec 1922 Ctee 1987-, sec Yorks Cons Membs Gp 1983-87, vice-pres Yorkshire Area Young Cons 1984-87; former memb N Yorks Co Cncl; JP 1975; memb UK Fedn of Business and Professional Women 1965-; pres Nat Assoc of Approved Driving Instrs, vice-pres Yorkshire Cons Trade Unionists 1988-; *Recreations* motoring, theatre, dressmaking; *Style*— Mrs Elizabeth J Peacock, MP; House of Commons, London SW1 (☎ 01 219 4092)

PEACOCK, Sir Geoffrey Arden; CVO (1977); s of Warren Turner Peacock (d 1966), of Crowthorne, and Elsie, *née* Naylor (d 1965); *b* 7 Feb 1920; *Educ* Wellington, Jesus Coll Cambridge (MA); *m* 1949, Mary Gillian Drew, da of Dr Harold Drew Lander (d 1967), of Cornwall; 2 da; *Career* served RA and Royal Lincoln Regt 1939-46, Lt-Col AA Cmd and Burma; pres War Crimes Ct Singapore; barr Inner Temple, legal asst Treasy Slr's Dept 1949, princ Treasy 1954, sr legal asst Treasy Slr's Dept 1958; Remembrancer City of London 1968-81, master: Co of Watermen and Lightermen of the River Thames 1986, Worshipful Co of Pewterers 1985, 1986 and 1988; kt 1981; *Recreations* sailing, rowing, beagling; *Clubs* Leander, London Rowing, Cruising Assoc, City Livery; *Style*— Sir Geoffrey Peacock, CVO; Haymarsh, Duncton, nr Petworth, West Sussex GU28 0JY

PEACOCK, Graham John; s of John Eward Peacock (d 1946), of 60 Herne Hill Rd, London, and Grace Hendry, *née* Samdison; *b* 21 Dec 1944; *Educ* Sedgehill Sch Beckenham Kent; *m* 26 April 1969 (m dis 1981), Outi-Maija, da of Paavo Hietanen (d 1970); 2 s (John Edward b 19 Dec 1969, Angus Graham b 14 July 1971); m 2, 23 March 1985, Georgina Barbara, da of Walter Albert Lloyds (d 1984); 1 s (Ross Graems Mathew b 13 June 1982), 1 da (Hannah Rose Grace b 12 Sept 1986); *Career* memb Met Police 1964-; memb: London branch Royal Order of St George, Farringdon Without Ward; Police Long Serv and Good Conduct Medal; Freeman City of London 1976, Liveryman Worshipful Co Loriners 1977; *Recreations* rugby, shooting; *Clubs* City Livery, United Wards; *Style*— Graham Peacock, Esq; 80 Chapel Green, Reedham Drive, Purley, Surrey CR2 4DS (☎ 01 660 5497); Norbury Police Station, 1516 London Rd, Norbury SW16 4EU (☎ 01 680 6100)

PEACOCK, Prof Joseph Henry; s of Harry James Peacock, OBE (d 1975), and Florence, *née* Milton (d 1979); *b* 22 Oct 1918; *Educ* Reading Sch, Bristol GS, Univ of Birmingham (MB, ChB); *m* 24 June 1950, Gilliam Frances, da of Frederick George Augustus Pinckney (d 1951), of The Old Vicarage, Fisherton De La Mere, Wylye Wilts; 1 s (Colin Henry b 1954), 1 da (Christabel Phyllis b 1958); *Career* WWII RAMC 1942-47, RMO 19 Royal Fus 1943, served hosps in India and Malaya; demonstrator in anatomy Univ of Birmingham 1947, prof of surgical sci Univ of Bristol 1972 (lectr 1953, reader 1965); conslt surgn: Utd Bristol Hosps 1955, SW Regnl Hosp Bd 1960; memb Gen Med Cncl 1975-85 (chm overseas sub-ctee F 1980-85), memb SW Regnl Hosp Bd 1975-84 (chm res ctee 1981-84), pres Vascular Surgical Soc GB 1976 (fndr memb), memb Surgical Res Soc and Euro Soc of Surgical Res; Rockefeller Fell Ann Arbor Michigan 1950; examiner LDS 1958-63, primary FRCS 1965-71 (memb ct of examiners 1976-82, chm 1982); examiner in surgery: Univ of Bristol, Univ of Birmingham, Univ of London, Univ of Wales, Univ of Liverpool, Univ of Ghana, Univ of Sudan; Jacksonian Prize RCS 1954 and 1967, Hunterian prof 1956, Arris and Gale lectr 1960; memb of ct: Univ of Bath, Univ of Bristol; MRCS 1941, LRCP 1941, FRCS 1949, memb BMA, fell Assoc Surgns GB, hon memb Coller Surgical Soc USA; *Books* Liver Transpantation & Vascular Surgery (contrib 1960), Colston Symposium (1967), Liver Transplantation (1988); *Recreations* short wave radio, gardening, travel; *Clubs* Army and Navy; *Style*— Prof Joseph Peacock; The Old Manor, Ubley, Nr Bristol BS18 6PJ (☎ 0761 62733)

PEACOCK, (Ian) Michael; s of Norman Henry Peacock; *b* 14 Sept 1929; *Educ* Kimball Union Acad USA, Welwyn Garden City GS, LSE; *m* 1956, Daphne Lee; 2 s, 1 da; *Career* md Video Arts TV Ltd 1978-, chm Monitor Enterprises Ltd 1970-; dir: Video Arts Ltd, Greater Manchester Ind Radio Ltd; *Style*— Michael Peacock, Esq; 21 Woodlands Rd, Barnes, London SW13 (☎ 01 876 2025)

PEACOCKE, Rev Dr Arthur Robert; s of (Arthur) Charles Peacocke (d 1961), of Watford, Herts, and Rose Elizabeth, *née* Lilly (d 1967); *b* 29 Nov 1924; *Educ* Watford Boys' GS, Exeter Coll Oxford (BA, BSc, MA, DPhil, DSc, DD), Univ of Cambridge (ScD by incorporation), Univ of Birmingham (BD); *m* 7 Aug 1948, Rosemary Winifred, da of Edgar Mann (d 1970), of Cheltenham; 1 s (Christopher b 1950), 1 da (Jane b 1953); *Career* asst lectr, lectr and sr lectr Birmingham Univ 1948-59, lectr in biochemistry Univ of Oxford, fell and tutor St Peter's Coll Oxford 1959-73, dean, fell, tutor and dir of studies in theology Clare Coll Cambridge 1973-84, prof Judeo-Christian Studies Tulane Univ 1984; dir Ian Ramsey Centre St Cross Coll Oxford 1985-88; lay reader Oxford Dio 1960-71, ordained 1971, vice pres Science and Religion Forum 1978- (chm 1972-78), warden Soc of Ordained Scientists 1987-; Oxford Univ: Bampton lectr 1978, select preacher 1973 and 1975; Hulsean preacher Cambridge Univ 1976; sec, 2 chm Br Biophysical Soc 1965-69; Lecomte du Nouy Prize 1983; Hon DSc De Pauw Univ Indiana 1983; *Books* Molecular Basis of Heredity (with JB Drysale 1965), Science and the Christian Experiment (1971), Osmotic Pressure of Biological Macromolecules (with MP Tombs 1974), From Cosmos to Love (with J Dominian 1974), Creation and the World of Science (1974), Intimations of reality (1984), God and the New Biology (1986), The Physical Chemistry of Biological Organization (1983) ; *Recreations* music, hill walking, churches; *Style*— Rev Dr Arthur Peacocke, SOSc; 55 St John St, Oxford, OX1 2LQ (☎ 0865 512 041); St Cross College, Oxford, OX1 3LZ

PEAKE, Brig (Anthony) Brian Lowsley; QHS (1983-85); s of Col Henry Gilbert Peake (d 1972), and Ethel Ruie, *née* Lowsley (d 1977); *b* 18 Mar 1925; *Educ* Epsom Coll, Univ of Cambridge (MA), St Thomas's Hosp; *m* 23 May 1959, Barbara Grace, da of Dr William Alexander Lister (d 1981); 1 s (David b 1960), 3 da (Dinah b 1961, Gillian b 1966, Rachael b 1968); *Career* RAMC 1953-85, Brig, CO BMH Hannover 1972-73, CO LMMH Aldershot 1983-85, conslt advsr to MOD in Obstetrics and Gynaecology; memb Postgrad Ctee Royal Coll of Obstetricians and Gynaecologists 1983-85; MRCS, LRCP, FRCOG; *Recreations* fly fishing, game shooting, stalking; *Style*— Brig Brian Peake, QHS; Parsonage House, Hampstead Norreys, nr Newbury, Berks

PEAKE, David Alphy Edward Raymond; s of Sir Harald Peake (d 1978), and his 1 w Resy, OBE, *née* Countess de Baillet Latour; *b* 27 Sept 1934; *Educ* Ampleforth, Ch Ch Oxford; *m* 1962, Susanna, da of Sir Cyril Kleinwort (d 1980); 1 s, 1 da; *Career* 2 Lt Royal Scots Greys 1953-55; banker; chm: Hargreaves Gp plc, Kleinwort Benson Gp plc 1989-; dir: Kleinwort Benson Ltd, BNP plc, M & G Gp plc; *Clubs* Brooks's, Cavalry and Guards', Pratt's; *Style*— David Peake, Esq; Sezincote House, Moreton-in-Marsh, Glos (☎ 0386 700 444); 15 Ilchester Place, London W14 (☎ 01 602 2375)

PEAKE, Air Cdre Dame Felicity Hyde; (Lady Peake); DBE (1949, MBE 1941), AE, JP; da of late Col Humphrey Watts, OBE, TD; *b* 1 May 1913; *Educ* St Winifred's Eastbourne, Les Grands Huguenots (Vaucresson, Seine et Oise, France); *m* 1, 1935, John Charles Mackenzie Hanbury (ka 1939); m 2, 1952, as his 2 w, Sir Harald Peake, AE (d 1978); 1 s (Andrew, b 1956); *Career* joined ATS Co of RAF 1939, cmmnd WAAF 1939, served at home and M East; dir: WAAF 1946-49, WRAF (from its inception) 1949-50; ret 1950; Hon ADC to King George VI 1949-50; memb RAF Benevolent Fund 1946- (vice-pres 1978), tstee Imperial War Museum 1963-85, re-elected govr London House 1978-; pres and fndg memb The Friends of the Imperial War Museum 1988- (chm 1986-88); *Style*— Air Commodore Dame Felicity Peake, DBE, AE, JP; 2 Shepherd's Close, Shepherd's Place, Upper Brook St, London W1Y

3RT (☎ 01 629 1264); Court Farm, Tackley, Oxford OX5 3AQ (☎ 086 983 221)

PEAKE, Hon Henrietta Cecilia Imogen; da of 2 Viscount Ingleby; *b* 1961; *Style—* The Hon Henrietta Peake

PEAKE, John Morris; CBE (1986); s of Albert Edward Peake (d 1977), of Cambridge, and Ruby, *née* Morris (d 1978); *b* 26 August 1924; *Educ* Repton, Clare Coll Cambridge (MA), RNC Greenwich (Dip Naval Arch); *m* 9 May 1953, Elizabeth, da of Arthur Rought, MC (d 1972), of Lympstone, Devon; 1 s (Christopher b 1956), 1 da (Catharine b 1954); *Career* RCNC 1944-50; with Personnel Admin Ltd 1950-51, dir Baker Perkins 1956-63 (joined 1951), jt md Baker Perkins Ltd 1963-66, md Baker Perkins PTY Aust 1969-74, pres Baker Perkins Inc USA 1975-77, md Baker Perkins Hldgs 1980-85 (dep md 1978-79), chm Baker Perkins plc 1984-87; memb Chemicals and Minerals Requirements Bd 1978-81; CBI Cncl 1980: chm overseas scholarships bd 1981-87, chm educn and trg ctee 1986-88, chm bd for engrg BTEC 1985 (memb BTEC Cncl 1986); memb RSA Peterborough 1988; chm Nene Tst Peterborough 1988; hockey Silver Medal London Olympics 1948; Hon DTech CNAA 1986; FInstD 1956, FIMA 1967, FIMechE 1969, CBIM 1978, FRSA 1984; *Recreations* sport, travel; *Clubs* East India, MCC; *Style—* John Peake, Esq, CBE; Old Castle Farmhouse, Stibbington, Peterborough PE8 6LP (☎ 0780 782683)

PEAKE, Hon Katherine Emma Charlotte; da of 2 Viscount Ingleby; *b* 1963; *Style—* The Hon Katherine Peake

PEAKE, Michael I'Anson; s of Arthur I'Anson Peake (d 1981), of Hillside, Benllech, Anglesey, and Eileen Constance Peake; *b* 25 Nov 1949; *Educ* Rydal Sch, Univ of London (LLB); *m* 11 July 1981, Mrs Dilys Shone; 2 s (Christopher I'Anson b 1981, Daniel Michael b 1984), 1 step s (Richard Arthur Shone b 1977); *Career* slr, ptnr Spittle & Howard; memb: contentious sub-ctee of local Law Soc, Slrs' Complaints Panel; *Recreations* golf; *Clubs* Warrington Golf; *Style—* Michael Peake, Esq; Norton House, Hobb Lane, Moore, Warrington (☎ 0925 74 645); Spittle & Howard, 16 Walton Rd, Stockton Heath, Warrington, Cheshire (☎ 0925 68483)

PEAKE, Peter Lowsley; s of Col Henry Gilbert Peake (d 1973), of Parsonage House, Hampstead Norreys, Berks, and Mary Ethel Ruie, *née* Lowsley (d 1977); *b* 15 July 1923; *Educ* Haileybury ISC, Sandhurst; *m* 1 March 1952, Mary Gildroy, da of Edward Philip Shaw (d 1970), of Commoners, Englefield Green, Surrey; 2 s (Simon b 1953, Anthony b 1960), 1 da (Philippa b 1957); *Career* cmmnd The Life Gds 1943, ret 1955 Maj; ptnr stockbroking firm, Menter of London; memb Stock Exchange 1960, ret 1983; memb Worshipful Co of Blacksmiths 1968; Chevalier of the Order of the Dannebrog Denmark 1951; *Style—* Peter Lowlsey Peake, Esq; Chantry Dene, Fort Rd, Guildford, Surrey (☎ 0483 60697)

PEAKER, Prof Malcolm; s of Ronald Smith Peaker, of Stapleford, Nottingham, and Marion, *née* Tomasin; *b* 21 August 1943; *Educ* Henry Mellish GS Nottingham, Univ of Sheffield (BSc), Univ of Hong Kong (PhD); *m* 23 Oct 1965, Stephanie Jane, da of Lt-Cdr J G Large, DFC; 3 s (Christopher James Gordon, Alexander John, Nicholas Edward) ; *Career* ARC Inst of Animal Physiology 1968-78, head physiology dept Hannah Res Inst 1978-81, dir and Hannah prof Univ of Glasgow 1981-; FZS 1969, FIBiol 1979, FRSE 1983; *Books* Salt Glands in Birds and Reptiles (1975), Avian Physiology (ed 1975), Comparative Aspects of Lactation (ed 1977), Physiological Strategies in Lactation (ed); *Recreations* zoology, natural history, golf; *Clubs* Farmers, Turnberry GC, Zoological; *Style—* Prof Malcolm Peaker; 13 Upper Crofts, Alloway, Ayr KA7 4QX; Hannah Research Inst, Ayr KA6 5HL (☎ 0292 76013, 0292 671052)

PEARCE, (John) Allan (Chaplin); s of John William Ernest Pearce (d 1951), of South Villa, Vale of Health, London, and Irene Kate, *née* Chaplin (d 1962); *b* 21 Oct 1912; *Educ* Charterhouse, Brasenose Coll Oxford (BA), Univ of London (LLB); *m* 18 Nov 1948, Raffaella Elizabetta Maria, da of Avv Umberto Baione, of 85 Via Cavour, Florence; 2 s (Laurence b 1949, Charles b 1952); *Career* cmmnd Lt Co of London Yeo, serv Libya, Egypt, Sicily, Italy 1941-44, Maj, mil mission to Italian Army Rome 1945-46; admitted slr 1947, Sandilands Williamson Hill & Co London 1952-70, Church Cmmrs for England Legal Dept 1970-78; ctee memb Br Italian Soc 1967, hon tres of Venice in Peril Fund 1970-86, fndr memb, chm & vice-pres Turner Soc 1976-85 (whose call for a Turner Gallery was answered in 1987); Liveryman Worshipful Co of Skinners 1937; memb Law Soc 1947; kt of the Order of Merit (Italy) 1978; *Recreations* travel, reading, painting; *Clubs* Travellers, Hurlingham; *Style—* Allan Pearce, Esq; 32 Brompton Sq, London SW3 2AE (☎ 01 584 9429)

PEARCE, Andrew; MEP (C) Cheshire West 1979-; s of Henry Pearce (d 1964); *b* 1 Dec 1937; *Educ* Rydal Sch Colwyn Bay, Univ of Durham; *m* 1966, Myra, da of Kevin Whelan, of Co Wexford; 3 s, 1 da; *Career* formerly mgmnt servs exec; princ admin Cmmn of the Euro Communities Brussels 1974-79, contested (C) Islington North 1969 and 1970; *Style—* Andrew Pearce, Esq, MEP; 30 Grange Rd, W Kirby, Wirral, L48 4HA (☎ 051 625 1896)

PEARCE, Sir Austin William; CBE (1974); s of William Thomas Pearce (d 1970); *b* 1 Sept 1921; *Educ* Devonport HS for Boys, Univ of Birmingham (BSc, PhD); *m* 1, 1947, Maglona Winifred Twinn (d 1975); 3 da; m 2, Dr Florence Patricia Grice, da of John Walter Forsythe; *Career* chm and chief exec Esso Petroleum Co Ltd 1972-80 (joined Esso when called Agwi Petroleum 1945, dir 1963, md 1968-71), dir Williams & Glyn's Bank 1974-85 (chm 1983-85), Royal Bank of Scotland Gp 1978- (vice-chm 1985-); chm: Br Aerospace 1980-87 (dir 1977-, memb organising ctee 1976), Oxford Instruments 1987-, CBI Industl Policy Ctee 1982-86; non-exec dir: Pearl Assur plc 1985-, Jaguar plc 1986-, Smiths Industs plc 1986-; former pres Inst of Petroleum, chm UK Petroleum Indust Assoc, pt/t memb NRDC 1973-76, memb Standing Cmmn on Energy and Environment 1978-81, pres Soc of Br Aerospace Cos 1982-83, pro chllr Univ of Surrey 1985-, chm bd of tstes Sci Museum 1986-, tres Royal Soc of Arts Mfrs and Commerce (RSA) 1988-; Br Assoc of Industl Eds Communicator of the Year Award 1983; Hon DSc Southampton 1978, Hon DSc Exeter 1985; Hon DEng Birmingham 1986, Hon DSc Salford 1987, Hon DSC Cranfield 1987; kt 1980; *Clubs* Athenaeum, Royal Wimbledon GC, R & A GC; *Style—* Sir Austin Pearce, CBE; c/o Royal Bank of Scotland, 67 Lombard St, London EC3 (☎ 01 623 4356)

PEARCE, Brian Harold; s of (John) Harold George Pearce (d 1982), of Sevenoaks, and Dorothy Elsie; *b* 30 July 1931; *Educ* Tonbridge, UCL (BEng); *m* 1, 3 Sept 1955, Jean Isabel, *née* Richardson (d 1985); 2 s (Nicholas Michael John b 1959, Jonathan Brian Miles b 1966), 1 da (Gillian Sarah (Mrs Mueller-Pearce) b 1961); m 2, 2 Aug 1988, Veronica Mary, *née* Maund, formerly Mrs Magraw; *Career* Nat Serv RE 1953-55 (cmmnd 2 Lt 1954); gp chm Pearce Signs Ltd and subsidiaries 1981- (gp md 1975); vice chm Royal London Soc for the Blind, bd memb Deptford Enterprise Agency; cncl memb: Goldsmith Coll London, Business in the Community; various offices London C of C & Indust, pres Br Sign Assoc, pres Euro Fedn of Illuminated Signs; Freeman: City of London, Worshipful Co of Lightmongers; *Recreations* sailing; *Clubs* RAC, Little Ship, Royal Cornwall YC; *Style—* Brian Pearce, Esq; Pearce Signs Ltd, Insigna House, London SE14 6AB

PEARCE, (John) Brian; s of George Frederic Pearce (d 1963), of Wakefield and Sidmouth, and Constance Josephine, *née* Seed (d 1967); *b* 25 Sept 1935; *Educ* Queen Elizabeth GS Wakefield, Brasenose Coll Oxford (BA); *m* 30 June 1960, Michelle, da of Alfred Starr Etcheverry (ka 1944); 4 s (Christoper David b 1963, Colin Alexander b 1965, Jonathan Edward b 1969, James Frederic Lauriston b 1970); *Career* Nat Serv RAF 1954-56, Pilot Offr 1955-56; Miny of Power 1959-60, Colonial Off 1960-67, Dept of Econ Affrs 1967-69, Civil Serv Dept 1969-81, HM Treasy 1981-84 (under sec 1976-84), dir Inter Faith Network for UK 1987-; *Recreations* reading (mainly theology), travel; *Style—* Brian Pearce, Esq; 124 Court Lane, London SE21 7EA; 5-7 Tavistock Place, London WC1 (☎ 01 388 0008)

PEARCE, Hon Mrs; Hon Constance Ada; *née* Caulfield; da of late 11 Viscount Charlemont; *b* 1918; *m* 1943, Henry Edward Pearce; 2 s, 3 da; *Style—* The Hon Mrs Pearce; 254 Mooroondu Rd, Thorneside, Queensland 4158, Australia

PEARCE, David John; s of Dr Raymond Maplesden Pearce (d 1976), and Ivy, *née* Shingler (d 1960); *b* 25 Mar 1928; *Educ* Manchester GS, Univ of Manchester (BSc); *m* 1, 24 Feb 1954, Doreen (d 1977), da of John Valentine (d 1964), of Brindle Heath, Salford; 1 s (Andrew b 1959), 1 da (Shiela b 1962); m 2, 7 June 1986, Eileen, da of John Alfred Corlett (d 1961), of Wigan; 2 step s (Paul b 1953, Barry b 1954), 1 step da (Tina-Ann b 1959); *Career* Nat Serv Lance Corpl HQ RE BAOR 1951-53; graduate engr Oscar Faber and Ptnrs consulting engrs 1949-51, res engr Spillers Ltd 1949-51, asst engr Mrez and McLlelan 1953-54, sr devpt engr Matthews and Mumby Ltd (asst engr, pt/t lectr) 1954-71, ptnr Dennis Matthews and Ptnrs 1972-79 (sr engr 1971-72), ptnr Pearce Matthews Ptnrship 1979-88; res ptnr Wallace Evans and Ptnrs Northern off (incorporating Pearce Matthews) 1988-; chm Lancs and Ches branch IStructE 1983; AMIStructE 1953, MICE 1958, FIStructE 1969, MConsE 1970; *Recreations* travel, walking, swimming, crafts; *Clubs* Rotary (Worsley); *Style—* David Pearce, Esq; 16 Chaseley Road, Pendleton, Salford M6 7DZ (☎ 061 736 5045); Wallace Evans and Ptnrs, Bruntwood Hall, Schools Hill, Cheadle, Cheshire SK8 1JD (☎ 061 491 1608, fax 061 491 3151)

PEARCE, Baron (Life Peer UK 1962); Edward Holroyd Pearce; PC (1957); s of late John W E Pearce; *b* 9 Feb 1901; *Educ* Charterhouse, Corpus Christi Coll Oxford (hon fell 1950); *m* 1927, Erica Doris (d 1985), da of late Bertram Priestman; 2 s (1 decd); *Career* barr Lincoln's Inn and Middle Temple 1925; KC 1945, bencher Hon Soc of Lincoln's Inn 1948, tres 1966; High Ct judge (probate, divorce and Admty) 1948-54, Queen's Bench 1954-57; lord justice of Appeal 1957-62, lord of appeal in Ordinary 1962-69; chm: Press Cncl 1969-74, Appeals Ctee Takeover Panel 1969-76; RBA 1940; kt 1948; *Style—* The Rt Hon the Lord Pearce, PC; Sweethaws, Crowborough, Sussex (☎ 089 26 61520)

PEARCE, Sir Eric Herbert; OBE (1970); s of Herbert Clement Pearce; *b* 5 Mar 1905; *Educ* Raynes Sch Hants; *m* 1956, Betty Constance Ham; 1 da; *Career* radio announcer; dir of programmes Major Broadcasting Network 1955-56, newsreader/chief announcer HSV7, then GTV 9, dir Community Affrs Gen TV Corpn Channel Nine 1979-; kt 1979; *Clubs* Athenaeum, Toorak Services (Melbourne); *Style—* Sir Eric Pearce, OBE; GTV Channel Nine, 22 Bendigo St, Richmond, Vic 3121, Australia

PEARCE, Dr John Dalziel Wyndham; s of John Alfred Wyndham Pearce (d 1951), of Edinburgh, and Mary Logan, *née* Dalziel (d 1933); *b* 21 Feb 1904; *Educ* George Watson's Coll, Univ of Edinburgh (MA, MB ChB, MD); *m* 1, 19 Oct 1929 (m dis), Grace, da of Robert Fowler (d 1959), of Edinburgh; m 2, 20 March 1964, (Ellinor) Elizabeth Nancy Draper, da of Ernest Isaac Lewis (d 1961), of Harrow; *Career* Lt-Col RAMC 1940-45, cmd psychiatrist NI, cmd psychiatrist Northern Cmd, OC Northfield Mil Hosp, advsr in psychiatry AFHQ CMF (despatches); former: physician i/c depts of psychiatry St Mary's Hosp and Queen Elizabeth Hosp for Children, conslt psychiatrist Royal Masonic Hosp, hon physician Tavistock Clinic and W End Hosp for Nervous Diseases, med co-dir Portman Clinic (Inst for Study and Treatment of Delinquency), medico-psychologist LCC remand homes; memb academic bd: Inst of Child Health, St Mary's Hosp Med Sch (Univ of London); examiner in med: RCP, Univ of London, Royal Coll of Psychiatrists; consulting psychiatrist: St Mary's Hosp, Queen Elizabeth Hosp for Children; chm advsy ctee on delinquent and maladjusted children Int Union for Child Welfare; memb: cncl Nat Assoc for Mental Health, Home Sec's Advsy Ccnl on Treatment of Offenders; FRCP, FRCPE, FRCPsych, FBPsS; *Books* Juvenile Delinquency (1952); *Recreations* golf, painting; *Clubs* Caledonian, New (Edinburgh); *Style—* Dr John Pearce; Flat 28, 2 Barnton Avenue West, Edinburgh EH 6EW (☎ 031 317 7116)

PEARCE, John Trevor Archdall; CMG (1964); s of Rev Canon W T L A Pearce, of NSW, Australia (d 1949), and Nona Bertha, *née* Langley (d 1964); *b* 7 May 1916; *Educ* The King's Sch Parramatta Aust, Keble Coll Oxford (MA); *m* 1948, Isabel Bundey (d 1983), da of James Rankine, of Hindmarsh Island, South Australia (d 1933); m 2, 1984, Judith Burland, da of G Kinvin Lotherington, of Harrison Street, Cremorne, NSW; *Career* WWII served Kenya, Ethiopia, Ceylon, India, Burma 1940-46, Major RE; colonial admin serv: Tanganyika, dist offr 1939, dist cmmr 1950, provincial cmmr 1959, perm sec (Admin) off of the vice pres 1961; chm Public Serv Cmmn Basutoland 1963, Swaziland 1965; registrar Papua New Guinea Univ of Technol 1969-73; *Recreations* golf; *Clubs* Headland GC (Queensland); *Style—* John Pearce, Esq, CMG; Clippings, 14 Golf St, Buderim, Qld 4556, Australia (☎ 071 452 120)

PEARCE, Maj-Gen Leslie Arthur; CB (1973), CBE (1971, OBE 1964, MBE 1956); *b* 22 Jan 1918; *Educ* N Zealand; *m* 1944, Fay Mattocks, of Auckland, NZ; 2 s, 1 da; *Career* Ch of Gen Staff, NZ Army, 1971-73; chm, Vocational Training Council 1975-82; co dir, dep chm NZ Cncl for Educational Research 1977-85; *Style—* Major-General Leslie Pearce, CB, CBE; 1064A Beach Road, Torbay, Auckland, New Zealand

PEARCE, (George) Malcolm; MBE (1987), JP; s of (Edward) Ewart Pearce, MBE, JP (d 1963), Lord Mayor of Cardiff 1961-62, and Winifred Constance, *née* Blackmore (d 1970); *b* 3 Feb 1926; *Educ* Howard Gardens HS; *m* 4 June 1949, Thelma Mavis, da of Albert John Jones (d 1987), of Cardiff; 2 s (Lester b 1954, Mark b 1967), 3 da (Patricia b 1950, Christine b 1951, Carol b 1958); *Career* Lt Paymaster RAPC Palestine 1945-47; CA; hon vice pres Boys Bde, pres Cardiff Bde 1960-87, tres Wales Festival of Remembrance 1980-; *Recreations* golf, bridge; *Clubs* Cardiff and County,

Cardiff Golf, Cardiff E Rotary; *Style—* Malcom Pearce, Esq, MBE, JP; Whitefriars, Westminster Crescent, Cardiff CF2 6SE (☎ 0222 754339)

PEARCE, Neville John Lewis; s of John Pearce (d 1940), of Bristol, and Ethel Annie Pearce ; *b* 27 Feb 1933; *Educ* Queen Elizabeth's Hosp Bristol, Silcoates Sch Wakefield, Univ of Leeds (LLB, LLM); *m* 12 April 1958, Eileen Frances, da of Herbert Francis Potter (d 1982), of Bath; 2 da (Deborah Susan (Mrs Storey) b 1961, Lindsey Jacqueline (Mrs Rich) b 1963); *Career* Nat Serv 1955-57, KOYLI 1955, cmmnd 2 Lt 1955, RASC 1955-57, Lt 1957; asst slr: Wakefield City and CBC 1955-57, Darlington CBC 1957-59; sr asst slr Grimsby CBC 1959-62, dep town clerk Grimsby CBC 1962-66, dep town clerk and dep clerk of the peace Blackpool CBC 1966-67, chief exec and town clerk Bath City and CBC 1967-73, dir of admin and co slr Avon CC 1973-82, chief exec Avon CC 1982-; lay preacher All Saints Church Weston Bath PCC, chm Bath and Wells Diocessan Social Responsibility Gp; CBIM 1987; *Recreations* work, wife, family, garden, church; *Style—* Neville Pearce, Esq; Penshurst, Weston Lane, Bath, Avon BA1 4AB (☎ 0225 26925); Avon House, Haymarket, Bristol BS99 7DE (☎ 0272 290777 ext 6251, fax 0272 250831)

PEARCE, (Ann) Philippa; da of Ernest Alexander Pearce; *Educ* Perse Girls' Sch Cambridge, Girton Coll Cambridge; *m* 1963, Martin James Graham Christie (decd); 1 da; *Career* prodr/scriptwriter Sch Broadcasting BBC Radio 1945-58; ed Educn Dept Clarendon Press 1958-60, children's ed Andre Deutsch Ltd 1960-67, freelance writer of children's fiction 1967-; *Books Incl:* Tom's Midnight Garden (Carnegie Medal 1959), A Dog So Small, The Elm Street Lot, The Battle of Bubble and Squeak (Whitbread Award 1978), The Way to Sutton Shore (1983); *Style—* Miss Philippa Pearce; c/o Kestrel Books, 27 Wrights Lane W85TZ

PEARCE, Thomas Neill; OBE (1979), TD; s of Thomas Henry Pearce (d 1944), and Amelia Harriet, *née* Neill (d 1954); *b* 3 Nov 1905; *Educ* Christ's Hosp; *m* 1935, Stella Mary (d 1978), da of Thomas Rippon (d 1934), of Chelmsford; 1 s (Christopher), 2 da (Valerie, Rosemary); *Career* Maj RA ADGB; capt Essex Co Cricket Club 1933-50; mangr MCC to India, Pakistan and Ceylon 1961-62; dir Finsbury Distillery Co Ltd; rugby football Middlesex and London Counties int referee, Old Blues RFC; *Recreations* watching cricket and rugby football; *Clubs* MCC, Essex CCC, Lord's Taverners, Br Sportsman's (hon sec); *Style—* Thomas Pearce, Esq, OBE; 10 Fontwell Close, Findon Valley, Worthing, Sussex BN14 0AD

PEARCEY, Leonard Charles; s of Leonard Arthur Pearcey, of Dorset, and Jessie Sinclair, *née* Millar (d 1965); *b* 6 June 1938; *Educ* Christ's Hosp, CCC Cambridge (MA); *Career* PA MD Hargreaves Gp 1957-59, dir studies Rapid Results Corr Coll 1962-63, teacher Wimbledon 1964-65, arts admin Harold Holt Ltd 1965-66, music dir Guildhall Sch of Music and Drama 1966-70, competition sec Int Violin Competition 1966-70, dir Merton Festival 1972-76, involved in numerous major arts and religious programmes, also own series singer/guitarist, composer numerous songs and arrangements, prodr/presenter maj presentations, conferences, award ceremonies, admin BBC Radio Times Drama Awards and Comedy Awards, stage coordinator/ compere World Travel Mkt (memb advsy cncl), ed Music Teacher Magazine 1980-85, featured columnist Classical Music Magazine 1979-85; pres Polruan Regatta Carnival and Children's Sports; Mayoress (sic) London Borough of Merton 1973-74; memb Actors Equity; *Books* The Musician's Survival Kit (1979), contrib Radio Times; *Recreations* travel; *Style—* Leonard Pearcey, Esq; 53 Queens Rd, London SW19 8NP (☎ 01 947 2555)

PEAREY, Capt Michael Alan; s of William Scott Pearey (d 1940), of Newcastle Upon Tyne, and Harriet Pringle, *née* Rochester (d 1972); *b* 3 June 1933; *Educ* Christ's Hosp, Britannia RNC Dartmouth; *m* 1957, Thelma Joy, da of Edward Hugh Owen, of Portsmouth; 3 s (Michael Scott b 1959, Richard Pringle b 1960, Alan Quentin b 1964),2 da (Susan Adrienne (Mrs White) b 1957, Julia Heriot b 1966); *Career* joined RN 1951, HMS Theseus 1953, RNC Greenwich 1954, HMS Dryad 1955-56, Lt 1956, HMS Sheffield 1957-58, RN Engrg Coll Manadon 1958-59, staff C-in-C Portsmouth 1960-61, staff Second Sea Lord 1962-63, HMS Lynx 1964-65, Lt Cdr 1964, HMS Neptune Clyde Submarine Base 1966-68, staff Flag Offr Malta 1969-71, Cdr 1970, Trg Cdr RN Supply Sch 1971-74, HMS Fearless 1974-75, Catering Advsr RN 1976-78, Cmd Supply Offr Naval Home Cmd 1978-79, Capt 1979, Chief Staff Offr (personal and admin) to Flag Offr Naval Air Cmd 1980-81, dir Fleet Supply Duties 1982-84, dir Naval Offr Appts (S and S Offrs and WRNS), dir Naval Manpower and Trg 1984-86, ret 1986; clerk Christ's Hosp Horsham 1986-; chm London HCIMA 1983-85; vice pres RFU 1987- (ctee memb 1968-); represented at rugby: RN, Combined Servs, Northumberland, Hants, Devon, Barbarians; Freeman: Newcastle Upon Tyne 1952, City of London 1986; MHCIMA 1978; *Recreations* rugby union, tennis; *Clubs* Devonshire, East India and Public Sch Sports; *Style—* Capt Michael Pearey; Itchingfield, W Sussex; Christ's Hosp, Horsham, W Sussex (☎ 0403 211297, fax 0403 211580)

PEARL, David Brian; s of Leonard Pearl (d 1983); *b* 6 August 1944; *Educ* Wellington; *m* 1972, Rosamond Mary Katharine, da of Lt-Cdr C G de L'isle Bush, of Frampton-upon-Severn, Glos; 2 s, 1 da; *Career* chm London Securities plc and assoc cos 1970-85; Lloyd's underwriter; Medway Ports Authy 1987-; memb Westminster City Cncl 1974-81, dep Lord Mayor 1979-80, chief whip 1980-81, vice-chm Fin and Scrutiny 1981; Westminster City Cncl memb of London Tourist Bd 1980-81; chm: St Marylebone Cons Assoc 1981-83, London Central Euro Constituency 1982-85; vice-pres Westminster South Cons Assoc 1983-; FCA; MInstM; *Recreations* sports, travel; *Clubs* Reform, MCC, Guards Polo, Royal St George's Golf; *Style—* David Pearl, Esq; Mill Ride Estate, Mill Ride, North Ascot, Berks SL5 8LT (☎ 0344 88 5444)

PEARL, Prof David Stephen; s of Chaim Pearl, and Anita, *née* Newman; *b* 11 August 1944; *Educ* George Dixons Birmingham, Univ of Birmingham (LLB), Queens Coll Cambridge (LLM, MA, PhD); *m* 1, 7 April 1967 (m dis 1983), Susan, da of Joseph Roer, of Croydon, Surrey; 3 s (Julian Kim b 1969, Daniel Benjamin Meir b 1971, Marcus Alexander Jethro b 1974); m 2, 4 Oct 1985, Gillian, da of Ryzard Maciejewski, of Melbourne, Royston, Herts; *Career* barr Gray's Inn 1968, fell and dir studies in law Fitzwilliam Coll Cambridge 1969-, univ lectr 1972-89, prof law Univ of E Anglia 1989-; city cllr Cambridge 1972-74, co cllr Cambridge 1974-77; asst rec 1985-, pt/t adjudicator Immigration Act 1980-, asst dep coroner Cambridge 1978-, gen sec Int Soc on Family Law 1985-; *Books* A Textbook on Muslim Personal Law (1979, second edn 1987), Social Welfare Law (1981), Interpersonal Conflict of Laws (1981), Family, Law and Society (with B Hoggett 1983, second edn 1987), Family Law and Immigrant Communities (1986); *Recreations* longdistance (badly); *Style—* Prof David Pearl; 183 Huntingdon Road, Cambridge CB3 ODL; Fitzwilliam College, Cambridge (☎ 0223 332 000)

PEARL, Prof Valerie Louise; da of Cyril R Bence and Florence Bence (d 1974); *b* 31 Dec 1926; *Educ* King Edward VI HS Birmingham, St Anne's Coll Oxford (BA, MA, DPhil); *m* 1949, Morris Leonard Pearl, s of Nathan Pearl (d 1961); 1 da; *Career* prof of history of London UCL 1976-81, pres New Hall Cambridge 1981-; govr Museum of London 1978-; syndic: Cambridge Univ Library 1983-, Cambridge Univ Press 1984-; cmmr Royal Cmmn on Historical Manuscripts 1984-; *Style—* Professor Valerie Pearl; The President's Lodge, 16 Madingley Rd, Cambridge CB3 0EE (☎ 0223 63 621)

PEARLMAN, Hon Mrs (Esther); *née* Jakobovits; 4 da of Baron Jakobovits (Life Peer), Chief Rabbi of the British Cwlth, *qv*; *m* 21 Feb 1971, Rev Rabbi Chaim Zundel Pearlman, s of Ralph David Pearlman, of 11 Langport Road, Sunderland; 5 s (Yehuda b 2 Oct 1972, Eliezer b 24 Feb 1974, Ephraim b 20 June 1978, Eliyohu b 2 April 1982, Daniel b 31 July 1985), 3 da (Zipporah b 9 March 1976, Adina b 20 Jan 1980, Sarah b 10 Sept 1988); *Style—* The Hon Mrs Pearlman; 14 Mayfield Gardens, London NW4 2QA (☎ 01 202 8864)

PEARLMAN, Her Honour Judge; Valerie Anne Pearlman; da of Sidney and Marjorie Pearlman; *b* 6 August 1936; *Educ* Wycombe Abbey; *m* 1972; 1 s, 1 da; *Career* barr 1958, rec SE Circuit 1982-85, circuit judge 1985-; *Style—* Her Honour Judge Pearlman; Lamb Building, Temple, EC4Y 7AS (☎ 01 353 0774)

PEARMAN, Sir James Eugene; CBE (1960); s of Eugene Charles Pearman, and Kate, *née* Trott; *b* 24 Nov 1904; *Educ* Saltus GS Bermuda, Bromsgrove Sch Worcs, Merton Coll Oxford; *m* 1, 1929, Prudence Tucker Appleby (d 1976); 2 s (James, Richard); m 2, 1977, Mrs Antoinette Trott, da of Dr James Aiguier, of Philadelphia; *Career* barr Middle Temple; memb Colonial Parl Bermuda 1943-72, MLC 1972-, sr ptnr Conyers Dill & Pearman; hon consul for Bolivia; kt 1973; *Clubs* Royal Bermuda Yacht, Midocean; *Style—* Sir James Pearman, CBE; Tideway, Point Shares, Pembroke 557, Bermuda (☎ 2 1125, 5 1422); Bank of Bermuda Ltd, Hamilton 5, Bermuda, PO Box 3011

PEARSE, William Richard George (Bill); s of Richard John Pearse (d 1946), of Taunton, and Daisy May, *née* Thomas (d 1982); *b* 23 Feb 1924; *Educ* Taunton Sch; *Career* RASC 1944-46; CA 1951, memb exec ctee Robson Rhodes 1981-84, managing ptnr Apsleys 1987-; pres and co-fndr SW Soc of CAs 1978-79, rec Taunton Ct, govr Bishop Foxes Sch, cncl memb Taunton Sch, vice pres Somerset CCC, memb mgmnt ctee Somerset Co RFU, chm SW div RFU, Somerset rep RFU; Freeman: City of London 1978, Worshipful Co of Chartered Accountants in England & Wales 1978; ACA 1951, FCA 1961; *Recreations* sport, cricket, rugby football; *Clubs* East India, Victory Services; *Style—* Bill Pearse, Esq; 11 Highlands, Taunton, Somerset TA1 4HP (☎ 0823 284 701); Apsleys, Apsley House, Billet St, Taunton, Somerset TA1 3TX (☎ 0823 259 101, fax 0823 334 459)

PEARSON, Brig Alastair Stevenson; CB (1958), DSO, OBE (1953), MC, TD; *b* 1 June 1915; *Educ* Kelvinside Acad, Sedbergh; *m* 1944, Mrs Joan Morgan Weld-Smith; 3 da; *Career* farmer; Ld-Lt of Dunbartonshire 1979-; keeper Dunbarton Castle 1981-; KStJ 1980; *Style—* Brig Alastair Pearson, CB, DSO, OBE, MC, TD; Tullochan, Gartocharn, by Alexandria, Dunbartonshire (☎ Gartocharn 205)

PEARSON, Brig Barclay Andrew; DSO (1945), DL (Stirlingshire 1965); s of Andrew Pearson, WS (d 1921), of Johnston Lodge, Laurencekirk, Kincardineshire, and Mary Henrietta Dorothea, *née* Bowden-Smith; *b* 13 Jan 1912; *Educ* Sherborne, Brasenose Coll Oxford (BA); *m* 5 April 1944, Heather, da of Lewis Campbell Gray (d 1947), of Newcastle, Co Down, NI; 1 da (Richenda b 1953); *Career* 2 Lt Argyll & Sutherland Highlanders 1934, WWII served ME and NW Europe (despatches thrice), ME Staff Coll 1942, DAQMG HQ 30 Corps 1942-44, 2 i/c 2 Bn Argyll & Sutherland Highlanders, Lt-Col 1944, Cmd 8 Bn The Royal Scots 1944-45, AA QHG HQ 51 Div 1945-46, AQMG HQ BAOR 1946, GSOII (Intelligence) BJSM Washington USA 1946-48, GSO1 (asst mil attache) Br Embassy Paris 1948-50, GSO1 (Ops and SD) HQ Scottish Cmd Edinburgh 1950-51, Col (SD) HQ AFCENT Fontainebleau 1951-53, cmd 1 Bn Argyll & Sutherland Highlanders 1954-57 (British Guyana, Berlin, Suez Campaign), cmd 154 Highland Bde 1957-60; ret 1960; sec Territorial Assoc Stirlinghsire 1960-68, Lanarkshire Productivity Assoc 1968-69; Scottish sec Public Schs Appts Bureau (ISCO) 1969-78; chm: regtl museum ctee Stirling Castle 1975-89, Stirling Dist Scout Cncl 1965-85; awarded Silver Acorn (for servs to scouting) 1985; Chevalier French Legion of Honour (1949); *Recreations* shooting, golf, curling, gardening, croquet; *Clubs* Army and Navy; *Style—* Brig Barclay Pearson, DSO, DL; Spinneyburn, Rumbling Bridge, Kinross-Shire (☎ 05774 270)

PEARSON, Barrie; s of Albert James Pearson (d 1987), of Selby, Yorks, and Mary Pearson (d 1980); *b* 22 August 1939; *Educ* King's Sch Pontefract Yorks, Univ of Nottingham (BSc); *m* 1, 1962 (m dis) Georgina Ann; 1 s (Gavin b 1968), 1 da (Philippa b 1965); m 2, 1983, Catherine Campbell; *Career* The De la Rue Co, The Plessey Co, Dexion-Comino Int Ltd, non exec chm Info Transmission Ltd 1985-87; md Livingstone Fisher Assoc plc 1976-; visiting fell in corporate aquisitions and disposals City Univ Business Sch; seminar presenter for: Inst of CAs, City Univ, Strategic Planning Soc, Ashridge Mgmnt Coll; CIMA; *Books* Successful Acquisiton of Unquoted Cos (1983, third edn 1989), Common Sense Business Strategy (1987), Common Sense Time Management for Personal Success (1988); *Recreations* food guide inspector, theatre, outstanding hotels, travel; *Style—* Barrie Pearson, Esq; Campbell Ho, Weston Turville, Bucks HP22 5RQ (☎ 0296 613 828); Acre Ho, 69-76 Long Acre, London WC2E 9JW (☎ 01 379 3461)

PEARSON, Hon Charles Anthony; s (by 2 m) of 3 Viscount Cowdray, TD, qv; *b* 5 Mar 1956; *Style—* The Hon Charles Pearson; 14 Markham Sq, London SW3

PEARSON, David; s of Maurice Judge Pearson, of Saltburn, Cleveland; *b* 7 Mar 1942; *Educ* Sir William Turner's Sch Redcar Yorks, King's Coll London; *m* 1972, Christine Faith, da of Douglas Littlejohn, of Wadhurst, Sussex; 3 children; *Career* md Chetwynd Haddons Ltd; MIPA; *Recreations* skiing; *Style—* David Pearson, Esq; Coleswood Ho, Little Lane, Eastmoor Park, Harpenden, Herts

PEARSON, David Compton Froome; s of Compton Edwin Pearson, OBE (d 1977); *b* 28 July 1931; *Educ* Haileybury, Downing Coll Cambridge; *m* 1966, Venetia Jane, *née* Lynn; 2 da; *Career* slr 1957, Linklaters & Paines 1957-69 (ptnr 1961-69), dep chm Robert Fleming Hldgs Ltd 1986-; dir: Robert Fleming & Co Ltd 1969-, The Fleming Enterprise Investmt Tst plc 1971-84, Blue Circle Industs plc 1972-1987, Robert Fleming Hldgs Ltd 1974-, Lane Fox & Ptnrs Ltd 1987-; chm: The Fleming Property Unit Trust 1971-, Channel Tunnel Investmts plc 1981-1986, Gill & Duffus Gp plc

1982-85 (dir 1973-85), Robert Fleming Securities 1985-; dep chm Austin Reed Gp plc 1977- (dir 1971-), memb Fin Act 1960 Tbnl 1978-84; *Recreations* gardening; *Clubs* Brooks's; *Style—* David C F Pearson, Esq; The Manor, Berwick St John, Shaftesbury, Dorset SP7 0EX (☎ 074 788 363); c/o Robert Fleming Holdings Ltd, 25 Copthall Ave, London EC2R 7DR (☎ 01 638 5858)

PEARSON, Sir (James) Denning; JP; s of James Pearson and Elizabeth Henderson; *b* 8 August 1908; *Educ* Canton Secdy Sch Cardiff, Cardiff Tech Coll (BSc); *m* 1932, Eluned Henry; 2 da; *Career* chief exec Rolls-Royce Ltd 1958-70, chm Gamma Assocs 1972-80; pres SBAC 1963, memb NEDC 1964-67; govr: Repton Coll until 1982, Trent Coll, Manchester Business Sch; kt 1963; *Style—* Sir Denning Pearson, JP; Green Acres, Holbrook, Derbyshire (☎ Derby 881137)

PEARSON, Derek Leslie; CB (1978); s of late George Frederick Pearson and Edith Maud, *née* Dent; *b* 19 Dec 1921; *Educ* William Ellis Sch, LSE (BSE); *m* 1956, Diana Mary, da of Sir Ralph Freeman (d 1950); *Career* WWII Fleet Air Arm and subsequently Channel Air Div, Lt Cdr (A) RNVR 1955; joined Colonial Off 1947, seconded to Kenya 1954-56, dep sec Cabinet Off 1975-77, Miny of Overseas Devpt 1977-81; *Clubs* Naval, Civil Service; *Style—* Derek Pearson, Esq, CB; Langata, Little London Road, Horam, Heathfield, E Sussex TN21 OBG

PEARSON, Lady Frances Elizabeth Ann; *née* Hay; da of 11th Marquess of Tweeddale (d 1967), by his 1 w Marguerite; *b* 1926; *m* 1956, Nigel Arthur Pearson (d 1975), s of Sir Neville Arthur Pearson, 2 Bt; *Style—* Lady Frances Pearson

PEARSON, Hon Mrs (Francesca Mary); *née* Charteris; da of Baron Charteris of Amisfield, GCB, GCVO, QSO, OBE, PC (Life Peer), *qv*; *b* 27 Sept 1945; *m* 1977, Malcolm Everard MacLaren Pearson; 2 da (Marina b 1980, Zara Alexandra Mary b 1984); *Style—* The Hon Mrs Pearson; 3 Shepherd's Close, London W1Y 3RT (☎ 01 629 2569)

PEARSON, Sir Francis Fenwick; 1 Bt (UK 1964), of Gressingham, co Palatine of Lancaster Francis Fenwick; MBE (1945), DL (1966); s of Frank Pearson (d 1917), of Lonsdale, and Susan Mary Palmer; *b* 13 June 1911; *Educ* Uppingham, Trinity Hall Cambridge; *m* 1938, Katharine Mary, da of Rev David Denholm Fraser (d 1948), of Kelso; 1 s (Francis), 1 da (Susan); *Heir* Francis Nicholas Fraser; *Career* cmmnd 1 Gurkha Rifles 1932, ADC to Viceroy of India 1934-36, Indian Political Serv 1936-47, under sec Foreign and Political Dept Govt of India 1943-45; chief min Manipur State 1945-47; MP (C) Clitheroe Div 1959-70, parly sec to PM 1963-64; chm Central Lancs Devpt Corpn 1971-86; *Recreations* fishing, walking; *Clubs* Carlton; *Style—* Sir Francis Pearson, Bt, MBE, DL; Beech Cottage, Borwick, Carnforth, Lancs (☎ 0524 734191)

PEARSON, Graham Scott; s of Ernest Reginald Pearson, and Alice, *née* Maclachlan (d 1987); *b* 20 July 1935; *Educ* Woodhouse Grove Sch Bradford Yorks, Univ of St Andrews (BSc, PhD); *m* 10 Sept 1960, Susan Elizabeth, da of Dr John Meriton Benn, CB; 2 s (Gavin b 1963, Douglas b 1965); *Career* Univ of Rochester NY 1960-62, princ scientific offr Rocket Propulsion Estab 1967-69 (sr sci off Westcott 1962-67), explosives and propellants liason offr Br Embassy Washington DC 1969-72, asst dir Naval Ordnance Servs Bath 1973-76, tech advsr explosives and safety Chevaline 1976-79, princ superintendent Perme Westcott 1979-80, dep dir 1 and 2 Rarde Fort Halstead 1980-83, dir gen R & D Royal Ordnance Factories 1983-84, dir Chemical Def Estab Porton Down 1984-; FBIS 1967, CChem, FRSC 1985; *Books* contrib: Advances in Inorganic and Radiochemistry Vol 8 (1966), Advances in Photochemistry Vol 3, (1964), Oxidation and Combustion Reviews Vol 3 and 4 (second edn 1969); *Recreations* reading, long distance walking, foreign travel; *Style—* Dr GS Pearson; MOD Chemical Def Estab, Porton Down, Salisbury, Wilts SP4 OJQ (☎ 0980 610211)

PEARSON, Hon Graham Thomas; s of Baron Pearson, CBE, PC (Life Peer, d 1980); *b* 1935; *m* 1963, Diana, da of Vice Adm Sir Maxwell Richmond, KBE, CB, DSO; *Style—* The Hon Graham Pearson; 856 The Street, Old Basing, Basingstoke, Hampshire

PEARSON, Air Cdre Herbert Macdonald; CBE (1944); s of John Charles Pearson; *b* 17 Nov 1908; *Educ* Cheltenham Coll, Cranwell; *m* 1, 1939, Jane Leslie (d 1978); 1 s, 2 da; m 2, 1982, Elizabeth Anne, JP, wid of Eric Griffiths; *Career* cmd RAF Kai Tak, Hong Kong 1951-53, asst COS Intelligence HQ of AAFCE Central Europe 1953-55, Air Cdre 1953, ret 1955; *Clubs* Naval and Military; *Style—* Air Commodore Herbert Pearson, CBE; Mapleridge Barn, Horton, Chipping Sodbury, Bristol BS17 6QH (☎ 0454 312160)

PEARSON, John C; s of Francis John Pearson (d 1978), of Newick House, Rottingdean, Sussex, and Mabel Alice, *née* Turley (d 1960); *b* 11 Nov 1932; *Educ* King's Sch Canterbury, Trinity Coll Dublin (MA, LLB); *Career* admitted slr 1960; sr ptnr John Pearson; involved: Malden and Dist C of C, CAB, old peoples welfare orgns, Mid-Surrey Law Soc, Kingston Heritage; memb Law Soc 1960; *Recreations* walking, rowing, canoeing, opera; *Clubs* London Rowing; *Style—* John Pearson, Esq; 4 Kingston Rd, New Malden, Surrey (☎ 01 942 9193); 2 Kingston Rd, New Malden, Surrey (☎ 01 942 9191)

PEARSON, (Hugh) John Hampden; s of Lt-Col Hugh Henry Pearson, RA (d 1975), and Sybil Monica, *née* Dunn; *b* 22 Mar 1947; *Educ* Charterhouse, King's Coll London (LLB); *m* 12 Oct 1974, Jacqueline Anne, da of Maj Harold Arthur Bird, of Goring, Sussex; 1 s (Daniel b 1982), 2 da (Alice b 1976, Juliet b 1978); *Career* admitted slr 1971, Stephenson Harwood 1971-73, Coward Chance 1973-86; ptnr: Durrant Piesse 1986-88, Lovell White Durrant 1988-; memb S African Townships Health Fund; memb City of London Slrs Co 1982; memb: Law Soc, Assoc of Pension Lawyers; *Recreations* reading, hill walking, squash, bridge, opera; *Clubs* MCC, Roehampton; *Style—* John Pearson, Esq; 15 Howard's Lane, London SW15 6NX; Providence Cottage, Buckland Newton, Dorset DT2 7BU; Lovell White Durrant, 21 Holborn Viaduct, London EC1A 2DY (☎ 01 236 0066, fax 01 248 4212, telex 887122)

PEARSON, (Dominic) Michael; s of Arthur Anselm Pearson (d 1954); *b* 18 Sept 1921; *Educ* Ampleforth, Peterhouse Cambridge (MA); *m* 1955, Carmen, da of Manuel Sanfeliu Galcerán (d 1968); 3 s, 3 da; *Career* served UK and India 1941-46, Capt REME; Metropolitan Vickers Electrical Co Ltd 1947, Sovex Ltd 1949, British Belting & Asbestos Ltd 1951, chm BBA Group plc 1974-84, ret 1984; pres Yorkshire Regnl Soc, Inst of Linguists; memb: Fortress Study Gp, Newcomen Soc; fell Inst of Linguists, CEng, FIMechE; *Clubs* Magic Circle, Leeds Magical Assoc; *Style—* Michael Pearson, Esq; Daisy Hill, Cliffe Drive, Rawdon, Leeds LS19 6LL (☎ 0532 502 501)

PEARSON, Hon Michael Orlando Weetman; s and h of 3 Viscount Cowdray, TD, DL, and his 1 w, Lady Anne, *née* Bridgeman, da of 5 Earl of Bradford; *b* 17 June 1944; *Educ* Gordonstoun; *m* 1, 1977 (m dis), Ellen (Fritzi), da of Hermann Erhardt, of Munich; m 2, 1 July 1987, Marina Rose, da of John Howard Cordle, of Malmesbury House, The Close, Salisbury, and Mrs Venetia Caroline Ross Skinner, *née* Maynard; 1 da (Eliza Anne Venetia b 31 May 1988); *Career* non-exec dir Bardsey Gp; *Clubs* White's; *Style—* The Hon Michael Pearson; Greenhill House, Varr Road, Fernhurst, W Sussex (☎ 0428 53725)

PEARSON, Capt (Francis) Nicholas Fraser; s and h of Sir Francis Fenwick Pearson, 1 Bt, MBE; *b* 28 August 1943; *Educ* Radley; *m* 1978, Henrietta, da of Cdr Henry Pasley-Tyler, of Coton Manor, Guilsborough, Northants; *Career* cmmnd 3 Bn RB 1961-69 (ADC to C in C Far East 1969); co dir Cons parly candidate Oldham West 1975-78; *Recreations* shooting, fishing, tennis, opera; *Clubs* Carlton; *Style—* Captain Nicholas Pearson; 9 Upper Addison Gardens, Holland Park, London W14 8AL

PEARSON, Richard John Crewdson; s of Maj R A R B Pearson (d 1983), and Evelyn Katherine, *née* Crewdson; *b* 4 May 1940; *Educ* Packwood Haugh, St Edwards Oxford, Univ of St Andrews (MA); *m* 30 Nov 1968, Catriona Wallace, da of Robert S Angus; 1 s (Richard b 25 Sept 1971), 1 da (Sarah Catriona b 13 April 1973); *Career* CA; ptnr Pannell Kerr Forster 1962-; auditor Corpn of London; Cmmr of Taxes 1988; Freeman City of London, Liveryman Worshipful Co of Barbers 1971; FCA 1975 (ACA 1965), ICEAW; *Recreations* windsurfing, walking, sporting and country pursuits; *Clubs* Reform; *Style—* Richard Pearson, Esq; 6 The Lindens, Stock, Essex; 78 Hatton Garden, London EC1 (☎ 01 831 7393)

PEARSON, Maj-Gen Ronald Matthew; CB (1985), MBE (1959); s of Dr John Pearson (d 1958), and Sheila MacKinnon, *née* Brown (d 1937); *b* 25 Feb 1925; *Educ* Glasgow Acad, Univ of Glasgow, Glasgow Dental Hosp (LDS RFPS); *m* 1956, Florence Eileen, da of William John Jack (d 1967); 2 da (Carol b 1957, Shirley b 1959); *Career* dental surgn in civilian practice 1948-49; cmmnd RADC 1949, RWAFF 1950-53, UK 1953-57, BAOR 1957-60, UK 1961-67; CO No 1 Dental Gp BAOR 1967-70, CO Dental Centres Cyprus 1970-73, CO No 8 Dental Gp UK 1973-75, Co No 4 Dental Gp UK 1975-76, dep dir Dental Serv UKLF 1976-78, dep dir Dental Serv BAOR 1978-82, Maj-Gen 1982, dir Army Dental Serv 1982-85, ret; Queen's Honorary Dental Surgeon 1978-85; CStJ 1983; *Recreations* trout fishing, photography, gardening, caravanning; *Style—* Maj-Gen Ronald Pearson, CB, MBE; c/o The Royal Bank of Scotland plc, Holts Farnborough Branch, Victoria Rd, Farnborough, Hants GU14 7PA

PEARSON, Baroness - Sophie Grace Hermann; da of Arthur Hermann Thomas, MC, of Worthing; *m* 1931, Baron Pearson, CBE, PC (Life Peer, d 1980); 1 s, 1 da; *Style—* The Rt Hon the Lady Pearson

PEARSON, (Geoffrey) Stuart; s of Geoffrey William Pearson, of Chapel House, Chantry Drive, Ilkley, W Yorkshire, and Joan, *née* Richardson; *b* 17 August 1947; *Educ* Bradford GS; *m* 27 June 1970, Jean Barbara, da of Capt Charles Raymond Clegg, of Ilkley; 1 s (James Stuart b 1974), 1 da (Emma Jane b 1972); *Career* sr ptnr Rawlinsons CAs 1976-85; chm: Moss Tst 1986-, Curtain Dream plc 1987-; govr Bradford Girls GS; FCA 1970, FCCA 1974;; *Recreations* reading, music, squash; *Style—* Stuart Pearson, Esq; Glenside, Askwith, nr Otley, West Yorkshire (☎ 0943 466565); Openstead House, Wells Promenade, Ilkley, W Yorkshire LS29 9JD (☎ 0943 816357, fax 0943 601900)

PEARSON, Gen Sir Thomas Cecil Hooke; KCB (1967, CB 1964), CBE (1959, OBE 1953), DSO (1940, and bar 1943), DL (Hereford and Worcester 1983); s of Vice Adm J L Pearson, CMG (d 1965), and Phoebe Charlotte, *née* Beadon (d 1973); *b* 1 July 1914; *Educ* Charterhouse, RMC Sandhurst; *m* 1947, Aud, da of Alf Skjelkvale (d 1953), of Oslo; 2 s (Anthony, Thomas); *Career* cmmnd RB 1934, staff coll 1942, Cdr 2 Bn RB 1942-43, Dep Cdr 2 Para Bde and 1 Airlanding Bde 1944-45, Cdr 1 and 7 Para Bde 1945-47, dir staff Jt Servs Staff Coll 1950, Cdr 45 Para Bde (TA) 1955-56, Nat Def Coll Canada 1957, 16 Para Bde 1957-59, chief Br Mil Mission to Soviet Forces in Germany 1960-61, Maj-Gen cmd 1 Div BAOR 1961-63, COS Northern Army Gp 1963-67, Cdr FARELF 1967-68, mil sec MOD 1969-72, C-in-C Allied Forces Northern Europe 1972-74, Col Cmdt Royal Green Jackets 1973-77, ADC Gen to HM The Queen 1974, ret; fisheries memb Welsh Water Authy 1980-83; Haakon VII Liberty Cross 1945, Norwegian Defence Association Medal 1973; *Recreations* yachting, shooting, fishing; *Clubs* Naval and Military, Island Sailing, Kongalig Norsk Seilforenning; *Style—* General Sir Thomas Pearson, KCB, CBE, DSO, DL; Streete House, Weston-under-Penyard, Ross-on-Wye, Herefordshire HR9 7NY (☎ 0989 62608)

PEARSON LUND, Peter Graham; s of Douglas Pearson Lund, CBE (d 1974), of Springfields, Fetcham, Surrey, and Honor Winifred; *b* 9 Sept 1947; *Educ* Shiplake Coll Henley, Guildford Sch of Art; *m* 16 Nov 1968, Isabelle McLachlan, da of late William Henderson, of Brighton; 2 s (Piers b 19 Oct 1969, Oliver b 10 Dec 1971); *Career* Tilney & Co 1969-70, Cazenove and Co 1970-73, Antony Gibbs 1973-75; md: Henderson Unit Tst Mgmnt (dir Henderson Admin Ltd) 1975-85, Gartmore Fund Mgmnt Ltd (dir Gartmore Investmt Mgmnt Ltd) 1985-; *Recreations* tennis, skiing, sailing; *Style—* Peter Pearson Lund, Esq; (☎ 01 623 1212); Gartmore Investment Management Ltd, Gartmore House, Monument St, London EC3R 8QQ (fax 01 283 6070)

PEART, Hon Emerson Frederick; o s of Baron Peart, PC (Life Peer, d 1988); *m* m; *Style—* Hon Emerson Peart

PEART, Baroness; Sarah Elizabeth; da of Thomas Lewis, of Aberystwyth; *m* 1945, Baron Peart, PC (Life Peer, d 1988); 1 s; *Style—* The Rt Hon Lady Peart

PEASE, Hon Mrs; Hon Elizabeth Jane; *née* Ormsby-Gore; da of 4 Baron Harlech, KG, GCMG, PC (d 1964); *b* 1929; *m* 1962, Hon William Simon Pease, *qv*; *Style—* The Hon Mrs Pease; 29 Upper Addison Gardens, London W14 8AJ; Lepe House, Exbury, Southampton

PEASE, Hon George; s of 2 Baron Gainford, TD (d 1971), and Veronica, Baroness Gainford, *qv*; hp of bro, 3 Baron Gainford; *b* 20 April 1926; *Educ* Eton, Edinburgh Coll of Art (DipTP); *m* 1958, Flora Daphne, da of Dr Neville Dyce Sharp; 2 s, 2 da; *Career* served WW II RNVR; county planning offr Ross and Cromarty; Scottish Off inquiry reporter; chm The Saltire Soc; memb Lothians Bldg Preservation Tst; ARIBA, MRTPI, ARIAS; *Style—* The Hon George Pease; Naemoor Gardens, Rumbling Bridge, Kinross KY13 7PY (☎ 05774 261)

PEASE, Hon Joanna Ruth Miriam; da of 3 Baron Gainford; *b* 22 August 1959; *Style—* The Hon Joanna Pease; c/o 1 Dedmere Court, Marlow, Bucks SL7 1PL (☎ 062 84 4679)

PEASE, Hon John Michael; s of 2 Baron Gainford, TD, and Veronica, Baroness Gainford, *qv*; *b* 22 Sept 1930; *Educ* Gordonstoun; *m* 1962, Catherine, da of Duncan

Shaw; 3 s (David b 1964, Andrew b 1967, Daniel b 1973); *Career* farmer and property developer; *Recreations* shooting, amateur drama; *Style—* The Hon John Pease; Auchentenavil, Tayvallich, Lochgilphead, Argyll

PEASE, Joseph Gurney; s of Sir Alfred Edward Pease, 2 Bt (d 1939), and hp of bro, Sir (Alfred) Vincent Pease, 4 Bt; *b* 16 Nov 1927; *Educ* Bootham Sch York; *m* 1953, Shelagh Munro, da of Cyril G Bulman; 1 s, 1 da; *Career* memb Guisborough UDC 1950-53; Lib candidate (gen elections): Bishop Auckland 1959, Darlington 1964, Westmorland 1970, Penrith and the Border 1974; pres NE Young Lib Fedn 1961, memb Lib Pty Cncl 1969, pres NW Regnl Lib Pty 1970 and 1971; *Style—* Joseph Pease, Esq; Greenbank, Grasmere, Cumbria LA22 9RW

PEASE, Dr Rendel Sebastian; s of Michael Stewart Pease, OBE (d 1966), and Hon Helen Bowen Wedgwood (d 1981), eld da of 1 Baron Wedgwood, PC, DSO; *b* 2 Nov 1922; *Educ* Bedales, Trinity Coll Cambridge; *m* 1952, Susan, da of Sir Frank Todd Spickernell, DSO, RN (d 1956); 2 s, 3 da; *Career* dir: Culham Laboratory UK AEA 1967-81, Fusion Res Programme UK AEA 1981-87; chm: Int Fusion Res Cncl IAEA 1976-83, Br Pugwash Gp 1988-; pres Inst of Physics 1978-80; FRS 1977 (vice pres 1986-87; *Recreations* music; *Clubs* Royal Society; *Style—* Dr Rendel Pease; The Poplars, West Ilsley, Newbury, Berks RG16 0AW

PEASE, Richard Peter; s and h of Sir Richard Thorn Pease, 3 Bt, of Hindley Ho, Stocksfield, Northumberland and Anne, *née* Heyworth; *b* 4 Sept 1958; *Educ* Eton, Univ of Durham; *Career* investmt fund mangr with Central Bd of Fin for the C of E; *Recreations* chess, bridge, backgammon, tennis, squash; *Clubs* Queens; *Style—* Richard Pease, Esq; 7 St Dionis Rd, London SW6; Central Bd of Finance, Winchester Ho, 77 London WC11 EC2 (☎ 01 588 1815)

PEASE, Sir Richard Thorn; 3 Bt (UK 1920); s of Sir Richard Arthur Pease, 2 Bt (d 1969); *b* 20 May 1922; *Educ* Eton; *m* 9 March 1956, Anne, o da of Lt-Col Reginald Francis Heyworth (d 1941), and formerly w of David Henry Lewis Wigan; 1 s, 2 da; *Heir* s, Richard Peter Pease b 4 Sept 1958; *Career* served WW II, 60 Rifles 1941-46; vice-chm Barclays Bank Ltd 1970-82, (currently dir), vice-chm Barclays Bank UK Mgmnt 1971-82, chm Yorkshire Bank, dir Grainger Tst plc; *Recreations* fishing; *Clubs* Brooks's, Pratt's; *Style—* Sir Richard Pease, Bt; Hindley House, Stocksfield-on-Tyne, Northumberland (☎ 0661 842361)

PEASE, Hon Mrs; Hon Rosemary; *née* Portman; da of 5 Viscount Portman (d 1942); *b* 1931; *m* 1951, Derrick Allix Pease, s of Sir Richard Arthur Pease, 2 Bt (d 1969); 3 s, 1 da; *Style—* The Hon Mrs Pease; 2 Britten St, SW3; Upper Woodcott, Whitchurch, Hants

PEASE, Dr (Rendel) Sebastian; s of Michael Stewart Pease, OBE, JP (d 1966), of Reynolds Close, Girton, Cambridge, and Helen Bowen, *née* Wedgwood, JP (d 1981); *b* 2 Nov 1922; *Educ* Bedales, Trinity Coll Cambridge (MA, ScD); *m* 9 Aug 1952, Susan, da of Capt Sir Frank Spickernel, KBE, CB, CVO, DSO, RN (d 1956), of Deane, Kintbury, Berkshire; 2 s (Christopher b 1956, Roland b 1959), 3 da (Rosamund (Mrs Chalmers) b 1953, Sarah (Mrs Kimbell) b 1955, Rowan b 1963); *Career* asst sci offr op res Miny Aircraft Prodn 1942-46, sci offr UKAEA 1954-61 (Sci Civil Serv Harwell 1947-54), dir Culham laboratories UKAEA 1967-81 (div head 1961-67), dir fusion res UKAEA 1981-87; conslt: Progressive Engrg Consltts, Pease Ptnrs 1988-; playing memb Newbury Symphony Orch, chm Br Pugwash Gp 1988-; memb: Euro Physical Soc, Royal Soc, Fabian Soc; D Univ Surrey 1973, ScD Aston 1981, DSc City 1987; Hon FINucE; memb Inst of Physics 1967 (pres 1978-80), C phys, FIEE 1978, FRS 1977; *Recreations* music; *Style—* Dr Sebastian Pease; The Poplars, W Ilsley, Newbury, Berks, (☎ 063528 237)

PEASE, Sir (Alfred) Vincent; 4 Bt (UK 1882); s of Sir Alfred (Edward) Pease, 2 Bt (d 1939), of Pinchinthorpe House, Guisborough, Cleveland, and Emily Elizabeth, *née* Smith (d 1979); half-bro of Sir Edward Pease, 3 Bt (d 1963); *b* 2 April 1926; *Educ* Bootham Sch York, Durham Sch of Agric; *Heir* bro, Joseph Gurney Pease; *Style—* Sir Vincent Pease, Bt; Flat 13, Hamilton House, Belgrave Road, Seaford, E Sussex BN25 2EL

PEASE, Hon Virginia Claire Margaret; da of 3 Baron Gainford; *b* 13 Oct 1960; *Style—* The Hon Virginia Pease; 1 Dedmere Court, Marlow, Bucks SL7 1PL (☎ 062 84 4679)

PEASE, Hon William Simon; s of 1 Baron Wardington (d 1950), and Dorothy Charlotte (d 1983), da of 1 Baron Forster (d 1936, when title became extinct); hp of bro, 2 Baron Wardington; *b* 15 Oct 1925; *Educ* Eton, New Coll Oxford (MA), St Thomas's Hosp Medical Sch (MB, BS); *m* 27 Oct 1962, Hon Elizabeth Jane Ormsby-Gore, *qv*, da of 4 Baron Harlech, KG, GCMG, PC (d 1964); *Career* Capt Grenadier Gds 1944-47; conslt surg ENT Dept Central Middx and Northwick Park Hosps; FRCS; *Recreations* sailing (yacht Leviathan), gardening; *Clubs* Royal Yacht Sqdn; *Style—* The Hon William Pease, FRCS; 29 Upper Addison Gardens, London W14 8AJ (☎ 01 371 1776); Lepe House, Exbury, Southampton (☎ 0703 893724); 10 Upper Wimpole Street, London W1M 7TD (☎ 01 935 0147)

PEAT, Sir Gerrard Charles; KCVO (1988); s of Charles Urie Peat, MC, MP (d 1979), and Ruth Martha, *née* Pulley (d 1979); *b* 14 June 1920; *Educ* Sedbergh; *m* 17 June 1949, Margaret Josephine Collingwood, da of Cyril Wylam-Walker (d 1965); 1 s (Michael Charles Gerrard b 1949); *Career* served WW II pilot RAF and ATA 1940-45, pilot 600 City of London Aux Sqdn 1948-51; ptnr Peat Marwick Mitchell & Co 1956-87, underwriting memb Lloyds 1973-, auditor to Queen's Privy Purse 1980-88 (asst auditor 1969-80); memb: Ctee of Assoc of Lloyds Membs 1983-, Corpn of City of London 1973-78, hon tres Assoc of Cons Clubs 1971-79; Liveryman Worshipful Co of Turners; FCA 1951; *Recreations* travel, shooting, fishing, golf, flying; *Clubs* Boodle's, City Livery; *Style—* Sir Gerrard Peat, KCVO; Home Farm, Mead Lane, Upper Basildon, Berks RG8 8ND (☎ 0491 671241); Flat 10, 35 Pont Street, London SW1X 0BB (☎ 01 245 9736); Suite 607, Britannia House, Glenthorne Rd, London W6 0LF (☎ 01 748 9898, telex 916107, fax 01 748 4250)

PEAT, Sir Henry; KCVO (1980, CVO 1973), DFC; s of late Sir Harry (William Henry) Peat, GBE, KCVO; *b* 1913; *Educ* Eton, Trinity Coll Oxford; *Career* served WWII, Flt Lt RAF Bomber Cmd Europe 1939-45; FCA; *Style—* Sir Henry Peat, KCVO, DFC; 48 Roebuck House, Palace St, Westminster, London SW1E 5BB

PEAT, William Wood Watson; CBE (1972), JP (Stirlingshire, 1963); s of William Peat, of Kirkland Farm, Denny, and Margaret Peat; *b* 14 Dec 1922; *Educ* Denny Public Sch; *m* 1955, Jean Frew Paton, da of James McHarrie, JP (d 1966), of Westwood, Stranraer; 2 s, 1 da; *Career* served Lt RCS 1941-46; farmer; chm Scottish Assoc of Young Farmers Club 1953-54 (pres 1979-81); gen cmmr of Income Tax 1962-; pres Nat Farmers Union of Scotland 1966-67, vice convenor Stirling CC 1967-70, chm BBC Scottish Agric Advsy Cmmn 1971-77; dir: FMC Ltd 1974-83, Islay Farmers Ltd 1974-86; pres Cncl Scottish Agric Orgns Ltd 1974-77, vice pres Assoc of Agric 1978-; chm: West of Scotland Agric Coll 1983-88 (govr 1964), Scottish Agric Coll 1986-; memb: Scottish River Purification Advsy Cmmn 1960-79, cncl Hannah Res Inst 1963-82, Br Farm Produce Cncl 1964-87 (vice-chm 1974), Central Cncl for Agric and Horticultural Co-operation 1967-83, Br Agric Cncl 1974-83, Co-operative Devpt Bd Food From Britain 1983-88; BBC nat govr for Scotland, chm Broadcasting Cncl for Scotland 1984-; FRAgS 1987; *Recreations* amateur radio, flying; *Clubs* Farmers; *Style—* Watson Peat, Esq, CBE, JP; Carbro, 61 Stirling Rd, Larbert, Stirlingshire FK5 4SG (☎ 0324 562420)

PECHELL, Dora, Lady; Dora Constance; da of late John Crampthorne; *m* 1949, Sir Ronald Horace Pechell, 9 and last Bt (d 1984); *Style—* Dora, Lady Pechell; 26 Burley Road, Summerley Private Estate, Felpham, West Sussex PO22 7NF

PECHELL, Doris, Lady; Doris Margery; da of late T Drewitt Lobb ; *m* 1 (m dis), Lt-Col Arthur Thomas Begg Green, ED (d 1982); 1 da (Felicity Ann (Mrs Irwin), *qv*); m 2, 1971, as his 2 w, Sir Paul Pechell, 8 Bt, MC (d 1972); *Style—* Doris, Lady Pechell; 25 Marchwood, 8 Manor Rd, Bournemouth, Dorset

PECK, Antony Dilwyn; CB (1965), MBE (1945); s of late Sir James Peck, CB; *b* 10 April 1914; *Educ* Eton, Trinity Coll Oxford; *m* 1, 1939, Joan de Burgh Whyte (d 1955); 1 s, 1 da; m 2, 1956, Sylvia Glenister; 1 s, 2 da; *Career* dep sec DTI 1970-73, ret; *Style—* Antony Peck, Esq, CB, MBE; 45 Argyll Rd, W8 (☎ 01 937 2869)

PECK, David Arthur; s of Frank Archibald Peck, of Sunningdale, Hatton Park, Wellingborough, Northants, and Molly, *née* Eyels; *b* 3 May 1940; *Educ* Wellingborough Sch, Univ of Cambridge (MA); *m* 3 Feb 1968, Jennifer Mary, da of Frederick William Still, of 7 Locke Rd, Liphook, Hampshire; 1 s (Mark b 12 June 1975), 2 da (Emma b 2 Oct 1970, Sophie b 11 Oct 1973); *Career* admitted slr 1966, sr ptnr Birkbeck Montagu's 1985- (ptnr 1967-); memb: Law Soc, Euro GP, Int Bar Assoc; *Recreations* cricket, golf, tennis, walking; *Clubs* Hawks, MCC, Hampstead, Free Forestar, Cryptics, Royal W Norfolk Golf, Camden Hill Tennis; *Style—* David Peck, Esq; 26 Rhepshow Place, London W2 (☎ 01 229 9674); Pages, Brinton, Norfolk; 7 St Bridge St, London EC4 (☎ 01 353 3222, fax 01 353 4761, telex 265068 BIRMON G)

PECK, His Honour Judge; David Edward; s of late William Edward Peck; *b* 6 April 1917; *Educ* Charterhouse, Balliol Coll Oxford; *m* 1, 1950 (m dis), Rosina Seton Glover Marshall; 1 s, 3 da; m 2, 1973, Frances Deborah Redford, *née* Mackenzie; 1 s; *Career* served WW II Cheshire Regt; barr Middle Temple 1949, circuit judge (formerly judge of Co Courts) 1969-; chm County Court Rule Ctee 1981- (memb 1978-); *Style—* His Honour Judge Peck; 8 New Square, Lincoln's Inn, WC2A 3QP

PECK, Sir Edward Heywood; GCMG (1974, KCMG 1966, CMG 1957); s of Lt-Col Edward Surman Peck, IMS (d 1934), and Doris Louise Heywood (d 1934); *b* 5 Oct 1915; *Educ* Clifton, Queen's Coll Oxford (MA); *m* 1948, Alison Mary, da of late John MacInnes, of Sevenoaks; 1 s, 2 da; *Career* entered Consular Serv 1938, served Turkey, Greece, India and Singapore 1940-60 (dep cmdt Br Sector Berlin 1955-58), asst under-sec state for SE Asia and Far Eastern Affrs FCO 1960-65, high cmmr Kenya 1966-68, dep under-sec state FCO 1968-70, Br perm rep to N Atlantic Cncl 1970-75, ret; hon visiting fell Def Studies Aberdeen Univ 1976-85; memb Cncl of Nat Tst for Scotland 1982-87; *Publications* North-East Scotland, Avonside Explored; *Recreations* hill walking, skiing, reading history, writing guide-books; *Clubs* Alpine, Royal Geographical Soc; *Style—* Sir Edward Peck, GCMG; (☎ 080 74 318)

PECK, Sir John Howard; KCMG (1971, CMG 1956); s of late Howard Peck, and Dorothea Peck; *b* 16 Feb 1913; *Educ* Wellington, Corpus Christi Coll Oxford; *m* 1, 1939, Mariska Caroline (d 1979), da of Josef Somlo; 2 s; m 2, 1987, Catherine, yst da of Edward McLaren; *Career* asst private sec to: First Lord of the Admty 1937-39, Min for Co-ordination of Def 1939-40, PM 1940-46; UK perm rep to the Cncl of Europe, consul-gen Strasbourg 1959-62; ambass to: Senegal 1962-66, Mauritania 1962-65; asst under-sec of state FO then FCO 1966-70; ambass to the Republic of Ireland 1970-73; *Books* Dublin from Downing Street (memoirs, 1978); *Style—* Sir John Peck, KCMG; Stratford, Saval Park Road, Dalkey, Co Dublin (☎ 0001 806315)

PECK, Stanley Edwards; CBE (1974), BEM (1954), QPM (1964), DL (Staffs 1962); s of Harold Edwards Peck, of Shanghai and Edgbaston (d 1962), and Mabel Beatrice Bevan, *née* Bell (d 1966); *b* 24 Jan 1916; *Educ* Solihull Sch, Univ of Birmingham; *m* 1939, Yvonne Sydney Edwards, da of John Edwards Jessop (d 1965); 2 s (John, Timothy), 2 da (Josephine, Angela); *Career* Fl Lt RAF 1941-45; Met Police 1935-54; supt New Scotland Yard 1950; asst and dep chief constable Staffs 1954-60 (chief constable 1960-64); HM inspector of constabulary 1964-78; pres Royal Life Saving Soc (UK) 1969-74, memb Br Rail Bd Police Ctee 1978-87; OStJ; *Recreations* golf, dog walking; *Clubs* RAF; *Style—* Stanley Peck, Esq, CBE, BEM, QPM, DL; Lodge Gdns, Walnut Grove, Radcliffe-on-Trent, Notts (☎ 06073 2361)

PECKER, Morley Leo; s of Alec Pecker (d 1975), of London; *b* 7 April 1937; *Educ* Epsom Coll; *Career* Nat Serv 2 Lt RA 1960-63; CA; articles Charles Eves Lord and Co 1954-60, mangr RF Frazer & Co 1963-65, sr advsr accountant Bd of Inland Revenue 1965-73, princ admin Cmmn EEC Brussels 1973-; memb Int Hockey Fedn, hon tres Euro Hockey Fedn, memb Br Olympic Assoc, hon life memb The Cricket Soc, past hon tres Middx Cricket Union; Olympic Hockey judge: Munich 1972, Montreal 1976, Moscow 1980, Los Angeles 1984; FCA 1970 (Assoc 1960), MIT (1964); *Recreations* hockey, cricket, music, photography; *Clubs* Chateau St Anne Belgium, MCC, The Cricket Society ; *Style—* ML Forester; Le Grand Forestier, 26 Ave du Grand Forestier, 1160 Brussels, Belgium (☎ Brussels 672 57 85); Commission of the European Communities, 299 Rue de la Loi, 1049 Brussels, Belgium (☎ Brussels 235 53 79, fax Brussels 235 9585)

PECKHAM, Prof Catherine Stevenson; da of Dr Alexander King, CBE, CMG, of 168 Rue de Grenalle, Paris, and Sarah Maskell, *née* Thompson; *b* 7 Mar 1937; *Educ* St Pauls Girls Sch London, Univ of London (MB BS, MD); *m* 7 Oct 1958, Prof Michael John Peckham, qv, s of William Stuart Peckham (d 1981); 3 s (Alexander b 1962, Daniel Gavin b 1964, Robert Shannan b 1965); *Career* reader in community med Charing Cross Hosp Med Sch 1977-85, prof of paediatric epidemiology Inst of Child Health and hon conslt Hosp for Sick Children Great Ormond St 1985- (sr lectr and hon conslt 1975-77), hon conslt Public Health Laboratory 1985-; memb US Fulbright Cmmn 1987-; FRCP 1988, FFCM 1980; *Recreations* flute; *Style—* Prof Catherine Peckham; 35 Brook Green, London W6 7BL, (☎ 01 602 2347); Institute of Child Health, Guilford St, WC1

PECKHAM, Prof Michael John; s of William Stuart Peckham (d 1981), and Gladys Mary, *née* Harris; *b* 2 August 1935; *Educ* William Jones West Monmouthshire Sch, St Catharine's Coll Cambridge (MA, MD), UCH Med Sch; *m* 7 Oct 1958, Catherine Stevenson, qv, da of Dr Alexander King, CMG, CBE, of 168 Rue de Grenelle, Paris; 3 s (Alexander b 1962, Daniel Gavin b 1964, Robert Shannan b 1965); *Career* Capt RAMC 1960-62; clinical res cncl scholar MRC Paris 1965-67, dean Inst of Cancer Res London 1984-86 (sr lectr 1972-74, prof 1974-86), civilian conslt to RN 1975-, dir Br Postgrad Med Fedn 1986; pres; Euro Soc of Therapeutic Radiology and Oncology 1984-85, Br Oncology Assoc 1986-88; fndr Bob Champion Cancer Tst; memb special health authy: Hosps for Sick Children Gt Ormond St, Brompton and Nat Heart Hosp, Hammersmith Hosp Imperial Cancer Res Fund (vice chm cncl); FRCP, FRCR, FRCPG; *Recreations* painting; *Style*— Prof Michael Peckham; 35 Brook Gn, London W6 7BL (☎ 01 602 2347); Br Postgraduate Med Fedn, 33 Millman St, London WC1n 3EJ (☎ 01 831 6222)

PECKOVER, Richard Stuart; s of Rev Cecil Raymond Peckover, and Grace Lucy, *née* Curtis; *b* 5 May 1942; *Educ* King Edward VII Sch King's Lynn, Wadham Coll Oxford (MA), Corpus Christi Coll Cambridge (PhD); *Career* UKAEA 1969-: res scientist in computational physics and reactor safety Culham Lab 1969-81, res assoc MIT 1973-74, gp ldr Safety and Reliability Directorate 1982 (branch head 1983-87), dep dir Winfrith AEE 1989-(asst dir 1987-89); FIMA, FInstP, FRAS, FRMetS, FSaRS (Safety and Reliability Soc); *Recreations* walking, talking, listening to music; *Clubs* United Oxford and Cambridge; *Style*— Richard Peckover, Esq; 6 The Square, Puddletown, Dorset DT2 8SL; Atomic Energy Establishment, Winfrith, Dorchester, Dorset DT2 8DH (☎ 0305 251 888)

PEDDER, Vice Adm Sir Arthur (Reid); KBE (1959), CB (1956); s of Sir John Pedder, KBE, CB (d 1954, dep sec Home Off), and Frances Evelyn Sharpe (d 1952); *b* 6 July 1904; *Educ* RNC Osborne, RNC Dartmouth; *m* 1934, Dulcie, da of Oscar Bickford (d 1954); 2 s; *Career* joined RN 1917, naval observer 1930, Cdr Admty 1937-40, served HM Penelope, HM Mauritius, cmd HM Khedive, cmd HM Phoebe, Capt 1944, returned to Admty, dep dir of Plans 1949-50, fourth Naval Memb Aust Commonwealth Naval Bd 1950-52, Rear Adm 1953, Asst Chief of Naval Staff (Warfare) Admty 1953-54, Flag Offr Aircraft Carriers 1954-56, Vice-Adm 1956, Cdr Allied Naval Forces Northern Europe 1957-59; ran beef cattle farm in retirement; *Recreations* keeping alive; *Clubs* Athenaeum, Ski of GB; *Style*— Vice Admiral Sir Arthur Pedder, KBE, CB; Langhurst, Barn Cottage, Hascombe, Godalming, Surrey (☎ Hascombe 294)

PEDDER, Air Marshal Sir Ian Maurice; KCB (1982), OBE (1963), DFC (1949); s of Maurice Albert Pedder (d 1967), and Elsie Pedder (d 1981); *b* 2 May 1926; *Educ* Royal GS High Wycombe, Queen's Coll Oxford; *m* 1949, Jean Mary, da of Tom Kellett; 1 s, 2 da; *Career* served in sqdns in Far East, Germany and UK 1944-64, directing staff RAF Staff Coll 1964-67, staff and cmd appts 1967-80, dep controller Nat Air Traffic Servs 1977-81 (controller 1981-85); Air Marshal 1981, memb bd CAA 1981-85; co dir and dep chm Dan-Air Servs; *Clubs* Royal Air Force, Victory Services; *Style*— Air Marshal Sir Ian Pedder, KCB, OBE; DFC, The Chestnuts, Cheddar, Somerset

PEDDIE, Hon Ian James Crofton; s of Baron Peddie (Life Peer) (d 1978); *b* 1945; *Educ* Gordonstoun, UCL (LLB); *m* 1976, Susan Renée, da of Edmund John Brampton Howes; *Career* barr Inner Temple 1971; *Style*— The Hon Ian Peddie; 36 Chiswick Staithe, Hartington Road, London W4 3TP

PEDDIE, Peter Charles; CBE (1983); s of Ronald Peddie, CBE, JP (d 1986), of Springwater Farm, Mudgley, Wedmore, Somerset, and Vera, *née* Nicklin (d 1981); *b* 20 Mar 1932; *Educ* Canford, St John's Coll Cambridge (MA); *m* 25 June 1960, Charlotte Elizabeth, da of Ernest Pierce Ryan (d 1982), of Sunny Cottage, Betchworth, Surrey; 2 s (Andrew b 20 Sept 1963, Jonathan b 5 May 1968), 2 da (Emma b 20 June 1961, Rachel b 9 Aug 1965); *Career* admitted slr 1957, ptnr Freshfields 1960- (asst slr 1957-60); govr Canford Sch 1981-, special tstee Middx Hosp 1977-, memb cncl Middx Hosp Med Sch 1977-88; Freeman City of London Slrs Co; memb Law Soc, memb Slrs Benevolent Assoc; *Recreations* gardening; *Clubs* City of London; *Style*— Peter Peddie, Esq; Grindall House, 25 Newgate St, London EC1A 7LA (☎ 01 606 6677, fax 01 248 348 789, telex 889 292)

PEDDIE, Robert Allan; s of Robert Allan Peddie (d 1966), of Hillside, Sutton, Kingston upon Hull, and Elizabeth Elsie, *née* Sharp (d 1988); *b* 27 Oct 1921; *Educ* Hull Tech Coll, Univ of Nottingham (BSc); *m* 6 April 1946, Ilene Ivy, da of John Sillcock (d 1956); 1 da (Barbara Elizabeth b Jan 1952); *Career* CEGB: asst regnl dir NW regn 1962-65, dep dir gen Midland regn 1966-70, dir gen SE regn 1970-72, bd memb UKAEA 1973-75, chm South Eastern Electricity Bd 1977-83 (conslt 1983-); first station mangr Bradwell Nuclear Power Station, reactor design engr (all nuclear power stations) CEGB; chm Sovereign Youth and Community Centre; Freeman City of London 1981; FIMechE 1961, FInstE 1962, FIEE 1963; *Recreations* swimming, golf, DIY; *Style*— Robert Peddie, Esq; 5 The Mount Drive, Reigate, Surrey RM2 0EZ (☎ 0737 244996)

PEDERSEN, Vagn Sondergaard; s of Holger Pedersen (d 1988), of Denmark, and Dorthea, *née* Jensen; *b* 27 April 1943; *Educ* Arhus Graduate Sch of Mgmnt Denmark (Cand Merc); *m* 27 June 1970, Helle Skovridder, da of Albert Jorgensen, of Denmark; 2 s (Christian b 19 March 1972, Steffen b 4 Sept 1975); *Career* asst gen mangr and sec to bd of mgmnt Provinsbanken Denmark 1973-81, regnl gen mangr Sparekassen SDS Denmark 1981-84, md and chief exec SDS Bank Ltd London(formerly London Interstate Bank Ltd) 1987-(dir and gen mangr 1984, dep md 1985); memb: ctee Assoc of Int Savings Banks in London (chm 1987-88), Anglo-Danish Trade Advsy Bd; *Books* Fremtidens Sparekasse System (1972), Pantebreve Effektiv Rente for og Efter Skat (1973); *Recreations* skiing, tennis, family life; *Clubs* Danish, Foreign Bankers; *Style*— Vagn Pedersen, Esq; SDS Bank Ltd, Bastion Hse, 140 London Wall, London EC2Y 5DN (☎ 01 606 8899, fax 01 600 3967, telex 884161 SDSLDN G)

PEDLER, Sir Frederick Johnson; s of Charles Henry Pedler (d 1935), and Lucy Marian, *née* Johnson; *b* 10 July 1908; *Educ* Watford GS, Gonville and Caius Coll Cambridge; *m* 1935, Esther Ruth, da of Henry F Carling (d 1949), of Peppard Common, Oxon; 2 s (Robin, Martin), 1 da (Esther); *Career* chief Br econ rep Dakar 1942, Fin Dept Colonial Off 1944, chm Cncl for Tech Educn in Overseas Countries 1959-71, dep chm United Africa Co 1965-68; dir: Unilever Ltd and NV 1956-68, William Baird Ltd 1969-75; tres SOAZ 1969-81 (hon fell); kt 1969; *Books* West Africa (1951), Economic Geography of West Africa (1957), The Lion and the Unicorn in Africa (1974), Main Currents of West African History 1940-78 (1979), A Pedler Family History (1984); *Clubs* Reform; *Style*— Sir Frederick Pedler; 36 Russell Rd, Moor Park, Northwood, Middx

PEDLER, Garth; s of Thomas Wakeham Pedler (d 1984), of Exeter, and Ruby, *née* Cornish; the 2000 or so Pedlers/Pedlars alive today and scattered round the world descend from just three families in 1542 in Wadebridge, Boyton and Okehampton, all in turn descended from ancestors in Clawton, Devon in the 13th cent; the earliest record of the name is that of Roger Pedelevre (Pie-de-Lièvre) in 1148 (Buckfast Abbey cartulary); *b* 21 Feb 1946; *Educ* King's Coll Taunton; *Career* with Touche Ross & Co 1969-73, then self-employed as taxation cnslt; FCA, ATII; *Books* The 9.5 mm Vintage Film Encyclopaedia (ed and jt-author); regular contributor to Classic Images USA 1982-; *Recreations* vintage film research and associated journalism, genealogy, history of transport, alpine hiking in summer; *Style*— Garth Pedler, Esq; 37 Campden Rd, S Croydon, Surrey CR2 7ER (☎ 01 680 3355)

PEDLEY, Roger Keith; s of Thomas Kenneth Fitzgeorge Pedley (d 1976), and Winifred Gordon, *née* Smith; *b* 12 Oct 1944; *Educ* King's Sch Worcester; *m* 26 Oct 1970, Paula Lesley, da of George Holland; 1 s (Rupert b 1980), 1 da (Helen b 1977); *Career* CA; Peat Marwick Mitchell 1968-; PMM: Paris 1969-72, Nottingham 1973-75, London 1975-76, ptnr 1976 in Nottingham; managing ptnr Peat Marwick McLintock Derby off 1980; *Recreations* flyfishing, windsurfing; *Style*— Roger K Pedley, Esq; Pear Treehouse, Church Street, Ockbrook, Derbyshire DE7 3SL (☎ 0332 662368); Peat Marwick McLintock, 1/2 Irongate, Derby DE1 3FJ (☎ 0332 49268, car telephone 0860 712000)

PEEBLES, Hon Mrs; (Annabel); *née* Elton; da of 2 Baron Elton; *b* 24 Oct 1960; *m* 5 July 1986, Donald M Peebles, er s of Dr R Anthony Peebles, of Hampton Court, Surrey; 1 da (Emma Richenda b 11 July 1988); *Style*— Hon Mrs Peebles

PEECH, Neil Malcolm; s of Albert Orlando Peech; *b* 27 Jan 1908; *Educ* Wellington, Magdalen Coll Oxford; *m* 1932, Margaret Josephine, da of Richard Coningsby Smallwood, CBE (d 1933), of Mile Path House, Hook Heath, Surrey; 1 s, 1 da; *Career* Steetley Co Ltd: md 1935-68, chm 1935-76, pres 1976-; dir Albright & Wilson Ltd 1958-79; Lloyd's underwriter 1950-69; High Sheriff Yorks 1959; *Style*— Neil Peech, Esq; Park House, Firbeck, Worksop (☎ 0909 730338)

PEEK, Sir Francis Henry Grenville; 4 Bt (UK 1874); s of Sir Wilfrid Peek, 3 Bt, DSO (d 1927); *b* 16 Sept 1915; *Educ* Eton, Trinity Coll Cambridge; *m* 1, 1942 (m dis 1949), Ann, da of late Capt Gordon Duff and wid of Sir Charles Mappin (she m 1951, Sir William Rootes, later 1 Baron Rootes); m 2, 1949 (m dis 1967), Marilyn, da of Dr Norman Kerr (she m 1967, Peter Quennell); 1 s (decd); m 3, 1967, Mrs Caroline Kirkwood, da of Sir Robert Lucien Morrison Kirkwood, *qv*; *Heir* kinsman, William Grenville Peek; *Career* ADC to Govr of Bahamas 1938-39, served Irish Guards 1939-46; *Style*— Sir Francis Peek, Bt; Los Picos, Nagueles, Marbella, Spain (☎ 774736); 60 Grosvenor Close, Nassau, Bahamas

PEEK, Vice Adm Sir Richard Innes; KBE (1972, OBE 1944), CB (1971), DSC (1945); s of late James Norman Peek; *b* 30 July 1914; *Educ* RAN Coll; *m* 1, 1943, Margaret Seinor, *née* Kendall (d 1946); 1 s; m 2, 1952, Mary Catherine Tilley, *née* Stops; 2 da; *Career* Flag Offr cmd Aust Fleet 1967-68, Naval memb Aust Naval Bd 1968-70, Chief of Naval Staff Aust 1970-73; Legion of Merit (USA); *see Debrett's Handbook of Australia and New Zealand for further details*; *Style*— Vice Admiral Sir Richard Peek, KBE, CB; Rothlyn, RMB, Monaro Highway, via Cooma, NSW 2630, Australia

PEEK, Capt William Grenville; s of late Capt Roger Grenville Peek (2 s of 2 Bt) and hp of kinsman, Sir Francis Peek, 4 Bt; *b* 15 Dec 1919; *Educ* Eton; *m* 1950, Lucy Jane, da of late Maj Edward Dorrien-Smith; 1 s, 3 da; *Career* Capt late 9 Lancers WWII serv 1939-45 (despatches); *Clubs* Royal Western Yacht; *Style*— Capt William Peek; Weekemoor, Loddiswell, S Devon

PEEL, Hon Mrs (Ann Katharine); *née* de Yarburgh-Bateson; child of 6 Baron Deramore; *b* 10 August 1950; *m* 15 May 1982, Jonathan Henry Maconchy Peel, er s of Walter Peel, of Knockdromin, Lusk, Co Dublin; 1 s (Nicholas Richard b 1987), 1 da (Katherine Diana b 1985); *Style*— The Hon Mrs Peel; 2 High Street, Nash, Buckinghamshire

PEEL, (Edmund) Anthony; s of Sir Jonathan Peel, CBE, MC, DL (d 1979), and Daphne Margaret Holwell, *née* Pakenham; *b* 4 Feb 1933; *Educ* Malvern, Pembroke Coll Cambridge (BA, MA); *m* 30 May 1964, Marion Julia, da of Lister Percy Redfern Bass, of Fivecorners, Wickham Bishops, Essex; 1 s (Richard b 1969), 1 da (Verity b 1965); *Career* slr 1962, Asher Prior Bates & Ptnrs Colchester; memb: Maldon DC 1973-83, Essex CC 1981-85; dep chm Maldon and Rochford Cons Assoc 1975-77, tres S Colchester and Maldon Cons Assoc 1984-86, chm Colne Housing Soc 1988-; memb Law Soc 1962, legal memb Royal Town Planning Inst 1967; *Style*— Anthony Peel, Esq; Elm House, Tolleshunt Dárcy, Maldon, Essex; Blackburn House, 32 Crouch St, Colchester (☎ 0206 68 331, fax 0206 760 096)

PEEL, Gp Capt Geoffrey William; s of Capt Lawrence Peel (ka 1914), of Knowlmere Manor, Clitheroe, Lancs, and Hon Lady Ethel Laura (d 1967), da of 2 Baron Crawshaw; *b* 20 Dec 1913; *Educ* Winchester, Magdalene Coll Cambridge (MA); *m* 3 Aug 1938, (Grace) Marjorie, da of Rev Canon Frank Rupert Mills (d 1955), of The Vicarage, Liskears, Cornwall; 1 s (Anthony b 1941), 2 da (Anne b 1947, Rosemary b 1952); *Career* cmmnd pilot gen duties branch RAF 1935, 16 Sqdn (army co-operation) 1936-38, special engr course Home Aircraft Depot Henlow 1938-40, station engr offr RAF West Freugh 1940-41, Wing Cdr engr Air HQ Iraq 1941, chief tech offr Aircraft Depot Iraq 1942, CO HQ maintenance unit Iraq 1942, CO RAF Shaibah Iraq 1943, engr SO HQ 206 Gp Middle East 1943-45, Gp Capt engr HQ Bomber Cmd 1945, HQ 8 Gp (pathfinder) 1945, ret 1946; co dir 1947-55, freelance industl conslt 1955-60, sec and industl conslt to Trade Assoc 1960-85; *Recreations* rifle shooting, tennis, shooting, foreign travel; *Style*— Gp Capt Geoffrey Peel; The Mews, Sherbourne Ct, Bourton-On-The-Water, Gloucs GL54 2BY (☎ 0451 20881)

PEEL, Jack Armitage; CBE (1972), DL (W Yorks 1971); s of George Henry Peel, of 8 Locherbe Green, Allerton, and Martha Peel; *b* 8 Jan 1921; *Educ* Ruskin Coll Oxford (Dip SocSci); *m* 1950, Dorothy Mabel, da of Walter Dobson, of 18 Melton Terrace, Bradford; 1 s, 1 da; *Career* trade union offr National Union of Dyers Bleachers and Textile Workers 1951-73, TUC gen cnsllr 1966-73, pt/t dir NCB 1968-73; dir idustl rels in Social Affrs Directorate EEC 1973-79 (chief advsr 1979-81); writer, industl rels conslt 1981-; special advsr industl rels to Sec of State for Tport 1983-84; sr visiting fell Industl Rels Bradford Univ 1984-; hon MA Bradford 1979; JP Bradford 1960-72;

Style— Jack Peel, Esq, CBE, DL; Timberleigh, 39 Old Newbridge Hill, Avon, Bath (☎ (0225) 23959)

PEEL, Prof John David Yeadon; s of Prof Edwin Arthur Peel, of Birmingham, and Nora Kathleen, *née* Yeadon (d 1988); *b* 13 Nov 1941; *Educ* Kings Edward's Sch Birmingham, Balliol Coll Oxford (MA), LSE (PhD), Univ of London (DLit); *m* 4 Sept 1969, Jennifer Christine Ferial, da of Maj Kenneth Nathaniel Pare; 3 s (David Nathaniel Yeadon b 16 March 1972, Timothy James Olatokunbo b 30 Jan 1974, Francis Edwin b 27 March 1977); *Career* asst lectr and lectr in sociology Univ of Nottingham 1966-70, lectr in sociology LSE 1970-73, visiting reader in sociology and anthropology Univ of Ife Nigeria 1973-75, Charles Booth prof of sociology Univ of Liverpool 1975- (dean of faculty of social and environmental studies 1985-88), visiting prof of anthropology and sociology Univ of Chicago 1982-83; ed Africa (jl of Int African Inst) 1979-86, gen ed Int African Library 1985-, advising ed African Studies Series 1986-; writer of numerous scholarly articles in Africanist, anthropological and sociological jls; Amaury Talbot Prize for African Anthropology 1983, Herskovits Award for African Studies (USA) 1984; sidesman St Saviour's church Oxton Wirral; memb Assoc Social Anthropologists 1979; *Books* Aladura: A Religious Movement among the Yoruba (1968), Herbert Spencer: The Evolution of a Sociologist (1971), Ijeshas and Nigerians: The Incorporation of a Yoruba Kingdom (1985); *Recreations* gardening, walking, old churches; *Style—* Prof J D Y Peel; Bryn Tirion, 23 Mount Rd, Upton, Wirral, Merseyside L49 6JA (☎ 051 678 6783); Dept of Sociology, Univ of Liverpool, P O Box 147, Liverpool L69 3BX (☎ 051 794 2973)

PEEL, Sir John Harold; KCVO (1960); s of Rev John Edward Peel and Katherine Hannah Peel; *b* 10 Dec 1904; *Educ* Manchester GS, Queen's Coll Oxford (MA, BM BCh), King's Coll Hosp Med Sch; *m* 1, 1935 (m dis 1945), Muriel Elaine Pellow; 1 da; m 2, 1947, Freda Margaret Mellish; *Career* obstetric and gynaecological surgn King's Coll Hosp 1936-69, surgn-gynaecologist Princess Beatrice Hosp 1936-66, hon tres RCOG 1959-66 (pres 1966-69); emeritus lectr King's Coll Hosp Med Sch 1969-, surgn-gynaecologist to HM The Queen 1961-73; pres: BMA 1970-71, Int Fedn of Obstetrics and Gynaecology 1970-73; Hon DSc Birmingham 1971, Hon DM Southampton 1973, Hon DCh Newcastle 1980, Hon FACOG, Hon FACS, Hon FRCS (Canada), Hon FCM (SA), Hon FRSM; fell Kings Coll London, FRCS, FRCOG, FRCP; *Books* Textbook of Gynaecology (1943), Lives of the Fellows of Royal College of Obstetricians and Gynaecologists (1976); *Recreations* fishing, golf, gardening; *Clubs* Naval and Military; *Style—* Sir John Peel, KCVO; 78 Countess Rd, Amesbury, Wilts SP4 7AT

PEEL, Sir (William) John; s of late Sir William Peel, KCMG, KBE; *b* 16 June 1912; *Educ* Wellington, Queens' Coll Cambridge; *m* 1936, Rosemary Mia Minka, da of late Robert Readhead; 1 s, 3 da; *Career* colonial admin serv 1933-51, Br resident Brunei 1946-48, res Cmmr Gilbert and Ellice Islands 1949-57; contested (C) Meridan Div of Warwicks 1955, MP (C) Leicester SE 1957-74; pps to: Econ Sec to Treasy 1958-59, min state BOT 1959-60; asst govt whip (unpaid) 1960-61, Lord Cmmr Treasy Nov 1961-64; pres: N Atlantic Assembly 1972-73, WEU Assembly 1972-74; memb Br Delgn to Euro Parli 1973-74; hon dir Cons Party Int Off 1975-76; kt 1973; *Style—* Sir John Peel; 51 Cambridge St, London SW1 (☎ 01 834 8762)

PEEL, Jonathan Sidney; MC (1957), DL (1976); s of Maj David Arthur Peel (ka 1944, s of late Rev the Hon Maurice Berkeley Peel, MC, 4 s of 1 Visc Peel) and Hon Sara Vanneck, da of 5 Baron Huntingfield; *b* 21 June 1937; *Educ* Norwich Sch, Eton, St John's Coll Cambridge (MA); *m* 20 Jan 1965, Jean Fulton, da of Air Chief Marshal Sir Denis Hensley Fulton Barnett, GCB, CBE, DFC, *qv*; 1 s (Robert b 1976), 4 da (Ruth b 1966, Emily b 1967, Anne b 1970, Delia b 1974); *Career* cmmnd RB Royal Green 1956, served Malaya 1956-57, UN Forces Congo (Zaire) 1960-61, Cyprus 1962-63, Capt 1966, resigned; page of honour to HM King George VI 1951-52 and to HM the Queen 1952-53; dir Norwich Union Insur Gp 1973-, chm Pleasureworld 1985-; memb Nat Tst: Cncl, Exec Ctee, Properties Ctee, Ctee for E Anglia (chm 1980-); memb Norfolk CC 1974-; chm: How Hill Tst for Environmental Studies 1985-, Norwich Sch 1985-, Police Authy 1985-, Broad Authy 1985-; Vice Lord Lt Norfolk 1981-, High Sheriff; *Books* Towards a Rural Policy (with M J Saver, 1973); *Recreations* music, forestry; *Clubs* Norfolk, Boodle's; *Style—* Jonathan Peel, Esq, MC, DL; Barton Hall, Barton Turf, Norwich NR12 8AU

PEEL, Michael David; s of James Peel (d 1978), of Gildersome, Morley, Leeds, and Kathleen, *née* Horbury; *b* 29 April 1946; *Educ* Queen Elizabeth GS Wakefield; *m* 1973 (m dis 1981), Deirdre Burrows, da of Alec Harrowsmith; *Career* articled clerk Starkie and Naylor 1964-69, CA 1969, audit sr Price Waterhouse 1969-71, chief accountant Richmond Tool Co 1971-72, co sec River Don Stamping Ltd 1972-74, mgmnt conslt Peat Marwick Mitchell and Co 1974-77, ptnr Broadhead Peel Rhodes CAS 1978-; involved coaching and team selection Halifax RUFC; FCA; *Recreations* rugby union, cricket; *Style—* Michael Peel, Esq; 9 Dawson Lane, Tong, Bradford, BO4 OST; Albion House, Albion St, Morley, Leeds LS27 8DT (☎ 0532 526122)

PEEL, Hon Robert Michael Arthur; s of 2 Earl Peel (d 1969), and Kathleen, da of Michael McGrath, of Ballyculane, Co Cork; *b* 5 Feb 1950; *Educ* Eton, Hertford Coll Oxford, UCL; *m* 1973, Fiona Natalie, da of Charles Davidson, of Dunhampstead House, Droitwich, Worcs; 3 da; *Style—* The Hon Robert Peel; Berryhill Farm, Coedkernew, Newport, Gwent

PEEL, 3 Earl (UK 1929); Sir William James Robert Peel; 8 Bt (GB 1800); Viscount Peel (UK 1895) and Viscount Clanfield (UK 1929); s of 2 Earl Peel (d 1969, himself gs of 1 Viscount, who was in turn 5 s of Sir Robert Peel, 2 Bt, the distinguished statesman); *b* 3 Oct 1947; *Educ* Ampleforth, Tours Univ, RAC Cirencester; *m* 1, 1973, Veronica Naomi Livingston, da of Alastair Timpson; 1 s (Viscount Clanfield), 1 da (Lady Iona b 1978); m 2, 1989, Hon Charlotte, *née* Soames, da of Baron Soames, GCMG, GCVO, CH, CBE, PC (Life Peer, d 1987), and formerly w of (Alexander) Richard Hambro, *qv*; *Heir* s, Viscount Clanfield; *Clubs* Turf; *Style—* The Rt Hon the Earl Peel; Gunnerside Lodge, Richmond, N Yorks

PEERLESS, Brian Read; s of Gordon Read Peerless (d 1977), and Ida Constance Holdup (d 1965); *b* 8 August 1934; *Educ* Ampleforth; *m* 1 Feb 1964, Caroline Margaret, da of Richard Leather (d 1977), of Berks; 1 s (Charles b 1968), 1 da (Jane-Emma b 1965); *Career* ptnr: W M Morris & Whiteheads 1963-72, Scott Goff Layon 1973-86; dir Smithernew Court Agency 1986-; memb ctee Stock Exchange Members Mutual Reference Soc 1964- (chm 1982-85); FInstD; *Recreations* lawn tennis, music; *Clubs* Hurlingham; *Style—* Brian Peerless, Esq; 34 Smith Terrace, London SW3 4DH; Smith New Court plc, 24 St Swithens Lane EC4N 8AE (telex 9413941, fax 01-623 3213)

PEERS, Charles; s of (Charles John) Jack Peers (d 1977), of Stadhampton, Oxford, and Rotha, *née* de Selincourt; *b* 16 Oct 1937; *Educ* Wennington Sch Wetherby Yorks, Northamptonshire Coll of Agric; *m* 8 Oct 1963, Heather Myrtle, da of William James Ridgway (d 1975), of Waterstock, Oxon; 2 s (Robert b 1967, Thomas b 1973); *Career* Nat Serv NCO 1956-58; farmer 1963; chm Stadhampton and Great Milton Parish Cncls 1968-82, dist cncllr 1970-78, chm NFU Parly Ctee 1980-87 (branch chm 1979-80); govr Peers Sch Littlemore Oxford 1971-, chm bd of govrs 1978-; *Recreations* shooting, classic vehicle restoration, buildings; *Style—* Charles Peers, Esq; Views Farm, Great Milton, Oxford 0X5 7NW (☎ 0844 279 352)

PEET, Frank Antony (Tony); s of Brig Lionel Meredith Peet (d 1967), of The Old Rectory, Lesnewth, Boscastle, Cornwall, and Elinor Marian, *née* Hayward (d 1988); *b* 5 May 1922; *Educ* Charterhouse, St John's Coll Cambridge, Brasenose Coll Oxford (MA); *m* 25 Nov 1950, June Rosemary, da of Thomas Graham Weall (d 1969), of Foursome, Maple Ave, Cooden Beach, Sussex; 2 s (John Graham b 8 May 1954, Ronald Arthur b 28 June 1957), 1 da (Vanessa b 21 Oct 1951); *Career* WWII, cmmnd RE 1942, Capt 1945, serv Africa, 42 FD Co RE Italy 1944-45 (despatches 1945); Colonial Serv Kenya 1949-62, admin cadet 1949, dist cmmr Garissa 1951; dist off: Embu 1952, Wundanyi Voi Dist 1952-54; off Municipal African Affrs Mombasa 1954, dist off Kandara 1955, seconded to Sp B Nairobi 1956; dist cmmr: Nakuaru 1957-59, Kiambu 1959, Fort Hall 1960-62; sr dist cmmr Mombasa 1963; called to Bar Grays Inn 1952 (disbarred 1964), admitted slr 1964, ptnr Marshall & Galpin 1965-88; clerk cmmrs of taxes Oxfordshire West 1979-88, Under Sheriff Oxfordshire 1986-88; tres Stadhampton PCC 1964-87, churchwarden 1966-70 and 1987-; *Recreations* golf, riding; *Clubs* Pegasus AFC, Harlequins GC, Vincent's (Oxford), Huntercombe GC; *Style—* Tony Peet, Esq; The Mill House, Stadhampton, Oxford

PEET, Ronald Hugh; CBE (1974); s of Henry Leonard Peet, and Stella Peet, of Manchester; *b* 12 July 1925; *Educ* Doncaster GS, Queen's Coll Oxford; *m* 1, 1949, Winifred Joy (d 1979), da of late Ernest Adamson; 2 s, 2 da; m 2, 1981, Lynette Judy Burgess Kinsella; *Career* Legal & General Assur Soc Ltd: dir 1969- 1984, chief exec 1972-80, chm 1980- 1984; Legal & Gen Gp plc: gp chief exec 1979-84, dir 1979-84; chm Aviation & Gen Assur Soc Ltd 1978-80, dir Watling St Properties 1971-84, chm City Arts Tst Ltd 1980-87; dir: Royal Philharmonic Orch Ltd 1977-88, ENO 1978-; chm Stockley plc 1984-87, dir AMEC plc 1984-; chm The Howard Gp plc 1985-86, dep chm PWS Hldgs plc 1986-88, dir New Scotland Insur Gp plc 1987-; FIA; *Recreations* music, opera; *Clubs* Hurlingham, City of London; *Style—* Ronald Peet, Esq, CBE; 36 Shawfield St, Chelsea, London SW3 4BD (☎ 01 351 0307);

PEGG, Dr Michael Anstice; s of Benjamin Daniel Pegg (d 1951), and Rose, *née* Anstice; *b* 3 Sept 1931; *Educ* Burton-on-Trent GS, Univ of Southampton (BA, MA, PhD); *m* 1, 31 August 1955, Jean Williams; 3 s (Paul b 1957, Richard b 1959, Timothy b 1962); m 2, 1 April 1986, Margaret Rae; *Career* Capt RAEC Educn Off SHAPE Paris 1959-61; sec and estab offr Nat Library of Scotland Edinburgh 1967-76 (asst keeper 1961-67), librarian Univ of Birmingham 1976-80, dir and univ librarian John Rylands Univ Library of Manchester 1980-; memb: Br Library Bd 1981-84, Standing Conference of Nat and Univ Libraries Cncl 1981-83; *Books* Les Divers Rapports d'Eustorg de Beaulieu (1964), Catalogue of German Reformation Pamphlets in Libraries of Great Britain and Ireland (1973), Catalogue of Sixteenth-Century German Pamphlets in Collections in France and England (1977), Catalogue of Reformation Pamphlets in Swiss Libraries (1983), Catalogue of Early Sixteenth Century Books in the Royal Library Copenhagen (1989); *Recreations* tennis, cricket, music, railway modelling; *Style—* Dr M A Pegg; John Rylands Univ Library of Manchester, Oxford Rd, Manchester M13 9PP (☎ 061 275 3700)

PEGGIE, Robert Galloway Emslie; CBE (1956); s of John Masterton Peggie (d 1986), of Loanhead, Midlothian, and Euphemia Glendinning, *née* Emslie (d 1956); *b* 5 Jan 1929; *Educ* Lasswade HS; *m* 27 June 1955, Christine Jeanette, da of William Cumming Simpson (d 1943); 1 s (David b 11 Feb 1962), 1 da (Alison b 13 Feb 1958); *Career* Nat Serv RAF 1947-49; CA 1946, mgmnt accountant Brush Electrical Engrg 1955-57, dep city chamberlain Edinburgh Corpn 1966-72 (O & M team 1957), seconded to PA Mgmnt conslts 1972-74, chief exec Lothian Regnl Cncl 1974-86, cmmr local admin Scotland 1986-; memb: ct Heriot-Watt Univ, cncl Royal Scottish Geographical Soc, Devpt Ctee Scottish Museums Cncl;; *Style—* R G E Peggie, Esq, CBE; 54 Liberton Drive, Edinburgh EH16 6NW (☎ 031 664 1631); Princes House, 5 Shandwick Place, Edinburgh EH2 4RG (☎ 031 229 4472)

PEGLER, James Basil Holmes; TD (and bar 1946); s of Harold Holmes Pegler (d 1963), of Greystones, Heathhurst Rd, Sanderstead, Surrey, and Dorothy Cecil, *née* Francis (d 1957); *b* 6 August 1912; *Educ* Charterhouse, Open Univ (BA); *m* 11 Sept 1937, Enid Margaret, da of Leonard Dell (d 1952), of Sanderstead, Surrey; 1 s (Stephen b 1951), 3 da (Judith b 1939, Valerie b 1941, Audrey b 1945); *Career* cmmnd 2 Lt 4 Bn The Queen's Royal Regt TA 1935, Maj 4 Bn Queen's Royal Regt (63 Searchlight Regt RA) TA 1941, GSO 2 WO LM5 1944, 2 i/c 127 LAA Regt RA TA 1948-50; gen mangr and actuary Clerical Med and Gen Life Assur Soc 1950 (investmt sec 1948), chm Life Offs Assoc 1959-61, pres Comité Européen des Assurs Life Gp 1964-70, prof of actuarial sci City Univ 1975-79 (visiting prof 1980-86); govr Fyling Hall Sch Robin Hood's Bay 1977; FIA 1939 (hon sec 1951-59, pres 1968-70), FSS 1948, FIS 1951, FIMA 1971; *Recreations* mathematics, lawn tennis; *Clubs* Army and Navy; *Style—* James B H Pegler, Esq, TD; Dormers, 28 Deepdene Wood, Dorking, Surrey RH5 4BQ (☎ 0306 885955)

PEGNA, Hon Mrs Elizabeth Ruth Frances; da of 1 Baron Layton (d 1966); *b* 1923; *m* 1944 (m dis 1965), Edward William Guttiers (Bobbie) Pegna; 2 s, 2 da; *Style—* The Hon Mrs Pegna; Whitegates, Chedworth, Cheltehnam, Glos

PEIERLS, Sir Rudolf Ernst; CBE (1946); s of Heinrich Peierls (d 1945), of Berlin, and Elisabeth, *née* Weigert (d 1921); *b* 5 June 1907,Berlin; *Educ* Humboldt Sch Oberschöneweide Berlin, Berlin Univ, Munich Univ, Leipzig Univ (DPhil), (DSc Manchester, MA Cantab and Oxon); *m* 1931, Eugenia, da of late Nikolai Kannegiesser (d 1910), of St Petersburg; 1 s, 3 da; *Career* asst Fed Inst of Technol Zurich 1929-32, Rockefeller fell Rome and Cambridge 1932-33, hon res fell Univ of Manchester 1933-35, res asst Royal Soc Mond Laboratory Cambridge 1935-37, prof of applied maths (later mathematical physics) Univ of Birmingham 1937-63, worked on Atomic Energy Project 1940-43 (USA 1943-45), Wykeham prof of physics Univ of Oxford and fell New Coll 1963-74 (later hon fell); prof of physics pt/t Univ of Washington Seattle 1974-77; FRS, FInstP; kt 1968; *Clubs* Athenaeum; *Style—* Sir Rudolf Peierls, CBE; 2B

Northmoor Rd, Oxford OX2 6UP (☎ 0865 56497); Nuclear Physics Laboratory, Keble Rd, Oxford OX1 3RH

PEILE, George Howard; MC (1943 and bar 1944), TD, DL; s of Henry Peile, CBE (d 1935), of Broomshiels Hall, Satley, Co Durham, and Eva Ethel, *née* Beckingham (d 1964); *b* 10 Sept 1910; *Educ* Eton, Trinity Coll Cambridge (BA); *m* 23 March 1946, Rosemary Margherita Cecilia, da of Maj George Cecil Whitaker (d 1959), of Watlington, Oxon; 2 s (Charles b 1954, 1 s decd), 1 da (Margaret b 1949); *Career* WWII serv 1939-45: Surrey & Sussex Yeo (QMR) 98 FD Rgt RA France, Italy; barr 1932; dir The Priestman Collieries Ltd, asst md The Newcastle Breweries Ltd, ret 1956; JP Northumberland 1959-79, memb Northumberland CC 1968-84; *Recreations* shooting; *Clubs* Northern Counties; *Style*— George H Peile, Esq, MC, TD, DL; Kirsopp House, Great Whittington, Northumberland, Newcastle-upon-Tyne NE19 2HA (☎ 043 472 241)

PEILE, Vice Adm Sir Lancelot Arthur Babington; KBE (1960), CB (1957), DSO (1941), LVO (1947), DL (Devon 1969); s of late Basil Wilson Peile; *b* 22 Jan 1905; *Educ* RNCs Osborne and Dartmouth; *m* 1928, Gertrude Margaret, *née* Tolcher; 2 s; *Career* Cdr (E) 1939, Capt (E) 1947, Rear Adm 1955, Vice Adm 1958, Adm Superintendent Devonport Dockyard 1957-60, ret 1960; *Style*— Vice Admiral Sir Lancelot Peile, KBE, CB, DSO, LVO, DL; Strawberry How, Thurlestone, Kingsbridge, Devon (☎ Kingsbridge 560209)

PEIRSE, Air Vice-Marshal Richard Charles Fairfax; CB (1984); s of late Air Chief Marshal Sir Richard Peirse, KCB, DSO, AFC (d 1970), and late Lady (Mary Joyce) Peirse, *née* Ledgard; the Peirses were once great landowners in N Riding of Yorks, being descended from Peter Peirse, who fought for the House of York as a standard-bearer at Bosworth Field 1485 (where he lost a leg); the pedigree is first recorded in the Visitation of 1634; John Peirse (1593-1658) is thought to have been the purchaser of the manor of Bedale, where the family resided for many generations, until it descended through m to the Beresford-Peirse family, *qv*; *b* 16 Mar 1931; *Educ* Bradfield, RAF Coll Cranwell; *m* 1, 1955 (m dis 1963), Karalie Grace Cox; 2 da (Amanda, Susan); m 2, 1963, Deirdre Mary O'Donovan (d 1976); 1 s (Richard); m 3, 1977, Anna Jill Margaret Long, da of Rt Hon Sir John (Brinsmead) Latey, MBE, of Roehampton, qv; *Career* cmmnd 1952, serv various sqdns and HQ in Germany, UK, Malta 1952-68, cmd No 51 Sqdn 1968-69, Dep Capt of the Queens Flight 1969-72, cmd RAF Waddington 1973-75, MOD 1975-82, AOC and Cmdt RAF Coll Cranwell 1982-85, qualified Flying Instr and graduate RAF Staff Coll Andover 1963, Jt Servs Staff Coll 1968, RCDS 1972; Sec Def Servs MOD 1985-; *Clubs* RAF; *Style*— Air Vice-Marshal Richard Peirse, CB; 10 Pembroke Road, London W8 (☎ 01 602 5888); Ministry of Defence, Whitehall SW1

PEIRSON, Margaret Ellen; eld da of late David Edward Peirson, CBE, and Norah Ellen, *née* Corney; *b* 28 Nov 1942; *Educ* N London Collegiate Sch Canons Edgware Middx, Somerville Coll Oxford (BA), Yale Univ USA; *Career* joined HM Treasy 1965, seconded Bank of England 1982-84, under sec HM Treasy 1986-; *Recreations* choral singing, theatre; *Style*— Miss Margaret Peirson; HM Treasury, Parliament St, London SW1

PEIRSON, Richard; s of Geoffrey Peirson (d 1986), of Purley, Surrey, and Beryl Joyce, *née* Walder; *b* 5 Mar 1949; *Educ* Purley GS, Univ of Liverpool (BSc); *m* 31 May 1975 (sep), Jennifer Margaret, da of late F E Fernie; 1 s (James Richard b 1978), 1 da (Caroline Jane b 1980); *Career* Arthur Andersen & Co 1970-72, Colegrave & Co 1972-73, J & A Scrimgeour Ltd 1973-75, Carr Sebag & Co (formerly WI Carr Sons & Co) 1975-82, Grieveson Grant & Co 1982-86, Kleinwort Benson Investmt Mgmnt Ltd 1986-; govr Denmead Sch; memb Stock Exchange; *Recreations* tennis, squash, reading, collecting watercolours; *Style*— Richard Peirson, Esq; 51 Mount Ararat Rd, Richmond, Surrey TW10 6PL (☎ 01 940 2013); Kleinwort Benson Investment Management Ltd, 10 Fenchurch St, London EC3M 3LB (☎ 01 623 8000, fax 9413545)

PEISER, Graham Allan; s of Eric George Peiser, of Bucks, and Honor, *née* Greenwood (d 1988); *b* 26 Mar 1940; *Educ* Coll of Estate Mgmnt Aldenham; *m* 26 Sept 1970, Jennifer Ann, da of Dr John Richard Cooper, of W Sussex; 2 da (Georgina b 1972, Lucy b 1976); *Career* chartered surveyor; ptnr Fuller Peiser 1970-; FRICS; *Style*— Graham A Peiser, Esq; Pear Tree Cottage, The Green, Sarratt, Rickmansworth, Herts WD3 4BL (☎ 092 77 69136); Thavies Inn House, 3-4 Holborn Circus, London EC1N 2HL (☎ 01 353 6851)

PELHAM, Hon Mrs Anthony; Barbara Clare; da of former Col J E D Taunton, late DQMG, Aust Mil Forces; *m* 1928, as his 2 w, Hon Anthony Ashley Ivo Pelham, (s of 5 Earl of Chichester (d 1951); *Style*— The Hon Mrs Anthony Pelham; Halland Clyst St Mary, Exeter, Devon

PELHAM, Michael Alan; s of Harry Alan Pelham (d 1971), and Doris Millicent, *née* Taunton (later Mrs Eccles, d 1959); *b* 23 Sept 1926; *Educ* Sherborne, King's Coll Cambridge (BA, MA); *m* 25 Oct 1958, Lucy Helen, da of Cyril R Egerton, of Hall Farm, Stetchworth, Newmarket; 1 s (Charles Peregrine b 27 July 1959), 1 da (Laura Mary b 15 May 1962); *Career* Nat Serv Capt RE 1946-48, RAFVR (Cambridge Univ Air Sqdn); Wiggins Teape & Co 1951-58; md: Abitibi Sales Co UK 1958, Abitibi-Bathurst Ltd 1962, Consolidated Bathurst (Overseas) Ltd 1967, Bridgewater Paper Sales Ltd 1983-87, Bridgewater Newsprint Ltd 1988; JP Inner London Area 1961, London Juvenile Ct Panel 1961-78; vice chm London Fedn of Boy's Clubs 1963-66; Freeman City of London 1964, Liveryman Worshipful Co of Newspaper Makers & Stationers 1964; *Recreations* sailing, gardening, fishing, shooting, music; *Clubs* Brooks's, Hurlingham, Royal Yacht Squadron, Royal Ocean Racing; *Style*— Michael Pelham, Esq; Abbey Spring, Beaulieu, Hants SO42 7YT (☎ 0590 612 264); 41 Yeomans Row, London SW3; 195 Knightsbridge, London SW7 (☎ 01 581 7676, fax 01 589 6514, car tel 0836 260 832, telex 25863)

PELHAM, Richard Anthony Henry; s of Maj Anthony George Pelham (d 1969); kinsman and hp of 9 Earl of Chichester; *b* 1 August 1952; *Educ* Eton; *m* 1987, Georgina, da of David Gilmour, of Ringshall, Suffolk; 1 s (b 1987); *Recreations* vintage motor cycle racing; *Clubs* Vintage Motor Cycle; *Style*— Richard Pelham, Esq; c/o Coutts & Co, 162 Brompton Rd, London SW3

PELHAM, Hon Mrs (Valery); da of Baron Segal (Life Peer) and Molly, *née* Rolo; *b* 14 Feb 1943; *Educ* Badminton Sch Bristol; *m* 1967, Paul Nicholas David Pelham; 1 s, 3 da; *Career* SRN St Thomas' Hosp; *Style*— The Hon Mrs Pelham; 24 Frognal Lane, London NW3

PELHAM BURN, Angus Maitland; JP (Kincardine and Deeside 1984), DL (1978); s of Brig-Gen Henry Pelham Burn, CMG, DSO (d 1958), and Katherine Eileen, *née* Staveley-Hill; *b* 13 Dec 1931; *Educ* Harrow, N of Scotland Coll of Agric; *m* 19 Dec 1959, Anne Rosdew, da of Sir Ian Algernon Forbes-Leith, 2 Bt, KT, MBE (d 1973); 4 da (Amanda b 1961, Lucy b 1963, Emily b 1964, Kate b 1966); *Career* Hudson's Bay Co 1951-58; chm and dir: Macrobert Farms (Douneside) Ltd 1970-87, Pelett Admin Ltd 1973-; dir: Aberdeen and Northern Marts Ltd 1970-86 (chm 1974-86), Aberdeen Meat Mktg Co Ltd 1973-86 (chm 1974-86), Bank of Scotland 1977- (chm Aberdeen Local Bd 1973-), Scottish Provident Inst 1975-, Prime Space Design Ltd 1981-87, Taw Meat Co 1984-86, Skeendale Ltd 1987-88, Aberdeen Tst Hldgs Ltd (formerly Aberdeen Fund Mangrs) 1985-, Status Timber Systems 1986-; memb: Kincardine CC 1967-75 (vice convener 1973-75), Grampian Regnl Cncl 1974-; memb: Aberdeen Assoc for the Prevention of Cruelty to Animals 1975- (dir and chm 1984-), Accounts Cmmn 1980- (dep chm 1987-), cncl Winston Churchill Mem Tst 1984-; chm Aberdeen Airport Consultative Ctee 1986-; memb Queen's Body Guard for Scotland (Royal Co of Archers) 1968-; Vice Lord Lt for Kincardineshire 1978-; Liveryman Worshipful Co of Farmers until 1988; Hon FInstM 1987; *Recreations* vegetable gardening, stalking, shooting, fishing; *Clubs* New (Edinburgh), Royal Northern & Univ (Aberdeen); *Style*— Angus Pelham Burn, Esq, JP, DL; 68 Station Rd, Banchory, Kincardineshire AB3 3YJ (☎ 033 023343); Knappach, Banchory, Kincardineshire AB3 3JS (☎ 033 044 555)

PELHAM BURN, Michael Raleigh; s of Archibald Henry Pelham Burn (d 1969), and Robina Phyllis Evelyn, *née* Heinekey-Buxton (d 1968); *b* 22 May 1923; *Educ* Radley, Trinity Coll Oxford, RMA Sandhurst; *m* 23 May 1964, Diane, da of George Hess (d 1974), of Baltimore, Maryland USA; 1 s (James Fraser b 1968), 1 da (Robina Claire b 1966); *Career* Capt Royal Dragoons, N Africa, Italy, France, Holland, Germany, Denmark; Aide to C-in-C ME; dir J H Vavasseur & Co Ltd to 1968, Kandy Food Prods to 1976; dist cncllr S Bucks to 1988; *Recreations* travel, sailing; *Style*— Michael R Pelham Burn, Esq; Widgenton, Beaconsfield, Bucks HP9 1XA (☎ 0494 673856)

PELHAM-CLINTON-HOPE, Lady Patricia; *née* Pelham-Clinton-Hope; da of 9 Duke of Newcastle, OBE (d 1988); *b* 20 July 1949; *m* 1, 1971 (m dis 1974), Alan Pariser; resumed surname of Pelham-Clinton-Hope 1974; m 2, 1981 (m dis 1983), Nick Mancuso, of Toronto; resumed maiden name again; *Career* actress; film The Killing of a Chinese Bookie 1976; *Style*— Lady Patricia Pelham-Clinton-Hope; 8012 Happy Lane, Los Angeles, California 90046, USA

PELL, Marion Priscilla; *née* Leak; da of Anthony Edward Lear, and Elsie Ellen, *née* Chellingworth; *b* 5 July 1952; *Educ* Watford GS for Girls, Univ of Southampton (LLB); *m* 4 Aug 1973, Gordon Francis Pell, s of Lt-Col Denis Herbert Pell (d 1987); 2 s (Oliver b 3 May 1982, Nicholas b 1 Aug 1984), 1 da (Victoria b 12 May 1987); *Career* asst slr Herbert Smith 1976-84 (ptnr 1984-); memb Law Soc; *Recreations* music, walking; *Style*— Mrs Gordon Pell; Watling House, 35 Cannon St, London EC4M 5SD (☎ 01 489 8000, fax 01 239 0426)

PELLEREAU, Maj-Gen Peter John Mitchell; s of Col John Cyril Etienne Pellereau (d 1973), of Robertsbridge, Sussex, and Aileen Nora Vidal, *née* Betham, of Penshurst Kent; family became Br following ceding of Isle de France to Britain becoming Mauritius; *b* 24 April 1921; *Educ* Wellington, Trinity Coll Cambridge (BA, MA); *m* 1949, Rosemary, da of Sydney Robert Garnar (d 1981), of Wrotham, Kent; 2 s (Matthew, David); *Career* cmmnd RE 1942, served in NW Europe, Maj OC 26 Armd Engr Sqdn RE (Hameln) 1946-47, Tech Staff Offr Fighting Vehicles Design Estab Chobham 1948-49, Dep Cdr Engr Base Installations Singapore 1953-55, sec Def Res Policy Ctee MOD 1959-60, Lt-Col Mil Sec's Dept MOD 1960-62, cmdg 131 Parachute Engr Regt RE TA 1963-64, Col Mil Dir of Studies RMCS Shrivenham 1965-67, asst dir RE Equipment Devpt MOD 1967-70, Brig Sr Mil Offr Royal Armament Res and Devpt Estab Fort Halstead 1970-73, pres Ordnance Bd 1975-76; past pres: RE Lawn Tennis Club, Oxted Hockey Club; ctee memb Wolfe Soc, sec Assoc of Consulting Engr 1976-87; CEng, FIMechE, FBIM; *Style*— Maj-Gen Peter Pellereau; Woodmans Folly, Crockham Hill, Edenbridge, Kent (☎ 0732 866309)

PELLEW, Mark Edward; LVO (1980); s of Anthony Pownoll Pellew, of Wimbledon, and Margaret Julia Critchley, *née* Cookson; *b* 28 August 1942; *Educ* Winchester, Trinity Coll Oxford (BA); *m* 1965, Jill Hosford, da of Prof Frank Thistlethwaite, CBE, of Cambridge; 2 s (Adam Lee b 1966, Dominic Stephen b 1968); *Career* HM Dip Serv 1965-; FO 1965-67, Singapore 1967-69, Saigon 1969-70, FCO 1970-76, first sec Rome 1976-80, asst head Personnel Ops Dept FCO 1981-83; cnsllr (polit) Washington DC 1983-; *Recreations* tennis, singing, playing the horn; *Clubs* Hurlingham; *Style*— Mark Pellew, Esq, LVO; c/o Foreign and Cwlth Office, King Charles Street, London SW1A 2AH; British Embassy, 3100 Mass Avenue, Washington DC 20008, USA (☎ 202 898 4264)

PELLEW, Hon Mrs Mary Rose; *née* Pellew; da of 9 Viscount Exmouth (d 1970); *b* 1938; *m* 1974, D Roman Llanso, of Madrid; *Style*— The Hon Mary-Rose Pellew de Llanso; Urb. Los Pinos, 28220-Majadahonda, Madrid, Spain

PELLEW, Hon Patricia Sofia; da (by 1 m) of 10 Viscount Exmouth; *b* 1966; *Style*— The Hon Patricia Pellew; Paseo de Rosales, 3Z, Madrid, Spain

PELLEW, Hon Peter Irving; s of late 9 Viscount Exmouth and Maria Luisa (Marquisa de Olias), da of late Marques de Amurrio of Madrid; *b* 1942; *Educ* Downside; *Style*— The Hon Peter Pellew; c/o The Rt Hon the Viscount Exmouth, Canonteign, nr Exeter, Devon EX6 7RH

PELLING, Anthony Adair; s of Brian Pelling, and Alice, *née* Lamb; *b* 3 May 1934; *Educ* Purley GS, LSE (BSc), NW Poly London, Wolverhampton Coll of Technol (MIPM); *m* Margaret Rose, *née* Lightfoot; 1 s (Andrew John), 1 da (Sarah Margaret); *Career* ROAC WO 1955-57; NCB 1957-67, Civil Serv 1967-; Miny Public Bldgs & Works: princ 1967-69, asst sec 1969-81, undersec 1981; dep dir Business in the Community 1981-83; dir DTp Highways Contracts and Maintenance 1983-85, construction indust and sports and recreation directorate DOE 1985-87, dir London Region DOE 1987-;; *Clubs* Reform, Surrey CCC; *Style*— Anthony Pelling, Esq; London Region, Dept of the Enviroment, Millbank Tower, Millbank, London SW1P 4QU

PELLING, Dr Henry Mathison; s of late Douglas Langley Pelling, of Birkenhead, Ches, and late Maud Mary, *née* Mathison; *b* 27 August 1920; *Educ* Birkenhead Sch, St John's Coll Cambridge (BA, MA, PhD, LittD); *Career* RA 1941-42, cmmnd 2 Lt then Lt RE 1942, Capt Educn Corps 1945; fell Queen's Coll Oxford 1949-65 (tutor 1950-65, dean 1963-64, supernumerary fell 1980), St John's Coll Cambridge 1946- (asst dir of res history faculty 1966-77, reader in recent Br history 1977-80), Smith-Mundt Sch Univ of Wisconsin USA 1953-54, fell Woodrow Wilson Center Washington DC 1983;

Hon DLitt New Sch for Social Res NY 1983; *Books* Origins of the Labour Party (1954), Challenge of Socialism (1954), America and the British Left (1956), British Communist Party (1958, with Frank Bealey), Labour and Politics (1958), American Labour (1960), Modern Britain 1885-1955 (1960), Short History of the Labour Party (1961, 8 edn 1985), History of British Trade Unionism (1963, 4 edn 1987), Social Geography of British Elections (1967), Popular Politics and Society in Late Victorian Britain (1968, 2 edn 1979), Britain and the Second World War (1970), Winston Churchill (1974), The Labour Governments 1945-51 (1984), also pieces written for various jls; *Recreations* theatre, cinema; *Clubs* Nat Lib, Royal Cwlth Soc; *Style*— Dr Henry Pelling; St John's College, Cambridge CB2 1TP (☎ 0223 338600)

PELLY, Derek Roland (Derk); s of Arthur Roland Pelly (d 1966), of Ballygate House, Beccles, Suffolk, and Phyllis Elsie, *née* Henderson (d 1973); *b* 12 June 1929; *Educ* Marlborough, Trinity Coll Cambridge (MA); *m* 20 June 1953, Susan, da of John Malcolm Roberts (d 1986), of Felpham, Sussex; 1 s (Sam b 1960), 2 da (Rosemary b 1955, Catherine b 1958); *Career* 2 Lt RA 1947-49; Barclays Bank 1952-88: local dir Chelmsford Dist 1959-68 (asst to chm 1968-69), local dir Luton Dist 1969-79, dir Barclays Int 1974 (vice chm 1977-86, chm 1986-87), dir Barclays plc 1974 (vice-chm 1984-86, dep chm 1986-88); ctee memb Family Assur Soc 1988-; JP Chelmsford 1965-68, chm City Commuter Gp 1987-88; dir Milton Keynes Devpt Corpn 1976-85, cncl memb Overseas Devpt Inst 1984-, govr London House for Overseas Graduates 1985-, tres Friends of Essex Churches 1989-, memb Chelmsford Diocesan Bd of Fin 1989-; FCIB, FRSA; *Recreations* painting; *Clubs* Commonwealth; *Style*— Derk Pelly, Esq; The Bowling Green, The Downs, Gt Dunmow, Essex CM6 1DT (☎ 0371 2662)

PELLY, Sir John Alwyne; 6 Bt (UK 1840), of Upton, Essex, JP (Hants 1966), DL (Hants 1972); s of Sir (Harold) Alwyne Pelly, 5 Bt, MC (d 1981), and Caroline Earle, da of Richard Heywood-Jones (d 1976), of Badsworth Hall, Yorks; *b* 11 Sept 1918; *Educ* Canford, RMC, RAC; *m* 1, 1945, Ava Barbara Ann, da of Brig Keith Frederick William Dunn, CBE, DL; m 2, 1950, Elsie May (Hazel) (d 1987), da of late Louis Thomas Dechow, of Rhodesia (now Zimbabwe); 1 da (Margaret b 1952) and 2 da decd; *Heir* n, Richard John Pelly b 1951; *Career* Coldstream Gds 1938-50, serv WWII (Egypt and Libya) POW 1942, Malayan Campaign 1948-50, ret Maj; High Sheriff Hants 1970-71, memb Lands Tbnl 1982-88; *Recreations* shooting, skiing; *Clubs* Royal Overseas; *Style*— Sir John Pelly, Bt, JP, DL; Preshaw House, Upham, nr Southampton, Hants SO3 1HP (☎ 048 93 2531; office 048 93 2974)

PELLY, Peter Richard; s of Francis Brian Pelly, AFC (d 1984), and Edith Beatrice Packe (d 1984); ggggs of Elizabeth Fry; *b* 17 June 1916; *Educ* Mowden Sch Brighton, Bryanston; *m* 25 Aug 1945, Kathleen Irene, da of Sydney William Moorhouse (d 1962); 2 da (Lynda Ann b 1947, Kathleen Georgina b 1951); *Career* apprentice De Havilland aircraft Co Ltd 1934-39, planning engr De Havilland Engrg Co Ltd 1939-47, prodn engr 1947-49, conslt engr Assoc Indus Conslts 1949-54, chief prodn engr Rotal Ltd 1954-57, works mangr Hamworthy Engrg Ltd 1957-58, gen works mangr Cox & Co (Watford) Ltd 1958-62, dir and gen mangr Delaney Gallay Ltd 1962-69 (tech dir 1969-72), admin mangr Warne Surgical Products Ltd 1972-75, co-ordinating engr Marconi Defence Systems 1975-81; *Recreations* gardening, DIY, photography; *Style*— Peter Pelly, Esq; Green Farm, Bovingdon Green, Bovingdon, Herts HP3 0LF (☎ 0442 832 313)

PELTZER DUNN, Garry Ian Michael; s of Richard Michael Fallows Dunn, and Bettine *née* Primrose Smith; *b* 2 Feb 1943; *Educ* Hove Coll; *m* 9 April 1966, Elaine Louise Bole, da of Maj Anton Peltzer (d 1976); 2 da (Katharine b 1967, Elizabeth b 1971); *Career* chartered surveyor (ARICS), ex dir Newsstop Ltd, ldr Hove Borough Cncl, chm Policy & Resources Ctee, elected 1974; former vice-chm: Hove C Assoc, SE Area Young C; former memb E Sussex CC, life memb Hove Civic Soc, former ctee memb Hove Civic Soc; memb Preston Nomads CC,; *Recreations* animal welfare, sport, travel; *Clubs* Hove Conservative, Hove Deep Sea Anglers; *Style*— Garry Peltzer Dunn, Esq; 234 New Church Rd, Hove, E Sussex (☎ 0273 414615)

PEMBERTON, Capt Bertram Stote; s of Bertram Roper Stote Pemberton (d 1943), of The Dove House, Harleston, Norfolk, and Nina Augusta, *née* Lloyd (d 1968); *b* 20 Jan 1912; *Educ* Eton, Naval Cadet HMS Erebus; *m* 23 July 1937, Sheila Elizabeth, da of John Murray Naylor, of Easter Ogil, Forfar, Angus; 1 s (Ian b 1938), 1 da (Gillian b 1940); *Career* Naval Offr 1930-60 Capt serv WWII, Home Fleet Mediterranean, E Indies (Staff of C-in-C) Capt 3 Frigate Sqdn 1955-56; dir Underwater Warfare (Admty) 1957-59; *Recreations* shooting, gardening, ornithology; *Clubs* Army & Navy; *Style*— Capt Bertram Pemberton, RN; Holberry Cottage, Bishops Sutton, Alresford, Hants SO24 0AG (☎ 0962 732 751)

PEMBERTON, Sir Francis Wingate William; CBE (1970), DL (Cambs 1979); s of late Dr William Warburton Wingate (assumed Arms of Pemberton, by Royal Licence, 1921), and Viola Patience, *née* Campbell; *b* 1 Oct 1916; *Educ* Eton, Trinity Coll Cambridge; *m* 19 April 1941, Diana Patricia, da of late Reginald Salisbury Woods and late Irene Woods, CBE, TD; 2 s; *Career* sr conslt, Bidwells Chartered Surveyors; dir: Agric Mortgage Corpn Ltd 1969-, Barclays Bank UK Mgmnt Ltd 1977-81; High Sheriff Cambs and Isle of Ely 1965-66, FRICS; kt 1976; *Style*— Sir Francis Pemberton, CBE, DL; Trumpington Hall, Cambridge (☎ 0223 841941); Business: Bidwell House, Trumpington Rd, Cambridge (☎ 0223 841841)

PEMBERTON, Jeremy; s of Sidney Charles Pemberton (d 1974), and Levina Beatrice (d 1974); *b* 17 Oct 1948; *Educ* Hampton GS; *m* 25 July 1969, Anne Marie Therese Antoinette, da of Adrien Croughs; *Career* creative dir Yellowhammer plc 1972-87; dep chm Yellowhammer plc 1987-; *Recreations* squash, chess; *Clubs* RAC; *Style*— Jeremy Pemberton, Esq; Yellowhammer, 76 Oxford St, London W1

PEMBROKE, Ann Marjorie Francescia; *née* Gorman; da of Reginald William Gorman (d 1979), of Bromley, Kent, and Ethel, *née* Lamb-Shine (d 1979); *b* 1 Jan 1938; *Educ* Holy Trinity Convent, Sorbonne; *m* 18 June 1960, Mark Pembroke, s of Geoffrey Vernon Worth Pembroke (d 1983), of Bexhill-on-Sea, Sussex; 2 s (Guy Richard b 1963, James Robert b 1966); *Career* FO London and Paris 1956-58; Pembroke & Pembroke London 1969-; memb: Ct of Common Cncl City of London, Care, IOW Soc; Dep Ward of Cheap, asst Irish Soc, govr City of London Sch, tstee Dr Johnson's House, rep Nat Assoc for Maternal and Child Welfare; Freeman City of London 1977, Liveryman Worshipful Co of Horners 1980; *Recreations* travel, horticulture, country pursuits; *Clubs* City Livery, Guildhall; *Style*— Mrs Mark Pembroke

PEMBROKE AND MONTGOMERY, 17 Earl of (E 1551) and 14 Earl of (E 1605) respectively; Henry George Charles Alexander Herbert; also Baron Herbert of Cardiff (E 1551), Baron Herbert of Shurland (E 1605), and Baron Herbert of Lea (UK 1861); o s of 16 Earl of Pembroke and Montgomery, CVO (d 1969), and Mary Countess of Pembroke, *qv*; *b* 19 May 1939; *Educ* Eton, Christ Church Oxford; *m* 1, 1966 (m dis 1981), Claire Rose, o da of Douglas Gurney Pelly; 1 s, 3 da (Lady Sophia b 1966, Lady Emma b 1969, Lady Flora b 1970); m 2, 16 April 1988, Miranda J, da of Cdr J S K Oram, of Bulbridge House, Wilton, Salisbury, Wilts; *Heir* s, Lord Herbert, *qv*; *Career* hereditary grand visitor of Jesus Coll Oxford; Royal Horse Gds 1958-60; owner of Wilton House (Inigo Jones, built around 1650, with additional work by James Wyatt 1810); *Style*— The Rt Hon the Earl of Pembroke and Montgomery; Wilton House, Salisbury, Wilts (☎ 0722 743211)

PEMBROKE AND MONTGOMERY, Mary, Countess of; Lady Mary Dorothea; *née* Hope; CVO (1947) DL; da of 1 Marquess of Linlithgow, KT, GCMG, GCVO, PC (d 1908); *b* 31 Dec 1903; *m* 27 July 1936, 16 Earl of Pembroke and Montgomery, CVO (d 1969); 1 s (17 Earl of Pembroke), 1 da; *Career* hon first offr WRNS; lady-in-waiting to HRH the Duchess of Kent 1934-49, extra lady-in-waiting 1949-68; *Style*— The Rt Hon Mary, Countess of Pembroke and Montgomery, CVO DL; The Old Rectory, Wilton, Salisbury, Wilts SP2 0HT (☎ 0722 743157)

PENDER, 3 Baron (UK 1937); John Willoughby Denison-Pender; s of 2 Baron Pender, CBE (d 1965), and Camilla Lethbridge, da of late Willoughby Arthur Pemberton; *b* 6 May 1933; *Educ* Eton; *m* 1962, Julia, da of Richard Nevill Cannon, OBE, of Coombe Place, Lewes, Sussex; 1 s, 2 da (Hon Emma b 1964, Hon Mary b 1965); *Heir* s, Hon Henry John Richard Denison-Pender b 19 March 1968; *Career* formerly Lt 10 Royal Hussars and Capt City of London Yeo; former dir Globe Trust Ltd; chm J J & D Frost plc; sits as Cons in House of Lords; *Recreations* golf, racing, gardening; *Clubs* White's, Pratt's; *Style*— The Rt Hon the Lord Pender; North Court, Tilmanstone, Kent

PENDER, Reginald Robinson; s of Reginald George Pender (d 1967); *b* 23 Mar 1934; *Educ* Harrow; *m* 1958, Elizabeth, da of Charles Joseph Meager (d 1968); 2 s, 1 da; *Career* Nat Serv Capt (Army) 1952-54; maritime arbitrator; dir Standard Building Soc; sec Br Ports Fedn Ltd; FICS, ACIArb; *Recreations* gardening; *Clubs* Challoner; *Style*— Reginald Pender, Esq; 10 Beverley Gdns, Cullercoats, North Shields, Tyne & Wear NE30 4NS (☎ 091 2521282); Bark Mill, West Hall, Brampton, Cumbria (☎ 069 72 289)

PENDLEBURY, Edward; s of Thomas Cecil Pendlebury (d 1978), and Alice Sumner (d 1956); *b* 5 Mar 1925; *Educ* King George V Sch Southport, Magdalen Coll Oxford (BA, MA); *m* 1957, Joan Elizabeth, da of Ernest Bell (d 1983); 1 s (Timothy b 1963); *Career* RNVR 1943-46 Russian Convoys, N Atlantic, Med; Miny Food and Agric (later Miny of Fisheries and Food) 1949-56, Br Def Staff Washington 1957-60, MOD 1970-85 (asst under sec 1983-85); *Recreations* gardening, gramophone, gazing; *Style*— Edward Pendlebury, Esq; Bosworth House, Draycott, nr Moreton-in-Marsh, Gloucestershire GL56 9LF

PENDRY, Prof John Brian; s of Frank Johnson Pendry (d 1978), and Kathleen, *née* Shaw; *b* 4 July 1943; *Educ* Ashton under Lyne GS, Downing Coll Cambridge (BA, MA, PhD); *m* 15 Jan 1977, Patricia, da of Frederick Gard, of London; *Career* res fell in physics Downing Coll Cambridge 1969-75, sr res asst Cavendish Lab Cambridge 1973-75 (postdoctoral fell 1969-72), memb tech staff Bell Laboratories USA 1972-73, SPSO and head of theory gp SERC Daresbury Laboratory 1975-81, prof of theorotical solid state physics and assoc head of dept Imperial Coll London 1981-; memb SERC physics ctee (chm panel Y) 1985-88; FRS 1984, FInstP 1984; *Recreations* music, piano playing, gardening; *Style*— Prof John Pendry; Metchley, Knipp Hill, Cobham, Surrey KT11 2PE (☎ 0932 64306); The Blackett Laboratory, Imperial College, London SW7 2BZ (☎ 01 589 5111, fax 01 589 9463, telex 929484)

PENDRY, Thomas (Tom); MP (Lab) Stalybridge and Hyde 1970-; s of L E Pendry, of Broadstairs; *b* 10 June 1934; *Educ* St Augustine's Ramsgate, Oxford Univ; *m* 1966, Moira Anne, da of A E Smith, of Derby; 1 s, 1 da; *Career* serv RAF 1955-57; joined Lab Pty 1950, NUPE official 1960-70, memb Paddington Cncl 1962-65, chm Derby Lab Pty 1966; oppn whip 1971-74, lord cmmr of Treasy (govt whip) 1974-77 (when resigned), parly under-sec state NI Off 1978-79; oppn spokesman: NI 1979-81, Overseas Devpt 1981-82, Devolution and Regnl Affrs 1982; chm PLP Sports Ctee, All Pty Football Ctee, chm NUPE Gp of Lab MPs; steward of the BBB of C; *Recreations* sports of all kinds; *Clubs* Reform, Stalybridge Labour; *Style*— Tom Pendry, Esq, MP; 2 Cannon St, Hollingworth, Hyde, Cheshire

PENFOLD, David Jon; s of Maj Arthur Jon Penfold, RA (d 1978), and May Dalglish, *née* Wardrop; *b* 26 April 1935; *Educ* Highgate Sch, and in France; *m* 19 June 1968 (m dis 1980), Susan, da of William Elliott (d 1978); 1 s (Jonathan David b 1970); *Career* Nat Serv RA 1953-55, Lt 1955; dir WB Darley Ltd 1958-63, ptnr Thompson Scheduling Ltd 1964-75; conslt KH Publicity Ltd 1975-81, Streets Fin Ltd 1981-87; (assoc dir 1985-87), dir Mountain & Molehill Ltd 1988-; chm: Burton-on-Trent Constitutional Club 1960-63, W Midlands Area Young Cons 1960-63, Windsor and Maidenhead Cons Assoc 1986-89; party candidate (Cons): W Nottingham 1966, Derby N Feb and Oct 1974; cllr: Burton-on-Trent Cncl 1960-63 and 1967-71, Windsor and Maidenhead DC 1983-87; chm Colne Valley Groundwork Tst 1988-; *Books* The Young Idea, (co-author 1963); *Recreations* skiing, golf, gardening, reading; *Style*— David Penfold, Esq; 10 Courtenay Square, London SE11; The Thatch, Littlewick Green, Berkshire; Mountain & Molehill Ltd, 56 Britton St, London EC1 (☎ 01 253 2268, fax 01 251 1939)

PENFOLD, Derek John; s of Joseph Penfold, of Tiverton, Devon, and Catherine, *née* O'Sullivan; *b* 17 July 1948; *Educ* Clapham Coll, City of Westminster Coll, NW London Poly (LLB); *Career* features ed Estates times 1975-78, dep ed Estates Gazette 1980-86 (news ed 1978-80), property analyst Alexanders Laing & Cruickshank 1986-87, dir Streets Communications 1987-; chm Greenwich Theatre 1980-88 (dir 1975-88), dir Greenwich Young People's Theatre 1980-88; memb: Woolwich of Dist Antiquarian Soc, Greenwich AA Cncl; former chm Greenwich Festival, cncllr London Borough of Greenwich 1971-78, chm and chief whip Leisure Ctee; Freeman City of London; *Recreations* theatre; *Clubs* Wig & Pen; *Style*— Derek Penfold, Esq; 42 Owenite St, Abbey Wood, London SE2 0NQ (☎ 01 311 6039); 18 Red Lion Ct, Fleet St, London EC4A 3HT (☎ 01 353 1090, fax 01 583 0661, telex 21827)

PENFOLD, Maj-Gen Robert Bernard; CB (1969), LVO (1957); s of late Bernard Hugh Penfold, of Selsey, and Ethel Ives, *née* Arnold; *b* 19 Dec 1916; *Educ* Wellington, RMC Sandhurst; *m* 1940, Ursula, da of late Lt-Col E H Gray; 2 da; *Career* chief of def staff Kenya 1966-69, GOC SE Dist 1969-72, gen mangr Royal Hong Kong Jockey Club

1972-80, chm Horseracing Advsy Cncl 1980-86; *Recreations* shooting, golf, gardening; *Clubs* Army & Navy; *Style—* Maj-Gen Robert Penfold, CB, LVO; Park House, Amport, Andover, Hants (☎ 026 4772818)

PENLEY, Francis Charles; s of Reginald Herbert Penley, of Rockstowes Hill, Dursley, Glos, and Geraldine, *née* Murray-Browne; *b* 28 Dec 1915; *Educ* Marlborough, Christ's Coll Cambridge (BA, LLM); *m* 7 Dec 1940, Katharine, da of Lt Col Archibald Nelson Gavin-Jones, DSO (d 1967); 1 s (John b 1948), 2 da (Prudence b 1946, Nicola b 1953); *Career* WWII: Lt TA 1936, Capt 1940, Adj 73 Medium Regt RA 1940-41, GSO 3 8 Army HQ 1942, serv Western Desert 1941-42 (POW 1942-45); admitted slr 1945-, Notary Public 1957; clerk: Gen Cmmrs of Taxes 1950-80, Justices Dursley, Whit minister, Berkley divs 1951-67; Stroud Bldg Soc (now Stroud and Swindon Bldg Soc); dir 1970-86, chm 1982-86; town cncllr Dursley 1962-78; fndr pres Dursley Rotary Club 1952-53 (memb 1952-), tstee and chm Gloucs Historic Churches Preservation Tst 1982-, fnd tstee Stinchcombe Hill Recreation Ground Tst 1983-, Paul Harris fell 1988; *Recreations* book binding; *Style—* Francis Penley, Esq; 26 Long St, Dursley, Gloucs 9L11 5TE (☎ 0453 2357)

PENLEY, Maj John Francis; TD (1984); s of Capt Francis Charles Penley, RHA, of Pinnocks, Uley, Glos GL11 5TB, and Katharine, *née* Gavin-Jones; *b* 22 Dec 1948; *Educ* Marlborough, Coll of Law; *m* 26 Jan 1978, Caroline Anne Myfanwy, da of George William Harris James (surgn Lt RNVR); 1 s (Matthew John b 1982), 1 da (Eleanor Anne b 1984); *Career* cmmnd Wessex Yeo 1971, Capt 1978, Maj OC Royal Glos Hussars The Royal Wessex Yeo 1984, 2 i/c The Royal Wessex Yeo 1987; slr 1973, asst slr Clifford Turner 1973-78, ptnr Penley Milward Bayley 1978, NP 1979; sec: Stinchcombe Hill Recreation Ground Tst, Dursley United Charities, Dursley Church Houses and Torchacre Charity, Henry Vizard Charity; memb: Bow Gp 1975-80, exec Glos ctee Co Landowners Assoc 1987-; memb Law Soc 1974, Soc of Notaries 1979, Agric Lawyers Assoc 1984; *Recreations* hunting, shooting, walking, gardening; *Style—* Maj John Penley, TD; The Gables, Uley, Dursley, Glos GL11 5TB (☎ 0453 860241); Penley Millard and Bayley, 26 Long St, Dorsley, Glos GL11 4JA (☎ 0453 2357, fax 0453 48527)

PENLEY, William Henry; CB (1967), CBE (1961); s of late William Edward Penley; *b* 22 Mar 1917; *Educ* Wallasey GS, Liverpool Univ; *m* 1, 1943, Raymonde Evelyn (d 1975), da of late Frederick Richard Gough; 2 s, 1 da; m 2, 1977, Marion Claytor, da of late Joseph Enoch Airey; *Career* controller R & D Estabs and Res MOD, and professional head of sci gp Civil Serv 1976-77, dep dir Under Water Weapons Marconi Space and Def Systems Ltd 1979-82, chm Appleton Laboratory Estabs Ctee 1977-79, engrg dir Marconi Underwater Systems Ltd 1982-85; engrg conslt 1985-; *Style—* William Penley, Esq, CB, CBE; 28 Walrond Rd, Swanage, Dorset (☎ 0929 425042)

PENMAN, Caroline Elizabeth; da of Reginald Geoffrey Filmer (d 1967), and Lucy Kathleen, *née* Long (d 1982); *b* 4 Feb 1944; *Educ* Private Sch Dunnotar, Private Sch Trevelyan Hatchlands Farlington; *m* 28 June 1969, Richard Howard Browne Penman, s of Donald Penman; *Career* owner antiques shop 1964-74, organiser circuit of antiques fairs (incl S of England Antiques Trade Fair 1974-86) 1970-85, owner Chelsea Antiques Fair 1985-, organiser City of London Antiques Fair 1987-88; dir London and Provincial Antique Dealers Assoc 1983-; *Recreations* antiques; *Style—* Mrs Caroline Penman; Cockhaise Mill, Lindfield, Sussex (☎ 04447 2514); P O Box 114, Haywards Heath, Sussex (☎ 04447 4531, fax 04447 3412)

PENN, Christopher Arthur; s of Lt-Col Sir Eric Penn, GCVO, OBE, MC; *b* 13 Sept 1950; *Educ* Eton; *m* 1976, Sabrina Mary, 2 da of Timothy Colman, DCL, of Bixley Manor, Norwich; 1 s (Rory b 1980), 1 da (Louisa b 1983); *Career* chartered surveyor; ptnr Jones Lang Wootton; *Clubs* Buck's; *Style—* Christopher Penn, Esq; 70 Lyford Rd, London SW18 3JW (☎ 01 874 8200)

PENN, Christopher William Milner; s of William Henry Milner Penn, of Westholms, Bisley, nr Stroud, Glos, and Ruth Adeline Mary, *née* Pendleton; *b* 6 June 1937; *Educ* Sherborne; *m* 1, 12 Oct 1963 (m dis 1983), Angela Edith Margeret, da of Frederick James Goodrich (d 1978); 3 s (Jonathan b 1965, William b 1967, Edward b 1969); m 2, 16 Dec 1988, Maureen Janice, da of Larry Edward Reeve (d 1965); *Career* Nat Serv RN 1955-57, cmmnd 1956, RNR 1957-77; Gabriel Wade & English Ltd 1957-70, William Brown & Co (Ipswich) Ltd 1970-73, Paul Frost Ltd 1973-(dir 1975-); memb Ipswich Borough Cncl 1958-78, memb Suffolk CC 1979- (ldr 1986-); *Recreations* sailing, fishing; *Clubs* Waldringfield; *Style—* Christopher Penn, Esq; Cherry Bank, Church Lane, Playford, Ipswich IP6 9DS (☎ 0473 622 636); Paul Frost Ltd, Tolleshunt Major, Maldon, Essex CM9 8LW (☎ 0621 860 323)

PENN, David John; s of Surgn Capt Eric Arthur Penn, DSC, of 9 New Orleans, Coast Rd, W Mersea, Essex, and Catherine, *née* Dunnett; *b* 2 Jan 1945; *Educ* Dulwich, St Catherine's Coll Oxford (MA); *Career* keeper Imp War Museum: Dept of Info Retrieval 1970-77, Dept of Firearms 1973-76, Dept of Exhibits and Firearms 1976-; vice-chm Nat Pistol Assoc, vice-pres Muzzle-Loaders Assoc of GB, hon sec Hist Breechloading Smallarms Assoc, memb Br Shooting Sports Cncl; Freeman: City of London 1982, Worshipful Co of Gunmakers 1982; *Books* Imperial War Museum Film Cataloguing Rules (with R B N Smither, 1976); *Recreations* shooting; *Clubs* Reform; *Style—* David Penn, Esq; Imperial War Museum, Lambeth Rd, London SE1 6HZ (☎ 01 735 8922 ext 270, fax 01 582 5374)

PENN, Lt-Col Sir Eric Charles William Mackenzie; GCVO (1980, KCVO 1972, CVO 1965), OBE (1960), MC (1944); s of Capt Eric Frank Penn (ka 1915, eldest s of William Penn, of Taverham Hall, Norwich), by his w Gladys, yr da of Charles John Ebden, JP, DL, of Newton House, Lanarks; *b* 9 Feb 1916; *Educ* Eton, Magdalene Coll Cambridge; *m* 29 Jan 1947, Prudence Stewart-Wilson, da of Aubyn Wilson (d 1934), and Muriel Stewart-Stevens (d 1982), of Balnakeilly, Pitlochry, Perthshire; 2 s (David, Christopher, *qv*), 1 da (Fiona); *Career* Gren Gds 1938-60 serv: France and Belgium 1939-40, Italy and Austria 1943-45, Germany 1945-46, Libya, Egypt 1950-52, Germany 1954-55; comptroller Lord Chamberlain's Off 1964-81 (asst comptroller 1960-64), extra equerry to HM The Queen 1963-; *Clubs* White's, Pratts; *Style—* Lt-Col Sir Eric Penn, GCVO, OBE, MC; 6 Rosscourt Mansions, 4 Palace St, London SW1E 5HZ

PENN, Cdr Geoffrey Briscoe; s of Bertram Harley Penn (d 1973), and Emily Margaret, *née* Briscoe (d 1972); *b* 13 Mar 1919; *Educ* Hampton Sch, RN Engrg Coll Keyham; *m* 17 Dec 1955, Barbara Mary Beverley, da of Lt-Col Beverley Beverley-Robinson, DSO (d 1961); 3 s (William b 1956, Jeremy b 1959, Robert b 1961); *Career* RN, serv WWII; Atlantic, E Indies, Med; cadet to A/Capt 1937-64, engr offr HMS Eagle 1958-60, chief engr Chatham Dockyard 1961-64; dir Parsons Chain Co 1964-65, gen mangr Ruston & Hornsby Ltd 1965-68, md Cochran Thermak 1968; FIMechE, MRINA; *Books* Up Funnel-Down Screw (1955), Snotty-The Story of the Midshipman (1957), HMS Thunderer, The History of Royal Naval Engineering College (1984); *Recreations* writing, drinking and swearing; *Style—* Cdr Geoffrey B Penn, RN; Holmwood, Hindon, Salisbury (☎ 074 789 470)

PENN-SMITH, Derek John; s of Major Sydney Penn-Smith, RE, FRIBA (d 1987), of Leicester, and Olive Amelia, *née* Kinton; *b* 21 Feb 1934; *Educ* Wyggeston Sch Leics, Sch of Arch Leics (DipArch), Durham Univ (Dip Town Planning); *m* 1, 19 July 1968 (m dis), Eva Margaret; 2 da (Fiona b 1964, Sally b 1966); m 2, 2 Dec 1972, Molly, da of John Berkin (d 1985), of Leics; *Career* Nat Serv 2 Lt RE Gibraltar; town planner; ptnr and conslt: Penn-Smith & Wall Peterborough 1961-87, Penn-Smith & Weston Derby 1961-88; ptnr S Penn-Smith Son & Ptnrs Lecis 1961-88 (sr ptnr 1980-88), dir Douglas Smith Stimson Ptnrship Ltd (inc S Penn-Smith Son & Ptnrs) 1988-; Freeman City of London, memb Ct Worshipful Co of Pewterers; FRIBA, FRTPI; *Recreations* sailing, (Durham Univ colours), aviation, orchid growing; *Style—* Derek Penn-Smith, Esq; Delphi, High Street, Naseby, Northants; Casa Caldera, Yaiza, Lanzarote; 61 Regent St, Leicester (☎ 0533 548616)

PENNA, Colin Eric; s of John Henry Penna 9d 1988), of 16 Park St, Willington, Crook, Co Durham, and Ruth, *née* Collin (d 1966); *b* 1 Nov 1935; *Educ* King James I Sch, Bishop Auckland, Co Durham, King's Coll London (LLB); *Career* slr; ptnr Marquis Penna & Hewitt, Brown-Humes & Hare of Co Durham; HM coroner S Dist Durham Co 1980; *Recreations* music, theatre; *Clubs* RAC; *Style—* Colin Penna, Esq; 16 Park St, Willington, Crook, Co Durham (☎ 0388 746 429); 5 Market Place, Bishop Auckland, Co Durham (☎ 0388 604 691)

PENNANT, His Honour David Edward Thornton; s of David Falconer Pennant, JP, DL (d 1938); *b* 2 August 1912; *Educ* Charterhouse, Trinity Coll Cambridge; *m* 1938, Alice Catherine, da of John Frederick Randall Stainer, MBE; 3 s, 1 da; *Career* served 1939-45 with Royal Signals (TA), OC Signals Offrs' Trg Sch, Mhow, India 1944-45; barr Inner Temple 1935; chllr Dio Monmouth 1949-78, chm Radnorshire QS 1962-64; dep chm: Brecknockshire QS 1956-64, Flintshire QS 1962-71, Dorset QS 1971; a Circuit judge 1961-84; *Style—* His Honour David Pennant; Parkbury, Balcombe Rd, Branksome Park, Poole, Dorset (☎ 0202 765614)

PENNANT-REA, Hon Mrs (Helen); *née* Jay; er (twin) da of Baron Jay, PC (Life Peer), *qv*; *Educ* N London Collegiate Sch, Sussex Univ (BA); *m* 1, 1975 (m dis 1982), David Kennard; 2 da (Amanda b 1976, Juliet b 1979); m 2, 24 June 1986, Rupert Lascelles Pennant, *qv*; 1 s (Edward b 1986), 1 step s, 1 step da

PENNANT-REA, Rupert Lascelles; s of Peter Athelwold Pennant-Rea, MBE, of Guiting Power, Glos, and Pauline Elizabeth, *née* Creasy; *b* 23 Jan 1948; *Educ* Peterhouse Zimbabwe, Trinity Coll Dublin (BA), Univ of Manchester (MA); *m* 1, 3 Oct 1970 (m dis 1975), (Elizabeth) Louise, da of Rt Rev William Derrick Lindsay Greer (d 1972), sometime Bishop of Manchester; m 2, 18 Aug 1979 (m dis 1986), Jane (Trevelyan), da of John Hamilton, of Isles of Scilly; 1 s (Rory b 1983), 1 da (Emily b 1982); m 3, 24 June 1986, Hon Helen (*qv*), er (twin) da of Baron Jay, PC (Life Peer), and former w of David Kennard; 1 s (Edward b 1986), 2 step da; *Career* with Confedn of Irish Indust 1970-71, Gen & Municipal Workers Union 1972-73, Bank of England 1973-77; economics corr The Economist 1977-81: economics ed 1981-85, ed 1986-; *Books* Gold Foil (1978), Who Runs The Economy? (jtly, 1979), The Pocket Economist (jtly, 1982), The Economist Economics (jtly, 1986); *Recreations* music, tennis, fishing, family; *Clubs* MCC, Reform; *Style—* Rupert Pennant-Lea, Esq; 25 St James's St, London SW1

PENNEFATHER, Capt Richard (Dick) Randolph Somerset; s of William John Somerset Pennefather (d 1955), and Verena Vera, *née* Black Hawkins (d 1972); sr rep of line of Abraham Pennefather, of Hanbury-on-the Hill, Staffs (circa 1600) (*see* Burke's LG of Ireland, 1958); *b* 18 April 1909; *Educ* RNC: Dartmouth, Greenwich; *m* 19 Sept 1942, Rachel Ann (d 1983), da of Dr Richard Fawcitt (d 1964), of Isle of Mull; 2 s, 1 d; *Career* joined HMS Repulse (Home Fleet), later on cruiser and destroyers Far East, Torpedo Offr 1936; serv: HMS Ajax; (Battle of River Plate), HMS Indomitable (Far East and last Malta Convoy); coastal cmd RAF, HMS Largs (N Africa) HMS Mauritius (Overlord), HMS Kenya, HMS Osprey, Capt 1949, asst dir plans MOD, Cdr HMS Unicorn (Korea), Cdre, NATO COS to C in C Portsmouth, Cdr HMS Bermuda, ADC to HM The Queen, ret 1959; dir Reavells & Co Ipswich; Master Worshipful Co of Clockmakers 1975; *Clubs* Army & Navy, Royal Lymington YC; *Style—* Capt Dick Pennefather, RN; White Barn, Crow Hill, Ringwood, Hants (☎ 0425 43527); Broom Hill, Tobermory, Isle of Mull (☎ 0688 2349)

PENNEY, Hon Christopher Charles; s of Baron Penney, OM, KBE, FRS (Life Peer); *b* 1941; *Educ* Cranleigh, Gonville and Caius Coll Cambridge, Guy's Hosp; *m* 1968, Margaret, da of Henry Bell Fairley, of Stockport; 1 s; *Career* MRCP, FRCP; *Style—* The Hon Christopher Penney; 39 Beaulieu Ave, Sydenham SE26

PENNEY, Hon Martin Charles; s of Baron Penney, OM, KBE, FRS (Life Peer); *b* 13 Mar 1938; *Educ* Cranleigh, Gonville and Caius Coll Cambridge; *m* 1961, Margaret Heather, da of Sqdn-Ldr H Almond, DSO, DFC, of Ramsdell, nr Basingstoke; 2 da; *Career* headmaster Bearwood Coll, Wokingham 1980-; *Style—* The Hon Martin Penney; Bearwood College, Wokingham, Berks (☎ 0734 786915)

PENNEY, Flt Lt Ronald Frederick; s of John Henry Penney, of Belmont Lodge, Belmont Rd, Bushey, Herts, and Ivy Kathleen Penny; *b* 7 June 1924; *Educ* Glendale GS; *m* 26 July 1973, Mrs Joan Rebecca Jacobs; 1 da (by previous m, Marilyn (Mrs Bishop) b 1947), 1 step s (Jeremy Jacobs b 1955), 1 step da (Jacqueline (Mrs Barnett) b 1948, d 1988); *Career* cmmnd RAF 1941 as Pilot Offr, Flt Lt 1944 (demobilised 1946), joined RAFVR, ret 1951; navigator Lancaster Aircraft with 626 Sqdn on Bomber Cmd, and 100 Sqdn; held private pilot's licence until 1982; CA 1958, former ptnr F G Jenkins Wood Co, md Ewan Lewis Gp of Cos, dir PJB Ltd; memb: Sqdn Assoc, The Wickenby Register, Air Crew Assoc, Bomber Cmd Assoc, Hendon Old People's Welfare Ctee, Rotany Int; (chm Charity Ist (accommodation for elderly bureau); Liveryman: Poulterers' Co, Bakers' Co; Freeman City of London, memb Guild of Freemen; FICA, memb IOD; *Recreations* flying, sailing, riding; *Clubs* RAF, City Livery; *Style—* Fl Lt Ronald Penney, RAF; 5 March Close, Mill Hill, London NW7 4NY (☎ 01 959 4083)

PENNEY, Baron (Life Peer UK 1967); William George Penney; OM (1969), KBE (1952, OBE 1946); s of W A Penney; *b* 24 June 1909; *Educ* Sheerness Tech Sch, Imperial Coll London (MA, PhD, DSc), Melbourne (hon LLD), Durham (hon DSc), Oxford and Bath Univ of Technology, FRS; *m* 1, 1935, Adele Minnie Elms (d

1944); 2 s; m 2, 1945, Eleanor Joan Quennell; *Career* Dir Atomic Weapons Res Estab Aldermaston 1953-59, memb for Weapons R&D, UKAEA 1954-59, memb for res, UKAEA 1959-61, dep chm 1961-64, chm 1964-67, dir Tube Investmts 1968-79, Standard Telephones and Cables 1971-83, tres Royal Soc 1956-60, vice-pres 1957-60, rector Imperial Coll of Sci and Technol 1967-73; *Style—* The Rt Hon Lord Penney, OM, KBE; Cat St, East Hendred, Wantage, Oxon OX12 8JT

PENNIE, John Anthony; s of Terence Edward Pennie, of 9A Cavendish Avenue, Cambridge, and Denise Judith *née* Watkins; *b* 18 Feb 1955; *Educ* Marlborough, Cambridge Univ (MA), Universite Libre De Bruxelles; *m* 12 Feb 1983, Annette Francine, da of Raymond Charles Rendall (d 1981); 1 s (Wilfred Oscar Norleigh b 29 Oct 1987), 1 da (Celia Mary b 18 Nov 1984); *Career* slr; ptnr Dickinson Dees 1984; Sandhoe Parish cncllr, sch govr; memb Law Soc; *Recreations* gardening; *Style—* John Pennie, Esq; Beaufront Hill Head, Hexham, Northumberland (☎ 0434 603508); Cross House, Westgate Rd, Newcastle Upon Tyne (☎ 091 261 1911, fax 091 261 5855)

PENNINGTON, Prof Robert Roland; s of Roland Alexander Pennington, (d 1952), of Warley, W Mids, and Elsie Davis (d 1977); *b* 22 April 1927; *Educ* Holly Lodge Smethwick W Mids, Univ of Birmingham (LLB, LLD); *m* 14 March 1968, Patricia Irene, da of Cecil Allen Rook (d 1968), of Alcester, Worcs; 1 da (Elisabeth Anne b 1974); *Career* slr 1951, reader Law Soc's Sch of Law London 1955 (sr lectr 1951), memb bd of mgmnt Coll of Law London 1962, prof in commercial law Univ of Birmingham 1968- (sr lectr 1962-68), govt advsr company legislation Trinidad 1967 (Seychelles 1970), special legal advsr on commercial law Harmonisation Cmmn of the Euro Communities 1973-79; memb Law Soc 1951; *Books* Company Law (1959, 5 edn 1985), Companies in the Common Market (1962, 3 edn as Companies in the European Communities 1982), The Investor and the Law (1967), Stannary Law: A History of the Mining Law of Cornwall and Devon (1973), Commercial Banking Law (1978), The Companies Acts 1980 and 1981 - a practitioner's manual (1983), Stock Exchange Listing - the new requirements (1985), Directors' Personal Liability (1987), Company Liquidations: the Substantive Law, the Procedure (2 vols 1987); *Recreations* travel, walking, history, archaeology; Gryphon House, Langley Road, Claverdon, Warwicks (☎ 092 684 3235); Faculty of Law, Univ of Birmingham, Birmingham B15 2TT (☎ 021 414 6296)

PENNOCK, Hon David Roderick Michael; s of Baron Pennock (Life Peer); *b* 1944; *Educ* Rugby, Merton Coll Oxford; *m* 1969, Jane Pinhard; 3 s, 1 da; *Career* chm Astell Scientific Ltd; *Recreations* tennis, farming, theatre; *Style—* The Hon David Pennock; Iridge Place, Hurst Green, Sussex TN19 7PN

PENNOCK, Baron (Life Peer UK 1982), of Norton in the Co of Cleveland; Raymond William Pennock; s of Frederick Henry Pennock and Harriet Anne, *née* Mathieson; *b* 16 June 1920; *Educ* Coatham Sch, Merton Coll Oxford (MA); *m* 1944, Lorna Pearse; 1 s, 2 da; *Career* served RA 1941-46, Capt (despatches 1945); joined ICI 1947, dir 1972, dep chm 1975-80, chm BICC plc 1980-; dep pres CBI 1979-80, pres 1980-82; memb: Plessey Bd 1979-, Standard Chartered Bank Bd 1982-; hon fellow Merton Coll Oxford; kt 1978; *Recreations* tennis, music, ballet, travel; *Clubs* Queen's, Royal Tennis Court; *Style—* The Rt Hon the Lord Pennock; BICC plc, 21 Bloomsbury St, London WC1B 3QN (☎ 01 637 1300)

PENNY, Francis David; CBE (1982); s of late David Penny; *b* 20 May 1918; *Educ* Bromsgrove County HS, UCL (BSc, fell 1973); *m* 1949, Betty E, da of late Oswald C Smith; *Career* md Yarrow plc 83; chm: Control Systems Ltd 1979-83, Automatic Revenue Controls Ltd 1979-83; pres Inst of Mech Engrg 1981-82; private consultant in engrg 1983-; memb of bd Br Standards Instn; FEng, FRSE, FIMarE, FIMechE; *Style—* Francis Penny, Esq, CBE; The Park, Dundrennan, Kirkcudbright DG6 4QH (☎ 05575 244)

PENNY, Joseph Noel Bailey; QC (1971); s of Joseph A Penny, JP; *b* 25 Dec 1916; *Educ* Worksop Coll, Christ Church Oxford; *m* 1, 1947, Celia (d 1969), da of R H Roberts; 3 s, 1 da; m 2, 1972, Sara Margaret, da of Sir Arnold France; 1 da; *Career* Maj Royal Signals 1939-46; barr Gray's Inn 1948, a Nat Insurance (now Social Security) cmmr 1977-; *Style—* Joseph Penny, Esq, QC; Fair Orchard, Lingfield, Surrey (☎ 0342 832191)

PENNY, Hon Patrick Glyn; s of 2 Viscount Marchwood, MBE (d 1979); *b* 3 July 1939; *m* 1, 1968 (m dis 1974), Sue Eleanor Jane, da of late Charles Phipps Brutton, CBE; 1 da; m 2, 1979, Mrs Lynn Vanessa Knox, da of John Leslie Wyles, of Wimbledon; *Style—* The Hon Patrick Penny; 33 Wellington Sq, London SW3 4NR

PENNY, Hon Peter George Worsley; s and h of 3 Viscount Marchwood; *b* 8 Oct 1965; *Educ* Winchester; *Recreations* horse racing, tennis, cricket; *Style—* The Hon Peter Penny

PENRHYN, 6 Baron (UK 1866) Malcolm Frank Douglas-Pennant; DSO (1945), MBE (1943); s of 5 Baron Penrhyn (d 1967, himself gn of 17 Earl of Morton and ggs of Lady Frances Lascelles, da of 1 Earl of Harewood) and Alice Nellie (d 1965), da of Sir William Charles Cooper, 3 Bt; *b* 11 July 1908; *Educ* Eton, RMC Sandhurst; *m* 1954, Elisabeth Rosemary, da of late Brig Sir Percy Laurie, KCVO, CBE, DSO, JP; 2 da (*see* Thomas Richard Troubridge); *Heir* bro, Hon Nigel Douglas-Pennant; *Career* Col (ret) KRRC, serv WWII 1939-45 in N Africa and NW Europe; *Style—* The Rt Hon the Lord Penrhyn, DSO, MBE; Littleton Manor, Winchester, Hants SO22 6QU (☎ 0962 880205)

PENRICE, Geoffrey; CB (1978); s of Harry Penrice; *b* 28 Feb 1923; *Educ* Thornes House GS, LSE; *m* 1947, Janet Gillies Allardice; 3 s; *Career* dir of statistics and dep sec Dept of Employment 1978-; *Style—* Geoffrey Penrice Esq, CB; 10 Dartmouth Park Ave, NW5 (☎ 01 267 2175)

PENROSE, Roger Ian; s of Edward Charles Penrose, of Plymouth, and Grace Feltis, *née* Bond; *b* 15 Sept 1953; *Educ* Plymouth Coll, Bath Univ (BSc, BArch); *m* 7 Aug 1976, Janet Elaine, da of Richard Alan Harvey, RN; 2 s (Richard Merrick b 1984, Simon Tristan b 1987); *Career* princ Ian Penrose and Associates (chartered architects), dir Ian Penrose Architects Ltd 1987-; *Recreations* motorcycling, sailing, cycle, swimming; *Clubs* OPM, IMTC; *Style—* Roger I Penrose, Esq; Red Ridges, Cheriton Bishop, Devon (☎ 9424 435/ 0392 5300, fax 0392 410265); 25 Victoria Park Rd, St Leonards, Exeter, Devon EX2 4NT (car tel 0836 592070)

PENRY, William (Cedric) Rhys; s of Benjamin William Penry (d 1972), and Ethel Evelyn Penry (d 1972); descended from John Penry, Christian martyr (1563-1593); *b* 21 June 1927; *Educ* Gowerton GS, Univ of Wales (BSc), Stanford-Insead Fontainbleau; *m* 1952, Margaret Winifred, da of Charles Starvington Cetta (d 1978); 1 s, 1 da; *Career* RAF 1945-48; works mangr Richard Thomas and Baldwins 1951-63; dir: Halivourgiki Athens 1963-69, British Steel Corpn (Int) Ltd 1977-, British Steel Corpn (Overseas Services) 1976-87, Slater Steel Corpn Canada 1977-86; int business conslt 1987-; FIM; *Recreations* golf, gardening; *Clubs* Directors'; *Style—* Cedric Penry Esq; Swallows Corner, Islet Road, Maidenhead, Berks SL6 8LG (☎ 0628 72701)

PENRY-DAVEY, David Herbert; QC (1988); s of Samuel Saunders Watson Penry-Davey of Gwanda, Caldbee Hill, Battle, E Sussex, and Almary Lorna *née* Patrick; *b* 16 May 1942; *Educ* Hastings GS, King's Coll London (LLB); *m* 1970, Judith Ailsa Nancy, da of John Walter, of Firgrove, Morley St, Bofolph, Norfolk; 2 s (Matthew b 1972, James b 1979), 1 da (Caroline b 1974); *Career* called to the Bar Inner Temple 1965, rec Crown Ct 1986; *Recreations* music, golf, cycling; *Style—* David Penry-Davey, Esq, QC; 8 New Square, Lincoln's Inn, London WC2 3AQP (☎ 01 242 4986, fax 01 405 1166)

PENTELOW, Jack Owen; s of John Owen Pentelow (d 1959), of 321 Brincliffe Edge Rd, Sheffield, and Margaret Anne Scott, *née* Bailey (d 1951); *b* 29 Nov 1915; *Educ* King Edward VII Sch Sheffield; *m* 5 Oct 1940, Joan Elizabeth, da of John Hadfield Topham (d 1957), of 6 Kenwood Bank, Sheffield; 2 s (Michael b 1946, Guy b 1949); *Career* cmnd 1944, Flying Offr 1945 RAF Aircrew; asst cost accountant John Fowler & Co Ltd Leeds 1939, cost accountant Br Jeffrey Diamond Ltd 1940-47; Smiths Industs Ltd: chief cost accountant 1947, div chief acct clock and watch div 1948 (prodn dir 1957), dir and gen mangr 1967-80; Liveryman Worshipful Co Clockmakers 1970; FCMA; *Clubs* Hove Conservative, Hove Deep Sea Anglers; *Style—* Jack Pentolow, Esq; 11 Welbeck Ave, Hove, E Sussex BN3 4JP (☎ 0273 734 219)

PENTIN, David John; s of Sydney Edward Pentin (d 1971), of Canterbury, Kent, and Amelia, *née* Winkel; *b* 26 June 1935; *Educ* Kent Col Canterbury, London Univ (LLB); *m* 11 June 1960, Alicia, JP, da of Gp Capt Ivor Morgan Rodney, OBE, RAF (d 1954); 3 s (John b 11 Feb 1964, Richard b 16 Aug 1969, Edward b 23 Feb 1971), 1 da (Caroline b 23 April 1962); *Career* Nat Serv RAF; sr ptnr Pentins CAs; memb Canterbury City Cncl 1983-: chm fin and gen purposes ctee 1985-; dep ldr of the cncl 1987-; FCA 1959; *Recreations* walking, skiing, cycling, music; *Style—* David Pentin, Esq; Ashley House, Brewery Lane, Bridge, Canterbury, Kent CT4 5LD (☎ 0227 830278); Lullingstone House, 5 Castle St, Canterbury, Kent CT1 2QF (☎ 0227 763400, fax 0227 762416, telex 888781)

PENTLAND, Baroness; Lady Lucy Elisabeth Babington; *née* Babington Smith; da of Sir Henry Babington Smith; *m* 1941, 2 Baron Pentland, 1 da; *Style—* The Rt Hon Lady Pentland; 4670 Independence Ave, New York City 10471, USA

PENTON, John Howard; MBE (1987); s of Richard Howard Penton (d 1960), of 33 Clephane Rd, London N1, and Cicely Urmson, *née* Heinekey (d 1966); *b* 12 Feb 1938; *Educ* Merchant Taylors', Architectural Assoc Sch of Architecture (AAdip), Open Univ (BA); *m* 2 Nov 1963, (Elizabeth) Diana, da of (Henry) Harold King (d 1985), of 1 Summerhill Ct, Avenue Rd, St Albans, Herts; 1 da (Ciceley Rebecca Clare b 1975); *Career* chartered architect; assoc D E Pugh & Assocs 1963-72, fndr ptnr Penton, Smart & Grimwade 1972-; consultancies: LT, London Housing Consortium, Irish Nat Rehabilitation Bd, The Inst for Rehabilitation & Res Houston Texas, The English Tourist Bd, Perkins Sch & Inst for the Blind Boston USA, The Nordic Ctee on Deaf/ Blindness Dronninglund Denmark, St Alban's Cathedral; hon architect Herts Assoc for Disabled; fndr chm Herts and Beds Constructions Indust Liaison Gp, former chm Herts Assoc of Architects, chm Centre on Environment for the Handicapped, fndr memb The Access Ctee for England; Awards: RIBA/DOE Housing Design 1985 Special Award, RIBA Res Fellowship 1984-85; Liam McGuire Memorial Lecture Dublin 1986, res fell Hull Sch of Architecture 1987, expert witness damage actions of disabled; Under Renter Warden Worshipful Co of Merchant Taylors, Liveryman Worshipful Co of Chartered Architects, Freeman Worshipful Co of Constructors; RIAS, ACIArb, FCSD, FRSA; *Recreations* reading, sketching, swimming, target rifle shooting, carving chessmen; *Clubs* Reform, Nat Lib; *Style—* John Penton, Esq, MBE; 1 Batchwood Gardens, St Albans, Hertfordshire DL3 5SE (☎ 0727 53854); Penton, Smart, & Grimwade, 8 Spicer St, St Albans, Herts AL3 4PQ (☎ 0727 40911, fax 0727 36733); 4 Rutland Sq, Edinburgh EH1 2AS (☎ 031 228 4137, fax 031 228 4540)

PENTY, Michael Harvey; s of Arthur Joseph Penty (d 1937), of Church St, Old Isleworth, Middx, and Violet Leonard, *née* Pike (d 1978); *b* 6 Nov 1916; *Educ* St Benedict's Ealing; *m* da of Col Laurence Sebastian Cecil Roche, MC (d 1968), of Castle Barton, Tiverton, Devon; 3 s (John Christopher Mathew b 22 Sept 1950, Stephen Michael Philip b 2 May 1952, Andrew Penty Laurence b 29 June 1954, Blaise Gerard Nicholas b 30 April 1956) 2 da (Frances Mary Cecilia (Mrs Walker) b 22 Nov 1948, Joanna Hilary Ruth b 2 March 1965); *Career* RA 1940-46, Capt Adj 40 (Highland) LAA Regt 1942-43, jr staff course Sarafand 1943, GSO3 (SD) HQ 13 Corps 1945-46; slr 1939, attorney Supreme Ct SA 1949; co fndr Whitefriar's Sch Cheltenham 1957-58, ed Law and Justice (formerly Quis Custodiet?) 1964-84, hon sec Plowden Legal Soc 1969-75; vice pres Isleworth Civic Tst (memb 1960-, formerly chm and hon sec); sr vice pres Newman Assoc 1961-63 (memb 1955-); Lord of the Manor of the Rectory of Isleworth; memb Law Soc: KSG; *Recreations* lawn tennis, gardening; *Clubs* Victory Servs, Ealing Lawn Tennis; *Style—* Michael Penty, Esq; The Manor House, 59A Church St, Old Isleworth, Middx TW7 6BE (☎ 01 560 8524); 35 Ashley Road, Hampton, Middx TW12 2JA (☎ 01 979 4333, fax 01 979 1393)

PEPPER, Donald John; s of Cdr Frank Sydney Charles Pepper (d 1940), of Plymouth, and Beatrice Mary, *née* Trevor (d 1952); *b* 7 August 1921; *Educ* Devonport HS; *m* 7 June 1946, Maureen, da of Robert MacKenzie im Thurn (d 1956), of Friern Barnet; 3 s (John Robert b 1948, David MacKenzie b 1952, Mark im Thurn b 1957); *Career* RN 1939-47; Frobisher RN Coll Dartmouth 1939, RN Engrg Coll Plymouth 1940-43, HMS King George V serv Med and Home Flt 1943-44, RNC Greenwich 1944-46, HMS Indefatigable 1946-47, staff RN Engrg Coll 1947, invalided out 1947; designer naval and merchant ship propulsion Foster Wheeler Ltd 1950-55, head nuclear energy dept Foster Wheeler Ltd 1955-59, md Rolls Royce & Assocs 1962-66 (fndr dir 1959-62); Rolls Royce HQ: main bd 1969, reappointed dir 1974, vice-chm 1976, ret 1983; currently: chm Met Safe Deposits Ltd, chm Port Solent Ltd, dir Chilworth Centre Ltd, advsr to Lockheed Air Terminal Inc; memb: Def Industs Cncl 1977-81, cncl Royal Soc of Aerospace Contractors; devpt fund tstee Southampton Univ, memb exec ctee Hants Devpt Assoc; gold medal winner for paper on nuclear propulsion to NICES 1961; Freeman City of London 1982, memb Worshipful Co of Coach Makers and Coach Harness Makers 1982; MIMechE 1959, MIMarE 1960, memb NICES 1961, CBIM 1969; *Recreations* golf, sailing; *Clubs* Royal Mid-Surrey GC, Royal Southern YC, RNC and RAYC, Army and Navy; *Style—* Donald Pepper, Esq; Hard Cottage, Swanwick

Shore, Southampton SO3 7EF (☎ 048 95 2107)

PEPPER, Gordon Terry; s of Harold Terry Pepper (d 1973), and Jean Margaret Gordon, *née* Furness (d 1963); *b* 2 June 1934; *Educ* Repton, Trinity Coll Cambridge (MA); *m* 30 Aug 1958, Gillian Clare, da of Lt-Col William Helier Huelin (d 1978); 3 s (Alasdiar b 1960, Harry b 1967, Mark b 1969), 1 da (Linda (Ninna) b 1961); *Career* Nat Serv cmmnd RCS 1952-54; Equity of Law Life Assur Soc 1957-60, W Greenwell & Co 1960-86; ptnr 1962, mgmnt ctee 1970, jt sr ptnr 1980; chm Greenwell Montagu & Co 1986-87, dir and sr advsr Midland Montagu (Hldgs) Ltd 1987-, chm Payton Pepper & Sons Ltd 1987 (dir 1986), hon visting prof City Univ Business Sch 1987-, dir Midland Montagu Centre For Fin Mkts 1988-; articles in various econ and fin journals; FIA 1961, fell Soc Investmt Analysts, CBIM, memb Stock Exchange; *Recreations* sailing, tennis, skiing, walking, family; *Clubs* Royal Ocean Racing, Royal Channel Islands YC; *Style*— Gordon Pepper, Esq; Staddleden, Sissinghurst, Cranbrook, Kent TN17 2AN (☎ 0580 712852); Midland Montagu, 10 Lower Thames St, London (☎ 01 260 9000, fax 01 623 5452, telex 887213)

PEPPER, Hon Mrs (Elizabeth) Jane Graham; *née* Guest; o da of Baron Guest, PC (Life Peer); *b* 25 May 1945; *m* 8 June 1968, G Willing Pepper, of Philadelphia, USA; *Style*— The Hon Mrs Pepper; 128 Springton Lake Rd, Media, Pa, 19063, USA

PEPPER, John Douglas; s of Douglas Ernest Pepper (d 1979), and Kathleen Mary, *née* Taylor; *b* 11 Jan 1932; *Educ* Scarborough HS for Boys; *m* 9 April 1955, Shirley Mary, da of Jack Wade, of Barrington Ct, Staines, Middx; 2 s (David b 1956, Michael b 1965), 2 da (Brigitte b 1958, Vivien b 1959); *Career* dir Plaxtons (GB) plc 1972 (chm 1987); FCA; *Recreations* golf (Ganton and Filey Golf), rotary; *Clubs* Rotary (pres 1978-79) Filey; *Style*— John D Pepper, Esq; White Lodge, Gristhorpe, Filey, N Yorks (☎ 0723 512959); Plaxtons (GB) plc, Castle Works, Eastfield, Scarborough, N Yorks (☎ 0723 581500, fax 0723 581328)

PEPPER, Kenneth Bruce; CB (1965); s of late E E Pepper; *b* 11 Mar 1913; *Educ* County HS Ilford, LSE; *m* 1945, Irene Evelyn Watts; 2 s; *Career* cmmr of HM Customs and Excise 1957-73; *Style*— Kenneth Pepper, Esq, CB; Fairfield, Cae Mair, Beaumaris, Gwynedd

PEPPER, Prof Michael; s of Morris Pepper (d 1982), and Ruby, *née* Bloom; *b* 10 August 1942; *Educ* St Marlebone GS, Reading Univ (BSc, PhD); *m* 22 Oct 1973, Dr Jeannette Denise, da of Albert Josse, of London; 2 da (Judith Leah, Ruth Jennifer); *Career* res physicist The Piessey Co Ltd 1969-82, res Cavendish Lab 1973-, Warren res fell Royal Soc 1978-86, princ res fell GEC plc 1982-87, prof of physics Univ of Cambridge 1987-, fell Trinity Coll Cambridge 1982-; awarded: Guthrie Prize and Medal Inst of Physics 1985, Hewlett-Packard Europhysics Prize 1985, Hughes Medal of Royal Soc 1987; ScD Cambridge 1989, FRS 1983; *Recreations* travel, music, walking, whisky tasting; *Style*— Prof Michael Pepper; Cavendish Laboratory, Madingley Rd, Cambridge CB3 0HE (☎ 0223 337 330, fax 0223 632 63)

PEPPERCORN, David James Creagh; s of James Kenneth Peppercorn, and Ida Alice Knight (d 1985); *b* 25 August 1931; *Educ* Beaumont Coll, Trinity Coll Cambridge (MA); *m* 1, 11 April 1959, Susan Mary Sweeney; 3 da (Caroline b 1961, Sarah b 1963, Frances b 1964); m 2, 10 June 1977, Serena Gillian, da of Michael Sutcliffe; *Career* int wine conslt, dir: Wine Standards Bd of the Vintners Co 1987, Morgan Furze & Co Ltd 1958-74, Peter Dominic 1964-74, Gilbey Vintner 1969-79; Inst of Masters of Wine 1968-76; chm Inst of Masters of Wine 1968-70; judge at Premier Concours Mondial (Budapest 1972), Liveryman Worshipful Co of Vintners 1952; memb Worshipful Co of Watermans; *Books* Bordeaux (1982), Pocket Guide to the Wines of Bordeaux (1986), Translations into: German (1986), French (1987), Danish (1987), American Edition Simon & Schuster (1987); Drinking Wine (1979, jt author with Bryan Cooper); *Recreations* music, walking, travelling; *Clubs* Garrick, MCC; *Style*— David J C Peppercorn, Esq; 2 Bryanston Place, London W1H 7FN (☎ 262 9398)

PEPPERELL, Peter Frederick; s of Amos Victor Pepperell (d 1947), and Elizabeth Sarah Gower (d 1943); *b* 12 May 1926; *Educ* Newport GS, Leeds Univ; *m* 1 Oct 1955, Joyce Johnston, da of David Henderson Adamson (d 1975); 1 s (David 1958), 1 da (Susan b 1960); *Career* serv Royal Hampshire Regt 1944-48; with Duncan Bros & Co Ltd Calcutta 1950-73, with Walter Duncan Gp UK 1973-; dir: Western Dooars Hldgs plc 1973, Walter Duncan & Goodricke plc 1982, Lawrie Gp plc 1985, Assam-Dooars Hldgs plc 1986; chm Lawrie Plantation Servs Ltd 1979, etc; *Recreations* golf; *Clubs* Oriental, Bengal (Calcutta); *Style*— Peter Pepperell, Esq; Lawrie Plantation Service Ltd, Wortham Place, Wrotham, Sevenoaks, Kent TN15 7AE

PEPPIATT, Lady; Pamela; da of Capt E W Carter, MC; *m* 1929, Sir Kenneth Peppiatt, KBE (d 1983, sometime chief cashier and dir Bank of England and dir Coutts); 2 s, 1 da; *Style*— Lady Peppiatt; 7 Harvey Orchard, Beaconsfield, Bucks (☎ Beaconsfield 3158)

PEPPITT, John Raymond; QC (1976); s of Reginald Peppitt, MBE (d 1962), and Phyllis Claire, *née* French (d 1978); *b* 22 Sept 1931; *Educ* St Paul's, Jesus Coll Cambridge (BA); *m* 2 April 1960, Judith Penelope, da of Maj Lionel Frederick Edward James, CBE; 3 s (Matthew b 1962, William b 1964, Edward b 1968); *Career* 2 Lt RA (Nat Serv) 1950-51; barr Gray's Inn 1958, bencher 1982; rec Crown Ct 1976-; *Recreations* collecting watercolours, rearing sheep; *Style*— John Peppitt, Esq, QC; Chegworth Manor Farm, Chegworth, Harrietsham, Kent ME17 1DD (☎ 0622 859313); chambers: 3 Gray's Inn Place, London WC1 (☎ 01 831 8441, fax 01 831 8479, telex 295 119 LEXCOL G)

PEPYS, Hon Mrs (Pamela Sophia Nadine); *née* Stonor; da of 5 Baron Camoys (d 1968), and Mildred (d 1961), da of William Watts Sherman, of New York; *b* 1917; *m* 1941, Lt-Col Charles Donald Leslie Pepys (King's Own Yorks LI; ggs of 1 Earl of Cottenham), eld s of late Col Gerald Leslie Pepys; *Style*— The Hon Mrs Pepys; 30/31 Lyefield Ct, Kidmore End Rd, Emmer Green, Reading, Berks RG4 8AP (☎ 0734 482981)

PEPYS, Lady Rachel; Lady (Mary) Rachel; *née* Fitzalan Howard; DCVO (1968, CVO 1954); da of 15 Duke of Norfolk, KG, PC, GCVO (d 1917); *b* 27 June 1905; *m* 1, 1939, Lt-Col Colin Keppel Davidson, CIE, OBE, RA (ka 1943), s of Col Leslie Davidson, CB, RHA, and Lady Theodora, da of 7 Earl of Albemarle; 1 s, 1 da; m 2, 1961, Brig Anthony Hilton Pepys, DSO (d 1967); *Career* lady-in-waiting to HRH Princess Marina, Duchess of Kent 1943-68; *Style*— Lady Rachel Pepys, DCVO; Highfield House, Crossbush, Arundel, W Sussex (☎ 0903 883158)

PEPYS, Lady Rose Edith Idina; da of late 6 Earl of Cottenham, and the Countess of Devon, *née* Sybil Venetia Taylor, of Powderham Castle, Exeter; ggggda of Capt William Bligh of Bounty; *b* 5 Nov 1927; *Educ* Latchington Court Seaford Sussex, St Mary's Hosp London; *Career* medical receptionist, formerly nurse; Dame of the Order of St Michael of the Wing (Portugal) 1988; *Recreations* reading, music, a little writing, theatres and films; *Clubs* RCN; *Style*— Lady Rose Pepys; Flat B, 101 Earls Court Road, London W8

PEPYS, Victoria; da of John Charles Geoffrey Pepys, of Kilpin, N Humberside, and Joyce Lillian, *née* Harvey; *b* 14 July 1955; *Educ* Beverley HS for Girls, Goole GS, Hull Regnl of Art, St Martins Sch of Art (BA); *m* 23 May 1987, Simon Cranmer, s of Ernest Young, of Preston, Lancs; *Career* PA to Jasper Conran 1977-79, sr account exec Lynne Franks PR 1980-; *Style*— Miss Victoria Pepys; Lynne Franks PR, 6-10 Frederick Close, Stanhope Place, London W2 2HD (☎ 01 724 6777, fax 01 724 8484)

PERCEVAL, Lady Geraldine Elizabeth Ursula; da of 11 Earl of Egmont; *b* 1939; *Style*— Lady Geraldine Perceval

PERCEVAL, Hon Mrs; Hon Joanna Ida Louisa; er da of 5 Baron Hatherton (d 1969), by his 1 w, Ida Gwendolyn (d 1969), formerly wife of Capt Henry Burton Tate and only child of Robin Legge; *b* 14 Oct 1926; *m* 1948, Robert Westby Perceval, s of Francis Westby Perceval (d 1956); 1 s, 2 da; *Style*— The Hon Mrs Perceval; Pillaton Hall, Penkridge, Stafford

PERCEVAL, John Dudley Charles Ascelin; s of Lt-Col John Francis George Perceval (d 1981), of Vancouver, Br Columbia, and Diana Madeleine Scott, *née* Pearce; *b* 8 April 1942; *Educ* Eton; *m* 11 Sept 1971, Tessa Mary, da of Geoffrey Bruce Dawson, OBE, MC (d 1984), of Caerlern; 2 s (Oliver Charles b 1972, Christopher Geoffrey John b 1978), 1 da (Candida Mary b 1974); *Career* Unilever 1961-69; exec dir Save & Prosper Gp Ltd 1985- (joined 1969); *Clubs* City of London; *Style*— John Perceval, Esq; The Forge House, Monk Sherborne, Basingstoke, Hants RG26 5HS (☎ 0256 850 073); Save and Prosper Gp Ltd, Finsbury Ave, London EC2 (☎ 01 588 1717)

PERCEVAL, Viscount; Thomas Frederick Gerald Perceval; s of 11 Earl of Egmont; *b* 17 August 1934; *Style*— Viscount Perceval

PERCEVAL MAXWELL, Gavin Richard; s of Maj John Robert Perceval-Maxwell (d 1963), of NI, and Phoebe Laura (d 1974), 2 da of Sir Benjamin Cherry, of Harmer Green, Herts; landowners in Co Down since 17th Century; descended from George Perceval, Registrar of the Prerogative Court, Dublin (d 1675), whose er bro, Sir John, was ancestor of Earls of Egmont; *b* 17 Feb 1924; *Educ* Stowe, Magdalene Coll Cambridge (MA); *m* 26 Sept 1962, Patricia Margaret, da of William Ponsonby Angley (d 1987); 1 s (John William b 1963); *Career* Army Serv 1943-48 cmmnd Lt KRCC attached Oxford and Bucks LI; at Archietectural Assoc 1948-51: High Sheriff of Co Durham 1968; *Recreations* gardening, painting; *Style*— Gavin Perceval Maxwell, Esq; Little Enton, Enton Green, Godalmng, Surrey GU8 5AG (☎ 04868 21255)

PERCHARD, Colin William; OBE (1985); s of William George Perchard, of La Chasse, St Martin, Jersey, Channel Islands, and Winifred Sarah, *née* Horn; *b* 19 Oct 1940; *Educ* Victoria Coll Jersey, Univ of Liverpool (BA), Int Inst for Educn Planning UNESCO Paris (advanced dip in educn planning and admin); *m* 4 April 1970, Elisabeth Penelope Glynis, da of Sir Glyn Jones GCMG, MBE, QV, of Brandfold Cottage, Goudhurst, Kent; 3 s (Nicholas b 1972, Jonathan b 1976, Adam b 1985); *Career* Br Cncl: asst rep Blantyre Malawi 1964-68, regnl offr Africa S of Sahara 1968-71, asst rep Calcutta 1971-72, offr i/c Dhaka 1972, rep Seoul 1973-76, dir Tech Coop Trg Dept 1976-79, Int Inst for Educn Planning Paris 1979-80, rep Harare 1980-86, controller Africa div 1986-; *Recreations* theatre, music, cooking; *Style*— Colin Perchard, Esq; The British Council, 10 Spring Gdns, London SW1A 2BN (☎ 01 930 8466, fax 01 839 6347, telex 8952201)

PERCIVAL, Allen Dain; CBE (1975); s of Charles Percival; *b* 23 April 1925; *Educ* Bradford GS, Magdalene Coll Cambridge; *m* 1952, Rachel Hay; *Career* principal Guildhall Sch of Music and Drama 1965-78, exec chm Stainer & Bell Publishers 1978-, Gresham Prof of Music City Univ 1980-; conductor, professional continuo player, broadcaster; *Style*— Allen Percival, Esq, CBE; 7 Park Parade, Cambridge (☎ 0223 353953)

PERCIVAL, Gordon Edward; s of Alan Percival (d 1981); *b* 20 Sept 1933; *Educ* Manchester GS; *m* 1956, Josephine Moira, 2 s (Nicholas, Mark), 1 da (Jacqueline); *Career* dir: Quartet plc, S & W Berisford Gp; md Sugar plc; dir of various other cos; landowner; *Style*— Gordon Percival, Esq; The Old Post House, Old Minster Lovell, nr Witney, Oxon OX8 5RN S & W Berisford plc, Berisford House, 50 Mark Lane, London EC3R 7QJ (☎ 01 481 9144; telex 884435 BERSFD G)

PERCIVAL, Rt Hon Sir Ian; PC (1983), QC (1963); s of Eldon Percival (d 1957), and Chrystyne, *née* Hoyle (d 1979); *b* 11 May 1921; *Educ* Latymer Upper Sch, St Catharine's Coll Cambridge (MA); *m* 1942, Madeline Buckingham, da of Albert Cooke (d 1928) and Nora (d 1970); 1 s (Robert), 1 da (Jane); *Career* serv WWII Maj The Buffs N Africa and Burma 1940-46; barr Inner Temple 1948, bencher 1970, rec of Deal, later of the Crown Ct 1971-, slr-gen 1979-83; memb Sidley & Austin USA and Int Attorneys; MP(c) Southport 1959-87; FTII, FCIArb, memb Royal Econ Soc; landowner; kt 1979; *Recreations* golf, parachuting, windsurfing, tennis; *Clubs* Carlton, Beefsteak, Royal Birkdale Golf, Rye Golf, City Livery; *Style*— The Rt Hon Sir Ian Percival, QC; home: Oxenden, Stone-in-Oxney, nr Tenterden, Kent (☎ 023 383 321); 9 King's Bench Walk, Temple, London EC4 (☎ 01 583 2939); work: 5 Paper Bldgs, Temple, London EC4 (☎ 01 583 4555, telex 8956431 ANTON G, fax 01 583 1926)

PERCIVAL, Michael John; s of John William Percival (d 1971), of Northampton, and Margery Edith, *née* Crawford; *b* 11 July 1943; *Educ* Berkhamsted Sch Herts; *m* 11 June 1966, Jean Margaret, da of Vincent Everard Dainty, of Northampton; 3 da (Katie b 1968, Alison b 1970, Linda b 1973); *Career* slr London 1966, ptnr Howes Percival Slrs (sr ptnr 1984); cncl of Northants Law Soc 1982, Pres Northampton and Dist Branch MS Soc 1988; tstee: Northants Nat Hist Soc and Field Club, St Christopher's Church of England Home for the Elderly, Northampton; server and asst at St Peter and St Paul's Church Abington, Northampton; High Ct and Co Ct Registrar 1983-88, memb of Northampton Dist Health Authy 1987, Clerk to Gen Commrs of Taxes for Northampton Dist 1 and 2 1988-; memb Law Soc 1966-; *Recreations* rugby, tennis, sailing; *Clubs* Northampton, Dallington LTC, Brancaster Staithe Sailing Club; *Style*— Michael Percival, Esq; Messrs Howes Percival Solicitors, Oxford House, Cliftonville, Northampton NN1 5PN (☎ 0604 230400, fax 0604 20956, telex 311445)

PERCY, Lady Richard; Hon Clayre; *née* Campbell; 2 da (by 1 m) of 4 Baron Stratheden and Campbell, CBE; *b* 1927; *m* 1, 17 Aug 1950 (m dis 1974), Rt Hon Nicholas Ridley, MP; 3 da (Jane b 1953, Susanna b 1955, Jessica b 1957); m 2, 1979, as his 2 w, Lord Richard Charles Percy, *qv*; *Style*— Lady Richard Percy; Lesbury

House, Alnwick, Northumberland NE66 3PT (☎ 0665 830 330); 212 Lambeth Rd, London SE1 (☎ 01 928 3441)

PERCY, Gerald; s of Lord William R Percy, CBE, DSO (d 1963) (5 s of 7 Duke of Northumberland), and Mary Swinton (d 1984); *b* 26 April 1928; *Educ* Eton, Christ Church Oxford (MA); *m* 1,1954, (m dis 1975), Jennifer, *née* Home-Rigg; 2 s , (Richard b 1957, Andrew b 1963), 2 da (Katherine b 1955, Diana b 1965); m 2, 1983, Victoria, da of Dr R Roger Henderson; *Career* Lt Royal Northumberland Fusiliers 1946-48; lived in Africa 1950-83: sec N Rhodesia Lib Pty 1961-63, dep man dir Lonrho Ltd 1963-73; *Recreations* ornithology, gardening, philately; *Clubs* Muthaigna, Nairobi, Inanda, Johannesburg; *Style—* Gerald Percy, Esq; The Granary, Nunnery Pl, Thetford, Norfolk IP24 2PZ (☎ 0842 761427)

PERCY, Humphrey Richard; s of Adrian John Percy of Wadhurst E Sussex and Maisie, *née* Gardener; *b* 2 Oct 1956; *Educ* Winchester; *m* 27 April 1985, Suzanne Patricia Spencer, da of Maj Bruce Holford- Walker of London SW3; 2 s (Luke, Christopher), 2 da (Daisy, Emma); *Career* J Henry Schroder Wagg & Co Ltd 1974-80, dir Barclays Merchant Bank Ltd 1985-86 (joined 1980); dir Barclays de Zoete Wedd Ltd 1986-; *Recreations* squash, reading, travel; *Clubs* Cannons; *Style—* Humphrey Percy, Esq; 2 Granville Rd, London SW18 5SL (☎ 01 870 4818); Barclays de Zoete Wedd ltd, Ebbgate House, 2 Swan Lane, London EC4R 3TS (☎ 01 623 2323, fax 01 623 6075, telex 923120)

PERCY, Lord James William Eustace; 3 and yst s of 10 Duke of Northumberland, KG, GCVO, TD, PC (d 1988); *b* 18 June 1965; *Educ* Eton, Bristol Univ; *Style—* Lord James Percy; Alnwick Castle, Alnwick, Northumberland

PERCY, Prof John Pitkeathly (Ian); s of John Percy (d 1984), of Edinburgh, and Helen Glass, Pitkeathly (d 1988); *b* 16 Jan 1942; *Educ* Edinburgh Acad, Edinburgh Univ; *m* 26 June 1965, Sheila Isobel Horn, da of Roy Toshack Horn (d 1957), of Edinburgh; 2 da (Jill Sheila b 12 April 1969, Sally Charlotte b 24 dec 1972); *Career* CA; asst Graham Smart & Annan 1960-68, ptnr Martin Currie & Scott 1969-71 (mangr 1968-69); Grant Thornton (London): (ptnr 1971-81, managing 1981-88, sr ptnr 1988-); vice-pres Inst CAs of Scotland 1988-; elder St Columbas Church of Scotland; hon prof of accountancy Aberdeen Univ; Freeman: City of London 1982, Worshipful Co of Painter Stainers 1982; MICAS 1967; *Recreations* golf, trout fishing; *Clubs* Hon Co of Edinburgh, RAC, Hazard's Golfing Soc, Royal and Ancient GC, New Club (Edinburgh), Caledonian; *Style—* Prof John Percy; 16 Elgood Ave, Northwood, Middx (☎ 09274 21293); Fionn Cottage, Badachro, Gairloch, Rosshire; Grant Thornton, Grant Thornton, Grant Thornton House, Melton St, Euston Square, London (☎ 01 383 5100, fax 01 383 4334, car tel 0836 516 227, telex 28984 GT LDN G)

PERCY, Hon Mary Edith; da of 1 and last Baron Percy of Newcastle (d 1958); *b* 24 Oct 1919; *Educ* Bristol Univ; *Style—* The Hon Mary Percy; Glebe Orchard, Etchingham, Sussex

PERCY, Lady Geoffrey; Mary Elizabeth; *née* Lea; o da of Ralph Lea, of Teddington, Middx; *m* 27 May 1955, Lord Geoffrey William Percy (d 1984), 4 and yst s of 8 Duke of Northumberland (d 1930); 1 da (Diana Ruth b 1956); *Style—* Lady Geoffrey Percy

PERCY, Lord Ralph George Algernon; 2 s of 10 Duke of Northumberland, KG, GCVO, TD, PC (d 1988); hp of bro 11 Duke of Northumberland, *qv*; *b* 16 Nov 1956; *Educ* Eton, Christ Church Oxford; *m* 1979, (Isobel) Jane, da of John Walter Maxwell Miller Richard, of Edinburgh; 1 s (George Dominic b 1984), 2 da (Catherine Sarah b 1982, Melissa Jane b 1987); *Career* land agent, landowner (12,000 acres); *Recreations* shooting, fishing, painting, skiing, tennis, snooker; *Style—* Lord Ralph Percy; Chatton Park, Chatton, nr Alnwick, Northumberland

PERCY, Lord Richard Charles; DL (Northumberland 1968); 3 s of 8 Duke of Northumberland, KG, CBE, MVO (d 1930) and Lady Helen Gordon Lennox, da of 7 Duke of Richmond (d 1965, as Dowager Duchess of Northumberland, GCVO, CBE, JP); bro of 9 and 10 Dukes; *b* 11 Feb 1921; *Educ* Eton, Christ Church Oxford, Durham Univ; *m* 1, 1966, Sarah Jane Elizabeth (d 1978), da of Petre Norton, of The Manor House, Whalton, Northumberland; 2 s (Algernon b 1969, Josceline b 1971); m 2, 1979, as her 2 husb, Hon Mrs Clayre Ridley, *qv* (above); *Career* Capt Grenadier Gds, serv WWII France and Germany, Lt-Col cmdg Northumberland Hussars TA 1959-61; lectr Dept of zoology Univ of Newcastle upon Tyne 1951-86; ret; *Style—* Lord Richard Percy, DL; Lesbury House, Alnwick, Northumberland NE66 3PT (☎ 0665 830 330); Kirkville, Fochabers, Morayshire IV32 7DQ (☎ 0343 820269)

PERCY, His Hon Judge; Rodney Algernon; 3 s of late Hugh James Percy, solicitor, of Alnwick; *b* 15 May 1924; *Educ* Uppingham, Brasenose Coll Oxford (MA); *m* 1948, Mary Allen, da of late J E Benbow, of Aberystwyth; 1 s, 3 da; *Career* Lt Royal Corps of Signals 1942-46, serv: Burma, India, Malaya, Java; barr Middle Temple 1950 (Lincoln's Inn 1987), dep coroner N Northumberland 1957, asst rec Sheffield QS 1964, dep chm Co Durham QS 1966-71, rec Crown Ct 1972-79, Circuit judge NE Circuit 1979-; pres Northumberland and Tyneside Marriage Guidance Cncl 1983; fndr memb Conciliation Service for Northumberland and Tyneside 1982; *Publications* editor: Charlesworth on Negligence (4th edn 1962, 5th edn 1971, 6th edn 1977), Charlesworth & Percy on Negligence (7th edn 1983); *Recreations* golf, gardening, hill walking, beachcombing, King Charles Cavalier spaniels; *Style—* His Honour Judge Percy; Brookside, Lesbury, Alnwick, Northumberland NE66 3AT (☎ 0665 830326)

PEREIRA, Sir (Herbert) Charles; s of Herbert John Pereira (d 1952); *b* 12 May 1913; *Educ* St Alban's Sch, London Univ (BSc, PhD, DSc); *m* 1941, Irene Beatrice, da of David James Sloan (d 1916); 3 s, 1 da; *Career* RE 1939-46; Colonial Serv 1946-67; dep dir E Africa Agric and Forestry Res Orgn 1955-61; dir: ARC of Rhodesia and Nyasaland 1961-63, ARC of Central Africa (Rhodesia Zambia and Malawi) 1963-67; chm ARC of Malawi 1967-74, dir E Malling Res Station 1969-72, chief scientist (dep sec) MAFF 1972-77, res conslt in tropical agric to World Bank and other orgns, memb bd of trustees Royal Botanic Gdns Kew 1983-86; Haile Selassie Prize for Res in Africa 1966; FRS; kt 1977; *Books* Land Use and Water Resources (1973), Policy and Practice in the Management of Tropical Watersheds (1989); *Recreations* sailing, swimming, mountain walking; *Clubs* Athenaeum, Harare; *Style—* Sir Charles Pereira; Peartrees, Nestor Ct, Teston Maidstone, Kent ME18 5AD (☎ 0622 813333)

PERELMAN, Alan Steven; s of Arthur Perelman, of 12 Woodlands Close, Harrogate, Yorks, and Evelyn *née* Beraha; *b* 30 April 1948; *Educ* Ashville Coll Harrogate, Christ's Coll Cambridge (MA), London Business Sch (MBA); *m* 30 Jan 1977, Christine, da of Godfrey Thomas; 1 s (Richard b 1 March 1978), 1 da (Elizabeth); *Career* Controller Bougainville Copper 1980-82, Controller ops, Hamersley Iron 1982-84, Dep Gen Mangr mktg and devpt Hamersley Iron 1984-85, fin dir The Gateway Corpn 1986-; govr Tetherdown Primary Sch; *Recreations* theatre, bridge, squash; *Style—* Alan Perelman, Esq; The Gateway Corporation Plc, Silbury Ct, 418 Silbury Boulevard, Milton Keynes, Beds MK9 2NB (☎ 0908 607 171)

PERERA, S Brandon Jayalath; s of Edward A Perera (d 1956), of Sri Lanka, and Elsie Lilian; *b* 2 Jan 1938; *Educ* St Benedict's Coll Colombo; *m* 13 Oct 1962, Ingrid Helen, da of Alfred Bohm (d 1972), of Switzerland; 2 s (Eugene b 1965, Adrian b 1970), 1 da (Sonia b 1967); *Career* CA in private practice; co dir and investor; FCA (1974); *Recreations* tennis, travel, languages; *Style—* Brandon Perera, Esq; Caerleon, Ruxley Crescent, Claygate, Esher, Surrey KT10 0TZ (☎ 0372 64432); Perera Fraser & Reeves, 6 Harwood Rd, London SW6 4PH (☎ 01 731 3462)

PERFECT, Geoffrey William; s of Frank George Perfect (d 1976), and Miriam Agnes, *née* Evans (d 1969); *b* 4 Feb 1922; *Educ* Royal GS, High Wycombe Bucks; *m* 8 April 1930, Eileen Mary, da of Lawrence Liddall (d 1970); 2 da (Anna (Mrs Duncan) b 1954, Sarah b 1955); *Career* WWII RAF 1940-45; engr asst Amersham Rural Dist Cncl 1945; chm: Frank Perfect & Sons Ltd (dir 1950), Frank Perfect & Sons Retail Ltd 1965, Glenmore Records Ltd 1965, Perfect Hotels Newquay Ltd 1965, Raphael cars Ltd 1965; chm 1987: Geoffrey Perfect Ltd: Hldgs, Homes, Investmts, Film and TV Prodns; govr Sports Aid Fndn Southern; chm: Alde House, Elderley Persons Home Bucks, Village Recreation Tstees, Methodist Church Tstees; JP 1972; Freeman City of London 1981, Liveryman Worshipful Co of Fanmakers 1982, Frreeman Worshipful Co of Constructors 1981 (Sr Warden 1988-); FCIOB 1980, FFB 1982; *Recreations* collector of vintage and sports cars; *Clubs* RAC; *Style—* Geoffrey Perfect, Esq; Glenore, Church Rd, Penn, Bucks (☎ 049481 2579); Casa Volante, Los Mojones, Puerto del Carmen, Lanzarote; Geoffrey Perfect Holdings Ltd, Church Rd, Penn, Bucks HP10 3LY (☎ 049481 4123)

PERHAM, Dr Richard Nelson; s of Cyril Richard William Perham (d 1948), of London, and Helen Harrow, *née* Thornton; *b* 27 April 1937; *Educ* Latymer Upper, St John's Coll Cambridge (BA, MA, PhD, ScD), MRC scholar MRC Laboratory of Molecular Biology Cambridge; *m* 22 Dec 1969, Nancy Jane, da of Maj Temple Haviland Lane; 1 s (Quentin Richard Haviland b 1973), 1 da (Temple Helen Gilbert b 1970); *Career* Nat Serv RN 1956-58; fell St John's Coll Cambridge 1964- (res fell 1964-67, tutor 1967-77), Helen Hay Whitney fell Yale Univ 1966-67; Cambridge Univ: lectr in biochemistry 1969-77 (demonstrator 1964-69), reader biochemistry of macro molecular structures 1977-, head of dept 1985- pres St John's Coll Cambridge 1983-87; govr Bishop's Stortford Coll, Syndic CUP, sr tres Lady Margaret Boat Club; memb: Sci Bd, SERC; chm: Biological Sci Ctee, SERC; pres Section D Br Assoc for Advancement of Sci 1987-88; memb: Biochemical Soc 1965, Euro Molecular Biology Orgn 1983, Royal Inst of GB 1986; FRS 1984, FRSA 1988; *Books* Instrumentation in Amino Acid Sequence Analysis (ed 1975), numerous papers in scientific jls; *Recreations* gardening, theatre, rowing, nosing around in antique shops; *Clubs* Hawks (Cambridge); *Style—* Dr Richard Perham; 107 Barton Rd, Cambridge CB3 9LL (☎ 0223 63752); Dept of Biochemistry, Univ of Cambridge, Tennis Ct Road, Cambridge CB2 1QW (☎ 0223 333663/7, fax 0223 333345, telex 81240 CAMSPL G)

PERKINS *see also*: Steele-Perkins

PERKINS, Hon Mrs (Celia Mary); *née* Sandys; da (by 1 m) of Baron Duncan-Sandys, CH, PC (d 1987), and Diana Churchill (d 1963); da of Sir Winston Churchill; *b* 18 May 1943; *m* 1, 1965 (m dis 1970), George Michael Kennedy; 1 s (Justin b 1967); m 2, 1970 (m dis 1979), Dennis Walters, MBE, MP, *qv*; 1 s (Dominic b 1971); m 3, 1985, Maj-Gen Kenneth Perkins, CB, MBE, DFC, *qv*; 1 s (Alexander b 1986), 1 da (Sophie b 18 May 1988) ; *Style—* Hon Mrs Perkins; Combe Head, Bampton, Devon EX16 9LB

PERKINS, Christopher Edwin Shuttleworth; s of Col George Forder Perkins, CBE, DSO (d 1972), of Salisbury, Wilts, and Nora Christine, *née* Shuttleworth (d 1975); *b* 5 May 1921; *Educ* Cheltenham, RMC Sandhurst; *m* 24 April 1948, Sheila Florence, da of Maj Gen E T L Gurdon, CB, MC (d 1959), of Woodbridge, Suffolk; 1 s (Timothy b 1956), 2 da (Sally b 1949, d 1976, Joy b 1950); *Career* WWII cmmnd Hampshire Regt 1939, co cdr N Africa and Italy 1942-45; staff HQ FARELF 1949-52, Territorial Adj 4 Royal Hampshire Regt Winchester 1953-54, ret 1955; gen mangr: JW French & Co Flour Millers 1955-61, WH Smith & Sons 1961-62; ptnr sec and accountancy business 1962-70, bd memb and non-exec dir Southern Newspapers 1966-81, chm Southern Newspapers plc Southampton 1981-; memb: Eastern Wessex TAVR Assoc, Salisbury Spire Appeal; *Recreations* shooting, fishing; *Clubs* Army and Navy; *Style—* Maj Christopher Perkins; Baverstock, Dinton, Salisbury, Wilts SP3 5EN (☎ 07227 6383); Southern Newspapers plc, 45 Above Bar, Southampton SO9 7BA

PERKINS, Francis Layton; CBE (1977), DSC (1940); s of Montague Thornton Perkins, and Madge Perkins; *b* 7 Feb 1912; *Educ* Charterhouse; *m* 1, 1941 (m dis 1971), Josephine Brice Miller; 1 s, 2 da; m 2, 1971, Jill Patricia Greenish; *Career* slr 1937; ptnr Clifford Turner & Co 1946, dir Hogg Robinson & Capel-Cure 1962; chm Hogg Robinson Gp, dir Transport Hldg Co, pres Corpn Insur Brokers, chm UK Insur Brokers European Ctee; memb Cncl and tres Industl Soc 1976-; chm Br Insur Brokers' Assoc 1976-80; chm Insur Brokers' Registration Cncl 1977-83; chm Barts (Hosp) Fndn for Res Ltd 1980-; cncl memb Common Law Inst of Intellectual Property 1983-; *Style—* Francis Perkins, Esq, CBE, DSC; Flat 4, 34 Sloane Court West, London SW3

PERKINS, Maj-Gen Kenneth; CB (1977), MBE (1955), DFC (1953); s of George Samuel Perkins and Arabella Sarah, *née* Wise; *b* 15 August 1926; *Educ* Lewes Co Sch for Boys, New Coll Oxford; *m* 1, 1949 (m dis 1984), Anne Theresa, da of John Barry (d 1960); 3 da; m 2, 1985, Hon Celia Mary Sandys, 2 da of Baron Duncan-Sandys (Life Peer); 1 s (b 1986), 1 da (b 1988); *Career* enlisted in the ranks 1944, cmmnd RA 1946, held various appointments worldwide 1946-66 (including army aviation during Korean War and Malayan Emergency); commanded: 1 Regt Royal Horse Artillery 1967-69, 24 Airportable Bde 1971-72, Sultan of Oman's Armed Forces 1975-77; ACDS (Operations) 1977-79, dir Mil Assistance Off 1980-82, Col Cmdt RA 1980-82, ret 1982; Order of Oman 1977, Hashemite Order of Independence 1975, Selangor Distinguished Conduct Medal 1955; *Books* Weapons and Warfare (1987), A Fortunate Soldier (1988); *Recreations* physical exercise, painting; *Clubs* Army and Navy; *Style—* Maj-Gen Kenneth Perkins, CB, MBE, DFC; Combe Head, Bampton, Devon EX16 9LB

PERKINS, Michael John; s of Phillip John Broad Perkins, OBE, DL (d 1982), of Lymington, Hants, and Jane Mary, *née* Hope; *b* 31 Jan 1942; *Educ* Eton, Dartmouth RNC; *m* 9 Nov 1968, Nicola Margaret, da of Air Cdre William Vernon Anthony Denney, RAF, of Amersham, Bucks; 1 s (Robert b 1971), 1 da (Caroline b 1973);

Career RN 1961-66, Sub Lt 1963, Lt 1965; ptnr Westlake Clerk CA's 1981, dir Southern Newspapers plc 1981; Freeman City of London 1956, Liveryman Worshipful Co of Haberdashers 1964; FCA (Canada) 1973, FCIS 1982; *Recreations* sailing, skiing, shooting; *Clubs* Royal Lymington YC; *Style*— Michael Perkins, Esq; Critchells Farmhouse, Lockerley, Romsey, Hants SO51 0JD (☎ 0794 402 81); Westlake Clark & Co, CAs, Newcourt House, New St, Lymington, Hants SO41 9BQ (☎ 0590 726 74, fax 0425 621 220)

PERKINS, Patricia; da of Charles Henry Victor Brown (d 1980), and Sarah Elizabeth, *née* Jones (d 1984); *b* 24 May 1935; *Educ* Putney HS for Girls, Girls Public Day Sch Tst; *m* 1, June 1960 (m dis), Stanley Edward Stewart Perkins (d 1984), s of Stanley Perkins (d 1968), of London; 1 s (Shane Charles Stewart b 22 July 1961), 1 da (Samantha Elizabeth Stewart b 21 Sept 1963); m 2, June 1982, Beau Maurice Gill Jnr; *Career* md Harlee Ltd 1979- (dir 1969-79), dir Helene plc 1979-; chm Nat Childrens Wear Assoc of GB and NI 1981-84, cncl memb Br Knitting Export Cncl 1983-85; *Recreations* sailing, riding, fishing; *Style*— Mrs Patricia Perkins; 407/409 Hornsey Rd, London N19 4DZ (☎ 01 272 4331, fax 281 4298, telex 8951059)

PERKINS, Robert James; s of John Howard Audley Perkins, MBE (d 1969), of Bristol, and Muriel May, *née* Bates (d 1957); *b* 27 June 1942; *Educ* Clifton, Fitzwilliam Coll Cambridge (MA); *m* 3 Aug 1968, Catherine Elizabeth, da of Nicol Robertson, of Milford on Sea, Hants; 1 s (Matthew b 1972), 1 da (Clare b 1971); *Career* qualified slr 1967, managing ptnr Moore and Blatch Lymington Hants 1976-, dir John Perkins and Son Ltd 1968-, NP 1986; ctee memb Hants Law Soc 1984-88 (hon sec New Forest area ctee (1984-88); chm: Milford on Sea Neighbourhood Cncl 1974-76, Milford on Sea Parish cncl 1976-78 (memb 1976-87); memb: Law Soc 1967, Int Bar Assoc 1978; *Recreations* sailing, singing, rowing; *Clubs* Bristol Commercial Rooms, Stewards Enclosure Henley, Keyhaven YC; *Style*— Robert Perkins, Esq; Rahere, Milford on Sea, Lymington, Hants SO41 OPE (☎ 0590 42542); Moore and Blatch, 48 High St, Lymington, Hants SO41 9ZQ (☎ 0590 72371, fax 0590 71224)

PERKS, Hon Mrs (Betty Quenelda); *née* Butler; 2 da of 28 Baron Dunboyne, *qv* ; *b* 23 June 1956; *Educ* Benenden, Girton Coll Cambridge (BA, MA); *m* 1985, Edward Roland Haslewood Perks, s of Judge Clifford Perks MC, of 32 Melbury Close, Chislehurst, Kent; 1 da (Candida Anne Quenelda b 1986); *Career* teacher: at Francis Holland London 1980-83, Headington Sch Oxford 1983-85; *Recreations* photography, tennis, swimming, skiing, squash; *Clubs* Hurlingham; *Style*— Hon Mrs Perks; 45 Heathfield Rd, London SW18 2PH

PERKS, His Honour (John) Clifford; MC (1944), TD; s of late John Hyde Haslewood Perks; *b* 20 Mar 1915; *Educ* Blundell's, Balliol Coll Oxford; *m* 1940, Ruth Dyke, *née* Appleby; 2 s (1 s and 2 da decd); *Career* barr Inner Temple 1938, dep chm Devon QS 1965-71, circuit judge 1970-85; *Style*— His Honour Clifford Perks, MC, TD; 32 Melbury Close, Chislehurst, Kent

PERLIN, Howard Stephen; *b* 23 Dec 1946; *m* 23 Oct 1988, Stephanie Lyn; *Career* dir Sears plc 1984-; FCA 1970; *Style*— Howard Perlin, Esq; Sears plc, 40 Duke St, London W1A 2HP (☎ 01 408 1180)

PEROWNE, Hon Lady (Agatha Violet); *née* Beaumont; da of 1 Viscount Allendale (d 1923); *b* 1903; *Educ* privately; *m* 1933, Sir John Victor Thomas Woolrych Tait Perowne, KCMG (d 1951); 1 s (John Florian Canning b 1942); *Career* OStJ; *Recreations* music, reading; *Style*— The Hon Lady Perowne; 1 Sandringham Court, Norwich, Norfolk NR2 2LF (☎ 0603 624746)

PEROWNE, Rear Adm Benjamin Cubitt; CB (1978); s of late Bernard Cubitt Perowne and Bertrude Dorothy Perowne; *b* 18 Feb 1921; *Educ* Culford Sch; *m* 1946, Phyllis Marjorie, da of late Cdre R D Peel, RNR, of Southampton; 2 s, 1 da; *Career* RN; dir mgmnt and support intelligence 1976-78, chief Naval supply and secretariat offr 1977-78, dir Royal UK Beneficent Assoc 1978-88;; *Recreations* shooting, gardening, fishing; *Clubs* Army & Navy; *Style*— Rear Adm Benjamin Perowne, CB; c/ o Barclays Bank, Haslemere, Surrey

PEROWNE, John Florian Canning; s of Sir Victor Perowne, KCMG (d 1951), and Hon Agatha, *née* Beaumont, da of 1 Viscount Allendale; *b* 20 August 1942; *Educ* Eton, Corpus Christi Coll Cambridge (MA); *m* 12 Oct 1968, Elizabeth Mary, da of Rev S B Freeman,a formerly Rector of Long Bredy, Dorset; 1 s (Matthew b 1983), 2 da (Anastasia b 1975, Clementine b 1979); *Career* admitted slr 1968, ptnr Daynes Hill & Perks Norwich; *Clubs* Norfolk (Norwich); *Style*— John Perowne, Esq; The White House, Bramerton, Norwich NR14 7DW (☎ 050 88 673), Paston House, 13 Princes St, Norwich NR31 1BD (☎ 060 366 0241)

PEROWNE, Stewart Henry; OBE (1943); s of Arthur William Thomson, Bishop of Worcester, and the late Helena Frances, *née* Oldnall-Russell; *b* 17 June 1901; *Educ* Haileybury, Corpus Christi Coll Cambridge (BA), Harvard (MA); *m* 10 Oct 1947, Freya Madeleine Stark, DBE, qv; *Career* joined Palestine Govt Educn Serv 1927, Admin Serv 1930 (pres offr 1931), asst dist cmmr Galilee 1934, asst sec Malta 1934, political ofr Aden Prot 1937, arabic programme organiser BBc Radio 1938, info offr Aden 1939, PR attaché Br Embassy Baghdad 1941, oriental cnsllr 1944, colonial sec Barbados 1947-51, seconded as princ advst (interior) Cyrenaica 1950-51, ret 1951; discovered ancient city of Ajiris 1951, advst UK Delgn to UN Assembly Paris 1951, designer and supervisor of refugee model villages; helped in the design of stamps and backnotes for various countries; hon fell Corpus Christi Coll Cambridge 1981; memb C of E Foreign Relations Cncl; Coronation Medal 1937, FRSA; Iraq Coronation Medal 1953; *Books* The One Remains (1954), Herod the Great (1956), The Later Herods (1958), Hadrian (1960), Caesars and Saints (1962), The Pilgrim's Companion in rome (1964), The Pilgrim's Companion in Jerusalem (1964), End of the Roman World (1966), The Death of the Roman Republic (1969), The Journeys of St Paul (1973), Roman Mythology (second edn 1983); *Recreations* archaeology of Greece and the Aegean, Holy Places of Christendom ; *Clubs* Travellers', London; *Style*— Stewart Perowne, Esq, OBE; Vicarage Gate House, Vicarage Gate, London W8 4AQ (☎ 01 229 1907)

PERRETT, Desmond Seymour; QC (1980); s of His Honour Judge Perrett *qv*; *b* 22 April 1937; *Educ* Westminster; *m* 1961, Pauline Merriel, da of late Paul Robert Buchan May, ICS; 1 s, 1 da; *Career* RN 1955-57; barr Gray's Inn 1962, bencher 1989; rec Crown Ct 1978-; *Style*— Desmond Perrett, Esq, QC; The Old Tap House, Upper Wootton, Basingstoke, Hants (☎ 0256 850027); 2 Crown Office Row, Temple, London EC4Y 7HJ (☎ 01 353 9337)

PERRETT, His Honour Judge; John Perrett; JP Warwicks 1970; s of late Joseph Perrett; *b* 22 Oct 1906; *Educ* St Anne's RC, Stratford Rd Schs Birmingham, King's Coll London; *m* 1933, Elizabeth Mary, da of late William Seymour; 2 s, 2 da; *Career* RAPC 1939-45, RASC 1945, barr Gray's Inn 1946, dep chm Warwicks QS 1970-71, a Circuit judge 1969-, JP; *Style*— His Honour Judge Perrett, JP; 9 The Close, Lichfield, Staffs (☎ Lichfield 52320); Farrar's Building, Temple, EC4 (☎ 01 583 9241)

PERRIN, Arthur Stanley; s of Walter William Perrin (d 1961); *b* 7 April 1920; *Educ* Southgate Co Sch; *m* 1954, Enid Beatrice, *née* Harvey; 1 s, 1 da; *Career* Sgt RASC WWII; md: Diecasting Machine Tools Ltd 1973-83, Lone Star Products Ltd 1973-83 Wheatrade Ltd 1983-84; chm: Californian Screen Blocks Ltd 1974- 83, 1974-83, Eaglet Industs Ltd 1975-, Br Toy & Hobby Mfr's Assoc 1980-82 (remains memb); chm Mayfield Athletic Club Ltd 1970-; *Recreations* golf; *Clubs* Brookman's Park GC, Mayfield Athletic, The Sportsman's, Hadley Wood GC; *Style*— Arthur Perrin, Esq; 34 Claremont Rd, Hadley Wood, Herts EN4 0HP (☎ 01 440 2309)

PERRIN, Charles John; s of late Sir Michael Perrin, CBE, of London (d 1988), and Nancy May, *née* Curzon; *b* 1 May 1940; *Educ* Winchester, New Coll Oxford; *m* 1966, Gillian Margaret, da of Rev M Hughes-Thomas (d 1969); 2 da (Felicity Margaret Roche b 1970, Nicola b 1973); *Career* joined Hambros Bank 1963- (dir 1973, dep chm 1986-); dir: Hambros plc, Hambro Pacific Ltd Hong Kong (chm), Harland & Wolff plc Belfast (non exec), Hambros Bank Executor & Tstee Co Ltd; memb exec ctee UK Ctee UNICEF 1970- (vice-chm 1972-); hon tres UK Int Year of the Child 1979, memb cncl or mgmnt ctee; Zoological Soc of London 1981-88, govr Queen Anne's Sch Caversham 1981-; *Clubs* Athenaeum; *Style*— Charles Perrin, Esq; 4 Holford Rd, Hampstead NW3 1AD (☎ 01 435 8103); 41 Towerhill, London EC3N 4HR (☎ 01 480 5000, telex 883851)

PERRING, John Raymond; TD (1965); s and h of Sir Ralph Edgar Perring, 1 Bt, by his w Ethel Mary, da of Henry Theophilus Johnson, of Putney; *b* 7 July 1931; *Educ* Stowe; *m* 1961, Ella Christine, da of late Maj Anthony George Pelham; 2 s (John b 1962, Mark b 1965), 2 da (Emma b 1963, Anna b 1968); *Career* chm: Perring Furnishings Ltd 1981-88, Perrings Fin Ltd, Ave Trading Ltd 1986-; chm Non-Food Ctee of Retail consortium; Master Worshipful Co of Merchant Taylors' 1988-89; one of HM Lts of City of London 1963-; FRSA; *Style*— John Perring, Esq, TD; 21 Somerset Rd, Parkside, Wimbledon, London SW19 5JZ

PERRING, Sir Ralph Edgar; 1 Bt (UK 1963) JP (London 1943); s of Col Sir John Ernest Perring, JP, DL (d 1948), and Florence, *née* Higginson (d 1960); *b* 23 Mar 1905; *Educ* Univ Coll Sch London; *m* 20 June 1928, Ethel Mary, OStJ, da of late Henry Theophilus Johnson; 2 s (and 1 s decd); *Heir* s John Raymond Perring, *qv*; *Career* Lt RA (TA) 1938-40; memb Ct of Common Cncl (Ward of Cripplegate) 1948-51, alderman City of London (Langbourn Ward) 1951-75, one of HM Lts of City of London and Sheriff 1958-59, lord mayor of London 1962-63, chm Perring Furnishings Ltd 1948-81, memb bd of govrs E-SU 1976-81, dir Confedn Life Insur Co of Canada 1969-82, vice-pres: Royal Bridewell Hosp 1964-73; tstee Morden Coll Blackheath 1970-, chm 1979-; former Master Worshipful Co of: Tin Plate Workers, Painters-Stainers, Furniture Makers; FeSA, KStJ; kt 1960; *Clubs* City Livery (sr former pres); *Style*— Sir Ralph Perring, Bt, JP; 15 Burghley House, Somerset Rd, Wimbledon, London W19 (☎ 01 946 3433)

PERRIS, Sir David Arthur; MBE (1970), JP (Birmingham 1961); s of Arthur Perris; *b* 25 May 1929; *Educ* Sparkhill Commercial Sch Birmingham; *m* 1955, Constance Parkes; 1 s, 1 da; *Career* chm W Midlands RHA 1974-82, sec TUC W Midlands Rgnl Cncl 1974-, sec Birmingham Trades Cncl 1966-83; chm NHS nat trg cncl 1975-82; vice-chm ATV Midlands Ltd 1980-81; dir Central Independent TV plc and vice-chm W Midlands Regnl Bd 1981-83; chm Birmingham Hosp Saturday Fund 1985-; pres Community Media Assoc 1983-; pres Birmingham Magistrates Assoc 1986 (chm 1975-86) chm Central Telethon Tst 1988-, Hon LLD Birmingham; kt 1977; *Style*— Sir David Perris, MBE, JP; Broadway, Highway Rd, Moseley, Birmingham B13 9HJ (☎ 021 449 3652)

PERROT, Emile Georges; s of Emile Georges Adolphus Perrot (d 1978), and Lilian May de Carteret, *née* Liebestraum; *b* 9 Mar 1949; *Educ* Guernsey GS, Univ of Hull (Dip Arch); *m* 24 Nov 1979, Carole Ann; 1 s (Emile b 1981), 1 da (Adele-Marie b 1978); *Career* States of Guernsey Civil Serv Architects Dept 1966-70, Deneuil Marty & Paoli Paris 1974-75, Krikor Baytarian London 1976-77, D Y Davies Assoc Richmond Surrey 1977-79, princ Emile Perrot Chartered Architects 1979-; FRIBA; *Style*— Emile G Perrot, Esq; 2 Clifton, St Peter Port, Guernsey, CI; Les Buttes, Rue De L'Eglise, St Pierre Du Bois, Guernsey

PERROTT, Sir Donald Cyril Vincent; KBE (1949); s of late Frederick John Perrott and late Alice Louisa Farwell; *b* 12 April 1902; *Educ* Tauntons' Sch Southampton, Univ Coll Southampton; *m* 1, 7 Sept 1925, Marjorie May (d 1969), da of late William Holway; 1 s; m 2, 26 Sept 1969, Mrs Lillian Lucinda Byre; *Career* sec Dept of Atomic Energy 1954 and memb for Fin and Admin of Atomic Energy Authy 1954-60, memb governing bd of Nat Inst for Res in Nuclear Sci 1957-60; *Style*— Sir Donald Perrott, KBE; 5 Plane Tree House, Duchess of Bedford's Walk, London W8 7QT

PERRY, Alan Joseph; s of Joseph George Perry (d 1957), of London, and Elsie May, *née* Lewis (d 1963); *b* 17 Jan 1930; *Educ* John Bright Sch, LLandudno Dartford GS, Kent; *m* 1961, Vivien Anne, da of Lt Col Ernest Charles Ball, of London (d 1968); 2 s (Howard b 1968, Myles b 1974); *Career* serv RE 1948-50; HM Treasy 1951-86, (princ 1968, asst sec 1976), cnsllr (Econ) Br Embassy Washington 1978-80, chm Review of BBC Ext Serv 1984; Adv on Govt Affairs, Ernst & Whinney, Accts and Conslts 1986-; *Recreations* tennis, painting; *Style*— Alan Perry, Esq; c/o Ernst & Whinney, 1 Lambeth Palace Rd, London SE1 7EV (☎ 01 928 2000)

PERRY, Hon Alan Malcolm; s of Baron Perry of Walton (Life Peer) of Walton House, Whittlebury, Northants, and Anne Elizabeth, *née* Grant; *b* 6 Feb 1950; *Educ* George Heriot's Sch Edinburgh, Trinity Coll Oxford (MA); *m* 1976, Naomi Melanie, da of Dr Abraham Freedman, MD, FRCP, of 21b Chesterford Gardens, London NW3; 2 s (Daniel b 1980, Guy b 1982); *Career* slr; *Recreations* painting, making music, gardening; *Style*— The Hon Alan Perry; 6 Sydney Grove, London NW4; Slaughter and May, 35 Basinghall St, London EC2 (☎ 01 600 1200, telex 883486/888926)

PERRY, Barrie Edward; s of Edward Perry; *b* 5 June 1933; *Educ* Surbiton Modern Sch, King's Coll Durham; *m* 1961 (m dis); 1 s; *Career* naval architect; former chm and md Proctor Masts; md Hamble Yacht Servs 1983-; dir: Marina Devpts Ltd, Penton Hook Marinas Ltd, Bray Marina Ltd, Cobb's Quay Ltd, Hartford Marina Ltd, Torquay Yacht Harbours Ltd; MDL Boat Sales Ltd; md The Marine Dvpt Gp plc; *Recreations* sailing; *Clubs* Royal Southern YC; *Style*— Barrie Perry, Esq; The Forge, Hook by Warsash, Southampton

PERRY, Colin Heywood; s of John Philip Perry (d 1972), and Barbara, *née* Heywood;

b 14 Dec 1940; *Educ* Winchester, Clare Coll Cambridge (MA), INSEAD Fontainebleau (MBA); *m* 1966, Rebecca Mary, da of John S Barclay (d 1968); 1 s (Alexander b 1970), 1 da (Georgina b 1968); *Career* chm and md Birmingham Mint Gp plc; *Style*— Colin Perry, Esq; Birmingham Mint Gp plc, Icknield St, Birmingham B18 6RX (☎ 021 236 7742, telex 336991); Great Blakes, Shelsley Beauchamp, Worcester WR6 6RB

PERRY, David Gordon; s of Elliott Gordon Perry, of Kemble, nr Cirencester, and Lois Evelyn, *née* Allen; *b* 26 Dec 1937; *Educ* Clifton, Christ's Coll Cambridge; *m* 16 Sept 1961, Dorne Mary, da of Edwin Timson Busby (d 1980), of Braybrooke, Market Harborough; 4 da (Belinda b 1963, Philippa b 1964, Rebecca b 1967, Joanna b 1970); *Career* Nat Serv 2 Lt Parachute Regt 1956-58; Br Printing Corpn (BPC) Ltd: md Fell & Briant Ltd (subsid) 1966-78, chief exec packaging and paper products div 1978-81, dir 1981; chief exec John Waddington plc 1988- (md 1981-88); Cambridge Rugby Blue 1958, fifteen caps England Rugby XV 1963-66, Capt 1965; CBIM 1986; *Recreations* golf, tennis, music; *Clubs* Utd Oxford & Cambridge, MCC; *Style*— David Perry, Esq; Deighton House, Deighton, Nr Escrick, York YO4 6HQ (☎ 090 487 257); John Waddington Plc, Wakefield Rd, Leeds LS10 3TP (☎ 0532 712244, fax 0532 713503, car tel 0860 311872)

PERRY, Sir David Howard; KCB (1986); s of Howard Dace Perry (d 1971), and Annie Evelyn (d 1976); *b* 13 April 1931; *Educ* Berkhamsted Sch, Pembroke Coll Cambridge (MA); *m* 1961, Rosemary, da of Alfred Seymour Grigg (d 1982); 1 s, 2 da; *Career* Royal Aircraft Estab 1954-78, MOD (Procurement Exec) Air Systems Controllerate 1978-82, chief of Def Procurement MOD 1983-85; chief of Def Equip Collaboration MOD 1985-87; FRAeS; *Style*— Sir David Perry, KCB

PERRY, Dr Ian Charles; s of Capt Sidney Charles Perry (d 1984), of Bush Hill Pk, Enfield, Middx, and Marjorie Ellen, *née* Elliott; *b* 18 April 1939; *Educ* Highgate, Guy's Hosp (MB, BS), RAF Inst of Aviation Med (DAV Med), Univ of London (MFom), RCP; *m* 27 July 1963, Janet Patricia, da of Maj Albert Edward Watson, of Burton Bradstock, Dorset; 2 da (Johanna Elizabeth b 18 Oct 1964, Helen b 7 July 1967); *Career* Lt RAMC 1963, Capt 2 i/c 24 Field Ambulance Aden 1965 and 1967 (sr MO Aden Bde 1966), sr MO (specialist Aviation Med) Army Air Corps Centre 1967-68, 200 Army Pilots Course 1968-69, Maj sr MO Conslt Aviation Med Army Air Corps Centre 1969, chm NATO (AG ARD) Aircrew Fatigue Panel 1969-72, ret 1973, RARO 1973-; princ aviation med practice (accident and explosion investigator incl Manchester Boeing 1985-86) 1973-75-; sr conslt Avimed Ltd, dir Aviation Conslts Ltd, sr conslt Occumed Ltd, chm Fireseal Ltd; currently: chm Aviation Conslts Assoc, hon con Br Helicopter Advsy Bd; former chm: Grateley PC, Grateley PTA; memb: Army air Corps Museum Friends, Preservation of Rural Eng; sec Nurdling Assoc of England; Freeman City of London 1973, Ct Asst Guild of Air Pilots and Navigators 1984; LRCP, MRCS, FRSM, FRAeS, FAMA, MBIM 1986; *Books* numerous papers on Aviation Med; *Recreations* golf, shooting; *Clubs* Sloane, Helicopter Club GB, Tidworth GC; *Style*— Dr Ian Perry; The Old Farm House, Garateley, Hants SP11 8JR (☎ 026488659/639, fax 026488 639, mobile 0836 664670); 19 Cliveden Place, London SW1W 8HD (☎ 01 730 8045/9328, fax 01 730 1985)

PERRY, Prof Jack; s of Abraham Perisky, and Rebecca Goldstein; *b* 31 Mar 1915; *Educ* Dame Alice Owen GS; *m* 5 Feb 1939, Doris Kate, da of Maurice Shaer, of Myddleton Rd, Golders Green; 3 s (Graham, Stephen, Jonathan); 2 da (Julian, Vivien); *Career* chm London Export Corpn Hldgs Ltd 1952-88; vice pres: 48 Gp of Br Traders with China 1978-, Soc for Anglo-Chinese Understanding 1988-; prof of business studies univ of Int Business and Econs Beijing 1986, visiting prof Foreign Trade Univ Tietsin 1988-; *Recreations* football, golf, cricket; *Clubs* Wentworth GC, RAC; *Style*— Prof Jack Perry; 49 Fairacres, Roehampton Lane, London SW15; Weavers, Down House, Liphook, Hants (☎ 878 20171); London Export Corporation (Holdings) Ltd, 7 Swallow Place, London W1 (☎ 01 493 7083, fax 01 629 5585, telex 297335 LLCM G)

PERRY, Margaret Strachan; *née* Maclaren; da of William Anderson Maclaren, of Inverness, Scotland, and Elizabeth, *née* Strachan; *b* 7 Mar 1934; *Educ* Inverness Royal Acad, Edinburgh Univ (MA); *m* 14 Feb 1964 (m dis 1988), Brian Evelyn Perry, s of Arthur Raymond Perry (d 1983), of Arborfield Cross, Berks; 2 s (Guy Robert Maclaren b 17 June 1966, Gregory Stuart b 10 Nov 1968); *Career* teacher London and Scotland 1954-64, dir Liftrucs Ltd 1970-(md 1984-); *Recreations* the arts, good food and wine, motor racing; *Style*— Mrs Margaret Perry; The Smithy, The Cross, Bramhope, Leeds (☎ 0532 842 791); Liftrucs Ltd, Gelderd Rd, Gildersome, Morley, Leeds LS27 7JX (☎ 0532 537 735, fax 0532 521 773, telex 557515)

PERRY, Ven Michael Charles; s of Charlie Perry (d 1972), and Kathleen Farmer; *b* 5 June 1933; *Educ* Ashby-de-la-Zouch Boys' GS, Trinity Coll Cambridge (MA), Westcott House Cambridge; *m* 13 July 1963, Margaret, da of Maj J M Adshead (d 1965); 2 s (Andrew b 1965, David b 1968), 1 da (Gillian b 1973); *Career* archdeacon of Durham and canon residentiary of Durham Cathedral 1970-, sub-dean 1985-; chm: Churches' Fellowship for Psychical and Spiritual Studies, Lord Crewe's Charity; memb: cncl Soc for Psychical Research, General Synod; author, editor; *Books* incl The Easter Enigma (1959), Sharing in One Bread (1973), The Resurrection of Man (1975), The Paradox of Worship (1977), Handbook of Parish Finance (1981), Psychic Studies (1984), Deliverance (1987); *Clubs* Royal Commonwealth Soc; *Style*— The Ven the Archdeacon of Durham; 7 The College, Durham DH1 3EQ (☎ 091 386 1891)

PERRY, Hon Michael John; s of Baron Perry of Walton (Life Peer); *b* 1948; *m* 1970, Kathleen Elliott; *Style*— The Hon Michael Perry; 5 Corstorphine Park Gdns, Edinburgh

PERRY, Michael Sydney; OBE (1973); s of Lt Cdr Sydney Albert Perry, RNVR (d 1979), of Douglas, IOM, and Jessie Kate, *née* Brooker; *b* 26 Feb 1934; *Educ* King William's Coll IOM, St John's Coll Oxford (MA); *m* 18 Oct 1958, Joan Mary, da of Francis William Stallard (d 1948), of Worcester; 1 s (Andrew b 1967), 2 da (Carolyn b 1962, Deborah b 1963); *Career* Nat Serv RN 1952-54; Unilever plc 1957-: chm Lever Bros (Thailand) Ltd 1973-77, pres Lever Y Asociados Argentina 1977-81, chm Nippon Lever KK Japan 1981-83, chm Utd Africa Co Int Ltd 1985-87, dir Unilever plc and NV 1985-, personal products coordinator worldwide Unilever 1987-; memb Br Overseas Trade Bd 1986-; chm: Japan Trade Advsy Gp BOTB 1986-, chm: Int Shakespeare Globe Centre Ltd 1986-, Argentine Diocesan Assoc 1988-; dir Netherlands Br C of C 1988-; *Recreations* music (choral), golf; *Clubs* Oriental; *Style*— Michael Perry, Esq, OBE; Bridges Stone Mill, Alfrick, Worcs WR6 5HR (☎ 0886 332 90); 35/3 Queen's Gate Gdns, London SW7 5RR (☎ 01 581 9839); Unilever plc, Unilever House, Blackfriars, London EC4P 4BQ (☎ 01 822 5252 telex 28395)

PERRY, Hon Niall Fletcher; s of Baron Perry of Walton (Life Peer); *b* 1953; *m* 1978, Sandra Buchanan; *Style*— The Hon Niall Perry; 57 Rowney Croft, Hall Green, Birmingham

PERRY, Dr Norman Henry; s of Charles Perry (d 1984), of London, and Josephine, *née* Ehrlich (d 1986); *b* 5 Mar 1944; *Educ* Quintin Sch London, University Coll London: (BA, PhD); *m* 7 Aug 1970, Barbara Ann, da of James Harold Marsden and Margaret, *née* Lithemeyer, of Sheffield; 2 s (Ben 1974, Tom 1977); *Career* lectr in geography UCL 1965-69, sr res offr GLC 1969-73, sr res fell Social Sci Res Cncl Survey Unit 1973-75; DOE: princ London & Birmingham 1975-79, princ London 1979-80, asst sec W Midlands 1980-86; grade 4 head of inner cities unit Dept of Employment and DTI 1986-88, grade 3 regnl dir DTI W Midlands 1988-; chm Third Olton (Solihull) Scout Gp 1985-88; FBIM 1983, RIPA 1979; *Books* Demands for Social Knowledge (with Elisabeth Crawford, 1976) Vols in European Glossary of Legal and Administrative Terminology: German/English, Vol 18 Regional Policy (1974), Vol 29 Environmental Policy (1979), Public Enterprise (1989); *Recreations* reading, history, gardening, occasional jogging; *Clubs* Civil Service; *Style*— Dr Norman Perry; DTI West Midlands, Ladywood House, Stephenson St, Birmingham B2 4DT (☎ 021 631 6000, fax 021 643 5500)

PERRY, Pauline; *née* Welch; da of John George Embleton Welch (d 1963), of Sunderland, and Elizabeth, *née* Cowan (d 1982); *b* 15 Oct 1931; *Educ* Girls HS Wolverhampton, Girton Coll Cambridge (BA, MA); *m* 26 July 1952, George Walter Perry, s of Percy Walter Perry (d 1939), of Wolverhampton; 3 s (Christopher b 1952, Timothy b 1962, Simon b 1946), 1 da (Hilary (Mrs Hayward) b 1955); *Career* teacher various secdy schs UK USA and Canada 1953-56 and 1959-61; lectr in philosophy: Univ of Manitoba 1956-59, Univ of Massachusetts 1961-62; lectr in educn: Univ of Exeter (pt/t) 1963-66, Univ of Oxford 1966-70; Access Course tutor 1966-70, HM Chief Inspr Schs 1981-86 (inspr 1970-74, staff inspr 1975-81), dir South Bank Poly 1987- freelance journalist and broadcaster; memb: ESRC, bd of Open Coll Educn Advsy Cncl IBA, examinations cncl RSA, bd IDS Br cncl CICHE, chm teacher educn gp SRHE, bd of South Bank Technoparts Ltd; conslt to OECD on Higher Educn and professional devpr of teachers 1976-81, nat corres in in-serv trg Cncl of Europe; hon FCP 1987, FRSA 1988; *Books* Your Guide to the Opposite Sex (1970), Case-Studies in Adolescence (co-author with G Perry 1970), Case-Studies in Teaching (co-author with G Perry 1969); *Recreations* music, walking; *Clubs* Nat Liberal; *Style*— Pauline Perry; South Bank Polytechnic, Borough Road, London SE1 0AA (☎ 01 928 8989, fax 01 261 9115)

PERRY, Peter George; CB (1983), JP (City of London 1974-); s of Joseph George Perry (d 1958), and Elsie Lewis (d 1963); *b* 15 Dec 1923; *Educ* Dartford GS, London Univ (LLB); *m* 1957, Marjorie Margaret, da of J J Stevens (d 1970); *Career* civil service 1947-84, under sec DHSS 1974-84; memb Indust Tribunals 1984-; *Recreations* sailing (Hestia of Hamble), opera, theatre, skiing; *Clubs* Little Ship; *Style*— Peter Perry, Esq, CB, JP; 50 Great Brownings, College Rd, Dulwich, London SE21

PERRY, Rodney Charles Langman; s of Thomas Charles Perry, of 60 Felpham Way, Felpham, Bognor Regis, West Sussex, and Kathleen Mary, *née* Moojen; *b* 23 July 1941; *Educ* Peter Symonds Sch Winchester; *m* 5 March 1965, Susan Geraldine, da of John Reginald Quertier, of 24 Wellington Court, Spencers Wood, Reading; 1 s (James Quertier b 20 Sept 1968), 1 da (Sarah De Moulpied b 23 Feb 1967); *Career* CA; articles Charles Comins & Co 1960-65, Coopers & Lybrand Zimbabwe 1965-69, ptnr Coopers & Lybrand UK 1976; ICAEW: memb cncl 1984-86, chm technology gp 1984-86; Freeman City of London, Worshipful Co of Information Technologists; FCA 1975; *Books* An Audit Approch To Computers (1986); *Recreations* squash, golf, boating, painting; *Clubs* Royal Lymington; *Style*— Rod Perry, Esq; Orchard House, Swallowfield St, Swallowfield, Reading, Berks; Flat 19, 87 St George's Court, St George's Drive, Pimlico, London SW1 (☎ 0734 883 666, 01 630 7968); Coopers & Lybrand, Plumtree Court, London (☎ 01 822 4575, telex 887470)

PERRY, Prof Roger; s of Charles William Perry, of Newquay, Wales, and Gladys, *née* Cooper; *b* 21 June 1940; *Educ* King Edward's GS Birmingham, Univ of Birmingham (BSc, PhD); *m* 13 Aug 1964, (Agnes) Joyce, da of John Houston; 1 s (Jonathan b 1965), 1 da (Deborah b 1968); *Career* appts in chem industry until 1964, dept of chem and chem engng Univ of Birmingham 1964-70, prof of public health and water technol Imp Coll 1981- (memb academic staff 1970-); conslt to: UK and int chem and engrg insts, WHO, UNEP; memb senate and academic cncl Univ of London 1984-; FRSH 1984, FIEWM 1972, FRCS 1970, CChem; *Books* Handbook of Air Pollution Analysis (1977, 2 edn 1986); *Recreations* cooking, gardening, building and travel; *Style*— Prof Roger Perry; Civil Engineering Department, Imperial College, London SW7 2BU (☎ 01 589 5111, fax 01 584 7596, telex 918351)

PERRY, Stephen Laurence Andrew; s of Jack Perry, of London, and Doris Kate Perry (d 1985); *b* 12 Sept 1948; *Educ* UCL (LLB); *m* 24 Dec 1980, Wendy Janet, da of Joseph Bond (d 1957); 1 s (Jack b 1984), 1 da (Jodie b 1981); *Career* md London Export Corpn (Hldgs) Ltd; dir: London Export Corpn (Mktg) Ltd, Tienshan Ltd, China Business Servs Ltd; memb: Sino-British Trade Cncl, Mgmnt Ctee of 48 Gp; chm: China Ctee London C of C, Academicals Football Club; dir Int Shakespeare Globe Tst Ltd; *Recreations* football, tai-chi; *Clubs* RAC, Wentworth, IOD; *Style*— Stephen Perry, Esq; 7 Swallow Place, London W1 (☎ 01 493 7083, telex 297335)

PERRY OF WALTON, Baron (Life Peer UK 1979); Walter Laing Macdonald Perry; OBE (1957); s of Fletcher Smith Perry (d 1960), and Flora Macdonald Macdonald (d 1966); *b* 16 June 1921; *Educ* Ayr Acad, Dundee HS, St Andrews Univ; *m* 1, 1946 (m dis 1971) Anne Elizabeth Grant; 3 s (Hon Michael John b 1948, Hon Alan Malcolm b 1950, Hon Niall Fletcher b 1953); m 2, 1971, Catherine Hilda, da of Ambrose Crawley; 2 s (Hon Robin Charles Macdonald b 11 June 1973, Hon Colin Stuart Macdonald b 12 Aug 1979), 1 da (Hon Jennifer Joan b 6 Feb 1981); *Career* dep leader SDP in House of Lords 1981-83; dir Dept of Biological Standards, Nat Inst for Med Res 1952-58; prof of pharmacology Univ of Edinburgh 1958-68, vice-principal 1967-68; vice-chllr The Open Univ 1969-80, fellow 1981-; FRCPE, FRCP, FRSE, FRS; kt 1974; *Recreations* making music and playing games; *Clubs* Savage, Scottish Arts; *Style*— The Rt Hon the Lord Perry of Walton, OBE, FRS; the Open Univ Scotland, 60 Melville St, Edinburgh EH3 7HF (☎ 031 226 3851)

PERSSE, Richard Henry; s of Brig Reginald Barry Lovaine Persse, KSLI (d 1985), of Taunton, Somerset, and Sheeleh Patricia, *née* Battersby (d 1979); *b* 22 Oct 1937; *Educ* Eton; *m* 3 May 1969, Susan Royale, da of Cdr Anthony Kennett, RN (ret), of Somerset; 2 s (Edward b 1971, James b 1972); *Career* cmmnd 1 Kings Dragoon Gds, served Malaya 1957-58; dir: Morgan Furze & Co (wine merchants) 1968-79, Morans of Bristol 1979-84; md J B Reynier Ltd (wine shippers) 1987-; *Recreations* fishing; *Clubs* Flyfishers; *Style*— Richard Persse, Esq; 64a Tachbrook St, Pimlico, London SW1V 2NA (☎ 01 630 8639); JB Reynier Ltd, 16-18 Upper Tachbrook St, London SW1 (☎ 01 834 2917)

PERSSON, Rt Rev William Michael Dermot; *see*: Doncaster, Bishop of

PERT, (Thomas) John; VRD; s of Thomas Richard Pert (d 1962), of Sleaford, and Henrietta Kate, *née* Cooke (d 1968); *b* 12 July 1915; *Educ* Carr's GS Sleaford, Nottingham Univ Coll of Law, Coll of Law London; *m* 1 Sept 1949, Dorothy Rachel, da of Thomas Hawley (d 1924), of Buckminster, Lincs; 2 s (John Richard William b 1952, Nicholas James b 1954); *Career* Lt Cdr RNR; HMS Calcutta 1939, HMS Iron Duke 1939, HS Rodney 1939-43; serving North Sea, Channel, South Atlantic, Arctic, Mediterranean; combined ops 1943-46; slr and NP coroner for Grantham District 1949; *Recreations* golf, skiing, swimming, cricket; *Clubs* The Naval, Belton Park, Ranceby and Stoke Golf; *Style*— John Pert, Esq, VRD; Glenrise, Old Somerby, nr Grantham (☎ 0476 63426); 79 Westgate, Grantham (☎ 0476 61631, fax 0476 73274)

PERT, Keith Giscard; TD; s of Earnest Morgan Pert (d 1955), of Norwich, and Mabel Giscard, *née* Barrow; *b* 11 Sept 1919; *Educ* Norwich GS, Norwich Sch of Arch (Dip Arch); *m* 16 March 1946, Audrey Joan, s of Alfred Lloyd (d 1933); 3 s (Christopher, Michael, Jeremy); *Career* WWII: RE Services ME; architect: fndr & ptnr Hare Pert & Ptnrs; past: pres E Anglian Soc of Architects, memb RIBA Cncl; FRIBA; memb of Livery Woolmens Co; WW II Star: 39/45, Italian; *Recreations* sailing, languages, ancient history; *Clubs* Ipswich and Suffolk; *Style*— Keith Pert, Esq, TD; Church Crescent, Sproughton, Ipswich, Suffolk (☎ Ipswich 461797); 18 Museum Street, Ipswich (☎ 0473 58311)

PERTH, 17 Earl of (S 1605); (John) David Drummond; PC (1957); also Lord Drummond of Cargill and Stobhall (S 1488), Lord Maderty (S 1609), Viscount Strathallan (S 1686), and Lord Drummond of Cromlix (S 1686); s of 16 Earl of Perth, GCMG, CB, PC (d 1951), and Hon Angela Constable-Maxwell (d 1965), da of 11 Lord Herries of Terregles; *b* 13 May 1907; *Educ* Downside, Trinity Coll Cambridge; *m* 4 Aug 1934, Nancy Seymour, da of Reginald Fincke, of New York City; 2 s; *Heir* s, Viscount Strathallan; *Career* Lt Intelligence Corps, seconded to War Cabinet Offices 1942-43 and to min of Production 1944-45; a representative peer for Scotland 1952-63, Hereditary Thane of Lennox and Hereditary Steward of Menteith and Strathearn; min of State for Colonial Affairs 1957-62, first crown estate cmmr 1962-77, chm of the Reviewing Ctee on the Export of Works of Art 1972-76, tstee Nat Library of Scotland, Hon LLD St Andrew's Univ; Hon FRIBA 1978, Hon FRIAS 1988; *Clubs* White's, Puffin's (Edinburgh); *Style*— The Rt Hon the Earl of Perth, PC; 14 Hyde Park Gardens Mews, London W2 (☎ 01 262 4667); Stobhall, by Perth (☎ (082 14) 332)

PERTWEE, Anthony Nigel Ferens; s of Norman Frank Pertwee; *b* 4 Nov 1942; *Educ* Tonbridge; *m* 1965, Margaret Joan, da of Ronald George Gammer; 1 s, 2 da; *Career* chm Pertwee Anfood Ltd, dir Pertwee Holdings Ltd; *Recreations* sailing, hot air ballooning, water sports, skiing; *Style*— Anthony Pertwee Esq; 5 Baynards Crescent, Frinton-on-Sea, Essex CO13 0QS (☎ 0255 673 709)

PERTWEE, Christopher Ferens; s of Norman Frank Pertwee, of Frinton-on-Sea, Essex, and Eileen Pertwee (d 1982); *b* 25 Nov 1936; *Educ* Tonbridge; *m* 1960, Carole, da of Alfred George (Jim) Drayson, of Sutton Valence, Kent; 3 s (Mark, Julian, Nicholas); *Career* chm and co dir Pertwee Hldgs Ltd, pres United Kingdom Agric Supply Trade Assoc 1982-83; dir: Colchester Oaks Hospital Ltd, Rosenlew MimiBulk Ltd; East Tst Ltd; memb Ct Worshipful Co of Farmers; *Recreations* hunting, tennis, ski-ing, gardening, antiques; *Clubs* Farmers; *Style*— Christopher Pertwee, Esq; The Bishops House, Frating, Colchester, Essex CO7 7HQ (☎ 0206 250706); office: Harbour House, Colchester, Essex CO2 8JF (☎ 0206 577991, telex 98121)

PERTWEE, Desmond Brian; s of Frank Pertwee (d 1964); *b* 26 April 1911; *Educ* King's Sch Canterbury; *m* 1, 1935 (w d 1949); m 2, 1950, Margaret Angela Clare, da of Vice Adm Charles Round-Turner (d 1953); 5 c; *Career* chm Frank Pertwee & Sons Ltd, Stimpson Pertwee Ltd, dir Pertwee Holdings Ltd (ret); *Recreations* ocean racing, sailing, horse trials (past); *Style*— Desmond Pertwee, Esq; Rookery House, Gt Horkesley, nr Colchester C06 4EJ (☎ 0206 271213)

PERUTZ, Gerald; s of Dr Georg Perutz (d 1935); *b* 8 Sept 1929; *Educ* Loughborough Coll; *m* 1953, Dinah Fyffe, *née* Pope; 3 children; *Career* gen mangr Rank Precision Industs 1957-63; chm Bell & Howell Co Chicago USA to 1983 (ret); chm Nimlor Gp Chicago USA; *Recreations* tennis, skiing; *Clubs* Glenview; *Style*— Gerald Perutz Esq; c/o National Westminster Bank Ltd, 115 Old Brompton Rd, London SW7; 223 Melrose, Kenilworth, Illinois USA

PERUTZ, Max Ferdinand; OM (1988), CH (1975), CBE (1963); s of Hugo and Adele Perutz; *b* 19 May 1914; *Educ* Theresianum, Vienna, Vienna Univ, Peterhouse Cambridge (hon fell 1962); *m* 1942, Gisela Peiser; 1 s, 1 da; *Career* chm Medical Research Council Laboratory of Molecular Biology Cambridge 1962-79, memb Scientific Staff 1979-, Fullerian prof of physiology at the Royal Institution 1973-79, Nobel Prize for Chemistry 1962, Royal Medal of Royal Society 1971; Copley Medal of Royal Soc 1979; OM; *Style*— Dr Max Perutz, OM, CH, CBE, FRS; 42 Sedley Taylor Rd, Cambridge CB2 2PN (☎ 0223 246041); MRC Laboratory of Molecular Biology, Cambridge CB2 2QH (☎ 0223 248011, telex 81532)

PERY, Hon Michael Henry Colquhoun; s of 5 Earl of Limerick, GBE, CH, KCB, DSO, TD (d 1967), and Angela Olivia, GBE, CH (d 1981), da of Lt-Col Sir Henry Trotter, KCMG, CB; bro of 6 Earl, *qv*; *b* 8 May 1937; *Educ* Eton, New Coll Oxford (BA); *m* 1963, Jennifer Mary, eldest da of John Anthony Stuart-Williams (d 1978), of Braughing, Herts; 2 s, 2 da; *Career* Lt XII Royal Lancers; Inns of Court, City Yeomanry; md: Alginate Industries Ltd 1974-82, Sifam Ltd 1983-; dir London Life Assoc 1983-; *Recreations* sailing, skiing, tennis; *Clubs* Garrick; *Style*— The Hon Michael Pery; Ardtur, Appin, Argyll PA38 4DD (☎ (063 173) 223); Sifam Ltd, Woodland Rd, Torquay, Devon (☎ (0803) 63822)

PERYER, Roger Norman; s of Frederick Grey Peryer (d 1988), and Edna, *née* Watt (d 1987); *b* 27 Feb 1937; *Educ* King's Coll Sch Wimbledon, Coll of Law; *m* 1, 6 Oct 1973 (m dis 1989), Joan Juliet, da of Peter Landymore Green; 1 s (Guy Roger Frederick b 2 Sept 1977), 1 da (Holly Juliet b 25 March 1975); *Career* admitted slr 1959; ptnr: Stileman Neate & Topping 1961-75, D J Freeman & Co 1975-; memb Slrs Complaint Bureau negligence panel 1978; Freeman City of London 1984, Liveryman Worshipful Co of Slrs 1985; memb Law Soc 1960, CIArb 1987; *Recreations* golf, shooting, boating; *Clubs* RAC, Leander, MCC, Temple GC, memb Stewards Enclosure Henley Royal Regatta; *Style*— Roger Peryer, Esq; 43 Fetter Lane, London EC4 A 1NA (☎ 01 583 4055, fax 01 353 7377, telex 894 579); 185 Kings Rd, Reading, Berks RG1 4EX (fax 0734 504 150, telex 848 740)

PESCHARDT, Michael Mogens; s of Mogens Jan Hagbarth Peschardt, and Betty Joyce, *née* Foster; *b* 17 Nov 1957; *Educ* Merchant Taylors', Univ of Sussex; *m* 9 July 1977, Sarah Louise, da of Tom James Vaughan; 3 s (Joseph Mogens b 1980, Jack Oliver b 1982, Samuel Thaddeus b 1984); *Career* news prodr BBC Radio Manchester 1980-82, chief parly journalist BBC Regnl Broadcasting until 1986, sports reporter BBC TV News, stories incl: 1986 World Cup England v Argentina, Umpire Rhana's row with Mike Gatting (lead story), 1988 Olympics; contributor to the Listener and New Statesman; *Recreations* walking, children, holidays; *Style*— Michael Peschardt, Esq; Holly Cottage, N Chailey, E Sussex; Social Affrs Unit, BBC TV Centre, London W12 (☎ 01 743 8000)

PESCOD, Prof (Mainwaring Bainbridge) Warren; OBE (1977); s of Bainbridge Pescod (d 1979), and Elizabeth, *née* Brown (d 1973); *b* 6 Jan 1933; *Educ* Stanley GS Co Durham, King's Coll Univ of Durham (BSc), MIT (SM); *m* 16 Nov 1957, (Mary) Lorenza, da of John Francis Coyle (d 1970); 2 s (Duncan Warren b 1959, Douglas James b 1961); *Career* teaching and res assoc MIT 1954-56, res assoc dept of civil engrg King's Coll Univ of Durham 1956-57, lectr and actg head dept of engrg Fourah Bay Coll, Univ Coll of Sierra Leone W Africa 1957-61, asst Babtie Shaw and Morton Glasgow 1961-64, prof and chm environmental engrg div Asian Inst of Technol Bangkok 1964-76; Univ of Newcastle upon Tyne: Tyne & Wear prof of environmental control engrg 1976-, head dept of civil engrg 1983-; memb Northumbrian Water Authy 1986-; CEng, FICE 1973, FIWEM (formerly FIPHE) 1962, MIWM 1985, MRSH 1964; *Books* Water Supply and Wastewater Disposal in Developing Countries (ed 1971), Treatment and Use of Sewage Effluent for Irrigation (ed with A Arar, 1988); *Recreations* squash, golf, reading; *Clubs* British and Royal Bangkok Sports (Bangkok); *Style*— Professor Warren Pescod, OBE; Tall Trees, High Horse Close Wood, Rowlands Gill, Tyne & Wear NE39 1AN (☎ 0207 542 104); Dept of Civil Engrg, University, Newcastle upon Tyne NE1 7RU (☎ 091 232 8511 ext 6410, fax 091 261 1182, telex 53654 UNINEW G)

PESKETT, (Stanley) Victor; s of Sydney Timber Peskett (d 1931), of Upper Norwood Kent, and Mary Havard, *née* Newell (d 1974); *b* 9 May 1918; *Educ* Whitgift Sch, St Edmund Hall Oxford (MA); *m* 14 Aug 1948, Prudence Eileen Peskett, OBE (1974), da of Cyril Reginald Alban Goatly (d 1930); 2 s (William b 1952, Roger b 1956), 2 da (Clare Veronica b 1949, Deborah Mary Elizabeth b 1954, d 1981); *Career* Royal Marines 1939-46 (Lt-Col 1944), despatches; snr English Master The Leys Sch 1946-59; princ The Royal Belfast Academical Institution 1959-78; Headmasters' Conference memb ctee 1976; memb of cncl Headmasters' Assoc (now Secondary Heads' Association) 1973-75; pres Ulster Headmasters' Assoc 1973-75; chm NI Ctee VSO 1969-78; chm NI Branch Irish Schools Swimming Assoc 1964-73; govr Belfast Sch of Music 1974-77; memb advsy cncl UDR 1975-78; *Recreations* local history, hand-loom weaving, wine-growing, transport admin; *Style*— Victor Peskett, Esq; Huntsman and Hounds Cottage, Metfield, Harleston, Norfolk IP20 0LB (☎ 0379 86425)

PESKIN, Richard Martin; s of Leslie Peskin (d (1980), and Hazel Pauline Peskin (d 1980); *b* 21 May 1944; *Educ* Charterhouse, Cambridge (MA,LLM); *m* 6 Feb 1979, Penelope Ann Elizabeth Howard; 1 s (Michael b 1966), 2 da (Elizabeth b 1969, Virginia b 1979); *Career* Great Portland Estates plc: dir 1968, dep md 1972, md 1985, chm and md 1986; FRSA 1989; *Recreations* golf, theatre, wine ; *Clubs* MCC, RAE, Mark's, Annabel's; *Style*— Richard Peskin, Esq; 41 Circus Rd, London NW8 9JH (☎ 01 289 0492); Knighton House, 56 Mortimer St, London WIN 8BD (☎ 01 580 3040)

PESTELL, Catherine Eva; CMG (1984); da of Edmund Ernest Pestell (d 1965), and Isabella Cummine, *née* Sangster (d 1987); *b* 24 Sept 1933; *Educ* Leeds Girls' HS, St Hilda's Coll Oxford (MA); *Career* 3 sec The Hague 1958, 2 sec Bangkok 1961, FO 1964, 1 sec UK Delgn to OECD Paris 1969, FCO 1971, St Antony's Coll Oxford 1974, cnsllr E Berlin 1975-78, Cabinet Off 1978-80, Diplomatic Serv inspector 1980-82, min (economic) HM Embassy Bonn 1983-87, auss (public depts) FCO 1987-89; *Style*— Miss Catherine Pestell, CMG; c/o Foreign and Commonwealth Office, London SW1A 2AH

PESTELL, John Edmund; s of Edmund Ernest Pestell (d 1965), and Isabella Cummine, *née* Sangster (d 1987); *b* 8 Dec 1930; *Educ* Roundhay Leeds, New Coll Oxford (MA); *m* 19 April 1958, Muriel Ada, da of William Norman Whitby (d 1971); 3 s (James b 1962, Hugh b 1963, Charles b 1966); *Career* Jt Intelligence Bureau 1953-57, Admin Staff Coll Henley 1963; WO MOD 1957-72: private sec to Parly Undersec of State 1958-60, private sec dto Min of Equipment 1969-70; pres sec (co-ordination) PMs Off 1972-74, under sec CSD 1976-81 (asst sec 1974-76), HM Treasy 1981-84, MOD 1984-88, chm CS selection bd, Cabinet Off 1988-; govr Cranleigh Sch 1975-; *Style*— John Pestell, Esq; c/o Cabinet Office, London SW1

PESTELL, Sir John Richard; KCVO (1969); s of late Lt-Cdr Frank Lionel Pestell, RN (d 1947), and Winifred Alice Pestell (d 1983); *b* 21 Nov 1916; *Educ* Portsmouth Northern Secdy Sch; *m* 1951, Betty, da of Reuben Parish (d 1955); 3 da; *Career* British South Africa Police S Rhodesia 1939-65, Cyrenaica Defence Force 1944-49, Major, sec/comptroller to Govr of S Rhodesia, Rt Hon Sir Humphrey Gibbs 1965-69, an adjudicator Immigration Appeals Harmondsworth 1970-87; *Recreations* walking; *Style*— Sir John Pestell, KCVO; Monks Walk, Ferry Lane, Medmenham, Marlow Bucks (☎ (0491) 571295)

PESTON, Baron (Life Peer UK 1987), of Mile End, Greater London Maurice Harry Peston; s of Abraham Peston; *b* 19 Mar 1931; *Educ* Bellevue Bradford, Hackney Downs London, LSE (BSc), Princeton Univ USA (BScEcon); *m* 17 Nov 1958, Helen Conroy; 2 s (Robert b 1960, Edmund b 1964), 1 da (Juliet b 1961); *Career* prof of economics Queen Mary Coll, Univ of London; *Style*— The Rt Hon Lord Peston; c/o Queen Mary College, Mile End Road, London E1 (☎ 01 980 4811)

PETCH, Barry Irvine; s of Charles Reginald Petch and Edith Anne, *née* Fryer (d 1952); *b* 12 Oct 1933; *Educ* Doncaster GS; *m* 1966, Anne Elisabeth, da of Dr F Johannessen, of Trondheim, Norway; 2 s, 1 da; *Career* RAPC (Capt) 1957-59; former finance dir IBM United Kingdom Holdings Ltd and subsidiaries; vice pres finance IBM Europe; FCA; *Recreations* sailing, golf; *Clubs* Reform, Country Club de Fourqueux; *Style*— Barry Petch, Esq; Les Moukelins, Chemin des Hauts de Grisy, St Nom La Breteche, France; IBM Europe, Tour Pascal, 22 route de la Demi-Lune, Puteaux - Hauts de Seine, France (☎ (767) 78 40)

PETCH, Simon Geoffrey Filby; s of Eric Petch (d 1986), of Cirencester, Glos, and

Nancy Mary, *née* Lamplough; *b* 6 May 1943; *Educ* Dean Close Sch Cheltenham, St Peter's Coll Oxford; *m* 1969, Patricia Ann, da of William James Burton (d 1983); 1 s (Jack b 1975); *Career* research offr Union of Construction Allied Trades and Technicians 1969-73, research Nat offr Electrical Power Engrs Assoc 1973-76; dep gen sec: Engrs Managers Assoc, Electrical Power Eng Assoc 1976-85; gen sec Soc of Telecom Executives 1986; *Recreations* horse racing, reading, walking; *Style*— Simon Petch, Esq; 3 Walpole Gardens, Strawberry Hill, Twickenham, Middx (☎ 01 894 1316); 1 Park Road, Teddington, Middx TW11 0AR (☎ 01 943 5181, telex 927162 STE G)

PETERBOROUGH, 36 Bishop of (cr 1541), 1984-; Rt Rev William John Westwood; patron of 101 livings, the chancellorship, the archdeaconries of Northampton and Oakham, and the canonries of his cathedral; Bishopric created by Henry VIII from the proceeds of the dissolved land holdings of the Abbey of St Peter (founded by Saxulf, a Thane of Mercia, 653), whose last Abbot became the first Bishop of the new see; s of Ernest, and Charlotte Westwood; *b* 28 Dec 1925; *Educ* Grove Park GS Wrexham, Emmanuel Coll Cambridge (MA), Westcott House Cambridge; *m* 1954, Shirley Ann, yr da of Dr Norman Jennings; 1 s, 1 da; *Career* rector of Lowestoft 1957-65, vicar of St Peter Mancroft Norwich 1965-75, hon canon Norwich Cathedral 1969-75, rural dean of Norwich 1966-70, city dean of Norwich 1970-73, area bishop of Edmonton 1975-84; memb Archbishop's Cmmn on Church and State 1966-70, church cmmr 1973-78 and 1985-; memb Press Cncl 1975-81, chm of govnrs, Coll of All Saints Tottenham 1976-78, chm C of E Ctee for Communications 1979-86; memb IBA Panel of Religious Advrs 1983-87; pres Church Housing Assoc (formerly chm 3 housing assocs), memb: BBFC Video Consultative Cncl, Broadcasting Standards Cncl; freeman of the City of London; *Recreations* the countryside, wine bars, reading; *Style*— The Rt Rev the Lord Bishop of Peterborough; The Palace, Peterborough PE1 1YA (☎ 0733 62492)

PETERKEN, Hon Mrs - Hon (Hyacinthe Ann); da of 7 Baron Hatherton, TD; *b* 1934; *m* 1954, Patrick Peterken; 2 s, 1 da; *Career* LLB Newcastle, solr 1978; *Style*— The Hon Mrs Peterken; Claypool Farm, Hutton Henry, Castle Eden, Durham

PETERKEN, Laurence Edwin; s of Edwin James Peterken (d 1971), of Banstead, Surrey, and Constance Fanny, *née* Giffin (d 1973); *b* 2 Oct 1931; *Educ* Harrow, Peterhouse Cambridge (MA); *m* 10 Dec 1955, (Hanne) Birgithe (d 1968), da of Harald von der Recke (d 1960), of Copenhagen; 1 s (Oliver b 1956), 1 da (Camilla b 1959); m 2, 29 May 1970, Margaret Raynal Blair; 1 s (Alexander b 1974), 1 da (Jemima b 1977); *Career* Nat Serv 1950-52, Pilot Offr RAF Regt, Sqdn Adjt No 20 LAA Sqdn 1952; mangr serv divn 1961-63 and commerical dir Hotpoint Ltd 1963-66, gp managing dir Br Domestic Appliances 1966-68, dir Br Printing Corpn Ltd 1969-73, md Debenhams Fashion Multiple Divn 1974-75 and mgmnt auditor 1975-77; controller of operational servs GLC 1977-85, gen mangr Greater Glasgow Health Bd 1986-; *Recreations* golf, opera; *Clubs* Athenaeum; *Style*— Laurence Peterken, Esq

PETERKIN, Hon Sir Neville Allan Mercer; s of Joseph and Evelyn Peterkin; *b* 27 Oct 1915; *Educ* Wellington Sch Somerset; *m* 1942, Beryl Thompson; 2 s, 1 da; *Career* barr Middle Temple 1939, registrar St Lucia 1943, magistrate Trinidad and Tobago 1944, res magistrate Jamaica 1954, High Ct judge Trinidad 1957; West Indies Associated States: High Ct judge 1967, Justice of Appeal 1975, Chief Justice 1980-88; kt 1981; *Style*— The Hon Sir Neville Peterkin; Requit, St Lucia, West Indies

PETERS, Brian Henry; s of Harry Peters; *b* 13 June 1933; *Educ* Edmonton County GS; *m* 1957, Moyra Bowes; 2 s; *Career* admin dir Allied Hambro Unit Trust Gp; *Recreations* badminton, motoring, compiling crossword puzzles; *Style*— Brian Peters, Esq; 74 Mayfield Rd, Writtle, Chelmsford, Essex (☎ 0245 420936)

PETERS, Hon Mrs (Corynne Lesley); 2 da of 2 Baron Burden; *b* 1 April 1955; *Educ* La Retrait W-S-M, St Brandons Clevedon, Taunton Sch; *m* 1977, William D-Day Peters s of late Leonard Thomas Peters; 1 s (Alexander b 1983), 1 da (Lindsey Jane b 1988); *Career* nurse; *Style*— The Hon Mrs Peters; Greenland, Royston Water, Churchinford, Taunton, Somerset TA3 MEF (☎ 0823 60 484)

PETERS, Lady; Frances Williamina; da of Francis William Vérel, of Glasgow; *m* 1917, Sir Rudolph Peters, MC, MD, FRCP, FRS, FRSE, sometime Whitley Prof of Biochemistry at Oxford (d 1982); 2 s; *Style*— Lady Peters; 3 Newnham Walk, Cambridge (☎ (0223) 50819)

PETERS, Kenneth Jamieson; CBE (1979), JP (City of Aberdeen 1961), DL (Aberdeen 1978); s of William Jamieson Peters (d 1966), and Edna Rosa, *née* Hayman (d 1980); *b* 17 Jan 1923; *Educ* Aberdeen GS, Aberdeen Univ; *m* 1951, Arunda Merle Jane Jones; *Career* serv WWII, Capt/Adj 2 Bn King's Own Scottish Borderers; editor: Evening Express Aberdeen 1953-56, The Press and Journal Aberdeen 1956-60; dir Highland Printers Ltd (Inverness) 1968-83, md Aberdeen Journals Ltd 1960-80, chm 1980-81; dir: Thomson Regional Newspapers 1974-81, Thomson North Sea 1981-88 and Thomson Scottish Petroleum Ltd 1981-86, Aberdeen Journals Ltd 1960-, National Girobank Scotland 1984-; chm Aberdeen and NE Scotland Ctee The Scottish Cncl Devpt and Industry 1982-88; memb bd: British Rail (Scotland) 1982-, Peterhead Bay Authority 1983-; assoc memb CInstT 1985, FSA (Scot) 1980; *Clubs* MCC, Royal Northern & University (Aberdeen); *Style*— Kenneth Peters Esq, CBE, JP, DL; 47 Abergeldie Rd, Aberdeen AB1 6ED (☎ 0224 587647)

PETERS, Mary Elizabeth; MBE (1973); da of Arthur Henry Peters, of Australia, and Hilda Mary Ellison (d 1956); *b* 6 July 1939; *Educ* Ballymena Acad, Portradown Coll, Belfast Coll of Domestic Science; *Career* former Home Economics teacher Graymunt Girls' Secondary Sch; Int athlete 1961-74, represented N Ireland at every Cwlth Games 1958-, 1964 Olympics (Pentathlon 4th), 1966 Cwlth games (Shot 2nd), 1970 Cwlth games (Pentathlon 1st, Shot 1st), 1972 Olympics (Pentathlon 1st, world record), 1974 Cwlth Games (Pentathlon 1st); memb NI Sports Cncl 1973-, vice-chm NISC 1977-80, chm NI Ctee of Sport for the Disabled 1984-, memb Sports Cncl (GB) 1974-77, re-elected 1987, memb Sports Aid Fndn, Patron NI amateur Athletic Assocn, pres NI Womens' AAA, team mgr British Womens' Athletics Team 1979-84 (inc Moscow and LA Olympic Teams); md Mary Peters Sports Ltd, Tstee Ulster Sports & Recreation Trust; hon DSc New Univ of Ulster (1974); *Recreations* swimming, weight training; *Style*— Mary E Peters, MBE; Willowtree Cottage, River Rd, Dunmurry, Belfast; Mary Peters Health Club, 37 Railway Street, Lisburn (☎ 084 62 76411)

PETERS, Michael Edmund du Thon; s of Edmund Lind du Thon Peters (d 1986), of Ryde, IOW, and Raymonde Marie, *née* Stempfer (d 1985); *b* 19 Mar 1939; *Educ* Clayesmore, Dorset Coll of Agric (NCA); *m* 1964, Judith Joy, da of Donald George Harris (d 1982), of Minehead, Somerset; 2 da (Emma, Charlotte); *Career* agric journalist, farmer and stockbreeder 1959-62, fndr and jt md Agripress Publicity Ltd 1963-70 (relinquished directorship 1975), md A O Smith Harvestore Products Ltd 1971-86, fndr and chm Merston Peters Ltd mgmnt and recruitment conslts; *Recreations* shooting, gardening, livestock, writing; *Style*— Michael Peters, Esq; Mead House, Drinkstone Green, Bury St Edmunds, Suffolk IP30 9TL (☎ 044 93 570); Merston Peters Ltd, Newman House, Northgate Avenue, Bury St Edmunds, Suffolk IP32 6BB (☎ 0284 752945, fax 0284 701155, telex 818321)

PETERS, Robert Byron; MBE (1977); s of Geofrey Halsted Peters, of Eddington Mill House, Hungerford, Berks RG17 0HL, and Edith Frances *née* Scott; *b* 3 May 1926; *Educ* Marlborough, RAF Short Course Trinity Coll Oxford; *m* 15 Jan 1959, Jean Eileen Meredith, da of George Thomas Edwards, of Hornsey; 1 s (Laurence Geofrey Byron b 1963); 2 da (Rebecca Frances b 1965, Victoria Louise b 1967); *Career* served RAF aircrew cadet (pilot) 1942-47; chief exec and sec Institute of Advanced Motorists, dir and sec: Advanced Mile-Posts Publications Ltd, IAM Fleet Training Ltd; chm Holborn & Metropolitan Counties Friendly Soc, chm: Kentex Estates Ltd, PIM Board Co Ltd (Gp), Pressboard Ltd, Sundeala Bd Co Ltd, Sundeala Bd (Scotland) Ltd, Sundeala Ceilings Ltd, Perforations (Sunbury) Ltd; *Books* amateur radio, swimming, tennis, computers, travel, aviation; *Style*— Robert Peters, Esq; IAM House, 359 Chiswick High Rd, London W4 4HS (☎ 01 994 4403, fax 01 994 9274, car ☎ 0860 516 313)

PETERS, Stanley Eric; s of late Thomas Peters, of Glos, and Fanny Ethel, *née* Hawtin; *b* 4 May 1918; *Educ* private; *m* 1952, Pauline, da of Mr Besson, of Dublin; *Career* Capt Royal Warwicks Regt; design conslt in: historic domestic architecture, decoration and gardens; advsr on architecturally famous houses; *Recreations* music, literature, travel, arts; *Style*— Stanley Peters, Esq; 26A Camberwell Road, London SE6 0EN (☎ 01 703 0150)

PETERS, Theophilus; CMG (1967); s of late Mark Peters, and Dorothy Peters, *née* Knapman; *b* 7 August 1921; *Educ* Exeter Sch, St John's Coll Cambridge (MA); *m* 1953, Lucy Bailey, da of late Lionel Morgan Summers; 2 s, 3 da; *Career* counsellor and consul-gen Buenos Aires 1971-73, consul-gen Antwerp 1973-78; *Recreations* Chinese art, flowers, music especially opera (and a lecturer on all these subjects); *Style*— Theophilus Peters, Esq, CMG; Henlopen House, Church Rd, Ketton, Stamford PE9 3RD

PETERS, William; CMG (1980), LVO (1961), MBE (1959); s of John William Peters (d 1983), of Morpeth, Northumberland, and Louise, *née* Woodhouse (d 1965); *b* 28 Sept 1923; *Educ* King Edward VI GS Morpeth, Balliol Coll Oxford (MA), LSE, Sch of Oriental and African Studies; *m* 1944, Catherine Bertha, da of Daniel Bailey (d 1928), of Edinburgh and Paisley; *Career* WWII serv Britain and Far East, Queen's Royal Rifles, KOSB, 9 Gurkha Rifles, demob as Capt 1946; joined Colonial Serv, asst dist cmmr Gold Coast (now Ghana) 1950, ret as acting sec regnl cmmr (Cabinet rank) Northern Ghana; joined CRO as asst princ 1959, princ 1959; 1 Sec: Dacca 1960-63, Cyprus 1963-67; head Zambia and Malawi Dept CRO 1967-68, head Central African Dept FCO 1968-69, dir Int Affrs Div Cwlth Secretariat 1969-71, cnsllr and head Chancery Canberra 1971-73, dep high cmmr Bombay 1974-77, ambass Uruguay 1977-80, high cmmr Malawi 1980-83; chm: LEPRA, Tibet Soc of UK, Br Uruguayan Soc; pres Royal Br Legion (Downs Branch), hon tres Deal Summer Music Fest; *Books* Diplomatic Service Formation and Operation (1972); *Recreations* music, walking, archaeology; *Clubs* Oxford & Cambridge, Royal Commonwealth Soc, Royal Soc for Asian Affairs; *Style*— William Peters, Esq, CMG, LVO, MBE; 12 Crown Court, Middle St, Deal, Kent (☎ 030 4362822);

PETERSEN, Sir Jeffrey Charles; KCMG (1978, CMG 1968); s of Charles Petersen; *b* 20 July 1920; *Educ* Westcliff HS, LSE; *m* 1962, Karin Kristina Hayward; 2 s, 4 da; *Career* amb to Republic of Korea 1971-74, to Romania 1975-77, to Sweden 1977-80, ret; Kt Grand Cross Royal Order of the Polar Star (Sweden) 1984, Order of Diplomatic Merit (South Korea) 1984; chm: British Materials Handling Board, Anglo-Korean Soc; pres: Anglo-Swedish Soc; vice-pres: Swedish Chamber of Commerce for the UK; various directorships; *Clubs* Travellers, Kent & Canterbury; *Style*— Sir Jeffrey Petersen, KCMG; 32 Longmoore St, SW1 (☎ 01 834 8262); Crofts Wood, Petham, Kent (☎ 022 770 537)

PETERSHAM, Viscount; Charles Henry Leicester Stanhope; s and h of 11 Earl of Harrington and Eileen, *née* Grey; *b* 20 July 1945; *Educ* Eton; *m* 1, 1966 (m dis), Virginia Alleyne Freeman, da of Capt Harry Freeman Jackson, of Cool-na-Grena, Co Cork; 1 s (William b 1967), 1 da (Serena b 1970); m 2, 1984, Anita, formerly w of 21 Earl of Suffolk and Berkshire, and yr da of Robin Fuglesang, of Lacock, Wiltshire; *Recreations* sailing (circumnavigation 1983-85 sy Surama), hunting (Master of the Limerick Hounds 1974-77), skiing, shooting, fishing; *Clubs* House of Lords Yacht, Antigua Yacht, Bora Bora Yacht; *Style*— Viscount Petersham; Baynton House, Coulston, Westbury, Wiltshire (☎ 0380 830273); 10 Stanhope Mews, West London SW7 (☎ 01 370 5191, telex 8950480)

PETERSON, Col Christopher Matthew; CBE (1983), TD (1956), JP (1973), DL (1978); s of Oscar Peterson (d 1923); *b* 22 Feb 1918; *Educ* St Illtyds Coll Cardiff; *m* 1945, Grace Winfred, da of John McNeil (d 1940); 3 children (and 1 child decd); *Career* co dir; Lloyd's underwriter; High Sheriff S Glamorgan 1981; *Clubs* Cardiff County, Army and Navy; *Style*— Col Christopher Peterson, CBE, TD, JP, DL; 51 Rannoch Drive, Cyncoed, Cardiff CF2 6LP (☎ (0222) 754062); 15 Castle Pill Crescent, Milford Haven

PETERSON, Colin Vyvyan; CVO (1982); s of late Sir Maurice Drummond Peterson, GCMG; *b* 24 Oct 1932; *Educ* Winchester, Magdalen Coll Oxford; *m* 1966, Pamela Rosemary Barry; 2 s, 2 da; *Career* HM Treasury 1959, sec for appointments to the Prime Minister and ecclesiastical sec to the Lord Chancellor 1974-82, under-sec Management and Personnel Off 1985-, lay asst to Bp of Winchester 1985-; *Style*— Colin Peterson, Esq, CVO; 87 Christchurch Rd, Winchester, Hants (☎ 0962 3784)

PETERSON, Lady Mary Isabel; *née* Maples; *m* 1940, Arthur William Peterson, KCB, MVO (d 1986); 1 s, 2 da; *Style*— Lady Peterson; Norton Mill House, Nortonbury Lane, Baldock, Herts (☎ (0462) 892353)

PETERSSON, Lars Urban Leonard; s of Robert Leonard Petersson, and Birgit Valborg Petersson; *b* 29 Oct 1938; *Educ* Stockholm Univ (MA), Harvard Bus Sch (MBA); *m* 10 Sept 1965, Elisabeth Margaret, da of Erik Rutger Smith (d 1970), of Sweden; 3 s (Magnus b 1966, Thomas b 1968, Philip b 1973); *Career* mgmnt conslts McKinsey & Co (London, NY, Zurich) 1965-72, dir: ITEL Corp 1972-73, Hunter Douglas dir of corporate diversification 1973-75, vice pres Trans Ocean Leasing 1975-83, Fndr and md Leasing Ptnrs Int 1983-; *Recreations* golf, boating; *Clubs* Harvard,

Harewood Down (Gerrards Cross), Britannia (Grand Cayman); *Style*— Lars Petersson, Esq; The Third House, West Witheridge, Beaconsfield (☎ 0494 676 537); Villa 142, Britannia, Grand Cayman

PETHERICK, Christopher; DL (1982); yr s of George Gerald Petherick (d 1946), and his w, Lady Jeane Pleydell-Bouverie (d 1976), eldest da of 6 Earl of Radnor; *b* 29 Mar 1922; *Educ* Harrow; *m* 1951, Countess Charlotte Raben-Levetzau, da of Count Raben-Levetzau (d 1965; cr as Lehnsgreve of Christiansholm, by Christian VI, King of Denmark 1734); 2 s (Martin, Thomas), 2 da (Catherine, Harriet); *Career* served in WW II as Capt Life Gds; High Sheriff of Cornwall 1978-79; *Clubs* White's; *Style*— Christopher Petherick, Esq, DL; Tredeague, Porthpean, St Austell, Cornwall (☎ 0726 72888)

PETHICK, Jan Stephen; s of Maj Thomas Francis Henry Pethick (d 1981), of Trewartha, Ventnor, IOW, and Denise Joyce, *née* Clark; *b* 16 Sept 1947; *Educ* Clifton, Jesus Coll Oxford (MA); *m* 20 Dec 1974, Belinda Patricia, da of Douglas Collins, of Hare Hatch House, Hare Hatch, Reading, Berks; 1 s (Benjamin b 18 May 1981), 2 da (Emily b 26 May 1975, Nancy b 15 April 1977); *Career* stock jobber trader Pinchin Denny & Co 1969-74, Midland Doherty Eurobond Trading 1975-77, head of Eurobond sales Lehman Bros Kuhm Leob 1974-84, md Shearson Lehman Hutton Int Inc 1986-; tstee The Peper Harow Foundation; *Recreations* golf, tennis, squash; *Clubs* NZ Gold, Roehampton; *Style*— Jan Pethick, Esq; 71 Kew Green, Kew, Richmond, Surrey TW9 3AH (☎ 01 940 2426); Shearson Lehman Hutton International, One Broadgate, London EC2M 7HA (☎ 01 260 3123, fax 01 382 9598, telex 888881)

PETHICK, Katharine Elizabeth; da of Robert Wentworth Pethick (d 1983), and Beryl Winifred, *née* Reid; *b* 6 Sept 1961; *Educ* Putney HS for Girls, Bransons Cwlth Coll, Kingston Poly (Art Fndn course), London Coll of Printing (Graphic Design Degree); 1 s (Frederick b 27 April 1986); *Career* ptnr Pethick & Money Design Consultants Fulham 1984, 5 design projects published in World Packaging Design Annual 1988; *Recreations* photography; *Style*— Ms Katharine Pethick; Finlay St, London SW6 (☎ 01 736 8056); Overstrand, Feock, Cornwall; Studios 4 & 5, 75 Filmer Rd, London SW6 7JF (☎ 01 384 1298, fax 01 731 8314)

PETHYBRIDGE, Frank; CBE (1977); s of late Frank Pethybridge, and late Margaret, *née* Priestnell; *b* 19 Jan 1924; *Educ* William Hulme's GS Manchester, Manchester Univ (BA); *m* 1947, Jean, da of late William Harold Gladstone Ewing; 1 s (Eldon), 1 da (Lynne); *Career* Flt-Lt RAF 1942-47; sec Manchester Regnl Hosp Bd 1965-73; Regnl Admin North Western Regnl Health Authy 1973-82; chm Lancs Family Practitioner Ctee 1985-89; FHSM, FRSH; *Style*— Frank Pethybridge Esq, CBE; 12 The Leylands, West Beach, Lytham St Annes FY8 5QS

PETHYBRIDGE, Hon Mrs (Olivia Mary); *née* Hawke; da of 9 Baron Hawke (d 1985); *b* 5 April 1955; *Educ* Heathfield; *m* 1983, Timothy John Pethybridge, s of J H Pethybridge, of Barn Park, Bodmin, Cornwall, 2 da (Maryrose b 1985, Flora b 1987); *Style*— The Hon Mrs Pethybridge; 64 Hendham Rd, London SW17 7DQ (☎ 01 682 0680)

PETIT, (Joseph) Adrien Letieré; s of Capt Joseph Paris Sydney Petit (d 1967), and Florence Georgina May, *née* Hawthorne (d 1959); *b* 6 May 1921; *Educ* Warwick Sch, Nottingham Univ (BSc), Birmingham Univ (Dip Eng); *m* 25 April 1959, Carroll Foster, da of Henry Alan Gould (d 1986); 1 s (Adam b 6 Nov 1963), 1 da (Marie-Louise b 9 Dec 1961); *Career* regnl dir PE Consulting Gp 1971-73 (1952-73); chm: C Brandauer & Co 1959-, Brandauer Holdings Ltd 1964-, Assmann Electronics Ltd 1985-; former cncllr Leamington Borough Cncl (vice-chm various ctees including fin), chm men's branch Leamington Cons Party, fell Huguenot Soc GB, tres Inst of Mgmt Conslts (pres 1979-80); memb Soc of Genealogists, FCIS, FIMC; *Recreations* travel, music, genealogy; *Clubs* IOD; *Style*— Adrien Petit, Esq; C Brandager & Co Ltd, 401-414 New John St West, Birmingham B19 3PF (☎ 021 359 2822)

PETIT, Sir Dinshaw Manockjee; 4 Bt (UK 1890), of Petit Hall, Island of Bombay; né Nasserwanjee Dinshaw Petit but obliged, under a trust created by Sir Dinshaw Manockjee Petit, 1 Bt, to adopt the name of the first Bt; s of Sir Dinshaw Manockjee Petit, 3 Bt, (d 1983), and Sylla (d 1963); *b* 13 August 1934; *m* 1, 1964 (m dis 1985), Nirmala Mody (surname of stepfather assumed by Deed Poll 1964), *née* Nanavati; 2 s, (Jehangir b 1965, Framjee b 1968); m 2, Elizabeth Maria Tinkelenberg; *Heir* s, Jehangir b 21 Jan 1965; *Career* Pres: NM Petit Charities, Sir D M Petit Charities, F D Petit Sanatorium, Persian Zoroastrian Amelioration fund, Petit Girls' Orphanage, D M Petit gymnasium, JN Petit Inst, Native Gen Dispensary; tstee Soc for Prevention of Cruelty to Animals and memb managing ctee B D Petit Parsi Gen Hosp; *Style*— Sir Dinshaw Petit, Bt; Petit Hall, Nepean Sea Rd, Bombay

PETIT, Jehangir; s and h to Sir Dinshaw Manockjee Petit, 4 Bt, *qv*; *b* 21 Jan 1965; *Style*— Jehangir Petit, Esq

PETO, Barbara, Lady - Barbara; da of Edwyn Thomas Close, of Woodcote, Camberley, Surrey; *m* 1935, Sir Christopher Henry Maxwell Peto, DSO, 3 Bt (d 1980); *Style*— Barbara, Lady Peto; The Granary, Dean, Charlbury, Oxford

PETO, Henry Christopher Morton Bampfylde; s and h of Sir Michael Henry Basil Peto, 4 Bt, of Childesden, Basingstoke, and Sarah Susan Worthington, *née* Stucley; *b* 8 April 1967; *Educ* Eton; *Recreations* tennis, psychology, football; *Style*— Henry Peto, Esq; Court Hall, North Molton, Devon EX36 3HP (☎ (059 84) 224)

PETO, Sir Henry George Morton; 4 Bt (UK 1855); s of Cdr Sir Henry Francis Morton Peto, 3 Bt, RN (d 1978); *b* 29 April 1920; *Educ* Sherborne, CCC Cambridge; *m* 1947, Frances Jacqueline, JP, da of late Ralph Haldane Evers; 2 s; *Heir* s, Francis Michael Morton Peto; *Career* RA 1939-46; manufacturing industry 1946-80; *Style*— Sir Henry Peto, Bt; Stream House, Selborne, Alton, Hants (☎ 042 050 246)

PETO, Sir Michael Henry Basil; 4 Bt (UK 1927); s of Brig Sir Christopher Henry Maxwell Peto, 3 Bt, DSO (d 1980); *b* 6 April 1938; *Educ* Eton, Ch Ch Oxford (MA); *m* 1, 1963 (m dis 1970), Sarah Susan, da of Maj Sir Dennis Stucley, 5 Bt; 1 s, 2 da; m 2, 1971, Lucinda Mary, da of Maj Sir Charles Douglas Blackett, 9 Bt; 2 s; *Heir* s, Henry Christopher Morton Bampfylde Peto b 8 April 1967; *Career* barr Inner Temple 1960, memb Stock Exchange 1965-; dir Barnett Consulting Gp 1985-; *Clubs* Pratt's; *Style*— Sir Michael Peto, Bt; Lower Church Cottage, Cliddesden, Basingstoke, Hants

PETO, Hon Mrs (Selina Lillian); *née* Hughes-Young; da of late 1 Baron St Helens, MC; *b* 1944; *m* 1969, Jonathan Basil Morton Peto (gs of Sir Basil Edward Peto, 1 Bt); 2 s, 3 da; *Style*— The Hon Mrs Peto

PETRE, His Hon Judge; Francis Herbert Loraine; s of Maj-Gen R L Petre, CB, SDO, MC (decd); *b* 9 Mar 1927; *Educ* Downside, Clare Coll Cambridge; *m* 1958, Mary Jane, da of Everard White, of Masterton, NZ; 3 s, 1 da; *Career* barr Lincoln's Inn 1952, dep chm E Suffolk QS 1970, dep chm Agricultural Lands Tribunal (Eastern Area) 1972, a Circuit Judge 1972-; regular judge central criminal court 1982; *Style*— His Honour Judge Petre; The Ferriers, Bures, Suffolk CO8 5DL (☎ 0787 227254)

PETRE, 18 Baron (E 1603); John Patrick Lionel Petre; o s of 17 Baron Petre (d 1989), and Marguerite Eileen, *née* Hamilton; *b* 4 August 1942; *Educ* Eton, Trinity Coll Oxford (BA); *m* 16 Sept 1965, Marcia Gwendolyn, o da of Alfred Plumpton, of Portsmouth; 2 s (Hon Dominic William, Hon Mark Julian b 1969), 1 da (Hon Clare Helen b 1973); *Heir* s, Hon Dominic William Petre b 9 Aug 1966; *Style*— The Rt Hon Lord Petre; Writtle Park, Essex

PETRE, Marguerite, Baroness; Marguerite Eileen; *née* Hamilton; da of late Ion Wentworth Hamilton, of Nettlebed, Oxon; *m* 25 Oct 1941, 17 Baron Petre (d 1989); 1 s (18 Baron, *qv*); *Style*— The Rt Hon Marguerite, Lady Petre; Ingatestone Hall, Essex

PETRIE, Charles James; s and h of Sir Peter Petrie, 5 Bt, CMG; *b* 16 Sept 1959; *Educ* American Coll Paris (BA), INSEAD Fontainebleau (MBA) ; *m* 1981, France, yr da of Comte Bernard de Hauteclocque, of Châ- teau d'Etrejust, Picardie; 1 s (Arthur Cecil b 15 Feb 1987), 1 da (Cecilia Marie Bernard b and d 1985); *Career* 2 Lt 67 French Inf Regt; *Style*— c/o Sir Peter Petrie, Bt, CMG; c/o Sir Peter Petrie, Bt, CMG, 16a Cambridge Street, London SW1

PETRIE, Dowager Lady; Jessie Ariana Borthwick; *née* Campbell; da of late Cdr Patrick Straton Campbell, JP, RN, of Westleton, Saxmundham, Suffolk; *m* 27 Nov 1962, Lt-Col Sir (Charles) Richard Borthwick Petrie, 4 Bt, TD (d 1988); *Style*— Dowager Lady Petrie; 3 Northmoor Road, Oxford

PETRIE, Sir Peter Charles; CMG (1980); 5 Bt (UK 1918); s of Sir Charles Petrie, 3 Bt (d 1977), and of Cecilia, Lady Petrie (d 1987); suc his half-bro, Sir Richard Petrie, 4 Bt 1988; *b* 7 Mar 1932; *Educ* Westminster, Ch Ch Oxford (MA); *m* 1958, Countess Lydwine Maria Fortunata, da of Count Charles Alphonse Oberndorff, of The Hague and Paris; 2 s, 1 da; *Heir* s, Charles James Petrie b 16 Sept 1959; *Career* 2 sec UK Delegation NATO Paris 1958-61, 1 sec New Delhi 1961-64, chargé d'affaires Katmandu 1963, Cabinet Office 1965-57, UK Mission to UN (NY) 1969-73, cnsllr (head of Chancery) Bonn 1973-76, head of Euro Integration Dept (Int) FCO 1976-79, min Paris 1979-85; ambass to Belgium 1985-; *Clubs* Brooks's, Jockey (Paris); *Style*— Sir Peter Petrie, Bt, CMG; 16A Cambridge St, London SW1V 4QH

PETSOPOULOS, Lady Charlotte Mary Roberte Paul; *née* Ponsonby; da of 10 Earl of Bessborough; *b* 1949; *m* 1974, Yanni Petsopoulos; 1 s; *Style*— Lady Charlotte Petsopoulos; 43 Pembridge Villas, London W11 (☎ 01 727 8809)

PETTER, Michael Gordon; s of Ernest Gordon Petter, of Victoria BC, and Mary Beresford-Jones, *née* Wanklyn; *b* 14 Sept 1933; *Educ* Rendcomb Coll, Queen's Coll, Oxford (MA); *m* 15 May 1965, Evelyn Mary, da of Douglas Gray Bazett Leakey (d 1980); 2 s (Hugh b 1986, John b 1970); *Career* princ Miny of Supply 1962-73 (asst princ 1959-62); grade 5 civil servant DTI 1973-; *Recreations* gardening, walking, family, local history; *Style*— Michael Petter, Esq; Dept of Trade and Industry, 1 Victoria Street, London SW1

PETTIFER, Brian Warren Bowers; s of Fred Tyler Pettifer (d 1965), of Alfryn House, Grimsby, S Humberside, and Chrystine, *née* Thompson; *b* 10 Oct 1935; *Educ* Oundle; *m* 2 Oct 1965, Veronica Mary, da of Dr Georg Tugendhat (d 1973), of Greensted Hall, Greensted, Ongar, Essex; 3 s (Crispin b 1967, Adam b 1969, Daniel b 1970), 1 da (Teresa b 1974); *Career* slr 1963, fndr own practice 1966, underwriter Lloyds 1977-; county cnsllr: Lindsey 1970-74, Humberside 1974-77; chief Whip Cons Pty and shadow chm for planning 1974-77; chm: Humberside Youth Assoc 1974-75, Barton on Humber Youth Centre Mgmnt Ctee 1974-88, Humberside Euro Cons Cncl 1983-86; capt Law Soc GC 1985-86; *Recreations* skiing, golf, tennis; *Clubs* Oriental; *Style*— Brian Pettifer, Esq; Cob Hall, Priestgate, Barton-on-Humber, S Humberside DN18 5ET (☎ 0652 32248); Pettifer & Co, 26 Priestgate, Barton-on-Humber, S Humberside DN18 5ET (☎ 0652 660660, fax 0652 660077)

PETTIFER, Julian; s of Stephen Henry Pettifer (d 1980), of Malmesbury, Wilts, and Diana Mary, *née* Burton; *b* 21 July 1935; *Educ* Marlborough, St John's Coll Cambridge (BA); *Career* nat serv 1953-55, basic tning with Rifle Bde, cmmnd Northamptonshire Regt, served as 2 Lt in Korea and Hong Kong; tv broadcaster and author, tv series include: BBC Tonight, Panorama, 24 Hours, Diamonds in the Sky, The Living Isles and ITV's Nature Watch Automania; awarded BAFTA Reporter of the Year 1968-69; memb cncl World Wide Fund for Nature; vice-chm British Wildlife Appeal; hon pres Malmesbury Civic Tst; *Books* Diamonds in the Sky (with Kenneth Hudson, 1979), Automania (with Nigel Turner, 1984), Nature Watch (with Robin Brown, 1981); *Recreations* music, theatre, tennis, gardening, books; *Clubs* Queen's; *Style*— Julian Pettifer, Esq; c/o Curtis Brown, 162-168 Regent St, London W1R 5TB

PETTINGELL, (Peter) John Partington; s of Hubert Edmund Pettingell (d 1980), and Avril Leah Nancy Pettingell (d 1975); *b* 28 Jan 1934; *Educ* Leeds GS, London Univ (BD); *m* 31 July 1965, Phyllis Margaret, da of Charles Chamberlain (d 1983); 1 s (John Stephen Edmund b 3 Jan 1973), 2 da (Julie Margaret b 5 Oct 1966, Susan Jane b 2 April 1968); *Career* Nat Serv RAF 1956-58; audit mangr WL Gallant & Co 1958-60, audit supervisor Price Waterhouse 1960-63, chief accountant GLC London 1963-65, sr lectr SW London Coll 1973-77, princ lectr Hong Kong Poly 1977-80, sr lectr Dorset Inst Higher Educn 1980-86, princ Partington Pettingell & Co 1983-; min Stockwell Baptist Church 1973-77; FCA 1956; *Books* Then the Spirit Came (1975), Jesus is Coming (1974); *Recreations* sailing, badminton, tennis; *Style*— John Pettingell, Esq; 41A Southern Rd, Bournemouth, Dorset (☎ 0202 431 406)

PETTIT, Sir Daniel Eric Arthur; s of Thomas Edgar Pettit (d 1940), of Liverpool, and Pauline Elizabeth, *née* Kerr (d 1957); *b* 19 Feb 1915; *Educ* Quarry Bank HS Liverpool, Fitzwilliam Coll Cambridge (MA); *m* 1940, Winifred, da of William Standing Bibby of Liverpool (d 1951); 2 s (Richard, Michael); *Career* military service 1940-46, RA; serv: UK, Africa, India, Burma; Major (RA) TA, Hon Col (movement); UK team Olympic Games 1936; sch master 1938-39, 1946-47; Unilever MGT 1948-59; chm: SPD Ltd (Unilever) 1960-70, Nat Freight Corpn 1970-78; memb: Freight Integration Cncl 1971-78, Fndn of Mgmnt Educn 1973-78; chm econ devpt ctee for Distributive Trades 1974-78, chm Post Office Staff Superannuation Fund 1979-83; chm Postel Investmnt Ltd 1982-83; memb Nat Ports Cncl 1971-80, dir: Bransford Farmers Ltd 1973-, Bransford Leisure Pursuits Ltd 1973-; dir Lloyd's Bank Ltd 1977-78, chm Birmingham and W Midlands Bd Lloyds Bank Ltd 1978-85, dir Lloyd's Bank (UK) Ltd 1979-85, chm: Incpen 1979-, RDC Properties Ltd 1987-; pres Chartered Inst of Transport 1972; dir: Lloyd's Bank Unit Tst 1984-85; Black Horse Ltd 1984-85; hon fell Fitzwilliam Coll Cambridge 1985; CBIM, FCIT, FRSA, MIPM; kt 1974;

Recreations cricket, football, fishing, shooting; *Clubs* Hawks (Cambridge), MCC, Farmers'; *Style*— Sir Daniel Pettit; Bransford Court Farm, Worcester WR65 5JL (☎ 0905 830098)

PETTIT, Richard William; s of Sir Daniel Pettit *qv*, and Winifred, *née* Bibby; *b* 11 Nov 1941; *Educ* Westminster, St John's Coll Oxford (MA); *m* 1967, Jane Anne, da of Wing Cdr Duncan Basset McGill, of Ruthin Castle, Clwyd; 1 s, 1 da; m 2, Alicia Margaret, da of Albert Ernqst Stone, of Bristol; *Career* md Vaux Brewery Sunderland (formerly operations dir); md DRG Cartons Bristol, memb CBI northern regn Cncl 1978-83; CEng, MIMechE, MIProdE, MBIM; *Recreations* farming, fishing, model railways; *Clubs* RAC; *Style*— Richard Pettit Esq; Blackmountain Farm, Newcastle-on-Clun, Craven Arms, Shropshire SY7 8PL

PETTMAN, Prof Barrie Owen; s of Matthew Mark Pettman (d 1967), and Ivy, *née* Warcup; *b* 22 Feb 1944; *Educ* Hull GS, Hull Tech Coll (BSc), City Univ Business Sch (MSc, PhD); *m* 1, 1970 (m dis 1986), Heather Richardson; m 2, 1987, Norma, da of Walter Albert Bonser (d 1974); *Career* lectr Dept of Social Admin Hull Univ 1970-82, registrar Int Mgmnt Centres 1983-; dir: MCB Univ pres 1970-; Int Inst of Social Econ 1972-; ed: Mgmnt Res News 1981-, Int Journal of Sociology & Social Policy 1984-, Int Journal of Social Economics 1973-79, Int Journal of Manpower 1980-84, Industrial Relations News 1982-84; jt ed Managerial Law 1975-, asst ed Equal Opportunities International 1982-; vis prof Canadian Sch of Mgmnt 1983-, hon vice pres Br Soc of Commerce 1975-, chm Inst of Sci Business 1972-79, memb Manpower Soc 1977-; FCI, FRGS, FRSA, FITD, MBIM; Int Inst of Social Econs; *Books* Training and Retraining (1973), Labour Turnover and Retention (1975), Equal Pay (1975), Manpower Planning Workbook (1976, 1984), Industrial Democracy (1984), Discrimination in the Labour Market (1980), Management: A Selected Bibliography (1983); *Recreations* golf, shooting; *Clubs* The Reform; *Style*— Prof Barrie Pettman; Enholmes Hall, Payrington, Hull HU12 0PR (☎ 0964 630033); MCB University Press, 62 Toller Lane, Bradford, W Yorkshire BD8 9BY (☎ 0274 499821, telex 51317, fax 0274 547143, car telephone 0860 813688)

PETTY, Christine Ann; *née* Durell; da of Richard Collier Durell, of Saltdean, nr Brighton, Sussex, and Lilian Adelaide Hilder; *b* 10 July 1931; *Educ* Hove Acad GS 1942-48, Brighton Coll of Art 1948-53; *m* 2 Sept 1963, Clive Anthony Michael Petty, s of Clive George Petty (d 1961), of Minstead, Hampshire; 2 da (Yvonne b 1967, Marie b 1968); *Career* registered arch, arch Black, Bayes & Gibson 1957-67 (assoc ptnr 1964-67); work inc: Charles Clore Pavilion for Small Mammals with Sir Misha Black, which received a civic Tst commendation award; MRIBA; *Recreations* family, theatre, music; *Style*— Mrs Christine Petty; Curtle, Blackhill-Lindfield, Sussex RH16 2HF (☎ 04447 3612);

PETTY, Very Rev John Fitzmaurice; s of Dr Gerald Fitzmaurice Petty, TD, MRCS, LRCP, FRCGP (d 1986), and Edith Stuart, *née* Knox (d 1977); *b* 9 Mar 1935; *Educ* King's Sch Bruton, RMA Sandhurst, Trinity Hall Cambridge (MA), Cuddesdon Theol Coll Oxford; *m* 10 Aug 1963, Susan, da of Sir Geoffrey Peter Shakerley (d 1982); 3 s (Simon b 1967, Mark b 1969, Jeremy b 1972), 1 da (Rachel b 1965); *Career* cmmnd RE 1955, seconded Gurkha Engrs Malaya/Borneo 1959-62, resigned cmmn as Capt 1964; ordained Sheffield Cath: deacon 1966, priest 1967; curate St Cuthbert's Fir Vale Sheffield 1966-69, p-in-c Bishop Andrewes' Church Southwark 1969-75, vicar St John's Hurst Ashton-under-Lyne 1983-87, hon canon Manchester Cath 1986, provost of Coventry 1988-; hon chaplain RAPC (Offrs Accounts) Ashton-under-Lyne 1977-87; memb ctee St Helier Artificial Kidney Fund (SHAK) 1967-69, chm Tameside Aids and Services for the Handicapped (TASH) 1981-87; co-ordinator: Home for Homeless Girls Tameside 1977-87, Ambulance for the Elderley 1976-87, Holidays for Belfast Families 1977-86; *Recreations* squash, skiing; *Style*— The Very Rev the Provost of Coventry; 10A Priory Row, Coventry CV1 5ES (☎ 0203 221835); Coventry Cathedral, 7 Priory Row, Coventry CV1 5ES (☎ 0203 227 597)

PETTY, Maj William Walford; s of Lt-Col W Petty, DSO (d 1963), of Helsington Lodge, Brigsteer, Westmorland, and Helen Edith Petty, *née* Walford (d 1955); *b* 15 Oct 1916; *Educ* Wellington, RMC Sandhurst; *m* 1, 31 Aug 1957, Barbara Joan (d 1962), da of Christian Hoyer Millar (d 1970); 1 da (Clare b 1959), m 2, 21 Nov 1964, Kathie Emilie Marianne, da of Wilhelm Röpert (d 1957), of Hamburg; 1 s (James b 1965); *Career* Maj Dogra Regt Indian Army and RA, served Malaya 1941-42, (POW 1942-45), Staff Coll Camberley 1949 (ret 1958); range offr Otterburn Trg Area, Northumberland 1957-82; *Recreations* shooting, gardening; *Clubs* Victory Services; *Style*— Maj William Petty; Aiket House, Aiketgate, Armathwaite, Carlisle

PETTY-FITZMAURICE, Lady Arabella Helen Mary; da of Earl of Shelburne, *qv*; *b* 30 August 1966; *Style*— Lady Arabella Petty-Fitzmaurice

PETTY-FITZMAURICE, Lady Georgina Elizabeth; only surv da of 8 Marquess of Lansdowne, PC, by his 1 w; *b* 10 Jan 1950; *Style*— Lady Georgina Petty-Fitzmaurice; Meikleour House, Perthshire

PETTY-FITZMAURICE, Lady Rachel Barbara Violet; da of Earl of Shelburne, *qv*; *b* 30 Jan 1968; *Style*— Lady Rachel Petty-Fitzmaurice

PEVSNER, Dieter; s of Sir Nikolaus Pevsner, CBE (d 1983); *Career* jt dep md André Deutsch Ltd 1981-; formerly sr ed Penguin; fndr and jt owner Wildwood House (publishers) 1971-81; *Style*— Dieter Pevsner, Esq; c/o André Deutsch Ltd, 105 Gt Russell St, WC1 (☎ 01 580 2746)

PEYRONEL, Alexandra Louise; *née* Rubens; da of Col Ralph Alexander Rubens, of 27 Gertrude St, London SW10, 3 husb of Lady Rosemary (d 1963), *née* Eliot, er da of 6 Earl of St Germans, MC, and Lady Blanche Douglas, *née* Somerset, da of 9 Duke of Beaufort; through Lady Blanche she is co-heiress (with Samantha Cope and Lady Cathleen Hudson, *qqv*) to the Baronies of Botetourt and Herbert, which went into abeyance on the death of 10 Duke of Beaufort, KG, GCVO, PC (1984); *b* 9 Oct 1951; *Educ* St Martin's and Byam Shaw Schs of Art (BA); *m* 1976, Daniel Augusto Peyronel, s of HE Vice-Adm Aldo Peyronel, of Buenos Aires and Mar del Plata; 1 s; *Recreations* tennis, swimming, riding, hunting; *Style*— Mrs Daniel Peyronel

PEYSSON, Hon Mrs (Elizabeth Cecilia); *née* Shaw; *née* Shaw yst da of Baron Kilbrandon, PC (Life Peer), *qv*; *b* 1948; *m* 1984, Jean-Marc Peysson; 1 s (Jean-Christophe b 1986); *Style*— The Hon Mrs Peysson; La Gautrivière, 03160 Bourbon l'Archambault, Allier, France

PEYTON, Hon Thomas; s of Baron Peyton of Yeovil (Life Peer); *b* 5 April 1950; *m* 1981, Vivien Birks; 1 s (Joseph b 1986); *Style*— The Hon Thomas Peyton; BP Oil Middle East, PO Box 299, Manama, Bahrain

PEYTON OF YEOVIL, Baron (Life Peer UK 1983); Rt Hon John Wynne William Peyton; PC (1970); s of late Ivor Eliot Peyton, of Englemere Wood, Ascot, and Dorothy Helen Peyton (d 1977); *b* 13 Feb 1919; *Educ* Eton, Trin Coll Oxford (MA); *m* 1, 1947 (m dis 1966), Diana, da of Douglas Clinch, of Durban, S Africa; 1 s, 1 da (and 1 s decd); m 2, 1966, Mary Constance, only da of Col Hon Humphrey Wyndham, MC (6 s of 2 Baron Leconfield), by his w Ruth, *née* Astley (great niece of 16 Baron Hastings and sis-in-law of the actress Madeleine Carroll), and formerly 2 w of Ralph Cobbold (2 cous of 1 Baron Cobbold); *Career* served 15/19 Hussars WWII (POW 1940-45); barr Inner Temple 1945; MP (C) Yeovil 1951-83, parly sec Miny Power 1962-64, min of Transport 1970, min for Transport Industries DOE 1970-74, chm Texas Instruments Ltd 1974-; *Clubs* Boodle's; *Style*— The Rt Hon the Lord Peyton of Yeovil, PC; The Old Malt House, Hinton St George, Somerset (☎ 0460 73618); 6 Temple West Mews, West Sq, London SE11 (☎ 01 582 3611)

PHAIR, Michael Keith; s of George Carlton Phair, of Ontario, Canada, and Mary Lucille, *née* Munro; *b* 24 June 1950; *Educ* Univ of Western Ontario (BA), Graduate Sch of Business Univ of Western Ontario (MBA); *m* 21 July 1973, Margaret Noreen (Margot), da of Charles Alexander Joseph Rogers, of Buenos Aires; 1 s (Nicholas b 20 Aug 1982), 1 da (Stephanie b 16 Aug 1978); *Career* sr rep Mexico Toronto Dominion Bank 1975-79, pres Banque Avual S America Panama 1979-84, sr invstmts offr Capital Mkts Dept Int Fin Corp Washington DC 1984-87, dir corporate fin NM Rothschild & Son Ltd 1988-; memb: Latin American Ctee London C of C, Canning Club, Canada and UK C of C; *Recreations* squash, tennis, sailing; *Style*— Michael K Phair, Esq; PO Box 185, New Court, St Swithins Lane, London EC4P 4DN (☎ 01 280 5494, fax 01 626 0799)

PHARO-TOMLIN, Col John Axel; s of Axel Christian Pharo-Tomlin (d 1965), of Dane Court, St Peters-in-Thanet, Kent, and Edith Madelaine Quayle, *née* Tomlin (d 1974); *b* 8 April 1934; *Educ* Radley Coll, RMA Sandhurst; *m* 19 Dec 1964, Joanna Marguerite Kate, da of Lt Col John Boileau Pemberton (d 1974), of Coaxdon Hall, Axminster, Devon; 1 s (Edward b 1968), 2 da (Sally b 1965, Alice b 1975); *Career* cmmnd 14/20 King's Hussars 1954, Adj 1961, instr RMA Sandhurst 1963, RNSC 1966, Sqdn Ldr 14/20 King's Hussars 1967, GSO 2 Singapore Dist 1968, Second-in-Command Duke of Lancaster's Own Yeo 1971, Bde Major 11 Armoured Bde 1972, GSO 1 Operational Requirements MOD 1975, CO 14/20 King's Hussars 1977 (despatches 1979), Col AG 16/17/18 MOD 1980, Col M1 (A) MOD 1984, ret 1986; mangr Banque Paribas London 1986-; Freeman City of London 1987; FBIM 1984; *Recreations* country pursuits, music; *Clubs* Cavalry and Guards, City Univ; *Style*— Col John Pharo-Tomlin; Banque Paribas, 68 Lombard St, London EC3V 9EH (☎ 01 9294545/01 9555367, fax 01 7266761, telex 945881/886055)

PHAROAH, Prof Peter Oswald Derrick; s of Oswald Higgins Pharoah (d 1941), and Phylis Christine, *née* Gahan; *b* 19 May 1934; *Educ* Lawrence Meml Royal Mil Sch Lovedale India, Palmers Sch Grays Essex, Univ of London (MD, MSc); *m* 17 May 1960, Margaret Rose, da of James McMinn (d 1979); 3 s (Paul b 1962, Mark b 1966, Timothy b 1975), 1 da (Fiona b 1961); *Career* med offr Dept of Public Health Papua New Guinea 1963-74, sr lectr London Sch of Hygiene and Tropical Med 1974-79, prof community health Univ of Liverpool 1979-; FFCM 1980; *Recreations* philately, squash, walking; *Style*— Prof Peter Pharoah; 11 Fawley Road, Liverpool L18 9TE (☎ 051 724 4896); Dept of Community Health, University of Liverpool, Liverpool L69 3BX (☎ 051 794 5577)

PHAYRE, Col (Robert) Desmond Hensley; s of Lt-Col Robert Bernard Phayre, MC (d 1966), of Collatons, Bow, Devon, and Joan Margaret, *née* Hensley (d 1977); Gen Sir Robert Phayre, GCB (d 1897), was ADC to Queen Victoria 1968; Lt-Gen Sir Arthur Phayre, GCMG, KCSI, CB (d 1885), 1st chief cmmr of Br Burma and gov of Mauritius; *b* 1 Oct 1915; *Educ* Rugby, RMA Woolwich; *m* 16 April 1940, Barbara Charlton, da of Maj Gen Sir Charlton Spinks, Pasha, KBE, DSO (d 1959), last Sirdar in Egypt; 1 s (Robert b 1949), 2 da (Marguerite Berthoud b 1941, Hilary (Mrs Nicholson) b 1943); *Career* cmmnd RA 1935, serv in Burma, Indian, Palestine 1947-48 (despatches), Cyprus 1956 (Suez); asst MA Helsinki 1949-50, Greece 1951-3; MA Tehran 1957-60, Amman 1963-66, sec of staff HQ allied forces Central Europe, NATO 1967-70; sr ptnr Collatons Enterprises; vice pres (Devon) SSAFA, warden SW; Freeman of England Assoc; chm Taw Fishing Club; Order of Humayun (Iran) 1959; Freeman of Shrewsbury; *Recreations* fishing, shooting, languages; *Style*— Col Desmond Phayre; Collatons House, Bow, Crediton, Devon (☎ 03633 242)

PHAYRE, Maj Robert Dermot Spinks (Robin); s of Col Robert Desmond Hensley Phayre, and Barbara Charlton, *née* Spinks; gggggggggf Col Robert Phayre (Phaire) 1619-82 was an addressee (1 of 3) on warrant for execution of King Charles 1, gggf Gen Sir Robert Phayre, GCB was ADC to HM Queen Victoria; *b* 3 Nov 1949; *Educ* Rugby, Trent Poly (BA); *m* 11 Dec 1976, Jane Elisabeth Stirling, da of Maj Michael Ranulph Vincent; 2 da (Katherine b 1980, Jemma b 1983); *Career* Adjt LI Depot 1978-80, platoon instr RMA Sandhurst 1980, Army Staff Coll Camberley 1981-82, Co Cdr 2 Bn LI 1983-84, S02 GI OPS HQ (BR) Corps 1985-86; 2 i/c 1 Bn LI 1987-89; chief instr Signal Wing Sch of Inf 1989-; Freeman: City of London, City of Shrewsbury; Liveryman Worshipful Co of Haberdashers; *Recreations* sailing, tennis, squash; *Clubs* Liveryman Worshipful Co of Haberdashers; *Style*— Major Robin Phayre; c/o Lloyds Bank, 30 High St, Crediton, Devon

PHEASANT, Victor Albert; MBE (1983); s of Albert George Pheasant (d 1976), of Bexleyheath, Kent, and Margaret, *née* Williams; *b* 2 July 1940; *Educ* Erith Technical Sch; *m* 21 Oct 1961, Susan Mary, da of Arthur Waldron Slade, of Rothwell, Northamptonshire; 2 s (Andrew Victor b 1962, Richard Michael b 1965); *Career* RAF 1960-84: air crew Strike Cmd 1960-80, RAF Central Tactics and Trials Orgn CTTO 1980-84, ret as Sqdn Ldr; projects dir Chemring Gp plc 1985-; *Recreations* carpentry; *Clubs* RAF; *Style*— Victor A Pheasant, Esq, MBE; Heathcote, Purbrook Heath, Portsmouth, Hants PO7 5RX (☎ 0705 263249); Chemring Gp plc, Rodney Rd, Fratton, Portsmouth, Hants (☎ 0705 735457, fax 0705 817509)

PHEASEY, Michael; s of Reginald Sidney Pheasey (d 1987), of Buxton, Derbyshire, and Harriet Annie, *née* Finlow; *b* 12 May 1944; *Educ* Buxton Coll; *m* 31 July 1965, Raynor Anne, da of George Smedley Mather (d 1961), of Buxton; 2 s (Robert b 1967, Nicholas b 1975), 1 da (Alison b 1968); *Career* Bradford & Bingley Bldg Soc: Sec 1980, gen mangr 1983, dep chief exec 1988, dir 1988 (title still dep chief exec); FCIS; *Recreations* golf, squash; *Clubs* Shipley GC, Heaton Squash; *Style*— Michael Pheasey, Esq; Bradford & Bingley Bldg Soc, PO Box 2, Bingley, West Yorks (☎ 0274 568 111)

PHELAN, His Hon Judge Andrew James; s of Cornelius Phelan, of Clonmel, Ireland; *b* 25 July 1923; *Educ* Clongoweswood Co Kildare, Nat Univ of Ireland, Trinity

Coll Cambridge; *m* 1950, Joan Robertson, da of John McLagan (d 1978), of Callender, Perthshire; 1 s, 2 da; *Career* barr (Ireland) King's Inn 1945, Gray's Inn 1949, jr fell Bristol Univ 1948-50, circuit judge 1974-; *Recreations* skiing, sailing (yacht 'Sarakiniko'); *Clubs* Royal Cruising, Bar YC; *Style*— His Hon Judge Phelan; 17 Hartington Rd, Chiswick, London W4 3TL (☎ 01 994 6109)

PHELIPS, David Edward; s of Cdre Harry Phelips, of Southampton, and Irene Woolcock (d 1943); formerly of Montacute House (considered about the finest Elizabethan House in Eng), Somerset, built by Sir Edward Phelips (1588-1603) Speaker of House of Commons and Master of the Rolls; *b* 6 Dec 1924; *Educ* Taunton Sch; *m* 4 Dec 1965, Claudie, da of Marcel Cambier, of Paris; *Career* RNVR 1943-46; dir: Drix Plastics Ltd 1964-79, Montacute Est Ltd 1979-; *Recreations* sailing; *Clubs* Naval, Master Mariners (Southampton); *Style*— David E Phelips, Esq; Barn Close, House, Itchen Abbas, Hampshire (☎ (096278) 464); Montacute Estate Office

PHELPS, Anthony John; CB (1976); s of John Francis Phelps, of Oxford; *b* 14 Oct 1922; *Educ* City of Oxford HS, Univ Coll Oxford; *m* 1, 1949, Sheila Nan (d 1967), da of late Colin Benton Rait, of Edinburgh; 1 s, 2 da; m 2, 1971, Janet M T, da of late Charles R Dawson, of Edinburgh; *Career* H M Treasury 1946-73; dep chm Bd of Customs and Excise 1973-82; *Clubs* MCC, City Livery; *Style*— Anthony Phelps Esq, CB; 1 Woodsyre, Sydenham Hill, SE26 6SS (☎ 01 670 0735)

PHELPS, Charles Frederick; s of Capt Seth Arthur Rose Phelps, MBE (d 1978) of Peaslake Surrey, and Rigmor Louise, *née* Kaae (d 1984); *b* 18 Jan 1934; *Educ* Bromsgrove, Brasenose Coll Oxford (BSc, MA, D Phil); *m* 29 Feb 1960, Joanna, da of Eric Lingeman, CBE (d 1966), of Eaton Square, London; 1 s (Anthony John Rose b 8 Sept 1960), 1 da (Amanda Louise Barnet b 20 Sept 1962); *Career* Univ of Bristol: lectr in chemical physiology 1960-63, reader in biochemistry 1970-74 (lectr 1963-70); prof of biochemistry Univ of Lancaster 1974-80, princ Chelsea coll Univ of London 1980-84, pro rector Imp Coll of Sci Technol and Medicine 1984-; memb: res ctee Arthritis and Rheumatism Cncl 1974-78, ctee Br Biophysical Soc 1974-84 (chm 1983-84), ed bd Biochim Biophys ACTA 1976-80, ctee Biochemical soc 1980-84, ed bd Int Res Common Systems 1980-; govr: Furzedown Sch Battersea 1980-85, King Edward's Sch Witley 1984-, Mill Hill Sch 1985-, Royal GS Guildford 1988-, Royal Postgraduate Med Fndn 1986-; Fell King's Coll London 1985; *Books* Messenger RNA (co ed H R V Arnstein), Biotechnology (co ed P Clarke) Molecular Variants of Proteins (P Campbell); *Recreations* landscape gardening, cooking, birdwatching; *Clubs* Athenaeum; *Style*— Prof Charles Phelps; 47 St Dionis Rd, London SW6 4UB; Brockhurst, The Green Chiddingfold Surrey GU8 4TU (☎ 042 879 3092); Imp Coll of Sci Technol and Medicine London SW7 2AZ (☎ 01 589 511 ext 3002, fax 01 584 7596, telex 929484 IMPCOL G)

PHELPS, Hon Mrs (Helen Rosemary); da of late 3 Baron Cozens-Hardy; *b* 1918; *m* 1953, Brig Douglas Vandeleur Phelps, TD, JP, DL (d 1988); 1 da Laura Douglas b 1959; 1 s (John Edward b 1961) adop; *Style*— The Hon Mrs Phelps; Grove Farm House, Langham, Holt, Norfolk

PHELPS, Howard Thomas Henry Middleton; s of Ernest Henry Phelps (d 1981), of Gloucester and Harriet Maria Ann, *née* Middleton (d 1978); *b* 20 Oct 1926; *Educ* Crypt GS Gloucester, Hatfield Coll Univ of Durham (BA); *m* 1949, Audrey, da of Thomas Ellis (d 1972); 1 da; *Career* dep dir industl relations NCB to 1972; dir of ops BA 1979-86 (personnel dir 1972-79), dir of operations 1979-86; dir: Peninsula and Oriental Steam Navigation Co chm Earls Court and Olympia Ltd, FRAeS, FIPM, FCIT, CBIM; *Recreations* music, gardens; *Clubs* Royal Overseas; *Style*— Howard Phelps, Esq; Tall Trees, Chedworth, nr Cheltenham, Glos (☎ 0285 72324); Earls Court Warwick Rd London

PHELPS, Maj-Gen Leonard Thomas Herbert; CB (1973), OBE (1963); s of Abijah Phelps; *b* 9 Sept 1917; *m* 1945, Jean Irene, da of R Price Dixon; 1 s, 1 da; *Career* 2 Lt Indian Army 1941, Brig 1967, Cdr Base Organisation RAOC 1970-71, Maj-Gen 1970, DGOS MOD 1971-73, ret, Col Cmdt RAOC 1976-78; dir: Warrior Gp 1974-78, Leon Davis & Co 1974-81, Greens Business Systems Ltd 1982-84; *Style*— Maj-Gen Leonard Phelps, CB, OBE; South Port Cottage, Sutton Courtenay, Oxon

PHELPS, Maurice; s of Harry Thomas Phelps (d 1973), and Lilian Carter; *b* 17 May 1935; *Educ* Wandsworth Sch, CCC Oxford (BA); *m* 1960, Elizabeth Anne; 2 s, 1 da; *Career* personnel dir Heavy Vehicle Div Leyland Vehicles 1977-80, bd memb for Personnel British Shipbuilders 1980-87; Dir Personnel and Employee Relations, Sealink UK Ltd; Non-Exec Board Memb, British Shipbuilders; *Recreations* surfing, sailing, squash; *Style*— Maurice Phelps, Esq; Abbotsfield, Goring Heath, South Oxfordshire (☎ (0491) 681916); Sealink UK Ltd, 20 Upper Ground, London SE1 9PF (☎ 01 928 5550)

PHELPS, Richard Lawson; s of John Graham Phelps, and Barbara Phelps; *b* 19 April 1961; *Career* athlete (modern pentathlon), jr nat champion: 1979, 1981, 1982; sr nat champion: 1979, 1981-84, 1986, 1988; Bronze Medalist (team modern pentathlon) Seoul Olympics 1988; life memb: Modern Pentathlon Assoc of GB 1984, Gloucester City Swimming Club 1988; *Style*— Richard Phelps, Esq; c/o British Olympic Assoc, 1 Wandsworth Plain, London SW18 1EH

PHELPS, Richard Wintour; CBE (1986); s of late Rev H Phelps, of Sidmouth, Devon, and Elsie, *née* Pearce; *b* 26 July 1925; *Educ* Kingswood Sch Bath, Merton Coll Oxford (MA); *m* 12 Feb 1955, Pamela Marie Phelps; 2 da (Hilary Susan b 25 Oct 1957, Diana Gillian b 15 March 1961); *Career* Lt 14 Punjab Regt Indian Army 1944-46; HM Overseas CS Nigeria 1948-57 and 1959-61, princ Home CS HM Treasy 1957-59 and 1961-65, gen mangr Skilmersdale New Town Devpt Corpn 1967-71, gen mangr Central Lancs Devpt Corpn 1971-86; sr admin Hants CC 1963-65, pt/t advsr on housing to Govt of Vanuatu 1986-, pt/t advsr on housing to Falkland Islands Govt 1988; Parly candidate (Alliance) Barrow-in-Furness Div 1987; *Recreations* travel, reading, bridge; *Clubs* Royal Cwlth Soc; *Style*— Richard Phelps, Esq, CBE; Fell Foot Hse, Newby Bridge, Ulverston, Cumbria LA12 8NL (☎ 053 95 312 74)

PHILIP SORENSEN, Nils Jorgen (Philip); s of Erik Philip Sorgensen Consul General, of Lillön, Skone, Sweden, and Brita Hjordis Bendix *née* Lundgren (d 1984); established Modern Security Indust in Europe (*see Enc Britannica*); *b* 29 Sept 1938; *Educ* Herlufsholm Kostskole, Naerstved, Denmark; Niels Brock Commercial Sch, CPH; *m* 1962, Ingrid, da of Eigil Baltzer-Andersen (d 1965); 1 s (Mark b 1973), 3 da (Annette b 1963, Christina b 1965, Louisa b 1968); *Career* dirships: TNT Security Pty (Australia); Gp 4 Securities SA (Belgium); Danskring A/S, Fiskerestauranten A/S Gp 4 Denmark A/S, Strandhotellet AS (Denmark); Securite Protection Surveillance (France); Gp 4 Securities SA Security Systems (Greece); Gp 4 Securitas Ireland ltd (Ireland); Secom Ltd (Japan); Securitas SA (Luxembourg); Gp 4 Securitas (Intemat) BV, Gp 4 Securitas (Nederland) BV (Nederlands); Securitas AS, (Norway); Grupo Quatro Securitas ETC (Portugal); has dirships in Thailand, Spain and the UK; memb of Cncl BSIA (UK); chm and memb of Bd of numerous security cos; hon citizen of Cork 1985, Soldier of the Year Award (Sweden); *Recreations* fishing vessel "Oke", photography; *Clubs* Bucks, Eccentric; *Style*— Nils Philip Sorensen, Esq; Winchcombe Abbey, Winchcombe, Gloucestershire; Farncombe House, Broadway, Worcestershire (☎ (0386) 858585, fax (0386) 858254)

PHILIPP, Elliot Elias; s of Oscar Isaac Philipp (d 1965), of Geneva, Switzerland, and Clarisse Weil (d 1971); *b* 20 July 1915; *Educ* St Paul's Sch, Cambridge Univ (MA); *m* 22 March 1939, Lucie Ruth (d 1988), da of Zacharias Max Hackenbroch (d 1937); 1 s (Alan Henry b 1943), 1 da (Ann Susan b 1941); *Career* Sqdn Ldr RAFVR, Bomber Cmd (despatches twice); conslt obstetrician and gynaecologist: Romford Hosps 1952-64, Royal Northern Hosp and City of London Maternity Hosp and Whittington; FRCS, FRCOG; *Books* The Scientific Foundations of Obstetrics and Gynaecology (ed), Near The Sun (war memoir); *Recreations* walking, travel, mountaineering, theatre, book collecting; *Clubs* Int Pen, Royal Soc of Med; *Style*— Elliot Philipp, Esq; 78 Nottingham Terrace, York Gate, London NW1 4QE (☎ 01 486 1075); 94 Harley St, London W1N 1AF (☎ 01 935 5007)

PHILIPPE, André J; Hon GCVO 1972; *b* 28 June 1926,Luxembourg City; *Career* barr Luxembourg 1951-52, Luxembourg ambass to UK, perm rep to Council of WEU, and concurrently ambass to Ireland and Iceland 1972-78, ambass to France 1978-84; ambass United Nations New York 1984-; Cdr Order of Adolphe of Nassau and Order of Oaken Crown (Lux), Cdr Légion d'Honneur (Fr); *Style*— His Excellency M André Philippe, GCVO; 801 Second Avenue, New York, NY 10017 USA (☎ (212) 370 9850)

PHILIPPS, Hon Colwyn Jestyn John; s (by 1 m) and h of 2 Viscount St Davids, *qv*; *b* 30 Jan 1939; *m* 1965, Augusta Victoria Correa Larrain, da of late Don Estantislao Correa Ugarte of Santiago, Chile; 2 s; *Style*— The Hon Colwyn Philipps

PHILIPPS, Hon Mrs (Elizabeth Joan); da of 1 Baron Kindersley, GBE (d 1954); *b* 1911; *m* 1930, Maj the Hon James Perrott Philipps, TD; *Style*— The Hon Mrs Philipps; Dalham Hall, Newmarket, Suffolk

PHILIPPS, Hon Gwenllian; OBE (1962); da of 1 Baron Milford (d 1962); *b* 1916; *Career* Subaltern, ATS; JP Radnorshire; CC Radnorshire 1959-64; High Sheriff 1970-71; *Style*— The Hon Gwenllian Philipps, OBE; The Old Rectory, Boughrood, Llyswen, Brecon

PHILIPPS, Hon (Richard) Hanning; MBE (1945); s of 1 Baron Milford (d 1962), and Ethel Georgina, JP, only da of late Rev Benjamin Speke; *b* 14 Feb 1904; *Educ* Eton; *m* 1930, Lady Marion, JP, *qv*, da of 12 Earl of Stair; 1 s, 1 d; *Career* served NW Europe 1944-45; Maj Welsh Gds (Reserve); Hon Col Pembroke Yeo; chm: Schweppes Ltd 1940-68, Northern Securities Trust Ltd 1950-80, chm Milford Haven Conservancy Bd 1963-75; memb Civic Tst for Wales and JP; Lord-Lt for: Pembrokeshire 1958-74, Dyfed 1974-79 and keeper of the Rolls for Dyfed 1974-; contested (Nat) Brecon and Radnor 1939; *Recreations* painting, forestry, gardening; *Clubs* Boodle's; *Style*— The Hon Hanning Philipps, MBE; Picton Castle, The Rhos, Haverfordwest, Dyfed SA62 4AS (☎ 043 786 201)

PHILIPPS, Hon Hugo John Laurence; s and h of 2 Baron Milford; *b* 27 August 1929; *Educ* Eton, King's Coll Camb; *m* 1, 1951 (m dis 1958), Margaret, da of Capt Ralph Heathcote, DSO, RN; 1 da; m 2, 1959 (m dis 1984), Hon Mary Makins, da of 1 Baron Sherfield; m 3 s, 1 da; 3, 26 Jan 1989, Mrs Felicity Leach; *Career* memb Lloyd's; farmer; *Books* Boodles; *Style*— The Hon Hugo Philipps; Llanstephan House, Llanstephan, Brecon, Powys

PHILIPPS, Lady Jean (Meriel); *née* McDonnell; da of 7 Earl of Antrim (d 1932); *b* 1914; *m* 1939, Capt the Hon William Speke Philipps, CBE (d 1975); 2 s, 2 da; *Style*— Lady Jean Philipps; Slebech Park, Haverfordwest, Dyfed

PHILIPPS, Lady Marion Violet; *née* Dalrymple; JP (Dyfed 1965); da of 12 Earl of Stair, KT, DSO (d 1961); *b* 1 Feb 1908; *Educ* privately; *m* 1930, Hon (Richard) Hanning Philipps, MBE, *qv*; 1 s, 1 da; *Career* memb Narberth Rural Dist Cncl 1970-73, chm Picton Land & Investment Pty Ltd WA, trustee Picton Castle Trust (Graham Sutherland Gallery) 1976-, founder memb and first pres British Polled Hereford Soc 1950; FRAgS; CStJ; Order of Mercy 1926; *Style*— Lady Marion Philipps, JP; Picton Castle, The Rhos, Haverfordwest, Dyfed SA62 4AS (☎ 043 786 201)

PHILIPPS, Hon Mrs Mary; *née* Makins; da (twin) of 1 Baron Sherfield, GCB, GCMG; *b* 1935; *m* 1959, as his 2 w (m dis 1984), Hon Hugo John Laurence Philipps, *qv*; *Style*— The Hon Mrs Mary Philipps

PHILIPS, Prof Sir Cyril Henry; s of William Henry Philips; *b* 27 Dec 1912; *Educ* Rock Ferry HS, Liverpool Univ (MA), London Univ (PhD); *m* 1, 1939, Dorcas (d 1974), da of John Rose Wallasey; 1 d (1 s decd); m 2, 1975, Joan Rosemary, da of William George Marshall; *Career* chm Police Complaints Bd, prof of oriental history London Univ 1946-, dir Sch of Oriental and African Studies London 1957-76, dep vice-chllr London Univ 1969-70, vice-chllr 1972-76; chm Cncl on Tribunals 1986-; kt 1974; *Clubs* Athenaeum; *Style*— Professor Sir Cyril Philips; Sch of Oriental and African Studies, Malet St, WCIE 7HP (☎ 01 637 2388)

PHILIPSON, Major Christopher Roland; s of Major Thirlwell Philipson, MC (d 1952), of Fordham Abbey, Cambridgeshire, and Daphne, *née* Gladstone (d 1971); *b* 4 Mar 1929; *Educ* Eton, Sandhurst; *m* 1 Jan 1958, Mary, da of Sir Reginald MacDonald-Buchanan, KCVO, MC (d 1981), of Cottesbrooke Hall, Northampton; 2 da (Caroline b 1959, Joanna b 1961); *Career* Major Life Guards, served in Germany, Cyprus, Egypt, Aden 1947-61; md Br Bloodstock Agency plc 1980-; *Recreations* shooting, gardening; *Clubs* Turf; *Style*— Major Christopher R Philipson; Queensberry House, Newmarket, Suffolk (☎ 0638 665021)

PHILIPSON, Garry; DFC (1944); s of George and Marian Philipson, of Stockton-on-Tees; *b* 27 Nov 1921; *Educ* Stockton GS, Durham Univ (BA); *m* 27 Aug 1949, June Mary Miller, da of Lt-Col James Miller Somerville (d 1975); 1 da (Diana Chloe Joan b 9 Sept 1952); *Career* Fl Lt RAFVR 1941-46, 2 Gp Bomber Cmd; in Overseas Civil Service 1949-60, princ Scottish Office 1961-66, under sec RICS 1966-67, dir Smith & Ritchie Ltd 1967-70, sec New Towns Assoc 1970-74, md Aycliffe and Peterlee Devpt Corpn 1974-85; vice-chm North Housing Assoc 1985-, tstee Dales Care 1988-; *Books* Aycliffe and Peterlee: Swords into Ploughshares and Farewell Squalor (1988); *Recreations* country pursuits, history, archaeology; *Clubs* RAF; *Style*— Garry Philipson, Esq, DFC; Tunstall Grange, Tunstall, Richmond, N Yorks (☎ 0748 833327)

PHILIPSON, Sir Robin (Robert James); s of James Philipson; *b* 17 Dec 1916; *Educ*

Whitehaven Secdy Sch, Dumfries Acad, Edinburgh Coll of Art; *m* 1, 1949, Brenda Mark; m 2, 1962 (m dis 1975), Thora Clyne; m 3, 1976, Diana Mary Pollock; *Career* head of sch of drawing and painting The College of Art Edinburgh 1960-, pres Royal Scottish Academy 1973-; FRSA, FRSE, Hon RA, PRSA, DUniv Stirling 1976, Hon LLD Aberdeen 1977; kt 1976; *Style*— Sir Robin Philipson; 23 Crawfurd Rd, Edinburgh EH16 5PQ (☎ 031 667 2373)

PHILIPSON-STOW, Sir Christopher; 5 Bt (UK 1907), of Cape Town, Cape of Good Hope, and Blackdown House, Lodsworth, Co Sussex, DFC; s of late Henry Matthew Philipson Philipson-Stow, JP (3 s of Sir Frederic Philipson-Stow, 1st Bt) by his w Elizabeth (herself da of Sir Thomas Chitty, 1st Bt); suc 1 cous, Sir Edmond Cecil Philipson-Stow, 4th Bt, MBE, 1982; *b* 13 Sept 1920; *Educ* Winchester; *m* 1952, Elizabeth Nairn, da of late James Dixon Trees, of Toronto, and widow of Maj Frederic George McLaren, of the Canadian 48 Highlanders; 2 s (Robert Matthew b 29 Aug 1953, Rowland Frederic b 2 Sept 1954); *Heir* er s, Robert; *Career* late Fl-Lt RAFVR, served WWII; *Style*— Sir Christopher Philipson-Stow, Bt, DFC; RR2, Port Carling, Ontario, Canada POB 1JO

PHILIPSON-STOW, Lady; Cynthia Yvette; da of late William Robertson Jecks, of Johannesburg, S Africa, and formerly w of Francis Romaine Govett; *m* 1951, as his 2 w, Sir Frederic Lawrence Philipson-Stow, 3 Bt (d 1976); *Style*— Lady Philipson-Stow; Na Xencha, Villa Carlos, Menorca, Spain; Apartado 211, Mahon, Menorca, Spain

PHILIPSON-STOW, Robert Nicholas; o s of Guyon Philipson Philipson-Stow (d 1983), and Alice Mary, *née* Fagge; *b* 2 April 1937; *Educ* Winchester; *m* 25 Sept 1963, Nicolette Leila, er da of Hon Philip Leyland Kindersley, *qv*; 2 s (Robert Rowland b 23 Sept 1970, Edward Miles b 30 April 1972), 1 da (Georgina Mary b 26 Oct 1976); *Career* 2 Lt RHG 1955-57 (Nat Serv); co sec Miles Druce & Co Ltd 1966-68; ptnr: George Henderson & Co, stockbrokers 1970-74, Henderson Crosthwaite & Co, stockbrokers 1974-86; compliance dir Guinness Maho n Holdings plc 1986-; exec chm Crown & Manor Boys' Club, Hoxton; memb HAC 1983; FCA 1963; *Clubs* White's; *Style*— Robert Philison-Stowe Esq;; Priors Court, Long Green, Gloucester (☎ 068481221); c/o Guinness Mahon Holdings plc, 32 St Mary-at-Hill, London EC3

PHILLIMORE, Hon Mrs Anthony; Anne Julia; da of Maj-Gen Sir Cecil Edward Pereira, KCB, CMG; *m* 1934, Capt the Hon Anthony Francis Phillimore (ka 1940, s of 2 Baron Phillimore); 1 s (3 Baron Phillimore), 1 da; *Style*— The Hon Mrs Anthony Phillimore; Coppid Hall, Henley-on-Thames, Oxon

PHILLIMORE, Hon Claud Stephen; 2 s of 2 Baron Phillimore, MC (d 1947); hp of nephew, 3 Baron; *b* 15 Jan 1911; *Educ* Winchester, Trinity Coll Cambridge (BA); *m* 1944, Anne Elizabeth, eldest da of late Maj Arthur Algernon Smith-Dorrien-Smith, DSO; 1 s (Francis), 1 da (Miranda); *Career* Capt and acting Maj 11 (City of London Yeo) Light Anti-Aircraft Brig RA (TA); architect; *Style*— The Hon Claud Phillimore; 39 Ashley Gdns, London SW1; Rymans, Apuldram, Chichester, W Sussex

PHILLIMORE, John Gore; CMG (1946); s of Adm Sir Richard Phillimore (d 1940), of Shedfield, Hants, and Violet Turton (d 1963); *b* 16 April 1908; *Educ* Winchester, Christ Church Oxford (MA); *m* 1951, Jill, da of Capt Mason Scott, RN (d 1975); 2 s (John, Hugh), 2 da (Louisa, Polly); *Career* ptnr Roberts Meynell & Co Buenos Aires 1936-48, md Baring Brothers London 1949-72, rep HM Treasy and Bank of England in S America 1940-45, High Sheriff of Kent 1975; *Clubs* White's; *Style*— John Phillimore, Esq, CMG; Brooklyn House, Kingsclere, Newbury, Berks RG15 8QY (☎ 0635 298321)

PHILLIMORE, Cdr Richard Augustus Bagot; s of Adm Sir Richard Fortescue Phillimore, GCB, KCMG, MBO (d 1940), and Violet Gore, *née* Turton (d 1963); *b* 9 Jan 1907; *Educ* RNS Osborne and Dartmouth; *m* 28 June 1948, Pamela Mary, da of Lt Col John A Darlington, DSO; 4 s (Peter Richard b 10 Feb 1950, Roger Henry b 28 Aug 1951, Charles Robert b 28 June 1953, Mark Augustus b 26 April 1956); *Career* RN: HMS Frobisher 1924-25, HMS Hood 1925-27, Sub Lt courses 1928, HM Yacht Victoria & Albert 1929, HMS Repulse 1930, HMS Dragon 1930-32, HMS Vortigern 1933, observers' course 1934, HMS Eagle 1934, HMS Hermes 1935-37, RAF Sch of Photograhy Farnborough 1937, HMS Cornwall 1938, HMS Rodney 1939, 3 Bomber Fp RAF Mildenhall 1939-40, trg naval observers 1940-41, HMS Biter 1942, staff of C in C Western Approaches 1943, jt A/U Sch Maydown 1943-44, staff Flag Offr Air East Indies 1945, cmd HMS Argonaut 1946, cmd HMS Dido 1947, fleet aviation offr Staff of C in C Med 1948-50, naval air div Admty 1951-53, ret 1953; church warden 1954-79, deanery rep 1979-85; pres Waltham Chase Boys Motor Cycle Club 1971-; High Sheriff and DL Hants 1960; *Style*— Cdr Richard Phillimore; Shedfield House, Shedfield, Southampton SO3 2HQ (☎ 0329 833 116)

PHILLIMORE, 3 Baron (UK 1918); Sir Robert Godfrey Phillimore; 4 Bt (UK 1881); s of Capt Hon Anthony Francis Phillimore (ka 1940), and gs of 3 Baron Phillimore (d 1947); *b* 24 Sept 1939; *Educ* Winchester; *Heir* unc, Maj Hon Claud Stephen Phillimore; *Career* late 2 Lt 9/12 Royal Lancers; *Style*— The Rt Hon the Lord Phillimore; Coppid Hall, Henley-on-Thames, Oxon

PHILLIMORE, Hon Mrs Robert; (Sheila Bruce); da of John Farquhar MacLeod, JP; *m* 1944, Hon Robert George Hugh Phillimore (d 1984), s of late 2 Baron Phillimore, MC; 4 da; *Style*— The Hon Mrs Robert Phillimore; Brook Cottage, Mill Road, Shiplake, Oxon RG9 3LW

PHILLIPPS, Ian Hugh; s of Dr Frederick Alfred Phillipps, MBE, (d 1975), of Jersey, and Gwendolen Herbert Smith, *née* Smith (d 1980); *b* 15 Nov 1924; *Educ* Winchester, Trinity Coll Cambridge (MA); *m* 14 Oct 1958, Jennifer, da of Capt Harold Freeman Robinson, of Little Hallingbury, Essex; 1 s (Vere b 1961), 2 da (Victoria (Mrs Sargent) b 1959, Christina b 1968); *Career* dir: Humphreys & Glasgow Ltd 1960-67, Radiation Gp Ltd 1967-70, Tube Investmts 1970-81; chm and chief exec Raleigh Industs Ltd Nottingham 1974-81; chm: Wests Gp Int plc 1983-86, The BSS Gp plc 1986-Chamberlain Phipps plc 1982-; cncl chm Soc of Br Gas Industs 1970-72, pres The Bicycle Assoc of GB 1977-79, chm CBI Regnl Cncl E Midlands 1983-84, memb of CVI Grand Cncl 1980-, cncl memb Nottingham Univ 1979-, govr Welbeck Coll MOD 1987-, chm Indust Year E Mids 1986, memb Pay Review Body for Nurses Midwives and the Professions Allied to Medicine 1984-, tres Quorn Hunt 1978-, pres CUBC 1945; FEng 1982, FICE 1950, FIGE 1950; *Recreations* hunting, fishing, brass band playing; *Clubs* Leander, London Rowing; *Style*— Ian Phillipps, Esq; Grange Farm, Rempstone, Loughborough, Leics LE12 6RW (☎ 0509 880071); The BSS Group Plc, Fleet House, Lee Circle, Leicester LE1 3QQ (☎ 0533 23232, telex 342761 BSS G)

PHILLIPS, Adrian Alexander Christian; s of Eric Lawrance Phillips, CMG, of 46 Platts Lane, London, and Phyllis Mary, *née* Bray; *b* 11 Jan 1940; *Educ* The Hall Sch, Westminster, Ch Ch Oxford (MA), UCL (DipTP); *m* 16 Feb 1963, Cassandra Frances Elais, da of David Francis Hubback, CB, of 4 Provost Rd, London; 2 s (Oliver b 1965, Barnaby b 1968); *Career* planning serv Miny of Housing 1962-68, sr res offr then ast dir Countryside Cmmn 1968-74, exec dir then head Programme Co-ordination Univ UN Environment Programme Nairobi 1974-78, programme dir Int Union for Conservation of Nature & Natural Resources Switzerland 1978-81, dir gen Countryside Cmmn 1989- (dir 1981-), dep chm Int Cmmn on Nat Parks and Protected Areas 1988-; MRTPI 1966, RSA 1982, FRGS 1983; *Recreations* walking, stroking the cat; *Clubs* Royal Overseas League; *Style*— Adrian Phillips, Esq; 2 The Old Rectory, Dumbleton, nr Evesham WR11 6TG (☎ 0386 881 973); The Countryside Commission, John Dower House, Crescent Place, Cheltenham GL50 3RA (☎ 0242 521 381, fax 0242 224 962)

PHILLIPS, His Hon Judge (David) Alan Phillips; s of Stephen Thomas Phillips, MC (d 1971), and Elizabeth Mary Phillips, *née* Williams (d 1963); *b* 21 July 1926; *Educ* Llanelli GS, Univ Coll Oxford (MA); *m* 1960, Jean Louise, da of Frederick Edmund Godsell (d 1963); 2 s (Stephen, David); *Career* served WW II 1944-48, Capt GS (Far East), lecturer 1952-59, barr 1960-75; arr Gray's Inn 1960, a rec of the Crown Court 1974, stipendiary magistrate for Mid-Glamorgan 1975-83; Circuit judge Wales and Chester Circuit 1983-; *Recreations* music, computers, swimming; *Style*— His Honour Judge Alan Phillips; The Crown Court, The Castle, Chester CH2 2PA

PHILLIPS, Rev Canon Dr Anthony Charles Julian; s of Arthur Reginald Phillips (d 1965), of Trevelyn, Mawnan Smith, nr Falmouth, Cornwall, and Esmee Mary, *née* Aikman (d 1987); *b* 2 June 1936; *Educ* Kelly Coll Tavistock, King's Coll London (BD, ADC), Gonville and Caius Coll Cambridge (PhD), Coll of the Resurrection Mirfield; *m* 11 April 1970, Victoria Ann, *née* Stainton; 2 s (Christopher b 6 Aug 1971, James b 27 June 1973), 1 da (Lucy b 10 Feb 1975); *Career* curate The Church of the Good Shepherd Cambridge 1966-69, dean chaplain and fell Trinity Hall Cambridge 1969-74, chaplain and fell St John's Coll Oxford 1975-86, headmaster The Kings Sch Canterbury 1986-; memb Soc for Old Testament Study; *Books* Ancient Israel's Criminal Law (1970), Deuteronomy (Cambridge Bible Commentary, 1973), God BC (1977), Lower than the Angels (1983), Israel's Prophetic Tradition (ed, 1982); *Recreations* gardening, beachcombing; *Clubs* Athenaeum; *Style*— The Rev Canon Dr Anthony Phillips; The King's School, Canterbury, Kent CT1 2ES (☎ 0227 475501)

PHILLIPS, Arthur; OBE (1957), JP (Hants); s of Albert William Phillips (d 1955); *b* 29 May 1907; *Educ* Highgate Sch, Trinity Coll Oxford; *m* 1934, Kathleen, da of Thomas Henry Hudson (d 1937); 2 s, 2 da; *Career* Maj, E African Campaign; barr Middle Temple, HM Colonial Service (Kenya) 1931-47, prof of english law Southampton Univ 1956-67, dep vice-chllr 1961-63, dep chm Hants QS 1956-71, a rec 1972-79; chllr Diocese of Winchester 1964-84; *Clubs* Royal Commonwealth Soc; *Style*— Arthur Phillips Esq, OBE, JP; 10 Old Parsonage Ct, Otterbourne, Winchester, Hants (☎ 0962 714945)

PHILLIPS, (William) Bernard; s of Stanley George Phillips (d 1968), of Sutton Coldfield, and Enid Effie, *née* Eades; *b* 26 April 1944; *Educ* Bishop Vesey GS Sutton Coldfield, Hertford Coll Oxford (MA); *m* 1, 13 May 1967 (m dis 1986), Christine Elizabeth, da of Arthur Charles Wilkinson, of Maidstone; 3 s (Andrew b 1968, Simon b 1972, William b 1974); m 2, 1 Aug 1987, Deborah Grace, da of Ellis Green (d 1975), of Sheffield; *Career* schoolmaster 1966-67, lectr 1967-70, called to the Bar Inner Temple 1970, in practice NE circuit 1971-, asst rec 1984-; memb: Inner Temple 1964; *Recreations* cookery, woodwork, collecting books; *Style*— Bernard Phillips, Esq; 25 King Ecgbert Road, Dore, Sheffield (☎ 0742 364682); 12 Paradise Square, Sheffield (☎ 0742 738951, fax 0742 760848)

PHILLIPS, Brian Harold; s of Charles Douglas Phillips (d 1958); *b* 30 August 1930; *Educ* Luton GS; *m* 1952, Margaret June, da of Stanley Archibald Wilkins (d 1977); 1 s, 1 da; *Career* sr local govt financial appts to 1967, finance controller Nationwide Bldg Soc 1967-71, gen mangr (Finance and Mgmnt Servs 1982-85, dir 1985, dep chief gen mangr 1986), dir and dep chief exec Nationwide Anglia Bldg Soc 1987; cncl memb Assoc of Certified Accountants 1985; FCCA, FRSA, IPFA, FBIM; *Style*— Brian Phillips, Esq; Treetops, 17 Silverthorn Drive, Longdean Park, Hemel Hempstead, Herts HP3 8BU

PHILLIPS, Prof Calbert Inglis; s of Rev David Horner Phillips, and Margaret Calbert Phillips; *b* 20 Mar 1925; *Educ* Glasgow HS, Robert Gordon's Coll Aberdeen, Aberdeen Univ Edinburgh (MB, ChB, MD), Edinburgh Univ (DPH), Bristol Univ (PhD), Manchester Univ (MSc); *m* 1962, Christina Anne, *née* Fulton; 1 s; *Career* Lt and Capt RAMC 1947-49; house surgeon: Aberdeen Royal Infirmary 1946-47 (house physician 1951), Aberdeen Maternity Hosp 1949, Glasgow Eye Infirmary 1950-51; asst anatomy dept Glasgow Univ 1951-52, resident and sr registrar St Thomas' Hosp 1953-54, Moorfileds Eye Hosp (and res asst Inst of Ophthalmology 1954-58, conslt surgn Bristol Eye Hosp 1958-63, Alexander Piggott Wernher travelling fell dept of ophthalmology Harvard Univ 1960-61, conslt ophthalmic surgn St Goerge's Hosp 1963-65, prof of ophthalmology Manchester Univ 1965-72, hon conslt ophthalmic to Uts Manchester Hosps 1965-72, prof of ophthalmology Edinburgh Univ 1972-, ophthalmic surgn Royal Infirmary Edinburgh 1972-; Hon FBOA 1975; FRCS 1955, FRSCE 1973; *Books* Clinical Practice and Economics (jt ed, 1977), Basic Clinical Ophthalmology (1984), author of numerous eye related papers for Br and American jls; *Style*— Prof Calbert Phillips; Princess Alexandra Eye Pavilion, Chalmers St, Edinburgh, Lothian EH3 9HA (☎ 031 229 2477)

PHILLIPS, Capt Christmas (Chris); s of Albert Phillips, and Mary Ann, *née* Stephens; *b* 25 Dec 1920; *Educ* Porth Co Sch, Birmingham Centl Tech Coll (BSc); *m* 20 March 1945, Mary, da of Edward Williams, of Mansfield, Notts; 2 s (Christoper b 1949, Ian b 1958), 2 da (Carol b 1949, Anne b 1961); *Career* Capt REME, cmmnd 1943; serv: Syria, Lebanon, Palestine, N Africa, Italy, France, Belgium, Holland, Germany demoblised 1947; jt md Redman Tools Worcester, md John Barnsley Ltd Netherton, dep chm Williams (Hldgs) plc Caerphilly, chm Holdens Bromyard, ret; pres Worcester & Hereford C of C and Indust, chm Mercia Industrialists Assoc, pres Worcester Industrialists Assoc; CEng, FIMechE, FIProdE; *Recreations* mountaineering, swimming; *Style*— Capt Chris Phillips; Severncroft, 95 Park Ave, Worcester NR3 7AQ (☎ 0905 21386)

PHILLIPS, Prof David; s of Stanley Phillips (d 1979), of South Shields, Tyne and Weir, and Daphne Ivy, *née* Harris; *b* 3 Dec 1939; *Educ* South Shields Grammar-Tech Sch, Univ of Birmingham (BSc, PhD); *m* 21 Dec 1970, (Lucy) Caroline, da of Clifford John Scoble, of Plymouth, Devon; 1 da (Sarah Elizabeth b 1975); *Career* Fullbright fell

Univ of Texas Austin USA 1964-66, exchange fell Royal Soc/Acad of Sciences; Univ of Southampton: lectr 1967-73, sr lectr 1973-76, reader 1976-80; The Royal Inst of GB: Wolfson prof of natural philosophy 1980-, actg dir 1986, dep dir 1986-; res scientist in applications of lasers in chemistry biology and medicine, author of 280 scientific papers reveiws and books in this field, various appearences on BBC TV and Radio incl Royal Inst Christmas Lectures for Young People with JM Thomas 1987 and 1988; vice pres and gen sec Br Assoc for the Advancement of Science 1988; FRSC 1976; *Books* Time-correlated single-photon counting (with DV O'Connor), Time-resolved vibrational spectroscopy (with GH Atkinson); *Recreations* music, theatre, popularisation of science; *Clubs* Athenaeum; *Style*— Prof David Phillips; 195 Barnett Wood Lane, Ashtead, Surrey KT21 2LP (☎ 0372 274385); The Royal Institution of Great Britain, 21 Albemarle Street, London W1X 4BS (☎ 01 409 2992, fax 01 629 3569)

PHILLIPS, Prof Sir David Chilton; KBE (1989); s of Charles Harry Phillips (d 1963), of Ellesmere, Shropshire (d 1963) and Edith Harriet, *née* Finney (d 1972), da of Samuel Finney, MP 1916-22; *b* 7 Mar 1924; *Educ* Oswestry Boys' HS, Univ Coll Cardiff (BSc, PhD); *m* 1960, Diana Kathleen, da of Maj Edward Maitland Hutchinson, RA (d 1957), of Chalfont St Giles; 1 da (Sarah); *Career* Sub-Lt RNVR 1944-47, post-doctoral fell Nat Res Cncl of Canada 1951-53, res offr Nat Res Labs Ottawa Canada 1953-55, res worker Royal Instn London 1956-66, prof of molecular biophysics Oxford Univ 1966-, fell CCC Oxford 1966-, biological sec The Royal Soc 1976-83, memb Medical Research Cncl 1974-78, Royal Soc assessor 1976-83, Fullerian prof physiology Royal Instn 1979-83, chm advsy bd res cncls 1983-; dir Celltech Ltd 1982-; Hon DSc: Leicester 1974, Univ of Wales 1975, Chicago 1978, Warwick 1982; Hon DSC Exeter 1982, Hon DUniv Essex 1983; Hon DSc Birmingham 1987; Biochemical Soc CIBA Medal 1971, Royal Soc Royal Medal 1975, Prix Charles Léopold Mayer French Académie des Sciences (jointly 1979), Wolf Prize (jtly 1987); hon memb American Soc Biological Chemists, foreign hon memb American Acad Arts and Sciences; foreign associate, US Nat Acad of Sciences; FInstP, FRS 1967 (vice pres 1972-73 and 1976-83); kt 1979; *Style*— Professor Sir David Phillips, KBE; 3 Fairlawn End, Upper Wolvercote, Oxford OX2 8AR (☎ 0865 55828); Laboratory of Molecular Biophysics, Dept of Zoology, Rex Richards Building, South Parks Road, Oxford OX1 3QU (☎ 0865 275 365)

PHILLIPS, David John; s of Arnold Phillips, and Sylvia Marie Phillips, *née* Mendoza; *b* 5 May 1952; *Educ* William Hulme's GS Manchester, Leeds Univ (LLB); *m* 23 June 1974, Ruth, da of Elias Edelstein; 2 s (Daniel b 1979, Richard b 1981), 1 da (Emma b 1983); *Career* slr (admitted 1978); proprietor: Phillips & Co, Slrs Manchester, Phillips Import Agents; dir Briton Finance Ltd; cncl memb Hale Synagogue; *Recreations* backgammon, bridge, watching Manchester City FC; *Clubs* Valley Lodge Country, Wilmslow; *Style*— David J Phillips, Esq; 8A Talbot Road, Old Trafford, Manchester (☎ 061 872 1458, telex via Prestel 618721458)

PHILLIPS, Prof Dewi Zephaniah; s of David Oakley Phillips (d 1978), of 70 Bath Rd, Morriston, Swansea, and Alice Frances, *née* Davies; *b* 24 Nov 1934; *Educ* Swansea GS, Univ Coll of Swansea (BA, MA), St Catherine's Oxford (BLitt); *m* 2 Sept 1959, (Margaret) Monica, da of Frederick John Hanford (d 1951), of Swansea; 3 s (Aled b 1962, Steffan b 1965, Rhys b 1971); *Career* lectr in philosophy: Queen's Coll Dundee 1964-65 (asst lectr 1963-64), Univ Coll Bangor 1963-65, Univ Coll of Swansea 1965-67 (sr lectr 1967-70, prof 1971-); *Books* The Concept of Prayer (1969), Faith and Philosophical Enquiry (1970), Death and Immortatily (1970), Moral Practices (with H O Mounce, 1970), Sense and Delusion (with Ilham Dilman, 1971), Athroyddo and Grefydd (1974), Religion Without Explanation (1976), Through a Darkening Glass (1982), Dramau Guenlvn Parry (1982), Belief Change and Forms of Life (1986), R S Thomas: Poet of the Hidden God (1986), Faith After Foundationalism (1988); *Recreations* lawn tennis, supporting Swansea City AFC; *Style*— Prof Dewi Phillips; 45 Queen's Rd, Sketty, Swansea (☎ 203 935); Dept of Philosophy, Univ Coll of Swansea, Singleton Park, Swansea (☎ 29 5189)

PHILLIPS, Lt-Col Edward Courtenay; MC (1945), JP (Hereford 1965, DL Hereford 1987); s of Gerald Courtenay Phillips (d 1938), of St Ct, Kingsland, Leominster, Hereford, and Dorothy Phillips (d 1975); *b* 6 June 1922; *Educ* Marlborough; *m* 9 Aug 1947, Anthea Mary, da of Capt R F J Onslow, MVO, DSC, RN, of The Cat and Fiddle, Presteigne, Radnorshire; 2 da (Sarah (Mrs Robert Corbett) b 1948, Harriet (Mrs Peter Cheney) b 1953); *Career* KRRC: joined 1940, cmmnd 1941, Capt 1945, Temporary Maj 1946-54, military attache Kharthoum 1959-61, ret 1961, Co Cmdt ACF Hereford 1970-75; conslt dir Sun Valley Poultry 1987- (joined 1961, chm 1983-87); chm: Herefordshire Co PSD 1987, South Hereford PSD 1988-; chm Hereford Diocesan Appeal 1976-81; High Sheriff Hereford and Worcester 1977-78; *Recreations* field sports, racing; *Clubs* Army and Navy, MCC; *Style*— Lt-Col Edward Phillips, MC, JP, DL; Chase House, Monnington-on-Wye, Hereford HR4 7NL (☎ 098 17 282); Sun Valley Poultry Ltd, Hereford HR4 9PB (☎ 0432 276432)

PHILLIPS, Edward Thomas John (Jack); CBE (1985); s of Edward Emery Kent Phillips (d 1984), and Margaret Elsie, *née* Smith (d 1986); *b* 5 Feb 1930; *Educ* Exmouth GS Devon, UCL (BA), Inst of Educn London Univ (postgraduate Cert Ed), SOAS (Dip Linguistics); *m* 27 Sept 1952, Sheila May, da of Thomas Henry Abbott (d 1978); 2 s (Christopher b 11 Dec 1957, Jonathan b 8 May 1965), 2 da (Nicola b 11 Sept 1960, Deborah b 3 July 1962); *Career* Nat Serv RAF 1948-49; educn offr Colonial Serv Nigeria 1953-62; The British Council: head of centre unit London overseas students dept 1962-65, trg at SOAS 1965-66, english language offr Enugu Nigeria 1966-67, sr lectr dept of educn Lagos Univ Nigeria 1967-70, english language teaching advsr Miny of Educn Nicosia Cyprus 1970-72, chief inspr english teaching div inspectorate 1974-75 (inspr 1972-74), rep Bangladesh 1975-77, dir personnel dept and dep controller personnel and staff recruitment div 1977-80, rep Malaysia 1980-85, controller english language and lit div 1985-; memb IATEEL; *Books* Organised English Books I and II (jt ed 1973); *Recreations* sport, music, theatre; *Style*— Edward Phillips, Esq, CBE; 1 Bredune, Kenley, Surrey; Westcott, Westwood, nr Starcross, Devon; The British Council, 10 Spring Gardens, London SW1A 2NB (☎ 01 389 4090, fax 01 839 6347, telex 8952201 BRICON G)

PHILLIPS, Edwin William; MBE (1946); s of Charles Edwin Phillips (d 1979), of Chiswick; *b* 29 Jan 1918; *Educ* Latymer Upper Sch; *m* 1951, Pauline Mary Matusch; 2 s; *Career* dir Lazard Bros & Co Ltd 1960-, chm Lazards Property Unit Trusts Ctee to 1983; dir: BR Property Bd 1970, Phoenix Assurance 1975, Woolwich Equitable Building Soc 1977; chm Friends Provident Life Office 1968-, Higgs and Hill 1975-; *Style*— Edwin Phillips Esq, MBE; Send Barns, Send, Surrey (☎ 0483 223305)

PHILLIPS, Eric Lawrance; CMG (1963); s of L Stanley Phillips and Maudie *née* Elkan; *b* 23 July 1909; *Educ* Haileybury Coll, Balliol Coll Oxford; *m* 1938, Phyllis Bray; 2 s, 1 step-da; *Career* under-sec BOT 1964-69, sec Monopolies Cmmn 1969-74, conslt to Monopolies and Mergers Cmmn 1974-75; chm Abbeyfield West London Soc 1980-86; *Clubs* RAC; *Style*— Eric Phillips, Esq, CMG; 46 Platts Lane, London NW3 (☎ 01 435 7873)

PHILLIPS, Sir Fred Albert; CVO (1966); s of Wilbert A Phillips, of Brighton, St Vincent; *b* 14 May 1918; *Educ* London Univ (LLB), Toronto Univ, McGill Univ (MCL); *Career* barr Middle Temple; cabinet cec West Indies Fedn 1958-62, govr St Kitts, Nevis & Anguilla 1967-69; sr legal advsr Cable & Wireless 1969-; dir: Trinidad External Telecommunications 1970-, Jamaica External Communications 1971- Barbados external telecommunications, Barbados Telephone Co, Telecommunications of Jamaica, Jamaica telephone Co, Granada Telecommunicatoins Ltd, Offshore Keyboarding Corpn; KSt J 1968; kt 1967; *Recreations* writing; *Style*— Sir Fred Phillips, CVO; P O Box 206, Bridgetown, Barbados (☎ 42 90448/42 90427)

PHILLIPS, Mrs Harold (Georgina); *née* Wernher; er da of Maj-Gen Sir Harold Augustus Wernher, 3 and last Bt, GCVO, TD (d 1973), and Lady Zia Wernher, CBE, *née* Countess Anastasia de Torby (d 1977), da of HIH Grand Duke Mikhail Mikhailovitch of Russia; *b* 17 Oct 1919; *m* 10 Oct 1944, Lt-Col Harold Pedro Joseph Phillips, Coldstream Gds (d 1980), 2 s of Col Joseph Harold John Phillips (d 1953), of Broome Cottage, Sunningdale, Berks; 1 s (Nicholas Harold b 1947), 4 da (Alexandra Anastasia (Duchess of Abercorn) b 1946, Fiona Mercedes (Mrs Burnett of Leys) b 1951, Marita Georgina (Mrs Randall Crawley) b 1954, Natalia Ayesha (Duchess of Westminster) b 1959); *Career* ch pres St John Ambulance; DGStJ (1987); *Recreations* racing; *Style*— Mrs Harold Phillips; 13 Burton Court, Franklins Row, London SW3; Ardhuncart Lodge, Alford, Aberdeenshire

PHILLIPS, (Gerald) Hayden; s of Gerald Phillips, of 30 Rydal Drive, Tunbridge Wells, and Dorothy Florence *née* Joyner; *b* 9 Feb 1943; *Educ* Cambridgeshire HS Clare Coll Cambridge (MA) Yale USA (MA); *m* 1, 23 Sept 1967, Dr Ann Watkins, da of Prof S B Watkins (d 1966); 1 s (Alexander b 1970); 1 da (Rachel b 1974); m 2, 11 July 1980, The Hon Laura Grenfell, da of 2 Baron St Just, of Wilbury House, Newton Tony, Wilts (d 1984); 1 s (Thomas Peter b 1987), 2 da (Florence b 1981, Louisa Henrietta b 1984); *Career* princ private sec to Home Sec 1974-76, dep chef de Cabinet to Pres the Euro Communities 1977-79, asst sec Home Off 1979-81, under sec of state Home Off 1981-86, dep under sec of state Cabinet Off 1986-88, dep sec HM Treasy 1988; *Clubs* Brooks's; *Style*— Hayden Phillips, Esq; HM Treasury, Parliament St, London SW1 (☎ 01 270 4390)

PHILLIPS, Lady; Hazel Bradbury; JP (1961); only da of Thomas John Evans, OBE, (d 1972), of Stavros, Cyncoed Crescent, Cardiff, and Elsie Rosina Evans, *née* Bradbury (d 1985); *b* 26 Nov 1924; *Educ* Howell's Sch Llandaff, Roedean, King's Coll London (LLB); *m* 8 Aug 1951, Sir (John) Raymond Phillips, MC (Hon Mr Justice Phillips, d 1982), s of Rupert Phillips, JP (d 1952), of The Greenway, Radyr, nr Cardiff; 2 s (David b 4 May 1953, Richard b 26 April 1955); *Career* barr Inner Temple 1948, memb Wales and Chester Circuit, lawyer memb London Rent Assessment Panel 1966- (vice pres 1972, pres 1973-79), memb Parole Bd 1979-82, chm Richmond upon Thames PSD 1985-88; *Recreations* walking, reading, gardening; *Clubs* Utd Oxford & Cambridge; *Style*— Lady Phillips, JP; The Elms, Park Rd, Teddington, Middx TW11 0AQ (☎ 01 977 1584)

PHILLIPS, Capt Hedley Joyce; OBE (1980), QPM 1972, DL Hants 1987); s of Francis Hedley Joyce Phillips (d 1928), and Constance Daisy, *née* Bigg (d 1986); *b* 12 Mar 1925; *Educ* Aldworth's Hosp (Reading Blue Coat Sch); *m* 22 March 1947, Brenda Marjorie, da of Herbert Walter Horner (d 1968); 1 s (Michael Hedley Joyce Phillips b 1948); *Career* WWII serv: enlisted RM 1942, cmmnd 1944, 48 RM Commando NW Europe 1944-45, 44 RM Commando SE Asia 1945-46, demobbed with rank of Capt 1946; cmmnd RM Forces Vol Res 1948, ret Capt 1953; Berks Constabulary 1946-64, asst chief constable Hants Constabulary 1964-67 (dep chief constable 1967-83), ret 1983; chm: Winchester & Dist VSO Ctee 1965-70, S Region Royal Life Saving Soc 1980-; tres Southampton Traveller's Aid 1972-80; *Recreations* golf, swimming, chess, military history; *Clubs* Naval & Military, Bramshaw Golf; *Style*— Capt Hedley Phillips, OBE, QPM, DL

PHILLIPS, Sir Henry Ellis Isidore; CMG (1960), MBE (Mil 1946); s of Harry Joseph Phillips, MBE (d 1961), and Rachel Love Trachtenberg (d 1961); *b* 30 August 1914; *Educ* Haberdashers' Sch Hampstead, UCL (MA), Inst of Historical Res; *m* 1, 1941 (m dis 1965), Vivien, da of Albert M Hyamson, OBE (d 1954); 2 s, 1 da; m 2, 1966, Philippa, da of Michael Cohen (d 1965); *Career* cmmnd Beds and Herts Regt 1939, Capt and Adj 5 Bn, (POW Singapore 1942-45); Colonial Admin Serv 1946: devpt sec Nyasaland 1952, seconded to federal treasy Rhodesia and Nyasaland 1953-57 (dep sec 1956-57); fin sec Nyasaland Govt 1957-64, min of finance Nyasaland 1961-64; md Standard Bank Fin and Devpt Corpn 1966-72, dir SIFIDA Investmt Co SA 1970-;chm: Assured Property Tst plc 1988- chm Ashley Industl Tst 1986-88; advsr Air Tport Users Ctee 1981-; bd memb: Civil Aviation Authy 1975-80, Nat Bank of Malawi 1983-88; vice chm Stonham Housing Assoc, hon tres Stonham Meml Tst 1977- hon tres SOS Sahel Int Britian 1987-, memb fin ctee UCL 1986-; kt 1964; *Clubs* MCC, Royal Cwlth; *Style*— Sir Henry Phillips, CMG, MBE; 34 Ross Ct, Putney Hill, London SW15 (☎ 01 789 1404); c/o Standard Chartered Bank, London EC4 (☎ 01 280 7500)

PHILLIPS, Herbert Moore; CMG (1949); s of Herbert Charles Phillips; *b* 7 Feb 1908; *Educ* St Olave's, Wadham Coll Oxford; *m* 1, 1934, Martha (decd), da of Karl Loffler, of Graz, Austria; 1 da; m 2, 1952, Doris Rushbrooke; *Career* asst sec Miny of Lab 1942, cnsllr for economic and social affrs to Perm UK Delegation to UN 1946-49, memb of UK delegation to various int organisations; consultant to: OECD, UNESCO, UN, UNICEF, World Bank, Ford and Rockefeller Fndns; *Books* Literacy and Development (1970), Basic Education, a World Challenge (1975), Educational Cooperation between Developed and Developing Countries (1976); *Clubs* United Oxford and Cambridge Univ; *Style*— Herbert Phillips, Esq, CMG; 9 rue de Mézières, 75006 Paris, France (☎ 5480944) Haneau du Plan, Plan de la Tour, France 83120 (☎ 94437802)

PHILLIPS, Sir Horace; KCMG (1973), CMG (1963); s of Samuel Phillips; *b* 31 May 1917; *Educ* Hillhead HS Glasgow; *m* 1944, Idina Doreen Morgan; 1 s, 1 da; *Career* Br later Indian Army (Maj) 1940-47; entered Dip Serv 1947; ambass to Indonesia 1966-68, high cmmr in Tanzania 1968-72, ambass to Turkey 1973-77; resident rep Taylor Woodrow Int Ltd: Iran 1978-79, Hong Kong 1979-83, Bahrain 1983-84, China (at

Peking) 1985-87; visiting lectr in diplomacy at Bilkent Univ Ankara (Turkey) 1988-; Hon LLD Glasgow 1977; Order of the Taj (Iran) 1961; *Recreations* languages, long distance car driving; *Clubs* Travellers'; Hong Kong; *Style*— Sir Horace Phillips, KCMG,CMG; 34a Sheridan Rd, Merton Park, London SW19 3HP (☎ 01 542 3836)

PHILLIPS, Ian; s of Wilfrid Phillips (d1976), and Dorothy McLellan, *née* Taylor (d 1963); *b* 16 July 1938; *Educ* Whitgift Sch Croydon; *m* 21 Oct 1961, Fay Rosemary, da of George Sharpe Stoner (d 1986); 2 s (Jonathan Peter b 13 April 1964, Simon James b 3 Sept 1966); *Career* bd memb (fin) London Tport Exec 1980-84, dir fin and planning BR Bd 1985-88, dir fin BBC 1988-; FCA; *Recreations* golf; *Style*— Ian Phillips; 113 Lower Camden, Chislehurst, Kent BR7 5JD (☎ 01 467 0529); Bakers Cottage, Church Rd, Quenington, Cirencester, Glos; BBC, Broadcasting House, London W1A 1AA (☎ 01 927 4312, fax 01 580 9455, telex 265781); car ☎ 0860 748109

PHILLIPS, Prof Ian; s of Stanley Phillips (d 1942), of Whitworth, Lancashire, and Emma, *née* Price (d 1960); *b* 10 April 1936; *Educ* Bacup and Rawtenstall GS, St John's Coll Cambridge (MA, MD), St Thomas's Hosp Med Sch; *Career* prof med microbiology Utd Med and Dent Schs of Guy's and St Thomas's Hosps, hon conslt microbiologist St Thomas's Hosp, civil conslt microbiology RAF 1979-; memb cncl Royal Coll of Pathologists 1974-76 and 1987-90, chm dist med team St Thomas's Hosp 1978-79, chm Br Soc for Antimicrobial Chemotherapy 1979-82, memb Veterianry Products Ctee 1981-85, chm elect Assoc of Med Microbiologists 1989; memb S London Botanical Inst; Freeman City of London 1975, Liveryman Worshipful Soc of Apothecaries; FRCP, FRCPath; *Books* Laboratory Methods in Antimicrobial Chemotherapy (ed with D S Reeves, J D Williams and R Wise, 1978), Microbial Disease (with D A J Tyrell, GS Goodwin and R Blowers, 1979); *Clubs* Royal Soc of Med; *Style*— Prof Ian Phillips; Dept of Microbiology, St Thomas's Hospital, Lambeth Palace Rd, London SE1 7EH (☎ 01 928 9292)

PHILLIPS, John; s of John Tudor Phillips (d 1981), of Finchley, London N12, and Bessie Maud, *née* Cork; *b* 25 Nov 1926; *Educ* Christ's Coll Finchley, Northern Poly Holloway; *m* 24 Sept 1955, Eileen Margaret, da of Lt Col Robert Fryer (d 1946), of Finchley; *Career* Nat Serv 1945-48, cmmnd 2 Lt RE 1947; studied under Romilly B Craze Architect 1948-52; surveyor to the fabric: Truro Cathedral 1960-79 (conslt architect 1979-), Westminster Cathedral 1976-; RIBA 1979-; conslt architect Brisbane Cathedral 1988-; pres Ecclesiastical Architects' and Surveyors' Assoc 1982; chm Christian Enterprise Housing Assoc 1964-82; RIBA 1954; *Recreations* steeple crawling, choral singing; *Style*— John Phillips, Esq; 8 Friary Way, N Finchley, London N12 9PH (☎ 01 445 3414); 55 Britton St, London EC1M 5NA (☎ 01 253 4340, fax 01 253 3707)

PHILLIPS, John Christopher; s of James Stacey Phillips (d 1980), of Torquay, Devon, and Emma, *née* England (d 1976); *b* 26 June 1935; *Educ* Sherborne; *m* 19 April 1969, Judith Ann, da of Thomas Ronald Biggart, MBE, TD; 2 s (David b 1972, Mark b 1974); *Career* fin dir Tarmac Bricks & Tiles Ltd (formerly Westbrick Ltd) 1979, cmmr Income Tax, chm Exeter and East Devon Local Employer Network, pres South Western Soc of Chartered Accountants 1985-86; FLA 1958; *Recreations* golf, sailing, gardening; *Style*— John Phillips, Esq; Willowgarth, Sunhill Lane, Topsham, Exeter (☎ 0392 873 828); Tarmac Bricks & Tiles Ltd, Pinhoe, Exeter (☎ 0392 66 749)

PHILLIPS, John Douglas Parnham; s of Maj Douglas Middleton Parnham Phillips, (d 1958), and Sheila Esme, *née* Wilkinson; *b* 3 May 1934; *Educ* Harrow, Pembroke Coll Cambridge (BA, MA); *m* 30 March 1968, Diana Phyllis Frances, da of John Stratton, of Badger Hill, York; 2 s (Douglas Hugh Parnham b 27 March 1970, Alexander Patrick Middleton b 31 Jan 1972); *Career* conslt in wildlife mgmnt concerned with uplands - Europe; MIBiol 1988; *Recreations* field sports, countryside, dogtraining; *Style*— John Phillips, Esq; Eccles House, Thornhill, Dumfrieshire, DG3 4LU (☎ 0848 31480)

PHILLIPS, John Edward; s of Stanley Edward Phillips (d 1987), of London, and Elsie Evelyn Ruth, *née* Wilson; *b* 12 May 1938; *Educ* Haileybury ISC; *m* 29 Dec 1967, Mary Isabelle, da of Colin Bootra-Taylor; 1 s (Michael John b May 1972, d 16 Oct 1980), 1 da (Sarah Jane b 14 Sept 1969); *Career* Trade Indemnity plc: joined 1961, mangr Aust 1969-73, dep gen mangr UK 1973-78, gen mangr and dir 1978- (amended dir and chief gen mangr 1987); dir: Gen Surety & Guarantee Co Ltd, Trade Indemnity Aust Ltd, Trade Indemnity Heller Ltd; pres Int Credit Insur Assoc 1986-88; memb bd mgmnt Nat head Injuries Assoc (Headway), tstee Old Haileyburians RFC; Freeman City of London 1980, memb ct assts Worshipful Co of Insurers; FBIM, fell Inst of Credit Mgmnt, memb IOD 1987; *Recreations* tennis, golf; *Clubs* MCC, Worplesdon GC, Royal Melbourne GC, Athenaum Melbourne; *Style*— John Phillips, Esq; Trade Indemnity plc, Trade Indemnity House, 12-34 Great Eastern St, London EC2A 3AX (☎ 01 739 4311, fax 01 739 4397, telex 21227)

PHILLIPS, John Fleetwood Stewart; CMG (1965); s of late Maj Herbert Stewart Phillips and Violet, da of Sir Alexander Pinhey, KCSI, and of Violet, da of Sir Henry Gordon, KCB, eldest bro of Gen Charles Gordon of Khartoum; kinsman of Earls of Galloway; *b* 16 Dec 1917; *Educ* Brighton, Worcester Coll Oxford; *m* 1948, Mary Gordon Shaw, MB, BS; 2 s, 2 da; *Career* serv Argyll and Sutherland Highlanders 1940-45 (wounded and captured 1941); Sudan Political Serv 1945-54; Dip Serv 1955-77; ambass to: S Yemen 1969-70, Jordan 1970-72, Sudan 1973-77, ret; *Clubs* Travellers'; *Style*— John Phillips, Esq, CMG; Southwood, Gordon Rd, Horsham, Sussex RH12 2EF (☎ 0403 52894)

PHILLIPS, John Francis; CBE (1977, OBE 1957), QC (1981); s of late F W Phillips; *b* 1911; *Educ* Cardinal Vaughan Sch, London Univ, Trinity Hall Cambridge (LLB, LLM); *m* 1937, Olive M Royer; 1 s, 2 da; *Career* arbitrator; barr Gray's Inn 1944; chm London Ct of Int Arbitration 1985-; pres (formerly chm) Private Patients Plan 1977-, dep chm Eggs Authority 1971-80; DCL 1985, OStJ 1985; *Clubs* Athenaeum, Oxford and Cambridge; *Style*— John Phillips, Esq, CBE, QC; 17 Ossulton Way, Hampstead Gdn Suburb, London N2 0DT (☎ 01 455 8460)

PHILLIPS, Sir John Grant; KBE (1972, CBE 1968); s of Oswald Phillips, of Sydney; *b* 13 Mar 1911; *Educ* C of E GS Sydney, Sydney Univ (BEc); *m* 1935, Mary W Debenham; 2 s, 2 da; *Career* govr and chm of Bd Reserve Bank of Australia 1968-75, dir Lend Lease Corpn Ltd 1976-81 (ret), chm Aust Stats Adv Council 1976-81; *Style*— Sir John Phillips, KBE; 2/25 Marshall St, Manly, NSW 2095, Australia

PHILLIPS, Lady Katharine (Mary); *née* Fitz-Alan-Howard; da of 15 Duke of Norfolk, KG, PC, CVO (d 1917); *b* 1912; *m* 1940, Lt-Col Joseph Anthony Moore Phillips, DSO, MBE, DL; 1 s (Anthony Bernard Moore Phillips b 1953); *Career* Order of Mercy; *Clubs* Royal Corinthian Yacht, Burnham on Crouch, Royal Thames YC London; *Style*— Lady Katharine Phillips; Lund House, Lund, Driffield, East Yorks

PHILLIPS, Hon Mrs; Hon Laura Claire; *née* Grenfell; da of 2 and last Baron St Just (d 1984) and his 1 w Leslie, da of Condé Nast; *b* 17 July 1950; *Educ* London Univ (BA); *m* 1980, Hayden Phillips, *qv*; 1 s (Thomas Peter b 1987), 2 da (Florence b 1981, Louisa Henrietta b 1984); *Career* with Private Office of Rt Hon Lord Jenkins of Hillhead Brussels Euro Cmmn 1977-79, dir Becket Pubns (Beckets Directory of the City of London); *Style*— The Hon Mrs Phillips

PHILLIPS, Hon Mrs (Margaret Askew Alexander); da of 2 Baron Harmsworth; *b* 31 Oct 1928; *m* 1, Wendell Holmes McCulloch; 2 s; m 2, 1960, Frank Gibson Phillips, s of late Henry Gibson Phillips, of Windmill Hill, Alton, Hants; *Style*— The Hon Mrs Phillips

PHILLIPS, Dr Marisa; da of Dr Joseph Fargion (d 1963), of Rome, and Bice, *née* Sacerdoti (d 1963); *b* 14 April 1932; *Educ* Henrietta Barnett Sch Rome Univ (PhD), Redlands Univ USA; *m* 1 Dec 1956, Philip Harold; 1 s (Adrian Brune 21 July 1963), 2 da (Suzanne Julia 29 June 1959); *Career* US Info Serv 1957-59, Penguin Books, sr legal asst dir Public Prosecutions 1970-77 (legal asst 1964-70), legal advsr Police Complaints Bd 1977-81, princ asst dir Public Prosecutions 1984-87 (asst dir 1981-), dir of legal Servs in Crown Prosecution Serv; memb: NSPCC, Anglo-Italian Soc; memb Hon Soc Lincoln's Inn; *Recreations* music, travel, theatre; *Style*— Dr Marisa Phillips; Dame Court, Kidderport Avenue, Hampstead, London NW3; Les Galeb D'Or, Ville Prauche-sur-Mer, Cote D'Azur, France; Crown Prosecution Service, 4-12 Queen Anne's Gate, London SW1

PHILLIPS, Capt Mark Anthony Peter; CVO (1974), ADC(P); s of Maj Peter William Garside Phillips, MC, late 1 King's Drag Gds, and Anne Patricia, *née* Tiarks; *b* 22 Sept 1948; *Educ* Marlborough, RMA Sandhurst; *m* 1973, HRH The Princess Royal (*see* Royal Family section); 1 s (Peter b 15 Nov 1977), 1 da (Zara b 15 May 1981); *Career* 1 The Queen's Dragoon Gds 1969, Regtl Duty 1969-74, co instr RMA Sandhurst 1974-77, Army Trg Directorate MOD 1977-78, ret; student RAC Cirencester 1978-79; personal ADC to HM The Queen 1974-; in Three Day Equestrian Event, GB winning teams; team championships: World 1970, European 1971, Olympic Gold Medallists (Team) Olympic Games Munich 1972, memb Equestrian Team (Reserve) Olympic Games Mexico 1968 and Montreal 1976, dir Gleneagles Mark Phillips Equestrian Centre 1988-, second person ever to win Badminton Horse Trials four times; chm Glos Assoc Youth Clubs; memb Royal Caledonian Hunt; patron: Everyman theatre, Cheltenham, British Assoc of Fitness Promotion Agencies; farmer; Liveryman, Worshipful Co of Farriers', Farmers', Saddlers', Loriners'; Freeman Worshipful Co of Carmen, Freeman City of London; *Clubs* Buck's (hon memb); *Style*— Captain Mark Phillips, CVO, ADC(P); Gatcombe Park, Minchinhampton, Stroud, Glos

PHILLIPS, Max; *b* 31 Mar 1924; *Educ* Colston's Sch Bristol, Christ's Hosp, Magdalene Coll Cambridge (MA); *m* 1953, Patrica, da of Cecil Moore (decd); 2 s (Nicholas b 1953, James b 1962), 2 da (Alison b 1955, Gillian b 1959); *Career* WWII RA 1943-46; asst princ, Colonial Off 1949-53, princ, Colonial Off 1953-59, sec Nigeria Fiscal Cmmn 1957-58, UKAEA: Overseas Relations Branch 1959-61, Health and Safety Branch 1961-64, Economics and Programming Branch 1964-69 (dep head 1967-69); chief personnel offr AWRE Aldermaston 1969-74, asst sec HM Treasy 1974-77, asst under sec State MOD 1977-84, sec AWRE 1984-87; Govnr and Almoner of Christ's Hosp; *Recreations* walking, swimming, travel; *Style*— Max Phillips, Esq; 2 Wilderness Farm, Onslow Village, Guildford, Surrey

PHILLIPS, Michael David; s of Frank Philips, and Cynthia Margaret, *née* Bond; *b* 22 June 1955; *Educ* Rickmansworth GS, Bath Univ (BSc), PCL (DipArch), RIBA; *m* 23 Aug 1986, Jane Louise; *Career* architect - DeVerre Urban Design Prize PCL 1981; Casson Conder 1974, Ralph Erskine 1975, Moxley Jenner 1978, Powell Moya 1978-79, Hutchison Locke & Monk 1981-85; ptnr Michael Phillips Assocs 1985-; prize winner IBA Internat Soc Housing Competition Berlin; *Style*— Michael Phillips, Esq; 286 Upper Richmond Road, Putney, London SW15 6TH (☎ 01 789 4063)

PHILLIPS, Michael George; s of Walter George Phillips (d 1958); *b* 31 Oct 1931; *Educ* Steyning GS; *m* 1957, Elizabeth Ann, da of Harold Stanley Batten (d 1959); 1 da; *Career* chm and md UBM Group Ltd 1975-82, dep chm MK Electric Group 1976-88; *Style*— Michael Phillips, Esq; Maysmead Place, Langford, nr Bristol BS18 7HX (☎ 0934 862343)

PHILLIPS, Michael Lothian Elliott; s of Cdre Joseph Allan Phillips, RN (d 1985), of the old Forge, West Mean, nr Petersfield, Hants, and Pansy Myra Edith, *née* Bonham Carter; *b* 30 Jan 1940; *Educ* Westbury House, Winchester ; *m* 6 Dec 1975, Sarah Lindsay, da of James Palmer Tomkinson (d 1953); 2 s (Patrick James Elliott b 8 June 1980, David William b 11 Nov 1984), 1 da (Rebecca Jane b 7 Feb 1979); *Career* Short Serv Cmmn with KRRC, later 2 Greenjackets Lt 1958-61; Warren hill Sporting Life 1962-65, racing corr The Times 1965-84 (Mandarin 1984-); *Recreations* gardening, tennis, skiing, shooting; *Clubs* Jockey Club Rooms; *Style*— Michael Phillips, Esq; Barndown House, Shefford Woodland, Nr Newbury, Berks RG16 7AE (☎ 048839 260); C/O The Times - Racing Desk, PO Box 481, Virgina Street, London E1 9BD

PHILLIPS, Hon Morgan David; s of Baroness Phillips; *b* 1939; *Educ* St Paul's, Downing Coll Cambridge, London U; *Style*— The Hon Morgan Phillips

PHILLIPS, Prof Neville Crompton; CMG (1973); 2 s of Samuel and Clara Phillips, of Christchurch, NZ; *b* 7 Mar 1916; *Educ* Dannevirke HS, Palmerston North Boys' HS, Canterbury Univ Coll NZ, Merton Coll Oxford; *m* 1940, Pauline Beatrice, 3 da of Selby Palmer, of Havelock North, NZ; 1 s, 2 da; *Career* served RA 1939-45, Maj, N Africa, Italy (despatches); prof of history Univ of Canterbury (Christchurch, NZ) 1949-66, vice-chllr and rector 1966-77, prof emeritus 1966, ret; chm Mgmnt Ctee Canterbury Archaeological Tst 1980-83; Hon LittD Univ of Canterbury NZ 1977; presented with Festschrift 1984; *Books* Italy, vol I (Sangro to Cassino), NZ Official War Histories (1957), History of University of Canterbury (ed & contrib 1973), Yorkshire and English National Politics 1783-84 (1961); *Style*— Professor Neville Phillips, CMG; Tyle House, Hackington Rd, Tyler Hill, Canterbury, Kent CT2 9NF (☎ 0227 471708)

PHILLIPS, Hon Mr Justice; Sir Nicholas Addison; QC (1978); *b* 21 Jan 1938; *Educ* Bryanston Sch, King's Cambridge; *m* 1972, Christylle Marie-Thérèse Rouffiac, nee Doreau; 2 da, and 1 step s, 1 step da; *Career* RNVR 1956-58; barr Middle Temple 1962, jr counsel to MOD and to Treasy in Admty matters 1973-78, govr Bryanston Sch 1975- (chm 1981), rec Crown Ct 1982-, judge of High Ct, Queen's Bench Divn 1987-; kt 1987; *Style*— The Hon Mr Justice Phillips; The Royal Courts of Justice, Strand, London WC2

PHILLIPS, Baroness (Life Peer UK 1964); Norah Phillips; JP (Co of London); da of William and Catherine Lusher, of Fulham; *b* 1910; *Educ* Marist Convent, Hampton Trg Coll; *m* 1930, Morgan Phillips (d 1963; sometime Gen Sec Labour Pty); 1 s, 1 da; *Career* sits as Labour Peer in House of Lords; a baroness-in-waiting (Govt whip) 1965-70; dir Assoc for the Prevention of Theft in Shops; pres: Nat Assoc of Women's Clubs, Inst of Shops Health and Safety Acts Admin, Assoc for Res into Restricted Growth, Keep Fit Assoc, Industl Catering Assoc, Int Professional Security Assoc, Small Appliance Mktg Assoc, Pre-Retirement Assoc; vice pres: Nat Chamber of Trade, Greater London Home Safety, Fair Play for Children; HM Lord-Lt of Greater London 1978-85; *Style*— The Rt Hon the Baroness Phillips, JP; 115 Rannoch Rd, London W6

PHILLIPS, (Jeremy) Patrick Manfred; QC (1980); s of Manfred Henry Phillips (d 1963), and Irene Margaret, *née* Symondson (d 1970);; *b* 27 Feb 1941; *Educ* Charterhouse; *m* 1970, Virginia Gwendolyn Dwyer; 2 s (Rufus b 1969, Marcus b 1970); 1976, Judith Gaskell Hetherington; 2 s (Tobias b 1982, Seamus b 1985), 2 da (Rebekah b 1979, Natasha b 1980); *Career* barr 1964; owner of Kentwell Hall; contributor to successive editions of Coopers Manual of Auditing and Coopers Students Manual of Auditing; deviser and originator of Kentwell Hall's Annual Re-Creation of Tudor Domestic Life 1978-; landowner (130 acres), dir Care Br (pt of Care Int (the Third World devpt agency)); *Books* author of various articles and pamphlets on Kentwell Hall Tudor Domestic Life and Heritage Educn; *Recreations* Kentwell Hall, Tudor bldgs, Tudor domestic life; *Style*— Patrick Phillips, Esq, QC; Kentwell Hall, Long Melford, Suffolk; 2 Temple Gardens, London EC4

PHILLIPS, Percy; s of Harry Phillips (d 1963); *b* 1 May 1900; *Educ* Grove Park County Sch Wrexham; *m* 1924, Gertrude, nee Nelken; 2 children; *Career* certified accountant and chartered sec, co dir; *Recreations* reading, bridge; *Style*— Percy Phillips Esq; Bracken Knoll, Courtenay Av, N6

PHILLIPS, (Ian) Peter; JP (Inner London); s of Bernard Phillips, of 7 South Drive, Ferring-on-Sea, Sussex, and Constance Mary Clayton (d 1984); *b* 13 Oct 1944; *Educ* Highgate Sch London, Sorbonne; *m* 2 May 1970, Wendy, da of Maurice Samuel Berne, of London NW11; 1 s (Leo b 1972), 1 da (Kira b 1974); *Career* ptnr Bernard Phillips & Co London 1968-82, ptnr Arthur Andersen & Co 1982-88, UK head corporate recovery services Arthur Andersen 1982-88, sr ptnr Buchler Phillips 1988-; tres North Kensington Neighbourhood Law Centre 1972, pres Insolvency Practitioners Assoc 1988-89; FCA 1968, FIPA 1981, FCCA 1983, MICM 1974; *Recreations* horse riding, skiing, modern jazz, baroque music, photography; *Style*— Peter Phillips, Esq, JP; Buchler Phillips, 43/44 Albermarle St, W1X 3FE (☎ 01 493 2550, fax 01 629 6444)

PHILLIPS, Peter John; s of Walter Alfred Phillips (d 1972), of Cardiff, and Victoria Mary Phillips (d 1974); *b* 18 June 1930; *Educ* Radley, Pembroke Coll Oxford (MA); *m* 9 June 1956, Jean Gwendoline, da of Sydney Essex Williams of Cardiff; 1 s (Jeremy Essex b 30 May 1957), 1 da (Louise Victoria b 7 May 1960); *Career* Nat Serv 2 Lt Welch Regt 1948-49; md Aberthaw & Bristol Channel Portland Cement plc 1964-83, chm AB Electronic Prods Gp plc 1987-, dep chm Principality Bldg Soc 1988, bd memb South Wales Electricity, chm CBI Wales 1982-83 (cncl memb); chm Welsh Indust Devpt Advsy Bd, cncl memb Univ of Wales Coll of Cardiff; *Recreations* fishing, walking, reading; *Clubs* Cardiff & County; *Style*— Peter Phillips, Esq, OBE; Beverley Lisvane Rd, Llanishen, Cardiff CF4 5SB (☎ 0222 762 078); AB Electronic Prods Gp plc, Abergynon, Mid Glam CF45 4SF (☎ 0443 740 331, fax 0443 741 676, telex 498606)

PHILLIPS, Surgeon Rear-Adm Rex Philip; CB (1972), OBE (1963); s of William John Phillips; *b* 17 May 1913; *Educ* Epsom Coll, Coll of Med Newcastle upon Tyne, Durham Univ; *m* 1939, Gill Foley; 2 s; *Career* MO i/c, RN Hosp Plymouth 1969-72; QHS 1969-72, CStJ 1970; *Style*— Surgn Rear-Adm Rex Phillips, CB, OBE; Langstone House, 25 Langstone High Street, Havant, Hants PO9 1RY (☎ 0705 484668)

PHILLIPS, Sir Robin Francis; 3 Bt (UK 1912); s of Sir Lionel Francis Phillips, 2 Bt (d 1944); *b* 29 July 1940; *Educ* Aiglon Coll Switzerland; *Heir* none; *Style*— Sir Robin Phillips, Bt; 12 Manson Mews, Queen's Gate, SW7

PHILLIPS, Sian (Mrs Robin Sachs); da of David Thomas Phillips (d 1961), and Sally Thomas (d 1985); *Educ* Pontardawe GS, Cardiff Coll Univ of Wales (BA), RADA (Meggie Albanesi Scholarship, Bancroft Gold Medal); *m* 1 1959 (m dis 1979), Peter O'Toole,*qv* ; 2 da (Kate b 1961, Pat b 1964); m 2 24 Dec 1979, Robin David, s of Leonard Sachs; *Career* actress; BBC News reader/announcer Wales 1953-55; London prodns incl: Hedda Gabler 1959, Ondine, Duchess of Malfi 1966, Lizard on the Rock 1961, Gentle Jack 1963, Maxibules 1964, Night of the Iguana 1964 (best actress nomination), Ride a Cock Horse 1965, Man and Superman (best actress nomination), Man of Destiny 1966, The Burglar 1967, Epitaph for George Dillon 1972, A Nightingale in Bloomsbury Square 1973, The Gay Lord Quex 1975, Spinechiller 1978, You Never Can Tell 1979, Pal Joey 1979-80, Dear Liar 1982, Major Barbara (NT) 1983, Peg 1984, Gigi 1985, Thursday's Ladies, Brel 1987; TV drama series incl: Shoulder to Shoulder, How Green was my Valley (BAFTA Best Actress Award), Crime and Punishment, Tinker Tailor Soldier Spy, Barriers, The Oresteiaa of Aescylus, I Claudius (BAFTA Best Actress Award and Best Performance Royal TV Soc); *Films*: Becket 1963, Goodby Mr Chips 1968, Murphy's War 1970, Under Milk Wood 1971, Dune 1984, Valmont 1989; Welsh Arts Cncl, BBC Rep Co, ITV, BBC; former memb Drama Ctee Arts Cncl 1970-75, former govr St David's Theatre Tst; hon Dlitt Univ of Wales 1983; memb Gorsedd of Bards 1960; hon fell: Cardiff Coll Univ of Wales 1980, Polytechnic of Wales 1988; *Books* Sian Phillips' Needlepoint (1987); *Recreations* gardening, drawing, needlepoint; *Style*— Miss Sian Phillips; Saraband Ltd, 265 Liverpool Rd, London N1 (☎ 01 609 5313)

PHILLIPS, Dr Simon Jeremy; s of Basil Montagu Phillips, MVO, MRCS, LRCP, DA, of Astley Close, Pewsey, Wilts, and Sheila Monica, *née* Redding; *b* 13 April 1943; *Educ* Sherborne, St Bartholomews Hosp and Univ of London (MB BS, DCH, DRCOG); *m* 30 Sept 1967, (Susan) Jennifer, da of Albert Hugh Thompson (d 1969), of Leeds, Yorkshire; 2 s (Jeremy David Hugh b 29 Oct 1970, Charles James Aston b 24 Oct 1973); *Career* GP 1970-; currently ptnr in practice with Dr's S J Phillips, D A N Twiner, B J Jones and E A Madigan; res grant from Bath Area Med Res Tst 1981-83 for work with refugees from Indo-China; author of numerous papers, articles in maj journals and contribs to med books; Freeman City of London 1968, Liveryman Worshipful Co of Gardeners 1976 (Freeman 1968); memb: BMA 1966, Clinical Soc of Bath; MRCS, LRCP; *Recreations* cooking, fishing, walking and mountaineering, backpacking, cross country skiing, photography, painting; *Style*— Dr Simon Phillips; Church Hldg, Etchilhampton, Devizes, Wilts SN10 3JL (☎ 038 086 291); Lansdowne Surgery, Waiblingen Way, Devizes (☎ 0380 2278)

PHILLIPS, Hon Mrs; Hon Sophia Rosalind; *née* Vane; 3 da of 11 Baron Barnard, TD, JP, *qv*; *b* 24 Jan 1962; *Educ* Cobham Hall, Westfield Coll London Univ (BSc); *m* 20 Sept 1986, Simon Benjamin Phillips, yst s of late Peter J Phillips, of Gustard Wood, Wheathampstead, Herts; *Style*— The Hon Mrs Phillips

PHILLIPS, Thomas Bernard Hudson; s of Prof Arthur Phillips OBE, of Otterbourne nr Winchester, Hants, and Kathleen, *née* Hudson; *b* 12 August 1938; *Educ* King's Sch Canterbury; *m* 14 July 1979, Rosemary Eleanor, da of Maj RAD Sinclair (ret), of Burnham-on-Crouch, Essex; 1 s (Roland b 12 Dec 1980), 1 da (Laura b 9 May 1982); *Career* slr; State Counsel Kenya 1967-70, Herbert Smith 1970- (Ptnr 1977-) memb Law Soc; *Recreations* sailing, skiing, golf; *Style*— Tom Phillips, Esq; Watling House, 35 Cannon St, London EC4M 5SD (☎ 01 489 8000)

PHILLIPS, Trevor Thomas (Tom); s of David John Phillips, and Margaret Agnes, *née* Arnold; *b* 24 May 1937; *Educ* Henry Thornton GS, St Catherines Coll Oxford (MA), Camberwell Sch of Arts and Crafts (NDD); *m* 12 Aug 1961 (m dis 1988), Jill Purdy; 1 s (Conrad Leofric (Leo) b 26 Jan 1965), 1 da ((Eleanor) Ruth b 25 Jan 1964); *Career* artist; works in collections of: Tate Gallery, V & A Museum, Br Museum, Nat Portrait Gallery, Br Cncl, MOMA NY, Philadelphia Museum, Library of Congress, Bibliotheque Nationale Paris, Aust Nat Gallery Canberra; exhibitions worldwide since 1969 incl retrospective exhibition 1974-75: Kunsthalle Basel, Germeente Museum, The Hague, Serpentine Gallery London; designer of tapestries: St Catherine's Coll Oxford, HQ Channel 4, Morgan Grenfell Offs; book artist: translated, illustrated, printed and published Dantes Inferno 1983; composer of the opera IRMA (recorded twice by Obscure Records 1977 and Matchless Recordings 1988), performed at Bordeaux Festival, Istanbul Festival, ICA; writer and critic for TLS and regular writer for The Independent and RA Magazine; TV dir for A TV Dante for Channel 4 with Peter Greenaway; chm Royal Academic Library, vice chm copywright Cncls 1984-88, hon pres S London Art Soc 1988-; ARA 1984, RE 1987; *Books* Trailer (1971), Works and Texts to 1974 (1975), A Humument (revised edn, 1987), Heart of a Humument (1985); *Recreations* watching cricket, collecting African art; *Clubs* Chelsea Arts, Grouchos, SCCC; *Style*— Tom Phillips, Esq; 57 Talfourd Rd, London SE15 (☎ 01 701 3978)

PHILLIS, Michael John; s of Francis William Phillis, and Gertrude Grace, *née* Pitman; *b* 6 Mar 1948; *Educ* Archbishop Tennysons GS Croydon; *m* 30 Aug 1969, Janice Susan, da of George Horne (d 1963); 1 s (Marc Weston b 26 Aug 1973), 1 da (Michelle b 18 Feb 1976); *Career* Bank of London & S America Ltd 1967-73, asst dir London & Continental Bankers 1973-81, regnl vice pres Marine Midland Bank 1981-83, asst gen mangr Kansallis Osake Pankki 1983-, dir Kansallis Gota Securities Ltd 1989-; *Recreations* golf, music, family, gardening; *Clubs* Warley Park GC, St James; *Style*— Michael Phillis, Esq; Kansallis-Osake-Pankki, Kansallis House, 80 Bishopsgate, London EC2N 4AU (☎ 01 256 7575, fax 01 256 5412, telex 267 173 KOPLON)

PHILLIS, Robert Weston; s of Francis William Phillis, and Gertrude Grace Phillis; *b* 3 Dec 1945; *Educ* John Ruskin GS, Nottingham Univ; *m* 16 July 1966, Jean, da of Herbert William Derham; 3 s (Martin b 1971, Benjamin b 1974, Timothy b 1974); *Career* lectr Edinburgh Univ and Scottish Business Sch 1971-75; md: Sun Printers Ltd 1976-79, Independent TV Pubns Ltd 1979-81, Central Independent TV plc 1981-87; dir: ITCA 1982-87; chm: Zenith Prodns Ltd 1984-, ITV Network Programming Ctee 1984-86, gp md Carlton Communications plc 1987-; dir and tstee TV Tst for the Environment 1984-, dir int cncl of Nat Academy of TV Arts and Socs 1985-, vice chm Royal TV Soc; *Recreations* golf, home and garden, theatre; *Style*— Robert Phillis, Esq; The Old Vicarage, High St, Wargrave, Berks; Carlton Communications plc, 15 St George St, Hanover Sq, London W1R 9DE (☎ 01 499 8050, fax 01 895 9575, telex 28177)

PHILLPOTTS, Simon Vivian Surtees; s of Christopher Louis George Phillpotts, CMG (d 1985), and Vivian Chanter, *née* Bowden; *b* 9 Feb 1947; *Educ* Abberley Hall, Harrow, Georgetown Univ USA; *Career* mangr: Shiro (China) Ltd Hong Kong 1968-74, Jardine Matheson & Co Hong Kong 1974-82; gen mangr Anglo Swiss Trading Hong Kong 1982-84, dir Daks-Simpson Ltd UK 1985-; *Clubs* Whites; *Style*— Simon Phillpotts, Esq; 11 Hanbury House, Regents Bridge Gdns, Rita Rd, London SW8 (☎ 01 735 6323); Daks-Simpson, 34 Jermyn St, London SW1 6HS (☎ 01 439 8781, fax 01 437 3633, telex 22466 DAKS M)

PHILO, Gordon Charles George; CMG (1970), MC (1944); s of Charles Gilbert Philo, and Nellie, *née* Pinnock; *b* 8 Jan 1920; *Educ* Haberdashers' Aske's Sch, Wadham Coll Oxford; *m* 1952, Mavis (Vicky) Ella (d 1986), da of John Ford Galsworthy; *Career* joined Dip Serv 1951; consul-gen Hanoi 1968-69, FCO 1969-78, ret; KMN (Hon) of Malaysia 1968; *Clubs* Athenaeum; *Style*— Gordon Philo, Esq, CMG, MC; c/o Athenaeum, Pall Mall, London SW1

PHILPOT, Elizabeth; *née* Massey; da of William Edmund Devereux Massey, CBE, of Dorking, Surrey, and Ingrid, *née* Glad-Block; *b* 8 April 1943; *Educ* Heathfield Sch Ascot, Courtauld Inst Univ of London (BA), Johann Wolfgang Goethe-Universität, Frankfurt Am Main (Dip); *m* 10 Sept 1977, Timothy Stephen Burnett Philpot, s of Christopher Burnett Philpot (d 1971), of Pickering, Yorks; *Career* local govt offr LCC (later GLC and ILEA) 1962-65, asst keeper of muniments Westminster Abbey 1968-69, admin asst Bedford Coll Univ of London 1969-70; Dip Serv 1970-82: third sec Brasilia Embassy, info attaché Paris Embassy; lectr and art historian 1982-; memb Reigate branch Nat Cncl of Women of GB; Freeman City of London 1975, Liveryman Worshipful Co of Clockmakers 1983 (Steward 1989); *Recreations* art history, travel, photography, horology, theatre, swimming, sailing, skiing; *Style*— Mrs Timothy Philpot; Rutlands, Reigate Rd, Dorking, Surrey RH4 1SP (☎ 0306 882739)

PHILPOT, John Stewart; s of Clifford Needham Philpot (d 1944), of Bungay, Suffolk, and Marjorie Emily Sophia, *née* Stewart (d 1980); *b* 22 May 1913; *Educ* Marlborough; *m* 12 April 1947, Pauline, da of Thomas Hopkins Bowman (d 1969), of Seacroft, Skegness, Lincolnshire; 2 da (Angela Frances b 1952, Jennifer Caroline b 1954); *Career* Lt RA TA, with Hon Artillery Co 1939, BEF and Dunkirk 1939-40, Egypt, Libya, Sicily and Italy 1943-45; slr and NP, admitted 1937, ret 1978; *Recreations* travel, gardening, photography, local history; *Style*— John Philpot, Esq; 121 Spilsby Rd, Boston, Lincolnshire PE21 9QN; Flat 4, The Homestead, South Green, Southwold, Suffolk IP18 6EX (☎ 0205 68486)

PHILPOT, Oliver Lawrence Spurling; MC (1944), DFC (1941); s of Lawrence Benjamin Philpot; *b* 6 Mar 1913; *Educ* Queen Mary Sch, N Vancouver, Aymestrey Ct

Worcester, Radley, Worcester Coll Oxford; *m* 1, 1938 (m dis 1951); 1 s, 2 da; m 2, 1954, Rosl Widhalm; 1 s, 1 da; *Career* md: Remploy Ltd 1974-78, exec Union Int Ltd 1962 (incl dep chm & chief exec Fropax Eskimo Food 1965-67), Venesta (later Aluminium) Foils Ltd 1959; chm and md Spirella Co of Great Britain Ltd, 1956; dir A Woollacott & Rappings Ltd 1953, Unilever Ltd from 1934 (mgmnt trainee - chm Trufood Ltd, 1948); *Style—* Oliver Philpot Esq, MC, DFC; 30 Abingdon Villas, Kensington W8 6BX (☎ 01 937 6013)

PHILPOT, Robert James; s of Maj R H Philpot, MC (Queens Royal Regt, d 1969), of Sherfield Manor, Romsey, Hants, and Miriam, *née* Hopkinson (d 1979); *b* 24 Oct 1925; *Educ* Wellington Coll; *m* 8 Sept 1956, Sylvia Mavis Rita, da of (William Alexander) Thomas (d 1934); *Career* served 1943-47, cmmnd Queens Royal Regt; dir Asprey plc 1983- (gen mangr 1975); *Recreations* gardening, sport; *Style—* Robert Philpot, Esq; Madeira Rd, Mitchum, Surrey; Asprey plc, 165-169 New Bond St, London W1Y OAR (☎ 01 493 6767, fax 01 491 0384, telex 25110)

PHILPOTT, Brian; s of Harold Edmund Philpott (d 1961), of London, and Nellie Edith Philpott (d 1986); *b* 22 June 1933; *Educ* Roan Sch for boys Greenwich, Nat Coll for heating, ventilating, refrigeration and fan engrg (grad 1957); *m* 12 June 1959, Vivienne Joan, da of Horace Percy Winder (d 1949), of Dorking; 1 s (David b 1963), 2 da (Diane b 1962, Sally b 1966); *Career* Nat Serv RAF 1951-53; trg Benham & Sons Ltd 1949-51 (1953-55), project engr Matthew Hall & Co Ltd 1955-61, sr design engr (later head of Environment Engrg Dept) WS Atkins & Ptnrs 1961-68, ptnr Bldg Design Partnership 1973- (joined 1968, appointed assoc 1969); memb assoc Inst Heating and Ventilating Engrs 1961; FCIBSE 1969, MConsE 1981; *Recreations* badminton, gardening, photography, walking; *Style—* Brian Philpott, Esq; Watchwood House, Watchwood Drive, Lytham St Annes, Lancs FY8 4NP (☎ 0253 735385); Building Design Partnership, Vernon St, Moor Lane, Preston, Lancs PR1 3PQ (☎ 0772 59383, fax 0772 201378 GROUP 3, telex 677160)

PHIPP, Peter John; s of Reginald John Phipp, and Hilda Emily Silk, *née* Edwards; *b* 4 Mar 1942; *Educ* Bournemouth GS; *Career* BBC TV 1962-72; 1972-: advertising photographer at studios in Bedford Gardens Kensington specialising in work for beauty and cosmetics indust and travel indust; dir Bartok Mgmnt; ACTT; *Recreations* tennis; *Style—* Peter Phipp, Esq; 30 Lansdowne Walk, London W11 3LT; Studio 11A, 79 Bedford Gardens, London W8 7EG (☎ 01 727 0100)

PHIPPIN, Eric Thomas; s of Thomas William Phippin (d 1979), and Margaret Anne, *née* Preston; *b* 9 Oct 1931; *Educ* Loughborough Central Sch London, City of London Coll; *m* 18 July 1953, Patricia Ann, da of Sidney Henry Collins (d 1982), of London; 3 s (Paul Jeremy b 31 Aug 1957, Stephen Christopher b 2 May 1960, Andrew Michael b 7 Sept 1966); *Career* Nat Serv RAF (movement control) 1950-52; RAFVR: Pilot Offr 1952, Flying Offr (org and supply) 1955; mgmnt trainee Union-Castle Mail Steamship Co Ltd 1952-63 (seconded to S and E Africa 1956-58); dir: Ocean Travel Devpt 1967-77, Chandris Cruises Ltd 1970-77 (passenger mangr 1963), Chandris Tours 1971-77, CTC Lines 1977-, CTC (Air Sea Holidays) Ltd 1977-, CTC (Hellas) SA 1984-; Freeman: City of London 1974, Worshipful Co of Basket Makers 1974; FCIT 1963; *Recreations* tennis, cricket, opera; *Style—* Eric Phippin, Esq; CTC Lines, 1 Regent St, London SW1 4NN (☎ 01 930 9963, fax 01 839 2483, telex 917193 LONDON)

PHIPPS, Lady Anne Elizabeth Grania; da of 4 Marquess of Normanby, KG, CBE; *b* 1965; *Style—* Lady Anne Phipps

PHIPPS, Antony Bourne; s of Maj Thomas Edward Phipps (d 1971), of Farndish Manor, Wellingboro, N Hants and Cicely Radcliffe, *née* Bourne (d 1988); *b* 18 Feb 1931; *Educ* Radley; *m* 30 Aug 1958, Virginia Margaret Jimpson, da of Harry Jimpson Greenhalgh (d 1966), of Santon House, Holmrook, Cumbria; 2 da (Cicely b 27 June 1959, Elizabeth b 11 Aug 1960); *Career* Nat Serv RN; chm and md: Storland plc, Skeltools Ltd, Noroguage Ltd, Swissonic Ltd, Acro Ltd, Storland Astronautics Ltd, EMC Engrg Co (London) Ltd, Medifield Ltd; Tstee Letchworth centre of Holistic Med Rosehill Hosp Hitchin; *Recreations* breeding racehorses, farming, hunting; *Clubs* Worcst Hunt; *Style—* Antony Phipps, Esq; Skeltools Ltd, Unit 1, Jubilee Trdg Estate, Letchworh, Herts (☎ 046 268 2518, fax 0462 480 192)

PHIPPS, Dr Colin Barry; s of Edgar Reeves Phipps; *b* 23 July 1934; *Educ* Acton Co Sch, Swansea GS, UCL, Birmingham Univ; *m* 1956, Marion May, da of Clifford Harry Lawrey; 2 s, 2 da; *Career* dep chm and chief exec Clyde Petroleum Ltd 1979-83, non-exec chm Clyde 1983-, MP (C) Dudley W Feb 1974-79; memb Cncl of Europe 1976-79, Western Euro Union 1976-79; FGS 1956, FInstPet 1972, memb Inst of Geologists 1978; *Clubs* Reform; *Style—* Dr Colin Phibbs; Mathon Ct, Mathon, Malvern WR13 5NZ (☎ 0684 892267); 38 Cheyne Walk, London SW3 (☎ 01 352 5381)

PHIPPS, Lord Justin Charles; s of 4 Marquess of Normanby, CBE; *b* 1958; *m* 1985, Rachel, da of Charles Stainsby, of The Manse, Chadlington, Oxon; 1 s (b 1986); *Style—* Lord Justin Phipps

PHIPPS, Air Vice-Marshal Leslie William; CB (1983), AFC (1959); s of late Frank Walter Phipps; *b* 17 April 1930; *Educ* SS Philip and James Sch Oxford; *Career* dir of Air Def and Overseas Ops 1978-79, dir-gen Personnel Mgmnt RAF 1980-82, sr directing staff RCDS 1983-; British Aerospace (mil aircraft div) 1984-; *Style—* Air Vice-Marshal Leslie Phipps, CB, AFC; 33 Knole Wood, Devenish Rd, Sunningdale, Berks SL5 9QR

PHIPPS, Lady (Evelyn) Patricia Mary; *née* Scudamore-Stanhope; da of late 12 Earl of Chesterfield; *b* 7 May 1917; *m* 1, 28 Sept 1938 (m dis 1947), Lt Cdr Ian McDonald, RAN; m 2, 24 Oct 1947, as his 3 w, John Harford Stanhope Lucas-Scudamore, DL (d 1976); 1 s, 1 da; m 3, 1983, Leckonby John Alexander Phipps; *Style—* Lady Patricia Phipps; Newcote, Moccas, Hereford (☎ 09817 291)

PHIPPS, Lady Peronel Katharine; da of 4 Marquess of Normanby, CBE; *b* 1959; *Style—* Lady Peronel Phipps; 72 Glebe Place, London SW3

PHIPPS, Vice-Adm Sir Peter; KBE (1964, CBE 1962), DSC (1941, Bar 1943), VRD (1945); *b* 7 June 1909; *Educ* Christchurch Boys' HS; *m* 1937, Jean Hutton; 2 s, 1 da; *Career* Chief of Defence Staff NZ 1963-65, Vice-Adm 1964, ret 1965; *Style—* Vice-Adm Sir Peter Phipps, KBE, DSC, VRD; 126 Motuhara Rd, Plimmerton, New Zealand (☎ Plimmerton 331240)

PHIPPS, Lady Phoebe; *née* Pleydell-Bouverie; 3 da of 7 Earl of Radnor, KG, KCVO, JP, DL, by his 1 w; *b* 25 Jan 1932; *Educ* Greenvale Sch Long Island, USA, Godolphin Sch Salisbury, Queen's Secretarial Coll, Powderham Castle Sch of Domestic Sci; *m* 1955 (m dis 1963), Hubert Beaumont, s of John Sheaffer Phipps, of Long Island; 1 s, 1 da; *Career* artist; *Clubs* Lansdowne; *Style—* Lady Phoebe Phipps; Water's Edge, 1 New Bridge Rd, Salisbury, Wilts (☎ 0722 28978)

PHIPPS, Rosemary Carolanne Tecla; da of James Fawcett Shirtcliffe (d 1985), and Tecla Lilli, *née* Behrmann; *b* 3 August 1944; *Educ* Parktown Girls High Pharmacy Sch SA (DMS), Newland Park (DHS, DipM); *m* 1975 (m dis 1987), John-Francis Phipps, s of late Sir Eric Phipps; 1 s (William b 1978), 1 da (Sophie b 1976); *Career* business mgmnt mktg conslt, lectr; author and publisher; dir: Phipps Radburn Publishing Ltd 1986-, The Oxford Coll for Business Studies Ltd 1988-; memb Oxford area bd Young Enterprise 1988-; *Books* Coming up Trumps (1986); *Recreations* painting, music, gardening; *Style—* Ms Rosemary Phipps; 43 Leckford Rd, Oxford OX2 6HY

PHIPPS, Rt Rev Simon Wilton Phipps; MC (1945); s of Capt William Duncan Phipps, CVO, RN (d 1967); *b* 6 July 1921; *Educ* Eton, Trinity Coll Cambridge; *m* 1973, Mary, widow of Rev Dr James Welch and da of Sir (Charles) Eric Palmer (d 1948); *Career* ordained 1950, curate Huddersfield Parish Church 1950-53, chaplain Trinity Coll Cambridge 1953-58, industl chaplain Coventry Diocese and chaplain Coventry Cathedral 1958-68 (Hon Canon 1965-68), first Bp Suffragan of Horsham (diocese of Chichester) 1968-74, Bp of Lincoln 1974-86; *Style—* The Rt Rev Simon Phipps; Sarsen, Shipley, West Sussex RH13 8PX

PHIPPS, Lady Sybil Anne; *née* Montagu Douglas Scott; da of 7 and 9 Duke of Buccleuch & Queensberry, KT, GCVO, and Lady Margaret Bridgeman (da of 4 Earl of Bradford by his w, Lady Ida Lumley, 2 da of 9 Earl of Scarbrough); *b* 14 July 1899; *m* 1919, Charles Bathurst Hele Phipps, Lt 1 Life Gds (d 1960); 1 s, 3 da; *Style—* Lady Sybil Phipps; 8 Cumberland Mansions, George St, London W1 (☎ Paddington 3339)

PHIPSON, John Norman; TD (1975); s of N H W Smith, and Margaret Helen, *née* Brown; descendant of Oliver Cromwell, via mothers family; *b* 29 Nov 1940; *Educ* Rugby Sch; *m* 2 Feb 1984, Harriet Jane Maxwell, da of late Hugh Hamilton McCleery; 2 s, 2 da; *Career* slr; Maj HAC (TA) 1959-75, Court of Assts HAC 1972, tres 1984-87, vice-pres 1988; ptnr Linklaters & Paines Slrs, London, Paris, New York, Hong Kong, Brussels, Tokyo; *Recreations* family; *Clubs* Players Theatre; *Style—* John N Phipson, Esq, TD; Barrington House, 59-67 Gresham St, London EC2V 7JA (☎ 01 606 7080, fax 606 5113, telex 884 349)

PHIZACKERLEY, Ven Gerald Robert; s of John Dawson Phizackerley (d 1980), and Lilian Mabel Ruthven, *née* Falloon (d 1983); *b* 3 Oct 1929; *Educ* Queen Elizabeth GS Penrith, Univ Coll Oxford (MA), Wells Theol Coll; *m* 1959, Annette Catherine, da of Cecil Frank Baker, MBE (d 1982); 1 da (Mary b 1961), 1 s (David b 1963); *Career* curate St Barnabas Carlisle 1954-57, chaplain Abingdon Sch 1957-64, rector Gaywood with Bawsey & Mintlyn Norwich 1964-78, rural dean Lynn 1968-78, hon canon Norwich Cathedral 1975-78, archdeacon Chesterfield and hon canon of Derby Cathedral 1978-; fell Woodard Corpn 1981-; JP Norfolk 1972-78; *Recreations* theatre, travel; *Style—* The Ven the Archdeacon of Chesterfield; The Vicarage, Ashford in the Water, Bakewell, Derbyshire DE4 1QN (☎ 062 981 2298)

PHYSICK, Dr John Frederick; CBE (1984); s of Nino William Physick (d 1946), of London, and Gladys, *née* Elliott (d 1978); *b* 31 Dec 1923; *Educ* Battersea GS, (DrRCA); *m* 28 May 1954, Eileen Mary, da of Cyril Walter Walsh (d 1970), of London; 2 s (Alastair b 2 Dec 1955, Nigel b 9 June 1958), 1 da (Helen b 6 Jan 1960); *Career* WWII RN 1942-46, AFHQ Algiers/Caserta 1942-45, RNVR until 1956; V & A Museum 1948-83: sec to advsy cncl 1973-83, asst to dir 1974-83, keeper of museum servs 1975-83, dep dir 1983; memb: drawings ctee RIBA 1975, memb Cathedrals Advsy Ctee 1977-81; pres Church Monuments Soc 1984-86, chm monuments sub-ctee Cncl for the Care of Churches 1984- (memb 1978-), memb Westminster Abbey Architectural Ctee 1985-, memb Rochester Cathedral Fabric Ctee 1987-(memb 1965-), vice chm Rochester Diocesan Advsy Ctee for the Care of the Churches 1987-; FSA, FRSA; *Books* Catalogue of the Engravings of Eric Gill (1965), Designs for English Sculpture 1680-1860 (1969), The Wellington Monument (1970), Marble Halls (1975), The Victoria and Albert Museum, the History of its Building (1982), Sculpture in Britain 1530-1830 (second edn, 1988), The Royal College of Art (contrib, 1987); *Style—* Dr John Physick, CBE; 49 New Rd, Meopham, Kent

PICK, Charles Samuel; s of Samuel Pick; *b* 22 Mar 1917; *Educ* Masonic Sch Bushey; *m* 1938, Hilda Beryl Hobbs; 1 s, 1 da; *Career* serv war 1939-46, cmmnd RA, AA Cmd, apptd Staff Capt, served ALFSEA, India Ceylon and Singapore; started in publishing with Victor Gollancz Ltd 1933, fndr memb Michael Joseph Ltd 1935, jt md 1959-62, md William Heinemann Ltd 1962, dir Heinemann Gp of Publishers 1962, (md 1979-), dir Pan Books 1968, chm Secker & Warburg 1973, ret from Heinemann in 1985; started Charles Pick Consultancy 1985 acting as sole literary agent for Wilbur Smith; chm and pres Heinemann Hldgs Inc 1980-85, memb Cncl Publishers' Assoc 1950-83; *Recreations* walking, reading, theatre; *Clubs* Savile, MCC; *Style—* Charles Pick, Esq; Littlecot, Lindfield, Sussex (☎ 2218); 3 Bryanston Place W1 (☎ 01 402 8043)

PICK, Dr David Hessel; s of Norris Pick, MB, ChB (d 1962), of Bank House Monk Bretton Barnsley, and Ada Mary, *née* Hessel (d 1941); *b* 25 July 1922; *Educ* The Wells Sch Ilkley, Sedberg Sch, Leeds Univ (MB, ChB); *m* 18 Aug 1948, Kathleen Mary, da of John Lawton (d 1972); 1 s (Mark b 1955), 1 da (Mary b 1949); *Career* served 1943-46 RAF Bomber Cmd, Warrant Offr; med practitioner 1952-83, hosp practitioner Otolarynology Barnsley Health Authy 1953-83, memb Med Bds DHSS 1967-87, hon sec Barnsley Local Med Ctee 1962-83, rep Barnsley Div BMA 1962-82; licence holder public trainer Coursing Greyhounds, coursing inspector Nat Coursing Club; *Recreations* horse racing, hare coursing, greyhound racing; *Style—* Dr David Pick; 419 Rotherham Rd, Barnsley, W Yorks

PICK, Joan Margaret; da of William Pick (d 1985), of Cumbria, and Harriet Rhodes, *née* Bancroft; *b* 9 Dec 1940; *Educ* Barrow-in-Furness County GS for Girls, Bristol Univ (BSc); *Career* scientific writer Understanding Science 1962-64, market researcher/business planner conslt Product Planning Ltd 1964-67, business planning conslt and dir of Interplan 1967-73; *Books* The Earth Enterprise Project (1973); *Recreations* keeping mentally and physically fit for the job; *Clubs* Mensa; *Style—* Miss Joan Pick; 24 Maybourne Grange, Turnpike Link, Croydon CR0 5NH (☎ 01 686 5089)

PICK, Prof John Morley; s of John Mawson Pick, of Ripon, Yorks, and Edith Mary, *née* Morley; *b* 12 Oct 1936; *Educ* King Edward VI Sch Retford, Leeds Univ (BA, PGCE), Birmingham Univ (MA), City Univ London (Phd); *m* 19 April 1960, Ann Clodagh, da of Sydney Simmons Johnson (d 1983), of Eastbourne; 1 s (Martyn b 1963), 1 da (Catherine b 1965); *Career* dir Dillington House Coll of Adult Educn and Arts Centre 1973-76, head arts policy and govt studies City Univ 1976-, Gresham prof rhetoric Gresham Coll City Univ 1983-88, prof arts mgmnt City Univ 1985-, dir Gresham Coll Res Project 1988-; FRSA 1987; *Books* Arts Administration (1980), The

State of The Arts (1981), The West End: Mismanagement And Snobbery (1983), The Theatre Industry (1984), The Modern Newspeak (1985), Managing The Arts? (1987), Arts in a State (1988); *Recreations* gardening, theatre, writing, comedy; *Style—* Prof John Pick; Spindlewood, Winthorpe, Newark NG24 2NL, (☎ 0636 77512); Department Arts Policy And Management, Level 12, Frobisher Cres, The Barbican, Silk St, London EC2 Y 8HB, (☎ 01 253 4399, 01 628 5641/2)

PICK, (Frederick) Michael; s of Frederick William Leopold Walter Pick (d 1949), and Helene Alice, *née* Julissen; *b* 21 June 1949; *Educ* England and Germany, Gonville and Caius Coll Cambridge (MA); *Career* civil servant 1975-77; dir Stair & Co Ltd (London and NYC); antique dealer and decorator; hon UK advsr to Permanent Consulate Gen and Legation of Republic of Estonia in USA; fndr ctee memb The Thirties Soc 1979; lectr and broadcaster; contrib to numerous periodicals and newspapers; author; *Books* The English Room, The National Tst Guide to Antiques, The English Country Room (1988); *Recreations* pottering to music, conversation; *Clubs* Lansdowne; *Style—* Michael Pick, Esq; 120 Mount St, London W1Y 5HB (☎ 01 499 1784)

PICK, (Rachel Anne); *née* Bridge; 2 da of Baron Bridge of Harwich, PC; *b* 15 April 1946; *Educ* BA (Hons); *m* 1975, Martin Pick; 1 s (Oliver b 1984), 1 da (Katharine b 1977); *Career* child psychotherapist; *Style—* Mrs R Pick

PICKARD, Brian Harold; s of Alfred Harold Pickard (d 1954), of London, and Winifred Sarah, *née* Cockrill (d 1982); *b* 14 Feb 1922; *Educ* Eltham Coll, Guy's Hosp and London Univ (MB BS, DLO); *m* 1, 13 May 1944, Joan Daisy, da of Harry Packham, of London; 2 s (Geoffrey b 1952, William b 1958), 2 da (Diane (Mrs Yeo) b 1945, Celia (Mrs Greetham) b 1947); m 2, Diana Sylvia, da of John William Stokes, of Frinton; 1 da (Lucy b 1981); *Career* RAF 1948-50, ENT specialist RAF Hosp Cosford; Sqdn Ldr RAFVR 1950-55; sr registrar ENT: Hosp for sick children Great Ormond St, Kings Coll Hosp London; conslt surgn ENT: St Georges Hosp London, Moorfields Eye Hosp London, Dreadnought Seamans Hosp London, Dispensaire Francais London visiting ENT specialist St Helena; med advsr Guild of Air Pilots and Air Navigators, conslt Br Airways; private pilot 1948-, colours for swimming Guy's and King's (cap Guy's swimming club); memb med panel CAA; Freeman: City of London, Worshipful Soc of Apothecaries; Past Master Guild of Air Pilots and Air Navigators; FRCS, LMSSA, FRSM, FRSA, MRAeS, memb Br Med Pilots Assoc (former pres); Chevalier de l'ordre National du Merite; *Recreations* sailing, flying; *Clubs* RAF, RAC, Utd Hosps SC (vice cdre), St Georges Hosp SC (former cdre); *Style—* Brian Pickard, Esq; Shandon, 19 Waltham Way, Frinton-on-Sea Essex CO13 9JE, (☎ 0255 674808); Cromwell Hospital, Cromwell Rd, SW5; Blackheath Hospital, 40 Lee Terrace, SE3, (☎ 0255 674808 telex 8951182 GECOMS G)

PICKARD, Sir Cyril Stanley; KCMG (1966, CMG 1964); s of G W Pickard; *b* 18 Sept 1917; *Educ* Alleyn's Sch Dulwich, New Coll Oxford; *m* 1, 1941, Helen Elizabeth (d 1982), da of G F Strawson, of Horley, Surrey; 3 s, 1 da (and 1 s decd); m 2, 1983, Mary Cecilia Rosser, widow of David Rosser, of Crawley and da of Basil Cozens-Hardy of Leatheringsett; *Career* served RA 1940-41, Capt; British high cmmr Pakistan 1966-71, British high cmmr in Nigeria 1971-74, ret; *Style—* Sir Cyril Pickard, KCMG; 37a Brodrick Rd, London SW17

PICKARD, (John) Michael; s of John Stanley Pickard (d 1979), of Epsom Surrey, and Winifred Joan; *b* 29 July 1932; *Educ* Oundle; *m* 1959, Penelope Jane, da of Christopher Catterall; 3 s, 1 da; *Career* fin dir Br Printing Corpn Ltd 1965-68, md Trust House Forte 1968-71; chm: St Paul's Fin Investmt Co Ltd 1963-86, Michael Pickard Ltd 1972-86, Happy Eater Ltd 1972-86, Grattan PLC; chm and chief exec Imperial Brewing & Leisure Ltd, dir Imperial Gp plc 1981; chief exec Sears plc 1986-, non-exec dir: Brown Shipley Hldgs Ltd 1986-, Electra Investmt Tst 1988-; chm Roedean Cncl 1981-, govr Oundle 1987-; FCA; *Recreations* sport, education; *Clubs* Walton Heath, MCC, Pilgrims; *Style—* Michael Pickard, Esq; 40 Duke St, London W1A 2HP (☎ 01 408 1180)

PICKARD, Michael John; s of Denis Luther Pickard; *b* 9 July 1939; *Educ* Christ's Hosp; *m* 1965, Heather Jill, da of John Hallsworth (d 1969); 1 s, 1 da; *Career* The Royal London Mutual Insurance Soc Ltd: actuary 1974-82, dir 1977-, chief gen mangr 1983-87, chm 1988-; FIA; *Recreations* squash, golf, reading; *Style—* Michael Pickard, Esq; Tyndals, Groton, nr Boxford, Suffolk CO6 5EE (☎ 0787 210692); The Royal London Mutual Insurance Soc Ltd, Royal London House, Middlesborough, Colchester, Essex CO1 1RA (☎ 0206 44155)

PICKEN, Ralph Alistair; s of Col David Kennedy Watt Picken, TD, JP, DL, of Cardiff, and Liselotte Lore Inge, *née* Regensteiner; *b* 23 May 1955; *Educ* Shrewsbury, Univ of Birmingham (LLB); *Career* admitted slr 1980, ptnr Trowers & Hamlins London 1984- (joined 1981); memb Law Soc 1980; *Recreations* bridge, Baroque, Bangkok, Bordeaux; *Style—* Ralph Picken, Esq; 3 Gloucester Cres, London NW1 7DS (☎ 01 485 5121); 6 New Sq, Lincoln's Inn, London WC2A 3RP (☎ 01 831 6292, fax 01 831 8700, telex 21422)

PICKERILL, Dame Cecily Mary Wise; *née* DBE (1977, OBE 1958); da of Rev Percy Wise Clarkson; *b* 9 Feb 1903; *Educ* Diocesan H for Girls Auckland NZ, Otago Univ Med Sch Dunedin NZ (MB, ChB); *m* 1934, Henry Percy Pickerill, CBE, MD, MDS (d 1956); 1 da; *Career* specialist plastic surgeon Wellington NZ 1935-68; *Style—* Dame Cecily Pickerill, DBE; Beech Dale, 50 Blue Mountains Rd, Silverstream, NZ (☎ Upper Hutt 284542)

PICKERILL, Reginald James; s of Sidney Pickerill (d 1957), of Cheshire, and Beatrice Pickerill, *née* Ashton (d 1970); *b* 17 Oct 1923; *Educ* King's Sch Macclesfield; *m* 27 Sept 1947, Peggy Evelyn, da of Fred Cronshaw (d 1959), of Cheshire; 1 s (Geoffrey Martin b 1948), 1 da (Diana Michelle b 1954); *Career* RA 1942-47; serv NW Europe; CA; asst to Controller of Income Tax Jersey CI 1952-55, tech asst Taxation Publishing Co 1956-61, tax mangr BAC 1962-65, tax exec The Plessey Co plc 1966-80 (tax conslt 1980-85); cncl memb Inst of Taxation 1969-83 (pres 1976-78); lectr: taxation Inst CA 1965-72, Inst of Tax 1967-76; former memb CBI tax panel & ctee, Beama Tax Ctee, Tax Ctee Int C of C; FCA, FTII; *Books* Capital Allowances in Law and Practice; *Recreations* golf, swimming, walking; *Style—* Reg Pickerill, Esq; Morwenstow, 61 Chyngton Way, Seaford, E Sussex (☎ 0323 895015)

PICKERING, Donald Ellis; s of John Joseph Pickering (d 1978), of Newcastle-upon-Tyne, and Edith, *née* Ellis (d 1983); *b* 15 Nov 1933; *Educ* private; *Career* actor; trained Old Vic Theatre Sch under Michel St Denis 1950-52, Old Vic Co 1952, Stratford 1954, Bristol Old Vic 1957-59; West End appearances incl: Poor Bitos, School for Scandal (and NY), Case in Question, Conduct Unbecoming (nominated Tony Award), Male of the Species, Hay Fever; Nat Theatre 1987-89; TV appearances incl: The Pallisers, Private Lives, Irish RM, Yes Prime Minister, Return to Treasure Island; films incl: Nothing but the Best, Thirty Nine Steps, Half Moon St; *Recreations* gardening, riding, tennis ; *Style—* Donald Pickering, Esq; Back Court, Manor House, Eastleach Turville, Cirencester, Glos GL7 3NQ; (☎ 036 785 476)

PICKERING, Prof John Frederick; s of William Frederick Pickering (d 1973), of Slough, and Jean Mary, *née* Clarke; *b* 26 Dec 1939; *Educ* Slough GS, UCL (BSc, PhD, DSc); *m* 25 March 1967, Jane Rosamund, da of Victor William George Day of Bristol; 2 da (Rachel b 1970, Catherine b 1974); *Career* industl mkt res exec 1961-62; lectr: Univ of Durham 1964-66, Univ of Sussex 1966-73; sr directing staff Admin Staff Coll Henley 1974-75, prof industl econ UMIST 1975-88 (vice princ 1983-85, dean 1985-87); vice pres Portsmouth Poly 1988-; Chm Cmmr 1983-; memb: Gen Synod C of E 1980-, Retail Prices Index Advsy Ctee 1974-; pres Bible Churchmen's Missionary Soc 1986-; FBIM 1987, memb Royal Econ Soc 1973; *Books* Resale Price Maintenance in Practice (1967), The Small Firm in the Hotel and Catering Industry (with others, 1971), Industrial Structure and Market Conduct (1974), The Acquisition of Consumer Durables (1977), The Economic Management of the Firm (jt ed, 1984); *Recreations* family life, cricket, classical music; *Clubs* Royal Cwlth Soc; *Style—* Prof J F Pickering; 1 The Fairway, Rowlands Castle, Hants PO9 6AQ (☎ 0705 412 007); Portsmouth Poly, Ravenlin House, Museum Rd, Portsmouth, Hants PO1 2QQ (☎ 0705 843 203, fax 0705 843 319)

PICKERING, His Hon Judge; John Robertson; s of late J W H Pickering; *b* 8 Jan 1925; *Educ* Winchester, Magdalene Cambridge; *m* 1951, Hilde, widow of E M Wright; 1 s, 2 step s; *Career* barrister Inner Temple 1949, dep chm NE London QS 1971, circuit judge 1972-; *Clubs* MCC; *Style—* His Honour Judge Pickering; 35 Eaton Terrace, London SW1 (☎ 01 730 4271)

PICKERING, His Honour Judge; Richard Edward Ingram Pickering; s of Richard Pickering (d 1961), and Dorothy Pickering; *b* 16 August 1929; *Educ* Birkenhead Sch, Magdalene Coll Cambridge (MA); *m* 1962, Jean Margaret, da of Mrs Alice Eley; 2 s; *Career* barrister Lincoln's Inn 1953, elected jr of N Circuit 1960, cllr Hoylake UDC 1961-64, legal chm Miny of Pensions and Nat Insurance Appeals Tbnl Liverpool 1967-77, hon memb Manx Bar (Summerland Fire Enquiry) 1973-74, pt-time chm Liverpool Industl Tbnl 1977-79, rec Crown Ct 1977-81, regnl chm Merseyside Mental Health Review Tbnl 1979-81, circuit judge (N Circuit) 1981-, N Circuit rep on Cncl HM Circuit Judges 1984-, nominated judicial memb Merseyside Mental Health Review Tbnl 1984-; *Recreations* study of military history, gardening; *Clubs* Athenaeum (Liverpool), United Oxford & Cambridge Univ; *Style—* His Hon Judge Pickering; Crown Court, Derby Square, Liverpool

PICKERING, Hon Mrs (Veronica Mary); da of Baroness Fisher of Rednal (Life Peeress) and Joseph Fisher (d 1978); *b* 24 Nov 1944; *Educ* Rednall Hill Jr Sch, Bournville Grammar Tech Sch, Bordesley Coll of Educn; *m* 1968, John Adrian Pickering, s of Alfred Walter Pickering, of Birmingham; 1 s (John Joseph b 1979), 1 da (Lyndsey Jane b 1974); *Career* teacher; *Style—* The Hon Mrs Pickering; Redlands, 8 Marlborough Ave, Bromsgrove, Worcs (☎ 0527 75190)

PICKERING, William Roy; s of Ernest Stanley Pickering (d 1977); *b* 21 Feb 1927; *Educ* Merchant Taylors' Sch Gt Crosby Lancs, Univ Coll of N Wales Bangor; *m* 1949, Carmen Fay, da of late Herbert Hawley, OBE, MSc, FRIC of India; 1 s, 3 da; *Career* dir of Tube Production Planning, Tube Investments STD 1962-64, dir and gen mangr Parkinson Cowan Appliances Ltd 1967-70, chm and md: Bryan Donkin Ltd 1970-79, Hopkinsons Ltd 1977-79; chm and md Padley & Venables Ltd 1979-, chm Bedford Steels Ltd 1979-; *Recreations* skiing, swimming shooting; *Style—* William Pickering, Esq

PICKETT, Hon Mrs (Patricia Margaret); da of 2 Baron Kershaw (d 1961); *b* 1943; *m* 1968, David Anniss Pickett, BSc, BMus; 2 da; *Style—* The Hon Mrs Pickett; 13 Wood End, Park St, St Albans, Herts

PICKETT, Hon Mr Justice; Thomas Pickett; CBE (1972); s of John Joseph Pickett (d 1985), and Caroline, *née* Brunt (d 1970); *b* 22 Nov 1912; *Educ* Glossop GS, London Univ (LLB); *m* 29 June 1940, (Winifred) Irene, yr da of Benjamin Buckley (d 1945); *Career* serv Army 1939-50, Maj; dep asst dir Army Legal Servs 1948, barr Lincoln's Inn 1948; Judge Pres of Ct of Appeal for Zambia 1965-71; sr regional chm NW Area Industl Tbnls (England and Wales) 1972-85 (ret); *Recreations* walking, swimming; *Clubs* County (Llandudno), Victoria (Llandudno); *Style—* Hon Mr Justice Pickett, CBE; Bryn Awelon, Aber Place, Craigside, Llandudno, Gwynedd LL30 3AR (☎ 0492 44244)

PICKFORD, Anthony James; s of Frederick Pickford, and Ethel Alice, *née* Hart; *b* 12 May 1925; *Educ* Univ Coll Sch Hampstead, King's Coll London (LLB); *m* 1 Sept 1956, Bettine Eleanor Marion Casson, da of Kenneth Casson Smith; *Career* Serv Army 1943-49; barr Lincoln's Inn 1951, practise in London 1951-57 (Nigeria 1957-59), legal asst George Wimpey & Co Ltd 1959-64, legal advsr Smithkline & French Laboratories Ltd 1964-; dir: Smithkline & French Laboratories Ltd Smithkline Beckman Int Ltd, Penn Chemicals BV; memb: standing advsy ctee (trade marks) DTI 1970- (former chm Trademart ctee), ABPI ctees 1964-, UNICE ctees Assoc memb chartered inst of Patent Agents; memb (formerley sec) of the ctee for W Africa affairs of the cons party contested E Ham (C) Gen Election 1955, chm Harlow (C) Assoc (former pres); *Recreations* conservative politics; *Clubs* East India; *Style—* Anthony Pickford, Esq; Alton House, 174-177 High Holborn, London, WC1V 7AA, (☎ 02 379 3161, fax 01 831 1435)

PICKFORD, David Michael; s of Aston Charles Corpe Pickford (d 1945); *b* 25 August 1926; *Educ* Emanuel Sch London, Coll of Estate Mgmnt; *m* 1956, Elizabeth Gwendoline, da of John Hooson, of Segrwyd Hall, Denbigh (d 1972); 1 s (Charles b 1960), 2 da (Penelope b 1952, Elizabeth b 1958); *Career* chartered surveyor; chm: Haslemere Estates plc 1983-86 (md to 1983), Lilliput Property Unit Tst, Exeter Park Estates plc, Compco plc Gulliver Devpts Property Unit Tst, The Rehabilitation Gp Ltd; dir City of Met Bldg Soc, Youth with a Mission (YWAM); vice pres Drug and Alcohol Fndn, dir Prison Fellowship; chm: Christian Union for the Estate Profession, Mission to London; *Recreations* farming, youth work; *Style—* David Pickford, Esq; Elm Tree Farm, Mersham, nr Ashford, Kent TN25 7HS (☎ 023 372 200); 33 Grosvenor Sq, London W1X 9LL (☎ 01 493 1156)

PICKFORD, Hon Mrs (Felicity Jane); *née* Mills; er da of 2 Viscount Mills (d 1988); *b* 21 June 1947; *m* 1970, Roger B Pickford; *Career* MB, ChB, FFARCS; *Style—* Dr the Hon Felicity Pickford; Heddfan, Ffawyddog, Llangattock, Crickhowell, Powys

PICKFORD, Robert William Granville; s of Col Richard Ellis Pickford, TD, DL, of Hathersage, Derbyshire, and Mary Avice, *née* Glossop; *b* 26 Nov 1941; *Educ* Rugby,

Sheffield Univ (LL B); *m* 11 Oct 1980, Heather Elizabeth, da of Francis Ernest Woodings, of Chesterfield, Derbyshire; 1 s (Bartholomew b 9 Sept 1985), 1 da (Olivia b 21 Dec 1981); *Career* slr 1966, ptnr W & A Glossop Sheffield; dir The Notaries Soc 1979-; Notary Public 1966; former chm RNLI Sheffield Branch; memb: Law Soc, The Notaries Soc, Slrs Benevolent Assoc; *Style*— Robert Pickford, Esq; 68 Wilkinson St, Sheffield S10 2GQ (☎ 0742 737776)

PICKLES, His Honour Judge; James; s of Arthur Pickles, OBE, JP; *b* 18 Mar 1925; *Educ* Worksop Coll, Leeds Univ, Ch Ch Oxford; *m* 1948, Sheila Ratcliffe; 2 s, 1 da; *Career* barr Inner Temple 1948, rec Crown Ct 1972-76, circuit judge 1976-; contested (Lib) Brighouse and Spenborough 1964; *Books* Straight from the Bench (1987); *Style*— His Honour Judge Pickles; c/o Leeds Crown Court, Leeds

PICKLES, John George; s of William Pickles (d 1972), of N Wales, and Kathleen Pickles, *née* Cathcart; *b* 29 Nov 1935; *Educ* Ruthin Sch, Univ of Liverpool (MCD, BArch); *m* 15 July 1961, Susan Rosemary (d 1985), da of Dr William Webb (d 1955), of Liverpool; 1 s (Charles b 1965), 1 da (Caroline b 1962); *Career* architect and town planner; ptnr in Holford Associates 1972-, dir Meridian Office Servs; artist exhibitions in NW England 1984-; ARIBA, MRTPI, MSAI, FRSA; *Recreations* watercolour painting, skiing, travel; *Style*— John G Pickles, Esq; Derby Cottage, 29 Derby Road, Formby, Merseyside; Holford Associates, Queen Building, 8 Dale Street, Liverpool (☎ 051 227 2881, fax 051 236 1329)

PICKSTOCK, Sam - Samuel Frank; s of Francis John Pickstock (d 1981), of Stafford, and Hilda Jane, *née* Billington; *b* 10 August 1934; *Educ* King Edward VI GS Stafford; *m* 1957, Edith, da of Joseph Lawton (d 1980) of Hanley; *Career* dir Tarmac plc 1984, md John McLean & Sons Ltd 1981 and chm of its subsidiary cos 1981; dir: Tarmac Properties Ltd 1976 (also subsidaries), Tarmac East Bute Dvpts Ltd 1985; *Recreations* weeding and thinking (occasionally); *Style*— Sam Pickstock, Esq; The Crows Nest Holding, Coton End, Gnosall, Stafford (☎ 0785 822755); Crestwood House, Birches Rise, Willenhall, West Midlands, (☎ 0902 368511

PICKTHORN, Sir Charles William Richards; 2 Bt (UK 1959); s of Rt Hon Sir Kenneth William Murray Pickthorn, 1 Bt (d 1975); *b* 3 Mar 1927; *Educ* Eton, CCC Cambridge; *m* 1951, Helen Antonia, da of late Sir James Mann, KCVO; 1 s, 2 da; *Heir* s, James Francis Mann Pickthorn; *Career* barr Middle Temple 1952, dir J Henry Schroder Wagg & Co Ltd 1971-79, memb editorial bd The Salisbury Review 1982-, chm R S Surtees Soc 1980-; *Style*— Sir Charles Pickthorn, Bt; Manor House, Nunney, nr Frome, Somerset (☎ 037 384 574); 3 Hobury St, London SW10 (☎ 01 352 2795)

PICKTHORN, Lady Helen Antonia; da of Sir James Gow Mann, KCVO (d 1961), and Mary, *née* Cook (d 1956); *b* 31 July 1927; *Educ* privately, Firtox Coll Cambridge (MA); *m* 4 July 1951, Charles William Richards Pickthorn, 2 Bt, gv; s of Rt Hon Sir Kenneth Pickthorn; 1 s (James b 1955), 2 da (Caroline b 1958, Frances b 1960); *Career* teacher Fidelis Sch London 1950-56, dir of Studies Kensington Sch of Languages 1956-61, res asst Lord Gladwyn House of Lords 1963-83; ed newsletter Cncl for Educn in the Cwlth 1956-76, Cwlth and Party Liaison offr 1974-, memb and ball chm Br-Italian Soc 1976-86; govr and chm More House Sch 1972-75, life memb Chelsea Soc; *Books* Student Guide to Britain (1965), Locked Up Daughters (1967), Alexander Mann: Sketches and Correspondence (1985); *Recreations* design and decoration; *Clubs* National Liberal (non political memb); *Style*— Lady Helen Pickthorn; C/O National Liberal Club, Whitehall Place, London SW1

PICKTHORN, Henry Gabriel Richards; s of Rt Hon Sir Kenneth William Murray Pickthorn, 1 Bt (d 1975), and Nancy Catherine Lewis, *née* Richards (d 1982); *b* 29 Sept 1928; *Educ* Eton, Trinity Coll Camb (BA); *m* 9 July 1955, Mary, da of Juxon Barton, CMG, OBE (d 1980); 3 s (John b 1957, Andrew b 1961, Thomas b 1967), 1 da (Henrietta b 1959); *Career* Nat Serv 1946-48, 2 Lt Northants Regt; TA 1952-61, Capt Queen's Westminsters (KRRC); slr; ptnr Linklaters & Paines 1957-; *Style*— Henry Pickthorn, Esq; 54 Chelsea Park Gdns, London SW3 6AD (☎ 01 352 8905); Barrington House, 59-67 Gresham St, London EC2 7JA (☎ 01 606 7080)

PICKTHORN, James Francis; s and h of Sir Charles William Richards Pickthorn, 2 Bt; *b* 18 Feb 1955; *Educ* Eton; *Style*— James Pickthorn Esq; c/o Manor House, Nunney, nr Frome, Somerset

PICTET, His Excellency Francois Charles; s of Charles Pictet (d 1984), of Geneva, Switzerland, and Elisabeth, *née* Decazes, of France; *b* 21 July 1929; *Educ* Calvin Coll Geneva, Univ of Geneva; *m* 1, 1954, Elisabeth (d 1980), da of Dr Robert Choisy (d 1985), of Geneva, Switzerland; 3 s (Nicolas b 1956, Horace b 1958, Charles b 1963); m 2, 1983, Countess Marie-Thérèse Althann, of Austria; *Career* joined Swiss Federal Dept of For Affrs 1956, served as Attaché Vienna 1957, sec Moscow 1958-60, first Sec Ankara 1961-66, Dept of For Affrs Berne 1966-75, ambass to Canada 1975-79, ambass and perm rep to Int Orgns in Geneva 1980-83, ambass of Switzerland to the Ct of St James's 1984-; *Recreations* music, walking; *Clubs* Hurlingham; *Style*— His Excellency François Pictet; Swiss Embassy Residence, 21 Bryanston Sq, London W1H 7FG; Swiss Embassy, 16-18 Montagu place, London W1H 2BQ (☎ 723 0701, telex 28212)

PICTON, Dr Arthur (Dyce); MBE, MC; s of Dr Lionel James Picton OBE (d 1949), and May Emma Binney (d 1954); *b* 12 April 1911; *Educ* Epsom Coll, Merton Coll Oxford (MA, BM, Bch) Kings Coll Hosp; *m* 19 July 1939, Sheila Pauline, *née* McCarthy; 1 da (Dinah b 1940); *Career* WWII Capt RAMC served RMO 2 Bn Rife Bde 1940-43; house surgn KCH 1937-38, gen practice Holmes Chapel Cheshire 1939-77; MRCS, LRCP, MRCGP; *Recreations* gardening, shooting, country life; *Style*— Dr Arthur Picton, MBE, MC; The Vineyard, W Hoathly, E Grinstead, Sussex RH19 4PP (☎ 0342 810 227)

PICTON, Jacob Glyndwr (Glyn); CBE (1972); s of David Picton (d 1960), of Aberdare, and Elen Picton (d 1937); *b* 28 Feb 1912; *Educ* Aberdare Boys' County Sch, Univ of Birmingham (MCom); *m* 2 Sept 1939, Rhiannon Mary (d 1978), da of late Arthur James, of Swansea; 1 s (Arthur b 1943), 1 da (Eira b 1946); *Career* Chance Bros Ltd 1933-47 (asst sec 1945-47); Univ of Birmingham: sr lectr in industl econs 1947-79, sub-dean faculty of commerce and social sciences 1952-58; govr United Birmingham Hosps 1953-74 (vice-chm 1958-74), chm Birmingham Children's Hosp 1956-66; pres W Midlands Rent Assessment Panel, teaching hosps rep on Whitley Cncls of NHS, vice-chm Nat Staff Ctee NHS; chm Birmingham Industl Therapy Assoc Ltd, chm several wages cncls; sole cmmr of enquiry into S Wales Coalfield Dispute 1965; *Books* South Wales Coalfield Strike (1965); *Recreations* music, gardening, Pembrokeshire history; *Clubs* Univ of Birmingham Academic Staff; *Style*— Glyn Picton, Esq, CBE

PICTON TURBERVILL, Richard Charles Quintin; DL (Mid Glamorgan); s of Col Charles Thomas Edmondes, TD (d 1969), of Ewenny Priory, Bridgend, Mid Glamorgan, and Eleanor Mary Turbervill; *b* 21 Oct 1924; *Educ* Radley RAC Cirencester (MRAC); *m* 1, 29 July 1950 (m dis 1971); m 2, 18 Jan 1972, Ann Elizabeth, da of Geoffrey Field Arthur (d 1960), of Ranskill, Notts; 3 s (Jeremy, Simon, Hugh);; *Career* mobile radar RA 1942-46; cncllr 1951-; pres: Bridgend Show soc, Political Pty Assoc, memb: River Aughys Agric Tbnl (Wales); chm Gen Cmmrs of Income Tax, High Sheriff Glamorgan 1965; *Recreations* shooting, stalking, sailing, gardening, skiing (in past); *Clubs* Royal Overseas Leasue, farmers Cardiff and County; *Style*— RCQ Picton Turbervill, Esq, JP; Ewenny Priory, Bridsend, Mid Glamorgan, CF35 5BW, (☎ 0656 652913)

PICTON-TURBERVILL, Richard Charles Quentin; JP (Glamorgan 1959), DL (Mid Glamorgan 1982); s of Col Charles Thomas Edmondes, of Old Hall, Cowbridge, Glam, by his w Eleanor, o child of Charles Grenville Turbervill, JP, Lord of the Manor of Ewenny (whose maternal gf was Sir Grenville Temple, 10 Bt, of the family which at one time enjoyed the Dukedom of Buckingham and a branch of which still has the Earldom of Temple of Stowe); *b* 6 July 1924; *Educ* Radley, RAC Cirencester; *m* 1, 1950 (m dis 1971), Catherine Vivian Lindsay, da of Col E D Corkery; 3 s; m 2, 1972, Ann Elizabeth, da of Geoffrey Field Arthur (d 1960), of Ranskill, Notts; *Career* served WWII RA Europe; farmer; High Sheriff Glamorgan 1965, memb Land Tbnl, Cmmr of Taxes; *Clubs* Royal Overseas, Farmers', County (Cardiff); *Style*— Richard Picton-Turbervill Esq, JP, DL; Ewenny Priory, Bridgend, Mid Glamorgan CE35 5BW (☎ 0656 2913)

PIERCY, 3 Baron (UK 1945); James William Piercy; s of 2 Baron Piercy (d 1981), and Oonagh Lavinia, JP, da of late Maj Edward John Lake Baylay, DSO; *b* 19 Jan 1946; *Educ* Shrewsbury, Univ of Edinburgh (BSc); *Heir* bro, Hon Mark Edward Pelham Piercy; *Career* AMIEE, ACCA; *Style*— The Rt Hon the Lord Piercy; 13 Arnold Mansions, Queen's Club Gdns, London W14

PIERCY, Hon Mark Edward Pelham; s of 2 Baron Piercy (d 1981), and hp of bro, 3 Baron; *b* 30 June 1953; *Educ* Shrewsbury, New Coll Oxford (BA); *m* 1979, Vivien Angela, da of His Hon Judge Monier-Williams, *qv*; 1 s (William Nicholas Pelham b 1989), 3 da (Katherine Henrietta, b 1982, Olivia Charlotte b 1984, Harriet Lavinia b 1987); *Career* barr Lincoln's Inn; *Style*— The Hon Mark Piercy; 39 Carson Rd, W Dulwich, London SE21 8HT

PIERCY, Baroness; Oonagh Lavinia; JP; da of late Maj Edward John Lake Baylay, DSO; *m* 1944, 2 Baron Piercy (d 1981); 2 s, 3 da; *Style*— The Rt Hon the Lady Piercy, JP; The Old Rectory, Elford, Tamworth, Staffs B79 9DD (☎ 082 785 233)

PIERCY, Hon Penelope Katherine; CBE (1968); da of 1 Baron Piercy, CBE (d 1966), and Mary Louisa, OBE (d 1953; da of Hon Thomas Pelham, CB, who was 3 s of 3 Earl of Chichester); *b* 15 April 1916; *Educ* St Paul's Girls' Sch, Somerville Coll Oxford (MA); *Career* under-sec Miny of Technol 1964-68, ret; *Recreations* gardening; *Style*— The Hon Penelope Piercy, CBE; Charlton Cottage, Tarrant Rushton, Blandford Forum, Dorset (☎ 0258 52072)

PIERCY, Baroness; Veronica; da of late John Hordley Warham; *Educ* St Paul's Girls Sch; *m* 1964, as his 2 w, 1 Baron Piercy, CBE (d 1966); *Style*— The Rt Hon Veronica, Lady Piercy; 7 Milborne Grove, SW10

PIERRE, Lady; Marjorie; *m* 1962, as his 2 w, Sir (Joseph) Henry Pierre (sometime conslt surgn Gen Hosp Port of Spain Trinidad; d 1984), s of late Charles Henry Pierre; 1 s, 1 step s; *Style*— Lady Pierre; St Florian, Fishery Rd, Bray, nr Maidenhead, Berks SL6 1UN

PIERS, Sir Charles Robert Fitzmaurice; 10 Bt (I 1661) VRD; s of Sir Charles Piers, 9 Bt (d 1945); *b* 30 August 1903; *Educ* RNCs Osborne and Dartmouth; *m* 1936, Ann Blanche Scott (d 1975), da of late Capt Thomas Ferguson; 1 s, 1 da (decd); *Heir* s, James Desmond Piers; *Career* mangr Midland Doherty Ltd of Duncan BC, ret; *Style*— Sir Charles Piers, Bt; PO Box 748, Duncan, British Columbia V9L 3Y1, Canada

PIERS, Rear Adm Desmond William; DSC (1943), CM (1982), CD; seventh in descent from Sir Henry Piers, 1 Bt (NS 1660/61) and fifth in descent from Lewis Piers who arrived in Halifax, Nova Scotia, at its founding 1749; s of William Harington Piers (d 1938), and Dr Florence Maud O'Donnel Piers (d 1958); *b* 12 June 1913; *Educ* Halifax County Acad, RMC of Canada, RN Staff Coll, Nat Def Coll of Canada; *m* 1941, Janet, da of Dr Murray Macneill (d 1956), of Halifax, NS; 1 step da; *Career* served Royal Canadian Navy 1932-67, Escort Gp Cdr in Battle of Atlantic 1941-43, destroyer Capt for Murmansk Convoys and Invasion of Normandy 1944-45, Canadian Fleet Cdr 1956-57, Cmdt RMC Canada 1957-60, chm Canadian Def Liaison Staff Washington DC and Canadian rep on NATO mil ctee 1962-66, ret 1967; Agent Gen of Nova Scotia in the UK and Europe 1977-79; Hon Doctorate Mil Science RMC Canada 1978; memb Order of Canada 1982; hon-life memb Nat Tst for Scotland 1984; Freeman City of London 1978; *Recreations* golf, tennis, figure skating, photography; *Clubs* Halifax, Ashburn GC (Halifax), Chester GC, Curling, Tennis Figure Skating; *Style*— Rear Adm Desmond Piers, DSC, CM, CD; The Quarter Deck, Chester, Nova Scotia BOJ IJO, Canada (☎ 902 275 4462)

PIERS, James Desmond; s and h of Sir Charles Robert Fitzmaurice Piers, 10 Bt, *qv*; *b* 24 July 1947; *m* 1975, Sandra Mae Dixon; 1 s (Stephen James b 1979); 1 da (Christine Sarah b 1976); *Style*— James Piers, Esq

PIGGOTT, Donald James; s of James Piggott (d 1962), and Edith, *née* Tempest (d 1968); *b* 1 Sept 1920; *Educ* Bradford, Christs Coll Cambridge (MA), LSE; *m* 15 June 1974, Kathryn Jessie Courtenay-Evans, *née* Eckford; *Career* Army Serv 1941-46, NW Europe and India; PA to fin dir London Tport 1947-50, distributor mgmnt Shell-Mex and BP Ltd 1951-58, mktg devpt BP Co Ltd 1958-73, dir gen Br Red Cross Soc 1980-85 (int dir 1973- 80); memb centl appeals advsy ctees BBC and IBA 1980-83, tstee memb Jt Ctee of St John and Red Cross 1980, dep pres Suffolk Branch Br Red Cross 1987; OStJ 1983; Freeman City of London 1988, Liveryman Worshipful Co of Carmen 1988; FRSM 1982; *Recreations* music, theatre; *Style*— Donald Piggott, Esq; 18 Elm Lodge, River Gardens, London SW6 6NZ (☎ 01 385 5588); Beech House, The Green, Tostock, Bury, St Edmunds

PIGGOTT, Maj-Gen Francis James Claude; CB (1964), CBE (1961), DSO (1945); s of Maj Gen Francis Stewart Gilderoy Piggott, CB, DSO (d 1966), and Jane Smith (d 1955); *b* 11 Oct 1910; *Educ* Cheltenham, RMC Sandhurst; *m* 19 July 1940, Muriel Joan, da of Wilfred E Cottam (d 1959), of Rotherham, S Yorks; 1 s (Richard), 1 da (Jane); *Career* 2 Lt the Queen's Royal Regt 1931, language offr Japan 1935-37, serv

WWII: France (despatches), NZ, Indian, Burma (DSO); in Japan, UK, Egypt 1946-52, CO 1st Bn The Queens Royal Regt 1952-54 in ROAR and Malaya, DDM1 1958-61, asst COS (Intelligence), SHAPE Paris 1961-64, Maj-Gen 1961, ret 1964; served with Army Security Vetting Unit 1965-75; *Clubs* Army and Navy; *Style—* Maj-Gen Francis Piggott, CB, CBE, DSO; c/o Army and Navy Club, 36-39 Pall Mall, London SW1

PIGGOTT, Harold Ebenezer; s of Percy Henry Heath Piggott (d 1979), and Mary Gertrude, *née* Saunders (d 1962); *b* 14 April 1937; *Educ* Worthing HS for Boys, Brighton Tech Coll (City & Guilds); *m* 5 Sept 1959, Barbara Ethel, da of William John Tunbridge, of Cornwall; 3 da (Susan b 17 July 1960, Clare b 8 Aug 1965, Amanda b 29 April 1968); *Career* fndr Harold E Piggott Ltd 1962, dir Hearts of Oak Benefit Soc 1978- (former chm Staff pension scheme), Hearts of Oak Tstee Ltd London 1982-, dir Aberdeen & Northern Mutual Assur Soc Ltd, investmt dir Hearts of Oak Insur Gp 1983-; pres Worthing Hard of Hearing Club, govr C of E Sch; chm: Sussex Parkinson Disease Soc, City of London Freeman Assoc of Sussex; Rotarian life memb: Guild of Freeman of City of London Nat Tst, Worthing Civic Soc 1987-; elected exec bd Nat Conf Friendly Socs, sec Sussex regn Assoc of Cost & Exec Accountants; memb: Sussex Mayors Assoc, Worthing Borough Sussex Police Conslt Ctee; vice-chm Worthing Borough Cncl Mgmnt Bd (fndr emergency ctee); co cncllr W Sussex 1974-85, chm catering Co Hall 1980-85, cncllr Worthing Borough (dep ldr cncl), Mayor of Worthing 1982-83, chm Policy & Resources Ctee, Property & Estates, Worthing Centenary; memb: Assoc of Dist Cncls W Sussex Branch, DHSS Appeals Tbnl 1975-87; Worthing Heene Cons auditor; Liveryman City of London 1977 (Freeman 1972), Steward Worshipful Co of Basketmakers 1988; fell IOD 1965, FBIM 1983, FCEA 1983, FFA 1987, FRSA 1988; Lord of the Manor of Netherhall Old Newton Sussex; *Books* Beauty & History in the South East (article in Hearts of Oak Magazine, 1978); *Recreations* swimming, chess, snooker, golf, reading; *Clubs* The Manorial Soc of GB United Wards, The City of London; *Style—* Harold Piggott, Esq; Netherhall, Upper Brighton Rd, Worthing, W Sussex BN14 9HY (☎ 0903 35510); Apartment at Playa Sol, Avenida Gola Diestany, 11-15 Santa Margarita, Rosas; Hearts of Oak House, Registered Office, 84 Kingsway, London WC2B 6NF (☎ 01 404 0393)

PIGGOTT, (Francis John) Richard; s of Maj-Gen F J C Piggott, CB, CBE, DSO, *qv*; *b* 8 Mar 1943; *Educ* Ullenwood Manor, Battisborough; *m* 2, 1980, Jennifer Anne; 2 s (James b 1970, Benjamin b 1981), 1 da (Sarah b 1968); *Career* chm and fndr Guildbourne Hldgs Gp (UK), Sociètè Immobilière de Guildbourne SARL (France), Guildbourne Hldgs RV (Holland), Guildbourne Texas (USA); *Recreations* shooting, fishing; *Clubs* Army and Navy; *Style—* Richard Piggott, Esq

PIGOT, His Hon Judge Thomas Herbert; QC (1967); s of late Thomas Pigot, and late Martha Ann Pigot; *b* 19 May 1921; *Educ* Manchester GS, Brasenose Coll Oxford (BA, BCL, MA); *m* 19 Aug 1950, Zena Marguerite, da of Thomas Wall; 3 da (Diana Marguerite b 1953, Clare Rowena b 1956, Anne Rosalind b 1959); *Career* 2 Lt Welsh Regt 1941, transfrd to Lincs Regt 1942, served N Africa (POW 1943-45); barr 1947, Northern circuit, circuit judge 1972, dep sr judge in Sovereign Base areas of Cyprus 1971, sr judge (chief justice), Common SJT in City of London 1984, HM Lt in the City of London 1984, bencher of the Inner Temple 1985; memb Worshipful Co of Cutlers 1985; *Style—* His Hon Judge Pigot, QC; c/o Central Criminal Court, London EC4M 7EH

PIGOTT, David John Berkeley; er s and h of Sir Henry Pigott, 5 Bt; *b* 16 August 1955; *Educ* Moor Park; *m* 1, 1981 (m dis 1984), Alison Fletcher; m 2, 1986, Julie Wiffen; *Style—* David Pigott, Esq; c/o Brook Farm, Shobley, Ringwood, Hants

PIGOTT, Sir (Berkeley) Henry Sebastian; 5 Bt (UK 1808), of Knapton, Queen's County; s of Maj Sir Berkeley Charles Pigott, 4 Bt (d 1982), and Christabel, *née* Bowden-Smith (d 1974); *b* 24 June 1925; *Educ* Ampleforth; *m* 4 Sept 1954, (Olive) Jean, o da of John William Balls (d 1975), of Holly Lodge, Surlingham, Norfolk; 2 s (David John Berkeley b 1955, Antony Charles Philip b 1960), 1 da (Sarah Jane Mary b 1964); *Heir* s, David John Berkeley Pigott, *qv*; *Career* served WWII RM 1944-45; farmer; Freeman of City of Baltimore USA; *Recreations* sailing (in Guinness Book of Records (1988 edn) for smallest single-handed circumnavigation); *Style—* Sir Henry Pigott, Bt; Brook Farm, Shobley, Ringwood, Hants BH24 3HT

PIGOTT, Hugh Sefton; s of Alfred Sefton Pigott, OBE (d 1979), of Dean Hill, Wilmslow, Cheshire, and Frances Ann, *née* Mills (d 1984); *b* 21 Dec 1929; *Educ* Oundle, King's Coll Cambridge (BA, MA); *m* m 1, 31 Aug 1957 (m dis 1984), Venetia Caroline Mary, da of Derric John Stopford Adams, of Ansty Hall, Coventry, Worcs; 4 s (Charles b 1958, Francis b 1960, Edward b 1963, Philip b 1966); m 2, 1 Nov 1986, Fiona Margaret Miller, da of John McDermid, of The Old Rectory, Hickling, Norfolk; *Career* Clifford Chance (formerly Coward Chance): articled clerk 1952-55, asst 1955-60, ptnr 1960-; memb Law Soc's standing ctee on co law 1972-85, memb advsy working pty on Europe 1976-79, hon legal advr to Accounting Standards Ctee 1986, memb top salaries review bdy 1988; Liveryman Worshipful Co of Slrs; *Recreations* poetry, the visual arts, piano playing, cooking; *Style—* Hugh Pigott, Esq; Clifford Chance, Royex House, Aldermanbury Sq, London EC2V 7LD (☎ 01 600 0808, fax 01 726 8561)

PIHL, Brig the Hon Dame Mary Mackenzie; *née* Anderson; DBE (1970, MBE 1958); da of 1 Viscount Waverley, PC, GCB, GCSI, GCIE (d 1958), and Christina, *née* Mackenzie (d 1920); *b* 3 Feb 1916; *Educ* Sutton HS, Villa Brillantmont Lausanne Switzerland; *m* 8 July 1973, Frithjof Pihl, s of Carl Pihl (d 1936); *Career* joined ATS 1941, transfrd WRAC 1949; dir WRAC 1967-70; Hon ADC to HM The Queen 1967-70; *Clubs* Naval, English Speaking Union; *Style—* Brig the Hon Dame Mary Pihl, DBE

PIKE, Claude Drew; OBE (1970), DL (Devon 1979); s of Ivan Samuel Pike (d 1934), and Alice, *née* Goodhead (d 1956); bro of Baroness Pike of Melton (Life Peer), *qv*; *b* 4 July 1915; *Educ* Silcoates Sch Wakefield, Jesus Coll Cambridge (MA, LLM); *m* 23 May 1941, Margaret, da of George Thomas Hirst (d 1965); 1 s (John), 1 da (Penelope); *Career* WWII serv 1940-45, promoted Capt Paymaster; chm Watts Blake Bearne plc 1964-86 (dir 1945); dir: Hepworth Ceramic Hldgs plc 1974-87, Lloyds Bank (Devon and Cornwall) 1973-86, Morwellham Recreational Tst; chm Exeter Cathedral Preservation Tst, pres Men of the Trees Devon, chm Trobay Hosp Med Res Tst, govr Blundell's; pres: Devon Historic Bldgs Tst Ltd, Devon Co Agric Assoc 1988-; landowner; CBIM 1976; *Recreations* forestry, dendrology; *Clubs* Oxford & Cambridge Univ; *Style—* Claude Pike, Esq, OBE, DL; Dunderdale Lawn, Penhurst Rd, Newton Abbot TQ12 1EN (☎ 0626 544 04); Manwood, Heathercombe, Newton Abbot, Devon TQ 13 9XE; Watts Blake Bearne & Co plc, Park House, Courtenay Park, Newton Abbot, Devon TQ 12 4PS (☎ 0626 523 45, telex 428 24 WBB G)

PIKE, Prof Edward Roy; s of Anthony Pike (d 1968), of Abercarn, Monmouth, and Rosalind Pike (d 1982); *b* 4 Dec 1929; *Educ* Southfield Sch Oxford, Univ Coll Cardiff (BSc, PhD); *m* 1955, Pamela, da of William Henry Spearing Sawtell (d 1978); 1 s, 2 da; *Career* serv RCS (SHAPE HQ France) 1948-50; Fulbright scholar faculty of physics MIT (USA) 1958-60, chief scientific offr Scientific Civil Serv 1960-, Clerk Maxwell prof of theoretical physics King's Coll London 1986-; chm Adam Hilger Ltd, dir Richard Clay plc 1985-66; vice-pres Inst of Physics 1981-85; FRS, FRSA; *Recreations* languages, music; *Style—* Prof E R Pike; 8 Bredon Grove, Malvern, Worcs WR14 3JR (☎ 0684 574910)

PIKE, Francis Bruce; s of Esmund Francis Victor Wallace Pike, of Old Brow, Bimport, Shaftesbury, Dorset, and Elizabeth Rosemary, *née* Dun; *b* 13 Feb 1954; *Educ* Uppingham, Univ of Paris, Selwyn Coll Cambridge (MA); *Career* md MIM Tokyo KK 1983-87; dir: OUB Investmt Mgmnt Ltd 1986-, MIM Britannia Okasan Investmt Mgmnt Ltd 1986-, MIM Ltd 1987-, Nippon Warrant Fund 1987-, Drayton Far Eastern Tst plc 1988-; chm Asia Supergrowth Fund 1987-; *Recreations* reading; *Style—* Francis Pike, Esq; 23 Elder Street, Spitalfields, London E1 (☎ 01 377 1442); MIM Ltd, 11 Devonshire Square, London EC2 (☎ 01 626 3434, fax 01 623 3339, telex 886108)

PIKE, Baroness (Life Peer UK 1974); Irene Mervyn Parnicott Pike; DBE (1981); da of Ivan Samuel Pike (d 1934), and Alice Pike (d 1956); sis of Claude Drew Pike, *qv*; *b* 16 Sept 1918; *Educ* Hunmanby Hall, Univ of Reading; *Career* MP (C) Melton, Leics Dec 1956-Feb 1974, asst postmaster-gen 1959-63, jt parly under-sec state Home Off 1963-64; chm: IBA gen adv cncl 1974-79, WRVS 1974-81 broadcasting complaints ctee 1981-; dir: Watts Blake Bearne & Co Ltd, Dunderdale Investmts; *Style—* The Rt Hon the Lady Pike, DBE; Hownam, nr Kelso, Roxburgh

PIKE, Air Cdre James Maitland Nicholson; CB (1963), DSO (1942), DFC (1941); s of Frank Pike (d 1966), and Daphne, *née* Kenyon Stow (d 1953), of Co Mayo, Eire; *b* 8 Feb 1916; *Educ* Stowe, RAF Coll Cranwell; *m* 1, 1942, Mary Bettina Dell; 1 da; m 2, 1955, Amber Pauline Bettesworth Hellard; 1 s, 1 step da; m 3, 1972, Dorothy May Dawson, *née* Holland; 1 step da; *Career* cmmnd RAF 1937, served WWII, Aden, Middle East, UK Coastal cmd, Malta, Azores; directing staff RAF Staff Coll 1945-47, Gp Capt 1955, Cdr RAF St Mawgan and RAF Kinloss 1955-57, SASO RAF Malta 1958-60, Air Cdre 1961, AOC RAF Gibraltar 1961-62, IDC 1963, dir Security RAF 1964-69, ret; civil serv MOD 1969-78; *Recreations* shooting, fishing; *Style—* Air Cdre James Pike, CB, DSO, DFC; The Hyde, 31 Brookside, Watlington, Oxford, OX9 5AQ (☎ 049161 2634)

PIKE, Michael Edmund; CMG (1984); *b* 4 Oct 1931; *Educ* Wimbledon Coll, LSE, Brasenose Coll Oxford (MA); *m* 1962, Catherine, *née* Lim; 1 s, 2 da; *Career* former cnsllr Washington and Tel Aviv, RCDS, ambass to Vietnam 1982-85; *Style—* Michael Pike, Esq, CMG; 5 Grooms Hill, London SE10 8ER

PIKE, Peter Leslie; MP (Lab) Burnley 1983-; s of Leslie Henry Pike (d 1980), and Gladys Pike (d 1971); *b* 26 June 1937; *Educ* Hinchley Wood Secdy Sch; *m* 1962, Sheila Lillian, da of Hubert John Bull (d 1964); 2 da; *Career* served RM 1955-57; with Midland Bank 1954-62, pty organiser Lab Pty 1963-73, with Mullard (Simonstone) 1973-83; patron Burnley Youth Theatre; memb: National Tst, CND, Anti-Apartheid; *Recreations* Burnley FC supporter; *Clubs* Byerden House Socialist, Mullard Sports and Social; *Style—* Peter Pike, Esq, MP; 75 Ormerod Rd, Burnley, Lancs BB11 2RU (☎ 0282 34719); House of Commons, London SW1A 0AA (☎ 01 219 3000)

PIKE, Sir Philip Ernest Housden; s of Rev Ernest Benjamin Pike (d 1959), and, Dora Case, *née* Lillie (d 1958); *b* 6 Mar 1914; *Educ* De Carteret Sch, Munro Coll Jamaica; *m* 1, 1943 (m dis 1959), Phyllis Kelvin, da of late Kelvin S Calder; 1 s, 1 da; m 2, 1959, Millicent Locke, da of late George Staples; *Career* barr Middle Temple 1938; legal draughtsman Kenya 1949-52, crown counsel Jamaica 1947-49, solicitor-gen Uganda 1952-58, QC Uganda 1953 and Sarawak 1958, attorney-gen Sarawak 1958-65, chief justice Borneo High Ct 1965-68, high ct judge Malawi 1969-70 (actg chief justice 1970), chief justice Swaziland 1970-72; kt 1969; *Recreations* golf; *Clubs* Clovelly Country (Cape); *Style—* Sir Philip Pike; 30 Berg Rd, Fish Hoek, Cape, 7975, S Africa (☎ 021 82 4119)

PIKE, Lady Romayne Aileen; *née* Brabazon; da of 14 Earl of Meath, and his w Elizabeth Mary, only da of Capt Geoffrey Vaux Salvin Bowlby, RHG; *b* 1943,May; *m* 1968, Robert Eben Neil, s of Lt-Col Godfrey Eben Pike (d 1967); 1 s (Harry), 1 da (Tamsin); *Career* sculptor; *Style—* Lady Romayne Pike; Kidborough House, Danehill, Sussex RH17 7HQ

PIKE, Rt Rev St John Surridge; s of the Rev Canon William Pike (d 1934), of Thurles, Co Tipperary, Ireland; *b* 27 Dec 1909; *Educ* The Abbey Tipperary, Bishop Foy School Waterford, Univ of Dublin (MA, DD); *m* 1958, Clare, da of William Henry Jones; 2 s, 1 da; *Career* ordained 1932, asst curate Taney (dioc of Dublin) 1932-37, head of Southern Church Mission Ballymacarrett Belfast 1937-47, SPG missionary Gambia 1947-52, rector St George's Belfast 1952-58, bishop of Gambia and the Rio Pongas 1958-63, vicar of Ewshot (dioc of Guildford) 1963-71, asst bishop of Guildford 1963-83, vicar of Holy Trinity Botleys and Lyne and Christ Church Longcross 1971-83; *Style—* St John Pike; Wisteria Cottage, Old Rectory Lane, Twyford, nr Winchester, Hants SO21 1NS

PIKE, Rt Rev Victor Joseph; CB (1953), CBE (1950, OBE 1944); s of Rev Canon William Pike (d 1934), and Florence, *née* Surridge (d 1967); *b* 1 July 1907; *Educ* Bishop Foy Sch Waterford, Trinity Coll Dublin (MA), DD (hc) 1955; *m* 1937, Dorothea Elizabeth, da of late Capt W R Frend; 1 s, 2 da; *Career* sr chaplain 43 Div 11 Armd Div 1940-42, dep asst chaplain-gen 5 Corps CMF 1942-44 (despatches), dep chaplain-gen MELF 1946, asst chaplain-gen Western Cmd 1947-49, asst chaplain-gen BAOR 1950-51, chaplain-gen to the Forces 1951-60 (archdeacon 1958-60); prebend of Fordington with Writhlington in Salisbury Cathedral 1960, bishop suffragan of Sherborne 1960-76, hon canon of Canterbury 1951-60, QHC 1948-53, chaplain to HM The Queen 1953-60; *Recreations* fishing, watching rugby (played rugby for Ireland 1931-35); *Clubs* Cavalry; *Style—* The Rt Rev Victor Pike, CB, CBE; 53 The Close, Salisbury, Wilts SP1 2EN (☎ 0722 5766)

PIKE, Lt-Gen Sir William Gregory Huddleston; KCB (1961, CB 1956), CBE (1952), DSO (1943); s of Capt Sydney Royston Pike, RA (d 1907), and Sarah Elizabeth, *née* Huddleston (d 1963); bro of Marshal of the RAF Sir Thomas Pike (d 1983); *b* 24 June 1905; *Educ* Bedford Sch, Marlborough, RMA Woolwich; *m* 1939, Josephine Margaret, da of Maj-Gen Reginald Henry Dalrymple Tompson, CB, CMG, DSO (d 1937); 1 s, 2 da; *Career* Br and Indian Artillery 1925-36, Staff Coll Camberley 1937-38, cmd and staff appts in France, Belgium, N Africa, UK, USA, Far East 1939-

50, CRA 1 Cwlth Div Korea 1951-52, dir staff duties WO 1954-57, COS FARELF 1957-60, Vice CIGS 1960-63, Hon Col 277 Highland Field Rgmt RA (TA) 1960-67, Col Cmdt RA 1962-70; Lieut of HM Tower of London 1963-66; jt hon pres Anglo Korean Soc 1963-69, chief cdr St John Ambulance 1969-75; chm Lord Mayor Treloar Trust and governing body Treloar Coll until 1982; memb Hon Artillery Co, govr Corps of Commissionaires; Legion of Merit (USA) 1953; GCStJ 1976; *Recreations* field sports, gardening; *Style*— Lt-Gen Sir William Pike, KCB, CBE, DSO; Ganwells, Bentley, Hants (☎ 0420 22152)

PIKESLEY, Richard Leslie; s of Leonard Leslie Pikesley, and Gwendolen Eleanor, *née* Read; *b* 8 Jan 1951; *Educ* St Nicholas GS Northwood, Harrow Sch of Art, City of Canterbury Coll of Art, Univ of London; *m* 4 May 1974, Susan Margaret, da of Sidney James Stone; 2 da (Caroline b 1984, Elzabeth b 1987); *Career* artist; contributions to mixed exhibitions incl: Royal Acad Summer Exhibition, Royal Inst of Oil Painters, Laing Prize exhibition, Royal Inst of Painters in Watercolours, New Grafton Gallery London, WH Patterson Fine Art London, Minton Fine Art Toronto; one man and small gp shows incl: Butlin Gallery Somerset, Linfield Gallery, St James's Gallery Bath; rep in various collections incl: St Johns Coll Cambridge, Hambro's Bank, S G Warburg; awards: finalist Hunting Gp Prize 1981 and 1989, EF Hutton Prize 1987, W H Patterson Prize 1988; memb NEAC 1974; *Recreations* horses, riding; *Style*— Richard Pikesley, Esq; Middlehill Farm, Marrowbone Lane, Bothenhampton, Bridport, Dorset DT6 4BU (☎ 0308 221 81)

PIKETT, Christopher; s of Maj Cecil Charles Pikett, and Joan Madeleine Pikett; *b* 15 Oct 1952; *Educ* West Bridgford GS Nottingham, Univ of Southhampton (LLB); *m* 18 Sept 1976, Geraldine Barbara, da of Derek Alan Stopps; 2 s (Oliver James b 1980, Edward Guy b 1983); *Career* barr middle Temple 1976, legal advsr in indust 1976-82; dir legal servs and co sec Varity Hldgs and subsidaries 1987-; memb Hon Soc of Middle Temple; FRSA; *Style*— Christopher Pikett, Esq; Varity Holdings Ltd, 35 Davies St, London W1Y 2EA (☎ 01 491 7000, fax 01 491 5271

PILBROW, Richard Hugh; Cranbrook Sch, Central Sch of Speech and Drama; s of Arthur Gordon Pilbrow; *b* 28 April 1933 Cranbrook Sch, Central Sch of Speech and Drama; *m* 1, 1958, Viki Brinton; 1 s, 1 da; m 2, 1974, Molly Friedel; 1 da; *Career* chm Theatre Projects Gp of Cos 1957-, lighting designer for prods in London, Moscow, New York, Paris; vice pres: Assoc of Br Theatre Technicians, Art Youth Theatre; memb: Arts Cncl of GB 1968-70, Soc of West End Theatre, Cncl London Acad of Music and Drama; FRSA; *Books* Stage Lighting (1970); *Clubs* Garrick; *Style*— Richard Pilbrow, Esq; Theatre Projects Conslts Ltd, 3 Apollo Studios, Charlton Kings Rd, London NW5 2SW (☎ 01 482 4224, fax 01 284 0636)

PILCH, Anthony Michael; CBE (1984); s of Lt-Col George Harold Pilch (d 1943); *b* 6 July 1927; *Educ* Shrewsbury, Balliol Coll Oxford (BA); *m* 1950, Betty Christine, da of Franklin John Skinner (d 1976); 1 da; *Career* dir Noble Lowndes & Partners Ltd 1968-85, ret; chm: National Assoc of Pension Funds 1979-81 (vice pres 1981-83), New Horizon Tst; *Recreations* theatre, photography, writing; *Style*— Michael Pilch, Esq, CBE; 10 Timber Hill Rd, Caterham, Surrey CR3 6LD (☎ 0883 46671)

PILCHER, Anthony David; s of Lt-Col William Spelman Pilcher, DSO (d 1970), and Diana, *née* Lawrence (d 1987); *b* 7 Sept 1935; *Educ* Eton; *m* 4 Feb 1964 (Margaret) Ann, da of Maj Gerald Borland Walker (ka 1941); 2 s (Harry b 4 Oct 1968, Sam b 16 Oct 1973); *Career* sr ptnr FLP Secretan 1977-87 (previously ptnr), chm FLP Secretan & Co Ltd 1987, dir Secretan (underwriting agencies) Ltd; Freeman: City of London, Worshipful Co of Pewterers; Liveryman and memb Ct Worshipful Co of Haberdashers; *Recreations* fishing, sailing, viticulture; *Clubs* Bembridge SC; *Style*— Anthony D Pilcher, Esq; 8 Victoria Rd, Kensington, London W8 5RD (☎ 01 937 3711); Upper North Wells House, Bembridge, IOW PO35 5NF; F L P Secretan & Co Ltd, Suite 776, Lloyd's, Lime St, London EC3M 7DQ (☎ 01 623 8084, fax 01 626 8066, telex 987321 LLOYDS G)

PILCHER, Sir (Charlie) Dennis; CBE (1968); s of Charlie Edwin Pilcher; *b* 2 July 1906; *Educ* Clayesmore Sch; *m* 1929, Mary Allison, da of William Aumonier; 2 da (*see* The Earl of Straffor); *Career* served RA 1940-45, Normandy 1944 (despatches), Maj; chartered surveyor; conslt Graves Son & Pilcher Chartered Surveyors (ptnr 1930 subsequently sr ptnr), Hemel Hempsted Devpt Corpn 1949-56, Bracknell Devpt Corpn 1956-71 (chm 1968-71), chm Cmmn for the New Towns 1971-78; advsr to govt on: housing rent assessment, control of business rents, commercial property devpt 1965-76; dir: Sun Life Assur Soc 1968-77, Save and Prosper Gp Ltd 1970-80; memb cncl Glyndebourne Festival Opera 1969-; FRICS; kt 1974; *Style*— Sir Dennis Pilcher, CBE; Brambles, Bats Lane, Mare Hill, Pulborough, W Sussex (☎ 079 82 2126)

PILCHER, Graham Hope; MC (1944), TD; s of William Hope Pilcher (d 1971), of Monorgan Farm, Longforgan, Dundee, and Eileen Beatrice Margaret, *née* Cox (d 1986); *b* 16 June 1916; *Educ* Dunfirmline, Clifton; *m* 7 Dec 1946, Rosamunde Evelyna Montague Lawrence, da of Cdr Charles Montague Lawrence Scott, RN, of Green Loaning, Lelant, St Ives, Cornwall; 2 s (Robin b 1950, Mark b 1958), 2 da (Fiona b 1948, Philippa b 1953); *Career* cmmnd TA Maj 4th Black Watch (Royal Highland Reg) TA, BEF France, Belgium 1940, Gibraltar 1940-43, UK 1943-44, 5th Black Watch 1944-45 NW Europe; dir: Jute Industs Ltd, Sidlaw Industs 1948-79; Dundee Rep Theatre Ltd 1957-, memb: Bd Dundee Approved Schs 1947-67, ctees of Episcopal Church of Scotland 1946-; *Recreations* golf, shooting; *Clubs* Royal and Ancient GC of St Andrews, Royal Perth Golfing Soc; *Style*— Graham Pilcher, Esq; Over Pilmore, Invergowrie, by Dundee DD2 5EL

PILCHER, Sir John Arthur; GCMG (1973, KCMG 1966, CMG 1957); s of late Lt-Col A J Pilcher; *b* 16 May 1912; *Educ* Shrewsbury, Clare Coll Cambridge; *m* 1942, Delia Margaret Taylor; 1 da (Julia, the Hon Mrs Seymour Fortescue); *Career* ambass: Philippines 1959-63, Austria 1965-67, Japan 1967-72; dir For & Colonial Investmt Tst 1973-82, advsr on Far Eastern affrs Robert Fleming & Co 1973-86; chm Japan Soc of London, patron Inst of Linguists (chm treasure trove review ctee), memb cncl Soc for Protection of Ancient Buildings; Grand Cross Order of Merit (Austria), Rising Sun First Class (Japan), Order of Merit (Italy); *Clubs* Brooks's; *Style*— Sir John Pilcher, GCMG; 33 The Terrace, Barnes, London SW13 0NR (☎ 01 876 9710)

PILCHER, (Anthony) Julian; s of Col Alan Humphrey Pilcher, CIE, MC, ED (d 1957), and Dorothy Eileeen, *née* Parrington; *b* 7 Feb 1936; *Educ* Shrewsbury; *m* 26 Oct 1963, Sally Louise, da of Herbert John Murray Cook, of Tilford, Surrey; 1 s (Simon b 1966), 2 da (Rebecca b 1967, Sophie b 1969); *Career* qualified CA 1959; ptnr: Harmood Banner & Co 1963-74, Deloitte Haskins & Sells 1974-82; fndg ptnr Lyon Pilcher & Co 1983-, dir Coll Servs Ltd Solent Pensions Ltd; pres Southampton C of C, govr Rookesbury Pk Sch; *Recreations* sailing, shooting, skiing; *Clubs* Cavalry and Guards, Royal Southern YC; *Style*— Julian Pilcher, Esq; Waynflete House, St Swithun St, Winchester (☎ 0962 54693); Lyon Pilcher & Co, 102-108 Above Bar, Southampton (☎ 0703 636915, fax 0703 339369)

PILCHER, Roger Anthony; s of Walter Pilcher (d 1967); *b* 11 April 1931; *Educ* Tonbridge, RMA Sandhurst; *m* Lydia; 5 s , 1 da; *Career* Maj The Buffs; mgmnt Int Factors Ltd (md 1967-68), md Credit Factoring Int Ltd 1968-84, chief exec The Export Fin Co Ltd 1984-; MIEX 1975; *Recreations* wildlife, hillwalking, photography; *Style*— Roger Pilcher, Esq; Ash House, Lea, Malmesbury, Wilts (☎ 0666 824 884); The Export Finance Co Ltd, Exfinco House, Swindon SN1 1QQ (☎ 0793 614 404)

PILDITCH, James George Christopher; CBE (1983); s of Frederick Henry Pilditch (d 1952), and his w, Marie-Thérèse, *née* Priest (d 1982); *b* 7 August 1929; *Educ* Slough GS, Univ of Reading, INSEAD; *m* 1, 1952 (m dis) Molly; m 2, 1970, Anne Elisabeth, da of Osborne Wilhemson Johnson, of Stockholm; 1 da; *Career* Nat Serv RA and RCA (Res); fndr AIDCOM Int plc; chm: design bd BTEC, cncl Mktg Gp of GB; memb Design Cncl; cncl memb Royal Soc of Arts 1984, former memb Heritage of London Tst 1986; chm: Furniture EDC NEDO 1985, design working pty, NEDO 1985; memb: and chm design panel Br Airports Authy 1987, Advsy Panel Design Mgmnt Unit London Business Sch 1982 (chm Financial Times Award 1987) first fell Design Mngmt Inst USA; FRSA, Hon FCSD; *Publications* The Silent Salesman, The Business of Product Design, Communication by Design, Talk about Design, winning ways; *Recreations* writing, drawing, watching the Lord's Test; *Clubs* MCC, Army & Navy, Leander; *Style*— James Pilditch, Esq, CBE; 62 Cadogan Sq, London SW1 (☎ 01 584 9279); Brookhampton House, N Cadbury, Somerset (☎ 096 340 225)

PILDITCH, John Richard; s and h of Sir Richard Edward Pilditch, 4 Bt , qv; *b* 24 Sept 1955; *Style*— John Pilditch, Esq; c/o 4 Fisherman's Bank, Mudeford, Christchurch, Dorset

PILDITCH, Sir Richard Edward; 4 Bt (UK 1929); s of Sir Philip Harold Pilditch, 2 Bt, and bro of Sir Philip John Frederick Pilditch, 3 Bt (d 1954); *b* 8 Sept 1926; *Educ* Charterhouse; *m* 7 Oct 1950, Pauline Elizabeth Smith; 1 s, 1 da; *Heir* s, John Richard Pilditch, qv; *Career* RN 1944-45 India and Ceylon; *Style*— Sir Richard Pilditch, Bt; 4 Fishermans Bank, Mudeford, Christchurch, Hants

PILE, Anthony John Devereux; er s of Sir John Pile (d 1982), and Lady Pile, *qv*; hp to unc, Sir Frederick Pile, 3 Bt; *b* 7 June 1947; *Educ* Durham Sch; *m* 1977, Jenny Clare, da of Peter H Youngman, of Fenn St, Westleton, Suffolk; 2 s (Thomas b 6 April 1978, Hugh b 1980), 1 da (Harriet b 1983); *Career* cmmnd Durham LI 1966, served in Dhofar, Oman (despatches), NI, Cyprus, GSO3 (Ops) HQ 3 Armd Div 1979-80, Maj 1980, ret; attended Sloan Fellowship Programme London Business Sch, prodn mangr Hygrade (Meats) London 1982-85, prodn dir Mayhew Foods Ltd Uckfield E Sussex 1985-, md Crossley Ferguson Ltd Stockholm-on-Tees; *Recreations* squash, politics; *Style*— Anthony Pile, Esq; 23 The Green, Norton, Cleveland; Crossley Ferguson Ltd, Riverside House, 33 Bridge Rd, Stockton-on-Tees, Cleveland TS18 3AE (☎ 0642 612592)

PILE, Col Sir Frederick Devereux; 3 Bt (UK 1900), of Kenilworth House, Rathgar, Co Dublin; MC (1945); s of Gen Sir Frederick Alfred Pile, 2 Bt, GCB, DSO, MC (d 1976), and his 1 w Vera, da of Brig-Gen Frederick Lloyd, CB; *b* 10 Dec 1915; *Educ* Weymouth Coll, RMC Sandhurst; *m* 1, 1940, Pamela (d 1983), da of late Philip Henstock; 2 da; m 2, 1984, Violet Josephine Andrews, da of Alfred Denys Cowper; *Heir* n, Anthony John Devereux Pile; *Career* served 1939-45 War, Col Royal Tank Regt; Br Jt Serv Mission Washington DC 1957-60, Cmdt RAC Driving and Maintenance Sch 1960-62; *Recreations* fishing, cricket, travelling; *Clubs* MCC; *Style*— Col Sir Frederick Pile, Bt, MC; Brookfield House, Dallington, Sussex

PILE, Lady; Katharine Mary; er da of Austin George Shafe, of Henley-on-Thames; *m* 1946, Sir John Pile (d 1982), sometime chm Imperial Gp; 2 s (Anthony John Devereux, *qv*; Timothy b 1953), 2 da (Jennifer b 1950, Sarah b 1960); *Style*— Lady Katharine Pile; Munstead, Godalming, Surrey (☎ 048 68 4716)

PILE, Sir William Dennis; GCB (1978, KCB 1971, CB 1968), MBE (1944); s of James Edward Pile; *b* 1 Dec 1919; *Educ* Royal Masonic Sch, St Catharine's Coll Cambridge; *m* 1, 1939 (m dis 1947) Brenda Skinner; m 2, 1948, Joan Marguerite Crafter; 1 s, 2 da; *Career* chm Bd of Inland Revenue 1976-79, dir Nationwide Bldg Soc 1980-, Distillers' Co Ltd 1980-; *Clubs* United Oxford & Cambridge, Hawks (Cambridge); *Style*— Sir William Pile, GCB, MBE; The Manor House, Riverhead, nr Sevenoaks, Kent (☎ 0732 54498)

PILGRIM, John Brian Neil; s of Frank Edwin Booth Pilgrim (d 1983), of 35 Douglas Rd, Long Eaton, Notts, and Ida Lilian, *née* Pickavance; *b* 19 Feb 1909; *Educ* Trent Coll; *m* 6 June 1970, Susan Wendy, da of Sydney W Adams (d 1968), of Stoneleigh, Lyddineton, Uppingham, Rutland; 2 da (Sarah b 25 Jan 1973, Emma b 28 Sept 1975); *Career* articled clerk Ellis Kenewell 1956-60, md Pelerine Lingerie 1980- (joined 1961, dir 1972-80); memb Attenborough Tennis Club 1956-73, fndr memb Attenborough Badminton Club 1959-69, memb Long Eaton Round Table 1961-78; ACA 1960, FCA 1960; *Recreations* golf, bridge, gardening, reading, music; *Clubs* Beeston Fields GC; *Style*— Brian Pilgrim, Esq; Pelerine Lingerie, Queens Rd East, Beeston, Notts

PILKINGTON, Sir Alastair Lionel Alexander Bethune; s of Col Lionel George Pilkington, MC (d 1955), and Evelyn Carnegie (d 1985), da of Sir Alexander Sharp Bethune, 9 Bt; *b* 7 Jan 1920; *Educ* Sherborne, Trinity Cambridge; *m* 1, 1945, Patricia Nicholl (d 1977), da of Rear Adm Frank Elliott, OBE; 1 s, 1 da; m 2, 1978, Kathleen, wid of Eldridge Haynes; *Career* chm: Pilkington Bros Ltd 1973-80 (dir 1980-85, hon pres 1985-), Chloride Gp Ltd 1979-87; dir: Bank of England 1974-84, BP 1976-, Hambros Advanced Technol Tst, Banque Nationale de Paris Wellcome Fndn Ltd; memb bd of govrs Technical Change Centre, pro-chllr Lancaster Univ 1980-, chm cncl Nat Academic Awards 1984-87; Hon FUMIST 1969; hon fell: Imperial Coll 1974, LSE 1980, Poly of Wales 1988; FBIM, Hon DTech Loughborough 1968, CNAA, Hon DEng Liverpool 1971, Hon LLD Bristol 1979, Hon DSc (Eng) London 1979, Hon DSc East Anglia 1988, Hon Engr Birmingham 1988; FRS; kt 1970; *Clubs* Athenaeum; *Style*— Sir Alastair Pilkington; Goldrill Cottage, Patterdale, nr Penrith, Cumbria (☎ 085 32 263); 74 Eaton Place, London SW1X 8AU (☎ 01 235 5604)

PILKINGTON, Antony Richard; only s of Maj Arthur Cope Pilkington, MC (yr bro of late Sir Richard Pilkington, KBE, MC), and Otilia Dolores, *née* Reed-Cook; *b* 20 June 1935; *Educ* Ampleforth, Trinity Coll Cambridge; *m* 1960, Alice Kirsty, er da of Sir Thomas Calderwood Dundas, 7 and last Bt (d 1970), MBE; 3 s (Jerome b 1961, David b 1963, Simon b 1972), 1 da (Miranda b 1966); *Career* chm Pilkington Bros plc 1980-, non-exec dir Guest Keen & Nettlefolds 1982-, chm Community of St Helens Trust; dep chm supervisory bd: Flachglas AG (Germany), Dahlbusch AG (Germany); dir: Pilkington ACI Ltd (Australia), Pilkington Hldgs Inc (USA), Business in the Community; non-exec dir: Libbey-Owens-Ford Co (USA), Nat Westminster Bank plc; *Style—* Antony Pilkington, Esq; Pilkington Brothers plc, Prescot Rd, St Helens, Merseyside WA10 3TT (☎ 0744 28882)

PILKINGTON, (Richard) Godfrey; s of Col Guy Reginald Pilkington, DSO, TD (d 1970), of Fairfield, Crank, St Helens, Merseyside, and Margery, *née* Frost (d 1973); *b* 8 Nov 1918; *Educ* Clifton, Trinity Coll Cambridge (MA); *m* 14 Oct 1950, Evelyn Edith (Eve), da of Philip Robert Stanley Vincent (d 1933), of Gerrards Cross, Bucks; 2 s (Andrew b 1955, Matthew b 1964), 2 da (Penny b 1956, Dr Clarissa (Mrs Arscott) b 1958); *Career* WWII Lt (Temp Actg Capt) Anti-Tank and Medium Gunners RA, served BNAF (I Army) and CMF (Italy) 1940-46; art dealer Frost and Reed Ltd 1947-53, fndr and ptnr Piccadilly Gallery London 1953-, ed Pictures and Prints 1951-60, master Fine Art Trade Guild 1964-66, chm Soc London Art Dealers 1974-77; *Recreations* walking, gardening, tennis, golf, boating; *Clubs* Athenaeum, Hurlingham; *Style—* Godfrey Pilkington, Esq; 45 Barons Ct Rd, London W14 9DZ (☎ 01 385 8278); The Old Vicarage, Lamb Lane, Buckland, Faringdon, Oxfordshire; Piccadilly Gallery, 16 Cork St, London W1X 1PF (☎ 01 499 4632/01 629 2875)

PILKINGTON, Rev the Hon John Rowan; o s of Baron Pilkington (Life Peer, d 1983), and his 1 w, Rosamond Margaret, *née* Rowan (d 1953); *b* 15 Mar 1932; *Educ* Rugby, Magdalene Cambridge (MA); *m* 4 April 1964, Celia, da of Robert Ian Collison; 2 da, 1 adopted s; *Career* vicar of St Mark with St Paul Darlington Co Durham; *Style—* The Rev the Hon John Pilkington; St Mark's Vicarage, 394 North Rd, Darlington, Co Durham DL1 3BH

PILKINGTON, Lawrence Herbert Austin; CBE (1964), JP; s of Richard Austin Pilkington, and Hon Hope, da of late 1 Baron Cozens-Hardy, PC; *b* 13 Oct 1911; *Educ* Bromsgrove Sch, Magdalene Coll Cambridge; *m* 1936, Norah Holden; 2 da; *Career* dir Pilkington Bros Ltd 1935-81; JP Lancs 1942; Hon: LLD Sheffield 1956, DSc Salford 1970; *Style—* Lawrence Pilkington, Esq, CBE, JP; Coppice End, Colborne Rd, St Peter Port, Guernsey, CI

PILKINGTON, Baroness; Mavis Joy Doreen; er da of Gilbert Caffrey, of Woodleigh, Lostock Park, Bolton; formerly Mrs Wilding; *m* 2, 17 Feb 1961, as his 2 w, Baron Pilkington (Life Peer, d 1983); *Career* Dep Lt Merseyside 1985; vice-patron Nat Rose Soc; *Style—* The Rt Hon the Lady Pilkington; Windle Hall, St Helens, Merseyside

PILKINGTON, Rev Canon Peter; s of Frank Pilkington (d 1977), and Doris Pilkington (d 1985); *b* 5 Sept 1933; *Educ* Dame Allans Sch Newcastle on Tyne, Jesus Coll Cambridge (BA, MA); *m* 1966, Helen, da of Charles Wilson, of Risholme, Lincoln and Elleron Lodge, N Yorks; 2 da (Celia b 1970, Sarah b 1972); *Career* schoolmaster St Joseph's Coll Chidya Tanganyika 1955-58, ordained 1959, curate Bakewell Derbys 1959-62, schoolmaster Eton 1965-75, headmaster King's Sch Canterbury 1975-86, high master St Pauls Sch London 1986; hon canon Canterbury Cathedral 1975-; *Clubs* Athenaeum; *Style—* The Rev Canon Peter Pilkington

PILKINGTON, Dr Roger Windle; s of (Richard) Austin Pilkington (d 1951), of St Helens, and The Hon Hope Cozens-Hardy (d 1947); *b* 17 Jan 1915; *Educ* Rugby, Univ of Freiburg, Magdalene Coll Cambridge (MA, PhD); *m* 1, 27 July 1937 (m dis 1973), Theodore Miriam, da of Dr Farris Nasser Jaboor (d 1940); 1 s (Hugh Austin b 1942, d 1986), 1 da (Cynthia Miriam b 1939); m 2, 11 Oct 1973, Ingrid Maria, da of Herman Gustaf Geijer (d 1961), of Brattfors; *Career* res in genetics 1937-45; freelance writer and author of 56 books; contrib to: Time and Tide, Family Doctor, Sunday Telegraph; chm: London Missionary Soc 1962, Tstees Homerton Coll Cambridge 1962-74, The Hall Sch 1962-73; memb Worshipful Co of Glass Sellers 1957 (Master 1967); life memb Eugenics Soc 1951; Chevalier Confrèrie du Minervois (France 1987); *Books* incl: The Small Boat series in 20 volumes, Small Boat in the Midi (1988), Small Boat Down The Years (1988), for children: The Boy from Stink Alley (1966), The Ormering Tide (1974); scientific works incl: The Ways of the Sea (1957), Robert Boyle, Father of Chemistry (1959); *Recreations* inland navigation, walking; *Style—* Dr Roger Pilkington; La Maison Du Coti, St Aubin, Jersey (☎ 0534 43760); Les Cactus, Montouliers, France (☎ 01033 67 89 49 98)

PILKINGTON, Lady Sophia Frances Anne; *née* Vane-Tempest-Stewart; er da of 9 Marquess of Londonderry; *b* 23 Feb 1959; *m* m 24 Oct 1987, Jonathan Mark Pilkington, yst s of Ronald Charles Leslie Pilkington, of Hill House, Stanstead Abbots, Herts; 1 da (Hermione Alice b 10 Jan 1989); *Style—* Lady Sophia Pilkington

PILKINGTON OF REAY, Maj Thomas Douglas; s of Alan Douglas Pilkington, DL (d 1973), and Edith Winifred, *née* Turner (d 1937); land and titles confiscated after Battle of Bosworth 1485; *b* 23 Oct 1912; *Educ* Eton, Worcester Coll Oxford, RAC; *m* 1, 1931 (m dis 1961), Vivien Mary, da of Walter Bernard Baker (d 1955); 3 s (Ian b 1938, Christopher b 1947, Nigel b 1951), 2 da (Fiona b 1937, Jane b 1943); m 2, 1962, Jane St Clare Garden, da of Lt-Col Thomas Edward St Clare Daniell, OBE, MC (d 1948); *Career* served RE (TA) 1937-39, WWII Major RA in N Africa, Italy 1939-45 (despatches); stockbroker 1934-39; farmer; JP (Hants) 1954-62; Gen Cmmr Inland Revenue: Hants 1955-62, Glos 1962-87; *Recreations* fishing, shooting, cricket, point to point racing, NH racing since 1948 (twice winner Belgian Grand Nat and many other races); *Clubs* MCC; *Style—* Maj Thomas D Pilkington of Reay; Hyde Mill, Stow on the Wold, Cheltenham, Glos GL54 1LA (☎ 0451 30641)

PILL, Hon Mr Justice; Sir Malcolm Thomas; QC (1978); s of Reginald Thomas Pill, MBE (d 1987), and Anne Elizabeth, *née* Wright (d 1982); *b* 11 Mar 1938; *Educ* Whitchurch GS, Trinity Coll Cambridge (MA, LLM), Hague Acad of Int Law (Dip); *m* 19 March 1966, Roisin Mary, da of Dr Thomas Prior Riordan, of Swansea; 2 s (John b 1967, Hugh b 1968), 1 da (Madeleine b 1971); *Career* serv RA 1956-58, Glamorgan Yeo (TA) 1958-67; barr Gray's Inn 1962; rec Crown Ct 1976-87; QC 1978; bencher Gray's Inn 1987; judge of the High Ct (Queen's Bench Divn) 1988-; chm: UNA (Welsh Centre) Tst 1969-77 and 1980-87, Welsh Centre for Int Affairs 1973-76, UK Ctee Freedom from Hunger Campaign 1978-87; kt 1988; *Clubs* Royal Cwlth Soc, Cardiff and Co; *Style—* The Hon Mr Justice Pill; Royal Courts of Justice Strand London WC2A 2LL

PILLAI, Sir (Narayana) Raghavan; KCIE (1946, CIE 1939), CBE (1937); s of M C Narayana Pillai; *b* 24 July 1898; *Educ* Madras Univ, Trinity Hall Cambridge; *m* 1928, Edith Minnie Arthurs (d 1976); 2 s; *Career* sec gen Miny of External Affairs New Delhi 1952-60; hon fell Trinity Hall Cambridge 1970; *Clubs* Oriental; *Style—* Sir Raghavan Pillai, KCIE, CBE; Flat 4, 26 Hans Place SW1 (☎ 01 589 3116)

PILLAR, Rt Rev Kenneth Harold; *see*: Hertford, Bishop of

PILLAR, Adm Sir William Thomas; GBE (1983), KCB (1980); s of William Thomas Pillar (d 1960), of Dartmouth, and Lily, *née* Woolnough (d 1932); *b* 24 Feb 1924; *Educ* Blundell's Tiverton, RNEC; *m* 1946, Ursula Winifred, da of Arthur Benjamin Ransley, MC (d 1965); 3 s, 1 da; *Career* joined RN 1942, Capt RNEC 1973-75, Port Adm Rosyth 1976-77, Asst Chief Fleet Support 1977-79, Chief Fleet Support and Memb Admty Bd 1979-82, Adm 1982, Cmdt Royal Coll Def Studies 1982-83; Lt Govr and Cdr-in-Chief, Jersey 1985-; FIMechE, CEng, FIMarE; KStJ 1985; *Recreations* sailing (yacht 'Shrimp II'), rough gardening, fixing things; *Clubs* Army and Navy, Royal Naval Sailing Assoc (cdre 1980-83), Royal Yach Sqdn; *Style—* Admiral Sir William Pillar, GBE, KCB; Selwood, Zeals Row, Zeals, Warminster, Wilts BA12 6PE (☎ 0747 840577); Government House, Jersey, Channel Islands

PINCHES, Rosemary Vivian; *née* Bidder; da of Lt-Col Harold Francis Bidder, DSO, JP, FSA (d 1971), formerly of Ravensbury Manor, Mordern, Surrey, and Lilias Mary Vivian, *née* Rush (d 1973); ggf was George Parker Bidder 'The Calculating Boy', illustrious engineer with Robert Stephenson and others, pres Inst of Civil Engineers, etc (*see* DNB and *George Parker Bidder*, by E F Clark (1983); *b* 19 Jan 1929; *Educ* Glendower Sch London, Westonbirt Sch Glos; *m* 26 July 1952, John Harvey Pinches, MC, s of John Robert Pinches (d 1968), of 19 Holland Park Avenue, London W11; 2 da (Joanna Harriet (Hon Mrs Edward Orlando Charles Wood) b 1954, Sarah Carolann Rosemary b 1956); *Career* personal asst to Sir John Heaton-Armstrong Chester Herald Coll of Arms 1948-52; Heraldic publisher and author, genealogist, proprietor of Heraldry Today, London, a publishing house and bookshop specializing in heraldry and genealogy 1954-; memb: Heraldry Soc, AGRA, Wilts Archaeological Inst, Wilts Family History Soc; *Books* Elvin's Mottoes Revised (1971), (with Anthony Wood) A European Armorial (1971), The Royal Heraldy of England (with John H Pinches), 1974, A Bibliography of Burke's 1876-1976 (1976); *Recreations* horse-racing, browsing in old bookshops, playing bridge; *Style—* Mrs John Pinches; Parliament Piece, Ramsbury, Marlborough, Wiltshire SN8 2QH (☎ 0672 20613,20617); 10 Beauchamp Place, London SW3 1NQ (☎ 01 584 1656)

PINCKNEY, David Charles; s of Dr Charles Percy Pinckney (d 1982), of Park House, Ascot, Berks, and Norah Manisty, *née* Boucher (d 1988); *b* 13 Sept 1940; *Educ* Winchester, New Coll Oxford (MA); *m* 25 May 1974, Susan Audrey, da of Col Austin Richards (d 1974), of Pump House, Writtle, Essex; 1 s (Charles b 1977), 2 da (Katherine b 1974, Caroline b 1976); *Career* sr audit ptnr Peat Marwick Mitchell CAs France 1977-83 (London 1963-67, Paris and Lyons 1968-83), md Wrightson Wood Fin Servs Ltd 1984-86, gp fin dir Thornton and Co Ltd 1987-; govr Br Sch Paris 1981-83; ACA 1966; *Recreations* skiing, tennis, foreign travel, opera; *Clubs* Brooks's, The Hurlingham, Vincent's (Oxford); *Style—* David Pinckney, Esq; Rake Hanger House, Hill Brow, Liss, Hampshire (☎ 0730 893775); Thornton Management Ltd, 33 Cavendish Square, London W1M 7HF (☎ 01 493 7262, fax 01 409 0590, telex 923061 THORN G)

PINCKNEY, Jeremy Gerald; s of Gerald Henry Pinckney; *b* 17 Oct 1935; *Educ* Eton; *m* 1960, Helen Belinda, da of Maj M H Gold, MC; 2 s, 1 da; *Career* dir: Cowley Investmts Ltd, English Nat Investmt Co Ltd, The Mining Investmt Corpn Ltd, North Sea & Nat Gas Investmts Ltd, Oil & Energy Securities Ltd and other cos ; *Style—* Jeremy Pinckney Esq; 45 Black Lion Lane, London W6

PINCOTT, Leslie Rundell; CBE (1978); s of Hubert George Pincott; *b* 27 Mar 1923; *Educ* Mercers' Sch Holborn; *m* 1944, Mary Mae Tuffin; 2 s, 1 da; *Career* oil indust 1950-78, md Esso Petroleum Co Ltd 1970-78; dep-chm Price Cmmn 1978-80, pres Dist Heating Assoc 1977-79; vice-chm Remploy Ltd 1970-87, chm Edman Communications Gp plc 1983-87, tstee London Devpt Capital Fund (Guiness Mahon) 1985-, chm: Printing Indust Econ Devpt Ctee 1982-87, Stone-Platt Industs 1980-82; Canada Permanent Tst Co (UK) Ltd 1978-79, BR SR Bd 1977-; dir: George Wimpey & Co Ltd 1978-85, Highlands Fabricators Ltd 1985-, FCA, CBIM, MInstM; *Recreations* tennis; *Clubs* Hurlingham (chm 1988), Arts; *Style—* Leslie Pincott, Esq, CBE; 6 Lambourne Ave, Wimbledon, London SW19 7DW

PINCUS, George Bernard; s of Dr Joseph Victor Pincus (d 1946), of Brighton, and Ruth, *née* Burns; *b* 13 Nov 1942; *Educ* Epsom Coll; *m* 21 May 1965 (m dis); 2 s (Benjamin b 1969, Damian b 1970); *Career* md PAVF 1974-84 and BBDO Ltd 1984-; memb cncl Epsom Coll 1965-, chm devpt ctee Epsom Coll 1986-; *Recreations* visual arts, theatre, history, travel; *Style—* George B Pincus, Esq; Willoughbys West, Wrens Hill, Oxshott, Surrey; 10 Cambridge Terr, London NW1 4JA (☎ 01 486 1277, telex 266749)

PINDER, Margaret Lilian; o da of Brig Harold Senhouse Pinder, CBE, MC, Royal Leics Regt (d 1973), of Burghclere Grange, Newbury, Berks, and Lilian Edith Murray (d 1975); *b* 4 May 1920; *Educ* Privately; *Career* vice-chm and vice-pres Arthritis Care (formerly Br Rheumatism and Arthritis Assoc), memb since 1953; fndr of first recuperative holiday hotel for arthritis (later names Margaret Pinder House by Arthritis Care) 1960; fndr and tstee of Pinder Centre for the treatment of physically disabled 1973; tstee the Lady Hoare Tst 1985; *Recreations* painting, racing (first owner to have horses trained under Nat Hunt in France after war); *Style—* Margaret Pinder; Summerfield House, Hatt Common, Newbury, Berkshire G15 0NH (☎ 0635 254354); Pinder Centre, Old Coach House, Avington, nr Winchester, Hants SO21 1DD (☎ 096 278 498)

PINDLING, Rt Hon Sir Lynden Oscar; KCMG (1983), PC (1976); s of Arnold Franklin Pindling; *b* 22 Mar 1930; *Educ* Western Sr Sch, Nassau Govt HS, London Univ; *m* 1956, Marguerite McKenzie; 2 s, 2 da; *Career* barr Middle Temple 1953, PM and min of econ affairs The Bahamas 1969- ; *Style—* The Rt Sir Hon Lynden Pindling, KCMG; Office of the Prime Minister, Rawson Sq, Nassau, Bahamas

PINE-COFFIN, Lt-Col Trenchard John; OBE, DL (Devon 1982); s of Lt-Col Edward Claude Pine-Coffin (whose mother Louisa, *née* Beresford, ggda of Rt Hon John Beresford, yr bro of 1 Marquess of Waterford); *b* 12 June 1921; *Educ* Malvern, RMC Sandurst; *m* 1952, Susan Therese, er da of Col A D Bennett, OBE, MC; 1 s (John b 1961), 2 da (Julia b 1953, Sarah b 1956); *Career* serv WWII Para Regt; High Sheriff Devon 1973-74; *Style—* Lt-Col Trenchard Pine-Coffin, OBE, DL; Portledge, Fairy Cross, Bideford, Devon

PINHORN, Margaret (Maggie) (Mrs Martin Dyke-Coomes); *née* Pinhorn; da of George Herbert Pinhorn, of Woodside, Comp Lane, St Mary's Platt, nr Sevenoaks, Kent, and Mary Elizabeth Suther (d 1963); *b* 1 Nov 1943; *Educ* Walthamstow Hall Sch for Girls (Sevenoaks), Central Sch of Art and Design (London); *m* 24 June 1978, Martin Dyke-Coomes, *qv*, s of Ernest Thomas Dyke-Coomes, of 67 Furzefield, West Green, Crawley, Sussex; 1 s (Ned Alexander b 1981), 1 da (Amy Elizabeth b 1983), 2 adopted s (Anthony b 1967, Claude b 1973); *Career* artist, dir, designer, prodr; fndr of Alternative Arts and dir: Covent Garden St Theatre 1975-88, Soho St Theatre from 1988; stared career in films in 1968 at Pinewood Studios in Art Dept of James Bond movie; worked on Br feature films incl: Chitty Chitty Bang Bang, Otley, Till Death Us Do Part; ind film maker, made Dynamo (1970), and Tunde's Film (1973); started Basement Community Arts Workshop in Cable Street 1972; made one of the first 'Open Door' progs for BBC, TV and went on to res and present the first BBC TV series 'Grapevine' for Community Programmes Unit; nat co-ordinator of the Assoc of Community Artists 1974-79; vice-chm Tower Hamlets Arts Ctee 1975-79; memb: Arts Cncl Community Art Ctee 1975-79, Gtr London Arts Community Arts Ctee 1979-81; co-prodr of 'Circus Senso' for Circus UK; *Recreations* playing with my children, creative cooking, collecting wines, travel, the arts; *Clubs* West Ham Football, Covent Garden Community Centre; *Style*— Mrs Martin Dyke-Coomes; Alternative Arts, 49-51 Carnaby St, Soho, London W1V 1PF (☎ 01 287 0907)

PININSKI, Count Peter James; s of Count Stanislaw Hieronim Mieczyslaw Aleksander Pininski, of Firs Hill, High Road, Chipstead, Surrey, and Castle Hill Cottage, Branscombe, Devon, and Jean Isobel Margaret, *née* Graham; *b* 23 August 1956; *Educ* Downside, Whitgift Sch, Sotheby Arts Course; *m* 18 June 1983, Countess Mary Sophie Teresa Matylda, da of Sqdn Ldr Count Jan Jozef Badeni, of Norton Manor, Norton, Wilts; 1 s (Aleksander Leon Jan Stanislaw b 15 June 1988); *Career* jr ptnr Hoare Govett (stockbrokers) 1984; dir Laing & Cruickshank (stockbrokers) 1986; tstee Ciechanowiecki Fndn 1988; *Recreations* history, literature, collecting art and antiques; *Style*— Count Peter Pininski; 4 Campden Hill TGardens, London W8 (☎ 01 229 7263); Orchard House, Norton, Wilts (☎ 0666 837 851); Piercy House, 7 Copthall Avenue, London EC2 (☎ 01 588 2800)

PINK, Lady Dora Elizabeth; JP (London); raised to the rank of a Marquess's da 1973; da of George Leonard Tottenham, ggs of Rt Rev Lord Robert Ponsonby Tottenham, Bishop of Clogher (s of 1 Marquess of Ely); sis of 8 Marquess; *b* 9 Nov 1919; *Educ* Queen's Univ Kingston Ontario (BA); *m* 1, 1946, Lt (E) Bernard Edgar Hall, RN (d 1947); m 2, 1950, Sir Ivor Thomas Montague Pink, KCMG (d 1966), er s of Leonard Montague Pink, of Port Iona, Sandbanks, Bournemouth; 1 da (Celia Elizabeth b 1952); *Career* served as Lt WRCNS 1939-45; *Clubs* The Hurlingham; *Style*— Lady Dora Pink, JP; 24 The Gateways, Chelsea, London SW3 3JA

PINKER, George Douglas; CVO (1983); s of late Ronald Douglas Pinker; *b* 6 Dec 1924; *Educ* Reading Sch, St Mary's Hosp London Univ (MB BS), DObst; *m* Dorothy Emma, nee Russell; 3 s, 1 da; *Career* surgn-gynaecologist to the Queen 1973-, consulting gynaecological surgn and obstetrician St Mary's Hosp Paddington and Samaritan Hosp 1958-, consulting gynaecological surgeon Middx and Soho Hosps 1969-, consultant gynaecologist King Edward VII Hosp for Officers 1974-; chief med advsr BUPA 1983-; pres Royal Coll of Obstetricians and Gynaecologists 1987- (hon tres 1970-77, vice pres 1980-83), memb editorial bd Modern Medicine 1980 (chm 1988); cncl memb Winston Churchill Tst, vice pres London Choral Soc 1988; Hon FRCSI 1987, hon memb British Paediatric Assoc 1988; MRCOG, FRCS(Ed), FRCOG, FRSocMed, FRCS 1989; *Clubs* Garrick; *Style*— George Pinker, Esq, CVO; Top Flat, 96 Harley St, London W1N 1AF (☎ 01 935 2292)

PINKER, Maj Richard Walrond; s of Henry George Pinker (d 1961), and May Simcoe Pinker (d 1963); *b* 19 July 1913; *Educ* Wrekin Coll Sherborne; *m* 16 Sept 1940, Caroline Mary, da of Charles Gordon Darroch Farquhar (d 1946); 1 s (Charles), 1 da (Anne (wid of Lt-Col David Blair ka 1979 NI)); *Career* cmmnd Devonshire Regt 1932, served India, Malta, UK (acting Lt-Col), ret from Army 1947; in wine trade with Mentzendorff & Co, dir (late md) Simon Bros & Co Ltd, wine buyer NAAFI (ret 1973); *Recreations* shooting, golf, gardening; *Clubs* Army and Navy; *Style*— Maj Richard W Pinker; Pilgroves, Brasted Chart, Westerham, Kent TN16 1LY (☎ 0959 62579)

PINKER, Prof Robert Arthur; s of Joseph Pinker (d 1976), and Dora Elizabeth, *née* Winyard (d 1987); *b* 27 May 1931; *Educ* Holloway Co Sch, LSE (Cert Soc Sc), Univ of London (BSc, MSc); *m* 24 June 1955, Jennifer Farrington, da of Fred Boulton (d 1941); 2 da (Catherine b 1963, Lucy b 1965); *Career* 2 Lt Royal Ulster Rifles 1951-52, Lt London Irish Rifles 1952-54; head of sociology dept Goldsmiths Coll 1964-72, Lewisham prof of social admin Goldsmiths and Bedford Colls 1972-74, prof of social studies Chelsea Coll 1974-78, prof of social work studies LSE 1978- (pro-dir 1985-88), pro-vice chllr for social Sci London 1989-; chm: Social Admin Assoc 1974-77, Br Library Project on Family and Social REs 1983-86, advsy cncl Centre for Policy on Ageing 1971-81 (chm of govrs 1981-), Jl of Social Policy 1981-86 (ed 1977-81), editorial bd Ageing and Soc 1981; scientific advsr Nursing Res DHSS 1974-79 and 1980-82, advsy cncl mmeb Age Concern Ins tof Gerontology King's Coll London 1987; memb: Social Sci Res Cncl 1972-76, working pty on role and tasks of social workers Barclay Ctee 1981-82, cncl Advertising Standards Authy 1988-, CNAA 1988-; memb Social Admin Soc 1967; *Recreations* reading, writing, travel, unskilled gardening; *Style*— Prof Robert Pinker; 76 Coleraine Rd, Blackheath, London SE3 7PE (☎ 01 858 5320); LSE, Houghton St, Aldwych, London WC2A 2AE (☎ 01 405 7686)

PINNER, Hayim; s of late Simon Pinner, and Annie, *née* Wagner; *b* 25 May 1925; *Educ* Davenant Fndn Sch, London Univ, Yeshiva Etz Hayim, Bet Berl Coll Israel; *m* 1956 (m dis 1980), Rita, *née* Reuben; 1 s, 1 da; *Career* RAOC 1944-48; ed Jewish Vanguard 1950-74, exec dir B'nai B'rith 1957-77, hon vice pres Zionist Fedn of GB and Ireland 1975- (hon tres 1971-75), sec gen Bd of deputies of Br Jews 1977-, vice pres Lab Zionist Movement; memb: Jewish Agency and World Zionist Orgn, exec cncl Christians and Jews, Inter-Faith Network, advsy cncl World Congress of Faiths, Trades Advsy Cncl, Hillel Fndn, jt Israel Appeal, Lab party Middle East ctee, B List Parly Candidates, UNA; contrib to: BBC radio and TV, LBC, Radio London; Freeman City of London; *Recreations* travelling, swimming, reading, talking; *Style*— Hayim Pinner, Esq; c/o Board of Deputies of British Jews, Woburn House, Tavistock Square, London WC1 (☎ 01 387 3952)

PINNINGTON, Geoffrey Charles; s of Charles Pinnington; *b* 21 Mar 1919; *Educ* Harrow Co Sch, Rock Ferry HS Birkenhead, King's Coll London; *m* 1941, Beryl, da of Edward Clark; 2 da; *Career* serv WWII RAF, Sqdn Ld 1943; journalist; ed Sunday People 1972-82, ret; dir Mirror Gp Newspapers 1976-82; jt vice chm Press Cncl 1983- (memb 1982-); *Style*— Geoffrey Pinnington Esq; 23 Lauderdale Drive, Richmond, Surrey TW10 7BS

PINNINGTON, Roger Adrian; TD; s of William Austin Pinnington (d 1979), of Oakhurst Manor, Alderley Edge, Cheshire, and Elsie Amy Pinnington (d 1983); *b* 27 August 1932; *Educ* Rydal Sch Colwyn Bay, Lincoln Coll Oxford (MA); *m* 16 April 1961, (Marjorie) Ann, da of Maj George Alan Livingstone Russell, of Beverley, Yorks; 1 s (Andrew b 1967), 3 da (Suzanne b 1963, Sally-Ann b 1964, Nikki b 1975); *Career* 2 Lt RA 1952, Maj Royal Mil Police 1960; dir: William E Cary Ltd 1964-74, Jonas Woodhead & Sons plc 1968-74, Camgears Ltd 1974-82; vice-pres TRW Europe Inc 1980-82; dep chm and chief exec UBM Gp plc 1982-85; dir Norcros plc 1985-86; dir and chief exec: Royal Ordnance plc 1986-87, Pilgrim House Gp 1987-89; chm: Blackwood Hodge plc, Bath and Bristol Estates Ltd, Harford Consultancy Services Ltd, Petrocon plc; Freeman City of London, Liveryman Worshipful Co of Glaziers 1977; CBIM 1988, FRSA 1983; *Recreations* gardening, debate, collecting sad irons; *Clubs* Vincent's, RAC, St James's; *Style*— Roger Pinnington Esq, TD; Robingate, Letchworth, Herts SG6 3JY; Jardines del Puerto, Puerto Banos, Spain; 46 Willoughby Rd, Hampstead, London NW3 (☎ 01 431 3999); 2 Barrington Rd, Letchworth, Herts SG6 3JY (☎ 0462 670944, fax 0462 678233); car ☎ 0836 244464

PINNINGTON - HUGHES, Prof John; s of Joseph Henry Hughes, and Annie, *née* Hope; *b* 6 Jan 1942; *Educ* Chelsea Coll London (BSc), London Univ (PhD), Liege Belgium Dh Cavsa, Wolfson Coll Cambridge (MA); 2s (Joseph Francis b 10 Oct 1986, John Steven b 6 Sept 1988), 2 da (Katherine b 23 Aug 1967, Georgina Anne b 7 July 1984); *Career* post doc res `fell dept pharmacology Yale Univ Med Sch 1967-69; Aberdeen Univ: lectr dept pharmacology 1969-73, lectr and dept dir unit for res on addictive drugs 1973-77; Imperial Coll London Univ: reader in pharmacology biochem 1977-79, prof pharmacological biochem and dir undergraduate studies in biochem 1979-82, visiting prof 1983-85; Cambridge Univ: dir Parke - Davis Res Unit 1983-, vice pres Drug Discovery Europe Warner-Lambert/Parke-Davis 1988 (co ordinator 1987-); *Recreations* gardening, dogs and family; *Style*— Prof John Pinnington-Hughes; Parke-Davis Res Unit, Addenbrooke's Hosp Site, Hills Rd, Cambridge CB2 2QB (☎ 01 0223 210 929, fax 0223 249 106, telex 817 004)

PINNOCK, Trevor David; s of Kenneth Alfred Thomas Pinnock, of Canterbury, Kent, and Joyce Edith, *née* Muggleton; *b* 16 Dec 1946; *Educ* Canterbury Catheral Choir Sch, Simon Langton GS Canterbury, RCM; *m* 2 Aug 1988, Pauline Heather, *née* Nobes; *Career* London Debut with Galliand Harpsichord Trio (jt fndr) 1966; solo debut Purcell Room London 1968, formed The English Concert 1972, London debut English Bach Festival 1973; recordings: CRD Records 1974-78, Polydor (Archiv) 1978-; tours of Europe, USA, Japan, solo with The English Concert, and as orchestral conductor; Metropolitan Opera debut Handel; Gvilio Cesare 1988; hon RAM; *Style*— Trevor Pinnock, Esq; c/o Basil Dougals Artists' Management, 8 St George's Terr, London NW1 8XJ (☎ 01 722 7142, fax 01 722 1841, telex 295299 BASART G)

PINSENT, Sir Christopher Roy; 3 Bt (UK 1938); s of Sir Roy Pinsent, 2 Bt (d 1978); *b* 2 August 1922; *Educ* Winchester; *m* 27 June 1951, Susan Mary, da of John Norton Scorer, of Walcot Lodge, Fotheringhay; 1 s, 2 da; *Heir* s, Thomas Benjamin Roy Pinsent b 21 July 1967; *Career* lecturer Camberwell Sch of Art; *Style*— Sir Christopher Pinsent, Bt; The Chestnuts, Castle Hill, Guildford, Surrey

PINSENT, David Hume; s of Basil Hume Pinsent, of Lingfield, Surrey, and Patricia Arbery Mary, *née* Atteridge; fifth in descent from David Hume, the Scottish philosopher; *b* 2 April 1943; *Educ* Downside, Imperial Coll London; *m* 1974, Alexandra Therese Emblyn, da of Capt Charles Edward Kendall (d 1978), of Gt Nineveh, Benenden, Kent; 2 s, 1 da; *Career* chm and md Anglo American Agric plc 1981-; dir: David Hume Securities, Cronite Gp plc, The Plantation Tst Co plc 1985-88, United California Farms Inc; *Recreations* hunting, bridge, music, politics; *Style*— David Pinsent, Esq; Old Chellows, Crowhurst, Lingfield, Surrey RH7 6LU (☎ 0342 832049)

PINSON, Barry; QC (1973); s of Thomas Alfred Pinson; *b* 18 Dec 1925; *Educ* King Edward's Sch, Birmingham Univ; *m* 1, 1950, Miriam Mary; 1 s, 1 da; m 2, 1977, Anne Kathleen Golby; *Career* barr Gray's Inn 1949, bencher 1981; tstee RAF Museums 1980-, Sadler's Wells Devpt Capital Ctee 1985-; *Publications* Revenue Law (17 edns); *Recreations* music, photograpy; *Clubs* Arts; *Style*— Barry Pinson, Esq, QC; 11 New Sq, Lincoln's Inn, London WC2 (☎ 01 242 3981, fax 01 831 2391, telex 894189)

PINTER, Harold; CBE (1966); s of J Pinter; *b* 10 Oct 1930; *Educ* Hackney Downs GS; *m* 1, 1956 (m dis 1980), Vivien Thompson (Vivien Merchant) (d 1982); 1 s; m 2, 1980, Lady Antonia Fraser, *qv*; *Career* actor 1949-57; directed: The Collection (Aldwych) 1962, The Birthday Party (Aldwych) 1964, Exiles (Mermaid) 1970, Butley 1970 (film 1973), Next of Kin (NT) 1974, Otherwise Engaged (Queens) 1975, (NY 1977), Blythe Spirit (NT) 1977, The Rear Column 1978 (Globe), Close of Play (NT) 1979, The Hothouse (Hampstead) 1980, Quartermaine's Terms (Queens) 1981, Incident at Tulse Hill (Hampstead) 1981, The Trojan War Will Not Take Place (NT) 1983, The Common Pursuit (Lyric, Hammersmith) 1984, Sweet Bird of Youth (Haymarket) 1985; *Plays* The Room (1957), The Birthday Party (1958), The Dumb Waiter (1957), The Hothouse (1958), A Night Out (1961), The Caretaker (1960), Night School (1960), The Collection (1961), The Lover (1963), Tea Party 91964), The Homecoming (1964), Landscape (1968), Silence (1969), Old Times (1971), Monologue (1972), No Man's Land (1975), Family Voices (1982), Victoria Station (1982), A Kind of Alaska (1982), One For the Road (1984); *Screenplays* The Caretaker (1962), The Servant (1966), The Pumpkin Eater (1963), The Quiller Memorandum (1966), Accident (1967), The Birthday Party (1968), The Homecoming (1968), The Go-Between (1969), Langrishe (1970), Go Down (1970), A la Recherche du Temps Perdue (1972), The Last Tycoon (1974), The French Lieutenant's Woman (1981), Betrayal (1981), Turtle Diary (1985), The Handmaid's Tale (1987); has also published volumes of poetry; *Clubs* Grouchos; *Style*— Harold Pinter, Esq, CBE; Judy Daish Associates Ltd, 83 Eastbourne Mews, London W2 6LQ

PINTO, George Richard; s of Maj Richard James Pinto, MC (d 1969), of London, and Gladys, *née* Hirsch (d 1985); *b* 11 April 1929; *Educ* Eton, Trinity Coll Cambridge (MA); *Career* 2 Lt Coldstream Gds 1947-49; Cooper Bros and Co (now Coopers & Lybrand) 1953-56, Model Roland & Store 1957-58, banker Kleinwort Benson Ltd 1958- (dir 1968-85, advsr 1985-); jt hon tres Anglo-Israel Assoc 1987-, chm Centl Cncl for Jewish Soc Serv 1975-78 (vice-chm 1972-75), chm of fin ctee Jewish Blind Soc 1962-; govr Oxford Centre for Postgraduate Hebrew Studies 1987-; FCA; *Recreations* reading, listening to classical music, golf, bridge; *Clubs* Brooks's, Cavalry and Guards', Portland; *Style*— G R Pinto, Esq; 20 Fenchurch St, London EC3P 3DB (☎ 01 623

8000, telex 888531, fax 01 623 5535)

PIPER, Sir David Towry; CBE (1969); s of Prof Stephen Harvey Piper, DSO, DSC, (d 1963), and Mary Joyce, *née* Casswell (d 1973); *b* 21 July 1918; *Educ* Clifton, St Catharine's Coll Cambridge; *m* 1945, Anne Richmond; 1 s, 3 da; *Career* serv WWII Indian Army (Japanese POW); dir, keeper and sec Nat Portrait Gallery 1964-67, dir and Marlay curator Fitzwilliam Museum Cambridge 1967-73, Slade prof Fine Art Oxford 1966-67, Clark lectr Cambridge 1977-78, dir Ashmolean Museum Oxford 1973-85; fell Worcester Coll Oxford 1973-85 (emeritus fellow 1985-); memb Royal Fine Art Commission 1970-86; tstee Pilgrim Tst 1973-; kt 1982; *Style—* Sir David Piper, CBE; Overford Farm, Wytham, Oxford OX2 8QN

PIPER, Geoffrey Steuart Fairfax; s of Sqdn Ldr Donald Steuart Piper (d 1972), of Bakewell, and Nancy Fairfax, *née* Robson; *b* 8 June 1943; *Educ* Repton, Pembroke Coll Cambridge (MA); *m* 29 July 1967, Susan Elizabeth, da of Roswell Douglas Arnold; 1 s (Charles b 1980), 3 da (Jennifer b 1968, Angela b 1970, Caroline b 1973); *Career* ptnr i/c Deloitte Haskins & Sells: Channel Islands 1980-86, Liverpool 1986-; pres Jersey Soc of Chartered and Certified Accountants 1983-85, chm Business Opportunities on Merseyside 1987-, dir Eldonian Devpt Tst 1988-; FCA 1973; *Recreations* golf, cricket, choral music; *Clubs* Royal and Ancient, MCC; *Style—* Geoffrey Piper, Esq; The Croft, Thornton Hough, Wirral, Merseyside L63 1JA (☎ 051 336 4830); Richmond House, Rumford Place, Liverpool 3 (☎ 051 227 4242, fax 051 227 4575)

PIPER, John Egerton Christmas; CH (1972); s of late C A Piper; *b* 13 Dec 1903; *Educ* Epsom Coll, RCA; *m* 1937, Mary Myfanwy Evans; 2 s, 2 da; *Career* painter and writer, memb Oxford Diocesan Adv Ctee 1950-; vice pres Turner Soc; Hon ARIBA 1957, Hon FRIBA 1971, Hon ARCA 1959; Hon DLitt: Leics 1960, Oxon 1966, Sussex 1974, Reading 1977, Cardiff 1981; *Clubs* Athenaeum; *Style—* John Piper Esq, CH; Fawley Bottom Farmhouse, nr Henley-on-Thames, Oxon (☎ 0491 572494)

PIPER, Peter (Bright Harold); CBE (1979); s of Robert Harold Piper; *b* 22 Sept 1918; *Educ* Maidstone GS; *m* 1, 1945, Marjorie Joyce, da of Capt George Arthur; 1 s, 1 da; m 2, 1979, Leonie Mary, da of Maj C V Lane; *Career* WWII RN 1939-46; dir Lloyds Bank plc 1970-83, gp chief exec Lloyds Bank Gp 1973-78 (chief gen mangr 1973), dir Lloyds and Scottish 1970-75, chm Lloyds First Western (USA) 1973-78; Freeman City of London, Liveryman Worshipful Co Spectacle Makers'; *Clubs* Overseas Bankers Australia; *Style—* Peter Piper, Esq, CBE; Greenways, Hawkshill Close, Esher, Surrey

PIPKIN, Maj Charles Harry Broughton; CBE (1973); s of Charles Pipkin, and Charlotte Phyllis, *née* Viney; *b* 29 Nov 1913; *Educ* Christs Coll Blackheath London; *m* 1941, Viola, da of Albert Byatt; 1 s (Charles b 1949), 1 da (Fiona b 1946); *Career* Maj REME 14 Army (despatches); electrical engr; various appointments BICC 1936-73, dep chm and chief exec 1973-77, chm 1977-80; pres: British Non-Ferrous Metals Assoc 1965-66, Electric Cable-Makers Fedn 1967-68, Br Electrical and Allied Manufacturers Assoc 1975-76; *Recreations* travel, reading, horse-racing; *Clubs* City Livery (Horner); *Style—* Major Charles Pipkin, CBE; Pegler's Barn, Bledington, Oxon OX7 6XQ (☎ 060 871 304)

PIPPARD, Prof Sir (Alfred) Brian; s of Prof Alfred John Sutton Pippard (d 1969), and Frances Louisa Olive Field (d 1964); *b* 7 Sept 1920; *Educ* Clifton, Clare Coll Cambridge (MA, PhD, ScD, hon fell 1973); *m* 1955, Charlotte Frances, da of Francis Gilbert Dyer (d 1948); 3 da; *Career* Cambridge Univ demonstrator, lectr, reader, J H Plummer Prof, Cavendish prof of physics 1971-82, pres Clare Hall Cambridge 1966-73; FRS; kt 1975; *Recreations* music; *Style—* Prof Sir Brian Pippard; 30 Porson Rd, Cambridge CB2 2EU (☎ 0223 358713)

PIPPET, Gp Capt Edward Francis; OBE (1955); s of Wilfrid Francis Pippet (d 1958), and Mildred Mary, *née* Keogh (d 1962); *b* 23 Oct 1915; *Educ* Douai Sch; *m* 28 April 1950, Wilhelmina Georgina Leonora, da of Dr Jonkheer Jelle Roelof Clifford Kocq van Breugel (d 1957); *Career* RAF 1935-70, France 1949-40, Atlantic and N Sea 1940-42; (despatches 1942) combined ops HQ 1943, W Africa 1943-44, NW Europe 1944-46, air attache Rangoon 1957-60, The Hague 1968-70; *Recreations* carpentry, gardening, reading; *Style—* Gp Capt Edward F Pippet; De Kleine Os, Zijdeweg 57B, 2245 BZ Wassenaar, Netherlands (☎ 01751 79839)

PIRIE, Douglas Gordon; ERD; s of Duncan Vernon Pirie Lt-Col (d 1931), of Chateau de Varennes, Anjou, France, and The Hon Evelyn Courtenay Forbes-Sempill (d 1934); *b* 21 Oct 1910; *Educ* Winchester, Edinburgh Univ; *m* 24 Sept 1954, Jean Frances Caroline Carmicheal, da of Carmichael of Carmicheal, of Berrington Hall, Shrewsbury (d 1959); 1 s (Alastair b 1957); *Career* 2 Lt Coldstream Guards (SR) 1935; ADC & priv sec: Govr of Mauritius 1937-40; served 1940-46 Coldstream Guards and on staff (despatches) Western Desert, Madagascar, Sicily, Italy, France, Belgium, Germany; Lt Col priv sec to Govr of Kenya 1946-47; Col Off 1947-50, Foreign Serv 1950-53; Gold Staff Offr Coronation of HM the Queen 1953; memb Queen's Bodyguard for Scotland Royal Co of Archers, Legion d'Honneur; *Recreations* gardening, travel; *Style—* Douglas Pirie, Esq; The Old House, Milland, Nr Liphook, Hampshire GU30 7LX (☎ 042 876 360)

PIRIE, Gp Capt Sir Gordon Hamish; CVO (1987), CBE (1946), JP (London 1962), DL (London 1962); s of Harold Victor Campbell Pirie; *b* 10 Feb 1918; *Educ* Eton, RAF Coll Cranwell; *m* 1, 1953, Margaret Joan Bomford (d 1972); m 2, 1982, Joanna Marian, wid of John C Hugill; *Career* perm cmmn RAF 1938, serv WWII (despatches), Gp Capt 1946, ret; contested (LNat&U) Dundee W 1955; memb Westminster City Cncl 1949-82: Mayor 1959-60, ldr of Cncl 1961-69, alderman 1963-78, Lord Mayor 1974-75; dep high bailiff Westminster 1978-87; chm Servs Sound and Vision Corpn 1979-, dir Parker Gallery; KStJ 1969; Cdr Cross of Merit SMO Malta 1971; kt 1984; *Recreations* motoring, bird-watching; *Clubs* Carlton, RAF; *Style—* Gp Capt Sir Gordon Pirie, CVO, CBE, JP, DL; Cottage Row, Tarrant Gunville, Blandford, Dorset DT11 8JJ (☎ 025 889 212)

PIRIE, Sheriff Henry Ward; s of William Pirie (d 1922), of Leith; *b* 13 Feb 1922; *Educ* George Watson's Coll Edinburgh, Edinburgh Univ (MA, LLB); *m* 1948, Jean Marion, da of Frank Jardine (d 1956), former pres RCS Edinburgh; 4 s; *Career* cmmnd Bombay Grenadiers 1944; advocate 1947; jr counsel to the Admiralty in Scotland 1950; sheriff-substitute of Lanarkshire at Airdrie 1954-55; sheriff-substitute (later sheriff) of Lanarkshire at Glasgow 1955-74, ret 1974; crossword compiler, journalist and broadcaster; OStJ 1967; *Recreations* opera, bridge, walking; *Style—* Sheriff H W Pirie; 16 Poplar Drive, Lenzie, Glasgow G66 4DN (☎ 041 776 2494)

PIRIE-GORDON OF BUTHLAW, (George) Patrick; yr s of Lt-Col Charles Pirie-Gordon, OBE, DSC, GCStJ, FSA, FRGS, sometime ed *Burke's Landed Gentry* and Director of Ceremonies Venerable Order of St John, by his w Mabel, CStJ, herself da of George Buckle, sometime ed *The Times*; suc er bro as 15th laird of Buthlaw 1980; *b* 24 May 1918; *Educ* Winchester, Oriel Oxford; *m* Catherine Grace, da of Alfred Rickard Taylor, of Lymington, and widow of Maj Jack Childerstone Colebrook; 2 da (Penelope b 1948, Jean b 1950); *Career* served WWII RA, rising to Lt-Col 2 Survey Regt (despatches twice); local dir Glyn Mills & Co bankers (now Royal Bank of Scotland) 1949-78; dir: Anglo-American Securities Corpn 1973-80, Montagu Boston Investment Tst 1982-; tstee Transantarctic Assoc 1962-, chm Mount Everest Fndn 1966-, vice pres Queens Nursing Inst 1980, hon vice pres Royal Geographical Soc 1982 memb Royal Co Archers (Queen's Bodyguard for Scotland) 1948-; Master Worshipful Co of Skinners 1963-64; hon fell Oriel Coll Oxford 1988; CStJ, FRGS; *Recreations* gardening, cooking, bird-watching; *Style—* Patrick Pirie-Gordon of Buthlaw; Waterton, Paddock Field, Chilbolton, Stockbridge, Hants SO20 6AU; c/o Montagu Boston Investment Trust, 117 Old Broad St, EC2 (T 01 588 1750)

PITBLADO, Sir David Bruce; KCB (1967, CB 1955), CVO (1953); s of Robert Bruce Pitblado and Mary Jane Sear; *b* 18 August 1912; *Educ* Strand Sch, Emmanuel Coll Cambridge (hon fell 1972); *m* 1941, Edith (d 1978), da of Capt J T and Mrs Rees Evans; 1 s, 1 da; *Career* civil servant 1935-71: Dominions Off, Treasy, private sec to PM 1951-56, Miny of Power (perm sec); Comptroller and Auditor general 1971-76, ret; hon tres SSAFA 1978-, chm Davies's 1979-; memb Middle Temple; *Clubs* Athenaeum; *Style—* Sir David Pitblado, KCB, CVO; 23 Cadogan St, London SW3 2PP (☎ 01 589 6765); Pengoitan, Borth, Dyfed

PITCHER, Desmond Henry; s of George Charles Pitcher (d 1968), of Liverpool, and Alice Marion, *née* Osborne (d 1985); *b* 23 Mar 1935; *Educ* Liverpool Coll of Technol; *m* 1, 1961 (m dis 1973), Patricia, *née* Ainsworth; 2 da (Stephanie b 18 May 1965, Samantha (twin) b 18 May 1965); m 2, 1978 (m dis 1984), Carol Ann, *née* Rose; 2 s (George b 1 Oct 1978, Andrew b 1 March 1981); *Career* devpt engr A V Roe & Co 1957-58, systems engr Automatic Telephone & Electrical Co 1958-60, nat mangr engrg Sperry Univac Ltd 1961-66 (md 1971-73), md MDS (Data Processing) Ltd 1966-71, dir Sperry Rand Ltd 1971-73 (dep chm 1973-76), vice pres euro div Sperry Univac Corpn 1973-76, md truck and bus div BL Ltd 1976-78, md Plessey Telecommunications and Office Systems 1978-83, dir Plessey Co 1979-83, chief exec The Littlewoods Orgn 1983-, chm Mersey Barrage Co Ltd 1986-, Faraday lectr 1973-74; Freeman: City of London 1987, Worshipful Co of Info Technologists 1987; CEng, FIEE 1968, FBCS 1975, HFIDE 1977, CBIM 1985, FRSA 1987; *Recreations* music, opera, golf; *Clubs* Brooks's, Royal Birkdale Golf; *Style—* Desmond Pitcher, Esq; Aguarda, 4 Granville Rd, Birkdale, Southport, Merseyside (☎ 0704 63531); Middle Dell, Bishopsgate Road, Englefield Green, Egham, Surrey; The Littlewoods Organisation, JM Centre, Old Hall Street, Liverpool (☎ 051 235 2222, fax 051 235 4900, telex 628501)

PITCHFORD, His Hon Judge; Charles Neville; *Career* barr Middle Temple 1948, circuit judge Wales and Chester Circuit 1972-; *Style—* His Honour Judge Pitchford; Llanynant, Coed Morgan, Abergavenny, Gwent

PITCHFORD, John Hereward; CBE (1971); s of John Pitchford; *b* 30 August 1904; *Educ* Brighton Coll, Christ's Coll Cambridge; *m* 1930, Teresa Agnes Mary Pensotti; 1 s, 2 da (one of whom, Elizabeth m Sir John Leahy, KCMG, *qv*); *Career* chm Ricardo Consulting Engrs Ltd 1962-76, pres 1976-; *Clubs* RAC; *Style—* John Pitchford, Esq, CBE; Byeways, Ditchling, E Sussex (☎ 079 18 2177)

PITCHFORD, Margot Walker; da of James Riley, (d 1985), of Chelsea, London SW3, and Joanna, *née* Walker; *b* 1 July 1943; *Educ* Queenswood, Sch Herts; *m* 1, 1965 (m dis 1975), David Robert Wilkinson; m 2, John Pitchford; 3 s (Piers, Adam, Guy); *Career* fashion model 1962-67, restauranteur Edwards Restaurant Bristol 1982-88; hotelier Penhallow Manor 1989-; *Recreations* ballet, needlepoint, interior design; *Style—* Mrs John Pitchford; Penhallow Manor, Altarnun, nr Launceston, Cornwall (☎ 0566 86206)

PITCHFORK, Group Capt Graham Ralph; MBE (1972); s of Ralph Pitchfork, of Sheffield, and Margaret Agnes, *née* Wragg; *b* 4 Feb 1939; *Educ* High Itorrs GS Sheffield, RAF Coll Cranwell (BA); *m* 5 June 1965, Marlane Margaret-Rose, da of Gareth Weasick (d 1939), of Dublin; 1 s (Paul b 1971), 2 da (Siobhan b 1966, Joanna b 1968); *Career* RAF: navigator, gp capt; Malay Peninsula 1965-66; S Arabia 1965-66; CO 208 Sqdn 1979-81; RAF Finningley 1987-; *Recreations* gliding, ornithology; *Clubs* RAF; *Style—* Group Capt Graham R Pitchfork, MBE; Barclays, Commercial Street, Sheffield 1

PITE, Hugh Stanley; s of The Rev George Stanley Pite (d 1952), and Olive Pite, *née* Legg (d 1943); *b* 21 Nov 1909; *Educ* Monkton Combe Sch, Bath; *m* 6 Sept 1952, Margaret Susan, da of Cecil Harry Kew (d 1938), of Barton-Under-Needwood, Staffs; 1 s (David Hugh Beresford b 1959), 3 da (Julia b 1955, Rosemary b 1957, Elizabeth b 1965); *Career* architect in private practice; landseer silver medal principal Hugh Pite & Assocs; Royal Acad Schs; work for private clients and public authorities: schs, libraries, clinics; FRIBA; *Recreations* painting, reading; *Style—* Hugh Pite, Esq; Yew Tree House, Dorking, Surrey RH4 1NE

PITHER, Jon Peter; s of Philip John Pither (d 1965), and Vera, *née* Roth (d 1980); *b* 15 June 1934; *Educ* Dauntsey's, Queens' Coll Cambridge (MA); *m* 1961, Karin Jutta, da of Werner Gropp; 1 s (Michael Gordon Carsten b 1963), 1 da (Brigitte Clare b 1965); *Career* cmmnd Royal Sussex Regt 1969-; md Amari plc, non-exec dir London Metal Exchange, underwriter Lloyds of London; *Recreations* sailing, skiing, golf; *Clubs* Athenaeum, Royal Thames Yacht, N Z Golf; *Style—* Jon P Pither, Esq; South House, Claremont Park, Esher, Surrey; Tides Reach, Rookwood, Sussex; Amari plc, Amari House, 52 High St, Kingston upon Thames KT1 1HN (☎ 01 549 6122, telex 262937, fax 01 546 0637, car tel 0836 220426)

PITHER, Hon Mrs (Pauline Ruth); da of 1 and last Baron Lambury (d 1967); *b* 1931; *m* 1954 (m dis 1972), John Pither; 2 s (Steven Edward b 1957, Gary John b 1959); *Style—* The Hon Mrs Pither; Appletree Farm House, Chorley Wood Common, Herts (☎ 260 2118)

PITMAN, Brian Ivor; s of Ronald Ivor Pitman, and Doris Ivy Pitman, *née* Short; *b* 13 Dec 1931; *Educ* Cheltenham GS; *m* 1954, Barbara Mildred Ann; 2 s (Mark, David), 1 da (Sally); *Career* chief exec and dir Lloyds Bank plc 1983-, dep chief exec: Lloyds Bank plc 1982-83, Lloyds Bank International Ltd 1978-81; dir: Lloyds Bank California 1982-86, The National Bank of New Zealand 1982-, Lloyds Bank International Ltd 1985-87, Lloyds Merchant Bank Hldgs Ltd 1985-88; *Recreations* golf, cricket, music;

Style— Brian Pitman, Esq; Lloyds Bank plc, 71 Lombard Street, London EC3P 3BS (☎ 01 626 1500)

PITMAN, Giles William; s of Capt John Pitman (ka 1943), and Elizabeth Cattanach Pitman; *b* 5 Sept 1938; *Educ* Eton, Christ Church Oxford (BA); *m* 1961, da of Maj George De Pree; 2 s, 1 da; *Career* jt gp md Pitman plc 1981-85; dir: Marine & General Mutual Life Assur Soc 1976, Bath Press Ltd 1981; Sir Isaac Pitman Ltd 1985; dep chm Pitman Examinations Inst 1985; *Style*— Giles Pitman, Esq; Heath House, Albury, Ware, Herts SG11 2LX (☎ 027 974 293);

PITOI, Sir Sere; CBE (1975); s of Pitoi Sere Orira; *b* 11 Nov 1935; *Educ* Sogeri, Queensland Univ, Birmingham Univ; *m* 1957, Daga Leva; 2 s, 3 da; *Career* chm Public Services Commission of Papua New Guinea 1971-; fell PNG Inst of Management MACE; kt 1977; *Style*— Sir Sere Pitoi, CBE; P O Box 6029, Boroko, Papua New Guinea

PITT, Barrie William Edward; yr s of John Pitt, and Ethel May, *née* Pennell; *b* 7 July 1918; *Educ* Portsmouth Southern GS; *m* 1, 1943, Phyllis Kate, *née* Edwards; 1 s (decd); m 2, 1953 (m dis 1971), Sonia Deirdre, *née* Hoskins; m 3, 1983, Frances Mary, *née* Moore; *Career* WWII Army 1939-45; bank clerk 1935, surveyor 1946, info offr UKAEA 1961, historical conslt to BBC Series The Great war 1963; author and ed of mil histories, contrib to Enclycopaedia Britannica and The Sunday Times; *publications*: The Edge of Battle (1958), Zeebrugge, St George's Day 1918 (1948), Coronel and Falkland (1960), 1918 The Last Act (1962), Purnells History of the Second World War (ed 1964), Ballantine's Illustrated History of World War 2 (ed-in-chief 1967), Purnell's History of the First World War (ed 1969), Ballantine's Illustrated History of the Violent Century (ed-in-chief 1971), British History Illustrated (ed 1974-78), The Battle of the Atlantic (1977), The Crucible of War: Western Desert (1941, 1980), Churchill and the Generals (1981), Year of Alamein 1942 (1982), Special Boat Squadron (1983), The Military History of World War II (1986), The Chronological Atlas of World War II (1989); *Recreations* golf; *Clubs* Savage; *Style*— Barrie Pitt, Esq; Fitzhead Ct, Fitzhead, Somerset TA4 3JP (☎ 0823 400923)

PITT, Barry Winston; s of Charles William Pitt, and Rhoda Grace, *née* Fenn; *b* 16 August 1942; *Educ* Dane Sch Nat Coll (Dip Environmental Studies); *m* 22 Aug 1967, Yvonne Dianne, da of Arthur Henry, of Woking, Surrey; 2 s (Anthony Arthur Charles Winston, James Alexander Winston); *Career* sr ptnr The BPA Partnership 1983-, md CJ Jeffries Ltd until 1986 (chm until 1987); chm: Coastal and Countryside plc 1987-, QA Servs Ltd 1988-, Wocad Ltd 1988-; former chm Bisley Cons Assoc; Freeman City of London, Liveryman Worshipful Co of Feltmakers; FCIBSE, MIHospE, MIP; *Recreations* yachting; *Clubs* Wig and Pen; *Style*— Barry Pitt, Esq; Vinyard Haven, 5 Allen House Park, Hook Heath, Woking, Surrey GU22 ODB; Chester House, Chertsey Rd, Woking, Surrey (☎ 04862 72053, fax 04862 29200, car phone 0836 702218)

PITT, Hon Bruce Michael David; o s of Baron Pitt of Hampstead (Life Peer), *qv*; *b* 18 June 1945; *Educ* King Alfred Sch Hampstead, Univ Coll London (LLB); *Career* barr Gray's Inn 1970; memb sub-ctee Criminal Bar Assoc Advsy Body to Law Cmmn on Special Def - Duress and Entrapment Coercion 1974; memb Bar Cncl Young Barristers' Ctee 1974-75; memb Senate Inns of Court and Bar Cncl 1975-76; memb Attorney-Gen's List of Counsel 1981-; asst recorder South Eastern Circuit 1985-; memb Hampstead Lab Pty 1960-; memb Campaign Against Racial Discrimination 1964-67; memb bars of Jamaica, Trinidad and Tobago, Barbados, and West Indies Associated States; *Recreations* swimming, arts, watching cricket; *Clubs* MCC, St Katherine's Yacht; *Style*— The Hon Bruce Pitt; 39 Cranes Park Crescent, Surbiton, Surrey (☎ 01 399 9720); 3 Temple Gardens, Temple, London EC4 (☎ 01 583 0010)

PITT, David Arthur; s of Frank Arthur Pitt (d 1954), of Alderley Edge, and Beatrice Ellen Pitt (d 1956); *b* 4 Oct 1927; *Educ* St Edward's Sch Oxford, Queens' Coll Cambridge (MA); *m* 30 May 1964, Margaret Helen Crichton, da of James Burnett Budge (d 1962), of Tanganyika; 3 s (James David Crichton, Andrew Alan, Jonathan Michael); *Career* RN 1946-48; Credit Insur Assoc 1954-56, Henry Cooke Lumsden plc 1956-89, (dep chm 1981-88); memb Lords Taverners NW Ctee; Assoc of Soc Investment Analysts 1961; *Recreations* real tennis, lawn tennis, sailing, skiing; *Clubs* MCC, St James's (Manchester), Manchester Tennis and Racquet; *Style*— David Pitt, Esq; Thornycroft Lodge, Pexhill, Macclesfield, Cheshire SK11 9PT; Henry Cooke, Lumsden plc, Stockbrokers, PO Box 369, No 1 King St, Manchester M60 3AH

PITT, Hon Mrs (Deborah Elspeth); da of 2 Viscount Leathers; *m* 1, 1966 (m dis), Thomas Richard Chadbon; 2 s (Dominic Thomas b 1966, Nicholas Richard b 1968); m 2, 1980, Richard William Pitt, yst s of late George Stanhope Pitt, of Rowbarns Manor, Horsley, Surrey; 1 da (Isabelle b 1981); *Style*— The Hon Mrs Pitt; 6 Bassingham Road, London SW18 3AG

PITT, Peter Clive Crawford; TD (1976); s of Norman Pitt (d 1987), of High Trees Ct, High Trees, Riegate, and Emily, *née* Crawford; *b* 7 Sept 1933; *Educ* Epsom Coll, Guy's Hosp (MB BS, DTM&H, MRCP); *m* 23 Jan 1965, Anna Catherine, da of Frederick William Markham Pratt (d 1965), of Pewsey, Wilts; 2 s (James Peter William b 22 Jan 1966, Daniel Crawford b 12 Sept 1969), 1 da (Rachel Louise b 6 Sept 1967); *Career* QA Mil Hosp 1959-61; surgical specialist Br Mil Hosp Kaduna Nigeria 1961-63, Cambridge Mil Hosp Aldershot 1963-65; sr surgical specialist: Br Mil Hosp Rinteln BAOR 1965-66, Br Mil Hosp Dharan Nepal 1966-68; Regtl MO TA 1969-; house surgn: Guy's 1957, (Paediatric) Guy's 1958; house physician Addenbrooks Cambridge 1958, registrar Redmill 1968-70, sr registrar Guy's and Chase Farm 1970-72, conslt surgn Oldchurch Hosp 1972-, dir Garnish Hall Tutorial Centre 1983-; pres Barking and Brentwood branch BMA 1981; cmmr Inland Revenue 1988; memb BMA, Hunterian Soc; FRCS 1963; *Books* Surgeon in Nepal: John Murray (1970); *Recreations* gardening, tennis; *Style*— Peter Pitt, Esq, TD; Garnish Hall, Margaret Roding, Dunmow, Essex (☎ 024 531 209); 3 Lake Rise, Romford, Essex (☎ 0708 47255)

PITT, William; *b* 17 July 1977; *Educ* London Nautical Sch, South Bank Poly London (BA); *m* 1967, Janet, *née* Wearn; 1 da; *Career* housing offr Lambeth Borough Cncl 1975-81; joined Lib Party 1959; contested: Croydon NW 1974, 1979, MP (SDP-Liberal Alliance) Croydon North-West 1981-83; *Style*— William Pitt Esq; 9 Queens Road, Broadstairs, Kent

PITT OF HAMPSTEAD, Baron (Life Peer UK 1975); David Thomas Pitt; JP (1966); s of Cyril S L Pitt, of St David's Grenada, WI; *b* 3 Oct 1913; *Educ* St David's RC Sch Grenada, Grenada Boys' Secdy Sch, Edinburgh Univ; *m* 1943, Dorothy Elaine, da of Aubrey Alleyne; 1 s (Hon Bruce), 2 da (Hon Phyllis, Hon Amanda); *Career* takes Labour Whip in House of Lords; GP London 1947-, pres W Indian Nat Party (Trinidad) 1943-47, memb LCC 1961-64, GLC 1964-77, for Hackney (dep chm 1969-70, chm 1974-75), chm Campaign Against Racial Discrimination 1965, dep chm Community Relations Commission 1968-77 (chm 1977-), memb Standing Adv Council on Race Relations 1977-79, part time memb PO Bd 1975-77, chm Shelter 1979, contested (L) Hampstead 1959, Clapham (Wandsworth) 1970; Hon DSc U of WI 1975, Hon DLitt Bradford 1977, Hon LLD Bristol 1977, Hon LLD Hutt 1983, Hon H D Shaw Univ N Carolina 1985; *Style*— The Rt Hon Lord Pitt of Hampstead JP; 6 Heath Drive, London NW3

PITT-RIVERS, Dr Rosalind Venetia; da of Hon Anthony Morton Henley, CMG, DSO (d 1925), and Hon Sylvia Laura, *née* Stanley, da of Lord Sheffield;; *b* 4 Mar 1907; *Educ* Notting Hill HS, Bedford Coll London Univ (MSc, PhD); *m* 1931, Capt George Henry Lane Fox Pitt-Rivers (d 1966); 1 s; *Career* memb: scientific staff Nat Inst for Med Res 1942-72, dept of pharmacology UCL 1972-85; hon res fell dept of pharmacology UCL; FRS 1954;; *Style*— Dr Rosalind Pitt-Rivers, FRS; The Old Estate Office, Hinton St Mary, Sturminster Newton, Dorset DT10 1NA (☎ 0258 72885)

PITTAM, Robert Raymond; s of Rev Raymond Gerald Pittam (d 1986), and Elsie Emma, *née* Sale (d 1978); *b* 14 June 1919; *Educ* Colne GS, Bootle GS, Pembroke Coll Cambridge (MA); *m* 14 Sept 1946, Gwendoline Lilian, da of Albert George Brown (d 1967); 1 s (Michael Robert b 1948), 1 da (Christine Margaret (Mrs Richardson) b 1953); *Career* WWII RAOC 1941-42; temp serv with Civil Serv during war; joined Home Off 1946, princ private sec to Home Sec 1955-57, serv Treasy and Civil Service Dept 1966-72, asst under sec of state Home Off 1972-79, fndr chm Home Off Retired Staff Assoc; lay preacher and chm Gp of Churches Welfare Orgn; FBIM 1965; *Recreations* cricket, reading; *Style*— Robert Pittam, Esq; 14 Devonshire Way, Shirley, Croydon CR0 8BR

PITTOM, L(ois) Audrey; CB (1979); da of Thomas Pittom; *b* 4 July 1918; *Educ* Laurels Sch Wroxall Abbey Warwick, St Anne's Oxford; *Career* under sec Health and Safety Executive, Dept of Employment 1975-78; ret; *Style*— Miss L Audrey Pittom, CB; 1 Rectory Lane, Barby, Rugby, Warwicks (☎ 0788 890424)

PITTS, David; JP (1967); s of Tom Farrar Pitts (d 1974), and Florence Pitts, *née* Crossley (d 1983); *b* 27 April 1929; *Educ* Woodhouse Gr, Bradford Coll; *m* 6 July 1957, Shirley Moira, da of Percy William Walker (d 1974); 1 s (William D b 1926); *Career* dir: David Pitts & Holt Ltd, P M Electronics Ltd, Pitts Energy Ltd; pres Electrical Contractors Assoc 1979-80; chm Northmidland Centre IEE 1973-74; freeman City of Bradford, FIEE; *Recreations* yachting, golf, opera; *Clubs* Lightmonger, Bradford; *Style*— David Pitts, Esq, JP; 'Miramar', Ryelands Grove, Bradford BD9 6HJ (☎ 0274 491223); 413 Cutler Heights Lane, Bradford BD4 9JL (☎ 0274 662871, fax 0274 660 686, car tel 0860 621 343)

PITTS, John Kennedy; s of Thomas Alwyn Pitts (d 1968); *b* 6 Oct 1925; *Educ* Trowbridge, Bristol Univ; *m* 1957, Joan Iris (d 1986), da of Henry Charles Light (d 1963); *Career* dir ICI Mond Division 1969-71, chm Richardson Fertilizers Ltd 1972-76, dep chm ICI Agricultural Div 1972-77, vice-pres Compagnie Neerlandaise de l'Azote 1975-77, chm Hargreaves Fertilizers Ltd 1975-77, chm and chief exec Tioxide Group plc 1978-87, memb Tees and Hartlepool Port Authority 1976-78; pres Chemical Industries Assoc 1984-86, vice chm Shildon and Sedgefield Devpt Agency Ltd 1986, chm Legal Aid Board 1988-; *Clubs* RAC; *Style*— John Pitts Esq

PITTS, (James) Michael; s of James Walter Pitts (d 1956); *b* 20 July 1929; *Educ* Shrewsbury; *m* 1955, Jean Hilarie; 2 s, 1 da; *Career* CA, sr ptnr Hodgson Impey; pres Birmingham & W Midlands Soc of CAs 1979-80; memb ct Birmingham Univ 1980, churchwarden St Laurence's Rowington, vice-chm Cannon Hill Tst; *Recreations* gardening, golf, sailing; *Clubs* RAC, The Birmingham; *Style*— Michael Pitts, Esq; Hickecroft, Mill Lane, Rowington, Warwick

PITTS-TUCKER, Robert St John; CBE (1975); s of Walter Greame Pitts-Tucker (d 1948); *b* 24 June 1909; *Educ* Haileybury, Clare Coll Cambridge; *m* 1942, Joan Margery, da of Frank Furnivall (d 1936); 3 s, 1 da; *Career* asst master Shrewsbury Sch 1931-44, headmaster Pocklington Sch 1945-66, gen sec HMC and HMA 1966-74; *Recreations* gardening, music, country walks; *Clubs* Royal Commonwealth Soc, East India and Sports; *Style*— Robert Pitts-Tucker Esq, CBE; Hillside, Toms Hill Rd, Aldbury, Tring, Herts HP23 5SA

PIXLEY, Sir Neville Drake; MBE (1944), VRD (1941); s of Arthur Pixley; *b* 21 Sept 1905; *Educ* C of E GS Brisbane; *m* 1938, Lorna, da of Llewellyn Stephens; 3 da; *Career* RANR WWII, Cdr 1945; ADC to King George VI and to HM The Queen 1951-54; chm P & O Australia 1956-70, dir Burns Philp & Co Ltd 1962-80, chm Aust Ctee Lloyds Register of Shipping 1967-80, dir Mauri Bros to 1968; memb bds of advice: Nat Bank of Aust (NSW), Elder Smith G M Ltd (ret); Order of St John in Australia, chm Royal Humane Soc of NSW; KStJ 1963, FCIT; kt 1976; *Style*— Sir Neville Pixley, MBE; Koiyong, 335 New South Head Rd, Double Bay, Sydney, NSW 2028, Australia (☎ 3262676)

PIZEY, Admiral Sir (Charles Thomas) Mark; GBE (1957, KBE 1953), CB (1942), DSO (and bar, 1942), DL (Somerset 1962); s of late Rev C E Pizey; *b* 1899; *m* Phyllis, da of Alfred D'Angibau; 2 da; *Career* WWII joined RN 1916, served HMS Revenge Battle of Jutland, HMS Danae Special Serv Sqdn World Cruise 1921-22, Flag Lt to Vice Adm Sir Howard Kelly Med Fleet 1929-30, cmd destroyers Med and Home fleets 1930-39, WWII Capt HMS Campbell Channel and North Sea op 1940-42 (despatches twice), Capt HMS Tyne and chief staff offr to Rear Adm Destroyers Russian Convoys 1942-43 (despatches twice), dir Ops (Home) Admty Naval Staff 1944-45, chief of staff to C-in-C Home Fleet 1946, chief UK servs liaison staff Aust 1948-49, Flag Offr cmdg 1 Cruiser Sqdn Med Fleet 1950-51, chief of naval staff and C-in-C Indian Navy 1951-55, Admiral 1954, C-in-C Plymouth 1955-58, ret; *Style*— Admiral Sir Mark Pizey, GBE, CB, DSO; 1 St Ann's Drive, Gore Rd, Burnham on Sea, Somerset TA8 2HR (☎ 0278 785 770)

PLACE, Rear Adm (Basil Charles) Godfrey; VC (1944), CB (1970), DSC (1943); s of Maj Charles Godfrey Morris Place, DSO, MC, (d 1931), and Anna Margaret, *née* Stuart-William (d 1949); descended from Archbishop Ussher (17th century), who dated bible and aquired Book of Kells for Trinity Dublin; *b* 19 July 1921; *Educ* The Grange Folkestone, RNC Dartmouth; *m* 1943, Althea Anningson, da of late Harry Tickler; 1 s (Charles), 2 da (Andrea, Melanie); *Career* Capt 1958, Adm cmdg Reserves, and dir-gen Naval Recruiting 1968-70, chm VC and GC Assoc 1971-, lay observer 1975-78; Polish Cross of Valour 1941; *Style*— Rear Adm Godfrey Place, VC, CB, DSC; The Old Bakery, Corton Denham, Sherborne, Dorset

PLACE, John Bassett Moore; s of Herman and Angela Place; *b* 21 Nov 1925; *Educ*

The Citadel, New York Univ, Sch of Mines Pace Univ; *m* 1952, Katherine Smart; 1 s (John), 2 da (Marian, Judith); *Career* chm, pres and chief exec offr Anaconda Co 1971-77; chm and chief exec: Crocker Nat Corp, Crocker Bank; dir Midland Bank 1981-; *Clubs* Stock Exchange, Pacific Union, Burlingame Country, California, San Francisco Golf, Links; *Style—* John Place Esq; Crocker National Corporation, One Montgomery St, San Francisco, California 94104, USA; c/o Crocker National Bank, 34 Great St Helens, EC3 (☎ 01 283 8111)

PLAISTER, Sir Sydney; CBE (1972); s of Herbert Plaister; *b* 15 Jan 1909; *Educ* Acton and Chiswick Poly, Coll of Estate Mgmnt; *m* 1937, Coralie Fraser Steele; 1 s, 1 da; *Career* chartered quantity surveyor 1930-, pres W Midlands Cons Cncl 1980-83, chm Midlands Central Cons Euro-Constituency Cncl 1978-83, memb exec ctee Nat Union of Cons Assocs 1967-82; Freeman City of London; FRSA, FRICS; kt 1980; *Style—* Sir Sydney Plaister, CBE; Turnpike Close, Old Warwick Rd, Lapworth, Warwicks B94 6AP (☎ 056 43 2792)

PLAISTOWE, Alan David; s of David Plaistowe, of Connemara, Co Galway, and Rhona Elizabeth, *née* French; *b* 18 June 1932; *Educ* Marlborough, Ramsey Labs UC London (BSc); *m* 14 June 1957, Jane, da of Donovan Candler, of London; 1 da (Victoria b 1966); *Career* Lt RE Libya 1950-52; with Design Engrs (gas processing, oil refining) 1955-58; Stone and Webster Engrg 1958-65; fndr and md Chem Systems Int 1965, pres Chem Systems Gp 1986-; FIChemEng, FIPet; *Recreations* flying, golf, gardening, jazz; *Clubs* RAC; *Style—* Alan Plaistowe, Esq; Wanden, Egerton, Kent; Chem Systems Ltd

PLANE, Marjorie; da of Reginald Shepherd, and Frances Miriam, *née* Wren; *b* 18 Feb 1950; *Educ* Rochdale Girls' Central Sch; *m* 18 Feb 1950, Geoffrey James Plane, s of Fred Plane (d 1970); 1 s (Garry James b 21 Dec 1950); *Career* jr clerk 49 Eclipse Mill Co Ltd 1947-49, costing clerk Samuel Heap & Sons Ltd 1949-50, payroll supervisor Samuel O'Neill Ltd 1951-52; Ratcliffe Industs plc: cashier bookeeper 1952-56, co sec 1956-77, main bd dir 1977-88; pres Rochdale C of C 1980-82, devpt dir Rochdale C of C Trade & Indust 1988-; chm Rochdale Enterprise Tst; memb: Rochdale Health Authy, Rochdale Employer Network, Cncl Rochdale Engr Employers' Assoc, Safe City Steering Gp, Saiwbal Rochdale twinning Ctee, Rochdale Econ Generation Advsy Panel, TVEI Steering Gp, VETAG Mgmnt Ctee; chm Friends of High Birch Ctee, local gp chm Indust Matters, co delegate CBI 1965-66, sec Rochdale Contintental Travellers Club 1965-; MBIM 1967; *Recreations* sailing, travel; *Clubs* Home Base-Glass Glasson Yacht Basin, Misty Tow Lancaster; *Style—* Mrs Marjorie Plane; Knowlewood, 68 Woodhouse Lane, Norden, Rochdale OL12 7SD (☎ 0706 41407); Co Ct Gldg, Town Hall Sq, Rochdale OL16 1NF(☎ 0706 343810, fax 59486)

PLANK, Hon Mrs (Marion Rose); *née* Blyton; 2 da of Baron Blyton (Life Peer; d 1987); *b* 1926; *m* 1948, John Plank; children; *Style—* The Hon Mrs Plank; 36 Gerald St, S Shields, Tyne and Wear

PLANT, Hon Christopher Victor Howe; s of Baron Plant (d 1986, Life Peer); *b* 1945; *m* 1966 (m dis 1980), Marian, da of John Parkes; m 2, 1986, Linda Louisa, da of Albert Pike, 2 da; *Style—* The Hon Christopher Plant; Laural Bank, 7 St Michael's Terrace, Lewes, E Sussex BN7 2HX

PLANT, (Ronald Arthur) Derek; s of Arthur Plant (d 1982), and Edith Frances, *née* Brock (d 1985); *b* 13 Jan 1935; *Educ* Rothesay Acad Isle of Bute, Scottish Hotel Sch Glasgow (Dip Hotel Mgmnt); *m* 22 Dec 1960, Christina Ann Murray, da of John Craig, of Cardross, Scotland; 2 da (Alison Christina (Mrs Carlton) b 1964, Isla Edith b 1966); *Career* Nat Serv 1955-57; Br Tport Hotels Ltd 1957-83: hotel gen mangr 1964-79, div dir 1979-80, company ops dir 1980-83; joint md Compass Hotels Ltd 1983-; Freeman: City of London 1978, Worshipful Co of Distillers 1979-; FHCIMA 1975; *Recreations* music, cricket, travel, reading; *Clubs* MCC; *Style—* Derek Plant, Esq 21 Godfries Close, Tewin, Herts AL6 OLQ (☎ 043 871 7761); Compass Hotels Ltd, Great Northern Hotel, Kings Crosss, London N1 9AN (☎ 01 837 4421, fax 01 837 7251, telex 299041)

PLANT, Baroness Gladys; *née* Mayers; Sampson Mayers; *m* 1931, Baron Cyril Thomas Howe Plant, CBE (Life Peer UK 1978), (d 1986); 2 s, 1 da; *Style—* Lady Gladys Plant; 8 Apple Tree Close, North Street, Barming, Maidstone, Kent ME16 9HQ

PLANT, Keith Forrester; s of Edwin James Plant, and Rhoda Plant (d 1986); *b* 12 Oct 1936; *Educ* Royal Wolverhampton Sch ; *m* 26 May 1960, Monica Anne, da of Arthur David Sheasby (d 1986); 1 s (Mark b 11 April 1962), 1 da (Sally b 10 Sept 1964); *Career* Nat Serv with RAF 1959-61; joined Tioxide as accountant 1961 (fin dir 1978, chief exec Tioxide Gp 1987-), dir of Tioxide Gp subsidiarie; FCA, Fndn Fell Corporate Treasurers (FCT), CBIM; *Recreations* badminton, gardening; *Style—* Keith Plant, Esq; Tioxide Group plc, Tioxide House, 137-143 Hammersmith Rd, London W14 0QL (☎ 01 602 7121, fax 01 784 0019, telex 920900)

PLANT, (Edward) Nicholas; s of Maj Raymond Plant, of St Georges Meadows, West Drayton, Middx, and Margery Grace, *née* Windsor; *b* 11 Oct 1941; *Educ* Prior Park Coll Bath, Kings Sch Chester, Sheffield Univ (LLB); *m* 30 March 1967, Patricia Mary, da of Percival Lee (d 1978), of Liverpool; 2 s (Edward b 1970, James b 1972); *Career* slr admitted 1966, Middleton & Upsall 1968- (managing ptnr Trowbridge off), Notary Public 1974; former: sec Trowbridge C of C, memb Round Table, Cons branch sec and pres, sec Trowbridge Rotary Club, GDBA branch; govr St Augustines Sch; memb: Law Soc 1966, Br Legal Assoc, Provincial Notaries Soc 1974; *Recreations* antiques, reading, things French, working; *Clubs* Royal Overseas League; *Style—* Nicholas Plant, Esq; 2 Fore St, Trowbridge, Wiltshire (☎ 0225 762 683, fax 0225 760 555)

PLASKETT, Maj-Gen Frederick Joseph; CB (1980), MBE (1966); s of Frederick Joseph Plaskett (d 1982), and Grace Mary Plaskett (d 1988); *b* 23 Oct 1926; *Educ* Wallasey GS, Chelsea Poly; *m* 1, 9 Sept 1950, Heather (d 1982), da of Maurice William Kington (d 1976), of Salisbury, Wilts; 4 da (Helen b 1951, Wendy b 1954, Kate b 1960, Lucy b 1965); m 2, 1984, Mrs Patricia Joan Healy, da of Richard Upton, of Wimborne, Dorset; *Career* Army 1945-81; regimental and staff appts: India, Korea, Japan, Malaya, W Africa, Germany, UK; ret as Maj-Gen dir-gen Tport and Movements (Army) 1981; Col Cmdt RCT 1981-; cmmr Royal Hosp Chelsea 1985-; dir-gen Road Haulage Assoc Ltd 1981-88; dir: Paccar UK (Fodern Trucks) 1981-, British Rail Midland Region 1986-; FCIT; *Recreations* sailing, fishing, gardening; *Clubs* Army and Navy; *Style—* Maj-Gen Frederick Plaskett, CB, MBE; c/o National Westminster Bank plc, The Commons, Shaftesbury, Dorset SP7 8JY

PLASTOW, Sir David Arnold Stuart; s of James Stuart Plastow (d 1987), of Grimsby, Lincs, and Marie Plastow (d 1975); *b* 9 May 1932; *Educ* Culford Sch Bury St Edmunds; *m* 1954, Barbara Ann, da of Ralph May, of Luton, Beds; 1 s, 1 da; *Career* mktg dir Motor Car Div Rolls-Royce Ltd 1967-70 (md 1971), md Rolls-Royce Motors Ltd 1972 (gp md 1974-80); chief exec Vickers plc 1980- (chm 1987-, non-exec dir 1975-80), pres: Soc of Motor Manufacturers and Traders 1976-78, Motor Indust Res Assoc 1978-81; non-exec dir: GKN plc 1978-84, Legal and Gen Gp plc 1985-87, memb: Bd Tenneco Inc Houston 1985-, Offshore Energy Technol Bd 1985-86, Engrg Cncl 1980-83; non-exec dir Guinness plc 1986- (dep chm 1987); dep chm Listed Cos Advsy Ctee 1987-; chm Cncl Indust Soc 1983-87; Hon DSc Cranfield 1978; kt 1986; *Recreations* golf, music; *Clubs* Royal and Ancient (St Andrews), Royal St George's (Sandwich); *Style—* Sir David Plastow; Vickers plc, Vickers House, Millbank Tower, Millbank, London SW1P 4RA (☎ 01 828 7777, telex 27921)

PLASTOW, Norman Frederick; s of Frederick Stephen William Plastow (d 1958), and Helena Florence Plastow (d 1974); *b* 27 Mar 1929; *Educ* Kings Coll Sch Wimbledon; *m* 4 April 1953, Audrey Ruth, da of Donald S Prosser (d 1977); 2 da (Hazel Anne b 1958, Wendy Jane b 1961); *Career* RAF (F/O) 1953-55; architect works incl: schs for Notts CC, Cornwall CC, ILEA (Finsbury Coll of Advanced Technol 1962), offices for Weidenfeld & Nicholson (1978) and Dominion Ins Co (1985); memb SIAD 1953-83; Wimbledon and Putney Commons Conservator 1979-, vice-pres and chm Wimbledon Soc 1975-, hon curator Wimbledon Windmill Museum 1976-, local sec Surrey Archaeological Soc 1978-, memb Conservation Areas Advsy Ctee to Borough of Merton; Time/RICS Conservation Award 1972; FRIBA, FBIS; *Books* ed Architects Standard Catalogue (annual); books inc: Safe as Houses (1972), The Trees of Wimbledon (1975), Wimbledon Windmill (1977), A History of Wimbledon and Putney Common (1986); *Recreations* archaeology, local history, photography, writing; *Style—* Norman Plastow, Esq; Far House, Hillside, Wimbledon, London SW19 4NL (☎ 01 947 2825)

PLATT, Adrian; s of Clifford Lowe Platt, OBE (d 1982), of Chislehurst, Kent, and Katharine Eileen, *née* Everington (d 1975); *b* 28 Nov 1935; *Educ* Marlborough, Grenobles Univ; *m* 24 Sept 1960, Valerie, da of Richard Bois (d 1956); 2 da (Emma b 1965, Katie b 1967); *Career* Nat Serv 4 RHA 1954-56, TA HAC 1956-62; dir Sedgwick Collins Ltd 1964-; chm: Sedgwick Forbes Marine Ltd 1968-69, Sedgwick Forbes Bland Payne Marine Ltd 1969-; dir Sedgwick Gp plc 1981, chm: Sedgwick Marine and Aviation Gp 1986-88, Sedgwick Ltd Devpt Gp 1988-; tstee Mary Rose Tst; Liveryman: Worshipful Co of Vinters 1956, Worshipful Co of Shipwrights 1988; *Recreations* skiing, tennis, golf, shooting, reading; *Clubs* Honourable Artillery Co, Inst of Directors; *Style—* Adrian Platt, Esq; Rosehill, Ockham Rd Sth, E Horsley, Surrey KT24 6SL (☎ 04865 3448); Sedgwick Ltd, Sedgwick House, 10 Whitechapel High St, London E1 (☎ 01 377 3411, car 0836 236 879, telex 882131)

PLATT, Prof Colin Peter Sherard; s of James Westlake Platt, CBE (d 1972), of Jersey, CI, and Veronica Norma Hope, *née* Arnold (d 1987); *b* 11 Nov 1934; *Educ* Collyers Sch Horsham Sussex, Balliol Coll Oxford (BA, MA), Univ of Leeds (PhD); *m* 8 Feb 1963, Valerie, da of Thomas Ashforth (d 1976), of Cannock, Staffs; 2 s (Miles b 9 April 1965, Theo b 20 Dec 1971), 2 da (Emma b 17 July 1963, Tabitha b 3 Jan 1967); *Career* Nat Serv RN Leading Coder Special 1953-54; lectr medieval archaeology Univ of Leeds 1962-64; dept of history Univ of Southampton: lectr 1964-74, sr lectr 1974-79, reader 1979-83, prof 1983-; FSA 1968, FRHistS 1971; *Books* The Monastic Grange in Medieval England (1969), Medieval Southampton: The Port and Trading Community, A D 1000-1600 (1973), Excavations in Medieval Southampton 1953-1969 (1975), The English Medieval Town (1976), Medieval England, A Social History and Archaeology from the Conquest to 1600 AD (1979), The Parish Churches of Medieval England (1981), The Castle in Medieval England and Wales (1982), The Abbeys and Priories of Medieval England (1984), Medieval Britain from the Air (1984), The Traveller's Guide to Medieval England (1985), The National Trust Guide to Late Medieval and Renaissance Britain (1986); *Recreations* reading fiction, visiting antiquitigs; *Style—* Prof Colin Platt; Department of History, Univ of Southampton, Southampton SO9 5NH (☎ 0703 595 000, fax 0703 593 939, telex 47661)

PLATT, David Wallace; s of Christopher Platt, of Knock, Ulster, and Susan Harriette La Nauze, *née* Wallace; *b* 13 Sept 1964; *Educ* Campbell Coll, Trinity Hall Cambridge (MA); *Career* barr Middle Temple 1987, chm CUCA 1986; vice-chm Westminster Cons Assoc, former political res asst and aide House of Commons and Cons Central Off, memb exec Cncl for Protection of Rural England; *Books* Educating Our Future (1986); *Recreations* politics, skiing, hunting, architecture, conservation; *Clubs* O & C; *Style—* David Platt, Esq; 44 Denbigh St, London SW1 (☎ 01 630 7089); 1 Harcourt Bldgs, Temple, London EC4 (☎ 01 353 0375, fax 01 583 5816)

PLATT, Derek William; s of Thomas Platt (d 1933), and Eliza, *née* Ford (d 1947); *b* 30 Dec 1927; *Educ* London Univ (BSc); *m* 30 July 1949, Barbara Mary, da of Wilfred Walker (d 1973); 2 s (Derek Andrew Jonathan b 1954, Michael William b 1955), 1 da (Penelope Mary Jane b 1951); *Career* chartered engr civil, mechanical and electrical; chm Highplaced Ltd 1963-; FICE, FIMechE, FIEE; *Recreations* sailing; *Clubs* Royal Thames YC, Royal Ocean Racing; *Style—* Derek Platt, Esq; The Old Vicarage, Hambledon, Hants PO7 6RP (☎ 070 132 432)

PLATT, Eleanor Frances; QC (1982); er da of Dr Maurice Leon Platt (d 1966), of Sussex, and Sara, *née* Stein (d 1983); *b* 6 May 1938; *Educ* London Univ (LLB); *m* 1963, Frederick Malcolm; 1 s (Jonathan b 1969), 1 da (Amanda b 1965); *Career* barr Gray's Inn 1960, rec SE circuit 1982-, memb Matrimonial Causes Rule Ctee 1986-; *Recreations* the arts, travel, skiing; *Style—* Miss Eleanor Platt, QC; 6 Pump Ct, Temple, London EC4Y 7AP (☎ 01 583 6013)

PLATT, Martin Philip; s and h of Hon Prof Sir Peter Platt, 2 Bt; *b* 9 Mar 1952; *m* 1971, Frances Corinne Moana, da of Trevor Samuel Conley; 2 s, 2 da; *Style—* Martin Platt, Esq; 25 Manchester St, Dunedin, New Zealand

PLATT, Norman; OBE (1985); s of Edward Turner Platt (d 1956), and Emily Jane Platt (d 1972); *b* 29 August 1920; *Educ* Bury GS, King's Coll Cambridge (BA); *m* 1, 1942, Diana Franklin, da of Sir Charles Travis Clay, CB (d 1975); 1 s (Tristan), 1 da (Marianna); m 2, 1963, Johanna Sigrid, da of Jesse Stewart Bishop; 1 s (Benjamin b 1965), 2 da (Rebecca b 1966, Lucinda b 1969); *Career* singer, actor, translator, opera producer; princ Sadler's Wells Opera 1946-48, and English Opera Gp 1948, memb Deller Consort, fndr and artistic dir Kent Opera 1969-; Hon DCL Kent; chm Canterbury Festival Planning Ctee 1984-86; *Recreations* looking at pictures, listening to music, being read to me by my wife; *Style—* Norman Platt, Esq; Pembles Cross, Egerton, Ashford, Kent TN27 9EN (☎ 023 376 237/406)

PLATT, Hon Mrs (Pauline Mary); da of Baroness Fisher of Rednal and Joseph Fisher; *b* 1940; *m* 1961, Michael James Platt; *Style*— The Hon Mrs Platt

PLATT, Hon Sir Peter; 2 Bt (UK 1959); s of Baron Platt (Life Peer and 1 Bt) (d 1978), and Margaret Irene, *née* Cannon (1987); *b* 6 July 1924; *Educ* Abbotsholme Sch Derbyshire, Magdalen Coll Oxford (MA, BMus, BLitt), RCM; *m* 1948, Jean Halliday, da of late Charles Philip Brentnall, MC; 1 s (Martin), 2 da (Margaret, Katherine); *Heir* s, Martin Philip Platt, b 9 March 1952; *Career* serv WWII (despatches); prof of music: Otago Univ NZ 1957-75, Sydney Univ 1975-; Hon FGSM 1973; *Style*— The Hon Sir Peter Platt, Bt; 1 Ellison Place, Pymble, NSW 2073, Australia (☎ 02 4494372); Dept of Music, University of Sydney, NSW 2006, Australia (☎ 02 6922923)

PLATT, Hon Roland Francis; s of Baroness Platt of Writtle (Life Peer); *b* 1951; *Educ* Felsted Sch; *m* 1982, Louise, yr da of L B B Jackson, of The Coppice, Hutton, Essex; 1 s (James b 1987), 1 da (Ann b 1985); *Career* FCA (ACA 1976); *Style*— The Hon Roland Platt; Fremnells, 10 Westbury Rd, Brentwood, Essex

PLATT, Ronald Thomas George; OBE (1969); s of Arthur Thomas Platt (d 1986), of Torquay (d 1986), and Henriette Jessie, *née* Collins; *b* 18 Sept 1926; *Educ* Bancrofts Sch, Glasgow Univ, LSE (BSc) ; *m* 4 Aug 1953, Kathleen; 4 s (Simon b 1957, David b 1962, Stephen b 1964, Andrew b 1960 (decd)); 2 da (Johanna b 1963, Alison b 1968); *Career* dir Iveco Ford Ltd; dir Ford cos in: Belgium, Finland, France, Ireland, Italy, Netherlands, Portugal, Switzerland; English Ford line mangr Ford US 1963-70, dir car sales Ford of Britain, vice pres Euro sales ops and export Ford of Europe 1974- (mktg dir 1973-74);; *Recreations* sailing, crosswords, grass cutting; *Style*— Ronald T Platt, Esq; Higher Barton, Hallwood Crescent, Brentwood, Essex (☎ 0277 223172); Ford of Europe Inc, Eagle Way, Brentwood, Essex

PLATT, Sylvia, Lady; Sylvia Jean; da of late Sidney Charles Caveley, and formerly w of John Alfred Haggard; *m* 1974, as his 2 w, 1 Baron Platt (Life Peer and 1 Bt; d 1978); *Style*— The Rt Hon Sylvia, Lady Platt; 53 Heathside, Hinchley Wood, Esher, Surrey

PLATT, Hon Victoria Catherine; da of Baroness Platt of Writtle; *b* 1953; *Educ* Marlborough, Girton Coll Cambridge (MA); *m* 1984, Rhodri, s of His Hon Judge John Davies, QC, of Teddington, Middx; 2 da (Rachael Catherine b 1985, Joanna Megan b 1987); *Career* ACA, ATII, accountant and lectr in private practice; *Recreations* running, hill walking, sailing; *Clubs* Thames, Hare and Hounds; *Style*— The Hon Vicky Platt

PLATT OF WRITTLE, Baroness (Life Peer UK 1981); Beryl Catherine; CBE (1978), DL (Essex 1983); da of Ernest Myatt (d 1950); *b* 18 April 1923; *Educ* Westcliff HS for Girls, Girton Coll Cambridge (MA); *m* 1949, Stewart Sydney, s of Sydney Rowland Platt (d 1946); 1 s, 1 da; *Career* aeronautical engr; tech asst Hawker Aircraft Ltd 1943-46, BEA 1946-49; Chelmsford RDC 1959-74; Essex CC elected 1965 (alderman 1969-74, vice-chm 1980-83, vice-chm educn ctee 1969-71, chm 1971-80, chm further educn sub-ctee 1969-71); non exec dir Br Gas plc 1988, fell Smallprice Tst 1988; memb: court Essex and City Univ 1968-78, cncl City and Guilds of London Inst 1974-, Cambridge Univ appts bd 1975-79, Engrg Cncl 1982-, cncl Royal Soc of Arts 1983-88, cncl Careers Res and Advsy Ctee 1983-; chm Equal Opportunities Cmmn 1983-88; memb ct Brunel Univ 1985, vice pres UMIST 1985-; hon fell: Womens Engrg Soc 1988, Girton Coll Cambridge, Poly of Wales; Hon Insignor Award City and Guilds London Inst 1988; Hon LLD Cambridge Univ 1988, Hon DSc Cranfield Inst City of London; Hon D: Univ of Salford, Open Univ, Univ of Bradford (Eng), Univ of Essex, Brunei Univ (Tech); FEANI 1988, Hon FCP, FIMechE, FEng, FRAeS, FRSA, FITD; *Recreations* reading, gardening, cooking, (yacht 'Corydalis'); *Style*— The Rt Hon the Baroness Platt of Writtle, CBE, DL; House of Lords, London SW1; Equal Opportunities Commission, Overseas House, Quay St Manchester M3 3HN (☎ (061 833) 9244)

PLATTS, David Ernest; s of John Ernest Platts (d 1977), of Halifax, Yorks, and Emma Crossley, *née* Crossland; *b* 8 July 1936; *Educ* Crossley and Porter GS Halifax; *m* 20 June 1959, Judith Beryl, da of Stanley Priestly, of Halifax, Yorks; 1 s (Charles John Savile b 1962, Mark Howard David b 1967), 1 da (Sarah Judith Rachel b 1966); *Career* slr; currently sole practioner on own account, former legal asst to registrar-gen Hon Kong former in house lawyer: Abbey Nat Bldg Soc, Trafalgar House Gp, Hammerson Gp; *Recreations* gardening, sailing, wine; *Clubs* Rotary; *Style*— David Platts, Esq; Seeleys Orchard, Penn Rd, Beaconsfield, Bucks HP9 2LN (☎ 0494 673 933, fax 0494 674 971)

PLATTS-MILLS, John Faithful Fortescue; QC (1964); s of John F W Mills and Dr Daisy Platts-Mills, NZ; *b* 4 Oct 1906; *Educ* Nelson Coll Victoria Univ NZ (LLM), Balliol Coll Oxford (MA, BCL); *m* 1936, Janet Katherine Cree; 6 s; *Career* serv WWII, pilot offr RAF; barr Inner Temple, bencher Inner Temple 1970; collier 1944; MP (Lab) Finsbury 1945-48, (Ind L) 1948-50, pres Haldane Soc; vice-pres Int Assoc of Democratic Lawyers; memb TGWU; *Clubs* Athenaeum, Vincent's (Oxford), Leander; *Style*— John Platts-Mills, Esq, QC; Cloisters, Temple, London EC4 (☎ 01 353 7705); Terrible Down Farm, Halland, E Sussex (☎ (082 584) 310)

PLAYER, Edward; s of Edward Player, CBE (d 1968), and Mary Edith; *b* 25 Mar 1920; *Educ* Wrekin, Birmingham Univ (Dip Engrg Prodn Mgmnt); *m* 15 Dec 1945, Joan, da of Walter Guy (d 1934), of Fiji; 2 da (Susan b 1947, Virginia b 1952); *Career* Capt RTR 1941-50, serv WWII N Africa (POW); chm Sterling Metals Ltd 1973-74 (md 1962-73); dir many assoc cos incl: Birmid Industries 1964-69, Birmid Qualcast (Foundries) Ltd 1969-73; mgmnt conslt (specialising Ferrows and non Ferrows industries) 1975-; fell Inst of Br Foundrymen, Liveryman Worshipful Co of Coachmakers' and Coach Harness Makers'; *Recreations* fishing, shooting; *Style*— Edward Player, Esq; 9 The Maltings, Lillington Ave, Leamington Spa (☎ 0926 339378)

PLAYFAIR, Sir Edward Wilder; KCB (1957), CB (1949); s of late Dr Ernest Playfair; *b* 17 May 1909; *Educ* Eton, King's Coll Cambridge; *m* 1941, Dr Mary Lois Rae; 3 da; *Career* serv Treasy 1934-46 and 1947-56, control off Germany and Austria 1946-47, perm under-sec of state for war 1956-59, perm sec MOD 1960-61; chm Int Computers and Tabulators Ltd 1961-65; tstee National Gallery 1967-74 (chm 1972-74), fell Imperial Coll of Science and Technol 1972; hon fell: UCL 1969, King's Coll Cambridge; Hon FBCS; *Clubs* Brooks's; *Style*— Sir Edward Playfair, KCB; 62 Coniger Rd, London SW6 3TA (☎ 01 736 3194)

PLAYFAIR, Acting Lt-Col TA (CCF) Hugh George Lyon; OBE (1989); s of John Maxwell Playfair (d 1983), of Baltilly, Ceres, Fife, and Majory Jean Playfair-Hannay, MBE, *née* Armour-Hannay; *b* 5 Dec 1939; *Educ* Oundle, King's Coll Cambridge (MA), New Coll Oxford (Dip Ed); *m* 22 Aug 1970, Bridget Ingledew Jane, da of Edward Andrew Garland (d 1953), of India; 2 s (Patrick b 1971, Edward b 1972), 1 da (Elizabeth b 1974); *Career* Nat Serv 2 Lt King's Own Scottish Borderers attached to Somaliland Scouts 1957-59; asst master: Marlborough Coll 1960-68, Cranbrook Sch Sydney 1969-73, (housemaster, sr history master 1970-73), Canford Sch 1974-; lay reader Diocese of Bath and Wells, MBIM 1979; *Books* The Playfair Family (1984); *Recreations* golf, gardening, shooting, stamp collecting; *Clubs* Royal & Ancient, Sherborne Golf; *Style*— Lt-Col Playfair, OBE; Canford School, Wimborne, Dorset (☎ 0202 881 254)

PLAYFAIR - HANNAY OF KINGSMUIR, Patrick Armour; s of John Maxwell Playfair (d 1983), of Baltilly, Ceres, Fife, and Majory Jean *née* , Armour-Hannay, MBE (d 1983); *b* 12 July 1929; *Educ* Oundle; *m* 15 May 1954, Frances Ann, da of Robert James Roberton, of Morebattle Tofts, Kelso; 1 s (James Patrick Lyon b 4 March 1957), 1 da (Freda Mary Caroline b 27 April 1962); *Career* Nat Serv 2 Lt RASC 1946-48 (Suez Canal zone with Air Despatch Co); tea and rubber planter Rosehaugh & Co Ltd Ceylon 1948-55, landowner and farmer at Clifton-on-Bowmont Kelso Fife 1956-; chm Assoc for Protection of Rural Scotland, ctee memb Nat Sheep Assoc, elder Church of Scotland; *Recreations* shooting, archery; *Clubs* Royal Company of Archers, Farmers; *Style*— Patrick Playfair - Hannay of Kingsmuir, Esq; Clifton-on-Bowmont, Kelso (☎ 057 382 227)

PLAYFORD, Jonathan Richard; QC (1982); s of Maj Cecil Roche Bullen Playford (d 1977), of London, and Euphrasia Joan, *née* Cox; *b* 6 August 1940; *Educ* Eton, London Univ (LLB); *m* 1978, Jill Margaret, da of William Herbert Dunlop, MBE (d 1982), of Doonside, Ayr; 1 s (Nicholas b 1981), 1 da (Fiona b 1985); *Career* barr Inner Temple 1962; recorder Crown Ct 1985; *Recreations* golf, gardening, country pursuits; *Clubs* Garrick; *Style*— Jonathan Playford, Esq, QC; 2 Harcourt Buildings, Temple EC4X 9DB (☎ 01 583 9020)

PLEASANCE, Roy Thomas; s of James Harold Pleasance (d 1981), and Mary Catherine, *née* Harris (d 1982); *b* 11 Feb 1926; *Educ* Rutlish Sch Merton; *m* 1, 12 June 1948, Gwendoline May; m 2, 3 Oct 1964, Anne; m 3, 29 June 1984, Norman Mary Germaine, da of Sir Norman King (d 1963); *Career* CA Taxation specialist; head of taxation dept BP Co Ltd 1958-73, chm UK Oil Ind Taxation Ctee 1964-74; *Books* UK Taxation of Offshire Oil and Gas (1977, with R Hayllar); *Recreations* opera, architecture, history; *Style*— Roy Pleasance, Esq; Arden's House, Abbey St, Faversham, Kent ME13 7BH (☎ 0795 534 124); 80 Preston St, Faversham, Kent (☎ 0795 535 249)

PLENDERLEITH, Ian; s of Raymond William Plenderleith, and Louise Helen, *née* Martin; *b* 27 Sept 1943; *Educ* King Edwards Sch Birmingham, Christ Church Oxford (MA), Colombia Business Sch NY (MBA); *m* 1 April 1967, Kristina Mary, da of John Hardy Bentley, OBE (d 1980); 1 s (Giles b 1972), 2 da (Melanie b 1969, Cressida b 1976); *Career* joined Bank of Eng 1965, seconded as tech ass to UK exec dir Int Monetary Washington DC 1972-74, private sec to govr 1976-79, head Gilt-Edged Div 1982- (asst dir 1986-); hon sec Tillington CC; memb advsy bd inst of archaeology devpt tst Univ Coll London; Liveryman Worshipful Co of Innholders 1977-; *Recreations* archaeology, theatre, cricket; *Clubs* Tillington CC; *Style*— Ian Plenderleith, Esq; Bank of England, London EC2R 8AH (☎ 01 601 4444)

PLESS, Mary, Princess of; (Dorothea) Mary Elizabeth; da of Lt-Col Richard George Edward Minchin (d 1985), of Busherstown, Co Offaly and Annagh, Co Tipperary, and Elizabeth Eve, *née* McKerrell-Brown; *b* 2 Jan 1928; *Educ* St Leonards Sch St Andrews; *m* 23 July 1958 (m dis 1971), Henry, Prince of Pless (d 1984), eld s of Hans Heinrich XIV, 3 Prince of Pless, Imperial Count of Hochberg by his 1 w Daisy, *née* Cornwallis-West; *Recreations* theatre, animal life; *Style*— Mary, Princess of Pless; 14 Campden House, Sheffield Terrace, London W8

PLESTED, Keith Harley; JP (1971); s of Harry Plested (d 1956), of Glos, and Florence Weller (d 1955); *b* 15 Mar 1923; *Educ* Wycliffe Coll, Stonehouse Glos; *m* 18 Sept 1952, Jean, da of C H Turner; 1 s (Julian b 1953), 1 da (Susan b 1958); *Career* chartered surveyor, FRICS, ret; chm South Gloucestershire Petty Sessional Div; memb govrs Wycliffe Coll Cncl; *Style*— Keith H Plested, Esq, JP; Nastend Court, nr Stonehouse, Glos (☎ 045 382 2516)

PLEYDELL-BOUVERIE, Hon Mrs Edward; Alice Pearl; da of Maj Edward Barrington Crake, Rifle Bde, by his 2 w, Clara Alice (da of George William Plunkenett Woodroffe, RHG); *m* 1, 1920 (as his 2 w), 2 Baron Montagu of Beaulieu, KCIE, CSI, JP, DL (d 1929); 1 s (3 Baron *qv*), 3 da (Anne Rachel Pearl, m 1 Howelmore Gwyn (d 1948); m 2, Sir John Chichester, Bt; Caroline Cecily m Grainger Weston; Mary Clare m 1, Viscount Garnock, m 2, Timothy Horn); m 2, 1936, Hon Edward Pleydell-Bouverie, MVO, DL, RN (d 1951), 2 s of 6 Earl of Radnor; 1 s (Robin); *Style*— The Hon Mrs Edward Pleydell-Bouverie; The Lodge, Beaulieu, Hampshire SO42 7YB (☎ 0590 612356)

PLEYDELL-BOUVERIE, Hon Mrs Peter; Audrey; *née* Kidston; yst da of Capt Archibald Glen Kidston, JP, of Breconshire; *b* 11 July 1906; *Educ* private; *m* 1, 1929 (m dis 1946), Anthony Seymour Bellville; m 2, 1947, as his 2 w, Maj Hon Peter Pleydell-Bouverie (d 1981), late KRRC and 5 s of 6 Earl of Radnor; 1 s (James b 1950); *Style*— The Hon Mrs Peter Pleydell-Bouverie; Bodenham House, Bodenham, Salisbury, Wilts (☎ 0722 29735)

PLEYDELL-BOUVERIE, Lady Belinda; da of 8 Earl of Radnor by his 2 w Margaret; *b* 9 Nov 1966; *Style*— Lady Belinda Pleydell-Bouverie; Longford Castle, Salisbury, Wilts SP5 4EF

PLEYDELL-BOUVERIE, Lady Frances; da of 8 Earl of Radnor by his 2 w Margaret; *b* 24 Oct 1973; *Style*— Lady Frances Pleydell-Bouverie; Longford Castle, Salisbury, Wilts SP5 4EF

PLEYDELL-BOUVERIE, Lady Lucy; twin da of 8 Earl of Radnor by his 2 w Margaret; *b* 6 May 1964; *Style*— Lady Lucy Pleydell-Bouverie; Longford Castle, Salisbury, Wilts SP5 4EF

PLEYDELL-BOUVERIE, Lady Martha; twin da of 8 Earl of Radnor by his 2 w Margaret; *b* 6 May 1964; *Style*— Lady Martha Pleydell-Bouverie; Longford Castle, Salisbury, Wilts SP5 4EF

PLEYDELL-BOUVERIE, Hon Peter John; 2 s of 8 Earl of Radnor and his 1 w Anne, *née* Seth-Smith; *b* 14 Jan 1958; *Educ* Harrow, Trinity Coll Cambridge; *m* 14 June 1986, Jane Victoria, da of Rt Hon Sir Ian Hedworth John Little Gilmour, 3 Bt, MP; 1 s (Timothy b 1987); *Career* dir: Fidelity Investment Services Ltd, Fidelity Pension Ltd (Investment Management Co); *Recreations* fishing, skiing, shooting, photography; *Style*— The Hon Peter Pleydell-Bouverie; Longford Castle, Salisbury, Wilts; 38 Queensdale Road, London W11 4SA (☎ 01 602 0394)

PLEYDELL-BOUVERIE, Hon Reuben; 2 s of 7 Earl of Radnor, KG, KCVO, JP, DL (d 1968), and his 1 w Helena Olivia, *née* Adeane; *b* 30 Dec 1930; *Educ* Harrow; *m* 28 Jan 1956, Bridget Jane, da of Maj John Fowell Buxton (ggs of Sir Thomas Buxton, 1 Bt); 2 s, 1 da; *Career* late 2 Lt Royal Scots Greys; prospector; industrial designer; *Recreations* beekeeping, windsurfing, sailing, shooting, fishing; *Style*— The Hon Reuben Pleydell-Bouverie; The Dower House, Slindon, Arundel, Sussex BN18 0RP

PLEYDELL-BOUVERIE, Hon Richard Oakley; s of 7 Earl of Radnor, KG, KCVO, JP, DL (d 1968), by his 2 w Isobel, OBE, da of Lt-Col Richard Oakley, DSO, JP; *b* 25 June 1947; *Educ* Harrow, RAC Cirencester; *m* 1978, Victoria, yr da of late Frank Waldron, of Pond House, Kidmore End, nr Reading; 2 s (David b 1979, Bartholomew b 1981); 1 da (Harriot b 1984); *Style*— The Hon Richard Pleydell-Bouverie; Lawrence End, Peters Green, Luton,

Beds (☎ 0582 21082)

PLIATZKY, Sir Leo; KCB (1977), CB (1972); s of Nathan Pliatzky; *b* 1919; *Educ* Manchester GS, City of London Sch, Corpus Christi Coll Oxford; *m* 1948, Marian Jean (d 1979), da of late Capt James Elias, MN; 1 s, 1 da; *Career* Sgt REME and Capt RAOC in Middle E and Cent Med 1940-45 (despatches); second perm sec Treasy 1976-77, perm sec Dept of Trade 1977-79, ret, retained for special duties 1979-80; non-exec dir: BA 1980-85, Assoc Communications Corpn plc 1980-82, Cent Independent TV 1981-, Ultramar plc 1981-; visiting prof City Univ 1980-84, assoc fell LSE 1982-85; hon fell Corpus Christi Coll Oxford 1980; *Books* Getting and Spending (Whitehall memoirs; revised edn 1984), Paying and Choosing - The Intelligent Person's Guide to the Mixed Economy (1985), The Treasury Under Mrs Thatcher (1989); *Clubs* Reform; *Style*— Sir Leo Pliatzky, KCB; 27 River Ct, Upper Ground, London SE1 9PE (☎ 01 928 3667)

PLIMMER, Sir Clifford Ulric; KBE (1967); s of late Arthur Bloomfield Plimmer; *b* 25 July 1905; *Educ* Scots Coll Wellington, Victoria Univ of Wellington; *m* 1935, Letha May, *née* Port; 3 s (and 1 s decd); *Career* chm: Lion Breweries Ltd, Utd Dominions Corpn Fin Ltd; chm and md Wright, Stephenson & Co Ltd to 1970, dir: Cable Price Downer Ltd, McKechnie Bros (NZ) Ltd, Nat patron Intellectually Handicapped Children's Soc Inc; memb: Dr Barnardos in NZ, Wellington Med Res Fndn; *Style*— Sir Clifford Plimmer, KBE; PO Box 106, Wellington, New Zealand

PLINCKE, John Richard; s of John Frederick Plincke (d 1969), and Norah Mary, *née* Pollard; *b* 29 Oct 1928; *Educ* Stowe, Arch Assoc Sch of Arch; (AA Dip); *m* 5 Dec 1970, Rosemary Drummond, da of Col Peter Halley Ball, of Hants; 2 da (Katherine b 1971, Anna b 1974); *Career* architect; set up practice 1961; ptnr in Plincke, Leaman and Browning Architects and Project Mgmnt Consultants (Wincheser) 1971-87; Civic Tst Awards 1984 and 1986; professional artist, memb Royal Inst of Painters in Water Colours, notable works incl Runic Cross I II III IV, Mexican Memory, Stained Glass Windows, St Marks Church Kempshott (1987); dir: Tropical Plants Display Ltd 1977; Liveryman Worshipful Co of Plasterers1975-; freeman of City of London 1959; RIBA; *Recreations* sailing, skiing; *Style*— John Plincke, Esq; P L and B, The Square, Winchester, Hants SO23 9ES (☎ 0962 67555)

PLINSTON, John Anthony; s of Capt Harold Plinston, RAMC, and Ruth, *née* Mihalop; *b* 9 Jan 1947; *Educ* Battersea GS; *m* 24 May 1969, Jean Barbara, da of Percy Valentine Candy (d 1988), of Wallington, Surrey; 1 s (Adam b 7 Feb 1972), 1 da (Sharon b 20 Oct 1969); *Career* articled clerk: Burgess Hodgson & Co 1964-70, Coopers & Lybrand 1971-73; ptnr: Daeche Dubois & Plinston 1974-, Burgess Hodgson & Co 1981-, Westbury Schotness & Co 1988-; dir Ibex Hldgs Ltd and subsid cos 1988-, Merlin Fin Conslts Ltd 1988-; chm SP Assoc Ltd and subsid 1986-; FCA 1971; *Recreations* sport, music, travel; *Style*— John Plinston, Esq; 94 Aveling Close, Purley, Surrey CR2 4DW (☎ 01 668 8352); 45 Bedford Row, London WC1R 4LR (☎ 01 242 8381, fax 01 405 1904, telex 27460)

PLOUVIEZ, Peter William; s of Charles Plouviez; *b* 30 July 1931; *Educ* Sir George Monoux GS, Hasting GS; *m* 1978, Alison Dorothy Macrae; 2 da (by former m); *Career* gen sec Br Actors' Equity Assoc 1974-; chm: Radio and TV Safeguards ctee 1974-, Festival of Br Theatre 1983-; vice chm Confedn of Entertainment Unions 1974-, vice-pres Int Fedn of Actors, tres Entertainment Charities Fund, memb Theatres Tst; Parly candidate (Lab) St Marylebone by-election 1963, cncllr St Pancras 1962-65; *Style*— Peter Plouviez, Esq; 8 Harley St, London W1 (☎ 01 637 9311)

PLOWDEN, Hon Anna Bridget; da of Baron Plowden (Life Peer); *b* 1938; *Educ* Newhall Chelmsford, Inst of Archeology London Univ; *Career* md Plowden & Smith Ltd 190 St Ann's Hill London SW18 2 RT, dir Recollections Ltd; chm conservation ctee Crafts Cncl 1979-83, memb ctee conservation unit Museums and Galleries Cmmn, assessor of the ceramic restoration course West Dean Coll Sussex; tstee St Andrews Conservation Tst Wells; *Books* Looking after Antiques (co-author, 1987); *Style*— The Hon Anna Plowden; 46 Brixton Water Lane, London SW2

PLOWDEN, Baroness; Bridget Horatia; *née* Richmond; DBE (1972); da of late Adm Sir Herbert Richmond, KCB, and Elsa Florence, 2 da of Sir Hugh Bell, 2 Bt, CB, JP, DL, by his 2 w Florence, DBE, JP, of Sir Joseph Olliffe; *Educ* Downe House; *m* 1933, Baron Plowden, *qv*; 2 s, 2 da; *Career* dir Trust Houses Forte Ltd 1961-72; govr and vice-chm BBC 1970-75, chm IBA 1975-80; vice-chm ILEA Schools Sub-Ctee 1967-70; advsy ctee for the Educn of Romany and Other Travellers: memb 1969- (chm 1969-84, pres 1984); pres: Pre-School Playgroups Assoc 1972-82 (vice-pres 1982-), Nat Assoc of Adult Educn 1980-88, Nat Marriage Guidance Cncl 1983-, Voluntary Orgn Liaison Cncl for Under-Fives 1984 (chm 1974-83); memb Nat Theatre Bd 1976-88; pres Br Accreditation Cncl for Independent Further and Higher Educn 1985-; Liveryman Worshipful Co of Goldsmiths' 1979-, vice-pres Coll of Preceptors 1983 (pres 1987), JP Inner London Area Juvenile Panel 1962-71, fell Royal TV Soc 1980; Hon LLD: Leicester 1968, Reading 1970, London 1976; Hon DLitt Loughborough 1976, DUniv Open 1974; *Style*— The Rt Hon the Lady Plowden, DBE; Martels Manor, Dunmow, Essex (☎ 0371 2141); 11 Abingdon Gdns, Abingdon Villas, London W8 6BY (☎ 01 937 4238)

PLOWDEN, Baron (Life Peer UK 1959), of Plowden, Co Salop; Edwin Noel Plowden; GBE (1987, KBE 1946), KCB (1951); s of late Roger H Plowden; *b* 6 Jan 1907; *Educ* Switzerland, Pembroke Coll Cambridge (hon fell 1958); *m* 1933, Bridget Horatia (*see* Plowden, Baroness); 2 s, 2 da; *Career* sits as Independent in House of Lords; temp civil servant Miny of Econ Warfare 1939-40, Miny Aircraft Prodn 1940-46 (chief exec and memb Aircraft Supply Ctee 1945-46), chief planning offr and chm Econ Planning Bd, HM Treasy 1947-53, vice-chm temp cncl Ctee of NATO 1951-52; chm: UKAEA 1954-59, various Ctees of Inquiry 1959-79, Tube Investmts Ltd 1963-76 (pres 1976-), London Graduate Sch of Business Studies 1964-76 (pres 1976-), Equity Capital for Indust Ltd 1976-83, Police Complaints Bd 1976-81, Top Salaries Review Body 1981- (memb 1977-); independent chm Police Negotiating Bd 1979-83; memb: Ford Euro Advsy Cncl 1976-83, Engrg Industs Cncl 1976, int advsy bd Southeast Bank NA 1982-86; visiting fell Nuffield Coll 1956-64, hon fell Pembroke Coll Cambridge; Hon DSc Pennsylvania State Univ 1958, Aston 1972, Hon DLitt Loughborough 1976; *Style*— The Rt Hon the Lord Plowden, GBE, KCB; Martels Manor, Dunmow, Essex (☎ 0371 2141); 11 Abingdon Gardens, Abingdon Villas, London W8 6BY (☎ 01 937 4238)

PLOWDEN, Hon Francis John; s of Baron Plowden (Life Peer); *b* 1945; *Educ* Eton, Trinity Coll Cambridge; *m* Geraldine *née* Wickman; *Career* CA 1969, dir Coopers Lybrand Associates Ltd 1983-, div dir responsible for policy and mgmnt work for govt 1986-; *Style*— The Hon Francis Plowden; 63 St John's Avenue, London SW15 6AL

PLOWDEN, William Francis Godfrey; JP (1953 Shropshire); o s of Roger Edmund Joseph Plowden, JP (d 1946), and his 1 w, Mary Florence, *née* Cholmondeley (d 1930); the Plowden family has been seated at Plowden since the C12, when Roger de Plowden is believed to have been present at the siege of Acre 1191 (*see* Burke's Landed Gentry, 18 edn, vol III, 1972); *b* 4 Dec 1925; *Educ* Beaumont, RAC Cirencester; *m* 17 July 1951, Valerie Ann, o da of Cdr Athelstan Paul Bush, DSO, RN (d 1970), of Tockington Court, nr Bristol; 3 s (Roger Godfrey Paul b 8 Feb 1953, Francis Richard Piers b 12 Jan 1957, Charles Edward Philip b 31 Dec 1960), 1 da (Jacqueline Mary Prudence b 27 Feb 1954); *Career* serv WWII in Rifle Bde 1943-46; farmer on family estate; High Sheriff of Shropshire 1967; *Recreations* hunting, fishing, shooting; *Style*— William Plowden, Esq, JP; Plowden Hall, Lydbury North, Shropshire (☎ 058 88246)

PLOWDEN, Hon William Julius Lowthian; s of Baron Plowden (Life Peer); *b* 1935; *Educ* Eton, King's Coll Cambridge, California Univ; *m* 1960, Veronica Mary, da of Lt-Col Derek Ernest Frederick Orby Gascoigne; 2 s, 2 da; *Career* under sec Dept of Indust 1977-78, dir-gen Royal Inst of Public Adm 1978-; visiting prof dept of govt LSE 1982-; *Style*— The Hon William Plowden; 49 Stockwell Park Rd, London SW9 (☎ 01 274 4535)

PLOWDEN ROBERTS, (Hugh) Martin; s of Stanley Plowden Roberts, OBE (d 1968), and Joan Aline Mary, *née* Mawdesley; *b* 6 August 1932; *Educ* St Edwards Sch Oxford, St Edmund Hall Oxford (BA, MA); *m* 22 Sept 1956, Susan Jane, da of Andrew Patrick (d 1979), of Melton Grange, Ferriby, Humberside; 2 da (Alexandra b 1961, Caroline b 1964); *Career* dir Payne & Son Meat Gp Ltd 1958-60, asst gen mangr CWS Meat Gp 1960-67; dir: Allied Suppliers Ltd 1967-82, Cavenham Ltd 1979-82 (chm 1981-82); dep chm Argyll Stores Ltd 1983-85, chm Dairy Crest Ltd 1987-88; dir: Lawson Mardon Gp Ltd 1987-, Argyll Gp Plc 1983-, Plowden Roberts Assocs Ltd 1984-; memb Milk Mktg Bd 1983-; Liveryman Worshipful Co of Butchers 1958; fell Inst of Grocery Distribution 1983; *Clubs* Farmers; *Style*— Martin Plowden Roberts, Esq; The Boxes, Ockham Lane, Hatchford, Cobham, Surrey, KT11 1LN (☎ 0932 62669); Argyll Group plc, 6 Millington Rd, Hayes, Middx UB3 4AY (☎ 01 848 8744, fax 01 573 1865, telex 934888)

PLOWMAN, Sir John Robin; CBE (1970, OBE 1949); s of Owen Plowman; *b* 18 Sept 1908, Bermuda; *Educ* Bermuda and England; *m* 1936, Marjorie Hardwick; 2 s; *Career* Miny of Marine and Air Services Bermuda 1977-, MLC (1966), govt ldr on Legislative Cncl 1968-; kt 1979; *Style*— Sir John Plowman, CBE; Chiswick, Paget, Bermuda

PLOWRIGHT, David Ernest; s of William Ernest Plowright; *b* 11 Dec 1930; *Educ* Scunthorpe GS; *m* 1953, Brenda Mary, *née* Key; 1 s, 2 da; *Career* joined Granada TV as news ed 1958 (from Yorkshire Post), programme producer 1960, exec producer of news and current affrs 1966 (in charge World In Action), programmes controller 1969-79, jt md Granada TV Ltd 1976-81 (md 1981-87, chm 1987-), dir Granada Gp 1981- (exec responsibility for drama including Brideshead Revisited and Laurence Olivier's King Lear); dir: Br Satellite Ltd, Br Screen Ltd, Merseyside Tourism Bd; *Recreations* sailing, theatre, television; *Style*— David Plowright, Esq; Westways, Wilmslow Rd, Mottram St Andrew, Prestbury, Cheshire; Granada TV Ltd, Manchester M60 9EA (☎ 061 832 7211); Granada TV, 36 Golden sq, W1 (☎ 01 734 8080)

PLOWRIGHT, Joan Ann; (Lady Olivier), CBE (1970); da of William Ernest Plowright; *b* 28 Oct 1929; *Educ* Scunthorpe GS, Laban Art of Movement Studio, Old Vic Theatre Sch; *m* 1, 1953 (m dis) Roger Gage; m 2, 1961, Sir Laurence Olivier, later Baron Olivier; 1 s, 2 da; *Career* leading actress with the Nat Theatre 1963-74, memb RADA Cncl; *Recreations* reading, music, entertaining; *Style*— Miss Joan Plowright, CBE; c/o LOP Ltd, 33-34 Chancery Lane, WC2A 1EN (☎ 01 836 7932)

PLOWRIGHT, Dr Walter; CMG (1974); s of Jonathan Plowright; *b* 20 July 1923; *Educ* Moulton and Spalding GS, RVC London; *m* 1959, Dorothy Joy, *née* Bell; *Career* with Colonial Vet and Res Servs (Kenya and Nigeria) 1950-63, Animal Virus Res Inst Pirbright 1963-71; prof of vet microbiology RVC 1971-78, head of dept of microbiology Inst for Res on Animal Diseases 1978-83; King Baudouin Inter Dev Prize 1984, Hon DSc: Univ of Nairobi 1984, Univ of Reading 1986; Gold Award Off Int de Epizooties 1988; FRCVS, FRS; *Style*— Dr Walter Plowright, CMG; Whitehill Lodge, Reading Rd, Goring, Reading RG8 OLL ☎(0491 872891)

PLOWS, Fiona Kay; da of Harold William Plows (d 1984), of Bournemouth, and Sarah, *née* Burgess; *b* 3 May 1938; *Educ* Bromley HS, UCL (LLB); *m* 1, 4 Sept 1965 (m dis 1972), (Michael) Jeremy Brown, s of Norman Marcus Brown (d 1969), of Chislehurst, Kent; m 2, 14 July 1977, David Michael Huntington Alderson, s of Nathan Alderson (d 1984), of Burnley, Lancs; *Career* admitted slr 1963, currently sr ptnr Godfrey Davis & Baldwin (Mitcham); memb Law Soc; *Recreations* travel, theatre, wining, dining, opera, history, archaeology; *Style*— Miss Fiona Plows; 19a Upper Green East, Mitcham, Surrey (☎ 01 648 5221)

PLUMB, Baron (Life Peer UK 1987), of Coleshill, Co Warwicks; (Charles) Henry Plumb; DL (Warwicks 1977), MEP (EDG) The Cotswolds 1979-; s of Charles Plumb, of Ansley, Warwicks, and Louise, *née* Fisher; *b* 27 Mar 1925; *Educ* King Edward VI Sch Nuneaton; *m* 1947, Marjorie Dorothy, da of Thomas Victor Dunn, of Bentley, Warwicks; 1 s (Hon John Henry b 1951), 2 da (Hon Mrs Holman, Hon Mrs Mayo, *qqv*); *Career* ldr (Cons) EDG Euro Parl 1982-87, pres Euro Parl 1987-; pres Nat Farmers Union 1970-79 (dep pres 1966-69, vice-pres 1964-66, memb cncl 1959-), chm Br Agric Cncl 1975-79; pres Warwicks County Fedn of Young Farmers' Clubs 1974- (pres Nat Fedn 1976-86); memb cncl: CBI, Animal Health Tst; COPA 1975-77; Royal Agric Soc England 1977 (dep pres 1978); pres: Int Fedn of Agric Prodrs 1979-; chm Agric Ctee Euro Parl 1979-82, hon pres Ayrshire Cattle Soc; dir: Utd Biscuits, Lloyds Bank, Fisons; Liveryman Worshipful Co of Farmers; Hon DSc Cranfield 1983; FRSA 1970, FRAgS 1974; Order of Merit of German Fed Republic; kt 1973; *Clubs* Farmers', Coleshill Rotary (hon memb); *Style*— The Rt Hon Lord Plumb, DL; The Dairy Farm, Maxstone, Coleshill, Warwickshire B46 2QJ (0675) 63133); 2 Queen Anne's Gate, London SW1 (☎ 01 222 0411)

PLUMB, Prof Sir John Harold; s of late James Plumb, of Leicester; *b* 20 August 1911; *Educ* Alderman Newton's Sch Leicester, Univ Coll Leicester, Christ's Coll Cambridge (PhD, LittD); *Career* historian; prof of modern english history Cambridge Univ 1966-74, master Christ's Coll Cambridge 1978-82, chm Centre of E Anglian Studies 1979-82; tstee Nat Portrait Gallery 1961-82; Hon DLitt Leicester Univ 1968, E Anglia 1973, Bowdoin Coll 1974, Univ of S Calif 1978, Westminster Coll 1983, Washington Univ 1983, St Louis 1983; FRHistS, FSA, FRSL; kt 1982; *Clubs* Brooks's, Beefsteak; *Style*— Prof Sir John Plumb; Christ's College, Cambridge (☎ 0223 334900); The Old Rectory, Westhorpe, Stowmarket, Suffolk (☎ 0449 781235)

PLUMBE, (Edwin) John Astley; s of Edwin Raymond Plumbe (d 1963), and Jessie Louisa, *née* Avis (d 1964); *b* 24 Dec 1914; *Educ* Weymouth Coll; *m* 1, 29 Dec 1948, Eleanor Burleigh (d 1956), da of Harry L Pope (d 1956), of Fairhaven, USA; 1 s (John Lawrence b 26 Oct 1952), 1 da (Robin Cornelia (Mrs Wood) b 25 Nov 1949); m 2, 2 Dec 1960, Katherine Bethune, *née* Macdonald; 2 da decd; *Career* Lt-Col 4/10 Baluch 1A, AA and QMG 10 Indian Div; former: exec insur co, conslt Antigua Singapore Jamaica and Kenya, dir Onello Apuzza SPA Milan; dir Norfolk Boat (Sail Trg) Ltd, sec Wells Art Centre, pres Wells branch Cons

Assoc; *Recreations* enjoying old age; *Clubs* HAC, Oriental, Norfolk; *Style*— John Plumbe, Esq; Yew Tree House, Wells-next-the-Sea, Norfolk NR23 1EZ (☎ 0328 710357)

PLUMBLEY, Philip Rodney; s of Alfred Daniel Plumbley (d 1970), of Freshwater, and Emily Amelia, *née* Jackson (d 1962); *b* 29 August 1931; *Educ* Co GS Newport IOW, Univ of Bristol (BA); *m* 13 April 1957, Shelagh Morell, da of Capt Howard Morell Holmes (d 1963); 1 s (Peter b 1964), 1 da (Rachel b 1962); *Career* Sgt Air Signaller 220 Sqn RAF Coastal Cmd 1951-53; NIIP 1964-65, MSL/ASL 1965-70, md Compton Ptnrs Recruitment and Fin Advertising and Consultancy Div 1970-72, co founder and dir Plumbley Endicotte Assoc Ltd (1973) Executive Search Consultancy; chm high Wycombe Operatic Soc 1985-; *Recreations* music, sailing; *Clubs* IOD; *Style*— Philip R Plumbley, Esq; Easterton, Ellesborough Rd, Wendover, Bucks (☎ 0296 622116); Premier House, 150 Southampton Row, London WC1B 5AL (☎ 01 278 3117)

PLUME, John Trevor; s of William Thomas Plume, and Alice Gertrude, *née* Edwards; *b* 5 Oct 1914; *Educ* City of London Sch; *m* 5 April 1947, Christine Mary, da of Samuel Albert Wells; 1 da (Katherine Mary); *Career* Enlisted Army 1940, demob Capt RA 1946; called to the Bar Grays' Inn 1936, bencher Grays' Inn 1969; regnl chm Indust Tbnls 1984-87 (chm from 1966), Liveryman Worshipful Co of Clockmakers 1977; Legal Assoc Memb Royal Town Planning Inst 1939; *Recreations* bee keeping, gardening, fishing, carpentry; *Style*— John Plume, Esq; Mulberry Cottage, Forest Side, Epping, Essex CM16 4ED (☎ 0378 72389)

PLUMMER, Maj-Gen Leo Heathcote; CBE (1974); s of Lt-Col Edmund Waller Plummer, DSO (d 1958), of Farnham, Surrey, and Mary Dorothy, *née* Brookesmith (d 1984); *b* 11 June 1923; *Educ* Canford Sch, Queen's Coll Cambridge; *m* 13 April 1955, Judyth Ann, da of Edward Victor Dolby, OBE (d 1973), of Eardisley, Hereford & Worcester; 3 da (Virginia, Sara, Nicola); *Career* cmmnd RA 1943, 17 Field Regt served N Africa, Sicily, Italy, Austria 1943-47, Adj LAA Regt RA TA 1947-49, 66 Airborne Light Regt 1949-50, 4 RHA 1950-51, Staff Coll Camberley 1952, GSO 2 HQ Anti-Aircraft Cmd 1953-54, BMRA 7 Armd Div 1957-59, Jt Servs Staff Coll 1959, battery cdr 39 Missile Regt 1960-61, brevet Lt-Col 1961, directing staff Staff Coll Camberley 1961-63, Cmdt Sudan Armed Forces Staff Sch 1963-65, CO 20 Heavy Regt 1965-67, Col Gen Staff MOD 1967, Brig Cdr 1 Artillery Bde 1967-70, dep dir Manning Army MOD 1971-74, asst chief staff ops HQ Northern Army Gp 1974-76, ADC to HM the Queen 1974-76, Maj-Gen chief Jt Servs Liaison Orgn Bonn 1976-78, ret 1979; chm Civil Serv Cmmn Panel 1983-; churchwarden: All Saints' Cologne 1976-78, All Saints' Icklesham E Sussex 1981-85; memb SSAFA Canterbury 1987-; *Recreations* gardening; *Clubs* Army and Navy; *Style*— Maj-Gen Leo Plummer, CBE; 1 High St, Wingham, Canterbury, Kent CT3 1AY (☎ 0227 720 538)

PLUMMER, Hon Sally Jane; da of Baron Plummer of St Marylebone (Life Peer); *Educ* Francis Holland Sch for Girls, Roedean, London Univ; *Career* human resources mgmnt conslt; *Recreations* animal welfare; *Style*— The Hon Sally Plummer; 33 Huntsworth Mews, Regent's Park, London NW1 6DD

PLUMMER OF ST MARYLEBONE, Baron (Life Peer UK 1981); Sir (Arthur) Desmond (Herne) Plummer; TD (1950), JP (London 1958), DL (Greater London 1970); s of late Arthur Herne Plummer, and late Janet McCormick; *b* 25 May 1914; *Educ* Hurstpierpoint Coll, Coll of Estate Mgmnt; *m* 1941, Pat, da of Albert Holloway, of Epping; 1 da; *Career* sits as Cons peer in House of Lords; Mayor St Marylebone Borough Cncl 1958-59 (memb 1952-65), LCC St Marylebone 1960-65, ILEA 1964-76, GLC (memb for Cities of London and Westminster 1964-73, for St Marylebone 1973-76), ldr of Oppn 1966-67, ldr of cncl GLC 1967-73, chm Portman Bldg Soc 1983- (vice-chm 1979-83), Nat Employers' Life Assur Co 1983-88; chm: Horserace Betting Levy Bd 1974-82, Epsom and Walton Downs Trg Grounds Man Bd 1974-82, Nat Stud 1975-82, pres: Met Assoc of Bldg Socs 1983-, London Anglers' Assoc 1976-; FAI 1948, FRICS 1970, FRSA 1974, Hon FFAS 1966, KStJ 1986; kt 1971; *Clubs* Carlton, RAC; *Style*— The Rt Hon the Lord Plummer of St Marylebone, TD, DL; 4 The Lane, Marlborough Place, St Johns Wood, London NW8 0PN

PLUMPTON, Alan; CBE (1980), JP (Monmouthshire 1971); s of John Plumpton (d 1978), of Sunderland, Northumberland, and Doris, *née* Barrett; *b* 24 Nov 1926; *Educ* Sunderland Tech Sch, Durham Univ (BSc), Henley Admin Staff Coll; *m* 8 Dec 1950, Audrey; 1 s (Nigel b 5 July 1953), 1 da (Jill (Mrs Stiel) b 3 Oct 1956); *Career* N Eastern Electricity Bd: grad engr 1948-49, asst distribution engr 1949-57, dist commercial engr Stockton 1957-60; S Wales Electricity Bd: dist mangr E Monmouthshire Dist 1961-64, dep chief commercial engr 1964-67, chief commercial engr 1967-72; London Electricity Bd: dep chm 1972-76, chm 1976-80; dep chm Electricity Cncl 1981-86, dir Schlumberger Measurement and Control (UK) Ltd 1985-87; chm: Manx Electricity Cncl 1985-, Ewbank Preece Gp Ltd 1986-, Schlumberger Measurement and Control (UK) Ltd 1988-; memb: cncl Inst of Electrical Engrs UK 1983-87, jt ctee of princs Electricity Bd/Br Electrical & Allied Mfrs Assoc UK 1981-86, Br Nat Ctee of CIGRE 1981-85, directing ctee of UNIPEDE 1975-81, br nat ctee and exec ctee World Energy Conf 1981-, industl policy ctee Confedn of Br Industs 1981-85; chm Euro Panel of Nationalised Industs 1983-85; past chm Pontypool Rural DC, former memb Gwent Water Authy; Freeman and Liveryman Worshipful Co of Gardeners 1978; FIEE, FCIBSE, CBIM, FRSA; *Recreations* golf, gardening; *Clubs* City Livery, IOD, Harewood Downs GC; *Style*— Alan Plumpton, Esq, CBE, JP; Lockhill, Stubbs Wood, Amersham, Bucks HP6 6EX (☎ 024 03 3791); Ewbank Preece, North Street, Brighton BN1 1RW (☎ 0273 724533, 0273 205635, telex 878102 EPLBTN G)

PLUMPTRE, Hon Francis Charles; yst s of 21 Baron FitzWalter, and Margaret Melisina, *née* Deedes; *b* 30 May 1963; *Educ* St Edmund's Sch Canterbury Kent; *Style*— The Hon Francis Plumptre; Goodnestone Park, Canterbury, Kent

PLUMPTRE, Hon (Wyndham) George; s of FitzWalter Brook Plumptre, 21 Baron FitzWalter, of Goodnestone Park, Canterbury, Kent and Margaret Melesina FitzWalter *née* Deedes; *b* 24 April 1956; *Educ* Radley, Jesus Coll Cambridge; *m* 1984, Alexandra Elizabeth, da of Prince Michael Cantacuzene, Count Speransky and Mrs James Edwards; 2 s (Wyndham James Alexander b 1986, Piers Harry Constantine b 1987); *Career* author; Royal Gardens (1981), Collins Book of British Gardens (1985), The Fast Set (1985), Homes of Cricket (1988), The Latest Country Gardens (1988), Cricket Caricatures and Cartoons (1989), Garden Ornament (1989), ed: Barclays World of Cricket (1986), Back Page Cricket (1987), Back Page Racing (1989); *Clubs* Beefsteak; *Style*— The Hon George Plumptre; Rowling House, Canterbury, Kent CT3 1QB (☎ 0304 813287)

PLUMPTRE, Hon Henry Bridges; 2 s of 21 Baron FitzWalter; *b* 18 Feb 1954; *m* 1981, Susie, only da of F T Payne, of Waverley Station, Scone, NSW; 1 s (Sam b 1982), 1 da (Camilla b 1984); *Style*— The Hon Henry Plumptre; Lordship Stud, Newmarket, Suffolk

PLUMPTRE, Hon Julian Brook; s and h of 21 Baron FitzWalter, and Margaret Melesina, *née* Deedes; *b* 18 Oct 1952; *Educ* Radley, Wye Coll London (BSc); *m* March 1988, Sally, *née* Quiney; *Career* estate agency; *Style*— The Hon Julian Plumptre; Goodnestone Park, Canterbury, Kent

PLUMPTRE, Hon William Edward; s of 21 Baron FitzWalter, and Margaret Melesina, *née* Deedes; *b* 23 July 1959; *Educ* Milton Abbey Sch Dorset; *Style*— The Hon William Plumptre; Fell Yeat, Martsop, Patterdale, Penrith, Cumbria

PLUMTREE, Air Vice-Marshal Eric; CB (1974), OBE (1946, DFC 1940); s of William Plumtree; *b* 9 Mar 1919; *Educ* Eckington GS; *m* 1942, Dorothy Patricia, *née* Lyall; 2 s (and 1 s decd); *Career* RAF, served WW II, Air Cdre 1966, dir Air Plans MOD (Air) 1968-69, AOC 22 Gp RAF 1970-71, Air Vice-Marshal 1971, Cdr Southern Maritime Air Region 1971-73, economy project offr (RAF) MOD 1973-74, co-ordinator of Anglo-American Relations MOD (Air) 1977-84; *Style*— Air Vice-Marshal Eric Plumtree CB, OBE, DFC; Wings Cottage, Ditchling, Sussex (☎ Hassocks 07918 5539)

PLUNKET, Aileen Sibell Mary; resumed use of first husband's surname; da of Arthur Ernest Guinness, JP, DL (d 1949, 2 s of 1 Earl of Iveagh, KP, GCVO), and Marie Clotilde (d 1953), da of Sir George Russell, 4 Bt; Mrs Aileen Plunket's wedding present from her f was Lutrellstown Castle and estate, in Co Dublin, Ireland, which she sold at auction in Oct 1983; *b* 16 May 1904; *m* m 1, 16 Nov 1927 (m dis 1940), Fl Lt Hon Brinsley Sheridan Bushe Plunket, RAFVR (ka 1941), 2 s of 5 Baron Plunket, GCMG, KCVO, KBE; 3 da (1 decd); m 2, 1956 (m dis 1965), Valerian Stux-Rybar, s of Geza Stux-Rybar; *Style*— Mrs Aileen Plunket

PLUNKET, Hon Mrs (Denis) Kiwa; Pamela Mary; da of late James Watherston, of Christchurch, NZ; *m* 1962, the Hon (Denis) Kiwa Plunket (d 1970), s of 5 Baron Plunket, GCMG, KCVO, KBE (d 1920); *Style*— The Hon Mrs Kiwa Plunket; 16 Town Hill, W Malling, Kent ME19 6QN (☎ (0732) 1197)

PLUNKET, 8 Baron (UK 1827); Robin Rathmore Plunket; s of 6 Baron Plunket (d 1938), and bro of 7 Baron (d 1975); *b* 3 Dec 1925; *Educ* Eton; *m* 1951, Jennifer, da of late Bailey Southwell, of S Africa; *Heir* bro, Hon Shaun Albert Frederick Sheridan Plunket; *Career* formerly Capt Rifle Bde; *Style*— The Rt Hon the Lord Plunket; Rathmore, Chimanimani, Zimbabwe; 39 Lansdowne Gdns, London SW8 (☎ 01 622 6049)

PLUNKET, Hon Shaun Albert Frederick Sheridan; s of 6 Baron Plunket, and Dorothé, *née* Lewis (both died in aircrash in USA 1938); hp of bro, 8 Baron Plunket; *b* 5 April 1931; *Educ* Eton, L'Institut de Touraine; *m* 1, 1961, Judith Ann, er da of late Gerard Patrick Power, of Lapworth, Warwickshire; 1 s (Tyrone Shaun Terence b 1966), 1 da (Loelia Dorothé Alexandra b 1963); m 2, 1980, Mrs Elisabeth de Sancha, da of late Helge Drangel, of Stockholm, formerly w of T de Sancha (d 1986); *Career* formerly Lt Irish Gds, ADC to GOC Rhine Army 1951-52, dist cmdt Kenya Police Res (Mau Mau) 1953; Hambros Bank, dir Garrod & Lofthouse Ltd 1956-66, chm and md Wilmington Overseas Security Ltd 1978, memb Lloyds, vice-chm Arthritis Care; chm Lady Hoare Tst; fell IOD; *Clubs* White's, Vanderbilt, Racquet; *Style*— The Hon Shaun Plunket; 11 Ennismore Gardens, London SW7 5AA (☎ 01 584 1099)

PLUNKETT, Hon Beatrice Mary; da (by 2 m) of 19 Baron Dunsany; *b* 1948; *Style*— The Hon Beatrice Plunkett

PLUNKETT, Hon Edward Carlos; s (by 1 m) and h of Randal Arthur Plunkett, 19 Baron Dunsany, and Vera de Sa Soutto Maj; *b* 10 Sept 1939; *Educ* Eton, Slade Sch, Ecole des Beaux Arts Paris; *m* 1982, Maria Alice Villela de Carvalho; 2 s (Randal b 1983, Oliver b 1985); *Career* artist and architectural designer, princ de Marsillac Plunkett Architecture PC (architects); *Recreations* chess; *Style*— The Hon Edward Plunkett; 45 East 89th St, New York, NY 10028 (☎ 212 410 0795); office: 38 East 57th St, New York, NY 10022 (☎ 212 750 6145, fax 212 980 1025)

PLUNKETT, Hon Jonathan Oliver; s and h of 16 Baron Louth; *b* 4 Nov 1952; *Educ* De La Salle Coll Jersey, Hautlieu Sch Jersey, Hull Univ (BSc); *m* 1981, Jennifer, da of Norman Oliver Hodgetts, of Coventry; 1 s (Matthew Oliver b 22 Dec 1982), 1 da (Agatha Elizabeth b 14 Aug 1985); *Career* electronics engr; AMIEE; *Style*— The Hon Jonathan Plunkett; Les Sercles, La Grande Pièce, St Peter, Jersey, CI

PLUNKETT, Hon Olivia Jane; da of 16 Baron Louth; *b* 1953; *Style*— The Hon Olivia Plunkett; The Lodge, Blanc Pignon, Beaumont, St Breiade, Jersey

PLUNKETT, Hon Otway Jeremy Oliver; s of 16 Baron Louth; *b* 1954; *Style*— The Hon Otway Plunkett

PLUNKETT, Patrick Trevor; s of Oliver Plunkett (d 1971), and Cordelia Edme, *née* Wheler (d 1988); *b* 13 June 1908; *Educ* St Gerards Bray Co Wicklow Ireland, Douai Sch Woolhampton Berks; *m* 18 May 1939, Penelope Mary, da of Raymond Dumas, of Hill Deverill Manor, Hill Deverill, Wilts; 2 s ((Oliver) David b 1939, Peter b 1948), 3 da (Davinia b 1945, Rosalyn b 1947, Georgina b 1949); *Career* IA 1940-45, Scinde Horse, ADC to GOC Waziristan Dist NW Frontier, Staff Capt Br Tank Bde, staff mountain warfare trg centre, Major DAA GHQ; farmer, memb Cornwall Milk Mktg Bd 1958, mangr Bachelor Robinson & Co Ltd Birmingham 1965-73, dir 1973 hldg co, ret 1973; hon vice pres Somerset Co BRCS; *Recreations* reading, contemplation of pretty girls!; *Clubs* Army and Navy; *Style*— Patrick Plunkett, Esq; Wyatts Leaze, Seend, Melksham, Wiltshire SN12 6PN (☎ 0380 828330)

PLUNKETT, Hon Stephanie Patricia; da of 16 Baron Louth; *b* 1963; *Style*— The Hon Stephanie Plunkett; Les Sercles, La Grande Piece, St Peter, Jersey CI

PLUNKETT, Hon Timothy James Oliver; s of 16 Baron Louth; *b* 1956; *Educ* de la Salle Coll Jersey; *m* 20 Oct 1984, Julie Anne Cook; 1 da (Sophie Louise b 7 Sep 1987); *Recreations* Sailing, Diving (Sub Aqua); *Style*— The Hon Timothy Plunkett

PLUNKETT-ERNLE-ERLE-DRAX, Henry Walter; JP (1971), DL (1979); s of Adm the Hon Sir Reginald Aylmer Ranfurly Plunkett-Ernle-Erle-Drax (2 s of 17 Baron Dunsany); *b* 18 Mar 1928; *Educ* RNC Dartmouth; *m* 1957, Hon Pamela Rose, *qv*; 5 s; *Career* served RN 1945-68; landowner, farmer, forester; co dir; govr: Milton Abbey Sch, Canford Sch; *Recreations* skiing, shooting, fishing, tennis, golf; *Style*— Henry Walter Drax, Esq JP, DL; Charborough Park, Wareham, Dorset BH20 7EW (☎ 0258 857368, office: 0258 857484)

PLUNKETT-ERNLE-ERLE-DRAX, Hon Mrs (Pamela Rose); *née* Weeks; da of Lt-Gen 1 and last Baron Weeks, KCB, CBE, DSO, MC, TD (d 1960), and his 2 w, Cynthia Mary, *née* Irvine (d 1985); *b* 9 Nov 1931; *m* 6 April 1957, Lt-Cdr Henry Plunkett-Ernle-Erle-Drax, RN, *qv*; 5 s; *Style*— The Hon Mrs Plunkett-Ernle-Erle-Drax; Charborough Park, Wareham, Dorset BH20 7EW (☎ 0258 857368)

PLURENDEN, Baroness; Dorothee Monica; da of Maj Robert Bateman Prust, OBE, of Vancouver, BC, Canada; *m* 1951, 1 and last Baron Plurenden (d 1978); 2 da (Rosanne, Francesca); *Style*— The Rt Hon the Lady Plurenden; Plurenden Manor, High Halden, Ashford, Kent; Lidostrasse 63, 6314 Unterägeri, Switzerland

PLYMOUTH, Archdeacon of; see: Ellis, The Ven Robin Gareth Archdeacon of; *see*: Ellis, Ven Robin Gareth

PLYMOUTH, 3 Earl of (UK 1905); Other Robert Ivor Windsor-Clive; DL (Salop

1961); Viscount Windsor (UK 1905), Baron Windsor (E 1529); s of 2 Earl of Plymouth, DL, PC (d 1943, ggs of Hon Robert Clive, gs of 1 Earl of Powis and gs of Clive of India), and Lady Irene Corona, *née* Charteris (d 1989), da of 11 Earl of Wemyss; *b* 9 Oct 1923; *Educ* Eton; *m* 1950, Caroline Helen, da of Edward Rice, of Dane Court, Eastry, Kent; 3 s, 1 da; *Heir* s, Viscount Windsor; *Career* late Coldstream Gds; memb Standing Cmmn on Museums and Galleries 1972-82, chm Reviewing Ctee on Export of Works of Art 1982-85; FRSA; KStJ; *Style*— The Rt Hon the Earl of Plymouth, DL; Oakly Park, Ludlow, Shropshire (☎ 0584 77243)

PLYMOUTH, Bishop of 1988-; Rt Rev Richard Stephen Hawkins; s of John Stanley Hawkins (d 1965), and Elsie, *née* Briggs; *b* 2 April 1939; *Educ* Exeter Sch, Exeter Coll Oxford (MA), St Stephen's House Oxford, Exeter Univ (BPhil); *m* 1966, Valerie Ann, da of Leonard William Herneman; 2 s (Simon b 1967 decd, Daniel b 1973), 2 da (Rebecca b 1968, Caroline b 1972 decd); *Career* team vicar Clyst Valley Team Ministry 1966-78, jt dir Exeter-Truro Min Training Sch and Bishop of Exeters Offr for Ministry 1978-81, Diocesan dir of Ordinands 1979-81, archdeacon of Totnes 1981-88; *Style*— The Rt Rev the Bishop of Plymouth; 15 Stoneleigh Close, Highweek, Newton Abbot, Devon TQ12 1PX (☎ 0626 63860)

POANANGA, Maj-Gen Brian Matauru; CB (1980), CBE (1977, OBE 1967, MBE 1962); s of Henare Poananga; *b* 2 Dec 1924; *Educ* RMC Duntroon Aust; *m* 1948, Doreen Mary Porter; 2 s, 1 da; *Career* Chief of Gen Staff New Zealand Army 1978-81; (despatches twice); deer farmer; *Style*— Major-General Brian Poananga, CB, CBE; PO Box 397, Taupo, New Zealand

POCHIN, Sir Edward Eric; CBE (1959), MD (1945); Charles Davenport Pochin (d 1910), of Sale, Cheshire, and Agnes, *née* Collier (d 1953); descends from Richard Pochin, of Barkby (1447; previously of Wissendine, Rutland); *b* 22 Sept 1909; *Educ* Repton, St John's Coll Cambridge (MA, MD, MB, BChir); *m* 1940, Constance Margaret Julia (d 1971), da of Tobias Harry Tilly (d 1930); 1 s, 1 da; *Career* memb Scientific Staff of MRC 1941, dir MRC Dept of Clinical Res UCH Med Sch 1946-74, Horton Smith Prize 1945, Antoine Béclère Lectr 1979; memb Int Cmmn on Radiological Protection 1959-77, vice-chm 1959-62, chm 1962-69, emeritus memb 1977-; rep UN scientific ctee on Effects of Atomic Radiation 1958-82, conslt to the dir Nat Radiological Protection Bd (memb 1970-82;) Coronation Medal 1952; FRCP; kt 1975; *Books* Nuclear Radiation: risks and benefits (Clavendon Press, Oxford 1983); *Recreations* fellwalking, travel; *Clubs* Athenaeum, Oriental; *Style*— Sir Edward Pochin, CBE, MD; c/o National Radiological Protection Board, Chilton, Didcot, Oxon (☎ 0235 831600, telex 837124 RADPRO)

POCKNEY, Penrhyn Charles Benjamin; s of Maj Ronald Penrhyn Pockney (d 1969), of Bishopthorpe, York, and Catherine Helen Margaret, *née* Dodsworth; *b* 22 May 1940; *Educ* Winchester; *m* 15 May 1965, (Patricia) Jane, da of Sir Richard William de Bacquencourt des Voeux, Bt (d 1944), of Burghclere, Newbury, Berks; 2 s (Richard b 1968, James b 1969); *Career* dir J & A Scrimgeour Ltd 1972- (ptnr 1968-72), ptnr Mullens & Co 1980-86, dir S G Warburg Akroyd Rowe & Pitman Mullens Securities Ltd 1986-; Liveryman Worshipful Co Skinners 1977 (Freeman 1963); FCA; *Recreations* gardening, fishing, golf; *Clubs* Boodles, Lansdowne, MCC; *Style*— Penrhyn Pockney, Esq; 1 Finsbury Ave, London EC2M 2PA (☎ 01 606 1066)

POCOCK, Air Vice-Marshal Donald Arthur; CBE (1975, OBE 1957); s of Arthur Pocock (d 1970), of Hampstead, and E Pocock, *née* Broad; *b* 5 July 1920; *Educ* Crouch End; *m* 1947, Dorothy Monica, da of D Griffiths; 2 s, 3 da; *Career* cmmnd RAF 1941; cmd RAF Regt Wing 1957-58, MOD 1958-59, HQ Allied Air Forces Central Europe 1959-62, sr ground defence SO NEAF 1962-63, MOD 1963-66, sr ground def SO FEAF 1966-68, ADC to HM The Queen 1967, Cmdt-Gen RAF Regt 1973-75; gen mangr (Iran) Br Aerospace Dynamics Gp 1976-79; dir Br Metallurgical Plant Constructors' Assoc 1980-85; *Style*— Air Vice-Marshal Donald Pocock, CBE; Brincliffe, Dence Park, Herne Bay, Kent (☎ 0227 374773)

POCOCK, Gordon James; s of Leslie Pocock; *b* 27 Mar 1933; *Educ* Royal Liberty Sch Romford, Keble Coll Oxford; *m* 1959, Audrey Singleton; *Career* sr dir mktg Br Telecom 1979-; *Style*— Gordon Pocock, Esq; 2 Queensberry Place, Friars Lane, Richmond, Surrey TW9 1NW (☎ 01 940 7118)

PODMORE, William; OBE (1985), JP (1965); s of William Podmore, JP, (d 1958), of Consall Hall, Wetley Rocks, Stoke-on-Trent, and Alberta, *née* Grainger (d 1958); *b* 12 Nov 1918; *Educ* Leek HS, Loughborough Univ DLC (Hons, CEng, MIMechE); *m* 30 Aug 1947, Edna May, da of Benjamin Atkinson (d 1966); 1 s (William b 1948), 1 da (Helen b 1952); *Career* mechanical engrg dir, test engr Power Jets Ltd 1941-46; chm: Podmores (Engrs) Ltd 1946, Consall (Hldgs) Ltd 1965; memb: Institution of Quarry Engrs 1948-65, Stoke-on-Trent Assoc of Engrs 1947-, exec ctee N Staffs C of C 1965, (pres 1973-74); chm: Cheadle RDC 1966-67, Staffs Moorlands (Cons) Assoc 1965-; tax cmmr 1967; pres Cheadle Rotary Club 1958-59; memb exec ctee CPRE Staffs Branch 1970-; memb Nat Tst Ctee for Mercia 1982-; MInst MechE 1941; *Recreations* landscape gardening, photography; *Style*— William Podmore, Esq, OBE, JP; Consall Hall, Weyley Rocks, Stoke-on-Trent (☎ (0782) 550203); Winton House, Stoke Rd, Stoke-on-Trent (☎ (0782) 45361)

POETT, Gen Sir (Joseph Howard) Nigel; KCB (1959, CB 1952), DSO (1944) and bar (1945); s of Maj-Gen Joseph Howard Poett, CB, CMG, CBE (d 1929), and Julia Caswell (d 1937), of Providence, Rhode Island, USA; *b* 20 August 1907; *Educ* Downside, RMC Sandhurst; *m* 1937, Ethne Julia, da of late Edward Jasper Herrick, of Hawkes Bay, NZ; 2 s, 1 da; *Career* cmmnd Durham LI 1927, Cdr 11 Bn Durham LI 1942, Cdr 5 Para Bde 1943-46; ops: Normandy to the Baltic 1944-45, Far East 1945-46, dir of Plans WO 1946-48, COS Far East LF 1950-52, Maj-Gen 1951, GOC 3 Inf Div 1952-54, dir Military Ops War Office 1954-56, Cmdt Staff Coll Camberley 1957-58, Lt-Gen 1958, GOC-in-C Southern Cmd 1958-61, Gen 1962, C-in-C Far East Land Forces 1961-63; Col Durham LI 1956-65; dir Br Productivity Cncl 1966-72; Silver Star (USA) 1944; *Clubs* Army and Navy; *Style*— Gen Sir Nigel Poett, KCB, DSO; Swaynes Mead, Great Durnford, Salisbury, Wilts

POHL, Erich Harald; s of Erich Franz Adolf Pohl, of Wiesbaden, Germany, and Kreszeuz, *née* Dolp; *b* 7 Nov 1956; *Educ* Werner-von-Siemens-Schule Wiesbaden Germany, Bankakademie Mainz-Frankfurt Germany; *Career* Deustsche: private accts and cashier Wiesbaden 1975-76 (bank trg 1973-75), investmt advsr and security salesman Russelsheim 1976-81, bond trader and salesman DM Bonds Frankfurt 1981-84; Morgan Stanley London: DM bond trader 1984-85, vice pres 1985-, sr trader in non US dollar currencies, exec dir 1986-; *Style*— Erich Pohl, Esq; Morgan Stanley Int, Kingsley Hse, 1a Wimpole St, London, W1M 7AA (☎ 01 493 1617, telex 01 881 2564)

POINTER, Simon Nicholas Peter; s of Peter Albert Pointer, of Shillingford Court, Shillingford, Oxon, and Mary Rosamund, *née* Slay; *b* 15 July 1950; *Educ* St Paul's, Exeter Coll Oxford (BA); *Career* dir The Map House 1978-; *Books* author of numerous articles in arts jls on the subject of antique maps and engravings; *Style*— Simon Pointer, Esq; 35 Cornwall Gdns, Kensington, London SW7 4AP (☎ 01 937 1382); The Map House, 54 Beauchamp Place, Knightsbridge, London SW3 1NY (☎ 01 589 4325/9821)

POIRIER, Lady Anne Thérèse; *née* Bennet; da of 9 Earl of Tankerville (d 1980); *b* 18 Oct 1956, (twin sis of 10 Earl); *m* 1981, Timothy, s of Joseph Poirier, of Comox, BC, Canada; *Style*— Lady Anne Poirier

POLAND, Rear Adm (Edmund) Nicholas; CB (1967), CBE (1962); s of Maj Raymond Alfred Poland, RMLI (ka 1918), and Frances Olive Bayly Jones, *née* Weston (d 1976); *b* 19 Feb 1917; *Educ* RNC Dartmouth; *m* 1 Sept 1941, Pauline Ruth Margaret, da of Maj Hugh Charles Pechell (d 1955), of Manor Close, Felpham, Bognor Regis, Sussex; 3 s (Raymond Anthony b 1942, Roger b 1949, Andrew b 1960), 2 da (Elizabeth b 1944, d 1948, Celia b 1947); *Career* Midshipman HMS Hood and Shropshire 1935-37, Sub Lt HMS Beagle and Hermes 1938-40, Lt HMS Eclipse Norwegian Campaign 1940, MTB serv in Channel and Med 1940-43, qualified torpedo offr HMS Vernon 1943, HMS Furious 1943-44, staff offr ops to Naval Force Cdr Burma HMS Nith 1944, HMS Royalist 1945, MTB's HMS Hornet 1945-46, Lt-Cdr HMS Osprey 1946, Flotilla Torpedo Anti-Submarine Offr 3 Submarine Flotilla 1947-50, Cdr 1950, Naval Staff Course Admty Naval Staff AW Warfare Div 1950-53, Br Jt Servs Mission Washington DC 1953-55, Jt Servs Staff Course 1956, Admty Tactical and Ship Requirements Div 1957, Capt 1957, Cmd RN Air Station Abbotsinch 1957-59, NATO Standing Gp Washington DC 1959-62, dir of underseas warfare MOD 1963-66, Rear Adm 1966, Chief of Staff to C in C Western Fleet 1966-68, ret 1968; md: Wellman Incandescent (Africa) pty Ltd Johannesburg 1968-70, John Bell Fabrics of Scot Ltd Biggar Lanarkshire 1970-72; dir Scottish Assoc for the Care and Resettlement of Offenders 1974-79 (vice pres 1979), vice pres Int Prisoners Aid Assoc 1980; pres local branch Royal Br Legion 1982-88; Alliance candidate CC; FBIM 1958-70, MBIM 1958-70; *Recreations* golf; *Style*— Rear Adm Nicholas Poland, CB, CBE; Yew Tree Lodge, Shaftesbury Rd, Wilton, Wilts, SP2 0DR (☎ 0722 742 632)

POLAND, Richard Domville; CB (1973); s of late Maj R A Poland, RMLI; *b* 22 Oct 1914; *Educ* RNC Dartmouth; *m* 1948, Rosalind Frances, da of late Surgn-Capt H C Devas; 1 s, 1 da; *Career* under-sec Min of Tport 1964-70, DOE 1970-74, sec Int Maritime Industry Forum 1976-78, chm Kent branch CPRE 1980-; *Style*— Richard Poland, Esq, CB; 63 Alexandra Road, Kew, Surrey TW9 2BT

POLE *see also*: Carew Pole

POLE, Prof Jack Richon; s of Joseph Pole (d 1985), and Phoebe Louise, *née* Rickards; *b* 14 Mar 1922; *Educ* King Alfred Sch London, Kings Coll London, Queen's Coll Oxford (BA), Princeton Univ (PhD); *m* 31 May 1952 (m dis 1988), Marilyn Louise, da of John Glenn Mitchell (d 1968); 1 s (Nicholas), 2 da (Ilsa, Lucy); *Career* RCS 1941-42, 2 Lt RA 1942, served E Surrey Regt seconded to Somali Scouts 1944-46, ret Capt; instr in history Princeton Univ 1952-53, asst lectr (later lectr) in american history UCL 1953-63, Commonwealth Fund American Studies 1957, visiting prof Berkeley 1960-61 (Jefferson Meml lectr 1971), visiting prof Ghana 1966, Chicago 1969, fell Center for Advanced Study in Behavioural Sciences Stanford California 1969; Cambridge Univ: reader in american history and govt 1963-78, fell Churchill Coll 1968-78, vice master 1975-78, memb cncl of senate 1970-74; guest scholar Woodrow Wilson Int Center Washington 1978-79, visiting prof Peking 1984; Oxford Univ: Rhodes prof of american history and visits and fell of St Catherine's Coll 1979-; memb Amnesty Int; Hon Fell Historical Soc of Ghana 1967; Jersey Prize Princeton Univ 1953, Ramsdell Prize Southern Hist Assoc USA 1960 FBA 1985, FRHistS; *Books* Political Representation in England & The Origins of the American Republic (1966), The Advance of Democracy (ed 1967), The Seventeenth Century: The Origins of Legislative Power (1969), Foundations of American Independence (1972), The Revolution in America: Documents of the Internal Development of America in the Revolutionery Era (1971), The Decision for American Independence (1975), The Pursuit of Equality in American History (1978), Paths to the American Past (1979), The Gift of Government (1983), Colonial British America (co-ed 1983), The American Constitution For and Against (ed 1987); *Recreations* cricket-playing, organising, writing about; painting; *Clubs* MCC, Trojon Wanderers Cricket; *Style*— Prof Jack Pole; 20 Divinity Rd, Oxford OX4 1LJ, (☎ 0865 246950); St Catherine's Coll, Oxford OX1 3UJ (☎ 0865 271 744)

POLE, Leslie Hammond; s of Reginald Hammond Pole (d 1978), of Syston, Leics, and Harriet, *née* Taylor (d 1985);; *b* 10 Dec 1930; *Educ* Loughborough Coll; *m* 26 Aug 1961, Kay, da of Walter Kenneth Bentley (d 1984); 2 s (Timothy Bentley b 1962, Michael Hammond b 1966), 1 da (Nicola Lesley b 1970); *Career* Actg Pilot Offr RAF 1954-56; CA; sr ptnr Pole Arnold (largest ind Leicester firm); tres Br Show Pony Soc, sec Leics Pharmaceutical Contractors Ctee, chm Raithby Lawrence & Co Ltd Printers 1978-; FCA 1954; *Recreations* motor rallies (incl Monte Carlo), horses, soccer; *Style*— Leslie H Pole, Esq; The Homestead, Old Woodhouse, Leicester (☎ 0509 890038)

POLE, Peter John Chandos; s and h of Sir Peter Van Notten Pole, 5 Bt; *b* 27 April 1952; *m* 1973, Suzanne Norah, da of Harold Raymond Hughes; 2 s (Michael b 1980, Andrew b 1986), 1 da (Naomi b 1983); *Style*— Peter Pole, Esq; 41 Webster St, Nedlands 6009, W Australia

POLE, Sir Peter Van Notten; 5 Bt (GB 1791); s of late Arthur Chandos Pole and kinsman of Sir Cecil Pery Van-Notten-Pole, 4 Bt (d 1948); *b* 6 Nov 1921; *Educ* Guildford GS; *m* 1949, Jean Emily, da of late Charles Douglas Stone; 1 s, 1 da; *Heir* s, Peter John Chandos Pole; *Career* 1939-45 war as Flt-Sgt RAAF; accountant; FASA, ACIS; *Style*— Sir Peter Pole, Bt; 5 Sandpiper Mews, 10 Perina Way, City Beach, WA 6015, Australia

POLIZZI DI SORRENTINO, Hon Mrs (Olga); *née* Forte; eldest da of Baron Forte (Life Peer), *qv*; *b* 1947,; *Educ* St Mary's Ascot; *m* 26 Sept 1966, Marchese Alessandro Polizzi di Sorrentino, s of Gen Polizzi di Sorrentino (d 1980); 2 da (Alexandra b 28 Aug 1971, Charleotte b 8 April 1974); *Career* dir Trusthouse Forte plc; tstee Royal Opera House; govr St Mary Sch Ascot; *Style*— The Hon Mrs Polizzi di Sorrentino; 166 High Holborn, London WC1 (☎ 01 836 7744)

POLKINGHORNE, Rev Dr John Charlton; s of George Baulkwill Polkinghorne (d 1981), and Dorothy Evelyn, *née* Charlton (d 1983); *b* 16 Oct 1930; *Educ* Elmhurst GS Street Somerset, Perse Sch Cambridge, Trinity Coll Cambridge (BA, PhD, MA, ScD), Westcott House Cambridge; *m* 26 March 1955, Ruth Isobel, da of Hedley Gifford Martin (d 1979); 2 s (Peter b 1957, Michael b 1963), 1 da (Isobel Morland b 1959); *Career* Nat Serv RAEC 1948-49; fell Trinity Coll Cambridge 1954-86; lectr: Univ of Edinburgh 1956-58, Univ of Cambridge 1958-65 (reader 1965-68, prof mathematical physics 1968-79); ordained: deacon 1981, priest 1982; curate: Cambridge 1981-82, Bristol 1982-84; vicar Blean Kent 1984-86, fell dean and chaplain Trinity Hall Cambridge 1986-; chm: Govrs of Perse Sch 1972-81, Nuclear Physics Bd 1978-79, Ctee on Use of Foetal Material 1988-; memb 1975-79; FRS 1974; *Books* The Analytic S-Matrix (1966), The Particle Play (1979), Models of High Energy Processes (1980), The Quantum World (1984), The Way the World Is (1983),

One World (1986), Science and Creation (1988); *Recreations* gardening; *Style*— The Rev Dr John Polkinghorne; 74 Hurst Park Ave, Cambridge CB4 2AF (☎ 0223 607 43); Trinity Hall, Cambridge CB2 1TJ (☎ 0223 332 525)

POLLARD, Andrew Garth; s of Rev George Pollard, of 44 Vernon Rd, Sheffield and Elizabeth Beatrice, *née* Briggs; *b* 25 April 1945; *Educ* Queen's Coll Taunton, King's Coll London (LLB, AKC); *m* 26 May 1973, Lucy Petica, da of Prof Charles Martin Robertson, of Cambridge; 3 s (Finn b 1978, Tam b 1980, Liam b 1982); *Career* slr 1969; ptnr: Clifford-Turner 1975-87 (slr 1969-75), Clifford Chance 1987-; *Recreations* music, walking; *Style*— Garth Pollard, Esq; Clifford Chance, Royex House, Aldermanbury Sq, London EC2V 7LD (☎ 01 600 0808, fax 01 726 8561, telex 895991)

POLLARD, Prof Arthur; s of George Arthur Pollard, of Clitheroe, Lancs, and Nellie, *née* Smith (d 1977); *b* 22 Dec 1922; *Educ* Clitheroe Royal GS, Univ of Leeds (BA), Lincoln Coll Oxford (BLitt); *m* 1, 2 Sept 1948, Ursula Ann Egerton (d 1970), da of Nathan Jackson (d 1973), of Congleton, Cheshire; 2 s (John Stanley b 1952, Andrew Michael b 1958); m 2, 9 April 1973, Phyllis Mary, da of John Richard Pattinson (d 1958), of Cartmel, Cumbria; *Career* 161 (RMC) OCTU 1943, cmmnd E Lancs Regt, served 1 Bn 1943; overseas serv, seconded on intelligence to FO 1943-45, Staff Capt (Movements), Kilindini, E Africa 1945-46; Univ of Manchester: asst lectr in eng literature 1949-52 (lectr 1952-64, sr lectr 1964-67), dir of gen studies Faculty of Arts 1964-67; Univ of Hull: prof of eng 1967-84, dean faculty of arts 1976-78; consIt prof of eng Univ of Buckingham 1983-; Congleton BC: cnllr 1952-65, alderman 1965-67, ldr 1963-67; ccnllr Humberside CC 1979-(Cons educn spokesman 1981-); memb: Secdy Examinations Cncl 1983-88, Assoc of CCs Educn Ctee 1985-; contrib to Black Papers on educn; reader: St Peter's Congleton 1951-67, All Saints Ferriby 1968-74, All Saints South Cave 1974-; Hon DLitt Buckingham 1982; *Books* Charles Simeon 1759-1836 (with MM Hennell, 1959), New Poems of George Crabbe (1960), English Hymns (1960), English Sermons (1963), Mrs Gaskell Novelist and Biographer (1965), Richard Hooker (1966), The Letters of Mrs Gaskell (with JAV Chapple, 1966), The Victorians (1970, revised and enlarged 1987), Satire (1970), Crabbe: The Critical Heritage (1972), Anthony Trollope (1978), The Landscape of the Brontes (1988), Complete Poetical Works of George Crabbe, 3 vols (with Norma Dalrymple-Champneys, 1988); *Recreations* cricket, railway history; *Style*— Prof Arthur Pollard; Sand Hall, North Cave, Brough, North Humberside (☎ 0430 422 202); County Hall, Beverley, North Humberside

POLLARD, Maj-Gen (Charles) Barry; s of Leonard Charles Pollard (d 1980); *b* 20 April 1927; *Educ* Ardingly, Selwyn Coll Cambridge; *m* 1954, Mary, da of Jack Sydney Heyes (d 1970); 3 da; *Career* RE 1947, GSO 1 MOD 1967, DSD Staff Coll 1967-68, CRE 3 Div 1969-71, Col GS 3 Div 1971-72, CCRE 1 (Br) Corps 1972-74, RCDS 1975, chief engr BAOR 1976-79; nat dir Project Trident (Trident Tst) 1980-84, dir Solent Business Fund 1984-, Col Cmdt RE 1982-87; md Westgate Fund Mgmnt Ltd 1985-;; chm Douglas Haig Memorial Homes; *Recreations* ocean sailing, golf; *Clubs* Army and Navy; *Style*— Major-Gen Barry Pollard; Yateley, Coombe Rd, Salisbury, Wilts (☎ 0722 335493)

POLLARD, Christopher Leslie; OBE; s of Sidney Samuel Pollard (d 1975), and Gertrude Winifred, *née* Skipper (d 1987); *b* 18 June 1939; *Educ* Thames Valley GS Twickenham, Acton Sch of Hotel and Catering Mgmnt; *m* 13 April 1963, Vivien Mary, da of Edwin Hornby (d 1982); 1 da (Rebecca b 27 June 1966); *Career* lectr hotel mgment Studies Cardiff 1960-63, propietor Mount Sorrel Hotel Barry 1963-74, md Hamard Catering Gp 1968-86 (chm 1974-86), di r Hamard Catering Saudi Arabia Ltd 1978, chm and md Dramah Investmts Ltd and Dramah Devpts ltd 1986, dir: Middlepatch Ltd 1987, Cardiff Mktg Bureau Ltd 1987, Channel Cement Ltd 1988; memb Wales Tourist Bd appointed by Sec of State for Wales 1983-; chm: Taste of Wales - Blas ar Gymru Ltd, attractions advsy ctee Wales Tourist Bd 1986, hotels advsy ctee Wales Tourist Bd 1986; memb Help the Aged Jubilee Appeal for Wales 1986, hon tres UK Freedom from Hunger Campaign 1977-87; Freeman City of London 1986, Citizen and Memb of Tinplate Workers alias Wire Workers Livery Co 1986; MHCI; *Style*— Christopher Pollard, Esq, OBE; Penarth House, Cliff Parade, South Glamorgan CF6 2BP (☎ 0222 709065; Wellesley House, 11 Ennismore Mews, Knightsbridge London SW7 1AP (☎ 01 584 1530; Hamard House, Cardiff Rd, Barry, South Glamorgan CF6 7XW (☎ 0446 743558, fax 0446 749803;

POLLARD, Eve (Mrs Nicholas Lloyd); da of Ivor Pollard, and Mini Pollard; *m* 1, 8 Dec 1968, (m dis), Barry Lester David Winkleman; 1 da (Claudia b 15 Jan 1972); m 2, 23 May 1978, Nicholas Markley Lloyd; 1 s (Oliver b 6 Aug 1980); *Career* fashion ed: Honey 1967-68, Daily Mirror Magazine 1968-69; womens ed: Observer Magazine 1970-71, Sunday Mirror 1971-81; asst ed Sunday People 1981-83, features ed and presenter TV-AM 1983-85; ed: Elle (USA) 1985-86, Sunday Magazine (News of the World) 1986, You Magazine (Mail on Sunday) 1986-88; Sunday Mirror and Sunday Mirror Magazine; devised two series Frocks on the Box for ITV 1985; *Books* Jackie: Biography of Mrs J K Onassis (1971); *Style*— Miss Eve Pollard; Sunday Mirror, 33 Holborn Circus, London EC1P 1DQ (☎ 01 353 0246, fax 01 822 3405, telex 27286 MIRROR G)

POLLARD, George; s of George Charles William Pollard (d 1935), and Thirza Elizabeth, *née* Wilson (later Mrs Walter Leonard Freeman; d 1979); *b* 12 Nov 1929; *Educ* St Pauls; *m* 22 May 1956, Jean Eileen, da of William George Simmonds (d 1970), of London SW14; 2 da (Barbara Ann b 27 Feb 1957, Sally Jane b 14 June 1960); *Career* Nat Serv 2 Lt Northants Regt served Greece 1948-49; slr 1955; sr ptnr Shoosmiths & Harrison 1981-; conservative memb Northampton Co Borough 1962-71, 1972-74, Northampton Borough Cncl 1974-79; Cons memb Northamptonshire CC 1973 (chm 1987); chm Northampton South Cons Assoc 1982-86 (pres 1986); chm Northampton Central Cons Cncl 1985-88; *Recreations* snooker, swimming, gardening, walking; *Clubs* Northampton and County; *Style*— George Pollard, Esq; 5 Favell Way, Weston Favell, Northampton (☎ 0604 405924); Shoosmiths & Harrison, PO Box 2, Compton House, Abington Street, Northampton (☎ 0604 29977, fax 0604 20229, telex 32167 SAND HG)

POLLARD, Sir (Charles) Herbert; CBE (1957, OBE 1946, MBE 1943); s of late Charles Pollard; *b* 23 Oct 1898; *Educ* Blackpool; *m* 1, 1922, Elsie (d 1970), da of Charles Crain; 1 da; m 2, 1971, Hilda M Levitch; *Career* city tres Kingston upon Hull 1929-61, fin advsr Assoc of Municipal Corpns 1951-61, memb ctees and working parties arranged by govt depts on: educn, housing, police, local authy fin; OStJ 1962, kt 1962; *Style*— Sir Herbert Pollard, CBE; St Peter's Court, St Peter's Grove, York, Y03 6AQ (☎ 0904 641827)

POLLARD, Ian Douglas; s of Douglas Pollard, DFC (d 1945), and Peggy, *née* Murfitt (d 1989); *b* 9 June 1945; *Educ* Perse Sch Cambridge; *m* 25 July 1964, Dianna, da of Prof Alexander Deer, of Cambridge; 3 da (Juliette b 1964, Samantha b 1966, Arushka b 1987); *Career* chm and md Flaxyard plc 1972-; architectural designer of: Marcopolo (Observers Bldg) 1987, Sainsbury's Homebase Kensington 1988; memb Nat Gdns Scheme, regnl appeal ldr PYBT; ARICS; *Recreations* gardening, cycling, diving; *Style*— Ian Pollard, Esq; Hazelbury Manor, Nr Box, Corsham, Wilts SN14 9HU (☎ 0225 810715)

POLLARD, John Stanley; s of Prof Arthur Pollard, of Sand Hall, Station Rd, N Cave, Humberside, and Ursula Ann Eggerton, *née* Jackson (d 1970); *b* 4 Jan 1952; *Educ* Kings Sch Macclesfield, Hymers Coll Hull, Univ of Leeds (LLB); *m* 14 Sept 1974, Clare Judith, da of Arnold Walter George Boulton, of White House, Winter Hill, Cookham Dean, Borkshire; 3 s (Samuel John b 1979, Joseph William b 1981, Edward George b 1984); *Career* slr 1977; HM dep coroner (West and Central Cheshire); memb Congleton Borough Cncl (elected as SDP candidate 1987), memb Congleton Town Cncl (5 yrs), SDP Parly Candidate for Crewe and Nantwich 1983; *Recreations* walking, gardening, politics; *Style*— John Pollard, Esq; Toft Green Cottage, Toft Green, Congleton, Cheshire; Hibbert & Co Slrs, 144 Nantwich Rd, Crewe, Cheshire

POLLARD, Kenneth Charles; s of Hubert George Pollard (d 1970), and Georgina Elizabeth, *née* Durman; *b* 21 Dec 1945; *Educ* Saltash S M; *m* 5 Oct 1974 (m dis 1986); 1 s (James b 1981); *Career* with RAF 1961-74: active serv 8 and 208 Sqdns, 2 tours of duty para test unit RAE Farnborough; sr ptnr Air Decor, aircraft interior conslts 1987-; *Recreations* sailing, (flying fifteen) golf; *Style*— Kenneth Pollard, Esq; Willow Cottage, Water End, Cople, Beds (☎ 02303 559, fax 02303 8121, car tel 0860 382796)

POLLARD, Michael Trent; s of George Edward Pollard (d 1974), and Flora, *née* Wise (d 1985); ggf Midshipman (later Lt) John Pollard serv in Victory at Trafalgar and shot dead the French sniper who had killed Nelson, John Pollard was known as 'Nelson's Avenger'; *b* 16 June 1931; *Educ* Queen Elizabeth's GS Wimborne, Westminster, London Univ; *m* 1, 1957, Joyce; 2 s (Nicholas b 1958, Simon b 1964); m 2, 1969, Anna Jane; *Career* Nat Serv RAF 1949-51; teacher 1956-66; ed: Read Magazine 1967-69, Pictorial Education 1969-71; dep ed Teachers World 1969-71, ed Resources in Education 1971-72; freelance journalist, author 2nd PR Conslt 1972-; dir Topic Records Ltd 1966-73; *Books* North Sea Surge (1978), Walking the Scottish Highlands: General Wade's Military Roads (1984), The Hardest Work Under Heaven (1984), and numerous non-fiction books for children; *Recreations* writing unpublishable novels; *Style*— Michael Pollard, Esq; Orchard House, Gt Cressingham, Thetford, Norfolk IP25 6NL (☎ 076 06 297)

POLLARD, Walter; s of David Pollard (d 1976), and Jane, *née* Hammond (d 1981); *b* 18 Nov 1927; *Educ* Clitheroe Royal GS, Dublin Univ (BA, MB, BCh); *m* 1, 23 Aug 1956, Rosemary Ann, da of F F Pinnock, CMG (d 1979), of Charlwood; 1 s (Rupert Francis b 1958), 2 da (Sophia Jane b 1957, Rebecca Mary b 1982); m 2, 29 Oct 1982, Joy Yvonne, da of S Pegler (d 1948), of Stroud; 1 da (Victoria Jane b 1983); *Career* RA 1946-47, RANC 1947-48; obstetrician and gynaecologist 1968-; examiner: Southampton Univ, Bristol Univ, Gen Medical Cncl, Royal Coll of Obstetricians and Gynaecologists; main interests: new surgical techniques, cynosurgery and laser in gynaecology; *Recreations* gardening, carpentry, travel; *Clubs* Fothergill; *Style*— Walter Pollard, Esq; Fosse House, Midford Road, Combe Down, Bath, Avon (☎ 0225 835312); Royal United Hospital Bath (☎ 0225 28331)

POLLEN, Sir John Michael Hungerford; 7 Bt (GB 1795), of Redenham, Hampshire; s of late Lt-Cdr John Francis Hungerford Pollen, RN; suc father's 2 cous, Sir John Lancelot Hungerford Pollen, 6 Bt, 1959; *b* 6 April 1919; *Educ* Downside, Merton Coll Oxford; *m* 1, 1941 (m dis 1956), Angela Mary Oriana, da of Maj F J Russi, MC; 1 s, 1 da; m 2, 1957, Mrs Diana Alice Jubb, da of late A E Timbrell; *Heir* s, Richard John Hungerford Pollen; *Career* served WW II (despatches), Capt RA; *Style*— Sir John Pollen, Bt; Manor House, Rodbourne, Malmesbury, Wilts; Lochportain, Isle of North Uist, Outer Hebrides

POLLEN, Peregrine Michael Hungerford; s of Sir Walter Michael Hungerford Pollen, MC, JP (d 1986); 1 cous of Sir John Pollen, 7 Bt; *b* 24 Jan 1931; *Educ* Eton, Ch Ch Oxford; *m* 26 June 1958, Patricia Helen, 3 da of Lt-Col Gerald Barry, MC; 1 s, 2 da; *Career* exec dep chm Sotheby Parke Bernet & Co 1975-82 (joined 1957, dir 1961), with former responsibility for Sotheby Parke Bernet New York (pres 1965-72); ADC to Sir Evelyn Baring as govr of Kenya 1955-56; *Clubs* Brooks's, Beefsteak; *Style*— Peregrine Pollen, Esq; Norton Hall, Mickleton, Glos (☎ 0386 438 218)

POLLEN, Richard John Hungerford; s and h of Sir John Michael Hungerford Pollen, 7 Bt, *qv*; *b* 3 Nov 1946; *Educ* Worth Abbey; *m* 2 Oct 1971, Christianne Mary, da of Sir (William) Godfrey Agnew, KCVO; 4 s (William b 1976, Jonathan b 1979, Andrew b 1982, Alexander b 1986), 2 da (Isabel b 1975, Alice b 1984); *Career* with Capel-Cure Myers 1964-68; overseas 1969-70; with Charles Barker 1971-79; Valin Pollen (VPI Gp plc) 1979; BHS, CGA, IPA; *Recreations* riding (eventing); *Style*— Richard Pollen Esq; Dunsfold Ryse, Chiddingfold, Surrey GU8 4YA (☎ 048 649 354); The VPI Gp, 32 Grosvenor Gardens, London SW1W ODH (☎ 01 730 3456)

POLLINGTON, Viscount; John Andrew Bruce Savile; s and h of 8 Earl of Mexborough; *b* 30 Nov 1959; *Style*— Viscount Pollington; Arden Hall, Hawnby, York YO6 5LS

POLLINS, Martin; s of Harry Pollins (d 1969), of London, and Hetty Pollins; *b* 11 Dec 1938; *Educ* Brighton Tech Sch; *m* 1, March 1963 (m dis 1980), m 2, 13 Dec 1980, Susan Elizabeth, da of Arthur Edwin Hines, of Brighton; 4 s (Andrew Martin, Richard Anthony, Nicholas, Matthew), 1 da (Anna); *Career* CA, ptnr PRB Parker Pollins 1968, chm The Charter Gp Ptnrship plc 1986-; cncl memb ICAEW 1987-, memb C of C; FCA 1964, ATII 1964; *Recreations* spectator of sport; *Style*— Martin Pollins, Esq; Forest Ridge, Maresfield, W Sussex TN22 3ER (☎ 0825 713 115); PRB Parker Pollins, Cornelius Hse, 178/180 Church Rd, Hove, E Sussex BN3 2DJ (☎ 0273 202 211, fax 0273 204 773, car tel 0836 587 142 or 0860 354 503)

POLLITT, Dr Norman Travers; s of Ellis Pollitt (d 1949), of Palmers Green, London N13, and Rose Malvina, *née* Graves (d 1962); *b* 25 May 1918; *Educ* Southgate Co Sch, St Mary's Hosp Med Sch and London Univ (MB BS); *m* 5 June 1953, Rosemary Lucy, da of Herbert Bexon Spencer, of Manor Cottage, Horton, Wimborne, Dorset; 2 s (Michael b 1955, Timothy b 1959), 1 da (Clare b 1963); *Career* Friends' Ambulance Unit 1940-46: Ethiopia 1942-45, NW Europe 1945-46; princ gen practice NHS 1956-60, med advsr Vitamins Gp 1961-68, res physician Roche Products 1968-79, conslt in vitaminology Hoffmann-La Roche 1979-82; chm med bds DHSS 1979-89; med ed Pears Cyclopaedia 1980-86; author of numerous pubns on nutrition and vitaminology; memb Med Journalists Assoc; Freeman City of London 1979, Liveryman Worshipful Soc of Apothecaries 1978; MRCS, LRCP 1952, FRSM 1960, MRCGP 1961; *Books* Which? Guide to Family Health (jt author, 1980); *Recreations* musical appreciation, photography, oenology; *Style*— Dr Norman Pollitt; 70 Royston Park Rd, Hatch End, Pinner, Middx; Springhead Cottage, Swallowcliffe, Salisbury, Wilts

POLLOCK; *see*: Montagu-Pollock

POLLOCK, Alexander; s of Robert Faulds Pollock, OBE, and Margaret Findlay, *née* Aitken; *b* 21 July 1944; *Educ* Rutherglen Acad, Glasgow Acad, BNC Oxford (MA), Edinburgh Univ (LLB), Perugia Univ; *m* 1975, Verena Francesca Gertraud Alice Ursula, da of J Reginald Critchley, of Patmore Lodge, Patmore Heath, Albury, Ware, Herts; 1 s (Andrew b 1979), 1 da (Francesca b 1976); *Career* slr 1970-73, advocate Scottish Bar

1973-, MP (C) Moray and Nairn 1979-1983, Moray 1983-87; memb commons select ctee on Scottish Affrs 1979-82; pps to George Younger: as Sec of State for Scotland 1982-86, as Sec of State Def 1986-87; sec Br Austrian Parly Gp 1979-87; memb Queen's Bodyguard for Scotland (Royal Company of Archers) 1984-; *Clubs* New (Edinburgh); *Style*— Alexander Pollock, Esq; Drumdarrach, Forres, Moray, Scotland IV36 ODW

POLLOCK, David (Charles) Treherne; s of Brian Treherne Pollock, and Helen Evelyn, *née* Holt-Wilson; *b* 7 April 1938; *Educ* StnAndrew's Pangbourne, Nowton Ct, St Lawrence Coll; *m* 2 Sept 1961, Lisbeth Jane, da of Maj Peter Scratchley; 2 s (Piers James Treherne b 16 March 1964, (Alexander) Blair Treherne b 2 July 1967), 1 da (Sophie-Jane Eleanor Treherne b 31 Jan 1969); *Career* 2 Lt The Gordon Highlanders 1956-59; int mktg exec The Economist 1961-69; dir: Mathers & Streets Ltd 1968-69, Charles Barker (City) Ltd 1969-70, Dewe Rogerson Ltd 1970-, Dewe Rogerson Gp Ltd 1975-, Dewe Rogerson Aust 1985-87, Dewe Rogerson Japan 1987-; memb Crafts Cncl sponsorship ctee 1988-; *Recreations* lawn tennis, skiing, shooting; *Clubs* City of London; *Style*— David Treherne Pollock, Esq; 9 The Chase, London SW4 0NP; Dewe Rogerson Ltd, 3 London Wall Bldgs, London Wall, London EC2M 5SY (☎ 01 638 9571)

POLLOCK, David Frederick; s and h of Sir George Frederick Pollock, 5 Bt, *qv*; *b* 13 April 1959; *m* 14 Sept 1985, Helena R, o da of L J Tompsett, OBE, of Tadworth, Surrey; *Career* md Pollock Audio Visual Ltd 1983-; dir Cloud 9 (Video Film Prodns) Ltd 1977; *Style*— David Pollock, Esq; Camelot Cottage, 43 Chequers Lane, Walton-on-the-hill, Surrey KT20 7SF (☎ 0737 81 3155)

POLLOCK, David Raymond John; s of Eric John Frank Pollock, of Dulwich, and Beryl Olive, *née* Newens (d 1982); *b* 22 Oct 1949; *Educ* Dulwich, Univ of Keele (BA); *m* 30 July 1975, Barbara Ann, da of Henry Chambre, MBE, of Hendon; 1 s (Thomas Hugo John b 19 March 1984), 1 da (Sarah Charlotte Chambré b 23 Aug 1980); *Career* MOD: admin trainee 1972, higher exec offr 1975 (private sec to Chief Sci Advsr), princ 1978; head of mgmnt primary mkts div Int Stock Exchange 1989- (head of industry policy unit 1986, head of business devpt primary mkts div 1988); memb; fin ctee Royal Inst of GB, City of London branch Ctee BIM; *Recreations* squash, walking, drawing and painting, books, convivialty; *Clubs* Snuffers Dining; *Style*— David Pollock, Esq; 46 Dacres Rd, London SE23 (☎ 01 699 3883); The International Stock Exchange, Old Broad St, London SE23 (☎ 01 588 2355, telex 886557)

POLLOCK, Hon David Stephen Geoffrey; s of 2 Viscount Hanworth; *b* 16 Feb 1946; *Educ* Wellington Coll, Guildford Tech Coll, Sussex Univ; *m* 1968, Elizabeth Vambe; 2 da; *Career* lectr, QMC, Univ of London; *Style*— The Hon David Pollock

POLLOCK, Ellen Clara; da of Hedwig Elizabeth Kahn (d 1958); *Educ* St Mary's Coll W2, Convent of The Blessed Sacrament Brighton; *m* 1, 13 July 1928, Lt Col Leslie Frank Coventry Hancock OBE (d 1944); 1 s (Michael Coventry); m 2, 1945, James Proudfoot, RP, ROI, (d 1971); *Career* 1920-; theatre incl: Hit the Deck 1927, Her First Affaire 1930, The Good Companions 1931, Finished Abroad 1934, The Dominant Sex 1935; seasons of Shaw's plays 1944-53, Six Characters in Search of an Author 1963, Lady Frederick 1969-70, Pygmaluin 1974, Tales from Vienna Woods 1976, The Dark Lady of the Sunnets 1977, The Woman I Love 1979, Country Life 1980; has appeared in numerous films and tv incl: Forsyte Saga, The Pallisers, The Nightingale Saga; pres the Shaw Soc; *Recreations* antiques; *Style*— Miss Ellen Pollock; 9 Tedworth Square, Chelsea, London SW3 4DU (☎ 01 352 5082)

POLLOCK, Sir George; QC (1951); s of William Mackford Pollock; *b* 15 Mar 1901; *m* 1, 1922, Doris Evelyn (d 1977), da of Thomas Main, of Leamington Spa, Warwicks; 1 s, 1 da; m 2, 1977, Mollie, *née* Pedder, (d 1988) wid of J A Van Santen; *Career* barr Gray's Inn 1928, bencher 1948, recorder of Sudbury 1946-51, dir Br Employers' Confedn 1954-65, sr consult to CBI on Int Labour Affrs 1965-69; kt 1959; *Style*— Sir George Pollock, QC; 62 Staveley Court, Eastbourne, East Sussex

POLLOCK, Sir George Frederick; 5 Bt (UK 1866), of Hatton, Middx; s of Sir (Frederick) John Pollock, 4 Bt (d 1963); *b* 13 August 1928; *Educ* Eton, Trinity Coll Cambridge (MA); *m* 1951, Doreen Mumford, da of Norman Ernest Keown Nash, CMG (d 1966); 1 s, 2 da; *Heir* s, David Frederick Pollock b 13 April 1959; *Career* 2 Lt 17/21 Lancers 1948-49; slr 1956; artist-photographer and audio-visual creator 1963-; Hon FRPS (pres 1978), FBIPP, FRSA, AFIAP; *Clubs* DHO; *Style*— Sir George F Pollock, Bt; Netherwood, Stones Lane, Westcott, nr Dorking, Surrey RH4 3QH

POLLOCK, John Craig Stuart; s of Ian Stuart Pollock (d 1954), and Lois, *née* Harris (d 1956); family has been in the Paper Trade, f to s for five generations; *b* 1 July 1927; *Educ* Dane Ct Prep Sch, Pyrford Surrey, Selwyn House Canada, Lower Merion Sr HS USA; *m* 21 Jan 1961, da of Margaret Elizabeth, da of Ernest George Willmot, of W Sussex; 1 s (David John Stuart b 1962), 1 da (Katharine Lois Milton b 1963); *Career* pres (formerly chm) Pollock & Searby Ltd; co fndr (with wife) and proprietor of The Penny Royal Open-Air Theatre Bosham, Sussex 1983; trained as journalist 1944 on The Philadelphia Enquirer, asst ed 'American Outlook'; *Recreations* sailing, theatre; *Clubs* Lansdowne; *Style*— John C S Pollock, Esq; Trippet Meadow, Canute Rd, Bosham, Chichester, W Susses (☎ 0243 573288); Pollock & Searby Ltd, 9/10 Mill Lane, Alton, Hants (☎ 0420 86404, telex 858889, fax 0420 83285)

POLLOCK, Adm of the Fleet Sir Michael Patrick; GCB (1971, KCB 1969, CB 1966), LVO (1952), DSC (1944); s of Charles Albert Pollock (d 1937), of The Lane House, Lydham, Shrops, and Gladys Mason; *b* 19 Oct 1916; *Educ* RNC Dartmouth; *m* 1, 1940, Margaret Steacy (d 1951); 2 s, 1 da; m 2, 1954, Marjory Helen Reece, *née* Bisset; 1 step da; *Career* RN 1930, Cdr 1950, Capt 1955, Rear Adm 1964, Vice Adm 1968, Adm 1970; cmd HMS Ark Royal 1963-64, asst chief of Naval Staff 1964-66, 2 i/c Home Fleet 1966-67, flag offr Submarines and NATO Cdr Submarines Eastern Atlantic 1968-69, controller of the Navy 1970-71, chief of Naval Staff and first sea lord 1971-74, first and princ naval ADC to The Queen 1972-74; chm Naval Insur Tst 1975-85; Bath King of Arms 1976-85; *Style*— Adm of the Fleet Sir Michael Pollock, GCB, MVO, DSC; The Ivy House, Churchstoke, Montgomery, Powys SY15 6DU (058 85 426)

POLLOCK, Peter Glen; s of Jack Campbell Pollock (d 1953), and Rebecca Shields Marshall, *née* Clarke (d 1985); *b* 6 Sept 1946; *Educ* Nautical Coll Pangbourne, St Andrews Univ (MA); *m* 3 Sept 1977, Nicola Sara, da of Derek William Bernard Clements, of Cirencester, Glos; 2 s (Jonathan William Campbell b 1982, Matthew Charles Simon b 1984); *Career* gp chief exec ML Hldgs plc 1985; fin dir: Fisher Controls Ltd 1983-85, Hawker Siddeley Power Transformers Ltd 1978-83; ctee memb Royal Utd Kingdom Beneficient Assoc 1985-, FICA; *Recreations* golf, shooting, skiing, sailing; *Clubs* Knole Park Golf; *Style*— Peter Pollock, Esq; ML Holdings Plc, Ajax Ave, Slough (☎ 0753 23838)

POLLOCK, Hon Richard Charles Standish; TD (1986); yr s of 2 Visc Hanworth; *b* 6 Feb 1951; *Educ* Wellington Coll, Trinity Coll Cambridge (MA); *m* 1982, Annette Louise, da of Peter Lockhart, of Daisy Cottage, Studham, Common Lane, nr Dunstable, Beds; 2 s (Harold William Charles b 30 April 1988, Frederick Thomas Charles b (twin) 30 April 1988); *Career* Maj Royal Yeo TAVR; slr; *Recreations* TAVR; *Style*— The Hon Richard Pollock, TD; 89 Kyrle Rd, London SW11 6BB; office: 14 Dominion St, London EC2M 2RJ (☎ 01 628 2020, telex 888562)

POLLOCK, Hon Mrs (Rosemary Tyrwhitt); da and co-heiress of Baroness Berners, *qv*; *b* 20 July 1931; *Educ* Stonar Sch Cottles Park nr Melksham Wilts; Dorset House Sch of Occupational Therapy Oxford; *m* 1959, Kelvin Alexander, s of Kelvin Clayton Pollock; 2 s; *Career* practising occupational therapist 1952-59; *Recreations* outdoor pursuits; *Style*— The Hon Mrs Pollock; Malt House, Hollingbourne, Kent

POLLOK-MCCALL, Maj Robert George; JP (1960), DL (Ross-shire 1964); s of Brig-Gen John Buchanan Pollok-McCall CMG, DSO, DL, JP (d 1951), of Kindeace, and Frances Catrina, *née* McCall; *b* 22 Mar 1912; *Educ* Harrow, Sandhurst; *m* 1, 26 July 1941, Pamela Mary (d 1983), da of Sir Kenneth Lloyd Gibson, Bt (d 1967), late of Gt Warley; 1 s (Angus John Kenneth), 2 da (Camilla b 1942, Juliet Fiona b 1946 decd); m 2, 21 Aug 1986, Jeanette Karen Julie, da of Baron Juel Brockdorff, of Hindemaye Fyn, Denmark; *Career* The Black Watch (ret 1954) served in Palestine (despatches); and in WWII; Queens Body Gd for Scotland (Royal Co of Archers); DL (Ross-shire 1964); *Recreations* shooting, fishing, skiing; *Clubs* Army and Navy, Royal Perth Golfing Soc; *Style*— Maj Robert Pollok-McCall, JP; Machany, Auchterarder, Perthshire (☎ 076 481343)

POLWARTH, Master of; Hon Andrew Walter Hepburne-Scott; s and h of 10 Lord Polwarth; *b* 30 Nov 1947; *Educ* Eton, and Trinity Hall Cambridge; *m* 1971, (Isabel) Anna, da of Maj John Freville Henry Surtees, OBE, MC; 2 s, 2 da; *Career* asst dir Baring Bros 1982-; *Style*— The Master of Polwarth; 72 Cloncurry St, London SW6

POLWARTH, 10 Lord (S 1690); Henry Alexander Hepburne-Scott; TD, DL (Roxburgh 1962); s of Master of Polwarth, JP, DL (d 1942), and Elspeth, JP (da of Rt Rev Archibald Campbell, DD, DCL, sometime Bishop of Glasgow and Galloway, by his w, Hon Helen, *née* Brodrick, da of 8 Visc Midleton, JP); suc gf (9 Lord Polwarth, CBE, JP, DL) 1944; *b* 17 Nov 1916; *Educ* Eton, King's Coll Cambridge; *m* 1, 1943 (m dis 1969), Caroline (d 1982), da of Capt Robert Hay (d 1939), er bro of Sir Bache Hay, 11 Bt (d 1966, since when Btcy dormant); 1 s, 3 da; m 2, 1969, Jean, da of Adm Sir Angus Cunninghame Graham of Gartmore and of Ardoch, KBE, CB, and formerly w of Charles Jauncey, QC; 2 step s, 1 step da; *Heir* s, Master of Polwarth; *Career* sits as Cons Peer in House of Lords, Rep Peer for Scotland 1945-63; Maj Lothians and Border Horse NW Europe 1944-45; CA; govr Bank of Scotland 1966-72 (dir 1974-), chm General Accident Gp 1968-1972, min of State for Scotland 1972-74; dir: ICI 1974-81, Canadian Pacific Ltd 1975-, Sun Life Assur of Canada 1975-84, Halliburton Co (USA) 1974-; memb Royal Co of Archers (Queen's Bodyguard for Scotland), Vice Lord-Lieut Borders Region (Roxburgh, Ettrick and Lauderdale) 1975-, chllr Aberdeen Univ 1966, memb Franco-Br Cncl (Br section); Hon LLD: St Andrews, Aberdeen; Hon DLitt Heriot-Watt, DUniv Stirling, FRSE, FRSA, Hon FRIAS; *Recreations* country pursuits and the arts; *Clubs* Brooks's, Pratt's, Army and Navy, New (Edinburgh); *Style*— The Rt Hon the Lord Polwarth, TD, DL; Harden, Hawick, Roxburghshire TD9 7LP (☎ (0450) 72069); 37 St James's Place, London SW1 (☎ 01 499 9789)

POMEROY, Brian Walter; *b* 26 June 1944; *Educ* The King's Sch Canterbury, Magdalene Coll Cambridge (MA); *m* 7 Aug 1974, Hilary Susan; 2 da (Gabriela b 1975, Alisa b 1977); *Career* ptnr Touche Ross & Co 1975; seconded as under sec in Dept of Indust 1981-83; ptnr i/c of Touche Ross Mgmnt Conslts 1987-; dir Centrepoint Soho; non-exec dir BL 1985-88 (now known as The Rover Gp plc); nominated memb of Cncl of Lloyd's 1987; FCA 1978; *Recreations* photography, tennis, running; *Style*— Brian Pomeroy, Esq; c/o Touche Ross & Co, Hill House, 1 Little New St, London EC4 3TR (☎ 01 353 8011)

POMEROY, Maj Hon Robert William; yst s of 8 Viscount Harberton, OBE (d 1956), and Mary Katherine, *née* Leatham (d 1971); bro of 9 Visc (d 1980) and bro and hp of 10 Visc; *b* 28 Feb 1916; *Educ* Eton; *m* 28 April 1953, (Winifred) Anne, da of Sir Arthur Colegate, MP (d 1956); 2 s (Hen ry Robert b 1958, Richard Arthur b 1960); *Career* Major Welsh Gds 1945, ret 1960; *Books* Nunney Church; *Recreations* beagling; *Clubs* Boodle's, Cavalry and Guards'; *Style*— Maj The Hon Robert Pomeroy; Rockfield House, Nunney, nr Frome, Somerset (☎ (037 384) 208)

POMEROY, Hon Rosamond Mary; da of 8 Viscount Harberton, OBE (d 1956); *b* 29 Feb 1916; *Career* served WWII 1944-45 with ATS; *Clubs* Sailing; *Style*— The Hon Rosamond Pomeroy; 38 Thurloe Sq, SW7; The Cottage in the Lane, Swaines Lane, Bembridge, IOW

POND, Lady Margaret Helen; *née* Jordan; da of Louis Arnold Jordan, CBE, of Surbiton; *m* 1945, Sir Desmond Arthur Pond (d 1986); 3 da; *Style*— Lady Pond; Welcombe, Bridford, Exeter, Devon EX6 7JA (☎ (0647) 52645)

PONSONBY, Arthur Mountifort Longfield; s of late Maj the Hon Cyril Myles Brabazon Ponsonby, MVO, Grenadier Gds (ka 1915, 2 s of 8 Earl of Bessborough) and his 1 w, Rita Narcissa (d 1977), da of late Lt-Col Mountifort John Courtenay Longfield (to all titles except UK Earldom) of 10 Earl of Bessborough; *b* 11 Dec 1912; *Educ* Harrow, Trinity Coll Cambridge; *m* 1, 1939, Patricia (d 1952), da of Col Fitzhugh Lee Minnigerode, of Virginia, USA; 1 s (Myles), 1 da (Sarah); m 2, 1956 (m dis 1963), Princess Anne Marie Galitzine, da of late Lt-Gen Sir Rudolf Carl Slatin (Baron von Slatin), GCVO, KCMG, CB; m 3, 1963, Madeleine Lola Margaret, da of Maj-Gen Laurence Douglas Grand, CB, CIE, CBE; 2 s (Matthew, Charles); *Career* served Welsh Gds 1940-46, Capt; company dir, ret; *Clubs* White's; *Style*— Arthur Ponsonby, Esq; Roche Court, Winterslow, Salisbury, Wilts (☎ 0980 862204)

PONSONBY, Sir Ashley Charles Gibbs; 2 Bt (UK 1956), of Wootton, Co Oxford; MC (1945); s of Col Sir Charles Edward Ponsonby, 1 Bt, TD, DL (d 1976), and Hon Winifred Gibbs, da of 1 Baron Hunsdon (d 1935); *b* 21 Feb 1921; *Educ* Eton, Balliol Coll Oxford; *m* 14 Sept 1950, Lady Martha, *qv*, *née* Butler, da of 6 Marquess of Ormonde, CVO, MC (d 1971); 4 s; *Heir* s, Charles Ashley Ponsonby b 10 June 1951; *Career* Schroder Wagg & Co Ltd (dir 1962-80); chm Colville Estate Ltd; dir: Equitable Life Assur Soc 1980-86, Rowntree Mackintosh Ltd 1974-86, Schroder Global Tst plc 1963- (chm 1964-87); memb Cncl Duchy of Lancaster 1979-; Lord-Lieut of Oxfordshire 1980-; *Clubs* Pratt's; *Style*— Sir Ashley Ponsonby, Bt, MC; Woodleys, Woodstock, Oxon (☎ 0993 811422); 120 Cheapside, London EC2V 6DS (☎ 01 382 6000)

PONSONBY, Hon Carolyn Mary; da of late 2 Baron Sysonby, DSO; *b* 1938; *Style*— The Hon Carolyn Ponsonby

PONSONBY, Charles Ashley; s and h of Sir Ashley Charles Gibbs Ponsonby, 2 Bt, MC, of Woodleys, Woodstock, Oxford, and Lady Martha Ponsonby, yr da of 6 Marquess of Ormonde; *b* 10 June 1951; *Educ* Eton, Christ Church Oxford (MA); *m* 1983, Mary Priscilla, yr da of Arthur Bromley Davenport (d 1982); 2 s (Arthur Ashley b 1984, Frederick Edward b 1986), 1 da (Alice Elizabeth b 1988); *Heir* s, Arthur Ashley Ponsonby; *Career* CA: Deloitte

Haskins & Sells 1973-77, Price Waterhouse 1977-79, Kleinwort Benson 1980-87, Barclays de Zoete Wedd 1987-; chm (non exec) S Dist Estates Ltd 1985-; FCA; *Clubs* Pratt's, Beefsteak; *Style*— Charles Ponsonby, Esq; 59 Lillieshall Rd, London SW4 0LW (☎ 01 622 5303); Barclays de Zoete Wedd Ltd, Ebbgate House, 2 Swan Lane, London EC4R 3TS (☎ 01 623 2323; Fax 01 895 1523; Telex 923141)

PONSONBY, Hon Mrs Bertie B; Constance Evelyn; da of late Rev Horace Rollo Meyer, Hon Canon of St Albans, and Arabella (d 1960), da of John Hamilton Ward (who was ggs of 1 Viscount Bangor); *b* 17 Nov 1907; *m* 1933, Hon Bertie Brabazon Ponsonby (d 1967), s of late 8 Earl of Bessborough, KP, CB, CVO; *Career* vice-pres SSAFA (Herts); *Style*— The Hon Mrs Bertie Ponsonby; 44 Hallmores, St Catharine's Rd, Broxbourne, Herts (☎ 0992 465676)

PONSONBY, Hon Frederick Matthew Thomas; s and h of 3 Baron Ponsonby of Shulbrede; *b* 27 Oct 1958; *Educ* Holland Park Sch, Cardiff Univ; *Style*— The Hon Frederick Ponsonby; 95 Elgin Cres, London W11

PONSONBY, Hon Julia Mary; eldest da of 3 Baron Ponsonby of Shulbrede; *b* 8 May 1960; *Style*— The Hon Julia Ponsonby

PONSONBY, Hon Laura Mary; da of 2 Baron Ponsonby of Shulbrede (d 1976); *b* 1935; *Educ* Langford Grove, Guildhall Sch of Music (AGSM); *Career* guide lectr Royal Botanic Gdns Kew; pres Haslemere Natural History Soc 1983-, vice pres Haslemere Recorded Music Soc 1986-; hon botanist Haslemere Educnl Museum; *Books* A List of Flowering Plants and Ferns of Haslemere and District (1978); *Recreations* music, gardening, natural history; *Style*— The Hon Laura Ponsonby; 17 South End, Kensington Sq, London W8

PONSONBY, Lady Martha; *née* Butler; da of 6 Marquess of Ormonde, CVO, MC (d 1971), and Jessie Carlos (d 1969), da of late Charles Carlos Clarke, of Sunninghill, Berks; *b* 14 Jan 1926; *m* 1950, Capt Sir Ashley Charles Gibbs Ponsonby, 2 Bt, MC, *qv*; *Style*— Lady Martha Ponsonby; Woodleys, Woodstock, Oxon

PONSONBY, Myles Walter; CBE (1966); s of Victor Coope Ponsonby, MC (d 1966), of Tackley, nr Oxford, and Gladys Edith, *née* Walter, ggda of John Walter, fndr The Times; *b* 12 Sept 1924; *Educ* St Aubyn's Rottingdean, Eton; *m* 20 May 1950, Anne Veronica Theresa, da of Brig Francis Herbert Maynard, CB, DSO, MC (d 1979), of London; 1 s (Sqdn-Ldr John Ponsonby b 1955), 2 da (Belinda (Mrs Mitchell) b 1951, Emma (Mrs Parry) b 1959); *Career* cmmnd KRRC 1943; active serv: Normandy 1944 (wounded), Tripolitania 1945-46, Palestine 1946-47, GHQ M East (Canal Zone) 1947-49; HMFO (later HM Dip Serv) 1951-80; served in: Egypt, Cyprus, Beirut, Indonesia, Kenya, N Vietnam (consul-gen), Rome, Mongolia (HM ambass); hon sec Sailsbury branch RUKBA; memb advsy cncl for CARE Br, chm Salisbury branch CRUSE Bereavement Care, cncllr Wilts CC 1988; *Style*— Myles Ponsonby, Esq, CBE; The Old Vicarage, Porton, nr Salisbury, Wilts SP4 0LH

PONSONBY, Hon Rachael Elizabeth Emma; da of 3 Baron Ponsonby of Shulbrede; *b* 25 June 1964; *Style*— The Hon Rachael Ponsonby

PONSONBY, Robert Noel; CBE (1985); s of Noel Edward Ponsonby (d 1928), and Mary Adela White-Thomson; *b* 19 Dec 1926; *Educ* Eton, Trinity Coll Oxford (MA); *Career* Glyndebourne 1951-55, dir Edinburgh Festival 1955-60; gen mangr Scottish Nat Orchestra 1964-72, controller music BBC 1972-85; artistic dir Canterbury Festival 1986-88; *Recreations* walking, bird watching, photography, music; *Clubs* Oriental; *Style*— Robert Ponsonby, Esq, CBE; Flat 4, 11 St Cuthbert's Rd, London NW2 3QJ (☎ 01 452 1715)

PONSONBY, Hon Thomas Maurice; TD, DL (Glos); s of 5 Baron de Mauley; hp to bro, 6 Baron; *b* 2 August 1930; *Educ* Eton; *m* 1956, Maxine Henrietta, da of late William Dudley Keith Thellusson; 2 s; *Career* Lt-Col The Royal Wessex Yeo 1970-72, Brevet Col TA 1972-; High Sheriff of Glos 1978; *Style*— The Hon Thomas Ponsonby, TD, DL; The Common, Little Faringdon, Lechlade, Glos

PONSONBY OF SHULBREDE, 3 Baron (UK 1930); Thomas Arthur Ponsonby; s of 2 Baron Ponsonby of Shulbrede (d 1976, whose f, the 1 Baron, was (i) bro of 1 Baron Sysonby, (ii) gn on his f's side to 1 Baron de Mauley, (iii) paternally ggs of 3 Earl of Bessborough and 3 Earl Bathurst, and (iv) maternally ggs of 2 Earl Grey, by his wife Mary Elizabeth, da of 1 Baron Ponsonby) by his wife Hon Elizabeth Bigham (d 1985), da of 2 Visc Mersey, CMG, CBE, PC (d 1956); *b* 23 Oct 1930; *Educ* St Ronan's Sch, Bryanston, Hertford Coll Oxford; *m* 1, 1956 (m dis 1973), Ursula Mary, da of Cdr Thomas Stanley Lane Fox-Pitt, OBE, RN; 1 s, 3 da (1 decd); m 2, 1973, Maureen Estelle Campbell-Tiech, da of Alfred William Windsor; *Heir* s, Hon Frederick Matthew Thomas Ponsonby; *Career* sits as Lab Peer in House of Lords; cllr 1956-65, alderman 1964-74, Royal Borough of Kensington and Chelsea, ldr Labour Gp 1968-73, alderman GLC 1970-77; chm of Council 1976-77; oppn ch whip (Lords) 1982- (previously dep chief whip); chm: London Tourist Bd 1976-80 (vice-pres 1986-), London Convention Bureau 1977-85, bd of tstees Community Projects Fndn 1978-82; Lord Chllrs Advsy Ctee on JPs for Inner London 1987-, memb Football Pools Panel 1987-, gen sec Fabian Soc 1964-76, pres Galleon World Travel Assoc Ltd 1977-80, govr LSE 1970-, pres Tourism Soc 1984- (chm 1980-83) contested (Lab) Heston and Isleworth, gen election 1959; *Style*— The Rt Hon the Lord Ponsonby of Shulbrede; 261 Kennington Rd, London SE11 6BY (☎ 01 582 0377)

PONTE, Lady Jennifer Jane; *née* Curzon; da of 6 Earl Howe, CBE; *b* 1941; *m* 1962, Alan Joseph Ponté; 4 s, 1 da; *Style*— Lady Jennifer Ponté; Ardeley Bury, nr Stevenage, Herts

PONTEFRACT, Bishop of 1971-; Rt Rev (Thomas) Richard Hare; *b* 29 August 1922; *Educ* Marlborough, Trinity Coll Oxford, Westcott House Cambridge; *m* 1963, Sara, da of Lt Col J E Spedding, OBE, (d 1969), of Keswick; 1 s (William), 2 da (Rosamund, Alice); *Career* RAF 1942-45; curate Haltwhistle 1950-52, domestic chaplain to Bishop of Manchester 1952-59, canon residentiary Carlisle Cathedral 1959-65, archdeacon of Westmorland and Furness 1965-71; vicar: St George with St Luke Barrow in Furness 1965-69, Winster 1969-71; *Style*— The Rt Rev the Bishop of Pontefract; 306 Barnsley Road, Wakefield WF2 6AX

PONTIFEX, Brig David More; CBE (1977, OBE 1965, MBE 1956); s of Cdr John Weddall Pontifex, (d 1977), of Cloudes Lodge, Lilliput, Poole, Dorset, and Monica Melangell Rosewall, *née* Matthews (d 1970); *b* 16 Sept 1922; *Educ* Downside Sch; *m* 6 Aug 1968, Kathleen Betsy (Kate), da of Maxwell Heron Matheson (d 1978), of Widelands, Waldringfield, Woodbridge, Suffolk; 1 s (John b 1975), 4 da (Catherine b 1969, Emily b 1971, Louise b 1973, Rosalind b 1975); *Career* cmmnd Rifle Bde 1942, Lt then Capt 10 and 2 Bn Italy 1944-45 (despatches 1945), Capt adjt 2 Bn BAOR 1946-48, Capt instr Eaton Hall OCS 1948-50, Staff Coll Camberley 1951, Maj DAA and QMG 16 Ind Para Bde Gp Egypt 1952-54, WO (MO 4) 1956-58, Armed Forces Staff Coll Norfolk Virginia 1958-59, 1 Bn BAOR 1959-61, Bde Maj 63 Gurkha Bde Gp Malaya 1961-62, Lt-Col 1 Bn Fed Regular Army Aden 1962-64, GSO1 2 Div BAOR 1965-67, Col GS Staff Coll Camberley 1967-69, Brig the Light Div Winchester 1969-73, DSD Army 1973-75, Dep Cdr and COS SE Dist Aldershot 1975-77; ADC to HM The Queen 1975-77, gen sec ACF Assoc, sec CCF Assoc, ed The Cadet Journal 1977-87; govr Farnborough 6 Form Coll 1977-81; *Recreations* travel, history; *Clubs* Naval and Military; *Style*— Brig David Pontifex, CBE; 68 Shortheath Rd, Farnham, Surrey (☎ 0252 723 284)

PONTIN, Sir Fred - Frederick William (Fred); *b* 24 Oct 1906; *Educ* Sir George Monoux GS Walthamstow; *m* Dorothy Beatrice Mortimer; 1 da; *Career* work in catering and welfare for Admty WWII; Pontins Ltd: 1946 (chm and jt md 1946-79) hon pres 1987; Pontinental Ltd 1963 1972-79); exec dir Belhaven Brewery to Dec 1981; dep chm Kunick Leisure Gp plc 1985-87 (chm 1983-85); memb: Variety Club of GB chief barker 1968, Grand Order of Water Rats; first pres Hotel and Catering Benevolent Assoc 1979; Lloyd's underwriter; memb IOD; kt 1976; *Clubs* Eccentric, Farmers Club; *Style*— Sir Fred Pontin; Flat 64, 3 Whitehall Court, London SW1A 2EL (☎ 01 839 5251); work: 92-94 Tooley Street, London SE1 2TH (☎ 01 403 7314)

POOLE, Hon Mrs (Anne Rosemary Dorothea); da of 1 Baron Croft, CMG, TD, PC (d 1947), and Hon Nancy, da of 1 Baron Borwick; *b* 2 April 1918; *Educ* private; *m* 1946, Flt Lt (Herbert) Edmund Poole, RAF (d 1984), s of Herbert Poole (d 1966), of Norwich; 3 s; *Career* nursing 1939-46; social work 1966-83; *Style*— The Hon Mrs Poole; Knight's Hill, Sawbridgeworth, Herts (☎ 0279 723146)

POOLE, David Anthony; QC (1984); s of William Joseph Poole (d 1956), and Lena Thomas; *b* 8 June 1938; *Educ* Ampleforth, Jesus Coll Oxford (MA), Univ of Manchester (Dip Tech Sc); *m* 1974, Pauline, da of James O'Flaherty; 4 s (William, Alexander, Gareth, Simon); *Career* barr; recorder 1982, chm Assoc of Lawyers for the Def of the Unborn, govr St Bede's Coll Manchester; *Recreations* reading, walking, watching rugby; *Clubs* Vincents, London Irish, Northern Lawn Tennis, Heaton Mersey CC; *Style*— David Poole, Esq, QC; 1 Priestnall Rd, Stockport, Cheshire SK4 3HR; 1 Deans Ct, Crown Sq, Manchester 3; 1 Crown Office Row, Temple, London EC4Y 7HH

POOLE, Hon David Charles; s and h of 1 Baron Poole, CBE, TD, PC; *b* 6 Jan 1945; *Educ* Gordonstoun, Ch Ch Oxford, Insead Fontainebleau; *m* 1, 21 Sept 1967, Fiona, da of John Donald; 1 s (Oliver John); m 2, 1975, Philippa, da of late Mark Reeve; *Career* memb Stock Exchange; *Clubs* Brooks's, Buck's, Royal Yacht Squadron, Groucho's; *Style*— The Hon David Poole; Rectory Farm, East Woodhay, nr Newbury, Berks (☎ 0635 253923); Invest International Holdings SA, 31 Grande Rue, Luxembourg

POOLE, David James; s of Thomas Herbert Poole (d 1978), and Catherine, *née* Lord (d 1980); *b* 5 June 1931; *Educ* RCA; *m* 5 April 1958, Iris Mary, da of Francis Thomas Toomer (d 1968); 3 s (Edward b 1959, Vincent b 1960, Bruce b 1964); *Career* served RE 1949-51; sr lectr of painting and drawing, Wimbledon Sch of Art 1961-77; portraits incl: HM The Queen, HRH Prince Philip, HM Queen Elizabeth the Queen Mother, HRH the Princess Royal, HRH Prince Charles, HRH Prince Andrew, HRH Prince Edward, Lord Mountbatten, distinguished membs of govt, HM Forces, industry, commerce, med, the academic and legal professions; featured in BBC TV series Portrait 1976; cmmnd by the City of London Corp to paint the Official Portrait Gp of the Royal Family to commemorate Her Majesty Queen Elizabeth II's Silver Jubilee Luncheon; one man exhibition: London 1978, Zürich 1980; featured in magazine 'Frankfurter Allgemeine' W Germany 1986; work in private collections: Her Majesty The Queen, Aust, Bermuda, Canada, France, W Germany, Italy, S Africa, Saudia Arabia, Switzerland, USA; ARCA 1954; RP (pres 1983); *Recreations* travel, being in the country; *Style*— David J Poole, Esq; The Granary, Oxton Barns, Kenton, Exeter, Devon EX6 8EX (☎ 0626 891611); Studio 6, Burlington Lodge, Rigault Rd, Fulham, London SW6 4JJ (☎ 01 736 9288)

POOLE, Henry Michael (Francis); s of Charles Frederick John Kaitting Poole (d 1976), of Mixtow House, Lanteglos-By-Fowey, Cornwall and Stella Mary Grant *née* Morris; *b* 23 Sept 1949; *Educ* Summer Fields Oxford, Eton Coll Windsor, Trinity Hall, Cambridge (MA); *m* 20 Sept 1975, Diana Mary Olga, da of Eric Arthur Parker; 1 s (Henry b 1983), 2 da (Lucy b 1978, Antonia b 1980); *Career* joined Laing & Cruickshank 1971 (ptnr 1979), dir cl Alexanders Institutional Equities 1987, non-exec dir Rockware Gp 1986-87; *Books* European Paper directory (1988); *Recreations* bridge, mountain walking, history; *Style*— Henry Poole, Esq; CL Alexanders Laing Cruickshank, Piercy House, Coptuall Ave, London EC2R 7BE, (☎ 01 588 2800)

POOLE, Sheriff Isobel Anne; da of John Cecil Findlay Poole, DM (Oxon) (d 1985), and Constance Mary, *née* Gilkes; *b* 9 Dec 1941; *Educ* Oxford HS for Girls, Edinburgh Univ (LLB); *Career* advocate 1964, former standing jr cncl to the Registrar Gen for Scotland; Sheriff of: the Lothian and Borders 1979-, at Edinburgh 1986, memb Sheriffs' Cncl 1980-85; *Recreations* country, the arts, house, gardens, friends; *Clubs* Scottish Arts; *Style*— Sheriff Isobel Poole

POOLE, Hon Mrs; Hon Jean; *née* Bruce; da of late 7 Lord Balfour of Burleigh; *b* 1924; *m* 1, 1949 (m dis 1971), John Shirley Ward; 1 s, 2 da; m 2, 1974, John Herbert Poole; *Style*— The Hon Mrs Poole; 1030 South El Molino Ave, Pasadena, Calif 91106, USA (☎ 213 796 4905)

POOLE, Michael John Ruscombe; s of John Chichester Poole, MC, CBE (d 1968); *b* 15 Mar 1930; *Educ* Downside; *m* 1959, Pamela Nicola, da of Evan Jones (d 1967); 2 c; *Career* dir: Hawkes Wills Ltd, F J Hawkes and Co (NZ) Ltd; *Recreations* tennis, gardening; *Style*— Michael Poole Esq; 1 Park Barn, Ditcham Park, Petersfield, Hants GU31 SRL (☎ Harting 437)

POOLE, 1 Baron (UK 1958); Oliver Brian Sanderson Poole; CBE (1945), TD (1945), PC (1963); s of late Donald Louis Poole, whose family connections with Lloyd's stretch back two centuries to when Henry Poole (d c 1793) did business at Lloyd's Coffee House; *b* 11 August 1911; *Educ* Eton, Ch Ch Oxford; *m* 1, 1933 (m dis 1951), Betty Margaret, da of Capt Dugald Gilkison and Janet, *née* Harcourt Vernon (ggggda of 1 Baron Vernon); 1 s, 3 da; m 2, 1952 (m dis 1965), Daphne Wilma Kenyon, da of late Eustace Bowles (himself gs of 6 Earl of Macclesfield), and formerly w of Brig Algernon Heber Percy, DSO; m 3, 1966, Barbara Ann, da of E A Taylor; *Heir* s Hon David Charles Poole; *Career* Warwicks Yeo 1934, MP (C) Oswestry Div of Salop 1945-50; chm Cons Pty Orgn 1955-57 (vice-chm 1963-64); memb of Lloyd's, formerly dir S Pearson & Son Ltd, Hon DSc City Univ 1970; *Style*— The Rt Hon The Lord Poole, CBE, TD; 24 Campden Hill Gate, Duchess of Bedford's Walk, W8 (☎ 01 937 6466)

POOLE-WILSON, Denis Smith; CBE (1969); s of Alexander Poole Wilson, MBE (d 1934), and Jessie Maude, *née* Smith (d 1960); *b* 22 Sept 1904; *Educ* St Andrew's Coll Dublin, Trinity Coll Dublin, Middx Hosp, London Hosp (BA), Dublin (MB, Bch, BAO); *m* 14 Oct 1939, Monique Michell, da of Charles Philip Goss (d 1959), of The Home Farm, Sunningdale, Berks; 2 s (Peter Nicholas b 1941, Philip Alexander b 1943); *Career* Lt-Col RAMC 1939-45, N Africa and Italy; conslt urological surgn Royal Manchester Children's Hosp 1935-69, Salford Royal Hosp 1935-69, Christie Hosp and Holt Radium Inst 1946-69, N Manchester Gen Hosp 1939-69; lectr in urology Univ of Manchester 1951-69; Hunterian prof RCS 1946; fell RSM (pres section of urology 1959-60); fndn and hon memb The Br Assoc of Urological Surgns (pres 1965-67); St Peter's Medal for notable contribs to urology 1971; Int Soc Urology 1947-69; hon memb Manchester Med Soc 1934- (pres 1967-68); fndr memb The Urological Club 1946-; FRCS (Eng) 1931, FRCS (I) 1931; *Recreations* gardening, fishing, reading; *Style*— Denis Poole-Wilson, CBE; Cockspur Thorns, Berwick St James, Salisbury, Wilts SP3 4TS (☎ 0722 790445)

POOLE-WILSON, Prof Philip Alexander; s of Denis Smith Poole-Wilson, CBE, and Monique Michelle Poole-Wilson (d 1985); *b* 26 April 1943; *Educ* Marlborough, Trinity Coll Cambridge (MA), St Thomas's Med Sch (MB, BChir, MD); *m* 25 Oct 1969, Mary Elizabeth, da of Dr William Horrocks Tattersall; 2 s (William, Michael), 1 da (Oenone); *Career* prof cardiology Cardiothoracic Inst (re named Nat Heart and Lung Inst) 1984-(sr lectr and reader 1976-84, vice-dean 1981-84), Simon Marks Br Heart Fndn prof cardiology 1988-, hon conslt physician Nat Heart Hosp 1976-; memb: cncl Br Heart Fndn, bd Euro Soc of Cardiology 1988-; visiting prof Charing Cross and Westminster Med Sch 1988-; FRCP 1978; *Recreations* sailing, gardening, countryside, opera; *Style*— Prof Philip Poole-Wilson; 174 Burgbage Rd, London SE21 7AG (☎ 01 274 6742); National Heart and Lung Institute, Dovehouse St, London SW3 6LY (☎ 01 352 8121, fax 01 376 3442)

POOLEY, Dr Derek; s of Richard Pike Pooley (d 1988), of Port Isaac, Cornwall, and Evelyn, *née* Lee (d 1985); *b* 28 Oct 1937; *Educ* Sir James Smiths Sch, Camelford; Univ of Birmingham (BSc, PhD); *m* 1961, Jennifer Mary, da of William Arthur Charles Davey (d 1980), of Birmingham; 2 s (Michael Bruce b 1967, Benjamin John b 1969), 1 da (Miriam Jane b 1973); *Career* head materials devpt Div Harwell 1976-81, dir energy res Harwell 1981-83, chief scientist Dept of Energy 1983-86, dir AEE Winfrith 1989 (dep dir 1986-89); *Recreations* photography, walking, gardening; *Style*— Dr Derek Pooley; 19A Park Homer Drive, Wimborne Minster, Dorset BH21 2SR (☎ 0202 841741); Atomic Energy Establishment, Winfrith, Dorchester, Dorset (☎ 0305 251888)

POOLEY, Graham Howard John; s of John Henry William Pooley, of Loughton, Essex, and Joan Margaret, *née* Price (d 1983); *b* 11 Mar 1949; *Educ* Brentwood Sch, Oriel Coll Oxford (MA); *m* 8 May 1971, Moira Helen *qv* da of Roger Francis Lewis (d 1978), of Chadwell Heath; 1 s (Oliver b 1973), 1 da (Laura b 1976); *Career* Nat & Grindlays Bank 1970-73, asst dir Chem Bank Int Ltd 1974-80, head Syndicate and Trading County Bank Ltd 1980-82, exec dir Bank of America Int Ltd 1982-86, dir and head int primary mkts Barclays de Zoete Wedd Ltd 1986-; *Recreations* bridge, croquet, ski-ing, home improvement, music; *Style*— Graham Pooley, Esq; Barnston Old Rectory, nr Gt Dunmow, Essex CM6 3PA (☎ 0371 820 329); Barclays De Zoete Wedd Limited, Ebbgate House, 2 Swan Lane London EC4R 3TS (☎ 01 623 2323)

POOLEY, Moira Helen; *née* Lewis; da of Roger Francis Lewis (d 1978), of Chadwell Heath, Essex, and Kathleen, *née* Kingseller; *b* 17 June 1950; *Educ* Ursuline Convent Brentwood Essex, QMC London (LLB); *m* 8 May 1971, Graham Howard John *qv*, s of John Henry William Pooley, of Loughton, Essex; 1 s (Oliver Edward b 24 March 1973), 1 da (Laura Kathleen May b 10 Nov 1976); *Career* barr Middle Temple 1974; memb local govt and planning bar assocs; vice-chm: Little Baddow Parish Cncl 1981-84, Barnston Parish Cncl 1988-; chm: Social Security Appeal Tbnl 1986-, Nat Insur Tbnl 1986-; *Recreations* poultry keeping, archeology, cookery; *Style*— Mrs Moira Pooley; Barnston Old Rectory, Great Dunmow, Essex CM6 3PA (☎ 0371 820329); Temple Gardens, London EC4Y 9AU (☎ 01 353 0832)

POOLEY, Peter; *b* 1936; *m* 1966, Janet Mary, er da of Jack Pearson, of Banbury; 1 s, 1 da; *Career* agric min Off of UK Perm Rep to Euro Community Brussels 1979-82, fisheries sec Miny of Agric London 1982-83, dep dir-gen (Agric) Euro Cmmn Brussels 1983-; *Style*— Peter Pooley, Esq; Commission of the European Communities, Rue de la Loi 200, B1049, Brussels, Belgium; Dereymaekerlaan 53, 1980 Tervuren, Belgium

POOLEY, Robert John; s of Sydney John Pooley (d 1972), and Hilda Vera, *née* Salmon; *b* 9 Feb 1935; *Educ* Medburn Sch; *m* 1, 24 Feb 1962 (m dis 1973), Yvonne Margaret, da of William Pereiva (d 1976), of Hatfield, Herts; 1 s (Julian David b 26 Feb 1964), 1 da (Katharine Yvonne 12 March 1966); m 2, 5 July 1974, Carolyn, da of Dr J Alfred Lee, of Westcliff, Essex; 1 s (Sebastian Robert John b 3 May 1979), 1 da (Samantha Carolyn Merlyn b 30 July 1974); *Career* RAF SAC 4 Sqdn 1953-57; De Havilland Aircraft Co 1957-61, chm Airtour Int Gp, Airtour Flight Equipment Ltd, Airlife Publishing Ltd, Robert Pooley Ltd, World Expeditions Ltd, Airtour Baloon Co Ltd, ed and publisher Pooley Flight Guides 1961; chm Soc of the St John Opthalmic Hosp Jerusalem, tstee Museum of Army Flying Devpt Tst; vice-pres: Helicopter Club of GB, Guild of Aviation Artists, Br Precision Pilots Assoc; vice-chm Royal Aero Club, tstee Boxmoor Tst, pres 1187 Sqdn ATC, St Johns Ambulance Bde Hemel Hampstead; memb St Johns Cncl for Herts OStJ 1986; Freeman City of London 1971, Liveryman Guild of Air Pilots and Air Navigators 1971 (Master 1987-88); FRIN 1979, FRAS 1981; *Books* Air Touring Flight Guides 1962-1989, Pilots Information Guide 1982 and 1986; *Recreations* flying, ballooning, riding, sub-aqua, skiing; *Clubs* Royal Aero, City Livery; *Style*— Robert Pooley, Esq; Felden Grange, Felden, Herts HP3 0BL (☎ 0442 65764); Airtour International, Elstree Aerodrome Herts WD6 3AW (☎ 01 953 4870/6064, fax 01 953 5219, car telephone 0860 643203)

POORE, Lady; Amelia; da of Senor Santiago Guliemone, of Estancia La Blanca, Estacion Acuna, Corrientes, Argentine Republic; *m* 1922, Sir Edward Poore, 5 Bt (d 1938); *Style*— Lady Poore; Curuzu Cuatia, Corrientes, Argentina

POORE, Dr (Martin Edward) Duncan; s of Thomas Edward Deverell Poore (d 1966), of Coshieville, Aberfeldy, and Elizabeth, *née* MacMartin (d 1965); *b* 25 May 1925; *Educ* Trinity Coll Glenalmond, Clare Coll Cambridge (MA, PhD), Oxford (MA by incorpn); *m* 3 Sept 1948, Judith Ursula (Judy), da of Gen Sir Treffry Thompson KCSI, CBI, (d 1979), of Chulmeigh, N Devon; 2 s (Robin b 1952, Alasdair b 1954); *Career* prof of botany Univ of Malaya 1959-65, dir Nature Conservancy 1966-74, sci dir then dir gen IUCN 1974-78, prof of forest sci and dir Cwlth Forestry Inst Oxford Univ 1980-83, conslt in land use and conservation 1983-, sr fell IIED; Thames Water Authy 1981-84, Nature Conservancy Cncl 1982-84 (chm advsy ctee on sci), chm Cwlth Forestry Assoc 1986-88; FRSA 1974, FRGS 1967; *Recreations* gardening, hill walking, music; *Clubs* Royal Cwlth Soc; *Style*— Dr Duncan Poore; Evenlode, Stonesfield, Oxon (☎ 099 389 246); Balnacarn, Glenmoriston Inverness-shire (☎ 0320 40261)

POORE, Sir Herbert Edward; 6 Bt (GB 1795); s of Sir Edward Poore, 5 Bt (d 1938); *b* 1930, April; *Heir* unc, Nasionceno Poore; *Style*— Sir Herbert Poore, Bt; Curuzu Cuatia, Corrientes, Argentine Republic

POORE, Nasionceno; s of Herbert Poore (d 1905) and bro of 5 Bt (d 1938); hp of n, Sir Herbert Edward Poore, 6 Bt; *b* 1900; *m* Juana Borda (d 1943); 3 s, 3 da; *Style*— Nasionceno Poore Esq

POOT, Anton; *b* 23 Nov 1929; *Educ* High Sch, Holland; *m* 1983, Jesmond, *née* Masters; by former m 1 s (Anton b 1958), 1 da (Marietta b 1954); *Career* worked for: NV Phillips Holland 1946-51, Phillips S Africa and Fedn of Rhodesia and Nyasaland 1951-63, NV Phillips Eindhoven Holland 1963-66; chm and md Phillips E Africa 1967-71, md: Ada (Halifax) Ltd, Phillips Electrical Ltd UK 1971-76; divnl md NV Phillips Holland 1976-78, chm and md: Phillips Appliances Div Holland 1978-83, Phillips Electronics and Assoc Industs Ltd 1984-; FBIM, FRSA; *Recreations* golf, sailing, skiing; *Clubs* Buck's, Wimbledon Park Golf; *Style*— Anton Poot, Esq; Arundel Great Court, 8 Arundel Street, London WC2R 3DT (☎ 01 689 2166, telex 267518, fax 01 379 0992)

POPE, Andrew Lancelot; CMG (1972), CVO (1965), OBE (1959); s of Maj Andrew Noble Pope, OBE (d 1941); *b* 27 July 1912; *Educ* Harrow; *m* 1, 1938 (m dis); m 2, 1948, Ilse, da of late K Pipperger, of Frayn, Austria (d 1988); 1 step da; *Career* cncllr Bonn 1962-72, dir conf bd NY Gerling Global Gen and Reinsur Co Ltd; *Style*— A Lance Pope Esq, CMG, CVO, OBE; Goldhill Grove, Lower Bourne, Farnham, Surrey (☎ 0252 721662)

POPE, Anthony; s of Lt Col Albert Victor Pope (d 1976), and his w, Barbara, *née* Shaw (d 1982); *b* 25 April 1933; *Educ* Melbourne GS Victoria Aust; *m* 1965, Cynthia Margaret, da of Wing-Cdr Alexander Walker (d 1976); 1 s, 1 da; *Career* dir: Eldridge Pope & Co plc 1960-, Hants & Dorset Mineral Water Co Ltd 1977-, Barnham Broom Golf and Country Club 1979-; FHCIMA, FRSH; *Recreations* shooting, farming; *Clubs* Cavalry and Guards; *Style*— Anthony Pope, Esq; Hamlet House, Chetnole, nr Sherborne, Dorset (☎ 0935 872325); Eldridge Pope & Co plc, Dorchester Brewery, Dorchester, Dorset (☎ 0305 251251)

POPE, Dudley Bernard Egerton; s of Sidney Broughton Pope (d 1932), and Alice Egerton, *née* Meehan; *b* 29 Dec 1925; *Educ* Ashford GS; *m* 17 March 1954, Kathleen Patricia, da of Edward Reginald Hall (d 1983); 1 da (Jane Clare Victoria b 17 Feb 1965); *Career* Midshipman MN 1942-43 (wounded invalided); naval corr, sub-ed, dep foreign ed London Evening News 1944-59; naval historian and author 1959-; *Books* non-fiction: Flag 4, the Battle of Coastal Forces in the Mediterranean (1954), The Battle of the River Plate (1956), 73 North (1958), England Expects (1959), At 12 Mr Byng Was Shot (1962), The Black Ship (1963), Guns (1965), The Great Gamble (1972), Harry Morgan's Way (1977), Life in Nelson's Navy (1981), The Devil Himself (1987); fiction: the Ramage series: Ramage (1965), Ramage and the Drum Beat (1967), Ramage and the Freebooters (1969), Governor Ramage, RN (1973), Ramage's Prize (1974), Ramage and the Guillotine (1975), Ramage's Diamond (1976), Ramage's Mutiny (1977), Ramage and the Rebels (1978), The Ramage Touch (1979), Ramage's Signal (1980), Ramage and the Renegades (1981), Ramage's Devil (1982), Ramage's Trial (1984), Ramage's Challenge (1985), Ramage at Trafalgar (1986), Ramage and the Saracens (1988), Ramage and the Dido (1989); The Yorke Series: Convoy (1979), Buccaneer (1981), Admiral (1982), Decoy (1983), Galleon (1986), Corsair (1987); *Recreations* sailing, shell collecting; *Style*— Dudley Pope, Esq; Le Pirate 379, BP 296, 97150 Marigot, St Martin, French West Indies (☎ 590 87 78 37)

POPE, Vice Adm Sir (John) Ernle; KCB (1976); s of Cdr R K C Pope; *b* 22 May 1921; *Educ* RNC Dartmouth; *Career* RN 1935, Capt 1960, Flag Offr Flotillas Western Fleet 1969-71, COS to C-in-C Western Fleet 1971-74, Rear Adm 1969, Vice Adm 1972, COS to Cdr Allied Naval Forces S Europe 1974; *Clubs* Army and Navy; *Style*— Vice Admiral Sir Ernle Pope, KCB; Homme House, Much Marcle, Herefordshire

POPE, Dr Geoffrey George; CB (1986); s of Sir George Reginald Pope (d 1982), and Lady Pope, *qv*; *b* 17 April 1934; *Educ* Epsom Coll, Imperial Coll London (MSc, PhD); *m* 1961, Rosemary Frances Harnden; 2 s; *Career* dep dir (Weapons) Royal Aircraft Estab 1979-81, asst chief scientific advsr (Projects) MOD 1981-82, dep controller and advsr (Res and Technol) MOD 1982-84; dir Royal Aircraft Estab (nom Royal Aerospace Estab) 1984-89; dep chief scientific advsr MOD 1989-; FEng; FRAeS, FCGI; *Recreations* music, photography, walking; *Style*— Dr Geoffrey Pope; Royal Aerospace Establishment, Farnborough, Hants GU14 6TD (☎ Aldershot 24461 Ext 2000)

POPE, Hon Mrs; Hon Jacqueline Dorothy Mametz; *née* Best; yr da of 8 Baron Wynford, MBE, DL; *b* 9 Nov 1946; *Educ* St Mary's Wantage; *m* 7 June 1969, Jeremy James Richard Pope, s of Philip Pope, of Dorchester; 3 s; *Career* social sec to Lady Erskine of Rerrick 1966-68 (wife of former govr of NI); internal and external landscape gardener and horticulturist; *Recreations* gardening, skiing; *Style*— The Hon Mrs Pope; Field Cottage, Compton Abbas West, Maiden Newton, Dorset (☎ 030 02 20469); work: The Winterbourne Hospital, Dorchester, Dorset (☎ 0305 63252)

POPE, Jeremy James Richard; OBE (1985); s of Philip William Rolph Pope, of Dorset, and Joyce Winifred Harcourt, *née* Slade; *b* 15 July 1943; *Educ* Charterhouse, Trinity Coll Cambridge (MA); *m* 1969, Jacqueline Dorothy Mametz, da of Lt Col the Lord Wynford Bt, MBE, DL, of Dorchester; 3 s (Rory b 1970, Rupert b 1973, Toby b 1977); *Career* slr 1969-; dir: Eldridge Pope & Co plc 1969- (md 1988, dep chm 1987-), Winterbourne Hosp plc 1981- (fndr chm), JB Reynier Ltd 1984-; memb exec ctee Brewers' Soc 1977-88, memb Dept of Trade Advsy Panel on Co Law 1980-81, chm Smaller Firms' Cncl CBI 1981-84, memb NEDC 1981-85, govr Forres Sch Swanage 1983-; memb: Royal Cmmn on Environmental Pollution 1984-, exec ctee Food and Drinks Fedn (dep-pres 1987-), Top Salary Review Body 1986-; memb Law Soc, FRSA 1989; *Recreations* gardening, field sports, cooking; *Style*— Jeremy Pope, Esq, OBE; Field Cottage, West Compton, nr Dorchester, Dorset DT2 0EY; Eldridge, Pope & Co plc, The Dorchester Brewery, PO Box 2, Dorchester, Dorset DT1 1QT (☎ 0305 251251)

POPE, Air Vice-Marshal John Clifford; CB (1963), CBE (1959); s of George Newcombe Pope (d 1938), and Lora Newcombe-Pope (d 1976); *b* 27 April 1912; *Educ* Tiverton Sch, RAF Coll Cranwell, RAF Tech Coll; *m* 1950, Christine Agnes (d 1982), da of Alfred Hames; 1 s, 2 da; *Career* cmmnd RAF 1932, served No 3 (Fighter) Sqdn, Nos 27 and 39 (Bomber) Sqdns NW Frontier 1933-36, Middle E 1943-47, sr tech staff offr No 3 Gp Bomber Cmd 1957-59 and Flying Trg Cmd 1960-61, Gp Capt 1956, Air Cdre 1961, AOC and Cmdt RAF Tech Coll Henlow 1961-63, sr tech staff offr Tport Cmd 1963-66, Air Vice-Marshal 1964; life vice-pres RAF Boxing Assoc; CEng, FIMechE; *Recreations* scale model steam engrg; *Clubs* RAF; *Style*— Air Vice-Marshal John Pope, CB, CBE; Dilston, 47 Oxford Rd, Stone, nr Aylesbury, Bucks (☎ 0296 748467)

POPE, Sir Joseph Albert; s of Albert Henry Pope and Mary Pope; *b* 18 Oct 1914; *Educ* Sch of Arts and Crafts Cambridge, King's Coll London; *m* 1940, Evelyn Alice, da of Rev Robert Henry Gallagher; 1 s, 2 da; *Career* Whitworth Scholarship 1935, prof of mechanical engrg Nottingham Univ 1949-60, vice-chllr Univ of Aston in Birmingham 1969-79, chm TecQuipment Gp Nottingham 1975-88; dir John Brown plc 1970-82, gen tres Br Assoc 1975-82, chm W Midlands Econ Planning Cnl 1977-79, dir Royal Worcester plc 1979-84; Hon LLD Birmingham Univ 1979, Hon DUniv Heriot-Watt 1979; Hon DSc: Aston 1979, Belfast 1980, Salford 1980, Nottingham 1987; FBIM, CEng, FIMechE; kt 1980; *Style*— Sir Joseph Pope; 3 Mapperley Hall Drive, Nottingham NG3 5EP (☎ 0602 621146); TecQuipment Ltd, Bonsall St, Long Eaton, Nottingham NG10 2AN (☎ 0602 722611, telex

377 828)

POPE, Michael Henry Burges; s of Maj John Edward Buckingham Pope (d 1978), and Elizabeth Burges, *née* Watson; *b* 28 June 1940; *Educ* Aiglon Coll Switzerland; *m* 1, 6 Feb 1969, Edwina Elizabeth, da of Maj John Francis Yates, of Codsall Wood, nr Wolverhampton; 2 s (Henry b 1972, Charles b 1973); 2, 17 Aug 1982, Jane Philippa, da of George Raikes, of The Ark, Coleman's Hatch, nr E Grinstead, Sussex; *Career* sales dir Golf-o-Tron UK Ltd 1964-66; mktg field promotions: md FPS Field Mktg 1977-87, conslt Ulysses Gp 1972-77, chm Swiftwash Ltd 1962-87; memb of Lloyds (1973); team mangr Br World Gliding Team 1983; MInstM; *Recreations* gliding, skiing (Ski Club of GB golf, Kandahar gold); *Clubs* Lansdown, Ski of GB, Avon Gliding; *Style—* Michael Pope, Esq; 123 Woodsford Square, Addison Road, London W14 8DT (☎ 01 603 8769; FPS Field Marketing, 261 Goldhawk Road, London W12 8EU (☎ 01 741 2194, telex 934031, fax 01 846 9253)

POPE, Philip William Rolph; s of Alfred Rolph Pope (d 1951), of Dorchester, and Kate Rendall (d 1967); *b* 19 Mar 1907; *Educ* Charterhouse Trinity (Cantab BA); *m* 1939, Joyce Winifred, James Harcourt Slade (d 1962); 1 s (Jeremy James Richard b 1943), 2 da (Philippa Rachel b 1940, Nicola Jane b 1948); *Career* actg Capt RA 1939 1946, Capt (acting), ADGB England, Main HQ BAOR Belgium and Germany; slr 1931; Eldridge Pope & Co plc: dir 1931, md 1951, chm 1974, pres 1982; dir Co of Proprietors Weymouth Waterworks; chm Weymouth Waterworks until taken over by Water Bd; cmmr for taxes Dorchester; chm Weymouth Div; *Clubs* ESJ; *Style—* Philip Pope, Esq; The Garden House, Tenantrees, West Stafford, Dorchester, Dorset DT2 8AW (☎ 0305 62811); The Brewery, Dorchester (☎ 251251)

POPE, Very Rev Robert William; OBE (1970); s of Jonas George Pope (d 1970), and Marjorie Mary, *née* Coates (d 1978); *b* 20 May 1916; *Educ* Harvey GS Folkestone, Maidstone GS, St Augustine Coll Canterbury, Durham Univ (LTh); *m* 12 Aug 1941, Elizabeth Beatrice Matilda, da of Robert James Bressey; 2 s (David Robert b 1942, Patrick John b 1943), 1 da (Hilary Mary Elizabeth b 1948); *Career* curate: Holy Trinity Gravesend 1939-41, St Nicholas Guildford 1942-43, Peaslake Parish of Shere 1943-44; chaplain RN 1944-71, HMS Chinkara 1944-46, HMS Daedalus 1946-47, RM Barracks Chatham 1947-50, HMS Gambia 1950-52, RM Commando 1955-57, RM Barracks ITC Lympstone 1957-59, HMS Tiger 1959-60, HMS Sultan 1960-63, HMS Phoenecia 1963-65, HMS Dockyard Chatham 1965-67, RM Barracks Eastney 1967-69, HM Dockyard Portsmouth 1969-71; ordained Rochester Cath: deacon 1939, priest 1940; vicar Whitchurch Hants 1971-77, dean of Gibraltar 1977-82; memb Third Order Soc of St Francis 1963 (minister provincial Euro Province 1985-, minister gen 1987-); *Style—* The Very Rev Robert Pope, OBE; West Wood, Wreath Green, Tatworth, Chard, Somerset TA20 2SN (☎ 0460 209 87)

POPE, Lady; Susie Annie; *née* Hendy; da of John O Hendy, of Clapham; *b* 26 August 1895; *m* 1930, Sir George Pope (d 1982, sometime gen mangr Times Newspapers); 1 s (Geoffrey, *qv*); *Style—* Lady Pope; Furze Hill Lodge, Kingswood, Surrey KT20 6EP (☎ 07373 56827)

POPE-HENNESSY, Sir John Wyndham; CBE (1959, MBE 1944); s of Maj-Gen Ladislaus Herbert Richard Pope-Hennessy, CB, DSO (d 1942), and late Dame Una Pope-Hennessy, DBE; *b* 13 Dec 1913; *Educ* Downside, Balliol Coll Oxford; *Career* dir and sec V and A Museum 1967-73, dir Br Museum 1974-76, consultative chm Dept of Euro Paintings Metropolitan Museum New York 1977-86, prof of fine arts New York Univ 1977-; FBA, FSA, FRSL; kt 1971; *Style—* Sir John Pope-Hennessy, CBE; 28 via de' Bardi, 50125 Florence, Italy

POPHAM, Maj-Gen Christopher John; CB (1982); s of Gordon F B Popham (d 1949), and Dorothy A L, *née* Yull; *b* 2 April 1927; *Educ* Merchant Taylors'; *m* 1950, Heather Margaret, da of Lt-Col H Reginald W Dawson (d 1937); 2 s; *Career* asst COS (Intelligence) Supreme HQ Allied Powers Europe 1979-82, ret 1982; Col Cmdt Corps of RE 1982-87; dir Br Atlantic Ctee 1982-; *Recreations* photography, railways, music; *Style—* Maj-Gen Christopher Popham, CB; c/o Barclays Bank plc, High St, Andover, Hants

POPPER, Prof Sir Karl Raimund; CH (1982); s of Dr Simon Siegmund Carl Popper, of Vienna, and Jenny, *née* Schiff; *b* 28 July 1902; *Educ* Vienna Univ (PhD); *m* 1930, Josefine Anna, da of Josef Henninger (d 1985), of Vienna; *Career* prof of logic and scientific method LSE 1949-69, emeritus prof 1969-; memb Acad Int de Philosophie des Sciences 1949, hon memb Royal Soc of NZ 1965, foreign hon memb American Acad of Arts and Sciences 1966, assoc memb Académie Royale de Belgique 1976, memb d'Honneur Académie Int d'Histoire des Sciences 1977, hon memb Deutsche Akademie für Sprache and Dichtung 1979, memb de l'Académie Europëene des Sciences 1980, hon fell Darwin Coll Cambridge, memb de l'Institut de France 1980, Socio Straniero dell'Accademia Nazionale dei Lincei 1981, hon memb Austrian Akademie der Wissenschaften 1982; Foreign Associate of the Nat Acad of Sciences, Washington; sr res fell of the Hoover Inst Stamford Univ; Hon LittD Cantab 1980, Hon DLitt Oxon 1982 and many other hon degrees from British, NZ, US, Canadian, Austrian and German Univs; Grand Decoration of Honour in Gold (Austria) 1976, Ehrenzeichen für Wissenschaft & Kunst (Austria) 1980, Order Pour le Mérite (W Germany) 1980, Grand Cross with Star of the Order of Merit (W Germany) 1983; FBA, FRS; *Publications incl*: The Logic of Scientific Discovery, The Open Society and Its Enemies, Conjectures and Refutations, Objective Knowledge, Unended Quest, The Self and Its Brain (with Sir John Eccles), Postcript to the Logic of Scientific Discovery (3 vols, ed W W Bartley III); *Style—* Prof Sir Karl Popper, CH; c/o London School of Economics and Political Science, Houghton St, London WC2A 2AE

POPPLEWELL, Hon John Arnold; s of Baron Popplewell (Life Peer) (d 1977); *b* 1928; *m* 1951; *Style—* The Hon John Popplewell

POPPLEWELL, Hon Mr Justice; Hon Sir Oliver Bury Popplewell; s of Frank Popplewell, OBE (d 1965), and Nina Sydney (d 1979); *b* 15 August 1927; *Educ* Charterhouse, Queens' Coll Cambridge Univ (MA, LLB); *m* 1954, Catharine Margaret, da of Alfred John Storey (d 1941); 4 s (and 1 s decd); *Career* serv RN 1946-48; barr Inner Temple 1951, QC 1969, dep chm Oxon QS 1970-71; rec: Burton-on-Trent 1970-71, Crown Court 1972-83, bencher Inner Temple 1978, High Court Judge (Queen's Bench) 1983-; memb of Home Office Advsy Bd on Restricted Patients 1980-82, chm and independent memb Wages Cncls, memb of Parole Bd 1985, vice-chm of Parole Bd 1986-1987, pres Employment Appeal Tbnl 1986-88, chm Ctee of Inquiry into Crowd Control Safety and Control at Sports Grounds 1985; kt 1983; *Recreations* sailing, tennis, bridge; *Clubs* MCC (ctee memb 1972/87, tstee 1983-1987), Hawks (Cambridge), Blakeney Sailing; *Style—* The Hon Mr Justice Popplewell; Royal Courts of Justice, Strand, London WC2

PORCHER, Michael Somerville; CMG (1962), OBE (1960); s of late Geoffrey Lionel Porcher; *b* 9 Mar 1921; *Educ* Cheltenham, St Edmund Hall Oxford; *m* 1955, Mary Lorraine, *née* Tweedy; 2 s; *Career* dep chief sec Br Guana 1956, colonial sec Br Honduras 1960, chief sec 1961, ret 1964, sec (Operations Div) Royal Nat Life-Boat Inst 1964-; *Style—* Michael Porcher Esq, CMG, OBE; Bladon, Worth Matravers, nr Swanage, Dorset

PORCHESTER, Lord; George (Geordie) Reginald Oliver Molyneux Herbert; s and h of 7 Earl of Carnarvon, *qv*; *b* 10 Nov 1956; *Educ* St John's Coll Oxford (BA); *Career* a page of honour to HM The Queen 1969-73; computer conslt and horticulturalist 1976-79; *Style—* Lord Porchester

PORRITT, Baron (Life Peer UK 1973); Brigadier Sir Arthur Espie Porritt; 1 Bt (UK 1963), GCMG (1967), GCVO (1970), CBE (1945); s of Ernest E Porritt, VD, MD, FRCS (d 1950), of NZ; *b* 10 August 1900; *Educ* Wanganui Collegiate Sch NZ, Otago Univ NZ, Magdalen Coll Oxford, St Mary's Hosp London; *m* 1, 1926, Mary Frances Wynne, da of William Bond; m 2, 1946, Kathleen Mary, da of late A S Peck and Mrs Windley; 2 s, 1 da; *Heir* (to Btcy only) s, Hon Jonathon Espie Porritt; *Career* sits as Independent in House of Lords; Sgt Surgn to HM The Queen 1952-67, Govr-Gen of New Zealand 1967-72; pres: RSM 1966-67, RCS 1960-63, BMA 1960-61; formerly hon surgn: St Mary's Hosp, Royal Masonic Hosp (chm 1973-82; Grand Master's Order of Service to Masonry 1981), King Edward VII Hosp for Offrs, Hosp of St John and Elizabeth; consulting surgn: King Edward VII Convalescent Home for Offrs, Osborne and Royal Hosp Chelsea; hon consulting Surgn to the Army 1954-67, chm Medical Advisory Ctee Miny of Overseas Devpt, memb Int Olympic Ctee 1934, chm Empire Games Fedn 1948-67, vice-pres 1968-; Red Cross cmmr for NZ in UK; chm African Med and Res Fndn 1973-, Arthritis and Rheumatism Cncl 1973-; KStJ; Order Legion of Merit (USA); *Clubs* Buck's; *Style—* Brig The Rt Hon the Lord Porritt; 57 Hamilton Terrace, NW8 (☎ 01 286 9212)

PORRITT, Hon Jeremy Charles; s of Baron Porritt, GCMG, GCVO, CBE (Life Peer and 1 Bt); *b* 19 Jan 1953; *Educ* Eton; *m* 1980, Penny, da of J H Moore, of London, Ontario; 1 s (Andrew, b 1981); *Style—* The Hon Jeremy Porritt

PORRITT, Hon Jonathon Espie; s and h of Baron Porritt, GCMG, GCVO, CBE (Life Peer and 1 Bt); *b* 6 July 1950; *Educ* Eton, Magdalen Coll Oxford; *m* 1986, Sarah, da of Malcolm Staniforth, of Malvern, Worcs ; *Career* dir Friends of the Earth; author; *Books* Seeing Green: the Politics of Ecology Explained, The Friends of the Earth Handbook; *Style—* The Hon Jonathon Porritt; 17a Laurier Road, London NW5 1SD

PORTAL, Sir Jonathan Francis; 6 Bt (UK 1901), of Malshanger, Church Oakley, Co Southampton; s of Sir Francis Spencer Portal, 5 Bt (d 1984), and his 2 w, Jane Mary, da of late Albert Henry Williams, OBE; *b* 13 Jan 1953; *Educ* Marlborough, Edinburgh Univ (BCom); *m* 9 Oct 1982, Louisa Caroline, er da of John Hervey-Bathurst, *qv* 1 s (William Jonathan Francis); *Heir* s, William Jonathan Francis Portal b 1 Jan 1987; *Career* chartered accountant (ACA); chief accountant Seymour Int Press Distributors; govr Old Malthouse School, Swanage, Dorset; Liveryman Clothworkers Co; *Recreations* travel, sailing, country sports; *Style—* Sir Jonathan Portal, Bt; 21 Yeomans Row, London SW3 2AL; office: (☎ 01 733 0022)

PORTAL OF HUNGERFORD, Baroness (UK 1945); Rosemary Ann Portal; da of 1 Viscount Portal of Hungerford, KG, GCB, OM, DSO, MC (d 1971, when the Viscountcy became extinct), and Joan Margaret, da of late Sir Charles Glynne Earle Welby, 5 Bt; suc to Barony of f 1971; *b* 12 May 1923; *Heir* none; *Career* formerly section offr WAAF; *Style—* The Rt Hon the Lady Portal of Hungerford; West Ashling House, Chichester, West Sussex

PORTARLINGTON, 7 Earl of (I 1785); George Lionel Yuill Seymour Dawson-Damer; Baron Dawson (I 1770), Viscount Carlow (I 1776); s of Air Cdre Viscount Carlow (k on active ser 1944) and gs of 6 Earl of Portarlington (d 1959); *b* 10 August 1938; *Educ* Eton; *m* 26 July 1961, Davina, eldest da of late Sir Edward Henry Windley, KCMG, KCVO; 3 s (Viscount Carlow, Hon Edward Lionel Seymour b 1967, Hon Henry Lionel Seymour b 1971), 1 da (Lady Marina Davina b 1969); *Heir* s, Viscount Carlow; *Career* Page of Honour to HM The Queen 1953-55; dir: G S Yuill & Co Ltd Sydney, Aust Stock Breeders Co Ltd Brisbane, Yuills AustLtd Sydney; pres Aust Malaysia Singapore Assoc; *Recreations* skiing, fishing; *Clubs* Union (Sydney); *Style—* The Rt Hon the Earl of Portarlington; 19 Coolong Rd, Vaucluse, NSW 2030, Australia (☎ Sydney 337 3013)

PORTEOUS, George Ross Dalziel; s of Prof Alexander James Dow Porteous (d 1981), of Birkenhead, Merseyside, and Eliza Murray Dalziel, *née* Ross (d 1972); *b* 19 July 1934; *Educ* Birkenhead Sch, Univ of Liverpool (LLB); *m* 23 Feb 1963, (Constance) Ursula, da of Hubert Kerridge (d 1969), of Irby Wirral, Merseyside; 1 s (Michael b 1965), 2 da (Lyn b 1963, Fiona b 1968); *Career* slr 1960, sr ptnr Warburton Porteous and Co; NP; pres The Cheshire Co Lawn Tennis Assoc, rep Lawn Tennis Assoc Cncl; memb: Law Soc, Liverpool Law Soc, Soc of Notaries; *Recreations* tennis, squash, photography; *Clubs* Heswall Lawn Tennis, Heswall Squash Racquets; *Style—* George Porteous, Esq; Kinross, 8 Church Meadow Lane, Heswall, Wirral, Merseyside L60 4SB (☎ 051 342 1713); 90-92 Telegraph Rd, Heswall, Wirral, Merseyside L60 0AQ (☎ 051 342 6116)

PORTEOUS, John (Robin); s of Charles Frederick Porteous (d 1941), of London, and Mary Grace, *née* Wooster; *b* 29 July 1934; *Educ* Westminster, Christ Church Oxford (MA); *m* 16 June 1956, Catherine Eleanor, da o John Traill Christie (d 1980); 2 s (Matthew b 1957, Tom b 1960), 1 da (Rebecca b 1969); *Career* Baring Bros & Co Ltd 1955-57, Philip Hill Higginson Ltd 1957-60, ptnr Pember & Boyle Stockbrokers 1966-86 (joined 1960), dir Morgan Grenfell Govt Securities Ltd 1986; memb Stock Exchange 1966-87, fell and sr bursar Gonville and Caius Coll Cambridge 1987-; memb: Cncl of Ancient Monuments Soc, Royal Mint Advsy Ctee 1968, syndic of Fitzwilliam Museum Cambridge 1989; Liveryman Worshipul Co of Skinners 1956; FSA 1980; *Books* Coins (1963), Coins in History (1969), Aangemunt En Nagemunt (Amsterdam 1970); *Recreations* numisatics, foreign travel, second hand bookshops; *Clubs* Groucho; *Style—* John Porteous, Esq; 52 Elgin Cres, London W11 (☎ 01 727 6915); 7 Summerfield, Newnham, Cambridge (☎ 0223 63947); Gonville and Caius Coll, Cambridge CB2 1TA (☎ 0223 332455, fax 0223 332456)

PORTEOUS, Col Patrick Anthony; VC (Dieppe 1942); s of Brig-Gen C McL Porteous (d 1936); *b* 1 Jan 1918; *Educ* Wellington, RMA Woolwich; *m* 1, 1943, Lois Mary (d 1953), da of Maj-Gen Sir Horace Roome, KCIE (d 1970); 1 s, 1 da; m 2, 1955, Deirdre, da of late Eric King; 3 da; *Career* 2 Lt RA 1937, 6 AA Regt 1938, served France, Belgium, Dunkirk 1939-40, joined Commandos 1940, Dieppe 1942, Normandy 1944; instr RMA Sandhurst 1950-53, DAQMG FARELF 1953-56, 14 Field Regt RA 1956, RAF Staff Coll 1958, AMS HQ Southern Cmd 1959-60, Col Junior Leaders Regt RA 1960-63, Col Gen Staff War Off later MOD 1963-66, Cdr Rheindahlen Garrison 1966-69, ret 1970; *Recreations* sailing, gardening; *Style—* Col Patrick Porteous, VC; Christmas Cottage, Funtington, Chichester, W Sussex (☎ Chichester 58315)

PORTER *see also*: Horsbrugh-Porter

PORTER, Alastair Robert Wilson; CBE (1985); s of James Porter (d 1974), of 40 Backwoods Lane, Lindfield, Haywards Heath, Sussex, and Olivia, *née* Duncan (d 1968); *b* 28 Sept 1928; *Educ* Irvine Royal Acad, Glasgow Acad, Merton Coll Oxford Univ (MA); *m* 28 Aug 1954, Jennifer Mary Priaulx, da of Capt Philip Charles Forman, RN (d 1965); 2 s (Angus b 1957, Duncan b 1961), 1 da (Francis b 1955); *Career* Nat Serv Royal Scot Fus and RASC

1947-49 (2 Lt 1948); barr 1952-54, res magistrate N Rhodesia 1954-61, registrar of High Ct of N Rhodesia 1961-64, perm sec Min of Justice N Rhodesia (later Zambia) 1964-65, sec and registrar RCVS 1966-; Haywards Heath Round table until 1968, class ldr Perrymount Road Methodist Church; sec-gen Fedn of Veterinarians of the EEC 1973-79, chm EEC'S Advsy Ctee on Veterinary Training 1986; hon Akademische Ehrenbürger Hanover Veterinary Sch 1988; memb Gray's Inn 1952; *Books* An Anatomy of Europe (jtly 1972); *Recreations* watching soccer; *Clubs* Caledonian; *Style*— Alastair Porter, Esq; 4 Savill Rd, Lindfield, Haywards Heath, Sussex, RH16 2NX (☎ 04447 2001), Royal College of Veterinary Surgeons, 32 Belgrave Sq, London, SW1X 8QP (☎ 01 235 4971, fax 01 245 6100)

PORTER, Alistair Campbell; s of Robert William Porter, OBE, of 73 Beaumont Rd, Cambridge, and Marion Audrey, *née* Glascock; *b* 26 Mar 1950; *Educ* The Leys Sch, Exeter Univ (LLB), Coll of Law; *m* 31 Aug 1985, Leila, da of Adel Assassa (d 1972); 1 da (Francesca Lauren b 1987); *Career* sr ptnr Alistair Porter & Co slrs 1981-; memb Law Soc; *Recreations* sailing; *Clubs* Royal Ocean Racing, Royal Corinthian YC; *Style*— Alistair Porter, Esq; 1 Lincoln's Inn Fields, London WC2 (☎ 01 405 8855, fax 01 831 6794, car tel 0836 711 030)

PORTER, Arthur Thomas; s of Guy Hazeley Porter (d 1982), of Sierra Leone, and Aoina Agnes, *née* Cole (d 1949); *b* 26 Jan 1924; *Educ* Fourah Bay Coll (BA), Cambridge Univ (BA, MA), Boston Univ USA (PhD); *m* 1 Sept 1953, Rigmor Sondergaard, da of Christian Malling Rasmussen (d 1971); 1 s (Arthur Thomas b 1956), 1 da (Emma Adina b 1958); *Career* asst lectr Edinburgh Univ 1952-53; Univ of Sierra Leone: lectr Fourah Bay Coll 1953-58 (sr lectr 1958-61), prof 1962-64, vice chllr 1974-84; princ Univ Coll Nairobi Kenya 1964-70, staff memb UNESCO 1970-74, Fulbrigh scholar USA 1986-87; memb Sierra Leone Historical Soc; Hon Citizen Kansas City Kansas Missouri USA; Hon LHD Boston Univ USA 1969, Hon LLD Univ of Malta 1969, Hon DLitt Univ of Sierra Leone 1988; memb Order of the Republic of Sierra Leone (MRSL) 1978; *Books* Creoledom (1963); *Clubs* Royal Cwlth Soc; *Style*— Arthur Porter, Esq; 81 Fitzjohn Ave, Barnet, Herts EN5 2HN; 266 Spur Rd, PO Box 1363, Freetown, Sierra Leone

PORTER, David John; MP (C) Waveney 1987-; s of George Edward Porter (d 1964), of Lowestoft, and Margaret Elizabeth, *née* Robinson; *b* 16 April 1948; *Educ* Lowestoft GS, New Coll of Speech and Drama London; *m* 25 March 1978, Sarah Jane, da of Rev Peter Shaw (d 1979); 2 s (Thomas Edward b 1982, Samuel George b 1986), 2 da (Victoria Louise b 1979, Alice Elizabeth b 1988); *Career* Dist Cncllr Waveney; *Recreations* writing, Waveney past, present and future, family; *Style*— David Porter, Esq, MP; House of Commons, Westminster, London SW1A OAA (☎ 01 219 6235)

PORTER, Prof Sir George; s of late John Smith Porter; *b* 6 Dec 1920; *Educ* Thorne GS, Leeds Univ (BSc), Radar Offr RNVR Western Approaches and Med; Emmanuel Coll Cambridge (MA, PhD, ScD); *m* 1949, Stella Jean, da of late G A Brooke; 2 s; *Career* prof of physical chem Sheffield Univ 1955-63 (Firth prof of chemistry 1963-66); prof of chemistry Royal Inst 1963-66, dir Royal Inst of GB and Fullerian prof of chem 1966-85; pres: Assoc for Science Educn 1985, Br Assoc for Advancement of Science 1985-86; hon fell Emmanuel Coll Cambridge 1967-; visiting prof Dept of Chem UCL 1967-, Imperial Coll London 1978-; hon liveryman Salters' Co; pres: Nat Assoc for Gifted Children 1975-80, Jt Nobel Prize for Chem 1967, The Royal Soc 1985; hon fellow and research prof of Imperial Coll London 1987; has appeared on TV series giving 100 lectures on scientific subjects; chllr Univ of Leicester 1986; FRS 1960, Hon Doctorate of 25 Univs; kt 1972; *Books* Chemistry for the Modern World 1962, over 300 scientific papers in the Proc Royal Soc J C S Transactions; *Recreations* sailing, gardening; *Clubs* Athenaeum; *Style*— Prof Sir George Porter; The Royal Institution, 21 Albemarle St, London W1X 4BS (☎ 01 409 2992)

PORTER, George Barrington; MP (C) Wirral South 1983-; s of Kenneth William Porter; *b* 11 June 1939; *Educ* Birkenhead Sch, Univ Coll Oxford; *m* 1965, Susan Carolyn James; 2 s, 3 da; *Career* slr 1965, cncllr Birkenhead County Borough Cncl 1967-74, Wirral Borough 1975-79, MP (C) Bebington and Elsmere Port 1979-1983; *Clubs* RAC, Artists (Liverpool); *Style*— George Porter, Esq, MP; House of Commons, London SW1 (☎ 01 219 3000)

PORTER, Henry Christopher Mansel; s of Maj Harry Robert Mansel Porter, MBE, of Pershore, and Anne Victoria, *née* Seymour; *b* 23 Mar 1953; *Educ* Wellington, Manchester Univ (BA), Perugia Univ Italy; *m* 2 da (Miranda Victoria Elliot b 30 Oct 1985, Amelia Charlotte Seymour Elliot b 22 Oct 1988); *Career* journalist; feature writer: Sunday Times 1981-83, Evening Standard, Liverpool Daily Post; columnist Sunday Times 1983; dir of Media Interviews 1985-; ed Illustrated London News 1987-; *Books* Lies, Damned Lies and Some Exclusives (1984); *Recreations* sailing, sleeping in the afternoon; *Style*— Henry Porter, Esq; The Illustrated London News, 91-93 Southwark Street, London SE1 (☎ 01 928 2111)

PORTER, Ivor Forsyth; CMG (1963), OBE (1944); s of Herbert Porter; *b* 12 Nov 1913; *Educ* Barrow GS, Leeds Univ; *m* 1951, Ann (m dis 1961), da of late Dr John Speares; m 2, 1961, Katerina, da of A T Cholerton; 1 s, 1 da; *Career* formerly dir Atlantic Region Res Dept FCO; ambass: UK Delegation to Geneva Disarmament Conf 1968-71, Senegal, Guinea, Mali and Mauritania 1971-73; *Clubs* Travellers', PEN; *Style*— Ivor Porter, Esq, CMG, OBE; 17 Redcliffe Rd, SW10

PORTER, James (Henry) Newton; TD; s of Col James Herbert Porter, CBE, DSO (d 1973), of Pigdon Hall, Morpeth, Northumberland, and Ellen, *née* Newton (d 1947); *b* 23 Feb 1926; *Educ* Eton; *m* 12 April 1950, Violet Anne Bates (Wendy), da of Sir Ralph George Elphinstone Mortimer, KT, OBE (d 1955), of Milbourne Hall, Ponteland, Newcastle upon Tyne; 1 s (Timothy b 1952), 1 da (Lucinda b 1954); *Career* Capt Grenadier Gds 1944-47, Maj Northumberland Hussars 1948-59; dir: John Rowell & Sons Ltd 1959, Scottish & Newcastle Breweries Ltd 1960; The Newcastle Breweries Ltd: joined 1947, asst md 1954, jt md 1961, md 1964, chm and md 1967, ret 1976; farmer 1976-; memb: Ct Univ of Newcastle upon Tyne, Cncl for the Disabled Newcastle upon Tyne; Northumberland Boy Scouts: chm fin ctee, chm West Castle Dist; *Recreations* shooting; *Clubs* Northern Counties (Newcastle upon Tyne); *Style*— Henry Porter, Esq, TD; The Woll, 46 Runnynede Rd, Ponteland, Newcastle upon Tyne NE20 9HG (☎ 0661 227 42); Pigdon Farm, Morpeth, Northumberland NE61 3SE (☎ 0670 513 511)

PORTER, James Forrest; s of Ernest, and Mary Violetta Porter; *b* 2 Oct 1928; *Educ* Salford GS, Dudley Trg Coll, LSE, London Univ Inst of Educn; *m* 1952, Dymphna, da of Leo Francis Powell; 2 da (Louise, Alison); *Career* princ Bulmershe Coll of Higher Educn 1967-78, dir Cwlth Inst 1978-; chm World Educ Fellowship 1979-, Cwlth fell Aust 1977, UN conslt 1975-; memb: UGC 1970-76, James Ctee on Teacher Educn 1972-, memb IBA 1973-80, BBC Educn Cncl 1987-; chm Newsconcern Int 1983-, bd memb Cwlth Magazine; FRSA, Hon FCP, FRGS; *Clubs* Royal Commonwealth Soc; *Style*— James Porter, Esq; Commonwealth Institute, Kensington High St, London W8 6NQ (☎ 01 602 3252); House by the Water, Bolney Ave, Shiplake, Oxon (☎ 073 522 2187)

PORTER, James William; MC (1945); s of Edward William (d 1932), of 14 Ernest Place, Fenton, Stoke-on-Trent, and Annie Louisa (d 1977); *b* 22 Sept 1910; *Educ* St Thomas RC Stoke-on-Trent; *m* 1937, Mabel (d 1961), da of Herbert Brittan (d 1964), of Stoke-on-Trent; 2 da (Patricia, June); *Career* Capt, served Dunkirk, N Africa, Italy, Austria; exec company relations 1970, dir Michelin Tyre UK Gp 1975; vice-pres Staffs Assoc of Boys Clubs; *Style*— James Porter, Esq, MC; 425 New Inn Lane, Trentham, Stoke-on-Trent ST4 8BN (☎ 0782 657965); Michelin Tyre plc, Campbell Rd, Stoke-on-Trent ST1 4EY (☎ 0782 48101, telex 36299)

PORTER, Air Vice-Marshal John Alan; OBE (1971); s of Alan Porter (d 1979), and Etta, *née* Ward (d 1952); *b* 29 Sept 1934; *Educ* Lawrence Sheriff Rugby, Bristol Univ (BSc), Southampton Univ; *m* 2 s (Alan, David); *Career* procurement exec MOD 1984-89; dir CE56 GC HQ 1989-; *Recreations* the arts, skiing; *Style*— Air Vice-Marshal John Porter, OBE; GC HQ, Oakley, Cheltenham, Glos

PORTER, John Andrew; JP, DL (Kent, TD); s of Horace Augustus Porter, DFC, JP (d 1948), of Kent, and Vera Marion, *née* Andrew (d 1967); *b* 18 May 1916; *Educ* Radley Coll, Sidney Sussex Coll Cambridge (MA); *m* 1941, Margaret Isobel, da of Samuel Alexander Wisnom (d 1944), of London; 2 da (Jocelyn, Angela); *Career* served WWII, Lt Col RA; past chm: Anglia Bldg Soc, Hastings and Thanet Bldg Soc, Gravesham Justices; sr ptnr Porter & Cobb Chartered Surveyors 1948-81, chm Gravesham PSD 1976-83; pres Gravesend Cons Assoc 1966-78, cmmnr of Income Tax; pres Kent County Cricket Club 1985-86; FRICS; *Recreations* cricket, gardening, reading; *Clubs* RAC, Hawks (Cambridge); *Style*— John Porter Esq, JP, DL, TD; Leader, Hodsoll Street, nr Wrotham, Kent TN15 7LH (☎ 0723 822260); 178-182 Parrock St, Gravesend, Kent (☎ 0474 64400)

PORTER, Air Marshal Sir (Melvin) Kenneth Drowley; KCB (1967, CB 1959), CBE (1945, OBE 1944); s of Flt Lt Edward Ernest Porter, MBE, DCM (d 1927), and Helen Porter (d 1920); *b* 19 Nov 1912; *Educ* No 1 Sch of Tech Trg Halton, RAF Coll Cranwell; *m* 1940, Elena, da of F W Sinclair (d 1961); 2 s, 1 da; *Career* RAF 1928, cmmnd 1932, served WW II 1939-45 (despatches 3); chief signals offr: Balloon Cmd 11 Gp, 2 Tactical AF 1943-45 (Actg Air Cdre 1944), Bomber Cmd 1945-46, 2 TAF 1955-56, Fighter Cmd 1956-59 (Air Cdre 1958); IDC 1959, Cmdt No 4 Sch of Tech Trg RAF St Athan and Air Offr Wales 1960-61, dir-gen of Ground Trg Air Miny 1961-63, Air Vice-Marshal 1962, dir-gen of Signals (Air) MOD 1963-66, AOC-in-C Maintenance Cmd 1966-70, Air Marshal 1966, ret 1970; dir Tech Educ Projects Dept of Educ Univ Coll Cardiff 1970-74, conslt 1975; CEng, FRAeS, FICE, CBIM; Offr Legion of Merit (USA); *Recreations* reading; *Clubs* RAF; *Style*— Air Marshal Sir Kenneth Porter, KCB, CBE; c/o Lloyds Bank, Redland Branch, 163 Whiteladies Rd, Clifton, Bristol BS8 8RW

PORTER, Sir Leslie; s of Henry Alfred Porter (d 1955), and Jane, *née* Goldstein (d 1983); *b* 10 July 1920; *Educ* Holloway Co Sch; *m* 1949, Shirley, da of Sir John Edward Cohen (d 1980); 1 s (John), 1 da (Linda); *Career* WWII Army 1 Bn KRRC TQMS; served: Egypt, Greece, Lybia, Algeria, Sicily, Italy; chm: Tesco plc 1973-85 (pres 1985-), hon vice pres Sports Aid Fndn, chm bd of govrs Tel Aviv Univ, govr Hong Kong Baptist Coll and Cranfield Inst, vice-pres Age Concern NPFA, pres UK Boys' Town Jerusalem; memb Lloyds 1964- (John Poland and other syndicates); past pres Inst of Grocery Distribution, CBIM, FIGD; landowner (8200 acres); *Recreations* yachting, golf, bridge, swimming; *Clubs* City Livery, Coombe Hill, Dyrham Park, Frilford GC, RAC Country and GC; *Style*— Sir Leslie Porter; Tesco plc, Hammond House, 117 Piccadilly, London, W1V 9FJ (☎ 01 629 2484 telex 291015, fax 01 491 2367)

PORTER, Hon Sir Murray Victor; s of late V Porter; *b* 20 Dec 1909; *Educ* Brighton (Victoria) G S, Aust; *m* 1932, Edith Alice Johnston, da of late C A Johnston; 2 da; *Career* 2 AIF 1941-45, MLA (Lib) Sandringham Victoria 1955-70, govt whip 1955-56, asst min 1956-58; min for: Forests 1958-59, Local Govt 1959-64, Public Works 1964-70, agent-gen for Victoria in London 1970-76; kt 1970; *Clubs* Melbourne Cricket, Royal Melbourne GC, Royal Automobile of Victoria; *Style*— The Hon Sir Murray Porter; Flat 7, The Point, 405 Beach Rd, Beaumaris, Vic 3193, Australia

PORTER, Rt Hon Sir Robert Wilson; PC (NI 1969), QC (NI 1965); s of late Joseph Wilson Porter; *b* 23 Dec 1923; *Educ* Model Sch, Foyle Coll Londonderry, Queen's Univ Belfast (LLB); *m* 1953, Margaret Adelaide, da of late F W Lynas; 1 s, 1 da (and 1 da decd); *Career* RAFVR 1943-46, RA (TA) 1950-56; barr NI 1950, barr Repub of I 1975, counsel to Attorney-Gen for NI 1963-64 and 1965; min of Health and Social Services NI 1969, parly sec 1969 and min of Home Affairs NI 1969-70; vice-chm 1959-61, and chm 1961-66 War Pensions Appeal Tbnl for NI; MP (U) Queen's Univ of Belfast 1966-69, Lagan Valley 1969-73; County Court Judge NI 1978-; kt 1971; *Clubs* RAF; *Style*— The Rt Hon Sir Robert Porter, QC; Larch Hill, Ballylesson, Belfast, NI, BT8 8JX

PORTER, Ronald Robert; s of Maj Kenneth Russell Porter, of 34 Dawson Ave, Brighton, Vic, Australia, and Laura Maria, *née* Terenzi; *b* 10 Nov 1951; *Educ* Melbourne C of E Boys GS, Securities Inst of Australia (Cert, Dip), Coll of Mktg UK, Australian Admin Staff Coll (Advanced Mgmnt); *m* 2 Feb 1974, Helen Mary, da of Dr John J Bourke (d 1985); 2 s (Nicholas James b 1979, William Charles b 1986), 2 da (Stephanie Jane b 1980, Alexandra Elizabeth b 1984); *Career* ptnr and dir JB Were & Son 1983, memb Melbourne Stock Exchange 1983, md JB Were & Son Ltd London 1987-; ASIA, memb ASX; *Recreations* tennis, golf, rugby, rowing; *Clubs* Riverside Old Oarsmen's Assoc, NSW GC, White City TC (NSW); *Style*— Ronald Porter, Esq; JB Were & Son Ltd, 10 Old Jewry, London TW10 6HG (☎ 01 606 2261, fax 01 606 2452, telex 885201)

PORTER, Prof The Rev Canon (Joshua) Roy; s of Joshua Porter (d 1945), of Marple, Cheshire, and Bessie Evelyn, *née* Earlam (d 1976); *b* 7 May 1921; *Educ* King's Sch Macclesfield, Merton Coll Oxford (BA), St Stephen's House Oxford (BA, MA); *Career* ordained: deacon 1945, priest 1946; curate St Mary Portsea 1945-47, resident chaplain to Bishop of Chichester 1947-49, fell chaplain and tutor Oriel Coll Oxford 1949-62, prof of theology and head of dept Univ of Exeter 1962-86 (emeritus prof 1986-), dean of arts Univ of Exeter 1968-71, canon and prebendary Wightring and theol lectr Chichester Cath 1965-88, Wiccamical canon and prebendary of Exceit 1988-, visiting prof South Eastern Seminary Wake Forest N Carolina 1967, Ethel M Wood lectr Univ of London 1979, Michael Harrah Wood lectr Univ of the S Sewanee 1984, examining chaplain to Bishop of London, vice-chm St Mary's Ward Cons Ctee Islington; Proctor in Convocation Canterbury Exeter Diocese 1964-75 (and other Univs incl Canterbury) 1975-; memb: Gen Synod 1970- (Panel of chm 1984-86), Soc for Old Testament Study 1952 (pres 1983), Folklore Soc (hon memb 1988), Soc of Biblical Literature 1967, Anglican Assoc (pres), Prayer Book Soc (vice-chm); *Books* World in the Heart (1944), Moses and Monarchy (1963), The Extended Family in the Old Testament (1967), Proclamation and Presence (with J I Durham 1970), The Non-Juring Bishops (1973), Leviticus (1976), Animals in Folklore (with W M S Russell 1978); *Recreations* theatre, opera, book collecting, travel; *Clubs* Royal Over-Seas League; *Style*—

Prof The Rev Canon Roy Porter; 36 Theberton St, Barnsbury, London N1 0QX (☎ 01 354 5861)

PORTER, Lady Shirley; da of Sir John Edward Cohen (d 1980), and Sarah Fox; *b* 29 Nov 1930; *Educ* Warren Sch Worthing, La Ramee Lausanne Switzerland; *m* 1949, Sir Leslie Porter, s of Henry Alfred Porter (d 1955); 1 s (John), 1 da (Linda); *Career* bd memb: LFB (London Festival Ballet), KBT (Keep Britain Tidy); dir Capital Radio; vice-pres LUYC; dep master Worshipful Co of Environmental Cleaners; memb Consumer Forum; JP (Inner London) 1972-84; bd memb Money Mgmnt Cncl; ldr WCC 1983-; *Recreations* golf, boating, ballet, theatre, travel, efficiency in local govt; *Clubs* Queen's, Coombe Hill, Frilford Heath, Dyrham Park Golf, RAC; *Style*— Councillor Lady Porter; 19 Chelwood Ho, Gloucester Sq, London W2; Westminster City Cncl, City Hall, Victoria St, London SW1 (☎ 01 828 8070)

PORTER (MRS HENSON), Marguerite Ann; da of William Albert Porter, and Mary Maughan; *b* 30 Nov 1948; *m* 1, 1970 (m dis 1978) Carl Myers; m 2, 1 Aug 1986, Nicholas Victor Leslie Henson, s of Leslie Henson; 1 s (Keaton Leslie b 24 March 1988); *Career* Royal Ballet Co 1966-: soloist 1973, princ 1978-85, guest artist 1985-; *Recreations* motherhood, reading, friends; *Style*— Ms Marguerite Porter; Studio D, 404 Fulham Rd, London SW6

PORTES, Prof Richard David; s of Herbert Portes; *b* 10 Dec 1941; *Educ* Yale Univ, Balliol and Nuffield Colls Oxford; *m* 1963 (m dis 1988) Barbara Frank; children; *Career* fell Balliol Coll 1945-69; econ prof; Princeton Univ 1969-72; London Univ 1972-, head econ dept Birkbeck Coll 1975-77 and 1980-83; dir Centre for Economic Policy Res 1983-; *Books* Planning and Market Relations (1971), Deficits and Detente (1983), Threats to Int Financial stability (1987), Global Macroeconomics (1987); *Recreations* swimming, squash; *Clubs* Groucho; *Style*— Prof Richard Portes; Department of Economics, Birkbeck College, 7-15 Gresse St, London W1P 1PA

PORTILLO, Michael Denzil Xavier; s of Luis Gabriel Portillo, and Cora Waldegrave, *née* Blyth; *b* 26 May 1953; *Educ* Harrow, Peterhouse Cambridge (MA); *m* 12 Feb 1982, Carolyn Clair, da of Alastair G Eadie; *Career* Ocean Transport and Trading Co 1975-76, cons Res Dept 1976-79, special advsr to sec of State for Energy 1979-81, Kerr McGee Oil (UK) Ltd 1981-83, special advsr to sec of State for Trade and Indust 1983, Special Advsr to Chancellor of the Exchequer; MP (cons) Enfield Southgate 1984, asst govt whip 1986-87, Parly Under-Sec of State for Health and Social Security 1987-88, Min of State for Tport 1988-; *Clubs* Charlton; *Style*— Michael Portillo, Esq; House of Commons, Westminster, London SW1A 0AA (☎ 01 219 6595)

PORTLAND, Gwyneth, Duchess of; Gwyneth Ethel; MBE; da of late John Wesley Edward, of Chettlewood Estate, and Montpellier, Jamaica, BWI, and widow of Col David Alexander John Bowie, MC, RA; *m* 1950, as his 2 w, 8 Duke of Portland, KBE, CMG, MC (d 1980); *Style*— Her Grace Gwyneth, Duchess of Portland, MBE; Muthaiga, PO Box 47311, Nairobi, Kenya

PORTLAND, 9 Duke of (GB 1716); (Victor Frederick) William Cavendish-Bentinck; CMG (1942); also Baron Cirencester, Viscount Woodstock, Earl of Portland (E 1689), and Marquess of Titchfield (GB 1716); prior to succession, His Grace was granted in 1977 the same title and precedence that would have been his had his f suc to the Dukedom; 3 s of (William George) Frederick Cavendish-Bentinck, JP (d 1948, gs of Maj-Gen Lord Frederick Cavendish-Bentinck, CB, MP, 4 s of 3 Duke, KG, by his w Lady Dorothy Cavendish, only da of 4 Duke of Devonshire; His Grace assumed the surname of Cavendish as a prefix to Bentinck by Royal Licence of 1801, and served as George III's Viceroy of Ireland and Home Secretary, and was twice appointed PM in 1783 and 1807), and Ruth Mary (d 1953), da of Edward Earl St Maur; suc bro 1980; *b* 18 June 1897; *Educ* Wellington; *m* 1, 1924 (m dis 1948) Clothilde Bruce, da of late James Bruce Quigley, of Dallas, Texas; 1 da (and 1 s decd); m 2, 1948, Kathleen Elsie, yr da of Arthur Barry, of Montreal, and formerly w of Arthur Ritchie Tillotson; *Heir* (to all honours save the Dukedom and Marquessate), kinsman, Count (Henry Noel) Bentinck; *Career* sits as Cons in House of Lords; late 2 Lt Gren Gds 1918; entered Diplomatic Service, served: Oslo 1915, Warsaw 1919, FO 1922, Lausanne Conference 1922-23, 2 Sec Paris 1923, The Hague 1924, FO 1925, Locarno Conference 1925, 1 Sec Paris 1928, Athens 1932, Santiago 1934; FO 1937, chm Jt Intelligence Ctee of Chs of Staff 1939-45, FO advsr to dir of Plans 1942-45, asst under-sec of state 1944; ambass to Poland 1945-47, ret 1947; pres of Cncl Br Nuclear Forum, Grosses Verdienstkreuz, Germany; *Clubs* Turf, Beefsteak; *Style*— His Grace the Duke of Portland, CMG; 21 Carlyle Square, London SW3

PORTMAN, Hon Christopher Edward Berkeley; s and h of 9 Viscount Portman; *b* 30 July 1958; *m* 30 July 1983, Caroline, da of Terence Ivan Steenson, of Caversham, Berks; 1 s (Luke Oliver Berkeley b 31 Aug 1984); m 2, 7 Dec 1987, Patricia Martins, da of Bernardino Pim, of Rio de Janeiro, Brazil; *Style*— The Hon Christopher Portman; Clock Mill, Clifford, Herefs

PORTMAN, 9 Viscount (UK 1873); Edward Henry Berkeley Portman; Baron Portman (UK 1873); s of Hon Michael Berkeley Portman (d 1959) (yr s of 7 Viscount) and n of 8 Viscount (d 1967); *b* 22 April 1934; *Educ* Canford, RAC Cirencester; *m* 1, 1956 (m dis 1965) Rosemary Joy, er da of Charles Farris, of Combe Bissett, Wilts; 1 s, 1 da; m 2, 1966, Penelope Anne Hassard, yr da of Trevor Robert William Allin, of Combe Bissett, Wilts; 4 s (Hon Alexander b 1967, Hon Justin b 1969, Hon Piers b 1971, Hon Matthew b 1973); *Heir* s, Hon Christopher Edward Berkeley Portman, *qv*; *Career* farmer; *Recreations* music, motorsport, fishing, shooting; *Clubs* White's, British Racing Drivers'; *Style*— The Rt Hon the Viscount Portman; Clock Mill, Clifford, Herefordshire (☎ Clifford 235)

PORTMAN, Hon Mrs Michael; Marjorie Karr; da of late Frederick William Harris; *m* 1938, as his 2 w, the Hon Michael Berkeley Portman (d 1959); 1 s, 1 da; *Books* Bryanston, Picture of a Family; *Style*— The Hon Mrs Michael Portman; Portman Lodge, Durweston, Blandford, Dorset

PORTMAN, Viscountess Nancy Maureen; da of Capt Percy Herbert Franklin, RN (ret); *m* 1946, as his 2 w, 8 Viscount Portman (d 1967); *Style*— The Rt Hon Nancy, Viscountess Portman; Sutton Waldron House, Blandford, Dorset

PORTMAN, Rodney John Berkeley; s of Berkeley Charles Berkeley Portman, and Sheila Margaret Penelope, *née* Mowat; *b* 15 Dec 1947; *Educ* Wellington, Trinity Coll Cambridge (MA); *m* 9 March 1976, Angela Theresa, da of Major John Pringle, MC; 2 s (Guy Seymour Berkeley b 12 Sept 1977, John Berkeley b 21 Aug 1982), 1 da (Oliva Joan b Nov 1979); *Career* land agent 1970-73; established Mander Portman Woodward Independent Sixth Form Coll 1973; established Berkeley Reafforestation Tst 1987 (charity dedicated to promoting Third World tree planting and tree mgmnt); Freeman City of London 1977, Liveryman Worshipful Co of Gunmakers; ARICS 1972; *Recreations* forestry, travel, countryside; *Clubs* Chelsea Arts; *Style*— Rodney Portman, Esq; 3 Harley Gdns, London SW10 9SW

PORTNOY, Leslie Reuben; s of Israel Portnoy, and Miriam Portnoy; *b* 27 May 1939; *Educ* Manchester GS, University of Manchester (LLB); *m* 7 March 1961, Stephanie, da of Nathan Swift; 1 s (Jonathan J b 10 May 1966), 1 da (Naomi M b 25 Oct 1969); *Career* called to the Bar Grays Inn 1961, dep circuit Judge 1978, memb Panel and Jewish Tribunal (Shops Act) 1980, asst rec 1981, rec 1988; govr King David Schs Manchester; *Style*— Leslie Portnoy, Esq; 95 Cavendish Rd, Salford (☎ 061 740 2286); Crown Square Chambers, 1 Deans Court, Crown Sq, Manchester M3 3HA (☎ 061 833 9801, fax 061 835 2483)

PORTSMOUTH, Archdeacon of; *see*: Crowder, Ven Norman Harry

PORTSMOUTH, Bishop of (RC) 1988-; Rt Rev (Roger Francis) Crispian Hollis; s of (Maurice) Christopher Hollis (d 1977), of Mells Somerset, and Margaret Madelaine, *née* King (d 1984); *b* 17 Nov 1936; *Educ* Stonyhurst, Balliol Coll Oxford, Pontifical Gregorian Univ Rome; *Career* Nat Serv 2 Lt Somerset LI 1954-56; ordained priest 1965, asst priest Amesbury Wilts 1966-67, asst RC chaplain Oxford Univ 1967-70 (sr RC chaplain 1970-77), RC asst to head of religious broadcasting BBC 1977-81, admin Clifton Cath and vicar-gen Clifton Diocese 1981-87, auxiliary bishop Archdiocese of Birmingham 1987-88; *Recreations* golf, cricket-watching; *Style*— The Rt Rev the Bishop of Portsmouth; Bishops House, Edinburgh Rd, Portsmouth PO1 3HG (☎ 0705 820 894)

PORTSMOUTH, 10 Earl of (GB 1743); Quentin Gerard Carew (Wallop); also Baron Wallop (GB 1720), Viscount Lymington (GB 1720); Hereditary Bailiff of Burley in the New Forest; s of Viscount Lymington (d June 1984) and his 2 w Ruth Violet, née Sladen (d 1978); suc gf 9 Earl (d Sept 1984); *b* 25 July 1954; *Educ* Eton, Millfield; *m* 1981 (m dis 1985), Candia Frances Juliet, only da of Colin McWilliam and Margaret, *née* Henderson; 1 s (Oliver Henry Rufus b 1981), 1 da (Lady Clementine Violet Rohais b 1983); *Heir* s, Viscount Lymington, *qv*; *Career* vice-pres Basingstoke Cons Assoc; patron SE Regnl Ctee of Nat Childrens' Home; dir Grainger Tst plc; *Recreations* shooting, sailing; *Clubs* Bucks, Royal Yach Sqdn, Int Assoc of Cape Horners; *Style*— The Rt Hon the Earl of Portsmouth; Estate Office, Farleigh Wallop, Basingstoke, Hants RG25 2HS (☎ 0256 21026)

PORTSMOUTH, Bishop of 1985-; Rt Rev Timothy John Bavin; s of Lt-Col Edward Sydney Durrance Bavin (RASC, d 1979), and Marjorie Gwendoline, *née* Dew; *b* 17 Sept 1935; *Educ* St George's Sch Windsor Castle, Brighton Coll, Worcester Coll Oxford, Cuddesdon Coll Oxford; *Career* Nat Serv RASC 1957-59, cmmnd 1958, Platoon Offr (2 Lt) 90 Co Aden 1958-59; curate St Alban's Cath Pretoria SA 1961-63, chaplain St Alban's Coll Pretoria 1963-69, curate Uckfield with Litte Horsted 1969-71, vicar Parish of the Good Shepherd Brighton 1971-72, dean of Johannesburg and rector of the Cathedral Parish 1971-74, bishop of Johannesburg 1974-84; *Books* Deacons in the Ministry of the Church (ed 1988); *Recreations* music, victoriana, country life; *Clubs* Royal Yacht Squadron (Cowes), Royal Naval (Portsmouth); *Style*— The Rt Rev the Bishop of Portsmouth; Bishopswood, Fareham, Hants PO14 1NT (☎ 0329 280 247)

PORTWIN, Guy Lister; s of Edwin Thomas Portwin, of Herts, and Elizabeth Emily Louise, *née* Gadd; *b* 28 Dec 1949; *Educ* Merchant Taylors' Sch; *m* 6 May 1979, Kathleen, da of John Joseph Skerritt, of Eire; 2 da (Liza, Emma), 2 s (Guy, John); *Career* dir: Wheatland Journals Ltd 1973-, Turret Press (Hldgs) Ltd 1979-84; md Turret-Wheatland Ltd 1984-; *Recreations* riding, reading; *Clubs* Durrants; *Style*— Guy L Portwin, Esq; Beechwood Farm, Buckland Common, nr Tring, Herts HP23 6PB (☎ 024 029 281); Turret-Wheatland Ltd, Turret House, Rickmansworth, Herts WO3 1SN (☎ 0923 777000)

POSFORD, John Albert; s of Capt Benjamin Ashwell Posford (d 1915); *b* 3 Sept 1914; *Educ* The Oratory Sch, King's Cambridge; *m* 1, 1940, Nell Margaret (d 1966), da of Capt Augustus Knight (d 1950); 1 s, 4 da; m 2, 1970, Jean Davidson, da of Col Alastair Gordon, MC, Royal Scots Fus (d 1968); 2 s; *Career* sr ptnr and fndr (1944) Posford, Pavry & Ptnrs, (consulting engrs to the ports of Felixstowe, Milford Haven and Sheerness); Queen's Award for Export Achievement 1979; chm Maritime Gp Br Conslts Bureau 1979; FRSA; *Recreations* gardening; *Clubs* United Oxford and Cambridge Univ; *Style*— John Posford Esq; Falkenham Lodge, Ipswich, Suffolk (☎ 039 48 246); 49 Eaton Mews South, SW1 (☎ 01 235 7446)

POSNER, Michael Vivian; CBE (1983); s of Jack Posner; *b* 1931; *Educ* Whitgift Sch, Balliol Coll Oxford; *m* 1953, Prof Rebecca (Prof of Romance Languages Oxford), da of William and Rebecca Reynolds; 1 s, 1 da; *Career* fell Pembroke Coll Cambridge 1960-83, economic dir Nat Economic Devpt Off, 1984-; reader economics Cambridge 1974-75; dir Economics Miny of Power 1966-67, econ advsr Treasury 1967-69 (econ conslt 1969-71), conslt IMF 1971-72, dep chief econ advsr Treasury 1975-76; memb: BR Bd 1976-, Energy Conservation Advsy Cncl 1974-, Standing Cmmn Energy and Environment 1978-; chm SSRC 1979-1983, dir Tech Change Centre 1981-; *Style*— Michael Posner, Esq, CBE; Rushwood, Jack Straw's Lane, Oxford

POSNER, Richard Max Stanley; JP (Middx Cmmn Area 1988); s of Claude Joseph Posner (d 1969), and Betty, *née* Lee; *b* 16 August 1944; *Educ* Christ's Coll Finchley; *m* 30 Aug 1974, Barbara Susan, da of Jan Konrad Szwenk (d 1971), of London; *Career* dir F66 Danish Design Ltd 1973-76; md: Richard Posner Assocs 1970-75, Baric Clothing Ltd 1976-80, Pappagalli's Pizza Inc Ltd 1980-89; dir Pozzitive TV Productions Ltd 1988; vice-chm Cunningham Ct Residents Assoc; *Recreations* sport fishing, winter sports, food and wine, pistol and clay Pigeon shooting; *Clubs* RAC, Marylebone Rifle & Pistol, Restauranteurs Assoc; *Style*— R M S Posner, Esq, JP; 30 Cunningham Ct, Blomfield Rd, Little Venice, London W9 1AE (☎ fax 01 286 0816, car tel 0860 541 589)

POSNETT, Sir Richard Neil; KBE (1980, OBE 1963), CMG (1976); s of Rev Charles Walker Posnett, K-I-H of Medak, India, and Phyllis, *née* Barker; *b* 19 July 1919; *Educ* Kingswood, St John's Coll Cambridge (MA); *m* 1; 2 s, 1 da; m 2, 1959, Shirley Margaret, da of Claude Hudson; 2 s, 1 da; *Career* lawyer, colonial admin, diplomat; barr Gray's Inn 1951, Colonial Office London 1958, perm sec for External Affrs Uganda 1962-63; joined Foreign Serv 1964, govr and C-in-C of Belize 1972-76, Dependent Territories advsr FCO 1977-79, Br high cmmr Kampala 1979, govr and C-in-C of Bermuda 1980-83, ret; UK Cmmr Br Phosphate Cmmrs 1978, pres Kingswood Assoc 1980; govr Kingswood Sch 1985; memb: Royal Forestry Soc, Royal African Soc, Lord Chllr's Panel of Independent Inspectors 1984; KStJ 1972; *Recreations* skiing, golf, trees; *Clubs* RIIA, Royal Commonwealth Soc, Achilles, Mid-Ocean, West Surrey GC, Privateers Hockey; *Style*— Sir Richard Posnett, KBE, CMG; Timbers, Northway, Godalming, Surrey GU7 2RE (☎ 048 68 6869)

POSNETTE, Dr Adrian Frank (Peter); CBE (1976); s of Frank William Posnette, (d 1956), of Cheltenham, Glos, and Edith Mary, *née* Webber (d 1969); *b* 11 Jan 1914; *Educ* Cheltenham GS, Christ's Coll Cambridge (BA, MA, ScD), Imp Coll of Tropical Agric (AICTA), London (PhD); *m* 15 July 1937, Isabelle, da of Dr Montgomery De Forest La Roche (d 1958), of New York City; 1 s (John b 1950), 2 da (Jane b 1939, Suzanne b 1942); *Career* Colonial Agric Serv Gold Coast 1937-55: appointed botanist 1937-44, head botany and plant pathology W African Cocoa Res Inst 1944-49, seconded to E Malling Res Station

Maidstone Kent 1949, appointed princ scientific offr 1955; dir E Malling Res Station 1972-79, (head plant pathology section 1957-69, dep dir 1969-72), prof of plant sciences Wye Coll Univ of London 1971-78; author of series of eight res pubns on virus diseases of cocoa trees 1947-55, and numerous pubns on virus diseases of fruit trees and strawberries 1953-80; govr Redhill Sch E Sutton; awarded Ridley Medal of the Worshipful Co of Fruiterers 1978 (Hon Freeman 1982); FIBiol 1963, FRS 1971, VMH 1982;; *Recreations* ornithology; *Clubs* Farmers, CU Hawks; *Style*— Dr Adrian Posnette, CBE; Walnut Tree, East Sutton, Maidstone, Kent ME17 3DR (☎ 0622 843282)

POSTAN, Lady Cynthia Rosalie; *née* Keppel; da (by 1 m) of late 9 Earl of Albemarle, MC; *b* 25 June 1918; *m* 1944, Prof Sir Michael Moissey Postan (d 1981, prof of economic history Cambridge and fell of Peterhouse), s of Efim Postan, of Tighina, Bessarabia; 2 s (Basil David b 1946, Alexander Henry Keppel b 1948); *Style*— Lady Cynthia Postan; 84 Barton Road, Cambridge CB3 9LH

POSTANS, Richard Crispin; s of Frederic Holmes Postans (d 1964), of Bowes Park, London, and Gladys, *née* Cooper (d 1983); *b* 25 Oct 1916; *Educ* Sch of The Worshipful Co of Stationers and Newspaper Makers, Open Univ (BA); *m* 9 April 1941, Ivy Joan, da of Lewis Making, MSM (d 1964), of Lower Quinton, Warwickshire; 1 s (Rod Making-Postans b 1949), 1 da (Elizabeth b 1946, d 1965); *Career* RAPC 1940-43; official: Canadian Nat Railway 1935-40, Royal Masonic Benevolent Inst 1945-79; Freeman City of London 1938, Liveryman of The Worshipful Co of Stationers and Newspaper Makers 1976; *Recreations* freemasonry, railways, cycling, geneaology, history, literature; *Style*— Richard Postans, Esq

POSTGATE, Prof John Raymond; s of Raymond William Postgate (d 1971), of Canterbury, and Daisy (d 1971); *b* 24 June 1922; *Educ* Kingsbury Co Sch, Balliol Coll Oxford (BA, MA, DPhil, DSc); *m* 20 Oct 1948, (Muriel) Mary, da of Leslie Gordon Stewart (d 1963), of Whetstone, London; 3 da (Selina b 1955, Lucy b 1956, Joanna b 1958); *Career* Nat Chemical Laboratory: sr res investigator 1949-50, sr and later princ sci offr 1950-59; princ then sr princ sci offr Microbiological Res Estab 1959-63, asst dir ARC Unit of Nitrogen Fixation Royal Veterinary Coll 1963-65 (Sussex Univ 1965- 80); Sussex Univ: dir AFRC unit of nitrogen fixation 1980-87, prof of microbiology 1965-87 (emeritus 1987-); visiting prof: Univ of Illinois 1962-63, Oregon State Univ 1977-78; Hon Memb: Soc for applied Bacteriology 1981, Soc for Gen Microbiology 1988; FIBiol (pres 1982-84), FRS 1977; *Books* Microbes and Man (1969, 1986), The Fundamentals of Nitrogen Fixation (1982), The Sulphate - Reducing Bacteria (1979, 1984), A Plain Man's Guide to Jazz (1973); *Recreations* hearing and playing jazz music, scientific, jazz and biographical writing, reviewing records; *Style*— Prof John Postgate; Houndean Lodge, 1 Houndean Rise, Lewes, E Sussex BN7 1EG (☎ 0273 472 675)

POSTLETHWAITE, William; s of William Postlethwaite (d 1971), and Alice Julia, *née* Bernie; *b* 28 Dec 1932; *Educ* St Anselm's Coll Cheshire; *m* 6 Sept 1958, Mary Louise, da of Eric Apter (d 1978); 1 s (John Andrew b 1962), 1 da (Diana Mary b 1961); *Career* md Kwik Save Gp plc 1983-88, chm Plastech Ext Co Ltd; FInstM; *Recreations* reading, sport, gardening; *Clubs* Lancs CC, pres Rotary West Wirral, St Melyd GC; *Style*— William Postlethwaite, Esq; Plastech ExturSions Ltd, The Barkin Centre, Widnes, Cheshire (☎ 051 495 1424, fax 051 495 1727)

POSWILLO, Prof David Ernest; s of Ernest Joseph Poswillo, JP (d 1979), of Gisborne, NZ, and Amelia Mary, *née* McCormick; *b* 1 Jan 1927; *Educ* Gisborne Boys' HS, Univ of Otago NZ (BDS, ODS, DSc), Westminster Med Sch Univ of London, Univ of Zurich (MDhc); *m* 27 June 1956, Elizabeth Alison, da of John Whitworth Russell (1982), of Nelson, NZ; 2 s (Stephen b 22 Nov 1962, Mark b 10 Dec 1964), 2 da (Jane b 13 Oct 1958, Jill (Mrs Battye) b 8 Jan 1960); *Career* OC Southern Dists Hosp RNZDC 1948-50, 30 Field Ambulance RAMC BAOR 1951; dir oral surgery N Canterbury Hosp Bd NZ 1953-68, prof of teratology RCS 1969-77, conslt oral surgn Queen Victoria Hosp E Grinstead 1969-77, prof of oral pathology and oral surgery Univ of Adelaide South Aust 1977-79, sr oral and maxillofacial surgn Royal Adelaide and Childrens Hosp South Aust 1977-79, prof of oral Surgery Royal Dental Hosp London 1977-83, prof of oral and maxillofacial surgery Guy's Hosp London 1983-; memb Human Task Force WHO 1976-78, cncl memb Royal Dental Hosp London 1977-83, conslt advsr to chief MO DHSS 1979-86, memb bd of faculty of Dental Surgery RCS 1981; tstee Tobacco Prods Res Tst 1980-, vice pres and cncl memb Med Def Union 1983 - (chm dental ctee), sec gen Int Assoc of Oral and Maxillofacial Surgeons 1983-, memb govrs cncl UMDS of Guys and St Thomas' Hosps 1983-; Hunterian Prof RCS 1968 and 1976, Regent's Prof Univ of California 1987; lectures: Arnott Demonstrator 1972, Erasmus Wilson 1973, Darwin-Lincoln and Johns Hopkins 1975, Waldron (Harvard) 1976, Richardson (Harvard) 1981, Tomes RCS 1982, President's BAOMS 1985 Sarnat (UCLA) 1989; RNZADC prize 1948, Tomes prize 1966, Down medal 1973, Kay-Kilner prize 1975, ASOMS res award 1976, Hunter medal and Triennial prize 1976, Orthog Surgery award Univ of Texas 1982, Edison award Univ of Michigan 1987; FDSRCS 1952, FRACDS 1966, FIBiol, CBiol, MRCPath 1975, FRC Path 1981; Hon FFDRCSI 1974; German Acad of Natural Scis (Leopoldina) 1988; *Recreations* gardening, DIY, skiing, sailing; *Style*— Prof David Poswillo; Ferndale, Oldfield Rd, Bickley, Kent BR1 2LE (☎ 01 467 1578); Floor 24 Guy's Hosp Tower, London SE1 9RT (☎ 01 407 7600 ext 3539, 01 378 6918)

POTEZ, Richard Julian; s of Andrew Louis Potez, (d 1977), of Knights Manor, Dedham, Essex, and June Rosemary, *née* Avila; *b* 14 July 1949; *Educ* Ampleforth; *m* 6 Aug 1977, Mary Josephine, da of Geoffrey Peter Rickards, of Bijou, Church Street, Willingdon, Eastbourne, Sussex; 1 s (Christopher b 1980), 1 da (Rebecca b 1982); *Career* RN 1967-88, Lt-Cdr Far East, Middle East, Europe, Falklands; with Citicorp Scrimgeour Vickers Stockbrokers and mkt makers 1988-; MNI, MBIM, MIAM, MISM; *Recreations* 12 bore shooting, dinner parties; *Style*— Richard Potez, Esq; Sharnden Manor, Rushers Cross, Mayfield, Sussex; Citicorp Scrimgeour Vickers, Cottons Centre PO Box 200, Hays Lane, London SE1 2QT

POTTER; *see*: Lee Potter

POTTER, Arthur Kingscote; CMG (1957), CBE (1946); s of Richard Ellis Potter (d 1947), and Harriott Isabel, *née* Kingscote (d 1940); *b* 7 April 1905; *Educ* Charterhouse, New Coll Oxford; *m* 1950, Hilda, da of late William Arthur Butterfield, OBE, of Hong Kong; 1 da; *Career* ICS (Burma) 1928, fin advsr (Brig) 11 Army Gp and then Allied Land Forces SE Asia 1943-44, chief fin offr (Brig) Mil Admin of Burma 1944-47, HM Treasury rep in India, Pakistan and Burma 1947-50, asst sec HM Treasury 1950-56, cnsllr UK Delegation to NATO Paris 1956-65; *Style*— Arthur Potter, Esq, CMG, CBE; Lower House Barns, Bepton, Midhurst, W Sussex GU29 0JB

POTTER, David Roger William; s of William Edward Potter, of Durweston Dorset, and Joan Louise, *née* Frost; *b* 27 July 1944; *Educ* Bryanston Sch, Univ Coll Oxford (MA); *m* 1985, Mary, da of W J Irwin (d 1984); 2 da (Louise b 1969, Antonia b 1971); *Career* md: Credit Suisse First Boston 1969-81, Samuel Montagu and various subsidiaries 1981-87, Midland Montagu Corporate Banking 1987-; dir: (non exec) Maybox 1987-; *Recreations* shooting, theatre, wine; *Clubs* Oxford and Cambridge, City, Vincents Oxford; *Style*— David R W Potter, Esq; 16 William Mews, London SW1; Midland Montagu, Suffolk House, Lawrence Poultney Hill, London EC4 (☎ 01 260 5412, fax 01 260 5048)

POTTER, Donald Charles; QC (1972); s of late Charles Potter; *b* 24 May 1922; *Educ* St Dunstan's Coll, LSE; *Career* barr Middle Temple 1948, bencher Lincoln's Inn 1979, asst lectr in Law LSE 1947-49; *Clubs* Garrick; *Style*— Donald Potter Esq, QC; 37 Tufton St, SW1P 3QL

POTTER, Edward; s of Flt-Lt Edward Josef Data (d 1974), of Krakow, Poland, and Eleanor, *née* Bolton (d 1976); *b* 15 Sept 1941; *Educ* Bolton Tech Sch, Manchester Regnl Coll of Art, Oxford Sch of Arch (Dip Arch); *Career* architect; RIBA Thesis Prize Winner 1968; ptnr Benthall Potter Assocs (architects), specialists in restoration of Historic Buildings; RIBA, FFAS; *Recreations* railways; *Clubs* Chelsea Arts; *Style*— Edward Potter, Esq; 59 Westover Rd, London SW18 2RF (☎ 01 870 8683, telex 261234 (TLSYT) GH5967, 01 870 7595)

POTTER, Ernest Frank; s of Frank William Potter; *b* 29 April 1923; *Educ* Dr Challoner's GS Amersham; *m* 1945, Madge, nee Arrowsmith; 1 s; *Career* dir mgmnt consulting servs Coopers & Lybrand 1959-71, head of information servs Br Steel Corpn 1972, dir fin Cammell Laird Shipbuilders Ltd 1973-76, dir of finance and corporate planning Cable and Wireless Ltd 1977-79, dir finance 1979-87; dir: General Hybrid Ltd 1987-, The Telecom Corpn 1988-, Bahrain Telecommunications Corpn 1981; memb Accountancy Standards Ctee 1985-; FCMA, FCIS, MIMC; *Clubs* Wentworth, RAF; *Style*— Ernest Potter, Esq; Long Meadow, Gorse Hill Rd, Virginia Water, Surrey GU25 4AS

POTTER, Miss Felicite; MBE (1944); da of Frederick Felix Potter, CBE (d 1955), of Holmwood, Walmer, Kent, and Emily Caroline, *née* Buckle (d 1967); *b* 10 May 1916; *Educ* Cheltenham Ladies Coll; *Career* second offr WRNS W Hartlepool 1939, admin duties HMS Victory Portsmouth 1940, first offr 1941, chief offr 1943, ret 1944; barr Lincoln's Inn 1951, Chancery Bar 1951-53; Govt Legal Serv: Miny of Housing and Local Govt (later The DOE) 1953-56 and 1959-71, off of Registration of Restrictive Trading Agreements 1956-59; *Recreations* painting, gardening; *Style*— Miss Félicité Potter, MBE; Goonpiper Hse, Feock, Truro, Cornwall, TR3 6RA (☎ 0872 862 475)

POTTER, His Hon Judge Francis Malcolm; s of Francis Martin Potter; *b* 28 July 1932; *Educ* Rugby, Jesus Coll Oxford; *m* 1970, Bertha Villamil; 1 s, 1 da; *Career* barr Lincoln's Inn 1956, rec of the Crown Ct 1974-78, circuit judge 1978-; *Style*— His Honour Judge Potter; 5 Fountain Court, Steelhouse Lane, Birmingham B4 6DR

POTTER, Sir (William) Ian; s of James William Potter and Maria, *née* McWhinnie; *b* 25 August 1902; *Educ* Sydney Univ; *m* 1975, Primrose C Dunlop; 2 da (by former m); *Career* princ ptnr Ian Potter & Co 1935-67, fndr and govr of Ian Potter Fndn Ltd, chm Aust Elizabethan Theatre Tst 1968-, economist Fed Treasy Canberra 1933-35; chm: ASEA Electric (Aust) Pty Ltd, Atlas Copco Aust Pty Ltd, Associated Steamships Pty Ltd, Aust Utd Investmt Co Ltd, Bulkships Ltd, McIlwraith McEacharn Ltd, Time-Life Int (Aust) Pty Ltd, Tricontinental Ltd; kt 1962; *Style*— Sir Ian Potter; 30 Sargood St, Toorak, Vic 3142, Australia (☎ 24 4308)

POTTER, (Ronald) Jeremy; s of Alistair Richardson Potter; *b* 25 April 1922; *Educ* Clifton, Queen's Coll Oxford; *m* 1950, Margaret, da of Bernard Newman; 1 s, 1 da; *Career* formerly dep chm New Statesman, md ITV Pub Ltd 1970-79, chm ITV Books Ltd 1971-79, gp dir of Corporate Affrs LWT 1979-; dir Hutchinson Ltd 1978- (dep chm 1980-81, chm 1981-); pres Periodical Publishers Assoc 1978-79, chm Richard III Soc 1971-; author; FRSA; *Books* Hazard Chase, Death in Office, Foul Play, The Dance of Death, A Trail of Blood, Going West, Disgrace and Favour, Death in the Forest, Good King Richard?; *Style*— Jeremy Potter Esq; 41 Woodsford Sq, London W14 8DP (☎ 01 602 0982)

POTTER, John McEwen; Dr; s of Alistair Richardson Potter, JP (d 1951), of Hazeldene, Bexley, Kent, and Mairi Chalmers, *née* Dick (d 1954); *b* 28 Feb 1920; *Educ* Clifton, Emmanuel Coll Cambridge (BA, MB BChir, MA) Univ of Oxford (MA, BM, BCh, DM); *m* 21 April 1943, Kathleen, da of Rev Dr Herbert Shaw Gerrard (d 1969), of Manchester; 3 s (James b 1944, Andrew b 1949, Simon b 1953) ; *Career* RAMC 1944-47, Lt 1944, active serv 8 Army Europe, Capt 1945, serv India and Burma, graded neurosurgeon 1946; lectr in physiology and jr chief asst surgical professional unit St Barts Hosp 1948-51, graduate asst to Nuffield prof of surgery Oxford 1951-56, EG Fearnsides scholar Cambridge 1954-56, Hunterian prof RCS 1955; conslt neurosurgeon: Manchester Royal Infirmary 1956-61, Radcliffe Infirmary Oxford 1961-87; clinical lectr in neurosurgery Oxford Univ 1962-68, fell Linacre Coll 1967-69, univ lectr in neurosurgery 1968-87; Wadham Coll Oxford: fell 1969, professorial fell 1974-87, sub-warden 1978-81, dean of degrees 1983-, emeritus fell 1987-; dir of postgrad med educn Oxford Univ 1972-87, memb bd of govrs Utd Oxford Hosps 1973; memb: Gen Med Cncl 1973-89 (chm registration ctee 1979-89), Gen Bd of Faculties Oxford Univ 1975-83, Oxfordshire Health Authy 1982-89, Hebdomadal Cncl Oxford Univ, 1983-89 Med Appeals Tbnl 1987; former examiner Universities of Oxford and Cambridge; vice pres Fourth Int Congress of Neurological Surgery; FRCS 1951, memb BMA, FRSM (pres neurology section 1975-76), memb Soc of Br Neurological Surgns, corr memb American Assoc of Neurological Surgns, hon memb Egyptian Soc of Neurological Surgns; *Books* The Practical Management of Head Injuries (fourth edn 1984), contrib to Books and Journals on subjects mostly relating to Neurology and Med Educn; *Recreations* fishing; *Style*— John Potter, Esq; 47 Park Town, Oxford OX2 6SL (☎ 0865 57875); Myredykes, Newcastleton, Roxburghshire TD9 O5R

POTTER, Maj-Gen Sir (Wilfrid) John; KBE (1968, CBE 1963, OBE 1951), CB (1966); s of late Maj Benjamin Henry Potter, OBE, MC; *b* 18 April 1913; *m* 1, 1943, Vivienne Madge (d 1973), da of late Capt Henry D'Arcy Medlicott Cooke; 1 s, 1 da; m 2, 1974, Mrs D Ella Purkis; 1 step s, 1 step da; *Career* Maj-Gen 1962, dir of Supplies and Tport (Army) 1963-65, Tport Offr in Chief (Army) 1965-66, dir of movements (Army) MOD 1966-68, ret; chm Traffic Cmmrs and Licensing Authy Western Traffic Area 1973-83; *Style*— Maj-Gen Sir John Potter, KBE, CB; Orchard Cottage, The Orchard, Freshford, Bath, Avon (☎ 022 122 2594)

POTTER, Jon Nicholas; s of Robert Edward Potter, and June, *née* Rosemeyer; *b* 19 Oct 1963; *Educ* Burnham GS, Univ of Southampton (BA), Univ of Aston (MBA); *Career* product mangr KP Foods; hockey player: Olympic Bronze LA 1984, World Cup Silver London 1986, Euro Cup Silver Moscow 1987, Olympic Gold Seoul 1988, Capt Barcelona 1988, 116 int caps, Hockey Player of the Year 1987-88; *Recreations* most sports, films, music; *Clubs* Hounslow Hockey, Ladykillers; *Style*— Jon Potter, Esq; Flat 5, 7 Tierney Rd, Streatham Hill, London SW2 (☎ 01 674 4767); KP Foods Ltd, Heathgate House, 57 Colne Rd,

Twickenham, Middx (☎ 01 894 5600, fax 01 894 6715, telex 936246)

POTTER, Leila Oriel; da of Leslie Gordon McConomy (d 1964), of London, and Amelia Kessler; *Educ* Birkenhead High Sch (GPDST); *m* George Potter s of Patrick Potter (d 1970); 3 da (Sarah b 1954, Lucy b 1965, Emily b 1967); *Career* md Bunbury Domestic/ Equestrian Employment Agency 1968-; chm Ladies Circle 1964-65, cncllr Crewe and Nantwich Borough and Dist 1968-75, chm Local Govt Advsy Ctee 1988-89, memb Women's Enterprise Network (WEN) and Women Into Business 1988-89; govr Kingsway Sch Crewe 1970-75; *Style*— Mrs Leila Potter; Foxdale, Bunbury, Nr Tarporley, Cheshire (☎ 0829 260 357); Foxdale, Bunbury, Nr Tarporley, Cheshire (☎ 0829 260 148/357)

POTTER, Hon Mr Justice; Hon Sir Mark Howard Potter Mark Howard; QC (1980); s of Prof Harold Potter (d 1951), and Beatrice Spencer, *née* Crowder (d 1978); *b* 27 August 1937; *Educ* Perse Sch Cambridge, Gonville and Caius Coll Cambridge (BA); *m* 1962, Undine Amanda Fay, da of Maj James Eric Miller, of 40 Bracondale, Norwich; 2 s (Nicholas b 6 Sept 1969, Charles b 27 Dec 1978); *Career* cmmnd 15 Medium Regt RA 1958, Lt Para Regt RHA (TA) 1960-65; asst supervisor legal studies Cambridge Univ (Gonville and Caius, Queen's, Sydney Sussex) 1961-68; called to the bar Gray's Inn 1961, QC 1980, bencher 1987, judge of the High Ct Queen's bench Div 1988; chm bar Public Affrs Ctee 1987; memb: Cncl of Legal Educn 1982-, advsy ctee Lord Civil Justice Review 1985-88; kt 1988; *Recreations* family, sport; *Clubs* Garrick, RAC; *Style*— The Hon Mr Justice Potter; Royal Courts of Justice, Strand, London WC2 (☎ 01 936 6000)

POTTER, Sir (Joseph) Raymond Lynden; s of Rev Henry Lynden Potter and Mabel Boulton Potter; *b* 21 April 1916; *Educ* Haileybury (life govr), Clare Coll Cambridge; *m* 1939, Daphne Marguerite, da of Sir Crawford Douglas-Jones, CMG; 3 s, 1 da; *Career* served WWII Queen's Own Royal W Kent Regt, UK and Middle East, subsequently Asst QMG WO; chm Halifax Bldg Soc 1974-83 (joined 1951, gen mangr 1956, chief gen mangr 1960-74, dir 1968-83); vice-pres Bldg Socs Assoc 1981- (formerly memb of cncl then chm 1974-83); memb bd: Warrington and Runcorn New Town Devpt Corpn 1969-, Wakefield Diocesan Bd of Finance 1960-65; sec RIIA 1947-51; Freeman City of London 1981; kt 1978; *Clubs* Hawks (Cambridge); *Style*— Sir Raymond Potter; Oakwood, Chilbolton, Stockbridge, Hants SO20 6BE (☎ 026 474 523)

POTTER, Hon Mrs (Vanessa Jane); *née* Robson; da of Sir Lawrence William Robson (d. 1982), and Baroness Robson of Kiddington, J P; *b* 2 Sept 1949; *Educ* Wycombe Abbey, St Thomas's Medical Sch; *m* 1973, Jonathan Martin Potter; 1 s, 2 da; *Career* medical practitioner; *Style*— The Hon Mrs Potter; Tyler Hall, Tyler Hill, Canterbury, Kent

POTTERTON, Homan; s of Thomas Edward Potterton (d 1960), and Eileen, *née* Tong; *b* 9 May 1946; *Educ* Kilkenny Coll, Trinity Coll Dublin (BA, MA); *Career* cataloguer Nat Gallery of Ireland 1971-73, asst keeper Nat Gallery London 1974-80, dir Nat Gallery of Ireland 1980-, FSA, HRHA; *Books* Irish Church Monuments 1570-1880 (1975), A Guide to the National Gallery (1976), The National Gallery, London (1977), Reynolds and Gainsborough: themes and painters in the National Gallery (1976), Pageant and Panorama: the elegant world of Canaletto (1978), Irish Art and Architecture (1978), Venetian Seventeenth Century Painting (1979), Dutch Seventeenth and Eighteenth Century Paintings in the National Gallery of Ireland a complete catalogue (1986); The Golden Age of Dutch Paintings from the National Gallery of Ireland (exhibition catalogue) (1986), contributions to Burlington Magazine, Apollo, Connoisseur, Country Life; *Style*— Homan Potterton Esq; National Gallery of Ireland, Merrion Sq, Dublin 2, (☎ 615133)

POTTINGER, Alan Derek; JP (1985); s of Dr JH Pottinger (d 1961), and Winifred, *née* Bradley (now Lady Kirby, wid of Sir Arthur Kirby, KBE, CMG); *Educ* Taunton Sch, Exeter Coll Oxford (MA); *m* 15 Aug 1953, Elizabeth Jean Laurie, *née* Gay; 1 s (Timothy Stuart b 8 Dec 1956), 1 da (Sally Anne Laurie b 16 Aug 1959); *Career* serv 44 Commando RM 1944-46; Smith Mackenzie & Co Ltd E Africa 1949-62 (latterly shipping mangr), Shell Mex & BP Ltd 1962-76, Shell UK Oil Ltd 1976-84 (latterly mangr distribution planning); FCIS 1954; *Recreations* sailing; *Clubs* Naval; *Style*— Alan Pottinger, Esq, JP; 2 Church Cottages, Aldbury, Nr Tring, Herts HP23 5RS (☎ 044 285 207)

POTTS, Archibold; s of Ernest Wilkinson Potts (d 1979), of Sunderland, Tyne and Wear, and Ellen, *née* Simpson (d 1980); *b* 27 Jan 1932; *Educ* Monkwearmouth Central Sch Sunderland, Ruskin Coll Oxford, Oriel Coll Oxford (MA), London Univ (external PGCE), Durham Univ (external MEd); *m* 17 Aug 1957, Marguerite Elsie (d 1983), da of Gabriel Elliot (d 1983), of Sunderland; 1 s (Michael b 1965), 1 da (Margaret b 1963); *Career* RAF corpl 1950-53, serv with Second Tactical Air Force in Germany 1951-53; railway clerk 1947-50 and 1953-56; lectr in economics and econ history: N Oxfordshire Tech Coll 1961, York Tech Coll 1962- 65, Rutherford Coll of Tech and Newcastle Upon Tyne Poly 1965-80; hd of sch of business admin 1980-86 and associate dean Faculty of Business and Professional Studies 1987; p/t case worker Nat Prices and Income Bd 1967-68, and Cmmn on Indust Rels 1970, dir Town Teacher Ltd 1986-, dir Business Travel Servs Ltd 1987-; vice chm NE Labour History Soc 1987-, memb exec ctee Assoc of Northumberland Local History Socs 1987-, sec Newcastle and Gateshead Co-op Pty 1988- (tres 1983-88), sec Newcastle TS Nelson Sea Cadet Corps 1988-; Lab Candidate Westmorland constituency (Gen Election) 1979; CC Tyne and Wear 1979-86-, vice chm 1983-84, chm 1984-85; memb exec ctee Soc for Study of Lab History 1987-; *Books* Stand True (1976), Bibliography of Northern Labour History (ed 1982), Shipbuilders and Engineers (1988), Contributor to Dictionary of Labour Biography Vol 2 1974, Vol 4 1977, and Vol 5 1979); *Recreations* local history and military modelling; *Clubs* Victory Service, London; *Style*— Archie Potts, Esq; 41 Kenton Avenue, Kenton Park, Newcastle upon Tyne NE3 4SE (☎ 091 2856361)

POTTS, Michael Stuart; s of Thomas Edmund Potts, ERD, of Bray on Thames, and Phyllis Margaret, *née* Gebbie; *b* 2 Sept 1938; *Educ* Hilton Coll S Africa, Repton; *m* 23 May 1964, Virginia May Lindsay, da of Gp Capt Hugh Whittall Marlow, OBE, AFC, of Cape Town, S Africa; 3 s (Andrew b 1966, Alexander b 1968, Rupert b 1970); *Career* CA; ptnr Coopers & Lybrand: Eire 1968-70, UK 1970- (sr ptnr) Liverpool Off 1971-; pres Liverpool Soc of CA's 1982-83; cncl memb: ICAEW 1988-, Merseyside C of C and Indust 1974- (hon tres 1974-82), Univ of Liverpool 1979- (dep tres 1986-); *Recreations* sailing, golf, motoring, horology; *Clubs* Dee Sailing (Commodore 1979-80), Royal Liverpool GC, Aston Martin Owners; Antiquarian Horological Soc; *Style*— Michael Potts, Esq; Brooke House, The Parade, Parkgate, Cheshire L64 6RN (☎ 051 336 1494); Coopers & Lybrand, State House, 22 Dale St, Liverpool L2 4UH (☎ 051 236 7351)

POTWOROWSKI, Tadeusz Krzysztof; s of Jan Jozef Zygmunt Potworowski, and Jadwiga Stefania, *née* Jaroszynska; family landowners in Poland since 14th centry, gf Senator Tadeusz Potworowski memb of Upper House in 1930s; *b* 10 Jan 1947; *Educ* Gunnersbury Catholic GS; *m* 28 Dec 1974, Irena Izabella, da of Count Konstanty Lukasz Maria Bninski, of Warsaw, Poland; 1 s (Dominik b 1980), 1 da (Gabriela b 1983); *Career* CA; princ Tad Potworowski & Co (formerly Jeffreys, Ubysz & Co) 1973-; dir: Robinski & Co Ltd 1986-88, Andrews Delicacies Ltd 1986-88; chm W London 1986-; FCA; *Recreations* travelling, skiing, swimming, gardening; *Style*— Tadeusz K Potworowski, Esq; Copperfield, Wayside Gardens, Gerrards Cross, Bucks SL9 7NG; 2 Bamborough Gardens, London W12 8QN (☎ 01 749 2821)

POUGATCH, Michael Seymour; s of Col M Pougatch (d 1969), of London, and Audrey Henrietta, *née* Cooper (d 1984); *b* 9 August 1933; *Educ* Malvern, Corpus Christi Coll Cambridge (MA); *m* 31 March 1962, Pauline Sonia, da of Reginald Percy Clifton, of Hever, Kent; 1 s (Mark b 1968), 2 da (Katrina b 1964, Anneli b 1965); *Career* Lt 13/18 Royal Hussars (QMO), Capt Fife and Forfar Yeomanry/Scottish Horse TA; merchant banker, dir Singer & Friedlander 1973; memb Malvern Coll Cncl 1982-, a fndr Grannies Cricket Club; Liveryman Worshipful Co of Broderers; *Recreations* cricket; *Clubs* MCC, Cavalry & Guards; *Style*— Michael Pougatch, Esq; Witherenden Mill, Stonegate, Wadhurst, Sussex TN5 7EU (☎ 0435 883444); 21 New Street, Bishopsgate EC2M 4HR (☎ 01 623 3000)

POULETT, Countess; Margaret Christine; *née* Ball; da of Wilfred John Peter Ball, of Reading; *m* 12 Sept 1968, as his 3 w, 8 Earl Poulett (d 1973, when the Earldom became ext, and the Barony became ext or dormant); *Style*— The Rt Hon the Countess Poulett; Le Cercle, Rue du Croquet, St Aubin, Jersey, C I

POULTER, Graham George; s of George Henry Poulter (d 1980), and Mavis Kathleen, *née* Shipman; *b* 5 May 1942; *Educ* Art Coll Wakefield; *m* 29 March 1967, Patricia Ann, *née* Dickinson; 2 s (Jason b 1970, James b 1975); *Career* art dir/copywriter Kidds Avertising, account mangr Cravens Advertising, branch mangr Taylor Advertising (London), dir Leeds Office Goddard Watts; chm and chief exec Graham Poulter Ptnrship plc (fndr memb 1969); *Recreations* skiing, squash, gym; *Style*— Graham G Poulter, Esq; Flat 1, The Mews, Oakhampton Court, Park Avenue, Roundhay, Leeds 8 (☎ 0532 733011); Poulter House, 2 Burley Road, Leeds LS3 1NJ (☎ 0532 469611, fax 0532 448796)

POULTON, Christopher Geoffrey; s of Sqdn Ldr Geoffrey Poulton, DFC, and Margery, *née* Hillman; *b* 4 June 1943; *Educ* Dulwich Coll, Churchill Coll Cambridge (MA); *m* 2 Sept 1967, Judith, *née* Barton; 3 da (Annabel, Rebecca, Victoria); *Career* Baring Bros & Co 1972-75, asst dir Charterhouse Japhet 1975-84, dir Cadogan Oakley 1984-86, divnl md CL-Alexanders Laing & Cruickshank 1986-; *Recreations* fishing, music, sailing; *Style*— Christopher Poulton, Esq; The Manor House, Sundridge, Kent; Piercy Hse, Copthall Ave, London, EC2R 7BE

POULTON, Richard Christopher; s of Rev Christopher John Poulton (d 1988), and Aileen Muriel, *née* Sparrow (d 1977); *b* 21 June 1938; *Educ* Kings Coll Taunton, Wesleyan Univ Middleton Conneticut USA, Pembroke Coll Cambridge Univ (DipEd, MA); *m* 3 April 1965, Zara Irene Mary, da of Prof Peter Charles Crossley-Holland of Llangeler, Llandysul; 2 s (Anthony b 1969, Benedict b 1971), 1 da (Elizabeth b 1966); *Career* asst master: Bedford Sch 1962-63, Beckenham and Penge GS 1963-66; head of dept and housemaster Bryanston Sch 1966-80; headmaster: Wycliffe Coll 1980-86, Christs Hosp 1987-; JP S Glos 1985-86, govr Oxford and Cambridge Exam Bd 1987; memb Head Masters Conf 1980, Secdy Heads Assoc 1980; Freeman City of London 1987; *Books* Victoria, Queen of a Changing Land (1975), Kings and Commoners (1977), A History of the Modern World (1980); *Recreations* choral music, walking, watching sport, writing; *Clubs* East India, Public Schs; *Style*— Richard Poulton, Esq; The Head Master's House, Christ's Hospital, Horsham, W Sussex RH13 7LS (☎ 0403 52547); Christ's Hospital, Horsham, W Sussex RH13 7LS (☎ 0403 52547)

POULTON, William Dacres Campbell; s of Maj Arthur Stanley Poulton (d 1981), of Battle, Sussex, and Winifred Evelyn, *née* Montgomery Campbell; *b* 15 Dec 1937; *Educ* Dover Coll, New Coll Oxford (BA, MA); *m* 3 Jan 1970, Carolyn Frances, da of Flt Lt Francis Macken (d 1961); 2 s (Charles b 1970, Andrew b 1976), 1 da (Elinor b 1972); *Career* Nat Serv 1956-58, 2 Lt Royal Sussex Regt 1957, Samaliland Scout 1957 -58;lectr in law New Coll Oxford 1963-68; called to the Bar 1965 Middle Temple, asst rec 1987, S E circuit, memb Sevenoaks Deanery Synod; *Recreations* gardening, walking, skiing; *Style*— William Poulton, Esq; Quarry Chase, Seal Hollow Rd, Sevenoaks, Kent (☎ 0732 451 389); 12 New Square, Lincolns Inn, London WC2 (☎ 01 405 3808, fax 01 831 7376)

POUNCEY, Philip Michael Rivers; CBE (1987); s of Rev George Ernest Pouncey (d 1929), and Madeline Mary Roberts (d 1956); *b* 15 Feb 1910; *Educ* Marlborough, Queens' Coll Cambridge; *m* 1937, Myril, da of late Lt-Col Albert Gros; 2 da; *Career* hon attaché Fitzwilliam Museum 1931-33; asst keeper: Nat Gallery 1934-45, Br Museum 1945-66 (dep keeper 1954-66); dir Sothebys 1966-82, conslt 1983-, hon keeper of Italian drawings Fitzwilliam Museum 1975-; FBA; *Books* (co-author) catalogues of Italian Drawings in the British Museum (1950, 1962, 1983); *Style*— Philip Pouncey, Esq, CBE; 5 Lower Addison Gdns, London W14 8BG (☎ 01 603 3652)

POUND, Guy Peter; s of Ernest John Pound of Poole, Dorset; *b* 26 Jan 1933; *Educ* Brentwood Public Sch, Bartlett Sch of Arch, UCL (Dip Arch); *m* 8 March 1982, Deborah, *née* Hall; *Career* architect; md of The Guy Pound Gp Practice (Arch and Planners) Ltd 1986, dir Anglo Continental Casinos Ltd 1987, chm Macs Rainwear Ltd 1983; works inc: Hythe Marina Village Hampshire, Milbay Docks Plymouth, Supreme Law Cts Canberra; competitions inc: runner up Cwlth Bank Canberra; assoc RIBA, fell RAIA; lawn tennis umpire all major tournaments inc centre ct Wimbledon, Wembley, Davis Cup etc; *Recreations* squash, tennis; *Clubs* Royal Southampton Yacht, Lawn Tennis Umpires Assoc of GB; *Style*— Guy Pound, Esq; The Studio, 11 Ravine Rd, Canford Cliffs, Poole, Dorset BH13 7HS; The Loft, Rear of 13 Ravine Rd, Canford Cliffs, Poole, Dorset BH13 (☎ 0202 707655, fax 0202 707076)

POUND, Joan, Lady; Joan Amy; da of James Woodthorpe; *m* 1942, Sir Derek Allen Pound, 4 Bt (d 1980); *Style*— Joan, Lady Pound; Saham Grove Hall, Shipdham, Thetford, Norfolk

POUND, Sir John David; 5 Bt (UK 1905), of Stanmore, Co Middlesex; s of Sir Derek Allen Pound, 4 Bt (d 1980); Sir John Pound, 1 Bt, was head of the firm John Pound & Co, Portmanteau Manufacturers, and lord mayor of London 1904-05; *b* 1 Nov 1946; *m* 1, 20 July 1968 (m dis 1978), Heather Frances O'Brien, o da of Harry Jackson Dean; 1 s; *m* 2, 1978, Penelope Ann, da of Grahame Arthur Rayden; 2 s (Christopher b 1982); *Heir* s, Robert John Pound b 2 Feb 1973; *Career* Liveryman Leathersellers' Co; *Style*— Sir John Pound, Bt; 6 Fetcham Park Drive, Fetcham, nr Leatherhead, Surrey

POUNDER, Rafton John; s of Cuthbert C Pounder (decd); *b* 13 May 1933; *Educ* Charterhouse, Christ's Coll Cambridge; *m* 1959, Valerie Isobel, da of late Robert Stewart, MBE; 1 s, 1 da; *Career* MP (UU) Belfast S Oct 1963-Feb 1974, sec N Ireland Bankers' Assoc 1977-; *Style*— Rafton Pounder, Esq; Gunpoint, Coastguard Lane, Orlock, Bangor, Co Down BT19 2LR

POUNDS, Maj-Gen (Edgar George) Derek; CB (1975); s of Edgar Henry Pounds, MBE, MSM; *b* 13 Oct 1922; *Educ* Reading Sch; *m* 1944, Barbara Winifred May Evans; 1 s, 1 da;

Career served Royal Marines 1940-76: Acting Maj-Gen 1973, Maj-Gen 1974, Cmdt Commanding Commando Forces RM 1973-76, ret; chief exec British Friesian Cattle Soc 1976-, exec Ctee Nat Cattle Breeders' Assoc 1978-; *Style*— Major-General Derek Pounds, CB; Scotsbridge House, Rickmansworth, Herts WD3 3BB

POUNDS, Prof Kenneth Alwyne; CBE (1984); s of Harry Pounds (d 1976), and Dorothy Louise, *née* Hunt (d 1981); *b* 17 Nov 1934; *Educ* Salt Sch Shipley Yorks, Univ Coll London (BSc, PhD); *m* 1, 29 Dec 1961, Margaret Mary (d 1976), da of Patrick O'Connell (d 1969); 2 s (David Edwin b 12 May 1963, John Michael b 13 April 1966), 1 da (Jillian Barbara b 12 June 1964); m 2, 10 Dec 1982, Joan Mary, da of Samuel Millit (d 1983); 1 s (Michael Andrew b 5 Aug 1983), 1 da (Jennifer Ann b 22 Feb 1987); *Career* Univ of Leciester: asst lectr 1960, lectr 1962, dir X-Ray astronomy gp 1969-, sr lectr in physics 1969, reader in physics 1971, prof of space physics 1973-, hd of physics 1986-; author of over 100 publications worldwide; playing memb: Oadby Town CC, Oadby Wyvern FC; fndr memb BNSC Mgmnt Bd, memb SERC Cncl (chm Astronomy, Space & Radio Bd 1980-84), memb Cncl Royal Soc 1986-87; hon Dr Univ of York 1984; FRS 1981; *Recreations* cricket, football, music; *Style*— Prof Kenneth Pounds, CBE; 12 Swale Close, Oadby, Leics (☎ 0533 719 370); Dept of Physics, Univ of Leics LE1 7RH (☎ 0533 523 509, telex 341664)

POUNTAIN, Christopher Charles; s of Charles Alfred Pountain, of Edinburgh, and Jean Mary *née* Stanfield; *b* 4 May 1953; *Educ* Royal High Sch Edinburgh, St Andrews (BSc); *m* 29 July 1988, Joyce Margaret, da of William Thomson, of Balrownie nr Brechin; *Career* actuary student Scottish Widows Fund 1975-79, insur analyst Wood Mackenzie 1979 (dir 1985, merger with County Nat West 1988), with London Office County Nat West 1988; FFA 1978; *Recreations* hill walking, skiing, cinema going, reading; *Style*— Christoher Pountain, Esq; County Nat West Securities, Drapers Gardens, 12 Throgmorton Ave, London, EC2P 2ES (☎ 01 382 1549, fax 01 382 1001)

POUNTAIN, Eric John; *b* 5 August 1933; *Educ* Queen Mary's GS Walsall; *m* 1960, Joan Patricia, 1 s, 1 da; *Career* chm Tarmac plc, James Beattie plc; non exec dir: Glynwed Int plc, Midland Bank plc; Staffordshire Agric Soc, tstee Ironbridge Gorge Museum Tst; DL of Staffordshire, ASVA, MFB, MBIM, FIHE; *Style*— Eric Pountain, Esq, DL; Edial House, Edial, nr Lichfield, Staffordshire; c/o Tarmac plc, Hilton Hall, Essington, Wolverhampton WV11 2BQ

POUNTNEY, David Willoughby; s of Edward Willoughby Pountney, of Clevedon, Avon, and Dorothy Lucy, *née* Byrt (d 1984); *b* 10 Sept 1947; *Educ* St Johns Coll Choir Sch Cambridge, Radley, St Johns Coll Cambridge (MA); *m* 23 Feb 1980, Jane Rosemary, da of Maj James Emrys Williams (d 1978); 1 s (James b 1984), 1 da (Emilia b 1981); *Career* dir of productions: Scottish Opera 1976-80, ENO 1983-; dir operas Ireland, Holland, Germany, Italy, Aust and USA, all maj Br cos; princ productions include: the Janacek cycle (Scottish Opera, WNO), Bussonis, Dr Faust (ENO, Deutsche Opera), The Lady Macbeth of Mtensk (ENO) Humperdink's Hansel and Gretel (ENO, received The Evening Standard Award); *Books* numerous opera translations inc Smetana's The Bartered Bride, Two Widows, Die Fledermaus, From the House of the Dead, The Flying Dutchman, La Traviata, Christmas Eve, Sefaglio; *Recreations* croquet, cooking, gardening; *Clubs* Garrick; *Style*— David Pountney, Esq; 142 Hemingford Rd, London N1 1DE (☎ 01 700 5555); ENO, London Coliseum, St Martin's Lane WC2 (☎ 01 836 0111)

POUT, Harry Wilfred; CB (1978), OBE (1959); *b* 11 April 1920; *Educ* East Ham GS, Imperial Coll London; *m* 1949, Margaret Elizabeth, *née* Nelson; 3 da; *Career* dep controller (MOD): Guided Weapons 1973, Guided Weapons and Electronics 1973-75, Air Systems 1975-79, Aircraft Weapons and Electronics 1979-80; def conslt 1980-82, Marconi Underwater Weapons Systems Ltd 1982-1986; def conslt 1986-; *Recreations* mountaineering, geology; *Style*— Harry Pout, Esq, CB, OBE; Oakmead, Fox Corner, Worplesdon, nr Guildford, Surrey GU3 3PP (☎ 0483 232223)

POVER, Hon Mrs (Joan Vera); *née* Brockway; 3 da of Baron Brockway (Life Peer), and his 1 w, Lilla, *née* Harvey-Smith; *b* 1921; *m* 29 April 1944, Capt Everett Samuel Pover, s of Samuel Pover, of Bushey, Herts; 3 s, 1 da; *Style*— The Hon Mrs Pover

POVEY, Robert Frederick Donald; s of Donald James Frederick Povey (d 1987), and Ellen Lillian, *née* Nye (d 1987); *b* 8 July 1944; *Educ* Strand GS, Brixton Sch of Bldg; *m* 23 March 1966 (m dis 1970), Pauline, da of Ernest John Wise; m 2, 22 June 1974, Karen Moira, da of late Arthur Reginald Whitfield; *Career* engr; ptnr Mitchell McFarlane and Ptnrs (dir and co sec); former chm Surrey Branch of Inst Structural Engrs, memb ctees of CIRIA and SCI producing pubns for structural engrs; FIStructE, MConsE; *Recreations* golf, amateur dramatics; *Clubs* Puttenham GC; *Style*— Robert Povey, Esq; Mitchell McFarlane & Ptnrs, Old Inn Ho, 2 Carshalton Rd, Sutton, Surrey SM1 4RA (☎ 01 661 6565, fax 01 643 9136)

POWDITCH, Alan Cecil Robert; MC (1944); s of Cecil John Powditch (d 1968), and late Annis Maudie, *née* Allen; *b* 14 April 1912; *Educ* Mercers Sch; *m* 8 Aug 1942, Barbara, da of John Leggat (d 1943); 1 s (Michael b 25 Oct 1950), 1 da (Frances Valerie b 2 April 1947); *Career* WWII Royal Tank Regt: Trooper 1941, Lance Corpl 1942, 2 Lt 1942, Lt 1943, Capt 1944, Maj 1944, demob 1946; hosp serv 1933-77; sec to bd of govrs St Mary's Hosp London 1950-74 (accountant 1938-41 and 1946-47, dep house govr 1947-50), dist admin NW dist Kensington Chelsea and Westminster AHA 1974-77; memb nat staff ctee Miny of Health 1964-72; JP Middx 1965-82 (supplemental list 1982-), chm juvenile panel Gore Div 1973-76 (dep chm 1976-82); *Recreations* golf; *Style*— Alan Powditch, Esq, MC; 27 Gateway Close, Northwood, Middlesex HA6 2RW (☎ 092 74 27488)

POWELL, Albert Edward; JP (1961); s of Albert Edward Powell (d 1938), of Morden Surrey, and Mrs Mary Daisy Fewtrell; *b* 20 May 1927; *Educ* Holy Family RC Sch Morden Surrey; *m* 1947, Margaret da of Thomas Neville (d 1942); 1 s (Michael), 2 da (Susan, Deirdre); *Career* London organiser Nat Union Printing, Bookbinding and Paperworkers 1957, organising sec SOGAT 1967 (gen pres 1973-83); dep chm Bexley Magistrates and Bexley Juvenile Bench of Magistrates; memb: Indust Trng Bd 1968 (chm 1974), Central Arbitration Ctee 1978, Industl Tribunal 1984, Parole Bd 1986, Socl Security Appeal Tribunal 1985; MTM Assoc of UK; former govr London Coll of Printing, tstee: Bookbinders Charitable Assoc, Mgmnt Ctee of Printers Charitable Assoc; former memb: London Electricity Consultative Ctee, NEDO Printing Industs Ctee; FIMS, HM The Queens Silver Jubilee Medal; *Recreations* golf, chess, gardening, music (classic); *Style*— Albert Powell Esq, JP; 31 Red House Lane, Bexley Heath, Kent DN6 8JF (☎ 01 304 7480)

POWELL, Albert Paul; s of late Albert Edward Powell; *b* 1 Mar 1940; *Educ* St Luke's Portsmouth, Law Society's Coll; *m* 1972, Avril Moira, nee Wylie; 1 s, 2 da; *Career* Capt Mid & Near E; slr; co dir: Trafalgar House Offshore & Structural Ltd, Br Bridge Builders Ltd, Cleveland Alloys Ltd, Cleveland Engineering Design Services Ltd; Freeman of the City of London; *Recreations* rifle shooting, medal collecting; *Clubs* English XX; *Style*— Albert Paul Powell, Esq; 20 Edinburgh Dve, Darlington, Co Durham (☎ 0325 57909)

POWELL, Anthony Dymoke; CH (1988), CBE (1956); s of late Lt-Col P L W Powell, CBE, DSO; *b* 21 Dec 1905; *Educ* Eton, Balliol Coll Oxford; *m* 1934, Lady Violet Pakenham, 3 da of 5 Earl of Longford, KP, MVO (ka 1915); 2 s (Tristram, John); *Career* served Welch Regt and Intelligence Corps WW II, Maj; tstee Nat Portrait Gallery 1962-76; hon fell: Balliol Coll Oxford 1974, Modern Language Assoc of America 1981; hon memb American Acad of Arts and Letters 1977; Hon DLitt: Sussex 1971, Leicester 1976, Kent 1976, Oxon 1980, Bristol 1982; Order of the White Line (Czech), Order of the Oaken Crown and Croix de Guerre (Luxembourg), Order of Leopold II (Belgium); *Books Incl:* Agents and Patients (1936), Music of Time (12 Vol series), A Question of Upbringing (1951), At Lady Molly's (1957, James Tait Black Memorial Prize), Temporary Kings (1973, W H Smith Prize), Hearing Secret Harmonies (1975), To Keep the Ball Rolling (memoirs; 4 Vol series, Vol I 1976, Vol IV 1982), The Fisher King 1986; *Plays* Afternoon Men (adapted from book of 1931), Arts Theatre Club, The Garden God, The Rest I'll Whistle, The Album of Music of Time (ed Violet Powell) 1987; *Clubs* Travellers', Pratt's; *Style*— Anthony Powell, Esq, CH, CBE; The Chantry, nr Frome, Somerset (☎ 037 384 314)

POWELL, Arthur Barrington; CMG (1967); s of late Thomas Powell; *b* 24 April 1918; *Educ* Cowbridge, Jesus Coll Oxford; *m* 1945, Jane, da of late Gen Sir George Weir, KCB, CMG, DSO; 4 s, 1 da; *Career* ICS 1939-47, Miny of Fuel and Power 1947, princ private sec to Min 1949-51, petroleum attaché HM Embassy Washington 1962-64, Gas Div 1968-72, Reg Finance Div DOI 1972-76, exec dir Welsh Devpt Agency 1976-83; *Clubs* United Oxford and Cambridge; *Style*— A B Powell Esq, CMG; The Folly, Newchurch West, Chepstow, Gwent

POWELL, Hon Mrs; Hon Beryl; *née* Davies; da of Baron Davies of Penrhys (Life Peer); *b* 1947; *m* 1965, Colin James Powell; children; *Style*— The Hon Mrs Powell; Maesgwyn, Ton Pentre, Rhondda

POWELL, Dr Brian David; s of T D L Powell (d 1970); *b* 20 Feb 1926; *Educ* Saltley Birmingham, Coleshill Warwicks, Trinity Coll Cambridge (MA, PhD), Univ of NSW Australia; *m* 1957, Jean Mary, *née* Stephenson; 3 da; *Career* Nat Res Cncl of Canada 1952-53; fell Royal Soc of Chemistry 1962, fell Inst of Food Science & Technol 1971; mastership in Food Control 1980; dir: Cadbury Ltd 1969-86 (Int Scientific Standards) Cadbury Shweppes plc 1980-86, Ghana Cocoa Growing Research Assoc Ltd 1980-1986; vice-pres Int Office of Cocoa & Chocolate 1976-1986; dir Edgbaston Church of England Coll for Girls 1985-, memb cncl Br Industl Biological Res Assoc 1966-1986; *Recreations* silversmithing, ind archaeology, walking, photography, community services; *Style*— Dr Brian D. Powell; 427 Heath Rd South, Northfield, Birmingham B31 2BB (☎ 021 475 4983)

POWELL, Charles David; s of John Frederick Powell, and Geraldine Ysolda Moylan; *b* 6 July 1941; *Educ* Kings Sch Canterbury, New Coll Oxford (BA); *m* 24 Oct 1964, Carla, da of Domingo Bonardi, of Italy; 2 s (Hugh b 1967, Nicholas b 1968); *Career* memb HM Dip Serv, Helsinki, Washington, Bonn and EEC Brussels, private sec to PM 1984- (under sec 1987); *Recreations* walking; *Clubs* Turf; *Style*— Charles Powell, Esq; c/o No, 10 Dowing St, London SW1

POWELL, David Beynon; s of David Eynon Powell (d 1942), and Catherine Ada, *née* Beynon; *b* 9 Feb 1934; *Educ* Gowerton GS, Christ's Coll Cambridge (MA, LLB), Yale Law Sch (LLM), Harvard Business Sch (SMP 18); *m* 18 Sept 1973 (m dis 1983), Pamela Susan, *née* Turnbull; *Career* Nat Serv Flying Offr RAF 1952-54; slr Supreme Ct, dep legal advsr BLMC Ltd 1970-73, dir legal servs BL Ltd 1974-83, gp legal dir Midland Bank plc 1984-; *Recreations* reading, music, bridge; *Style*— David Powell, Esq; 20c Randolph Crescent, London W9 1DR (☎ 01 289 2326); Midland Bank plc, Head Office, Poultry, London EC2P 2BY (☎ 01 260 8239, fax 01 260 8461)

POWELL, His Honour Judge Watkin Dewi Watkin; JP (Dyfed); s of W H Powell; *b* 29 July 1920; *Educ* Penarth GS, Jesus Coll Oxford; *m* 1951, Alice, da of William Williams; 1 da; *Career* called to the Bar Inner Temple 1949, dep chm Merioneth and Cardigan QS 1966-71; dep rec 1965-71: Cardiff, Birkenhead, Merthyr Tydfil, Swansea; a circuit judge and official referee for Wales and Chester 1972-, liaison judge for Dyfed 1974-84 and Mid Glamorgan 1984-, designated judge for Merthyr Tydfil 1986-; Univ Coll Cardiff: memb of ct and cncl 1976-88, vice pres 1982-88, hon fell and chm of cncl 1987-88; hon fell and vice-chm of cncl University of Wales Coll Cardiff 1988- (formerly memb of ct and cncl); memb: ct and cncl Univ Coll of Wales Aberystwyth, cncl Univ of Wales Coll of Med, ct Univ of Wales; chm Cncl of Hon Soc of Cymmrodorian 1979-86 (vice-pres 1986-, pres Theatr Cymro Soc 1983-; *Style*— His Honour Judge Watkin Powell, JP; Crown Court, Law Courts, Cathays Park, Cardiff

POWELL, (Elizabeth) Dilys; CBE (1974); da of late Thomas Powell and late Mary Powell; *b* 20 July 1901; *Educ* Bournemouth HS, Somerville Coll Oxford; *m* 1, 1926, Humfry Payne (d 1936); m 2, 1943, Leonard Russell (d 1974); *Career* film critic The Sunday Times 1939-76, TV film critic 1976-; film critic Punch 1979-; FRSL; *Books* Publications Descent from Parnassus, Remember Greece, The Traveller's Journey is Done, Coco, An Affair of the Heart, The Villa Ariadne; *Style*— Miss Dilys Powell, CBE; 14 Albion St, Hyde Park, London W2 (☎ 01 723 9807)

POWELL, Rt Hon (John) Enoch; MBE (1943), PC (1960); s of Albert Enoch Powell; *b* 16 June 1912; *Educ* King Edward's Birmingham, Trinity Coll Cambridge (MA); *m* 1952, Margaret Pamela, *née* Wilson; 2 da; *Career* fell of Trinity Coll Cambridge 1934-38, prof of greek Sydney Univ NSW 1937-39; serv Royal Warwickshire Regt WWII, Brig 1944; MP (C) Wolverhampton SW 1950-74, Down S 1974-83; S Down 1983-87; parly sec Miny of Housing and Local Govt 1955-57, fin sec to the Treasy 1957-58, min of Health 1960-63; author; *Style*— The Rt Hon Enoch Powell, MBE, PC; 33 South Eaton Place, SW1 (☎ 01 730 0988)

POWELL, Geoffrey; s of Owen Thomas Powell, of Stoke-on-Trent, and Ethel Mary, *née* Woollam; *Educ* Stanfield HS Stoke-on-Trent, London Univ (BSc, MSc); *m* 30 Nov 1968, Penelope Elizabeth, da of Maj George Eastlake; 1 s (Adam b 1971), 1 da (Nina b 1973); *Career* chief exec Imperial Foods (General Products) Ltd 1984-86 (personnel dir 1979-82, planning dir 1982-84); md: Granada TV Rental Ltd 1986-88, Granada UK Rental and Retail Ltd 1988-; dir Granada Gp plc 1987; *Recreations* skiing, squash, reading; *Style*— Geoffrey Powell, Esq; Granada TV Rental Ltd, PO Box 31, Ampthill Rd, Bedford MK42 9QQ (☎ 0234 55233, fax 0234 226006, telex 82303)

POWELL, Col Geoffrey Stewart; MC (1944); s of Owen Welch Powell (d 1964), of Scarborough, and Ada Jane, *née* King (d 1968); *b* 25 Dec 1914; *Educ* Scarborough Coll, Open Univ (BA); *m* 7 July 1944, (Anne) Felicity, da of Maj Walter William Wadsworth, MC (d 1972), of West Grimstead; 1 s (Lt-Col John Stewart Wadsworth), 1 da (Rosemary Anne Felicity (Mrs Anderson)); *Career* 2 Lt 5 Bn The Green Howards (TA) 1936-39, 2 Lt The Green Howards (regular army) 1939; WWII serv 1939-45: 2 Lt (later Lt-Col) The Green Howards and Parchute Regt (active serv India, ME, NW Europe); Staff Coll Camberley 1946, Bde Maj Java and Malaya 1946-49 (despatches) 1949), regtl duty Austria 1949-50, graduated US Cmd and Gen Staff Coll Fort Leavenworth 1951, WO 1951-53, regtl duty Egypt and Cyprus 1954-55, GSO1 WO 1955-57, CO II Bn KAR Kenya 1957-59, Col gen staff WO 195-62, Bde Col Yorks Bde 1962-64, ret 1964; dep col The Green Howards 1982-84, MOD 1964-76; chm Campden and Dist Hist and Archaeological Soc, Cncl memb Bristol and Gloucs Archaeological Soc; *Books* The Green Howards (1968), The Kandyan Wars: The British Army in Ceylon 1803-1818 (1973), Men at Arnhem (1976), Suez: The Double War (with Roy Fullick 1979), The Book of Campden: History in Stone (1982), The Bridges to Arnhem (1984); *Recreations* hill walking, history, books, beagling; *Clubs* Army & Navy; *Style*— Col Geoffrey Powell, MC

POWELL, (Richard) Guy; s of Richard Albert Brakell Powell (d 1957), and Stella Float, *née* Young; *b* 28 April 1927; *Educ* The King's Sch Canterbury, Hertford Coll Oxford (MA); *Career* admitted slr 1953; ptnr: Rooper & Whately 1960-70, LEE & Pembertons 1970-; clerk Prowdes Educnl Fndn 1974-; memb Cncl of Private Libraries Assoc 1963-; Freeman City of London 1948, Liveryman Worshipful Co of Drapers' 1952; FRSA 1952, memb Vereinigung Der Freunde Antiker Kunst (Switzerland) 1960; *Recreations* book collecting, gardening; *Clubs* Travellers, United Oxford and Cambridge; *Style*— R Guy Powell, Esq; 45 Pont St, London SW1X 0BX (☎ 01 589 1114, fax 01 589 0807)

POWELL, James Richard Douglas; s and h of Sir Nicholas Folliott Douglas Powell, 4 Bt; *b* 17 Oct 1962; *Style*— James Powell Esq

POWELL, Air Vice-Marshal John Frederick; OBE (1956), AE (1946); s of Rev Morgan Powell (d 1951), of Limpley Stoke nr Bath, and Edith Susannah, *née* David (d 1964); *b* 12 June 1915; *Educ* King's Coll Choir Sch Cambridge, Lancing Coll, King's Coll Cambridge (BA, MA); *m* 16 Sept 1939, (Geraldine) Ysolda, da of Sir John Moylan, CB, CBE (d 1967), of Church Lane Cottage, Bury, Sussex; 4 s (Charles b 1941, Christopher b 1943, Roderick b 1948, Jonathan b 1956) ; *Career* lectr RAF Coll Cranwell 1938, controller coastal cmd (ops) RAFVR 1939-45, (despatches), RAF (Educn Branch) 1946, instr later sr tutor RAF Coll 1946-59, educn staff FEAF 1959-62, MOD 1962-64, Gp Capt 1964, cmd educn offr HQ Bomber Cmd 1964-66, OC RAF Sch of Educn 1966-67, Air Cdre 1967, Dir RAF Educn Servs 1967-72, Air Vice- Marshal 1968; warden and dir of studies Moor Park Coll Farnham 1972-77; *Recreations* choral music, gardening, walking; *Clubs* RAF; *Style*— Air Vice-Marshal John Powell, OBE, AE; Barkers Hill Cottage, Donhead St Andrew, Shaftesbury, Dorset SP7 9EB (☎ 074 788 505)

POWELL, (Geoffrey) Mark; s of Francis Turner Powell, MBE, of Tanglewood, Oak Grange Rd, West Clandon, Surrey, and Joan Audrey, *née* Bartlett; *b* 14 Jan 1946; *Educ* Tonbridge, St Chad's Coll Durham Univ (BA); *m* 24 July 1971, Veronica Joan, da of Paul Frank Rowland, of Langford, Clymping, Sussex; 2 da (Jessica b 1973, Catriona b 1976); *Career* memb Int Stock Exchange 1971; ptnr Powell Popham Dawes & Co 1972-77; dir: Laing & Cruickshank 1977-86, CL-Alexanders Laing & Cruickshank Hldgs Ltd 1986-, chief exec 1987-; Freeman City of London 1967, Liveryman Worshipful Co of Haberdashers 1968; *Clubs* MCC, City of London; *Style*— Mark Powell, Esq; Creedhole Farm, High Button, Thursley, Surrey GU8 6NR (☎ 042 879 3163); 32 Canonbury Sq, London N1 2AL (☎ 01 226 8236);

POWELL, Sir Nicholas Folliott Douglas; 4 Bt (UK 1897); s of Sir Richard George Douglas Powell, MC, 3 Bt (d 1980); descends from Walter Powell (d 1567), descendant of Rhys ap Tewdwr Mawr, King of South Wales (*see also* William R Powell, MP); *b* 17 July 1935; *Educ* Gordonstoun; *m* 1, 26 May 1960 (m dis 1987), Daphne Jean, yr da of Maj George Henry Errington, MC; 1 s, 1 da; m 2, 10 July 1987, Davina Hyacinth Berners, er twin da of Michael Edward Ranulph Allsopp; 1 s (b 5 Jan 1989); *Heir* s, James Richard Douglas Powell; *Career* Lt Welsh Gds 1953-57; co dir; *Style*— Sir Nicholas Powell, Bt; Petrunella Coffee Estate, Box 58, Chipinga, Zimbabwe

POWELL, Peter William George; s of Albert Victor Powell (d 1960), of London, and Jessie May Graveney (d 1981); *b* 18 Feb 1926; *Educ* Christ's Coll London, Northern Poly (Dip Arch), UC London (Dip Civic Arch and Town Planning); *m* 16 Feb 1962, Jamila Akhter Jabeen, da of Mohd Amin Malik (d 1987); 1 s (William Ahmed b 1964), 2 da (Jessima Elizabeth b 1968, Sophia Elizabeth (twin) b 1968); *Career* chartered architect and chartered town planner (FRIBA, FRTPI) 1950-; private practice London and Govt Service 1959-66, advsr town planning and housing to the Govt of Pakistan under the Tech Co operation Scheme of the Columbo Plan, author of two reports for Pakistan govt on urban improvements and housing legislation; fndr memb Pakistan Inst of Architects 1959 and the Pakistan Inst of City of Regnl Planning 1960; professional service: Overseas Relations Ctee RIBA 1967-73, Hertfordshire Assoc of Architects, cncl memb and hon tres 1973-80, RIBA Eastern Region, cncl memb and hon tres 1979-84, memb cncl of Architects Registration Cncl of the UK 1987-89, memb of Organising Ctee of RTPI 1970 to estabish a Cwlth Assoc of Planners; *Recreations* watching cricket, book collecting; *Clubs* Marylebone Cricket, Middlesex CCC and Surrey CCC, Cricketers (London); *Style*— Peter Powell, Esq; 8 Longdean Park, Hemel Hempstead, Herts HP3 8BS (☎ 0442 54824)

POWELL, Sir (Arnold Joseph) Philip; CH (1984), OBE (1957); yr s of Rev Canon Arnold C Powell (d 1963), and Mary Winnifred, *née* Walker (d 1954); *b* 15 Mar 1921; *Educ* Epsom Coll, AA Sch of Architecture; *m* 1953, Philippa, da of Lt-Col Charles Chevalier Eccles, of Tunbridge Wells; 1 s, 1 da; *Career* architect in private practice, as ptnr in Powell Moya and Ptnrs; works incl: Churchill Gdns housing Pimlico and 'Skylon' for 51 Festival of Britain (both of which won in open competition), new buildings at St John's and Queens' Colls Cambridge, Wolfson Coll Oxford, Chichester Festival Theatre, Museum of London, Queen Elizabeth II Conf Centre, Westminster and several new hosps; memb: Royal Fine Art Cmmn 1969-, RA 1977; FRIBA (Royal Gold Medal for Architecture, RIBA 1974); kt 1975; *Style*— Sir Philip Powell, CH, OBE; 16 The Little Boltons, London SW10 9LP (☎ 01 373 8620); office: 21 Upper Cheyne Row, London SW3 (☎ 01 351 3881)

POWELL, Raymond; MP (Lab) Ogmore 1979-; s of Albert Powell; *b* 19 June 1928; *Educ* Pentre G S, Nat Cncl of Labour Colls, LSE; *m* 1951, Marion Grace Evans; 1 s, 1 da; *Career* chm Lab Pty Wales 1977-78, chm S Wales Euro-Constituency Lab Pty 1979-80, sec Anglo-Bulgaria All Pty Parly Gp 1982-, sec Welsh Gp Lab MP's 1985-, vice-chm PLP Agriculture Ctee 1987-88, Paiting Whip 1987-; *Style*— Raymond Powell Esq, MP; 8 Brynteg Gdns, Bridgend, Mid-Glam (☎ 0656 2159)

POWELL, Sir Richard Royle; GCB (1967), KCB (1961, CB 1951, KBE 1954, CMG 1946); s of Ernest Hartley Powell; *b* 30 July 1909; *Educ* Queen Mary's GS Walsall, Sidney Sussex Coll Cambridge (hon fellow 1972); *Career* dep sec: Admty 1948-50, MOD 1950-56; perm sec: MOD 1956-59, BOT 1960-68; dep chm Perm Ctee on Invisible Exports 1968-76; chm: Alusuisse (UK) Ltd 1969-84, Sandoz Gp of cos 1972-1987, Wilkinson Match Ltd 1979-80 (hon pres 1981-83); dir: Whessoe plc 1968-87, Ladbroke Gp plc 1980-1986, Bridgewater Paper Co Ltd 1983-, Aero-Print Ltd 1969-84, Clerical, Medical and Gen Life Assurance Soc 1972-85, BPB Industries plc 1973-83, Philip Hill Investmt Tst until 1981, Philip Hill & Partners 1981-1986; chm Civil Service Security Appeals Panel until 1982; *Clubs* Athenaeum; *Style*— Sir Richard Powell, GCB, KCB, CB, KBE, CMG; 56 Montagu Sq, London W1H 1TG (☎ 01 262 0911)

POWELL, Tim (Harry Allan Rose); MBE (1944), TD (1973); s of William Allan Powell (d 1954); *b* 15 Feb 1912; *Educ* Winchester, Pembroke Coll Cambridge; *m* 1936, Elizabeth North, da of Leonard W North Hickley (d 1932); 2 da; *Career* Herts Yeo 1938, Col 1944-45 S E Asia (head of Secretariat to Supreme Allied Cdr); md Massey-Ferguson Hldgs Ltd 1962-78 (chm 1970-80), chm Holland & Holland Ltd 1983-87; *Recreations* fishing, lapidary; *Clubs* Bucks, MCC; *Style*— Tim Powell Esq, MBE, TD; Ready Token, nr Cirencester, Gloucs (☎ 028 574 219); 12 Shafto Mews, Cadogan Sq, SW1 (☎ 01 235 2707)

POWELL, Victor George Edward; s of George Richard Powell; *b* 1 Jan 1929; *Educ* Beckenham GS, Durham Univ, Manchester Univ; *m* 1956, Patricia Copeland Allen; 3 s, 1 da; *Career* sr ptnr Victor G Powell Assocs, Mgmnt Consits 1963-, dir and chief advsr ILO 1977-, dir Mosscare Housing Assoc Ltd 1974-; Assoc memb BIM 1957; MIMC 1968; *Style*— Victor Powell Esq; Inglewood, Coppice Lane, Disley, Stockport, Cheshire SK12 2LT (☎ Disley 2011)

POWELL, Lady Violet (Georgiana); *née* Pakenham; da of 5 Earl of Longford, KP, MVO (d 1915); *b* 1912; *m* 1934, Anthony Dymoke Powell, CH, CBE; 2 s; *Style*— Lady Violet Powell; The Chantry, Nr Frome, Somerset

POWELL, William Rhys; MP (C) Corby 1983-; yst s of Rev Canon Edward Powell, formerly Vicar and Lord of the Manor of Belchamp St Paul, Sudbury, Suffolk, and Anne Woodhouse, *née* Mirton; descends from Walter Powell (d 1567), of Bucknell, Salop who descended from Rhys ap Tewdwr Mawr, King of South Wales; *see also* Sir Nicholas Powell, 4 Bt; *b* 3 August 1948; *Educ* Lancing, Emmanuel Coll Cambridge (MA); *m* 1973, Mary Elizabeth, da of Adolphus Henry Vaudin, of Garlands, Leatherhead Rd, Great Bookham, Surrey; 3 da; *Career* barr Lincoln's Inn 1971; *Clubs* Corby Cons; *Style*— William Powell Esq, MP; House of Commons, London SW1; Lynch House, Fowlmere, Cambs; 1 Crown Office Row, Temple, London EC4 (☎ 01 583 3724)

POWELL-COTTON, Christopher; CMG (1961), MBE (1951, MC 1945, JP); s of Maj P H G Powell-Cotton; *b* 23 Feb 1918; *Educ* Harrow, Trinity Coll Cambridge; *Career* Uganda Admin: district cmmr 1950, prov cmmr 1955, min of security and external relations 1961, ret; dir Powell-Cotton Museum of Nat History and Ethnography; landowner; *Clubs* MCC; *Style*— Christopher Powell-Cotton, Esq, CMG, MBE, MC, JP; Quex Park, Birchington, East Kent CT7 0BH (☎ 0843 41836)

POWELL-JONES, John Ernest; CMG (1974); s of late Walter James Powell-Jones and Gladys Margaret, *née* Taylor; *b* 14 April 1925; *Educ* Charterhouse, Univ Coll Oxford; *m* 1, 1949 (m dis 1967), Ann Murray; 2 s, 1 da; m 2, 1968, Pamela Sale; *Career* HM Foreign Serv 1949-; ambass at Phnom Penh 1973-75, RCDS 1975; ambass to: Senegal, Guinea, Mali, Mauritania and Guinea-Bissau 1976-79, Cape Verde 1977-79; ambass and perm rep UN Conference on Law of the Sea (concluded Dec 1982) 1979-82; ambass Switzerland 1982-85, ret 1985; chm Inter Counsel (UK) Ltd 1986; elected cncllr Waverley Borough 1987; *Clubs* Travellers'; *Style*— John Powell-Jones, Esq, CMG; Gascons, Gaston Gate, Cranleigh, Surrey (☎ 0483 274313)

POWER, Sir Alastair John Cecil; 4 Bt (UK 1924), of Newlands Manor, Milford, Southampton; s of Sir John Patrick McLannahan Power, 3 Bt (d 1984), and Melanie, adopted da of Hon Alastair Erskine (d 1987; s of 6 Baron Erskine) ; *b* 15 August 1958; *Style*— Sir Alastair Power, Bt; c/o Ashwick House, Dulverton, Som

POWER, Lady; Barbara Alice Mary; *née* Topham; elder da of His Honour Judge Alfred Frank Topham, KC, of Cracknells, Yarmouth, IOW; *b* 14 Dec 1904; *Educ* Manor House Sch Lympsfields; *m* 1930, Adml Sir Manley Power, KCB, CBE, DSO*, DL (d 1981), sometime C-in-C Portsmouth Allied C-in-C Channel and C-in-C Home Station designate (RN), seventh in descent from John Power (d 1659), whose elder bro Sir Henry Power, PC, was 1 & last Viscount Valentia of the 1620 cr; (1 s decd), 1 da; *Recreations* reading, conservation; *Clubs* Royal Solent Yacht; *Style*— Lady Power; Norton Cottage, Yarmouth, IOW (☎ 760401)

POWER, Christopher Danvers (Kit); s of Piers Danvers Power (d 1960), and Margaret, *née* Chilton; *b* 5 May 1934; *Educ* Eton, Trinity Coll Cambridge (MA); *m* 26 March 1968, Penelope Joyce, da of Capt Robert Shaw, RN; 2 s (Nicholas b 1973, Julian b 1975); *Career* Nat Serv RN; Rootes Motors Ltd 1958-69, Spencer Stuart and Assocs Ltd 1969-(md 1975-81, chm 1981-); *Recreations* sailing; *Clubs* Royal Cruising; *Style*— Kit Power, Esq; Dudley Ho, Montpelier Row, Twickenham, Middx; Brook Ho, Park Lane, London W1 (☎ 01 493 1238, fax 01 491 8068)

POWER, Eugene Barnum; Hon KBE (1977); s of Glenn Warren Power (d 1955), and Annette Barnum Power (d 1941); *b* 4 June 1905; *Educ* Michigan Univ (AB, MBA, LHD), St John's Univ (LHD); *m* 1929, Sadye Lillian, da of Clarence Abraham Harwick (d 1949); 1 s (Philip Harwick); *Career* microphotographer, ret 1970; organised 1936 first large microfilming project for libraries, to copy all books printed in England before 1640; dir of first large-scale copying operation of important Br MSS during WWII, also enemy documents; special rep, co-ordinator of info and of Library of Congress London 1942, Off of Strategic Services 1943-45; fndr Univ Microfilms Ann Arbor Michigan (merged with Xerox Corpn 1962, sold to Bell & Howell 1986) 1938-70, fndr Univ Microfilms Ltd London 1952; dir Xerox Corpn 1962-68; dir Domino's Pizza Inc 1978-, pres: Eskimo Art Inc 1953-, Power Fndn 1967-; chm and tstee Ann Arbor Summer Festival Inc 1978-(chm emeritus 1988), regent Univ of Michigan 1956-66; memb Cncl of Nat Endowment for the Humanities 1968-74; co-fndr and first pres and fell Nat Microfilm Assoc (now Assoc for Info and Image Mgmnt), co-fndr and first pres Int Micrographic Congress (now Int Info Mgmnt Congress) 1964-65; hon fell Magdalen Coll Cambridge 1967; *Recreations* water polo, swimming, music, theatre, sailing, fishing; *Clubs* The American (London), Ann Arbor Rotary (Ann Arbor Michigan); *Style*— Mr Eugene Power, KBE; 989 Forest Rd, Barton Hills, Ann Arbor, Mich 48105, USA (☎ 313 662 2886); 2929 Plymouth Rd, Suite 300, Ann Arbor, Mich 48105, USA (☎ 313 769 8424)

POWER, John Christopher; TD (1980); s of Geoffrey William Power; *b* 7 Dec 1945; *Educ* BA (Hons); *m* 1969, Ann Marie; 1 da; *Career* Maj Para Regt (TA); formerly dir NEI Parsons Peebles Transformers Ltd 1980, dir Hawker Siddeley Petter Diesels Ltd & Petter Diesels Inc (USA) 1984; Nin of Def 1987; hon tres Round Table; CDipAF, FBIM, FIMEMME, FIElecIE; *Recreations* squash, running, swimming, parachuting, shooting; *Style*— John Power, Esq, TD; Harwood, 2 Oakwood Ave, Purley, Surrey

POWER, Jonathan Richard Adrian; s of Patrick Power, of Little House, Lincombe Lane, Boars Hill, Oxford, and Dorothy Power (d 1984); *b* 4 June 1941; *Educ* Liverpool Inst HS, Univ of Manchester (BA), Univ of Wisconsin (MA); *m* 22 Dec 1964 (m dis 1988), Anne Elizabeth, da of Dennis Hayward, of Southampton; 3 da (Carmen b 18 Jan 1966, Miriam b 23

May 1968, Lucy b 24 Nov 1978); *Career* columnist: International Herald Tribune (column syndicated to 24 princ US and Canadian papers 20 African and Asian papers) 1973-; film: It's Ours Whatever They Say (silver medal Venice Film Festival 1972); memb Int Inst for Strategic Studies 1980; *Books* Development Economics, World of Hunger, The New Proletariat, Against Oblivion; *Recreations* walking, cycling, opera; *Style*— Jonathan Power, Esq; Houseboat Esperance, 106 Cheyne Walk, London SW10 (☎ 01 351 6344)

POWER, Michael George; s of Adm of the Fleet, Sir Arthur John Power, and Amy Isobel, *née* Bingham; *b* 2 April 1924; *Educ* Rugby; *m* 1954, Kathleen Meave, *née* McCaul; 1 s, 2 da; *Career* WWII Rifle Bde 1942-46, M East Centre Arab Studies 1946-47, Col Admin Serv Kenya, Malaya 1947-63; Home CS 1963-81; under sec MOD 1973-81; dir Greenwich Hosp 1982-87; *Recreations* carpentry, gardening; *Style*— Michael Power, Esq; Wancom Way, Puttenham Heath Rd, Compton, Guildford GU3 1DU

POWER, (Ann) Prunella; OBE (1980); da of Capt Edward Hugh Bagot Stack, 8 Gurkha Rifles (d 1914), and Mary Meta Bagot Stack (d 1935), fndr Women's League of Health and Beauty 1930; *b* 28 July 1914; *Educ* The Abbey Malvern Wells; *m* 1, 15 Oct 1938, Lord David Douglas-Hamilton (ka 1944), yst s of 13 Duke of Hamilton and 10 Duke of Brandon (d 1940); 2 s (Diarmaid Hugh b 17 June 1940, Iain b 16 Aug 1942); m 2, 22 July 1950, Alfred Gustave Albers, FRCS (d 1951), o s of late N W Albers, of Newlands, Cape, S Africa; m 3, 15 May 1964, Brian St Quentin Power, 2 s of late Stephen St Quentin Power, of Guerrin, Co Clare; *Career* pres The Women's League of Health and Beauty 1982- (memb of cncl 1950-); vice-pres Outward Bound Tst 1980-; memb Nat Fitness Cncl 1937-39; *Books* The Way to Health and Beauty (1938), Movement is Life (1973), Island Quest (1979), Zest for Life (1988); *Recreations* poetry, music, travel; *Style*— Mrs Brian St Quentin Power, OBE; 14 Gertrude St, London SW10 (☎ 01 351 3393)

POWERS, George Dale; s of George Powers, of Chicago, Illinois, USA, and Harriette Elizabeth, *née* Bonyata (d 1977); *b* 13 Dec 1941; *Educ* Art Inst of Chicago (Interior Design), Univ of Chicago; *m* 20 June 1964, Enid, da of John Wilson-Willison (d 1975), of New Farm, Worksop, Notts; 2 da (Caroline b 1965, Alexandra b 1969); *Career* interior designer, trainee Jack Denst Designs 1962-63; interior designer: John M Smyth & Co 1963-64, Sir Percy Thomas & Son 1965-66, William McCarty Assocs 1966-67; freelance 1967-71 clients incl: David Hicks, Billy McCarty, Colefax and Fowler, private clientele; George Powers Assocs 1971-, clients incl: Schlumberger Oil, NBC News (offices), restoration work St James Ch Piccadilly, Ferguson & Partners, state bedroom Hatfield Ho for Marchioness of Salisbury, interior for Lord Charles Cecil; churchwarden St James Church Piccadilly 1982-87; IDDA 1979, ASID 1986, Nat Tst for Historic Preservation 1986; *Books* The Revolving Kitchen (1966); *Recreations* reading, swimming, cooking, ecclesiastical architecture, music, historic restoration; *Clubs* East India, Lansdowne; *Style*— George Powers, Esq; George Powers Assocs, 27 Rosebury Rd, London SW6 2NQ (☎ business: 01 736 9016, home: 01 731 4547)

POWERS, Dr Michael John; s of Reginald Frederick Powers, of Parkstone, Poole, and Kathleen Ruby, *née* Whitmarsh; *b* 9 Feb 1947; *Educ* Poole GS, London Univ, The Middx Hosp Med Sch (BSc, MB BS, DA), Poly Poly of Central London (Dip Law); *m* 16 Nov 1968, Meryl Julia, da of Frank Edward Hall of Queen's Park Bournemouth; 1 s (Andrew b 1982), 1 da (Julia b 1972); *Career* registered med practitioner 1972-, house surgn Middx Hosp 1972-73, house physician Royal S Hants Hosp 1973-74, sr house offr Royal Utd Hosp Bath 1974-75, registrar (anaesthetics) Northwick Park Hosp Harrow 1975-77; barr Lincoln's Inn 1979, practising at Common Law Bar specialising in med and pharmaceutical law, pres SE Eng Coroners Soc 1987-88; students cnsllr to Hon soc Lincoln's Inn 1983-, HM asst dep coroner Westminster 1981-87; memb: BMA, Medico-Legal Soc; FRSM 1972; *Books* The Law and Practice on Coroners (with Paul Knapman 1985); *Recreations* sailing, hill walking, painting, and music; *Clubs* Bar YC, Royal Yachting Assoc; *Style*— Dr Michael Powers; 1 Paper Buildings, Temple, London, EC4Y 7EP, (☎ 01 583 7355, fax 01 353 2144)

POWERS, William; MBE (1982); s of Capt John Powers (d 1974), and Doris Gladys, *née* Rickard; *b* 2 Sept 1924; *m* 27 June 1953, Janet Elsie Elisabeth, da of Archibald Fletcher; 2 da (Lynda Elisabeth b 1954, Jane Alison b 1956); *Career* Beds & Herts Regt 1942, 9 Commando 2 Special Serv Bde 1942-45 (despatched 1943), Mounted Police Palestine 1945-47, appt Dist Supt 1947, Trans-Jordan Frontier Force 1947-49, seconded Maj; chief exec Shaw & Kilburn Luton 1968-86, chm Station Motors Gp 1986-; patron: Luton & Dist Royal Br Legion, Luton & Dunstable Burma Star Assoc; vice-pres: Luton Household Div Assoc, Luton Royal Naval Assoc; dir Luton Musical Pageant, pres Luton & Dunstable Operatic Soc, JP dep chm Luton Magistrates Ct, chm S Beds Cmmrs of Taxes, memb The Lord Chancellors Advsy Ctee, High Sheriff of Beds; FIMI 1965, MIRTE 1965, MBIM 1969; *Clubs* The Household Div Luton; *Style*— William Powers, Esq, MBE; Old Bedford Rd, Luton, Beds, LU2 7BL; Chairman, Station Motors Gp, Beds, Midland Rd, Luton, Beds LU2 0HR (☎ 0582 31084)

POWERSCOURT, 10 Viscount (I 1743); Mervyn Niall Wingfield; also Baron Wingfield (I 1743), and Baron Powerscourt (UK 1885, title in House of Lords); s of 9 Viscount Powerscourt (d 1973), and Sheila, Viscountess Powerscourt *qv*; *b* 3 Sept 1935; *Educ* Stowe; *m* 1, 1962 (m dis 1974), Wendy Ann Pauline, da of Ralph C G Slazenger; 1 s, 1 da; m 2, 1979, Pauline, da of W P Van, of San Francisco, Calif; *Heir* s, Hon Mervyn Anthony Wingfield; *Style*— The Rt Hon the Viscount Powerscourt

POWERSCOURT, Sheila, Viscountess - Sheila Claude; da of Lt-Col Claude Beddington (who fought, and was wounded, in the Boer War, and WWI and who was ka in WWII in 1939), of London, Italy and Hampshire, and late (Frances) Ethel, er da of Francis Berry Homan-Mulock, JP; *b* 23 May 1906; *Educ* Roedean Sch; *m* 1932, Hon Mervyn Wingfield, later 9 Viscount Powerscourt (d 1973); 2 s (10 Viscount, Hon Guy Wingfield), 1 da (Hon Lady Langrishe); *Career* writer of poetry and prose (all as Sheila Wingfield, with one exception); *Prose Publications* Real People (1952), Sun Too Fast (1978, as Sheila Powerscourt); *Poetry* Poems (1938), Beat Drum, Beat Heart (1946), A Cloud Across The Sun (1949), A Kite's Dinner (1954), The Leaves Darken (1964), Her Storms (1974), Admissions (1977), Collected Poems of Sheila Wingfield (1983), Ladder to the Loft (1987); *Recreations* country pursuits, sailing (small boats), travelling, voracious reading; *Style*— The Rt Hon Sheila, Viscountess Powerscourt; Palma au Lac, CH-6600 Locarno, Switzerland (☎ 093 33 01 71)

POWIS, 7 Earl of (UK 1804); George William Herbert; Baron Powis, of Powis Castle, Co Montgomery, Baron Herbert of Chirbury, Co Salop, and Viscount Clive, of Ludlow, Co Salop (all UK 1804; Baron Clive, of Walcot, Co Salop (GB 1794); Baron Clive of Plassey, Co Limerick (I 1762); eldest s of Rt Rev Percy Mark Herbert, KCVO, DD, sometime Bishop of Norwich (d 1968), and Hon Elaine Letitia Algitha Orde-Powlett (d 1984), o da of 5 Baron Bolton; ggs of 2 Earl of Powis; s his kinsman the 6 Earl 1988; *b* 4 June 1925; *Educ* Eton, Trinity Coll Cambridge (BA); *m* 26 July 1949, Hon Katharine Odeyne de Grey, yst da of 8 Baron Walsingham, DSO, OBE; 4 s (Viscount Clive, Hon Michael Clive b 1954, Hon Peter James b 1955, Hon Edward David b 1958), 2 adopted da (Lorraine Elizabeth b 1961, Nicola Wendy b 1962); *Heir* s, Viscount Clive, *qv*; *Career* served army 1943-47; former chartered land agent; farmer; FRICS; patron of twelve livings; Marrington Hall, Chirbury, Montgomery, Powis (☎ 093 872 256)

POWLES, Sir Guy Richardson; KBE (1961), CMG (1954, ED 1944); s of Col (Charles) Guy Powles, CMG, DSO, NZ Staff Corp (d 1951), and Jessie Mary, *née* Richardson; *b* 5 April 1905; *Educ* Wellington Coll NZ, Victoria Univ, (Hon LLD); *m* 1931, Eileen, da of Alfred James Nicholls; 2 s; *Career* barr Supreme Court, NZ 1929, high cmmr Western Samoa 1949-60, for NZ in India 1960-62, Ceylon 1960-62, ambass of NZ to Nepal 1960-62, first ombudsman of NZ 1962-75, chief ombudsman 1975-77, pres NZ Inst of Int Affairs 1967-71, NZ cmmr Cmmn of the Churches on Int Affairs, World Council of Churches 1971-, cmmr Int Cmmn of Jurists Geneva 1975-; patron NZ Found for Peace Studies 1975-; *Style*— Sir Guy Powles, KBE, CMG, ED; 34 Wesley Rd, Wellington, New Zealand

POWLETT; *see*: William-Powlett

POWLETT, Rear-Adm Philip Frederick; CB (1961), DSO (1941, and bar 1942, DSC 1941, DL (Norfolk 1974)); s of Vice-Adm Frederick Armand Powlett, CBE (d 1964), and Nora Powlett, *née* Chaplin (d 1934); *b* 13 Nov 1906; *Educ* RNCs Osborne and Dartmouth; *m* 1935, Frances Elizabeth Sykes (d 1987), da of Edward Elwell (d 1917); 2 s, 1 da; *Career* Cmdg Offr HMS Shearwater, Blankney, Cassandra, Dauntless (operations Atlantic, Malta Convoys, Arctic Convoys, E Coast UK), Capt 6 Frigate Sqdn Home Fleet 1955-56, Dir (RN) Joint Anti-Submarine Sch and sr naval officer N Ireland 1956-58, Flag Officer and Adm Superintendent Gibraltar 1959-62; Polish Cross of Valour 1942; ret 1962; *Clubs* Naval; *Style*— Rear-Admiral Philip Frederick Powlett, CB, DSO, DSC, DL; The Mill House, Lyng, Norwich, Norfolk NR9 5QZ (☎ 0603 872334)

POWLEY, John Albert; s of Albert Powley (d 1984), of 151 Green End Rd, Cambridge, and Evelyn Mary, *née* Fulcher; *b* 3 August 1936; *Educ* Cambridge Central Sch, Cambs Coll of Arts and Technol; *m* 13 July 1957, Jill, da of Lt Cdr Herbert Henry Palmer, RNVR (d 1985), of Fen Ditton, Cambridge; 2 s (Stephen John b 1961, Stewart Wayne b 1965), 1 da (Amanda Jane b 1963); *Career* Nat Serv 1957-59; radio and tv service engr with Pye Ltd Cambridge 1959-60, md John Powley (Radio & TV) Ltd 1960-84; memb: Cambs CC 1967-77, Cambridge City Cncl 1967-79 (ldr 1976-79); contested (C) Harrow 1979; MP (C) Norwich South 1983-87; *Recreations* golf; *Style*— John Powley, Esq; 32 Sunningdale, Eaton, Norwich, Norfolk NR4 6AN (☎ 0603 504437)

POWLING, Wing Cdr Ronald Henry Charles; DL; s of George William Powling (d 1987) of Tankerton, Kent and Amelia Powling (d 1968); *b* 2 Nov 1920; *Educ* Simon Langton Sch Canterbury; *m* 15 Nov 1941, Silvia, da of Harold Marshall (d 1973) of Southport; 3 s (Neil Patrick, Nicholas Michael, Mark Adrian Rufus), 1 da (Katrina Beverley); *Career* WWII Fighter Pilot RAFVR 1939-46, Flying and Admin Cmd RAF 1946-53; chm: Kent CC, SE Provincial Cncl of Local Authorities; memb joint cncl Local Authorities; pres Tankerton Con Assoc; *Recreations* golf, gardening, swimming, walking; *Style*— Wing Cdr Ronald Powling, DL; Browndown, 73 Bennells Ave, Tankerton, Whitstable, Kent CT5 2HP (☎ 0227 274 893)

POWNALL, Henry Charles; QC (1979); s of John Cecil Glossop Pownall, CB (d 1967); *b* 25 Feb 1927; *Educ* Rugby, Trin Cambridge; *m* 1955, Sarah Bettine, da of Maj John Latham Deverell (d 1978); 1 s, 1 da (and 1 da decd); *Career* barr Inner Temple 1954, bencher 1976, junior prosecuting counsel to the Crown at the Central Criminal Ct 1964-71, sr and second sr prosecuting counsel 1976-79, recorder of the Crown Ct 1972-84, hon legal adviser ABA 1976-, judge Cts of Appeal of Jersey and Guernsey 1980-86, circuit judge 1984 pres Orders and Medals Research Soc 1971-75, 1977-81; memb of ctee 1961-69, 1970-71 and 1981-; *Recreations* travel, medals and medal ribbons; *Clubs* Pratt's, Hurlingham, Ebury Court; *Style*— His Honour Judge Henry Pownall QC; Central Criminal Court, Old Bailey, London EC4M 7EH

POWNALL, Brig John Lionel; OBE (1972); s of John Cecil Glossop Pownall, CB (d 1967), and Margaret Nina, *née* Jesson; *b* 10 May 1929; *Educ* Rugby, RMA Sandhurst; *m* 1962, Sylvia Joan Cameron, da of James Cameron Conn, WS (d 1957), of Hawick, Roxburghshire; 2 s (Richard b 1967, Edward b 1972); *Career* enlisted 1947, cmmd 16/5 Lancers 1949, served in Egypt, Cyrenaica, Tripolitania, BAOR, Hong Kong, Cyprus cmd 16/5 The Queen's Royal Lancers 1969-71, Adj-Gen's Secretariat 1971-72, offr i/c RAC Manning and Records 1973-75, Col GS Near East Land Forces/Land Forces Cyprus 1975-78, asst dir def policy MOD 1978-79, Brig RAC UK Land Forces 1979-82, Brig MOD 1982-84, ret 1984, Col 16/5 The Queen's Royal Lancer's 1985-; dep chm Police Complaints Authy 1986-(memb 1985-); *Recreations* country pursuits, opera, arts; *Clubs* The Cavalry and Guards; *Style*— Brig John Pownall, OBE; Police Complaints Authority, 10 Great George St, London SW1

POWNALL, Philip John; s of Alexander Pownall, and Lilian Pownall; *b* 22 Feb 1937; *Educ* Lymm GS, Manchester Univ (MB, ChB); *m* 20 April 1963, Margaret, da of E G Sadler, of Cheshire; 2 s (Christopher Alexander b 1969, Timothy Philip b 1983), 2 da (Helen Margaret b 1964, Suzanne b 1970); *Career* tutor Orthopaedic Surgery Leeds Univ 1972-75, conslt Orthopaedic Surgn Bolton Hosps 1975-; vice-chm Bolton Ind Hosp 1984-87 ("The Beaumont") (dir 1983-87); pres Bolton and District Med Soc 1986-88; memb Manchester Med Soc 1961-; FRCS (1971 London, Edinburgh 1972); *Recreations* photography, engrg, boats; *Clubs* The Country Gentlemans, Gourmet; *Style*— Philip J Pownall, Esq; The Beeches, 44 Albert Road West, Heaton, Bolton, Gtr Mancheter; Consulting Rooms, 11 Chorley Hill Road, Bolton (☎ 0204 384404 & 0204 22444)

POWYS, Hon Clare Lynette; da of 7 Baron Lilford; *b* 1962; *Style*— The Hon Clare Powys

POYNDER, Col Anthony John Irvine (Tony); s of late Lt-Col Frederick Sinclair Poynder, DSO, HVO, OBE, MC, and Grace Muriel, *née* Campbell; *b* 10 Feb 1920; *Educ* Wellington Coll, RMA Woolwich, Peterhouse Cambridge (MA); *m* 15 Dec 1945, Anne, da of late Maj-Gen James Francis Harter, DSO, MC, DL; 2 da (Jennifer (Mrs Parks) b 28 Nov 1946, Patricia (Lady Francis Seymour) b 7 oct 1958), 2 step s (Charles David Stancomb b 30 April 1942, Anthony James Stancomb b 2 Feb 1944); *Career* cmmnd 3 July 1939 RE, WWII served France, North Africa, NW Europe, 6 Armd Div RE and 82 Assault Engrs Sqdn RE (MC and despatches); 1945-66: staff coll, jt servs staff coll appointments incl Cdr Para Sqdn RE, asst to Adj Gen Cdr 4 Div Engrs, chief Instr Field Engrg RSME 1963, sr Army Memb Defence Operational Requirements Staff MOD; mktg mangr Br Hovercraft Corpn 1966-70, sr mktg devpt exec Westland Aircraft 1970-71, head crane dept Sea Containers Gp 1971-81; dir: Sea Container Servs Ltd 1972-74, md Sea Container Atlantic Servs Ltd 1974-81, Sea Co Hldgs Ltd 1981-85, Orient Express Hotels Hldgs Ltd; Freeman City of London, Liveryman Worshipful Co of Coachmakers and Coach Harness Makers; *Books* Wahid The Little Camel; *Clubs* Hawks, Army and Navy, REYC; *Style*— Col Tony Poynder, MC; Gassons, Slindon Village, Arundel, W Sussex (☎ 0243 65 395)

POYNTER, Kieran Charles; s of Kenneth Reginald Poynter, of Sanderstead, Surrey, and

Catherine Elizabeth, *née* Reilley; *b* 20 August 1950; *Educ* Salesian Coll, Imp Coll of Sci and Technol, Univ of London (BSc, ARCS); *m* 20 Aug 1977, Marylyn, da of Cmdt Thomas Melvin (d 1968), of Athlone, Ireland; 3 s (Dominic b 1979, Benedict b 1980, Andrew b 1983), 1 da (Louise b 1981); *Career* CA 1974, ptnr Price Waterhouse 1982 (joined 1971, now responsible for servs to insur sector in UK and memb PW World Firm Insur Gp); memb: insur ctee ICAEW 1983-, standing inter professional liaison gp Accounting and Actuarial Professions 1987-, accounting and auditing standards ctee Lloyd's of London; memb Catenian Assoc; FCA 1979; *Recreations* golf, skiing, tennis; *Clubs* Surrey Tennis and Country; *Style—* Kieran Poynter, Esq; Cranbrook, The South Border, Woodcote, Purley, Surrey CR2 3LL (☎ 01 660 4723); Price Waterhouse, Southwark Towers, 32 London Bridge St, London SE1 9SY (☎ 01 407 8989, fax 01 378 0647, telex 884657/8)

POYNTON, Lady Finola Dominique; *née* Fitz-Clarence; da of 7 Earl of Munster by his 1 w; *b* 6 Dec 1953; *m* 1981, Jonathan Terence Poynton, s of Lt Col D R Poynton, of Woodford, Cheshire; 1 s (Oliver Maximillian Christo b 1984), 1 da (Chloë Nona b 1982); *Style—* Lady Finola Poynton; 153 Wellfield Road, London SW16

POYNTON, Sir (Arthur) Hilton; GCMG (1964), KCMG (1949, CMG 1946); s of Arthur Blackburne Poynton (d 1944, formerly master of Univ Coll Oxford), and Mary (d 1952), da of late J Y Sargent, fell of Hertford Coll Oxford; *b* 20 April 1905; *Educ* Marlborough, Barenose Coll Oxford; *m* 1946, Elisabeth Joan, da of late Rev Edmund Williams; 2 s, 1 da; *Career* entered Civil Serv 1927, Dept of Scientific and Industl Res, transferred to Colonial Off 1929; private sec to: min of Supply (Lord Beaverbrook) 1941, min of Production (Oliver Lyttelton, later Lord Chandos) 1942-43, reverted to Colonial Off 1943, dep under-sec state 1948-59, perm under sec state 1959-66; hon fell Brasenose Coll Oxford 1964, KStJ 1968; *Recreations* music, travel, gardening; *Style—* Sir Hilton Poynton, GCMG, KCMG, CMG; Craigmillar, 47 Stanhope Rd, Croydon CRO 5NS (☎ 01 688 3729)

POYNTON, Robert Alan (Joe); s of Alan Poynton, of Lelant, Cornwall, and Mabel Winifred, *née* Evans; *b* 28 Jan 1943; *Educ* King Edwards Sch Bath, Bath Univ BSc Architecture; *m* 14 Aug 1970, Jane Elizabeth, da of Leonard East, of The Manor, Cannington, Somerset; 3 da (Susan b 1971, Jenny b 1973, Sally b 1976); *Career* architect; sr ptnr Poynton Bradbury Assocs St Ives Cornwall; architect: the Barbara Hepworth Museum 1975, Lands End Visitor Centre 1982, Isles Of Scilly Centre 1984, Nat Lighthouse Museum 1987; architect to Curry Mallet Village Community Project initiated by HRH The Prince of Wales 1985; memb The Nat Community Architecture Gp 1982-87, chm Cornwall Branch RIBA 1984-86, winner CPRE/RIBA Housing Design Award (1987), winner Cwlth Fndn Award (1989); *Recreations* sailing, wind surfing; *Clubs* ST Ives Sailing (pres), RIBA Sailing; *Style—* Robert Poynton, Esq; Tregender Vean, Ludgvan, Cornwall (☎ 0736 796791); Poynton Bradbury Associates, Tregenna Place, St Ives, Cornwall TR26 1SD (☎ 0736 797828)

POYNTZ, Lt-Col John Mackay Brace; OBE (1950); s of Col Hugh Stainton Poyntz, DSO, OBE (d 1955), of Winchester, and Hilda Gwendoline, *née* Thackeray (d 1958); (*see* Burke's Landed Gentry, 18 edn, Vol 1) ; *b* 12 July 1916; *Educ* Stowe and RMC Camberley; *m* 26 July 1940, Joan Stewart Menzies, da of Charles B Ogilvie (d 1945), of Kent; 2 adopted da (Jane Caroline Ogilvie b 1958, Jocelin Georgina Massey b 1958); *Career* joined Seaforth Highlanders 1936, served WWII, cmmnd (Lt-Col) 3 Gold Coast Regt 1946 (despatches 1949), Mil Asst to Maj-Gen i/c Admin MELF 1954-57, served Hongkong, Shanghai, Malaya, Burma, India, Egypt, Cyprus, Germany (ret 1960); Queen's Messenger 1961-78; *Recreations* motorised golf only (due to disability); *Clubs* Army & Navy; *Style—* Lt-Col John Poyntz, OBE; Stowey House, Liphook, Hampshire GU30 7EQ

PRAG, Derek Nathan; MEP (EDG) Herts 1979-; s of Abraham J Prag; *b* 6 August 1923; *Educ* Bolton Sch, Emmanuel Coll Cambridge (BA); *m* 1948, Dora Weiner; 3 s; *Career* economic journalist Reuters 1950-55, freelance ed Financial Times Business Letter from Europe 1975-76, in charge of Anglo-American Section of High Authority Information of the European Coal and Steel Community 1955-59, head Publications Div European Communities 1959-67, dir London Office Jt Info Serv of European Communities 1965-73; ran own consultancy on relations with EEC 1973-79; cons spokesman EDG Instl Ctee 1982-84 and 1987-, cons spokesman Political Affairs Ctee 1984-86, sr vice-chm Ctee of Enquiry into Facism and Racism, alternate memb Social Affairs and Employment Ctee, alternate memb Political Affrs Ctee, memb European Parl ASEAN Delgn, rapporteur on Seat of the EC Iusts and working-place of the European Parliament, chm European Parl's All-Party Gp on Disablement; chm London Europe Soc; hon dir EEC Cmmn, Silver Medal of European Merit for 20 yrs service to European Union; *Recreations* listening to music, reading, swimming, gardening; *Clubs* Carlton; *Style—* Derek Prag, Esq, MEP; Pine Hill, 47 New Rd, Digswell, Herts AL6 0AQ (☎ 043781 2999)

PRAGNELL, Anthony William; CBE (1982), OBE (1960, DFC 1944); s of late William Hendley Pragnell, and the late Sylvia Mary Pragnell; *b* 15 Feb 1921; *Educ* Cardinal Vaughan Sch London, London Univ (LLB Ext); *m* 1955, Teresa Mary (d 1988), da of the late Leo Francis Monaghan, of Maidstone; 1 s, 1 da; *Career* served RAF 1942-46, Fl-Lt Bomber Cmd; civil serv 1939-54 (asst examiner Inland Revenue 1939-50, GPO 1950-54); Independent TV Authy 1954: sec 1955-61, dep dir-gen 1961-83 (became Independent Broadcasting Authority 1972); dir Channel Four Television 1983-88; fell: Royal TV Soc 1980, European Inst for the Media, Manchester Univ 1983-; Emile Noël European Prize 1987; *Recreations* reading, listening to music, watching TV; *Clubs* RAF; *Style—* Anthony Pragnell Esq, CBE, OBE, DFC; Ashley, Grassy Lane, Sevenoaks, Kent TN13 1PL (☎ 0732 451463)

PRAIN, Philip James Murray; s of (John) Murray Prain, DSO, OBE, TD, DL (d 1985), and Lorina Helen Elspeth, *née* Skene; *b* 14 Nov 1936; *Educ* Eton, Clare Coll Cambridge (MA); *m* 28 Sept 1972, Susan Ferrier, da of Andrew Munro Marr (d 1955); 1 da (Philippa Victoria b 1975); *Career* 2 Lt Black Watch 1955-57, Lt TARO, memb The Queen's Body Guard for Scotland, Royal Co of Archers 1966; Kleinwort Benson Ltd 1962-; asst dir, dir (Hong Kong) 1979-83; barr Inner Temple 1963; chm Manor Gardens Enterprise Centre Islington; tstee: Westminster Amalgamated Charity, All Saints' Fndn Margaret Street; Freeman City of London 1978, Liveryman Worshipful Co of Founders 1978; *Recreations* travel, photography; *Clubs* MCC, Royal and Ancient GC, Leander (Assoc), Hong Kong, Royal Hong Kong Jockey; *Style—* Philip Prain, Esq; 73 Woodsford Square, London W14 8DS (☎ 01 603 7767); Kleinwort Benson Ltd, 20 Fenchurch St, London EC3P 3DB (☎ 01 623 8000, telex 888531)

PRAIN, Sir Ronald Lindsay; OBE (1946); s of Arthur Lindsay Prain, and Amy Gertrude, *née* Watson; *b* 3 Sept 1907,, Iquiqui, Chile; *Educ* Cheltenham Coll; *m* 1938, Esther Pansy (d 1987), da of late Norman Brownrigg; 2 s (Graham b 1940, Angus b 1952); *Career* controller Miny of Supply: diamond die and tool control 1940-45, quartz crystal control 1943-45; chm exec Roan Selection Tst (RST) Int Gp of Copper Mining Companies 1943-68 (chm 1950-72); dir: Metal Market & Exchange Co Ltd 1943-65, Selection Trust Ltd 1944-78, San Francisco Mines of Mexico Ltd 1944-68, Int Nickel Co of Canada Ltd 1951-72, Wankie Colliery Co Ltd 1953-63, Monks Investment Tst 1960-83, Minerals Separation Ltd 1962-78, Foseco Minsep Ltd 1969-80, Barclays Bank Int 1971-77, Pan-Holding SA and other cos; first chm: Agric Research Cncl of Rhodesia and Nyasaland 1959-63, Merchant Bank of Central Africa Ltd 1956-66, Merchant Bank (Zambia) Ltd 1966-72; pres: Br Overseas Mining Assoc 1952, Inst of Metals 1960-61, Cheltenham Coll 1972-80; memb cncl Overseas Devpt Inst 1960-80; tstee Inst for Archaeo-Metallurgical Studies; hon pres Copper Dvpt Assoc; Hon FIMM; kt 1956; *Publications* Selected Papers (4 vols), Copper, The Anatomy of an Industry (1975, Japanese edn 1976, Spanish edn 1981), Reflections of on Era (1981); *Recreations* cricket, real tennis, travel; *Clubs* White's, MCC; *Style—* Sir Ronald Prain, OBE; Waverley, Granville Rd, St George's Hill, Weybridge, Surrey KT13 0QJ; (☎ 0932 842776)

PRANCE, Prof (Ghillean) Iain Tolmie; s of Basil Camden Prance, CIE, OBE (d 1947), and Margaret Hope, *née* Tolmie (d 1970); *b* 13 July 1937; *Educ* Malvern, Oxford Univ (BA, MA, DPhil); *m* 13 July 1961, Anne Elizabeth, da of The Rev Archibald MacAlister Hay (d 1980); 2 da (Rachel b 1963, Sarah b 1966); *Career* NYBG: res asst 1963-68, BA Krukoff curator Amazonian Botany 1968-75, dir res 1975-81, vice pres 1977-81, sr vice pres 1981-88, dir Inst Econ Botany 1981-88; adjunct prof City Univ NY 1968-; visiting prof: tropical studies Yale Univ, Reading Univ 1988-; dir Royal Botanic Gdns Kew 1988-; author of numerous papers and books; exec dir Orgn Flora Neotropica (UNESCO) 1975-88, memb Mayor's cmmm on Cable TV White Plains NY 1981-88, tstee Au Sable Inst of Enviromental Studies 1984-, ldr Amazonian exploration prog 1965-88; FIL, DR (hc) Goteborgs Univ 1983; FLS 1963, Foreign memb Royal Danish Acad sciences and letters 1988, corr memb Brazilian Acad of sciences 1976; *Books* Arvores De Manaus (1975), Extinction is forever (1977), Biological Diversification in the Tropics (1981), Leaves (1986), Amazonia (1985), Flowers for all Seasons (1988); *Recreations* squash, music; *Clubs* Explorers (Fell 1978); *Style—* Prof Iain Prance, Esq; Royal Botanic Gardens, Kew, Richmond, Surrey, TW9 3AB, (☎ 01 940 1171 fax 01 948 1197)

PRATLEY, David Illingworth; s of Arthur George Pratley, of Dorset, and Olive Constance, *née* Illingworth; *b* 24 Dec 1948; *Educ* Westminster Abbey Choir Sch, Westminster Sch, Bristol Univ (LLB); *Career* PR offr Thorndike Theatre Leatherhead 1970-71, press & publicity offr Queen's Univ of Belfast 1971-72, dep dir Merseyside Arts Assoc 1972-76, dir Gtr London Arts Assoc 1976-81, regnl dir Arts Cncl of GB 1981-86, arts mgmnt conslt 1986-87, chief exec Royal Liverpool Philharmonic Soc 1987-88, chm Nat Campaign for the Arts 1988-, dir Dance Umbrella Ltd 1986-, md Trinity Coll of Music; memb SDP Arts Ctee (1987 chm, Alliance Arts & Broadcasting Panel) 1986-88; *Books* Culture for All (Geothe Inst 1981), Cumbria Arts & Museums Strategy (Cumbria Co Cncl, 1987), The Pursuit of Competence - the Arts and the European Community (ICA, 1987); *Recreations* arts, travel, gardens, countryside; *Clubs* Athenaeum; *Style—* David Pratley, Esq; 13 St James St, London W6 9RW (☎ 01 741 3513); Trintiy Coll of Music, Mandeville St, London W1M 0AU (☎ 01 935 5773)

PRATT, (Richard) Camden; s of Richard Sheldon Pratt, of 108 Manthorpe Rd, Grantham, Lincs, and Irene Gladys, *née* Whalley; *b* 14 Dec 1947; *Educ* Boston GS, Westcliff HS, Lincoln Coll Oxford (MA); *m* 4 Aug 1973, Dorothy Jane Marchia, da of Capt William Paul Allsebrook, of Tichis 15, Glyfada, Athens, Greece; *Career* called to the Bar Grays Inn 1970; *Recreations* sailing, shooting, walking, theatre; *Style—* Camden Pratt, Esq; 1 Kings Bench Walk, Temple, London EC4 (☎ 01 583 6266, fax 01 583 2068)

PRATT, George Henry; s of Joseph Henry Pratt, and Hannah Carruthers, *née* Briggs (d 1949); *b* 15 Jan 1929; *Educ* Whitehaven GS; *m* 20 Sept 1952, Elsie, da of John Lawson (d 1955), of Glenesk, Vulcans Lane, Workington; 1 s (Michael J b 26 Jan 1956); *Career* sr ptnr R Gibbons & Co CAs 1955, sec & chief exec W Cumbria Bldg Soc 1963, memb local tbnl of Dept of Health & Social Security; former pres: Cumberland Soc of CAs, Round Table, Rotary Club, pres Cumbria Union of GCs 1989; former capt and pres Workington GC; FICA 1952;; *Recreations* gardening, golf, all sports; *Clubs* Workington Golf; *Style—* George Pratt, Esq; Lynthwaite, 45 Stainburn Rd, Workington, Cumbria CA14 1SW (☎ 0900 3119); Messrs R Gibbons & Co, Carleton House, 136 Gray St, WorkingtonC Cumbria CA14 2LU (☎ 0900 68311)

PRATT, Michael John; QC (1976); o s of W Brownlow Pratt; *b* 23 May 1933; *Educ* West House Sch Edgbaston, Malvern Coll (LLB Birmingham); *m* 1960, Elizabeth Jean Hendry; 2 s, 3 da; *Career* 2 Lt 3 Carabiniers (Prince of Wales's Dragoon Gds), Staff Capt; barr Mid Temple 1954, a recorder of the Crown Ct 1974-, bencher 1986; *Clubs* Cavalry and Guards, Birmingham Conservative; *Style—* Michael Pratt Esq, QC; South Hill, 170 Oak Tree Lane, Bournville, Birmingham B30 1TX (☎ (021 472) 2213)

PRATT, Lord Michael John Henry; s of 5 Marquess Camden (d 1983), and 2 w, Averil (d 1977), da of late Col Henry Sidney John Streatfield, DSO (through whom she was ggda of 2 Earl of Lichfield); *b* 15 August 1946; *Educ* Eton, Balliol Coll Oxford; *Career* author and researcher; *Clubs* White's, Pratt's, MCC, Beefsteak; *Style—* Lord Michael Pratt; 16 Coulson St, London SW3 (☎ 01 581 2200); Bayham Manor, Lamberhurst, Kent (☎ 0892 890500)

PRATT, Peter Charles; s of Charles Frederick Pratt (d 1982), of Sunningdale, and Edith Hilda, *née* Appleton (d 1983); *b* 24 Sept 1931; *Educ* Salesian Coll, Clapham Coll, Univ of Reading (BSc); *m* 1 29 Sept 1956, Pamela Mary (d 1969), da of Alfred Smith (d 1960) of Colchester; 1 s (Julian b 1957), 1 da (Nicola b 1961); m2, 8 July 1982, Fay Jameson, *née* Wright; *Career* Nat Serv L Cpl RE 1950-52 (works servs Cyprus 1951-52); Overseas Civil Serv 1955-60: trainee surveyor Sch of Mil Survey 1955-56, surveyor dept of lands and surveys Govt of Tanganyika 1956-60; Ellerman Lines plc 1960-84: investmt mgmnt and admin 1960-74, co sec 1967-79, divnl chief exec 1979-82, main bd dir 1982-84; dir New Cavendish St Investmt Co Ltd 1984; memb: investmt ctee Merchant Navy Ratings Pension Fund 1982-, MNOPF Ctees; trustee: Moorgate Tst Fund, New Moorgate Tst Fund; Freeman City of London 1967, Liveryman Worshipful Co of Shipwrights 1968; FRGS 1952, FCIS 1966; *Recreations* swimming, clay-pigeon shooting, theatre, music, reading, watching cricket; *Clubs* Carlton, RAC, Surrey CCC; *Style—* Peter Pratt, Esq; 25 Willoughby Rd, Hampstead, London NW3 1RT (☎ 01 794 9040); 1 South Audley St, London W1Y 5DQ (☎ 01 491 4606)

PRATT, Lord Roderic Arthur Nevill; s of 4 Marquess of Camden (d 1943); *b* 1915; *Educ* Eton, Trinity Cambridge; *m* 1945, Ursula Eva, da of Capt the Hon Valentine Maurice Wyndham-Quin, RN (d 1983, s of late 5 Earl of Dunraven and Mount-Earl); 1 s (Capt Adrian Pratt b 1952, m 1984, Leonora Murray Lee), 1 da (Zara b 1955, m 1988, John Weir Johnstone); *Career* Maj late Life Gds; underwriting memb Lloyd's ; *Style—* Lord Roderic Pratt; The Garden House, Dewhurst, Wadhurst, E Sussex TN5 6QB (☎ 089 288 3179)

PRATT, Lady Samantha Caroline; da of 6 Marquess Camden; *b* 5 Oct 1964; *Style*— Lady Samantha Pratt

PREECE, Andrew Douglas; s of Bernard Charles Preece, 2 Knowle Rd, Weeping Cross, Stafford, and Joyce Mary, *née* Clayton; *b* 28 Sept 1944; *Educ* King Edward V1 GS Stafford, Selwyn Coll Cambridge (MA); *m* 5 Oct 1968, Caroline Jane, da of Edmond Arthur Bland (d 1988); 2 da (Victoria Jane b 31 March 1972, Joanna Mary b 19 Jan 1981), 1 s (James Douglas b 4 Aug 1976); *Career* articled clerk asst slr Hall Collins 1968-71, ptnr Herbert Smith 1978- (asst slr 1971-74, assoc ptnr 1974-77); Freeman Worshipful Co of Slrs; memb Law Soc, IBA, UK Oil Lawyers Gp; *Recreations* sailing, golf; *Clubs* Moor Park GC, RAF YC; *Style*— Andrew Preece, Esq; The Red House, Dog Kennel Lane, Chorleywood, Hertforshire WD3 5EL; Flat 20, Presidents Quay House, 72 St Katherines Way, London E1; Watling House, 35 Cannon St, London EC4M 5SD (☎ 01 489 8000, fax 01 329 0426 telex 886633)

PREECE, Anthony John; s of John Henry Preece (d 1977), and Ivy, *née* Rhodes; *b* 11 May 1945; *Educ* Batley GS, Loughborough Univ; *m* 1, 30 Sept 1967 (m dis 1986), Caroline Betty, da of Thomas Harold Keston Edwards (d 1962); 3 s (David b 23 Nov 1971, Christopher b 6 Mar 1975, Adam b 23 Mar 1977); m 2, 25 May 1986, Esme Irene, da of Jacques Sadler (d 1971); 1 da (Sarah b 18 June 1986) ; *Career* asst dir Stock Exchange 1972-85, md Scrimgeour Vickers Servs 1985-86; ops dir Citicorp Scrimgeour Vickers 1986-; *Recreations* wine, food, travel, theatre ; *Clubs* Royal Institution, IOD; *Style*— Anthony J Preece, Esq; Bowman Lodge, Warren Lane, Oxshott, Surrey, KT22 0ST (☎ 0372 842461); Citicorp Scrimgeour Vickers, Cotton Centre, Hays Lane, London SE1 (☎ 01 234 5555)

PREECE, David Henry Gunston; s of Reginald Preece (d 1935), and Elizabeth Gwen, *née* Jenkins (d 1981); *b* 4 August 1933; *Educ* Barry GS, Welsh Sch of Architecture, UWIST (DipArch with Distinction 1956); *m* 27 Aug 1983, Denise Celia, da of Bill Upward (d 1982); 1 step s (Marcus Livermore b 1971); *Career* CA, princ ptnr David Preece Assocs; import major cmmns include: New Civic Centres for Boroughs of Islwyn, Vale of Glam, Lliw Valley, Afan and HQ for SW Water Authy Exeter, Welsh Water Brecon, Palace for Sheikh Mohammed Bin Saleh in Riyadh; currently engaged on projects in Hong Kong, China and SE Asia; *Recreations* sketching, travel; *Clubs* IOD; *Style*— David H G Preece, Esq; Cliff House, Cliff Walk, Penarth, S Glamorgan; 48 Elm Grove Road, Dinas Powys, S Glamorgan CF6 4AB (☎ (0222) 514037, fax (0222) 514120)

PREECE, Michael John Stewart; s of Lt-Col James Preece, OBE, TD, of Broadeaves, Les Ruisseaux, St Brelade, Jersey, CI, and Margaret, *née* Paterson; *b* 29 Dec 1934; *Educ* Rugby, Emmanuel Coll Cambridge (MA); *m* 20 Sept 1958, Tessa Gillian Rosamond, da of Sir Francis John Watkin Williams, BT, QC, of Llys, Middle Lane, Denbigh, Clwyd; 2 s (James b 1964, Hugh b 1969), 2 da (Emily b 1961, Rosamund b 1963); *Career* Nat Serv 2nd Lt 1953-55 (Korea, Hong Kong), Capt Cheshire Yeo 1963-70; slr; registrar Diocese of Bangor, clerk to Dean and Chapter Bangor Cathedral; under sheriff Anglesey; *Recreations* shooting, squash, golf, Roman remains; *Clubs* Lansdowne; *Style*— Michael Preece, Esq; Plas Llanddyfnan, Talwrn, Llangefni, Anglesey, Gwynedd LL77 7TH (☎ 0248 750659); 282A High Street, Bangor, Gwynedd LL57 1UL (☎ 0248 352387)

PREECE, William Royston; s of Horace Preece, and Gladys, *née* Gravenor; *b* 26 April 1933; *m* 8 Nov 1958, Dorothy Vivien Carrington, da of Herbert Kitchener Evans, DCM; 1 s (Jeffrey b 1960), 1 da (Diana b 1964); *Career* Steel Co of Wales 1951-58, chm and md A Watkinson Ltd (footwear retailers) 1960-, chm Independent Footwear Retailers Assoc (Northern England) 1975-76 (exec memb Nat Assoc 1975-80); memb: City of York Guild of Codwainers (clerk 1977-79, master 1980-81), Guild of Merchant Taylors; FID; *Recreations* gardening, spectator sports, family, dogs, photography; *Clubs* Royal Overseas League, York GC, York 41; *Style*— William Preece, Esq; c/o A Watkinson Ltd, 53 Goodramgate, York (☎ 0904 23388)

PREEDY, Ronald Alan; OBE (1977); s of William Frank Preedy (d 1969), of St Agnes, Cornwall, and Rose Esther, *née* Chubb; *b* 30 Sept 1935; *Educ* Truro Sch; *m* 20 June 1959, (Lillian) Mary, da of late Henry Russell Richards, of St Agnes, Cornwall; 1 s (Mark b 1960); *Career* cmmnd RA 1954, posted 33 Para Lt Regt 1954-61, Troop Cdr 45 Fd Regt BAOR 1961-63, Gunnery Staff Course Larkhill 1963-64 (Instr-in-Gunnery 1964-66), Bde Maj RA 5 Div Wrexham 1968-70, Battery Cdr 29 Commando Regt RA Poole 1970-73, Instr Jr Div Staff Coll Warminster 1974-75, CO 29 Commando Regt Plymouth 1975-77, Princ Staff Offr (Ops) Royal Brunei Malay Regt 1977-80, ret (voluntary) 1980; commenced yacht delivery 1981-, completed single-handed double transatlantic in aid of RNLI 1984-85, awarded Alex Rose trophy and RNVR Cruise Challenge Cup by RN Sailing Assoc; SDLJ Brunei 1980; *Books* Sail and Deliver (1989); *Recreations* sailing, golf, drawing, painting; *Clubs* RN Sailing Assoc, Ocean Cruising; *Style*— Ronald Preedy, Esq, OBE; 34 Trevaunance Rd, St Agnes, Cornwall TR5 0SQ (☎ 087 255 3110)

PRENDERGAST, (Christopher) Anthony; CBE, DL (1980); s of Maurice Prendergast; *b* 4 May 1931; *Educ* Falmouth GS; *m* 1959, Simone Ruth Laski, DBE, OBE, JP, DL; 1 s; *Career* chm Dolphin Sq Tst Ltd 1967-, Lord Mayor and dep high steward of Westminster 1968-69, High Sheriff of Gtr London 1980; DL Gtr London 1988; Lloyd's underwriter; *Recreations* shooting, fishing, photography; *Clubs* Carlton, Brooks's, Irish, MCC; *Style*— Anthony Prendergast, Esq, CBE, DL; Flat C, 52 Warwick Sq, London SW1V 2AJ (☎ 01 821 7653)

PRENDERGAST, Brig John Hume; DSO (1946), MC (1937, bar 1940); s of Maj-Gen Charles Gordon Prendergast, CB (d 1930), of Jersey, and Marguerite Eghertha, *née* Hume (d 1973); *b* 15 Nov 1910; *Educ* Victoria Coll Jersey; *m* 3 April 1939, (Rose Ann) Peggy, da of Henry Norton Hutchinson, OBE, ICS (d 1947); 2 s (John b 1942, Rollo b 1947), 1 da (Caroline (Mrs Priestly) b 1944); *Career* cmmnd Royal Sussex Regt 1931, 4/15 Punjab regt Rajmak Wajiristan 1932, seconded N Wajiristan Transborder Armed Police 1936-39, active serv Ipi Ops, Capt 1939, mountain warfare advsr Norway Expedition 1940, returned IA 1940, Maj 1940, instr in mountain warfare Sch of Inf Poona 1941-42, 2 i/c 1/15 Punjab Regt in first Arakan ops 1943-45, joined 19 (Dagger) Indian Div in reconquest of Burma 1944, cmd first river recrossing of Irawaddy (despatches), recapture of Mandalay, CO 3/6 Rajputana Rifles 1945, continued in Burma until 1947, Staff Coll Quetta 1947, 1 Yorks and Lancaster Regt 1948, mil attaché kabul embassy Afghanistan 1948-50, 1 Yorks and Lancaster Regt Brunswick 1951 (cmd 1952), served Khartoum and Canal Zone 1952, GSO1 BAOR 1955, cmd 1947 Midland Bde TA 1958-60, ret 1960; long distance motor exploration (incl voluntary work for wild life conservaton): Iran, Afghanistan, Pakistan, India; pres 15 Punjab Regt Assoc 1983-88; *Books* The Road to India (1977), Prender's Progress (1979); *Recreations* long distance motor travel, fly fishign, painting, writing, landscape; *Style*— Brig John Prendergast, DSO, MC; Barton Mead, Tisbury, Wilts SP3 6JU (☎ 0747 870542)

PRENDERGAST, Sir John Vincent; KBE (1977), CBE (1960, CMG 1968, GM 1955, CPM 1955, QPM 1963); yst s of late John and Margaret Prendergast; *b* 11 Feb 1912; *Educ* Ireland, London Univ (extnl); *m* 1943, Enid Sonia, yr da of Percy Speed; 1 s, 1 da; *Career* served WWII, Maj; local govt London 1930-39, asst dist cmmr Palestine 1946-47, Palestine and Gold Coast 1947-52, seconded Army Canal Zone 1952-53, Colonial Police Serv Kenya 1953-58 (dir of Intelligence and Security 1955-58), chief of Intelligence Cyprus 1958-60, dir Special Branch Hong Kong (ret as Dep Cmmr of Police) 1960-66, dir Intelligence Aden 1966-67, dep cmmr and dir of operations Ind dir G Heywood Hill ltd 1982-; Cmmn Against Corruption, Hong Kong 1973-77;; *Clubs* East India London, Hong Kong, Royal Hong Kong Jockey; *Style*— Sir John Prendergast, KBE, CMG, GM CPM, QPM; 20 Westbourne Terrace, London W2 3UP (☎ 01 262 9514)

PRENDERGAST, (Walter) Kieran; s of Lt Cdr Joseph Henry Prendergast, and Maj, *née* Hennessy (d 1988); *b* 2 July 1942; *Educ* St Patrick's Coll Sydney Aust, Salesian Coll Chertsey Surrey, St Edmund Hall Oxford; *m* 10 June 1967, Joan da of Patrick Reynolds (d 1974); 2 s (Damian b 1968, Daniel b 1976) 2 da (Siobhain b 1971, Brigid b 1973); *Career* FO 1962, Istanbul (Turkish language student) 1964, Ankara 1965, FO 1 967, second sec Nicosia 1969, Civil Serv Coll 1972, first sec FCO 1972, first sec (info later econs), The Hague 1973, asst private sec to 2 foreign secs (Rt Hon Anthony Crosland, MP, and Rt Hon Dr David Owen, MO) 1976, UK Minion to UN New York 1979, cnsllr head of chancery and consul- gen Tel Aviv 1982, head of Southern African dept FCO 1986-89; *Recreations* family, walking, reading, sport, wine; *Clubs* Travellers'; *Style*— Kieran Prendergast, Esq; c/o Foreign and Commonwealth Office, King Charles St, London SW1A 2AH

PRENDERGAST, Robert James Christie Vereker; s of Capt Richard Henry Prendergast (d 1965), of Roehampton, London, and Jean *née* Christie (d 1988); *b* 21 Oct 1941; *Educ* Downside, Trinity Coll Cambridge (MA); *m* 16 Apr 1971, Berit, da of Wilburg Thauland (d 1982), of Oslo Norway; 1 da (Victoria b 1973); *Career* barr 1964, South Eastern ct rec 1987; *Recreations* keeping friends mildly amused; *Style*— Robert Prendergast, Esq; 9 King's Bench Walk, Temple, London EC4, (☎ 01 353 5638, fax 01 353 6166); 24 Latham Rd, Twickenham, Middx; The Croft, Semley, Shaftesbury, Dorset

PRENDERGAST, Simone Ruth; DBE (1986), OBE (1981, DL (Greater London 1982), JP (Inner London 1971)); Dame; da of Norman Laski (d 1968), and Elaine Blond, *née* Marks, OBE (d 1985); *b* 2 July 1930; *Educ* Queens College London, Cheltenham Ladies Coll; *m* 1, 1953 (m dis 1957), Albert Kaplan; m 2, 21 Sept 1959, (Christopher) Anthony Prendergast, CBE, *qv*, s of Maurice Anthony Prendergast (d 1961); 1 s (Christopher Hugh b 6 June 1960); *Career* chm: cities London and Westminster Cons Assoc 1971075, London Centl Euro Constituency 1976, Greater London Area (Nat Union of Cons Assocs) 1984-87, dep chm Greater London Area Cons Party Non union 1981-84; pres Westminster Homes 1985-; chm: Blond McIndee Centre Med Res 1986-, Jewish Refugees Ctee 1980-, Westminster Childrens Soc 1980-; vice chm Age Concern Westminster 1988; memb: Cncl Centl Br Fund for Jewish Relief 1969, memb St John Cncl for London 1975-82; Lady Mayoress Westminster 1968, Lord Chancellors Advsy Ctee 1981-, Slrs Disciplinary Tribunal 1986-; Asst Com St John 1982; memb ct of patrons RCS 1987, hon FRSA 1988; *Recreations* reading, gardening; *Style*— Dame Simone Prendergast, DBE, JP, DL; 52 Warwick Square, London SW1V 2AJ (☎ 01 821 7653); Quilter Cottage, Broadway, Worcs

PRENTICE, Hon Mrs (Eve-Ann); da of Baron Whaddon (Life Peer); *b* 1952; *m* 1972, Patrick Prentice; *Career* journalist Guardian 1978-87, production ed Sunday Telegraph 1988- (dep prodn ed 1987-88); *Recreations* science, foreign affairs; *Style*— The Hon Mrs Prentice

PRENTICE, Graham Noel; *b* 7 Mar 1955; *Educ* Peter Symonds Winchester, Churchill Coll Cambridge (BA); *m* 15 Sept 1975, Beverley Annette Prentice; 1 da (Katy b 1987); *Career* articled clerk Wragge & Co 1978-80, admitted slr 1980, Freshfields 1981 (ptnr 1986-); *Pubns* Irregular Resolution of Unincorporated Association May Not be a Nullity (1980), The Enforcement of Outsider Rights (1980), Protected Shorthold Tenancies: Traps for the Unwary (I, II, III, 1982), Remedies of Building Sub-Contractors against Employers (1983); *Recreations* photography, reading; *Style*— Graham Prentice, Esq; Freshfields, Grindall House, 25 Newgate St, London EC1A 7LH (☎ 01 606 6677, fax 01 248 2435)

PRENTICE, Hon Mrs (Helen); *née* Chilver; er da of Baron Chilver (Life Peer), *qv*; *b* 30 May 1960; *Educ* Bedford HS; *m* 1982, Geoffrey Prentice; *Style*— The Hon Mrs Prentice; c/o The Rt Hon Lord Chilver, Cayley Lodge, Cranfield, Bedford MK43 0SX

PRENTICE, James Kniveton; s of Oscar Prentice, FRGS (d 1959), of Birkenhead, Ches, and Hester Alice Owen, *née* Kniveton (d 1987); *b* 21 Jan 1937; *Educ* Bradfield Coll, Liverpool Univ (LLB); *m* 27 April 1957, Maria Theresa, da of Rosiland Porter (d 1930), of Godalmin; 2 s (David James Kniveton b 20 Feb 1958, Peter Hugh b 15 Jan 1961), 1 da (Tessa Mary b 3 Sept 1959); *Career* served HAC 1951-55; dir Bleichroeder Bing & Co 1956-69, exec dir Willis Faber & Dumas Ltd 1970-87; dir: Willis Faber (Int) Ltd 1985-87, Willis Faber Hellas 1982-87, Willis Faber Belgium Ltd 1974-87, Kentriki Insurance Co Ltd Nicosia 1987-; Freeman City of London, Liveryman Worshipful Co of Insurers (1984); *Books* Time Chance and Change (1984), The Memory is Green (1987); *Recreations* sailing, music, writing, photography; *Clubs* Travellers, Anglo-Belgian, Ithchenor SC, Emsworth SC; *Style*— James Prentice, Esq; Cranberry, Westbourne, Elsworth, Hants; 312 Willoughby House, Barbican, London EC2 (☎ 01 623 0478); Kentriki Ins Co Ltd, 312 Willoughby House, Barbican, London EC2Y 8BL (☎ 01 623 0428)

PRENTICE, John Oscar; s of Oscar Prentice (d 1957), of The Green Cottage, Langstone, Hants, and Hester Alice Owen, *née* Kniveton (d 1987); *b* 15 Dec 1925; *Educ* Bradfield, Clare Coll Cambridge; *m* 1, 5 Feb 1954, Geraldine Ildiko, da of Capt Humphrey Ridley Tomalin (d 1976), of London; 3 da (Juliet b 1956, Kate b 1959, Jessica b 1961); m 2, 1987, Catherine; *Career* Lloyd's broker and underwriter; dep chm Willis Faber plc 1972-84, chm: Willis Faber & Dumas (Agencies) Ltd 1977-85, Wellington Underwriting Agencies Ltd 1985-; yachtsman; Britannia Cup (Royal Yacht Sqdn) 1974, Admiral's Cup (Victorius Br Team) 1975, second Euro Championship (Int 6 Metre Class) 1988; FRGS; *Recreations* yacht racing (yacht 'Battlecry'), fishing, farming, music; *Clubs* Royal Thames YC, City of London, Imperial Poona YC, Royal Southern YC; *Style*— John Prentice, Esq; Gentilshurst, Fernhurst, Haslemere, Surrey GU27 2HG (☎ 0428 53010); 29 Wilton Row, London SW1; Wellington, 120 Fenchurch St, London EC3M 5BA (☎ 01 929 2811, car tel 0836 204 4611, telex 268892 WELTN g)

PRENTICE, Rt Hon Sir Reginald Ernest; PC (1966), JP (Croydon 1961); s of Ernest George Prentice; *b* 16 July 1923; *Educ* Whitgift Sch, LSE; *m* 1948, Joan Godwin; 1 da; *Career* MP (Lab): East Ham North 1957-74, Newham North East 1974-77; MP (C) Newham North East 1977-79; min of state Dept of Educn and Science 1964-66, min Public Building and Works 1966-67, min Overseas Devpt 1967-69, alderman GLC 1970-71, oppn spokesman on Employment 1972-74, sec of state Educn and Science 1974-75, min Overseas Devpt 1975-76, min of state (min for Social Security) DHSS 1979-81; MP (C) Daventry 1979-87 (ret 1987 election); memb exec ctee Nat Union of Conservative Assocs, pres Assoc of Buisiness Executives, co dir and conslt on public affairs; kt 1987; *Clubs* Marlborough GC; *Style—* The Rt Hon Sir Reginald Prentice, PC, DL

PRENTICE, Hon Sir William Thomas; MBE (1945); s of Claud Stanley Prentice (d 1931); *b* 1 June 1919; *Educ* St Joseph's Coll Sydney, Sydney Univ; *m* 1946, Mary Elizabeth Beresford, da of Frank Beresford Dignam (d 1946); 3 s, 1 da; *Career* Staff Capt 7 Aust Inf Bde Bougainville campaign 1944-45; barr NSW 1947-70, Judge Supreme Ct Papua New Guinea 1970, sr puisne judge 1975, dep chief justice on independence Papua New Guinea 1975, chief justice 1978-80; kt 1977; *Recreations* bush walking, swimming, reading; *Clubs* Tattersall's (Sydney); *Style—* The Hon Sir William Prentice, MBE; 16 Olympia Rd, Naremburn, NSW 2065, Australia

PRENTICE, Dame Winifred Eva; DBE (1977), OBE (1972); da of Percy John Prentice, and Anna Eva Prentice; *b* 2 Dec 1910; *Educ* Northgate Sch for Girls Ipswich E Suffolk and Ipswich Hosp, W Middx Hosp, Queen Elizabeth Coll London Univ; *Career* principal tutor Stracathro Hosp 1947-61, matron 1961-72; pres Royal Coll of Nursing 1972-76; *Style—* Dame Winifred Prentice, DBE, OBE; Marleish, 4 Duke St, Brechin, Angus (☎ 035 62 2606)

PRENTIS, Henry Barrell; s of Stanley William Prentis (d 1974), of London, and Elizabeth Maxwell, *née* MacDonald (d 1970); *b* 16 Oct 1944; *Educ* St Olaves & St Saviour's GS; *m* 1 July 1967, Lilia Doris Nelson, da of Efstratios Kyriacou Sotirkati, of London; 1 s (Henry b 14 May 1975), 1 da (Miranda b 15 July 1975); *Career* dir Frank B Hall (Hldgs) olc 1981, dep chm Leslie & Goodwin (Lloyds insur brokers), dir Leslie & Goodwin Ltd and subsidiaries 1975-80; Freeman: City of London 1983, Worshipful Co of Insurers 1983; FCA 1969; *Recreations* numismatic, bibliophile, fishing; *Clubs* RAC; *Style—* Henry Prentis, Esq; Cherry Lawn, Nunnery St, Castle Hedingham, Essex CO9 3DP (☎ 0787 61100); Leslie & Godwin Ltd, 6 Braham St, London E1 8ED (☎ 01 480 7200, fax 01 480 7450, car tel 0836 741 353, telex 8950221 CORPCO G)

PRENTIS, Nigel Anthony; s of James Martin Prentis, and Megan, *née* Jones; *b* 2 Dec 1951; *Educ* Perse Sch Cambridge; *m* 9 March 1974, Caroline Sylvia, da of Victor Stephen Plumb (d 1985); 2 s (Daniel b 1979, Matthew b 1982), 1 da (Louisa b 1977); *Career* trg Spicer & Pegler 1969-75, audit mangr Charter & Myhill 1975-77, fndr Prentis & Co 1977; FCA 1974; *Books* Self Employment Fact Book (1982); *Recreations* soccer, voluntary work with children; *Style—* Nigel Prentis, Esq; 115c Milton Rd, Cambridge CB4 1XE (☎ 0223 352024, fax 0223 64317, telex 817936 CAMTEL)

PRESCOT, Kenrick Warre; s of late Brig C P Prescot, CBE; *b* 21 Nov 1920; *Educ* Eton, Worcester Coll Oxford; *m* 1948, Angharad Joanna, da of Brig C R M Hutchison, DSO, MC (ka 1942); 2 s, 1 da; *Career* served WWII RA, India, Burma and UK 1942-46, Capt; Bank of England 1947-59, vice-pres Bankers Tst Company 1959-83; dir: Bankers Trust Int Ltd 1970-76, Amev Life Assurance Ltd 1973-80, Amev (UK) Ltd 1980-, Bankers Tstee Co Ltd 1983-; *Recreations* tennis, beagling, croquet; *Clubs* Gresham, MCC, Hurlingham; *Style—* Kenrick Prescot, Esq; 13 The Little Boltons, London SW10

PRESCOTT, John Leslie; MP (Lab) Kingston upon Hull, E 1970-; s of John Herbert Prescott, JP, of Chester, by his w Phyllis; *b* 31 May 1938; *Educ* Ellesmere Port Secondary Modern, WEA, Ruskin Coll Oxford, Hull Univ; *m* 1961, Pauline, da of Ernest Tilston, of Chester; 2 s; *Career* joined Lab Pty 1956; former trainee chef & merchant seaman (NUS official 1968-70); contested (Lab) Southport 1966, PPS to Sec of State for Trade 1974-76, ldr Lab Pty Delegn European Parl 1976-79 (memb 1975-79); oppn spokesman: on Tport 1979-81, Regional Affrs 1981-Nov 1983; memb shadow cabinet and front bench spokesman Tport Nov 1983-84; front bench spokesman Employment 1984-; *Style—* John Prescott, Esq, MP; 365 Saltshouse Rd, Sutton-on-Hull, North Humberside (☎ 702698)

PRESCOTT, Sir Mark; 3 Bt (UK 1938), of Godmanchester, Co Huntingdon; s of Maj (William Robert) Stanley Prescott (d 1962, yr s of Col Sir William Prescott, 1 Bt), by his 1 w Gwendolen, *née* Aldridge, and n of Sir Richard Stanley Prescott, 2 Bt (d 1965); *b* 3 Mar 1948; *Educ* Harrow; *Career* racehorse trainer; *Style—* Sir Mark Prescott, Bt; Heath House, Moulton Rd, Newmarket, Suffolk CB8 8DU (☎ 0638 662117)

PRESCOTT, Peter John; s of Wentworth James Prescott (d 1983), and Ellen Marie, *née* Burrows; *b* 6 April 1936; *Educ* Windsor GS, Pembroke Coll Oxford (MA); *m* 15 Sept 1971, Gillian Eileen, da of late Harold Lowe, and of Eddie Lowe, *née* Pennack; *Career* Nat Serv 2 Lt RA 1957-59; asst cultural attaché HM Embassy Cairo 1964 (London 1967-70), Univ of Sussex 1970-71; Br Cncl: asst then dep rep Paris 1971-75, dir E Europe and N Asia dept London 1975-79, seconded to dept of educn and sci 1979-81, rep Aust 1981-84, rep and cultural cnsllr HM Embassy Paris 1984-; *Recreations* reading, music, walking, swimming; *Style—* Peter Prescott, Esq; British Council, 9/11 Rue de Constantine, 75007 Paris, France (☎ 45 559 595, fax 47 057 702, telex 250912F)

PRESCOTT, Peter Richard Kyle; s of Capt Richard Stanley Prescott (d 1987), of Cordoba, Argentina, and Sarah Aitchison, *née* Shand; *b* 23 Jan 1943; *Educ* St George's Coll Argentina, Dulwich, UCL (BSc), QMC (MSc); *m* 23 Sept 1967, Frances Rosemary, da of Wing Cdr Eric Henry Bland (d 1980), of Tonge Corner, Sittingbourne; 2 s (Richard Julyan Kyle b 1973, Thomas Alexander Kyle b 1975), 1 da (Miranda Katherine b 1971); *Career* called to Bar Lincoln's Inn 1970; *Books* The Modern Law of Copyright (with Hugh Laddie & Mary Victoria, 1980); *Recreations* flying, music, reading, sub-aqua diving; *Clubs* Comton Abbas Flying; *Style—* Peter Prescott, Esq; Arlington Square, London N1 (☎ 01 359 4580); Isle of Purbeck, Dorset; Francis Taylor Bldg, The Temple, London EC4 (☎ 01 353 5657, fax 01 353 3588, 01 353 8715)

PRESLAND, John David; s of Leslie Presland; *b* 3 July 1930; *Educ* St Albans Sch, LSE; *m* 1969, Margaret Brewin; *Career* exec vice-chm Port of London Authy 1978-82; memb Br Computer Soc; FCA, IPFA; *Clubs* Oriental; *Style—* John Presland, Esq; c/o Br Ports Assoc, Cwlth House, 1-19 New Oxford St, London WC1A 1DZ (☎ 01 242 1200)

PRESS, John Bryant; s of Edward Kenneth Press (d 1951), and Gladys Mary Smith, *née* Cooper (d 1980); *b* 11 Jan 1920; *Educ* King Edward VI Sch Norwich, CCC Cambridge (MA); *m* 20 Dec 1947, Janet Nellie, da of Oliver Crompton (d 1982), of Cardiff; 1 s (Roger b 1948), 1 da (Judith b 1953); *Career* WWII RA 1940-45: Gunner 1940-41, 2 Lt 1942, Lt 1943, Staff Capt 1944-45; Br Cncl 1946-80: Athens 1946, Salonika 1947-50, Madras 1950-51, Colombo 1951-52, Birmingham 1952-54, Cambridge 1955-62, London 1963-64, Paris 1965-71, Oxford 1972-78, London 1979-80; FRSL 1959; *Books* The Fire and the Fountain (1955), Uncertainties (1956), The Chequer'd Shade (1958), Guy Fawkes Night (1959), Rule and Energy (1963), A Map of Modern English Verse (1969), The Lengthening Shadows (1971), A Girl with Beehive Hair (1986); *Recreations* the arts, travel; *Style—* John Press, Esq; 5 South Parade, Frome, Somerset BA11 1EJ (☎ 0373 611 42)

PREST, (Edward) Charles; OBE (1986), DFC (1944); s of Gerald Stanley Prest (d 1956), of Eastbourne, and Margaret Sabine Prest, *née* Pasley (d 1967); *b* 11 May 1920; *Educ* Rugby Sch, RMA Woolwich; *m* 6 Nov 1944, Joyce Marjorie, da of John Perks (d 1969), of London; 1 s (Richard Jullion b 1946), 1 da (Jennifer Mary b 1957); *Career* cmmnd in RA 1939, served with 99 Field Regt (Royal Bucks Yeomanry) RA in France (until Dunkirk) and England 1939-42, Army (Air Observation Post) pilot 1942; flying instructor 1942-43, Flight Cdr in 659 AOP Sqdn RAF Attached to 11 Armoured Divn Normandy to the Rhine 1943-45 (Capt 1945); joined the Slag Reduction Co Ltd (now Faber Prest plc) 1946 (sec 1948, dir 1952, md 1963-83, chm 1966-86, pres 1986); dir of all subsidiary and associated cos The Slag Reduction Co NZ Ltd 1979-84, Appleby Slag Reduction Co Ltd 1976-83, Appley Slag Co Ltd 1981-84; *Recreations* golf, walking, computers; *Clubs* Army and Navy, Lindrick GC, Sea View Yacht; *Style—* Charles Prest, Esq, OBE, DFC; Victoria High St, Seaview, Isle of Wight PO34 5EU (☎ 0983 617310)

PREST, Nicholas Martin; s of Prof Alan Richmond Prest (d 1984), of Wimbledon, and Pauline Chasey, *née* Noble; *b* 3 April 1953; *Educ* Manchester GS, Christ's Church Oxford (MA); *m* 1985, Anthea Joy Elisabeth, da of Stuart John Guthrie Neal, of Wales; 1 da (Clementine Joy Chasey b 1987); *Career* entered civl service, MOD 1974, admin trainee, princ offr 1979; joined Utd Scientific Instruments Ltd 1982, dir United Scientific Hldgs plc 1985; *Recreations* tennis; *Style—* Nicholas Prest, Esq; 16 Leamington Rd Villas, London W11 1HS (☎ 01 727 7704); United Scientific Hldgs plc, United Scientific House, 215 Vauxhall Bridge Rd, London SW1 (☎ 01 821 8080)

PRESTIGE, Colin Gwynne; s of Harold Haldane Calder Prestige, CBE (d 1982), of Chislehurst, Kent, and Lydia Ellen Neville, *née* Edwards (d 1983); *b* 19 Nov 1926; *Educ* Bradfield Coll, Oriel Coll Oxford (BA, MA); *Career* Supply and Secretarial Div RN 1945-48; slr 1954; ptnr Lawrence Graham London 1959- (second sr ptnr 1987-); chm Young Slrs Gp Law Soc 1960-61, cncl memb Law Soc 1967-, chm Non-contentious Business Ctee 1974-77, vice chm Professional Purposes Ctee 1980-82 and 1983-84 (father of cncl 1987-), memb Holborn Law Soc 1962 (memb ctee 1962-, hon tres 1963-71, vice-pres 1971-73, pres 1973-74); chm Rent Assesment Appeals Ctee Greater London 1965-68; cncl memb: Incorporated Cncl of Law Reporting Eng and Waıes 1984-, The Selden Soc 1988-; dir Royal Theatrical Fund 1967-79; tstee: D'Oyly Carte Opera Tst 1964-, Friends of D'Oyly Carte 1981-; memb Worshipful Co of Slrs 1988; FRSA 1967; *Books* D'Oyly Carte and the Pirates; Original New York Productions 1875-96 (1971), Conveyancing; Who Buys Your House ? (1977); *Recreations* Gilbert and Sullivan, literary research; *Clubs* Garrick; *Style—* Colin Prestige, Esq; c/o Lawrence Graham, 190 Strand, London WC2R 1JN (☎ 01 379 0000, fax 01 379 6854, telex 22673 LAWGRA G)

PRESTON, Hon Mrs (Caroline Anne); *née* Cecil; er da of 3 Baron Rockley; *b* 27 Mar 1960; *m* 1985, Mark G Preston, yr s of Simon Preston, of Lowfield Farm, Tetbury, Glos; 1 s (Hugh Simon b 1987); *Style—* Hon Mrs Preston; 5 South Park Mews, London SW6

PRESTON, Ella, Lady; Ella Henrietta; da of late Friedrich von Shikendantz; *m* 1913, Sir Thomas Hildebrand Preston, OBE, 6 Bt (d 1976); 1 s (Sir Ronald 7 Bt, *qv*), 1 da (Tatiana Stella Gertrude b 1920); *Style—* Ella, Lady Preston; Beeston Hall, Beeston St Lawrence, Norwich, Norfolk NR12 8YS

PRESTON, (John) Hugh (Simon); s of Rev Cecil George Armitage Preston (d 1966), and Dr Maureen Evans; *b* 28 April 1937; *Educ* Marlborough; *m* 10 Oct 1964, Julia Deborah, da of Richard Glover Hubbard (d 1969); 1 s (Guy b 1968), 1 da (Olivia b 1972); *Career* chartered surveyor, ptnr Strutt & Parker; FRICS; *Recreations* reading, gliding, gardening, music; *Clubs* Farmers'; *Style—* Hugh Preston, Esq; Summerdown House, Malshanger, Basingstoke, Hampshire; 55 Northbrook St, Newbury, Berks

PRESTON, Jeffrey William; s of William Preston, and Sybil Grace Preston *née* Lawson; *b* 29 Jan 1940; *Educ* Liverpool Collegiate Sch, Hertford Coll Oxford (MA); *Career* dept sec Welsh Off 1985, asst princ Miny of Ariation 1963, priv sec Permanent Sec, Bd of Trade 1966; pncpl: Bd of Trade 1967, HM Treasury 1970; DTI 1973; asst sec Dept of Trade 1975-82, under-sec and regnl dir Yorks and Humberside Regnl; DTI 1982-85; *Recreations* motoring, opera, swimming; *Clubs* Utd Oxford and Cambridge Univs; Leeds (Leeds); *Style—* Jeffrey Preston, Esq; The Welsh Office, Cathays Park, Cardiff CB1 3NQ (☎ 823579)

PRESTON, Hon Mrs (Judith Susanna); *née* Briggs; yr da of Baron Briggs (Life Peer); *b* 1961; *m* 1985, Philip G F Preston, only s of W Preston, of Folkestone, Kent; *Style—* Hon Mrs Preston

PRESTON, Sir Kenneth Huson; s of late Sir Walter Preston; *b* 19 May 1901; *Educ* Rugby, Trinity Oxford; *m* 1, 1922, Beryl Wilmot (d 1979), da of Sir William Wilkinson; 1 s, 1 da; m 2, 1984, Mrs Violet Evelyn Dumont; *Career* dir Midland Bank Ltd 1945-76, pres Stone-Platt Industries Ltd 1968-82; memb: S Area Bd BR, Br Olympic Yachting team 1936 and 1952, Capt 1960; kt 1959; *Clubs* Royal Yacht Sqdn (V-Cdre 1965-71), Thames Yacht (V-Cdre 1953-56); *Style—* Sir Kenneth Preston; Court Lodge, Avening, Tetbury, Glos (☎ 045 383 4402)

PRESTON, Michael David; s of Richard Preston, and Yetta, *née* Young (d 1958); *b* 12 Dec 1945; *Educ* Hazelwood Sch, St Paul's, Exeter Coll Oxford (MA); *m* 13 April 1969, Stephanie Ann, *née* Levy; 2 s (Matthew b 1972, Robert b 1975); *Career* articled clerk Price Waterhouse London; fndr shareholder and dir: The Sterling Publishing Gp plc, Broad St Gp plc, Pacific Agric Hldgs Inc, Corporate Data Sciences Inc; dir Debrett's Peerage Ltd; playing memb Royal Amateur Orchestra; former pres Oxford Univ Cons Assoc; FCA 1971; *Recreations* music, wine, tennis, squash, golf; *Clubs* Utd Oxford and Cambridge; *Style—* Michael Preston, Esq; 91 Redington Rd, London NW3 7RR (☎ 01 431 2530); 30 Furnival St, London EC4A 1JE

PRESTON, Michael Richard; s of Maj Frederick Allen Preston, MC, TD (d 1972), of Carshalton, Surrey, and Winifred Gertrude, *née* Archer (d 1987); *b* 15 Oct 1927; *Educ* Whitgift Sch, Sutton and Cheam Sch of Art Surrey, Guildford Sch of Art (NDD), Goldsmith's Coll London (ATD, Dip Humanities); *m* 1, 13 Aug 1955 (m dis 1975), Anne, da of Dr Ralph Gillespie Smith (d1959), of Kirdford, Sussex; m 2, 22 Aug 1980, Judith Gaye James, da of Alec Warden Hopkins, of Blenheim, NZ; *Career* volunteer Queen's Royal Regt 1944-48, Queen's Royal Regt TA 1948-52, HAC 1952-61; asst master Whitgift Sch 1954-55, drawing master Dulwich Coll 1955-64, head of design and later keeper dept of museum servs Science Museum 1964-87; exhibitions designed include: Centenary of Charles Babbage (1971), A Word to the Mermaid's (1973), Tower Bridge Observed (1974), The Breath of Life (1974), Science and Technology of Islam (1976), Stanley Spencer in the Shipyard (1979), Science and Technology of India (1982), The Great Cover-Up Show (1982), Beads of Glass (1983), Louis Pasteur and Rabies; many permanent galleries in: Science Museum 1964-86, Nat Railway Museum York 1971-75, Wellcome Museum of the History of Medicine 1975-80, Nat Museum of Photography, Film and Television Bradford 1977-83; advsy assignments on museum projects: Iran 1976-79, Spain 1977-80, Germany 1978-79, Canada 1979-82, Expo '86 Vancouver BC 1984-86, Trinidad 1982-83, Turkey 1984-, Hong Kong 1985; conslt designer 1987-; consultancies to: The Wellcome Fndn 1986-, Dean &

Chapter Canterbury Cathedral 1987, TAVRA 1988-, Design Expo '89 Nagoya Japan 1988-; National Institute of Design India 1989-; chm Greenwich Soc 1961-64, examiner UEI 1959-64, examiner first degrees Univ of London 1970-74, panel memb BTEC 1982-, memb int advsy panel Tubitak (Sci Res Cncl of Turkey) 1984-; FRSA 1955-68, memb ICOM 1964-, memb CSD 1953 (fell 1972-), hon memb Guild Glass Engineers 1976- (hon fell 1980-, pres 1986-); *Recreations* looking at buildings, travel, food, jazz; *Clubs* Arts; *Style—* Michael Preston, Esq; 37 Walham Grove, London SW6 1QR (fax 01 381 6955, telex 23491 DOON G)

PRESTON, (Bryan) Nicholas; OBE (1985); s of Bryan Wentworth Preston, MBE (d 1965); *b* 6 Feb 1933; *Educ* Eton, RAC Cirencester; *m* 1955, Elsbeth, *née* Hostettler; 1 s, 2 da; *Career* farmer; dir Stone Manganese Marine Ltd, chm Br Marine Equipment Cncl 1966-68 and 1976-78; memb: BOTB E Euro Trade Cncl 1979-82, BOTB Euro Trade Ctee; *Recreations* field sports, skiing; *Clubs* Boodle's, Farmers'; *Style—* Nicholas Preston, Esq, OBE; Park Farm, Beverston, nr Tetbury, Glos GT8 8TT (☎ 0666 526880)

PRESTON, Peter John; s of John Whittle Preston; *b* 23 May 1938; *Educ* Loughborough GS, St John's Coll Oxford; *m* 1962, Jean Mary Burrell; 2 s, 2 da; *Career* editor The Guardian 1975-; *Style—* Peter Preston Esq; The Guardian, 119 Farringdon Rd, London EC1 (☎ 01 278 2332)

PRESTON, Sir Peter Sansome; KCB (1978), CB (1973); s of Charles Guy Preston; *b* 18 Jan 1922; *Educ* Nottingham HS; *m* 1951, Marjory Harrison; 2 s, 3 da; *Career* served WW II RAF; joined BOT as exec offr 1947, trade cmmr New Delhi 1959, under-sec BOT (subsequently DTI) 1969-72, dep sec Dept of Trade 1972-76, perm sec Miny of Overseas Devpt (subsequently Overseas Devpt Admin FCO) 1976-82; int advsr Land Rover-Leyland 1983-87, dir Wellcome Int Trading 1985-; vice-chm CARE Br 1985-; *Style—* Sir Peter Preston, KCB; 5 Greville Park Avenue, Ashtead, Surrey (☎ 0372 72099)

PRESTON, Hon Robert Francis Hubert; s of late 15 Viscount Gormanston; *b* 1915; *Educ* Downside; *m* 1, 1941 (m dis 1955), Jean Helen o child of late Capt Charles Shaw, 15 Hussars; 2 da; m 2, 1970, Daphne Helen Anne, da of late Col Robert Hanbury Brudenell-Bruce, DSO (*see* Peerage Marquess of Ailesbury), and formerly w of (1) late Lt-Cdr Reginald Hughes-Onslow, RN (*see* Peerage Earl of Onslow), and (2) late Maj John Edward Mountague Bradish-Ellames; *Career* formerly Capt 11 Hussars, served WWII (wounded); hon sec Northamptonshire Branch CPRE; *Style—* The Hon Robert Preston; Thatched Cottage, Dingley, Market Harborough, Leics

PRESTON, Sir Ronald Douglas Hildebrand; 7 Bt (UK 1815); s of Sir Thomas Hildebrand Preston, OBE, 6 Bt (d 1976), and Ella Lady Preston, *qv*; *b* 9 Oct 1916; *Educ* Westminster, Trinity Cambridge, Ecole des Sciences Politiques Paris; *m* 1, 1954 (m dis 1971), Smilya Stefanovic; m 2, 1972, Pauleen Jane, da of late Paul Lurcott; *Heir* kinsman, Philip Charles Henry Hulton Preston; *Career* served WW II, with 8 Army in Mid East and Italy, Austria and Allied Control Cmmn to Bulgaria, late Maj Intelligence Corps; Reuters correspondent in Belgrade 1948-53; Times correspondent: Vienna and E Europe 1953-60, Tokyo 1960-63; HM Diplomatic Serv 1963-76; *Recreations* tennis, shooting; *Clubs* Travellers', Norfolk (Norwich), Tokyo (Tokyo); *Style—* Sir Ronald Preston, Bt; Beeston Hall, Beeston St Lawrence, Norwich NR12 8YS (☎ 0692 630771)

PRESTON, Simon Douglas Nelson; s of Jocelyn Panizzi Preston (d 1970), of Romsey, and Emily Geraldine Morval Kirby, *née* Nelson; *b* 5 August 1933; *Educ* Sherborne, Trinity Coll Cambridge (MA); *m* 30 June 1962, Celia Mary, da of Frank Bodenham Thornely, MC (d 1958), of Tunbridge Wells; 4 s (Rupert b 1963, Adam b 1966, John b 1975, Charles b 1975), 1 da (Emma b 1965); *Career* Nat Serv Lt RM Commandos Austria special duties 1952-54; PR off Stock Exchange 1959-64, info off Lazard Bros & Co Ltd 1964-66; dir: Fin PR Ltd 1966-68, Charles Barker City Ltd 1968-71; fin dir Leo Burnett Ltd 1971-74, md and dir Dewe Rogerson Ltd 1974-81, dir Mixed Media Ltd 1982-87; chm City Liason Gp 1973-74 and 1979-83, memb cncl Assoc Ind Business 1978-79, chm Br Enterprise Award Ctee 1981-84, dir Think Br Campaign 1982-; memb Inst PR (hon tres 1981-82); *Recreations* farming, sailing, entomology; *Clubs* Travellers; *Style—* Simon Preston, Esq; Badsell Park Farm, Matfield, Tonbridge, Kent (☎ 0892 832 549); St James PR Ltd, 4 Red Lion Ct, London EC4 (☎ 01 583 2525, fax 01 583 3948, telex 883 934 FINADA)

PRESTON, Thomas Davis; s of Thomas William Samuel Lane Preston (d 1952), of Eastbourne, Sussex, and Madeleine Irene, *née* Davis (d 1966); *b* 1 Dec 1932; *Educ* Gillingham; *m* 23 March 1963, Jennifer Katherine, da of Dr James Anderson, OBE; 2 da (Carolyn b 1969, Lesley b 1971); *Career* Colonial Serv Kenya: dist offr 1954-62, dist cmmr 1962-63 ret 1963; Phillips Harrisons & Crosfield Kenya: mktg mangr 1963-69, mktg dir 1970-73, chm and md 1974-79, chm 1979-88; dir Harrisons & Crosfield plc London 1981-, chm and chief exec Harrisons & Crosfield Aust 1982-; chm: Harcros Chemicals Aust 1982-, Harcros Timber Aus 1982-, Linatex Aust 1984-, Harrisons & Crosfield Papua New Guinea 1982-, New Britain Palm Oil Devpt Papua New Guinea 1982-, Kapiura Plantations Papua New Guinea 1986-; *Recreations* golf; *Style—* Thomas Preston, Esq; High St, Sevenoaks, Kent; Melbourne Mansion Queens Club Gardens, London; Clark Road, Neutral Bay, Sydney, Australia; 1 Gt Tower St, London EC3R 5AB (☎ 01 626 4333, fax 929 3785, telex 885 636)

PRESTON, Timothy William; s of Charles Frank Preston LDS, RCS; *b* 3 Nov 1935; *Educ* Haileybury, Jesus Coll Oxford; *m* 1965, Barbara Mary Haygarth; *Career* barr Inner Temple 1964, a rec of the Crown Ct 1979-; *Clubs* Cavalry and Guards; *Style—* Timothy Preston, Esq; 2 Temple Gdns, London EC4Y 9AY (☎ 01 583 6041)

PRESTON-DUNLOP, Dr Valerie Morthland; *née* Preston; da of Arthur Llewellyn Preston (d 1936), Bishop of Woolwich, and Nancy Robina, *née* Napier (d 1977); *b* 14 Mar 1930; *Educ* Downe House Newbury, Art of Movement Studio (Dip), London Univ (Dip Ed), London Univ (MA), Laban Centre (PhD); *m* 16 Sept 1961, John Henderson Dunlop, s of Sir John Kinninmont Dunlop, KBE, CMG, MC (d 1976), of Ridge Lea, Sevenoaks; 1 s (Roger Napier b 1965), 1 da (Emma Preston b 1971); *Career* sr lectr Dartford Coll of PE 1954-63, dir Beechmont Movement Study Centre 1965-73, sr post grad tutor Laban Centre for Movement and Dance 1978-, int lectr and writer on dance (princ areas of res Rudolf Laban and Choreology), pioneer of dance scholarship, fndr Beechmount Action Centre Tst for the Disadvantaged, govr Walthamstow Hall Sch; FICKL 1961, fndr memb Dance Res Soc 1982; *Books* Practical Kinetography (1969), Dancing and Dance Theory (1979), Dance in Education (1980), Point of Departure (1984); *Recreations* gardening, music; *Clubs* Royal Society of Arts; *Style—* Dr Valerie Preston-Dunlop; Corners, The Street, Ightham, Kent (☎ 0732 884882); Laban Centre, Newcross, London SE14 (☎ 01 692 4070)

PRESTT, His Honour Judge; Arthur Miller; s of Arthur Prestt (d 1959); *b* 23 April 1925; *Educ* Bootham Sch York, Trinity Hall Cambridge; *m* 1949, Jill Mary, da of Graham Richards Dawbarn, CBE (d 1977); 1 s, 1 da; *Career* served WWII 13 Bn Parachute Regt (NW Europe, Malaya, Java); war crimes prosecutor Far E, Hon Maj Parachute Regt; barr Mid Temple 1949, JP Cumberland 1966, dep chm Cumberland QS 1966-69 (chm 1970-71), QC 1970, circuit judge 1971-, sr circuit judge Manchester (N Circuit) and recorder of Manchester 1982-; previously active in Scout Assoc (Silver Acorn 1970); *Recreations* golf, gardening; *Style—* His Honour Judge Prestt, QC; Glebe House, Eccleston, Chorley, Lancs PR7 6LY (☎ 0257 431 397)

PRESTT, Ian; CBE (1986); s of Arthur Prestt (d 1959), and Jessie, *née* Miller (d 1978); bro of His Hon Judge Prestt QC, circuit Judge, Hon Rec of Manchester and Sr Circuit Judge, Manchester 1982; *b* 26 June 1929; *Educ* Bootham Sch York, Liverpool Univ (BSc, MSc, FIBiol); *m* 8 Sept 1956, Jennifer Ann, da of Reginald Wagstaffe, of Southport, Lancs (d 1983); 1 s (Duncan b 1 March 1959, d 1979), 2 da (Julie b 1959, Alexandra b 1968); *Career* 2 Lt RA 1947-49; joined Nature Conservancy 1956, dep dir Central Unit Environmental Pollution Cabinet Off & DoE 1968, dept dir NCC 1974; dir gen RSPB 1975-, chm Int Cncl for Bird Preservation 1982-; memb: exec Ctee Wildfowl Tst 1976-; NCC Advsy Ctee Birds 1981-; *Recreations* sketching, reading, architecture; *Clubs* Athenaeum; *Style—* Ian Prestt, Esq, CBE; Eastfield Ho, Tuddenham Rd, Barton Mills, Bury St Edmonds IP28 6AG (☎ 0638 715139); RSPB, The Lodge, Sandy, Beds SG19 2DL (☎ 0767 80551)

PRETOR-PINNEY, Anthony Robert Edmund; o s of Lt Cdr Giles Robert Pretor-Pinney, RN (ka 1942), and Lucy Theodosia Gascoigne, *née* Fowle (who m 2, Capt John Domvile Auchmulty Musters, DSC, RN, and d 1980); descended from John Pretor (d 1818), who assumed the additional surname and arms of Pinney by Royal Licence on succeeding to the estates of his kinsman John Frederick Pinney (d 1762), of Bettiscombe, Dorset (*see* Burke's Landed Gentry, 18 edn, vol I, 1965); *b* 7 May 1930; *Educ* Winchester, RNC Dartmouth, RAC Cirencester (MRAC 1957); *m* 22 Aug 1963, Laura Uppercu, eldest da of George Winthrop Haight (d 1983), of New York, USA; 2 s (Giles b 3 July 1964, Gavin b 11 May 1968), 1 da (Jennifer b 11 March 1966); *Career* RN 1947-1954; agric; memb Lloyd's 1955; MSTA 1987; *Style—* Anthony Pretor-Pinney, Esq; Somerton Erleigh, Somerset; 25 Church Road, London SW13

PREVETT, John Henry; OBE (1974); s of Frank George Harry Prevett (d 1981), and Florence Emily, *née* Wilson (d 1968); *b* 6 April 1933; *Educ* Oxted Co GS, John Ruskin GS; *m* 28 March 1959, Joy Maureen, da of Martin Josiah Goodchild (d 1947); 2 s (David b 1961, Steven b 1962); *Career* actuary; ptnr Bacon & Woodrow Conslts 1962-; chm: Assoc of consulting Actuaries 1983-85, Br Def and Aid Fund for Southern Africa 1983-; memb: (lab) Reigate Borough Cncl 1963-69 and 1971-73, Reigate and Banstead Borough cncl 1973-84 and 1986-; Freeman: City of London 1980, Worshipful Co of Actuaries 1980; FIA 1955, FPMI 1977; *Books* Actuarial Valuations of Interests in Settled Property (with C O Beard, 1973); *Recreations* wining and dining; *Clubs* Lunchtime Comment; *Style—* John Prevett, Esq, OBE; 62 Gatton Rd, Reigate, Surrey (☎ 0737 246629); Bacon 7 Woodrow, Empire House, St Martins-le-Grand, London EC1A 4ED (☎ 01 600 2747, fax 01 726 6519)

PREVETTE, Kenneth George Charles; OBE (1983); s of George William Prevette (d 1966), and Rosina Hannah, *née* Gray (d 1966); *b* 17 May 1917; *Educ* Cottingham Coll; *m* 1946, Sheila, da of Herbert Henry Spencer (d 1949), of North Shore, Blackpool; 1 s (Martin), 1 da (Linda); *Career* TA (Royal W Kent Regt) 1939-46, Colour Sgt 1939, (POW 1940-45); sec The Pharos Press 1946-83, clerk Golders Green Fndn 1959-83, gen sec Cremation Soc of GB 1964-83 (exec sec 1963-64), sec The Pharos Assur Friendly Soc 1967-72 (chm 1978-80); dir: The London Cremation Co plc 1971-, Kent Co Crematorium plc 1973-, Norwich Crematorium plc 1978-83, Golders Green Crematorium Ltd 1984-; tstee Golders Green Fndn 1983; Int Cremation Fedn: sec gen 1979-81, vice pres 1981-84, hon life memb 1984; Freeman of the City of London 1974; *Recreations* photography, growing trees from seeds, roses; *Style—* Kenneth Prevette, Esq, OBE; 80 Ware St, Bearsted Green, Maidstone, Kent ME14 4PG (☎ 0622 38261)

PREVITE, Hon Mrs; Hon Phyllida; *née* Browne; da of 6 Baron Kilmaine, CBE (d 1978); *b* 1935; *m* 1959, John Edward Previté; 2 s; *Style—* The Hon Mrs Previté; The Wilderness, Hampton Wick, Kingston upon Thames, Surrey

PREVOST, Brian Trevor George; s of Raymond George Prevost (d 1974), and (Winifred) Grace, *née* White (d 1981); *b* 2 May 1932; *Educ* Bradfield, Imede Lausanne Switzerland; *m* 16 June 1956, Margaret Anne, da of Lt-Col John Douglas Allder Vincent (d 1964); 3 da (Sally b 1958, Wendy b 1960, Jacky b 1964); *Career* 2 Lt RA 1951-53, Lt HAC (RHA) 1955-63; dir Sedgwick Collins & Co Ltd 1964-72, underwriting memb Lloyds 1969-79, dir Sedgwick Forbes Ltd and chm Sedgwick Forbes Reins Brokers Ltd 1972-79; Swiss Reins Co (UK) Ltd: dep chief exec 1979-83, dir and gen mangr 1983-89, md 1989-; chm and chief exec Swiss Re GB Mgmnt Ltd 1989-; chm Reins Off Assoc 1989- (memb exec ctee 1983-, dep chm 1987-88); *Recreations* yachting, golf, bridge; *Clubs* Royal Southern YC, Little Ship, Lloyds YC, Insurance Golfing Soc Of London; *Style—* Brian T G Prevost, Esq; Rickstones, 8 Orchard Way, Esher, Surrey KT10 9DY (☎ 0372 62 318); Swiss Re House, 71-77 Leadenhall St, London EC3A 2PQ (☎ 01 623 3456, fax 01 929 4282, telex 884380)

PREVOST, Sir Christopher Gerald; 6 Bt (UK 1805); s of Sir George James Augustine Prevost, 5 Bt (d 1985), and Muriel Emily, *née* Oram (d 1939) ; *b* 25 July 1935; *Educ* Cranleigh; *m* 1964, Dolores Nelly, o da of Dezo Hoffmann; 1 s, 1 da; *Heir* s, Nicholas Marc Prevost b 13 March 1971; *Career* late 60 Regt; fndr Mailtronic Ltd, manufacturers and suppliers of mailroom equipment, chm and md 1977-; memb Business Equipment Trade Assoc 1982-; *Recreations* squash, skiing; *Style—* Sir Christopher Prevost, Bt; Highway Cottage, Berry Grove Lane, Watford, Herts WD2 8AE

PRICE *see also*: Rugge-Price, Tudor Price

PRICE, (Alan) Anthony; s of Walter Longsdon Price (d 1942), and Kathleen Lawrence (d 1937); *b* 16 August 1928; *Educ* The King's Sch Canterbury, Merton Coll Oxford (MA); *m* 1953, Ann, da of Norman George Stone (d 1968); 2 s (James, Simon), 1 da (Katherine); *Career* mil service 1947-49, Capt; journalist and author; ed The Oxford Times 1972-; *Books* The Labyrinth Makers (1970, CWA Silver Dagger), The Alamut Ambush (1971), Colonel Butler's Wolf (1972), October Men (1973), Other Paths to Glory (1974, CWA Gold Dagger 1974, Swedish Acad of Detection Prize 1978), Our Man in Camelot (1975), War Game (1976), The '44 Vintage (1978), Tomorrow's Ghost (1979), The Hour of the Donkey (1980), Soldier No More (1981), The Old Vengeful (1982), Gunner Kelly (1983), Sion Crossing (1984), Here Be Monsters (1985), For the Good of the State (1986), A New Kind of War (1987), A Prospect of Vengenance (1988); *Recreations* military history; *Clubs* Detection; *Style—* Anthony Price, Esq; Wayside Cottage, Horton-cum-Studley, Oxford OX9 1AW (☎ 086 735 326)

PRICE, Barrie; s of Albert Price (d 1978), of Bradford and Mary, *née* Melvin (d 1982); *b* 13 August 1937; *Educ* St Bede's GS Bradford; *m* 15 April 1963, Elizabeth, da of William Murphy (d 1979); 4 s (Nicholas Becket b 1963, Joseph b 1965, Gerard b 1968, Mark b 1974), 1 da (Catherine b 1966); *Career* trainee acct 1953-58, qual CA 1959; sr ptnr Lishman Sidwell Campbell and Price 1974- (joined 1962); chm and md: Slouand Ltd (mgmnt conslts)

1968-; chm: Ripon Life Care and Housing Tst, Ripon City and Dist Devpt Assoc 1969-; govr: St Wilfrids RC Sch Ripon, St John Fisher RC Sch Harrogate; memb: Ripon City Cncl (Mayor 1980-81, dep Mayor 1974-75, 1982-83, 1987-88), memb Harrogate Boro DC (dep leader 1987-88, chm Econ Devpt Ctee); tstee City of Ripon Festival (chm 1981), Yorks Film Archive, Ripon Cathedral Appeal; memb: Friends of the Venerable, Harrogate Int Festival; ICA 1959, FCA 1968, FCCA, FBIM; *Recreations* opera, theatre, football, racing; *Clubs* Opera North, Bradford City AFC Exec, Ripon Race Course Members; *Style*— Barrie Price, Esq; Prospect House, Palace Road, City of Ripon, North Yorks HG4 1HA (☎ 0765 2058); Becket's House, Market Place, Ripon (☎ 0765 700681)

PRICE, Bernard Albert; s of Albert Price (d 1952), of Calverhall, Shrops, and Doris, *née* Whittingham (d 1959); *b* 6 Jan 1944; *Educ* Whitchurch GS Shrops, Kings Sch Rochester Kent, Merton Coll Oxford (MA); *m* 4 June 1966, Christine Mary, da of Roy William Henry Combes (d 1979), of Chelmsford, Essex; 2 s (David b 1971, John b 1976), 1 da (Emma b 1973); *Career* co clerk and chief exec Staffs CC 1983- (sr dep clerk 1980-83), clerk to the Lieutenancy Staffs 1983-, sec W Mids Forum of Strategic Local Authys 1985-, chm Soc of Local Authy Chief Execs Mgmnt Practices Panel 1987-; *Recreations* sailing, walking; *Style*— Bernard Price, Esq; The Cottage, Yeatsall Lane, Abbots Bromley, Rugeley, Staffs (☎ 0283 840269); County Buildings, Martin St, Stafford, Staffs (☎ 0785 223121)

PRICE, Brian Derek; s of Gp Capt Derek Price (d 1988), and Lorna Mary MacMullen, *née* Bulleid; *b* 2 Oct 1939; *Educ* Tonbridge; *m* 18 June 1966, Juliet Elisabeth Rosamund, da of Maj Sir Reginald Lawrence William Williams, Bt, MBE, ED (d 1970); 2 s (Edmund Hugh Owain b 1969, Henry William Frederick b 1973); *Career* CA, ptnr Hodgson Impey (formerly Hodgson Harris) 1974-, seconded DOE 1988; chm London Soc of CAs 1979-80 (ctee memb 1967-80); cncl memb ICEAW 1987; govr Royal Nat Coll for the Blind Hereford 1982, tstee and tres Fight for Sight 1980-; ACA 1962, FCA 1967; *Recreations* history, walking; *Clubs* City of London, London Rowing; *Style*— Brian Price, Esq; 52 Hazlewell Rd, Putney, London SW15 6LR; Hodgson Impey, Spectrum House, 20-26 Cursitor St, London EC4A 1HY (☎ 01 405 2088, fax 01 831 2206)

PRICE, Rear-Adm Cecil Ernest; CB (1978), AFC (1953); s of Ernest C Price; *b* 29 Oct 1921; *Educ* Bungay G S; *m* 1946, Megan Morgan; 1 s, 1 da; *Career* RN 1941, Capt 1966, Rear-Adm 1976, Dep Asst Chief of Staff (Operations) SHAPE 1976-80; *Style*— Rear-Admiral Cecil Price, CB, AFC; Low Farm, Mendham, Harleston, Norfolk (☎ Harleston 852676)

PRICE, The Hon Charles; s of Charles Harry Price and Virginia, *née* Ogden; *b* 1 April 1931; *Educ* Univ of Missouri; *m* Carol Ann, *née* Swanson; 2 s, 3 da; *Career* pres Linwood Securities 1960-81; chm: Price Candy Co 1969-81, American Bank Corpn 1973-81, American Bank and Tst Co 1973-81 American Mortgage Co 1973-81; dir of Ameribanc Inc; US Ambassador: Belgium 1981-83, UK 1983-89; Hon Fell Regent's Coll 1986, Hon Dr Westminster Coll Missouri; Salvation Army's William Booth Award 1985; Tstee Citation Award Midwest Res Inst 1987; *Recreations* golf; *Clubs* White's, Mark's, Swinley Forest Golf, Metropolitan (Washington); *Style*— The Hon Charles H Price II; 5049 Wornall Rd, Apt 1011 C-D, Kansas City, Missouri 64112, USA

PRICE, Christopher; s of Stanley Price (d 1988), of Sheffield, and Katherine Phyllis, *née* Thornton; *b* 26 Jan 1932; *Educ* Leeds GS, Queen's Coll Oxford; *m* 26 June 1956, Annie Greirson, da of James Ross (d 1987), of Edinburgh; 2 s (Anthony Ross b 1959, Michael John b 1962), 1 da (Jennifer Margaret b 1957); *Career* ed New Education 1966-68, educn corr New Statesman 1968-74, dir Leeds Poly 1986-; MP (Lab): Birmingham Perry Barr 1966-70, Lewisham West 1974-83; chm Select Ctee on Educn Sci and the Arts 1979-83; fell Inst of Biotechnological Studies 1984, FRSA 1987; *Books* The Confait Confessions (1979); *Clubs* Athenaeum; *Style*— Christopher Price, Esq; Churchwood, Beckett Park, Leeds LS6 3QS (☎ 0532 755508); Leeds Polytechnic, Leeds, LS1 3HE (☎ 0532 462313)

PRICE, Christopher J S; s of John Eric Price, of Salcombe, and Mary Stuart Price; *b* 16 Mar 1939; *Educ* Brentwood Sch; *m* 1962, da of Geoffrey Egerton Gilbert AIEE; 1 s (Mathew b.1965), 1 da (Emma 1967); *Career* chm Sedgwick Credit, dir Sedgwick Ltd; *Recreations* sailing, gardening, opera, theatre; *Clubs* Carlton, City of London; *Style*— Christopher Price, Esq; CBIM, Sedgwick Ltd, Sedgwick House, The Sedgwick Centre, 10 Whitechapel High St, London E1 8DX

PRICE, Lt-Col Christopher Keith; s of Col David Keith Price, MC, TD (d 1981), of Upper Sydenhurst, Chiddingfold, Surrey, and Barbara Christian, *née* Naumann; *b* 12 July 1947; *Educ* Charterhouse; *m* 6 April 1974, Michele, da of Edward Asa-Thomas, TD (d 1983), of Whitethorn House, Crawley Winchester, Hants; 1 s (Andrew b 2 Nov 1980); *Career* cmmnd 4/7 Royal Dragoon Guards 1966, Troop Ldr 1966-70, Regtl Signals Offr/Asst Adj 1970-71, ADC to Cdr Land Forces NI 1971-73, 2 i/c Sqdn 4/7 DG 1973-75, GSO3 3 Div 1975-77, Staff Offr to Res Cmmr Designate to Rhodesia 1977-78, chief of staff HQ 33 Amd Bde 1980-81, Sqdn Cdr 4/7 DG 1982-83, Directing Staff Army Coll 1984-86, CO 14/20 King's Hussars 1987-; memb Grand Mil Race Ctee; Freeman: City of London, Worshipful Co of Grocers 1977; *Recreations* hunting, shooting, polo, fishing; *Clubs* Cavalry & Guards; *Style*— Lt-Col Christopher Price; 38 Micklethwaite Rd, London SW6 (☎ 01 395 1858); 14/2OH, BFPO 17 (☎ 01049 251 681 420)

PRICE, Cyril; s of Ieuan Penry Price (d 1975), and Elsie (d 1980); *b* 26 Feb 1924; *Educ* Cathays, Cardiff; *m* 1946, Nancy Joy, da of Fredric Seaton, JP, of Australia (d 1966); 1 s, 1 da; *Career* Fleet Air Arm Lt RNVR (A) 828 Sqdn HMS Formidable, HMS Implacable; dir: Tennant Guaranty Ltd 1964-83 (renamed The Royal Bank of Canada Trade & Finance Ltd 1982), Orford Trading Co Ltd 1964-83, Tennant Guaranty Trust Ltd 1969-83, Tennant Guaranty Int Ltd 1976-83; sr int exec AMCA Netherlands BV 1983-84; int business consult 1984-; chm High Wycombe Centre Inst of Dir's 1988-; cncl memb Economic League (SE Region) 1985-; *Clubs* Hazlemere Golf and Country, IOD; *Style*— Cyril Price, Esq; 11 Hubert Day Close, Beaconsfield, Bucks HP9 1TL (☎ 0494 670321)

PRICE, Sir David Ernest Campbell; DL (Hants 1982), MP (C) Eastleigh 1955-; s of Maj Villiers Price (d 1982), and Margaret Campbell Currie (d 1930); *b* 20 Nov 1924; *Educ* Eton, Trinity Cambridge, Yale Univ USA; *m* 1960, Rosemary Eugénie Evelyn, da of Cyril F Johnston, OBE, (d 1950); 1 da (Arabella); *Career* WWII served 1 Bn Scots Guards, HQ 56 (London) Div, Italy; ICI 1949-62; parly sec BOT 1962-64, oppn front bench spokesman on Sci and Technol 1964-70, parly sec Miny of Technol June-Oct 1970, parly sec Miny of Aviation Supply 1970-71, parly under-sec state Aerospace DTI 1971-72; memb select ctee on Tport 1979-83, and Social Servs 1984-; conslt Union Int plc 1973-, vice-pres Inst of Industl Mangrs 1973-, chm Parly & Scientific Ctee 1973 and 1979-82; kt 1980; *Recreations* wine, history of art, music, cooking, gardening; *Clubs* Beefsteak; *Style*— Sir David Price, DL, MP; 16 Laxford House, London SW1W 9JU; Forest Lodge, Moonhills Lane, Beaulieu, Hampshire SO42 7YW; The House of Commons, London SW1

PRICE, Lt-Col David Everard Crossley; OBE, TD (1944); s of Capt Athelstan Elder, of Culverwood House, Hertford, and Mary Winifred, *née* Crossley; *b* 18 Mar 1907; *Educ* Lancing; *m* Joan Voase, da of John Hutchinson; 2 s (Robert Athelstan b 1949, John Aiden Joseph b 1952), 1 da (Joanna Margaret b 1956); *Career* Royal Gloucs Hussars 1935-43, Dep Provo Marshal 1943-47; underwriter Lloyds 1928-88; master: Scarteen Black & Tan Hounds 1933-38, VWH Cricklade 1939-43, Limerick Hounds 1947-48, Wexford Hounds 1948-52; Liveryman Worshipful Co of Merchant Taylors; *Clubs* Kildare Street Dublin; *Style*— Lt-Col David Price; Kilmokea House, Campile, New Ross, Co Wexford, Ireland (☎ 051 88109)

PRICE, David George; s of Lt Cdr Rodney Athelstan Price, RN (ka 1943), and Elizabeth Peace, *née* Cole-Hamilton; *b* 22 Mar 1940; *Educ* Wellington, Cambridge Univ (MA), London Coll Estate Mgmnt; *m* 14 March 1970, Diana Catherine, da of T A S Davie (d 1978), of Grangehill, Beith, Ayrshire; 2 s (Toby Charles Rodney b 18 Oct 1972, Simon James Edward b 26 June 1974); *Career* 2 Lt Black Watch (TA) 1964, Lt 1966; md Titan Tanks Ltd 1966-74, chm and md Power Plastics Ltd 1974-87; Liveryman Worshipful Co Merchant Taylors; pres Made Up Textiles Assoc 1989; *Recreations* tennis, opera, gardening; *Style*— David Price, Esq; Woodcock, Thirsk, N Yorks YO7 2AB; Power Plastics Ltd, Horn Beam Pk, Harrogate, N Yorks YO7 2AB (☎ 0423 879007, fax 0423 871050, car 0860 200301, telex 57745)

PRICE, David William James; s of Richard J E Price (d 1983), of Quinta da Romeira, Bucelas, Portugal, and Miriam Joan, *née* Dunsford; *b* 11 June 1947; *Educ* Ampleforth, CCC Oxford (MA); *m* 1971, Shervie Ann Lander, da of Sir James Whitaker, 3 Bt, *qv*; 1 s (William b 1973), 1 da (Hesther b 1971); *Career* merchant banker; dir: Mercury Warburg Investmt Mgmnt Ltd 1978-, S G Warburg & Co Ltd 1982-87; cncllr London Borough of Lambeth 1979-82; chm Mercury Asset Mgmnt Ltd 1983-, dep chm Mercury Asset Mgmnt plc 1987-; *Clubs* Oriental, Brooks's; *Style*— David Price, Esq; 39 Old Town, Clapham, London SW4 (☎ 01 720 4359); Mercury Asset Management Ltd, 33 King William St, London EC4 (☎ 01 280 2800)

PRICE, Eric Hardiman Mockford; s of Frederick Hardiman Price, and Florence Nellie Hannah; *b* 14 Nov 1931; *Educ* St Marylebone GS, Christ's Coll Cambridge (BA, MA); *m* 3 Feb 1963, Diana Teresa Anne Mary Stanley, da of Stanley Joseph Leckie Robinson (d 1962), of Harbury Hall, Warwicks; 1 s (Julian b 27 Feb 1969), 3 da (Caroline b 29 Jan 1964, Nichola b 28 Mar 1966, Ashling b 6 July 1970); *Career* Nat Serv Army 1950-52, HAC 1952-57; Economist: Central Electricity Authy Electricity Cncl 1957-58, Br Iron and Steel Fedn 1958-62; chief economist Port of London Authy 1962-67; Miny of Transport: sr econ advsr 1966-69, chief econ advsr 1967-71, dir of econs 1971-75; DOE: undersec econs 1972-76, dir of econs and statistics 1975-76; undersec econs and statistics: Depts of Trade Indust and Consumer Protection 1977-80, Dept of Energy 1980-; dir Robinson Bros Ltd Ryders Green 1985-; Br Isnt of Energy Econs: cncl memb 1980-, vice chm 1981-82 and 1988-89, chm 1982-85; memb: FREconS, FSS, BIEE (British Institute of Energy Economics); *Recreations* squash, tennis, local history; *Clubs* Moor Park GC; *Style*— Eric Price, Esq; Batchworth House, Batchworth Heath Farm, London Road, Rickmansworth, Herts WD3 1QB (☎ 09274 24471); Department of Energy, Thames House South, Millbank, London SW1 (☎ 01 211 3440)

PRICE, Lady; Eva Mary; *née* Dickson; *m* 1939, as his 2 w, Sir Henry Philip Price, 1 and last Bt (d 1963); *Career* chm Nat Liberal Cncl 1952-53 and cr. Bt 1953; *Style*— Lady Price; c/o Midland Bank, 60 Broadway, Hayward's Heath, Sussex

PRICE, Sir Francis Caradoc Rose; 7 Bt (UK 1815); s of Sir Rose Francis Price, 6 Bt (d 1979) and Kathleen June, yr da of Norman William Hutchinson, of Melbourne, Aust; *b* 9 Sept 1950; *Educ* Eton, Trinity Coll Univ of Melbourne, Univ of Alberta; *m* 1975, The Hon Madam Justice Marguerite Jean, da of Roy Samuel Trussler, of Victoria, BC; 3 da; *Heir* bro, Norman William Rose Price; *Career* barr and slr Canada, ptnr Reynolds, Mirth, Richards & Farmer; *Books* Pipelines in Western Canada (1975), Mortgage Actions in Alberta (1985); *Recreations* cricket, jogging, theatre, opera; *Clubs* Centre, Faculty; *Style*— Sir Francis Price, Bt; 9677 95 Ave, Edmonton, Alberta T6C 2A3, Canada (☎ home 403 469 9555, work 403 425 9510)

PRICE, Sir Frank Leslie; DL (Hereford and Worcs and Co of W Midlands, 1977); s of George Frederick Price (d 1978), and Lucy Price (d 1978); *b* 26 July 1922; *Educ* St Matthias Church Sch Birmingham, Vittoria St Arts Sch; *m* 1, 1944 (m dis), Maisie Edna, da of Albert Davis, of Handsworth, Birmingham; 1 s (Noel); m 2; *Career* md Murrayfield Real Estate Co Ltd 1959-66; fndr chm Midlands Art Centre for Young People 1960-66; chm: Br Waterways Bd 1968-84, Telford Newtown 1968-72, Elite Design and Security Ltd 1983-, Sir Frank Price Assoc SA 1986-; pres BAIE 1979-83; chm Swansong Devpts Ltd 1985; FSVA, FCIT, FRSA, kt 1966; *Clubs* Reform; *Style*— Sir Frank Price, DL; c/o Reform Club, 104 Pall Mall, London SW1; Cresta Montona Turee Almeria Spain; Apartado 438 Garrucha, Almeria, Spain

PRICE, Frederick Enoch; s of Frederick William Rayner Price (d 1975), and Gladys May, *née* Shingleton (d 1979); *b* 4 May 1930; *Educ* Dudley GS Worcs, Hertford Coll Oxford (BA, MA); *m* 19 June 1965, Margaret Ann, da of Norman Forsyth Wilson (d 1961); 1 s (Christopher Forsyth b July 1966), 1 da (Joanna b Sept 1970); *Career* graduate trainee Martins Bank 1953- 57, articled clerk Cooper Bros and Co 1957-60, sr ptnr Blackham Cox Taylor and Co 1971-, underwriting memb Lloyds 1981-; memb Edgbaston Rotary Club; FCA, ACMA; *Style*— Frederick Price, Esq; Blackham Cox Taylor and Co, Third Floor, 36 Bennetts Hill, Birmingham B2 5SU (☎ 021 236 3974, fax 021 233 1816)

PRICE, Rt Hon George Cadle; PC (1982); s of William Price by his w Irene Cecilia Escalante de Price; *b* 15 Jan 1919; *Educ* Holy Redeemer Primary Sch Belize City; *Career* city cncllr Belize City 1947-65 (intermittently mayor), fndr People's Utd Pty 1950 (leader 1956-), memb Nat Assembly 1954-, PM Belize 1981- (Premier 1964-81 when independence granted); *Style*— The Rt Hon George Price; Office of The Prime Minister, Belmoplan, Belize

PRICE, Hugh Maxwell; s of Capt Denis Lewin Price, of Crossways House, Cowbridge, South Glamorgan, and Patricia Rosemary, *née* Metcalfe; *b* 25 April 1950; *Educ* Haileybury; *m* 14 June 1975, Sarah Anne, da of Royden Eric Snape; 1 s (Andrew b 17 March 1979), 1 da (Emma b 10 May 1982); *Career* admitted slr 1975; ptnr Morgan Bruce & Hardwickes (previously Hardwickes) Cardiff 1978-; hon asst sec Cardiff Law Soc, dep registrar High Ct; memb Law Soc; *Recreations* squash, tennis, gardening; *Clubs* Cardiff Athletic, Cowbridge Squash and Tennis; *Style*— Hugh Price, Esq; Orchard House, Llanblethian, nr Cowbridge, South Glamorgan C87 7EY (☎ 04463 3590); Morgan Bruce & Hardwickes, 1 Musuem Place, Cardiff CF1 3TX (☎ 0222 233 677, fax 0222 399 288)

PRICE, J(ohn) Maurice; QC (1976); s of Edward Samuel Price; *b* 4 May 1922; *Educ* Grove Park Sch Wrexham, Trinity Coll Cambridge; *m* 1945, Mary, da of Dr Horace Gibson, DSO; 2 s; *Career* RN 1941-46, Lt RNVR, barr Gray's Inn 1949, memb Senate of Inns of Ct and the

Bar 1975-78; *Clubs* Flyfishers'; *Style*— J Maurice Price, Esq, QC; Bowzell Place, Weald, Sevenoaks, Kent TN14 6NF; 2 New Sq, Lincoln's Inn, WC2A 3RU (☎ 01 242 6201)

PRICE, Hon Mrs (Joanna Mary); *née* Cavendish; da of 5 Baron Chesham; *b* 1938; *m* 1960, Peter Henry Mabille Price; 1 s, 1 da; *Style*— The Hon Mrs Price; Avington Manor, Alresford Road, Winchester, Hants

PRICE, John Alan; QC (1980); s of Frederick Leslie Price (d 1976); *b* 11 Sept 1938; *Educ* Stretford GS, Manchester Univ; *m* 1964, Elizabeth Myra, da of Stanley Priest; 1 s, 1 da; *Career* barr Gray's Inn 1961, in practice on Northern Circuit, dep circuit judge 1975-, rec Crown Ct 1980-; *Recreations* tennis, squash, golf, football; *Clubs* Northern Lawn Tennis, Wilmslow Golf; *Style*— John Price, Esq, QC; 15 Carrwood Rd, Wilmslow, Cheshire (☎ Wilmslow 523532); Byrom House, Quay St, Manchester (☎ 061 834 5238); 5 Essex Ct, Temple

PRICE, John Philip; s of Eifion Wyn Price, of Rhayader, Powys, and Kathleen, *née* Woodfield; *b* 11 Dec 1949; *Educ* Monmouth Sch, Corpus Christi Oxford (MA, BPhil); *Career* barr Inner Temple 1974-; dir gen, Dairy Trade Fedn 1986-; *Books* The English Legal System (1979); *Style*—John Price, Esq; 36 Rossmore Court, Park Road, London NW1 6XX (☎ 01 402 6658); Dairy Trade Federation, 19 Cornwall Terrace, London NW1 4QP (☎ 01 486 7244, fax 01 487 4734, telex 262027)

PRICE, Air Vice-Marshal John Walter; CBE (1979, OBE 1973); s of Henry Walter Price (d 1984), and Myrza, *née* Griffiths (d 1958); *b* 26 Jan 1930; *Educ* Solihull, RAF Col Cranwell; *m* 1956, Margaret Sinclair, da of John McIntyre (d 1960), of Sydney Aust; *Career* cmmnd from RAF Coll Cranwell 1950, Sqdn flying appts in Germany (Vampires & Venoms), Korea (Meteors with 77 Sqdn RAAF (despatches 1953), Aust (Vampires and Meteors); cmd No 110 Sqdn 1964-66 (Sycamores and Whirlwinds) in Malaya and Borneo, No 72 Sqdn 1970-72 (Wessex) in UK; RAF Station Laarbruch 1976-78 (Buccaneers and Jaguars), Germany; staff appts in Air Miny 1961-64, PSO to CAS 1968-70, MOD (Air) 1973-75 Dep Dir Ops, HQ Strike Cmd 1979 Gp Capt Ops, MOD (Air) 1980-82 dir of ops (Strike) and as ACAS (Ops) 1982-84, ret as Air Vice-Marshal 1984; joined Clyde Petroleum plc 1984- (mangr external rels, 1986); joined bd of govrs Solihull Sch 1979, (elected chm 1982); *Recreations* golf, cabinet making; *Clubs* RAF; *Style*— Air Vice-Marshal John Price, CBE; 2 Palace Yard, Hereford (☎ 0432 272292); Coddington Ct, Coddington Ledbury, Herefordshire (☎ 053 186811)

PRICE, June, Lady; Kathleen June; da of late Norman W Hutchinson, of Toorak, Melbourne, Australia; *m* 1949, Sir Rose Francis Price, 6 Bt (d 1979); 2 s; *Style*—June, Lady Price; Dormer Cottage, Park Rd, Stoke Poges, Bucks

PRICE, (Arthur) Leolin; QC (1968, NSW 1987); s of Evan Price (d 1959) and Ceridwen Price (d 1974); *b* 11 May 1924; *Educ* Judd Sch Tonbridge, Keble Coll Oxford (MA); *m* 1963, Hon Rosalind, *qv*; 2 s, 2 da; *Career* barr: Mid Temple 1949, Lincoln's Inn 1959, QC Bahamas 1969, bencher 1970; govr Gt Ormond St Hosp for Sick Children 1972-, chm Ctee of Management Inst of Child Health 1976-, govr Christ Coll Brecon 1977-, dir Child Health Res Investment Tst Co plc 1980- (chm 1987-), chllr Diocese of Swansea and Brecon 1982-, dir Marine Adventure Sailing Tst plc 1982-, vice chm Soc of Cons Lawyers 1987-; *Clubs* Carlton; *Style*— Leolin Price, Esq, QC; 32 Hampstead Grove, London NW3 6SR (☎ 01 435 9843); 10 Old Sq, Lincoln's Inn, London WC2A 3SU (☎ 01 405 0758); Moor Park, Llanbedr, Crickhowell, Powys NP8 1SS (☎ 0873 810443)

PRICE, Leonard Sidney; OBE (1974); s of late William Price, and late Dorothy Price; *b* 19 Oct 1922; *Educ* Central Fndn Sch London; *m* 1958 Adrienne Mary, *née* Wilkinson; *Career* WWII 1942-45; Dip Serv 1939-81; FO 1939-42 and 1945-48, Chungking (later vice consul) 1948, Mexico City 1950, Rome 1953, vice consul (later second sec) Katmandu 1954, FO 1957, consul Split 1960, consul and first sec Copenhagen 1963, FO (later FCO) 1967, first sec Kuching 1970, Suva 1972, parly clerk FCO 1975, cnsllr (admin) Canberra 1977-81, ret 1981; hon tres St John Ambulance in Somerset 1983-88; *Recreations* carpentry; *Clubs* Civil Serv; *Style*— Leonard Price, Esq, OBE; 5 Staplegrove Manor, Taunton, Somerset TA2 6EG (☎ 0823 337 093)

PRICE, Sir Leslie Victor; OBE (1971); s of late H V L Price; *b* 30 Oct 1920; *m* 1941, Lorna D Collins; 1 s, 2 da; *Career* chm Australian Wheat Bd 1977- (memb 1971-); kt 1976; *Clubs* Queensland, Melbourne; *Style*— Sir Leslie Price, OBE; 6 Alayne Court, Toowoomba, Queensland, Australia

PRICE, Lionel Dennis Dixon; s of Flt Lt Harold Price (d 1988), of Birkenhead, and Florence Mitchley, *née* Thompson; *b* 2 Feb 1946; *Educ* Bolton Sch, CCC Cambridge (MA); *m* 19 Oct 1968, Sara Angela, da of Flt Lt Ronald William Holt, of Gerrards Cross, Bucks; 3 s (Matthew b 1972, Edward b & d 1974, James b 1975); *Career* Bank of England 1967-79, alternate exec dir Int Monetary Fund 1979-81; Bank of England: head of info div 1981-84, head int div 1985-; *Recreations* genealogy, golf; *Clubs* Overseas Bankers; *Style*— Lionel D D Price, Esq; 102 Clarence Rd, St Albans, AL1 4NQ; Bank of England, London EC2R 8AH (☎ 01 601 3347, fax 01 601 5561)

PRICE, Margaret Berenice; CBE (1982); da of late Thomas Glyn Price; *b* 13 April 1941; *Educ* Pontllanfraith Secondary Sch, Trinity Coll of Music London (hon fellow); *Career* opera singer; debut 1962 with Welsh Nat Opera, since then has appeared in all the major opera houses: La Scala, Vienna State, Munich, Paris, Hamburg, San Francisco, Metropolitan (New York), Chicago; also concert and Lieder career, renowned for her interpretation of Mozart; Elizabeth Schumann Prize for Lieder, Ricordi Prize for Opera Silver Medal Worshipful Co of Musicians; Bayerische Kammersängerin 1979; Hon DMus Wales 1983; *Style*— Miss Margaret Price, CBE; Bayerisch Staatsoper München, Max-Joseph-Platz 2, 8000 München 22, W Germany

PRICE, Hon Mrs (Margaret Joan); *née* Nelson; JP (Warwicks); da of 1 Baron Nelson of Stafford (d 1962); *b* 1915; *m* 1941, Edward Michael Price; 3 da; *Style*— The Hon Mrs Price, JP; Frankton Manor, Frankton, Warwickshire

PRICE, travel, fitness trg (Rhys) Michael John; s of Lt-Col Rhys Neville Griffiths Price, MBE, ERD, of 30 Chancellor House, MT Ephraim, Tunbridge Wells, Kent, and Marjory, *née* Body; *b* 25 Feb 1944; *Educ* Blundells, Selwyn Coll Cambridge (MA), Middx Hosp Med Sch (MB BChir); *m* 21 Aug 1968, Hilary, da of Norman Butters, TD (d 1979), of Aldeburgh, Suffolk; 2 s (Rupert b 1970, Jeremy b 1973); *Career* Surgn Lt Cdr HMS President RNR 1977-83; princ gen practice 1970-, memb Herts Local Med Ctee 1974-77, assoc regnl advsr gen practice NW Thames 1982-; RCGP: hon sec and chm Herts and Beds faculty 1978-84, ed News and Views RCGP journal 1983-84, memb occasional papers ed bd 1983-; Freeman City of London 1976, Liveryman Worshipful Co Apothecaires; 1972; MRCGP 1976, FRCGP 1984; *Recreations* travel, ftiness training; *Clubs* BMA, Royal Naval Med; *Style*— Dr Michael Price; 38 Oakwood, Berkhamsted, Herts (☎ 0442 866871); The Surgery, Parkwood Drive, Hemel Hempstead, Herts (☎ 0442 50117)

PRICE, Norman George; JP (1961); s of George Strongitharm Price (d 1942); *b* 14 Nov 1922; *Educ* Rockferry HS, Liverpool Univ, London Univ (MSc); *m* 1945, Grace Dorothy, *née* Melling; 2 da; *Career* Merchant Navy 1940-46, Miny of Supply 1950-54, Colonial Serv Fiji 1954-58, Granada Gp Ltd 1958-62; personnel dir: Carreras Ltd 1962-71, J Bibby Sons Ltd 1971-81; educ conslt Assoc of Business Exec 1981-82; dep chm Dunmow Bench, chm Domestic Ct; sec Donkey Breed Soc 1982-85; Dr res LSE 1985-; *Recreations* racing, gardening, reading; *Clubs* Reform; *Style*— Norman Price Esq, JP; Boleyns, Duton Hill, Dunmow, Essex CM6 2DU (☎ 037 184 419)

PRICE, Norman William Rose; s of Sir Rose Francis Price, 6 Bt (d 1979) and Kathleen June, yr da of Norman William Hutchinson, of Melbourne, Australia; hp of bro, Sir Francis Caradoc Rose, 7 Bt; *b* 17 Mar 1953; *Educ* Eton, Gordonstoun; *m* Charlotte Louise, da of Mr and Mrs Randolph Rex Bivar Baker, of Yelverton, Devon; *Career* Restauranteur; *Style*— Norman Price Esq; 73 Fawnbrake Avenue, London SE24 0BE

PRICE, Peter Nicholas; MEP (EDG) Lancs W 1979-84, London SE 1984-; s of Rev Dewi Emlyn Price, of Worcester; *b* 19 Feb 1942; *Educ* Worcester Royal GS, Aberdare Boys' GS, Southampton Univ; *Career* slr; sr ptnr Peter Price & Ptnrs 1964-80; MEP for Lancs W 1979-84, vice-chm Budgetary Control Ctee Euro Parl 1979-84, EDG Spokesman on Legal Affairs Ctee 1984-, rapporteur Legal Affairs Ctee; former Nat vice-chm: Young Cons, Cons Political Centre; former sec Foreign Affairs Forum; former memb Cons Nat Exec Ctee; memb EDG South Asia Delgn, RIIA; *Recreations* theatre, music, photography; *Style*— Peter Price, Esq, MEP; 7 Juniper Close, Biggin Hill, Westerham, Kent TN16 3LZ (☎ 0959 76161); European Parliament, 97-113 rue Belliard, 1040 Bruxelles, Belgium (☎ 010 32 2 234 2351)

PRICE, (Llewelyn) Ralph; CBE (1972); s of Llewelyn David Price (d 1962); *b* 23 Oct 1912; *Educ* Quarry Bank Sch Liverpool; *m* 1939, Vera Patricia, da of C H Harrison (d 1935); 1 s, 2 da; *Career* dir Honeywell Ltd 1972-; chm: ML Hldgs Ltd 1975-87, Honeywell Advsy Cncl 1981-; dir American Chamber of Commerce 1976-81; former memb NEDC Electronics Ctee, pres Br Indust Measurement and Control Trade Assoc 1972-77; FCA; *Recreations* golf, music, bridge; *Clubs* RAC, Temple Golf; *Style*— Ralph Price, Esq, CBE; Nascot, Pinkneys Drive, Pinkneys Green, Maidenhead, Berks (☎ 0628 28270)

PRICE, Richard Henry; s of Henry George Price, of Monmouth, Gwent, and Nesta Suzanne, *née* Jones (d 1986); *b* 13 July 1944; *Educ* Monmouth Sch, Univ Coll London (BSc Econ), Univ of Cambridge (PGCE); *m* 29 March 1969, Sally Josephine, da of Col John Lewis McCowen, of Devon; 3 s (Guy b 1970, Toby b 1972, Tom b 1980); *Career* sch master Queens Coll Taunton 1968-70; CBI 1970-: head of indust trends dept 1973-79, dep then dir of regions 1979-83, dir of employment affrs 1983-87, exec dir for govt relations 1987-; memb cncl of ACAS 1984-, MSC Trg Cmmn 1988-, Soc of Business Economists; *Recreations* golf, bridge, skiing, cricket, gardening; *Clubs* Oxford and Cambridge; *Style*— Richard Price, Esq; 10 Beechwood Grove, East Acton Lane, London W3 (☎ 01 740 8357); Kingscot, The Parade, Monmouth, Gwent; CM Centre Point, 103 New Oxford Street, London WC1A 1DU (☎ 01 379 7400)

PRICE, Air Vice-Marshal Robert George; CB (1983); *b* 1928; *Career* RAF Coll Cranwell 1950; AOA HQ Strike Command 1981-; *Style*— Air Vice-Marshal Robert Price, CB; c/o Barclays Bank, Easingwold, Yorks

PRICE, Sir (James) Robert; KBE (1976); s of Edgar James Price (d 1937), and Mary Katherine Price (d 1937); *b* 25 Mar 1912; *Educ* St Peter's Coll Adelaide, Adelaide Univ, Oxford Univ; *m* 1940, Joyce Ethel, *née* Brooke; 1 s, 2 da; *Career* scientist; chief div of organic chemistry CSIRO 1961-66, chm exec CSIRO (memb 1966-70) 1970-77, former dir Humes Ltd; FAA 1959; *Clubs* Sciences (Melb); *Style*— Sir Robert Price, KBE; Yangoora, 2 Ocean View Ave, Red Hill South, Vic 3936, Australia

PRICE, Robert Thomas; s of Richard James Price (d 1978), of Monfa, Beach Bank, Criccieth, Gwynedd, and Laura Jane, *née* Thomas; *b* 10 Oct 1932; *Educ* Porthmadog GS, Univ Coll of Wales Aberystwyth (LLB Hons); *m* 14 Oct 1978, Ann Wyn, da of Hugh John Hughes (d 1978), of Bryneglwys Ynys Talsarnau Gwynedd; 1 da (Anna Eluned b 1981); *Career* RAF 1958-60; admitted slr 1957, ptnr William George & Son Porthmadog Gwynedd, coroner Lleyn and Eifion Dist of Gwynedd 1984-; capt Criccieth GC 1968, chm Dwyfor Dist Cncl 1980, chm Criccieth Town Cncl 1967, 1973, 1980; memb Gwynedd Law Soc; *Recreations* yachting, golf, angling; *Style*— Robert Price, Esq; Monfa, Beach Bank, Criccieth, Gwynedd LL52 0HW (☎ 0766 522717); 103 High St, Porthmadog, Gwynedd (☎ 0766 512474, fax 0766 514363)

PRICE, Robin John; JP (1980); s of Lt-Col Kenrick Jack Price, DSO, MC (d 1982), of Bala Gwynedd, and Juliet Hermione de Laszlo, *née* Slessor; *b* 7 Mar 1947; *Educ* Millfield; *m* 15 April 1972, Diana Mary, da of William Paige Gilbert Lyon, of Victoria, Australia; 1 s (Richard b 1976), 2 da (Annabel b 1974, Charlotte b 1982); *Career* chm Merioneth Branch CLA 1973-75, pres Int Sheep Dog Soc 1980; landowner; *Recreations* shooting, fishing, tennis; *Clubs* MCC, Turf; *Style*— Robin Price, Esq, JP; Rhiwlas, Bala, Gwynedd LL23 7NP (☎ Bala 520612); Estate Office, Rhiwlas, Bala, Gwynedd LL23 7NP (☎ Bala 520387)

PRICE, Roland John Stuart; s of Philip Stuart Price, of Tamworth, and Rowena Mary, *née* Jones; *b* 29 July 1961; *Educ* Sydney GS Aust, Royal Ballet Sch London; *Career* ballet dancer; Gold Medal Adeline Genée Award 1978, Sadler's Wells Royal Ballet 1979- (princ dancer 1984-); princ roles incl: The Two Pigeons, La Fille Mal Gardee, Coppelia, Swan Lake, The Sleeping Beauty, The Snow Queen, many one act ballets incl creations by Macmillan and Bintley; *Style*— Roland Price, Esq; 111 Fairbridge Rd, London N19; Sadler's Wells Royal Ballet, Sadler's Wells Theatre, Rosebery Ave, London EC1R 4TN (☎ 01 263 6451)

PRICE, Brig Rollo Edward Crwys; CBE (1967), DSO (1961); s of Eardley Edward Carnac Price, CIE (d 1972), and Frances Louisa, *née* Crwys (d 1980); *b* 6 April 1916; *Educ* Canford, RMC Sandhurst, Staff Coll Camberley; *m* 28 July 1945, Diana, da of Maj John Austen Budden (d 1967), of Sutton, Bincarn Monor, nr Yeovil, Somerset; 3 da (Angela b 1947, Gillian b 1951, Tessa b 1955); *Career* cmmn 2 Lt 24 Regt S Wales Borderers 1936; WWII Serv 1939-45, Actg Capt 1 SWB: Palestine 1945-46, Cyprus 1946-47; Maj DAAG HQ Western Cmd 1949-51, Maj 1 SWB Eritrea and BAOR 1954-55, Maj 1 SWB active Serv Malaya 1956-58, Lt-Col 4 Bn Queen's Own Nigeria Regt UN force (Nigeria, S Cameroons, Belgian Congo), Lt-Col AA & QMG HQ 43 Inf Div UK 1962-63, Actg Brig cdr 160 inf Bde S Wales 1964-66, Brig cdr Br T ps Malta 1967-69, ret 1969; *Recreations* travel, reading, writing; *Style*— Brig Rollo Price, CBE. DSO; Elsford, Netherton, Yeovil, Somerset

PRICE, Hon Mrs (Rosalind Helen Penrose); *née* Lewis; da of 1 Baron Brecon, PC (d 1976, when title became extinct), and Baroness Brecon, CBE, *qv*; *b* 1938; *Educ* Cheltenham Ladies' Coll; *m* 1963, (Arthur) Leolin Price, QC, *qv*; 2 s, 2 da; *Career* Conservative Central Office Radio and TV Dept 1959-61; Br Consul-Generals Office NY 1962; dir: Bulldog Manpower Servs Ltd 1975-87, Norland Nursery Trg Coll 1964-86; chm: Powys Dist Health Authy 1986-, Governing Body of N London Collegiate Sch 1968-87; co chm of the Fndn 1975-87; memb: Social Security Advsy Ctee DHSS 1987-, midwifery ctee of UK Central Cncl 1983-88, Governing Body of the Frances Mary Buss Fndn 1969-87, Police Complaints Bd 1983-85, Cons Party Ctee 1977, memb and vice-chm Jellicoe Ctee 1974-75, Cncl of Nat Assoc for the Care and Resettlement of Offenders 1974-79, Parole Bd for England and Wales 1969-74, The Griffins Soc 1965-79 (Hon Sec 1966-70, vice-chm 1970-74, chm 1974-79); dep chm Camden Sch for Girls 1981; memb 1972-80 and later chm Bd of Visitors, Brixton Prison; co-opted memb Inner London Probation Ctee 1971-; sub ctees regarding community service; *Style*— The Hon Mrs Price; 32 Hampstead Grove, London NW3 6SR (☎ 01 435 9843); Moor Park, Llanbedr, Crickhowell, Powys NP8 1SS (☎ 0873 810443)

PRICE, Roy Kenneth; CB (1980); s of Ernest Price and Margaret, *née* Scott; *b* 16 May 1916; *Educ* Eltham Coll; *m* 1948, Martha, *née* Dannhauser; 1 s, 1 da; *Career* slr 1937, under-sec (legal) in office of HM Treasy Slr 1972-81; memb of exec cncl RNIB; pres: Richmond Assoc for the Nat Tst, chm Portcullis Tst, vice-chm Friends of the Museum of Richmond; *Clubs* Law Soc; *Style*— Roy Price, Esq, CB; 6 Old Palace Lane, Richmond, Surrey TW9 1PG (☎ 01 940 6685)

PRICE, Hon Mrs (Sarah Theresa Mary); *née* Butler; da of Baron Butler of Saffron Walden, KG, CH, PC (Life Peer, d 1982) and his 1 w, Sydney Elizabeth (d 1954); *b* 1944; *m* 1969, Anthony John Willis Price; 3 s; *Style*— The Hon Mrs Price

PRICE, Lady Susan; *née* Murray; da of 10 Earl of Dunmore; *b* 1949; *m* 1980, Graham Price of Bunbury, W Australia; *Style*— Lady Susan Price; 15 Wandoo Rd, Duncraig, W Australia 6073

PRICE, (Benjamin) Terence; s of Ben Price (d 1955), of Gloucester, and Nelly Elizabeth Caroline, *née* Barnes (d 1973); *b* 7 Jan 1921; *Educ* Crypt Sch Gloucester, Queens' Coll Cambridge (MA); *m* 9 July 1947, Jean Stella, da of John Vidal (d 1971); 1 s (Jeremy b 1951), 1 da (Nicola b 1954); *Career* Lt RNVR 1945-46; head reactor devpt div Atomic Energy Res Estab Harwell 1947-60, asst chief scientific advsr MOD 1960-65, dir Def Operational Analysis Estab 1965-68, chief scientific advsr Miny of Tport 1968-71, dir of devpt Vickers Ltd 1971-73, sec-gen Uranium Inst 1974-87; Int Inst for Strategic Studies, Int Sci Policy Fndn; *Books* Radiation Shielding (1954); *Recreations* making music, flying, skiing; *Clubs* Athenaeum; *Style*— Terence Price, Esq; Seers Bough, Wilton Lane, Jordans, Beaconsfield, Bucks HP9 2RG (☎ 02407 4589)

PRICE, Hon Mrs (Virginia Yvonne Lloyd); *née* Lloyd-Mostyn; da of 5 Baron Mostyn, MC; *b* 24 Mar 1946; *m* 1, 1973, John Robert Hodgkinson; 2 s (Dominic, Thomas b 1976); m 2, 1983, James R K Price; *Style*— The Hon Mrs Price; c/o Capt Rt Hon Lord Mostyn, MC, Mostyn Hall, Mortyn, Flintshire

PRICE, Vivian William Cecil; QC (1972); s of late Evan Price; *b* 14 April 1926; *Educ* Judd Sch Tonbridge, Trinity Coll Cambridge, Balliol Coll Oxford; *m* 1961, Elizabeth Anne, da of late Arthur Rawlins; 3 s, 2 da; *Career* RN 1946-49; barr Mid Temple 1954, Hong Kong 1975, Singapore 1979, bencher Mid Temple 1979, dep high ct judge (Chancery Div) 1975-; *Clubs* Travellers'; *Style*— Vivian Price, Esq, QC; Redwall Farmhouse, Linton, Kent (☎ Maidstone 43682); New Court, Temple, London EC4 (☎ 01 353 1769)

PRICE, William Barclay; s of Edward Cuthbert Barclay Price (d 1968), and Doris, *née* Thompson (d 1975); *b* 21 Nov 1931; *Educ* Marling Sch Stroud Gloucs, Wycliffe Coll Stonehouse Gloucs; *m* 29 Oct 1955, Rosemary Joyce, da of James William Vaile (d 1972); 1 s (Stephen b 1959), 1 da (Jacqueline b 1956); *Career* Nat Serv cmmnd Pilot Off 1954 RAF 1954-56, Pilot Off 501 (County of Gloucester) Sqdn Royal Auxiliary Air Force 1956-57; CA 1953; ptnr 1953; ptnr S J Dudbridge & Sons 1964- (articled clerk 1948-53, rejoined 1956); tstee Stroud United Charities; former: hon tres Stroud Branch CAB, hon tres South Cerney Sailing Club, memb Minchinhampton PCC; FCA 1953; *Recreations* sailing, reading; *Style*— William Price, Esq; Jastene, 33 Sheppard Way, Minchinhampton, Stroud, Gloucs GL6 9BZ (☎ 0453 883114); Dudbridges Chartered Accountants, 8/9 Lansdown, Stroud, Gloucs GL5 1BD (☎ 04536 4488)

PRICE, William Frederick Barry; OBE (1976); s of William Thomas Price (d 1984), of Hanley Swan, and Vera Evelyn, *née* Burt; *b* 12 Feb 1925; *Educ* King Edward's Sch Birmingham, Worcester Royal GS; *m* 20 March 1948, Lorraine Elisabeth Susanne, da of Maj Archibald Hoather (d 1960), of Epsom; 3 s (Adam b 1956, Matthew b 1963, Ashley b 1967), 2 da (Caroline b 1949, Amanda b 1960); *Career* joined Bd of Trade 1950: asst trade cmmr Delhi 1954-57 (Nairobi 1958-61, Dar es Salaam 1961-63), trade cmmr Accra 1963-67; FCO: first sec Sofia 1967-71, consul gen Rotterdam 1973-77, cnsllr British Embassy Bangkok 1981-83, consul gen Amsterdam 1983-85, ret 1985; sec William and Mary Tercentenary Tst 1986-; *Recreations* Open Univ student, cycling, computers; *Clubs* Oriental; *Style*— Barry Price, Esq, OBE; 46 Finchley Park, London N12 9JL (☎ 01 445 4642)

PRICE, William Frederick Ernest; *b* 25 Nov 1947; *Educ* Durrants Sch Croxley Green; *m* 1 s (Alexander b 1980), 2 da (Victoria b 1978, Charlotte b 1982); *Career* chm and md Avica Equipment Ltd 1970-80; gp md: Balterley Bathrooms plc 1981-, chm Arrowhead Properties Ltd; *Style*— William Price Esq; c/o Balterley Bathrooms plc, Silverdale Rd, Newcastle-under-Lyme, Staffs ST5 6EL (☎ 0782 711118)

PRICHARD, Brian Justin; s of Bernard A'Bear Prichard (d 1957), of Epsom, and Florence Eveline, *née* Smith (d 1966); *b* 2 Sept 1925; *Educ* Wimbledon Coll, Keble Coll Oxford, King's Coll London (LLB); *m* 1 May 1954, Patricia Margaret Oldham, da of Reginald Garforth Cooke, of Christchurch; 1 s (Jonathan Mark b 1957), 3 da (Gillian Mary (Mrs Theokritoff) b 1956, Nicola Anne (Mrs Boath) b 1960, Susan Elizabeth b 1964); *Career* Sub-Lt RNVR 1944-47; slr; sr ptnr Rooks Rider; chm Walter Lawrence plc 1964-; fndr memb Westminster Advsy Ctee on Alcoholism; memb Law Soc 1951; Freeman: City of London, Worshipful Co of Barbers; *Recreations* travel, reading; *Clubs* City Livery; *Style*— Brian Prichard Esq; Drakes Hide, Windsor Bridge Court, Brocas St, Eton, Windsor, Berks (☎ 0753 856015); 8 and 9 New Square, Lincoln's Inn, London WC2A 3QJ (☎ 01 242 8023)

PRICHARD, Mathew Caradoc Thomas; s of Maj Hubert de Burgh Prichard, of Pwllywrach, Cowbridge (ka 1944), and Rosalind Margaret Clarissa Hicks, *née* Christie; *b* 21 Sept 1943; *Educ* Eton, New Coll Oxford (BA); *m* 20 May 1967, Angela Caroline, da of Thomas Craddock Maples, of Symonds Farm House, Childrey, nr Wantage; 1 s (James b 1970), 2 da (Alexandra b 1968, Joanna b 1972); *Career* chm Agatha Christie Ltd and Bookers Authors Div; chm Welsh Arts Cncl 1986-, memb Arts Cncl GB 1983-, advsr local div Barclays Bank S Wales; High Sheriff Co of Glam 1973-74; *Recreations* golf, cricket, bridge; *Clubs* Boodle's, Cardiff and County, Royal Ancient GC, Royal Porthcawl GC, MCC; *Style*— Mathew Prichard, Esq; Bookers plc, Portland, House Stag plc, London SW1E 5AY (☎ 01 828 9850)

PRICHARD, Sir Montague Illtyd; CBE (1965), MC (1944); s of George Montague Prichard (d 1929), and Elsie Honoriah, *née* Farrow (d 1968); *b* 26 Sept 1915; *Educ* Felsted Sch Essex; *m* 1942, Kathleen Georgiana Hamill; 2 s (James, Roger), 1 da (Anne); *Career* served RE, India, Somaliland, Malaya, Burma, Lt-Col as CRE 20 Indian Div; chm and chief exec Perkins Engine Gp Ltd and subsids 1957-75, chm Brothers Corpn 1977-82, chm Tozer Kemsley & Millbourn (Holdings) plc 1982-85, dir Polysius Ltd, chm Scientific Applied Res plc 1984, Belgrave Holdings plc 1985-; FBIM, FIPE, FInstMSM; kt 1972; *Recreations* work, people, gardening; *Clubs* East India, Sports, Devonshire; *Style*— Sir Montague Prichard, CBE, MC; Willowdale House, Apethorpe, Peterborough, Cambs

PRICHARD, Air Cdre Richard Julian Paget; CB (1963), CBE (1958), DFC (1942), AFC (1941); s of Maj W O Prichard; *b* 4 Oct 1915; *Educ* Harrow, St Catharine's Coll Cambridge; *Career* RAF 1937, dir Air Plans Air Miny 1960-63, AOC No 13 Scottish Sector Fighter Command 1963-64, AOC Northern Sector of Fighter Command 1965-66; US Legion of Merit; *Clubs* RAF; *Style*— Air Commodore Richard Prichard, CB, CBE, DFC, AFC; c/o Lloyds Bank Ltd, 6 Pall Mall, London SW1Y 5NH

PRICHARD, Robert David Caradoc; s of Lt-Col David Prichard and Elizabeth , 2 da of Sir David Llewellyn, 1 Bt; Col Prichard is ninth in descent from Matthew Prichard, whose epitaph claims him to be desended from 'Cradocke Vraich Vras, Earle of Hereford, and Prince between Wye and Seaverne'; *b* 17 Nov 1947; *Educ* Wellington, CCC Cambridge; *Career* merchant banker; asst dir Kleinwort Benson Investment Management 1981-; *Recreations* bridge, croquet; *Style*— Robert Prichard Esq; 25 Longmoore St, SW1 (☎ 01 828 0919)

PRICHARD-JONES, David John Walter; s and h of Sir John Prichard-Jones, 2 Bt, by his 1 w, Heather, da of Sir Walter Nugent, 4 Bt; *b* 14 Mar 1943; *Educ* Ampleforth, Ch Ch Oxford (BA); *Style*— David Prichard-Jones, Esq

PRICHARD-JONES, Lady; Heather Vivian Mary; da of Sir Walter Richard Nugent, 4 Bt, MP (d 1955) and sis of Sir Peter Nugent, 5 Bt, *qv*; *m* 1937, Sir John Prichard-Jones, 2 Bt, *qv*; 1 s (David); *Style*— Lady Prichard-Jones

PRICHARD-JONES, Sir John; 2 Bt (UK 1910); s of Sir John Prichard-Jones, JP, DL, 1 Bt (d 1917); *b* 20 Jan 1913; *Educ* Eton, Christchurch Oxford (MA); *m* 1, 1937, Heather (m dis 1950), da of late Sir Walter Nugent, 4 Bt; 1 s; m 2, 1959, Helen Marie Thérèse, da of J F Liddy; 1 da (Susan); *Heir* s, David John Walter Prichard-Jones; *Career* barr Gray's Inn 1936; former Capt The Queen's Bays; farmer and bloodstock breeder; Hon LLD Univ of Wales; *Style*— Sir John Prichard-Jones, Bt; Allenswood House, Lucan, Co Dublin, Eire

PRICKETT, Air Chief Marshal Sir Thomas Other; KCB (1965, CB 1957), DSO (1943), DFC (1942); s of Eric G Prickett, of Bedford; *b* 31 July 1913; *Educ* Stubbington House Sch, Haileybury Coll; *m* 1942, Elizabeth Gratian (d 1984), da of late William Galbally, of Laguna Beech, California, USA; 1 s, 1 da; m 2, 1985, Shirley Westerman, w of William Westerman; *Career* joined RAF 1937, served 1939-45 (Desert Air Force and Bomber Cmd), Gp Capt 1952, Air Cdre 1956, COS special air task force (Suez Operations), SASO 1 Group, Air Vice-Marshal 1960, asst chief Air Staff (Ops) Air Miny 1960-63 (Policy and Planning 1963-64); AOC-in-C NEAF and cdr Br Forces Cyprus (admin Sovereign Base Area) 1964-66, Air Marshal 1966, AOC-in-C RAF Transport and Air Support Cmds 1967-68, Air Chief Marshal 1969, Air memb for Supply and Organisation MOD (RAF) 1968-70, ret; *Clubs* RAF; *Style*— Air Marshal Sir Thomas Prickett, KCB, DSO, DFC; East House, Petworth, West Sussex (☎ Petworth 0798 43382)

PRICKMAN, Air Cdre Thomas Bain; CB (1953), CBE (1945); s of Thomas Prickman; *b* 1902; *Educ* Blundells and RAF Coll Cranwell; *m* 1, 1938, Ethel Serica (d 1949), da of John Cubbon; m 2, 1952, Dorothy (wid of Gp Capt Frederick Charles Read, d 1949), da of John Charles Clarke; *Career* joined RAF 1923, Fighter Cmd 1939-50, AOA RAF Home Cmd 1950-54, ret 1954; *Style*— Air Cdre Thomas Prickman, CB, CBE; Tilsmore Cottage, Cross-in-Hand, Heathfield, Sussex (☎ 043 52 3273)

PRIDAY, Christopher Bruton; QC (1986); s of Arthur Kenneth Priday (d 1968), of Cheltenham, and Rosemary, *née* Bruton (d 1982); *b* 7 August 1926; *Educ* Radley, Univ Coll Oxford (MA); *m* 24 Oct 1953, Jill Holroyd, da of John Holroyd Sergeant, MC (d 1965), of Rotting Dean, Susex; 2 s (Edward b 1957, Charles b 1959); *Career* called to the Bar Gray's Inn 1951 (hon ad eundum Middle Temple 1985); fell Central Assoc of Agric Valuers 1988, Assoc RICS 1987-; *Books* jt author: Milk Quotas: Law and Practice (1986), A Handbook of Milk Quota Compensation (1987); *Recreations* opera, golf; *Clubs* St Ednodoc GC; *Style*— Christopher Priday, Esq, QC; 29 Tedworth Square, London SW3 (☎ 01 352 4492); 11 Kings Bench Walk, Temple, London EC4 (☎ 01 353 2484, fax 01 353 1261)

PRIDDEN, Lady Maria; *née* Noel; da of 5 Earl of Gainsborough, JP; *b* 3 Feb 1951; *Educ* St Mary's Convent, Ascot; *m* 1971, Robert Pridden; 1 s, 1 da; *Style*— Lady Maria Pridden; Fort Henry House, Exton, Oakham, Leics

PRIDEAUX, Sir Humphrey Povah Treverbian; OBE (1945), DL (Hants 1983-); s of Walter Treverbian Prideaux; bro of Sir John Prideaux and Walter Prideaux, *qqv*; *b* 13 Dec 1915; *Educ* St Aubyns Rottingdean, Eton, Trinity Coll Oxford; *m* 1939, Cynthia, da of late Lt-Col H Birch Reynardson, CMG; 4 s; *Career* Jt Planning Staff War Off 1945, Naval Staff Coll 1948, Cmdt Sch of Admin 1948, Chiefs of Staff Secretariat 1950-53, ret; dir: NAAFI 1956-73 (chm 1963-73), The London Life Assoc Ltd 1964-88 (vice-pres 1965-72, pres 1973-84), Brooke Bond Liebig Ltd 1968-81 (chm 1972-81), W H Smith & Son Ltd 1969-77 (vice-chm 1977-81), Morland & Co 1981- (chm 1983-), Grindlays Bank 1982-85; chm Lord Wandsworth Fndn 1966-; kt 1971; *Clubs* Cavalry & Guards; *Style*— Sir Humphrey Prideaux, OBE, DL; Summers Farm, Long Sutton, Basingstoke, Hants (☎ 0256 862295)

PRIDEAUX, Sir John Francis; OBE (1945), DL (Surrey 1976); s of Walter Treverbian Prideaux, of Elderslie, Ockley, Dorking, Surrey (d 1958), and Marion Fenn, *née* Arbuthnot (d 1958); bro Sir Humphrey Prideaux and Walter Prideaux, *qqv*; *b* 30 Dec 1911; *Educ* St Aubyn's Rottingdean, Eton; *m* 1934, Joan Terrell, da of Capt Gordon Hargreaves Brown, MC, Coldstream Gds (missing, presumed ka 1915), of Doddershall Park, Quainton, Aylesbury, Bucks; 2 s (Michael, *qv*), 1 da; *Career* joined Middx Yeo 1933, served WWII, Col Q, 2 Army 1944; joined Arbuthnot Latham & Co Ltd Merchant Bankers 1930 (dir 1936-69, chm 1964-69), dir Arbuthnot Latham Holdings 1969-82 (chm 1969-74), chm Arbuthnot Latham Bank 1983-85; memb London Advsy Bd Bank of New South Wales 1948-74; dir: Westminster Bank Ltd (later National Westminster Bank Ltd) 1955-81 (chm 1971-77), Westminster Foreign Bank Ltd (later Int Westminster Bank Ltd) 1955-81 (chm 1969-77); chm Ctee of London Clearing Banks 1974-76, dir Dow Scandia Banking Corpn 1982-, vice-pres British Bankers Assoc 1972-77, pres Inst of Bankers 1974-76, memb Wilson Ctee to review functioning of fin insts in the City 1977-80; dep chm Cwlth Devpt Corpn 1960-70, chm Victoria League for Cwlth Friendship 1977-82, memb Lambeth Southwark and Lewisham AHA (T) 1974-82 (cmmr 1979-1980); tres and chm bd of govrs St Thomas' Hosp 1964-74 and chm Special Tstees 1974-, prime warden Goldsmiths' Co 1972; - Legion of Merit USA 1945; kt 1974; *Recreations* all country pursuits; *Clubs* Brooks's; *Style*— Sir John Prideaux, OBE, DL; Elderslie, Ockley, Dorking, Surrey RH5 5TD (☎ 0306 711263)

PRIDEAUX, Michael Charles Terrell; s of Sir John Francis Prideaux, *qv*; *b* 23 Oct 1950; *Educ* Eton, Trinity Coll Cambridge (BA); *m* 1975, Susan Henriette, da of Charles Peto Bennett (d 1977); 1 s (John b 1979), 1 da (Laura b 1976); *Career* fin advertisment mangr Financial Times 1979-80 (UK advertisment dir 1980-83), chief exec Charles Barker City 1983-, dir Charles Barker Gp 1983-, dir Charles Barker plc 1987-; *Recreations* gardening, shooting; *Style—* Michael Prideaux Esq; Selehurst, Lower Beeding, nr Horsham, Sussex (☎ 0403 76501); 30 Farringdon St, London EC4 (☎ 01 634 1000)

PRIDEAUX, Walter Arbuthnot; CBE (1973), MC (1945), TD (1948); eldest s of Walter Treverbian Prideaux (d 1958), and Marion Fenn, *née* Arbuthnot (d 1958); bro of Sir John Francis Prideaux and Sir Humphrey Povah Treverbian Prideaux, *qqv*; *b* 4 Jan 1910; *Educ* Eton, Trinity Coll Cambridge; *m* 4 Feb 1937, Anne, 2 da of Francis Stewart Cokayne; 2 s (Walter Michael Cokayne, *qv*, Francis Martin b 17 Oct 1945), 1 da (Sarah (Mrs David Marcus Knight) b 7 Jan 1940); *Career* served Kent Yeo 1936-48; slr 1934, clerk of the Goldsmiths' Co 1953-75, chm City Parochial Fndn 1972-80; *Style—* Walter A Prideaux, Esq, CBE, MC, TD; 16 Tanbridge Place, Horsham, W Sussex RH12 1RY (☎ 0403 58891)

PRIDEAUX, Walter Michael Cokayne; er s of Walter Arbuthnot Prideaux, CBE, MC, TD, *qv*; *b* 19 Nov 1937; *Educ* Eton, Trinity Coll Cambridge (BA, MA); *m* 19 Sep 1964, Lenore Mary Jaqueline, da of Brig Richard Hugh Rossiter Cumming (d 1982), of Abbotswood Lodge, Weybridge, Surrey; 1 s (Walter Edward Cumming b 25 July 1971), 2 da (Rebecca Lenore b 20 Aug 1965, Belinda June b 20 June 1969); *Career* 2 Lt Queen's Royal Rifles (TA) 1961, Lt 1963, TARO 1964-87; admitted slr 1964, asst slr White, Brooks & Gilman of Winchester Southampton, Eastleigh and Fair Oak 1964, ptnr 1966, sr ptnr 1983; memb Winchester City Cncl 1976-; govr: Perin's Community Sch, Alresford 1976- (chm 1981-88), Peter Symond's Sixth Form Coll Winchester 1981-; Freeman City of London 1958, Liveryman Worshipful Co of Goldsmiths 1961; memb Law Soc 1964; *Clubs* Hampshire; *Style—* Walter Prideaux, Esq; High Stoke, Beauworth, Alresford, Hants (☎ 096 279 434); 19 St Peter St, Winchester, Hants (☎ 0962 844440, fax 0962 842300, telex 47396)

PRIDEAUX-BRUNE, Peter John Nicholas; s of John Charles Fulke Prideaux-Brune (d 1988), of Prideaux Place, Padstow, Cornwall, and Margaret Mary, *née* Hearne (d 1982); *b* 21 August 1944; *Educ* Downside, Christ Church Oxford (MA); *m* 1, 14 Oct 1971, Vivien Patricia (d 1983), da of Maj Arthur Creagh Gibson, MC (d 1970), of Glenburn Hall, Jedburgh, Roxburghshire; 2 s (Nicholas Pagan b 2 May 1975, William Anthony b 4 Nov 1978); m 2, 27 Oct 1988, Elizabeth, da of Maj William Canon Grant Peterkin (d 1978), of Hillside House, Ceres, Fife; *Career* called to the Bar Inner Temple 1972, practises Western circuit, underwriting memb Lloyd's 1977; landowner Prideaux Place (family estate); pres Padstow branch RNLI; Freeman City of London 1972, Liveryman Worshipful Co of Vintners 1972; memb Criminal Bar Assoc; kt SMOM 1983; *Recreations* skiing, music; *Clubs* Turf; *Style—* Peter Prideaux-Brune, Esq; Prideaux Place, Padstow, Cornwall (☎ 0841 532411); 24 Chiddingstone St, London SW6; Queen Elizabeth Building, Temple, London EC4 (☎ 01353 7181, car tel 0836 715399)

PRIDHAM, Kenneth Robert Comyn; CMG (1976); s of Col G R Pridham, CBE, DSO (d 1951), and Mignonne M H Cumming (d 1964); *b* 28 July 1922; *Educ* Winchester, Oriel Coll Oxford (MA); *m* 1965, Rosalind, da of Edward Gilbert Woodward (d 1949) of London, Metropolitan Magistrate; *Career* served in WW II 1942-45, Lt King's Royal Rifle Corps (despatches); served N Africa, Mid East, Italy; dip serv: cncllr Copenhagen 1968-72, asst under-sec FCO 1974-78, ambass to Poland 1978-81; ret 1982; *Clubs* Travellers, Hurlingham; *Style—* Kenneth Pridham, Esq, CMG; Lloyds Bank Ltd, 16 St James's St, London SW1

PRIEST, Prof Robert George; s of James George Priest (d 1945), of South Benfleet, Essex, and Pheobe, *née* Logan; *b* 28 Sept 1933; *Educ* Westcliff HS, Univ Coll London (MB BS, MD); *m* 24 June 1955, Marilyn, Baden Roberts Baker, JP (d 1979), of Westcliff-on-Sea; 2 s (Ian b 1956, Roderick b 1960); *Career* Capt RAMC 1958-61 (acting Maj 1960-61), Sch of Infantry Warminster 1958-59, GHQ Far Elf Singapore 1960-61; house physician to Lord Amulree 1956-57, house surgn Edgware Gen Hosp 1957, SHO registrar Royal Edinburgh Hosp 1961-64, lectr in psychiatry Univ of Edinburgh 1964-67, visiting lectr Univ of Chicago 1966-67, sr lectr St Georges Hosp Med Sch Univ of London 1967-73, prof of psychiatry St Mary's Hosp Med Sch Imperial Coll Univ of London 1979-; chm Psychiatric Advsy Ctee NW Thames RHA 1976-79, memb cncl Br Assoc for Psychopharmacology (chm membership ctee) 1977-81, pres Soc for Psychosomatic Res 1980-81, vice chm Regnl Manpower Ctee NW Thames RHA 1980-83, chm Mental Health Gp Ctee BMA 1982-85, memb ctee World Psychiatric Assoc 1985-; Int Coll of Psychosomatic Med: fell 1977, memb governing body and UK delegate 1978-81, tres 1981-83, sec 1981-85, vice pres 1985-87; Royal Coll of Psychiatrists: memb of cncl 1982-88, registrar 1983-88, chm public policy ctee 1983-88, memb ct of efectors 1983-88, chm gen psychiatry ctee 1985-88 (chm fellowship sub-ctee); memb Central Ctee for Hosp Med Servs 1983-(chm Psychiatric Sub Ctee 1983-87); FRCP (Edin) 1974, FRCPsych 1974; *Books* Insanity: A Study of Major Psychiatric Disorders (1977), Sleep Research (jt ed, 1979), Benzodiazepines Today and Tomorrow (jt ed, 1980), Psychiatry in Medical Practice (ed, 1982), Anxiety and Depression (1983), Sleep: An International Monograph (1984), Nomifesine Pharmacologial and Clinical Profile (jt ed, 1984), Psychological Disorders in Obstetrics and Gynaecology (ed, 1985), Handbook of Psychiatry (jtly, 1986); *Recreations* squash, tennis, foreign languages, nature study; *Style—* Prof Robert Priest; Academic Dept of Psychiatry, St Mary's Hosp, Praed St, London W2 1NY (☎ 01 725 1648)

PRIESTLEY, Clive; CB (1983); s of Albert Ernest Priestley (d 1985), of Bournemouth, Dorset, and Annie May Priestley (d 1974); *b* 12 July 1935; *Educ* Loughborough GS, Nottingham Univ (BA MA), Harvard Univ; *m* 1, 1961 (m dis 1984), Barbara Anne, da of George Gerard Wells; 2 da (Rebecca, Alison); m 2, 1985, Daphne June Challis, da of Walter Challis Franks, JP (d 1969); *Career* HM Home Civil Service 1960-63 (under sec PM's off 1979-83); HQ dir Br Telecom plc 1983-; *Clubs* Army and Navy; *Style—* Clive Priestley, Esq, CB; Br Telecom plc, Bond Street, Bristol BS1 3TD (☎ 0272 272800, telex 44881)

PRIESTLEY, (Jessie) Jacquetta; OBE (1952); da of Sir Frederick Gowland Hopkins OM, FRS (d 1947), and Jessie Anne Stephens; f second cousin of Gerard Manley Hopkins the poet; *b* 5 August 1910; *Educ* Parse Girls Sch Cambridge, Newnham Coll Cambridge (MA); *m* 1, 1933 (m dis 1953), Prof Christopher Hawkes; 1 s (Charles Nicolas b 1937); m 2, 1953, J B Priestley, OM (d 1984); *Career* author and archaeologist; entered admin grade of Civil Serv 1941, princ and sec of the UK Nat Cmmn of UNESCO 1943-49, archaelogical advsr Festival of Britain 1951, formerly archaeological corr to The Observer and Sunday Times; has excavated in England, Ireland, France and Palestine; Hon D Litt Warwick Univ; FSA; *Books* as Jacquetta Hawkes: Archaeology of Jersey (1939), Prehistoric Britain (with Christopher Hawkes), A Land (Kensley award, 1951), Fables (1953), Man on Earth (1954), Journeys Down a Rainbow (with J B Priestley, 1955), Providence Island, Man and the Sun (1962), UNESCO History of Man Kind Vol 1, Part 1 (1963), The Dawn of the Gods (1968), The First Great Civilizations (1973), Atlas of Early Man (1976), A Quest of Love (1980), Mortimer Wheeler: An Adventurer in Archaeology (1982); *Recreations* natural history, walking; *Style—* Jacquetta Priestley, OBE; Littlecote, Leysbourne, Chipping Campden, Gloucs GL55 6HL

PRIESTLEY, James Frederick; MC (1944); s of Hugh William Priestley, MC (d 1932), and Elizabeth Grainger, *née* Hall (d 1974); *b* 22 Feb 1915; *Educ* Horris Hill, Winchester, Western Reserve Acad Ohio USA; *m* 9 Sept 1939, Honor Purefoy, da of Robert Pollock (d 1957); 2 s (Hugh b 1942, Richard b 1947), 2 da (Sarah (Mrs Bond) b 1945, Julia b 1952, d 1975); *Career* 1 Bn Herts Regt (TA) 1939, 1 Bn Coldstream Guards 1940, Maj and Co Cdr Guards Armoured Div from formation until 1945; jobber Wedd Jefferson (later Wedd Durlacher) 1933 (ptnr 1944-74), ret; pres NW Hants Cons Assoc 1958-62; *Recreations* shooting, fishing; *Style—* James Priestley, Esq; Invergeldie, Comrie, Perthshire; Little Blackhall, Banchory, Kincardineshire; Upton Manor, Upton, nr Andover, Hampshire (☎ 026 476 250)

PRIESTLEY, Leslie William; TD (1974); s of George Priestley (d 1947), and Winifred, *née* Young; *b* 22 Sept 1933; *Educ* Shooters Hill GS; *m* 8 Oct 1960, Audrey Elizabeth, da of Sidney Humber (d 1978); 1 s (Ian b 1967), 1 da (Jane b 1970); *Career* hd mktg Barclaycard 1966-73, local dir Barclays Bank 1978-79 (asst gen mangr 1974-77), sec gen ctee of London Clearing Bankers 1979-83, dir Banker's Automated Clearing Servs Co 1983-84, regnl gen mangr Barclays Bank 1984-85; chief gen mangr: TSB Eng & Wales, Central TSB; dir LEB 1984-, dir TSB Gp 1985 (Trustcard 1985-); chm: Hill House Hammond Ltd 1988-, Mortgage Express 1988-; dir Hill Samuel Gp PLC 1988-, chief exec TSB England & Wales plc; conslt ed Bankers Magazine 1972-81; FCIB, CBIM, FInstM; *Recreations* reading, gardening, swimming, theatre; *Clubs* Wig and Pen, RAC; *Style—* Leslie Priestley, Esq, TD ; 60 Lombard St, London EC3V 9EA (☎ 01 600 6000, fax 01 626 1250, telex 945131)

PRIESTLEY, Prof Maurice Bertram; s of Jack Priestley, of Manchester, and Rose Priestley (d 1966); *Educ* Manchester GS, Jesus Coll Cambridge (MA, Dip Math Stat), Manchester Univ (PhD); *m* 24 June 1959, Nancy, da of Ralph Norman Nelson (d 1959); 1 s (Michael Richard b 1963), 1 da (Ruth Nicola b 1961); *Career* scientific offr Royal Aircraft Estab 1955-56, lectr Univ of Manchester 1960-65 (asst lectr 1957-60), prof UMIST 1970- (sr lectr 1965-70, hd dept of Mathematics 1973-75, 1980-85, 1986-), dir of Manchester-Sheffield Sch of Probability and Statistics 1976-79 and 1988-, visiting prof Univs of Princeton and Stanford USA 1961-62; cncl memb Manchester Statistical Soc; hon prof of probability and statistics Univ of Sheffield; fell of Royal Statistical Soc 1955, memb Int Statistical Inst 1972, fell Inst of Mathematical Statistics 1978; *Books* Spectral Analysis and Time Series (vols I and II, 1981), Essays in Time Series and Allied Processes (jt ed 1986), Non-Linear and Non-Stationary Time Series Analysis (1988); *Recreations* music, Hi-Fi, amateur radio, golf; *Style—* Prof Maurice Priestley; Department of Mathematics, UMIST, Manchester, M60 1QD (☎ 061 236 3311)

PRIESTLEY, Robert Hugh; MBE (1945), TD (1945); s of Hugh William Priestley (d 1932), and Elizabeth Grainger, *née* Hall (d 1975); *b* 23 Nov 1911; *Educ* Horris Hill, Winchester Coll, Trinity Coll Cambridge; *m* 24 April 1935, Mary Hermia, da of Sir George Menteth Boughey, Bt (d 1959); 1 s (John Charles Robert b 1945), 2 da (Anthea Mary b 1948, Lavinia Jane b 1950); *Career* Maj, served Mid East, Sicily, Italy, France and Germany (despatches); stockbroker, Mullens and Co 1932-75, ptnr 1945-75; cricket Winchester Coll XI 1929-30, rackets Winchester Coll Pair 1929-30, Cambridge rackets pair 1931-32; Bronze Star Medal (USA) 1945; *Recreations* shooting, golf; *Style—* Robert Priestley, MBE, TD; The Manor, Church Oakley, Basingstoke, Hants (☎ 0256 780333)

PRIESTMAN, Richard John; s of Cecil Priestman, of Liverpool, and Mary, *née* Gray; *b* 16 July 1955; *Educ* Maghull GS, Liverpool Poly; *Career* bank clerk Nat West Bank plc, Br record holder 1988, Olympic Games Seoul 1988 Bronze Medallist Archery Team Event; *Clubs* Nethermoss Archers, Grand National Archery Soc; *Style—* Richard Priestman, Esq; 20 Haymans Green, Maghull, Liverpool L31 6DA (☎ 051 526 6523)

PRIMAROLO , Dawn; MP (Lab Bristol South 1987-); *b* 2 May 1954; *Educ* Thomas Bennett Comprehensive Sch Crawley, Bristol Poly (BA), Bristol Univ; *m* 7 Oct 1972 (sep), Michael Primarolo; 1 s (Luke b 24 Jan 1978); *Career* legal sec and advice worker 1972-75, sec resources for learning Avon CC 1975-78 (cncllr 1985-87); *Style—* Ms Dawn Primarolo, MP; 272 St Johns Lane, Bedminster, Bristol BS3 5AU (☎ 0272 635 948)

PRIME, Brian Salisbury; s of George Henry Luke Prime (d 1975), of Northwood Middx, and Dilys Salisbury, *née* Jones (d 1978); *b* 14 August 1932; *Educ* Harrow GS, LSE (BSc); *m* 10 March 1962, Susan Mary Eveline, da of Thomas Holdstock (d 1983), of Redhill; 2 s (Jonathan b 1965, Richard b 1967), 1 da (Sally-Ann b 1963); *Career* Lt RA 1954-56; trained as CA and mgmnt accountant; md Kingsway Gp plc (dir 1967-), (fin) Celcon Blocks Ltd 1975-, Ryarsh Brick Ltd 1980-, Nymoelle Stenindustri Ltd 1986-, Eurospace Furniture Packs Ltd 1983-, New Horizon Furniture Ltd 1985-, Busboard Parker Ltd 1986-, Contrology Products Ltd 1987-, Brantham Engrg Ltd 1987-, Elremco Products Ltd 1987-, Compton Aggregates Ltd 1978-; memb: cncl Chartered Inst of Mgmnt Accountants, Lloyds 1982; CBIM, FCA, FCMA; *Recreations* skiing, gardening; *Clubs* Directors, Danish; *Style—* Brian S Prime, Esq; White Gables, 18 Bromley Common, Bromley, Kent (☎ 01 460 9245); Kingsway Gp plc, Celcon House, 289-d293 High Holborn, London WC1V 7HU

PRIME, Derek Arthur; s of Thomas Beasley Prime (d 1970), of 11 Cecilly Terr, Cheadle, Staffs, and Lucy, *née* Beardmore (d 1980); *b* 16 July 1932; *Educ* Alleynes Uttoxeter, N Staffs Tech Coll (HNC); *m* 9 Nov 1963, Pamela, da of Arthur Dix, 24 Vicarage Crescent, Upper Tean, Staffs; 1 s (Christopher b 1965), 1 da (Carol b 1964); *Career* engrg apprentice Thomas Bolton & Sons Ltd Staffs 1948-53, designer JC Bamford Excavators Ltd 1953-59; JCB res: asst chief designer 1959-64, chief designer 1964-70, tech dir 1970-73, md 1973-; product dir Back-Hoe Loaders 1986; Queens

Award for Technological Innovation 1973, RSA Award for Design Mgmnt 1979, Design Cncl Awards for Engrg Products 1973 (1975 and 1984), former memb Engrg Advsy Cncl 1975-82; RDI 1982, FRS 1983, FCSD 1979, MIED 1964, REng Des 1986; *Recreations* gardening, photography; *Style*— Derek Prime, Esq; Bladon House, Lodge Hill, Tutbury, Burton-on-Trent, Staffs DE13 9HF (☎ 0283 813839); JCB Research, Rocester, Uttoxeter, Staffs ST14 5JP (☎ 0889 590312, fax 591287, telex 36372)

PRIMROSE, Lady Caroline Sara Frances; da of 7 Earl of Rosebery, DL; *b* 20 Nov 1964; *Educ* Royal Agric Coll Cirencester; *Career* slr; *Recreations* racing, music; *Style*— Lady Caroline Primrose

PRIMROSE, James Smith Arthur; s of James Smith Arthur Primrose, and Emily, *née* Sturdy; *b* 1 July 1924; *Educ* Kelvinside Acad, Glasgow Acad, Glasgow Univ (BSc); *m* 19 Feb 1952, Bethia Smart Anderson, da of late Thomas Forrest Mathieson Leishman; 2 s (Haold Robert Stuart b 2 April 1954, Robert Thomas Anderson b 20 July 1960), 1 da (Catherine Bethia Mary b 16 Feb 1956); *Career* RE Trg Unit 1944, cmmd 2 Lt off trg QVO Sappers and Miners Bangalore 1945-46, Lt 1 Indian Sapper & Miners M&E Burma Meiktila 1946-47, Capt GHQ Singapore 1947; precedent ptnr Ramsay & Primrose Consulting Engrs, Scotland Curling Team Switzerland 1980; St Pauls Church of Scotland, Soc Building Contracts Ctee, Nat Cncl for Electrical Contractors, Glasgow High/Kelvinside RFC; memb Incorporation of Bakers; CEng, FIEE, FCIBS, MConsE; *Recreations* yachting, curling, golf; *Clubs* Royal Northern & Clyde YC, Glasgow Rotary, Buchanan Castle GC; *Style*— James Primrose, Esq; Carfax, 14 Baldernock Rd, Milngavie G62 8DU (☎ 041 956 2095); 18 Lynedoch St, Glasgow G3 6EY (☎ 041 332 4015, fax 041 333 9197)

PRIMROSE, Lady Jane Margaret Helen; da of 7 Earl of Rosebery, DL; *b* 11 July 1960; *Educ* New Coll Oxford (BA); *Career* slr; *Recreations* racing, art, music, photography; *Style*— Lady Jane Primrose; 137 Holland Park Avenue, London W11

PRIMROSE, John Ure; s and h of Sir Alasdair Primrose, 4 Bt, and Elaine Noreen, da of Edmund Cecil Lowndes, of Buenos Aires, Argentina; *b* 1960; *Style*— John Primrose Esq

PRIMROSE, Sir (Alasdair) Neil; 4 Bt (UK 1903), of Redholme, Dumbreck, Govan, co of City of Glasgow; s of Sir John Ure Primrose, 3 Bt (d 1984), and Enid, da of Late James Sladen, of Br Columbia, Canada; *b* 11 Dec 1935; *Educ* St Georges Coll, Teachers Trg Coll; *m* 1958, Elaine Noreen, da of Edmund Cecil Lowndes, of Buenos Aires, Argentina; 2 s (John, Andrew), 2 da (Doris, Deborah); *Heir* s, John Ure, *qv*; *Career* teacher; head master St Peter's 1965-72; head of Middle Sch St Andrews 1973-; landowner (200 acres); *Recreations* bowls, golf; *Clubs* Old Georgian, Boulogne Golf, San Isidro Bowls; *Style*— Sir Alasdair Primrose, Bt; Ada Elflein 3155, 1642 San Isidro, Buenos Aires, Argentina (☎ 766 9438); St Andrew's Scots School; R S Pena 691, 1636 Olivos, Buenos Aires, Argentina (☎ 781 8031/2/3)

PRIMROSE, Robert William; ISO (1977), MBE (1969); s of Neville Arthur Primrose (d 1972), of Trunch, Norfolk, and May Edith, *née* Martin (d 1951); *b* 3 July 1921; *Educ* Co Sch for Boys Gillingham Kent; *m* 28 Dec 1948, Elizabeth Katherine Maud, da of Preston Wong (British Army Aid Gp, executed by Japanese 1943); *Career* Civil Serv (Admty) 1938-44, Lt RNVR, Br Assault Area Normandy 1944, Br Pacific Fleet 1945, Hong Kong 1946; admin offr Colonial Admin Serv Hong Kong 1947-77 (appts included clerk of exec and legislative cncls, first admin sec UMELCO off, staff grade admin offr), ptnrship sec Johnson Stokes and Master Slrs Hong Kong 1977-88, ret; FCIS 1955; *Recreations* music, philately, reading; *Clubs* Royal Commonwealth Soc; *Style*— Robert Primrose, Esq, ISO, MBE; 52 Beechwood Ave, Kew Gardens, Surrey TW9 4DE (☎ 01 878 6756)

PRIMROSE LISTON FOULIS, Sir Iain; 13 Bt (NS 1634); s of Lt-Col James Alastair Liston Foulis (d 1942, s of Lt-Col Archibald Primrose Liston-Foulis (ka 1917), 4 s of 9 Bt), by his w Kathleen, da of Lt-Col John Moran and Countess Olga de la Hogue, yr da of Marquis De La Hogue (Isle of Mauritius); suc kinsman, Sir Archibald Charles Liston-Foulis, 12 Bt (d 1962); Sir James Foulis, 2 Bt, was actively engaged in the wars of Scotland after the death of Charles I and was knighted during his f's lifetime; *b* 9 August 1937; *Educ* Stonyhurst, Cannington Farm Inst Bridgewater Somerset; *Career* Nat Serv Argyll and Sutherland Highlanders 1957-59, Cyprus 1958; language tutor Madrid 1959-61 and 1966-; trainee exec Bank of London and S America 1962, Bank of London and Montreal Ltd Bahamas, Guatemala and Nicaragua 1963-65, sales Toronto Canada 1966; landowner since 1962; *Recreations* mountain walking, swimming, camping, travelling, car racing and rallies, looking across the plains of Castille to the mountains; *Clubs* RACE, Friends of the Castles, Friends of the St James' Way (all in Spain); *Style*— Sir Iain Primrose Liston Foulis, Bt; Residencial Urbenova, Calle Soledad 11, Portal 5-2-C, San Agustin de Guadalix, 28750 Madrid, Spain (☎ 91 8418978)

PRINCE, Dr John Anthony; s of Fl-Lt Allan Leslie Prince (ka 1944), and Mary Pamela, *née* Paul; *b* 5 Nov 1941; *Educ* Giggleswick, Christ Church Oxford (MA, BM BCh, DIH); *Career* conslt occupational physician: Occidental Oil Inc 1977-83, News Int 1985-86, London Borough of Tower Hamlets 1983-, Tower Hamlets Health Authy London Hosp 1983; memb Tower Hamlets DHA; memb; BMA, Soc of Occupational Med; MRCGP, MFOM; *Recreations* literature, history, antiquarianism, natural history, walking; *Style*— Dr John Prince; 57 Philpot St, London E1 2JH

PRINCE, Michael Eliot Gerald; s of Leslie Barnett Prince, CBE (d 1985; s of Sir Alexander Prince, KBE (fndr of NAAFI)), of London, and Norah Millie, *née* Lewis (d 1979); *b* 16 Dec 1927; *Educ* Marlborough, Magdalene Coll Cambridge; *m* 1, 2 May 1955 (m dis), Lore, da of Henry Meyer (d 1948), of London; 1 s (Andrew b 1957), 2 da (Carolyn b 1956, Jennifer b 1960); m 2, 10 June 1969, Rosemary June (Tremayne), da of Sir Oliver Hart Dyke, 8 Bt (d 1969); *Career* CA; co-fndr Target Tst Gp (dir 1962-84); chm: Dulwich Coll Prep Sch 1986-, Bembridge Sch 1977-; FCA; *Recreations* walking; *Clubs* Carlton, City Livery, MCC; *Style*— M E G Prince, Esq; 5 Knott Park House, Wrens Hill, Oxshott, Leatherhead, Surrey KT22 0HW

PRINCE, Roger Graham; s of Graham Stanley Prince, of Norwich, and Lilian Mary, *née* Gee; *Educ* City of Norwich Sch, Downing Coll Cambridge (MA, LLB); *Career* called to the Bar Inner Temple 1977, assoc Prince de Pinna foreign and int lawyers 1988-; practice devoted to establishing rule of law over judiciary and govt and so the independence of the Bar from the judiciary and the judiciary from itself; teaching 1987; fndr World Law Centre 1988; MENSA 1983; *Recreations* instr Amateur Rowing Assoc, riding, skiing; *Clubs* Downing Coll Boat, London Rowing, Bar YC, Inner Temple Boat; *Style*— Roger Prince, Esq; 76B Chancery Lane, Lincoln's Inn, London WC2A 1AA (☎ 01 404 5053)

PRINCE, William Herbert Carriss; s of Charles William Carriss Prince (d 1972), and Mary, *née* Redden (d 1983); *b* 8 Feb 1934; *Educ* Denstone, Univ of Birmingham (BSc Mech Eng); *m* 1959, Janet Christine Mary, da of Frank Livingstone Haworth (d 1984); 1 s (Christopher b 1963), 1 da (Nicola b 1965); *Career* Lt REME, Nat Serv BAOR; dep md Walsall Conduits Ltd 1988-; *Recreations* sailing; *Style*— William Prince, Esq; 125 Little Sutton Rd, Four Oaks, Sutton Coldfield, W Midlands (☎ 021 308 5174); Walsall Conduits Ltd, Dial Lane, Hill Top, West Bromwich, W Midlands (☎ 021 557 1171)

PRINCE-SMITH, James William; s and h of Sir (William) Richard Prince-Smith, 4 Bt, *qv*; *b* 2 July 1959; *Educ* Wellesley House, Gresham; *Career* Lt 13/18 Royal Hussars (Queen Mary's Own); *Recreations* mountaineering, photography, riding, hang-gliding; *Clubs* Cavalry and Guards; *Style*— James Prince-Smith, Esq; Morton Hall, Morton-on-the-Hill, Norwich (☎ Norwich 880165); 13/18 Royal Hussars, BFPO 15

PRINCE-SMITH, Sir (William) Richard; 4 Bt (UK 1911), of Hillbrook, Keighley, W Riding of Yorks; s of Sir William Prince-Smith, 3 Bt, OBE, MC (d 1964), and Marian Marjorie (d 1970); *b* 27 Dec 1928; *Educ* Charterhouse, Clare Coll Cambridge (MA); *m* 1, 11 Oct 1955, Margaret Ann, da of late Dr John Carter; 1 s (James, *qv*), 1 da; m 2, 1975, Ann Christina, da of Andrew Faulds, OBE, of Lee Wick Farm, St Osyth, Colchester, Essex; *Career* former farmer and agric landowner; co dir and property owner; *Clubs* The Springs (Rancho Mirage), Thunderbird (Rancho Mirage); *Style*— Sir Richard Prince-Smith, Bt; 40-735 Paxton Drive, Rancho Mirage, Calif 92270, USA (☎ (619) 321 1975)

PRING, David Andrew Michael; CB (1980), MC (1943); s of Capt John Arthur Pring (d 1957), of Rochester, Kent, and Gladys Pring (d 1955); *b* 6 Dec 1922; *Educ* King's Sch Rochester, Magdalene Coll Cambridge (MA); *m* 1962, Susan Margaret, da of A W B Brakspear (d 1972), of Henley; 1 s, 1 da; *Career* serv RE 1941-46, N Africa, Sicily, Italy, Austria, Capt 1945; clerk of the House of Commons 1948-87, clerk of ctees House of Commons 1976-87; *Books* Parliament and Congress (1972); *Clubs* Athenaeum; *Style*— David Pring, Esq, CB, MC; Bushy Platt, Stanford Dingley, nr Reading, Berks RG7 6DY (☎ 0734 712585)

PRINGLE, Air Marshal Sir Charles Norman Seton; KBE (1973, CBE 1967); s of Seton Pringle, OBE (d 1957), of Dublin, and Ethel Louisa, *née* McMunn; *b* 6 June 1919; *Educ* Repton, St John's Coll Cambridge (MA); *m* 1946, Margaret Elisabeth, da of Bertie Sharp (d 1956), of Baildon, Yorks; 1 s; *Career* joined RAF 1941, dir-gen of Engrg (RAF) MOD 1969-70, Air Offr Engrg Strike Cmd 1970-73, dir-gen Engrg (RAF) 1973, controller Engrg and Supply (RAF) 1973-76, ret 1976; sr exec Rolls Royce Ltd 1976-78, dir Soc of Br Aerospace Cos 1979-85, dir F R Gp plc 1985-; pres RAeS 1975-76; chm: CEI 1977-78, body govnrs Repton Sch 1985-; *Recreations* photography, ornithology; *Clubs* Buck's, RAF, Inst of Dir; *Style*— Air Marshal Sir Charles Pringle, KBE; K9 Sloane Avenue Mansions, London SW3 3JP; Appleyards, Fordingbridge, Hants SP6 3BP (☎ 0425 52357); Flight Refuelling (Holdings) plc, Wimborne, Dorset BH21 2BT (☎ 0202 882121, telex 41247)

PRINGLE, Hamish Patrick; s of Robert Henry Pringle, of Nassau, Bahamas, and Pamela Ann, *née* Molloy; *b* 17 July 1951; *Educ* Trinity Coll Glenalmond Perthshire, Trinity Coll Oxford (BA); *m* 24 July 1977, Vivienne Elizabeth, da of Dr H Michael Lloyd (d 1976), of West Byfleet, Surrey; 3 s (Sebastian b 1983, Benedict b 1985, Tristan b 1989); *Career* assoc dir Boasc Massimi Pollitt 1978-79, new business dir McCormick Publicis 1979-82, dir Abbott Mead Vickers 1982-86, md Madell Willmot Pringle 1986-; cncl memb IPA 1985-86, memb IPA Advertising Effectiveness Awards ctee 1985-; MIPA 1985; ctee memb Hartswood Tennis Club; *Recreations* sport, gardening, property development, art, family; *Style*— Hamish Pringle, Esq; Madell Wilmot Pringle & Ptnrs Advertising Ltd, 140 Gt Portland St, London W1N 5TA (☎ 01 631 4464, fax 01 631 0361)

PRINGLE, (Arthur) Michael; TD (and bar 1951); s of Dr John Pringle (d 1953), of 153 Withington Rd, Manchester, and Dorothy Emily, *née* Beney, MBE (d 1985); *b* 11 Feb 1914; *Educ* Rugby; *m* 17 May 1941, Ruth Margaret (Peggy), da of Cdr Alfred Bernard Stairs Townend, OBE, RN; 2 da (Katherine Margaret (Mrs Thorogood) b 23 Jan 1945, Harriet Mary (Mrs Cripps) b 10 Aug 1948); *Career* cmmnd 42 E Lancs Divn RASC TA 1936, served France and Belgium 1940, Normandy Landing 1944; jt fndr and dir Br Trufting Machinery Ltd 1954-61; farmer at Gt Leigh 1962-; underwriting memb Lloyd's 1971-; *Style*— Michael Pringle, Esq, TD; Longlands Farm, Gt Leighs, Chelmsford, Essex CM3 1PR (☎ 0245 361 274)

PRINGLE, Dr Robert William; OBE (1967); s of Robert Pringle (d 1973), of Edinburgh, and Lillias, *née* Hair (d 1976); *b* 2 May 1920; *Educ* George Heriot's Sch Edinburgh, Univ of Edinburgh (BSc, PhD); *m* 1948, Carol, da of John Foster Stokes (d 1937), of Ontario, Canada; 3 s (Robert, David, Andrew), 1 da (Vivien); *Career* prof and chm of physics Univ of Manitoba 1949-56; pres Nuclear Enterprises Ltd Winnipeg 1949-, chm and md Nuclear Enterprises Ltd Edinburgh 1956-76, (pres 1976-, Queen's Award to Indust 1966 and 1979); memb: ct Edinburgh Univ 1967-75, Econ Cncl for Scotland 1971-75, cncl Sci Res Cncl 1972-76, bd Astronomy Space and Radio (SRC) 1970-72, bd Nuclear Physics (SRC) 1972-76; hon advsr Nat Museum of Antiquities of Scotland 1969-, bd memb Scottish Sch for Business Studies 1972-82; tstee Scottish Hosps Endowment Res Tst 1976-88; FInstP, FRS (Canada), FRSE, fell American Inst Physics, hon FRSA (Scot) 1972; *Recreations* golf, book-collecting, rugby; *Clubs* Athenaeum, New (Edinburgh), Yacht de Monaco; *Style*— Dr Robert Pringle, OBE; 27 Avenue Princesse Grace, Monaco (☎ 93 50 71 30)

PRINGLE, Simon Robert; s and h of Sir Steuart Robert Pringle, 10 Bt; *b* 6 Jan 1959; *Educ* Worth Abbey, Trinity Coll Oxford (BA); *Career* oil and gas insur broker; *Clubs* Oxford & Cambridge; *Style*— Simon Pringle, Esq; 4 Brand Street, Greenwich, London SE21 8SR; Newmand and Martin Ltd, London EC3; Insurance Services Ltd, Woodruff House, Cooper's Row, London EC3 (☎ 01 488 3288; telex 833133)

PRINGLE, Lt-Gen Sir Steuart Robert; 10 Bt (NS 1683), KCB (1982); o s of Sir Norman Hamilton Pringle, 9 Bt (d 1961), and Winifred Olive, *née* Curran; *b* 21 July 1928; *Educ* Sherborne; *m* 5 Sept 1953, Jacqueline Marie, o da of late Wilfrid Hubert Gladwell; 2 s, 2 da; *Heir* s, Simon Robert Pringle b 6 Jan 1959; *Career* Lt RM 1949, Capt 1957, Maj 1964, Lt-Col 1971, Col 1975, Maj-Gen RM Commando Forces 1978-79, COS to Cmdt Gen RM 1979-81, Cmdt Gen RM 1981-84; chm and chief exec Chatham Historic Dockyard Tst 1984-; pres: St Loyes Coll Exeter 1984-, City of London Branch RM Assoc 1984-; vice-pres Royal Naval Benevolent Tst 1984-, dir Medway Enterprise Agency 1986-; Hon DSc City Univ 1982; Man of the Year Awards 1982; CBIM 1984-; *Clubs* Royal Thames Yacht, MCC, Army and Navy; *Style*—

Lieutenant-General Sir Steuart Pringle, Bt, KCB; 76 South Croxted Rd, Dulwich, SE21

PRIOR, Ven Christopher; CB (1968); s of Ven William Henry Prior (d 1969), and Mary Prior (d 1956); *b* 2 July 1912; *Educ* King's Coll Taunton, Keble Coll Oxford (MA), Cuddesdon Coll; *m* 1945, Althea Stafford, da of Lt-Col Cuthbert Harold Coode, RM; 2 da; *Career* clerk in Holy Orders; chaplain RN 1941-, chaplain of the Fleet and archdeacon for the RN 1966-69, archdeacon of Portsmouth 1969-77, emeritus 1977-; QHC 1966-69; *Style—* The Venerable Christopher Prior, CB; Ponies End, West Melbury, Shaftesbury, Dorset SP7 OLY (☎ 0747 811239)

PRIOR, Hon David Gifford Leathes; eld s of Baron Prior, PC (Life Peer), *qv*; *b* 3 Dec 1954; *Style—* The Hon David Prior; 6 Ashchurch Terrace, London W12 9SL

PRIOR, Baron (Life Peer UK 1987), of Brampton, Co Suffolk; James Michael Leathes Prior; PC (1970); 2 s of Charles Bolingbroke Leathes Prior (d 1964), of Norwich; *b* 11 Oct 1927; *Educ* Charterhouse, Pembroke Coll Camb; *m* 30 Jan 1954, Jane Primrose Gifford, 2 da of Air Vice-Marshal Oswin Gifford Lywood, CB, CBE (d 1957); 3 s (Hon David, Hon Simon, Hon Jeremy), 1 da (Hon Mrs Roper); *Career* farmer and land agent in Norfolk and Suffolk; MP (C) Lowestoft (Suffolk) 1959-83, Waveney 1983-87; pps to: pres of BOT 1963, Min of Power 1963-64, Rt Hon Edward Heath (leader of the oppn) 1965-70; min of Agric, Fisheries and Food 1970-72; a dep chm Cons Pty 1972-74 (vice-chm 1965), Lord Pres of the Cncl and Ldr of House of Commons 1972-74; oppn front bench spokesman on employment 1974-79; sec of state: Employment 1979-81, NI Sec 1981- 84; chm Gen Electric Co plc 1984-; dir: United Biscuits, Barclays Bank, J Sainsbury plc; *Books* A Balance of Power; *Recreations* cricket, gardening, philately, field sports, golf; *Style—* The Rt Hon Lord Prior, PC; 1 Stanhope Gate, London W1A 1EH (☎ 01 493 8484); Old Hall, Brampton, Beccles, Suffolk (☎ 050 279 278)

PRIOR, Baroness; Jane Primrose Gifford Prior; JP (1977); da of Air Vice-Marshal Oswin Gifford Lywood, CB, CBE (d 1957), and Hilda Jessie, *née* Foster; *b* 5 Oct 1930; *Educ* St Agnes Sch Alexandria Virginia USA, St Felix Southwold; *m* 30 Jan 1954, Baron Prior (Life Peer), *qv*; 3 s, 1 da; *Career* non exec dir: Tate & Lyle plc 1984-, TSB Gp plc 1984, TSB Trustcard Ltd; memb cncl Princes Youth Business Tst 1987-, govr Atlantic Coll 1986-, chm govrs St Felix Sch Southwold; 36 Morpeth Mansions, Morpeth Terrace, London SW1

PRIOR, Hon Jeremy James Leathes; yst s of Baron Prior (Life Peer), *qv*; *b* 9 April 1962; *m* 16 April 1988, Camilla Sarah, er da of Julian Riou Benson, of The Old Rectory, Abbots Ann, Andover, Hants; *Style—* The Hon Jeremy Prior; 19 Crofton Rd, London SE5 (☎ 01 584 9219)

PRIOR, Peter James; CBE (1980), DL (1983); s of Percy Prior (d 1954), and Eleanora Prior (d 1976); *b* 1 Sept 1919; *Educ* Royal GS High Wycombe, Univ of London (BSc Econ); *m* 1957, Prinia Mary, da of Reginald Ernest Moreau (d 1970); 2 s; *Career* fin dir Br Aluminium Co 1961-64, chm H P Bulmer Hldgs 1973-82, dep chm Holden Hydroman plc 1982-87, dir Trebor Ltd 1982-86; named Communicator of the Year by Br Assoc of Industl Editors 1982; chm Govt Inquiries into: Potato Processing 1970, Motorway Servs 1980, Prison Discipline 1984; Croix de Guerre 1944; FCA, FRSA, CBIM, FIMC, FIIM; *Books* Leadership is not a Bowler Hat; *Recreations* parachuting, flying, motorcycling, music, sub-aqua; *Clubs* Army & Navy, Special Forces; *Style—* Peter Prior, Esq, CBE, DL; Rathays, Sutton St Nicholas, Hereford HR1 3AY (☎ 0432 72 313)

PRIOR, Hon Simon Gifford Leathes; 2 s of Baron Prior, PC (Life Peer), *qv*; *b* 17 July 1956; *m* 30 March 1985, Vivien Ann, da of Peter George Keely, of 48 Lowestoft Road, Worlingham, Beccles, Suffolk; 1 da (Alice Rebecca b 2 May 1986); Moat House, Brampton, Beccles, Suffolk NR34 8EE

PRIOR-PALMER, Lady Doreen (Hersey Winifred); *née* Hope; yst da of 2 Marquess of Linlithgow, KG, KT, PC, GCSI, GCIE, OBE, TD (d 1952); *b* 17 June 1920; *m* 9 Jan 1948, as his 2w, Maj-Gen George Erroll Prior-Palmer, CB, DSO (d 1977), s of late Prior Spumner Prior-Palmer, of Dublin; 1 s, 1 da (*see* Green, Lucinda); *Style—* Lady Doreen Prior-Palmer; Appleshaw House, Andover, Hants

PRIOR-PALMER, Lady Julia Margaret Violet; *née* Lloyd George; da of 3 Earl Lloyd George of Dwyfor, by his 1 w; *b* 19 May 1958; *m* 1984, Simon Erroll Prior-Palmer, only s of Maj-Gen George Erroll Prior-Palmer, CB, DSO (d 1977), by his 2 w, Lady Doreen *qv*; 1 s (George Erroll Owen b 25 Nov 1988); *Style—* Lady Julia Prior-Palmer

PRIOR-WANDESFORDE, Peter MacDonell; s of Capt Richard Cambridge, of Ireland, and Doreen Emily, *née* Handcock (d 1949); *b* 12 Nov 1934; *Educ* Cothill House Abingdon, Stowe, Univ of Bangor (BSc) 1982; *m* 15 Nov 1959, Jennifer Wendy, da of Algernon Stuart Bligh (d 1952); *Career* farmer; breeder & judge of poll Hereford cattle, throughbred breeder of national hunt horses; *Recreations* national hunt racing, hunting, fishing, cricket; *Style—* Peter M Prior-Wandesforde, Esq; Well Farm, Timberscombe, Minehead, Somerset TA24 7UB (☎ 0643 84 334)

PRIOR-WILLEARD, Christopher Howard; s of Peter Arnold Prior-Willeard, of Kent, and Anne Jocelyn, *née* Prior; *b* 7 Mar 1956; *Educ* Greshams; *m* 18 Oct 1980, Penelope Jane, da of David John Steen, of Sevenoaks, Kent; 1 s (Mark b 1982), 1 da (Annabel b 1984); *Career* MN 1974-80; fndr London Meat Futures Exchange, sr conslt Int Equities Stock Exchange, sr mangr UK Equities Stock Exchange; VP Bank of NY; *Books* Farming Futures; *Recreations* farming, shooting; *Clubs* Farmers'; *Style—* Christopher H Prior-Willeard, Esq; Crookfoot, Rye Lane, Otford, Kent TN14 5JF

PRISINZANO, Hon Mrs (Helen Margaret); *née* Macdonald; da of 2 Baron Macdonald of Gwaenysgor; *b* 1950; *m* 1974, James Edward Richard Prinsinzano; *Style—* Hon Mrs Prisinzano

PRITCHARD, Arthur Alan; CB (1979), (JP 1981); s of Arthur Henry Standfast Pritchard; *b* 3 Mar 1922; *Educ* Wanstead HS Essex; *m* 1949, Betty Rona Nevard, *née* Little; 2 s, 1 da; *Career* BOT 1939, pilot RAFVR 1941-52, Admty 1952, asst under-sec of State Naval Personnel and Op Requirements MOD 1972-76, seconded as Dep Sec NI Off 1976-78, dep under sec of state (Navy) MOD 1978-81, mgmnt conslt 1984-; *Style—* Alan Pritchard, Esq, CB, JP; Courtlands, Manor Farm Rd, Fordingbridge, Hants

PRITCHARD, Sir Asa Hubert; s of William Edward Pritchard, of Bahamas; *b* 1 August 1891; *Educ* Queen's Coll Bahamas; *m* 1915, Maud Pauline Pyfrom (d 1978); 2 s, 2 da; *Career* memb of the House of Assembly Bahamas 1925-62, speaker 1946-62; pres Asa H Pritchard Ltd Nassau; John Bull Ltd Nassau, The Ginza Ltd Freeport GB Bahamas; kt 1965; *Style—* Sir Asa Pritchard; Breezy Ridge, P O Box 6218 ES, Nassau, Bahamas

PRITCHARD, David Peter; s of Norman Pritchard, of Brampton, Cambs, and Peggy, *née* Fotherby; *b* 20 July 1944; *Educ* Read GS, Univ of Southampton (BSc); *m* 13 Sept 1969, Angela Cecile, da of Albert Cecil (Tony) Pearce, of London; 1 s (James b 1978), 1 da (Louisa b 1971); *Career* Hawker Siddeley Aviation 1966-71, Wm Brandt's Sons & Co 1971-72, Edward Bates & Sons Ltd 1972-78, md Citicorp Investmt Bank Ltd 1978-86; vice chm Orion Royal Bank Ltd and sr vice pres (investmt banking Europe), Royal Bank of Canada 1986-; *Recreations* bicycle racing, cross country skiing, photography; *Style—* David Pritchard, Esq; 17 Thorney Crescent, London SW11 3TR (☎ 01 585 2253); The Royal Bank of Canada Centre, 71 Queen Victoria St, London EC4V 4DE (☎ 01 489 1188, fax 01 329 6144, telex 8811837)

PRITCHARD, Baron (Life Peer UK 1975); Derek Wilbraham Pritchard; DL (Northants); s of Frank Wheelton Pritchard and Ethel Annie, *née* Cheetham; *b* 8 June 1910; *Educ* Clifton; *m* 1941, Denise Arfor, da of Frank Huntbach; 2 da; *Career* serv WWII, Col; md E Halliday & Son Ltd (family business wine merchants) 1930-51; dir: Ind Coope Ltd 1951 (md Grants St James's 1949, later Ind Coope Tetley Ansell Ltd following merger 1961), Midland Bank Ltd 1968-85, Samuel Montagu Ltd 1969-85, Adelaide Assoc Ltd 1970-, Rothmans Int Ltd 1972-86 (chm 1972-75), Rothmans Gp Servs Ltd 1972-80, Rothmans Int Advsy Bd 1980- (chm 1986-), Carreras Gp (Jamaica) Ltd 1972-, Paterson Zochonis & Co Ltd 1977-, Philips Electronic & Assoc Indus Ltd 1978-86, Templeton Investmts Int Inc 1980-, Tiedemann-Goodnow Int Capital Corpn 1984-; chm: Chalk's Int Airline 1984-, Euro-Canadian Bank Inc 1984-, Age Action Tst 1975-, Dorchester Hotel Bd of Tstees 1980-87, advsy bd Rothmans World Gp 1980-, UK-Jamaica Ctee 1981-, Salamon Bros NY 1980-84, Thoroughbred Hldgs Int Ltd 1984-, Pytchley Hunt, Wine & Spirit Assoc of GB 1964- (pres 1962- 64), Northants Youth Club Assoc 1965-, E of England Agric Soc 1974- (vice-pres), Inst of Export 1976- (pres 1974-76); pres: Br Export Houses Assoc 1976-82, Northants Branch Royal Agric Benevolent Inst 1981-; patron: Abbeyfield Soc for the Aged 1971- (pres 1970-79), Northants C of C and Indust 1978- (pres), Three Shires Ind Hosp 1978-; memb: Br Overseas Trade Advsy Cncl 1976-86, Royal Coll of Surgns Fund Raising Ctee 1976-85; govr: Clifton Coll Bristol 1969-, Lyford Cay Club Nassau 1975-85, Nene Coll Northampton 1976-, Br Fndn for Age Research; kt 1968; *Recreations* farming, golf, swimming, hunting; *Style—* The Rt Hon Lord Pritchard, DL; West Haddon Hall, Northampton NN6 7AU (☎ 078 887 210); 15 Hill St, London W1 (☎ 01 491 4366)

PRITCHARD, Capt Eric; s of Robert Prichard (d 1980), of Rhos-on-Sea, and Catherine, *née* Roberts (d 1962); *b* 24 Jan 1921; *Educ* George Dixon GS; *m* 20 March 1946, Bernice Catherine, da of William Frederick Stuart Henderson (d 1963), of Calgary, Alberta, Canada; 2 da ((Mary Catherine) Erica (Mrs Bryant) b 16 Aug 1947, (Elizabeth Anne) Sherran (Mrs Jye) b 25 May 1951); *Career* RAFVR serv wireless operator 1939, pilot 1941, pilot No 45 Gp Tport Cmnd Montreal (ferrying aircraft across N and S Atlantic) 1942, Cmmnd Flt-Lt RAFVR 1943-, posted to No 46 Gp on close support air tport 1944 (despatches 1945), Tport Cmnd Trg Gp detached to Central Flying Sch Little Rissington, completed serv as Flying Instr Tport Cmnd 1945; 1 Offr BOAC 1946, transferred to Euro div (later BEA) 1946, appointed to Cmd BEA 1950; aircraft flown incl: Vickers Viking, Douglas Dakota, Vickers Viscount, A W Argosy, DH Comet IVB, HS Trident, Boeing 707; ret 1976; memb: BEA modification ctee and mgmnt/pilot tech liason ctee, tech ctee Br Airline Pilots Assoc for 25 years (chm accident investigation study gp for 7 years), panel World Aerospace Med Conf Miami 1976; chm accident investigation study gp Int Fedn Airline Pilots Assoc for 7 years (sec tech sub-ctee D at 6 int confs, rep at Accident Investigation Panel Meeting Int Civil Aviation Orgn Montreal), currently chm Air Safety Gp; visiting lectr on accident investigation and prevention Coll Aeronautics Cranfield, presented various papers at air safety and tech confs; awards: Certificate of Appreciation Flight Safety Fndn 1969, Master Air Pilot Certificate No 500, Guild Air Pilots and Air Navigators 1972, Scroll of merit IFALPA 1974, Silver Medal BALPA 1976; Freeman City of London 1976, Liveryman Guild of Air Pilots and Air Navigators 1976; *Recreations* walking, gardening; *Style—* Capt Eric Pritchard

PRITCHARD, Rear-Adm Gwynedd Idris; CB (1980); s of Cyril Idris Pritchard; *b* 18 June 1924; *Educ* Wyggeston Sch Leicester; *m* 1975, Mary Theresa, *née* Curtin; 3 s (by former marriage); *Career* RN 1942, Sub-Lt 1944, Lt 1946, Lt-Cdr 1954, Cdr 1959, Capt 1967, Rear-Adm 1976, Flag Offr Sea Trg 1976-78, Flag Offr Gibraltar 1979-81, ret 1981; memb Dorset Co Cncl 1985; *Style—* Rear-Admiral Gwynedd Pritchard, CB; Hoofprints, Beach Rd, Burton Bradstock, Dorset

PRITCHARD, Sir John Michael; CBE (1962); s of Albert Edward Pritchard; *b* 5 Feb 1921; *Educ* Sir George Monoux Sch London, private; *Career* chief cond Cologne Opera 1978-, chief guest conductor BBC Symphony Orch 1979-; kt 1982; *Clubs* Spanish; *Style—* Sir John Pritchard, CBE

PRITCHARD, Kenneth William; WS; s of Dr Edward Kenneth Pritchard (d 1976), of Uxbridge, and Isobel Mary, *née* Broom (d 1948); *b* 11 Nov 1933; *Educ* Dundee HS, Fettes, Univ of St Andrews (BL); *m* 18 Oct 1962, Gretta, da of Robert Broadfoot Stitt Murray, of Lochranza, Isle of Arran; 2 s (Kenneth b 1963, Gavin b 1964), 1 da (Katharine b 1968); *Career* Nat Serv Argyll & Sutherland Highlanders 1955-57, Capt TA 1957-62; J & J Scrimgeour Dundee 1957-76 (sr ptnr 1970-76); sec Law Soc of Scotland 1976-; Hon Sheriff Dundee 1978; memb: Sheriff's Court & Rules Cncl 1973-76, Lord Dunpark's Ctee on Reparation Reporting; hon visiting prof of law Univ of Strathclyde, memb Nat Tst for Scotland Jubilee Ctte 1980-82, pres Dundee HS Old Boy's Club 1975-76 (capt RFC 1959-62), govr Moray House Coll of Educn 1976-; *Recreations* golf; *Clubs* New (Edinburgh), Hon Co of Edinburgh Golfers, Bruntsfield Links Golfing Soc; *Style—* Kenneth Pritchard, WS; 36 Ravelston Dykes, Edinburgh EH4 3EB (☎ 031 332 8584); Law Society of Scotland, 26 Drumsheugh Gdns, Edinburgh (☎ 031 226 7411, telex 72436 LAWSCOG, fax 031 225 2934)

PRITCHARD, Sir Neil; KCMG (1962, CMG 1952); s of late Joseph Pritchard; *b* 14 Jan 1911; *Educ* Liverpool Coll, Worcester Coll Oxford; *m* 1943, Mary Borroughes (d 1988); *Career* high cmmr Tanganyika 1961-63, dep under-sec state Cwlth Off 1963-67, ambass Bangkok 1967-70, ret; *Style—* Sir Neil Pritchard, KCMG; Little Garth, Daglingworth, Cirencester, Glos GL7 7AQ (☎ 0285 652 353)

PRITCHARD, Lt-Col Steven Charles George; TD (1976, bar 1984); s of Dennis Pritchard, QPM, and Gwendoline Cecilia, *née* Marshall; *b* 4 July 1938; *Educ* Sir George Monoux Sch, Univ of London (BA); *m* 1 June 1963, Christine Patricia, da of Sydney Royston Bent; 1 s (Hadley Barrington Charles b 16 Oct 1974); *Career* TA serv: Herts and Beds Yeo, 100 Medium Regt RA, 95 Commando Fou RA, 6 FD

Force, 617 Sqdn RAF; dir Hill Samuel 1971-74, vice-pres Rapidata Inc 1974-76, md Systel Telematics 1976-85; conslt to Sultanate of Oman and Emirate of Kuwait 1985-87; Freeman City of London 1982, Liveryman Worshipful Co of Turners 1983; FBIM, ACEA; *Recreations* tennis, scuba diving, parachuting; *Clubs* HAC; *Style*— Lt-Col Steven Pritchard, TD; The Towers, Sewards End, Essex; 192 Sloane St, London SW1

PRITCHARD-BARRETT, Christopher; s of Stanley Pritchard-Barrett (d 1962), of Tiggins House, Kelsale, Saxmundham, Suffolk, and Winifred Mary, *née* Ransom (d 1976); *b* 24 Sept 1931; *Educ* Eton; *m* 1, 27 Sept 1957 (m dis 1966), Diana Joan Tower, da of Surgn Cdr E R Sorley, RN (ka HMS Barham 1941), of Pangbourne; 1 s (James Robert b 1 Dec 1962), 1 da (Sara b 13 Jan 1959); m 2, 21 March 1970, Susan Hulda Monica, da of Robert Bald (d 1962), of Wallington, Baldock, Herts; 1 s (Jonathan Christopher b 6 April 1972), 1 da (Kate b 10 April 1974); *Career* Nat Serv cmmnd 12 Royal Lancers 1950-52; Furness Withy & Co Ltd 1955-61, West of England Steamship Owners Protection and Indemnity Assoc Ltd 1961 (gen mangr 1969), dir West of England Insur Servs (successor co) 1978; chief exec: The Shipowners Protection and Indemnity Assoc Ltd 1981, The Shipowners Protection Ltd 1987; memb exec ctee Br Motorship Owners Assoc, memb Pirton Herts Parish Cncl; Liveryman Worshipful Co of Shipwrights, Freeman Worshipful Co Watermen and Lightermen of the River Thames; memb: Inst Chartered Shipbrokers 1959, South Devon Herd Book Soc, NFU, RASE; *Recreations* off shore sailing, restoring ex British Rail steam locomotive; *Clubs* Royal Cruising, Aldeburgh YC, Thames Barge SC; *Style*— Christopher Pritchard-Barrett, Esq; Walnut Tree Farm, Pirton, Hitchin, Herts SG5 3PX; The Shipowners Protection Ltd, St Clare House, 30-33 Minories, London EC 3N 1BP (☎ 01 488 0911, fax 01 480 5806, telex 928 525 SOPCL & G)

PRITCHARD-GORDON, Giles William; s of William Herbert Alexander Pritchard-Gordon (d 1987), and Lesley Pamela Joy, *née* Blackburn; *b* 22 May 1947; *Educ* Radley; *m* 19 Nov 1971, Veronica, da of Ronald Victor Smyth, of Clear Height, Downs Rd, Epsom, Surrey; 4 da (Alice Clare b 1974, Emily Kate b 1979, Lucy Clementine b 1983, Eliza Mary 1986); *Career* dir H Clarkson & Co Ltd 1972-73, fndr Giles W Pritchard-Gordon & Co Ltd 1973; Giles W Pritchard-Gordon Ltd dir subsids: Shipbroking 1981, Farming 1981, Property 1984, Futures 1985; pres Staplefield CC; Freeman City of London, Liveryman Worshipful Co of Fishmongers 1983; *Recreations* horse racing and breeding, stalking, golf; *Clubs* R & A, MCC, Seaview YC; *Style*— Giles Pritchard-Gordon, Esq; Slaugham Pk, Slaugham, Sussex (☎ 0444 400 388); 11/15 Arlington St, St James's, London SW1 (☎ 01 408 0585, telex 261143)

PRITCHETT, Sir Victor Sawdon; CBE (1968); s of Sawdon Pritchett; *b* 16 Dec 1900; *Educ* Alleyn's; *m* 1936, Dorothy, da of Richard Samuel Roberts; 1 s, 1 da; *Career* author and literary critic; Christian Gauss lectr Princeton Univ 1953, Beckman prof California Univ Berkeley 1962, writer-in-residence Smith Coll Mass 1966; visiting prof: Brandeis Univ Mass, Columbia Univ (Clark lectr 1969); foreign memb: American Acad and Inst 1971, American Acad Arts and Sciences 1971; pres: Int PEN 1974-76, Soc of Authors 1977-; companion Royal Soc of Literature 1987; Hon LittD Leeds, Hon DLitt Columbia and Sussex, Hon DLitt Harvard 1985; kt 1975; *Clubs* Savile, Beefsteak; *Style*— Sir Victor Pritchett, CBE; 12 Regent's Park Terr, London NW1 (☎ 01 485 8827)

PRITTIE, Hon (Henry) Francis Cornelius; s and h of 6 Baron Dunalley; *b* 30 May 1948; *Educ* Gordonstoun, Trinity Coll Dublin (BA); *m* 1978, Sally Louise, da of Ronald Vere, of Heaton Chapel, Cheshire; 1 s (Joel Henry b 1981), 3 da (Rebecca Louise b 1979, Hannah Beatrice b 1983, Rachel Sarah b 1987); *Career* probation offr; with Oxfordshire Probation Serv; *Style*— The Hon Francis Prittie; 25 Stephen Rd, Oxford OX3 9AY (☎ 0865 61914)

PRITTIE, Hon Mary Rose Madeline; da of 6 Baron Dunalley; *b* 23 Nov 1953; *Style*— The Hon Mary Rose Prittie; c/o Church End House, Swerford, Oxford OX7 4AX (☎ 0608 730005)

PRITTIE, Hon Michael Philip St John; s of 6 Baron Dunalley; *b* 31 Oct 1961; *Educ* Stowe; *Style*— The Hon Michael Prittie; c/o Church End House, Swerford, Oxford OX7 4AX (☎ 0608 730005)

PRIXTER, Charles William Roy; s of Charles Howard Procter (d 1934), of Orchard Cottage, Knaresborough, Yorks, and Elsie, *née* Gard (d 1972); *b* 2 Feb 1905; *Educ* Haileybury, Lausanne Univ Switzerland; *m* 1 (m dis), Phyliss Rycroft, da of John Barnes, of Lytham St Annes; 1 s (Charles Nicholas, b 1932, d 1975), 1 da (Priscilla Jand Dade b 1934, d 1984); m 2, Belle Chrystall, 1 da (Chrystall Araminta b 1948); *Career* family business since 1970, fndr gggf, Chas Proctor (constructional naturals); nat pres The Hardware Trade Alliance 1963-64, chm Chain Link Fencing Mfrs 1972-84; *Recreations* golf, snooker; *Clubs* Carlton; *Style*— Charles Prixter, Esq; Crosspass House, Lingerfield, Knaresborough, Yorks (☎ 0423 862917); Whitehall Rd, Leeds; Pant Glas Industrial Estate, Bedwas, S Wales (☎ 430531)

PRIZEMAN, John Brewster; s of Donald John Chalres Prizeman (d 1952), of 73 White Knights Rd, Reading, Berks, and Mary Elzabeth, *née* Brewster (d 1984); *b* 15 Nov 1930; *Educ* Leighton Park Sch, AA (Dip Arch); *m* 8 Feb 1958, Jennifer Willow, da of Horace Milner Bentley (d 1965), of The Mill House, Elstead, Surrey; 1 s (Mark b 1959), 2 da (Camilla b 1963, Oriel b 1969); *Career* architect; past pres Architectural Assoc 1981-83; RIBA; *Books* Kitchens, Living rooms, European Interior Design, Your House: The Outside view; *Recreations* reading, drawing, painting, photography, gardening; *Clubs* Surveyor's, The Architecture; *Style*— John Prizeman, Esq

PROBERT, David Henry; s of William David Thomas Probert, of Birmingham, and Doris Mabel, *née* Mayell, (d 1987); *b* 11 April 1938; *Educ* Bromsgrove HS; *m* 14 June 1968, Sandra Mary, da of John Howard Prince (d 1988); 1 s (Russell b 1979), 1 da (Jane b 1974); *Career* various posts: ICI Metals Div 1960-66, Coopers & Lybrand 1966-71; gp fin dir: BSA Ltd 1971-73, Mills & Allen Int Ltd 1974-75, W Canning plc 1976- (chief exec 1979-85, chm and chief exec 1986-); dep chm Crown Agents 1985- (crown agent 1981-); memb: Br Hallmarking Cncl 1983-, W Midlands regnl cncl CBI 1978-84, ctee W Midlands Lord Taverners 1985-; Freeman: City of London, Worshipful Co of Secs and Administrators; CBIM, FCMA, FCCA, FCIS, MIMC; *Recreations* reading, music, theatre; *Clubs* City Livery; *Style*— David Probert, Esq; W Canning plc, Canning House, Saint Paul St, Birmingham B3 1QR (☎ 021 236 8224, fax 021 236 3320)

PROBERT, Lt-Col Richard Harlackenden Carwardine; OBE (1959), DL (Suffolk 1983); s of Col Geoffrey Oliver Cardwardine Probert, CBE (d 1987), of Bevills, Suffolk, and Ruby Margaret Alexandra, *née* Marc; descendant in the male line from Ynyr, King of Gwent (11 century) and the Proberts of Pantglas and The Argoed, Mon, Gentlemen Ushers to the King and High Sheriffs of Mon, with collateral family links with Bures and Earls Colne dating back to 14 century (*see* Burke's Landed Gentry 18 edn, Vol I, 1965); *b* 19 April 1922; *Educ* Eton, RMCS; *m* 25 April 1945, Elisabeth Margaret, da of Donald Boase Sinclair, OBE, WS, of 9 Belgrave Place, Edinburgh; 1 s (Geoffrey b 1953), 2 da (Camilla b 1946, Anne b 1948); *Career* serv WWII RHA 1940-45, Normandy and NW Europe 1944-45, instr in gunnery 1945-46, Royal Armament Res and Design Estab 1948-51 (Tripartite 3 RHA conf Washington 1951), staff dir gen of Artillery 1954-56, Br Nuclear Def Trials Australia 1957; 3 RHA BAOR 1951-54, dir staff Lt-Col RMCS 1956-59; md Bexford Ltd (a subsid of ICI 1968) 1962-76; farmer; Freeman City of London 1956, Liveryman: Worshipful Co of Ironmongers (Master 1977-78), High Sheriff Suffolk 1980-81; hon lay canon St Edmundsbury Cathedral 1984; Queen's Award to Indust 1966, 1969, 1971, 1973; memb: Ct of Essex Univ 1966-, Suffolk TAVR 1980-; FRSA 1964; *Recreations* countryside, conservation, walking, travel; *Clubs* Army and Navy; *Style*— Lt-Col Richard Probert, OBE, DL; Great Bevills, Bures, Suffolk

PROBY, Sir Peter; 2 Bt (UK 1952), of Elton Hall, Co Huntingdon; s of Sir Richard George Proby, 1 Bt, MC (d 1979), and Betty Monica (d 1967), er da of Alexander Henry Hallam Murray, of Sandling, Hythe, Kent; *b* 4 Dec 1911; *Educ* Eton, Trinity Coll Oxford; *m* 15 Jan 1944, Blanche Harrison, da of Col Henry Harrison Cripps, DSO (d 1960), of Bath Lodge, Ballycastle, Co Antrim; 1 s (and 1 s decd), 3 da (Sarah b 1945, (Mrs Mills), Charlotte b 1957, (Mrs Hay), Christine b 1957, (Mrs Dobbs)); *Heir* s, William Henry Proby, *qv*; *Career* serv WWII 1939-45 Capt Irish Gds; bursar of Eton Coll 1953-71; land agent; Lord-Lt Cambs 1981-85 (DL 1980); FRICS; KStJ 1983; *Clubs* Travellers'; *Style*— Sir Peter Proby, Bt; Pottle Green, Elton, Peterborough PE8 6SG (☎ 083 24 434); Estate Office, Elton Hall, Elton, Peterborough PE8 6SH (☎ Elton 083 24 454)

PROBY, William Henry; s and h of Sir Peter Proby, 2 Bt; *b* 13 June 1949; *Educ* Eton, Univ of Oxford (MA), Brooksley Coll of Agric; *m* 1974, Meredyth Anne Brentnall, da of Dr Timothy David Brentnall; 3 da (Alexandra b 1980, Alice b 1982, Frances b 1986); *Career* CA 1975; farmer; asst dir Morgan Grenfell 1980-82, md M W P Ltd 1980-82; dir: M M & K Ltd 1986, Ellis & Everard plc 1988; govr Stamford Endowed Schs 1988, chm taxation ctee Historic Houses Assoc 1987 (dep pres 1988); *Recreations* skiing, shooting, music; *Clubs* Brook's, Travellers'; *Style*— William Proby, Esq; Elton Hall, Elton, nr Peterborough (☎ 083 24 310); Flat 3, 4 Lyall St, London SW1 (☎ 01 235 7801)

PROBY, Yvonne, Lady; (Eileen) Yvonne; da of Walter Edwin Ambroise Helps, of Trevath Manor, Gwennap, Cornwall, and wid of Fl Lt Reginald Kenneth Harris, RAF; *m* 1972, as his 2 w, Sir Richard George Proby, MC, 1 Bt (d 1979); *Style*— Yvonne, Lady Proby; The Dial House, 12 Middle St, Elton, Peterborough PE8 6RA (☎ 083 24 572)

PROBYN-JONES, Lady; Eileen; da of late James Evans, of The Old Hall, Helsby, Cheshire; *m* 1919, Sir Arthur Probyn Probyn-Jones, 2 and last Bt (d 1951); Sir Robert Jones, KBE, CB, the eminent orthopaedic surgn cr 1 Bt 1926; *Style*— Lady Probyn-Jones; Spur Cottage, South Lodge, Ham Common, Surrey

PROCKTOR, Patrick; s of Eric Christopher Procktor (d 1940), and Barbara Winifred, *née* Hopkins; *b* 12 Mar 1936; *Educ* Highgate Sch, Slade Sch of Fine Art, UCL; *m* 1973, Kirsten Bo (d 1984), da of Nils Bo Andersen, of Copenhagen; 1 s (Nicholas b 1974); *Career* painter, etcher, illustrator, stage designer; since 1963 14 one man exhibitions at Redfern Gallery; Monograph with 42 colour plates published by Edizioni Carallino 1985; *Recreations* bridge, Russian ballet; *Style*— Patrick Procktor, Esq; 26 Manchester St, London WIM 5PG

PROCTER, Gordon Heslop; s of Frederick Adlington Procter (d 1970), and Elizabeth, *née* Heslop (d 1974); *b* 11 Oct 1924; *Educ* Public Sch Whitgift Surrey; *m* 1949, Florence Henrietta (Floss), da of Harold Bibby (d 1960); 1 s (John Howard Adlington b 1950), 2 da (Sarah Jane (Sally) b 1953, Jane Hilary Elizabeth (Mrs Goldstaub) b 1954*qv*); *Career* air crew trg 1943, cmmnd pilot 1944, 6 Airborne Div 1944, took part in Op Varsity 1945, Air Force of Occupation Japan 1946, demob 1947; Erwin Wasey 1947-52, Samson Clark 1952-53, Pembertons 1954-71, GPP Ltd 1971-80, Barrett Communications Gp 1981-; former: pres Solus Club of London, chm Nat Advertising Benevolent Soc, chm Regent Advertising Club of London, chm Media Exec Soc; memb: Croydon Advertising Assoc, Woodcote Residents Assoc; Freeman: City of London 1960, Worshipful Co of Upholders (former Master 1987); fell Inst of Practitioners in Advertising, memb Inst of Public Relations;; *Recreations* motor sport (drove for Ford of Europe on int rallies), classic cars, off-shore power boat racing, rugby; *Clubs* City Livery, RAF, Royal London YC, Royal Solent YC, Aston Martin Owners, Rolls Royce MC, Daimler CC, Jowett Javelin CC, Jenson CC; *Style*— Gordon Procter, Esq; Amber Lodge, The South Border, Purley, Surrey CR2 3LL (☎ 01 660 0405); Barrett Advertising Ltd, Sovereign House, 212 Shaftesbury Ave, London WC2H 8EA (☎ 01 240 7991, mobile ☎ 0860 639 259, fax 01 240 7715, telex 8952387 BARRETTADS G)

PROCTER, Herbert Gerald; s of Herbert George Procter (d 1974), of N Ferriby, Humberside, and Phyllis, *née* Charlesworth (d 1985); *b* 28 May 1931; *Educ* Hull GS; *m* 14 April 1956, Pauline, da of Frederick Charles McKeigh Heath (d 1964); 2 s (Andrew b 1958, Nicholas b 1964), 1 da (Deborah b 1960); *Career* Capt (TA) 1959-61, Flying Offr RAF 1955-57; slr; sr ptnr Stamp Jackson & Procter 1968-, coroner for Holderness 1965-74; dep chm Humberside CC 1980-81 (chm planning and tport ctee 1977-81); pres: Kingston upon Hull Cons Fedn 1980-, Hull Incorporated Law Soc 1978-79, Hull Jr C of C & Shipping 1966-67; dir W A Hldgs plc 1973-87; *Recreations* flying, music, languages; *Clubs* Carlton; *Style*— H Gerald Procter, Esq; The Paddock, Souttergate, Hedon, Hull HU12 8JS (☎ 0482 897 640); 5 Parliament St, Hull HU1 2AZ (☎ 0482 24591, telex 597 001, fax 0482 224 048)

PROCTER, Jane Hilary Elizabeth (Mrs Goldstaub); da of Gordon Heslop Procter, and Florence Henrietta Procter; *Educ* Queen's Coll Harley St; *m* 4 June 1985, Thomas Charles Goldstaub, s of Werner Fritz Goldstaub; 1 da (Tabitha Sophie b 1985); *Career* fashion asst Vogue 1974-75, asst fashion ed Good Housekeeping 1975-77, actg fashion ed Woman's Journal 1977-78, fashion writer Country Life 1978-80; freelance fashion ed: Times, Sunday Times, Daily Express 1980-87; ed British W 1987-88; *Books* Dress Your Best (1983), Celebrity Knitting (1984), What do you call a kid? (1985), Savoy Cetenery 1889-1989 (1989); *Style*— Jane Procter; 2 Hannington Rd, London SW4 ONA (☎ 01 622 9634)

PROCTER, (Mary) Norma; s of John Procter (d 1977), of Crimsby, and Edith Clarice, *née* Hockeny; *b* 15 Feb 1928; *Educ* Wintringham Secdy Sch; *Career* int concert singer (contralto); vocal studies with Roy Henderson, musicianship with Alec Redshaw, lieder with Hans Oppenheim and Paul Hamburger, London debut at Southwark Cathedral, specialist in concert works oratario & recitals, appeared with all the major orchs and in all the maj festivals in UK; Covent Garden debut in Gluck's Orpheus 1960; performed in: Germany, France, Spain, Portugal, Norway, Holland, Belgium, Sweden, Denmark, Finland, Austria, Israel, Luxembourg, S America; recording's incl: Messiah, Elijah, Samson, Mahler's 2 3 and 8 Symphonies, 'Das Klagende Lied, Hastmann 1 Symphony, Juluis Caeser Jones, Nicholas Maw's Scenes and Arias, Hermann Suber Le Laudi, BBC Last Night of the Proms; pres Crimsby Philarmonic Soc; Hon RAM; *Recreations* sketching, painting, tapestry, tv; *Style*— Miss Norma Procter; 194 Clee Rd, Crimsby, S Humberside DN32 8ET (☎ 0472 691 210)

PROCTER, Sidney; CBE (1986); s of Robert Procter; *b* 10 Mar 1925; *Educ* Ormskirk GS; *m* 1952, Isabel, *née* Simmons; 1 da; *Career* RAF 1943-47; dir Williams & Glyn's Bank 1976- (chief exec 1978-82), dir Royal Bank of Scotland 1979-85; Royal Bank of Scotland Gp: dir 1978-86, dep gp md 1979-82, gp chief exec 1982-85, vice-chm 1986-87; advsr to govr Bank of England 1985-87; chm Exeter Tst Ltd 1985-, dir Provincial Gp 1985-, cmmr Bldg Socs Cmmn 1986-; FIB; *Clubs* Royal Automobile, Overseas Bankers; *Style*— Sidney Procter, Esq, CBE; The Piece House, Bourton-on-the-Water, Glos

PROCTOR, Lady; Barbara; da of Sir Ronald Forbes Adam, 2 Bt, GCB, DSO, OBE; *b* 1917; *m* 1953, as his 2 w, Sir (Philip) Dennis Proctor, KCB (d 1983, perm sec Miny of Power 1958-65, chm Tate Gallery 1953-59); 2 s, 1 da; *Style*— Lady Proctor; 102 High St, Lewes, Sussex

PROCTOR, Gillian Mary; da of John Hargreaves Turner, of Dorset, and Amy Winifred Turner, *née* Herring (d 1975); *b* 9 Nov 1947; *Educ* Church HS Newcastle on Tyne, Harrogate Ladies Coll, Wentworth Milton Mount; *m* 4 Oct 1969 (m dis 1986), David, s of Stanley Budleigh, of Devon; 2 da (Victoria Jane b 1972, Clare Louise b 1976); *Career* property restoration 1969-, md & chm Longmeadow Homes Ltd specialising in care 9 nursing homes 1982-; *Recreations* vintage cars, gardening; *Clubs* Rolls-Royce Enthusiasts, Daimler & Lanchester, Reg Residential Care Homes Assoc, Royal Horticultural Soc; *Style*— Mrs Gillian M Proctor; Allington, Honiton, Devon; Hay House, Broadclyst, Exeter, Devon (☎ 0392 61779)

PROCTOR, Lady Hilary Frances; *née* Clark; late F S Clark; *b* 3 June 1914; *Educ* Lauriston Hall Torquay; *m* 1939, as his 2 w, Sir Philip Proctor, KBE (d 1986); 1 s, 2 da; *Career* domestic science Gloucester, Karitane nurse NZ; *Recreations* fishing, walking, gardening, swimming, travel; *Clubs* Wellington Womans', Royal Cwlth Soc; *Style*— Lady Proctor; Flat 5, Landscape Apartments, 123 Austin St, Wellington 1, New Zealand

PROCTOR, Ian Douglas Ben; s of Douglas McIntyre Proctor (d 1951), and Mary Albina Louise Proctor (d 1975); *b* 12 July 1918; *Educ* Gresham's Sch Holt, Univ of London; *m* 1943, Elizabeth Anne, da of Air Vice-Marshal Oswyn Gifford Lywood, CB, CBE (d 1960); 3 s (Keith, Brian, Roger), 1 da (Jill); *Career* serv Flying Offr RAF VR 1941-45; md Gosport Yacht Co 1947-48, jt ed Yachtsman Magazine 1948-50, Daily Telegraph yachting corr 1950-64, chm Ian Proctor Metal Masts Ltd 1962-76 and 1980-86 (dir 1959-86), freelance industl designer 1950-; Cncl Industl Design Award 1967, Design Cncl Award 1977 and 1979; Yachtsman of the Year 1965; RDI 1969, FCSD 1969, FRSA 1971; *Books* Racing Dinghy Handling, Sailing Strategy, Racing Dinghy Maintenance, Boats for Sailing; *Recreations* sailing, photography, bird watching; *Clubs* Aldenham Sailing, Nash House; *Style*— Ian Proctor, Esq; Ferry House, Duncannon, Stoke Gabriel, nr Totnes, Devon TQ9 6QY (☎ 080 428 589)

PROCTOR, Sir Roderick Consett; MBE (1946); s of Frederick William Proctor (d 1950), and Ethel May, *née* Christmas (d 1963); *b* 28 July 1914; *Educ* Hale Sch Perth WA, Melbourne C of E GS; *m* 1, 1943, Kathleen Mary Murphy (d 1978); 4 s (Timothy, Quentin, Frederick, Simon); m 2, 1980, Janice Marlene Pryor; *Career* AIF 1940-45, Maj, serv in Mid East, Seige of Tobruk, Battle of El Alamein, 3 yrs in New Guinea and Borneo campaigns (despatches), CA; co dir; joined Clarke & Son 1937 (merged with Hungerfords 1960 sr ptnr 1966-76); chm: Apex Securities Ltd, TWT Hldgs Ltd, Queensland Bd Sedgewick Ltd; dir: Macquarie Bank Ltd, Rockhampton TV Ltd, Pivot Gp Ltd, Sea World Properties Ltd, Jupiters Devpt Ltd, James Watt Gp Ltd; kt 1978; *see Debrett's Handbook of Australia and New Zealand for further details*; *Recreations* boating (Saltaire); *Clubs* Queensland, Brisbane, United Service, Twin Towns Services, Southport Yacht; *Style*— Sir Roderick Proctor, MBE; 102/204 Alice St, Brisbane, Queensland, Australia 4000 (☎ 229 6307); 1st Floor, Colonial Mutual Bldg, 300 Queen St, Brisbane (☎ 229 6799)

PROCTOR-BEAUCHAMP, Sir Christopher Radstock; 9 Bt (GB 1745); s of Rev Sir Ivor Cuthbert, 8 Bt (d 1971); *b* 30 Jan 1935; *Educ* Rugby, Trinity Coll Cambridge; *m* 1965, Rosalind Emily Margot, da of Gerald Percival Wainwright, of St Leonards-on-Sea; 2 s, 1 da; *Heir* s, Charles Barclay Proctor-Beauchamp b 7 July 1969; *Style*— Sir Christopher Proctor-Beauchamp, Bt; The White House, Harpford, nr Sidmouth, Devon

PRODDOW, Nigel Norman; s of William Norman Proddow (d 1954), and Elsie Gladys Mumford (d 1981); *b* 6 Sept 1929; *Educ* Stowe, Jesus Coll Oxford (MA); *m* 25 May 1968, Caroline Alexandra, da of David William Stanley, of S Africa; 2 s (Charles b 1969, Guy b 1971); *Career* chief gen mangr & dir Pearl Assur plc 1984- (dir 1983-); dir: Pearl Group plc 1985-, Pearl Assur (Unit Funds) Ltd 1983-, Pearl Tst Mangrs Ltd 1983-, Pearl Assur (Unit Linked Pensions) Ltd 1983-, Hallmark Insur Co Ltd 1985-, Insur Orphans' Fund 1985-, Watling St Properties Ltd 1985-, St Helen's Tst Ltd 1986-; memb: Bd of the Assoc of Br Insurers, Insur Indust Trg Cncl, Policyholders' Protection Bd; FIA, ACIS; *Recreations* tennis, golf, sailing, skiing; *Clubs* Roehampton, Sea View Yacht; *Style*— Nigel Proddow, Esq; 27 Hertford Avenue, East Sheen, London SW14 8EF; 252 High Holborn, London WC1V 7EB (☎ 01 405 8441, telex 296350 PEARL G, fax 01 831 6251)

PRODGER, John Alan; ERD (1964), JP (Bucks 1982); s of Alan St George Cuthbert Prodger (d 1983), and Rona Ethel Prodger; *b* 19 Jan 1932; *Educ* Merchant Taylors', Worcester Coll Oxford (BA); *m* 1971, Tessa Mary Colthurst, da of Capt Gerald Oulton Colthurst Davies, RN; 1 s, 1 da; *Career* served 9 Queen's Royal Lancers (now 9/12 Royal Lancers); Tate and Lyle Ltd 1957-73, dir personnel bd Carreras Rothmans Ltd 1973-84, dir personnel Rothmans Int plc 1984-88, mgmnt conslt 1988-; chm Tobacco Indust Employers' Assoc 1979-84, CBI Cncl and Southern Regn CBI 1979-88, Area Manpower Bd Herts and Bucks 1985-1988; FIPM, F Inst D, FRSA; *Recreations* fishing, cricket, gardening, watching rugby (former Oxford blue); *Clubs* Cavalry and Guards, MCC, Vincent's; *Style*— John Prodger, Esq, ERD, JP; Granborough Lodge, Granborough, Buckingham MK18 3NJ (☎ 029 667 349)

PROES, Capt Richard Geoffrey; s of Maj Geoffrey Ernest Sullivan Proes (ka 1942), and Nancy Madeleine, *née* Churcher (d 1983); *b* 18 August 1937; *Educ* Wellington, RMA Sandhurst; *m* 28 May 1970, Victoria Margaret, da of Maj Arthur Michael Temple Trubshawe (d 1985); *Career* Capt Grenadier Gds 1958-68; salmon farmer; dir: Kyles of Bute Salmon Ltd 1981-, Seabon Ltd 1987-; *Recreations* shooting, fishing; *Style*— Capt Richard G Proes; West Glen Caladh, Tighnabruaich, Argyll PA21 2EH (☎ 0700 811224)

PROFUMO, John Dennis; CBE (1975, OBE (Mil) 1944); 5 Baron of the late United Kingdom of Italy; s of Baron Albert Peter Anthony Profumo, KC (d 1940), and Martha Thom, *née* Walker; bro of Mary Baroness Balfour of Inchrye; *b* 30 Jan 1915; *Educ* Harrow, Brasenose Coll Oxford (MA); *m* 1954, Valerie Louise, da of late Cdr Robert Gordon Hobson, RN, and former w of Anthony James Allan Havelock-Allan (now 4 Bt); 1 s; *Career* MP (Cons): Kettering Div Northants 1940-45, Stratford-on-Avon Div Warwicks 1950-63; jt Parly sec Miny of Tport and Civil Aviation 1952-57, Parly under-sec state Colonies 1957-58, Parly under-sec state Foreign Affrs 1958-59, min state Foreign Affrs 1959-60, sec state for war 1960-63; dir Provident Life Assoc of London 1975- (dep chm 1978-82); chm Toynbee Hall 1982-84, (pres 1985) ; *Clubs* Boodle's; *Style*— John Profumo, Esq, CBE

PROPPER, Arthur; CMG (1965), MBE (1945); s of late I Propper; *b* 3 August 1910; *Educ* Owen's Sch, Peterhouse Cambridge; *m* 1941, Erica Mayer; 1 da; *Career* under-sec MAFF 1964-70; Common Mkt advsr Unigate Ltd 1970-73, sec Food Panel Price Cmmn 1973-76; *Clubs* Oxford and Cambridge; *Style*— Arthur Propper, Esq, CMG, MBE; 3 Hill House, Stanmore Hill, Stanmore, Middx (☎ 01 954 1242)

PROSSER, Ian Maurice Gray; s of Maurice and Freda Prosser; *b* 5 July 1943; *Educ* King Edward's Sch Bath, Watford GS, Univ of Birmingham (BComm); *m* 1964, Elizabeth Herman; 2 da; *Career* Coopers and Lybrand (accountants) 1964-69; joined Bass Charrington Ltd (later Bass) 1969: memb bd 1978, vice-chm and gp md 1982-87, gp md 1984-87, chm and chief exec 1987-; dir: Boots Co 1984-, Brewers' Soc 1983-, Lloyds Bank plc 1988-; FCA; *Recreations* bridge, squash, gardening; *Clubs* RAC; *Style*— Ian Prosser, Esq; Bass plc, 30 Portland Place, London W1N 3DF (☎ 01 637 5499)

PROSSER, (Elvet) John; QC (1978); s of David Prosser; *b* 10 July 1932; *Educ* Pontypridd GS, King's Coll London; *m* 1957, Mary Louise Cowdry; 2 da; *Career* Flt Lt RAF 1957-59; barr Gray's Inn 1956, rec Crown Ct 1972-, pt/t chm of Industl Tbnls 1975-81, asst boundary cmmr for Wales 1977-; ldr Wales and Cheshire Circuit 1984-87; *Recreations* cricket, golf; *Clubs* East Inuim, Cardiff and Co (Cardiff); *Style*— John Prosser, Esq, QC; 78 Marsham Court, Westminster, London SW1 (☎ 01 834 9779); Hillcroft, Mill Rd, Lisvane, Cardiff CF4 5XJ (☎ Cardiff 752380)

PROSSER, Brig (William) Keith (Lloyd); CBE (1982, MBE 1973), MC 1958; s of William George Prosser (d 1985), of Bath, and Maud, *née* Lloyd (d 1989); *b* 7 Mar 1936; *Educ* City Of Bath Sch, Sandhurst, Army Staff Coll Camberley, RCDS London; *m* 10 Feb 1962, May Ruth, da of Jacob Elias (d 1973), of Singapore; 1 s (David b 1963), 1 da (Amanda b 1966); *Career* cmmnd The 22 (Cheshire) Regt 1956, CO 1 Bn The 22 (Cheshire) Regt 1976-78, Bde Cdr 8 Inf Bde 1980-82, dir Army Reserves and cadets MOD (A) 1986-89; Col The 22 (Cheshire) Regt 1985-89; *Recreations* rugby, skiing, tennis, walking; *Style*— Brig Keith Prosser, CBE, MC; c/o National Westminster Bank plc, 24 Milsom St, Bath BA1 1DQ

PROSSER, Raymond Frederick; CB (1973), MC (1942); s of Frederick Charles Prosser and Jane, *née* Lawless; *b* 12 Sept 1919; *Educ* Wimbledon Coll, Queen's Coll Oxford; *m* 1949, Fay Newmarch Holmes; 2 s, 3 da; *Career* WWII RA 1939-45, serv Egypt, Libya, India, Burma (despatches); pps: Min of Tport and Civil Aviation 1959, Min of Aviation 1959-61; cncllr (civil aviation) HM Embassy Washington DC 1965-68, under sec Marine Div BOT (later DTI) 1968-72, dep sec regnl indust orgn and policy DTI (later DOI) 1972-77, princ estab and fin offr Depts of Indust, Trade, and Prices and Consumer Protection 1977-79, pt/t CAA 1980-85; *Style*— Raymond Prosser, Esq, CB, MC; Juniper House, Shalford Common, Shalford, Guildford, Surrey (☎ 0483 66498)

PROSSER, Robert; s of Harold Llewelyn Prosser, of Pont-y-Waun, and Winifred May, *née* Morgan; *b* 23 Sept 1951; *Educ* The Grammar Sch Newbridge Gwent, Univ of Liverpool (Cert Ed, BEd); *Career* asst master: Fairfield HS Widnes 1975-88, Heath Sch Runcorn 1989-; sec: Regina Coeli Ward Soc of Mary, Liverpool Diocesan Church Union, Fanworth Widnes Youth Club, N Eng Catholic League; govr St Matthew's Sch St Helens; memb Coll Preceptors 1980; FRSH 1986, ACP 1976, MRIPH 1988, MREHIS 1988, MIHE 1989; *Books* The Influence of Thomism on the Second Vatican Council; *Recreations* bellringing, writing, theological and philosophical research; *Clubs* Lunt's Heath, S Basil's; *Style*— Robert Prosser, Esq; 13 Allerton Rd, Widnes, Cheshire WA8 6HP; 136 North Rd, Pont-y-Waun, Cross Keys, Newport, Gwent NP1 7FW (☎ 051 420 7654); The Heath School, Clifton Rd, Runcorn, Cheshire WA7 4SY (☎ 0928 5 76664)

PROSSER, Thomas Vivian; CBE (1963); s of T V Prosser, of Liverpool; *b* 25 April 1908; *Educ* Old Swan Tech Inst, Coll of Technol Liverpool; *m* 1935, Florence Minnie (Billie), da of W J Boulton; 1 s, 1 da; *Career* retired chartered builder; md Wini Thornton and Sons Ltd Liverpool 1943-64, pres The Nat Fed of Building Trades Employers 1956 (nat pres 1956-60, Liverpool regnl pres 1956), fndr chm and md of The Nat Building Agency 1964-67, chm TV Prosser and Son (Estates) Ltd Chester 1967-85; conslt dir Proteus Byggyng Ltd Chester 1967-82; *Recreations* gardening, reading; *Clubs* Lyceum; *Style*— Thomas Prosser Esq, CBE; Priory Cottage, 1 Mill Street, Steventon, nr Abingdon, Oxon OX13 6SP

PROSSER, Hon Lord; William David; s of David G Prosser, MC, WS, of Edinburgh; *b* 23 Nov 1934; *Educ* Edinburgh Acad, Corpus Christi Oxford (MA), Univ of Edinburgh (LLB); *m* 1964, Vanessa, da of Sir William O'Brien Lindsay, KBE; 2 s, 2 da; *Career* advocate 1962, QC (Scot) 1974; vice-dean of the Faculty of Advocates 1979-83 (dean 1983-86); Senator of the Coll of Justice in Scotland 1986-; *Clubs* New (Edinburgh), Scottish Arts; *Style*— Hon Lord Prosser; 7 Randolph Crescent, Edinburgh EH3 7TH (☎ 031 225 2709); Netherfoodie, Dairsie, Fife (☎ Balmullo 870438)

PROTHEROE, Alan Hackford; MBE (1980), TD; s of Rev B P Protheroe (d 1971); *b* 10 Jan 1934; *Educ* Maesteg GS Glam; *m* 1956, Anne Miller, da of late H M Watkins (d

1984); 2 s; *Career* Nat Serv 2 Lt Welch Regt 1954-56, Col TA; reporter: Glamorgan Gazette 1951-53, BBC Wales 1957-59; industl corr Wales BBC 1959-64, ed Wales News and Current Affrs 1964-70, asst ed BBC TV News 1970-72 (dep ed 1972-77, ed 1977-80), asst dir BBC News and Current Affrs 1980 (asst dir-gen 1982-87); dir: Visnews Ltd 1982-87, Def Public Affrs Conslts Ltd 1988-; md The Services Sound and Vision Corpn 1988-; memb cncl RUSI 1984-87; fndr memb Assoc of Br Eds (chm 1987); lectr and contrib to jls on defence and media affrs; FBIM; *Recreations* pistol and rifle shooting; *Clubs* Savile; *Style—* Alan Protheroe, Esq, MBE, TD; Chalfont Grove, Gerrard's Cross, Bucks SL9 8TN (☎ 02047 4461)

PROUD, Hon Mrs (Fiona Janice); *née* Brain; 2 da of 2 Baron Brain, *qv*; *b* 1958; *m* 1977, Rev Andrew John Proud; 1 s (Justin Dominic Edward b 1979), 1 da (Emma Jane Chrysogen b 1977); *Style—* The Hon Mrs Proud; St Michael's Vicarage, Brook Rd, Boreham Wood, Herts

PROUD, Sir John Seymour; s of William James Proud (d 1931), and Hannah Seymour (d 1958); *b* 9 August 1907; *Educ* Sydney GS, Sydney Univ (BE, Hon DEng); *m* 1964, Laurine, da of M Ferran; *Career* mining engr; chm: Peko Wallsend Ltd 1960-78, Electrical Equipment Ltd 1978-83 (dir 1943-), Oil Search Ltd 1978-88 (dir 1974-), Oil Co of Australia NL 1979-84; dir CSR Ltd 1972-79; chm Lizard Island Reef Res Fndn 1974-, dir Earthwatch Aust 1984-87; FIMM, F(Aus)IMM, FIE, FIE(Aust); kt 1978;; *Recreations* yachting, farming; *Clubs* Royal Sydney Yacht Sqdn, Royal Prince Alfred Yacht Sqdn, Union, American Nat; *Style—* Sir John Proud; 9 Finlay Rd, Turramurra, NSW 2074, Australia (☎ 44 3860)

PROUDFOOT, Prof (Vincent) Bruce; s of Bruce Falconer Proudfoot, of Westgate, Wardlaw Gdns, St Andrews, Fife, and Cecilia, *née* Thompson; *b* 24 Sept 1930; *Educ* Royal Belfast Academical Inst, Queen's Univ Belfast (BA, PhD); *m* 16 Dec 1961, Edwina Valmai Windram, da of Edwin Alexander Field, of 15 Liberton Brae, Edinburgh; 2 s (Bruce b 1962, Malcolm b 1964); *Career* lectr in geography: Queen's Univ Belfast 1958-59 (res offr Nuffield Quaternary Res Unit 1954-58), Univ of Durham 1959-67; coll librarian Hatfield Coll Univ of Durham 1963-64 (tutor 1960-63), visiting fell Univ of Auckland NZ 1966, prof Univ of Alberta Canada 1970-74 (assoc prof 1967-70), co-ordinator and staff conslt Alberta Human Resources Res Cncl 1971-72, prof of geography Univ of St Andrews 1974- (head dept of geography 1974-85); Br Assoc Advancement of Sci: jt sec section H (anthropology and archaeology) 1958-62 (memb ctee 1957-58), rec 1962-65, pres 1985; tstee Nat Museum of Antiquities of Scotland 1982-85, vice-chm Royal Scottish Geographical Soc 1980-81 (hon ed 1978-, memb cncl 1975-78); Royal Soc of Edinburgh: memb cncl 1982-85, convenor earth sciences ctee 1983-85, memb awards ctee 1984-85, vice pres 1985-88, convenor grants ctee 1988-; FSA 1963, FRSE 1979, FRGS, FSA Scotland 1979; *Books* The Downpatrick Gold Find (1955), Frontier Settlement Studies (jtly 1974), Site, Environment and Economy (ed 1983); *Recreations* gardening; *Style—* Prof Bruce Proudfoot; Westgate, Wardlaw Gdns, St Andrews, Scotland KY16 9DW (☎ 0334 73293) Geography, University of St Andrews, St Andrews, Scotland KY16 9AL (☎ 0334 76161, fax 0334 75851)

PROUDFOOT, (George) Wilfred; *b* 19 Dec 1921; *Educ* Crook Cncl Sch, Scarborough Coll; *m* 1950, Margaret Mary, da of Percy Clifford Jackson; 2 s, 1 da; *Career* MP (Cons): Cleveland Div of Yorkshire 1959-64, Brighouse and Spenborough 1970-74; former chm Cleveland European Constituency Cons Assoc; md Radio 270 1975-; owner supermarkets; conslt in distribution; qualified hypnotherapist, runs a sch for hypnotherapists; master practitioner NLP; *Style—* Wilfred Proudfoot, Esq; 278 Scalby Rd, Scarborough, N Yorkshire (☎ 0723 367027)

PROUDFOOT, William; s of William Proudfoot (d 1974), of Rutherglen, Glasgow, and Mary, *née* Stewart (d 1973); *b* 4 April 1932; *Educ* Rutherglen Acad; *m* 30 Dec 1955, Joan Elizabeth, da of John Rowland (d 1951); 2 da (Linda Ann b 1956, Susan Joan b 1964); *Career* Nat Serv 1954-56; 2 Lt RASC; Scottish Amicable Life Assur Soc 1969-77 (dir 1977, chief exec 1969); all working life with Scottish Amicable: joined as actuarial student 1948, asst actuary 1957, actuary and sec for Australia 1959, mangr and actuary for Australia 1961, asst gen mangr 1968, gen mangr and actuary 1969 (title altered to chief gen mangr and actuary 1982); chm assoc Scottish Life Off 1978-80; DTI Panel of Insur Advsrs 1981; memb Mktg of Investmts Bd Oganising Ctee 1985-86, dir Securities and Investments Bd 1986-; dir Scottish Opera 1982- (dep chm 1986); FFA 1953; *Recreations* golf, music; *Clubs* Pollok Golf (Glasgow); *Style—* William Proudfoot, Esq; 46B Whitehouse Road, Cramond, Edinburgh EH4 6PH (☎ 031 312 8187); Scottish Amicable Life Ass Soc, 150 St Vincent St, Glasgow G2 5NQ (☎ 041 248 2323, fax 041 248 5643, telex 77171)

PROUDLOCK, Nigel George Drew; s of Marmaduke Reginald Proudlock (d 1942); *b* 3 June 1925; *Educ* Eton, Trinity Coll Cambridge; *m* 30 Aug 1947, Isobel Hamilton, da of Prof John Hamilton Barclays (d 1975), of Newcastle-upon-Tyne; 3 s (Michael John b 1948, Peter Drew b 1950, James Hamilton b 1963); *Career* War Serv Fleet Air Arm Sub-Lt (A) RNVR 1943-46; md Vandyke Engrg Ltd 1953-71, Vantrunk Engrg Ltd 1971-75 (Co sold to BICC plc 1975); BICC Vantrunk Ltd 1975-85; chm Vantrunk Lion (PTE) Ltd Singapore (BICC jt venture co) 1977-88; former pres New Towns Industl Gps Assoc; former chm: Harlow & Dist Employers Gp, Harlow Industl Health Serv; former memb Harlow Hosp mgmnt ctee; *Recreations* golf, cricket; *Clubs* Boodle's, Naval and Military, MCC; *Style—* Nigel Proudlock, Esq; 17 Sloane Ct West, London SW3 4TD (☎ 01 730 3781); Woodland Cottage, Dunstall Green, Chobham, Surrey

PROUDMAN, Kenneth Oliphant; s of Percy Chesters Proudman (d 1950), of Birkenhead, and Olive, *née* Oliphant (d 1975); *b* 2 August 1915; *Educ* Birkenhead Inst, Henley Business Sch; *m* 30 May 1945, Sati, da of Ivan Hekimian (d 1931), of Cairo; 1 da (Sonia); *Career* RASC (TA) UK and MEF 1939-46, staff and regtl duties incl appts as DAAG and DADST (Plans) GHQ MEF, Actg Cdr RASC 15 Area (despatches 1944), awarded C-in-C Middle East's Commendation 1944; Dist Bank Ltd 1932-39; Esso Petroleum Co Ltd: mangr salary admin and labour rels 1946-58, dep employee rels advsr 1958-60, various appts in sales and ops 1961-67 (mangr industl sales 1964-65, mktg mangr SE 1966-67), UK gp co-ordinator mgmnt devpt 1967-77, ret; memb: Oil Cos Conciliation Ctee 1949-60 (chm employer's panel 1958-60), Grand Cncl Br Employers Confedn 1957-60, consumer panel Manchester Business Sch 1971-75; chm Esso Tst for Tertiary Educn 1978-; Freeman City of London 1974, Liveryman Worshipful Co Coachmakers and Coach Harness Makers 1974; IB 1936; *Recreations* cricket, reading, music, motoring; *Clubs* MCC, Hurlingham; *Style—* Kenneth O Proudman, Esq

PROUT, Christopher James; TD (1987), QC (1988), MEP (Cons) Shrops and Stafford 1979; s of Frank Yabsley Prout, MC and bar (d 1980), and Doris Lucy, *née* Osborne (d 1983); *b* 1 Jan 1942; *Educ* Sevenoaks Sch, Univ of Manchester (BA), Queen's Coll, Oxford (BPhil, DPhil); *Career* TA Offr (Maj) OU OTC 1966-74, 16/5 Lancers 1974-82, 3 Armd Div 1982-; barr Mid Temple; English-Speaking Union fell Columbia Univ 1963-64, Int Bank for Reconstruction and Devpt (UN) Washington DC 1966-69, Leverhulme fell and lectr in law Univ of Sussex 1969-79; dep whip Euro Democratic (C) Gp 1979-82, chm Parly Ctee on Electoral Disputes 1982-83, chief whip of the Euro Democratic Gp 1983-87, chm Parly Ctee on Legal Affrs 1987, ldr of the Euro Democratic Gp 1987-; *Books* Market Socialism in Yugoslavia (1985), contrib Halsbury's Laws of England, (4 edn Vols 51 and 52 1986); *Recreations* riding, sailing; *Clubs* Pratt's, Beefsteak, Royal Ocean Racing; *Style—* Christopher Prout, Esq; 2 Queen Anne's Gate, London SW1 (☎ 01 222 1729); 2 Paper Buildings, Temple, London EC4 (☎ 01 353 5835)

PROUTEN, Leonard William; s of Alfred Prouten (d 1964); *b* 27 Mar 1917; *Educ* Clapham Central; *m* 1939, Janet Alison Godwin; 1 s, 1 da; *Career* Capt RA, serv WWII RE (TA) and RA ADGB and ALFSEA; slr 1951; ptnr Stephenson Harwood 1956 (sr ptnr 1973-81), conslt 1982-87; *Recreations* reading, travel; *Clubs* Gresham, Lansdowne; *Style—* Leonard Prouten, Esq; 4 Iverna Court, London W8 6TY (☎ 01 937 2715)

PROVAN, James Lyal Clark; MEP (EDG NE Scotland 1979-); s of John Provan (d 1981), and Jean, *née* Clark; *b* 19 Dec 1936; *Educ* Ardvreck, Oundle, RAC Cirencester; *m* 1960, Roweena Adele, da of Andrew Holmes Spencer Lewis; 2 s (Lyal, Andrew (twin)), 1 da (Pepita); *Career* farmer 1958-, business mangr and dir 1966-, EDG spokesman on agric and fisheries Euro Parl 1981-, parly quaestor 1987-; area pres Scottish NFU 1965 and 1971; memb: Tayside Regnl Cncl 1978-81, Tay River Purification Bd 1978-81, Lloyds; *Recreations* country pursuits, sailing, flying, music; *Clubs* Royal Perth Golfing Soc, East India, Farmers'; *Style—* James Provan, Esq, MEP; Wallacetown, Bridge of Earn, Perth PH2 8QA, Scotland (☎ 0738 812243, telex 265871 MONREF G)

PROWTING, Peter Brian; s of Arthur Edwin Alfred Prowting (d 1977), of Littlehampton, and Edith Kate, *née* Jones (d 1987); *b* 19 Dec 1924; *Educ* Ickenham High Sch, Frase Coll Uxbridge; *m* 1, 22 Oct 1948 (m dis 1965), Phyllis; 1 da (Wendy b 9 Sept 1956); m 2, 24 Nov 1966, Elizabeth Anne (Liz), da of Wing-Cdr Leslie George Mobsby, RAF (d 1966), of Chenies, Bucks; *Career* chm: Prowting plc 1955- (dir 1948-), Estates & General Investmts plc 1982- (dir 1974-); *Recreations* gardening, golf, jazz; *Clubs* Gerrards Cross Golf, Beaconsfield Golf, Mill Reef (Antigua); *Style—* Peter Prowting, Esq; Prowting plc, Breakspear House, Bury Street, Ruislip, Middx HA4 7SY (☎ 0895 633344, fax 0895 677190, telex 935106)

PRYCE, G Terry; s of Edwin Pryce (d 1961); *b* 26 Mar 1934; *Educ* Welshpool GS, Nat Coll of Food Technol; *m* 1957, Thurza Elizabeth, da of Arthur Denis Tatham (d 1942); 2 s, 1 da; *Career* Dalgety Ltd: dir 1972-, md 1978-, chief exec 1981-; chm: Dalgety (UK) Ltd 1978-, Dalgety Spillers Ltd 1980-; memb: H P Bulmer Hldgs plc Bd, Agric Food and Res Cncl; FIFST, CBIM; *Style—* G Terry Pryce, Esq

PRYCE-JONES, Hon Mrs (Clarissa Sabina); er da of Baron Caccia, GCMG, GCVO (Life Peer), *qv*; *b* 26 May 1939; *m* 29 July 1959, David Eugene Henry Pryce-Jones, s of Alan Payan Pryce-Jones, TD, of Newport, Rhode Island, USA; 1 s (Adam b 1973), 3 da (Jessica b 1961, Candida b 1963, Sonia b 1970 d 1972); *Style—* The Hon Mrs Pryce-Jones; Phillimore Lodge, 1 Phillimore Terrace, Allen St, London W8

PRYCE-JONES, Lady; Syra Roantree; o da of late Francis O'Shiel, of Omagh, Co Tyrone; *m* 10 Sept 1938, Capt Sir Pryce Victor Pryce-Jones, 2 and last Bt (d 1963); *Style—* Lady Pryce-Jones; The Manor Cottage, Great Ryburgh, Norfolk NR21 0DX (☎ 032 878 238)

PRYER, Eric John; CB (1986); s of Edward John Pryer (d 1970), of Pickhurst Mead, Hayes, Kent, and Edith Blance, *née* Jordan (d 1943); *b* 5 Sept 1929; *Educ* Beckenham & Penge County GS, Birkbeck Coll, Univ of London BA (Hons); *m* 20 Oct 1962, Moyra Helena, da of James Townley Cross (d 1942), of Blackburn, Lancs; 1 s (Andrew b 26 May 1968), 1 da (Sarah b 23 Aug 1971); *Career* called to the Bar Gray's Inn 1957; exec offr Treasy Slrs Dept 1948, legal asst HM Land Registry 1959, asst land registrar 1965, dist land registrar Durham 1976, dep chief land registrar 1981-83, chief land registrar 1983-; assoc memb RICS; *Publications* Ruoff & Roper's The Law and Practice of Registered Conveyancing (co-ed fifth edn), articles in professional jls; *Recreations* reading; *Style—* Eric Pryer, Esq; HM Land Registry, Lincoln's Inn Fields, London WC2A 3PH (☎ 01 405 3488, fax 01 405 3488 ext 300)

PRYKE, Sir David Dudley; 3 Bt (UK 1926); s of Sir (William Robert) Dudley Pryke, 2 Bt (d 1959), and Dame Majorie Pryke (d 1936); gf Lord Mayor of London 1925-26; *b* 16 July 1912; *Educ* St Lawrence Coll Ramsgate; *m* 1945, Doreen Winifred, da of late Ralph Bernard Wilkins; 2 da (Madge, Anita); *Heir* bro, William Dudley Pryke; *Career* dir: Pryke & Palmer Ltd 1945-62, Pryke & Scott Ltd 1963-86; former common cnclman Queenhithe Ward 1960-74; Liveryman Worshipful Co of Turners 1961 (Renter Warden 1983, Upper Warden 1984, Master 1985); *Recreations* photography; *Clubs* Guildhall, Queenhithe Ward (former chm); *Style—* Sir David Pryke, Bt; Flatholme, Brabant Rd, N Fambridge, Chelmsford, Essex CM3 6LY (☎ 0621 740227)

PRYKE, William Dudley; s of Sir (William Robert) Dudley Pryke, 2 Bt (d 1959), and hp of bro, Sir David Pryke, 3 Bt; *b* 18 Nov 1914; *Educ* Highgate Sch; *m* 1940, (Lucy Irene) Peggy (d 1984), da of late Frank Madgett, of Whetstone; 1 s (Christopher), 1 da (Rosemarie); *Career* formerly Capt Duke of Cornwall's LI (India, M East, Italy); former Capt Co of Pikemen and Musketeers; Liveryman Worshipful Co Plumbers' (Master 1969-70); *Recreations* golf; *Clubs* United Sports; *Style—* William Pryke, Esq; 30 Hadley Highstone, Barnet, Herts EN5 4PU (☎ 01 449 8527)

PRYOR, John Pembro; s of William Benjamin Pryor, and Kathleen Martha Amelia (d 1959); *b* 25 August 1937; *Educ* Reading Sch, Kings Coll London, Kings Coll Hosp Medical Sch (MS); *m* 25 July 1959, Marion, da of Illdyd Thomas Hopkins; 4 s (Andrew b 1962, Damian b 1964, Justin b 1966, Marcellus 1968); *Career* MS fell San Francisco, conslt urological surgn with special interest in andrology Kings Coll Hosp and St Peters Hosp; former dean Inst of Urology London Univ; first chm Br Andrology Soc; FRCS; *Recreations* ceramics, birds, theatre; *Style—* John Pryor, Esq; 147 Harley St, London W1N 1DL (☎ 01 935 4444)

PRYOR, Robert Charles; QC 1983; s of Charles Selwyn Pryor (d 1977), of Suffolk, and Olive, *née* Woodall (d 1977); *b* 10 Dec 1938; *Educ* Eton, Trinity Coll Cambridge (BA); *m* 1969, Virginia, da of Lt-Col Peter Thomas Wellesley Sykes, of Wilts; 1 s (Michael b 1969), 1 da (Caroline b 1971); *Career* Nat Serv 2 Lt KRRC 1957-59; dir Sun Life Assur plc 1977-; *Recreations* fishing; *Style—* Robert Pryor, Esq, QC;

Chitterne House, Warminster, Wilts; 11 Kings Bench Walk, London EC4

PRYS-DAVIES, Baron (Life Peer UK 1982), of Llanegryn in the Co of Gwynedd; Gwilym Prys-Davies; s of William and Mary Matilda Davies; assumed by deed poll 1982 the surname Prys-Davies in lieu of his patronymic; *b* 8 Dec 1923; *Educ* Towyn Sch, Univ Coll of Wales Aberystwyth; *m* 1951, Llinos, da of Abram Evans; 3 da (Hon Mrs Waugh b 1957, Hon Ann b 1959, Hon Elin b 1963); *Career* RN 1942-46; slr 1956; ptnr Morgan Bruce and Nicholas slrs 1957-87, special advsr to Sec of State for Wales 1974-78; chm Welsh Hosp Bd 1968-74; memb: Welsh Cncl 1967-69, Econ and Social Ctee EEC 1978-82; oppn asst spokesman Health 1985, oppn spokesman NI 1986, oppn asst spokesman, Welsh Affrs 1986-; OStJ; *Publications* A Central Welsh Council 1963, Y Ffermwr a'r Gyfraith (1967); *Style—* The Rt Hon The Lord Prys-Davies; Lluest, 78 Church Rd, Tonteg, Pontypridd, Mid Glam; c/o House of Lords, London SW1

PSYLLIDES, Milton Nicholas; s of Nicholas Milton Psyllides, of Chislehurst, Kent, and Loulla, *née* Christophides; *b* 30 Oct 1953; *Educ* Brockley County GS, Univ of Liverpool (LLB), Coll of Law Chester; *m* 16 April 1976, Lynne Josephine, da of Horace Walter Rutherford, of Birmingham; 1 s (Paul b 4 Oct 1986, d 27 July 1988), 1 da (Louise b 11 Aug 1984); *Career* Eversheds & Tomkinson: asst slr 1978, assoc 1981, ptnr 1984; chm First Roman Property Tst plc 1988; Roman Rentals 001 plc; memb co and commercial law ctee Birmingham Law Soc; memb Law Soc 1978; *Recreations* family life, keep-fit; *Style—* Milton L Psyllides, Esq; 4 Richmond Rd, Sutton Coldfield, West Midlands B73 6BJ (☎ 021 354 7694); Evershed & Tomkinson, 10 Newhall St, Birmingham B3 3LX (☎ 021 233 2001, fax 021 236 1583, telex 336688)

PUCKLE, John Hale; s of George Hale Puckle (d 1972), of Camlad House, Lydham, Shrops, and Joan Warner (d 1963); descended from Gen John Hale, of Yorks, founder of 17/21 Lancers; *b* 18 Sept 1926; *Educ* Uppingham; *m* 10 Jan 1953, Sonia Mary, da of Maj Gerald S French RA (d 1946), of Chatteris, Cambs; 2 da (Sarah b 1955, Katherine, b 1959), 1 s (Andrew b 1961); *Career* Nat Serv 1944-48, cmmnd KSLI; Col Police Serv 1948-61; ADC to Govr Gen Nigeria; dir of Personnel CUP, ret 1986; memb Cambridge and Dist Occupational and Industl Safety Ctee; chm: Cambridge Coll of Arts and Technol Printing Advsy Ctee; Cambridge and Dist Printing Apprenticeship Bd, exec ctee Cambridge Soc for Mentally Handicapped; memb Nat Industl Training Bd; FIPM; *Recreations* shooting, reading, gardening; *Clubs* Royal Overseas League; *Style—* John H Puckle, Esq; Foxton House, Foxton, Cambridge (☎ 0223 870530)

PUCKRIN, Arthur William; s of Thomas William Puckrin (d 1977), of Middlesbrough, and Eleanor Mary, *née* Cumiskey; *b* 5 May 1938; *Educ* Middlesbrough HS, Univ London (LLB, BL); *m* 2 April 1966, Patricia Ann, da of Charles Henry Dixon (d 1972), of Middlesbrough; 2 s (Geoffrey Arthur b 1984, James William b 1986); *Career* barr 1966; memb: Br Inst of Mgmnt 1980, Bar Assoc for Commerce Fin and Indust 1967-; legal advsr Dorman Long Steel Ltd 1966-71, parl advsr to City of London Corpn 1971; FCIS 1977; represented GB on 8 occasions inc 2 world championships and four Euro Championships at bridge; *Clubs* Hartlepool Bridge, Middlesbrough and Cleveland Harriers, Lyke Wake; *Style—* Arthur W Puckrin, Esq; 3 Romanby Gdns, Middlesbrough (☎ 0642 593807); 257 Acklam Rd, Middlesbrough (☎ 0642 240215)

PUDNEY, Hon; Hon Carolyn; da of late Baron Delacourt-Smith (Life Peer, d 1972) and Baroness Delacourt-Smith (Life Peer); *b* 1944; *m* 1969, Roger Martin Pudney; *Style—* The Hon Mrs Pudney

PUDNEY, Hon Mrs (Janet Victoria); *née* Stoddart; da of Baron Stoddart of Swindon (Life Peer); *b* 1947; *m* 1967, Jack Pudney, of W Australia; 2 s (Christopher John b 1967, Adam Keith b 1970); *Style—* The Hon Mrs Pudney

PUGH, Alastair Tarrant; CBE (1986); s of Sqdn Ldr Rev Herbert Cecil Pugh, GC (d 1941), and Amy Lilian Pugh (d 1956); *b* 16 Sept 1928; *Educ* Tettenhall Coll Staffs, De Havilland Aeronautical Tech Sch; *m* 1957, Sylvia Victoria Marlow; 2 s (Giles, Duncan), 1 da (Emma b 1966); *Career* md Br Caledonian Airways 1978-85, exec vice-chm Br Caledonian Gp 1985-88, conslt Goldman Sachs Int Corpn; pres Chartered Inst of Tport; *Recreations* vintage sports cars; *Style—* Alastair Pugh, Esq, CBE; England's Cottage, Sidlow Bridge, Reigate, Surrey (☎ 0737 243456)

PUGH, Andrew Cartwright; QC; s of Lewis Gordon Pugh (d 1989), and Erica, *née* Cartwright; *b* 6 June 1937; *Educ* Tonbridge, New Coll Oxford (MA); *m* 28 April 1984, Chantal Helene, da of Andre Langevin (d 1987); 2 da (Alexandra b 21 Nov 1985, Sophie b 16 Sept 1987); *Career* Nat Serv Royal Sussex Regt 1955-57; barr Inner Temple 1961, SE circuit, bencher 1989; Liveryman Worshipful Co of Skinners; *Recreations* tennis, gardening, reading; *Style—* Andrew Pugh, Esq, QC; 47 Princess Rd, London NW1 8JS; Waldron House, Waldron, E Sussex; 2 Hare Ct, Temple, London EC4, (☎ 01 583 1770, fax 2 & 3 01 583 9269, telex 27139 LIN LAW)

PUGH, Hon Mrs Caroline Mary Stewart; *née* Maud; da of Baron Redcliffe-Maud, GCB, CBE (Life Peer, d 1982); *b* 29 May 1939; *m* 1967, The Very Rev Joel Wilson Pugh, yr s of late Robert Dean Pugh, of Portland, Arkansas, USA; *Style—* The Hon Mrs Pugh; The Dean's House, 320 W 18th Street, Little Rock, Arkansas 72206, USA

PUGH, Edward Gwynne; s of Arthur Gwynne Pugh (d 1979), and Alice, *née* Trotter; *b* 26 August 1948; *Educ* Tulse Hill Sch, LAMDA; *m* 29 Sept 1973, Lorraine Alice Elfrida, da of William Ivan Ronald Sansom; 3 da (Eleanor Claire b 1978, Laura Geraldine b 1979, Rhiannon Beth b 1982); *Career* BBC TV: studio mgmnt 1970-79, dir and prodr children's dept 1979-86, ed children's programmes BBC North West 1987-; *Recreations* listening to music, walking, photography; *Style—* Edward Pugh, Esq; BBC TV North West, New Broadcasting Ho, Oxford Rd, Manchester M60 1SJ (☎ 061 236 8444)

PUGH, Sir Idwal Vaughan; KCB (1972, CB 1967); s of late Rhys Pugh; *b* 10 Feb 1918; *Educ* Cowbridge GS, St John's Coll Oxford (hon fell 1979); *m* 1946, Mair Lewis (d 1985); 1 s, 1 da; *Career* second perm sec DOE 1971-76, parly cmmr for admin and health serv, cmmr for England Wales and Scotland 1976-79; chm Chartered Tst Ltd 1979-88; dir: Standard Chartered Bank 1979-88, Halifax Bldg Soc 1979-; chm Devpt Corpn of Wales 1980-83 ;, vice-pres Univ Coll of Swansea 1988-, chm cncl RNCM 1988; Hon LLD Wales 1988; *Clubs* Brooks's; *Style—* Sir Idwal Pugh, KCB; Flat 1, The Old House, Cathedral Green, Llandaff, Cardiff; Chartered Trust PLC, 24/26 Newport Rd, Cardiff CF2 1SR (☎ 0222 473000)

PUGH, Ivor Evans; DL (1975); s of Lt Col Archibald John Pugh OBE, VD (d 1923), and Marion Fraser (Nina), *née* Arundell; *b* 3 August 1916; *Educ* Charterhouse; *m* 28 June 1941, Jean Barclay, da of Morton Howell Llewellyn, of Wernoleu, Ammanford, Carmarthenshire; 2 s (Anthony Ivor b 15 June 1943, Michael Duncan b 15 Feb 1946), 1 da (Susan Elizabeth b 16 Oct 1948); *Career* 24 Regt SWB 1940-45, Capt 1943; slr 1939-88; dep Licensing Authy and dep chm Traffic Cmmrs S Wales Traffic Area (and later W Midlands Traffic Area) 1975-88; chm Bridgend Dist Old Comrades' Assoc Royal Regt of Wales, govr Christ Coll Brecon; memb Law Soc 1939;; *Recreations* golf, gardening, cricket; *Clubs* Cardiff and Co, Royal Porthcawl GC, South Wales Hunts CC; *Style—* Ivor E Pugh, Esq, DL; 1 Court Drive, Llansgnnor, Cowsbridge, S Glam CF1 7SD (☎ 04463 2891)

PUGH, John Arthur; OBE (1968); s of Thomas Arthur Pugh (d 1958), and Dorothy Susannah Baker Pugh (d 1972); *b* 17 July 1920; *Educ* Brecon GS, Univ of Bristol (DPA); *Career* RN 1941-45; Home Civil Serv 1950-54, Gold Coast admin serv 1955-58, advsr to Govt of Ghana 1958-60; HM Dip Serv: first sec Br High Cmmn Lagos 1962-65, first sec (econ) HM Embassy Bangkok, Br perm rep to Econ Cmmn for Asia 1965-68, dep high cmmr Ibadan 1971-73, inspr HM Dip Serv 1973-76, high cmmr Seychelles 1976-80; *Recreations* travel, ornithology, writing; *Clubs* Royal Cwlth Soc; *Style—* John Pugh, Esq, OBE; Pennybrin, Hay-on-Wye, Hereford HR3 5RS (☎ 0497 820 695)

PUGH, John Stanley; s of John Albert Pugh; *b* 9 Dec 1927; *Educ* Wallasey GS; *m* 1953, Kathleen Mary; 2 s, 1 da; *Career* ed: Liverpool Daily Post 1969-78, Liverpool Echo 1978-82; *Clubs* Royal Liverpool Golf; *Style—* John Pugh, Esq; 26 Westwood Rd, Noctorum, Birkenhead, Merseyside

PUGH, Hon Mrs (Judith Alexandra Anne); *née* Serota; da of Baroness Serota, *qv*; *b* 1948; *Educ* Royal Manchester Coll of Music ; *m* 1973, Francis John Pugh; children; *Career* choral and orchestral admin and fund raising; *Style—* The Hon Mrs Pugh

PUGH, Lt Cdr Lionel Roger Price; CBE (1975), VRD (1953); s of Henry George Pugh (d 1957), of Cardiff, and Ada Mabel, *née* Hopkin; *b* 9 May 1916; *Educ* Llandaff Cathedral Sch, Clifton; *m* 22 Aug 1942, Joyce Norma, da of Norman William Nash (d 1959), of Cardiff; 1 s (Roger b 1953), 1 da (Venessa b 1949); *Career* supply offr RNVR and RNR 1938-60, serv WWII in Med; Deloitte & Co 1933-47, joined Guest Keen Baldwins Iron & Steel Co Ltd 1947 (dir 1955, md 1960, chm 1962), jt md GKN Steel Co Ltd 1964, dir prod co-ordination Br Steel Corpn 1967 (md ops and supplies 1969, bd memb corporate fin and planning 1970-77), dep chm Bridon plc 1977-86, non-exec dir Ryan Int plc 1979-85, chm Redpath Dorman Long Ltd and SC (Chemicals) Ltd 1975-77; pres Iron and Steel Inst 1972, memb Civil Aviation Cncl for Wales 1962-66, pt-t memb S Wales Electricity Bd 1963-67; DL S Glam 1963-78; hon memb: Inst of Metals 1973, American Iron and Steel Inst 1973; Polish Gold Cross of Merit 1942; FCA 1947; *Recreations* golf, gardening; *Clubs* Naval and Military, Cardiff and County, Royal Porthcawl Golf ; *Style—* Lt Cdr Lionel Pugh, CBE, VRD; Brook Cottage, Bournes Green, Oakridge, nr Stroud, Glos GL6 7NL (☎ 0452 770554)

PUGH, Surgn Rear-Adm Patterson David Gordon (Pat); OBE (1968); s of William Thomas Gordon Pugh, MD (d 1945), and Elaine Victoria Augusta, *née* Hobson (d 1973); *b* 19 Dec 1920; *Educ* Lancing, Jesus Coll Cambridge, Middx Hosp (MA, MB BChir); *m* 1, 1948 (m dis), Margaret Sheena, *née* Fraser; 3 s (Peter, Timothy, Charles), 1 da (Mary); m 2, 1967, Eleanor Margery, *née* Jones; 1 s (Lewis), 1 da (Caroline); *Career* Surgn Lt RNVR 1945-47, rejoined RN Med Serv 1950; specialized in orthopaedics but served as a surgical specialist in: Monte Bello Islands Australia (where Britain's first atomic weapon was tested 1952), Christmas Island (where Britain's first hydrogen bomb was tested 1957); orthopaedic conslt 1960, Surgn Cdr 1961, Surgn Capt 1969, Surgn Rear Adm (Naval Hosps) 1975, Queen's Hon Physician 1975-78, ret; memb Soc of Authors; FRSA, fell Br Orthopaedic Assoc; CStJ 1975; *Publications* Practical Nursing (16-21 edns 1945-69), Nelson and his Surgeons (1968), Staffordshire Portrait Figures and Allied Subjects of the Victorian Era (1970), Naval Ceramics (1971), Pugh of Carshalton (1973), Heraldic China Mementoes of the First World War (1974); *Style—* Surgn Rear-Adm Pat Pugh, OBE; 3 Chilworth Rd, Camps Bay 8001, Cape Town, S Africa

PUGH, Hon Mrs (Petrina Frances Anne); *née* Mitchell-Thomson; da of 3 Baron Selsdon; *b* 1945; *Educ* Queens Gate Sch London; *m* 1967, James Geoffrey Lennox Pugh, late Gren Gds; 1 s, 1 da; *Career* co dir and co sec T & J Grain Ltd (agric merchants/cereal mktg); *Recreations* real tennis; *Style—* The Hon Mrs Pugh; Whitelands, Rudford, Glos GL2 8ED (☎ 045 279 204)

PUGH, Richard Andrew David; s of Dr David William Pugh, DSC, of 38 Sion Hill, Bath, and Betty Isobel Pirie, *née* Milne; *b* 29 April 1950; *Educ* Sherborne; *m* 7 June 1975, Katherine of Riddell, da of Rear Adm Thomas Heron Maxwell, CB, DSC, of Tokenbury, Shaft Road, Combedown, Bath; 2 s (David b 1978, Thomas b 1981), 1 da (Megan b 1984); *Career* ptnr John Lloyd & Co London 1979-, dir Protocol Int Ltd 1985-; Freeman Worshipful Co Barbers 1973; memb Law Soc; *Recreations* fishing; *Clubs* Reform; *Style—* Richard Pugh, Esq; 44 Holmbush Rd, London SW15 3LE (☎ 01 788 6054); 7 Maiden Lane, London WC2E 7JS (☎ 01 836 4571, fax 01 379 4561)

PUGH, Richard Henry Crommelin; s of John James Edgar Pugh (d 1944), of Buxton, Derbyshire, and Charlotte Winifred Crommelin, *née* Sadler (d 1977); *b* 9 Sept 1927; *Educ* Buxton Coll, Univ of London (LLB); *m* 15 Aug 1953, Ann, da of Roy Waddington Swales (d 1979), of Fernilee, Derbyshire; 1 s (Stephen b 1958), 1 da (Helen b 1956); *Career* Nat Serv RAF 1947-49; CA, Grattan Warehouses Ltd 1951-56, chm home shopping div Great Universal Stores 1956-; govr and fell Worcester Coll of FE, chm Worcester Cathedral Appeal; memb Worshipful Co of Chartered Secretaries 1984, Freeman City of London 1984; FCA 1951, ACIS 1951, ACMA 1959; *Recreations* golf, swimming, motor cruising, genealogy; *Clubs* City Livery; *Style—* Richard Pugh, Esq; Elgar House, Worcester (☎ 0905 23411)

PUGH, Sheenagh Myfanwy; da of John Richard Pugh, of Swansea, and Moira Eveleen Sara, *née* Neil; *b* 20 Dec 1950; *Educ* Mundella GS Nottingham, Univ of Bristol (BA); *m* 17 Sept 1977, Michael John Hugh Burns, s of Daniel Burns (d 1980), of Chester-Le-Street; 1 s (Anthony b 1979), 1 da (Samantha b 1980); *Career* writer; awards: Br Comparative Literature Assoc Translation Prize 1986, Cardiff Int Poetry Competition 1988, Nat Poetry Competition (commended) 1987 and 1988; *Books* Crowded by Shadows (1977), What a Place to Grow Flowers (1979), Earth Studies and Other Voyages (1982), Prisoners of Transience (1985), Beware Falling Tortoises (1987); *Recreations* reading, playing pool, watching snooker; *Style—* Ms Sheenagh Pugh; Maengwyn, Bridge St, Lower St Clears, Dyfed SA33 4EN (☎ 0994 230945)

PUGH-COOK, Richard Gerald; s of Cdr George Garnet Pugh-Cook, OBE, RN (d 1969); *b* 15 Dec 1937; *Educ* Felsted; *m* 1963, Elizabeth Ann, da of Capt Michael William Allday; 2 s, 1 da; *Career* dir: Mid-Wales Yarns Ltd, Steeles Carpets Ltd; gp mktg dir Tomkinsons Carpets Ltd; *Recreations* tennis, cricket; *Style—* Richard Pugh-Cook, Esq; The Old Vicarage, Elmbridge, Droitwich, Worcs (☎ 029 923 214, office:

0562 820006, telex 337577, fax 0562 820030)

PUGSLEY, Sir Alfred Grenvile; OBE (1944); s of Herbert William Pugsley, of Wimbledon, and Marion, *née* Clifford; *b* 1903,May; *Educ* Rutlish Sch, Univ of London; *m* 1928, Kathleen Mary (d 1974), da of Laban Warner, of Aldershot; *Career* Royal Airships Works Cardington 1926-31, RAE Farnborough 1931-45, prof of civil engrg Bristol Univ 1944-68 (pro-vice-chllr 1961-64, emeritus prof); Hon DSc: Belfast 1965, Cranfield 1978; Hon DUniv Surrey 1968, Hon fell Bristol Univ; Structural Engrs Gold Medal 1968, Civil Engrs Ewing Gold Medal 1979; FRS 1952; hon: FRAeS 1963, FICE 1981; kt 1956; *Clubs* Athenaeum; *Style—* Sir Alfred Pugsley, OBE; 4 Harley Ct, Clifton Down, Bristol BS8 3JU (☎ 0272 739400)

PUGSLEY, Peter Vivian Rupert; s of Vivian Stanley Pugsley; *b* 2 Mar 1933; *Educ* Cranleigh; *m* 1971, Carolyn, da of Sidney Francis Morgann; 1 child; *Career* md Green Shield Trading Stamp Co Ltd; *Recreations* hockey, golf; *Clubs* MCC; *Style—* Peter Pugsley, Esq; Herons Hollow, North St, Westbourne, Emsworth, Hants PO10 85N (☎ 0243 377529)

PULESTON JONES, Haydn; s of Iago Oliver Puleston Jones (d 1971), and Elizabeth Ann, *née* Morris; *b* 16 Sept 1948; *Educ* Welshpool HS, Kings Coll London (LLB, AKC); *m* 9 June 1973, Susan Elizabeth, da of Lt Cdr George Karn (d 1970); 2 s (Simon b 1975, Nicholas b 1978); *Career* Linklaters & Paines 1971-79 (ptnr 1979-); memb: banking law sub- ctee City of London Law Soc 1980-, Montgomery Soc (ctee memb) 1974-; tstee Montgomeryshire Charitable Tsts 1983-; memb: Law Soc 1973, The City of London Slrs' Co 1980-; *Recreations* gardening, classical music, genealogy; *Style—* Haydn Puleston Jones, Esq; Ducks Farm, Dux Lane, Plaxtol, nr Sevenoaks, Kent TN15 ORB; Linklaters & Paines, Barrington House, 59/67 Gresham St, London EC2V 7JA (☎ 01 606 7080, fax 01 606 5113, telex 884349)

PULFER, Hon Mrs (Margaret Hilary Diana); *née* Brooke; da of Baron Brooke of Cumnor, CH, PC (Life Peer); *b* 1944; *m* 1971, James Douglas Pulfer; *Style—* The Hon Mrs Pulfer; c/o University of Swaziland, Swaziland

PULL, William; s of Stanley Herbert Pull, and Suzanne, *née* Birnie; *b* 5 May 1942; *Educ* Malvern, Oriel Coll Oxford (MA); *m* 1981, Andrea, da of Henry Michael Cairns-Terry; 2 s (Richard b 1983, Jonathan b 1985); *Career* Baring Bros & Co Ltd 1969-79, Harrisons & Crosfield plc 1979-87 (dir 1985-87), head of corporate fin Italian Int Bank 1988-; *Recreations* history, walking, paintings; *Clubs* Savile; *Style—* William Pull, Esq; 30 Poplar Grove, London W6 (☎ 01 602 7833)

PULLEN, Dr (Donald) Michael Philip; s of Arthur Philip Pullen, OBE (d 1967) and Isobel Hunter *née* Mann; *b* 23 Mar 1922; *Educ* Kings Sch Canterbury, Middx Hosp; *Career* jr appts Middx Hosp 1948-52, gen practice, surgn Cunard SS Co, admin med off Newcastle RHA, specialist community med, ret 1983; assoc with hospital planning and construction N Region; MRCS, LRCP; *Recreations* music, literature, cats, gardening; *Style—* Dr D M P Pullen; 6 Winston Way, New Ridley, Stocksfield, Northumberland NE43 7RF (☎ 0661 843486)

PULLEN, Sir (William) Reginald James; KCVO (1987, MVO 1966, CVO 1975), JP (Inner London); s of William Pullen (d 1964), of Falmouth, and Lily Rhoda Chinn; *b* 17 Feb 1922; *Educ* Falmouth GS, King's Coll London (LLB); *m* 1948, Doreen Angela, da of Tom Hebron, CBE, MVO; 2 da (Rosalind b 1951, Sandra b 1953); *Career* Fl Lt RAFVR (admin and special duties SE Asia); asst to chief accountant Westminster Abbey 1947 (receiver gen 1959-87, chapter clerk 1963-87, dep registrar 1951-64, registrar 1964-84); memb Westminster City Cncl 1962-65; clerk to tstees of the Utd Westminster Almshouses Gp of Charities 1987-, tstee The Passage RC Pay Centre for Homeless People 1983-, jt hon tres cncl Christians and Jews 1988-; Dep High Bailiff Westminster 1987-; OStJ 1969, CStJ 1981, KStJ 1987; Freeman: City of London, Worshipful Co of Waxchandlers; Liveryman Worshipful Co of Fishmongers; FICSA; *Recreations* reading, walking, cooking; *Clubs* MCC, Royal Air Force; *Style—* Sir Reginald Pullen, KCVO, JP; 42 Rochester Row, London SW1P 1BU (☎ 01 828 3131)

PULLEN, Trevor Keith; s of Ronald Pullen, of Bexley, Kent, and Pamela Ann *née* Berry; *b* 22 Nov 1948; *Educ* Roan GS Greenwich, Lanchester Poly Coventry (BA); *m* 1, 13 Sept 1969 (m dis 1980), Glenise May; 1 s (Andrew b 1973), 1 da (Samantha b 1971); m 2, 31 March 1988, Pauline; *Career* Prudential Portfolio Mangrs: UK equity dir 1982, global securities dir 1988; investmt dir Prudential Holborn 1987, chm Barnard Enterprises 1987; *Recreations* golf, squash, skiing ; *Clubs* Addington GC; *Style—* Trevor Pullen, Esq; 9 Prince Consort Drive, Chislehurst, Kent (☎ 01 467 952); 142 Holborn Bars, London EC1N 2NH (☎ 01 936 0751, car tel 0860 527 092, telex 265082)

PULLEY, (Henry John) Campbell; s of William Laurie Pulley, of Shenfield, Essex, and Janet Fairley, *née* Jackson (d 1985); *b* 26 Oct 1939; *Educ* Lancing, Magdalene Coll Cambridge (MA); *m* 25 April 1964, Margaret Anne (Nan), da of Walter Roy Nieland (d 1962), of Hutton, Essex; 2 da (Nicola b 8 April 1965, Deborah b 3 Nov 1967); *Career* memb Lloyd's 1972-; dir Anderson Finch Villiers Ltd 1977-80, dir gp insur Minet Gp 1985-; former chm Hutton Mount Assoc, dir Hutton Mount Ltd; Freeman City of London 1961, Memb Ct Worshipful Co of Saddlers 1988 (Liveryman 1961); FCII 1975; *Style—* H J C Pulley, Esq; Bow End, 9 Bowhay, Hutton Mount, Brentwood, Essex CM13 2JX (☎ 0277 214 072), Minet House, 100 Leman St, London E1 8HG (☎ 01 481 0707, fax 01 488 9786, telex 8813901)

PULLEY, Brig (Harry) Christopher; CBE (1967), MC (1944); s of Maj Harry Cuthbert Pulley, OBE (d 1925), of Baghdad, Iraq, and Norah Kathleen Olive, *née* Cullin (d 1963); *b* 17 August 1914; *Educ* Wellington, RMC Sandhurst; *m* 28 May 1947, Betty Jean Fyers, da of Robert Phillip Martin (d 1953); 1 s (Christopher David b 1950, d 1962), 2 da (Alison Mary Jean b 1948, d 1950, Rosemary Jean b 1952); *Career* IA cmmnd 3 QAO Gurkha Rifles served NWF, India, Burma, Java and Malaya, Br Army 7 DEO Gurkha Rifles, served Malaya, Nepal as Cmd Br Gurkha L of C, Brig, (despatches twice); *Style—* Brig Christopher Pulley, CBE, MC; Meadow End, East Grimstead, Salibury, Wilts SP5 3RT (☎ 072 272 761)

PULLIN, Peter Charles; s of William John Pullin (d 1984), and Dorothy Hilda Pullin; *b* 3 May 1952; *Educ* Cheltenham GS; *m* 26 April 1980, Shane, da of Harold Heyes; *Career* Marcus Hazlewood and Co Certified Accountants 1970-76, asst mangr Chelsea Bldg Soc 1976-80 (accountant 1980-81), treasy accountant TSB Tst Co Ltd 1981-84; tres: Derbyshire Bldg Soc 1984-86, Cheltenham and Gloucester Bldg Soc 1986-; FCCA 1975, MCT 1987; *Recreations* golf, photography; *Style—* Peter Pullin, Esq; Cranlea, Malleson Rd, Gotherington, Cheltenham, Glos (☎ 0242 67 6322); Cheltenham and Gloucester Bldg Soc, Cheltenham House, Clarence St, Cheltenham, Glos GL50 3JR (☎ 0242 36161)

PULLINGER, Sir (Francis) Alan; CBE (1970), DL (Herts 1982); s of William Pullinger; *b* 22 May 1913; *Educ* Marlborough, Balliol Coll Oxford; *m* 1, 1946, Felicity Charmian Gotch Hobson (decd); 2 s, 1 da; m 2, 1966, Jacqueline Louise Anne Durin; *Career* chm Haden Carrier Ltd 1961-79, pres Inst of Heating and Ventilating Engrs 1972-73; Hhn FCIBS 1977; vice-chm cncl of Benenden Sch; chm Herts Scout Cncl; kt 1977; *Recreations* mountaineering, sailing, beagling; *Clubs* Alpine, Travellers'; *Style—* Sir Alan Pullinger, CBE, DL; Barnhorn, Meadway, Berkhamsted, Herts (☎ 04427 3206)

PULLINGER, Anthony Giles Broadbent; s of Sir Alan Pullinger, CBE, *qv*, of Barnhorn, Meadway, Berkhamstead, Herts, and Felicity Charmian Gotch, *née* Hobson (d 1964); *b* 24 May 1955; *Educ* Dragon Sch, Marlborough, Balliol Coll Oxford; *m* 2 Oct 1982, Henrietta Mary, da of Maj Richard Conyngham Corfield, of Hill Cottage, Radway, Warwicks; 1 s (Jack b 1985), 1 da (Rosanna b 1988); *Career* stockbroker Laing & Cruickshank 1978-, seconded to the take-over panel 1982-84, ptnr Laing & Cruickshank 1984-, dir Alexanders Laing & Cruickshank 1985-; Freeman: City of London 1986, Worshipful Co of Grocers 1986; *Recreations* fishing, shooting, walking, music, travel, natural history; *Style—* Anthony Pullinger, Esq; 3 Thurleigh Ave, London SW1Z 8AN (☎ 01 673 3724); Alexanders Laing & Cruickshank, Piercy House, 7 Copthall Ave, London EC24 7BE (☎ 01 588 2800, fax 01 256 9545)

PULLMAN, Bruce John; s of Bernard John Pullman, of Brockenhurst, Hants, and Dorothy Jean, *née* Hayes; *b* 4 April 1957; *Educ* Canford, Merton Coll Oxford (BA); *m* 14 July 1979, Joanna Alexis Hamilton, da of John Edward Hamilton Davies, of Whitby, N Yorks; 2 da (Rebecca b 1984, Abigail b 1985); *Career* NM Rothschild & Sons Ltd 1979-81, dir County NatWest Investmt Mgmnt (CNIM) 1987- (joined 1981-, responsible for quantitave investmt res); *Books* contrib Portfolio Insur (ed Donald L Luskin 1988); *Recreations* Baptist Church; *Style—* Bruce Pullman, Esq; County Natwest Investment Management Ltd, Fenchurch Exchange, 43/44 Crutched Friars, London EC3N 2NX (☎ 01 374 3000, fax 01 373 3277)

PULVERMACHER, (Francis) Michael; s of Francis Howard Pulvermacher (d 1978), of Pentyrch, Glamorgan, and Marjorie Constance Denman, *née* Wheatley; *b* 26 June 1938; *Educ* Framlingham, Univ of London (LLB, LLM); *m* 17 Sept 1966, Diana, da of Lt-Col James William Randall Penrose (d 1966), of Shernal Green, Droitwich, Worcs; 1 s (Francis b 1975), 3 da (Joanna b 1968, Isobel b 1969, Helen b 1971); *Career* notary public 1961, slr 1961, ptnr Alms and Young 1968-; hon sec Law Soc 1971-84, lectr Notaries Soc 1983-; memb: Scout Assoc, Lord Chllrs Legal Aid Advsy Ctee 1986-; pres Assoc of SW Law Socs 1977-78, tstee St James Pool Taunton Charity; memb Law Soc 1961; *Recreations* hill walking, sailing, beekeeping, campanology; *Style—* Michael Pulvermacher, Esq; Causeway Cottages, West Buckland, Wellington, Somerset

PUMPHREY, Christopher Jonathan; TD; s of Col Jonathan Moberly Pumphrey, OBE, TD, DL, and Violet Frances, *née* Bosanquet (d 1984); *b* 2 Nov 1933; *Educ* Winchester, Magdalene Coll Cambridge (MA); *m* 1960, Joanna Jane, da of (Frederic) Howard Aykroyd (d 1978), of The Lodge, Kirkby Overblow, nr Harrogate; 2 s (Edward b 1963, Andrew b 1965), 1 da (Sara Rose (Mrs Alexander) b 1962); *Career* chm Wise Speke & Co stockbrokers 1987- (ptnr 1960-87); *Clubs* Northern Counties (Newcastle-upon-Tyne), Leander; *Style—* Christopher Pumphrey, Esq, TD; Bolam West Houses, Middleton, Morpeth, Northumberland (☎ 066 181 232)

PUMPHREY, Sir (John) Laurence; KCMG (1973, CMG 1963); s of late Charles Ernest Pumphrey (d 1950), of W Bitchfield, Belsay, Northumberland, and Iris Mary, *née* Moberly-Bell (d 1968); *b* 22 July 1916; *Educ* Winchester, New Coll Oxford; *m* 1945, Jean, da of Sir Walter Riddell, 12 Bt, of Hepple, Morpeth, Northumberland; 4 s (Matthew b 1946, Charles b 1948, Jonathan b 1954, James b 1965), 1 da (Laura b 1951); *Career* served WWII, Lt Northumberland Hussars (POW 1941-45); joined Foreign Serv 1945, dep high cmmr Nairobi 1965-67, high cmmr Zambia 1967-71, ambass to Pakistan 1971-76, ret; *Recreations* walking, fishing; *Clubs* Royal Cwlth Soc; *Style—* Sir Laurence Pumphrey, KCMG; Caistron, Thropton, Morpeth, Northumberland NE65 7LG (☎ 0669 40244)

PUMPHREY, Capt (Edward) Nigel; DSC (1941), DSO (1942, bar 1942 and 1943); s of Charles Ernest Pumphrey (d 1950), and Iris Mary, *née* Bell (d 1966); *b* 27 July 1910; *Educ* RNC Dartmouth; *m* 5 June 1940, Frances Mary, da of late Maj Carleton Salked; 1 s (Michael b 1941), 1 da (Philipa b 1943); *Career* Naval Offr 1927-56 (Capt RN 1952-56), WWII served MTB and Destroyers; farmer 1956-77; *Recreations* golf, gardening, reading; *Style—* Capt Nigel Pumphrey, DSC, DSO; Greatham Mill, Liss, Hampshire (☎ 04207 219)

PUNCH, Michael Richard Talbot; s of James William Punch of Newnham, nr Daventry, Northants, and Madeline Mary Punch, MBE, *née* Talbot; *b* 22 May 1944; *Educ* Magdalen Coll Sch Brackley, Magdalen Coll Oxford (BA); *m* 7 June 1973, Johanna Catherine, da of Richard Patrick Lowe (d 1987); 1 s (Thomas Richard Talbot b 8 Jan 1981), 1 da (Lucy Alice Talbot b 30 Dec 1977); *Career* copywriter: Foote Cone & Belding, London Press Exchange, Grey Advertising 1965-73; dep creative dir: Lonsdale Crowther Osborn 1973-76, David Williams & Ketchum 1976-78; creative dir and dep md JR Foote Cone & Belding Hong Kong 1979-82, creative dir Nicklin Advertising 1983-; *Style—* Michael Punch, Esq; Nicklin Advertising Ltd, 56 Marsh Wall, London E14 (☎ 01 538 5521)

PURBECK, Luca G; s of Herbert Gutmann (d 1942, former dir of Dresdner Bank Berlin, and London stockbroker), and Daisy (d 1959), da of Maj Kurt von Frankenberg und Ludwigsdorf (d 1932); Mr Purbeck's (1) paternal gf Gutmann founded Dresdner Bank 1872; (2) maternal gggf Gen von Porbeck was ka at Talavera on Napoleon's side, whilst (3) maternal gggf Frankenberg fought under the Duke of Brunswick with Wellington in Spain and at Waterloo and was severely wounded; *b* 13 July 1914; *Educ* Realgymnasium Potsdam, Berlin Univ; *m* 1, 1954, Vera (d 1979), da of Arthur Doughty, of London (d 1961); 1 s (and 1 s decd); m 2, 1982, Monica Pelissier, da of Arthur Greey (d 1974), of Birmingham; *Career* Hambros Bank Ltd London 1936-37, dir Brieger & Co Ltd London 1938-39, news ed Associated Press of America (London) 1944-46, fndr md Mayborn Prods Ltd London and Dylon Int Ltd, pres Dylon-France Safco SA; dir: Dylon-Japan KK, Dylon-Nederland NV 1946-79, Mayborn Gp Ltd 1983-86 (non-exec vice-chm 1980-82); silver medallist Soc of Dyers and Colourists; paintings and sculpture accepted by Royal Acad; FInstM; *Publications* Selected Poems (1982), Ausgewaehlte Gedichte (1982); *Recreations* golf, painting, sculpting, writing; *Clubs* Wentworth, RAC, Directors'; *Style—* Luca Purbeck, Esq; 14 Langford Place, St Johns Wood, London NW8 (☎ 01 624 9492)

PURCELL, (John) Denis; s of John Poyntz Purcell (d 1963), of Midhurst, and Dorothy, *née* Branston (d 1968); *b* 7 Dec 1913; *Educ* Marlborough, Wadham Coll Oxford (MA); *m* 7 April 1951, Pauline Mary, da of Rev Hiram Craven (d 1962), of Painswick; 2 s (Rupert b 1959, Edmund b 1961); *Career* HAC 1938, cmmnd Shrops Yeo 1940, ADC Gen Off C-in-C Western Cmd 1941, G3 ALO England and Italy 1942-44, Maj DAAG Haifa and Jerusalem 1944-46; barr 1938, SE circuit, acting dep chm London QS 1962-63; Met stipendiary magistrate: Bow Street 1963, Clerkenwell Magistrates Ct 1963-86, ret; Liveryman Worshipful Co of Armourers and Braziers 1948; *Recreations* racing, gardening; *Style—* Denis Purcell, Esq; 1 Cheltenham Terr, London SW3 4RD (☎ 01 730 2896)

PURCELL, Robert Michael; CMG (1983); s of late Lt-Col Walter Purcell; *b* 22 Oct 1923; *Educ* Ampleforth; *m* 1965, Julia Evelyn, da of late Brig Edward Marsh-Kellett; 2 da; *Career* cnsllr and dep high cmmr Malta 1977-80, ambass to Somali Democratic Republic 1980-83, ret; KSG 1976; *Clubs* Naval and Military; *Style—* Robert Purcell, Esq, CMG; Lythe House, Selborne, Hants (☎ 042 050 231)

PURCELL, Roger Bernard Allan; s of Bernard George Purcell (d 1982), of Leatherhead, and Hazel Cecily, *née* Roseberry; *b* 27 April 1945; *Educ* Shrewsbury, Pembroke Coll Cambridge (MA); *Career* CA, Binder Hamlyn 1966-72, First Investors and Savers 1972-74, Save & Prosper Gp 1974-86; dir: County Securities 1986-87, Securities and Investmts Bd 1987-; FCA 1969; *Recreations* walking, jogging, bridge, golf; *Style—* Roger Purcell, Esq; 202 Old Brompton Rd, London SW5 (☎ 01 370 3028); 3 Royal Exchange Buildings, London EC3 (☎ 01 283 2474, fax 01 628 1227)

PURCHAS, Rt Hon Lord Justice; Sir Francis Brooks Purchas; PC (1982); s of late Capt Francis Purchas; *b* 19 June 1919; *Educ* Summerfields Sch Oxford, Marlborough, Trinity Coll Cambridge; *m* 1942, Patricia Mona Kathleen, *née* Milburn; 2 s (Robin, *qv*); *Career* barr Inner Temple 1948, QC 1965, bencher 1972; rec: Canterbury 1969-72, London SE circuit 1972-74; High Court judge (Family Div) 1974-82, presiding judge S Eastern circuit 1977-82, Lord Justice of Appeal 1982-; kt 1974; *Recreations* shooting, golf, fishing; *Clubs* Hawks (Cambridge); *Style—* The Rt Hon Lord Justice Purchas; Parkhurst House, nr Haslemere, Surrey GU27 3BY (☎ 0428 78280); 1 Temple Gdns, Temple, London EC4Y 9BB (☎ 01 353 5124)

PURCHAS, Robin Michael; QC (1987); s of Rt Hon Sir Francis Brooks Purchas, *qv*; *b* 12 June 1946; *Educ* Marlborough, Trinity Coll Cambridge (MA); *m* 3 Sept 1970, (Denise) Anne Kerr, da of Capt David Finlay, RN; 1 s (James Alexander Francis b 27 Sept 1973), 1 da (Charlotte Robin b 3 Nov 1975); *Career* barr Inner Temple 1968; *Recreations* tennis, skiing, sailing, opera, theatre, shooting; *Clubs* Queens, Lansdowne; *Style—* Robin M Purchas, QC; The Old Rectory, Ashen, Sudbury, Suffolk; 2 Harcourt Buildings, Temple, London EC4 (☎ 01 353 8415, fax 01 353 7622)

PURDEN, Roma Laurette (Laurie); MBE (1973); da of George Cecil Arnold Purden (d 1964), and Constance Mary Sheppard (d 1952); *b* 30 Sept 1928; *Educ* Harecroft Sch Tunbridge Wells; *m* 1957, John Keith Kotch (d 1979), s of Harold James Kotch, OBE (d 1962); 2 da (Emma, Sophie); *Career* fiction ed Homes Notes 1948-51 (asst ed 1951-52), asst ed Woman's Own 1952, sr asst ed Girl 1952-54; ed: Housewife 1954-57, Home 1957-62, House Beautiful 1963-65, Good Housekeeping 1965-73; ed-in-chief: Good Housekeeping and Womancraft 1973-77, Woman's Journal 1978- (Woman's Journal won Periodical Publishers Assoc Consumer Magazine of the Year award 1985), Woman & Home 1982-83; dir Brickfield Pubns Ltd 1978-80; Magazine Editor of the Year 1979 (Br Soc of Magazine Editors); *Style—* Laurie Purden, MBE; 174 Pavilion Road, London SW1 (☎ 01 730 4021); IPC Magazines, King's Reach Tower, Stamford Street, London SE1 9LS (☎ 01 261 6622, telex 915748 MAEDIVG)

PURDIE, Robert Anthony James; s of Red Anthony Watson Purdie, of Shearwater, Popes Lane, Colyford, Colyton, Devon, and Erica Margaret Gertrude Helen, *née* Roberts; *b* 15 April 1956; *Educ* Harrow, Seaford Coll, Univ Coll Cardiff (LLB); *m* 5 Feb 1983, Elisabeth Jean, da of Roy Maclean Calman (d 1976); *Career* barr Middle Temple 1979, practicing South Eastern circuit; churchwarden Parish of St Cross or Holywell with St Peter-in-the-East cum St John Baptist Oxford 1988; memb Family Law Bar Assoc; *Books* Matrimonial and Domestic Injunctions (jtly, second edn 1987), contrib to Atkins Encyclopedia of Court Forms, Husband and Wife (1985); *Recreations* fishing, collecting books and antiques; *Clubs* Lansdowne; *Style—* Robert Purdie, Esq; Cloisters, 1 Pump Court, Temple, London EC4Y 7AA (☎ 01 583 5123, fax 01 353 3383)

PURDON, Maj-Gen Corran William Brooke; CBE (1970), MC (1945), CPM (1982); s of Maj-Gen (William) Brooke Purdon, DSO, OBE, MC, and Dorothy Myrtle, *née* Coates; *b* 4 May 1921; *Educ* Rokeby Sch Wimbledon, Campbell Coll Belfast, RMC Sandhurst; *m* 28 July 1945, (Maureen) Patricia, da of Maj James Francis Petrie (d 1952); 2 s (Patrick b 1947, Timothy b 1949), 1 da (Angela b 1958) ; *Career* cmmnd Royal Ulster Rifles 1939, Army Commandos, France and Germany 1940-45 (wounded, MC), Palestine Emergency 1945-46, Egypt 1949-51, Malayan Emergency 1956-58, Cyprus Emergency 1958; CO 1 Bn Royal Ulster Rifles, BAOR and Borneo War 1962-65, GSO1 and chief instr Sch of Inf Warminster 1965-67, Cdr Sultan's Armed Forces Sultanate of Oman and Dir of Ops Dhofar War 1967-70, Cmdt Sch of Inf Warminster 1970-72; GOC: NW Dist 1972-74, Near East Land Forces 1974-76, ret as Maj-Gen; dep cmmr Royal Hong Kong Police 1978-81; dir Falconstar Ltd (Mil Trg Teams) 1983-85, dir Def Systems Ltd 1985-; govr Royal Humane Soc 1984-, Hon Col Queen's Univ Belfast OTC 1975-78, pres Army Gymnastic Union 1973-76, patron Small Arms Sch Corps Old Comrade Assoc 1985-; cncl memb St John Ambulance Bde Wiltshire 1981-86; Hon Col D Co (London Irish Rifles) 4 (V) Bn Royal Irish Rangers 1986-; KStJ 1983; MBIM; Bravery Medal (Oman) 1968, Distinguished Service Medal (Oman) 1969; *Recreations* physical fitness, running, swimming, military biographies, reviewing military books; *Clubs* Army and Navy, Hong Kong; *Style—* Maj General Corran Purdon, CBE, MC, CPM; Old Park House, Devizes, Wiltshire SN10 5JR (☎ 0380 4876); Defense Systems Ltd, Bank House, 247 Cromwell Rd, Lonodn SW5 0WB; Titan International Gp, 5 Arlington St, St James's, London SW1A 1RA (☎ 01 493 5212, telex 21330 TITAN G)

PURDY, (Robert) John; CMG (1963), OBE (1954); s of late Lt-Col Thomas Woods Purdy (d 1961), of Woodgate House, Aylsham, Norfolk, and Nona Isabel, *née* Hunt (d 1958); *b* 2 Mar 1916; *Educ* Haileybury, Jesus Coll Cambridge (BA); *m* 1957, Elizabeth, da of Richard Matthew Sharp (d 1975); 2 s (Robert, Andrew), 1 da (Susanna); *Career* served 3 and 4 Burma campaigns 1943-45, Maj; Colonial Admin Serv N Nigeria 1939; sr resident: Adamawa Province 1957-59, Plateau Province 1959-61, Sokoto Province 1961-63, ret; bursar Gresham's Sch Holt 1965-81; *Recreations* shooting, fishing, gardening; *Clubs* Hawks (Cambridge); *Style—* John Purdy, Esq, CMG, OBE; Spratt's Green House, Aylsham, Norwich NR11 6TX (☎ 0263 732147)

PUREFOY, Geoffrey; GSM Malay (1949); s of Rev Canon Brian Purefoy (d 1963), and Mary Lillias Geraldine Purefoy; family connected with Shalstone Manor since 1400 AD, see Purefoy Letters, Eland Sidgwick and Jackson 1931; *b* 3 Mar 1929; *Educ* Rugby, Coole Hoteliere, Lausanne; *m* 1, 28 April 1956, Marcia Lamond; m 2, 1 March 1984, Wendy Allison; 2 da (Caroline Mews, Alison Bryony), 1 s (Simon Henry); *Career* farmer, vice chm Nat Sheep Assoc 1973-76; memb Ct of Assts Worshipful Co of Clothworkers; *Style—* Geoffrey Purefoy, Esq; Shalstone Manor, Buckingham MK18 5LT (☎ 0280 704854)

PURNELL, Kenneth Benjamin; CBE (1970); s of Sidney Harold Purnell (d 1934), of Birmingham, and Edith, *née* Bevan (d 1962); *b* 21 August 1923; *Educ* Blue Coat Sch Birmingham, Commercial Coll Birmingham; *m* Beryl, da of W Bradburn (d 1942); 2 s (Andrew b 1962, Trevor b 1962), 1 da (Jacqueline b 1964); *Career* memb Lloyds; chm: KBP Hldgs Ltd 1962-86, Rentcroft Investmts Ltd 1964-, Peter Reeves Co Ltd 1970-; dir: Nationwide Rental Gp plc 1986, Westmead Ltd 1986-, Birmingham Midland Investments, Merchant Bankers 1964-72, Birmingham Freehold Investmts Ltd 1964-72; Birmingham Leasehold Investmts Ltd 1964-72; chm dvpt ctee Birmingham Assoc of Youth Clubs 1963-66 (memb exec cncl 1963-72), vice-pres Br Olympic Assoc 1965; pres: W Midlands Sports Cncl 1965-72, Birmingham Radio Cncl 1972-74, Birmingham Sporting Club 1965-80, vice-pres Cwlth Games Ctee Scotland 1970, pres Birmingham Engrg & Building Centre 1971-82; ldr Trade Missions to: Far East 1974 (1979 and 1982), America 1976, S America 1977, Zimbabwe, S Africa and Kenya 1980; cncl memb Birmingham Chamber of Industry & Commerce 1971-83; vice-chm Variety Club of GB, memb Midland Region Ctee 1971-75 (chm Appeals Ctee 1977-79, sec 1980-86), dir Sports Aid Fndn 1977, chm W Midlands Regnl Sports Cncl 1977-80; dir Malvern Festival 1978, govr The Birmingham Blue Coat Sch 1971, pres Haematology Unit E Birmingham Hosp 1979-84; Liveryman Worshipful Co of Patternmakers, Freeman City of London; *Recreations* all sports; *Clubs* Reform, RAC, Lloyds; *Style—* Kenneth Purnell, CBE; 54 Somerset Road, Edgbaston, Birmingham B15 2PD

PURSEGLOVE, Prof John William; CMG (1973); s of late Robert Purseglove; *b* 11 August 1912; *Educ* Lady Manners Sch Bakewell, Univ of Manchester, Gonville and Caius Coll Cambridge, Imperial Coll of Tropical Agric Trinidad; *m* 1947, Phyllis Agnes Adèle, da of late George Turner, of Falkland Islands; 1 s, 1 da; *Career* tropical crops specialist Overseas Dvpt Admin E Malling Research Station Kent 1967-75; FLS 1944, FIBiol 1970; *Books* Tobacco in Uganda (1951), Tropical Crops and Dicotyledons (2 vols, 1968), Monocotyledon (2 vols, 1972), Spices (1981); Japanese Editio (1986); *Recreations* natural history; *Style—* Prof John Purseglove, CMG; Walnut Trees, Sissinghurst, Cranbrook, Kent TN17 2JL (☎ Cranbrook 712836)

PURSER, George Robert Gavin; s of Dr Joseph Alexander Purser (d 1968), of Charlwood, Surrey, and Constance Katherine, *née* Back; *b* 31 May 1936; *Educ* Lancing; *m* 4 June 1966, Mary-Ruth, da of Harold Lowe, of Charlwood Surrey; 2 da (Harriet b 1968, Philippa b 1969); *Career* Lt served Cyprus; sr ptnr Lawrence Graham slrs; dir: Woodward Schs (S Div) Ltd, Woodward Corpn; *Recreations* tennis, golf, shooting, gardening; *Clubs* Athenaeum; *Style—* G R G Purser, Esq; Telvet Cottage, Dolby Green, Ifield Rd, Charlwood, Surrey; Lawrence Graham, 190 Strand, London WC2R 1JN (☎ 01 379 0000, fax 01 379 6854, telex 22673)

PURSER, Simon Edmund Kinross; s of Lt Edmund Kinross Purser, RN (ret), of Exeter Devon, and Pamela Mary, *née* Scanes; *b* 21 Feb 1947; *Educ* Sherborne; *Career* audit supervisor Cooper Bros 1971-73, exec Old Broad St Securities 1973-75, dir County NatWest Ltd 1975-; tstee the John McCarthy Fndn; FCA 1970; *Recreations* sailing, squash, skiing, flying; *Style—* Simon Purser, Esq; 10 Belvedere Drive, Wimbledon, London SW19 (☎ 01 947 4224); 16 Monmouth Hill Topsham Devon; County NatWest Ltd, Drapers Gardens, 12 Throgmorton Ave, London EC2 (☎ 01 826 8245, fax 01 638 660)

PURSSELL, Anthony John Richard; *b* 5 July 1926; *Educ* Oriel Coll Oxford; *m* 1952, Ann Margaret Batchelor; 2 s, 1 da; *Career* jt vice chm Arthur Guinness Son & Co Ltd 1981-83 (md 1975-81), regnl dir Lloyds Bank (S Midlands bd) 1981-; hon tres Oxfam 1987-; memb: IBA 1976-81, bd CAA 1984-; *Clubs* Leander (Henley); *Style—* Anthony Purssell, Esq; Allendale, Bulstrode Way, Gerrards Cross, Bucks SL9 7QT

PURTON, Peter John; s of Arthur John Purton (d 1970), of Watford, Herts, and Olive May Purton; *b* 18 July 1933; *Educ* Aldwickbury Harpenden Herts, Aldenham Elstree Herts; *m* 6 Sept 1958, Mary, da of Lawrence Fone, of Chipperfield, Herts; 2 s (William b 1962, Thomas b 1965), 1 da (Catherine b 1960); *Career* 3 Regt RHA 2 Lt Germany 1951-53, 290 (City of London) Field Regt RATA, Capt UK 1953-60; admitted slr 1958, Norton Rose 1953- (ptnr 1961-); chm: Law Reform Ctee 1972-75, Planning and Devpt Law Ctee 1979-86; memb: Scott Ctee on Property Linked Unit Tsts 1973, Lord Chllrs Law Reform Ctee 1975-, American Bar Assoc, Cncl of the Law Soc of England and Wales 1969-86, Int Bar Assoc; hon tres Family Welfare Assoc 1979-83, (chm 1983-), vice chm bd of govrs Aldenham Sch 1983-; former Master Worshipful Co of Slrs 1983-84, Liveryman Worshipful Co of Tallow Chandlers 1983; FRSA, LMRTPI; *Books* The Organisation and Management of a Solicitors Practice (gen ed 1979); *Recreations* swimming, shooting, stalking, walking, heritage, jigsaw puzzles and family; *Clubs* Union Soc of Westminster; *Style—* Peter Purton, Esq; The Old Rectory, Dunton, nr Winslow, Bucks MK18 3LW (☎ 0525 240 228); Kempson House, Camomile Street, London EC3A 7AN (☎ 01-283 2434, fax 01-588 1181)

PURVES, Dame Daphne Helen; DBE (1979); da of Irvine Watson Cowie; *b* 8 Nov 1908; *Educ* Otago Girls' HS Dunedin NZ, Otago Univ; *m* 1939, Herbert Dudley Purves; 1 s, 2 da; *Career* sr lectr in French Dunedin Teachers Coll 1967-73, pres Int Fedn of Univ Women 1977-80, vice-pres for Women Global Co-operation Soc Club 1980; *Style—* Dame Daphne Purves, DBE; 12 Grendon Court, 36 Drivers Rd, Dunedin, New Zealand (☎ Dunedin 779 105)

PURVES, Elizabeth Mary (Libby); da of James Grant Purves, CMG (d 1984), of Suffolk, and Mary, *née* Tinsley; *b* 2 Feb 1950; *Educ* Sacred Heart Tunbridge Wells, St Annes Coll Oxford; *m* 1980, Paul Heiney, s of Norbert Wisniewski (d 1970), of Sheffield; 1 s (Nicholas b 1982), 1 da (Rose b 1984); *Career* journalist & broadcaster; former presenter BBC TV: Radio 4 Today, Midweek; radio documentaries incl Street Gospel, Holy Bones; *Books* Britain at Play (1982), Adventures Under Sail (1982), Sailing Weekend Book (with Paul Heiney, 1985), How Not To Be A Perfect Mother (1986), Where Did you Leave the Admiral? (1987); *Recreations* yachting, walking, cycling; *Clubs* Roy Thames YC, Ocean Cruising, Royal Cruising; *Style—* Ms Libby Purves; Pattles Farm, nr Saxmundham, Suffolk; c/o A P Watt, 26-28 Bedford Row, London WC1

PURVES, (Andrew) Geoffrey; s of Maj Andrew Purves (d 1967), of 9 Winchcombe Place, High Heaton, Newcastle upon Tyne, and Blanche, *née* Lawson; *b* 12 June 1944; *Educ* Heaton GS, Univ of Durham Univ (BA), Univ of Newcastle (BArch); *m* 12 Oct 1968, (Elizabeth) Ann, da of James Campbell Finlay, of 20 Lodore Rd, Newcastle upon Tyne; *Career* sr ptnr Geoffrey Purves and Ptnrs, chm: Northumbria branch RIBA 1981-83, Northern regn RIBA; dir: Newcastle Arch Workshop Ltd, Saunders and Purves Ltd, Power Factors Ltd, Purves Nixon Ltd, Geoffrey Purves and Ptnrs (project mgmnt) Ltd; RIBA, ARIAS, FRSA ; *Recreations* sailing; *Clubs* Royal Cwlth Soc, Clyde Cruising; *Style—* Geoffrey Purves, Esq; Hawthorn House, Kirkwhelpington, Northumberland NE19 2RT (☎ (0830 40376); 8 North Terrace, Newcastle upon Tyne NE2 4AD (☎ 091 232 0424, fax 091 232 8131)

PURVES, William; CBE (1988), DSO (1951); s of Andrew Purves (d 1943), and Ida Purves; *b* 27 Dec 1931; *Educ* Kelso HS; *m* 1958 (m dis 1988), Diana Troutbeck, da of Nicholas Gosselin Pepp Richardson (d 1944); 2 s, 2 da; m 2, 9 Feb 1989, Rebecca Jane, *née* Lewellen; *Career* chm: The Hongkong and Shanghai Banking Corpn, The Br Bank of The Mid East; tres Univ of Hong Kong; Hon Doctor Stirling Univ; vice pres and fell Chartered Inst of Bankers, ACIB (Scotland); *Recreations* golf; *Clubs* Hong Kong, Royal Hong Kong Jockey, Royal Hong Kong GC, New (Edinburgh); *Style—* William Purves, Esq, CBE, DSO; The Hongkong and Shanghai Banking Corpn, PO Box 64, Hong Kong (☎ 5 8221122, telex 73201 HKBG HX)

PURVIS, Ian Whitelaw; MC (1945); s of Maj Murray Purvis (d 1971), and Hilda Whitelaw, *née* Hamilton (d 1981); *b* 26 Oct 1922; *Educ* Glenalmond Coll, Queens' Coll Cambridge (BA); *m* 6 June 1952, Winifred Margaret Anne, da of Charles Reginald Clapperton (d 1939); 1 s (Alan b 1953), 3 da (Lindsay b 1955, Lorna b 1956, Hilary b 1962); *Career* served WWII 6th Gurkha Rifles (A/Maj) India & Burma 1942-46; estate mangr and farmer 1950-83; *Recreations* hill walking, painting, archaeology, gardening; *Style—* Ian W Purvis, Esq; Tornaveen, Clachan, Tarbert, Argyll (☎ 088 04 646)

PURVIS, John Robert; s of Lt-Col Robert William Berry Purvis, MC; *b* 6 July 1938; *Educ* Cargilfield Barnton Edinburgh, Glenalmond Coll Perths, St Salvator's Coll, Univ of St Andrews; *m* 1962, Louise S Durham; 1 s, 2 da; *Career* md Gilmerton Mgmnt Servs Ltd 1973-, managing ptnr Purvis & Co 1986-, dir James River (UK) Hldgs Ltd 1988-; MEP (EDG) Mid Scotland and Fife 1979-84; memb IBA London (chm for Scotland) 1985-, chm SCUA econ employment and industry ctee 1986-, vice pres Scottish Cons & Unionist Assoc 1987-; *Clubs* Cavalry and Guards, Farmers', New (Edinburgh), Royal and Ancient (St Andrews); *Style—* John Purvis, Esq; Gilmerton, Dunino, St Andrews, Fife KY16 8NB (☎ 0334 73275)

PURVIS, Brig Richard Hopkins (Dick); CBE; s of Albert Hopkins Purvis (d 1968), and Mabel Hope, *née* Fendick (d 1931); *b* 16 Dec 1920; *Educ* Aldenham; *m* 2 Oct 1948, Jean, da of William Douglas Walker (d 1957); 2 s (Nicholas Hopkins b 1952, Paul Richard b 1956); *Career* memb HAC 1938-40, cmmnd Royal Regt of Artillery 1940, Royal Artillery Pilot Air Observation Post Sqdn RAF 1942-44, graduate ME Staff Coll 1945, Royal Naval Staff Coll 1957; CO 1963-65, Cmdt Sch of Artillery Manorbier 1969-70, def sales orgns MOD 1970-75; fndr Def Mfrs Assoc of GB 1976, (dir gen 1976-87, life vice pres 1987); Freeman City of London 1947, Liveryman Worshipful Co of Painters and Stainers 1947-88; MInstD, RUSI; *Clubs* Army & Navy; *Style—* Brig Dick Purvis, CBE; The Defence Manufacturers Assoc, Pk House, Shalford, Guildford, Surrey GU4 8DW

PURVIS, Stewart Peter; s of Peter Purvis, and Lydia, *née* Stewart; *b* 28 Oct 1947; *Educ* Dulwich, Univ of Exeter (BA); *m* 2 Sept 1972, Mary, da of Arthur Presnail; 1 da (Helen b 1974); *Career* dep ed ITN 1986- (joined 1972, prog ed News at Ten 1980, ed Channel Four News 1983, dep ed ITN 1983), prof 2 exclusive documentaries about Prince and Princess of Wales; winner: of two Royal TV Soc awards, Broadcasting Press Guild Award for Best News or Current Events Prog (Channel Four News), BAFTA award for Best News or Outside Broadcast (Channel Four News) 1987 and 1988; *Style—* Stewart Purvis, Esq; ITN, 48 Wells St, London W1 (☎ 01 637 2424, fax 01 636 0349, telex 22101)

PUSINELLI, (Frederick) Nigel Molière; CMG (1966), OBE (1963, MC 1940); s of Siegfried Jacques Pusinelli (d 1963), and Theresa May Pusinelli (d 1981); *b* 28 April 1919; *Educ* Aldenham Sch, Pembroke Coll Cambridge (BA); *m* 1941, Joan Mary Chaloner, da of Cuthbert Bede Smith (d 1963); 1 s, 1 da; *Career* served RA 1939-45, Maj BEF 1940, India and Burma 1942-45; Colonial Admin Serv 1946-68, dist cmmr Gilbert and Ellice Islands Colony 1946-57, dir of establishments and asst high cmmr Aden and S Arabia 1963-68, ret; chm Chichester Harbour Conservancy, RYA Southern Region, Overseas Services Pensioners' Assoc; *Recreations* dinghy racing (Nosloa); *Clubs* Royal Cwlth Soc, Emsworth Sailing; *Style—* Nigel Pusinelli, Esq, CMG, OBE, MC; Routledge Cottage, Westbourne, Emsworth, Hants PO10 8SE (☎ 0243 372915)

PUTTERGILL, Graham Fraser; s of Henry William Puttergill (d 1984), of Gonubie, SA, and Elizabeth Blanche, *née* McClelland; *b* 20 Mar 1949; *Educ* St Patrick's Coll Port Elizabeth SA; *m* 7 Aug 1976, Susan Jennifer, da of Victor James Wilkinson, of Dorchester; 2 s (Miles b 1982, David b 1987), 1 da (Robyn b 1985); *Career* 1 Lt Capt Town Highlanders 1967-68; chm Antony Gibbs Pension Servs Ltd 1982- (md 1977-82), exec chm Gibbs Hartley Cooper Ltd 1985-, dir HSBC Hldgs UK Ltd 1986; ACII 1973, FPMI 1983; *Style—* Graham Puttergill, Esq; Kisdon, Puers Lane, Jordans, Bucks; Bishops Ct, Artillery Lane, London E1

PUTTICK, Richard George; s of George Frederick Puttick (d 1918), and Dorothea Puttick (d 1979); *b* 16 Mar 1916; *Educ* St Mark's Teddington; *m* 1943, Betty Grace, da of Herbert Folbigg (d 1967); 2 s; *Career* chm Taylor Woodrow plc 1974-85 (ch exec 1978-85); memb CBI Cncl 1967-69; govr London Business Sch 1977-85; Liveryman Worshipful Co of Joiners and Ceilers; CBIM, FCIOB; *Recreations* music, reading, gardening, supporting sports; *Clubs* Surrey County Cricket; *Style—* Richard Puttick Esq; Woodlawn, Hanger Hill, Weybridge, Surrey KT13 9XU

PUTTNAM, David Terence; CBE (1983); s of Capt Leonard Arthur Puttnam, RA (d 1981), of Winchmore Hill, and Marie Beatrice, *née* Goldman; *b* 25 Feb 1941; *Educ* Minchenden GS London; *m* 22 Sept 1961, Patricia Mary, da of John Frederick Jones, of Folkestone, Kent; 1 s (Alexander David b 5 April 1966), 1 da (Deborah Jane (Mrs Grossman) b 25 Jan 1962); *Career* film producer; dir: Br Film & TV Producers Assoc Ltd, Enigma Prodns Ltd, Hamuni Ltd, Nat Film & TV Sch Ltd, Anglia TV Gp plc; pres Cncl for Protection of Rural England 1985; Special Jury Prize for The Duellists Cannes 1977, two Academy Awards and four Br Academy Awards for Midnight Express 1978, four Acadamy Awards (incl Best Film) and three Br Academy Awards (incl Best Film) for Chariots of Fire 1981, three Academy Awards and eight Br Academy Awards for The Killing Fields 1985, Michael Balcon Award for outstanding contribution to the BFI, Br Academy Award 1982, Hon LLD Bristol 1983, Hon DLitt Leicester 1986; Chevalier des Arts et des Lettres (France) 1986; chm and chief exec offr Columbia Pictures 1986-87; special lectr in the department of drama (film studies), Univ of Bristol 1986; FRGS; *Books* The Third Age of Broadcasting (co-author, 1982), Rural England (co- author, 1988); *Recreations* fishing, reading, cinema, watching cricket ; *Clubs* MCC; *Style—* David Puttnam, Esq, CBE; Enigma Productions, 11 Queen's Gate Place Mews, London SW7 SBG (☎ 01 581 8238, fax 01 225 2230)

PUXLEY, James Christopher Lavallin; s of Capt William Lavallin Puxley, RN (d 1969), and Margaret Jessie Lavallin Puxley, *née* Burgess, of Dunboy Castle, Co Cork; *b* 24 Dec 1930; *Educ* Upper Canada Coll, RN Coll Dartmouth; *m* 1955, Alys Jean Marie, da of Dr Cyril Rickword Lane (d 1984); 1 s (Patrick), 1 da (Victoria); *Career* chm: County Bisgood Ltd, Bisgood Int Ltd, Bisgood Int Futures Ltd; dir: County Hldgs Ltd, County Bank Ltd; memb: Stock Exchange 1963, cncl of Stock Exchange, (Cncl's vice-chm membership ctees); vice-chm Cncl's Markets Ctee; *Recreations* animal husbandry; *Style—* James Puxley Esq; Charity Farm, Goring Heath, Oxon (☎ 0491 680331); County Bisgood & Co Ltd, Copthall House, 48 Copthall Avenue, London EC2R 7DN (☎ 01 628 3033)

PUXLEY, Maj John Philip Lavallin; TD (with two clasps); s of Rev H L Puxley (d 1950), of The Whitehouse, Chaddleworth, Newbury, Berks, and Dorothy Florence Mary, *née* Wroughton (d 1971); *b* 28 June 1915; *Educ* Eton, Brasenose Coll Oxford (BA); *m* 21 June 1947, Aline Carlos, da of Carlos Butler Wilson (d 1934), Of Welford Farmhouse, Newbury, Berks; 2 s (James Henry Lavallin b 1948, Charles John Lavallin b 1950); *Career* Berkshire Yeo 1939-60, WWII served India, Malaya and Java; slr of the Supreme Ct 1947; High Sheriff of Berkshire 1971 gen cmmr of Income Tax 1982-; pres Newbury Agric Soc 1969, life memb Royal Agric Soc of Eng; *Recreations* stamp collecting; *Style—* Maj John Puxley, TD; Llethr Llestry, Carmarthen, Dyfed (☎ 048 838 203); Welford Park Newbury, Berks

PYBUS, William Michael; s of Sydney James Pybus (d 1972), and Evelyn Mary, *née* Wood (d 1976); *b* 7 May 1923; *Educ* Bedford Sch, New Coll Oxford (MA); *m* 12 Sept 1959, Elizabeth Janet, da of Peter Percy Whitley (ka 1942); 2 s (Peter b 1961, Charles b 1965), 2 da (Sarah b 1962, Elizabeth b 1967); *Career* WWII cmmnd 1 King's Dragoon Gds 1942, attached II Hussars: Normandy (wounded), Egypt, Middle East; slr 1950; ptnr Herbert Oppenheimer Nathan & Vandyk 1953-88; chm: AAH Hldgs plc 1968-, Br Fuel Co 1968-88, Inter-Continental Fuels Ltd 1975-88, Overseas Coal Devpts Ltd 1979-88, Siebe plc (formerly Siebe Gorman Hldgs Ltd) 1980- (dir 1972-); dep chm R Mansell Ltd 1980-85; chm Br Rail (London Midland) 1977-89 (pt/t memb BR Midlands and West Bd 1975- 77); dir: NatWest Bank plc (Outer London Region) 1977-88, Cornhill Insur plc 1977-; dir Coal Trade Benevolent Assoc 1969-, pres Coal Indust Soc 1976-81; conslt Denton Hall Burgin & Warrens 1988-; Master Worshipful Co of Pattenmakers 1972-73, Liveryman Worshipful Co of Fuellers; CBIM, FInstM, FRSA; *Recreations* fishing; *Clubs* Cavalry and Guards', MCC, RAC, YCCC ; *Style—* William Pybus, Esq; 5 Chancery Lane, London WC2A 1LF (☎ 01 242 1212; fax, 01 831 0668; telex, 263567)

PYE, Prof (John) David; s of Wilfred Frank Pye (d 1972), of Mansfield, Notts, and Gwenllian, *née* Davies; *b* 14 May 1932; *Educ* Queen Elizabeths GS for Boys Mansfield, Univ Coll of Wales Aberystwth (BSc), Bedford Coll for Women London Univ (PhD); *m* 27 Dec 1958, Ade, da of August Kuku, of Valga, Estonia; *Career* Univ of London: res asst inst laryngology and otology 1958-64, lectr zoology King's Coll 1964-70, reader zoology King's Coll 1970-73, prof zoology Queen Mary Coll 1973-, head dept zoology and comparative physiology Queen Mary Coll 1977-82; fndr dir QMC Instruments Ltd 1976-, delivered the six televised Royal Inst Christmas Lectures 1985-86 and two Friday Evening Discourses 1979 and 1983, memb IEE professional gp ctee E15 (Radar, Sonar, Navigation and Avionics) 1983-86; ed boards Zoologic Soc 1985-(1972-77, 1978-83), Journal of Experimental Biology 1974-78, Journal of Comparative Physiology 1978-, Bioacoustics 1987-; Linnean Soc ed of the Zoological Journal 1981-85 (ed sec 1985-, vice-pres 1987-); memb: Zoological Soc 1957, Soc for Experimental Biology 1958, Assoc for Study of Animal Behaviour 1963, Mammal Soc 1964, Royal Hort Soc 1988; *Books* Bats (1968), Ultrasonic Communication by Animals (with G D Sales, 1974), Sound Reception in Mammals (ed with R J Bench and A Pye, 1975); *Recreations* brewing, baking, DIY, arts and travel; *Style—* Prof David Pye; 24 St Mary's Ave, Finchley, London N3 1SN (☎ 01 346 6869); Sch of Biological Sciences, Queen Mary Coll, Mile End Rd, London E1 4NS (☎ 01 980 4811 ext 4102)

PYE, (William) Roger; s of William Ernest Pye, (d 1985) of Staunton-on-Arrow, Hereford, and Daisy Grace, *née* Lewis; *b* 6 Dec 1938; *Educ* Hereford Cathedral Sch; *m* 28 Oct 1961, Barbara Ann Juanita, da of Arthur Edgar Wall (d 1988); 2 da (Nicola Susan b 26 Jan 1963, Dawn Louise b 21 June 1967); *Career* forestry conslt and nurseryman, md WE Pye (Forestry) Ltd 1985-88 (dir 1961-85); capt Kingston CC 1960; fndr: Silurians RFC 1961, Radnorshire Soc Field Res Section: (chm 1976-80, ed 1988); fndr memb and chm Woolhope Archaeological Field Section 1973, vice chm Gp II CBa 1980-83, liaison offr CBA Gp II, tstee Rankin Lecture Tst 1974-81 (sec 1976-81); memb Kingston Twinmart Assoc, chm Kingston Primary Sch PTA 1976; *Recreations* country pursuits, archaelogy, folklore; *Style—* Roger Pye, Esq; The Cressyn, Old Radnor, Presteign, Radnorshire (☎ 054421/634); Beech Grove Nursey, Rushock, Kington, Herefordshire (☎ 0544 231422)

PYM, Hon Andrew Leslie; yr s of Baron Pym (Life Peer), *qv*; *b* 30 Nov 1954; *m* 1976, Ruth, da of Peter Skelton; 1 s, 1 da; *Style—* The Hon Andrew Pym; c/o The Rt Hon Lord Pym, PC, MC, DL, Everton Park, Sandy, Beds SG19 2TE

PYM, Rt Hon Baron (Life Peer UK 1987), of Sandy, Co Beds; Francis Leslie Pym;; PC (1970), MC (1945), DL (Cambs 1973); Lord of the Manor of Sandy and Girtford, and patron of one living (Sandy); o s of late Leslie Ruthven Pym, JP, DL (d 1945), (sometime MP for Monmouth and Lord Cmmr of the Treasy), and Iris Rosalind (d 1982), da of Charles Somerville Orde; *b* 13 Feb 1922; *Educ* Eton, Magdalene Coll Cambridge (hon fell); *m* 25 June 1949, Valerie Fortune, er da of Francis John Heaton Daglish; 2 s (Hon (Francis) Jonathan, Hon Andrew Leslie, *qv*), 2 da (Hon Charlotte, see Hon Mrs Lightbody, Hon Sarah, see Hon Mrs Walton); *Career* served WW II, 9 Queen's Royal Lancers (despatches twice), Capt; former gen mangr Merseyside Dairies Ltd, then ran tent-making co in Hereford; memb Herefordshire CC 1958-62;

contested (C) Rhondda 1959, MP (C) Cambs 1961-83 and SE Cambs 1983-87; parly sec to the Treasy and govt chief whip 1970-73, sec of state NI 1973-74; oppn spokesman: agric 1974-76, House of Commons affrs and devolution 1976-78, for and cwlth affrs 1978-79, sec of state for Def 1979-81; chllr of the Duchy of Lancaster, paymaster gen and ldr House of Commons 1981, lord pres of the cncl and ldr of House of Comm'ns 1981-82, for sec 1982-83; pres Atlantic Treaty Assoc 1985-, chm English Speaking Union 1987-; *Books* The Politics of Consent (1984); *Clubs* Cavalry and Guards, Buck's; *Style*— The Rt Hon Lord Pym, PC, MP, DL; Everton Park, Sandy, Beds SG19 2DE (☎ 0767 87640)

PYM, Hon (Francis) Jonathan; er s of Baron Pym (Life Peer), *qv*; *b* 21 Sept 1952; *Educ* Eton, Magdalene Coll Camb (BA); *m* 20 June 1981, Laura Elizabeth Camille, yr da of Robin Alfred Wellesley, *qv*; 2 s (Matthew b 1984, Oliver b 1988), 1 da (Katie b 1985); *Career* ptnr Travers Smith Braithwaite (slrs) 1984-; memb: Law Soc, City of London Law Soc; *Recreations* gardening; *Clubs* Garrick; 53 Ridgway Place, London SW19 4SP (☎ 01 946 3583); 6 Snow Hill, London EC1A 2AL (☎ 01 248 9133; fax, 01 236 3728; telex, 887117 TRAVER-G)

PYMAN, Lancelot Frank Lee; CMG (1961); s of late Dr F L Pyman; *b* 8 August 1910; *Educ* Dover Coll, King's Coll Cambridge; *m* 1936, Sarah Woods Gamble; *Career* Levant Consular Serv 1933; HM consul-gen: Zagreb 1957-61, Basra 1961; ambass to the Somali Repub'1961-63, consul-gen San Francisco 1963-66; *Style*— Lancelot Pyman Esq, CMG; c/o National Westminster Bank, 66 Trafalgar Square, London WC2

PYTCHES, Rt Rev (George Edward) David; 6 s of Rev Thomas Arthur Pytches (d 1953), of The Little Grange, Woodbridge, Suffolk (see Burke's Landed Gentry 1937 edn), and Eirene Mildred, *née* Welldon (d 1947); *b* 9 Jan 1931; *Educ* Old Buckenham Hall Norfolk, Framlingham Coll Suffolk, Univ of Bristol (BA), Univ of Nottingham (MPhil), Trinity Coll Bristol; *m* 8 Jan 1958, Mary, da of Albert Trevisick (d 1984), of Highclere, Chestwood, Bishopstawton, N Devon; 4 da (Charlotte Mary (m Rev Dr Christopher John Cocksworth) b 24 Dec 1958, Deborah Jane (m Clifford John Wright) b 13 Dec 1961, Rebecca Anne (m Robert Hopper) b 10 July 1963, Natasha Clare (m Michael Shaw) b 18 Feb 1965); *Career* ordained: deacon 1955, priest 1956; asst curate: St Ebbe's Oxford 1955-58, Holy Trinity Wallington 1958-59; missionary priest: Chol Chol Chile 1959-62, Valparaiso Chile 1962-68 (rural dean 1966-70); asst bishop Diocese of Chile Bolivia and Peru 1972-77, vicar St Andrew's Chorleywood 1977; *Books* Come Holy Spirit (1985); *Recreations* travel, pottering about, collecting semi-precious stones; *Style*— The Rt Rev David Pytches; The Vicarage, Quickley Lane, Chorleywood, Herts WD3 5AE (☎ 092 78 2391)

PYTEL, Walenty; s of Wladislaw Pytel, of Bath, and Jadwiga Pytel Lives; *b* 10 Feb 1941; *Educ* Leominster, Minster Sch, Hereford Coll of Art; *m* 7 Oct 1963, Janet Mary, da of William Sidney Spencer (d 1973), of Westington Court; 1 s (Jeremy Walenty Spencer b 1964), 1 da (Victoria Catharine Mary b 1968); *Career* sculptor, works in steel, bronze, bone china; works incl: sculpture cmmnd by MPs to commemorate Queens Silver Jubilee 1977 (New Palace Yard Westminster), Take Off Birmingham Int Airport 1985, Unicorn HRH Princess Anne's to the Portuguese Govt 1979, Mural Lord Montague Beaulieu 1972, Chanel Perfume Paris 1975, Le Perroquet Berkeley Hotel London 1973; exhibitions: New Jersey 1987, San Diego 1987, Tokyo 1987, Marbella 1985; *Recreations* salmon fishing, game shooting, sailing; *Style*— Walenty Pytel, Esq; Terrace Hall, Woolhope, Hereford HR1 4QJ (☎ 043277 373)

Q

QUAGLIA, Pietro Giovanni Battista; s of Giovanni Quaglia (d 1966), of Turin, Italy, and Margherita Garelli Quaglia (d 1985); *b* 30 Nov 1937; *Educ* Turin Business Mgmnt Sch, Int Univ of Social Studies Turin; *m* 1964, Maria, da of Cav Antonio Troso, of Pescara; 2 da (Gianna b 1968, Silvana b 1969); *Career* md Fiat Auto (UK) Ltd, dir Fiat Fin Ltd; formerly: vice pres Fiat USA Inc, dir Hesston Corpn, chm and md Fiat Aust Pty Ltd, pres Italian C of C (Sydney Aust); FInstD; Kt of Order of Italian Repub 1987; *Recreations* riding, tennis, fencing; *Clubs* Guards Polo; *Style*— Pietro Quaglia Esq ; 63A Princes Gate, Exhibition Rd, London SW7; Fiat Auto (UK) Ltd, Bakers Ct, Bakers Rd, Uxbridge, Middx UB8 1RG (☎ 0895 51212, telex 261719)

QUAILE, Peter; s of Charles Thompson Quaile (d 1958), of Birkenhead, Cheshire, and Elsie May, *née* Crickmore (d 1958); Manx family, Sir William Quaile Lord Mayor of Dublin 1700, s-in-law Sir James Sumerville 1 Bt, Lord Mayor of Dublin 1736, Mark Hildesley Quaile of Castletown was elected memb of House of Keys 1842; *b* 4 Mar 1927; *Educ* Birkenhead Sch; *m* 3 Nov 1951, Eileen Elizabeth Olive, da of Aubrey Alford Gifford Toone (d 1963), of Bowden, Cheshire; 2 s (Andrew b 1954, Michael b 1958), 2 da (Helen b 1957, Penelope b 1960); *Career* Alliance of Liverpool & Manchester: asst underwriter 1948, marine rep 1951, underwriter 1959; mangr and underwriter Sea Elders of Liverpool 1971 (dep mangr 1967), dep chief gen mangr of Sun Alliance Insur Gp 1984 (asst gen mangr 1975, gen mangr 1979), chm DAS Legal Expenses Insur Co Ltd 1985; dir: London and Co Glazing Co Ltd 1985, Fire Protection Assoc 1985, Br Aviation Insur Co Ltd 1987, Sun Insur Co (Bermuda) Ltd 1987, Sun Insur Co (NY) 1987, McGee (New York) 1987, Alliance Assur Co Ltd 1980, Sun Alliance and London Insur plc 1980, Phoenix Assur plc, Sun Alliance and London Assur Co Ltd 1980, Sun Insur Off Ltd 1980, The London Insur 1980; JP (Surrey); FCII; *Recreations* shooting, fishing, rugby; *Style*— Peter Quaile, Esq; Springfold, Lawbrook Lane, Peaslake, Guildford, Surrey GU5 9QW (☎ 048 681 2501); Sun Alliance Insurance Gp, 1 Bartholomew Lane, London EC2N 2AB (☎ 01 588 2345, fax 638 3728 1103, telex 888310-G, car ☎ 0860 314 503)

QUAILE, Capt Roger Thompson; TEM (1950); s of Charles Thompson Quaile (d 1958), of Birkenhead, and Elsie May, *née* Crickmore (d 1958); *b* 6 Oct 1920; *Educ* Birkenhead Sch, Park High Sch Birkenhead; *m* 31 May 1952, Patricia Elizabeth, da of Robert Beck Jones (d 1952); 2 s (Jonathan Robert Charles b 1958, William Roger b 1964), 1 da (Elizabeth Mary b 1953); *Career* TA 1939, RA 1939, cmmnd 2 LT 1941, 1 Lt 8 Army Western Desert 1942-43, 2 Bn King's (Liverpool) Regt Italy and Greece 1944-46 (Capt 1945-46 Raiding Support Regt Land Forces Adriatic 1944); md WT Oversy and Co Ltd 1963 (dir 1954-), dir Morice Tozer and Beck Ltd 1967, dep chm Morice Tozer and Beck Hldgs Ltd 1970, md Alexander Howden Insur Brokers Ltd 1976-78, underwriting memb Lloyds 1976, chm and dir various minor co's; pres Warlingham Rugby FC; FCII 1950, FInstD 1956, FCIB 1967, FCIArb 1971; *Recreations* shooting, rugby football administration, gardening; *Clubs* Gresham; *Style*— Capt Roger Quaile, TEM; Hillsborough, 8 Searchwood Rd, Warlingham, Surrey CR3 9BA (☎ 08832 2413)

QUANCE, Gordon William; s of Frederick William Quance (d 1984), and Alice May, *née* Holden; *b* 7 Mar 1931; *Educ* Queen Marys GS W Midlands, Univ of Birmingham (LLB, LLM); *m* 30 Aug 1962, Sylvia, da of John Bertram Grice (d 1969); *Career* admitted slr 1956, private practice 1956-; memb Law Soc; *Recreations* music, books; *Style*— Gordon Quance, Esq; Talbot House, Talbot Ave, Little Aston Park, Streetly, Staffordshire; 31 High St, West Bromwich, W Midlands (☎ 021 553 0314/2681)

QUANT, Air Cdre (John) Antony; s of John Henry Quant (d 1968), and Mildred Gwenllian, *née* Jones; *b* 19 Jan 1933; *Educ* Taunton Sch, Eltham Coll, Univ of London and Guy's Hosp (BDS, MB, BS); *m* 11 Feb 1956, Valerie Kathleen, da of Ernest James Goose (d 1970); 2 da (Sarah (Mrs Allen) b 1958, Amanda (Mrs Chandler) b 1961); *Career* Nat Serv RAF 1957, perm cmmn Dental Offr 1958, Prince Rupert Sch Wilhelmshaven 1958, RAF Sundern 1959, RAF Guterslah 1961, RAF Halton 1961, oral surgn PMRAF Hosp Halton 1962, RAF Hosp Nocton Hall 1962, registrar oral surgn RAF Hosp Cosford 1963, sr registrar TPH RAF Hosp Akrotiri 1965; med student Guy's Hosp 1966-70, house surgn Guy's Hosp 1971, house physician Willesborough Hosp Ashford Kent, sr registrar/conslt (oral surgery and med) RAF Hosp Wegberg 1972, conslt PM RAF Hosp Halton 1978, conslt advsr (oral surgery and md) RAF 1979-; memb (former sec and chm) Def Med Servs Post Grad Cncl Speciality Bd in Oral Surgery and Oral Med, dental advsr RAF Aviation Forensic Pathology Team, chm RAF LTA 1985-88; C St J 1987; FDSRS 1963, MRCS 1970, LRCP 1970, fell BAOMS, memb Oral Surgery Club of GB; *Recreations* tennis, shooting, bridge; *Clubs* RAF; *Style*— Air Cdre Antony Quant; Witsend, Clay Lane, Wendover, Bucks HP22 6NS (☎ 0296 624714); Marina del Sol, Mijas Costa, Espagne; Princess Mary's Royal Air Force Hospital, Halton, Nr Aylesbury, Bucks HP22 5PS (☎ 0296 623535 ext 759); The Paddocks Private Hosp, Princes Risborough, Bucks HP17 0JS (☎ 08444 6951)

QUANT, Mary (Mrs A Plunket Greene); OBE (1966); da of Jack Quant and Mildred Quant; *b* 11 Feb 1934; *Educ* Goldsmiths' Coll of Art; *m* 1957, Alexander Plunket Greene; 1 s; *Career* fashion designer, dir Mary Quant Gp of Cos 1955-, memb Design Cncl 1971, Br and USA Bicentennial Liaison Ctee 1973, adv cncl V and A Museum 1976-78; Maison Blanche Rex Award 1964, Sunday Times Int Award 1964, Piavola d'Oro Award 1966, Annual Design Medal Inst of Industrial Artists and Designers 1966; FSIA 1967, RDI 1969; *Style*— Miss Mary Quant, OBE; 3 Ives St, London SW3 (☎ 01 584 8781)

QUANTRILL, Prof Malcolm William Francis; s of Arthur William Quantrill (d 1976), of Norwich, and Alice May, *née* Newstead (d 1979); *b* 25 May 1931; *Educ* City of Norwich Sch, Univ of Liverpool (BArch), Univ of Pennsylvania (MArch), Tech Univ of Wroclaw (DSc); *m* 1, (m dis 1965), Arja Irmeli Nenonen; m 2, 18 Dec 1971, Esther Maeve, da of James Brignell Dand (d 1983), of Chester; 2 s (Christopher b 1961, Jan b 1962), 2 da (Francesca b 1974, Alexandra b 1978); *Career* dir The Architectural Assoc London 1967-69, dean sch of architecture London Poly 1973-80, prof of architecture Univ of Jordan Amman 1980-83, distinguished prof of architecture Texas A & M Univ 1986-; dep ed Art International Lugano 1978-83, ed-in-chief The Cubit 1988-; fndr memb The Thomas Cubitt Tst London (tstee 1977, sec 1977-80), memb Rotary Int 1988; memb RIBA 1961; Cdr of the Order of Knights of the Finnish Lion 1988; *Books* Gotobed Dawn (1962), Gotobedlam (1964), John Gotobed Alone (1965), Ritual and Response in Architecture (1974), Monuments of Another Age (1976), On the Home Front (novel, 1977), Alvar Aalto: a critical study (1983), Reima Pietilä: architecture, context and modernism (1985), The Environmental Memory (1987), Reimě Pietilä: One Man's Odyssey in Search of Finnish Architecture (1988); *Recreations* photography, travel, tennis, broadcasting; *Clubs* Garrick; *Style*— Prof Malcolm Quantrill; College of Architecture, Texas A & M Univ, Texas 77843-3137 (☎ 409 845 7878, fax 409 845 4491)

QUARMBY, Arthur; s of Harold Quarmby (d 1981), of Lane House, Holmfirth, and Lucy May, *née* Barrow; *b* 18 Mar 1934; *Educ* Pocklington Sch, Leeds Sch of Architectural Town Planning (Dip Arch); *m* 13 Aug 1957, Jean Valerie, da of Herbert Mitchell, of Hebble Drive Holmfirth; 1 s (Jonathan Hugh, b 1961), 1 da (Rachel Jane b 1964); *Career* architect; plastics structures in Europe and the Antartica, worlds largest transparent inflated dome (for 20 Century Fox), assault craft for Rotork Marine, conslt on structural plastics, world authy on earth-sheltered architecture, architectural journalist; chief constable of the Graveship of Holme; memb; Huddersfield Choral Soc, Colne Valley Male Voice Choir, Holme Valley Choir; memb RIBA 1959, FRIBA 1985, FRSA; *Books* The Plastics Architect (1974); *Recreations* music, archeology, watersports, hill walking; *Clubs* Inigo Jones; *Style*— Arthur Quarmby, Esq; Underhill, Holme, W Yorks (☎ 0484 682372); 83 Fitzwilliam St, Huddersfield (☎ 0484 536553, fax 0484 514199 for AQP, 51458 COMHUD G for AGP)

QUARMBY, David Anthony; s of Frank Reginald Quarmby (d 1983); *b* 22 July 1941; *Educ* Shrewsbury, King's Coll Cambridge (MA), Univ of Leeds (PhD, Dip Industl Mgmnt); *m* 1968, Hilmary, da of Denis Hilton Hunter; 4 da; *Career* memb London Tport Exec 1975-84 (md LTE Buses 1978-84), dir J Sainsbury plc 1984- (jt md 1988)); FCIT, FIRTE, FILDM, FRSA; *Recreations* music, singing; *Style*— David Quarmby, Esq; 13 Shooters Hill Rd, Blackheath, London SE3 7AR (☎ 01 858 7371); J Sainsbury plc, Stamford St, London SE1 9LL (☎ 01 921 6000)

QUARREN EVANS, His Hon Judge; John Kerry; s of Hubert Royston Quarren Evans, MC (d 1967), and Violet Soule Quarren Evans; *b* 4 July 1926; *Educ* King Henry VIII Sch Coventry, Cardiff HS, Trinity Hall Cambridge (MA, LLM); *m* 1958, Jane Shaw, da of Neil Lawson (d 1985); 1 s, 1 da; *Career* Army 1944-48, Capt Royal Welch Fus; slr of Supreme Ct 1953; ptnr: Lyndon Moore & Co of Newport Gwent 1954-71, T S Edwards & Son 1971-80; rec Wales and Chester circuit 1974-80, a circuit judge S Eastern circuit 1980-; *Recreations* music, golf, rugby football, staurologosophy, oenology, old things; *Clubs* Denham Golf, Newport Golf, Royal Porthcawl Golf, Crawshays Welsh RFC; *Style*— His Honour Judge Quarren Evans; c/o Acton Crown Ct, Armstrong Rd, London W3 7BJ (☎ 01 740 8888)

QUAYLE, Anthony John; *b* 3 Mar 1946; *Educ* King's Coll London, Sloan Sch of Mgmnt (BSc), MIT (SM); *Career* appts in BR Engrg Ltd 1968-76, mfrg mangr Brush Electrical Machines Ltd 1976-79, md Alvis Ltd 1979- (a United Scientific Gp Co; mfr of armoured vehicles, Scorpion range best known; Queen's Award for Export 1982), dir United Scientific Holdings PLC 1981-; CEng, MIMechE; *Style*— Anthony Quayle, Esq; Alvis Ltd, Holyhead Rd, Coventry CV5 8JH, W Midlands (☎ 0203 595501, telex 31459); Miralago, Church Lane, Norton Lindsey, Warwick CV35 8JE (☎ Claverdon 092684 2842)

QUAYLE, Sir (John) Anthony; CBE (1952); s of Arthur Quayle and Esther, *née* Overton; *b* 7 Sept 1913; *Educ* Rugby; *m* 1947, Dorothy Hyson; 1 s, 2 da (of whom 1, Rosanna, m Richard Astley, ggs of Francis L'Estrange Astley, bro of 16 Baron Hastings; 2 s, 1 da); *Career* served WW II RA; actor 1931, dir Shakespeare Meml Theatre Stratford 1948-56, prodns incl King Lear (with John Gielgud); roles incl Antony (1950), Falstaff in Henry IV Parts I and II (1951), took Shakespeare Memorial Co to Australia (1949, 1953); other appearances incl: Tamburlaine NY (1956); Titus Andronicus, Eurotour (1957); West End appearances incl: View From the Bridge (1956), Long Day's Journey Into Night (1958), Incident at Vichy (1966), Sleuth (1970); dir: The Relapse, Tiger at the Gates (New York), The Rules of the Game; Hon DLitt Hull 1987; kt 1985; *Books* Eight Hours from England (1945), On Such a Night (1947); *Clubs* Special Forces; *Style*— Sir Anthony Quayle, CBE; 49b Elystan Place, London SW3 3JY

QUAYLE, Maj-Gen (Thomas) David Graham; s of Dr Thomas Quayle, CIE (d 1962), and Phyllis Gwendolen, *née* Johnson (d 1977); *b* 7 April 1936; *Educ* Repton, Trinity Coll Oxford (BA); *m* 2 Aug 1962, Susan Jean, da of Brig FWP Bradford, MBE (d 1977); 3 da (Lucy b 1963, Sophie b 1964, Emma b 1966); *Career* cmmnd RA 1958, served in Germany, Kenya, Aden and UK 1958-66, RMCS 1967, IA Staff Coll 1968, Staff HQ 1 Br corps 1969-70, cmdg The Chestnut Troop RHA 1971-72, Staff MOD 1972-74, instr Staff Coll Camberley 1974-76, cmdg 40 Field Regt (The Lowland Gunners) RA 1976-79, Royal Sch of Artillery 1979-81, Cdr artillery 4 Armd Div and Herford Garrison 1981-83, def Attaché Br Embassy Bonn 1983-86, Cdr Artillery 1 Br

Corps 1986-; *Recreations* shooting, fishing, racing, bridge, travel; *Style*— Maj-Gen David Quayle; HQ 1st British Corps, BFPO 39 (☎ 01049 521293 2243)

QUAYLE, John Douglas Stuart; s of Douglas Quayle (d 1957), of London, and Katherine, *née* Parke; *b* 21 Dec 1937; *Educ* Challoners St Albans, RADA; *m* 20 Oct 1966, Petronell Emily, da of Arthur Thomas Pickard (d 1972), of Torquay; *Career* Nat Serv RCS 1956-58, Cyprus and NI; Pitlochry Festival Theatre 1966; repertory: in Colchester, Salisbury, Richmond, Tours, London plays incl Donkeys Years and Habeas Corpus 1967-78; Nat Theatre player 1980-82, Noises Off Savoy Theatre 1983-85, Theatre of Comedy Ambassadors and Criterion 1986-88; various radio, tv and film performances; *Recreations* riding, shooting, walking; *Clubs* Garrick, Farmers; *Style*— John Quayle, Esq; C/o Barry Burnett, Suite 42/43, Grafton House, 2/3 Golden Sq, London W1

QUAYLE, Prof (John) Rodney; s of John Martin Quayle, and Mary Doris Quayle; *b* 18 Nov 1926; *Educ* Alun GS, UCNW Bangor (BSc, PhD), Univ of Cambridge (PhD); *m* 1951, Yvonne Mabel, da of Albert Sanderson; 1 s, 1 da; *Career* West Riding prof of microbiology Univ of Sheffield 1965- (sr lectr biochemistry 1963-65), vice-chllr Univ of Bath 1983-; FRS; *Style*— Prof Rodney Quayle; The Lodge, North Rd, Bath BA2 6HE; Bath Univ, Claverton Down, Bath, Avon BA2 7AY

QUEENSBERRY, 12 Marquess of (S 1682); Sir David Harrington Angus Douglas; 11 Bt (S 1668); also Viscount Drumlanrig, Lord Douglas of Hawick and Tibbers (both S 1628), and Earl of Queensberry (S 1633); s of 11 Marquess (d 1954), by his 2 w Cathleen, *née* Mann; *b* 19 Dec 1929; *Educ* Eton; *m* 1, 1956 (m dis 1969), Ann, da of Maurice Jones and formerly w of George Radford; 2 da; m 2, 1969, Alexandra, da of Guy Wyndham Sich; 2 s (Viscount Drumlanrig, Lord Milo b 1978), 1 da (Lady Kate b 1969); *Heir* s, Viscount Drumlanrig; *Career* late 2 Lt RHG; prof of ceramics RCA 1959-83; pres Design and Industs Assoc 1976-78; *Style*— Prof the Most Hon the Marquess of Queensbury; 24 Brook Mews North, London W2 3BW (☎ 01 724 3701, telex 24224 REF 750)

QUEENSBERRY, Mimi, Marchioness of; Muriel Beatrice Margaret Françoise; da of Arthur John Rowe-Thornett (d 1936), of Villa Ginetta, Monte Carlo, and Ella Margaret Teresa, *née* March (d 1961); *b* 5 April 1911; *Educ* Inst Massena Nice, Inst des Essarts Montreux Switzerland, Broomfield Hall Sunningdale; *m* 1, Albert Sydney Gore Chunn; 1 da (Yosky Rowena b 1931); m 2, 1947, as his 3 wife, Francis Archibald Keihead, 11 Marquess of Queensberry (d 1954), s of Percy Sholta Douglas, 10 Marquess of Queensberry; 1 s (Lord Gawain Douglas, *qv*); *Style*— The Most Hon Mimi, Marchioness of Queensberry; c/o Standard Chartered Bank (IOM) Ltd, 64 Athol St, Douglas, IOM

QUELCH, Basil Herbert; DFC (1945); s of Herbert James Quelch (d 1961), and Alice Quelch (d 1967); *b* 8 April 1919; *Educ* Southfield Sch Oxford; *m* 24 Aug 1940, Maureen Patricia, da of George Campbell Jones (d 1955); 1 s (Christopher b 1945), 1 da (Anne b 1952); *Career* Fl Lt RAF 1939-46, Europe (coastal cmd), Pilot Battle of Britain (fighter cmd), Germany BAFO dir Saccone & Speed Ltd Wine & Spirit Merchants 1970-74, md Arthur Cooper (Wine Merchants) Ltd 1970-73, mktg dir Courage Ltd 1973-79 (ret); dir: Harp Lager (sales) Ltd 1973-79, Taunton Cider Ltd 1975-79; *Recreations* sailing, civilian flying; *Style*— Basil Quelch, Esq; 114 Oaktree Rd, Tilehurst, Reading, Berks RG3 6JY (☎ 0734 428023)

QUENBY, John Richard; s of Richard Quenby (d 1942), of Bedford, and Margaret, *née* Wyse; *b* 30 Oct 1941; *Educ* Bedford Modern Sch, Open Univ (BA); *m* 9 April 1965, Sandra, da of Col Noel Frederick Charles King (d 1974), of Sydney, Aust; 2 da (Georgia Margaret b 1970, Fiona Elizabeth b 1971); *Career* dir Granada Computer Servs Ltd 1983-85, md Granada Overseas Hldgs Ltd 1985-, chm GL Distrib France 1986-; dir and chm: Granada France SA 1986-87, Telerent Italiana SPA 1986-87, Telerent Iberica 1986-87, Telerent Denmark 1986-87; dir Kapy SA Spain 1988-; *Recreations* rowing, photography; *Clubs* Bedford, Bedford Rowing; *Style*— John Quenby, Esq; 22 St Georges Rd, Bedford (☎ 0234 62192); PO Box 31, Ampthill Rd, Bedford (☎ 0234 328111, fax 0234 46350, car telephone 0836 617200)

QUENINGTON, Viscount; Michael Henry Hicks Beach; s and h of 2 Earl St Aldwyn, KBE, TD, PC; *b* 7 Feb 1950; *Educ* Eton, Univ of Oxford (MA); *m* 1982, Gilda Maria, o da of Barão Saavedra, of Rua Paula Freitas 104, Copacabana, Rio de Janeiro, Brazil; 2 da (Atalanta Maria b 1983, Aurora Ursula b 1988); *Career* commodity broker; *Clubs* Leander, Whites; *Style*— Viscount Quenington; Box 609, Bedford Hills, NY 10019, USA (☎ 914 241 1746); Farr Man & Co Inc, 2 World Trade Center 3050, New York, NY 10048

QUIBELL, Baroness; Catherine Cameron Rae; *m* 1954, as his 2 w, 1 Baron (d 1962, when title became extinct); *Career* pres Scunthorpe and Dist Spastic Soc; *Style*— The Rt Hon The Lady Quibell; 38 Exeter Rd, Scunthorpe, Lincs

QUICK, Anthony Oliver Hebert; s of Rev Prof Oliver Chase Quick (d 1944), of Christ Church, Oxford, and Frances Winifred, *née* Pearson; *b* 26 May 1924; *Educ* Shewsbury, SOAS London, Univ of Oxford (MA); *m* 20 Dec 1955, (Eva) Jean, da of Walter Carruthers Sellar (d 1951); 3 s (Oliver b 1959, James b 1962, Jonathan b 1968), 1 da (Ruth b 1957); *Career* RNVR 1943-46, Midshipman, Lt; asst master Charterhouse 1949-61; headmaster: Rendcomb Coll 1961-71, Bradfield Coll 1971-85; *Books* Britain 1714-1851 (1961), Britain 1851-1945 (1967), 20th Century Br (1968); *Style*— Anthony Quick, Esq; Corbin, Scorriton, Buckfastleigh, Devon TQ11 OHU (☎ 036 43 383)

QUICK, Brian; s of Stanley James Quick (d 1973); *b* 26 May 1933; *Educ* Devonport HS; *m* 1964, Anne Vivien, da of George Ernest Fowler; 1 s, 1 da; *Career* chm: Island Int Ltd, Island Pictures Inc, HSIS Int SA, Hill Samuel Personal Fin Ltd, Universal Credit Ltd; *Recreations* tennis, golf; *Style*— Brian Quick, Esq; 45 Beech St, London EC2P 2LX (☎ 01 628 8011, telex 888822); 2 Wheatfield Rd, Harpenden, Herts (☎ 0582 460425)

QUICKE, Sir John Godolphin; CBE (1978), DL (Devon 1985); s of Capt Noel Arthur Godolphin Quicke (d 1943), and Constance May Quicke; *b* 20 April 1922; *Educ* Eton, New Coll Oxford; *m* 1953, Prudence Tinné, da of Rear Adm Charles Pierre Berthon, CBE (d 1965); 3 s, 3 da; *Career* farmer and landowner; chm Miny of Agric SW regnl panel 1972-75, pres CLA 1975-77, memb SW regnl bd Natwest Bank 1973-, chm Exeter local bd Commercial Union Assur Co 1980-; memb: consultative bd Jt Consultative Orgn for R & D, Food & Agric 1980-84, Countryside Cmmn 1981-88, properties ctee Nat Tst 1984-; vice-chm N Devon Meat Ltd 1982-86; chm: Agric EDC, NEDO 1983-88, agric sector gp NEDO, RURAL (Soc for the Responsible Use of Resources in Agric and on the Land) 1983-, estates panel Nat Tst 1984-; RASE Bledisloe Gold Medal 1985; kt 1988; *Recreations* music, trees, travel; *Clubs* Boodle's; *Style*— Sir John Quicke, CBE, DL; Sherwood, Newton St Cyres, Exeter, Devon (☎ 039 2851 216)

QUIGLEY, Desmond Francis Conor; s of Dr Thomas Francis Quigley, and Eleanor, *née* Blachford; *b* 20 May 1947; *Educ* Downside, The Coll Swindon; *m* 6 Jan 1973, Johanna Mary, da of John Foley; *Career* Fin Times 1973-75, The Times 1975-79, Fin Weekly 1979-81, Grandfield Rork Collins Fin 1981-82, Streets Fin 1982-86, md Quigley & Assoc 1986-; *Style*— Desmond Quigley, Esq; 16-18 St Johns La, London EC1M 4BS (☎ 01 253 4242)

QUILLEY, Denis Clifford; s of Clifford Charles Quilley (d 1968), and Ada Winifred, *née* Stanley; *b* 26 Dec 1927; *Educ* Bancroft's Sch Woodford Essex; *m* 1949, Stella Jean, *née* Chapman; 1 s, 2 da; *Career* actor; first stage appearance Birmingham Rep Theatre 1945; Nat Theatre 1971-76; Privates on Parade Aldwych 1977 (SWET Award 1977), Piccadilly 1978, Morell in Candida Albery Theatre 1977, Deathtrap Garrick 1978, title role in Sondheim's Sweeney Todd Drury Lane (SWET Award) 1980, Molokov in Chess Barbican 1985, Antony in Antony and Cleopatra Chichester 1985; Fatal Attraction Haymarket 1985; La Cage aux Folles Palladium 1986; films incl: Murder on the Orient Express, Evil Under the Sun, Privates on Parade; TV plays and series incl: The Merchant of Venice, The Crucible, Masada, Anno Domini; *Recreations* playing the piano, flute and cello, walking; *Style*— Denis Quilley, Esq; c/o Bernard Hunter Associates, 13 Spencer Gdns London SW14

QUILLIAM, Prof Juan Pete (Peter); OBE (1986); s of Thomas Alfred Quilliam (d 1953), of N Finchley, London, and Caroline Maude, *née* Pavitt (d 1958); *b* 20 Nov 1915; *Educ* Univ Coll Sch Hampstead, Univ Coll London (BSc, MSc, MB, BS, DSc); *m* 1, Melita Kelly (d 1957); 1 s (Jonathan Peter b 1953), 1 da (Penelope Sally Ann (Mrs Walker) b 1950); m 2, 28 March 1958, Barbara Lucy, da of Rev W Kelly, of Pelynt, Cornwall; *Career* MO RAFVR 1942-46; Univ of London: prof of pharmacology St Bartholomew's Hosp Med Coll 1962-63, memb Senate 1968-, and ct 1973-, memb Mil Educn ctee, chm Convocation 1973-, chm Convocation Tst 1973-, memb advertising advsy ctee IBA 1984-, jt charity appeals advsy ctee IBA/BBC 1987-; dep chm General Optical Cncl 1975-88 (memb 1960-88), tstee City Parochial Fndn 1977-89, chm Crouch Habour Authy 1988-, tstee and co-chm Help the Hospices Tst 1988; BMA: chm of med academic staff ctee 1978, 1980, 1982, memb cncl 1971-85, chm bd of sci 1982-85, vice-pres 1988-; memb: Physiological Soc 1948, Br Pharmacological Soc 1950; Univ of London Rowing Purple 1938-40, pres Univ of London Boat Club 1939-40; FRCP (London) 1975; *Books* Experimental Pharmacology (1954, second edn); *Recreations* sailing; *Clubs* United Hosps SC (Essex); *Style*— Prof Peter Quilliam, OBE; Convocation, Univ of London, Senate House, Malet St, London WC1E 7HU (☎ 01 636 8000)

QUILTER, David Cuthbert Tudway; DL (Somerset 1970); s of Percy Cuthbert Quilter (d 1947), and Gladys Clare Alice, *née* Tudway (d 1973); *b* 26 Mar 1921; *Educ* Eton; *m* 1, 30 Oct 1953, Elizabeth Mary, da of Sir John Carew Pole, Bt, OBE (d 1977), of Antony House, Torpoint, Cornwall; 1 s (Simon b 26 March), 2 da (Susan b 9 July 1957, Lucy b 6 May 1961); m 2, 1979, Joan, wid of Lt-Col Anthony Fulford; *Career* served WWII, Coldstream Gds, Capt; Barclays Bank Ltd: local dir Pall Mall Dist 1957-62, Bristol Dist 1962-84, dir 1971-81; dir Bristol Evening Post 1982-; chm of tstees Wells Cathedral Preservation Tst 1976-; tres Bristol Univ 1976-88; govr Wells Cathedral Sch 1968-; memb: cncl Outward Bound Tst 1959-, Garden Soc 1973-; life tstee Carnegie UK Tst 1981-, tstee The America Museum in Br 1986-; JP London Juvenile Courts 1959-62, Mayor of Wells 1974-75, High Sheriff Somerset 1974-75, Vice Lord-Lt Somerset 1978-; Liveryman Fishmongers Co 1964; *Books* No Dishonourable Name (1947), History of Wells Cathedral Sch (1985); *Recreations* gardening, shooting, tennis, golf; *Clubs* Boodle's, Pratt's; *Style*— David Quilter, Esq, DL; Milton Lodge, Wells, Somerset (☎ 0749 72168)

QUIN, Joyce Gwendolen; MEP (Lab) S Tyne and Wear 1979-; *b* 1944; *Style*— Miss Joyce Quin, MEP; 5 Grange Crescent, Sunderland, Tyne and Wear

QUINE, Hector; s of Herbert Leigh Quine (d 1951), of London, and Gladys, *née* Foster (d 1934); *b* 30 Dec 1926; *Educ* Hextable Coll Kent; *m* 10 Oct 1960, Penelope Mary, da of Francis Henry Arnold Engleheart (d 1963), of Stoke-by-Nayland, Suffolk; 1 s (Adrian b 1967), 1 da (Francesca b 1972); *Career* serv RASC 1944-48, Norway, Egypt, Palestine; guitarist Royal Opera House Covent Gdn 1958-; prof: RAM 1959-87, Guildhall Sch of Music and Drama 1967-78, Trinity Coll of Music London 1958-78; advsr Assoc Bd of the Royal Schs of Music 1967- (examiner); Hon RAM, Hon FTCL; *Recreations* cricket, carpentry, photography; *Clubs* Chelsea Arts, Royal Philharmonic Soc, Royal Soc of Musicians, Performing Rights Soc; *Style*— Hector Quine, Esq; 22 Limerston Street, Chelsea, London SW10 0HH (☎ 01 352 4419)

QUINLAN, Sir Michael Edward; KCB (1985, CB 1980); s of late Gerald Andrew Quinlan, of Hassocks, Sussex, and late Roseanne Quinlan; *b* 11 August 1930; *Educ* Wimbledon Coll, Merton Coll Oxford; *m* 1965, Margaret Mary, *née* Finlay; 2 s, 2 da; *Career* RAF 1952-54; civil servant 1954-: def cnsllr UK delgn to NATO 1970-73, under sec Cabinet Office 1974-77, dep under sec of State (policy and programmes) MOD 1977-81; dep sec Treasy 1981-82, perm sec Dept of Employment 1983-88, MOD 1988-; author of various articles on nuclear deterrence; *Recreations* cricket, squash, listening to music; *Clubs* RAF; *Style*— Sir Michael Quinlan, KCB; c/o Dept of Employment, Caxton House, Tothill Street, London SW1H 9NF

QUINLAN, Timothy Edward; s of Edward John Quinlan (d 1959), of Essex, and Emma Louise, *née* Norrie (d 1974); *b* 12 August 1935; *Educ* St Ignatius Coll Harvard Business Sch; *m* 1961 (m dis 1981), Maryann, da of Arthur Barron (d 1976), of Essex; 2 s (James b 1962, Edward b 1975), 1 da (Sarah b 1964); m 2, 22 July 1988, Susan, da of Raymond Lindley, of Moorland House, Epworth, nr Doncaster, South Yorkshire; *Career* dir and gp gen mangr: Brent Walker Gp plc, Basildon Astrodome Ltd, Radio Mercury, Essex Radio, Widcombe Basin Ltd, Brent Walker Hldgs plc, Brent Walker Ltd 1978, Brent Walker Casinos Div Ltd, Brent Walker Catering Div Ltd, Brent Walker Film Distributors Ltd, Brent Walker Film Prodns Ltd, Brent Walker Restaurants Ltd, Curzon Restaurants Ltd, Peter Evans Hldgs Ltd, Peter Evans Eating Houses Ltd, La Boheme (Chelsea) Ltd, Focus Cinemas Ltd, Garons Agencies Ltd, Isow's Restaurants Ltd, Marlowe Rooms Ltd, Network Cinema (UK) Ltd, Waldair (Chancery Lane) Ltd, Waldair (Foster Lane) Ltd, Waldair (High Holborn) Ltd, Waldair (Tower Hill) Ltd, Westcliff Leisure Centre Ltd, Brent Walker Concessionaires Ltd, Manorlike Ltd, Brent Walker Finance Ltd, Brent Walker Casinos Northern Ltd, Fillfore Ltd; *Recreations* skiing, golf, tennis; *Clubs* Thorpe Hall GC, Thorpe Bay

Tennis, St James's; *Style—* Timothy Quinlan, Esq; 121 Thorpe Bay Gdns, Thorpe Bay, Southend on Sea, Essex SS1 3NW (☎ 0702 296310); Knightsbridge House, 197 Knightsbridge, London SW7 1RB (telex 23639, fax 01 225 1835)

QUINN, Francis; s of John Quinn (d 1959), of 12 Milwood Drive, Bellshill, and Mary Tinney (d 1969); *b* 22 July 1927; *Educ* Our Lady's High, Motherwell, Glasgow Univ (MA, BL, LLB); *m* 26 Dec 1955, Maureen Teresa, da of Daniel Doherty (d 1941), of Roslea Drive, Glasgow; 3 s (Antony b 1956, John b 1958, Paul b 1965), 1 da (Jane b 1961); *Career* served RAF, LAC (gliding instructor); slr; sr ptnr Quinn Martin & Lawgan, specialising in ct work; NP; *Recreations* bridge, golf, soccer, gliding; *Clubs* Glasgow Bridge, Hamilton Bridge, Uddingston Bridge (fndr), Bothwell Castle GC; *Style—* Francis Quinn, Esq; Loancroft, 2 Castle Ave, Uddingston, Glasgow (☎ 031 813474); 87 Carlton Rd, Glasgow (☎ 031 429 4354)

QUINN, James Charles Frederick; s of Rev Chllr James Quinn (d 1962), and Muriel Alice May, *née* MaGuire (d 1973); *b* 23 August 1919; *Educ* Shrewsbury, Trinity Dublin, Christ Church Oxford (MA); *m* 1941, Hannah, da of Rev Robert Malcolm Gwynn, Vice-Provost Trinity Dublin; 1 s (Gough), 1 da (Christina); *Career* served WWII Maj Irish Gds Italy and NW Europe 1941-46, Br Army Staff, France, and Town Major Paris 1946, film prodr and exhibitor; dir Br Film Inst 1955-64, memb BBC Gen Advsy Cncl 1960-64; Foreign Leader award US State Dept 1962; Cncl of Europe Fellowship 1966; tstee: Imperial War Museum 1968-78, Nat Life Story Collection 1986-; chm Nat Panel for Film Festivals 1966-83; films produced incl: Herostratus 1966, Overlord 1975 (Silver Bear Berlin Film Festival); memb Br Cncl Film TV and Video Advsy Ctee 1984-; chm The Minema Ltd 1984-; Chevalier de l'Ordre des Arts et des Lettres (France 1979); *Recreations* lawn tennis; *Clubs* Cavalry and Guards, Vincents (Oxford); *Style—* James Quinn, Esq; 108 Marine Parade, Brighton, Sussex

QUINN, James Steven Brian; s of James Joseph Quinn (d 1977), of Lancs, and Elizabeth Thomas ; *b* 16 June 1936; *Educ* Waterpark S Ireland, Univ Coll Dublin, Kings Inn Dublin (LLB, BCL); *m* 1963, Blanche Cecilia, da of Richard Francis James (d 1986), of Spain; 2 s (James b 1963, Alexander b 1969), 1 da (Susannah b 1965); *Career* head of Industl Activities Prices and Incomes Bd 1969-71, dir M L H Conslts 1971-79, corporate devpt advsr Midland Bank Int 1977-80, chief industl advsr Price Cmmn 1977-80; chm: Brightstar Communications 1983-85, B A J Hldgs 1985-87, Harmer Holbrook 1987-88; Int Inst of Communication Tstee 1982-87; Inst of Euro Trade and Technol: memb exec ctee 1983- chm exec ctee 1984-87, pres 1988-; *Recreations* golf, reading; *Clubs* Athenaeum; *Style—* Brian Quinn, Esq; Craiglea House, Austenwood Lane, Gerrards Cross, Bucks; Network House, Oxford Rd, Uxbridge, Middx (☎ 0895 74141)

QUINN, Dame Sheila Margaret Imelda; DBE (1987, CBE 1978); da of Wilfred Amos Bairstow Quinn (d 1963); *b* 16 Sept 1920; *Educ* Layton Hill Convent Sch Blackpool, London Univ; *Career* regnl nursing offr Wessex Regnl Health Authy 1978-83, UK rep Standing Ctee of Nurses EEC 1979-, pres Royal Coll of Nursing 1982-86 (chm cncl 1974-79, dep pres 1980-82), nursing advsr Br Red Cross 1983-88; memb EEC Advsy Ctee on Trg in Nursing 1983- (pres 1979-82), first vice-pres Int Cncl of Nurses 1981-85 (memb bd of dirs 1977-81); Hon DSc Southampton Univ 1986; *Recreations* reading, walking, gardening; *Clubs* New Cavendish, St Johns House; *Style—* Dame Sheila Quinn, DBE; 48 Glenwood Avenue, Bassett, Southampton, Hants SO2 3QA (☎ 0703 766 843)

QUINNEN, (Paul) Nigel Andrew; s of John Norman Quinnen (d 1986), of Ealing, London, and Elisabeth, *née* Clarke; *b* 10 Oct 1953; *Educ* St Benedict's Ealing, Wadham Coll Oxford; *m* 16 Dec 1977, Dinah Mary, da of Rear Adm Derek Hetherington, of Christmas Common, Oxon; 1 s (Bruno b 1986), 1 da (Romy b 1987); *Career* articles Coopers & Lybrand 1976-80, fund mangr J Henry Schroder Wagg 1980-85, investmt dir Lazard Investors 1985; Oxford rugby blue 1974-75; ACA 1980; *Recreations* golf; *Clubs* Royal Mid Surrey GC; *Style—* Nigel Quinnen, Esq; 15 Grove La, Kingston, Surrey, KT1 2ST (☎ 01 549 8540); Lazard Investors, 21 Moorfields, London, EC2P 2HT (☎ 01 588 2721)

QUINNEN, Peter John; s of John Norman Quinnen (d 1986), of Ealing London, and Mabel Elizabeth, *née* Clark; *b* 4 April 1945; *Educ* St Benedict's Sch Ealing, Christ Church Oxford (MA); *m* 26 Aug 1972, Pammy, da of Gordon Urqhart, of Ayr, Scotland; 2 s (Thomas b 1974, Henry b 1977); *Career* stockbroker; dir James Capel and Co 1982-, chm and chief exec James Capel and Co 1986-; *Recreations* golf, opera, music; *Clubs* RAC, St George's Hill Wednesday; *Style—* Peter Quinnen, Esq; James Capel & Co, James Capel House, PO Box 551, 6 Bevis Marks, London EC3A 7JQ (☎ 01 621 0011)

QUINTON, Baron (Life Peer UK 1982), of Holywell in City of Oxford and Co of Oxfordshire; Anthony Meredith Quinton; s of Surgn Capt Richard Frith Quinton, RN (d 1935), and Gwenllyan Letitia Quinton; *b* 25 Mar 1925; *Educ* Stowe, Christ Church Oxford (BA); *m* 1952, Marcelle, da of late Maurice Wegier, of New York; 1 s, 1 da; *Career* RAF, served WW II; fell: All Souls Coll Oxford 1949-55, New Coll Oxford 1955-78; pres Trinity Coll Oxford 1978-87, memb Arts Cncl of GB 1979-82; vice-pres Br Acad 1985-86, chm Br Library Bd 1985-; FBA; *Books* Political Philosophy (ed, 1967), The Nature of Things (1973), Utilitarian Ethics (1973), K Ajdukiewicz - Problems and Theories of Philosophy (trans with H Skolimowski, 1973), The Politics of Imperfection (1978), Francis Bacon (1980), Thoughts and Thinkers (1982); *Clubs* Garrick, Beefsteak, United Oxford and Cambridge Univ; *Style—* The Rt Hon the Lord Quinton; The Mill House, Turville, Henley-on-Thames, Oxon RG9 6QL

QUINTON, Hon Edward Frith; o s of Baron Quinton (Life Peer), *qv*; *b* 24 Dec 1957; *Educ* Winchester, Imperial Coll of Science and Technol London (BSc); *m* 22 June 1987, Sarah Eve, da of A W Travis, of Western Samoa; *Career* mechanical engr; *Recreations* vintage motoring; *Style—* The Hon Edward Quinton; Leslie Hartridge Ltd, Buckingham MK18 1EF (☎ 0280 813661)

QUINTON, John Grand; s of William Grand Quinton (d 1968), and Norah May Quinton, *née* Nunn (d 1969); Freemen of City of Norwich since 1702; *b* 21 Dec 1929; *Educ* Norwich Sch, Cambridge (MA); *m* 1954, Jean Margaret, da of Donald Chastney (d 1950); 1 s (Michael), 1 da (Joanna); *Career* Barclays Bank: sr gen mangr 1982-84, dep chm 1985-87, chm 1987-; *Recreations* tennis, gardening, opera; *Clubs* Reform; *Style—* John Quinton, Esq; Chenies Place, Chenies, Bucks; Barclays Bank, 54 Lombard St, London EC3P 3AH (☎ 01 626 1567)

QUIRICI, Daniel; s of Ernest Quirici, of Cannes, France, and Candice, *née* Postai; *b* 8 June 1948; *Educ* Ecole des Hautes Etudes Commerciales Paris (MBA), Stanford Univ California (PhD); *m* 1 Sept 1972, Margaret, da of Donald Wright Mann, of NY; 2 s (Alexandre b 15 Aug 1973, Francois b 23 May 1979), 1 da (Florence b 14 Feb 1978); *Career* assoc prof HEC 1970-76, assoc Arthur D Little 1976-82, sr vice pres Credit Commercial de France Paris 1983-, md Laurence Prust & Co Ltd (a subsidiary of CCF) 1986-; memb traffic ctee Knightsbridge Assoc; *Recreations* tennis, golf; *Clubs* RAC; *Style—* Daniel Quirici, Esq; 8 Montpelier Square, London SW7; Laurence Prust & Co Ltd, 27 Finsbury Square, London EC2 1LP (☎ 01 982 7531, 01 628 1111, fax 01 638 7660)

QUIRK, Hon Mrs (Carol Ann); *née* Penny; da of 2 Viscount Marchwood, MBE (d 1979); *b* 1948; *m* 1978, Patrick J Quirk; 2 s; *Style—* The Hon Mrs Quirk; 9 Lambourn Rd, London SW4 OLX

QUIRK, (Jonathan) Piers; s of Dudley Cecil Quirk, JP, of Chiddingstone, Kent, and Joan Mary, *née* Salmon; *b* 27 Dec 1943; *Educ* Winchester, Coll of Estate Mgmnt, Univ of London (BSc); *m* 3 Sept 1983, Sally, da of (Arthur) Richard Kemp, of Chiddingstone, Kent; 1 s (Frederick b 1986), 1 da (Zoe b 1988); *Career* ptnr Messrs Parris & Quirk Chartered Surveyors of Tunbridge Wells and London 1971-87; pres Royal Tunbridge Wells C of C 1986, Freeman City of London 1984, Liveryman Worshipful Co of Chartered Surveyors 1984; FRICS 1974; *Recreations* photography, woodwork, paintings, rugs; *Style—* Piers Quirk, Esq; The Oasts, Chiddingstone, Kent TN8 7AQ (☎ 0892 870 701); Fox & Sons, 27 Mount Pleasant, Tunbridge Wells, Kent TN1 1PP (☎ 0892 515 252, fax 0892 515 868)

QUIRK, Prof Sir (Charles) Randolph; CBE (1976); s of Thomas Quirk; *b* 1920; *Educ* Cronk y Voddy Sch, Douglas HS IoM, UCL (MA, PhD, DLit), Yale Univ; *m* Prof Gabriele Stein; *Career* prof of Eng language Durham Univ 1958-60, London Univ 1960-68, Quain prof of Eng language and lit UCL 1968-81, vice-chllr London Univ 1981-85; memb: bd Br Cncl 1983-, cncl RADA; govr the Eng-Speaking Union, hon master of Bench Gray's Inn 1983; pres: Br Acad 1985-, Inst of Linguists; chm: Br Library Advsy Ctee, Hornby Educnl Tst; tstee Wolfson Fndn; ed English Language Series (Longman); hon doctorates: Lund, Uppsala, Paris, Liège, Nijmegen, Salford, Reading, Leicester, Newcastle, Durham, Bath, Open, Essex, Bar Ilan, Southern California, Brunel, Glasgow; for fell: Royal Belgian Acad of Sci, Royal Swedish Acad; fell and res fell UCL; FBA; kt 1985; *Books* A University Grammar of English (1973), Style and Communication in the English Language (1982), English in the World (1985), A Comprehensive Grammar of the English Language (1985), Words at Work (1986); *Clubs* Athenaeum; *Style—* Prof Sir Randolph Quirk, CBE; The British Academy, Cornwall Terrace, London NW1 4QP (☎ 01 487 5966)

QUIRKE, Patrick Adair; s of John Patrick Quirke, of Augustine Rd, London W14, and Elizabeth, *née* Naismith; *b* 26 June 1951; *Educ* Westminster, Kingston Coll of Technol; *m* 15 Oct 1988, Suzanna Angela, da of John David Anthony Willis, of The Coach House, Bailbrook Lane, Bath, Avon; *Career* film dept BBC TV: asst sound recordist 1973-85, film sound recordist 1985-, BAFTA award for film sound The Duty Men 1988; ptnr The Chance Band (high soc dance band) 1974-; *Recreations* tennis, skiing, sub-aqua; *Clubs* Roof Garden; *Style—* Patrick Quirke, Esq; BBC TV, Ealing Film Studios, Ealing Green, London W5 (☎ 01 567 6655 ext 647)

QUITMAN, Harold Channing; s of Ernest Arthur Quitman (d 1944); *b* 28 May 1918; *Educ* Malvern; *m* 1950, Jean Jacqueline da of Lt-Col Sir Roland Lawrence, Bt, MC; 1 s (Jeremy Roland Channing b 6 June 1953), 1 da (Annabel Susan Maude b 16 Dec 1951); *Career* Inf Bn HAC 1939, BEF 1940, Maj 21 Army Gp 1944-46; Aquis Property Co Ltd: dir 1954, chm and md 1960-64; Aquis Securities plc: chm 1964-84, md 1964-79; memb Worshipful Co Haberdashers (master 1979-80); Wine Warden (Haberdashers) 1984-; memb Presidential cncl City of Westminster C of C (chm 1965-67); gen cmmr of Taxes; Cdr of Merit SMOM; FRSA; *Recreations* gardening, painting, wine; *Clubs* Garrick, MCC; *Style—* Harold Quitman Esq; Rookley Farmhouse, Upper Somborne, Stockbridge, Hants SO20 6QX (☎ 07947 388338)

QUYSNER, David William; s of Charles William Quysner, of Mildenhall, Suffolk, and Marjorie Alice, *née* Partington; *b* 29 Dec 1946; *Educ* Bolton Sch, Selwyn Coll Cambridge (MA), London Business Sch; *m* 11 Sept 1971, Lindsay Jean Parris, da of Sir Norman Biggs, of Hurstpierpoint, Sussex; 1 s (Simon James b 1980), 2 da (Sarah Louise b 1976, Deborah Helen b 1977); *Career* Investors in Indust plc 1968-82, dir Abingworth plc 1982-, non exec dir The Melville Gp plc 1986-; *Recreations* opera, golf; *Style—* David Quysner, Esq; Abingworth PLC, 26 St James's St, London SW1A 1HA (☎ 01 839 6745, fax 01 930 1891)

R

RABEN-LEVETZAU, Lady Rosanagh Mary; *née* Crichton; Baroness Michael Raben-Levetzau; da of late 5 Earl of Erne and Lady Davidema Katherine Cynthia Mary Millicent Bulwer Lytton, da of 2 Earl of Lytton; *b* 12 August 1932; *m* 1956, Baron Michael Paul Raben-Levetzau of Rathmore Park, Tullow, Co Carlow; 4 s (Matthew b 1962 m Sarah Jane Stratton 1987, Alexander b 1964, Victor b 1968, Seamus b 1970); *Style*— Baroness Michael Raben-Levetzau; Rathmore Park, Tullow, Co Carlow, Eire (☎ 0503 61179)

RABIN, Prof Brian Robert; s of Emanuel Rabin (d 1973), and Sophia, *née* Neshaver (d 1982); *b* 4 Nov 1927; *Educ* Latymer's, UCL (BSc, MSc, PhD); *m* 29 Aug 1954, Sheila Patricia, da of Charles Patrick George (d 1972); 1 s (Paul Robert b 27 Jan 1958), 1 da (Carol (Mrs Costa) b 23 Sept 1959); *Career* UCL 1954-: asst lectr (later lectr) 1954-63, reader in biochemistry 1963-67, prof of enzymology 1967-70, head of biochemistry dept 1970-88, fell UCL 1984, prof of biochemistry 1988-; fndr dir London Biotechnology Ltd 1985-; dir Cogent Ltd and Cogents Hldgs Ltd 1986-; FZS 1972, FIBiol 1972, EMBO 1980, memb Academie FurUmuweltfragen 1987; *Recreations* travel, carpentry; *Clubs* Athenaeum; *Style*— Prof Brian Rabin; 34 Grangewood, Potters Bar, Herts EN6 1SL (☎ 0707 54576); Dept of Biochemistry, Univ Coll, Gower St, London WC1E 6BT (☎ 01 380 7039)

RABINOWITZ, Harry; MBE (1978); s of Israel Rabinowitz (d 1960), and Eva, *née* Kirkel (d 1971); *b* 26 Mar 1916; *Educ* Athlone HS S Africa, Witwatersrand Univ, London Guildhall Sch of Music; *m* 15 Dec 1944, Lorna Thurlow, da of Cecil Redvers Anderson (d 1970); 1 s (Simon Oliver b 1951), 2 da (Karen Lesley b 1947, Lisa Gabrielle b 1960); *Career* Cpl SA Forces 1942-43; conductor BBC radio 1953-60; head of music: BBC TV Light Entertainment 1960-68, London Weekend TV 1968-77; now freelance conductor/composer; conductor: Hollywood Bowl 1983-84, Boston Pops 1985-88, London Symphony Orchestra, Royal Philharmonic Orchestra; conductor films: Chariots of Fire, Manhattan Project, Heat & Dust, The Bostonians, Maurice, Time Bandits, Return to Oz, L'Argent, Camile Claudel, etc; TV: New Faces 1987/8, Paul Nicholas Special 1987, Julia MacKenzie Special 1986, Nicholas Nickleby, Drummonds, The Insurance Man, Absent Friends, Simon Wiesenllal Story; composer TV: Agatha Christie Hour, Reilly Ace of Spies; conductor theatre: World Premieres of "Cats" and "Song and Dance"; awards: Br Acad of Songwriters, Composers and Authors (BASCA) Gold Award 1986, Radio and TV Industries Award 1986; *Recreations* wine tasting, gathering edible fungi; *Clubs* Holmbury St Mary Village; *Style*— Harry Rabinowitz, Esq, MBE; Hope End, Holmbury, St Mary, Dorking, Surrey RH5 6PE (☎ 0306 730 605)

RABSON, John; s of Rev Alban Rabson (d 1966), and Kathleen Muriel, *née* Blackshaw; *b* 8 Sept 1942; *Educ* Newport GS Essex, Colchester Royal GS, Harlow Tech, Enfield Tech, Univ of Essex (MPhil, Dip EE); *m* 9 Dec 1972, Rosemary Margaret, da of Thomas Border (d 1985); 1 s (Hugo b 1975); *Career* chartered electrical, electronic and radio engr; res offr Univ of Essex Jan-Sept 1973; exec engr PO (now BT) 1973-; CEng, MIEE, MIERE; *Recreations* amateur radio (licence G3PAI held since 1961), codes and ciphers, science fiction; *Style*— John Rabson, Esq; Limes Farm House, Eyke, Woodbridge, Suffolk (☎ 0394 460298); BTRL, Martlesham, Ipswich (☎ 0473 643210, telex 98376)

RABUKAWAQA, Sir Josua Rasilau; KBE (1977, CBE 1974, MBE 1968), MVO (1970); s of Dr Aisea Rasilau; *b* 2 Dec 1917; *Educ* Suva Methodist Boys' Sch, Queen Victoria Sch, Teachers' Training Coll Auckland (NZ); *m* 1944, Mei Tolanivutu; 3 s, 2 da; *Career* served Fijian Armed Forces 1953-55; ambass-at-large Fiji & chief Protocol 1978-; first high commnr Fiji to UK 1970-76, awarded R B Bennett Cwlth Prize 1981 by RSA; *Style*— Sir Josua Rabukawaqa, KBE, MVO; 6 Vunivivi Hill, Nausori, Fiji

RABY, Derek Graham; s of Sir Victor H Raby, KBE, CB, MC, of Bishopsteignton, S Devon, and Dorothy Alys, *née* Buzzard; *b* 18 May 1927; *Educ* King's Sch Bruton, Somerset; *m* 14 July 1956, Elsa Jean, da of H White, ARIBA (d 1969), of Felpham, Sussex; 1 s (Charles b 1959); *Career* RAF 1945-48; appeals dir PDSA, dir PDSA Trading Ltd; Freeman City of London; writer of plays, articles, and occasional broadcaster 1973-, pubns incl We Need a Man (1975); *Recreations* gardening, wine; *Style*— Derek Raby, Esq; The Little House, Elm Grove Rd, Cobham, Surrey KT11 3HB (☎ 0932 64465, 0306 888291); PDSA House, South St, Dorking, Surrey RH4 2LB (☎ 0306 888291)

RABY, Sir Victor Harry; KBE (1956), CB (1948), MC (1918); s of Harry Raby, of Menheniot Cornwall; *b* 1897; *Educ* Grey Coll Bloemfontein S Africa; *m* 1921, Dorothy Alys, da of Rodney Buzzard, of Ditchling, Sussex; 1 s; *Career* served WW I with London Regt; under-sec Air Miny 1946, dep under-sec 1954, ret 1957; *Clubs* RAC; *Style*— Sir Victor Raby, KBE, CB, MC; New Way, Forder Lane, Bishopsteignton, Devon

RACE, Stephen Russell (Steve); s of Russell Tiniswood Race (d 1926), of Lincoln, and Robina Race (d 1964); *b* 1 April 1921; *Educ* Christ's Hosp Sch (formerly Lincoln Sch), RAM; *m* 1, 7 June 1944 Clair Leng (d 1969); 1 da (Nicola b 1946); m 2, 14 April 1970, Leonie Rebecca Govier Mather; *Career* RAF 1941-46; free lance pianist arranger and composer 1946-55, light music advsr Assoc-Rediffusion Ltd 1955-60, TV conductor Tony Hancock and Peter Sellers Shows; appeared radio and TV: My Music, A Good Read, Jazz in Perspective, Any Questions?, Music Now, Music Weekly, Kaleidoscope, Look What they've done to my Song, Jazz Revisited, With Great Pleasure, Desert Island Discs, Steve Race Presents the Radio Orch Show, Gershwin Among Friends, Irving Berlin Among Friends; radio reviews in The Listener 1975-80; memb Royal Albert Hall Cncl of Arts and Sci 1976-, exec cncl memb Musicians' Benevolent Fund 1985-, Govr of Tokyo Metropolis Prize for Radio 1979, Wavendon Allmusic Media Personality of the year 1987, TV and Radio Industs Club Award 1988; compositions incl: Nicola (Ivor Novello Award), Faraway Music, The Pied Piper, incidental music for Richard III, Cyrano de Bergerac, Twelfth Night (BBC); Cantatas: Song of King David, The Day of the Donkey, Song of Praise, My Music - My Song; numerous other works incl: ITV advertising sound-tracks (Venice Award 1962, Cannes Award 1963); film music: Calling Paul Temple, Three Roads to Rome, Against The Tide, Land of Three Rivers; dep chm Performing Rights Soc 1966-68; Freeman City of London 1982; FRSA 1975, FRAM 1978, ARAM 1968; *Books* Musician at Large (autobiography 1979), My Music (1979), Dear Music Lover (1981), Steve Race's Music Quiz (1983), The Illustrated Counties of England (1984), You Can't be Serious (1985), The Penguin Masterquiz (1985), With Great Pleasure (1986), The Two Worlds of Joseph Race (1988); *Style*— Steve Race, Esq; Martins End Lane, Great Missenden, Bucks HP16 9HS

RACKHAM, Reginald Colmer; s of Percy Chester Rackham (d 1968), of Haywood Close, Pinner, Middx, and Mabel Violet, *née* Dinsmore (d 1976); *b* 27 Jan 1913; *Educ* Berkhamstead Sch Herts; *m* 12 Sept 1942, (Elizabeth) Pamela, da of Donald Jervis Molteno, JP (d 1969), of Glenlyon House, Fortingall, Perthshire; 2 s (Anthony b 1946, Allan b 1948), 1 da (Alison b 1951); *Career* WWII serv RE: Sapper Newark 1940, 2 Lt garrison engr Perth 1941, Lt garrison engr Kirkcaldy 1942-44, Capt Halifax and Normandy 1944, Maj Brussels 1945; jr asst engr and surveyor Hendon RDC 1930-35; Beddington & Wallington UDC and Borough 1935-40, E Cornwall JPC 1946-47, Devon CC 1947-51; area planning offr Somerset CC 1957-73; former pres Mendip Rotary Club, vice chm Winscombe Probis Club; FRICS 1940, FRTPI 1940; *Recreations* motor sports, walking, photography; *Style*— Reginald Rackham, Esq; Church Paddock, Winscombe Hill, Winscombe, Avon (☎ 093 484 3170)

RADCLIFFE, Hugh John Reginald Joseph; MBE (1944); s of late Sir Everard Radcliffe, 5 Bt; hp of nephew, Sir Sebastian Radcliffe, 7 Bt; *b* 3 Mar 1911; *Educ* Downside; *m* 15 April 1937, Marie Thérèse, yst da of Maj-Gen Sir Cecil Edward Pereira, KCB, CMG; 5 s, 1 da; *Career* served WW II, Lt-Col Scottish London; company dir; dep chm London Stock Exchange 1967-70; Kt Order of St Gregory the Great (Papal) 1984; Kt Cdr Order of St Silvester (Papal) 1965; *Style*— Hugh Radcliffe, Esq, MBE; The White House, Stoke, Andover, Hants

RADCLIFFE, Julian Guy Yonge; TD; s of Maj G L Y Radcliffe MBE; *b* 29 August 1948; *Educ* Eton, New Coll Oxford; *m* Francis Harriet Thompson (princ Min of Agriculture); 2 s, 1 da; *Career* Lloyd's broker and underwriting memb of Lloyd's; md: Investmt Insurance Int 1973, Control Risks Ltd; dir: Credit Insurance Assoc Ltd 1975, Hogg Robinson Gardner Mountain plc; cmmnd Royal Yeomanry 1971, Maj 1980; *Recreations* farming, shooting, military and strategic studies; *Clubs* City of London, Carlton, Cavalry & Guards; *Style*— Julian Radcliffe, Esq, TD; 32 Brynmaer Rd, SW11 4EW; Lower Stanway, Much Wenlock, Shropshire TF13 6LD (☎ 0865 223)

RADCLIFFE, Mark Hugh Joseph; s of Hugh John Reginald Joseph Radcliffe, MBE, of Andover, Hants, and Marie Therese, *née* Pereira; *Educ* Downside; *m* 20 Feb 1963, Anne, da of Maj-Gen A E Brocklehurst, CB, DSO; 3 da (Lucinda b 1964, Emily Marie Louise b 1968, Camilla Mary b 1971); *Career* 2 Lt Coldstream Gds 1956-58; Mktg mangr Cape Asbestos Ltd plc 1958-68, chief exec Lancer Boss Gp Ltd 1968-74, md Triang Pedigree Ltd 1974-78, dir TI Gp plc 1978-, currently pres and md John Crane Int; FInstD; *Recreations* shooting, golf, tennis, gardening; *Clubs* Guards and Calvalry; *Style*— Mark Radcliffe, Esq; The Malt House, Upton, nr Andover, Hants (☎ 026 476 266); 50 Curzon St, London W1 (☎ 01 499 9131); Crossburn House, Liverpool Rd, Slough (☎ 0753 822 512); 6400 Oakton, Morton Grove, Illinois (☎ 0101 312 967 2403, fax 0753 691 405)

RADCLIFFE, Michael Francis; s of John Maurice Radcliffe (d 1949), of Almondsbury, nr Bristol, and Margery Bloomfield, *née* Lumsden (d 1974); *b* 8 Mar 1940; *Educ* Cheltenham, Clare Coll Cambridge (MA), Carnegie Mellon Univ Pittsburgh USA (MSc); *m* 13 June 1964, Gillian Mary, da of Reginald Harvey (d 1985), of Bishops Cleeve; 2 da (Abigail Sarah b 20 Sept 1968, Jessica Jane b 21 May 1970); *Career* Br Oxygen Co Ltd 1962-71, fin controller Plessey Telecommunications Ltd 1971-78, fin dir Brush Electrical Machines Ltd 1978-85, md Brush Transformers Ltd 1985-; dir: Crompton Greaves Ltd Bombay 1986-, Brush Electrical Engrg Co Ltd 1989-; FBIM 1979, FIMEMME 1985, FInstD 1986; *Recreations* golf; *Style*— Michael Radcliffe, Esq; 1 Manor Park, Ruddington, Nottingham NG11 6DS (☎ 0602 213776); Brush Transformers Ltd, PO Box 20, Loughborough, Leics LE11 1HN (☎ 0509 611411, fax 0509 610721, telex 341094 BTZ G)

RADCLIFFE, (Walter) Nicholas; s of Maj Walter Henry Radcliffe (d 1967), of Plymouth, and Katharine Agnes, *née* Lewarne; *b* 21 Sept 1939; *Educ* Sherborne; *m* 26 June 1980, Elaine Louise, da of Ralph Quartly Mallett, of Newbury, Berks; 2 s (Julian b 1981, Michael (twin) b 1981); *Career* Hon Artillery Co 1958-63, cmmd RA TA Capt, ret 1971; slr, landowner; *Recreations* tennis, skiing; *Style*— Nicholas Radcliffe, Esq; Warleigh Park House, Tamerton Foliot, Plymouth (☎ 0752 773195)

RADCLIFFE, Percy; JP; s of Arthur and Annie Radcliffe; *b* 14 Nov 1916; *Educ* Ramsey GS; *m* 1942, Barbara Frances, da of William Cannell Crowe; 2 s, 1 da; *Career* farmer; elected IOM govt 1963, chm local govt bd 1966-76, chm finance bd 1976-81, chm govt exec cncl (prime minister) Isle of Man 1981-; *Recreations* horse driving (Holypark Sensation); *Style*— Percy Radcliffe Esq, JP, MLC; Kellaway, Sulby, Isle of Man (☎ 064 89 7257); Government Office, Douglas, Isle of Man (☎ 0786 26262)

RADCLIFFE, Sir Sebastian Everard; 7 Bt (UK 1813); s of Capt Sir (Joseph

Benedict) Everard Henry, 6 Bt, MC (d 1975); *b* 8 June 1972; *Heir* unc, Hugh Radcliffe, MBE; *Style*— Sir Sebastian Radcliffe, Bt

RADCLYFFE, Sarah; da of Capt Charles Raymond Radclyffe, of Lew House, Lew, Nr Bampton, Oxon, and Helen Egerton, *née* Coton; *b* 14 Nov 1950; *Educ* Heathfield Sch Ascot Berks; *Career* film prodr 1978-; films incl: My Beautiful Laundrette 1985, Caravaggio 1985, Wish You Were Here 1986, Sammy and Rosie Get Laid 1987, A World Apart 1987, Paperhouse 1987; *Style*— Miss Sarah Radclyffe; 15 Shirlock Rd, London NW3 2HR; 10 Livonia St, London W1 (☎ 01 439 2424, fax 01 437 9964, telex 914 106 WORKING)

RADFORD, David Wyn; s of Robert Edwin Radford, CB, of Guildford, Surrey, and Eleanor Margaret, *née* Jones; *b* 3 Jan 1947; *Educ* Cranleigh Sch, Selwyn Coll Cambridge (MA, LLM); *m* 23 Sept 1972, Nadine, da of Joseph Poggioli, of London; 2 s (Simon b 1982, Peter b 1983), 2 da (Carine b 1975, Lauren b 1986); *Career* called to the Bar Gray's Inn 1969, asst rec 1988-; Liberal Pty Parly Candidate Hampstead Constituency 1975-83; *Recreations* following soccer, politics, theatre; *Style*— David Radford, Esq; 1 Gray's Inn Sq, Gray's Inn, London WC1R 5AG (☎ 01 404 5416, fax 01 405 9942)

RADFORD, (Guy) Harold Richard; s of Walter Guy Wolfe Radford (d 1947); *b* 26 Sept 1908; *Educ* Marlborough; *m* 1948, Joanna Laetitia, *née* Wardle-Smith; *Career* former owner Harold Radford & Co Ltd (mfr private fleet of vehicles, designing and converting vehicle bodies for special purposes and for Special Branch Combined Forces of the Secret Serv, WWII), chm Staley Radford & Co Ltd, former chm Carroll Radford Holder Ltd; dir Wainwright Radford Ltd; memb of Lloyd's; conslt to motor indust; Freeman of the City of London; FIMechE, MICBM; *Recreations* lawn tennis, rackets, squash rackets, horse riding & driving in harness; *Clubs* MCC, RAC, Queen's, Jester's; *Style*— Harold Radford, Esq; The Old Forge Farm, Conford, Liphook, Hants GU30 7QW (☎ 0428 77 214); Staley Radford & Co Ltd, 100 Whitechapel Rd, London E1 1JE (☎ 01 377 9717, telex 8811557), Wainwright Radford Ltd, 20 Moorfields High Walk, London WC2Y 9DN (☎ 01 628 2373, telex 883128)

RADFORD, John Davenport; s of Vaughan Nattrass Radford (d 1988), of Epperstone, Notts, and Beatrice Mary, *née* Bullivant; *b* 8 Sept 1923; *Educ* Oundle; *m* 10 Nov 1948, Angela, da of Maj Frederick William Cooper (d 1960), of Carcolston Notts; 1 s (Stephen b 1959), 2 da (Diana b 1952, Philippa b 1954); *Career* RN 1943-46; md Stag Furniture plc 1970-83 (joined 1947); chm Convent Hosp Nottingham, cncl memb Southwell Minster; High Sheriff Notts; Master Worshipful Company of Furniture Makers 1987; *Recreations* yachting, country sports; *Clubs* Royal Thames Yacht, Royal Lymington Yacht, Nottingham & Notts United Services; *Style*— John D Radford, Esq; Stag Furniture Holdings plc, Haydn Road, Nottingham (☎ 0602 605007)

RADFORD, Patrick Vaughan; CBE (1983), MC (1945), TD, DL (1987); s of Vaughan Nattras Radford (d 1988), and Beatrice Mary, *née* Bullivant (d 1978); *b* 16 Nov 1926; *Educ* Oundle; *m* 1, 1945 (m dis 1956), Nancy Madeline, *née* Shaw; 1 da (Carol b 1946); m 2, 1956, Evelyn Lily, da of George Herbert Wilkinson (d 1971); 4 s (Nicholas b 1957, Jonathan b 1959, Timothy b 1960, Anthony b 1962), 1 step da (Anthea b 1947); *Career* served WWII, joined RAC 1941, cmmnd 2 Lt 1942, served 1 Derby Yeo in UK, N Africa, Italy, Austria 1942-46, joined Derby (Yeo TA 1947 (Maj), 2i/c Leics and Derbys Yeo TA 1956, Lt-Col 1958-61; barr Grays Inn 1954; chm Stag Furniture Hldgs plc 1971-; govr Trent Coll; gen cmmr for Income Tax; Liveryman Worshipful Co of Furniture Makers 1963 (Master 1982/83); FCIS; *Recreations* country sports, fishing, shooting; *Clubs* Cavalry & Guards, Nottingham Utd Services; *Style*— Patrick Radford, Esq, CBE, MC, TD, DL; Langford Hall, Newark, Notts N823 7RS (☎ 0636 76802); Stag Furniture Holdings PLC, Haydn Rd, Nottingham (☎ 0602 605007)

RADFORD, Sir Ronald Walter; KCB (1976, CB 1971), MBE (1947); s of George Leonard Radford (d 1959), and Ethel Mary Radford (d 1971); *b* 28 Feb 1916; *Educ* Southend-on-Sea HS, St John's Coll Cambridge (MA); *m* 1949, Jean Alison Dunlop, da of Lawrence Harold Strange (d 1954); 1 s, 1 da; *Career* served with Indian Civil Serv 1939-47; HM Customs and Excise: asst princ 1947, princ 1948, asst sec 1953-65, cmmr and sec 1965-70, dep chm 1970-73, chm 1973-77; sec-gen Customs Co-op Cncl 1978-83 (hon sec gen 1983-); *Clubs* Reform, MCC, Civil Service; *Style*— Sir Ronald Radford, KCB, MBE; 4 Thomas Close, Brentwood, Essex CM15 8BS (☎ 0277 211567)

RADICE, Giles Heneage; MP (Lab) North Durham 1983-; s of Lawrence Radice (himself s of Evadio Radice) and Patricia (eldest da of Sir Arthur Pelham Heneage, DSO, JP, DL, sometime MP for Louth); *b* 4 Oct 1936; *Educ* Winchester, Magdalen Coll Oxford; *m* 1959, Penelope, er da of late Robert Angus, JP, DL, of Ladykirk, Ayrshire, by his w (subsequently Lady Moore); 2 da (Adele b 1961, Sophia b 1964); *Career* former head GMWU Res Dept, MP (Lab) Chester-le-Street March 1973-1983, chm Manifesto Gp in Labour Party, memb Cncl Policy Studies Institute 1978-, oppn front bench spokesman: Employment 1981-Nov 1983, memb Shadow Cabinet Nov 1983-; *Style*— Giles Radice Esq, MP; 40 Inverness St, London NW1

RADLEY, (Herbert) Arthur Farrand; MBE (1946); s of John Charles Radley (d 1927), of Rusholme, Manchester, and Helen Louise, *née* Howell (d 1959); *b* 16 June 1916; *Educ* Friends' Sch Saffron Walden, Leighton Park, St Edmund Hall Oxford (BA, Sorbonne; *m* 17 May 1947, (m dis 1950), Gisela, da of Stefan Fritz Ingenieur (d 1980), of Weiz, Austria; *Career* english asst Lycée Lakanal Sceaux Paris 1938-39, asst modern language master Watford GS 1939; enlistment TA, Rifleman (Artists Rifles) 1939, serv Malta GC 1941-44 (incl ADC to GOC), memb Special Forces Exec SOE ops in France and Italy 1944-45, HQ Eighth Army and V Corps; involved: Mil Govt Land Steiermark 1945-46, Allied Cmmn for Austria, political div Vienna 1946-47, released as Maj 20 The Lancs Fus 1947; asst head visitors dept Br Cncl 1947-50; BBC 1950-76: orgn and methods 1950-60, organiser TV music 1960-65, TV gen features 1965-70, mgmnt services 1970-76; has broadcast on: French radio, BBC German Serv, BBC World Serv; lectr 1976, subjects incl: architecture (Georgian and Euro baroque), industl archaeology (Royal Dockyards and Victualling Yards); Grosses Goldenes Ehrenzeichen (Grand Gold Medal) of Styria Austria 1985; memb: Nat Assoc of Decorative and Fine Arts Socs 1987, Railway and Canal Historical Soc; vice pres London branch Inland Waterways Assoc; FBCS (fndr memb 1957), MIPM (exec cncl memb 1952-55), FInstAM 1967 (chm London branch 1961-63); *Recreations* travel and photography, chess, chamber music and choral singing, archiving, protocol; *Clubs* Special Forces; *Style*— Arthur Farrand Radley, Esq, MBE; 157 Holland Park Ave, London W11 4UX (☎ 01 603 6062)

RADLEY, Eric John; s of Rev John Benjamin Radley (d 1942), and Florence Sophia, *née* Roberts; *b* 12 June 1917; *Educ* Eltham Coll, London Univ (BA); *m* 28 Aug 1948, Margaret Elisabeth, da of Leonard Munro Cobb (d 1958), of Cliftonville; 1 s (Peter Benjamin b 1949), 3 da (Helen Margaret (Mrs Penfold) b 1953, Mary Elisabeth b 1954, Rosemary Ann (Mrs Whittle) b 1959); *Career* farm business Elton Newham Glos, lectr W Glos Coll 1962-79; sec: Littledean Utd Reform Church 1951-88, Forest of Dean Utd Reform Church 1962-88; parly candidate 1959; memb: Glos RDC 1955-62, Glos CC 1981- (chm 1985-); *Books* Notes on Economic History (1967), Objective Tests in Economic History (1979), A Country Diary from the Forest of Dean (1984); *Recreations* gardening for flowers, literature, theatre, cricket; *Style*— Eric Radley, Esq; Elton Farm, Newnham on Severn, Glos GL14 1JJ (☎ 045 276 239)

RADNOR, Dowager Countess of; Anne Isobel Graham Pleydell-Bouverie; OBE (1961), DL (Wiltshire 1987); da of Lt-Col Richard Oakley, DSO, JP (d 1948), and Enid Elizabeth (d 1980), da of James Noble Graham, JP, DL (of the senior cadet branch of the Ducal family of Montrose); *b* 6 Sept 1908; *m* 1, 1931, Richard Sowerby (d 1939), er s of Lt-Col Thomas Sowerby, JP, of The Manor House, Lilley, Herts; m 2, 1943, as his 2 w, 7 Earl of Radnor, KG, KCVO, JP, DL (d 1968); 1 s (Richard Oakley); *Career* memb: Historic Buildings Cncl for England 1953-68, advsy bd for Redundant Churches 1969-79; tstee Historic Churches Preservation Tst; pres: Health Visitors' Assoc 1963-84, Wilts Tst for Nature Conservancy, Wilts Community Cncl, Salisbury-South Wilts Museum; past-pres Assoc of Wilts Parish Cncls; *Style*— The Rt Hon the Dowager Countess of Radnor, OBE, DL; Avonturn, Alderbury, Salisbury (☎ 0722 710235)

RADNOR, 8 Earl of (GB 1765); Sir Jacob Pleydell-Bouverie; 11 Bt (GB 1714); also Viscount Folkestone, Baron Longford (both GB 1747), and Baron Pleydell-Bouverie (GB 1765); patron of two livings; s of 7 Earl of Radnor, KG, KCVO (d 1968), and his 1 w, Helena (who m 2, 1943, Brig Montacute William Worrell Selby-Lowndes, and d 1985), da of late Charles Adeane, CB (whose w Madeline, CBE, JP, was gda of 1 Baron Leconfield); *b* 10 Nov 1927; *Educ* Harrow, Trinity Coll Cambridge; *m* 1, 1953 (m dis 1962), Anne, da of Donald Seth-Smith, MC; 2 s; m 2, 1963 (m dis 1985), Margaret, da of Robin Fleming, of Catter House, Drymen; 4 da; m 3, 1986, Mrs A C Pettit; *Heir* s, Viscount Folkestone; *Career* landowner and farmer; chm Br Dyslexia Assoc 1971-76, pres Dyslexia Fndn 1975-; *Recreations* field sports; *Clubs* White's, Farmers; *Style*— The Rt Hon the Earl of Radnor; Longford Castle, Salisbury, Wilts SP5 4EF (☎ 0722 29732)

RADOMIR, Hon Mrs (Sarah Elizabeth); *née* Marks; da of 2 Baron Marks of Broughton; *b* 1953; *m* 1979, Nicholai Radomir; *Style*— The Hon Mrs Radomir

RAE, Allan Alexander Sinclair; CBE (1973); s of John Rae (d 1969), of Ayr, and Rachel Margaret, *née* Sinclair (d 1969); *b* 26 Nov 1925; *Educ* Ayr Acad, Glasgow Univ (LLB); *m* 1, 1 June 1955, Shelia Grace (d 1985), da of Capt Geoffrey Saunders, OBE, RN (d 1948); 2 s (Nigel b 1956, David b 1961), 1 da (Susan b 1962); m 2, 7 April 1986, Gertrud, da of Arnold Dollinger (d 1972), of Basle, Switzerland; *Career* Staff Capt RA JAG Dept 1944-47; slr; sr ptnr Crawford Bayley & Co Bombay 1959-64 (joined 1948, ptnr 1950-59), dir and head of legal and patents dept CIBA Ltd Basle 1964-69, dir and head of regnl servs CIBA-GEIGY Ltd Basle 1969-72, chm CIBA-GEIGY Gp of Cos UK 1972-, Ilford Ltd 1972-88; dir: ABB Power Ltd 1973-, Williams & Glyn's Bank 1974-85, T & N plc 1979-, ABB Kent (hldgs) plc 1980-, Mettler Instruments Ltd 1985-89, Riggs AP Bank Ltd 1986-; pres Chemical Industs Assoc Ltd 1986-88 (vice pres 1984-86, memb cncl 1975-); companion BIM; *Recreations* sailing, skiing, golf; *Clubs* Buck's, Royal Thames YC, Sunningdale GC; *Style*— Allan Rae, Esq, CBE; Bryn Dulas, Llanddulas, Clywd LL22 8NA; 30 Buckingham Gate, London SW1E 6LH (☎ 01 828 5676, fax 01 828 4743, telex 917011)

RAE, John; s of John Rae (d 1976), of Rutherglen, Lanarkshire, and Marion, *née* Dow; *b* 29 Sept 1942; *Educ* Rutherglen Acad Univ of Glasgow (BSc, PhD); *m* 11 May 1968, Irene Isabella, da of William Cassels, of Glasgow; 1 s (Philip John b 23 March 1974), 2 da; *Career* teaching and res in theoretical physics: Univ of Glasgow 1964-68, Univ of Texas Austin 1968-70, Univ Libre Brussels 1970-72, QMC London 1972-74; acting div head theoretical physics div Harwell 1985 (industl fell 1974-76, gp leader theory of fluids 1976-86), chief scientist Dept of Energy 1986-; BNES 1985, FInstE 1986, SERC 1986, NERC 1986; *Recreations* music (singing), gardening; *Style*— Dr John Rae; Dept of Energy, Thames House South, Millbank, London SW1P 4QJ (☎ 01 211 4137, fax 01 834 3771, telex 918777 ENERGY G)

RAE, Dr John Malcolm; s of Dr Lawrence John Rae, of Walton on the Hill, Surrey, and Annie Blodwen, *née* Williams (d 1977); *b* 20 Mar 1931; *Educ* Bishop's Stortford Coll, Sidney Sussex Coll Cambridge (MA), King's Coll London (PhD); *m* 31 Dec 1955, Daphne Ray, da of John Phimester Simpson (d 1939), of Edinburgh, 2 s (Shamus, Jonathan (twins)), 4 da (Siobhan, Penelope, Alyce, Emily); *Career* 2 Lt Royal Fus 1950-51; history master Harrow 1955-66, headmaster Taunton Sch 1966-70, headmaster Westminster Sch 1970-86, dir The Laura Ashley Fndn 1986-, Gresham prof of rhetoric 1988-, dir The Observer Ltd; JP Middx 1961-66, memb Ethics Ctee Humana Hosp London, govr of Schs and Colls; Freeman City of London; hon FCP [illegible]4, FRSA 1988; *Books* The Custard Boys (1960), Conscience and Politics (1970), [illegible] Public School Revolution (1980), Letters from School (1987); five books for children, film script Reach for Glory 1961 (UN award), contributor to nat newspapers; *Recreations* cinema, swimming; *Clubs* Hawks (Cambridge), RAC; *Style*— Dr John Rae; 101 Millbank Court, 24 John Islip St, London SW1P 4LG (☎ 01 828 1842); The Laura Ashley Foundation, 33 King St, London WC2E 8JD (☎ 01 487 2503)

RAE, John William; s of Lt-Col William Rae, DSO, VD, CD (d 1973), and Edith Marion, *née* Brodrick (d 1988); *b* 16 Dec 1938; *Educ* Charterhouse, Queen's Coll Oxford (MA); *Career* TA: 2 Lt 5 Bn Queen's Royal Regt 1959-60, Lt 3 Bn Queen's Royal Surrey Regt 1961-63; TA Reserve of Offrs 1963-67; Regular Army Reserve of Offrs (II) 1967-85 and 1988-, HAC (HSF) 1985-88; called to the Bar Inner Temple 1961, worked way around world 1962-64, int commercial lawyer 1965-78, practising barr 1979-; memb exec ctee Oxford Soc (chm West London branch 1968-); memb Guild Church Cncl and ctee of friends of St Botolph-without-Aldersgate Church London; memb: Aldersgate Ward Club, ctee of Friends of Holland Park Kensington; Freeman City of London; Master Worshipful Co of Plumbers 1982-83, Liveryman Worshipful Co of Painter-Stainers; memb: Gen Cncl of the Bar, Bar Euro Gp (German speaker), Criminal Bar Assoc; *Recreations* beagling, cycling, tennis, skiing, walking, travel, current affairs, music, photography; *Clubs* Beefsteak, Coningsby, Canada; *Style*— John W Rae, Esq; 16A Campden Hill Court, Campden Hill Road, London W8

7HS (☎ 01 937 3492); 2 Paper Buildings, Temple, London EC4Y 7ET (☎ 01 353 0826, fax 01 583 3423, telex 885358 TEMPLE G)

RAE, Kenneth St John; s of Lt Col William Rae, DSO (d 1973), and Edith Marion, *née* Brodrick (d 1988); *b* 2 Oct 1940; *Educ* Charterhouse, Univ of Br Columbia (BCom); *m* 21 March 1969, Sarah Hine, da of Lt Col Phillip Anthony Egerton Dumas, of Matfield, Kent; 1 s (Angus William Brodrick b 1970), 1 da (Isobel Julie Egerton b 1972), 1 step s (James Henry George Pollard b 1964); *Career* Sub Lt Univ Naval Trg Div Canada 1962; economist P & O 1964-68; PA to: chm Anglo Norness 1968-70, gen md JH Fenner 1970-71; dir Davies & Newman 1977- (joined 1971); Freeman: City of London, Worshipful Co of Plumbers (1965); *Recreations* gardening; *Style—* Kenneth Rae, Esq; Wyck House, Wood's Green, Wadhurst, Sussex TN5 6QS (☎ 089 288 2609); Davies & Newman Ltd, New City Ct, 20 St Thomas St, London (☎ 01 378 6867, fax 403 2025, telex 892141)

RAE, Hon Mrs (Penelope Ann); *née* Rippon; yst da of Baron Rippon of Hexham, PC, QC (Life Peer); *b* 5 Oct 1953; *m* 1984, Simon Rae; 1 da (Albertine Helen Yorke b 1985); *Style—* The Hon Mrs Penelope Rae

RAE, Hon Sir Wallace Alexander Ramsay; s of George Ramsay Rae; *b* 31 Mar 1914; *Educ* Sydney Tech Coll; *Career* Flt lt UK, OC Test Flight Amberley Qld; grazier; MLA (Nat Party of Australia) for Gregory Qld 1957-74, minister for: Local Govt and Electricity 1969-74, Lands and Forestry Qld 1974, agent-gen for Qld in London 1974-80; kt 1976; *Style—* The Hon Sir Wallace Rae; 6 Ondine St, Mermaid Waters, Gold Coast, Queensland 4218, Australia

RAE SMITH, David Douglas; CBE (1976), MC (1945); s of Sir Alan Rae Smith, KBE (d 1961), of Copynsfield, Westerham, Kent, and Mabel Grace *née* Eales (d 1963); *b* 15 Nov 1919; *Educ* Radley, ChCh Oxford (MA); *m* 12 April 1947, Margaret Alison, da of James Watson (d 1968), of Holyrood House, Hedon, E Yorks; 3 s (James b 1949, John b 1952, Alan b 1960), 1 da (Katherine b 1957); *Career* Capt RA 1939-46, MC (despatches), ME, Italy, France and Germany; CA; ptnr Deloitte Haskins & Sells 1954-82, sr ptnr 1973-82; hon tres Royal Inst of Int Affairs 1961-81; memb cncl Radley Coll 1966- (chm 1976-), Thomas Tilling plc 1982-83, Sandoz Products Ltd 1983-, Bankers Tstee Co Ltd 1984-, memb Licensed Dealers Tribunal 1974-88; *Recreations* horseracing, golf; *Clubs* Gresham; *Style—* David Rae Smith, Esq, CBE, MC; Oakdale, Crockham Hill, Edenbridge, Kent (☎ 0732 866220)

RAEBURN, Ashley Reinhard George; CBE (1976); s of Dr Adolf Alsberg (d 1933), of Kassel, Germany, and Elisabeth, *née* Hofmann (d 1949); *b* 23 Dec 1918; *Educ* UCS, Balliol Coll Oxford (MA); *m* 6 Nov 1943, Esther Letitia Vivonne, da of Alfred Johns, of Goodwick, Pembs (d 1957); 1 s (Richard b 1946), 3 da (Ursula b 1944, Joanna b 1949, Charlotte b 1954); *Career* WWII RA (Capt) served in UK and India 1940-46; MOF and HM Treasy 1946-54, Royal Dutch Shell Gp 1955-77 (gp tres 1962), dir Shell Int Petroleum Co Ltd (responsible for Africa and India and Pakistan) 1968-72, chief rep Shell Cos in Japan 1972-77, dir Rolls Royce Ltd 1978-82 (vice-chm rep 1979-), dir Boosey & Hawkes plc 1983-88 (chm 1984-86), dir Amalgamated Metal Corpn plc 1983-; endowment tstee Balliol Coll Oxford 1965-, memb Cncl of Management Studies 1965- (now Templeton Coll) Oxford (chm 1978-85); *Recreations* walking, gardening, music; *Clubs* United Oxford and Cambridge; *Style—* Ashley Raeburn, Esq

RAEBURN, David Antony; s of Walter Augustus Leopold Raeburn, QC (d 1972), of London, and Dora Adelaide Harvey, *née* Williams; *b* 22 May 1927; *Educ* Charterhouse, Christ Church Oxford (MA); *m* 8 April 1961, Mary Faith Fortescue, da of Arthur Hubbard (d 1977), of Harare, Zimbabwe; 2 s (Mark b 1965, Martin b 1967), 1 da (Fiona b 1964); *Career* Nat Serv 1949-51, (cmmnd RAEC 1950); asst master: Bristol GS 1951-54, Bradfield Coll 1955-58, head of classics Alleyns Sch Dulwich 1958-62; headmaster: Beckenham and Penge GS (renamed Langley Pk Sch for Boys 1969), 1963-70, Whitgift Sch Croydon 1970-; tres of HMC 1983-89, pres Jt Assoc of Classical Teachers 1983-85 (dir summer sch in ancient greek 1968-85); FRSA 1969; *Recreations* play production; *Style—* David Raeburn, Esq; Haling House, 38 Haling Park Rd, S Croydon CR2 6NE (☎ 01 688 8114); Whitgift Sch, Haling Park, S Croydon, CR2 6YT (☎ 01 688 9222)

RAEBURN, Maj-Gen Sir (William) Digby (Manifold); KCVO (1979), CB (1966), DSO (1945), MBE (1941); s of late Sir Ernest Manifold Raeburn, KBE, s of 1 Bt; *b* 6 August 1915; *Educ* Winchester, Magdalene Cambridge; *m* 1960, Adeline Margaret, da of late Thomas Selwyn Pryor, MC; *Career* Maj-Gen (ret) late Scots Gds; dir of Combat Devpt (Army) 1963-65, Chief of Staff Allied Forces N Europe 1965-68, Chief Army Instructor Imperial Defence Coll 1968-70, resident govr and keeper of Jewel House of HM Tower of London 1971-79; *Style—* Maj-Gen Sir Digby Raeburn, KCVO, CB, DSO, MBE; 25 St Ann's Terrace, London NW8

RAEBURN, (Sir) Michael Edward Norman; (4 Bt, UK 1923, but does not use his title); s of Sir Edward Alfred Raeburn, 3 Bt (d 1977), and Joan, da of Frederick Hill, of Boston, USA; *b* 12 Nov 1954; *m* 1979, Penelope Henrietta Theodora, da of Alfred Louis Penn (d 1963), of London; 1 s, 2 da; *Heir* s, Christopher Edward Alfred Raeburn, b 4 Dec 1981; *Career* civil servant; *Style—* Michael Raeburn, Esq; Little Spring Cottage, Fletching Street, Mayfield, East Sussex TN20 6TN; HM Land Registry, Curtis House, Forest Rd, Hawkenbury, Tunbridge Wells, Kent

RAFFAN, Keith William Twort; MP (Cons Delyn 1983-); s of Alfred William Raffan, TD, MB, ChB; *b* 21 June 1949; *Educ* Robert Gordon's Coll Aberdeen, Trinity Coll Glenalmond, Corpus Christi Coll Cambridge (MA); *Career* parly corr Daily Express 1981-83; parly candidate (C), Dulwich Feb 1974-, E Aberdeenshire Oct 1974; memb select ctee on Welsh Affrs 1983-, introduced Controlled Drugs (Penalties) Act 1985-; pres Young Cons 1987-; memb NUJ; *Clubs* Carlton, Flint Cons, Prestatyn Cons; *Style—* Keith Raffan, Esq, MP; House of Commons, London SW1A 0AA

RAGLAN, 5 Baron (UK 1852); FitzRoy John Somerset; JP (Monmouthshire, now Gwent, 1958), DL (1971); s of 4 Baron Raglan, JP (d 1964; who was descended from 5 Duke of Beaufort), and Hon Julia Hamilton, da of 11 Lord Belhaven and Stenton; *b* 8 Nov 1927; *Educ* Westminster, Magdalen Coll Oxford, RAC Cirencester; *m* 1973 (m dis), Alice (who m 1981, Ian, s of Capt Evan Williams, of Co Limerick), yr da of Peter Baily, of Gt Whittington, Northumberland; *Heir* bro, Hon Geoffrey Somerset; *Career* sits as SDP peer in House of Lords; Capt Welsh Gds; chm: Cwmbran New Town Devpt Corpn 1970-83, Courtyard Arts Tst 1974-, Bath Preservation Trust 1975-77, Bath Soc 1977-, Bugatti Owners' Club 1988-; pres: Bath Centre Nat Tst, UK Housing Trust 1982- (chm S Wales Regn 1976-89), Usk Civic Soc; memb sub-ctee D (food and agric) of House of Lords ctee on European Communities 1974-85 and 1987- (chm 1976-78); patron: Usk Farmers' Club, Raglan Baroque Players; *Style—* The Rt Hon the Lord Raglan, JP, DL; Cefntilla, Usk, Gwent (☎ 029 13 2050)

RAIKES, Lady Audrey Elizabeth Joyce; *née* Wilson; da of A Wilson, of Repton, Derbys; *m* 1940, Sir Victor Alpin MacKinnon Raikes, KBE (d 1986); 2 da; *Style—* Lady Raikes; 9 Gledhow Gardens, London SW5 (☎ 01 373 7865)

RAIKES, Vice Adm Sir Iwan Geoffrey; KCB (1976), CBE (1967, DSC 1943), DL (Powys 1983)); s of Adm Sir Robert Henry Taunton Raikes, KCB, CVO, DSO (d 1953), and Ida Guinevere, *née* Evans (d 1983); *b* 21 April 1921; *Educ* RNC Dartmouth; *m* 1947, Cecilia Primrose, da of Philip Gerald Benedict Hunt (d 1958), of Woodhayes, Woodlands, Southampton; 1 s, 1 da; *Career* RN 1935, HMS Beagle Atlantic convoys 1941, submarines Atlantic, Mediterranean and North Sea 1942-45, cmd HM Submarines: H43 1943-44, Varne 1944-45, Virtue 1945-46, Talent 1948-49, Aeneas 1951-52; Cdr 1952, staff of C-in-C Allied Forces Mediterranean 1953-55, exec offr HMS Newcastle (Far East) 1955-57, JSSC 1957, Capt 1960, cmd HMS Loch Insh (Persian Gulf) 1961-62, dep dir Undersurface Warfare MOD 1962-64, dir plans and Operations (Singapore) on staff of C-in-C Far East 1965-66, IDC 1967, cmd HMS Kent 1968-69, ADC to HM The Queen 1969-70, Rear Adm 1970, naval sec MOD 1970-72, flag offr First Flotilla 1973-74, flag offr Submarines and Cdr Submarines Eastern Atlantic 1974-76, Vice Adm 1973, ret 1977; *Recreations* fishing, shooting, gardening; *Clubs* Naval & Military; *Style—* Vice Adm Sir Iwan Raikes, KCB, CBE, DSC, DL; Aberyscir Ct, Brecon, Powys

RAILTON, Dame Ruth; DBE (1966), OBE (1954); da of Rev David Railton, MC (d 1955; rector of Liverpool and originator of the idea of the Unknown Warrior Tomb, his flag, used in WW I, hangs in the Warriors Chapel in Westminster Abbey), and Ruby Marion de Lancey Willson; *b* 14 Dec 1915; *Educ* St Mary's Sch Wantage, Royal Acad of Music London; *m* 1962, Cecil Harmsworth King (d 1987); *Career* dir of music or choral work for many schools and societies 1937-49, adjudicator Fedn of Music Festivals 1946-74, fndr and musical dir of the Nat Youth Orchestra of GB and Nat Jr Music Sch 1946-65, pres Ulster Coll of Music 1960-, govr Royal Ballet Sch 1966-74, fndr and pres Irish Children's Theatre 1978-81, vice-pres Cork Int Fest 1975, memb bd of dirs Nat Concert Hall Dublin 1981-86; patron European Pianoforte Teachers Assoc; hon prof: Chopin Conservatoire Warsaw 1960, Conservatoire of Azores (Lisbon) 1966; FRAM, FRCM, Hon RMCM, FTCL, Hon LLD Aberdeen Univ 1960; *Style—* Dame Ruth Railton, DBE; 54 Ardoyne House, Pembroke Park, Dublin 4 (☎ 0001 617262)

RAINBOW, (James) Conrad Douglas; CBE (1979); s of Jack Conrad Rainbow (d 1956), of Edgware, Middx, and Winifred Edna, *née* Mears (d 1973); *b* 25 Sept 1926; *Educ* William Ellis Sch Highgate London, Selwyn Coll Cambridge (MA); *m* 13 April 1974, Kathleen Margaret, da of Robert Holmes (d 1947); 1 s (James b 14 April 1975), 1 da (Nicola b 8 June 1977); *Career* Nat Serv 1946-48, Flt-Lt RAF VR (T); asst master St Paul Sch London 1951-60, HM inspr of schs 1960-69, chief educn offr Lancs 1974-79 (dep chief 1969-73), princ private tutorial coll 1979-, visiting prof Univ of Wisconsin; former: memb of ct and cncl Lancs Univ, memb advsy ctee Duke of Edinburgh Awards Scheme, chm steering gp of Understanding Br Industry; currently memb exec ctee Cncl of Br Int Schs in the Euro Commununity; *Recreations* music, rowing (now as observor); *Clubs* Leander, IOD; *Style—* Conrad Rainbow, Esq, CBE; Freefolk Ho, Laverstoke, Whitchurch, Hants RG28 7PB (☎ 0256 892 634)

RAINE, Craig Anthony; s of Norman Edward Raine, and Olive Marie Raine, *née* Cheeseborough; *b* 3 Dec 1944; *Educ* Barnard Castle Sch, Exeter Coll Oxford; *m* 1972, Elisabeth Ann Isabel (pasternak Slater), da of Dr Eliot Slater, OBE (d 1982); 3 s (Isaac b 1979, Moses b 1984, Vaska b 1987), 1 da (Nina b 1975); *Career* poet; The Onion Memory (1978), A Martian Sends A Postcard Home (1979), Rich (1984), The Electrification of the Soviet Union (1986); *Recreations* publishing; *Clubs* Groucho; *Style—* Craig Raine, Esq; c/o Faber and Faber, 3 Queen Sq, London WC1 (☎ 01 278 6881)

RAINE, George Edward Thompson; s of Reginald Thompson Raine MC, (d 1960), of Stocksfield, Northumberland, and Mary Dorothy, *née* Tomlinson (d 1976); *b* 1 August 1934; *Educ* Rugby, Emmanuel Coll, Cambridge, St Thomas' Hosp Med Sch (MA, MB, B Chir, FRCS); *m* 11 June 1960, Ena Josephine, da of Joseph Noble, of Ashington, Northumberland; 1 da (Meriel b 1965); *Career* sr conslt Orthopaedic Surgn W Middlesex Univ Hosp 1974-, assoc surgn Royal Masonic Hosp London; formerly sr Orthopaedic Registrar: St George's Hosp London, Rowley Bristow Orthopaedic Hosp Pyrford Surrey, Centre for Hip Surgery Wrightington; orthopaedic surgn to Rambert Dance Co Sch; orthopaedic surgn Crystal Palace Football Club; govr The Lady Eleanor Holles' Sch Hampton; freeman City of London 1987; *Recreations* English lake district, foreign travel; *Style—* George E T Raine, Esq; Pelham's View, 32 Pelhams Walk, Esher, Surrey KT10 8QD (☎ 0372 66656); 144 Harley Street, London W1N 1AH (☎ 01 935 0023)

RAINE, (Harcourt) Neale; s of Harold Raine (d 1966), and Gertrude Maude, *née* Healey (d 1972); *b* 5 May 1923; *Educ* Dulwich, London Univ (MSc); *m* 1947, Eileen; 1 s (Antony b 1954); *Career* divnl md and board memb Associated Engrg Ltd 1965-70; md Alfred Herbert Ltd, 1971-75, consultant engr 1975-; chm Technician Educn Cncl 1976-82; chm Business & Technician Education Cncl 1983-; dir Stothert & Pitt plc 1978-; MInstD; CEng, MICE, FIMC, FIProdE, FRSA; *Recreations* saloon car racing, painting (pastels); *Style—* Neale Raine Esq; Penn Lea, The Avenue, Charlton Kings, Cheltenham, Glos GL53 9BJ (☎ 0242 526185)

RAINEY, Hon Mrs (Jane Teresa Denyse); *née* Ormsby Gore; da of 5 Baron Harlech, PC, KCMG (d 1985); *b* 1942; *m* 1966 (m dis 1984), Michael Sean O'Dare Rainey, s of Maj Sean Rainey, and Mrs Marion Wrottesley; 2 s, 2 da; *Style—* The Hon Mrs Rainey; Brogyntyn Home Farm, Oswestry, Salop

RAINEY, Simon Piers Nicholas; s of Peter Michael Rainey, of Calverley Park Crescent, Tunbridge Wells, and Theresa Cora, *née* Heffernan; *b* 14 Feb 1958; *Educ* Cranbrook Sch Kent, Corpus Christi Coll Cambridge (MA), Univ of Brussels (Lic Sp Dr Eur); *m* Pia Maria Clemence Fulbert, da of Karel Johanna Maria Witlox, of Taalstraat, Vught, The Netherlands; 1 da (Venetia b 1988); *Career* called to the Bar Lincoln's Inn 1982, in practice 1984-, advsr to UN Ctee for Trade and Devpt (Minconmar Project) 1984-85; *Publications* Halsbury's Laws: European Communities (jtly), Marsden: Law of Collisions at Sea (jtly), Maritime Laws of Anglophone Countries of West Africa (1985); *Recreations* classical music, opera, drawing, riding, Italy; *Style—* Simon Rainey, Esq; 38 Halton Rd, London N1 2EU; 2 Essex Ct, Temple, London EC4 (☎ 01 583 8381, 353 2918, fax 01 353 0998, telex 8812528 ADROIT)

RAINEY, (John) Stanley; s of John Rainey (d 1987), of Belfast, and Mary Lilian, *née* Ross (d 1971); *b* 30 August 1923; *Educ* Royal Belfast Academical Inst, Queen's Univ Belfast (BSc); *m* 21 Aug 1951, (Margaret) Ann Bruce, da of Bruce Slipper (d 1966), of Groomsport, Co Down; 4 s (John b 1952, David b 1954, Stephen, Neil (twins) b 1958); *Career* Capt RE 1944-47; John Rainey & Son Ltd 1948-: dir 1948-, md and chm 1968-87, chm 1987-; chm TSB NI 1983-86 (dep chm 1977-78 and 1980-83); dir: TSB Gp plc 1983-, TSB Pension Tst Ltd 1984-, TSB Trustcard Ltd 1985-; chm TSB NI plc 1986-; Capt Instonians CC 1956-57; pres: Rotary Club Belfast 1969-70, Ulster Reform Club 1983; C Eng, MIMechE 1958, MIProdE 1964; *Recreations* golf, shooting, music, painting; *Clubs* Royal Co Down GC, Malone GC, Ulster Reform; *Style*— Stanley Rainey, Esq; Long Thatch, 33 Bally Morran Rd, Co Down, N Ireland (☎ 0238 541302); TSB Northern Ireland plc, 4 Queen's Sq, Belfast (☎ 0232 325599, telex 743665, fax 0232 221754)

RAINFORD, John; s of Robert Sutter Rainford (d 1959), of Nelson Ho, The Beacon, Exmouth, Devon, and Monica, *née* Tamblyn (d 1987); *b* 20 July 1935; *Educ* Exeter Sch, Pembroke Coll Cambridge (BA, LLB); *m* 9 Sept 1959, Shelia, da of Reginald Walter Charles Pile, (d 1975), of Parkway, Exmouth, Devon; 2 s (Justin b 1965, Kyle b 1966), 1 da (Helen b 1963); *Career* Nat Serv RA 1954-56, cmmnd 2 Lt 20 Field Regt 1956; slr, ptnr Messrs Richards Butler 1967-; memb Law Soc 1963; *Clubs* United Oxford & Cambridge University; *Style*— John Rainford, Esq; The Courtyard, Windhill, Bishop's Stortford, Herts CM23 2NG (☎ 0279 52854); 5 Clifton St, London EC2A 4DQ (☎ 01 247 6555, fax 01 247 5091, telex 949494)

RAINGER, Peter; CBE (1982); s of Cyril Frederick Rainger (d 1973), and Ethel, *née* Wilson (d 1983); *b* 17 May 1924; *Educ* Northampton Engrg Coll, Univ of London (BSc REng); *m* 1, 1953, the late Josephine Dorothy, da of Joseph Campbell, of Northolt London; 2 s (John b 1957, David b 1960); m 2, Barbara Gibson; 1 step da (Pamela b 1946); *Career* Nat Serv RAF 1942-47; engr BBC 1951-; designer TV equipment 1951-69, Head Designs Dept 1969-71, Head Res Dept 1971, ret Dep Dir Engrg responsible for all R & D 1984 (devpts incl: conversion of TV pictures between different tech standards, introduction of teletext broadcasting); currently conslt to broadcasting indust; Freeman City of London, Worshipful Co of Engineers; FRS, FEng, FIEE, FRTS, SMPTE; *Books* Satellite Broadcasting (1985); *Recreations* computing, model engineering, sailing; *Style*— Peter Rainger, Esq, CBE; Applehurst, West End Ave, Pinner HA5 1BJ; Denham Court, 4 Wortley Rd, Highclyffe BH23 5DT

RAINGOLD, Gerald Barry; s of Henry Raingold (d 1979), of 19 Hanover House, London NW8, and Francis Raingold; *b* 25 Mar 1943; *Educ* St Paul's, Inst of CAs, London Graduate Sch of Business Studies (MBA); *m* 14 July 1978, Aviva, da of Henry Petrie (d 1962), of London; 1 s (Andrew b 18 Sept 1981), 2 da (Nina b 2 Aug 1979, Karen b 23 July 1983); *Career* CA; Cole Dicken & Hills (articles) 1963-68, Cooper Bros 1968-72 (mangr 1972), sr mangr corporate finance Wallace Brothers Bank 1972-76, sr conslt Midland Montagu Gp 1976-78, dep md (formerly mangr, sr mangr, asst gen mangr) Banque Paribas London 1978-; memb: London Business Sch Alumni, city ctee Inst of Mgmnt 1980-83, Inst of Dirs city branch, Royal Inst Int Affairs, Bus Graduates Assoc; dir Br Francophone Business Gp (trade assoc); Freeman City of London 1987; FCA 1968, FInstD 1987; *Recreations* opera, ballet, tennis, reading; *Clubs* Overseas Bankers; *Style*— Gerald Raingold, Esq; 12 Marston Close, London NW6 4EU (☎ 01 328 5800); Banque Paribas, 68 Lombard St, London EC3V 9EH (☎ 01 929 4545, fax 01 726 6761, car 0860 622149, telex 945881 PARIBA G)

RAINS, Prof Anthony John Hardins; CBE (1986); s of Robert Harding Rains (Capt RAMC, d 1920), of Bexhill, and Florence Eleanor, *née* Rapson (d 1962); *b* 5 Nov 1920; *Educ* Christs Hosp, St Marys Hosp Med Sch, Univ of London (MBBS, MS); *m* 30 Oct 1943, Mary Adelaide, da of Edward Henry Lillywhite (d 1963), of London; 3 da (Margaret b 1944, Diana b 1948, Charlotte b 1963); *Career* med offr RAF 1944-47; lectr in surgery Univ of Birmingham 1950-59, hon conslt surgn Utd Birmingham Hosps 1954-59, prof of surgery Charing Cross Hosp Med Sch (Univ of London) 1959-81, hon conslt surgn Charing Cross, West London and Fulham Hosps 1959-81, dean Inst Basic Med Sci Royal Coll of Surgns 1976-83, postgrad dean SW Met RHA 1981-85, asst dir Br Post grad Med Fedn 1981-85, ed Jl Royal Soc of Med 1986-; chm Med cmmn Accident Prevention 1972-84, tstee Smith and Nephew Fndn 1974; first chm Child Accident Prevention ctee cncllr Kings Norton Birmingham 1953-59; Freeman Worshipful Soc of Apothecaries 1965; FRCS 1948; *Books* The Treatment of Cancer in Clinical Practice (with PB Kunkler, 1959), Bailey and Loves Shorts Practice of Surgery (ed 13-20 edns 1965-88), Joseph Lister and Antisepsis (1977); *Recreations* reading; *Style*— Prof Anthony Rains; 42 Sydney Buildings, Bath BA2 6 DB (☎ 0225 63148)

RAINSFORD, Surgn Rear Adm Seymour Grome; CB (1955); s of Dr Frederick Edward Rainsford (d 1923), of Co Dublin, and Eleanor *née* Douglas (d 1955); *b* 24 April 1900; *Educ* Dublin (MD, ScD), (DPH); *m* 1974, Caroline Mary Herschel, da of Sir Denis Hill (d 1982); 2 s (Edward, Simon); *Career* surgn Rear Adm RN 1953-56; conslt pathologist; factory inspectorate Min of Lab 1956-66; conslt coagulation disorders Wessex Regnl Hosp Bd 1966-80; res fell Arthritis & Rheumatic Cncl 1980-83; FRCP, FRCPath; *Clubs* Army and Navy; *Style*— Surgn Rear Adm Seymour Rainsford; 25 Colletts Close, Corfe Castle, Wakeham BH20 5HG (☎ 0929 480 822)

RAISMAN, John Michael; CBE (1983); s of Sir Jeremy Raisman GCMG, GCIE, KCSI (d 1978), and Renee Mary, *née* Kelly; *b* 12 Feb 1929; *Educ* Dragon Sch Oxford, Rugby, Queen's Coll Oxford (MA); *m* 1953, Evelyn Anne, da of Brig James Ingram Muirhead, CIE, MC (d 1964); 1 s, 3 da; *Career* dep chm Br Telecom plc, chm Shell UK Ltd 1979-85 (chief exec 1978-85); dir: Vickers plc 1981-, Glaxo Hldgs plc 1982, Lloyds Bank plc 1985-; chm: Oil Indust Emergency Ctee 1980-85, advsy cncl London Enterprise Agency 1980-85, cncl Indust for Mgmnt Educ 1979-85; CBI: memb cncl, chm Europe ctee 1980-88, memb Presidents ctee 1980-88; memb: governing Body Business in the Community 1982-85, cncl Inst for Fiscal Studies , Royal Cmmn on Environmental Pollution 1985-87; chm: Electronics EDC 1985-87; bd of tstees Royal Acad, investmt bd Electra Candover ptnrs; govr Henley Mgmnt Coll, pro chllr Aston Univ; Hon D Univ Stirling 1983; Hon LLD Aberdeen 1985; Hon LLD Manchester 1986; *Recreations* golfing, skiing, music; *Clubs* Brooks's, Royal Mid-Surrey, Sunningdale; *Style*— John Raisman, Esq, CBE; c/o British Telecom, BT Centre, 81 Newgate St, London EC1A 7AJ

RAISON, Dr John Charles Anthony; s of Cyril Alban Raison (d 1948), and Ceres Constance Mary Raison; *b* 13 May 1926; *Educ* Malvern, Trinity Hall Cambridge (MA, MD), Birmingham Univ; *m* 1, 3 April 1951, Rosemary, da of Edgar Padmore, MC (d 1962); 1 s (Charles Christopher John b 1957), 2 da (Marie Louise b 1953, Camille Annette b 1954); m 2, 13 Sept 1983, Ann Alexander, da of Capt (John Henry) Roy Faulkner, MN (d 1982); 3 step da (Kate Helen Alexander b 1964, Jane Susan Alexander b 1966, Lucy Ann Alexander b 1969); *Career* Sqdn Ldr Royal Auxiliary Air Force 605 Sqdn 1950-52; visiting prof in cardiac surgery Golbenkian Fndn Lisbon 1962, conslt clinical physiologist regnl cardiothoracic surgical unit Birmingham Regnl Hosp Bd 1962-66, clinical physiologist and chief planner cardiac surgical unit Presbyterian Pacific Med Cantre San Francisco USA 1966-69, sr princ med offr then chief sci offr, Dept of Health London 1969-79, dep dir Nat Radiological Protection Bd 1978-81, specialist in community med Wessex Regnl Health Authy 1982-; memb Southern Warwicks RDC 1955-60; MFCM 1972, FFCM, FRCP 1987; *Recreations* gardening, theatre, tennis, sailing; *Style*— Dr John Raison; 14 Kingsway, Chandlers Ford, Hants SO5 1BX (☎ 0703 253627); Wessex Regional Health Authority, Highcroft, Romsey Road, Wincyhester, Hants (☎ 0962 63511)

RAISON, Patrick Nicolas; s of Rev Herbert Chaplin Raison (d 1952); *b* 30 Oct 1933; *Educ* Harrow, Magdalen Oxford, Sch of Business Stanford Univ USA; *m* 1962, Françoise Yvonne, da of Maitre Fernand Haissly of Switzerland; 1 s, 2 da; *Career* barr Grays Inn, md Oxford Controls Co Ltd; *Recreations* travel, aviation (Cessna GBFGY); *Clubs* Carlton; *Style*— Patrick Raison Esq; Farncombe Hill, Broadway, Worcs (☎ 852465)

RAISON, Rt Hon Timothy Hugh Francis; PC (1980), MP (C) Aylesbury 1970-; s of Maxwell Raison, of Theberton; *b* 3 Nov 1929; *Educ* Eton, Christ Church Oxford; *m* 1956, Veldes Julia, er da of John Arthur Pepys Charrington (himself yr s of Arthur Charrington by Dorothea Lethbridge, ggda of Sir Thomas Lethbridge, 2 Bt); 1 s, 3 da; *Career* Min for Overseas Devpt 1983-, Min of State Home Off 1979-83, Oppn Spokesman Environment 1975-76, Parly Under-Sec DES 1973-74, PPS to NI Sec 1972-73; memb ILEA 1967-70, Richmond Cncl 1967-71, Home Office Advsy Cncl Penal System 1970-74, Central Advsy Cncl Educn 1963-66, Cncl Policy Studies Institute 1978-79; former journalist with *Picture Post, New Scientist*, former ed *Crossbow* and *New Society*; *Clubs* Beefsteak, MCC; *Style*— The Rt Hon Timothy Raison, MP; 66 Riverview Gdns, SW13 (☎ 01 748 4724)

RALLI, David Charles; s and h of Sir Godfrey Ralli, 3 Bt, TD; *b* 5 April 1946; *Educ* Eton; *m* 1975, Jacqueline Cecilia, da of David Smith; 1 da, 1 s; *Career* farmer; chm Dereham Farm Servs 1985-87, dir Mid Norfolk Farmers 1985-, cncllr Breckland DC 1987-; *Recreations* golf, shooting, fishing; *Clubs* White's, Farmers; *Style*— David Ralli Esq; Hunts Farm, Saham Toney, Thetford, Norfolk

RALLI, Sir Godfrey Victor; 3 Bt (UK 1912), TD; s of Sir Strati Ralli, 2 Bt, MC (d 1964); *b* 9 Sept 1915; *Educ* Eton; *m* 1, 24 June 1937 (m dis 1947), Nora Margaret, o da of late Charles Forman, of Lodden Court, Spencers Wood, nr Reading; 1 s, 2 da; m 2, 24 March 1949, Jean, da of late Keith Barlow; *Heir* s, David Charles Ralli; *Career* Ralli Brothers Ltd 1936-62 (apart from army service 1939-45); chm: G & L Ralli Investment & Tstee Co Ltd 1962-75, Greater London Fund for the Blind 1962-82; *Recreations* golf, fishing, gardening; *Clubs* White's, Naval and Military; *Style*— Sir Godfrey Ralli, Bt, TD; Great Walton, Eastry, Sandwich, Kent CT13 0DN

RALPHS, Lady; Enid Mary; CBE (1984), JP, DL (Norfolk 1981); da of Percy William Cowlin (d 1929), and Annie Louise, *née* Willoughby (d 1977); *b* 20 Jan 1915; *Educ* Camborne GS, Exeter Univ (BA; DipEd Cambridge); *m* 1938, Sir Lincoln Ralphs (d 1978), sometime chief educn offr Norfolk; 1 s, 2 da; *Career* teacher Penzance GS 1937-38; staff tutor Oxford Univ 1942-44, pt-time sr lectr Keswick Hall Coll of Educn 1948-80; chm: Norwich Bench 1977, vice-pres Magistrates' Assoc of England and Wales, chm Cncl of Magistrates' Assoc 1981-84, memb Home Office Advisory Bd on Restricted Patients 1985-; ret; *Books* co author The Magistrate as Chairman (1987); *Recreations* gardening, travel; *Clubs* Royal Overseas League; *Style*— Lady Ralphs, CBE, JP, DL; Jesselton, 218 Unthank Rd, Norwich NR2 2AN (☎ Norwich 53382); The Magistrates' Association, 28 Fitzroy Sq, London W1P 6DD (☎ 01 387 2353)

RALSTON, Gavin Ronald; s of Charles Wallace Ralston (d 1948), and Helen Ripley Ker, MBE (d 1975); *b* 18 Dec 1912; *Educ* Lancing; *m* 9 June 1943, Charity, da of Cyril Ralph Snowden CBE (d 1962); 2 da (Patricia Ann b 1945, Carolyn b 1947), 1 s (Andrew b 1950); *Career* James & Co Colombe Ceylon 1934-49, commerce mangr Manchester Ship Canal 1959-72; Ceylon Planters Rifle Corps, Rifle Brigade (2nd Bn); Major RE, served RE (Movement Control) Ceylon and Middle East, Western Desert & GHQ/Cairo; vice-chm High Peak Conservative Assoc 1962-67; *Recreations* Reading; *Clubs* St James's (Manchester); *Style*— Gavin Ralston, Esq; Hornwich Lodge, Eccles Rd, Whaley Bridge, Ches

RAM, Edward (Ned) David Abel; s of Sir Lucius Abel John Granville Ram, KCB, QC (d 1952), and Elizabeth Lady Ram, *née* Mitchell-Innes; *b* 5 Dec 1934; *Educ* Eton Coll Oxford (BA), Worcester Coll Oxford; *m* 2 Dec 1960, Sheliagh Ann, da of Lt Col James Albert Lewis MC (ka 1942); 1 s (Henry b 1967); *Career* slr, ptnr Withers 1962; dir Daily Mail and General Tst 1977-; Nat Serv 2 Lt Rifle Brigade; *Recreations* shooting, sailing; *Clubs* Brooks's, Royal Fowey Yacht; *Style*— Ned Ram, Esq; 52 St Augustines Road, London NW1 9RN (☎ 01 485 3255); Messrs Withers, 20 Essex Street, Strand, London NC2

RAMAGE, Richard; s of Richard Ramage (d 1971), of London, and Elizabeth Maud, *née* Sims (d 1982); *b* 13 August 1927; *Educ* Haberdashers' Askes's, Cubitt Town Sch; *m* 15 March 1952, Sylvia Mavis, da of Sydney John Eary (d 1986); 3 s (Colin Richard b 1953, Kevin John b 1957, Christopher James b 1968); *Career* Esso Petroleum Gp 1948-64, dir and controller Conoco Europe 1964-72, dep md Conoco Ltd 1972-; memb Tport Users Consultative Ctee for Eastern England; FCIS, ATII; *Style*— Richard Ramage, Esq; 3 Roundwood Grove, Hutton Mount, Shenfield, Brentwood, Essex CM13 2NE (☎ 0277 219128); Conoco Ltd, 230 Blackfriars Rd, London SE1 (☎ 01 408 6192)

RAMEL, Baron (Axel) Knut Stig Malte; yr (twin) s of Baron Stig Urban Malte Ramel, of Stockholm, Sweden, and Ann-Marie, *née* Countess Wachtmeister; *b* 4 April 1954; *Educ* Stockholm Sch of Economics; *Career* Beijen Invest AB Stockholm 1978-80, Credit Suisse First Boston Ltd 1980-84, exec dir Merrill Lynch Int & Co 1984-; *Style*— Baron Knut Ramel; 49A Britannia Rd, London SW6 (☎ 01 384 1081); 25 Ropemaker St, London EC2 (☎ 01 867 2805, fax 01 867 2040)

RAMM, Rev Canon Norwyn MacDonald; s of Rev Ezra Edward Ramm, and Dorothy Mary Ramm; *b* 8 June 1924; *Educ* Berkhamstead Sch Herts, St Peter's Coll Jamaica WI, Univ of Oxford (MA); *m* 23 June 1962, Ruth Ellen, da of Robert James Kirton, CBE (d 1988), of Byron Cottage, North End Ave, London; 2 s (Peter Kay MacDonald b 1965, David Oliver Kirton b 1967), 1 da (Selina Angela Susan b 1963); *Career* curate

St James Montego Bay Jamaica 1951-53, rector Stony Hill with Mount James Jamaica 1953-57, curate St Michael at the North Gate Oxford 1957-61, p-in-c St Martin and All Saints Oxford 1961-71, vicar St Michael at the North Gate Oxford 1961-88; chaplain to HM The Queen 1985, hon canon Christ Church Cathedral Oxford 1985-88 (hon canon emeritus 1988); chaplain: Br Fire Servs Assoc 1980, Oxford City Police Assoc; pres Isis Dist Scout Assoc 1984, fndr and pres Samaritans of Oxford; *Recreations* gardening, skiing, collecting graces; *Clubs* Clarendon (Oxford), Frewen (Oxford), Oxford Rotarian; *Style*— The Rev Canon N M Ramm; Fairlawn, Church La, Harwell, nr Abingdon, Oxon OX11 0EZ (☎ 0235 835 454)

RAMPHAL, Sir Shridath Surendranath; CMG (1966), QC (Guyana 1965); s of James I Ramphal and Grace Ramphal; *b* 3 Oct 1928; *Educ* Queen's Coll Georgetown, King's Coll London, Harvard Law Sch; *m* 1951, Lois Winifred, *née* King; 2 s, 2 da; *Career* barr Gray's Inn 1951, crown counsel Br Guiana 1953-54, asst to attorney-gen 1954-56, legal draftsman Br Guiana 1956-58, slr-gen 1959-61, asst attorney-gen W Indies 1961-62, attorney-gen Guyana 1965-73, memb Nat Assembly 1965-75, min state External Affrs 1967-72, min For Affrs 1972-75 (held concurrently with attorney-generalship -1973), min Justice 1973-75, sec-gen Cwlth 1975-; memb: South Cmmn, Brandt Cmmn on Int Devpt Issues, Palme Cmmn on Disarmament and Security Issues, Independent Cmmn on Int Humanitarian Issues, World Cmmn on Environment and Devpt, Int Cmmn Jurists, and many other bodies; chllr Univ of Guyana 1988; hon master of bench Gray's Inn 1981; Hon FRSA 1981; hon fell: King's Coll London 1975, LSE 1979, Magdalen Coll Oxford 1982; visiting prof: Univ of Exeter 1986, faculty of laws Kings Coll London 1988; Hon LLD: Southampton 1976, Aberdeen 1979, Hull 1983; Cambridge 1985, Warwick 1988; Hon DLitt Bradford 1985; Hon DUniv: Surrey 1979, Essex 1980; Hon DCL: Oxford 1982, East Anglia 1983; Durham 1985; Hon DSc Cranfield Inst of Technol 1987; and hon degrees from many Cwlth univs; RSA Albert Medal 1988; (sr Counsel Guyana) 1966, Hon AC 1982, Order of Excellence Guyana 1983, kt 1970; *Books* One World to Share: selected speeches of the Commonwealth Secretary-General 1975-79, Inseparable Humanity: An Anthology of Reflections of Shridath Ramphal (ed R Sanders, 1988), *Recreations* photography, cooking; *Style*— Sir Shridath Ramphal, CMG, QC; Commonwealth Secretariat, Marlborough House, Pall Mall, London SW1Y 5HX (☎ 01 839 3411, telex 27678)

RAMPLY, David Temple; s of George Temple Ramply, OBE, and Mary Betty Grosvenor, *née* Jarvis (d 1962); *b* 1 Mar 1944; *Educ* Oundle; *m* 4 July 1968, Patricia Jane, da of Capt Gavin Miller Hunter (d 1978), of Huntingdon, Cambs; 3 da (Katherine Jane b 1970, Emma Clare b 1971, Suzanna Elizabeth b 1976); *Career* md R & T Agric Gp of Cos 1972-; dir: R & T Agric Ltd, R & T Cropcare Ltd, R & T Agric Liming Ltd, Anglia Bulk Servs Ltd; *Recreations* rugby, tennis; *Clubs* Huntingdon RUFC (pres); *Style*— David T Ramply, Esq; Paxton Place, Gt Paxton, Huntingdon, Cambs PE19 4RG (☎ 0480 72123); Wheatsheaf House, Alconbury Hill, Huntingdon, Cambs PE17 5UD (☎ 0480 57661, telex 32510, fax 0480 52125)

RAMPTON, Sir Jack Leslie; KCB (1973, CB 1969); s of Leonard Wilfrid Rampton, and Sylvia, *née* Davies; *b* 10 July 1920; *Educ* Tonbridge, Trinity Coll Oxford (MA); *m* 1950, Eileen Joan, *née* Hart; 1 s, 1 da; *Career* joined Treasy 1941, asst private sec to Chllrs of the Exchequer 1942-43, private sec to fin sec 1945-46, econ and fin advsr to cmmr-gen SE Asia and Br high cmmr Malaya 1959-61, under-sec 1964-68, dep sec DTI 1970-72, second perm sec DTI 1972-74, perm under-sec Dept of Energy 1974-80; dir: London Atlantic Investmt Tst 1981-, Sheerness Steel Co 1982-87 (dep chm 1985-87), ENO 1982-88, Carnarvon Mining 1984, Flextech 1985-; memb: Honeywell Advsy Cncl 1981-, cncl Victoria League (dep chm 1985-), Cook Soc 1977 (chm 1987-88), cncl Br-Aust Soc 1986-; govr Cwlth Tst 1988-; pt/t conslt Sun Oil 1982-87; Hon DSc Aston; CBIM; *Recreations* gardening, travel, photography; *Style*— Sir Jack Rampton, KCB; 17 The Ridgeway, Tonbridge, Kent (☎ 0732 352117); work: c/o Britain Australia Society, 19 St James's SW1 (☎ 01 930 5123)

RAMSAY, Alexander William; s of Sir William Clark Ramsay, CBE (d 1973), and Sarah Nora, *née* Evans (d 1982); *b* 3 August 1931; *Educ* Mill Hill, BNC Oxford (MA); *m* 15 Aug 1957, Patricia, da of late William Hague; 2 s (William Alexander b 26 Dec 1958, Sholto David Hague b 7 May 1965), 2 da (Araminta Mary b 24 June 1961, Bonella Ann b 11 March 1964); *Career* 2 Lt Middx Regt, served in Korea 1950, Capt TA; barr Gray's Inn; company dir, vice-chm Portman Building Soc; Westminster City cncllr for six years, dep Lord Mayor of Westminster, JP (resigned), High Sheriff of Gtr London 1976-77; Freeman of City of London, Liveryman of Worshipful Co of Fuellers; pres The Rugby Football Union 1979-81; *Recreations* sport, reading; *Clubs* Carlton, East India, City University, Vincent's, RLYC; *Style*— Alexander Ramsay Esq; Etna House, 350 Kennington Rd, London SE11 4LG (☎ 01 735 8811, fax 01 820 1936, telex 919349); car ☎ 0836 242308

RAMSAY, Sir Alexander William Burnett; 7 Bt (UK 1806); s of late Sir Alexander Burnett Ramsay, 6 Bt (d 1965); is the presumed heir to the Baronetcy of Burnett of Leys (cr 1626); *b* 4 August 1938; *m* 1963, Neryl Eileen, da of J C Smith Thornton Trangie; 2 s; *Heir* s, Alexander David Ramsay b 20 Aug 1966; *Style*— Sir Alexander Ramsay, Bt; 30 Brian St, Balgownie, NSW 2519, Australia

RAMSAY, Hon Anthony; s of 16 Earl of Dalhousie, KT, GCVO, GBE, MC; *b* 1949; *Educ* Ampleforth, Magdalen Coll Oxford; *m* 1973 (m dis), Georgina Mary, da of the late the Hon Michael Langhorne Astor (s of late 2 Visc Astor); 1 s; *Style*— The Hon Anthony Ramsay

RAMSAY, Maj-Gen Charles Alexander; OBE (1979); s of Adm Sir Bertram Home Ramsay, KCB, KBE, MVO (allied Naval C in C invasion of Europe 1944, ka 1945), and Helen Margaret Menzies; descended from Sir Alexander Ramsay, 2nd Bart of Balmain; *b* 12 Oct 1936; *Educ* Eton, Sandhurst; *m* 1967, Hon Mary Margaret Hastings, da of 1 Baron MacAndrew, TD, PC (d 1979); 2 s, 2 da; *Career* cmmnd Royal Scots Greys 1956, Staff Coll, Canada 1967-68, cmd Royal Scots Dragoon Gds 1977-79, Cdr 12 Armd Bde 1980-82, dep DMO MOD 1983-84, GOC Eastern Dist 1984-87; dir gen TA and Army Orgn 1987-; memb Royal Co of Archers (Queen's Body Gd for Scotland); *Recreations* field sports, equitation, travel, farming; *Clubs* Boodle's, Cavalry & Guards, New (Edinburgh), Farmers, Pratt's; *Style*— Maj Gen C A Ramsay, OBE; (☎ 089 084 221); Chesthill, Glenlyon, Perthshire (☎ 088 77 224)

RAMSAY, Col George Patrick Maule; s of Capt Archibald Henry Maule Ramsay (d 1955), and Ismay Lucretia Mary Ramsay, *née* The Hon Ismay Preston (d 1975); *qv* Dalhousie; *b* 15 Nov 1922; *Educ* Eton, RMA Sandhurst; *m* 1, 1947; 2 s (Alexander, Patrick), 3 da (Catherine, Diana, Fiona); m 2, 1980, Bridget, da of Ronald Hornby (d 1984); *Career* WWII serv Scots Gds: Italy (wounded), Malaya, Egypt, Kenya, Germany; Col Cmdg Scots Gds 1964-67; dir: Hill Samuel 1968-79, Kornferry Int 1979-82, Goddard Kay Rogers 1982-87; memb Royal Co of Archers Queens Body Gd for Scotland; *Recreations* shooting, fishing, gardening; *Clubs* Boodle's, Army & Navy, Pratt's, Beefsteak; *Style*— Col George Ramsay; The Old School House, The Square, Elham, Canterbury, Kent CT4 6TJ

RAMSAY, Lord; James Hubert Ramsay; s and h of 16 Earl of Dalhousie, KT, GBE, MC, by his w Margaret, da of late Brig-Gen Archibald Stirling of Keir (2 s of Sir John Stirling-Maxwell, 10 Bt, KT, DL, which Btcy has been dormant since 1956) and Hon Margaret Fraser, OBE, da of 13 Lord Lovat; *b* 17 Jan 1948; *Educ* Ampleforth; *m* 1973, Marilyn, yr da of Maj David Butter, MC, and Myra (da of Sir Harold Wernher, 3 and last Bt, GCVO, TD, by his w Lady Zia, *née* Countess Anastasia Mikhailovna, er da of HIH Grand Duke Mikhail of Russia; Lady Ramsay is hence 1 cous of the Duchesses of Abercorn and Westminster, *qqv*); 1 s, 2 da (Hon Lorna b 1975, Hon Alice b 1977); *Heir* s, Hon Simon David Ramsay b 18 April 1981; *Career* cmmnd 2 Bn Coldstream Gds 1968-71; dir Hambros Bank 1981-82 when left to set up a subsidiary of Skandiaviska Enskilda Banken which was to handle activities in int capital mkts previously dealt with by parent bank in Stockholm; *Clubs* White's, Pratt's, Turf; *Style*— Lord Ramsay; Dalhousie Lodge, Edzell, Angus; 3 Vicarage Gdns, London W8 (T 01 727 2800)

RAMSAY, Hon John Patrick; yst s of 16 Earl of Dalhousie, KT, GCVO, GBE, MC, *qv*; *b* 9 August 1952; *Educ* Ampleforth; *m* 1981, Louisa Jane, only da of late Robert Erland Nicolai d'Abo, of W Wratting Park, Cambs; 1 s (Christopher b 1984), 1 da (Lucy b 1985); *Heir* Christopher Ramsay; *Clubs* Turfs, Whites; *Style*— The Hon John Patrick Ramsay; 1 Kassala Rd, London SW11

RAMSAY, Norman James Gemmill; WS (1939); s of James Ramsay (d 1940), of Buenos Aires, and Kilmarnock, Scotland, and Christina Emma, *née* Sheppard (d 1950); *b* 26 August 1916; *Educ* Merchiston Castle Sch, Univ of Edinburgh (MA, LLB); *m* 5 Jan 1952, Rachael (Ray) Mary Berkeley, da of Sir Herbert Charles Fahie Cox; 2 s (David James b 10 Jan 1954, Alexander Malcolm b 4 March 1957); *Career* WWII RN 1940-46 (serv E Indies Station, Eastern Fleet Aden), writer, leading writer, Petty Offr Writer, Paymaster Sub-Lt, Paymaster Lt, Lt (S) RNVR; admin-gen Northern Rhodesia 1947-56, advocate (Scotland) 1956-, res magistrate 1956-58, sr res magistrate 1958-64, puisne judge High Ct of Northern Rhodesia (later Zambia) 1964-68; Sheriff: S Strathclyde, Dumfries and Galloway 1971-85; *Recreations* gardening; *Clubs* Royal Cwlth Soc; *Style*— Sheriff Norman Ramsay; Mill of Borgue, Kirkcudbright DG6 4SY (☎ 05577 211)

RAMSAY, Patrick George Alexander; s of Rt Rev Ronald Erskine Ramsay (d 1953), and Winifred, *née* Partridge (1985); *b* 14 April 1926; *Educ* Marlborough, Jesus Coll Cambridge (MA); *m* 22 Dec 1948, Hope Seymour Dorothy, da of Rt Rev Algernon Markham (d 1948); 2 s (Alexander b 1950, Jamie b 1953); *Career* RN Fleet Air Arm 1944-46; BBC: report writer Eastern Euro Desk, Monitoring Serv 1949, liason offr US for broadcasts info serv Cyprus 1951-52, sr admin asst external broadcasting 1956-58, head of news admin 1958-64, planning mangr to programme planning 1964-66, controller prog servs 1972-79 (asst controller 1966-69), asst controller programme planning 1969-72, controller BBC Scotland 1979-83; mgmnt advsr Oman Broadcasting Servs 1984-85; chm Windsor and Eton Soc 1971-76; FRSA; *Clubs* National Liberal, New (Edinburgh); *Style*— Patrick Ramsay, Esq; Abcott Manor, Clungunford, Shrops

RAMSAY, Raymond; MBE (1946); s of Alexander Ramsay (d 1963), of Cape Province, S Africa, and Florence E Ramsay, MBE, *née* Tanner (d 1957); *b* 19 August 1916; *Educ* St Marylebone GS, St Barts Hosp Med Coll (LRCP); *m* 4 Oct 1952, Lillian Jane, da of Lt-Col WH Bateman, MC, TD, of Little Court, Batheaston, Bath; 3 s (Jonathan b 1953, William b 1956, Alasdair b 1961); *Career* vol RAMC 1939, cmmnd Lt 1939, Capt 1940, Maj 1942; active serv: Burma 1940, retreat to India 1942, sr MO first Wingate Expdn (wounded POW, i/c Hosp Barracks no 6 Block Rangoon Central Jail 1943-45); demonstrator in anatomy St Barts Hosp Med Coll 1946-47, jr surgical registrar St Barts Hosp 1947-48, surgical registrar Norfolk and Norwich Hosp 1948-51, sr surgical registrar Bristol Royal Infirmary 1951-53, conslt surgn to E Berks Dist (formerly Windsor Gp of Hosps) 1953; FRCS, fell Hunterian Soc, memb RSM; *Recreations* sailing; *Clubs* Royal Solent YC; *Style*— Raymond Ramsay, Esq, MBE

RAMSAY, Richard Alexander McGregor; s of Alexander John McGregor (d 1986), of Ramsay, and Beatrice Kent, *née* De La Nauze; *b* 27 Dec 1949; *Educ* Trinity Coll Glenalmond, Univ of Aberdeen (MA); *m* 19 July 1975, Elizabeth Catherine Margaret, da of Robert Cecil Blackwood (d 1969); 1 s (Alistair Robert Blackwood b 19 Feb 1983), 1 da (Catherine Anne Blackwood b 1 Feb 1981); *Career* CA; articled clerk Price Waterhouse 1972-75, exec mangr Grindlay Brandts Ltd 1975-78, Hill Samuel and Co Ltd 1979-88 (dir 1984-88 seconded dir industl devpt unit DTI 1984-86), dir Barclays de Zoete Wedd Ltd 1988-; FCA; *Recreations* skiing, mountain walking, gardening, historic cars; *Style*— Richard Ramsay, Esq; Ebbgate house, 2 Swan Lane, London EC4R 3TS (☎ 01 623 2323, 0738 822329)

RAMSAY, Sir Thomas Meek; CMG (1965); s of William Ramsay (d 1914), and Annie Elizabeth Ramsay (d 1953); *b* 24 Nov 1907; *Educ* Malvern GS, Scotch Coll Melbourne, Melbourne Univ (BSc); *m* 1942, Catherine Anne, da of John William Richardson; 4 s, 1 da; *Career* chm Kiwi Int Co Ltd 1966-80; memb Mfrg Indust Advsy Cncl 1964-77, chm Indust Design Advsy Cncl of Australia 1969-76; kt 1972; Debrett's Handbook of Australia and New Zealand for further details; *Style*— Sir Thomas Ramsay, CMG; 23 Airlie St, South Yarra, Vic 3141, Australia

RAMSAY, William Marcus Raymond; s of Raymond Ramsay, MBE, of Long Meadow, Farnham Common, Bucks, and Lillian, *née* Bateman; *b* 24 July 1956; *Educ* Univ of London (BA); *m* 11 Oct 1980, Fiona, da of P H Gray, of Lothersdale, N Yorks; 2 s (William b 1981, James b 1985); *Career* asst dir Morgan Grenfell & Co Ltd 1985 (grad entrant 1979, mangr 1984), memb exec ctee N M Rothschild Asset Mgmnt 1988 (joined 1986, dir 1987); dir: Capoco Ltd, The Theatre Royal Windsor 1987-; Freeman City of London 1980-, Worshipful Co of Fletchers 1980-; *Recreations* The Theatre; *Clubs* Brooks's; *Style*— William Ramsay, Esq; Five Arrows Ho, St Swithin's Lane, London EC4N 8NR (☎ 01 280 5000, fax 01 929 1643, telex 888031)

RAMSAY OF MAR, Capt Alexander Arthur Alfonso David Maule; DL (Aberdeenshire 1971); s of Adm Hon Sir Alexander Ramsay, GCVO, KCB, DSO (d 1972; s of 13 Earl of Dalhousie), and Lady Patricia (d 1974, da of HRH 1 Duke of Connaught and Strathearn, 3 s of Queen Victoria), who on her marriage renounced, by Royal permission, the style and title of HRH and Princess and assumed that of Lady; *b* 21 Dec 1919, (King Edward VIII and King Alfonso XIII of Spain sponsors); *Educ* Eton,

Trinity Coll Oxford (MA); *m* 1956, Lady Saltoun, *qv*; 3 da; *Career* Grenadier Gds 1938-47 (wounded N Africa 1943), Capt 1941, ADC to HRH the Duke of Gloucester 1944-47; page of honour at Coronation of George VI 1937; chartered surveyor; memb Forestry Soc of GB 1957- (now Inst of Chartered Foresters), vice-patron Braemar Royal Highland Soc 1959-, Laird of Mar 1963, chm exec ctee Scottish Life Boat Cncl RNLI 1965-, memb Nat Bd SWOA (later TGUK) 1966- (chm NE Region 1967-82); FRICS; *Recreations* shooting, sailing, travel, Scottish and family history, heraldry; *Clubs* Cavalry and Guards', Turf (London), Royal Northern and Univ (Aberdeen), New (Edinburgh), Household Div YC (Warsash), Island SC (Cowes); *Style—* Capt Alexander Ramsay of Mar, DL; Cairnbulg Castle, Fraserburgh, Aberdeenshire AB4 5TN (☎ 0346 23149); Inverey House, Braemar, Aberdeenshire AB3 5YB; Flat 8, 25 Onslow Sq, London SW7 3NJ

RAMSAY OF MAR, Hon Alice Elizabeth Margaret; 2 da of Lady Saltoun, *qv*; *b* 8 July 1961; *Style—* The Hon Alice Ramsay of Mar

RAMSAY OF MAR, Hon Elizabeth Alexandra Mary; yst da of Lady Saltoun, *qv*; *b* 15 April 1963; *Style—* The Hon Elizabeth Ramsay of Mar

RAMSAY RAE, Air Vice-Marshal Ronald Arthur; CB (1960), OBE (1947); s of George Ramsay Rae (d 1949), of Lindfield, NSW, Aust, and late Alice Ramsay, *née* Haselden; *b* 9 Oct 1910; *Educ* N Sydney HS, Sydney Tech Coll; *m* 19 Sept 1939, Rosemary Gough, da of Charles Gough Howell, QC, Attorney General of Singapore; 1 s (Ian Wallace b 1956), 1 da (Philippa Anne b 1958); *Career* Cadet RAAF 1930, cmmnd 1931, transfrd RAF 1932, 33 Sqdn Bicester 1932-1936, 142 Sqdn Air Armament Sch Eastchurch 1936, Singapore 1937 (POW Java 1942-45, despatches 1946), Empire Air Arm Sch 1946, CO Centl Gunnery Sch 1946-47, RAF Staff Coll Andover 1948, ME 1948-50, CO N Luffenham 1950, CO Oakington 1951-53, Air Min DD of Flt Trg 1954-55, Cmdt Aircraft and Arm Ex Estab Boscombe Down 1955-57, Air Min Dep Air Sec 1957-59, AOC 224 GP Malaya Singapore 1957-62 (ret 1962); gen sec Nat Playing Fields Assoc 1962-71, sec St Moritz Tobogganing Club 1971-78, memb Royal Aero Soc 1956; MRAES; *Recreations* cricket, golf, cresta; *Clubs* RAF, St Moritz Tobaganing (pres 1978-84), MCC, W Sussex GC (Pulborough); *Style—* Air Vice-Marshal Ramsay Rae, CB, OBE; Little Wakestone, Fittleworth, W Sussex RH20 1JR (☎ 079 882 217)

RAMSAY-FAIRFAX-LUCY, Hon Lady; *see*: Fairfax-Lucy

RAMSAY-STEEL-MAITLAND, Lady; Matilda Brenda; *née* Doughty; da of late Thomas Doughty, of Coalbrookdale; *b* 2 Dec 1907; *Educ* Clewer Coalbrokkdale Sch of Art; *m* 1942, as his 2 w, Sir (Arthur) James (Drummond) Ramsay-Steel-Maitland, 2 Bt (d 1960); *Career* served Dept of Lab 1939-45, Nat Serv Melbourne Aust; county cmdt Scottish Girls Trg Corps; exhibited pictures in Africa, Edinburgh, London and Paris, gave 1 man exhibition, Edinburgh 1980, past pres Corstophine Art Gp; owned and controlled an orange grove Marrakesh Maroc, until liberation; *Style—* Lady Ramsay-Steel-Maitland; Castle Gogar, Edinburgh 12 9BQ (☎ 031 339 1234); Royal Bank of Scotland, 36 St Andrews Sq, Edinburgh

RAMSBOTHAM, Lt-Gen Sir David John; KCB (1987), CBE (1980, OBE 1974); s of Rt Rev Bishop John Alexander Ramsbotham, of W Lindeth, Silvervale, Lancs, and Eirian Morgan, *née* Morgan Owen (d 1987); *b* 6 Nov 1934; *Educ* Haileybury, CCC Cambridge (BA, MA); *m* 26 Sept 1958, Susan Caroline, da of Robert Joicey Dickinson, of Corbridge, Northumberland (d 1980); 2 s (James David Alexander b 30 Aug 1959, Richard Henry b 8 June 1962); *Career* cmmnd Rifle Bde 1958, Royal Green Jackets Co 2 RGJ 1974-76, Cdr 39 Inf Bde 1978-80, RCDS 1981, dir PR (Army) 1982-84, Cdr 3 Armd Div 1984-87, Cdr UK Field Army and inspr gen TA 1987-; *Recreations* shooting, gardening, sailing; *Clubs* MCC; *Style—* Lt-Gen Sir David J Ramsbotham, KCB, CBE

RAMSBOTHAM, Hon Sir Peter Edward; GCMG (1978, KCMG 1972, CMG 1964), GCVO (1976); yr s of late 1 Viscount Soulbury, GCMG, GCVO, OBE, MC, PC (d 1971), and his 1 w, Doris Violet (d 1954), da of Sigmund de Stein; hp of bro, 2 Viscount; *b* 8 Oct 1919; *Educ* Eton, Magdalen Coll Oxford; *m* 1, 30 Aug 1941, Frances Marie Massie (d 1982), da of late Hugh Massie Blomfield; 2 s, 1 da; m 2, 1985, Dr Zaïda Hall, da of Maurice Henry Megrah, QC; *Career* For Off 1950, Br high cmmr Cyprus 1969-71, ambass to Iran 1971-73, ambass to USA 1974-77, govr Bermuda 1977-80; dir: Commercial Union Assur Co 1981-, Lloyds Bank plc 1981-; chm Southern regn bd Lloyds Bank 1983-, tstee Leonard Cheshire Fndn 1981-; chm Ryder-Cheshire Mission for Relief of Suffering 1982-; KStJ 1976; *Style—* The Hon Sir Peter Ramsbotham, GCMG, GCVO; East Lane, Ovington, nr Alresford, Hants SO24 0RA (☎ 096 273 2515)

RAMSBOTTOM, Roy Frederic; s of Harry Ramsbottom, of The Paddocks, Davenham, Northwich, Cheshire, and Stella, *née* Walton; *b* 11 August 1943; *Educ* Sir John Deanes GS Northwich; *m* 21 Oct 1972, Susan Mary (Su); *Career* sr ptnr Marray Smith and Co CAs Northwich Ches 1985- (ptnr 1970-85), dir Walthamstow Building Soc 1985-; hon tres Ches Agric Soc 1977, chm Chester and N Wales Soc of CAs; memb ICEAW; *Recreations* cricket; *Style—* Roy Ramsbottom, Esq; Helensmere, Little Budworth, Cheshire; Murray Smith and Co, Darland House, 44 Winnington Hill, Northwich, Cheshire CW8 1AU (☎ 0606 7941, fax 0606 782878)

RAMSDEN, Anne, Lady; Anne; *née* Wickham; er da of Lt-Col Sir Charles George Wickham, KCMG, KBE, DSO (d 1971), and his 1 w, Phyllis Amy, *née* Rose (d 1924); *m* 6 Oct 1945, Sir Caryl Oliver Imbert Ramsden, 8 Bt, CMG, CVO (d 1987); 1 s (Sir John, 9 Bt, *qv*); The Old Brewery, Helperby, York

RAMSDEN, Sir Geoffrey Charles; CIE (1942); s of Col H F S Ramsden, CBE (d 1931), and Hon Edwyna Fiennes (d 1931), da of 17 Baron Saye and Sele; *b* 21 April 1893; *Educ* Haileybury, Sidney Sussex Coll Cambridge (MA); *m* 1930, Margaret Lovell (d 1976), da of late Rev John Robinson, of Downtown, Wilts; *Career* served WWI with 1 Bn The Royal Sussex Regt on N W Frontier (India), Capt 1917; entered ICS 1920, sec Indian Tariff Bd 1923, dep cmmr of various dists 1926-36, cmmr 1936-44, devpt advsr to govr 1945, fin cmmr 1944 and 1946-47, ret 1948; kt 1948; *Style—* Sir Geoffrey Ramsden, CIE; Fynescourt, Grayshott, Hindhead, Surrey (☎ Hindhead 4499)

RAMSDEN, Rt Hon James Edward; PC (1963); only s of Capt Edward Ramsden, MC, JP, and Geraldine Ramsden, OBE, yst da of Brig-Gen John Wilson, CB, JP, DL, and great n of 13 Baron Inchiquin; *b* 1 Nov 1923; *Educ* Eton, Trinity Coll Oxford; *m* 1949, Juliet Barbara Anna, yst da of Col Sir Charles Ponsonby, 1 Bt, TD, by his w Hon Winifred Gibbs, eld da of 1 Baron Hunsdon; 3 s (Thomas b 1950, George b 1953, Richard b 1954), 2 da (Emma b 1957, Charlotte b 1960); *Career* KRRC, served WW II NW Europe, with RB (despatches); MP (C) for Harrogate 1954-74, pps to Home Sec 1959-60, under-sec and fin sec WO 1960-63, sec State War 1963-64, min Def (Army) April-Oct 1964; dir: Colonial Mutual Life Assur (UK Bd) 1966-72, Standard Telephones & Cables 1971-81, Prudential Assur 1972- (dep chm 1976-82), London Clinic 1973- (chm 1984-), Prudential Corpn 1979- (dep chm 1979-82); memb Historic Bldgs Cncl England 1971-72; *Recreations* foxhunting, forestry, woodturning; *Clubs* Pratts; *Style—* The Rt Hon James Ramsden; Old Sleningford Hall, Ripon, N Yorks (☎ 85229)

RAMSDEN, Sir John Charles Josslyn; 9 Bt (E 1689), of Byram, Yorks; o s of Sir Caryl Oliver Imbert Ramsden, 8 Bt, CMG, CVO (d 1987), and Anne, Lady Ramsden, *qv*; *b* 19 August 1950; *Educ* Eton, Trinity Coll Cambridge (MA); *m* 14 Dec 1985, (Jennifer) Jane, da of Rear Adm Christopher Martin Bevan, CB; 1 da (Isobel Lucy b 1987); *Heir* undetermined; *Career* Dawnay Day & Co Ltd (merchant bankers) 1972-74, entered HM Dip Serv 1975; second Sec Dakar 1976-78, first Sec Delgn to MBFR Talks Vienna 1979, head of chancery and HM consul Hanoi 1980-82, FCO 1982-; *Clubs* Pratt's, RAC; *Style—* Sir John Ramsden, Bt; c/o Foreign and Commonwealth Office, King Charles St, London SW1

RAMSDEN, Veronica Mary; da of James Edgar Ramsden, and Pamela Mary, *née* Cox; *b* 15 Oct 1956; *Educ* Ursuline Convent Brentwood Essex, Univ of Wales (LLB); *Career* barr 1979, practising barr 1982-; *Recreations* chess, horse-racing, reading, pool, snooker, fringe theatre; *Clubs* Presscala, Fleet St; *Style—* Miss Veronica Ramsden; Blounts Court Lodge, Potterne, Wiltshire (☎ 0380 71705); 4 Studley Rd, London E7 (☎ 01 472 6522); 59 Temple Chambers, Temple Ave, London EC4Y OHP (☎ 01 353 3111, fax 01 353 4581)

RAMSEY, Rt Rev Kenneth Venner; s of Jmaes Ernest Ramsey (d 1935), of 6 Nettlestone Rd, Southsea, Hants, and Laura Rebecca, *née* Reeves (d 1927); *b* 26 Jan 1909; *Educ* Portsmouth GS, Univ Coll Oxford (BA, MA), Univ of Manchester (BD); *Career* ordained: deacon 1933, priest 1934; curate St Matthew Stretford 1933-35, vice princ Egerton Hall Theol Coll Manchester 1935-38, lectr in Christian ethics Univ of Manchester 1935-38, vice princ Bishop Wilson Coll IOM 1938-39, princ Egerton Hall Manchester 1939-41, vicar St Paul Peel Little Hulton Lancs 1941-48, rector Emmanuel Church Didsbury Manchester 1948-55, hon canon Manchester Cathedral 1950-53, proctor in convocation and memb Church Assembly 1950-55, rural dean Heaton 1950-53, bishop suffragan Hulme 1953-75, bishop Manchester 1975-; chm: Cncl of Christians and Jews, Missions to Seaman Manchester; memb Manchester Educn Ctee; *Style—* The Rt Rev Kenneth Ramsey; 41 Bradwell Drive, Heald Green, Cheadle, Cheshire SK8 3BX (☎ 061 437 8612)

RAMSEY, Vivian Arthur; s of Ian Thomas Ramsey (d 1972 former Bishop of Durham), and Margretta, *née* McKay; *b* 24 May 1950; *Educ* Abingdon Sch, Harley Sch Rochester NY USA, Oriel Coll Oxford (MA), City Univ (Dip Law); *m* 14 Aug 1974, Barbara, da of Lt-Col Gerard Majella Walker, of Farnborough, Hants; 2 s (Nicholas b 1981, James b 1986), 2 da (Helen b 1980, Katharine b 1984); *Career* grad engr Ove Arup & Ptnrs 1972-77, barr Middle Temple 1979, practising barr 1981-, ed Construction Law Jnl 1984-; tres: St Swithuns Hither Green 1977-84, Swanley Village Sports and Social Club 1986-; MICE 1977; *Recreations* pantomime, building renovation; *Style—* Vivian Ramsey, Esq; 10 Essex St, Outer Temple, London WC2R 3AA (☎ 01 240 6981, fax 01 240 7722, telex 8955650)

RAMSEY-FAIRFAX-LUCY; *see*: Fairfax-Lucy

RAMSHAW, Alec; JP (1982); s of John Robert Ramshaw (d 1969), of Beverley, E Yorks, and Olive, *née* Ackrill (d 1968); *b* 4 July 1931; *Educ* St Mary's Beverley, Woods Coll Hull; *m* 1, (m dis), Patricia Margaret; m 2, 4 Dec 1980, Sheila Patricia, da of Alfred Aldous Fox, (d 1964); 2 s (Simon James, Nicholas Mark), 1 da (Claire Alexandra); *Career* Nat Serv RAF; estate agent and insur broker 1963-, insur inspr 1963-52; memb Humberside fin ctee Br Red Cross Soc 1963 (chm 1976), fndr memb Hull Hosp League of Friends; cncllr for Swanland Beverley Borough Cncl, ccllr for S Hunsley Humberside CC (ldr Cons Gp); FNAEA 1977; *Recreations* golf; *Style—* Alec Ramshaw, Esq, JP; Owl Cottage, Spinney Croft Close, N Ferriby, Hull HU14 3EQ (☎ 0482 631 421); 3 Spinney Croft Close, N Ferriby, Hull HU14 3EQ (telex V 0836 264944, C 0860 537694)

RANASINHA, Sir Arthur Godwin; CMG (1949), CBE (1948); s of W P Ranasinha, and Mary Ann, *née* de Alwis; *b* 24 June 1898; *Educ* St Thomas' Coll Colombo, Trinity Hall Cambridge, Ceylon Univ, Univ of London (BA); *m* 1921, Annette Hilda (d 1968), da of Mudalyar de Alwis, of Negombo, Ceylon; 1 s (decd), 2 da; *Career* entered Ceylon Civil Serv 1921, police magistrate 1923-26, dist judge 1928-30, asst govt agent Colombo 1932, sec to Min for Agric and Lands 1933, public tstee 1936, custodian of Enemy Propert supt 1939, Supt of Census 1944, sec to Ldr of State Cncl on political mission to London 1945, cmmr of Lands 1946, perm sec Min of Ag and Lands 1947-50, sec to Cabinet and dep sec Treasy 1950-51, perm sec Miny of Fin and sec to Treasy and Cabinet 1951-54, govr Central Bank of Ceylon and for Ceylon, IMF 1954-59, ambass for Ceylon in Greece and Italy 1959-61; chm: fin ctee FAO 1961, People's Bank Cmmn 1965-66, Taxation Cmmn 1966-67, Tea Cmmn 1967-68; Knight Grand Cross Order of Merit of Italy, kt 1954; *Style—* Sir Arthur Ranasinha, CMG, CBE; 99/1 Rosmead Place, Colombo 7, Sri Lanka

RAND, Gerald Frederick; s of William Frederick Rand (d 1960), of Herts, and Elsie Mary White (d 1926); *b* 10 Nov 1926; *Educ* Merchant Taylors' Sch; *m* 1, 13 July 1949, Eileen Margaret, da of William Alexanda Winson (d 1975), of Herts 1 s (Stephen b 1953); m 2, 1 Nov 1972, Clarissa Elizabeth, da of Thomas William Barker (d 1956), of Hull; *Career* landowner and master builder, ret, owner of The Lynford Hall Estate Norfolk, Lord of the Manors of Lynford, Mundford, Cranwich Norfolk; chm Rand Contractors Ltd 1952-68, md Power Plant Int 1962-71, chm Manor Minerals (UK) Ltd 1985-; elected to Société Jersiaise 1967, memb governing cncl The Manorial Soc of GB 1985, regnl chm Domesday Nat Ctee 1986, memb Country Landowners Assoc; *Recreations* shooting, hunting, studies in medieval history, historic buildings; *Style—* Gerald F Rand, Esq; Lynford Hall, Thetford, Norfolk IP26 5HW (☎ 0842 878351); Westmill, Ashwell, Herts (☎ 046 274 2568)

RANDALL, John Spencer; *Career* chm (1981-) and md Avana Gp Ltd; dir D Jones Dickinson & Co, R F Brookes Ltd; non-exec dir Northern Foods Dec 1981; *Style—* John Randall Esq; c/o Avana Group Ltd, Avana Buildings, Pendyris St, Cardiff, Wales (☎ (0222) 25521)

RANDALL, Stuart Jeffrey; MP (Lab) Kingston upon Hull W 1983-; *b* 22 June 1938; *Educ* Univ of Wales (BSc); *m* 1963, Gillian Michael, 3 da (Jennifer, Joanna, Emma); *Career* pps to Roy Hattersley, dep ldr of the Lab Pty and shadow chllr of the

Exchequer, front bench spokesman for Agric 1987-; fisheries & food front bench spokesman for Home Affrs 1987-; *Style*— Stuart Randall, Esq, MP; House of Commons, London SW1 (☎ 01 219 3583/6359)

RANDALL, William Edward; CBE (1978), DFC (1944), AFC (1945); s of William George Randall, and Jane Longdon, *née* Pannell; *b* 15 Dec 1920; *Educ* Tollington Sch London; *m* 1, 1943, Joan Dorothea Way; 2 s, 1 da; m 2, 1975, Iris Joyce Roads; *Career* chm: Chubb & Son plc 1981-84, The British Security Indust Assoc 1981-85; *Style*— William Randall Esq, CBE, DFC, AFC; c/o Chubb & Son plc, Manor House, Manor Lane, Feltham, Middx (☎ 01 751 5021)

RANDLE, Guy Hawksworth; s of James Randle (d 1965), and Emma, *née* Hawksworth (d 1978); *b* 10 July 1937; *Educ* Hitchin GS, Gt Bartholomew's Hosp Med Coll (MB BS), Liverpool Mod Sch; *m* 26 June, Diana Suzanne, da of Brian Wright (d 1971); 1 s (Marcus b 1970), 2 da (Katherine b 1966, Louisa b 1975); *Career* conslt obstetrician and gynacologist Beverley E Yorks; MRCS (Eng), LRCP (Lond), LMSSA (London), DOSSE RCOG, MRCOG, FRCOG; *Recreations* squash, golf; *Clubs* Squash (Beverley), Golf (Beverley and Ganton); *Style*— Guy Randle, Esq; Brimley Close, Movescroft, Beverley, E Yorks HU17 7EE; 61 North Bar, within Beverley

RANDLE, Prof Sir Philip John; s of Mr Alfred John Randle (d 1952), of Nuneaton, and Nora Annie, *née* Smith (d 1968); *b* 16 July 1926; *Educ* King Edward VI GS Nuneaton, Univ of Cambridge (MD), UC Hosp Med Sch (MA, PhD); *m* 1952, Elizabeth Ann, da of Dennis Arthur Harrison (d 1974); 1 s (Peter d 1971), 3 da (Rosalind, Sally, Susan); *Career* res fell Sidney Sussex Coll Camb 1954-57, fell Trinity Hall Camb 1957-64, lectr in biochemistry Univ of Cambridge 1955-64, prof of biochemistry Univ of Bristol 1964-75, prof of clinical biochemistry Univ of Oxford (fell Hertford Coll 1975-); FRCP, FRS; kt 1985; *Style*— Prof Sir Philip Randle; 11 Fitzherbert Close, Iffley, Oxford (☎ 0865 773115); Dept of Clinical Biochemistry, John Radcliffe Hospital, Oxford (☎ 0865 817395)

RANDOLPH, Denys; s of Harry Beckham Randolph (d 1980); *b* 6 Feb 1926; *Educ* St Paul's, Queen's Univ Belfast; *m* 1951, Marjorie, *née* Hales; 2 da; *Career* chm: Wilkinson Sword 1972-1980 (pres 1980-85), Wilkinson Match Ltd 1974-80, Woodrush Investmts 1980-; chm IOD 1976-79; Master: Worshipful Co of Scientific Instrument Makers 1977, Worshipful Co of Cutlers 1985; CEng, AFRAeS, FIProdE, CBIM, FIOD; *Recreations* viticulture, golf, boating (La Russhe); *Clubs* Army & Navy, City Livery, Little Ship; *Style*— Denys Randolph, Esq; 6 Atherstone Mews, London SW7 (☎ 01 584 5121); The Cottages, Rush Court, Wallingford, OX10 8JJ (☎ 0491 36586)

RANDOLPH, Hugh Thomas; s of The Ven Thomas Berkeley Randolph (d 1987), and Margaret, *née* Jenner; for Randolph and Jenner families (see Burke's Landed Genrrey 18th Ed vol III); *b* 27 Sept 1936; *Educ* Marlborough, Sidney Sussex Coll Cambridge (MA); *Career* asst master: King Edward VI Sch Southampton 1959-63, Abingdon Sch 1963- (housemaster 1978-); *Recreations* history, music, rural, pursuits, theology; *Style*— Hugh Randolph, Esq; 20 Park Rd, Abingdon, Oxfordshire OX14 1DS (☎ 0235 22887); Abingdon Sch, Abingdon, Oxfordshire OX14 1DE (☎ 0235 21563)

RANFURLY, 7 Earl of (I 1831); Gerald Francoys Needham Knox; also Baron Welles (I 1781), Viscount Northland (I 1791), and Baron Ranfurly (UK 1826, which he sits as in House of Lords); er s of Capt John Needham Knox, RN (d 1967, ggs of Hon John Knox, 3 s of 1 Earl of Ranfurly), and Monica, *née* Kitson (d 1975); suc kinsman, 6 Earl of Ranfurly, KCMG 1988; *b* 4 Jan 1929; *Educ* Wellington; *m* 22 Jan 1955, Rosemary Beatrice Vesey, o da of Air Vice-Marshal Felton Vesey Holt, CMG, DSO (d 1931); 2 s (Viscount Northland, *qv*, Hon Rupert Stephen b 5 Nov 1963), 2 da (Lady Elizabeth Marianne (Mrs Empson) b 24 Feb 1959, Lady Frances Christina (Mrs Gordon-Jones) b 13 Feb 1961); *Heir* s, Viscount Northland, *qv*; *Career* former Lt Cdr RN; memb London Stock Exchange 1963-, chm Brewin Dolphin & Co Ltd Stockbrokers; *Style*— The Rt Hon the Earl of Ranfurly; Maltings Chase, Nayland, Colchester, Essex (☎ 0206 262224)

RANFURLY, Dowager Countess of; Hermione; *née* Llewellyn; OBE (1970); eldest da of Griffith Robert Poyntz Llewellyn, of Baglan Hall, Abergavenny, Mon (er bro of Sir Godfrey Llewellyn, 1 Bt, CB, CBE, MC, TD, JP, DL); *m* 17 Jan 1939, 6 Earl of Ranfurly, KCMG (d 1988); 1 da (Lady Caroline Simmonds, *qv*); *Career* WWII PA to Supreme Allied Cdr Med; fndr pres Ranfurly Library Serv, which sends donated books to developing countries; received Rotary Award for World Understanding 1987; CStJ; *Style*— The Hon Dowager Countess of Ranfurly; Great Pednor, Chesham, Bucks HP5 2SU (☎ 024 06 2155)

RANGER, Sir Douglas; s of William Ranger, and Hatton Thomasina Ranger; *b* 5 Oct 1916; *Educ* Brisbane CEGS, Middx Hosp Med Sch (MB, BS); *m* 1943, Betty, da of Capt Sydney Harold Draper; 2 s; *Career* surgical registrar Middx Hosp 1942-44; otolaryngologist: Middx Hosp 1950-82, Mt Vernon Hosp 1958-74, London Chest Hosp 1952-75; dean Middx Hosp Med Sch 1974-83; memb: cncl RCS 1967-72, Ct of Examiners 1966-72; civil conslt in otolaryngology RAF 1965-83, advsr in otolaryngology to DHSS 1971-83, hon conslt RAF 1983-; hon sec Br Assoc of Otolaryngologists 1965-71, dir Ferens Inst of Otolaryngology 1965-83; FRCS; kt 1978; *Books* The Middlesex Hospital Medical School, Centenary to Sesquicentary; *Style*— Sir Douglas Ranger; The Tile House, The Street, Chipperfield, King's Langley, Herts WD4 9BH

RANK, Sir Benjamin Keith; CMG (1955); s of Wreghitt Rank (d 1939), and Bessie, *née* Smith (d 1955); *b* 14 Jan 1911; *Educ* Scotch Coll Melbourne, Ormond Coll Melbourne Univ (MB, BS, MS); *m* 1938, Barbara Lyle, da of Harold Lyle Facy; 1 s, 3 da; *Career* Lt Col AAMC 1940-46; hon plastic surgn Royal Melbourne Hosp 1946-66; pres: Br Assoc Plastic Surgns 1965, Royal Aust Coll of Surgns 1966-68, Fifth Int Congress of Plastic Surgns 1971; vice-pres bd of mgmnt Royal Melbourne Hosp 1980-82, memb Motor Accident Bd of Vic 1980-, pres Interplast Aust 1985-; C St J 1981; kt 1971; *see Debrett's Handbook of Australia and New Zealand for further details*; *Books* Melbourne; *Style*— Sir Benjamin Rank, CMG; 12 Jerula Ave, Mt Eliza, Vic 3930, Aust

RANK, John Rowland; s of Capt Rowland Rank, RFA (d 1939), of Aldwick Place, W Sussex, and Margaret, *née* McArthur (d 1988); n of late J Arthur Rank (Baron Rank, d 1972), fndr of Rank Orgn, and gs of late Joseph Rank, fndr of Rank Flour Milling; *b* 13 Jan 1930; *Educ* Stowe; *Career* property owner; Lord of Manor of Saham Toney Norfolk; with Rank Ltd 1948-50; patron Pallant House Gallery Tst; tstee: Stanstead Park Fndn, Chichester Festival Theatre; chm tstees Chichester Centre of Arts; sometime on Ct: of Corpn of Sons of Clergy, of Sussex Diocesan Cncl; former cncl memb Friends of Chirchester Cathedral, memb Sennicotts Church Advsy Cncl; *Recreations* theatre, architectural, gardening, travelling, art exhibitions; *Clubs* Georgian Gp, Regency Soc of Brighton and Hove; *Style*— John Rank, Esq; Sennicotts, Chichester

RANK, Joseph McArthur; s of late Rowland Rank and Margaret McArthur, of Montreal; nephew of 1 and last Baron Rank; *b* 24 April 1918; *Educ* Loretto Sch Musselburgh; *m* 14 Feb 1946, Hon Moira Hopwood, *qv*, da of 3 Baron Southborough; 1 s, 1 da; *Career* Fl Lt RAFVR UK, France, Germany and Burma, personal pilot to Air C-in-C SE Asia; flour miller; chm Ranks Hovis McDougall Ltd 1969-81; pres Nat Assoc of Br & Irish Millers 1957 (centenary pres 1978), chm Millers Mutual Assoc 1969-; dir Royal Alexander and Albert Sch 1952-; first High Sheriff E Sussex 1974; Hon FRCP; *Recreations* boating, travelling; *Clubs* RAF, Bembridge Sailing; *Style*— Joseph Rank, Esq; Landhurst, Hartfield, E Sussex TN7 4DH (☎ 089 277 293)

RANK, Hon Mrs (Moira); *née* Hopwood; only da of 3rd Baron Southborough (d 1982); *b* 13 Dec 1919; *m* 1, 1940, Fl Lt Peter Anthony Stanley Woodwark (ka 1943), s of late Col Sir (Arthur) Stanley Woodwark, CMG, CBE; 1 s (Colin b 1948), 2 da (Caroline b 1943; m 2, 1946, Joseph McArthur Rank, *qv*; Camilla Moira b 1953); *Recreations* gardening; *Style*— The Hon Mrs Rank; Landhurst, Hartfield, Sussex TN7 4DH (☎ 089 277 293)

RANK, Nicholas John; s of John Stephen Rank, OBE, of Ches, and Hilda, *née*, Hammerton; *b* 5 Nov 1950; *Educ* Stockport Sch, Univ of Manchester (BA, BArch); *m* 28 July 1973, Janet Elizabeth, da of Sidney Silcock, of Ches; 3 da (Naomi b 1976, Anna b 1978, Sarah b 1981); *Career* architect, ptnr Nicholas Rank Assocs (architects, designers, historic bldgs conslts) 1983, conslt architect Manchester diocese; chm Assoc of Christians in Planning and Architecture, memb Ecclesiastical Architects and Surveyors Assoc, sr lectr in architecture Manchester Poly 1978-; memb RIBA; *Recreations* music, reading; *Style*— Nicholas Rank, Esq; 8 Grenfell Rd, Didsbury, Manchester M20 0TQ (☎ 061 434 3199, 061 228 7414)

RANKEILLOUR, Baroness; Mary Sibyl; da of Lt-Col Wilfred Ricardo, DSO (gn of David Ricardo, the celebrated political economist); *b* 5 April 1910; *m* 1933, 3 Baron Rankeillour (d 1967); 1 s (4 Baron), 1 da (Hon Mrs Dobson); *Style*— The Rt Hon Lady Rankeillour; 106 Headley Road, Liphook, Hants GU30 7PT (☎ 0428 722177)

RANKEILLOUR, 4 Baron (UK 1932); Peter St Thomas More Henry Hope; s of 3 Baron Rankeillour (d 1967; he descended from Gen the Hon Sir Alexander Hope, GCB, 4 s of 2 Earl of Hopetoun, ancestor of the Marquesses of Linlithgow), and Baroness Rankeillour, *qv* formerly of Mapledurham House, nr Reading, and Mary Sybil Hope, da of late Col Wilfred Ricardo, DSO; *b* 29 May 1935; *Educ* Ampleforth and privately; *Heir* kinsman, Michael Hope; *Career* former dep chm Br Sailors' Soc (Scotland), currently rear cmdr House of Lords YC; *Style*— The Rt Hon The Lord Rankeillour; Achaderry House, Roy Bridge, W Inverness-shire (☎ 039 781 206); House of Lords, London

RANKIN, Alick Michael; CBE (1987); s of Col Niall Rankin (d 1965), and Lady Jean Margaret Rankin, *qv*, da of late 12 Earl of Stair; *b* 23 Jan 1935; *Educ* Eton, Univ of Oxford; *m* 1, 1958 (m dis 1976), Susan, da of Hugh Dewhurst, of Dungarthill, Dunkeld; 1 s, 3 da; m 2, 1976, Suzetta, da of Patrick Nelson, of Seafield, IOM; *Career* served Scots Gds 1953-55; investmt banking Toronto Canada 1956-59, joined Scottish & Newcastle Breweries 1960 (gp md 1983-, chief exec 1985, deputy chm 1987); dir: Bank of Scotland 1987, Christian Salveson plc 1986; vice chm The Brewers Soc 1987; *Recreations* fishing, shooting, golf, tennis; *Clubs* Royal and Ancient (St Andrews), Hon Co of Edinburgh Golfers, New (Edinburgh), I Zingari (cricket), Eton Ramblers, Butterflies, Lansdowne; *Style*— Alick Rankin Esq, CBE; 3 Saxe Coburg Place, Edinburgh (☎ 031 332 3684); Scottish & Newcastle Breweries, Abbey Brewery, Holyrood Rd, Edinburgh EH8 8YS (☎ 031 556 2591)

RANKIN, Andrew; QC; s of William Locke Rankin (d 1963), and Mary Ann, *née* McArdle; *b* 3 August 1924; *Educ* Roy HS Edinburgh, Univ of Edinburgh (BL), Downing Coll Cambridge (BA); *m* 1, 1944 (m dis 1963), Winifred, da of Frank McAdam, of Edinburgh; 5 children, 1 decd; m 2, 1964, Veronica, da of George Aloysius Martin, of Liverpool (d 1965); *Career* lectr faculty of law Liverpool Univ 1948-52; barr Gray's Inn 1950, rec of the Crown Ct 1970-; *Style*— Andrew Rankin, Esq, QC; Chelwood, Pine Walks, Prenton, Birkenhead, Merseyside L42 8LQ; 69 Cliffords Inn, Fetter Lane, London EC4A 1BZ (☎ 01 405 2932); 2 Strand Chambers, 218 Strand, London WC2R 1AP (☎ 01 353 7825, telex 265871, fax 5832073)

RANKIN, Antony Colin Deans; s of Maj-Gen Henry Charles Deans Rankin, CIE, OBE (d 1965), and Edith Watson Rankin (d 1988); *b* 5 Feb 1923; *Educ* Loretto Sch Musselburgh; *m* 1950, Barbara, da of Desmond Vernon; 1 s (b 1956), 1 da (b 1954); *Career* Capt 12 Lancers 1941-46; dir: ICI plc mond div 1970-81, Ellis & Everadd plc 1979-81; *Recreations* golf, gardening, watching sport; *Clubs* MCC, Army & Navy; *Style*— Antony Rankin, Esq; Peacock Cottage, Manton, Marlborough, Wilts SN8 4HQ (☎ 0672 52362)

RANKIN, Gavin Niall; s and h of Sir Ian Niall Rankin, 4 Bt; *b* 19 May 1962; *Educ* Eton, Buckingham Univ (LLB); *Career* 2 Lt Scots Gds 1981; Price Waterhouse 1984-88, CA Panfida Gp 1989-; page of Honour to HM Queen Elizabeth The Queen Mother 1977-79; memb ICA, FRGS; *Style*— Gavin Rankin, Esq; 52 Bassett Rd, London W10 6JL

RANKIN, Sir Ian Niall; 4 Bt (UK 1898), of Bryngwyn, Much Dewchurch, Co Hereford; s of late Lt-Col (Arthur) Niall Talbot Rankin, yr s of 2 Bt; s unc, Sir Hugh Rankin, 3 Bt 1988; *b* 19 Dec 1932; *Educ* Eton, Ch Ch Oxford (MA); *m* 1, 1959 (m dis 1967), Alexandra, da of Adm Sir Laurence George Durlacher, KCB, OBE, DSC; 1 s (Gavin Niall), 1 da (Zara Sophia b 1960); m 2, 1980, June, er da of late Capt Thomas Marsham- Townshend, and former w of Bryan Montagu Norman; 1 s (Lachlan John b 1980), 1 step da; *Heir* s, Gavin Niall Rankin b 19 May 1962; *Career* Lt Scots Gds (Res); dir of Indust Cos; FRGS; *Recreations* tennis, shooting, yachting; *Clubs* Royal Yacht Sqdn, Pratt's, Beefsteak, White's; *Style*— Sir Ian Rankin, Bt; 63 Marlborough Place, London NW8 0PT (☎ 01 625 5330)

RANKIN, Lady Jean Margaret; *née* Dalrymple; DCVO (1969), CVO (1957); da of late 12 Earl of Stair, KT, DSO; *b* 15 August 1905; *m* 1931, Lt-Col (Arthur) Niall Talbot Rankin, Scots Gds (d 1965), s of Lt-Col Sir (James) Reginald (Lea) Rankin, 2 Bt; 2 s (*see* Rankin, Ian Niall and Rankin, Alick Michael); *Career* woman of the bedchamber to HM Queen Elizabeth The Queen Mother 1947-; govr: Thomas Coram Fndn, Magdalen Tst; *Style*— Lady Jean Rankin, DCVO; 3 Catherine Wheel Yard, St James's St, London SW1 (☎ 01 493 9072); House of Treshnish, Dervaig, Isle of Mull (☎ 068 84 249)

RANKIN, Robina, Lady; Robina; da of Stewart Finlay, of Comrie, Perthshire; *m*

1946, as his 2 w, Sir Hugh Charles Rhys Rankin, 3 Bt (d 1988); *Career* SRN, Swedish masseuse, ret; FSA (Scot); *Style—* Robina, Lady Rankin; Bracken Cottage, Kindallochan, Pitlochry, Perthshire

RANKIN-HUNT, Capt David; s of James Rankin-Hunt, of Wales, and Edwina Anne, *née* Blakeman; *b* 26 August 1956; *Educ* Christ Coll Brecon, St Martin's Sch; *Career* Lt Scots Gds, Capt The London Scottish Regt (51 Highland Vol) 1984-; Lord Chamberlain's Off 1981-: registrar 1987-89, employed in The Royal Collection 1989-; dir The Highland Soc, lay steward St George's Chapel Windsor Castle; FSA (Scotland); Order of Isabella The Catholic Fifth Class Spain;; *Recreations* military history, heraldry, conservation issues, Welsh affairs; *Clubs* Army and Navy, Highland Brigade; *Style—* Capt David Rankin-Hunt; Flat 5, Henry III Tower, Windsor Castle, Berkshire, SL4 1NJ (☎ 0753 851408) The Royal Collection, Stable Yard House, St James' Palace, London SW1 (☎ 01 930 4832)

RANKINE, Jean Morag; da of Alan Rankine (d 1988), of Whitley Bay, and Margaret Mary Sloan, *née* Reid; *b* 5 Sept 1941; *Educ* Central Newcastle HS, UCL (BA, MPhil), Copenhagen Univ; *Career* British Museum: res asst dept of printed books 1967-73, asst keeper dir's off 1973-78, head of public servs 1978-83, (dep dir 1983-); *Recreations* rowing, skiing, walking, opera; *Clubs* Thames Rowing; *Style—* Miss Jean Rankine; British Museum, London WC1B 3DG (☎ 01 323 8490, fax 01 323 8480)

RANKING, His Hon Judge; Robert Duncan; s of Robert Maurice Ranking (d 1939); *b* 24 Oct 1915; *Educ* Cheltenham, Pembroke Coll Cambridge; *m* 1949, Evelyn Mary, nee Walker; 1 da; *Career* dep chm Sussex QS Sessions 1962-68, county ct judge 1968, circuit judge 1971-88; dep chm Agric Land Tbnl SE area; judge of the Mayor's & City of London Ct 1979-88; *Style—* His Hon Judge Ranking; Little Oakfield, Camden Hill, Tunbridge Wells, Kent (☎ Tunbridge Wells 27551)

RANNIE, Prof Ian; s of James Rannie (d 1954), of Troon, and Nichola Denniston, *née* McMeekan (d 1971); *b* 29 Oct 1915; *Educ* Ayr Academy, Univ of Glasgow (Bsc, MB ChB, BSc); *m* 3 July 1943, Flora, da of William Welch (d 1954), of Gateshead; 2 s (Bruce b 1944, Gordon b 1946); *Career* lectr in pathology med sch Univ of Durham 1942-, prof of pathology dental sch: Univ of Durham 1960-63, Univ of Newcastle 1963-81; conslt pathologist Royal Victoria Infirmary Newcastle-upon-Tyne 1948-81; active in Univ affairs and NHS, memb BMA Ctees (cncl and jt conslt ctee), chm Central Manpower Ctee 1976-81, pres Int Soc of Geographical Pathology 1970-73, vice-pres Int Angiology Soc 1970-77; hon membership awarded by Hungarian Atherosclerosis Soc 1976; FRCPath 1963, FIBiol 1963; *Recreations* golf; *Clubs* East India, Royal Overseas League; *Style—* Prof Ian Rannie; 5 Osborne Villas, Newcastle upon Tyne NE2 1JU (☎ 091 281 3163)

RANSFORD, Andrew Oliver; s of Doctor Oliver Neil Ransford, of Bulawayo Zimbabwe, and Doris Irene, *née* Galloway; father medical and historical author (publishers John Murray); gf missionary in India; *b* 25 April 1940; *Educ* Emmanuel Coll Cambridge (BA, MB, BChir), UCH; *m* 21 Sept 1968, Penelope Jane, da of Peter A N Milmo (d 1969), of Caterham, Surrey; 2 s (Mark b 1971, Christopher b 1977), 2 da (Philippa b 1969, Helen b 1980); *Career* conslt orthopaedic surgn (appointed 1978): UCH, Royal Nat Osrthopaedic Hospital; FRCS; *Books* multiple orthopaedic publications in journals and medical text books; *Recreations* antiques; *Clubs* British Medical Assoc, Royal College of Surgeons; *Style—* Andrew Ransford, Esq; 5 Fordington Rd, London N6 4TD (☎ 01 883 3317); 107 Harley St, London W1N 1DG (☎ 01 486 1088)

RANSOM, Robert Stephen; s of Donald Hibbert Ransom (d 1963), of Bushey, and Dora Millicent, *née* Lewis, (d 1970); *b* 26 Nov 1929; *Educ* Bradfield; *m* 28 Dec 1963, Alice, da of Poul Emil Kronmann (d 1979), of Copenhagen; 2 da (Anne-Marie b 1966, Julia b 1970); *Career* Lt RA 1948-50; CA 1957, sr ptnr Macnair Mason 1980- (ptnr 1958-80-); FCA; *Recreations* literature, travel, gardening; *Clubs* City of London, City Univ; *Style—* Robert Ransom, Esq; Rampyndene House, Burwash, Sussex (☎ 0435 882248); Macnair Mason, 30-33 Minories, London EC3N 1DU (☎ 01 481 3022, fax 01 488 4458, telex 886189)

RANSOME, Hon Mrs; Hon (Shirley) Elizabeth; *née* Macpherson; da of 2 Baron Macpherson of Drumochter by his 1 w Ruth; *b* 31 Mar 1953; *m* 1978, Mark William Ransome; *Style—* The Hon Mrs Ransome; 101, 18th Street, Parkhurst 2193, Johannesburg, S Africa

RANT, His Hon Judge James William; QC (1980); s of Harry George Rant, of Gerrards, Cross Bucks, and Barbara Veale; Grant of Arms to William Rant of Yelverton 1574 (Robert Cooke, Clarenceaux King of Arms); *b* 16 April 1936; *Educ* Stowe, Univ of Cambridge (MA, LLM); *m* 1963, Helen, da of Percyval George Adnams (d 1964), of IOM; 1 s (Charles Freston); *Career* barr Grays Inn 1961, pupillage with the late J N Dunlop 1962-63, in chambers of Dorothy Waddy QC until 1968, head of Chambers 1968-84, dep circuit judge 1975, rec of the Crown Ct 1979, circuit judge 1984, judge of Central Criminal Ct 1986; Freeman of the City of London; *Recreations* cookery, music, family life; *Style—* Judge James William; 3 Temple Gdns, Middle Temple Lane, Temple, London EC4

RAPER, Dr Alan Humphrey; s of Frederick George Raper (d 1977); *b* 11 August 1927; *Educ* Acklam Hall Middlesborough, Univ of Leeds; *m* 1955, Audrey, *née* Baker; 1 s, 2 da; *Career* dir: Glaxo Holdings Ltd, Glaxo Nigeria Ltd, Glaxo Gp Ltd, Glaxochem (Pte) Ltd Singapore, Glaxo Nigeria Ltd, Glaxo Labs (India) Ltd, Glaxo Far East (Pte) Ltd, Glaxo Orient (Pte) Ltd, Glaxo Australia Pty Ltd, Glaxo Bangladesh Ltd, Glaxo Canada Ltd, Glaxo Labs (Pakistan) Ltd, Glaxo Philippines Inc, Glaxo NZ Ltd, Glaxo (1972) Charity Tst, Scholeds Ltd; chm Macfarlan Smith Ltd; memb of cncl Chemical Industs Assoc 1974-, memb Health and Safety Cmmn 1983-; *Recreations* skiing, hill walking, history; *Style—* Dr Alan Raper; Church Cottage, 126 High St, Lindfield, Sussex; Mews Cottage, Low Startforth Hall, Barnard Castle, Co Durham

RAPER, Vice Adm Sir (Robert) George; KCB (1971, CB 1968); s of late Maj Robert George Raper, of Battle, Sussex; *b* 27 August 1915; *Educ* RNC Dartmouth, RNEC Keynham, RNC Greenwich; *m* 1940, (Frances) Joan St John, da of C St John Phillips; 1 s, 2 da; *Career* joined RN 1929, HMS Edinburgh 1940-42 (despatches), turbine res section Admty 1942-45; engr offr: HMS Broadsword, HMS Battleaxe, HMS Crossbow 1945-47; Cdr 1947, Engr-in-Chief's Dept Admty 1948-51, engr offr HMS Birmingham 1952-54, loaned to RCN set up NEDIT 1954-55, tech sec to Engr-in-Chief of the Fleet 1955-57, Capt 1957, Cmd HMS Caledonia 1959-61, dep dir of Marine Engrg Admty 1961-63, CSO to Flag Offr Sea Trg 1963-65, Rear Adm 1966, dir Marine Engrg MOD (RN) 1966-68, chief naval engr offr and dir-gen Ships MOD 1968-74, Vice Adm 1968, ret 1974; FEng, FIMechE, FRINA, FIMarE, FRSA; *Style—* Vice Adm Sir George Raper, KCB; Oast Cottage, Chitcombe, Broadoak, nr Rye, E Sussex TN31 6EX

RAPER, John Baldwin; DFC (1944); s of Alfred Baldwin Raper, MP (ka 1941), of Bucks, and Elizabeth Alice, *née* Tobin, formerly Marchiness of Conynham (d 1928), of Aust; *b* 5 Mar 1923; *Educ* Nautical Coll Pangbourne, Trinity Coll Oxford; *m* 1947 (m dis 1968), Joy Katherine, *née* Garraway; 1 da (Amanda b 1949); *Career* FL Lt RAF Bomber Cmd 1941-46; dep dir sales Assoc Rediffusion Ltd 1961-63, md Chapman Raper & Assocs Ltd 1963-70, Times Newspapers Ltd 1971-74, FCO 1975-88; Liveryman Worshipful Co of Vintners; *Recreations* golf, writer, antiques; *Clubs* RAF, NZ GC; *Style—* John Raper, Esq, DFC; Flat 10, 52 Elm Park Rd, London SW3 6AU (☎ 01 352 0175); FCO, Whitehall, London SW1 2AH

RAPHAEL, Adam Eliot Geoffrey; s of Geoffrey George Raphael (d 1969), of London, and Nancy May, *née* Rose; *b* 22 April 1988; *Educ* Charterhouse, Oriel Coll Oxford (MA); *m* 16 May 1970, Caroline Rayner, da of George Ellis (d 1954), of Cape Town, USA; 1 s (Thomas Geoffrey b 1971), 1 da (Anna Nancy b 1974); *Career* 2 Lt RA 1956-58; political corr The Guardian 1974-76 (for corr Washington 1969-73 and S Africa 1973), exec ed The Observer 1988- (political corr 1976-81, political ed 1981-87), presenter Newsnight BBC TV 1987-88; *Recreations* tennis, skiing; *Clubs* RAC, Hurlingham, Ski (GB); *Style—* Adam Raphael, Esq; 50 Addison Ave, London W11 4EP (☎ 01 603 9133); The Observer, Chelsea Bridge House, Queenstown Rd, London SW8 4NN (☎ 01 350 3435)

RAPHAEL, Frederic Michael; s of Cedric Raphael Raphael, TD (d 1979), and Irene Rose, *née* Mauser; *b* 14 August 1931; *Educ* Charterhouse, St John's Coll Cambridge (MA); *m* 17 Jan 1955, Sylvia Betty, da of Hyman Glatt; 2 s (Paul b 1958, Stephen b 1967), 1 da (Sarah b 1960); *Career* author; *Books* Obbligato (1956), The Earlsdon Way (1958), The Limits of Love (1960), A Wild Surmise (1961), The Graduate Wife (1962), The Trouble with England (1962), Lindmann (1963), Orchestra and Beginners (1967), Like Men Betrayed (1970), Who Were You With Last Night? (1971), April, June and November (1972), Richard's Things (1973, screenplay 1981), California Time (1975), The Glittering Prizes (1976, TV plays 1976, Writer of the Year Award), Heaven and Earth (1985), After The War (1988); short stories: Sleeps Six (1979), Oxbridge Blues (1980, TV plays 1984), Think of England (1986); screenplays: Nothing but the Best (1964), Darling (Acad Award 1965), Two for the Road (1967), Far From the Madding Crowd (1967), A Severed Head (1972), Daisy Miller (1974), Rogue Male (1976), Something's Wrong (dir 1978), School Play (1979), The Best of Friends (1979); biography: Somerset Maugham and his World (1977), Byron (1982); essays: Bookmarks (ed 1975), Cracks in the Ice (1979); From the Greek (play) 1979; translations (with Kenneth McLeish): Poems of Catullus (1976), The Oresteia (1978, televised as The Serpent Son BBC 1979); FRSL 1964; *Recreations* tennis, skiing; *Clubs* Savile, The Queen's; *Style—* Frederic Raphael, Esq; The Wick, Langham, Colchester, Essex CO4 5PE; Lagardelle, St Laurent-La-Vallée 24170 Belves, France; c/o A P Watt Ltd, 20 John St, London WC1

RAPLEY, Hon Mrs Heather; *née* McLeavy; da of Baron McLeavy (Life Peer, d 1976); *b* 1929; *m* 1955, Patrick William Rapley; *Style—* The Hon Mrs Rapley; 7 Salcombe Drive, Earley, Reading

RAPLEY, Raymond Herbert; s of Richard Herbert Rapley (d 1928), and Olive Evelyn, *née* Riddiford (d 1979); *b* 13 Jan 1929; *Educ* Huntingdon GS, Open Univ (BA); *m* 5 May 1950, Betty, da of Harry Gregory, MM (d 1946) of Dronfield, Derbys; 2 s (David b 1965, Martin b 1957), 2 da (Elizabeth Frances, b 1956, Yvonne Linda b 1958); *Career* Rapleys Surveyors and Planning Conslts London 1951-, md Yelcon Ltd Housebuilders Cambs 1961-; former cncl memb Inc soc of Valversand Auctioneers 1968-69, regnl pres Housebuilders Fed (E Anglia regn) 1986-87, pres Bldg Employers Confedn (Cambridge branch) 1986-87; *Style—* Raymond Rapley, Esq; Misty Meadows, Gore Tree Rd, Hemingford Grey, Cambs

RAPPORT, Cecil Herbert; OBE, JP; s of Maurice Aaron Rapport (d 1953), and Phoebe Annie, *née* Jacobs (d 1960); *b* 12 Oct 1915; *Educ* Monkton House Coll Cardiff, City of Cardiff Tech Coll; *m* 25 Nov 1942, Audrey Rachel, da of Sidney Fligelstone; 1 s (Derek Ivor), 2 da (Valerie Avery Gee, Heather Hockley); *Career* Welch Regt 1939-45; pres: Cardiff Inst for the Blind, Royal Br Legion Cardiff, Friends of Cardiff Royal Infirmary, Cardiff Central Cons Assoc; chm Wales Festival of Remeberance; High Sheriff S Glamorgan 1984-85, former Dep Lord Mayor City of Cardiff; former Alderman City Cardiff, Freeman City of London 1959; memb: Worshipful Co of Horners 1958, Guild of Freemen of the City of London 1969; memb IOD; KStJ; *Recreations* swimming, sailing, music; *Clubs* City Livery, RAC; *Style—* Cecil Rapport, Esq, OBE, JP; Cefn Coed House, Cefn Coed Rd, Cyncoed, Cardiff, South Glam CF2 6AP (☎ 2222 757375); Ivor House, Bridge St, Cardiff, South Glam CF1 2TH (☎ 02222 373737/02222 231444, fax 0222 220121)

RASCH, Sir Richard Guy Carne; 3 Bt (UK 1903); s of Brig Guy Elland Carne Rasch, CVO, DSO (d 1955; s of 1 Bt), and Phyllis Dorothy Lindsay, *née* Greville (d 1977); s unc, Col Sir Frederic Carne, 2 Bt, TD, 1963; *b* 10 Oct 1918; *Educ* Eton, RMC Sandhurst; *m* 1, 1947 (m dis 1959), Anne Mary, eld da of late Maj John Henry Dent-Brocklehurst, OBE, of Sudeley Castle, Glos; 1 s, 1 da; m 2, 1961, Fiona Mary, eld da of Robert Douglas Shaw, and former w of Humphrey John Rodham Balliol Salmon; *Heir* s, Simon Anthony Carne Rasch, *qv*; *Career* former Maj Grenadier Gds; memb HM Body Guard of Hon Corps of Gentlemen-at-Arms 1968-88; memb London Stock Exchange; *Recreations* fishing, shooting; *Clubs* White's, Pratt's, Cavalry & Guards; *Style—* Sir Richard Rasch, Bt; 30 Ovington Sq, London SW3 1LR; The Manor House, Lower Woodford, Salisbury, Wilts SP4 6NQ

RASCH, Simon Anthony Carne; s and h of Sir Richard Rasch, 3 Bt, by his 1 w, Anne Mary, eld da of late Maj John Henry Dent-Brocklehurst, OBE, of Sudeley Castle, Winchcombe, Glos; *b* 26 Feb 1948; *Educ* Eton, RAC Cirencester; *m* 31 Oct 1987, Julia, er da of Maj Michael, and Lady Joanna Stourton, *qv*; *Career* page of honour to HM 1962-64; chartered surveyor; *Style—* Simon Rasch Esq; The White House, Manningford Bruce, nr Pewsey, Wilts (☎ 098 063 0200)

RASHLEIGH, Jonathan Michael Vernon; s of Nicholas Vernon Rashleigh, of Rodmell, Lewes, Sussex, and Rosalie Mary, *née* Matthews; *b* 29 Sept 1950; *Educ* Bryanston; *m* 5 April 1975, Sarah, da of John Norwood, of Knowle, Solihull, W Midlands; 3 s (Charles b 1979, Hugh b 1986, Philip b 1988), 1 da (Julia b 1982); *Career* Ernst and Whinney 1968-76, dir 3i plc 1986- (joined 1976); Freeman City of London, Liveryman Worshipful Co of Tobacco Pipe Makers and Tobacco Blenders 1972; ACA 1974, FCA 1979; *Recreations* chess, theatre, cricket, music; *Style—* Jonathan Rashleigh, Esq; Longeaves, Norton Lindsey, Warwick CV35 8JL (☎ 092684 2523); 91 Waterloo Rd, London SE1 8XP (☎ 01 928 7822)

RASHLEIGH, Peter; s of Harry Rashleigh, JP, 3 s of 3 Bt; h of nephew, Sir Richard Rashleigh, 6 Bt; *b* 1924; *m* 1949, Lola, *née* Edmonds, of NSW, Australia; 3 da (Margaret, Bettine, Jill); *Career* master mariner; *Style*— Peter Rashleigh Esq; 8A Frederick St, Gosford, NSW, Australia

RASHLEIGH, Sir Richard Harry; 6 Bt (UK 1831); s of Sir Harry Rashleigh, 5 Bt (d 1984), and Honora Elizabeth (Lady Rashleigh), *qv*; *b* 8 July 1958; *Educ* All Hallows Sch Dorset; *Heir* unc, Peter Rashleigh; *Career* mgmnt accountant; with Arthur Guinness Son & Co plc 1980-82, Dexion-Comino Int Ltd 1982-84, United Biscuits plc 1985-; *Recreations* sailing, tennis, shooting; *Clubs* Naval; *Style*— Sir Richard Rashleigh, Bt; Stowford Grange, Lewdown, nr Okehampton, Devon EX20 4BQ; office: UBFF, North Rd Industrial Estate, Okehampton, Devon (☎ 0837 3261)

RASHLEIGH BELCHER, John (Jack); s of Dr Ormonde Rashleigh Belcher (d 1961), of Liverpool, and Ruth Stephens (d 1960); nine generation of doctors - father to son; *b* 11 Jan 1917; *Educ* Epsom Coll, Univ of London (MB, BS, MRCS, LRCP, MS); *m* 1940, Jacqueline Mary, da of Cyril Paul Phillips (d 1964); 2 s (Ormonde, Henry), 1 da (Sarah); *Career* MO RAF 1940-46, Sqdn MO 42 Sqdn, surgical specialist, Sqdn Ldr; served in Canada 1943; res and asst surgical posts St Thomas's Brompton Middx and London Chest Hosps 1939-40 and 1946-51; conslt cardio-theracic surgn: London Chest Hosp 1951, Middx Hosp 1955-82; memb: Soc of Thoracic and Cardiovascular Surgns of GB and Ireland (pres 1980), Thoracic Soc, Cardiac Soc, American Coll of Chest Physicians, bd of Govrs of the Hosps for the Diseases of the heart and Chest 1961-82; Hunterian prof RCS; lecture tours for Br cncl to: Japan, Indonesia, Singapore, Malaysia, Afghanistan, Cyprus, Greece, Yugoslavia and Hong Kong; toured Indonesia and Bolivia for FCO; personal lecture tours to India, Nepal, Afghanistan, Jamaica and the USA; *Books* Thoracic Surgical Management (jtly 1953), Br Journal of Diseases of the Chest (co-ed 1955-78), papers in medical journals notably on bronchial cancer and mitral value surgery; *Recreations* picture framing, photography, gardening, ski-ing, golf; *Style*— Jack Rashleigh Belcher Esq; 23 Hornton Court, Hornton St, London W8 7RT

RASKIN, Susan; da of John Cary Abbatt, of Bath, and Sybil Eileen, *née* Lympaney; *b* 28 Mar 1942; *Educ* Plymouth HS, Tiffin Girls' Sch, Kingston upon Thames; *m* 18 Aug 1966, James Leo Raskin, s of Meyer Raskin (d 1971); 2 s (Benjamin Leo 1969, Thomas John b 1972), 1 da (Joanna b 1967); *Career* admitted slr 1967; ptnr: Raskin & Raskin 1969-88, Russell Jones & Walker 1988-; Bristol Poly law lectr 1974-80 (sr law lectr 1980-83); memb Women's Nat Cmmn, govr Bath HS, GPDST 1983-; *Recreations* singing, foreign languages, reading, hill-walking, swimming; *Clubs* Bath Assoc of Graduate Women, Assoc of Women Solicitors, Bristol Medico-Legal Assoc; *Style*— Mrs Susan Raskin; Tanglewood, Claverton, Bath (☎ 022122 3366, 0225 337642); Raskin & Raskin, Scarborough House, 29 James St West, Bath

RASTALL, (Walter) Guy; s of Herbert Guy Rastall (d 1968), and Madge Eveline Rastall, *née* Haggar (d 1985); gs of Walter Haggar the S Wales film pioneer; *b* 29 April 1938; *Educ* Lydney GS, Univ of Birmingham (BA); *m* 5 Sept 1966, Jane, da of Hector Ardern, MBE (1981), of Gwent; 1 s (Andrew b 1967), 2 da (Felicity b 1969, Penelope b 1972); *Career* CA; sr lectr Bristol Poly 1965-70, chief cost and mgmnt acct (military engines) Rolls-Royce plc 1970-; *Recreations* golf; *Clubs* St Pierre Golf & Country; *Style*— Guy Rastall, Esq; Keep House, Castle View, Tutshill, Chepstow, Gwent (☎ 02912 2680); Rolls Royce plc, Filton, Bristol (☎ 0272 797734)

RATCLIFFE, Frederick William; JP (Cambridge 1981); s of Sidney Ratcliffe (d 1964), of Leek, Staffs, and Dora, *née* Smith (d 1975); *b* 28 May 1927; *Educ* Leek HS, Univ of Manchester (BA, MA, PhD), Univ of Cambridge (MA); *m* 20 Aug 1952, Joyce, da of Thomas Edwin Brierley, of Harrogate; 2 s (R George, R John), 1 da (Helen L); *Career* WWII N Staffs Regt 1945-48; asst librarian Univ Library of Manchester 1954-62, sub librarian Glasgow Univ Library 1962-63, dep univ librarian Univ of Newcastle-Upon-Tyne 1963-65, librarian Univ of Manchester 1965-80 (dir John Rylands Univ Library of Manchester 1972-80), hon lectr historical bibliography Univ of Manchester 1970-80, univ librarian Univ of Cambridge and fell Corpus Christi Coll 1980-, visiting prof Univ of Loughborough 1982-86, Sandars reader bibliography Cambridge Univ 1989; JP: Stockport 1972-80; memb Manchester City Cultural Soc 1970-80; tstee: St Denions Library Hawarden, George Fearn Tst Stockport, FC Pybus Tst Newcastle Cambridge Fndn; fell Woodard Corp 1981-; chm: Cambridgeshire Library and Info jt ctee, advsy ctee Nat Preservation Off, Weffcome Inst for the History of Med Library Panel; memb UK Delgn CSCE Cultural Forum Budapest 1985, patron Soc of Bookbinders and Restorers; memb: Library Assoc, Bibliographical Soc, Cambridge Bibliographical Soc; hon FLA 1987; FRSA 1986; Comendador de la Orden del Merito Civil (Spain) 1988; *Books* numerous articles in literary jnls; *Recreations* book collecting, walking, gardening, handprinting; *Clubs* Sette of Odd Volumes; *Style*— Dr Frederick Ratcliffe, JP; Ridge House, Rickinghall Superior, Diss, Norfolk IP22 1DY (☎ 0379 898 232); 84 Church Lane, Girton, Cambridge CB3 0JP (☎ 0223 277 512); University Library, West Rd, Cambridge CB3 9DR (☎ 0223 62496/0223 333 045, fax 0223 334 748, telex 81395); Corpus Christi College, Cambridge

RATCLIFFE, Maj James Charles; s of Charles Ratcliffe (d 1933), and Dorothy Gladys, *née* Pigott (d 1988); *b* 11 June 1916; *Educ* Rydal Sch Colwyn Bay; *m* 2 July 1955, Ylva Mary Violet Augusta, da of Casper Rudolf Leopold Brunnström; 1 s (Christopher Charles Leopold b 1956, d 1976); *Career* cmmnd Maj RA 1938, served: BEF France and Belgium 1939 and 1940, ME 1942-44, Italy 1944-45, Home and ME 1945-58; *Recreations* racing, hunting, shooting, tennis; *Clubs* Army and Navy, Pall Mall; *Style*— Maj James Ratcliffe; Tremynfa, Bwlch, Breconshire (☎ 0874 730445)

RATCLIFFE, Col Peter Jocelyn Carne; OBE (1972); s of Jocelyn Vivian Ratcliffe (d 1973), of Helston, Cornwall, and Daphne Naylor, *née* Carne; *b* 17 Nov 1926; *Educ* Harrow; *m* 7 Oct 1950, Ann Pamela, da of Leonard Forsell, of Bosrhyn, Port Navas, Cornwall; 1 s (David b 1953), 1 da (Susan b 1956); *Career* Grenadier Gds 1944, cmmnd 2 Lt 1945; serv: Germany, Egypt, Cyprus (despatches 1958), Belgium; Adj Gds Depot 1952, Adj 2 Bn Gren Gds 1954, SD Directorate WO and MOD 1962-64, Regtl Adj Gren Gds 1964, 2 i/c 1 Bn 1967, Cmdt Gds Depot 1967, GSOI HQ London Dist 1970, Dep Cdr 3 Inf Bde 1973, chief mil personnel branch SHAPE 1974, ret 1974; City Marshal 1974; stock exchange firm (admin) 1978, exec dir Cinema and TV Benevolent Fund 1983-; Freeman City of London 1974; *Recreations* sailing, gardening, radio; *Clubs* Royal Yacht Sqdn, Household Division YC; *Style*— Col Peter J C Ratcliffe, OBE; c/o Barclays Bank Ltd, 1 Chertsey Rd, Woking, Surrey GU21 5AA; 72 Dean St, London W1V 6LT

RATCLIFFE, (James) Terence; MBE (1987), JP (1972); s of Jack Ratcliffe, Bury, and Alice, *née* Bennet (d 1981); *b* 9 Feb 1987; *Educ* Bury HS, Univ of Manchester (DipArch); *m* 8 Sept 1956, Mary Grundy (Molly), da of Reginald Victor Adlem, of Bury; 3 s (Mark b 1961, Jonathon b 1964, Nicholas b 1965), 1 da (Elisabeth (twin) b 1965); *Career* architect, sr ptnr Ratcliffe Groves Partnership; pres Euro Area of YMCA's; ARIBA; *Recreations* athletics, YMCA; *Style*— Terence Ratcliffe, Esq, MBE, JP; Ivy House, Bolton Rd, West, Holcombe Brook, Bury, Lancs (☎ 020 488 2519); 105 Manchester Rd, Bury, Lancs (☎ 061 797 6000); 174 High Holborn, London (☎ 01 528 8048)

RATFORD, David John Edward; CMG (1984), CVO (1979); s of late George Ratford, and Lilian, *née* Jones; *b* 22 April 1934; *Educ* Whitgift Middle Sch, Selwyn Coll Cambridge; *m* 1960, Ulla Monica, da of late Oskar Ratford, of Stockholm, and Gurli, *née*, Jerneck; 2 da; *Career* Nat Serv Intelligence Corps 1953-55; FO 1955, third sec Prague 1959-61, second sec Mogadishu 1961-63, second then first sec FO 1963-68, first sec (commercial) Moscow 1968-71; FCO 1971-74, cnsllr (agric and econ) Paris 1974-78, cnsllr Copenhagen 1978-82, min Moscow 1983-86, dep political dir (Europe), FCO 1986-; Cdr Order of The Dannebrog (Denmark 1979); *Recreations* music, tennis; *Clubs* Travellers'; *Style*— David Ratford, Esq, CMG, CVO; c/o Foreign & Commonwealth Office, London SW1A 2AH

RATH, James Winston; s of Maj Joseph Rath (d 1983), and Mary, *née* Futterweit (d 1988); *b* 12 May 1944; *Educ* St Marylebone GS, Univ of St Andrew (MA); *Career* CA; Coopers & Lybrand 1969-73, sec Assoc Investment Tst Cos 1988- (asst sec 1973-88); vice-chm exec ctee Wembley Jewish Youth Club; ACA 1972, FCA 1978; *Style*— James Rath, Esq; 6 Atherton Heights, Bridgewater Rd, Wembley, Middx HA0 1YD (☎ 01 902 3123); Park House, 16 Finsbury Circus, London EC2M 7JJ (☎ 01 588 5347, fax 01 638 1803)

RATHBONE, Bertram Lyle; s of Francis Warre Rathbone (d 1939), and Edith Bertha, *née* Hampshire; *b* 28 June 1913; *Educ* Marlborough, LSE; *m* 1, 1939 (m dis 1945), Joan Duckworth; 1 da; m 2, 1949, Elizabeth Eleanor, da of Lt-Col Thomas Coulson Leah, DSO, RA (d 1927); 1 s, 1 da; *Career* cmmnd RAC 1941, 2 Lt 4/7 DG ME 1942, Staff Capt GHQ MEF subsequently DAQMG (Plans) Staff Coll Haifa 1944-45; ptnr Rathbone Bros & Co 1939-79; dir: Albany Investmt Tst, Norton Megaw & Co (and assoc cos); hon tres Liverpool Univ 1972-81 (pres of cncl 1981-84 and 1985-89); Hon LLD Liverpool Univ 1981; *Recreations* travel; *Clubs* Travellers'; *Style*— Bertram Rathbone, Esq; Park Lodge, Sefton Park Rd, Liverpool L8 3SL (☎ 051 727 5006)

RATHBONE, Tim - John Rankin (Tim); MP (C) 1974-; s of J Rathbone, MP (ka 1940), and Beatrice, later Lady Wright (m Sir Paul Wright, *qv*); *b* 17 Mar 1933; *Educ* Eton, Ch Ch Oxford, Harvard Business Sch; *m* 1, 1960 (m dis 1981), Margarita Sanchez y Sanchez; 2 s (John Paul, Michael), 1 da (Tina); m 2, 1982, Susan Jenkin, da of Jenkin Coles (d 1969) and former w of Lionel Geoffrey Stopford Sackville, *qv*; 2 step s (Charles, Thomas), 1 step da (Lucinda); *Career* 2 Lt KRRC 1951-53; Robert Benson Lonsdale & Co 1956-58, trainee to vice-pres Ogilvy & Mather Inc NY 1958-66, chief publicity & PRO Cons Central Off 1966-68; dir: Charles Barker Gp 1968-87, Ayer Barker Ltd (md 1970-74, dep chm 1974-79), Charles Barker City 1981-87, Ayer Barker Ltd (md 1970-74, dep chm 1974-79), Charles Barker City 1981-87; PPS to: Min of Health 1979-82, Min for Trade (consumer affrs) 1982-83, Min for the Arts 1985; chm advsy ctee Inst of Mtgmnt Resources 1987-; fndr memb and chm All Pty Drug Misuse Gp 1984, fndr memb Cons Gp for Fundamental Change in SA 1985, vice chm Br-Japanese Gp; memb All: Pty Franchise Gp, Br-SA Gp, Br South American Gp, Engrg Gp; FRSA (cncl memb 1984-88); *Clubs* Brooks's, Pratts, Sussex, Soc of Sussex Downsmen; *Style*— Tim Rathbone, Esq, MP; House of Commons, London SW1A 0AA (☎ 01 219 3460)

RATHBONE, Sebastian David; s of Richard Reynolds Rathbone (d 1969); *b* 6 Jan 1932; *Educ* Rugby, Trinity Coll Cambridge; *m* 1964, Susan Kennedy, da of late Robert Kennedy Rathbone; 4 s, 1 da; *Career* CA, ptnr Rathbone Bros & Co 1960-88, dep chm Rathbone Bros plc 1988-; *Recreations* sport; *Clubs* Athenaeum (Liverpool), Nat Lib; *Style*— Sebastian Rathbone, Esq; c/o Rathbone Bros & Co, Port of Liverpool Bldg, Pier Head, Liverpool

RATHBONE, Tim; *see*: Rathbone, John Rankin

RATHCAVAN, 2 Baron (UK 1953); hon Phelim Robert Hugh O'Neill; 2 Bt (UK 1929), PC (NI 1969); er s of 1 Baron Rathcavan (d 1982), by his w Sylvia (d 1972), da of Walter Sandeman of the sherry and port family; 1 Baron Rathcavan was only surv s of 2 Baron O'Neill, JP, DL (descended from the O'Neills who, as High Kings of Ireland, are the earliest traceable family in Europe); *b* 2 Nov 1909; *Educ* Eton; *m* 1, 1934 (m dis 1944), Clare Désirée (d 1956), er da of Detmar Jellings Blow, JP (d 1910), of Carlos Place, Mayfair, and Hilles House, Stroud (sometime Lord of the Manor of Painswick) by his w Winifred, ggda of 1 Baron Tollemache; 1 s, 1 da; m 2, 1953, Bridget Doreen, yst da of late Maj Hon Richard Coke (3 s of 2 Earl of Leicester) and formerly w of Thomas Ewards-Moss (yr bro of Sir John E-M, 4 Bt); 3 da (1 da decd); *Heir* s, Hon Hugh O'Neill; *Career* Maj RA; MP (UU) for N Antrim (UK Parl) 1952-59, NI Parl (U and later Alliance) 1959-73 (Parl suspended March 1972); min: of Educn 1969, of Agric 1969-71; *Clubs* Brooks's; *Style*— Maj the Rt Hon the Lord Rathcavan, PC; Killala Lodge, Killala, Co Mayo, Ireland

RATHCREEDAN, 2 Baron (UK 1916); Charles Patrick Norton; TD; s of 1 Baron Rathcreedan (d 1930), by his 2 w, Marguerite, da of Sir Charles Huntington, 1 Bt (Btcy extinct on death of 3 Bt 1928); *b* 26 Nov 1905; *Educ* Wellington, Lincoln Coll Oxford; *m* 1946, Ann, da of Surgn-Capt William Bastian, RN; 2 s, 1 da; *Heir* s, Hon Christopher Norton; *Career* former Maj 4 Bn Oxford & Bucks LI (TA), POW WWII; barr 1931, slr 1936; Master Worshipful Co of Founders 1970; *Style*— The Rt Hon The Lord Rathcreedan, TD; Church Field, Fawley, Henley-on-Thames, Oxon (☎ 4160)

RATHDONNELL, 5 Baron (I 1868); Thomas Benjamin McClintock-Bunbury; s of 4 Baron Rathdonnell (d 1959); *b* 17 Sept 1938; *Educ* Charterhouse, RNC Dartmouth; *m* 2 Oct 1965, Jessica Harriet, o da of George Gilbert Butler (eighth in descent from 2 Baron Dunboyne) and Norah Pomeroy Colley, gggda of 4 Viscount Harberton; 3 s (Hon William, Hon George b 26 July 1968, Hon James b 21 Feb 1972), 1 da (Hon Sasha b 1976); *Heir* s, Hon William Leopold McClintock-Bunbury, b 6 July 1966; *Style*— The Rt Hon the Lord Rathdonnell; Lisnavagh, Rathvilly, Co Carlow, Republic of Ireland (☎ 0503 61104)

RATTEE, Donald Keith; QC (1977-); *b* 9 Mar 1937; *Career* barr, bencher Lincoln's Inn 1985, attorney gen of the Duchy of Lancaster 1986-, rec Crown Ct 1989-; *Style*— Donald Rattee, Esq; 7 New Sq, Lincoln's Inn, London WC2A 3QS (☎ 01 405 1266, fax 01 405 0554, telex 24216)

RATTRAY, Andrew; s of James Dewar Rattray (d 1971), and Martha Topley, *née* Gray (d 1966); *b* 14 April 1925; *Educ* Leith Acad Edinburgh, Heriot Watt Coll Edinburgh, Glasgow Coll of Commerce; *m* 21 July 1953, Margaret Ann Todd, da of John Burns (d 1966);; *Career* Sgt Queens Own Cameron Highlanders 1943-47; co sec Rest Assured (Northern) Ltd 1964-79, md Airsprung Scotland Ltd 1981- (dir gen mangr 1979-81); FSCA 1972, MBIM 1979; *Recreations* hill walking, music, theatre; *Style*— Andrew Rattray, Esq; 6 Fair Oaks, Carmunnock, Glasgow G76 (☎ 041 644 3913); Stepps Rd, Queenslie Industrial Estate, Glasgow G33 (☎ 041 744 3442, fax 041 744 8935)

RATTRAY OF RATTRAY, Hon Mrs Elizabeth Sophia; *née* Sidney; da (by 1 m) of 1 Visc De L'Isle, VC, KG, GCMG, GCVO, PC; *b* 1941; *m* 1, 1959 (m dis 1966), George Silver Oliver Annesley Colthurst; m 2, 1966 (m dis 1971), Sir (Edward) Humphry Tyrell Wakefield, 2 Bt; m 3, 1972, Capt James Silvester Rattray of Rattray; 1 s; *Style*— The Hon Mrs Rattray of Rattray; Craighall-Rattray, Blairgowrie, Perthshire

RAVEN, (Anthony) David; s of Harry Raven (d 1967), of Bournemouth, and May Louise, *née* Fletcher (d 1982); *b* 12 July 1934; *Educ* Ermysted's, Yeovil Technical Coll, Univ of London (BSc); *m* 3 April 1965, Elizabeth, da of Ronald Spence Allen (d 1969), of Loughborough; 2 da (Louisa Elizabeth b 21 July 1971, Natasha Mary b 11 Aug 1977); *Career* with Westland Aircraft Ltd, English Electric Co Ltd, Perkins Ltd 1965-68, Jaguar Cars Ltd 1968-71, tech dir Willowbrook Ltd 1971-73; chm and md: Diplomat Technico Ltd 1973-, Diplomat Projects Ltd 1986-88, Debdale Consultancy Ltd 1984-, C H Technology Ltd 1988-; chm: Bruce Engrs Ltd 1986-88, Hallite Diplomat Ltd 1988-, Milsco Diplomat Ltd 1987-; dir Remora Textiles Ltd 1980-82, non-exec dir Roger Staton Assocs Ltd 1978-; govr Lutterworth HS; CEng, MIMechE, MBIM, FInstD; *Books* Profit Improvement by Value Analysis Value Engineering and Purchase Analysis (1971); *Recreations* antique clocks, choral singing, historic buildings, pretending to garden; *Style*— David Raven, Esq; c/o Debdale Consultancy Ltd, Shawell, Lutterworth, Leics LE17 6AL

RAVEN, Ronald William; OBE (Mil 1946), TD (1953); s of Fredric William Raven (d 1952), and Annie Williams Raven, *née* Mason (d 1973), who was a direct descent of Miles Mason (1752-1822), originator of Mason's Patent Ironstone China; bro of Dame Kathleen Raven, *qv*; *b* 28 July 1904; *Educ* Ulverston GS, St Bartholomew's Hosp and Med Coll London; *Career* RAMC 1941-46 served: N Africa, Italy, Malta (despatches); Hon Col RAMC 1946-; consulting surgn Westminster and Royal Marsden Hosp 1969-; vice-pres and chm: Epsom Coll 1954-, Marie Curie Memorial Fndn 1957-; fndr pres: Br Assoc Surgical Oncology 1973-77, Assoc Head and Neck Oncologists for GB 1968-71, World Fedn for Cancer Care 1982-87; memb ct of patrons RCS 1976- (memb cncl 1968-76), vice-pres Malta Meml Dist Nursing Assoc 1982-; created the Ronald William Room Museum Royal Crown Derby Porcelain Co 1987 (hon life memb Derby Porcelain Int Soc 1988); O St J 1946; Master Worshipful Co of Barbers 1980-81; Hon MD Cartagena 1949, foreign memb Acad of Athens 1983-; hon FRSM, FRSA, MRCS, LRCP 1928, FRCS 1931; Chev Légion d'Honneur 1952; *Publications* author of: Treatment of Shock (trans Russian, 1942), Surgical Care (second edn 1952), Cancer and Allied Diseases (1955), Cancer of Larynx, Pharynx and Oesophagus and its Surgical Treatment (1958), Cancer (ed and contrib, 7 vols 1958-60), Modern Trends in Oncology (1973), The Dying Patient (trans Dutch and Japanese, 1975), Principles of Surgical Oncology (1977), Foundations of Medicine (1978), Rehabilitation and Continuing Care in Cancer (1986), The Gospel of St John (1987), papers on surgical subjects, especially relating to Cancer in British and foreign jls; *Recreations* philately (medallist int stamp exhib 1950), music, ceramics, paintings, travel; *Clubs* MCC, Pilgrims; *Style*— Ronald Raven Esq, OBE, TD; 29 Harley St, London W1N 1DA (☎ 01 580 3765)

RAVEN, Capt Simon Arthur Noël; s of Arthur Godart Raven, and Esther Kate, *née* Christmas; *b* 28 Dec 1927; *Educ* Charterhouse, King's Coll Cambridge (MA); *m* 1951 (m dis), Susan Mandeville, *née* Kilner; 1 s (Adam); *Career* novelist, dramatist & critic; The Pallisers (BBC); Edward & Mrs Simpson (Thames); *Books* Arms for Oblivion (10 vols), The First-Born of Egypt (7 vols, 5 vols complete); *Clubs* Brooks, Reform, MCC; *Style*— Simon Raven, Esq; c/o Curtis Brown, 162-168 Regent St, London W1R 5TB

RAVEN (INGRAM), Dame Kathleen Annie; DBE (1968); da of Fredric William Raven (d 1952), and Annie Williams, *née* Mason (d 1973); sis of Ronald William Raven, *qv*; *b* 9 Nov 1910; *Educ* Ulverston GS, privately, St Bartholomew's Hosp London, City of of London Maternity Hosp; *m* 1959, Prof John Thornton Ingram (d 1972); *Career* asst matron St Bartholomews Hosp 1946-49, matron The General Infirmary Leeds 1949-57, chief nursing offr DHSS 1958-72; memb: Gen Nursing Cncl for England and Wales 1950-57, exec ctee for Assoc of Hosp Matrons for England and Wales 1955-57, cncl Royal Coll Nursing 1950-57, cncl Central Health Services 1957-58, cncl and nursing advsy bd BRCS 1958-72, Nat Florence Nightingale Meml Ctee of GB and NI 1958-72, WHO Expert Advsy Panel on Nursing 1961-79 (fell 1960); vice-pres Royal Coll of Nursing 1972-, chm Interviewing Panels Civil Serv cmmn 1974-80, fndn govr Aylesbury GS 1986-, memb Distressed Gentlefolks Aid Assoc 1973- (chm exec ctee 1981-87); Hon Freewoman Worshipful Co of Barbers 1981, Freeman City of London 1986; SRN 1936, SCM 1938, FRSA 1970 FRCN 1986; OStJ 1963; *Recreations* painting, reading; *Clubs* Royal Commonwealth Soc; *Style*— Dame Kathleen Raven, DBE; Jesmond, Burcott, Wing, Leighton Buzzard, Beds (☎ 0296 688 244); 29 Harley St, London W1

RAVENSCROFT, Mark Henry; s of Thomas Benson Ravenscroft, of The Forge, Bird Lip, Gloucestershire, and Patricia Ann, *née* Hewit; family name and coat of arms awarded after defeating the Danes in 800 AD at the battle of the Dec; *b* 31 Oct 1959; *Educ* Whiteffriars Cheltenham, Royal Agricultural Coll Cirencester, MRAC; *m* 1 March 1986, Amanda Katherine, da of Jonathan Gervais Browne; 1 da (Laura Jane b 1987); *Career* contracter; *Recreations* shooting, painting; *Clubs* CGA; *Style*— Mark Ravenscroft, Esq; Straw Collage, The Burgage, Prestbury, Cheltenham, Glos

RAVENSDALE, 3 Baron (UK 1911); Sir Nicholas Mosley; 7 Bt (GB 1781), of Ancoats, Lancashire, and of Rolleston, Staffordshire, MC (1944); s of Sir Oswald Mosley, 6 Bt (d 1980), and (first w) Lady Cynthia Blanche, *née* Curzon, da of 1 Marquess of Curzon and Kedleston and 1 Baron Ravensdale (she d 1933); suc aunt, Baroness Ravensdale (who was also cr a Life Peer as Baroness Ravensdale of Kedleston 1958) 1966; suc father as 7 Bt 1980; *b* 25 June 1923; *Educ* Eton, Balliol Coll Oxford; *m* 1, 1947 (m dis 1974), Rosemary, da of Marshal Sir John Salmond, GCB, CMG, CVO, DSO, RAF, by his 2 w, Hon Monica Grenfell (da of 1 Baron Desborough and Ethel, da of Hon Julian Fane, 4 s of 11 Earl of Westmorland, by Julian's w Lady Adine Cowper, da of 6 Earl Cowper); 3 s, 1 da; m 2, 1974, Verity, 2 da of John Raymond, of Winslade House, Basingstoke, and former w of John Bailey; 1 s (Hon Marius b 1976); *Heir* s, Hon Shaun Mosley; *Career* Capt Rifle Bde WW II; author (as Nicholas Mosley); *Books Incl:* Accident (1964, filmed by Joseph Losey), The Assassination of Trotsky (1972, also filmed), Rules of the Game: Sir Oswald and Lady Cynthia Mosley 1896-1933 (1982), Beyond the Pale, Sir Oswald Mosley 1933-80 (1983); *Style*— The Rt Hon the Lord Ravensdale, MC; 2 Gloucester Crescent, London NW1 7DS (☎ 01 485 4514)

RAVENSWORTH, 8th Baron (UK 1821); Sir Arthur Waller Liddell; 13th Bt (E 1642), JP (Northumberland 1959); s of Hon Cyril Liddell, JP, DL (2 s of 5th Baron Ravensworth); suc cous, 7th Baron, 1950; is 2 cous once removed of late Guy Liddell, CB, CBE, MC, sometime civil asst War Office. Lord Ravensworth's gf, the 5th Baron, was second cousin to Alice Liddell, whose Adventures in Wonderland and through the Looking Glass were immortalised by Lewis Carroll; *b* 25 July 1924; *Educ* Harrow; *m* 1950, Wendy, adopted da of J Stuart Bell, of Cookham; 1 s, 1 da; *Heir* s, Hon Thomas Liddell; *Career* former radio engr BBC; *Style*— The Rt Hon The Lord Ravensworth, JP; Eslington Park, Whittingham, Alnwick, Northumberland (☎ 066 574 239)

RAW, Peter Michael; s of George Raw, of Ewell, and Florence May, *née* Elliott; *b* 17 May 1939; *Educ* Queen Elizabeth's GS Wakefield, Downing Coll Cambridge (BA, MA); *m* 1 July 1972, Mary Angela, da of John Smith (d 1977), of Leicester; 3 s (James Edward b 1973, Simon David b 1975, John Peter b 1977), 1 da (Catherine Jane b 1981); *Career* prodn and tech dir Engelhard Ltd Chessington Surrey 1983-; vice pres Esher RFC; MIM 1970, CEng 1984; *Recreations* long distance running, cricketer, scouting; *Clubs* London Road Runners; *Style*— Peter Raw, Esq; Orchard House, Bushy Rd, Bookham, Surrey KT22 9SX (☎ 0372 57546) Engelhard Ltd, Engineered Materials Division, Davis Rd, Chessington, Surrey KT9 1TD (☎ 01 397 5292, fax 01 914 1412, telex 28720)

RAWCLIFFE, Rt Rev Derek Alec; *see*: Glasgow and Galloway, Bishop of

RAWCLIFFE, James Overbury; s of Brig James Maudsley Rawcliffe, OBE, MC, TD (d 1965), and Margaret Duff, *née* Capron (d 1982); *b* 8 Nov 1930; *Educ* Rossall; *m* 1957, Jutta Maria Edith, *née* Heinisch; 1 s (Rupert b 1965), 3 da (Susan, Jutta, Charlotte); *Career* dir and vice pres RHM Hldgs (USA) Inc dir Red Wing Co Inc; FCA, FCMA; *Clubs* Canning, MCC; *Style*— James Rawcliffe Esq; 45 Rosalyn Drive, Fredonia, New York 14063, USA; 707 Skokie Blvd, Suite 520, Northbrook, Illinois 60062, USA

RAWDON-LEEFE, Christopher Timothy; s of Maj Thomas Leefe (d 1968), of Langton, Malton, Yorks, and Sylvia Paola, *née* Roden, TD; *b* 7 Oct 1926; *Educ* Branksome Hall, Worksop Coll; *m* 1, 1952 (m dis 1963), Dorothé Gisela (d 1970), da of Dr Paul Goerz; m 2, 18 April 1964, Joanna Elizabeth, da of John Edward Buxton (d 1981), of Surrey; 2 s (Mark, Tom); *Career* Army 1944-62, 1 Bn Green Howards, RASC NW Egypt, Europe, Far East, ret Maj 1962; tport mangr Br Oxygen 1964-67, personnel and admin mangr RF White 1967-70, gen mangr Advertising Euromoney Pubns Ltd 1970-84, chm Money Media 1984-; dir Rolls-Royce Enthusiasts' Club; Freeman City of London 1977, memb Worshipful Co of Coachmakers and Coach Harness Makers 1977; *Books* Rolls-Royce Alpine Compendium (1973); *Recreations* restoration of vintage Rolls-Royce cars, music, antiques, opera, travel; *Clubs* RREC, RROC of America, 20 Ghost, Silver Ghost Assoc; *Style*— Christopher Rawdon-Leefe, Esq; West Farm House, Harrlotts Lane, Ashtead, Surrey KT21 2QE (☎ 0372 275337, office 0372 278127)

RAWLENCE, Lorna Marjorie; da of Henry Augustus Ralph Chapman, CBE (d 1958), and Hilda Winifred, *née* Barfoot (d 1970); *Educ* Cheltenham Ladies' Coll; *m* 5 May 1945 (m dis 1973), Michael Fitzgerald Rawlence, s of (George) Norman Rawlence, MBE (d 1967); 2 s (Simon Edward Fitzgerald b 5 Aug 1947, Nigel John Randal b 6 Sept 1954), 2 da (Justine Diana b 31 March 1946, d 11 Jan 1950, Anthea Justine b 14 Oct 1950); *Career* barr Inner Temple 1979; practising: Southampton 1981-87, Portsmouth 1987-; memb Inner Temple 1963; *Recreations* riding, theatre, travel; *Style*— Ms Lorna Rawlence; 22 Ennismore Gdns, London SW7 1AB; The Bell House, Charlton All Saints, Salisbury SP5 4HQ (☎ 0725 20089); 24 Hampshire Terrace, Portsmouth, Hants (☎ 0705 826636, fax 0705 291262)

RAWLENCE, Simon Edward Fitzgerald; s of Michael Fitzgerald Rawlence, and Lorna Marjorie Rawlence; *b* 5 August 1947; *Educ* Eton, Chace Coll Cambridge; *m* 26 July 1969, Suzanna Elaine, da of Cuthbert Neil Kirkus; 2 s (Ben b 1974, Leo b 1976), 2 da (Eleanor b 1982, Zoe b 1979); *Career* CA; sole practitioner 1977-87, sr ptnr Rawlence & Browne 1987-; *Recreations* tennis, amateur dramatics; *Style*— Simon Rawlence, Esq; Riversfield, 159 Lower Rd, Bemerton, Sandbury, Wilts SP2 9NL; Rawlence & Browne, 15 St Edmunds Church St, Samsbury SP1 1EF (☎ 0722 24853)

RAWLINGS, Keith John; s of Jack Frederick Rawlings (d 1985), and Eva, *née* Mullis; *b* 24 April 1940; *Educ* Kent Coll Canterbury; *m* 21 Dec 1965, Susan Mary, da of Thomas Johnson (d 1967); 1 s (Jonathan b 1965), 1 da (Sarah b 1967); *Career* insur broker and ind fin advsr, chm Burlington Insur Servs Ltd 1969-; dir: London & Edinburgh Tst plc 1986-87, Rutland Tst plc 1986-; *Recreations* tennis, golf, sailing, travel; *Clubs* St James's; *Style*— Keith Rawlings, Esq; Summerhayes, Cliff Rd, Hythe, Kent CT21 5XQ (☎ 0303 67014); Burlington House, Manor Rd, Folkestone, Kent CT20 2SD (☎ 0303 850555, fax 0303 44914, telex 96240, car 0836 274010)

RAWLINS, Colin Guy Champion; OBE (1965), DFC (1941); s of Capt Richard Seymour Champion Rawlins, DCM (d 1949), and Yvonne Blanche, *née* Andrews (d 1925); *b* 5 June 1919; *Educ* Prince of Wales Sch Nairobi Kenya, Charterhouse, Queen's Coll Oxford (BA, MA), LSE; *m* 25 May 1946, Rosemary, da of Capt Jens Jensen (d 1972); 2 s (Robert Champion b 1949, Andrew Champion b 1957), 1 da (Susan Champion b 1947); *Career* Pilot Offr RAFVR 1938, WWII Actg Sqdn Ldr 1941, served in 5 Gp Bomber Cmd, Fl Cdr 144 Sqdn (shot down Holland 1941, POW Germany 1941-45); HM Overseas Civil Service served in N Rhodesia and Zambia, cadet provincial admin 1946, dist offr 1948, res cmmr 1963-66, other appts in field and Govt HQ; dir of zoos and chief exec Zoological Soc of London 1966-84, pres Int Union of Directors of Zoological Gdns and Aquaria 1977-80, chm and memb many statutory and voluntary orgns in N Rhodesia and Zambia, dir and assoc ed Aircraft Owners and Pilots Assoc of UK 1985-; chm and pres local branch of Amersham and Chesham Cons Assoc 1967-; FCSA; *Recreations* gardening, aviation, travel; *Style*— Colin Rawlins, Esq, OBE, DFC; Birchgrove, 64 Earl Howe Rd, Holmer Green, nr High Wycombe, Bucks HP15 6QT (☎ 0494 712249)

RAWLINS, Gordon John; OBE (1986); s of Arthur James Rawlins, of New Milton, Hants, and Joyce Rosemary, *née* Smith; *b* 22 April 1944; *Educ* Welbeck Coll, RMA Sandhurst, RMCS (BSc); *m* 1, 28 Aug 1965, Ann Rose (d 1986), da of Alfred George Beard (d 1981); 1 s (Richard James b 1968); m 2, 25 Oct 1986, Margaret Anne (Meg), da of James Martin Edward Ravenscroft; 1 step s (Hamish Richmond Haddow b 1970), 1 step da (Islay Elizabeth Haddow b 1972); *Career* cmmnd REME 1964; recent career: Staff Coll (Maj) 1977-78, Maj GSO2 ASD 1 MOD 1978-80, Maj 21C 5 ARMD WKSP 1981-82, Lt-Col CO 7 ARMD WKSP 1982-84, Lt-Col mil asst to MGO MOD 1984-86, Col PB21 MOD 1986, Col Sec to COS ctee MOD 1987, Brig Comd Maint 1 (BR) Corps 1988, serv Aden, Oman, Jordan, UK, Hong Kong and BAOR, ret 1989 as Brig; sec ProdE and chief exec Inst of Indust Mangrs 1988-; MRAeS, CEng 1982; *Recreations* rugby, cricket, music; *Clubs* Army and Navy; *Style—* Gordon Rawlins, Esq, OBE; Instns of Prodn Engrs and Industl Mngrs, Rochester House, 66 Little Ealing Lane, London W5 4XX (☎ 01 579 9411, fax 01 579 2244)

RAWLINS, Surgn Vice Adm Sir John Stuart Pepys; KBE (1978, OBE 1960, MBE 1956); s of Col Cmdt Stuart William Hughes Rawlins, CB, CMG, DSO (d 1927), and Dorothy Pepys, *née* Cockerell (d 1937); *b* 12 May 1922; *Educ* Wellington, Univ Coll Oxford (MA), St Bartholomew's Hosp (BM, BCh); *m* 1944, Diana Margaret Freshney, da of Charles Freshney Colbeck, ISO (d 1966); 1 s, 3 da; *Career* Surgn Lt RNVR 1947, Surgn Lt RN, RAF Inst Aviation Med 1951, RN Physiology Laboratory 1957, Surgn Cdr RAF Inst Aviation Med 1961, HMS Ark Royal 1964, US Naval Med Res Inst 1967, Surgn Capt 1969, Surgn Cdre dir of health and res (Naval) 1973, Surgn Rear Adm 1975, dean of Naval Medicine and MO i/c Inst of Naval Medicine 1975-77, Actg Surgn Vice Adm 1977, med dir-gen (Navy) 1977-80; Queens Hon Physician 1975-80; chm; Deep Ocean Technology Inc, Deep Ocean Engineering Inc, Trident Underwater (systems) Ltd, Medical Express Ltd; dir: Under Sea Industs Inc 1981-83, Diving Unlimited Int Ltd; past pres Soc for Underwater Technology; conslt: in underwater technol to MOD, Hon fell Univ of Lancaster Soc for Underwater Technology, chm external advsy ctee, Centre for Offshore Health (Robert Gordons Tst); CStJ, FRCP, FFCM, FRAeS; *Recreations* stalking, shooting, riding, judo; *Clubs* Vincent's (Oxford), Army & Navy, Explorer's (New York); *Style—* Surgn Vice-Adm Sir John Rawlins, KBE; Wey House, Standford Lane, Headley, Bordon, Hants GU35 8RH (☎ 042 03 2830)

RAWLINS, Peter Jeremy; s of Leslie Rawlins; *b* 14 May 1941; *Educ* Warwick Sch, Univ of Nottingham (BA); *m* 1967, Gillian Lister, da of Cyril Goddard (d 1980); 4 s (Thomas b 1970, James b 1973, John b 1980, Tim b 1982); *Career* div md BTR plc, dir Graham Bldg Servs Ltd; chm: F J Reeves Ltd, Goodman Croggan Ltd; FCA; *Recreations* sport; *Style—* Peter Rawlins Esq; Beech Cottage, Apperley Lane, Rawdon, Leeds LS19 6LW (☎ 0532 502363); Graham Specialist Division, PO Box B120, Reliance House, 140 Leeds Rd, Huddersfield HD1 6PZ (☎ 0484 533555, fax 0484 435174)

RAWLINS, Hon Mrs (Rachel Elizabeth Cecily); *née* Irby; eld da of 7 Baron Boston (d 1958); *b* 30 August 1914; *m* 15 June 1940, Lt Darsie Rawlins, RNVR, s of George Edward Hawkes Rawlins, of King's Lane, Great Missenden, Bucks; 2 s (Adrian b 1942, Anthony b 1944), 2 da (Diana b 1949, Christina b 1955); *Style—* The Hon Mrs Rawlins; Red Tiles, Kingswood Ave, Penn, Bucks

RAWLINSON, Alexander Noel; s and h of Sir Anthony Rawlinson, 5 Bt; *b* 15 July 1964; *Style—* Alexander Rawlinson Esq

RAWLINSON, Hon Angela Lorraine; *née* Rawlinson; da of Baron Rawlinson of Ewell, PC, QC, by his 2 w and 1 cous, Elaine; *b* 3 Sept 1962; *Style—* The Hon Angela Rawlinson; 9 Priory Walk, London SW10

RAWLINSON, Sir Anthony Henry John; 5 Bt (UK 1891); s of Sir (Alfred) Frederick Rawlinson, 4 Bt (d 1969), and Bess, Lady Rawlinson, *qv*; *b* 1 May 1935; *Educ* Millfield; *m* 1, 1960 (m dis 1967), Penelope Byng, da of Rear-Adm Gambier John Byng Noel, CB; 1 s, 1 da; m 2, 1967 (m dis 1976), Pauline Strickland, da of John Holt Hardy, of Sydney NSW; 1 s; m 3, 1977, Helen Leone, da of Thomas Miller Kennedy, of Glasgow; 1 s; *Heir* s, Alexander Rawlinson; *Career* fashion photographer (portraits); *Recreations* tennis, cricket; *Style—* Sir Anthony Rawlinson, Bt; Heath Farm, Guist, Dereham, Norfolk

RAWLINSON, Hon Anthony Richard; 2 s of Baron Rawlinson of Ewell, PC, QC, by his 2 w, Elaine; *b* 28 Dec 1963; *Educ* Georgetown Univ (BSc), Worth School; *Career* merchant banker with N M Rothschild & Sons Ltd; *Recreations* theatre, music and cricket; *Style—* The Hon Anthony Rawlinson; 9 Priory Walk, London SW10

RAWLINSON, Hon Mrs (Catherine Julia); da of Baron Trend (Life Peer); *b* 1950; *m* 1966, Colin James Rawlinson; *Style—* The Hon Mrs Rawlinson

RAWLINSON, Charles Frederick Melville; s of Capt Rowland Henry Rawlinson (d 1980); *b* 18 Mar 1934; *Educ* Canford, Jesus Coll Cambridge; *m* 1962, Jill Rosalind, da of John Wesley; 3 da (incl Julia Caroline b 1964, m 1988, James Ogilvy, s of Hon Angus Ogilvy, and HRH Princess Alexandra); *Career* banker; chm Assoc Paper Indust plc 1979-, dir Willis Faber plc 1981-, jt chm Morgan Grenfell & Co Ltd (London) 1983-87 (dir 1970-85, former vice-chm); vice-chm Morgan Grenfell Gp plc 1985-1987; FCA, FCT; *Recreations* music, sailing; *Clubs* Brooks's, City of London, Leander; *Style—* Charles Rawlinson, Esq; 23 Great Winchester St, London EC2P 2AX (☎ 01 588 4545)

RAWLINSON, Hon Michael Vincent; er s of Baron Rawlinson of Ewell, PC, QC, and his 2 w, Elaine; *b* 24 Jan 1957; *m* 1982, Maria Alexandra Madeline de Lourdes (b 14 Dec 1953), only da of late Anthony Garton, by his w Hilda Isabella Maria (Anita), whose bro Juan m HRH Princess Hilda of Bavaria, and who was herself da of Garstang Bradstock Lockett, of Lima, Peru, by his w Hilda Luz Dora (yr da of late Juan Leovigilde de Loayza, of Lima and Santiago, Chile); *Style—* The Hon Michael Rawlinson; The Willowpond, 314 Fulham Rd, London SW10

RAWLINSON, William; CBE (1978); s of David Rawlinson (d 1950), of London, and Ann Markus (d 1974); *b* 10 Sept 1916; *Educ* Balliol Coll Oxford (MA); *m* 29 July 1954, Marietta, *née* Pordes; *Career* Flt Lt RAF 1941-46; barr Inner Temple 1939; memb Govt Legal Serv 1948-81; since 1972 dealing with EEC Law and policy, lectr on EEC Civil Serv Coll, lectr Univ of Southern California, California State Univ 1982, barr Ilan Univ; contrib Int Fin Law Review, sitting periodically stipendiary Metropolitan Magistrate London; *Recreations* reading, music; *Clubs* Reform; *Style—* William Rawlinson, Esq, CBE; 11 Kings Bench Walk, Temple, London EC4Y 7EQ (☎ 01 583 0610, fax 01 583 9123)

RAWLINSON OF EWELL, Baron (Life Peer UK 1978); Peter Anthony Grayson Rawlinson; PC (1964), QC (1959, NI 1972); s of Lt-Col Arthur Rawlinson, OBE, and Ailsa, eldest da of Sir Henry Grayson, 1 Bt, KBE; *b* 26 June 1919; *Educ* Downside, Christ's Coll Cambridge (exhibitioner 1938, hon fellow 1981); *m* 1, 1940 (m annulled by Sacred Rota Rome, 1954), Haidée, da of Gerald Kavanagh, of Dublin; 3 da; m 2, 1954, his 1 cous, Elaine, da of Vincent Dominguez, of Rhode Island, and Angela, 6 da of Sir Henry Grayson, 1 Bt, KBE; 2 s, 1 da; *Career* sits as Cons peer in House of Lords; Maj Irish Gds WWII (despatches); barr 1946; MP (C): Epsom 1955-74, Epsom and Ewell 1974-78; slr-gen 1962-64, attorney gen 1970-74; rec Kingston 1975-, chm of the Bar 1975-76, ldr Western Circuit 1975-82, reader Inner Temple 1983, tres Inner Temple 1984; pres Senate Inns of Courtland Bar 1986-87; kt 1962; *Clubs* White's, Pratt's, MCC; *Style—* The Rt Hon the Lord Rawlinson of Ewell, PC, QC; Priory Walk, London SW10;

RAWNSLEY, Andrew Nicholas James; s of Eric Rawnsley, and Barbara, *née* Butler; *b* 5 Jan 1962; *Educ* Rugby, Sidney Sussex Coll Cambridge (MA); *Career* writer and broadcaster: BBC 1983-85, The Guardian 1985- (political columnist 1987-); Student Journalist of the Year 1983, Young Journalist of the Year 1987; *Recreations* House of Commons; *Style—* Andrew Rawnsley, Esq; The Guardian Newspaper, 119 Farringdon Rd, London EC1R 3ER (☎ 01 278 2332, fax 01 837 2114, telex 8811746 GUARDN G)

RAWSON, Christopher Selwyn Priestley; s of Cdr S G C Rawson, OBE, RN (d 1974), and Dr Doris, *née* Brown (d 1979); *b* 25 Mar 1928; *Educ* The Elms Sch Colwall Worcs, The Nautical Coll Pangbourne; *m* 24 Jan 1959, Rosemary Ann, da of Alex R Focke (d 1983); 2 da (Gina b 16 Jan 1961, Caroline b 22 March 1964); *Career* navigating apprentice Merchant Serv T & J Brocklebank Ltd 1945-48, mangr John Crossley & Sons Ltd Halifax 1948-53, London rep of Milford Docks Ltd 1953-60, chm and md Christopher Rawson Ltd 1960-80, dir London Underwriters First Fin Servs Ltd 1983-; underwriting memb Lloyds 1973; JP City of London Bench 1972- (Inner London 1967-72), Sheriff City of London 1961-62, common councilman Ward of Bread St 1963-72, Alderman Ward of Lime St 1972-83, HM Lt City of London 1980-83, CSt J; Master Clothworkers Co 1988 (Liveryman 1962, Asst 1977), Master Watermens Co 1982-84 (Freeman 1966, Asst 1974), Younger Brother Trinity House 1988; Assoc Textile Inst; Cdr of the Order of Senegal 1961, Cdr of the Order of Ivory Coast 1961, Cdr of the Order of Liberia 1962; *Recreations* shooting, sailing; *Clubs* Garrick, Royal London YC (rear cdre); *Style—* Christopher Rawson, Esq; 56 Ovington St, London SW3 2JB; Prince Rupert House, 64 Queen St, London EC4R 1AD

RAWSON, Jessica Mary; *née* Quirk; da of Roger Nathaniel Quirk, CB (d 1964), and Paula, *née* Weber; *b* 1 Jan 1943; *Educ* St Paul's Girls Sch Hammersmith, New Hall Cambridge (BA), SOAS London (BA); *m* May 1968, John Graham, s of Graham Stanhope Rawson (d 1953); 1 da (Josephine b 1972); *Career* asst princ Miny of Health 1965-67; Dept of Oriental Antiquities Br Museum: asst keeper II 1967-71, asst keeper I 1971-76, dep keeper 1976-87, keeper 1987-; *Books* Animals in Art (1977), Ancient China, Art and Archaeology (1980), Chinese Ornament, the Lotus and the Dragon (1984), Chinese Bronzes, Art and Ritual (1987), Ancient Chinese Bronze in the Collection of Bella and PP Chiu (1988); *Style—* Mrs John Rawson; 3 Downshire Hill, London NW3 1NR (☎ 01 794 4002); Dept of Oriental Antiquities, British Museum, Great Russell St, London WC1 (☎ 01 323 8444, fax 01 323 8480)

RAWSON, Prof Kenneth John; s of Arthur William Rawson (d 1949), and Beatrice Annie, *née* Standing; *b* 27 Oct 1926; *Educ* Northern GS Portsmouth, RNC Greenwich, Univ Coll London, Brunel Univ (MSc); *m* 29 July 1950, Rhona Florence, *née* Gill, da of William Henry Gill MBE, of Manor Farm House, Norton St Philip; 2 s (Christopher John b 1955, Timothy James b 1981), 1 da (Hilary Anne b 1958); *Career* at sea 1950-51, structural res 1951-53, forward design Admty 1953- 57 with Lloyds Shipping Register 1957-59, ship designer MOD 1959- 69, naval staff 1969-72, prof Univ Coll London 1972-77, head of forward design MOD 1977-79, chief naval architect MOD 1979-83; Brunel Univ 1983-: prof, dean of educn and design, pro vice-chllr, vice pres RINA 1982; FEng 1983, FRINA 1961, FCSD 1984, FRSA 1984; *Style—* Prof Kenneth Rawson; Moorlands The Street, Chilcompton, Bath BA3 4HB (☎ 0761 232 793); Brunel Universtiy, Englefield Green, Egham, Surrey TW20 OJZ (☎ 0784 31341 or 37201)

RAWSON OF SOWERBY, John Hugh Selwyn; er s of Frederick Philip Selwyn Rawson, JP (d 1947), of Brockwell, Triangle, Sowerby, and Sarah Katharine, *née* Mitchell (d 1960); descended from John Rawson, of Ingrow, Yorks (b 1505) (*see* Burke's Landed Gentry, 18 edn, vol III, 1972); *b* 28 April 1915; *Educ* Loretto, Huddersfield Tech Coll; *m* 1, 30 Jan 1939 (m dis), Mary Elizabeth (d 1980), o da of Harold Whitaker, PhD (d 1955), of Hopewell House, Lightcliffe, Halifax; 1 da (Margaret Elizabeth Ann b 1945); m 2, 25 March 1965, Marjorie Louis, 2 da of George Nelson Bories (d 1930), of The Stubbins, Triangle; *Career* Lt 4 Duke of Wellington's Regt, 58 Anti-Tank Regt 1935-38, 3/7 How Mountain Battery FMSVF 1939-40, 1 Perak Bn FMSVF 1940-41, escaped after fall of Singapore, invalided; rubber planter in Malaya 1939- 42; agriculture and property owner 1942-; shipping mangr 1958-75; memb: Royal Br Legion, British Field Sports Soc, Sowerby Conservative Assoc, Yorks Agric Soc, Lorettonian Soc; Master of Otterhound Assoc; *Recreations* hunting, gardening, writing, building; *Style—* John Rawson, Esq; The Stubbins, Triangle, Sowerby Bridge, West Yorks HX6 3DR

RAWSTORNE, Joyce; *née* Priestley; da of Maj William Priestley (d 1966), of Rovie Lodge, Rogart, Sutherland, and Joan, *née* Baring-Gould (d 1967); *b* 10 June 1909; *Educ* West Heath Sevenoaks Kent; *m* 25 July 1933, Brig George Streynsham Rawstorne, CBE, MC, Lord Lieut of Co Sutherland 1950, 2 s of Rt Rev Atherton Gwillym Rawstorne, DD (d 1948), late Bishop of Walley; 2 da (Jean (decd), Diana Claire); *Career* pres: SSAFA for Sutherland 1952-86, Garden Scheme in aid of the Queen's Nurses 1948-86; *Recreations* shooting, fishing, gardening; *Style—* Mrs Joyce Rawstorne; Seaforth Hall, Rogart, Sutherland, Scotland IV28 3UA (☎ 040 84210)

RAY, Cyril; s of Albert Benson Ray, and Rita, *née* Caminetsky; *b* 16 Mar 1908; *Educ* Manchester GS, Jesus Coll Oxford; *Career* war corr Manchester Guardian 1939-45: 5 Destroyer Flotilla 1940, HMS Victorions N African Landings 1942, 8 Army Italy 1942-3 (despatches) war corr BBC: US 82 Airborne Div (US Army citation Nijmegen 1944, US 3 Army 1944-45; trustee of Albany 1967- (chm 1981-86); Freeman City of London, Liveryman Worshipful Co of Fanmakers 1975, hon Citizen of Cognac 1985, Burgess of St Emilion 1973; hon life memb: NUJ, Circle of Wine Writers (fndr and former pres); Commendatore Italian order of merit 1981 (Cavaliere 1972), Chevalier, French order of merit 1985 (Méite Agricole 1974); *Books* Scenes and Characters from

Surtees (ed 1948) From Algiers to Austria The History of 78 Division in Italy (1952), The Pageant of London (1958), Merry England (1960), Regiment of the Line: The Story of the Lancashire Fusiliers (1963), The Gourmet's Companion (ed 1963), Morton Shand's Book of French Wines (ed 1964), Best Murder Stories (ed 1965), The Wines of Italy (1966, Bologna Trophy 1967), In a Glass Lightly (1967), Mouton: The Story of Mouton Rothschild (1974), Wine and Food (with Elizabeth Ray 1975), The Wines of France (1976), The Wines of Germany (1977), The Complete Book of Spirits and Liqueurs (1978), The Saint Michael Guide to Wine (1978), Ruffino: The Story of a Chianti (with C Mozley 1979), Lickerish Limericks with Filthy Pictures by Charles Mozley (1979), Ray on Wine (Glenfiddich Wine Book of the Year, 1979), The New Book of Italian Wines (1982), Bollinger: The Story of a Champagne (revised edn 1982) Lafite: The Story of Château Lafite - Rothschild (revised edn 1985), Cognac (revised edn 1985); *Recreations* riding (until 1985); *Clubs* Athenaeum, Brook's, MCC, Special Forces; *Style*— Cyril Ray, Esq; K 1 Albany, Piccadilly, London W1V 9RQ (☎ 01 734 0270)

RAY, Edward Ernest; CBE (1988); s of Walter James Ray (d 1968), of London, and Cecilia May, *née* Hampton; *b* 6 Nov 1924; *Educ* Holloway Co Sch, London Univ (BCom); *m* 2 July 1949, Margaret Elizabeth, da of (Stanley) George Bull (d 1964), of Kettering, Northants; 2 s (Andrew John b 26 Nov 1952, Patrick Charles b 17 March 1956); *Career* Petty Offr RN 1943-46; CA, sr ptnr Spicer and Oppenheim (formerly Spicer and Pegler) 1984-88 (ptnr 1957-88), chm London CAs 1972-73, inspr DTI, bd memb Securities and Investmt Bd 1984-, chm Investors Compensation Scheme 1988-; memb: Worshipful Co of CAs 1975-, Freeman City of London; FCA (pres 1982 and 1983); *Books* VAT for Businessmen (1972), Partnership Taxation (3 edn 1987); *Recreations* golf, tennis, walking and bird watching; *Clubs* City of London; *Style*— Edward Ray, Esq, CBE; Southgate, Wiveton Rd, Blakeney, Norfolk NR25 7NJ (☎ 01 360 0028)

RAY, Elizabeth Mary; JP (Kent 1968-81; E Sussex 1981-); da of Rev Henry Cleeve Brocklehurst (d 1942), of Chalfont St Giles, Bucks, and Gwenna Maud, *née* Jones (d 1971); *b* 1 Oct 1925; *Educ* Private, LSE (Dip Soc Sci and Admin 1956); *m* 22 May 1953, Cyril Ray, s of Albert Benson Ray (d 1954), of Lytham St Annes; 1 s (Jonathan Cleeve b 1960); *Career* social worker LCC 1956-60, GLC 1964-68; Kent CC Social Servs 1972-83; freelance study supervisor Social Servs Course 1983-87; memb: bd of visitors HM Prison Lewes 1984-, mgmnt cncl Kent Opera 1970-; author (with husband): Wine with Food (1976), Best of Eliza Acton (1968), Resourceful Cook (1975), Country Cooking (1978); contrib: Homes and Gardens, A La Carte, and many other magazines; cookery corr Observer 1969-79; *Recreations* travel, listening to music, cooking; *Clubs* Lansdowne; *Style*— Mrs Elizabeth Ray, JP; K I Albany, Piccadilly, London W1V 9RQ (☎ 01 734 0270)

RAY, George William; s of late George William Ray, of High Wycombe, and Agnes Mary, *née* Pryke (d 1973); *b* 6 May 1905; *Educ* Royal GS High Wycombe; *m* 31 Aug 1940, (Ellen) Eileen, da of Harry Saunders (d 1974); 1 s (John Stewart); *Career* Furniture Industs Ltd (later Ercol Furniture Ltd) 1923-: co sec 1932, dir 1944; dir and sec Ercol Hldgs Ltd; dir and sec; vice-chm Govrs Royal GS High Wycombe, memb High Wycombe CC, cncl memb Thames Chiltern C of C and Indust, nat vice-pres Furnishing Trades Benevolent Assoc (nat pres 1989), formerly memb Nat Savings Ctee; chm: Consultative Ctee of TSB, Mgmnt and Languages Consultative Ctee of Bucks Coll; Warden of local church; Freeman City of London, Liveryman Worshipful Co of Furniture Makers 1963; FInstD; *Style*— George Ray, Esq; Ramsdale, 8 Sch Close, High Wycombe, Bucks HP11 1PH (☎ 0494 206 55); Ercol Hldgs Ltd, London Rd, High Wycombe, Bucks HP13 7AE (☎ 0494 212 61, fax 0494 462 467, telex 83616)

RAY, Malcolm John; s of George Henry Ray (d 1985), and Lucy, *née* Roberts (d 1985); *b* 27 August 1938; *Educ* Bilston GS, Univ of Aston (BSc, MSc); *m* 6 Sept 1962, Betty Maria, da of Whitmore Nicholls (d 1968), of Staffs; 1 s (Jonathan b 1974); *Career* md Rylands Whitecross Ltd Warrington (sales dir) 1976-81, md Catton & Co Ltd Leeds 1981-87, chm and md Birmid Qualcast Indust Ltd 1987-; chm: Darcast Components Ltd 1987, Birmas Components Ltd 1987, PBM Components Ltd 1987, Sterling Int Components Ltd 1987; MIBF 1964, MBIM 1974, FIM 1975, C Eng 1976, MInst M 1976; *Recreations* game fishing, walking; *Style*— Malcolm Ray, Esq; Thatched Cottage, Hill Wootton, Warwick CN35 7PP (☎ 0926 50 309); Birmid Quacoast Indust Ltd, Dartmouth Rd, Smethwick, Warley West Midlands B (☎ 021 558 1431, fax 021 565 4718, telex 335423)

RAY, Robin; s of Ted Ray, and Sybil, *née* Stevens; *Educ* Highgate Sch, RADA; *m* 1960, Susan, da of Alan Stranks; 1 s (Rupert b 1979); *Career* actor, author, broadcaster; West End debut 'The Changeling' Royal Ct Theatre 1960; extensive work in radio and TV, especially music and arts; stage play 'Cafe' 'Puccini' Wyndham's Theatre 1986; drama critic Punch 1986-87; *Books* Words on Music (1985); *Style*— Robin Ray, Esq; c/o David Wilkinson Associates, 24 Denmark St, London WC2H 8NJ (☎ 01 240 0451)

RAYLEIGH, 6 Baron (UK 1821) John Gerald Strutt; s of Hon Charles Richard Strutt (d 1981; s of 4 Baron Rayleigh), and Hon Mrs Charles Strutt, *qv*; suc uncle 5 Baron Rayleigh 1988; *b* 4 June 1960; *Educ* Eton, RAC Cirencester; *Heir* uncle, Hon Hedley Vicars Strutt, *qv*; *Career* Lt Welsh Guards (ret); Terling Place, Chelmsford, Essex

RAYMENT, Lt-Col Clifton Herbert; MBE (1951); s of Lionel Herbert Rayment (d 1979), and Mary Charlotte Gertrude, *née* Clifton (d 1972); *b* 24 Dec 1919; *Educ* Berkhamsted Sch, Coll of Estate Mgmnt, Quetta Staff Coll; *m* 1, 14 Feb 1942, Patricia; 1 da (Sarah b 1945); m 2, 21 Sept 1957, Aileen, da of William Vans Agnew, of Fairacre, Shermanbury, W Sussex; 1 s (Alastair b 1958), 1 da (Lucinda b 1960); *Career* Probyn's House (Indian Army) 1939-46, Royal Tank Regt 1946-62, Regimental sec, Royal Tank Regt 1962-86; sec RAC Benevolent Fund; *Recreations* shooting, beagling, sailing, cricket, tennis, squash; *Clubs* Army and Navy, MCC, Parkstone YC; *Style*— Lt-Col Clifton Rayment, MBE; Briarswood House, Wareham, Dorset (☎ 09295 2993)

RAYMENT, William Alfred; s of William Charles Rayment (d 1958), of Finchley London, and Daisy Catherine Rayment (d 1976); *b* 23 Jan 1917; *Educ* Tollington Park Central, Northern Poly; *m* 1, 25 Jan 1941 (m dis 1946), Gladys Florence, da of late George Stockham, of Islington, London; m 2, 28 Aug 1948, Mariorie Lily, da of William Whiteway (d 1924), of Hornsey, London; 1 da (Margaret Ann b 7 June 1949); *Career* WWII RA, enlisted 1940, cmmnd 1944, seconded IA 1945, Maj 1 Indian anti-Tank Regt 1946, hon Capt 1946; nat pres Display Prodrs and Screen Printers Assoc 1967-69, pres Fedn of Euro Screen Printers Assoc 1975-79, memb Lloyds 1977; Freeman: City of London 1977, Worshipful Co of Farriers 1977; FInstD 1965; *Recreations* flat green bowls; *Style*— William A Rayment, Esq; Kerswell, 4 Upland Dr, Brookmans Pk, Hatfield, Herts AL9 6PS (☎ 0707 53056)

RAYMER, Garth Anthony; s of Charles Robert Peyton Raymer (d 1968), and Christine Joyce, *née* Spaul; *b* 28 August 1945; *Educ* Prince Henry's GS Evesham; *m* 5 Sept 1970, Lynne Margaret; 3 s (Martin b 1973, Peter b 1975, Michael b 1976); *Career* CA; ptnr Rabjohns Worcester and Evesham 1970-; *Recreations* sport, public service, architecture; *Style*— Garth Anthony, Esq; Vine Cottage, Great Comberton, Pershore, Worcestershire; 113 High St, Evesham, Worcs (☎ 0386 49424)

RAYMOND, Hon Mrs (Gay); da of 4 Visc Hardinge (d 1979); *b* 1938; *m* 1963, Pierre Raymond; 1 s; *Style*— The Hon Mrs Raymond; Stage Coach Road, Brome, Québec J0E 1K0, Canada

RAYMOND, Michael Murray John; MC (1945), DL (Essex 1982); only s of Samuel Raymond; *b* 9 Jan 1923; *Educ* Sherborne, Trinity Coll Oxford; *m* 1, 1951 (m dis 1960), Madeline June, da of Brig Sidney Lucey, MC; 2 s (Richard b 1952, Philip b 1953), 1 da (Virginia b 1955); m 2, 1962, Daphne, da of R Alexander, of Worcs; 1 s (Charles b 1965); *Career* served as Capt WW II 60 Rifles and Rifle Bde; dir Henry Head & Co 1964-73; memb Lloyd's; *Style*— Michael Raymond Esq, MC, DL; Belchamp Hall, Belchamp Walter, Sudbury, Suffolk (☎ 0787 72744)

RAYMOND, Paul; *b* 15 Nov 1925; *Educ* St Francis Xaviers Coll Liverpool, Glossop GS Glossop Derbyshire; 1 s (Howard b 23 Nov 1959), 1 da (Deborah b 28 Jan 1956); *Career* RAF 1944-47; musician, music hall artiste, impresario, night club proprietor, publisher, West End property owner; memb Grand Order of Water Rats; *Style*— Paul Raymond, Esq; 96 Arlington House, Arlington St, London SW1; Paul Raymond Organisation Ltd, 2 Archer St, London W1V 7HE (☎ 01 734 9191, fax 01 734 5030, telex 22638)

RAYMOND, William Francis (Frank); CBE (1978); s of Capt Leonard William Raymond, ISO (d 1973), of Maidenhead, Berks, and May, *née* Bennett MBE (d 1973); *b* 25 Feb 1922; *Educ* Bristol GS, Queen's Coll Oxford (BA, MA); *m* 13 Aug 1949, Amy Elizabeth (Betty), da of Maj Charles Kingston Kelk, of Ludshott Manor, Liphook, Hants; 3 s (Christopher b 1950, Robin b 1954, Charles b 1959), 1 da (Karen b 1952); *Career* res scientist: MRC 1943-45, Grassland Res Inst 1945-72 (asst dir 1962-72); agric sci conslt (EEC, FAO, World Bank); visiting prof of agric Wye Coll Univ of London 1978-83, chief scientist MAFF London 1980-82 (dep chief scientist 1972-80); hon tres Soc for the Responsible use of Resources in Agric and on the Land (Rural), chm Stapledon Meml Trst; FRSC, CCHEM 1962; *Books* Forage Conservation and Feeding (with Redman and Waltham, fourth edn 1987); *Recreations* gardening; *Clubs* Farmers; *Style*— Frank Raymond, Esq, CBE; Periwinkle Cottage, Christmas Common, Watlington, Oxon OX9 5HR (☎ 0491 612 942)

RAYMONT, Timothy; s of Richard Kenneth Raymont (d 1970), and Patricia Parris, *née* Goodenough; *b* 26 July 1946; *Educ* Radley Coll, Univ of East Anglia (BA); *Career* jt md Holmes of Reading Ltd 1972-; dir GG Furniture Ltd 1979-82 (chm 1980-81), Minty plc and subsidiaries 1983-88; memb of Design Index Selection Ctee 1978-88; *Recreations* opera, squash, motor cycling; *Style*— Timothy Raymont, Esq; 32 Hartismere Rd, London SW6 7UD (☎ 01 381 1134); Chatham St, Reading RG1 7JX (☎ 0734 586421)

RAYNAR, Hon Mrs (Sarah Elizabeth Ann); *née* Butler; da of 16 Viscount Mountgarret (d 1966); *b* 1932; *m* 1955 (m dis 1976), Geoffrey Kenneth Raynar; 2 s; *Style*— The Hon Mrs Raynar; 52 St Anne's Road, Headingley, Leeds LS6 3NX

RAYNAUD, Simon Lewis John; s of Gabriel Raynaud (d 1976), of France, and Sarah Dorothy, *née* Stiller; *b* 26 April 1935; *Educ* Harvey GS; *m* 1 July 1962, Estelle Naomi, da of Heim Golding (d 1986); 2 s (Jonathan b 1965, Daniel b 1970); *Career* certified accountant; FCCA; *Recreations* music, theatre, tennis, travel in Australia; *Clubs* Arts; *Style*— Simon Raynaud, Esq; Montazel, 4 Halland Way, Northwood, Middx HA6 2AG (☎ 09274 24684, car tel 0836 607323)

RAYNE, Sir Edward; CVO (1977); s of Maj Joseph Edward Rayne (d 1951), of Park Lane, London, and Meta Elizabeth, *née* Reddish (d 1967); *b* 19 August 1922; *Educ* Harrow; *m* 10 Oct 1952, Phyllis, da of William Cort (d 1977), of Worcester Park, Surrey; 2 s (Edward Anthony Claude b Sept 1953, Nicholas Edward b 3 June 1957); *Career* ladies shoe mfr & retailer; chm & md H & M Rayne Ltd 1951-87, pres Rayne-Delman Shoes Inc 1961-72, exec chm Rayne-Delman Shoes Inc 1972-87, dir Debenhams plc 1975-88, pres Debenhams Inc 1976-87; exec chm Harvey Nichols & Co Ltd 1978-88; chm: Lotus Ltd 1978-86, Br Fashion Cncl 1985-; pres Royal Warrant Holders Assoc 1964, hon tres 1974-; Master Worshipful Co of Patten Makers 1981; FRSA 1971; Chevalier de l'Ordre National du Méite (France) 1984; kt 1988; *Recreations* bridge, golf; *Clubs* Portland, White's, Brooks's, Travellers (Paris); *Style*— Sir Edward Rayne, CVO; Flat 16, 15 Grosvenor Square, London W1X 9LD (☎ 01 493 2871); 29 Hartfield Rd, Cooden, nr Bexhill-on-Sea, Sussex (☎ 04243 2175)

RAYNE, Baroness; Lady Jane Antonia Frances; *née* Vane-Tempest-Stewart; da of 8 Marquess of Londonderry (d 1955); *b* 1932; *m* 1965, as his 2 w, Baron Rayne (Life Peer), *qv*; 2 s, 2 da; *Style*— The Rt Hon the Lady Rayne; 33 Robert Adam St, London W1M 5AH

RAYNE, Baron (Life Peer UK 1976); Max; er s of Phillip and Deborah Rayne; *b* 8 Feb 1918; *Educ* Central Fndn Sch, UCL; *m* 1, 1941 (m dis 1960), Margaret, da of Louis Marco; 1 s, 2 da; m 2, 1965, Lady Jane Antonia Frances Vane-Tempest-Stewart *qv*, da of 8 Marquess of Londonderry, JP, DL; 2 s (Hon Nicholas b 1969, Hon Alexander b 1973), 2 da (Hon Natalie b 1966, Hon Tamara b 1970); *Career* served WWII RAF; chm: London Merchant Securities plc 1960-, Westpool Investmt Tst plc 1980-, London Festival Ballet Tst 1967-75, Nat Theatre Bd 1971-88; dep chm First Leisure Corpn plc 1984-; govr: St Thomas' Hosp 1962-74 (special tstee 1974-), Royal Ballet Sch 1966-79, Yehudi Menuhin Sch 1966-88 (vice pres 1987-), Malvern Coll 1966-, Centre for Environmental Studies 1967-73; memb: gen cncl King Edward VII's Hosp Fund for London 1966-, cncl of govrs United Medical Sch of Guy's and St Thomas' Hosps 1982-, international cncl Salk Inst 1982-88; hon vice-pres Jewish Welfare Bd 1966-; fndr patron Rayne Fndn 1962-; hon fellow: Darwin Coll Cambridge 1966, UCL 1966, LSE 1974, King's Coll Hosp Med Sch 1980, Univ Coll Oxford 1982; Hon FRCPsych 1977, Hon LLD London 1968; Officier Legion d'Honneur 1987 (Chevalier 1973); kt 1969; *Style*— The Rt Hon the Lord Rayne; 33 Robert Adam St, London W1M 5AH (☎ 01 935 3555)

RAYNE, Hon Robert Anthony; s of Baron Rayne by his 1 w, Margaret; *b* 1949; *m* Jane, da of late Robert Blackburn, the aviation pioneer; 1 s; *Career* memb bd London Merchant Securities 1983-; *Recreations* collecting paintings; *Style—* The Hon Robert Rayne

RAYNER, Claire Berenice; *b* 2 Jan 1931; *Educ* City of London Sch for Girls, Royal Northern Hosp Sch of Nursing (SRN 1954; awarded hosp Gold Medal for outstanding achievement), Guy's Hosp; *m* 1958, Desmond Rayner; 2 s (Adam, Jay), 1 da (Amanda); *Career* sister, Paediatric Dept, Whittington Hosp; writer; public speaker, Ruth Martin of Woman's Own 1966-75; regular radio appearance Mike Aspel Show Capital Radio London 1982-85, frequent appearances for BBC, HTV, Anglia, Thames and LWT, 10 weekly series Claire Rayner's Casebook BBC 1980 (repeated in 1981, 1982, 1983, and 1984); advice columnist The Sunday Mirror (previously with The Sun); Freeman City of London 1987; *Books* Over 70 books (some under the pseudonym of Sheila Brandon), including The Meddlers, A Time to Heal, The Performers (12 vol family saga, translated into several languages), For Children, contributor: Design magazine (the journal of the Design Council), The Lancet, Medical World, Nursing Times, Nursing Mirror, UK National newspapers and leading magazines; *Clubs* Royal Soc of Medicine; *Style—* Mrs Claire Rayner; PO Box 125, Harrow, Middx HA1 3XE

RAYNER, Baron (Life Peer UK 1983), of Crowborough in Co of East Sussex; Derek George Rayner; s of George William Rayner; *b* 30 Mar 1926; *Educ* City Coll Norwich, Selwyn Cambridge; *Career* adviser to PM on improving efficiency in Civil Service 1979-82; jt md Marks & Spencer 1973 and jt vice-chm 1982, chm 1984- (dir 1967-, joined 1953); special advsr to Govt 1970, ch exec Procurement Exec Mgmnt Bd MOD 1971-72, memb UK Perm Security Cmmn 1977-; dep chm Civil Service Pay Board 1978-80, former memb Design Cncl, Cncl of Royal Coll of Art; kt 1973; *Style—* The Rt Hon the Lord Rayner; c/o Marks & Spencer, Michael House, Baker St, London W1; 29 Connaught Sq, London W2 (☎ 01 935 4422)

RAYNER, Hon Mrs; Hon Madeleine; *née* Rayne; da of Baron Rayne by his 1 w, Margaret; *b* 1943; *m* 1964, Alan Rayner; *Style—* The Hon Mrs Rayner

RAYNER, Major Michael Staney; s of Rupert Rayner (d 1934), and Ida Feodora, *née* Pickles (d 1977); *b* 11 July 1916; *Educ* Roundhay Sch Leeds; *m* 12 June 1941, Margaret Olivia, da of Frederick Owen Lighton (d 1967); 2 s (John Michael b 1942, Paul Rupert b 1946); *Career* enlisted RA 1940, cmmnd 2nd Lt RA 1941-47, London Div 1941-42, transferred to RE 1942, Capt India Cmd RE 1943, XIV Army Burma 1943-46, Arakan Burma Campaign 1944, Imphal to Rangoon Campaign 1944-45, Maj RE 1945 (despatches twice 1946); dir: R M Thompson Ltd 1950-, R M Thompson (Hldgs) Ltd 1982-, Victoria Court Mgmnt (Filey) Ltd 1982-; chm Yorkshire Region Chartered Inst of Bldg 1967-68, chm Bd of govrs 1976-80; FCIOB; *Recreations* sailing; *Clubs* Ullswater YC; *Style—* Maj Michael Rayner; 5 Victoria Court, Filey, N Yorks YO14 9LJ (☎ 0723 514748); Smithy Cottage, Stainton, Penrith Cumbria CA11 (☎ 0768 64200); R M Thompson Ltd, Leeds (☎ 0532 491194)

RAYNER, Maj Ranulf Courtauld; s of Brig Sir Ralph Herbert Rayner, MBE (d 1977), of Ashcombe Tower, nr Dawlish, S Devon, and Edith Elizabeth, *née* Courtauld; *b* 25 Feb 1935; *Educ* Eton, RMA; *m* 2 July 1970, Annette Mary, da of Brig Angus Binny, CBE, MICE, of Skilgate, Somerset; 2 s (Ralph b 8 Sept 1971, Giles b 25 June 1975); *Career* cmmnd 9 Queen's Royal Lancers 1955, instr RMA Sandhurst 1962, Army FLying Sch 1964, Royal Horse Gds 1965, cmd Independent Sqdn Cyprus 1967, ret 1969; local steward Devon and Exeter Steeplechases; represented Army at: Polo, Skiing, Cresta run (capt Cresta Team 1959-69); *Books* The Painting of the America's Cup (1986), The Story of Yachting (1988), The Story of Skiing (1989); *Recreations* yachting, shooting, fishing, flying, skiing, tobogganing, painting; *Clubs* Starcross; *Style—* Maj Ranulf Rayner; Ashcombe Tower, nr Dawlish, S Devon EX7 0PY (☎ 0626 863 178, office 0626 862 484, fax 0626 867 011)

RAYNES, Dr (Edward) Peter; s of Edward Gordon Raynes, and Ethel Mary, *née* Wood; *b* 4 July 1945; *Educ* St Peter's York, Cambridge Univ (MA, PhD); *m* 19 Sept 1970, Madeline, da of Cecil Ord; 2 s (Michael b 1974, Andrew b 1977); *Career* Royal Signals and Radar Estab 1971- (currently dep chief scientific offr); FRS 1987, MInstP; *Books* Liquid Crystals: Their Physics, Chemistry and Applications (with C Hilsum); *Recreations* choral and solo singing; *Style—* Dr Peter Raynes; 23 Leadon Rd, Malvern, Worcs WR14 2XF, (☎ 0686 565 497); Royal Signals and Radar Establishment, Malvern, Worcs WR14 3PS, (☎ 0684 892 733 ext 2873, fax 0684 892 733 ext 2540)

RAYNES, Lady (Frederica) Rozelle (Ridgway); *née* Pierrepont; da of 6 Earl Manvers (d 1955); *b* 1925; *Educ* Queen Elizabeth's GS, Mansfield Notts; *m* 1, 1953 (m dis 1961), Maj Alexander Mongomerie Greaves Beattie; m 2, 1965, Richard Hollins Raynes, MB, BS, DPH, MFCM; *Career* served 1939-45 war as Leading Wren Stoker WRNS; writer, school care worker (ILEA), asst purser Merchant Navy; *Books* North in a Nutshell, Maid Matelot, The Sea Bird; *Recreations* sailing; *Clubs* Royal Cruising, Royal Naval Sailing Assoc; *Style—* Lady Rozelle Raynes; Dolphin's Leap, St Margaret's Bay, Kent; 88 Narrow St, London E14

RAYNHAM, Viscount; Charles George Townshend; s and h of 7 Marquess Townshend; *b* 6 Sept 1945; *Educ* Eton, Royal Agricultural College Cirencester; *m* 1975, Hermione, da of Lt-Cdr Robert Martin Dominic Ponsonby; 1 s, 1 da (Hon Louise b 1979); *Heir* s, Hon Thomas Charles Townshend b 2 Nov 1977; *Style—* Viscount Raynham; 22 Ebury St, SW1 (☎ 01 730 3388/4466)

RAYNSFORD, Hon Mrs (Joan Rosemary); *née* Wakefield; OBE (1981); eldest da of 1 and last Baron Wakefield of Kendal (d 1983), and Rowena Doris, *née* Lewis (d 1981); Henry Raynsford of Rainford Hall, Lancs, m Elizabeth Wilcotes, heiress of the Manor of Great Tew, Oxon, circa 1430 and their son, William, was Lord of the Manor of Great Tew and High Sheriff of Berks and Oxon 1464. Great Tew remained the home of the main branch of the Raynsford family for 200 years. The family continued in Northamptonshire and are descended from the elder brother, John, of Sir Richard Raynsford of Dallington, who was Lord Chief Justice of England, 1676-78. The Wakefield family can trace its lineage to Roger Wakefield of Challon Hall, near Kendal, Westmorland, temp. Elizabeth I. The family recorded in the first generation of Kendal money men and the was contemporary with first London Bankers listed in the first London Directory of 1677. Wakefield's Bank was established in 1788 in the Old House, Kendal, which the family still occupies, and subsequently became the Kendal Bank. This was taken over by the Bank of Liverpool in 1831 which amalgamated with Martins Bank in 1918 and is now Barclays Bank; *b* 18 Nov 1920; *Educ* Francis Holland Sch London, Downe House Newbury, Berlin Univ; *m* 18 March 1944, Capt Antony Edward Montague Raynsford, DL, RN (ret), er s of Lt-Col Richard Raynsford, DSO, JP, DL; 1 s (Richard), 1 da (Julia); *Career* chm: Battlefields (Hldgs) Ltd, Shapland & Petter Hldgs Ltd, Lake District Estates Co Ltd, Ullswater Navigation & Transit Co Ltd, Ravenglass & Eskdale Railway Co Ltd; vice-chm Cons National Women's Ctee 1971-72 (chm Gter London Women's Ctee 1968-71); memb international exec ctee European Union of Women 1979-81; vice-pres British Ski Fedn 1966-69; *Recreations* skiing, walking in mountains; *Clubs* Lansdowne, Ski of GB (chm 1972-75, pres 1981), Kandahar Ski (chm 1977-82); *Style—* The Hon Mrs Raynsford, OBE; Milton Malsor Manor, Northampton NN7 3AR (☎ 0604 858251); The Old House, Kendal, Cumbria LA9 4QG (☎ 0539 20861)

RAYNSFORD, Wyvill Richard Nicolls (Nick); s of Wyvill John Macdonald Raynsford (Capt Northants Yeo, ka 1944), and Patricia Howell, *née* Dunn (d 1956); *b* 28 Jan 1945; *Educ* Repton, Sidney Sussex Coll Cambridge (MA), Chelsea Sch Art (Dip Art and Design); *m* 30 Aug 1968, Anne Elizabeth, da of Col Marcus Jelley, of Northampton; 3 da (Catherine Patricia b 1979, Laura Anne b 1982, Helen Daphne b 1984); *Career* mkt res A C Neilson Co Ltd 1966-68, Student Co-operative Dwellings 1972-73, SHAC (London Housing Aid Centre) 1973-86 (dir 1976-87), ptnr Raynsford & Morris housing and parly consits 1987-; cncllr London Borough of Hammersmith and Fulham 1971-75; MP (Lab Fulham 1986-87; memb Inst of Housing 1978; *Books* A Guide to Housing Benefit (1982); *Style—* Nick Raynsford, Esq; 31 Cranbury Rd, Fulham, London SW6 2NS (☎ 01 731 0675); London House, 271-3 King St, Hammersmith, London W6 9LZ (☎ 01 741 8011)

RAZZALL, (Edward) Timothy; s of Leonard Humphrey Razzall, of Barnes, London, a Master of the Supreme Court 1954-81, and Muriel, *née* Knowles (d 1968); *b* 12 June 1943; *Educ* St Paul's, Worcester Coll Oxford (BA); *m* 1 (m dis); 1 s (James Timothy b 1972), 1 da (b 1970); m 2, 30 Sept 1982, Deirdre Bourke, da of Duncan Taylor-Smith (d 1985); m dis; 1 s, 1 da; *Career* slr; ptnr in Frere Cholmeley 1973-, chm Abaco Investments plc 1975-; dir: Cala plc 1973-, Harper and Row Ltd, Wea Records Ltd, Gower Medical Publishing Ltd, ISS Holdings Ltd; cllr London Borough of Richmond upon Thames 1974-; chm Policy and Resources Ctee and dep ldr 1983-; tres Liberal Party 1987-88; tres Social and Liberal Democrats 1988-; memb Law Soc 1969- ; *Recreations* sport, food and wine; *Clubs* National Liberal; *Style—* Timothy Razzall, Esq; 110 Station Rd, London SW13 (☎ 01 878 7122; office 01 405 7878; fax, 01 405 9056)

REA, Charles Julian; s of Hon James R Rea (d 1954), and Betty Marion Rea, *née* Bevan (d 1965); *b* 7 June 1931; *Educ* Bryaston, Downing Coll Cambridge (MA); *m* 1, 1952, Bridget, da of Montague Slater (d 1956); 1 da (Julia b 1952), 1 s (Steven b 1956); m 2, 1963, Anne, da of William Robson (d 1978); 2 s (William b 1965, James b 1968), 2 da (Lucy b 1966, Kate b 1972); *Career* publisher; dir: Addison-Wesley-Longman Gp Ltd (formerly Longman Hldgs), Longman Gp (Overseas Hldgs) Ltd, Longman Gp (UK) Ltd, Longman Gp Far East Ltd, Longman Nigeria Ltd, Maskew Miller Longman (Pty) Ltd SA, Pitman Examinations Inst; chm: The Egyptian Int Publishing Longman Egypt, Book Devpt cncl, Good Life Whole Foods Ltd; *Recreations* fishing, sailing, pottery, theatre, music; *Clubs* Garrick; *Style—* Julian Rea, Esq; 62 Dukes Avenue, London N10 2PU; Mitchells, West Chiltington, Pulborough, Sussex; Longman Gp UK Ltd, Longman House, Burnt Hill, Harlow, Essex CM20 2JE (☎ 0279 26721, telex 81259, fax 0279 310 60)

REA, Hon Daniel William; s of 3 Baron Rea; *b* 30 Dec 1958; *Educ* William Ellis Sch, Bristol Univ, Univ Coll Hosp London; *m* 1983, Hon Rebecca, *qv*, da of Baron Llewelyn Davies; *Style—* The Hon Daniel Rea; 3 Benn St, London E9

REA, Hon Mrs Findlay; Helen Margaret; *née* Richardson; da of Bernhard Hermann Richardson (decd), of Edinburgh; *m* 1, 1936, Donald Crawford Reid; m 2, 1959, as his 3 w, Hon Findlay Russell Rea (d 1984), 3 and yst s of 1 Baron Rea; *Style—* Hon Mrs Findlay Rea; Weald Cottage, Weald, Sevenoaks, Kent

REA, Hon Matthew James; s and h of 3 Baron Rea; *b* 28 Mar 1956; *Educ* William Ellis Sch, Sheffield Univ; *Style—* The Hon Matthew Rea; 12 St Leonards Bank, Edinburgh

REA, Hon (John Silas) Nathaniel; s of 3 Baron Rea; *b* 16 Oct 1965; *Educ* William Ellis Sch; *Style—* The Hon Nathaniel Rea; 15 Tanza Rd, London NW3

REA, 3 Baron (UK 1937); Sir (John) Nicolas Rea; 3 Bt (UK 1935); s of Hon James Rea (d 1954; 2 s of 1 Baron Rea), by his 1 w, Betty, *née* Bevan (d 1965); suc unc, 2 Baron, 1981; *b* 6 June 1928; *Educ* Dartington Hall, Dauntsey's Sch, Christ's Cambridge (MA, MD), Univ Coll Hosp London; *m* 1951, Elizabeth Anne, da of William Robinson (d 1944), of Woking; 4 s (Matthew, Daniel, Quentin, Nathaniel); *Heir* s, Hon Matthew Rea; *Career* Actg Sergeant Suffolk Regt; sits as Labour peer in House of Lords; research fellow Paediatrics Ibadan Univ Nigeria 1952-55, lectr in Social Medicine St Thomas's Hosp Med Sch 1966-68, medical practitioner in NHS general practice (Kentish Town Health Centre); DPH, DCH, DObst; MRCGP; *Recreations* music (bassoon), travel, maintaining crumbling houses; *Clubs* Royal Soc of Medicine; *Style—* The Rt Hon the Lord Rea; House of Lords, London SW1

REA, Hon Quentin Thomas; s of 3 Baron Rea; *b* 8 Mar 1961; *Educ* William Ellis Sch, Manchester and Southampton Univs; *Style—* The Hon Quentin Rea; c/o 15 Tanza Rd, London NW3

REA, Hon Mrs (Rebecca); da of Baron Llewelyn-Davies, PC (Life Peer); *b* 1957; *m* 1983, Hon Daniel William, *qv*, s of 3 Baron Rea; *Style—* The Hon Mrs Rea; 3 Benn St, London E9

READ, Prof Alan Ernest; CBE (1988); s of Ernest Arthur Read, BEM (d 1957), of Wembley, Middx, and Annie Lydia Read (d 1971); *b* 15 Nov 1926; *Educ* Kilburn GS, Wembley Co GS, Preston Manor Co GS, St Marys Hosp Med Sch London (MB, BS, MD) MRCP 1952, FRCP 1965; *m* 9 Aug 1952, Enid, da of Harold Arthur Malein, of Bristol; 1 s (Simon Andrew b 4 April 1956) 2 da (Sara Jane b 11 May 1957, Lousia Mary b 28 Dec 1965); *Career* Nat Serv med specialist BMH Trieste 1952-54; Univ of Bristol: reader in medicine 1965-69, prof of medicine 1969, head of academic med unit 1969-, dean of faculty of medicine 1984-86; vice pres RCP (sr censor) 1985-86; memb: Assoc of Physicians, Br Soc of Gastroenterology; Freeman City of London, Liveryman Worshipful Co Apothecaries; MRCP 1952, FRCP 1965; *Books* Basic Gastroenterology (jtly 1965), The Clinical Apprentice (1966), Modern Medicine (1975), The Liver (jtly 1984), Gastroenterology (jtly 1988); *Recreations* riding, boating, fishing, golf; *Style—* Prof Alan Read, CBE; Riverbank, 77 Nore Rd, Portishend, Bristol, Avon BS20 9JZ (☎ 0272 843 543); Dept of Medicine, Univ of Bristol, Bristol Royal Infirmary, Avon (☎ 0272 279 220)

READ, Bryan Colman; CBE (1984), JP (1965, DL 1986); s of L Hector Read (d 1963), of Norwich, and Ena P Read (d 1985); *b* 1 Oct 1925; *Educ* Bishops Stortford Coll, St Johns coll Cambridge (MA); *m* 1949, Sheila Mary, da of Frank Oliver Winter, of Norwich; 1 s (James b 1953), 3 da (Joanna b 1950, Susan b 1950, Rebecca b 1960); *Career* Flour Miller, R J Read (Hldgs) Ltd 1954-57, Pasta Foods Ltd 1955-85; pres Nat Assoc of British and Irish Flour Millers 1968-83; chm: Nat Institute of Agricultural Botany 1976-78, Research Ctee, Flour Milling and Baking Research Assoc 1984, Gt Yarmouth Port and Haven Cmmnrs River Ctee; memb: Home Grown Cereals Authy 1966, Agricultural and Food Research Cncl 1985; *Recreations* sailing, music; *Clubs* Farmers; *Style—* Bryan Read, Esq; 21 Upton Close, Norwich NR4 7PD (☎ 0603 54281)

READ, Air Marshal Sir Charles Frederick; KBE (1976), CBE (1964, CB 1972, DFC 1942, AFC 1958); s of Joseph Francis Read (d 1941), and Ethel Mary Read (d 1950); *b* 9 Oct 1918; *Educ* Sydney GS; *m* 1946, Betty Elsie, da of Aubrey Victor Bradshaw; 3 s; *Career* RAAF, served Pacific; Air Marshal, Dep Chief of Air Staff RAAF 1968-72, Chief of Air Staff 1972-75, ret; *Style—* Sir Charles Read, KBE, CB, CBE, DFC, AFC; 2007 Pittwater Rd, Bayview, NSW 2104, Australia (☎ 997 1686)

READ, Charles Patrick Wilson; s of Sir Charles David Read (d 1957), of London, and Frances Edna, *née* Wilson; *b* 17 Mar 1942; *Educ* Harrow; *m* 1966, Susan Viner, da of Brian Viner Edsall, of Wisborough Green, W Sussex; 1 s (Jason b 1968); *Career* md Young & Co's Brewery plc 1976-, dir B Edsall & Co Ltd 1984-; *Recreations* shooting, fishing; *Style—* Charles Read Esq; Malthouse Cottage, Little Bognor, nr Fittleworth, Pulborough, W Sussex (☎ 079 882 260); Young & Co's Brewery plc, Ram Brewery, Wandsworth, London SW18 (☎ 01 870 0141, telex 8814530)

READ, Prof Frank Henry; s of Frank Charles Read (d 1976), and Florence Louise, *née* Wright; *b* 6 Oct 1934; *Educ* Haberdashers' Aske's Hampstead Sch, RCS (BSc), Univ of Manchester (PhD, DSc); *m* 16 Dec 1961, Anne Stuart Wallace; 2 s (Jonathon Hugh Tobias b 1965, Sebastian Timothy James b 1970), 2 da (Kirsten Victoria b 1962, Nichola Anne b 1964); *Career* prof of physics Univ of Manchester 1975, vice-chm Inst of Physics 1985, chm IOP Publishing Ltd 1985; memb: cncl of Royal Soc 1987, sci bd Sci and Engrg Res Cncl 1987; FRS 1984; *Books* Electrostatic Lenses (1976), Electromagnetic Radiation (1980); *Recreations* farming, stone-masonry, shooting; *Style—* Prof Frank Read; Hardingland Farm, Macclesfield Forest, Cheshire SK11 0ND (☎ 0625 257 59); Schuster Laboratory, Univ of Manchester, Manchester M13 9PL (☎ 061 275 4125, fax 061 273 5867, telex 668932 MCHRULG)

READ, Gen Sir John Antony Jervis; GCB (1972), KCB (1967, CB 1965, CBE 1959, OBE 1957, DSO 1945, MC 1941); s of John Dale Read, of Heathfield, Sussex (d 1940), by his w Evelyn Constance Bowen; *b* 10 Sept 1913; *Educ* Winchester, RMC Sandhurst; *m* 14 June 1947, Sheila, da of Frederick G C Morris, of London NW8; 3 da; *Career* 2 Lt Oxford and Bucks LI 1934, served Africa and Burma WWII, dep asst mil sec WO 1947-49, Co Cdr Sandhurst 1949-52, Lt-Col 1952, Temp Brig 1957, Cmdt Sch of Inf Warminster 1959, Brig 1961, GOC 50 Inf Div TA and Northumbrian Dist 1962-64, Maj-Gen 1962, Vice QMG 1964-66, Lt-Gen 1966, GOC-in-C Western Cmd 1966-69, Gen 1969, QMG 1969-72, ADC (Gen) to HM The Queen 1971-73, Cmdt Royal Coll of Def Studies 1973-74; Col Cmdt: Army Catering Corps 1966-76, Light Div 1968-73, Small Arms Sch Corps 1970-75; special cmmr Duke of York's Royal Mil Sch 1974-; pres: Ex-Services Fellowship Centre 1974-, TA Rifle Assoc; chm: Army Cadet Force Assoc 1973-82 (pres 1982-), Royal Sch for Daughters of Offrs 1975-82 (govr 1966); govr: St Edward's Sch Oxford 1972-87, Royal Hosp Chelsea 1975-81; *Clubs* Army & Navy; *Style—* Gen Sir Antony Read, GCB, KCB, CB, CBE, OBE, DSO, MC; Brackles, Little Chesterton, nr Bicester, Oxon OX6 8PD (☎ 0869 252189)

READ, Sir John Emms; s of William Emms Read, of Brighton (d 1952); *b* 29 Mar 1918; *Educ* Brighton Hove and Sussex GS, Admin Staff Coll Henley; *m* 1942, Dorothy Millicent, da of Thomas Alfred Berry; 2 s; *Career* Cdr (S) RN 1939-46; CA; Ford Motor Co Ltd 1946-64 (dir of sales 1961-64), dir EMI Ltd 1965-; EMI Gp: jt md 1967, ch exec 1969-79, dep chm 1973-74, chm 1974-79; dep chm Thorn-EMI 1979-81; dir: Thorn EMI plc 1981-1987, Capital Industs-EMI Inc 1970-83, dep chm Thames TV 1981- (dir 1973-), Wonder World; chm: Fin & GP CBI 1978-84, TSB Hldgs Ltd 1980-, central bd TSB 1980-, Utd Dominions Tst 1981-85; chm cncl of mgmnt Inst of Neurology, memb Governing Body The Br Post Grad Med Fedn London Univ, pres Sussex Assoc of Boy's Clubs, govr Henley Mangl Coll 1974-; tstee: Westminster Abbey Tst 1979-86, Charities Aid Fndn, London Symphony Orchestra Tst 1985-, Community Action Tst, Utd Westminster Almshouses, Brighton Festival Tst 1985-; memb ct Surrey Univ 1986-; FCA, FRSA, CBIM, FIB ComplERE; kt 1976; *Recreations* music; *Clubs* MCC; *Style—* Sir John Read; Muster House, 12 Muster Green, Haywards Heath, W Sussex RH16 4AG; TSB Group, 25 Milk Street, London EC2V 8LU (☎ 01 606 7070)

READ, Martin; s of Charles Enderby Read, of Nine Acres, Ulceby, Alford, Lincs, and Lillian Clara, *née* Chambers; *b* 24 July 1938; *Educ* Queen Elizabeth's GS, Alford, Wadham Coll Oxford (MA); *m* 27 April 1963, Laurette, da of J T Goldsmith (d 1960), of Green Walk, Hendon, London; 2 da (Robyn Lisa b 7 Sept 1966, Abigail Kim b 14 May 1970); *Career* articled clerk A V Hammond & Co Bradford 1959-62, ptnr with Slaughter and May 1971 - (asst slr 1963-70); vice chm Law Soc standing ctee on coy law, past chm coy law sub-ctee City of London law soc; memb City of London Slrs Co; memb Law Society 1963; *Recreations* theatre, literature, golf, cricket and tennis; *Clubs* MCC, Royal St George's; *Style—* Martin Read, Esq; Michaelmas House, Bois Avenue, Chesham Bois, Amersham, Bucks HP6 5NS; 35 Basinghall St, London EC2V 5DB (☎ 01 600 1200, fax 01 726 0038, 01 600 0289, telex 883486, 88889260)

READ, Martin Peter; s of Philip Peter Lennox Read, and Patricia Mary, *née* Ireland; *b* 22 Oct 1944; *Educ* St Marys Sch Nairobi, Bexhill-on-Sea GS; *m* 14 June 1975, Nicolette Evelyn Marianne, da of Guy William Willett, of Alderney, Channel Islands; 3 da (Isabel b 1979, Louise b 1981, Juliet b 1984); *Career* Private (later Lance Corpl) Royal Sussex Regt 1963-66, served Aden, Lt RA BAOR 1966-69; asst appeals sec Help the Aged 1969, md Petty Wood & Co Ltd 1985 (dir 1979), ptnr Skyfires Fireworks; MICM 1977, FBIM 1984; *Recreations* admiring beauty, lateral thought, sailing, fireworks; *Style—* Martin Read, Esq; The Telegraph House, Pains Hill, Lockerley, Hants SO51 0JE (☎ 0794 41082); Petty, Wood & Co Ltd, BO Box 66, Andover, Hants (☎ 0264 66111, fax 0264 332025)

READ, Michael Philip; s of Leslie Gustave Read, of Essex, and Joyce Eleanor, *née* Barker (d 1974); *b* 3 Feb 1944; *Educ* Westcliff-on-Sea GS, Southend Sch of Architecture; *m* 11 Aug 1973, Sandra Jean, da of Frederick George Hedges, of Herts; 2 s (Robert b 1974, Simon b 1976); *Career* chief exec Harpenden Building Soc; lectr on Building Soc Law at Luton Coll of Higher Educn and refresher courses for the Chartered Building Societies Inst; MBIM, FCBSI; *Recreations* sailing, fish breeding; *Style—* Michael Read, Esq; Aberdeen House, 14/16 Station Rd, Harpenden, Herts AL5 4SE (☎ 05827 65411)

READ, Paul Graham; s of Henry Graham Read (d 1968), and Norah Lilian, *née* Barnett; *b* 4 April 1947; *Educ* Prices GS; *m* 15 April 1972, Patricia Jacqueline, George Henry Lovell, of Hampshire; 1 s, (Matthew Paul Henry b 1988), 1 da (Natalie b 1985); *Career* CA; commercial dir and co sec The Berkeley Gp plc 1983-, commercial dir and md Camper & Nicholas Ltd 1974-80, md Berkeley Homes (N London) Ltd 1980-83; FCA; *Recreations* sailing, music, karate, photography; *Clubs* Porchester Sailing; *Style—* Paul Read, Esq; Greenhill Cottage, Stoner Hill Road, Froxfield, Hampshire GU32 1DX (☎ 0730X 65 475); 4 Heath Rd, Weybridge, Surrey KT13 8TB (☎ 0932 847 222, fax 0932 858 596)

READ, Piers Paul; s of Sir Herbert Edward Read DSO, MC (d 1968), and Margaret *née* Ludwig; *b* 7 Mar 1941; *Educ* Ampleforth, St John's Coll Cambridge (BA, MA); *m* 29 July 1967, Emily Albertine, da of E B Boothby, KCMG, of 23 Holland Park Avenue, London W11; 2 s (Albert b 1970, William b 1978), 2 da (Martha b 1972, Beatrice b 1981); *Career* author; artist in residence Ford Fndn Berlin 1963-64, sub-ed Times Literary Supplement London 1965, Harkness fell Cwlth fund NY 1967-68, adjunct prof of writing Columbia Univ 1980; govr Cardinal Manning Boys Sch London 1971-75, ctee of mgmnt Soc of Authors 1973-76 literature panel Arts Cncl London 1975-77; FRSL 1972; *Books* Games in Heaven with Tussy Marx (1966), The Junkers (1968), Monk Dawson (1969), The Professor's Daughter (1971), The Upstart (1973), Polonaise (1976), A Married Man (1979), The Villa Golitsyn (1981), The Free Frenchman (1986), A Season in The West (1988); *Style—* Piers Read, Esq; 50 Portland Rd, London W11 4LG (☎ 01 727 5719)

READE, Sir Clyde Nixon; 12 Bt (E 1661); s of late Sir George Reade, 10 Bt; suc bro, Sir John Stanhope Reade, 11 Bt, 1958; *b* 1906; *m* 1, 1930, Trilby (d 1958), da of Charles McCarthy; m 2, 1960 (m dis 1968), Alice Martha, da of Joseph Asher, of Ohio; *Heir* kinsman, Robert Reade; *Style—* Sir Clyde Reade, Bt; 408 East Columbia St, Mason, Michigan 48854, USA

READE, Robert Ward; s of late Leverne Elton Reade, 5 s of 9 Bt; hp of kinsman, Sir Clyde Reade, 12 Bt; *b* 11 Oct 1923; *Style—* Robert Reade Esq

READER, Dame Audrey Tattie Hinchcliff; DBE (1978), OBE (1966, JP 1963); da of William Henry Nicholls (d 1928), and Mabel, *née* Mallet (d 1944); *b* 9 Dec 1903; *Educ* Malvern Coll Melbourne; *m* 1928, Reginald John (d 1986), s of John Montague Reader (d 1946); 1 da; *Career* voluntary charity worker; state exec memb Lib Party of Australia 1951-77 (memb 1945-), hon sec Nat Cncl of Women (Vic) 1964-67 (memb 1955, exec memb 1958-70); *Recreations* gardening, reading, writing; *Clubs* Royal Soc of St George; *Style—* Dame Audrey Reader, DBE, OBE, JP; 68 Millewa Ave, Chadstone, Vic 3148, Australia (☎ 568 8716)

READER HARRIS, Dame (Muriel) Diana; DBE (1972); da of Montgomery Reader Harris (d 1945), and Frances Mabel Wilmot, *née* Wilkinson (d 1915); (*see also* Hon Mrs Reader-Harris); *b* 11 Oct 1912; *Educ* Sherborne Sch for Girls, London Univ (BA); *Career* asst mistress Sherborne Sch for Girls 1934, house mistress 1938, headmistress 1950-75, i/c group evacuated from Sherborne to Canada 1940); asst educn sec and dep gen sec National Assoc of Youth Clubs 1943-49; pres: Assoc of Headmistresses 1964-66, Church Missionary Society 1969-82; chm: Christian Aid 1978-83, Royal Foundation St Katharine 1979-, Royal Soc of Arts 1979-81 (vice-pres 1981-) and various other organizations; FRSA; *Clubs* University Women's; *Style—* Dame Diana Reader Harris, DBE; 35 The Close, Salisbury, Wilts SP1 2EL (☎ 0722 26889)

READER-HARRIS, Hon Mrs (Henrietta Marguerite Jean); *née* Loder; da of 2 Baron Wakehurst (d 1970), and Dame Margaret Wakehurst, *née* Tennant; *b* 5 Feb 1922; *Educ* Sydney Univ (Dip Soc Studies); *m* 1953, John Wilmot Reader-Harris (d 1975), s of Montgomery Reader-Harris (d 1945) (*see also* Dame Diana Reader-Harris); 1 s (Michael), 1 da (Sarah Van Hove); *Career* hosp almoner; voluntary social servs; *Recreations* visiting places of historical and archaeological interest; *Clubs* ECU; *Style—* The Hon Mrs Reader-Harris; 35 The Close, Salisbury, Wilts SP1 2EL (☎ 0722 26889)

READING, Dr James Henry; s of Henry Reading (d 1968), and Elizabeth Reading, *née* Smith (d 1948); *b* 26 April 1926; *Educ* Roan Sch, London Univ (MB, BS), St Bartholomew's Hosp; *m* 30 Dec 1950, Ena Rhianon Josephine, da of Thomas Jones (d 1970), of Dyfed; 1 s (Anthony b 1954), 1 da (Ann b 1955, Sián b 1964); L.....; *Career* Wing Cdr RAF (ret); med practioner; DTM & H (London) and DTM & H (England); MRCS, RCP; *Recreations* astronomy, photography, travel; *Clubs* RAF; *Style—* Dr James Reading; The Gables, Rushden, Northants (☎ 0933 312965); Medical Centre, Rushden, Northants (☎ 0933 314836)

READING, Dowager, Marchioness of; Margot Irene; da of Percival Augustus Duke, CBE, of Walton-on-the-Hill, and Violet Maud, *née* Mappin; *b* 11 Jan 1919; *Educ* Benenden; *m* 7 June 1941, 3 Marquess of Reading, MBE, MC (d 1980); 3 s (4 Marquess, Lord Anthony Rufus-Isaacs, Lord Alexander Rufus-Isaacs), 1 da (Lady Jacqueline Thomson); *Style—* The Most Hon the Dowager Marchioness of Reading; Glebe Farm House, Cornwell, nr Chipping Norton, Oxon (☎ 060 871 523); 3 Tyrawley Rd, SW6 (☎ 736 0361)

READING, 4 Marquess of (UK 1926); Simon Charles Henry Rufus Isaacs; also Baron Reading (UK 1914), Viscount Reading (UK 1916), Earl of Reading and Viscount Erleigh (both UK 1917); s of 3 Marquess of Reading, MBE, MC (d 1980); *b* 18 May 1942; *Educ* Eton, Univ of Tours; *m* 1979, Melinda, yr da of Richard Dewar; 1 s, 2 da (Lady Sybilla b 3 Nov 1980, Lady Natasha b 24 April 1983); *Heir* s, Julian Michael Rufus, Viscount Erleigh b 26 May 1986; *Career* Lt 1 Queen's Dragoon Gds 1961-64; chm and chief exec: Abbey Sports and Events Ltd, Abbey Corporate Events Ltd; dir Shepherd Insur Hldgs, memb Stock Exchange 1971-74; vice-pres: Boys Bde, Dean Close Sch; *Clubs* Cavalry & Guards, MCC Queen's; *Style—* The Most Hon The Marquess of Reading; Jayne's Court, Bisley, Glos GL6 7BE

READMAN, Eleanor Maysie Hope; *née* Bowser; Voluntary Med Serv Medal (1975, 3 bars); da of David Charles Bowser, CBE, JP (d 1979), of Argaty and The Kings Lundies, Doune, Perthshire, and Maysie Murray, *née* Henderson (d 1974); *b* 18 April 1929; *Educ* privately in Scotland, Southover Manor Sch Sussex; *m* 29 April 1950, Lt-Col Ian Richard Readman, MC, JP (d 1980), s of Lt-Col John Jeffrey Readman, DSO (d 1951), of Broadholm, Lockerbie, Dumfrieshire; 2 s (John Charles Jeffrey b 1951, Alexander Hubert (Sandy) b 1954), 1 da (Jane (Mrs Hope) b 1958); *Career* Br Red

Cross Soc: memb Perth branch 1959, pres Perth and Kinross branch 1974-84, chm cncl Scottish Central branch 1986-(vice chm 1984-86); elder and choir memb Dunblane Cathedral, memb Perth ctee Scottish Veterans Garden Assoc 1981-; Jubilee Medal 1980; *Recreations* music, reading, sewing; *Clubs* Cavalry and Guards, Royal Perth County and City; *Style—* Mrs I R Readman; Gateside of Glassingall, Dunblane, Perthshire FK15 0JG (☎ 0786 824 248); Scottish Branch British Red Cross Society, Alexandra House, 204 Bath St, Glasgow G2 4HL (☎ 041 332 9591)

READY, Nigel Peter; s of Colin Peter Ready, FICE (d 1986), and Monica Isabel Elms, *née* Tapper; *b* 13 July 1952; *Educ* Wycliffe Coll, Jesus Coll Cambridge (MA); *m* 29 Dec 1973, Marisa, da of Germano Brignolo, of Asti, Italy; 2 s (Oliver James b 1976, Thomas Nigel b 1985), 1 da (Natasha Isabella b 1975); *Career* ptnr Cheeswright Murly & Co 1981-, NP 1980; hon sec Soc of Public Notaries of London 1988-; special agent for Dep Cmmnr of Maritime Affairs Republic of Vanuatu 1986-; Freeman City of London, Liveryman Worshipful Co Scriveners; *Books* The Greek Code of Private Maritime Law (jtly 1982), Brooke's Notary (tenth edn 1988); *Recreations* wine, opera, reading; *Style—* Nigel Ready, Esq; 206 Denmark Hill, London SE5 8DX; c/o Cheeswright Murly & Co, 24 St Mary Ave, London EC3A 8HD (☎ 01 623 9477, fax 01 623 5428, telex 883806)

REARDON, Rev Canon Martin Alan; s of Ernest William Reardon, CBE (d 1981), and Gertrude Mary, *née* Pyne; *b* 3 Oct 1932; *Educ* St Edward's Sch Oxford, Selwyn Coll Cambridge (BA, MA), Cuddesdon Coll; *m* 22 July 1964, Ruth Maxim, da of (Henry) George Slade; 1 s (John Paul b 1970), 1 da (Sarah Mary b 1972); *Career* ordained: deacon 1958, priest 1959; curate: Rugby St Andrew Coventry 1958-62, Wicker with Neepsend Sheffield 1962-65; sec Sheffield Cncl of Churches 1962-71, licence to officiate 1965-71, sub-warden Lincoln Theol Coll 1971-78, sec Gen Synod Bd for Mission and Unity C of E 1978-, canon and prebendary Lincoln Cath 1979-89, rector Plumpton Dio of Chichester 1989-; *Style—* The Rev Canon Martin Reardon; The Rectory, Plumpton, Lewes, E Sussex BN7 3BU

REARDON SMITH, (William) Antony John; s and h of Sir William Reardon-Smith, 3 Bt; *b* 20 June 1937; *Educ* Wycliffe Coll; *m* 1962, Susan, da of Henry W Gibson, of Cardiff; 3 s, 1 da; *Style—* Antony Reardon Smith, Esq; 26 Merrick Sq, London SE1 4JB

REARDON-SMITH, Sir William Reardon; 3 Bt (UK 1920); s of Sir Willie Reardon-Smith, 2 Bt (d 1950); *b* 12 Mar 1911; *Educ* Blundell's Sch; *m* 1, 1935 (m dis 1954, she d 1959), Nesta, da of Frederick J Phillips; 3 s, 1 da; m 2, 1954, Beryl, da of William H Powell; 1 s, 3 da; *Heir* s, (William) Antony Reardon-Smith; *Career* Maj RA (TA); *Style—* Sir William Reardon-Smith, Bt; Rhode Farm, Romansleigh, South Molton, N Devon

REASON, Eric Frank; s of Frank Wesley Reason (d 1937), of 15 Evelyn Rd, Worthing, and Agnes, *née* Anders (d 1955); *b* 24 August 1904; *Educ* Steyning GS Sussex; *m* 7 Feb 1942, Violet Edith, da of Robert Richard Walker (d 1939), of 1 A'Becket Gdns, West Worthing; 1 s (David b 1947), 1 da (Janet b 1942); *Career* RA 1942, FD security section Sgt Intelligence Corps 1944; dep overseas mangr Guardian Assurance Co Ltd 1950-65 (asst mangr Paris branch 1931-45, overseas inspector 1945-50); chm and md: Reason & Ptnrs Ltd 1965-, Pendle Insurance Co Ltd 1971-78, Insurance Consultancy Servs Ltd Gibraltar 1978-; dir and registrar Inst Insur Conslts 1978-; Friendship Assoc for the Blind; memb: Br Tunisian Soc; Freeman City of London 1959, Liveryman Worshipful Co Wheelwrights 1959; FCII; *Clubs* City Livery, British Commonwealth; *Style—* Eric Reason, Esq; 83 The Chine, Grange Park, London N21 2EG (☎ 01 360 9413 and 01 360 0374)

REAY, Master of; Hon Aeneas Simon Mackay; also Baron Aeneas Mackay; s and h of 14 Lord Reay (and h to S Btcy, Netherland Baronies and Jonkheership), and his 1 w, Hon Annabel Thérèse Fraser, da of 17 Lord Lovat; *b* 20 Mar 1965; *Educ* Westminster Sch, Brown Univ USA; *Style—* The Master of Reay

REAY, Lt-Gen Sir (Hubert) Alan John; KBE (1981); s of Rev John Reay; *b* 19 Mar 1925; *Educ* Lancing, Edinburgh Univ; *m* 1960, Ferelith Haslewood Deane; 2 s (and 1 s decd), 2 da; *Career* formerly post-graduate dean Royal Army Med Coll, dir Medical Services HQ BAOR 1979-81, dir-gen Army Medical Services 1981-85; chief hon steward Westminster Abbey 1985-, govr and chm med ctee Royal Star and Garter Home Richmond 1986-; QHP, FRCP, FRCP (Edin); *Style—* Lt-Gen Sir Alan Reay, KBE; 63 Madrid Rd, Barnes, London SW13 4PQ

REAY, Charlotte, Lady; Charlotte Mary; *née* Younger; da of William Younger, of Ravenswood, Melrose (d 1925, 4 s of James Younger, of Alloa; bro of George Younger, cr a Bt and 1 Viscount Younger of Leckie); sis of Sir William Younger, 1 Bt, DSO, of Fountainbridge, and Maj-Gen Ralph Younger, CB, CBE, DSO, MC, JP, DL; 1 cous twice removed of Rt Hon George Younger, Sec of State for Scotland; *m* 14 April 1936, 13 Lord Reay (d 1963); 1 s, 2 da; *Style—* The Rt Hon Charlotte, Lady Reay; Southbank, Melrose, Roxburghshire

REAY, Christopher John; s of Wing-Cdr Stanley Basil Reay OBE (d 1987), of East Molesey, Surrey, and Beatrice, *née* Levene; *b* 5 July 1937; *Educ* Tiffin Sch, King's Coll Cambridge (MA); *m* 30 March 1963, Elaine Patricia, da of Fl-Lt Arthur Walter Barnes (ka 1942); 2 s (Timothy b 1963, Ian b 1966), 1 da (Annabel b 1965); *Career* CA; ptnr: Reay & King 1981-, Josolyne Layton-Bennett 1965-81; dir Decorative Specialists Ltd 1985-; chm Horsley Cons Assoc 1972-74, pres Wimbledon Village Rotary Club 1988-; London Soc of CA: memb main ctee 1979-, tres 1985-86; FCA; *Recreations* tennis, travel, Wimbledon FC; *Clubs* St George's Hill Lawn Tennis; *Style—* Christopher J Reay, Esq; Foresters, Manor Close, East Horsley, Surrey KT24 6SB (☎ 04865 4153); 39 Queens Gate, London SW7 5HR; Admel House, 24 High St, Wimbledon, London SW19 5DX (☎ 01 947 1719, fax 01 879 0461)

REAY, 14 Lord (S 1628); Sir Hugh William Mackay; 14 Bt (NS 1627); also Chief of Clan Mackay, Jonkheer Mackay (Netherlands 1816), Baron Mackay van Ophemert (Netherlands 1822), and Baron Mackay (Netherlands 1858); s of 13 Lord Reay (d 1963, having been naturalised a British subject 1938) by Charlotte, da of William Younger (bro of 1 Viscount Younger of Leckie); *b* 19 July 1937; *Educ* Eton, Ch Ch Oxford; *m* 1, 1964 (m dis 1978), Hon Terese Fraser, da of 15 Lord Lovat; 2 s (Master of Reay b 1965, Hon Edward b 1974), 1 da (Hon Laura b 1966); m 2, 1980, Hon Victoria Isabella Anne, *née* Warrender, da of 8 Baron Bruntisfield; 2 da (Hon Antonia b 1981, 1 da b 1985); *Heir* s, Master of Reay; *Career* memb of European Parly 1973-79; vice-chm Cons Gp European Parl; delegate to Cncl of Europe and WEU 1979-; sits as Conservative in House of Lords; *Clubs* Turf, Beefsteak, Pratts; *Style—* The Rt Hon The Lord Reay; Kasteel Ophemert, Ophemert in Gelderland, The Netherlands; House of Lords, London SW1

REAY, William Robert; s of Michael Errington Reay (d 1979), and Agnes Clara, *née* Heslop; *b* 15 Mar 1925; *Educ* Heaton GS Newcastle-Upon-Tyne; *m* 20 Sept 1952, Mary Alison, da of Charles Lane (d 1928); 1 da (Susan Margaret b 1956); *Career* Sub Lt RNVR 1943-46 (combined ops and minesweeping); Joseph Miller and Co CA's: ptnr 1952-73, sr ptnr 1973-87, conslt 1987-; Tynemouth Bldg Soc: dir 1978-85, chm 1985-; dir Northern Indust Improvement Tst plc 1987-, dir Talawakelle Estates Hldgs Ltd 1987-, dir Talawakelle Hldgs Ltd 1987-; Warden St Mary's Church, Monkseaton, Whitley Bay; ACA 1952, FCA 1957; *Recreations* painting, music, caravanning; *Clubs* Pen & Palette (Newcastle), Constitutional (Newcastle); *Style—* William Reay, Esq; 5 Grasmere Cres, Monkseaton, Whitley Bay NE26 3TB (☎ 091 252 4265); Joseph Miller & Co, 31 Mosley St, Newcastle-Upon-Tyne (☎ 091 232 8065, fax 091 222 1554)

REBBECK, Lady; Clara Margaret Allen; da of R G Coombe, of Ceylon; *m* Rear-Adm Sir (Leopold) Edward Rebbeck, KBE, CB (d 1983); 2 s, 2 da; *Style—* Lady Rebbeck; Stubb Hill House, Iping, nr Midhurst, W Sussex

REBBECK, Dr Denis; CBE (1952), JP (1949, DL (Belfast 1960)); s of Sir Frederick Ernest Rebbeck, KBE, JP, DL (d 1964), of Belfast and Amelia Letitia, *née* Glover (d 1955); *b* 22 Jan 1914; *Educ* Campbell Coll Belfast, Cambridge Univ (MA), Dublin (MA, BLitt), Belfast (MSc, PhD); *m* 1938, Rosamond Annette Kathleen, da of Henry Boal Jameson (d 1932); 4 s; *Career* shipbuilder; dir: Harland and Wolff Ltd Belfast 1946-70 (md 1962-70, chm 1965-66), Iron Trades Insur Gp 1950-84 (chm 1972-84), Nat Shipbuilders Security Ltd 1952-58, Colvilles (Scottish steelmakers) 1963-67, Shipbuilding Corpn Ltd 1963-73, John Kelly Ltd shipowners Belfast 1968-79 (chm 1969-79), Royal Bank of Scotland 1969-84 (Nat Comm Bank 1965-69), Belships Co Ltd 1970-76 (chm 1972-76), Nordic Business Forum for Northern Britain 1980-84, Nationwide Building Soc 1980-, General Underwriting Agencies Ltd (chm); pres Shipbuilding Employers Fedn 1962-63, cmmr Belfast Harbour 1962-85; memb: gen ctee Lloyds Register of Shipping 1962-85, mgmnt bd Engrg Employers Fedn 1963-75, NI Econ Cncl 1965-70, research cncl Br Ship Research Assoc 1965-73, pres World Ship Society 1978-81, chm Pilotage Cmmn 1979-83, prime warden Worshipful Co of Shipwrights London 1980-81; *Recreations* sailing (10 ton sloop 'Drommedaris'); *Clubs* Royal Yacht Sqdn, Royal Norwegian Yacht, City Livery; *Style—* Dr Denis Rebbeck, CBE, JP, DL; The White House, Craigavad, Holywood, Co Down BT18 0HE (☎ 023 17 2294); General Underwriting Agencies Ltd, 33 Massey Ave, Belfast BT4 2JT (☎ 0232 760725, telex 747478)

RECKITT, Basil Norman; TD (1946); s of Maj Frank Norman Reckitt (d 1940); *b* 12 August 1905; *Educ* Uppingham, King's Coll Cambridge; *m* 1, 1928, Virginia, da of late Maj Meredith Carre-Smith; 2 da; m 2, 1966, Mary, *née* Peirce, wid of Paul Holmes, OBE; *Career* Lt-Col Home & Germany (Mil Govt); co dir; chm Reckitt & Colman Ltd 1966-70; Sheriff of Kingston upon Hull 1970-71; pro-chllr Hull Univ 1971-; Hon LLD Hull 1967; *publications*: Charles I and Hull, The History of Reckitt & Sons Ltd, Diary of Military Government in Germany, The Journeys of William Reckitt; *Recreations* hunting, ornithology; *Style—* Basil Reckitt, Esq, TD; Haverbrack, Milnthorpe, Cumbria; Holoman Hse, Isle of Raasay, Off Kyle of Lochalsh, Ross-shire, Scotland

RECKITT, Charles Lennard Hay; s of Charles Edward Hay Reckitt (d 1971), and Edith Margaret, *née* Barrett (d 1969); *b* 28 July 1916; *Educ* Bishops Stortford Coll; *m* 29 May 1943, Betty, da of Col J W F Brittlebank (d 1944), of Herts; 2 da (Jennifer Margaret b 1944, Valerie Anne b 1945); *Career* WWII Capt, London Scottish Regt and Royal Leics Regt 1939-46; farmer 1949-69; accountant 1949-; *Recreations* sailing, gardening, natural history, beer and wine, local govt; *Style—* Charles Reckitt, Esq; Blindwells, Strete, Dartmouth, Devon (☎ 0803 770 433, 08043 5555); Ernst & Whinney, 3 The Quay, Dartmouth, Devon

RECORD, Norman John Ronald; s of George Ronald Record (d 1967), of 26 Windsor Ave, Newton Abbot, Devon, and Dorothy Millie Rowland; *b* 19 May 1934; *Educ* Wembley Co GS, Univ Coll London (BSc); *m* 1 April 1961, Susan Mary, da of Ernest Samuel Weatherhead (d 1969), of Grosvenor Rd, Paignton, Devon; 2 s (Guy b 1964, Justin b 1966); *Career* 2 Lt RAOC 1955-57; economist, corp planning dir C & J Clark Ltd 1980-; formerly held planning and mkting posts in C & J Clark Ltd since 1964, and Perkins Engines Ltd 1957-64; CBE: cncl memb 1982-, SW regnl cncl memb 1979-85, econ situation ctee memb 1973-83, SW econ planning cncl 1973-79; memb: The Strategic Planning Soc, The Mktg Soc, The Labour Fin and Indust Gp, The Labour Econ Strategies Gp, ct of govrs Bath University; Fell Soc Business Economists, FBIM; author of papers on Macro-Economics; originator of The Theory of Capacity Utilisation in the Control of The Economy; *Recreations* current affairs, theatre, local history, swimming; *Clubs* Royal Overseas League; *Style—* Norman Record, Esq; The Old Vicarage, Wedmore, Somerset BS28 4AA (☎ 0934 712326); C & J Clark Ltd, Street, Somerset BA16 0YA (☎ 0458 43131, telex 44102)

RECORDON, Hon Mrs (Dinah); da of Baron Baker, OBE (Life Peer), and Fiona Mary MacAlister Baker (d 1979); *b* 2 April 1936; *Educ* Perse Sch for Girls, Homerton Coll Cambridge; *m* 1960, Nigel Esmond Recordon, s of Esmond Gareth Recordon (d 1958); 1 s, 3 da; *Style—* The Hon Mrs Recordon; Bush Farm, Colwall, nr Malvern, Worcs WR13 6HH (☎ 0684 40393)

RECORDON, Nigel Esmond; s of Esmond Gareth Recordon (d 1957), of Cambridge, and Frieda, *née* Robertson (d 1973); *b* 5 Mar 1934; *Educ* Oundle, St John's Coll Cambridge (MA); *m* 25 June 1960, Hon Dinah, yr da of late Baron Baker, OBE, (Life Peer), Cambridge; 1 s (Benedict), 3 da (Emma, Clare, Martha); *Career* Nat Serv 2 Lt RA 1952-54, TA Suffolk Yeo; admitted slr 1960, ptnr Recordon & Lister; *Recreations* farmer, beekeeper, long distance walking; *Style—* Nigel Recordon, Esq; Bush Farm, Colwall, Malvern (☎ 0684 40393); 12 Worcester Rd, Malvern, Worcs WR14 4QU (☎ 0684 892939)

REDCLIFFE-MAUD, Baroness; Jean; yr da of late John Brown Hamilton, of Melrose, Roxburghshire; *m* 1932, Baron Redcliffe-Maud, GCB, CBE (d 1982), sometime Master of Univ Coll Oxford; 1 s (Hon Humphrey Maud), 2 da (Hon Mrs Pugh, Hon Mrs Nicholls); *Clubs* University Women's; *Style—* The Rt Hon the Lady Redcliffe-Maud; 221 Woodstock Rd, Oxford (☎ 0865 515354)

REDDAWAY, Prof (William) Brian; CBE (1971); s of William Fiddian Reddaway (d 1949), of 2 Buckingham Rd, Cambridge, and Kate Waterland, *née* Sills (d 1966); *b* 8 Jan 1913; *Educ* King's Coll Sch Cambridge, Lydgate House Hunstanton, Oundle, King's Coll Cambridge (BA, MA); *m* 17 Sept 1938, Barbara Augusta, da of Edward Bennett (d 1916), of Lydbrook, Glos; 3 s (Peter b 1939, Stewart b 1941, Lawrence b

1943), 1 da (Jacqueline b 1947); *Career* asst Bank of Eng 1934-35, res fell Univ of Melbourne 1936-37, prof of econs Cambridge 1970-80, fell Clare Coll 1938-, lectr 1939-55, dir dept of applied Econs 1955-70, statistician Bd of Trade 1940-47; memb Royal Cmmn on the Press 1961-62; FBA 1967; *Books* Russian Financial System (1935), Ecomonics of a Declining Population (1939), Measurement of Production Movements (1948), Development of the Indian Economy (1962), Effects of UK Direct Investment Overseas (1968), Effects of the Selective Employment Tax (1973), Some Key Issues for the Development of the Economy of Papua New Guinea (1986); *Recreations* squash, tennis, walking; *Style—* Prof Brian Reddaway, CBE; 12 Manor Ct, Grange Rd, Cambridge CB3 9BE (☎ 0223 350041); Clare Coll, Cambridge (☎ 0223 333200)

REDDAWAY, Jean Muriel; OBE (1979); da of William Harold Brett (d 1981), and Agnes Rosina Lucy, *née* Buckley (d 1930); *b* 10 August 1923; *Educ* Orme Girls' Sch Newcastle-under-Lyme, Penrhos Coll, Slade Sch of Art (diploma of art, art teachers dip), London Univ; *m* 19 Feb 1944, George Frank Norman Reddaway, s of William Fiddian Reddaway (d 1949), of Cambridge; 2 s (John b 1946, David b 1953), 3 da (Helene b 1948, Catharine b 1951, Lucy b 1960); *Career* teacher of art, Impington Village Coll 1944-46, exhib at RRA 1946, exhibitions of paintings Beirut 1962-65, Khartoum 1968-69, Poland 1974-78; Polish OM (1980); *Recreations* painting, embroidery, gardening; *Style—* Mrs Jean M Reddaway, OBE; 51 Carlton Hill, London NW8 0EL (☎ 01 624 9238)

REDDAWAY, (George Frank) Norman; CBE (1965, MBE (Mil) 1946); s of William Fiddian Reddaway (d 1949), of King's College, Cambridge, and Kate Waterland, *née* Sills (d 1965); *b* 2 May 1918; *Educ* Oundle, King's Coll Cambridge (MA), Staff Coll Camberley, IDC; *m* 19 Feb 1944, Jean Muriel, OBE, da of (William) Harold Brett (d 1981), of Southport; 2 s (John b 1946, David b 1953), 3 da (Helen b 1948, Catharine b 1951, Lucy b 1960); *Career* Lance-Corpl Suffolk Regt 1939, 2 Lt No 3 Mil & Air Mission 1940, Capt GHQ Liaison Regt (Phantom) 1941-44, Maj Military Govt 1944, maj/actg Lt-Col Greater Berlin Mil Govt 1945-46; FO German Dept 1946, priv sec to Parly under-sec 1947-49, HM Embassy Rome 1949-52, UK High Cmmn Ottawa 1952-55, Info Res Dept FO 1955-59, IDC 1960, regnl info offr HM Embassy Beirut 1961-65, Singapore 1965-66, Khartoum 1967-69, asst under-sec FCO 1970-74, HM Ambass Warsaw 1974-78; chm Int House, dir Stearns Catalytic Int Ltd, tstee Thomson Fndn; Cdr Order of Merit (Polish People's Republic) 1985; *Recreations* int affairs, gardening, family history; *Clubs* Athenaeum, Oxford and Cambridge, Royal Cwlth Soc; *Style—* Norman Reddaway, Esq, CBE; 51 Carlton Hill, London, NW8 (☎ 01 624 9238)

REDDY, Thomas; s of Thomas Reddy (d 1973), of Poulton-le-Fylde, and Charlotte Winifred Teresa, *née* Hickey (d 1987); *b* 6 Dec 1941; *Educ* Baines's Sch Poulton; *m* 30 Aug 1969, Phyllis Wendy, da of Stanley Smith (d 1969), of Manchester and Lytham St Annes; 1 s (Christian b 1973), 1 da (Verity b 1971); *Career* journalist 1968-70; dir and exec creative dir Royds McCann 1970-87, chief exec Tom Reddy Advertising 1987-; broadcaster on adveritising TV and radio; chm Creative Club Manchester, fndr Manchester Creative Circle; guest lectr on advertising Univ of Manchester Inst of Sci and Technol; memb Br Direct Marketing Assoc (BDMA), Manchester Publicists Assoc (MPA); *Recreations* book collecting; *Clubs* Portico Library, Manchester Literary and Philosophical Society; *Style—* Thomas Reddy, Esq; Byeways, White House Lane, Great Eccleston, Lancs (☎ 0995 70568); Tom Reddy Advertising, Old Colony House, 6 South King St, Manchester (☎ 061 832 0182)

REDESDALE, 5 Baron (UK 1902); Clement Napier Bertram Mitford; s of Hon Rupert Freeman-Mitford (d 1939; bro of 2, 3 and 4 Barons); suc unc, 4 Baron, 1963; *b* 28 Oct 1932; *Educ* Eton; *m* 1958, Sarah, da of Brig Alston Cranstoun Todd, OBE; 1 s, 6 da; *Heir* s, Hon Rupert Bertram Mitford b 18 July 1967; *Career* sits as Cons in House of Lords; vice-pres and dir corporate communications (Europe, Africa and ME), Chase Manhattan Bank; govr Yehudi Menuhin Sch 1973-; *Recreations* walking; *Clubs* Lansdowne; *Style—* The Rt Hon the Lord Redesdale; The School House, Rochester, Newcastle-upon-Tyne; 2 St Mark's Sq, London NW1 (☎ 01 722 1965); The Chase Manhattan Bank NA; Woolgate House, Coleman St, London EC2T 2HD (☎ 01 726 7630)

REDFORD, Donald Kirkman; CBE (1980), DL (Lancs 1983); s of Thomas Johnson Redford (d 1965), of Whetstone, London; *b* 18 Feb 1919; *Educ* Culford Sch, King's Coll London Univ (LlB); *m* 1942, Mabel, 2 da of Wilfrid Wilkinson, of Humberston, Lincs; 1 s, 1 da; *Career* Wing Cdr RAFVR; practising barrister to 1946; Manchester Ship Canal Co: joined 1946, md 1970, chm 1972-86; chm Nat Assoc of Port Employers 1972-74, chm British Ports Assoc 1974-78; ctee of mgmnt RNLI 1977-; Manchester Univ court and cncl: dep tres 1980-82, tres 1982-83, chm of cncl 1983-87; *Clubs* Oriental; *Style—* Donald Redford Esq, CBE, DL; 8 Harrod Drive, Birkdale, Southport, Lancs PR8 2HA

REDGRAVE, John Albert Bryan; s of John Albert Redgrave (d 1985), of Felixstowe, Suffolk, and Lily Maria Redgrave (d 1986); *b* 2 August 1931; *Educ* Holloway GS, Reading Univ (BA); *m* 27 March 1954, May Florence Lillian, da of Walter Jennings (d 1955); 2 d (Lynn b 1958, Jane b 1966); *Career* served RAF (Bomber Commd) 1955-57; md & chm Bellrock Gypsum Ind 1958-70, chief exec Powell Duffryn Pollution Control & Powell Duffryn Process Engrg 1970-72, chm & chief exec Grimshaw Hldngs 1972-74, chm & chief exec Walter Lawrence plc 1974-85; chief exec Hunting Gate Grp 1985-; JP (Bucks) 1971-76; Ct of Assts the Fletchers' Co, Freeman City of London 1972; *Recreations* golf, archery, swimming, game fishing; *Clubs* Carlton, City Livery, Royal Toxophilite Society, Flempton Golf, Sheringham Golf, Cromer Golf; *Style—* John Redgrave, Esq; The Old Rectory, Flempton, Bury St Edmunds, Suffolk IP28 6RQ; Hunting Gate Group, 4 Hunting Gate, Hitchin, Herts, SG4 0TB (☎ 0462 34444, fax 0462 55924)

REDGRAVE, Maj Gen Sir Roy Michael Frederick; KBE (1979), MC (1945); s of Robin Roy Redgrave (d 1972), of Rye, Sussex, and Jean Michelene, *née* Capsa (d 1977); *b* 16 Sept 1925; *Educ* Sherborne; *m* 1953, Valerie, da of Maj (Richard) Arthur Colley Wellesley (d 1984); 2 s (Alexander, Robin); *Career* joined RHG as trooper 1943, Commanded RHG 64-67; National Defence Coll Canada 1973, Cmdt RAC Centre 1974-75, British Cmdt Berlin 1975-78, Cdr British Forces Hong Kong and Maj-Gen Bde of Gurkhas 1978-80; FRGS; dir-gen Winston Churchill Memorial Trust 1980-82, chm Hammersmith and Fulham Dist Health Authority 1981-85; special tstee Charing Cross Hosp, cncl Victoria League for Cwlth Friendship, FRGS, Council Medical Sch Charing & Westminster Bri Nepal Society; Hon Col 31 Signal Regt (Volunteers); *Style—* Maj Gen Sir Roy Redgrave, KBE, MC; c/o Lloyd's Bank, Wareham, Dorset BH20 4LX

REDGRAVE, Steven Geoffrey; MBE (1986); s of Geoffrey Edward Redgrave, of Marlow Bottom, Bucks, and Sheila Marion, *née* Stevenson; *b* 23 Mar 1962; *Educ* Marlow C of E First Sch, Holy Trinity Sch Marlow, Burford Sch Marlow Bottom, Great Marlow Sch; *m* 12 March 1988, (Elizabeth) Ann, da of Brian John Callaway, of Cyprus; *Career* sports conslt, amateur rower; notable achievements: Olympic gold coxed pairs 1988, Olympic bronze coxed pairs 1988, World Champs winner coxless pairs and second coxless pairs 1987, World Champs winner coxless pairs Cwlth Games gold single sculls, gold coxed fours, gold coxless pairs 1986, Olympic gold coxed fours 1984, Jr World Champs second double sculls 1980, 8 wins Henley Royal Regatta 1981-87, Wingfield Sculls Champ 1985-88; *Clubs* Marlow Rowing, Leander Henley; *Style—* Steven G Redgrave, Esq, MBE; c/o Olympic British Assoc, 1 Wandsworth Plain, London, SW18 1EH

REDGRAVE, Vanessa; CBE (1967); da of Sir Michael Redgrave (d 1985), and Rachel, *née* Kempson; sis of Corin Redgrave, actor, and Lynn Redgrave, actress; *b* 30 Jan 1937; *Educ* Queensgate Sch, Central Sch of Speech and Drama; *m* 1962 (m dis 1967), Tony Richardson (*qv*), s of Clarence Albert Richardson; 2 da; *Career* actress, numerous stage and film performances; memb WRP; *Style—* Miss Vanessa Redgrave, CBE; c/o James Sharkey Assocs Ltd, 3rd Floor Suite, 15 Golden St, London W1R 3AG

REDGROVE, Peter; s of Gordon James Redgrove and late Nancy Lena, *née* Cestrilli-Bell; *b* 2 Jan 1932; *Educ* Taunton Sch Somerset, Queen's Coll Cambridge; *m* 2, Penelope Shuttle; *Career* scientific journalist and editor 1954-61, won Fulbright Award to travel to US as visiting poet to Buffalo Univ NY 1961, Gregory fell in poetry Leeds Univ 1962-65, resident author and sr lectr in complementary studies Falmouth Sch of Art Cornwall 1966-83, O'Connor prof of Literature Colgate Univ NY 1974-75, freelance writer, poet; analytical psychologist; broacaster BBC 1956-, writer radio and television drama (won Imperial Tobacco Prize for Radio Drama 1978, Giles Cooper Award for Radio Drama 1981, Prix Italia 1982), FRSL; *Books* playbooks include: Miss Carstairs Dressed for Blooding and Other plays (1976), In the Country of the Skin (1973); psychology and sociology: The Wise Wound (with Penelope Shuttle, 1978), The Black Goddess and the Sixth Sense (1987); novels include: The Beekeepers (1980), The Facilitators (1982); poetry includes: The Collector and Other Poems (1960), Penguin Modern Poets II (1968), Dr Faust's Sea-Spiral Spirit and Other Poems (1972), The Apple-Broadcast and Other New Poems (1981), The Working of Water (1984), The Mudlark Poems and Grand Buveur (1986), The Moon Dispores: Poems 1954-87, In the Hall of the Saurians (1987); anthologies include Lamb and Thundercloud (1975), Poets' Playground (1963); reviewer for the Guardian 1975-, numerous prose articles for other journals; contributor to: The Times Literary Supplement, the Spectator, The New Statesman, the Observer and the Listener; *Recreations* work, photography, judo; *Style—* Peter Redgrove, Esq; c/o David Higham Associates, 5-8 Lower John Street, Golden Square, London W1R 4HA

REDHEAD, Prof Michael Logan Gonne; Prof; s of Robert Arthur Redhead, of Oak Cottage, Cooden Beach, Sussex, and Christabel Lucy Gonne, *née* Browning (d 1966); *b* 30 Dec 1929; *Educ* Westminster, UCL (BSc, PhD); *m* 3 Oct 1964, Jennifer Anne, da of Montague Arthur Hill; 3 s (Alexander b 1965, Julian b 1968, Roland b 1974); *Career* dir Redhead Properties Ltd 1962, ptnr Galveston Estates 1970; prof: philosophy of physics Chelsea Coll London 1984-85, philosophy of physics King's Coll London 1985-87, history and philosophy of sci Univ of Cambridge 1987-; fell Wolfson Coll Cambridge 1988, pres Br Soc Philosophy of Sci 1989; Lakatas Award 1988, FInstP; *Books* In Completeness, Nonlocality and Realism (1987); *Recreations* tennis, music, poetry; *Clubs* Hurlingham, Queen's; *Style—* Prof Michael Redhead; 34 Coniger Rd, London SW6 (☎ 01 736 6767); Dept of Sci, Univ of Cambridge, Free Sch Lane, Cambridge (☎ 0223 334540, car ☎ 0865 263199)

REDMAN, Lady (Barbara Ann); *née* Wharton; da of late J R Wharton, of Haffield, nr Ledbury, Herefordshire; *b* 15 April 1919; *Educ* Benenden; *m* 1953, as his 2 w, Lt-Gen Sir Harold Redman, KCB, CBE (d 1986); 1 s, 1 da; *Career* 3 offr WRNS Lord Mountbatten's staff SACSEA; priv sec to Capt Anthony Kimmins (author and film producer); patron Royal Homeopathic Soc; *Recreations* gardening, environmental protection, painting, music; *Style—* Lady Redman; Stair House, West Lulworth, Dorset

REDMAN, Maurice; s of Herbert Redman (d 1974), and Olive, *née* Dyson; *b* 30 August 1922; *Educ* Hulme GS Oldham, Univ of Manchester (BSc); *m* 17 Sept 1960, Dorothy, da of James Appleton (d 1936); 2 da (Pamela b 19 July 1961, Philippa b 2 March 1964); *Career* various appts Co Borough of Oldham Gas Dept 1943, dep (formerly asst) prodn engr N Western Gas Bd 1957, dir of engrg Southern Gas Bd 1970 (chief engr 1966), dep chm Scottish Gas Bd 1970, chm Scottish Regn Br Gas Corpn 1974 (dep chm 1973); various offices Methodist Church; CEng, FIGasE, MRSC, MIChemE; *Recreations* music, gardening, swimming, photography; *Clubs* New (Edinburgh); *Style—* Maurice Redman, Esq; Avington, Cramond Regis, Edinburgh EH4 6LW (☎ 031 312 6178)

REDMAN, Timothy Stewart; s of Dudley Stewart Redman (d 1960), and Josephine Mary (d 1952), *née* Baker; *b* 4 June 1940; *Educ* Cheltenham; *m* 23 May 1964, Gillian Judith, da of John Pillar (d 1974); 2 s (Jonathan Stewart b 1967, Nicholas Timothy b 1970); *Career* Brewer; dir Greene King & Sons plc 1975-; memb Lloyd's of London 1984-; *Recreations* gardening, fishing, shooting; *Style—* Timothy Redman, Esq; Orchard House, Comberton, Cambridge CB3 7EE; Chalet le Caribou, Les Carroz d'Araches, France; Westgate Brewery, Bury St Edmunds, Suffolk IP33 1QT (☎ 0284 63222, telex 817589, fax 0284 706502)

REDMAN-BROWN, Geoffrey Michael; s of Arthur Henry Brown, of Newport, Gwent, and Marjorie Frances Joan, *née* Redman (d 1969); *b* 30 Mar 1937; *Educ* Newport HS, Balliol Coll Oxford (MA); *m* 23 Feb 1988, Jean Rose, da of Leslie James Wilkinson (d 1986), of Essex; *Career* Nat Serv RAF 1956-58; memb Stock Exchange 1967, ptnr Phillips & Drew 1970 (joined 1961-), dir pres and PR UBS Phillips & Drew Ltd 1989; prov Grand Master Oxford's Grand Lodge Ancient and Accepted Masons Eng; Freeman City of London, Liveryman Worshipful Co Broderers; assoc Soc Investment Analysts 1972; *Recreations* swimming, gardening, travel; *Clubs* City of London, RAC; *Style—* Geoffrey Redman-Brown, Esq; 5 Three Kings Yard, Mayfair, London W1 (☎ 01 629 2638); Priestfield, Hook Norton, Banbury, Oxon (☎ 0608 737 738); UBS Phillips & Drew, 100 Liverpool St, London EC2M 2RH (☎ 01 901 3333, car tel 0860 321 072)

REDMAYNE, Clive; s of Procter Hubert Redmayne (d 1965), of 9 Grenville Rd, Hazel Grove, Stockport, Cheshire, and Emma, *née* Torkington (d 1976); *b* 27 July 1927; *Educ* Stockport Sch, London (BSc); *m* 19 July 1952, Vera Muriel, da of Wilfred Toplis, MM (d 1983), of 35 Wellfield Rd, Stockport, Cheshire; 1 s (John Clive James b 27 July 1959), 1 da (Jane Susan (Mrs Goodwin) b 6 April 1956); *Career* apprentice Fairey Aviation Co Stockport 1944-48; stress off: Fairey Aviation Co 1948-50, Eng Electric Co Warton 1950-51, A V Roe & Co Chadderton 1951-55; head of structural analysis weapons div Woodford 1955-62, structures dept Royal Aircraft Estab Farnborough 1962-67, asst dir Miny of Technol 1967-70, AD/MRCA MOD(PE) 1970-74, div ldr systems engrg Namma Munich 1974-76, chief supt A & AEE Boscombe Down 1976-78, dir Harrier MOD(PE) 1978-80, dir gen future projects MOD (PE) 1980-81, dir gen Aircraft 3 MOD(PE) 1981-84, conslt aeronautical engr 1985-; MIMechE 1956, CEng 1970, FRAeS 1981; *Recreations* caravanning, walking, skiing, chess, bridge, reading; *Clubs* Caravan; *Style*— Clive Redmayne, Esq; Pennycot, 47 Old Bisley Rd, Frimley, Camberley, Surrey (☎ 0276 21610)

REDMAYNE, Hon Sir Nicholas John; 2 Bt (UK 1964); s of Baron Redmayne, DSO, TD, PC, DL (Life Peer and 1 Bt, who d 1983); *b* 1 Feb 1938; *Educ* Radley, Sandhurst; *m* 1, 7 Sept 1963 (m dis 1976), Anne (d 1985), da of Frank Birch Saunders, of Kineton, Warwicks; 1 s, 1 da; m 2, 1978, Mrs Christine Diane Wood Hewitt, da of late Thomas Wood Fazakerley; *Heir* s, Giles Martin Redmayne b 1 Dec 1968; *Career* cmmnd Grenadier Gds 1958-62; stockbroker; dir Kleinwort Benson Ltd; *Recreations* shooting, tennis, skiing; *Style*— The Hon Sir Nicholas Redmayne, Bt; Walcote Lodge, Walcote, Lutterworth, Leics (☎ 045 55 2637, business ☎ 01 623 8000)

REDMOND, Geraldine Melaine; da of Jerome Anthony Wilson, of Liverpool, and Dorothy Kathleen, *née* Hoult; *b* 20 Jan 1953; *Educ* Notre Dame Convent Woolton, Upton RC Convent Wirral, Cygnets House London; *m* 19 July 1985, Keith Redmond, s of Joseph Redmond, of Liverpool; 1 da (Melaine Francesca); *Career* md Famous Army Stores Ltd; dir Limocoat Ltd, Famous Army Stores (Holdgs) Ltd, SA Draughting Services (NW) Ltd, Tenglow Ltd, Betterpoise Ltd, Harmond Investments Ltd; chp Garston OAP Club; *Recreations* cookery, swimming, classic vintage car driving; *Style*— Mrs G M Redmond; Sunbeam House, Woolton Rd, Garston, Liverpool L19 5PH (☎ 051 427 5151, fax 051 427 3918, 0836 505 105)

REDMOND, Sir James; s of Patrick and Marion Redmond; *b* 8 Nov 1918; *Educ* Graeme HS Falkirk; *m* 1942, Joan Morris; 1 s, 1 da; *Career* radio offr Merchant Navy 1937-38 and 1939-45; BBC Television Alexandra Palace 1937-39; BBC: installation engr 1949, supt engr Television Recording 1960, sr supt engr TV 1963, asst dir of engrg 1967, dir of engrg 1968-78; pres IEE 1978-79; memb: Cncl Brunel Univ 1980-, Cncl Open Univ 1981-, bd Services Sound & Vision Corpn 1983-; FEng, FIEE; kt 1979; *Recreations* golf; *Clubs* Athenaeum; *Style*— Sir James Redmond; 43 Cholmeley Crescent, Highgate, London N6 (☎ 01 340 1611)

REDMOND, John Vincent; s of Maj Robert Spencer Redmond, TD, of Knutsford, Cheshire, and Marjorie Helen, *née* Heyes; *b* 10 April 1952; *Educ* Wrekin Coll, Western Reserve Acad Ohio USA, Univ of Kent at Canterbury (BA); *m* 21 May 1977, Tryphena Lloyd (Nina), da of Jenkin John Lloyd Powell, of Carmarthen, Dyfed; 2 s (William b 1981, Samuel b 1985); *Career* admitted slr 1976; Cobbetts Manchester 1974-75, Clyde & Co Guildford and London 1975-78, Laytons Bristol and London (ptnr) 1978-; memb: Bristol Jr Chamber 1978-, Bristol Festival for Children, Bristol-Oporto Assoc; memb Law Soc 1976; *Recreations* squash, sailing; *Style*— John Redmond, Esq; Hafod, Scot Lane, Chew Stoke, Avon BS18 8UW (☎ 0272 333181); Laytons, St Bartholomews, Lewins Mead, Bristol BS1 2NH (☎ 0272 291626, fax 0272 293369, car tel 0836 533382)

REDMOND, Martin; MP (Lab) Don Valley 1983-; *b* 15 August 1935; *Style*— Martin Redmond Esq, MP; House of Commons, London SW1

REDMOND, Robert Spencer; TD; s of Frederick Redmond (d 1937), of Croxteth Rd, Liverpool, and Eliza, *née* MacKenzie (d 1976); *b* 10 Sept 1919; *Educ* Liverpool Coll; *m* 19 May 1949, Marjorie Helen, da of Abraham Vincent Heyes, of Tanhouse Lane, Parbold, N Wigan, Lancs; 1 s (John Vincent b 10 April 1952); *Career* Liverpool Scottish (TA) 2 Lt 1938, RASC 1941, Special Operations 1943-45, ME Staff Coll 1943, Released with Rank Major 1946; Cons constituency agent: Wigan 1947-49, Knutsford 1944-56; md Heyes & Co Ltd 1956-66, md Ashley Associates 1969-70 (commercial mangr 1966-69 and p/t commercial dir 1970-72), MP (Con) Bolton West 1970-74 (vice chm Employment Ctee, memb Select Ctee on Nat Industs a spokesman on problems of small business), pte practise as exec selection conslt 1972-76, dir Nat Fedn of Clay Industs 1976-84; free lance journalist 1984-; fndr (and chm) NW Export Club 1960, NW regnl cncllr FBI and CBI 1958-66 memb and cncl CBI 1976-844; *Books* How to Recruit Good Managers (1989); *Recreations* writing, gardening; *Clubs* Army and Navy; *Style*— Robert S Redmond, Esq, TD; 194 Grove Park, Knutsford, Cheshire WA16 8QE (☎ 0565 2657)

REDSHAW, Sir Leonard; s of Joseph Stanley Redshaw, of Barrow-in-Furness; *b* 15 April 1911; *Educ* Barrow GS, Liverpool Univ (Naval Architecture degree); *m* 1939, Joan Mary, da of William White, of London; 1 s, 1 da; *Career* apprentice Ship Drawing Office Vickers Ltd 1927, joined mgmnt staff Vickers-Armstrong Ltd 1936, personal asst to Shipbuilding mangr 1950, special dir 1953; Shipbuilding gen mangr of Shipyards Vickers-Armstrong (Shipbuilders) Ltd in Barrow-in-Furness and Newcastle-upon-Tyne 1955, dir 1956, dep gen mangr 1961, md Vickers Ltd Shipbuilding Gp 1964; ch exec and dir i/c of Shipbuilding 1967, dir Vickers Ltd 1967, asst md 1968-76; chm: Vickers Ltd Shipbuilding Gp 1968-76, Vickers Oceanics Ltd 1972-78, Vickers Offshore Engrg Gp 1975-78; memb Lloyds Gen Ctee 1972-81; dir: Rolls Royce & Assocs Ltd 1966-77, Brown Bros & Co Ltd 1970-77 (chm 1973-77), Fillite (Runcorn) Ltd 1971-, Silica Fillers Ltd 1971-85, Cockatoo Docks & Engrg Co Pty Ltd 1972-76; CEI John Smeaton Medal 1977, RINA William Froude Medal 1978; FRINA, FWeldI (past pres), FoEng; kt 1972; *Style*— Sir Leonard Redshaw; Netherclose, Ireleth, Askam-in-Furness, Cumbria LA16 7EZ (☎ 0229 62529)

REDWAY, Maj Paul Warwick; TD (1950); s of Warwick Richard Redway, FAI (d 1958), of Princes Risborough, and Eva Gladys, *née* Burr; *b* 7 June 1918; *Educ* Royal GS High Wycombe; *m* 22 June 1940, Jacqueline Kelleway, da of John Paul Line (d 1959); 2 s (Marcus Vaughan b 15 Nov 1943, Hugh Warwick b 1 Oct 1948), 1 da (Robina Paulina b 25 Jan 1946); *Career* TA 2 Lt Queen Victoria's Rifles 1937, Maj 1942, served with KRRC (UK and Normandy); md Skinningrove Iron Co Ltd 1966-; JP 1955; *Recreations* skiing, shooting, fishing; *Clubs* London, The Royal Green Jackets; *Style*— Maj Paul Redway, TD; Bugle Cottage, Egton, Whitby, North Yorks YO21 1UT (☎ 0947 85 363)

REDWOOD, John Alan; MP (C) Wokingham 1987-; s of William Charles, Kent, and Amy Emma Champion; *b* 15 June 1951; *Educ* Kent Coll Canterbury, Magdalen Coll Oxford (BA Hons), St Anthony's Coll 1971-72 (DPhil, MA); *m* 1974, Gail Felicity, da of Robert Stanley Chippington; 1 s (Richard b 1982), and 1 da (Catherine b 1978); *Career* fell All Soul's Coll Oxford 1972-87; investmt analyst Robert Fleming & Co 1974-77; Oxfordshire County Cncllr 1973-77; clerk mangr dir NM Rothschild Asset Mgmnt 1977-83; hd Prime Ministers Policy Unit 1983-86; dir Overseas Corporate Finance NM Rothschilds 1986-87; non-exec dir Norcros 1986-87;; *Recreations* village cricket, water sports; *Style*— John Redwood, Esq, MP; 506 Queen's Quay, Upper Thames Street, London EC4V 3EH; House of Commons SW1

REDWOOD, Sir Peter Boverton; 3 Bt (UK 1911); s of Sir Thomas Boverton Redwood, 2 Bt (d 1974); *b* 1 Dec 1937; *Educ* Gordonstoun; *m* 22 Aug 1964, Gilian Waddington, o da of John Lee Waddington Wood, of Limuru, Kenya; 3 da; *Heir* half-bro, Robert Redwood; *Career* Col KOSB, ret 1987; *Recreations* shooting; *Style*— Sir Peter Redwood, Bt; c/o National Westminster Bank, Millbank Branch, Thames House, Millbank, SW1

REDWOOD, Robert Boverton; s of Sir Thomas Boverton Redwood, 2 Bt (d 1974); hp of half-bro, Sir Peter Redwood, 3 Bt; *b* 24 June 1953; *Educ* Truro Cathedral Sch; *m* 1978, Mary Elizabeth Wright; 1 s (James b 1985), 1 da (Morwenna b 1982); *Career* police offr; *Style*— Robert Redwood Esq; Charnwood, 11 Deans Park, South Molton, Devon EX36 4JY

REECE-SMITH, Gregory; s of Gordon Reece-Smith, of Spain, and Joyce Constance, *née* Baxter; *b* 22 Mar 1948; *Educ* KCS Wimbledon, LSE (BSc); *m* 22 June 1973, Caroline Mary, da of Basil Arthur Buche, of Surrey; 2 s (Gavin Robert b 1977, Duncan Paul b 1980); *Career* CA; joined Peat Marwick Mitchell 1970 (resigned as sr mangr 1983), chief fin offr Dubilier America Inc NY 1984, mgmnt engr to medium sized cos facing the problems of high growth and change 1985-; dir: Blue Chip Systems Gp plc, Blue Chip Microsystems Ltd, Overview Films Ltd, St Christopher's Sch Tst (Epsom) Ltd; *Recreations* squash, rugby, educn; *Clubs* RAC; *Style*— Gregory Reece-Smith, Esq; 2 The Ridings, Epsom, Surrey KT18 5JQ (☎ 03727 25437); work: 01-434-9829)

REED, April Anne; Air Cdre; RRC (1981); da of Capt Basil Duck Reed, RN (d 1969), and Mignon Ethel Nancy, *née* Neame (d 1976); *b* 25 Jan 1930; *Educ* Sherborne House Chandlersford and Channing Sch Highgate, Middx Hosp London, Royal Maternity Hosp Belfast; *Career* Princess Mary's RAF Nursing Serv: joined as Flying Offr 1954, Flt Offr 1958, Sqdn Ldr dep matron 1970, Wing Cdr sr matron 1976, Gp Capt princ matron 1980, Air Cdre dir nursing servs 1984; ret due to serv reorganistaion 1985; memb charity exec Raf Benevolent Fund 1985; *Recreations* gardening, wildlife, hill walking, antiques, oriental rugs; *Clubs* RAF; *Style*— Air Cdre April Reed, RRC; 3 Edieham Cottages, Angle Lane, Shepreth, Royston, Herts (☎ 0763 61329); 3 Garners Row, Burnham Thorpe, Norfolk; 2 Murlaggan, Roy Bridge, By Fort William, Inverness; 67 Portland Place, London W1N 4AR

REED, Barry St George Austin; CBE (1988), MC (1951), DL (Gtr London 1977-); s of Douglas Austin Reed (d 1988), and Mary Reed (d 1973); gs of fndr of Austin Reed, the tailors and outfitters; *b* 5 May 1931; *Educ* Rugby; *m* 1956, Patricia, *née* Bristow; 1 s, 1 da; *Career* Maj (Korea); exec chm Austin Reed Gp plc 1973-; chm: Chester Barrie Ltd 1978-, Stephens Bros Ltd 1977-, Br Knitting and Clothing Export Cncl 1985-; dir Nat West Bank plc; (chm of its Eastern Advsy Bd 1987-); pres Menswear Assoc of Br 1966-67; memb: Consumer Protection Advsy Ctee 1973-79, Euro Trade Ctee of BOT Bd 1975-84, cncl Royal Warrant Hldrs Assoc 1979-; Clothing EDC 1986-, cncl Br Textile Confedn 1986-, Br Fashion Cncl 1986-; Master Worshipful Co of Glovers of London 1980-81; FRSA, CBIM; *Recreations* gardens, travel; *Clubs* Marylebone Cricket, Naval and Military, City Livery; *Style*— Barry Reed Esq, CBE, MC, DL; Crakehall House, Bedale, N Yorks (☎ 0677 22 743); 103 Regent St, London W1 (☎ 01 734 6789)

REED, Bernard William Douglas; *b* 21 August 1935; *Educ* Sutton GS Surrey, St Peter's Coll Oxford (MA), City of London Coll, Harvard Business Sch (MBA); *m* 25 March 1961, Ann Helen Terry, 3 s (Ian Michael b 1963, Neil Malcolm b 1966, Duncan James b 1969), 1 da (Julia Louise b 1964); *Career* Sub Lt RN 1954-56; Phillips & Drew 1959-62, McKinsey & Co 1964-68, BOC Gp 1973-78, London Int Fin Futures Exchange 1981-84, exec dir of mktg Int Stock Exchange 1985-; ctee memb Harvard Business Sch Club of London; Freeman Worshipful Co of Wheelwrights; AMSIA 1961; *Recreations* squash, windsurfing, running; *Style*— Bernard Reed, Esq; The International Stock Exchange, London EC2N 1HP (☎ 01 588 2355)

REED, David; s of Dr George Norman Reed (d 1954), Surg Lt Cdr RN, and Phyllis Maude, *née* Cave (later Mrs Dawson: d 1969); *b* 31 July 1947; *Educ* St Edward's Sch Oxford; *m* 19 Jan 1974, Jennifer Carol, da of Dennis George Sandford Loudon, of Michael Bournes, West Meston, Sussex; 3 s (Jonathan b 16 Jan 1977, Nicholas b 8 March 1982, Bemjamin b 17 Jan 1987), 1 da (Emily b 3 Sept 1979); *Career* with Whinney Murray (now Ernst and Whinney) 1967-71; ACA 1971; with Peat Marwick Mitchell and Co Sydney 1972-73; County Bank Ltd (now County Nat West Ltd) 1974-; (dir 1979, md 1986); memb: FCA 1976; *Recreations* shooting, sailing, tennis; *Style*— David Reed, Esq; 8 Holtwood Road, Oxsholt, Surrey (☎ 0372 842180); County Natwest Ltd, Drapers Gardens, 12 Throgmorton Avenue, London EC2 (☎ 01 382 1000)

REED, Derek Sydney; s of Sydney Richard Reed, of Town Barton, Ilsington, Devon, and Margaret Annie Reed; *b* 8 Sept 1946; *Educ* Newton Abbot GS, Liverpool Univ (LLB); *m* 26 May 1973, Carole, da of William Brunswick Whiting; 2 s (James b 1976, Mark b 1980), 1 da (Vanessa b 1974); *Career* slr of the Supreme Ct, ptnr Woollcombe Watts; *Recreations* walking, gardening, sport, music; *Style*— Derek Reed, Esq; Church House, Newton Abbot, Devon (☎ 0626 52661)

REED, Gavin Barras; s of Lt-Col Edward Reed (d 1953), and Greta Milburn, *née* Pybus (d 1964); *b* 13 Nov 1934; *Educ* Eton, Trinity Coll Cambridge (BA); *m* 28 June 1957, Muriel Joyce, da of late Humphrey Vaughan Rowlands; 1 s (Christopher b 1964), 3 da (Fiona b 1958, Joanna b 1960, Lucinda b 1962); *Career* Nat Serv Pilot Fleet Air Arm; dir Scottish & Newcastle Breweries plc; other directorships incl: Newcastle Breweries (chm), McEwan Younger (chm), Matthew Brown plc (chm), Thistle Hotels Ltd, Milburn Estates Ltd, Selective Assets Tst; *Recreations* shooting, tennis; *Clubs* Naval, New (Edinburgh); *Style*— Gavin Reed, Esq; Whitehill, Aberdour, Burntisland, Fife KY3 0RW; Broadgate, West Woodburn, Northumberland; Scottish & Newcastle

Breweries plc, 111 Holyrood Rd, Edinburgh EH8 8YS (☎ 031 556 2591)

REED, Jane Barbara; da of William Charles Reed and Gwendoline Laura, *née* Plaskett; *b* 31 Mar 1940; *Educ* Royal Masonic Sch for Girls; *Career* editor Woman's Own 1969-79, publisher Quality Monthly Gp, IPC 1979-81; editor-in-chief Woman 1981-83, md Holborn Publishing Gp IPC 1983-85, managing editor (features) Today Newspaper 1985-86, managing editor News UK Ltd 1986-, chm Editorial Ctee Fedn of Periodical Publishers 1978-85, memb Ctee for the Public Understanding of Science (Copus) Royal Society 1986-; *Books* Girl about Town (1964), Kitchen Sink or Swim (1981, with Dierdre Saunders); *Recreations* music, hockey, work; *Clubs* Groucho's; *Style*— Miss Jane Reed; 41 Chipstead Street, London SW6 3SR; New UK Ltd, 70 Vauxhall Bridge Road, London SW1

REED, John Edward; s of John William Reed (d 1982), of Devon, and Gladys Lavinia Williams, *née* Silk (d 1982); *b* 7 April 1946; *Educ* Dulverton Secondary, Aston Univ (BSc Hons) Architecture, Dipl Arch, RIBA; *m* 7 Aug 1976, Christine Anne, da of Richard Foley (d 1966), of Worthing; 2 da (Joai Jane b 1983, Chloë Yi-Fen b 1985); *Career* Chartered Architect ptnr; Reed Holland Associates 1981-; *Recreations* family and christian orientated; *Style*— John E Reed, Esq; Reed Holland Associates, Chartered Architects, 2 Half Acre, Williton, Taunton, Somerset (☎ 0984 33433)

REED, Dr John Langdale; s of John Thompson Reed (d 1966), of Northampton, and Elsie May, *née* Abbott (d 1962); *b* 16 Sept 1931; *Educ* Oundle, Cambridge Univ (MA, MB, BChir), Guy's Hosp; *m* 7 Jan 1959, Hilary, da of Lt-Col John Freeman Allin, MC (d 1976), of Kings Norton; 1 s (John Richard b 1967), 1 da (Alison b 1960); *Career* Nat Serv RAMC 1958-60; conslt psychiatrist St Bart's Hosp London 1967-, sr lectr St Bart's Hosp Med Coll 1967-; dir Community Psychiatry Res Unit 1979-86, sr princ med offr mental health and illness div Dept of Health London 1986-: chm Vanguard Housing 1981-86; FRCP 1974, FRCPsych 1974; *Books* Psychiatric Services in the Community (jtly 1984); *Recreations* genealogy, bridge, walking; *Style*— Dr John Reed; Dept of Health, Alexander Fleming House, Elephant & Castle, London SE1 (☎ 01 407 5522)

REED, Dr May; da of Joseph Henry George Reed (d 1970), of The Grange, Ingatestone, Essex, and Edith May, *née* Leech (d 1966); *b* 22 April 1914; *Educ* Brentwood Co HS, Bedford Coll London Univ (BSc, PhD); *Career* WWII nurse Br Red Cross 1939-42; res sci MRC 1958-77, sr res fell Somerville Coll Oxford 1972-79; hon res advsr Chartered Soc of Physiotherapy 1966-75, fndr memb and first hon sec The Brill Soc; vice-chm: Brill Royal Br Legion Women's Section, Vale of Aylesbury Decorative and Fine Arts Soc; pres Brill Sports and Social Club; memb: Soc for Endocrinology, Soc for Study of Fertility 1960; FRSA 1959, FRSM 1965; *Recreations* fly fishing; *Clubs* Royal Commonwealth Soc; *Style*— Dr May Reed; Old Post Office House, Brill, Bucks HP18 9RP (☎ 0844 238226)

REED, Sir Nigel Vernon; CBE (1967, MBE (Mil) 1944), TD (1950); s of Vernon Herbert Reed, of Paihia NZ (d 1963, former MP and MLC NZ), and Eila Mabel Reed (d 1959); *b* 31 Oct 1913; *Educ* Wanganui Collegiate, Univ of NZ (LLB), Jesus Coll Cambridge (LLB); *m* 1945, Ellen Elizabeth, da of Dr Lewis Garibaldi Langstaff, of Toronto, Canada (d 1917); 1 s, 2 da; *Career* Mil Serv 1939-45, Lt-Col 1944; joined Colonial Legal Service 1946, magistrate Nigeria 1946, chief magistrate Nigeria 1951; High Ct of the Northern Regn of Nigeria: chief registrar 1955, judge 1956, sr Puisne judge 1964; chief justice of the Northern States of Nigeria 1968-75, ret; appointed cmmr for Law Revision of the States of Northern Nigeria 1988; kt 1970; *Recreations* gardening; *Clubs* Royal Commonwealth Soc; *Style*— Sir Nigel Reed, CBE, TD; Paihia, Bay of Islands, New Zealand

REED, Paul Charles Rowe; s of Capt Charles Henry Rowe Reed, MC (d 1969), and Irene Millicent, *née* Alderton (d 1988); *b* 24 Feb 1942; *Educ* Gaveney House Sch Exmouth, Reigate GS; *m* 7 June 1974, Catherine, da of Michael O'Connell (d 1971), of Ballynoe, Co Cork; 2 s (Mark b 1975, Lawrence b 1977); *Career* with Friends Provident Life Office 1958-82, Merchant Navy Officers Pension Fund 1982- (dep investmt mangr 1985); dir: Merchant Navy Investmt Mgmnt 1985-, Transcapital BV 1986-, Dublin City Properties 1988-; AIA 1970; *Recreations* racehorses; *Style*— Paul Reed, Esq; 21 Crescent Road, Reigate, Surrey RH2 8HT (☎ 0737 245491); Merchant Navy Investment Management Ltd, 30 Finsbury Circus London EC2M 7QQ (☎ 01 588 6000, fax 01 588 1224)

REED, Dr William Leonard; s of William Alfred Reed (d 1949), of Dulwich, and Alice Kate, *née* Bloxam (d 1964); *b* 16 Oct 1910; *Educ* Dulwich, Guildhall Sch of Music, Jesus Coll Oxford (MA, DMus), RCM; *Career* Nat Fire Serv 1941-44; music lectr Br Cncl in Scandinavia and Finland 1937-39, music master Sloane Sch Chelsea 1945, tutor adult educn classes in music appreciation for Oxford delegacy for extra mural studies ILEA, and WEA 1962-, dir music Westminster Theatre Arts Centre 1967-80; compositions (with date of first BBC broadcasts) incl: Idyll for Small Orchestra (1936), Saraband for Orchestra (1936), Hornpipe for Orchestra (1938), Six Facets for Orchestra (1939), Fantasy for Piano Quartet (1940), Waltz Fantasy for Orchestra (1949), Scherzo for Orchestra (1970), Concert Overture for Orchestra (1981), Five Spiritual Songs for Baritone and Piano (1981), Fantasy for String Quartet (1985), Three Surrey Impressions for Two Pianos (1985), Prelude, Nocturne and Rhapsody for Piano (1988); Musicals: Annie (1967), Love All (1978); with other composers: The Vanishing Island (1955), The Crowning Experience (1958), High Diplomacy (1969); Freeman Worshipful Co of Musicians 1944; PRS; soc memb: Elgar, Delius, Sibelius, Dvorak, Sullivan, Haydn, Grainger, Johnson, Howells; *Books* ed: The Treasury of Christmas Music (1950), Music of Britain (1952), The Treasury of Easter Music (1963), The Second Treasury of Christmas Music (1967), jt ed: The Treasury of English Church Music (1965), The Treasury of Vocal Music (1969), National Anthems of the World (1978, 1985, 1987); *Recreations* photography; *Style*— Dr William Reed; Upper Suite No 7, The Quadrangle, Morden Coll, London SE3 OPW (☎ 01 305 0380)

REED-PURVIS, Air Vice-Marshal Henry; CB (1982), OBE (1972); *b* 1 July 1928; *Educ* King James I Sch, Durham Univ (BSc); *m* 1951, Isabel Price; 3 da (Jane, Sara, Shona); *Career* served RAF Regt in Iraq, Persian Gulf, Oman, Malaya, Borneo, Europe and N America; dir RAF Regt 1976-79; Cmdt-Gen RAF Regt and Dir-Gen Security (RAF) 1979-83, ret; sales dir British Aerospace Army Weapons Div 1983-; vice-pres: Cncl for Cadet Rifle Shooting; memb Exec Ctee The Forces Help Soc; Lord Roberts' Workshops; *Recreations* golf, archaeology, bridge; *Clubs* RAF; *Style*— Air Vice-Marshal Henry Reed-Purvis, CB, OBE; Westbury House, Ashwell, Herts (☎ 046 274 2075)

REEDAY, Thomas Geoffrey; s of Thomas Cockcroft Reeday (d 1947), and Marion, *née* Johnson (d 1975); *b* 20 July 1924; *Educ* Queen Elizabeth GS Wakefield, London Univ (LLB); *Career* WWII Army 1943-47; banker, lawyer, lectr; barr Lincoln's Inn 1954, head dept law PCL 1977-85, chief examiner in law relating to banking Inst of Bankers 1973-86; Liveryman Worshipful Co of Chartered Secs and Administrators 1978; FCIS 1978, FCIB 1982; *Books* Law Relating to Banking (fifth edn 1985), Legal Decision Affecting Bankers (co-ed vols 9 and 10 1988); *Recreations* railway preservation; *Style*— Geoffrey Reeday, Esq; 66 Lamorna Grove, Stanmore, Middx HA7 1PG (☎ 01 952 4591)

REEDER, Frederick John; s of Frederick Reeder, of Gravesend, Kent, and Susan Elizabeth, *née* Evans (d 1982); *b* 19 Nov 1936; *Educ* Coopers' Company's Sch; *m* 31 March 1962, Judy Barbara, da of Frank William Smith; 2 s (Paul b 1968, Mark b 1974), 1 da (Tracy b 1965); *Career* Nat Serv Br Army Singapore Malaya 1955-57; Commercial Union Properties Ltd: dir 1974-82, chm 1976-82 (UK); dir property invstmt Postel Invstmt Mgmnt 1982-; FRICS 1974, FSVA 1986; *Recreations* sailing; *Clubs* Les Ambassadeurs; *Style*— Frederick Reeder, Esq; Rocklands, Whitton, Twickenham; Standon House, 21 Mansell St, London E1 8AA (☎ 01 702 0888, fax 01 702 9453, telex 8956577 and 888947)

REES, Allen Brynmor; s of Allen Brynmor Rees, 74 Coleridge Ave, Penarth, S Glamorgan (d 1941), and Elsie Louise, *née* Hitchcock, (d 1956); *b* 11 May 1961; *Educ* Monmouth Sch, Univ of Wales Aberystwyth (LLB); *m* 26 Aug 1961, Nerys Eleanor, da of Wynne Evans, (d 1977), of Upper Maen, Meifod, Powys; 2 da (Meriel Anne Brynmor b 7 Oct 1968, Eleanor Haf Brynmor b 22 Aug 1975); *Career* sr ptnr: Darbey-Scott-Rees Slrs, Pages (incl internal legal dept of Midland News Assoc), Skidmore Hares and Co; chm W Mids Rent Assesment Panel 1968-, hd off slr to Birmingham Midshires Building Soc 1976-; chm: Socl Security Tbnls 1980-, Industl Tribunals 1982- (pt/t); writer of The Solicitors Notebook for the Slrs Jl 1968-, chm Bilston Round Table 1974 (memb 1966-77), pres exec ctee Old Monmothians 1977 (memb 1966-), pres Bilston Rotary Club 1984 and 1985 (memb 1974-); memb Legal Aid Area Ctee 1975-, Negligence Panel rep for Wolverhampton Area of Law Soc 1982-; memb Law Soc 1962; *Recreations* squash, canoeing, shooting, skiing, gardening; *Style*— Allen Rees, Esq; Rossleigh, Shaw Lane, Albrighton, Wolverhampton WV7 3DS; Yr Hen Ystabl, Meifod, Powys (☎ 090 722 2423); 17 Wellington Rd, West Midlands WV14 6AD; 44 Queen St, Wolverhampton WV1 3BN (☎ 0902 353535/0902 21241, fax 0902 353088/0902 25136, telex 338490 CHACOM G)

REES, Andrew Merfyn; s of Peter Donald Rees, and Rita Clarice, *née* Coleshaw;; *b* 20 July 1954; *Educ* Culford Sch, FitzWilliam Coll Cambridge (MA); *m* 11 Sept 1981, Monica, da of Rosman Gordon; 2 s (Richard b 1983, Charles b 1987); *Career* slr; Head of Corporate Services Evershed & Tomkinson 1988 (associate 1983, ptnr 1985); Law Soc; *Recreations* shooting, travel; *Style*— A M Rees, Esq; 10 Newhall St, Birmingham B3 3LX (☎ 021 233 2001, fax 021 236 1583)

REES, Arthur Morgan; QPM (1970), OBE (1963, CBE 1960), DL (Staffs 1967); s of Thomas Rees, of S Wales; *b* 20 Nov 1912; *Educ* Llandovery Coll, St Catharine's Coll Cambridge (rugby blue, BA, MA); *m* 1943, Dorothy, *née* Webb (d 1988); 1 da (Rosemary); *Career* RAF Pilot 1941-46, Substantive Sqdn-Ldr and actg Wing Cdr; chief constable: Denbighshire Constabulary 1956-64, Staffordshire & Stoke on Trent Police 1964-77; chm Midlands Sport Cncl 1967-77 (life memb Midlands Sports Advsy Cncl), conslt dir: Wales Britannia Building Soc 1983-87, Inter Globe Security Services Ltd 1985-; pres: (fndr) Ex Police in Indust and Commerce Soc, Queen's Silver Jubilee Appeal UK; chm: Crayshay's Welsh RFC 1962-, Staffs St John Cncl 1967-, Prince's Tst 1984-88, English Karati Bd, Br Karati Bd, Hawks Dinner Ctee 1986; pres: Eccleshall Rugby Club, Staffs Playing Fields Assoc 1986, Eccleshall RFC 1979-; dep pres Staffs Boys Club 1970-; former Rugby int (Wales), former sr rugby referee London Soc; KStJ; *Recreations* rugby, karate, hockey; *Clubs* RAF, Hawks Cambridge; *Style*— Wing Cdr Arthur Rees, CBE, QPM, DL; The Old Vicarage, Ellenhall, Stafford ST21 6JQ (☎ 0785 850789)

REES, Brian; s of Frederick Thomas Rees (d 1966), of Ashbrooke Road, Sunderland, and Anne, *née* Keedy (d 1976); *b* 20 August 1929; *Educ* Bede GS Sunderland, Trinity Coll Cambridge; *m* 1, 17 Dec 1959, Julia (d 1978), da of Sir Robert Birley, KCMG, FSA (d 1983), of Somerton, Somerset; 2 s (Robert Hugh Corrie b 13 April 1961, Philip Timothy b 28 Aug 1964), 3 da (Jessica Margaret Anne b 19 April 1963, Natalia Rachel b 24 Jan 1966, Camilla Marion b 2 April 1969); m 2, 3 Jan 1987, Juliet Mary Akehurst, da of C d'O Gowan; *Career* nat serv with RASC 1948-49; asst master Eton 1952-63, housemaster 1963-65; headmaster: Merchant Taylors' 1965-73, Charterhouse 1973-81, Rugby 1981-84; chm ISIS 1982-83; patron Conference for Independent Education 1983- (formerly pres); Liveryman Worshipful Co of Merchant Taylors; *Books* A Musical Peacemaker (Biography of Sir Edward German) (1987); *Recreations* music, painting, travel; *Clubs* Beefsteak; *Style*— Brian Rees Esq; 52 Spring Lane, Flore, Northants NN7 4LS (☎ 0327 41330); Le Manoir de Subarroques, Viens, 84750 Vaucluse, France

REES, Prof Brinley Roderick; s of John David Rees (d 1947), of Port Talbot, Wales, and Mary Ann, *née* Roderick (d 1976); *b* 27 Dec 1919; *Educ* Christ Coll Brecon, Merton Coll Oxford (MA, PhD); *m* 24 Aug 1951, Zena Muriel Stella, da of Alfred Reginald Mayall, of Leominster; 2 s ((Idris John) Mark b 1954, (Alan) Hugh b 1957); *Career* Welch Regt 1940-45, Capt 4 Welch Regt 1943, Capt/Adj 15 Welch Regt 1945; Univ Coll Cardiff: prof of Greek 1958-70, dean of arts 1963-65, dean of students 1968-69, hon lectr 1980-88, vice pres 1986-88; Univ of Birmingham: prof of Greek 1970-75, dean of arts 1973-75, life memb Univ Ct 1982-; St David's Univ Coll Lampeter: princ 1975-80, pres classical assoc 1978-79; emeritus prof 1981; Rotarian 1966-75, hon Rotarian 1975-; Hon LLD Univ of Wales 1981, Leverhulme emeritus fell 1984-86; *Books* The Merton Papyri, II (with Bell and Barns 1959), Papyri from Hermopolis and Elsewhere (1964), Lampas (with Jervis 1970), Classics for the Intending Student (ed 1970), Pelagius: A Reluctant Heretic (1988); *Recreations* walking, theology; *Style*— Prof Brinley Rees; 31 Stephenson Ct, Wordsworth Ave, Cardiff, S Glam CF2 1AX (☎ 0222 472 058)

REES, Prof Charles Wayne; s of Percival Charles Rees (d 1963), and Daisy Alice, *née* Beck (d 1941); *b* 15 Oct 1927; *Educ* Farnham GS, Univ Coll Southampton, Univ of London (BSc, PhD, DSc); *m* 19 Dec 1953, Patricia Mary, da of George Walter Francis; 3 s (David Charles b 1958, George Wayne b 1959, Michael Francis b 1961); *Career* lectr in organic chemistry: Birkbeck Coll London 1955-57, King's Coll London 1957-63 (reader 1963-65); prof of organic chemistry: Univ of Leicester 1965-69, Univ of Liverpool 1969-77 (Heath Harrison prof 1977-78); Hofman prof of organic chemistry

Imperial Coll London 1978-, visiting prof Univ of Würzburg 1968, lectr Royal Soc of Chemistry Tilden 1973-74 (Pedler lectr 1984-85), Award in Heterocyclic Chemistry 1980; Andrews lectr Univ NSW 1988, lectured widely in Australia, China, Japan and USA; pres Perkin Div 1981-83, pres chemistry section Br Assoc for the Advancement of Sci 1984; written and edited about 20 books and 300 res papers on organic chemistry; FRSC 1966, FRS 1974; *Recreations* food and wine, music, London; *Style*— Prof Charles Rees; 67 Hillgate Pl, London W8 7SS (☎ 01 229 5507); Chemistry Deptmt, Imperial Coll, London SW7 2AY (☎ 01 589 5111)

REES, Harland; s of Dr David Charles Rees, of Port Elizabeth, SA, and Myrtle May, *née* Dolley (d 1950); *b* 21 Sept 1909; *Educ* St Andrews Coll Grahamstown SA, Oxford Univ (BA, BM BCH, MA, MCH); *m* 20 May 1950, Helen Marie, da of John Ronald Tulloch Tarver (d 1963), of Wing, Buckinghamshire; 2 s (David b 1951, Martin b 1956), 1 da (Annabel b 1954, d 1976); *Career* Capt RAMC 1942, Maj 1944, Lt-Col 1945 (served India, Burma, Thailand); conslt surgn: St Peters Hosp 1947-62, Hampstead Gen Hosp 1947-74, King's Coll Hosp 1948-74; S Beds DC: parish cncllr, dist cncllr, chm 1986; chm Kensworth Cons Assoc; FRCS, BAUS; *Recreations* golf, previously rugby Oxford Univ; *Clubs* Vincents (Oxford); *Style*— Harland Rees, Esq; Kensworth Gorse, Kensworth, nr Dunstable, Bedfordshire LU6 3RF (☎ 0582 872 411)

REES, (Thomas Morgan) Haydn; CBE (1975), JP (Mold 1977), DL (Flints 1969, Clwyd 1974); s of late Thomas Rees, of Gorseinon, Swansea, and Mary, *née* Bowen; *b* 22 May 1915; *Educ* Swansea Business Coll; *m* 12 July 1941, Marion, da of A B Beer, of Mumbles, Swansea; 1 da ((Elizabeth) Maryon Haydn (Mrs Hughes)); *Career* served WWII 1939-45; slr 1946, se asst slr Caernarvonshire CC 1947; Flints CC 1948-74: dep clerk, Clerk of the Peace (until office abolished 1971, formerly dep clerk), clerk Police Authy (until merger with N Wales Police Authy 1947, formerly dep clerk), clerk Magistrates Cts Ctee (formerly dep clerk), clerk Probation Ctee (formerly dep clerk), clerk Justices Advsy Ctee, chief exec, Clerk to Lieutenancy; Clwyd CC 1974-77: chief exec, clerk Magistrates Cts Ctee, clerk Justice Advsy Ctee, Clerk to Lieutenancy; clerk N Wales Police Authy 1967-77, sec Welsh Counties Ctee 1968-77, asst cmmr Royal Cmmn on Constitution 1969-73; memb: Welsh Cncl 1968-79, Welsh Arts Cncl 1968-77 (memb regal ctee 1981-), Lord Chllr's Ctee for Wales and Chester circuit 1972-77, Prince of Wales Ctee 1976-79, Gorsedd Royal National Eisteddfod of Wales, Nat Water Cncl 1977-82, Water Space Amenity Cmmn 1977-82, Severn Bridge Ctee 1978-81, Theatre Clwyd Govrs 1983-(clerk 1974-77); pt/t memb bd BSC (Indust) Ltd 1979-83; chm Govt Quality of Life Experiment in Clwyd 1974-76, Welsh Water Authy 1977-82, New Jobs Team Shotton Steelworks 1977-82, N Wales Arts Assoc 1981-, Deeside Enterprise Tst Ltd 1982-; *Recreations* the arts, golf; *Clubs* Mold GC; *Style*— Hadyn Rees, Esq, CBE, JP, DL; Cefn Bryn, Gwernaffield Rd, Mold, Clwyd CH7 1RQ (☎ 0352 2421)

REES, Prof Hubert; DFC (1944); s of Owen Rees (d 1970), and Evelyn Togela, *née* Bowen; *b* 2 Oct 1923; *Educ* Llandovery and Llenelli Co Sch, Univ Coll Wales (BSc), Univ Birmingham (PhD, DSc); *m* 26 Dec 1946, Mavis Rosalind, da of Roland Hill; 2 s (Wynne d 1977, Hubert), 2 da (Gwyneth, Judith); *Career* RAFVR 1942-46; lectr genetics dept Univ of Birmingham 1950-59; dept of agric botany Univ Coll of Wales: sr lectr 1959, reader 1966, prof 1967-; FRS 1976; *Recreations* fishing; *Style*— Prof Hubert Rees, DFC; Irfon, Llanbadarn Rd, Aberystwyth (☎ 0970 623 668); Univ Coll of Wales, Abertstwyth (☎ 0970 623 111)

REES, Very Rev (John) Ivor; s of David Morgan Rees (d 1928), and Cecilia Maria Perrott (d 1955), *née* Evans; *b* 19 Feb 1926; *Educ* Llanelli GS; Univ Coll of Wales (BA); Westcott House Cambridge; *m* 5 Aug 1954, Beverley, da of Henry Albert Richards, Co Sergeant-Major, (d 1946); 3 s ((Christopher) Meirion b 1956, (David) Mark b 1958, Stephen Wynne b 1963); *Career* RN, Coastal forces and Pacific fleet 1943-7; curate: Fishguard 1952-5, Llangathen 1955-7; vicar: Slebech & Uzmarton 1957-65 (p in c 1957-9), Llangollen 1965-74; rector Wrexham 1974-6; canon St Asaph 1975-6; Dean of Bangor Cathedral 1976-, vicar of the cathedral parish of Bangor 1979-; OStJ 1981; *Books* The Parish of Llangollen and its Churches (1971); *Recreations* good music, light reading; *Style*— The Rt Rev the Dean of Bangor; The Deanery, Bangor, Gwynedd LL57 1LH (☎ 0248 370693)

REES, Jeremy John; s of John Louis Rees, of Gloucs, and June Rosamond, *née* Lloyd; *b* 13 Feb 1955; *Educ* Felsted, Univ of Southampton (LLB); *m* 26 April 1980, Fiona Michelle, da of Michael Hudelist, of Perth, Aust; 2 s (James b 1984, David b 1987); *Career* Peat Marwick Mitchell & Co 1976-81, dir IBJ Int Ltd 1986-(joined 1981); ACA 1979; *Recreations* cricket, hockey, squash, skiing (snow and water), gardening; *Style*— Jeremy Rees, Esq; Bucklersbury House, 3 Queen Victoria St, London EC4N 8HR (☎ 01 236 1090)

REES, John Samuel; s of John Richard Rees and Mary Jane Rees; *b* 23 Oct 1931; *Educ* Cyfarthfa Castle GS Merthyr Tydfil; *m* 1 June 1957, Ruth Jewell; 1 s (Paul b 1961), 1 da (Diane b 1962); *Career* Nat Serv Welsh Regt and RAEC 1950-52, sports ed Merthyr Express 1952-54 (reporter 1948-50); The Star Sheffield: reporter 1954-56, sub-ed 1956-58, dep chief sub-ed 1958-60, dep sports ed 1960-62, asst ed 1962-66, dep ed Evening Echo, Hemel Hempstead 1966-69; ed: Evening Mail Slough & Hounslow 1969-72, The Journal Newcastle-upon-Tyne 1972-76, Evening Post-Echo Hemel Hempstead 1976-79; asst md Evening Post-Echo Ltd 1979-81, ed Western Mail Cardiff 1981-88, editorial conslt 1988-; *Recreations* marquetry, watching cricket and rugby, walking, gardening; *Style*— John Rees, Esq; Timbertops, St Andrew's Road, Dinas Powys, S Glam CF6 4HB (☎ 0222 513254)

REES, Rt Rev (Leslie) Lloyd; s of Rees Thomas Rees (d 1939), of Trebanos, Swansea, Glam, and Elizabeth Rees (d 1965); *b* 14 April 1919; *Educ* Pontardawe GS, Kelham Theol Coll; *m* 5 Feb 1944, Rosamund, da of Thomas Smith (d 1960); 2 s (Christopher Michael b 1946, Gerald Hugh b 1948); *Career* curate St Saviour's Roath Cardiff and asst chaplain HM Prison Cardiff 1942-45; chaplain: HM Prison Durham 1945-48, HM Prison Dartmoor (and vicar of Princetown) 1948-55, HM Prison Winchester 1955-62; chaplain gen of Prisons, hon canon of Canterbury, chaplain to HM The Queen 1962-80, bishop of Shrewsbury 1980-86, hon canon Lichfield 1980-86, asst bishop diocese of Winchester 1986-; chaplain OStJ; Freedom of the City of London; Hon DLitt Geneva Theol Coll; *Recreations* music; *Style*— The Rt Rev L Lloyd Rees; Kingfisher Lodge, 20 Arle Gardens, Alresford, Hants (☎ 0962 734619)

REES, Prof Martin John; s of Reginald Jackson Rees, and Harriete Joan, *née* Bett (d 1985); *b* 23 June 1942; *Educ* Shrewsbury, Trinity Coll Cambridge (MA, PhD); *Career* prof Sussex Univ 1972-73, Plumian prof of astronomy and experimental philosophy Cambridge Univ 1973-, dir Cambridge Inst of Astronomy 1977-, Regents fell Smithsonian Inst Washington 1984-, visiting prof Harvard Univ; FRS, For Assoc US Nat Acad Sci; *Recreations* rural pursuits; *Style*— Prof Martin Rees; c/o King's Coll, Cambridge, Cambs CB2 1ST

REES, Rt Hon Merlyn; PC (1974), MP (Lab) Morley and Leeds South 1983-; s of L Rees; *b* 18 Dec 1920; *Educ* Harrow Weald GS, Goldsmiths' Coll London Univ, LSE, London U Inst of Educn; *m* 1949, Colleen Faith, *née* Cleveley; 3 s; *Career* served WW II RAF; schoolmaster (economics and history) 1949-60, economics lecturer 1962-63; fought (Lab) Harrow E 1955, 1959 (twice: general and by-election); MP (Lab) S Leeds 1963-1983, PPS to chllr Exchequer 1964, parly under-sec MOD (Army) 1965-66 and (RAF) 1966-68, Home Off 1968-70; memb Shadow Cabinet 1972-74 and again 1980-, oppn spokesman NI 1972-74, NI Sec 1974-76, Home Sec 1976-79, shadow Home Sec 1979-81, oppn front bench spokesman Energy 1981-83, memb: Franks Ctee on Official Secrets Act 1972, Franks Ctee on Falklands 1982; Published Northern Ireland, A Personal Perspective (1985); hon DLL Univ of Wales; *Style*— The Rt Hon Merlyn Rees, MP; House of Commons, London SW1A 0AA

REES, Rev (Richard) Michael; s of Rev Richard Rees (d 1975), of Bedford, and Margaret Patricia, *née* Head; *b* 31 July 1935; *Educ* Brighton Coll, St Peter's Coll Oxford (MA), Tyndale Hall Bristol; *m* 6 Sept 1958, Yoma Patricia, da of Maj the Rev Cyril Herbert Hampton, of Branksome Park; 2 s (Timothy b 1960, Killadeas b 1961); *Career* editor Missionary Mandate 1956-69; curate: All Saints Crowborough Sussex 1959-62, Christ Church with Emmanuel Clifton Bristol 1962-64; chaplain Bristol ATC 1963-64, vicar Christ Church Clevedon Avon 1964-72, chaplain Clevedon Maternity Hosp, vicar Holy Trinity Church Cambridge 1972-84, chm Cambridge Cncl of Churches, chief sec Church Army 1984-; tstee: Disabled Christians Fellowship 1962-(chm 1962-72), Cambridge Work Relations Gp 1984-, Simeon's Tstees 1969-; govr St Brandon's Sch Clevedon 1969-87; *Recreations* photography, tropical fish, classical music; *Style*— The Rev Michael Rees; 6 Pickwick Way, Chislehurst, Kent BR7 6RZ (☎ 01 467 9167); The Chief Secretary, Church Army, Independents Road, Blackheath, London SE3 9LG (☎ 01 318 1226, fax 01 318 5258)

REES, Owen; s of John Trevor Rees (d 1970), of Trimsaran Dyfed, and Esther (d 1977), *née* Phillips; *b* 26 Dec 1934; *Educ* Llanelli GS, Manchester Univ (BA); *m* 17 May 1958, Elizabeth, da of Harold Frank Gosby (d 1955), of Henley-on-Thames and Trimsaran; 1 s (David), 2 da (Philippa, Helen); *Career* civil servant: Bd of Trade 1959-69; Cabinet Off 1969-71; Welsh Off 1971-; head of Euro Div Welsh Off 1972-75; sec for Welsh Educn 1977-78; head of Educn Dept 1978-80; dir Indust Dept 1980-85; head of Econ and Regnl Policy Gp 1985-; *Style*— Owen Rees, Esq; Welsh Office, Cathays Park, Cardiff (☎ 0222 825245)

REES, Baron (Life Peer UK 1987), of Goytre, Co Gwent; Peter Wynford Innes Rees; PC (1983), QC (1969); s of Maj-Gen Thomas Wynford Rees, CB, CIE, DSO, MC, Indian Army (d 1959), of Goytre Hall, Abergavenny, and Rosalie, da of Hon Sir Charles Alexander Innes, KCSI, CIE (d 1959); *b* 9 Dec 1926; *Educ* Stowe, Ch Ch Oxford; *m* 1969, Mrs Anthea Wendell, da of late Maj J M Hyslop, Argyll & Sutherland Highlanders; *Career* served Scots Gds 1945-48; barr 1953, practised Oxford circuit; contested (C) Abertillery 1964 and 1965, Liverpool, West Derby, 1966; MP (C) Dover 1970-74, Dover and Deal 1974-83, Dover 1983-87; pps to solicitor-gen 1972; min state HM Treasury 1979-81; min for Trade 1981-83, ch sec to Treasury and memb Cabinet 1983-85; memb court and cncl Museum of Wales; *Clubs* Boodle's, Beefsteak; *Style*— The Rt Hon Lord Rees, PC, QC; Goytre Hall, Abergavenny, Gwent; 39 Headfort Place, London SW1A 0AA

REES, Philip; s of John Trevor Rees, of Ebbw Vale, Gwent, and Olwen Muriel, *née* Jones (d 1982); *b* 1 Dec 1941; *Educ* Monmouth Sch, Bristol Univ (LLB Hons); *m* 6 Aug 1969, Catherine, da of Joseph Stephen Good, of Cardiff; 1 s (David Stephen b 27 Aug 1970), 1 da (Siân Catrin b 1 Oct 1973); *Career* barr; Recorder of the Crown Ct 1983-; *Recreations* music, sport; *Clubs* Cardiff and County; *Style*— Philip Rees, Esq; 35 South Rise, Llanishen, Cardiff CF4 5RF (☎ 0222 754364); 34 Park Place, Cardiff CF1 3BA (☎ 0222 382731, fax 0222/22542)

REES, Dr Richard John William; CMG (1979); s of William Rees, MVO (d 1952), of London, and Gertrude Ethel, *née* Smith (d 1959); *b* 11 August 1917; *Educ* E Sheen County Sch, London Univ, Guys Hosp, Med Sch (BSc, MB, BS, FRC, Path, FRCP); *m* 1942, Kathleen, da of Joseph Harris, MVO (d 1967), of Yorks; 3 da (Lorna, Hazel, Diana); *Career* Capt RAMC Army Blood Transfusion Service, served in N Africa and Italy campaigns 1942-46; asst clinical pathologist Guy's Hosp 1946-49, memb Scientific Staff Nat Inst of Med Res London 1949-69, head of laboratory for Leprosy and mycubacterial res Nat Inst Med Res 1969-82, chm Lepra Med Advsy Bd 1963-1987; pres Section of Comparative Med Royal Soc of Med 1975; vice-pres: Lepra Exec Ctee 1964-87, Int Leprosy Assoc 1988; memb MRC Tropical Med Res Bd 1968-72, WHO, Advsy Panel on leprosy 1969-, editorial bd of Leprosy Reviews 1960-; Section of Comparative Med 1983; hon fell RSM; *Publications* more than 200 Scientific papers on: basic and applied studies on animals and man relevant to pathology, immunology and chemotherapy of leprosy and tuberculosis; *Recreations* theatre, gardening; *Style*— Dr Dick Rees, CMG; Highfield, Highwood Hill, London NW7 4EU (☎ 01 959 2021)

REES, Dr (Robert) Simon Owen; s of Edward Bertram Rees (d 1985), of Carmarthen, Dyfed, and Dorothy, *née* Owen; *b* 24 May 1933; *Educ* Harrow, Gonville and Caius Coll Cambridge (MA, MB, BChir), Westminster Med Sch London Univ; *m* 13 Dec 1958, Dr Jacqueline Jane, da of James Layton, of Hampstead, London; 3 s (Rupert b 18 Aug 1962, Jasper b 7 Dec 1964, Sheridan b 13 March 1967); *Career* conslt radiologist Nat Heart Hosp London W1 1966-, conslt radiologist St Bartholomews Hosp London EC1 1967-88, dean inst of cardiology Univ of London 1969-72, hon sr lectr nat heart and lung inst Univ of London 1972-, chm med ctee Nat Heart Hosp 1982-84, conslt radiologist magnetic resonance unit Nat Heart and Chest Hosps 1985-(chm scientific advsy and policy ctee 1983-), conslt radiologist Brompton Hosp London SW3 1988-, govr Med Coll St Bartholomew's Hosp 1988-, dir of radiology Brompton and Nat Heart Hosps 1988-; Freeman City of London 1964, Liveryman Worshipful Co of Apothecaries 1964; memb Br Cardiac Soc, Br Inst of Radiology; FRCP, FRCR, FRSM; *Books* Clinical Cardiac Radiology (1973, 2 ed 1980); *Recreations* riding, hunting, real tennis, choral singing, skiing ; *Clubs* Boodle's, MCC; *Style*— Dr Simon Rees; Rubbin Cottage, Treyford, Midhurst, West Sussex GU29 0LD (☎ 0730 825444; 121 Harley St, London W1 (☎ 01 935 1918, 01 935 7541)

REES, Sir (Charles William) Stanley; TD (1950), QC (1957), DL (Sussex 1968); s of Dr David Charles Rees (d 1917); first supt and med tutor to London Sch of Tropical

Medicine (went to S Africa in 1901 at invitation of Cape Govt to deal with outbreak of bubonic plague, where he remained until his death from typhus), and Myrtle May, *née* Dolley (d 1950); *b* 30 Nov 1907; *Educ* St Andrew's Coll Grahamstown S Africa, Univ Coll Oxford (BA, BCL); *m* 1934, Jean Isabel (d 1985), da of Laurence Henry Munro (d 1906), of Melbourne, Aust; 1 s; *Career* 2 Lt 99 Anti-Aircraft RA Regt (London Welsh) 1939, Capt 1940, JAG's Office in Home Cmd 1940-43, Lt-Col 1943, i/c JAG's branch HQ Palestine Cmd 1944-45, ret as Hon Lt-Col 1945; barr Inner Temple 1931, rec of Croydon 1961-62, bencher 1962, Judge of the High Ct of Justice Family Div (formerly Probate, Divorce and Admty Div) 1962-77, chm E Sussex QS 1964-70 (dep chm 1959-64); vice patron Brighton Coll 1983- (govr 1954-83, pres 1974-83), chm Statutory Pharmaceutical Soc of GB 1980-81; kt 1962; *Recreations* walking, gardening; *Clubs* United Oxford and Cambridge, Sussex; *Style*— Sir Stanley Rees, QC, TD, DL; Lark Rise, Lyoth Lane, Lindfield, Haywards Heath, Sussex RH16 2QA (☎ 044 47 2049)

REES, William Howard Guest; CB (1988); s of Walter Guest Rees (d 1967), of S Wales, and Margaret Elizabeth, *née* Harries (d 1978); *b* 21 May 1928; *Educ* Llanelli GS, Royal Veterinary Coll, London Univ (BSc, MRCVS, DVSM); *m* 1952, Charlotte Mollie, da of Enoch Collins (d 1979), of S Wales; 3 s (Michael, Nicholas, Alan), 1 da (Amanda); *Career* veterinary surg; chief veterinary offr; min of agric fisheries & food 1980-88; *Recreations* golf; *Clubs* Pennard Golf (S Wales), Tyrrells Wood (Leatherhead); *Style*— Howard Rees, Esq, CB; Tallesin, Paddocks Way, Ashtead, Surrey (☎ 0372 276 522)

REES, William Hurst; s of Richard Rees (d 1956), of Bushey, Herts, and Florence Ada, *née* Bonner (d 1975); *b* 12 April 1917; *Educ* Watford GS, Coll Estate Mgmnt London (BSc); *m* 15 Feb 1941, Elizabeth Mary, da of Dr A Wight (d 1975), of Reading; 2 s (William Andrew b 6 Feb 1944, John Hurst b 12 Feb 1948), 1 da (Jacqueline (Mrs Padley) b 8 Feb 1950); *Career* Army 1940-46, cmmd 2 Lt RA 1941, transferred RE 1943, liaison offr Belgian Army Engrs SO 2 RE, Maj RE 1946; head valuation dept Coll of Estate Mgmnt 1946-51; princ in private practice: Richard Ellis & Son London 1951-61, Turner Rudge & Turner E Grinstead Sussex 1961-73; memb Lands Tbnl 1973-; hon FSVA, hon memb Rating Surveyor's Assoc; FRICS; *Books* Modern Methods of Valuation (co-author, 6 edn 1970), Valuation: Principles into Practice (ed, 3 edn 1988); *Recreations* music, opera; *Style*— W H Rees, Esq; Brendon, Carlton Rd, S Godstone, Surrey RH9 8LD (☎ 0342 892 109)

REES, Prof William Linford Llewelyn; CBE (1977); s of Edward Parry Rees (d 1947), and Mary Rees (d 1952); *b* 24 Oct 1914; *Educ* Llanelli GS, Univ Coll Cardiff (BSc), Welsh Nat Sch of Medicine (MB, BCh), London Univ (DSc); *m* 1940, Catherine Magdalen, da of David Thomas Alltwen (d 1941); 2 s, 3 da; *Career* emeritus prof of Psychiatry London Univ, conslt physician St Barts Hosp 1980-, civilian conslt psychiatry to RAF to 1983; tres World Psychiatric Assoc 1966-78, vice pres Psychiatric Rehabilitation Assoc, pres Royal Coll of Psychiatrists 1975-78, pres BMA 1978-79, chm Stress Fndn (vice pres) and Medico-Pharmaceutical Forum 1980, psychiatrist in chief and executive medical dir to Charter Medical 1984-; Liveryman Barber Surgeons Worshipful Co, Worshipful Soc Apothecaries; Hon FRCPsych, distinguished fell American Psychiatric Assoc 1968, hon fell American Coll of Psychiatrists 1977; Hon LLD Univ of Wales; FRCP; *Recreations* photography, entertaining grandchildren, gardening, swimming; *Clubs* Athenaeum; *Style*— Prof William Rees, CBE; 62 Oakwood Ave, Purley, Surrey; 27 Speed House, Barbican, London EC1 (☎ 01 588 4881)

REES ROBERTS, Tristan William Otway; s of Peter William Rees Roberts, of Hants, and Ursula Vivien, *née* McCannell; *b* 11 April 1948; *Educ* Frensham Heights, Farnham GS, Trinity Hall Cambridge (MA, BArch, Dip Arch); *m* 21 March 1970, Anna Ingelin, da of Edmund George Noel Greaves, of Cambridge; 1 s (Marcus Lucien Branch b 1975), 2 da (Saria Mona Natascha b 1973, Ariana Lucia Katrina b 1979); *Career* architect in private practice with Henry Freeland 1980-; most important cmmns: Kings Coll, Temple Bar, Thorpe Hall, Bishop's Palace Ely; Freeman City of London 1986; *Books* painting, hill walking; *Style*— Tristan Rees Roberts, Esq; 13 Caius Terr, Glisson Rd, Cambridge CB1 2HJ (☎ 0223 68101); Freeland Rees Roberts Architects, 25 City Rd, Cambridge (☎ 0223 66555)

REES-DAVIES, William (Billy) Rupert; QC (1973); s of Sir William Rees-Davies, KC, JP, DL (sometime Lib MP for Pembroke and chief justice Hong Kong, d 1939); *b* 19 Nov 1916; *Educ* Eton, Trinity Coll Cambridge; *m* 1, 1959, Jane Lesa, yr da of Henry Mander, of Kensington; 2 da; m 2, 1982, Sharlie Kingsley; *Career* served WW II Welsh Gds; barr Inner Temple 1939; MP (C): Isle of Thanet 1953-74, Thanet W 1974-83; chm: All Party Ctee Tourism 1965-68, Cons Ctee Tourism; Cons ldr Select Ctee Health and Social Services 1980-83; *Clubs* MCC, Hawks; *Style*— William Rees-Davies Esq, QC; 5 Paper Buildings, Temple, London EC4 (☎ 01 583 3724); 5 Lord North St, London SW1

REES-MOGG, Baron Rees-Mogg (Life Peer UK 1988), of Hinton Blewitt, Co Avon; William Rees-Mogg; s of late Edmund Fletcher Rees-Mogg, JP (of a Somerset family of landowners extant since the thirteenth century), and Beatrice, da of Daniel Warren, of New York State, USA; *b* 14 July 1928; *Educ* Charterhouse, Balliol Coll Oxford; *m* 1962, Gillian Shakespeare Morris, da of T R Morris; 2 s, 3 da; *Career* dir: GEC, M & G Group; chm: Pickering & Chatto (antiquarian booksellers & publishers); Sidgwick & Jackson (publishers) 1985-88; editor The Times 1967-81; dir: The Times 1968-, Times Newspapers Ltd 1978, GEC; vice-chm BBC 1981-; chm: Arts Cncl 1982-; Broadcasting Standards Cncl 1988-; High Sheriff Somerset 1978; kt 1981; *Books* An Humbler Heaven (1977), The Reigning Error: The Crisis of World Inflation (1974), Blood in the Streets (1987); *Clubs* Garrick, Carlton; *Style*— The Rt Hon Lord Rees-Mogg; The Old Rectory, Hinton Blewitt, nr Bristol, Avon (☎ 0761 52489); 3 Smith Sq, London SW1; Pickering & Chatto Ltd, 17 Pall Mall, London SW1Y 5NB (☎ 01 930 2515)

REES-WILLIAMS, Hon Morgan; s of 1 Baron Ogmore, TD, PC (d 1976) and hp of bro, 2 Baron; *b* 19 Dec 1937; *Educ* Mill Hill Sch; *m* 1, 1964 (m dis 1970), Patricia, da of C Paris Jones; m 2, 1972 (m dis 1976), Roberta, da of Capt Alec Stratford Cunningham-Reid, DFC; *Career* Lt R Regt of Wales (TA); *Style*— The Hon Morgan Rees-Williams; Flat 6, 98 Elm Park Gdns, SW10

REESE, Dr Alan John Morris; TD (1958; clasps: 1964, 1970, 1976), JP (Middx 1974);; s of Joseph Reese (d 1968), of Plymouth, Devon, and Emily, *née* Brand (d 1984); *b* 26 August 1920; *Educ* Plymouth Coll, St Barts Hosp Med Coll Univ of London (MB, BS, MD) ; *m* 24 Jan 1959, Margaret Denise, da of Ernest George Turner (d 1969), of Battersea, London; 1 s (Charles b 1962), 1 da (Victoria b 1960); *Career* emergency cmmn RAMC 1945; served: Egypt, Cyrenaica, Palestine, Malta; war substantive Capt 1946, released 1948; TA: Capt 1948, Maj 1953, Lt Col 1966; TAVR 1967, Lt Col RARO; sr registrar in pathology St Georges Hosp London 1950-54; lectr in Pathology Univ of Bristol 1954-56, sr lectr in pathology Inst of Basic Med Scis Univ of London, RCS 1956-82; WHO prof of pathology Univ of Mandalay Burma 1963-64, hon cnslt in morbid anatomy Whittington Hosp 1966-82, senate of Univ of London 1974-83; examiner in pathology: RCS 1973-79, RCS Ed 1978-; barr Middle Temple: memb Islington Cons Assoc 1960-, contested seats on Islington Borough Cncl, vice pres Islington S and Finsbury Cons Assoc 1987-, contested Lewisham W on ILEA 1986, Cons Chcllr and chm health ctee Met Borough of St Pancreas 1959-62; govr Godolphin and Latymer Sch 1976-85 OSTJ 1974; Freeman City of London 1944, Liveryman Worshipful Soc of Apothecaries 1948- (Yeoman 1943-48); MRC Path 1963, FRC Path 1968, LMSSA 1943; *Books* The Principles of Pathology (1981); *Recreations* fishing; *Clubs* Army and Navy; *Style*— Dr Alan Reese, TD, JP; 9 Hopping La, Canonbury, London N1 2NU (☎ 01 226 2088); 14 Herd St, Marlborough, Wilts SN8 1DF (☎ 0672 52339)

REESE, Colin Bernard; s of Joseph Reese (d 1968), of London, and Emily Reese (d 1984); *b* 29 July 1930; *Educ* Dartington Hall Sch, Clare Coll Cambridge (BA, PhD, MA, ScD); *m* 29 June 1968, Susanne Leslie, da of Joseph Charles Henry Bird (d 1985); 1 s (William Thomas b 11 July 1972), 1 da (Lucy b 13 Aug 1970); *Career* res fell: Clare Coll Cambridge 1956-59, Harvard Univ 1957-58; Univ demonstrator in chemistry Cambridge Univ 1959-63, official fell and dir of studies in chemistry Clare Coll 1959-73; Cambridge Univ: asst dir of res 1963-64, lectr in chemistry 1964-73; Daniell prof of chemistry King's Coll London 1973-; FRS 1981; *Style*— Prof Colin Reese; 21 Rozel Rd, London SW4 0EY (☎ 01 498 0230); Dept of Chem, King's Coll London, Strand, London WC2R 2LS (☎ 01 836 5454)

REEVE, Anthony; CMG (1986); s of Sidney Reeve, of Cheltenham, Glos, and Dorothy, *née* Mitchell; *b* 20 Oct 1938; *Educ* Queen Elizabeth GS Wakefield, Marling Sch Stroud, Merton Coll Oxford (MA); *m* 1 Feb 1964 (m dis 1988) Pamela Margaret Angus; 1 s (James b 1968), 2 da (Emily b 1972, Anna b 1977); *Career* Lever Bros and Assoc 1962-65; joined HM Dip Serv 1965: MECAS 1966-68, asst political agent Abu Dhabi 1968-70, FCO 1970-73, first sec (later cnsllr) Washington 1973-78, cnsllr: FCO 1978-81, Cairo 1981-84 (asst under sec of state) FCO 1984-88, HM ambass to the Hashemite Kingdom of Jordan 1988-; *Recreations* writing, music; *Clubs* United Oxford and Cambridge, Leander; *Style*— Anthony Reeve, Esq, CMG; c/o FCO (Amman), King Charles St, London SW1A 2AH

REEVE, Carol Ann; da of John Reeve, and Hilda, *née* Foxall; *b* 26 May 1950; *Educ* Westcliff HS For Girls; *Career* dir and co sec Talk of the South Ltd 1986- (joined 1972), dir Essex Radio plc 1979-, co sec Manzi Leisure Ltd 1986-; *Style*— Ms Carol Reeve; 42 Springfield Drive, Westcliff On Sea, Essex SSO ORA (☎ 0702 348 707); Talk Of The South, Lucy Rd, Southend-on-Sea SS1 2AN (☎ 0702 679 21); Essex Radio, Clifftown Rd, Southend-on-Sea SS1 1SX

REEVE, James Ernest; CMG (1982); s of Ernest Stanley Reeve (d 1970), of Surrey, and Margaret Anthea, *née* James (d 1939); *b* 8 June 1926; *Educ* Bishop's Stortford Coll Herts; *m* 20 Aug 1947, Lillian Irene, da of Capt Albert Edward Watkins, OBE, of Epsom, Surrey; 1 s (Christopher b 30 April 1953), 1 da (Sandra b 8 Oct 1955); *Career* HM Dip Serv 1949-83: HM vice-consul Ahwaz and Khorramshahr Iran 1949-51, UN Gen Assembly Paris 1951, private sec to Rt Hon Selwyn Lloyd FO 1951-53, HM Embassy Washington 1953-57, HM Embassy Bangkok 1957-59, Northern Dept FO 1959-61, HM consul Frankfurt W Germany 1961-65, sec HM Embassy Libya 1965-69, 1 sec HM Embassy Budapest 1970-72, chargé d'affaires and csllr for estab of first Br Embassy to GDR E Berlin 1973-75, HM consul gen Zurich and Liechtenstein 1975-80, HM min and consul gen Milan 1980-83; dir Sprester Investmts Ltd 1983-; memb secretariat int of Aluminium Inst London 1983-; *Recreations* theatre, tennis, skiing, travel; *Clubs* RAC; *Style*— James Reeve, Esq, CMG; 20 Glenmore House, Richmond Hill, Richmond, Surrey (☎ 01 948 3153); c/o New Zealand House, (PAI), Haymarket, London SW1 (☎ 01 930 0528)

REEVE, Michael Arthur Ferard; s of Maj Wilfrid Norman Reeve, OBE, MC (d 1976), of 6 Bramerton St, London, and Agnes Bourdon, *née* Ferard; *b* 7 Jan 1937; *Educ* Eton, Univ Coll Oxford (MA); *m* 30 Dec 1970, Charmian Gay, da of David Roydon Rooper, of 5 Albert Place London; 2 s (Hugo b 10 Dec 1973, Luke b 15 Sept 1977); *Career* dir: Elliott Gp of Peterborough 1969-83, Charterhouse Bank 1970-74, Rea Bros 1977-80, Collins Collins & Rawlence (Hamptons estate agents) 1982-85, underwriter Lloyds 1978; md Copley & Bank 1974-80, Greyhound Bank 1981-87; pres Laneast & Truin Cons Assoc; memb: Royal Inst of Int Affairs, The Pilgrims; FCA 1964; *Recreations* horses, gardening, reading; *Clubs* Institute of Directors, Overseas League; *Style*— Michael Reeve, Esq; Tregeare, Launceston, Cornwall (☎ 056 686 732)

REEVE, Robin Martin; s of Percy Martin Reeve, of Lancing, W Sussex, and Cicely Nora, *née* Parker; *b* 22 Nov 1934; *Educ* Hampton Sch, Gonville and Caius Coll Cambridge (BA, MA), Univ of Bristol (PGCE); *m* 25 July 1959, Brianne Ruth, da of Leonard Stephen Hall (d 1953), of Ashford, Middx; *Career* asst master: Kings Coll Sch 1958-62 (headmaster 1980-), Lancing Coll 1962-80 (head of history dept 1962-80, dir of studies 1975); chm govrs of Rosemead Sch W Sussex; HMC 1980-, SHA; *Recreations* gardening, architecture, reading; *Clubs* East India, Public Schs; *Style*— Robin Reeve, Esq; 20 Burghley Rd, London SW19 5BH (☎ 01 947 3190); King's Coll Sch, Southside, Wimbledon Common, London SW19 4TT (☎ 01 947 9311)

REEVE, Sir (Charles) Trevor; QC (1965); s of William George Reeve (d 1918), and Elsie *née* Bowring (d 1952), of Wokingham, Berks (d 1918); *b* 4 July 1915; *Educ* Winchester, Trinity Coll Oxford; *m* 1941, Marjorie, da of Charles Evelyn Browne, of Eccles, Lancs; *Career* served WWII, Maj 10 Royal Hussars (PWO), BEF, MEF and CMF, GSO (2) (SD) 10 Corps (despatches), Staff Coll Camberley 1945; barr Inner Temple 1946, bencher 1965, county ct judge 1968, circuit judge 1972, judge of the High Court of Justice (Family Div) 1973-88; kt 1973; *Clubs* Garrick, Royal North Devon GC, Sunningdale GC; *Style*— Sir Trevor Reeve, QC; 95 Abingdon Rd, Kensington, London W8 6QU

REEVES, Anthony Alan; s of Allen Joseph Reeves, MBE, (d 1976), and Alice Turner, *née* Pointon (d 1966); *b* 5 Mar 1943; *Educ* Hanley HS, Coll of Law; *m* 19 Aug 1967, Jane, da of William Thowless (d 1942); 1 s (Max b 1972), 2 da (Rachel b 1969, Ruth b 1974); *Career* slr 1965, managing ptnr Kent Jones and Done Slrs 1978; non-exec dir: Steelite Int plc 1983-, Bullers plc 1984-86, PMT Ltd 1987-; chm The CAS

Gp plc 1985-; sr tstee The Beth Johnson Fndn 1972-, memb N Staffs Med Inst Cncl 1979-82, non-exec dir Stoke City FC 1984-85, chm Law Soc Woking Party Coal Mining Subsidence 1985-; Law Soc; *Recreations* fishing, shooting, ballet, contemporary art; *Style*— Anthony Reeves, Esq; Churchill House, 47 Regent Road, Hanley, Stoke-on-Trent ST1 3RQ (☎ 0782 202020, fax 0782 202040, car 0836 726633, telex 36468)

REEVES, Anthony Henry; s of Herbert Henry Reeves, of Limpsfield Chart, Surrey, and Kathleen Norah Reeves (d 1963); *b* 8 Sept 1940; *Educ* Sir Walter St Johns; *m* 1972, Jacqueline, da of Herbert Mitchell Newton-Clare, of Edgeworth, Cirencester; 2 s, 1 da; *Career* former dir Alfred Marks Bureau Ltd, founded Graphics Staff Agency, estab ORS (Overseas Recruitment Servs) Ltd (acquired HCC 1984) as part of Alfred Marks Gp which had acquired the staff agency, purchased ORS Ltd 1981, exec md Hosp Capital Gp 1984-86, pres and chief exec Lifetime Corpn USA (acquired HCC 1986) 1986-; *Recreations* golf, squash, tennis; *Clubs* RAC, Royal Wimbledon GC, Reform, Arts; *Style*— Anthony Reeves Esq; Spur Lodge, 142 Upper Richmond Road West, London SW14 8DS (☎ 01 878 4738)

REEVES, Christopher Reginald; s of Reginald Raymond Reeves, and Dora Grace, *née* Tucker (d 1962); *b* 14 Jan 1936; *Educ* Malvern; *m* 1965, Stella Jane, da of Cdr Patrick Whinney, RN, of Guernsey; 3 s; *Career* merchant banker; Bank of England 1958-63, Hill Samuel & Co Ltd 1963-67, Hill Grenfell & Co Ltd: dir 1970, dep chm and dep chief exec 1975, jt chm and gp chief exec 1980-87; dep chm and bd memb Morgan Grenfell Gp plc 1983-87, sr advsr Merrill Lynch Capital Mkts 1988, vice chm Merrill Lynch Europe Ltd 1989; dir: Alliary Int Insur Co Ltd, BICC plc, Andrew Weir & Co Ltd, Westpac Banking Corpn (dep chm London bd), Oman Int Bank, Int Freehold Properties SARL; govr Dulwich Coll Prep Sch; *Recreations* sailing, shooting, skiing; *Clubs* Boodle's, Royal Southern YC; *Style*— Christopher Reeves Esq; 64 Flood St, London SW3

REEVES, (Charles) Christopher Seward; s of late Maj Charles Westcott Reeves, OBE, of Enfield, Middx, and Winifred Mary Reeves; *b* 6 Oct 1917; *Educ* Aldenham; *m* 1, 3 April 1948, Betty Rosanne Roberts (d 1987); 1 s (Robert Christopher b 1952), 1 da (Bettina b 1949); m 2, 10 Dec 1988, Elizabeth Mary (Bunty), da of late Arthur Brown; *Career* WWII Home Guard 1941-45; selling and admin Fitch and Son Ltd (now Fitch Lovell Gp) 1939-53, selling EM Denny Ltd 1953-55, selling Danish Bacon Co Ltd 1955-63, sales mangr Mathews and Skailes Ltd London 1963-73, mangr Atalanta (UK) Ltd London (subsid of Atlanta Corpn NY USA), now ret; fndr chm Enfield Young Cons 1946, memb local cons pty 1946-, pres Chislehurst Cons Commons Branch, chm Bromle Youth Tst, govr four local schs, chm of govrs Kemnal Manor Sch 1982-88; cncllr London Borough of Bromley 1967-, Mayor of Bromley 1986-87, memb Bromley Family Practitioners Ctee, chm Nat Benevolent Inst; Liveryman Worshipful Co of Skinners; *Recreations* bridge, sailing, petanque; *Style*— Christopher Reeves, Esq; 6 Manor Place, Chislehurst, Kent BR7 5QH (☎ 01 467 5247); 114 Bay View, Hermanus Cape, RSA

REEVES, Helen May; OBE (1986); da of Leslie Percival William Reeves, (d 1967), and Helen Edith, *née* Brown; *b* 22 August 1945; *Educ* Dartford Girls GS, Univ of Nottingham; *Career* probation offr (later sr probation offr) Inner London Probation Serv 1967-79, dir Nat Assoc of Victims Support Schemes 1980-; *Recreations* gardening, food, architecture; *Clubs* Soc of Friends; *Style*— Ms Helen Reeves; Victim Support, Cranmer House, 39 Brixton Rd, London SW9 6DZ (☎ 01 735 9166)

REEVES, Maj Jonathan Harvey William; s of Lt-Col William Robert Reeves, DSO, of Cefnisa, Conwy, N Wales, and Joan Riddell Scudamore, *née* Jarvis; *b* 9 August 1937; *Educ* Monkton Combe, RAC Cirencester; *m* 1, 29 July 1961, Daphne Susan, da of Col Brian Pierson Doughty-Wylie, MC, (d 1981), of Pen-y-Graig, St Asaph; 1 s (Thomas b 1969), 2 da (Emma b 1963, Katherine b 1966); m 2, 9 Sept 1974, Susan Elizabeth, da of Maj John Frederick Mowat, of Lake House, Ellesmere, Salop; *Career* served RWF 1960-70, Queen's Own Mercian Yeo 1971-74, cmd Shropshire Yeo Sqdn; ptnr Fisher Hoggarth land agents and chartered surveyors 1983-, surveyor to Diocese of Worcester 1986-; FRICS 1984; *Recreations* shooting, fishing, skiing, gardening; *Clubs* Army and Navy; *Style*— Jonathan Reeves, Esq; Southern Mythe Ct, Tewkesbury, Gloucestershire (☎ 0684 292178); Fisher Hoggarth, The Estate Office, Dumbleton, Evesham, Worcestershire (☎ 0386 881214)

REEVES, Dr Marjorie Ethel; da of Robert John Ward Reeves (d 1935), and Edith Saffrey, *née* Whitaker (d 1980); *b* 17 July 1905; *Educ* Trowbridge Girls HS Wilts, St Hugh's Coll Oxford (BA, MA, DLitt), Westfield Coll London (PhD); *Career* history teacher Roan Sch Greenwich 1927-29, lectr St Gabriel's Coll of Educn London 1932-38, vice princ St Anne's Coll Oxford 1938-72 (former tutor and fell); hon warden House of St Gregory & St Macrina Oxford, church warden Univ Church Oxford, memb Dante Soc, corr fell Medieval Acad of America; hon fell: St Annes Coll Oxford, St Hugh's Coll Oxford; former memb: Central Advsy Cncl for Educn, academic planning bds Univ of Kent and Univ of Surrey, Br Cncl of Churches; former chm Higher Educn GP; FR HistS 1945, FBA 1972; *Books* The Influence of Prophecy in the Later Middle Ages (1969), The Figurae of Joachim of Fiore (1972), Then and Then Series (gen ed), Why History? (1980), The Myth of the Eternal Evangel in the Nineteenth Century (1987), The Crisis in Higher Education (1988), The Diaries of Jeffrey Whitaker (1989); *Recreations* gardening, music; *Clubs* Univ Womans; *Style*— Dr Marjorie Reeves; 38 Norham Rd, Oxford OX2 6SQ, (☎ 0865 57039)

REEVES, Prof Nigel Barrie Reginald; OBE (1987); s of Capt Reginald Arthur Reeves, of Battle, E Sussex, and Marjorie Joyce, *née* Pettifer; *b* 9 Nov 1939; *Educ* Merchant Taylors', Worcester Coll Oxford (BA), St John's Coll Oxford (DPhil); *m* 1, 1964 (m dis 1976), Ingrid, *née* Söderberg; 1 s (Dominic Hans Adam b 1968), 1 da (Anna b 1973); m 2, 3 April 1982, Minou, da of Sadegh Samimi (d 1978); *Career* lectr: in english Univ of Lund 1964-66, in german Univ of Reading 1968-74; Alexander von Humboldt fell Univ of Tübingen 1974-75, dean faculty of human studies Univ of Surrey 1986- (prof of german 1975-, head linguistic and int studies dept 1979-), visiting prof and cncl memb Euro Business Sch London 1983-, chm Inst of Linguists 1985-88; pres: Nat Assoc of Language Advsrs 1986-, Assoc of Teachers of German 1987-; chm Nat Congress on Languages in Educn 1986-; FIL 1981, FRSA 1986, CIEx 1986; *Books* Heinrich Heine, Poetry and Politics (1974), Fr Schiller, Medicine, Psychology and Literature (with K Pewhurst, 1978), The Marquise of O and Other Short Stories by Heinr Kleist (with F D Luke, 1978), Business Studies, Languages and Overseas Trade (with D Liston, 1985), The Invisible Economy, A Profile of Britains Invisible Exports (with D Liston, 1988); *Style*— Prof Nigel Reeves, OBE; Dept of Linguistic and International Studies, University of Surrey, Guildford GU2 5XH (☎ 0483 571281 ext 9174, fax 0483 300803, telex 859 331)

REEVES-SMITH, Leonard Edward; OBE (1977); s of Edward Kitchener Reeves-Smith (d 1975), of Mitcham, and Rose, *née* Reeves (d 1979); *Educ* Hampton GS; *m* 6 Feb 1952, Jeannette Avril, da of Henri Askew (d 1981); 1 s (Gary b 22 Feb 1953); *Career* WWII enlisted RAC 1944 served Italy, demob Capt 1948; buyer and gen mangr family retail grocery business 1948-62, chief exec Nat Grocers Fedn 1965 (exec asst 1962, nat sec 1963), dir gen Nat Grocers Benevolent Fund 1980-, dir Nat Grocers Benevolent Fund (Properties) Tst Ltd; gen sec: Grocers Fedn Benevolent Fund, London Grocers and Tea Dealers Benevolent Soc, Grocery Employees Nat Benefits Soc; JP 1970; dep chm Farnham Petty Sessional Div 1975 (Juvenile Panel and Domestic Panel); Freeman City of London 1978, Liveryman Worshipful Co of Chartered Secs and Admins 1978; MIGD 1963, FCIS 1970, FRSA 1970, MBIM 1970; *Recreations* walking, birdwatching, conservation; *Style*— Leonard Reeves-Smith, Esq, OBE; Marralomeda, 25 Mount Pleasant Close, Lightwater, Surrey; National Grocers Benevolent Fund, 17 Farnborough St, Farnborough, Hampshire (☎ 0252 515946)

REFFELL, Vice Adm Derek Roy; KCB (1984); s of Edward Pomeroy Reffell (d 1974), and Murielle Frances (d 1975); *b* 6 Oct 1928; *Educ* Culford Sch, RNC Dartmouth; *m* 1956, Janne Marilyn Gronow, da of Capt William Gronow Davis, DSC, RN (d 1946); 1 s (David, b 1960), 1 da (Jane, b 1962); *Career* Capt HMS Hermes 1974-76, Rear Adm 1980, asst chief Naval Staff (Policy) 1980-81, flag offr Third Flotilla (cdr Naval Task Gp South Atlantic July-Oct 1982) 1982-83, flag offr Naval Air Cmd 1983-84, controller of the Navy 1984, Adm 1988; Asst Coachmakers and Coach Harness Makers of London; FNI, CBIH; *Recreations* golf, wine making; *Style*— Adm Sir Derek Reffell, KCB; c/o Ministry of Defence, Whitehall, London SW1 2HB

REFSHAUGE, Maj-Gen Sir William Dudley; AC (1980), CBE (1959, OBE 1944), ED (1965); s of Francis Christopher Refshauge (d 1930), and Margaret Isobel Craig (d 1971); *b* 3 April 1913; *Educ* Hampton HS, Scotch Coll Melbourne, Melbourne Univ (MB BS); *m* 1942, Helen Elizabeth Stanfield, da of Richard Everett Allwright (d 1953); 4 s, 1 da; *Career* dir-gen Aust Army Med Servs 1955-60; dir-gen Aust Dept of Health 1960-73, pres World Health Assembly 1971, sec-gen World Med Assoc 1973-76, dir Walter and Eliza Hall Inst of Med Res 1977-85, memb nat ctee Sir Robert Menzies Fndn 1979-; kt 1966; *see Debrett's Handbook of Australia and New Zealand for further details*; *Style*— Maj-Gen Sir William Refshauge, AC, CB; 26 Birdwood St, Hughes, ACT 2605, Australia (☎ 81 0943)

REGAN, Jack; s of John Regan (d 1973), of Edinburgh, and Molly, *née* Sommerville; *b* 10 Jan 1942; *Educ* Scotus Acad Edinburgh, Edinburgh Univ (MA); *m* 2 Oct 1965, Katrina Isabel, da of Stanley Thewlis, of Lancs; 2 s (Dominic b 1967, Quentin b 1980), 3 da (Jane b 1968, Tessa b 1972, Anna-Louise b 1975); *Career* sub ed The Scotsman Edinburgh 1960-68, chief sub ed The Daily Nation Nairobi Kenya 1968-70; BBC: TV news reporter 1971-76, prodr Radio Aberdeen 1976, reporter Radio Scotland 1976-78, Scottish affrs corr Radio 4 1978-84, home news ed BBC Radio News London 1984-87, ed news and current affrs Radio Scotland 1987-; *Recreations* reading, writing, sampling scotch whisky; *Style*— Jack Regan, Esq; 51 Newark Drive, Pollokshields, Glasgow G41 4QA (☎ 041 423 2647); BBC Radio Scotland, Queen Margaret Dr, Glasgow G12 8DG (☎ 041 330 2658, 041 339 8844, fax 041 337 1402, telex 777746)

REGAN, Dr Nils Albert; s of Dr Kenneth Martin Regan (d 1976), of London and Lausanne, and Ruth, *née* Boss (d 1988); *b* 19 Feb 1925; *Educ* Kings Coll Wimbledon, Aberdeen Univ (MB ChB, DObst); *m* 22 Nov 1956, Doreen Thelma, da of Dr Norman S Gurrie (d 1981), of London; 1 s (Andrew b 1967), 2 da (Carolyn b 1957, Gillian b 1959); *Career* Sqdn Ldr RAF med branch 1949-52; princ in gen practice 1957-; hosp practitioner G/U med and family planning: Westminster Hosp, St Stephens Hosp; advsr family planning Riverside Health Authy, memb Kensington and Chelsea Family Practitioner Ctee and Med Servs Ctee; memb BMA, FRCOG; *Recreations* theatre, music, tennis; *Clubs* Hurlingham; *Style*— Dr Nils Regan; 11 Ranelagh House, Elystan Place, London SW3 3LE (☎ 01 581 2558); 15 Denbigh St, London SW1V 2HF (☎ 01 834 6969)

REGER, Janet; da of Hyman Phillips (d 1981), of Reading, Berks, and Rachel, *née* Leven; *b* 30 Sept 1937; *Educ* Kendrick Sch Reading, Leicester Coll of Arts & Technol (Dip); *m* 1 Jan 1961, Peter Reger (d 1985), s of Josef Reger, (d 1955), of Munich; 1 da (Aliza b 1961); *Career* freelance designer Zurich 1960-67, fndr Janet Reger exclusive designer lingerie and night wear 1967-, own boutique Beauchamp Place Knightsbridge 1974-; *Clubs* Aquilla Health; *Style*— Mrs Janet Reger; 2 Beauchamp Place, London SW3

REGESTER, Paul John Dinsmore; OBE (1944), TD (1947); s of William Regester, JP (d 1930), Moorside, Westfield, Sussex, and Rose, *née* Horton (d 1919); *b* 14 Jan 1911; *Educ* Oundle; *m* 1, July 1940 (m dis 1960), Barbara, da of Edward Stern (d 1963), of Claydon, Suffolk; 1 s (Michael b 1942); m 2, 1960, Margaret Audrey Constance, da of Maj Frank Naumann, MC (d 1947), of Rydenwood, Cranleigh, Surrey; *Career* cmmnd RA (TA) 1929, TA Res 1932, active list 1939 (Straits Settlement Volunteer Force 1932-39), France 1940, Staff Capt Q HQ 5 Corps 1940 (DAAG Tport 1940, DAQMG 1941), serv N African invasion 1942; AAG: 1 Army 1943, 2 Army 1943; serv Normandy 1944, Col A Orgn HQ 21 Army Gp 1944, CSO Br Mil Admin Singapore 1945-46; slr 1932, advocate slr Pemang 1932-39, advocate and slr Kuala Lumpu 1946-59, judge advocate gen Fedn Malaya Armed Forces 1957-59, ctee memb Straits Racing Assoc 1954-59, returned UK and recommenced practice 1959; memb Dummer Parish Cncl 1963-71; *Recreations* horse racing and gardening; *Clubs* East India; *Style*— Paul Regester, Esq, OBE, TD; Thatch Cottage, Farley Green, Albury, Guildford, Surrey GU5 9DN (☎ 0486 41 2274)

REGIS, John Paul Lyndon; s of Tony Regis, and Agnes Regis; *b* 13 Oct 1966; *Educ* St Austins RC Boys Sch; *Career* sprinter; Euro Jr Champs 1985: Bronze Medallist 100m, Gold Medallist 4x100m; Euro Indoor Champs Bronze Medallist 200m (Br record), World Championships Bronze Medallist 200m, Olympic Games Seoul 1988 Silver Medallist 4x100m (Br record), 300 indoor record holder; *Recreations* golf, tennis; *Clubs* Queens Tennis, Sundridge Park GC; *Style*— John Regis, Esq; 67 Fairby Rd, Courtlands Estate, Lee, London SE12 8JP (☎ 01 852 3670)

REGIS, Thomas Henry; s of Thomas Regis (d 1974), and Hannah Helen, *née* Tape; *b* 21 Mar 1936; *Educ* Kings Bruton Sch; *m* 16 June 1962, Deirdre Patricia Gordon; 2 s (Thomas b 1966, William b 1968), 1 da (Lucilla b 1964); *Career* chm Asphaltic Hldgs plc; md: Asphaltic Roofing Supplies Ltd, Asphaltic Investmt Ltd, Asphaltic Land Ltd, Russell Asphalt Ltd, Chartives Asphalt Ltd, Philmatic Roofing Ltd, Snorscombe Farm Ltd, Modern Bldg Supplies Ltd, Asphaltic Contracts Ltd, Barrier Insulation Ltd;

Liveryman Worshipful Co of Makers of Playing Cards; *Recreations* hunting, point-to-point racing, shooting, squash, tennis; *Clubs* Lansdowne; *Style*— Thomas Regis, Esq; The Dell, Rose Lane, Wheathampstead, Herts; Asphaltic Roofing Supplies Ltd, Regis Rd, Kentish Town, London NW5 2UN (☎ 01 485 5600, fax 01 485 3383)

REHAAG, Godfrey Claude; s of Claus Walter Rehaag (d 1984), and Hollis Maud, *née* Lehmann; *b* 6 June 1948; *Educ* Harvey GS Folkestone, Univ of Kent (MA); *m* 10 May 1980, Jane, da of Raymond Peter Hitchings, of Cornwall; 1 s (Thomas b 1982), 3 da (Natalie b 1980, Lucie b 1985, Emily b 1988); *Career* CA; sr ptnr Rehaag McGuire & Co 1987, dir Biotech Ind Products Ltd 1987; cncl memb: Sterts Arts and Environmental Centre 1986, Gaia Tst 1987, Marine Biological Assoc UK 1987; memb MENSA; *Recreations* gardening, DIY, Rambling, reading, voluntary work; *Clubs* British Mensa, Sterts Theatre Co; *Style*— Godfrey Rehaag, Esq; Frogs Meadow, Milton Combe, Yelverton, Devon PL20 6HP (☎ 0822 854926, 0566 3830/3831); 22 Broad St, Launceston, Cornwall PL15 8AE

REHDER, Frank Ernest; CVO (1976); s of Ernest A Rehder (d 1955), of Dulwich, London, and Julia Clara Dorothea, *née* Lienau (d 1959); *b* 4 August 1918; *Educ* Charterhouse, Corpus Christi Coll Oxford (MA); *Career* WWII Capt RA 1940-45, Capt Royal Northumberland Fus 1945-46; slr 1948, ptnr Sinclair Roche & Temperley London 1953-83 (conslt 1984-), maritime and commercial arbitrator 1975; memb and hon slr: London Maritime Arbitrators Assoc 1960 (hon memb 1977-), London Ct of Int Arbitration 1975-; chm: CIArb 1984-86, Dulwich Cons Assoc 1963-67; cncllr Camberwell Borough Cncl 1960-65; Freeman City of London, Liveryman Worshipful Co of Arbitrators (Master 1985-86); FCIArb 1972; *Recreations* gardening, walking; *Style*— Frank E Rehder, Esq, CVO; 152 Court Lane, Dulwich, London SE21 7EB (☎ 01 693 6240)

REID, (Philip) Alan; s of Philip Reid (d 1981), of Glasgow, and Margaret, *née* McKerracher (d 1976); *b* 18 Jan 1947; *Educ* Fettes Coll, St Andrews Univ (LLB); *m* 14 July 1971, Maureen Anne Reid, da of Alexander Petrie, of Cupar, Fife, Scotland; 1 s (Richard b 1984), 1 da (Caroline b 1981); *Career* ptnr Peat Marwick McLintock 1979-; chm int tax ctee Inst of CAs of Scotland 1982-; memb: tax steering ctee Consultative Ctee of Accountancy Bodies 1982-85, tax practices ctee Inst of CAs of Scotland 1982-; govr Eton End Sch Berks; ACA 1973, FTII 1981; *Recreations* family, skiing, theatre, travel; *Clubs* RAC; *Style*— Alan Reid, Esq; 1 Puddle Dock, Blackfriars, London EC4V 3PD (☎ 01 236 8000, 01 248 6552, telex 8811541)

REID, Sir Alexander James; 3 Bt (UK 1897), of Ellon, Aberdeenshire, JP (Cambs and Isle of Ely 1971), DL (1973); s of Sir Edward Reid, 2 Bt, KBE (d 1972, through whose sis, Victoria, Sir Alexander is 1 cous of Richard Ingrams, ed of Private Eye, and 1 cous once removed to the ha of the Barony of Darcy de Knayth), and Tatiana, Lady Reid, *qv*; *b* 6 Dec 1932; *Educ* Eton, Magdalene Coll Cambridge; *m* 1955, Michaela, da of Olaf Kier, CBE, of Royston; 1 s, 3 da; *Heir* s, Charles Reid; *Career* 2 Lt 1 Bn Gordon Highlanders 1951 served Malaya; Capt 3 Bn Gordon Highlanders TA, ret 1964; chm: Ellon Castle Estates Co Ltd 1965-, Cristina Securities Ltd 1970-; govr Heath Mount Prep Sch 1970- (chm 1976-); chm Cytozyme (UK) Ltd 1985-; High Sheriff of Cambridge 1987-88; landowner (1200 acres); *Recreations* shooting, all country pursuits; *Clubs* Caledonian; *Style*— Sir Alexander Reid, Bt, JP, DL; Kingston Wood Manor, Arrington, Royston, Herts (☎ 095 44 231)

REID, Alexander Maynard; s of Alexander Simpson Reid (d 1985), of London, and Kathleen Irene, *née* Maynard; *b* 3 May 1943; *Educ* Highgate Sch, Fitzwilliam Coll Cambridge (MA); *Career* admitted slr 1970, ptnr Milne Moser & Sons Kendal 1983, clerk to Gen Cmmrs of Income Tax for S Westmorland Div, Notary Public 1982; govr Brewery Arts Centre Kendal; memb Law Soc 1970; *Recreations* fellwalking, running, horseriding, tennis, golf, cinema; *Style*— Alexander Reid, Esq; 16 Serpentine Rd, Kendal, Cumbria CA9 4PD (☎ 0539 22 990); Milne Moser, 100 Highgate, Kendal, Cumbria LA9 4HE (☎ 0539 29 786)

REID, Andrew Milton; s of late Rev A A R Reid, DD; *b* 21 July 1929; *Educ* Glasgow Acad, Jesus Coll Oxford; *m* 1953, Norma MacKenzie, da of late Norman Davidson; 2 s; *Career* asst md John Player Sons 1975-77, dir Imperial Gp Ltd 1978-, chm Imperial Tobacco Ltd 1979-, full-time chm and chief exec 1983,dep chm Imperial Gp 1986-; dir: Trade Indemnity plc 1982-, Renold plc until 1983; memb: cncl Royal Sch of Church Music 1986-, Tobacco Advisory Cncl 1977-87, Bristol Urban Devpt Bd, Bristol Univ Cncl; *Recreations* fishing, golf, sailing; *Clubs* Clifton (Bristol), Utd Oxford and Cambridge; *Style*— Andrew Reid, Esq; Parsonage Farm, Publow, Pensford, nr Bristol; Imperial Tobacco Ltd, Hartcliffe, Bristol BS99 7UJ (☎ 0272 781 111, telex 44744)

REID, Hon Mrs (Angela Margaret Amherst); *née* Cecil; o da of 3 Baron Amherst of Hackney, CBE (d 1980), and Margaret Eirene, *née* Clifton Brown; *b* 16 May 1955; *Educ* St Mary's Sch Calne, Froebel Inst Roehampton; *m* 7 June 1980, (Gavin) Ian Reid, s of Col (Percy Fergus) Ivo Reid, of Hill House, Somerton Oxford; 1 s (Nicholas Andrew b 1985), 2 da (Susanna Claire b and d 1987, Jessica Mary b 1988); *Career* primary teacher; *Style*— The Hon Mrs Reid; Lower Dean Farm, Watlington, Oxford OX9 5ET (☎ 049 161 2886)

REID, Beryl Elizabeth; OBE (1986); da of late Leonard Reid, and Anne Burton McDonald Reid (d 1962); *b* 17 June 1921; *Educ* Withington Girl's Sch; *m* 1, 1950, Bill Worsley; m 2 1954, Derek Franklin; *Career* actress; in pantomime and variety 1941-; After the Show (St Martin's 1951), Watergate Revues (March-Nov 1954), Rockin' The Town (Palladium 1956), The Killing of Sister George (Duke of York's 1965, NY 1966, Tony Award for Best Actress, film of same 1969), Entertaining Mr Sloane (film 1970, play Royal Court 1975), Spring Awakening, and Romeo and Juliet (Nat Theatre 1974), Il Campiello, and Counting the Ways (Nat Theatre 1976-77), The Way of the World (RSC Aldwych 1978), Born in the Gardens (Bristol Old Vic 1979-80, SWET Award), Joseph Andrews (film 1977), Smiley's People (1982, BAFTA Award for Best TV Actress), The Sch for Scandal (Haymarket and Duke of York's 1983-84), Gigi (Lyric 1985-86); *Books* So Much Love (autobiog, 1984); *Recreations* painting, cooking, surfing, flying, intensive driving; *Style*— Beryl Reid, OBE; Honeypot Cottage, Wraysbury, nr Staines, Middx; c/o Eric Braun (☎ 01 892 6795)

REID, Charles Edward James; s and h of Sir Alexander Reid, 3 Bt; *b* 24 June 1956; *Educ* Rannoch, RAC Cirencester; *Recreations* shooting, fishing; *Clubs* Clifton, Caledonian; *Style*— Charles Reid, Esq

REID, Dr Daniel; OBE (1989); s of John Dinsmore Reid (d 1972), of Glasgow, and Ethel, *née* Cheyne (d 1978); *b* 5 Feb 1935; *Educ* Allan Glen's Sch Glasgow, Univ of Glasgow (MB ChB, MD), Royal Inst of Public Health and Hygiene (DPH); *m* 3 Aug 1963, Eileen, da of William James Simpson (d 1939), of Greenock, Renfrewshire; 2 da (Anne Cheyne b 21 April 1965, Jane Anderson b 25 July 1967); *Career* Nat Serv Capt RAMC 1960-62, attached Northumberland Fus; registrar univ dept of infectious diseases Ruchill Hosp Glasgow 1963-65, sr registrar epidemiological res laboratory Central Public Health Laboratory London 1965-69, dir communicable diseases (Scotland) unit Ruchill Hosp Glasgow 1969-; chm: advsy gp on infection Scottish Health Servs Planning Cncl 1983-, Glasgow Assoc for the Welfare of the Disabled 1983-87; FRCP (Glasgow) 1983, FFCM 1977, FRSH 1976; Encomienda con placa de la Orden Civil de Sanidad Spain 1975; *Books* Injections in Current Medical Practice (jt ed, 1986); *Style*— Dr Daniel Reid, OBE; 29 Arkleston Rd, Paisley, Strathclyde PA1 3TE (☎ 041 889 4873); Communicable Diseases (Scotland) Unit, Ruchill Hospital, Glasgow G20 9NB (☎ 041 946 7120, fax 041 946 4359, telex 776373)

REID, Hon Sir George (Oswald); QC (1971); s of George Watson Reid (decd), and Lillias Margaret, *née* Easton; *b* 22 July 1903; *Educ* Scotch Coll Melbourne, Melbourne Univ (LLB); *m* 1, 1930, Beatrix Waring (d 1972), da of late Lt-Gen Hon Sir James Whiteside McCay, KCMG, KBE, CB, VD; 1 da; m 2, 1973, Dorothy, da of C W F Ruttledge (decd); *Career* MLA Vic (Lib) for Box Hill 1947-52 and 1955-73, min without portfolio 1955-56; min: of Lab and Indust and Electrical Undertakings 1956-65, for Fuel and Power 1965-67, Immigration 1967-70; attorney-gen 1967-73, ret; chm Middle Yarra Advsy Cncl 1975-81; kt 1972; *see Debrett's Handbook of Australia and New Zealand for further details*; *Clubs* Melbourne, RACV, Melbourne Savage; *Style*— The Hon Sir George Reid, QC; Nilja, Alexander Rd, Warrandyte, Vic 3113, Australia

REID, Very Revd Dr George Thomson Henderson; MC (1945); s of Rev Dr David Reid, DD (d 1933), and Georgina Stuart (d 1946); *b* 31 Mar 1910; *Educ* George Watsons Boys' Coll, Edinburgh Univ (MA, BD), Aberdeen Univ (DD); *m* 1938, Watt, da of Very Rev Prof Hugh Watt, DD (d 1968), of Edinburgh; 3 s (David, Hugh, George), 1 da (Mary); *Career* WWII sr chaplain to the Forces: 3 Bn Scots Gds 1940-45, 15 (S) div 1945; min of Church of Scotland: min of Cockenrie 1935-38, St Andrews Juniper Green 1938-49, Claremont Glasgow 1949-55, W Church of St Andrews Aberdean 1955-75; religious advsr to Grampian TV 1968-73; convener of Church of Scotland Ctee on Christians Aid 1954-64; moderator of Gen Assembly 1973-74; *Recreations* golf, water colour, sketching; *Clubs* Monton Hall GS Edinburgh; *Style*— Dr George Reid; 33 Westgarth Avenue, Edinburgh EH13 0BB (☎ 031 441 1299)

REID, Very Rev (William) Gordon; s of William Albert Reid, of Roxburghshire, and Elizabeth Jean, *née* Inglis; *b* 28 Jan 1943; *Educ* Glashiels Acad, Edinburgh Univ (MA), Keble Coll Oxford (MA), Cuddesdon Coll; *Career* provost of St Andrews Cathedral Inverness 1984-, curate St Salvadors Edinburgh 1967-69, chaplain and tutor Salisbury Theol Coll 1969-72, rector of St Michael and All Saints Edinburgh 1972-84; cncllr Lothian Regnl Cncl 1974-84, chm Lothian and Borders Police Bd 1982-84; *Clubs* New (Edinburgh); *Style*— The Very Rev the Provost; St Andrews Hse, 15 Andross St, Inverness IV3 5NS (☎ 0463 233 535)

REID, Sir Hugh; 3 Bt (UK 1922); s of Sir Douglas Neilson Reid, 2 Bt (d 1971); *b* 27 Nov 1933; *Educ* Loretto; *Style*— Sir Hugh Reid, Bt; Caheronaun Park, Loughrea, Co Galway, Ireland

REID, Col (Percy Fergus) Ivo; OBE (1953), DL (Northants 1969); er s of Col Percy Lester Reid, CBE, JP, DL (d 1968), of Thorpe Mandeville Manor, Northants, and Katharine Marjorie Elizabeth, *née* Fergusson; *b* 2 Nov 1911; *Educ* Stowe, Pembroke Coll Oxford; *m* 1940, Mary Armida, da of Col James Douglas Macindoe, MC; 2 s, 1 da; *Career* served Irish Gds 1933-59; WWII, Staff Coll, cmdt Gds Depot, cmd Irish Gds and Regt Dist 1955-59; memb HM Body Guard Hon Corps Gentlemen at Arms 1961, Harbinger 1979-81; High Sheriff Northants 1967; *Recreations* shooting, racing, travelling; *Clubs* White's; *Style*— Col Ivo Reid, OBE, DL; The Glebe House, Marston St Lawrence, Banbury, Oxon

REID, John (Robson); *b* 1 Dec 1925; *Educ* Wellingborough GS, Sch of Architecture The Poly (Dip Arch); *m* 1948, Sylvia Mary, *née* Payne; 1 s (Dominic), 2 da (Suzannah, Victoria); *Career* WWII Capt The Green Howards 1944-47, served Middle East; architect and industl designer 1950-; architecture incl: Westminster Theatre, Savoy Grill, Barbican Centre Exhibition Halls; industl design incl: furniture and lighting fittings, road and rail tport, consumer durables; ldr Br Delgn on Design Educn USSR 1967, dean art and design Middx Poly 1975-78, Pageantmaster to the Lord Mayors of London 1972-; UNIDO conslt on industl design 1977-79: in India, Pakistan, Egypt, Turkey; advsr to Nat Inst of Design India 1979-, specialist Br Cncl India 1985; pres: Soc of Industl Artists and Designers 1966-66, Int Cncl of Socs of Industl Design 1969-71, vice pres The Illuminating Engrg Soc 1969-71, chm Nat Inspection Bd for Electricity Installation Contracting; memb advsy ctee: Central Sch of Art and Design, Leeds Coll of Art and Design, Newcastle upon Tyne Sch of Art and Design, Carleton Univ; govr Hornsey Coll of Art and Design; lectr for Design Cncl in: Canada, Czechoslovakia, Eire, Hungary, Japan, Poland, USA, USSR; Master: Worshipful Co of Furniture Makers, Worshipful Co of Chartered Architects; 4 Design Cncl awards, 2 Milan Trienalle Silver Medals; RIBA, PPSCD, FCIBSE; *Books* incl: International Code of Professional Conduct for Industrial Design (1969), A Guide to Conditions of Contract for Industrial Design (1969) Industrial Design in India, Pakistan, Egypt and Turkey (1978); *Recreations* music, swimming; *Clubs* City Livery; *Style*— John Reid, Esq; Arnoside House, The Green, Old Southgate N14 7EG; 5 The Green, London N14 5EG (☎ 01 882 1083/4)

REID, Sir John James Andrew; KCMG (1985), CB (1975), TD (1958); s of Mr Alexander Scott Reid (d 1966), of Fife, and Mary Cullen Andrew Reid (d 1970); *b* 21 Jan 1925; *Educ* Bell-Baxter Sch Cupar, Univ of St Andrews (BSc, MB ChB, DSc, MD, DPH); *m* 1949, Marjorie, da of Cyril Robins Crumpton (d 1952); 1 s (Jonathan), 4 da (Joanna, Lucinda, Nicola, Morag); *Career* Nat Serv 1948-50; Lt-Col TA; med practitioner; currently conslt advsr on Int Health (DHSS); hon conslt in communtiy med to the Army; MOH Northamptonshire, MOH Buckinghamshire 1967-72, dep chief MD DHSS 1972-77, visiting prof of health serv admin London Sch of Hygiene and Tropical Med 1973-78, chief MD Scottish Off 1977-85; memb of exec bd WHO (ex-chm 1973-75, 1976-79, 1980-83, 1984-87); Hon LLD Dundee; FRCP, FRCPE, FRCPG, FFCM; *Style*— Sir John Reid, KCMG, CB, TD; The Manor House, Oving, Aylesbury, Bucks HP22 4HW (0296 641 302); c/o Room D313, DHSS, Alexander Fleming House, Elephant & Castle, London SE1 6BY (☎ 01 407 5522)

REID, Rev Prof John Kelman Sutherland; CBE (1970), TD (1961); s of David Reid (d 1933), of 11 Braid Rd, Edinburgh, and Georgina Thomson, *née* Stuart (d 1946); *b* 31 Mar 1910; *Educ* George Watson's Boys' Coll Edinburgh, Univ of Edinburgh (MA, BD); *m* 3 Jan 1950, Margaret Winnifrid, da of Rev WS Brookes (d 1958), of Corrie,

Isle of Arran; *Career* Royal Army Chaplains Div, Chaplain Class 4 Royal Signals 1942-43, Parachute Regt 1943-46, TA 1946-62; prof of philosophy Univ of Calcutta 1936-38, min of religion Craigmillar Park Church Edinburgh, prof of theology Univ of Leeds 1952-61, prof of systematic theology Univ of Aberdeen 1961-76; ed (and emeritus) Scottish Jl of Theology 1948-, sec New English Bible 1949-82; memb: World Cncl of Churches Faith and Order Cmmn 1961-82, Br Cncl of Churches 1961-68, Soc for Study of Theology, Societas NT Studiorum, Scottish Church Theology Soc, Church Serv Soc, Scottish Church Soc; Hon DD Edinburgh Univ 1957; *Books* The Authority of Scripture (third edn 1981), Presbyterians and Unity (1962), Life in Christ (1963), Christian Apologetics (1969), Calvin's Concerning the Eternal Predertination of God (trans, second edn 1982), Oscar Cullmann: Baptism in the New Testament (trans 1950); *Style—* The Rev Prof John Reid, CBE, TD; 8 Abbotsford Court, 18 Colinton Road, Edinburgh EH10 5EH (☎ 031 447 6855)

REID, Prof John Low; s of James Reid (d 1961), of Glasgow, and Irene Margaret; *b* 1 Oct 1943; *Educ* Kelvinside Acad Glasgow, Fettes Coll Edinburgh, Univ of Oxford (MA, BM, BCh, DM); *m* 2 May 1964, Randa, da of Naguib Aref Pharaon (d 1987), of London; 1 s (James b 1965), 1 da (Rebecca b 1967); *Career* house offr Radcliffe Infirmary Oxford and Brompton Hosp London 1968-70, res fell sr lectr and reader Royal Postgrad Med Sch London 1970-78, visiting scientist Nat Inst of Health Bethesola Maryland USA 1973-75; Univ of Glasgow: regius prof materia medica 1978-89, regius prof med and therapeutics 1989-; memb med advsy ctee BBC Scotland; FRCPG 1979, FRCP 1987; *Books* Handbook of Hypertention (1981), Lecture Notes on Clinical Pharmacology (1981), Clinical Science (ed 1982-84), Journal of Hypertension (ed 1987); *Recreations* gardening, books, outdoors; *Style—* Prof John Reid; 1 Whittingehame Gardens, Glasgow G12 (☎ 041 339 4034); Stobhill Hosp, Glasgow (☎ 041 558 0111)

REID, Lady Laura Louise; *née* Meade; da of 6 Earl of Clanwilliam; *b* 11 Mar 1957; *m* 25 April 1981, W Scott B Reid, s of Howard A Reid, of Bronxville, NY; 1 s (Nicholas b 1982), 2 da (Amelia b 1984, Clementine b 1988); *Style—* Lady Laura Reid; 524 Purchase St, Rye, New York 10580, USA

REID, Sir (Harold) Martin (Smith); KBE (1987), CMG (1978); s of Marcus Reid (d 1948), and Winifred Mary Reid, *née* Stephens (d 1969); *b* 27 August 1928; *Educ* Merchant Taylors', BNC Oxford (MA); *m* 1956, Jane Elizabeth, da of Frank Lester Harwood (d 1975), of Hants; 1 s (Thomas), 3 da (Philippa, Emily, Alice); *Career* RN 1947-49; entered For Serv 1953; served: in London, Paris, Rangoon, London; political advsr to govr Br Guiana 1965-66, dep high cmmnr Guyana 1966-68, No 2 in Bucharest and Blantyre Malawi 1968-73, princ private sec to successive Secs of State for NI 1973-74, head Central and S African dept FCO 1974-79, min Pretoria 1979-82, seconded as Dip Serv res chm Civil Serv Selection Bd 1983, Br high cmmnr Kingston 1984-87, ambassador (non-res) Port au Prince 1984-87, special res advsr FCO 1987-88, ret 1988; *Recreations* painting, chess; *Clubs* Royal Cwlth Soc; *Style—* Sir Martin Reid, KBE, CMG; 43 Carson Road, London SE21 8HT

REID, Michael Herbert; s of John Lillingstone Reid (d 1958); *b* 25 Feb 1925; *Educ* Radley, Trinity Coll Oxford; *m* 1970, Caroline Jane Jefferson, *née* Bell; 1 s, 2 da; *Career* RAF and RAuxAF Middle East; landowner and farmer; cncl memb: South of England Agric Soc (pres 1985-86), Cridmore Farm Co; High Sheriff E Sussex 1981-82; *Recreations* fishing; *Clubs* RAF; *Style—* Michael Reid Esq; Maplesden, Stonegate, Wadhurst, Sussex TN5 7EL (☎ 0580 200295)

REID, Sir Norman Robert; s of Edward Daniel Reid (d 1956); *b* 27 Dec 1915; *Educ* Wilson's GS Camberwell, Edinburgh Coll of Art, Edinburgh Univ (DA); *m* 1941, Jean Lindsay, da of Alexander Taylor Bertram, of Brechin; 1 s, 1 da; *Career* WWII served A & SH, Maj 1946; Tate Gallery: joined 1946, dep dir 1954, keeper 1959, dir 1964-79; memb: cncl Friends of the Tate Gallery 1958-79, Arts Cncl Panel 1964-74, advsy panel Inst of Contemporary Arts 1965-, advsy ctee Paintings in Hosps 1965-69, Br Cncl Fine Arts Ctee 1965-77 (chm 1968-75), cultural advsy ctee UK Nat Cmmn for UNESCO 1966-70, Studies in History of Art Bd London Univ 1968, The Rome Centre 1969-77 (pres 1975-77), Burlington Magazine Bd 1971-75, advsy cncl Paul Mellon Centre 1971-78, cncl of mgmnt Inst of Contemporary Prints 1972-78, Contemporary Arts Soc Ctee 1973-77 and 1965-72, cncl RCA 1974-77; pres Penworth Soc of Arts, tstee Graham and Kathleen Sutherland Fndn 1980-86; Hon LittD UEA; FMA, FIIC; Offr of the Mexican Order of the Aztec Eagle; kt 1970; *Clubs* Arts; *Style—* Sir Norman Reid; 50 Brabourne Rise, Park Langley, Beckenham, Kent

REID, Maj Gen Peter Daer; CB (1981); s of Col Spence Daer Reid (d 1954), Dorothy Hungerford Reid, *née* Jackson; *b* 5 August 1925; *Educ* Cheltenham, Wadham Coll Oxford; *m* 1958, Catherine Fleetwood, da of Wilfred Andrew Carmichael Boodle (d 1961); 2 s (Duncan, Jamie), 2 da (Penelope, Philippa); *Career* cmmnd Coldstream Gds 1945, transferred Royal Dragoons 1947, Staff Coll Camberley 1959, CO Royal Dragoons 1965-68, RCDS 1973, CRAC 3 Div 1974-76, Maj-Gen, dir RAC 1976-78, chief exec MBT 80 PE 1979-81, dir Armd Warfare Studies 1981; served: Germany, Egypt, Gibraltar, Morocco, Malaya, Singapore, ret 1981; def advsr GKN, mil advsr Howden Airdynamics Ltd, assoc memb Burdeshaw Assoc Ltd Washington USA; *Recreations* sailing, skiing, fishing, bird watching; *Clubs* Army & Navy; *Style—* Maj Gen P D Reid, CB; The Border House, Cholderton, Salisbury, Wilts

REID, Air Vice-Marshal Sir (George) Ranald McFarlane; KCB (1945, CB 1941), DSO (1919), MC (and Bar); s of late George MacFarlane Reid, and Gertrude Macquisten; *b* 1893; *Educ* Routenburn and Malvern; *m* 1934, Leslie Livermore, da of Dr Hamilton Wright (decd); 1 s, 1 da; *Career* cmd British Forces Aden 1938-41, Air Cdre 1939, AOC W Africa 1944-45, ret 1946; Gentleman Usher to HM King George VI 1952 and to HM The Queen 1952-59, extra Gentleman Usher 1959; *see Debrett's Handbook of Australia and New Zealand for further details*; *Style—* Air Vice-Marshal Sir Ranald Reid, KCB

REID, Sir Robert Basil; CBE (1980); s of Sir Robert Neil Reid, KCSI, KCIE (d 1963), and Amy Helen Disney (d 1980); *b* 7 Feb 1921; *Educ* Malvern, BNC Oxford (hon fell 1985); *m* 1951, Isobel Jean (d 1976), da of Robert McLachlan (d 1942), of Coruannan, Giffnock, Glasgow; 1 s, 1 da; *Career* WWII cmmnd RTR 1941-46, Capt; joined London and NE Railway as traffic apprentice (later goods agent, asst dist goods mangr, dist passenger mangr and commercial offr), planning mangr Scottish region BR 1967, divnl mangr Doncaster Eastern Region 1968, dep gen mangr Eastern Region, gen mangr Southern Region 1974; BR bd: full-time memb 1977, chief exec (Railways) 1980, vice chm 1983, chm 1983-; pres Chartered Isnt of Tport 1982-83, chm Nationalised Industs Chm's Gp 1987, rep Br Railways Bd on Managing Bd of the Union of Int Railways, chm Community of Euro Railways, vice pres Inst of Materials Handling 1987, doctor of business admin (honoris ausa) Int Mgmnt Centre Buckingham; memb: Business in the Community, cncl Princes Youth Business Tst, CBI Pres Ctee; Freeman City of London, Junior Warden Worshipful Co of Carmen, Master Worshipful Co of Information Technologists; hon fell BNC Oxford 1984; CBStJ 1986; CBIM, FInstM; kt 1985; *Recreations* golf, sailing, shooting, fishing, mountaineering; *Clubs* Naval & Military; *Style—* Sir Robert Reid, CBE; c/o Euston House, 24 Eversholt Street, PO Box 100 London NW1 1DZ (☎ 01 299 431)

REID, (James) Robert; s of His Hon Judge John Alexander Reid, MC (d 1969), and Jean Ethel, *née* Ashworth; *b* 23 Jan 1943; *Educ* Marlborough, New Coll Oxford, (MA); *m* 25 May 1974, Anne Prudence, da of John Arkell Wakefield; 2 s (Edward b 1976, David b 1978), 1 da (Sarah b 1980); *Career* barr Lincoln's Inn 1965, QC 1980, rec 1985, jt tres Barr Benevolent Assoc 1986, bencher 1988; *Style—* Mr Robert Reid; 9 Old Square, Lincoln's Inn, London WC2

REID, Sue; da of Peter Reid, DSC (d 1971), and Vera Reid; *b* 20 May 1950; *Educ* Casterton Sch Cumbria, Brunel Univ; *m* 26 Oct 1974 (m dis 1982), Simon Fulfora-Brown; 1 s (Harry Reid Kemble b 19 Nov 1988); *Career* asst ed Mail on Sunday; *Books* Labour of Love (1988); *Style—* Ms Sue Reid; 12 Burnaby Street, London SW10; Mail on Sunday, Northcliffe House, London EC4

REID, Tatiana, Lady; Tatiana; da of Col Alexandre Fenoult, late of the Russian Imperial Gd; *m* 1930, Sir Edward Reid, 2 Bt, KBE (d 1972), sometime Page of Honour to George V; 1 s (Sir Alexander Reid, 3 Bt, JP, DL), 1 da (decd); *Style—* Tatiana, Lady Reid; 16 Buckingham Terr, Edinburgh EH4 3AD

REID, Flt Lt William; VC (1943); s of William Reid (d 1941), and Helena, *née* Murdoch (d 1972); *b* 21 Dec 1921; *Educ* Baillieston Sch, Coatbridge Secdy Sch, W of Scotland Agric Coll, Glasgow Univ (BSc); *m* 28 March 1952, Violet Campbell, da of William George Gallagher (d 1976); 1 s (William Graeme b 1961), 1 da (Susan May b 1963); *Career* RAFVR Bomber Cmd 1941-46: 61 Sqdn 1943, 617 sqdn 1944 (POW 1944), demob 1946; farms mangr Macrobert Farms Douneside Ltd 1950-59, nat cattle and sheep advsr Spillers Ltd 1959-81; hon pres Br Legion (Crieff), bd memb BLESMA, pres Strathallan Aircraft Assoc, hon life pres Air Crew Assoc (chm Scottish branch); Freeman City of London 1988;; *Recreations* golf, fishing, shooting; *Clubs* RAF; *Style—* Flt Lt William Reid, VC; Cranford Ferntower Place, Crieff, Perthshire, Scotland PH7 3DD (☎ 0704 2462)

REID ENTWISTLE, Dr Ian; s of John Morton Entwistle, and Mary, *née* Reid; *b* 29 Sept 1931; *Educ* Rivington and Blackrod Sch, Liverpool Univ Med Sch (MB ChB); *m* 1, 15 May 1969, Anthea Margaret (d 1979), da of Kenneth Evans, of Norfolk House, Meols Dr, West Kirby, Wirral; 2 s (John b 1972, Alexander b 1973); m 2, Rosemary Elizabeth, *née* Harrison; *Career* Surgn Lt HMS Eaglet RNR 1962-65; princ med offr RMS Queen Mary, Queen Elizabeth and Queen Elizabeth II 1961-; casualty offr David Lewis Northern Hosp Liverpool 1957, house physician to prof of child health Royal Liverpool Children's Hosp 1957, princ in private and NHS practice 1958-, med supt Cunard Steam Ship plc 1966-; pt/t med conslt: Whitbread (Northern) Ltd, Spillers Foods Ltd, Hanson Engrg Ltd, BHS plc, BASS Northern; pt/t authorised assessor and examiner: CAA, Gen Cncl of Br Shipping, Gen Foods Ltd, Trafalgar House plc; conslt Pre-Retirement Assoc; formerly med conslt Br Eagle Int Airlines 1966-68, sr gp med conslt Utd Gas Industs 1971-80; tres and sec Merseyside and N Wales RCGP 1973-80 (bd memb 1963-), jt tres and sec Soc of Occupational Med (Merseyside) 1961-67, chm Brewing Indust Med Advsrs 1987-, cncl memb Birkenhead Med Soc 1986-, memb aerospace physiology and med working pty Cncl of Europe 1974-, memb NASA 1969-, med advsr West Kirby Swimming Club for Disabled; underwriting memb Lloyd's 1978-, assoc fell Aerospace Med Assoc USA 1973-, memb Soc of Occupational Med, memb Assur Med Assoc; FBIM 1988, memb RAe Soc; *Books* Exacta Medica (ninth edn, 1989), Exacta Mecanix (fifth edn, 1988); *Recreations* motor racing, horticulture, boating, horology, photography, railway modelling; *Clubs* Mid Cheshire Pitt, Manchester Naval Offrs Assoc; *Style—* Dr Ian Reid Entwistle; Knollwood, Well Lane, Gayton, Wirral L60 8NG (☎ 051 342 2332); consultation suite, 27 Banks Rd, West Kirby, Wirral L48 0RA (☎ 051 625 6600)

REID SCOTT, David Alexander Carroll; s of Maj Alexander Reid Scott, MC (d 1960), and Ann, *née* Mitchell (d 1953); *b* 5 June 1947; *Educ* Eton, Lincoln Coll Oxford Univ (MA); *m* 23 April 1972, Anne (d 1988), da of Phillipe Clouet des Pesruches (d 1977); 3 da (Iona b 1975, Camilla b 1976, Serena b 1979); *Career* first vice-pres White Weld & Co 1969-77, seconded sr advsr Saudi Arabian Monetary Agency 1978-83, md Merrill Lynch & Co 1983-84, exec dir Phoenix Securities Ltd 1984-, non exec dir Merrett Hldgs plc 1986-; *Recreations* Irish country life, farming, arts, antiques; *Clubs* Turf, Kildare St, Coningsby; *Style—* David Reid Scott, Esq; 2 Brunswick Gardens, London W8 4AJ (☎ 01 221 8004); Ballynure, Grange Con, Co Wicklow, Ireland; Phoenix Securities Ltd, 99 Bishopsgate, London EC2 (☎ 01 638 2191, fax 01 638 0707, car tel 0836 732 963)

REID SCOTT, Malise; s of Maj Alexander Reid Scott, MC (d 1960), and Ann Mitchell (d 1953); *b* 28 Sept 1948; *Educ* Eton; *m* 11 Sept 1978, Verity Fleur, da of Dudley Austell Comonte (d 1983), of 13 Upper Belgrave St, London SW1; 1 s (Hugo Alexander Carroll b 5 Sept 1985), 1 da (Rebecca (Mrs Star) b 10 Feb 1981); *Career* 11 Hussars (PAO) 1967-70; Watney Mann Ltd 1970-72, Laurence Prust & Co 1972-86 (ptnr 1983-86), ptnr Laurence Keen & Co 1986-; *Recreations* country pursuits, painting; *Clubs* Hurlingham; *Style—* Malise Reid Scott, Esq; 48 Lyford Rd, London SW18 3LS (☎ 01 874 1629); 49-51 Bow Lane, Cheapside, London EC4M 9LX (☎ 01 489 9493)

REIDHAVEN, Viscount; James Andrew Ogilvie-Grant; also Master of Seafield; er s and h of 13 Earl of Seafield; *b* 30 Nov 1963; *Educ* Harrow; *Style—* Viscount Reidhaven

REIDHAVEN, Viscount; Hon James Andrew Ogilvie-Grant; Master of Seafield; s (by 1 m) of Earl of Seafield (13 in line); *b* 30 Nov 1963; *Educ* Harrow; *Style—* Viscount Reidhaven; Old Cullen, Cullen, Buckie, Banffshire AB5 2XW

REIDY, Dr John Francis; s of Frederick Cyril (d 1957), and Marie Isobel, *née* Smith; *b* 25 August 1944; *Educ* Stonyhurst, St Georges Hosp Med Sch and Kings Coll London (MB BS); *m* 25 Nov 1978, Dianne Patricia, da of Gerald Eugene Murphy, of Launceston, Tasmania, Australia; 1 s (Thomas Edward b 19 Nov 1980), 1 da (Laura Eugenie b 1 June 1982); *Career* conslt radiologist Guys Hosp 1980-; Liveryman Worshipful Soc of Apothecaries; MRCS, LRCP 1967, MRCP 1971, FRCR 1975, FRCP 1988; *Books* numerous pubns on cardiovascular and interventional radiology; *Style—* Dr

John Reidy; 19 Cumberland St, London SW1V 4LS (☎ 01 834 3021); Radiology Dept, Guys Hosp, London SE1 (☎ 01 407 7600)

REIGATE, Baron (Life Peer UK 1970); Sir John Kenyon Vaughan-Morgan; 1 Bt (UK 1960), PC (1961); yr s of Sir Kenyon Pascoe Vaughan-Morgan, OBE, DL, sometime MP Fulham East, n of Sir Walter Vaughan Morgan, 1 and last Bt (cr 1906, extinct 1916); *b* 2 Feb 1905; *Educ* Eton, Christ Church Oxford; *m* 1940, Emily, da of William Redmond Cross, of New York; 2 da; *Heir* none; *Career* WWII served Welsh Gds; sits as Cons peer in House of Lords; MP (C) Reigate 1950-70, Min of State BOT 1957-59; late memb LCC and pres E Fulham Con Assoc; former co dir; *Clubs* Brooks's, Beefsteak, Hurlingham; *Style*— The Rt Hon The Lord Reigate, PC; 36 Eaton Sq, SW1 (☎ 01 235 6506)

REILLY, Brian Thomas; s of Thomas Joseph Reilly, OBE (d 1978), and Eugene Reilly (d 1963); *b* 9 Dec 1924; *Educ* Mount St Mary's Coll Sheffield; *m* 1952, Jean Cynthia, da of Hugh Gilbey (d 1968); 1 s, 4 da; *Career* md GEC Radio & TV Ltd 1968-74, assoc dir GEC 1976-79, chm Panasonic (UK) Ltd 1979-; *Recreations* golf, bridge, theatre; *Clubs* St James's, Annabel's; *Style*— Brian Reilly, Esq; Nutfield, The Fair Mile, Henley-on-Thames, Berks (☎ (0491) 578956); Panasonic UK Ltd (☎ Slough 34522, telex 847652)

REILLY, Hon Mrs; Hon (Brigid Margaret); *née* Campbell; only da of 3 Baron Glenavy (Patrick Campbell, the raconteur and wit, d 1980) by his 2 w, Cherry, da of Maj George Monro; *b* 8 May 1948; *Educ* Godstowe, Pipers Corner Sch Naphill, E Berks Coll of Further Educn; married; *Style*— Hon Mrs Reilly; 2535 Panorama Drive, N Vancouver, BC, Canada

REILLY, Lt-Gen Sir Jeremy Calcott; KCB (1987), DSO (1973); s of Lt-Col Julius Frank Calcott Reilly (d 1984), of Chilbolton, Hants, and Eileen Norah, *née* Moreton; *b* 7 April 1934; *Educ* Uppingham, RMA Sandhurst; *m* 12 Nov 1960, Julia Elizabeth, da of William Forrester (d 1984), of Weymouth, Dorset; 3 da (Katherine b 1961, Penelope b and d 1964, Brigid b 1965); *Career* cmmnd Royal Warwicks Regt 1954, CO 2 Bn Royal Regt of Fusiliers 1971-73, instr Staff Coll 1974-75, Col GS MOD 1975-77, PSO to FM Lord Carver and attached to FCO (Rhodesia) 1977-79, Brig 1979, Cdr 6 Field Force and UK Mobile Force 1979-81, Maj-Gen 1981, GOC 4 Armd Div BAOR 1981-83, Dep Col Royal Regt Fusiliers 1981-86, ACDS MOD 1985-86, Col Royal Regt Fusiliers 1986-, Lt-Gen 1986, CTAD 1986-89; Col Cmdt Queen's Div 1988; *Style*— Lt-Gen Sir Jeremy Reilly, KCB, DSO; c/o Royal Regt Fusiliers, HM Tower of London, London EC3N 4AB

REILLY, Michael Charles Tempest; s of Hugh Tempest Reilly (d 1943), and Jessie Margery, *née* Dunthorne (d 1958); *b* 30 August 1913; *Educ* Haileybury, St Mary's Hosp and Univ of London (MB BS, MS); *m* 12 Dec 1945, Katharine Joyce (Joy), da of Gilbert Petrie (d 1955); 3 s (David b 1947, Christopher b 1953, Timothy b 1956), 1 da (Susan b 1946); *Career* WWII med branch RAFVR 1940-46, station med offr UK 1940-44, Station MO Ceylon 1944 and 1945, SMO Cocos Islands Expeditionary Force, HQ 222 Gp Columbo, demob war-substantive Sqdn Ldr; surgical first asst The London Hosp 1950-54, conslt surgn Plymouth and Dist Hosps 1954-78, emeritus conslt surgn SW RHA; initiator of new op sigmoid myotomy for diverticular disease 1964, author of numerous articles in med press on diverticular disease and chapters in three surgical textbooks; pres: section of proctology RSM 1972 (life memb), SW Surgns 1976; memb GMC 1979-83, memb cncl RCS of England 1973-85 (Bradshaw lectr 1985), former memb Plymouth Hosp Mgmnt Ctee (former chm med advsy ctee), sec Plymouth Med Soc 1960-65, pres Devon and Cornwall Ileostomy Assoc 1970-75; hon fell: Medico-Chirugical Soc of Jordan 1978, Medico-Chirugical Soc of Bologna 1980; memb BMA 1938, MRCS 1947, LRCP 1947, FRCS 1949, sr fell Assoc of Surgns of GB and Ireland 1978; *Recreations* pestering politicians about the decline of the NHS; *Style*— Michael Reilly, Esq; Magnolia Cottage, Harrowbeer Lane, Yelverton, Devon PL20 6EA (☎ 0822 852636)

REILLY, Sir (D'Arcy) Patrick; GCMG (1968), OBE (1942); s of Sir D'Arcy Reilly (d 1948), and Margaret Florence, *née* Wilkinson; *b* 17 Mar 1909; *Educ* Winchester, New Coll Oxford (MA); *m* 1, 27 July 1938, Rachel Mary (d 1984), da of Brig-Gen Sir Percy Sykes, KCIE, CB, CMG; 2 da (Jane b 1939, Sarah b 1941); m 2, 23 Oct 1987, Ruth Margaret, wid of Sir Arthur Norrington; *Career* joined Dip Serv 1933; second sec FO 1938, Miny Econ Warfare 1939-42, first sec Algiers 1943 and Paris 1944, cnsllr Athens 1947, Imp Def Coll 1949, asst under sec 1950-53, min Paris 1953-56, third sec Tehran 1955, dep under sec FO 1956, ambassador to USSR 1957-60, dep under sec FO 1960-64, ambassador to France 1965-68; chm Banque Nationale de Paris plc 1969-80, United Bank for Africa (Nigeria) 1969-74, pres London Chamber of Commerce and Indust 1972-75; chm: cncl Bedford Coll Univ of London 1970-75, N Kensington Amenity Tst 1971-74; fell All Souls Coll Oxford 1932-34 and 1969-, hon fell New Coll Oxford 1972; Hon LittD Univ of Bath 1982; Commandeur Legion d'Honneur France 1979; *Recreations* gardening, travel; *Clubs* Athenaeum; *Style*— Sir Patrick Reilly, GCMG, OBE; 75 Warrington Cres, London W9 1EH (☎ 01 289 5384); Grenville Manor, Haddenham, Bucks HP17 8AF (☎ 0844 291 496)

REILLY, Baron (Life Peer UK 1978); Paul Reilly; s of Prof Sir Charles Reilly, OBE, FRIBA, sometime head Liverpool Sch Architecture; Lord Reilly is 1 cousin to Sir Patrick Reilly, GCMG, sometime ambassador to Paris and USSR; *b* 29 May 1912; *Educ* Winchester, Hertford Coll Oxford, LSE; *m* 1, 1939, Pamela Foster; 1 da; m 2, 1952, Annette, da of Brig-Gen Clifton Inglis Stockwell, CB, CMG, DSO; *Career* dir Design Cncl to 1977, memb Royal Fine Art Commn until 1981; memb cncl: BTA 1960-70, RCA 1963-80, BBC Gen Advsy 1964-70, BR Bd Design Panel 1966-88, Environment Panel 1977-85, GLC Historic Bldgs Ctee, stamp advsy ctee PO; former journalist with News Chronicle; dir Conran Design Gp, Bldg Trades Exhibition Ltd; kt 1967; *Books* An Introduction to Regency Architecture (1948), An Eye on Design - an Autobiography (1987); *Clubs* Arts; *Style*— The Rt Hon the Lord Reilly; 3 Alexander Place, London SW7 2SG (☎ 01 589 4031)

REILLY, Lady; Ruth Margaret; *née* Cude; yst da of Edmund Cude (d 1970), and Alice Marian Haswell (d 1974); *b* 17 May 1922; *m* 1, 1947, Frank Davies (d 1959), s of Frederick Davies; 1 da; m 2, 1963, (Peter) Rupert Waterlow (d 1969), s of Sir Philip Waterlow; m 3, 1969, as his 2 w, Sir Arthur Norrington, JP (d 1982), sometime pres Trinity Coll Oxford, vice-chllr Oxford Univ and warden Winchester Coll; m 4, Sir D'Arcy Patrick Reilly, GCMG, OBE, former Ambassador in Moscow and Paris; *Career* physiotherapist, writer; *Books incl:* In the Shadow of a Saint (1983), The Household of St Thomas More (1985); *Recreations* music, painting, reading; *Style*— Lady Reilly; 3 Beach Cottages, Fishguard, Dyfed; Grenville Manor, Haddenham, Bucks HP17 8AF; 75 Warrington Crescent, London W9

REILLY, Wyn Anthony Prowse; s of Dr Noel Marcus Prowse Reilly, CMG, of N Sandwich, USA, and Dolores Albra Thompson, *née* Pratten (d 1982); *b* 17 Mar 1930; *Educ* Leighton Park Sch, Trinity Hall, Cambridge (MA), Univ Coll Oxford; *m* 4 Sept 1965, Annuschka Maria, da of Capt Peterpaul Maria Pilarski (d 1970); 2 s (J Alyosha J b 1968, P M Julian P b 1971), 1 da (S Natasha S b 1972); *Career* ADC & private sec to HE Govr The Gambia 1953-54, admin offr Tanganyika HMOCS 1956-62; sr lectr in public admin Univ of Manchester 1962-; on secondment from Manchester Univ: prof of admin Univ of Mauritius 1969-71, princ Admin Coll of Papua New Guinea 1973-75, sr planning offr local govt Botswana 1978-79, dir-gen Mgmnt Devpt Inst The Gambia 1984-85; *Recreations* sailing, skiing, walking, music; *Style*— Wyn Reilly, Esq; West Cottage, Birtles Rd, Macclesfield, Cheshire SK10 3JG (☎ 0625 31114); IDPM, Crawford Hse, University of Manchester, Precinct Centre, Oxford Rd, Manchester M13 9QS (☎ 061 275 2817)

REINDORP, Rt Rev George Edmund; s of Rev Hector William Reindorp, of Goodmayes, Essex, and Dora Lucy, *née* George; *b* 19 Dec 1911; *Educ* Felsted Sch, Trinity Coll Cambridge (MA), Westcott House Cambridge; *m* 1, 1943, Alix Violet (d 1987), da of Alexander Edington, MD, of Durban SA; 3 s, 1 da and 1 da decd; m 2, 6 Jan 1988, Lady (Bridget) Mullens, wid of late Sir William Mullens, DSO, TD; *Career* ordained: deacon 1937, priest 1939; chaplain RNVR 1938-46; curate St Mary Abbots Kensington 1937-39, vicar St Stephen with St John Westminster 1946-57, provost of Southwark and rector St Saviour with All Hallows Southwark 1957-61, bishop of Guildford 1961-73, bishop of Salisbury 1973-81, asst bishop Diocese of London 1982-; memb House of Lords 1970; arranger/prodr/performer Religious Dept BBC Radio 1982-83; chaplain RCGP 1965; Hon DD Lambeth Univ 1961, DUniv Surrey Univ 1971; *Books* What about You? (1956), No Common Task (1957), Putting it Over: ten points for preachers (1961), Over to You (1964), Preaching through the Christian Year (1973); *Recreations* skiing, radio and television, avoiding committees; *Clubs* Ski Club of Great Britain, Kandahar; *Style*— The Rt Rev George Reindorp; 17 Vincent Square, Westminster, London SW1P 2NA

REINERT, Richard Arnim; s of Dr Harald Herman Richard Reinert (d 1981), of Le Pinede, Frejuś, France, and Irene Mary, *née* Bridge; *b* 8 August 1956; *Educ* Dover Coll, Tours Uinv Tours France (Dip), Southampton Univ; *m* 27 April 1979, Brigitte Edgard Therese, da of Dr Hendrik Rene Firmin Verhamme; 2 s (Alexander H R b 24 Oct 1981, Scott R H b 8 Oct 1987), 1 da (Stephanie B M 10 Jan 1983); *Career* dir REFCO SA Paris 1983-, md REFCO Overseas London 1988-; *Recreations* golf, squash, tennis, sailing; *Clubs* Royal St Georges GC; *Style*— Richard A Reinert, Esq; REFCO Overseas Ltd, Europe House, World Trade Centre, London, E1 9AA (☎ 01 488 3232, fax 480 7069, telex 887438)

REINHARDT, Max; s of Ernest Reinhardt (d 1942), of Istanbul, Turkey, and Frieda Reinhardt, *née* Darr (d 1960); *b* 30 Nov 1915; *Educ* English HS Istanbul, Ecole Des Hautes Etudes Commerciales Paris, LSE; *m* 1957, Joan Dorothy, da of Carlisle MacDonald (d 1972), of NY, USA; 2 da (Alexandra, Veronica); *Career* book publisher; chm: Reinhardt Books Ltd, The Nonesuch Press Ltd; cncl memb RADA; *Recreations* swimming, bridge, reading for pleasure; *Clubs* Garrick, Savile, Beefsteak, RAC; *Style*— Max Reinhardt, Esq; 16 Pelham Crescent, London SW7 2NR (☎ 01 589 5527)

REISS, Sir John Anthony Ewart; BEM (1941); s of late James Arthur Reiss; *b* 8 April 1909; *Educ* Eton; *m* 1, 1938, Marie Ambrosine Phillpotts; 1 s, 1 da; m 2, 1951, Elizabeth Booth-Jones, da of Air Vice-Marshal Sir Norman MacEwen, CB, CMG, DSO (d 1953); 2 da; *Career* joined Associated Portland Cement Manufacturers 1934, dir 1952, chm 1956-74; pres of tstees Fndn for Business Responsibilities; pres Aims of Industry 1978-; kt 1967; *Style*— Sir John Reiss, BEM; Barrow House, Barrow, Oakham, Leics

REITER, Glenn Mitchell; s of Bernard Leon Reiter (d 1968), and Helene Gloria, *née* Edson; *b* 1 Feb 1951; *Educ* Yale Univ (BA), Yale Law Sch (JD); *m* 5 Sept 1976, Marilyn, da of Edward John Beckhorn, of Marco Island, Florida, USA; 1 s (Benjamin Bernard b 1980), 1 da (Diana Elizabeth b 1983); *Career* ptnr Simpson Thacher & Bartlett 1984- (assoc 1978-84); *Clubs* RAC; *Style*— Glenn M Reiter, Esq; Simpson Thacher & Bartlett, 99 Bishopsgate, London EC2M 3XD (☎ 01 638 3851, fax 01 628 0977)

REITH, Barony of (UK 1940);; *see*: Reith, Christopher John

REITH, Christopher John; s of 1 Baron Reith, KT, GCVO, GBE, CB, TD, PC (Dir-Gen BBC 1926-38); suc f 1971 but disclaimed Peerage for life 1972; *b* 27 May 1928; *Educ* Eton, Worcester Coll Oxford; *m* 1969, Ann (Penelope Margaret), da of Henry Morris, of Notts; 1 s (James b 1971), 1 da Julie b 1972); *Heir* s, Hon James Harry John Reith b 2 June 1971; *Career* served RN 1946-48, subsequently farmer; *Style*— Christopher Reith, Esq; Whitebank Farm, Methven, Perthshire (☎ 333)

REITH, Robert Davidson; s of Alexander Davidson Reith (d 1974), and Margaret, *née* Hunter (d 1979); *b* 25 July 1938; *Educ* Dulwich; *m* 30 Sept 1961, Stella Ann, da of Francis Joseph Lewis (d 1984); 1 s (Martin Robert Davidson b 1965), 1 da (Catherine Ann b 1963); *Career* dir: Oscar Faber plc, Oscar Faber Consulting Engrs Ltd 1986; ptnr Oscar Faber Partnership 1974; memb: Cncl of Assoc of Consulting Engrs, Watford Borough Cncl 1967-72, memb Worshipful Co of Plumbers 1980, Worshipful Co of Engrs 1988; CEng, FICE, FIStructE, MConsE; *Recreations* golf, tennis, riding, private flying; *Clubs* Caledonian; *Style*— Robert Reith, Esq; Oscar Faber plc, Marlborough House, St Albans AL1 3UT (☎ 01 784 5784, fax 01 784 5700)

RELLIE, Alastair James Carl Euan; CMG (1987); s of Lt Cdr William Rellie (d 1943), and Lucy Rellie, *née* Mobin (d 1974); *b* 5 April 1935; *Educ* Michaelhouse S Africa, Harvard Univ USA (BA); *m* 1961, Annalisa, da of Maj Clive Modin (d 1944); 1 s (Euan b 1968), 2 da (Jemima b 1970, Lucasta b 1972); *Career* Lt Rifle Bd 1958-60; second sec FCO 1963-64, vice consul Geneva 1964-67, first sec FCO 1967-68, (commercial) Cairo 1968-70, Kinshasa 1970-72, FCO 1972-74; counsellor: UK Mission to UN, NewYork 1974-79, FCO 1979-; *Recreations* travel, talk, newspapers; *Clubs* Brooks's; *Style*— Alastair Rellie, CMG; 50 Smith St, London SW3 (☎ 01 352 5734); FCO, King Charles St, London SW1 (☎ 01 270 0813)

RELLY, Gavin Walter Hamilton; *b* 6 Feb 1926, of Stellenbosch SA; *Educ* Trinity Coll Oxford (MA); *m* 1951, Jane Margaret, *née* Glenton; 1 s, 2 da; *Career* chm: Anglo-American Corpn of S Africa, AECI Ltd; dir: Anglo-American Industl Corpn Ltd, Anglo-American Coal Corpn Ltd, Anglo-American Farms Ltd, Anglo-American Gold Investmt Co Ltd, Anglo-American Investmt Tst Ltd, Boart Int Ltd, De Beers Consolidated Mines Ltd, Highveld Steel and Vanadium Corpn Ltd, Minerals and

Resources Corpn Ltd, Mondi Paper Co Ltd, The South African Motor Corpn (Pty) Ltd, S African Eagle Insur Co Ltd, Standard Bank Investmt Corpn Ltd, Zambia Copper Investmts Ltd, Vaal Reefs Exploration and Mining Co Ltd; chm SA Nature Fndn; *Recreations* golf, fishing; *Clubs* Rand, River, Country, Western Province; *Style—* Gavin Relly, Esq; c/o Anglo-American Corporation of South Africa Ltd, 40 Holborn Viaduct, London EC1P 1AJ (☎ 01 353 1545); 44 Main St, Johannesburg, South Africa

RELPH, Michael Leighton George; s of George Relph (CBE), and Deborah Caroline, *née* Nanson; *Educ* Bembridge Sch Isle of Wight; *m* 1, 1940 (m dis 1948), Doris, *née* Ringwood; 1 s (Simon); m 2, 1950, Maria Rose, *née* Barry; 1 da (Emma); *Career* stage designer West End 1940-50, asst art dir (originally apprentice) Gaumont Br Studios, art dir Warner Bros Studios, art dir Ealing Studios 1942; assoc prodr to Michael Balcon 1945, prodr-writer in partnership with Basil Dearden (dir) until his death in 1972; Ealing prodns incl: The Captive Heart, Kind Hearts and Coronets, The Blue Lamp (Best Film Award Br Film Acad); also produced and/or wrote, directed for: Ealing MGM, Rank Orgn, Br Lion, United Artists, Paramount, EMI; fndr dir Allied Film Makers produced: League of Gentlemen, Victim, Man in the Moon; chm Film Prodn Assoc of GB 1971-76, memb Cinematograph Films Cncl 1971-76, govr Br Film Inst (chm prodn bd) 1971-78; *Style—* Michael Relph, Esq; The Lodge, Primrose Hill Studios, Fitzroy Rd, London NW1 (☎ 01 586 0249)

RELPH, Simon George Michael; s of Michael George Leighton Relph, and Doris, *née* Ringwood (d 1978); *b* 13 April 1940; *Educ* Bryanston, King's Coll Cambridge (MA); *m* 14 Dec 1963, Amanda Jane, da of Col Anthony Grinling, MC (d 1981), of Hinds Cottage, Dyrham Park, Avon, Wilts; 1 s (Alexander James b 16 June 1967), 1 da (Arabella Kate b 17 Sept 1975); *Career* asst dir feature films 1961-73, prodn admin Nat Theatre 1974-78, prodn supervisor Yanks 1978, exec prodr Reds 1979-80; prodr/co-prodr 1981-85: The Return of the Soldier, Privates on Parade, The Ploughman's Lunch, Secret Places, Wetherby, Comrades; chief exec Br Screen Fin Ltd 1986-88; cncl memb: BAFTA, Br Screen Advsy Cncl; exec memb Br Film and TV Producers Assoc; *Recreations* golf, photography, fishing; *Style—* Simon Relph, Esq; 37 Oxford St, London, W1 1RE (☎ 01 434 0291, fax 01 434 9933, telex 888694 BRISCR G)

REMINGTON-HOBBS, Lady Clare Charlotte Rosemary; *née* Finch-Knightley; yr da of 11 Earl of Aylesford, *qv*; *b* 13 Sept 1959; *m* 1985, James Remington-Hobbs, s of C Remington-Hobbs, of Normandy, France; 2 s (Johnathon b 1986, Alexander Charles b 1988); *Style—* Lady Clare Remington-Hobbs

REMINGTON-HOBBS, Col Edward; DSO (1945), OBE (1947); s of A Remington-Hobbs, MD (d 1928), and gs of Sir Joseph Wilkinson (d 1902); *b* 7 Feb 1916; *Educ* Westminster, RMC Sandhurst; *m* 1, 1950, Angela Susan (k in air crash 1953), only da of Capt Marshall Owen Roberts (d 1931), of 15 Grosvenor Sq, W1; 1 da (Julie Marguerite b 1951); m 2, 1957 (m dis 1967) Ann; m 3, 1972, Susan Mary Sheila, da of Hon Charles Winn (2 s of 2 Baron St Oswald JP, DL), and his 1 w, Hon Olive Paget (da of 1 and last Baron Queenborough, GBE, JP, gs of 1 Marquess of Anglesey by his 2 w); 3 s (David Whitney Erskine b 1947, James Nicholas Geoffrey b 1949, d 1969, Anthony John Mark b 1952), 1 da (Vanessa Mary Linda b 1960); *Career* Argyll and Sutherland Highlanders; serv WWII: UK, BNAF, NW Europe (wounded), SEAC; instr Staff Coll Camberley 1944, ret 1950, gold staff offr Coronation of HM The Queen 1953, usher (silver stick) Silver Jubilee Thanksgiving Serv 1977, underwriting memb of Lloyd's 1959-; chm & md: Polyseal Ltd 1960-75, Bellfax Int Ltd 1975-84; chm Snuffers Ltd 1984-; memb Order of St John Cncl for Sussex 1965-69, Order Cross Bearer 1966-; memb Chapter General 1972-, KStJ (1976); Freeman City of London 1960, memb Guild of Freemen 1987, Liveryman Worshipful Co of Gunmakers 1988-; memb The Pilgrims 1971-; *Recreations* cricket, shooting, golf; *Clubs* Boodle's, Pratt's, MCC, I Zingari, Swinley Forest; *Style—* Col Edward Remington-Hobbs, DSO, OBE; The Maidens' Tower, Leeds Castle, Maidstone, Kent ME17 1PL (☎ 062 780 272); 3 Lyall Mews, London SW1X 8DJ (☎ 01 235 0930); 123-124 Newgate St, London EC1A 7AA (☎ 01 600 8387)

REMINGTON-HOBBS, Susan Mary Sheila; *née* Winn; da of Hon Charles Winn (2 s to Baron Sir Oswald JF DL), by his 1 w, Hon Olive, da of last Baron Queenborough gs 1 Marquess of Anglesea by 1 w; *b* 27 April 1923; *Educ* Owleston Croft, Cambridge, French Sch Paris; *m* 1, 20 July 1946, Hon Geoffrey Denis Erskine Russell, (now Baron Ampthill); 3 s (David Whitney Erskine b 1947, James Nicholas Geoffrey b 1948, d 1969, Anthony John Mark b 1952), 1 da (Vanessa Mary Linda b 1960); m 2, 19 Dec 1972, Col Edward Remington-Hobbs DSO, OBE; *Career* joined Red Cross 1939, serv VAD 1941-45; *Recreations* reading, walking, photography; *Style—* Susan Remington-Hobbs; The Maidens Tower, Leeds Castle, Maidstone, Kent ME17 1PL (☎ 062780 272); 3 Lyall Mews, London SW1X 8DJ (☎ 01 235 0930)

REMNANT, Hon Hugo Charles; 3 s of 3 Baron Remnant, CVO; *b* 28 Nov 1959; *Educ* Eton, Newcastle Univ (BSc), RAC Cirencester; *Career* land agent; *Style—* The Hon Hugo Remnant; c/o Bear Ash, Hare Hatch, Reading RG10 9XR (☎ 073 522 2639)

REMNANT, 3 Baron (UK 1928); Sir James Wogan Remnant; 3 Bt (UK 1917), CVO (1979); o s of 2 Baron Remnant, MBE (d 1967), and Norah Susan, *née* Wogan-Browne; *b* 23 Oct 1930; *Educ* Eton; *m* 24 June 1953, Serena Jane, o da of Cdr Sir Clive Loehnis, KCMG, RN (ret), and his w, Rosemary Beryl, o da of Maj Hon Robert Dudley Ryder, 4 s of 4 Earl of Harrowby; 3 s, 1 da; *Heir* s, Hon Philip John Remnant, *qv*; *Career* ptnr Touche Ross & Co 1958-70; dir Australian Mercantile Land and Fin 1957-69, Australia & NZ Banking Gp 1965-81; chm: Touche, Remnant & Co 1980- (md 1970-80), TR City of London Tst 1978- (dir 1973-), TR Pacific Investmt Tst 1987-, TR Energy 1980-, Bank of Scotland London Bd 1979- (dir 1973-); dep chm Ultramar 1981 (dir 1970-); dir: Nat Provident Inst 1963, Union Discount Co of London 1969- (dep chm 1970-86) and other Cos; pres Nat Cncl of YMCAs 1983- (previously govr and pres London Central YMCA); tstee The Royal Jubilee Trusts 1989- (chm 1980-88, hon tres 1972-80); chm Assoc of Investmt Tst Cos 1977-79; Church Cmmr 1976-84; FCA; *Clubs* White's; *Style—* The Rt Hon the Lord Remnant, CVO; Bear Ash, Hare Hatch, Reading, Berks RG10 9XR (☎ Wargrave 073 522 2639)

REMNANT, Hon Melissa Clare; da of 3 Baron Remnant, CVO; *b* 20 May 1963; *Educ* Wycombe Abbey; *Career* mgmnt information conslt; *Style—* The Hon Melissa Remnant

REMNANT, Dowager Baroness; Norah Susan; *née* Wogan Browne; Dowager Baroness; da of Lt-Col Alexander John Wogan-Browne, 33 Indian Light Cavalry (direct descent from Sir John Wogan, Judiciary of Ireland 1295-1312), and Caroline Marcia, da of Gen James Primrose CSI (ggggf of Sir Archibald Primrose, 1 Bt, whose ers was created 1 Earl of Rosebery 1703) by his w, Elizabeth de la Poer Beresford (ggggs of Sir Marcus Beresford, 1 Earl of Tyrone); *b* 18 July 1900; *Educ* private sch; *m* 1924, 2 Baron Remnant, MBE; 1 s (3 Baron), 1 da (Hon Mrs (Susan) Alan Tyser), *qv*; *Style—* The Rt Hon the Dowager Lady Remnant; 131 Cranmer Court, Sloane Ave, London SW3 (☎ 01 589 5018)

REMNANT, Hon Philip John; s and h of 3 Baron Remnant, CVO; *b* 20 Dec 1954; *Educ* Eton, New Coll Oxford; *m* 1977, Caroline, da of Capt Godfrey Cavendish; 1 s (b 1981), 2 da (b 1983, b 1986); *Career* merchant banker, dir Kleinwort Benson Ltd; *Style—* The Hon Philip Remnant; 36 Stevenage Rd, London SW6 6ET

REMNANT, Hon Robert James; 2 s of 3 Baron Remnant, CVO; *b* 10 Oct 1956; *Educ* Eton; *m* 1981, Sherrie, da of Frederick Cronn and Mrs Michael Watson, of Los Angeles; 1 s (Christopher Michael b Oct 1982); *Style—* The Hon Robert Remnant; c/o Jardine Matheson & Co Ltd, PO Box 70, GPO, Hong Kong

RENALS, Sir Stanley; 4 Bt (UK 1895); s of Sir James Herbert Renals, 2 Bt (d 1927), and Susan Emma, *née* Crafter (d 1957); suc bro, Sir Herbert Renals, 3 Bt (d 1961); *b* 20 May 1923; *Educ* City of London Freemen's Sch; *m* 2 Jan 1957, Maria Dolores Rodriguez Pinto, da of José Rodriguez Ruiz (d 1948); 1 s; *Heir* s, Stanley Michael Renals, *qv*; *Career* serv Merchant Navy 1938-60, entered as apprentice and ret with Master Mariner (FG) Certificate World Wide; *Style—* Sir Stanley Renals, Bt; 47 Baden Rd, Brighton, E Sussex BN2 4DP (☎ 0273 693993)

RENALS, Stanley Michael; s and h of Sir Stanley Renals, 4 Bt of Brighton, Sussex, and Maria Dolores Rodriguez, *née* Pinto; *b* 14 Jan 1958; *Educ* Falmer HS, Brighton Poly (BSc); *m* 1982, Jacqueline Ann, da of Roy Denis Riley, of 26 Uplands Rd, Hollingdean, Brighton, Sussex; 1 s (Lloyd James b 1985) 1 da (Frances Emma b 1986); *Career* design engr Kulicke & Soffa 1983-85, sales mangr Alpha Metals 1988 (area mangr 1985); CEng, MIMechE, MIProdE; *Recreations* squash, DIY; *Clubs* Dragons Health and Leisure; *Style—* Stanley Renals, Esq; 72 Sunninghill Ave, Hove, Sussex BN3 8JA; Alpha Metals, 1 The Broadway, Tolworth, Surbiton, Surrey KT6 7DQ (☎ 01 390 7011, 01 399 6252, telex 929818)

RENDALL, Peter Godfrey; s of Godfrey A H Rendall (d 1961), of Bushey Heath, Herts, and Mary Whishaw, *née* Wilson (d 1946); *b* 25 April 1909; *Educ* Rugby, Corpus Christi Coll Oxford (BA, MA); *m* 6 Feb 1944, Ann, da of Edward McKnight Kauffer (d 1956), of London and NY; 2 s (Jonathan Godfrey, Edward Simon), 1 da (Helen Grace); *Career* Flt Lt RAF 1943-46; Upper Canada Coll Toronto 1934-35, sr classics master and housemaster Felsted Sch 1935-43 (sr classics master 1931-34), second master St Bees Sch Cumberland 1946-48, headmaster Aichimota Sch Gold Coast Ghana 1948-53, classics master Lancing Coll 1954-59, headmaster Bembridge Sch IOW 1959-74; town clerk Burford Oxon 1977-85; asst co cmmr Boys Scouts 1947-48, chm Lancing branch UNO 1956-59, chm Tolsey Museum Burford 1976-; Coronation Medal 1951; *Recreations* reading, carpentry, gardening; *Clubs* Royal Cwlth Soc, Oxford Union Soc; *Style—* Peter Rendall, Esq; Chippings, The Hill, Burford, Oxon (☎ 099 382 3033)

RENDELL, Ruth Barbara; da of Arthur Grasemann (d 1973), and Ebba Elise Grasemann, *née* Kruse (d 1963); *b* 17 Feb 1930; *m* 1950 and 1977 (m and re-m), Donald John Rendell (d 1954); 1 s (Simon b 1953); *Career* writer; awards: Arts Cncl Nat Book Award Genre Fiction (1981), Crime Writers' Assoc 3 Gold Dagger Awards (1976, 1987 and 1987), 1 Silver Dagger (1984), Mystery Writers of America 3 Edgar Allen Poe Awards (1974, 1984 and 1987); *Books* incl From Doon with Death (1964), The Face of Trespass (1971), A Judgement in Stone (1976), Master of the Moor (1982), The Killing Doll (1984), An Unkindness of Ravens (1985), The New Girlfriend (1985), Live Flesh (1986), Talking to Strange Men (1987); under pseudonym Barbara Vine: A Da rk-Adapted Eye (1986), A Fatal Inversion (1987); *Recreations* reading, walking, opera; *Clubs* Groucho's, Detection; *Style—* Mrs Ruth B Rendell; Nussteads, Polstead, Suffolk; 31 Clanricarde Gardens, London W2

RENDER, Phillip Stanley; s of Stanley Render, of Bransholme, Hull, and Bessie, *née* Bestwick; *b* 15 Jan 1944; *Educ* Malet Lambet HS Hull; *m* 21 Oct 1967, Patricia Mary, da of Alfred Bernard Rooms, of Parkstone Rd, Hull; 2 s (Adrian b 1973, Andrew b 1978), 1 da (Suzanne b 1982); *Career* chartered surveyor in own practice 1982-, surveyor to tstees of Beverley Consolidated Charity 1973-, dir Beverley Bldg Soc 1986-, memb sub-ctee Northern Assoc of Surveryors 1988-; sec West Beck Preservation Soc 1982-, memb exec ctee Salmon and Trout Assoc (E Yorks Branch) 1982-; CS 1961-71; FRICS 1968; *Recreations* salmon and trout fishing, badminton; *Clubs* West Beck Preservation Soc, Hull and East Riding Sports; *Style—* Phillip Render, Esq; 6 West End Rd, Cottingham, N Humberside (☎ 0482 848 327); 7 North Bar Within, Beverley, N Humberside (☎ 0482 860 169); fax 0482 472 340)

RENDLE, Michael Russel; s of H C R Rendle (decd), of Kuala Lumpur, and Valerie Patricia, *née* Gleeson; *b* 20 Feb 1931; *Educ* Marlborough, New Coll Oxford (MA); *m* 1957, Elisabeth Heather, da of J W J Rinkel; 2 s, 2 da; *Career* joined Anglo-Iranian Oil Co (now BP) 1954; md: BP Trinidad 1967-70, BP Australia Ltd 1974-78, chm BP Chemicals Int Ltd 1981-83, chm BP Coal Ltd 1983-86, md BP Co plc 1981-86; memb London advsy bd Westpac Banking Corpn (Australia), dir Willis Faber plc 1985-; memb BOTB 1982-; chm: European Trade Ctee 1982-86, BP Trading Ltd 1978-81; INSEAD Int Cncl and UK Advisory Bd 1984-86; UNICE Social Affairs Ctee 1984-87; *Recreations* golf, music, outdoor sports, gardening; *Clubs* Vincent's (Oxford); Australian (Melbourne), Royal Melbourne Golf; *Style—* Michael Rendle, Esq; Bridgetts, Widdington, nr Saffron Walden, Essex CB11 3SL (☎ 0799 40470); Willis Faber plc, Ten Trinity Sq, London EC3P 3AX

RENDLE, Timothy John; s of Morgan Rendle, RI, RBA, ARWA, ARWS, vice princ Brighton Coll of Art (d 1952), of Hove, Sussex, and Joy, *née* Griffith (d 1975); *b* 25 Mar 1924; *Educ* Brighton Coll, British Columbia, Brighton Coll of Art; *m* 13 Sept 1975, Judith Anne, da of Robert Chalenor Freeman (d 1983), of Liverpool; 1 da (Claudia b 1976); *Career* architect, interior and furniture designer, architectural asst Louis de Soissons & ptnrs 1950-52, architectural assoc to Sir Hugh Casson 1953-60; formed architectural practice 1958; chm WLAS 1983 and WLAS Planning 1984-; ARIBA; *Recreations* music (violin) painting, photography; *Style—* Timothy J Rendle, Esq; 54 Britannia Rd, London SW6 (☎ 01 736 9744)

RENDLESHAM, 8 Baron (I 1806); Charles Anthony Hugh Thellusson; s of Lt-Col Hon Hugh Thellusson, DSO, 3 s of 5 Baron Rendlesham, JP, DL, by his w Lady Egidia Montgomerie (da of 13 Earl of Eglinton and Winton, KT); Hugh was bro of 6 and 7 Barons Rendlesham and m Gwynnydd, da of Brig-Gen Sir Robert Colleton, 1 and last Bt, CB; suc unc 1943; the Thellussons descend from an eighteenth century Swiss Ambass to the court of Louis XV of France, one Isaac de Thellusson; *b* 15 Mar 1915; *Educ* Eton; *m* 1, 1940, Margaret (m dis 1947), da of Lt-Col Robin Rome, MC; 1 da (Hon Lady Goring, *qv*); m 2, 1947, Clare (d 1987), da of Lt-Col Douglas McCririck, of Wiveliscombe, Somerset; 1 s, 3 da; *Heir* s, Hon Charles Thellusson; *Career* late Royal Corps of Signals, Capt, served WW II; *Style—* The Rt Hon The Lord Rendlesham; 100b Eaton sq, SW1

RENFREW, Prof (Andrew) Colin; s of Archibald Renfrew (d 1978), and Helena Douglas *née* Savage; *b* 25 July 1937; *Educ* St Albans Sch, St John's Coll Cambridge (BA, PhD, ScD); *m* 21 April 1965, Jane Margaret, da of Ven Walter F Ewbank; 2 s (Alban b 24 June 1970, Magnus b 5 Nov 1975), 1 da (Helena b 23 Feb 1968); *Career* Nat Serv Flying Offr (Signals) RAF 1956-58; reader prehistory & archaeology Univ of Sheffield 1965-72 (formerly lectr and sr lectr), res fell St Johns Coll Cambridge 1965-68, Bulganian Govt Scholarship 1966, visiting lectr Univ of California (Los Angeles) 1967, prof of archaeology and head of dept Univ of Southampton 1972-81, Disney prof of archaeology and head of dept Univ of Cambridge 1981-, fell St John's Coll Cambridge 1981-86, master Jesus Coll Cambridge 1986-; memb: Royal Cmmn for Historic Monuments of England 1977-87, Historic Bldgs of Monuments Commn Advsy Bd 1983-, Historic Bldgs & Monuments Cmmn Sci Panel 1983-; Freeman City of London; Hon DLitt Sheffield Univ 1987; FSA 1968, FSA Scotland 1970, FBA 1980; *Books* The Explanation of Culture Change: Models in Prehistory (ed 1973), Br Prehistory, a new Outline (ed 1977), Problems in European Prehistory (1979), Approaches to Social Archaeology (1984), The Archaeology of Cult: The Sanctuary at Phylakopi (1985), Archaeology and Language: The Puzzle of Indo-European Origins (1987); *Recreations* modern art, numismatics, travel; *Clubs* Athenaeum, Utd Oxford and Cambridge Univ; *Style—* Prof Colin Renfrew; The Master's Lodge, Jesus Coll, Cambridge CB5 8QL (☎ 0223 323 934) University of Cambridge, Department of Archaeology, Downing Street, Cambridge CB2 3DZ (☎ 0223 333 520)

RENFREW, Glen McGarvie; *b* 15 Sept 1928; *m* Daphne; 1 s (Barry), 3 da (Susan, Judy, Pamela; also 1 da, Ann, decd); *Career* jt dep md Reuters Ltd to 1981, md Feb 1981-; dir IDR Inc (USA); *Style—* Glen Renfrew Esq; c/o Reuters Ltd, 1700 Broadway, NY 10019, USA; c/o Reuters Ltd, 85 Fleet St, EC4 (☎ 01 353 6060/836 2567); Shorewood Drive, Sands Point, New York, USA

RENNELL, 3 Baron (UK 1933); (John Adrian) Tremayne Rodd; 2 but only surviving s of Cdr Hon Gustaf Rodd (bro of: (1) 2 Baron Rennell, KBE, CB, JP, DL, who d 1978, (2) Hon Peter Rodd, who d 1968, husb of late Nancy Mitford and allegedly the model for Evelyn Waugh's character Basil Seal, (3) late Baroness Emmet of Amberley, and (4) late Hon Mrs (Lt-Col Simon) Elwes, wife of the former Official War Artist); *b* 28 June 1935; *Educ* Downside, RNC Dartmouth; *m* 1977, Phyllis, da of Thomas Neill, of Co Armagh; 1 s, 1 da (Hon Sophie b 1981, Hon Rachel b 1987); *Heir* s, Hon James Roderick David Tremayne Rodd b 9 March 1978; *Career* served RN 1952-62; Morgan Grenfell & Co 1963-66, former freelance journalist & Scottish Rugby International; dir Tremayne Ltd 1980-; *Clubs* White's, Brooks, Portland, Queens, Sunningdale; *Style—* The Rt Hon Lord Rennell; 3 Briar Walk, Putney, London SW15 6UD (☎ 01 785 2338)

RENNERT, Jonathan; s of Sidney Rennert, of London, and Patricia, *née* Clack; *b* 17 Mar 1952; *Educ* St Paul's, RCM, St John's Coll Cambridge (MA); *Career* dir of music: St Jude's Church London 1975-76, St Matthew's Ottawa Canada 1976-78, St Michael's Cornhill City of London 1979-; organ recitalist on four continents, lectr; recordings, radio and TV broadcasts as conductor, solo organist, organ accompanist, harpsichord continuo player; conductor: Cambridge Opera 1972-74, St Jude's Singers 1975-76, St Michael's Singers 1979-, The Elizabethan Singers 1983-88, English Harmony 1988-; fndr and dir Cornhill Festival of Br Music and Lloyds Bank Nat Composers' Award 1982-; examiner: Assoc Bd of the Royal Schs of Music, Royal Coll of Organists; adjudicator Thames TV, course dir Royal Sch of Church Music, admin and chm Exec Ctee Int Congress of Organists 1987; memb: Incorporated Soc of Musicians, Musicians' Union, Royal Coll of Organists and Organists' Benevolent League; former pres The Organ Club; hon fell Royal Canadian Coll of Organists 1987; Liveryman Worshipful Co of Musicians; FRCO, ARCM, LRAM,; *Books* William Crotch 1775-1847 Composer Artist Teacher (1975), George Thalben-Ball (1979); *Style—* Jonathan Rennert, Esq; 74 Pembroke Rd, Kensington, London W8 6NX (☎ 01 602 7483)

RENNIE, Archibald Louden; CB (1980); s of John Rennie Lindores (d 1974), of Fife, and Isabella Mitchell, *née* Louden (d 1979); *b* 4 June 1924; *Educ* Madras Coll St Andrews, Univ of St Andrews (BSc); *m* 14 Setp 1950, Kathleen, da of John James Harkess (d 1955), of Chingford, Essex; 4 s (Adam b 1951, John b 1953, David b 1956, Simon b 1959); *Career* temp experimental offr mine design dept and minesweeping res div Admty 1944-47; princ Dept of Health for Scotland 1954-62 (asst princ 1947-54), private sec to Sec of State for Scotland 1962-63, asst sec Scottish Home and Health Dept 1963-69, registrar gen for Scotland 1969-73, under sec Scottish Econ Planning Devpt 1973-77, sec Scottish Home and Health Dept 1977-84, ret 1984; vice chm NHS Advsy Ctee on Distinction Awards 1985; assessor St Andrew's Univ Ct 1984- (chllrs assessor 1986-); memb: Scottish Records Advsy Cncl 1985-, Cncl on Tbnls (and Scottish Ctee) 1987-88; chm Hong Kong Disciplined Servs Pay Review Ctee 1988-; chm Blacket Assoc (local conservation soc) 1970-73, memb Elie and Earls Ferry SC ctee 1984; tstee Lockerbie Disaster Appeal Fund; *Recreations* sailing, sea-fishing, gardening, golf, scottish literature; *Clubs* Scottish Arts (Edinburgh), Elie Golf House; *Style—* Archibald Rennie, Esq, CB; Baldinnie, 10 Pk Pl, Elie, Leven, Fife (☎ 0333 630741)

RENNIE, Lady; Jean Marcella; *née* Huggins; *m* 1929, Sir Gilbert Rennie, GBE, KCMG, MC, sometime High Commissioner in UK for Fedn of Rhodesia & Nyasaland (d 1981); 2 s, 1 da; *Style—* Lady Rennie; 7 Beech Hill, Hadley Wood, Barnet, Herts EN4 0JN (☎ 01 449 1503)

RENNIE, Sir John Shaw; GCMG (1968, KCMG 1962, CMG 1958), OBE 1955; s of late John Shaw Rennie, of Saskatoon, Saskatchewan, Canada; *b* 12 Jan 1917; *Educ* Hillhead HS Glasgow, Glasgow Univ, Balliol Coll Oxford; *m* 1946, Mary Winifred Macalpine, da of James Bryson Robertson, of Hillhead, Glasgow; 1 s; *Career* entered Colonial Civil Serv Tanganyika 1940, asst dist offr 1942, (dist offr 1949), dep colonial sec Mauritius 1951, Br res cmmr New Hebrides 1955-62, govr and CIC Mauritius 1962-68, (govr-gen 1968), dep cmmr gen UN Relief and Works Agency for Palestine Refugees 1968-71, (cmmr gen 1971-77); Hon LLD Glasgow; *Clubs* Royal Cwlth Soc; *Style—* Sir John Rennie, GCMG, OBE; 26 College Cross, London N1 1PR; Via Roma 33, 06050 Collazzone (PG), Italy

RENNY, Hon Mrs (Nicola Gladys); *née* Moncreiff; da of 4 Baron Moncreiff (d 1942); *b* 1917; *m* 1, 1940, Capt Frederick W Gifford, RA (ka 1943); 1 s; m 2, 1946, Charles John Derek Renny (d 1970); 1 s, 2 da; *Clubs* Royal Channel Islands Yacht (RCIYC); *Style—* The Hon Mrs Renny; Greenways, Les Vardes, St Peter Port, Guernsey

RENOUF, Sir Francis Henry; s of Francis Charles Renouf (d 1983), of NZ, and Mary Ellen, *née* Avery (d 1983); *b* 31 July 1918; *Educ* Wellington Coll NZ, Victoria Univ of Wellington (M Com), Oxford Univ (Dip PL); *m* 1, 7 Aug 1954, Anne Marie Harkin; 1 s (John b 1962), 3 da (Paula b 1955, Frances b 1957, Katy b 1957); m 2, 2 Sept 1985, Susan Rossiter, da of Sir John Rossiter (d 1988); *Career* 2 Lt (later Capt) NZEF 1940, (POW Greece 1941-45); chm Renouf Gp 1950-87, ret; Lawn Tennis Victoria Univ blue 1938-40, Oxford blue 1948 and 1949; Order of Merit (first class) West Germany 1986; *Recreations* lawn tennis; *Clubs* Cavalry and Guards'; *Style—* Sir Francis Renouf; 37 Eaton Sq, London SW1 (☎ 01 235 1124)

RENOWDEN, Very Rev Charles Raymond; s of Rev Canon Charles Renowden (d 1964), and Mary Elizabeth, *née* Williams (d 1974); bro of Ven Glyndwr Rhys Renowden, *qv*; *b* 27 Oct 1923; *Educ* Llandysil GS, St David's Univ Coll Lampeter (BA), Selwyn Coll Cambridge (BA, MA); *m* 1951, Ruth Cecil Mary, da of George Edward Cecil Collis (d 1969); 1 s, 2 da; *Career* ordained: deacon 1951, priest 1952; lectr in philosphy and theology St David's Univ Coll Lampeter 1955-57 (head dept of philosophy 1957-69, sr lectr philosphy and theology 1969-71); dean of St Asaph 1971-; *Recreations* music, ornithology; *Style—* The Very Rev the Dean of St Asaph; The Deanery, St Asaph, Clwyd, N Wales LL17 0RL (☎ 0745 583597); St Asaph Cathedral Office (☎ 0745 583429)

RENOWDEN, Rev Canon; Air Vice-Marshal (Ret) Glyndwr Rhys; CB (1987), QHC (1980); s of Rev Canon Charles Renowden (d 1964), and Mary Elizabeth Renowden (d 1972); *b* 13 August 1929; *Educ* Llanelli GS, St David's Univ Coll Lampeter (BA, LTh); *m* 1956, Mary Kinsey-Jones; 1 da; *Career* Chaplain in Chief RAF 1983-88; *Clubs* RAF; *Style—* The Rev Canon Glyndwr R Renowden, CB, QHC; Red Cedars, Kenystyle, Penally, nr Tenby, Dyfed

RENSHALL, (James) Michael; OBE (1977); s of Arthur Renshall (d 1973), and Ethel, *née* Gardner (d 1970); *b* 27 July 1930; *Educ* Rydal Sch, Clare Coll Cambridge (MA); *m* Aug 1960, Kathleen Valerie, da of Harold Tyson, of Liverpool; 1 da (Susan b 1961); *Career* CA ptnr with Peat Marwick McLintock, chm Accounting Standards Ctee 1986-; memb Cncl of Inst of CA England and Wales; FCA; *Recreations* theatre, art, economic and military history, gardens; *Clubs* Utd Oxford and Cambridge, City Livery; *Style—* Michael Renshall, Esq; 5 Ferrings, London SE21 7LU (☎ 01 693 3190); 1 Puddle Dock, Blackfriars, London EC4U 3PD (☎ 01 236 8000, telex 8811541 PMMLONG, fax 248 6552)

RENSHAW, (John) David; s and h of Sir (Charles) Maurice Bine Renshaw, 3 Bt, and Isobel Bassett Popkin (now Mrs L E S Cox); *b* 9 Oct 1945; *Educ* Ashmole Sch, Southgate N14; *m* 1970 (m dis 1988) Jennifer, da of Gp Capt Fredrick Murray, RAF (ret), 1 s (Thomas b 1976), 2 da (Joanna b 1973, Catherine b 1978); *Career* Army 1960-69 Corporal; fatstock offr with the meat and livestock cmmn 1974-88; *Recreations* skiing, upholstery, DIY; *Style—* John Renshaw Esq; Kestral, Black Prince Hols Ltd, Festival Gdn Marina, Eturia, Stoke-on-Trent; c/o HO Bromsberrow Way, Meir Park, Meir, Stoke-on-Trent, (☎ 0782 393408)

RENSHAW, Sir (Charles) Maurice Bine; 3 Bt (UK 1903); s of Capt Sir (Charles) Stephen Bine Renshaw, 2 Bt (d 1976), and Edith Mary, 4 da of Rear-Adm Sir Edward Chichester, 9 Bt, CB, CMG; *b* 7 Oct 1912; *Educ* Eton; *m* 1, 1942 (m dis 1947), Isobel Bassett, da of late Rev John L T Popkin; 1 s, 1 da; m 2, Winifred Mary, da of H F Gliddon, and formerly w of of James H T Sheldon; 3 s, 3 da; *Heir* s, (John) David Renshaw; *Career* late Flying Offr RAF; *Style—* Sir Maurice Renshaw, Bt; Tom-na-Margaidh, Balquhidder, Perthshire; Linwood, Instow, N Devon

RENSHAW, Peter Bernard Appleton; NP (1988); s of Bernard Artoune Renshaw, Flat 3, Wrayton Lodge, Whitehall Rd, Sale, Ches, and Elsie Renshaw, *née* Appleton (d 1954); *b* 23 July 1954; *Educ* Charterhouse, Selwyn Coll Cambridge; *m* 16 Oct 1982, Patricia Ann, da of Robert Vernon Caffrey, of 26 Avonlea Rd, Sale, Ches; 1 s (Thomas Peter b 1987); *Career* ptnr Slater Heelis Slrs Manchester 1982- (articled clerk 1977-79, slr 1979-82); memb Law Soc; *Recreations* walking, squash, DIY; *Style—* Peter Renshaw, Esq, NP; Slater Heelis, 71 Princess St, Manchester, Greater Manchester M2 4HL (☎ 061 228 3781, fax 061 236 5282, telex 669568)

RENTON, Hon Clare Olivia; 2 da of Baron Renton, KBE, TD, PC, QC, DL (life peer); *b* 23 August 1950; *Educ* St Mary's Wantage, Birkbeck Coll London; *m* 1982, Timothy John Whittaker Scott, s of J D Scott (d 1980); 1 s (Duncan b 1984), 1 da Helen b 1983); *Career* barr Lincoln's Inn 1972; *Recreations* opera, history, the country; *Style—* The Hon Clare Renton; 5 Raymond Buildings, Gray's Inn, London WC2 (☎ 01 831 0720)

RENTON, Baron (Life Peer UK 1979); David Lockhart-Mure Renton; PC (1962), KBE (1964), TD, QC (1954), DL (Hunts 1962, Huntingdon & Peterborough 1964, Cambs 1974); s of Dr Maurice Waugh Renton; *b* 12 August 1908; *Educ* Oundle, Univ Coll Oxford (MA, BCL); *m* 1947, Claire Cicely (d 1986), yst da of late Walter Atholl Duncan; 3 da; *Career* sits as Cons peer in House of Lords; barr 1933; Maj RA; MP Hunts (Nat Lib 1945-50, Nat Lib & C 1950-68, C 1968-79); min state Home Off 1961-62; memb Cmmn on the Constitution 1971-74, chm ctee on preparation of Legislation 1973-75; pres: Conservation Soc 1971-72, Statute Law Soc 1980-, Nat Cncl for Civil Protection 1980-, Nat Soc Mentally Handicapped Children 1982-88 (chm 1978-82); dep speaker House of Lords 1982-88, bencher Lincoln's Inn 1963 (tres 1979); patron: Hunts Cons Assoc, Nat Law Library, Ravenswood Fndn, Design and Mfr for Disability (DEMAND), Greater London Assoc for the Disabled; *Recreations* shooting, tennis, gardening; *Clubs* Carlton, Pratt's; *Style—* Rt Hon Lord Renton, PC, KBE, TD, QC, DL; Moat House, Abbots Ripton, Huntingdon, (☎ 048 73 227); 22 Old Buildings, Lincoln's Inn, WC2 3TL (☎ 01 242 8986)

RENTON, Air Cdre Helen Ferguson; CB (1982); da of John Paul Renton (d 1973), and Sarah Graham Renton, *née* Cook (d 1986); *b* 13 Mar 1931; *Educ* Stirling HS, Glasgow Univ (MA); *Career* RAF Offr cmmnd 1955 (Admin Branch); serv UK 1955-60, Cyprus 1960-62, UK 1962-67, HQ Staff Germany 1967 MOD Staff 1968-71, HQ NEAF 1971-73, HQ Trg Cmd 1973-76, MOD Staff 1977-78, 1980-86; dir WRAF 1980-86; vice pres RAF Assoc 1982-; Hon LLD Glasgow Univ; *Publications* Service Women (1977); *Recreations* needlework, travel, gardening; *Clubs* RAF; *Style—* Air Cdre Helen Renton; c/o Royal Bank of Scotland, 14-15 Hereward Centre, Broadway, Peterborough, Cambridgeshire PE1 1TB

RENTON, (Robert) Ian; s of Col Robert Donald Alexander Renton, MBE, MC (d 1976), and Susan Marion Langdon, *née* Studdy; *b* 1 Nov 1958; *Educ* Shrewsbury, Magdalene Coll Cambridge (MA); *m* 28 Sept 1985, Claire Lindsay, da of Dr James

Woods Rentoul, of Cornwall; 1 da (Ailsa b 9 Jan 1989); *Career* racecourse mangr; asst mangr Cheltenham Racecourse 1985-88, racecourse mangr Warwick Racecourse 1986-88, gen mangr and clerk of course Wincanton Racecourses 1988-; *Recreations* skiing, tennis, wine; *Style—* Ian Renton, Esq; Holywell Farmhouse, Holywell, Dorchester, Dorset DT2 0LQ

RENTON, Ronald Timothy (Tim); MP (C) Mid-Sussex 1974-; yr s of Ronald Kenneth Duncan Renton, CBE (d 1980), by his 2 w Eileen, MBE, yst da of Herbert James Torr, of Morton Hall, Lincs, and gda of John Torr, MP for Liverpool 1873-80; *b* 28 May 1932; *Educ* Eton, Magdalen Coll Oxford (MA); *m* 1960, Alice Blanche Helen, da of Sir James Ferugsson of Kilkerran, 8 Bt; 2 s (Alexander b 1961, Daniel b 1965 (twin)), 3 da (Christian b 1963, Chelsea b 1965 (twin), Penelope b 1970); *Career* dir Silvermines Ltd 1967-84, former md Tennant Trading, memb APEX; contested (C) Sheffield Park 1970, pres Cons Trade Unionists 1980-84 (vice-pres 1978-80), chm Cons Employment Ctee, PPS to John Biffen (as chief sec to Treasy) 1979-81, PPS to Sir Geoffrey Howe (as chllr and foreign sec) 1983-84, parly under sec FCO 1984, Min of State FCO 1984-87, Min of State Home Off 1987-; memb: advsy cncl BBC 1982-84, governing cncl Roedean Sch 1982-; chm Cons Foreign and Cwlth Cncl 1983-84, tstee Mental Health Fndn 1985-; *Recreations* gardening, growing amenity trees, sea fishing (mv Porage); *Clubs* Garrick; *Style—* Tim Renton, Esq, MP; Mount Harry House, Offham, Lewes, E Sussex (☎ 0273 47 4456); c/o House of Commons, London SW1A OAA

RENWICK, Diana, Lady; Diana Mary; da of Col Bernard Cruddas, DSO, of Middleton Hall, Morpeth; *m* 1934, Sqdn Ldr Sir Eustace Renwick, 3 Bt (d 1973); 2 s, 1 da; *Style—* Diana, Lady Renwick; Whalton, Northumberland

RENWICK, George Frederick; s of George Russell Renwick (d 1984), of The Old Parsonage, Sidlesham, Sussex, and Isabella Alice, *née* Watkins; *b* 27 July 1938; *Educ* Charterhouse, New Coll Oxford (MA); *m* 16 March 1974, Elizabeth Zoe, da of Strathearn Gordon, CBE (d 1983); 1 d (Helen b 1978); *Career* Nat Serv Lt RA 1957-59; teaching assoc N Western Univ Sch of Law Chicago 1962-63; admitted slr 1966; ptnr Slaughter and May 1970- (joined 1963); memb: Law Soc 1966, Int Bar Assoc, Addington Soc; *Clubs* Athenaeum, MCC; *Style—* George Renwick, Esq; c/o Slaughter and May, 35 Basinghall St, London EC2V 5DB (☎ 01 600 1200, fax 01 726 0038, telex 883486)

RENWICK, 2 Baron (UK 1964), of Coombe, Co Surrey; Sir Harry Andrew Renwick; 3 Bt (UK 1927); s of 1 Baron Renwick, KBE (d 1973), by his 1 w, Dorothy, *née* Parkes; *b* 10 Oct 1935; *Educ* Eton; *m* 1965, Susan, da of Capt Kenneth Lucking (decd), and Mrs M Stormonth Darling; 2 s (Hon Robert, Hon Michael b 26 July 1968); *Heir* s, Hon Robert James Renwick b 19 Aug 1966; *Career* dir Gen Technology Systems 1975-, vice-pres Br Dyslexia Assoc 1982- (chm 1977-82), ptnr W Greenwell and Co 1963-80; chm Dyslexia Educnl Tst 1986-; memb House of Lords Select Ctee on the European Communities 1988-; *Clubs* White's, Turf; *Style—* The Rt Hon Lord Renwick; House of Lords, Westminster SW1A 0PW

RENWICK, Prof James Harrison; s of Ray Renwick, MBE, (d 1974), of Otley Yorks, and Edith Helen, *née* Harrison (d 1988); *b* 4 Feb 1926; *Educ* Sedbergh, St Andrews Univ (MB, ChB), UCL (Phd, DSc); *m* 1, 2 April 1959 (m dis 1979), Helena, da of Albert Verheyden (d 1986), of Ghent; 1 s (Arnold James b 1962), 1 da (Sonia Ruth b 1963), m 2, Kate, da of Vincent James Salafia (d 1967), of Philadelphia; 2 s (Douglas Raymond b 1982, Gregory Hugh b 1984); *Career* Nat Serv Capt RAMC 1951-53, serv Korean War, seconded Atomic Bomb Casualty Cmmn Hiroshima Japan; prof human genetics Univ of Glasgow 1967-68, reader then prof human genetics and teratology Univ of London 1977-; Freeman Worshipful Co of Stationers and Newspaper Makers; FRCP, FRCPath; *Books* contrib scientific appendix to report Royal Cmmn on Civil Liability and Compensation for Personal Injury; *Recreations* music, walking; *Style—* Prof James Renwick; 5 Speed House, Barbican, London, EC2Y 8AT; London School of Hygiene & Tropical Medicine, Keppel St, London WC1E 7HT (☎ 01 637 2839, fax 01 436 5389, telex 8953474)

RENWICK, Joan, Baroness; (Edith) Joan; da of Sir Reginald Clarke, CIE; *m* 1, Maj John Ogilvie Spencer (decd); m 2, as his 2 w, 1953, 1 Baron Renwick, KBE (d 1973); *Style—* The Rt Hon Joan, Lady Renwick; Herne's Cottage, Windsor Forest, Berks

RENWICK, Lady; Margaret Rachel; da of Alfred Stanley and Rachel Fawcett; *m* 1933, Sir John Renwick, JP; 1 s, 1 da; vice-pres Girl Guides Assoc; chm Sheffield Cheshire Home; *Style—* Lady Renwick; Saint Cross, Ridgeway, Sheffield S12 3YA (☎ 0246 433114)

RENWICK, Sir Richard Eustace; 4 Bt (UK 1921), of Newminster Abbey, Morpeth, Northumberland; s of Sir Eustace Renwick, 3 Bt (d 1973), and Diana, Lady Renwick, *qv*; *b* 13 Jan 1938; *Educ* Eton; *m* 1966, Caroline, da of Maj Rupert Milburn, JP (2 s of Sir Leonard Milburn, 3 Bt, JP), and Anne, da of Maj Austin Scott Murray, MC; 3 s; *Heir* s, Charles Richard Renwick b 10 April 1967; *Career* late Capt Northumberland Hussars; md & proprietor Master Saddlers Co; *Recreations* tennis, hunting, point-to-pointing; *Clubs* Northern Counties (Newcastle); *Style—* Sir Richard Renwick, Bt; Whalton House, Whalton, Morpeth, Northumberland (☎ 065 075 383; office: 067089 732

RENWICK, HE Sir Robin William; KCMG (1989, CMG 1980); s of Richard Renwick, of Edinburgh, and Clarice Renwick, *née* Henderson (d 1958); *b* 13 Dec 1937; *Educ* St Paul's, Cambridge Univ (MA); *m* 1965, Annie Colette, da of Jean-Jacques Giudicelli (d 1985); 1 s (John), 1 da (Marie); *Career* HM Ambass SA July 1987-; HM Dip Serv: first sec New Delhi 1966-70, Paris 1972-76; cnsllr Cabinet Off 1976-78; head Rhodesia Dept FCO 1978-79; poltical advsr to Lord Saomes as Govr of Rhodesia 1979-80; head of Chancery Washington 1971-84; asst under sec FCO 1984-; *Books* Economic Sanctions (Harvard 1981); *Recreations* tennis, islands; *Clubs* Hurlingham, Travellers; *Style—* HE The Br Ambass to SA; c/o Foreign and Commonwealth Office; Foreign and Commonwealth Office, King Charles St, London SW1

REPARD, Hon Mrs Peggy; *née* Bowyer; da of late 1 Baron Denham (d 1948); *b* 18 May 1925; *m* 24 April 1947, Cdr John David Latimer Repard, OBE, DSC, RN; s of late William John Repard, of Many Waters, Bexhill; 3 da; *Style—* The Hon Mrs Repard; 18 Friars Field, Northchurch, Berkhamsted, Herts HP4 3XE (☎ 0442 864375)

REPTON, Rt Rev the Bishop of 1986-; (Francis) Henry Arthur Richmond; s of Francis Richmond (d 1985), of Newtown Butler, Co Fermanagh, N Ireland, and Lena, *née* Crawford; *b* 6 Jan 1936; *Educ* Portora Royal Sch Enniskillen, Trinity Coll Dublin (BA, MA), Strasbourg Univ, Linacre Coll Oxford (M Litt), Wycliffe Hall Oxford; *m* 10 Sept 1966, Caroline Mary, da of Herbert Siegmund Berent (d 1988), of Bletchingley, Surrey; 2 s (Patrick b 1969, Gerald b 1971), 1 da (Harriet b 1974); *Career* curate All Saints Woodlands Dorset 1963-66, Sir Henry Stephenson res fell and hon lectr Dept of Biblical Studies Sheffield Univ 1966-69, vicar St George's Sheffield 1969-77, hon lectr on New Testament dept of biblical studies Sheffield Univ 1969-77, anglican chaplain Sheffield Univ 1974-77, warden Lincoln Theol Coll 1977-85, proctor in convocation 1980-85; *Recreations* music, gardening, walking; *Style—* The Rt Rev the Bishop of Repton; Repton House, Lea, Matlock, Derbyshire DE4 5JP (☎ 0629 534644)

RETTIE, (James) Philip; CBE (1987), TD (1964); s of James Low Rettie (d 1962), of Balcairn, Dundee , and Josephine Rachel, *née* Buist; *b* 7 Dec 1926; *Educ* Trinity Coll Glenalmond, Manchester Univ; *m* 1, 1955 Helen Grant; 2 s (Andrew, Simon), 1 da (Sarah); m 2, 1980, Diana Mary, da of Col Colin John Ballantyne TD, DL, (d 1981); *Career* RE 1945-48, Maj RETA 1949-65 ; William Low & Co plc 1948-85 (chm 1980-85), chm Sea Fish Indust Authy 1981-87; tstee: TSB 1967-88, Scottish Civic Tst 1983-; Highland TA Assoc 1975-, Hon Col 117 Field Sqn RETA 1982-87, Hon Col 277 Fd Sqn RETA 1983-; farmer 1964-, landowner (380 acres); *Recreations* shooting, hill walking; *Clubs* Caledonian (London); *Style—* Philip Rettie, Esq, CBE, TD; Wester Ballindean, Inchture, Perthshire, PH14 9QS (☎ 0828 86337)

REUBEN, Arnold; JP (1971); s of Jack Reuben (d 1971); *b* 19 Dec 1929; *Educ* King George V Sch Southport, Exeter Coll Oxford; *m* 1954, Audrey, *née* Cussins; 1 s, 2 da; *Career* dir Waring & Gillow Hldgs Ltd, chm Leeds United Devpt Co Ltd, govr Leeds Playhouse, pres Leeds Jewish Welfare Bd; *Recreations* theatre, lit, wine and food, travel, walking; *Clubs* Royal Cwlth Soc; *Style—* Arnold Reuben, Esq, JP; Stone Acre, Leeds LS17 8EP (☎ 0532 683222)

REVANS, Reginald William; s of Thomas William Revans (d 1936), of London, and Ethel Amelia Charlotte Mary, *née* Evans (d 1966); *b* 14 May 1907; *Educ* Battersea GS, UCL (BSc), Emmanuel Coll Cambridge; *m* 1, June 1932 (m dis 1948), Ann-Ida Margareta Aqvist, of Sweden; 3 da (Marina b 31 March 1933, Vendela b 5 June 1935, Barbara b 8 Dec 1938); m 2, 30 Sept 1955, Norah Mary, da of Harold Merritt (d 1950), of Chelmsford, Essex; 1 s (Andrew b 24 Aug 1957); *Career* reserved occupation Essex Civil Def Servs; educn offr: Essex CC 1935-45, Mining Assoc of GB 1945-47, NCB 1947-50; res advsr NCB and Nat Assoc of Colliery Mangrs 1950-55, prof of indust admin Univ of Manchester 1955-65, res advsr Fondation Industrie-Universite Bruxelles Belgium 1965-75; memb Br Olympic Team Amsterdam 1928, Cambridge Univ Long Jump record 1929, Cwlth Games Hamilton Ont Canada 1930 (two silver medals); pres Euro Assoc of (Univ) Mgmnt Trg Centres 1962-64, fndr memb Br Inst of Mgmnt, hon professorial fell Univ of Manchester; Chevalier of the order of Leopold (Belgium) 1972; Hon MSc Univ of Manchester 1965, Hon DSc Univ of Bath 1973; CBIM 1947-; *Recreations* formerly athletics; *Style—* Reginald Revans, Esq; 8 Higher Downs, Altrincham, Cheshire WA14 2QI

REVELL, Stephen Michael; s of Alfred Vincent Revell, of Beardwood Meadow, Blackburn, Lancs, and Doris, *née* Peaty (d 1985); *b* 20 Dec 1956; *Educ* St Mary Coll Blackburn, Christ's Coll Cambridge (MA); *m* 10 Nov 1979, Anne Marie, da of Brian Higgins, of Whitefield, Greater Manchester; *Career* ptnr Freshfields 1987- (asst slr 1979-87); and Worshipful Co of Slrs 1988; memb Law Soc; *Recreations* skiing, fell walking, sugar lamp collecting, travelling; *Style—* Stephen Revell, Esq; Chantry St, London N1; Freshfields, Grindall House, 25 Newgate St, London EC1A 7LH (☎ 01 606 6677, fax 01 489 9565, telex 889292)

REVELSTOKE, 4 Baron (UK 1885); Rupert Baring; s of 3 Baron Revelstoke (d 1934, through whose sis Susan, the present Lord R is 1 cous once removed to Richard Ingrams, ed of Private Eye); also 1 cous twice removed of HRH The Princess of Wales, n to late Countess (w of 5 Earl) of Kenmare, and bro-in-law of late Guy Liddell, CB, CBE, MC; *b* 8 Feb 1911; *Educ* Eton; *m* 1934 (m dis 1944), Hon Flora Fermor-Hesketh (d 1971; da of 1 Baron Hesketh by his w Florence, gda of Gen J C Breckinridge, sometime Vice-Pres of the USA), sis of Hon Lady Stockdale; 2 s; *Heir* s, Hon John Baring; *Career* late 2 Lt RAC (TA); *Style—* The Rt Hon Lord Revelstoke; Lambay Island, Rush, Co Dublin, Eire

REX-TAYLOR, David; s of William Walter Taylor (d 1953); *b* 25 Jan 1947; *Educ* Jt Servs Sch Linguists, Birkbeck Coll London; *Career* asst mangr (Russia) BEA 1969-71, regnl organiser London Nat Fund Res into Crippling Diseases 1971-72; fndr: Bibliagora Publishers and Int Book Mail Order Co (1973), Bridge Book Club and Lineage Res Unit; exec ed Int Bridge Press Assoc (md inc USA) FInst SMM; *Recreations* snooker, bridge (fndr Evening Standard Bridge Congress) Br Rubber Bridge Championship; Greater London bridge clubs; *Style—* David Rex-Taylor, Esq; PO Box 77, Feltham TW14 8JF (☎ 01 898 1234, Cellnet 0860 518507, fax 01 844 1777, telex 935918 BRIDGE G)

REYNOLDS, Dr (Eva Mary) Barbara; da of Alfred Charles Reynolds (d 1969), and Barbara, *née* Florac (d 1977); *b* 13 June 1914; *Educ* St Paul's Girls' Sch, UCL (BA, BA, PhD), Cambridge Univ (MA); *m* 1, 5 Sept 1939, Lewis Guy Melville Thorpe (d 1977); 1 s (Adrian b 1942), 1 da (Kerstin b 1949); m 2, 30 Oct 1982, Kenneth Robert Imeson; *Career* asst lectr in italian LSE 1937-40, lectr in italian Univ of Cambridge 1940-62, reader in italian Univ of Nottingham 1966-78 (warden of Willoughby Hall 1963-69); visiting prof in italian: Univ of Calif Berkeley 1974-75, Wheaton Coll Illinois 1977-78, Trinity Coll Dublin 1980 and 1981, Hope Coll Michigan 1982; hon reader Warwick Univ 1975-80; managing ed Seven an Anglo-American Literary Review 1980-; chm Univ Women's Club 1988-; Hon DLitt Wheaton Coll Illinois 1979, Hon DLitt Hope Coll Michigan 1982; Silver Medal for servs to Italian culture 1964, Silver Medal for servs to Anglo-Veneto cultural rels 1971, Cavaliere Ufficiale al Merito Della Repubblica Italiana 1978; *Books* The Linguistic Writings of Alessandro Manzoni (1952), The Cambridge Italian Dictionary (gen ed Vol I 1962, Vol II 1981), Dante: Paradise (trans with Dorothy L Sayers), Guido Farina, Painter of Verona (with Lewis Thorpe, 1967), Dante: Poems of Youth (trans 1969), Concise Cambridge Italian Dictionary (1975), Ariosto: Orlando Furioso (trans Vol I 1975, Vol II 1977), The Passionate Intellect: Dorothy L Sayers' Encounter with Dante (1989); *Recreations* travel; *Clubs* University Women's, Authors; *Style—* Dr Barbara Reynolds; 220 Milton Rd, Cambridge CB4 1LQ (☎ 0223 357 894)

REYNOLDS, Brian Edwin Albert; s of Walter Albert Reynolds (d 1942), and Ann Margaret, *née* Boyce; *b* 5 Mar 1938; *Educ* Leyton Co HS, West Ham Coll Of Technol; *m* 28 July 1962, Mary Christine, da of William Horace Sherman, of Parkstone, Poole, Dorset; 3 da (Amanda Jennifer b 1964, Sarah Gillian b 1968, Janine Verity b 1979); *Career* prod mangr Berk Ltd 1963-65, mangr wax dept Wynmouth Lehr Fatoils Ltd

1965-70, supervisor BDH Chemicals 1973-75, md Poth Hille & Co Ltd 1989 (gen mangr 1975-77, dir 1977-88), dir Holroyds Oil & Ceresine Co Ltd; church warden (formerly dep church warden) St Marys and All Saints Langdon Hills Essex 1975; Freeman City of London 1980, Liveryman Worshipful Co of Wax Chandlers 1981; *Recreations* music, philately, railways; *Style—* Brian Reynolds, Esq; 28 New Ave, Langdon Hills, Basildon, Essex SS16 6BT (☎ 0268 42566); Poth Hille & Co Ltd, 37 High St, Stratford, London E15 2QD (☎ 01 534 7091, fax 01 534 2291, telex 897300)

REYNOLDS, Sir David James; 3 Bt (UK 1923); s of Lt-Col Sir John Francis Roskell Reynolds, 2 Bt, MBE (d 1956), and Millicent Orr-Ewing (d 1932); gda of 7 Duke of Roxburgh, and ggda of 7 Duke of Marlborough; *b* 26 Jan 1924; *Educ* Downside; *m* 1966, Charlotte Baumgartner; 1 s (James Francis), 2 da (Lara Mary b 1 March 1967, Sofie Josefine b 5 May 1968); *Heir* s, James Reynolds b 10 July 1971; *Career* serv WWII Capt 15/19 Hussars Italy; *Style—* Sir David Reynolds, Bt; Blanchepierre House, rue de la Blanchepierre, St Lawrence, Jersey, CI

REYNOLDS, Graham; OBE (1984); s of the late Arthur Thomas Reynolds, and Eva Mullins; *b* 10 Jan 1914; *Educ* Highgate Sch, Queens' Coll Cambridge (BA hons); *m* 6 Feb 1943, Daphne, da of Thomas Dent of Huddersfield; *Career* asst keeper V & A Museum 1937, seconded to Miny of Home Security 1939, princ 1942; dep keeper V & A (dept of paintings) 1947-58; keeper V & A (dept of prints, drawings and paintings) 1959-74; tstee William Morris Gallery Walthamstow 1972-75, chm Gainsborough's House Soc Sudbury 1977-79, memb Reviewing Ctee on Export of Works of Art 1984-; Leverhulme Emeritus fellowship 1980-81; *publications incl* Nicholas Hilliard and Issac Oliver (1947,1971), English Watercolours (1959, revised 1988), English Portrait Miniatures (1952, rev 1988), Painters of the Victorian Scene (1953), Constable the Natural Painter (1965), Victorian Paintings (1966,1987), Turner (1969), Catalogue of the Constable Collection V & A Museum (1960, rev 1973), Concise History of Watercolour Painting (1972), Catalogue of Portrait Miniatures Wallace Collection (1980), The Later Paintings and Drawings of John Constable (1984, awarded Mitchell prize 1984), Constable's England (1983); *Clubs* Athenaeum; *Style—* Graham Reynolds, Esq, OBE; The Old Manse, Bradfield St George, Bury St Edmunds, Suffolk IP30 0AZ (☎ 028 486610)

REYNOLDS, John Arthur; s of Arthur Reynolds (d 1986), of Buntingford, Herts, and Beatrice Mary, *née* Darton; *b* 23 May 1930; *Educ* Hertford GS; *m* 1, 9 Feb 1952, Joyce Florence (d 1979), da of Arthur James Harvey (d 1986); 1 s (Geoffrey Arthur b 1955), 1 da (Kathryn Louise b 1959); m 2, 18 Oct 1980, Olive, da of Flt Offr W C Rasbary (ka 1941); *Career* master builder and shopkeeper; memb Buntingford Town Cncl 1961 (chm 1973-76 and 1979), memb Braughing RDC 1964 (chm housing ctee 1970-74), E Herts DC 1973: vice-chm 1976-79, vice-chm planning ctee 1979-83, chm appeals ctee 1983-; fndr memb and first hon pres Buntingford Civic Soc, ind cncllr on all cncls; JP 1972; *Recreations* travel, music, theatre; *Style—* John Reynolds, Esq, JP; Aspenden Cottage, Aspenden, Buntingford, Herts SG9 9PE (☎ 0736 71507); 10 High Street, Buntingford, Herts SG9 9AG (☎ 0763 71309)

REYNOLDS, John Roderick; s of David Reynolds (d 1988), of Peterborough, and Gwen Reynolds, *née* Roderick; *b* 11 Oct 1948; *Educ* Oundle Sch, Imperial Coll London (BSc); *m* 7 Sept 1974, Jane Elizabeth, da of David Berridge, of Cambs; 2 s (Henry b 1980, Guy b 1982), 1 da (Daisy b 1985); *Career* Price Waterhouse 1970-76, dir J Henry Schroder Wagg and Co Ltd 1976-; FCA, ARCS; *Recreations* shooting, tennis, shooting, opera, bridge; *Clubs* Hurlingham, RAC; *Style—* John Reynolds, Esq; The Manor House, Weston-Sub-Edge, Chipping Campden, Glos; 32 Winchendon Rd, London SW6; 120 Cheapside, London EC2 (☎ 01 382 6000, fax 01 382 6459)

REYNOLDS, Lady Kathleen (Marie Gabrielle); *née* Pelham-Clinton-Hope; yr da of 9 Duke of Newcastle, OBE (d 1988); *b* 1 Jan 1951; *m* 27 Feb 1970, Edward Vernon Reynolds, s of Henry Reynolds, of The Mall, Kenton, Middlesex; *Style—* Lady Kathleen Reynolds

REYNOLDS, (James) Kirk; s of The Hon Mr Justice James Reynolds, of Helen's Bay, Co Down, N Ireland, and Alexandra Mary Erskine, *née* Strain; *b* 25 Mar 1951; *Educ* Campbell Coll Belfast, Peterhouse Cambridge (MA); *Career* called to the Bar Middle Temple 1974; *Books* Handbook of Rent Review (1981), Renewal of Business Tenancies (1984); *Style—* Kirk Reynolds, Esq; 46 St John's Villas, London N19

REYNOLDS, Martin Paul; s of Sqdn Ldr Cedric Hinton Fleetwood Reynolds, of 38 West Hill Way, Totteridge London N 20, and Doris Margaret, *née* Bryan (d 1982); *b* 25 Dec 1936; *Educ* Univ Coll Sch, St Edmund hall Oxford (MA); *m* 17 June 1961, Gaynor Margaret, da of Stuart Morgan Phillips (d 1957); 3 s (Simon Stuart Hinton b 1964, Peter Bryan b 1966, Thomas Edward Barnsbury b 1969); *Career* qualified teacher 1961, barr Inner Temple 1962, asst rec 1988; cncllr London Borough of Islington 1968-71 and 1973-82; Parly candidate Harrow W Oct 1974; ACIARB 1986; *Books* Negotiable Instruments for Students (1964); *Recreations* sailing, travel in France, music; *Style—* Martin Reynolds, Esq; 3 Mountfort Crescent, Barnsbury Square, London N1 1JW (☎ 01 607 7357); 1 Paper Buildings, Temple, London EC4 (☎ 01 583 7355, fax 01 353 2144)

REYNOLDS, Dr Mary Angela; da of Dr William Henry Reynolds, of Ladycroft, 118 Marsh Lane, Mill Hill, London NW7 4PE, and Mary Angela, *née* Keane (d 1989); *Educ* St Mary's Convent Shaftesbury Dorset, Charing Cross Hosp Med Sch (MB BS); *Career* MO to US Public Health Serv American Embassy 1967-68, asst gen mangr chief underwriter and chief med offr Canada Life Assur Co (UK and Ireland) 1978-; first lady pres Assur Med soc 1989, chm med affrs ctee Assoc of Br Insurers, vice-pres London Insur Inst (former cncl memb), dep chm Life Underwriters Club 1988-; memb: steering ctee Women in Mgmnt Insur Project MSC and Industl Soc, gen ctee Insur Benevolent Fund (dir Insur Orphans Fund), Perm Health Insur Club; Assur Med Soc: memb working pty for Chartered Insur Insts Underwriting Dip, first ed bulletin; Freeman City of London 1983, Liveryman Worshipful Co of Insurers 1983; FBIM 1980, FAMS; *Books* Your Health is Your Wealth 1978, Ethics of Modern Life Underwriting 1978; *Recreations* opera, tennis; *Style—* Dr Mary Reynolds; Canada Life Assurance Co, Canada Life Place, Potters Bar Herts 5BA (☎ 0707 51122, fax 0707 46088, telex 25376)

REYNOLDS, Michael Arthur; s of William Arthur Reynolds (d 1981), of Hakin, Milford Haven, Dfyed, Wales, and Violet Elsie, *née* Giddings, (d 1978); *b* 28 August 1943; *Educ* Milford Haven GS, Cardiff Coll of Art (Dip Ad); *m* 1, (m dis 1971), Patricia; 1 s (Joseph Michael b 1970); m 2, (m dis 1974), Judith; m 3, 15 April 1983, Jill Caroline, da of Derek Holmes ; *Career* creative dir KPS Ltd Nairobi 1968, copywriter J Walter Thompson 1971, gp head Benton & Bowles 1973; creative dir: ABM 1975, McCann Errickson 1979, Interlink 1981, MWK (and shareholder) 1983, Pearson Partnership 1987; MIPA; *Recreations* gardening, archery, rare books; *Clubs* Chelsea Arts; *Style—* Michael Reynolds, Esq; Winwick Manor, Winwick, Northants NN6 7PD (☎ 078 887 502); Flat 3, 19 Hanson St, London W1; Cinema Ho, 93 Wardour St, London W1V 3TE (☎ 01 494 2305, fax 01 494 2695, car tel 0836 293 820, telex 24842 CINHSE)

REYNOLDS, Michael Emanuel; CBE; s of Isaac Mark Rosenberg (d 1959), of 16 Palace Ct, Finchley Rd NW3, and Henrietta, *née* Woolf (d 1977); *b* 22 April 1931; *Educ* Haberdashers' Askes' Sch; *m* 1 (m dis 1961), Hazel, *née* Fishberg; m 2, 28 Aug 1964, Susan Geraldine, da of Mervyn Clement Scott Yates (d 1967), of 22 Albany Park Rd, Kingston, Surrey; 2 da (Amanda Jane 4 July 1965, Michelle B 7 March 1967); *Career* Nat Serv RASC; with Marks & Spencer plc 1951-61, controller Br Home Stores plc 1961-64; Spar UK Ltd: trading controller 1964-67, chm and md 1967-77; BV Intergroup Trading (IGT): fndr memb Bd of Admin, dir 1974-75, chm and dir 1975-77; fndr and owner Susan Reynolds Books Ltd 1977-84; pres Nat Grocers Benevolent Fund 1976-77; FRSA; *Recreations* bridge; *Style—* Michael Reynolds, Esq, CBE; 55 Newlands Terrace, 155 Queenstown Rd, London SW8 3RN (☎ 01 627 5862)

REYNOLDS, Patrick John; s of James Reynolds (d 1969); *b* 20 August 1929; *Educ* Latymer Sch Edmonton; *m* 1959, Pauline Claire, *née* Farmer; 2 da; *Career* chm Reynolds Medical Ltd; Queen's Award for Export 1980 and 1988, Queen's Award for Technol 1988; *Recreations* cricket, badminton, tennis; *Style—* Patrick Reynolds, Esq; Old Manor, Little Berkhamsted, Hertford, Herts (☎ 0707 874 071)

REYNOLDS, (Arthur) Paul; s of Capt A C J Reynolds (d 1954), of Cornwall, and Voilet Emma, *née* Tuttle (d 1966); *b* 1 May 1917; *Educ* St Austell GS Cornwall, Coll of Estate Mgmnt London; *m* 1, 1945, Joyce (d 1979), da of FlLt Harold Arthur Rolls of Leighton Buzzard (d 1980); m 2, 1981, Diana, da of Edward John Pyman (d 1985), of Leighton Buzzard; 1 s (Christopher b 1946), 1 da (Elizabeth b 1950); *Career* Capt RA 1940-46 attached to Indian Artillery; ptnr HA Rolls & Ptnrs specialist in the care & restoration of Churches (St Albans & Oxford Dioceses), surveyor to the fabric of All Saints Church, Leighton Buzzard; FRICS, MIAS, EASA; *Recreations* music - choral singing, oil painting, golf, cricket, swimming; *Style—* Paul Reynolds, Esq; Sandy Mount, Plantation Road, Leighton Buzzard, Beds LU7 7HR (☎ 0525 373307); HA Rolls & Ptnrs, 15 Bridge Street, Leighton, Buzzard, Beds LU7 7AH (☎ 0525 373209)

REYNOLDS, Sir Peter William John; CBE; s of Harry Reynolds, of Amersham, and Gladys Victoria French (decd); *b* 10 Sept 1929; *Educ* Haileybury Coll; *m* 1955, Barbara Anne, da of Vincent Kenneth Johnson OBE, 2 s (Mark, Adam); *Career* Nat Serv 2 Lt RA 1948-50; chm Rank Hovis McDougall plc 1981-; Unilever Ltd 1950-70; trainee md then chm Walls (Meat & Handy Foods) Ltd; Rank Hovis McDougall plc 1971-; asst gp md 1971; gp md 1972-81; memb Consultative Bd for Resources Devpt in Agri 1982-84; dir Ind Dvpt Bd for NI 1982-; chm Resources Ctee Food & Drink Fed 1983-; fndr memb of Ctee 1974-; dir: Hovis Ltd, Ranks Pension Ltd, RHM Overseas Ltd, RHM Res Ltd, RHM Overseas Fin BV (Holland), RHM Int Fin NV, RHM Hldgs (USA) Inc, Purchase Fin Co Ltd, RHM Operatives Pensions Ltd, Cerebos Pacific Ltd; kt 1985; *Recreations* gardening, beagling; *Clubs* Naval & Military, Farmers; *Style—* Sir Peter Reynolds, CBE; Rignall Farm, Great Missenden, Bucks; PO Box 178, Windsor, Berks SL4 3ST (☎ Windsor (0753) 857123)

REYNOLDS, Richard Christopher; s of Stanley Reynolds (d 1960), and Christine, *née* Barrow ; *b* 2 June 1945; *Educ* Peter Simmons Sch Winchester, Croydon Tech Sch, Croydon Tech Coll; *m* 2 March 1968, Sharon, da of Peter Bragg, of Great Bookham, Surrey; 1 s (Paul), 1 da (Julia); *Career* md: Barratt E London Ltd 1983-, Barratt Urban Renewal E London Ltd 1983-, Barratt Urban Construction E London Ltd 1983-; dir: Barratt Southern Ltd 1983-, Barratt Rosehaugh Co-Ptnrship Ltd 1988-; *Recreations* clay pigeon shooting; *Style—* Richard Reynolds, Esq; Barratt East London Ltd, Warton House, 150 High St, Stratford E15 2NE (☎ 01 555 3242, fax 01 519 5536)

REYNOLDS, Ruth Evelyn Millicent; da of Lt-Col Charles Ernest White-Spunner Fawcett, Croix-de-Guerre Avec Palme (d 1944), of Littlewood, Ganghill, Guildford, and Millicent Aphrasia, *née* Sullivan (d 1971); *b* 4 Oct 1915; *Educ* Conamur Sandgate Kent, Guildford Sch of Art, Wycombe Coll of Art; *m* 4 Nov 1939, Lt-Col Dudley Lancelot Collis Reynolds, OBE, s of Maj James Christopher Reynolds (d 1923), of The Lawns, Alveston, Glos; 1 s (John b 1950), 2 da (Jenny b 1941, Diana b 1946); *Career* WWII WAAF Bomber Cmd HQ Langley Bucks 1939; J Stanley Beard & Bennet Architects 1934-37, BBC admin dept 1937-39, six month in News Talks run by Richard Dimbleby, later talks dept and Features and Drama; sculptor and artist in oil and water-colour, one man exhibitions incl: Halifax House, Oxford Univ Grad Centre 1965, ESU Oxford 1967, Co Museum Aylesbury 1976, Loggia Gallery London 1982, Century Galleries Henley-on-Thames 1986; gp exhibitions: Loggia Gallery, Amnesty Int Sculpture Exhibition Bristol and London 1979; work in private collections incl: Anne Duchess of Westminsters Arkle Collection, Rev J Studd, Guinness (Park Royal) Ltd, Mrs Jenny Hopkinson (California), Fuad Mulla Hussein Kuwait Planning Bd, RAF Hatton Bucks, G Wright (Minnesota), M Bolshi (Berne Switzerland), St Dunstans Church Aylesbury, Welsh Regt Museum Cardiff Castle, P Van Kuran dir Tandem Computers inc (California), A Jarret vice-pres Syntex Corp (California), BBONT Oxford, Dr T J Goodwin Chorleywood, Mrs M Bohli Berne (Switzerland), Wing Cdr V Thomas, OBE curator Chequers, Maj E Golding Litton Cheyney Dorset, Maj and Mrs D N Philip (Mauritius), Diana R Room Mountain View (California), G P Peuschel, FSAI, GMW Ptnrship Manchester, Lambeth Palace; fndr memb Aylesbury Decorative and Fine Arts Soc, memb Buckinghamshire Art Soc; asst organizer Millenium Art Exhibition St Dunstan's Church Monks Risborough Aylesbury 1988; MFPS, AFAS, FRSA 1980; *Recreations* sketching, dog-walks in Chilterns, travel; *Clubs* International Lyceum; *Style—* Mrs Ruth Reynolds; Chiltern Retreat, Princes Risborough, Bucks HP17 OJR (☎ 08444 3115)

REYNOLDS, Simon Anthony; s of Maj James Reynolds (d 1982), of Leighton Hall, Carnforth, Lancs, and Helen Reynolds (d 1977); *b* 20 Jan 1939; *Educ* Ampleforth, Heidelberg Univ; *m* 1970, Beata Cornelia, da of Baron Siegfried von Heyl zu Herrnsheim (d 1982), of Schlosschen, Worms, Germany; 2 s, 2 da; *Career* dealer in Fine Art; *Books* The Vision of Simeon Solomon; *Recreations* writing, collecting fine art, travelling; *Style—* Simon Reynolds, Esq; 64 Lonsdale Rd, Barnes, London SW13 (☎ 01 748 3506)

REYNTIENS, (Nicholas) Patrick; OBE (1976); s of Nicholas Serge Reyntiens, OBE (d 1951), and Janet Isabel, *née* MacRae (d 1975); *b* 11 Dec 1925; *Educ* Ampleforth, Regent St Poly Edinburgh Coll of Art (DA); *m* 8 Sep 1953, Anne Mary, da of Brig-

Gen Ian Bruce DSO, MBE (d 1956); 2 s (Dominick Ian, John Patrick), 2 da (Edith Mary, Lucy Anne); *Career* WWII Lt 2 Bn Scots Guards 1943-47; artist specialising in stained glass, work includes: Coventry Cathedral, Liverpool Met Cathedral, Derby Cathedral, Eton Chapel, Great Hall Christ Church Oxford, Washington DC Episcopalean Cathedral; other works included in private collections; memb panel architectural advsrs to: Westminster Abbey, Westminster Cathedral, Brompton Oratory; Fellow Br Soc Master Glass Painters; *Books* The Technique of Stanined Glass (third edn 1982); *Style—* Patrick Reyntiens, Esq; Ilford Bridges Farm, nr Stocklinch, Ilminster, Somerset (☎ 0460 522 41)

RHEAD, David Michael; s of Harry Bernard Rhead, JP; *b* 12 Feb 1936; *Educ* St Philips GS Edgbaston; *m* 1958, Rosaleen Loretto, *née* Finnegan; 4 da; *Career* chm: LCP Hldgs plc 1975-87 (dep chm 1973, fin dir 1968), Wilson Gp Ltd, Hickman Boswell Gp Ltd; Freeman: City of London, Worshipful Co of CAs in England & Wales; FCA, CBIM; *Recreations* fishing, golf; *Style—* David Rhead Esq; Cherry Trees, 62 Little Sutton Lane, Sutton Coldfields, W Midlands B75 6PE (☎ 021 308 4762)

RHIND, Prof David William; s of William Rhind (d 1976), and Christina, *née* Abercombie; *b* 29 Nov 1943; *Educ* Berwick GS, Univ of Bristol (BSc), Univ of Edinburgh (PhD); *m* 27 Aug 1966, Christine, da of William Frank Young, of Berwick upon Tweed; 1 s (Jonathan b 1969), 2 da (Samantha b 1972, Zoe b 1979); *Career* res offr Univ of Edinburgh 1968-69, res fell RCA 1969-73, reader (former lectr) Univ of Durham 1973-81, prof of geography Birkbeck Coll Univ of London 1982-; visiting fell: Int Trg Centre Netherlands 1975, Aust Nat Univ 1979; author of around 100 tech papers; hon sec RGS; chm: Bloomsbury Computing Consortium Mgmnt Ctee, Royal Soc Ordnance Survey Sci Ctee; vice pres Int Cartographic Assoc; advsr House of Lords Select Ctee Sci of Technol 1984-85, memb Govt Ctee of Enquiry on Handling of Geographic Info 1985-87; FRGS 1970, MIBG; *Books* Land Use (with R Hudson, 1980), A Census User's Handbook (1983), An Atlas of EEC Affairs (with R Hudson and H Mounsey, 1984); *Clubs* Athenaeum; *Style—* Prof David Rhind; 7 New Place, Welwyn, Herts AL6 9QA (☎ 043 871 5350); Dept of Geography, Birkbeck Coll, Univ of London, Malet St, London (☎ 01 631 6474, fax 01 631 6498)

RHODES, Anthony John David; s of John Percy Rhodes (d 1985), of Leigh-on-Sea, Essex, and Eileen Daisy, *née* Frith (d 1984); *b* 22 Feb 1948; *Educ* Westcliff GS, Corpus Christi Coll Cambridge (MA); *m* 14 Dec 1974, Elisabeth Marie Agnes Raymonde, da of Lt-Col Pierre Fronteau (ret French Army), of Lisieux, France; 1 s (Christophe b 1978), 1 da (Sophie b 1984); *Career* project mangr Shell Int Petroleum Co 1969-73, dep tres Ocean Tport & Trading Ltd 1975-80, exec dir Bank of America Int Ltd 1980-; *Recreations* opera, music, golf, shooting, philately; *Style—* Anthony Rhodes, Esq; 1 Watling St, London EC4P 4BX; (☎ 01 634 4556, fax 01 634 4532, telex 884552)

RHODES, Sir Basil Edward; CBE (1981), OBE (1945, MBE 1944, DL (S Yorks 1975)); s of Col Harry Rhodes, TD, of Lane End House, Rotherham, S Yorks, and Astri Alexandra, *née* Natvig (d 1969); *b* 8 Dec 1915; *Educ* St Edwards Sch Oxford; *m* 21 Sept 1962, Joëlle, da of Robert Vilgard; 1 s (Charles Edward Robert Christian); *Career* serv WWII: W Desert, Greece, Crete, Burma (wounded and mentioned in despatches); Yorks Dragoons and Queen's Own Yeo (Hon Col 1973-81) TA; admitted slr 1946, ptr Gichard & Co Rotherham) 1946-; dir: Carlton Main Brickworks Ltd, S H Ward & Co, Wessex Fare Ltd, Duncan Millar & Assocs Ltd; pres Rotherham Cons Assoc, chm S Yorks Cons Fedn; Mayor of Rotherham 1970-71, High Sheriff S Yorks 1982-83, Pres of Sheffield & Dist Law Soc 1983-84; Cons Pty area tres for Yorks 1983-88; *Recreations* field-sports, skiing, gardening; *Clubs* Cavalry and Guards, Sheffield; *Style—* Sir Basil Rhodes, CBE, TD, DL; Bubnell Hall, Baslow, Derbys (☎ 024 688 3266); 31/33 Doncaster Gate, Rotherham S65 1DF (☎ 0709 365 531, fax 0709 829 752)

RHODES, Sir John Christopher Douglas; 4 Bt (UK 1919); s of Lt-Col Sir Christopher George Rhodes, 3 Bt (d 1964); *b* 24 May 1946; *Heir* bro, Michael Rhodes; *Style—* Sir John Rhodes, Bt

RHODES, John Ivor McKinnon; CMG (1971); s of Joseph Thomas Rhodes (d 1922); *b* 6 Mar 1914; *Educ* Leeds Modern Sch; *m* 1939, Eden Annetta, *née* Clark; 1 s, 1 da; *Career* Maj ME, fin staff WO 1933-46; princ and asst sec HM Treasy 1947-66, min UK mission to UN 1966-73, memb UN Ctee on Contributions and UN Pensions Bd 1966-71, chm UN Advsy Ctee on Admin and Budget Questions 1971-74, sr conslt (asst sec gen) to administrator UN Dvpt Programme 1979-80; *Recreations* gardening, playing electronic organ; *Style—* John Rhodes, Esq, CMG; Quintins, Watersfield, Pulborough, W Sussex (☎ 0798 831634)

RHODES, Hon Mrs; Hon Margaret; *née* Elphinstone; da of late 16 Lord Elphinstone, KT, and Lady Mary Bowes-Lyon, DCVO, da of 14 Earl of Strathmore, whereby Mrs Rhodes is first cous of HM The Queen (at whose wedding Mrs Rhodes was a bridesmaid); *b* 9 June 1925; *m* 1950, Denys Gravenor Rhodes (d 1981), er s of Maj Tahu Rhodes, Gren Gds, and Hon Helen (eldest da of 5 Baron Plunket); 2 s, 2 da; *Style—* The Hon Mrs Rhodes; The Garden House, Windsor Great Park, Windsor, Berks (☎ Egham 34617)

RHODES, Marion; da of Samuel Rhodes (d 1930), of Huddersfield, Yorks, and Mary Jane, *née* Mallinson (d 1956); *b* 17 May 1907; *Educ* Greenhead GS, Huddersfield, Huddersfield Art Sch, Leeds Coll of Art, The Central Sch of Arts and Crafts London (Art Teachers Cert Univ of Oxford); *Career* teacher 1930-67, pt/t lectr art Berridge House Trg Coll 1947-55; Paris Salon: hon mention 1952, bronze medal 1956, silver medal 1961, gold medal 1967; exhibited at: Royal Acad 1934-, Royal Scottish Acad, The Paris Salon, Walker Art Gallery, Towner Art Gallery, Atkinson, Southport, Brighton, Bradford, Leeds, Manchester, USA, SA; works purchased by Br Museum (amongst many others); memb: Soc of Graphic Artists 1936 (hon life memb 1969), Acad of Fine Art 1955-81, Accademia Delle Arti E De Lavoro Parma 1979-82; fell Ancient Monuments Soc, Assoc Artistes Francois 1971-79, hon memb Tommasso Campanella Acad Rome (silver medal 1979), Academiy of Italy (gold medal 1979), Certificate of Merit Dictionary St Internat Biography 1972, fell Royal Soc of Painter - Etchers & Engravers; life FRSA; *Recreations* gardening, geology; *Clubs* ESU; *Style—* Miss Marion Rhodes; 2 Goodwyn Ave, Mill Hill, London NW7 3RG (☎ 01 959 2280)

RHODES, Michael Philip James; s of late Lt-Col Sir Christopher Rhodes, 3 Bt; hp of bro, Sir John Rhodes, 4 Bt; *b* 3 April 1948; *m* 1973, Susan, da of Patrick Roney-Dougal; 1 da; *Style—* Michael Rhodes Esq

RHODES, Sir Peregrine Alexander; KCMG (1984, CMG 1976); s of Cyril Edmunds Rhodes (d 1966), and Elizabeth Frances (d 1962); *b* 14 May 1925; *Educ* Winchester, New Coll Oxford; *m* 1, 1951 (m dis), Jane Hassell; 2 s, 1 da; m 2, 1969, Margaret Rosemary, da of Eric Page (d 1980); *Career* Coldstream Gds 1944-47; Isnt For Study of Int Orgn Sussex Univ 1968-69; Dip Serv: Rome 1970-73, chargé affaires 1973-74, cnsllr E Berlin 1973-75, seconded under-sec Cabinet Off 1975-78, high cmmr Cyprus 1979-82, ambass Cyprus 1982-85; dir gen Br Property Fndn 1986-; chm Anglo Hellenic League 1986-, vice pres Br Sch Athens; FRSA 1988; *Recreations* photography, reading; *Clubs* Travellers'; *Style—* Sir Peregrine Rhodes, KCMG

RHODES, Prof Philip; s of Sydney Rhodes (RSM, d 1962), of Sheffield, and Harriett May, *née* Denniff (d 1981); *b* 2 May 1922; *Educ* King Edward VII Sch Sheffield, Clare Coll Cambridge (BA, MA), St Thomas's Hosp Med Sch (MB, BChir); *m* 26 Oct 1946, Mary Elizabeth, da of Rev John Kenneth Worley, MC (d 1957), of Gt Addington, Northants; 3 s (Richard, David, Kenneth), 2 da (Susan (Mrs Lutwyche), Frances (Mrs Marshall); *Career* Maj RAMC 1949-51; St Thomas's Hosp: obstetric physician 1958-64, prof of gynaecology 1964-74, dean med sch 1968-74; dean faculty of med Univ of Adelaide S Aust 1974-77, postgrad dean of med Univ of Newcastle upon Tyne 1977-80, postgrad dean and prof of postgrad med educn Univ of Southampton 1980-87; Brontë Soc Prize 1972, chm educn ctee of King Edward's Hosp Fund for London, memb Gen Med Cncl 1979-89; FRCS, FRCOG, FRACMA; *Books* Fluid Balance in Obstetrics (1960), An Introduction to Gynaecology and Obstetrics (1967), Woman: A biological study (1969), Reproductive Physiology for Medical Students (1969), The Value of Medicine (1976), Doctor John Leake's Hospital (1977), Letters to a Young Doctor (1983), An Outline History of Medicine (1985); *Recreations* writing, reading; *Clubs* Utd Oxford and Cambridge; *Style—* Prof Philip Rhodes; Fairford Hse, Lyndhurst Rd, Brockenhurst, Hants, SO42 7RH (☎ 0590 22251)

RHODES, Philip John; s of (Osmond) Cyril Rhodes, of Lincoln, and Dorothy, *née* Ibbetson; *b* 23 August 1937; *Educ* City Sch Lincoln; *m* 11 Sept 1965, Madeleine Ann, da of Samuel Edward Blaza, of Waltham, Lincs; 2 da (Jane b 1966, Judith b 1969); *Career* Nat Serv: Sherwood Foresters 1956, Intelligence Corps 1957; asst gen mangr General Accident plc 1988- (city mangr 1985-87); pres Perth C of C 1982-83, vice pres The Insur Inst of London 1988; Freeman of City of London, Liveryman Worshipful Co of Insurers 1988; ACII; *Recreations* music, golf, tennis; *Clubs* Royal Cmwlth Soc; *Style—* Philip Rhodes, Esq; Dixon House, 1 Lloyds Avenue, London, EC3N 3DH (☎ 01 626 8711, fax 01 481 8403, telex 885372)

RHODES, Richard David Walton; JP (Fylde, 1978); s of Harry Walton Rhodes (d 1966), of 38 Hill Road, Penwortham, Preston, Lancs, and Dorothy Fairhurst (d 1986); *b* 20 April 1942; *Educ* Rossall Sch Fleetwood, St John's Coll Durham (BA), Hertford Coll (Dip Ed); *m* 11, Aug 1966, Stephanie, da of Frederic William Heyes (d 1978), of 6 Hollinhurst Ave, Penwortham, Preston, Lancs; 2 da (Deborah b 1968, Victoria b 1971); *Career* asst master St John's Sch, Leatherhead 1964-75; headmaster: Arnold Sch Blackpool 1979-87 (dep Headmaster 1975-79), Rossall Sch Fleetwood 1987-; *Recreations* sports, photography, public speaking, gardening; *Clubs* East India, Devonshire, Sports and Public Schs; *Style—* Richard Rhodes, Esq; The Hall, Rossall Sch, Fleetwood, Lancs FY7 9JW (☎ 03917 3849)

RHODES, Robert Elliott; s of Gilbert Gedalia Rhodes (d 1970), of London, and Elly Brook, *née* Feingold; *b* 2 August 1945; *Educ* St Paul's, Pembroke Coll Oxford (MA); *m* 16 March 1971, Georgina Caroline, da of Jack Gerald Clarfelt, of Linhay Meads, Timsbury, Hants; 2 s (Matthew b 1973, James b 1975), 1 da (Emily b 1983); *Career* called to Bar Inner Temple 1968, 1 prosecuting counsel to Inland Revenue at Centl Criminal Ct and Inner London Crown Cts 1981 (2 prosecuting counsel 1979), rec Crown Ct 1987; *Recreations* reading, listening to opera, watching cricket, playing real tennis; *Clubs* MCC; *Style—* Robert Rhodes, Esq; 2 Crown Office Row, Temple, London, EC4Y 7HJ (☎ 01 583 2681, fax 01 583 2850. telex 8955733 INLAWS)

RHODES, Zandra Lindsey; da of Albert James Rhodes (d 1988), of Chatham, Kent, and Beatrice Ellen, *née* Twigg (d 1968), fitter at Worth, Paris; *b* 19 Sept 1940; *Educ* Medway Technical Sch for Girls Chatham, Medway Coll of Art Rochester Kent, Royal Coll of Art (DesRCA); *Career* started career as textile designer 1964, set up print factory and studio with Alexander McIntyre 1965, transferred to fashion indust 1966, ptnrship with Sylvia Ayton producing dresses using own prints, opened Fulham Rd clothes shop (fndr ptnr and designer) 1967-68, first solo collection US 1969 (met with phenomenal response from Vogue and Women's Wear Daily), thereafter established as foremost influential designer (developed unique use of printed fabrics and treatment of jersey), prodr annual spectacular fantasy shows USA; fndr with Anne Knight and Ronnie Stirling: Zandra Rhodes (UK) Ltd, Zandra Rhodes Shops 1975-86 (md 1975-); first shop London 1975 (others opened in Bloomingdales NY and Marshall Field Chicago), shops and licencees now world wide; Zandra Rhodes designs currently incl: interior furnishing, sheets and pillowcases, sarees, jewellry, rugs, kitchen accessories, fine china figurines; launched fine arts and prints collections Dyanssen Galleries USA 1989; solo exhibitions incl: Texas Gallery Houston 1981, La Jolla Museum of Contemporary Art San Diego 1982, Barbican Centre 1982, Parson's Sch of Design NY 1982, Art Museum of Santa Cruz Co California 1983; work represented in numerous permanent costume collections incl: V & A, City Museum & Art Gallery Stoke-on-Trent, Royal Pavilion Brighton Museum, City Art Gallery Leeds, Met Museum NY, Museum of Applied Arts & Scis Sydney, Nat Museum of Victoria Melbourne; acknowledged spokeswoman and personality of 60s and 70s (famous for green and later pink coloured hair), frequent speaker on fashion and design, subject of numerous documentaries and films; Designer of the Year English Fashion Trade UK 1972, Emmy Award for Best Costume Design Romeo and Juliet on Ice CBS TV 1984, Best Show of the Year New Orleans 1985, Woman of Distinction Award Northwood Inst Dallas Texas 1986; key to City of Miami and City of California; hon DFA Int Fine Arts Coll Miami, hon DRCA Royal Coll of Art, hon DD Cncl for Nat Acad Awards 1987; RDI 1977, FSIAD 1982; *Books* The Art of Zandra Rhodes (1984, US ed 1985); *Recreations* gardening, travelling, drawing, watercolours; *Style—* Miss Zandra Rhodes; 85 Richford St, London W6 7HJ (☎ 01 749 9561, fax 01 749 6411, telex 946561 ZANDRA G)

RHODES JAMES, Robert Vidal; MP (C) Cambridge Dec 1976-; s of William Rhodes James, OBE, MC (d 1972), Indian Army; *b* 10 April 1933,Murree India,; *Educ* Sedbergh, Worcester Coll Oxford; *m* 1956, Angela Margaret, eldest da of late Ronald Robertson; 4 da; *Career* clerk House of Commons 1955-64; fell All Souls Coll Oxford 1964-68; dir Inst for Study of Int Orgn Univ of Sussex 1968-73; pa to UN sec-gen 1973-76; PPS FCO 1979-82, Cons liaison offr for higher educn 1979-87, vice-chm Home Affrs and constitutional ctees; chm History of Parly Tst 1983-; memb Chairman's Panel of House of Commons 1987-; chm Cons Friends of Israel 1988-; Hon

DLitt; FRSL, FRHistS; *Books* Lord Randolph Churchill (1959), An Introduction to the House of Commons, 1961, Rosebery (1963), Gallipoli (1965), Chips: The Diaries of Sir Henry Channon (1967), JCC Davidson: Memoirs of a Conservative (1968), Churchill, A Study in Failure 1900-1939 (1970), Ambitions and Realities (1972), The Complete Speeches of Sir Winston Churchill (eight volumes, 1974), Victor Cazalet, A Portrait (1975), The British Revolution 1880-1939 (two volumes, 1976, 1977), Albert, Prince Consort (1983), Anthony Eden (1986); *Recreations* sailing; *Clubs* Travellers', Grillions, Pratt's; *Style*— Robert Rhodes James, Esq, MP; The Stone House, Great Gransden, Nr Sandy, Beds

RHYL, Baroness; Hon Esmé Consuelo Helen; *née* Glyn; OBE (1946); 2 da of 4 Baron Wolverton, JP, DL, by his w, Lady Edith Ward, CBE (da of 1 Earl of Dudley); sis of 5 Baron Wolverton and late Lady Hyde (mother of 7 Earl of Clarendon); *b* 20 Sept 1908; *m* 1950, Baron Rhyl, OBE, PC (Life Peer, d 1981), s of Gen Sir Noel Birch, GBE, KCB, KCMG, and Florence (3 da of Sir George Chetwode, 6 Bt, and sis of 1 Baron Chetwode; *Style*— The Rt Hon Lady Rhyl, OBE; Holywell House, Swanmore, Hants;

RHYS, Lady Anne Maud; *née* Wellesley; da of 5 Duke of Wellington and Hon Lilian Coats, da of 1 Baron Glentanar; *b* 2 Feb 1910; *m* 1933 (m dis 1963), Hon David Rhys, 3 s of 7 Baron Dynevor; 1 s, 1 da; *Career* inherited Duchy (Sp) of Ciudad Rodrigo and Grandeeship of 1 Class on death of her bro, 6 Duke, 1943, but ceded them to unc, 7 Duke, 1949; *Style*— Lady Anne Rhys; Le Bourg, Rue de Tertrie, Castel Parish, Guernsey

RHYS, Col David Lewellin; OBE (1950), MC (1937), DL (Gwent 1975-); s of Owen Lewellin Rhys; *b* 2 April 1910; *Educ* Epsom, RMC Sandhurst; *m* 1949, Doreen, *née* Giles; 2 s; *Career* cmmnd S Wales Borderers 1930, Palestine 1936, Waziristan 1937, Burma 1942-43, Italy 1944-45, Malaya 1955-56, Col; mil attaché Netherlands East Indies 1947-49; sec: Monmouth T and AFA 1957-68, Wales TA and VRA 1968-75, DL Monmouthshire 1963-75; chief cmmr St John Ambulance Bde Wales 1975-79; CStJ 1975, KStJ 1978; *Recreations* fishing, shooting, golf; *Clubs* Army and Navy, Cardiff and Country; *Style*— Colonel David Rhys, OBE, MC, DL; Paradwys, Aberthin, Cowbridge, S Glamorgan (☎ 044 632 056)

RHYS, Hon David Reginald; s of 7 Baron Dynevor (d 1956), and Lady Margaret Child-Villiers (d 1960), da of 7 Earl of Jersey; *b* 18 Mar 1907; *Educ* Eton, Tours, Frankfurt AM; *m* 1, 1933 (m dis 1963), Lady Ann Maud Wellesley, da of 5 Duke of Wellington; 1 s, 1 da; m 2, 1963, Sheila Mary d'Ambrumenil (MTC AAGB 1943-46), da of D J Phillips; 1 s; *Career* late Capt Welsh Gds, served 1939-45 war (wounded, Normandy); hotel dir; *Recreations* racing; *Clubs* Farmers'; *Style*— The Hon David Rhys; Southwick Ct, Trowbridge, Wilts BA14 9QB (☎ 022 14 2469)

RHYS, Hon Mrs Elwyn; Diana Sloane; da of Maj Roger Cyril Hans Sloane Stanley, DL, JP of Paultons Park, Hants; *m* 1931, Capt the Hon Elwyn Villiers Rhys (2 s of 7 Baron Dynevor and who d 1966); 1 da; *Style*— The Hon Mrs Elwyn Rhys

RHYS, (William Joseph) St Ervyl-Glyndwr; s of Edward John Rhys (d 1955) and Rachel, *née* Thomas (d 1986); *b* 6 July 1924; *Educ* Newport HS, Univ of Wales, Guy's Hosp London Univ, St John's Coll Cambridge (MA, MB, BS); *m* 1961, Ann, *née* Rees; 6 da; *Career* Sqdn Ldr RAF Inst Aviation Med & Empire Test Pilot Sch; MRCOG, DPH, MFCM; gynaecology Welsh Hosp Bd 1962, MOH Cardiganshire 1966-74, conslt physician community med (Dyfed) 1974-82, hon med advsr Welsh Nat Water Devpt Authy 1966-82, hon memb (White Robe) Gorsedd of Bards of Wales; Lord of the Barony of Llawhaden, Lord of the Manor of Llanfynydd (Celtic, pre-Norman); Freeman, City of London, Camb Univ rep on Cncl and Court of Govrs of Univ Coll Wales 1979-86; chm tstees St John's Coll Dyfed 1987- (memb 1979-); High Sheriff Co of Dyfed 1979-80, cmmr St John Ambulance Bde Ceredigion 1982-, pres Scout Assoc Ceredigion 1983-, chm Hospitallers' Club Dyfed 1983-; memb: exec ctee Assoc of Friends of Nat Library of Wales 1984-; chm Governing Body Ceredigion Schs 1987- (memb 1985-); tstee The Two Red Dragons Educn Tst (promotes Japanese in Europe) 1988-; CStJ; *Recreations* medical history, genealogical research, local history, walking; *Clubs* RAF; *Style*— St Ervyl-Glyndwr Rhys, Esq; Plas Bronmeurig, Ystrad Meurig, Dyfed (☎ (09745) 650); Minffordd, Llangadog, Dyfed (☎ 777496)

RHYS, Hon Susannah Mair Elizabeth; 3 and yst da of 9 Baron Dynevor

RHYS, William Escott; s of Hubert Ralph John Rhys (d 1972), and Ethel Violet, *née* Sweet-Escott (d 1949); *b* 13 July 1924; *Educ* Shrewsbury; *m* 1 July 1950, Yvette Dorothy Mary, da of Frederick James Box (d 1952); 1 s (John Frederick William b 1958), 2 da (Jane Caroline b 1953, (Yvette) Julia b 1955); *Career* WWII serv RN 1943-46: cmmnd Midshipman 1943, Sub Lt 1944, CO LCT 7092 1944, Temp Lt (CW List) 1946; SA Brain & Co: asst brewer 1946-52, dir 1952-65, head brewer 1965-68, jt md 1968-71, chm and md 1971-79, chm and chief exec 1979-; regnl dir Lloyds Bank 1985-, chm S Wales Brewers Assoc 1973-76; memb: Inst of Brewing, Freeman Worshipful Co of Brewers; *Recreations* golf, shooting; *Clubs* MCC, Royal Porthcawl GC, Cardiff & Co; *Style*— Mr William Rhys; 20 Hollybush Td, Cyncoed, Cardiff CF2 6TA (☎ 0222 762127); S A Brain & Co Ltd, The Old Brewery, St Mary St, Cardiff CF1 1SP (☎ 0222 399022, fax 0222 383 127)

RHYS JONES, Griffith (Griff); s of Elwyn Rhys Jones and Gwyneth Margaret Jones; *b* 16 Nov 1953; *Educ* Brentwood Sch Essex, Emmanuel Coll Cambridge (MA); *m* 21 Nov 1981, Joanna Frances, da of Alexander James Harris; 1 s (George Alexander b 1985), 1 da (Catherine Louisa b 1987); *Career* actor and writer; BBC radio producer 1976-79; TV Comedy Series: Not The Nine O'Clock News 1979-82, Alas Smith and Jones 1984-, The World According to Smith and Jones 1986-87; TV play: A View of Harry Clarke 1989; theatre: Charley's Aunt 1983, Trumpets and Raspberries 1985, The Alchemist 1986, Arturo Ui 1987; Film: Morons From Outer Space; dir: Talkback, Playback; *Books* The Lavishly Tooled Smith and Jones (1986), Janet Lives with Mel and Griff (1988); *Clubs* Groucho; *Style*— Griff Rhys Jones, Esq; 33 Percy Street, London W1 (☎ 01 637 5302, fax 01 631 4273)

RHYS WILLIAMS, Caroline Susan; *née* Foster; eldest da of Ludovic Anthony Foster, of Greatham Manor, Pulborough, Sussex; *m* 14 Feb 1961, Sir Brandon Meredith Rhys Williams, 2 Bt, MP (d 1988); 1 s (Sir Gareth, 3 Bt, *qv*), 2 da (Elinor Caroline b 21 Oct 1964, Miranda Pamela Cariadwen b 5 Nov 1968); *Style*— Lady Rhys Williams; Gadairwen, Groes Faen, Glamorgan; 32 Rawlings Street, London SW3

RHYS WILLIAMS, Sir (Arthur) Gareth Ludovic Emrys; 3 Bt (UK 1918), of Miskin, Parish of Llantrisant, Co Glamorgan; s of Sir Brandon Rhys Williams, 2 Bt, MP (d 1988) and Caroline Susan , eldest da of Ludovic Anthony Foster, of Greatham Manor, Pulborough , Sussex; *b* 9 Nov 1961; *Educ* Eton, Durham Univ; *Heir* none; *Recreations* Bow Group, target shooting, TA, conjuring, travel; *Style*— Sir Gareth Rhys Williams, Bt; Gadairwen, Groes Faen, Mid Glamorgan; 32 Rawlings St, SW3 (☎ 01 584 0636)

RICARDO, Lady Barbara Maureen; *née* Montagu Stuart Wortley Mackenzie; da of 3 Earl of Wharncliffe (d 1953), of Wortley Hall, later Carlton House, Wortley, and Lady Maud Lilian Elfreda Mary Wentworth Fitzwilliam (d 1979); *b* 26 August 1921; *Educ* privately; *m* 1943, David Cecil Ricardo, s of Maj Louis Ferdinand Ricardo, 8 Hus of Tanganyika, East Africa; 2 s (Dorrien, Richard); *Career* served WW II Women's Land Army, remount depot rider Melton Mowbray Leicestershire 1941-55; *Style*— Lady Barbara Ricardo; Carlton Lodge, Wortley, Sheffield S30 7DG (☎ 0742 882584)

RICE, Arthur Gorton; s of Arthur Edwin Rice (d 1967), of Birmingham; *b* 8 April 1929; *Educ* St Georges in the Field Birmingham; *m* 6 June 1953, Joan, da of Thomas Rollason; 3 s (Michael b 23 March 1956, Jonathan b 7 April 1962, Ian b 30 Dec 1967), 2 da (Pamela b 20 Sept 1958, Sarah b (twin) 7 April 1962); *Career* nat serv with RAF, Berlin airlift 1948-49; sr ptnr Rice & Co Bank House Cannock Staffs; FCA; *Recreations* squash rackets, golf, tennis; *Clubs* Moor Hall GC, Four Oaks; *Style*— Arthur Rice, Esq; Bank House, Mill Street, Cannock, Staffs WS11 3OW (☎ 05435 3846, fax 05435 74250, telex 335622 SPETAL G)

RICE, Clive Edward Butler; s of Patrick Edward Butler Rice, of Johannesburg, and Angela Viviene Syndercomb; *b* 23 July 1949; *Educ* St Johns Coll Johannesburg, Natal Univ Pietermaritzburg; *m* 1975, Susan Elizabeth, da of Kenneth Vaughan-Davies (d 1985); 1 s (Mark), 1 da (Jackie); *Career* 2 Lt SA Def Force; capt: Notts CCC, Transvaal, and currently the Springboks; *Books* Clive Rice Cricket Coaching Tips; *Clubs* Nottinghamshire CCC; *Style*— Clive Rice Esq; 83 Selby Rd, West Bridgeford, Nottingham; Notts CCC, Trent Bridge, Nottingham

RICE, Maj-Gen Desmond Hind Garrett; CVO (1985), CBE (1976, OBE 1970); s of Arthur Garrett Rice (d 1948), of Battle, Sussex; *b* 1 Dec 1924; *Educ* Marlborough; *m* 1954, Denise Anne, da of Stanley Ravenscroft (d 1956), of Budleigh Salterton, Devon; 1 da; *Career* served in: Italy, Egypt, Germany and W Berlin; vice adj gen 1978-79, Col 1 The Queen's Dragoon Gds 1980-86, Maj-Gen; sec The Centl Chancery of The Orders of Knighthood 1980-; *Recreations* field sports, gardening; *Clubs* Cavalry and Guards'; *Style*— Maj-Gen Desmond Rice, CVO, CBE; Fairway, Malacca Farm, West Clandon, Guildford, Surrey (☎ 0483 222677)

RICE, His Hon Judge Gordon Kenneth; s of Victor Rice (d 1947); *b* 16 April 1927; *Educ* BNC Oxford; *m* 1967, Patricia Margaret; *Career* barr Middle Temple 1957, Crown Court judge 1980-; *Style*— His Hon Judge Gordon Rice; 83 Beach Ave, Leigh-On-Sea, Essex (☎ 0702 73485)

RICE, Kenric Garrett; s of Charles Robert Rice (d 1958), and Winifred Margaret, *née* Hill (d 1976); *b* 9 Oct 1918; *Educ* Stowe; *m* 1, 23 Nov 1940 (m dis 1978), Rachel Barbara, da of George Robinson (d 1955); 1 s (Nigel b 4 Oct 1945), 2 da (Amanda b 5 June 1948, Nicola b 19 March 1956); m 2, 29 Sept 1978, Anna, da of Edward William Minton Beddoes (d 1952); 1 da (Emma b 21 July 1980); *Career* Princess Louise Regt (Middx Regt) TA, cmmnd 5th BN Argyll and Sutherland Highlanders 1940, Staff Offr GSOIII Air 2nd Army 1944, GSO III 1 56 Ind Bde 1945; Boar, Int staff The Hong Kong and Shanghai Banking Corpn (Shanghai, Singapore, Peking, Hong Kong, Calcutta, Rangoon, Borneo and London) 1946-71, gp tres Babcock & Wilcox Ltd 1971-78, chm advsr Guinness Mahon Bankers 1979-82, dir Wintrust Securities Ltd Bankers 1982-85, non exec dir Regency W of England Building Soc 1980-; MCT 1980; *Recreations* sailing, golf, skiing; *Clubs* MCC, Overseas Bankers (and GC) East India, Island Sailing; *Style*— Kenric Rice, Esq; The Old Well House, Lodsworth, Petworth, West Sussex GU28 9BZ (☎ 07985 216)

RICE, Ladislas Oscar; *b* 20 Jan 1926; *Educ* Reading Sch, LSE (BSc), Harvard Grad Sch of Bus Admin (MBA); *m* ;1 s (Sebastian b 1970), 1 da (Valentina b 1973); *Career* W H Smith & Son Ltd 1951-53, sr ptnr Urwick Orr & Ptnrs 1953-66, md Minerals Separation 1966-69, chm Burton Gp plc 1969-80; current directorships incl: Burton Gp plc (dep chm), Huntingdon Int Hldgs plc, Drayton Japan Tst plc, Drayton Cons Tst plc, Polymark Int plc, Heredities Ltd, Stanley Gibbons Hldgs plc, Nat Tst (Enterprises) Ltd, Fndn for Mgmnt Educn; CBIM, FIMC; *Recreations* travel, books, pictures; *Clubs* Brooks's London, Harvard of New York City; *Style*— Ladislas Rice, Esq; 19 Redington Rd, London NW3 (☎ 01 435 8095); La Casa di Cacchiano, Monti in Chianti, Siena, Italy

RICE, Michael Penarthur Merrick; s of Arthur Vincent Rice (d 1969), of Penarth, Glam, and Dora Kathleen, *née* Blacklock (d 1980); *b* 21 May 1928; *Educ* Challoner Sch; *Career* Nat Serv Royal Norfolk Regt 1946-48; chm Michael Rice Gp Ltd 1955-, dir Eastern England TV Ltd 1969-83; conslt: Govt of Saudi Arabia 1960-, Govt of Bahrain 1963-71, Govt of Egypt, Jamaica, Oman, Carreras Mktg Ltd 1965-75, chm The PR Conslts Assoc 1978-81; The Aga Khan Award for Architecture 1980; museum planning and design for: Qatar Nat Museum, The Museum of Archaeology and Ethnography Riyadh Saudi Arabia, 8 prov museums in Saudi Arabia, Oman Nat Museum, The Museum of the Sultan's Armed Forces Oman; co-fndr The PR Conslts Assoc (memb Honoris Causa 1985), tstee The Soc for Arabian Studies; FIPR 1975, FRSA 1987; *Books* Dilmun Discovered The First Hundred Years of the Archaeology of Bahrain (1984), The Temple Complex at Barbar Bahrain (1983), Search for the Paradise Land: the Archaeology of Bahrain and the Arabian Gulf (1985), Bahrain Through the Ages: The Archaeology (1985), The Excavations at Al-Hajjar Bahrain (1988); *Recreations* collecting English watercolours, antiquarian books and early Egyptian artefacts, embellishing a garden, the opera and listening to music, writing poetry, the company of friends and animals; *Clubs* Athenaeum; *Style*— Michael Rice, Esq; Odsey Hse, Baldock Rd Odsey, nr Baldock, Herts SG7 6SD (☎ 0462 74 2706); The Glassmill, 1 Battersea Bridge Rd, London SW11 3BG (☎ 01 223 3431, fax 01 228 4229, telex 917343 ORYZA G)

RICE, Peter Anthony; s of John Daniel Rice (d 1981), of Newry, Co Down, NI, and Brigid Tina, *née* McVerry; *b* 25 June 1950; *Educ* Abbey GS Newry, Univ of Lancaster (BA); *Career* ptnr Wood Mackenzie & Co 1981- (joined 1974), dir Hill Samuel & Co 1986-87, gp corporate fin and planning mangr Commercial Union Assur plc 1988-; chm Edinburgh Centl Cons Assoc 1977-79, fndr chm Scottish Bow Gp 1980-82; memb Stock Exchange 1981, FIA 1974; *Style*— Peter Rice, Esq; The Old Rectory, 6 Redington Rd, Hampstead, London NW3 7RS (☎ 01 431 3176); Commerical Union, St Helens, Undershaft, London EC2 (☎ 01 283 7500)

RICE-OXLEY, James Keith; CBE (1981); s of Montague Keith Rice-Oxley (d 1956), and Marjorie, *née* Burrell (d 1929); *b* 15 August 1920; *Educ* Marlborough, Trinity Coll

Oxford (MA); *m* 1949, Barbara Mary Joan, da of Frederick Parsons (d 1957), of Bull Lane, Gerrards Cross; 2 da; *Career* Maj (despatches) 1944; chm Nat Sea Trg Tst 1965-80, dir Gen Cncl of Br Shipping 1965-80, dir Int Shipping Fedn 1969-80, chm Shipowners Gp ILO 1969-1980; memb: cncl Dr Barnardo's 1981- (vice chm 1988-), Industl Tribunals (Eng and Wales) 1981-88; chm MN Trg Bd 1981-, memb engrg bd Business and Technician Educn Cncl 1983-87, UK govr World Maritime Univ 1983-; Gen Cmmr of Income Tax 1986-; *Recreations* ceramics, squash; *Style—* James Rice-Oxley, Esq, CBE; Ox House, Bimport, Shaftesbury, Dorset SP7 8AX (☎ 0747 2741)

RICH, John Rowland; CMG (1978); s of Rowland William Rich (d 1981), of Leeds and Winchester, and Phyllis Mary, *née* Chambers; *b* 29 June 1928; *Educ* Sedbergh, Clare Coll Cambridge (MA); *m* 1956, Rosemary Ann, da of Bertram Evan Williams (d 1974), of Dorset; 2 s (Anthony, Stephen), 1 da (Alison); *Career* Nat Serv (Army) 1949-51; joined FO (later FCO) 1951; served in FO and FCO: Addis Ababa 1953-56, Stockholm 1956-58, Bahrain 1963-66, Prague 1969-72; inspr Dip Serv 1972-74, cnsllr commercial Bonn 1974-78; consul gen Montreal 1978-80; HM ambass: Czechoslovakia 1980-85, Switzerland 1985-88; *Recreations* tennis, walking, european wild orchids; *Clubs* Travellers'; *Style—* John Rich, Esq; c/o National Westminster Bank plc, 13 Bridge Rd, East Molesey, Surrey KT7 9EZ

RICH, Michael Samuel; QC (1980); s of Sidney Frank Rich, OBE, JP (d 1985), of Streatham, and Erna Babette, *née* Schlesinger (d 1988); *b* 18 August 1933; *Educ* Dulwich, Wadham Coll Oxford (MA); *m* 31 July 1983, Janice Sarita, da of Henry Jules Benedictus; 3 s (Benedict b 1966, Jonathan b 1969, Edmund b 1970), 1 da (Sara b 1964); *Career* Lt RASC 1954; called to Bar Middle Temple 1959, bencher 1985, rec 1986, memb Hong Kong Bar; chm Southwark Playgrounds Tst; tstee: Brixton Village, S London Liberal Synagogue; *Books* Mills Law of Town and County Planning (1968); *Style—* Michael Rich, Esq, QC; 18 Dulwich Village, London SE21 7AL (☎ 01 693 1957); 2 Paper Bldgs, Temple, London EC4 (☎ 01 353 5835, fax 01 583 1390)

RICH, Owen James; CBE (1987); s of John Alan Frank Rich (d 1953), and Lilian Frances, *née* Mounty (d 1978); *b* 22 Sept 1925; *Educ* Midsomer Norton GS; *m* 12 Nov 1949, Dorothy Edith, da of Samuel Philip Gordon (d 1945); 1 s (Matthew Ashman b 24 May 1960), 1 da (Christine Frances b 11 Dec 1950); *Career* WWII Capt IA served India, Burma, French Indo China (Vietnam), Celebs New Guinea; Alfred McAlpine plc 1941-; pupil civil engr 1941-43, contracts engr 1947-58, contracts dir 1958-72, md main subsidiary 1972-76, pg md 1976-85, dep chm 1985-87; chm of tstees Alfred McAlpine Pension Co 1987-; involved with Third World Orgns homeless in Eng; chm cncl Fed of Civil Engrg Contractors 1988-89, memb cncl CBI 1988-89; FCIOB (1978), FRSA (1987); *Recreations* walking, fishing, gardening; *Clubs* RAC; *Style—* Owen Rich, Esq, CBE; Alfred McAlpine plc, Hooton S Wirral, Ches L66 7ND (☎ 051 339 4141)

RICHARD, Cliff; OBE (1980); s of Rodger Oscar Webb (d 1961), and Dorothy Marie Bodkin (formerly Webb), *née* Beazley; *b* 14 Oct 1940; *Educ* Riversmead Sch Cheshunt; *Career* singer and actor; first hit record Move It 1958; 12 gold records, 33 silver records; own series on BBC and ITV; various repertory and variety seasons; films: Serious Charge 1959, Expresso Bongo 1960, The Young Ones 1961, Summer Holiday 1962, Wonderful Life 1964, Finders Keepers 1966, Two a Penny 1968, His Land 1970, Take Me High 1973; vice-pres: PHAB, Tear Fund; singer, entered show business 1958; 11 gold and 32 silver discs, three BBC Cliff Richard TV series; 2 stage plays; 9 films; 1 stage musical; twice represented UK in Eurovision Song Contest; regular concert tours worldwide; *Books* Which One's Cliff (1977), Happy Christmas from Cliff (1980), You, Me and Jesus (1983), Jesus, Me and You (1985), Single-Minded (1988); *Recreations* tennis; *Style—* Cliff Richard, Esq, OBE; PO Box 46C, Esher, Surrey KT10 9AA (☎ 0372 67752, fax 0372 62352)

RICHARD, Ivor Seward; QC (1971); s of Seward Thomas Richard, of Rhiwbina, Cardiff; *b* 30 May 1932; *Educ* St Michael's Sch Llanelly, Cheltenham, Pembroke Coll Oxford; *m* 1; 1 s; m 2, 1962, Alison, da of J Imrie of Alverstoke, Hants; 1 s, 1 da; *Career* barr Inner Temple 1955, Parly candidate (Lab) S Kensington gen election 1959 and LCC election 1961, MP (Lab) Barons Court 1964-74, PPS to Sec State Def 1966-69, Parly under-sec state Def (Army) 1969-70, oppn spokesman Posts and Telecommunications 1970-71, dep oppn spokesman Foreign Affrs 1971-74; UK perm rep at the UN 1974-79, chm Rhodesia Conference Geneva 1976; UK cmmr to the Cmmn of the European Communities 1981-85 responsible for: employment, social affrs, the Tripartite Conf (formed 1975, policy forum between workers, employers and the cmmn), educn and vocational trg; former govr Atlantic Inst; memb: Fabian Soc, Lab Lawyers; *Style—* Ivor Richard, Esq, QC; 11 South Square, Gray's Inn, London WC2

RICHARD, John Walter Maxwell Miller; s of Col J E M Richard, OBE, of Kaizle, Peebles, and Gaynor Richard (d 1933); *b* 19 April 1933; *Educ* Cargilfield, Eton, Trinity Coll Cambridge (BA); *m* 1977, Christine Margaret, da of Ludwig Christian Saam (d 1954); 1 s, 3 da; *Career* ptnr Bell, Lawrie, Macgregor & Co; memb: Stock Exchange 1959, Cncl of Stock Exchange, Cncl's Markets Ctee; *Style—* John Richard Esq; 8 Braid Hills Approach, Edinburgh EH10 6JY (☎ 031 447 9313); Bell, Lawrie, Macgregor & Co, PO Box No 8, Erskine House, 68-73 Queen St, Edinburgh EH2 4AE (☎ 031 225 2566; telex 72260)

RICHARD, Pierre Ernest Charles Laurent (Peter); DFC (1945); s of Ernest Adolph Richard, MM (d 1960), of London, and Ivy Lilian, *née* Payne (d 1968); *b* 11 April 1921; *Educ* Univ Coll Sch Hampstead, RADA; *m* 14 Dec 1968, Ann Josephine; 2 s (Stephen b 1969, Christopher b 1977), 1 da (Louise b 1972); *Career* WWII serv: flying offr RAF 1941-46, navigator and bombaimner 8 (PFF) Gp, Bomber Cmd 1944-45; importer clock and watch indust 1946-, dir subsidiary co of Gt Univ Stores; chm Nat Benevolent Soc Watch and Clock Makers, former chm Watch and Clock Importers Assoc of GB; sec Hampstead Garden Suburb Free Church 1986-, pres The Pathfinder Assoc 1987-; Freeman City of London, Liveryman Worshipful Co of Clockmakers; Cross of Merit Gold Class Poland; *Clubs* Royal Air Force; *Style—* Peter Richard, Esq, DFC; 2 Leeside Crescent, London NW11 0DB (☎ 01 455 2905)

RICHARD, Ralph Henry; s of Dr Kurt Simon Richard (d 1958), and Emmy Rose, *née* Levi; *b* 24 Dec 1912; *Educ* Aylesford House PS, Sandridgebury Herts, Bryanston Sch Blandford Forum Dorset; *m* 1, 21 May 1964 (m dis 1972), Vivienne Elspeth da of the late Harold Bradley; 2 s (Daniel b 1968, Simon b 1968), 1 da (Debbie b 1966); m 2, 4 Sept 1975, Erica Robyn, *née* Greet; 2 s (Timothy b 1982, Zacharias b 1983); *Career* sales dir Allied Mills Ltd 1978-; dir: Flour Advsy Bureau 1980-, ABR Foods Ltd 1984-, Bakery Exhibitors Ltd 1988-; md Westmill Foods 1988-; Freeman: City of London, Worshipful Co of Bakers (1982), Tradesman City of Glasgow (1988); *Style—* Ralph Richard, Esq; 31 Grand Ave, Muswell Hill, London N10 3BD (☎ 01 883 1295); Westmill Foods Ltd, 52 Mark Lane, London EC3R 7PE (☎ 01 488 1593, fax 01 488 2974, car tel 0860 350 280, telex 888115)

RICHARDS, (Joseph) Alan; s of Albert John Knight-Richards (d 1967), of Whites Drive, Sedgley, Dudley, Worcs, and Sarah, *née* Jones (d 1968); *b* 23 Mar 1930; *Educ* Dudley GS, Birmingham Sch of Architecture (Dip Arch); *m* 20 Dec 1952, Tess, da of Frederic Dutton Griffiths (d 1981), of The Quadrant, Sedgley, Dudley, Worcs; 2 da (Julia, Wendy); *Career* princ asst architect Co Borough of Wolverhampton 1952-58, co fndr and jt sr ptnr Mason Richards Partnership 1958- (fndr consultancy serv for expert witness 1977-); Freeman City of London 1983; Liveryman: Worshipful Co of Arbitrators 1983, Worshipful Co of Architects 1988; FRIBA 1952, FCIArb 1979, memb Br Acad of Experts 1988; *Recreations* power boating, cruising, travel; *Clubs* City Livery, RYA; *Style—* Alan Richards, Esq; Salisbury House, Tettenhall Rd, Wolverhampton WV 4SG (☎ 0902 771331, fax 0902 21914)

RICHARDS, Archibald Banks; s of Charles Richards (d 1941); *b* 29 Mar 1911; *Educ* Daniel Stewart's Coll Edinburgh; *m* 1941, Edith Janet, *née* Sinclair (d 1987); 1 s, 1 da; *Career* CA Scot 1934, ptnr: A T Niven & Co 1939-64, Touche Ross & Co 1964-78; pres Institute Chartered Accountants Scotland 1976-77; *Style—* Archibald Richards, Esq; 7 Midmar Gardens, Edinburgh EH10 6DY (☎ 031 447 1942)

RICHARDS, Sir (Francis) Brooks; KCMG (1976, CMG 1963), DSC and bar (1943); s of Francis Bartlett Richards (d 1955), of Little Court, Cobham, Surrey, and Mary Bertha Richards, *née* Street (d 1974); *b* 18 July 1918; *Educ* Stowe, Magdalene Coll Cambridge (MA); *m* 1941, Hazel Myfanwy, da of Lt-Col Stanley Price Williams, CIE, of London (d 1977); 1 s (Francis Neville, *qv*), 1 da; *Career* served WW II RN (Lt-Cdr RNVR), Br Embassy Paris 1944-48; entered Foreign Service 1946: German Political Dept FO 1948-52, first sec Athens 1952-54, Political Residency Bahrain 1954-57, asst private sec to Foreign Sec 1958-59, cnsllr Paris 1959-64, head of Info Policy Dept FCO/CRO 1964, seconded to Cabinet Office 1966, HM min Bonn 1969-71, ambass to Vietnam 1972-74, to Greece 1974-78; dep sec Cabinet Office 1978-80, security co-ordinator N Ireland 1980-81; chm Ctee of Mgmnt Br Inst Paris 1979-88; chm CSM European conslts 1983-, chm CSM Parly Conslts 1983-; Friends of the Imperial War Museum; Chevalier de la Légion d'Honneur, Croix de Guerre; *Recreations* gardening, drawing, collecting, sailing; *Clubs* Traveller's (London), Royal Ocean Racing, Special Forces (chm 1983-86, pres 1986-89); *Style—* Sir Brooks Richards, KCMG, DSC; The Ranger's House, Farnham, Surrey (☎ 0252 716764)

RICHARDS, Christopher John D'Arcy; s of Kenneth Richards, MBE, LDS, of Heswall, Wirral, and Winifred Enid; *b* 29 August 1946; *Educ* Oundle Sch, St Andrews Univ; *m* Ruth Irene, da of Alan Gilroy, JP, of Heswall, Wirral; 2 s (John, Nicholas), 1 da (Claire); *Career* main bd dir Tysons plc (dep man of the gp); dir Dental Designs Ltd; sch gov; FCIOB; memb Nat Cncl, chm professional practice bd; *Recreations* sailing; *Clubs* The Athenaeum; *Style—* Christopher J D Richards, Esq; Lingcroft, Tower Road North, Heswall, Wirral, Merseyside (☎ 051 342 2470)

RICHARDS, David Gordon; s of Mr Gordon Charles Richards (d 1956), and Vera Amy Richards, *née* Barrow (d 1962); *b* 25 August 1928; *Educ* Highgate Sch; *m* 1960, Catherine Stephanie, da of Edward Gilbert Woodward (d 1949); 1 s (Edwin), 2 da (Victoria, Katharine); *Career* 8 RTR 1947-49; CA; ptnr: Harmood Banner & Co 1955-74, Deloitte Haskins & Sells 1974-84; ICEAW: cncl memb 1970-87, vice pres 1977-78, dep pres 1978-79, centenary pres 1979-80, memb gen purposes and fin ctee 1977-83, chm int affrs ctee 1980-83, chm Cons of Accountancy Bodies 1979-80, dep chm Monopolies and Mergers Cmmn 1983-; memb: Ctee of London Soc of CAs 1966-70 and 1981-82 (chm 1969-70), ctees of investigations under Agric Mktg Act 1972-88, Cncl for Securities Indust 1979-80, panel on Take Overs and Mergers 1979-80, Review Body of Doctors' and Dentists' Remuneration 1984-; Uk and Ireland rep Cncl Int Fedn of Accounts 1981-83, memb disciplinary bd Inst of Actuaries 1986, chm disciplinary bd Br Psychological Bd 1988-; govr Highgate Sch 1982- (chm 1983-), tstee the Bob Champion Cancer Tst 1983-, jr warden Worshipful Co of CAs 1984-85, (sr Warden 1985-86, Master 1986-87); tstee Princes Youth Business Tst 1986-; hon tres Royal Acad of Music Appeal Fund 1985-; ACA 1951, FCA; *Recreations* gardening, silviculture, tennis, golf, shooting; *Style—* David Richards, Esq; Eastleach House, Eastleach, Glos GL7 3NW (☎ 036 785 416); MMC, New Court, 48 Carey Street, London WC2A 2JT (☎ 01 831 6111)

RICHARDS, Derek James; s of William Richards, of Kenmore, Cricket Lane, Lichfield, Staffs, and Grace Winifred, *née* Funnell; *b* 12 Nov 1934; *Educ* King Edward VI Sch Lichfield, Jesus Coll Cambridge (BA, MA), Guys Hosp Med Sch (MB, BChir); *m* 22 Sept 1962, Angela, da of William Hugh Maton, 4 High View Ct, Silverdale Rd, Eastbourne; 2 s (Michael John b 29 July 1964, Simon William b 11 Jan 1969), 2 da (Elizabeth Jane b 21 April 1966, Alice Louise b 16 April 1978); *Career* house offr registrar Guys Hosp, sr house offr Bristol Royal Infirmary, sr registrar Univ Coll Hosp, conslt surgn Eastbourne Health Authy; memb ctee of mgmnt Horder Centre (Crowborough, E Sussex), pres League of Friends Uckfield Hosp (Uckfield, E Sussex), memb BMA; fell BOA, FRCS 1964, MRCS, LRCP; *Recreations* golf, shooting, following Grand Prix racing; *Style—* Derek Richards, Esq; Clare Glen, High Hurstwood, Nr Uckfield, East Sussex TN22 4BN (☎ 082 581 3306); 28 Lushington Rd, Eastbourne BN21 4LL (☎ 0323 34030)

RICHARDS, Hon Sir Edward Trenton; CBE (1967); s of late George Richards, of British Guiana; *b* 4 Oct 1908; *Educ* Collegiate Sch, Queen's Coll Guyana; *m* 1940, Madree Elizabeth, da of Graham Williams, of Warwick Bermuda; 1 s, 2 da; *Career* secdy school teacher 1930-43; barr Middle Temple 1946; MP (House of Assembly) Bermuda 1948-76, govt leader Bermuda 1971 (dep leader 1968-71), pm of Bermuda 1972-75; kt 1970; *Style—* Hon Sir Edward Richards, CBE; Wilton, Keith Hall Rd, Warwick East, Bermuda (☎ 2 3645)

RICHARDS, Francis Neville; o s of Sir (Francis) Brooks Richards, KCMG, DSC, *qv*; *b* 18 Dec 1945; *Educ* Eton, King's Coll Cambridge (MA); *m* 16 Jan 1971, Gillian Bruce, da of I S Nevill, MC (d 1948); 1 s (James b 1975), 1 da (Joanna b 1977); *Career* Royal Green Jackets 1967-69, invalided following accident; third sec to second sec Br Embassy Moscow 1971-73; second sec to first sec UK Delgn to MBFR talks Vienna 1973-76, FCO 1976-85, asst private sec to sec of state 1980-82, cnsllr (econ and commercial) Br High Cmmn New Delhi 1985-88, head of S Asian Dept FCO 1988-; *Recreations* riding, walking, travel; *Clubs* Travellers', President's Estate Polo (New Delhi); *Style—* Francis Richards, Esq; c/o Foreign and Commonwealth Office, London SW1

RICHARDS, Hon Mrs (Gillian Mary); da of Baron Hunt of Fawley, CBE (Life Peer); *b* 1951; *m* 1972, Paul Andrew Richards; 3 s, 1 da; *Style—* The Hon Mrs Richards; Arborfield, Belmont, Wantage, Oxon

RICHARDS, Hon Mrs; Hon Irene Mary; *née* Leatherland; da of Baron Leatherland (Life Peer); *b* 1923; *Educ* Brentwood Co HS; *m* 1961 (m dis 1977), Douglas Richards; 1 s (David), 1 da (Jennifer); *Career* conference offr; *Style—* The Hon Mrs Richards; 19 The Greens Close, Loughton, Essex IG10 1QE

RICHARDS, Sir James Maude; CBE (1959); s of Louis Saurin Richards (d 1935), and Lucy Denes Clarence (d 1955); *b* 13 August 1907; *Educ* Gresham's Sch, Architectural Assoc Sch London (AADipl); *m* 1, 1936 (m dis 1948), Margaret, da of late David Angus; 1 s (decd), 1 da; m 2, 1954, Kathleen Margaret, da of Henry Godfrey-Faussett-Osborne, of Queendown Warren, Sittingbourne, Kent (d 1948); 1 s (decd); *Career* architectural writer, critic and historian; ed The Architectural Review 1937-71, dir of pubns Miny of Information (Middle East, Cairo) 1943-46, architectural corr The Times 1947-71, memb Royal Fine Art Cmmn 1951-66, prof of architecture Leeds Univ 1957-59, ed Euro Heritage 1973-75; author of numerous books on art, architecture and travel; Order of the White Rose Finland (Chevalier 1 Class 1959, promoted Cdr 1985), Gold Medal Mexican Inst of Architects 1963, Bicentenary Medal RSA 1971; hon fell American Inst of Architects 1985; ARIBA, FSA; kt 1972; *Recreations* travel; *Clubs* Athenaeum, Beefsteak; *Style—* Sir James Richards, CBE; 29 Fawcett St, London SW10 (☎ 01 352 9874)

RICHARDS, Ven John; s of William Richards, of 14 Premier Place, Exeter, and Ethel Mary Coates (d 1966); *b* 4 Oct 1933; *Educ* Reading Sch, Wyggeston GS Leicester, Sidney Sussex Coll Cambridge (MA), Ely Theological Coll; *m* 2 Sept 1958, Ruth, da of Wilfred Haynes (d 1985), of Heavitree, Exeter; 2 s (Peter b 1961, David b 1968), 3 da (Elizabeth b 1962, Rachel b 1964, Bridget b 1968); *Career* asst curate St Thomas Exeter 1959-64; rector: Holsworthy with Hollacombe and Cokebury 1964-74, Heavitree Exeter 1974-81; archdeacon of Exeter and canon of Exeter Cathedral 1981-; church cmmr 1988-; *Recreations* gardening, walking, fishing; *Style—* The Ven the Archdeacon of Exeter; 12 The Close, Exeter EX1 1EZ (☎ 0392 75745)

RICHARDS, Lt-Gen Sir John Charles Chisholm; KCB (1980); s of Charles Richards and Alice Milner; *b* 21 Feb 1927; *Educ* Worksop Coll Notts; *m* 1953, Audrey Hidson; 2 s, 1 da; *Career* joined RM 1945, Cdr 3 Commando 1975-76, Cmdt Gen RM 1977-81; HM Marshal of the Dipl Corps 1982-, Rep Col Cmdt RM 1989; Freeman City of London 1982; CBIM 1980; *Recreations* golf, gardening, swimming; *Clubs* Army and Navy; *Style—* Lt-Gen Sir John Richards, KCB; St James's Palace, London SW1

RICHARDS, John Deacon; CBE (1978); s of William John Richards (d 1985), and Ethel, *née* Waggott (d 1971); *b* 7 May 1931; *Educ* Geelong GS Aust, Cranleigh Sch, Architectural Assoc Sch of Architecture (AA Diploma); *m* 1958, Margaret, da of William Brown (d 1983); 1 s (Alan), 3 da (Kathleen, Lucy, Jessica); *Career* architect; sr conslt Robert Matthew, Johnson-Marshall and Ptnrs (architect and planner of Stirling Univ); bd memb and chm Scottish Ctee of the Housing Corpn 1982-, bd memb Scottish Homes 1988-; *Recreations* country life; *Clubs* Athenaeum, Scottish Arts; *Style—* John Richards Esq; Robert Matthew, Johnson-Marshall and Ptnrs, 10 Bells Brae, Edinburgh (☎ 031 225 2532)

RICHARDS, John William; s of John Richards (d 1979), of Leicester, and Florence Lillian, *née* Wilcox; *b* 3 Jan 1924; *Educ* Newbold; *m* 24 Aug 1946, Glady Ethel, da of John Howard (d 1983), of Cambs; 1 s (Anthony John Wilfred b 1958); *Career* fndr memb Jack Richards & Son Ltd 1956 (chm); *Recreations* touring with caravan, charity working, gardening; *Style—* John W Richards, Esq; St Audrey Lodge, 1 Harp Close Fakenham, Norfolk NR21 9HN (☎ 0328 4665); 2 Garrood Drive, Industrial Estate, Fakenham, Norfolk NR21 8NL (☎ 0328 3111, telex 818238)

RICHARDS, Brigadier Joseph Harold William Garner; OBE (1943), DL (Huntingdon 1952, Cambs 1974); s of Rev Joseph Richards (d 1941); *b* 29 August 1897; *Educ* Newcastle GS, RMA; *m* 1932, Enid Clunes, da of Patrick C C Mackay (d 1980), of Boree, Walcha, NSW, Australia; 1 da; *Career* joined RA as 2 Lt, served France 1917 (despatches), NW Frontier Province 1919 and 1924, on Staff Sch Artillery 1928-32, instructor Gunnery Coast Artillery Sch 1935-40, Lt-Col 1940, cdr Cross Channel Guns Dover 1941-45, Col 1944, chief instr Sch of AA Artillery 1945-47, Brig 1947, cdr Highland AA Bde 1947-49, ret; County Civil Defence offr Huntingdon and Peterborough 1952-67; *Recreations* heavy horses, gardening, antiques; *Style—* Brigadier Joseph Richards, OBE, DL; Old House, 48 High St, Brampton, Cambs PE18 8TH (☎ 0480 53677)

RICHARDS, Hon Juliet Elizabeth; da of 2 Baron Milverton; *b* 1964; *Style—* The Hon Juliet Richards

RICHARDS, Brig Leslie Frederick; CBE (1971, OBE 1963, MBE 1959); s of Frederick William Richards (d 1960), of Essex, and Edith Anne, *née* Orme (d 1971); *b* 12 April 1915; *Educ* CFS London; *m* 15 June 1945, Winifred Marjorie, da of Thomas Hyde (d 1974), of Essex; 2 s (Frederick Thomas b 1948, Phillip James b 1951); *Career* (Brig, formerly II Sikh Regt and RMO), cmmnd Indian Army 1941; served: India, Iraq, Persia, Syria, Burma, Egypt, NW Europe; fndr memb Indian Parachute Bde 1942-47, Brig, formerly 2 Sikh Regt and RMP; Marshal (Army) and inspr Mil Corrective Estabs 1968-71; *Recreations* field and mounted sports, sailing; *Clubs* Cwlth Tst; *Style—* Brig Frederick Richards, CBE; The Old Stables, Stratford Rd, Dedham, Essex, Colchester (☎ 0206 322211)

RICHARDS, Martin Edgar; s of Edgar Lynton (Tony) Richards, CBE, MC, TD (d 1983), and Barbara, *née* Lebus; *b* 27 Feb 1943; *Educ* Harrow; *m* 30 Jan 1969, Caroline, da of Edwin Billing Lewis (d 1948); 1 s (Charles b 1975), 1 da (Catherine b 1972); *Career* slr 1968; ptnr Clifford Chance (formerly Clifford-Turner) 1973-; *Style—* Martin Richards, Esq; Royex House, Aldermanbury Sq, London EC2V 7LD (☎ 01 600 0808, fax 01 726 8561)

RICHARDS, Michael Anthony; s of Edward Albert Richards (d 1975), of Argentina and UK, and Clara Muriel, *née* Webb (d 1970); *b* 12 Oct 1926; *Educ* St Alban's Coll Argentina, St Georges Coll Argentina, J M Estrada Coll Argentina, Royal Vet Coll; *m* 14 April 1956, Sylvia Rosemary, da of Geoffrey Charles Pain, JP (d 1986); 2 da (Claire Penelope b 3 Nov 1957, Sally Veronica (Mrs Wilson) b 18 Jan 1961); *Career* Br Latin American Vol Scheme Br Army 1945, Sgt Intelligence Corps Middle East 1945-47; gen veterinary practice 1953-59; lectr: veterinary medicine London Univ 1961-65, veterinary pathology Univ of Edinburgh 1967-69; author various scientific pubns on veterinary medicine and pathology; chief inspr: Cruelty to Animals Act (1987) 1982-86 (inspr 1969-82), Animals (Scientific Procedures) Act (1986) 1986-87; CBiol, FIBiol 1985, MRCVS; *Recreations* philately; *Clubs* RSM; *Style—* Michael Richards, Esq; Hill View, Back Row, Charleston, By Glamis, Forfar, Angus DD8 1UG (☎ 030 784 231)

RICHARDS, Hon Michael Hugh; s of 1 Baron Milverton, GCMG (d 1978); hp of bro, 2 Baron Milverton; *b* 1 August 1936; *Educ* Ridley Coll Ontario, Clifton Coll; *m* 1960, Edna Leonie B, da of Col Leo Steveni, OBE, MC, IA (ret); 1 s; *Career* Capt (ret) Rifle Bde; Malaya 1957 (despatches); attached Royal Nigerian Army 1962, memb UN Congo Force, 1963-65; md Philip Morris Nigeria Ltd 1972-, dir Africa Carreras-Rothmans Ltd 1978-82, md Murray Son & Co, dir personnel Rothmans Int Tobacco; *Clubs* Naval and Military; *Style—* The Hon Michael Richards; Lovelynch House, Middleton Stoney Rd, Bicester, Oxon

RICHARDS, Prof Peter; s of Dr William Richards (d 1981), and Barbara Ashton, *née* Taylor (d 1971); *b* 25 May 1936; *Educ* St George's Hosp Med Sch, Royal Postgraduate Med Sch London (PhD), Monkton Combe Sch, Emmanuel Coll Cambridge (MA, MBBCh, BCh); *m* 1, 6 July 1959 (m dis 1986), Anne Marie, da of Svend Larsen (d 1964), of Odense, Denmark; 1 s (Allan), 3 da (Marianne, Annette, Christina); m2, 26 July 1987, Dr Carol Anne, da of Dr Raymond Seymour, Wendlebury; *Career* hon sr lectr St Marys Hosp Med Sch 1970-73 (lectr in med 1967-70), conslt physician St Peters Hosp Chertsey 1970-73, sr lectr and conslt physician St Georges Hosp and Med Sch 1973-79, dean and prof of med St Mary's Hosp Med Sch 1979- (hon conslt physician), pro-rector (med educn) Imp Coll of Sci Technol and Med; cncl memb Anglo-Finnish Soc; Liveryman Worshipful Co of Apothecaries 1984, Freeman City of London 1985; FRCP 1976; *Books* The Medieval Leper and His Northern Heirs (1977), Understanding Water, Electrolyte and Acid Base Metabolism (jointly 1983), Wasser-und Elektrolythaushalt: Diagnostik und Therapie (jointly 1985), Learning Medicine (5 ed 1988), Living Medicine (1989); *Recreations* social history, walking, listening to music; *Clubs* Garrick; *Style—* Prof Peter Richards; St Mary's Hospital Medical School, Norfolk Place, London W2 1PG (☎ 01 723 1252 ext 5009, fax 01 724 7349)

RICHARDS, Philip Brian; s of Glyn Bevan Richards (d 1976), of Ynysybwl, and Nancy Gwenhwyfar, *née* Evans of Bargoed; *b* 3 August 1946; *Educ* Cardiff HS, Univ of Bristol (LLB); *m* 17 July 1971, Dorothy Louise, da of Victor George, of Ystrad Mynach; 2 da (Rhuanedd b 1974, Lowri b 1978); *Career* called to Bar Inner Temple 1969, in practice 1970-; pt/t chm Soc Sec Appeal Tbnl 1987-, Plaid Cymru parly candidate 1974 and 1979; vice pres: Mountain Ash RFC, Neyland RFC; tstee Welsh Writers' Tst, memb mgmnt ctee Cynon-Taf Housing Assoc; *Recreations* music, sport, literature, walking; *Clubs* Cardiff and County, Newport and County; *Style—* Philip Richards, Esq; Cwm Pandy, Llanwynno Rd, Cwmaman, Aberdare CF44 6PG (☎ 0685 870 864); 30 Park Place, Cardiff CF1 3BA (☎ 0222 398 421, fax 0222 398 725)

RICHARDS, Sir Rex Edward; s of late Harold William Richards, of Colyton, Devon; *b* 28 Oct 1922; *Educ* Colyton GS Devon, St John's Coll Oxford (DSc); *m* 1948, Eva Edith, da of Paul Vago, of London (d 1948); 2 da; *Career* fell and tutor Lincoln Coll Oxford 1947-64, Dr Lee's prof of chemistry and fellow Exeter Coll Oxford 1964-69, warden Merton Coll 1969-84, vice-chllr Oxford Univ 1977-81; dir Leverhulme Tst 1985-; non exec dir: IBM-UK 1978-83, Oxford Instruments Gp 1982-; memb: scientific advsy ctee Nat Gallery 1978-, advsy bd Research Cncls 1980-83; Advsy Cncl for Applied Res and Devpt 1984-87; tstee: CIBA Fndn 1978-, Nat Heritage Memorial Fund 1980-84, Tate Gallery 1982-, Nat Gallery 1982-; Corday - Morgan Medal (Chemical Soc 1954, Dowy Medal (Royal Soc) 1976, Royal Medal (Royal Soc) 1986, Medal of Honour, Rheimiciche Friedrich, Wilhelm Univ, Bonn, 1983; Hon DSc: East Anglia, Exeter, Leicester, Salford, Edinburgh, Leeds, Cambridge, Kent; Hon LLD Dundee; hon FRCP, FRS, FRIC; kt 1977; *Recreations* twentieth century painting and sculpture; *Clubs* Royal Soc; *Style—* Sir Rex Richards

RICHARDS, Hon Susan Mary; da of 2nd Baron Milverton; *b* 1962; *Style—* The Hon Susan Richards

RICHARDS, (David) Wyn; s of Evan Gwylfa Richards (d 1987), of Llanelli, and Florence Margretta, *née* Evans (d 1988); *b* 22 Sept 1943; *Educ* Gwendraeth GS, Llanelli GS, Trinity Hall Cambridge; *m* 23 Dec 1972, Thelma Frances, *née* Hall; 5 s (Mark b 1974, Cennydd b 1976, Hywel b 1977, Daniel Owen b 1981, Aled Wyn b 1988); *Career* barr Inner Temple 1968, rec 1985; *Style—* Wyn Richards, Esq; 2 Queens Rd, Sketty, Swansea, W Glam SA2 0SD (☎ 0792 202 462); Iscoed Chambers, 86 St Helen's Rd, Swansea, W Glam SA1 4BQ (☎ 0792 6529 88, fax 0792 458 089)

RICHARDSON; *see*: Stewart-Richardson

RICHARDSON, (Henry) Anthony; s of Thomas Ewan Richardson (d 1974), of Batley, W Yorks, and Jessie, *née* Preston (d 1986); *b* 28 Dec 1925; *Educ* Giggleswick Sch, Univ of Leeds (LLB, LLM); *m* 8 May 1954, Georgina, *née* Lawford, step da of Gp Capt George Richard Bedford, RAF (ret), of Wetherby, W Yorks; *Career* barr Lincoln's Inn 1951; NE circuit: dep circuit judge 1972-78, rec of the Crown Ct 1978-; *Recreations* walking, gardening, listening to music; *Style—* Anthony Richardson, Esq; Grey Thatch, Wetherby Rd, Scarcroft, Leeds LS14 3BB (☎ 0532 892555); 38 Park Square, Leeds LS1 2PA (☎ 0532 439422)

RICHARDSON, Sir Anthony Lewis; 3 Bt (UK 1924); s of Sir Leslie Lewis Richardson, 2 Bt (d 1985), of Old Vineyard, Constantia, Cape Town, SA, and Joy Patricia, *née* Rillstone; *b* 5 August 1950; *Educ* Diocesan Coll Cape Town SA; *m* 1985, Honor Gillian, da of Robert Anthony Dauney, of 5 George St, Paddington, Sydney, Australia; *Heir* br, Charles John Richardson b 1955, *qv*; *Career* stockbroker S G Warburg Securities, London, memb London Stock Exchange; dir Potter Partners, Sydney, Australia; *Recreations* various sports, photography; *Clubs* Boodles, Hurlingham, Annabels; *Style—* Sir Anthony Richardson, Bt; 5 Marloes Rd, Kensington, London W8 6LQ (☎ 01 373 8960); c/o S G Warburg Securities, 1 Finsbury Ave, London EC2 (☎ 01 606 106)

RICHARDSON, Dr Arthur Tom (Tony); s of Arthur Whittaker Richardson, OBE (d 1985), of New Malden, Surrey, and Dora May, *née* Tattersall (d 1975); *b* 28 April 1923; *Educ* Caterham Sch, St Thomas Hosp Sch Univ of London (MB, BS) DPhys Med (RCP); *m* 1, 2 March 1946 (m dis 1964), Doreen Marie Jackson; 2 s (Raymond b 1947, Desmond b 1952); m 2, 10 July 1964, Janet Elizabeth, da of Donald MacPherson, CIE, of Cannon Hill, London NW6; 2 da (Catriona b 1965, Kirsty b 1968); *Career* Flt Lt (Med) RAF 1947-49; conslt rheumatologist: Royal Free Hosp 1953-88, Royal Masonic Hosp 1970-; hon memb American Acad of Physical Med and Rehabilitation 1953-; memb: bd of govrs Royal Free Hosp 1965-72, sch cncl Royal Free Hosp Med Sch 1967-71, NW Thames Regnl Hosp Bd 1972-76, Cncl of Professions Supplementary to Med 1976-; pres Br Assoc for Rheumatology and

Rehabilitation 1976-77; Freeman City of London 1952, Liveryman Worshipful Co of Apothecaries 1952; FRSM 1946, MRCS 1946, LRCP 1946, MRCP 1953, FRCP 1965; *Recreations* sailing; *Clubs* Savage, RAC, Royal Harwick YC; *Style—* Dr Tony Richardson; 8 Clifton Hill, London NW8 OQG (☎ 01 328 2665); 90 Harley St, London W1M 1AF (☎ 01 935 7637)

RICHARDSON, Hon Mrs (Averil Diana); *née* Betterton; da of 1 Baron Rushcliffe; *b* 1914; *m* 1, 1939, Maj Richard Wyndham-Quin Going, KOSB (ka 1944); 1 s, 1 da; m 2, 1946, Col Charles Walter Philipps Richardson, DSO and Bar, KOSB (b 8 Jan 1905, educ RNCs Osborne and Dartmouth and RMC Sandhurst, served NW Europe WW II and enjoys fishing); 2 s; *Style—* The Hon Mrs Richardson; Quintans, Steventon, Hants (☎ Dummer 473)

RICHARDSON, Charles John; s of Sir Leslie Lewis Richardson, 2 Bt (d 1985); hp of br, Sir Anthony Lewis Richardson, 3 Bt, *qv*; *b* 8 Dec 1955; *Educ* Diocesan Coll, Cape Town; *Style—* Charles Richardson Esq; 9 Eglantine Road, London SW18

RICHARDSON, Gen Sir Charles Leslie; GCB (1967, KCB 1962, CB 1957), CBE (1945), DSO (1943); s of Lt-Col Charles William Richardson, OBE, of Springfield, Lurgan, Co Down, and Evaline Adah, *née* Wingrove; *b* 11 August 1908; *Educ* St Ronans, Wellington, RMA Woolwich (King's Medal), Clare Coll Cambridge (BA); *m* 1947, Audrey Elizabeth, da of Capt C R E Jörgensen, of Bushby Ruff House, nr Dover; 1 s (and 1 s decd), 1 da, 1 step da; *Career* 2 Lt RE 1928, served India 1931-38, served 1939-45 in France, Belgium, Dunkirk, UK, Palestine, Africa, Sicily, Italy, NW Europe; Acting Brig 1943-47, Brig Gen Staff (Ops) Eighth Army 1943, dep COS Fifth US Army 1944, BGS (Plans) 21 Army Gp 1944, ch of Military Div Br Control Cmmn Berlin 1945-46, Lt-Col Co Engr Regt BAOR 1947-48, staff appts UK and Egypt 1949-52, cdr Inf Bde 1953-54, Maj-Gen Cmdt RMC of Science 1955-58, GOC Singapore District 1958-60, dir of Combat Devpt War Office 1960-61, dir-gen of Military Training War Office 1961-63, GOC-in-C Northern Cmd 1963-64, QMG Miny of Defence 1965-66, Gen 1965, master-gen of the Ordnance 1966-71, ADC Gen to HM The Queen 1967-70, Col Cmdt RAOC 1967-71, Chief Royal Engr 1972-77; consultant and dir of various cos 1971-76, tres Kitchener Nat Memorial Fund 1971-76, chm Gordon Boys Sch 1977-87; Legion of Merit USA 1944; *Books* Flashback (1985), Send for Freddie (1981); *Recreations* skiing, tennis; *Clubs* Army and Navy; *Style—* Gen Sir Charles Richardson, GCB, CBE, DSO; The Stables, Sandy Lane, Betchworth, Surrey RH3 7AA (☎ Betchworth 3314)

RICHARDSON, David; s of Harold George Richardson (d 1986), of Ewell, Surrey, and Madeleine Raphaële, *née* Lebret; *b* 24 April 1928; *Educ* Wimbledon Coll, King's Coll, Univ of London (BA); *m* 14 Feb 1951, (Frances) Jean, da of Ernest Pendrell Pring (d 1971), of Looe, Cornwall; 3 s (Stephen Michael b Dec 1951, Nicholas Henry b April 1954, Benedict Hugh b Sept 1965), 1 da (Catherine Anne b March 1957); *Career* RAF 1949-51: PO 1949, Flying Offr 1950; RAF Res 1951-56; HM inspr of taxes 1953-55; Miny of Lab (later Dept of Employment) 1956-82: chief exec Construction Industry Trg Bd 1964-66, chm Centl Youth Employment Exec 1969-71, under sec industl relations 1972-75, dir safety policy Health and Safety Exec 1975-77, dir ACAS 1977-82; dir: ILO (London) 1982-, Tablet Publishing Co Ltd 1985-, Industl Trg Serv Ltd 1986-; FIPM; *Recreations* music, landscape gardening; *Clubs* RAF; *Style—* David Richardson, Esq; 183 Banstead Road, Carshalton, Surrey SM5 4DP (☎ 01 642 1052); International Labour Office, Vincent House, Vincent Square, London SW1P 2NB (☎ 01 828 6401, telex 886836 INTLAB G)

RICHARDSON, Sir Egerton Rudolf; CMG (1959); s of James Neil Richardson; *b* 15 August 1912; *Educ* Calabar HS Kingston Jamaica, Oxford Univ; *Career* entered Jamaican Civil Service 1933, clerk to Treasury 1939-43, sr clerk 1943-44, asst sec 1947-50, permanent sec 1953-55, financial sec Jamaica 1956-62, ambass and permanent rep to UN 1962-67; Jamaican ambass to: USA 1967-72, Mexico 1967-75; permanent sec Miny of Public Service 1973-75, permanent rep of Jamaica to UN in NY 1981-; kt 1968; *Style—* Sir Egerton Richardson, CMG; 215E 68th St, New York, NY 10021, USA

RICHARDSON, Sir (John) Eric; CBE (1962); s of William Richardson, of Birkenhead (d 1952); *b* 30 June 1905; *Educ* Higher Elementary Sch Birkenhead, Liverpool Univ (BEng, PhD); *m* 1941, Alice May, da of Hugh Munro Wilson, of Hull (d 1979); 1 s, 2 da (and 1 da decd); *Career* engr and educationalist; hd of engrg dept Hull Municipal Tech Coll 1937; princ: Oldham Municipal Tech Coll 1942, Royal Tech Coll Salford 1944, Northampton Poly (now City Univ London) 1947; dir Poly of Central London 1957-70; Hon DSc (City Univ London); FIEE, MIMechE, FBHI, FBOA, FPS, FRSA, FCGI; kt 1967; *Recreations* photography, gardening; *Style—* Sir Eric Richardson, CBE; 73 Delamere Rd, Ealing, London W5 3JP (☎ 01 567 1588)

RICHARDSON, Garry Peter Alan; s of Claude Alan Richardson; *b* 6 Jan 1931; *m* 1961, Jill Rosemary Grenville, da of Robert Grenville Smith of Switzerland; 3 da; *Career* dir Mount House Ltd; *Recreations* tennis, golf, sailing; *Clubs* Lansdowne, Wentworth; *Style—* Garry Richardson, Esq; Mount House, Waverley Drive, Virginia Water, Surrey (☎ 099 04 4473)

RICHARDSON, Dr George Barclay; CBE (1978); s of George Richardson (d 1970), and Christina Richardson (d 1975); *b* 19 Sept 1924; *Educ* Aberdeen Central Secdy Sch, Aberdeen Univ (BSc), Oxford Univ (MA); *m* 21 Sept 1957, Isabel Alison, da of Laurence Chalk (d 1979); 2 s (Graham b 25 April 1960, Andrew b 25 July 1962); *Career* Lt RNVR 1945-46; third sec Dip Serv 1949-50, fell St John's Coll Oxford 1951, reader in econs Oxford 1959-74, chief exec and sec to the delegates OUP 1974-88 pro vice chllr Oxford Univ 1988-, vice pres Oxford Univ Appeal Campaign 1988-; Warden-Elect Keble Coll Oxford 1989; econ advsr UK AEA 1968-74; memb: Monopolies Cmmn 1969-74, Royal Cmmn on Enviromental Pollution 1973-74, econ devpt ctee for Electrical Engrg Ctee 1964-74; hon fell CCC 1986, hon DCL Oxford 1988; *Books* Information and Investment (1960), Economic Theory (1964); *Recreations* reading, music, swimming; *Clubs* Oxford and Cambridge United Univ; *Style—* Dr George Richardson, CBE; Wardens Lodgings, Keble College, Oxford; Ridgeway, 153 The Hill, Burford, Oxon OX8 4RE

RICHARDSON, Ian William; CBE (1989); s of John Richardson, and Margaret, *née* Drummond; *b* 7 April 1934; *Educ* Heriot's Sch Edinburgh, Tynecastle Edinburgh, Royal Scottish Acad of Music and Drama; *m* 2 Feb 1961, Maroussia, da of Alexei Simeonitch Frank (d 1967); (Jeremy b 24 Dec 1961, Miles b 15 July 1963); *Career* actor; joined Birmingham Repertory Co 1958, Hamlet 1959; RSC 1960-75: Arragon in Merchant of Venice, Malateste in Duchess of Malfi 1960, Oberon in a Midsummer Night's Dream 1961, Edmund in King Lear 1964, Herald and Merat in Marat/Sade 1964-65, Vendice in Revenger's Tragedy 1965 and 1969, Coriolanus 1966, Bertram in All's Well That Ends Well 1966, Cassuns in Julius Caesar 1968, Pericles 1969, Angelo in Measure For Measure 1970, Prospero in The Tempest 1970, Richard II and Bolingbroke 1973, Berowne in Love's Labours Lost 1973, Ford in The Merry Wives of Windsor 1975, Richard III 1975; Professor Higgins in My Fair Lady New York 1976-77 (Drama Desk Award), Man and Superman Show Festival Ontario 1977, Lolita (Broadway) 1981; Films incl: Man of La Manche 1972, The Sign of Four and The Hound of the Baskervilles (as Sherlock Holmes) 1982, Brazil 1984, Whoops Apocalypse 1987, The Fourth Protocol 1987; TV series incl: Tinker Tailor Soldier Spy 1979, Private Schulz 1981, The Woman in White 1982, The Master of Ballantrae 1984, Mistral's Daughter 1985, Porterhouse Blue 1987, Troubles 1988; TV plays incl: Danton's Death 1978, Monsignor Quixote 1985, Blunt 1987; RTS Award 1982, American Arts Club Gold Medal 1988; FRSAMD 1971; Publications: prefaces to Cymbeline (Folio Soc), Richard II (BBC Publications), Merry Wives of Windsor (Doubleday); *Recreations* history, music, reading; *Clubs* Garrick; *Style—* Ian Richardson, Esq, CBE; c/o London Mgmnt, 235-241 Regent St, London W1 (☎ 01 493 1610)

RICHARDSON, Jo(sephine); MP (Lab) Barking Feb 1974-; *b* 28 August 1923; *Career* memb Lab NEC 1979-; vice pres CND 1975-, memb: PLP Civil Liberties Gp 1979- (chm 1975-79), ASTMS, APEX; chm Lab Pty Women's Ctee 1981-82 and 1988-, memb shadow cabinet and spokesperson on women's rights 1983-; *Style—* Ms Jo Richardson, MP; House of Commons, London SW1A 0AA (☎ 01 219 5028)

RICHARDSON, John David Benbow; MC (and bar 1942), CBE (1988); s of His Hon Judge Richardson, OBE (d 1956); *b* 6 April 1919; *Educ* Harrow, Clare Coll Cambridge; *m* 1946, Kathleen Mildred, da of Dudley Charles Turner, CMG (d 1958); 4 s; *Career* Capt 1 Kings Dragoon Gds; barr, dep chm Durham County Quarter Sessions 1964-71, recorder 1972-73, pres North Rent Assessment Panel 1979-; *Recreations* fishing, gardening, golf; *Clubs* MCC, York County Stand, Northern Counties; *Style—* John Richardson Esq, MC, CBE; The Old Vicarage, Nine Banks, Whitfield, Hexham, Northumberland NE47 8DB (☎ 049 85 217)

RICHARDSON, Ven John Farquhar; s of William Henry Richardson and Gertrude Mary, *née* Walker; *b* 23 April 1905; *Educ* Winchester, Trinity Hall Cambridge; *m* 1936, Elizabeth Mary, da of Henry Roy Dean; 1 s (John), 2 da (Jane, Mary); *Career* archdeacon of Derry 1952-73; chaplain to: HM King George VI 1952, HM Queen Elizabeth II 1952-75; vice provost Woodard Schs Midlands Div 1969-80; dep chm Trent Coll 1975-85; *Recreations* golf; *Clubs* RAC, Jesters, Hawks; *Style—* The Ven John Richardson; 474 Kedleston Road, Derby DE3 2NE (☎ 0332 559 135)

RICHARDSON, John Francis; s of Francis Richardson (d 1957); *b* 16 June 1934; *Educ* Scarborough Coll, Wadham Coll Oxford; *m* 1960, Jacqueline Mary; 2 c; *Career* joined Burnley Bldg Soc 1959, asst gen mangr Burnley Bldg Soc 1972-76, dep gen mangr Burnley Bldg Soc 1976-80, chief gen mangr Burnley Bldg Soc 1980-; *Recreations* golf; *Clubs* Clitheroe Golf; *Style—* John Richardson Esq; 'Hammerton', Old Rd, Chatburn, Clitheroe, Lancs

RICHARDSON, Baron (Life Peer UK 1979); Sir John Samuel Richardson; 1 Bt (UK 1963), LVO (1943); s of Maj John Watson Richardson (ka 1917, formerly solicitor), of Sheffield, and Elizabeth Blakeney, da of Rt Hon Sir Samuel Roberts, 1 Bt, JP, DL; *b* 16 June 1910; *Educ* Charterhouse, Trinity Coll Cambridge (MA, MD); *m* 6 June 1933, Sybil Angela Stephanie, 3 da of Arthur Ronald Trist (d 1971), of Stanmore; 2 da; *Heir* to Btcy, none; *Career* sits as an Independent peer in House of Lords; medical specialist RAMC 1939-45, Lt-Col; conslt physician St Thomas's Hosp 1947-75 and to Metropolitan Police 1957-80; hon consultant physician to Army 1963-75, emeritus 1976-; pres: Royal Soc of Med 1969-71, BMA 1970-71, Gen Medical Cncl 1973-80; FRCP; Hon FRCPE, G&I; Hon DSc: Nat University of Ireland 1975, Hull 1981; Hon DCL Newcastle 1980; Hon LLD: Nottingham 1981, Liverpool 1983; hon fellow Trinity Coll Cambridge 1979; Hon FRCS, FRCPy, FRCGP, FFCM, FPS, hon bencher Gray's Inn; CStJ; kt 1960; *Style—* The Rt Hon the Lord Richardson, LVO; Windcutter, Lee, Ilfracombe, Devon (☎ 0271 63198)

RICHARDSON, Joy, Lady Joy Patricia; *née* Rillstone; da of John Percival Rillstone, of Johannesburg, S Africa; *m* 1946, Sir Leslie Lewis Richardson, 2 Bt (d 1985); 2 s (Sir Anthony Lewis, 3 Bt, Charles John, *qqvv*), 1 da (Jennifer b 1947, m 1984, Richard Michael Fearon Gold); *Style—* Joy, Lady Richardson; Old Vineyard, Constantia, Cape Town, S Africa

RICHARDSON, Karen; *Educ* Somerville Coll Oxford (MA); *Career* admitted slr 1978, ptnr Travers Smith Braithwaite; memb ctee City of London Law Soc; chm Assoc Women Slrs; Liveryman Slrs Co; memb Law Soc; *Style—* Miss Karen Richardson; c/o Travers Smith Braithwaite, 6 Snow Hill, London EC1A 2AL

RICHARDSON, (William) Kenneth; s of James McNaughton Richardson, of Stirling, and Jane Ann McKay, *née* Monteith; *b* 16 Nov 1956; *Educ* High Sch of Stirling, St Andrews Univ (MA); *Career* mgmnt trainee: United Biscuits, Sue Ryder Fndn; planning asst Scottish Opera 1983-87, co mangr Royal Opera and admin Royal Opera House Garden Venture 1987-; *Recreations* cooking; *Style—* Kenneth Richardson, Esq; 58 Steele Rd, London, E11 3JA (☎ 01 555 9532); Royal Opera Hse, Covent Garden, London, WC2E 9DD (☎ 01 240 1200, fax 01 836 1762, telex 27988)

RICHARDSON, Lawford; CMG (1980); s of Lawford Richardson; *b* 3 Dec 1908; *Educ* Sydney C of E GS; *m* 1936, Marjorie, da of A Smith; 1 s, 1 da; *Career* chm A Buckle & Son Pty, Farley & Lewers, Friends' Provident Life Office, NBN Ltd; dep chm Ready Mixed Concrete 1981-, Davis Consolidated Industs, Fibre Containers Ltd; dir Canberra Quarries Pty, Friends' Provident Life Off (UK), Gravel & Sand Suppliers Ltd, Phoenix Assur Co of Australia, Southern Television Corpn; FCA; *Style—* Lawford Richardson, Esq, CMG; 19 Stanhope Rd, Killara, NSW 2071, Australia

RICHARDSON, Mark Rushcliffe; s of Brig Charles Walter Philipps Richardson, DSO, of Quintans, Steventon, Basingstoke, Hampshire, and Hon Averil Diana Richardson *qv*; *b* 17 Sept 1947; *Educ* Wellington, Christ Church Oxford (BA); *m* 28 Sept 1983, Cherry Victoria, da of Sidney Wallace Smart, of Oak Ash, Chaddleworth, Newbury, Berks; 1 s (Hugo b 24 Nov 1981), 2 da (Melanie b 13 Nov 1974, Davina b 19 Jan 1976); *Career* dir Lazard Bros & Co Ltd 1986- (fund mangr 1969-86), ctee chm Lazard Euro Exempt Fund and UK Equity Fund, ctee memb Lazard Far Eastern Exempt Fund and Aust Exempt Fund; hon tres Riding for the Disabled Assoc; *Recreations* country pursuits, skiing; *Clubs* Boodles; *Style—* Mark Richardson, Esq; Priors Court, West Hanney, Wantage, Oxon (☎ 023 587 210); 21 Moorfields, London EC21 2HT (☎ 01 588 2721, fax 01 638 5021, 0836 583 176, telex 886438)

RICHARDSON, Lady; Meriel; *née* Forbes-Robertson; da of Frank Forbes Robertson, stage and film actor, by his 1 w, Honore Helen McDermott, actress; *m* 1944, as his 2 w, Sir Ralph Richardson, actor (d 1983); 1 s; *Style—* Lady Richardson

RICHARDSON, Michael John; s of George Richardson; *b* 24 July 1936; *Educ* Heanor GS Derbys; *m* 1955, Janet Ruth, *née* Holmes; 2 da; *Career* auctioneer; memb Inst of Motor Auctioneers; former sec Society of Motor Auctioneers, jt md Br Car Auctions Ltd; *Recreations* golf, yachting, gliding; *Clubs* Royal Thames Yacht; *Style—* Michael Richardson Esq; The Hollies, 13 Holly Ave, Camberley, Surrey (☎ 0276 29039)

RICHARDSON, Michael John; s of George Frederick Richardson (d 1979), and Mabel Alice, *née* Cox; *b* 28 Mar 1935; *Educ* Epsom Coll; *m* 22 Aug 1959, Helen Patricia, da of Percival Bluett Bray (d 1942); 1 s (David b 16 Jan 1962), 1 da (Susan b 2 Jan 1965); *Career* CA; FW Smith Riches 1952-60, Price Waterhouse 1960-63, dir 3i Gp (3i Corp Fin Ltd) 1963-80, fin dir Shandwick Gp 1980-81, dir Standard Chartered Merchant Bank Ltd 1986- (joined 1981); ldr Sevenoaks Methodist Youth Club, vestry steward Sevenoaks Methodist Church; Freeman City of London, Liveryman Worshipful Co of CAs; FCA; *Books* Going Public (1973); *Recreations* singing, swimming, gardening; *Style—* Michael Richardson, Esq; 19 Mount Harry Rd, Sevenoaks, Kent TN13 3JJ (☎ 0732 453839); Standard Chartered Merchant Bank Ltd, 33-36 Gracechurch St, London EC3V 0AX (☎ 01 623 8711, fax 01 626 1610, telex 884689)

RICHARDSON, Michael John de Rougemont; s of Arthur Wray Richardson, of Hove, Sussex; *b* 9 April 1925; *Educ* Harrow, RMC Sandhurst; *m* 16 July 1949, Octavia, yr da of Arthur Joyce Mayhew, Capt Denbighshire Hus; 1 s, 2 da; *Career* dir: N M Rothschild & Sons Ltd, Drayton Far Eastern Tst plc, English & Int Tst plc, Anglo-Scottish Amalgamated Corpn Ltd, The Savoy Hotel plc, Shield Tst Ltd, chm: Hyde Park Fin Ltd, Hyde Park Fin (Hldgs) Ltd, Derby Tst Ltd, Brycourt Unit Tst Mgmnt Ltd Drayton Far Eastern Trust (Finance) Ltd, The Rank Fndn, Sedgwick Gp plc, Smith New Court, Rothschild North America, NMR Int NV;; *Recreations* sailing, foxhunting; *Style—* Michael Richardson, Esq; c/o N M Rothschild & Sons Ltd, New Court, St Swithin's Lane, London EC4 (☎ 01 280 5000)

RICHARDSON, Michael Norman; s of Norman Richardson (d 1965), and Ethel, *née* Spittle (d 1978); *b* 23 Feb 1935; *Educ* Dulwich Coll; *m* 13 April 1976, Rosemarie Christina, da of Emmerich von Moers (d 1946); 4 da (Penelope, Theresa, Christina, Alexandra); *Career* RAF 1958-60, PO and Flying Offr in Directorate of Legal Servs, Far E Air Force, Sword of Merit OCT course 1958; slr 1958; asst slr Coward Chance & Co 1960-63; ptnr: Jaques & Co 1963-73, Richardson & Oakley 1977-85, Lawrence Graham (specialising Int Corporte Fin) 1985-; dep chm Henry Ansbacher & Co Ltd 1970-77, non-exec dir Sarasota Technol plc 1985-87; dir: Amicus Investmts Ltd, Quadrant Assoc Ltd, Quadrant Investmts Ltd, Tech Casino Servs Ltd, Palladium Gp UK Companies; memb Law Soc 1958, Fell IOD 1987; *Recreations* all sports, gardening, art; *Clubs* Oriental, MCC; *Style—* Michael Richardson, Esq; Fernhill Cottage, Hatchet Lane, Windsor Forest, Berks SL4 2DZ (☎ 0344 882 635); 190 Strand, London WC2R 1JN (☎ 01 379 0000, fax 01 379 6854, telex 22673)

RICHARDSON, (William) Norman Ballantyne; DL (Greater London 1985); s of Robert Richardson (d 1974), of Wishaw, Lanarkshire, and Sarah Maddick, *née* Shields; *b* 8 Oct 1947; *Educ* King Edward VI GS Birmingham, Goldsmiths' Coll Univ of London (CertEd); *Career* dep head Emmanuel C of E Sch London NW6 1979-81; headmaster: All Saints' C of E Sch London SW6 1981-85, Christ Church C of E Sch London SW3 1985-; chm: ILEA Divnl Consultative Ctee of Headteachers 1985-86 and 1989-, Local Advsy Ctee on Primary/Secondary Transfer 1987-88, ILEA Central Consultative Ctee of Headteachers 1989-; memb: Colne/East Gade Advsy Ctee on Educn 1977-81, London Diocesan Headteachers' Cncl 1984-, ILEA Standing Advsy Ctee on Religious Educn 1985-; chm London (South) ctee Royal Jubilee and Prince's Tsts 1984-; sec: London Youth Involvement Ctee Queen's Silver Jubilee Tst 1981-83, Greater London Ctee Royal Jubilee and Prince's Tsts 1983-84; FRGS 1969, FRSA 1974, MCollP 1985, MBIM 1986; *Recreations* reading biographies, watching tv and generally recharging the batteries; *Clubs* Royal Cwlth Soc; *Style—* Norman Richardson, Esq, DL; 12c Treport St, London SW18 2BP; Christ Church School, 1 Robinson St, London SW3 4AR

RICHARDSON, Paul Michael; JP (co of Nottingham, 1978); s of George Herbert Richardson, Ravenshead, Nottingham and Evelyn *née* O'Neil ; *b* 4 Jan 1941; *Educ* West Bridgford HS, Alfreton HS; *m* 14 Nov 1970, Jacqueline Margaret da of John Sydney Edwards of Aspley, Nottingham; 2 s (Michael b 10 Nov 1972, William b 22 July 1975), 1 da (Joanne b 16 Aug 1971); *Career* md FW Buck and Sons Ltd 1977-, dir Long Eaton Advertiser co Ltd 1980-, Hd of weekly publications T Bailey Forman Ltd 1982-; memb Rotary Club Sutton-in-Ashfield 1977-; Lib cncllr Sutton-in-Ashfield urban 1967-70; *Recreations* sports enthusiast; *Style—* Paul Richardson, Esq, JP; Long Eaton Advertiser co Ltd, Newspaper Buildings, West Gate, Long Eaton, Nottingham, NG10 1EH

RICHARDSON, Philip Edward; s of Wilfrid Laurence Richardson (d 1983), of Solihull and Nellie Elizabeth, *née* Hands (d 1966); *b* 6 Oct 1945; *Educ* Tudor Grange GS, Solihull, Coll of Law; *m* 26 May 1969, Corrinne Mary, da of John Woodall (d 1983), of Flyford Flavell; 2 s (Toby b 1972, Tom b 1977), 2 da (Polly b 1975, Prue b 1980); *Career* slr; ptnr Dawkins and Grey 1971-, dir English String Orchestra Ltd 1984-; Jt Hon Sec Birmingham Law Soc 1980-87 (pr offr 1987-), chm of govrs Pershore HS 1988-, pres Birmingham Consular Assoc 1987-, vice-chm Hill and Moor pc 1987-, Hon Consul:- The Netherlands 1982-, Belgium 1984-; memb: Law Soc 1970, Birmingham Law Soc 1970; *Recreations* music, railways; *Clubs* The Birmingham; *Style—* Philip Richardson, Esq; Bluebell Cottage, Hill, Pershore, Worcs (☎ 0386 860664); 40 Great Charles Street, Queensway, Birmingham (☎ 021 233 1021, fax 021 200 1548, car 0860 202994)

RICHARDSON, Lt-Gen Sir Robert Francis; KCB (1982), CVO (1978), CBE (1975, OBE 1971, MBE 1965); s of Robert Buchan Richardson; *b* 2 Mar 1929; *Educ* George Heriot's Sch Edinburgh, RMA Sandhurst; *m* 1, 1956, Maureen Robinson (d 1986); 3 s, 1 da; m 2, 7 May 1988, Mrs Alexandra Inglis, *née* Bomford; *Career* Lt-Gen 1982-85; GOC NI 1982-85, V-Adj Gen/Dir Manning (Army) MOD 1980-82, GOC Berlin 1978-80, Dep Adj-Gen HQ BAOR 1975-78, Cdr 39 Inf Bde NI 1974-75, Col Gen Staff Staff Coll Camberley 1971-74, CO 1 Bn Royal Scots 1969-71, GSO 2 asst chief Def Staff Operations MOD 1968-69, Bde Maj Aden Bde 1967 (despatches); cmmnd The Royal Scots (The Royal Regiment) (Col 1980-) 1949; admin The MacRobert Tst; *Recreations* golf, outdoor sports, gardening; *Clubs* Caledonian, Royal Scots, Hon Co of Edinburgh Golfers (Muirfield); *Style—* Lt-Gen Sir Robert Richardson, KCB, CVO, CBE; c/o Lloyds Bank plc, Cox's & King's Branch, 6 Pall Mall, London SW1

RICHARDSON, Roger Hart; RD (1965); s of Justin Richardson, of Headley, Surrey (d 1975), and Margery, *née* Wolfe; *b* 13 August 1931; *Educ* Rugby, Christ's Coll Cambridge (MA); *m* 25 Oct 1967, Evelyn Louise, da of Dr Paul Kane, MD, of 24 Montagu Sq, London W1; 1 s (Matthew b 1967), 1 da (Lydia b 1970); *Career* Lt Cdr RNR 1949-70; chm and md Beaver & Tapley Ltd (furniture mfrs) Southall Middx 1975-; Liveryman Worshipful Co of Furniture Makers 1961- (memb of Ct of Assts 1974, Jt Warden 1987, Sr Warden 1987, Warden 1988); *Recreations* sailing, music, bird-watching, wine; *Clubs* RNSA; *Style—* Roger Richardson, Esq, RD; 11 Broom Water, Teddington, Middx (☎ 01 977 7921, 01 574 4311); Beaver & Tapley Ltd, Scotts Rd, Southall, Middx

RICHARDSON, Hon Mrs (Sarah Amy); da of 13 Baron Clifford of Chudleigh, OBE; *b* 22 June 1956; *Educ* Convent of the Sacred Heart Woldingham; *m* 25 April 1981, Robert Carwithen Richardson, s of C C Richardson; 2 da (Amy Natasha b 1984, Jessie Katharine b 1987); *Style—* The Hon Mrs Richardson; Greatcombe, Holne, Devon TQ13 7SP

RICHARDSON, Maj Gen Thomas Anthony; CB (1974), MBE (1960); s of Maj Gen Thomas William Richardson, OBE, of Norfolk (d 1968), and Josephine Mary Herbert Wickham Clarke (d 1973); *b* 9 August 1922; *Educ* Wellington, Military Coll of Science; *m* 1945, Katharine Joanna Ruxton (d 1988), da of Maj Charles Minto Roberts (d 1956), of Somerset; 1 s (Christopher), 1 da (Charlotte); *Career* CO 7 RHA 1964-67, Cdr RA 2 Div (Brig) 1967-69, Dir Operational Requirements (Brig) 1980-71, Dir Army Aviation (Maj Gen) 1971-74, Head Br Defence Liaison Staff India (Maj Gen) 1974-77; sec: Timbers Growers Eng and Wales 1978-84, Br Christmas Tree Growers Assoc, Chm Tree Cncl 1986, chm: Army Aviation Assoc, Army Gliding Assoc, RA Rugby Club, Rhine Army Free Fall Parachute Club, 2nd Div Ski Ctee; Cdre Army Sailing Assoc, vice cdre: RA Yacht Club, (and chm) RAYC Germany; hon sec RA Garrison Shoot Larkhill; *Recreations* fishing, shooting, travelling; *Clubs* Army and Navy; *Style—* Maj Gen Tony Richardson, CB, MBE; 12 Lauriston Rd, Wimbledon, London SW19 4TQ (☎ 01 946 2695)

RICHARDSON, Thomas Legh; s of Arthur Legh Turnour Richardson (d 1984), and Penelope Margaret, *née* Waithman; *b* 6 Feb 1941; *Educ* Westminster, Christ Church Oxford (MA); *m* 10 Feb 1979, Alexandra Frazier, da of John D Ratcliff (d 1974), of New York; *Career* joined FO 1962; serv in Accra, Dares Salaam, Milan, New York, Rome, head of econ relations FCO 1986-; *Recreations* reading, walking, music; *Clubs* United Oxford and Cambridge; *Style—* Thomas Richardson, Esq; c/o FCO, Whitehall, London

RICHARDSON, Tony; s of Clarence Albert Richardson (d 1969), and Elsie Evans Richardson (d 1974); *b* 5 July 1928; *Educ* Ashville Coll Harrogate, Wadham Coll Oxford; *m* 1962 (m dis 1967), Vanessa Redgrave (*qv*), da of Sir Michael Redgrave (d 1985); 3 da (Natasha, Joely, Katharine); *Career* artistic dir English Stage Co Royal Ct Theatre 1956-65, dir Woodfall Film Prodns 1958-; prods incl: Look Back in Anger, The Entertainer, Luther, The Seagull, Pericles and Othello (Stratford), Taste of Honey; films incl: Taste of Honey, The Loneliness of the Long Distance Runner, Tom Jones (20 Oscars), The Charge of the Light Brigade, The Border, The Hotel New Hampshire; *Recreations* tennis, travel, bird collecting; *Style—* Tony Richardson, Esq; 1478 N Kings Rd, Los Angeles, CA 90069 (☎ 213 656 5314)

RICHARDSON, Hon Mrs (Valentine Ellen MacDermott); *née* Crittall; da of 1 Baron Braintree (d 1961); *b* 1918; *m* 1939, Karl Stewart Richardson; 2 s; *Style—* The Hon Mrs Richardson; Hungry Hall, Witham, Essex

RICHARDSON, William; CBE (1981), DL (Cumbria 1982); s of Edwin Richardson; *b* 15 August 1916; *Educ* Jr Tech Coll, Tech Colls Barrow-in-Furness; *m* 1941, Beatrice Marjorie Iliffe; 1 s, 1 da; *Career* chm: Vickers Shipbuilding & Engrg 1976-83 (md 1969-76), Vosper Thornycroft UK 1978-83, Barclay Curle 1978-83, Brooke Marine 1981-83; dep chm Br Shipbuilders 1981-83 (memb bd 1977-83); dir Vickers Cockatoo Dockyard Pty (Australia) 1977-84, Vosper Shiprepairers 1979-82; memb res cncl and off bearer Br Ship Res Assoc 1976-78; chm mgmnt bd Shipbuilders and Repairers Nat Assoc 1976-78 (memb exec cncl 1969-77); pres Br Productivity Cncl Area Assoc 1969-72, shipbuilding indust rep on Def Industs Quality Assur Panel 1972-82; memb: Shipbuilding Indust Trg Bd 1979-82, NE Coast Inst Engrs and Shipbuilders 1967-; author of papers on various aspects of UK shipbuilding indust, contrib to tech journals; Silver Jubilee Medal (1977); CEng, FRINA 1970 (assoc memb 1950, memb 1955), FInstD, CBIM (fell 1977); Liveryman Worshipful Co of Shipwrights' 1978; *Recreations* sailing, small-bore shooting, golf, fishing; *Clubs* Grange-over-Sands Golf, Nat Small-Bore Rifle Assoc; *Style—* William Richardson Esq, CBE, DL; Hobroyd, Pennybridge, Ulverston, Cumbria LA12 7TD (☎ 0229 86226)

RICHARDSON, Air Marshal Sir (David) William; KBE (1986); *b* 10 Feb 1932; *Educ* Birmingham Univ, Cranfield Inst of Technol (MSc); *m* 1953, Mary Winifred, *née* Parker; 2 s (b 1956, b 1958), 1 da (b 1960); *Career* RAF 1953, AOC Maintenance Gp HQ RAF Support Cmd 1981-83, Air Offr Engrg RAF Strike Cmd 1983-86, RAF Chief Eng 1986, ret 1988; dir AIT Ltd; FRAeS; *Recreations* sailing; *Clubs* RAF; *Style—* Air Marshal Sir William Richardson, KBE; Bounds Cottage, Bidborough, Kent TN4 0XB

RICHARDSON OF DUNTISBOURNE, Baron (Life Peer UK 1983), of Duntisbourne in the Co of Gloucestershire; Gordon William Humphreys Richardson; KG (1983), PC (1976), MBE (1944), TD (1979); s of John Robert and Nellie Richardson; *b* 25 Nov 1915; *Educ* Nottingham HS, Gonville and Caius Coll Cambridge; *m* 1941, Margaret Alison, er da of late Very Rev Hugh Richard Lawrie Sheppard, Canon and Precentor of St Paul's Cathedral; 1 s, 1 da (*see* Sir John Buchanan Riddell, 13 Bt); *Career* govr Bank of England 1973-83 (memb Ct 1967-83), serv WWII S Notts Hussars Yeo and Staff Coll Camberley; barr 1946-55, memb Bar Cncl 1951-55; wih ICFC 1955-57; former chm: J Henry Schroder Wagg, Schroders Ltd, Schroders Inc; former chm Industl Devpt Advsy Bd, former chm Ctee on Turnover Taxation 1963-64; memb NEDC 1980-83 (and 1971-73); one of HM Lts City of London 1974-; former memb Ct London Univ, former tstee Nat Gallery, dep high steward Cambridge Univ 1982-; dir: Glyndebourne Arts Tst 1980-88, Royal Opera House 1983-88; *Clubs* Athenaeum, Brooks's; *Style—* The Rt Hon the Lord Richardson of Duntisbourne, KG, MBE, TD,; c/o Morgan Stanley International, Kingsley House, 1A Wimpole Street, London W1M 7AA

RICHARDSON-BUNBURY, Lt-Cdr Sir (Richard David) Michael; 5 Bt (I 1787), of Augher, Co Tyrone; s of Richard Richardson-Bunbury (d 1951); ggs of Sir James Richardson-Bunbury, 2 Bt), and Florence Margaret Gordon, da of Col Roger Gordon Thomson; suc kinsman, Sir Mervyn Richardson- Bunbury, 4 Bt (d 1953);; *b* 27 Oct

1927; *Educ* RNC Dartmouth; *m* 15 July 1961, Jane Louise, da of Col Alfred William Pulverman, IA (d 1938); 2 s (Roger Michael b 1962, Thomas William b 1965); *Heir* s, Roger Richardson-Bunbury; *Career* Midshipman RN (S) 1945, Sub Lt (S) 1947, Lt (S) 1948, Lt Cdr 1956, sec to Head of UK Serv Liaison Staff Australia 1956- 58, RN Staff Coll, Greenwich 1960-61, Capt's sec HMS Ark Royal 1961-64, sec to Flag Offr Naval Flying Trg 1964-67, ret 1967; entered computer servs indust 1967, ret 1987; dir Sandy Laird Ltd 1988; *Recreations* woodwork, gardening, reading, travel; *Style—* Lt Cdr Sir Michael Richardson-Bunbury, Bt, RN; Woodlands, Mays Hill, Worplesdon, Guildford, Surrey GU3 3RJ (☎ 0483 232034)

RICHARDSON-BUNBURY, Roger Michael; s and h of Lt Cdr Sir Michael Richardson-Bunbury, 5 Bt, RN; *b* 2 Nov 1962; *Educ* Sherborne, Manchester Univ (BA); *Style—* Roger Richardson-Bunbury, Esq

RICHARDSON-HILL, John William; *Career* dir Hill Samuel Securities, dir business dvpt Antony Gibbs & Sons 1981-; ACIS, AIB, AMBIM; *Style—* John Richardson-Hill Esq; c/o Antony Gibbs & Sons, 1 Fredericks Place, London EC2 (☎ 01-588 4111)

RICHES, Sir Derek Martin Hurry; KCMG (1963, CMG 1958); s of Claude W H Riches, of Cardiff (d 1947), and bro of Gen-Sir Ian Riches, *qv*; *b* 26 July 1912; *Educ* Univ Coll Sch, Univ Coll London; *m* 1942, Helen, da of George Washburn Hayes, of Poughkeepsie, NY, USA; 1 da; *Career* entered Foreign Service 1934, chargé d'affaires Jedda 1952, cnsllr and head of Eastern Dept Foreign Office 1955-59; ambass to: Libya 1959-61, Republic of Congo 1961-63, Lebanon 1963-67, ret; *Style—* Sir Derek Riches, KCMG; 48 The Ave, Kew Gardens, Surrey

RICHES, Gen Sir Ian Hurry; KCB (1969, CB 1959), DSO (1945); s of Claud W H Riches (d 1947), and Flora Martin (d 1962); bro of Sir Derek Riches, *qv*; *b* 27 Sept 1908; *Educ* Univ Coll Sch; *m* 1936, Winifred Eleanor, da of Adm Sir Geoffrey Layton, GBE, KCMG, KCB, DSO (d 1964); 2 s (Jeremy, Jonathan); *Career* joined RM 1927, serv 1939-45 in Italy, Yugoslavia and India, Maj 1946, Lt-Col 1949, Col 1953, cmd 3 Commando Bde RM (Actg Brig) 1954-55, cmd Inf Trg Centre RM 1955-57, Maj-Gen RM Portsmouth 1957-59, Cmdt-Gen RM 1959-62, Gen 1961, regnl dir of Civil Def 1964-68; Rep Col Cmdt RM 1967-68; *Clubs* IOD, Hampshire, Royal Naval and Royal Albert Yacht; *Style—* Gen Sir Ian H Riches, KCB, DSO; Leith House, Old Hillside Rd, Winchester, Hants (☎ 0962 54067)

RICHES, John Dansey Hurry; s of Norman Vaughan Hurry Riches (d 1975), and Nesta Strange, *née* South (d 1974); *b* 30 Dec 1920; *Educ* Repton; *m* 1948, Pearl, da of Samuel Joseph McIlveen (d 1969); 1 da (Jane); *Career* serv WWII Maj RA; slr, pres Incorporated Law Soc for Cardiff and Dist 1976; *Recreations* cricket, sports generally; *Clubs* MCC, Cardiff and Co; *Style—* John Riches, Esq; 9 Brynderwen Close, Cyncoed, Cardiff CF2 6BR (☎ 0222 754596); office: 26 West Bute St, Cardiff CF1 5UA (☎ 0222 29741)

RICHES, Roger John; s of Harry Watson Riches, of Burnham on Sea Somerset, and Joan, *née* Ratcliffe; *b* 12 Mar 1945; *Educ* Kettering Secondary Sch, Kettering Tech Coll, Sheffield Poly (Dip Mgmnt Studies); *m* 12 March 1974, Heather, da of Harvey Watson Tolley; 1 s (Mark b 1979), 1 da (Sarah b 1985); *Career* dist mangr Yorks Bldg Soc: Wakefield 1972-73, Leeds 1973-74, Doncaster 1975-78, trg mangr 1978-83, regnl exec Yorks 1983-; chm Bradford Centre CBSI 1984-85, vice-chm Yorks Gp CBSI 1988-89, educn liaison offr Yorks Gp CBSI 1982-, visiting lectr CBSI; FCBSI; *Recreations* sport, music, theatre; *Clubs* Grange Burley in Wharfedale; *Style—* Roger Riches, Esq; 27 Stirling Rd, Burley in Wharfedale, Ilkley, W Yorks LS29 7LH (☎ 0943 864 588); Yorkshire Bldg Soc, Regnl Off, 26 Church St, Dewsbury, West Yorks (☎ 0924 457 677)

RICHMOND, Archdeacon of; *see*: McDermid, The Ven Norman

RICHMOND, Sir Alan James; *b* 12 Oct 1919; *Educ* Les Rayons Switzerland, London Univ (BSc, PhD); *m* 1951, Sally; 1 step s, 1 step da; *Career* chartered mech engr; lectr Battersea Poly 1946-55, head dept of mech engrg Welsh Coll of Advanced Technol 1955-58, princ Lanchester Coll of Technol Coventry 1958-70, dir Lanchester Poly Coventry 1970-72, princ Strode Coll Street Somerset 1972-81, conslt, expert witness and commercial arbitrator 1982-; Hon DSc CNAA; CEng, FIMechE, FCIArb; kt 1969; *Recreations* law, gardening, reading; *Clubs* Royal Cwlth Soc; *Style—* Sir Alan Richmond; 6 Middle Lane, Upper East Hayes, Bath, BA1 6LS (☎ 0225 333393)

RICHMOND, (Francis) Henry Arthur; *see*: Repton, Bishop of

RICHMOND, Prof John; s of Hugh Richmond (d 1953), and Janet Hyslop, *née* Brown (d 1985); *b* 30 May 1926; *Educ* Doncaster GS, Univ of Edinburgh (MB, ChB, MD); *m* 2 Sept 1951, Jenny, da of Thomas Nicol (d 1977); 2 s (David b 1953, Michael b 1956), 1 da (Virginia b 1961); *Career* RAMC 1949-50 serv: Ethiopia, Kenya, N Rhodesia (MO 1 Bn KAR); jr hosp appt Edinburgh 1948-49, GP Galloway 1950-52, hosp appt Northants 1952-54, res fell N Gen Hosp Edinburgh 1955, lectr (later sr lectr and reader) Univ of Edinburgh 1956-73 (secondments: res fell Memorial Sloan Kettering Cancer Center NY 1958-59, Makerere Univ Med Sch Uganda 1965); prof of med Univ of Sheffield 1973-(dean med sch 1985-88); pres RCPEd 1988-, chm MRCP Examining Bd 1985-; memb: Sheffield Health Authy 1981-84, High Constables of Edinburgh 1962-71, bd of advsrs Univ of London 1984-, external advsr Chinese Univ Hong Kong 1982-; memb: Cncl of Mgmnt Yorks Cancer Res Campaign, Bd of Mgmnt St Luke's Hospice Sheffield; memb: Assoc Physicians GBI, Med Res Soc; *Style—* Prof John Richmond; Stumper Lea, 42 Stumperlowe Hall Rd, Sheffield S10 3QS (☎ 0742 301 395); Dept of Medicine, Royal Hallamshire Hospital, Sheffield S10 2JF (☎ 0742 766 222, fax 0742 721 104)

RICHMOND, Sir Mark Henry; s of Harold Sylvestor Richmond (d 1952), and dorothy Plaistowe (d 1976); *b* 1 Feb 1931; *Educ* Epsom Coll, Clare Coll Cambridge (BA, PhD, ScD); *m* 1958, Shirley Jean, da of Dr Vincent Townrow (d 1982); 1 s (Paul b 1964), 2 da (Clare b 1959, Jane b 1962, d 1987); *Career* scientific staff Med Res Cncl 1958-65; reader of molecular biology Univ of Edinburgh 1965-68; prof of bacteriology Univ of Bristol 1968-81; vice-chllr Univ of Manchester 1981-; chm ctee of Vice-Chllrs of Princs 1987-; kt 1986; *Recreations* walking, gardening; *Clubs* Athenaeum; *Style—* Sir Mark Richmond; Vice Chancellors Office, University of Manchester, Oxford Road, Manchester M13 9PL

RICHMOND AND GORDON, 9 (and 4 respectively) Duke of (E 1675, UK 1876 respectively); Frederick Charles Gordon Lennox; also Earl of March, Baron of Settrington (both E 1675), Duke of Lennox, Earl of Darnley, Lord of Torboulton (all S 1675), Duc d'Aubigny (Fr 1684), Earl of Kinrara (UK 1876), and Hereditary Constable of Inverness Castle; s of 8 Duke of Richmond and Gordon, DSO, MVO, JP, DL (d 1935), by his w, Hilda, DBE, JP (da of Henry Brassey, JP, DL, of Preston Hall, Kent, and sis of 1 Baron Brassey of Apethorpe, JP, DL, who m a da of the 7 Duke); His Grace descends from King Charles II by Louise de Kéroualle (da of Guillaume de Penancoët, Comte de Kérouallе, Brittany), cr Baroness Petersfield, Countess of Fareham and Duchess of Portsmouth for life by HM, and Duchesse d'Aubigny by Louis XIV; *b* 5 Feb 1904; *Educ* Eton, Christ Church Oxford; *m* 1927, Elizabeth, da of Rev Thomas Hudson, sometime vicar of Wendover; 2 s; *Heir* s, Earl of March and Kinrara; *Career* serv WWII as Flt Lt RAF; patron of five livings; late Lt Roy Tank Corps (TA); bore sceptre with dove at Coronations of King George VI and of HM Queen Elizabeth II; *Style—* His Grace The Duke of Richmond and Gordon; Carne's Seat, Goodwood, Chichester, Sussex; 29 Hyde Park St, W2; Seat: Goodwood, Chichester

RICHMOND BROWN, Hon Lady; Gwendolen Carlis; *née* Meysey-Thompson; da of 1 and last Baron Knaresborough (d 1929), and Ethel Adeline, only child of Sir Henry Pottinger, 3 Bt; *b* 10 April 1903; *m* 1951 (m dis 1968), as his 2 w, Lt-Col Sir Charles Frederick Richmond Brown, 4 Bt; *Career* lady-in-waiting to HRH Duchess of Gloucester 1938-45; *Style—* The Hon Lady Richmond Brown; Estate Office House, Birdsall, Malton, N Yorks (☎ 094 46 343)

RICHMOND-WATSON, Anthony Euan; s of Euan Owens Richmond-Watson (d 1954), and Hon Gladys Gordon, *née* Catto (d 1967); *b* 8 April 1941; *Educ* Westminster, Edinburgh Univ (BCom); *m* 1, 1966, Angela, da of John Broadley, of Somerset (d 1979); 1 s (Luke b 1971), 1 da (Tamsin b 1967); m 2, 1976, Geraldine Ruth Helen, da of Charles Barrington, of Cornwall (d 1966); 1 da (Alice b 1976); *Career* merchant banker; gp dir Morgan Grenfell & Co Ltd 1988- (joined 1968, dir 1975); non exec dir: Yule Catto & Co plc 1978, Norfolk Capital Gp plc 1985 (chm 1986); MICAS; *Style—* Anthony Richmond-Watson, Esq; 23 Great Winchester St, London EC2P 2AX (☎ 01 588 4545)

RICHTERICH, Pierre Albert Henri; s of Albert Richterich (d 1986), of Bingley, W Yorks, and Marguerite Anne, *née* Hoffmann; *b* 24 Mar 1934; *Educ* Bradford GS, Bradford Coll; *m* 26 Aug 1961, Patricia; 2 da (Carla b 1965, Annick b 1968); *Career* Nat Serv 1953-54: Intelligence Corps, RASC, posted to SHAPE HQ Paris; fndr chm and md PA Richterich & Co Ltd 1959-; former pres: Airedale Agricultural Soc, Rotary Club Bradford Blaize; formerly: chm and pres Bingley RT, chm Area 32, memb Nat Exec RTBI 1972-74; *Recreations* skiing, fellwalking, golf, windsurfing; *Clubs* Bradford, RAC, E India; *Style—* Pierre Richterich, Esq; P A Richterich Intl Ltd, Northvale Mills, Singleton St, Bradford BD1 4RF (☎ 0274 735 821, fax 0274 391 480, telex 51366)

RICKARD, Stephen Leslie; s of late Aubrey Rickard, of Ventnor, IOW, and (Evelyn) Gladys, *née* Naylor; *b* 9 May 1917; *Educ* Berkhamstead Sch Herts, Kingston-on-Thames Art Sch, Royal Acad Schs (dip and gold medal in sculpture); *m* 4 May 1940, Evelyn Norman, da of late Maj Norman Loring, of Hove, Sussex; 2 s (Jeremy b 1942, Simon b 1946), 2 da (Harriet b 1952, Judith b 1956); *Career* WWII, called up E Surrey Regt 1940, 2 Lt King's Own Royal Regt NI, transferred Indian Army 1942 (Capt and actg Maj), demob 1946; sculptor and glass engraver; sculptures incl three dimensional portrait heads of: Lord Fairhaven (Anglesey Abbey Cambs), Dr Margaret Murray (Univ Coll Lib London), Prof J D Bernal (Sci Museum Library London); glass engravings: Princess Alexandra's 21st Birthday, Princess Margarets Wedding, Winston Churchills 80th Birthday, gifts to HM the Queen and HRH The Prince of Wales, many gifts from FO to int heads of state, innumerable ret presents to Hosps; newspaper for Blind Cassette, memb Civic Tst, speaker on glass engraving to local gps; FRBS 1956, FSD-C 1966, FGE 1979; *Recreations* none to speak of - art & life being inseparable; *Clubs* Savage; *Style—* Stephen Rickard, Esq; 33 Winchilsea Ave, Newark, Notts NG24 4AD (☎ 0636 71674)

RICKARDS, John Ayscough; s of George Ayscough Rickards, MC, and Barbara Ramsey, *née* Smyth; *b* 7 July 1939; *Educ* Harrow, Cambridge; *m* 1, 1963 (m dis), Lindy, da of Alan Martinaeu, MBE, JP; 2 da (Anna b 1967, Clare b 1968); m 2, 1976, Joanna, da of William Quincey Roberts, CVO, CBE, DSO, TD; 1 s (William b 1982), 1 da (Harriet b 1983); *Career* Greenwell & Co 1963-85, Samuel Montagu & Co 1987-88, md Nomura Security 1988; *Recreations* shooting, fishing, skiing, tennis; *Clubs* Whites, City of London; *Style—* John A Rickards, Esq; West Stratton House, West Stratton, Michledever, Hants (☎ 096 289 266)

RICKETT, Sir Denis Hubert Fletcher; KCMG (1956, CMG 1947), CB (1951); s of Hubert Cecil Rickett, OBE, JP (d 1950); *b* 27 July 1907; *Educ* Rugby, Balliol Coll Oxford; *m* 1946, Ruth Pauline, MB, BS, MRCS, LRCP, da of late William Anderson Armstrong, JP; 2 s, 1 da; *Career* fell All Souls Coll Oxford 1929-49, joined staff of Economic Advsy Cncl 1931, Offs of War Cabinet 1939, PPS to Rt Hon Oliver Lyttelton, DSO, MC, MP (Min of Prodn, later Viscount Chandos) 1943-45, PA (for work on Atomic Energy) to Rt Hon Sir John Anderson, MP (Chllr of the Exchequer) 1945, transferred to Treasy 1947, PPS to Rt Hon Clement Atlee, OM, CH (PM) 1950-51, Economic Min Br Embassy Washington and head of UK Treasy and Supply Delegation 1951-54, third sec HM Treasy 1955-60, second sec 1960-68, vice-pres World Bank 1968-74; dir: Schroder Int 1974-79, De La Rue Co 1974-77; advsr J Henry Schroder Wagg & Co 1974-79; *Recreations* music, travel; *Clubs* Brooks's, Athenaeum; *Style—* Sir Denis Rickett, KCMG, CB; 9 The Close, Salisbury, Wiltshire SP1 2EB

RICKETTS, Cyril Lewis; OBE (1979); s of Matthew Edwin Ricketts (d 1972); *b* 10 Mar 1907; *Educ* Brentwood Sch; *m* 1939, Margaret Constance, *née* Townsend; 2 s and 1 da decd; *Career* chm and md Elephant Chemical Co Ltd 1933-72, High Sheriff Co Merioneth 1949-50, pres Industrial Assoc of Wales 1958-59, vice-pres Devpt Corpn for Wales 1958-83 (fndr dir); chm Transport Users Consultative Ctee for Wales 1968-79; *Recreations* cricket, music, gardening; *Style—* Cyril Ricketts, Esq, OBE; Ty Isaf, Llanbedr, Gwynedd LL45 2PA (☎ 034 123 253); office: 9 Princes Ave, Barmouth, Gwynedd (☎ 0341 280378)

RICKETTS, Sir Robert Cornwallis Gerald St Leger; 7 Bt (UK 1828), of The Elms, Gloucestershire, and Beaumont Leys, Leicestershire; s of Sir Claude Ricketts, 6 Bt (d 1937); *b* 8 Nov 1917; *Educ* Haileybury, Magdalene Coll Cambridge; *m* 1945, (Anne) Theresa, *qv*; 2 s, 2 da (*see* His Hon Judge Mason); *Heir* s, Tristram Ricketts; *Career* slr 1949, formerly ptnr Wellington and Clifford; pa to COS Gibraltar 1942-45 and ADC to Lt-Govr of Jersey 1945-46; hon citizen of Mobile Alabama USA; FRSA; *Recreations* books, history; *Style—* Sir Robert Ricketts, Bt; Forwood House, Minchinhampton, Stroud, Glos GL6 9AB (☎ 0453 882160)

RICKETTS, Lady; (Anne) Theresa; CBE (1983); da of late Rt Hon Sir Stafford Cripps, CH, PC, QC (chllr of the Exchequer in Attlee's Govt and 4 s of Baron Parmoor, KCVO, PC, JP); *b* 12 April 1919; *m* 1945, Sir Robert Ricketts, 7 Bt, *qv*; 2

s, 2 da; *Career* chm Nat Assoc of Citizens' Advice Bureaux 1979-84; memb: Elec Consumers Cncl 1978-; dir: Mail Services Standards Bd 1985-; *Style*— Lady Ricketts, CBE; Forwood House, Minchinhampton, Stroud, Glos (☎ 0453 882160)

RICKETTS, (Robert) Tristram; s and h of Sir Robert Ricketts, 7 Bt, of Forwood House, Minchinhampton, Glos, and Anne Theresa, *née* Cripps; *b* 17 April 1946; *Educ* Winchester, Magdalene Coll Cambridge (MA); *m* 1969, Ann, yr da of Eric William Charles Lewis, CB (d 1981), of 31 Deena Close, Queen's Drive, London W3; 1 s, 1 da; *Career* chief exec Horserace Betting Levy Bd 1980-; *Clubs* Athenaeum; *Style*— Tristram Ricketts, Esq; 47 Lancaster Ave, London SE27 9EL (☎ 01 670 8422); office: 52 Grosvenor Gardens, London SW1W OAU (☎ 01 730 4540)

RICKMAN, John Eric Carter; s of Maj Eric Roper Rickman (d 1976), of 40 Cumberland Terr, Regents Park, London, and Catherine Mary, *née* Carter (d 1964); *b* 28 May 1913; *Educ* Feltonfleet, Haileybury, Fleet St; Army; *m* 29 April 1939, Margaret Wood, da of Robert Oswald Law (d 1954), of 7 Princes Gate, London SW7; 1 s (Robin b 1942), 2 da (Jill b 1940, Rosemary b 1945); *Career* serv TA Commn, Glos and Reconaissance Regts 1931-46, serv WWII in NW Europe, 1 Canadian Air Staff, 84 Gp TAF (Maj) 1945; reporter; Bristol Evening World 1931, Glos Echo 1932, Daily Mail 1934 (reporter and zoo correspondent), succeeded from Robin Goodfellow, chief Daily Mail Horse Racing corr 1949, ITV horse racing commentator 1955-78 (front man famous for hat raising welcome to viewers); *publications* Homes of Sport: Horse Racing (1952), Eight Flat Racing Stables (1979); winner of showing awards with home bred Welsh Cobs (second) and faverolles poultry; *Recreations* golf, writing, Euro travel, country pursuits; *Clubs* Kennel, Derby, Twelve, Liphook GC; *Style*— John Rickman, Esq; Pheasants Walk, Copyhold Lane, Fernhurst, Haslemere, Surrey GU27 3DZ (☎ 0428 3197)

RICKS, David Trulock; OBE (1981); s of Percival Trulock Ricks 9d 1983), of Bromham, Beds, and Annetta, Helen, *née* Hood (d 1967); *b* 28 June 1936; *Educ* Kilburn GS, RAM, Merton Coll Oxford (MA), Univ of London Inst of Educn, Univ of Lille (Licence-es-Lettres); *m* 1 Aug 1960, Nicole Esteele Aimée, da of André Armand Chupeau (d 1973), of Marans, France; 2 s (Ralph Antoine b 1964, Quentin b 1969); *Career* teacher and lectr in London 1960-67; Br Cncl 1967-: dir of studies 1967-70, Univ of Essex 1970-71, dir State Inst of Language Studies Jaipur India 1971-74, dep rep Tanzania 1974-76, and cultural attache HM Embassy Iran 1979-80 (dep rep 1976-79), dir serv conditions dept London 1980-85, rep Italy 1985-; govr Br Inst of Florence 1985-, memb Rome Ctee Keats-Shelley Meml House Rome 1985-; *Books* Penguin French Reader (jt ed 1967); *Recreations* playing the piano, music, skiing; *Clubs* United Oxford and Cambridge; *Style*— David Ricks, Esq, OBE; c/o The British Council, 10 Spring Gdns, London SW1A 2BN (☎ 01 930 8466)

RICKS, Sir John Plowman; s of James Young Ricks (d 1949); *b* 3 April 1910; *Educ* Christ's Hosp, Jesus Coll Oxford (MA); *m* 1, 1936, May Celia (d 1975), da of late Robert William Chubb; 3 s; m 2, 1976, Doreen Ada, widow of Arthur Forbes Ilsley; *Career* solicitor to the Post Office 1953-72 (joined Post Office Solicitor's Dept 1935); kt 1964; *Style*— Sir John Ricks; 8 Sunset View, Barnet, Herts EN5 4LB (☎ 01 449 6114)

RICKS, Robert Neville; s of Sir John Plowman Ricks, of Sunset View, Barnet, Herts, and May Celia, *née* Chubb (1975); *b* 29 June 1942; *Educ* Highgate Sch, Worcester Coll Oxford (MA); *Career* admitted slr 1967; Treasury Slrs Dept: legal asst 1969-73, sr legal 1973-81, asst slr 1981-86, princ asst slr 1986; memb Gen Synod C of E 1980-85;; *Recreations* wine, collecting original cartoons; *Clubs* United Oxford and Cambridge; *Style*— Robert Ricks, Esq; 2 Eaton Terrace, AberavonRd, London E3 5AJ (☎ 01 981 3722); Treasury Solicitors Dept, 28 Broadway SW1 (☎ 01 210 3140)

RIDDELL, (William) James; MBE (1944); s of Col Archibald Riddell, DSO (d 1970), of Surrey, and Edith Mary, *née* Lawrie (d 1947); descended from Sir Walter Riddell, 2 Bt; *b* 27 Dec 1909; *Educ* Harrow, Clare Coll Cambridge; *m* 1, 1 Dec 1959, Jeannette Anne Oddie (d 1972), da of late Edward Kessler, of Manchester; m 2, 1972, Alison, da of Arthur Newton Jackson (d 1961), of Wilmslow; 1 da (Jemma Jeannette b 1976); *Career* WW II ADC to High Cmmnr of Palestine and Trans-Jordan 1939-41, political offr (Capt): Syria and Lebanon, Beirut, Homs, Damascus, frequently with French Foreign Legion 1941; started up organised and ran (as Maj) ME Mountain Warfare Ski Sch at Cedars of Lebanon 1941-44; led WO Team of 15 observers on exercise 'Polar Bear' crossing the coastal range of British Columbia, subsequently coordinated WO trg pamphlets 1-5 on snow and mountain warfare; author of 27 books, some self illustrated; worked with Baynard Press, Selfridges, de Havilland Aircraft, free-lance journalism etc 1930-37; skiing - first season 1920 (Mürren), subsequently memb Br Ski Team 1929-36, winner of 1929 'Inferno', winner of combined Anglo-Swiss 1931, Br ski champion 1934, vice-capt Br Olympic ski team 1936, awarded Pery Medal 1962, Arnold Lunn Medal 1979; *Books* Inside Britain, Outside Britain, Animal Lore and Disorder, In the Forests of the Night, Flight of Fancy, Dog in the Snow, The Holy Land, Ski Runs of Switzerland; *Recreations* landscape gardening, watercolours, anglo/swiss relationship; *Clubs* White's, Ski Club of GB, Kandahar Ski, Alpine Ski, DHO, Eagles, Martini Int, Swiss Academic Ski; *Style*— James Riddell, Esq, MBE; Foresters, Hightown Hill, Ringwood, Hants (☎ Ringwood (04254) 3593); 17 Hyde Park Gardens Mews, London W2 (☎ 01 723 2802)

RIDDELL, Sir John Charles Buchanan; 13 Bt (NS 1628), of Riddell, Roxburghshire; s of Sir Walter Riddell, 12 Bt (d 1934), and Hon Rachel Lyttelton, JP (d 1965) (yst da of 8 Viscount Cobham, JP, DL, and Hon Mary Cavendish, da of 2 Baron Chesham); *b* 3 Jan 1934; *Educ* Eton, Christ Church Oxford (BA, MA); *m* 1969, Hon Sarah, da of Baron Richardson of Duntisbourne, KG, MBE, PC, *qv*, sometime govr of Bank of England; 3 s (Walter b 1974, Hugh b 1976, Robert b 1982); *Heir* s, Walter John Riddell b 10 June 1974; *Career* 2 Lt 2KRRC; CA; banker; contested (C) Durham NW Feb 1974, Sunderland S Oct 1974; dir: UK Provident 1975-85, First Boston (Europe) Ltd 1975-78, dep chm IBA 1981-85, dir: Northern Rock Bldg Soc 1981-85, Credit Suisse First Boston 1978-85; priv sec and tres to TRH The Prince and Princess of Wales 1985-; memb Prince's Cncl; *Clubs* Garrick, Northern Countries; *Style*— Sir John Riddell, Bt; Hepple, Morpeth, Northumberland; Wien House, Kensington Palace, London W8 4PL

RIDDELL-WEBSTER, John Alexander; MC (1943); s of Gen Sir Thomas Sheridan Riddell-Webster, GCB, DSO, DL (d 1974), of Lintrose, Coupar Angus, and Harriet Hill, *née* Sprot (d 1977); *b* 17 July 1921; *Educ* Harrow, Pembroke Coll Cambridge; *m* 16 Jan 1960, Ruth, da of (Samuel Plenderleith) Laurence Lithgow (d 1972), of The Old House, Great Barton, Suffolk; 2 s (Michael b 1960, Thomas b 1962), 1 da (Caroline b 1964); *Career* serv Seaforth Highlanders 1940-46: UK, Madagascar, India, Paiforce, Syria, Sicily (wounded, MC), WO 1944-45, Staff Capt and DAQMG, BAOR 1945-46; joined Anglo-Iranian Oil Co (later BP) 1946 serv: in Iran, Iraq, Bahrain and London 1946-52, Aden and Basrah 1952-53, London 1954-56, Canada 1956-63 (vice-pres mktg BP Canada 1959-63), London 1963-66 (dir Shell Mex and BP 1965, md mktg 1971-75), md mktg BP Oil Ltd 1976-80, ret 1980; dir Scottish Affairs BP Edinburgh 1980-82; farmer 1982-; memb cncl: Incorporated Soc of Br Advertisers 1967-80, Advtg Assoc 1973-80, British Roads Fedn 1975-80, Royal Warrant Holders Assoc 1967 (pres 1980); memb Automobile Assoc Ctee 1980; pres Oil Industries Club 1977-78; chm Transport Action Scotland 1982; elected regnl cncllr Tayside 1986; CBIM, FInstPet; *Recreations* shooting, fishing, gardening; *Clubs* New (Edinburgh), Royal Perth Golfing Soc; Lintrose, Coupar Angus, Perthshire PH13 9JQ (☎ 0828 27472)

RIDDELSDELL, Dame Mildred; DCB (1972), CBE (1958); da of Rev H J Riddelsdell; *b* 1 Dec 1913; *Educ* St Mary's Hall Brighton, Bedford Coll London; *Career* asst sec Min of Nat Insur 1945, under sec 1950, loaned to UN 1953-56, sec Nat Incomes Cmmn 1962-65, second permanent sec DHSS 1971-73, chm CS Retirement Fellowship 1974-77; *Style*— Dame Mildred Riddelsdell, DCB, CBE; 26A New Yatt Rd, Witney, Oxon

RIDDICK, Graham Edward Galloway; MP (C) Colne Valley 1987-; s of John Julian Riddick, of Coldstream House, Shipton-under-Wychwood, Oxford OX7 6DG, and Cecilia Margaret, da of Sir Edward Ruggles-Brise, 1 Bt, MC, TD, MP for Maldon (Essex) 1922-42; *b* 26 August 1955; *Educ* Stowe, Warwick Univ; *m* 1988, Sarah Northcroft; *Career* chm: N Yorks Freedom Assoc (memb nat cncl), Cons Angola Study Gp; sec All Pty Wool Textile Parly Gp; *Recreations* shooting, fishing, tennis, squash, bridge; *Clubs* Carlton, Yorks Cricket; *Style*— Graham Riddick, Esq, MP; c/o House of Commons, Westminster, London SW1A 0AA (☎ 01 219 4215)

RIDDICK, Stewart Keith; s of Walter Claude Riddick, of Swindon, Wilts, and Margaret, *née* Lowman; *b* 17 Sept 1944; *Educ* Warneford Sch Highworth; *m* 2 Sept 1973, Victoria, da of Max Heliczer (d 1972), 2 s (Simon b 11 Oct 1979, Jonathan b 24 Sept 1983); *Career* chm SKR Group; mem: fin ctee Dacorum Volunteer Bureau, advsr Douglas Bader Fndn, Br Paraplegic Sports Assoc; Freeman City of London, Liveryman Worshipful Co of Joiners and Ceilers; FInstD; *Recreations* sailing, golf, shooting; *Style*— Stewart Riddick, Esq; Stewart House, 930 High Rd, London N12 9RT (☎ 01 446 4131, fax 01 291 801, car tel 0836 212 022, telex 24108 JAYBEE)

RIDDIOUGH, Maj Stanley Hyde; MBE (1945), TD (1945), JP (Lancs 1964), DL; s of Walmsley Riddiough JP; *b* 12 Sept 1915; *Educ* Oundle; *m* 1944, Suzanne, *née* Reynolds; 3 da; *Career* Maj RA 1939-46, chm & md John Riddiough & Co Ltd 1972-, dir Colne Bldg Soc 1970-, gen cmmr Income Tax 1975-, High Sheriff Lancs 1977-78; *Recreations* cinematography, amateur radio; *Clubs* Rotary; *Style*— Maj Stanley Riddiough, MBE, TD, JP, DL

RIDDLE, Howard Charles Frazer; s of Cecil Riddle (d 1987), of Sevenoaks, Kent, and Eithne, *née* McKenna; *b* 13 August 1947; *Educ* Judd Sch Tonbridge, LSE (LLB); *m* 31 Aug 1924, (Susan) Hilary, da of Dr André Hurst, of Ottawa, Canada; 2 da (Stephanie b 1979, Poppy b 1984); *Career* slr Edward Fail Bradshaw & Waterson; memb Law Soc 1978; *Recreations* rugby football; *Style*— Howard Riddle, Esq; 19 Danesdale Rd, London E9 (☎ 01 533 3348); Norton Cottages, Bethersden, Kent; Edward Fail, Bradshaw & Waterson, 402 Commercial Rd, Stepney, London E1 0LG (☎ 01 790 4032, fax 01 790 2739)

RIDDY, John Charles Philip; s of Prof Donald C Riddy, CBE (d 1979), and Kathleen Constance (d 1985); *b* 21 June 1934; *Educ* St Paul's, Hertford Coll Oxford (MA); *m* 2 Sept 1963, Felicity Jacqueline, da of Dr Kenneth John Maidment; 1 s (Gerson b 1964), 2 da (Francesca b 1966, Myrianthe b 1976); *Career* Flt Offr RAF 1955; buiness mangr Stirling Univ 1969-; pres Assocn of Self-Cater Operations, Scotland; co-fndr (with Stephen Ware) British Univs Accommodation Consortium (BUAC) 1970, fndr Open Univ Hosts Club; FPWI (1974), MHCIMA (1978); *Books* Hodson of Hodson's Horse (biog), Gen Sir John Cotton (biog), J G Farrell (study of writings), European Settlement in India 1780-1870; *Recreations* cricket, swimming, snooker; *Style*— John Riddy, Esq; Davidson Hall, Stirling Univ FK9 4CA (☎ 0786 64375); Gareth Lodge, Fortingall, Perthshire (☎ 08873 341); work: (☎ 0786 73171, ext 2497/2039, telex 77759 STUNIV-G)

RIDEOUT, Prof Roger William; s of Sidney Rideout (d 1949), of Bromham, Beds and Hilda Rose, *née* Davies (d 1985); *b* 9 Jan 1935; *Educ* UCL (LLB, PhD); *m* 1, 30 July 1960 (m dis 1978), Marjorie Roberts, da of Albert Roberts of Bedford; 1 da (Tania Mary b 1965); m 2, 24 Aug 1978, Gillian Margaret, *née* Lynch; *Career* Nat Serv Lt RAEC 1958-60; lectr: Univ of Sheffield 1960-63, Univ of Bristol 1963-64; barr Gray's Inn 1964; prof of lab law UCL 1973- (reader in Eng law 1965-73, sr lectr 1964-65); vice-dean and dep head dept of laws UCL 1982- (dean of faculty 1975-77); memb Phelps-Brown Ctee 1967-68, chm Indus Law Soc 1977-80 (vice-pres 1983-), pt/t chm Indus Tbnls 1983-, dep chm Central Arbitration Ctee 1978-; *Clubs* MCC; *Style*— Prof Roger Rideout; 255 Chipstead Way, Woodmansterng, Surrey SM7 3JW (☎ 0737 552 033); Faculty of Laws University College London, Bentham House, Endsleigh Gardens, London WC1H OEG (☎ 01 380 7022, 01 387 7050 ext 2113)

RIDGEON, David Cyril Elliot; s of Cyril Elliot Ridgeon (d 1973), and Kathleen Joan, *née* Miller; *b* 6 May 1935; *Educ* Monkton Combe Sch Bath; *m* 30 Sept 1961, Jill Elizabeth, da of Lewis Starling (d 1966); 2 da (Rachel b 1962, Anne b 1966); *Career* builders merchant and timber importer; dir: Cyril Ridgeen and Son Ltd 1960-, Ridgeons (Saffron Warden) Ltd 1986-, CRS (wholesale) Ltd 1976-, Saffron Walden Bldg Material Supply Co Ltd 1960-86, Saffron Walden & Essex Bldg Soc 1981-86; vice-pres Blders Merchant Fedn 1987-88, pres 1989-90; Liveryman Worshipful Co of Builders Merchants; *Recreations* tennis; *Clubs* Rotary; *Style*— David Ridgeon, Esq; Rectory Farm, Madingley Rd, Coton, Cambridge CB3 7PG; Tenison Rd, Cambridge (☎ 0223 61177)

RIDGEON, Mr Jonathan Peter; s of Peter James Ridgeon, of 60 Spring Close, Burwell, Cambridge, and Margaret Jane, *née* Allum; *b* 14 Feb 1967; *Educ* Newmarket Upper Sch, Magdalene Coll Cambridge; *Career* 110 hurdler, Euro jr champion 1985, second World Jr Championships 1986, second World Championships 1987 (Br record time), AAA champion 1987, World Student Games champion 1987, fifth Olympic Games Seoul 1988; *Recreations* tennis; *Clubs* Hawks, Achilles Athletics; *Style*— Jonathan Ridgeon, Esq; Magdalene College, Cambridge

RIDGEWAY, Lt Cdr Thomas Graeme; s of Charles Lennox Ridgeway (d 1957), and Dorothy Sydney, *née* Washbrough; *b* 29 Dec 1918; *Educ* RNC Dartmouth; *m* 17 July

1948 (m dis 1957), Jane, da of late Adm Sir Lewis Clinton-Baker, KCB, KCVO, CBE, of Bayfordbury, Herts; 1 s (Stephen b 18 Dec 1950); *Career* RN 1932-59; WWII submarines 1940-47, cmd HMS Templar 1944-46; post-war cmd: HMS Fame, HMS Ulysses, HMS Carisbrocke Castle; Admty 1957-59, ret 1959; fenced and shot for both the Navy and Devon; master mariner 1970-82; Hereditary Freeman City of Exeter; *Recreations* hunting, fishing, shooting, sailing; *Clubs* Royal Naval; *Style—* Lt Cdr Thomas Ridgeway; Higher Hill, Hittesleigh, nr Exeter (☎ 064 723 348)

RIDGWAY, (Charles) Ian; s of Harry Ridgway (d 1972),m of Hawthorn Cottage, Sandal, Wakefield, Yorks, and Eva, *née* Whitehead (d 1973); *b* 6 Jan 1934; *Educ* Queen Elizabeth GS Wakefield, Wakefield Tech Coll; *m* 22 Sept 1960, (Margaret) Heather, da of Reginald Arthur Wilkinson, of Pontefract, Yorks; 1 s (Mark b 1962), 1 da (Jacqui b 1964); *Career* Nat Serv 1951-53; jig and tool engr Slater and Crabtree Ltd 1956-57, sales dir Rhodes Cowlishaw Sales Co Ltd 1972-78, md Rhodes Interform Ltd 1978-84, md Joseph Rhodes Ltd 1989- (mgmnt apprentice 1954, commercial dir 1967-72, jt md 1984); chm Wakefield and Dist Engrs Employers Fedn 1965-69, chm Wakefield Sr C of C 1970-71, ecclesiastical tst Wakefield Cathedral 1969-; chm Metalforming Machinery Mfrs Assoc 1976-80, chm Europ Power Pres Mfs Panel 1977-81; FBIM 1969; *Recreations* restoration of vintage cars; *Style—* Ian Ridgway, Esq; Hawthorn Cottage, Sandal Ave, Wakefield, Yorks WF2 7LD (☎ 0924 255119); Joseph Rhodes Ltd, Belle Vue, Wakefield, Yroks WF1 5EQ (☎ 0924 371161, fax 0924 370928, car 0836 316695, telex 55339)

RIDGWAY, Laurence Victor; s of Hugh Bernard Ridgway (d 1956), of Spencer Rd, Harrow Weald, Middlx, and Leonora, *née* Herger (d 1962); *b* 18 Dec 1915; *Educ* Harrow Business Coll; *m* 9 Aug 1941, Marie, da of Franz Breier (d 1927), of Ybbs an der Donau, Austria; 1 da (Heather-Ann (Mrs Clint) b 22 Feb 1944); *Career* cmmnd 2 Bn The Hants Regt 1942, Liaison Offr 209 Bde HQ 1942 (camp cmdt 1943), Staff Capt Allied Cmmn for Auria 1944, Maj and dep dir Army Welfare Servs BTA HQ Vienna; sub-ed Industl Newspapers Ltd 1934-39, advertisement dir Tobacco magazine 1947-62, dir Trade Pubns Ltd 1962, md Int Trade Pubns Ltd 1963-80 (launched series of int business magazines, World Tobacco, Int Tax Free Trader, Tableware Int, Coffee Int, Marine Stores Int, ME Education), dir Industl Newspapers Ltd 1980, owner the Ridgway Press 1980-; churchwarden St Mary's Church Limpley Stoke; Freeman City of London 1966, Liveryman Worshipful Co of Tobacco Pipe Makers and Tobacco Blenders 1969; *Books* Stories of The Operas (co-ed, Vienna 1946); *Clubs* MCC; *Style—* Laurence Ridgway, Esq; Sunrise House, Midford Lane, Limpley Stoke, Bath BA3 6JR (☎ 0221 22 3502)

RIDGWELL, Patrick John; s of Joseph Thomas Ridgwell (d 1969), and Ida May Mann (d 1988); *b* 15 Mar 1930; *Educ* St David's Coll Lampeter, Corpus Christi Coll Cambridge (MA); *m* 1965, Maryla, da of Capt Maximillian Statter (d 1947); 1 s (Jolyon b 1967), 1 da (Caroline b 1965); *Career* chm The Association of Independent Investmt Mangrs 1976-; md Anthony Wieler & Co Ltd, dir Anthony Wieler Unit Tst Mgmnt; *Recreations* choral singing, mountain walking, architecture; *Clubs* United Oxford and Cambridge Univ, IOD; *Style—* Patrick Ridgwell, Esq; Providence Corner, Well Rd, Hampstead, London NW3 1LH (☎ 01 435 9711); 19 Widegate St, London E1 7HP (☎ 01 377 1010, telex 886307, fax 247 5000)

RIDING, Robert Furniss; s of William Furniss Riding (d 1985), of Manchester, and Winifred, *née* Coupe; *b* 5 May 1940; *Educ* Stockport GS, Christ Church Oxford (MA); *Career* dir and later chm Nat Commercial Devt Capital Ltd 1980-85, gen mangr Williams & Glyn's Bank plc 1982-85, tres and gen mangr The Royal Bank of Scotland plc 1985-86, dep chm and chief exec RoyScot Finance Gp plc 1986-; chm: RoyScot plc 1986-, Royal Bank Leasing Ltd 1986-, RoyScot Vehicle Contracts Ltd 1986-, RoyScot Factors Ltd 1986-, RoyScot Fin Servs Ltd 1988; dir: Int Commodities Clearing House Ltd 1985-86, Royal Bank of Scotland AG (Switzerland) 1985-86, Royal Bank of Scotland Gp Insur Co Ltd 1986-88, Royal Bank Gp Servs Ltd 1987-AT Mays Gp plc 1988; tstee and former chm Assoc of Sea Trg Orgns; memb cncl and chm trg The Royal Yachting Assoc; *Recreations* sailing; *Clubs* Island Cruising (cdre 1988-); *Style—* Robert Riding, Esq; Blandford House, Blandford Close, Maybury, Woking, Surrey GU22 7EJ (☎ 0483 70376); Middlewood, Old Banwell Road, Locking, Avon BS24 8BT (☎ 0934 822587); 2 Garden Close, Salcombe, S Devon TQ8 8DR

RIDLEY, (Hon) (Helen Laura) Cressida; *née* Bonham Carter; da of Baroness Asquith of Yarnbury (Life Peer, d 1969); *b* 1917; *m* does not use courtesy title; 1939, Jasper Alexander Maurice Ridley, Lt KRRC (d on active service 1943); 1 s; *Style—* Mrs Ridley; Keeper's Cottage, Great Bottom, Stockton, Warminster, Wilts

RIDLEY, Sir Adam Nicholas; s of Jasper Ridley (s of Maj Hon Sir Jasper Ridley, KCVO, OBE, 2 s of 1 Viscount Ridley, by the Maj's w Countess Nathalie, da of Count Benckendorff, sometime Russian ambass in London) and Cressida Bonham Carter (da of Baroness Asquith of Yarnbury and gda of H H Asquith the Lib PM); nephew by marriage of Baron Grimond, TD, PC, of Firth, Co Orkney; *b* 14 May 1942; *Educ* Eton, Balliol Coll Oxford, Univ of California Berkeley; *m* 1, 1970 (m dis), Lady Katharine Rose Celestine Asquith, 2 da of 2 Earl of Oxford and Asquith; m 2, 1981, Margaret Anne (Biddy), da of Frederic Passmore, of Virginia Water, Surrey; 2 s (Jasper and Luke (twins) b 29 May 1987), 1 s (b 1988); *Career* Dep of Economic Affairs 1965-69, HM Treasy 1970-71, Central Policy Review Staff 1971-74; former economic advsr and asst dir CRD, dir CRD 1979 election campaign, special advsr to the Chllr of the Exechequer 1979-84; special advisor to Chllr of the Duchy of Lancaster, Minister in charge of the office of Arts and Libraries (also mangr personnel office) 1985; appointments Exec Dir Hambro's Bank & Hambro's plc 1985, dir Strauss Turnbull 1986, dep chm SGST Securities 1988; kt 1985; *Style—* Sir Adam Ridley; 52 Novello St, London SW6 4JB

RIDLEY, Hon Mrs; Hon Annabel; da of 9 Baron Hawke (1985); *b* 27 August 1940; *Educ* Hatherop Castle Sch; *m* 1961, Nicholas Adam Ridley, s of Rev Michael Ridley (d 1953); 1 s, 2 da; *Career* artist, glass engraver; *Recreations* singing, tennis; *Style—* The Hon Mrs Ridley; 29 Richmond Hill, Richmond, Surrey (☎ 01 940 1732); Arsparfel, Køerarsbars, Crozon Morgat 29160, Finistøere, France

RIDLEY, Viscountess; Lady Anne Katharine; *née* Lumley; da of late 11 Earl of Scarbrough, KG, GCSI, GCIE, GCVO, TD, PC and Katharine, *née* McEwen, DCVO; *b* 16 Nov 1928; *m* 3 Jan 1953, 4 Viscount Ridley, *qv*; *Style—* The Rt Hon The Viscountess Ridley; Blagdon, Seaton Burn, Northumberland

RIDLEY, Dame (Mildred) Betty; DBE (1975); da of Rt Rev Henry Mosley (d 1948), sometime Bishop of Southwell, and Mildred, *née* Willis (d 1963); *b* 10 Sept 1909; *Educ* North London Collegiate Sch, Cheltenham Ladies' Coll; *m* 3 Sept 1929, Rev Michael Ridley (d 1953), Rector of Finchley, s of Samuel Forde Ridley (d 1942); 3 s (Simon b 1933, Adam b 1937, Giles b 1946), 1 da (Clare (Mrs West) b 1930); *Career* vice-pres Br Cncl of Churches 1954-56; a church cmmr 1958-81; memb Gen Synod of C of E 1970-81; Third Church Estates cmmr 1972-81; govr: King Alfred's Coll Winchester, St Gabriel's Sch Newbury; MA Lambeth 1958; *Recreations* making and listening to music; *Clubs* Reform; *Style—* Dame Betty Ridley, DBE; 6 Lions Hall, St Swithun St, Winchester SO23 9HW (☎ 0962 55009)

RIDLEY, Lt Cdr (Charles) David Matthew; s of Arthur Hilton Ridley, CBE (d 1974), of Park End, Simonburn, Hexham, and Kathleen Thelma (d 1982); *b* 27 June 1928; *Educ* RNC Dartmouth; *m* 1960, Alison Hay, da of Major David Hay Thorburn (d 1963), of Burnside, Fairlie, Ayrshire; 1 s; *Career* Lt Cdr Royal Navy (on staff of: SNO W Indies 1958-60, FOST 1960-62, HMS Ganges 1962-64, CINC S Atlantic 1964-66); farmer 1966-; High Sheriff Northumberland 1981; *Recreations* gardening, shooting; *Style—* Lt Cdr David Ridley; Little Park End, Simonburn, Hexham, Northumberland NE48 3AE (☎ 043 481 497)

RIDLEY, Jasper Godwin; s of Geoffrey William Ridley, OBE (d 1957), of The Manor House, W Hoathly, E Grinstead, Sussex, and Ursula Mary, *née* King; *b* 25 May 1920; *Educ* Felcourt Sch E Grinstead, Sorbonne, Magdalen Coll Oxford; *m* 1 Oct 1949, Vera, da of Emil Pollak (d 1974), of Malostranské, Nabrezí I, Prague, Czechoslovakia; 2 s (Benjamin b 1952, John b 1956), 1 da (Barbara b 1950); *Career* barr Inner Temple 1945, in practice 1946-52; cncllr St Pancras Borough Cncl 1945-49; chm Tunbridge Wells and Dist Writers' Circle, chm Tunbridge Wells gp of The Rambler's Assoc; Master Worshipful Co of Carpenters 1988 (Liveryman 1943, Warden 1985); FRSL 1963, vice pres English section of Int PEN 1985; *Books* Nicholas Ridley (1957), The Law of Carriage of Goods (1957), Thomas Cranmer (1962), John Knox (1968), Lord Palmerston (James Tait Memorial Prize 1970), Mary Tudor (1973), Garibaldi (1974), The Roundheads (1976), Napoleon III and Eugenie (1979), The History of England (1981), The Statesman and the Fanatic (1982), Henry VIII (1984), Elizabeth I (1987), The Tudor Age (1988); *Recreations* chess, walking; *Style—* Jasper Ridley, Esq; 6 Oakdale Rd, Tunbridge Wells, Kent (☎ 0892 22460); The Manor House, W Hoathly, Sussex

RIDLEY, Hon Mrs (Julia Harriet); *née* McLaren; er da of 3 Baron Aberconway by his 1 w; *b* 22 Sept 1942; *Educ* Grenoble Univ; *m* Charles Walter Hayes Ridley; 1 s (Casper Charles b 1977), 2 da (Emma Jane b 1970, Harriet Deirdre b 1971); *Style—* The Hon Mrs Ridley; c/o UPI, Rome, Italy

RIDLEY, (Edward Alexander) Keane; CB (1963); s of Maj Edward Keane Ridley (d 1947), of Dudswell House, nr Berkhamsted, Herts, and Ethel Janet, *née* Tweedie (d 1962); *b* 16 April 1904; *Educ* Wellington, Keble Coll Oxford (MA); *Career* admitted slr 1928, appt to Treasy Slrs Dept 1934 (princ asst slr 1956), ret 1969; Hon RCM 1977; *Recreations* Music; *Style—* E A K Ridley, Esq, CB; 407 Gilbert House, Barbican, London EC2Y 8BD (☎ 01 628 8578)

RIDLEY, Malcolm James; s of Eric Malcolm Thomas Ridley (d 1972), and Pauline Esther, (d 1972); *b* 10 Mar 1941; *Educ* Trinity Sch Croydon, Bristol Univ (LLB); *m* 1, 14 July 1962 (m dis 1976), Joan Margaret, da of Stanley Charles Martin, of Alfriston, Sussex: 2 da (Camilla b 1970, Estelle b 1972); *m* 2, 9 April 1977, Bridget Mina, da of Charles Edward O'Keeffe (d 1963); 1 s (John b 1979), 1 da (Susannah b 1977); *Career* ca, Price Waterhouse Vancouver 1962-68, commerical experience 1968-74, Price Waterhouse London 1974-79, ptnr Deloitte Haskins & Sells London 1981- (joined 1979); memb Founders Co 1981; CA Canada 1966, FCA 1980, ATII 1974; *Recreations* tennis, bridge, theatre, opera; *Clubs* RAC; *Style—* Malcolm Ridley, Esq; Moor Lodge, South Holmwood, Dorking, Surrey RH5 4NA (☎ 0306 889 594); Hillgate House, 26 Old Bailey, London EC4M 7PL (☎ 01 248 3913)

RIDLEY, Mark; s of Francis Rex Ridley, of Thorpeness, Suffolk, and Ann, *née* Garrod; *b* 8 Sept 1956; *Educ* Stowe, New Coll Oxford (MA, DPhil); *Career* EPA Cephalosporin res scholar Linacre Coll Oxford 1978-81, Hayward res fell Oriel Coll Oxford 1981-83, Astor fell New Coll Oxford 1983-86, res fell St Catharines Coll Cambridge 1986-; Gibbs Prize (Oxford, 1978), Rolleston Memorial Prize (Oxford, 1982), Singer Prize (Br Soc for History of Sci, 1980); FLS; *Books* The Explanation of Organic Diversity (1983), The Problems of Evolution (1985), Evolution and Classification (1986), Animal Behaviour (1986), The Essential Darwin (ed 1987); *Style—* Mark Ridley, Esq; St Catharines College, Cambridge (☎ 0223 338353); Dept of Zoology, Downing Street, Cambridge CB2 3EJ (☎ 0223 336610, fax 0223 336676)

RIDLEY, Hon Mary Victoria; da of 4 Viscount Ridley, TD, JP, DL; *b* 30 Nov 1962; *Career* antiquarian bookseller; *Style—* The Hon Mary Ridley; Blagdon, Seaton Burn, Newcastle upon Tyne NE13 6DD

RIDLEY, Hon Matthew White; s and h of 4 Viscount Ridley, TD, JP, DL; *b* 7 Feb 1958; *Educ* Eton, Magdalen Coll, Oxford (DPhil); *Career* journalist; The Economist: sci ed 1984-87, Washington corr 1987-89; winner Glaxo Sci Journalism Award 1983; *Style—* The Hon Matthew Ridley; Blagdon, Seaton Burn, Newcastle upon Tyne NE13 6DD

RIDLEY, 4 Viscount (UK 1900); Sir Matthew White Ridley; 8 Bt (GB 1756), TD, JP (1957); also Baron Wensleydale (UK 1900); s of 3 Viscount Ridley, CBE (d 1964), and Ursula, OBE, 2 da of Sir Edwin Lutyens, OM, KCIE, the architect, by Sir Edwin's w Lady Emily Lytton (da of 1 Earl of Lytton, GCB, GCSI, CIE, PC, sometime Viceroy of India and s of the novelist Bulwer Lytton, cr Baron Lytton); *b* 29 July 1925; *Educ* Eton, Balliol Coll Oxford (BA); *m* 3 Jan 1953, Lady Anne Lumley, da of 11 Earl of Scarbrough, KG, GCSI, GCIE, GCVO, PC; 1 s, 3 da; *Heir* s, Hon Matthew Ridley; *Career* Lt-Col TA, Bt-Col, Hon Col Northumberland Hussars Sqdn Queen's Own Yeo RAC TA, Col Cmdt Yeo RAC TA 1982-86; chm Northumberland CC 1967-79, pres Assoc of CCs 1979-84, chm: Northern Rock Bldg Soc; dir: Tyne Tees TV, Barclays Bank NE, MMI Group Ltd; Lord-Lt for Northumberland 1984- (DL 1968); chm N of England TA&VRA 1980-84; pres Cncl of TAVRAS 1984-; hon fell ARICS; OM (W Germany); *Recreations* dendrology, shooting, fishing; *Clubs* Turf, Pratt's; *Style—* Col the Rt Hon the Viscount Ridley; Blagdon, Seaton Burn, Newcastle on Tyne NE13 6DD (☎ 067 089 236)

RIDLEY, Michael Kershaw; s of George K Ridley, of Eccleston, Chester, and Mary Partington; *b* 7 Dec 1937; *Educ* Stowe, Magdalene Coll, Cambridge (MA); *m* 1968, Diana Loraine, da of Roy A McLernon; of Knowlton PQ, Canada; *Career* Grosvenor Estate, Canada & US 1965-68 (London 1969-72); property mangr Br & Cwlth Shipping Co 1972-81; clerk of the Cncl Duchy of Lancaster 1981-; memb advisory panel Greenwich Hosp 1978-; FRICS; *Recreations* reading, golf, walking; *Clubs* Royal Mid-

Surrey (Golf); *Style*— Michael K Ridley, Esq; 37 Chester Row, London SW1

RIDLEY, Rt Hon Nicholas; PC (1982), MP (C) Cirencester and Tewkesbury 1959-; s of 3 Viscount Ridley, CBE; *b* 17 Feb 1929; *Educ* Eton, Balliol Coll Oxford; *m* 1, 1950 (m dis 1974), Hon Clayre Campbell, *see* Lady Richard Percy; 3 da; m 2, 1979, Judy, da of Dr E Kendall; *Career* formerly civil engrg contractor and dir various cos; contested (C) Blyth 1955, pps to Min Educn 1962-64, delegate to Cncl Europe and WEU 1962-66, parly sec Miny Technology 1970, parly under-sec DTI 1970, memb Royal Commission Historical Manuscripts 1967-79, min state FCO 1979-81, financial sec to Treasury 1981-Oct 1983, sec state Transport Oct 1983-; *Style*— The Rt Hon Nicholas Ridley, MP; Old Rectory, Naunton, Cheltenham, Glos; 50 Warwick Sq, London SW1

RIDLEY, Philip Waller; CB (1978), CBE (1969); s of Lt-Col Basil White Ridley, DSO, MC (d 1969), and Frida, *née* Gutknedt (d 1956); *b* 25 Mar 1921; *Educ* Lewes Co Sch for Boys, Trinity Coll Cambridge (BA); *m* 1942, Mary Foye, da of E K Robins; 2 s (Timonthy, Mark), 2 da (Helen decd, Diana); *Career* Army 1941-46 W Africa and NW Europe, Maj Int Corps; cnsllr Br Embassy Washington 1966-70; under-sec 1971-75; dep-sec Dept of Trade Indust 1975-80; Civil Serv 1948-80; dir Avon Rubber plc 1980-89, Fingerscan Dvpt Ltd 1987-; independant industl consIt; *Recreations* country pursuits, music, skiing; *Style*— Philip Ridley, Esq; Old Chimneys, Plumpton Green, Lewes, E Sussex BN8 4EN (☎ 0273 890342)

RIDLEY, Sir Sidney; s of John William Ridley, of Lancaster; *b* 26 Mar 1902; *Educ* Lancaster Royal GS, Sidney Sussex Coll Cambridge (MA); *m* 1929, Dorothy, da of Oswald Hoole, of Prestwich (d 1987); 3 da; *Career* entered ICS 1926, fin sec Govt of Sind 1936, sec to agent-gen for India in SA 1936-40, chief sec to Govt of Sind 1945, cmmr Ahmedabad 1946, cmmr Poona 1947, revenue cmmr Sind 1947-54; rep in Ghana of the W Africa Ctee 1957-60; fellow and domestic bursar St John's Coll Oxford 1960-68, emeritus fell 1969; kt 1953; *Style*— Sir Sidney Ridley; Lambrook Cottage, Waytown, Bridport, Dorset DT6 5LF (☎ 030 888 337)

RIDLEY, Rear Adm (William) Terence Colborne; CB (1968), OBE (1954); s of late W H W Ridley; *b* 9 Mar 1915; *Educ* RNC Dartmouth, RNEC Keyham; *m* 1938, Barbara, da of R L Allen; 1 s; *Career* serv: Atlantic, Mediterranean and Pacific, Capt RNEC 1962-64, Rear Adm 1966, Adm Superintendent HM Dockyard Rosyth 1966-71, Port Adm Rosyth 1971-72; chm ex serv Mental Welfare Soc 1973-83; *Recreations* gardening; *Style*— Rear Adm Terence Ridley, CB, OBE; 12 New King St, Bath, Avon BA1 2BL (☎ 0225 318371)

RIDLEY, Dr Tony Melville; CBE (1986); s of John Edward Ridley (d 1982), and Olive, *née* Armstrong; *b* 10 Nov 1933; *Educ* Durham Sch, Univ of Durham (BSc), Northwestern Univ Illinois (MS), Univ of California Berkeley (PhD); *m* 20 June 1959, Jane, da of John William Dickinson (d 1984); 2 s (Jonathan b 1963, Michael b 1966), 1 da (Sarah b 1962); *Career* Nuclear Power Gp 1957-62; Greater London Cncl 1965-69; dir-gen Tyne & Wear Passenger Transport Exec 1969-75; md Hong Kong Mass Transit Railway Corpn 1975-80; bd memb London Regnl Transport (formerly London Transport Exec) 1980-88, md (Railways) 1980-85; chm London Underground Ltd 1985-88; Docklands Light Railway 1982-88 (chm 1987-88); London Transport Int 1981-88 (chm 1982-87); md Eurotunnel project 1989-, m(dir 1987-); dir Halcrow Fox and Associates 1980-; visiting prof Univ of Newcastle-upon-Tyne 1985-; first recipient of Highways Award of Inst of Highways and Transportation 1988; Freeman City of London, Liveryman Worshipful Co of Carmen 1982; FCIT, FICE, Fell Hong Kong Inst of Engineers, Memb Inst of Transportation Engrs, FRSA; *Publications* articles in transport, engineering and other journals; *Recreations* theatre, music, international affairs, rejuvenation of Britain; *Clubs* IOD, Hong Kong, Hong Kong Jockey; *Style*— Dr Tony M Ridley, CBE; 77 Church Rd, Richmond, Surrey TW10 6LX (☎ 01 948 3898)

RIDLEY, William Patrick (Bill); s of Lt-Col J E Ridley, of Mill Moorings, Felsted, Essex, and Edith Maude, *née* Tilley; *b* 22 Mar 1935; *Educ* Wellington, Lincoln Coll Oxford; *m* 1, 11 July 1964 (m dis 1985), Regine Elizabeth Margarete, da of Dr Hans Doelle; 2 da (Stephanie b 16 May 1965, Kirstin b 10 Dec 1966), m 2, March 1986, Elizabeth Marie, da of Jan Chorosz; *Career* 2 Lt bomb disposal RE 1953-55, Capt RE Reserve 1955-65; CA; res dept Bank of London and of America 1962-65, sec and accountant to Devpt Co subsid of Cwlth Devpt Corpn 1965-68; ptnr: Merrett Cyriax Assoc Mgmnt consIts 1968-73, Wood MacKenzie and Co 1973-86; dir: Gower Press 1970-73, Hill Samuel and Co 1986-88, Co Natwest 1988; memb: Watt Ctee, Quality of Markets Ctee; ACA 1962, FCA 1973, memb Stock Exchange 1974; *Books* Making Use of Economics Statistics (1986), Company Administration Handbook (contrib, 1970), Finance and International Economy (contrib 1987); *Recreations* travel, archaeology; *Style*— Bill Ridley, Esq; 15 John Spencer Sq, London N1 (☎ 01 354 1828); County Natwest, Drapers Gardens, 12 Throgmorton Ave, London EC2 (☎ 01 382 1000)

RIDLEY-THOMAS, Roger; s of John Montague Ridley-Thomas, MB, ChB, FRCSE (d 1973), of Norwich, and Christina Anne, *née* Seex (d 1976); *b* 14 July 1939; *Educ* Greshams Sch; *m* 1962, Sandra Grace McBeth, da of William Morrison Young, OBE, of Gt Glen, Leics; 2 s (Christopher b 1964, Simon b 1966), 2 da (Philippa b 1970, Sarah b 1972); *Career* Royal Norfolk Regt 1958-60; newspaper publishing; Eastern Counties Newspapers Ltd 1960-65; advertisement mgmnt: Middlesbrough Evening Gazette 1965-67, Western Mail and Echo Ltd 1968-70, Newcastle Chronicle and Journal Ltd 1970-72; asst md The Scotsman Publications Ltd 1972-80, md Aberdeen Journals Ltd 1980-84, md The Scotsman Publns Ltd 1984-, dir: Radio Forth Ltd 1978-81, TRN Viewdata Ltd 1979-, Aberdeen Journals Ltd 1980-84, Aberdeen C of C 1981-84, Scottish Business in the Community 1984-, Thomson Scottish Orgn Ltd 1984-, Northfield Newspapers Ltd 1984-, The Scotsman Communications Ltd 1984-, Central Publns Ltd 1984-, Thomson Regional Newspapers Ltd 1985-, Scottish Business Achievement Award Tst Ltd 1985-, Edinbrugh C of C and Mfrs 1985-; pres Scottish Daily Newspaper Soc 1983-85; cncl memb CBI 1983-86; Scottish Wildlife Appeal Ctee 1985-; *Recreations* vegetable growing, shooting, fishing, golf, tennis, travel; *Clubs* New (Edinburgh); *Style*— Roger Ridley-Thomas, Esq; Cardrona Estate, Innerleithen, Peeblesshire (☎ 0896 830242); The Scotsman Publications Ltd, 20 North Bridge Rd, Edinburgh EH1 1YT (☎ 031 225 2468, telex 72255)

RIDLEY-THOMPSON, Lt-Col Aubrey Percy; TD (1959), DL (Leics 1978); s of Capt Thomas Percy Ridley-Thompson (d 1952), of Earl's Ct, London, and Kathleen Swire (d 1972); *b* 18 Oct 1921; *Educ* Westminster; *m* 11 June 1949, Jacqueline, da of Ronald Peake (d 1936), of Howard House, Ashtead, Surrey; 1 s (Timothy Percy b 16 May 1950), 1 da (Nicola Ann b 11 Jan 1954); *Career* Lt-Col cmdg Leicestershire and Derbyshire Yeo 1962-64; dir Boots The Chemists 1968-82; OStJ 1984; *Recreations* gardening; *Style*— Lt-Col Aubrey Ridley-Thompson, TD, DL; The Hermitage, Kegworth, Leicestershire DE7 2EU (☎ 67 2313)

RIDOUT, Maj Harry Leonard; s of Maj Henry Alfred Walter Ridout (d 1974), of Portsmouth, and Agnes Cuthill (d 1963); *b* 22 Jan 1911; *Educ* German Boarding Church Sch, Army Apprentice Tech Sch; *m* 24 March 1937, Eileen Florence Mary, da of John Francis Barry (d 1944), of Plumstead, London SE18; *Career* army offr: mgr REME 1926-64; serv: Gibraltar, N Africa, Italy (despatches), Austria, Germany, Singapore, Hong Kong; team man REME modern pentathlon team 1964-74 (Br & Army champions); ctee memb modern pentathlon assoc of GB 1964-74 (frequently team mgr GB Team) accompanied GB Team 1972 (Munich) and 1976 (Montreal - Gold Medal) Olympics; ret offr grade III REME offrs sch; ret; water colourist; works sold USA, Germany, Switzerland; *Recreations* rugby (Army and Blackheath), tennis, golf, army rugby refereeing; *Clubs* Farnham Art Soc, Assoc of Artificers RA, Shillinglee Park golf; *Style*— Maj Harry L Ridout; 10 Hanover Court, Tower Road, Liphook, Hants GU30 7AX (☎ 0428 724338)

RIDSDALE, Sir Julian Errington; CBE (1977), MP (C) Harwich Div of Essex 1954-; s of Julian Ridsdale, of Rottingdean, Sussex; *b* 8 June 1915; *Educ* Tonbridge, RMC Sandhurst; *m* 1942, Victoire Evelyn Patricia, da of Col J Benmnett, of Kensington; 1 da; *Career* serv WWII Royal Norfolk Regt, Royal Scots and Somerset LI, ret as Maj 1946; contested (C): SW Islington 1949, Paddington 1951; parly under-sec state for Air and vice-pres Air Cncl 1962-64, parly under-sec RAF MOD 1964, chm Br Japanese Parly Gp 1964-, vice-chm UN Parly Assoc 1966-82, ldr Parly Delgns to Japan 1973, 1975 and 1977-83; memb Trilateral Cmmn EEC, USA and Japan 1973-; memb N Atlantic Assembly 1979-; dep-chm Int Triangle USA, Japan and Europe 1981-; pres Political Ctee N Atlantic Assembly 1983-; chm All Party Gp Engrg Dvpt 1985-; Order of the Sacred Treasure (Japan); kt 1981; *Style*— Sir Julian Ridsdale, CBE, MP; 12 The Boltons, London SW10 (☎ 01 373 6159); Fiddan, St Osyth, Essex (☎ 0255 820367)

RIFKIND, Rt Hon Malcolm Leslie; PC (1986), QC (1985), MP (C) Edinburgh Pentlands Feb 1974-; s of Elijah Rifkind, of Edinburgh; *b* 21 June 1946; *Educ* George Watson's Coll Edinburgh, Edinburgh Univ (LLB, MSc); *m* 1970, Edith Amalia, *née* Steinberg; 1 s, 1 da; *Career* fought Edinburgh Central 1970, memb Select Ctee European Secondary Legislation 1975-76, oppn front bench spokesman Scottish Affrs 1975-76, chm Scottish Cons Devolution Ctee 1976, jt sec Cons Foreign and Cwlth Affrs Ctee 1978, memb Select Ctee on Overseas Dvpt 1978-79; parly under-sec state: Scottish Office 1979-82, FCO 1982-83; min state FCO 1983-86; Sec of State for Scotland 1986-; *Recreations* walking, reading; *Style*— Rt Hon Malcolm Rifkind, QC, MP; The House of Commons, London SW1

RIGBY, Anthony John; s and h of Sir John Rigby, 2nd Bt, ERD; *b* 3 Oct 1946; *Educ* Rugby; *m* 1978, Mary, da of Robert Oliver, of Cheshire; 3 s; *Career* sch teacher; *Style*— Anthony Rigby, Esq; Honeysuckle Cottage, Haughton, West Felton, Oswestry (☎ Queens Head 573)

RIGBY, Bryan; s of William George Rigby (d 1971), and Lily; *b* 9 Jan 1933; *Educ* Wigan GS, King's Coll London (BSc DipChemEng); *m* 1978, Marian Rosamund, da of David Ellis (d 1980); 1 s, 1 da; 1 step s, 1 step da; *Career* UKAEA Industl Gp (Capenhurst) 1955-60, Beecham Gp London and Amsterdam 1960-64, mktg dir Laporte Industs 1964-78, dep dir-gen CBI 1978-Jan 1984, md BASF UK Ltd 1984-86; Regnl MD BASF AG Jan 1987-, CEng, MIChemE, MInstM; *Recreations* music, golf, gardening; *Clubs* Reform; *Style*— Bryan Rigby, Esq; Cluny, 61 Penn Rd, Beaconsfield, Bucks (☎ 049 46 3206); BASF UK Ltd, BASF House, 151 Wembley Park Drive, Wembley, Middx HAP 8JG (☎ 01 908 3188)

RIGBY, Sir (Hugh) John Macbeth; 2 Bt (UK 1929), of Long Durford, Rogate, Co Sussex; ERD and two clasps; s of Sir Hugh Rigby, 1 Bt, KCVO (d 1944); *b* 1 Sept 1914; *Educ* Rugby, Magdalene Coll Cambridge; *m* 1946, Mary (d 1988), da of Edmund Erskine Leacock; 4 s; *Heir* s, Anthony Rigby; *Career* Lt-Col (ret) RCT, serv UK and SEAC; dir Executors of James Mills Ltd to 1977; *Style*— Lt-Col Sir John Rigby, Bt, ERD and two clasps; Casa das Palmeiras, Armação de P˜era, Algarve, Portugal (☎ 082 32548); 5 Park St, Macclesfield, Cheshire (☎ 0625 613959)

RIGBY, Maj Reginald Francis; TD (1950 and clasp 1952); s of late Reginald Rigby (d 1958), of Rudyard, Staffs, and Beatrice Mary, *née* Green (d 1934); *b* 22 June 1919; *Educ* Manchester GS; *m* 1949, Joan Edwina, da of Samuel E M Simpson, of Mayfield, Newcastle under Lyme; 1 s (and 1 s decd 1983); *Career* serv WWII Far E, Maj Staffs Yeo; slr; rec Crown Ct 1977-83;; *Recreations* fishing; *Clubs* Army and Navy, Flyfishers; *Style*— Maj Reginald Rigby, TD; The Rookery, Woore, Shropshire CW3 9RG (☎ 063 081414)

RILEY, Dr Alan John; s of Arthur Joseph Riley, of Chestfield, Kent, and Edith Ada, *née* Rashbrook; *b* 16 July 1943; *Educ* Bexley GS, Univ of London, Charing Cross Hosp Med Sch London Univ (MB, BS), Univ of Manchester (MSc); *m* 1, 14 Nov 1964 (m dis 1976), Pamela Margaret, da of Leonard George Allum, of London; 1 s (John b 1971), 1 da (Veronica b 1968), 2 adopted s (Grant b 1968, Robert b 1970); m 2, 11 Dec 1976, Elizabeth Jane, da of Capt Arthur Norman Robertson (d 1959); *Career* GP Bideford Devon 1970-76; specialist in sexual med 1972-, dir SMC Res Ltd 1982-; ed: Br Journal of Sexual Med 1983-, Sexual and Marital Therapy 1986-; author of over 100 pubns on aspects of sexual and reproductive med; dep co surgn St John Ambulance Bde (ret 1988); LRCP 1967, MRCS 1967, FZS 1977, memb Assoc Sexual and Marital Therapists 1979, OStJ 1983; *Recreations* woodwork, photography, natural history; *Clubs* RSM; *Style*— Dr Alan Riley; Field Place, Dunsmore, Bucks HP22 6QH (☎ 0296 622070, car 0836 213469)

RILEY, Barry John; s of Peter Riley (d 1978), and Barbara *née* Pitt; *b* 13 July 1942; *Educ* Jesus Coll Cambridge (BA); *m* 16 Aug 1969, Anne Geraldine; 2 s (Paul b 20 April 1971, Timothy b 16 April 1976), 1 da (Martha b 4 Nov 1972); *Career* ed asst Investors Chronicle 1964, dep city ed Morning Telegraph Sheffield 1966; Financial Times 1967-: ed Lex column 1978 (asst 1968, jt ed 1974), fin ed 1981, investmt ed and columnist 1987; memb domestic promotions ctee Br Invisible Exports Cncl; *Style*— Barry Riley, Esq; 17 Mount Pleasant Rd, London W5 1SG (☎ 01 998 5829); The Financial Times, 1 Southwark Bridge, London SE1 9HL (☎ 01 873 3000)

RILEY, Bridget; CBE (1972) ; da of John Fisher Riley, of Cornwall and Bessie Louise *née* Gladstone (d 1975); *Educ* Cheltenham Ladies Coll, Goldsmith's Coll of Art, RCA; *Career* Peter Stuyvesant Fndn Travel Bursary to USA 1964, Euro Touring Expdn to Hanover, Berne Dusseldorf, Turin, London, Prague 1970-71, UK Arts Cncl Tour to: Manchester, Sheffield, Durham, Edinburgh, Birmingham, Letchworth, Bristol 1973, World Tour to USA, Australia, Japan 1978-80, Colour Project for Royal Liverpool

Hosp 1980-83; tstee Nat Gallery 1981-88, participation with Ballet Rambert in Colour Moves 1983, colour project for St Mary's Hosp Paddington 1987-88, exhibitions in Stockholm, Zurich, Koln, pioneered with Peter Sedgeley. The Estab of Space 1969; Int Prize for painting XXXIV Venice 1968; *Style*— Miss Bridget Riley; 7 Royal Crescent, London W11 (☎ 01 603 4469); Mayor Rowan Gallery, 31a Bruton Place, London W1X 7AB (☎ 01 499 3011, fax 01 494 1377)

RILEY, (John) Derek; s of Alan Stanley Riley, of Northwood, Middx, and Joan Marjorie *née* Page; *b* 24 Jan 1950; *Educ* Henry Mellish GS, John Wilmott GS, Salford Coll of Technol; *m* 1 (m dis 1985) Elizabeth; 1 s (James Derek b 22 Nov 1980), 1 step s (James Lloyd Wooller b 8 Nov 1981); m 2, 28 June 1985, Deborah Louise da of Warrant PO Howard Martin Lloyd Jones (d 1987); 1 s (Alexander Thomas b 5 feb 1988), 1 da (Sasha Louise b 22 Feb 1986); *Career* area dir Hambro Life (Allied Dunbar) 1981, regnl dir Allied Hambro (Allied Dunbar) 1985, exec dir sales Allied Dunbar Gp 1987; FLIA 1978; *Recreations* tennis, music; *Clubs* Bath Rugby Football; *Style*— Derek Riley, Esq; Allied Dunbar Assur Plc, Allied Dunbar Centre, Station Road Swindon Station Wiltshire SN1 1EL (☎ 0793 28291, fax 0793 512371, car tel 0836 617117)

RILEY, Maj John Roland Christopher; s of Lt-Col Christopher John Molesworth Riley, MC (d 1958), of Trinity Manor, Jersey, and Betty Maisie, *née* Hanbury (d 1928); *b* 4 July 1925; *Educ* Winchester; *m* 14 April 1956, Penelope Ann (d 1978), da of late Lt-Col J F Harrison, of Kings Walden Bury, Hitchin, Herts; 2 da (Bridget, Anna); *Career* cmmnd Coldstream Gds 1944; serv: NW Europe, Palestine, Malaya, Instr Army Staff Coll 1960-62; dep States of Jersey 1963 (senator 1975, retired from govt 1981); dir: Air UK 1963-, Chase Bank CI 1975-; chm: Securicor Jersey 1982-, Channel TV 1983; dep chm: Royal Tst Fund Mgmnt CI 1987, Royal Tst Asset Mgmnt CI 1987, Jersey Gas Co 1970-, Fuel Supplies CI 1976-, Servisair Jersey 1976-; vice-pres Royal Jersey Agric & Hort Soc 1986-88; Master Jersey Drag Hunt 1962-; Seigneur de la Trinité; landowner; *Recreations* horse riding, yachting; *Clubs* Royal Yacht Sqdn, Guards; *Style*— Maj John Riley; Trinity Manor, Jersey CI (☎ 0534 61026)

RILEY, (John) Martin; s of Rev Lambert Riley (d 1948), of Roehampton, London, and Marjorie Grace, *née* Maton (d 1973); *b* 15 Nov 1931; *Educ* Bradfield, Queens' Coll Cambridge (MA); *m* 5 Oct 1963, Alison Rosemary, da of Col Gordon Dewar, CBE (d 1985), of Frensham, Surrey; 2 s (Charles b 1965, Hugh b 1968), 1 da (Philippa b 1970); *Career* slr 1963, sr ptnr Mercers of Henley-on-Thames 1977-(ptnr 1964);chm Turners Crt Boys Home 1976-; co cncllr Oxfordshire CC 1970-81; *Style*— Martin Riley, Esq

RILEY, Norman Robinson; s of James Herbert Riley (d 1979); *b* 20 July 1925; *Educ* Bury HS, QMC London, Oxford Univ; *m* 1956, Inger Clara, nee Linde; 1 da; *Career* legal adviser The Distillers Co Ltd 1955-62, legal advisor Kellogg Int Corpn 1962-65, legal dir STC plc 1965-85; *Recreations* tennis, golf, wines; *Style*— Norman Riley, Esq; 1 Macartney House, Chesterfield Walk, SE10

RILEY, Prof Patrick Anthony; s of Bertram Hurrell Riley (d 1961), and Olive, *née* Stephenson (d 1987); *b* 22 Mar 1935; *Educ* Manegg Sch Zurich, King Edward VII Sch King's Lynn, Univ Coll London, Univ Coll Hosp Med Sch London (MB, BS, PhD); *m* 5 July 1958, Christine Elizabeth, da of Dr Islwyn Morris (d 1972), of Treorchy, Rhondda, Glam; 1 s (Benjamin b 20 Feb 1968), 2 da (Sian b 12 Feb 1962, Caroline b 25 June 1963); *Career* Rockefeller res scholar 1962-63, MRC jr clinical res fell 1963-66, Beit meml res fell 1966-68, Wellcome res fell 1968-70, sr lectr biochemical pathology Univ Coll Hosp Med Sch 1974-76 (lectr 1970- 73), prof cell pathology Univ Coll London 1984- (reader 1976-84); sec and tres Euro Soc Pigment Cell Res, pres-elect Int Pigment Cell Soc, memb steering ctee NCUP; FIBiol 1876, FRCPath 1985; *Books* Faber Pocket Medical Dictionary (with PJ Cunningham first edn 1966), Hydroxyanisole: Recent Advances in Anti-Melanoma Therapy (1984); *Recreations* music, stereo photography; *Style*— Prof Patrick Riley; 15 Laurel Way, London N20 8HS (☎ 01 445 5687); Department of Chemical Pathology, University College and Middlesex School of Medicine, London W1P 6DB (☎ 01 636 8333 ext 3384)

RILEY, Peter Lawrence; s of Lawrence Joseph Riley (d 1957), and Freda, *née* Cronshaw (d 1985); *b* 10 May 1947; *Educ* St Joseph's GS Blackpool; *m* 16 Oct 1971, Sandra Carol, da of Tom Gartside (d 1974); 1 s (Mark b 2 July 1974), 1 da (Caroline Louise b 6 June 1977); *Career* CA; ptnr Condy & Co 1973-80, dir numerous Cos 1974-87, dir Plymouth Argyle Football Co Ltd 1977-81, sr ptnr Peter Riley & co 1981-; FCA 1970; *Recreations* yachting, squash; *Clubs* Royal Western YC, St Mellion Golf And Country; *Style*— Peter Lawrence Riley, Esq; 5, The Orchard, Yealmpton, Devon; Britannic House, 51 North Hill, Plymouth PL4 8HZ (☎ 0752 260451)

RILEY, Sir Ralph; s of late Ralph Riley, and late Clara Riley; *b* 23 Oct 1924; *Educ* Audenshaw GS, Univ of Sheffield (BSc, PhD, DSc); *m* 1949, Joan Elizabeth Norrington; 2 da (Susan, Jennifer); *Career* serv WWII Capt N Staffs Regt 1943-47, W Europe; Cambridge Univ: res worker 1952-78, head of cytogenetics dept 1954-72 (dir 1971-78); dep chm & sec Agric and Food Res Cncl fell 1978-85; Wolfson Coll Cambridge; Royal Medal 1981, Wolf Prize in Agric 1986, foreign memb: Indian Nat Sci Acad, Nat Sci Acad USA, Acad Agric France; memb Cambridge Phil Soc, William Bate Hardy Prize; Hon DSc: Edinburgh 1976, Hull 1982, Cranfield 1985; Hon LLD Sheffield 1984; Hon FRASE 1980; FRS 1967; kt 1984; *Clubs* Athenaeum; *Style*— Sir Ralph Riley; 16 Gog Magog Way, Stapleford, Cambridge CB2 5BQ (☎ 0223 843845)

RILEY, Hon Mrs (Ruth Margaret); da of 1 Baron Hives, CH, MBE (d 1965); *b* 1922; *m* 1941, Joseph Graham Riley; 3 s; *Style*— The Hon Mrs Riley; 7 Avenue Rd, Duffield, Derbys

RILEY, Major Timothy Richard; DL (Cumbria); s of Lt-Col Hamlet Lewthwaite Riley, DSO, OBE (d 1932), of Ennim, Penrith, Cumberland, and Joyce Nancy, da of Lt-Col Timothy Fetherstonhaugh, DSO; *b* 11 Dec 1928; *Educ* Shrewsbury, RMA Sandhurst; *m* 11 April 1955, Ankaret Tarn, da of Sir William Jackson, 7 Bt (d 1985); 2 da (Nicola Ankaret Katharine b 1959, Antonia Elizabeth Tarn b 1962); *Career* joined regular army 1946, cmmnd Rifle Bde 1948, served Germany, Middle East & UK, ret 1966; joined The Earl of Lonsdale's Estates 1966, dir: Lowther Wildlife Country Park Ltd 1969-79, Lowther Caravan Park Ltd 1970-, Lakeland Investmts Ltd 1972-82; show dir Lowther Horse Driving Trials 1973-; jt organiser Brougham Horse Trials 1974-80; dir Border Museum of Rural Life 1975-81, chm Skelton Horticultural & Agric Soc 1979-82; memb Penrith Rural District Cncl 1967-70, memb Cumberland CC 1969-74, memb Cumbria CC 1977-89; chm Cumbria Police Authy 1984-89; memb: ACC Police Ctee 1987-89, NW Eng & Isle of Man TA 1971-; chm Ullswater Sch (Penrith) 1978-85; clerk of the Course Cartmel 1978-; dir sec & gen mangr 1985-; clerk the Course Carlisle 1986-; memb HARP (Jump) 1986-, point to point course inspector 1969-; High Sheriff of Cumbria 1989; *Recreations* shooting, racing, travel; *Clubs* Naval and Military; *Style*— Major Timothy Riley, DL; Burbank House, Blencowe, Penrith, Cumbria CA11 0DB (☎ 08533 246); Lowther Estate Office, Penrith, Cumbria CA10 2HG (☎ 09312 09312 392)

RILEY-SMITH, Prof Jonathan Simon Christopher; s of Maj William Henry Douglas Riley-smith (d 1981), of Toulston Grange, Tadcaster, N Yorks and Brehurst, Loxwood, W Sussex, and Elspeth Agnes Mary, *née* Craik Henderson; *b* 27 June 1938; *Educ* Eton, Trinity Coll Cambridge (BA, MA, PhD); *m* 27 July 1968, Marie-Louise Jeannetta, da of Wilfred John Sutcliffe Field, of Chapel Field House, Norwich, Norfolk; 1 s (Tobias Augustine William b 19 Oct 1969), 2 da (Tamsin Elspeth Hermione b 10 Sept 1971, Hippolyta Clemency Magdalen b 10 Nov 1975); *Career* lectr in mediaeval history Univ of St Andrews 1966-72 (asst lectr 1964-65); Univ of Cambridge: asst lectr 1972-75, lectr 1975-78, Queens' Coll Cambridge, fell 1972-78, dir of Studies in history 1972-78, praelector 1973-75, librarian 1973 and 1977-78; head of dept of history Royal Holloway and Bedford New Coll Univ of London 1984- (prof of history 1978-); librarian Priory of Scotland Most Ven Order of St John 1966-78 (Grand Priory 1982-); KStJ 1969, CStJ 1966; FRHistS 1971; Knight of Magistral Grace, SMOM 1971 (Officer of Merit, Pro Merito Melitensi 1985); *Books* The Knights of St John in Jerusalem and Cyprus (1967), Ayyubids, Mamlukes and Crusaders (with U and M C Lyons 1971), The Feudal Nobility and The Kingdom of Jerusalem (1973), What Were The Crusades? (1977), The Crusades Idea and Reality (with L Riley-Smith 1981), The First Crusade and The Idea of Crusading (1986), The Crusades: A Short History (1987); *Recreations* the past and present of own family; *Style*— Prof Jonathan Riley-Smith; Dept of History, Royal Holloway and Bedford New College, Egham Hill, Egham, Surrey TW20 0EX (☎ 0784 34455)

RIMBAULT, Brigadier Geoffrey Acworth; CBE (1954), DSO (1954), MC (1963), DL (Surrey 1971); s of Arthur Henry Rimbault (d 1926), of London, and Sarah Elizabeth *née* Wilson (d 1945); *b* 17 April 1908; *Educ* Dulwich Coll; *m* 9 Sept 1933, Joan vera, da of Thomas Hallett-Fry (d 1912), of Beckenham, Kent; 1 s (Greville Hallet Lynden b 30 June 1935); *Career* cmmnd Loyal Regt N Lancs 1930, serv Wazisistan 1931-36, Palestine 1937, Staff Coll Camberley 1940, OC 1 Loyals Anzio Italy 1944 and Palestine 1945-46, chief instr RMA Sandhurst 1950-51, chief of staff E Africa 1952-54, cmd 131 Inf Bde 1955-57, cmd Aldershot Garrison 1958-61, Col 1959 (until amalgamation 1970); life vice-pres Surrey CC (pres 1982-83); Freeman City of London, Liveryman Worshipful Co Merciers 1961 (Master 1970-71); *Recreations* cricket; *Clubs* MCC, Free Foresters; *Style*— Brig Geoffrey Rimbault, CBE, DSO, MC, DL; 10 Clarke Place, Elmbridge, Cranleigh, Surrey GU6 8TH (☎ 0483 271207)

RIMELL, Mercy; *née* Cockburn; da of Samuel Crosby Cockburn (d 1967), of Budbrook Lodge, Warwick, and Elsie, *née* Simkin; *b* 27 June 1919; *Educ* privately; *m* 23 June 1937, Thomas Frederick (Fred) Rimell (race horse trainer), s of Thomas Devereux Rimell (d 1976), of Windsor Lodge, Lambourn; 1 s (Guy b 1938), 1 da (Scarlet b 1943); *Career* race horse trainer, farmer; trained champion hurdle winner Gaye Brief 1983; *Recreations* racing; *Clubs* Turf; *Style*— Mrs Fred Rimell; The Hill, Upton-upon-Severn, Worcestershire (☎ 06846 2623; The Racing Stables, Kinnersley, Severn Stoke, Worcester W18 9JR (☎ 090 567 233)

RIMER, Colin Percy Farquharson; QC (1988); s of Kenneth Rowland Rimer, of Beckenham, Kent, and Maria Eugenia, *née* Farquharson; *b* 30 Jan 1944; *Educ* Dulwich, Trinity Hall Cambridge (MA, LLB); *m* 3 Jan 1970, Penelope Ann, da of Alfred William Gibbs, of Beckenham, Kent; 2 s (David b 1972, Michael b 1974), 1 da (Catherine b 1971); *Career* legal asst Inst of Comparative Law Paris 1967-68, called to the Bar Lincoln's Inn 1968, practising since 1969; *Recreations* music, photography, novels, walking; *Style*— Colin Rimer, Esq, QC; 13 Old Square, Lincoln's Inn, London WC2A 3UA (☎ 01 404 4800)

RIMINGTON, Richard John; *Career* chm: Hollis Bros & ESA (timber importers and woodworkers) 1981-, AND Engrg, Data Dynamics Gp, Torkmatic, Torkmatic UK (Sales), West Mills Light Engrg, Young and Marten, Zenith Electric Co; dep chm James Clark & Eaton Ltd; dir: A W Metal Works, Eastern Tractors Hldgs, Middlesex Machine Tool, Nash & Hodge Engrs, Suter Electrical, W H Welding Equipment, Weyside Engrg (1926) Ltd; memb IOD; FCA; *Style*— Richard Rimington, Esq; c/o Dixon Wilson & Co, Gillett House, 55 Basinghall St, London EC2Y 5EA (☎ 01 628 7251/4321)

RIMMER, Kenneth Archibald; s of Archibald Rimmer (d 1988), of Woodford Green, Essex, and Eliza Rhoda, *née* Roe; *b* 30 Jan 1940; *Educ* Buckhurst Hill County HS Essex; *m* 7 May 1966, Janice Lynne, da of Frederick Thomas Pigrome, of Leigh-on-Sea, Essex; 1 s (Matthew b 1970), 1 da (Helen b 1972); *Career* Australia and New Zealand Bank 1956-69, Bank Julius Baer 1969-73; vice pres and mangr The Bank of California 1980- (joined 1973); ACIB 1972; *Recreations* piano, bowls, snooker; *Style*— Kenneth Rimmer, Esq; The Bank of California, 18 Finsbury Circus, London EC2M 7BP (☎ 01 628 1883, fax 01 628 1864, telex 8814323)

RING, Sir Lindsay Roberts; GBE (1975), JP (Inner London 1964); s of George Arthur Ring; *b* 1 May 1914; *Educ* Dulwich Coll, Mecklenburg Germany; *m* 1940, Hazel Doris, da of A Trevor Nichols, CBE; 2 s, 1 da; *Career* serv WWII Maj RASC; Freeman City of London 1935, memb Court of Common Cncl (Bishopsgate Ward) City of London 1964-68, alderman (Ward of Vintry) 1968, sheriff City of London 1967-68, Lord Mayor of London 1975-76; FCIS 1976; chm Ring & Brymer (Birchs) Ltd (caterers); memb Gaming Bd for GB 1977-; Hon DSc (City U) 1976, Hon DLitt (Ulster) 1976; KStJ 1976; *Style*— Sir Lindsay Ring, GBE, JP; Chalvedune, Wilderness Rd, Chislehurst, Kent BR7 5EY (☎ 01 467 3199); Ring & Brymer Ltd, 30 Sun St, London EC2 (☎ 01 377 2552)

RINGADOO, Hon Sir Veerasamy; s of Nagaya Ringadoo; *b* 1920; *Educ* Port Louis G S Mauritius, LSE (LLB, hon fellow 1976); *m* 1954, Lydie Vadamootoo; 1 s, 1 da; *Career* barrister 1949; MLC for Moka-Flacq 1951-67, min Labour and Social Security 1959-64, Min Education 1964-67, first MLA (Lab) for Quartier Militaire and Moka 1967-, min Natural Resources 1967-68, min Finance 1968-82; govr IMF; Hon LLD (Mauritius) 1975, Hon DLitt (Andhra) 1978; kt 1975; *Style*— Hon Sir Veerasamy Ringadoo; Port Louis, Mauritius

RINGROSE-VOASE, Lt Cdr Christopher John; MBE (1970); s of John Reginald Ringrose-Voase (d 1956), of Ceylon, and Florence Marjorie, *née* Grandage (d 1970); *b* 2 Nov 1929; *Educ* RNC Dartmouth; *m* 7 April 1958, Patricia Ann, da of Cdr Charles Skinner Bushe, CBE, RN, of Port of Spain, Trinidad; 2 s (Anthony b 1960,

Christopher b 1964), 2 da (Lucinda b 1961, Alexandra b 1962); *Career* RN worldwide submarine specialist, cmd of HMS Astute 1958-59 and 1962-64, HMS Finwhale 1966-67; asst dir Cncl for the Protection of Rural England 1981- (asst sec 1970-76, sec 1976-81); *Recreations* fishing; *Clubs* Naval and Military (tstee); *Style*— Lt Cdr Christopher Ringrose-Voase, MBE, RN; 4 Hobart Place, London SW1W 0HY (☎ 01 235 9481)

RINK, Paul James Ernest; s of Paul Lothar Max Rink (d 1978), and Mary Ida McCall, *née* Moore; *b* 18 Dec 1940; *Educ* Sedbergh; *m* 26 July 1969, Marlene Ann, da of Maurice Hughes, of Lostock, Lancs; 1 s (Nicholas b 1971), 1 da (Sally b 1973); *Career* sales dir Wolstenholme Bronze Powders Ltd 1967-73; joint md: Wolstenholme Bronze Powders Ltd 1973-78, Wolstenholme Rink plc 1978-; chm and md: Wolstenholme Bronze Powders Ltd 1978-, Makin Metal Powders Ltd 1985-; *Recreations* golf, rugby, football, cricket; *Clubs* Bolton GC, MCC; *Style*— Paul Rink, Esq; Wolstenholme Rink plc, Springfield House, Darwen, Lancs BB3 0RP (☎ 0254 873888, telex 63251)

RIPLEY, David; s of Arthur and Brenda; *b* 13 Sept 1966; *Educ* Royds Sch Leeds; *Career* cricketer; *Style*— Mr David Ripley; c/o Northants CCC; County Ground Northampton

RIPLEY, Sir Hugh; 4 Bt (UK 1880), of Rawdon, Yorks; s of Sir Henry Ripley, 3 Bt, JP (d 1956), and Dorothy, *née* Harley (d 1964); *b* 26 May 1916; *Educ* Eton; *m* 1, 1946 (m dis 1971), Dorothy Mary Dunlop, yr da of John Cumming Bruce-Jones, and Dorothy Euphemia Mitchell, da of Sir Thomas Dunlop, 1 Bt, GBE, JP, DL; 1 s, 1 da; m 2, 1972, Susan, da of William Parker, of Keythorpe Grange, E Norton, Leics; 1 da; *Heir* s, William, b 13 April 1950; *Career* farmer Maj, King's Shropshire LI, served WW II N Africa, Italy; dir John Walker & Sons 1956-81; *Recreations* fishing, shooting; *Clubs* Boodle's; *Style*— Sir Hugh Ripley, Bt; The Oak, Bedstone, Bucknell, Shrops; 20 Abingdon Villas, London W8

RIPLEY, William Hugh; s and h of Sir Hugh Ripley, 4 Bt; *b* 13 April 1950; *Educ* Eton, McGill Univ Canada; *Recreations* fishing, writing; *Style*— William Ripley, Esq; Dove Cottage, Bedstone, Bucknell, Salop

RIPON, 11 Bishop of 1977-; Rt Rev David Nigel de Lorentz Young; see founded AD 678 but merged in York till reconstituted 1836; patron of 38 livings and 20 alternately with others, all the Canonries in the Cathedral, the Archdeaconries of Richmond and Leeds and the chancellorship of the diocese; s of Brig Keith Young, CIE, MC; *b* 2 Sept 1931; *Educ* Wellington, Balliol Coll Oxford; *m* 1, 1962, Rachel (d 1965), da of Jack Lewis, of Liverpool; 1 s, 1 da; m 2, 1967, Jane, da of Lewis Collison, TD, JP; 3 s; *Career* lecturer Buddhist Studies Manchester Univ 1967-70; vicar of Burwell Cambridge 1970-75; chm: governing body Soc for the Promotion of Christian Knowledge 1978-, Partnership World Mission 1978-; archdeacon Huntingdon and hon canon Ely Cathedral 1975-77, bishop of Ripon 1977-; *Recreations* fell walking, sailing; *Clubs* Royal Commonwealth Soc; *Style*— The Rt Rev the Bishop of Ripon; Bishop Mount, Ripon, N Yorks HG4 5DP (☎ 0765 2045)

RIPPENGAL, Derek; CB (1982); s of William Thomas Rippengal (d 1972), of Middlesex, and Margaret Mary Rippengal, *née* Parry (d 1982); *b* 8 Sept 1928; *Educ* Hampton GS, St Catharine's Coll Cambridge (Scholar, MA); *m* 1963, Elizabeth (d 1973), da of Charles Gordon Melrose (d 1985), of East Lothian; 1 s (Robert b 1966), 1 da (Emma b 1970); *Career* barr Middle Temple 1953, QC 1980; counsel to chm of Ctees House of Lords 1977-; formerly: chancery bar and univ posts 1953-58; treasy slrs off 1958-72 (princ asst treasy slr 1971), slr & legal advsr to dept of trade & indust 1972-73, dep parliamentary counsel, law cmmn 1973-74, parliamentary counsel 1974-76; *Recreations* music, fishing; *Clubs* Athenaeum; *Style*— Derek Rippengal, Esq; 'Wychwood', Bell Lane, Little Chalfont, Bucks HP6 6PF (☎ Little Chalfont 2350); House of Lords (☎ 219 3211)

RIPPON OF HEXHAM, Baron (Life Peer UK 1987), of Hesleyside, Co Northumberland; (Aubrey) Geoffrey Frederick Rippon; PC (1962), QC (1964); o s of Arthur Ernest Sydney Rippon (d 1966); *b* 28 May 1924; *Educ* King's Coll Taunton, BNC Oxford (MA); *m* 1946, Ann Leyland, OBE, da of Donald Yorke, MC, of Birkenhead; 1 s (Hon Anthony Simon Yorke b 4 Oct 1959), 3 da (Hon Fiona Carolyn b 28 June 1947, Hon Sarah Lovell (*see* Hon Mrs Taylor, Hon Penelope Ann (*see* Hon Mrs Rae); *Career* contested (C) Shoreditch 1950, Finsbury 1951; MP (C) Norwich S 1955-64, Hexham 1966-87; PPS to: min Housing and Local Govt 1956-57, min Defence 1957-59; parly sec Miny Aviation 1959-61, jt parly sec Miny Housing and Local Govt 1961-62, min Public Bldgs and Works 1962-64 (with seat in Cabinet 1963-64); ch opposition spokesman: Housing, Local Govt and Land 1966-68, Defence 1968-70; min Technology 1970, chllr Duchy of Lancaster 1970-72, sec state for Environment 1972-74; ch oppn spokesman Foreign and Cwlth Affrs 1974-75, chm Cons Foreign Affrs Ctee 1970-81; ldr: Cons Delegn to Cncl Europe and WEU 1967-70, Cons Gp European Parl 1977-79; barr 1948; Mayor of Surbiton 1951-52, ldr Cons Gp LCC 1957-59 (memb LCC (Chelsea) 1952-61); memb Court London Univ 1958-; chm: Dun & Bradstreet 1976-, Britannia Arrow Hldgs 1977-, Robert Fraser Gp 1985-; dir: Fairey Co, Bristol Aeroplane Co, Hotung Estates, Singer & Friedlander; chm Br Section European League for Economic Cooperation; Grand Cross Order of Merit (Liechtenstein) 1967, Kt Grand Cross Royal Order of North Star (Sweden) 1982; *Clubs* White's, Pratt's, MCC; *Style*— The Rt Hon Lord Rippon of Hexham, PC, QC; The Old Vicarage, Broomfield, Bridgwater, Somerset; 2 Paper Buildings, Temple, London EC4 (☎ 01 353 5835)

RISK, Douglas James; s of James Risk (slr), of Glasgow, and Isobel Katherine Taylor, *née* Dow; *b* 23 Jan 1941; *Educ* Glasgow Acad, Gonville and Caius Coll Cambridge (BA, MA), Glasgow Univ (LLB 1965); *m* 4 Aug 1967, Jennifer Hood, da of John Howat Davidson (d 1985, schoolmaster), of Glasgow; 3 s (Kenneth b 1968, Malcolm b 1972, Colin b 1974), 1 da (Helen b 1970); *Career* admitted to faculty of Advocates 1966; standing jnr cncl Scottish Educn Dept 1975; sheriff of Lothian and Borders at Edinburgh 1977-79, sheriff of Grampian, Highland and Island at Aberdeen 1979-; hon lectr faculty of Law Aberdeen Univ 1980-; *Clubs* Royal Northern and Univ, Aberdeen; *Style*— Douglas J Risk, Esq; Sheriffs Chambers, Sheriff Court House, Exchequer Row, Aberdeen AB9 1AP

RISK, Sir Thomas Neilson; s of late Ralph Risk, CBE, MC; *b* 13 Sept 1922; *Educ* Kelvinside Acad, Glasgow Univ (BL, LLD); *m* 1949, Suzanne Eiloart; 4 s; *Career* serv WWII RAF, RAFVR 1946-53; ptnr Maclay Mruuay & Spens, slrs 1950-81; govr Bank of Scotland 1981- (dir 1971-, dep govr 1977-81), Br Linen Bank (govr 1977-86), Merchants Tst plc 1973-, Shell UK 1982-, MSA (Britain) Ltd 1958-, Bank of Wales 1986-; former dir: Standard Life Assur Co 1965-88 (chm 1969-77), Howden Gp 1971-87, Barclays Bank 1983-85; memb: Scottish Industl Devpt Bd 1972-75, Scottish Econ Cncl 1983-, Nat Econ Devpt Cncl, kt 1984; *Style*— Sir Thomas Risk; Bank of Scotland, The Mound, Edinburgh EH1 1YZ (☎ 031 243 5511)

RISLEY, George Francis; s of Thomas Risley (d 1971); *b* 23 Dec 1929; *Educ* Doncaster GS, Coll of Technol Liverpool, IMEDE Lausanne Switzerland; *m* 1; 2 s, 1 da; m 2, 1976, Rosemary Wendy Pamela, da of Cecil Lionel Bell; 1 s, 1 da; *Career* dir: Hazlewood Foods plc, Sandyford Meats Ltd, Sweet Mate Ltd, California Car Care Ltd, Wendy Jane Ltd; exec memb: cncl of Inst of Grocery Distribution, British Frozen Foods Fedn; dir Campsie Springs (Scotland) Ltd; *Recreations* golf; *Clubs* RAC; *Style*— George Risley, Esq; Hazlewood Foods plc, Rowditch, Derby (☎0332 295 295, telex 377872)

RISNESS, Dr Eric John; CBE (1982); s of Kristen Riisnaes (sic) (d 1981), and Ethel Agnes, *née* Weeks, of 64 Leasway, Bedford; *b* 27 July 1927; *Educ* Stratford GS, Cambridge (MA, PhD); *m* 26 Jul 1952, Colleen Edwina, da of Reginald Edwin Armstrong (d 1975); 2 s (Michael b 1958, Stephen b 1972), 2 da (Susan b 1953, Julia b 1968); *Career* joined MOD 1954, various posts in res and devpt of naval equipment including: dir of res Undersea Warfare 1975-76, project mangr Sting Ray torpedo 1976-78, dir Naval Analysis 1982-83, dir gen Surface Weapons 1983-84, dep dir and md Admty Res Estab Portland 1984-87; md STC Technol Ltd 1987-; chm Shalford Choral Soc; FIEE 1963; *Recreations* genealogy, music, golf; *Clubs* Bramley GC; *Style*— Dr Eric Risness, CBE; 8 Orchard Rd, Shalford, Guildford, Surrey GU4 8ER (☎ 0483 34581); STC Technology Ltd, London Rd, Harlow, Essex CM17 9NA (☎ 0279 29531 ext 2370, telex 81151 STL HW G)

RISSON, Maj-Gen Sir Robert Joseph Henry; CB (1958), CBE (1945, DSO 1942 ED); s of Robert Risson (decd); *b* 20 April 1989; *Educ* Gatton H S, Qld U (BE); *m* 1934, Gwendolyn, da of C A Spurgin (decd); *Career* CMF memb Aust Military Bd 1957-58, chm Melbourne and Metropolitan Transportation Ctee 1949-70, exec dir Metropolitan Transportation Ct 197-75, conslt Miny of Transport 1975-77; OStJ 1967, kt 1970; *see Debrett's Handbook of Australia and New Zealand for further details*; *Style*— Maj-Gen Sir Robert Risson, CB, CBE, DSO, ED; 39 Somers St, Burwood, Vic 3125, Australia

RITBLAT, Jill(ian) Rosemary; da of Max Leonard Slotover, FRCS, of Monte Carlo, Monaco, and Peggy Cherna, *née* Cohen; *b* 14 Dec 1942; *Educ* Newcastle-upon-Tyne Church HS, Roedean; *m* 1, 21 April 1966, Elie A Zilkha, s of Abdalla K Zilkha, of Switzerland; 1 s (David b 1968), 1 da (Eliane b 1971); m 2, 27 Feb 1986, John Ritblat, s of Montie Ritblat, LDS (d 1984); *Career* barr 1963; alternative delegate UN Geneva for Int Cncl of Jewish Women 1977-79; Art History Degree, (BA 1983); events organiser, patrons of New Art, Tate Gallery 1984-87 (chm 1987), memb Cncl of Museum of Modern Art Oxford 1986-; *Recreations* people, travel, skiing, looking at art; *Style*— Mrs Jill Ritblat; Friends of the Tate Gallery, Tate Gallery, Millbank SW1P 4RG (☎ 0034 215 254)

RITCHIE, Alexander; s of William Ritchie (d 1964), and Janet Bogie, *née* Kilgour; *b* 8 Sept 1935; *Educ* Perth Acad, Univ of St Andrews, Queens Coll Dundee; *m* 15 May 1971, Beatrice Hume, da of Dr Thomas Hume Caulfield, Phd, BSc, FRIC, FMI (d 1986); 1 s (Kenneth William b 1974), 1 da (Fiona Hume b 1977); *Career* CA; snr ptnr W A Finlayson & Co 1974, dir Kenscott Inns Ltd 1983, McDonald award for history Perth Acad 1954, winner Sir William McLintock prize 1956, ICA (Scotland 1956); *Recreations* mountaineering, study of works of Robert Burns; *Style*— Alexander Ritchie, Esq; High Beeches, Lynedoch Road, Scone, Perth PH2 6RJ; 22 St John Street, Perth PH1 5SP (☎ 0738 23911)

RITCHIE, Dr Anthony Elliot; CBE (1978); s of Professor-Emeritus James Ritchie, CBE (d 1958), and Jessie Jane, *née* Elliot (d 1933); *b* 30 Mar 1915; *Educ* Edinburgh Acad, Aberdeen Univ (MA, BSc), Edinburgh Univ (MB, ChB, MD); 28 June 1941, Elizabeth Lambie, da of John Knox (d 1951), of Dunfermline; 1 s (James Knox b 1949), 3 da (Innes Elizabeth b 1945, Margaret b 1950, Alison b 1958); *Career* Carnegie res scholar and lectr physiology dept Univ of Edinburgh 1941-48, prof physiology Univ of St Andrews 1948-69, sec and tres Carnegie Tst for Univs of Scotland 1969-86; chm numerous govt educn and sci ctees, memb advsy ctee med res 1960-69, sci advsr civil defence 1961-80, memb Br Library Bd 1973-80; tstee Nat Lib of Scotland 1975-, Carnegie Tst 1986-; hon FCSP 1970, hon DSc St Andrews 1972, hon LLD Strathclyde 1985, hon FRCPEd 1986, FRSE 1952 (memb cncl 1952-78, gen sec 1966-76, bicentenary gold medal 1983); *Books* Clinical Electromyography (with Dr Jar Lenman, fourth edn 1986); *Recreations* hill-walking, literature, motor cars, electronics, DIY; *Clubs* New (Edinburgh), Caledonian; *Style*— Dr Anthony Ritchie; 12 Ravelston Park, Edinburgh, EH4 3DX (☎ 031 332 6560)

RITCHIE, Hon Charles Rupert Rendall; s and h of 5 Baron Ritchie of Dundee; *b* 15 Mar 1958; *m* 1984, Tara, da of Howard J Koch, Jr, of USA; *Style*— The Hon Charles Ritchie

RITCHIE, Douglas Malcolm; s of Ian David Ritchie, of Montreal, Canada, and Helen Mary, *née* Jamieson; *b* 8 Jan 1941; *Educ* McGill Univ Canada (BSc, MBA); *m* 11 Sept 1965, Cydney Ann, da of Raymond Brown, of Montreal, Canada; 3 s (Campbell, Raymond, Neill); *Career* exec vice pres Alcan Canada Prods Toronto 1975-78 (vice pres 1973-75), corporate vice pres Aluminium Co of Canada Ltd Montreal 1978-80, pres and chief exec Alcan Smelters & Chemicals Ltd 1982-86 (exec vice pres 1980-82), md and chief exec offr Br Alcan Aluminium plc 1986-; non exec dir: Ryan Int plc, The Laurentian Gp Corpn Montreal; memb Fndn for Canadian Studies in the UK; *Recreations* shooting, fishing, golf; *Style*— Douglas Ritchie, Esq; Chalfont Park, Gerrards Cross, Bucks SL9 0QB (☎ 0753 887373, fax 0753 889667, telex 847343)

RITCHIE, Graham; *b* 13 July 1948; *Educ* Jesus Coll Camb (MA); *m* 6 Feb 1971, Jacqueline Mary; 1 s (b 1983), 3 da (b 1974, twins b 1976); *Career* slr; sr ptnr Ritchie, Somerton Camb; articles and reports: International Child Kidnapping (1979), Domestic Violence and Womens Refuges (1979), report to Cwlth Law Mins Meeting 1983 International Aspects of Child Abuse; *Recreations* sailing, swimming, cycling, literature; *Style*— Graham Ritchie, Esq; 10 Milton Rd, Cambridge (☎ 355440, fax 358865)

RITCHIE, Ian Carl; s of Christopher Charles Ritchie (d 1959), and Mabel Berenice, *née* Long (d 1981); *b* 24 June 1947; *Educ* Varndean-Brighton Liverpool, Sch of Arch Poly Central London (Dip Arch); *m* Jocelyne Van den Bossche; 1 s (Inti b 1983); *Career* architect; principal Ian Ritchie Architects 1981-, ptnr Chrysalis Architects 1979-81, dir Rice Francis Ritchie (RFR) Paris 1981-86 (now conslt) (engineering design); designs exhibited at: ICA, Biennale de Paris, Centre Pompidou Paris; RIBA: external examiner 1983-, pres medal assessor 1987; work published in architectural books and magazines in UK, Europe, USA, Asia 1976-; taught at: Oita Univ 1970 Japan, Planning Sch PCL London 1972, Architectural Asso 1979-82, Visiting Critic Univ of Sheffield 1985-87; RIBA (awards 1988 nat chm), MCSD, Tableau de L'Ordre des Architectes Francais (1982), Silver Medal Architectural Design 1982 (for Eagle Rock House); *Recreations* art, swimming, reading, writing, film-making, lecturing on concept design; *Clubs* Architecture; *Style—* Ian C Ritchie, Esq; "O" Metro Wharf, Wapping Wall, London E1 9SS (☎ 481 4427, fax 481 8200)

RITCHIE, Sir James Edward Thomson; 2 Bt (UK 1918), of Highlands; TD (1943) and two clasps; s of Sir James William Ritchie, MBE, 1 Bt (d 1937), and Ada, da of Edward Bevan; *b* 16 June 1902; *Educ* Rugby, Queen's Coll Oxford; *m* 1, 1928 (m dis 1936), Esme (d 1939), only da of late James Montague Oldham, of Ormidale, Ascot; m 2, 1936, Rosemary, yr da of late Col Henry Sidney John Streatfeild, DSO, TD; 2 da; *Career* served WW II holding various staff and regimental appts (Central Med Force 1944-45); chm M W Hardy & Co Ltd 1948-78, dir William Ritchie & Son (Textiles) Ltd, patron of Ashford and Dist Caledonian Soc, memb Court of Assts Merchant Taylors' Co (master 1963-64), Hon Lt-Col late Inns of Court Regt RAC (TA), a selected mil memb Kent T&AFA 1953-68, pres Ashford Branch Royal British Legion 1951-75, jt hon tres and chm Finance and Gen Purposes Ctee London Sch of Hygiene and Tropical Medicine London Univ 1951-61, memb Finance and Gen Purposes Ctee and a co-opted memb of Bd of Management 1964-65; FRSA; *Style—* Sir James Ritchie, Bt, TD; 3 Farquhar Street, Bengeo, Hertford SG14 3BN

RITCHIE, James Walter; MC (1942 and bar 1943); s of Sir Adam Ritchie (d 1957), of Boreham Manor, Chelmsford, and Vivienne, *née* Lentaigne; *b* 12 Jan 1920; *Educ* Ampleforth, Clare Coll Univ of Cambridge; *m* 10 March 1951, Penelope June, da of late Thomas Lawrence Forbes, of Chilbolton Cottage, Stockbridge; 2 s (Michael b 3 Aug 1953, Peter b 21 Sept 1958), 2 da (Jennifer (Mrs Corry) b 3 March 1952, Vivienne (Mrs Brann) b 20 Sept 1956); *Career* ranks serv Oxford and Buckinghamshire LI !940-41, cmnd Intelligence Corps 1941, 2 Lt to Capt (Res) Adj 5/7 and 1 Bn Gordon Highlanders 1942-46, demobed 1946; Smith Mackenzie & Co Ltd: Tanzania Uganda Kenya 1946-61, dir Dares Salaam 1962, chm Nairobi 1970; md Inchcape plc 1976-84 (dir 1972-); jt master Tedworth Hunt 1986-; *Recreations* hunting, fishing, golf; *Clubs* Oriental, City of London; *Style—* James Ritchie, Esq; Lockeridge Down, Marlborough, Wilts SN8 4EL (☎ 0672 86244)

RITCHIE, Hon Mrs (Jean Davina); *née* Stuart; da of 1 Viscount Stuart of Findhorn, PC, CH, MVO, MC (d 1971); *b* 7 Jan 1932; *m* 1, 1951, John Reedham Erksine Berney, Lt Royal Norfolk Regt (ka Korea 1952), s late of Maj Sir Thomas Reedham Berney, 10 Bt, MC; 1 s; m 2, 1954, Percy William Jesson, s of Lt-Col Harold Jesson; 2 s, 1 da; m 3, 1985, Michael D Ritchie; *Style—* The Hon Mrs Jesson; c/o Rt Hon Viscount Stuart of Findhorn, 63 Wichenden Rd, London SW6

RITCHIE, Dr John Hindle; MBE (1985); s of Charles Ritchie, of Wylam, Northumberland (d 1983), and Bertha, *née* Hindle (d 1972); *b* 4 June 1937; *Educ* Royal GS Newcastle upon Tyne, Univ of Liverpool (BArch Hons), Univ of Sheffield (PhD); *m* 24 August 1963, Anne, da of John Leyland, of Upton Wirral; 2 da (Jane b 1968, Nicola b 1971); *Career* SRC 1963-66, Liverpool City Cncl 1966-69, Rowntree Housing Tst 1969-72, Cheshire CC 1972-74, Merseyside CC 1974-80, memb Merseyside Devpt Corpn 1980 (chief exec 1985), chm Merseyside Educn & Trg Enterprise Ltd; *Style—* Dr John Ritchie; Merseyside Devpt Corpn, Royal Liver Building, Pierhead, Liverpool L3 1JH (☎ 051 236 6090)

RITCHIE, Margaret Claire; da of Roderick Macintosh Ritchie (d 1975), of Edinburgh, and Ida, *née* Neal; *b* 18 Sept 1937; *Educ* Central Newcastle HS, Leeds Girls' HS, Univ of Leeds (BSc), Univ of London (PGCE); *Career* asst sci teacher St Leonard's Sch St Andrews 1960-64, head of sci dept Wycombe Abbey Sch 1964-71, headmistress Queenswood Sch Hatfield 1971-81, headmistress Queen Mary Sch Lytham 1981-; memb Soroptimist Int; memb: SHA, GSA; *Style—* Miss Margaret Ritchie; Queen Mary School, Lytham, Lancs FY8 1DS (☎ 0253 723246)

RITCHIE, (Thomas) Norman; TD (1950); s of Dr John Ritchie (d 1959), and Dorothy Anne, *née* Johnston (d 1968); *b* 9 June 1913; *Educ* Edinburgh Acad; *m* 25 Oct 1941, Margaret Armstrong, da of Col David Paterson, DSO, TD, DL (d 1971); 1 s (David b 1948), 1 da (Frances b 1942); *Career* WWII Maj London Scottish Regt served UK, Germany 1939-45; CA; ptnr Brown, Fleming & Murray (now Ernst & Whinney) 1950-78 (ret); chm ctee which distributed assets and allocated liabilities on dissolution Fedn of Rhodesia & Nyasaland 1963, dir Beagle Aircraft Co Ltd 1969-69; cmmnr Pub Works Loan Bd 1970-82, memb Gaming Bd for GB 1978-84; hon tres Alexandra Rose Day 1983-; Master Worshipful Co of Distillers 1985-86; *Recreations* bridge, reading, Times crossword; *Clubs* Caledonian, Hurlingham, Gresham; *Style—* Norman Ritchie, Esq, TD

RITCHIE, Hon Philippa Jane; da of 5 Baron of Ritchie of Dundee; *b* 14 August 1954; *Educ* St Mary's Convent Baldslow, UCL (BA Hons Eng Lit); *Career* actress; *Style—* The Hon Philippa Ritchie; 12 Oxford Gdns, London W4

RITCHIE, Shirley Anne; QC; da of James Ritchie, of Johannesburg S Africa, and Helen Sutherland, *née* Peters; *b* 10 Dec 1940; *Educ* St Mary's Diocesan Sch, Pretoria and Rhodes Univ (BA, LLB); *m* 23 May 1969, Robin Hamilton Corson Anwyl, s of Douglas Fraser Corson (d 1978); 2 s (Jonathan b 1973, James b 1975); *Career* called to S African Bar 1963 and Inner Temple 1966, rec of the Crown Ct 1981-; memb: Senate of Inns of Court and Bar 1978-81, Gen Cncl of the Bar 1987, Criminal Injuries Compensation Bd 1980-, Mental Health Review Tribunal 1983-; dep chm Barrister Benevolent Assoc 1980-; QC 1979; Master of the Bench of the Inner Temple 1985; *Recreations* theatre, music, sailing; *Style—* Shirley A Ritchie, QC; c/o 4 Paper Buildings, Temple EC4Y 7EX (☎ 01 353 1131, fax 01 353 4979)

RITCHIE, Rear Adm (George) Stephen; CB (1967), DSC (1942); s of Sir Douglas Ritchie, MC (d 1983), and Margaret Stephen, OBE, *née* Allan (d 1978); *b* 30 Oct 1914,,; *Educ* RNC Dartmouth; *m* 1942, Disa Elizabeth, da of Robert Morris Beveridge (d 1923); 3 s (John decd, Paul, Mark), 1 da (Tertia); *Career* hydrorapher; cmd 4 of HM Surveying ships World-Wide, N Africa, Italy, France during WWII; Rear Adm Hydrographer of the Navy (UK) 1966-71; pres Int Hydrographic Bureau Monaco 1972-82, Challenger (1956), The Admiralty Chart (1967); *Recreations* gardening, sea fishing, boules; *Clubs* Reform, Monte Carlo (Monaco), Emeritus; *Style—* Rear Adm Stephen Ritchie, CB, DSC; Seaview, Collieston, Ellon, Aberdeen, Scotland AB4 9RS (☎ 035 887 216)

RITCHIE OF DUNDEE, 5 Baron (UK 1905); (Harold) Malcolm Ritchie; s of 2 Baron Ritchie of Dundee; (d 1948), and Sarah Ruth, da of Louis Jennings MP; suc bro, 4 Baron 1978; *b* 29 August 1919; *Educ* Stowe, Trin Coll Oxford (MA); *m* 1948, Anne, da of Col Charles Johnstone, MC, of Durban; 1 s (Rupert), 1 da (Philippa); *Heir* s, Hon Charles Ritchie; *Career* served WW II as Capt KRRC, Middle East, Greece and Italy; headmaster Brickwall House Sch 1965-72; *Recreations* theatre, gardening; *Style—* Rt Hon Lord Ritchie of Dundee; The Garden House, Beckley, Rye, E Sussex (☎ Beckley 514)

RITCHIE-CALDER, Baroness; Mabel Jane Forbes; yr da of David McKail, MD, DPH, FRCPG, of Glasgow; *m* 11 Oct 1927, Baron Ritchie-Calder, CBE, sometime chm Metrication Bd and Prof of Int Rels Edinburgh Univ (d 1982); 3 s, 2 da; *Style—* The Rt Hon Lady Ritchie-Calder; 4/57 Gillsland Road, Edinburgh EH10 5BW (☎ 031 229 7653)

RITCHLEY, Martin Howard; s of Robert William Ritchley (d 1964), of Orpington, Kent, and Bertha Amy, *née* Jones; *b* 1 July 1946; *Educ* City of London Sch; *m* 3 July 1970, (Mary) Elizabeth, da of Albert William Burns (d 1969), of Stevenage; 1 s (David b 1975), 2 da (Catherine b 1971, Anna b 1980); *Career* articled to Barton Mayhew & Co CAs 1964-70; Coventry Econ Bldg Soc: chief accountant 1970-76, sec 1976-83; Coventry Bldg Soc: sec 1983-, dir 1985-; FCA 1979; *Recreations* golf; *Clubs* Coventry GC; *Style—* Martin Ritchley, Esq; 6 Cannon Hill Rd, Coventry CV4 7AZ (☎ 0203 418 148); Coventry Building Society, Economic House, P.O.Box 9, High St, Coventry CV1 5QM (☎ 0203 555 255, fax 0203 226 469)

RITTNER, Luke Philip Hardwick; *b* 24 May 1947; *Educ* Blackfriars Sch Northants, City of Bath Tech Coll, Dartington Coll of Arts, London Academy of Music and Dramatic Art; *m* 1974, Corinna Frances Edholm; 1 da; *Career* asst administrator Bath Festival 1968, admin dir Bath Festival 1974, dir and founder Association for Business Sponsorship of the Arts 1976, sec-gen Arts Council 1983-; *Clubs* Garrick; *Style—* Luke Rittner, Esq; 105 Piccadilly, London W1 (☎ 01 629 9495)

RIVERDALE, 2 Baron (UK 1935); Sir Robert Arthur Balfour; 2 Bt (UK 1929), DL (S Yorks 1959); s of 1 Baron Riverdale, GBE (d 1957); *b* 1 Sept 1901; *Educ* Oundle; *m* 1, 1926, Nancy, da of Engr Rear-Adm Mark Rundle, DSO; 1 s; m 2, 1933, Christian, da of Maj Arthur Hill (ka 1915, ggggs of Sir Rowland Hill, 1 Bt); 1 s, 1 da; *Heir* s, Hon Mark Balfour; *Career* former co dir; pres Br Assoc Chambers Commerce; chevalier Crown of Belgium, Order of Leopold Medaille Civique; *Recreations* yachting, shooting, stalking, fishing; *Clubs* Sheffield; *Style—* Rt Hon Lord Riverdale, DL; Ropes, Grindleford, via Sheffield SB0 1HX (☎ Hope Valley 30408)

RIVETT, Dr Geoffrey Christopher; s of Frank Andrew James Rivett (d 1970), of Salford, Lancs, and Catherine Mary, *née* Barlow (d 1973); *b* 11 August 1932; *Educ* Manchester GS, Brasenose Coll Oxford (MA), Univ Coll Hosp Med Sch (BM, BCh DObstRCOG); *m* 1, March 1958 (m dis 1976), Joan Dorothy Rivett, *née* Peacock; 2 s (John Graham b 1960, Barry Mark b 1963); m 2, 17 April 1976, (Elizabeth) Barbara, da of Maj William Alfred Hartman (d 1968), of Uckfield, Sussex; *Career* Nat Serv Capt RAMC 1958-60; GP Bletchley Bucks 1960-72, Dept of Health 1972 (currently princ st med offr); Freeman City of London 1981, Worshipful Co of Apothecaries 1981 (Liveryman 1985); ARPS 1970, FRCGP 1987; *Books* The Development of the London Hospital System 1823-1982 (1986); *Recreations* house conversion, photography; *Clubs* Royal Soc of Med, Wig and Pen; *Style—* Dr Geoffrey Rivett; 1 Speed Ho, Barbican, London EC2Y 8AT (☎ 01 628 5682); Shilling Orchard, Shilling St, Lavenham, Suffolk CO10 9RH (☎ 0787 247 808); Dept of Health, London

RIVETT-CARNAC, Cdr Miles James; s of Vice Adm James Rivett-Carnac (d 1970), and Isla Nesta, *née* Blackwood (d 1973); hp of bro, Rev Sir Nicholas Rivett-Carnac, 8 Bt; *b* 7 Feb 1933; *Educ* RNC Dartmouth; *m* 11 Oct 1958, April Sally, da of Maj Arthur Andrew Sidney Villar (d 1966), of 48 Lowndes Square, London SW1; 2 s (Jonathan b 1962, Simon b 1966), 1 da (Lucinda b 1960); *Career* Cdr RN 1965; cmd HMS Woolaston 1963-65 (despatches); armed forces staff coll Norfolk, Virginia, USA 1965; cmd HMS Dainty 1966-68; MOD 1968-70; ret 1970; joined Baring Bros & Co Ltd 1970 (dir 1975) md Outwich Ltd Johannesburg 1976-78, pres Baring Bros Inc 1978-81; memb exec ctee Baring Bros & Co 1981, dir Barings plc 1986-, ch exec Baring Investment Management Holdings 1986-; chm Tribune Investment Tst 1985-; chm Hampshire and IOW Boys' Clubs; memb exec ctee King Edward VII Hosp; memb cncl King George V Fund for Sailors; *Recreations* golf, tennis, stamps, racing; *Clubs* White's, Links (New York); *Style—* Cdr Miles Rivett-Carnac, RN; Martyr Worthy Manor, nr Winchester, Hants SO12 1DY (☎ 096 278 311); Baring Bros & Co Ltd, 8 Bishopsgate, London EC2 (☎ 01 283 8833)

RIVETT-CARNAC, Rev Canon Sir (Thomas) Nicholas; 8 Bt (UK 1836); s of Vice Adm James William Rivett-Carnac, CB, CBE, DSC (d 1970; 2 s of 6 Bt), and Isla Nesta, *née* Blackwood (d 1974); suc unc 1972; *b* 3 June 1927; *Educ* Marlborough; *m* 1977, Susan Marigold MacTier, yr da of late C Harold Copeland; *Heir* bro, Miles James Rivett-Carnac; *Career* ordained 1962, curate Holy Trinity Brompton 1968-72, priest-in-charge St Mark's Kennington Oval 1972-, rural dean of Lambeth 1978-82, hon canon Southwark Cathedral 1980-; *Style—* The Rev Canon Sir Nicholas Rivett, Bt; St Mark's Vicarage, Kennington Oval, London SE11 (☎ 01 735 1801)

RIVETT-DRAKE, Brig Dame Jean Elizabeth Rivett; DBE (1964), MBE (1947, JP 1965, DL (E Sussex 1983)); da of Cdr Bertram Gregory Drake and Dora Rivett-Drake; *b* 13 July 1909; *Educ* St Mary's Hall Brighton, Paris, RAM (LRAM piano); *Career* served WW II (despatches 1946), driver 1 London Motor Transport Co, Women's Transport Service (FANY) 1940, cmmnd ATS 1942, served with Br Liberation Army 1945-47, asst dir WRAC 1948-56, dep pres Regular Cmmns Bd 1948-49, London Dist 1952-54, asst dep dir FARELF 1954-56 dep dir War Office 1957-60, Eastern Cmd 1960-61, Dir WRAC, (Brig) 1961-64, ADC (Hon) to HM The Queen 1961-64; memb Hove Boro Cncl 1966-83, lay memb Press Cncl 1973-78, memb E Sussex CC 1973-77, mayor of Hove 1977-78; *Clubs* English Speaking Union; *Style—* Brig Dame Jean Rivett-Drake, DBE, MBE, JP, DL; c/o Barclays Bank, Town Hall Branch, 92 Church Rd, Hove, E Sussex

RIX, Bernard Anthony; QC (1981); s of Otto Rix (d 1982), of London, and Sadie Rix (Silverberg); *b* 8 Dec 1944; *Educ* St Paul's Sch London, New Coll Oxford (BA, MA), Harvard Law Sch (Kennedy Scholar, LLM); *m* 1983, Hon Karen, da of Baron Young of Graffham, PC; 1 da; *Career* barr Inner Temple 1970, QC, memb Senate of the Inns of the Ct and Bar 1981-83; dir London Philharmonic Orchestra (1986-); *Recreations* music, opera, Italy; *Style—* Bernard Rix Esq, QC; 3 Essex Court, London EC4 (☎ 01 583 9294)

RIX, Sir Brian Norman Roger; CBE (1977), DL (Greater London 1987); s of Herbert Dobson Rix (d 1966), of E Yorks, and Fanny Rix (Nicholson) (d 1976); *b* 27 Jan 1924;

Educ Bootham Sch York; (Hon MA: (Hull 1981, Open 1983), DSc (Nottingham), LLD (Manchester 1986), DUniv (Essex 1984); *m* 1949, Elspet Jeans MacGregor, da of James MacGregor (d 1954), of Surrey; 2 s (Jamie, Jonathan), 2 da (Shelley, Louisa); *Career* WW II RAF and Bevin Boy; actor-mangr 1948, ran repertory cos at Ilkley, Bridlington and Margate 1948-50, toured Reluctant Heroes and brought to Whitehall Theatre 1950-54, Dry Rot 1954-58, Simple Spymen 1958-61, One for the Pot 1961-64, Chase Me Comrade 1964-66; went to Garrick Theatre 1967: Uproar in the House, Let Sleeping Wives Lie; then followed: She's Done It Again 1969-70, Don't Just Lie There, Say Something! 1971-73 (filmed 1973), Robinson Crusoe 1973, A Bit Between the Teeth 1974, Fringe Benefits 1976, entered films 1951 and subsequently made 11 films including Reluctant Heroes 1951, Dry Rot 1956, BBC TV contract to present farces on TV 1956-72, first ITV series Men of Affairs 1973, A Roof Over My Head 1977; presenter Let's Go BBC TV series (first ever for mentally handicapped) 1978-83, disc jockey BBC Radio 2 Series 1978-80, dir and theatre controller Cooney-Marsh Gp 1977-80, sec gen Mencap (Royal Soc for Mentally Handicapped Children and Adults) 1980-87, tstee Theatre of Comedy 1983-, chm Ind Dvpt Cncl for People with Mental Handicap 1981-8; kt 1986; *Books* My Farce from My Elbow; an autobiography (1975); *Recreations* cricket, gardening, amateur radio; *Clubs* MCC, Lord's Taverners (past pres), (hon vice-pres RSGB); *Style*— Sir Brian Rix, CBE, DL; 3 St Mary's Grove, Barnes Common, London SW13

RIX, Sir John; MBE (1955), DL Hampshire (1985); s of Reginald Arthur Rix (d 1948), of Burnham, Bucks; *b* 30 Jan 1917; *Educ* Imperial Service Coll Haileybury, Southampton Univ; *m* 1953, Sylvia Gene, da of Capt Cecil Lewis Howe (d 1979); 2 s, 1 da; *Career* joined Vosper plc 1937, gen mangr 1955, dir 1958, md 1963-78, chm and chief exec 1978-82, chm 1982-85, md Vosper Thornycroft (UK) Ltd 1966-70, chm and chief exec 1970-77; chm: Vosper Ship repairs Ltd 1977-78, Vosper Hovermarine Ltd 1980-85; Mainwork Ltd 1980-85, dir Vosper Private Ltd Singapore 1966-85, Charismarine Ltd 1976-, Southampton Cable Ltd 1985, Chilworth Centre Ltd 1985-; chm Seahorse Int Ltd 1986-, dep chm Victorian Cruise Line Ltd 1988-; kt 1977; *Recreations* sailing, tennis, walking, golf; *Clubs* Royal Thames Yacht; *Style*— Sir John Rix, MBE, DL; Lower Baybridge House, Owslebury, Winchester, Hants (☎ 096 274 306

RIX, Hon Mrs (Karen Debra); *née* Young; er da of Baron Young of Graffham (Life Peer); *b* 1957; *m* 1983, Bernard Anthony Rix (*qv*); *Style*— Hon Mrs Rix

RIX, Timothy John; s of Howard Terrell Rix (d 1979), and Marguerite Selman, *née* Helps; *b* 4 Jan 1934; *Career* Sub Lt RNVR 1952-54; Mellon Fell Yale 1957-58; joined Longmans Green & Co Ltd 1958: overseas educnl publisher 1958-61, publishing mangr Far East and SE Asia 1961-63, hd of Eng Language Teaching Publishing 1964-68, divnl md 1968-72, jt md 1972-76, chief exec 1976, chm 1984; chm and chief exec Addison-Wesley-Longman Gp Ltd 1988-; dir: Pearson Longman Ltd 1979-83, Goldcrest TV 1982-83, Yale Univ Press 1984-; pres Publishers Assoc 1982-84, dep chm Nat Book League 1985-86, chm Book Tst 1986-88; memb: Br Cncl Publisher Advsy Panel 1978-, Br Cncl Bd 1988-, Arts Cncl Literature Panel 1983-87, Br Library Advsy Cncl 1982-86, Br Library Bd 1986-; chm Book House Training Centre 1986-89; CBIM, FRSA; *Recreations* reading, landscape, wine; *Clubs* Garrick; *Style*— Timothy Rix Esq; 24 Birchington Rd, London N8 8HP (☎ 01 348 4143); Addison-Wesley-Longman Gp Ltd, Burnt Mill, Harlow, Essex CM20 2JE (☎ 0279 26721)

RIXSON, Air Cdre Denis Fenn; CVO (1986), OBE (1944, DFC 1941, AFC 1960); s of George Herbert Rixson (d 1954), of Westminster, and Anne, *née* Fenn (d 1958); *b* 12 Dec 1918; *Educ* Christs Hosp; *m* 7 Sept 1946, (Elizabeth) Hope, da of George Douglas Budge (d 1957), of Monmouthshire and Fife; 2 s (Rhoderick Geroge John b 26 Jan 1948, d Jan 1953, Robert Denis James b 14 March 1952), 1 da (Elizabeth Ann Mary b 12 Dec 1953); *Career* cmmnd RAF 1936, WWII serv ME and Europe 1939-45, serv Rhodesia India and UK 1946-60, Gp Capt dep dir operational requirements Air Miny 1960, Cdr RAF Geilenkirchen Germany 1962-63, Air Cdre asst COS Intelligence AFCENT 1963-65, Air Offr i/c admin HQ Fighter Cmd Bentley Priory 1965-67, Cmdt ROC 1967-69; dir appeals and publicity Royal Hosp and Home for incurables 1970-83, vice chm and Trustee of Devpt Tst for the Young Disabled 1983-, vice pres Throgmorton Euro Med Gp 1985-, tstee Compaid Tst 1988-; tstee Amberley Chalk Pits Heritage Museum Tst 1983-, conslt Chasely Home for Disabled Ex-Servicemen Eastbourne 1987-; *Recreations* swimming, gardening, fishing, cricket; *Clubs* RAF, MCC, Pratts; *Style*— Air Cdre Denis Rixson, CVO, OBE, DFC, AFC; Hesworth, Close Walks Wood, Midhurst, W Sussex GU29 OET (☎ 073 081 4940)

RIZZA, George Joseph; s of James Rizza (d 1974), and Emily Neri (d 1943); *b* 5 Nov 1925; *Educ* Gordons Sch Huntly, Royal Scottish Acad of Music; *m* 25 March 1969, Margaret, da of Harvey Gibson (d 1947); 1 da (Jane Diane b 1971); *Career* Novello & Co Ltd 1973, Laurel Music 1970, Cinderella 1978, Lorna Music 1978, Woodside Music 1978-82, Mayheu Music 1978-82, Fairfield 1975, Goodwin & Tabb 1975, Elkin 1975, Mercury Music 1973, Paxton 1976, Performing Right Society 1973, Jazz Journal 1973-83, Austria Travel 1986, Park Lane Gp 1964-80, J W Chester Ltd 1962-72; ARCM; *Style*— George Rizza, Esq; 14 Vine Avenue, Sevenoaks, Kent (☎ 0732 452429); Novello & Co Ltd, Fairfield Road, Borough Green, Kent TN15 8DT (☎ 0732 883261, telex 95583)

ROACH, Prof Gary Francis; s of John Francis Roach (d 1982), Bertha Mary Ann, *née* Walters (d 1975); *b* 8 Oct 1935; *Educ* Univ Coll of S Wales and Monmouthshire (BSc), Univ of London (MSc), Univ of Manchester (PhD); *m* 3 Sept 1960, Isabella Grace Willins Nicol; *Career* Flying Offr Educn Branch RAF 1955-58; res Mathmatician BP 1958-61, lectr UMIST 1961-66, visiting prof Univ of Br Columbia 1966-67; Univ of Strathclyde: lectr 1967-70, sr lectr 1970-71, reader 1971-79, prof 1979-82, dean faculty of sci 1982-85; Incorporation of Bonnetmakers & Dyers Glasgow 1981; FRAS 1964, FIMA 1967, FRSE 1975; *Books* Green's Functions (second edn 1982); *Recreations* mountaineering, photography, philately, gardening, music; *Style*— Prof Gary Roach; 11 Menzies Ave, Fintry, Glasgow G63 0YE (☎ 036 086 335); Dept of Mathematics, Univ of Strathclyde, Livingstone Tower, 26 Richmond St, Glasgow G1 1XH (☎ 041 552 4400, ext 3800)

ROACH, Jill; da of Peter Roach, of the Cottage, Winthorpe, Notts, and Joan Catherine Roach; *b* 4 Sept 1946; *Educ* East Haddon Hall Sch Northants, Queen Mary Coll London U (BA); *m* 1974 (separated), Robert Hedley Llewellyn Watkins, s of Arthur Goronwy Watkins, CBE; 2 s; *Career* former sr producer BBC TV (former editor John Craven's Newsround); head production Blackrod (ind TV production subsid of TVS); *Recreations* the children; *Style*— Miss Jill Roach; Blackrod Ltd, 40-44 Clipstone St, London W1P 7EA (☎ 01 637 9376, telex 269859); 4 Old Forge Mews, London W12

ROAD, Christopher John; s of Alfred Sinclair Road, OBE, and Eve Helen, *née* Adlerova; *b* 7 May 1948; *Educ* St Paul's, Trinity Hall Cambrige (MA); *m* 5 June 1971, Zofia Alicja, da of Piotr Jan Pialucha (d 1972); 1 s (Thomas b 1980), 1 da (Katharine b 1974); *Career* admin offr Br Cncl 1971-78, Macfarlanes Slrs 1979-83 (ptnr 1983-); memb: City of London Slrs Co, memb Law Soc; *Style*— Christopher Road, Esq; 37 Ashlone Rd, London SW15 1LS (☎ 01 788 0386); 10 Norwich St, London EC4A 1BD (☎ 01 831 9222, fax 01 831 9607, telex 296381 MACFAR G)

ROADS, Dr Christopher Herbert; s of Herbert Clifford Roads (d 1963), of Kneesworth, Cambs, and Vera Iris, *née* Clark (d 1986); *b* 3 Jan 1934; *Educ* Cambridge & County Sch, Trinity Hall Cambridge (BA, MA, PhD); *m* 24 April 1976, Charlotte Alicia Dorothy Mary; da of Neil Lothian, of Mintern House, Minterne Magna, Dorchester, Dorset; 1 da (Cecilia Iris Muriel Lothian b 1981); *Career* Lt Royal Artillery Egypt 1952-54, advsr to War Office on Disposal of Amnesty Arms 1961-62; keeper of dept of records Imperial War Museum 1962-70 (deputy dir general 1964-79); fndr and dir: Cambridge Coral Starpon Research Group 1968-, Duxford Airfield Branch 1971-79; tstee later dir HMS Belfast Pool of London 1970-79; dir: National Sound Archive 1983-, Museums and Archives Dvpt Associates Ltd 1977-85, Historic Cable Ship John W Mackay 1986-, National Discography Ltd 1986-; UNESCO conslt in design and operation of audiovisual archives and museums in general 1976-; hon sec Cambridge Univ Long Range Rifle Club 1979; vice pres: World Expeditionary Society 1971, Duxford Aviation Soc 1974, English Eight 1980, Cambridge Univ Rifle Assoc 1987-; pres: Archive and Cataloguing Commission of Internat Film and TV Cncl 1970, Historical Breech Loading Small Arms Assoc 1973-, Cambridge Numismatic Soc 1964-66; memb: Council of Scientific Exploration Soc 1971-82, Cambridge Univ Rifle Assoc 1955-87; FRGS; Churchill Fellowship 1971; Visiting Fellow Centre of Internat Studies Cambridge Univ 1983-84; Order of Independence 2 class (Jordan) 1977; *Recreations* rifle shooting (winner of various competitions), flying, marine & submarine exploration, wind surfing, cine & still photography; *Clubs* Hawks (Cambridge), United Oxford and Cambridge University; *Style*— Dr Christopher Roads; The White House, 90 High Street, Melbourn, nr Royston, Herts SG8 6AL; National Sound Archive, 29 Exhibition Road, London SW7

ROAKE, John; s of the late Joseph Henry Roake, and the late Muriel Mary, *née* Edgson; *b* 20 Dec 1923; *Educ* Leighton Park Sch Reading, Poly N London (Dip Arch); *m* 6 Nov 1948, Bertha, da of Louis Press (d 1987); 2 s (Matthew b 4 Feb 1955, Adam b 21 May 1958), 1 da (Dinah b 16 Jan 1961); *Career* chartered architect; ptnr WS Hattrell & Ptnrs 1961-88 (conslt 1988-); FRIBA; Membre de l'Ordre des Architectes Francais; *Recreations* swimming, walking, reading, theatre, travel; *Clubs* Reform; *Style*— John Roake, Esq; 74 Victoria Drive, London SW19 6HL (☎ 01 788 6118); 22 St John's Rd, Bathwick, Bath, Avon BA2 6PX (☎ 0225 62726)

ROBARTS, Anthony Julian; s of Lt-Col Anthony Vere Cyprian Robarts (d 1982); *b* 6 May 1937; *Educ* Eton; *m* 1961, Edwina Beryl, da of the Rt Hon Sir John Gardiner Sumner Hobson, OBE, TD, QC, MP (d 1967); 2 s, 1 da; *Career* banker; dir (later md) Coutts & Co 1963-, dir Coutts Fin Co, rgnl dir NatWest Bank; dir The Int Fund for Insts Inc (USA), The F Bolton Gp Ltd; *Recreations* shooting, gardening, opera; *Clubs* MCC; *Style*— Julian Robarts, Esq; c/o Coutts & Co, 440 Strand, London WC2 (☎ 01 379 6262)

ROBB, Lady (Violet) Cynthia Lilah; *née* Butler; da of 7 Marquess of Ormonde, MBE; *b* 31 August 1946; *m* 1971, Donald Leroy Robb; *Style*— Lady Cynthia Robb; 2734 N Racine, Chicago, Ill. USA

ROBB, George Alan; WS (1968); s of George Robb (d 1969), of Inverdee, Cults, Aberdeen, and Phyllis Mary, *née* Allan (d 1966); *b* 20 May 1942; *Educ* Aberdeen GS 1946-60, Aberdeen Univ (MA), Edinburgh Univ (LLB); *m* 3 Aug 1973, Moira Ann, da of Sidney Milne Clark, of 12 Earlswells Drive, Bieldside, Aberdeen; 2 s (Andrew George b 19 Dec 1976, Michael Nicholas b 22 Dec 1984), 1 da (Judith Olivia b 30 May 1978); *Career* law apprentice Davidson and Syme WS Edinburgh 1966-68, asst: Davidson and Syme WS 1968-69, Edmonds and Ledingham Aberdeen 1969-71, Brander and Cruickshank Advocates Aberdeen 1971-73 (ptnr 1973-83); dir: Aberdeen Tst Hldgs Ltd 1983-89, Aberdeen Petroleum plc 1982, North of Scot Investment Co plc 1986, Multitrust plc 1988; memb: Law Soc of Scot 1966, WS Soc 1968, IOD 1984 (memb Aberdeen ctee 1984-88), FInst Pet 1983; *Recreations* riding, shooting, gardening; *Clubs* Royal Northern Univ, Aberdeen; *Style*— George A Robb, Esq, WS; Birchwood, 6 Hillhead Road, Bieldside, Aberdeen AB1 9EJ (☎ 0224 868358); Prince Arthur House, 10 Queen's Terr, Aberdeen AB9 1QJ (☎ 0224 631999, telex 73683)

ROBBINS, Baroness; Iris Elizabeth; da of A G Gardiner, of The Spinney, Whiteleaf, Bucks; *m* 1924, Baron Robbins, CH, CB (d 1984, economist, Prof of Economics LSE 1929-61, chm Financial Times 1961-70), s of late Rowland Richard Robbins, CBE, of Hollycroft, Sipson, Middx; 1 s (Hon Richard), 1 da (Hon Mrs (Anne) Robbins), *qqv*; *Style*— The Rt Hon the Lady Robbins; Southwood Hall, London N6

ROBBINS, John; s of Frederick Ernest Robbins, of Denham Gardens, Wolverhampton, and Dora Elizabeth Crump (d 1985); *b* 5 May 1933; *Educ* Wolverhampton GS, Birmingham Univ (LLB); *m* 4 Sept 1963, Maria Krystina, da of Frank Grzymek, of Wolverhampton; 1 s (Robert b 1966), 2 da (Lucy b 1970, Annalisa b 1975); *Career* slr 1957; sr ptnr Woolley Beavon Slrs Wolverhampton; govr Wolverhampton GS, pres Wolverhampton Law Soc 1985; memb Law Soc; *Recreations* cricket, music, local history; *Clubs* Wig and Pen, Old Wulfrunians; *Style*— John Robbins, Esq; George House, St John's Sq, Wolverhampton, West Midlands WV2 4BZ (☎ 0902 25733, fax 0902 311886)

ROBBINS, Prof Keith Gilbert; s of Gilbert Henry John Robbins and Edith May, *née* Carpenter; *b* 9 April 1940; *Educ* Bristol GS, Magdalen and St Antony's Coll Oxford (MA, D Phil), Glasgow Univ (DLitt); *m* 24 Aug 1963, Janet Carey, da of John Thomson, of Fulbrook, Oxon; 3 s (Paul b 1965, Daniel b 1967, Adam b 1972), 1 da (Lucy b 1970); *Career* lectr Univ of York 1963-71, dean of faculty of arts Univ Coll North Wales Bangor 1977-79 (prof of history 1971-79), prof of modern history Univ of Glasgow 1980-; vice pres Royal Historical Soc 1984-88; pres: Historical Assoc 1988-, Ecclesiastical History Soc 1980-81; Raleigh lectr Br Acad 1984, Ford lectr Oxford 1987, ed History 1977-86; fell of the Royal Historical Soc 1970; *Books* Munich 1938 (1968), Sir Edward Grey (1971), The Abolition of War (1976), John Bright (1979), The Eclipse of a Great Power: Modern Britain 1870-1975 (1983), The First World War (1984), Nineteenth Century Britain: Integration and Diversity (1988), Appeasement (1988); *Recreations* music; *Style*— Prof Keith Robbins; 15 Hamilton Drive, Glasgow

G12 8DN (☎ 041 33 7766); Dept of Modern History, University of Glasgow, Glasgow G12 8QQ (☎ 041 33 8855)

ROBBINS, Hon Richard; s of Baron Robbins, CH, CB (Life Peer, d 1984) and Baroness Robbins, *qv*; *b* 12 July 1927; *Educ* Dauntsey's Sch, New Coll Oxford; *m* 1, 1952 (m dis 1961), Wendy, da of Brig Nithsdale Dobbs; 2 s; m 2, 1961, Brenda, former w of A Rooker Roberts, and da of Douglas Edward Clark (d 1966), of Hong Kong; *Career* artist, teacher, painter, sculptor; princ lectr Middx Polytechnic; *Recreations* golf; *Clubs* Hampstead Golf, Lyme Regis Golf; *Style—* The Hon Richard Robbins; 50 Highbury Hill, London N5 1HP (☎ 01 226 1481); Fine Art Dept, Middlesex Polytechnic, Quicksilver Place, Western Rd, Wood Green, London N22

ROBBINS, Stephen Dennis; s of Lt-Col J Dennis Robbins, OBE, TD, FCA (d 1986), of Inworth Hall, Essex, and Joan, *née* Mason; *b* 11 Jan 1948; *Educ* Marlborough, Coll of Europe Bruges; *m* 28 Sept 1974, Amanda Robbins, JP, da of J Michael Smith, of Foden Bank Farm, Macclesfield, Ches; 3 da (Harriet b 1976, Victoria b 1979, Camilla (twin) b 1979); *Career* barr 1969, practice SE circuit 1972, rec Crown Cts 1987-(asst rec 1983-87), ctee memb London Common Law Bar Assoc and Senate Overseas Relations, chm disciplinary ctee Potato Mktg Bd 1988-; *Recreations* Scottish hill walking, fishing, shooting, music, collecting Sphemera; *Style—* Stephen Robbins, Esq; Hillcrest Farm, Sevington, nr Ashford, Kent (☎ 0233 629732); The Studios, Edge Street, London W8 (☎ 01 727 7216); 1 Harcourt Bldgs, Temple, London EC4 (☎ 01 353 9421)

ROBENS OF WOLDINGHAM, Baron (Life Peer UK 1961), of Woldingham, Co Surrey; Alfred Robens; PC (1951); s of George and Edith Robens, of Manchester; *b* 18 Dec 1910; *Educ* Manchester Secdy Sch; *m* 1937, Eva, da of Fred Powell, of Manchester; 1 adopted s; *Career* MP (Lab) Northumberland Wansbeck 1945-50, Blyth 1950-60; min Labour and Nat Service 1951; chm: NCB 1960-71, MLH Conslts 1971-83, Johnson Matthey & Co (precious metal refiners, traders and bankers) 1971-85, St Regis Newspapers Bolton 1975-80, St Regis Int 1976-80, Snamprogetti 1980-, Engrg Industs Cncl 1976-80, Guy's Hosp Med & Dental Sch 1974-86; dir: Bank of England 1966-80, Times Newspapers Hldgs 1980-83, Br Fuel Co 1967-85, AAH 1971-88, St Regis Paper Co (NY) 1976-80, THF 1971-86, AMI Europe Ltd 1980-; DCL, LLD; *Style—* The Rt Hon the Lord Robens of Woldingham, PC; Salcombe Court, Cliff Road, Salcombe, Devon TQ8 8JG

ROBERTS *see also*: Goronwy-Roberts, Hardy-Roberts

ROBERTS, Prof (Edward) Adam; s of Michael Roberts (d 1948), of London, and Janet,*née* Adam-Smith; *b* 29 August 1940; *Educ* Westminster, Magdalen Coll Oxford (BA); *m* 16 Sept 1966, Frances Primrose, da of Raymond Horace Albany Dunn (d 1951), of Ludham, Norfolk; 1 s (Bayard b 1972), 1 da (Hannah b 1970); *Career* asst ed Peace News 1962-65, lectr int rels LSE 1968-81 (Noel Buxton student 1965-68), Oxford Univ: Alastair Buchan reader int rels 1981-86, prof fell St Antonys Coll 1981-86, Montague Burton prof int refs 1986-; fell Balliol Coll 1986-, chm govrs William Tyndale Sch 1976-88; *Books* The Strategy of Civilian Defence: Non-violent Resistance to Aggression (ed 1967), Nations in Arms: The Theory and Practice of Territorial Defence (second edn 1986), Documents on the Laws of War (with Richard Guelff second edn 1989), United Nations, Divided World: The UN's Roles in International Relations (ed with Benedict Kingsbury 1988); *Recreations* rock-climbing, mountaineering, running; *Clubs* Alpine; *Style—* Prof Adam Roberts; Balliol College, Oxford OX1 3BJ (☎ 0865 277777)

ROBERTS, Hon Mrs David Aileen Mary; da of late Charles Burrow;; *m* 1936, Hon David Stowell Roberts (d 1956); 2 s, 1 da; *Style—* The Hon Mrs David Roberts; Box Cottage, Box, Stroud, Glos

ROBERTS, Allan; MP (Lab) Bootle 1979-; s of Ernest and Anne Roberts; *b* 28 Oct 1943; *Educ* Droylesden, Little Moss Boys' Co Secndy Sch, Didsbury Coll, Manchester Univ; *Career* former sch teacher and social worker, princ offr Salford Social Servs Dept 1976-79; *Style—* Allan Roberts Esq, MP; 12 Oxford Avenue, Bootle, Merseyside

ROBERTS, Andrew Denby; s of Sir James Roberts, OBE, 2 Bt (d 1973), and hp of bro, Sir William Roberts, 3 Bt; *b* 21 May 1938; *Educ* Rugby, Christ Church Oxford; *Style—* Andrew Roberts, Esq

ROBERTS, Air Vice-Marshal Andrew Lyle; CBE (1983), AFC (1969); s of Ronald Lyle Roberts, of 9 Mayfield Way, Ferndown, Wimborne, Dorset, and Nora, *née* Poole; *b* 19 May 1938; *Educ* Cranbook Sch, RAF Coll Cranwell; *m* 8 Nov 1962, Marcia Isabella, da of Lt-Col Christopher Lane Cecil Ward, of Bridge House, Buckland Newton, Dorchester, Dorset; 3 da (Katherine Lucy b 1963, Penelope Susan b 1965, Sarah Jane b 1968); *Career* RAF Coll Cranwell 1956-58, Pilot Offr 1958, 38 Sqdn RAF Luqa Malta 1959-61, Flying Offr 1960, Flt Lt 1961, Instr RAF Coll Cranwell 1962-64, ADC AOC 18 Gp RAF Pitreavie Castle 1965-66, Flt Cdr 201 Sqdn 1967-68, Sqdn Ldr 1967, student RN Staff Coll 1969, personal air sec to under sec of state RAF 1970-71, Wing Cdr OC 236 Operational Conversion Unit RAF St Mawgan 1972-73, US Armed Forces Staff Coll 1974, HQ SACLANT 1975-77, Gp Capt Station Cdr RAF Kinloss 1977-79, Gp Capt Ops HQ Strike Cmd 1980-82, student Royal Coll of Def Studies 1983, Air Cdre Dir Air Force Plans and Programmes MOD 1984-86, Air Vice-Marshal COS HQ 18 Gp 1987-; MBIM 1969-; *Recreations* walking, natural history, music (church organ), off-shore sailing; *Clubs* RAF; *Style—* Air Vice-Marshal Andrew Roberts, CBE, AFC; c/o Midland Bank, 61 High St, Staines, Middx TW18 4QW

ROBERTS, Anne Clark; da of William Cunningham (d 1972), of Scotland, and Ann Simpson Lyon, *née* Clark; *b* 11 Jan 1961; *Educ* Larbert HS, Univ of Aberdeen (MA); *m* 13 Aug 1988, Thomas John Blackham Roberts, s of Thomas Blackburn Roberts, CBE, TD, DL (d 1979), of Wattenwynch, Park Drive, Blundell Sands, Liverpool; *Career* Next plc 1984-88: personnel and training specialist, operations mangr Jewellery and retailer; dir Nat Tst (Enterprises) Ltd 1988-; winner: Nat Training Award 1987, Cosmopolitan Woman of Tomorrow Award (Indust and Commerce) 1989; *Recreations* antique collecting, interior decoration; *Style—* Mrs Anne C Roberts; The Lymes, Willoughby, Waterleys, S Leics; Nat Tst (Enterprises) Ltd, Heywood House, Westbury, Wilts BA13 4NA (☎ 0373 826826, telex 44268 ACORN G, fax 0373 827162)

ROBERTS, Bertie; s of Thomas Roberts (d 1947), of Blaengarw, S Wales, and Louisa Elizabeth Georgina, *née* Moore (d 1950); *b* 4 June 1919; *Educ* Garw GS S Wales; *m* 1, Aug 1946 (m dis 1961), Peggy Joan, da of George Clark (d 1971), of New Milton, Hants; 1 s (Andrew Mark); m 2, 10 Feb 1962, Catherine Watson, da of William Allardyce Matthew (d 1966), of Montrose, Scotland; *Career* Capt RAOC 1942-46, Civil Serv 1936-79; Miny of Public Bldg & Works: ldr study gp on feasibility of using computers 1958, comptroller of accounts 1963, dir of computer servs 1967, head of orgn and methods 1969; dir of estate mgmnt overseas DOE (with FCO) 1971, regnl dir DOE (Maj-Gen) Br Forces Germany 1976-79; memb: community health cncl Hastings DHA, St Leonards-on-Sea Rotary Club; *Recreations* travel, music; *Clubs* Civil Serv, Dickens Pickwick; *Style—* Bertie Roberts, Esq; Fairmount, 41 Hollington Pk Rd, St Leonards-on-Sea, E Sussex TN38 0SE (☎ 0424 714 177)

ROBERTS, Brian Reginald; *b* 3 Jan 1927; *Educ* Royal Liberty Sch Romford, Pembroke Coll Cambridge (MA); *Career* sr ptnr R A Coleman & Co; memb: Stock Exchange 1965, Cncl of Stock Exchange, Cncl's Infor Servs Ctee; *Clubs* Royal Anglesey Yacht; *Style—* Brian Roberts, Esq; Walnut Cottage, Llandegai, Nr Bangor, Gwynedd; R A Coleman & Co, 204 High St, Bangor, Gwynedd LL57 1NY (☎ 0248 353242)

ROBERTS, Sir Bryan Clieve; KCMG (1973, CMG 1964), QC, JP (Inner London 1975); s of Herbert Roberts and Doris Evelyn Clieve; *b* 22 Mar 1923; *Educ* Whitgift, Magdalen Coll Oxford; *m* 1, 1958 (m dis 1975), Pamela Campbell; m 2, 1976 (m dis 1985), Brigitte Reilly-Morrison; m 3, 1985, Mrs Barbara Forter; *Career* WWII served RA and RHA; barr Gray's Inn 1950; Nyasaland: dir of Public Prosecutions N Rhodesia 1960-61, MLC 1961-63, min Justice 1962-63, slr-gen 1961-64; Malawi: Attorney Gen 1964-72, head Civil Serv 1965-72, chm Army Cncl 1965-72; under sec Lord Chllr's Off 1977-82 (joined 1973); chm Cwlth Magistrates Assoc 1979-; Metropolitan stipendiary magistrate 1982-; *Style—* Sir Bryan Roberts, KCMG, QC, JP; 3 Caroline Place, London W2

ROBERTS, Christopher Keepfer; s of John Anthony Roberts, and Pauline Isobel, *née* Keepfer; *b* 26 Mar 1956; *Educ* Denbigh HS, Jesus Coll Cambridge (MA); *Career* ptnr slr 1980, Allen & Overy 1985-(asst 1978-85); memb Law Soc; *Recreations* sailing, squash; *Style—* Christopher Roberts, Esq; Allen & Overy, 9 Cheapside, London, EC2V 6AD (☎ 01 248 9898, fax 01 236 2192)

ROBERTS, Dr Colin Norman; s of late Norman Summerson Roberts, and late Agnes Fanny Smith; *b* 9 Jan 1936; *Educ* Chelsea Coll London (BPharm), Univ Coll Hosp Univ of London, Med Sch Birmingham Univ, Royal Veterinary Coll Univ of London (PhD); *m* 1972, Ann, *née* Blucher; 2 s (Alexander b 1977, Guy b 1981), 1 da (Jessica b 1978); *Career* sr scientific cncllr Biosafety Res Centre, Foods, Drugs and Pesticides, Fukude Japan 1979-, expert agrée French Govt Toxicology Pharmacology 1983-, export dir Life Science Res Ltd 1978- (subsid of APBI, NY); contract res and consultancy for medical pharmaceutical agrochemicl and food industs (Queen's Award for Export 1982) dep md 1987-; fell Pharmaceutical Soc of GB 1982; FRSM; fell Br Inst for Regulatory Affrs; scientific fell Zoological Soc; Liveryman Soc of Apothecaries; 1987- dep md; *Recreations* swimming, reading, music, history of medicine and pharmacy (esp toxicology); *Clubs* Athenaeum; *Style—* Dr C N Roberts; Life Science Research Ltd, Eye, Suffolk IP23 7PX (☎ 0379 4122, telex 975389 LIFSCI G, Fax 037971 427)

ROBERTS, David Edward Glyn; s of David Emlyn Roberts (d 1975), and Henrietta Liston, *née* Griffiths; *b* 29 Feb 1932; *Educ* Calday Grange GS; *m* 1, 13 Oct 1955, Beryl Shelia Price (d 1968); 3 da (Deborah Mary, Angela Margeret, Ruth Alexandra); m 2, 11 Aug 1972, Elizabeth Mary, *née* Grimwade; 2 steps (Adrian Edward Ainsworth Thorn, Richard Charles Ainsworth), 1 da (Patricia); *Career* Nat Serv 2 Lt RA 1955-57; actuary Royal Insur Co 1949-61, stockbroker Tilney and Co 1961-74, Roberts and Huish 1974-85, md Ashton Tod McLaren 1985-, md Quilter Goodison 1988-; Freeman Worshipful Co of Actuaries; FIA 1955, FCII 1959, memb stock exchange; *Style—* Glyn Roberts, Esq; Quilter Goodison & Co, Garrard Ho, 35-41 Gresham St, London (☎ 01 600 4177)

ROBERTS, His Hon Judge David Ewart; s of John Hobson Roberts (d 1969), of Birmingham, and Dorothy, *née* Rolason (d 1979); *b* 18 Feb 1921; *Educ* Abingdon Sch St John's Coll Cambridge (MA, LLB); *Career* WWII 1941-46, cmmnd RA; serv: Egypt, N Africa, Italy, Yugoslavia, Germany; called to the Bar Middle Temple, practised Midland circuit 1948, asst Rec Coventry QS 1966-71, rec Crown Ct Midland & Oxford circuit 1978-82, circuit judge 1982-; *Recreations* photography, skiing; *Style—* His Hon Judge David Roberts; 4 Greville Dr, Brimingham B15 2UU (☎ 021 440 3231)

ROBERTS, David Francis; s of Arthur Roberts; of Plealey, Shropshire, and Mary Kathleen, *née* Maddox; *b* 28 August 1941; *Educ* Priory GS Shrewsbury, Worcester Coll Oxford (MA); *m* 3 July 1974, Astrid Suhr, da of Ernest Suhr Henriksen, of Vancouver, Canada; 2 s (Peter b 21 July 1978, Mark b 24 July 1981), 1 da (Rachel b 1 July 1975); *Career* asst princ MAFF 1964, private sec to Parly Sec (John Mackie, MP) 1967-69, princ 1969, head of Branch Tropical Foods Div 1969-70, seconded as first sec (Agric) FCO Copenhagen 1970-74, private sec to Min of Agric (Fred Peart, MP) 1975-76, asst sec Head of Euro Community Div MAFF 1976, seconded as head of Agric Div HM Treasy 1979-80, head of Sugar Oils and Fats Div MAFF 1980-84, under sec, seconded to FCO as min (Agric) UK Representation to Euro Community 1985; *Recreations* squash, sailing; *Style—* David Roberts, Esq; c/o FCO, (UKREP BRUSSELS) King Charles St, London SW1A 2AH; UK Permanent Representation to the European Communities, Rond Point Robert Schumann 6, 1040 Brussels (☎ 02 230 6205, fax 02 2308379)

ROBERTS, Maj Gen David Michael; s of James Henry (d 1983), of London, and Agnes Louise; *b* 9 Sept 1931; *Educ* Emanuel Sch, Roy Free Hosp Sch of Medicine (MB, BSc, MD); *m* 1964, Angela Louise, da of Capt James Henry Squire, of Herefordshire; 1 s (Justin b 1965), 2 da (Katie b 1966, Eleanor b 1970); *Career* dir of Army Med and consit physician to the Army 1984-; jt prof of mil med Royal Army Med Coll and Royal Coll of Physicians 1975-81; Queen's hon physician 1984; examiner in tropical med RCP; published many papers in gastroenterology; Jubilee Medal; FRCP, FRCPE; *Recreations* squash, mixing concrete and making things; *Style—* Maj Gen David Roberts; Elmgrove, Normandy, Surrey GU3 2AS; Defence Medical Services Directorate, First Avenue House, High Holborn, London WC1V 6HE (☎ 01 430 5693)

ROBERTS, Prof (Edward Frederick) Denis; s of Herbert Roberts (d 1940), and Jane Spottiswoode, *née* Wilkinson (d 1979); *b* 16 June 1927; *Educ* Royal Belfast Academical Inst, Queen's Univ of Belfast (BA, PhD), Trinity Coll Dublin (MA); *m* 30 Oct 1954, Irene Mary Beatrice, da of Leander Murray Richardson (d 1948); 1 s (Patrick Denis b 1957), 1 da (Jane Anne b 1959); *Career* res asst, dept of history, Queen's Univ of Belfast 1951-55; Nat Library of Scotland: asst keeper, dep of manuscripts 1955-66, sec of the library 1966-67; librarian: Trinity Coll Dublin 1967-70, Nat Library of Scotland 1970-; hon prof Univ of Edinburgh 1975; FRSE 1980; Hon FLA 1983; *Clubs* New (Edinburgh); *Style—* Professor Denis Roberts; 6 Oswald Ct,

Edinburgh EH9 2HY (☎ 031 667 9473); National Library of Scotland, George IV Bridge, Edinburgh EH1 1EW (☎ 031 226 4531)

ROBERTS, Denis Edwin; CBE (1974), MBE (Mil) (1945); s of Edwin Roberts (d 1964), of Bromley, Kent, and Alice Gertrude, *née* West (d 1982); *b* 6 Jan 1917; *Educ* Holgate GS Barnsley; *m* 19 Oct 1940, Edith, da of Harry Whitehead (d 1946), of Barnsley Yorks; 2 s (David Harry b 1947, Andrew John b 1950); *Career* WWII serv Royal Signals France, N Africa, Italy, Austria 1939-46; PO 1933-80, numerous appts incl: dir operations 1971-75, sr dir postal servs 1975-77, md posts 1977-80; chm Br Philatelic Tst 1981-85, memb Industl Tbnl 1982-86; Freeman City of London 1978, Worshipful Co of Gardeners; *Clubs* City of London, City Livery; *Style*— Denis E Roberts, Esq, CBE; 302 Gilbert House, Barbican, London EC2Y 8BD (☎ 01 638 0881)

ROBERTS, Hon Mr Justice; Hon Sir Denys (Tudor Emil); KBE (1975, CBE 1970, OBE 1960); s of William David Roberts (d 1954), of St Albans; *b* 19 Jan 1923; *Educ* Aldenham, Wadham Coll Oxford (MA, BCL); *m* 1949 (m dis 1973), Brenda Dorothy, da of L Marsh; 1 s, 1 da; m 2, 1985, Anna Fiona Dollar, da of N G A Alexander; 1 s; *Career* WWII serv RA; barr London 1950-53, crown counsel Nyasaland 1953-59, QC Gibralter 1960, attorney-gen Gibralter 1960-62, slr-gen Hong Kong 1962-66, QC Hong Kong 1964, attorney-gen Hong Kong 1966-73, chief sec Hong Kong 1973-78, chief justice Hong Kong 1979-88, Chief Justice, memb Ct of Appeal for Bermuda 1988-; Brunei 1979-, hon bencher Lincoln's Inn 1978, hon fell Wadham Coll 1984; SPMB (Brunei) 1984; *Books* Smuggler's Circuit (1954), Beds and Roses (1956), The Elwood Wager (1958), The Bones of the Wajingas (1960), How to Dispense with Lawyers (1964); *Recreations* cricket, tennis, writing, walking; *Clubs* MCC, Hong Kong, Royal Commonwealth Soc; *Style*— The Hon Mr Justice Roberts, KBE; 52 Clarence Road, St Albans, Herts; The Supreme Court, Hong Kong

ROBERTS, Derek Franklyn; s of Frank Roberts, MBE (d 1981), of Wirral, Cheshire, and May Evelyn Roberts; *b* 16 Oct 1942; *Educ* Park High GS Birkenhead, Liverpool Coll of Commerce, Harvard Business Sch (AMP); *m* 6 Sept 1969, Jacqueline, da of Sylvio Velho; 2 s (Maxwell Franklyn b 9 March 1971, Daniel Downes b 29 Dec 1972), 1 da (Katy Jane b 3 Sept 1976); *Career* chief exec and dir Yorkshire Bldg Soc 1987, dir BWD Securities plc 1988, chm Yorkshire Bldg Soc Est Agents Ltd 1988; pres Huddersfield Dist Centre Chartered Bldg Socs Inst; FCII, FCBSI; *Recreations* golf, gardening, walking; *Clubs* Huddersfield GC, Huddersfield RUFC; *Style*— Derek Roberts, Esq; Yorkshire Bldg Soc, Yorkshire House, Westgate, Bradford, West Yorks (☎ 0274 734 822, fax 0274 306 031)

ROBERTS, Rt Rev Edward James Keymer; s of Rev Arthur Henry Roberts (d 1952), and Bertha Louisa Roberts (d 1984); *b* 18 April 1908; *Educ* Marlborough, Corpus Christi Coll Cambridge (MA); *m* 1, 1941, Dorothy Frances (d 1982), da of Rev Canon Edwin Bowser (d 1952); 3 s, 2 da; m 2, 1984, Diana, da of Ewen Cameron Bruce, DSO, MC, and widow of (i) Anthony Seymour Bellville and (ii) Arthur Christopher Grey; *Career* archdeacon of IOD 1948-52, archdeacon of Portsmouth 1952-56, bishop suffragan of Malmesbury 1956-62 and of Kensington 1962-64, bishop of Ely 1964-77, ret 1977; FRSCM; Hon DD Cambridge; *Recreations* walking; *Clubs* Leander; *Style*— The Rt Rev Edward Roberts; The House of the Marsh, Quay Lane, Brading, Isle of Wight (☎ 0983 407434)

ROBERTS, Hon Mrs; Hon (Elisabeth); da of Baron Edmund-Davies, PC (Life Peer); *b* 1939; *m* 1965, Richard Owen Roberts; *Style*— The Hon Mrs Roberts; 28 Rosehill Rd, Burnley, Lancs

ROBERTS, Ernest Alfred Cecil; MP (Lab) Hackney North and Stoke Newington 1979-; s of Alfred and Florence Roberts; *b* 20 April 1912; *m* 1953, Joyce Longley; *Career* former engineer, asst gen sec AUEW 1957-77; awarded Tom Mann Gold Medal for Trade Union Activity 1943; *Style*— Ernest Roberts Esq, MP; House of Commons, London SW1 (☎ 01 219 5066, 01 219 4609)

ROBERTS, Sir Frank Kenyon; GCMG (1963), GCVO (1965, KCMG 1953, CMG 1946); s of Henry George Roberts, of Preston, and Gertrude Kenyon, of Blackburn; *b* 27 Oct 1907,(in Buenos Aires);; *Educ* Bedales, Rugby, Trinity Coll Cambridge; *m* 1937, Celeste Leila Beatrix, da of Sir Said Shoucair Pasha, of Cairo, sometime financial advsr to Sudan Govt; *Career* entered FO 1930, serv Paris, Cairo, and as British min Moscow 1945-47, princ private sec to Foreign Sec 1947-49, dep high cmmr India 1949-51, dep under-sec state FO 1951-54, ambass Yugoslavia 1954-57, UK perm rep N Atlantic Cncl 1957-60; ambass: USSR 1960-62, W Germany 1963-68; dir: Hoechst UK, Mercedes-Benz, Amalgamated Metal Corpn; pres: Br-Atlantic Ctee 1968-81 (now vice-pres) European-Atlantic Gp 1973-, patron Atlantic Treaty Assoc (pres 1969-73); pres Anglo-German Assoc, vice-pres UK-USSR Assoc, vice-pres (former President German Chamber of Commerce UK); German Order of Merit (1965); *Clubs* Brooks', RAC; *Style*— Sir Frank Roberts, GCMG, GCVO, KCMG, CMG; 25 Kensington Ct Gdns, London W8 5QF (☎ 01 937 1140)

ROBERTS, Air Vice-Marshal (John) Frederick; CB (1967), CBE (1960); s of William John Roberts (d 1925), of Vine Villa, Brecon Road, Pontardawe, Swansea, and Catherine, *née* Hopkin (d 1959); *b* 24 Feb 1913; *Educ* Ponterdawe GS; *m* 1, Feb 1940, Mary Winifred (d 1968), da of late JE Newns; 1 s ((David) John b 1947); m 2, Dec 1976, Pamela Joy Roberts, da of Arthur Stiles, of Domewood, Copthorne, West Sussex; 2 step da (Gillian, Bryony); *Career* joined RAF 1938, ME 1942-45 (despatches), Staff Coll 1950, memb directing staff Staff Coll 1954-56, sr air staff offr Record Offr 1958-60, Comptroller Allied Air Forces Central Europe 1960-62, station cdr RAF Uxbridge 1963, dir personnel servs MOD (Air) 1964-65, dir gen RAF Ground Trg (RAF) 1966-68, ret 1968; articled clerk 1931-36, qualified CA 1936, Deloitte & Co Swansea 1937; played in various matches for Glamorgan CCC, played for RAF, 1939-48 and for Combined Servs 1946-47; involved with RAF Benevolent Fund 1968-87, pres Pontardawe GC;; *Recreations* cricket, golf; *Clubs* MCC, Pontardawe GC, RAF; *Style*— Air Vice-Marshal Frederick Roberts, CB, CBE; 1 Lon Cadog, Sketty, Swansea SA2 DTS (☎ 0792 203763)

ROBERTS, Prof Gareth Gwyn; s of Edwin Roberts (d 1974), of Penmaenmawr, N Wales, and Meri, *née* Jones (d 1959); *b* 16 May 1940; *Educ* John Bright GS Llandvdno, Univ Coll of N Wales Bangor (BSc, PhD, DSc); *m* 15 Aug 1962, Charlotte, da of Albert William Standen, of Bournemouth; 2 s (Peris, Daron), 1 da (Bronwen); *Career* lectr Univ Coll of N Wales 1963-66, res scientist Xerox Corpn Rochester NY 1966-68, prof of physics New Univ of Ulster Coleraine 1968-76, prof of applied physics Durham Univ 1976-85, prof of electronic engrg Oxford Univ 1985-, dir of res Thorn Emi plc 1985-; cncl memb Inst of Physics, physics pres, Br Assoc for the advancement of Sci; memb: Univ Grants Ctee, newly fnded Univ Funding Cncl, SERC Ctees, Royal Soc Ctees; Royal Inst BBC Christmas lectrs 1988, awarded Holweck Gold Medal and Prize 1986; author of 150 articles and patents, ed Jl of Molecular Electronics; Hon MA Oxford 1987; FRS 1984, FInstP 1972, FIEE 1974; *Books* Langmuir - Blodgett Films (1989); *Recreations* soccer, duplicate bridge, classical music; *Style*— Prof Gareth Roberts; Galleons Lap, Templewood Lane, Franham Common, Bucks SL2 3HF (☎ 02814 4430); Thorn EMI Central Research Laboratories, Dawley Rd, Hayes, Middx (☎ 01 848 6488)

ROBERTS, Prof Geoffrey Frank Ingleson; CBE (1978); s of Arthur Reginald Wilfred Roberts (d 1959), of Venns Lane, Hereford, and Laura, *née* Ingleson (d 1971); *b* 9 May 1926; *Educ* Hereford Cathedral Sch, HS for Boys Hereford, Leeds Univ (BSc); *m* 14 Sept 1949, Veronica, da of Capt John Busby, MN (d 1952); 2 da (Lesley Jane b 1952, Ellice Catherine b 1955); *Career* dep dir (ops) Gas Cncl 1968-71, full-time memb Gas Cncl/Br Gas Corpn: prod and supply 1972-78, external affairs 1979-81, ret 1988; chm Br Pipe Coaters; conslt prof of gas engrg Salford Univ 1983-; *Recreations* reading, DIY, gardening, caravan touring; *Clubs* RAC; *Style*— Prof Geoffrey Roberts, CBE; Ranmoor, St Nicholas Rd, Ilkley, W Yorks LS29 0AN (☎ 0943 608915); Department of Chemical and Gas Engineering, University of Salford, Salford M5 4WT (☎ 061 736 5843)

ROBERTS, Sir Gilbert Howland Rookehurst; 7 Bt (UK 1809), of Glassenbury, Kent, of Brightfieldstown, co Cork and of the City of Cork; s of Sir Thomas Langdon Howland Roberts, CBE, 6 Bt (d 1979); *b* 31 May 1934; *Educ* Rugby, Gonville and Caius Coll Cambridge; *m* 1958, Ines Eleonore, da of late A Labunski; 1 s, 1 da; *Heir* s, Howland Langdon Roberts; *Career* serv Kenya with RE (E African GS Medal); MIMechE; *Style*— Sir Gilbert Roberts, Bt; 3340 Cliff Drive, Santa Barbara, Cal 93109, USA

ROBERTS, Sir Gordon James; CBE (1975), JP (Northants 1952), DL (Northants 1984); s of Archie Roberts (d 1963), of Deanshanger, Milton Keynes, and Lily, *née* Maycock (d 1979); *b* 30 Jan 1921; *Educ* Deanshanger Sch Northants; *m* 1944, Barbara, da of Geoffrey Leach (d 1961), of Haversham, Milton Keynes; 1 s (Adrian), 1 da (Diane); *Career* ldr Northants CC 1974-77, dep chm Cmmn for the New Towns 1978-82; chm: Northants AHA 1973-78, Oxford Regnl Health Authy 1978-, computer policy ctee NHS 1981-84, supervisory bd mgmnt advsy serv NHS 1982-, Regnl Health Authy 1982-84; FRSA; kt 1984; *Recreations* local history, reading, walking; *Style*— Sir Gordon Roberts, CBE, JP, DL; 114 Ridgmont, Deanshanger, Milton Keynes, Bucks MK19 6JG (☎ 0988 562605); Oxford Regional Health Authority, Old Road, Headington, Oxford OX3 7LF (☎ 0865 64861)

ROBERTS, (David) Gwilym (Morris); CBE (1987); s of Edward Humphrey Roberts (d 1949), of Crosby, Merseyside, and Edith, *née* Roberts (d 1983); *b* 24 July 1925; *Educ* Merchant Taylors' Sch Crosby, Sidney Sussex Coll Cambridge (BA, MA); *m* 1, 16 Oct 1960, Rosemary Elizabeth Emily (d 1973), da of John Edmund Giles (d 1971), of Tavistock, Devon; 1 s ((Edward) Matthew Giles b 1963), 1 da (Annabel Elizabeth Giles b 1967); m 2, 14 Oct 1978, Wendy Ann, da of Dr John King Moore (d 1975), of Beckenham, Kent; *Career* Lt Cdr RNR, ret 1961; chartered civil engr; jt chm Acer Conslts Ltd 1987-, sr ptnr John Taylor & Sons 1981- (ptnr 1956-), dir Thomas Telford Ltd 1983-, pres ICE 1986-87; cncl memb NERC 1987-; govr: Chailey Sch 1987-, Roedean Sch 1987-; *Recreations* tennis, walking, local history, engineering archaeology of the Middle East; *Clubs* St Stephen's Constitutional, Utd Oxford and Cambridge, MCC; *Style*— Gwilym Roberts, Esq, CBE; North America Farm, Hundred Acre Lane, Westmeston, Hassocks, Sussex BN6 8SH (☎ 0273 890324); Acer Consultants Ltd, Artillery House, Artillery Row, London SW1P 1RY (☎ 01 222 8050, fax 01 222 7050, fax 01 222 0243, telex 918873 ACERA G)

ROBERTS, (Hywel) Heulyn; s of John Roberts (d 1949), of Aigburth, Liverpool, and Lily, *née* Jones (d 1955); *b* 16 Mar 1919; *Educ* Liverpool Inst; *m* 29 July 1944, Margaret Eluned, da of Griffith Llewelyn Davies (d 1940), of Llanarth, Cardiganshire; 1 s (Glyn Heulyn b 1961), 3 da (Meinir Heulyn b 1948, Rhian Heulyn b 1950, Mair Heulyn b 1956); *Career* memb: Cardiganshire CC 1952-74 (chm 1971-72), Dyfed CC 1973- (chm 1973-76); chm Dyfed-Powys Police Authority 1967-74, memb Welsh Counties Ctee 1973- (chm 1973-74), vice-chm Assoc of County Cncls (Wales & England) 1985-, memb Univ of Wales Ct and Univ of Wales Cncl 1974-, chm Welsh Folk Museum, St Fagans 1971-74, memb Sports Cncl for Wales 1972-84; High Sheriff of Dyfed 1982-83; admitted Druidic Order Gorsedd of Bards 1976; *Recreations* walking, reading; *Clubs* Farmers'; *Style*— David Osmond Davis Esq; Synod Parc, Synod, Llandysul, Dyfed (☎ 0545 580274)

ROBERTS, Hilary Llewelyn Arthur; s of Michael Hilary Roberts, MP (d 1983), of Cardiff, and Eileen Jean, *née* Billing; *b* 30 Sept 1953; *Educ* Whitchurch GS, Univ Coll of Wales Aberystwyth; *m* 5 Sept 1986, Shirley, da of Bryn Lewis, of Port Talbot; 1 s (Tom b 1986); *Career* barr 1978, head of chambers Newport 1985-; *Recreations* rugby; *Clubs* United Services Mess (Cardiff); *Style*— Hilary Roberts, Esq; 70 Brynteg, Rhiwbina, Cardiff (☎ 0222 610814); Westgate Chambers, Commercial St, Newport (☎ 0222 67403)

ROBERTS, Howland Langdon; s and h of Sir Gilbert Roberts, 7 Bt; *b* 19 August 1961; *Style*— Howland Roberts Esq

ROBERTS, Hugh Ashley; s of Rt Rev Dr Edward Roberts, *qv*, and Dorothy Frances, *née* Bowser (d 1982); *b* 20 April 1948; *Educ* Winchester, Corpus Christi Coll Cambridge (MA); *m* 13 Dec 1975, (Priscilla) Jane Stephanie, *qv*, er da of the Rt Hon The Lord Aldington, *qv*; 2 da (Sophie b 1978, Amelia b 1982); *Career* Christie Manson & Woods Ltd 1970-87 (dir 1978-87), dep surveyor of The Queen's Works of Art 1988-; *Recreations* gardening; *Clubs* Brooks's; *Style*— Hugh Roberts, Esq; Salisbury Tower, Windsor Castle, Berkshire (☎ 0753 855581)

ROBERTS, Ian; s of James William Roberts; *b* 23 Mar 1940; *Educ* Huddersfield Coll, Sheffield Univ; *m* 1966, Hilda Carole, *née* Bramwall; 2 s, 1 da; *Career* chm Wultex Machine Co Ltd 1978 (md 1974), dir Hampton Gold Mining Areas Ltd 1978; *Recreations* walking, music, english history; *Clubs* Marsden & Longwood Cons; *Style*— Ian Roberts Esq; 2 The Crescent, Filey, N Yorks

ROBERTS, Dame Jean; DBE (1963), JP, DL; *Educ* Albert Sch, Whitehill Sch; *m* 1922, Cameron Roberts (decd); 1 da; *Career* taught handicapped children; rep of Kingston Ward in Corpn of City of Glasgow 1929-1966; JP 1934, DL 1964, lord provost of the City of Glasgow and Ld-Lt of the Co of the City of Glasgow 1960-63; memb Scottish Arts Cncl 1963, memb Arts Cncl of Gt Britain 1965-68, chm Scottish Nat Orch Soc 1970-75; Hon LLD Glasgow 1977, Order of St Olav 1962; *Style*— Dame

Jean Roberts, DBE, JP, DL; 35 Beechwood Drive, Glasgow, G11 7ET (☎ 041-334 1930)

ROBERTS, Jeremy Michael Graham; QC (1982); s of Lt-Col John Michael Harold Roberts (d 1954), and Eileen Dora, (*née* Chaplin); *b* 26 April 1941; *Educ* Winchester Brasenose Coll Oxford (BA); *m* 25 July 1964, Sally Priscilla, da of Col Frederick Peter Johnson OBE, of Centre Cottage, Eversley Centre, Hants; *Career* barr Inner Temple 1965; recorder 1981; QC 1982; *Recreations* theatre, opera, reading, horse and dog racing, canals; *Style*— Jeremy Roberts, Esq, QC; 2 Dr Johnsons Buildings, Temple, London EC4 7AY (☎ 01 353 5371)

ROBERTS, Hon Mrs (Joan Mary); *née* Royle; da of Baron Royle (Life Peer d 1975); *b* 17 Dec 1920; *m* 1, 1942 (m dis 1963), Gordon Dixon; 1 s; m 2, 1975, Albert Roberts; *Style*— The Hon Mrs Roberts; Abbotswell, Frogham, Fordingbridge, Hants

ROBERTS, (Anthony) John; s of Leonard Douglas Treeweek Roberts, of Tavistock, Devon, and Margaret, *née* Long; *b* 26 August 1944; *Educ* Hampton Sch, Univ of Exeter (BA); *m* 3 Oct 1970, Diana June, da of Norman George Lamdin, of Bexhill-on-Sea, Sussex; 2 s (Ian, Neil); *Career* GPO: various posts incl PA to chief exec 1967-74, regnl bd memb for Personnel & Fin 1974-76, dir chms off 1976-80, sec of the PO 1980-82, dir Counter Servs 1982-85, md PO Counters Ltd 1985-; Freeman of The City of London 1982, Liveryman Worshipful Co of Gardeners 1988; CBIM 1986; *Recreations* watching rugby, squash, reading, music; *Clubs* Betchworth Park GC, Oxshott Squash; *Style*— John Roberts, Esq; Post Office Counters Ltd, Drury House, Blackfriars Rd, London SE1 9UA (☎ 01 922 1101)

ROBERTS, John Anthony; s of Walter Ben Roberts (d 1978), of Kirk Hammerton, Yorks, and Betty Joyce, *née* England; *b* 3 Dec 1940; *Educ* Harrow; *m* 9 Sept 1972, Margaret Mary, da of Maurice Houdmont, of Sheffied; 1 s (Piers b 1980), 2 da (Tabitha b 1973, Alexandra b 1975); *Career* HAC 1961-64; articled Mellors Basden & Co 1959-64; ptnr Coopers & Lybrand 1964-; memb: Trent Bus Sch Advsy Ctee, bd Prince's Youth Bus Tst (Nottingham area); pres: Notts Sco CA, Fransfield Horticultural Soc 1987-88; FCA 1964; *Recreations* wine, food, travel, music; *Clubs* Nottinghamshire United Services; *Style*— John Roberts, Esq; The Old Vicarage, Farnsfield, Nottinghamshire (☎ 0623 882 835); Coopers & Lybrand, 22a The Ropewalk, Nottingham NG1 5DT (☎ 0602 419 813, fax 0602 410 192, telex 377979)

ROBERTS, John Griffith; s of Griffith Roberts (d 1950), and Mary Ann Roberts (d 1942); *b* 10 June 1912; *Educ* Penygroes Co Sch; *m* 3 Nov 1948, Betty, da of David Thomas, MA (d 1963), of Maesyrhedyn, Pontardawe, Swansea; 1 da (Rhiannon b 1960); *Career* admitted slr 1934, in private practice 1935-, chm Rent Tbnl for N W Wales until ret 1982; memb: Caernarvonshire CC 1946-74 (chm 1965-66), Gwynedd CC 1974-, Pwllheli Town Cncl 1974- (former Mayor Pwllheli), Assoc of CCs and of Welsh Cos Ctee, Ct and Cncl of Univ of Wales, Court & Cncl of Univ Coll of N Wales; former chm: Gwynedd Educn Ctee, policy and resources ctee Gwynedd CC; chm: govrs Pwllheli Comprehensive Sch and Pwllheli Youth and Community Centre; rep Welsh Cos Ctee on Wales Advsy Body for local authy higher educn; memb Law Soc 1955; *Recreations* motoring, travel, billiards, bowls; *Clubs* Snooker Pwllheli, Clwb y Bont Literary Pwllheli; *Style*— John Roberts, Esq; Maesywern, Ffordd Talcymerau, Pwllheli, Gwynedd LL53 5PU (☎ 612 364); 26 Stryd Penlan, Pwllheli, Gwynedd (☎ 612 362)

ROBERTS, John Harvey Polmear; s of George Edward Polmear Roberts (d 1973), of Polmear, Illogan, Redruth, Cornwall, and Mary Harvey, *née* Sara (d 1975); *b* 11 June 1935; *Educ* Blundells Sch Tiverton Devon, Coll of Law; *m* 14 Jan 1961, (Mary) Patricia, da of Dr Richard Raphael Gamble, MB, BCh (d 1955), of Elm Tree House, Penkhull, Stoke on Trent, Staffs; 2 s (Hugh b 1962, Paul b 1963), 2 da (Emma b 1965, Louise b 1971); *Career* admitted slr 1957, HM Coroner for S Bucks 1980-, regnl chm Mental Health Review Tbnls for Oxford and Wessex Regions 1981-, managing ptnr Messrs Winter-Taylors 1984-; former pres and media spokesman Berks, Bucks and Oxon Inc Law Soc, memb Law Soc Negligence Panel; chm: Bucks Housing Assoc Ltd, Governing Cncl Pipers Corner Sch Ltd; dir: Wycombe Wanderers FC Ltd, Ercol Furniture Ltd, Ercol Hldgs Ltd; hon slr and tstee local St John Ambulance Bde, hon slr Welfare Offrs and local Royal Br Legion Branches and Clubs, legal cncllr Middle Thames Marriage Guidance Cncl; Freeman City of London, Liveryman and memb of Ct of Assts Worshipful Co of Feltmakers, Liveryman Worshipful Co of Coopers; memb: Law Soc, Coroners Soc of England and Wales, Medico-Legal Soc, Br Acad of Forensic Scis; SBStJ; *Recreations* golf, hill walking, reading; *Clubs* Oriental, Wig and Pen; *Style*— John Roberts, Esq; Badgers Hill, Speen, Aylesbury, Bucks HP17 0SP (☎ 024 028 289); Messrs Winter-Taylors, Park House, London Rd, High Wycombe, Bucks HP11 1BZ (☎ 0494 450 171 , fax 0494 441 815, telex 937217)

ROBERTS, John Herbert; s of John Emanuel Roberts (d 1970), and Hilda Mary, *née* Webb (d 1981); *b* 18 August 1933; *Educ* LSE (BSc), Univ of London; *m* 1965, Patricia Iris, da of John Duck (d 1977); 1 s (Matthew b 1974), 3 da (Catherine b 1966, Jessica b 1968, Emma b 1972); *Career* cmmnd RASC serv Suez and Cyprus 1955-56; tax inspr Inland Revenue 1957-81, under sec Dir of Ops Inland Revenue 1981-85; dir: Tech Div 2 Inland Revenue 1985-89, Compliance & Collection Div Inland Revenue 1988-; *Style*— John Roberts, Esq; New Wing, Somerset House, Strand, London WC2R 1LB (☎ 01 438 7649)

ROBERTS, John Lewis; CMG (1987); s of Thomas Hubert Roberts (d 1969), of Danygraig, Ynysmeudwy, Pontardawe, Swansea, and Hannah Meudwen, *née* Lewis (d 1967); *b* 21 April 1928; *Educ* Pontardawe GS, Trinity Hall Cambridge (BA); *m* 5 Dec 1952, Maureen Jocelyn, da of Lt-Col Denis Moriarty, IA (d 1985), of Eastbourne, Sussex; 2 s (Patrick b 4 Sept 1954, David b 31 Oct 1957); *Career* 2 Lt RA 1948-50; cnsllr Paris Embassy 1966-69; Civil Air Attaché Bonn Embassy 1959-62 and Def Supply; asst under sec of state for Equipment Collaboration MOD; ret 1988; FRSA 1988; *Recreations* angling, sailing, gardening; *Clubs* Piscatorial Society; *Style*— John Roberts, Esq, CMG; Ministry of Defence, Horse Guards Ave, London SW1 (☎ 01 218 3359)

ROBERTS, Lady Joya Mary Segar; da of Eric Scorer, OBE, and Maud Segar; *b* 27 July 1921; *Educ* St Marys Sch, Wantage Oxfordshire; *m* 1955, as his 2 w, Gen Sir Ouvry Lindfield Roberts, GCB, KBE, DSO (d 1986);; *Recreations* portrait artist (sketching animals), breeding Shetland Sheep dogs, Br white cats, gardening; *Style*— Lady Roberts; Upper Field House, 105 Church Way, Iffley, Oxford (☎ 0865 779 351)

ROBERTS, Hon Mrs Juliana Eveline; *née* Curzon; da of late 2 Viscount Scarsdale; *b* 1928; *Educ* Heathfield School Ascot; *m* 1, 1948 (m dis 1952), George Derek Stanley Smith (d 1963); 1 s, 1 da; m 2, 1953 (m dis 1956), Frederick Nettlefold; 1 da (Viscountess Windsor); m 3, 1956 (m dis 1962), as his 2 w, Sir Dudley Herbert Cunliffe-Owen, 2 Bt (d 1983); 1 da; m 4, 1962 (m dis 1972), as his 2 w, John Roberts; 1 s, 1 da; *Career* hotel mgmnt; *Recreations* sailing, fishing, gourment eating; *Clubs* LDYC (Ireland); *Style*— The Hon Mrs Juliana Roberts; Tomona, Bally Common, Nenagh, Co Tipperary; The Stables, Oakley Park, Ludlow, Shropshire

ROBERTS, Malcolm John Binyon; s of Sqdn Ldr Kenneth Arthur Norman Roberts (d 1973), and Greta Kathleen, *née* Cooper; *b* 3 July 1951; *Educ* St Edmund's Sch Canterbury; *m* 28 April 1984, Caroline Mary, da of John Harry Scrutton; 1 da (Iona Caroline b 27 March 1987); *Career* ptnr and dir Montagu Loebl Stanley 1979-86, dir Fleming Montagu Stanley 1986-; memb Stock Exchange 1978; *Recreations* tennis, gardening; *Clubs* City of London; *Style*— Malcolm Roberts, Esq; Bewley Lane House, Plaxtol, Kent TN15 0PS; 31 Sun St, London EC2 (☎ 01 377 9242)

ROBERTS, Hon (William Herbert) Mervyn; yst s of 1 Baron Clwyd (d 1955), and Hannah Rushton, *née* Sproston (d 1951); *b* 23 Nov 1906; *Educ* Trinity Coll Cambridge (BA); *m* 15 April 1947, Eileen Margaret, o da of late Alfred Thomas Easom, of Hillside, Abergele; 1 da (Catherine Angela b 14 Dec 1950); *Career* music teacher and composer; ARCM, LMusTCL, ALCM; *Style*— The Hon Mervyn Roberts; 17 Wimblehurst Road, Horsham, Sussex RH12 2EA

ROBERTS, Michael Curig; s of Thomas Curig Roberts, of 11 The Green, Caldy, Wirral, and Violet Evelyn Roberts; *b* 2 June 1938; *Educ* Shrewsbury; *m* 10 June 1967, Tessa Mary, da of Guy Hughes, of Yew Tree Plat, Winchester; 1 s (William Thomas Curig b 1971), 2 da (Phillippa Jill b 1969, Elizabeth Mary b 1974); *Career* ptnr Deloitte Haskins & Sells CAS, chm Mid Kent Water Co; chm Abbots Hill Sch Ltd, dir St James Malvern Ltd, memb London Residuary Body; tres Great Goddersden PCC; Freeman City of London, memb Worshipful Co of Gold and Silver Wyre Drawers; FCA; *Recreations* golf, tennis, reading, walking; *Clubs* Royal Liverpool GC, Ashridge GC, Gresham, RAC; *Style*— Michael Roberts, Esq; Lovatts Cottage, Gaddesden Row, Hemel Hempstead, Herts HP2 6HX; Deloitte Haskins & Sells, 128 Queen Victoria St, London EC4V 4DE (☎ 01 248 3913, fax 01 248 4897, telex 894941)

ROBERTS, Michael Victor; s of Ernest Alfred Roberts, of Waltham Abbey, Essex, and Lilian May, *née* Piper (d 1979); *b* 23 Sept 1941; *Educ* Cheshunt GS, Clare Coll Cambridge (BA, MA), Loughborough Tech Coll; *m* 6 July 1972, Jane Margaret, da of Francis Huddleston (d 1986); 1 s (Alfred b 1973), 1 da (Mary b 1975); *Career* asst librarian Loughborough Tech Coll 1964-66, asst cataloguer Leeds City Libraries 1966-68, dep bibliographical servs librarian City of London Libraries 1968-70; Guildhall Library: princ cataloguer 1970-73, keeper of enquiry servs 1973-82; dep dir City of London Libraries & Art Galleries 1982-; memb Harwich & Dover Ct Sailing Club; chm: Library Assoc Local Studies Gp, London & Home Countries branch; ctee memb Library Assoc London & Home Counties branch, memb Br Records Assoc Cncl; Freeman City of London 1983, Liveryman Worshipful Co of Fletchers 1984; assoc Library Assoc 1967; *Books* ed Guildhall Studies in London History 1973-81; *Recreations* fishing, walking, local history; *Style*— Michael Roberts, Esq; 13 Kings Head St, Harwich, Essex (☎ 0255 551 544); Guildhall Library, London EC2P 2EJ (☎ 01 260 1852)

ROBERTS, Paul Bartholemew; s of Joseph Roberts (d 1984), of London, and Angela, *née* Coletta; *b* 4 Sept 1941; *Educ* St Michael's Convent Finchley, St Aloyius Coll Highgate; *m* 1, 15 July 1972, Clare Celia Fay, da of Cochrane H Campbell, CBE, of Helensborough, Scotland; m 2, 10 Dec 1983 (m dis 1988), Nicola Anne, da of Dr Peter Stuart; 1 da (Lucy b 22 June 1984); *Career* dir John Rigby and Co Gunmakers 1984, chm Gun Trade Assoc 1986; memb Worshipful Co of Gunmakers 1980, Freeman City of London 1980; *Recreations* shooting, big game hunting, polo; *Clubs* Cowdray Park Polo; *Style*— Paul Roberts, Esq; Black Hall, Loxwood, W Sussex; 66 Great Suffolk St London SE1 0BU (☎ 01 620 0690, fax 01 928 9205, car tel 0836 283824)

ROBERTS, Peter David Thatcher; s of Leonard Charles Roberts (d 1978); *b* 1 Mar 1934; *Educ* Alleyns Sch Dulwich, Sir John Cass Coll, London Univ; *m* 1959, Elizabeth June Dodds; 1 s, 2 da; *Career* MN 1951-59, Lt RNR; Leinster/Hispania Maritime Ltd 1960-69: dir 1963, md 1965; Hays plc 1969 (dir 1983-); chm: Hays Marine Servs Ltd, Hays Commercial Servs Ltd, Hays Personnel Servs Ltd; dir Shipowners P & I Assoc Ltd; memb: gen ctee Lloyds Register of Shipping, Ct Watermen and Lightermen of River Thames; Liveryman Worshipful Co of Shipwrights; dir Shipowners P & L Assoc Ltd, memb gen ctee Lloyds Register of Shipping; *Recreations* offshore sailing, golf; *Clubs* Royal Ocean Racing, RAC, Wildernesse GC; *Style*— Peter Roberts, Esq; Callenders Cottage, Bidborough, nr Tunbridge Wells, Kent (☎ 0892 29053, office 0483 302203)

ROBERTS, Hon Mrs (Priscilla Jane Stephanie); *née* Low; MVO (1985); da of 1 Baron Aldington, KCMG, CBE, DSO, TD, PC, DL; *b* 4 Sept 1949; *Educ* Cranborne Chase, Westfield Coll and Courtauld Inst of Art London Univ; *m* 1975, Hugh Roberts, s of Rt Rev Edward Roberts, sometime Bishop of Ely; 2 da (Sophie Jane Cecilia, b 28 March 1978, Amelia Frances Albinia b 8 Feb 1982); *Career* curator of the Print Room Royal Library Windsor Castle 1975-; *Style*— The Hon Mrs Roberts, MVO; Salisbury Tower, Windsor Castle, Berks (☎ 0753 855581)

ROBERTS, Ven Raymond Harcourt; CB (1984), QHC (1980); s of Thomas Roberts (d 1981), and Caroline Maud, *née* Braine; *b* 14 April 1931; *Educ* Pontywaun GS Gwent, St Edmund Hall Oxford (BA MA); *Career* clerk in Holy Orders, Ordained Diocese of Monmouth, deacon 1956, priest 1957, curate of Bassaleg 1956-59, chaplain RNVR 1958-59, chaplain RN 1959-84; chaplain of the Fleet and archdn RN 1980-84; Hon Chaplain to The Queen 1980-84; hon canon of Gibraltar 1980-84; QHC 1980-84; gen sec Jerusalem and Middle East Church Assoc 1985; archdeacon Emeritus 1985; *Clubs* Royal Commonwealth Soc; *Style*— The Venerable Raymond H Roberts, CB; The Old Gatehouse, Castle Hill, Farnham, Surrey GU9 0AE

ROBERTS, Roger Hugh; JP; s of Norman Puleston Roberts, JP (d 1973), of Montmillan, Knowles Hill, Newton Abbot, Devon, and Marion Emily Louisa, *née* Crocker (d 1973); *b* 28 May 1934; *Educ* Kelly Coll, Guildford Law Coll; *m* 21 March 1959, Joan, da of Walter Blakeney Spencer; 1 s (Phillip b 1961), 4 da (Louise b 1960, Kathryn b 1963, Sally b 1967, Caroline b 1971); *Career* slr, chm bd of govrs Stover Sch; pres Newton Abbot YMCA; tstee Bearnes Charity; *Recreations* riding, skiing, boating; *Clubs* Rotary, Wessex Ski, SW Water Sports; *Style*— Roger Roberts, Esq, JP; Vikings, 22 Seymour Rd, Newton Abbot, Devon (☎ 0626 52359); Pidsley & Roberts, Slrs, 22 Union St, Newton Abbot, Devon (☎ 0626 54455)

ROBERTS, Rev Roger Lewis; CVO (1973); s of Robert Lewis Roberts, CBE (d 1956), and Muriel Grace, *née* Henderson (d 1945); *b* 3 August 1911; *Educ* Highgate,

Exeter Coll Oxford (MA); *m* 1935, Katie Agnes Mary, da of Ronald Perryman, of Chagford (d 1969); 1 s (John d 1977); *Career* Maj Army Educnl Corps 1942-43; headmaster Blundell's Sch 1943-47; ordained priest St Alban's 1948; ed Church Times 1960-68; chaplain: The Queen's Chapel of the Savoy, Royal Victorian Order 1961-73; Chaplain to HM The Queen 1969-81; *Clubs* Utd Oxford and Cambridge; *Style*— The Rev Roger Roberts, CVO; Thorn Farm Cottage, Chagford, Devon (☎ 064 73 2493)

ROBERTS, Roy Ernest James; CBE; *b* 14 Dec 1928; *Career* chm Simon Engrg plc, dep chm Dowty Gp plc; *Style*— Roy Roberts, Esq; Simon Engineering plc, Buchanan House, 3 St James's Square, London SW1Y 4JU (☎ 01 925 0666)

ROBERTS, Sir Samuel; 4 Bt (UK 1919); s of Sir Peter Roberts, 3 Bt (d 1985), and Judith Randall, *née* Hempson; *b* 16 April 1948; *Educ* Harrow, Sheffield Univ (LLB), Manchester Business Sch (MBA); *m* 1977, Georgina Ann, da of David Cory, of Bluetts, Peterston-super-Ely, nr Cardiff, S Glam; 3 da (Eleanor b 1979, Olivia b 1982, Amelia b 1985); *Career* barr Inner Temple 1972; chm Curzon Steels Ltd 1980-84; dir Cleyfield Properties Ltd; *Style*— Sir Samuel Roberts, Bt; 42 Markham Square, London SW3 4XA (☎ 01 589 3332)

ROBERTS, Dame Shelagh Marjorie; DBE (1981), MEP (EDG) London SW, by-election, Sept 1979-; da of Ivor Glyn Roberts (d 1937), of Ystalyfera, and Cecelia May Roberts (d 1963), of Liverpool; *b* 13 Oct 1924; *Career* memb: GLC 1970-81, Race Relations Bd 1973-78, Occupational Pensions Bd 1973-79, Port of London Authy 1975-79; *Recreations* swimming, skiing; *Clubs* Hurlingham, St Stephen's; *Style*— Dame Shelagh Roberts, DBE, MEP; 47 Shrewsbury House, Cheyne Walk, London SW3 5LW (☎ 01 352 3711)

ROBERTS, Sir (Edward Fergus) Sidney; CBE (1972); s of late E J Roberts; *b* 19 April 1901; *Educ* Scots Coll Sydney; *Career* pres Aust Country Party Qld 1967, chm Fed Cncl ACP 1969-74, memb Bd Qld Country Life Newspaper 1969-77, federal pres ACP 1969-; kt 1978; *see Debrett's Handbook of Australia and New Zealand for further details*; *Style*— Sir Sidney Roberts, CBE; 53 Eldernell Ave, Hamilton, Qld 4007, Australia

ROBERTS, Sir Stephen James Leake; s of Frank Roberts (d 1964), of Sandford Ave, Church Stretton, Shropshire, and Annie Leake (d 1933); *b* 13 April 1915; *Educ* Wellington GS; *m* 1940, Muriel, da of James Hobbins, of Rosedene, Lawley Bank, Shropshire; 2 s, 2 da; *Career* chm Milk Mktg Bd (W Midland regnl memb 1966-) 1977-; farmer (Salop delegate to NFU Cncl 1962-70); kt 1980; *Recreations* football; *Clubs* Farmers; *Style*— Sir Stephen Roberts; Little Worth, Little Wenlock, Telford, Shropshire TF6 5AX (☎ 0952 504569); Milk Marketing Board, Thames Ditton, Surrey (☎ 01 398 4101)

ROBERTS, Thomas Somerville; JP; s of Joseph Richard Roberts; *b* 10 Dec 1911; *Educ* Cardiff HS, Balliol Coll Oxford (BA); *m* 1, 1938, Ruth Moira Teasdale; 2 s; m 2, 1950, Margaret Peggy Anderson; *Career* port dir S Wales Ports 1970-75, chm S Wales Port Employers 1962-75, dir Dvpt Corpn Wales 1965-79, dep chm Welsh Dvpt Agency 1976-80, vice-pres Dvpt Corpn Wales 1979-83, chm Milford Haven Conservancy Bd 1976-82; hon fellow Univ Coll Cardiff; FCIT; *Recreations* TV; *Style*— Thomas Roberts, Esq, JP; Marcross Lodge, 9 Ely Rd, Llandaff, Cardiff (☎ 0222 561 153)

ROBERTS, Sir William James Denby; 3 Bt (UK 1909), of Milner Field, Bingley, WR of Yorkshire; s of Sir James Denby Roberts, OBE, 2 Bt (d 1973); *b* 10 August 1936; *Educ* Rugby, RAC Cirencester; *Heir* bro, Andrew Roberts; *Career* collector of vintage aircraft; fndr and former owner Strathallan Aircraft Collection; *Style*— Sir William Roberts, Bt; Strathallan Castle, Auchterarder, Perthshire; Combwell Priory, Flimwell, Wadhurst, Sussex

ROBERTS, William Morys; s of Gwilym James Roberts, MD (lately Maj Royal Army Med Corps 1945-46) Penarth, South Glamorgan, and Eileen Burford *née* Chivers; *b* 8 Dec 1934; *Educ* Kingswood Sch Bath Avon, Gonville and Caius Coll Cambs (BA, MA); *m* 29 July 1967, Patricia Anne, da of John Stratford Bettinson, of Ickleton, Cambridgeshire; 1 s (Simon b 1972), 2 da (Sarah b 1969, Alice b 1974); *Career* RA 1953-54, Intelligence Corps 1954-55, 2 Lt (later Lt RARO) 1955-67; CA Turquand, Youngs and Co 1958-61, dir: WM Brandt's Sons and Co Ltd 1971 (chief accountant 1965, sec 1970), Edward Bates and Sons Ltd 1973-75; ptnr Ernst and Whinney 1976 (head of London Insolvency 1987-); churchwarden All Saint's Church Great Chesterford 1976-; memb: Insolvency Rules Advsy Ctee 1984-; ACA 1961, FCA 1971; *Books* Insolvency Law and Practice (with J S H Gillies 1988); *Recreations* gardening; *Clubs* IOD; *Style*— W M Roberts, Esq; Brock House, Great Chesterford, Saffron Walden, Essex CB10 1PJ (☎ 0799 30470); Ernst and Whinney, Becket House, 1 Lambeth Palace Road, London SE1 7EU (☎ 01 928 2000, fax 01 928 1345, telex 885234)

ROBERTS, (Ieuan) Wyn Pritchard; MP (C) Conwy 1970-; s of Rev E P Roberts, of Anglesey; *b* 10 July 1930; *Educ* Harrow, Oxford Univ; *m* 1956, Enid Grace, da of W Williams, of Anglesey; 3 s; *Career* parly under-sec Welsh Office 1979-, oppn front bench spokesmman Welsh affrs 1974-75 and 1976-79, PPS to sec state Wales 1970-74; previously Welsh controller & exec producer TWW 1959-68, programme exec Harlech TV 1969; formerly journalist on Liverpool Post and news assist BBC; memb court of govrs Nat Museum and Nat Library Wales, Gorsedd Royal National Eisteddfod (1966); *Style*— Wyn Roberts, Esq, MP; Tan y Gwalia, Conway, Gwynedd (☎ 049 267 371)

ROBERTS-WRAY, Lady; Mary Howard; da of late Frank Howard Smith; *m* 1, 1935, Sir Ernest Hillas Williams, JP (d 1965); 1 da; m 2, 1965, as his 2 w, Sir Kenneth Roberts-Wray, GCMG, QC (d 1983); *Style*— Lady Roberts-Wray; The Old Golf House, Forest Row, Sussex

ROBERTSHAW, John Desmond; s of late Horace Robertshaw, and Elsie Robertshaw; *b* 19 Dec 1928; *Educ* Bembridge Sch, Oxford Univ; *m* 1961, Lesley Lynette, da of Harry Carter; 1 s, 2 da; *Career* York Tst Ltd, dep chm Utd Scientific Hldgs plc 1983- (dir 1965-); dir: Kode Int plc 1979-, Rights and Issues Investmt Tst Ltd 1962-, Safe Computing Ltd 1982-,Shorco Gp Hldgs plc, Assoc Farmers plc; memb Panel on Take-overs and Mergers; FCA, FIMBRA (dep chm); Panel on Take-overs and Mergers; FCA; *Recreations* golf; *Clubs* MCC; *Style*— John Robertshaw, Esq; Birches Farm, Isfield, Sussex (☎ 082 575 304); York Trust, Dauntsey House, Frederick Place, Old Jewry, London EC2R 8HN (☎ 01 606 2167, telex 889341)

ROBERTSON, Dr Alan; CBE; s of late William Arthur Robertson, and late Clarice Firby Robertson; *b* 15 August 1920; *Educ* Middlesbrough HS, Univ Coll Durham Univ, Balliol Coll Oxford (BSc, PhD); *m* 1948, Dorothy Eileen, da of late Frank Freeman; 2 s, 1 da; *Career* indust chemist; dir ICI 1975-82; chm Br Nutrition Fndn 1981-, memb cncl Pestalozzi Children's Village Tst, chm AGC (Agric Genetics Co) 1983-, vice-chm Br Waterways Bd 1983-; govr Lister Inst of Preventive Med 1985-; Royal Soc Chemistry Industl Medal 1982; Cncl China Soc; FRSC, CChem; *Recreations* all sports, gardening, biographical history; *Clubs* Farmers', Oriental; *Style*— Dr Alan Robertson, CBE; Woodlands, Tennysons Lane, Haslemere, Surrey GU27 3AF (☎ 0428 4196); British Waterways Bd, Melbury House, London NW1 6JX (☎ 01 725 8011)

ROBERTSON, Alastair Macdonald; s of John Robertson (d 1980), and Elizabeth Watt Robertson; *b* 4 Nov 1930; *Educ* George Heriot's Sch, Edinburgh Univ (MA, BSc); *m* 1969, Avril Margaret, *née* Willison; *Career* gen mangr and dir Scottish Equitable Life Assurance Soc ret 1982; chief exec and dir City of Edinburgh Life (formerly Stevenston Life) 1983-; non exec dir Edinburgh Money Mgmnt Ltd; FFA; *Recreations* golf, skiing, sailing (yacht 'Semlas' regd Leith); *Clubs* New (Edinburgh), Cullane Golf; *Style*— Alastair Robertson, Esq; 13 Cumlodden Ave, Edinburgh (☎ 031 337 4264); 43 Charlotte Sq, Edinburgh EH2 4HQ

ROBERTSON, Prof Sir Alexander; CBE (1963); s of Alexander Robertson and Barbara M Strath, of Netherley, Kincardineshire; *b* 3 Feb 1908; *Educ* Mackie Acad, Aberdeen Univ (MA, BSc), Royal Dick Veterinary Coll Edinburgh (MRCUS), Edinburgh Univ (PhD); *m* 1936, Janet Paul, da of John McKinlay, and Marion Gray, of Lanark; 2 da (Myra Gray, Barbara Ann); *Career* veterinarian; prof of hygiene Royal (Dick) Veterinary Coll Edinburgh 1944-53, prof animal health 1953-71, dean Faculty of Veterinary Med Edinburgh Univ 1964-70, dir Centre for Tropical Veterinary Med 1971-78, prof of tropical animal health 1971-78, emeritus 1978; pres Br Veterinary Assoc 1954; pres RCVS 1968; hon memb World Veterinary Assoc 1975; tstee Int Laboratory for Research in Animal Diseases 1973-82 (chm 1980-81); Hon LLD (Aberdeen) 1971, Hon DVSc (Melbourne) 1973, Hon FRCVS; FRSE, FRIC, FRSH, FRSZScot; kt 1970; *Books* Int Encyclopaedia of Veterinary Medicine (ed); *Style*— Prof Sir Alexander Robertson, CBE; 205 Mayfield Rd, Edinburgh EH9 3BD (☎ (031) 667 1242)

ROBERTSON, Alexander Hughes; s of Alexander Buchanan Robertson (d 1971), of Co Durham, and Anne, *née* Hughes (d 1977); *b* 20 Jan 1929; *Educ* Newcastle Royal GS, Durham Univ, Kings Coll (Dip Arch); *m* 17 Dec 1955, Pamela, da of James Foster Charlton, of Greasby, Wirral; 2 da (Sarah b 1957, Hilary b 1960), 1 s (Alexander b 1965); *Career* conslt architect; architect The Singapore Improvement Tst, sr ptnr The Alexander Robertson Ptnrship; FRIBA, FCIArb; Freeman City of London 1981, Liveryman Worshipful Co of Arbitrators 1982; *Recreations* study of historical bldgs, golf; *Clubs* Caledonian, Caldy Golf, Old Novocastrian Soc; *Style*— Alexander Robertson, Esq; 30 Darmonds Green, W Kirby, Wirral L48 5DU (☎ 051 625 5655); The Alexander Robertson Partnership, The Oaks, Village Rd, W Kirby, Wirral (☎ 051 625 9256)

ROBERTSON, Carol Anne; *née* Moseley; da of Kenneth Marsingall Moseley, of Northampton, and Agnes Beryl, *née* Pegler (d 1983); *b* 2 Sept 1935; *Educ* Northampton HS for Girls, Southampton Univ (BSc Hons); *m* 31 Aug 1961, John Corbett, s of John Corbett Robertson; 1 s (Jack b 1964), 2 da (Sophie b 1969, Bernadette b 1969); *Career* registered nurse Barts Hosp London 1959, registered midwife Radcliffe & Churchill Hosps Oxford 1959, registered health visitor Liverpool 1962, community health nurse tutor RCN London 1979; health visiting lectr South Bank Poly 1979-82; health visitor: Bootle Liverpool 1962-63, Ilford Essex 1963-64, Portsmouth 1977-78; ctee memb West Sussex HPR Trg Gp; memb: Warsash Theatre Gp, Warsash and Dist Art Gp; Portsmouth and SE Hants Health Authy 1983-86; *Books* Health Visiting in Practice (1987); *Recreations* walking, dog trg; *Style*— Mrs Carol Robertson; 14 Solent Dr, Hook Park, Warsash, Southampton SO3 9HB (☎ 04895 84788)

ROBERTSON, Brig Clive Henderson; DL (Dorset 1984); s of Lt-Col William Henderson Robertson, MC (d 1976), and Alice Maud, *née* Jackaman (d 1974); *b* 21 August 1927; *Educ* Radley; *m* 5 Sept 1959, Fiona Ann, da of Col Ronald Scott-Dempster; 1 s (Andrew b 19 May 1962), 1 da (Caroline b 22 June 1960); *Career* cmmnd 11 Hussars (PAO) 1947, ADC to GOC 7 Armd Div 1952-53 (despatches Malaya 1955 and 56), Staff Coll Camberley 1960, JSSC 1964, CO 11 Hussars 1968-69, CO Royal Hussars (PWO) 1969-71, mil asst to Mil Sec 1971-72, Col-Gen staff MOD 1972-74, Cmdt RAC Gunnery Sch 1974-75, Cdr RAC Centre Bovington 1975-78, vice-pres Reg Cmmns Bd 1978-80; asst priv sec to HRH The Duke of Edinburgh 1984-; chm: govrs Hardy's Sch 1982-83, Army Benevolent Fund Dorset 1983-; *Recreations* skiing, gardening, theatre; *Clubs* Cavalry & Guards; *Style*— Brig Clive Robertson, DL

ROBERTSON, Sheriff Daphne Jean Black; WS; da of Rev Robert Robert Black Kincaid (d 1980), and Ann Parker Collins,; *b* 31 Mar 1937; *Educ* Hillhead HS, Greenock Acad, Edinburgh Univ (MA), Glasgow Univ (LLB); *m* 1965, Donald Buchanan, s of Donald Robertson (d 1948), of Argyll; *Career* slr 1961; Sheriff of Glasgow and Strathkelvin 1979; *Style*— Sheriff Daphne Robertson, WS; Sheriff Court House, Glasgow (☎ 041 429 8888)

ROBERTSON, (James) Douglas Moir; DL (Surrey 1988); s of George Robertson (d 1984), and Jessie Barrie, *née* Brough; *b* 15 Nov 1938; *Educ* Trinity Acad Edinburgh, Herriot Watt Edinburgh; *m* 29 June 1963, Caroline Blanche, da of David Stephen Adams, of Edinburgh; 2 s (Graham b 1965, Brian b 1977), 1 da (Alison b 1970); *Career* princ Surveyors Collaborative 1969; exec dir: Bldg Cost Info Serv RICS 1962-, Bldg Maintenance Info Ltd 1970-; chm Bldg Data Banks Ltd 1985-; chm: Surrey CC 1987-, Nat Policy Brs Airports Consortium 1984-, Staines Preparatory Sch 1987-; memb ACC 1980-; FRICS 1969; FBIM 1971; *Recreations* golf; *Clubs* RAC; *Style*— Douglas Robertson, Esq, DL; 85/87 Clarence St, Kingston upon Thames, Surrey KT1 1RB (☎ 01 549 0102, fax 01 547 1238, car tel 0836 229 456)

ROBERTSON, Hon Mrs (Elizabeth Anne); *née* Bourne; da of Baron Bourne (Life Peer, d 1982), and Baroness Bourne, *qv*; *b* 1931; *m* 1952, Ian McKay Robertson (d 1984); children; *Style*— The Hon Mrs Robertson; Belmont House, Donhead St Mary, Shaftesbury, Dorset

ROBERTSON, Geoffrey Ronald; QC (1988); s of Francis Albert Robertson, of 20 Lucretia Ave, Longueville, Sydney, Australia, and Bernice Joy, *née* Beattie; *b* 30 Sept 1946; *Educ* Epping Boys' HS, Sydney Univ (BA, LLB), Oxford Univ (BCL); *Career* called to bar Middle Temple 1973; visiting fell: Univ of NSW Australia 1977, Univ of Warwick 1980-81; memb exec cncl ICA, exec memb Freedom of Info Campaign; *Books* Reluctant Judas (1976), Obscenity (1979), People Against the Press (1983), Media Law (1984), Hypotheticals (1986), Does Dracula Have Aids? (1987); *Recreations* tennis, opera, fishing; *Style*— Geoffrey Robertson, Esq, QC; 14 Thornhill Crescent,

London N1 (☎ 01 609 0554); 1 Dr Johnson's Buildings, Temple EC4 (☎ 01 353 9328, fax 01 353 4410)

ROBERTSON, George Islay MacNeill; MP (Lab) Hamilton 1978-; s of George and Marion Robertson; *b* 12 April 1946; *Educ* Dunoon GS, Dundee Univ; *m* 1970, Sandra Wallace; 2 s, 1 da; *Career* oppn front bench spokesman: Scottish Affrs 1979-80, Def 1980-81, Foreign and Cwlth Affrs 1981-; princ spokesman on Euro and Community Affrs 1985-; vice-chm Br Cncl 1985-; cncl memb RIIA 1984-; PPS to Social Servs Sec 1979; chm Scottish Cncl Lab Pty 1977-78, memb Lab Scottish Exec 1973-79; former bd memb: Scottish Devpt Agency, Scottish Tourist Bd, Police Advsy Bd Scotland; former Scottish organiser GMWU; *Style*— George Robertson, Esq, MP; 3 Argyle Park, Dunblane, Perths; c/o House of Commons, London SW1A 0AA

ROBERTSON, (Thomas) Iain; TD (1966); s of Thomas Herbert Robertson, BEM (d 1987), of Glasgow, and Jessie, *née* Watson (d 1988); *b* 2 Nov 1931; *Educ* Glasgow Acad; *m* 31 Aug 1956, Joyce Elizabeth, da of James Kinghorn (d 1970), of Glasgow; 4 da (Pauline b 1958, Sally b 1961, Nicola b 1963, Wendy b 1970); *Career* Nat Serv 12 Royal Lancers 1949, ret Maj RA TA 1966; joined Stock Exchange 1956, ptnr Campbell Neill & Co Glasgow (sr ptnr 1969, chm and chief exec 1986), memb Lloyds of London 1987; elder Church of Broom, dir Glasgow Bute Benevolent Soc; past deacon Incorpns of Gardeners of Glasgow, memb Incorpns of Bonnetmakers & Dyers of Glasgow; memb Stock Exchange, TSA, FIMBRA; *Recreations* sailing, fishing; *Clubs* RSAC, Western (Glasgow), Caledonian; *Style*— T Iain Robertson, Esq, TD; Ennismor, 25 Lethington Rd, Whitecraigs, Glasgow, G46 6TB (☎ 041 639 3048); Campbell Neill & Co Ltd, Stock Exchange House, Glasgow, G2 1JN (☎ 041 248 6271, fax 041 221 5962)

ROBERTSON, Maj-Gen Ian Argyll; CB (1968), MBE (1947), DL (Nairn 1973); s of John Argyll Robertson (d 1943), and Sarah Lilian Pitt Healing (d 1962); *b* 17 July 1913; *Educ* Winchester, Trinity Coll Oxford; *m* 1939, Marjorie Violet Isobel, da of Maj Malcolm Bedford Duncan (d 1956); 2 da; *Career* cmmnd Seaforth Highlanders 1934-, cmd 1 Bn Seaforth Highlanders 1954-57, cmd Sch Inf 1963-64, cmmd 51 Inf Div 1964-66 (ret 1968); HM Vice-Lord-Lt Highland Region 1973-; *Recreations* gardening, golf; *Clubs* Army and Navy, MCC, Vincent's (Oxford); *Style*— Maj-Gen Ian Robertson, CB, MBE, DL; Brackla House, Nairn (☎ 066 77 220)

ROBERTSON, Rear Adm Ian George William; CB (1974), DSC (1944); s of William Henderson Robertson MC (d 1978), and Alice Maud Jackerman (d 1974); memb of Clan Donnachaidh; *b* 21 Oct 1922; *Educ* Radley; *m* 1947, Barbara Irene, da Frank Hird Holdsworth (d 1970); 1 s (Mark), 1 da (Jennifer); *Career* CO: HMS Keppel 1960-62, HMS Mohawk 1963-65, HMS Seahawk 1965-67, HMS Eagle 1970-72; Adm cmd reserves and dir of Naval Recruiting 1972-74; Imperial Def Coll 1968; *Recreations* golf, sailing, DIY; *Clubs* Naval, Piltdown Golf; *Style*— Rear Adm Ian Robertson; Moons Oast, Barcombe, Rd, Piltdown, E Sussex TN22 3XG

ROBERTSON, Ian James; s of James Robertson (d 1986), of Drumfin, Killearn, Stirlingshire, and Mary Young Brown Steele; *b* 21 June 1937; *Educ* Merchiston Castle Sch, Edinburgh, Glasgow Univ (BA); *m* 14 Sept 1963, Fiona Elizabeth, da of Robert Bruce Mackinnon, of Bearsoen, Glasgow; 1 s (J I David), 2 da (Virginia, Victoria); *Career* dep chm Whatlings plc 1970-84; devpts dir: Whatlings, Alfred McAlpine Scotland 1984; dir Scottish Opera Theatre Royal Ltd; memb East End Exec Glasgow, incorporation of Wrights of Glasgow; FBIM 1984; *Recreations* opera, golf, fishing; *Clubs* Buchanan Castle, RSAC; *Style*— Ian Robertson, Esq; Whatlings plc, North Claremont St, Glasgow G3 7LF (☎ 041 331 2151)

ROBERTSON, Ian Macbeth; CB (1976), LVO (1956); s of Sheriff J A T Robertson (d 1942), of Edinburgh, and Brenda Robertson, *née* Lewis (d 1943); *b* 1 Feb 1918; *Educ* Melville Coll, Edinburgh Univ (MA); *m* 1947, Anne Stewart, da of John McMillan Marshall, CBE (d 1949); *Career* civil servant; private sec to min of State Scottish Off 1951-52 and to Sec of State for Scotland 1952-55; under sec Scottish Off 1963-78; sec of cmmns for Scotland 1978-83; JP Edinburgh 1978; memb Williams Ctee on Nat Museums and Galleries in Scotland 1979-81; chm bd of govrs Edinburgh Coll of Art 1981-88; hon DLitt Herriott-Watt Univ 1988; HRSA 1987; *Clubs* New (Edinburgh); *Style*— Ian Robertson, Esq, CB, LVO; Napier House, 8 Colinton Rd, Edinburgh EH10 5DS

ROBERTSON, Sir James Anderson; CBE (1963), QPM; s of James Robertson, of Glasgow (d 1934), and Mary Rankin Anderson (d 1950); *b* 8 April 1906; *Educ* Provanside Sch Glas, Glasgow Univ (BL); *m* 1942, Janet Lorraine Gilfillan, da of William MacFarlane (d 1952), of Largs, Ayrshire; 2 s, 1 da; *Career* chief constable Glasgow 1960-71, chm Glasgow Standing Conference of Voluntary Youth Orgn; kt 1968; *Recreations* gardening; *Style*— Sir James Robertson, CBE, QPM; 3 Kirklee Rd, Glasgow G12 (☎ 041 339 4400)

ROBERTSON, James Geddes; CMG (1961); s of Capt Alexander Myron Robertson (ka 1916), and Elspeth Duncan Robertson, *née* Geddes (d 1951); *b* 29 Nov 1910; *Educ* Fordyce Acad Banffshire, George Watson's Coll Edinburgh, Edinburgh Univ (MA); *m* 1939, Marion Mitchell, da of David Mitchell Black (d 1944), of Edinburgh; 1 s (Duncan), 1 da (Christine); *Career* WWII serv 1939-45, RAF 1942-44; civil servant entered Min of Labour 1933; asst sec 1956; on exchange to Australian Cwlth Dept of Labour 1947-49; overseas devpt Miny of Labour 1949-61; memb of govt delgns to ILO 1956-60, Social Ctee Brussels Treaty Orgn and Wester European Union 1950-61, Social Ctee Cncl of Europe 1953-61; safety and health dept Miny of Labour 1961-63; trg dept 1963-65; under-sec dept of econ affairs (subsequently dept of environment) 1965-71; chm Northern Econ Planning Bd 1965-71; ret 1971; memb: Industl Tbnls Panel 1971-73, Northern Rent Scrutiny Bd 1973-74, Rent Assessment Panel (Scotland) 1975-81; *Style*— James Robertson, Esq, CMG; 1/1 Wyvern Park, Edinburgh EH9 2JY

ROBERTSON, Maj James Pearce; s of Capt Ronald Douglas Robertson (d 1968), and Mary Pearce, *née* Wills (d 1963); *b* 7 July 1920; *Educ* Stowe, St Andrew's Univ, King Alfred's Coll Winchester; *m* 20 July 1957, June Mary O'Carroll, da of Maj-Gen Anthony Gerald O'Carroll Scott, CB, CBE, DL (d 1980); *Career* WWII cmmnd RA 1939, served Western Desert (invalided UK) 1941, NW Europe (wounded Holland) 1944, Liberation Norway 1945, Palestine 1946, Malta 1955, Cyprus 1959, Aden 1961 ret 1964; schoolmaster 1966-85, head of history dept, cncl head of house in Hants Comprehensive Schs; vice-chm parish cncl 1978-, memb PCC 1978-, fund raising Save the Children Fund 1978-, organiser Sealed Knot Soc, lectr to Womens' Inst; *Recreations* whipping-in to hounds, polo, all team games (regimental rugger player), historical research, carpentry, restoring old houses, gardening, photography, writing; *Style*— Major James P Robertson; Rose Cottage, Penton Mewsey, nr Andover, Hampshire (☎ 026 477 2772)

ROBERTSON, Jean; CBE (1986); da of Alexander Robertson (d 1967), and Jean Turmer, *née* McCartney (d 1987); *b* 21 Sept 1928; *Educ* Mary Erskine Sch for Girls; *Career* Queen Alexandra's Naval Nursing Serv: RN Hosp Chatham 1955, HMNAS Sanderline 1957, RN Hosp Haslar 1968 (1958, 1963), RN Hosp Hong Kong 1959, RN Hosp Plymouth 1959, HMS Terror Singapore 1961, RN Hosp Malta 1966, RN Hosp Gibraltar 1972, MOD (N) Empress State London 1974, RN Hosp Mauritius 1975, Matron RN Hosp Plymouth 1976, MOD (N) Matron-in-Chief's Dept 1979, Surg-Rear Adml Naval Hosp 1981, Matron-in-chief 1983-86; involved with Help the Aged; *Recreations* swimming, gardening, lace making; *Style*— Miss Jean Robertson; 14 The Haven, Gosport, Hants PO12 2BD (☎ 0705 582301)

ROBERTSON, Lady Joan Patricia Quirk; *née* Wavell; da of Field Marshal 1 Earl Wavell, GCB, GCSI, GCIE, CMG, MC, PC (d 1950), and Eugénie Marie, CI, DStJ, *née* Quirk (d 1987); *b* 23 April 1923; *m* 1, 27 Jan 1943, Maj Hon Simon Nevil Astley (d 1946), yr s of 21 Baron Hastings and Lady Marguerite Nevill (da of 3 Marq of Abergavenny); 1 da; m 2, 19 June 1948, Maj Harry Alastair Gordon, MC (d 1965); 2 da; m 3, 1973, Maj Donald Struan Robertson, Scots Gds, s of Rt Hon Sir Malcolm Robertson, GCMG, KBE (d 1951); *Style*— Lady Joan Robertson; Winkfield Plain Farm, Winkfield, Windsor, Berks SL4 4QU (☎ 0344 885360)

ROBERTSON, Maj-Gen John Carnegie; s of Sir William Charles Fleming Robertson, KCMG (d 1937), and Elizabeth Dora, *née* Whelan (d 1978); *b* 24 Nov 1917; *Educ* Cheltenham, Sandhurst; *m* 5 July 1961, Teresa Mary Louise (Tessa), da of Cecil Theodore Porter, of Heather Cottage, Sunningdale, Berks; *Career* cmmnd Glos Regt 1938, 2 Glos 1938-39, BEF 1940 (captured before Dunkirk POW 1940-45), Staff Capt NI 1947-48, Co Cdr 1 Wilts, Staff Capt 29 Bde 1948 (attached JAG Dept), Staff Capt Dir Army Legal Servs Egypt 1949-52; Maj Dep Asst Dir Army Legal Servs 1952-58: Kenya, London, Hong Kong; asst dir Army Legal Servs HQ BAOR 1958-60, Lt-Col 1960-62, OC Army Legal Aid (Civil UK) 1962-64, Col asst dir Army Legal Servs Kenya 1965-66, OC Civil Legal Aid Servs BAOR 1966- 69, dep dir Army Legal Servs HQ FARELF 1969-71, Col Legal Staff dir Army legal Servs HQ BAOR 1971-73, dir Army legal Servs 1973-76; called to the Bar Gray's Inn 1949; *Clubs* Huntercombe GC; *Style*— Maj-Gen John Robertson; Berry House, Nuffield, Nr Henley-on-Thames, Oxon RG9 5SS (☎ 0491 641 740)

ROBERTSON, John Davie Manson; OBE (1978); s of John Robertson (d 1972), and Margaret Gibson Wright (d 1987); *b* 6 Nov 1929; *Educ* Kirkwall GS, Univ of Edinburgh (BL); *m* 25 Feb 1959, Elizabeth Amelia, da of Donald William Macpherson (d 1987); 2 s (John b 1961, Sinclair b 1967), 2 da (Susan b 1959, Fiona b 1965); *Career* Anglo Iranian Oil Co (later BP) UK and M East 1953, Robertson Gp 1958- (chm 1980-), dir Stanley Servs Ltd 1987-; cross country and athletics Univ Blues, hon vice consul Denmark 1972-, hon consul W Germany 1976-, Hon Sheriff Grampian Highland and Islands 1977-, chm Orkney Health Bd 1983- (memb 1974, vice chm 1979-83), chm Scottish Health Mgmnt Efficiency Gp 1985-; memb: Highlands and Islands Devpt Consultative Cncl 1988-, Bd of Mgmnt Orkney Hosps 1970-74; chm: Orkney Savings Ctee 1974-78, Highland and Islands Savings Ctee 1975-78; memb Nat Savings Ctee for Scotland 1975-78, chm Childrens Panel Orkney 1971-76 (chm Advsy Ctee 1977-82); FSA Scot 1981; Royal Order of Knight of Dannebrog Denmark 1982, The Cavalier's Cross of the Order of Merit W Germany 1986; *Books* Uppies & Doonies (1967); *Recreations* rough shooting, fishing; *Clubs* New Edinburgh; *Style*— John D M Robertson, Esq, OBE; Shorelands, Kirkwall, Orkney, (☎0856 2530); S & J D Robertson Grp Ltd, Shore St, Kirkwall, Orkney, (☎0856 2961, fax Kirkwall 5043, telex 75498)

ROBERTSON, John Windeler; s of Maj John Bruce Robertson (d 1973); *b* 9 May 1934; *Educ* Winchester; *m* 1959 (m dis 1984), Jennifer-Ann, da of Gontran Gourdou, of Switzerland; 1 s, 1 da; m 2, 1987, Rosemary Helen Jane Banks; *Career* dep chm Stock Exchange 1976-79 (memb 1956-, memb cncl 1966-86), sr ptnr Wedd Durlacher Mordaunt & Co 1979-86; dir Securities Assoc 1986-88; dep chm Barclays de Zoete Wedd Securities Ltd (BZW) 1986-88; *Recreations* deer stalking, golf, powerboating; *Clubs* City of London; *Style*— John Robertson Esq; Flat 9, 4 Tedworth Square, London SW3 4DY (☎ 01 351 7918)

ROBERTSON, Lewis; CBE (1969); s of John Robertson (d 1976); *b* 28 Nov 1922; *Educ* Trinity Coll Glenalmond; *m* 1950, Elspeth, *née* Badenoch; 3 s, 1 da; *Career* served RAF; industrialist, administrator, accountancy; dir Scottish & Newcastle Breweries 1975-87; dep chm and chief exec: Scottish Devpt Agency 1976-81, Grampian Hldgs Ltd 1971-76; chm: F H Lloyd Hldg 1982-87, Triplex Foundries Gp 1983- (now Triplex Lloyd plc), Girobank Scotland 1984-, Borthwicks 1985-89, FJC Lilley plc 1986-; dir Whitman Int SA Geneva 1987-; tstee (and memb exec ctee) Carnegie Tst for Univs of Scotland 1963-; memb: Monopolies Cmmn 1969-76, Restrictive Practices Court 1983-; FRSE; *Recreations* work, reading, classical music, things italian, listmaking; *Clubs* Athenaeum, New (Edinburgh); *Style*— Lewis Robertson Esq, CBE; 32 Saxe-Coburg Place, Edinburgh EH3 5BP (☎ 031 332 5221)

ROBERTSON, Hon Mrs (Lucy); *née* Maclay; yr da of 2 Baron Maclay, KBE (d 1969), and Nancy, Baroness Maclay, *qv*; *b* 24 July 1938; *Educ* St Leonard's Sch; *m* 1966, James Ian Alexander Robertson, eld s of Capt Ian Greig Robertson, DSO, DSC, RN (d 1987), of Mallorca; 3 s, 1 da; *Clubs* Lansdowne; *Style*— The Hon Mrs Robertson; Glenside Farm, Plean, Stirlingshire (☎ 0786 816655)

ROBERTSON, Hon Mrs (Myrtle Olive Felix - Ziki); *née* Arbuthnot; da of Baroness Wharton in her own right (tenth holder of the title, cr E 1544-45; she d 1974, since when the Barony has fallen into abeyance between her 2 daughters; *see also* Hon Mrs Appleyard-List) by her 1 husb, David Arbuthnot, s of Maj John Arbuthnot, MVO (gn of Sir Robert Arbuthnot, 2 Bt); *b* 20 Feb 1934; *m* 1958, Henry Macleod, s of Henry Robertson, of Elgin; 3 s (Myles b 1964, Christopher and Nicholas, twins, b 1969), 1 da (Lesley b 1966); *Style*— The Hon Mrs Robertson; 9 Gipsy Lane, SW15 (☎ 01 876 8300)

ROBERTSON, Lady; Nancy; da of H S Walker, of Huddersfield; *m* 1926, Sir James Wilson Robertson, KT, GCMG, GCVO, KBE (d 1983, Govr-Gen and C-in-C Federation of Nigeria 1955-60); 1 s, 1 da; *Style*— Lady Robertson; The Old Bakehouse, Cholsey, nr Wallingford, Oxon

ROBERTSON, Cmdt Dame Nancy Margaret; DBE (1957, CBE 1953, OBE 1946); da of Rev William Cowper Robertson and Jessie, *née* McGregor; *b* 1 Mar 1909; *Educ* Esdaile Sch, Edinburgh, Paris; *Career* secretarial work in London and Paris 1928-39; WRNS 1939, dir of WRNS 1954-58 now retired; *Recreations* needlework, gardening;

Style— Cmdt Dame Nancy Robertson, DBE; 14 Osborne Way, Tring, Herts (☎ 044 282 2560)

ROBERTSON, Neil; JP, DL (1970); s of Ian Stephen Robertson (d 1956); *b* 13 Mar 1921; *Educ* Cargilfield Sch, Loretto Sch; *m* 1948, Marie Forbes, da of Maj Robert Young (d 1957); 1 s, 4 da; *Career* farmer, co dir, ccncllr 1955-75, cncllr regnl 1974-86; convener of Moray Co 1971-75; past pres: Elgin Branch NFU, Moray Area NFU; former memb Scottish Agric Advsy Ctee, former dir RHASS; past chm: Banff Moray & Nairn River Bd, Northeast River Purificationn Bd; chm Grampian Manpower Ctee 1974-82, memb of Cncl on Tbnls 1981-87; *Recreations* shooting, golf; *Style*— Neil Robertson, JP, DL; Millburn, Linkwood, Elgin, Moray (☎ 0343 2139, office 0343 2355)

ROBERTSON, Peter Duncan Neil; s of Laurence Neil Robertson, Flt Lt RAF (despatches, d 1961), and Edith Pamela, *née* Moorhouse; *b* 23 May 1940; *Educ* Sandroyd Sch Harrow; *m* 13 July 1962, Diana Helen, da of Dr R C Barbor, MRCP, of Rosefield Peldon, Nr Colchester, Essex; 1 s (Toby Neil b 1970), 1 da (Tania Gay b 1967); *Career* trainee R C Greig and Co 1958-61, private client and pension fund mgmnt dir: M & G Investment Mngmnt Ltd, External Investment Tst, Drayton Far East Tst 1965-; fund mangr and investment dir M & G Investment Management 1971-, investmt dir Japanese Dept and Pacific Basin; *Recreations* shooting, golf, tennis, cooking, racing; *Clubs* Turf; *Style*— Peter Robertson, Esq; 31 Dancer Road, London SW6 4DU (☎ 01 731 7118); M & G Investment Management Ltd, Three Quays, Tower Hill, London EC3 6BQ (car ☎ 0860 355619, office 01 626 4588, fax 01 623 8615, telex 887196)

ROBERTSON, Peter McKellar; OBE (1988), JP (Ayrshire 1976), DL (1960); s of John McKellar Robertson, CBE (d 1939); *b* 5 June 1923; *Educ* Marlborough, Royal Tech Coll Glasgow (BSc); *m* 1951, Elspeth Marion, da of late James Charles Hunter, of Glentyan, Kilbarchan, Renfrewshire; 1 s, 2 da; *Career* RN; landowner; memb: Ayrshire CC 1949-75, cmmn Local Authy Accounts Scotland 1974-87 (vice chm 1983-87); *Recreations* music; *Clubs* Western (Glasgow), Prestwick Golf; *Style*— Peter Robertson, Esq, OBE, JP, DL; Noddsdale, Largs, Ayrshire (☎ 0475 672382)

ROBERTSON, Robert; CBE (1967), JP (1958); s of Rev Wlliam Robertson, HCF s (d 1950), and Jessie Douglas (d 1961, authoress of Patchwork Quilt); *b* 15 August 1909; *Educ* Forres Acad, Royal Tech Coll Glasgow, Strathclyde Univ; *m* 1938, Jean, da of James Moffatt (d 1931), of Glasgow; 1 s (Struan), 1 da (Margaret); *Career* served WWII with jt responsibility for safe passage of special trains for important persons such as Churchill (code Rapier), Eisenhower (code Cutlass), Royalty (code Grove); ambulance trains for D day landings; civil engr; govr Jordanhill Coll of Educn 1960-83; memb: Scottish Cncl for Res in Educn, Scottish Cncl for Commercial Admin and Professional Educn 1962-68; chm: Renfrewshire Educn Ctee 1960-72, Sec of State for Scotland's standing ctee on Supply and Trg of Teachers for Further Educn 1963-72, Nat Ctee for In-service Trg of Teachers (Scotland) 1966-70, Renfrewshire CC 1972-75; govr Jordanhill Sch of Further Educn 1968-83; chm E Renfrewshire Cons Assoc 1971-74; memb Strathclyde Regnl Cncl 1974-; memb cncl: Glasgow Coll of Bldg and Printing, Langside Coll, Reid Kerr Coll 1974-86; FEIS Stirling Univ 1973-; *Publications* Robertson Report on Supply and Training of Teachers in Scotland (HMSO 1965); *Recreations* painting, fishing; *Style*— Robert Robertson, Esq, CBE, JP; 24 Broadwood Park, Alloway, Ayrshire (☎ 0292 43820); Castlehill, nr Maybole, Ayrshire (☎ 029 250 337)

ROBERTSON, Ronald Foote; CBE (1980); s of Thomas Robertson (d 1934), and Mary, *née* Foote (d 1968); *b* 27 Dec 1920; *Educ* Perth Acad, Univ of Edinburgh (MB ChB, MD); *m* 1949, Dorothy Tweedy, da of George Wilkinson (d 1983); 3 da (Muriel (decd), Alison, Diana); *Career* conslt physician Royal Infirmary of Edinburgh 1974-86, physician to The Queen in Scotland 1977-85; pres: Royal Coll of Physicians of Edinburgh 1976-79, BMA 1983-84; FRCP; *Recreations* curling, fishing, gardening; *Clubs* New (Edinburgh); *Style*— Dr R F Robertson; 15 Wester Coates Terr, Edinburgh EH12 5LR (☎ 031 337 6377)

ROBERTSON, Sir Rutherford Ness; AC (1980), CMG (1968); ....; s of Rev Joshua Robertson (d 1971), and Josephine, *née* Hogan (d 1939); *b* 29 Sept 1913; *Educ* St Andrew's Coll Christchurch NZ, Sydney Univ (BSc, DSc), St John's Coll Cambridge Univ (PhD); *m* 1937, Mary Helen Bruce, da of George Thomas Rogerson (d 1926); 1 s; *Career* res scientist Ctee Scientific and Res Organisation 1946-62; prof of botany Adelaide Univ 1962-69 (now emeritus), chm Aust Res Grants Ctee 1965-69, dir Res Sch of Biological Sciences Aust Nat Univ 1973-78, pro-chllr Aust Nat Univ 1984-86; dep chm Aust Science and Technol Cncl 1977-81; FRS 1961; kt 1972; *see Debrett's Handbook of Australia and New Zealand for further details*; *Books* Electrolytes in Plant Cells (co-author, 1961), Protons, Electrons, Phosphorylation and Active Transport (1968), The Lively Membranes (1983); *Recreations* reading, water colours; *Clubs* Union (Sydney); *Style*— Sir Rutherford Robertson, AC, CMG; PO Box 9, Binalong, NSW 2584

ROBERTSON, Brigadier Sidney Park; MBE (1962), TD (1967), JP (1968); s of John Davie Manson Robertson (d 1934); *b* 12 Mar 1914; *Educ* Kirkwall GS, Edinburgh Univ (BCom); *m* 1940, Elsa Miller, da of James Miller Croy (d 1943), 1 s, 1 da; *Career* Brig 51 Highland Div 1966-67 (cmmnd RA 1940, despatches NW Europe 1945; Lt-Col cmdg Lovat Scouts 1962-65); Hon Col Cmdt Royal Regt of Artillery 1977-80, Hon Col (Ulster and Scottish) Light Air Defence Regt 1975-80; mangr Anglo-Iranian Oil Co Middle East 1946-51; mangr operations/sales S Div Shellmex & BP 1951-54, fndr S & J D Robertson Gp Ltd 1954 (chm 1965-79); chm: Orkney Hosps Health Bd 1965-79, Royal Artillery Cncl of Scotland 1980-84; vice-pres Nat Artillery Assoc 1977-; Hon Sheriff Grampian Highlands and Islands 1969-; hon area vice-pres Royal Br Legion 1975-; hon pres Orkney Bn Boys' Brigade; vice-pres RNLI Inst 1985-; DL 1968, Vice Lord-Lt for the Islands Area of Orkney 1987-; MIBS 1936; *Recreations* travel, fishing; *Clubs* Army and Navy, Caledonian, New (Edinburgh); *Style*— Brig Sidney Robertson, MBE, TD, JP; Daisybank, Kirkwall, Orkney KW15 1LX (☎ 0856 2085)

ROBERTSON, Simon Manwaring; s of David Lars Manwaring Robertson, of Ketches, Newick, Sussex, and Pamela Lauderdale Manwaring, *née* Meares; *b* 4 Mar 1941; *Educ* Cothill Sch, Eton; *m* 26 June 1965, Virginia Stewart Manwaring, da of Mark Richard Norman, of Garden House, Much Hadham, Herts; 1 s (Edward Manwaring b 1968), 2 da (Selina Manwaring b 1969, Lorna Manwaring b 1973); *Career* dir: Kleinwort Benson Ltd 1976, Mowlem Gp plc 1987, Kleinwort Benson Gp plc 1988; *Recreations* being in the Prättigau, tennis; *Clubs* Boodles, Racquet (New York); *Style*— Simon Robertson, Esq; Kleinwort Benson Ltd, 20 Fenchurch St, London EC2 (☎ 01 623 8000)

ROBERTSON, (Charles) Speirs; s of Capt Charles Robertson, MC, CA (d 1952), of Hyndland, Glasgow, and Marion, *née* Sutter (d 1971); *b* 30 June 1924; *Educ* Glasgow Acad, Glasgow Univ (BSc); *m* 28 March 1953, Nora Beatrice, da of George Arthur Kearle (d 1978), of Hoole Chester; 2 s (Morven b 1954, Graham b 1959), 1 da (Lynne b 1962); *Career* chm Speirs Robertson & Co Ltd 1967-; MIMC; CEng; FIEE; FBIM; *Recreations* music reading photography; *Style*— Speirs Robertson, Esq; Molsiver House, Oakley Road, Bromham, Bedford (☎ 02302 3410)

ROBERTSON, Timothy Patrick Vyvyan (Tim); s of George Ernest James Robertson; *b* 7 Nov 1943; *Educ* Winchester, Trinity Coll Cambridge (MA), Cranfield Inst of Technol (MBA); *m* 22 March 1969, Anna C, da of Thomas Edward Ray Moore, DSC, of Thruxton, Hants; 1 s (Hugo Sam Moore b 1982), 2 da (Chloe Mary Jean b 1971, Gemma Frances Ray b 1974); *Career* dir: W B B & Co plc, W B B GmbH, W B B de France SA, W B B Clay Sales Ltd, Pacific Clay Sales Ltd, Teignbridge Enterprise Agency; cmmr Teignmouth Harbour; *Recreations* sailing, golf, skiing; *Clubs* Bembridge Sailing, Wykehamist Golfing Soc, DHO; *Style*— Tim Robertson, Esq; Mapstone, Lustleigh, S Devon TQ13 9SE; Park House, Courtenay Park, Newton Abbot, TQ12 4PS (telex 42824 WBBG, fax 0626 56425)

ROBERTSON, (Sholto David Maurice) Toby; OBE (1978); s of late Cdr David Lambert Robertson (RN), and Felicity Douglas, *née* Tomlin; *b* 29 Nov 1928; *Educ* Stowe, Trinity Coll Cambridge (BA, MA); *m* 1963 (m dis 1981), (Teresa) Jane, *née* McCulloch; 2 s (Sebastian James Lambert b 1964, Joshua David Nathaniel b 1969) 2 da (Francesca Kate Tomlin b 1965, Sasha Corinna Jane b 1967); *Career* dir first professional prodn The Iceman Cometh (New Shakespeare, Liverpool) 1958, dir TV plays ITV/BBC 1959-63; dir of over 40 prodns Pro Theatre Co incl: 1964: The Soldier's Fortune, The Confederacy, The Importance of Being Earnest; 1965: The Man of Mode; 1966: Macbeth, The Tempest; 1967: A Murder of No Importance, A Room with a View; 1968: Twelfth Night (1973-1978), No Man's Land, The Beggar's Opera (also for Phoenix Opera 1972), The Servant of Two Marters; 1969: Edward II; 1970: Boswell's Life of Johnson; 1971: King Lear (also 1978), Lovers Labour's Lost; 1972: Richard III, Ivanov (also 1978); 1973: Pencles Royal Hour of the Sun; 1974: The Pilgrims Progress (1977), Hamlet (1979), War Music, Anthony and Cleopatra, Smith of Smiths (1978, 1979), Buster; 1978: The Lunatic, The Lover and the Poet (1979); 1979: Romeo and Juliet, The Govt Inspector; 1980: Next Time I'll Sing to You, Pericles (NY, OBIE Award for outstanding director 1981); 1981: Measure for Measure (Peoples Arts Theatre, Peking), The Revenger's Tragedy (NY, Villager Award for outstanding treatment of classical text 1982); York Cycle of Mystery Plays (York Fest) 1984, Midsummer Nights dream 1985, Medea (1986), Taming of the Shrew (1986), You Never Can Tell (1987), Captain Canrallo (1988), The Glorious Years (1988), Richard II (Washington DC 1988), Kingsley Amis The Old Devils (adapted Robin Hawdon 1989), Othello (1989); opera incl: Marriage of Figaro 1977, Elisir d'Amore Opera Co of Philadelphia, Oedipus Rex 1982, Dido & Aeneas; asst dir Lord of the Flies (film) 1961; dir of more 25 TV prodns; dir: Old Vic Theatre 1977-80, Old Vic Co 1979-80; currently artistic dir Theatre Clwyd (leading Welsh-speaking theatre co); *Recreations* painting, sailing, bunburying; *Clubs* Garrick, Bunbury; *Style*— Toby Robertson, Esq; 210 Brixton Rd, London SW9; Theatre Clwyd, Mold, Clwyd, North Wales CH7 1YA (☎ 0352 56331)

ROBERTSON, Vernon Colin; OBE (1977); s of Lt Col Colin John Trevelyan Robertson, OBE, DSO (d 1959), and Agnes Muriel, *née* Dolphin (d 1968); *b* 19 July 1922; *Educ* ISC (now Haileybury), Univ of Edinburgh (BSc), Univ of Cambridge (Dip Agric, MA); *Career* enlisted RA 1941, cmmnd 1942, serv 12 (HAC) Regt RHA N Africa, Italy and Austria 1942-45, Adj 1 Regt RHA (T/Capt) 1945 (despatches) demobbed 1946; memb HAC 1942-; univ demonstrator Sch of Agric Cambridge Univ 1950-53; Hunting Aerosurveys Ltd: ecologist 1953, md new consulting div (Hunting Tech Servs Ltd) until 1977, dir until 1977, environmental conslt 1988-; Groundwater Conslt (Int) Ltd Cambridge 1975-85; bd memb Cwlth Devpt Corpn 1982, 1985 and 1988; chm: Tropical Agric Assoc (UK) 1981-85, Frinton Arts & Music Soc 1983-86; Freeman City of London 1977, Liveryman Worshipful co Painters-Stainers 1977; *Recreations* sailing, natural history, photography, music, gardening; *Clubs* Farmers; *Style*— Vernon Robertson, Esq; The Saltings, Manor Road, Great Holland, Frinton-on-Sea, Essex CO13 0JT (☎ 0255 674 585)

ROBERTSON, William Stewart; OBE (1983); s of William Robertson (d 1946), and Charlotte Ann, *née* Nairn; *b* 23 Feb 1902; *Educ* HS Pert, Glasgow Univ (BSc); *m* 6 Feb 1950, Phyllis Emily, da of John Henry Gaydon; 1 s (Martin); *Career* Sgt Inst Motor Transport RE 1944-47; Singer MFG Co Ltd: engr 1947-58, dir 1958, asst md 1962-66; tech dir Reid Gear Co 1966-69; Rediffusion Simulation: plant mangr 1969, md 1972, chm 1977; additional chm Rediffusion: Computers, Radio Systems, Television (Jersey), Simulation (FortWorth USA); external dir Evans & Sutherland Computers Utah USA; MIPE; memb: IOD, CBI; *Recreations* golf, model engineering, DIY, gardening; *Clubs* Athenaeum, Inst of Directors, Les Amassadors; *Style*— William Robertson, Esq, OBE; Flat 24, 39 Queensgate SW7; Roborough, Wyndhamlea, West Chiltington, Pulborough, Sussex (☎ 079 833 3085)

ROBERTSON OF OAKRIDGE, 2 Baron (UK 1961); Sir William Ronald Robertson; 3 Bt (UK 1919); s of Gen 1 Baron Robertson of Oakridge, GCB, GBE, KCMG, KCVO, DSO, MC (d 1974); *b* 8 Dec 1930; *Educ* Charterhouse; *m* 1972, Celia, da of William Elworthy; 1 s; *Heir* s, Hon William Brian Elworthy Robertson b 15 Nov 1975; *Career* sits as Independent peer in House of Lords; memb London Stock Exchange 1973-, late Maj Royal Scots Greys; memb of the Salters' Co (master 1985-86); *Style*— The Rt Hon Lord Robertson of Oakridge; Keith, Bayley, Rogers & Co, 93/95 Borough High Street, London SE1 1NL (☎ 01 378 0657, telex 888437 EBBARK)

ROBERTSON-GLASGOW, Robert Foxcroft; s of Robert Wilson Robertson-Glasgow (d 1976), of Hinton House, Hinton Charterhouse, Bath, and Phyllis Mary Helen (d 1971), of Hinton House, whose father Thomas Jones (d 1848) suc to Hinton in 1846 and was s of Thomas Jones, of Stapleton House, Glos, and Frances Foxcroft (*see* Burke's Landed Gentry, 18 ed, vol II, 1969); *b* 11 Sept 1935; *Educ* Radley, Lincoln Coll Oxford, RAC Cirencester; *m* 10 Sept 1983, Patricia Coleridge, da of Thomas Patrick Shevlin (d 1950), of Wallsend-on-Tyne; *Career* 2 Lt The Royal Scots (The Royal Regt) 1955-56; farmer; memb: Som CC, London Delgn of Som and S Avon branch Nat Farmers' Union; gen cmmr of taxes; *Recreations* shooting, gardening, art history; *Clubs* Army and Navy; *Style*— R F Robertson-Glasgow, Esq; Hinton House,

Hinton Charterhouse, Bath, Avon (☎ 022 122 2254)

ROBERTSON-PEARCE, Anthony Brian; s of John Gilbert Robertson-Pearce (d 1967), of Testwood House, Lynhurst, Hants, and Damaris Aubrey, *née* Wilce (d 1946); *b* 3 April 1932; *Educ* Chideock Manor Sch, Christ's Coll Cambridge (BA), Univ of Stockhom (Dip Archaeological Photography), Alliance Francaise Paris (Dip in French); *m* 1, 18 May 1956 (m dis 1973), (Ingrid) Christina da, of Erik Nystrom (d 1957), of Holo, Sweden; 1 s (Michael b 3 Aug 1960), 2 da (Pamela b 22 April 1957, Penelope b 3 Oct 1965); m 2, 7 June 1974 (m dis 1980), Catharina Carlsdotter, da of Capt Soldan Carl Fredrik Henningsson Ridderstad (d 1973), of Linkoping, Sweden; *Career* supervisor and photographer excavations Motya Sicily 1965, Br Sch of Archaeology Baghdad 1966, supervisor and MO Tell-A-Rimah N Iraq 1967, photographer and MO Br Excavations Tawilan Jordan 1968; Central Bd of Nat Antiquities (Riksantikvarieambetet) Stockholm: field archaeological photographer 1969, publishing dept 1972, second head of publishing; dep govr Bd of Govrs ABIRA (American Biographical Inst Res Assoc); PRO Sollentuna Kommun Stockholm 1983-; FRAI, FIBA; *Books* Dr James Robertson 1566-1652 (1972), The Prehistoric Enclosure of Ekornavallen Sweden (1974), The Ruins of Kromoberg Castle (1974), Kaseberg Ship-setting (1975) ; *Recreations* riding, golf; *Clubs* Naval, Sallskapet Stockholm; *Style—* Anthony Robertson-Pearce, Esq; Nybrogatan 54, S-11440, Stockholm, Sweden (☎ 08 661 0268); SFP & Co, Banergatan 55, 11526 Stockholm, Sweden (☎ 08 663 0555, fax 660 3817)

ROBEY, Ian Crake; OBE (1985), JP (1979),; s of Lt-Col A E L Robey, OBE (d 1973); *b* 4 July 1927; *Educ* Felsted Sch Essex; *m* 1, 1953 (m dis 1977), Pamela, *née* Elbourne; 2 s, 2 da; m 2, 1981, Sandra, *née* Levitt; *Career* builders' merchant; chm Cakebread Robey & Co plc 1965-; dir Assoc Builders' Merchants Ltd 1964-87; chm: National Home Improvement Council 1982-83, Neighbourhood Revitalisation Services 1984-86; pres Builders Merchants Fedn 1979-81; FInstBM (1972), vice-chm Nat Home Improvement Cncl; *Recreations* food, music, theatre; *Style—* Ian Robey, Esq, JP; The Willows, High St, Watton-at-Stone, Herts (☎ 0920 830 076)

ROBIN, Ian Gibson; s of Dr Arthur Robin (d 1956), of 8 Napier Rd, Edinburgh, and Elizabeth Parker, *née* Arnold (d 1953); *b* 22 May 1909; *Educ* Merchiston Castle Sch Edinburgh, Clare Coll Cambridge (MA, MB BCh); *m* 19 July 1939, Sheelagh Marian, da of Cyril Merton Croft (d 1951), of 19 Marryat Road, Wimbledon; 1 s (Graham Luke), 2 da (Shirley, Wendy); *Career* RNVR 1939 (invalided out); registrar and chief clinical asst Guy's Hosp 1935-36, private practice Harley St 1937-, conslt ENT surgn Royal Northern Hosp 1937-74, surgn EMS Sector 3 London Area 1939-45; conslt ENT surgn: St Mary's Hosp 1948-74, Princess Louise Hosp for Children 1948-68, Paddington Green Children's Hosp 1968-74; formerly: vice chm Nat Inst for the Deaf, pres Br Assoc of Otolaryngologists, pres laryngology section and vice pres otological section RSM, cncl memb Nat Deaf Children's Soc; memb: Med Soc of London 1947-67, Hunterian Soc 1948-; *Books* Diseases of Ear Nose and Throat (second edn 1961); *Recreations* golf, gardening, sketching; *Clubs* Hawks (Cambridge), Achilles, Hampstead Golf; *Style—* Ian Robin, Esq; Stowe House, 3 North End, Hampstead, London NW3 7HH (☎ 01 458 2292); 86 Harley Street, London W1N 1AE (☎ 01 580 3625)

ROBINS, (Robert Victor) Charles; s of (Robert) Walter Vivian Robins (d 1968), of London, and (Alice) Kathleen, *née* Knight (d 1979); *b* 13 Mar 1935; *Educ* Eton; *m* 6 Nov 1962 (m dis 1985), Vivian Mary, da of Alan Vivian Mackay, of Brazil; 3 s (Timothy b 1963, William b 1965, Archie b 1972); *Career* underwriting memb Lloyds 1951, chm Lloyds Brokers; former cricketer Middx (memb ctee 1963-); former memb ctee MCC 1973-79 and Cricket Cncl 1976-79, neutral observer Pakistan v West Indies Test Karachi 1981, memb organising ctee World Cup Cricket India and Pakistan 1987; Liveryman Worshipful Co of Glovers; *Recreations* golf; *Clubs* MCC, City of London; *Style—* Charles Robins, Esq; St Didier, Taggs Island, Hampton, Middx (☎ 01 941 027); c/o Stafford Knight & Co Ltd, 4/5 London Wall Bldgs, London EC2M 5NR (☎ 01 628 3135, fax 01 638 2510, telex 945846 SMALLT)

ROBINS, Daniel Gerard; QC (1986); s of William Albert Robins, of Malaga, Spain, and Hilda Marjorie Robins, JP, *née* Johnson; *b* 12 Mar 1942; *Educ* City of London Sch, LSE (BSc, LLB); *m* 25 May 1968, Hon Elizabeth Mary Gerran, da of Baron Lloyd of Kilgerran, CBE, QC, JP (Life Peer); 3 da (Charlotte b 1971, Sophie b 1974, Anneli b 1976); *Career* barr Lincolns Inn 1966, SE circuit; dir Educn Tst Ltd; Freeman Worshipful Co of Drapers 1978; FRAI 1963; *Recreations* golf, tennis, ornithology; *Clubs* Savile, Royal Naval (Portsmouth); *Style—* Daniel Robins, Esq, QC; 2 Harcourt Buildings, Temple, London EC4 (☎ 01 353 8415)

ROBINS, Hon Mrs (Elizabeth Mary Gerran); *née* Lloyd; da of Baron Lloyd of Kilgerran (Life Peer); *b* 1944; *m* 1968, Daniel Gerard Robins, QC; 3 da; *Style—* The Hon Mrs Robins; 66 Church Rd, Wimbledon, SW19

ROBINS, John Vernon Harry; s of Col W V H Robins, DSO, of Delamere, Cheshire, and Charlotte Mary, *née* Grier (d 1979); *b* 21 Feb 1939; *Educ* Winchester Coll, Stanford Univ USA (SEP); *m* 11 Aug 1962, Elizabeth Mary, da of Alex Banister, OBE, of Sussex; 2 s (Nicholas Vivian James b 1963, Michael Victor Andrew b 1973), 1 da (Tessa Vivienne Mary b 1965); *Career* Nat Serv 2 Lt 2/10 PMO Gurkha Rifles 1959-61; md SNS Communications Ltd 1966-74, chief exec Bally gp (UK) Ltd 1974-79, gp fin dir Fitch Lovell plc 1979-84, dir fin and mgmnt servs Willis Faber plc 1984-; chm Assoc Corporate Tresurers; Warden Worshipful Co of Glovers; FCT 1979; *Recreations* clocks, music; *Clubs* Brooks's; *Style—* John Robins, Esq; The Old Vicarage, Sawbridge Worth, Herts CM22 9AD; Willis Faber plc, 10 Trinity Sq, London EC3P 3AX (☎ 01 488 8578)

ROBINS, Gp Capt Leonard Edward; CBE (1979), AE (1958, clasps 1968, and 1978), DL (Gtr London 1978, Wandsworth 1979-); s of Joseph Robins (d 1957), of Mitcham, Surrey, and Louisa Josephine, *née* Kent (d 1963); *b* 2 Nov 1921; *Educ* Singlegate Mitcham Surrey, City Day Continuation Sch London; *m* 6 Aug 1949, Jean Ethelwynne (d 1985), da of Roy Augustus Searle (d 1970), of Ryde, IOW; *Career* WWII RAF served: UK, Ceylon, India, SEAC; Airman (Co of London) Radar Reporting Unit RAuxAF 1950, cmmnd 1953, Pilot Offr, transferred to 1 (Co of Hertford) Maritime HQ Unit RAuxAF 1960, Flying Offr 1955, Flt Lt 1963, Sqdn Ldr 1968, Wing Cdr 1969, OC 1 MHU 1969-73, Gp Capt and inspr RAuxAF MOD 1973-83, ret; ADC to HM the Queen 1974-83; civil servant: GPO 1936-48, Minys of Health, Housing, Planning, Local Govt and DOE 1948-80, ret; personal staff Lord Mayor of London: 1977-78, 1980-81, 1982-83, 1986-87, 1987-88, 1988-89; selected memb: Gtr London TAVRA 1973-83, City of London TAVRA 1980-84; pres Wandsworth Victim Support 1980-86, tstee Royal Fndn of Greycoat Hosp 1983-88; Freeman City of London 1976; Offr of Merit with Swords SMOM 1986; Coronation Medal 1953, Jubilee Medal 1977; FBIM 1977; *Recreations* military history, book hunting, kipping, speech writing; *Clubs* RAF; *Style—* Gp Capt Leonard Robins, CBE, AE, DL; 16 Summit Way, Upper Norwood, London SE19 2PU (☎ 01 655 3173); Higher Bosigran, Pendeen, Penzance, Cornwall TR20 8YX (☎ 0736 796884)

ROBINS, Malcolm Owen; CBE (1978); s of Owen Wilfred Robins (d 1961), and Amelia Ada, *née* Wheelwright (d 1966); *b* 25 Feb 1918; *Educ* King Edward VI Sch Stourbridge, Queen's Coll Oxford (MA); *m* 10 June 1944, Frances Mary, da of William Hand (d 1950); 1 s (David b 1946), 1 da (Sylvia b 1950); *Career* staff memb Royal Aircraft Estab 1940-57, asst dir MOS 1957-58, hon res assoc UCL and UK project mangr jt UK/USA Space Res Programme 1958-62, hd space res mgmnt Unit Miny of Science 1962-65, divnl hd SRC 1965-68, staff memb Miny of Technol 1968-72, dir SRC 1972-78, learned societies offr Royal Soc/Br Academy 1979-81; memb Anglo-Australian Telescope Bd 1973-78, memb (sometime chm) Steering Ctee Institut Laue Langevin Grenoble 1973-78, visiting prof UCL 1974-77; CPhys, FInstP, FRAS; *Recreations* gardening, golf, writing; *Style—* Malcolm Robins, Esq, CBE

ROBINS, Peter Marshall; OBE (1981); s of Henry Joseph Robins (d 1951), of Newent, and Maudie Theresa, *née* White; *b* 3 July 1952; *Educ* Newent GS; *m* 20 Sept 1958, Iona Naomi Irene Juliana, da of Edwin Jack Hill (d 1987); 2 s (Adrian Peter b 1963, Arlene b 1966); *Career* slr; dir Bentham Properties Ltd 1966; farmer; Mayor City of Gloucester 1975-76, chm Gloucester City Cncl 1973-74 (memb 1974-82, ldr 1973-82), dep mayor 1976-82; memb: Gloucester Co Borough Cncl 1965-74, Gloucester CC 1973-85; dir Crickley Hill Archaeological Tst; *Recreations* golf; *Style—* Peter Robins, Esq; Robins Farm, Matson Lane, Gloucester GL4 9DZ (☎ 0452 29681); York House, 94 Bath Rd, Cheltenham CL53 7JT (☎ 0242 525321, fax 0242 221080)

ROBINS, Sir Ralph Harry; s of Leonard Haddon Robins, and Maud Lillian Robins; *b* 16 June 1932; *Educ* Imperial Coll, Univ of London (BSc, ACEI); *m* 1962, Patricia Maureen, *née* Grimes; 2 da; *Career* devpt engr Rolls-Royce Derby 1955-56, exec vice-pres Rolls-Royce Inc 1971, md RR Indust & Marine Div 1973, chm Int Aero Engines AG 1983-84, md Rolls-Royce plc 1984-; chm Defence Industries Cncl 1986-, dep-pres Soc of Br Aerospace Cos 1987 (pres 1986-87); FEng, MIMechE; *Style—* Sir Ralph Robins; Rolls Royce plc, 65 Buckingham Gate, London SW1E 6AT (☎ 01 222 9020)

ROBINS, Prof Robert Henry; s of Dr J N Robins (d 1958), of Folkestone, Kent, and Muriel Winifred, *née* Porter (d 1960); *b* 1 July 1921; *Educ* Tonbridge Sch, New Coll Oxford (MA, BA); *m* 29 Aug 1953, Sheila Marie (d 1983), da of Arthur Fynn (d 1944), of Norwood; *Career* WWII Flt Lt RAFVR 1942-45; lectr in linguistics Sch of Oriental and African Studies Univ of London 1948-55, prof of gen linguistics Univ of London 1966-86 (reader 1955-65), prof emeritus 1987-; pres Int Ctee of Linguists 1977-; DLit London Univ; FBA; hon memb Lingustic Soc of America; Press Philological Soc 1988-, Int Ctee of Linguists 1977-; *Books* Ancient and Mediaeval Grammatical Theory in Europe (1951), The Yurok Language (1958), General Linguistics: an Introductory Survey (1964, 1989), A Short History of Linguistics (1967, 1979); *Recreations* gardening, travel; *Clubs* Royal Cwlth Soc, Athenaeum; *Style—* Prof Robert Robins; 65 Dome Hill, Caterham, Surrey CR3 6EF (☎ 0883 43778); School of Oriental and African Studies, Univ of London, London WC1H 0XG (☎ 01 637 2388)

ROBINSON; *see*: Lynch-Robinson

ROBINSON, (George) Adrian; s of Thomas Gerard Robinson, BEM, of Preston, Lancs, and Elizabeth, *née* Gillow; *b* 3 Nov 1949; *Educ* Preston Catholic Coll, Pembroke Coll Oxford (MA); *m* 6 April 1974, Susan Margaret, da of James Hopwood Edmondson, of Accrington, Lancs; 2 s (Philip Adrian b 9 Sept 1984, Andrew James b 3 May 1987); *Career* various appts Midland Bank Ltd 1971-80; Airbus Industrie: sales fin mangr 1980-82, dep sales fin dir 1982-84, sales fin dir 1984; corporate fin dir Midland Bank plc 1985, dir Aerospace Chemical Bank 1986-87 (md special fin gp 1987-); ACIB 1973; *Recreations* golf, tennis, shooting; *Style—* Adrian Robinson, Esq; 180 The Strand, London WC2R 1EX (☎ 01 380 5072, fax 01 380 5109, telex 264 766)

ROBINSON, Alwyn Arnold; *b* 15 Nov 1929; *Educ* Queen Elizabeth Sch Darlington; *m* 1953, Dorothy Heslop; 2 s, 1 da; *Career* md Daily Mail 1975- (joined 1951, features ed 1966, asst ed 1969, managing ed 1971, gen mangr 1972, exec dir 1974); dir: Associated Newpapers Holdings plc, Mail Newspapers plc, Daily Mail Ltd, The Mail on Sunday Ltd, Harmsworth Publishing Ltd; jt vice-chm Press Cncl 1982-83 (memb 1977-); *Style—* Alwyn Robinson, Esq; c/o The Daily Mail, New Carmelite House, London EC4 (☎ 01 353 6000)

ROBINSON, Andrew William Stafford; s of Joseph William Cyril Maitland-Robinson, MBE, of Jersey, and Hilda, *née* Powell; *b* 20 Oct 1946; *Educ* Dragon Sch, Radley, Downing Coll Cambridge (MA), Univ of Exeter; *m* 2, 30 Aug 1985, Patricia Margaret, da of David Quigg (d 1976), of Corby, Northants; 4 da by earlier m (Caroline b 1973, Miria b 1974, Daisy b 1980, Frideswide b 1984); *Career* slr 1974, Notary Public 1977, sole practitioner in Penzance 1982-; memb child care panel Law Soc, tres Penwith Youth for Christ, tstee Duchy Addiction Rehabilitation Tst; fndr Lawyers Support Gp 1983; memb: Law Soc, Notaries Soc, Alcohol Concern; *Style—* Andrew Robinson, Esq; 5 Princes St, Penzance, Cornwall (☎ 0736 68369)

ROBINSON, Arthur Geoffrey; CBE (1978); s of Arthur Robinson (d 1987), and Frances Mary Mason (d 1970); *b* 22 August 1917; *Educ* Lincoln Sch, Jesus Coll Camb (MA), SOAS London Univ; *m* 1, 1943, Patricia (d 1971), da of William MacAllister (d 1922), of Wetherby; 3 s (Matthew b 1944, Thomas b 1950, George b 1961), 1 da (Sophy b 1955); m 2, 1973, Gai Rencie, wid of Martin Treves and da of Baron Salmon of Sandwich; *Career* served RA Staff Capt 1939-46; slr 1948; Treasury Slrs Dept 1954-62; PLA 1962-66; md Tees and Hartlepool Port Authy 1966-77; Nat Ports Cncl 1980-81; chm Br Ports Assoc 1983-85, English Industl Estates Corpn 1974-84, Medway Ports 1978-87; *Books* Hedingham Harvest (1977); *Recreations* music; *Clubs* United Oxford and Cambridge Univ; *Style—* A G Robinson, Esq; Salts End, Gosshall Lane, Ash, Canterbury CT3 2AN (☎ 0304 812366); La Baume, Uzes 30700, Gard, France (☎ 66 22 55 44)

ROBINSON, Prof Sir (Edwin) Austin Gossage; CMG (1947), OBE (1944); s of Rev Albert Gossage Robinson (d 1948); *b* 20 Nov 1897; *Educ* Marlborough, Christ's Coll Cambridge (MA); *m* 1926, Joan, Prof of Economics Cambridge Univ 1965-71, da of Maj-Gen Sir Frederick Maurice; 2 da; *Career* economic section Cabinet Office 1939-42, Min of Production 1942-45, economic advsr Bd of Trade 1945-46, attached to Central Economic Planning Staff Treasury 1947-48; prof of economics Cambridge 1950-65, prof emeritus 1966-; sec Royal Economic Soc 1945-70, pres Int Economic Assoc 1959-62; Fell Sidney Sussex Coll Cambridge 1931-; FBA; kt 1975; *Style—* Prof Sir Austin Robinson, CMG, OBE; 62 Grange Rd, Cambridge (☎ 0223 357548); Sidney Sussex College, Cambridge

ROBINSON, Hon Mrs; Hon Betty Mary a Court; *née* Holmes à Court; da of 4 Baron Heytesbury (d 1949); assumed additional surname à Court 1946; *b* 1902; *m* 1, 1923 (m dis 1946), Cdr Vivian John Robinson, RN; 2 s, 1 da; m 2, 1956, Alfred Esmond Robinson, CBE, MC (d 1975); *Style—* The Hon Mrs` Court Robinson; Combe House, 62 Church Lane, Backwell, Bristol BS19 3JJ (☎ 027 583 2732)

ROBINSON, Gp Capt (Donald) Brian; s of Maj Dudley Clare Robinson, MC (d 1970), of Balvonie, 1 Shimna Pk, Newcastle, Co Down, NI, and Margaret, *née* Moore; *b* 26 July 1927; *Educ* Wellington, Oxford Univ, RAF Coll Cranwell, Royal Canadian Air Force Staff Coll, Jt Servs Staff Coll; *m* 9 Oct 1957, Rosabelle Ileene Zahra, da of Maj Edward Archibald Theodore Bayly, DSO (d 1959), of Ballyarthur, Woodenbridge, Co Wicklow, Ireland; 2 s (Colan b 1958, Tim b 1965), 1 da (Judy b 1962); *Career* RAF 1949-82; served: Korean War on Sunderland Flying Boats (despatches 1954), NATO staff SACLANT 1966-69, directing staff RAF Staff Coll Bracknell 1969-72, HQ Strike Cmd High Wycombe 1972-76, sr Air SO (formerly Wing Cdr ops and plans) HQ Cyprus 1976-79, NATO staff AIRSOUTH 1979-82, ret Gp Capt 1982; memb design staff Ferranti Computer Systems Ltd Gwent 1983-87; official helper RAF Benevolent Fund Gwent; memb: Border Ctee of TAVR Assoc for Wales, Gwent Nat Tst Assoc, Chepstow Soc, Shirenewton Village Produce Assoc (chm 1986-); *Recreations* walking, horticulture, the countryside; *Clubs* RAF; *Style—* Gp Capt Brian Robinson; Green Acres, Shirenewton, Chepstow, Gwent NP6 6BU (☎ 02917 539)

ROBINSON, Maj (Alfred) Christopher; s of Col Annesley Robinson, DSO (d 1976), of Long Melford, Suffolk, and Doris Lilian, *née* Barrett (d 1988); *b* 18 Nov 1930; *Educ* Wellington, RMA Sandhurst; *m* 1, 17 Aug 1957 (m dis 1961), Caroline Stafford, da of Maj Christopher Scott-Nicholson (ka 1945), of Ruthwell, Dumfriesshire; m 2, 31 March 1962 (m dis 1978), Amanda, da of Paul Boggis-Rolfe (d 1988), of Bampton, Oxon; 2 s (Charles b 1964, Barnaby b 1970), 2 da (Nicola b 1963, Polly b 1964); *Career* 16/5 The Queen's Royal Lancers 1951-65; Trade Imdemnity Co Ltd 1966-70, Glanvill Enthoven & Co Ltd 1970-73, The Spastics Soc 1973-; chm Ferriers Barn Disabled Centre; memb: ctee Colne Stour Countryside Assoc, Sudbury Deanery Synod; memb ICFM 1986; *Recreations* country pursuits, travel, wine appreciation; *Clubs* Essex; *Style—* Maj Christopher Robinson; Water Lane Cottage, Bures, Suffolk CO8 5DE (☎ 0787 227179); The Spastics Soc, 12 Park Crescent, London W1N 4EQ (☎ 01 636 5020, fax 01 436 2601)

ROBINSON, Christopher John; LVO (1986); s of Rev Preb John Robinson (d 1974), of 40 Mathon Road, West Malvern, and Esther Hilda, *née* Lane (d 1983); *b* 20 April 1936; *Educ* Rugby, Christ Church Oxford (MA, B Mus), Birmingham Univ (Cert Ed); *m* 6 Aug 1962, Shirley Ann, s of Harry Frederick Churchman, of 36 Mill Lane, Sauston, Cambridge; 1 s (Nicholas b 3 June 1970), 1 da (Elizabeth b 27 Sept 1968); *Career* asst organist: Christ Church Oxford 1955-58, New Coll Oxford 1957-58; music master Oundle Sch 1959-62; organist: Worcester Cathedral 1963-74 (asst organist 1962-63), St George's Chapel Windsor Castle 1975-; conductor: City of Birmingham Choir 1964- (princ conductor 3 choir festivals 1966, 1969, 1972), Leith Hill Festival 1977-80, Oxford Bach Choir 1977-; pres RCO 1982-84, chm Elgar Soc 1988-; Hon: RAM 1980, MMus Birmingham Univ 1987; FRCO 1954; *Recreations* cricket, foreign travel; *Clubs* L.....; *Style—* Christopher Robinson, Esq, LVO; 23 The Cloisters, Windsor Castle, Berks SL4 1NJ (☎ 0753 864529)

ROBINSON, Christopher Philipse; s of late Christopher Robinson, QC; hp of kinsman, Sir John Robinson, 7 Bt; *b* 10 Nov 1938; *m* 1962, Barbara Judith, da of Richard Duncan, of Ottawa; 2 s; *Style—* Christopher Robinson Esq; 5 Bedford Cres, Ottawa, Ontario, Canada

ROBINSON, Hon Mrs (Claire Elizabeth); *née* Portman; da of 9 Viscount Portman and Rosemary Joy (Farris) Maitland; *b* 1 Oct 1959; *Educ* St Mary's Wantage, Winkfield Place, Marlborough Secretarial Coll Oxford; *m* 1983, Anthony Henry Robinson, only s of Anthony Leonard á Court Robinson, of Blagdon, Avon; 3 s (Anthony b 1984, James b 1985, Patrick b 1987); *Style—* The Hon Mrs Robinson; Pinkneys Court, Pinkneys Green, Maidenhead, Berks (☎ 0628 27300)

ROBINSON, David Foster; s of Arthur Robinson, of New Milton, Hants, and Ellen Robinson, *née* Jackson; *b* 29 May 1936; *Educ* Kings Sch Macclesfield, Manchester Univ (BA); *m* 5 Nov 1966, Hannah, da of Roger Alan Watson (d 1979), of Edinburgh; 2 s (William b 1968, Edward b 1970), 1 da (Caroline b 1971); *Career* Nat Serv 2 Lt RAPC 1960-62; ptnr Spicer & Oppenheim 1974- (prev Spicer & Pegler, joined 1962); dir: Spicers Consulting Gp 1969- (prev Spicer & Pegler Assocs), Sulaiman Assocs 1979- (prev Egunjobi & Sulaiman Conslts (Nigeria) Ltd); memb Langford & Ulting PC 1978-; FCA, FIMC; *Books* Human Asset Accounting (1972), Key Definitions in Finance (1980), Managing People (1984), Getting the Best out of People (1988); *Recreations* gardening, walking, tennis; *Clubs* City of London; *Style—* Daivd Robinson, Esq; Luards, Langford, Maldon, Essex; 35 Taeping St London E14 (☎ 0621 54242); Spicer & Oppenheim Friary Ct, 65 Crutched Friars EC3N 2NP (☎ 01 480 7766, fax 01 480 6958, telex 884257 ESAND G)

ROBINSON, Prof David Julien; s of Edward Robinson (d 1973), of Lincoln, and Dorothy Evelyn, *née* Overton (d 1979); *b* 6 August 1930; *Educ* Lincoln Sch, King's Coll Cambridge (BA); *Career* assoc editor Sight and Sound 1956-58, editor Monthly Film Bulletin 1956-58, programme dir Nat Film Theatre and London Film Festival 1959, editor Contrast 1962-63; film critic: The Financial Times 1959-74, The Times 1974-; prodr and dir films: Hetty King- Performer 1969, Keeping Love Alive (co-dir Stephen Garrett) 1987; memb: Williams Ctee on Obscenity and Film Censorship, numerous film festival juries incl Cannes; *Books* Hollywood in the Twenties (1969), Buster Keaton (1969), The Great Funnies (1972) World Cinema (1973, 1980), Chaplin, The Mirror of Opinion (1983), Chaplin His Life and Art (1985); *Recreations* collecting, music hall, prehistory of cinema; *Style—* Prof David Robinson; 96-100 New Cavendish St, London WIM 7FA (☎ 01 580 4959); The Times, 1 Virginia St, London E19XN (☎ 01 782 5000, fax 01 583 9519, telex)

ROBINSON, Ven (William) David; s of William Robinson (d 1969), of Blackburn, and Margaret, *née* Bolton (d 1982); *b* 15 Mar 1931; *Educ* Queen Elizabeth GS Blackburn, Durham Univ (BA, Dip Theol, MA); *m* 30 Jul 1955, Carol Averil Roma, da of Norman William Edward Hamm, of Blackburn; 1 s (Christopher), 1 da (Catherine b 1960); *Career* pilot offr RAF 1949-51; curate St Wilfrid Standish 1958-61, sr curate Lancaster Priory (priest i/c St George) 1961-63, vicar St James Blackburn 1963-73, diocesan stewartship advsr and priest-i/c St James Shireshead 1973-86, hon canon Blackburn Cathedral 1975-86, vicar of Balderstone 1986-87, archdeacon of Blackburn 1986-; *Recreations* fell-walking; *Style—* The Ven the Archdeacon of Blackburn; 7 Billinge Close, Blackburn, Lancs BB2 6SB (☎ 0254 53442)

ROBINSON, Derek Hugh; s of Cyril Thomas John Robinson (d 1967), of Derby, and Doris Isabel, *née* Garrett (d 1960); *b* 5 June 1929; *Educ* Bemrose Sch Derby, Tech Coll Derby, Univ of Southampton, Univ Coll London (BSc); *m* 15 Dec 1958, Heather Margaret Anne, da of Reginald Walter Merrick (d 1962), of Midsomer Norton, Somerset; 2 s (Ian, Edward), 1 da (Fiona); *Career* offr US Army Corps of Engrs Labrador 1954; engr: John Laing & Son Ltd 1950-52, Ontario Dept of Highways Toronto 1952-54, Turriff Construction Corpn Warwick 1954-55, E W H Gifford & Ptnrs Southampton 1957-63; consulting engr: D H Robinson Assocs Winchester 1963-87, Allott & Lomax Winchester 1987-; CEng, FICE, FIStructE, MConsE; *Recreations* walking, photography, nature study, family life, motoring, travel; *Style—* Derek Robinson, Esq; 6 Palmerston Court, Barnes Close, Winchester, Hants (☎ 0962 549 05); Haven Lights, Castle Rd, Dartmouth, S Devon (☎ 08043 4382); Bridge House, East Hill, Winchester, Hants (☎ 0962 610 77, fax 0962 616 55)

ROBINSON, Eaton Holroyd (Robin); s of Frederick Eaton Robinson, OBE (d 1964), and Mary Adams, *née* Mackintosh (d 1957); *b* 29 Nov 1915; *Educ* Merchant Taylors' Sch, Imp Coll London Univ (ACGI, BSc); *m* 1, 21 July 1956, Shirley Callcott (d 1985), da of Peter Charles Callcott Reilly, OBE (d 1966); 1 s (Anthony Nigel b 3 Feb 1963), 2 da (Tessa Jane b 6 March 1965, Sarah Anne b 7 Jan 1966); m 2, 21 Feb 1987, June Elisabeth Micklem; *Career* O/Cdt London Univ OTC, Pilot Civil Airguard, Sgt Home Guard 1940-45; graduate trainee Rolls-Royce Bristol 1938-39, devpt engr Power Jets 1940-45, tech sales Shell Petroleum Ltd and sales tech advsr Burham-Shell Ltd (India) 1945-49, ptnr Urwick Orr & Ptnrs Ltd 1950-55, dep chm Leslie Hartridge Ltd 1973- (md 1956-72); memb Friends Ctee Univ of Buckingham, vice pres Imperial Coll Alumni; FIMechE; *Recreations* golf, fishing; *Style—* E H Robinson, Esq

ROBINSON, Hon Mrs (Gai Rencie); da (by 1 m) of Baron Salmon (Life Peer); *b* 1933; *m* 1, 1955, Martin Treves (d 1970); 3 s, 1 da; m 2, 1973, Geoffrey Robinson, CBE, *qv*; *Style—* The Hon Mrs Robinson; 19 Millers Court, Chiswick Mall, London W4 (☎ 01 748 2997); Salts End, Ash, nr Canterbury, Kent (☎ 0304 812366)

ROBINSON, Geoffrey; MP (Lab) Coventry NW 1976-; s of Robert Robinson; *b* 25 May 1939; *Educ* Emanuel Sch, Cambridge Univ, Yale Univs; *m* 1967, Marie Elena Giorgio; 1 s, 1 da; *Career* Lab Pty res asst 1965-68, sr exec Industl Reorganisation Corpn 1968-70, fin controller BL 1971-72, md Leyland Innocenti Milan 1972-73; chief exec: Jaguar Motor Cars Coventry 1973-75, Meriden Co-Op 1979-80; oppn spokesman: Regnl Affairs 1983-84, Indust 1984-86; *Style—* Geoffrey Robinson, Esq, MP; House of Commons, London SW1A 0AA

ROBINSON, Sir George Gilmour; s of late George Thomas Robinson; *b* 30 August 1894; *Educ* Repton, Trinity Coll Oxford (MA); *m* 1942, Muriel Alice, da of W E Fry, of Kent; *Career* served WW I RASC; barr Inner Temple 1924, resident magistrate Kenya 1930-37, Puisne judge N Rhodesia 1938-46 and Nigeria 1947-52, chief justice Zanzibar 1952-55, ret; Order of the Brilliant Star (Zanzibar); kt 1955; *Style—* Sir George Robinson; The Old House, Southwold, Suffolk (☎ 0502 722374)

ROBINSON, Ian; s of Thomas Mottram Robinson (d 1972), and Eva Iris, *née* Bird (d 1984); *b* 3 May 1942; *Educ* Univ of Leeds (BSc), Harvard Univ (SMP); *m* 28 Oct 1967, Kathleen Crawford, da of James Leay, of Edinburgh; 1 s (Andrew John b 1977), 1 da (Caroline Anne b 1973); *Career* Ralph M Parsons Co Ltd: dir of ops 1979, vice pres (USA) 1983, md 1985; md John Brown Engrg Constructors Ltd 1986-; FIChE, CEng; *Recreations* gardening, tennis, golf; *Clubs* Les Ambassadeurs; *Style—* Ian Robinson, Esq; John Brown Engrs & Constructors Ltd, 20 Eastbourne Terr, London W2 6LE (☎ 01 262 8080)

ROBINSON, Jancis Mary (Mrs N L Lander); da of Thomas Edward Robinson, of Eden House, Kirkandrews-on-Eden, Cumbria, and Ann, *née* Conacher; *b* 22 April 1950; *Educ* Carlisle HS, St Annes Coll Oxford (MA); *m* 22 Oct 1981, Nicholas Laurence Lander, s of Israel Lennard Lander, of Flat 4, Wedderburn House, Wedderburn Rd, London; 1 s (William Isaac b 5 Sept 1984), 1 da (Julia Margaux b 10 July 1982); *Career* mktg and producing skiing holidays Thomson Holidays 1971-74, odd jobs whilst writing for Good Food Guide 1975, ed (formerly asst ed) Wine and Spirit 1975-80, founder Drinker's Digest (1977) to become Which? Wine Monthly (1980), ed Which? Wine Monthly and Which? Wine Annual Guide 1980-82; Sunday Times: wine corr, food corr, gen features 1980-86; wine corr The Evening Standard; Broadcasting: presenter and writer The Wine Programme (1983, 1985 and 1987), presenter Jancis Robinson's Christmas Wine List 1985, commentary writer and narrator 40 Minutes (Nuclear Dumps) 1986, presenter BBC Design Awards 1986-87, narrator Design Classics 1987, presenter and writer Jancis Robinson Meets 1987, lectures incl: Christie's and Sotheby's wine courses, Gleneagles Wine Weekend; wine judging Britain and abroad; Glenfiddich Award: best book on wine (The Great Wine Book) 1983, Wine and Food Writer/Broadcaster of the Year 1984, Wine Writer 1986, Food Writer 1986; winner: Marques de Caceres Award 1985, Wine Guild of UK Premier Award 1986, Andre Simon Meml Award 1987, Wine Guild Award for ref book 1987, Clicquot Book of the Year (Vines, Grapes and Wines) 1987, Silver Medal German Academy of Gastronomy 1988; memb Inst of Masters of Wine 1984; Jurade de St Emilion, Commanderie de Bontemps de Médoc et Graves; *Books* The Wine Book (1979), The Great Wine Book (1982), Masterglass (1983), How to Choose and Enjoy Wine (1984), Vines, Grapes and Wines (1986), Jancis Robinson's Food and Wine Adventures (1987), Jancis Robinson on The Demon Drink (1988); *Style—* Ms Jancis Robinson

ROBINSON, Joan Elizabeth; *née* Moore; da of Percy Moore of Ledbury, and Florence, *née* Dudfield; *b* 12 Nov 1947; *Educ* Newent Comprehensive Sch Glos, Eaton Hall Coll of Educ Notts; *m* 25 July 1980, Richard Anthony, s of Lt Cdr James Valentine Robinson RNR, (d 1982), of Brockweir, Gwent; 2 da (Clare b 1978, Jane b 1980); *Career* teacher: W Lavington Comp Sch 1969-71, Howtown Outdoor Activity Centre Ullswater 1971-77;memb: Eden DC 1983-, Cumbria CC 1985-, (ldr Lib Gp on CC 1986-), ACC 1985-, social advsy panel for the Rural Devpt Cmmn 1986-; lib spokesperson on nat parks ctee of the ACC 1986-; *Recreations* sailing (ocean sailing - dinghy sailing); *Clubs* Ullswater; *Style—* Mrs Joan Robinson; 27 Monnington Way, Penrith Cumbria, CA11 8QJ (☎ 0768 65430)

ROBINSON, Prof John; s of William Clifford Robinson (d 1982), and Annie, *née* Banks; *b* 11 July 1933; *Educ* Little Lever Secondary Sch, Radcliffe Jr Tech Coll, Salford Tech

Coll (HND), Cranfield Inst of Tech (MSc), Inst of Sound and Vibration Res Univ of Southampton (PhD); *m* 1, 3 Aug 1957 (m dis 1980), Cynthia, da of late Eric Nicholls; 2 s (Gary Edward b 16 Aug 1958, Lee John b 16 May 1961); m 2, 12 Sept 1984, Shirley Ann, da of Roland Walter Bradley, of Bidford-on-Avon, Warwicks; *Career* Br and USA Aerospace Indust 1949-71, head Robinson and Assocs 1971-; conslt organiser World Congress and Exhibition on Finite Element Methods 1975- (ed and publisher World Congress Proceedings 1975-), ed and publisher Finite Element News 1976-, lectr of worldwide courses on Understanding Finite Element Strees Analysis 1980-, fndr and memb steering ctee Nat Agency for Finite Element Methods and Standards 1983-, dir Robinson FEMInst 1986-, industl res prof Univ of Exeter 1986-; MRAES 1962, MIMechE 1964, CEng; *Books* Structural Matrix Analysis for the Engineer (1966), Integrated Theory of Finite Element Methods (1973), Understanding Finite Element Stress Analysis (1981), Early Fem Pioneers (1985) articles; *Style*— Prof John Robinson; Great Bidlake Manor, Bridestowe, Okehampton, Devon EX20 4NT (☎ 083 786 220)

ROBINSON, John Barrie; s of Reginald Thomas Robinson (d 1988), of 197 Carleton Rd, Pontefract, W Yorks, and Constance Helen, *née* Sykes; *b* 15 Oct 1934; *Educ* Normanton GS; *m* 11 June 1960, (Margaret) Jill, da of Robert Victor Fisher (d 1976), of 7 Mount St, Walsall; 2 s (Andrew b 1961, Jonathan b 1964), 1 da (Helen b 1968); *Career* Nat Serv 1953-55; Parker Pen Co UK Ltd: sales mangr 1968-79, sales and mktg dir 1979-83, gen mangr 1983-; area dir (Europe, Africa, Middle East) Parker Pen plc 1986-; FInstD; *Recreations* golf; *Clubs* Royal Eastbourne Golf; *Style*— J Barrie Robinson, Esq; 2 Summerdown Close, Eastbourne, E Sussex BN20 8DW (☎ 0323 30693); Parker Pen plc, Parker House, Newhaven, E Sussex BN9 0AU (☎ 0273 513 233, ext 268)

ROBINSON, Sir John James Michael Laud; 11 Bt (E 1660), of London, DL (Northants); s of Michael Frederick Laud-Robinson (d 1971), and Elisabeth Bridge (d 1977); suc gf, Maj Sir Frederick Robinson, 10 Bt, MC (d 1975, descended from Sir John Robinson, 1 Bt, Lord Mayor of London 1662-63 and s of Ven William Robinson, sometime Archdeacon of Nottingham and half-bro of Archbishop Laud); *b* 19 Jan 1943; *Educ* Eton, Trinity Coll Dublin (MA); *m* 1968, (Kathryn) Gayle Elizabeth, da of Stuart Nelson Keyes, of Orillia, Ontario, Canada; 2 s, 1 da; *Heir* s, Mark Christopher Michael Villiers Robinson b 23 April 1972; *Career* chartered financial analyst; chm: Celebrity Fabrics Ltd, Waterslides plc; landowner; pres British Red Cross (Northants Branch), chm St Andrews Hosp Northampton; *Clubs* L .....; *Style*— Sir John Robinson, Bt, DL; Cranford, Kettering, Northants (☎ 053 678 248)

ROBINSON, John Martin; s of John Cotton Robinson, of Hill Top Farm South, Whittle-le-Woods, Lancs, and Ellen Anne Cecilia, eld da of George Adams, of Cape Town, S Africa; *b* 10 Sept 1948; *Educ* Fort Augustus Abbey St Andrews, Oriel Coll Oxford (MA, DPhil); *Career* librarian to Duke of Norfolk 1978-; GLC Historic Buildings Div 1974-86; memb exec ctee Georgian Gp, Fitzalan Pursuivant of Arms Extraordinary 1982-88, Donat of SMO Malta, memb cncl Br Records Assoc 1986-, Maltravers Herald 1989-; FSA; *Books* The Wyatts (1980), Observations of Humphry Repton (1981), Royal Residences (1982), The Dukes of Norfolk (1983), Georgian Model Farms (1983), The Latest Country Houses (1984), The Architecture of Northern England (1986), Cardinal Consalvi (1987), The English Country Estate (1988), Guide for Heraldry (jtly with Thomas Woodcock 1988); *Clubs* Travellers'; *Style*— John Robinson, Esq, Maltravers Herald; Beckside House, Barbon, Via Carnforth, Lancs (Barbon 300); 8 Doughty Mews, London WC1 (☎ 01 405 2856)

ROBINSON, John Stephen; s of Hon Richard Anthony Gasque Robinson, of 382 Russell Hill Rd, Toronto, Ontario (d 1979), and Hon Mrs (Wendy Patricia) Robinson, *qv*; gs and h of 1 Baron Martonmere, GBE, KCMG, PC; *b* 10 July 1963; *Educ* Lakefield Coll Sch, Seneca Coll; *Style*— John Robinson Esq; 382 Russell Hill Rd, Toronto M4V 2V2, Ontario, Canada (☎ 416 485 3077)

ROBINSON, Rev Canon Joseph; s of Thomas Robinson (d 1967), of Wigan Lancs, and Maggie, *née* Wright (d 1981); *b* 23 Feb 1927; *Educ* Upholland GS, King's Coll London (BD, MTh, FKC); *m* 5 Sept 1953, Anne, da of James Antrobus (d 1978), of Wigan, Lancs; 2 s (Michael Francis b 1954, Christopher John b 1959), 2 da (Gillian Elizabeth b 1956, Katherine Mary b 1961); *Career* ordained: deacon 1952, priest 1953; curate Tottenham 1952-55, minor canon St Paul's Cathedral 1955-68, lectr in Old Testament studies King's Coll London 1959-68, canon of Canterbury 1968-80, master of the Temple 1980-; govr: Sons of the Clergy, Queen's Coll Harley St; fell Woodward Fndn; Liveryman Worshipful Co of Waxchandlers, Chaplain Worshipful Co of Cutlers, former Master Worshipful Co of Parish Clerks; Hon LLD Simon Greenleafe Law Sch Anaheim California USA; *Books* Cambridge Bible Commentary on 1 Kings (1972), Cambridge Bible Commentary on 2 Kings (1976); *Recreations* reading, gardening; *Clubs* Athenaeum; *Style*— The Rev Canon Joseph Robinson; The Master's Hse, Temple, London EC4Y 7BB (☎ 01 353 8559)

ROBINSON, Keith; s of Wilfrid Robinson, of Acklam, Middlesbrough, and Florence Marshall, *née* Gray; *b* 8 Dec 1947; *Educ* Acklam Hall GS, Univ of London (BA); *m* 8 Sept 1979, Janet Wilson, da of Archibald Black, of Yarm, Cleveland; 2 s (William James b 1982, Richard Alexander b 1985); *Career* CA; dir York Planetarium Co Ltd 1983-; *Recreations* travel, eating out; *Style*— Keith Robinson, Esq; 54 Mount Leven Rd, Yarm, Cleveland TS15 9RJ (☎ 0642 785628); Keith Robinson & Co, 4 Woodlands Rd, Middlesbrough, Cleveland TS1 3BE (☎ 0642 225325)

ROBINSON, (Leonard) Keith; CBE (1981), DL (Hampshire 1985); s of Cuthbert Lawrence Robinson and Hilda Robinson; *b* 2 July 1920; *Educ* Queen Elizabeth's GS Blackburn, Victoria Univ Manchester (LLB); *m* 1948, Susan May, da of the late Vice-Adm W Tomkinson; 2 s, 2 da; *Career* WWII RAFVR Sqdn Ldr Coastal Cmd 1940-46; slr Bristol 1948-55; dep town clerk Birkenhead Co Borough Cncl 1955-65, town clerk Stoke on Trent City Cncl 1966-73, co chief exec Hants CC 1973-85; chm Assoc of Co Chief Execs 1975-77, a princ advsr to Assoc of CCs 1974-85, memb W Midlands Econ Planning Cncl 1967-73, former memb Central Ctee for Reclamation of Derelict Land, memb Advsy Cncl for Energy Conservation 1982-84; mgmnt conslt 1985-87; dir Salisbury Playhouse Bd 1978-; vice chm: Nuffield Theatre 1985-, Southern Arts Man Cncl 1985-; asst cmmr Local Govt Boundary Cmmn 1987-; pres: The Castle CC Winchester 1977-, Winchester Dramatic Soc; mgmnt ctee memb: Hants Devpt Assoc 1985-, Hants Gdn Tst 1984-; *Recreations* theatre, fly fishing, gardening, cricket; *Clubs* National Liberal, MCC; *Style*— Keith Robinson Esq, CBE, DL; Bransbury Mill Cottage, Bransbury, Barton Stacey, Winchester, Hants S021 3QL

ROBINSON, Keith Thomas; s of Leslie Robinson (d 1986), of Brook House, North End, Great Dunmow, Essex, and Dorothy Elizabeth, *née* Gregson; *b* 27 Feb 1944; *Educ* Tonbridge, Royal Aric Coll Cirencester (Dip Estate Mgmnt); *m* 4 Oct 1969, Penelope Jane, da of Norman Eustace Scott Miller, OBE; 1 s (Thomas), 3 da (Joanna, Catherine, Georgina); *Career* chartered surveyor; Bidwells of Cambridge 1965-67, ptnr Gunton & Gunton (architect and surveyors) 1967-81, chm and md of family property cos and farming co; pres High Easter CC, govr St Cedds Sch Chelmsford Essex; memb Worshipful Co of Glaziers; ARICS, Assoc Chartered Land Agents Soc; *Recreations* sailing, golf, tennis, fell walking, swimming; *Clubs* Farmers, Channels GC, Royal Windermere YC; *Style*— Keith Robinson, Esq; The Parsonage, High Easter, Chelmsford, Essex CM1 4QZ; Crummocks, Ecclerigg, Windermere, Cumbria LA23 1LJ (☎ 0245 31291)

ROBINSON, Prof Kenneth; s of James Robinson (d 1977), of Liverpool, and Ethel, *née* Allen; *b* 4 Mar 1950; *Educ* Liverpool Collegiate GS, Wade Deacon GS, Bretton Hall Coll, Univ of Leeds (BED), Univ of London (PhD); *m* 30 Jan 1982, Marie-Thérèse, da of Frederick George Watts, of Leamington Spa; 1 s (James b 11 Oct 1984); *Career* educationist: dir Nat Curriculum Cncl arts in schools project 1985-89, chm Artswork 1987-, prof arts educn Univ of Warwick 1989-; FRSA; *Books* Learning Through Drama (1977), Exploring Theatre and Education (ed 1980), The Arts in Schools (princ author, 1982), The Arts and Higher Education (ed 1983); *Recreations* theatre, music, cinema, snooker; *Style*— Prof Ken Robinson; Univ of Warwick, Westwood, Coventry CV4 7AL (☎ 0203 523 523)

ROBINSON, Rt Hon Sir Kenneth; PC (1964); s of Dr Clarence Robinson (d 1923); *b* 19 Mar 1911; *Educ* Oundle; *m* 1941, Helen Elizabeth Edwards; 1 da (Hester b 1955); *Career* serv WWII Lt-Cdr RNVR; MP (Lab) St Pancras N 1949-70, asst whip 1950-51, oppn whip 1951-54, min of Health 1964-68, min for Planning & Land (min of Housing & Local Govt) 1968-69; md personnel BSC 1972-74; former Lloyd's insurance broker; chm: LTE 1975-78, ENO 1972-77, Arts Cncl of Gt Britain 1977-82, Young Concert Artists Tst 1983-; Hon DLitt Liverpool; FCIT, Hon FRCGP; kt 1983; *Books* Wilkie Collins: a Biography (1951, republished 1974); *Recreations* music, visual arts, reading, playgoing; *Clubs* Arts; *Style*— The Rt Hon Sir Kenneth Robinson; 12 Grove Terrace, London NW5 (☎ 01 267 0880)

ROBINSON, Prof Kenneth Ernest; CBE (1971) ; s of Ernest Robinson (d 1917), of Plumstead, Kent, and Isabel May, *née* Chalk, (d 1954); *b* 9 Mar 1914; *Educ* Sir George Monoux GS London, Hertford Coll Oxford (BA, MA), LSE; *m* 4 Nov 1938, Stephanie Christine Sara, da of William Wilson (d 1951), of Westminster; 1 s (Julian b 1944), 1 da (Miranda b 1947); *Career* Home Civil Serv Admin Class: asst princ Colonial Off 1936, Princ 1942, asst sec 1946, resigned 1948; official fell Nuffield Coll Oxford 1948-57 (hon fell 1984), reader in cwlth govt Univ of Oxford 1948-57; Univ of London: dir inst of cwlth studies, prof cwlth affrs 1957-65 (hon life memb 1979-); Reid lectr Acadia Univ Canada 1963, vice-chllr Univ of Hong Kong 1965-72, hallsworth fell Univ of Manchester 1972-74, Callander lectr Univ of Aberdeen 1979; vice-pres: Royal Cwlth Soc, Royal African Soc; govr LSE 1959-65; JP Hong Kong 1967-72; Hon LLD Chinese Univ of Hong Kong 1968, Hon DLitt Univ of Hong Kong 1972, Hon Dr Open Univ 1978, corresponding memb Academie des Sciences D'Outre-Mer Paris 1959-; FRHistS 1959; *Books* Five Elections in Africa (with WJM McKenzie, 1960), Essays in Imperial Government (with A F Madden, 1963), The Dilemmas of Trusteeship (1965); *Clubs* United Oxford and Cambridge Univ, Lansdowne, Hong Kong; *Style*— Prof Kenneth Robinson, CBE; The Old Rectory, Church Westcote, Oxford OX7 6SF (☎ 0993 830 586)

ROBINSON, Kent Seafield; s of Maj Geoffrey Seafield Robinson, (d 1974), of E Grinstead, Sussex, and Irene Marian, *née* Valpy; *b* 1 May 1938; *Educ* Kings Sch Canterbury, Sandhurst RMA; *m* 1, 12 March 1960 (m dis 1985), Cicelie Amanda Stewart, da of Sqdn Ldr Ronald Ernest Cheesman, of Hartley Wintney, Hants; 2 s (Mark b 1961, Andrew b 1963); m 2, 20 June 1985, Carol Patricia Palmer, da of Eric Dean, CB, CBE, of Hove, Sussex; *Career* RMA Sandhurst 1956-58, RASC 1958-65; Army Cross Country Driving Champion Team 1963, Far E Army Rally Champion 1964, medically ret 1965; int money broker 1969-79; opened offs: Jersey 1972, Kuwait 1976, Tokyo 1978; currently chm Lional Robinson & Co (electrical wholesalers and distributors), chm Basingstoke IOD 1985-87, pres Electrical Wholesalers Fedn 1989; FInstD 1974; *Recreations* squash, vintage motor cars, continental tours; *Style*— Kent Robinson, Esq; Wedmans Farm, Rotherwick, Basingstoke, Hants RG27 9BX; Lionel Robinson & Co Ltd, 163 Eldon St, Preston, Lancs PR2 2AD (☎ 0772 57975, fax 0772 204168, telex 67442)

ROBINSON, (Thomas) Lloyd; TD (1945); s of Thomas Rosser Robinson (d 1927), of Swansea, and Rebe Francis-Watkins (d 1962); *b* 21 Dec 1912; *Educ* Wycliffe Coll Glos; *m* 1939, Pamela Rosemary, da of William Henry Foster (d 1960), of Four Oaks, Warwicks; 1 s (Anthony), 2 da (Angela, Juliet); *Career* Maj Royal Warwickshire Regt 1939-45, 61 Divn PSC 1943, SHAEF; chm Dickinson Robinson plc 1974-77, (dep chm 1968), hon vice-pres 1978-88; hon pres 1988-; dir Legal & General Group 1970-83, vice-chm 1978-83; dir: Van Leer Group Holland 1977-81, Bristol Waterworks Co 1978-84; chm: Legal and General Western Advsy Bd 1972-84, chm Cncl of govrs Wycliffe Coll 1970-83 (pres 1988-), Cncl Bristol Univ 1977- (pro-chllr 1984-); LLD 1985; High Sheriff Avon 1978-79; master Soc of Merchant Venturers 1977-78; pres: Gloucestershire CCC 1980-83, Warwicks Old County Cricketers Assoc 1988; *Recreations* music, golf; *Clubs* Army & Navy, Marylebone Cricket, R and A Clifton (Bristol); *Style*— Thomas Lloyd Robinson, Esq; Lechlade, Stoke Bishop, Bristol BS9 1DB (☎ 0272 681957); 1 St, Bristol (☎ 0272 294294)

ROBINSON, Gp-Capt Marcus; CB (1956), AFC (1941, and bar 1944), AE (1942), DL (1953); s of Wilson Robinson (d 1953), of Glasgow, and Eileen Charlotte, *née* Colvil (d 1959); *b* 27 May 1912; *Educ* Rossall; *m* 1, 4 April 1941 (m dis 1950), Mary Playfair; 1 s (Ainslie b 18 April 1942), 1 da (Elaine b 26 Nov 1944); m 2, 25 Sept 1953, Joan Elizabeth Weatherlake, da of O C Carter (d 1964), of Bournemouth; *Career* cmmnd 602 Sqdn Aux Air Force 1934, Fl Cdr 1938-40, Sqdn Ldr i/c 616 Sqdn 1940, Sqdn Ldr flying instr 1940, Wing Cdr 1942, chief instr 15 Pilot Advanced Flying Unit, Gp Capt 1945, i/c 20 and 21 Flying Trg Schs 1945, Sr Air SO 23 Gp RAF, demob 1946, reformed 602 City of Glasgow Fighter Sqdn 1946-51; memb air advsy cncl Air Min 1952-56, chm Glasgow Territorial & Aux Forces Assoc 1952-56; Robinson Dunn & Co Ltd: dir 1939-66, chm and md 1966-77, ret 1977; chm: Glasgow Rating & Valuation Appeals Ctee 1963-77 (dep chm 1958-63), Earl Haig Fund Scotland 1974-78 (vice pres 1978); awarded Silver Jubilee Medal 1977; *Recreations* skiing, sailing, golf; *Clubs* Western, Royal Northern & Clyde YC; *Style*— Gp-Capt Marcus Robinson, CB, AFC,

AE, DL; Rockfort, Helensburgh G8A 7BA (☎ 0436 72097)

ROBINSON, Mark Noel Foster; s of John Foster Robinson, CBE, DL (d 1988), and Margaret Eva Hannah, *née* Paterson (d 1977); *b* 26 Dec 1946; *Educ* Harrow, Christ Church Oxford (MA); *m* 1982, Vivien Radclyffe, da of Alan Roger Douglas Pilkington (d 1968); 1 s (James b 1986), 1 da (Alice b 1983); *Career* barr Middle Temple; UN Off 1972-, exec off of UN Sec-Gen as second offr 1975-77, asst dir Dip Staff Cwlth Secretariat 1977-83, MP (C) Newport W 1983-87, pps to Rt Hon Nicholas Edwards, MP (Welsh sec) 1984-85, parly under-sec of state Welsh Off 1985-87; dir Leopold Joseph & Sons Ltd 1988-, bd memb Cwlth Devpt Corpn 1988-; fell Indust and Parl Tst; memb: RIIA, RUSI, FBIM; *Recreations* fishing, country pursuits; *Clubs* Travellers'; *Style—* Mark Robinson, Esq; 33 Clarendon Rd, London, W11 4JB

ROBINSON, Air Vice-Marshal Michael Maurice Jeffries; CB (1982), DL (Hampshire); s of Dr Maurice Robinson (d 1983), and Muriel Maud, *née* Jeffries (d 1981); *b* 11 Feb 1927; *Educ* Kings Sch Bruton, Queen's Coll Oxford, RAF Coll Cranwell; *m* 19 April 1952, Drusilla Dallas, da of Dr Harry Julius Bush (d 1962); 1 s (Ian), 2 da (Jennie, Sarah); *Career* RAF Coll Cranwell 1946-48, No 45 Sqdn (Malaya/ Singapore) 1948-51, Nottingham Univ Air Sqdn 1951-53, Central Flying Sch 1953-55, No 213 & 88 Sqdns RAF Germany 1956-57, Sqdn Cdr RAF Coll Cranwell 1958-60, RAF Staff Coll Bracknell 1961, No 100 Sqdn (Cdr) Victor nuclear bomber 1962-64, JSSC Latimer 1964-65, HQ FEAF/FE Cmd Jt HQ 1965-67, air staff MOD (Air) 1967-70, ops HQ Strike Cmd 1970-72, Cdr RAF Lossiemouth 1972-74, Asst Cmdt RAF Coll Cranwell 1974-77, sr air SO HQ No 1 Gp 1977-79, dir gen of Orgn (RAF) MOD (Air) 1979-82; chm: Housing Assoc for Offrs Families, mgmnt ctee Basingstoke CAB; dir Church Urban Fund Appeal Diocese of Winchester; govr: King's Sch Bruton, Duke of Kent Sch (RAF Benevolent Fund) Ewhurst, Gordons Sch Woking; *Recreations* golf, gardening, going to the opera; *Clubs* RAF; *Style—* Air Vice-Marshal Michael Robinson, CB, DL

ROBINSON, Michael Perkin; OBE (1984), TD (1948), DL (1971); s of Cecil Hall Robinson (d 1949), and Doris Mary Robinson (d 1973); *b* 12 April 1919; *Educ* Stowe; *m* 22 June 1946, Barbara Helen, da of Dr Cecil Ernest Clay (d 1962); 3 da (Shirley Rozanne (Mrs Stephen), Jennifer Jane Brionry (Mrs Hill), Alexandra Clare); *Career* Col, Dep Bde Cdr 146 Bde TA; pres Newspaper Soc 1968-69, chm Yorkshire Weekly Newspaper Gp Ltd; Hon Col 5 LI 1982-85; *Recreations* golf, fishing, photography; *Style—* Michael Robinson, Esq, OBE, TD, DL; Carleton Lodge, Carleton, Pontefract W Yorks (☎ 0977 703 818)

ROBINSON, Ven Neil; s of James Neesom Robinson (d 1972), and Alice Carter, *née* Harness (d 1976); *b* 28 Feb 1929; *Educ* Penistone GS, St John's Coll Univ of Durham (BA, Dip Theol); *m* 3 April 1956, Kathlyn, da of Thomas Williams (d 1951); 2 s (Peter b 1957, John b 1965), 2 da (Anne b 1958, Susan b 1962); *Career* Nat Serv RA 1947-49; curate and precentor Holy Trinity Hull 1954- 58, vicar Glen Parva with S Wigston Leicester 1958-69, hon canon Leicester Cathedral 1968-83, rector and rural dean Market Bosworth 1969-83, residentiary canon Worcester Cathedral 1983-87, archdeacon of Suffolk 1987-; chaplain Hereford and Worcester CC; chm: Worcester Trg Centre, Suffolk Clergy Charity, Church Men in the Midlands; *Recreations* hill walking; *Style—* The Ven the Archdeacon of Suffolk; 38 Saxmundham Rd, Aldeburgh, Suffolk OP15 5JE

ROBINSON, Nicholas Ambrose Eldred; s of late Gerard Robinson; *b* 26 July 1941; *Educ* Birkenhead Sch; *m* 1977, Annie Georgette Gabrielle, *née* Barada; 2 s, 2 da; *Career* chartered surveyor; ptnr Eddisons (Bradford), dir Bradford Property Tst plc; FRICS, ACIArb; *Recreations* sailing; *Clubs* Bradford; *Style—* Nicholas Robinson, Esq; 6 Strayside Mews, 2 Leeds Rd, Harroage HG2 8AA; (☎ 0423 502 530); 5 Rothwell St, London NW1 8YH (☎ 01 722 5107)

ROBINSON, Nicholas Johnson; s of Johnson Robinson (d 1941), and Eleanor Robinson (d 1958); the family shipowning firm Stag Line (*see below*) was founded in North Shields 1817 by Capt James Robinson (gggf) and bought out by Hunting Gibson plc; *b* 15 May 1918; *Educ* Loretto Sch, Musselburgh, Trinity Hall Cambridge (MA); *m* 1948, Dorothy Evelyn, *née* Dixon; 3 da; *Career* RCS, Maj, serv France, UK, India 1939-46; shipowner, chm Stag Line Ltd 1976-82 (dir 1953-82, ret 1983); pres Tyne & Wear C of C 1973-75, JP for borough of Tynemouth 1954-66, High Sheriff County of Tyne & Wear 1981-82; *Recreations* gardening, concerts; *Clubs* Army & Navy; *Style—* Nicholas J Robinson, Esq; 42 The Grove, Gosforth, Newcastle-upon-Tyne NE3 1NH (☎ 091 285 1770)

ROBINSON, Patrick William; s of Lyell Bryant Robinson (d 1961); *b* 23 July 1927; *Educ* Rugby, Trinity Hall Cambridge; *m* 1952, Ann Dorothea, *née* Fletcher; 1 s (Fletcher), 2 da (Lorraine, Georgina); *Career* Pilot offr (Post-War Nat Serv); dir: Rio Tinto Zinc Corpn 1965-68, Kleinwort Benson Ltd 1969-72; chm Herbert Morris Ltd 1969-79; *Recreations* fishing, painting; *Clubs* Boodle's, India House (NY), Melbourne (Australia); *Style—* Patrick Robinson, Esq; Lovington Mill, Castle Cary, Somerset (☎ 096 324 243); 3 East 71st St, New York 10021, USA (☎ 628 7906); 127 Swan Court, Flood St, London SW3 (☎ 01 352 9089)

ROBINSON, Paul Heron; Jr; s of Paul Heron Robinson, of Hinsdale, Illinois; *b* 22 June 1930; *Educ* Univ of Illinois Coll of Commerce and Business Admin (BD); *m* 1953, Martha Courtney, da of Edgar Merritt Bidwell (d 1967); 1 da; *Career* serv 1953-55 Korea as Lt USNR, Active Naval Res 1955-61; fndr and pres Robinson Inc 1960, Robinson Admin Servs Inc 1971, Robinson Coulter (London) 1972, Robinson Thomson (NZ) 1980, Robinson Thomson (Aust) 1980; US ambass to Canada 1981-; *Recreations* ranching, riding, sailing, history; *Clubs* Chicago, Shoreacres (Illinois), Capitol Hill, Army-Navy (both Washington DC), Mount Royal (Montreal); *Style—* HE Mr Paul Heron Robinson, Jr; US Embassy, 100 Wellington St, Ottawa, Ontario, Canada K1P 5T1 (☎ 613 238 5335)

ROBINSON, (Kenneth) Paul; s of John Robert Robinson (d 1965), of Skegness, Lincs, and Gertrude, *née* Major (d 1972); *b* 5 Feb 1925; *Educ* Skegness GS, Hatfield Coll Durham Univ (BSc); *m* 30 June 1951, Helen Elizabeth, da of George McKissock (d 1980); 5 s (Ian Paul b 1957, Douglas Stewart b 1959, Nicholas Duncan b 1962, Andrew Simon b 1965, Robin Neil b 1966); *Career* GEC England: joined 1950, divnl mangr of Applied Electronics Labs 1960, gen mangr GEC Road Signals 1964; joined Plessey 1966, gen mangr Plessey Controls, joined Marconi Space & Defence Systems 1973, gen mangr Frimley Unit 1974-81, md Marconi Compensation Systems Ltd 1984, md Marconi Command & Control Systems Ltd 1984-, asst md GEC Marconi Co 1984-; CEng, FIEE; *Recreations* golf, swimming, DIY; *Clubs* Inst of Directors, Royal Commonwealth Soc; *Style—* Paul Robinson, Esq; Frenchmans, 33 High St, Odiham, Hants

ROBINSON, Peter Damian; CB (1983); s of John Robinson (d 1957), and Florence Eleanor, *née* Easten (d 1972); *b* 11 July 1926; *Educ* Corby Sch Sunderland, Lincoln Coll Oxford (MA); *m* 1, 1956, Mary Katinka (d 1978), da of Dr William Percy Bonner (d 1960), of Peterborough; 2 da; m 2, 1985, Sheila Suzanne Gibbins, da of Charles Gorguet Guille (d 1966), of Finchley, London; *Career* RM Commandos 1944-46; barr Middle Temple 1951, Common Law Bar 1952-59, clerk of Assize NE circuit 1959-70, admin NE circuit 1970-74, SE circuit 1974-80, dep sec Lord Chancellor's Dept 1980-, dep clerk of the Crown in Chancery 1982-86, int cnslt in judicial admin 1987-; *Recreations* books, walking, theatre, music, travel; *Clubs* Athenaeum; *Style—* Peter Robinson Esq, CB; 6 Morpeth Mansions, Morpeth Terr, London SW1

ROBINSON, Peter David; MP (UDUP) Belfast E 1979-; s of David and Sheliah Robinson; *b* 29 Dec 1948; *Educ* Annadale GS, Castlereagh Coll of Further Educn; *m* 1979, Iris Collins; 2 s, 1 da; *Career* gen sec UDUP 1975-79 (dep ldr 1980-); memb NI Assembly 1982-; Alderman Castlereagh Boro Cncl 1977-; *Style—* Peter Robinson Esq, MP; 51 Gransha Rd, Dundonald, Belfast (☎ 0232 56418)

ROBINSON, Peter Frank; s and h of Sir Wilfred Robinson, 3rd Bt, *qv*; *b* 23 June 1949; *Style—* Peter Robinson, Esq; 9 Bingham St, London N1

ROBINSON, Prof Peter Michael; s of Maurice Allan Robinson, and Brenda Margaret, *née* Ponsford; *b* 20 April 1947; *Educ* Brockenhurst GS, UCL (BSc), LSE (MSc), Australian Nat Univ (PhD); *m* 27 Feb 1981, Wendy Rhea, da of Morris Brandmark; *Career* lectr LSE 1969-70; assoc prof: Harvard Univ 1977-79 (asst prof 1973-77), Univ of Br Columbia 1979-80; prof Univ of Surrey 1980-84, prof of econometrics LSE 1984-; pubns incl numerous articles in learned jnls and books; memb ed bd various jnls; *Recreations* walking; *Style—* Prof Peter Robinson; Dept of Economics, London Sch of Economics, Houghton St, London WC2A 2AE (☎ 01 405 7686)

ROBINSON, (Henry) Richard Gwynne; s of Dr Henry Robinson, JP, DL (d 1960), and Margaret, *née* Barnes (d 1963); *b* 25 Oct 1916; *Educ* Radley; *m* 10 Jan 1959, Rose Mary, da of Col Leslie Herbert Queripel, CMG, DSO (d 1962), of Tunbridge Wells; 2 s (David b 1964, Philip b 1965); *Career* Gunner HAC TA 1939, HAC and RA 1939-46, Maj 1945, instr in gunnery; Prudential Assurance Co Ltd 1934-67; Lawn Tennis Assoc: cncl memb 1954, chm 1973, vice-pres 1974, hon life vice-pres 1987; sports cncl: memb 1979-88, memb govrng bodies of sport consultative gp 1989-; Central Cncl of Physical Recreation: rep memb 1973, memb exec ctee 1979-, chm major spectator sports div 1983-; ctee memb: Wimbledon Championships 1972-87, Wimbledon Lawn Tennis Museum 1975-; Kent Co Lawn Tennis Assoc: memb cncl 1950, hon sec 1953, jt hon sec 1967, vice pres 1977-; ctee memb: Tunbridge Wells Lawn Tennis Club 1947-65 (chm 1962-65), Tunbridge Wells Lawn Tennis Tournament 1948-85 (chm 1956-59 and 1967-85); memb HAC 1939, Freeman City of London 1946, Liveryman Worshipful Co of Skinners 1946; FCII 1950; *Recreations* lawn tennis, squash rackets, shooting, sports, administration; *Clubs* All England Lawn Tennis & Croquet; *Style—* Richard Robinson, Esq; Long View, Limes Lane, Buxted, nr Uckfield, E Sussex TN22 4PB (☎ 082581 2551)

ROBINSON, Robert Henry; s of Ernest Redfern Robinson (d 1962), and Johanna Hogan (d 1978); *b* 17 Dec 1927; *Educ* Raynes Park GS, Exeter Coll Oxford (MA); *m* 1958, Josephine Mary, da of Paul Richard; 1 s (Nicholas), 2 da (Lucy, Suzy); *Career* writer and broadcaster; *Books* Landscape with Dead Dons (1956), The Conspiracy (1968), Inside Robert Robinson (1965), The Dog Chairman (1982), The Everyman Book of Light Verse (1984); *Clubs* Garrick; *Style—* Robert Robinson, Esq; 16 Cheyne Row, London SW3; Laurel Cottage, Buckland St Mary, Somerset

ROBINSON, Prof Roger James; s of Albert Edward Robinson, of Axmouth, Devon, and Leonora Sarah, *née* Potts; *b* 17 May 1932; *Educ* Poole GS, Balliol Coll Oxford (BA, MA, DPhil, BM, BCh); *m* 1962, Jane Hippisley, da of John Douglas Packham (d 1941); 2 s (Andrew b 1964, James b 1971), 1 da (Sarah b 1965); *Career* lectr Ch Ch Oxford 1953-56; med appts 1960-67: Radcliffe Infirmary, Hammersmith Hosp, Nat Hosp Queen Square; sr lectr Inst Child Health 1967-71, conslt paediatrician Guy's Hosp 1971-75, Ferdinand James de Rothschild prof of paediatrics Guy's Hosp Med Sch (now Guy's and St Thomas's 1975-; FRCP 1975,; *Books* Medical Care of Newborn Babies (jtly 1972); *Recreations* walking, canoeing; *Clubs* RSM; *Style—* Prof Roger Robinson; Guy's Hospital, London SE1 9RT (☎ 01 407 7600)

ROBINSON, Prof Ronald Edward; CBE (1971), DFC (1944); s of William Edward Robinson (d 1969), and Ada Teresa, *née* Goldsmith; *b* 3 Sept 1920; *Educ* Battersea GS, St John's Coll Cambridge (BA, MA, PhD); *m* 14 Aug 1948, Alice Josephine, da of Ludwell Howard Denny (d 1976), of Washington DC; 2 s (Peter Denny b 1950, Mark David Cudwell b 1958), 2 da (Alice Star Teresa b 1951, Kristin Day b 1954); *Career* res off African div Colonial Off 1947-49, fell St Johns Coll Cambridge 1948-71 (res fell 1948-51); Cambridge Univ: lectr hist 1951-66, Smuts reader Cwlth studies 1966-71; visiting fell Inst Advanced Studies Princeton 1959-61, Beit prof hist of Br Empire and Cwlth Oxford Univ 1971-87, emeritus prof and fell Balliol Coll 1987; FRCSoc; *Books* Developing The Third World (1971), Africa and The Victorians (second edn 1981) Bisharck, Europe and Africa (1988); *Recreations* room cricket; *Clubs* Hawks, Gridiron; *Style—* Prof Ronald Robinson, CBE, DFC; 79 Mill Rd, Cambridge; Balliol College, Oxford (☎ 0223 357 063)

ROBINSON, Sheriff Stanley Scott; MBE (1945), TD 1950; s of William Scott Robinson (d 1962), of Edinburgh, and Christina Douglas, *née* Wallace (d 1989); *b* 27 Mar 1913; *Educ* Boroughmuir Sch Edinburgh, Univ of Edinburgh (BL); *m* 14 April 1937, Helen Anne, da of John Hardie, of Edinburgh; 3 s (Derek John b 1938, Alastair Stanley b 1942, Ian George b 1951); *Career* RA (TA): cmmnd 1935, Capt 1939, Maj 1942, Lt Col 1947, ret 1953; slr 1935, slr Supreme Cts 1962; Sheriff of Grampian Highlands and Islands 1972 (ret 1985), Hon Sheriff of Inverness 1985; Hon Sheriff of Forfarshire, vice pres Law Soc Scotland 1969-72, former dean of faculty of slrs Slrs of Forfarshire (now Angus); govr Eden Ct Theatre Inverness; chm: Highland Club Inverness, regnl advsy ctee Forestry Cmmn (Highland); memb Soc of Slrs in Supreme Ct 1962;; *Books* Law of Interdict in Scotland 1987, contrib Stair Encyclopaedia of Laws of Scotland 1987 (law of crofting, law of railways and canals, law of game); *Recreations* bowling, caravaning; *Clubs* Highland, Inverness; *Style—* Sheriff Stanley Robinson MBE, TD; Drumalin House, 16 Drummond Rd, Inverness (☎ 0463 233488)

ROBINSON, Hon Mrs; Stella Hope; 2 da of Hon Claude Hope-Morley (d 1968), and sis of 3 Baron Hollenden; raised to the rank of a Baron's da; *b* 15 April 1919; *m* 21 Oct 1950, Neville Whiteoak Robinson, yr s of late David Whiteoak; 2 s, 1 da; *Career* 1939-45 WWII as 2 Offr WRNS; *Style—* The Hon Mrs Robinson; 107 Old Church St,

Chelsea, London SW3 6DX

ROBINSON, Stephen Joseph; OBE (1971); s of Joseph Alan Robinson, of Leicester, and Ethel Bunting (d 1962); *b* 6 August 1931; *Educ* Sebright Sch, Univ of Cambridge (MA); Harvard Business Sch; *m* 13 April 1957, Monica Mabs, da of John Scott (d 1986); 1 da (Marion Jean b 1961); 1 s (Peter Joseph b 1962); *Career* Pilot Offr RAF 1950; Mullard Research Lab 1954-71, MEL Equipment Ltd 1971-79, product dir MEL Bd 1973, md Pye TVT Ltd 1980-84, dep dir Royal Signals and Radar Establishment MOD 1985-; S G Brown Medal 1972; FRS; FEng; FIEE; *Recreations* saling, skiing, walking; *Style*— Stephen Robinson, Esq; 140 The Street, Kirtling, Newmarket, Suffolk CB8 9PD (☎ 9638 730104); Royal Signals and Radar Establishment, St Andrews Rd, Great Malvern (☎ 0684 892 733)

ROBINSON, Rev Thomas Hugh (Tom); s of Lt Col James Arthur Robinson, OBE (d 1944), and Maud Loney, *née* Trayer (d 1980); *b* 11 June 1934; *Educ* Bishop Foy Sch Waterford, Trinity Coll Dublin (BA, MA); *m* 9 July 1959, Mary Elizabeth Doreen, da of Richard Edmund Clingan (d 1988), of Portadown; 2 s (Peter b 1962, Keith b 1964), 1 da (Katherine b 1967); *Career* cmmnd Royal Army Chaplains' Dept 1966, dep asst chaplain Gen 2 Armd Div 1977-80, chaplain Royal Mil Coll of Sci 1980-82; sr chaplian: Eastern Dist 1982-84, 1 Br Corps 1984-85, BAOR 1985-86; dep chaplain Gen 1986-; ordained: deacon 1957, priest 1958; curate asst St Clements Belfast 1957-60, chaplain Missions to Seamen Mombasa 1961-64, rector St Mary's Youghal Co Cork 1964-66; *Recreations* winemaking, social golf; *Style*— The Rev Tom Robinson; Duke's House, Duke of Connaught's Rd, Aldershot, Hants GU11 2LR (☎ 0252 23671); Ministry of Defence Chaplains (Army), Bagshot Park, Bagshot, Surrey GU19 5PL (☎ 0236 71717 ext 2832)

ROBINSON, Thomas Lloyd; TD (1946); s of Thomas Rosser Robinson (d 1928), of Swansea, and Rebe, *née* Francis-Watkins (d 1962); *b* 21 Dec 1912; *Educ* Wycliffe Coll; *m* 6 Sept 1939, Pamela Rosemary, da of William Harry Foster, of Four Oaks, Warwickshire; 1 s (Anthony b 13 Aug 1948), 2 da (Angela b 1 Jan 1940, Juliet b 10 Jan 1947); *Career* WWII Royal Warwicks Regt (TA) 1939-45: Staff Coll Camberley 1943, 61 Div 1943-44, Gen Staff Sch Fort Leaveworth USA 1944-45, SHAEF 1945; dir Esta Robinson Ltd 1952-58, md Esta Robinson (Hldgs) Ltd 1958-66 (dep chm 1963-66), chm DRG 1974-77 (vice chm and md 1968-74, dir Rompus 1988-), dir Van Leer Gp Stichting Holland 1977-81, dir Bristol Waterworks Co 1978-84, vice chm Legal and General Gp plc 1978-83 (dir 1976-83); pro chllr cncl Univ of Bristol 1983-(memb 1977-83), pres Wycliffe Coll 1988-(chm 1970-83); High Sheriff of Avon 1979-80; pres Gloucestershire CC 1980-83; Freeman: City of Swansea 1934, City of Bristol 1963; Master Soc of Merchant Venturers Bristol 1977-78; Hon LLD Bristol 1985; CBIM 1965; *Recreations* music, golf; *Clubs* Army and Navy, MCC, Royal and Ancient Clifton Bristol; *Style*— Lloyd Robinson, Esq, TD; Lechlade, Stoke Bishop, Bristol BS9 1DB (☎ 0272 681 987); DRG plc, Bristol (☎ 0272 294 294)

ROBINSON, (Robert) Timothy (Tim); s of Eddy Robinson and Christine Verley; *b* 21 Nov 1958; *Educ* Dunstable GS, High Pavement Coll, Sheffield Univ (BA); *Career* prof cricketer; memb: England Team, Nottinghamshire CCC; *Style*— Tim Robinson, Esq; Nottinghamshire CCC, County Ground, Trent Bridge, Nottingham

ROBINSON, Timothy Morgan; s of Kenneth Hubert Robinson (d 1983), of Porthcawl, S Wales, and Winfred Glenice Mary, *née* Rees; *b* 17 May 1944; *Educ* Taunton Sch; *m* 8 Feb 1981, (Caroline Jane) Binna, da of Alexander Nicol, of Badgeworth, Glos; 3 s (Tom b 1977, Toby b 1978, Edward b 1986), 1 da (Holly b 1984); *Career* admitted slr 1968; sr lectr in law Gloucester Coll 1971-72, pt/t immigration act judge 1973-76, sr ptnr Robinsons (criminal law specialists) 1976-; chief exec: Bristol Law Servs Ltd 1985, Robinsons Law Servs 1980-; memb: Cheltenham Round Table 1978-, Glos and Dist Rugby Referees Soc; co rugby referee, Wales schs rugby cap; memb Law Soc 1968; *Recreations* rugby football, making money, family life; *Style*— Timothy Robinson, Esq; The Old Vicarage, Badgeworth, Glos (☎ 0242 529 410); Whaddon Chambers, Whaddon Rd, Cheltenham Spa, Glos (☎ 0242 517 876, fax 222 246, car tel 0860 824 538)

ROBINSON, Vivian; QC (1986); s of William Robinson (d 1986), of Wakefield, and Ann, *née* Kidd; *b* 29 July 1944; *Educ* Queen Elizabeth GS Wakefield, The Leys Sch Cambridge, Sidney Sussex Coll Cambridge (BA); *m* 19 April 1975, (Nora) Louise, da of Maj Peter Duncan Marriner, TD (d 1988), of Rayleigh; 1 s (Edward Duncan b 30 Jan 1980), 2 da (Katherine Anne b 12 Sept 1977, Anna Ruth b 12 July 1981); *Career* called to the bar Inner Temple 1967, rec of the Crown Court 1986-; Liveryman Worshipful Co of Gardeners; *Recreations* gardening, reading; *Clubs* Arts, MCC; *Style*— Vivian Robinson, Esq, QC; Queen Elizabeth Building, Temple, London, EC4Y 9BS (☎ 01 583 5766)

ROBINSON, Hon Mrs Richard; Wendy Patricia; da of James Cecil Blagden (d 1973), of Bapchild Court, nr Sittingbourne, Kent, and Audrey Cecily Yeatman, *née* Small; *b* 3 Feb 1939; *m* 1959, Hon Richard Anthony Gasque Robinson (d 1979), s of 1 Baron Martonmere, of Romay House, Tuckers Town, Bermuda; 2 s (*see* Robinson, John Stephen, David), 1 da (Carolyn b 1969); *Career* dir Heart and Stroke Fndn of Ontario, several private Corpns and Cos; *Style*— The Hon Mrs Richard Robinson; 382 Russell Hill Rd, Toronto, Ontario, Canada (☎ 416 485 3077)

ROBINSON, Sir Wilfred Henry Frederick; 3 Bt (UK 1908), of Hawthornden, Wynberg, Cape Province, S Africa, and Dudley House, City of Westminster; s of late Wilfred Henry Robinson (3 s of 1 Bt), and late Eileen, *née* St Leger; suc unc, Sir Joseph Benjamin Robinson 1954; *b* 24 Dec 1917; *Educ* Diocesan Coll Rondesbosch, St John's Coll Cambridge; *m* 1946, Margaret Alison Kathleen, da of late Frank Mellish, MC, of Bergendal, Cape Province, S Africa; 1 s, 2 da; *Heir* s, Peter Robinson; *Career* former Maj Para Regt; vice-princ of Diocesan Coll Sch Rondebosch Cape S Africa; fin offr Soc of Genealogists; *Style*— Sir Wilfred Robinson, Bt; Society of Genealogists, 14 Charterhouse Bldgs, London EC1M 7BA; 24 Ennismore Gdns, London SW7 1AB

ROBJANT, Peter; s of Roland Walter Donald Robjant (d 1961), and Kathleen Elizabeth Florence, *née* Hagger; *b* 31 May 1942; *Educ* Buckhurst Hill Co HS, St Catherines Coll Cambridge (MA, LLM); *m* 14 Aug 1971, Jean Sheila, da of Maj Allan Forbes Malcolmson (d 1985), 1 s (David Allan b 1973), 1 da (Mary b 1975); *Career* articled clerk Church Adams Tatham & Co 1966-68, asst slr Wild Hewitson & Shaw 1968-71, ptnr Sylvester & Mackett 1972- (asst slr 1971-72), chm W Wilts CAB 1983-88 (memb legal servs gp NACAB); memb Law Soc; *Recreations* walking; *Style*— Peter Robjant, Esq; 32 Hilperton Rd, Trowbridge, Wilts; 39 Castle St, Nether Stowey, Bridgwater, Somerset (☎ 0225 765 903); Sylvester & Mackett, Castle House, Trowbridge, Wilts BA14 8AX (☎ 0225 755 621, fax 0225 769 055, telex 444 258)

ROBOROUGH, 2 Baron (UK 1938); Sir Massey Henry Edgcumbe Lopes; 5 Bt (UK 1905), JP (Devon 1951); s of 1 Baron Roborough (d 1938) and Lady Albertha Edcumbe, da of 4 Earl of Mount Edgcumbe, GCVO, PC, JP, DL, by his w Lady Katherine Hamilton (da of 1 Duke of Abercorn, KG); *b* 4 Oct 1903; *Educ* Eton, Ch Ch Oxford; *m* 1936, Helen, da of Lt-Col Edward Dawson, JP; 2 s (and 1 da decd); *Heir* s, Hon Henry Lopes; *Career* served Royal Scots Greys 1925-38 and 1939-45; DL Devon 1946, vice-lieut 1951-58, lord-lieut 1958-78, high steward Barnstaple, county alderman Devon 1956-74; chm: SW Devon Div Educn Exec 1952-74, Dartmoor Nat Park 1965-74, Devon Outward Bound Sch; ADC to Earl of Clarendon as Govr-Gen Union of S Africa 1936-37; memb Duchy of Cornwall Cncl 1958-68; Hon Col Devon Army Cadet Force 1967-78; KStJ; *Style*— The Rt Hon the Lord Roborough, JP; Seat: Maristow, Roborough, S Devon; Residence: Bickham Barton, Roborough, S Devon (☎ Yelverton 2478)

ROBOTHAM, Maj (Alpheus) John; OBE (1972), JP (Derby 1956), DL (1968); s of late William Blews Robotham; *b* 9 Mar 1905; *Educ* Clifton Coll Bristol, Jesus Coll Cambridge (MA); *m* 1932, Gwendolyn Constance, *née* Bromet; 2 s, 1 da; *Career* WW II 2 Derbyshire Yeo 1939-45, Maj served Alamein, NW Europe (despatches); slr; *Clubs* County (Derby); *Style*— Maj John Robotham, OBE, JP, DL; Brambles, Woodlands Lane, Quarndon, Derby (☎ 0332 596558)

ROBOTHAM, (John) Michael; s of Alpheus John Robotham, OBE, JP, DL, of Quarndon, Derby, and Gwendolyn Constance, *née* Bromet; *b* 27 Mar 1933; *Educ* Clifton; *m* 29 June 1963 (m dis 1989), Diana Elizabeth, da of Alfred Thomas Webb (d 1967); 2 s (Guy Thomas Blews b 1967, Adam John Blews b 1971 d 1982); *Career* 2 Lt 12 Royal Lancers 1957-59; memb Stock Exchange 1963; dir: Western Selection plc 1969-, The Kwahu Co plc 1970-, Creston plc 1976-, NMC Investments plc 1976-, Afex Corpn plc 1983-, London Finance & Investment Co plc 1983-; hon tres Inst of Advanced Motorists 1963-88 (chm 1989), chm Mile-Posts Publications 1975-; FCA, FIMBRA; *Recreations* tennnis, shooting, skiing; *Clubs* Cavalry and Guards', HAC, City of London; *Style*— Michael Robotham, Esq; Brickwall Farm House, Clophill, Bedford MK45 4DA (☎ 0525 61333); J M Finn & Co, Salisbury House, London Wall, London EC2M 5TA (☎ 01 628 9688, fax 01 628 7314); City Group Ltd, 25 City Road, London EC1X 1BQ (☎ 01 628 9371, fax 01 633 9426); car ☎ 0836 726960

ROBSON, Air Vice-Marshal (Robert Michael) Bobby; OBE (1971); s of Dr John Alexander Robson, of Dorset, and Edith, *née* Knape; *b* 22 April 1935; *Educ* Sherborne, RMA Sandhurst; *m* 4 April 1959, Brenda Margaret, da of Leslie Clifford Croysdill, MBE (d 1970), of Dorset; *Career* cmmnd 1955, RAF Regt 1958, navigator trg 1959, strike sqdns 1985, Sqdn Cdr RAF Coll 1968, def advsr Br High Cmmr Sri Lanka 1972, Nat Def Coll 1973, CO 27 Sqdn 1974-75, MOD staff duties 1978, CO RAF Gatow 1978-80, RCDS 1981, dir of initial Offr Trg RAF Coll 1982-84, dir of PR (RAF) 1985-87, head of study into Offrs Terms of Service 1987; ADC to the Queen 1979-80; ret 1987; sheep farmer, freelance journalist 1987-; *Recreations* reading, opera, fishing; *Clubs* RAF; *Style*— Air Vice-Marshal Bobby Robson, OBE; Long Row Cottage, N Rauceby, Sleaford, Lincolnshire NG34 8QP (☎ 0529 98631)

ROBSON, Brian Ewart; CB (1985); s of Walter Ewart Robson Esq, of Hove, Sussex (d 1976); and Lily May Drain (d 1987); *b* 25 July 1926; *Educ* Varndean Sch Brighton, Queen's Coll Oxford (MA); *m* 17 March 1962, Cynthia Margaret, da of William James Scott, of Natal, Brazil; 2 da (Suzanne b 13 Nov 1965, Vanessa b 18 Feb 1969); *Career* Lt Royal Sussex and Kumaon Regts (attached Indian Army) 1944-48; civil servant, dep under sec of State MOD 1982-86; *Books* The Swords of the British Army (1976), The Road to Kabul (1986); *Recreations* military history, cricket, travel; *Clubs* Naval and Military, Oxford Union; *Style*— Brian Robson, Esq, CB; 17 Woodlands, Hove, E Sussex (☎ 0273 505803)

ROBSON, Christopher William; s of Leonard Robson (d 1970), of Egglescliffe, Cleveland, and Irene Beatrice, *née* Punch (d 1984); *b* 13 August 1936; *Educ* Rugby; *m* 17 July 1965, Susan Jane, da of Maj John Davey Cooke-Hurle (d 1979), of Startforth Hall, Barnard Castle, Co Durham; 1 s (Andrew Leonard Feilding b 1973), 2 da (Sarah Louise b 1966, Lydia Katharine b 1969); *Career* Nat Serv Lt RASC 1955-57; slr 1962, sr ptnr Punch Robson Gilchrist Smith (formerly JWR Punch and Robson) 1971- (joined 1962); fell Woodard Schs (Northern div) Ltd 1974-85, cncl memb Queen Marys Sch N Yorks, govr Aysgarth Sch N Yorks; memb: Law Soc, Br Astronomical Soc; *Recreations* astronomy, skiing, shooting, walking; *Style*— Christopher Robson, Esq; Rudd Hall, E Appleton, Richmond, N Yorks DL10 7QD (☎ 0748 811 339); 35 Albert Rd, Middlesbrough, Cleveland TS1 1NU (☎ 0642 230 700, fax 0642 218 923)

ROBSON, David Ernest Henry; QC (1980); s of Joseph Robson (d 1979), and Caroline, *née* Bowmaker; *b* 1 Mar 1940; *Educ* Robert Richardson GS Ryhope, Ch Ch Oxford (MA); *Career* alled to the Bar Inner Temple 1965, memb NE circuit 1965, rec of the Crown Ct (NE circuit) 1979-; pres Herrington Burn (Sunderland) YMCA 1986-, artistic dir Royalty Studio Theatre Sunderland 1986-; as actor: Rhineland Tour 1960, The Crucible Lyric Hammersmith 1961, Italian Straw Hat (dir Theater Der Jugend Essen Germany), The Master Builder 1974, Prime of Miss Jean Brodie 1975, Twelfth Night 1978, She Stoops to Conquer 1979, guest dir in various provincial theatres, Midsummer Nights Dream 1979, Taming Of The Shrew 1980, Merchant of Venice 1981, Romeo and Juliet 1982, Journeys End 1978, The Vortex 1980; *Recreations* acting, Italy; *Clubs* County Durham; *Style*— David Robson, Esq, QC; Whitton Grange, Rothbury, Northumberland NE65 7RL (☎ 0669 209 29); Victoria Buildings, Grainger Street, Newcastle-on-Tyne (☎ 091 232 2392)

ROBSON, (William) David; s of (William) Michael Robson, of Hales Place, Tenterden, Kent, and Audrey Isobel Wales, *née* Dick (d 1964); *b* 28 Jan 1944; *Educ* Eton; *m* 27 Sept 1975, (Anne) Helen, da of Cecil Seymour Gosling (d 1974); 1 s ((William) Henry b 1979), 1 da (Emma Lucy b 1977); *Career* Lloyd's managing agent; dir Merrett Hldgs plc 1985-; Freeman of City of London, Liveryman Worshipful Co of Vintners; *Recreations* golf, opera; *Clubs* White's, Pratt's; *Style*— David Robson Esq; The Woods, Hatfield Broad Oak, Bishops Stortford, Herts CM22 7BU (☎ 027970 452); Arthur Castle House, 33 Creechurch Lane, London EC3A 5AJ (☎ 01 283 3434)

ROBSON, Edward Stephen; s of John Arthur Robson (d 1931); *b* 15 July 1923; *Educ* Pitmans Coll Putney; *m* 1968, Joan Barbara; 1 s, 1 da; *Career* Warrant Offr RAF; md: Nickerson Fuel Oils Ltd, Nickerson Lubricants Ltd; dir: Nickerson Investmts Ltd, Nickerson Tport Ltd 1971-; *Recreations* golf, cricket; *Clubs* Pathfinder, Albany Halifax, Sicklehome GC; *Style*— Edward Robson Esq; Barnbrook, Hope, via Sheffield S30 2RA

ROBSON, Hon Mrs Elizabeth; *née* Atkin; da of Baron Atkin (Life Peer, d 1944); *m* 1, 1932, John Kennedy Cockburn Millar (d 1952); m 2, 1960, His Hon Judge Denis Hicks

Robson, QC (d 1983); *Career* barr Gray's Inn 1955; *Style*— The Hon Mrs Robson; Woodford, Dreemskerry, Isle of Man

ROBSON, Col Felix Guy; s of Guy Coburn Robson (d 1945), of Belsize Ave, London NW3, and Beryl Sinclair, *née* Nicholson (d 1980); *b* 20 July 1921; *Educ* Merchant Taylors; *m* 10 Aug 1954, Elizabeth Winifred, da of Cdr William Trinick, OBE (d 1957), of Falmouth; 2 s (Rupert b 1959, Angus b 1961); *Career* war emergency cmmn RA field branch 1941, Capt and Air Observer Pilot Italy 1944-46, cmmnd 3 RHA 1947, Staff Coll Camberley PSC 1951, Army Pilot and Fl-Cdr Malaya 1954-56, Mil Asst on MOntgomery's personal staff Paris 1956, GSO2 Allied Forces Fontainebleau 1957-59, GSO2 Intelligence War Off 1961-62, Staff Offr to Commandant Army Intelligence Centre 1963-64, Lt-Col Mil Attaché Br Embassy Cambodia 1964-66, Lt-Col Cmd-Offr HQ Intelligence Corps UK 1966-69, Col Gen Staff for Security at HQ BAOR 1970-73, Col Gen Staff for Public Info HQ Allied Forces Central Euro 1973-76; ret 1976, re-employed as Ret Offr HQ Intelligence Corps 1976-86; village & church affrs, tstee of two local museums; memb RUSI 1962, MBIM 1973; *Books* Short History & Guide To Church Of St Mary Westwell (1988); *Recreations* country pursuits, military & local history; *Clubs* United Service, Naval & Mititary; *Style*— Col Felix Robson; Dunn St Cottage, Pilgrams Way, Westwell, Ashford, Kent TN25 4NJ (☎ 023371 2521)

ROBSON, Frank Alexander; OBE (1982); s of Herbert Edward Robson (d 1951), and Sutherland Murray Stanford (d 1964); *b* 4 July 1916; *Educ* Wyggeston GS for Boys Leicester; *m* 1939, Mary Lilian, da of Pastor George Wallace Harris (d 1957), of London; 3 s (David b 1942, James b 1954, Peter b 1947), 1 da (Elizabeth b 1946); *Career* army serv Royal Leicester 1940, 50 Div of 8 Army N Africa and Middle East 1942, (POW in Italy and Germany 1942-45), Lt 1946; chm Ladies Pride plc 1937-(later chm of Gp and all subsidiaries, ret 1970); former pres: Leicester and District Knitting Industs Assoc 1974-75, Leicester branch Chartered Inst of Secretaries; memb cncl of Confedn of Br Indust; county chm Leicestershire Scout Cncl 1970-85, chm Lorraine Charity Club Leicester; FCIS; *Recreations* ocean sailing, horseracing (as owner and modest punter); *Clubs* Leicester racecourse; *Style*— Frank Robson, Esq, OBE; 48 St James Rd, Leicester LE2 1HQ (☎ Leic 545110)

ROBSON, Prof Sir (James) Gordon; CBE (1977); s of James Robson; *b* 18 Mar 1921; *Educ* Stirling HS, Univ of Glasgow; *m* 1, 1945, Dr Martha Kennedy (d 1975); 1 s; m 2, 1984, Jennifer Kilpatrick; *Career* prof of anaesthetics Royal Postgrad Medical Sch London Univ 1964-86, ret; hon conslt Hammersmith Hosp 1964-86, conslt advsr anaesthetics DHSS 1975-84; hon memb USA Assoc University Anaesthetists; memb: Physiological Soc, cncl Assoc Anaesthetists of GB and Ireland 1973-84, editorial bd and consulting ed Br Journal Anaesthesia 1965-85; hon sec Conf of Med Royal Colls and Their Faculties in UK 1976-82; master Hunterian Inst RCS 1982-88, hon conslt in Anaesthetics to the Army 1983-87, chm Advsy Ctee on Distinction Awards 1984-; pres: Scottish Soc of Anaesthetists 1985-86, Royal Soc of Medicine 1986-88; memb: Ctee of Automobile Assoc 1979-, memb ctee of mgmnt RNLI 1988-, chm Medical and Survival Ctee RNLI 1988- (memb 1981-); MB, ChB, FRCS, FRSM, DSc McGill, FFARCS, Hon FFARACS, Hon FFARCSI, Hon FDSRCS; hon fellowship Royal Coll of Physicians and Surgeons of Canada 1987, hon fell Royal Med Soc (Edinburgh) 1987, Kt 1982; *Recreations* golf, wet fly fishing; *Clubs* Denham Golf, Council of Royal College of Surgeons; *Style*— Prof Sir Gordon Robson, CBE; Brendon, Lyndale, London NW2 2NY

ROBSON, James Scott; s of William Scott Robson (d 1950), of Hawick, and Elizabeth Hannah, *née* Watt (d 1974); *b* 19 May 1921; *Educ* Hawich HS, Univ of Edinburgh (MB, ChB, MD), New York Univ; *m* 2 March 1948, Mary Kynoch, da of Alexander Knight MacDonald (d 1960), of Perth; 2 s (Michael Knight b 1952, Christopher James b 1957); *Career* RAMC: Lt (India) 1945, Capt (Palestine) 1946, Capt (Egypt) 1947-48, MO i/c med div BMH Suez; Rockefeller Studentship NY 1942-44, Rockefeller res fell Harvard 1949-50; Univ of Edinburgh: sr lectr therapeutics 1959-60, reader therapeutics 1959-60, reader therapeutics 1961-68, reader medicine 1968-76, prof medicine 1977-86; hon assoc prof med Harvard Univ 1962, visiting prof Merck Sharp & Dome Australia 1968; pres Renal Assoc London 1977-80, memb biomedical res ctee SH & H Dept, chm Nat Med Consultative Ctee in Med, memb ed bd and dep ed chm Clinical Science; FRCP (Edin) 1948; hon memb Australasian Renal Assoc 1969; FRCP (London) 1977; *Books* Companion to Medical Studies (co ed 1968-88), contrib numerous medical publication; *Recreations* gardening, theatre, travel, reading; *Clubs* New (Edinburgh); *Style*— Prof James Robson; 1 Grant Ave, Edinburgh EH13 0DS (☎ 031 441 3508)

ROBSON, John Malcolm; s of Edward Stephen Robson, of Barnbrook, Aston Lane, Hope, Derbys, and Joan Barbara, *née* Burchett; *b* 16 Mar 1952; *Educ* King's Coll Sch Wimbledon, London Tech Coll (LLB); *m* 22 July 1982, Jennifer Lillias, da of Bernard Seed, of Sutton, Surrey; 2 s (David, Aidan), 1 da (Lillias); *Career* called to the bar Inner Temple 1974; memb Wallington and Carshalton Round Table 1979-; *Recreations* swimming, ceramics, wines; *Style*— John Robson, Esq; 47 Egmont Rd, Sutton, Surrey SM2 5JR (☎ 01 642 5746); 2 Gray's Inn Square, Gray's Inn, London WC1R 5AA (☎ 01 405 1317, fax 01 405 3082)

ROBSON, John Robert; s of Maj William Michael Robson, of Hales Place, Tenterden, Kent, and Audrey Isabel Dick (d 1962); *b* 12 Jan 1947; *Educ* Eton; *m* 21 Jan 1969, Tessa Diana, da of Capt William J Straker-Smith, of Carham, Cornhill on Tweed, Northumberland; 1 s (James b 30 Oct 1975), 1 da (Claire b 2 Jan 1972); *Career* dir Merrett Hldgs plc; chm: Merrett Syndicates Ltd, Anton Underwriting Agencies Ltd; dir Concept Marketing and Communications Ltd; underwriting memb Lloyds 1969, govr Wellesley House and St Peters Ct Sch; Freeman City of London 1977, Liveryman Worshipful Co of Vintners 1982; MRPS; *Recreations* sailing, golf, zululand, philately; *Clubs* Pratts, Honourable Company Edinburgh Golfers, Rye GC Bembridge Sailing; *Style*— John Robson, Esq; Arthur Castle House, 33 Creechurch Lane, London EC3 5AJ (☎ 01 283 3434, fax 01 621 1406, car tel 0860 350 453, telex 885986)

ROBSON, Hon (Erik) Maurice William; s of Sir Lawrence William Robson (d 1982), and Baroness Robson of Kiddington (Life Peeress) (*qv*); *b* 1943; *Educ* Eton, Ch Ch Oxford; *m* 7 Sept 1985, Chloë Annabel, elder da of Richard Arthur Edwards, and Eileen Daphne, *née* Joliffe (ggd of 1 Baron Hylton); *Career* CA, ptnr Robson Rhodes; tres Highland Soc of London and Anglo-Swedish Soc; memb of Lloyds, dir Nat Liberal Club Ltd; FCA; *Recreations* sailing, skiing, stalking, fishing, shooting, hunting; *Clubs* Leander, Boodles, National Libeal, Royal Lymington Yacht, etc; *Style*— Hon Maurice Robson; Flat 2, 12 St Catherines Mews, Milner St, London SW3 2QB (☎ 01 584 3819)

ROBSON, Michael Anthony; s of Thomas Chester Robson, MM, CDM (d 1984), of Sunderland, and Gertrude Edith, *née* Thomas (d 1975); *b* 29 Nov 1931; *Educ* W Hartlepool GS, St Edmund Hall Oxford (MA); *m* 1, 6 Dec 1952, Cicely, da of James Frederick Bray (d 1934), of Hull; 1 s (Jake b 1957), 1 da (Zuleika b 1953); m 2, 10 Oct 1977, Judith, da of James Francis Smithies (d 1979), of Woolpit, Suffolk; *Career* writer and film dir: Anglia TV 1963-69, BBC2 1970; freelance; radio plays incl: Landscape with Lies (1974), Weekend at Montacute (1976), Welcome, These Pleasant Days! (1981), Intent to Deceive (1988); TV plays incl: An Adventure in Bed (1975), No Name, No Packdrill (1977), Heart to Heart (1979), Swallows and Amazons Forever! (1984), This Lighting Strikes Twice (1985), Hannay (series 1988-89), Handles, Ship of Adventure (1989); feature films incl: Got it Made (1974), The Water Babies (1978), Holocaust 2000 (jtly, 1978), The Thirty-Nine Steps (1979); *Books* incl The Beargarden (1958), Time After Rain (1962), On Giant's Shoulders (jtly, 1976); *Recreations* riding, reading; *Clubs* Oxford and Cambridge; *Style*— Michael Robson, Esq; Shave Hill Cottage, Buckhorn Weston, Gillingham, Dorset SP8 5HY (☎ 07476 2271)

ROBSON, Nigel John; s of Col Hon Harold Burge Robson TD, DL, JP (d 1964, s of Baron Robson, Life Peer, who d 1918), and Iris Emmeline, *née* Abel Smith (d 1984); *b* 25 Dec 1926; *Educ* Eton; *m* 28 Sept 1957, Anne, da of Stephen Deinol Gladstone (d 1965), of Lewins, Crockham Hill, Edenbridge, Kent; 3 s (Andrew b 1958, William b 1960, Hugo b 1962); *Career* serv Grenadier Gds 1945-48, Lt Palestine 1946-47; banker, joined Arbuthnot Latham & Co Ltd 1949, (dir 1953, chm 1969-75), dir Grindlays Bank 1969, (vice-chm 1970, dep chm 1975, chm 1977-83), dir Ottoman Bank 1959, (dep chm 1983-, chm 1987-), fell Chartered Inst of Bankers 1980- (vice pres 1980-83), dir Br Sugar plc 1982-86; chm F & GPC Br Heart Fndn 1984-, (tres 1986-), London advsr The Bank of Tokyo Ltd 1984-, chm Royal Tst Bank 1984-; dir Roy Trustco Ltd (Canada) 1985-, dir TSB Gp plc 1985-, chm TSB England & Wales plc 1986-, memb bd of Banking Supervision 1986-; tres: The Automobile Assoc 1986-, Univ of Surrey 1986-; dir Bank of Tokyo Int Ltd 1987-; govr: St Aubyns Sch Tst Ltd, King Edward's Sch Witley; FCIB 1980; *Recreations* music, walking; *Clubs* Brooks's, MCC, City of London; *Style*— Nigel Robson Esq; Pinewood Hill, Wormley, Godalming, Surrey GU8 5UD; office: 60 Lombard St, London EC3V 9EA (☎ 01 600 6000)

ROBSON, Lady (Jane) Penelope Justice; *née* Shirley; da of late 12 Earl Ferrers; *b* 1925; *m* 1944, Rev Canon John Maurice Robson, TD, canon emeritus of Derby Cathedral (hon canon 1975); 1 s, 1 da; *Style*— Lady Penelope Robson; Bristow's Close, Southrop, Lechlade, Glos GL7 3QA

ROBSON, Peter; s of Tom Baker Robson (d 1979), of Redcar, Cleveland, and Elizabeth (d 1949), *née* Ord; *b* 6 July 1926; *Educ* St Peter's Sch York, Brasenose Coll Oxford (MA); *m* 1, 21 June 1952, Kari, da of Dialmar Petersen (d 1968), of Norway; 1 s (Eirik b 1958), 1 da (Annelise b 1960); m 2, 11 Feb 1984, Betty Mildred, da of John Sydney Hurford (d 1948), of St Leonards-on-Sea; *Career* slr, sr ptnr Maxwell Batley 1970-85, currently conslt; *Recreations* golf, cricket administration; *Clubs* Oriental; *Style*— Peter Robson, Esq; 14 Rochester Gardens, Hove, E Sussex

ROBSON, Peter Gordon; s of Donald Robson (d 1981), and Lette, *née* Brewer; *b* 5 Nov 1937; *Educ* Scarborough HS; *Career* asst master Marton Hall Bridlington 1962-70, head of maths Cundall Manor York 1972-89; *Books* Between the Laughing Fields (poems, 1968), Maths Dictionary (1979), Maths for Practice and Revision (4 vols, 1982-87), Fountains Abbey, a Cistercian Monastery (1983); *Recreations* music, genealogy, photography; *Style*— P G Robson, Esq; 31 Red Scar Lane, Scarborough, N Yorks YO12 5RH; Cundall Manor, Helperby, York YO6 2RW

ROBSON, Prof Peter Neville; OBE (1983); s of Thomas Murton Robson (d 1956), of Botton, Lancs, and Edith, *née* Gresty (d 1980); *b* 23 Nov 1930; *Educ* Bolton Sch, Univ of Cambridge (BA), Univ of Sheffield (PhD); *m* 4 May 1957, Anne Ross, da of William Semple (d 1964), of Glasgow; 1 d (Fiona Susan b 1963); *Career* res engr Metropilitan Vickers Electrical Co Ltd Manchester 1954-57, reader (lectr, sr lectr) Univ of Sheffield 1957-68 (prof of electronics and electrical engrg 1968-); FIEE, FEng 1983, FRS 1987; *Style*— Prof P N Robson; 46 Canterbury Ave, Sheffield S10 3RU, S Yorks; Dept of Electronic and Electrical Engineering, Univ of Sheffield, Sheffield S1 3JD (☎ 0742 768555 ext 5131, telex 547216 UGSHEF G)

ROBSON, Stephen Arthur; s of Arthur Cyril Robson, ISO, of Scruton, N Yorks, and Lilian Marianne, *née* Peabody (d 1972); *b* 30 Sept 1943; *Educ* Pocklington Sch Yorks, St Johns Coll Cambridge (BA, MA, PhD), Stanford Univ California (MA); *m* 14 Dec 1974, Meredith Hilary, da of Ernest Lancashire (d 1982); 2 s (David Robert b 1 March 1978, Andrew Luke b 8 Sept 1979); *Career* under sec HM Treasy; *Recreations* sailing; *Clubs* Boshan SC; *Style*— Stephen Robson, Esq; H M Treasury, Parliament St, London SW1 (☎ 01 270 4510)

ROBSON, Sir Thomas Buston; MBE (1919); s of Thomas Robson (d 1928); *b* 4 Jan 1896; *Educ* Rutherford Coll Newcastle, Armstrong Coll Durham Univ (MA); *m* 1936, Roberta Cecilia Helen (d 1980), da of late Rev Archibald Fleming; 2 da; *Career* WWI RGA Capt 1918 (despatches); ptnr Price Waterhouse & Co 1934-66, chm Renold Ltd 1967-72; memb: cncl Inst of CA's 1941-66 (pres 1952-53), Central Valuation Bd for Coal Indust 1947, cos act accountancy advsy ctee Bd of Trade 1948 (chm 1955-68), MOT Advsy Ctee on replacement of 'Queen' ships 1959, Tport Tbnl 1963-69; chm EDO Ctee on Paper and Bd Indust 1964-67; vice-pres Gtr London Central Scout Cncl; ACA 1923, FCA 1939; kt 1954; *Style*— Sir Thomas Robson, MBE; 3 Gonville House, Manor Fields, London SW15 3NH (☎ 01 789 0597)

ROBSON, Prof (William) Wallace; s of Wilfrid Rosbon (d 1935), of London, and Kathleen, *née* Ryan (d 1961); *b* 20 June 1923; *Educ* New Coll Oxford (BA, MA); *m* 18 Aug 1962, Anne Varna, da of Capt Robert Moses, MC, of Stockton-on-Tees; 1 s (Hugh Wallace b 1965), 1 adopted s (Robert b 1959); *Career* asst lectr Kings Coll London 1946-48, fell Lincoln Coll Oxford 1948-70, prof of English lit Univ of Sussex 1970-72, Masson prof of English Lit Univ of Edinburgh 1970-; FRSE 1987-; *Books* Critical Essays (1966), The Signs Among Us (poems 1968), Modern English Literature (1972), The Definition of Literature (1982), A Prologus to English Literature (1986); *Style*— Prof Wallace Robson; Dept of English Literature, Univ of Edinburgh, David Hume Tower, George Sq, Edinburgh EH8 9JX (☎ 031 667 1011)

ROBSON OF KIDDINGTON, Baroness (Life Peeress UK 1974); Inga-Stina Robson; JP (Oxon 1955); da of Erik Arvidsson, of Stockholm; *b* 20 August 1919; *Educ* Stockholm; *m* 1940, Sir Lawrence Robson (d 1982), sometime sr ptnr Robson Rhodes & Co (accountants); 1 s, 2 da; *Career* sits as Lib in House of Lords; chm: SW Thames RHA 1974-82, bd govrs Queen Charlotte's and Chelsea Hosps 1970-84, Midwife Teachers Training Coll; Swedish For Off 1939-40, min of Info1942-43;

contested (Lib): Eye 1955 and 59, Gloucester 1964 and 1966; pres Lib Pty Orgn 1970-71; chm: Anglo-Swedish Soc 1982, Nat Assoc of Leagues of Hosp Friends 1986; *Recreations* skiing, sailing, fishing; *Clubs* Nat Liberal, Boodle's; *Style*— The Rt Hon the Lady Robson of Kiddington, JP; Kiddington Hall, Woodstock, Oxon (☎ 060 872 398)

ROCH, Mr Justice; Sir John Ormond; QC (1976); s of Frederick Ormond Roch (d 1973), and Vera Elizabeth Roch, *née* Chamberlain; *b* 19 April 1934; *Educ* Wrekin Coll, Clare Coll Cambridge (BA, LLB); *m* 1967, Anne Elizabeth, da of Dr Willoughby Hugh Greany; 3 da (Joanna b 1968, Lucinda b 1970, Charlotte b 1972); *Career* rec 1968-85, high ct judge Queens Bench Div, tres Wales and Chester circuit 1980-84; *Recreations* music, reading, sailing (Cantabile of Dale); *Clubs* Dale Yacht; *Style*— The Hon Mr Justice Roch, QC; Roy Cts of Justice, The Strand, London

ROCHDALE, Archdeacon of; see: Bonser, The Ven David

ROCHDALE, Archdeacon of; *see*: Bonser, Ven David

ROCHDALE, 1 Viscount (UK 1960); John Durival Kemp; OBE (1945), TD (1943), DL (Cumbria 1948); also Baron Rochdale (UK 1913); s of 1 Baron Rochdale, CB (d 1945), and Lady Beatrice Egerton, MBE, da of 3 Earl of Ellesmere, JP, DL (by his w Lady Katherine Phipps, 2 da of 2 Marquess of Normanby); *b* 5 June 1906; *Educ* Eton, Trinity Coll Cambridge; *m* 1931, Elinor, CBE, JP, da of Capt Ernest Pease, of Darlington; 1 s (and 1 da decd); *Heir* s, Hon St John Kemp; *Career* served 1939-45, Europe, UK, Pacific, India, Brig (despatches), Hon Col 251 Westmorland and Cumberland Yeo, Field Regt RA (TA), later 2 Battery RA (TA) 1959-67; joined Kelsall & Kemp Ltd Rochdale Woollen Mfrs 1928 (chm 1952-71); dir: Consett Iron Co Ltd 1956-67, Geigy (Hldgs) Ltd 1959-64, Williams Deacon's Bank Ltd 1960-70; dep chm W Riding Worsted & Woollen Mills Ltd 1969-72, chm Harland & Wolff Ltd Belfast 1971-75, dir Nat & Commercial Banking Gp 1971-77, dep chm Williams & Glyn's Bank Ltd 1973-77; memb Central Tport Consultative Ctee for GB 1952-57, pres Nat Union of Mfrs 1953-56, memb Dollar Exports Cncl 1953-60, govr BBC 1954-59, vice-pres Br Productivity Cncl 1955-56, pres Br Legion NW area 1955-60; chm: Cotton Bd 1957-62, Ctee of Inquiry into Major Ports of GB 1961; memb: Western Hemisphere Exports Cncl 1960-64, Textile Inst 1962; chm Nat Ports Ncl 1963-67, pres Econ League 1964-67, chm Ctee of Inquiry into Shipping Ind 1967-70, pres NW Industl Devpt Assoc 1974-84, dir Cumbria Rural Enterprise; Textile Inst Medal 1986; upper bailiff Worshipful Co of Weavers 1956-57; MinstT; *Recreations* forestry, gardening, music; *Clubs* Lansdowne; *Style*— The Rt Hon Viscount Rochdale, OBE, TD, DL; Lingholm, Keswick, Cumbria CA12 5UA (☎ 07687 72003)

ROCHE, Hon Lady; Hon (Helen) Alexandra Briscoe; *née* Gully; JP (1984); JP; da of 3 Viscount Selby; *b* 1934; *Educ* Paris; *m* 1, 1952 (m dis 1965), Roger Moreton Frewen (d 1972); 3 s, 2 da; m 2, 1971, Sir David O'Grady Roche, 5 Bt, *qv*; Justice of the Peace 1984-; *Recreations* sailing, gardening; *Clubs* RYS; *Style*— The Hon Lady Roche, JP; Bridge House, Starbotton, Skipton, N Yorks BD23 5HY

ROCHE, Sir David (O'Grady); 5 Bt (UK 1838), of Carass, Co Limerick; s of Lt-Cdr Sir Standish O'Grady Roche, 4 Bt, DSO, RN, (d 1977), and Evelyn Laura, only da of late Maj William Andon, of Jersey; *b* 21 Sept 1947; *Educ* Wellington, Trinity Coll Dublin; *m* 1971, Hon (Helen) Alexandra Briscoe Gully, JP, da of late 3 Viscount Selby (*see* Hon Lady Roche), and formerly w of late Roger Moreton Frewen; 2 s (David b 1976, 1 s decd), 1 da (Cecilia b 1979); *Heir* s, David Alexander O'Grady Roche, b 28 Jan 1976; *Career* CA; formerly with Peat Marwick Mitchell & Co, mangr Samuel Montagu Ltd; chm: Carlton Real Estates plc 1978-82, Roche & Co Ltd (The Securites Assoc), Carass Property Ltd, Echo Hotel plc; *Recreations* shooting, sailing (yacht Lady Nicola); *Clubs* Bucks, Kildare St, University (Dublin), Royal Yacht Squadron; *Style*— Sir David Roche, Bt; Bridge House, Starbotton, Skipton, N Yorks (☎ 075 676 863); 36 Coniger Rd, London SW6 (☎ 01 736 0382); 45 Albemarle St, London W1X 3FG (☎ 01 499 5651)

ROCHE, Hon Frances Caroline Burke; da of 5 Baron Fermoy (d 1984); sis of 6 Baron Fermoy, *qv*; *b* 31 Mar 1965; *Style*— The Hon Frances Roche; Axford House, Marlborough, Wiltshire

ROCHE, Francisco; s of Antonio Roche, of Granada, Spain, and Catalina Roche; *b* 3 August 1946; *Educ* Univ of Madrid; *m* 9 Feb 1974, Angela, da of Virgilio Riesco, of Leon, Spain; 1 s (Francisco b 31 Oct 1978), 1 da (Angela b 31 July 1975); *Career* Banco Hispano Americano Ltd: mangr BHA SA 1977-83, gen mangr BHA NY 1983-86, md BHA Ltd 1988-(chief exec 1986-); memb Spanish C of C; *Style*— Francisco Roche, Esq; Banco Hispano Americano Ltd, 15 Austin Friars, London EC2N 2DJ (☎ 01 628 4499, fax 01 588 5825, telex 8813971)

ROCHE, Hon Thomas Gabriel; QC (1955); s of Baron Roche, PC (Life Peer, d 1956); *b* 1909; *Educ* Rugby, Wadham Oxford; *Career* WW II as Lt-Col RA; barr 1932, rec Worcester 1959-71; church cmmr 1961-65; *Style*— The Hon Thomas Roche, QC; Ashcroft House, Chadlington, Oxford (☎ 060 876 421)

ROCHE-GORDON, Delphine Mary; da of Thomas William Edgar Roche (d 1972), of Cambridge, and Henrietta Laure Lea, *née* Bopp; *b* 2 April 1945; *Educ* Dover GS, Slough HS, Ealing Sch of Art; *m* 1, 27 Feb 1967 (m dis 1972), Norman Wynne Griffith; m 2, 28 Oct 1972, Campbell Munro Gordon, s of Murdoch Campbell Gordon (d 1973); 2 s (Christopher, Nicholas), 1 da (Amy); *Career* owner of and designer for The Bunny Shop Eton Bucks 1967, BBC TV costume asst on The First Churchills 1968; BBC costume designer 1969-, programmes incl: Black & White Minstrels, Val Doonican series, Harry Secombe series, Shirley Bassey special, Perry Como special, Royal Command Performance with Dad's Army, Weir of Hermiston, Secret Servant, All Creatures Great and Small 1985, Tutti Frutti (BAFTA nomination) 1986, The Dark Room 1987, Dunroamin' Rising, The Justice Game, The Shawl 1988; involved with: Gartmore Conservation Soc, The Princess of Wales Hospice; *Recreations* cycling, horse riding, sewing, reading, animals; *Style*— Mrs Delphine Roche-Gordon; Drummit Ho, Gartmore, Stirling, Scotland (☎ 08772 456); BBC TV Broadcasting House, Queen Margaret Drive, Glasgow (☎ 041 330 272)

ROCHESTER, David John; s of Edward Rochester (d 1983), and Anne Edna, *née* Raine; *b* 29 Dec 1939; *Educ* The Reigate Sorbonne Paris; *m* 31 Dec 1977, Shannon Marie, da of Joseph Clements, of Twin Falls, Idaho, USA; 2 da (Raine Elizabeth b 1981, Hailey Clements b 1984); *Career* ptnr Cazenove & Co 1961-81, pres Wedd Durlacher Mordaunt Inc 1981-83, md Merrill Lynch Ltd 1983-; *Recreations* shooting, tennis golf; *Clubs* Racquet & Tennis (NY), Royal Sydney (Australia); *Style*— David Rochester, Esq; 61 St George's Drive, London SW1; Blue Doors, South Stoke, Arundel, W Sussex; Merrill Lynch Limited, Ropemaker Place, Ropemaker Street, London EC2Y 9LY

ROCHESTER, 2 Baron (UK 1931) Foster Charles Lowry Lamb; s of 1 Baron Rochester, CMG, JP, sometime MP Rochester and paymaster-gen in 1931 Nat Govt (d 1955); *b* 7 June 1916; *Educ* Mill Hill, Jesus Coll Cambridge (MA); *m* 12 Dec 1942, Mary, da of Thomas Benjamin Wheeler, CBE (d 1981); 2 s, 1 da (and 1 da decd); *Heir* s, Hon David Lamb; *Career* sits as Soc and Lib Dem in House of Lords; former Capt 23 Hussars WWII; personnel mangr Mond ICI; pro-chllr Keele Univ; DL (Cheshire) 1979; Hon D Univ Keele 1986; *Clubs* Reform; *Style*— The Lord Rochester; The Hollies, Hartford, Cheshire (☎ 0606 74733)

ROCHESTER, 105 Bishop of 1988-; Rt Rev (Anthony) Michael Arnold Turnbull; patron of seventy-six livings, of the Archdeaconries of Rochester, Tonbridge and Bromley, two Residentiary Canonries, and of all the Honorary Canonries; s of George Ernest Turnbull (d 1954), and Adeline Turnbull; *b* 27 Dec 1935; *Educ* Ilkley GS, Keble Coll Oxford (MA), St John's Coll Durham (DipTh); *m* 25 May 1963, Brenda (JP), da of Leslie James Merchant; 1 s (Mark b 1966), 2 da (Rachel b 1964, Rebecca b 1970); *Career* curate Middleton and Luton 1960-65; chaplain: Archbishop of York 1965-69, Univ of York: rector of Heslington 1969-76, chief sec Church Army 1976-84, archdeacon of Rochester and canon residentiary Rochester Cathedral 1984-88; memb Gen Synod; *Books* Gods Front Line (1978), Parish Evangelism (1980); *Recreations* cricket, books, walking; *Clubs* Athenaeum, MCC; *Style*— The Rt Rev the Bishop Rochester; Bishopscourt, Rochester, Kent ME1 1TS (☎ 0634 42721)

ROCK, David Annison; s of Thomas Henry Rock (d 1964), of Sunderland, Co Durham, and Muriel Rock, *née* Barton (d 1964); *b* 27 May 1929; *Educ* Bede GS Sunderland, Univ of Durham, (B Arch); *m* 18 Dec 1954 (m dis 1985), Daphne Elizabeth Richards; 3 s (Adam b 1960, Jacob b 1961, Mark b 1963), 2 da (Felicity b 1957, Alice b 1963); *Career* 2 Lt BAOR RE 1953-55; sr architect Sir Basil Spence 1952-55 and 1955-58, ptnr and fndr London Gp Bldg Design Partnership 1959-71, fndr ptnr Rock Townsend 1971, co fndr Workspace Business Centre Concept in UK 1971, fndr dir Barley Mow Workspace 1974-; fndr chm Dryden Street Collective 1971-78; vice-pres RIBA 1987-88 (memb cncl 1970-76, 1986-88), chm Soc of Architect Artists 1986-; cncl Nat Acad Awards; awards inc: The Soane Medallion, the Owen Jones Studentship, RIBA Bldg Industry Tst Fellowship, The Glover Medal; FIBA, FCSD; *Books* Vivat Wave: Strategies to Enhance an Historic Town (1974), The Grassroot Developers (1980); *Recreations* painting, illustration, work; *Style*— David Rock, Esq; 27 Roupell Street, London SE1 8TB (☎ 01-928 8738); Rock Townsend, 35 Alfred Place, WC1 (☎ 01 637 5300, fax 01-580 6080)

ROCK, Michael John; s of Arthur Edward Rock (d 1984), of Worcestershire, and Edna Davis; *b* 18 May 1942; *Educ* Halesowen GS, Birmingham Poly, Cologne Univ, Univ of London (BA, DipM); *m* 1, 11 Sept 1971 (m dis 1978), Zofia Kamilla, da of Rev Frederick Arlt, of Birmingham; m 2, 1 June 1979 (m dis 1983), Margaret; *Career* student apprentice Rheinisch Stahlwerke AG 1960-65, prod mgmnt Baker Perkins Int Germany 1965-66, (Austria 1966-70), commercial dir G D Peters Ltd 1970-73; dir: ITS Ltd 1973, Riehle-Iwa Ltd 1985; memb: Nat Cncl IMRA (Industrial Market Research Assoc) 1983-86, BIM Cncl Slough 1985-; Farnham Royal Parish cncllr 1987; Freeman City of London 1986, Liveryman Worshipful Co of Marketers; FInstM, FIEx, FBIM, MIM, MIMC, FRSA, FRGS; *Recreations* walking, languages, music, books, painting, travel, geography, ind archaeology, following rugby; *Clubs* RAC, Directors, Stoke Poges Golf; *Style*— Michael Rock, Esq; 7 Sospel Court, Farnham Royal, Bucks SL2 3BT; ITS Ltd, PO Box 331, Slough SL2 3DQ (fax 02814 6461, telex 848314)

ROCKER, David; s of Richard Frederick Rocker (d 1984), of Hatfield Peverel, Essex, and Elizabeth Ellen, *née* Lewis; *b* 9 June 1944; *Educ* King Edward VI Sch Chelmsford; *m* 1972, Jacolyn Jane, da of John Geoffry Matthews, of Finchingfield, Essex; *Career* slr, ptnr Leonard Gray & Co 1968-71; legal advsr: Hawker Siddeley Gp Ltd 1971-73, Trident TV 1973-79; dir legal affrs Guinness plc 1982-86; chm: Guinness Superlatives Ltd 1984-85, Guinness Overseas Ltd 1985-86; princ David Rocker & Co 1986-; *Recreations* motor-racing, squash, riding; *Style*— David Rocker, Esq; The Maltings, The Green, Writtle, Essex (☎ 0245 420141)

ROCKLEY, 3 Baron (UK 1934); James Hugh Cecil; s of 2 Baron Rockley (d 1976, whose f, 1 Baron, was er s of Lord Eustace Cecil, 3 s of 2 Marquess of Salisbury by his 1 w, Frances, the Gascoyne heiress), and Anne, da of Adm Hon Sir Herbert Meade-Fetherstonhaugh, GCVO, CB, DSO, yr bro of 5 Earl of Clanwilliam; *b* 5 April 1934; *Educ* Eton, New Coll Oxford; *m* 1958, Lady Sarah Primrose Cadogan, eldest da of 7 Earl Cadogan, MC, DL; 1 s, 2 da; *Heir* s, Hon Anthony Robert Cecil b 29 July 1961; *Career* vice-chm Kleinwort Benson Gp; dir: Kleinwort Benson Ltd 1970-, Equity & Law plc 1980-, Christies Int plc 1989-; tstee Nat Portrait Gallery 1981-88, chm Issuing Houses Assoc 1987-89; *Style*— The Rt Hon the Lord Rockley; Lytchett Heath, Poole, Dorset (☎ 0202 2228)

ROCKLEY, Baroness; Lady Sarah Primrose Beatrix; da (by 1 w) of 7 Earl Cadogan; *b* 1938; *m* 1958, 3 Baron Rockley; 1 s, 2 da; *Style*— The Rt Hon the Lady Rockley; Lytchett Heath, Poole, Dorset

ROCKSAVAGE, Earl of; David George Philip; s and h of 6 Marq of Cholmondeley, GCVO, MC; *b* 27 June 1960; *Educ* La Sorbonne; *Career* a page of honour to HM the Queen 1974-76; *Style*— Earl of Rocksavage

RODD, Michael Philip; s of Howard Philip Rodd, of San Jose, Ibiza, and Jean Dunn Rodd, *née* Allon; *b* 29 Nov 1943; *Educ* Trinity Coll Glenalmond, Univ of Newcastle upon Tyne (LLB); *m* 1966, Nita Elizabeth, da of Dr Donald Robert Cubey, of Whitley Bay, Tyne and Wear; 3 s (Benjamin b 1968, Jonathan b 1971, Owen b 1978); *Career* broadcaster, TV prodr Border TV 1965-67, BBC Newcastle 1967-71, BBC London 1971-81; presenter BBC TV's Tomorrow's World and The Risk Business; Industrial Broadcaster of Year (Brit Instit of Mngmt 1980); co-fndr (with Michael Blakstad) and exec dir of Blackrod (ind TV productn subsid of TVS) 1980, specialists in developing use of TV by business and industry; *Recreations* music, home decorating; *Style*— Michael Rodd, Esq; Blackrod, Threeways House, 40-44 Clipstone St, London W1P 7EA, (☎ 01 637 9376, telex 269859)

RODDICK, Winston; QC (1986); s of William Daniel Roddick (d 1977), of Caernarfon, and Aelwen, *née* Hughes; *b* 2 Oct 1940; *Educ* Caernarfon GS, Tal-Handak Malta, UCL; *m* 24 Sept 1966, Cennin, da of James Parry, BEM (d 1986) of Caernarfon; 1 s (Daniel b 1977), 1 da (Helen b 1979); *Career* barr Gray's Inn 1968, rec 1986; chm Lloyd George Soc; memb of the Welsh Language Bd, dir Welsh Diabetes Res Tst; *Recreations* walking the countryside; *Clubs* Cardiff & County, Nat Lib, Caernarfon

Sailing; *Style*— Winston Roddick, Esq, QC; 1 Harcourt Buildings (3rd Floor), Temple, London (☎ 01 353 2214)

RODDIE, Prof Ian Campbell; CBE (1987), TD (1967); s of Rev John Richard Wesley Roddie (d 1953), of Belfast, NI, and Mary Hill, *née* Wilson (d 1973); *b* 1 Dec 1928; *Educ* Methodist Coll Belfast, Queen's Univ of Belfast (MB, BCh, BAO, MD, DSc); *m* 1, 15 Feb 1958, Elizabeth (Betty) Ann Gillon (d 1974), da of Thomas Honeyman, of Cheltenham, Glos; 1 s (Patrick b 1965), 3 da (Mary b 1960, Catherine b 1963, Sarah b 1964); m 2, 29 Nov 1974 (m dis 1983), Katherine Anne, da of Edward O'Hara, of Belfast, NI; 1 s (David b 1977), 1 da (Claire b 1975); m 3, 14 Nov 1987, Janet Doreen, da of Thomas Russell Lennon (d 1978), of Larne, NI; *Career* RAMC and T and AVR 1951-68, Queen's Univ Belfast, OC med subunit, ret Maj 1968; res med offr Royal Victoria Hosp Belfast 1953-54; Queen's Univ Belfast: reader (lectr and sr lectr) in physiology 1954-64, Dunville prof of physiology 1964-87, dean of the med faculty 1976-81, pro-vice chllr 1984-87, prof emeritus 1988-; Harkness fell Univ of Washington Seattle USA, staff conslt Asian Devpt Bank Manila 1978-; visiting prof Univ of NSW Sydney Aust 1983-84, The Chinese Univ of Honk Kong 1988-; conslt physiologist Eastern Health and Social Servs Bd NI 1957-88 (bd memb 1976-81); memb: NI Postgraduate Med Cncl 1976-81, Home Def Scientific Advsy Ctee (chief-regnl scientific advsr) 1977-88, Gen Dental Cncl 1978-81, Royal Irish Acad 1978-, GMC 1979-81; pres Royal Acad of Medicine in Ireland 1985-87, chm of ctee The Physiological Soc (UK) 1986-88; memb Physiological Soc 1956, MRCPI 1957, FRCPI 1965, MRIA 1978; *Books* Physiology for Practitioners (1971), The Physiology of Disease (1975); *Recreations* reading, travel, work; *Clubs* Royal Cwlth Soc; *Style*— Prof Ian Roddie, CBE, TD; Dept of Physiology, Shatin, New Territories, Hong Kong (☎ 0 695 2877, fax 0 695 4234, telex 50301 CUHK HX)

RODDIE, Dr (Thomas) Wilson; s of Rev John Richard Wesley Roddie (d 1953), and Mary Hill, *née* Wilson (d 1974); *b* 19 August 1921; *Educ* The Methodist Coll Belfast, Queen's Univ Belfast (MB, BCh, BAO); *m* 21 April 1949, Alix Pauline Mary, da of Rev Canon Frank Hurst (d 1973); 2 da (Elisabeth Margaret Anne (Mrs Nicholls) b 13 April 1950, Alexandra Frances Mary b 24 Sept 1953); *Career* RNVR; Surgn Lt: Ulster Div 1951-55, Malayan Div Singapore 1955-59; Surgn Lt Cdr Ulster Div 1959-72; resident obstetrical offr Princess Mary Maternity Hosp Newcastle-upon-Tyne 1947, sr house offr Jessop Hosp for Women Sheffield 1948, sr registrar Royal Maternity and Royal Victoria Hosps Belfast 1950-55; conslt obstetrician and gynaecologist: Kandang Kerbau Hosp Singapore (and sr lectr Univ of Malaya) 1955-59, Eastern Health and Social Servs Bd Belfast 1959-86 (ret); civilian conslt gynaecologist UKLF (NI) 1969-86, examiner Royal Coll of Midwives 1959-86; MRCOG 1949, FRCOG 1961; fell: Ulster Med Soc, Ulster Obstetrical and Gynaecological Soc (pres) 1969; memb: BMA, North of England Obstetrical and Gynaecological Soc; *Recreations* travel; *Clubs* RNR; *Style*— Dr Wilson Roddie; Lodge Farm, Kirkby Fleetham, North Yorks DL7 0SN (☎ 0609 748673)

RODEN, Nina Joy; *née* Blatt; da of Samuel Blatt (d 1980), of 50 Green Walk, Hendon, and Rose, *née* Meisler (d 1978); *b* 19 April 1934; *Educ* The Skinners Co Sch for Girls, City of London Coll Moorgate; *m* 17 Sept 1973 (m dis 1986), (Joseph) Peter Roden, s of Gregory Roden (d 1974), of Brinscall, Lancs; *Career* PA to head of publicity Hulton Press (Picture Post) 1949-56, freelance writing travel featurs for various magazines, PA to first Sec HM Embassy Paris 1956-58, prodr ATV Network Ltd 1958-71 (formerly: prodn asst, asst prod, assoc prodr), dir Nina Blatt Ltd (representing prodrs/dirs in media (TV)); memb The Samaritans; memb BAFTA 1971-; *Recreations* theatre, music, writing, literary persuits; *Style*— Mrs Nina Roden; The Coach House, 1A Larpent Ave, Putney, London SW15 6UP (☎ 01 788 9971, 01 788 5602/3)

RODEN, 9 Earl of (I 1771); Sir Robert William Jocelyn; 13 Bt (E 1665); also Baron Newport (I 1743) and Viscount Jocelyn (I 1755); s of 8 Earl of Roden, DL (d 1956), and Elinor Jessie, da of Joseph Charlton Parr, JP, DL of Grappenhall Heyes, Cheshire; *b* 4 Dec 1909; *Educ* RNC Dartmouth; *m* 1937, Clodagh, da of Edward Kennedy (gs of Sir John Kennedy, 1 Bt); 3 s; *Heir* s, Viscount Jocelyn; *Career* served WWII (despatches three times) 1939-45, Capt RN, ret; *Style*— Capt The Earl of Roden, RN; 75 Bryansford Village, Newcastle, Co Down, N I BT33 0PT (☎ 23469)

RODGER, Alan Ferguson; QC (1985); s of Prof Thomas Ferguson Rodger, CBE (d 1978), of Glasgow, and Jean Margaret Smith, *née* Chalmers (d 1981); *b* 18 Sept 1944; *Educ* Kelvinside Acad Glasgow, Univ of Glasgow (MA, LLB), New Coll Oxford (MA, DPhil); *Career* jr res fell Balliol Coll 1969-70, fell and tutor in law New Coll Oxford 1970-72, memb faculty of advocates 1974 (clerk 1976-79), standing jr counsel (Scotland) to Dept of Trade 1979, advocate depute 1985-88, home advocate depute 1986-88, Slr Gen Scotland 1989-; memb mental welfare cmmn for Scotland 1982-85; *Books* Owners and Neighbours in Roman Law (1972), Introduction to the Law of Scotland (asst ed ninth edn 1987); *Recreations* writing, walking; *Clubs* Athenaeum; *Style*— Alan Rodger, Esq, QC; The Crown Office, Regent St, Edinburgh, Lothian (☎ 031 557 3800)

RODGER, George William Adam; s of George F Eck Rodger (d 1956), and Hilda Seebohm Rodger (d 1961); *b* 19 Mar 1908; *Educ* Privately, St Bees Coll; *m* 1, 1942, Cicely Joane Hussey-Freke (decd); m 2, 1953, Lois Witherspoon; 2 s (Jonathan George b 1962, Peter Anthony b 1965), 1 da (Jennifer b 1959); *Career* war corr Life magazine 1940-45; service inc: W Africa (Free French), Eritrea (For Legion), Ethiopia (Indian Army), (American Army); photographer BBC 1936-39, staff photographer Life 1945, fndr memb Magnum Photos Inc 1947; in 1978 started 2 yr Cape-Cairo expedition resulting in the famous pictures of Kordofan; 1 man exhibitions inc: Photographers Gallery London 1974, 1979 and 1987, S Africa 1978, Grenoble 1982, Marseilles 1984, Gerona 1986, Cyprus 1987; won first prize Peace to the World exhibition Moscow 1985; *Books* Red Moon Rising (1943), Desert Journey (1943), Far on the Ringing Plains (1943), Les Villages des Noubas (1955), World of the Horse (1977), George Rodger en Afrique by Carole Naggar (1984), George Rodger - Magnum Opus by Dirk Nishen (1987); *Style*— George Rodger, Esq; Waterside House, Smarden, Kent (☎ 023 377 322)

RODGER, Dr Nicholas Andrew Martin; s of Lt-Cdr Ian Alexander Rodger RN, of Arundel, Sussex, and Sara Mary *née* Perceval; *b* 12 Nov 1949; *Educ* Ampleforth, Univ Coll Oxford (BA, MA, DPhil); *m* 28 Aug 1982, Susan Eleanor, da of Henry Meigs Farwell, of Irkenham, Middlesex; 1 s (Christopher b 1987), 1 da (Ellen b 1984); *Career* asst keeper of Public Records 1974-, hon sec Navy Records Soc 1976-; *Books* The Admiralty (1979), The Wooden World an Anatomy of the Georgian Navy (1986); *Recreations* hill walking, magiology, music, history of weights and measures; *Style*— Dr Nicholas Rodger, Esq; Public Record Office, Chancery Lane, London WC2A 1LR

RODGER, Rt Rev Patrick Campbell; s of Patrick Wylie Rodger; *b* 28 Nov 1920; *Educ* Rugby, Ch Ch Oxford; *m* 1952, Margaret, da of Dr William Menzies Menzies, of Edinburgh; 1 s (and 1 s decd); *Career* served WWII; ordained 1949, rector St Fillan's Kilmacolm with St Mary's Bridge of Weir 1958-61, exec sec Faith and Order in World Cncl of Churches 1961-66, vice-provost St Mary's Cathedral Edinburgh 1966-67 (provost 1967-70); 8 bishop of Manchester 1970-78, bishop of Oxford 1978-86; asst bishop, Diocese of Edinburgh 1986-; memb: House of Lords 1974-86, Praesidium Conf of Euro Churches 1974-86; *Style*— The Rt Rev Patrick Rodger; 12 Warrender Park Terrace, Edinburgh EH9 1EG (☎ 031 229 5075)

RODGERS, David Ernest; s of Ernest Rodgers, of Sutton, nr Peterborough, and Pamela Anne, *née* Wilkins; *b* 1 Feb 1942; *Educ* King Edward VII Sch Sheffield, St John's Coll Cambridge (BA, MA); *Career* art asst York City Art Gallery 1963-65, dep dir Sheffield City Art Galleries 1965-68; curator: Old Battersea House 1968-69, Wolverhampton Art Gallery and Museums 1969-81; dir: Exeter Museums 1981-86, Geffrye Museum 1986-; tutor Open Univ 1976-78, external assessor in history of art NCAA 1977-79; memb bd of mgmnt Ikon Gallery Birmingham 1976-81 (vice chm 1979-81), govr Wolverhampton Poly 1978-81, hon sec Exeter Festival Ctee 1981-86, served on Arts Cncl Panels and working parties; *Books* Coronation Souvenirs and Commemboratives (1976); author of articles for Burlington Magazine, Apollo, Antique collector; *Recreations* collecting, cooking, gardening, theatre; *Style*— David Rodgers, Esq; Clevedon Lodge, 15C Stockwell Pk Rd, London SW9 0AP; The Geffrye Museum, Kingsland Rd, London E2 8EA

RODGERS, Sir John Charles; 1 Bt (UK 1964), of Groombridge, Kent, DL (Kent 1973); s of Charles Rodgers, of York, and Maud Mary Hodgson; *b* 5 Oct 1906; *Educ* St Peter's York, Ecole des Roches France, Keble Coll Oxford (MA); *m* 1930, Betsy, JP, MA, PhD, da of Francis Aikin-Sneath, JP, of Burleigh Court, Glos (d 1939); 2 s (Tobias and Piers); *Heir* s, Tobias Rodgers, b 2 July 1940; *Career* MP (C) Sevenoaks 1950-79, pps to Rt Hon Viscount Eccles at Ministries of Works, Education and BOT 1951-57, parly sec BOT and min Regnl Devpt and Employment 1958-60; formerly FO during WW II; fndn govr Admin Staff Coll, exec Council memb Foundn for Management Educn 1959-, BBC Gen Advsy Council 1946-52, govr BFI 1958, memb Council Nat Trust 1978-; chm Radio Luxembourg London, Cocoa Merchants Ltd; formerly: dep chm J Walter Thompson, chm British Market Research Bureau, chm New English Libary; CBIM, FSS, FIS, FRSA; awarded high honours from Spain, Portugal, Belgium, Taiwan, Sweden, Finland, Luxembourg, Liechtenstein; Cncl of Europe Medal of Merit; *Recreations* travel, theatre; *Clubs* Brooks's, Pratt's, Royal Thames Yacht; *Style*— Sir John Rodgers, Bt, DL; The Dower House, Groombridge, Kent (☎ 089 276 213); 72 Berkeley House, Hay Hill, London W1 (☎ 01 629 5220)

RODGERS, (Doris) June (Mrs Roger Evans); da of James Alfred Rodgers, JP, of Craigavad, Co Down, Northern Ireland, and Margaret Doris, *née* Press; *b* 10 June 1945; *Educ* Victoria Coll Belfast, Trinity Coll Dublin (MA), Lady Margaret Hall Oxford (MA); *m* 6 Oct 1973, Roger Kenneth *qv* s of Gerald Raymond Evans, of Mere, Wilts; 2 s (Edward Arthur b 13 May 1981, Henry William b 8 Feb 1983); *Career* called to Bar Middle Temple 1971; memb Ct Common Cncl City of London Ward Farringdon without 1975-, former memb City & East London Area Health Authy; Freeman City of London 1975; memb: Hon Soc Middle Temple, Ecclesiastical Law Soc; *Books* Financing Strikes (jtly); *Recreations* architectural history, Anglo-Normandy; *Clubs* United Oxford & Cambridge Universities; *Style*— Miss June Rodgers; 2 Harcourt Buildings, The Temple, London EC4 (☎ 01 353 6961, fax 01 353 6968)

RODGERS, Peter David; s of Francis Norman Rodgers, of Glemsford, Suffolk, and Margaret Elizabeth, *née* Harte; *b* 8 Oct 1943; *Educ* Finchley Catholic GS, Trinity Coll Cambridge (MA); *m* 14 Sept 1968, Christine Mary Agnes, da of Dr Duncan Primrose Wilkie, OBE, of Epping, Essex; 2 s (Benedict b 3 Nov 1980, William b 18 Jan 1982), 2 da (Susannah b 29 May 1974, Georgia b 17 Oct 1985); *Career* trainee Oxford Mail 1966-67, features ed Industry Week 1967-69, industl corr The Guardian 1970-76, energy ed The Sunday Times 1976-81; The Guardian: fin corr 1981-84, city ed 1984-; *Recreations* offshore cruising and racing, fell walking, reading, music, rebuilding old houses; *Style*— Peter Rodgers, Esq; 163 Liverpool Rd, Islington, London N1 (☎ 01 278 5628); The Guardian, 119 Farringdon Rd, London EC1 (☎ 01 278 2332, 01 239 9587, fax 01 837 2114, 01 833 8342, telex 8811746)

RODGERS, (Andrew) Piers Wingate; yr s of Sir John Charles Rodgers, 1 Bt, DL, *qv*; *b* 24 Oct 1944; *Educ* Eton, Merton Coll Oxford (BA); *m* 9 Sept 1979, Marie-Agathe, da of Charles-Albert Houette, Croix de Guerre (d 1989), of Langeais, France; 2 s (Thomas b 1979, Augustus b 1983); *Career* with J Henry Schroder Wagg & Co Ltd 1967-73 (pa to chm 1970-73), dir Int Cncl on Monuments & Sites Paris 1973-79, UNESCO Expert (Implementation of World Cultural Heritage Convention) 1979-80, sec of Royal Academy London (also sec of Chantrey Bequest and British Inst Fund) 1981-; Freeman of City of London, Liveryman of Worshipful Co of Masons; memb Co of Merchant Adventurers of City of York; FRSA; Chevalier Ordre des Arts et des Lettres (France); *Clubs* Brooks's, Pratt's, MCC; *Style*— Piers Rodgers, Esq; Peverell House, Bradford Peverell, Dorset; 18 Hertford Street, London W1; Royal Academy of Arts, Piccadilly, London W1

RODGERS, (John Fairlie) Tobias; s and h of Sir John Rodgers, 1 Bt, DL; *b* 2 July 1940; *Educ* Eton, Worcester Coll Oxford; *Career* bookseller and publisher; *Clubs* Brooks's, Garrick, Pratt's; *Style*— Tobias Rodgers Esq; 34 Warwick Ave, W9

RODGERS, Rt Hon William Thomas; PC (1975); s of William Rodgers by his w Gertrude Helen; *b* 28 Oct 1928; *Educ* Quarry Bank HS Liverpool, Magdalen Oxford; *m* 1955, Silvia, da of Hirsch Szulman; 3 da; *Career* MP (L to 1981, thereafter SDP) Teesside Stockton 1962-79, Stockton N 1979-83; fndr memb and vice pres SDP 1981-87, in Lab Govts: trport sec 1976-79, min state Treasy 1969-70, MOD 1974-76, BOT 1968-69, parly under-sec DEA 1964-67, FO 1967-68, fought Bristol W March 1957; gen sec Fabian Soc 1953-60 (remained memb till 1981), ldr UK Delegn Cncl Europe & WEU 1967-68, chm Expenditure Ctee Trade & Industry 1971-74; dir gen RIBA 1987-; *Books* Hugh Gaitskell (1963), The People into Parliament (1966), The Politics of Change (1982), Government and Industry (1986); *Style*— The Rt Hon William Rodgers, PC; 48 Patshull Rd, NW5 2LD (☎ 01 485 9997)

RODIN, Jack; s of Mark Rodin (d 1966), of London, and Sarah, *née* Zeff (d 1960); *b* 2 Feb 1926; *Educ* Raines Fndn London, London Univ (BSc); *m* 14 Feb 1964, (Marie) Elizabeth, da of Charles Paddison, of Newtown, Llantwit, S Glam; 1 s (Jonathan), 2 da (Penelope, Sarah); *Career* engr Sir Alexander Gibb and Ptnrs Consulting Engrs 1947-

54, sr engr specialist conslts (chief engr, dir) 1954-60, jt fndr Lowe and Rodin Consulting Engrs 1960 (merged with Bldg Design Ptnrship 1970), currently sr ptnr and chief exec Bldg Design Partnership; pres Concrete Soc 1988-; MConsE 1964, FICE 1968, FIStructE 1974; *Recreations* music, tennis; *Clubs* Arts; *Style*— Jack Rodin, Esq; 109 Blackheath Pk, Blackheath, London SE3 OEY (☎ 01 852 8048); Bldg Design Ptnrship, 16 Gresse St, London W1A 4WD (☎ 01 631 4733, fax 01 631 0393, telex 25322)

RODNEY, Hon Anne; da of 9 Baron Rodney *qv*; *b* 27 June 1955; *Educ* Lycée Français de Londres, Convent of the Sacred Heart, Woldingham, King's Coll London Univ; *Career* snr account exec Hill & Knowlton (UK) Ltd; *Style*— The Hon Anne Rodney

RODNEY, Hon Diana Rosemary; da of 8 Baron Rodney; *b* 19 April 1924; *Educ* McGill Univ; *Career* serv WWII WRCNS; agricultural writer, info office Alberta Agriculture Edmonton Alberta; *Style*— The Hon Diana Rodney; 5222 Sark Rd, Victoria, British Columbia V8Y 2M3, Canada

RODNEY, Hon George Brydges; s and h of 9 Baron Rodney; *b* 3 Jan 1953; *Educ* Eton; *Style*— The Hon George Rodney; 23 Hornton St, London W8

RODNEY, 9 Baron (GB 1782); Sir John Francis Rodney; 9 Bt (GB 1764); s of 8 Baron Rodney (d 1973; descended from the celebrated Admiral who won the decisive victory over the French in the Battle of the Saints 1782; the Admiral's gggf, Sir John Rodney, m Jane Seymour, niece of the Queen of the same name and 1 cous of King Edward VI), and Lady Marjorie Lowther (d 1968), da of 6 Earl of Lonsdale, OBE; *b* 28 June 1920; *Educ* Stowe, McGill Univ (Montreal); *m* 3 Nov 1951, Régine Elisabeth Lucienne Jeanne Thérèse Marie Ghislaine, yr da of late Chevalier Robert Egide Marie Ghislain Pangaert d'Opdorp, of Château Rullingen, Looz, Belgium; 1 s, 1 da; *Heir* s, Hon George Brydges Rodney; *Career* sits as Cons in House of Lords (maiden speech 1982); serv WWII as Lt Commandos (despatches); formerly with Rootes and the Portals Gp of cos; cncl memb Br Fedn of Printing Machinery & Supplies (former pres), chm Printers Educnl Equipment Tst, chm Standing Conference on Drug Abuse, chm FAIR (concerned with pseudo religious cults), sec All Party Ctee on Drug Abuse, chm All Party Ctee on Cults, memb House of Lords select ctee and sub-ctee on Energy, Transport & Technol; delegate to Cncl of Europe and Western European Union; memb of Sci & Technol, and Agric Ctees; *Recreations* sailing (yacht Corise of Canford), shooting, gardening; *Clubs* White's, Royal Yacht Sqdn, Royal Southampton Yacht; *Style*— The Rt Hon the Lord Rodney; 38 Pembroke Rd, London W8 6NU (☎ 01 602 4391)

RODNEY, Hon Michael Christopher; s of 8 Baron Rodney; *b* 26 June 1926; *Educ* McGill Univ; *m* 1, 1953 (m dis 1973), Anne, da of David Yuile, of Montreal; 3 da; m 2, 1974, Penelope, da of the late Capt E S Garner (ret) of Easton-on-the-Hill, Northamptonshire; *Career* serv WWII RCN; barr Canada 1950; *Style*— The Hon Michael Rodney; 11683-72 Ave, Edmonton, Alberta, Canada

RODNEY BENNETT; *see*: Bennett

RODRIGUE, Claude; s of Ezra Rodrigue (d 1946), of Cairo, and Bella, *née* Semah; *b* 17 April 1930; *Educ* English Sch Cairo, Imperial Coll London (SIMechE); *m* 17 Oct 1958, Ann, da of Lt-Col Sir John Rhodes, Bt, DSO (d 1954), of Westminster Gardens; 2 s (Philip b 24 March 1960, Michael b 16 Oct 1966), 1 da (Carolyn b 10 Oct 1962); *Career* memb: London Stock Exchange 1966, Dunkley Marshall and Co 1960-81 (ptnr 1975-81), Strauss Turnbull and Co Ltd 1981-88, Jacobson Townsley and Co Ltd 1988-; memb Br Bridge Team 1960-82, Euro Champion 1960, World Olympic par point Champion, 3 Olympic Championship 1976, multi-winner Camrose Trophy; invited commentator to first bridge match between nationalist and socialist China (Hong Kong) 1982; Freeman of the City of London 1977; IBPA; *Recreations* good food and wine, bridge, opera; *Clubs* St James' Bridge, Stock Exchange Bridge (pres); *Style*— Claude Rodrigue, Esq; Flat 1, 18 Hyde Park Gate, London SW7 5DH (☎ 01 225 2252); 44 Worship St, London WC2A 2JT (☎ 01 377 6161, fax 01 375 1380, telex 888 948)

RODRIGUES, Sir Alberto Maria; CBE (1964), OBE (1960, MBE 1948, ED); s of late Luiz Gonzaga Rodrigues; *b* 5 Nov 1911; *Educ* St Joseph's Coll, Univ of Hong Kong (MB, BS); *m* 1940, Cynthia Maria de Silva; 1 s, 2 da; *Career* Med Offr Hong Kong Defence Force (POW 1940-45); general medical practitioner 1953-; MLC Hong Kong 1953-60, MEC Hong Kong 1960-74 (sr unofficial memb 1964-74); pro-chancellor Hong Kong Univ 1968-; dir: Jardine Securities 1969-, Hong Kong & Shanghai Hotels 1969-, Lap Heng Co 1970-, Peak Tramways Co 1971-, Computer Data (Hill) 1973-, Hong Kong Commercial Broadcasting Co 1974-, Jardine Strategic Hldgs 1987; Li & Fung Co Ltd 1970; kt 1966; *Style*— Sir Alberto Rodrigues, CBE, OBE, MBE, ED; St Paul's Hospital Annexe, Causeway Bay, Hong Kong (☎ 760017)

RODWELL, Andrew John Hunter; er s of Col Evelyn John Clive Hunter Rodwell, MC, TD, JP (d 1981), of Woodlands, Holbrook, Suffolk, and Martha, *née* Girdlestone; the Rodwells have lived in Suffolk since the early 18 century and acquired Woodlands in 1840 (*see* Burke's Landed Gentry, 18 edn, vol II, 1969); *b* 23 Dec 1938; *Educ* Eton; *m* 20 July 1963, Susan Eleanor, da of Peter Comley Pitt, of Frensham Manor, Rolvenden, Cranbrook, Kent; 3 da (Camilla Eleanor Hunter b 21 July 1964, Miranda Harriet Hunter b 29 May 1967, Patricia Louise Hunter b 17 May 1971); *Career* short service cmmn with RWAFF 1957-60; farmer; md SCH (Supplies) Ltd; *Recreations* country pursuits, photography; *Style*— Andrew Rodwell, Esq; Woodlands, Holbrook, Suffolk (☎ 0473 328800/328272)

RODWELL, Hon Mrs; Hon Christine Maralyn; *née* Woolley; da of Baron Woolley, CBE, DL (Life Peer); *b* 1946; *m* 1, 1970 (m dis 1980), Dr Barrie Scott Morgan; m 2, Cdr David Rodwell, RN; *Style*— The Hon Mrs Rodwell; 35 Northumberland Avenue, Wanstead, London E12

RODWELL, His Hon Judge Daniel Alfred Hunter; QC (1982); s of Brig Reginald Mandeville Rodwell, AFC (d 1974), and Nellie Barbara, *née* D'Costa (d 1967); *b* 3 Jan 1936; *Educ* Munro Coll Jamaica, Oxford Univ (BA); *m* 1967, Veronica Frances Ann, da of Robin Cecil, CMG, of Hants; 2 s (William b 1967, Thomas b 1970), 1 da (Lucy b 1974); *Career* Nat Serv in W Yorks Regt, 2 Lt, TA (Capt); barr, rec Crown Ct 1980, circuit judge 1986; circuit Judge July 1986; *Recreations* hunting, sailing (Antalya), gardening; *Clubs* Pegasus, Bar Yacht; *Style*— His Hon Judge Rodwell, QC; St Albans Crown Court, The Civil Centre, St Albans, Herts AL1 3XE

RODWELL, Dennis Graham; s of Albert James Rodwell, MBE, and Constance Edith Rodwell, *née* Scaddan, of Hampshire; *b* 24 Jan 1948; *Educ* Kingswood Sch Bath, Clare Coll Cambridge (BA, MA, Dip Arch); *m* 10 May 1975, Rosemary Ann, da of Donald Ramsey Rimmer, of Somerset; 2 s (Nicholas b 1978, Christopher b 1979), 1 da (Melanie b 1982); *Career* architect 1973-; own practice 1975; architectural works include an extensive variety and scale of conversion, rehabilitation and restoration projects in housing and commercial uses in Edinburgh, Glasgow, Dundee and the Scottish Borders; projects include restorations of: The Signal Tower Leith parts of St Mary's Street Edinburgh, Commendation 1987 from Edinburgh Architectural Assoc, Greenside Park, St Boswells, Commendation 1985, from Assoc for Protection of Rural Scotland, restoration of Melrose Station and its mgmnt as the Scottish Borders Crafts Centre 1986; occasional lecturing: conservation and restoration subjects; *published articles include*: historical, travel and architectural conservation subjects in The Daily Telegraph, European Heritage, Architectural Conservation in Europe, Country Life, Scottish Field, Prospect, Craftwork, The Scotsman; chm The Trimontium Tst 1988-, memb The Edinburgh New Town Conservation Ctee 1987-90; served on the Ctees: The Scottish Georgian Soc, The Borders Architects Gp, The Cncls of the Royal Incorpn of Architects in Scotland, The Edinburgh Architectural Assoc; *Recreations* travel, walking, reading, photography; *Style*— Dennis Rodwell, Esq; Greenside Park, St Boswells, Melrose, Roxburghshire TD6 0AH (☎ 0835 23289); 8 Dundas St, Edinburgh EH3 6HZ (☎ 031 556 6710)

ROE, Rt Rev (William) Gordon; *see*: Huntingdon, Bishop of

ROE, James Kenneth; s of Kenneth Alfred Roe (d 1988), and Zirphie Norah, *née* Luke (d 1940); *b* 28 Feb 1935; *Educ* King's Sch Bruton; *m* 1958, Marion Audrey (MP for Broxbourne, and parly under sec of state for DOE 1987-88), da of Mr William Keyte (d 1977), of Devon; 1 s (William b 1969), 2 da (Philippa b 1962, Jane b 1965); *Career* banker; dir N M Rothschild & Sons Ltd 1970-; chm: Equity Consort Investmt Tst plc (dir 1977-), N M Rothschild & Sons Channel Islands Ltd (dir 1981-); dir: Kleeneze Hldgs plc 1985, Tokyo Pacific Hldgs NV 1969-; *Clubs* Carlton, MCC; *Style*— James Roe Esq; New Ct, St Swithin's Lane, London EC4P 4DU (☎ 01 280 5000, telex 88031)

ROE, Marion Audrey; MP (C) Broxbourne 1983-; da of William Keyte (d 1977), and Grace Mary, *née* Bocking (d 1983); *b* 15 July 1936; *Educ* Bromley HS, Croydon HS (both GPDST), English Sch of Languages Vevey, Switzerland; *m* 1958, James Roe, s of Kenneth Roe; 1 s (William b 1969), 2 da (Philippa b 1962, Jane b 1965); *Career* parly under sec of state DOE 1987-88; pps: Sec of State for Tport 1986-87, Min of State for Tport 1986, to Under Secs of State for Tport 1985-86; memb: select ctee on Agric 1983-85,Social Servs 1988-; sec of Cons Parly Hort Ctee 1983-85, jt sec Cons Parly Party Orgn Ctee 1984-85; vice chm Cons Parly Social Security Ctee 1988-, succeeded in bringing into law private membs act 'Prohibition of Female Circumcision' 1985; contested Barking 1979 general election; GLC memb for Ilford North 1977-86, Cons dep chief whip GLC 1978-82, leading Cons spokesman GLC Police Ctee 1982-83, cncllr London Borough of Bromley 1975-78, vice-pres Women's Nat Cancer Control Campaign 1985-87; memb: London Advsy Ctee IBA 1978-81, gen advsy cncl BBC 1987, bd of govrs St Peters Hosp 1978-82; govr St Olave's GS for Boys Orpington 1975-80, memb SE Thames Regnl Health Authy 1978-84, patron UK Nat Ctee for the UN Dvpt Fund for Women 1985-87; Freeman City of London; *Books* The Labour Left in London - A Blueprint for a Socialist Britain (1985); *Recreations* opera, ballet, theatre; *Clubs* Carlton (lady assoc memb); *Style*— Mrs Marion Roe, MP; House of Commons, London SW1A 0AA (☎ 01 219 3464)

ROE, Dame Raigh; DBE (1980), CBE (1975, JP 1966); da of A C Kurts (decd); *b* 12 Dec 1922; *Educ* Perth Girls' Sch; *m* 1941, James Arthur Roe; 3 s; *Career* world pres Assoc Country Women of the World 1977-80 (hon life memb 1972); Australian of the Year 1977; dir: ABC 1978-, Queen Elizabeth II Silver Jubilee Trust for Young Australians 1978, Airlines of WA 1981-, Hospital Benefits Fund of WA 1982-; memb Honour Deutscher Landfrauenverband 1980; *Style*— Dame Raigh Roe, DBE, CBE, JP; 76 Regency Drive, Crestwood, Thornlie, W Australia 6108 (☎ 459 8765)

ROE, Air Ch Marshal Sir Rex David; GCB (1981), KCB (1977, CB 1974, AFC); *b* 1925; *Educ* City of London Sch, London Univ; *m* 1948, Helen, *née* Nairn (d 1981); 1 s, 2 da; *Career* Air Memb Supply & Orgn 1978-81, when ret, AOC-in-C: Support Cmmd 1977-78, Trg Cmmd 1976-77; SASO HQ Near East AF 1972-76; RCDS 1971, commanded RNZAF Centl Flying Sch 1956-58, joined RAF 1943; *Style*— Air Chief Marshal Sir Rex Roe, GCB, KCB, CB, AFC; c/o Lloyds Bank, 6 Pall Mall, SW1

ROE, Hon Susan; only da of Baron Lewin, GCB, MVO, DSC; *b* 1949; *m* 1969, Peter Roe; *Style*— The Hon Mrs Roe; c/o Adm of the Fleet The Rt Hon The Lord Lewin, KG, GCB, MVO, DSC, House of Lords, London SW1

ROEBUCK, Christina Rowena Margaret; da of Rev Eric Stopford, of Blanefield, Glasgow, and Christina Heather Liddle, *née* Muir; *b* 28 Feb 1943; *Educ* Orme Girl's GS Staffs, Harper & Adams Agric Coll (Nat Dip Poultry Husbandry); *m* 1, 1968 (m dis 1985), Ian Patrick, s of Edward Caudwell, of Culter, Kincardineshire; 2 da (Charlotte b 1971, Rosalind b 1973); m 2, 1986, Simon John, s of John Frederick Roebuck, of Walton, Derbys; 1 s (Harry b 1987); *Career* farmer; agricultural advsr Br Egg Mktg Bd 1962-68; memb c Arab Horse Soc (judge on the judges panel); conf co-ordinator World Arabian Horse Org Conf London 1988; *Recreations* breeding arabian horses, shooting; *Style*— Mrs Christina R M Roebuck; Harthill Hall, Alport, Bakewell, Derbyshire DE4 1LH (☎ 062 986 203)

ROEBUCK, Roy Delville; *b* 25 Sept 1929; *m* 27 March 1957, Dr Mary Ogilvy, *née* Adams; 1 s (Gavin Macgregor b 1957); *Career* Nat Serv RAF 1947-50; journalist: Stockport Advertiser, Northern Daily Telegraph, Yorkshire Evening News, News Chronicle, Daily Express, Manchester Evening Chronicle, Daily Herald 1950-66; contested (Lab) Altrincham and Sale gen election 1964 and by-election 1965, MP (Lab) Harrow East 1966-70, contested (Lab) Leek gen election 1974; called to the Bar Gray's Inn 1974; govr Moorfields Eye Hosp 1984-88, memb Islington Community Health Cncl 1988-; *Recreations* reading Hansard, music, walking; *Clubs* RAC; *Style*— Roy Roebuck, Esq; 12 Brooksby St, London N1 1HA (☎ 01 607 7057); 5 Pump Court, The Temple, London EC4Y 7AP (☎ 01 353 2532, fax 01 353 5321)

ROEG, Nicolas Jack; s of Jack Nicolas Roeg (d 1952), and Mabel Gertrude Silk (d 1985); *b* 15 August 1928; *Educ* Mercers Sch; *m* 1, 1957, Susan Rennie, da of Maj F W Stephen MC; 4 s (Joscelin, Nicolas, Lucien, Sholto); m 2, 1986, Theresa Russell; 2 s (Statten Jack, Maxmilian Nicolas Sextus); *Career* film dir: Performance, Walkabout, Don't Look Now, The Man Who Fell to Earth, Bad Timing, Eureka, Insignificance, Castaway, Track 29; *Style*— Mr Nicolas Roeg

ROFE, Brian Henry; s of Henry Alexander Rofe (d 1979), and Marguerite, *née* Browne; *b* 7 Jan 1934; *Educ* Shrewsbury, St John's Coll Cambridge (BA, MA); *m* 26 May 1962, (Margaret) Anne, da of Rev Phillip R Shepherd; 2 s (Christopher b 16 Jan 1965, Andrew b 1 April 1968), 1 da (Katharine b 1 July 1963); *Career* Nat Serv RA

1952-54, 2 Lt 1953, Actg Lt TA 1955; chartered engr, asst civil engr John Laing Construction 1957-63, asst/sr engr Rofe and Rafety 1963-69, res engr Draycote Reservoir 1967-69; ptnr Rofe Kennard and Lapworth 1970- (consulting water engrs) contracts incl: Thames Groundwater Scheme 1971-76, Iraq Rural Water Supply 1975-77, Sherbourne and Wyre Flood Schemes, Blashford Lakes Scheme; memb Church Cncl St Marys Walton on Thames, Guildford Diocesan Steward ship Advsy Ctee; Freeman: City of London, Worshipful Co of Grocers; FIWES (vice pres 1986-87), FIWEM (vice pres 1988-89), FICE 1972, FGS, MConsE; *Books* Kempe's Engineers Year Book (Water Supply Chapter 1970-), Civil Engineering Reference Book (Water Supply Section); *Recreations* sailing, bridge, golf; *Clubs* Royal Cwlth Soc, Cambridge Cruising; *Style*— Brian Rofe, Esq; Laleham Cottage, 40 Churchfield Rd, Walton-on-Thames, Surrey KT12 2SY (☎ 0932 223147); Raffety House, 2-4 Sutton Ct Rd, Sutton SM1 4SS (☎ 01 643 8201, fax 01 642 8469, telex 946688 ARKELL G)

ROFFE, Clive Brian; JP 1987; s of Philip Roffe (d 1961); *b* 4 June 1935; *Educ* Brighton Coll; *m* 1966, Jacqueline Carole, *née* Branston; 2 da (Danielle Philippa Geraldine b 1970, Natasha Nicole b 1974); *Career* Llyod's underwriter 1966, fin conslt; chm: Melbo Petroleum Ltd 1970, Edinburgh Insur Servs 1971, Offshire Investmts Ltd 1968, dir other companies; Freeman of City of London; *Recreations* organ, philately, jogging; *Clubs* MCC, Guards Polo, Hurlingham, City Livery, Lloyd's Yacht; *Style*— Clive Roffe Esq, JP; 50 Kingsway Court, Hove, Sussex (☎ 0273 737 044)

ROGER, Alan Stuart; MBE (Mil) 1943; s of Sir Alexander Forbes Proctor Roger, KCLE (d 1961), and Helen Stuart, *née* Clark; *b* 27 April 1909; *Educ* Loretto, Trinity Coll Oxford (BA); *Career* war serv in France, India, Iraq, Persia, Hong Kong; chm of Bonsaikai of London 1964, memb of Cncl of Contemporary Art Soc 1980, Floral Ctee B of RHS, Scotlands Gdns Ctee; vice-pres Nat Tst for Scotland (1983-), tstee Nat Galleries of Scotland 1967-82, author Wisley Handbook on Bonsai; *Recreations* gardening; *Style*— Alan S Roger, Esq, MBE; Dundonnell, by Garve, Koss & Cromarty IV23 2QW; 81 Elms Road, London

ROGER, Peter Charles Marshall; s of Matthew McCargo Roger (d 1977), and Muriel Ethel, *née* Morrison; *b* 11 April 1942; *Educ* Glasgow HS; *m* 21 April 1972, Fiona Ann, da of James Murray (d 1986); 2 s (Kenneth b 1975, Andrew b 1979), 1 da (Alison b 1982); *Career* AC, Thompson McLintock & Co 1964-71, Speirs & Jeffrey 1971-, dep chm Stock Exchange Scottish Unit; pres Newlands South Church, memb Inst CA Scotland 1964; *Recreations* golf; *Clubs* Prestwick, Pollok, Boat of Garten; *Style*— Peter Roger, Esq; 36 Renfield St, Glasgow G2 1NA (☎ 041 248 4311, fax 041 221 4764, telex 777 902)

ROGERS, Allan Ralph; MP (Lab) Rhondda 1983-, MEP; s of John and Madeleine Rogers; *b* 24 Oct 1932; *Educ* University Coll of Swansea; *m* 1955, Ceridwen James; 1 s, 3 d; *Career* sometime geologist, teacher; MEP (Lab) SE Wales 1979-84; *Style*— Allan Rogers Esq, MP, MEP; 70 Cemetery Road, Porth, Rhondda, Mid-Glamorgan

ROGERS, Prof (Claude) Ambrose; s of Sir Leonard Rogers, KCSI, CIE, FRS (d 1962), and Una Elsie North (d 1951); *b* 1 Nov 1920; *Educ* Berkhamsted Sch, UCL, Birkbeck Coll London (BSc, PhD, DSc); *m* 1952, Joan Marian, widow of W G Gordon and da of F North; 2 da; *Career* experimental offr Miny of Supply 1940-45; lecturer and reader UCL 1946-54, prof of Pure Mathematics Birmingham Univ 1954-58, Astor prof of mathematics UCL 1958; pres London Mathematical Soc 1970-72; chm Jt Mathematical Cncl 1981-84; prof emeritus Univ of London 1986; FRS; *Books* Packing and Covering (1964), Hausdorff Measures (1970), Analytic Sets (1980); *Style*— Prof Ambrose Rogers; 8 Grey Close, London NW11 6QG (☎ 01 455 8027); Department of Statistical Science, University College, London WC1E 6BT (☎ 01 387 7050)

ROGERS, Ms Barbara; *b* 21 Sept 1945; *Educ* Univ of Sussex (BA); *Career* writer, researcher, journalist, ed Everywoman Magazine 1985-; cllr London Borough of Islington 1982-86; *Recreations* gardening, music; *Style*— Ms Barbara Rogers; Everywoman Magazine, 34 Islington Green, London N1 8DU (☎ 01 359 5496)

ROGERS, Lady; Brenda Mary; CBE (1964); da of late Ernest Thompson Sharp; *m* 1939, Sir Philip James Rogers, CBE, *qv*; *Career* joined British Red Cross Somerset 1936, former cmdt First Lagos (Nigeria) Detachment, pres Nairobi Div 1953, dep pres Kenya Branch British Red Cross 1956, Red Cross rep Mauritius Hurricane Disaster Relief Ctee 1960, Red Cross organiser of refugees from Belgian Congo 1960, dep pres Sussex Counties Branch British Red Cross 1968-, memb nat exec ctee BRCS 1964-67 and 1969-73 (hon vice pres 1980-); govr Delamere Girls Sch Kenya 1960-62; *Clubs* New Cavendish; *Style*— Lady Rogers, CBE; Church Close, Newick, Sussex (☎ 082 572 2210)

ROGERS, Ven David Arthur; s of Rev Canon Thomas Godfrey Rogers (d 1974), and Doris Mary Cleaver, *née* Steele (d 1977); *b* 12 Mar 1921; *Educ* St Edward's Sch Oxford, Christ's Coll Cambridge (MA), Ridley Hall Cambridge; *m* 1951, Joan, da of Philip Malkin (d 1956); 1 s (Jeremy Peter b 1952), 3 da (Janet Elizabeth b 1954, Katharine Rosemary b 1956, Anne Sarah b 1960); *Career* Lt Green Howards and Royal Armd Corps, NW Europe 1945; rector St Peter Levenshulme 1953-59, vicar of Sedbergh, Cautley and Garsdale 1959-79, rural dean of Sedbergh and then Ewecross 1959-77, archdeacon of Craven 1977-86, archdeacon Emeritus 1986-; *Style*— The Venerable D A Rogers; Borrens, Leck, Carnforth, Lancs LA6 2JG (☎ 05242 71616)

ROGERS, David Bryan; CB (1984); s of Frank and Louisa Rogers; *b* 8 Sept 1929; *Educ* Grove Park Wrexham, Univ Coll London (BA); *m* 1955, Marjory Geraldine Gilmour Horribine; 1 s, 2 da; *Career* inspr of taxes 1953, principal inspr 1968, sr princ inspr 1976, under sec and dir of Operations Bd of Inland Revenue 1978-81, dep sec and dir gen Bd of Inland Revenue 1981-; memb UCL 1983-; *Recreations* piano, organ, singing; *Style*— Bryan Rogers, Esq, CB

ROGERS, David Owen; s of Alan Edgar Rogers (d 1983), of Haslemere, Surrey, and Joan Grace, *née* Thornhill; *b* 5 May 1952; *Educ* Royal GS Guildford Surrey, Kingston-Upon-Hull Coll of Commerce (Higher Nat Dip Business Studies); *m* 21 Aug 1982, Deborah June, da of Brian Geoffrey Sharp, of Godalming Surrey; 2 da (Jennifer Clare b 1984, Josephine Kate b 1986); *Career* Rank Leisure Servs Ltd 1973-77, EMI Records Ltd 1978-79, Office of Population Censuses and Surveys 1980-84, House Husband 1984-; longstanding memb Lib Party, fndr memb Social and Liberal Democrats, elected to East Sussex CC 1977 as memb for Brighton (St Nicholas) 1977 and 1981 and Brighton Borough Cncl St Nicholas Ward 1979 and Seven Dials Ward 1983 and 1987, memb Democrat Gp (formerly Liberal, then Alliance) 1977-; ASLDC (formerly ALC) 1977-; *Style*— David Rogers, Esq; 74 Fort Rd, Newhaven, East Sussex BN9 9EJ (☎ 0273 512 172)

ROGERS, Dr Eric William Evan; s of William Percy Rogers (d 1978), of Southgate, London, and Margaret, *née* Evans (d 1988); *b* 12 April 1925; *Educ* Southgate Co Sch, Imp Coll Univ of London (DIC, BSc, MSc, DSc); *m* 1 April 1950, (Dorothy) Joyce, da of Alan Charles Loveless (d 1973), of Tankerton, Whitstable, Kent; 2 s (Christopher b 1958, Andrew b 1965), 1 da (Margaret b 1960); *Career* with Aerodynamics Div Nat Physical Lab 1945-70, dep dir (Aircraft) Royal Aircraft Estab, Farnborough 1978-85 (joined 1970, Hhd of Aerodynamics Dept 1972-74), aeronautical res conslt 1985-; CEng 1970, FRAeS 1960, FCGI 1976; *Recreations* music, history; *Style*— Dr Eric Rogers; 64 Thetford Rd, New Malden, Surrey KT3 5DT (☎ 01 942 7452)

ROGERS, Sir Frank Jarvis; s of Percy Rogers (d 1960); *b* 24 Feb 1920; *Educ* Wolstanton GS; *m* 1949, Esma Sophia, *née* Holland; 2 da; *Career* journalist 1937-49; Military Service 1940-46; gen manager Nigerian Daily Times 1949-52, manager Argus Melbourne 1952-55, md Overseas Newspapers 1958-60, dir Daily Mirror 1960-65, md IPC 1965-70, chm Nat Newspaper Steering Gp 1970-72, dir Newspaper Publishers Assoc 1971-73, chm British Exec Ctee Int Press Inst 1978-88, chm Exec Ctee Industrial Soc 1976-79, chm EMAP plc (formerly East Midlands Allied Press Ltd) 1973-, dir Plessey New Jersey Inc, adviser Corporate Affairs Plessey Co Ltd 1973-81, chm Ansafone Ltd 1981-85, dep chm The Daily Telegraph plc 1986-; kt 1988; *Recreations* golf, travel; *Clubs* Moor Park Golf; *Style*— Sir Frank Rogers, Esq; Greensleeves, Loudwater Drive, Loudwater, Rickmansworth, Herts; c/o East Midland Allied Press Ltd, Scriptor Court, 155 Farringdon Rd, London EC1R 3AD (☎ 01 837 2285)

ROGERS, Geoffrey; s of Arthur Frank Rogers (d 1967), and Florence Annie (died 1980); *b* 24 Nov 1946; *Educ* Bideford GS; *m* 19 April 1969, Janet Anne, da of Cyril John Langman; 1 s (Timothy b 1979), 2 da (Rebecca b 1973, Nicola b 1974); *Career* CA; sr ptnr Atkey Goodman Accountants Taxation and Mgmnt Conslts Plymouth 1975-, ptnr Barretts Restaurents Plymouth 1988-; sec IOD Plymouth Centre 1981-, memb Devon and Cornwall Branch Ctee IOD 1983-, pres elect SW Soc of Certified Accountants 1989; FIOD, MBIM, FCA, FCCA; *Recreations* yachting; *Clubs* Royal Western YC of England; *Style*— Geoffrey Rogers, Esq; The Manor House, Chapel Street, Devonport, Plymouth PL1 4DS (☎ 0752 558141)

ROGERS, Hugh Anthony Edmund; s of Lt Col Wilfred Edmund Rogers (d 1970), and Elizabeth Susan, *née* Kidd; *b* 23 June 1937; *Educ* Marlborough Coll; *m* 12 Nov 1966, Fiona Linday, da of Richard Hughes, Newnham Hall, Nr Baldock, Herts (d 1979); 2 da (Anabel b 1970, Charlotte, b 1975), 2 s (Peverell b 1971, Saltren b 1974); *Career* Nat Serv Cmmnd into the 4 Hussars 1956, Lt Inns of Court and City Yeomanary 1957-64; *Recreations* gardening; *Style*— Hugh Rogers, Esq; Carwinion, nr Falmouth, Cornwall (car ☎ 0326 25058)

ROGERS, (Leonard) John; OBE (1979); s of Leonard Samuel Rogers, JP (d 1964) of Croydon, Surrey, and Amy Mary, *née* Martlew (d 1958); *b* 30 Oct 1931; *Educ* Whitgift Sch Croydon, Städtisches und Staatliches Gymnasium Neuss am Rhein, Trinity Coll Cambridge (MA); *m* 16 July 1955, Avery Janet, da of Hugh Griffith Ernest Morgan (d 1968), of Croydon, Surrey; 4 s (Paul b 1956, Nicholas b 1958, Jonathan b 1962, Crispin b 1966); *Career* Nat Serv, E Surrey Regt 1950, Eaton Hall OCS 1951, Lt Intelligence corps BAOR 1951-52; export contracts administrators (Guided Weapon) Bristol Aircraft Ltd 1958-60, asst sec Bristol Aeroplane Plastics Ltd 1960-62, export contracts mangr (Comm Aircraft Div) Br Aircraft Corpn 1965-73, business dir BAC Commercial Acft Div 1973 (mktg dir 1977), divnl mktg dir British Aerospace 1978-79, aviation conslt Roconsult AG Zug Schweiz 1980-84; dir: AIM GP plc 1984-, AIM Aviation Ltd 1984-; md Henshalls Ltd; Methodist Church: Dorking and Horsham circuit steward 1977-82, memb Euro Affairs Ctee 1980-86, sec Connexional 1988 Steering Ctee 1986-89, led Wesley 250 Anniversary Pilgrimage to Moravian Church in Herrnhut GDR 1988; memb: Gen purposes ctee London Voluntary Serv Cncl 1980-83, Romanian Trade Ctee London C of C Comm 1975-83; Freeman City of London 1979, Liveryman Worshipful Co of Coachmakers and Coach Harness Makers 1979; Fell IOD 1978; *Recreations* european languages, opera, roses, mountain-walking; *Clubs* IOD; *Style*— John Rogers, Esq; Willow Pool, Effingham, Surrey KT24 5JG (☎ 0372 583 59); Henshalls Ltd, Abbot Close, Oyster Lane, Byfleet, Surrey KT14 7JT (☎ 09323 510 11, fax 09323 527 92, telex 928460 WHS G)

ROGERS, John Michael Thomas; s of Harold Stuart Rogers, and Sarah Joan Thomas, *née* Bibby; *b* 13 May 1938; *Educ* Rydal Sch, Birkenhead Sch, Fitzwilliam House Cambridge (MA, LLB); *m* 1971, Jennifer Ruth; 1 da (Caitlin Sarah b 1981); *Career* called to Bar Gray's Inn 1963, rec 1976; QC 1979; *Recreations* farming, sailing (Minerua, Mew Tow); *Clubs* Reform, Pragmatists, Bristol Channel, Yacht, Ruthin, RFC; *Style*— John Rogers Esq, QC; 2 Dr Johnson's Building, Temple, London EC4Y 7AY (☎ 01 353 5371)

ROGERS, Air Chief Marshal Sir John Robson; KCB (1981), CBE (1971); s of B Rogers; *b* 11 Jan 1928; *Educ* Brentwood Sch, RAF Coll Cranwell; *m* 1955, Gytha, *née* Campbell; 2 s, 2 da; *Career* dir-gen Orgn RAF 1977-79, AOC Trg Units HQ RAF Support Cmmd 1979-81, Air memb Supply and Orgn 1981-83, Controller Aircraft 1983-, Air Vice-Marshal 1977, Air Marshal 1981, Air Chief Marshal 1984; dir: Br Car Auctions Ltd, First Technology Gp; chm RAC Motor Sports Assoc; FRAeS, CBIM; dep chm First Security Group; *Recreations* motor sport; *Clubs* RAF, RAC; *Style*— Air Chief Marshal Sir John Rogers, KCB, CBE; c/o Lloyds Bank, 27 High St, Colchester, Essex

ROGERS, John Willis; QC (1975); s of Reginald John Rogers (d 1940); *b* 7 Nov 1929; *Educ* Sevenoaks Sch, Fitzwilliam Cambridge; *m* 1952, Sheila Elizabeth, nee Cann; 1 s, 1 da; *Career* barr 1955, 1 Prosecuting Cncl to Inland Revenue SE Circuit 1969-75, rec 1974-, QC 1975, hon rec for City of Canterbury 1985-; *Recreations* cricket, gardening, music, change-ringing; *Clubs* Garrick, Marylebone Cricket, Band of Brothers; *Style*— John W Rogers, Esq, QC; 3 Serjeants' Inn, London, EC4Y 1BQ (☎ 01 353 5537)

ROGERS, Hon Mrs (Loretta Anne); *née* Robinson; da of 1 Baron Martonmere, GBE, KCMG, PC; *b* 1939; *m* 1963, Edward Samuel Rogers; 1 s, 3 da; *Style*— The Hon Mrs Rogers; 3 Frybrook Rd, Toronto, Ontario M4V 1Y7 , Canada

ROGERS, Martin John Wyndham; s of John Frederick Rogers (d 1985), of Oxshott, Surrey, and Grace Mary, *née* Stride (d 1971); *b* 9 April 1931; *Educ* Oundle, Heidelberg Univ, Trinity Hall Cambridge (MA); *m* 31 August 1957, Jane, da of Harold Arthur Cook (d 1978), of Cobham, Surrey; 2 s (Mark Wyndham Edward b 31 May 1959, Stephen James Wyndham b 17 June 1961), 1 da (Sarah Lucy b 24 June 1965); *Career* Henry Wiggin & Co 1953-55; under master and master of Queen's Scholars Westminster Sch 1967-71 (asst master 1955-60, sr chem master 1960-64, housemaster 1964-66); head master Malvern Coll 1971-82, chief master King Edwards

Sch Birmingham and head master of the Schs of King Edward VI in Birmingham 1982-; seconded as Nuffield res fell (O level chem project) 1962-64, Salters Co fell dept of chem engrg and chem technol, Imperial Coll London 1969; chm: Curriculum Ctees of HMC, GSA and IAPS 1979-86, Headmasters' Conference 1987; memb Cncl Birmingham Univ 1985, govr Oundle Sch 1988-; *Books* John Dalton and the Atomic Theory (1965), Chemistry and Energy (1968),Foreground Chemistry Series (ed 1968), Gas Syringe Experiments (1970), Facts, Patterns and Principles (jtly 1970), Francis Bacon and the Birth of Modern Science (1981); *Recreations* family life, history of science in 16th and 17th cents; *Clubs* East India; *Style*— Martin Rogers, Esq; Vince House, 341 Bristol Road, Birmingham B5 7SW (☎ 021 472 0652); Bray Cottage, Hockworthy, nr Wellington, Somerset; King Edward's Sch, Edgbaston Park Road, Birmingham B15 2UA (☎ 021 472 1672)

ROGERS, Nicholas Emerson (Nick); s of Reginald Emerson Rogers (d 1983), of 3 Fairfield Rd, Petts Wood, Kent, and Doreen, *née* Burbidge; *b* 15 Mar 1946; *Educ* Charterhouse, Orpington Secdy Sch; *m* 26 Oct 1973, Linda Jane, da of Reginald Douglas Bracey, of Little Tubbs, 19 Gifford Close, Thordun park, Chard, Somerset; *Career* photographer The Sunday Independent Plymouth 1968-70 and The Evening Post Reading 1970-72, staff photographer The Daily Mail 1973-78, dep picture ed The Observer 1984-86, feature photographer The Times 1986; Kodak Indusl and Commercial Photographer of the Year 1987, Feature Photographer of the Year Br Press Award 1988; memb: RBS, NUJ, BPPA; *Recreations* photography, sailing, walking, travel; *Style*— Nick Rogers, Esq; The Pound House, Wadstray, Blackawton, South Devon TQ9 7DE (☎ 080421 421); The Times, 1 Pennington St, London E19XN (☎ 01 782 5877, car tel 0860 380 347)

ROGERS, Nigel David; s of Thomas Rogers (d 1980), of Wellington, Shropshire, and Winifred May, *née* Roberts; *b* 21 Mar 1935; *Educ* Wellington GS, King's Coll Cambridge (BA, MA), Hochschule für Musik Munich; *m* 14 Oct 1961 (m dis 1974), Frederica Bement, da of Edmund Parker Lord (d 1985), of Framingham, Mass,USA; 1 da (Lucasta Julia Webster b 26 May 1970); *Career* singer and conductor; début Studio der Frühen Musik, Munich 1961, specialised as leading exponent of baroque style of singing 1964-; performances of baroque operas in England, Germany, Holland, Poland, Switzerland and Austria, world-wide concerts and recitals; numerous recordings incl: Monteverdi 1610 Vespers, Monteverdi "Orfeo", songs of John Dowland, Schütz, Christmas Story; Schubert, Die Schöne Mullerin; 17 C Airs de Cour etc; founder: Chiaroscuro Vocal Ensemble 1979, Chiaroscuro Baroque Orch 1987; conducted baroque orchs in Milan, Venice, Padua; teacher Schola Cantorum Basilienses Bâle 1972-76, prof of singing RCM London 1979-; Hon FRCM 1981; *Books* Everyman's Companion to Baroque Music (Chapter on Voice, 1989); *Recreations* walking, country life, drinking wine, travel(Italy); *Style*— Nigel Rogers, Esq; Chestnut Cottage, East End, near Newbury, Berks RG15 0AF (☎ 0635 253 319); Royal College of Music, Prince Consort Rd, London SW7; Robert White Artist Management, 182 Moselle Ave, London N22 6EX (☎ 01 881 6914, fax 01 889 3113)

ROGERS, (Thomas Gordon) Parry; s of Victor Frank Rogers (d 1947), of Harrow, Middx, and Ella Mary Rogers; *b* 7 August 1924; *Educ* West Hartlepool GS, St Edmund Hall Oxford (MA); *m* 1, 9 April 1947 (m dis 1973), Pamela Mary, da of J Leslie Greene (d 1950); 1 s (Michael b 1951), 7 da (Mary b 1948, Natalie b 1949, Patricia b 1955, Barbara b 1957, Bernadette b 1957, Frances b 1962, Philippa b 1964); m 2, 15 Sept 1973, (Patricia) Juliet, da of Richard D Curtis (d 1986); 1 s (Benedict b 1974), 1 da (Ruth b 1979); *Career* WWII 1944-47 RAC and RAEC; personnel mangr Procter & Gamble 1948-54, chief personnel offr Mars 1954-56, personnel dir Hardy Spicer 1956-61, dir of external affrs IBM (UK) 1971-74 (personnel dir 1961-71); Plessey: personnel dir 1974-78, dir personnel and Europe 1978-86, chm Plessey Pension Tst 1978-86; chm: Percam Ltd, Prima Europe Ltd, Future Perfect Ltd; dir: Hobsons Publishing plc, Ocean Tport & Trading plc, Butler Cox & Ptnrs Ltd, Norman Broadbent Int; chm: Salisbury Health Authy 1985-, Business and Technician Educn Cncl 1986-, SW London Coll HEC 1988-; memb: Clegg Cmmn, Butcher Ctee, DHSS Review, Employment Apppeal Tbnl; Freeman City of London 1987, memb Worshipful Co of Information Technologists; CBIM 1980, CIPM 1980, FRSA 1978; *Books* Recruitment and Training of Graduates (1967); *Recreations* golf, tennis, birdwatching, music; *Clubs* Savile, Royal Wimbledon GC, Sherborne GC; *Style*— Parry Rogers, Esq; St Edward's Chantry, Bimport, Shaftesbury, Dorset (☎ 0747 2789); 32 Romulus Court, Justin Close, Brentford, Middx (☎ 01 568 6060)

ROGERS, Rev Percival Hallewell (Val); MBE (1945); s of Percy Charles Rogers (1956), of Brentwood, Essex, and Olivia Jane, *née* Horne (d 1970); *b* 13 Sept 1912; *Educ* Brentwood Sch, St Edmund Hall Oxford (MA, DipEd), Bishops' Coll Cheshunt, Int Acad for Continuous Educn Sherborne; *m* 1 Jan 1940, (Annie) Mary Stuart, da of Lt Col James Morwood, IMS ((d 1946), of 4 Malone Park, Belfast; 2 s (Julian Hallewell James b 1941, Bruce Henry Arthur b 1946, k Alpine climbing 1969), 1 da (Olivia Mary b 1948); *Career* Nat Serv TA 1939, RA 1940, cmmnd 1941 2 Lt RA 1941, War Substantive Lt 1942, Actg Capt 1943, Temp Capt 1944, Actg Maj DAA and QMG Milan 1945, War Substantive Capt and temp Maj 1945 (despatches twice), Maj released 1946; head of english dept Haileybury Coll 1936-54, ordained priest at St Albans 1948, chaplain Haileybury Coll 1948-54, headmaster Portora Royal Sch Enniskillen 1954-73, chaplain Gresham's Sch Holt 1974-75. dean Int Acad Sherborne 1975-76, asst priest Trinity Church New Orleans 1976-80, dir of ordinands and lay readers Diocese of Clogher 1980-84, priest i/c St Andrew's Sandford on Thames 1985-87; memb: Exec Ctee C of I Bd of Educn 1956-73, Alliance Party for Reconciliation NI 1970-84 (chm Fermanagh Assoc 1983-84); chm Student Christian Movement in Schs Ireland 1956-64, sec UNICEF Co Fermanagh 1982-84, schools lectr for UNICEF Oxford 1987-; memb HMC 1954-73; *Books* A Guide to Divinity Teaching (1962), The Needs of the Whole Man (1971); *Recreations* sailing, boating, chess, music; *Clubs* East India Public Schools and Sports, Union Soc (Oxford); *Style*— The Rev P H Rogers, MBE; 7 Eyot Place, Oxford OX4 1SA (☎ 0865 244 976)

ROGERS, Sir Philip; GCB (1975, KCB 1970, CB 1965), CMG (1952); s of William Edward Rogers (d 1951), and Sara Jane Rogers (d 1954); *b* 19 August 1914; *Educ* William Hulme's GS, Emmanuel Coll Cambridge (MA); *m* 1940, Heather Mavis, da of George Hall Gordon (d 1943); 1 s, 1 da; *Career* civil servant; perm sec DHSS 1970-75, chm Outward Bound 1975-80, chm Univ Superannuation Scheme 1975-84, chm London Sch Hygiene and Tropical Med 1976-82, pres Reading Univ Cncl 1980-87, dep chm Hammersmith Special Health Authy; memb Ct London Univ; non-exec dir: Glaxo 1977-84, Lloyds Bank Regnl Bd 1979-85; *Recreations* gardening; *Clubs* East India, Phyllis Court; *Style*— Sir Philip Rogers, GCB, CMG; 96 King's Rd, Henley-on-Thames, Oxon RG9 2DQ (☎ 0491 575 228)

ROGERS, Sir Philip James; CBE (1952); s of late James Henry Rogers; *b* 19 Sept 1908; *Educ* Blundells; *m* 1939, Brenda Mary, CBE, *qv*; *Career* Capt Frontier Force; MLC Nigeria 1947-51, Kenya 1957-62; chm: E African Tobacco Co Ltd 1951-63, Rift Valley Cigarette Co Ltd 1956-63; memb E A Industl Cncl 1954-63; chm: Kenya Ctee on Trg and Study in USA 1958-63, African Teachers Serv Bd 1956-63; chm of govrs Univ of Kenya 1958-63, tstee Outward Bound Tst of Kenya 1959-63, memb E A Air Cncl 1958-63, chm bd of govrs Coll of Social Studies 1960-63, chm Kenya Special Loan Cncl 1960-63, rep for Kenya E A Centl League Assembly 1962-63, chm Tobacco Res Cncl 1963-71, govr Plumpton Agric Coll 1967-72, chm Fedn of Sussex Amenity Socs 1968-80, memb E Sussex Co Cncl Educn Ctee 1967-77; kt 1961; *Style*— Sir Philip Rogers, CBE; Church Close, Newick, Sussex (☎ 082 572 2210)

ROGERS, Richard George; *b* 23 July 1933; *Educ* Architectural Assoc London (AA Dip), Yale Univ (MArch, Fulbright and Yale Scholar); *m* 1, 1960, Su Brumwel; 3 s; m 2, 1973, Ruth Elias; 2 s; *Career* dir: Richard Rogers Partnership Ltd; winner of int competition for Pompidou Centre Paris 1977, winner of Lloyd's int competition for Headquarters London 1978; Projects include PA Technol Centre phases 1, 2, 3 Cambridge 1970-84, Music Res Centre for Pierre Boulez and Miny Cultural Affairs Paris 1977, Cummins Fleetguard Factory France 1980, Inmos Microprocessor Factory Newport 1982, World Headquarters for Wellcome Fndn UK 1986, PA Technol Science Lab Princeton USA 1984, London Docklands Devpt 1984, Billingsgate Market Conversion 1985; visiting lectr at UCLA Princton Columbia, Harvard & Cornell Univs USA; Saarinen prof Yale Univ 1985; chm tstees Tate Gallery 1984, memb RIBA Cncl, UN Architects' Ctee; RIBA Hon Dr (RCA)S RA, Royal Acad London, Royal Acad of Art, The Hague; Royal Gold Medal, RIBA 1985; Chevalier l'Order National de la Legion d'Honneur 1986; Hon FAIA 1986; exhibition Royal Acad London 1986; *Books* By Their Own Design 1980 Rogers; *Style*— Richard Rogers, Esq; Thomas Wharf, Rainville Road, London W6 9HA (☎ 01 385 1235)

ROGERS, Stuart Peter; s of Alfred Rogers, and Hannah, *née* Glicksman; *b* 12 Mar 1947; *Educ* Latymer Upper Sch; *m* 18 Sept 1979, Judith Frances, da of Harry Jacobs; 1 s (Nicholas Charles b 26 Sept 1983), 1 da (Sophie Esther b 12 June 1985); *Career* md: Contract Mail Ltd 1972-85, CM Direct Ltd 1985-88, dir CM Direct a div of The Hilton Taylor Partnership Ltd 1988-; co chm Variety Club of GB Sandown Park Brochure Ctee, memb mktg ctee Variety Club of GB; *Recreations* theatre, golf; *Style*— Stuart Rogers, Esq; 13 Dorset Dr, Edgware, Middx HA8 7NT (☎ 01 952 6354); 1 Livonia St, London WIV 3PG (☎ 01 734 1640, fax 01 434 4284)

ROGERS, Thomas Edward; CMG (1960), MBE (1945); s of Thomas Edward Rogers, MBE (d 1958); *b* 28 Dec 1912; *Educ* Bedford Sch, Emmanuel Coll Cambridge, SOAS; *m* 1950, Eileen Mary, *née* Speechley; *Career* ICS 1936-41, IPS 1941-47, For Pakistan Cabinet Off; serv 1949-73: min Ottawa 1966-70, acting high cmmr 1967 and 1968, ambassador Colombia 1970-73; chm Anglo-Colombian Soc 1981-; Grand Cross Order of San Carlos 1974 Colombia; *Recreations* travel; *Clubs* United; *Style*— Thomas Rogers, Esq, CMG, MBE; Chintens, Grayshott, Hants (☎ 0428 714 145)

ROGERS, Victor Alfred Baden; CBE (1986); s of Henry George Rogers (d 1963), of Norwood Green, Southall, Middx, and Louisa May, *née* Hall (d 1983); *b* 8 Mar 1926; *Educ* Cranfield Inst of Tech (MSc); *m* 1 April 1950, Jean Valentine, da of Joseph Franklin Stokes (d 1969); 2 s (David Edward b 1954, Peter John b 1962); *Career* Westland Helicopters Ltd: chief designer 1966-72 (Lynx Helicopter 1969-72), tech dir 1972-81 (RAeS Silver Medal 1979), dir 1981-84; gp dir and tech dir Westland plc Helicopter and Hovercraft Gp 1984-86; former chm SBAC (tech bd), chm AECMA (CTI) Europe, local pres RAeS (Yeovil Branch); FRAeS 1963, FIMechE 1972, FEng 1979; *Recreations* music, computers, golf; *Style*— Victor Rogers, Esq, CBE; Wrenfield, Bradford Rd, Sherborne, Dorset DT9 6BW (☎ 0935 81 2007)

ROGERS-COLTMAN, Charles Hugh; s of Lt Cdr Julian Rogers-Coltman OBE (d 1944); *b* 25 April 1930; *Educ* Radley Coll, Selwyn Coll Cambridge; *m* 1955, Olive Teresa Margaret, da of Lt-Col W H Bamfield; 1 s, 3 da; *Career* land agent, farmer, co dir; High Sheriff of Shropshire 1964, govr Wrekin Coll; *Recreations* shooting, fishing, skiing; *Clubs* Turf, MCC; *Style*— Charles Rogers-Coltman Esq; The Home, Bishop's Castle, Shropshire (☎ Linley 233)

ROGERSON, Michael Anthony; s of Peter Anthony Rogerson (d 1984), of Virginia Water, Surrey, and Yvonne Marie, *née* Kennedy; *b* 19 Feb 1941; *Educ* Harrow; *m* 27 Sept 1969, Margaret Jane, da of Keith Gordon Blake, CBE (d 1982), of Guildford; 1 s (Richard Pierce Gordon b 1974), 1 da (Belinda Jane b 1971); *Career* Spicer and Pegler: UK 1960-65, Australia 1965-67; Ernst Whinney 1967-73, ptnr Grant Thorton 1973-, non exec chm Tech PR Ltd; CBI: chm London Regn (chm Urban Regeneration Task Force), memb cncl, memb pres ctee; vice chm: Catholic Marriage Advsry Cncl, exec memb Sheriff and Recorders Fund; memb Advsry Cncl Catholic Soc Serv for Prisoners; memb Worshipful Co of Skinners 19714; FCA 1965, FBIM 1982; *Recreations* golf, bridge, gardening, racing; *Clubs* Boodles, Worplesdon Golf; *Style*— Michael Rogerson, Esq; Millcroft, Mill Lane, Pirbright, Surrey GU24 0BN (☎ 0486 781426); Grant Thornton House, Euston Square, London NW1 2EP (☎ 01 383 5100, fax 01 383 4715, telex 28984)

ROGERSON, Michael Cunliffe; TD (1966); s of Gordon Cunliffe Rogerson (d 1981), and Nora Margaret Stewart, *née* Boot (d 1984); *b* 30 Mar 1933; *Educ* Magdalen Coll Sch Brackley; *m* 4 April 1959, Sheila, da of Sidney Hugh Hyndman (d 1982), of Lichfield; 2 da (Catherine b 1962, Louise b 1964); *Career* mil serv Seaforth Highlanders 1951-54, Argyll & Sutherland Highlanders TA 1954-67; various mgmnt appts Clarks Ltd Somerset 1954-78, dir various cos 1978-; *Recreations* local politics, golf; *Style*— Michael C Rogerson, Esq, TD; Coopers, Coopers Hill, Eversley, Hampshire (☎ 0252 873583); SP Ltd, 41 Market Place, Henley-on-Thames (☎ 0491 576803, fax 0491 579694)

ROGERSON, Michael Dennis; s of Frank Rogerson (d 1944), and late Florence Emmely, *née* Allanby; *b* 26 July 1910; *Educ* Marlborough, Univ of Cambridge (BA); *m* 15 April 1939, (Hilda) Marion, da of Norman Graham Brownrigg (d 1936), of Fernden Sch, Haselmere, Surrey; 2 s (Mark b 1942, Matthew b 1950), 1 da (Mary Louise b 1945); *Career* Capt RASC 1941-45; headmaster Cottesmore Prep Sch 1936-71, farmer 1951-72, golf course architect 1972-; FRGS 1933; *Books* In And Out Of School (1989); *Recreations* hockey, tennis, golf; *Clubs* Seniors GC; *Style*— Michael Rogerson, Esq; Buchan House, Peasepottage, Crawley, Sussex (☎ 0293 28316); Cottesmore Golf and Country Club, Peasepottage, Crawley, Sussex (☎ 0293 28256)

ROGERSON, Philip Graham; s of Henry Rogerson, and Florence, *née* Dalton; *b* 1 Jan 1945; *Educ* William Hulmes GS Manchester; *m* 21 Dec 1968, Susan Janet, da of Jack Kershaw, of 12 Brampton Ave, Cleveleys, nr Blackpool, Lancs; 1 s (Simon Andrew b 19 July 1974); 2 da (Penelope Rose b 2 Dec 1971, Hannah Rosemary b 7 April 1988); *Career* various appts with the ICI Gp 1978-, gp tres ICI plc 1986-; FCA, MCT; *Recreations* golf, tennis, theatre; *Style—* Philip Rogerson, Esq; Baywood, 4 New Beacon Bungalows, Brittains Lane, Sevenoaks, Kent TN13 2ND (☎ 0732 461 402); Imperial Chemical Industries plc, 9 Millbank, London SW1P 3JF (☎ 01 834 4444, fax 01 834 2042, telex 21324)

ROKEBY-JOHNSON, (Henry) Ralph; s of Henry Spencer Rokeby-Johnson (d 1977); *b* 2 April 1931; *Educ* Eton, Brasenose Coll Oxford; *m* 1, 1958, Rosemary Ann, *née* Halford; m 2, 1965, Billinda Jessie Forster, *née* Pharazyn; 1 s (Rupert b 1966,); m 3, 1979, Cecilia Bridget, *née* Cavendish; 1 s (Henry b 1979); *Career* non-marine underwriter R W Sturge & Co 1974-, dir A L Sturge (Mgmnt) Ltd 1966-, ptnr R W Sturge & Co 1968-88, dir A L Sturge (Hldgs) Ltd 1971-88; *Recreations* motoring, golf; *Clubs* City of London, Mark's, Sunningdale; *Style—* Ralph Rokeby-Johnson, Esq; Arthingworth, P O Box 1513, Rancho Santa Fe, California 92067

ROLF, Percy Henry; s of Percy Algernon Rolf, of Ryde, Isle of Wight, and Lydia Kate, *née* Arnold; *b* 25 Dec 1915; *Educ* Sandown GS, London Univ (LLB); *m* 1939, Cecilia Florence, da of Frederick Thomas Cooper, of Fishbourne, IOW; 1 s (Clive Frederick b 1940), 1 da (Mary Cecilia b 1946); *Career* slr; Crown Ct rec 1978-; *Recreations* golf, gardening; *Style—* Percy Rolf, Esq; Ashlake Water, Fishbourne, Isle of Wight

ROLFE, Hon Mrs (Louise Jane Denholm); da of Baron William Denholm Barnetson (d 1981), and Joan Fairley Barnetson, *née* Davidson; *b* 24 Dec 1952; *Educ* Eothen Sch for Girls Caterham; *m* 1982, Bernard Rolfe; 1 s (Guy b 1983), 1 da (Florence b 1985); *Career* PR conslt; *Style—* The Hon Mrs Rolfe; 5 St Ann's Crescent, London SW18 2ND

ROLL, Rev Sir James William Cecil; 4 Bt (UK 1921), of The Chestnuts, Wanstead, Essex; s of Sir Cecil Ernest Roll, 3 Bt (d 1938), and Mildred Kate (d 1926), da of William Wells, of Snaresbrook, Essex; *b* 1 June 1912; *Educ* Chigwell Sch, Pembroke Coll Oxford, Chichester Theol Coll; *Heir* none; *Career* curate: St James the Great Bethnal Green 1937-39, St Matthews Custom House 1940-44; hon curate East Ham Parish Church 1944-58, vicar of St John The Divine Becontree from 1958-83 (ret); *Style—* The Rev Sir James Roll, Bt; 82 Leighcliff Rd, Leigh on Sea, Essex (☎ 0702 76177)

ROLL, Hon Joanna; da of Baron Roll of Ipsden, KCMG, CB; *b* 1944; *Style—* The Hon Joanna Roll

ROLL OF IPSDEN, Baron (Life Peer UK 1977); Eric Roll; KCMG (1962, CMG 1949), CB (1956); yr s of Mathias Roll and Fany Roll; *b* 1 Dec 1907; *Educ* Birmingham Univ (PhD); *m* 1934, Winifred, da of Elliott Taylor; 2 da; *Career* sits as Independent in House of Lords; prof econs and commerce Univ Coll Hull 1935-46, under-sec Treasy 1948, dep sec MAFF 1959-61; dep head UK Delgn negotiating EEC entry 1961-63, UK Delgn NATO Paris 1952; exec dir UK IMF and IBRD 1963-64; hon chm Book Devpt Cncl 1967-; dir Bank of Eng 1968-77; chm: S G Warburg & Co 1974-84 (jt chm 1983-87), Mercury Securities 1974-84; currently pres S G Warburg Gp plc; dir Times Newspapers Hldgs 1966-83; appeal chm Loan Fund for Musical Instruments; chllr Southampton Univ 1974-84; Grosses Goldene Ehrenzeichen mit Stern Austria, Cdr 1 Class Order of the Dannebrog (Denmark), Offr Legion of Honour; *Style—* The Rt Hon the Lord Roll of Ipsden, KCMG, CB; 2 Finsbury Ave, London EC2M 2PA

ROLL PICKERING, John Anthony; s of Lt Cdr Thomas George Pickering, RN ret, of Pentland Newtake, 34 Frogston Rd West, Edinburgh EH10 7AR, and Nora, *née* Roll; *b* 1 Nov 1949; *Educ* Edinburgh Acad, Trinity Coll Glenalmond; *m* 28 April 1973, Rosemary Anne, da of Maj Kenneth Aubrey Hearson, of Hordlea, Wigmore Lane, Halfway House, nr Shrewsbury, Salop SY5 7DZ; 1 s (Timothy b 1980), 1 da (Amanda b 1977); *Career* joined Queen's Own Lowland Yeo 1968, cmmnd 1970, transferred London Scottish/51 Highland Volunteers 1972, RARO 1976; trainee Bell Lawrie Robertson & Co stock brokers Edinburgh 1968-72, with various firms London Stock Exchange 1972-82, exec Hill Samuel Investmt Servs 1982-85, sr conslt C Howard & Ptnrs 1986-88, conslt James Capel Fin Servs 1988-; dir Highland Soc of london 1984-, memb cncl Br Deer Soc 1981-88 (hon tres 1984-88); contested (Con) Epsom and Ewell Borough Cncl 1976 and 1979, Freeman City of London 1978, Liveryman Worshipful Co of Horners (1978); ALIA 1986; *Recreations* shooting, photography, deer; *Clubs* Cavalry & Guards; *Style—* John Roll Pickering, Esq; Waldhaus, 79 College Rd, Epsom, Surrey KT17 4HH (☎ 0372 725099); c/o James Capel Financial Servs Ltd, PO Box 551, 6 Bevis Marks, London EC3A 7JQ (☎ 01 588 0998, fax 01 588 6240, telex 888866)

ROLLAND, Lawrence Anderson Lyon; s of Lawrence Anderson Rolland (d 1959), of Leven, and Winifred Anne, *née* Lyon (d 1978); *b* 6 Nov 1937; *Educ* George Watsons Coll Edinburgh, Duncan of Jordanstone Coll of Art Dundee (Dip Arch); *m* 30 April 1960, Mairi, da of John McIntyre Melville (d 1980), of Kirkcaldy; 2 s (Michael b 1963, Douglas b 1966), 2 da (Gillian b 1961, Katie b 1967); *Career* sole ptnr L A Rolland 1960; jt sr ptnr Robert Hurd & ptnr and L A Roland & Ptnr 1965, sr ptnr Hurd Rolland Ptnrship; awards and commendations incl: Satire Soc Civic Tst, RIBA, Europa Nostra, Times Conservation, Stone Fedn; fndr memb Scottish Construction Indust Gp 1980; memb: E Neok of Fife Preservation Tst, N E Fife Preservation Soc; sec Kinghorn Singers; elder Largo Parish Church, gen tstee C of S 1979-, convenor advsy ctee for artistic matters for C of S 1975-80; govr Duncan of Jordonstone Coll of Art Dundee; Hon Fell Bulgarian Inst of Architects 1987; RIAS (pres 1979-81), RIBA 1960 (pres 1985-87), FRS 1988; *Recreations* music, fishing, shooting and more architecture; *Clubs* Reform, Commonwealth; *Style—* Lawrence Rolland, Esq; School House, Newburn, Upper Largo, Fife (☎f 03333 6383); Rossend Castle, Burntisland, Fife (☎ 031 226 6555); 25A Fitzroy Sq, London W1 (☎ 01 387 9565, fax 01 388 1848)

ROLLETT, David Ian; s of Cyril Wells Rollett (d 1978), and Mildred Ada, *née* Moss; *b* 17 May 1924; *Educ* Lincoln GS, Magdalen Coll Cambridge (MA); *m* 7 Feb 1948, Patricia Diana, da of Charles Hubert Walters (chief constable of Lincoln, d 1982), of Tollerton, Nottingham; 1 da (Anthea b 1948); *Career* WWII REME 1943-47, Capt served England and India; divnl and regnl mangr Anglia Water Authy 1974-83; FICE, FIWEM; *Recreations* photography, walking, DIY; *Clubs* Rotary Huntingdon (Rotary dist govr Dist 107 1988-89); *Style—* David Rollett, Esq; 11 Beech Ave, Great Stukeley, Huntingdon, Cambridgeshire PE17 5AX (☎ 0480 55820)

ROLLIN, Charles Austin Noble; s of Philip Talbot Noble Rollin (d 1985), of Val Plaisant, Jersey, CI, and Edith May *née* Austin; *b* 14 Jan 1943; *Educ* St Edwards Sch Oxford; *m* 12 Oct 1963, Catherine (m dis 1977), da of John William Nash; 3 da (Jeannette b 1967, Anne b 1970, Pamela b 1972); *Career* CA; proprietor Greenhow & Co; *Recreations* music, theatre, squash; *Style—* Charles Rollin, Esq; Greenhow & Co, 71 St Peters Rd, Reading RG6 1PD (☎ 0734 664 020)

ROLLIN, Dr Henry Rapoport; s of Aaron Rapoport Rollin (d 1973), of 35 Heathfield Gdns, London, and Rebecca, *née* Sorkin (d 1975); *b* 17 Nov 1911; *Educ* Central HS Leeds, Univ of Leeds (MB ChB, MD); *m* 27 July 1973, Dr (Anna) Maria, da of George Tihanyi, of 21 St Agnes Close, London; 1 s (Aron David Rapoport b 1976), 1 da (Rebecca Ilona b 1979); *Career* Wing-Cdr and sr neuropsychiatric specialist RAFVR 1942-47; Fulbright fell Temple Univ Hosp Philadelphia USA 1953-54, Gwilyn Gibbon res fell Nuffield Coll Oxford 1963-64, emeritus conslt psychiatrist Horton Hosp Epsom, Surrey 1977 (conslt psychiatrist 1948-77), conslt forensic psychiatrist Home Off 1977-86; memb: Mental Health Review Tbnls 1960-83, Parole Bd 1970-73; hon librarian RCPsych 1975-85, hon conslt psychiatrist Queen Elizabeth Fndn for the Disabled, hon med advsr Nat Schizophrenia Fellowship; Hon FRCPsych 1989; FRSM 1943, FRCPsych 1971, MRCP 1975; *Books* The Mentally Abnormal Offender and the Law (1969), Coping with Schizophrenia (1980); *Recreations* music, history of medicine, theatre; *Style—* Dr Henry Rollin; 101 College Rd, Epsom, Surrey KT17 4HY (☎ 0372 24772)

ROLLIN, Peter Hamilton; s of Lawrence Hamilton Rollin, of Hamilton House, Diss, Norfolk, and Hedy, *née* Gutgiser; *b* 13 Nov 1942; *Educ* Bedford Mod Sch, The Coll of Law; *m* 6 April 1976, Elizabeth Mary, da of Maj John Kellock Corbitt, of 8 Frenze Rd, Diss, Norfolk; 1 s (Matthew b 1977), 1 da (Rachael b 1974); *Career* slr 1969, dep registrar Co Ct 1986; former pres Diss Chamber of Trade and Commerce; memb Diss Urban Dist Town Cncl 1971-77, memb Norfolk CC 1973- (ldr 1987); memb The Law Soc 1970; *Recreations* choral singing, philately; *Style—* Peter Rollin, Esq; Jacques, Back St, Garboldisham, Diss, Norfolk (☎ 095381 362); Park House, Mere St, Diss, Norfolk IP22 3JY (☎ 0379 643 555, fax 0379 652 221, telex 975640 ROLLIN G)

ROLLO, (Peter) Andrew; MBE (1945); s of William Hereward Charles Rollo, MC (d 1962), and Kathleen Nina Asquith Rollo, *née* Hill (d 1960); *b* 6 July 1919; *Educ* Eton; *m* 1953, Patricia Mary Best (d 1985); 1 s (William Raoul b 1955), 1 da (Susan Rose b 1957); *Career* Lt RN 1938-47; slr 1950-85; *Recreations* gardening, fishing; *Clubs* Turf, RYS; *Style—* Andrew Rollo, MBE; Cold Blow, Oare, Marlborough, Wiltshire SN8 4JL (☎ 0672 63205)

ROLLO, Hon Mrs William; Diana Joan; da of Edward Castell Wrey, 7 s of Sir Henry Wrey, 10 Bt, and bro of 11, 12 and 13 Bts; sis of Sir Bourchier Wrey, 14 Bt; *m* 1, 1932 (m dis 1946), Jocelyn Abel Smith (d 1966, of the Abel Smiths of Woodhill); 2 s; m 2, 1946, as his 2 w, Hon William Hereward Charles Rollo, MC (k out hunting 1962), bro of 12 Lord Rollo; *Style—* The Hon Mrs William Rollo; Barleythorpe, Oakham, Rutland LE15 7EQ

ROLLO, 13 Lord (S 1651); Eric John Stapylton Rollo; JP (Perthshire 1962); also Baron Dunning (UK 1869); s of Maj 12 Lord Rollo (d 1947), and his 1 w, Helen, da of Frederick Chetwynd-Stapylton (gggs of 4 Viscount Chetwynd); *b* 3 Dec 1915; *Educ* Eton; *m* 1938, Suzanne, da of William Hatton, of Broome House, Broome, Worcs; 2 s, 1 da; *Heir* s, Master of Rollo; *Career* farmer; *Style—* The Rt Hon the Lord Rollo, JP; Pitcairns, Dunning, Perthshire (☎ 076 484 202)

ROLLO, Hon James Malcolm; 2 s of 13 Lord Rollo, JP; *b* 25 Sept 1946; *Educ* Eton, Christ Church Oxford; *m* 14 Sept 1968, Henrietta Elizabeth Flora, da of Maj Alasdair Boyle; 1 s (Malcolm b 1981), 1 da (Helen b 1985); *Style—* The Hon James Rollo

ROLLO, Hon John Dunning; s of 12 Lord Rollo by his 2 w Phyllis; half-bro of 13 Lord Rollo; *b* 16 July 1931; *Style—* The Hon John Rollo; Pitcairns, Dunning, Perthshire

ROLLO, Hon Simon David Paul; s of 12 Lord Rollo (d 1947) by his 3 w Lily, nee Seiflow; half-bro of 13 Lord Rollo and Hon David (decd) and Hon John Rollo; *b* 4 Oct 1939; *Educ* Eton; *m* 1964, Valerie Ernestine, yr da of Robert William Gaspard Willis, of Sudbury; 2 da; *Style—* The Hon Simon Rollo; Biffens Boatyard, Staines, Middx

ROLLS, John Lawrence; s of Capt George Henry Rolls; *b* 14 Jan 1930; *Educ* Sherborne, Loughborough Univ; *m* 1970, Maura Catherine, *née* Tunney; 5 children; *Career* dep chm Oil Mop (UK) Ltd, chm Aquaflite Ltd, chm Marine Auctions Ltd, chm Ravenscourt Devpts Ltd; *Recreations* shooting, golf; *Style—* John Rolls, Esq; Ravenscourt, Lymington, Hants (☎ 73132)

ROLT, David Anthony; Dr Frederick Henry Rolt, OBE (d 1973), and Florence Mary, *née* Edwards (d 1968); *b* 30 Jan 1926; *Educ* Kingston GS, Imperial Coll of Sci and Technol; *m* 30 April 1949, Nettie Winifred, da of Herbert Charles Kinns (d 1953) 2 s (Anthony b 1951, Timothy b 1953); *Career* Royal Norfolk Regt 1945-46, cmmnd 2 Lt RE 1947, demob 1948; dir construction bd Sir Rob McAlpine and Sons Ltd (joined 1948); FCIOB 1973; *Recreations* boating; *Clubs* Royal Dorset YC (currently Commodore of the Assoc of Dunkirk Little SMPS); *Style—* David Rolt, Esq; Hartlebury Cottage, 1 Trinity Terrace, Weymouth, Dorset DT4 8JW (☎ 0305 777 786); 40 Bernard St, London Wc1N 1LG (☎ 01 837 3377, fax 01 833 4102, car tel 0860 250 720, telex 22308)

ROMAIN, Richard David Anidjah; s of Philip Isaac Anidjah Romain, of Stanmore, Middx, and Joan, *née* Rose; *b* 10 August 1958; *Educ* City of London Sch, Loughborough Univ (BSc); *m* 12 March 1989, Juliet Barbara, da of Gerald Michael Raeburn, of Edgware, Middx; *Career* md John Morley Presentations Ltd 1985 (dir 1983), main bd dir John Morley Jewellery Gp 1987; cncllr London Borough of Harrow 1982-, (chief whip); main bd memb West London Waste Authy, memb Lord-Lieut's ctee (Harrow), nat exec memb Aid for Addicts and Family, memb Nat Assoc of Goldsmiths, chm ed bd The Harrow Magazine; Freeman City of London 1981, Liveryman Worshipful Co of Bakers; *Recreations* snooker, swimming, motor cruising; *Style—* Richard Romain, Esq; 106/108 High St, Watford, Herts WD1 2BW (☎ 0923 226 883, fax 0923 249 136, car tel 0836 223 637)

ROMANES, Constance Margaret; OBE (1981), JP (1965); da of Claud Valentine Gee (d 1951), and Hilda Bentham (d 1968); *b* 9 August 1920; *Educ* St Leonard's Sch, Girton Coll Cambridge; *m* 29 June 1943, Giles John, s of Capt Francis John Romanes (d 1944); 1 s (Julian b 1951), 2 da (Jane b 1946, Rosalind b 1947); *Career* dep chm Magistrates Assoc 1981-87; chm: Dorset branch Magistrates' Assoc 1981-, Weymouth and Portland Bench 1985-; memb James Ctee (an interdepartmental ctee on distribution of criminal business) and various govt working parties, Lord Chllr's nominee on Legal Aid Duty Slr ctee 1986, memb Portland Borstal 1971-86, YCC Bd of

Visitors (chm 1976-81), chm Dorset Care Tst 1984-, memb Local Parole Review Ctee 1984-86, memb Salisbury Dioc Synod 1976-84, Bishops selector for ACCM 1976-83; contrib to various jls and has read papers at various int conferences; *Recreations* music (active memb of orchestras and chamber groups), gardening; *Clubs* RSM; *Style*— Mrs Constance Romanes, OBE, JP; Portesham House, nr Weymouth, Dorset (☎ 0305 871300)

ROMANES, Giles John; s of Francis John Romanes (d 1944), of Brick House, Duton Hill, Dunmow, Essex, and Doris Helena McNaughton, *née* Wright; gfs were George John Romanes, FRS, biologist, and Sir Almroth Edward Wright, FRS, bacteriologist; *b* 8 Dec 1918; *Educ* Eton, Cambridge (MA); *m* 29 June 1943, Constance Margaret, da of Rev Claud Valentine Gee; 1 s (Julian b 1951), 2 da (Geraldine b 1946, Rosalind b 1947); *Career* consIt ophthalmic surgn W Dorset Hosps 1960-84; KStJ (1987); FRCS; *Books* Traction Engines in Retirement (1962); *Recreations* skiing, traction engine operation and threshing, flying; *Clubs* RSM, Ski of GB, Nat Traction Engine; *Style*— Giles Romanes, Esq; Portesham House, nr Weymouth, Dorset DT4 3HE (☎ 0305 871 300); 20 Dukes Ave, Dorchester, Dorset DT1 1EN (☎ 0305 63774)

ROME, Alan Mackenzie; s of John Mackenzie Rome (d 1969), and Evelyn Anne, *née* Rae (d 1978); *b* 24 Oct 1930; *Educ* Kings Sch Bruton, RWA (Dip Arch); *m* 8 Sept 1956, Mary Lilyan, da of Thomas William Barnard (d 1984); 1 s (Timothy b 1961), 1 da (Judith b 1963); *Career* Nat Serv RE 1949-50; in off of Sir George Oatley, FRIBA 1947-49, asst to architect Westminster Abbey 1955-60; own practice (initially with Michael Torrens, FRIBA, and Rolfe & Crozier-Cole) 1960-; cathedral architect to Dean and Chapter of: Bristol, Peterborough, Salisbury, Wells; memb: Cncl for the Care of Churches, Redundant Churches Fund, Bath and Wells Diocesan Advsy Ctee, SPAB; occasional lectr Bristol Univ; FRIBA, FSA; *Recreations* walking, sketching; *Style*— Alan Rome, Esq; 11 Mayfair Ave, Nailsea, Bristol BS19 2LR (☎ 0272 853215)

ROME, Maj Patrick Leslie; MC (1944); s of Brig-Gen Charles Leslie Rome, DSO (d 1936), of Godalming, Surrey, and Mary Ethel Phyllis Illingworth (d 1963); *b* 22 June 1921; *Educ* Charterhouse; *m* 31 Oct 1946, Clare Pauline Mary, da of George 5 Duke de Stacpoole (d 1965), of Tobertynan, Co Meath, Eire; 2 s (Derek b 1949, Andrew b 1959), 2 da (Lavinia b 1947, Susan b 1953); *Career* offr DLI 1941-58: served 2 DLI India and Burma 1942-45 (wounded 1944), BAOR 1948-51, Staff Coll Camberley 1954, Gold Coast Ghana 1955-57 (ret 1958); joined the Morgan Crucible Co 1958-72, dir Morganite Int Ltd 1968, md Morganite Int Ltd 1972 (ret 1982); *Recreations* shooting, sailing, skiing; *Clubs* Army and Navy, Ski of GB; *Style*— Maj Patrick Rome, MC; Pitts House, Chitterne, Warminster, Wilts (☎ 0985 50416); Prince's House, Roundstone, Co Galway (☎ 095 35850)

ROMER, Hon Lady (Frances Evelyn Lebeau); da of Alfred Kemp, of Epping; *m* 1925, as his 2 w, Rt Hon Sir Charles Romer, OBE (d 1969), s of Baron Romer, PC (Life Peer, d 1944); 2 s; *Style*— The Hon Lady Romer; Orchard House, Littlestone, Kent

ROMER, Ian Lebeau Ritchie; s of Rt Hon Sir Charles Robert Ritchie Romer (d 1969), of Littlestone, Kent, and The Hon Lady Frances Evelyn Lebeau, *née* Kemp; previous 3 direct generations (and present) were all educated at Trinity Hall, went to the Chancery Bar and were benchers of Lincoln's Inn; *b* 26 Dec 1929; *Educ* Bryanston, Trinity Hall Cambridge (BA); *m* 1, 1952, Elizabeth, da of James Dales of Vancouver, 1 s (James b 1955 decd), 1 da (Jane b 1956); m 2, 1960, Mary Rose, da of Col W H Crichton (d 1984), of Polstead, Suffolk, 1 s (Caspar b 1970), 1 da (Emma b 1961); *Career* barr; bencher Lincoln's Inn 1981; *Clubs* Garrick; *Style*— Ian L R Romer, Esq; High Barn, Hawkley, Hants GU33 6NJ (☎ Hawkley 301); 17 Old Buildings, Lincolns Inn, London WC2 (☎ 01 405 9653)

ROMER, Mark Lemon Robert; eld s of Sir Charles Robert Ritchie Romer (d 1969; Lord Justice of Appeal), of Littlestone, and Frances Evelyn Lebeau, *née* Kemp; f, gf and ggf all members of Court of Appeal, gf going on to House of Lords where he sat with two brothers-in-law (Viscount Maugham, Lord Russell of Killowen); *b* 12 July 1927; *Educ* Bryanston, Trinity Hall Cambridge (MA, LLM); *m* 1953, Philippa Maynard, da of Maj Maynard Tomson, MC (d 1984) of Hitchin; 1 s (Stephen b 1957), 2 da (Caroline b 1955, Eugénie b 1961); *Career* served KRRC UK 1945-48; barr 1952; met stipendiary magistrate 1972-; *Recreations* bird-watching, travel, looking at pictures, painting watercolours; *Style*— Mark Romer, Esq; c/o National Westminster Bank Ltd, 95 Chancery Lane, London WC2; Clerkenwell Magistrates Court, Kings Cross Rd, London WC1

ROMER, Cdr (Robert) Mark; s of Robert Parbury Romer (d 1927), and Evelyn Margaret Wall (d 1986); ggf Sir Robert Romer, Lord Justice of Appeal, gggf Mark Lemon first ed of Punch; *b* 31 July 1924; *Educ* Sherborne, Corpus Christi Coll Cambridge (BA); *m* 31 March 1948, Fay Patricia Wade, da of Maj Patrick Wade Gardner, MC (d 1970), of 32 Connaught Sq, London; 3 da (Sally-Fay b 1957, Caroline b 1960, Melanie b 1963); *Career* RN 1944-74, Cdr WWII, Korean War 1950, Malaya 1964; MOD 1974-84, asst dir Standardization (Navy); consulting engr 1984-; FIEE; *Recreations* gardening, music, reading; *Style*— Cdr Mark Romer, Esq, RN; Sion Lodge, 34 Sion Hill, Bath BA1 2UW (☎ 0225 22430)

ROMER-LEE, Robin Knyvett; s of Knyvett Romer-Lee, OBE, of Green Farm, Hickling, Norfolk, and Jeanne Pamela, *née* Shaw (d 1982); *b* 27 Oct 1942; *Educ* Eton; *m* 30 March 1968, Annette Millet, da of George Henry Brockle Hurst (d 1972); 2 s (Benjamin b 1971, Edward b 1973); *Career* insur broker and memb of Lloyds; dir Sedgwick Ltd 1987, chm Sedgwick Assoc Risks Ltd 1985; *Recreations* sailing, fishing, gardening; *Style*— Robin Romer-Lee, Esq; The Old Rectory, Groton, nr Colchester CO6 5EE (☎ (0787) 210710); Sedgwick House, Sedgwick Centre, London E1 8DX

ROMNEY, 7 Earl of (UK 1801); Sir Michael Henry Marsham; 13 Bt (E 1663); also Baron of Romney (GB 1716) and Viscount Marsham (UK 1801); s of Lt-Col Hon Reginald Marsham, OBE (2 s of 4 Earl of Romney), and Dora, 4 da of Charles North, JP, DL (5 in descent from Hon Roger North, the memoirist and 6 s of 4 Baron North); suc first cous, 6 Earl, 1975; *b* 22 Nov 1910; *Educ* Sherborne; *m* 28 June 1939, Aileen, o da of Lt-Col James Russell Landale;; *Heir* first cous once removed, Julian Marsham; *Career* late Maj RA, served WW II; *Recreations* foxhunting; *Style*— The Rt Hon the Earl of Romney; Wensum Farm, W Rudham, King's Lynn, Norfolk (☎ E Rudham 249)

ROMSEY, Lord; Norton Louis Philip Knatchbull; s and h of Countess Mountbatten of Burma and of 7 Baron Brabourne; *b* 8 Oct 1947; *Educ* Gordonstoun, Kent Univ; *m* 1979, Penelope Meredith, only da of Reginald and Marian Eastwood of Palma de Mallorca, Spain; 1 s, (Hon Nicholas b 1981), 2 da (Hon Alexandra b 1982, Hon Leonora b 1986); *Heir* s, Hon Nicholas Louis Charles Norton Knatchbull b 15 May 1981; *Career* film and TV prodr 1971-80; dir: Southern Sound plc, Radio Mercury plc, Suffolk Gp Radio plc, Satellite TV plc (Sky Channel), Chalford Communications Ltd, Friday Prodns Ltd; chm Britt Allcroft Ltd (Thomas the Tank Engine and Friends), High Steward Romsey 1980, vice adm Royal Motor YC 1985, vice-pres Mary Rose Tst; memb ct of Southampton Univ; *Clubs* Royal Motor Yacht; *Style*— Lord Romsey; Broadlands, Romsey, Hants SO51 9ZD (☎ (0794) 517888)

ROMYN, Conrad; MC (1946); s of Conrad Richardson (d 1936), and Anne Elizabeth Romyn (d 1918); *b* 18 Nov 1915; *Educ* St Lawrence Coll Geneva Univ Vienna; *m* Ann Dorothea, da of the late Isak Bergson; 1 da (Jenny Ann) ; *Career* Maj IA Regt attached to D Force Burma, on loan to 20 Indian Div 1939-46; author illustrated book on St Lucia (cmmnd by St Lucian Govt), Timothy Bhalu-Children's Book; painter; exhibitions in: RA London, Ecole de Paris, Salons de la Societé Francaise Paris, Prix Othon Friels Paris, Salon des Surindepandts Paris, Nyköping Museum Sweden; works purchased by: Museum of Modern Art Stockholm, Swedish Banks, Leicester Yorks and Surrey Depts of Educn; in private collections in: England, France, Holland, Sweden, Norway, Denmark, Canada, USA; *Recreations* music, visiting museums, antique books and maps, travel; *Style*— Conrad Romyn, Esq, MC; 1 North Cottage, Hampton Court, Surrey (☎ 01 977 5890); Royal Bank of Scotland, Kingston upon Thames

RONALDSHAY, Earl of; Lawrence Mark; s and h of 3 Marquess of Zetland, DL; *b* 28 Dec 1937; *Educ* Harrow, Christ's Coll Cambridge; *m* 1964, Susan, da of Guy Chamberlin, of Shefford House, Great Shefford, Newbury; 2 s (Lord Dundas b 5 Mar 1965, Hon James Edward b 2 May 1967), 2 da (Lady Henrietta Kate b 9 Feb 1970, Lady Victoria Clare b 2 Jan 1973); *Heir* s, Lord Dundas; *Career* late 2 Lt Grenadier Gds; landowner; dir: Redcar Racecourse, Catterick Racecourse, Tocketts Mill Devpt Co, Escor Toys Ltd, Barony Fishing Co Ltd, Racing Five Ltd; *Recreations* tennis (lawn and Royal), squash, racing (racehorses: Foggy Buoy, Tatiana, Chance Command); *Clubs* All England Lawn Tennis, Jockey; *Style*— Earl of Ronaldshay; Copt Hewick Hall, Ripon, N Yorks HG4 5DE (☎ 0765 3946); 10 Crescent Place, SW3 (☎ 01 584 6840)

RONEY, Richard Esmond Barham; s of Esmond Richard Roney (d 1979), of London NW6, and Muriel, *née* Barham; gs of Sir Ernest Roney, on mother's side descended from Fitzurse (first knight to kill Thomas A Becket) Admiral Lord Barham and Rev Richard Harris Barham (Thomas Ingoldsby); *b* 17 April 1943; *Educ* St Paul's; *m* 1, 28 Nov 1964, Georgina, da of Richard Wykes Stephens, of Henley-on-Thames; 1 s (Esmond b 1969), 1 da (Charlotte b 1972); m 2, 1 June 1981, Danielle, da of Marcel Bloch (d 1985); 1 step da (Karen); *Career* slr; dir: Denison Mines (North Sea) Ltd, LL & E (UK) Inc, Oranje Nassau (UK) Ltd, Pennozil Ltd; *Recreations* skiing, golf, theatre, music, reading, good food and wine, cinema, sightseeing; *Clubs* Boodles, Wentworth; *Style*— Richard Roney, Esq; 15 Queens Gate Gardens, London SW7 (☎ 01 584 6076); 84 Brook St, London W1Y 1YG (☎ 01 629 2382; fax: 01 629 0027; telex: 8954320)

RONSON, Gerald Maurice; *b* 27 May 1939; *m* Gail; 4 da; *Career* chm and chief exec Heron Int plc; tstee: Ronson Fndn (and fndr), Br Museum (natural hist) 1987-; a vice pres NSPCC 1985-; memb: governing cncl Business in the Community, cncl Princes Youth Business Tst; CBIM 1982; *Recreations* yachting, shooting; *Clubs* Royal Southern YC, One Per Cent; *Style*— Gerald Ronson, Esq; c/o Heron International plc, Heron House, 19 Marylebone Rd, London NW1 (☎ 01 486 4477)

ROOKE, Sir Denis Eric; CBE (1970); s of F G Rooke; *b* 2 April 1924; *Educ* Westminster City Sch, Addey and Stanhope Sch UCL (BSc); *m* 1949, Elizabeth Brenda, *née* Evans; 1 da; *Career* Maj REME 1944-49; joined S Eastern Gas Bd 1949 (devpt engr 1959); memb: advsy cncl for R&D 1972-77, advsy cncl for energy conservation 1974-77, offshore energy tech bd 1975-78, Brit Nat Oil Corpn (pt/t) 1976-82, NEDC 1976-80, Energy Cmmn 1977-79; pres IGasE 1975, chm Br Gas plc 1986- (chm Br Gas Corpn 1976-86, dep chm 1972-76); pres Welding Inst 1981-; pres Pipeline Industs Guild 1981-83; FEng 1986; chm CNAA 1978-83; tstee Sci Museum 1984-, cmmr Royal Cmmn for the Exhibition of 1851-1984; Hon DSc: Salford Univ 1978, Leeds 1980, The City Univ 1985, Univ of Durham 1986, Cranfield Inst of Technol 1987; Hon DTech CNAA 1986, Hon LLD Univ of Bath 1987; FRS 1978, FEng 1977; kt 1977; *Recreations* listening to music, photography; *Clubs* Athenaeum, English-Speaking Union; *Style*— Sir Denis Rooke, CBE; 23 Hardy Rd, Blackheath, SE3 7NS (☎ 01 858 6710)

ROOKE, His Honour Judge; Giles Hugh; TD (1963), QC (1979); s of Charles Eustace Rooke, CMG (d 1947), and Irene Phyllis (d 1969), da of Thomas Main Patterson, and former w of 3 Baron Borwick; *b* 28 Oct 1930; *Educ* Stowe, Exeter Coll Oxford; *m* 1968, Anne Bernadette Seymour, da of His Hon John Perrett; 3 s (Alexander b 1969, Nicholas b 1970, George b 1979), 1 da (Elizabeth b 1972); *Career* Maj (TA) Kent Yeo 1951-61, KCLY 1961-65; barr 1957, Crown Ct rec 1975-81, circuit judge (SE Circuit, on which practised as barr from 1957) 1981-; hon rec of Margate 1980-; *Recreations* cultivant son jardin; *Style*— His Honour Judge Rooke, TD, QC; St Stephen's Cottage, Bridge, Canterbury CT4 5AH (☎ 0227 830298)

ROOKE, James Smith; CMG (1961), OBE (1950); s of Joseph Nelson Rooke (d 1964); *b* 6 July 1916; *Educ* Workington Gs, Univ Coll London, Vienna Univ; *m* 1938, Maria Theresa, da of Franz Rebrec, of Austria; 3 children; *Career* Dip Serv 1938-76: cnsllr: Berne, Rome, commercial min Canberra 1966-68, econ min Paris 1968-72; chief exec Br Overseas Trade Bd 1972-76, co dir and industl and banking conslt 1976-80, lectr Dip Acad Vienna 1980-; Grand Decoration of Honour in Gold of the Austrian Republic 1981; *Books* english translations of Rilke and Holderlin; *Recreations* skiing, tennis, climbing, swimming; *Clubs* Devonshire; *Style*— James Rooke Esq, CMG, OBE; c/o Midland Bank Ltd, 165 Kilburn High Road, London NW6; Kreuzwiesengasse 4, Vienna XV11, Austria (☎ 0222 465123)

ROOKE, Brig Vera Margaret; CB (1984), CBE (1980), RRC (1973); da of late William James Rooke, and Lily Amelia, *née* Cole; *b* 21 Dec 1924; *Educ* Girls' County Sch Hove, Addenbrooke's Hosp Cambridge (SRN), Royal Alexandra Children's Hosp Brighton (RSCN), St Helier Hosp Carshalton; *Career* cmmnd Queen Alexandra's Royal Army Nursing Corps 1951, liaison offr QARANC MOD 1973-74; asst dir Army Nursing Services and matron: Mil Hosp Hong Kong 1975, Royal Herbert Hosp and Queen Elizabeth Mil Hosp Woolwich 1976-78; dep dir Army Nursing Servs HQ UKLF 1979-80, Lt-Col 1972, Col 1975, Brig 1981, matron-in-chief and dir Army Nursing Serv 1981-84, Queens Hon Nursing Sister 1981-84; *Style*— Brig Vera Rooke, CB, CBE, RRC,; 6 Carpenters, Alresford, Hampshire SO24 9HE

ROOKER, Jeffrey William; MP (Lab) Birmingham, Perry Barr Feb 1974-; *b* 5 June 1941; *Educ* Handsworth Tech Sch, Handsworth Tech Coll, Warwick Univ (MA), Aston Univ (BScEng); *m* 1972, Angela; *Career* oppn front bench spokesman: social security 1981-Nov 1983, Treasy and Econ Affrs Nov 1983-; *Style*— Jeffrey Rooker Esq, MP; House of Commons, London SW1

ROOKLEDGE, Gordon Charles; s of Charles Harcourt Rookledge Collett (d 1954), of Johanesburg, SA, and Elsie Alicia, *née* Goodwin (d 1976); *b* 3 Dec 1933; *Educ* Stanley Park Secdy Sch; *m* 1 April 1960, Jennifer Mary, da of Robert Dampier Lush, of Carshalton, Surrey; 1 s (Gavin Alistair b 1964), 2 da (Sarah Louise b 1962, Emma Constance b 1966); *Career* Nat Serv RA 1952-54; sales rep: Austin Miles Ltd 1954-58, Eros Engraving Ltd 1958-64; sales mangr Westerham Press 1964-68; chm and md: Gavin Martin Ltd (fndr 1968), Sarema Press (Publishers) Ltd (fndr 1973), KGM (Offset) Ltd (fndr 1983); pt/t tutor RCA 1974-84, visiting lectr E Ham Coll of Technol and Middx Poly; chm Carshalton Soc; memb: Friends of the Earth, Media Natura; *Books* Rookledge's International Typefinder (ed);; *Recreations* film and video, collecting print ephemera, paintings, swimming, squash; *Clubs* Groucho, Chelsea Arts, Wynkyn De Worde Soc, Galley; *Style*— Gordon Rookledge, Esq; Gavin Martin Ltd, KGM House, 26-34 Rothschild St, West Norwood, London SE27 0HQ (☎ 01 761 3077, fax 01 761 6319)

ROOLEY, George Arthur; CBE (1972); s of Richard Arthur Rooley (d 1932), of Leicester, and Edith Mary Rooley (d 1931); *b* 16 Feb 1911; *Educ* Leicester Coll Art and Technol, Bath Univ (MSc); *m* 1 June 1935, Valeria, da of Herbert Green (d 1966), of Leicester; 1 s (Richard Herbert b April 1940); *Career* chartered engr; fndr ptnr D Smith Seymour & Rooley Consulting Engrs 1945, chm Assoc of Conslt Engrs 1970-71, pres Int Fedn of Hosp Engrg 1972-74, sr ptnr DSSR 1981 (retd); Freeman: City of London 1977, Worshipful of Co of Engineers 1984, Worshipful Co of Constructors 1977; FICE, FIMechE, MConsE, Hon FCIBSE, SFInstE; *Recreations* golf, gardening; *Clubs* Stoke Poges GC (former capt and pres), Royal Overseas; *Style*— George Rooley, Esq, CBE; Greenways, Church Lane, Stoke Poges, Bucks SL2 4PB (☎ 028 14 3339)

ROOLEY, Richard Hebert; s of George Arthur Rooley, CBE, qv, of Stoke Poges, Bucks, and Valeria Rooley; *b* 24 April 1940; *Educ* Glasgow Acad, Morrisons Acad, Trinity Coll Dublin (BA, BAI); *m* 25 July 1964, (Ismena) Ruth, da of George Young (d 1956), of Carlow, Eire; 1 s (George b 1966), 1 da (Ismena b 1968); *Career* Donald Smith & Rooley conslt engrs 1964-: assoc 1968-, ptnr 1971-, ptnr project mgmnt ptnrship 1978-; memb cncl CIBSE 1972-81, chm Bldg Servs Res and Info Assoc 1984-86; church warden Stokes Poges 1980-86, lay chm Burnham Deanery Synod 1985-86; Liveryman Worshipful Co of Engrs (memb ct of Assts 1989), Jr Warden Worshipful Co of Constructors 1988; C Eng, FICE, FIMechE, FCIBSE, MConsE, Fell American Soc of Heating Refrigerating and Air Conditioning Engrs (memb bd of dir 1980-83); *Recreations* golf; *Clubs* RAC; *Style*— Richard Rooley, Esq; 31 Oakfield Rd, Clifton, Bristol BS8 2AT (☎ 0272 733 655); Crusader House, St Stephens St, Bristol BS1 (☎ 0272 279 419, fax 0272 276 159)

ROOME, Capt David Gordon; LVO (1962); s of Maj-Gen Sir Horace Eckford Roome, KCIE, CB, CBE, MC, DL, late RE (d 1964), late of IOW, and Helen Isabel Roome, *née* Walford (d 1970); *b* 8 Feb 1923; *Educ* Wellington; *m* 25 Jan 1949, Anne Patricia, da of Rear Adm Humfrey John Bradley Moore, CBE (d 1985), of Kent; 2 s (Geoffrey b 1951, Rowland b 1956), 1 da (Julia b 1950); *Career* RN 1940-72; WWII served: N Atlantic, Med, Far East; Royal Yacht 1960-62, IDC 1963, sr Naval Offr W Indies 1970-72 (as Cdre), ret as Capt RN; ADC to HM The Queen 1971; *Recreations* sailing; *Clubs* Civil Serv; *Style*— Capt David Roome, LVO; East Hall, Boughton Monchelsea, Maidstone, Kent ME17 4JX (☎ 0622 43410)

ROOME, John Walford; s of Maj-Gen Sir Horace Eckford Roome, KCIE, CB, CBE, MC, DL, late RE (d 1964), and Helen Isabel, *née* Walford (d 1970); *b* 19 Feb 1928; *Educ* Wellington, Clare Coll Cambridge (MA, LLM); *m* 2 July 1955, (Mary) Katherine, da of James Douglas (d 1958); 1 s (James Henry b 7 Oct 1958), 3 da (Christian b 19 Feb 1957, Frances b 3 July 1960, Annabel b 3 Sept 1964); *Career* RN 1946-48; slr Withers Crossman Block 1953- (sr ptnr 1986-); Cdre: Royal Yacht Sqdn 1986-, Royal Ocean Racing Club 1976-78; chm Offshore Racing Cncl 1978-87, Younger Brother Trinity House 1984 Portsmouth Naval Base Property tstee 1986-; memb: Law Soc, Slrs Disciplinary Tbnl 1987-; *Recreations* sailing (yacht 'Flycatcher'); *Clubs* Royal Yacht Sqdn, Royal Cruising, Royal Ocean Racing, Royal Lymington YC; *Style*— John Roome, Esq; Riversdale House, Boldre, Lymington, Hants; 20 Essex St, London WC2

ROOME, Maj-Gen Oliver McCrea; CBE (1973), DL (Isle of Wight, 1981); s of Maj-Gen Sir Horace Roome, KCIE, CB, CBE, MC, DL late RE (d 1964), and Helen Isabel, *née* Walford (d 1970); *b* 9 Mar 1921; *Educ* Wellington; *m* 1947, Isobel Anstis, da of Rev A B Jordan (d 1981), of Nottingham; 2 s (Peter b 1951, Harry b 1954), 1 da (Melanie b 1960); *Career* cmmnd RE 1940; WWII served: UK, Western Desert, Sicily, Italy; various appts 1946-68; Uk, Far East, Middle East, Berlin; IDC 1969, dir of army recruiting 1970-73, chief Jt Servs Liaison Orgn Bonn 1973-76, ret; Col Cmdt RE 1979-84; co cmmr Scouts IOW 1977-85; High Sheriff IOW 1983-84; Vice Lord-Lieut IOW 1987; *Recreations* sailing (yacht 'Morning Sky'), youth activities; *Clubs* Army and Navy, Royal Yacht Sqdn, Royal Cruising, Royal Ocean Racing; *Style*— Maj-Gen Oliver Roome, CBE, DL; c/o Lloyds Bank, 6 Pall Mall, London SW1

ROONEY, Denis Michael Hall; CBE (1977); s of Frederick Joseph Rooney (d 1955), of Calcutta and Bognor Regis, and Ivy Anne, *née* Hall (d 1985); *b* 9 August 1919; *Educ* Stonyhurst, Downing Coll Cambridge (BA, MA); *m* 1, 29 Aug 1942, (Ruby) Teresa (d 1984), da of Thomas Frederick Lamb (d 1946), of Plymouth; 3 s (Nicholas b 30 Nov 1950, Simon b 15 May 1958, Damian b 20 Jan 1963), 3 da (Caroline b 25 Jan 1945, Alison 9 Nov 1947, Amanda 23 Nov 1959); m 2, 7 April 1986, Muriel Edith, wid of Bernard Franklin; 1 step da (Tilly b 2 Feb 1972); *Career* Lt (E) RN 1941-46, served maj war vessels and latterly staff engr offr to Admty German Mine Sweeping Admin Hamburg; apprentice Met Vickers 1937-38, exec dir and chief exec BICC Construction Ltd 1958-72 (engr and contract mangr 1946-54), regnl export mangr BICC Ltd 1955-57; chm: Balfour Beatty Ltd 1975-80 (md 1973-77), BICC Int Ltd 1978-80, Nat Nuclear Corpn 1980-81, (industl conslt and non-exec dir 1981-86), SE Asia Trade Advsy Gp BOTB 1975-79; memb: BOTB and BOTAC 1976-80, Cncl Christian Assoc of Business Execs, W London Ctee for Protection of Children, Inst of Business Ethics; Freeman of City of London 1974, Liveryman of Worshipful Co of Turners 1974; FEng 1979, FIMechE 1960, FIEE 1965, CBIM 1978; USSR Jubilee Medal 1988; *Books* IEE Journal Railway Electrification in Brazil (1953); *Recreations* golf, visiting historic buildings; *Clubs* Roehampton, IOD; *Style*— Denis Rooney, Esq, CBE; 36 Edwardes Sq, London W8 6HH (☎ 01 603 9971)

ROONEY, Oswald Basil Nick (Mickey); s of Basil Oswald Rooney (d 1986), and Laura Amy, *née* Franks (d 1970); *b* 19 Nov 1916; *Educ* Ampleforth; *m* 2 June 1941, Rachel Margery, da of Arthur Blair White, MBE, of Co Dublin; 5 s (1 s d at birth, Roger Michael Basil b 1942, Robert Christopher Blair b 1947, Patrick John Brian b 1951, Gavin Charles b 1958), 1 da (Gabriel Ann b 1953); *Career* WWII Maj Army 1939-46, served OCTU, 5 Scots Gds, Inniskilling Fus, Commandos 1940, SAS 1943; md RA Rooney & Sons Ltd; ret 1983; *Recreations* gardening, racing; *Clubs* Harlequins, EI & S Cuntill, Lloyds; *Style*— Oswald B Rooney, Esq; The Rectory, Edgcote, nr Banbury, Oxon

ROOSE, Christopher Sturt (Chris); s of Arnold Roose, and Olive Lesley, *née* Sturt (d 1969); *b* 22 April 1946; *Educ* Univ Coll Sch Hampstead, St John's Coll Cambridge (MA); 1, 10 Aug 1968 (m dis 1976), Judith Ann Muriel Blackett; partner, Ann Patricia (Mel) Churcher; 1 s (Ben b 1979); *Career* exec gp head Lintas 1969-73, sr writer Saatchi & Saatchi Garland Compton 1973-75, creative dir and head TV D'Arcy MacManus & Masius 1976-81, creative ptnr Thorne Roose Georgiades 1981-82, creative dir Broadbents 1982-; author: Gentlemen and Players (TV 1988), The Big Hand (short story 1988); *Recreations* opera, music, theatre; *Style*— Christopher Roose, Esq

ROOSE-EVANS, James Humphrey; s of Jack Roose-Evans, and Catharina Primrose, *née* Morgan; *b* 11 Nov 1927; *Educ* Crypt GS Gloucester, St Benet's Hall Oxford (MA); *Career* plays: Cider with Rosie (adapted from Laurie Lee's novel, 1962), 84 Charing Cross Rd (1981), Re Joyce! (1988); prodns in West End incl: and Ideal Husband, The Happy Apple, Private Lives, Cider with Rosie, Under Milk Wood, Mate!, The Seven Year Itch, A Personal Affair, The Best of Friends; dir chester Mystery Plays Chester Festival 1973, winner 7 awards incl Best Dir and Best Author (84 Charing Cross Rd); fndr: Hampstead Theatre 1959, Bleddfa Trust-Centre for Caring and the Arts 1974; former memb: drama panel Welsh Arts Cncl, SE Wales Arts Assoc; has taught regularly at: RADA, Julliard Sch of Music New York, Homerton Coll Cambridge; ordained non-stipendiary Anglican priest 1981 (first Br theatre dir to be also ordained priest); *Books* Directing a Play (1968), Experimental Theatre (fourth edn 1988), London Theatre (1977), The Adventures of Odd and Elsewhere (new edn 1988), The Secret of the Seven Bright Shiners (new edn 1989), Odd and the Great Bear (1973), Elsewhere and the Gathering of the Clowns (1974), The Return of the Great Bear (1975), The Secret of Tippity witchit (1976), The Lost Treasure of Wales (1977), Inner Journey, Outer Journey (1987), Darling Ma (letters of Joyce Grenfell to her mother, ed 1988), The Time of My Life ENSA (memoirs of Joyce Grenfell, ed 1989); *Clubs* Garrick, Dramatist's; *Style*— James Roose-Evans, Esq; c/o David Higham Assoc, 5-8 Lower John St, Golden Square, London W1 (☎ 01 437 7888)

ROOT, Alan George; s of George Root, of Holyport, Berks (d 1966), and Lottie, *née* Singleton-Hayes (d 1975); *b* 16 Nov 1923; *Educ* Maidenhead Sch and privately; *m* 11 June 1949, Margaret Dorothy, da of Sidney Kentish (d 1981), of Holmer Green, Bucks; 4 da (Amanda b 1958, Sarah b 1959, Penelope b 1964, Emma b 1966); *Career* RAF 1941-46, 29 Sqdn Mosquito Night Intruders; gen mangr Newsweek int edns 1953-67, dir Life Magazine, int edns 1967-71; free house owner 1971-78; md Penthouse Gp of Cos 1978-80, dir Publishing Conslt Co 1981-82; antiques and art collator for Trusthouse Forte plc 1983-; *Recreations* cricket, gardening, cooking and wine, photography, antiques; *Clubs* Carlton, MCC; *Style*— Alan Root, Esq; Thornwell Cottage, Thornwell Lane, Wincanton, Somerset BA9 9DY (☎ 0963 34211); Trusthouse Forte plc, 166 High Holborn, London WC1V 6TT (☎ 01 836 7744)

ROOT, Hilary Margaret; da of Frederick James Root (d 1982), and Margaret Eleanor Root; *b* 7 July 1945; *Educ* Sherborne Sch for Girls, Trinity Coll Dublin (BA); *Career* fund mangr Sheppards stockbrokers; *Recreations* travel, tennis, entertaining; *Style*— Miss Hilary Root; c/o Sheppards, No.1 London Bridge, London SE1 9QU (☎ 01 378 7000, telex 888282); 18 Bywater St, London SW3 4XD (☎ 01 584 3810)

ROOT, Neville Douglas; s of Neville Ernest Arthur Root, and Ada Jackson, *née* Shipley; *b* 17 Mar 1939; *Educ* Pinner GS; *m* 15 July 1961, Betty Vivienne, da of Rowland Twine (d 1983); 2 s (Neville b 1963, David b 1967), 1 da (Sally b 1964); *Career* dir: Black Clawson Int Ltd 1975-86, Greenbank Gp plc 1984-86, NW Elec Bd 1984-, Walker Green Bank plc 1986-; *Recreations* sailing, golf; *Clubs* St James (Manchester); *Style*— Neville Root, Esq; 16 South Downs Road, Hale, Altrincham, Cheshire (☎ 061 928 2496); Walker Greenbank plc, Manor Rd, Manchester M19 3EJ (☎ 061 224 6224, fax 061 224 2098)

ROOTES, Hon Mrs Brian (Elizabeth Margaret); da of Rev Humphrey Barclay, CVO, MC (of the Essex banking family, being s of Henry Barclay, CVO, JP, DL, who was himself gs of Robert Barclay by his w Elizabeth, nee Gurney, a member of the extensive Norfolk family); *b* 11 April 1916; *m* 1, 1939, Norman (ka 1940), s of Brig-Gen Lewis Philips, CB, CMG, CBE, DSO; 1 s; m 2, 1944, Hon Brian Rootes (d 1971), s of 1 Baron Rootes; 1 s; *Style*— The Hon Mrs Brian Rootes; The Old Farmhouse, Ramsbury, Wilts

ROOTES, 2 Baron (UK 1959); (William) Geoffrey Rootes; s of 1 Baron Rootes (d 1964), and his 1 w, Nora (d 1964), da of Horace Press; *b* 14 June 1917; *Educ* Harrow, Christ Church Oxford; *m* 1946, Marian, da of Lt-Col Herbert Roche Hayter, DSO, of Newbury, Berks, and wid of Wing Cdr James Hogarth Slater, AFC; 1 s, 1 da; *Heir* s, Hon Nicholas Rootes; *Career* served WWII RASC; sits as Cons in House of Lords; chm Chrysler UK (formerly Rootes Motors) 1967-73; dir: Rank Hovis McDougall 1973-84, Joseph Lucas Industs 1973-86; late memb NEDC for Motor Mfrg Indust, memb Cncl IOD 1953-78; vice-pres: Br Field Sports Soc 1978-, Game Conservancy 1979-; county pres Berks St John Ambulance; FBIM, FRSA; CStJ 1983; *Recreations* shooting, fishing; *Clubs* Buck's, Flyfishers'; *Style*— The Rt Hon the Lord Rootes; North Standen House, Hungerford, Berks RG17 0QZ (☎ (0488) 82441)

ROOTES, Hon Nicholas Geoffrey; s and h of 2 Baron Rootes; gf founded Rootes Motors; *b* 12 July 1951; *Educ* Harrow; *m* 1976, Mrs Dorothy Anne Burn-Forti, da of Cyril Walter James Wood (d 1979), of Swansea; 1 step s (Dante Burn-Forti b 1965), 1 step da (Lucinda Burn-Forti b 1963); *Career* writer; *Recreations* flyfishing, skiing, tennis; *Style*— The Hon Nicholas Rootes

ROOTHAM, Col Jasper St John; s of Dr Cyril Bradley Rootham (d 1938); *b* 21 Nov 1910; *Educ* Tonbridge, St John's Coll Cambridge; *m* 1944, Joan, *née* McClelland; 1 s, 1 da; *Career* WWII 1941-45 served: Middle East, Yugoslavia, France, Germany (despatches 1944), Col; Civil Serv 1933-41: Miny of Agric, Colonial Off, Treasy, 10

Downing St; Bank of England 1946-67: asst chief cashier, advsr to govr, asst to govr; sr banking dir Lazard Bros & Co Ltd 1967-75; poet and prose writer; *Publications* Miss Fire, Demi-Paradise, Verses 1928-72, The Celestial City and Other Poems, Stand Fixed in Steadfast Gaze, Affirmation, Lament for a Dead Sculptor and other Poems (1985); *Recreations* music, country life; *Clubs* United Oxford & Cambridge; *Style*— Col Jasper Rootham; 30 West St, Wimborne Minster, Dorset

ROPER, John Charles Abercromby; CMG (1969), MC (1945); s of Charles Roper (d 1950); *b* 8 June 1915; *Educ* Harrow, Cambridge Univ, Princeton; *m* 1, 1945 (m dis), Valerie Muir, *née* Wilson (d 1978); 2 da; m 2, 1960, Kathryn, *née* Bibas (d 1984); m 3, 1986, Phoebe, *née* Foster; *Career* Maj Scots Gds; Dip Serv 1946 (ret); dep cmdt NATO Def Coll 1960-62, asst sec Cabinet Off 1962-64, cnsllr UK Delgn OECD 1964-70, ambassador Luxembourg 1970-75; *Recreations* travel, the arts; *Clubs* Special Forces; *Style*— John Roper, Esq, CMG, MC; Tenuta di Monteverdi, 58048 Paganico, Prov of Grosseto, Italy

ROPER, John Francis Hodgess; s of Rev Frederick Mabor Hodgess Roper by his w Ellen Frances, *née* Brockway; *b* 10 Sept 1935; *Educ* William Hulme's GS Manchester, Reading Sch, Magdalen Coll Oxford, Univ of Chicago; *m* 1959, Valerie, da of Rt Hon John Edwards, OBE, sometime MP; 1 da; *Career* former econs lectr Manchester Univ; Parly candidate: (Lab) Derbyshire High Peak 1964, (SDP) Worsley 1983, MP (Lab and Co-op 1970-81, SDP 1981-83) Farnworth 1970-83; PPS to Min of State for Indust 1978-79, Lab oppn spokesman Def (front bench), SDP chief whip 1981-; sec Anglo-Benelux Parly Gp 1974-, vice-chm GB East Europe Centre 1974-, Anglo-German Parly Gp 1974-, memb WEU 1973-, hon tres Fabian Soc 1976-; memb: gen advsy cncl IBA 1974-, Cncl Inst Fiscal Studies 1975-; res fell and ed Int Affrs Royal Inst of Int Affrs 1983-; vice-pres Manchester Statistical Soc 1971-, tstee History of Parliament Tst 1974-; *Style*— John Roper, Esq; House of Commons, SW1

ROPER, Mark; s of Geoffrey Desmond (d 1982), of Forde Abbey, and Diana charlotte, *née* king (d 1988); *b* 27 June 1935; *Educ* Bradfield, Magdalene Coll Cambridge (MA); *m* 30 Sept 1967, Elizabeth Dorothy, da of Oliver Robin Gagot; 3 da (Alice b 1 Aug 1968, Victoria b 9 Feb 1970, Lucinda b 29 Aug 1972); *Career* Nat Serv 2 Lt Rifle Bde 1954-56; farmer Forde Abbey and lands (specialising in forest nursery and fruit growing); chm Dorset Country Landowners 1985-88, memb regnl advsy ctee The Forestry Cmmn 1972-88; High Sheriff Dorset 1984; *Style*— Mark Roper, Esq; Forde Abbey, Chard, Somerset

ROPER, (Mervyn Edward) Patrick; s of Capt Nigel Edward Godfrey Roper, DSO, RN (d 1983), and Marjorie Pamela, *née* Wrench; *b* 5 Oct 1954; *Educ* Marlborough, Coll of Law Surrey; *m* 17 Sept 1977, Sarah-Rose Mary, da of Dr D C Wilkins, CBE, TD; 1 s (Francis b 23 March 1987); *Career* mangr corp servs Turner Kenneth Brown Slrs London; Liveryman Worshipful Co of Drapers 1980; *Recreations* gardening, cooking; *Clubs* Naval and Military; *Style*— Patrick Roper, Esq; 19 Criffel Ave, London SW2 4AY (☎ 01 674 4541); 100 Fetter Lane, London EC4A 1DD (☎ 01 242 6006, fax 01 242 3003, telex 29796 TKBLAW G)

ROPER, Hon Mrs (Sarah-Jane Leathes); *née* Prior; o da of Baron Prior, PC (Life Peer), *qv*; *b* 5 Sept 1959; *m* 4 Sept 1982, David Alexander Roper; 3 da (Lucy Victoria b 10 March 1987, Alexandra Florence b (twin) 10 March 1987, Rosanna Jane b 16 Jan 1989); *Style*— The Hon Mrs Roper; 122 Lower Ham Road, Ham, Kingston, Surrey KT2 5BD

ROPER, Stephen John; s of Stanley Dunham Roper, of Lucy's Mill, Mill Lane, Stratford-on-Avon, Warwicks, and Kathleen Nora Theresa, *née* Barry; *b* 14 April 1943; *Educ* Wimbledon Coll, Durham Univ (BA); *m* 4 May 1969, Sophie Jaqueline, da of Georges Alex, Cmdt (ret) French Army; 2 da (Stephanie b 1970, Joanna b 1971); 1 s (Tristan b 1977); *Career* CA; Pannell Fitzpatrick & Co Kingston Jamaica WI 1971-75, ptnr Eacott Worrall & Co (Wokingham, Maidenhead, Burnham) 1975-; *Recreations* reading, squash; *Clubs* Royal Ascot Squash; *Style*— Stephen Roper, Esq; Lavendale House, Broomfield Park, Sunningdale, Berkshire SL5 0JS (☎ 0990 24032); Lisa House, 11-15 Peach St, Wokingham, Berks (☎ 0734 781714)

ROPER-CURZON, Hon David John Henry Ingham; s and h of 20 Baron Teynham; *b* 5 Oct 1965; *Educ* Radley; *m* 1985, Lucinda Airy, da of Maj Gen Christopher Airy; 1 s (b Feb 1986); *Style*— The Hon David Roper-Curzon

ROPER-CURZON, Hon Henrietta Margaret Fleur; da of 19 Baron Teynham, DSO, DSC (d 1972), and his 2 w, Anne, *née* Curzon-Howe; *b* 25 August 1955; *Educ* Warwick Univ; *Career* TV prodr; *Style*— The Hon Henrietta Roper-Curzon; Inwood House, Holly Hill Lane, Sarisbury Green, Hants

ROPER-CURZON, Hon Holly Anne-Marie; da of 19 Baron Teynham, DSO, DSC (d 1972), and his 2 w, Anne, *née* Curzon-Howe; *b* 1963; *Educ* Nottingham Univ; *Career* slr; *Style*— The Hon Holly Roper-Curzon; Inwood House, Holly Lane, Sarisbury Green, Hants

ROPER-CURZON, Hon Michael Henry; s of 19 Baron Teynham, DSO, DSC (d 1972); *b* 1931; *m* 1964 (m dis 1967), Maria, da of late Maj R V Taylor, 16/5 Queen's Royal Lancers; *Career* Lt (ret) RN; OStJ; *Style*— The Hon Michael Roper-Curzon; 75 Eccleston Sq Mews, London SW1 (☎ 01 828 9559)

ROPNER, (William Guy) David; s of Sir William Guy Ropner, JP (d 1971), and Margarita (d 1973), da of Sir William Cresswell Gray, 1 Bt; *b* 3 April 1924; *Educ* Harrow; *m* 1, 10 Sept 1955, (Mildred) Malise Hare, da of Lt-Col George Armitage, MC, TD (d 1977); 3 s (Guy b 1959, Roderick b 1962, Peter b 1964), 1 da (Lucy (Mrs Goelet) b 1957); m 2, 1985, Hon Charlotte Mary Piercy, da of 2 Baron Piercy (d 1981), and formerly w of Paolo Emilio Taddei; 1 s (Nicholas b 1986); *Career* WWII 2 Lt RA, Capt 3 Regt RHA Europe and UK 1942-47; dir Br Shipowners Assoc 1954-, pres Gen Cncl of Br Shipping 1979-80; chm: Lights Advsy Ctee 1978-87, MN Welfare Bd 1980-, Cleveland & Durham Industl Cncl 1980-; FICA; *Clubs* St Moritz Tobogganing; *Style*— David Ropner, Esq; 1 Sunningdale Gdns, Stratford Rd, London W8 6PX (☎ 01 937 3862); The Lodge, Accommodation Rd, Longcross, Surrey; office: Boundary House, 7/17 Jewry St, London EC3N 2HP (☎ 01 488 4533)

ROPNER, Jeremy Vyvyan; s of John Raymond Ropner (s of William Ropner (d 1947), who was 3 s of Sir Robert Ropner, 1 Bt), and Joan, *née* Redhead; *b* 3 May 1932; *Educ* Harrow, RNC Dartmouth; *m* 1955, Sally, da of Maj George Talbot Willcox, MC, and Constance (da of William Ropner *ante*); 1 s (and 1 s decd), 2 da; *Career* shipowner; dir Ropner Hldgs plc, dir Nat West Bank (East Regnl Bd); chm: Hartlepools Water Co, Ropner Shipping Co Ltd, Ropner plc; *Recreations* forestry, golf; *Clubs* Brooks's; *Style*— Jeremy Ropner, Esq; Firby Hall, Bedale, N Yorks (☎ 22345)

ROPNER, Sir John Bruce Woollacott; 2 Bt (UK 1952), of Thorp Perrow, N Riding of Yorks; s of Sir Leonard Ropner, 1 Bt, MC, TD (d 1977). Sir Leonard's f, William, was 3 s of Sir Robert Ropner, JP, DL, cr a Bt 1904 (*see* Ropner, Bt, Sir Robert); *b* 16 April 1937; *Educ* Eton, St Paul's Sch USA; *m* 1, 1961 (m dis 1970), Anne Melicent, da of late Sir Ralph Delmé-Radcliffe; 2 da (Jenny b 1963, Katherine b 1964); m 2 , 1970, Auriol Veronica, da of Capt Graham Lawrie Mackeson-Sandbach, of Caerllo, Llangernyw, Abergele, Denbighshire; 1 s (Henry), 2 da (Carolyn b 1971, Annabel b 1974); *Heir* s, Henry John William Ropner, b 24 Oct 1981 (godparents include Earl of Shelburne, Count Colloredo-Mansfeld, Countess Peel); *Career* dir Ropner plc; *Books* Brooks's; *Style*— Sir John Ropner, Bt; Thorp Perrow, Bedale, Yorks

ROPNER, Robert Clinton; s and h of Sir Robert Ropner, 4 Bt; *b* 6 Feb 1949; *Educ* Harrow; *Style*— Robert Ropner, Esq

ROPNER, Sir Robert Douglas; 4 Bt (UK 1904), of Preston Hall, Stockton-on-Tees, Co Palatine of Durham, and Skutterskelfe Hall, Hutton Rudby, North Riding of Yorks; s of Sir (Emil Hugo Oscar) Robert Ropner, 3 Bt (d 1962); *b* 1 Dec 1921; *Educ* Harrow; *m* 1943, Patricia Kathleen, da of William Edward Scofield, of West Malling, Kent; 1 s, 1 da; *Heir* s, Robert Clinton Ropner; *Career* formerly Capt RA; *Style*— Sir Robert Ropner, Bt

ROSCOE, Sir Robert Bell; KBE (1981); s of T B Roscoe; *b* 7 August 1906; *Educ* Central Tech Coll Brisbane; *m* 1931, Daphne, da of G Maxwell; 1 da; *Career* dir Chase NBA Gp Ltd Aust & NZ 1969-80; chm Melbourne Underground Rail Loop Authy 1971-81; *for further details see Debrett's Handbook of Australia and New Zealand*; *Style*— Sir Robert Roscoe, KBE; 833 Burwood Rd, Hawthorn East, Victoria 3123, Australia

ROSE, Sir Alec Richard; s of Ambrose Rose, of Canterbury (d 1954); *b* 13 July 1908; *Educ* Simon Langton Boys' Sch Canterbury; *m* 1, Barbara Kathleen, *née* Baldwin; 2 s, 2 da; m 2, Dorothy Mabel, *née* Walker; *Career* WWII Lt RANVR Atlantic Convoys; self employed nuseryman and fruit merchant; sailed round world in ketch 'Lively Lady' in 354 days; hon rear-cdre RNSA, hon life govr RNLI; Freeman: City of Portsmouth, City of London; memb: Hon Co of Basketmakers, Worshipful Co of Furiterers, Hon Co of Shipwrights; kt 1968; *Books* My Lively Lady, My Favourite Tales of the Sea; *Recreations* sailing; *Clubs* Royal Yacht Sqdn, Royal Thames YC, Royal Cruising; *Style*— Sir Alec Rose; Woodlands Cottage, Eastleigh Rd, Havant, Hants (☎ Havant 477124)

ROSE, Barry; MBE (1981); s of William George Rose, of Essex and Beatrice Mary, *née* Castle; *b* 17 July 1923; *m* 18 May 1963, (Dorothy) Jean Colthrop, da of Lt-Col Walter Reginald Bowden; 1 da (Diana b 1964); *Career* ed and publisher; chm own gp of cos 1970-; memb: Chichester RDC 1951-61, W Sussex CC 1952-73 (ldr Cons Gp 1967-72, aldeman 1972), Bognor Regis UDC 1964-68; hon ed Rural Dist Review 1959-63; memb: RDCA 1960-63, CCA 1968-72; chm SE Area Conservation Local Govt Advsy Ctee 1969-73; fndr Assoc of Cncllrs 1960 (pres 1975-86); memb: Medico Legal Soc, Br Soc of Criminology; hon life memb Justices' Clerks Soc 1985, hon memb American Soc of Criminology; memb Pagham Parish Cncl 1951-62; *Books* A Councillor's Work (1971), England Looks at Maud (d 1972); plays: Change of Fortune (1950), Funny Business (1951); *Recreations* talking politics; *Clubs* Athenaeum, Garrick, Utd Oxford and Cambridge, West Sussex County; *Style*— Barry Rose, Esq; Courtney Lodge, Sylvan Way, Bognor Regis, West Sussex (☎ 0243 829902)

ROSE, Brian; s of Edwin Rose George (d 1984), and Emily (d 1967); *b* 26 Jan 1952; *Educ* Canford; *m* 4 Oct 1952, Audrey, da of Henry Barnes (d 1966); 1 da (Fiona Jane b 19 Dec 1965); *Career* Intelligence Corps 1948-50; Miny of Food 1950-54, CRO 1954; Dip Serv: Peshawar 1955-56, Ottawa 1958-61, Kingston Jamaica 1962-65, Rome 1966, Zagreb 1966-68, Zomba and Malawi 1968-71, FCO 1971-74, Dusseldorf 1974-77, E Berlin 1977-78, Zurich 1978-82, consul gen Stuttgart 1982-85, cnsllr Br Embassy Helsinki 1985-88; memb Inst of Linguists; *Recreations* squash, tennis, music, reading; *Clubs* Travellers'; *Style*— Brian Rose, Esq; c/o Travellers Club, Pall Mall, London

ROSE, Hon Mr Justice; Sir Christopher Dudley Roger; s of Roger Rose (d 1987), of Morecambe, and Hilda, *née* Thickett (d 1986); *b* 10 Feb 1937; *Educ* Morecambe GS, Repton, Univ of Leeds (LLB), Wadham Coll Oxford (BCL); *m* 5 Aug 1964, Judith, *née* Brand; 1 s (Daniel b 1967), 1 da (Hilary b 1970); *Career* lectr law Wadham Coll Oxford 1959-60, Bigelow teaching fell Law Sch Univ of Chicago 1960-61, barr 1960, QC 1974, rec Crown Ct 1978-85, bencher Middle Temple 1983, judge High Ct Queens Bench Div 1985-, presiding judge Northern circuit 1987- (practised 1961-85); govr Pownall Hall Sch 1977-89; memb senate Inns of Ct and Bar 1983-85; kt 1985; *Style*— Hon Mr Justice Rose; Royal Cts of Justice, Strand, London WC2A 2LL

ROSE, Dr (Frank) Clifford; s of James (d 1956), and Clare (d 1960); *b* 29 August 1926; *Educ* Kings Coll London, Westminster Medical Sch (MB BS); *m* 16 Sept 1963, Angela Juliet, da of Eric Halsted (d 1976); 3 s (Sebastian b 1964, Jolyon b 1966, Fabian b 1968); *Career* conslt neurologist; dir Acad Unit of Neuroscience Charing Cross and Westminster Med Sch Univ of London, physician i/c dep of neurology regnl Neurosciences Centre Charing Cross Hosp; chm scientific advsy ctee: Int MND/ALS Res Fndn, Motor Neurone Disease Assoc, Assoc for Res into Multiple Sclerosis; chm: Headache and Migrane Res Gp, Migraine Tst, World Fedn Neurology; vice pres Neurology Section Royal Soc of Soc, tres Med Soc of London; ed, co-ed, author of over 40 books on: neurology, migraine, stroke, speech and language, Parkinsons disease; Harold Wolff Award 1981 and 1984, Distinguished Clinical Award 1986 American Assoc for Study of Headache; *Recreations* reading; *Clubs* RSM; *Style*— Dr Clifford Rose; Dept of Neurology, Charing Cross Hosp, London W6 8RF (☎ 01 741 7833)

ROSE, Sir Clive Martin; GCMG (1981, KCMG 1976, CMG 1967); s of Rt Rev Alfred Rose (d 1971, sometime Suffragan Bishop of Dover), and Lois, *née* Garton (d 1978); *b* 15 Sept 1921; *Educ* Marlborough, Christ Church Oxford; *m* 1946, Elisabeth Mackenzie, da of Rev Cyril Lewis; 2 s, 3 da; *Career* Rifle Bde (Maj) 1941-46; served: UK, Europe, India, Iraq; Dip Serv 1948: served India, Germany, France, US, Uruguay; head UK Delgn Negotiations on Mutual Reduction of Forces and Armaments 1973-76, dep sec Cabinet Off 1976-79, ambassador and UK perm rep The N Atlantic Cncl 1979-82, ret 1982; chm cncl Royal Utd Servs Inst 1983-86 (vice-pres 1986-); conslt Control Risks 1983-; dir: Control Risks (GS) Ltd 1985-, Control Risks Info Servs Ltd 1986-; memb RCDS Advsy Bd 1985-, chm Suffolk Preservation Soc 1985-; pres Assoc of Civil Def and Emergency Planning Offrs 1987-; FRSA; *Publications* Campaigns against Western Defence; NATO's Adversaries and Critics (1985); *Clubs* Army & Navy; *Style*— Sir Clive Rose, GCMG; Chimney House, Lavenham, Suffolk

ROSE, Eliot Joseph Benn (Jim); CBE (1979); s of Col Ernest Albert Rose, CBE (d

1976), of Old Kiln, Churt, Surrey, and Julia, *née* Levy (d 1969); *b* 7 June 1909; *Educ* Rugby, New Coll Oxford; *m* 1, 1940 (m dis 1945), Mollie Lipscombe; m2, 14 Feb 1946, Susan Pamela, da of Thornely Carbutt Gibson; 1 s (Alan b 1949), 1 da (Harriet b 1950); *Career* WWII 1939-45: RAF 1939-41, Govt CCs Bletchley, Wing-Cdr Dep Dir Intelligence Air Ministry 1945; sec Lord Baldwin's Fund for German Refugees 1938-39, literary ed The Observer 1948-51, first dir Int Press Inst 1951-62, dir Nuffield Survey of Race Relations in Br 1963-69, ed dir Westminster Pres 1970-73, chm and chief exec Penguin 1974-80; sec Lord Baldwin's Fund for German Jewish Refugees 1988-89, memb Rampton ctee of enquiry into Educn of Ethnic Minority Children 1979-81; fndr 33 club for German Jewish Refugees 1933-39, co-fndr and chm The Runnymede Tst, chm Inter-Action Tst, 1968-84, tstee Writers and Scholars Tst, memb bd UNICEF UK; US Legion of Merit 1945; *Books* Colour and Citzenship (1969); *Recreations* music and walking; *Clubs* Garrick; *Style*— Eliot Rose, Esq; 37 Pembroke Square, London W8 (☎ 01 937 3772); Rocks Farm, Groombridge, Kent (☎ 0892 864 223)

ROSE, Dr Frank Clifford; s of James Rose (d 1958), and Clare Rose (d 1960); *b* 29 August 1926; *Educ* Kings Coll London, Westminster Med Sch (MBBS); *m* 16 Sept 1963, Angela Juliet, da of Eric Halsted (d 1979); 3 s (Sebastian b 1964, Jolyon b 1966, Fabian b 1968); *Career* conslt neurologist Charing Cross Hosp 1965- physician i/c dept of neurology 1978-, dir academic neuroscience unit Charing Cross and Westminster Med Sch 1985-; dir Princess Margaret Migraine Clinic; chm: headache and migraine res gp World Fedn of Neurology, sec advsy ctee Int ALS/MND Res Fnd, med patron Motor Neurone Disease Assoc, formerly pres Med Soc of London; Liveryman of the Worshipful Soc of Apothecaries 1965; FRSM; *Books* jt author numerous books on neurology incl Advances in Sinove Research (1985), Advances in Headache Research (1987); *Recreations* travellling; *Style*— Dr Clifford Rose; 109 Harley St, London W1N 1DG (☎ 01 741 7833)

ROSE, Lt-Col Hugh Vincent; s of Col Hugh Rose (d 1957), and Emma Maria (d 1951), *née* Knowles; *b* 11 April 1905; *Educ* Belgrave House Sch, Aldenham, RMC Sandhurst (Army Crammer, Carlisle and Gregson); *m* 6 Jan 1954, Susan Muriel, da of Capt Guy Sclater, RN (killed 1914 when cmdg HMS Bulwark); 2 s (Hugh Michael b 1940, Philip Timothy b 1960), 1 da (Elizabeth b 1938); *Career* cmmnd offr Indian Army 1924, seconded Foreign and Political Serv Govt of India 1930, Staff Coll Quetta 1939, served NW Frontier M East, CO 3 Gurkhas in 1947 Calcutta riots, cmd 33 Bde Malaya dep dir ops Eritrea 1950, Cdr Perak Howe Gd 1952, serv rep on jt intelligence ctee Far East 1954; asst def sec North Borneo 1955; dir Indr Hugh Rose Properties Ltd first euro to climb Kuh-i-Taftan an active volcano in Persian Baluchistay 1933, discovered unknown pass from Hoti area into Tibet in Himalayas; Chevalier Order of Menelik II; *Recreations* formerly polo, pig sticking, squash, writing, skiing; *Clubs* The Kandahar Ski, Naval & Military; *Style*— Lt-Col Hugh Rose, FRGS; 7 Harbour Way, Emsworth, Hants PO10 7BE (☎ 0243 373907)

ROSE, Hon Mrs (Irené Phyllis); *née* Hirst; CBE (1961); da of 1 Baron Hirst of Witton (d 1943, title extinct); *b* 1901; *m* 1922, Gp Capt Trevor Felix David Rose, RAFVR and late Maj RFA and RHA (d 1946); 2 da; *Career* admin WVS 1940-46; memb LCC 1952-58 and 1961-65 (North Lewisham constituency); chm Greater London area and London area of Cons Women's Nat Advsy Ctees 1954-57 and 1959-62, memb Cons Nat Exec Ctee 1959-62; *Style*— The Hon Mrs Rose, CBE; Pear Tree Cottage, Cranleigh, Surrey

ROSE, Lady Jean; *née* Ramsay; da of late 14 Earl of Dalhousie; *b* 1909; *m* 1945, Lt-Col David McNeil Campbell Rose, DSO, Black Watch; 1 s, 1 da; *Style*— Lady Jean Rose; Trian, Comrie, Perthshire

ROSE, Joyce Dora Hester; CBE (1981), JP (Herts 1963); da of Abraham (Arthur) Woolf, of Hampstead, London (d 1972), and Rebecca, *née* Simpson (d 1985); *b* 14 August 1929; *Educ* King Alfred Sch London, Queen's Coll, London; *m* 6 Oct 1953, Cyril, s of Benjamin Rose, of Bedford (d Jan 1971); 1 da (Gillian b 1955); 2 s (Stephen b 1957, Andrew b 1959); *Career* dep chm Watford Adult Ct and Juvenile and Domestic Panels memb of Herts: Magistrates Cte Ctee, Probation Ctee, Police Ctee; co-dep chm Magistrates Assoc; memb of Nat Exec and Cncl Magistrates Assoc (chm Herts branch); Lib Pty: pres 1979-80, chm 1982-83, chm Womens Fedn 1987- (pres 1972 and 1973), memb nat exec and home affrs panel; pres: Herts Area Lib Orgn, Home Counties Union of Women's Lib Assocs, Hampstead Highgate Womens Lib Assoc; memb Women's Nat Cmmn; previously long term memb nat exec UK ctee of UNICEF (vice chm 1968-70); *Clubs* Nat Lib; *Style*— Mrs Joyce Rose; 38 Main Avenue, Moor Park, Northwood, Middx HA6 2LQ (☎ Northwood 21385)

ROSE, Sir Julian Day; 4 Bt (UK 1909), of Hardwick House, Whitchurch, Oxon and 5 Bt (UK 1872), of Montreal, Dominion of Canada; s of Sir Charles Henry Rose, 3 Bt (d 1966), by his w, Hon Phoebe Margaret Dorothy Phillimore, da of 2 Baron Phillimore; also suc kinsman, Sir Francis Rose, 4 Bt 1979; *b* 3 Mar 1947; *Educ* Stanbridge Earls Sch Romsey; *m* 1976, Elizabeth Goode Johnson, of Columbus Ohio, USA; 1 s (Lawrence Michael b 6 Oct 1986), 1 da (Miriam Margaret b 1984); *Career* co fndr and asst dir Inst for Creative Devpt, Antwerp; commenced organic farming enterprise Hardwick Estate 1983; memb: Soil Assoc Cncl 1984, bd UK Register of Organic Food Standards; *Style*— Sir Julian Rose, Bt; Hardwick House, Whitchurch, Oxon

ROSE, Martin John; s of John Ewert Rose, of Chandlers Ford, Hants, and Margaret Mary, *née* Eames; *b* 21 Mar 1956; *Educ* St Mary's Coll Southampton, Univ of Warwick (LLB); *m* 7 May 1988, Emma Margaret Havilland, da of Robert Bernard Hutchinson, of Wimborne, Dorset; *Career* barr Middle Temple 1979, practising barr Western circuit 1980-86, legal conslt The Stock Exchange 1986, sr legal advsr The Securities Assoc 1986-; dir Kensquare Ltd; memb Law Reform Ctee, Bar Assoc for Commerce, Fin and Indust; *Recreations* riding, cooking, mil history; *Style*— Martin Rose, Esq; The Stock Exchange Building, Old Broad St, London EC2 (☎ 01 256 9000, fax 01 628 1644)

ROSE, Paul Bernard; s of Arthur Rose (d 1974), and Norah, *née* Helman; *b* 26 Dec 1935; *Educ* Bury GS, Manchester Univ (LLB), Inst of Advanced Legal Studies, Sorbonne; *m* 13 Sept 1957, Eve Marie Thérèse, da of Jean Lapu, of 8 rue Boucry, Paris; 2 s (Howard Imre b 25 Jan 1961, Daniel Dean b 18 Oct 1970), 1 da (Michelle Alison b 11 Oct 1964) ; *Career* barr Gray's Inn 1958; legal advsr Cooperative Union Ltd 1958-61; lectr Salford Univ 1961-63; MP (Lab) Manchester, Blackley 1964-79; asst recorder 1975-88; pt/t immigration adjudicator 1987-; HM Coroner Gtr London Southern Dist 1988-; chm NW Sports Cncl 1966-68; fndr and first sec Brent SDP; patron St Lucia Soc; AIL fndr memb SDP, frontbencher; memb Cncl of Europe, Inst of Linguists, Bar Cncl; *Recreations* sport, the arts, computers, writing, travel; *Style*— Paul Rose, Esq; 47 Lindsay Drive, Kenton, Harrow, Middlesex HA3 0TA (☎ 204 3076); Coroner's Office, The Law Courts, Barclay Road, Croydon CR9 3NE (☎ 01 681 5019)

ROSE, Hon Lady (Phoebe Margaret Dorothy); *née* Phillimore; da of 2 Baron Phillimore, MC (d 1947), and (1 w) Dorothy Barbara (d 1915), er da of Lt-Col Arthur Balfour Haig, CVO, CMG, JP; *b* 28 Feb 1912; *m* 1937, Sir Charles Henry Rose, 3 Bt (d 1966); 1 s (and 1 decd), 2 da; *Style*— The Hon Lady Rose; Hardwick House, Whitchurch, Reading, Oxon RG8 7RB (☎ 073 57 2955)

ROSE, (Thomas) Stuart; CBE (1974); s of Thomas Rose (d 1967); *b* 2 Oct 1911; *Educ* Magdalen Coll Sch Oxford, Central Sch of Arts and Crafts London; *m* 1940, Dorothea Winifred, *née* Ebsworth; 2 da; *Career* designer and print conslt FBI 1948-68, art ed Design Magazine 1962-68, first design dir PO 1968-76, typographic advsr to PMG 1962-68; memb: industl design ctee FBI 1948-65 (chm 1965-68), cncl of Industl Design Stamp Design Ctee 1960-62, PO Stamp Advsy Ctee 1968-76; PPCSD, FSTD; *Books* Royal Mail Stamps: a survey of Br Stamp design (1980); *Recreations* drawing, music and the country; *Clubs* The Arts (chm 1982-85); *Style*— Stuart Rose, Esq, CBE; Walpole House, East Street, Coggeshall, Essex CO6 1SH (☎ 0376 62409)

ROSE, Hon Mrs (Susan Jane); *née* James; da of 4 Baron Northbourne; *b* 1936; *m* 1961, Michael Hugh Rose, s of late Rt Rev Alfred Carey Wollaston Rose, formerly Bishop of Dover; 1 s, 3 da; *Style*— The Hon Mrs Rose; Le Sirondole, Panzano-in-Chianti, Florence, Italy

ROSE OF KILRAVOCK, (Anna) Elizabeth Guillemard; 25 of Kilravock and Chief of Clan Rose; da of Lt-Col Hugh Rose of Kilravock, CMG, JP, DL (d 1946), and Ruth Antoinette, *née* Guillemard; suc f 1946; *b* 28 May 1924; *Educ* St Leonard's Sch; *Career* served with WRNS 1944-46; *Style*— Miss Elizabeth Rose of Kilravock; Kilravock Castle, Croy, by Inverness

ROSE PRICE, Hon Mrs (Maureen Maude Tower); *née* Butler; da of late 27 Baron Dunboyne; *b* 1919; *m* 1946, Lt-Col Robert Caradoc Rose Price, DSO, OBE, late Welsh Gds (d 1988); 1 s, 1 da; *Clubs* The Arts; *Style*— The Hon Mrs Rose Price; Tetworth Hall, Ascot, Berks SL5 7DU (☎ 0990 21155)

ROSEBERY, 7 Earl of (S 1703); Sir Neil Archibald Primrose; 9 Bt (S 1651), DL (Midlothian 1960); also Viscount of Rosebery, Lord Primrose and Dalmeny (both S 1700), Viscount of Inverkeithing, Lord Dalmeny and Primrose (both S 1703), Baron Rosebery (UK 1828), Earl of Midlothian, Viscount Mentmore, and Baron Epsom (all UK 1911); s of 6 Earl of Rosebery, KT, DSO, MC, PC (d 1974, the celebrated race horse owner and s of the Lib PM and Hannah, da of Baron Meyer de Rothschild, through whom Mentmore came into the family), by his 2 w, Hon Dame Eva, *née* Bruce, DBE, JP (da of 2 Baron Aberdare and former w of 3 Baron Belper); *b* 11 Feb 1929; *Educ* Stowe, New Coll Oxford; *m* 1955, (Alison Mary) Deirdre, da of Ronald William Reid, MS, FRCS; 1 s, 4 da; *Heir* s, Lord Dalmeny; *Style*— The Rt Hon The Earl of Rosebery, DL; Dalmeny House, South Queensferry, West Lothian (☎ 031 331 1784/1785)

ROSEHILL, Lord; David John MacRae Carnegie; s and h of 13 Earl of Northesk; *b* 3 Nov 1954; *Educ* Eton; *m* 1979, Jacqueline, da of David Reid, by his w Elizabeth, of Sarasota, Florida; 1 s, 2 da (Hon Sarah Louise Mary b 29 Oct 1982, Hon Fiona Jean Elizabeth b 24 March 1987); *Heir* s, Hon Alexander Robert MacRae Carnegie b 16 Nov 1980; *Career* farmer and company dir; *Recreations* shooting; *Clubs* Kennel Club; *Style*— Lord Rosehill; Fair Oak, Rogate, Petersfield, Hants (☎ 073 080 508)

ROSEMONT, David John; s of Leslie Rosemont (d 1964), of Oxted, Surrey, and Elizabeth, *née* Williams (who m 2, 1974, Air Cdre Philip E Warcup); *Educ* Lancing, Architectural Assoc Sch of Architecture; *m* 8 Aug 1975, Elizabeth Abbott (Abbey), da of Frederick Milne Booth Duncan, of Ayr, Scotland; 2 s (Hugo David b 3 March 1979, Jonathan Duncan b 22 Dec 1980); *Career* architect 1971, assoc: Fairhursts Manchester 1975-77, SKP Architects London 1977-81, commenced private practice David Rosemont Assocs 1981, sr ptnr David Rosemont Stuart Passey and Ptnrs 1985-, dir Alliance Property and Construction plc 1987-, memb Br Acad of Experts 1988; co chm Inner Cities Ctee Assoc of Ind Businesses 1988; memb AA, RIBA; *Recreations* opera, photography, gastronomy, classic cars, places; *Clubs* Carlton; *Style*— David Rosemont, Esq; 7 Trinity Crescent, London SW17 7AG (☎ 01 672 7117); David Rosemont, Stuart Passey and Partners, 212 St Ann's Hill, London SW18 2RU (☎ 01 870 8622, 01 870 9824, fax 01 870 9885)

ROSEN, Albert; s of Dr Lazar Rosen (d 1951), and Terezie, *née* Ruzickova (d 1971); *b* 14 Feb 1924; *Educ* Vienna Gymnasium, Bratislava Gymnasium, Vienna Music Acad, Prague Conservatory; *m* 1, 1955 (m dis 1961), Anna, *née* Hartlová; 1 s (Alexander b 1956); m 2, 1962 (m dis 1975), Blahoslava, *née* Markvartova; 1 da (Susana b 1964); *Career* conductor: State Opera Dilsen 1949, Prague Nat Opera 1959; chief conductor: Prague Smetana Theatre 1965, Radio TV Symphonia Orchestra Dublin 1969, Perth Aust 1981, Adelaide Aust 1986; Wexford Festival Opera 1965-88, San Francisco Opera 1980, Opera du Rhin Strasburg 1982, ENO 1987; *Recreations* travel; *Style*— Albert Rosen, Esq; 70 Haddingon Road, Dublin 4, Ireland (☎ 0001 687876)

ROSEN, Anthony; s of Maurice Rosen (d 1971); *b* 19 Dec 1930; *Educ* Framlingham Coll; *m* 1954, Hilary June, da of Comins Mansfield (d 1983), of Paignton, Devon; 2 s (Andrew b 1956, Howard b 1958), 1 da (Philippa b 1965); *Career* Capt RA (Air OPs) 1950-52; chm: Fordson Estates Ltd, Earnison plc: chief exec Feenix Farming, ptnr Second Opinion Assocs; Rosen and Luckin Assocs, memb Agric Forum and 75 Club; political and econ columnist Farming News;; *Books* Englands Present Land-Vision and Reality Farming and the Nation; *Recreations* work, photography, travel; *Clubs* Farmers'; *Style*— Anthony Rosen, Esq; Foxhill, Elstead, Surrey GU8 6LE (☎ 0252 703 600/703 607, telex 858623)

ROSEN, Hon Mrs (June Avis); *née* Lever; da of Baron Lever (Life Peer, d 1977); *b* 4 June 1940; *Educ* Cheltenham Ladies' Coll, Sch of Physiotherapy, Ancoats Hosp, Manchester; *m* 1962, Emanuel, s of Lionel Rosen, MBE, of Hull; 3 children; *Career* physiotherapist; *Recreations* choral singing, sewing, reading, ctee work; *Style*— The Hon Mrs Rosen; 18a Torkington Rd, Wilslow, Cheshire (☎ 522768)

ROSENBERG, Jenifer Bernice; da of Philip Levene (d 1966), of London, and Jane-Sarah, *née* Kent (d 1982); *b* 1 Oct 1942; *Educ* Our Lady of Zion GS; *m* 1, 1 Aug 1975, Jack Goldstein (d 1975); m 2, 8 Feb 1982, Ian David Rosenberg, s of Alfred Rosenberg (d 1984), of London; *Career* sr buyer Marks and Spencer plc 1960-74, fndr and md J and J Fashions Ltd 1974-; memb: Clothing and Allied Products Trg Bd Design 2000 Ctee, cncl Academic for Nat Awards, governing body of London Inst; hon conslt to Bournemouth and Poole Coll of Art and Design, orgnr of the Woman of Distinction luncheon for the Jewish Blind Soc, fndr of JIA Woman in Business Ctee (former chm), memb Dr Barnardo's Ball ctee and ctee for Ravenswood Village home for the mentally handicapped; winner: Twice Award from Tyne and Wear cncl for Industl and Commercial Enterprise, Veuve Clicquot/Inst of Dirs Business Woman of the Year Award 1986; Br Inst of Mgmnt; *Recreations* theatre, photography, music, travelling, bridge; *Style—* Ms Jenifer Rosenberg; 48 Queen's Grove, St John's Wood, London NW8 6HH; J and J Fashions Ltd, 260 York Way, London N7 9PQ (☎ 01 609 6261, fax 01 609 9845, car 0860 821194/0836 202623, telex 23512)

ROSENBERG, John; s of Jacob Rosenberg (d 1961), of NY, and Dorothy Rosenberg (d 1965); *b* 25 Sept 1931; *Educ* Columbia GS NY, Columbia Coll Columbia Univ (BA); *m* 19 Dec 1953, Elizabeth Ann, da of EAC King (d 1936), of India; 2 da (Laura b 1961, Catherine b 1963); *Career* London story ed Metro-Goldwyn Mayer 1961-65, script and prodn exec Romulus Films and Anglia TV 1965-76, head of drama Anglia TV 1976-; originator and prodr of over 100 films, series and plays for the Ind TV Network incl: Alternative Three 1977, The Atom Spies 1978, Miss Morison's Ghosts 1981, (Int Emmy Nomination and Sid Roberts Award), The Kingfisher 1982, Death of an Expert Witness 1983, Edwin 1984, Shroud for a Nightingale 1984, Love Song 1985, Cover her Face 1985, Inside Story 1986, A Killing on the Exchange 1987, Cause Célèbre 1987, Menace Unseen 1988 (Sid Roberts Award), A Taste for Death 1988; co-originator of Tales of the Unexpected and prodr of 70 Tales 1977-87; *Books* The Desperate Art (1955), A Company of Strangers (1957), Mirror and Knife (1961), The Double Darkness (1965), The Savages (1971); detective novels (with Elizabeth Rosenberg): Out Brief Candle (1959), Murderer (1961); Dorothy Richardson (biography 1973); *Recreations* walking; *Style—* John Rosenberg, Esq; Anglia Television Ltd, 48 Leicester Square, London WC2H 7FB

ROSENBERG, Michael; s of Emanuel Rosenberg (d 1963), of London, and Hetty Rosenberg (d 1975); *b* 2 August 1935; *Educ* Wykeham Tech Sch Neasden; *m* Marlene Suzanne, da of Anthony Spears, of London; 2 s (Robert, Paul), 1 da (Caroline); *Career* dir Windsor Hosiery Co 1970-73; sales exec: Condax Agenices Ltd 1966-70, Gt Universal Stores Ltd 1960-66; sales/gen mangr Menwear Gp 1950-60; current chm and md: Unidoor Ltd, Dominex Ltd, David James Int, Uniport Shipping, Uniwell Knitwear Mfrg Co Ltd; *Recreations* golf, tennis; *Clubs* Hartsbourne Country; *Style—* Michael Roston, Esq; 4 Sunningdale Rd, Stanmore, Middx HA7 3QL (☎ 01 954 5448); Unidoor Hse, 137-139 Essex Rd, Islington N1 2XT (☎ 01 359 8261, fax 01 354 3595, car tel 0860 324 259, telex 265980 UNIDOR G)

ROSENHEAD, Martin David; s of Louis Rosenhead, CBE (d 1984), of Liverpool, and Esther, *née* Brostoff, JP; *b* 19 May 1935; *Educ* Quarry Bank HS Liverpool, St John's Coll Cambridge (MA); *m* 20 Jan 1961, Lindsay Margaret, da of Stanislas Eugene Meunier, of Epping, Essex; 1 da (Annabel b 26 Jan 1967); *Career* various mgmnt appts ICI 1956-68, business devpt dir construction sector Foseco-Minsep plc 1969-70, dir Redland plc 1970-74, non-exec dir Royal Brierley Crystal Ltd 1974-84, business devpt dir Wallpaper Mfrs Ltd 1974-79, dir Arthur Sanderson and Sons Ltd 1974-79, chm Thomson Shepherd Ltd 1976-78, md Bradfield Brett Hldgs Ltd 1978-79; chm: Royal Stafford China Ltd 1980-83, Spartan Hldgs Ltd 1980-84, Teakspire Ltd 1980-86; non exec dir Cowan De Groot plc 1983-84, dir Profile Consulting Ltd 1988-; dir Home Off policy advsy bd Sci and Technol Gp Directorate of Telecommunications 1986-; former parly candidate (Lib); FIOD 1970, FBIM 1980; *Recreations* music, walking, talking, skiing, Europe, hypnosis; *Style—* Martin Rosenhead, Esq; 6A St Peters Rd, St Margarets-on-Thames, Twickenham, Middx TW1 1QX, (☎ 01 892 7464); 12 Latham Rd, Twickenham, Middx TW1 1BN, (☎ 01 891 3705, fax 01 892 1459 (ROS), car phone 0860 396 388, telex 934968 FAXTEL G (ROS))

ROSENTHAL, Thomas Gabriel (Tom); s of Dr Erwin Isak Jacob Rosenthal, and Elizabeth Charlotte, *née* Marx; *b* 16 July 1935; *Educ* Perse Sch Cambridge, Pembroke Coll Cambridge (MA); *m* Ann Judith, *née* Warnford-Davis; 2 s (Adam, Daniel); *Career* 2 Lt RA 1954-56, Lt Cambridgeshire Regt TA 1956-80; md: Thames and Hudson Int 1966 (joined Thames and Hudson 1959), Martin Secker and Warburg Ltd 1971 (chm 1980); chm William Heinemann 1980-84, chm and md various subsid cos 1980-84, chm and md Andre Deutsch Ltd (joined 1984); chm Soc of Young Publishers 1961-62; memb: Cambridge Univ Appts Bd 1967-71, exec ctee Nat Book League 1971-74, ctee of mgmnt and tstee Amateur Dramatic Club Cambridge, cncl RCA 1982-87, exec cncl ICA 1987-; *Books* A Reader's Guide to Modern European Art History (1962), A Reader's Guide to Modern American Fiction (1963), Monograph on Jack B Yeats (1964), Monograph on Ivon Hitchens (with Alan Bowness, 1973), Monograph on Arthur Boyd (with Ursula Hoff, 1986); introductions to: The Financier, The Titan, Jennie Gerhardt (Theodore Dreiser); articles in: The Times, The Guardian, TLS, London Magazine, Encounter, New Statesman, Spectator, Jnl of Br Assoc for American Studies, Studio International, Dictionary of National Biography, Nature, The Bookseller; *Recreations* bibliomania, opera, looking at pictures, reading other publishers' books, watching cricket; *Clubs* Garrick, MCC; *Style—* Tom Rosenthal, Esq; c/o Andre Deutsch Ltd, 105-106 Great Russell St, London WC1B 3LJ (☎ 01 580 2746, fax 01 631 3253, telex 261026 ADLIB G)

ROSEVEARE, Lady; Olivia Margaret; da of Samuel Montgomery (d 1929), of Dublin; *m* 1958, as his 2 w, Sir Martin Pearson Roseveare d 1985, sometime sr chief inspr Miny of Educn, sometime princ Soche Hill Coll Malawi); s of Canon Richard Polgreen Roseveare, Vicar of Lewisham (d 1924); *Style—* Lady Roseveare; Box 29, Mzuzu, Malawi, Africa

ROSHIER, Christopher Edward; s of Edward Cecil Roshier (d 1974), of Exeter, and Muriel Gertrude, *née* Stratford (d 1978); *b* 30 Mar 1946; *Educ* Heles Sch Exeter, Fitzwilliam House Cambridge (MA); *m* 20 Sept 1969, Adrienne Mary, da of Harry James Langdon, of Richmond; 1 s (Giles b 1974), 2 da (Annabel b 1971, Holly b 1978); *Career* merchant banker, dir: Hill Samuel & Co Ltd 1977-87, Sharpe & Fisher plc (non-exec) 1986-, St Modwen Properties (non-exec) 1987-; md Drexel Burnham Lambert 1987-; FCA; *Recreations* bridge; *Style—* Christopher Roshier; 120 Strawberry Vale, Twickenham TW1 4SH (☎ 01-892 5376)

ROSIER, (Frederick) David Stewart; s of Air Chief Marshal Sir Frederick Rosier, GCB, CBE, DSO, ret *qv* and Hettie Denise, *née* Blackwell; *b* 10 April 1951; *Educ* Winchester, Keble Coll Oxford (BA, MA), RMA Sandhurst; *m* 27 Sept 1975, Julia Elizabeth, da of David Leslie Gommie ; *Career* cmmnd The Queens Dragoon Gds 1973-78, served: Germany, N Ireland, UK (Troop Ldr, Intelligence Offr, sqdn 2i/c; resigned Capt 1978); exec dir S G Warburg & Co Ltd 1984 (joined 1978), dir Warburg Investmt Mgmnt Ltd Jersey 1982, dir Mercury Asset Mgmnt Gp plc 1987, chm Mercury Rowan Mullen Ltd 1988-; Cncllr Wandsworth Borough Cncl 1982-86; Liveryman Worshipful Co of Coachmakers; *Recreations* squash, cricket, golf, skiing, shooting; *Clubs* Cavalry & Guards, Hurlingham, Fantasians; *Style—* David Rosier, Esq; 1 Kyrle Rd, London SW11 6BD (☎ 01 228 3800); 33 King William St London EC4R 9AS (☎ 01 280 2900, fax 280 2515, car tel 0836 538 549)

ROSIER, Air Chief Marshal Sir Frederick Ernest; GCB (1972, KCB 1966, CB 1961), CBE (1955, OBE 1943), DSO 1942; s of Ernest George Rosier (d 1942), and Frances Elisabeth, *née* Morris (d 1934); *b* 13 Oct 1915; *Educ* Grove Park Sch Wrexham; *m* 30 Sept 1939, Hettie Denise, da of William Herbert Blackwell (d 1965); 3 s (David b 1951, Nicholas b 1953, John b 1961), 1 da (Elisabeth b 1943); *Career* cmmnd RAF 1935, 43 (F) Sqdn 1936-39, served UK, Western Desert and Europe 1939-45, OC Horsham St Faith 1947, Exchange Duties with USAF 1948-50, DSD Joint Servs Staff Coll 1950-52, Gp Capt Ops Central Fighter Estab 1952-54, Gp Capt Plans Fighter Cmd 1955-56, IDC 1957, Dir Joint Plans Air Miny 1958, chm Joint Planning Staff 1959-61, AOC Air Forces Middle East 1961-63, SASO Tport Cmd 1964-66, AOC in C Fighter Cmd 1966-68, perm mil dep CENTO 1968-70, Dep C in C Allied Forces Central Europe 1970-73, ADC to HM the Queen 1956-58, Air ADC to HM the Queen 1972-73; mil advsr and dir BAC 1973-77, dir i/c BAC Saudi Arabia 1977-80; pres Victory Servs Club 1980-, vice pres 8 Army Veterans 1977-, chm of appeals Polish Air Force Benevolent Fund 1975-; Liveryman Worshipful Co of Coachmakers and Harnessmakers 1976, Freeman City of London 1976; Order of Orange Nassau Netherlands 1946, Order of Polonia Restituta Poland 1987; *Clubs* RAF; *Style—* Air Chief Marshal Sir Frederick Rosier, GCB, CBE, DSO; 286 Latymer Ct, London W6 7LJD (☎ 01 741 0765); Ty Haul, Llangollen, Clwyd

ROSKILL, Ann Julia Scott; JP (Inner London) 1978-; da of Harold Edward Cooke (d 1968), and Dorothy Margaret, *née* Key (d 1987); *b* 24 Oct 1933; *Educ* Christ's Hosp HS Lincoln, Girton Coll Cambridge (MA); *m* 10 April 1965, Nicholas Wentworth Roskill, s of Capt Stephen Wentworth Roskill, CBE, DSC, RN, DLitt, LittD; 1 s (Edward Stephen Wentworth b 1968), 1 da (Sybil Margaret Julia b 1971); *Career* Queen's Coll (Harley St): tutor in history 1964-67, co-librarian 1974-86; memb Cncl Fairbridge-Drake Soc (formerly Fairbridge Soc) 1969- (chm: Future Policy Ctee 1983-86, Housing Ctee 1986-), memb-at-large Nat Cncl for Eng and Wales ESU 1983-, memb cncl Queen's Coll 1987-; *Recreations* music, gardening; *Clubs* ESU; *Style—* Mrs Ann Roskill, JP

ROSKILL, Sir Ashton Wentworth; QC (1949); el s of John Roskill, KC (d 1940), and bro of Baron Roskill, *qv*, and Sybil Mary Wentworth Dilke; mother's f Ashton Dilke, MP, bro of Rt. Hon Sir Charles Dilke Bt, MP; *b* 1 Jan 1902; *Educ* Winchester Coll, Exeter Coll Oxford (MA); *m* 1, 1932, Violet Willoughby (d 1964), da of Lt-Col Charles W Waddington CIE, MVO (d 1946), 1 s (John), 1 da (Susannah, m Mr Justice Hobhouse, *qv*); m 2, 1965, Phyllis, yr da of Sydney Burney, CBE; *Career* Cert of Hon Cncl of Legal Educ 1925; attached WO (mil intelligence) 1940-45; KC then QC 1949; barr Inner Temple 1925, bencher 1958, tres 1980; chm Monopolies and Mergers Cmmn 1965-75; hon bencher Middle Temple 1980; kt 1967; *Clubs* Reform; *Style—* Sir Ashton Roskill, QC; Heath Cottage, Newtown, Newbury, Berkshire, RG15 9DA (☎ Newbury 40328)

ROSKILL, Baron (Life Peer UK 1980), of Newtown in Co of Hampshire; Eustace Wentworth Roskill; PC (1971), JP (1950), DL (Hants 1972); yst s of John Roskill, KC, and Sybil Mary Wentworth, *née* Dilke (niece of Sir Charles Dilke, 2 Bt); bro of Sir Ashton Roskill, QC, *qv*; *b* 6 Feb 1911; *Educ* Winchester, Exeter Coll Oxford; *m* 1947, Elisabeth, 3 da of Thomas Frame Jackson; 1 s, 2 da; *Career* Middle Temple: barr 1933 bencher 1961, reader 1978, dep tres 1979, tres 1980; hon bencher Inner Temple 1980; with ministries of shipping and war tport 1939-45; QC 1953, chm Hants QS 1960-71 (dep chm 1951-60), cmmr of Assize Birmingham 1961, judge of High Court Queen's Bench Divn 1962-71, Lord Justice of Appeal 1971-80, a Lord of Appeal in Ordinary 1980-86; vice-chm Parole Bd 1967-69, chm Cmmn of Third London Airport 1968-70, pres Senate of Four Inns of Court 1972-74 (hon memb 1974); life memb Canadian Bar Assoc 1974; chm: London Int Arbitration Tst 1981-, Fraud Trials Ctee 1983-85, Appeal Ctee of Panel on Take-overs and Mergers 1987-; hon fell Exeter Coll Oxford 1963; fell Winchester Coll 1981-86; kt 1962; *Style—* The Rt Hon the Lord Roskill, PC, DL; New Court, Temple, EC4 Y9BE (☎ 01 353 8870); Heatherfield, Newtown, Newbury, Berks RG15 9DB (☎ 0635 40606)

ROSKILL, Hon Julian Wentworth; s of Baron Roskill, PC, QC, JP, DL (Life Peer), and Elisabeth Wallace, *née* Jackson; *b* 22 July 1950; *Educ* Horris Hill, Winchester Coll; *m* 1975, Catherine Elizabeth, 2 da of Maj William Francis Garnett, of Quernmore Park, Lancaster; 2 s (Matthew b 1979, Oliver b 1981); *Career* slr 1974; *Recreations* photography, music, theatre, squash, swimming; *Style—* The Hon Julian Roskill; 8 Leigh Road, London N5 1SS (☎ 01 359 0628)

ROSLING, Derek Norman; CBE (1988); s of Norman Rosling (d 1984), and Jean, *née* Allen (d 1957); *b* 21 Nov 1930; *Educ* Shrewsbury; *m* (m dis); 2 s (Alan b 1962, John b 1964), 1 da (Jean b 1961); *Career* vice-chm Hanson plc 1973-; FCA; *Recreations* sailing, golf, theatre; *Clubs* Royal Channel Island, Palm Valley Country, Lymington Town, Roehampton; *Style—* Derek N Rosling, Esq, CBE; 388 Via Las Palmas, Palm Springs, California 92262, USA

ROSLING, Peter Edward; LVO (1972), CMG (1987); s of Peregrine Starr Rosling (d 1980), of Surrey, and Jessie, *née* Birtles (d 1980); *b* 17 June 1929; *Educ* GS; *m* 2 Sept 1950, Kathleen, da of Francis Theodore Nuell (d 1973), of Saltford, Bath; 3 s(Michael b 1957, Christopher b 1962, John b 1965); *Career* HM Dip Serv RN 1948-50; Br Embassy, Belgrade 1946-48 and 1952-56; vice-consul Innsbruck 1956-58; FO 1958-62; vice-consul (info) Cape Town 1962-67; first sec: FCO 1967-72, Belgrade, 1971-75; FCO 1975-79; NATO Def Coll Rome 1979-80; consul-gen Zagreb 1980-83; high cmmr Lesotho 1984; *Recreations* bridge, hill walking, tennis; *Clubs* Royal Cwlth Soc; *Style—* Peter Rosling, Esq, LVO, CMG; Kent House, Pioneer Rd, Maseru, Lesotho (☎ 313567); British High Commission, Box MS 521, Maseru, Lesotho Telex (☎ 313961)

ROSOMAN, Leonard Henry; OBE (1981); s of Henry Edward Rosoman (d 1979), of Cambridge Drive, Lee, London, and Lillian Blanch, *née* Spencer (d 1954); *b* 27 Oct 1913; *Educ* Deacons Sch Peterborough, Durham Univ, Royal Acad Schs, Central Sch of Arts & Crafts; *m* 21 June 1963 (m dis 1969), Jocelyn, da of late Bertie Rickards, of Melbourne, Aust; *Career* Aux Fire Serv 1939-43, Home Off 1943-45, official war artist Admty 1945-46; artist; lectr Reimann Sch London 1937-39, Camberwell Sch of Art 1946-47, Edin Coll of Art 1948-56, Chelsea Sch of Art 1956-57; tutor RCA 1957-78;

exhibitions in London incl: St Georges Gallery 1949, Roland Browse & Delbanco Gallery 1954, 1957, 1959, 1965, 1969, The Fine Art Soc 1974, 1978, 1983, Oldham Art Gallery 1977; exhibitions USA incl: Lincoln Centre NY 1968, State Univ of NY at Albany 1971, Touchstone Gallery NY 1975; major murals incl: Festival of Br 1951, Diaghilev Exhibition 1954, Brussels World Fair 1958, Shakespeare Exhibition 1964, Royal Acad of Arts 1986, vaulted ceiling Lambeth Palace Chapel 1988; Winston Churchill Fell 1966; FRSA 1968, RA 1969, Hon ARCA 1978, Hon RSWS 1979, Hon RWA 1984; *Books* Painters on Painting, Bruegel's Mad Meg (1969); *Recreations* travelling and painting as much as possible; *Clubs* Arts; *Style—* Leonard Rosoman, Esq, OBE; 7 Pembroke Studios, Pembroke Gardens, London W8 6HX (☎ 01 603 3638)

ROSPIGLIOSI, Hon Francesco; Prince Francesco Rospigliosi; 2 s of 11 Earl of Newburgh; *b* 1947; *m* 1974, Countess Clothilde, da of Count Henri Rival de Rouville ; 1 s (Prince Alessandro b 1978); *Style—* Prince Francesco Rospigliosi; via Modestino 3, 20 144, Milano, Italy

ROSPIGLIOSI, Princess Helen; Hon Helen Mary Grace; *née* Lyon-Dalberg-Acton; da of 2 Baron Acton, KCVO (d 1924); *b* 21 May 1910; *m* 1933 (m dis 1958) Prince Guglielmo Rospigliosi (s of Prince Ludovico Rospigliosi, 4 s of Princess Elena Giustiniani-Bandini, da of Sigismund Prince Giustiniani-Bandini who was also 8 Earl of Newburgh, by her husb Camillo Prince Rospigliosi); 2 s, 1 da; *Style—* Princess Helen Rospigliosi; 602 Park West, London W2

ROSPIGLIOSI, Princess Margherita Maria Francesca; da of late Prince Giambattista Pia Sigismondo Francesco Rospigliosi (s of Lady Elena Maria Concetta Isabella Gioacchina Giuseppa Giustiniani-Bandini *Princess Camillo Rospigliosi* 3 da of late 8 Earl of Newburgh) and sis of 11 Earl of Newburgh; *b* 1909; *Style—* Princess Margherita Rospigliosi

ROSS, Alan; CBE (1982); s of John Brackenridge Ross CBE (d 1958), and Clare Margaret Fitzpatrick (d 1979); *b* 6 May 1922; *Educ* Haileybury, St John's Coll Oxford; *m* 1949, Jennifer (m dis 1985), da of Sir Geoffrey Fry KCB CVO (d 1959), of Wiltshire 1 s (Jonathan Timothy de Beaurepaire b 1953); *Career* RN 1942-47; asst staff offr Intelligence 16 Destroyer Flotilla 1944; on staff of Flag Offr W Germay 1945, interpreter Br Naval CinC Germay 1946; Br Cncl 1947-50; staff memb The Observer 1952-72, ed London Magazine 1961-, md London Magazine Edns 1961-; Atlantic Award for Literature 1946; FRSL; *Books* Open Sea (1975), Death Valley (1980), Colours of War (1983), Ranji (1983), Blindfold Games (1986), The Emissary (1986); *Recreations* the turf; *Clubs* Vincents Oxford, MCC; *Style—* Alan Ross, Esq, CBE; 30 Thurloe Place, London SW7

ROSS, Alastair Robertson; s of Alexander James Ross (d 1985), and Margaret Elizabeth McInnes, *née* Robertson (d 1983); *b* 8 August 1941; *Educ* McLaren HS Callander Perthshire, Duncan of Jordanstone Coll of Art Dundee (Dip Art); *m* 12 April 1975, Kathryn Margaret-Greig, da of John Ferrier Greig Wilson, of Birmingham; 1 da (Alexandra b 1981); *Career* artist, lectr Duncan of Jordanstone Coll of Art 1969- (p/t 1966-69); recent works incl: bronze for Blackness devpt project Dundee, portrait in bronze of Sir Ian Moncreiffe of that Ilk at HM New Register House Edinburgh 1988 (awarded Sir Otto Beit Medal of Royal Soc Br Sculptors 1988), cmmn for new Rank Xerox HQ Marlowe Bucks 1988-89; awarded: Dickson Prize for Sculpture 1962, Holo-Krome (Dundee) Sculpture Prize & Cmmn 1962, Scottish Educn Dept Travelling Scholarship 1963, Royal Scottish Acad Chalmers Bursary 1964, Royal Scottish Acad Carnegie Travelling Scholarship 1965, Duncan of Dumfork Scholarship 1965, award winner in sculpture Paris Salon Exhibition 1967, awarded medailles de bronze 1968, and d'argent 1970 Societe des Artistes Francais (elected membre associé 1970), Sir William Gillies Bequest Fund Award RSA 1989; memb exec ctee Fife branch St John Assoc 1979-; memb Soc Portrait Sculptors 1966; SBStJ 1979, OStJ 1984; Freeman City of London 1989; FRSA 1966, ARBS 1968 (vice pres 1988-, Scottish rep on cncl 1972-), professional memb SSA 1969 (cncl memb 1972-75), FSA Scot 1971, FRBS 1975, ARSA 1980; *Recreations* heraldry, genealogy, Scottish history; *Clubs* St Johns House; *Style—* Alastair Ross, Esq; Ravenscourt, 28 Albany Terr, Dundee DD3 6HS Tayside (☎ 0382 24 235)

ROSS, Sir Alexander; s of William Alexander Ross (d 1947), and Kathleen Ross (d 1974); *b* 2 Sept 1907; *Educ* Mt Albert GS NZ, Auckland Univ (Dip Banking); *m* 1, 1933, Nora Bethia Burgess (d 1974); 2 s, 2 da; m 2, 1975, Cynthia Alice, da of Arthur Francis Barton (d 1946); *Career* dep govr Res Bank of NZ 1948-55 (joined 1934), mangr NZ team to Empire Games Vancouver 1954, selector for NZ rowing team Empire and Olympic Games, chm Utd Dominions Tst Ltd 1963-74, memb Br Nat Export Cncl 1965-69, memb NRDC 1966-74, chm East Euro Trade Cncl 1967-69, vice-pres Br Export Houses Assoc 1968-71; chm Br Cwlth Games Fedn 1968-82, life vice-pres Cwlth Games Fedn; chm ANZ Banking Gp 1970-75, dep chm Eagle Star Insur Co (ret from bd Eagle Star Insur Co and Eagle Star Hldgs 1983), dir Drayton East Investmt Tst 1975-, dir Power Components 1976-; dep chm Royal Overseas League, life vice-pres; dir Whitbread Investmt Tst, tstee Aust Musical Fndn; Queensland pres St John Ambulance Bde; Hallway Int, dir Doug Moran Nat Portrait Prize Ltd, chm Queensland Community Fndn; patron Gold Coast Heart Foundation; chm Asiaciti Investmt Hldgs Pty Ltd; chm Criterion Capital Mgmnt Pty Ltd; *Recreations* walking; *Clubs* Hurlingham; *Style—* Sir Alexander Ross; 20 Compass Way, Tweed Heads West, NSW 2485, Australia

ROSS, Sir Archibald David Manisty; KCMG (1961, CMG 1953); s of John Archibald Ross, ICS; *b* 12 Oct 1911; *Educ* Winchester, New Coll Oxford; *m* 1939, Mary Melville, da of Melville Macfadyen; 1 s (and 1 s decd), 1 da; *Career* HM Dip Serv 1936-71: Berlin, Stockholm, Tehran, min Rome 1953-56, asst under-sec of state for Foreign Affrs 1956-60; ambass: Portugal 1961-66, Sweden 1966-71; chm: Alfa-Laval 1972-1982, Saab (GB) 1972-82, Scania (GB) 1972-82, Datasaab (later Ericsson Information Systems) 1976-86; memb cncl RASE 1980-85; *Clubs* Travellers', Leander, Lansdowne; *Style—* Sir Archibald Ross, KCMG; 17 Ennismore Gdns, London SW7

ROSS, Hon Sir (Dudley) Bruce; s of William Alexander Ross (decd), and Annie Isabella Ross; *b* 21 May 1892; *Educ* St Peter's Coll Adelaide, Adelaide Univ (LLB); *m* 1, 1920, Margaret Eleanor (decd); 1 s, 3 da; m 2, 1954, Agnes Jessie Linklater, da of H C Fletcher; *Career* Div AIF WW I; barr 1914; KC 1945, pres Law Soc of SA 1947-49, judge of Supreme Court of S Aust 1952-62, ret; kt 1962; *Style—* The Hon Sir Bruce Ross

ROSS, Carl Philip Hartley; s of John Carl Ross (fndr Ross Foods Ltd); *b* 3 May 1943; *Educ* Shrewsbury Sch; *m* 1, 1968, Pamela Jean, *née* Dixon; 3 da (Rachel b 1969, Kathryn b 1971, Amanda b 1975); m 2, 1985 Joanna Louise, *née* Norton; *Career* CA: Peat Marwick Mitchell & Co, Forrester Boyd & Co; dir Cosalt Ltd 1971-75, md Orbit Hldgs Ltd 1972-75, chm Bristol & West Cold Stores Ltd 1974-83, Philip Ross & Co CAs 1982-; FCA; *Recreations* foxhunting, golf; *Style—* Philip Ross, Esq; 42 Crabtree Lane, Sutton-on-Sea, Lincolnshire LN12 2RA (☎ 0521 41811)

ROSS, Lt-Col (Charles) Christopher Gordon; s of Maj Charles Gordon Ross, MC (d 1964), of Moor Park, Herts, and Iris Jefford, *née* Fowler (d 1976); *b* 8 July 1931; *Educ* Marlborough, RMA Sandhurst; *m* 27 April 1963, Fiona Mary Ghislaine, da of Gp-Capt Albert Peter Vincent Daly, AFC (d 1985), of Garryannagh, Urra, Nenagh, Co Tipperary, Ireland; 1 s (Alastair b 1964), 1 da (Geraldine b 1965); *Career* cmmnd 14/20 King's Hussars 1951, Troop Ldr ADC, Capt 1956, Adj Sqdn 2 i/c, Maj 1963, Sqdn Ldr, Staff Offr, Regt 2 i/c, Lt-Col 1974 Staff Offr, resigned 1978, chm 14/20 Regt Assoc 1986- (vice chm 1982-85); sec to The Diocese of Salisbury 1979-; churchwarden, tres Royal Br Legion Branch; FBIM 1980; *Recreations* shooting, gardening, reading; *Clubs* Army and Navy, St Moritz Tobogganing; *Style—* Lt-Col Christopher Ross; Wishford Hse, nr Salisbury, Wiltshire SP2 0PQ (☎ 0722 790 486); Church Hse, Crane St, Salisbury SP1 2QB (☎ 0722 333 074/335 876, fax 0722 334 062)

ROSS, David Thomas Mcleod; s of David Ross, and Margert, *née* Mcleod; *b* 3 June 1949; *Educ* Boroughmuir Secdy Sch Edinburgh; *m* 25 Aug 1973, Margaret Gordon Sharpe Ross, da of Robert Charters Russell, of Loanhead; 3 da (Lindsay b 1976, Louise b 1978, Heather b 1984); *Career* CA 1976; md Ivory and Sime plc 1988- (dir 1982, joined 1968); memb: Co of Merchants of the City of Edinburgh, FCCA; *Recreations* shooting; *Style—* David Ross, Esq; The Avenue, 40 Greenhill Gardens, Edinburgh, EH10 4BJ (☎ 031 447 4970); Ivory and Sime plc, One Charlotte Square, Edinburgh EH2 4DZ (☎ 031 225 1357, fax 031 225 2375, telex 727242 IVORYS G)

ROSS, Donald Campbell Mackay; s of Donald Campbell Ross, of Cromarty, Ross & Cromary (provost of Ross and Cromarty 1966-72 as was gf 1947-48), and Elizabeth *née* Macleod); *b* 19 August 1941; *Educ* Fortrose Acad Ross & Cromarty, Heriot Watt Univ Edinburgh (B Arch); *m* 1 Jan 1968, Hilary, da of Frederick William Boulton, of Wigan, Lancashire (d 1959); 2 da (Zoe Karen b 1970, Sasha Victoria b 1976); *Career* architect, princ of Campbell Ross, chartered architect Inverness, 1971-; *Recreations* windsurfing, sailing, painting; *Clubs* Rotary of Inverness, The Highland; *Style—* Donald Ross, Esq; 20 Church St, Inverness IV1 1EB (☎ 0463 236903)

ROSS, The Rt Hon Lord; Donald MacArthur Ross; PC (1985); s of John Ross, slr; *b* 29 Mar 1927; *Educ* Dundee HS, Edinburgh Univ; *m* 1958, Dorothy, *née* Annand; 2 da; *Career* dean Faculty of Advocates 1973-76, senator of Coll of Justice, Scotland (Lord of Session) 1977-85, Lord Justice Clerk of Scotland 1985-, QC (Scot) 1964; sheriff princ Ayr & Bute 1972-73; dep chm Scottish Boundary Cmmn 1977-85, chm of Court Heriot-Watt Univ 1984-; hon LLD Edinburgh 1987; *Recreations* gardening; *Clubs* New; *Style—* The Rt Hon Lord Ross, PC; 33 Lauder Rd, Edinburgh (☎ 031 667 5731)

ROSS, Donald Nixon; s of Donald Ross (d 1942), of Kimberley, South Africa, and late Jessie Ross; *b* 4 Oct 1922; *Educ* Kimberley HS South Africa, Univ of Capetown (BSc, MB, ChB), RCS London; *m* 5 Feb 1953, Dorothy Maud, da of late James Curtis, of Chepstow; 1 da (Janet Susan b 1958); *Career* res fell Guy's Hosp 1953-58; conslt surgn: Guy's Hosp 1958-63, Nat Heart Hosp 1963-68, Middx Hosp 1968-70; sr surgn Inst of Cardiology 1970-; Freeman Worshipful Soc Apothecaries London 1968; hon: FACS 1976, FACC 1973, FRCS (Thailand) 1987, FRCS Ireland 1984, DSC CNAA 1982; FRSM, FRCS 1949, MInstD; memb Order Cedars of Lebanon 1975, Offrs Cross Order Merit FRG 1981; *Books* Hypothermia (1960), Surgeons Guide To Card Diagnosis (1962), Surgical Cardiology (1969), Biol Tissue In Heart Valve Repl (1972), Surgery And Your Heart (1982), contrib numerous scientific journals and books; *Recreations* horse riding, breeding arabian horses; *Clubs* Kimberley, S Africa, Garrick; *Style—* Donald Ross, Esq; 69 Gloucester Cres, London NW1; Rumbolds, Flanders Green, Cottered, Herts (☎ 01 482 0322); 25 Upper Wimpole St, London WIM 7TA (☎ 01 935 8805, fax 01 935 9190, telex 263 449)

ROSS, Duncan Alexander; s of William Duncan Ross (d 1982), and Mary, *née* Maciver (d 1985); *b* 25 Sept 1928; *Educ* Dingwall Acad, Glasgow Univ (BSc); *m* 17 May 1958, Mamie Buchanan Clark, da of Harold Parsons (d 1978); 1 s (Alastair b 1962), 1 da (Deborah b 1959); *Career* various engrg posts S Scotland Electricity Bd 1952-57, engrg commercial and mgmnt posts Midlands Electricity Bd 1957-77 (dep chm 1981-84), South Wales Electricity Bd 1977-80, chm Southern Electricity Bd 1984-; FIEE, CBIM; *Recreations* golf, skiing, bridge; *Style—* Duncan Ross, Esq; Holly House, Canon Hill Way, Bray, Berkshire SL6 2EX (☎ 0628 782753); Southern Electricity Board, Southern Electricity House, Littlewick Green, Maidenhead, Berks SL6 3QB (☎ 0682 82 2166)

ROSS, Ernest; MP (Lab) Dundee West 1979-; *b* 1942; *Educ* St Johns Jr Secdy Sch; *m* ; 2 s, 1 da; *Career* quality control engr Timex Ltd; joined Lab Pty 1973; memb AUEW; *Style—* Ernest Ross, Esq; House of Commons, London SW1

ROSS, Harry Edward Thomas; TD (1945); s of Harry Ross (d 1958), and Rhoda, *née* Smith (d 1941), of Beckenham, Kent; *b* 3 June 1903; *Educ* St Dunstans Coll; *m* 16 Sept 1937, Vera Elizabeth, da of James Robert Davis, of Lahloo Hayes, Kent; 2 s (Robert b 1941, Timothy b 1948), 1 da (Elizabeth b 1953); *Career* ret md Port Line (Cunard); former dir: Montreal Aust New Zealand Line, London Steam-ship Owners Mutual Insur Assoc Ltd, Port of London Authy, Cunard House Ltd, Shipowners rep on pilotage ctee of Trinity Ho; chm London Gen Shipowners Soc 1964-65; London Shipowners Dock Labour Ctee; Lloyds Register of Shipping Gen Ctee; memb Chamber of Shipping; *Recreations* gardening, philately, rugby, football; *Style—* Harry Ross, Esq, TD; 12 Kirk Court, Sevenoaks TN13 3JW (☎ 0732 454 724)

ROSS, Hon Huw Weston; yr s of Baron Ross of Newport (Life Peer), *qv*; *b* 15 June 1960; *Style—* The Hon Huw Ross; 61 Pyle Street, Newport, Isle of Wight

ROSS, Ian Henry; s of Maj Cecil Henry Ross (d 1986), of Edinburgh, and Margaret Elliot, *née* Armour; *b* 13 Oct 1942; *Educ* Merchiston Castle Sch, Edinburgh; *m* 12 May 1973, Patricia Mary (Trishia), da of Col Peter Tooley Willcocks, MBE, MC (d 1967); 2 s (Alastair b 1977, Neil b 1980), 1 da (Nicola b 1984); *Career* sr export dir White Horse Distillers Ltd 1976-82 (joined 1960, dir 1972-76), md MacDonald Greenlees Ltd 1982-86, memb cncl Scotch Whisky Assoc 1983-, chm John Walker & Sons Ltd 1988- (md John Walker & Sons Ltd 1986-87), memb cncl Royal Warrant Holders Assoc 1988-; *Recreations* sailing, fishing; *Clubs* New Edinburgh, Royal Highland YC; *Style—* Ian Ross, Esq; Woodhill, Tilford, nr Farnham, Surrey GU10 2BW (☎ 025 18 2431);

Landmark House, Hammersmith, London (☎ 01 748 5041)

ROSS, His Hon James; s of John Stuart Ross (d 1943), and Maude Mary, *née* Cox (d 1966); *b* 22 Mar 1913; *Educ* Glenalmond, Exeter Coll Oxford (BA); *m* 16 Sept 1939, Clare Margaret, da of Alderman Robert Cort-Cox, of Stratford-upon-Avon; 1 da (Heather); *Career* slr 1938, asst prosecuting slr Birmingham 1941-45, barr Grays Inn 1945, legal memb Mental Health Review Tbnl (Birmingham) 1962, dep chm Agric Land Tbnl (E Midlands) 1963, QC 1966, dep chm Lincs (Lindsay) Quarter Sessions 1967-71, rec Coventry 1968-71, judge Co Ct 1971, circuit judge 1972, memb Parole Bd 1974-77, hon rec of Coventry 1979-85, sr circuit judge and rec order Birmingham 1985-87; QC; *Recreations* sailing, walking; *Style*— His Hon James Ross, QC; 45 Avenue Rd, Dorridge, Solihull, W Midlands; 2 Dr Johnsons Bldgs, Temple, London

ROSS, Hon James Gibb; er s of Baron Ross of Newport (Life Peer), *qv*; *b* 1 Mar 1956; 65 Brocklehurst Street, London SE19

ROSS, Rear Adm (Maurice) James; CB (1962), DSC (1940); s of late Basil James Ross; *b* 31 Oct 1908; *Educ* Charterhouse; *m* 1946, Helen Matheson, *née* McCall; 1 da; *Career* joined RN 1927, WWII 1939-45 served Home and Med Waters, ret Rear Adm 1964; Master Worshipful Co of Gardeners 1983-84; *Books* Ross in the Antarctic 1839-43 (1982); *Recreations* gardening; *Clubs* Army and Navy; *Style*— Rear Adm James Ross, CB, DSC; The School House, Chippenham, Ely, Cambs CB7 5PP (☎ 0638 720 180)

ROSS, James McConville; s of Dr David Sloan Ross, of Elderslie, Renfrewshire, and Maureen, *née* McConville (d 1979); *b* 29 Sept 1960; *Educ* Glasgow HS, St Andrews Univ (MA); *Career* business ed Reid Business Publishing 1984-85, sr electronics analyst James Capel & Co 1987- (analyst 1986-87); *Recreations* skiing, windsurfing, reading, theatre; *Style*— James Ross, Esq; 73 Canon Beck Rd, London SE16 (☎ 01 232 1842); James Capel & Co, 6 Bevis Marks, London EC3A 7JQ (☎ 01 621 0011)

ROSS, John Gordon; JP (1966), DL (1986); s of Maj William Gordon Ross (d 1953), of Two Shires Yew, Chinnor Hill, Oxon, and Louisa, *née* Horn (d 1948); *b* 2 Feb 1921; *Educ* Dragon Sch Oxford, Bedford Sch, Imperial Coll of Sci and Technol (BSc, DIC); *m* 1, 20 Dec 1951, Cynthia Abel (d 1987), da of Reginald Macauley Abel Smith, MC, JP, DL; 1 s (Christopher Lumsden Gordon Ross b 22 Oct 1952, d 12 Dec 1974), 2 da (Jennifer Louisa Ross b 2 Feb 1954, Mary Elizabeth Ross b 17 Sept 1958); m 2, 23 Jan 1989, Veronica June, da of Sqdn-Ldr Bernard Dudley Fletcher Austen; *Career* sci offr Royal Aircraft Estab Farnborough 1941-48; lectr and examiner UCL 1948-52, asst dir RA Lister & Co Ltd Dursley Gloucs 1959-64, conslt engr and poultry farmer 1963-77, asst gen mangr overseas ops RA Lister & Co Ltd 1977-84; diocesan lay reader 1964-; memb: Bishop of Gloucester's Cncl, Horsley PCC (churchwarden 1964-); Gloucs lay rep on the Gen Synod of the C of E, added memb Gloucs CC educn ctee, chm Forest Dean Devpt Assoc; govr; Dursley Tech Coll, Forest of Dean Tech Coll; mangr Horsley Aided Primary Sch, chm Horsley Sch Tstees, fndr chm Yercombe Tst; Dursley Bench 1966 (former dep chm, former chm of the Juvenile & Domestic Benches chm 1977-85); chm Gloucs Magistrates' Cts Ctee 1985-; Gloucs rep: Central Cncl of Probation & After-Care Ctees 1973-76, Central Cncl of Magistrates Cts Ctee 1986-; memb Gloucs Police Ctee 1972-77, gen cmmr of Income Tax Berkley Upper Div 1967-; CEng, MAReS 1946, FIMechE 1963; *Recreations* music, photography, gardening; *Clubs* Naval & Army; *Style*— John Ross, Esq, JP, DL; Horsley Ct, Horsley, Stroud, Glos GL6 OPW (☎ 045 383 2060)

ROSS, John MacDonald; CBE (1968); s of Sir James Stirling Ross, KBE, CB (d 1961), and Christina Macdonald, *née* Ross (d 1922); *b* 31 Mar 1908; *Educ* Highgate Sch, Wadham Coll Oxford; *m* 1932, Helen Margaret, da of George Wilson Wallace (d 1928); 2 s, 3 da; *Career* asst princ Home Office 1930, asst sec General Register Office 1946, Home Office 1951-68; Faith and Order Cmmn of World Cncl of Churches 1964-76; *Recreations* Greek New Testament, early piano, bookbinding; *Clubs* Athenaeum; *Style*— John Ross, Esq, CBE; 64 Wildwood Rd, London NW11 6UU (☎ 01 455 7872)

ROSS, John Malcolm Thomas; s of John Carl Ross; *b* 7 Oct 1934; *Educ* Shrewsbury, Clare Coll Cambridge; *m* 1, 1958, Gillian Mary Hampton; 1 s, 1 da; m 2, 1964, Linda Susan Thomas; 1 s, 2 da; m 3, 1981, Jennifer Mary Fawcett, née Clark; *Career* chartered accountant Peat Marwick Mitchell & Co, dir Ross Gp Ltd 1964-68; Cosalt Ltd: md 1968-73, chm and chief exec 1973-85, dep chief and chief exec 1985-86, FCA; *Recreations* golf, gardening; *Style*— John M T Ross, Esq; Five Gables, 27 Ferriby Lane, Grimsby, South Humberside DN33 3NS

ROSS, Sir (James) Keith; 2 Bt (UK 1960), of Whetstone, Middx, RD (1967); s of Sir James Paterson Ross, 1 Bt, KCVO, FRCS (d 1980; Surgn to HM 1952-64), and Marjorie Burton, *née* Townsend (d 1978); *b* 9 May 1927; *Educ* St Paul's, Middx Hosp London (MB, BS, MS); *m* 24 Nov 1956, Jacqueline Annella, da of Francis William Clarke (d 1971); 1 s, 3 da (Susan b 1958, Janet b 1960, Anne b 1962); *Heir* s, Andrew Charles Paterson Ross b 18 June 1966; *Career* Surgn Lt RNVR 1952-54, Surgn Lt Cdr RNR 1954-72; conslt cardio thoracic surg Harefield Hosp 1964-67; conslt cardiac surgn: Nat Heart Hosp London 1967-72, Wessex regn Southampton 1972-, King Edward VII Hosp Midhurst 1979-; pres Soc of Cardiothoracic Surgns 1987-88; memb cncl RCS 1986-; FRCS 1956, FRCS Ed 1989, FRSM; *Recreations* fly fishing, sailing, painting; *Clubs* MCC, Army and Navy, Royal Lymington YC; *Style*— Sir Keith Ross, Bt, RD; Moonhills Gate, Hilltop, Beaulieu, Hants SO42 7YS (☎ 0590 612104); Southampton General Hospital, Southampton, Hants (☎ 0703 777222)

ROSS, Lt-Col (Walter Hugh) Malcolm; OBE (1988); s of Col Walter John Macdonald Ross, CB, OBE, MC, TD, JP, DL (d 1982), of Netherhall, Bridge-of-Dee, Castle-Douglas, Kirkcudbrightshire, and Josephine May, *née* Cross (d 1982); *b* 27 Oct 1943; *Educ* Eton, RMA Sandhurst; *m* 31 Jan 1969, Susan (Susie) Jane, da of Gen Sir Michael Gow, GCB, Long Vere House, Hascombe, Godalming, Surrey; 1 s (Hector b 1983), 2 da (Tabitha b 1970, Flora b 1974); *Career* cmmd Scots Gds 1964-87; asst comptroller Lord Chamberlain's Off 1987, mgmnt auditor The Royal Household 1987-, Extra Equerry to HM The Queen 1988-; memb Queen's Body Gd for Scotland Royal Co of Archers 1981-; *Clubs* Pratt's, New (Edinburgh); *Style*— Lt-Col Malcolm Ross, OBE; Netherhall, Bridge-of-Dee, Castle-Douglas, Kirkcudbrightshire

ROSS, Hon Mrs Charles; Mary Margaret; da of late Thomas Graham and late Margaret Graham, of Swan Park, Monaghan, Republic of Ireland; *m* 1953, as his 2 w, Hon Charles Dudley Anthony Ross (d 1976), yr s of Una Mary, Baroness de Ros; 1 s; *Style*— The Hon Mrs Charles Ross; 67 Seafield Rd, Southbourne, Bournemouth, Dorset (☎ 0202 428149)

ROSS, Nick (Nicholas) David; s of John Caryl Ross, Surrey, and Joy Dorothy, *née* Richmond; paternal gf (Pinhas Rosen) Signatory to Israel's Declaration of Independence, and first Min of Justice; *b* 7 August 1947; *Educ* Wallington Co GS, Surrey; Queen's Univ Belfast (BA); *m* 1 March 1985, Sarah Patricia Ann, da of Dr Max Caplin OBE, FRCP, of London; 3 s (Adam Michael b 1985, Samuel Max b 1987, Jack Felix b 1988); *Career* BBC freelance reporter and presenter N Ireland 1971-72; presenter radio: Newsdesk, The World Tonight 1972-74, World at One 1972-75, Call Nick Ross 1987-; presenter TV: Man Alive, Out of Court, Fair Comment 1975-78; producer and dir: documentaries, The Fix, The Biggest Epidemic of Our Times 1981; fndr presenter BBC breakfast TV 1983; presenter: Sixty Minutes 1983-84, Watchdog, Star Memories, Drugwatch 1985-86; Crimewatch UK (1984-); occasional BBC radio presenter: World at One, You the Jury, Any Questions, The Radio 4 Generation; presenter company videos; chm corporate conferences; *Recreations* scuba diving, skiing; *Style*— Nick Ross, Esq; c/o Jon Roseman Associates, 103 Charing Cross Rd, London WC2H 0DT (☎ 01 439 8245)

ROSS, Peter Angus; s of Maj John Milner Ross (d 1979), and Evangeline Joyce, *née* Robertson (d 1982); *b* 25 Feb 1936; *Educ* Glasgow Acad; *m* 16 Aug 1962, Elliot Wallace, da of James Allan Baillie Montgomery (d 1982), of Glasgow; *Career* Nat Serv RA 1954-56; with sis managed farm 1956-58, asst tea taster and rep Wm Wright & Co (Pekoe) Ltd 1958-63, chm Burnthills Gp Ltd (fndr dir Burnthills (Contractors) Ltd - first memb of the gp 1963) dir: Goldenbolt Int Ltd and assoc cos, Huewind Ltd and assoc cos, Stonefield Hotel Ltd, Castle, Ross Hotels Ltd, Covenanters Inn Ltd, Mull & West Highland Narrow Gauge Rlwy Co Ltd; farms as Ladyland Estates (in ptnrship with wife) and Grangehill Estates; fndr memb and past pres Johnstone Rotary Club 1975-, memb Garnock Valley Neighbourhood Tst 1983-85; received Aims of Indsut Award for Scotland 1982; *Clubs* RNVR Carrick Glasgow; *Style*— Peter Ross, Esq; Grangehill, Beith, Ayrshire, Scotland (☎ 05055 3040); 84 High St, Johnstone, Renfrewshire (☎ 0505 24461)

ROSS, Hon Mrs (Roxana Rose Catherine Naila); *née* Lampson; da of 1 Baron Killearn, GCMG, CB, MVO, PC (d 1964); *b* 1945; *m* 1966, Ian Cowper Ross; 2 s, 2 da; *Style*— The Hon Mrs Ross

ROSS, (Alexander) Sandy; s of Alexander Coutts Ross (d 1978), and Charlotte Edwardes, *née* Robertson (d 1979); *b* 17 April 1948; *Educ* Grangemouth HS, Edinburgh Univ (LLB), Moray House Coll Edinburgh; *m* Alison, *née* Fraser; 1 s (Andrew b 1983), 1 da (Frances b 1986); *Career* slr 1970-75, prodr Granada TV 1978-86, controller of entertainment Scottish TV 1986-; memb: Edinburgh Town Cncl 1971-74, Edinburgh DC 1973-76; memb BAFTA; *Recreations* golf, music, reading; *Style*— Sandy Ross, Esq; 7 Murray Field Ave, Edinburgh EH12 6AU (☎ 031 337 3679); Scottish Television, Cowcaddens, Glasgow G2 3PR (☎ 041 332 9999, fax 041 332 6982)

ROSS, Stephen Lawrence; s of Julian Ross (d 1988) of London and Miriam *née* Gimmack; *b* 11 Dec 1950; *Educ* Woodhouse GS; *m* (m dis); 1 s (Daniel Paul b 20 Feb 1979), 1 da (Nicola Jane b 2 Oct 1981); *Career* CA 1974; audit mangr Deloitte Haskin Sells (London) 1976, ptnr Keane Shaw & Co (London) 1978, sr ptnr Ross Bennet-Smith (London) 1983; FCA; *Recreations* tennis, horse racing, bridge ; *Style*— Stephen L Ross, Esq; 46/47 Upper Berkeley St, London W1 (☎ 01 724 7724, fax 01 724 7070)

ROSS, William; MP (UU) Londonderry East Feb 1974-; s of Leslie Alexander Ross (d 1973); *b* 4 Feb 1936; *m* 1974; 3 s, 1 da; *Recreations* shooting, fishing; *Clubs* Northern Counties, Londonderry; *Style*— William Ross, Esq, MP; Hillquarter, Turmeel, Dungiven, N Ireland (☎ 050 47 41428); House of Commons, London SW1 (☎ 01 219 3571)

ROSS MARTYN, John Greaves; s of Dr William Ross Martyn, of Wilmslow, Cheshire, and Ida Mary Martyn, *née* Greaves; *b* 23 Jan 1944; *Educ* Repton, Cambridge Univ (BA, LLM); *m* 4 Aug 1973, Pauline, da of Ronald Jennings (d 1979), of Morley, Yorks; 1 s (Philip b 1978), 1 da (Elizabeth b 1975); *Career* asst lectr Birmingham Coll of Commerce 1966-68, barr Middle Temple 1969, in practice at Chancery Bar 1970-, asst recorder 1988, SE circuit; tres Bromley Parish Church Youth Centre; memb Chancery Bar Assoc; *Books* Williams, Mortimer and Sunnucks on Executors, Administrators and Probate (jt ed, 1982), Family Provision: Law and Practice (1985); *Recreations* gardening, skiing; *Style*— John Ross Martyn, Esq; 5 New Square, Lincoln's Inn, London WC2A 3RJ (☎ 01 404 0404, fax 01 831 6016)

ROSS OF NEWPORT, Baron (Life Peer UK 1987), of Newport, Co Isle of Wight; Stephen Sherlock Ross; s of Reginald Sherlock Ross and Florence Beryl, *née* Weston; *b* 6 July 1926; *Educ* Holmwood Sch Finchley, Bedford Sch; *m* 8 Oct 1949, Brenda Marie, da of Arthur Ivor Hughes, of Stanmore, Middx; 2 s (Hon James Gibb b 1 March 1956, Huw Weston b 15 June 1960), 2 da (Hon Lesley Priscilla (Hon Mrs O'Sullivan) b 2 Oct 1950, Hon Judith Caroline (Hon Mrs Kiendl) b 1 Oct 1952); *Career* WWII 1939-45, RN 1944-48; asst Nock & Joseland Kidderminster 1948-53; ptnr Sir Francis Pittis & Son, Newport, IOW 1958-73 (joined 1953) conslt Fox & Sons Newport IOW 1987-89; memb IOW CC 1967-74 and 1981-85 (leader 1981-83), chm Policy and Resources Ctee 1973-74 and 1981-83; MP (L) IOW 1974-87; FRICS; *Recreations* cricket, collecting ceramics; *Clubs* Royal Commonwealth; *Style*— The Rt Hon Lord Ross of Newport

ROSS OF THAT ILK, David Campbell; s of Sheriff Charles Campbell Ross of Shandwick, QC; suc kinswoman Miss Rosa Ross Williamson Ross of that Ilk and Pitcalnie in 1968 as Chief of Clan Ross; *b* 1934; *m* 1958, Eileen, da of Lawrence Cassidy; *Heir* s, Hugh Andrew Campbell (b 1961); *Style*— David Ross of that Ilk; Old School House, Fettercairn, Laurencekirk AB3 1DL

ROSS ROZYCHKI, Andrew (Zbigniew Jan); s of Lt-Col K Rozychki (d 1969), and Wanda Redlich (d 1939); *b* 23 Oct 1930; *Educ* Stonyhurst Coll, Balliol Coll Oxford (MA); *m* 1955, Marysia, da of Count Tadeusz von Grodkow Los (decd, cr. Emperor King Franz Joseph 1861); 1 da (Izabella); *Career* md: NTP Business Journals Ltd 1968-70, F T Business Publications Ltd 1970-72; dir Morgan-Grampian plc 1973-82, md: Morgan-Grampian Professional Press Ltd 1972-76, Fleet Financial Publishing Ltd 1978-80; chm: The Countryman Ltd 1983-, Geographical Press Ltd 1983-; dir Punch Pubns Ltd 1987-; MIOD; *Style*— Andrew Ross Rozychki, Esq; 23-27 Tudor Street, London EC4Y 0HR (☎ 01 583 9199)

ROSS RUSSELL, Graham; *b* 3 Jan 1933; *Educ* Loretto, Trinity Hall Cambridge, Harvard Business Sch; *m* 1963, Jean Margaret, da of the late Col K M Symington; 4 children; *Career* chm Laurence Prust Hldgs Ltd, memb: Stock Exchange 1965-, Stock Exchange Cncl 1973-; dep chm Stock Exchange 1984-88, cmmr of Public Works Loan Bd 1981-; dir of Securities and Investmts Bd 1989-; dir of a number of industl cos; *Style*— Graham Ross Russell, Esq; 30 Ladbroke Sq, London W11; Laurence, Prust &

Co, Basildon House, 7-11 Moorgate, London EC2R 6AH (☎ 01 606 8811; telex 888570)

ROSS SKINNER, Harry John Crawley; VRD; s of Lt Col Harry Crawley Ross Skinner, DSO, MC (d 1972), of Warmwell House, Dorchester, Dorset, and Joan, *née* Crawley; *b* 6 Feb 1932; *Educ* Eton, RAC Cirencester; *m* 1, 21 May 1955, Rosemary, da of Anthony Freestone-Barnes, of Winchester; 4 s (Andrew Harry b 1956, Sambrooke Anthony b 1958, Paul Stuart b 1960, Simon Francis b 1963); m 2, 13 Sept 1971, Venetia Caroline *née* Maynard qv; 4 step children; *Career* Lt Cdr RN (Res); farmer; dir: Winchmore plc, Blaircourt Investmts Ltd, Woodstock Estates Ltd; *Recreations* sailing, skiing, shooting; *Clubs* Royal Cruising; *Style*— Harry J C Ross Skinner, Esq, VRD; Warmwell House, Dorchester DT2 8HQ

ROSS SKINNER, Venetia Caroline; *née* Maynard; da of Lt-Col Alister Cecil Maynard, MBE (d 1975), descended from a collateral branch of the Viscounts Maynard (ext 1865), and Muriel Violet, *née* Wingfield (d 1986), descent of 4 Viscount Powerscourt; *b* 22 Mar 1936; *Educ* Queen's Coll, Harley St; *m* 1, 21 June 1957 (m dis 1969), John Howard Cordle; 1 s (Rupert b 1959), 3 da (Sophie b 1958, Marina b 1960 m Hon Michael Pearson *qv*, Rachel b 1963); m 2, 13 Sept 1971, Harry John Crawley Ross Skinner *qv*; *Career* Welsh pony breeder; building co dir; *Recreations* yachting; *Style*— Mrs Venetia C Ross Skinner; Warnwell House, nr Dorchester, Dorset (☎ 0305 852269, car telephone 0863 245687)

ROSS STEWART, David Andrew; OBE (1985); s of Maj-Gen W Ross Stewart CB, CIE (d 1966), of Blakehope, Caddonfoot, Galashiels, Scotland, and Margaret Jean Denholm, *née* Fraser; *b* 30 Nov 1930; *Educ* Rugby, Clare Coll Cambridge (BA); *m* 23 May 1959, Susan Olive, da of Lt Col W H F Routh (d 1964), of Hillside, Kingston St Mary, Taunton, Somerset; 2 s (James b 20 Sept 1961, Charles b 15 May 1964); *Career* mgmnt trainee Alex Cowan & Sons Ltd 1952-55, asst to gen mangr Alex Cowan & Son (NZ) Ltd 1959-62; gen mangr: Alex Cowan & Sons (Stationery) Ltd London 1962-66, Spicers (Stationery) Ltd Sawston 1966-68; md John Bartholomew & Son Ltd Edinburgh 1968-; chm: Confedn of Scottish Business Sch Cncl, SCDI Trade Devpt Ctee; convener Edinburgh Univ Advsy Ctee on Business Studies, chm New Club Edinburgh, dep chm Scot Provident Inst, chm St Andrew Tst plc, dir East of Scotland Industl Investmts Ltd, memb Scottish advsy bd Abbey Nat Bldg Soc; *Recreations* fishing, gardening, golf; *Clubs* New (Edinburgh), Hon Co of Edinburgh Golfers, Muirfield GC; *Style*— David Ross Stewart, Esq, OBE; 13 Blacket Place, Edinburgh EH9 1RN (☎ 031 667 3221); John Bartholomew & Son Ltd, 12 Duncan St, Edinburgh EH9 1TA (☎ 031 667 9341, fax 031 662 4282, telex 728134 BARTS G)

ROSSDALE, Fleur Viola; da of John Spencer Rossdale, and Lucie Marcelle Louise, *née* Bourcier; *b* 20 Mar 1957; *Educ* Francis Holland Sch, Florence Univ (Dip); *m* 11 Dec 1982, Fletcher Freeland Robinson, s of Patrick William Robinson, of London; 2 s (George b 1984, William b 1986); *Career* originator of The Br Interior Design Exhibition, co-originator with Weidenfeld & Nicolson of 'The Interior Design Yearbook'; *Recreations* walking, gardening; *Style*— Ms Fleur Rossdale; 3 Pembroke Sq, London, W8 6PA, (☎ 01 938 4759/0)

ROSSE, Anne, Countess of; Anne; da of Lt-Col Leonard Messel, OBE, TD (s of Ludwig Messel, of Nymans, Handcross, Sussex and 3 Hyde Park Gdns, London W2, s of Simon Messel of Darmstadt and gs of Simon Lindheim, private sec to the Grand Duke of Hesse and sec of the WO in Darmstadt), and of Maud Frances, MBE (da of (Edward) Linley Sambourne, the Punch cartoonist, of 18 Stafford Terrace, London W8, s of Francis Linley, of the Linleys of Bath); sis of Linley Francis Messel and of late Oliver Messel, the portraitist and set designer; *m* 1, 1925 (m dis 1934), Ronald, s of Sir Robert Armstrong-Jones, CBE, of Plas Dinas, Caernarvonshire; 1 s (Earl of Snowdon, *qv*), 1 da (Viscountess de Vesci, *qv*); m 2, 1935, 6 Earl of Rosse, KBE (d 1979); 2 s (7 Earl and Hon Desmond Parsons, *qqv*); *Career* dir for the Nat Tst of Nymans Gardens; founder of The Victorian Soc at 18 Stafford Terrace; *Style*— The Rt Hon Anne, Countess of Rosse; Nymans, Handcross, Sussex; Womersley Park, Doncaster, Yorks; Birr Castle, Co Offaly, Eire; 18 Stafford Terrace, London W8

ROSSE, 7 Earl of (I 1806); Sir William Brendan Parsons; 10 Bt (I 1677); Lord of the Manors of Towton and Womersley; s of 6 Earl of Rosse, KBE (d 1979), and Anne, Countess of Rosse, *qv*; *b* 21 Oct 1936; *Educ* Eton, Grenoble Univ, Ch Ch Oxford; *m* 1966, Alison, da of Maj John Cooke-Hurle, of Startforth Hall, Barnard Castle; 2 s (Lord Oxmantown, Hon Michael b 1981), 1 da (Lady Alicia b 1971); *Heir* s, Lord Oxmantown; *Career* late 2 Lt Irish Gds; UN official: Ghana, Dahomey, Mid-W Africa, Iran, Bangladesh, Algeria 1963-80; dir: Agency for Personal Services Overseas, The I am Gp, the Historic Irish Houses and Gardens Assocs, Br Scientific Heritage Fndn; memb of Irish Govts Advsy Cncl on Devpt Co-operation; patron: Nat Science and Engrg Centre, Halley's Comet Soc; tstee Edward de Bono Fndn; *Clubs* The International; *Style*— The Rt Hon the Earl of Rosse; Birr Castle, Co Offaly, Eire (☎ 353 509 20023)

ROSSER, Sir Melvyn Wynne; DL (West Glam 1986); s of David John Rosser of Swansea; *b* 11 Nov 1926; *Educ* Glanmor Secdy Sch, Bishop Gore GS Swansea; *m* 1959, Margaret Mary; 1 s, 2 da; *Career* ptnr Deloitte Haskins & Sells: Swansea 1961-66, Cardiff 1966-79, London 1979-80; memb: Land Cmmn 1965-69, Welsh Econ Cncl 1964-72; chm Welsh Cncl 1972-80; dir: Nat Bus Co 1969-72, Wales Telecommunications Bd 1970-80, Br Steel Corpn 1972-80, Nat Coal Bd 1980-; chm Manpower Services Ctee for Wales 1980-; memb: Royal Cmmn on Standards of Conduct in Public Life 1974, and Cmmn 1970-73, PM's Advsy Ctee on Outside Business Appts 1976-83; pres Univ Coll of Wales Aberystwyth 1985- (vice-pres 1977-85); memb Cncl and Ct of Univ of Wales; Hon LLD Univ of Wales; Hon Fell Polytechnic of Wales; memb Gorsedd of Bards; FCA; kt 1974; *Recreations* gardening; *Clubs* Reform, Cardiff and County; *Style*— Sir Melvyn Rosser, DL; Corlan, 53 Birchgrove Road, Lonlas, Swansea

ROSSI, Sir Hugh Alexis Louis; MP (C) Hornsey and Wood Green 1983-; *b* 21 June 1927; *Educ* Finchley Catholic GS, King's Coll London; *m* 1955, (Philomena) Elizabeth, barr, da of Patrick Jennings (d 1951); 1 s, 4 da; *Career* MP (C) Hornsey 1966-1983; min of state for Social Security and the Disabled DHSS 1981-83, Min of State NI office 1979-81, oppn spokesman Housing and Land 1974-79, parly under-sec Environment Jan-March 1974, lord cmmr Treasy 1972-74, govt whip 1970-72; memb UK Delegn to Cncl Europe and WEU 1970-73 (dep leader 1972-73, Euro whip 1971-73); Kt of Holy Sepulchre (1966 Papal); slr 1950 (LLB London), former memb Hornsey & Haringey Cncl and Middx CC; KCSG (1985 Papal); fell Kings College London (1986); kt 1983; *Style*— Sir Hugh Rossi, MP; House of Commons, London SW1 (☎ 01 219 3000)

ROSSITER, Rt Rev (Anthony) Francis; s of Leslie Anthony Rossiter (d 1952), and Winifred Mary, *née* Poppitt; *b* 26 April 1931; *Educ* St Benedict's Ealing, Sant Anselmo (LCL) Rome, Lateran Univ; *Career* ordained priest 1955, dep head St Benedict's Sch 1960-67, pres Conf of Major Religious Superiors of Eng and Wales 1970-74, vicar Religious Archdiocese of Westminster 1969-89, abbot pres Eng Benedictine Congregation 1985- (second asst 1976-85), abbot of Ealing 1967-; Hon DD St Vincent Coll Pensylvania 1988; *Style*— The Rt Rev the Abbot of Ealing; Ealing Abbey, London W5 2DY (☎ 01 998 2158)

ROSSITER, Richard Wellsted; s of William Rossiter (d 1959), of Bristol, and Christabel Ida Rossitca, JP; *b* 30 Oct 1934; *Educ* Bristol GS; *m* 30 Sept 1966, Susan Jennifer, da of Reginald Brookes; 2 da (Emily, Charlotte); *Career* Nat Serv cmmnd Sub Lt RN 1957-59; sr ptnr Rossiter & Co Chartered Acountants; chm: Fromedale Estates Ltd, Westcare Discounts; past capt and chm Clifton RFC; played cricket for: RN, MCC, Free Foresters, Glos CCC (memb ctee); former chm Clifton LTC; vice chm Bristol cncl Disabled Adults; FCA 1957; *Recreations* cricket, tennis, sport generally, skiing; *Clubs* Clifton, Lansdowne, MCC, Free Foresters; *Style*— Richard Rossiter, Esq; Lougwood, Tickenham, Avon BS21 6SW (☎ 0272 730863); 63 Whiteladies Rd, Bristol BS8 2HT

ROSSLYN, Athenaïs, Countess of; Comtesse Athenaïs; *née* de Rochechouart-Mortemart; da of Louis Victor de Rochechouart-Mortemart, Duc de Vivonne (d 1938 , bro of 13 Duc de Mortemart), and Mme Michel Valery Ollivier, *née* d'Harcourt; Lords of Mortemart 1205, the Marquessote of Mortemart was erected into a Duchy Peerage in 1650 by King Louis XIV; *m* 1955 (m dis 1962), 6 Earl of Rosslyn (d 1977); 1 s (7 Earl of Rosslyn), 1 da (Lady Caroline St Clair-Erskine); *Style*— Athenaïs, Countess of Rosslyn; 64 Avenue Henri-Martin, Paris XVI, France

ROSSLYN, 7 Earl of (UK 1801); Sir Peter St Clair-Erskine; 10 Bt (S 1666); also Baron Loughborough (GB 1780); s of 6 Earl of Rosslyn (d 1977), and Athenaïs, Countess of Rosslyn, *qv*; *b* 31 Mar 1958; *Educ* Eton, Bristol Univ; *m* 1986, Helen, el da C R Watters of Sussex; 1 s (Lord Loughborough), 1 da (Lady Alice b 14 June 1988); *Heir* s, Hon Jamie William St Clair-Erskine, Lord Loughborough, b 28 May 1986; *Career* tstee Dunimarle Museum, Metropolitan Police 1980-; *Clubs* Whites; *Style*— The Rt Hon the Earl of Rosslyn

ROSSMORE, 7 Baron (I 1796 & UK 1838) William Warner Westenra; s of 6 Baron Rossmore (d 1958); *b* 14 Feb 1931; *Educ* Eton, Trinity Cambridge; *m* 1982, Valerie Marion, da of Brian Tobin, of Riverstown, Birr, Ireland; 1 s, 1 step da; *Heir* s, Hon Benedict William Westenra, b 6 March 1983; *Career* 2 Lt Somerset LI; co-fndr Coolemine Therapeutic Community Dublin (Psychotherapeutic Counselling); *Recreations* drawing and painting; *Clubs* Kildare St & Univ Dublin; *Style*— The Rt Hon Lord Rossmore; c/o Lloyds Bank plc, 6 Pall Mall, London SW1

ROSSWICK, (Robert) Paul; s of John Rosswick (d 1959), and Phoebe, *née* Fagin (d 1982); *b* 1 June 1932; *Educ* Malvern Coll, London Hosp Med Coll (MB, BS); *m* 25 March 1962, Elizabeth Rita, da of Horace Cooper; 1 s (Jonathan b 1965), 1 da (Sarah b 1966); *Career* conslt surgn St Georges Hosp London 1970, surgn Royal Masonic Hosp London 1977; *Recreations* music, photography; *Clubs* Savage, RSM; *Style*— Paul Rosswick, Esq; 10 Lorian Close, London N12 7DZ (☎ 01 445 4792); 79 Harley St, W1N 1DE (☎ 01 935 3046, car tel 0836 202657)

ROST, Peter Lewis; MP (C) Erewash 1983-; s of Frederick Rost, formerly Rosenstiel (d 1971), of NY, and Elisabeth Merz; *b* 19 Sept 1930; *Educ* Aylesbury GS, Birmingham Univ (BA); *m* 1961, Hilary, da of Arthur Mayo (d 1971), of Boxmoor, Herts; 2 s, 2 da; *Career* RAF 1948-50; stockbroker, investment analyst and fin journalist; MP (C) Derbyshire S E 1970-1983; Grand Cross Order of Merit Germany 1979; *Style*— Peter Rost, Esq, MP; Norcott Court, Berkhamsted, Herts (☎ 044 27 6123)

ROSTEN, Leonard; *b* 5 Jan 1929; *Educ* Regent Poly London, Northampton Engrg Coll, London Univ (BSc); *m* 5 June 1956, Jeanette, *née* Jacobs, 2 da (Susan b 1959, Deborah b 1963); *Career* sr scientific Intelligence Offr CD Corps 1962-68; assoc W V Zinn and Assocs 1968-70 (engr 1955-68), fndr ptnr Cooper Macdonald and Ptnrs 1970-, chm ACE Midland Gp 1981-82 (tres 1984); FIStructE 1973, FICE 1986, MConsE, FRSA; papers: Detailing by Computer (with W V Zinn), Civil Engineering (1971); *Recreations* music, ancient history; *Clubs* RAC; *Style*— Leonard Rosten, Esq; 23 Poolfield Drive, Solihull, Midlands B91 1SH (☎ 021 705 9620); Cooper Macdonald and Ptnrs, Bank House, Cherry St, Birmingham B2 5SF (☎ 021 643 7891, fax 021 643 5156, car 0836 769 483, telex 928439 COMACE G)

ROSTRON, Sir Frank; MBE (1954); s of late Samuel Ernest Rostron, of Oldham, and late Martha *née* Jagger; *b* 11 Sept 1900; *Educ* Oldham HS, Manchester Coll Science and Technol (HNC Elec Eng); *m* 1929, Helen Jodrell (d 1984), da of late Thomas Owen, of Manchester; 1 s (David), 1 da (Barbara); *Career* RAF 1941-45, electrical engr offr (Bomber Cmd) Eng, Pilot Offr to Sqdn Ldr (despatches twice); chartered electrical engr pres Manchester C of C 1955-56; Ferranti Ltd 1917-70 (dir 1958-70), dir: Nat and Vulcan Boiler and Gen Insur Co Ltd 1958-70, McKechnie Bros Ltd 1966-71; chm: Cotton Bd 1963-68, Cotton and Allied Textiles Indust Trg Bd 1966-68 (fndr); CEng, FIEE; kt 1967; *Recreations* reading, walking, gardending; *Style*— Sir Frank Rostron, MBE; 5 Brocklehurst Drive, Prestbury, Macclesfield, Cheshire SK10 4JD (☎ 0625 829577)

ROTBLAT, Prof Joseph; s of late Zygmunt & Sonia Rotblat; *b* 4 Nov 1908; *Educ* Free Univ of Poland (MA), Univ of Warsaw (DPhys), Univ of Liverpool (PhD), Univ of London (DSc); *Career* res fell Radiological Lab Warsaw 1933-39, asst dir Atomic Physics Inst Warsaw 1937-39, Oliver Lodge fell Univ of Liverpool 1939-40, lectr (later sr lectr) Univ of Liverpool 1940-49; worked on atom bomb Liverpool and Los Alamos New Mexico 1939-45; dir of nuclear physics res Univ Liverpool 1945-49, prof Univ of London and chief physicist St Bart's Hosp 1950-76; editor-in-chief Physics in Medicine 2nd Biology 1960-72; vice dean faculty of sci Univ of London 1974-76, tres St Bart's Med Coll 1973-76; govr: St Bart's Med Coll 1977-, St Bart's Hosp 1978-; pres: Hosp Physicists Assoc 1969-70, Br Inst of Radiology 1971-72, Youth Sci Fortnight 1972-74, Pugwash Conferences on Sci and World Affairs 1988-; Hon DSc (Bradford) 1973, hon fell UMIST 1985, Dr Honoris Causa (Lomonosov Univ) Moscow 1988, Polish Acad of Scis (1966), American Acad Arts & Scis (1972), Czechoslovak Acad of Scis (1988); Order of Merit, Polish Peoples Republic (1987); *Books* Atoms and The Universe (1956), Science and World Affairs (1962), Aspects of Medical Physics (1966), Scientists in the Quest for Peace (1972), Nuclear Reactors - To Breed or not to Breed (1977), Nuclear Radiation in Warfare (1981), Scientists, The Arms Race and

Disarmament (1982), The Arms Race at a Time of Decision (1984), Nuclear Strategy and World Security (1985), Strategic Defence and the Future of the Arms Race (1986); *Recreations* walking, travel; *Clubs* Atheneaum; *Style*— Prof Joseph Rotblat, CBE; 8 Asmara Rd, West Hampstead, London NW2 3ST (☎ 01 435 1471); Flat A, Museum Mansions, 63A Great Russell St, London WC1B 3BJ (☎ 01 405 6661, fax 01 831 5651)

ROTH, Andrew; s of Emil Roth, (d 1963), of New York, and Bertha, *née* Rosenberg (d 1984); *b* 23 April 1919; *Educ* De Witt Clinton HS NY, Coll of City of New York (BSS), Columbia Univ (MA), Michigan Univ, Harvard Univ; *m* 1, 2 Nov 1941 (m dis 1949), Renee Louise, da of Otto Knitel (d 1962), of NY; m 2, 30 June 1949 (m dis 1984), Mathilda Anna, *née* Friederich; 1 s (Bradley Neil Adrian b 1950), 1 da (Susan Teresa (Terry) b 1953); *Career* USNR Intelligence 1941-45; sr Lt 1945; reader history dept City Coll NY 1939-40, high school history teacher 1940-41; journalist, foreign corr, author 1945-; memb NUJ; *Books* Japan Strikes South (1941), French Interests and Policies in the Far East (1942), Dilemma in Japan (1945), The Business Background of MPs (1959-70), MP's Chart (1967-87), Enoch Powell Tory Tribune (1970), Can Parliament Decide? (1971), Heath and the Heathmen (1972), Lord on the Board (1972), The Prime Ministers Vol II (1975), Sir Harold Wilson Yorkshire Walter Mitty (1977), Parliamentary Profiles (1984-85, 1988); *Recreations* sketching, jazz-dancing, toin-chasing; *Style*— Andrew Roth, Esq; 34 Somali Rd, London NW2 3RL (☎ 01 435 6673); Trepwll, Cilreddin Bridge, Llanychaer, Pembrokeshire, Dyfed; 2 Queen Anne's Gate Buildings, Dartmouth St, London SW1H 9BP (☎ 01 222 5884, fax 01 222 5889)

ROTH, Prof Klaus Friedrich; s of Franz Roth (d 1937), and Mathilde, *née* Liebrecht; *b* 29 Oct 1925; *Educ* St Paul's, Peterhouse Cambridge (BA), UCL (MSc, PhD); *m* 29 July 1955, Melek, da of Mahmoud Khairy (d 1954), Pasha of Sultana Melek Palace, Heliopolis, Cairo, Egypt; *Career* asst master Gordonstoun 1945-46, memb dept maths UCL 1948-66, prof London Univ 1961-; Imperial Coll London Univ: prof pure maths 1966-88, (prof emeritus and visiting prof 1988-), MIT: visiting lectr 1956-57, visiting prof 1965-66; Fields medal awarded at Int Congress Mathematicians 1958, hon memb American Acad Arts and Scis 1966, fell UCL 1979; memb: London Math Soc 1951 (De Morgan Medal 1983), American Math Soc 1956; FRS 1960; *Books* Sequences (with H Halberstam, second edn 1983); *Recreations* chess, cinema, ballroom dancing; *Style*— Prof K F Roth; 24 Burnsall St, London SW3 3ST (☎ 01 352 1363); Dept of Mathematics, Imperial Coll, 180 Queen's Gate, London SW7 2BZ (☎ 01 589 5111)

ROTH, Prof Sir Martin; s of Samuel Simon Roth of London; *b* 6 Nov 1917; *Educ* London Univ, St Mary's Hosp Med Sch, McGill Univ Montreal; *m* 1945, Constance, da of Samuel Heller of Cockfosters, Herts; 3 da; *Career* prof psychological med Newcastle upon Tyne 1956-77, prof psychiatry Cambridge Univ 1977-85; MD, FRCP, FRCPsych (pres 1971), DPM; Freedom City of Salomanca 1975, Gold Florin City of Florence 1979; kt 1972; *Clubs* Athenaeum; *Style*— Prof Sir Martin Roth; Dept of Psychiatry, New Addenbrooke's Hospital, Cambridge University, Hills Road, Cambridge

ROTHENBERG, Hon Mrs; Hon Mary; *née* Sinclair; da of 2 and last Baron Pentland (d 1984) and Lucy Elizabeth, da of late Sir Henry Babington Smith; *b* 21 Nov 1942; *Educ* Mount Holyoke USA (BA); *m* 1976, Jon Anderson Rothenberg; 1 da (Laura); *Career* graphic designer; *Style*— The Hon Mrs Rothenberg; 131 East 66 St, New York, NY 10021, USA

ROTHENBERG, Robert Michael; s of Helmut Rothenberg, and Anna Amalia, *née* Hannes; *b* 10 August 1950; *Educ* Highgate Sch, Exeter Univ (BA); *m* 10 July 1981, Philippa Jane, da of Stephen Fraser White, of Great Doddington; 1 s (Simon b 1983), 2 da (Katie b 1982, Joanna b 1987); *Career* CA 1975-; ptnr Blick Rothenberg & Noble 1979-, dir Computastaff Hldgs Ltd 1987-, lectr to professional audiences on taxation and co law 1981-; hon tres Camden CAB 1982-87; FCA, ATII; *Recreations* travel, skiing, opera, theatre; *Clubs* Garrick, MCC; *Style*— Robert Rothenberg, Esq; 74 Hillway, Highgate, London N6 6DP (☎ 01 348 7771); Blick Rothenberg & Noble, 12 York Gate, London NW1 4QS (☎ 01 486 0111, fax 01 935 6852, telex 298982)

ROTHERA, Anthony Charles Graham; TD and Bar (1946); s of Wilfred Stewart Rothera (d 1951), and Dulcie Alice, *née* Lisser (d 1943); *b* 11 Feb 1913; *Educ* Nottingham HS, Canford Sch; *m* 10 Sept 1947, Phyllis, da of Claude Chadburn (d 1977), of Nottinghamshire; 3 s (Ian b 1950, Michael b 1952, Shane b 1957); *Career* HM coroner: Nottingham 1951-81, Notts 1981-83; pres: Notts C of C 1963-64, Notts Law Soc 1965, Coroners Soc of Eng and Wales 1966; hon coroner Nottingham 1983; chm Derbys, Leics and Notts Agric Wages Ctee; *Recreations* shooting, horticulture; *Clubs* Victory Services; *Style*— Anthony C G Rothera, Esq; Normanton Hall, Southwell, Notts NG25 0PS

ROTHERHAM, Miles Edward; s of Leonard Rotherham, CBE, of Horningsham, Wilts, and Nora Mary, *née* Thompson; *b* 23 Nov 1941; *Educ* Dulwich, Christ's Coll cambridge (BA, MA); *m* 8 April 1972, Anne Jennifer, da of Maj Alan Holier James, TD, DL (d 1983), of Northlands, Winterton, South Humberside; 1 s (James b 1976), 1 da (Joanna b 1978); *Career* tech offr INCO 1964-68, sales mangr Int Nickel 1968-78; dir: Amari World Metals 1978-, Br Petroleum Metals Mktg 1979-; princ rep Olympic Dam; friend of Battersea Park; Freeman City London 1978, Liveryman Worshipful Co of Goldsmith's 1981; CEng (1979), FIM (1979); *Recreations* antique collecting, boule; *Clubs* Athenaeum; *Style*— Miles Rotherham, Esq; Amari House, 52 Kingston upon Thames, Surrey (☎ 01 5496122, fax 01 730 3244, telex 886852)

ROTHERMERE, Mary, Viscountess; Mary; da of Kenneth Murchison, of Dallas, Texas, and formerly w of Richard Ohrstrom, of The Plains, Virginia; *m* 1966, as his 3 w, 2 Viscount Rothermere (d 1978); 1 s (Hon Esmond b 1967); *Style*— The Rt Hon Mary, Viscountess Rothermere; c/o Carmelite House, Carmelite St, London EC4

ROTHERMERE, 3 Viscount (UK 1919); Sir Vere Harold Esmond Harmsworth; 3 Bt (UK 1910); also Baron Rothermere (UK 1914); patron of three livings; s of 2 Viscount Rothermere (d 1978) and his 1 w Margaret Hunam, *née* Redhead; gn of 1 and last Viscount Northcliffe (d 1922) who founded the Daily Mail 1896, and also gs of 1 Viscount Rothermere who was first Air Sec 1917 and gave the RAF its first twin engine monoplane 1935; *b* 27 August 1925; *Educ* Eton, Kent Sch Conn USA; *m* 1957, Patricia Evelyn Beverley, da of John Matthews, and former w of Capt Christopher Brooks (gs of 2 Baron Crawshaw); 1 s, 2 da, 1 step da; *Heir* s, Hon Jonathan Harmsworth; *Career* chm & ch exec Associated Newspapers Gp 1971-; chm: Daily Mail and Gen Tst 1978-; dir Consolidated Bathurst (Canada); tstee: Reuters, Visnews; pres: Cwlth Press Union 1983-; FRSA, FBIM; Commendatore Ordine Merito Italia 1977, Cdr Lion of Finland 1978; *Recreations* reading, painting, walking; *Clubs* Royal Yacht Sqdn, Beefsteak, The Brook (NY), Boodles, Travellers (Paris); *Style*— The Rt Hon the Viscount Rothermere; 36 Rue du Sentier, Paris 75002, France; Associated Newspapers Holdings plc, New Carmelite House, Carmelite St, London EC4Y 0JA (☎ 01 353 6000)

ROTHERWICK, 2 Baron (UK 1939); Sir (Herbert) Robin Cayzer; 2 Bt (UK 1924); s of 1 Baron Rotherwick, JP, DL (d 1958 5 s of Sir Charles Cayzer 1 Bt, cr 1904) and Freda, da of Col William Rathborne, of Co Cavan; *b* 5 Dec 1912; *Educ* Eton, Ch Ch Oxford; *m* 1952, Sarah Jane (d 1978), da of Sir Michael Slade, 6 Bt; 3 s, 1 da; *Heir* s, Hon Herbert Cayzer; *Career* WW II Mid East 1939-45, late Maj The Greys (supp reserve); dep chm Br & Cwlth Shipping Co & Assoc Cos; *Recreations* racing, shooting; *Clubs* White's, Turf; *Style*— The Rt Hon Lord Rotherwick; Cornbury Park, Charlbury, Oxon (☎ 810311); 50 Eaton Mews North, SW1 (☎ 01 235 6314)

ROTHES, 21 Earl of (S before 1457); Ian Lionel Malcolm Leslie; also Lord Leslie and Ballenbreich; s of 20 Earl of Rothes (d 1975) and Beryl, Countess of Rothes, *qv*; 3 Earl k at Flodden 1513, 6 Earl one of first signatories of Nat Covenant 1638, 7 Earl was inprisoned during Cwlth for supporting the King but was rewarded with a Dukedom on the Restoration (regranted Earldom in default of male issue upon his el da and her descendants male and female 1663) d 1681 when suc by his da, w of 5 Earl of Haddington, on her d in 1700 Rothes passed to her eld s and Haddington to 2 s; *b* 10 May 1932; *Educ* Eton; *m* 8 July 1955, Marigold, o da of Sir David Martyn Evans-Bevan, 1 Bt; 2 s; *Heir* s, Lord Leslie; *Career* late Sub-Lt RNVR; *Style*— The Rt Hon the Earl of Rothes; Tanglewood, W Tytherley, Salisbury, Wilts

ROTHNIE, Sir Alan Keir; KCVO (1980), CMG (1967); s of John Rothnie (d 1962), of Aberdeen, and Dora Rothnie; *b* 2 May 1920; *Educ* Montrose Acad, St Andrews Univ; *m* 1953, Anne Cadogan, da of late Euan Cadogan Harris, 2 s, 1 da; *Career* RN (Atlantic and N Russia) WW II; FO 1945, 1 sec 1952, cnsllr Baghdad 1963-64, Moscow 1965-68, consul-gen Chicago 1969-72, ambassador to: Saudi Arabia 1972-76, Switzerland 1976-80; Hon LLD St Andrews 1981; *Clubs* White's, MCC, Royal and Ancient (St Andrews); *Style*— Sir Alan Rothnie, KCVO, CMG; Little Job's Cross, Rolvenden Layne, Kent TN17 4PP

ROTHSCHILD, Hon Amschel Mayor James; s of 3 Baron Rothschild, GBE, GM, and his 2 w, Teresa; *b* 18 April 1955; *Educ* Leys Sch Cambridge, City Univ London; *m* 1981, Anita, 3 da of James Guinness (s of Sir Arthur Guinness, KCMG, of the Irish brewing and banking family); 1 s (b 1985), 2 da (b 1982, b 1983); *Style*— The Hon Amschel Rothschild; 11 Herschel Rd, Cambridge CB3 9AG (☎ (0223) 350488)

ROTHSCHILD, Hon Elizabeth Charlotte; da of late Hon (Nathaniel) Charles Rothschild, 2 s of 1 Baron Rothschild; sister of 3 Baron; raised to rank of a Baron's da 1938; *b* 1909; *Style*— The Hon Elizabeth Rothschild

ROTHSCHILD, Hon (Nathaniel Charles) Jacob; s and h of 3 Baron Rothschild, GBE, GM by his 1 w; *b* 29 April 1936; *Educ* Eton, Ch Ch Oxford; *m* 1961, Serena, da of Sir Philip Dunn, 2 Bt, by Lady Mary St Clair-Erskine (da of 5 Earl of Rosslyn); 1 s (Nathaniel), 3 da (Hannah b 1962, Beth b 1964, Emily b 1967); *Career* chm: J Rothschild Hldgs plc, bd of Tstees Nat Gallery; *Clubs* White's; *Style*— The Hon Jacob Rothschild; Stowell Park, Marlborough, Wilts; 14 St James's Place, London SW1A 1NP

ROTHSCHILD, Leopold David de; CBE (1985); 2 s of Maj Lionel de Rothschild, OBE (*see* Edmund de Rothschild); *b* 12 May 1927; *Educ* Harrow, Trin Cambridge; *Career* dir: Sun Alliance & London Insur 1982-, N M Rothschild & Sons 1970-, Bank of Eng 1970-83; chm: Eng Chamber Orch & Music Soc Ltd, Bach Choir; FRCM; *Style*— Leopold de Rothschild Esq, CBE; New Court, St Swithin's Lane, London EC4P 4DU (☎ 01 280 5000, telex 888031)

ROTHSCHILD, Hon Miranda; da of 3 Baron Rothschild, GBE, GM, by his 1 w; *b* 25 Dec 1940; *Style*— The Hon Miranda Rothschild

ROTHSCHILD, Hon Sarah; da of 3 Baron Rothschild, GBE, GM, by his 1 w; *b* 13 Sept 1934; *Educ* St Hilda's Oxford; *Style*— The Hon Sarah Rothschild

ROTHSCHILD, 3 Baron (UK 1885); Sir (Nathaniel Mayer) Victor Rothschild; 4 Bt (UK 1847), GBE (1975), GM (1944); also a Baron of the Austrian Empire (1822); s of Hon (Nathaniel) Charles Rothschild (2 s of 1 Baron, who himself was gs of Nathan Mayer Rothschild, the first of the family of financiers to settle in the UK; the name comes from Nathan's f having lived at the sign of the Rot Schild, Judengasse, Frankfurt; *b* 31 Oct 1910; *Educ* Harrow, Trinity Coll Cambridge (PhD, ScD; prize fell, hon fellow); *m* 1, 28 Dec 1933 (m dis 1946), Barbara, o da of late St John Hutchinson, KC; 1 s (Hon Jacob *qv*), 2 da (Hon Sarah *qv*, Hon Miranda *qv*); m 2, 14 Aug 1946, Teresa Georgina, MBE, MA, 2 da of Robert John Grote Mayor, CB, and (Katharine) Beatrice, da of Daniel Meinertzhagen, of Mottisfont Abbey, Romsey, and Brockwood Park, Alresford, sr ptnr of Frederick Huth & Co Merchant Bankers; *see* Nicholas Meinertzhagen); 1 s (Hon Amschel *qv*) (and 1 s decd), 2 da (Hon Emma *qv*, Hon Victoria *qv*); *Heir* s, Hon (Nathaniel Charles) Jacob Rothschild; *Career* served WW II in Intelligence Corps (Lt-Col, despatches); (American Legion of Merit, American Bronze Star); fell Trinity Coll Cambridge 1935-39 (hon fell 1961), dir BOAC 1946-48, chm Agric Res Cncl 1948-58, chm Risby Fruit Farms Ltd 1949-, asst dir of Res Dept of Zoology Cambridge 1950-70, vice-chm Shell Research 1961-63, chm 1963-70, chm Shell Res NV 1967-70; dir Shell Internationale Research Mij 1965-70, Shell Chems UK 1963-70, Shell Int Gas 1969-70; res co-ordinator Royal Dutch Shell Gp 1965-70; dir-gen and first perm under-sec Centl Policy Review Staff Cabinet Office 1971-74; chm: Rothschilds Continuation 1976-, Biotechnology Investments Ltd 1981-, Rothschilds Continuation Hldgs A G 1982-; dir: N M Rothschild & Sons (chm 1975-76), Rothschild Inc 1976-85; memb: BBC Gen Advsy Cncl 1952-56, Cncl for Scientific Policy 1965-67, Central Advsy Cncl for Science & Technol 1969; chm Royal Cmmn on Gambling 1976-78, head of independent review SSRC 1981; hon fellowships: Wolfson Coll Cambridge, Inst of Biol, Imperial Colol; recipient of many hon degrees incl: Hon DSc (Newcastle Univ, Manchester Univ, City Univ London, Univ of Bath), Hon LLD London, Hon DUniv York; Melchett Medal, RSA Medal; Hon Fellow: Bellairs Research Inst of McGill Univ, Barbados, Weizmann Inst of Science, Rehovoth; Hon PhD Tel Aviv, Hebrew Univ of Jerusalem, Bar-Ilan, Israel; Lectures: 4 Royal Soc Technology Lecture 1970; Trueman Wood Lecture RSA, 1972; Dimbleby Lecture 1978; KStJ 1948; FRS 1953, FSS 1984, FRSE 1986; - Wolfson Coll Cambridge, Inst of Biol, Imperial Coll; recipient of many hon degrees incl: Hon DSc (Newcastle Univ, Manchester Univ, City Univ London, Univ of Bath), Hon LLD London, Hon DUniv York; Melchett Medal, RSA Medal; Hon Fellow: Bellairs Research Inst of McGill Univ, Barbados, Weizmann Inst of Science, Rehovoth; Hon PhD Tel Aviv, Hebrew

Univ of Jerusalem, Bar-Ilan, Israel; Lectures: 4 Royal Soc Technology Lecture 1970; Trueman Wood Lecture RSA, 1972; Dimbleby Lecture 1978; KStJ 1948; *Books* Fertilization (1956), A Classification of Living Animals (1961), The History of Tom Jones, a Changeling (1951), The Rothschild Library (1954, 1969), A Framework for Govt Research and Development (1971), The Rothschild Family Tree (1973 and 1981), Meditations of a Broomstick (1977), You Have It, Madam (1980), An Enquiry into the Social Science Research Cncl (1982), The Shadow of a Great Man (1982), Random Variables (1984), Probability Distributions (with N Logothetis, 1986); *Clubs* Pratt's; *Style—* The Rt Hon the Lord Rothschild, GBE, GM

ROUBANIS, Lady Sarah Consuelo; *née* Spencer-Churchill; da of 10 Duke of Marlborough (d 1972); *b* 1921; *m* 1, 1943 (m dis 1966), Lt Edwin F Russell, USA Navy; 4 da; m 2, 1966 (m dis 1967), Guy Burgos, of Santiago, Chile; m 3, 1967, Theodorous Roubanis; *Style—* Lady Sarah Roubanis; 9454 Lloyd Crest Drive, Beverley Hills, Los Angeles, Calif 90210, USA

ROUECHÉ, Mossman (Jr); s of Col Mossman Roueché, of Sarabota, Florida, USA, and Elizabeth Molin, *née* Meier; *b* 14 Dec 1947; *Educ* Montgomery Blair HS Maryland USA, Kenyon Coll Ohio USA (BA), State Univ of NY at Buffalo (MA); *m* 29 July 1972, Charlotte Mary, da of Charles Percy Tunnard Wrinch, of Guernsey, CI; 1 s (Thomas b 1986), 1 da (Alice b 1979); *Career* trainee Standard Chartered Bank plc 1973-75, dir Samuel Montagu & Co Ltd 1986-; memb: cncl Soc for Premotion of Roman Studies, PCC St Magnus the Martyr Church; *Recreations* archaeology; *Style—* Mossman Roueché, Esq; 19 Bartholomew Villas, London NW5 2LJ; Box Cottage, Fisher's Lane, Charlbury, Oxon; 10 Lower Thames St, London EC2 (☎ 01 260 9170)

ROUGIER, Maj-Gen (Charles) Jeremy; CB (1986); s of Lt Col C L Rougier, MC (d 1940), and Marjorie Alice *née* Tanner (d 1981); *b* 23 Feb 1933; *Educ* Marlborough Coll; Pembroke Coll, Cambridge (MA); *m* 5 Dec 1964, Judith Cawood, da of Alan Wheen Ellis (d 1945); 3 s (Johnathan b 1966, Toby b 1967, Fergus b 1970); 1 da (Beth b 1971); *Career* Aden 1960; instr RMA Sandhurst 1961-62; psc 1963; MA to MGO 1964-66; Cdr 11 Engr Sqn, Cwlth Bde 1966-68; jssc 1968; Co Cdr RMA Sandhurst 1969-70; DSD, Staff College Camberley 1970-72; CO 21 Engr Regt BAOR 1972-4; staff of CDS 1974-77; Cmd Royal Sch of Mil 1977-79; RCDS 1980; COS HQ N I 1981; ACGS (Trg) 1982-83; dir of Army Trg 1983-84; chm Review of Offr Trg and Educn Study 1985; Engr-in-Chief (Army) 1985-88; ret; dir RHS Garden Rosemoor 1988-; FICE (1986); *Recreations* squash, hill walking, DIY, gardening; *Clubs* Army and Navy; *Style—* Maj-Gen Jeremy Rougier, CB; RHS Garden Rosemoor, Great Torrington, Devon EX38 7EG

ROUGIER, Sir Richard George; s of GR Rougier, CBE, QC (d 1977), and Georgette, *née* Heyer (d 1974); *b* 12 Feb 1932; *Educ* Marlborough, Pembroke Coll Cambridge (BA); *m* 2 June 1962, Susanna Allen, da of Harvey Allen Whitworth, MC (d 1959); 1 s (Nicholas Julian b 23 Feb 1966); *Career* QC 1972, rec 1973, high Ct Judge 1986; kt 1986; *Recreations* fishing, bridge, golf; *Clubs* Garrick, Rye GC; *Style—* Sir Richard Rougier, KB; Royal Courts of Justice, Strand, London WC2

ROUMANIA, HRH The Princess Helen of; 2 da of HM King Michael of Roumania, GCVO, and HM Queen Anne of Roumania, *née* HRH Princess Anne of Bourbon-Parma; *b* 15 Nov 1950; *Educ* in Switzerland and England; *m* 24 Sept 1983, Dr (Leslie) Robin Medforth-Mills, *qv*; 1 s (Nicholas Michael de Roumanie Medforth-Mills b 1 April 1985), 1 da (Elisabetta Karina b 4 Jan 1989); *Style—* HRH The Princess Helen of Roumania, Mrs Robin Medforth-Mills ; Flass Hall, Esh Winning, Durham DH7 9QD

ROUND, Ivan Frederick; s of Jame Round (d 1966), of 26 Newtown Lane, Cradley Heath, Warley, W Midlands, and Alice Beatrice, *née* Hickman (d 1960); *b* 9 Dec 1931; *Educ* King Edward The IV GS Stourbridge; *m* 10 May 1951, Margaret (d 1974), da of Ernest David Willetts, of Rowley Regis Watley, W Midlands; 2 s (Gary b 5 Oct 1963, Nigel b 12 May 1967); *Career* chm: J Round & Sons (H/F) Ltd 1960-, Sades of Brown Ltd 1984-; offr i/c Halesowen Rotaract Club; *Recreations* yacthing, racket ball, badminton, tennis; *Clubs* The Carton Halesowen; *Style—* Ivan Round, Esq; 41 Bromsgroe Rd, Romsley, Halesowen, Worcs B62 0LE (☎ 0562 710 779); La Luna, 130 St Anthoney St, Bugibba, St Pauls Bay, Malta; 7/10 High St, Cradley Heath, Warley, W Midlands (☎ 0384 66301)

ROUND, Prof Nicholas Grenville; s of Isaac Eric Round, and Laura Christabel, *née* Poole; *b* 6 June 1938; *Educ* Launceston Coll Cornwall, Pembroke Coll Oxford (BA, MA, DPhil); *m* 2 April 1966, Ann, da of Louis Le Vin; 1 da (Grainne Ann b 1968); *Career* Queen's Univ Belfast: lectr in spanish 1962-71, reader in spanish 1971-72, warden Alanbrooke Hall 1970-72; Stevenson prof of hispanic studies Univ of Glasgow 1972-; exec memb: Clydebank/Milngarie Constituency Lab Pty (former vice chm), Strathclyde West Euro - Constituency Lab Pty, Strathclyde Regal Lab Pty; memb: MLA, MHRA, SSMLL, AHGPI, AIM; *Books* Unamuno: Abel Sánchez (1974), The Greatest man Uncrowned: A Study of the Fall of Don Alvaro de Luna (1986), Tirso de Molina: Damned for Despair (1986); *Recreations* music, reading, drawing, hill walking, politics, all aspects of Cornwall; *Clubs* Queen's Univ Belfast Student's Union (hon life memb); *Style—* Prof Nicholas Round; 11 Dougalston Ave, Milngavie, Glasgow G62 (☎ 041 956 2507); Dept of Hispanic Studies, Univ of Glasgow, Glasgow G12 8QL (☎ 041 339 8855, ext 8665)

ROUNDELL, James; s of Charles Wilbraham Roundell, and Ann, *née* Moore; *b* 23 Oct 1951; *Educ* Winchester, Magdalene Coll Cambridge (BA); *m* 3 May 1975, Alexandra Jane, da of Sir Cyril Stanley Pickard; 1 s (Thomas b 1979), 1 da (Rebecca b 1982); *Career* Chrisites Fine Art Auctioneers 1973-: i/c of 18th and 19th Century English drawings and watercolours 1974-76, dir Old Master & Modern Prints 1976-86, dir Impressionist and Modern Pictures 1986- (during which time handled the sale of two of the three most expensive pictures ever sold; Cambridge Blue at Cricket; Liveryman Worshipful Co of Grocers 1981 (Freeman 1972); *Books* Thomas Shotter Boys (1975); *Recreations* cricket, opera; *Clubs* Hurlingham, MCC, 1Z + various cricket clubs; *Style—* James Roundell, Esq; Christie's, 8 King St, St James's, London SW1 (☎ 01 839 9060)

ROUNTHWAITE, Francis Anthony; s of George William Rounthwaite (d 1963), and Eileen May, *née* Jones; *b* 3 Jan 1941; *Educ* Newcastle-Upon-Tyne Royal GS, Univ of Durham (BA); *m* 19 March 1966, Shirley Mabel, da of Harold William Perkins, of Lanchester, Tyne & Wear; 1 s (Graham b 1969), 1 da (Julia); *Career* accountant Deloitte Haskins and Sells 1963-66, gen mangr for fin planning Euro operations Massey Ferguson (UK) 1967-70, memb nat mgmnt bd Robson Rhodes (apptd mangng ptnr West Midlands 1987) 1970-, capt Berkswell Tennis Club; FCA 1966; *Recreations* tennis, skiing, gardening; *Clubs* Balsall Common Lions; *Style—* Francis Rounthwaite, Esq; 62 Kelsey Lane, Balsall Common, Coventry CV7 7GL (☎ 0676 32451); Robson Rhodes, Centre City Tower, 7 Hill St, Birmingham B5 4UU (☎ 021 643 5494, fax 021 643 7738, car tel 0860 373 043)

ROUNTREE, His Hon Judge Peter Charles Robert; s of Francis Robert George Rountree, MBE (d 1986), of Sark, C I, and Mary Felicity Patricia Rountree, MBE (d 1983); *b* 28 April 1936; *Educ* Uppingham, St John's Coll Cambridge (MA); *m* 20 Dec 1968, Nicola Mary, da of Nicholas Norman Norman-Butler, TD, DL (d 1971), of Leez Priory, Hartford End, Essex; 1 s (James Alexander Francis b 7 Dec 1975); *Career* called to the Bar 1961, recorder 1986; Circuit judge 1986-; Inner Temple; *Recreations* sailing, golf, tennis; *Clubs* RYS, Bar Yacht (Cdre), New Zealand Golf, Rye Coy, RAC; *Style—* His Hon Judge Peter Rountree

ROUS, Lady Henrietta Elizabeth; da of 5 Earl of Stradbroke (d 1983), and The Hon Mrs Keith Rous, *qv*; *b* 1947; *Style—* Lady Henrietta Rous; Clovelly Court, Bideford, Devon

ROUS, Lady Ingrid Arnel; el da (by 1 m) of 6 Earl of Stradbroke, *qv*; *b* 1963; *Style—* Lady Ingrid Rous

ROUS, Hon John; s of 5 Earl of Stradbroke (d 1983), and his 2 wife, Hon Mrs Keith Rous, *qv*; *b* 31 July 1950; *Educ* Gordonstoun, Kent Univ; *m* 12 Nov 1984, Zeenat, da of Dr A Hameed (d 1976), of Lucknow; 1 da (Maha Magdalene b 1987); *Style—* The Hon John Rous; Clovelly Court, Bideford, Devon; 83 Flood St, London SW3

ROUS, Hon Mrs Keith; (April) Mary; does not use style of Mary, Countess of Stradbroke; da of Brig-Gen the Hon Arthur Melland Asquith, DSO (d 1939; s of 1 Earl of Oxford and Asquith, KG, PC), and Betty Constance (d 1962; da of Lord Manners); *b* 14 April 1919; *Educ* at home and in Paris, Vienna, Florence; *m* 1943, as his 2 w, Hon (William) Keith Rous, 5 Earl of Stradbroke (d 1983, 4 days after succeeding his brother, 4 Earl); 1 s, 3 da (and 1 da decd); *Recreations* reading, gardening, cooking for guests; *Style—* The Hon Mrs Keith Rous; Clovelly Court, Bideford, N Devon (☎ 023 73

ROUS, Lady Marye Violet Isolde; er da of 4 Earl of Stradbroke (d 1983); *b* 16 Mar 1930; *Style—* Lady Marye Rous; Sacaba Beach, Malaga 29004 (☎ 952 360979)

ROUS, Hon Peter James Mowbray; s of late 3 Earl of Stradbroke, KCMG, CB, CVO, CBE and Dame Helena, DBE, da of late Lt-Gen James Fraser, CMG; *b* 1914; *Educ* Harrow, Melbourne GS, Sandhurst; *m* 1942, Elizabeth Alice Mary (d 1968), da of late Maj the Hon Alastair Thomas Joseph Fraser, DSO, (s of 13 Lord Lovat), and Lady Sibyl, *née* Grimston, da of 3 Earl of Verulam; 6 s (and 2 s decd), 4 da; *Career* Maj (ret) 16/5 Lancers; *Style—* The Hon Peter Rous; c/o Drummond's Bank, 49 Charing Cross Rd, London SW1

ROUS, Lady Sophia Rayner; 2 da (by 1 m) of 6 Earl of Stradbroke, *qv*; *b* 1964; *Style—* Lady Sophia Rous

ROUS, Maj-Gen Hon William Edward; OBE (mil 1980, MBE mil 1974); s of 5 Earl of Stradbroke (d 1983), by 1 w, Pamela Catherine Mabell, later Hon Mrs Robert Pardoe (d 1972); bro of 6 Earl, *qv*; *b* 22 Feb 1939; *Educ* Harrow, RMA Sandhurst; *m* 1970, Judith Rosemary, da of Maj Jocelyn Arthur Persse, Rifle Bde (ka 1943); 2 s (James b 1972, Richard b 1975); *Career* cmmnd Coldstream Gds 1959, cmd 2 Bn 1979-81, Brig cmdg 1 Inf Bde 1983-84; dir of Public Relations (Army) 1985-87; Goc & Armd Div 1987-; *Style—* Maj-Gen the Hon William Rous, OBE; RHQ Goldstream Guards, Wellington Barracks, London SW1

ROUSE, Sir Anthony Gerald Roderick; KCMG (1969, CMG 1961), OBE (1945); s of Lt-Col Maxwell Emsley Rouse, JP, of Eastbourne, Sussex (d 1956), and Sybil Rose, *née* Thompson; *b* 1911; *Educ* Harrow; *m* 7 Sept 1935, Beatrice, da of Percival Ellis of Eastbourne (d 1962); *Career* HAC 1935, RA (TA) 1938, 2 Lt 1940 transferred Intelligence Corps served MEF and CMF on staff 3 Corps (commendation); Foreign Serv 1946, first sec (info) Athens 1946, transferred FO 1949, Br Embassy Moscow 1952-54, cnsllr 1955, off of UK high cmmr Canberra 1955-57, HM inspr Foreign Serv Estabs 1957-59, cnsllr (info) Br Embassy Bonn 1959-62, Br dep cmdt Berlin 1962-64, min Br Embassy Rome 1964-66, consul-gen NY 1966-71; *Style—* Sir Anthony Rouse, KCMG, OBE; St Ritas, Paradise Drive, Eastbourne, E Sussex

ROUSE, Clifford; s of Frank Leonard Rouse (d 1977), and May Theresa (d 1973); *b* 3 Sept 1930; *Educ* Malmesbury GS, St Luke's Coll Exeter; *m* 14 Aug 1952, Audrey Vera, da of William Foster (d 1972), of Exeter; 2 s (Andrew Clifford b 1955, Stephen Philip b 1957); *Career* dir of music Colfox Sch Bridport Dorset 1961-70, music advsr London Borough of Waltham Forest 1971-86 (ret); *Recreations* walking at home and abroad; *Style—* Clifford Rouse, Esq; Hill House, St Decumans Road, Watchet, Somerset TA23 0HR (☎ 0984 31668)

ROUSE, Lt Cdr (Derrick) Malcolm; MBE (1974); s of Claude Vernon Rouse, of Devon, and Beatrice Ada Saxby, *née* Wallacott (d 1984); *b* 14 Feb 1922; *Educ* UC Sch; *m* 30 July 1952, Eileen Patricia, da of Maj Arthur Douglas Ingrams (d 1988) 2 s (Justin b 1958, Benedict b 1965); 4 da (Corinne b 1953, Deborah b 1955, Arabella b 1956, Josephine b 1960); *Career* with Br Aeroplane Co 1939-42; RN 1942-77, Fleet Air Arm, Flag Lt and personal pilot to Flag Offr Naval Air Cmd 1963-66, Flag Lt to Dep Supreme Allied Cdr Atlantic 1966-69, CO 781 Sqdn 1970-76, dep dir Fleet Air Arm Museum 1976-77, ret; staff mangr Saccone and Speed Ltd Wine Merchants 1977-82, with David Burns Wine Merchants IOW 1982-85, ptnr in own Wine and Delicatessen Business 1985-; *Recreations* golf, fishing, sailing, theatre, photography; *Style—* Lt-Cdr Malcolm Rouse, MBE; The Dell, Bonchurch, IOW PO38 1NT (☎ 0983 852266); Benedict's, 28 Holyrood St, Newport, IOW PO30 5AU (☎ 0983 529596, telex 896466 TARVS)

ROUSE, Lt Cdr Peter James; s of Capt Norman S Rouse (d 1956), of Wilts, and Nancy A Campbell, *née* Johnston (d 1980); *b* 12 July 1922; *Educ* RNC Dartmouth; *m* 8 Sept 1951, Elizabeth Jeannette Stringer, da of P A S Sringer (d 1985), of Wilts; 1 s (Richard b 1956), 2 da (Nichola b 1953 (decd), Phillipa b 1954); *Career* ret RN 1954; Lloyds underwriter 1951-; *Recreations* sailing, general country recreations; *Clubs* Royal Lymington Yacht; *Style—* Lt Cdr Peter J Rouse; Tarrant House, Tiptoe, Lymington, Hants (☎ 0590 682213)

ROUSE, Richard Meadows; s of Philip Graves Rouse, and Maud, *née* Ellis; *b* 20 July 1931; *Educ* Uppingham, Christ's Coll Cambridge (BA); *m* 29 May 1965, Susan, da of Sidney Thomas Croker, of 48 Brim Hill, London; 2 s (William b 26 July 1966, James b 21 May 1969); *Career* 2 Lt Army 1950-51; int tax ptnr Arthur Young 1966- (joined 1963); churchwarden St Peters Church St Albans: FCA 1958; *Books* UK Taxation of Offshore Oil and Gas Butterworths (it author, 1980); *Recreations* sailing, stampcollecting; *Clubs* Reform; *Style—* Richard Rouse, Esq; Arthur Young, 7 Rolls

Biuldings, Fetter Lane, London EC4A 1NH (☎ 01 831 7130, fax 01 405 2147, telex 888604)

ROUSE-BOUGHTON, Lady; Elizabeth; *née* Hunter; da of late Ernest William Hathaway Hunter; *m* 1, 1933, Geoffrey Swaffer (d 1939); m 2, 1948, as his 2 wife, Maj Sir Edward Hotham Rouse-Boughton, 13 and last Bt (d 1963); *Style—* Lady Rouse-Boughton; Dickens Cottage, Seagrove Bay, Seaview, IOW

ROUSSEL, (Philip) Lyon; OBE (1974); s of Paul Marie Roussel (d 1958), and Lady Murray (Beatrice), *née* Cuthbert (d 1983); *b* 17 Oct 1923; *Educ* Hurstpierpoint Coll, St Edmund Hall Oxford (MA), Chelsea Sch of Art; *m* 18 July 1959, Elisabeth Mary, da of Kenneth Arnold Bennett (d 1988); 1 s (Edward b 1965), 1 da (Tanya b 1963); *Career* WWII Maj Indian Parachute Regt 1942-46, demob with hon rank of Maj; Sudan Political serv Kassala Upper Nile 1950-55, princ WO 1955-56, Assoc Newspapers 1956-57, Br Cncl 1960-83; India 1960-71: regnl rep Western and Central India 1964-71; rep and cultural attaché Br Embassy Belgium and Luxembourg 1971-76, "Europalia" Great Br Festival ctee 1973, cultural cnsllr and head cultural dept Br Embassy Washington 1976-79, controller arts div Br Cncl 1979-83, memb Festival of India ctee 1981-88, memb advsy ctee br Salutes NY 1981-83, sponsorship conslt Nat Theatre 1983-84, freelance artist 1984; memb: Br Legion Woodstock, common room Wolfson Coll Oxford; FRSA 1979; FRGS 1981; *Recreations* looking at and collecting pictures, travel, tennis; *Clubs* Athenaeum, Probus; *Style—* Lyon Roussel, Esq, OBE; 26 High St, Woodstock, Oxford OX7 1TG (☎ 0993 811 298); La Grange, Lacam, Loubressac, 46130, France

ROUT, Owen Howard; s of Frederick Owen Rout (d 1983), and Marion, *née* Salter (d 1972); *b* 16 April 1930; *Educ* Grey HS Port Elizabeth SA; *m* 27 Feb 1954, Jean, da of Alfred Greetham (d 1961); 2 da (Gillian (Mrs Catchpole) b 16 June 1959, Jacqueline b 26 Nov 1962); *Career* Barclays Bank: local dir York 1969-71, Chelmsford 1972-75, regnl gen mangr E Mids & E Anglia 1975-77, sr local dir Leeds dist 1977-81, chm W Yorks Local Bd 1977-81, dir Barclays Bank UK Ltd 1977-87, gen mangr Barclays Bank plc and Barclays plc 1982-87 (exec dir UK Ops 1987-), chm Barclays Insur Servs Co Ltd and Barclays Insur Brokers Int Ltd 1982-85, Barclays Fin Servs Ltd 1988-; dir: Baric Ltd 1982-84, Spreadeagle Insur Co Ltd 1983-85; cncl memb Chartered Inst of Bankers 1985-(tres 1986-), memb Supervisory Bd Banking World Magazine 1986-, dir Bankers Books Ltd 1986-; FCIB, ACIS; *Recreations* watching sport, playing golf, listening to music, gardening; *Clubs* Headingley Taverners (Leeds), Pannal GC (Harrogate), Saffron Walden GC; *Style—* Owen Rout, Esq; Barclays Bank plc, Head Office, 54 Lombard St, London EC3P 3AH (☎ 01 626 1567)

ROUTLEDGE, Alan; CBE (1979); s of George Routledge (d 1954), and Rose Routledge, *née* Briscoe (1986); *b* 12 May 1919; *Educ* Liscard HS, Wallasey; *m* 1949, Irene Jessie, da of David Hendry (d 1963), of Falkirk, Stirlingshire; 2 s; *Career* Control Cmmn Germany 1946-51, head cypher & signals branch Dip Wireless Serv FO 1962-73, head Communications Planning Staff FCO 1973-79, head Communications Ops Dept FCO 1979; ret; *Recreations* gardening, golf, watching cricket; *Clubs* Civil Service; *Style—* Alan Routledge, Esq, CBE; 15 Ilford Ct, Elmbridge, Cranleigh, Surrey GU6 8TJ

ROUTLEDGE, (Katherine) Patricia; da of Isaac Edgar Routledge (d 1985), of Birkenhead, Cheshire, and Catherine, *née* Perry (d 1957); *b* 17 Feb 1929; *Educ* Birkenhead HS, Univ of Liverpool (BA); *Career* actress and singer; trained Bristol Old Vic and with Walther Gruner Guildhall Sch of Music, first professional appearance as Hippolyta in A Midsummer Night's Dream Liverpool Playhouse 1952, first West End appearance in Sheridan's The Duenna Westminster Theatre 1954, first Broadway appearance in How's the World Treating You? Music Box New York 1966 (Whitbread Award), Darling of the Day Broadway 1968 (Antionette Perry Award), Love Match Ahmanson Theatre Los Angeles 1968-69, Cowardy Custard Mermaid Theatre 1972-73, Noises Off Savoy Theatre 1981, Queen Margaret in Richard III RSC 1984-85 (Laurence Olivier Award Nomination), The Old Lady in Candide Old Vic 1988-89 (Laurence Olivier Award Nomination), Come for the Ride (solo show) 1988; recent tv appearances incl: Sophia and Constance, A Woman of No Importance (Broadcasting Press Guild Critics Award), A Lady of Letters (BAFTA Nomination); *Style—* Miss Patricia Routledge; Marmont Management Ltd, Langham Ho, 308 Regent St, London W1R 5AL (☎ 01 637 3183)

ROUTLEDGE, Paul; s of John James Routledge, of Surrey, and Barbara, *née* Saxton; *b* 23 Sept 1950; *Educ* E Grinstead GS; *m* 15 Aug 1979, Susan Jean, da of John Arthur Ashley, of Surrey; 1 s (James b 12 July 1988, 1 da (Gemma b 1982); *Career* CA 1975-; est own practice 1979; *Recreations* golf, boating; *Style—* Paul Routledge, Esq; The Owls, Cudworth Lane, Newdigate, Surrey; Abacus House, Wickhurst Lane Broadbridge Heath RH12 3LY (☎ 0403 210165, fax 0403 65886, car phone 0860 330612)

ROUTLY, (Ernest) John; s of Dr Ernest Sydney Routly (d 1931); *b* 4 Sept 1914; *Educ* Radley Gonville and Caius Coll Cambridge; *m* 1939, Alice Janet, JP, *née* Bailey; 2 da; *Career* RAFVR; slr; dir various cos incl: Rootes Gp 1946-60, William Baird 1960-66; fin advsr Help the Aged and Action Aid 1975, dir Andrews Gp Hldgs 1987-; memb Bucks CC 1965-80 (vice-chm 1977-79), High Sheriff of Bucks 1972-73; chm Festiniog Rly Co 1954-, dir Romney Hythe and Dragonchurch Rly 1986-; *Recreations* railways; *Clubs* E India, RAF; *Style—* John Routly, Esq; Ormonde House, 18 St John's Hill, Shrewsbury SY1 1JJ (☎ 0743 231489)

ROUX, Michel André; s of Henri Roux (d 1983), and Germaine, *née* Triger; *b* 19 April 1941; *Educ* Ecole Primaire Saint St Mandé France, Brevet de Maitrise Patisserie; *m* 1, (m dis 1979), Francoise Marcelle Bequet; 1 s (Alain b 1968), 2 da (Christine b 1963, Francine b 1965); m 2, 21 May 1984 Robyn Margaret Joyce; *Career* French Mil Sev 1960-62; Versailles 1960, Colomb Bechar Algeria 1961-62, awarded the Medaille Commemorative des Operations de securité et de Maintien de L'Ordre en AFC avec Agiape Sahara BOPP no 42; commis patissier and cuisinier at Br Embassy Paris 1955-57, commis cook at Miss Cecile De Rothschild Paris 1957-59 (chef 1962-67); restaurants opened in England: Le Gavroche 1967, Le Poulbot 1969, Le Gamin 1971, The Waterside Inn 1972, Gavvers 1981, Le Gavroche (moved to Mayfair) 1981, Roux Britannia 1986, Les Trois Plats 1988; awards: Silver Medal des Cuisiniers Francais (Paris) 1963, Silver Medal Ville de Paris 1966, Silver Medal Sucre Tire et Souffle (London)1970, Prix International Taittinger (2nd, Paris) 1971, Gold Medal Cuisiniers Francais (Paris) 1972, Meilleur Ouvrier de France en Patisserie (Paris) 1976, Vermeil Medal du Prestige des Cuisiniers Francais (Paris) 1983, Lauréat Best Menu of the Year prepared for a Private Function (Caterer and Hotel keeper) 1984, Laureate Restauranteur of the Year (Caterer and Hotel keeper) 1985, Laureat du Premier Hommage Veuve Cliquot aux Ambassadeurs de la Cuisine Francaise dans le Monde (Paris) 1985, Laureat Personality of the Year Gastronomie dans le Monde (Paris) 1985, Laureat Culinary Trophy Personality of the Year in Patisserie (Assoc of French Patissiers de la Saint-Michel) 1986; memb: l'Acamedie Culinaire de France (UK branch), Assoc Relais et Desserts, Assoc Relais et Chateaux; Chevalier de l'Ordre National du Merite 1987, Officier du Merite Agricole 1987; *Books* New Classic Cuisine (1983), Roux Brothers on Patisserie (1986), At Home with the Roux Brothers (1987), French Country (1989); *Recreations* shooting, walking, skiing; *Clubs* The Benedicts; *Style—* Michel Roux, Esq; River Cottage, Ferry Rd, Bray, Berkshire SL6 2AT (☎ 0628 771966) The Waterside Inn, Ferry Rd, Bray, Berkshire SL6 2AT (☎ 0628 771966/20691, fax 0628 784710)

ROW, Hon Sir John Alfred; s of Charles Edward Row and Emily Harriet Row; *b* 1 Jan 1905; *Educ* Toowoomba GS, Trebonne State Sch; *m* 1, 1929, Gladys (decd), da of H E Hollins (decd); 1 da; m 2, 1966, Irene, da of F C Gough (decd); *Career* sugar cane farmer 1926-, memb Vic Mill Suppliers Ctee and Herbert River Cane Growers Exec 1932-60, rep Local Cane Prices Bd 1948-60, dir State Co-op Cane Growers' Store 1955-60; M:A (Country Pty) for Hinchinbrook Qld 1960-72, min for Primary Industs Qld 1963-72, ret; kt 1974; *Style—* The Hon Sir John Row; 10 Gort St, Ingham, Qld 4850, Australia

ROW, Cdr Sir Philip John; KCVO (1969, CVO 1965, MVO 1958), OBE (1944), RN; *Career* dep tres to HM the Queen 1958-68, extra equerry to HM the Queen 1969-; *Style—* Cdr Sir Philip Row, KCVO, OBE, RN; Warren Lodge, Warren Lane, Finchampstead, Berks RG11 4HR (☎ 0734 328835)

ROWALLAN, 3 Baron (UK 1911); Arthur Cameron Corbett; s of 2 Baron Rowallan, KT, KBE, MC, TD, DL (d 1977), and Gwyn, da of Joseph and sis of Rt Hon Lord Grimond, PC, *qv*; *b* 17 Dec 1919; *Educ* Eton, Balliol Coll Oxford; *m* 1, 1945 (m dis 1962), Eleanor, da of George Boyle (descent from David Boyle, Lord Justice Gen of Scotland *see* Peerage Earl of Glasgow by Mary, 2 da of Sir Peter Mackie, 1 and last Bt; 1 s (Maj-Gen Hon William, OBE *qv*), 3 da (Lady Christine Armstrong b 1946, Lady Henrietta b 1947, Lady Virginia Gibbs b 1954); m 2, 1963 (m annulled 1970), April Ashley; *Heir* s, Hon John Corbett; *Career* serv WWII, Capt Ayrshire Yeo; *Style—* The Rt Hon the Lord Rowallan; 22 Mediteranee, Torre de Marbella, Marbella, Spain

ROWAN, Jack; s of Harry Rowan (d 1955), of Abbeydale Road, Sheffield, and Mary, *née* Allen (d 1952); *b* 10 Feb 1927; *Educ* Greystones Intermediate Sch, Sheffield Commercial Coll; *m* 10 Oct 1959, (Constance) Shirley, da of William Barraclough (d 1980), of Bradford; 1 s (Steven b 12 March 1962), 1 da (Lisa b 25 Oct 1965); *Career* RNAS 1946-48; CA, sr ptnr Barber Harrison & Platt (ptnr 1955), dir Sheffield Refreshment Houses Ltd 1975-82; memb Accreditation bd Sheffield & Dist Soc of CAs, formerly area sec Round Tables of GB and Ireland, FCA 1950; *Recreations* golf, assisting daughter's equestrian activities; *Clubs* Sheffield, Abbeydale Golf; *Style—* Jack Rowan, Esq; 53 Heather Lea Ave, Dore, Sheffield (☎ 0742 366 050); Barber Harrison and Platt, 2 Rutland Park, Sheffield S10 2PD (☎ 0742 667 171, fax 0742 669 846)

ROWAN, Robert; s of Joseph Rowan, (d 1978), of Southend-on-Sea, and Anne, *née* Henderson; *b* 29 Nov 1934; *Educ* Westcliff-on-Sea HS, The Coll of Law; *m* 14 June 1958, Sandra Joyce, da of John Bertram Jackson (d 1974), of Ilford, Essex; 1 s (James Anthony Robert b 1965), 1 da (Claire b 1963); *Career* Nat Serv RAF 1953-55; inspr Guardian Royal Exchange Gp 1955-67, admitted slr 1970, sr ptnr Carter Faber 1970-; chm Writtle Cons Assoc 1982-86, memb Roywell Essex 1974-79; hon slr The Cruising Assoc 1985-; Freeman City of London, memb Worshipful Co of Carmen; memb Law Soc, FCII; *Recreations* sailing, shooting; *Clubs* RAC, Royal Harwich YC; *Style—* Robert Rowan, Esq; Ratcliffes, The green Writtle, Essex (☎ 0245 420918); Flat 46, St Georges Wharf, Shad, Thames, London SE1 (☎ 01 378 0161); Carter Faber, 10 Arthur St, London EC4R 9AY (☎ 01 929 5555, 01 929 3637, telex 887824)

ROWAN, Thomas Stanley; s of Thomas Rowan (d 1965); *b* 11 April 1935; *Educ* Wellington, Univ of Natal, Gonville and Caius Coll Cambridge (LLB); *m* 1964, Anne Strafford, *née* Sanderson; 1 s, 1 da; *Career* dir Singer & Friedlander Ltd 1975-; CA, FCA; *Recreations* golf; *Clubs* Leeds; *Style—* Thomas Rowan Esq; 2 St Leonards Rd, Harrogate, N Yorks (☎ home 0423 884588, office London (☎ 01 623 3000)

ROWAN-ROBINSON, Alan Francis Noel; s of Surgn Cdr The Rev Leslie Charles Rowan-Robinson, RN, MB, ChB (Edin) (d 1955), of Gt Houghton, Northamps, and Frances Dorothea, *née* Eteson (d 1964); *b* 23 Dec 1922; *Educ* Privately and Trinity Coll Cambridge (MA); *Career* headmaster Kingshott Sch, St Ippolyts, Hitchin, Hertfords 1959-80, ret (1980); *Recreations* train travel, walking, gardening; *Clubs* Utd Oxford and Cambridge, Naval; *Style—* Alan Rowan-Robinson, Esq; Round Hill, Ashbrook Lane, St Ippolyts, Hitchin, Herts SG4 7PB (☎ 0462 57419)

ROWAT, Lt Col David Peter; OBE (1972); s of Ernest Ivimy Rowat (d 1972), of Roquebrune, France, and Phyllis Esdon, *née* Rowat (d 1979); *b* 24 Nov 1928; *Educ* Charterhouse, RMA Sandhurst, Staff Coll Camberley, JSSC Latimer; *m* 11 May 1968, Elizabeth, da of Cdr Richard Paston Mack, MVO (d 1974), of West House, Droxford, Hants; 1 s (Peter b 1970), 1 da (Sarah b 1969); *Career* enlisted 1947, cmmnd 5 Royal Inniskilling Dragoon Guards 1949; served: Baor, Korea, Egypt, Aden, Bahrain, Cyprus; ADC to CINC MELF 1953-55, CO The Royal Yeomanry 1969-71; asst dir CLA Game Fair 1974-80; JP (1978); *Recreations* fishing, cricket, golf; *Clubs* MCC; *Style—* Lt Col David Rowat, OBE, JP

ROWBOTHAM, Graham William Henry; s of Frederick Rowbotham, of Canterbury, Kent, and Gladys Emma Ellen, *née* Andrews; *b* 25 June 1948; *Educ* The King's Sch Canterbury, St John's Coll Oxford (MA); *m* 7 Oct 1977, Susan (Sue), da of Anthony Thomas Gordon Turner (d 1980); 3 da (Sophie b 1978, Natasha b 1979, Gemma b 1983); *Career* slr; Srthur Andersen & Co 1969, Slaughter & May 1970-79, Simmons & Simmons 1980- (ptnr 1981-, head of Banking and Int Fin Gp 1985-); memb: editorial advsy bds Int Financial Law Review and Computer Law and Practice; memb Worshipful Co of Solicitors 1985; memb: Law Soc, Int Bar Assoc; *Recreations* lawn tennis, golf, real tennis, skiing, walking, reading; *Clubs* Roehampton, Royal Tennis Ct; *Style—* Graham W H Rowbotham, Esq; Simmons & Simmons, 14 Dominion St, London, EC2M 2RJ (☎ 01 628 2020, fax 01 588 4129 and 01 588 9418, telex 888562 SIMMON G)

ROWCLIFFE, Hon Mrs (Una Mary); *née* Slim; da of late 1 Viscount Slim, KG, GCB, GCMG, GCVO, GBE, DSO, MC; *b* 1930; *m* 1, 1953 (m dis 1979), Maj Peter Nigel Stewart Frazer, Gren Gds; 3 da; m 2, 1980, Ronald Rowcliffe; *Style—* The Hon Mrs

Rowcliffe; Bamson, Puddington, Tiverton, Devon

ROWE, Andrew John Bernard; MP (C) Mid-Kent 1983-; s of John Douglas Rowe (d 1960), and Mary Katherine Storr; *b* 11 Sept 1935; *Educ* Eton, Merton Coll Oxford (MA); *m* 1, 1960, Alison Boyd (m dis); 1 s (Nicholas); m 2, 1983, Sheila L Finkle; 2 step-da; *Career* tstee community serv volunteers, cncl memb Save the Children Fund; *Clubs* Carlton; *Style—* Andrew Rowe, Esq, MP; Tudor Milgate, Milgate Park, Thurnham, Maidstone, Kent ME14 4NN (☎ 0622 36809); House of Commons, London SW1A 0AA (☎ 01 219 3000)

ROWE, Sir Henry Peter; KCB (1978, CB 1971), QC (1978); 3 s of Dr Richard and Olga Röhr; *b* 18 August 1916; *Educ* Vienna, Gonville and Caius Coll Cambridge; *m* 1947, Patricia, da of R W King; 2 s, 1 da; *Career* first Parly counsel 1977-81; barr 1947, Parly counsel off 1947-, jt second Parly counsel 1973-76; *Style—* Sir Henry Rowe, KCB, QC; 19 Paxton Gdns, Woking, Surrey (☎ 91 43816)

ROWE, Ian Alastair; s of Albert Rowe, (d 1947), of Vienna, Austria, and Rose Marian, *née* Sheffield; *b* 23 June 1931; *Educ* Brentwood Sch; *m* 5 July 1971, Suzy Gay Denise, da of Howard Philip Baker (d 1984), of Knowle, Warwicks; 1 s (Alastair b 1975), 1 da (Samantha b 1972); *Career* Nat Serv 2 Lt army 1949-51, Capt AVR; articles 1952-57; Meridian Deposit Brokers: euro fin controller 1959-64, euro tresy mangr 1965-69, fin dir 1973-; memb: ACA 1958-62, FCA 1963-; *Recreations* amateur racing driving, vintage veteran car competitor; *Clubs* VSCC, VCC, RREC; *Style—* Ian Rowe, Esq; Meridian Deposit Brokers Ltd, Dark House, 16 Finsbury Circus, London EC2M 7DJ (☎ 01 588 1431)

ROWE, Jeremy; CBE (1980); s of Col Charles William Dell Rowe, CB, MBE (d 1954); *b* 31 Oct 1928; *Educ* Uppingham, Trinity Coll Cambridge; *m* 1957, Susan Mary, da of Cdr Richard Noel Johnstone, RN; 4 da; *Career* dep chm Abbey Nat Building Soc 1978-; chm: London Brick plc 1979-84, Peterborough Devpt Corp 1981-88, Occupational Pensions Bd 1987-, Family AssurSoc 1986-; dir: Sun Alliance Insur Gp W End Bd 1978-, John Maunders Gp plc 1984-; Telephone Rentals plc 1984-89, Kingsgrange plc 1987-; *Recreations* tennis, shooting, travel, music, history; *Clubs* All England Tennis, Buck's; *Style—* Jeremy Rowe, Esq, CBE; Woodside, Peasmarsh, Rye, Sussex (☎ 079 721 335)

ROWE, Norman Lester; CBE (1976); s of Arthur William Rowe, OBE (d 1957) and Lucy Lester, *née* Adams (d 1980); *b* 15 Dec 1915; *Educ* Malvern Coll & Guy's Hosp Univ of London; *m* 17 Sept 1938, Cynthia Mary, da of Augustus Morris Freeman (d 1948); 1 s (David b 1939), 1 da (Susan b 1941); *Career* WWII Capt RADC 1941-46 (France and Germany 1944-46); sr registrar plastic and jaw injuries unit Hill End Hosp St Albans 1947, conslt oral surgery plastic and oral surgery centre Rooksdown Ho Basingstoke and SW Met RHB 1948-59, conslt to RN 1955-80; conslt oral and maxillofacial surgery: Queen Mary's Hosp Roehampton 1959-80, The Westminster Hosp 1961-80, The Inst of Dental Surgery 1961-74, Eastman Dental Hosp London 1961-74; conslt to Army 1969-80, ret 1980, emeritus conslt 1981; visiting prof Univs: Seattle, Witswaterand, Hadesseh, Baghdad, Khartoum, Kuwait, Santiago, Montevideo; memb bd of faculty of dental surgery RCS 1956-74 (vice-dean 1967), Webb-Johnson Lectr 1967-69; former examiner RCS: England, Edinburgh, Glasgow, Ireland; sec gen Int Assoc of Oral and Maxillofacial Surgns 1968-71 (hon fell 1986), pres BAOMS 1969 (hon fell 1981), pres Europ Assoc for Cranio-Maxillo-Facial Surgery 1974-76 (hon member 1980); Down's Surgical Prize Medal (BAOMS) 1976, Colyer Gold Medal (RCS) 1981, Tomes' Medal (Br Dental Assoc) 1985; memb numerous overseas socs; hon FDSRCS: Glasgow 1979, Edinburgh 1981; hon FRCS Edinburgh 1986; memb: BDA, BMA, BAOMS, IAOMS, EACMFS, OSC (GB); *Books* Fractures of the Facial Skeleton (second edn 1968), Maxillofacial Injuries (1985); *Recreations* music and photography; *Clubs* Royal Naval Medical; *Style—* Norman Rowe, CBE; Brackendale, Holly Bank Rd, Hook Heath, Woking, Surrey GU22 0JP (☎ 0483 760008)

ROWE, Richard Brian (Dick); s of Charles Albert Rowe (d 1967), of Perivale, Middx, and Mabel Florence, *née* Waller (d 1971); *b* 28 April 1933; *Educ* Greenford Co GS, King's Coll London Univ (LLB); *m* 19 March 1959, Shirley Ann, da of William G Symons, of Alum Chine, Bournemouth, Hants; 2 da (Melissa Jane b 1965, Hollie Ann b 1968); *Career* Nat Serv RAF 1952-54; Land Cmmn 1966-69, Lord Chllrs Off house of Lords 1969-75, registrar family div High Ct 1979- (probate divorce and admty div 1954-66, sec family div 1975-79); *Books* Rayden on Divorce (ed 1967), Tristram and Coote's Probate Practice (ed 1978, 1983, 1989); *Recreations* most sports; *Clubs* MCC; *Style—* Mr Dick Rowe, Esq; Principal Registry Family Division (High Court), Somerset House Strand, London WC2 1LP

ROWE, Robert Stewart; CBE (1969); s of James Stewart Rowe, MBE (d 1960), and Anna Gray Gillespie (d 1973); *b* 31 Dec 1920; *Educ* private tutors, Downing Coll Cambridge (MA); *m* 1953, Barbara Elizabeth Hamilton, da of Thomas Austin Hamilton Baynes, OBE (d 1973); 1 s, 2 da; *Career* RAF 1941-46; asst keeper of art Birmingham Art Gallery 1950-56, dep dir Manchester City Art Galleries 1956-58, dir Leeds City Art Gallery, Temple Newsam House and Lotherton Hall 1958-83; memb art panel Arts Cncl of GB 1959-62 and 1969-74, memb advsy cncl V&A Museum 1969-74, pres Museums Assoc 1973-74, memb Arts Cncl of GB 1981-86, memb exec cncl Yorks Arts Assoc 1973-84, tstee Henry Moore Sculpture Tst 1983-, chm Bar Convent Museum York 1986; Hon DLitt Leeds; *Publications* Adam Silver (1965); *Recreations* reading, writing, gardening; *Style—* Robert Rowe, Esq, CBE; Grove Lodge, Shadwell, Leeds LS17 8LB (☎ 0532 656365)

ROWE-HAM, Sir David Kenneth; s of Kenneth Henry Ham, and Muriel Phyllis Rowe; *b* 19 Dec 1935; *Educ* Dragon,Charterhouse; *m* 1 (m dis 1980), Elizabeth, *née* Aston; 1 s (Adrian); m 2, 1980, Sandra Celia, widow of Ian Glover; 1 s (Mark b 1981), and 1 adopted (step)s (Gerald); *Career* CA since 1962; Lord Mayor of London 1986-87; conslt Touche Ross and Co 1984-; dir public and private cos including chm Asset Tst plc 1982-, cmmnd 3 King's own Hussars, sr ptnr Smith keen Cutler 1972-82; dir: The 1928 Investmt Tst 1984-86; regnl dir Lloyds Bank 1985-; dir W Canning plc 1981-86 (consultant 1986-); Savoy Theatre Ltd 1986; Advisory Panel Fund Mngrs Ltd 1986- (chm 1987); Alderman City of London Ward of Bridge and Bridge Without 1976-; Sheriff City of London 1984-85; chm: Birmingham municipal Bank 1970-72, political cncl jr Carlton Club 1977; dep chm political ctee Carlton Club 1977-79; chief Magistrate of the City of London 1986-87; Adm of the Port of London 1986-87; memb: Soc of Investment Analysists, Stock Exchange 1964-84, Crt memb City Univ 1981-86 (Chllr 1986-87); memb: Worshipful Co of CA in England and Wales (Master 1985-86), Worshipful Co of Wheelwrights; Hon memb Worshipful Co of Landerers, memb Ct HAC, memb Guild of Freeman; Princess Youth Tst 1986-87; Royal Shakespeare Theatre Tst; tstee Friends of D'oly Carte, memb: Lord Taveners, Utd Wards Club Govr Hosp, JP City of London 1976, FCA Hon DLitt City Univ 1986, Cdr O of the Lion of Malawi 1985; Commandeur de l'Ordre Me'rite France 1984, Order of the Aztec. Eagle (CI II) Mexico 1987; holder of the P Pedro Ernesto Medal (Rio de Janero) 1987; Order of Diego Losada of Caracas 1987; Her Majesty's Commn of Lieutenancy for City of London 1987; KJStJ 1986; - (Chancellor 1986-87) Worshipful Co of CA in England and Wales (master 1985-86) Woshipful Co of Wheelwrights; Hon memb Woshipful Co of lannderers, memb Ct HAC, memb Guild of freeman; Princes Youth Bus Tst 1986-87; Royal Shakespeare Theatre Tst; Tstee of the Friends of D'oly Carte, memb of the Lords Taveners, memb United Wards Club Govr Hosp, JP City of London 1976, FCA Hon D Litt City Univ 1986, Cdr O of the Lion of Malawi 1985; Commandeur de l'Ordre Mérite France 1984, Order of the Aztec. Eagle (CI II) Mexico 1987; holder of the Pedro Ernesto Medal (Rio de Janiero) 1987; Order of Diego Losada of Caracas 1987; Her Majesty's Commn of Lieutenancy for City of London 1987; KJStJ 1986; *Recreations* theatre, shooting; *Clubs* Carlton, Guildhall, City Livery; *Style—* Sir David Rowe-Ham, Esq

ROWELL, Sir John Joseph; CBE (1974), EM (1946); s of Joseph Alfred Rowell (d 1932), and Mary Lilian Rowell (d 1970); *b* 15 Feb 1916; *Educ* Brisbane GS, Queensland Univ; *m* 1947, Mary Kathleen, *née* de Silva; 5 children; *Career* NP, slr, tres Law Cncl of Australia 1961-63, pres Old Law Soc 1964-66, memb Law Reform Cmmn of Qld 1967-, chm Legal Aid Cmmn Qld 1978-; chm: Gas Corpn of Qld Ltd, Qld Bulk Handling, Concrete Constructions (Qld) Pty Ltd; kt 1980; *see Debrett's Handbook of Australia and New Zealand for further details*; *Recreations* golf, fishing, gardening; *Clubs* Brisbane, Union (Sydney), Indoorpilly Golf, United Service Australian (Sydney); *Style—* Sir John Rowell, CBE, EM; 'Edgecliffe', 48 Walcott St, St Lucia, Brisbane, Queensland, Australia

ROWLAND, (John) David; s of Cyril Arthur Rowland and Eileen Mary Rowland; *b* 10 August 1933; *Educ* St Paul's ,Trinity Coll Cambridge; *m* 1957, Giulia Powell; 1 s 1 da; *Career* chm Stewart Wrightson Hldgs plc (dep chm to 1981); Stwart Wrightson Gp Ltd 1972-, Stwart Wrightson Int Gp 1979-, Stwart Wrightson Ltd 1973-, Stwart Wrightson Australia Gp Ltd 1979-, Stewart Wrightson Underwriting Ltd 1978-, Ark Stewart Wrightson Nigeria 1980-, Nasco Karaoglan Gp Ltd 1977-, Westminster Insurance Agencies Ltd 1981-; chm non exec: Pinpoint Analysis Ltd 1983-, Project Fullemploy Ltd 1981-, Royal London Mutual Ins Soc Ltd 1985-86; vice pres Br Insurance Brokers Assoc 1980-, govr Coll of Insurance 1983-85; memb of cncl: Templeton Coll (Oxford Centre for Management Studies) 1980; (chm 1985-) Indus Soc 1983-, Contemporary Applied Arts 1985-, Business in the Community City of London section 1983-86 (dir and memb governing cncl 1986-), Lloyds 1987-; *Recreations* golf, running slowly; *Clubs* MCC; Royal & Ancient (St Andrews); Royal Worlington & Newmarket (Sunningdale), Royal St George's (Sandwich); *Style—* David Rowland, Esq; c/o Stewart Wrightson Hldgs, 1 Camomile St, EC3 (☎ 01 623 7511)

ROWLAND, Gilbert Raymond David; s of Capt Norman Denis Rowland, and Effy May, *née* McEwen; *b* 8 Oct 1946; *Educ* Catford Secdy Sch, RCM; *Career* harpsichordist; major performances include: Wigmore Hall 1973-75, Greenwich Festival 1975-84, Purcell Room 1979, 1983 and 1985, Berlin 1985, broadcasts for BBC Radio 3 1977, 1978, 1983, 1984, and 1985; various solo recordings for Nimbus Records, and Scarlatti Sonatas for Keyboard Records; piano teacher Epsom Coll 1969-; memb: ARCO 1967, ARCM; *Style—* Gilbert Rowland, Esq; 418 Brockley Road, London SE4 2DH (☎ 01 699 2549)

ROWLAND, HE Air Marshal Sir James Anthony; AC (1987), KBE (1977), DFC (1944), AFC (1953); s of Cdr Louis Claude Rowland (d 1954), and Elsie Jean Rowland, *née* Wright (d 1961); *b* 1 Nov 1922; *Educ* Cranbrook Sch Sydney, St Paul's Coll Sydney Univ (BEAero); *m* 1955, Faye Alison, da of David John Doughton (d 1971); 1 da (Ann); *Career* dir-gen Aircraft Engrg RAAF 1972, Air memb for Tech Servs 1973-74, Chief of Air Staff RAAF 1975-79, govr of New South Wales 1981-89; Hon DEng St Peter's Coll Sydney Univ; *see Debrett's Handbook of Australia and New Zealand for further details*; *Style—* HE Air Marshal Sir James Rowland, AC, KBE, DFC, AFC; 35 Trapper's Way, Clareville, NSW 2107, Australia

ROWLAND, John; s of Peter Rowland (d 1976) and Marion Agnes *née* Guppy; *b* 17 Jan 1952; *Educ* Aquinas Coll, Perth W Australia, Univ of W Australia (B Econs), Univ of London (LLB); *m* 8 Dec 1979, Juliet Claire da of Ernest John Hathaway, 2 s (Benjamin b 1985, Matthew b 1988); *Career* Pilot Offr RAAF 1971-72; tutor Kingswood Coll Univ of W Australia 1973-74; barr, Middle Temple, in practice 1979-, memb Bar of England and Wales 1979, London Common Law Bar Assoc 1984; *Recreations* cricket, walking, skiing; *Style—* John Rowland, Esq; 4 Pump Court, Temple, London, EC4Y 7AN, (☎ 01 353 2656 fax 01 583 2036)

ROWLAND, John David; s of Cyril Arthur Rowland, and Eileen Mary Rowland; *b* 10 August 1933; *Educ* St Paul's, Trinity Coll Cambridge (MA); *m* 18 May 1957, Eileen Giulia, da of Trevor Powell; 1 s (Mark Trevor b 25 Dec 1959), 1 da (Belinda Jane b 25 Aug 1961); *Career* Mathews Wrightson & Co Ltd 1956-72 (dir 1965), dir Mathew Wrightson Holdings 1972, chm Stewart Wrightson Holdings plc 1981-87 (dep chm 1978-81), dir Royal London Mutual Insur Soc 1985-86, chm Westminster Insur Agencies 1981-88, memb cncl Lloyd's 1987, dep chm Willis Faber plc 1987-88, Gp Chief Exec Sedgwick Gp plc 1988 (chm designate 1989), dir Sedgwick Lloyd's Underwriting Agencies Ltd 1988-; dir Project Fullemploy 1973, vice pres Br Insurance and Investmt Brokers' Assoc 1980, memb cncl Templeton Coll 1980 (chm 1985-), govr Coll of Insur 1983-85, memb cncl Industrial Soc 1983-88, memb pres ctee Business in the Community 1986-; memb Contemporary Applied Arts (formerly Br Crafts Centre) 1985-; memb Ct of Worshipful Co of Insurers; *Recreations* golf, running slowly; *Clubs* MCC, Royal & Ancient Golf, Royal St Georges (Sandwich), Royal Worlington & Newmarket, Sunningdale; *Style—* David Rowland, Esq; 6 Mountfort Crescent, London N1 1JW (☎ 01 609 2041); Sedgwick Group plc, Sedgwick House, Sedgwick Centre, London E1 8DX (☎ 01 377 3456, fax 01 377 3199, telex 882131)

ROWLAND, Mark Robert; s of John Reginald Rowland, of Watersfield, Sussex, and Roberta Teresa, *née* Heather; *b* 7 Mar 1963; *Educ* Midhurst GS; *m* 3 Sept 1983, (Louisa) Stephanie, da of Maj Harry James Marshall Graham, TD; 1 s (Martyn b 1984), 1 da (Suzanne b 1982); *Career* long distance runner; UK 1500m champion 1985, 4 Euro (indoor) championship 1987, 4 World (indoor) Championship 1987, 9 in World 1500m Rankings 1988, 3 in World 3000m Steeplechase Rankings 1988, champion AAA 3000m Steeplechase 1988, Olympic Bronze Medal 3000m Steeplechase Seoul 1988; *Clubs* Phoenix Athletic; *Style—* Mark Rowland, Esq; c/o British Olympic Assoc, 1

Wandsworth Plain, London SW18 1EH

ROWLAND, Peter Morton Bayard; s of Rev A Norman Rowland (d 1959), and Lydia Mary, *née* Strange (d 1952); *b* 25 Jan 1916; *Educ* Caterham Sch Surrey, Birkbeck Coll London (BA), King's Coll London (LLB); *m* 26 July 1969, (Ann) Clare Allingham, da of Sir Owen Arthur Aisher, *qv*; *Career* WWII T/Maj RASC 1939-46; with Farrow Bersey Gain Vincent CA 1933-40; barr 1947; practised at bar 1947-72 and 1987-; chm Rowland Debons Ltd 1972-, Project Fin Inst Ltd 1984-, Kelvingate Int Ltd 1985-; vice chm Construction Indust Advsy Gp Ltd 1988-; dir Anglo-Bahamian Bant Ltd 1985-EXA SARL 1985-, Manderstom Conslts Ltd 1986-, Just Unit Ltd 1988-; memb exec ctee Economic Res Cncl 1949-58, European Atlantic Gp 1954-; pt/t memb VAT Tbnl 1985-; govr: Caterham Sch 1956-62, Hurlingham Sch 1958-73; memb: Worshipful Co of Arbitrators 1985; FCA 1963, FCIA Arb 1978; *Books* Trust Accounts (1954, 1959, 1964), Corporation Tax (with John Talbot) (1965), Arbitration Law and Practice (1988); *Recreations* tennis, chess; *Clubs* City of London, Arts, Hurlingham; *Style*— Peter M B Rowland, Esq; 40 Green St, London W1Y 3FH (☎ 01 499 5904); 3 Temple Gardens, London EC4Y 9AU (☎ 01 353 7884, fax 01 583 2044)

ROWLAND PAYNE, Dr Christopher Melville Edwin; s of Major Edwin Rowland Payne, and Rosemary Ann *née* Bird BSc; *b* 19 May 1955; *Educ* Clifton, London Univ and St Bartholomew's Hosp (MB BS, MRCP); *Career* house surgn St Bart Hosp London 1978, house physician: med prof Unit Royal Infirmary Edinburgh 1978, Roy Marsden Hosp 1979 (sr); med registrar: St Thomas Hosp, London Hosp 1980; dermatological registrar St Thomas 1981-83, Westminster Hosp 1983-85; memb: Societé Francaise de Dermatologie, Br Assoc Dermatologists; Liveryman Worshipful Soc of Apothecaries, Freeman City of London; Roxburgh Prize 1977, Br Assoc Dermatologists Prizes 1984, 1985, 1986, Dawling Club Prizes 1985, 1986, 1876, HAC 1975-76; FRSM; *Books* contributor Br Med Journal, Journal Royal Soc Med; *Recreations* shooting, yachting, cycling, military history; *Style*— Dr Christopher Rowland Payne; 11 Hanson Street, London W1 (☎ 01 631 0193); Skin Research Laboratories, Westminster Hospital, London SW1 (☎ 01 352 8161)

ROWLANDS, Edward (Ted); MP (Lab) Merthyr Tydfil and Rhymney 1983-; s of William Samuel Rowlands (d 1966), of Rhondda; *b* 23 Jan 1940; *Educ* Rhondda GS, Wirral GS, King's Coll London; *m* 1968, Janice Williams; 2 s, 1 da; *Career* res asst History of Parly Tst 1963-65, lectr in modern history and govr Welsh Coll of Advanced Technol 1965-66; MP (Lab): Cardiff N 1966-70, Merthyr Tydfil 1972-1983; parly under-sec of state: for Wales 1969-70 and 1974-75, FCO 1975-76; min of state FCO 1976-79; oppn front bench spokesman Energy 1981-87; memb: select ctee For Affrs 1987-, academic cncl Wilton Park, FCO, exec of Cwlth Inst; judge: Booker McConnell Novel of the Year Competition 1984, Manchester Oddfellows Social Award Book; *Style*— Edward Rowlands, Esq, MP; 5 Park Crescent, Thomastown, Merthyr Tydfil, Mid Glamorgan (☎ 0685 4912)

ROWLANDS, John Kendall; s of Arthur and Margaret Rowlands; *b* 18 Sept 1931; *Educ* Chester Cathedral Choir Sch, King's Sch Chester, Gonville and Caius Cambridge (MA, MA); *m* 1, 1957 (m dis 1981), Else A H Bachmann; 1 s, 2 da; m 2, 1982, Lorna Jane Lowe; 1 da; *Career* dep keeper dept of prints and drawings Br Museum 1974-81, keeper 1981-; FSA 1976; *Books* The Paintings of Hans Holbein the Younger 1985; *Recreations* organ and piano playing; *Clubs* Beefsteak; *Style*— John Rowlands, Esq, FSA; British Museum, Department of Prints and Drawings, Great Russell St, London WC1 (☎ 01 636 1555)

ROWLANDS, Air Marshal Sir John Samuel; GC (1943), KBE (1971, OBE 1954); s of Samuel Rowlands (d 1919), and Sarah Rowlands (d 1943), of Ewloe Green, Ewloe, Chester; *b* 23 Sept 1915; *Educ* Hawarden GS, Bangor Coll Wales Univ; *m* 1942, Constance, da of Wing Cdr Harry R. Wight, MC (d 1947), of Codshall, Staffs; 2 da; *Career* joined RAFVR 1939, Gp Capt 1958, Air Cdre 1963, dir-gen of trg (RAF) MOD 1968-70, AOC-in-C Maintenance Cmd 1970-73, Air Vice-Marshal 1968, Air Marshal 1970, ret 1973; asst princ Sheffield Poly 1974-80; *Recreations* photography; *Clubs* RAF; *Style*— Air Marshal Sir John Rowlands, GC, KBE; 45 Lyndhurst Rd, Sheffield S11 9BJ (☎ 0742 554476)

ROWLANDS, (John) Martin; CBE (1980); s of John Walter Rowlands (d 1936), and Mary Ace (Mrs Maitland), *née* Roberts; *b* 20 July 1925; *Educ* Charterhouse, Selwyn Coll Cambridge (MA); *m* 29 Oct 1956, Christiane Germaine Madeleine, da of Justin Lacheny (d 1984); 2 da (Diane Mary b 1957, Noelle Lucy b 1966); *Career* Capt RA serv India and SE Asia 1943-47; Overseas Civil Serv: admin offr Hong Kong 1952-85, sec for Hong Kong Civil Serv 1978-85, memb Hong Kong Legislative Cncl 1978-84, ret 1985; *Recreations* railways, birdwatching; *Clubs* Hong Kong, Royal Hong Kong Jockey; *Style*— Martin Rowlands, Esq, CBE; Flat 3, 15 Collingham Rd, London SW5 ONU

ROWLANDSON, Hon Mrs (Antonia Jane Hamilla); *née* Inskip; da of 2 Viscount Caldecote; *b* 1952; *m* 1972, Piers Rowlandson; 1 s (Titus b 1973); *Career* journalist; *Style*— The Hon Mrs Rowlandson; 83 Disraeli Road, London SW15

ROWLANDSON, Jack William Dunn; s of Brig George Dobbie Rowlandson, and Violet May, *née* Hatchard-Smith; *b* 24 Sept 1910; *Educ* Charterhouse; *m* 8 July 1939, Mary Elizabeth, da of Alfred Hobson (d 1953), of Epsom; 1 s (James b 3 Jan 1950), 1 da (Jillian b 3 Oct 1943); *Career* Air Miny 1936-37, airfield operator Whitney Straight 1937-39, Sqdn Ldr RAF 1940-47; trainee accountant Ware Ward & Co Exeter 1928-35, CA 1936, Moore Stephens 1947, chief accountant St Barts Hosp 1947-62, Newton Armstrong Mgmnt Consits 1962-; hon sec Rahere Assoc 1950; FCA; *Recreations* sailing, gardening, swimming; *Clubs* Little Ship, Old Carthusian YC; *Style*— Jack Rowlandson, Esq; Peters Brae, Danehill, Sussex RH177EY, (☎ 0825 790 212); 4/8 Ludgate Circus, London EC4M74LD (☎ 01 583 9432)

ROWLATT, James Arthur; s of Arthur Rowlatt (d 1974), and Margaret Evangeline Rawlins (d 1977); *b* 27 June 1930; *Educ* Eton, Cambridge Univ (BA); *m* 12 Sept 1968, Vita Marie Koefoed (d 1987), da of Jacob Nikolai Wichmann (d 1967), of Denmark; 2 da (Sophie b 1969, Kate b 1973); *Career* dir: Portfolio Mgmnt 1961-77, Parambe Ltd 1971-; md Voyager Investmt; chm, Fleet Friendly Soc; *Books* Pan Guide to Saving and Investment (1965); *Recreations* other peoples' gardens, science fiction; *Style*— James Rowlatt, Esq; 18 Holland St, Kensington W8 4LT (☎ 01 937 5929); 213 St John St London EC1V 4LJ (☎ 01 253 4949, fax 01 253 6191)

ROWLEY, Hon Lady; Celia Ella Vere; *née* Monckton; da of 8 Viscount Galway, GCMG, DSO, OBE, PC (d 1943), and Hon Lucia Emily Margaret *née* White (d 1983), da of 3 Baron Annaly; *b* 1925; *m* 1959, Sir Joshua Francis Rowley, 7 Bt, *qv*; 1 da (Susan Emily Frances b 1965); *Style*— The Hon Lady Rowley; Holbecks, Hadleigh, Ipswich, Suffolk

ROWLEY, Sir Charles Robert; 7 Bt (UK 1836), of Hill House, Berkshire; s of Lt-Col Sir William Joshua Rowley, 6 Bt (d 1971); *b* 15 Mar 1926; *Educ* Wellington; *m* 1952, Astrid, da of late Sir Arthur Massey, CBE, MD; 1 s (Richard b 1959), 1 da (Mrs Edwin Phillipps de Lisle b 1955); *Heir* s; *Style*— Sir Charles Rowley, Bt; Naseby Hall, Northants; 21 Tedworth Sq, SW3

ROWLEY, Dr Donald; s of late Bertram Rowley; *b* 24 June 1926; *Educ* Selwyn Coll Cambridge (DSc Bristol); *m* 1950, Ruth Mary, *née* Dunkley; 1 s, 1 da; *Career* dir: BAC (Guided Weapons) Ltd 1967-77 (asst md 1975-77 Br Aerospace Dynamics Gp 1977-85, md naval weapons div Br Aerospace plc 1981-86; pres Electronic Engrg Assoc 1983-84; FEng,; *Recreations* photography, gardening, music; *Style*— Donald Rowley, Esq; Manor Farm House, Northwick, Pilning, Bristol (☎ 04545 2327)

ROWLEY, John Howard; s of Capt Charles Donovan Rowley (d 1935), and Hon Irene Evelyn Beatrice, *née* Molesworth (d 1949); *b* 5 Nov 1931; *Educ* Gresham's Sch Holt, Univ of Reading (BSc); *m* 9 Feb 1963, (Aileen) Margery, da of Capt Robert Clifford Freeman, MC (d 1973); 1 s (Charles b 24 Jan 1969), 1 da (Irene b 18 Aug 1965); *Career* Lt RA 1950-52 (Capt CCF); entered educn Jamaica 1957; headmaster: de Carteret Prep Sch 1963, Gresham's Sch Holt 1975 (mathematics dept i/c target rifle shooting); memb: ctee BSSRA, Fullbore ctee CCRS; Cmdt Cadet competitors Bisley NRA, pres OGRE; *Recreations* fishing, gardening, walking; *Clubs* N London Rifle (Bisley); *Style*— John Rowley, Esq; Monk's Orchard, Blakeney, Holt, Norfolk (☎ 0263 740 488); Dalnabreac, Acharacle, Argyll (☎ 096 785 668); Gresham's Sch, Holt, Norfolk (☎ 713271, fax 0263 712 028)

ROWLEY, Sir Joshua Francis; 7 Bt (GB 1786), of Tendring Hall, Suffolk; JP (Suffolk 1978); s of Col Sir Charles Samuel Rowley, OBE, TD, 6 Bt (d 1962); *b* 31 Dec 1920; *Educ* Eton, Trinity Coll Cambridge; *m* 1959, Hon Celia Ella Vere, *née* Monckton, da of 8 Viscount Galway (*see* Rowley, Hon Lady); 1 da; *Career* formerly Capt Gren Gds, dep sec Nat Trust 1952-55, chm W Suffolk CC 1971-74, Suffolk CC 1976-78, DL 1968, high sheriff 1971, Vice Lord-Lt 1973-78, Lord-Lt 1978-; *Clubs* Boodle's, Pratt's, MCC; *Style*— Sir Joshua Rowley, Bt, JP; Holbecks, Hadleigh, Ipswich, Suffolk (☎ 0473 823211, 0206 262213)

ROWLEY, Keith Nigel; s of James Rowley, of 21 Blackwood Close, West Byfleet, Weybridge, Surrey KT14 6PP, and Eva, *née* Swales; *b* 20 August 1957; *Educ* Woking Co GS for Boys, King's Coll London (LLB), Cncl Educn; *m* 2 Aug 1986, Chantal Anna, da of Dewar Cameron Mackenzie, of Newton's Hill Cottages, Hartfield, East Sussex; *Career* barr Gray's Inn 1979; *Recreations* classical music, theatre, fishing, shooting, wine; *Style*— Keith Rowley, Esq; 12 Hestercombe Ave, London SW6 5LL; 11 Old Square, Lincoln's Inn, London WC2A 3TS (☎ 01 430 0341. fax 01 831 2469, telex 940 14894 JPAR G)

ROWLEY, Baroness; Mary Elizabeth; da of Ernest Verrall Barnes, of N Finchley; *m* 1, Harold Gliksten (decd) of Florida USA; m 2, 1958, Baron Rowley (Life Peer, d 1968); 2 hus Arthur Henderson, PC, QC, bro 1 Baron Henderson, cr Life Peer 1966; *Style*— The Rt Hon Lady Rowley; PO Box 5, Miami Shores, Fla 33153, USA

ROWLEY, Peter; MC (1944); s of Roland Rowley, MC, of Wembley, Middx (d 1955), and Catherine Isobel Whitticks (d 1944); *b* 12 July 1918; *Educ* Wembley Sch, Univ Coll Oxford (MA); *m* 19 Oct 1940, Ethnea Louis Florence Mary, da of John Howard-Kyan of Newell House, Grimston Ave, Folkestone, Kent (d 1958); 4 da (Rosemary b 1942, Anne b 1946, Carolyn b 1949, Julia b 1951); *Career* WWII Maj Sherwood Foresters; serv Middle E, Italy, Germany; Bde Maj 13 Bde, GSO II 8 Corps; slr 1950-, snr ptnr Titmuss Sainer & Webb 1979-83; memb Law Soc Land Law & Conveyancing Ctee 1974-87; Liveryman Worshipful Co of Distillers'; chm Leonard Cheshire Fndn 1982-; *Recreations* opera, wine, carpentry; *Clubs* Royal Automobile; *Style*— Peter Rowley, Esq, MC; 38 Devonshire Place Mews, London W1N 1FJ (☎ 01 930 1003); 26/29 Maunsel St, London SW1P 2QN (☎ 01 828 1822)

ROWLEY, (William) Philip; MBE (1945); s of Capt William Thomas John Rowley (d 1960), of London, and Gertrude Julia, *née* Hart (d 1967); *b* 3 April 1915; *Educ* Mil Coll of Sci; *m* 21 July 1939, Viva Maude, da of George Bartling (d 1960), of London; 1 s (Timothy b 1950); *Career* Signals Offr Reconaissance Bn 51 Highland Div 1941-42; Staff Offr radio to: Signal Offr-in-Chief GHQ Home Forces 1942, Signal Offr-in-Chief 21 Army Gp HQ (Field Marshall Montgomery's HQ) 1942-43, COS Supreme Army Cdr 1943, Signal Offr-in-Chief Supreme HQ AEF (General Eisenhower's HQ) 1943-46; sec Br Jt Communications Bd (Br Armed Forces) 1942-46, sec Combined Signal Bd (W Allied Armed Forces) 1943-46, Br jt sec Multipartite Signal Bd (W Allies and Russian Armed Forces) 1946; educn offr Radio and TV Retailers Assoc 1949-59, offr Sci Instrument Mfrs Assoc 1953-53, gen mgmnt appts various int electronic cos 1957-71, chm Telemotive UK Ltd 1971-87 (fndr chm and md 1971-80), conslt Satellite tv engrg 1987-; memb Br Inst Radio Engrs: Educn Ctee 1948-52, Membership Ctee 1953-56; Corpn King's Coll Sch Wimbledon; CEng, FIEE 1988, FIERE 1965, MBrit IRE 1945; author of numerous TV trg courses (1949, further edns 1959); author of numerous tv training courses (1949, further edns 1959); *Recreations* tennis, music, performing arts; *Clubs* Ballpark (Eastbourne); *Style*— Philip Rowley, Esq, MBE; 11 Clifton House, Pk Ave, Eastbourne, E Sussex BN22 9QN (☎ 0323 503252)

ROWLEY, Richard Charles; s and h of Sir Charles Rowley, 7 Bt; *b* 14 August 1959; *Style*— Richard Rowley, Esq

ROWLEY, Samuel Arthur; s of Joshua Ernest Rowley (d 1968), of West Hagley, Worcs, and Nora Rowley, *née* Cheshire (d 1967); *b* 12 June 1928; *Educ* Sebright Sch, Birmingham Univ (LLM); *m* 25 May 1972, Brenda Maureen, da of Frank Lawson Musto GSM, of Worthing; *Career* slr; memb: Law Soc; *Recreations* gardening, travel, music, fine arts; *Style*— Samuel Rowley, Esq; Shannon Court, Corn St, Bristol, BS99 7JZ (☎ 0272 294861, fax 0272 298313, telex 44742 LAWILL)

ROWLEY, Lady Sibell; *née* Lygon; 2 da of 7 Earl Beauchamp KG, PC, KCMG (d 1938), and Lady Lettice Mary Elizabeth *née* Grosvenor (d 1936), sis of 2 Duke of Westminster; *b* 10 Oct 1907; *m* 11 Feb 1939, Flt Lt Michael Richard Bernard Rowley, AuxAF (d 1952), s of George Francis Richard Rowley; *Style*— Lady Sibell Rowley; 1 Stable Cottages, Barton House, Guiting Power, N Cheltenham, GL54 5UH

ROWLEY-CONWY, Hon John Seymour; s of 9 Baron Langford, OBE, DL; *b* 1955; *Educ* Marlborough, Magdalene Coll Cambridge (MA), Oriel Coll Oxford (MSc); *m* 1983, Emma Josephine, da of Maj Peter Brown, of 30 Bowbank, Longworth, Oxon; 1 s (William Geoffrey Peter b 1988), 1 da (Katherine Grete Claire b 1985); *Style*— The Hon John Rowley-Conwy; 66 Fentiman Rd, London SW8

ROWLEY-CONWY, Hon Owain Grenville; s and h of 9 Baron Langford, OBE, DL;

b 27 Dec 1958; *Educ* Marlborough, RAC Cirencester; *m* 3 May 1986, Joanna, da of Jack Featherstone, of Clwyd; 1 s (Thomas Alexander b 1987), 1 da (Magdalen Guinevere b 1988); *Style*— The Hon Owain Rowley-Conwy

ROWLEY-CONWY, Hon Peter Alexander; s of 9 Baron Langford, OBE; *b* 1951; *Educ* Marlborough, Magdalene Coll Cambridge (MA, PhD); *m* 1979, Deborah Jane, only da of Col J H G Stevens, of All Hallows Cottage, Brockham, Betchworth, Surrey; 2 da (Gabrielle Catrin b 1984, Eleanor Mavsli b 1986); *Books* Star Carr Revisited; a Re-Analysis of the Large Mammals (Univ of London 1987), Mesolithic Northwest Europe; Recent Developments (Dept of Archaeology, Univ of Sheffield, 1987)l; *Style*— The Hon Peter Rowley-Conwy; 147 Victoria Rd, Cambridge

ROWLINSON, Prof John Shipley; s of Frank Rowlinson (d 1986), of Wilmslow, Cheshire, and Winifred *née* Jones; *b* 12 May 1926; *Educ* Rossall Sch Fleetwood Lancs, Trinity Coll Oxford Univ (BSc, MA, DPhil); *m* 2 Aug 1952, Nancy, da of Horace Gaskell (d 1970), of Walkden, Lancs; 1 s (Paul b 1954), 1 da (Stella (Mrs Barczak) b 1956); *Career* res assoc Univ of Wisconsin USA 1950-51, sr lectr in chem Univ of Manchester 1957-60 (res fell 1951-54, lectr 1954-57), prof of chem technol London Univ 1961-73, Dr Lees prof of chem Oxford 1974- fell Exeter Coll Oxford 1974-; borough cncllr Sale 1956-59; hon fell City and Guilds Inst 1986; FRSC, FIChemE, FEng 1976, FRS 1970; *Books* Liquids and Liquid Mixtures (1959), The Perfect Gas (1963), Thermodynamics for Chemical Engineers (1975), Molecular Theory of Capillarity (1982); *Recreations* mountaineering; *Clubs* Alpine; *Style*— Prof John Rowlinson; 12 Pullen's Field, Oxford OX3 OBU (☎ 0865 67507); Physical Chemistry Laboratory, South Parks Road, Oxford OX1 3QZ (☎ 0865 275401)

ROWLINSON, Stephen Richard; s of Henry Robert Rowlinson (d 1988), of Godalming; *b* 25 Dec 1939; *Educ* Wanstead Co HS, Univ of Nottingham (BA); *m* 17 Aug 1967, Kathleen Ann (Kathy); 2 s (Benjamin Toby, Thomas Henry); 1 da (Emily Kate Louise); *Career* gen trainee Sullivan Stauffer Colwell Bayles FNC 1961-62, divnl gen mangr Marris Lebus Ltd 1962-67, conslt McKinsey and Co Inc 1967-74, chm TCK Gp Ltd 1974-77, chm Rowlinson Tomala and Assocs Ltd 1977-82, chm and chief exec Bickerfon Rowlinson Ltd 1982-84 (chief exec 1985), chm and chief exec Korn/Ferry Int Ltd 1989-; memb investmt ctee Lazards Unquoted Co's Fund, resident memb City of London Barbican Steening Gp; M Inst Dips; *Recreations* ridiang, bickerton, bicycles; *Clubs* RAC, Marry's Bar; *Style*— Stephen Rowlinson, Esq; 16 Wallside, Barbican, London EC2Y 8BM; Korniferry International Ltd, Norfolk House, 31 St James's Square, London SWLY 4JL (☎ 01 930 4334, fax 01 930 8085, car tel 0836 732562, telex 914860

ROWNTREE, Sir Norman Andrew Forster; s of Arthur Thomas Rowntree, of London; *b* 11 Mar 1912; *Educ* Tottenham Co Sch, London Univ; *m* 1939, Betty, da of William Thomas, of Stonehouse, Glos; 2 s, 1 da; *Career* consulting engr 1953-64, dir Water Resources Bd and visiting prof Resources Bd 1964-73, prof of civil engrg Manchester Univ Sci and Technol Ins 1975-79; CEng, FICE; kt 1970; *Style*— Sir Norman Rowntree; 97 Quarry Lane, Kelsall, Tarporley, Cheshire (☎ 0829 51195)

ROWORTH, Philip William; s of Leslie Norman Roworth (d 1964), and Marjorie Joan, *née* Wilcocks; *b* 16 Jan 1950; *Educ* Loughborough GS; *m* 1, 22 July 1972 (m dis 1985), Brenda, *née* Stekell; 1 s (Richard Alexander b 1977), 1 da (Deborah Louise b 1981); m 2, 5 April 1986, Laura Susan, da of Bernard Barker, of Woodthorpe, Nottingham; *Career* ptnr Rothmere & Co, CAs, 1982-; dir Dorson Financial Servs Ltd 1985-; ACA 1977, FCA 1983; *Recreations* swimming, sport and games in general; *Style*— Philip Roworth, Esq; 27 Nell Gwyn Crescent, Bestwood Lodge, Nottingham (☎ 0602 206036); 66 St James Street, Nottingham (☎ 0602 472949 or 412742 or 411101)

ROWSE, Dr (Alfred) Leslie; s of Richard Rowse, of St Austell, and Ann, *née* Vanson; *b* 4 Dec 1903; *Educ* St Austell GS, Christ Church Oxford (MA, DLitt); *Career* historian and poet; fell All Souls Coll Oxford 1925-74, FBA 1958-, FRSL, pres Eng Assoc 1951-52; Benson Medal RSL for serve to literature; DL (Hon), Jennez Medal Royal Inst Cornwall; author of numerous books on Shakespeare, the Elizabethan Age, the Churchills, Cornwall, English History and Literature, several volumes of poetry ; *Recreations* gardening; *Clubs* Athenaeum; *Style*— Dr A L Rowse; Trenarren House, St Austell, Cornwall PL26 6BH

ROWSE, Hon Mrs (Rosemary Sybella Violet); er da of 1 Baron Grimston of Westbury (d 1979), and Sybil Rose (d 1977), da of Sir Sigmund Neumann, 1 Bt; *b* 4 Mar 1929; *m* 1, 10 Feb 1953 (m dis 1964), (Charles) Edward Underdown, o s of late Harry Charles Baillie Underdown, JP; m 2, 29 March 1984, Antony Herbert David Rowse, s of late Herbert James Rowse; *Career* interior designer; *Style*— The Hon Mrs Rowse; 75B Flood Street, London SW3

ROWSON, Peter Aston; s of Lionel Edward Aston Rowson, OBE; *b* 8 Oct 1942; *Educ* St Edmunds Coll Ware; *m* 1967, Jennifer Mary, *née* Smyth; 1 s, 2 da; *Career* accountant; fin dir and co sec: Panther Securities plc, Panther Devpts Ltd, Panther Shop Investmts Ltd, Neil Martin Ltd, Ingrams Opticians Ltd, Saxonbest Ltd, MRG Systems Ltd; co sec: Yardworth Ltd, Excelchoice Ltd, Snowbest Ltd, Christchurch Park Properties Ltd, Westmead Building Co Ltd, A Brown & Sons plc; *Style*— Peter Rowson, Esq; 38 Mount Pleasant, London WC1X 0AP (☎ 01 278 8011)

ROXBEE COX, Hon Christopher Withers; s of Baron Kings Norton (Life Peer), *qv*; *b* 31 Oct 1928; *Educ* Westminster; *m* 3 Sept 1955, Rosemary Joyce, da of late Frederick Day Ardagh; 2 s; *Career* dir Reed Taylor Mgmnt Conslts 1981-; *Style*— The Hon Christopher Roxbee Cox; The Malt House, Kingsdown, Kent ME9 0RA (☎ Doddington 882)

ROXBURGH, Dr Ian Archibald; s of Archibald Cathcart Roxburgh (d 1954), of London NW3, and Grace Mary Blanche, *née* Lambert (d 1967); *b* 30 August 1917; *Educ* Stowe, Trinity Coll Cambridge (BA, MB BChir), Edinburgh Univ; *m* 1, 7 July 1951 (m dis 1985), Gilliam Frances, da of Roger Edward Norton, CMG, OBE (d 1978), of London; 1 s (Alan b 1967), 1 da (Frances b 1955); m 2, 18 Oct 1985, Patricia Jean, da of James Alexander Stanley Wilson (d 1959), of Totteridge, Ifield, Sussex; *Career* Surgn-Lt RNVR, RN Barracks Portsmouth 1944; RN Hosp: Haslar 1944, Sydney 1944-46, Devonport 1946; St Bartholomew's Hosp: house physician med professorial unit 1943, med registrar 1947; registrar skin dept Prince of Wales Gen Hosp Tottenham 1948-50, GP Chelsea 1951-, med advsr Cwlth Devpt Corpn 1967-76, ret 1988; memb: Suffolk Wildlife Tst, Suffolk Naturalist Soc, Suffolk Preservation Soc, Royal Br Legion; MRCS 1943, LRCP 1943, MRCGP 1953, memb BMA 1943, FRSM 1948; *Recreations* natural history, travel; *Clubs* Royal Commonwealth Soc; *Style*— Dr Ian Roxburgh; Brandon Lodge, Walberswick, Southwold, Suffolk (☎ 0502 724 741)

ROXBURGH, Rt Rev James William; *see*: Barking, Bishop of

ROXBURGH, Vice Adm Sir John Charles Young; KCB (1972, CB 1969), CBE (1967), DSO (1943), DSC (1942) and bar (1945); s of Sir (Thomas) James (Young) Roxburgh, CIE, ICS (d 1974), and Mona Gladys Mabel, *née* Heymerdinguer (d 1982); *b* 29 June 1919; *Educ* RNC Dartmouth; *m* 1942, Philippa, 3 da of Major Charles Montague Hewlett, MC (d 1944); 1 s, 1 da; *Career* joined RN 1933, psc 1955, idc 1962; joned Submarine Branch 1940; serv: Norway, Bay of Biscay, Med 1940-42; cmd HMS Submarines H43, Utd and Tapir 1942-45 (Med, Norway), Br Jt Servs Mission Washington 1958-60, dep dir Def Plans (Navy) MOD 1963-65, cmd HMS Eagle 1965-67, flag offr Sea Trg 1967-69, Flag Offr Plymouth 1969, Flag Offr Submarines and NATO Cdr Subs E Atlantic 1969-72, Vice Adm 1970, ret 1972; chm Grovebell Gp Ltd 1972-75, county councillor (Surrey) 1977-81, memb Cncl and Mgmnt Ctee of Freedom Assoc 1977-85, pres RN Benevolent Tst 1978-84; *Recreations* golf, sailing, walking, music; *Clubs* Army and Navy, Liphook GC; *Style*— Vice Admiral Sir John Roxburgh, KCB, CBE, DSO, DSC; Oakdene, Wood Rd, Hindhead, Surrey GU26 6PT (☎ 042 873 5600)

ROXBURGH, Dr Ronald Cathcart; s of Dr Archibald Cathcart Roxburgh (d 1954), and Grace Mary Blanche, *née* Lambert (d 1967); descent from Dr John Grieve, body surgn to Empress Elizabeth of Russia; *b* 16 August 1920; *Educ* Stowe, Trinity Coll Cambridge (MA, MD); *m* 21 March 1952, Angela Mary Elisabeth, da of Brig William Edward Harvey Grylls, OBE, and sis of Michael Grylls, MP, *qv*; 2 s (Andrew Cathcart b 1958, Alistair Michael b 1962), 2 da (Fiona Elisabeth b 1954, Penelope Alexandra b 1956); *Career* temp Surgn Lt RNVR 1945-47, house surgn Barts 1944-45, conslt paediatrician E Anglian RHA 1960-82; conslt memb W Norfolk Dist Health Authy 1983-88; chm: Wiggenhall branch NW Norfolk Cons Assoc 1986-, Norfolk branch NSPCC 1988-; FRCP; *Recreations* shooting, fishing, gardening; *Style*— Dr Ronald Roxburgh; Wiggenhall House, Wiggenhall St Mary, King's Lynn, Norfolk PE34 3DN

ROXBURGH, Willis; OBE (1971), DFC (1943 DL 1978); s of William (d 1950), of Stirlingshire, and Margaret Ewing, *née* Hunter (d 1971); *b* 3 June 1912; *Educ* Merchiston Castle, Kelvinside Acad; *m* 22 April 1947, Lillian Joan, da of John Percy Tilley (d 1951); 2 s (William b 1948, Peter Robert Hunter b 1951), 1 da (Jennifer Margaret Hunter b 1942); *Career* WWII pilot RAF, Atlantic, Biscay, Euro 1940-44, asst air attaché Lord Halifax Staff, Br Embassy Washington DC 1944-48; admin asst AIOC (now BP), Abadan Persia 1939, dir Astral Equipment Ltd Dundee 1046-50 (md 1950-55); md: Morphy Richards Astral Ltd Dundee 1955-60, Morphy Richards Ltd London 1960-65, chief exec Nairn Williamson Ltd 1966-70 (chm and chief exec 1970-75); contested (C) Gorbals Div Glasgow 1948, vice chm Scottish Cons Pty 1965-74; memb Toothill ctee of enquiry into the Scottish economy 1960-66; *Recreations* golf, skiing, shooting; *Clubs* RAF (London), R & A St Andrews, Hon Co Edinburgh Golfers (Muirfield), Sunningdale, Pine Valley (USA), Elie (Fife) Fife Hunt; *Style*— Willis Roxburgh, Esq, DFC, OBE, DL; 2 Montgomery Ct, 110 Hepburn Gdns, St Andrews, Fife KY16 9LT

ROXBURGHE, 10 Duke of (S 1707); Sir Guy David Innes-Ker; 11 Bt (Premier Bt of Scotland or Nova Scotia, S 1625); also Lord Roxburghe (S before 31 March 1600), Earl of Roxburghe, Lord Ker of Cessford and Cavertoun (both S 1616), Marquess of Bowmont and Cessford, Earl of Kelso, Viscount of Broxmouth (S, with the dukedom the last Peerages cr in the Peerage of Scotland, 1707), and Earl Innes (UK 1837); s of 9 Duke of Roxburghe (d 1974) and his 2 w (late Mrs Jocelyn Hambro); 1 Earl obtained a charter in 1648 of succession to the honour, to his gs 4 s of his da Countess of Perth, and after him the 3 s successively of his gda Countess of Wigton; Dukedom in remainder to whoever succeeds to Earldom; *b* 18 Nov 1954; *Educ* Eton, Magdalene Coll Cambridge; *m* 1977, Lady Jane *née* Grosvenor, da of 5 Duke of Westminster and Hon Viola Lyttelton (da of 9 Viscount Cobham) and sis of Countess of Lichfield, *qv*; 2 s (Marquess of Bowmont and Cessford, Lord Edward b 1984), 1 da (Lady Rosanagh b 16 Jan 1979); *Heir* s, Marquess of Bowmont and Cessford; *Career* formerly Lt RHG/1 Dragoons; landowner, co dir; *Recreations* fishing, shooting, golf, cricket, skiing; *Clubs* White's, Turf; *Style*— His Grace the Duke of Roxburghe; Floors Castle, Kelso, Roxburghshire (☎ 0573 24288); Roxburghe Estate Office, Kelso, Roxburghshire, Scotland (☎ 0573 23333)

ROXBURGHE, Mary, Duchess of; Lady Mary Evelyn Hungerford; *née* Crewe-Milnes; da (by 2 m) of first and last Marquess of Crewe; 1 Baron Houghton m sis 3 and Last Baron Crewe (extinct 1894), their s 2 Baron cr. Earl of Crewe 1895 and a Marquess 1911; *b* 1915; *m* 1935 (m dis 1953), 9 Duke of Roxburghe (d 1974); *Career* pres Nat Union of Townswomen's Guilds; bore HM the Queen's Canopy at Coronation of King George VI; *Style*— Mary, Duchess of Roxburghe; 15 Hyde Park Gdns, London W2 2LU (☎ 01 262 3349); West Horsley Place, Leatherhead, Surrey

ROY, Allan; TD; s of Harold William Roy (d 1951), of Hawes House, Ainsdale, Southport, and Kathleen, *née* McLaren (d 1945); *b* 13 May 1911; *Educ* Fettes Coll, Sch of Architecture Liverpool Univ; *m* 3 June 1939, Margaret Helen Nicoll (Peggy), da of James Nicoll (d 1951), of The Woodlands, Harpenden; 1 s (Niall b 27 April 1949), 2 da (Kirsty (Mrs Gjertsen) b 7 Nov 1942, Jeannie (Mrs Galdstone) b 17 Dec 1946); *Career* 2 Lt Liverpool Scottish 1932, Capt 1 Bn Queen's Own Cameron Highlanders 1940, Maj 1942, serv India and Burma; released from Army 1945; chm Chisholm & Co (Hldgs) Ltd 1951-; Scotland Rugby Int 1938-39; *Recreations* golf; *Clubs* Royal Ancient Golf, Formby Golf, Highland Brigade; *Style*— Allan Roy, Esq, TD; Hawes House, Ainsdale, Southport, Lancs PR8 2NZ (☎ 0704 77735); Chisholm & Co (Holdings) Ltd, 14/16 Derby Rd, Liverpool (☎ 051 207 6221, telex 629118 CHISOM)

ROY, Andrew Donald; s of Donald Whatley Roy (d 1960), of York, and Beatrice Anne, *née* Barstow (d 1963); *b* 28 June 1920; *Educ* Malvern, Sidney Sussex Coll Cambridge (BA, MA); *m* 22 Dec 1947, Katherine Juliet, da of James Herbert Grove-White (d 1979), of Cirencester and Perrots Brook; 1 s (Donald b 1948), 2 da (Juliet (Mrs Worboys) b 1950, Mary (Mrs Mitchell) b 1953; *Career* serv WWII RA 1939-46: 54 Heavy Regt UK 1940-41, 8 Medium Regt India and 14 Army 1941-44 (Adj 1942-44); Univ of Cambridge: econs lectr 1951- 64, fell Sidney Sussex Coll 1951-64 (tutor 1953-56, sr tutor 1956- 62), Govt Econ Serv 1962-80; under sec (econs) 1969-80: Treasy 1969-72, DTI 1972-74, MOD 1974076, chief econ advsr DHSS 1976-80, conslt NIESR 1981-83; memb: Royal Econ Soc, Royal Statistical Soc, Econometric Soc; *Books* British Economic Statistics (with CF Carter, now Sir Charles Carter, 1954); *Clubs* Utd Oxford and Cambridge Univ; *Style*— Andrew Roy, Esq; 15 Rusholme Rd, Putney, London SW15 3JX (☎ 01 789 3180)

ROYCE, David Nowill; s of Bernard Royce (d 1977), and Christine Ida, *née* Nowill (d

1958); *b* 10 Sept 1920; *Educ* Reading Sch, Univ of Vienna; *m* 24 July 1942, Esther Syvia, da of Rev Thomas Francis Yule (d 1939); 2 s (Robert b 1944, George b 1952), 1 da (Jacqueline b 1946); *Career* serv WWII Army 1940-46, Maj GSO2 Int HQ Br Troops Berlin; asst princ German section FO 1948, second sec 1949, private sec to Parly Under Sec for Affrs 1950-51; first sec: Athens 1953-55, Saigon 1955-57, FO (asst head econ relations dept) 1955-60, head chancery Caracus 1960-62, commercial cnsllr Bonn 1963-66, commercial inspr Helsinki 1967-71 (commercial cnsllr and consul-gen 1967-69), under sec DTI 1975-80 (asst sec 1971-73); dir gen Inst Export 1980-85 (hon fell), export conslt 1985-; lay reader Chelsea Old Church 1976-; FIEX 1985; *Recreations* swimming; *Style—* David Royce, Esq; 5 Sprimont Pl, London SW3 3HT (☎ 01 589 9148)

ROYCE, Norman Alexander; s of Joseph Samuel Royce (d 1960), of London, and Margaret, *née* Fraser (d 1954); *b* 4 Feb 1915; *Educ* Abbey Sch Beckenham, Bromley Coll of Art, Architectural Association (Dip Arch); *m* 10 Sept 1948, Molly Walden, da of late Alfred William Clarke, OBE; 3 s (Christopher b 1950, Darryl b 1952, Dominic b 1964), 1 da (Lesley b 1954); *Career* RAF 1940-46: Pilot Staff Offr 1945, Sqdn Ldr, served Europe and ME; sr ptnr Royce Hurley & Stewart Architects 1938-, pres CIArb 1942, vice-pres RIBA 1968 (fell 1960, assoc 1940), pres Concrete Soc 1977; chm: Joint Contracts Tribnl 1978-83, London Ct Int Arbitration 1980; chm: 444 (Shoveditch) Sqdn ATC, Biggins Hill Airport Consultative Ctee; memb: ctee Royal London Soc for the Blind, ctee Old peoples Home & Sheltered Housing Bencurtis House Beckenham; vice-chm Biggin Hill RAf Assoc; Freeman City of London 1952; Master: Worshipful Co of Gardeners 1973, Worshipful Co of Fanmakers 1979, Worshipful Guild Air Pilots & Air Navigators 1981, Worshipful Co of Arbitrators 1983; Master-Elect Worshipful Co of Chartered Architects; CIArb 1957 (former pres), FRIBA 1960, ARIBA; *Recreations* flying, gardening, cricket; *Clubs* Carlton, RAF, City Livery, MCC; *Style—* Norman Royce, Esq; 4 Waldon Gdns, Shortlands, Bromley, Kent BR2 0JR (☎ 464 3256); 3 Field Ct, Grays Inn, London WC1R 5EF (☎ 01 242 5957, fax 01 405 5724)

ROYCE, Roger John; QC (1987); s of J Roger Royce of Trig, Rock Cornwall, and Margaret, *née* Sibbald; *b* 27 August 1944; *Educ* The Leys Sch Cambridge, Trinity Hall Cambridge (BA); *m* 12 May 1979, Gillian Wendy, da of Geoffrey Guy Adderley, of High Trees, Whitedown Lane, Alton, Hants; 1 s (Andrew David Lyndon b 1986), 1 da (Joanna Katy Rachel b 1984); *Career* admitted slr 1969, called to the Bar 1970, rec 1986; sport: Cambridge Univ Hockey Blue,1965-66 East Hockey 1965-66, West Hockey 1972-73, capt Somerset Hockey 1976, qualified ski instr Austrian 1969; *Recreations* skiing, cricket, golf, collecting corkscrews,; *Clubs* Hawks, St Enodoc GC; *Style—* John Royce, Esq, QC; Guildhall Chambers, Broad St, Bristol (☎ 0272 273 366, fax 0272 298 941)

ROYDEN, Sir Christopher John; 5 Bt (UK 1905); s of Sir John Royden, 4 Bt (d 1976), of Netherfield Place, Battle, Sussex, and Dolores Catherine, da of Cecil Coward, of Lima; *b* 26 Feb 1937; *Educ* Winchester, Christ Church Oxford (MA); *m* 1961, Diana Bridget, da of Lt-Col Joseph Henry Goodhart, MC (d 1975), of Keldholme Priory, Kirkbymoorside, York, by Evelyn (yst da of Henry Beaumont, JP, DL); 2 s (John b 1965, Richard b 1967), 1 da (Emma b 1971); *Heir* s, John Michael Joseph Royden, b 17 March 1965; *Career* Nat Serv 2 Lt 16/5 The Queen's Royal Lancers 1955-57; stockbroker Spencer Thornton & Co 1971-86; *Recreations* shooting, fishing, gardening; *Clubs* Boodles; *Style—* Sir Christopher Royden, Bt; Bridge House, Ablington, Bibury, Glos

ROYDEN, Catherine, Lady (Dolores Catherine); da of Cecil Coward, of Lima; *m* 1936, Sir John Royden, 4 Bt (d 1976); 2 s, 2 da; *Style—* Catherine, Lady Royden; Netherfield Place, Battle, Sussex

ROYDEN, John Michael Joseph; s and h of Sir Christopher John Royden, 5 Bt,; *b* 17 Mar 1965; *Educ* Stowe, Univ of Reading (LLB); *Career* dir Petley & Co Ltd; fin futures broker; memb Soc Tech Analysts; *Recreations* shooting, fishing, backgammon, waterskiing, painting, bonking; *Style—* John Royden, Esq; Flat 2, 8 Nevern Sq, London SW5 9NW (☎ 01 370 2665)

ROYLE, Hon Lucinda Katherine Fanshawe; da of Baron Fanshawe of Richmond (Life Peer); *b* 1962; *Style—* The Hon Lucinda Royle

ROYLE, Peter Richard; s of Eric Vernon Royle, and Marjorie Ethel, *née* Tomlin; *b* 28 Jan 1935; *Educ* Haileybury; *m* 1 (m dis), Vanessa Susan Colman; 4 da (Lucinda Mary b 1962, Bettina Jane b 1964, Melissa Gail b 1965, Amanda Claire b 1969); m 2, 7 July 1982, Margaret Helen Scatliff; *Career* chm and chief exec W R Royle Gp Ltd and 9 Operating Busidiary cos; *Recreations* golf, photography; *Clubs* Reform, Royal Ashdown Golf, Piltdown Golf; *Style—* Peter Royle, Esq; W R Royle Gp Ltd, Wenlock Rd, London N1 7ST (☎ 01 253 7654)

ROYLE, Hon Susannah Caroline Fanshawe; da of Baron Fanshawe of Richmond (Life Peer); *b* 1960; *Style—* The Hon Susannah Royle

ROYLE, Timothy Lancelot Fanshawe; s of Sir Lancelot Carrington Royle, KBE (d 1978); *b* 24 April 1931; *Educ* Harrow, Mons Mil Acad; *m* 1959, Margaret Jill, da of Sir Ivan Rice Stedeford, GBE; 2 s, 1 da; *Career* church cmmr 1967-83; chm: Lindley Lodge Educn Tst 1970-, chm Christian Weekly Newspapers 1976-; md Hogg Robinson UK 1972-81, Hogg Robinson Ltd 1976-81, Hogg Robinson Gp 1980-81; chm: Control Risks Group 1974-, Westminster Property Gp 1983-84, Fin Strategy 1983-84; chm Berry Palmer & Lyle 1984-; dir Wellmarine Reinsurance Brokers 1975-; memb General Synod of C of E 1985-; FInstM, FBIBA; *Recreations* country pursuits, real tennis, skiing; *Clubs* Cavalry and Guards, MCC, St Moritz Tobogganing; *Style—* Timothy Royle, Esq; c/o National Westminster Bank, 11 Leadenhall St EC3

ROYLE, Col Vernon Fanshawe; ERD; s of Vernon Peter Royle (d 1944), of Stanmore Lodge, Lancaster, and Constance, *née* Stokes (d 1968); *b* 30 April 1915; *Educ* Harrow; *m* 2 Sept 1939, Bridget, da of Cecil Gwyn (d 1950), of Groveheath, Ripley, Surrey; 2 da (Susan b 1942, June b 1945); *Career* serv WWII, India, Burma 1940-45, CO King's Own (TA) 1947-52, Hon Col 1958-69, Dep Cdr 126 Inf Bde (TA) 1954-56; slr and insur exec; cmmr St John's Ambulance Bde Lancs 1954-69, DL Lancs 1961-70; *Recreations* genealogy, travel; *Style—* Col Vernon Royle, ERD; 39 Allestree Rd, London SW6 6AD

ROZYCKI; *see*: Ross, Andrew

RUBENS, Col (Ralph) Alexander; s of Capt Joshua Ernest Rubens (d 1985), of Henley-in-Arden, Warwicks, and Anna Louba, *née* Markova Klionsky; *b* 5 Feb 1920; *Educ* King Edwards Sch, RMC Sandhurst, RAF Staff Coll Bracknell, Jt Servs Staff Coll; *m* 1, 21 Dec 1949, Lady Rosemary Alexandra, *née* Eliot (d 1963), da of 6 Earl of St Germans (d 1968); 1 da (Alexandra Louise (Mrs Peyronel) b 9 Oct 1951); m 2, 23 Oct 1967, Joan, da of Reginald Wilson Hawkes, of Sholtery, Stratford upon Avon, Warwicks; *Career* cmmnd 1939, company cdr 2 Bn Sherwood Foresters served N Africa and Italy (Maj 1943), Anjio (wounded twice), staff appts attached RN and RAF, represented 3 Chiefs of Staff at 10 Downing St 1964-68 (Col), head of mgmnt info Army, ret 1974; clerk to Worshipful Co of Stationers and Newspaper Makers 1974-84, non-exec dir Graison (wine advsr) 1984-; vice-chm Chelsea Soc; fndr memb Consultative Ctee of the Livery Corpn of London; Freeman City of London 1976, Liveryman Worshipful Co of Stationers and Newspaper Makers 1976; *Recreations* wine, travel, theatre, reading, walking, swimming; *Clubs* Garrick, Saintsbury; *Style—* Col Alexander Rubens; 27 Gertrude St, Chelsea, London SW10 0JF; 45 Crag Path, Aldeburgh, Suffolk

RUBENS, Bernice Ruth; da of Eli Reuben (d 1958), of Cardiff, and Dorothy, *née* Cohen (d 1987); *b* 26 July 1928; *Educ* Cardiff HS for Girls, Univ Coll Cardiff (BA); *m* 29 Dec 1947 (m dis), Rudi Nassauer, s of Franz Nassauer; 2 da (Sharon b 1949, Rebecca b 1951); *Career* novelist; *Books* Set on Edge (1960), Madame Sousatzka (1962), Mate in Three (1965), The Elected Member (Booker Prize 1970), Sunday Best (1972), Go Tell The Lemming (1974), I Sent a Leter to My Love (1976), The Ponsonby Post (1978), A Five Year Sentence (1979), Spring Sonata (1981), Birds of Passage (1982), Brothers (1983), Mr Wakefield's Crusade (1985), Our Father (1987), Kingdom Come (1989); documentary film maker; Hon Fell Univ of Wales 1984; *Recreations* playing the 'cello; *Style—* Ms Bernice Rubens; 16A Belsize Park Gdns, London NW6 4LD (☎ 01 586 5365)

RUBENS, Robert David; s of Joel Rubens, of London N3, and Dinah, *née* Hasseck; *b* 11 June 1943; *Educ* Quintin GS, King's Coll London (BSc), St George's Hosp Med Sch (MB BS), Univ of London (MD) (1974); *m* 30 Oct 1970, Margaret, da of Alan Chamberlin, of Burncross, Yorks; 2 da (Abigail b 15 Nov 1971, Carolyn b 10 June 1974); *Career* house and registrar appts 1968-72: St George's, Brompton, Hammersmith & Royal Marsden Hosps 1968-72, conslt physician Guy's Hosp 1975-; conslt med offr: Mercantile & Gen Reinsurance Co plc 1977-(chief med offr 1987-), Legal & Gen Assur Soc Ltd 1978-; dir of oncology servs Guy's Hosp 1985, prof of clinical oncology United Med & Dental Schs of Guy's and St Thomas' Hosps 1985-; Imp Cancer Res Fund: scientific staff 1972-85, dep dir breast cancer unit 1982-85, dir clinical oncology unit 1985-; memb ed bd Cancer Treatment Reviews 1987-; examiner RCP 1987-, dir of studies for Br Cncl Course on Breast Cnacer 1989, chm dir of oncology United Med and Dental Schs of Guys' and St Thomas' Hosp 1989-; cncl memb Assur Med Soc 1982-, memb: SE Thames Regnl Cancer Ctee 1983-; Assoc of Cancer Physicians 1985; chm Fourth EORTC Breast Cancer Conf 1987, hon dir Incorporated Homes for Ladies with Limited Income 1983; Freeman: City of London 1979, Worshipful Soc of Apothecaries 1978-(Liveryman 1983-); MRCP 1969, memb BMA 1969, FRSM 1971; memb: British Breast Gp 1976, American Assoc for Cancer Res 1977, American Soc of Clinical Oncology 1977, Med Soc of London 1979; FRCP 1984; author of: A Short Textbook of Clinical Oncology (1980), numerous pubns on experimental and clinical cancer therapy and other med subjects; *Recreations* golf, music, reading; *Clubs* Athenaeum, Royal Wimbledon GC; *Style—* Prof Robert Rubens; 5 Currie Hill Close, Arthur Rd, Wimbledon, London SW19 7DX (☎ 01 946 0422); Guy's Hospital, London SE1 9RT (☎ 01 955 5000)

RUBIE, Hon Mrs (Jane Alice); *née* Liddell; da of 8 Baron Ravensworth and Wendy, adopted da of J Stuart Bell, of Cookham, Berks; *b* 1952; *m* 1984, Michael James Crowhurst Rubie; 2 da (Sophia Amy Elizabeth b 1986, Isabel Emma Mary b 1988); *Style—* THe Hon Mrs Rubie; Eslington Park, Whittingham, Alnwick, Northumberland

RUBIN, David (Antony); s of Leonard Rubin, and Sylvia Rubin (d 1987); *b* 11 Jan 1954; *Educ* Haberdashers Boys Sch; *m* 1 July 1982, Diana, da of Neville Curtis; 2 s (Guy Maurice b 1977, Scott James b 1987); *Career* CA; licenced insolvency practitioner and expert in insolvency matters; appointed in the High Ct in Insolvency matters, ACA; *Recreations* charity work, fund raising, golf, sport; *Clubs* Dyhram Park County; *Style—* David Rubin, Esq; Pearl Assurance House, 319 Ballards Lane N12 (☎ 01 446 8203, fax 01 446 29994)

RUBIN, Hon Mrs; Hon Susan; *née* Rayne; da of Baron Rayne by his 1 w, Margaret; *b* 1945; *m* 1965, John Rubin; *Style—* The Hon Mrs Rubin

RUBINSTEIN, Michael Bernard; s of late H F Rubinstein, and Lina, *née* Lowy; *b* 6 Nov 1920; *Educ* St Pauls; *m* 1955, Joy, *née* Douthwaite; 2 s, 2 da; *Career* serv WWII RE TA 1939, Capt RA 1945; admitted slr 1948; Rubinstein Callingham (formerly Rubinstein Nash & Co): sr ptnr 1976-86, conslt 1986-; memb Lord Chllr's Ctee on Defamation 1971-74, chm SPNM 1986 (tstee 1967-), tstee Aereopagitica Educnl Tst 1979-; occasional TV and radio broadcasting; *Books* Wicked, Wicked Libels (ed and contrib, 1972), Rembrandt and Angels (monograph, 1982), The Cart-Ruts on Malta and Gozo (with Roland Parker, 1982), Music to my Ear (1985); *Clubs* Garrick; 2 Raymond Bldgs, Gray's Inn, London WC1R 5BZ (☎ 01 242 8408)

RUCK, Adam; s of Andrew Ruck, of Wrotham, and Patricia Ruck, *née* Creasey; *b* 9 Oct 1952; *Educ* Haileybury, New Coll Oxford, Courtauld Inst of Art (MA); *Career* travel writer/columnist, author; *Books* The Holiday Which? Guide to France (3 edn, 1987), The Holiday Which? Guide to Italy (co-author 1987), The Good Skiing Guide 1985 (co-ed, 3rd edn 1987); *Recreations* tennis, skiing; *Clubs* Garratt Lane Snooker; *Style—* Adam Ruck, Esq; 29 Algarve Road, London SW18 (☎ 01 874 9491)

RUCK, Hon Mrs (Catherine Dorothy); *née* Neville; da of 7 Baron Braybrooke, JP, DL, by his 2 w, Dorothy, JP, da of late Sir George Lawson, KC; *b* 21 Jan 1922; *m* 1954, Gordon Alexander Egerton Ruck (d 1977); 1 da; *Style—* The Hon Mrs Ruck; Asherne, Strete, Dartmouth, Devon

RUCK KEENE, David Kenneth Lancelot; s of Thomas Ruck Keene, of Goulds Grove, Ewelme, Oxford, and Anne Coventry, *née* Greig; *b* 22 Sept 1948; *Educ* Eton; *m* 30 Oct 1976, Tania Caroline, da of William Anstey Preston Wild; 3 da (Katherine b 1981, Rosanna b 1983, Lucia b 1985); *Career* CA; Rowe & Pitman Stockbrokers 1977-82, (ptnr 1982-86), dir SG Warburg, Akroyd, Rowe & Pitman, Mullens Ltd 1986-; FCA 1974, memb Stock Exchange 1982; *Recreations* country pursuits, rackets, tennis, golf; *Clubs* White's, Queen's, MCC; *Style—* David Ruck Keene, Esq; Warburg Securities, 1 Finsbury Ave, London EC2M 2PA (☎ 01 606 1066, fax 01 382 4800)

RUCK KEENE, Thomas; s of Admiral William George Elmhirst Ruck Keene, MVO (d 1936), of Bicester, Oxon, and Violet Mary, *née* Hoare (d 1962); seventh child of eight (sixth son), all on active service WWII 3 brothers killed on active service; *b* 6 May 1922; *Educ* Twyford Sch, RNC Dartmouth; *m* 12 Oct 1945, Anne Coventry, da of

Capt Kenneth Beatson Septimus Greig, RN, of Ayr; 3 s (David b 1948, Simon b 1958, William b 1960), 2 da (Laura b 1946, Julia b 1950); *Career* RN 1936-48; Lt RN, Norwegian Campaign 1940, Med 1941, sunk HMS Southampton 1941, HMS Warspite, battles of Matapan, Crete; ship disabled; HM Submarines 1941-43; O i/c MTBr Coastal Cmnd 1944-45; Fleet Minesweepers 1945-48; ret 1948; ICI Export 1948-51; memb Int Stock Exchange London 1951-87 (ptnr Kitcat & Aitken 1982, conslt 1982-87); ret 1987; *Recreations* fishing, shooting, bridge; *Clubs* Brooks's, MCC, Swinley Forest & Huntercombe Golf, Castaways, Fox, City of London; *Style—* Thomas Ruck Keene, Esq; Goulds Grove, Ewelme, Oxford OX9 6PX (☎ (0491) 39200)

RUCKER, Sir Arthur Nevil; KCMG (1942), CB (1941), CBE (1937); only s of Sir Arthur William Rucker (d 1915), and his 2 w Thereza, *née* Story-Maskelyne; *b* 20 June 1895; *Educ* Marlborough, Trinity Coll Cambridge; *m* 1922, Elsie Marion, da of late George Broadbent; 2 s, 2 da; *Career* serv WWI Lt Suffolk Regt, private sec to Min of Health 1928-35, asst sec Min of Health 1935-37, dep sec 1941; dir Estabs 1937-39, princ private sec to PM 1939-41, sec off of Min State Cairo 1941-43, dep sec min health 1943-47, dep dir gen Int Refugee Orgn 1947, dep agent-gen of UN for Korea 1951, chm Tithe Redemption Cmmn 1954, memb Cwlth War Graves Cmmn 1955-69; vice-chm Stevenage Dvpt Corpn 1956, chm 1962-66; hon LLD (Wales); Korean Order of Diplomatic Merit (1974); *Clubs* Athenaeum; *Style—* Sir Arthur Rucker, KCMG, CB, CBE; Manor Farm House, Yattendon, Berks (☎ 0635 201205)

RUCKER, Brig James William Frederick; s of Charles Edward Sigismund Rucker (d 1965), of South's Farm, Ashmore, Salisbury, Wilts, and Nancy Winifred, *née* Hodgson; *b* 3 May 1936; *Educ* Charterhouse; *m* 14 Sept 1963, Caroline Lloyd, da of Raymond Wilson Sturge (d 1984), of Lord's Mead, Ashmore, Salisbury, Wilts; 2 s (Rupert b 1967, Jeremy b 1970), 1 da (Sara b 1964); *Career* Col The QOH, Cdr RAC, BAOR, Brig; DOR MOD; md NAAFI 1987-; *Recreations* shooting, cricket, tennis, gardening; *Clubs* Cavalry and Guards, MCC; *Style—* Brig James Rucker, Esq; Manor Farmhouse, Ashmore, Salisbury, Wilts; 6 Beechmore Rd, London SW11; Imperial Ct, Kennington Lane, London SE11

RUCKMAN, Robert Julian Stanley; s of William James Ruckman (d 1962), late of Sycamore Rd, Chalfont, and Ida Marjorie, *née* Woodward; *b* 11 May 1939; *Educ* Harrow Tech Coll, Cranfield Inst of Tech (MSc); *m* 16 Oct 1965, Josephine Margaret, da of Lieut RNVR George Colin Trentham, DSC (despatches) (d 1979); 1 s (Gordon b 1966), 1 da (Helen b 1973); *Career* chartered engr; systems analyst; Systems Sci Corp Virginia USA 1966, Tech Staff Kent Instruments 1968, sr Engr Dpmt Tport 1970; civil servant (computer mangr); pubns on digital systems; MIEE, MIEEE, MinstMC, MCIT, Comp IAP; *Recreations* hill walking, classical music, woodworking; *Clubs* CGA; *Style—* Robert Ruckman, Esq; Flamingo, 13 Alexander Ave, Droitwich, Worcs; Dept of Transport, Regnl Off, Room 105, 5 Broadway, Five Ways, Birmingham (☎ 021 631 8173)

RUDD, Hon Mrs (Fiona Catherine Ritchie); *née* Calder; da of Baron Ritchie-Calder, CBE; *b* 10 July 1929; *Educ* LSE; *m* 1949, Dr Ernest Rudd; 3 da; *Style—* The Hon Mrs Rudd; 19 South Parade, York YO2 2BA

RUDD, Hon Mrs (Hilary Aileen); *née* Peddie; da of Baron Peddie (Life Peer) (d 1978); *b* 1938; *m* 1959 (m dis), Christopher Geoffrey Rudd; 1 s, 1 da; *Style—* The Hon Mrs Rudd; 31 Nonsuch Court Ave, Ewell, Surrey

RUDD, Lewis Michael Cooper; s of Dr A S Rudd, and Mrs Rudd (d 1983); *b* 16 Sept 1936; *Educ* Highgate, Magdalen Coll Oxford (MA); *m* 1964, Joan Muriel, da of R N Bower, of Rushley Farm, Mansfield, Nott; 2 s, 1 da; *Career* head of children's programmes Rediffusion TV 1966-68, controller of children's programmes Thames TV 1968-72, asst controller of programmes Southern TV 1972-81, controller of young people's programmes Central Independent TV 1981-; credits incl: Do Not Adjust Your Set, Magpie, Spearhead, Worzel Gummidge, Your Mother Wouldn't Like It; *Style—* Lewis Rudd, Esq; c/o Central Independent Television, Lenton Lane, Nottingham NG7 2NA (☎ 0602 863322, telex 377696)

RUDDLE, Kenneth Anthony (Tony); s of Sir (George) Kenneth Fordham Ruddle (d 1979), of Islington Lodge, Langham, Oakham, Rutland, Lady Nancy Margaret Ruddle, *née* Allen; gf, George Ruddle, bought family brewery in 1911; *b* 12 April 1936; *Educ* Repton; *m* 1, 1959 (div 1976), Elizabeth Margaret Duff Brown; 1 s (Guy), 1 da (Caroline); m 2, 1976, Fiona Eileen Morse; *Career* joined family co 1959, md 1968, chm 1973-; *Recreations* hunting, golf, skiing; *Clubs* Luffenham Heath Golf; *Style—* K A Ruddle, Esq; c/o G Ruddle & Co plc, The Brewery, Langham, Oakham, Leics LE15 7JD (☎ 0572 56911, telex 341648); Leesthorpe Hall, Melton Mowbray, Leicestershire (☎ 066477 244)

RUDDLE, Peter; s of John Eric Ruddle, and Alice Emily, *née* Ambrose; *b* 16 May 1945; *m* 5 Oct 1968, Hazel Patricia, da of Sydney Robert Driscoll; 3 s (Simon Peter b 1970, Christopher John b 1972, William Edward b 1976); *Career* mangr Algemere Bank Nederland NV; *Recreations* swimming, gardening, DIY, bridge; *Clubs* Overseas Bankers; *Style—* Peter Ruddle, Esq; 3 Amherst Road, Benhill-on-Sea, E Sussex (☎ 0424 214823); 61 Threadneedle St, London EC2P 2HH (☎ 01 628 0846, fax 0424 212944, car tel 0860 396356)

RUDDOCK, Joan; MP (Lewisham-Deptford 1987-); da of Kenneth Charles Anthony (d 1981), and Eileen Messenger; *b* 28 Dec 1943; *Educ* Pontypool GS for Girls, Imperial Coll London (BSc); *m* 1963, Keith, da of Charles Ruddock (d 1966), of Cumbria; *Career* mangr Citizens Advice Bureau Reading (employment); chairperson CND 1981-85; currently memb nat cncl CND; *Style—* Ms Joan Ruddock, MP; House of Commons, Westminster, London SW1

RUDEBECK, Herman; s of Herr Andreas Rudebeck; *b* 7 June 1907; *Educ* Sonderborg, Statsskole; *m* 11 July 1931, Muriel Annie, da of Edward Gidley Lake; 2 s (Andrew Edward b 26 Oct 1944, Howard Alan b 27 Sept 1947), 2 da (Susan (Mrs Parker) b 16 Sept 1936, Tessa (Mrs Ryder Runton) b 1 Aug 1939); *Career* mangr OM Ltd 1928-30, md HR & Co Ltd 1934-84, chm Waycom Ltd 1959 (pres 1977); farmer 1953-; former chm Streat Parish Cncl; Liveryman Worshipful Co of Farmers 1960; memb: Lloyds, Baltic Exchange; *Recreations* tennis, shooting; *Clubs* Danish, Farmers; *Style—* Herman Rudebeck, Esq; The Gote House, Streat, nr Hassocks, Sussex BN6 8RN (☎ 01 890 328); HiRudebeck & Co Ltd, 2 Queens Rd, Haywards Heath, Sussex (☎ 0444 450 672)

RUDGE, Anthony John de Nouaille; s of John Edward Rudge (d 1970); *b* 17 Feb 1931; *Educ* Eton, Christ Church Oxford; *m* 1961, Kathleen Jill, da of George Craig Watson; 2 s (Anthony Alexander de Nouaille b 12 Feb 1963, Nicholas John de Nouaille b 15 July 1966); *Career* dir: Barclays Bank plc 1972- (chm Birmingham Region), Yorks Bank Ltd 1980-, Midland Radio Hldgs plc 1988-; dir W Midlands Industl Devpt Assoc, tstee Birmingham Hippodrome Theatre Devpt Tst, pres Evesham Rowing Club; *Recreations* travel, music, history; *Clubs* Travellers; *Style—* Anthony Rudge, Esq; Church Farm, Churchover, nr Rugby, Warwickshire

RUDGE, Peter John Harrington; s of William Charles Rudge London, and Edna May, *née* Brown; *b* 31 Jan 1934; *Educ* Lower Sch of John Lyon Harrow; *m* 1, 8 Aug 1961 (m dis 1980), Lisa Pauline Jean, da of John William Mackareth (d 1983), of Yorks; 1 s (Jeremy Charles Harrington b 9 Nov 1965); m 2, 14 July 1981, Tanis Shelmerdine, da of James Wells-Hunt; *Career* Nat Serv Sub Lt RN 1957-59 serv UK and Germany, Lt RNR 1959-62; CA; articled to Thornton and Thornton 1951-57, chief accoutant The Chequered Flag (SCS) Ltd 1959-65, fin dir London Lotus Centre Ltd 1965-88; chm Professional Acceptances Ltd 1965-88, EGO Computer Systems Ltd 1978-88; dir Forster and Hales Ltd 1980-88; chm W London Gp under Road Tport Indust Trg Bd, gen cmmr Income Tax; FCA; *Recreations* rugby, football, cricket, golf; *Clubs* MCC, Esher RFC, Richmond GC; *Style—* Peter Rudge, Esq; EGO Computer Systems Ltd, Stirling Way, Borehamwood, Herts WD6 2BT (☎ 01 207 4433, fax 01 207 6866, telex 261215)

RUDKIN, (James) David; s of David Jonathan Rudkin, of Westbourne, Emsworth, Sussex, and Anne Alice *née* Martin (d 1969); *b* 29 June 1936; *Educ* King Edward's Sch Birmingham, Oxford Univ (MA); *m* 3 May 1967, (Alexandra) Sandra Margaret, da of Donald Thompson (d 1969); 2 s (Jamie b 1973, Tom (twin) b 1973), 2 da (Sophie b 1977, Jess b 1978); *Career* RCS 1955-57; playwright; Afore Night Come 1960 (staged 1962), The Sons of Light 1964 (staged 1974), Ashes 1972 (staged 1974), Cries from Casement as his Bones are Brought to Dublin 1972 (radio 1973), Penda's Fen (TV film) 1972 (shown 1974), The Triumph of Death 1976 (staged 1981), The Saxon Shore 1983 (staged 1986), Testimony film screenplay 1984 (released 1988), auth/dir White Lady (TV film) 1986; translations: Hippolytus (Euripides) 1978, Peer Gynt (Ibsen) 1982; *Recreations* bridge, languages, geology, music, the sea; *Style—* David Rudkin, Esq; Margaret Ramsay Ltd, 14a Goodwin's Court, London WC2N 4LL (☎ 01 240 0691, fax 01 836 6807)

RUDKIN, (Malcolm) Spencer; s of Edward Shaw Rudkin (d 1967), of 11 Dovedale Drive, Grimsby, and Alice Lilian (d 1966); *b* 24 July 1931; *Educ* Humberside Fndn Sch Cleethorpes, Grimsby Coll of Tech, Bradford Tech Coll; *m* 29 Sept 1955, Judith Mary, da of William Humphrey (d 1965), of 95 Oxford St, Cleethorpes; 2 s (Malcolm Graham, Michael Charles), 2 da (Helen Judith, Karren Elizabeth); *Career* Nat Serv Royal Lincolnshire Regt 1952-53, Royal Mil Police 1953-54 serv: Berlin, Border Detachment Helmstedt, Autobahn crossing point to Berlin corridor; Acting Sgt i/c Helmstedt Detachment 247 Berlin Provost Co; md: ES Rudkin Ltd (family firm) 1966-, A Sutton & Sons (Builders) Ltd 1971-; track and cross country running referee (Grade 1), referee English Cross-Country Union Championships Luton 1975; Grimsby Harriers & Athletic Club: tres 1961-68, tstee and vice pres 1975-; Lincolnshire AAA pres and chm 1968-74, life vice pres Eastern Countries Cross Country Assoc 1975- (chm 1969-72, pres 1973-74); hon memb English Cross Country Union; memb: Grimsby Borough Cncl 1968-79, Humberside CC 1974- (ldr 1979-81 and 1985-86, ldr opposition 1981-85 and 1986), Assoc d CC 1977-81 and 1985 served on ctees inc: social servs, policy, Finance Planning and Transportation ctees, memb transportation sub-ctee; dep ldr cons gp 1978-79, cons gp spokesman planning and transportation 1987-, vice chm planning and transportation ctee 1988-; *Recreations* golf, swimming, athletics; *Clubs* Grimsby Cons, Grimsby GC; *Style—* Spencer Rudkin Esq DL; 5 East End Close, Scartho, Grimsby, South Humberside DN33 2HZ (☎ 0472 752192) E S Rudkin Ltd, 38-40 Louth Rd, Grimsby, South Humberside (☎ 0472 79102)

RUDKIN, Walter Charles; CBE (1981); s of Walter Rudkin (d 1970), of Sleaford, Lincs, and Bertha, *née* Charles (d 1985); *b* 22 Sept 1922; *Educ* Carres GS Lincs, Univ Coll Hull, London Univ (BSc); *m* 8 April 1950, Hilda Mary, da of George Hope (d 1975) of Sunderland; 2 s (Alistair b 1951, Ian b 1957); *Career* WWII Navigator RAF 1942-46; lectr Univ of the Witwatersrand Johannesburg SA 1948-52, MOD: joined 1954, Hong Kong 1956-59, jr directing staff IDC 1962-64, Cabinet Off 1968-71, dir econ Intelligence 1973-81, dir econ and logistic Intelligence 1981-82; advice worker Bromley CAB (hon sec mgmnt ctee), chm Bromley Police Community Consultative Gp 1986-88; *Recreations* fishing; *Clubs* Royal Commonwealth Soc; *Style—* Walter Charles, Esq, CBE; 85 Kingsway, Petts Wood, Orpington, Kent BR5 1PW (☎ 0689 22603)

RUDMAN, Michael Edward; s of Michael B Rudman, and Josephine, *née* Davis; *b* 14 Feb 1939; *Educ* St Mark's Sch Texas, Oberlin Coll (BA), St Edmund Hall Oxford (MA); *m* 1, 1963 (m dis 1981), Veronica Anne Bennett; 2 da; m 2, 1983, Felicity Kendal; *Career* pres OUDS 1963-64, asst dir and assoc producer Nottingham Playhouse and Newcastle Playhouse 1964-68, asst dir RSC 1968; artistic dir: Traverse Theatre Club 1970-73, Hampstead Theatre 1973-78; dir Lyttelton Theatre 1979-81; assoc dir Nat Theatre 1979-88; plays dir incl Nottingham Playhouse: Changing Gear, Measure for Measure, A Man for All Seasons, Julius Ceaser, Death of a Salesman, Lily in Little India; RSC Theatregoround: The Fox and the Fly 1968; Traverse Theatre: Curtains 1971, Straight Up 1971, Carravagro Buddy 1972, The Relapse 1972; Hampstead Theatre: Ride Across Lake Constance 1973, The Show-off 1974, Alphabetical Order 1975, Clouds 1977, Gloo Joo 1978; Nat Theatre: Gloo Joo 1978, Death of a Salesman 1979, Measure for Measure 1980, The Second Mrs Tanquery 1981, Brighton Beach Memoirs 1986, Fathers and Sons 1987; West End: Donkeys Years 1976, Clouds 1978, Taking Steps 1980, The Dragon's Tail 1985, Brighton Beach Memoirs 1987; New York: The Changing Room 1973, Hamlet 1976, Death of a Salesman 1984; memb Bd Dirs Hampstead Theatre 1979-; *Clubs* RAC, Dyrham Park Country, Cumberland LT, Roy Mid-Surrey Golf; *Style—* Michael Rudman, Esq; c/o Peter Murphy, Esq, Curtis Brown Group, 162-168 Regent St, London W1R 57A (☎ 01 872 0331)

RUFF, William Willis; CBE (1973), DL (Surrey 1964); s of William Ruff (d 1957); *b* 22 Sept 1914; *Educ* Durham Sch; *m* 1939, Agnes, *née* Nankivell; 2 s; *Career* serv Maj Royal Signal Corps (N Africa & India); slr; clerk Surrey Co Cncl 1952-74, chm Soc Clerks of Peace and Clerks of County Cncls 1969-72; memb Parly Boundary Cmmn for England 1974-83; *Recreations* music, watching cricket; *Style—* William Ruff Esq, CBE, DL; 3 Brympton Close, Ridgeway Rd, Dorking, Surrey (☎ 0306 882406)

RUFFER, Jonathan Garnier; s of Maj J E M Ruffer; *b* 17 August 1951; *Educ* Marlborough, Sidney Sussex Coll Cambridge; *m* 1982, Jane Mary, da of Dr P Sequeira; *Career* Myers and Co Stock Exchange; barr Middle Temple (jr Harmsworth exhibitioner), J Henry Schroder Wagg 1977-79, Dunbar Gp Ltd 1980-85, (dir Dunbar

Fund Mgmnt Ltd 1981-85); dir CFS (Investmt Mgmnt) Ltd 1985-88; md Rathbone Investmt Mgmnt 1988-;; *Books* The Big Shots (1977); *Recreations* shooting, opera, name-dropping; *Clubs* Athenaeum; *Style—* Jonathan Ruffer, Esq; Harewood Cottage, Ugley Green, Bishops Stortford, Herts CM22 6HW (☎ 0279 813105)

RUFUS, Michael John; s of James Henry Rufus (d 1969), and Maisie Priscilla Rufus; *b* 10 August 1938; *Educ* King Edward VI Edgbaston Birmingham, Southampton Univ (BSc, CBiol), Anglo European Coll of Chiropractice Bournemouth (DC); *Career* RN Aircrew (observer) 1958-71, serv Antarctic and Arctic in HMS Endurance 1968-70, Far E in HMS Victorious 1961-62, HMS Hermes 1966-68; Zoologist at Freshwater Biological Assoc River Lab Wareham 1974-77; established Sherborne Chiropractic Centre 1982; currently chm Dorset Working Spaniel Club (fndr ctee memb, former sec/tres); organiser, judge and commentator of numerous gundog competitions and events in SW England; *Style—* Michael Rufus, Esq; Tilly Whim, Bradford-Peverell, Dorchester, Dorset DT2 9SJ (☎ 0305 64084); Sherborne Chiropractic Centre, Half Moon St, Sherborne (☎ 0935 815660)

RUFUS ISAACS, Lord Alexander Gerald; s of 3 Marquess of Reading, MBE, MC (d 1980); *b* 25 April 1957; *Educ* St Paul's, Oriel Coll Oxford (MA), City Univ London; *Career* barr Middle Temple 1982; *Clubs* Dangerous Sports; *Style—* Lord Alexander Rufus Isaacs; 3 Tyrawley Rd, London SW6

RUFUS ISAACS, Lord Antony Michael; s of 3 Marquess of Reading, MBE, MC (d 1980); *b* 22 Sept 1943; *Educ* Gordonstoun; *m* 1, 1972 (m dis 1976), Anne Pugsley; m 2, 1983, Heide Lund, of Vancouver, BC; 1 da (Tallulah Elke Margot b 1987); *Style—* Lord Anthony Rufus Isaacs; 9723 Oak Pass Rd, Beverly Hills, California 90210, USA

RUGBY, 2 Baron (UK 1947); Alan Loader Maffey; s of 1 Baron Rugby, GCMG, KCB, KCVO, CSI, CIE (d 1969); *b* 16 April 1913; *Educ* Stowe; *m* 1947, Margaret, da of Harold Bindley; 3 s (and 1 s decd), 2 da; *Heir* s, Hon Robert Maffey; *Career* sits as Independent peer in House of Lords; serv WWII Flt Lt RAF; inventor Foldgate Herd Handler (RASE Silver Award 1974); farmer; *Style—* The Rt Hon Lord Rugby; Grove Farm, Frankton, Rugby, Warwicks

RUGGE-PRICE, Sir Charles Keith Napier; 9 Bt (UK 1804); s of Lt-Col Sir Charles James Napier Rugge-Price, 8 Bt (d 1966); *b* 7 August 1936; *Educ* Middleton Coll Ireland; *m* 1965, Jacqueline Mary, da of Maj Pierre Paul Loranger, MC, CD; 2 s (James b 1967, Andrew b 1970); *Heir* s, James Keith Peter Rugge-Price, b 8 April 1967; *Career* mangr Tomenson-Alexander Ltd Toronto 1971-76; supervisor Compensation City of Edmonton 1976-81; sr mgmnt conslt City of Edmonton 1982-; *Style—* Sir Charles Rugge-Price, Bt; 23 Lambert Crescent, St Albert, Alberta T8N 1M1, Canada; City of Edmonton, 16156 Centennial Bldgs, 10015-103 Avenue, Edmonton Alberta T5J 0K1 (☎ 403 428 5909)

RUGGE-PRICE, Maeve, Lady; Maeve Marguerite; da of Edgar Stanley de la Peña, of Hythe, Kent; *m* 1935, Lt-Col Sir Charles James Napier Rugge-Price, 8 Bt (d 1966); *Style—* Maeve, Lady Rugge-Price

RUGGLES-BRISE, Guy Edward; TD, DL (Essex 1967); s of Col Sir Edward Ruggles-Brise, 1 Bt, MC, TD, sometime MP Maldon, JP, DL (d 1942), by his 1 w, Agatha, *née* Gurney, of the Norfolk family; hp to bro, Sir John Ruggles-Brise, 2 Bt, CB, OBE, TD; *b* 15 June 1914; *Educ* Eton; *m* 7 Dec 1940, Elizabeth (d 1988), da of James Knox, of Smithstone House, Kilvinning, Ayrshire; 3 s (Timothy Edward b 1945, James Rupert b 1947, Samuel Guy b 1956); *Career* 104 Essex Yeo 1934-38, 147 Essex Yeo 1938-40, Capt, No 7 Commando 1940, POW Bardia 1941, escaped form Italy 1944; sr ptnr Brewin Dolphin & Co (Stockbrokers) 1973-79, memb Stock Exchange 1946-88; pres Pony Riding for the Disabled Tst 1983-84 (chm Exec Ctee 1968-78); High Sheriff Essex 1967-68; *Recreations* hunting, shooting, fishing; *Clubs* City of London; *Style—* Guy Ruggles-Brise, Esq, TD, DL; Ledgowan Lodge, Achnasheen, Ross (☎ 044 588 245); The Manor House, Housham Tye, Harlow, Essex (☎ 027 982 236); Brewin, Dolphin & Co, 5 Giltspur St, London EC1A 9DE (☎ 01 248 4400)

RUGGLES-BRISE, Sir John Archibald; 2 Bt (UK 1935), of Spains Hall, Finchingfield, Essex, CB (1958), OBE (Mil 1945), TD, JP (Essex 1946); s of Col Sir Edward Ruggles-Brise, 1 Bt, MC, TD, MP (d 1942); *b* 13 June 1908; *Educ* Eton; *Heir* bro, Guy Ruggles-Brise, TD, DL; *Career* Lloyd's underwriter; pres CLA 1957-59 (sponsored first CLA Game Fair 1958); Ld-Lt of Essex 1958-78, chm Standing Cncl Baronetage 1958-63, Church cmmnr 1959-64; pro-chllr Essex Univ 1964-74, hon DUniv Essex; hon freeman of Chelmsford; *Clubs* Carlton; *Style—* Col Sir John Ruggles-Brise, Bt, CB OBE, TD, JP; Spains Hall, Finchingfield, Essex CM7 4PF (☎ 0371 810266)

RUGGLES-BRISE, Rosemary Elizabeth; *née* Craig; da of John Sommerville Craig, of 1 Buckland Ct, 37 Belsize Park, London NW3 4EB, and Agnes Marchbank, *née* Marshall; *b* 23 Oct 1949; *Educ* St Leonards Sch St Andrews Fife; *m* 3 May 1975, Timothy Edward Ruggles-Brise, s of Capt Guy Edward Ruggles-Brise, of Housham Tye, Harlow, Essex; 2 s (Archie b 1979, Charlie b 1983), 2 da (Olivia b 1977, Felicity b 1984); *Career* Dip Serv 1971-75; ptnr Spains Hall Forest Tree Nursery 1979-; *Style—* Mrs Rosemary Ruggles-Brise; Spains Hall Farmhouse, Finchingfield, Essex CM7 4NJ (☎ 0371 810232)

RULE, Brian Francis; s of Sydney John Rule, Pen-Y-FFordd, Chester, and Josephine, *née* Hegarty; *Educ* Ysgol Daniel Owen Mold, Loughborough Univ of Technol (BSc, MSc); *m* 30 Aug 1963, Kay M, da of Dr Neville Alexander Dyce-Sharp; *Career* res asst Loughborough Univ 1963-65, project mangr Glasgow Univ 1965-67, dir of computing Univ of Aberdeen 1974-77 (lectr 1967-71, sr lectr 1971-74); dir: Honeywell Info Systems Ltd London 1977-79, Sci servs Natural Enviroment Res Cncl 1979-85; dir gen info Technol systems MOD 1985-; memb Antiquarian Horological Soc; dep chm City of Aberdeen Children's Panel 1971-74; *Recreations* antiquarian horology; *Clubs* Royal Cwlth Soc; *Style—* Brian Rule, Esq; c/o MOD, Whitehall, London (☎ 01 218 4828)

RULE, John Eric; s of Eric Houldsworth Rule, of Guildford, Surrey, and Alpha Rule (d 1988); *b* 15 Nov 1934; *Educ* John Bright GS Llandudno N Wales, Royal GS Guildford; *m* 5 Sept 1959, Georgina Frances, da of Frederick William Luck, of Guildford, Surrey; 1 s (Stephen b 1965), 1 da (Jane b 1961); *Career* Trooper Queen's Royal Lancers 1957, cmmnd 2 Lt RAPC 1958, Capt 1958-59; articled clerk Wrigley Cregan Todd & Co 1951-56; Arthur Anderson & Co: sr auditor 1960-63, audit mangr 1963-69, ptnr 1969-, euro banking co-ordination ptnr 1975-83, euro fin servs co-ordinator 1984-86; ICAEW: memb banking ctee, past chm auditing courses ctee, past chm auditing and accounting ed ctee; chm govrs Royal GS Guildford 1988-; ACA 1956, FCA 1966; *Recreations* gardening, golf, motor sailing; *Clubs* Naval & Military, NZ Golf; *Style—* John Rule, Esq; Fairwinds, 29 Warren Rd, Guildford, Surrey GU1 2HG (☎ 0483 63828); Arthur Andersen Ltd, 1 Surrey St, London WC2R 2PS (☎ 01 438 3908)

RULE, Hon Mrs (Miranda Jane Caroline); *née* Rhys; eldest da of 9 Baron Dynevor, *qv*; *b* 1960; *m* 1986, David Rule, 2 s of Ronald William Pritchard Rule, of Newcastle-under-Lyme, Staffs; 1 s (James Gareth b 1986), 1 da (Rhiannon b 1987); *Style—* The Hon Mrs Rule; c/o The Rt Hon Lord Dynevor, The Walk, Carmarthen Rd, Llandeilo, Dyfed

RUMBALL, Rev Frank Thomas; s of William Rumball (d 1979), of Shropshire, and Ethel Irine, *née* Peel; *b* 13 Jan 1943; *Educ* Ludlow GS, St Peter's Coll Saltley, Salisbury and Wells Theol Coll; *Career* hd of Music Walsall-Wood Secdy Sch 1963-69, hd of religious educn 1966-69, hd of music Ludlow Sch 1969-72; deacon Hereford Cathedral 1974, priest 1975, asst curate Bromyard 1974-78, team vicar Ewyas Marold Team Ministry 1978-81, Pastoral Care f Minsterly 1982-82, priest i/c Eye, Lucton, Croft with Yarpole 1982-; organist; *Recreations* shooting, fencing, yachting, giving organ recitals for charity; *Style—* The Rev Frank T Rumball; The Smithy, Acton Scott, Church Stretton, Shropshire SY6 6QN (☎ 069 46 339); Eye Vicarage, Leominster, Herefordshire HR6 0DP (☎ 0568 5710)

RUMBALL, (William) Norman; s of late Arthur Rumball; *b* 16 April 1906; *Educ* Mercers Sch; *m* 1935, Kathleen Ethel, *née* Le Rossignol; 1 s, 1 da; *Career* stockbroker, pres Le Masurier James & Chinn Ltd; *Recreations* golf; *Clubs* Victoria (Jersey), La Moye Golf (Jersey), Reform; *Style—* Norman Rumball, Esq; The Elms, Millbrook, Jersey, Channel Islands (☎ 0534 20244)

RUMBELOW, (Howard) Clive; s of Leonard Douglas Rumbelow (d 1980), of Cardiff, and Phyllis Mary Rumbelow (d 1984); *b* 13 June 1933; *Educ* Cardiff HS, Cambridge Univ (MA, LLM); *m* 29 June 1968, Carolyn Sandra, da of Dr Arthur Macdonald Macgregor (d 1963), of Epworth; 1 s (Michael b 1969), 2 da (Jane b 1970, Helen b 1972); *Career* RAF 1951-53; ptnr Slaughter and May 1968-; *Recreations* golf, squash; *Style—* Clive Rumbelow, Esq; 79 Princes Way, London SW19 6HY (☎ 01 789 4813); Slaughter & May, 35 Basinghall St, London EC2V 5DB (☎ 01 600 1200, fax 01 726 0038, telex 883 486)

RUMBLE, Capt John Bertram; s of Maj Leslie Rumble TD (d 1976), and Sybil Florence Leech-Porter (d 1988); *b* 30 Oct 1928; *Educ* Sherborne Sch; *m* 26 Sept 1952, Jennifer, da of Col R H Wilson, CIE, MC (d 1971); 1 s (Peter b 1956); 3 da (Sally-Anne b 1956, Nicola b 1959, Fiona b 1963); *Career* entered RN 1946, ADC (Lt) to Govr of Malta 1952-53, specialised in communications 1954; Signal Offr HMS Ark Royal 1959-61, cdr 1962, Co HMS Torquay 1964-66, staff communications offr to C in C Eastlant 1966-67, Exec Offr HMS Hermes 1967-69, Capt 1970, staff dir gen weapons 1970-71; Co HMS Fearless 1974-75; asst chief of staff Communications C in C South 1976-77 (Cdr); MOD Intelligence 1977-79; dir gen Royal Overseas League 1979-; memb Cncl Mayfair Picadilly and St James Assoc 1979 (chm 1980); FBIM, FIIM; *Recreations* fly fishing, shooting, goldleaf gilding, sailing; *Clubs* Farmers, Keyhaven Yacht, Milford-on-sea Tennis; *Style—* Capt J B Rumble, RN; 88 Wroughton Rd, London SW11 6AT (☎ 01 223 9413); Royal Overseas League, Overseas House, Park Place, St James's St, SW1

RUMBLE, Peter William; CB (1984); s of Arthur Victor Rumble and Dorothy Emily, *née* Sadler; *b* 28 April 1929; *Educ* Harwich County HS, Oriel Coll Oxford (MA); *m* 1953, Joyce Audrey Stephenson; 1 s, 1 da; *Career* entered Civil Service 1952, HM inspr of Taxes 1952, princ min of Housing and Local Govt 1963; Dept of the Environment: asst sec 1972, under sec 1977; chief exec Historic Buildings and Monuments Cmmn 1983-89, tstee American Friends of English Heritage 1988-, memb cncl Architectural Heritage Fund 1988-; *Recreations* music; *Style—* Peter Rumble, Esq, CB; 11 Hillside Road, Cheam, Surrey SM2 6ET (☎ 01 643 1752)

RUMBOLD, Sir (Horace) Algernon Fraser; KCMG (1960, CMG 1953), CIE (1947); s of Col William Rumbold, CMG, yr bro of Sir Horace Rumbold, 9 Bt; 1 cous of Sir Anthony Rumbold, 10 Bt (d 1983); hp of Sir Henry Rumbold, 11 Bt; *b* 27 Feb 1906; *Educ* Wellington, Christ Church Oxford; *m* 1946, Margaret Adel, da of Arthur Hughes; 2 da; *Career* India Off 1929-47, CRO 1947-66 (dep under sec of state 1958-66), advsr Welsh Off 1967; memb governing body SOAS 1965-80 (hon fell 1981), dep chm Air Tport Licensing Bd 1970-71; pres Tibet Soc of the UK 1977-88; *Books* Watershed in India (1979); *Style—* Sir Algernon Rumbold, KCMG, CIE; Shortwoods, W Clandon, Surrey (☎ 0483 222757)

RUMBOLD, Angela Claire Rosemary; CBE (1981), MP (C) Mitcham and Morden 1982-; da of late Prof Harry Jones, FRS, and his w Frances Molly; *b* 11 August 1932; *Educ* King's Coll London; *m* 1958, John Marix Rumbold, s of Marix Henry Branscombe Rumbold (d 1980); 2 s (Philip, Matthew), 1 da (Polly); *Career* former Pa to Sir Horace Cutler, ldr Cons GLC, chm AHA Educn Ctee 1978-79; chm: Nat Assoc for Welfare of Children in Hosp 1974-77, Policy and Resources Ctee (Kingston upon Thames Cncl) 1979-83, Cncl of Local Educn Authorities 1979-80; MP (C) Merton, Mitcham & Morden 1982; PPS to Nicholas Ridley, MP 1983-85; Parly under sec of state on environment 1985-, min of state DES 1986-; *Recreations* reading, swimming, music, gardening; *Style—* Mrs John Rumbold, CBE, MP; House of Commons, London SW1

RUMBOLD, Sir Henry John Sebastian; 11 Bt (GB 1779), of Wood Hall, Watton, Herts; s of Sir (Horace) Anthony Claude Rumbold, 10 Bt, KCMG, KCVO, CB (d 1983, formerly an ambass to Thailand and Austria), by his 1 w, Felicity (d 1984), da of late Lt-Col Frederick Bailey and Lady Janet, *née* Mackay (da of 1 Earl of Inchcape); *b* 24 Dec 1947; *Educ* Eton, William & Mary Coll, Virginia, USA; *m* 1978, Frances Ann, da of Dr Albert Whitfield Hawkes (decd), and formerly w of Julian Berry; *Heir* Sir Algernon Rumbold (cous); *Career* solicitor-ptnr Stephenson Harwood; *Recreations* riding, shooting, reading; *Style—* Sir Henry Rumbold, Bt; 19 Hollywood Rd, London SW10 9HT; Hatch House, Tisbury, Salisbury, Wilts SP3 6PA; 1 St Paul's Churchyard, London EC4M 8SH (☎ 01 329 4422)

RUMBOLD, Sir Jack Seddon; William Alexander Rumbold of Christchurch, NZ and Jean Lindsay Rumbold (*née* Mackay); *b* 5 Mar 1920,New Zealand; *Educ* St Andrew's College NZ, Canterbury Univ NZ (LLB 1940), Brasenose Coll Oxford Univ (Rhodes Scholar, BCL); *m* 1, Helen Suzanne Davis; 2 da; m 2 Veronica Ellie Hurt (*née* Whigham); *Career* RN Lt RNVR (despatches) 1941-45; called to Bar Inner Temple 1948, private legal practice; Colonial Legal Serv, Kenya 1957-62; attorney-general Zanzibar 1963-64; QC 1963; legal adviser Kenya Govt 1964-66; academic dir British Campus of Stanford Univ USA 1966-1972; chm of Industl Tbnls 1967-1979; pres of

Industl Tbnls England & Wales 1979-1984; *Recreations* books, music, formerly cricket (Oxford Blue 1946); *Clubs* Garrick, MCC; *Style—* Sir Jack Rumbold, QC

RUMBOLD, Pauline, Lady; Pauline Laetitia; da of late Hon David Francis Tennant, 3 s of 1 Baron Glenconner, and Hermione Youlanda Ruby Clinton (the actress Hermione Baddeley), da of late W H Clinton Baddeley, and Louise Bourdin; *b* 6 Feb 1929; *m* 1, 1946 (m dis 1953), Capt Julian Lane-Fox Pitt-Rivers; m 2, 1954, Euan Douglas Graham, yr s of Brig Lord Douglas Malise Graham, CB, DSO, MC, and n of 6 Duke of Montrose; m 3, 1974, (as his 2 w), Sir (Horace) Anthony Claude Rumbold, 10 Bt, KCMG, KCVO, CB (d 1983, former ambass to Thailand and Austria); *Style—* Pauline, Lady Rumbold; Hatch Cottage, Cokers Frome, Dorchester, Dorset

RUMGAY, Ian Charles; s of Alexander Edward Rumgay, and Violet Florence Emma, *née* Wright; *b* 26 May 1952; *Educ* Swanage GS; *Career* account mangr PR 1976-80, md Opinion PR 1980-82; dir: JPPR 1982-83, Shandwick PR Co 1983-; dept md Sandwick Communications Ltd 1989-; *Recreations* gardening, dining, tennis, skiing; *Style—* Ian Rumgay, Esq; Shandwick PR Co Ltd, 50 Upper Brook St, London W1N 1PG (☎ 01 491 4568/01 672 0986, fax 01 629 0425, telex 25914)

RUMSEY, (Raymond) Clive; s of Kenneth Walter Rumsey (d 1961), and Florence Alice, *née* Beveridge; *b* 21 Mar 1930; *Educ* Wimbledon Sch of Art (Nat Dip Design), RCA London (Graphic Design); *m* 4 Sept 1965, Lisa Anne, da of Patrick Vincent McGrath, of Chislehurst, Kent; 1 s (Julian St John b 17 Jan 1968); *Career* Nat Serv RCS 1949-51, NCO draughtsman Sch of Signals Catterick, HQ Southern Cmd Salisbury; Lintas Ltd London 1954-74: art dir, creative dir and head of dept (seven yrs spent in Europe as agency creative dir); ind advertising conslt 1974-75; McCann-Erickson Advertising: joined 1975, set up pan-Euro creative unit Euroteam, regnl creative dir (Europe) 1981-87 (responsible for creative standards of 22 offs across Europe), dep mangr McCann Erickson Paris, left agency 1988; conslt 1988-, lectr MIPA; *Recreations* travelling, collecting, objet d'art; *Style—* Clive Rumsey, Esq; The Old Cottage, Mount Lane, Barford St Martin, Salisbury, Wilts SP3 4AF (☎ 0722 743 236); c/o McCann-Erickson Advertising Ltd, 36 Howland St, London W1A 1AT (☎ 01 580 6690)

RUMSEY, Stephen John Raymond; s of John William Raymond Rumsey, of Hampstead, and May, *née* Blemings; *b* 6 Nov 1950; *Educ* Windsor GS, LSE (BSc); *m* 3 June 1978, Anne Christine Elaine, da of Arnold Williamson (d 1988) 2 s (James b 1979, Edward b 1981); *Career* investmt mangr Postel Investmt 1977-85, ptnr de Zoete of Bevan 1985-86, md fixed div Barclays de Zoete Wedd 1986-; fndr Wetland Tst, Churchill Fell 1970; cncllr Royal Borough of Kingston upon Thames 1978-82, dep chm Socl Serrs Ctee; memb Stock Exchange 1985; *Recreations* ornithology, agriculture, social servs; *Style—* Stephen Rumsey, Esq; Elms Farm, Pett Lane, Icklesham, Winchelsea, East Sussex, TN36 4AH (☎ 0797 226137) Barclays de Zoete Wedd Ltd, 2 Swan Lane, London EC4R 3TS (☎ 01 623 2323, fax 01 626 6106)

RUNCHORELAL, Sir Chinubhai Madhowlal; 2 Bt (UK 1913), of Shahpur, Ahmedabad, India; s of Sir Chinubhai Madhowlal Runchorelal, CIE (d 1916), whose name he then assumed in place of that of Girjaprasad; *b* 19 April 1906; *m* 1924, Tanumati Zaverilal Mehta, of Ahmedabad, India (d 1971); 3 s; *Style—* Sir Chinubhai Runchorelal, Bt; Shantikunj, Shahibag, Ahmedabad, India

RUNCHORELAL, Udayan Chinubhai Madhowlal; s and h of Sir Chinubhai Runchorelal, 2 Bt; *b* 25 July 1929; *m* 1953, Muneera Khodadad Foxdar, of Bombay; 1 s, 3 da; *Career* nat pres India Jr Chamber 1961-62, currently a Jaycee Senator; represented Gujarat in Ranji Trophy in Cricket and played the combined Univ XI against Pakistan; represented India in int events in target shooting on 4 occasions; awarded Arjun Award for Target shooting 1972-73; *Recreations* cricket, target shooting; *Style—* Udayan Runchorelal Esq

RUNCIE, Most Rev and Rt Hon Robert Alexander Kennedy; *see*: Canterbury, Archbishop of

RUNCIMAN, Hon Mrs (Anne Elizabeth); *née* Bewick-Copley; da of 6 Baron Cromwell (d 1982); *b* 1955; *Educ* Oxford HS; *m* 1982, David James McNaught Runciman; *Career* television prodr; *Style—* The Hon Mrs Runciman

RUNCIMAN, Hugh Leishman Inglis (Peter); s of Hugh Inglis Runciman (d 1950), of Aberdeen, and Gladys West, *née* Rowbotham (d 1986); *b* 9 Oct 1928; *Educ* St Alban's Coll Buenos Aires, King's Coll London (BSc); *m* 7 Aug 1957, Rosemary Janet, da of John Hadfield, of Sheffield; 3 da (Alison Jane b 1962, Rosemary Ann b 1964, Helen Mary b 1967); *Career* 2 Lt RE 1947-49; asst chief designer Chloride Batteries Ltd 1953-60, md Derbyshire Stone Quarries Ltd 1961-68, dir Tarmac Roodstone Hldgs Ltd 1969-79, chm Shanics & McEwan Gp plc 1980-; non exec dir Br Steel plc, Scottish Nat Tst plc; former pres Glasgow C of C; memb: Scottish Business Gp, cncl Aims of Indust, Scottish Economic Cncl; Freeman City of Glasgow, memb Incorpn of Hammermen 1988; FIQ; *Recreations* squash, fishing, shoting, gardening; *Clubs* Fly Fishers, Western; *Style—* Peter Runciman, Esq; Shoreacres, Rhu, Dunbartonshire (☎ 0436 820445); Shanics & McEwan Gp plc, 22 Woodside Pl, Glasgow G3 7QY (☎ 041 331 2614, fax 041 331 2071)

RUNCIMAN, Hon Sir Steven (James Cochran Stevenson); CH (1984); 2 s of 1 Viscount Runciman of Doxford; *b* 7 July 1903; *Educ* Eton, Trinity Cambridge; *Career* historian; prof of Byzantine history Istanbul Univ 1942-45, Br Cncl rep Greece 1945-47; recipient of Wolfson Literary Award 1982; Kt Cdr Order of the Phoenix (Greece) 1961; FBA; kt 1958; *Books Incl:* A History of the Crusades (in 3 vols); *Clubs* Athenaeum; *Style—* The Hon Sir Steven Runciman, CH; Elshieshields, Lockerbie, Dumfriesshire (☎ 038 781 0280)

RUNCIMAN, Hon Walter Garrison (Garry); CBE (1987); s and h of 2 Viscount Runciman of Doxford, OBE, AFC, AE, DL, by his 2 w, Katherine; *b* 10 Nov 1934; *Educ* Eton, Trinity Coll Cambridge; *m* 1963, Ruth, da of Joseph Hellman, of Johannesburg; 1 s, 2 da; *Career* fell Trinity Coll Cambridge 1959-63 and 1971-; chm Walter Runciman plc & subsids 1976- (joined firm 1964); sociologist, former pt/t reader in sociology Sussex Univ; tres Child Poverty Action Gp 1972-; vice-pres Gen Cncl Br Shipping 1985-86, pres 1986-87; memb Securities and Investmts Bd 1986-; FBA 1975; *Books* Plato's Later Epistemology (1962); Social Science and Political Theory (1963); Relative Deprivation and Social Justice (1966); A Critique of Max Weber's Philosophy of Social Science (1972); A Treatise on Social Theory Vol I (1983), Vol II (1989); *Clubs* Brooks's; *Style—* The Hon Garry Runciman, CBE; 36 Carlton Hill, NW8 (☎ 01 624 8419)

RUNCIMAN OF DOXFORD, 2 Viscount (UK 1937); Sir Walter Leslie Runciman; 3 Bt (UK 1906), OBE (1946), AFC (1937), AE, DL (Northumberland 1961); also Baron Runciman (UK 1933); s of 1 Viscount Runciman of Doxford, (shipowner, MP, pres BOT and head Mission Czechoslovakia 1938, d 1949) and Hilda Stevenson, MP, JP; bro of Sir Steven Runciman, the historian; *b* 26 August 1900; *Educ* Eton, Trinity Coll Cambridge (MA); *m* 1, 1923 (m dis 1928), Rosamond Lehmann (the writer), *qv*; m 2, 1932, Katherine Schuyler, da of William Garrison, of New York; 1 s; *Heir* s, Hon Walter Garrison Runciman; *Career* RAuxAF 1930-46, acting Air Cdre 1943-46; pres Marine Soc; shipowner, pres UK Chamber Shipping 1952; former banker; elder brother of Trinity House; Hon DCL Durham; *Recreations* sailing (yacht 'Virgo'), shooting; *Clubs* Brooks's, Royal Yacht Sqdn; *Style—* The Rt Hon the Viscount Runciman of Doxford, OBE, AFC, AE, DL; Doxford, Chathill, Northumberland (☎ Chathill (066 589) 223); 46 Abbey Lodge, Park Rd, London NW8 9AT (☎ 01 723 6882)

RUNCORN, Prof (Stanley) Keith; s of William Henry Runcorn (d 1966), of Southport, Lancs, and Lily Idina, *née* Roberts; *b* 19 Nov 1922; *Educ* King George V Sch Southport, Gonville and Caius Coll Cambridge (BA, MA, ScD), Manchester Univ (PhD); *Career* serv WWII: experimental offr Miny of Supply Air Def (later known as Radar Res and Devpt Estab) 1943-46; lectr physics Manchester Univ 1948-49 (asst lectr 1946-48), fell Gonville and Caius Coll Cambridge 1948-55, asst dir of res in geophysics Cambridge Univ 1950-55; prof of physics and head of dept: King's Coll Durham Univ 1956-63, Univ of Newcastle upon Tyne 1963-88; Royal Soc Rutherford Memorial lectr 1970, Halley lectr Oxford Univ 1973, Sydney Chapman prof of physical sci Univ of Alaska 1988-, sr res fell Imperial Coll of Sci & Technol London 1988-; visiting prof: California Inst of Technol 1958, UCLA 1975, Univ of California (Hitchcock prof) 1982, Univ of Queensland 1981; J Ellerton Becker visiting fell Aust Acad of Sci 1963; memb cncl Natural Environment Res Cncl 1965-69; hon DSc: Utrecht 1969, Ghent 1971, Paris 1979, Bergen 1980; FRS 1965, FRAS, FInstP, hon memb EGS, fel AGU, memb Pontifical Acad of Sci; foreign memb: Royal Netherlands Acad of Arts and Sci, Royal Norwegian Acad of Sci and Letters, Indian Nat Sci Acad; Vettesen Prize Columbia Univ & Vettesen Fndn New York 1971, Gold Medal Royal Astron Soc 1984, Wegener Medal European Union of Glosciences 1987; *Books* Dictionary of Geophysics (ed), Continental Drift (ed), Physics of the Earth and Planetary Interiors (ed 1967); *Recreations* squash rackets, swimming, hiking, rugby; *Clubs* Athenaeum, Union Soc (Newcastle upon Tyne); *Style—* Prof Keith Runcorn; c/o Dept of Physics, Univ of Newcastle, Newcastle upon Tyne NE17 7RU (☎ 091 222 7287, fax 091 2611182)

RUNDALL, Lady Rosalthé Frances; *née* Ryder; o da of 7 Earl of Harrowby, *qv*; *b* 1 May 1954; *Educ* Queensgate Sch London; *m* 1976, Francis Richard Seton Rundall, yr s of Frank Lionel Montagu Rundall, Dove House, Stutton, Ipswich, Suffolk, 3 s (Francis Thomas Mansell b 1981, Mark Dudley Ridgway b 1982, John William Nathaniel b 1987); *Style—* The Lady Rosalthé; Greater Aston Farmhouse, Aston Sub Edge, Chipping Campden, Glos

RUNGE, Charles David; s of Sir Peter Runge (d 1970), of Lane End, High Wycombe, Bucks, and The Hon Lady Fiona Margaret Stewart, *née* Macpherson, da of 1 Baron Strathcarron; *b* 24 May 1944; *Educ* Eton, Christ Church Oxford (MA), Manchester Business Sch; *m* 1, 28 July 1969 (m dis 1979), Harriet, da of late John Bradshaw, of Inkpen, Berks; 1 s (Tom b 1971), 1 da (Louise b 1973); m 2, 9 April 1981, Jil, da of John Liddell (d 1987), of Greenock, Scotland; 1 da (Emma b 1986); *Career* Tate & Lyle: md tport 1977-79, chief exec refineries 1979-81, md agribusiness 1983-86, dir corporate affrs 1986-87; chief exec Milk Mktg Bd 1988-; *Recreations* music, walking, fishing; *Clubs* Boodles; *Style—* Charles Runge, Esq; The Milk Marketing Bd, Thames Ditton, Kingston KT7 0EL (☎ 01 398 4101)

RUNGE, Hon Lady (Fiona Margaret); *née* Macpherson; er da of 1 Baron Strathcarron, KC, PC (d 1937), and Jill (d 1956), da of Sir George Wood Rhodes, 1 Bt, JP; *b* 9 Feb 1917; *m* 29 Oct 1935, Sir Peter Francis Runge (d 1970), 2 s of Julius Joseph Runge, of Seven Oaks, Kent; 3 s, 1 da; *Style—* The Hon Lady Runge; 4 Lammas Way, Lane End, High Wycombe, Bucks 4P14 3EX

RUOFF, Theodore Burton Fox; CB (1970), CBE (1962); s of Percy Otto Ruoff (d 1971), of Herts, and Edith, *née* Crane (d 1910); *b* 12 April 1910; *Educ* King Edward VI GS Bury St Edmunds Suffolk; *m* 1947, Marjorie Alice, da of George Mawson (d 1946), of Sussex; *Career* slr, Chief Land Registrar of England & Wales 1963-75; works: An Englishman Looks at the Torrens System (1957), Ruoff's Concise Land Registration Practice (co-author) 3 edn 1982), Rentcharges in Registered Conveyancing (1961), Ruoff's Land Registration Forms (co-author 3 edn 1983), The Law & Practise of Registered Conveyancing (5 edn with R B Roper and others 1986), Land Registration Handbook (with EJ Pryer, CB (1989), Legal Legends and other True Stories (1989); *Recreations* sketching, painting, gardening, golf, making cassettes for the blind; *Clubs* Travellers', MCC; *Style—* Theodore Ruoff, Esq; Flat One, 83 South Hill Park, Hampstead, London NW3 2SS (☎ 01 435 8014)

RUSBRIDGER, Hon Lindsay Mary; *née* Mackie; da of Baron Mackie of Benshie (Life Peer); *b* 1945; *m* 1982, Alan, yr s of G H Rusbridger, of Warren Rd, Guildford; *Style—* The Hon Mrs Rusbridger; c/o Ballinshoe, Kirriemuir, Angus DD8 5Q9

RUSBY, Vice-Adm Sir Cameron; KCB (1979), LVO (1965); s of Capt Victor Evelyn Rusby, CBE, RN, and Irene Margaret, *née* Gunn; *b* 20 Feb 1926; *Educ* RNC Dartmouth; *m* 1948, Marion Bell; 2 da; *Career* Dep Supreme Allied Cdr Atlantic 1980-82, ret 1982; cmd offr HMS Ulster 1958-59, exec offr HM Yacht Britania 1962-65, Dep Dir Naval Signals 1965-68, cmd offr HMS Tartar 1968-69, Dep Assist COS Plans and Policy on staff of Allied C in C Southern Europe 1969-72, Sr Naval Offr West Indies 1972-74, Rear Adm 1974, Asst Chief Dep Staff Ops 1974-77, Vice Adm 1977, Flag Offr Scotland and NI 1977-79; *Style—* Vice Adm Sir Cameron Rusby, KCB, LVO; c/o Bank of Scotland, 70 High St, Peebles EH45 8AQ

RUSH, Allen Frank; s of Colin Charles Rush (d 1968), of Richmond, Surrey, and Muriel Mary, *née* Hinds (d 1968); *b* 2 Jan 1933; *Educ* Kings Coll Sch Wimbledon, King's Coll Univ of London (BSc); *m* 1, 26 July 1958 (m dis 1979), Janet Larema, da of Lt Col David George Ogilvy Ayerst, of Burford, Oxon; 1 s (David b 1959), 2 da (Susan b 1961, Lindy b 1970); m 2, Linda Evelyn, da of Maurice Stratton Townsend, of High Wycombe; *Career* Flying Offr RAF 1954-56; mgmnt consIt A/C Inbucon 1961-65; WS Try Ltd: dir 1968, md 1972, chm of int subsid 1977, dep chm 1983; commenced Michael Rush Assoc 1985, project mangr Daily Mail & Evening Standard new devpt printing works 1985; MICE 1958, memb IOD 1975, FFB 1983; *Recreations* horse riding; *Clubs* RAF; *Style—* Allen Rush, Esq; Kingstreet End, Little Missenden,

Amersham, Bucks HP7 ORA (☎ 02406 6864); PO Box 137, Amersham, Bucks HP7 0RS (☎ 02406 6214, car tel 0836 233 674)

RUSHDIE, (Ahmed) Salman; s of Anis Ahmed Rushdie (d 1987), and Negin, *née* Butt; *b* 19 June 1947, (Bombay); *Educ* Rugby, King's Coll Cambridge; *m* 1, 1976 (m dis 1987), Clarissa Luard; 1 s; 2, 1988, Marianne Wiggins; *Career* former advertising copywriter; memb gen cncl Camden Ctee for Community Relations 1977-; novelist; *Books* Grimus (1975), Midnight's Children (winner of Booker Prize 1981), Shame (1983), The Jaguar Smile: a Nicaraguan Journey (1987), The Satanic Verses (1988); *Style*— Salman Rushdie, Esq; c/o Jonathan Cape Ltd, 30 Bedford Sq, WC1 (☎ 01 636 5674/9395)

RUSHFORD, Antony Redfern; CMG (1963); s of Stanley Rushford (d 1952), of New Milton Hants, and Sarah Beatrice, *née* Sould (d 1979); *b* 9 Feb 1922; *Educ* Taunton, Trinity Coll Cambridge (MA, LLM); *m* 1975, June Jeffery Wells, da of Charles Reginald Morrish, DSC, KPM (d 1952); 1 s (Simon), 1 da (Samantha), stepchildren; *Career* RAFVR 1943-77, Sqdn Ldr 1946; barr Inner Temple (formerly solicitor), asst slr EW Marshall Harvey & Dalton 1948, Home Civil Service CO 1949-68, joined HM Dip Serv 1968, CO, late FCO, ret as dep legal advsr (asst under-sec of State) 1982, Crown Counsel Uganda 1954-63, princ legal advsr Br Indian Ocean Territory 1983-, attorney-gen Anguilla and St Helena 1983, legal advsr for Cwlth Sec-Gen St Kitts and Nevis independence 1982-83, E Caribbean cts 1983; maritime legislation for Jamaica Int Maritime Orgn 1983 and 1984, special legal advsr Govt of St Lucia 1982-; has drafted many constitutions for UK dependencies and Cwlth countries attaining independence; presented paper on constitutional dvpt to meeting of Law Offrs from smaller Cwlth Jurisdications IOM 1983, UK del and advsr at many consititutional conferences and discussions; co rep Inst of Advanced Legal Studies, lectr Overseas Legal Offrs course, memb editorial bd Inst of Int Law and Econ Dvpt Washington 1977-82, fndr memb Exec Cncl Royal Cwlth Soc for the Blind 1969-81 and 1983- (hon legal advsr 1984-), memb: Glyndebourne Festival, Cwlth Lawyers Assoc, Cwlth Assoc of Legislative Counsel 1984-; govr Taunton Sch 1948-; OStJ; FRAS; *Clubs* Royal Cwlth Soc; *Style*— Antony Rushford, Esq, CMG; The Penthouse, 63 Pont St, Knightsbridge SW1X 0BD

RUSHMAN, Nigel John; s of Maj Frederick William Edward Henry Rushman of Lancs, and Irene Vera, *née* Beer; *b* 25 May 1956; *Educ* Gillingham Tech HS, Gravesend GS, Thanet Tech Coll; *m* 1, 21 Sept 1980 (m dis), Deborah Sally, da of Kenneth William White, of London; 1 da (Louise Amanda b 1986); *Career* md: Rushman Communications; currently dir: 4th Market Ltd, Rushman Investmts; MRSPHH, FInstSMM; *Recreations* motor polo, hunting, shooting, skiing; *Clubs* Royal Corithian YC, St James's; *Style*— Nigel Rushman, Esq; Breach Cottage, Easton Royal, Pewsey Wilts (☎ 0672 810497); Mayfair Chambers, 7 Broadbent St, London W1; Rusham Communications Ltd, Warmlake Estate, Sutton Valence, Kent (☎ 0622 842966, fax 0622 843202, car tel 0860 821 651)

RUSHMORE, Brigadier Frederick Herbert Margetson; CBE (1962, OBE 1956, MBE 1951); s of Frederick Margetson Rushmore, master of St Catharine's Coll Cambridge (d 1933), and Millicent Sarah, *née* Beck (d 1965); *b* 19 May 1915; *Educ* King's Sch Bruton, Christ's Coll Cambridge (BA); *Career* served RA 1935-70 (Burma 1943-44, Korea 1952-53), Brig; dir Nat Assoc of Leagues of Hospital Friends 1970-80, chm General Cmmrs for Income Tax (Holborn Div) 1979-; *Recreations* music, drama; *Clubs* London Rowing, Leander; *Style*— Brig Frederick Rushmore, CBE; 71 Lakeside House, Eaton Drive, Kingston upon Thames, Surrey (☎ 01 549 1877)

RUSHTON, James Edward; s of Edward Sydney Rushton (d 1983), of Wilmslow, Cheshire, and Stella Kathleen Joan Rushton; *b* 8 August 1936; *Educ* Repton; *m* 1, 6 June 1963, Fiona Patricia, da of George Stirling Tuite; 2 da (Emma b 1963, Sophie b 1965); m 2, 26 May 1972, Angela Christine, da of Harry Coupe Wrather; 1 s (Daniel b 1973); m 3, 24 June 1983, Marjorie Evelyn, da of James Eric Pickering (d 1958); *Career* chartered surveyor; ptnr Edward Rushton Son & Kenyon 1963 (sr ptnr 1978-); chm Gen Practice Div Educ Ctee 1980-83 (chm Gtr Manchester Branch 1987-88); MRICS Gen Practice Divnl Cncl 1976-84; ctee memb Greater Manchester branch IOD; *Recreations* golf, travel, photography; *Clubs* E India, St James's (Manchester); *Style*— James E Rushton, Esq; Legh House, Wilmslow Rd, Mottram-St-Andrew, Macclesfield, Cheshire (☎ 0625 828901); Edward Rushton Son & Kenyon, Kings Court, Exchange St, Manchester M2 3AX

RUSSELL; *see*: Hamilton-Russell

RUSSELL, Hon Mrs (Ann Bridget); *née* Parnell; 4 da of 6 Baron Congleton (d 1932); *b* 27 April 1927; *m* 5 Nov 1947 (m dis 1967), Major Derek Campbell Russell, RE; 3 children by adoption (2 s, 1 da); *Style*— The Hon Mrs Russell; Lyscombe Farm, Piddletrenthide, Dorset

RUSSELL, Rev Canon Dr Anthony John; s of Michael John William and Beryl Margaret Russell; *b* 25 Jan 1943; *Educ* Uppingham, Univ of Durham (BA), Univ of Oxford (DPhil), Cuddesdon Theological Coll; *m* 1967, Sheila Alexandra, da of Alexander Scott; 2 s (Jonathan b 1971, Timothy b 1981), 2 da (Alexandra b 1969, Serena b 1975); *Career* dir Arthur Rank Centre; chaplain to HM The Queen; canon theologian of Coventry Cathedral; examining chaplain to Bp of Hereford; chaplain: Royal Agric Soc of England, Royal Agric Benevolent Inst; *Books* Groups and Teams in the Countryside (1975), The Clerical Profession (1980), The Country Parish (1986); *Style*— The Rev Canon Anthony Russell; The Rectory, Whitchurch, Stratford-on-Avon, Warwickshire CV37 8NS; Arthur Rank Centre, National Agricultural Centre, Kenilworth, Warwickshire CV8 2LZ (☎ 0203 555100)

RUSSELL, Hon Anthony John Mark; yst s of 4 Baron Ampthill; *b* 10 May 1952; *Educ* Stowe; *m* 22 June 1985, Christine L, er da of John O'Dell; 1 s (William Odo Alexander b 10 May 1986); *Style*— The Hon Anthony Russell

RUSSELL, Anthony Patrick; s of Dr Michael Hibberd Russell (d 1987), of Little Sutton, S Wirral, and Pamela, *née* Eyre; *b* 11 April 1951; *Educ* The Kings Sch Chester, Pembroke Coll Oxford (BA, MA); *Career* barr Middle Temple 1974, Northern circuit 1974 (jr 1977), sec Manchester Middle Temple Soc 1986-, memb Bar Cncl 1988-; memb Cncl Guild of Church Musicians 1985-, sec Fabric Ctee Manchester Cathedral 1987-; *Recreations* music, singing, sailing, reading; *Clubs* Utd Oxford and Cambridge; *Style*— Anthony Russell, Esq; 37 Willow Park, Willow Bank, Fallowfield, Manchester M14 6XP (☎ 061 224 4413); Old Bank Chambers, 2 Old Bank St, Manchester M2 7PF (☎ 061 832 3791, fax 061 835 3054)

RUSSELL, Sir Archibald Edward; CBE (1955); s of Arthur Hallett Russell (d 1961); *b* 30 May 1904; *Educ* Fairfield GS, Bristol Univ (BSc); *m* 1929, Lorna Lillian, da of James J Mansfield (d 1932), of Newport; 1 s, 1 da; *Career* chief designer Bristol Aeroplane Co Ltd 1943, tech dir 1952; tech dir Br Aircraft Corpn 1960-66, md 1966-67, chm (Filton Div) 1967-69, ret 1971; memb Cncl Air Registration 1961-71; FRS, RAeS Gold Medal 1955, Daniel Guggenheim Medal 1971; Elmer A Sperry Medal 1983; kt 1972; *Style*— Sir Archibald Russell, CBE; Glendower House, Clifton Park, Bristol 8 (☎ 0272 739208)

RUSSELL, Rev Arthur Colin; CMG (1957), ED (1941); s of Arthur Walker Russell, OBE, WS (d 1967); *b* 2 Nov 1906; *Educ* Harrow, Brasenose Coll Oxford (MA); *m* 1939, Elma Isobel (d 1967), da of late Douglas Strachan (Hon RSA); 3 da (and 1 decd); *Career* Capt Gold Coast Regt, admin officer Colonial Serv 1929-57 (Gold Coast); Barr Inner Temple 1939; Chief Regnl Offr Ashanti, 1955-57, Parish min Church of Scotland Aberlemno, Angus 1959-76, dist cllr Angus Dist Cncl 1977-84; *Books* Stained Glass Windows of Douglas Strachan; *Recreations* hill walking, bird-watching, bridge, chess; *Style*— The Rev Arthur Russell, CMG, ED; Balgavies Lodge, by Forfar, Angus DD8 2TH (☎ 030 781 571)

RUSSELL, Arthur Mervyn; s of Sir Arthur Russell, 6 Bt (d 1964), and hp of half-bro, Sir George Russell, 7 Bt; *b* 7 Feb 1923; *Style*— Arthur Russell, Esq

RUSSELL, Hon Mrs Barbara; *née* Baroness Barbara Korff; da of Baron Serge Alexandrovitch Korff, of Russia; *b* 31 Jan 1911; *m* 1941, Hon Edward Wriothesley Curzon Russell, OBE (d 1982, sometime managing ed Morning Post), 3 s of 2 Baron Ampthill; 2 da (Diana b 1943, Angela b 1946); *Style*— The Hon Mrs Edward Russell; Tall Pines, 308 Hearthstone Ridge, Landrum, S Carolina 29356-9602, USA (☎ 803 457 4689); Pony's Point, Iona, CB1, Nova Scotia, (BOA 1LO) Canada (☎ 902 622 2766)

RUSSELL, Charles Dominic; s and h of Sir Charles Russell, 3 Bt, *qv*; *b* 28 May 1956; *Educ* Worth Abbey Sch; *m* 24 May 1986, Sarah Jane Murray, da of Anthony Chandor, of Blackdown Border, Haslemere, Surrey; *Career* antiquarian book dealer; *Style*— Charles Russell Esq; 3 Chartfield Sq, London SW15

RUSSELL, Sir Charles Ian; 3 Bt (UK 1916), of Littleworth Corner, Burnham, co Buckingham; s of Capt Sir Alec Charles Russell, MC, 2 Bt (d 1938); *b* 13 Mar 1918; *Educ* Beaumont Coll, Univ Coll Oxford; *m* 18 Jan 1947, Rosemary, da of late Maj Sir John Theodore Prestige, of The Court House, Bishopsbourne, Canterbury; 1 s, 1 da; m 2, 1986, Sarah Chandor; 1 s (Charles Williams b 1988); *Heir* s, Charles Dominic Russell; *Career* serv WWII Capt RHA (despatches); slr 1947, former sr partner Charles Russell & Co, of Hale Court, Lincoln's Inn, WC2, currently a conslt; *Clubs* Garrick, Army and Navy, Royal St George; *Style*— Sir Charles Russell, Bt; Hidden House, Strand St, Sandwich, Kent

RUSSELL, Christopher Garnet; s of George Percival Jewett (d 1948), of Michelgrove House, Michelgrove Rd, Boscombe, Hants, and Marjorie Alice Boddam-Whetham, *née* Keeling-Bloxam; *b* 6 April 1943; *Educ* Westminster, New Coll Oxford (MA); *m* 23 June 1973, Agatha Mary, da of Stephen Joseph Culkin (d 1984); 1 s (Charles b 1976), 2 da (Claire b 1974, Lucy b 1975); *Career* barr Middle Temple 1971, Lincoln's Inn 1985; *Style*— Christopher Russell, Esq; 11 Church St, Marcham, Oxon (☎ 0865 391 553); 86 Paramount Ct, University St, London WC1 (☎ 01 383 5943); 12 New Sq, Lincoln's Inn, London WC2 (☎ 01 405 3808, fax 01 831 7376)

RUSSELL, 5 Earl (UK 1861) Conrad Sebastian Robert; also Viscount Amberley (UK 1861); s of 3 Earl Russell, OM, FRS (d 1970, otherwise Bertrand Russell, the philosopher, writer and savant; himself ggs of Lord John Russell, of Great Reform Bill fame and twice PM, 6 3 s of 6 Duke of Bedford and 1 Earl Russell), by his 3 w, Patricia; suc half-bro, 4 Earl (d 1987); *b* 15 April 1937; *Educ* Eton, Merton Coll Oxford; *m* 1962, Elizabeth, da of Horace Sanders, of Chippenham, Wilts; 2 s (Nicholas Lyluph b 1968, John Francis b 1971); *Heir* s, Viscount Amberley; *Career* reader in history Bedford Coll London 1979; prof history Yale Univ USA 1979-84, Astor prof Br history Univ Coll London 1984-; *Books* The Crisis of Parliaments: English History 1509-1660 (1971), The Origins of the English Civil War (1973), Parliaments and English Politics 1621-1629 (1979); *Style*— The Rt Hon the Earl Russell; 43 Streatley Road, London NW6

RUSSELL, Cyril; s of Gerald Cyril Russell, MC (d 1962), of The Covert, Aldeburgh, Suffolk, and Barbara, *née* Reynolds; *b* 2 Oct 1924; *Educ* Beaumont Coll; *m* 30 June 1949, (Eileen Mary) Elizabeth, da of Maj William Douglas Grant Batten (d 1934); 3 s (Gerald b 1950, Patrick b 1952, Nicholas b 1958); *Career* cmmnd Irish Gds 1943, Serv 3 Bn: France, Belgium, Holland (wounded Sept 1944); admitted slr 1948, ptnr Charles Russell & Co 1951, sr ptnr Charles Russell Williams & James; memb Law Soc; *Recreations* golf, sailing; *Clubs* Boodle's, Swinley Forest Golf, MCC Aldeburgh Yacht, Aldeburgh Golf; *Style*— Cyril Russell, Esq; 42 Queensdale Rd, London, W11 (☎ 01 603 5828); The Covert, Aldeburgh, Suffolk; Hale Court, Lincoln's Inn, London, WC2 3UL (☎ 01 242 1031, fax 01 430 0388, telex 23521 LAWYER G)

RUSSELL, Hon (Francis) Damian; 2 s of Baron Russell of Killowen, PC (Life Peer d 1986) and Joan (d 1976), only child of James Aubrey Torrens, MD, FRCP, of Wimpole St, London W1; *b* 8 June 1947; *Educ* Beaumont, Trinity Coll Dublin; *Recreations* art, books, skiing, shooting; *Style*— The Hon Damian Russell; 17 Lurline Gdns, London SW11 (☎ 01 622 6820)

RUSSELL, Hon Daniel Charles Edward; yst s of Capt the Hon Langley Gordon Haslingden Russell, MC (d 1981), o s of 2 Baron Russell of Liverpool, CBE, MC; bro of 3 Baron; granted rank of a Baron's s 1983; *b* 8 Mar 1962; *Style*— The Hon Daniel Russell

RUSSELL, Lady Daphne Crommelin; da of 12 Duke of Bedford (d 1953); *b* 2 Sept 1920; *Style*— Lady Daphne Russell; Oak Cottage, Beckley, Rye, Sussex

RUSSELL, David Francis Oliphant; CBE (1969), MC (1942), DL (1955); s of Sir David Russell, LLD (d 1956), of Silverburn, Leven, Fife, and Deborah Margaret Alison Russell (d 1958); *b* 9 Sept 1915; *Educ* Sedbergh, St Andrews Univ (DSc, LLD); *m* 1945, Catherine Joan, *née* Robinson; 4 da (Margaret, Mary, Cecilia, Judy); *Career* serv WWII Maj: N Africa, Sicily, France; hon pres Tullis Russell Co Ltd (chm and md 1945-85), Chancellor's Assessor St Andrew's Univ 1963-75 (remained Ct memb); memb Royal Co of Archers (The Queen's Body Guard for Scotland) 1949, bd of tstees Nat Museum of Antiquities 1966-82; cncllr emeritus Nat Trust for Scotland 1976; FRSE; *Recreations* fishing, shooting; *Clubs* New (Edinburgh); *Style*— David Russell, Esq, CBE, MC, DL; Rossie, Collessie, by Ladybank, Fife (☎ 0337 28 300)

RUSSELL, David Wallace; s of Charles Henry William Russell (d 1982), and Violet Lilian Vida, *née* David; *b* 2 July 1936; *Educ* Dulwich; *m* 1, 19 Sept 1959 (d 1967), Julia Eleanor, da of Raywood Ingham of Eastbourne; 2 s (Simon b 1962, Timothy b 1963);

m 2, 12 July 1969, Irene, da of Dirk Marinus Uijl (d 1965), of Rotterdam; 2 da (Christina b 1970, Rebecca b 1972); *Career* Nat Serv cmmnd RASC 1959-60; slr 1958-, chm Portsmouth Bldg Soc (dir 1974-), ptnr Blake Lapthorn Slrs 1962-, clerk to Gen Cmmrs of Income Tax Portsmouth and Havant Dists 1974-; chm of govrs Portsmouth GS (govr 1980-); memb Law Soc; *Recreations* squash, skiing, walking, caravanning; *Style*— David Russell, Esq; Montgomery House, 11 Montgomery Rd, Havant, Hants PO9 2RH; Blake Lapthorn, 8 Landport Terr, Portsmouth PO1 2QW

RUSSELL, Hon David Whitney Erskine; s and h of 4 Baron Ampthill and his 1 w, Susan Mary, da of Hon Charles Winn (s of 2 Baron St Oswald, JP, DL); *b* 27 May 1947; *Educ* Stowe; *m* 15 Nov 1980, April McKenzie, yst da of Paul Arbon, of New York; 2 da (Christabel b 1981, Daisy b 1983); *Clubs* Turf, White's; *Style*— The Hon David Russell; 21 Albert Bridge Rd, London SW11 4PX (☎ 01 627 2080)

RUSSELL, Prof Donald Andrew Frank Moore; s of Samuel Charles Russell (d 1979), and Laura, *née* Moore (d 1966); *b* 13 Oct 1920; *Educ* King's Coll Sch Wimbledon, Balliol Coll Oxford (BA, DLitt); *m* 22 July 1967, Joycelyne Gledhill Dickinson (Joy), da of Percy Parkin Dickinson (d 1972); *Career* serv WWII: Royal Signals 1941-43, Intelligence Corps 1943-45; fell St John's Coll Oxford 1948-88; univ lectr classical languages and lit 1957-58, reader classical lit 1978-85, prof classical lit 1985-88; JH Gray Lectures Cambridge Univ 1981, Paddison visiting prof Univ of N Carolina 1985, emeritus fell St Johns Coll Oxford 1988-; FBA 1971; *Books* Longinus On the Sublime (1964), Plutarch (1972), Ancient Literary Criticism (with M Winterbottom 1972), Criticism in Antiquity (1981), Menader Rhetor (with NG Wilson 1981), Greek Declamation (1983); *Style*— Prof Donald Russell; 47 Woodstock Rd, Oxford OX2 6HQ (☎ 0865 56135); St John's Coll, Oxford OX1 3JP

RUSSELL, Prof Edward Walter; CMG (1960); s of Sir (Edward) John Russell, OBE, FRS (d 1965), and Elnor, *née* Oldham (d 1965); *b* 27 Oct 1904; *Educ* Oundle, Gonville and Caius Coll Cambridge (BA, MA, PhD); *m* 1933, Alice Margaret, da of Sir Hugh Calthrop Webster (d 1940); 1 s (John), 2 da (Ann, Sally); *Career* physicist Rothamsted experimental station 1930-48, reader in soil sci Oxford Univ 1948-55; dir East African Agric and Forestry Res Organ 1955-64, prof of soil sci Reading Univ 1964-70; *Books* Soil Conditions and Plant Growth, (tenth edn); *Style*— Prof Walter Russell, CMG; 31 Brooklyn Dr, Emmer Green, Reading RG4 8SR (☎ 0734 472 934)

RUSSELL, Edwin John Cumming; s of Edwin Russell, and Mary Elizabeth, *née* Cumming; *b* 4 May 1939; *Educ* Brighton GS, Brighton Art Sch, Royal Acad Schs; *m* 7 Nov 1964, Lorne, da of Lt Cdr J A H McKean (d 1981); 2 da (Rebecca b 21 Jan 1966, Tanya b 25 April 1968); *Career* sculpture for churches: Crucifix St Paul's Cathedral 1964, St Michael KCMG Chapel 1970, St Catherine Westminster Abbey 1966, Bishop Bubwith W Front Wells Cathedral; sundials incl: Jubilee Dolphin Dial Nat Maritime Museum Greenwich 1978, sundial Sultan Qaboos Univ Oman 1986, Botanical Armillary Sundial Kew Gardens 1987; forecourt sculpture Rank Xerox Int HQ 1989; shopping centre sculptures: Mad Hatters Tea Party Warrington 1984, Lion and Lamb Farnham 1987 (Best Shopping Centre Award); public works: Suffragette Meml London 1968, First Govr of Bahamas Sheraton Hotel Nassau 1968, Alice and the White Rabbit Guildford (Lewis Carroll commemorative sculpture) 1984, Panda World Wide Fund Int HQ 1988; private collections incl: Goodwood House, Arup Assocs, Trafalgar House plc, Cementation Int, John Mowlem & Co, City of London GS; FRBS 1970; *Recreations* philosophy; *Style*— Edwin Russell, Esq; Lethendry, Polecat Valley, Hindhead, Surrey GU26 6BE (☎ 042 873 5655)

RUSSELL, Hon Lady; Hon (Helen) Elizabeth; *née* Blades; da (twin) of 1 Baron Ebbisham, GBE (d 1953); *b* 27 July 1908; *m* 16 Feb 1939, Adm the Hon Sir Guy Herbrand Edward Russell, GBE, KCB, DSO (d 1977) s of late 2 Baron Ampthill, GCSI, GCIE and Lady Margaret Lygon, CI, GCVO, GBE, da of 6 Earl Beauchamp); 2 s, 1 da; *Style*— The Hon Lady Russell; Flat 8, 89 Onslow Square, London SW7 3LT

RUSSELL, Hon Mrs; Hon Elizabeth Mary Gwenllian Lloyd; *née* Lloyd Mostyn; da of 4 Baron Mostyn (d 1965); *b* 18 August 1929; *m* 1, 14 Sept 1950 (m dis 1957), David Nicholas Goldsmith Duckham; 1 da; m 2, 25 May 1957, John Henry Russell; *Career* hotel proprietor; *Style*— The Hon Mrs Russell; Kings of Kinloch, Meigle, Perthshire

RUSSELL, Hon Emma Kiloran; da of late Capt the Hon Langley Gordon Haslingden Russell, MC, only s of late 2 Baron Russell of Liverpool, CBE, MC; sis of 3 Baron; granted rank of a Baron's da 1983; *b* 15 June 1955; *Style*— The Hon Emma Russell

RUSSELL, Sir Evelyn Charles Sackville; s of Henry Frederick Russell, of Brentwood, Essex; *b* 2 Dec 1912; *Educ* Douai, Château de Mesnières (Seine Maritime, France); *m* 1939, Joan, da of Harold Edward Jocelyn Camps, of Coopersale, Epping; 1 da; *Career* joined HAC 1938, serv WWII RA: N Africa, Italy, Greece; called to the Bar Gray's Inn 1945, Met stipendiary magistrate 1961-78, chief chief Met stipendiary magistrate 1978-82, hon 1980; kt 1981; *Style*— Sir Evelyn Russell; The Gate House, Coopersale, Epping, Essex CM16 7QT (☎ Epping 72568)

RUSSELL, Hon Mrs (Frances Marian); da (by 1 m) of Lady Sempill, *qv*; *b* 1942; *m* 1976, David Ian Russell, s of Denis Russell, MBE, TD (unc of Sir Charles Russell, 3 Bt, *qv*); *Style*— The Hon Mrs Russell; 25 Eddiscombe Rd, SW10

RUSSELL, Lord Francis Hastings; s (by 2 m) of 13 Duke of Bedford, of Les Ligures, Monte Carlo, and Lydia, Duchess of Bedford, *née* Yarde-Buller; *b* 27 Feb 1950; *Educ* Eton, NE London Poly (BSc); *m* 1971, Mrs (Faith Diane) Anak Carrington, da of late Dr S I M Ibrahim, of Singapore; 1 da (Czarina b 1976); *Career* chartered surveyor 1979; *Recreations* skiing; *Clubs* Bucks; *Style*— Lord Francis Russell; Munster House, 46 Roland Way, London SW7 3RE (☎ 01 373 2345/2575); 26A Cadogan Sq, London SW1X 0JP (☎ 01 225 3344)

RUSSELL, George; CBE (1985); s of William Henry Russell (d 1972), of Gateshead, Co Durham, and Frances Annie, *née* Atkinson (d 1973); *b* 25 Oct 1935; *Educ* Gateshead GS, Durham Univ (BA); *m* 19 Dec 1959, Dorothy, da of Ernest Victor Brown (d 1969), of Gateshead, Co Durham; 3 da (Erica Frances b 1963, Livia Jane b 1966, Alison Victoria b 1969); *Career* gp chief exec Marley plc 1986-, chm Basys Int Ltd 1987-88; dep chm 4 TV Co Ltd 1987-88; dir: Alcan Aluminium Ltd 1987-, Northern Rock Building Soc 1985-, chm IBA 1989-, vice pres and gen mangr: Welland Chemical Co of Canada 1968 and St Clair Chemical Co Ltd 1968; md Alcan UK Ltd 1981-82, (asst md 1977-81; md Alcan Aluminium (UK) 1977-81; md and chief exec Br Alcan Aluminium 1982-86, chm Luxfer Hldgs Ltd 1976 and Alcan UK Ltd 1978, dir Alcan Aluminiumwerke GmbH Frankfurt 1982-86; visiting prof Univ of Newcastle upon Tyne 1978, memb: bd Northern Sinfonia Orchestra 1977-80, Northern Industl Bd 1977-80, Washington Corpn 1978-50, IBA 1979-86, bd Civil Serv Pay Res Unit 1980-81, Megaw Inquiry into Civil Serv Pay 1981-82, Widdicombe Ctee of Inquiry into Conduct of Local Authy Business 1985-86; tstee: Beamish Devpt Tst 1985-89, Thomas Bewick Birthplace Tst 1986-89; Hon DEng Newcastle-upon-Tyne 1985; *Recreations* tennis, badminton, bird watching; *Style*— George Russell, Esq, CBE; 46 Downshire Hill, Hampstead, London NW3 1NX; Marley plc, London Rd, Riverhead, Sevenoaks, Kent TN13 2DS (☎ 0732 455255, telex 95231, fax 0732 740694)

RUSSELL, Sir George Michael; 7 Bt (UK 1812), of Swallowfield, Berkshire; s of Sir Arthur Edward Ian Montagu Russell, 6 Bt (d 1964); *b* 30 Sept 1908; *Educ* Radley; *m* 1936, Joy Francis Bedford, da of late W Mitchell, of Irwin, W Australia; 2 da; *Heir* half-bro, Arthur Russell; *Style*— Sir George Russell, Bt

RUSSELL, Hon Georgiana Adeline Villiers; da of 3 Baron Ampthill, CBE, by his 3 w, Adeline; *b* 3 Jan 1952; *Style*— The Hon Georgiana Russell

RUSSELL, Prof Gerald Francis Morris; s of Maj Daniel George Russell, MC (d 1958), of Ventnor, IOW, and Berthe Marie Mathilde Ghislaine, *née* De Boe (d 1981); *b* 21 Jan 1928; *Educ* George Watson's Coll Edinburgh, Edinburgh Univ (MB, ChB, MD); *m* 8 Sept 1950, Margaret Euphemia, da of John Taylor (d 1956), of 50 Montpelier Pk, Edinburgh; 3 s (Malcolm b 1951, Nigel b 1956, Graham b 1957); *Career* Capt RAMC 1951-53, regtl med offr Queen's Bays; dean Inst of Psychiatry Univ of London 1966-70, prof of psychiatry Royal Free Hosp Sch of Med London Univ 1971-79, hon conslt psychiatrist Royal Free Hosp and Friern Hosp 1971-79, prof of psychiatry Inst of Psychiatry London Univ 1979-, hon conslt psychiatrist Bethlem Royal and Maudsley Hosp 1979-; FRCP, FRCPEd, FRCPsych; *Books* The Neuroses and Personality Disorders, vol 4 of the handbook of psychiatry (jtly 1983), Scientific and Clinical Articles on Eating Disorders; *Recreations* art galleries, photography, music; *Style*— Prof Gerald Russell; The Institute of Psychiatry, De Crespigny Pk, London SE5 8AF (☎ 01 703 8408)

RUSSELL, Hon Mrs Hon Catherine Virginia; *née* Ponsonby; yst da of 2 Baron Ponsonby of Shulbrede (d 1976); *b* 21 July 1944; *m* 1972, Ian Macdonald Affleck Russell; 2 da; *Style*— The Hon Mrs Russell; Shulbrede Priory, Lynchmere, Haslemere, Surrey

RUSSELL, Lord Hugh Hastings; yr s of 12 Duke of Bedford (d 1953), and Louisa Crommelin Roberta Jowitt, *née* Whitwell (d 1960); *b* 29 Mar 1923; *Educ* Christ's Coll Cambridge; *m* 7 Sept 1957, Rosemary, yr da of Keith Freeling Markby (d 1972), of Treworder, Blisland, Bodmin, Cornwall; 1 s, 1 da; *Career* ARICS; *Recreations* shooting, riding, ornithology; *Style*— Lord Hugh Russell; The Bell House, Dolan, Llandrindod Wells, Powys

RUSSELL, Lord James Edward Herbrand; s of Marquess of Tavistock; *b* 1975; *Style*— Lord James Russell

RUSSELL, Prof James Knox; s of James Knox Russell, and Jane Edgar *née* Younger; *b* 5 Sept 1919; *Educ* Aberdeen GS, Aberdeen Univ (BM ChB, MD); *m* 16 May 1954, Cecilia Valentine, MD, DCH, da of Patrick Urquhart MA, (d 1956); 3 da (Janice Valentine b 1950, Hilary Margaret b 1951, Sarah Younger b 1956); *Career* serv WWII; MORAF 1954-56 serv Bommber Cmd in England and W Europe (particular interest in early diagnosis of stress in operational aircrew), trained as obstetrician/gynaecologist under Prof Sir Dugald Baird in Aberdeen 1946-50, chief asst to Prof Harvey Evers Newcastle upon Tyne 1950-58, Prof Obstetrics/Gynaecology Univ of Newcastle upon Tyne 1958-82 (Emeritus 1982-), dean Post Graduate Medicine 1968-77, cnslt in human reproduction WHO 1960-82; examiner obst/gyn Univs: London, Birmingham, Manchester, Aberdeen, Belfast, Liverpool, Tripoli, Kuala Lumpur 1980-82; visiting prof: NY 1967 and 1974, SA 1971 and 1978, Univ of Oviedo 1982; Graham Waite Mem lectr AM Coll Obst/Gyn Dallas 1982; vice chm Mitford PC 1985-; FRCOG 1958 (memb 1949); *Books* Early Teenage Pregnancy (Churchill Livingstone) 1982; *Recreations* curing & smoking: bacon, salmon, eels, rainbow trout, chicken; *Clubs* Royal Overseas League; *Style*— Prof J K Russell; Newlands, Tranwell Woods, Morpeth, Northumberland NE61 6AG (☎ 0670 515 666)

RUSSELL, John Bayley; s of Frederick Charles Russell (d 1987), of Brisbane, Aust, and Clarice Emily Mander, *née* Jones (d 1959); *b* 22 Jan 1942; *Educ* C of E GS brisbane Aust, Univ of Queensland (BComm); *m* 27 Sept 1968, Virginia, *née* Winsome; 1 s (Simon b 1972); *Career* Bain and Co Securities: ptnr 1972, ptnr i/c London Off 1980-84, (and 1986-), ptnr i/c NY office 1984-86, memb Aust Br C of C; FIOD, memb Aust Stock Exchange; *Recreations* golf, reading; *Clubs* Univ and Schs (Sydney); *Style*— John Russell, Esq; Bain & Co, 115 Houndsditch, London EC3A 7BU (☎ 01 283 9133, fax 01 626 7090)

RUSSELL, John Harry; s of Joseph Harry Russell (d 1983), and Nellie Annie Russell (d 1976); *b* 21 Feb 1926; *Educ* Halesowen GS; *m* 1951, Iris Mary, da of Thomas Cook, of 20 Olive Hill Road, Blackheath, Birmingham; 1 s (David John b 24 Jan 1953), 1 da (Susan Jane b 14 July 1959); *Career* serv WWII RN; Joseph Lucas Ltd 1948-52, Vono Ltd (Duport Gp) 1952-59, Standard Motors Ltd 1959-61; Duport Gp 1961-86: md Foundries Engrg Div 1972-73, dep grp md 1973-75, gp md 1975-80, dep chm 1976-81, chm and chief exec 1981-86; dir Barclays Bank Birmingham local bd 1976-88; Liveryman Worshipful Co of Glaziers, Freeman City of London 1976; FCA, FBIM; *Recreations* reading, music, antiques; *Clubs* Annabel's, Mark's; *Style*— John H Russell, Esq; 442 Bromsgrove Rd, Hunnington, Halesowen, W Midlands B62 0JL

RUSSELL, Hon John Hugo Trenchard; s of 3 Baron Ampthill, CBE, by his 3 w, Adeline; *b* 13 Oct 1950; *Educ* Eton; *m* 1976, Susanna, da of Peter Merriam (s of Sir Laurence Merriam, MC, JP, DL, and Lady Marjory Kennedy, da of 3 Marquess of Ailsa; 2 s; *Career* dir Baring Brothers & Co Ltd; FCA; *Clubs* Turf; *Style*— The Hon John Russell; Ringstead Farm, Dorchester, Dorset DT2 8NF; 14 Brodrick Rd, London SW17 7DZ

RUSSELL, Hon Mrs Langley (Kiloran Margaret); *née* Howard; da of Hon Sir Arthur Howard, KBE, CVO (bro of 3 Baron Strathcona and Mount Royal), and Lady Lorna Baldwin, da of 1 Earl Baldwin of Bewdley, KG, PC (Stanley Baldwin, the PM); *b* 21 July 1926; *Educ* governess, Longstowe Hall, Cone Ripman Sch of Dancing; *m* 1951, Capt Hon Langley Russell, MC (d 1975), only s of 2 Baron Russell of Liverpool, CBE, MC; 3 s (3 Baron, Adam, Daniel), 3 da (Emma, Annabel, Lucy); *Career* serv WWII WRNS 1944-45; temporary work in the theatre, and as a model, a shop assistant and a receptionist; memb Canadian Red Cross; *Recreations* theatre, travelling; *Style*— The Hon Mrs Langley Russell; Ash Farm, Stourpaine, Blandford, Dorset (☎ Blandford 0258 52177)

RUSSELL, Hon Lucy Catherine; da of late Capt the Hon Langley Gordon Haslingden Russell, MC, only s of late 2 Baron Russell of Liverpool, CBE, MC; sis of 3 Baron;

granted rank of a Baron's da 1983; *b* 1968; *Style*— The Hon Lucy Russell

RUSSELL, Sir (Robert) Mark; KCMG (1985, CMG 1977); s of Sir Robert Russell CSI, CIE (d 1972), and Esther Rhona, *née* Murray (d 1983); *b* 3 Sept 1929; *Educ* Trinity Coll Glenalmond, Exeter Coll Oxford (MA); *m* 1954, Virginia Mary, da of George Swire de Moleyns Rogers (d 1957); 2 s (Neil, Alexander), 2 da (Claire, Lesley); *Career* 2 Lt RA 1952-54; Dip Serv 1954-: third sec FO 1954, second sec Budapest 1956, second sec Berne 1958, first sec FO 1961, first sec and head of chancery Kabul 1965, first sec FCO 1967 (cnsllr 1969), cnsllr (commercial) Bucharest 1970, cnsllr Washington 1974 (head of chancery 1977), chief inspr and dep chief clerk FCO 1978, ambassador ANkara 1983;; *Clubs* Royal Cmwlth Soc, New (Edinburgh); *Style*— Sir Mark Russell, KCMG; c/o Foreign and Cmnwlth Office, King Charles Street, London SW1A 2AH

RUSSELL, Lady Mary Katherine; *née* Baillie-Hamilton; da of 12 Earl of Haddington, KT, MC, TD; *b* 13 Jan 1934; *m* 1, 21 July 1954 (m dis 1965), (John) Adrian Bailey; 2 s (William Anthony b 1957, Philip Graham b 1959), 1 da (Arabella Sarah Lucy b 1955, now Viscountess Chandos); m 2, 1 Oct 1965, David Russell, s of Brig Hugh Edward Russell, DSO; 1 s (Jason Dominic b 1966), 1 da (Mariana b 1968); *Style*— Lady Mary Russell; 28 Northumberland Pl, London W2; Combe Manor, nr Newbury, Berks

RUSSELL, Sheriff (Albert) Muir (Galloway); CBE (1989), QC (Scotland 1965); s of Hon Lord Russell (d 1975), Senator of the Coll of Justice, and Florence Muir, *née* Galloway (d 1983); *b* 26 Oct 1925; *Educ* Edinburgh Acad, Wellington Coll, Brasenose Coll Oxford (BA 1945), Edinburgh Univ (LLB 1951); *m* 9 April 1954, Margaret Winifred, da of Thomas McWalter Millar, FRCS(E) (d 1970), of Edinburgh; 2 s (Douglas b 27 April 1958, Graham b 14 June 1962), 2 da (Anne b 1 Nov 1960, Jennifer b 22 Jan 1964); *Career* Lt Scots Guards 1944-47, serv BLA and BAOR; memb Faculty of Advocates (Edinburgh) 1951; standing jr counsel to BOT, Dept of Agric and Forestry Cmmn; Sheriff of Grampian Highlands and Islands at Aberdeen 1971-; memb Sheriff Ct Rules Cncl 1977-86; vice-chm bd of mgmnt Southern Gp of Hosps Edinburgh 1964; govr Moray House Coll of Educ 1966-70; *Recreations* golf, music; *Clubs* Royal Northern and Univ (Aberdeen); *Style*— Sheriff Muir Russell, QC; Easter Ord House, Skene, Aberdeenshire AB3 6SQ (☎ 0224 740228)

RUSSELL, Hon Mrs; Hon Nicole; *née* Yarde-Buller; da (by 1 m) of 4 Baron Churston; *b* 11 Mar 1936; *m* 1, 10 April 1958 (m dis 1962), Richard Wilfred Beavoir Berens; 1 s (Thomas), 1 da (Jessica); m 2, 6 Feb 1963, Michael Russell; 2 s (Francis, Alexander), 1 da (Lorna); *Style*— The Hon Mrs Russell; The Chantry House, Wilton, Salisbury, Wilts

RUSSELL, Lady; (Aliki) Olga; *née* Diplarakos; da of George Diplarakos, of Athens; *Educ* Lycee Victor-Duruy Paris, Piano Conservatoire; *m* 1, Cmdt Paul-Louis Weiller; 1 s (Paul-Annik b 1933, m 1965, Donna Olimpia Torlonia, gda of King Alfonso XIII of Spain and gggda of Queen Victoria); m 2, 1945, Sir John Wriothesley Russell, GCVO, CMG (d 1984); 1 s (Alexander b 1950, m 1986, Elizabeth Diana Manners), 1 da (Georgiana b 1947, m 1976 Brooke Boothby, *qv*); *Career* Order of Isabel la Catolica (Spain); *Recreations* sculpting, music; *Style*— Lady Russell; 80 Chester Sq, London SW1W 9DU; The Vine Farm, Northbourne, Kent (☎ 0304 374 794)

RUSSELL, Rt Hon Lord Justice; Rt Hon Sir (Thomas) Patrick; PC (1987); s of Sidney Russell (d 1953), and Elsie (d 1948); *b* 30 July 1926; *Educ* Urmston GS, Manchester Univ (LLB); *m* 1951, Doreen (Janie) Ireland; 2 da; *Career* barr Middle Temple 1949, prosecuting counsel to the Post Off Northern Circuit 1961-70, asst rec Bolton 1964-70, rec Barrow-in-Furness 1970-71, QC 1971, Crown Ct rec 1972-80, bencher 1978, ldr N Circuit 1978-80, High Ct judge (Queen's Bench) 1980-86, presiding judge N Circuit 1983-86; Lord Justice of Appeal 1987, Hon LLD Manchester Univ 1988; kt 1980; *Style*— The Rt Hon Lord Justice Russell; Royal Cts of Justice, The Strand, London WC2

RUSSELL, Peter John; s of Capt Raymond Colston Frederick Russell, of Bristol, and Marjorie Catherine, *née* Lock; *b* 14 Dec 1951; *Educ* Bedminster Down Sch Bristol, London Univ (BA, LLM); *m* 7 April 1979, Dr Evelyn Mary, da of Sqdn Ldr Lorence Alan Scott, of Bridport, Dorset; 1 s (Timothy Paul b 1985), 1 da (Sarah Anne b 1982); *Career* barr Inner Temple 1975, Northern Circuit 1975-, lectr in law Manchester Univ 1975-82; memb: Manchester Wine Soc, Manchester Medico-Legal Soc, Hon Soc of the Inner Temple;; *Recreations* wine tasting; *Style*— Peter Russell, Esq; 17 Victoria Avenue, Didsbury, Manchester M20 8GY (☎ 061 434 4306); 5 John Dalton St, Manchester M2 6ET (☎ 061 6875, fax 061 834 8557)

RUSSELL, Lord Robin Loel Hastings; s of Marquess of Tavistock; *b* 12 August 1963; *Style*— Lord Robin Russell

RUSSELL, Lord Rudolph; s (by 1 m) of 13 Duke of Bedford; *b* 7 Mar 1944; *Educ* Gordonstoun; *Style*— Lord Rudolph Russell

RUSSELL, Lady Sarah Elizabeth; da of 4 Earl Russell (d 1987); *b* 16 Jan 1947; *Style*— Lady Sarah Russell

RUSSELL, Susan McCarrison; da of Dr Alfred MacCarrison Russell, of Dalisbury, Wiltshire, and Dr Dorothy Hazel, *née* Webster; *b* 6 Dec 1947; *Educ* Upper Chine Sch Sandown IOW, Coll of Law, Inns of Ct Sch of Law; *m* 22 May 1976, Capt Mark Richard Glasgow, s of Richard Edwin Glasgow, of Ipswich, Suffolk; 2 s (Edward McCarrison b 26 Jan 1979, Simon Markby b 9 July 1981); *Career* called to the Bar Middle Temple 1972, practising John Rankin QC's chambers 1973-; memb Hon Soc Middle Temple 1969-; Freeman City of London 1982; *Recreations* tennis; *Clubs* RAC, Hurlingham; *Style*— Miss Susan Russell

RUSSELL, Thomas; CMG (1980), CBE (1970, OBE 1963); s of late Thomas Russell OBE, MC; *b* 27 May 1920; *Educ* Hawick HS, St Andrews Univ, Peterhouse Cambridge; *m* 1951, Andrée Irma, *née* Desfosses; 1 s; *Career* Capt Para Regt (N Africa, Italy), Colonial Admin Serv Solomon Islands 1948, dist cmmmr 1948-49 and 1954-56, seconded Colonial Office 1956-57 (fin sec 1965, chief sec 1970) govr Cayman Islands 1974-81, rep of Cayman Islands in UK 1982-; *Recreations* anthropology, archaeology; *Clubs* Royal Cwlth Soc; *Style*— Thomas Russell, Esq, CMG, CBE; 6 Eldon Drive, Farnham, Surrey GU10 3JE; office: CI Govt Office, Trevor House, 100 Brompton Rd, London SW3 1EX (☎ 01 581 9418)

RUSSELL, Hon Valentine Francis Xavier Michael; s of Baron Russell of Killowen, PC; *b* 1938; *Educ* Beaumont, Oriel Coll Oxford; *Style*— The Hon Valentine Russell

RUSSELL, Hon Mrs Victoria Anne; da of 4 Baron Mottistone; *b* 23 Dec 1957; *m* 1984, Christopher Russell, s of late John Russell and Lady Whitley, step s of Air Marshal Sir John Whitley; 1 da (Emily b 1985); 1 s (John Hugh b 1987); *Style*— The Hon Mrs Russell

RUSSELL, William Robert; s of William Andrew Russell (d 1932); *b* 6 August 1913; *Educ* Wakefield Central Sch; *m* 1940, Muriel Faith, *née* Rolfe; 1 s, 1 da; *Career* chm Shaw Savill & Albion Co Ltd 1968-73, chm Europe/Australis/Europe Conf 1957 and 1965-70, chm Cncl of European and Japanese Nat Shipowners Assoc 1969-71 and 1973-75, chm Aust Br Trade Assoc 1966-72 and 1975-77, vice-pres 1980-84, chm NZ UK C of C and Indust 1979-84, chm Bank of NZ (London Bd) 1981-83; *Recreations* golf, gardening, sailing (yachts 'Westland Voyager' Moody 346, 'Westland Venturer' Moody 37); *Clubs* Naval; *Style*— William Robert Russell, Esq; Westland, Uvedale Rd, Limpsfield, Oxted, Surrey

RUSSELL, Hon William Southwell; yr s (by his 1 w, Dorothy) of 26th Baron de Clifford, OBE, TD (d 1982); hp to bro, 27th Baron; *b* 26 Feb 1930; *Educ* Eton, King's Coll Cambridge, Princeton; *m* 1961, Jean Brodie, o da of Neil Brodie Henderson, and Conn, da of Adm of the Fleet Sir Charles Madden, 1st Bt, GCB, OM, GCVO, KCMG; 1 s (Miles Edward Southwell b 7 Aug 1966), 2 da (Mary-Jane Sophia b 13 March 1963, Joanna Clare b 23 Jan 1965); *Career* formerly with tea div of Tate & Lyle; master of Science in Engineering (US); *Style*— The Hon William Russell; Five Chimneys, Hadlow Down, Uckfield, Sussex (☎ (082 581) 3159)

RUSSELL OF KILLOWEN, Baroness; Elizabeth; *née* Foster; da of Air Vice-Marshal W McNeece Foster, CB, CBE, DSO, DFC; *m* 1, 1952, Judge Edward Laughton-Scott, QC (d 1978); 2 s, 1 da; m 2, 1979, as his 2 w, Baron Russell of Killowen, PC (Life Peer UK 1975) (d 1986); *Style*— The Lady Russell of Killowen; 8 Daisy Lane, London SW6

RUSSELL OF LIVERPOOL, 3 Baron (UK 1919); Simon Gordon Jared Russell; s of Capt Hon Langley Russell, MC, s of 2 Baron Russell of Liverpool, CBE, MC, by his 1 w Constance, *née* Gordon; suc gf 1981; *b* 30 August 1952; *Educ* Charterhouse, Trinity Coll Cambridge, INSEAD; *m* 1984, Gilda F, yst da of F Albano, of Salerno, Italy; 2 s (Edward Charles Stanley b 1985, William Francis Langley b 1988), 1 da (Hon Leonora Maria Kiloran b 1987); *Heir* s, Hon Edward Charles Stanley; *Career* mgmnt conslt; *Style*— The Rt Hon Lord Russell of Liverpool; c/o House of Lords, London SW1A 0PW

RUSSELL VICK, His Hon Judge Arnold Oughtred; QC (1980); s of His Hon Judge Sir Godfrey Russell Vick, QC (d 1958), and Marjorie Hester, JP (d 1985), yst da of John A Compston, KC; *b* 14 Sept 1933; *Educ* The Leys Sch, Jesus Coll Cambridge (MA); *m* 5 Sept 1959, Zinnia Mary, da of Thomas Brown Yates RBA, (d 1968) of Godalming, Surrey; 2 s (Philip b 1960, Mark b 1964), 1 da (Tessa b 1963); *Career* serv RAF 1952-54 qualified pilot (Flying Off); called to the Bar Inner Temple 1958, memb of Bar Cncl 1964-68, dep rec Rochester City QS 1971, memb Lord Chllr's Co Ct Rules Ctee 1972-80, rec of Crown Ct 1972-82, circuit judge 1982-; master Curriers' Co 1976-77; *Recreations* golf, cricket, gardening, bridge; *Clubs* MCC, Hawks (Cambridge); *Style*— His Hon Judge Russell Vick, QC; Law Courts, Barker Rd, Maidstone, Kent (☎ 0622 54966)

RUSSELL VICK, Mary; *née* de Putron; OBE (1980); da of Pierre de Putron, OBE (d 1950), of La Bertozerie, Guernsey, CI, and Christobel, *née* Whitehead (d 1982); *b* 16 July 1922; *Educ* The Beehive Bexhill-on-Sea, Somerville Coll Oxford (MA); *m* 2 Dec 1944, Clive Compston Russell Vick, s of His Hon Judge Sir Godfrey Russell Vick, QC (d 1958), 3 da (Rosemary (Mrs Scott) b 21 Sep 1945, Susan (Mrs Clear) b 28 Feb 1950, Christabel b 1 Sep 1956); *Career* 3 Offr WRNS 1943-45; played hockey for Sussex and England 1947-49 and 1951-53, pres All England Women's Hockey Assoc 1976-86, chm GB Women's Hockey 1981-, hockey rep Nat Olympic Ctee Br Olympic Assoc 1981-; vice pres Sevenoaks Hockey Assoc Sussex Ladies Hockey Assoc, Southern Counties Women's Hockey Assoc;; *Recreations* sport, gardening; *Style*— Mrs Clive Russell Vick, OBE; Ameroak, Seal, Sevenoaks, Kent TN15 0AG (☎ 0732 61 154)

RUSSELL-COBB, Trevor; s of Herbert Edmund Cobb (d 1939), and Valerie Cecil Russell (d 1950); *b* 3 Feb 1918; *Educ* Wellington, London Univ (BA, BSc); *m* 1, 8 May 1940, Suzanne, da of late Guy Chambers; 1 s (Rupert b 1943), 1 da (Theresa b 1947); m 2, 17 Dec 1952, Nan Piquet-Wicks, da of late John Stanley Hughes; 2 s (Piers b 1953, Fabian b 1955); *Career* Lt-Col Welsh Guards regtl and staff duty; chm and md Russell-Cobb Ltd (publication rels conslts) 1962-; dir Campbell Johnson Ltd (public rels conslts) 1955-62, dir U N Fellowship Dept Br Cncl London 1946-51, tech asst UN (Geneva) 1952-54; dir English Chamber Orchestra and Music Soc 1963-78; memb Victorian Soc 1970-74, cncl memb Tres Royal Soc of Arts 1972-83; sec Associates of the V & A 1978-82; tstee Sir John Soane's Museum 1978-; memb Police Studies Inst advsy ctee the Economics of Historic Country Houses 1980-81; chm Fndn for Ephemera Studies 1984-; *Books* Paying the Piper (1968); *Recreations* playing the piano, walking, reading; *Style*— Trevor Russell-Cobb, Esq; 25 Alderney St, London SW1V 4ES (☎ 01 834 0605)

RUSSELL-HOBBS, Ronald Arthur; s of Samuel George Hobbs (d 1955), of Hounslow, and Kate, *née* Waghorn (d 1987); *b* 10 Nov 1940; *Educ* Duke of York's Royal Mil Sch Dover Kent; *m* 1 (m dis), Susan Frances, *née* Martin; 1 s (Andrew Martin b 1967), 2 da (Sarah Jane b 1966, Emma Louise b 1968); m 2, 27 March 1981, Joy, da of Noel Russell, of Dublin; 2 da (Lucy b 1979, Kate b 1981); *Career* divnl md Longman Gp Ltd 1969-81, jt md Pergamon Press Ltd 1981-83, dir Br Printing & Communications Corpn plc 1981-83, md Millbank Publishing Gp ltd 1983-87, gp chief exec Dunn & Wilson Gp ltd 1988; *Recreations* cricket, rugby, antiques; *Style*— Ronald Russell-Hobbs, Esq; White Lodge, Tyringham, Rutland Drive, Harrogate, N Yorks HG1 2NX (☎ 0423 69183); Dunn & Wilson Ltd, Goodbard House, Infirmary St, Leeds LS1 2JS (☎ 0532 445 565, fax 0532 444 318, car tel 0860 227 363)

RUSSELL-SMITH, Dame Enid Mary Russell; DBE (1953); da of late Arthur Russell-Smith; *b* 3 Mar 1903; *Educ* St Felix, Newnham Coll Cambridge; *Career* asst princ Miny of Health 1925 (dep sec 1956-63), chm Sunderland Church Cmmn 1971, Durham Co Conservation Tst 1973-75, St Paul's Jarrow Devpt Tst 1975-80; assoc fell Newnham Coll Cambridge 1956-72, hon fell 1974, princ St Aidan's Coll Durham Univ 1963-70, hon pt/t lectr Univ Coll London 1964-; *Books* Modern Bureaucracy: the Home Civil Service (1974); *Style*— Dame Enid Russell-Smith , DBE; 3 Pimlico, Durham, DH1 4QW

RUSSETT, Alan William Frank; s of William Frank Russett (d 1958), and Grace Undine, *née* Stokes (d 1978); *b* 21 July 1929; *Educ* Bristol GS, Oxford Univ (MA); *m* 15 May 1954, Anne, da of Alexander Freyear Dickinson (d 1963), of Brazil; 1 da (Caroline); *Career* 2 Lt Somerset LI, King's African Rifles in E Africa; conslt and co dir in Oil Indust: Regional coordinator and gen mangr BP 1956-81, md Triton Europe plc 1983-87, dir Richships Ltd 1983-87; *Recreations* yachting, history of art; *Clubs* Oriental, Royal Southern Yacht; *Style*— Alan W F Russett, Esq; 5 Hobury Street, London SN10 0JA (☎ 01 352 0451)

RUSSO, Sir Peter George; CBE (1953, OBE 1939); s of George Russo; *b* 1898; *m* 1926, Margot, da of late John A Imossi of Gibraltar; 1 da; *Career* min housing and econ devpt Gibraltar 1964-68; kt 1964; *Style*— Sir Peter Russo, CBE; 2 Red Sands Road, Gibraltar

RUSTON, (Edward) Harold; s of Major Allpress Harold Ruston, DSO (d 1970), of Huntingdon, and Edith Gertrude, *née* Francis (d 1983); *b* 2 July 1933; *Educ* Huntingdon GS, Worksop Coll Notts; *m* 29 April 1950, Patricia Frances, da of John Albert Norman Perkins (d 1973), of Cambs; 1 s (Nicholas John b 1957), 1 da (Anne Francis b 1953); *Career* serv WWII RAF 1941-46: Flt Lt navigator 57 Sqdn, 5 Gp Bomber Cmd; (POW Stalag Luft I 1944); chm: Rustons Engrg Co Ltd 1970 (dir 1955), F T Ruston & Sons Ltd 1980 (dir 1950), Rustons Balsham Ltd (dir 1975), Ruston's Thrapston Ltd (dir 1960), Ruston's Ramsey Ltd (dir 1950), Ruston's Garden & Tool Hire Ltd; *Recreations* cricket, model engineering; *Clubs* MCC, Worcestershire CC, Middlesex CCC; *Style*— Harold Ruston, Esq; Ruston's Engineering Co Ltd, St Germain Street, Huntingdon, Cambs PE18 6JT (☎ 0480 55151, telex 32351, fax 0480 52116)

RUTHERFORD, Prof Andrew; s of Thomas Armstrong Rutherford (d 1935), of Helmsdale, Sutherland, and Christian Proudfoot Russell, MBE, JP (d 1973); *b* 23 July 1929; *Educ* Helmsdale Sch Sutherland, George Watson's Boys' Coll Edinburgh, Univ of Edinburgh (MA), Merton Coll Oxford (BLitt); *m* 4 Sept 1953, Nancy Milroy, da of Arthur Browning (Maj RAMC, d 1962), of Bathgate, W Lothian; 2 s (Richard Browning, John Arthur Thomas), 1 da (Alison Jean); *Career* Nat Serv cmmnd 2 Lt Seaforth Highlanders 1951-53, serv Somaliland Scouts, Lt 2 Bn Seaford Highlanders TA 1953-58; asst lectr Univ of Edinburgh 1956-65 (asst lectr 1955), visiting assoc prof Univ of Rochester NY 1963; Univ of Aberdeen: sr lectr 1964, second prof of english 1965-68, regius prof of england 1968-84, dean faculty of arts and social sci 1979-82, sr vice-princ 1982-84; Univ of London: warden Goldsmiths' Coll 1984- (prof 1988); chm of english bd CNAA 1966-73, Br Cncl Lecture Tours 1973-89, pres Int Assoc of Univ Profs of English 1977-80, memb BBC Gen Advsy Cncl 1979-84, chm literature advsy ctee British Cncl 1987-, memb various Scottish educn dept ctees on curriculum and examinations; *Books* Byron: A Critical Study, (1961), Kipling's Mind and Art (ed 1964), Byron: The Critical Heritage (ed 1970), The Literature of War (1979) Early Verse by Rudyard Kipling 1979-1989 (1986); *Recreations* shooting; *Clubs* Athenaeum, Royal Cwlth Soc; *Style*— Prof Andrew Rutherford; Goldsmiths' Coll, Univ of London, New Cross, London SE14 6NW (☎ 01 692 7171 ext 2001)

RUTHERFORD, David John Buckley; OBE (1987); s of Col Alexander John Buckley Rutherford, CVO, CBE (d 1979), of Assendon Lodge, Henley-on-Thames, Oxon, and Joan, *née* Begg (d 1979); *b* 27 July 1930; *Educ* Winchester, Trinity Coll Cambridge (MA); *m* 11 July 1959, Elisabeth Dagmar, da of Henri Thierry-Mieg (d 1938); 3 da (Virginia b 15 Aug 1960, Sophie b 19 Nov 1961, Alice b 21 Sept 1965); *Career* 2 Lt 9 Lancers 1949, City of London Yeo RR TA; chm Wine and Spirit Assoc GB 1974-76 and 1988-89; ct memb Vintners Co; Ordre National Du Merite France 1976, Ordem do Infante Dom Henrique Portugal 1977, Ordine Al Merito Della Republica Italiana 1982; *Recreations* golf; *Style*— David Rutherford, Esq, OBE; Martini & Rossi Ltd, New Zealand House, 80 Haymarket, London SW1Y 4TG (☎ 01 930 3543)

RUTHERFORD, John Malcolm Chalmers; s of John Rutherford Rutherford (d 1957), and Doreen, *née* Hilton (d 1957); Sir John Rutherford (Baronet) was both MP and Mayor of Blackburn; He purchased the estate of Rutherford in 1923, the family name having been associated with the lands of Rutherford and others since the derivation of the place name in the twelfth century and as such the family claims to be the second oldest landed family in the Scottish borders; Sir John Rutherford had the good fortune to own Solario, winner of the St Ledger in 1925, the Ascot Gold Cup and The Epsom Coronation Cup in 1926; He left his estate to his gnephew on condition that he change his name from Chalmers to Rutherford; This he did by deed poll in 1933; John Rutherford Rutherford was MP for the Edmonton Constituency in London before serving in WWII; *b* 29 Sept 1938; *Educ* Repton, East of Scotland Coll of Agric; *m* 14 April 1962, Jean Gavin, da of Henry Ballantyne (d 1983); 3 s (Johnny b 1963, Guy b 1969, Alexander b 1973), 1 da (Sara Jane b 1966); *Career* Nat Serv 1957-59 in KOSB as 2nd Lt; farmer; dir Border Archery Ltd, Mellerstain, Kelso 1975-; chm Glenteviot Farmers Ltd 1971-76; Nat Playfields Assoc (Scotland) Ctee 1967-; *Recreations* shooting, fishing, cricket; *Clubs* Puffin's (Edinburgh); *Style*— John Rutherford, Esq; Rutherford Lodge, Kelso, Roxburghshire TD5 8NW

RUTHERFORD, (Gordon) Malcolm; s of Gordon Brown Rutherford (d 1988), of Newcastle upon Tyne, and Bertha, *née* Browne; *b* 21 August 1939; *Educ* Newcastle Royal, GS, Balliol Coll Oxford; *m* 1, 1965 (m dis 1969), Susan Margaret, *née* Tyler; m2, 24 Feb 1970, Elizabeth Claude Rosemary Maitland, da of Pierre Pelen, of Paris; 3 da (Emma b 15 April 1973, Camilla b 10 Sept 1974, Laetitia b 6 July 1976); *Career* arts ed then foreign ed The Spectator 1962-65, fndr newsletter Latin America 1965; Financial Times: dip corr 1966-69, Bonn corr 1969-74, dep foreign ed 1974-77, chief political columnist and asst ed 1977-88, observer and asst ed 1988-; *Books* Can We Save the Common Market (1981); *Recreations* tennis, theatre, reading; *Clubs* Travellers; *Style*— Malcolm Rutherford, Esq; 89 Bedford Gardens, London W8 (☎ 01 229 2063); Financial Times, London

RUTHVEN-STUART, Dr Ian Alexander; s of Capt Alexander Whitewright Ruthven-Stuart, Gordon Highlanders and RFC (d 1974), and Stella Marion Grant Duff Ainslie (d 1979); *b* 5 July 1927; *Educ* Trinity Coll Glenalmond, Edinburgh Univ (MB, ChB); *m* 29 June 1953, Christina Adelaide, da of Capt Peter Tupper Carey (d 1976: RN); 3 s (Nicholas b 1955, David b 1961, Peter b 1967), 2 da (Sophie b 1967, Sarah b 1957); *Career* Surgn Lt RNVR 1952-54; med practioner; *Recreations* running, swimming, skiing, fishing, squash, tennis, golf, shooting, DIY, windsurfing, sailing; *Clubs* Naval; *Style*— Ian Ruthven-Stuart, Esq; Health Centre, Park Rd, Denmead, Portsmouth, Hants

RUTLAND, 10 Duke of (E 1703); Charles John Robert Manners; CBE (1962); also Earl of Rutland (E 1525), Baron Manners of Haddon (E 1679), Marquess of Granby (E 1703), and Baron Roos of Belvoir (UK 1896); s of 9 Duke of Rutland (d 1940), and Dowager Duchess of Rutland, *qv*; and fifteenth in descent from 1 Earl of Rutland's maternal grandmother Anne Plantagenet (sis of Edward IV); *b* 28 May 1919; *Educ* Eton, Trinity Coll Cambridge; *m* 1, 27 April 1946 (m dis 1956), Anne Bairstow, da of Maj William Cumming Bell, of Huddersfield; 1 da; m 2, 15 May 1958, Frances Helen, da of Charles Sweeny and Margaret Duchess of Argyll, *qv*; 2 s, 1 da (and 1 s decd); *Heir* s, Marquess of Granby; *Career* Cons memb Leics CC; proprietor of Belvoir Castle (remodelled by Wyatt in 1816) and the late medieval Haddon Hall in Derbyshire; late Capt Gren Gds; patron of 11 livings, owner of 18,000 acres, and possessor of minerals in Leics and Derbys; *Style*— His Grace the Duke of Rutland, CBE; Belvoir Castle, Grantham, Lincs; Haddon Hall, Bakewell, Derbys

RUTLAND, Hon Mrs; Hon Joan Claire Florence; *née* Milne; da of Field Marshal 1 Baron Milne, GCB, GCMG, DSO (d 1948); *b* 12 Mar 1907; *m* 16 March 1937, as his 2 w, James Hart Rutland (d 1954); *Style*— The Hon Mrs Rutland; Cromwell Cottage, Church St, Alresford, Hants

RUTLAND, Dowager Duchess of; Kathleen; JP; da of Francis John Tennant (bro of 1 Baron Glenconner and Margot Asquith); *b* 27 Jan 1894; *m* 27 Jan 1916, 9 Duke of Rutland (d 1940); 3 s, 2 da (10 Duke, Lord John Manners, Lord Roger Manners; Lady Ursula d'Abo, Lady Isabel Throckmorton, *qqv*); *Career* bore Queen's Canopy at Coronation of King George VI; pres Kathleen Rutland Home for the Leicestershire Inst for the Blind; *Style*— Her Grace The Dowager Duchess of Rutland; 21 Wilton St, SW1

RUTMAN, Laurence David; s of Sidney Rutman and Anne, *née* Smith; *b* 8 Oct 1937; *Educ* Hendon Co Sch, UCL (LLB), Yale (LLM); *m* 26 July 1964, Sandra Christine, da of Philip Colvin Rutman; 2 s (Simon b 1966, Paul b 1970), 1 da (Laura b 1968); *Career* ptnr: Paisner & Co. 1960-74, Ashurst Morris Crisp 1974-; *Recreations* farming, opera, books; *Style*— Laurence Rutman, Esq; Broadgate House, 7 Eldon St, London, EC2M 7HD, (☎ 01 247 7666, fax 01 377 5659, telex 887067)

RUTT, Rt Rev Cecil Richard; *see*: Leicester, Bishop of

RUTT, David Hare; s of Cecil Rutt (d 1957), and Mary Hare Turner; *b* 9 August 1931; *Educ* Nottingham Univ (BA); *m* 22 Aug 1956, Margaret Frances, da of John Lemuel Shaw; 1 s (Peter John b 1960), 1 da (Caroline Frances b 1964); *Career* HM Inspr of Schs 1967; FIOP 1984; *Recreations* calligraphy, printing, historical investigation; *Style*— David H Rutt, Esq; The Lodge, Market Place, Folkingham, Sleaford, Lincolnshire NG34 0SE

RUTTER, Rev Canon (Allen Edward Henry) Claude; s of Rev Norman Rutter (d 1967), and Hilda, *née* Mason (d 1979); *b* 24 Dec 1928; *Educ* Monkton Combe, Dauntsey's, Queens' Coll Camb (MA, DipAgric), Durham Univ (DipTh); *m* 26 April 1960, Elizabeth Jane, da of Rt Rev Martin Patrick Grainge Leonard, DSO, MA (d 1963), Bishop of Thetford; 2 s (Christopher b 1962, Timothy b 1965), 2 da (Patricia b 1961, Miranda b 1976); *Career* scientific liaison offr E Malling Res Station, Kent 1953-56; curate: Bath Abbey 1959-60, E Dereham, Norfolk 1960-64; rector: Cawston Gp and Chap Cawston Coll, Norfolk 1964-69, Gingindhlovu, Zululand (and Agric Sec Helwel, Diocese of Zululand) 1969-73, and Queen Thorne, Dorset 1973-, RD Sherborne Dorset 1976-; chm Salisbury Diocesan Lay Educl and Trg Ctee 1984-, Canon and Preb Salisbury Cathedral 1986-, Diocesan co-ordinator Rural Miny Devpt 1987-; Co Cricket for: Cambridge Univ 1953, Wilts CCC 1948-55, and Norfolk CCC 1961-65 (the only clergyman to have played in the Gillette Cup); hockey for Camb Univ Wanderers and Maidstone Clergy Golf Champ 1977; *Recreations* cricket, hockey, golf, farming, gardening, picture framing; *Clubs* Hawk's (Cambridge), MCC; *Style*— The Rev Canon Claude Rutter; Trent Rectory, Sherborne, Dorset DT9 4SL (☎ 0935 851049)

RUTTER, Hadyn Michael; s of Herbert Rutter (d 1985), of Winsford, Cheshire, and Mabel Rutter; *b* 29 Dec 1946; *Educ* Verdin GS Winsford, Lincoln Coll Oxford (BA); *m* 1 April 1970, Susan, da of Charles Robert Johnson, of Winsford; 3 da (Tanya b 1974, Amanda b 1977, Lisa b 1981); *Career* slr; Richards Butler & Co London 1969-72, Bruce Campbell & Co Cayman Islands 1972-80 (sr ptnr 1977-80), own practice 1980-; pres Cayman Islands Law Soc 1979 (sec 1975-79); dir: Golf Links Int Ltd, Golf Links Int Inc, Sun Centre Ltd; organiser World Pro-Am: Arizona, Acapulco, Bahamas; author Cayman Islands Handbook Tax Guide 1977; Duke of Edinburgh Award (Gold) 1965; *Recreations* cricket, golf, badminton, tennis; *Clubs* Utd Oxford and Cambridge; *Style*— Hadyn Rutter, Esq; The Mount, Cuddington Lane, Cuddington, Cheshire CW8 2SZ (☎ (0606) 883070, fax (0606) 783373)

RUTTER, His Hon Judge John Cleverdon; s of Edgar John rutter (d 1971), of Cardiff, and Nellie, *née* Parker (d 1928); *b* 18 Sept 1919; *Educ* Cardiff HS for Boys, Univ Coll of the SW of Eng Exeter (LLB), Keble Coll Oxford (MA); *m* 4 Sept 1951, Jill, da of Maxwell Duncan McIntosh; 1 s (Jeremy b 1953), 1 da (Philippa (Mrs James) b 1955); *Career* serv WWII RA 1939-46, cmmnd 1941, serv overseas; barr Lincoln's Inn 1948, practising Wales and Chester circuit 1948-66; rec: Cardiff 1962-66, Merthyr Tydfil 1962-66, Swansea 1965-66; legal memb Mental Health Review Tbnl Wales 1962-66, Stipendiary Magistrate Cardiff 1966-71, dep chm Glamorgan Quarter Sessions 1969-71, circuit judge Cardiff Crown Ct 1972-; *Recreations* golf, reading; *Style*— His Hon Judge Rutter; Law Courts, Cardiff

RUTTER, Trevor John; OBE (1976); s of Alfred Rutter (d 1974), of Gwent, and Agnes, *née* Purslow (d 1966); *b* 26 Jan 1934; *Educ* Monmouth Sch, Brasenose Coll Oxford (BA); *m* 1959, Jo, da of David Barrs Henson (d 1980); 1 s (Orlando); *Career* Br Cncl 1959-65, Indonesia, W Germany (Munich); FO 1967, first sec; Br Cncl 1968-; rep in Singapore 1968-71 and Bangkok 1971-75; HQ posts 1975-85 incl asst dir gen 1982-85; rep in Germany 1986-; *Style*— Trevor Rutter, Esq; West House, West St, Wivenhoe, Essex (☎ Wivenhoe 2562); The British Council, Hahnenstr 6, 5000 Köln 1, W Germany

RYAN, David Edward; s of Thomas Ryan (d 1986), and Janet Stafford Ryan; *b* 17 May 1946; *Educ* Hyde GS; *m* 21 Dec 1968, Susan, da of John Cooper (d 1987); 2 s (Mark b 29 Sept 1969, Andrew b 30 July 1971), 1 da (Anna b 21 Nov 1981); *Career* articled Shuttleworth & Haworth, CA 1968, joined Webb Hanson Bullivant & Co 1969 (ptnr 1972); Neville Russell: ptnr 1986, sr ptnr Stockport off 1987-; bd memb Manchester City Mission, involved with Stockport C of C and Stockport Luncheon Club; *Recreations* walking, cycling, being out of doors, listening to music, theatre; *Style*— David Ryan, Esq; Neville Russell, Regent House, Heaton Lane, Stockport SK4 1BS (☎ 061 477 4750, fax 061 477 4750 ext 150)

RYAN, Maj-Gen Denis Edgar; CB (1987); s of Reginald Arthur Ryan, of Westbury, Wilts, and Amelia, *née* Smith; *b* 18 June 1928; *Educ* Sir William Borlase Marlow Bucks, King's Coll London (LLB); *m* 6 Aug 1955, Jean Mary, da of Charles Waldemar Bentley (d 1963); 1 s (Mark b 1966), 1 da (Amanda b 1964); *Career* cmmnd RAEC 1950, instr 3 HEC BAOR 1950-52, SO3 HQ BAOR 1952-54, instr RMA Sandhurst

1954-56, adj Army Sch of Educn 1956-59, Staff Coll 1960, DAQMG HQ Near E Land Forces (Cyprus) 1961-62, SO2 Special Ops HQ E Africa Cmd (Kenya) 1962-64, SO2 AED 1 MOD 1964-66, GSO2 Intelligence Centre 1966-68, CAES HQ 4 Div BAOR 1968-70, GSO1 Cabinet Off 1970-72, trg devpt advsr Staff Coll 1972-75, Col GS DI4 MOD 1976-78, chief educn offr HQ SE Dist 1978-79, cdr educn HQ BAOR 1979-82 and UK 1982-84: dir of Army Educn MOD 1984-87; *Recreations* cricket, tennis, rugby, music, theatre; *Clubs* Army and Navy; *Style*— Maj Gen Denis Ryan, CB; c/ Royal Bank of Scotland, Holt's Whitehall Branch, Kirkland House, Whitehall, London SW1A 2EB

RYAN, Sir Derek Gerald; 3 Bt (UK 1919); s of Sir Gerald Ryan, 2 Bt (d 1947), of Hintlesham Hall, Ipswich, and Hylda, da of Maj Spencer Herapath; *b* 9 July 1922; *Educ* Harrow, Sandhurst; *m* 1, 1947 (m dis 1971), Penelope, da of Rex Hawkings, of New York; 1 s, 3 da; m 2, 1972, Katja, da of Ernst Best, of Kassel; *Heir* s, Derek Ryan; *Career* late Lt Gren Gds; admin dir Cabot Corpn Boston 1956-72; sch rep Harrow-W Germany and Austria; *Recreations* yachting, vintage cars, music, ornithology; *Clubs* First Guards; Adels Verein (Hessen); *Style*— Sir Derek Ryan, Bt; Scharfensteinstrasse 11, 6228 Eltville am Rhein 1 , W Germany (T 061 23 5333)

RYAN, Jennifer Mary; da of Arthur William Butterworth (d 1977), of Huddersfield, Yorks, and Elsie *née* Morton; *b* 2 April 1947; *Educ* Holme Valley GS, LSE (BSc), Harvard (MBA); *m* 12 Aug 1978, John Ryan; *Career* fin mgmnt Ford Motor Co 1968-83, fin dir TI Raleigh Industs 1983-86, distribution dir Ross Young's Ltd 1988- (fin dir 1986-88); memb cncl UK Article Number Assoc, former memb indust and employment ctee ESRC; *Recreations* travel, sports; *Clubs* Harvard Business Sch (London); *Style*— Mrs Jennifer Ryan; Kenilworth House, Top Rd, Worlaby, Brigg, S Humberside DN20 0NE; Ross Young's, Ross House, Grimsby DN31 3SW (☎ 0472 359 111, fax 0472 365 602, telex 52387)

RYAN, John Patrick; s of James Patrick Ryan (d 1960), of Rhos-on-Sea, N Wales, and Marie Elsie, *née* Gaines (d 1988); *b* 19 August 1943; *Educ* St Mary's Coll Rhos-on-Sea N Wales, Queen's Coll Cambridge (MA); *m* 8 Feb 1968, Verna Marguerite, da of Capt Charles Edward Henry Mytton, of Hampstead Garden Suburb; 2 s (Nicholas b 26 Feb 1972, Alastair b 13 Sept 1976), 1 da (Annabel b 22 March 1974); *Career* actuarial supt Guardian Royal Exchange 1968, ptnr James Capel & Co 1972-76, vice pres & princ Tillinghurst 1976-(part of Towers Perrin Co); cncl memb Inst of Actuaries 1986- (chm futures ctee 1988-); Freeman: City of London, Liveryman Worshipful Co of Needlemakers; FIA 1968, ASMIA 1973, Fell Inst of Risk Mgmnt 1987; Assoc Casualty Actuarial Soc USA 1979, memb American Acad of Actuaries USA 1979; *Recreations* travel, walking, theatre, old buildings; *Style*— John Ryan, Esq; 15 Priory Gdns, Highgate, London N6 5QY (☎ 01 348 0195); Old Mill House, West Row Fen, Mildenhall, Suffolk; Tillinghast, 1 Towers Perrin, Castlewood House, 77-91 New Oxford St, London WC1A 1PX (☎ 01 379 4000, fax 01 379 7478, telex 261 411)

RYAN, Peter Henry; s of John Ryan, CBE (d 1975), and Mabel Ryan; *b* 1 Oct 1930; *Educ* Harrow, Gonville and Caius Coll Cambridge (MA); *m* 1 (m dis 1980); 1 s (Mark b 1958), 2 da (Nicola b 1961, Jocelyn b 1965); m 2, 1986, Valerie Mary Bishop; 3 step s (Piers, Gavin, Warren); *Career* Nat Serv Flying Offr, RAF; Peter Ryan Associates 1986-; dir: Thomas Tilling Ltd 1979-83, Central & Sherwood plc 1983-87, Stag Furniture Hldgs plc 1984-, M Y Hldgs plc 1984-, Norbain Electronics plc 1987-, Inoco plc 1988-, Unistrut Europe plc; chm: Unistrut Europe plc 1988-, Elga Gp plc 1989-; memb bd of govrs Royal Marsden Hosp; CEng, MIMechE; *Recreations* golf, theatre, travel, DIY; *Clubs* RAF, MCC; *Style*— Peter Ryan, Esq; Peter Ryan Associates, Park Hse, Queens Drive, Oxsholt, Surrey KT22 0PF (☎ 0372 843 665)

RYAN, Richard Kevin de Burgo; s of Richard Jarlath de Burgo Ryan, and Ursula Clare, *née* Bradshaw; *b* 19 Oct 1957; *Educ* Bedford Sch, Leeds Univ (BA), RMA Sandhurst; *Career* cmmnd 1 Bn Royal Green Jackets 1979-82, serv London and NI, Capt 1982; 4 Bn Royal Green Jackets (TA) 1983-, Maj; insurance broker with Willis Faber & Dumas 1982-87; stockbroker with Capel- Cure Myers 1987-; *Recreations* shooting, fishing, music; *Clubs* Royal Green Jackets, Cavalry and Guards'; *Style*— Richard K de B Ryan, Esq; 87 Strathville Road, Earlsfield, London SW18 4QR (☎ 01 870 7754); Brookside, Cranbrook, Kent; 65 Holborn Viaduct, London EC1A 2EU (☎ 01 236 5101, telex 885556, fax 01 236 4558)

RYCROFT, Sir Richard Newton; 7 Bt (GB 1784), of Calton, Yorks; s of Sir Nelson Edward Oliver Rycroft, 6 Bt (d 1958); *b* 23 Jan 1918; *Educ* Winchester, Christ Church Oxford; *m* 1947, Ann, da of late Hugh Bellingham Smith; 2 da (Susan b 1948, m 1974 Ian Martell, 1 s 1 da; Viscountess FitzHarris, *qv*); *Heir* unc, Henry Rycroft, OBE, DSC, RN; *Career* master New Forest Foxhounds; memb The Badger Protection Gp; serv WWII Maj (Beds and Herts Regt) on special work in Balkans (despatches); kt of Order of the Phoenix of Greece (with swords); patron of one living; *Style*— Sir Richard Rycroft, Bt; Winalls Wood House, Stuckton, Fordingbridge, Hants (☎ (0425) 2263)

RYDE, Hon Mrs Hon; Mary Teresa; *née* Lister Robinson; da of 1 and last Baron Robinson, OBE (d 1952); *b* 1914; *m* 1, 1939 (m dis 1951), Wing Cdr Paul Richey, DFC; 2 s, 2 da; m 2, 1979, Peter Leighton Ryde; *Style*— The Hon Mrs Ryde; 4 Phene St, London SW3

RYDEN, Kenneth; MC (1944, and bar 1944), DL (City of Edinburgh 1978); s of Walter Ryden (d 1947), of Blackburn, Lancs, and Elizabeth, *née* Culshaw (d 1966); *b* 15 Feb 1917; *Educ* Queen Elizabeth's GS Blackburn; *m* 27 July 1950, Catherine Kershaw, da of Herbert Wilkinson (d 1936), of Oswaldtwistle, Lancs; 2 s (Nicholas Charles b 20 March 1953, Peter Anthony b 16 Sept 1956); *Career* serv WWII RA (V) 1939-45, cmmnd RE, attached Royal Bombay Sappers and Miners; serv: India, Assam and Burma (despatches 1944), ret Capt RE 1946; articled and professional trg 1936-39, asst estate surveyor HM Off of Works Edinburgh 1939; Miny of Works: estate surveyor Glasgow and Edinburgh 1946-47 (attached to UK High Cmmn India and Pakistan 1947-50), sr estate surveyor Scotland 1950-59; fndr and sr ptnr Kenneth Ryden & Ptnrs Edinburgh Glasgow and London 1959-74; memb bd Housing Corpn 1971-77; chm Chartered Auctioneer and Estate Agents Inst Scotland 1960-61; memb: Lothian Regnl Valuation Appeal Panel 1965-75 and 1981- (chm 1987-), Scottish Slrs Disciplinary Tbnl 1985-; Freeman City of London 1978, Master Worshipful Co of Merchants of The City of Edinburgh 1976-78 (tres 1974-76, memb 1959), Liveryman Worshipful Co of Chartered Surveyors 1978; FRICS 1950, FRVA 1959, FRCPE 1983; *Recreations* golf, fishing, scottish art; *Clubs* New (Edinburgh); *Style*— Kenneth Ryden, Esq, MC, DL; 19 Belgrave Cres, Edinburgh EH4 3AJ (☎ 031 332 5893)

RYDER, Edward Alexander; s of Alexander Harry Ryder, of 47 The Grove, Halesroad, Cheltenham, and Gwendoline Gladys, *née* Morris (d 1979); *b* 9 Nov 1931; *Educ* Cheltenham GS, Bristol Univ (BSc); *m* 24 March 1956, Janet, da of Alfred John Barribal (d 1973); 1 s (Clive b 1961), 1 da (Joanne (Mrs Rockley) b 1959); *Career* Nat Serv Flying Offr RAF 1953-55; civil servant; superintending inspr HM Nuclear Installations Inspectorate 1975-80, head of hazardous installations policy branch Health and Safety Exec 1980-85, HM chief inspr of nuclear intallations 1985-; FInstP; *Recreations* golf, concerts; *Style*— Edward Ryder, Esq; HM Nuclear Installations Inspectorate, 1 Chepstow Place, London W2 4TF (☎ 01 243 6000)

RYDER, Hon Jill Patricia; da of Baron Ryder of Eaton Hastings; *b* 1950; *Style*— The Hon Jill Ryder

RYDER, Dr (Arthur) John; s of Charles Foster Ryder (d 1942), of Thurlow, Suffolk, and Mabel Elizabeth, *née* Sims (d 1974); *b* 17 April 1913; *Educ* Radley, Oriel Coll Oxford (BA), LSE (MA); *m* 9 April 1946, Krystyna Karolina, da of Henry Reicher; *Career* lectr Br Cncl 1939-45, educn offr Br Control Cmmn Germany 1946-56, memb Cons Res Dept 1958-62, lectr, sr lectr and reader St David's Univ Coll Wales 1962-80, freelance translator 1980-(co recipient The Schlegel-Tieck Prize for translation from German 1983); Parly cand (C) Cardiganshire 1964; licensed reader, C of E 1966; Freeman Worshipful Co of Salters 1934; *Books* The German Revolution of 1918 (1967), Twentieth Century Germany: From Bismarck to Brandt (1973), pamphlet published by the Historical Assoc; *Recreations* travel, antiques; *Style*— Dr John Ryder; 74 Clifton Hill, St John's Wood, London NW8 (☎ 01 624 8221)

RYDER, Hon John Stuart Terrick Dudley; s of 6 Earl of Harrowby (d 1987); *b* 1924; *Educ* Eton; *m* 1946, Dorothy Ethel, da of J T Swallow, of Mansfield; 2 s; *Career* serv WWII RAF pilot 1942-46; *Style*— The Hon John Ryder; Sandon Hall, Stafford

RYDER, Hon Michael John; s of Baron Ryder of Eaton Hastings; *b* 1953; *Style*— The Hon Michael Ryder

RYDER, Richard Andrew; OBE (1981), MP (C) Mid-Norfolk 1983-; s of Richard Stephen Ryder, JP, DL, and Margaret MacKenzie; *b* 1949; *m* 1981, Caroline (private sec to Mrs Thatcher), o da of Sir David Stephens, *qv*; 1 da; *Career* political sec to PM 1975-81, PPS to: Fin Sec Treas 1984, Sec of State Foreign Affrs 1984-; chm Cons Foreign and Cwlth Cncl 1984-; govt whip 1986-88; Parly sec MAFF 1988-; *Style*— Richard Ryder, Esq, OBE, MP; The House of Commons, London SW1A 0AA

RYDER, Richard Hood Jack Dudley; s of Maj Dudley Claud Douglas Ryder (d 1986), of Rempstone Hall, and Vera Mary, *née* Cook; *b* 3 July 1940; *Educ* Sherborne, Pembroke Coll Cambridge (MA), Columbia New York (res fell), Edinburgh (DCP); *m* 24 April 1974, Audrey Jane, da of Frank Rae Arthur Smith; 1 s (Henry Arthur Woden Calcraft Dudley b 1981), 1 da (Emily Nancy Charlotte b 1978); *Career* sr clinical psychologist Oxford 1968-83, princ clinical psychologist Portsmouth 1983-84; memb DHSS health advsy serv 1976-78, chm cncl RSPCA 1977-79, memb cncl Lib Pty 1984-87 (contested Parl elections 1983 & 87), chm SLD Animal Protection Gp 1988-89; chm: Teignbridge NSPCC, Teignbridge Home Start; fell Zoological Soc; AFB PsS; *Books* Victims of Science (second edn 1983), Animal Revolution (1989), Animal Rights - A Symposium (ed 1979) rhododendroms; *Clubs* Nat Lib; *Style*— Richard D Ryder, Esq

RYDER, (Richard) Stephen; DL (1973); s of Charles Foster Ryder (d 1942), of Thurlow, Suffolk, and Mabel Elizabeth, *née* Sims (d 1974); *b* 6 Feb 1917; *Educ* Radley, Cambridge Univ (MA); *m* 12 April 1947, Margaret, da of Neil MacKenzie; 2 s (Richard b 1949, Charles b 1954); *Career* cmmnd KRRC 1940-46, serv UK and Middle E; farmer/landowner; former chm and pres Suffolk CLA, chm exec ctee Suffolk Historic Churches Tst 1982-, pres S Suffolk Cons Assoc 1983-87, Lay Canon St Edmundsbury Cathedral 1984- (Church Warden 1951-), vice-pres Suffolk Branch Magistrates Assoc (former cncl memb); JP 1956-87; vice-chm: W Suffolk CC 1970-74, Suffolk CC 1978-81; High Sheriff Suffolk 1975-76; Freeman City of London 1958, memb Worshipful Co of Salters Salters 1958; *Recreations* visiting old churches, travelling, shooting; *Clubs* Farmers and Landowners; *Style*— Stephen Ryder, Esq, DL; Great Bradley Hall, Newmarket, Suffolk, CB8 9LT (☎ 044083 294, 221)

RYDER OF EATON HASTINGS, Baron (Life Peer UK 1975); Don (Sydney Thomas) Ryder; s of John Ryder; *b* 16 Sept 1916; *Educ* Ealing Co GS; *m* 1950, Eileen, da of William Dodds; 1 s, 1 da; *Career* ed Stock Exchange Gazette 1950-60, jt md 1960-61, sole md 1961-63, Kelly Iliffe Holdings and Assoc Iliffe Press Ltd, dir Int Publishing Corp 1963-70, md Reed Paper Gp 1963-68, chm and chief exec Reed Int Ltd 1968-75, pres Nat Materials Handling Centre 1970-74, dir MEPC Ltd 1972-75; industl advsr to Govt 1974; memb ct and cncl Cranfield Inst of Technol 1970-74, vice pres ROSPA 1973-, chm NEB 1975-77; memb: cncl and bd bells BIM 1970, Br Gas Corpn 1973-79, cncl UK SA trade Assoc 197, Reserve Pension Bd 1973-, cncl Industl Soc 1971; kt 1972; *Style*— Rt Hon Lord Ryder of Eaton Hastings; House of Lords, London SW1

RYDER OF WARSAW, Baroness (Life Peer UK 1978); Sue (Margaret Susan) Ryder; CMG (1976), OBE (1957); da of Charles Ryder; *b* 3 July 1923; *Educ* Benenden; *m* 1959, Gp Capt Leonard Cheshire, VC, OM, DSO, DFC; 1 s, 1 da; *Career* serv WWII SOE & FANY; social worker, fndr Sue Ryder Fndn for Sick and Disabled All Age Gps; tstee Cheshire Fndn, tstee and co-fndr Ryder-Cheshire Mission for the Relief of Suffering; Hon LLD: Liverpool 1973, Exeter 1980, London 1981, Leeds 1984, Hon DLitt Reading 1982; Hon DCL Kent 1986 Pro Ecclesia et Pontifice award 1982; offs Cross, Order of Polonia Restituta 1965, Medal of Yugoslav Flag with Gold Wreath and Diploma 1971, Golden Order of Merit (Poland) 1976, Order of Smile (Poland) 1981; *Books* And the Morrow is Theirs (autobiog, 1985), Child of My Love (autobiog 1986), Remembrance (annual magazine of the Sue Ryder Foundation); *Clubs* SOE; *Style*— The Rt Hon Lady Ryder of Warsaw, CMG, OBE; Sue Ryder Home, Cavendish, Suffolk

RYDILL, Prof Louis Joseph; OBE (1962); s of Louis William Rydill (d 1975), and Queenie Elizabeth, *née* Gallagher (d 1974); *b* 16 August 1922; *Educ* Public Central Sch Plymouth, Dockyard Tech Coll Devonport, RNEC Keyham, RNC Greenwich; *m* 11 April 1949, Eva, da of Emanuel Newman (d 1961); 2 da (Sarah (Mrs Ash) b 1950, Jessica b 1959); *Career* asst constructor and constructor RCNC 1945-53, asst prof of Naval architecture RNC Greenwich 1953-56, constructor then chief constructor on design of HMS Dreadnought 1956-62, chief constructor on design of aircraft carrier CVAOI 1962-67; prof of naval architecture RNC Greenwich and Univ Coll London 1967-72, asst and dep to dir of submarine project team, dir of warship design and engrg 1976-81, prof of naval architecture Univ Coll London 1981-85, visiting prof of naval architecture at US Naval Acad Annapolis 1985, conslt in ship and submarine design 1985-; memb DSAC; Hon Res fell Univ Coll London 1985; FRINA 1967, FEng

1982; *Recreations* music, books, plays; *Style—* Prof Louis Rydill, OBE; The Lodge, Entry Hill Drive, Bath BA1 5NJ (☎ 0225 427 888)

RYE, Renny Michael Douglas; s of Douglas Rye, of 127 Union Street, Maidstone, Kent, and Pamela, *née* Whitmore; *b* 2 Dec 1947; *Educ* Maidstone GS, St Catherine's Coll Oxford (BA); *m* 8 Aug 1970, Ann, da of Andrew Frank (Peter) Lynn, of Maidstone, Kent; 1 s (Thomas b 1977), 1 da (Helen b 1974); *Career* BBC: prodn ops asst BBC radio 1971-73, asst floor mangr TV plays dept 1973-79, prodr and asst ed 1979-81; freelance drama dir: The Box of Delights (BBC) 1983-84, The December Rose (BBC) 1985, Casualty (BBC) 1986, The Gemini Factor (Thames) 1987, All our Childrem (BBC) 1987-89, Agatha Christie's Poirot (LWT) 1988; DGGB 1984; *Recreations* cricket, films, music; *Style—* Renny Rye, Esq; c/o Scott Marshall Personal Management, 44 Perryn Road, London W3 7NA (☎ 01 749 7692, 743 1669)

RYECART, Lady Marsha Mary Josephine; *née* Fitzalan Howard; da of 17 Duke of Norfolk, CB, CBE, MC; *b* 10 Mar 1953; *m* 1977, Patrick Geoffrey Ryecart, actor, s of Rev John Reginald Ryecart and Verena Maria Olga, da of Baron Hans Ludwig von Gablenz, of Schloss Weinberg, Austria; 1 s (Frederick b 1987) 2 da (Mariella b 1982, Jemima b 1984); *Career* actress; tv performances incl: Upstairs Downstairs, Duchess of Duke St, Pride and Prejudice, Nancy Astor, Pygmalion, Anna Karenina, Paradise Postponed, Inside Story, Hedgehog Wedding, The New Statesman; *Style—* Lady Marsha Ryecart; c/o Frazer & Dunlop Ltd, Chelsea Harbour, London SW10

RYLAND, Timothy Richard Godfrey Fetherstonhaugh; s of Richard Desmond Fetherstonhaugh Ryland (d 1983), and Frances Katharine Vernon, *née* Plummer; *b* 13 June 1938; *Educ* St Andrew's Coll, Trinity Coll Dublin (BA (Hons), LLB); *Career* barr Gray's Inn 1961; dep CJ 1978; rec Crown Ct 1983; *Recreations* opera, wine; *Clubs* Kildare St and Univ Dublin; *Style—* Timothy Ryland, Esq; Lamb Building, Temple, London EC4Y 7AS (☎ 01 353 0774)

RYLANDS, George Chapman; OBE (1976), TD (1959), DL (1975); s of Lt-Col Geoffrey Glazebrook Rylands JP (d 1957); *b* 16 Jan 1924; *Educ* Bromsgrove; *Career* JP 1959, CC 1969, chm Cheshire TA Assoc 1974, memb N W England and IOM TA & VR Assoc 1974, chm HM Prison Appleton Thorn Cheshire 1960, chm Cheshire Police Authy 1973, pres Runcorn Co Constituency Cons Assoc 1965-68; *Recreations* golf, reading; *Style—* George Rylands Esq, OBE, TD, DL; Woodstock, Tarporley Rd, Stretton, nr Warrington, Cheshire (☎ Norlott Brook 378)

RYLANDS, Lt-Col Joseph; DFC (1945), DL (Lancs 1967); s of Joseph T Rylands (d 1942), of Manchester, and Mary Agnes Rylands (d 1963); *b* 5 Dec 1914; *Educ* St Bede's Coll, Manchester Coll of Technol; *m* 1947, Lena Mary, da of Adam Goss (d 1953), of Manchester; 3 s, 4 da; *Career* serv WWII TA (RA) 1938-46, 7 Cheshire HG 1951-55, Lt-Col (Hon); memb E Lancs TA Assoc 1947; vice-chm TA & VRA NW England and IOM to 1979; a former co chm and md, ret 1980; awarded Jubilee Medal; *Recreations* gardening; *Style—* Lt-Col Joseph Rylands, DFC, DL; Brynwood, Wilmslow Rd, Alderley Edge, Cheshire SK9 7QL (☎ 0695 583233)

RYLE, Lt-Col Ian Nigel; OBE (1961), MC (1945, DL (Kent 1976)); s of Arthur John Ryle (d 1921); *b* 7 April 1914; *Educ* Epsom Coll; *m* 1, 1959 (m dis 1975), Jytte, da of Christian Skovby, of Denmark; 1 da (Jacqueline Lilian); m 2, 1976, Joanna, *née* Hawksworth (d 1977); *Career* Royal East Kent Regt 1940-46, Royal Tank Regt 1946, NW Europe 1944-45, Staff Coll 1947, Lt-Col 1956, ret 1964; sec Worcs Territorial and aux Forces Assoc 1965-68, sec SE Territorial & Aux Volunteer Reserve Assoc 1968-79; American Bronze Star 1944; Freeman City of London 1984; *Recreations* foxhunting, shooting, fishing; *Style—* Lt-Col Ian Ryle, OBE, MC, DL; 6 Ashlawn, The Green, Benenden, Cranbrook, Kent TN17 4DM (☎ 0580 240857)

RYMAN, John; MP (Lab) Blyth Valley 1983-; *b* 7 Nov 1930; *Educ* Leighton Park, Pembroke Coll Oxford; *Career* barr Middle Temple, 1957; MP (Lab) Blyth Oct 1974-1983; *Style—* John Ryman, Esq, MP; Lowstead Wark, Hexham, Northumberland

RYMAN, Hon Shirley; *see*: Summerskill, Hon Shirley

RYRIE, Sir William Sinclair; KCB (1982), CB (1979); s of Rev Dr Frank Ryrie; *b* 10 Nov 1928; *Educ* Mt Hermon Sch Darjeeling, Heriot's Sch Edinburgh, Edinburgh Univ; *m* 1, 1953 (m dis 1969), Dorrit Klein; 2 s, 1 da; m 2, 1969, Christine Gray Thomson; 1 s; *Career* Nat Serv, Intelligence Corps Malaya; Colonial Off 1953-63; asst sec int monetary affairs Treasy 1966-69, princ private sec to Chllr 1969-71, under-sec Public Sector Gp 1971-75, econ min and head UK Treasy and Supply Delegn Washington and UK exec dir IMF and IBRD 1975-79, second perm sec (Domestic Economy) Treasy 1980-82, perm sec Overseas Devpt Admin 1982-84, exec vice-pres and chief exec Int Fin Corp, WorkBank, Washington 1984-; *Clubs* Reform; *Style—* Sir William Ryrie, KCB, CB; 4840 Van Ness St, NW, Washington DC, 20016 USA (☎ 202 966 1139)

RYTON, Royce Thomas Carlisle; s of Reginald Thomas Ryton (d 1966), of Ferring, Sussex, and Olive Edwina (d 1963); *b* 16 Sept 1924; *Educ* Lancing, Webber Douglas Acad; *m* 6 Sept 1954, Morar Margaret, da of Capt Edward Coverley Kennedy, RN (ka 1939); 1 da (Charlotte Susan b 15 Oct 1955); *Career* serv WWII RN; actor-playwright: many years experience in rep tours all over the country incl Sheffield, Birmingham and Cambridge Theatre Cos, appeared in West End as Bill in own play, The Unvarnished Truth (Phoenix Theatre and Long US tour) 1978, Terry in The Other Side of the Swamp (Phoenix) 1979, also the author, toured UK and Hong Kong in Sir Anthony Quayle's Co in The Tempest and St Joan, author of Crowm Matrimonial which ran for over 500 performances at the Haymarket, London 1972-74, this play was also performed on Broadway 1973 and on TV; Motherdear (Ambassadors), The Anastasia File - New York and London and two UK tours, author The Royal Baccarat Scandal (Chichester Festival) 1988 and (Haymarket London) 1989; memb Br Actors Equity Assoc; *Books* Plays: Crown Matrimonial (1973), The Unvarnished Truth (1979), The Anastasia File (1986); *Recreations* geneaology, Victorian and Russian royalty; *Clubs* Dramatists; *Style—* Royce Ryton, Esq; 64 Kingfisher Drive, Ham, Richmond, Surrey TW10 7UE (☎ 01 940 8620)

S

SAATCHI, Charles; s of Nathan David and Daisy Saatchi, of London; *b* 9 June 1943; *Educ* Christ's Coll Finchley; *m* 1973, Doris Jean, da of Jack Lockhart of USA; *Career* dir Saatchi & Saatchi Co plc 1970- (largest advtg agency in the world); *Style*— Charles Saatchi, Esq; Saatchi & Saatchi Co plc, 80 Charlotte St, London W1A 1AQ (T 01 636 5060, telex 261580)

SAATCHI, Maurice; s of Nathan David Saatchi and Daisy Saatchi; *b* 21 June 1946; *Educ* LSE (BSc); *m* 1987, Josephine Hart; 1 s (Edward), 1 step s; *Career* chm: Saatchi & Saatchi Co plc; *Style*— Maurice Saatchi, Esq; Saatchi & Saatchi Co plc, 15 Lower Regent St, London SW1Y 4LR (☎ 01 930 2161)

SABATH, Hugo; s of Jacob Sabath (d 1934), of Prague, and Rose Sabath (d 1944); *b* 9 April 1910; *Educ* Real Gymnasium TG Masaryk (matric); *m* 1, 14 July 1945, Greta (decd); 2 s (Martin b 1947, Julian b 1949); m 2, 15 April 1987, Gillian Eugenie Louise Berkeley; *Career* serv WWII: BBC translator (translated Beveridge Plan in Czech for broadcasting to Czechoslovakia); dir Textile Exporters 1944-54 (co sec 1954-62); co sec Fin Co 1962-70; dir Merchant Bank 1970-80; ret; *Recreations* travel, music, theatre, reading; *Clubs* Czech; *Style*— Hugo Sabath, Esq; 41 Meadway, London NW11 (☎ 01 455 9225); Burnt Oak Cottage, Thruxton (☎ Andover 026477-3332)

SABATINI, (Lawrence) John; s of Frederick Laurence Sabatini, and Elsie May, *née* Friggens; *b* 5 Dec 1919; *Educ* Watford GS; *m* 19 July 1947, Patricia, da of William Lawty Dyson; 1 s (Richard John Lawty b 1950), 1 da (Nicola Patricia Anne b 1954); *Career* Army 1940-46, cmmnd RTR 1943, serv in NW Europe 5 RTR; HM Off of Works 1938, Miny of Works asst princ 1947 (asst private sec to minister 1948-49, princ 1949), Jt Servs Staff Coll 1955; MOD: transferred 1955, princ private sec to ministers 1958-60, asst sec 1960, def cnsllr to UK Delegation to NATO on secondment to Dip Serv 1963-67, asst undersec of state 1972-79; RHS, RZS; *Recreations* travel, gardening, photography; *Clubs* MCC; *Style*— John Sabatini, Esq; 44A Batchworth Lane, Northwood, Middx HA6 3DT (☎ 09274 23249)

SABBEN-CLARE, Ernest Elwin; s of James W Sabben-Clare, DSO (d 1968), and Gladys, *née* Dickson (d 1961); *b* 11 August 1910; *Educ* Winchester, New Coll Oxford (BA, MA), London Univ (BA); *m* 9 Dec 1938, Rosamond Dorothy da of Lt Col H C Scott (d 1958); 2 s (Timothy b Dec 1939, James b Sept 1941), 1 da (Penelope b June 1944); *Career* Colonial Serv Tanzania (formerly Tanganyika) 1935-740, Colonial off attache and cmmr Caribbean Cmmn, Br Embassy Washington 1940-50, Nigeria 1950-55, teaching 1955-70: under master (formerly asst master) Marlborough Coll 1955-60, headmaster Bishop Wordsworth Sch Salisbury 1960-63 and Leeds GS 1963-70; info offr Oxford Univ 1970-77; tres Oxford branch CRUSE (nat orgn for widows and bereved) 1979-87; chm of govrs:Bramcore Sch Scarborough 1970-80, Badminton Sch Bristol 1983-87; *Recreations* gardening, chess; *Clubs* Athenaeum; *Style*— Ernest Saben-Clare, Esq; 4 Denham Close, Abbey Hill Rd, Winchester SO23 7BL, (☎ 0962 55966)

SABBEN-CLARE, James Paley; s of Ernest Edwin Sabben-Clare, of Winchester, and Rosamund Dorothy Mary, *née* Scott; *b* 9 Sept 1941; *Educ* Winchester, New Coll Oxford (BA, MA); *m* 30 Aug 1969, (Geraldine) Mary, da of (Henry) Stuart Borton (d 1985), of Blandford; 1 s (Matthew b 1973), 1 da (Rebecca b 1971); *Career* Flt Lt RAFVR 1965-81; asst master Marlborough Coll 1964-68, visiting fell All Souls' Coll Oxford 1967-68, headmaster Winchester Coll 1985-(second master 1979-85, head of classics dept 1969-79); patron Winchester Samaritans, vice pres Winchester Gp for the Disabled; govr: The Pilgrims' Sch, St Swithun's Sch, King Edward VI Sch, Southampton, Northaw Sch, King Alfred's Coll, Westonbirt Sch; *Books* Caesar and Roman Politics (1971, 1981), Fables from Aesop (1976), The Culture of Athens (1978, 1980), Winchester Coll (1981, 1988), contrib to educnl and classical jnls; *Recreations* games, theatre, furniture-making, hill-walking; *Clubs* Jesters; *Style*— James Sabben-Clare, Esq; Headmaster's House, Winchester Coll, Winchester, Hampshire SO23 9NA (☎ 0962 54328)

SABIN, Frank Collins; s of Richard Stanley Sabin (d 1957), of Eastbourne, and Lillian Grace, *née* Bentley (d 1958); *b* 6 July 1905; *Educ* Merchant Taylors', UCL (Dip Civil Engrg, BSc); *m* 1, 1934, Cicely Marks (d 1956); m 2, 1957 Kathleen Gladys Smith; *Career* civil engr, local govt 1927-38, Miny of Works 1938-44, Miny of Housing and Local Govt, Regnl Planning 1944-47, sr inspr planning appeals 1948-67, private practise land surveyor 1967-74, ret 1974; FICE, MRTPI, MRSH; *Recreations* travelling, bridge, philately, gardening, ballroom and Latin American dancing; *Style*— Frank C Sabin, Esq; 50 Arkwright Road, Sanderstead, Surrey CR0 2LL (☎ 657 4670)

SABIN, Paul Robert; s of Robert Reginald Sabin (d 1988), and Dorothy Maude Sabin; *b* 29 Mar 1943; *Educ* Oldbury GS, Aston Univ; *m* 19 June 1965, Vivien, da of Harry Furnival; 1 s (Martin Lawrence b 1969), 2 da (Ann Hazel b 1973, Caroline Jane b 1978); *Career* West Bromwich CBC 1961-69, Redditch Devpt Corpn 1969-81 (chief fin offr 1975-81), City of Birmingham 1981-86 (city tres 1982-86, dep chief exec 1984-86), chief exec Kent CC 1986-; Hon Citizen of the City of Baltimore USA 1985; DMS, IPFA 1966, FBIM, FRSA; *Recreations* antique maps and books, music; *Style*— Paul Sabin, Esq; Chief Executive's Office, Kent County Council, County Hall, Maidstone, Kent ME14 1XQ (☎ 0622 671411, fax 0622 681097)

SABINE, Dr Peter Aubrey; s of Bernard Robert Sabine (d 1970), and Edith Lucy, *née* Dew; *b* 29 Dec 1924; *Educ* Brockley Co Sch, Chelsea Poly, Imperial Coll London (BSc, ARCS, PhD, DSc); *m* 13 April 1946, Peggy Willis, da of Harry Augustus Lambert (d 1958); 1 s (Cedric Martin Peter b 1952); *Career* Geological Survey 1945-; Geological Museum 1945-50, i/c petrographical dept 1950-, chief petrographer 1959-70, asst dir field staff 1970, chief geochemist 1977, dep dir (chief sci offr and chief geologist) 1977-84, geological advsr 1984-; chm Int Union Geological Sci Cmmn on Systematics in Petrology 1984- (memb sub cmmn Igneous Rocks 1969-, chief UK del 1980-84, cncl memb 1984-), chm Royal Inst 1979-82; memd: DTI chemical and minerals requirements bd 1973-82, Minerals Metals and Reclamation Ctee 1983-84, minerals and geochemistry Ctees EEC 1975-84 (advsr 1985-86), Ctee of Dirs of W Euro Surveys 1978-84, Mineral Indust Res Orgn 1983-86, Mineral Soc of America 1953 (Fell 1959), Mineral Soc 1945 (cncl memb 1950-53), Lyell Fund 1955- (cncl memb 1956-67, sec 1959-66, vice pres 1966-67 and 1982-84; FGS 1944, FRSE 1964, FIMM 1965 (cncl 1976-80), CEng 1971, FRSA 1975; *Books* Gemstones (jtly, 1983), Chemical Analyses of Igneous Rocks (jtly, 1956), Petrography of British Igneous rocks (jtly, 1982), plus many contribs to professional jls and geological maps; *Recreations* gardening, genealogy, antique furniture restoration; *Clubs* Athenaeum, Geological Soc (hon memb); *Style*— Dr Peter Sabine; 19 Beaufort Rd, Ealing, London W5 3EB (☎ 01 997 2360)

SACH, Keith Howard; s of Cyril James Sach, of Warwicks, and Jessie Annie Sach, *née* Andlaw; *b* 13 May 1948; *Educ* Strode's Sch, King George V Sch, St Peter's Coll Birmingham; *Career* asst master Solihull Sch 1970-79, dir RLSS UK 1979-88, (chief cwlth sec 1979-86, cwlth vice pres 1987), md S & P 1988-; broadcaster and writer on water safety and lifeguard; memb Health and Safety Exec Working Pty, author of Safety in Swimming Pools; Civil Criminal and Coroners' Ct expert witness on drowning and near drowning accidents; chm: Nat Water Safety Ctee 1980-83, Nat Rescue Trg Cncl 1981-88; *Recreations* theatre, music, travel, swimming; *Style*— Keith Sach, Esq; S & P House, 3/5 Charing Cross Rd, London WC2H OHA (☎ 01 925 0225/930 9010; fax 01 925 0219)

SACHER, Hon Mrs (Rosalind Eleanor Cameron); *née* Corbett; da of 3 Baron Rowallan by his 1 w, Eleanor; *b* 2 Jan 1958; *m* 1977, Jeremy Sacher; 1 s (Harry b 1987), 2 da (Chloe b 1979, Charlotte b 1982); *Style*— The Hon Mrs Sacher; 30 Lansdown Crescent, London W11 2NT

SACHS, Hon Lady ((Janet) Margaret); *née* Goddard; 2 da of Baron Goddard, GCB, PC, sometime Lord Chief Justice (Life Peer d 1971), and Mary Linda, da of Sir Felix Otto Schuster, 1 Bt; *b* 26 Oct 1909; *m* 12 May 1934, Rt Hon Sir Eric Sachs, MBE, TD, sometime Lord Justice of Appeal (d 1979); 1 s (Richard b 1935), 1 da (Katharine Frances b 1939, m 1, 1965, George Pulay, who d 1981; 2 da; m 2, 1987, Hon Mr Justice (Sir Jeremiah LeRoy) Harman, *qv*); *Style*— The Hon Lady Sachs; Walland Oast, Wadhurst, E Sussex (☎ 0892 88 2080)

SACHS, His Honour Judge Michael Alexander Teddes; s of Dr Joseph Sachs (d 1954), of Penrith, Cumbria, and Ruby Mary, *née* Ross (d 1957); *b* 8 April 1932; *Educ* Sedbergh, Univ of Manchester (LLB); *m* 13 July 1957, Patricia Mary, da of James Conroy (d 1968), of thrybergh, Yorkshire; 2 s (Hugh b 1964, Jeromy b 1966), 2 da (Madeline (Mrs Morgan) b 1959, Elizabeth b 1962); *Career* slr 1957; ptnr Slater Heelis Manchester 1962-84, rec Crown Ct 1980-84 circuit judge 1984-; memb no 7 (NW) legal aid ctee 1966-80 (chm 1975-76), chm Greater Manchester legal slrs ctee 1977-81, pres Manchester Law Soc 1978-79; memb ct Univ of Manchester 1977-84, memb cncl Law Soc 1979-84 (chm standing ctee on Criminal Law); kt of St Sylvester; *Style*— His Hon Judge Michael Sachs; c/o Circuit Administrator, Northern Circuit, Lord Chancellors Dept, Aldine House, New Bailey St, Salford M3 5EU (☎ 061 832 9571)

SACK, Barry Lawrence; s of Raphael Sack (d 1988), of Johannesburg, SA, and Daphne, *née* Shapiro (d 1980); *b* 3 Oct 1948; *Educ* Westminister City Univ of Witwatersrand SA (BCom); *m* (m dis); *Career* md Anglo Leasing 1973-78, fndr Aurit Serrs Ltd (a subsidiary of J Rothschilds Hldgs plc), md Target Unit Tsts 1980-; jt md: Comcap plc 1985, Summit Gp plc 1985; dir Atlantic Gp plc; *Recreations* music, art, sculpture; *Style*— Barry Sack, Esq; 49 Pall Mall, London SW1Y 5JG (☎ 930 7682)

SACKLOFF, Ms Gail Josephine; da of Myer Sackloff, of London, and Rachel, *née* Crivon; *b* 15 Dec 1944; *Educ* Norfolk Coll for Girls Dublin Ireland; *Career* Euro import co-ordinator for May Dept Stores USA Nigel French Fashion Consultancy 1970-78, merchandise mangr Batus Retail 1978-; *Recreations* theatre, weekends on my boat on the river Thames; *Clubs* Network; *Style*— Ms Gail Sackloff; Batus Retail, Elsley House, 24-30 Gt Titchfield St, London W1P 8ED (☎ 01 637 3931, fax 01 580 1628, telex 21854)

SACKMAN, Simon Laurence; s of Bernard Sackman (d 1986), and Mamie, *née* Epstein; *b* 16 Jan 1951; *Educ* St Pauls', Pembroke Coll Oxofrd (BA, MA); *m* 7 Feb 1982, Donna, da of Solomon Abraham Seruya, of Gilbraltar; 2 da (Sarah b 1984, Paloma b 1987); *Career* ptnr Norton Rose 1983- (articled clerk 1974-77, asst slr 1977-83); memb: City of London Slrs 1982, Law Soc 1977; *Recreations* theatre, music; *Style*— Simon Sackman, Esq; Norton Rose, Kempson House, Camomile St, London EC3A 7AN (☎ 01 283 2434, fax 01 588 1181, telex 883652)

SACKS, John Harvey; s of Joseph Gerald Sacks, of Dorset House, Gloucester Pl, London NW1, and Yvonne Sacks; *b* 29 April 1946; *Educ* Perse Sch, Cambridge, London Univ (LLB); *m* 1969, Roberta Judith, da of Archy Arenson, of Priory Dr, Stanmore; 1 s, 2 da; *Career* formerly chm London and SE Eng Furniture Mfrs Assoc; chief exec Arenson Gp plc, chm Arenson Int Ltd 1970-; FCA, FCCA, fell Assoc of Corporate Tres; *Recreations* tennis, bridge, walking, law; *Style*— John Sacks, Esq; Barlogan, Priory Dr, Stanmore, Middx (☎ 01 954 2042); Lincoln Hse, Colney St, St Albans, Herts (☎ 0923 857211, telex 922171)

SACKVILLE, 6 Baron (UK 1876); Lionel Bertrand Sackville-West; proprietor of Knole, one of the most spacious homes in private hands in the country, started, around 1456, by Thomas Bourchier, then Archbishop of Canterbury, and expanded in the early seventeenth century by Thomas Sackville, to whom it was made over by Elizabeth I; patron of eleven livings; s of late Hon Bertrand George Sackville-West (bro of 4 Baron and unc of Vita (Victoria) Sackville-West, w of Hon Sir Harold Nicolson, KCVO, CMG) and Eva, da of late Maj-Gen Inigo Richmond Jones, CB, CVO; suc cous 1965; *b* 30 May 1913; *Educ* Winchester, Magdalen Coll Oxford; *m* 1, 1953, Jacobine Napier (d 1971), da of J R Menzies-Wilson and widow of Capt John Hitchens, RA; 5 da; m 2, 1974 (m dis 1983), Arlie Roebuck, da of Charles Woodhead, of Romany Rye Brisbane Aust, widow of Maj Hugh Dalzell Stewart and formerly w of Maj-Gen Sir Francis Wilfred de Guingand, KBE, CB, DSO; m 3, Jean, JP, da of Arthur Stanley Garton (d 1963), and widow of Sir Edward Imbert-Terry, 3 Bt, MC (d 1978); *Heir* bro, Hugh Inigo Sackville-West; *Career* late Coldstream Gds, served WW II (POW); Lloyd's underwriter, ret; *Style*— The Rt Hon the Lord Sackville; Knole, Sevenoaks, Kent (☎ 0732 455694)

SACKVILLE, Hon Thomas Geoffrey; MP (C) Bolton W 1983-; yr s of 10 Earl De La Warr, DL (d 1988); *b* 26 Oct 1950; *Educ* Eton, Lincoln Coll Oxford (BA); *Career* formerly merchant banker; PPS to Min of State at the Treasy 1985-; govt whip 1988-; PPS Min of State for Social Security 1987-; *Style*— The Hon Thomas Sackville, MP; House of Commons, London SW1 (☎ 01 219 4050/3537)

SACKVILLE-WEST, Hon Catherine Jacobine; resumed use of maiden name 1984; da of 6 Baron Sackville, *qv*, and his 1 wife, Jacobine Napier (d 1971), da of J R Menzies-Wilson, of Fotheringhay Lodge, Nassington, Peterborough; *b* 10 Mar 1956; *Educ* Cranborne Chase Wilts, Queen's Coll London; *m* 1980 (m dis 1984), Stuart Cooper Bennett, er s of H M Bennett, of Pasadena, Calif, USA; *Style*— The Hon Catherine Sackville-West; 36 Iffley Rd, London W6 (☎ 01 748 1853)

SACKVILLE-WEST, Hugh Rosslyn Inigo; MC; s of late Hon Bertrand Sackville-West (bro of 4 Baron Sackville) and Eva, da of Maj-Gen Inigo Richmond Jones, CB, CVO; hp of bro, 6 Baron; *b* 1 Feb 1919; *Educ* Winchester, Magdalen Coll Oxford; *m* 1957, Bridget Eleanor, da of Capt Robert Lionel Brooke Cunliffe, CBE, RN (ggs of 3 Bt); 2 s, 3 da; *Career* Capt RTR, serv WWII (Croix de Guerre); admin offr N Nigeria 1946-59; ARICS; *Style*— Hugh Sackville-West Esq; Knole, Sevenoaks, Kent

SACKVILLE-WEST, Hon Sarah Elizabeth; da (by 1 m) of 6 Baron Sackville; *b* 14 Sept 1960; *Style*— The Hon Sarah Sackville-West; 36 Fentiman Rd, London SW8

SACKVILLE-WEST, Hon Victoria Mary; da (by 1 m) of 6 Baron Sackville; *b* 26 April 1959; *Style*— The Hon Victoria Sackville-West; 107 Ashley Gdns, Thirlebey Rd, London SW1P 1HJ

SADIE, Dr Stanley John; CBE (1982); s of David Sadie of London (d 1966), and Deborah, *née* Simons (d 1988); *b* 30 Oct 1930; *Educ* St Paul's, Gonville and Caius Coll Cambridge (BA, MA, MusB, PhD); *m* 1, 10 Dec 1953, Adèle (d 1978), da of Henry Bloom (d 1974), of London; 2 s (Graham b 1956, Stephen b 1963), 1 da (Ursula b 1960); m 2, 18 July 1978, Julie Anne, da of Walter McCornack, of Eugene, Oregon; 1 s (Matthew b 1983), 1 da (Celia b 1979); *Career* prof Trinity Coll of Music 1957-65, music critic The Times 1964-81, ed The Musical Times 1967-87; ed: The New Grove Dictionary of Music and Musicians and assoc pubns 1970 (1980, 1984, 1986, etc), Master Musicians series (1976-); author of Studies of: Handel (1962, 1972), Mozart (1966, 1983, 1986), Opera (1964), and others; *Recreations* watching cricket, reading, opera, canal boating; *Style*— Dr Stanley Sadie, CBE; 12 Lyndhurst Rd, Hampstead, London NW3 5NL (☎ 01 435 2482); c/o Macmillan, Stockton House, 1 Melbourne Place, London WC2B 4LF (☎ 01 836 6633, fax 01 379 4980, telex 914690)

SADLEIR, (Franc) Richard; s of Maj Franc Granby Sadleir, (ka 1944), of Paignton, Devon, and Josephine Ruth, *née* Hepburn; *b* 27 Dec 1944; *Educ* Marlborough, New Coll Oxford (MA); *m* 25 July 1970, Frances Judith, da of Edward John Wilson (d 1986), of St Agnes, Cornwall; 1 s (Timothy b 1975), 1 da (Rebecca b 1972); *Career* Bank of London and S America Ltd 1967-70, J Henry Schroder Wagg and Co Ltd 1970-(dir 1984-); dir The Securities Assoc Ltd 1986-88; *Recreations* walking, reading, sailing; *Style*— Richard Sadleir, Esq; Fair Winds, Golden Ball Lane, Pinkneys Green, Nr Maidenhead, Berks SL6 6NW (☎ 0628 31205); J Henry Schroder Wagg and Co Ltd, 120 Cheapside, London WC2V 6DS (☎ 01 382 6000, fax 01 382 3950, telex LONDON 885029)

SADLER, John Stephen; CBE (1982); s of Bernard Eustace Sadler (d 1982), of Bromley Kent, and Phyllis Dorothy Sadler, *née* Carey; *b* 6 May 1930; *Educ* Reading Sch, Corpus Christi Coll Oxford (BA, MA); *m* 1952, Ella, da of John McCleery, of Belfast; 3 s (Stephen, Hugh, Robert); *Career* Civil Serv 1952-66, princ BOT 1958, Br Trade Cmmnr Lagos 1960-64, dep chm John Lewis Ptnrship plc 1984- (joined 1966, fin dir 1971-87), memb Monopolies and Mergers Cmmn 1973-85, tstee Br Telecommunications Staff Superannuation Scheme 1983-, dir: Investmt Mgmnt Regulatory Orgn Ltd 1987-, Debenham Tewson & Chinnocks Hldgs plc 1987-; *Recreations* golf, rowing, walking; *Style*— John Stephen Sadler, Esq, CBE; Riverlea, The Warren, Mapledurham, Reading RG4 7TQ; 7 The Chilterns, 63 Chiltern St, London W1M 1HS (☎ 01 487 4452); John Lewis Partnership plc, 4 Old Cavendish St, London W1A 1EX (☎ 01 637 3434)

SADLER, Philip John; CBE (1986); s of Edward John Sadler (d 1977), and Adelaide Violet, *née* Parrish (d 1985); *b* 27 Jan 1930; *Educ* Enfield GS, LSE; *m* 11 July 1964, Teresa Jacqueline, da of Victor Coan (d 1949), of London; 2 s (Matthew John b 1965, Jonathan b 1968); *Career* princ scientific offr Civil Serv 1954-64, regnl dir Lloyds Bank plc 1985-, chief exec Ashridge Tst 1988-; dir: Williams Lea Gp Ltd 1983-, Broadway Lodge Ltd 1983-; vice pres: Euro Fndn for Mgmnt Devpt 1981-88, Strategic Planning Soc 1981-88, Assoc for Mgmnt Educn and Devpt 1988-; fell Int Acad of Mgmnt; CBIM; FIPM; FRSA; BIM Burnham Medal 1982; *Recreations* tennis, swimming, classical music; *Style*— Philip Sadler, Esq, CBE; Highfield, 115 Cross Oak Rd, Berkhamsted, Herts HP4 3HZ; Ashridge Management Coll, Berkhamsted, Herts HP4 1NS (☎ 044 284 3491, telex 826434, fax 044 284 2382)

SAFFORD, John Francis; s of Sir Archibald Safford, MC, QC (d 1961), of Richmond, and Nora Iris Leighton (d 1949); *b* 2 Jan 1927; *Educ* Winchester, Trinity Coll Oxford (MA); *m* 15 Feb 1958, Nancy Helen Dorothy, da of Henry Marshall, MC (d 1981), of St Neots, Cambs; 2 s (Nicholas b 1962, Roger b 1967), 1 da (Judith b 1960); *Career* Nat Serv Sgt Intelligence Corps Germany 1948-50; dir Br Iron and Steel Consumers Cncl 1977-; Nat Econ Devpt Off 1966-76, engrg dir 1974-76) Guthrie & Co (UK) Ltd 1959-66; CB 1953-59 (assist to Dep chm 1956-57) Bank of England 1951-52; *Recreations* bird watching, gardening; *Style*— John Safford, Esq; 16 Berwyn Rd, Richmond, Surrey TW10 5BS (☎ 01 876 5179, 01 878 4898)

SAGE, Morley William; OBE (1984); s of William George Sage (d 1968), of Worle, Weston Super Mare, and Grace Graves Age *née* Smith (d 1977); *b* 15 Jan 1930; *Educ* Blundells, Emmanuel Coll Cambridge (MA); *m* 30 April 1955, Enid Muriel, da of Herbert Sim Hirst (d 1987), of Ferndown, Dorset; 1 s (Morley b 1962), 2 da (Caroline b 1957, Fiona b 1960); *Career* chartered electrical engr conslt; lab and energ mangr Corporate Lab, ICI plc 1962-75; dir computing serv Univ of Southampton 1975-88, princ consit Systems Technol Conslt 1980-; visiting fell Clare Hall Cambridge 1967-69 (life fell 1986); memb Br Computor Soc 1967, Univ Grants Technol Sub-Ctee 1974-79 (Computor Systems and Electrical Bd 1973-77), Inst of Measurement and Control 1977 (cncl 1967-71); chm: Data Communications Protocol Steering Ctee CTI 1977-81, Inter Univ Ctees on Computing 1983-85; dep chm res resources and methods ctee, ESRC 1982-85; chm Integrated Prodn Systems, SERC 1975-76, control engrg ctee, SERC 1974-79, (computing sci ctee, 1976-79); CEng, FIEE 1972 (vice-pres 1984), FEng 1987; *Recreations* reading, gardening, caravanning, do it yourself, model railways; *Clubs* Royal Cwlth Soc; *Style*— Morley Sage, OBE; Wiltown Pl, Wiltown, Curry Rivel, Langport, Somerset TA10 0HE, (☎ 0458 251407)

SAGGERS, Lady Kirstie; Cairistiona Anne; *née* Graham; 2 da of 7 Duke of Montrose (but er da by 2 w), of Dalgoram, Baynesfield, Natal, S Africa, and Susan Mary Jocelyn, *née* Semple; *b* 7 Jan 1955; *Educ* Salisbury Girls' HS Rhodesia, Ruskin Sch of Drawing and Fine Art (Dip AD), Oxford; *m* 8 May 1982, Philip Patrick Saggers, slr, yst s of Gordon Francis Saggers, dental surgn, of Narrandera Rd, Lockhart, NSW; 2 da (Susanna Mary b 1984, Marina Lilias b 1986); *Career* patron and chieftain of Clan Graham of Australia, patron of Scottish Australian Heritage Council; *Style*— Lady Kirstie Saggers; c/o Narrandera Rd, Lockhart, NSW, Australia; office (☎ 02 2323533)

SAIDEMAN, Michael Allan; s of Morris Saideman, Bournemouth, Dorset (d 1983), Rachel Saideman, Bournemouth, Dorset (d 1985); *b* 3 Feb 1935; *Educ* Barking Abbey; *m* 27 Aug 1961 Pamela, Nathan Bloom London W2; 1s (Andrew b 1963), 1 da (Susan b 1965); *Career* CA; gp fin dir Campari Int plc 1973-; *Recreations* golf, bowls; *Style*— Michael Saideman, Esq; International House, Priestley Way, London NW2 7AZ (☎ 01 450 661, telex 923396, fax 01 452 0443)

SAIN, Hon Mrs (Harriet Mary); *née* Lawson; 2 da of 5 Baron Burnham, *qv*; *b* 5 Mar 1954; *m* 1984, Marino Sain, o s of Silvano Sain, of Trieste, Italy; 1 s (Thomas Andrea b 1987); *Style*— The Hon Mrs Sain

SAINER, Leonard; s of Archer Sainer (d 1974), and Sarah Sainer (d 1971); *b* 12 Oct 1909; *Educ* Central Fndn Sch, UCL, LSE; *Career* slr; former sr ptnr with Titmuss Sainer & Webb; life pres Sears plc; *Recreations* golf, horse racing; *Style*— Leonard Sainer, Esq; 8 Farm St, London W1X 7RE

SAINER, Leonard; s of late Archer Sainer, and late Sarah Sainer; *b* 12 Oct 1909; *Educ* Central Fndn Sch, Univ Coll London, LSE (LLB); *Career* sr ptnr Titmuss Sainer & Webb 1938-79, chj Sears plc 1979-86; memb Law Soc; *Style*— Leonard Sainer, Esq; 8 Farm St, London W1X 7RE (☎ 01 355 1125, car tel 0836 279444)

SAINSBURY, Baron (Life Peer UK 1962); Alan John Sainsbury; s of John Benjamin Sainsbury, and Mable Miriam, *née* Van Den Bergh; *see also* Sainsbury, Sir Robert; *b* 13 August 1902; *Educ* Haileybury; *m* 1, 1925 (m dis 1939), Doreen Davan, *née*, Adams (d 1988); 3 s; m 2, 1944, Anne Elizabeth, da of Paul Lewy; 1 da; *Career* jt pres J Sainsbury Ltd 1967 (joined 1921, chm 1956-67), contested (Lib) 1929, 1931, 1935, subsequently joined Lab Pty and SDP in 1981; *Style*— The Rt Hon the Lord Sainsbury; J Sainsbury plc, Stamford House, Stamford St, SE1 (☎ 01 921 6000)

SAINSBURY, Sir Robert; s of late John Benjamin Sainsbury, and late Mabel Miriam, *née* Van Den Bergh; *see also* Baron Sainsbury; *b* 24 Oct 1906; *Educ* Haileybury, Pembroke Coll Cambridge; *m* 1937, Lisa Ingeborg, *née* Van den Bergh (cousin); 1 s, 2 da (1 da decd); *Career* J Sainsbury: joined 1930, dir 1934, jt gen mangr 1938, dep chm 1956, chm 1967, jt pres 1969-; former tstee and chm Tate Gallery, memb Arts Panel Arts Cncl until 1974, memb mgmnt ctee Courtauld Inst of Art 1979-82, hon fell Pembroke Coll Cambridge 1983; Hon Dr RCA 1976, Hon LittD E Anglia 1977, Hon LLD Liverpool 1988; kt 1967; FCA, hon FRIBA 1986; *Style*— Sir Robert Sainsbury

SAINSBURY, Roger Norman; s of Cecil Charles Sainsbury, of Hitchin, Herts, and Ivy Evelyn *née* Pettengell; *b* 11 June 1940; *Educ* Eton, Keble Coll Oxford (MA); *m* 16 May 1969, Susan Margaret, da of Henry William Higgs (d 1981); *Career* chartered engr, dir John Mowlem & Co plc 1982-; awarded Inst of Civil Engrs: George Stephenson medal, Reed and Mallik medals; FEng, FICE; *Clubs* gardening, theatre; *Style*— Roger N Sainsbury, Esq; 88 Dukes Ave, Muswell Hill, London N10 2QA; John Mowlem & Co plc, Ealing Rd, Brentford, Middx (☎ 01 568 9111)

SAINSBURY, Hon Timothy Alan Davan; MP (Cons Hove 1973-); yst s (by 1 m) of Baron Sainsbury; *b* 11 June 1932; *Educ* Eton, Worcester Coll Oxford (MA); *m* 26 April 1961, Susan Mary, da of Brig James Alastair Harry Mitchell, CBE, DSO; 2 s (Timothy b 1962, Alexander b 1968), 2 da (Camilla b 1962, Jessica b 1970); *Career* dir J Sainsbury plc 1962-83; PPS to: sec state Environment 1979-83, Sec State Def 1983; asst govt whip 1983-, Lord Cmmr (Govt Whip) 1985-87; under-sec of State for Def Procurement at MOD 1987-; memb Cncl of RSA 1981-83; hon fell Worcester Coll Oxford 1982; *Style*— The Hon Timothy Sainsbury, MP; House of Commons, London SW1

SAINSBURY OF PRESTON CANDOVER, Baron (Life Peer UK 1989), of Preston Candover, Co Hants; Sir John Davan Sainsbury; eldest s (by 1 m) of Baron Sainsbury (Life Peer), *qv*; *b* 2 Nov 1927; *Educ* Stowe, Worcester Coll Oxford (hon fell 1982); *m* 8 March 1963, Anya (Anya Linden, the Royal Ballet ballerina), da of George Charles Eltenton, and former w of Igor Tamarin; 2 s, 1 da; *Career* chm J Sainsbury plc 1969- (dir 1958-, vice-chm 1967-69); chm Royal Opera House Covent Garden 1987- (dir 1969-85 and 1987-, tst dir 1974-84 and 1987-), cncl memb Friends of Covent Garden 1969- (chm 1969-81); dir The Economist 1972-80; tstee: National Gallery 1976-83, Westminster Abbey Tst 1977-83, Tate Gallery 1982-83, Rhodes Tst 1984-; govr Royal Ballet Sch 1965-76, 1987-; jt hon tres European Movement 1972-75 (a pres 1975-); memb: cncl Retail Consortium 1975-79, nat ctee for Electoral Reform 1976-85, president's ctee CBI 1982-84; assoc V & A 1976-85; fell Inst of Grocery Distribution 1973-; vice pres Contemporary Arts Soc 1984-, chm Benesh Inst of Choreology 1986-87; hon fell Worcester Coll Oxford 1982, hon bencher Inner Temple 1985, Hon DSc Econ (London) 1985; kt 1980; *Clubs* Garrick; *Style*— The Rt Hon Lord Sainsbury of Preston Candover; J Sainsbury plc, Stamford House, Stamford St, SE1 (☎ 01 921 6000)

SAINT, Lady (Josephine Sylvia) Rose; *née* Chetwynd-Talbot; da (by 1 m) of late 21 Earl of Shrewsbury and Waterford; *b* 23 May 1940; *m* 1965, (Stafford) Antony Saint, yr s of Stafford Eric Saint, CVO, FRCS, MRCP (d 1988); 1 s, 2 da; *Style*— Lady Rose

Saint

SAINT BRIDES, Baron (Life Peer UK 1977); John Morrice Cairns James; GCMG (1975, KCMG 1962, CMG 1957), CVO (1961), MBE (1944), PC (1968); s of Lewis Cairns James (d 1946) and Catherine Mary (d 1970); *b* 30 April 1916; *Educ* Bradfield, Balliol Coll Oxford (BA); *m* 1, 1948, Elizabeth Margaret Roper (d 1966), da of late Francis Piesse; 1 s, 2 da; m 2, 1968, Mme Geneviève Christiane Sarasin, da of Robert Henri Houdin (d 1960); *Career* serv WWII RN, Maj RM N Africa and Sicily, Lt-Col 1945; dep high cmmr: Lahore 1952-53, Karachi 1955-56; asst under-sec state CRO 1957-58, dep high cmmr New Delhi 1958-61, high cmmr Pakistan 1961-66, dep under-sec state CRO 1966-68, perm under-sec state Cwlth Affrs 1968; high cmmr: India 1968-71, Australia 1971-76; King of Arms Order of St Michael and St George 1975-86; former visiting fell Chicago Univ, fell Center for Int Affairs Harvard Univ 1979-80, distinguished diplomat in res Foreign Policy Res Inst Philadelphia 1981, visiting scholar Univ of Texas at Austin 1982, distinguished visiting prof of int studies Rhodes Coll Memphis Tennessee 1983-84, memb and visiting fell Center for Int Security and Arms Control Stanford Univ 1984-89; *Clubs* Oriental, Harvard (New York); *Style*— The Rt Hon the Lord Saint Brides, GCMG, CVO, MBE, PC; Cap Saint-Pierre, 83990 St Tropez, France (☎ 94 97 14 75)

ST ALBANS, Archdeacon of; *see*: Davies, Ven Philip Bertram

ST ALBANS, 8 Bishop of (cr 1887) 1980-; Rt Rev John Bernard Taylor; s of George Ernest Taylor and Gwendoline Irene Taylor; *b* 6 May 1929; *Educ* Watford GS, Christ's Coll Cambridge, Jesus Coll Cambridge (MA); *m* 1956, Linda Courtenay, da of Allan Dearden Barnes (d 1976); 1 s, 2 da; *Career* former examining chaplain to Bishop of Chelmsford, archdeacon of W Ham 1975-80; author; *Books* A Christian's Guide to the Old Testament, Tyndale Commentary on Ezekiel, Understanding the Old Testament: the Minor Prophets, Preaching through the Prophets; *Style*— The Rt Rev the Bishop of St Albans; Abbey Gate House, St Albans, Herts (☎ 0727 53305)

ST ALBANS, 14 Duke of (E 1684) Murray de Vere Beauclerk; Baron Hedington and Earl of Burford (E 1676), Baron Vere of Hanworth (GB 1750); Hereditary Grand Falconer and Hereditary Registrar of Court of Chancery; s of 13 Duke of St Albans, OBE (d 1988), and his 1 w, Nathalie Chatham (d 1985), da of Percival Walker; gggggs of 1 Duke of St Albans, who was natural s of King Charles II and Eleanor (Nell) Gwynn; *b* 19 Jan 1939; *Educ* Tonbridge; *m* 1, 31 Jan 1963 (m dis 1974), Rosemary Frances, o da of Francis Harold Scoones, MRCS, LRCP, JP; 1 s (Earl of Burford), 1 da (Lady Emma Caroline de Vere b 22 July 1963); m 2, 1974, Cynthia Theresa Mary, da of late Lt-Col William James Holdsworth Howard, DSO, and former w of late Sir Anthony Robin Maurice Hooper, 2 Bt; *Heir* s, Earl of Burford, *qv*; *Career* Freeman of City of London, Liveryman of the Drapers' Co; FCA; *Clubs* Hurlingham; *Style*— His Grace the Duke of St Albans; 3 St George's Ct, Gloucester Rd, London SW7 (☎ 01 589 1771); office: 7 Westminster Palace Gardens, Artillery Row, London SW1 (☎ 01 222 3804)

ST ALBANS, Suzanne, Duchess of; Suzanne Marie Adèle; *née* Fesq; da of late Emile William Fesq, of Le Mas Mistral, Vence, France; *m* 19 March 1947, as his 2 w, 13 Duke of St Albans, OBE (d 1988); 3 s, 1 da (and 1 da decd); *Career* author and painter; *Style*— Her Grace Suzanne, Duchess of St Albans; 207 Park Palace, Monte Carlo, Monaco (☎ (93) 50 87 39)

ST ALDWYN, 2 Earl (UK 1915); Sir Michael John Hicks Beach; 10 Bt (E 1619), PC (1959), GBE (1980, KBE 1964), TD (1949), JP (Glos 1952), DL (Glos 1950); also Viscount St Aldwyn (UK 1906), Viscount Quenington (UK 1915); s of Viscount Quenington (ka 1916, s of 1 Earl, chllr of Exchequer 1885-86 and 1895-1902) by his w Marjorie, da of Henry Dent Brocklehurst, bro of 1 and last Baron Ranksborough; suc gf 1916; *b* 9 Oct 1912; *Educ* Eton, Ch Ch Oxford; *m* 1948, Diana Mary Christian, formerly w of Maj Richard Smyly and da of late Henry Mills (gs of 1 Baron Hillingdon); 3 s; *Heir* s, Viscount Quenington, *qv*; *Career* sits as Conservative peer in House of Lords; parly sec Miny of Ag Fish and Food 1954-58; oppn chief whip House of Lords 1964-70 and 1974-78, govt chief whip 1958-64 and 1970-74, Capt Hon Corps of Gentlemen-at-Arms 1958-64 and 1970-74, Vice Lord Lieut of Glos 1981-87; GStJ (chllr 1978-87); *Recreations* shooting, fishing; *Clubs* Pratt's, Carlton, Beefsteak, Royal Yacht Squadron; *Style*— The Rt Hon the Earl St Aldwyn, PC, GBE, TD, JP, DL,; Williamstrip Park, Cirencester, Glos GL7 5AT (☎ 028 575 226); 13 Upper Belgrave St, London SW1X 8BA (☎ 01 235 8464)

ST ANDREWS, Earl of; George Philip Nicholas Windsor; er s and h of HRH The Duke of Kent, KG, GCMG, GCVO (*see Royal Family*); *b* 26 June 1962; *Educ* Eton, Downing Coll Camb; *m* 9 Jan 1988, Sylvana (b 28 May 1957), former w of John Paul Jones, and da of Max(imilian) Tomaselli and Josiane Preschez; 1 s; *Heir* e, Edward Edmund Maximilian George Windsor, Lord Downpatrick b 2 Dec 1988; *Style*— Earl of St Andrews

ST ANDREWS AND EDINBURGH, Archbishop of (RC) 1985-; Most Rev Keith (Michael) Patrick O'Brien; s of Mark Joseph O'Brien, DSM (d 1988), of Edinburgh, and Alice Mary, *née* Moriarty (d 1955); *b* 17 Mar 1938; *Educ* St Patrick's HS Dumbarton, Holy Cross Acad Edinburgh, Univ of Edinburgh (BSc), St Andrews Coll Drygrange, Moray House Coll of Educn, Univ of Edinburgh (Dip Ed); *Career* Holy Cross Parish Edinburgh 1965-66, sch chaplain and teacher St Columba's Secdy Sch Dunfermline 1966-71; asst priest: St Patrick's Parish Kilsyth 1972-75, St Mary's Bathgate 1975-78; spiritual dir St Andrew's Coll Drygrange 1978-80, rector St Mary's Coll Blairs 1980-85; *Recreations* music, walking; *Style*— The Most Rev the Archbishop of St Andrews and Edinburgh; St Bennet's, 42 Greenhill Gardens, Edinburgh EH10 4BJ (☎ 031 447 3337); Archdiocesan Centre, 106 Whitehouse Loan, Edinburgh EH9 1BD (☎ 031 452 8244)

ST ANDREWS, DUNKELD AND DUNBLANE, Bishop of 1969-; Rt Rev Michael Geoffrey Hare Duke; s of Arthur Robert Aubrey Hare Duke (d 1972), of United Service Club, Calcutta, India, and Dorothy Lee, *née* Holmes (d 1967); *b* 28 Nov 1925; *Educ* Bradfield Coll Berks, Trinity Coll Oxford, Westcott House Cambridge (MA); *m* 6 July 1949, Grace Lydia Frances McKane (Baa), da of Rev Walter Edward Fagan Dodd (d 1971); 1 s (Barnabas Martin b 1954), 3 da (Phillida Frances b 1950, Teresa Mary b 1956, Hilary Margaret b 1958); *Career* Sub Lt RNVR 1944-46; ordained: deacon 1952, priest 1953; curate St John's Wood Church 1952-56, Vicar St Mark's Bury 1956-62, pastoral dir Clinical Theol Assoc 1962-64 (pastoral conslt 1964-69), Vicar St Paul's 1964-69, OCF E Midland Dist HQ 1968-69; chm: Scottish Assoc for Mental Health 1978-85, Scottish Pastoral Assoc 1970-74; pres Br Region Christian Peace Conf 1982-, vice pres Scottish Inst of Human Relations 1974-76; *Recreations* broadcasting, writing; *Style*— The Rt Rev the Bishop of St Andrews, Dunkeld and Dunblane; Bishop's House, Fairmount Road, Perth PH2 7AP

ST AUBYN, Hon Giles Rowan; LVO (1977); yst s of 3 Baron St Levan (d 1978), and Hon Clementina Gwendolen Catharine, *née* Nicolson, da of 1 Baron Carnock; *b* 11 Mar 1925; *Educ* Wellington, Glasgow Univ, Trinity Coll Oxford; *Career* author, FRSL; *Books* Macaulay (1952), A Victorian Eminence (1957), The Art of Argument (1957), The Royal George (1963), A World to Win (1968), Infamous Victorians (1971), William of Gloucester: Pioneer Prince (1977), Edward VII, Prince and King (1979), The Year of Three Kings (1983); *Clubs* Beefsteak, The Royal Over-Seas League; *Style*— The Hon Giles St Aubyn, LVO; Cornwall Lodge, Cambridge Park, St Peter Port, Guernsey CI (☎ 0481 24157)

ST AUBYN, Hon (Oliver) Piers; MC (1944); s of late 3 Baron St Levan and Hon Clementina, *née* Nicolson, da of 1 Baron Carnock and sis of Harold Nicolson, the writer (*see* Nigel Nicolson); hp of bro, 4 Baron St Levan, DSC; *b* 12 July 1920; *Educ* Wellington, St James's Sch Maryland USA; *m* 1948, Mary Bailey (d 1987), da of Bailey Southwell, of Olievenhoortpoort S Africa; 2 s (James b 1950, Nicholas b 1955) 1 da (Fiona); *Career* served WW II, Capt 60 Rifles and Parachute Regt (despatches); memb Stock Exchange 1949-; ptnr W Greenwell & Co 1957-78; high sheriff E Sussex 1982-83; *Clubs* House of Lords Yacht, Brooks's; *Style*— The Hon Piers St Aubyn, MC; Hogus House, Ludgvan, Penzance, Cornwall TR20 8EZ (☎ 0736 740822)

ST AUBYN, Maj Thomas Edward; DL (1984); Maj; s of Capt The Hon Lionel St Aubyn, MVO (d 1964), and Lady Mary, *née* Parker (d 1932); *b* 13 June 1923; *Educ* Eton; *m* 21 Nov 1953 Henrietta Mary, da of Sir Henry Gray Studholme, 1 Bt, CVO (d 1987); 3 da (Sarah b 1955, Caroline b 1957, Clare b 1962) ; *Career* serv in KRRC 1941-62, Italian Campaign 1944-45, seconded to Sudan Def Force in rank of Bimbashi 1948-52, instru RMA Sandhurst 1955-56; ldr of Tibesti Mountain Expedition 1957 and other Sahara Expdn 1963-71; FRGS (1961), High Sheriff of Hants 1979-80, memb of HM Body Guard of the Hon Corps of Gentlemen at Arms 1973, Clerk of the Cheque and Adj 1986-; *Recreations* shooting, fishing, skiing, stalking, riding; *Clubs* Army and Navy; *Style*— Maj Thomas E St Aubyn; Dairy House Farm, Ashford Hill, Newbury, Berks RG15 8BL (☎ 0635 298493)

ST CLAIR-ERSKINE, Lady Caroline; da of 6 Earl of Rosslyn and Athenaïs, Countess of Rosslyn, *qv*; *b* 7 June 1956; *Style*— Lady Caroline St Clair-Erskine

ST CLAIR-FORD, Capt Sir Aubrey; 6 Bt (GB 1793), DSO (and bar 1942), RN; s of late Anson St Clair St Clair-Ford (s of late Capt St Clair St Clair-Ford, s of 2 Bt), and late Isabella Maria (Elsie), *née* Adams; suc kinsman, Sir (Francis Charles) Rupert Ford, 5 Bt, 1948; *b* 28 Feb 1904; *Educ* RNC Osborne, RNC Dartmouth; *m* 1945, Anne, da of Harold Cecil Christopherson; 1 s, 1 da; *Heir* s, James Anson St Clair-Ford; *Career* Cdr RN 1939, Capt HMS Kipling ops Atlantic, Crete and Mediterranean 1942 (sunk by enemy action), Capt HMS Belfast during Korean War (despatches twice, offr American Legion of Merit) 1951-52, ret Capt 1955; Tarmac Civil Engrg Ltd 1955-69; *Clubs* Army and Navy; *Style*— Capt Sir Aubrey St Clair-Ford, Bt, DSO, RN; Corner House, Sandle Copse, Fordingbridge, Hants (☎ 0425 523 28)

ST CLAIR-FORD, James Anson; s and h of Capt Sir Aubrey St Clair-Ford, 6 Bt, DSO, RN; *b* 16 Mar 1952; *Educ* Wellington, Bristol Univ; *m* 1977 (m dis 1985), Jennifer Margaret, da of Cdre J Robin Grindle, RN; m 2, 1987 Mary Ann, da of His Hon Judge Blaher QC; *Style*— James St Clair-Ford, Esq; c/o Corner House, Sandle Copse, Fordingbridge, Hants

ST CLAIR-FORD, Maj-Gen Sir Peter; KBE (1961, CBE 1953), CB (1954), DSO (1943) and Bar (1943); s of late Anson St Clair-Ford and bro of Capt Sir Aubrey St Clair-Ford, 6 Bt, *qv*; *b* 25 Nov 1905; *Educ* Dover Coll, RMC Sandhurst; *Career* King's Own Yorkshire LI 1925, GOC 1 Federated Div Malaya 1954-57, Dep Chief of Staff HQ Allied Land Forces Cent Europe 1958-60, ret; *Style*— Maj-Gen Sir Peter St Clair-Ford, KBE, CB, DSO; Cotswold Lodge, Littlestone, New Romney, Kent TN28 8QV (☎ 0679 62368)

ST CYRES, Viscount; John Stafford Northcote; s and h of 4 Earl of Iddesleigh; *b* 15 Feb 1957; *Educ* Downside, RAC Cirencester; *m* 14 May 1983, Fiona Caroline Elizabeth, da of Paul Alan Campbell Wakefield, of Barcelona, Spain; 1 s (Thomas b 1985), 1 da (Elizabeth-Rose Adele b 10 April 1989); *Heir* s, Hon Thomas Stafford Northcote, b 5 Aug 1985; *Career* farmer; *Recreations* shooting, sailing; *Style*— Viscount St Cyres; Lloyds Bank, 234 High St, Exeter, Devon; Hayne Barton, Newton St Cyres, Devon (☎ 0392 851311)

ST DAVIDS, 2 Viscount (UK 1918); Sir Jestyn Reginald Austen Plantagenet Philipps; 14 Bt (E 1621); also Baron Strange de Knokin (E 1299), Baron Hungerford (E 1426), Baron de Moleyns (E 1445); s of 1 Viscount (s of Rev Sir James Philipps, 12 Bt, and Hon Mary, da of Rev the Hon Samuel Best and sis of 5th Baron Wynford) and Baroness Strange of Knokin, Hungerford and de Moleyns in her own right, she being da of late Maj the Hon Paulyn Francis Cuthbert Rawdon-Hastings (bro of 11 Earl of Loudoun); suc to Viscountcy 1938, to mother's Baronies 1974; *b* 19 Feb 1917; *Educ* Eton, Trin Cambridge; *m* 1, 1938 (m dis 1954), Doreen Guinness, *née* Jowett (d 1956); 1 s, 4 da; m 2, 1954 (m dis 1959), Elisabeth Joyce, *née* Woolf; m 3, 1959, Evelyn Marjorie, da of late Dr John Harris of Bray, Berks; *Heir* s, Hon Colwyn Philipps; *Career* sits as Independent in House of Lords; Lt RNVR; *Style*— The Rt Hon The Viscount St Davids; 15 St Mark's Crescent, Regent's Park, London NW1 (☎ 01 485 9953)

ST EDMUNDSBURY AND IPSWICH, Bishop of 1986-; Rt Rev John Dennis; patron of sixty-one livings, three Archdeaconries and twenty-four honorary Canonries; the See was founded 1914; s of Hubert Ronald Dennis, of 4 Park Road, Ipswich IP1 3ST, and Evelyn Neville-Polley (d 1982); *b* 19 June 1931; *Educ* Rutlish Sch Merton, St Catharine's Coll Camb (MA); *m* 28 Aug 1956, Dorothy Mary, da of Godfrey Parker Hinnels (d 1975); 2 s (John David b 1959, Peter Hugh b 1962); *Career* RAF 1950-51; curate: St Bartholomew's Armley Leeds 1956-60, Kettering 1960-62; vicar: the Isle of Dogs 1962-71, John Keble Mill Hill 1971-79; area dean W Barnet 1979-86, prebendary St Paul's Cathedral 1977-79, bishop suffragan Knaresborough 1979-86; diocesan dir of Ordinands Diocese of Ripon 1980-86, episcopal guardian of Anglican Focolarini 1981-, chaplain Third Order of Soc of St Francis 1989-; *Recreations* cycling, walking, gardening, wood carving, reading; *Clubs* Royal Overseas League; *Style*— The Rt Rev the Bishop of St Edmundsbury and Ipswich; Bishop's House, 4 Park Road, Ipswich IP1 3ST (☎ 0473 52829)

ST GEORGE, Charles Reginald; s of William Acheson St George, of Morecombe, Lancs, and Heather Atwood, *née* Brown (d 1978); *b* 20 April 1955; *Educ* Henley GS,

Univ of Exeter (BA), Queens Univ Kingston Ontario Canada (MA); *m* 19 July 1980 (m dis 1989); 1 s (Michael John b 31 Dec 1985), 1 da (Imogen Margaret b 15 Jan 1984); *Career* CBI: sec Smaller Firms Cncl 1979-82, (hd of secretariat 1982-83), account mangr Ian Greer Assocs Ltd 1983-87, md Profile Political Rels Ltd 1989 (dir 1987-88); prospective Lib parly candidate Guildford 1980-82, Lib Alliance borough cnclr Guildford 1983-87; *Recreations* golf, tennis and skiing; *Style*— Charles St George, Esq; 107 Biggin Hill, Upper Norwood, London SE19 3HX (☎ 01 764 3155); Profile Political Relations, Assets House, 17 Elverton St, London SW1P 3QG (☎ 01 828 2905, fax 01 834 1440, car 0836 727787)

ST GEORGE, George Bligh; s of Sir Theophilus St George, 6, Bt; hp of bro, Rev Sir Denis Howard St George, 8 Bt; *b* 23 Sept 1908; *Educ* Univ of Natal (BA); *m* 1935, Mary Somerville, da of Francis John Sutcliffe; 2 s, 3 da; *Career* served WW II Lt Technical Services Corps; *Style*— George St George Esq; 4 Eastwood, 30 Springfield Cres, Durban 4001, Natal, S Africa

ST GEORGE, Lady Henrietta Fortune Doreen; *née* FitzRoy; da of 11 Duke of Grafton, KG; *b* 1949; *m* 1979, Edward G P St George; 1 s (Henry Edward Hugh b 1983); 1 da (Katherine Helen Cecilia b 1984); *Style*— Lady Henrietta St George; 1 Chelsea Sq, London SW1; P O Box F 2666, Grand Bahama, Bahamas

ST GEORGE, Rev Sir (Denis) Howard; 8 Bt (I 1766) of Athlone, Co Westmeath; s of Sir Theophilus John St George, 6 Bt (d 1943), and Florence Emma, *née* Vanderplank; suc bro Sir Robert St George, 7 Bt, 1983; *b* 6 Sept 1902; *Educ* Rand Univ (BSc); *Heir* bro, George Bligh St George; *Career* is in Holy Orders of Roman Catholic Church; *Books* Failure and Vindication, the unedited journal of Bishop Allard, OMI (1981); *Style*— The Rev Sir Howard St George, Bt, OMI; Nazareth House, 82 South Ridge Road, Durban, Natal, S Africa

ST GERMANS, Bridget, Countess of; (Mary) Bridget; o child of Sir (Thomas) Shenton Whitelegge Thomas, GCMG, OBE (d 1962), and Lucy Marguerite, *née* Montgomery; *m* 1 (m dis), Lt-Col Jack Leslie Larry Lotinga, MC; m 2, 15 Nov 1965, as his 3 w, 9 Earl of St Germans (d 1988); *Style*— The Rt Hon Bridget, Countess of St Germans; Penmadown, St Clement, Truro, Cornwall TR1 1SZ

ST GERMANS, 10 Earl of (UK 1815); Peregrine Nicholas Eliot; also Baron Eliot (GB 1784); s of 9 Earl of St Germans (d 1988), by his 1 w Helen Mary (who d 1951, having m 2, 1947, Capt Ralph Benson, Coldstream Gds), da of Lt Charles Walters Villiers, CBE, DSO; *b* 2 Jan 1941; *Educ* Eton; *m* 9 Oct 1964, Hon Jacquetta Jean Fredricka Lampson, da of 1 Baron Killearn; 3 s (Lord Eliot, Hon Louis b 11 April 1968, Hon Francis b 16 Nov 1971); *Heir* s, Lord Eliot b 24 March 1966; *Career* landowner; patron of three livings; *Recreations* sitting still; *Clubs* Pratt's, The Cornish; *Style*— Lord Eliot; Port Eliot, St Germans, Cornwall (☎ (0503) 30211)

ST GERMANS, Bishop of 1985-; Rt Rev (John) Richard Allan Llewellin; s of John Clarence Llewellin, of Long Compton, Warwicks, and Margaret Gwenllian, *née* Low; *b* 30 Sept 1938; *Educ* Clifton Coll Bristol, Fitzwilliam Coll Cambridge (MA), Westcott House Theol Coll; *m* 24 July 1965, Jennifer Sally, da of Edward Terence House (d 1981), of Chard, Somerset; 1 s (David b 1966), 2 da (Sarah b 1958, Helen b 1970); *Career* slr 1960-61; curate Radlett 1964-68, asst priest Johannesburg Cathedral 1968-71, vicar Waltham Cross 1971-79, rector Harpenden 1979-85; *Recreations* sailing, DIY; *Style*— The Rt Rev the Bishop of St Germans; 32 Falmouth Rd, Truro, Cornwall TR1 2HX (☎ 0872 73190, fax 0872 77883)

ST HELENS, 2 Baron (UK 1964); Richard Francis Hughes-Young; s of 1 Baron, sometime Dep Govt Ch Whip (d 1980), and Elizabeth, da of late Capt Richard Blakiston-Houston (ggs of Sir Matthew Blakiston, 2 Bt); *b* 4 Nov 1945; *Educ* Nautical Coll Pangbourne; *m* 1983, Mrs Emma R Talbot-Smith; 1 s, 1 da (b 1987); *Heir* s, Hon Henry Thomas Hughes-Young, b 7 March 1986; *Style*— The Rt Hon The Lord St Helens; Marchfield House, Binfield, Berks

ST JOHN, Edmund Oliver; WS; s of late Col Edmund Farquhar St John, CMG, DSO, s of late Rev the Hon Edmund Tudor St John (s of 14 Baron St John of Bletso) and Henrietta, da of late Col James Dalmahoy, MVO, WS; hp of cous, 21 Baron; *b* 13 Oct 1927; *Educ* Trinity Coll Glenalmond; *m* 1959, Elizabeth Frances, da of Lt-Col H R Nicholl, *qv*; 1 s (Charles b 1963), 2 da (Nicola b 1960, Emma b 1968); *Career* dir Benn Bhuidhe Hldgs Ltd; *Clubs* New (Edinburgh); *Style*— Edmund O St John, Esq, WS; Spittal, Biggar, Lanarkshire; 11 Atholl Crescent, Edinburgh EH3 8HE (☎ (031) 229 8851)

ST JOHN, Hon Helen Evelyn; da (by 1 m) of late 18 Baron St John; *b* 1906; *Style*— The Hon Helen St John; c/o Balfour & Manson, Solicitors, 58 Frederick St, Edinburgh EH2 1LS

ST JOHN, Hon Henry Fitzroy; s (by 1 m) and h of 7 Viscount Bolingbroke and St John; *b* 18 May 1957; *Style*— The Hon Henry St John

ST JOHN, Cdr Michael Beauchamp; DSC (1943); s of Major Beauchamp (d 1965), of Aberdeenshire, and Madeleine Ethel, *née* Goodbody (d 1982); *b* 13 May 1915; *Educ* RNC Dartmouth; *m* 7 Oct 1944, Pamela Patience, da of Sir Arthur Guinness, KCMG (d 1951), of Hants; 1 s (Andrew b 1945), 2 da (Clare b 1947, Hermione b 1951); *Career* joined RNC Dartmouth 1939, appt to submarine serv 1936, served throughout 1939-46 war (N Sea, Med, SE Asia, Far East), ret 1955; dir own Private Exempt Co -1962, staff mangr Nat Employers Mutual Assoc 1963-74; *Recreations* shooting, walking, drinking in good company; *Style*— Cdr Michael St John, DSC; The Old Thatch, Heyshott, Midhurst, W Sussex GU29 0DJ (☎ 073 081 3329)

ST JOHN, (Oliver) Peter; s of Lt-Col Frederick Oliver St John, DSO, MC (d 1977) and gs of late Sir Frederick Robert St John, KCMG (yst s of late Hon Ferdinand St John, 2 s of 3 Viscount Bolingbroke and St John); through Sir Frederick's w, Isabella Fitz-Maurice (gda of 5 Earl of Orkney, Peter is hp to his 2 cous once removed, 8 Earl of Orkney; *b* 27 Feb 1938; *m* 1963, Mary Juliet, da of W G Scott-Brown; 1 s, 4 da; *Career* assoc prof Political Science Manitoba Univ; *Style*— Peter St John Esq; 200 Dromore Ave, Winnipeg, Manitoba, Canada

ST JOHN, Hon Mrs (Sally Hayter); *née* Rootes; da of 2 Baron Rootes; *b* 12 Sept 1947; *m* 1968, Andrew St John, s of Cdr Michael St John, DSC, RN (ret), of Midhurst (gn of 15 and 16 Barons St John of Bletso) by Pamela, da of Sir Arthur Guinness, KCMG; *Style*— The Hon Mrs St John; Culnacloich, Glenalmond, Perth

ST JOHN, Hon Mrs (Vanessa Marguerite); *née* Palmer; da of 3 Baron Palmer, OBE, *qv*; *b* 15 Dec 1954; *m* 1977, Robert William St John, s of Lt-Col Carl St John, of Globe Manor, Pook Lane, Havant, Hants; 1 s, 3 da; *Style*— The Hon Mrs St John; 20 Sudbrooke Rd, London SW12 8TG

ST JOHN OF BLETSO, 21 Baron (E 1559); Sir Anthony Tudor St John; 18 Bt (E 1660); s of 20 Baron, TD (d 1978), and Katharine Emily, *née* von Berg; *b* 16 May 1957; *Educ* Diocesan Coll Cape Town, Cape Town Univ SA (BA, BSc, BProc), London Univ (LLM); *Heir* cous, Edmund St John; *Career* sits as Independent Peer in Lords; lawyer; former marketing network advsr Shell (SA) Pty Ltd; oil analyst stockbroker with County Securities 1986-; *Recreations* tennis, golf, windsurfing, running; *Clubs* Western Province Sports, Royal Cape; *Style*— The Rt Hon The Lord St John of Bletso; 46 Reporton Rd, Fulham, London SW6 (☎ 021 213111)

ST JOHN OF BLETSO, Baroness; Katharine; da of late Alfred von Berg; *m* 1955, 20 Baron St John of Bletso (d 1978); *Style*— The Rt Hon The Lady St John of Bletso; c/o Syfret's Trust Co Ltd, 24 Wale st, PO Box 206, Cape Town 8001, S Africa

ST JOHN OF FAWSLEY, Baron (Life Peer UK 1987), of Preston Capes, Co Northants Norman Antony Francis St John-Stevas; PC (1979); s of late Stephen Stevas and Kitty St John O'Connor; *b* 18 May 1929; *Educ* Ratcliffe, Fitzwilliam Coll Cambridge, Christ Church Oxford; *Career* former pres Cambridge Union, barrister 1952, former jurisprudence tutor; political correspondent The Economist 1959; author; contested (C) Dagenham 1951, MP (C) Chelmsford 1964-87; Min State Educn and Science with special responsibility for the Arts 1973-74, oppn spokesman the Arts 1974 and memb Shadow Cabinet; Min Arts 1979, leader House of Commons and chllr of Duchy of Lancaster 1979-81; vice-pres Theatres Advsy Cncl 1983-; OStJ 1980, Order of Merit (Italy) 1965, KSLJ 1963, FRSL 1966; *Clubs* White's, Garrick, Pratt's; *Style*— The Rt Hon the Lord St John of Fawsley, PC; 2 Ennismore Gardens, London SW7; The Old Rectory, Preston Capes, Daventry, Northamptonshire; Covel Lodge, Chelmsford, Essex

ST JOHN PARKER, Michael; s of Rev Canon John William Parker, of Lincoln, and Doris Edna, *née* Nurse; *b* 21 July 1941; *Educ* Stamford Sch, King's Coll, Cambridge; *m* 5 Aug 1965, Annette Monica, da of Leonard Drake Ugle (d 1976) of West Wickham, Kent; 2 s (Sebastian b 1969, Dominic b 1972), 2 da (Arabella b 1966, Sophia b 1967); *Career* asst master: Sevenoaks Sch 1962-63, King's Sch Canterbury 1963-69, Winchester 1969-70; head history Winchester 1970-75, Headmaster Abingdon Sch 1975- (schoolmaster student ChCh Oxford Trinity Term 1984); memb cncl Hansard Soc, chm Midland Div HMC 1984, memt jt standing ctee Oxford and Cambridge Schs Examination Bd; govr: St Helen's Sch Abingdon 1975-83, Christ Church Cathedral Sch, Colcethorpe Sch, Joscas Prep Sch ; *Books* The British Revolution - Social and Economic History 1750-1970 (co author 1972), Politics and Industry - the Great Mismatch (contrib 1979), numerous articles, pamphlets and reviews; *Recreations* mostly to do with buildings, books, music and gardens; *Clubs* East India, Leander; *Style*— Michael St John Parker, Esq; Lacies Court, Abingdon, Oxfordshire (☎ 0235 20 163); Abingdon School, Oxfordshire OX14 1DE (☎ 0235 21 563)

ST JOHN-BROOKS, Julian Gordon deRenzy; Major; s of Ralph Terence St John-Brooks (d 1963), of Dublin, and Julia Margaret, *née* Gordon (d 1965); *b* 31 August 1919; *Educ* Cheam Sch, Harrow RMA Woolwich; *m* 5 Jan 1946, Diana, da of Maj Henry Wintersladen, TD (d 1959), of Marton-in-Cleveland; 1 s (Justin b 1960), 3 da (Caroline b 1947, Irena b 1949, Katharine b 1952); *Career* cmmnd RA 1939, WWII served M East and Italy 1941-45, WO 1945; Major 1952, psc, ptsc, Tech SO Min of Supply 1946-55, ret 1955; service mangr (guided weapons) Bristol Aeroplane Co 1955-60, poultry farmer 1960-65, restaurateur-chef 1965-; CEng, MRAeS; *Recreations* gardening, reading; *Clubs* Gloucestershire CC,; *Style*— Maj Julian St John-Brooks; The Manor House, Gaunts Earthcott, Almondsbury, Bristol BS12 4JR (☎ 0454 772225)

ST JOHNSTON, Andrew; s of Dr Adrian St Johnston (d 1955), and Eleanor Margaret, *née* Andrewes (d 1953); *b* 28 August 1922; *Educ* Charterhouse, Imperial Coll (BSc); *m* 1, 1949 (m dis), Barbara, *née* Hemelryk; 2 da (Caroline b 1953, Harriet b 1955); m 2, 1958, Aldrina Nia (Dina), da of Clifford Vaughan (d 1985); *Career* WWII 1943-47 Lt Cdr RN served as radar offr; electronic engr Midgley Harmer Ltd 1947-49, computing div Elliott-Automation 1949-68 (project ldr for NRDC on 401 computer, the first plug-in unit machine), dir (formerly ptnr) Vaughan Systems & Programming Ltd 1968-; *Recreations* walking, countryside, food and drink, cooking; *Style*— Andrew St Johnston, Esq; Hedgegrove Farm, Pembridge Lane, Broxbourne, Herts EN10 7QR (☎ (0992) 463054); Vaughan Systems & Programming Ltd, The Maltings, Hoe Lane, Ware, Herts SG12 9LR (☎ (0992) 2282, telex 81516, fax (0992) 60902)

ST JOHNSTON, Colin David; s of James Hallewell St Johnston, MC, TD, MA (d 1963), and Sheilagh Cassandra, *née* Davidson (d 1973); *b* 6 Sept 1934; *Educ* Shrewsbury, Lincoln Coll Oxford; *m* 1958, Valerie, da of John Thomas Gerald Paget (d 1969); 3 s, 1 da; *Career* Nat Service North Staffs Regt 1953-55; md Ocean Cory Ltd 1976-, dir Ocean Transport and Trading plc 1974-, non-exec dir FMC plc 1981-83; cncl memb: Royal Cwlth Soc for the Blind 1966-, Industrial Soc 1981-; *Recreations* squash; *Clubs* MCC; *Style*— Colin St Johnston Esq; 30 Fitzroy Rd, London NW1 8TY (☎ 01 722 5932); 46/47 Russell Sq, London WC1B 4JP

ST JOHNSTON, Kerry; s of George Eric St Johnston (d 1978), and Viola Rhona, *née* Moriarty; *b* 30 July 1931; *Educ* Eton, Worcester Coll Oxford (MA Jurisprudence); *m* 1, 25 Feb 1960, Judith Ann, da of Peter Nicholls (d 1972); 2 s (James b 1963, Rory Tilson b 1966), 1 da (Claire Marie b 1961); m 2, 1980, Charlotte Ann, da of John Scott Limnell Lyon (d 1942); *Career* mil serv XI Hussars (Lt) 1950-51; with Ocean Steamship Co 1955-76 (md 1963-68), fndr dir overseas Containers 1965-70 (dep chm 1973-76), pres Private Investment Co for Asia, Singapore 1977-81; chm P & O Containers Ltd (formerly Overseas Containers Ltd) 1982-; dir: Royal Ins 1972-76, Lloyds Bank Int 1983-86, P & O Steam Navigation Co 1986-, Touche Remnant Investment Tst 1982-; *Recreations* fishing, racing, gardening; *Clubs* Boodles; *Style*— Kerry St Johnston, Esq; 5/53 Drayton Gardens, London SW10; Beagle House, Braham St, London E1

ST LEGER, Hon David Hugh; s of 9 Viscount doneraile (d 1983), and Melva, Viscountess Doneraile, *qv*; *b* 1950; *Style*— The Hon David St Leger

ST LEGER, Hon Edward Hayes; s of 9 Viscount doneraile (d 1983) and Melva, Viscountess Doneraile, *qv*; *b* 1960; *Style*— The Hon Edward St Leger

ST LEGER, Hon Elizabeth Adele; da of 9 Viscount Doneraile (d 1983), and Melva, Viscountess Doneraile, *qv*; *b* 12 Jan 1953; *Style*— The Hon Elizabeth St Leger

ST LEVAN, Dowager Baroness; Hon Clementina Gwendolen Catharine; *née* Nicolson; da of 1 Baron Carnock (d 1928), and Catharine, *née* Hamilton (d 1951); sis of Sir Harold Nicolson (d 1968), the author; *b* 3 July 1896; *m* 6 Oct 1916, 3 Baron St Levan (d 1978); 3 s, 2 da; *Career* wrote two books, edited one; *Style*— The Rt Hon the Dowager Lady St Levan; Avallon, Green Lane, Marazion, Cornwall (☎ 0736 710 508)

ST LEVAN, 4 Baron (UK 1887); Sir John Francis Arthur St Aubyn; 5 Bt (UK 1866), DSC (1942), DL (Cornwall 1977); s of 3 Baron (d 1978), and Hon Clementina Gwendolen Catharine, *née* Nicolson, da of 1 Baron Carnock and sis of Harold Nicolson, the author; *b* 23 Feb 1919; *Educ* Eton, Trin Cambridge; *m* 1970, Susan, da of late Maj-Gen Sir John Noble Kennedy, GCMG, KCVO, KBE, CB, MC; *Heir* bro, Hon Piers St Aubyn, MC; *Career* slr 1948, Lt RNVR, high sheriff of Cornwall 1974, fell of Royal Soc for Encouragement of Art; pres London Cornish Assoc; pres CPRE (Cornwall); pres Friends of Plymouth Museum; *Clubs* Brooks's, Royal Yacht Squadron; *Style—* The Rt Hon The Lord St Levan, DSC, DL; St Michael's Mount, Marazion, Cornwall

ST MAUR, Edward Adolphus Ferdinand; s of Capt Frederick Percy St Maur (d 1975), and Hope Wilhelmina Albemarle, *née* Blakeney (d 1974); gggs of 12 Duke of Somerset and gs of the Earl St Maur, he is a cousin of present Dukes of Somerset and Portland; *b* 26 May 1924; *Educ* Malvern, Sandhurst; *m* 10 March 1950, Sheila Matilda, da of Gen A V Hammond DSO (d 1980), of Ireland; 3 da (Caroline, Elizabeth, Philippa); *Career* Maj 1941-59; past pres of Br Inst of Prof Photography; now professional photographer; FBIPP, ARPS, MBKS, FRSA; *Recreations* travel, swimming, photography; *Clubs* Cavalry and Guards; *Style—* Edward St Maur, Esq; Flat 2, William IV Wing, Itton Court, Itton, Chepstow, Gwent (☎ 02912 79680); Town Gate House, Moor St, Chepstow, Gwent (☎ 0291 625329)

ST OSWALD, 5 Baron (UK 1885); Derek Edward Anthony Winn; s of 3 Baron St Oswald (d 1956) and Eve Carew Green (d 1976); suc bro, 4 Baron, MC (d 1984); *b* 9 July 1919; *Educ* Stowe; *m* 1954, (Charlotte) Denise Eileen, da of Wilfrid Haig Loyd (d 1971), of Oakhill, Seaview, Isle of Wight; 1 s, 1 da; *Heir* s, Hon Charles Rowland Andrew Winn, *qv*; *Career* formerly Lt King's Royal Rifle Corps (Supp Reserve), Capt Parachute Regt (Regular Army Reserve) 1939-46; ADC to govr-gen of NZ 1943-45; substantive Capt Western Desert and N Africa (wounded); asst supt Malayan Police Force 1948-51; pres: S and W Yorks Br Legion, S and W Playing Fields Assoc, Wakefield Hospice Appeal Fund; *Books* I Served Caesar (1972); *Recreations* shooting, walking, horse racing; *Clubs* Lansdowne, Special Forces; *Style—* The Rt Hon Lord St Oswald, DL; Nostell Priory, Wakefield, West Yorkshire; The Old Rectory, Bainton, Driffield, East Yorkshire YO25 9NG

ST PIERRE, Roger; s of Alexander Richard St Pierre, MBE, and Caroline Amelia Borrett (d 1985); *b* 8 Nov 1941; *Educ* Goodmayes Junior Sch, Ilford County HS; *m* 10 Nov 1974, Lesley, da of Bernard Constantine, of Sheffield; 1 s (Richard b 1976), 2 da (Danielle b 1978, Nicole b 1979); *Career* author and journalist; editor: Disco International 1977-79, Voyager Magazine; contrib: Toyota Today, Motorway Express, London Evening Standard, The Dorchester Magazine, Travel GBI, Renaissance, The Times, Financial Weekly; PR mangr for: Diana Ross, Glen Campbell, Jerry Lee Lewis, Don Williams, Frankie Lane; author of nearly 1,000 record/album sleeve notes; broadcaster BBC and other broadcasting stations; cycle racer in many countries, mangr of international cycle teams specialist writer: travel, music, motoring, cycling and leisure; *Books* incl: Books of the Bicycle (1973), The Rock Handbook (1986), Illustrated History of Black Music (1986), Marilyn Monroe (1987); *Recreations* cycling, music, travel; *Style—* Roger St Pierre, Esq; 24 Beauval Rd, Dulwich, London SE22 8UQ (☎ 01 6936463, 01 299 0719)

ST VINCENT, 7 Viscount (UK 1801); Ronald George James Jervis; s of 6 Viscount (d 1940, himself ggs of 2 Viscount, who was in his turn n of 1 Viscount and Earl of St Vincent, whose title commemorated his victory over the Soaniards in 1797 despite being outnumbered 27 to 15 - the name title was chosen by George III himself; St Vincent, more modestly, had suggested Yarmouth and Orford, which did not call to mind his successful action) and Marion, *née* Broun; *b* 3 May 1905; *Educ* Sherborne; *m* 2 Oct 1945, Constance Phillida Anne, da of Lt-Col Robert Hector Logan, OBE, late Loyal Regt; 2 s, 1 da; *Heir* s, Hon Edward Jervis; *Career* served WW II, acting Lt-Cdr RNVR; *Style—* The Rt Hon the Viscount St Vincent; Les Charrieres, St Ouen, Jersey, CI

SAINTY, Sir John Christopher; KCB; s of Christopher Lawrence Sainty (d 1977), of Hassocks, Sussex, and Nancy Lee, *née* Miller (d 1945); *b* 31 Dec 1934; *Educ* Winchester, New Coll Oxford (MA); *m* 1965, (Elizabeth) Frances, da of Gp Capt Derek James Sherlock, OBE (d 1977); 3 s; *Career* clerk House of Lords 1959, private sec to ldr of House and chief whip 1963, clerk of journals 1965, research asst Inst of Historical Res 1970, reading clerk House of Lords 1974, clerk of the Parliaments 1983-; *Style—* Sir John Sainty, KCB; 22 Kelso Place, London W8 5QG; House of Lords, London SW1

SAKZEWSKI, Sir Albert; s of O T Sakzewski; *b* 12 Nov 1905; *Educ* Ipswich HS Qld; *m* 1935, Winifred May (d 1972), da of W P Reade; 2 s (Bryan Paul b 25 Feb1939, Richard Anthony b 24 Feb 1941); *Career* CA, chm and govt nominee Totalisator Admin Bd Qld 1962-81, fndr Sir Albert Sakzewski Fndn, chm of dirs: Avanis Pty Ltd, Blend Investmts Pty Ltd, Commercial Fin Pty Ltd, Queensland Securities Pty Ltd, Southern Cross Products Pty Ltd; tstee Tattersall's Club Brisbane, memb: Roy Cwlth Soc, Aust/Br Soc, Aust Ballet Fndn, Queensland Art Gallery Fndn (fndr benefactor), fndr Sir Albert Sakzewski Fndn; FCA, FASA; kt 1973; *Recreations* horse racing and breeding, golf, billiards (Aust Amateur Billards Champion 1932 with a then Aust record break of 206, Qld Amateur Billiards Champion 6 times), snooker (Qld Amateur Snooker Champion 8 times); *Clubs* Brisbane, Tattersall's (Brisbane), Queensland Turf, Tattersall's Racing (life memb), Brisbane Amateur Turf (life memb), Rockhampton Jockey (life memb), Golf Coast Turf, Roy Qld Golf, Southport Golf (life memb); *Style—* Sir Albert Sakzewski; Ilya Lodge, Rossiter Parade, Hamilton, Qld 4007, Australia; National Bank House, 255 Adelaide Street, Brisbane 4000

SALAMAN, Hon Mrs (Nancy Adelaide); da of late 1 Viscount Samuel, GCB, OM, GBE, PC; *b* 1906; *Educ* Oxford Univ; *m* 1935, Arthur Gabriel Salaman, MB, BCh, MRCS, LRCP; 2 s, 2 da; *Style—* The Hon Mrs Salaman; 1 Belmont Hill, Newport, Saffron Walden, Essex

SALAMAN, (Frederick) Nicholas Paul; s of Sebastian Max Alexander Clement Salaman (d 1976), and Joan Elisabeth; *b* 4 Feb 1936; *Educ* Radley, Trinity Coll Oxford (MA); *m* 1, 1960 (m dis 1974), Elisabeth Cecila, da of Francis Sclater, of Bunces Farm, Newick, nr Uckfield, Sussex; 2 da (Sophia, Charlotte); m 2, 1983, Lyndsay Margaret, da of James Meiklejohn, of Wise Lane, Mill Hill; 2 da (Rose Clementine b 1983, Phoebe Joy b 1987); *Career* writer; advtg and mktg; dir London Herb & Spice Co Ltd 1978-; *Books* The Frights, Dangerous Pursuits, Falling Apart, Mad Dog (play), Forces of Nature;; *Recreations* harpsichords, tennis and unearthing old High Table recipes; *Clubs* Beefsteak, Chelsea Arts'; *Style—* Nicholas Salaman Esq; c/o Chelsea Arts Club, 143 Old Church St, London SW3

SALAMON, Julie Anne (Mrs Harrington); s of Jan Salamon, of Rickmansworth, Herts, and Jean Ada, *née* Dibbo; *b* 1 May 1960; *Educ* Rickmansworth GS, Casio Coll Watford; *m* 10 Aug 1985, Michael James Wiliam Harrington, s of Harold Harrington, of Residing, Otterbourne, Hants; *Career* sales exec: Daily Express 1980-82, Over 21 magazine 1982-84; dep advtg mangr Punch 1984-87, advertisement mangr World of Interiors 1987, publisher London Portrait magazine 1988-; *Style—* Miss Julie Salamon; Reed Publishing, London Portrait Magazine, 7-11 St Johns Hill, London SW11 1TE (☎ 01 924 3408)

SALE, Hon Mrs; Hon Ismay Hilda Margaret; *née* FitzRoy; da of 4 Baron Southampton (d 1958), and Lady Hilda Mary Dundas (d 1957), da of 1 Marquess of Zetland; *b* 3 Dec 1908; *m* 8 Feb 1928, Brig Walter Morley Sale, CVO, OBE, late Royal Horse Guards (d 1976), 3 s of Charles Vincent Sale, of Aston Rowant House, Oxon; 1 s, 1 da; *Style—* The Hon Mrs Sale; 15 St Paul's Mews, Ramsey, IOM (☎ 0624 815408)

SALE, Robert John; s of Lt Col John Walker Sale, OBE (d 1974), of Ilderton Glebe, Wooperton, Nr Alnwick, Northumberland, and Nancy Jaqueline Sale; *b* 24 Feb 1930; *Educ* RNC Dartmouth; *m* 14 Jan 1956, Susan, da of Richard Clement Parker (d 1955), of Redlands, Nr Cambridge; 1 s (John Richard (Dick) b 1963), 1 da (Lynda Katherine b 1957); *Career* HMS Britannia 1943-47, Midshipman HMS Forth Med Fleet 1947-49, Sub Lt HMS Crispin Home Fleet 1949-50, Lt HMS Consort (serv Far E Fleet and Korean War) 1950-53, HMS Diligence 1953-54, Flag Lt to Adm of the Fleet Sir George Creasy C-in-C Portsmouth 1972-77; Barclays Bank UK Ltd 1955-86, local dir 1962, gen mangr 1977, sr gen mangr 1985; dir: Halifax Building Soc, Ropner plc, Tees Towing Co Ltd, Whitehead Ltd, Newcastle Technol Centre; govr: Aysgarth Sch, Brathay Hall Tst; investmt advsr Dean and Chapter Durham Cathedral, chm NE Bd Prince's Youth Business Tst; FCIB; *Recreations* fishing, shooting, hill walking,, squash, tennis, gardening; *Clubs* Royal Ocean Racing; *Style—* Robert Sale, Esq; Eryholme Grange, Nr Darlington, Co Durham (☎ 060 981 401)

SALEM, Daniel Laurent Manuel; s of Raphael Salem (d 1963), and Adriana Gentili di Giuseppe (d 1976); *b* 29 Jan 1925; *Educ* Harvard (BA, MA); *m* 1950, Marie-Pierre, da of Rene Arachtingi (d 1975); *Career* chm: Condé Nast Int Inc 1970-, Condé Nast Pubns Ltd 1967-, Philharmonia Tst Ltd 1985-; dep chm Condé Nast Pubns Inc 1987-, dir of various other cos; Chevalier de la Legion d'Honneur April 1987; *Recreations* music, chess, bridge, backgammon, golf; *Clubs* White's, Portland, Harvard (NYC); *Style—* Daniel Salem, Esq; 3 Ennismore Gdns, London SW7 (☎ 01 584 0466); Condé Nast Publications Ltd; Vogue House, Hanover Sq, London W1 (☎ 01 499 9080)

SALES, Barry Edward; s of Lawrence Edward Sales, of Upwey, Dorset, and Doris May, *née* Heaton (d 1978); *b* 23 Oct 1933; *Educ* Sherborne and Corpus Christi Coll (MA); *m* 14 June 1958, Lois Marshall, da of Dr Roderick Marshall, (d 1975), of New York; 2 da (Catherine b 1962, Elizabeth b 1967); *Career* Lt King's African Rifles (Africa Serv Medal 1954); dir: Murco Petroleum Ltd 1964-, Utd Refineries Ltd 1985-; *Recreations* piano, squash, antiquarian books; *Style—* Barry E Sales, Esq; The Croft, Chalfont Lane, Chorleywood, Herts WD3 5PP; Winston House, Dollis Park, London N3 1HZ (☎ 01 349 9191)

SALES, Harry Brimelow; MBE (1973); s of Harry Thomas Sales (d 1939), of Northenden, Manchester, and Mary, *née* Brimelow (d 1940); *b* 13 Sept 1918; *Educ* Stockport GS, Univ of Manchester (LLM); *m* 2 s (John Roger b 26 Sept 1944, Robert Anthony b 10 Oct 1949), 2 da (Janet Margaret (twin) b 26 Sept 1944, Rosemary Anne b 7 Oct 1947); *Career* slr 1940-74; prosecuting slr Manchester 1942-44; town clerk: Tottenham (acting dep) 1944-47, Guildford (dep) 1947-52, Aldershot 1952-74; called to the Bar Inner Temple 1975; memb Admin Law Ctee of Justice; chm Free Painters and Sculptors; *Books* Halsbury's Laws of England (ed Housing vol and Public Health vol), Encyclopaedia of Rating and Local Taxation (ed); *Recreations* walking, climbing; *Clubs* Alpine, Climbers, Swiss Alpine; *Style—* Harry Sales, Esq; Little Yarrowfield, Guildford Rd, Mayford, Woking, Surrey (☎ 04862 70611); 2 Mitre Court Buildings, Temple, London EC4 (☎ 01 583 1380, fax 01 353 7772, telex 28916)

SALES, Hon Mrs Isobel Caroline; *née* Irby; da of 7 Baron Boston (d 1958); *b* 1917; *m* 1, 1946 (m dis 1950), Maj Vernon Owain Roberts; m 2, 1950, Edward Horatio Sales; 2 da (Christian b 1950, Alexandra b 1952); *Style—* The Hon Mrs Sales; 53 Stanhope Gdns, London SW7

SALIS; *see*: de Salis

SALISBURY, 76 Bishop of 1982-; Rt Rev John Austin Baker; patron of 63 livings, and 45 shared, the Precentorship, Chancellorship, Treasurership and Succentorship of his Cathedral and other Canonries and Archdeaconries of Dorset, Sarum, Wilts and Sherborne. The Bishopric was founded at Sherborne 705, Wells and Exeter were separated from it 905; in 1075 it was removed to Old Sarum, and in 1220 to Salisbury; s of George Austin Baker and Grace Edna; *b* 11 Jan 1928; *Educ* Marlborough, Oriel Coll Oxford; *m* 1974, Gillian Leach; *Career* ordained priest 1955, official fellow, chaplain and lectr in Divinity Corpus Christi Coll Oxford 1959-73, also lectr in theology Brasenose Coll Oxford and Lincoln Coll Oxford 1959-73, canon Westminster 1973-82, sub-dean and lector Theologiae 1978-82, rector St Margaret's Westminster and speaker's chaplain 1978-82; memb C of E Doctrine Cmmn 1967-87; *Books* The Foolishness of God (1970), Travels in Oudamoria (1976), The Whole Family of God (1981); *Clubs* Utd Oxford and Cambridge; *Style—* The Rt Rev the Lord Bishop of Salisbury; South Canonry, The Close, Salisbury, Wilts SP1 2ER (☎ 0722 334031)

SALISBURY, Mark Pryce; s of Andrew Salisbury, of Llandudno, and Iris Helen Salisbury, *née* Roberts; *b* 15 Oct 1955; *Educ* Sir Hugh Owen GS Caernarfon, Liverpool Univ (LLB); *m* 12 Dec 1981, Christine Anne, da of Thomas Gordon Morris, of Gwynedd; 1 s (Adam b 1986); *Career* slr; snr ptnr Gamlin Kelly & Beattie Slrs, Llandudno; *Recreations* golf, tennis, sailing; *Clubs* North Wales Golf; *Style—* Mark P Salisbury, Esq; Annedd Wen, 56 Deganwy road, Deganwy, Gwynedd (☎ 0492 84440); 14 Trinity Square, Llandudno, Gwynedd (☎ 0492 79733, fax 0492 75296)

SALISBURY, 6 Marquess of (GB 1789); Robert Edward Peter Gascoyne-Cecil; DL (Dorset 1974); also Baron Cecil (E 1603), Viscount Cranborne (E 1604), Earl of Salisbury (E 1605); patron of seven livings; s of 5 Marquess of Salisbury, KG, PC, FRS (d 1972); sometime acting foreign sec), and Elizabeth Vere (d 1982), da of Rt Hon Richard Cavendish, CB, CMG, PC, bro of 9 Duke of Devonshire; *b* 24 Oct 1916; *Educ* Eton; *m* 18 Dec 1945, Marjorie Olein, da of Capt the Hon Valentine Maurice

Wyndham-Quin, RN (d 1983, s of 5 Earl of Dunraven and Mount-Earl); 4 s (and 1 s decd), 1 da; *Heir* s, Viscount Cranborne, *qv*; *Career* Capt Gren Gds; takes Cons whip in the House of Lords; memb editorial bd The Salisbury Review 1982-; pres Royal Assoc British Dairy Farmers; MP (C) W Bournemouth 1950-54; pres Monday Club 1974-81; high steward of Hertford 1972-; *Style*— The Most Hon the Marquess of Salisbury, DL; Hatfield House, Hatfield, Herts

SALISBURY-JONES, Raymond Arthur; s of Maj Gen Sir Guy Salisbury-Jones GCVO, CMG, CBE, MC, DL of Hambledon, Marshal of Dip Corps, Ct of St James 1957-61; and Lady Hilda Violet Helena Cnec de Bunsen da of Sir Mourice de Bunsen HBM Ambass to Madrid 1906-1913, and Vienna 1913-14; *b* 31 July 1933; *Educ* Eton, Christ Church Oxford (MA); *Career* 2 Lt Coldstream Guards, serv Canal Zone 1951-53; export mktg mangr Rolls Royce Motors Ltd 1956-75; dir: RR Motors Int Ltd 1968-74, Daniel Thwaites plc, RSJ Aviation Int Ltd, Liveryman of City Co of Grocers; *Recreations* rowing, music, skiing; *Clubs* English Speaking Union, Pratt's; *Style*— R Salisbury-Jones, Esq; 4 Clifton Gardens, London W9 1DT (☎ 01 289 5169); Suite 635, 162-168 Regent Street, London W1R 5TB (☎ 01 434 1345)

SALISSE, John; CBE (1986); s of Joseph Salisse (d 1966), of Bournemouth, and Ann, *née* Hull (d 1976); *b* 24 Mar 1926; *Educ* Portsmouth GS; *m* 7 July 1949, Margaret, da of James Horsfield (d 1950); 1 da (Caroline b 1960); *Career* Marks & Spencer plc 1944-85 (dir 1968-85); chm: CBI Distributive Trades Survey 1983-86, St Enoch Mgmnt Centre Ltd 1986-, Jt London Tourism Forum 1986-, London Enterprise Agency 1983-88, Retcul Consortium 1988-; dir: London Tourist Bd 1984-, Project Fullempty 1984-86, vice-pres commerce and distribution ctee CECD 1986; memb: Cncl for Charitable Support 1984-, CBI ctee on commerce and distribution 1988 (cncl memb 1984-), jt tres Euro Movement 1982-86, tstee London Educn Business Ptnrship 1987-; hon sec The Magic Circle 1965-86 (hon vice-pres 1975-; fin ctee RCP 1986-; *Recreations* golf, theatre, history of magic; *Clubs* The Magic Circle, Highgate Golf, The Magic Castle (Los Angeles), IOD; *Style*— John Salisse, Esq, CBE; c/o Midland Bank, 90 Baker St, London W1M 2AX

SALLITT, Timothy William Baines; s of Brig William Baines Sallitt, OBE (d 1979), and Mary Elaine, *née* Whincup; *b* 21 Mar 1934; *Educ* Rugby, Bradford Poly, Borough Poly, Georgia Tech Atlanta USA; *m* 14 June 1958, Angela Mary, da of Dr Brian Laidlaw Goodlet, OBE (d 1961); 1 s (Henry b 1962), 2 da (Amelia b 1960, Lucinda b 1965); *Career* Nat Serv 2 Lt RE Cyprus 1955-57; BP 1957-59; divnl mangr: Brush Electrical Engrg 1959-66, Plessey Co 1966-70; sub-co md Hawker Siddeley Gp 1970-77; gp dir Hawker Siddeley Gp 1977-; memb cncl Electrical Res Assoc; former pres BEAMA; dep chm Export Guarantees Advsy Cncl; FIIM; *Recreations* sailing, gardening, Egyptology; *Clubs* Boodle's; *Style*— Timothy Sallitt, Esq; The Manor House, Harringworth, nr Corby, Northants (☎ 057 287 234); Hawker Siddeley Group plc, 32 Duke Street, St James's, London SW1Y 6DG (☎ 01 930 6177 and 0509 612898, fax 0509 611789)

SALMON, The Rev Anthony James Heygate; s of Sir Eric Cecil Heygate Salmon, MC, DL (d 1946), of 115 Old Church St, London SW3, and (Hilda) Marion, *née* Welch; *b* 20 August 1930; *Educ* Wellington, Corpus Christi Coll Oxford (MA, Dip Theol); *m* 18 Aug 1973, Anthea, da of Thomas Robert Calthorpe Blofeld, CBE, FSA, JP (d 1986), of Hoveton House, Wrotham, Norfolk (d 1986); *Career* curate St Mark's, S Norwood, Croydon 1956-59; Usuthu Mission, Swaziland 1959-61; rector Gingindholovu, Zululand 1961-69; chaplain Coll of the Agcension, Sellyoak 1969-74; rector St John The Baptist, Harrietsham 1974-85; vicar St Lawrence, Chobham, with St Saviour's, Valley End 1985-; *Recreations* walking, gardening; *Style*— The Rev Anthony Salmon; The Vicarage, Bagshot Rd, Chobham, Surrey GU24 8BY (☎ 09905 8187)

SALMON, Baron (Life Peer UK 1972); Cyril Barnet Salmon; PC (1964), JP (Kent 1949); s of late Montagu Salmon; *b* 28 Dec 1903; *Educ* Mill Hill, Pembroke Coll Cambridge; *m* 1, 1929, Rencie (d 1942), da of late Sidney Gorton Vanderfelt, OBE; 1 s (hon David *qv*), 1 da; m 2, 1946, Jean, Lady Morris, da of late Lt-Col David Edward Maitland-Makgill-Crichton (descent from of Lauderdale) and former w of 2 Baron Morris; *Career* barr 1925, QC 1945, judge High Ct of Justice, Queen's Bench Div 1957-64, a lord justice of appeal 1964-72, a lord of appeal in Ordinary 1972-80, kt 1957; hon fell Pembroke Coll Cambridge, hon DCL Kent 1978, hon LLD Cambridge 1982; *Recreations* fishing, golf; *Clubs* Brooks's (tstee), Athenaeum; *Style*— The Rt Hon The Lord Salmon, PC, JP; Manwood House, Sandwich, Kent (☎ 2244)

SALMON, Hon David Neville Cyril; s (by 1 m) of Baron Salmon (Life Peer) *qv*; *b* 1935; *m* 1, 1958 (m dis 1972), Heather Turner-Laing; m 2, 1973, Sarah Harrison; *Style*— The Hon David Salmon; Holne Cottage, Holne, nr Ashburton, Devon

SALMON, Baroness - Jean Beatrice; da of late Lt-Col David Edward Maitland-Makgill-Crichton *see* Peerage Earl of Lauderdale Colls; *b* 1912; *m* 1, 1933 (m dis 1946, he d 1975), 2 Baron Morris; 2 twin s (3 Baron Morris *qv*, hon Edward b 1937), 2 da (hon Mrs Hildyard, JP, b 1934, hon Mrs Farrell b 1936) m 2, 1946, Baron Salmon (Life Peer); *Style*— The Rt Hon the Lady Salmon; Manwood House, Sandwich, Kent

SALMON, Neil Lawson; s of Julius Salmon (d 1940), and Emma Constance, *née* Gluckstein (d 1979); *b* 17 Feb 1921; *Educ* Malvern, Institut Minerva Zürich Switzerland; *m* 18 March 1944, Yvonne Hélène, da of Arthur Danziger Isaacs; 1 s (Roger Bruce b 1946), 1 da (Zoë Hélène b 1948); *Career* dep chm J Lyons & Co Ltd 1972-81 (gen mangr 1946, dir 1965, md 1967); dir Allied Breweries Ltd (now Allied-Lyons plc) 1978-81; memb: Restrictive Practices Ct 1971-, Monopolies and Mergers Cmmn 1980-; memb cncl BIM 1974-88; chm Professional Standards Ctee 1982-88; CBIM 1970; *Recreations* opera, ballet, theatre, wine, food; *Clubs* Savile; *Style*— Neil Salmon, Esq; Eldon House, 1 Dorset Street, London W1H 3FB (☎ 01 581 4501)

SALMON, Col William Alexander; OBE (1956); s of Lt-Col William Harry Broome Salmon, Indian Army (d 1962), and Lillian Mabel (d 1963); *b* 16 Nov 1910; *Educ* Haileybury, RMC Sandhurst; *m* 1939, Jean Barbara (d 1982), da of late Rt Rev John Macmillan, OBE, DD (Bp of Guildford 1935-49); 1 s, 2 da; *Career* cmmnd 2 Lt HLI 1930, ADC to govr of Sind 1936-38; serv WWII: France 1939, Middle E, Italy, Greece, Bde Maj 1942, GSO2 HQ Aegean Force 1943, CO 2 Beds and Herts Regt 1945-46, CO 2 Royal Irish Fus 1946-47, GSO1 (Trg) HQ Scottish Cmd 1947-49, COS to Lt Gen Glubb Pasha HQ Arab Legion 1950-53, CO 1 Bn HLI 1953-55, Col General Staff (O & T Div) SHAPE 1957-59, AQMG (QAE2) W O 1959-62, AAG (AG14) W O 1962-63, ret 1963; asst ecclesiastical sec to lord chllr and PM 1965-77; *Books* Churches and Royal Patronage (1983); *Recreations* shooting, fishing, writing; *Clubs* Army & Navy; *Style*— Col W A Salmon, OBE; Apartment 1, Great Maytham Hall, Rolvenden, Kent TN17 4NE (☎ 0580 241239)

SALMOND, Alexander Elliot Anderson; MP (SNP) Banff and Buchan 1987; s of Robert Fyfe Findlay Salmond, of 101 Preston Rd, Linlithcow, Scotland, and Mary Stewart Milen (*née* Salmond); *b* 31 Dec 1954; *Educ* Linlithcow Acad, St Andrews Univ (MA); *m* 6 May 1981, Moira French McGlashan; *Career* assis economist Govt Econ Serv 1978-80; economist Royal Bank of Scotland 1980-87; vice-chm Scottish Nat Pty 1985-; *Publications* numerous articles and conference papers on oil and gas economics; *Recreations* reading, golf; *Style*— Alexander E A Salmond; House of Commons, London (☎ 01 219 4578)

SALT, Sir Anthony Houlton; 6 Bt (UK 1869) of Saltaire, Yorks; s of Cdr Sir John William Titus Salt, 4 Bt, RN (d 1952), and Stella Houlton, *née* Jackson (d 1974); suc bro, Sir David Salt, 5 Bt, 1978; *b* 15 Sept 1931; *Educ* Stowe; *m* 1957, Prudence Mary Dorothea Francis, da of late Francis Meath-Baker; 4 da (Fenell b 1959, Rebecca b 1961, Lucinda b 1964, Charlotte b 1967); *Heir* bro, Patrick Salt *qv*; *Career* memb Stock Exchange 1957; ptnr Hill Chaplin & Co (Stockbrokers) 1957-68, dir Williams de Broe Hill Chaplin & Co 1968-81 (chm 1981-84, associate 1984-); *Clubs* City of London, Oriental, City Univ; *Style*— Sir Anthony Salt, Bt; Dellow House, Ugley Green, Bishop's Stortford, Herts CM22 6HN (☎ 0279 813141); Williams de Broe Hill Chaplin & Co, 25 Grosvenor St, London W1X 9FE (☎ 01 629 2515; telex 887084 Willdebroe)

SALT, Anthony William David; s of late Lt-Col Sir Thomas Henry Salt, 3 Bt, JP, DL, and hp of bro, Sir Michael Salt, 4 Bt *qv*; *b* 5 Feb 1950; *Educ* Milton Abbey; *m* 1978, Olivia Anne, da of Martin Morgan Hudson; 1 s (Edward James Stevenson Salt, b 11 June 1981); *Career* bank official; *Recreations* veteran/vintage cars; *Clubs* Vintage Car of GB; *Style*— Anthony Salt Esq; 1 Titchwell Rd, SW18 (☎ 01 874 8888)

SALT, Julia Ann; da of Kenneth Gordon Richardson, and Nora *née* MacLachlan; *b* 4 May 1955; *Educ* St Mary's Senior HS Hull, St Hilda's Coll Oxford (BA); *m* 29 March 1980, David Sidney, s of John Frederick Salt (d 1987); 1 s (Frederick b 17 July 1985), 1 da (Freya b 12 Aug 1983); *Career* ptnr Allen & Overy 1985-; memb; City of London Slrs Co 1985, The Law Soc 1977; *Recreations* sailing, birdwatching, opera, languages; *Clubs* Royal York YC, Utd Oxford and Cambridge; *Style*— Mrs Julia A Salt; 32 Cromwell Tower, Barbican, London, EC2 (☎ 01 248 9898, fax 01 236 2192, telex 8812801)

SALT, Sir (Thomas) Michael John; 4 Bt (UK 1899) of Standon, and of Weeping Cross, Co Stafford; s of Lt-Col Sir Thomas Henry Salt, 3 Bt (d 1965); *b* 7 Nov 1946; *Educ* Eton; *m* 1971, Caroline, da of Henry Hildyard; 1 da (Henrietta Sophia b 1978); *Heir* bro, Anthony Salt *qv*; *Style*— Sir Michael Salt, Bt; Shillingstone House, Shillingstone, Dorset

SALT, Patrick Macdonnell; yr s of Cdr Sir John William Titus Salt, 4 Bt (d 1953); *b* 25 Sept 1932, heir bro 6 Bt *qv*; *Educ* Stowe; *m* 1976, Ann Elizabeth Mary, *née* Maclachlan; *Career* marine underwriter Lloyd's, dir: Grayston Rust & Salt Ltd, Cassidy David Members Agency Ltd; *Recreations* fishing, gardening; *Clubs* City Univ; *Style*— Patrick Salt, Esq; Hillwatering Farm House, Langham, Bury St Edmunds, Suffolk, IP31 3ED (☎ Walsham le Willows 367); St Helen's, 1 Undershaft, London EC3A 8JR (☎ 01 623 1026)

SALT, (Douglas) Roy; OBE (1969); s of Capt James Salt MN (d 1969), of 65 West St, Polruan, Fowey, Cornwall, and Daisy Melita, *née* Rundle (d 1987); *b* 18 April 1918; *Educ* Fowey GS; *m* 1 June 1940, Edna May, da of John William Davies (d 1946), of Harrow Weald; 1 da (Heather Valerie (Mrs Milton)); *Career* serv WWII RE 1940, RAOC 1941, REME 1942-46; apprenticeship (later printing mangr) HMSO 1933-40 and 1946-51, asst gen mangr (later gen mangr) Gaskiya Corpn Zaria Nigeria 1951-60, McCorquodale Printers 1960-77; md: Caxton Press Co Ltd Ibadan Nigeria 1960-74; Benhams Colchester 1974-77; memb Western region C of C Nigeria, sec to Zaria Race Club Zaria Nigeria; fell Inst of Industl Mangrs; *Recreations* sailing, golf, swimming; *Style*— Roy Salt, Esq, OBE; 1 The Ridings, Leavenheath, Colchester, Essex (☎ 0787 210 684); Salts Cottage, 65 West St, Polruan, Fowey, Cornwall

SALTER, Rev (Arthur Thomas) John; TD (1988); er s of Arthur Salter (d 1982), of The Tong-Norton Farm, Tong, nr Shifnal, Shropshire, and Dora May, *née* Wright (d 1985); the Salter family has been seated in Shropshire since the reign of King John, when John de le Sel is mentioned in the records of Shrewsbury Abbey 1211 (*see* Burke's Landed Gentry, 18 edn, vol III, 1972); *b* 22 Nov 1934; *Educ* Wellington GS, King's Coll London (AKC 1960), St Boniface's Theological Coll Warminster; *Career* serv Intelligence Corps 1954-55, RAMC 1955-56; ordained deacon 1961, priest 1962; asst priest: St Peter's, Mount Park, Ealing 1961- 65, St Stephen with St Thomas the Apostle, Shepherd's Bush 1965-66, St Alban the Martyr, Holborn with St Peter, Saffron Hill 1966-70; Vicar of St Silas with All Saints, Pentonville 1970-; priest-in-charge of St Clement, Barnsbury and St Michael the Archangel, Islington 1970-79; priest-in-charge of St Dunstan-in-the-West with St Thomas of Canterbury within the Liberty of the Rolls 1979-; gen sec The Anglican and Eastern Churches Assoc 1975-; chaplain Law Courts Branch of Edward Bear Fndn for Muscular Dystrophy; chm Wynford Estate's Old Peoples Club; Royal Army Chaplains Dept 1975-, CF IV (Capt) 1975-81, CF III (Maj); chaplain: 36 Signal Regt 1975-80, 257 (S) Gen Hosp RAMC (V) Duke of York's HQ 1980-; memb Societas Sanctae Crucis (SSC); Hon Kt Order of St Michael of the Wing (Royal House of Braganza, Portugal) 1984, Companion of Honour Order of Orthodox Hospitallers (Cyprus) 1985, Hon Archimandrite's Cross of Byelo-Russian Autocephalic Orthodox Church-in-Exile 1979, Archpriest's Cross of Ethiopian Catholic Uniate Church (Eparchy of Asmara, Eritrea) 1980, Archpriest's Cross Exarchate of Pope Shenouda III (Coptic Orthodox Patriarchate of Alexandria) 1981; *Recreations* travelling in Eastern Europe, genealogy, reading; *Clubs* Army and Navy, City Livery, Polish Hearth; *Style*— The Rev John Salter, TD; St Silas and James Vicarage, 87 Richmond Avenue, Islington, London N1 OLX (☎ 01 607 2865); St Dunstan-in-the-West Vestry, 184A Fleet Street, London EC4 (☎ 01 405 1929)

SALTER, Michael Anthony John; s of James Joseph Salter (d 1960), and Grace Elizabeth Salter (d 1978); *b* 21 May 1943; *Educ* Malvern; *m* 17 Aug 1968, Mary Elizabeth, da of Denis Oswald Feeny (d 1973); 1 s (Mark b 1969), 2 da (Helen b 1971, Jennifer b 1974); *Career* fin dir: Coral Racing Ltd 1980-85, Bass Wales and West Ltd 1985-, Welsh Brewers Ltd; FCA; *Recreations* classical music, opera, tennis; *Clubs* Rugby (London); *Style*— Michael Salter, Esq; 6 The Paddock, Cherry Orchard Rd, Lisvane, Cariff CF4 5UE (☎ 759519); Bass Wales and West Ltd, Mazes y Coed Rd, Cardiff CF4 4UW (☎ 61531)

SALTER, Richard Stanley; s of Stanley James Salter (d 1980), and Betty Maud, *née*

Topsom (d 1974); *b* 2 Oct 1951; *Educ* Harrow Co Sch, Balliol Coll Oxford (MA); *Career* called to Bar Inner Temple 1975, in practice 1975-; arbitration sec and membership sec London Common Law and Commercial Bar Assoc 1986-; ACI Arb 1983; *Recreations* books, music, theatre; *Clubs* Savile; *Style*— Richard Salter, Esq; 14 Addison Cres, London W14 8JR; 3 Gray's Inn Place, Gray's Inn, London WC1R 5EA (☎ 01 831 8441, fax 01 831 8479, telex 295 119 LEXCOL G)

SALTHOUSE, Dr Edward Charles; s of Edward Salthouse, MBE (d 1965), of Belfast, and Winifred Charles, *née* Boyd (d 1977); *b* 27 Dec 1935; *Educ* Campbell Coll Belfast, Queen's Univ Belfast (BSc, PhD); *m* 1961, Denise Kathleen Margot, da of Dr Joseph Reid (d 1963), of Ballymena, N Ireland; 2 s (Michael, Kevin); *Career* lectr Univ of Bristol 1962-67, Durham Univ: reader in electrical engrg sci 1962-79, master Univ Coll 1979-, dean faculty of sci 1982-85, pro-vice chllr 1985-88; FIEE 1980, FRSA (1986); *Recreations* photography, industl history; *Clubs* Royal Overseas League; *Style*— Dr Edward Salthouse; The Masters House, The Castle, Durham DH1 3RL; Shieldaig, Hume, Kelso TD5 7TR

SALTOUN, Lady (twentieth holder of title; S 1445); Flora Marjory; *née* Fraser; Chief of the Name of Fraser; family granted right to own Univ of Fraserburgh by King James VI; da of 19 Lord Saltoun, MC (d 1979), and Dorothy, da of Sir Charles Welby, 5 Bt, CB, by Maria, sis of 4 Marquess of Bristol; *b* 18 Oct 1930; *Educ* St Mary's Wantage; *m* 1956, Capt Alexander Ramsay of Mar, *qv*, *see* Peerage, Royal Family section; 3 da; *Heir* da, Hon Mrs Nicolson; *Career* sits as Independent in House of Lords; *Clubs* Turf; *Style*— The Rt Hon the Lady Saltoun; Cairnbulg Castle, Fraserburgh, Aberdeenshire AB4 5TN (☎ 0346 23149)

SALUSBURY-TRELAWNY, Sir John Barry; 13 Bt (E 1628), of Trelawny, Cornwall; s of Sir John William Robin Maurice Salusbury-Trelawny, 12 Bt (d 1956), by his 1 w, Glenys Mary, da of John Cameron Kynoch; *b* 4 Sept 1934; *Educ* HMS Worcester; *m* 1958, Carol Knox, yr da of C F K Watson, of The Field, Saltwood, Kent; 1 s, 3 da; *Heir* s, John Salusbury-Trelawny *qv*; *Career* Nat Serv RNVR; dir: Martin Walter Gp Ltd 1971-74, Korn/Ferry Int 1977-83, Goddard Kay Rogers & Associates 1984- (mgmnt conslts); JP Kent 1973-78; FInstM; *Clubs* Army & Navy, Buck's; *Style*— Sir John Salusbury-Trelawny, Bt; Beavers Hill, Saltwood, Hythe, Kent (☎ 0303 66476); 32 St James's Sq, London SW1 (☎ 01 930 5100)

SALUSBURY-TRELAWNY, John William Richard; s and h of Sir John Salusbury-Trelawny, 13 Bt *qv*; *b* 30 Mar 1960; *m* 16 Aug 1980, Anita, yr da of Kenneth Snelgrove and Mrs L E Thorpe, of Iver Heath, Bucks; 1 s (Harry John b 10 Dec 1982), 1 da (Victoria Hayley b 1981); *Style*— John Salusbury-Trelawny Esq; 45 St Leonard's Rd, Hythe, Kent (☎ 0303 65571)

SALUSBURY-TRELAWNY, Lt-Col Philip Michael; MC (1945), DL (Cornwall 1982); 2 s of Maj John Salusbury-Trelawny, MC (d 1954, himself ggs of Sir William Salusbury-Trelawny, 8 Bt), of Cotleigh House, Honiton, Devon, and Louisa Frederika, *née* Mainwaring (d 1985); *b* 11 Nov 1921; *Educ* Winchester; *m* 23 March 1946, Jean Mary (sometime Flight Offr WAAF, d 1988), only da of Col Herbert Cecil Fraser, DSO, OBE, TD (d 1940), of Redlands, Ilkley, Yorks; 1 s (Simon Jonathan b 1948, m 1978 Marian MacAuley), 1 da (Diana Jane b 1947, m 1970 Robert Blake); *Career* cmmnd Indian Army 1941, Frontier Force Rifles 1941-47, Maj, N Africa and Italy (MC) 1942-45, Duke of Cornwall's LI 1947-75, Lt-Col 1964, Regtl Sec Light Inf in Cornwall 1979-84; *Recreations* shooting, gardening; *Clubs* Army and Navy; *Style*— Lt-Col Philip Salusbury-Trelawny, MC, DL; Colgare House, Lanhydrock, Bodmin, Cornwall (☎ 0208 73887)

SALVESEN, Alastair Eric Hotson; s of Lieut Col Iver Ronald Stuart Salvesen (d 1957), and Marion Hamilton, *née* McClure; Fndr of family business, Christian Salvesen emigrated from Norway to Edinburgh 1836; bro Robin Salvesen *qv*; *b* 28 July 1941; *Educ* Fetters, Cranfield (MBA); *m* 18 July 1979, Elizabeth Evelyn, da of Patrick Murray (Cdr RNVR), of Hawick, Roxburghshire; *Career* chm and man dir Dawnfresh Seafoods Ltd 1981-; chm Starfish Ltd 1986-; dir Windsor Creameries Manufacturing Ltd 1985-; memb The Queen's Bodyguard for Scotland (The Royal Company of Archers); CA; MinstM; *Recreations* shooting, archery, farming and forestry; *Clubs* New (Edinburgh); *Style*— Alastair E H Salvesen, Esq; Rake Barn, Southwaite, Cockermouth, Cumbria (☎ 0900 824031); Westwater, Langholm, Dumfriesshire (☎ 0541 80462); Dawnfresh Seafoods Ltd, North Shore, Whitehaven, Cumbria CA28 7XQ (☎ 0946 61141, telex 64283, fax 0946 65027)

SALVESEN, Robin Somervell; s of Iver Ronald Stuart Salvesen, and Marion Hamilton, *née* McClure; bro Alastair Salvesen *qv*; *b* 4 May 1935; *Educ* Cargilfield Sch Edinburgh, Fettes Coll Edinburgh, Univ Coll Oxford (Engrg), Hendon Technical Coll; *m* 6 Aug 1960, Sari Frances Judith *née* Clarke; 3 s (Francis b 26 Oct 1965, Thomas b 16 June 1967, Iver b 31 Jan 1969); 4 da (Ferelith b 3 May 1961, Alice b 25 Dec 1962, Tabitha b 13 Feb 1964, Emily b 22 June 1970); *Career* 5 bat QO Nigeria Reg 1955-56, Royal Scots TA 52 Lowland Volounteers 1957-69; dir: Christian Salvesen (mangrs) 1968-, Christian Salvesen Ltd 1969-; memb: East Lothian CC 1965-68, Forth Ports Authy 1970-73; Gen Cncl of Br Shipping 1974-79, 1984-, chm Offshore Section 1976-79; dir Salvesen Offshore Hldgs 1974-; chm: Br Steamship Short Trader Assoc, N of England Protecting & Indemnity Assoc, Short Sea Bulk Section, gen cncl of Br Shipping, Leith Nautical Coll, Forth Pilotage Auth, Christian Salvesen (marine) Ltd, Scot Cncl King George's Fund for Sailors, Lights Advsy Ctee, Br Shipowners Assoc; dir: Christian Salvesen plc, Salvesen Offshire Hldgs Ltd, Marine Shipping Mutual Insurance, Furness & Salvesen (Agencies) Ltd, John Cook & Son Ltd, Br Shipowners Assoc, Headland Shipping Ltd, The Murrayfield plc, Gen Cncl of Br Shipping, Br Shipping Fedn; memb ctee of mgmnt Scottish Veterans Residences, Gen Ctee, Lloyds Register of Shipping; Hon Danish Consul for E Scotland 1972-; Silver Jubilee Medal 1977; Royal Order of the Knights of Dannebrog (Denmark) 1981; *Recreations* shooting with long bow and shotgun; *Clubs* New (Edinburgh); *Style*— Robin S Salvesen, Esq; 50 East Fettes Ave, Edinburgh EH4 1EQ (☎ 031 552 7101, fax 031 552 5809)

SALWEY, John David deGray; s of David Ernest Lifford Salwey (d 1957), of Brown St, Salisbury, Wilts, and Mary Kathleen, *née* Hughes (d 1978); *b* 10 Mar 1932; *Educ* Catherdral Sch Salisbury, Bryanston Sch Blandford; *m* 5 Jan 1957, Ann Margaret, da of Arnold Sprackling, of Manor Farm, Woolbeding, Midhurst, W Sussex; *Career* farms mangr Bighton Manor Estate 1960-72, estate mangr Letchworth Garden City Farms 1972-87, farm mangr course dir Shuttleworth Coll 1987; *Recreations* shooting, skiing, gliding, travel; *Clubs* Farmers; *Style*— John Salwey, Esq; Lakeside Cottage, Old Warden Park, Biggleswade, Beds (☎ 076 727 737); Shuttleworth Coll, Old Warden Park, Biggleswade, Beds (☎ 076 727 441)

SALZ, Anthony Michael Vaughan; s of Michael H Salz, of Yelverton, Devon, and Veronica, *née* Hall; *b* 30 June 1950; *Educ* Summerfields Sch, Radley Coll, Exeter Univ (LLB); *m* 17 May 1975, Sally Ruth, da of Harold J Hagger, of Broughton, Hants; 1 s (Christopher b 1978), 2 da (Emily b 1980, Rachel b 1982); *Career* slr, ptnr Freshfields 1980- (seconded to Davis Polk and Wardwell, NY 1977-78); memb: Law Soc; contrib to various learned jls; *Recreations* fly fishing, tennis, golf and the family generally; *Style*— Anthony Salz, Esq; 25 Newgate St, London EC1A 7LH (☎ 01 606 6677)

SALZ, Michael; s of Michael Salz (d 1950), of London, and Tania, *née* Wagner (d 1955); *b* 1 May 1916; *Educ* Cambridge (MA); *m* 24 July 1948, Veronica Edith Dorothea Elizabeth, da of the late (Frank) Francis Vaughan Hall; 1 s (Anthony Michael Vaughan b 1950), 1 da (Joanna Mary Vaughan (Mrs Leadbetter) b 1952); *Career* conslt orthopaedic surgn Cambridge and Middx Hosp; sec Br Rheumatoid Arthritis Surgical Soc, past pres Plymouth Med Soc; LRCP 1940, FRCS 1948, FRSM, fell Br Orthopaedic Assoc; *Recreations* flyfishing, skiing; *Style*— Michael Salz, Esq; Nuffield Hosp Plymouth (☎ 0752 790707), 144 Harley St, London W1 (☎ 01 935 0023, 0822 853633, 01 262 3860, 0841 520536)

SAMENGO-TURNER, Fabian Pius; s of late Joseph Frederick Samengo-Turner and Eva Turner; *b* 11 Feb 1931; *Educ* St Benedicts Sch, King's Coll London; *m* 1953, Maureen Ursula, *née* O'Connor; 3 s, 1 da; *Career* Lt Intelligence Corps, md Laurentide Fin Tst 1962-67, Citibank Fin Tst 1968-72, chm Citibank Fin Tst 1973-74, exec dir Citicorp Investmt Bank Ltd 1975-; *Recreations* squash, tennis, motor racing, sailing; *Clubs* RAC, Overseas Bankers; *Style*— Fabian Samengo-Turner, Esq; Chapel Row Farm, Bucklebury, Reading, Berks RG7 6PB (☎ 0734 712 109); Citicorp Investment Bank Ltd, 335 Strand, London WC2R 1LS (☎ 01 438 1283, telex 299831)

SAMMONS, Geoffrey Tait; s of Herbert Sammons, CBE (d 1967), and Elsie, *née* Kay (d 1951); *b* 3 July 1924; *Educ* Glenalmond, Univ Coll Oxford (MA); *m* 9 July 1949, Stephanie Anne, da of Stephen Hawley Clark (d 1961); 1 s (Timothy b 1956), 1 da (Anthea b 1952); *Career* RA 1943-45, Lt 8 Medium Regt RA Burma Campaign 1944-45; Allen and Overy Slrs London: joined 1946, ptnr 1953-86, sr ptnr 1981-86; cmmnr Bldg Socs Cmmn 1986-, non-exec dir Spirax Sarco Engrg plc; govr The Lister Inst of Preventative Med 1987-; memb Law Soc 1949; *Recreations* golf, gardening; *Clubs* Army & Navy; *Style*— Geoffrey Sammons, Esq

SAMPLES, Reginald McCartney (Mac); CMG (1970), OBE (1962), DSO (1942); s of William, of N Wales, and Jessie Samples, *née* McCartney (d 1980); *b* 11 August 1918; *Educ* Rhyl County Sch, Liverpool Univ (B Com); *m* 1947, Elsie Roberts Hide, 2 s (Graeme, William), 1 step da (Murcia); *Career* served WWII 1940-46 with RNAS (Fleet Air Arm), Lt (A) RNVR; Central Office of Information 1946-48, Cwlth Relations Office 1948-78 (ret), dir Br Info Servs in India, Pakistan and Canada, asst under-sec of state Cwlth Office London 1968, sr trade cmmr and Brit consul-gen Toronto 1969; asst dir Royal Ontario Museum 1978-83; dir: National Ballet of Canada 1970-, Canadian Aldeburgh Foundation 1973-, Canadian/Scottish Philharmonic Fndn 1980-; *Recreations* tennis, watching ballet; *Clubs* Naval (London), RCS (London), York (Toronto), Queens (Toronto); *Style*— Reginald McCartney Samples, CMG, OBE, DSO; Jackes Ave, Apt 1105 Toronto, Canada, M4T 1E5 (☎ 416 962 1208)

SAMPSON, JP (1975) Ian Godfrey; s of Maj Geoffrey Morgan Sampson (d 1978) of Peterborough Cambs and Dorothy Louise, *née* Dufty; *b* 29 May 1941; *Educ* Taunton Sch; *m* 11 July 1964, Wendy Celia Anne, da of Neil Cecil Alister Simon (d 1985), of Poole Dorset; 2 da (Jacqueline b 1970, Philippa b 1972); *Career* HAC TA 1963 (ret 2 Lt); gen mangr Target Unit Tst Gp 1975-80, md NM Schroder Unit Tst Gp 1980-, dir NM Shroder Life Assur Co Ltd 1987-; vice chm Painshill Park Tst Ltd; borough cncllr 1974-76; *Recreations* restoration of Painshill Park, travel; *Clubs* HAC, RAC, United (Guernsey); *Style*— Ian Sampson, Esq, JP; 10 Crossway, Walton on Thames, Surrey KT12 3JA (☎ 0932 221 363); 14 James Street, London WC2E 8BT (☎ 01 836 8731, fax 01 240 7884, telex 296299)

SAMPSON, Maj Richard Claude; s of Evelyn Sampson, eld s of Canon Gerald Sampson; *b* 5 May 1916; *Educ* St Hugh's Prep Sch, privately, Exeter Coll Oxford; *m* 1947, Rosemary Anne, da of W B Collingridge, of Billing Manor and Mauritius; 1 s, 1 da (Mary, m Dan Shorland Ball); *Career* cmmnd 2 Lt 1937 Wilts Regt (Duke of Edinburgh's) later Royal Regt, served in WW II mostly with KAR (E Africa, Ethiopia, Madagascar and Europe), Br Military Mission to Ethiopia 1946-47, local Lt-Col (advsr to late Emperor Hailé Selassie on offr trg), personal staff offr and ADC to govr (also C-in-C) Nyasaland, rep Kenya on E Africa Security Conf, served as acting supt of Colonial Police and instr at Police Training Sch during Mau-Mau campaign in E Africa, ret 1969; formerly appeals dir with Richard Maurice Ltd, charities' conslt; former: pres Royal Br Legion N Norfolk, chm N Norfolk Army Benevolent Fund, vice-pres Norfolk Red Cross, memb appeal ctee Sue Ryder Fndn; *Recreations* shooting, gardening, history and labradors; *Clubs* Naval & Military, Norfolk; *Style*— Maj Richard Sampson; c/o National Westminster Bank, London St, Norwich

SAMSON, Greta Edith May; da of Charles Dudley Franks (d 1958), of Totnes, Devon, and Lilian Florence, *née* May (d 1974); *b* 3 July 1926; *m* 13 Sept 1952, John Louis Rumney Samson (d 1988), s of Air-Cdre Charles Rumney Samson, CMG, DSO, AFC (d 1931), of Cholderton, Wilts; 2 da (Sally b 1954, Frances b 1955); *Career* dir Samson Books Ltd; *Recreations* gardening, walking, food, reading; *Style*— Mrs Greta Samson; Down Hse, Redlynch, Salisbury, Wilts SP5 2JP (☎ 0725 203 47)

SAMUEL, Andrew William Dougall; s of Capt Andrew Samuel RN (d 1952), and Letitia Shearer Samuel; *b* 12 July 1937; *Educ* Hutchesons' Boys GS, Glasgow; Glasgow Sch of Architecture; *m* 1, 20 Feb 1962 (div 1981), Sybille Marie Luise; 1 s (Craig Andrew Alexander Porter Samuel b 1966), 1 da (Katja b 1969); m 2, 2 Oct 1981, Mary Carswell, da of John Bisset CA (d 1978), of Homeglen, Carmunock, Glasgow; *Career* CA; principal/dir Andrew Samuel & Co Ltd 1968; dir: Gavin Watson Ltd 1983, Townhead Properties Ltd 1980, Clouston Securities Ltd 1985; holder: World Canoeing Record Loch Ness 1975-85 (Guinness Book of Records), World Canoeing K2 (Doubles Record English Channel 1980-86 (Guinness Book of Records), World Canoeing Record for English Channel 1976 (Guinness Book of Records); Scottish Nat Canoeing Racing Coach 1976-83; chm former E Central Tourist Assoc (Scotland); former chm Central Scotland Tourist Assoc; Festival dir Trossachs Water Festival 1973-76; sec Trossachs Tourist Assoc 1969-76 with Lord Home of The Hirsel as pres; upon retiral made hon vice pres; FRIAS, RIBA, FIPD, FFB; *Recreations* boating, travel, canoeing, photography; *Clubs* Trossachs Canoe and Boat, Bowfield Country; *Style*— Andrew Samuel, Esq; Woodside Farm, By Beith, Ayrshire, Scotland KA15 1JF

SAMUEL, Hon Anthony Gerald; s of 2 Viscount Bearsted, MC (d 1948), and

Dorothea Montefiore, *née* Micholls (d 1949); *b* 18 Feb 1917; *Educ* Eton, New Coll Oxford; *m* 1, 1946 (m dis 1961), Mary Eve, da of late John Comyn Higgins, CIE, of Alford, Lincs; 2 da (Jacqueline Eve (Mrs Robert Rusk) b 1948, Daphne Lavinia (Mrs Leo Petro) b 1951); m 2, 1962 (m dis 1966), Jenifer, da of Maj Kenneth Alfred Bridge Puckle, RM (ret), of Farnham; m 3, 1966, (Jean) Mercy, da of M C Haystead; *Career* Lt and Acting Capt Intelligence Corps WWII; *Clubs* White's; *Style—* The Hon Anthony Samuel; Arndilly House, Craigellachie, Banffshire; 29 St Leonard's Terrace, London SW1 (☎ 01 730 9089)

SAMUEL, Anthony John Fulton; s and h of Sir Jon Samuel, 5 Bt; *b* 13 Oct 1972; *Style—* Anthony Samuel Esq; c/o PO Box F 904, Freeport, Grand Bahama, Bahamas

SAMUEL, Hon Dan Judah; s of late 2 Viscount Samuel; hp of bro, 3 Viscount; *b* 25 Mar 1925; *Educ* Rugby, Balliol Coll Oxford, Sch of Advanced Int Studies (Johns Hopkins) Washington DC; *m* 1, 1957 (m dis 1977), Esther (Nonni), da of late Max Gordon of Johannesburg; 1 s (Jonathan b 1965), 2 da (Lia b 1961, Maia b 1963); m 2, 1981, Heather, da of Angus Cumming, of Haywards Heath; 1 s (Angus b 1983), 1 da (Sasha b 1982); *Career* late Maj Yorks Hussars; dir Shell Petroleum Co 1973-81; gp personnel co-ordinator Shell Chemical Co London 1976-77, regional co-ordinator W Hemisphere 1977-; pres Scallop Corpn (NY) 1981-; UK tstee Asian Inst of Technol Bangkok; memb Cncl of the Americas (NY); *Recreations* sailing (yacht 'Limajo'); *Clubs* Hurlingham, Chichester Yacht, Westhampton Yacht Sqdn (Long Island); *Style—* The Hon Dan Samuel; 812 Park Ave, New York; The Barns, Old Mill Farm, Mill Hamlet, Sidlesham, Sussex (☎ 024 356 513)

SAMUEL, 3 Viscount (UK 1937), of Mount Carmel, and Toxteth in the City of Liverpool; David Herbert Samuel; s of 2 Viscount, CMG (d 1978, gs of Edwin Samuel, whose yr bro Montagu cr Lord Swaythling), and Hadassah, Viscountess Samuel, *née* Goor-Grasovsky, *qv*; *b* 8 July 1922; *Educ* High Sch Jerusalem, Balliol Coll Oxford (MA), Hebrew Univ (PhD); *m* 1, 1950 (m dis 1957), Esther Berelowitz; 1 da (hon Judith b 1951); m 2, 1960 (m dis 1978), Rinna Dafni, *née* Grossman; 1 da (hon Naomi b 1962); m 3, 1980, Veronika Grimm, da of Ernest Engelhardt, of 555 Sheppard Ave West, Downsview, Ontario Canada; *Heir* bro, Hon Dan Samuel; *Career* Capt RA, served India, Burma, Sumatra 1942-45 (despatches); Sherman prof of physical chemistry Weizmann Inst Israel 1949-, head Center for Neurosciences and Behavioral Research 1979-, post-doctoral fell Chemistry Dept Univ Coll London 1956; research fell: Chemistry Dept Harvard Univ Cambridge Mass 1957-58, Lab of Chemical Biodynamics (Lawrence Radition Lab) Univ of Calif Berkeley USA 1965-66; chm Bd of Studies on Chemistry at Feinberg Grad Sch 1968-74, head Chemistry Group Science Teaching Dept 1967-84, visiting prof Sch of Molecular Sciences Warwick Univ 1967; memb: bd Bat-Sheva de Rothschild Fndn for Advancement of Science in Israel 1970-84, bd US-Israel Educnl (Fulbright) Fndn 1969-74 (chm 1974-75), bd Israel Center for Scientific and Technol Info 1970-74, Scientific Advsy Ctee, bd of Tstees Israel Center to Psychobiology 1973-; dean Faculty of Chemistry Weizmann Inst of Science 1971-73; titular memb Ctee for Chemical Educn of Int Union of Pure and Applied Chemistry (IUPAC) 1982- (nat rep 1973-82); Visiting Prof MRC Neuroimmunology Unit Zoology Dept UCL 1974-75, memb Acad Advsy Ctee Everyman's (Open) Univ 1976-84; memb: Israel Chem Soc (cncl 1976-84), Int Brain Res Orgn (IBRO), bd Shenkar Coll for Textile Technol and Fashion (hon fell), Israel Exec Ctee American-Israel Cultural Fndn, bd of govrs Tel Aviv Museum, Alzheimer Disease and Associated Disorders, Journal of Labelled Compounds and Radiopharmaceuticals; *Recreations* etching; *Style—* The Rt Hon the Viscount Samuel; Isotope Dept, Weizmann Institute of Science, Rehovot, Israel (☎ 8483117); 11 Meonot Shine, Neve Weizmann, Rehovot, Israel (☎ 8482892)

SAMUEL, Sir John (Jon) Michael Glen; 5 Bt (UK 1898), of Nevern Square, St Mary Abbots, Kensington; s of Sir John Oliver Cecil Samuel, 4 Bt (d 1962), and Charlotte Mary Desmond; *b* 25 Jan 1944; *Educ* Radley, London Univ (BSc); *m* 1, 24 Sept 1966, Antoinette Sandra, da of late Capt Anthony Hewitt, RE; 2 s (Anthony, Rupert); m 2, March 1982, Mrs Elizabeth Ann Molinari, yst da of Maj R G Curry, of Bournemouth; *Heir* s, Anthony Samuel; *Career* chm: Electric Auto Corporation (Detroit USA) 1978-82, Silver Volt Corpn (Freeport Bahamas 1980-82, Whisper Electric Car A/S (Denmark) 1985-, Synergy Research Ltd (UK) 1983-; *Recreations* motor racing; *Style—* Sir Jon Samuel, Bt; The Old Bakehouse, Loxwood, W Sussex RH14 0SW

SAMUEL, Hon Judith; da (by 1 m) of 3 Viscount Samuel; *b* 29 Jan 1951; *Educ* Technion-Israel Inst of Technol, Barch (Architectural Assoc London); *Career* Israel Defence Forces 1969-70; *Style—* The Hon Judith Samuel; 11 Lessin St, Tel Aviv, Israel; 5 Lipsky Street, Tel Aviv, Israel

SAMUEL, Hon Michael John; yr s of 4 Viscount Bearsted, MC, TD, *qv*; *b* 2 Nov 1952; *Educ* Eton; *m* 1980, Julia Aline, yst da of James Edward Alexander Rundell Guinness, *qv*; 3 da (Natasha Vivienne b 1981, Emily Elizabeth b 1983, Sophie Alexandra b 1986); *Recreations* shooting, fishing, riding, golf; *Clubs* White's; *Style—* The Hon Michael Samuel; 24 Hyde Park Gate, London SW7

SAMUEL, Hon Naomi Rachel; da (by 2 m) of 3 Viscount Samuel; *b* 27 May 1962; *Educ* Hebrew Univ, Jerusalem Sch of Law; *Career* Israel Defence Forces 1 Lt 1980-83; *Style—* The Hon Naomi Samuel; 47 Ha'rav Berlin, Jerusalem 92505, Israel

SAMUEL, Hon Nicholas Alan; er s and h of 4 Viscount Bearsted, MC, TD, *qv*; *b* 22 Jan 1950; *Educ* Eton, New Coll Oxford; *m* 1975, Caroline Jane, da of Dr David Sacks; 1 s (Harry Richard b 23 May 1988), 4 da (Eugenie Sharon b 1977, Natalie Naomi b 1979, Zöe Elizabeth b 1982, Juliet Samantha b 1986)); *Style—* The Hon Nicholas Samuel; 9 Acacia Road, London NW8

SAMUEL, Hon Philip Ellis Herbert; s of late 1 Viscount Samuel, GCB, OM, GBE, PC, and Beatrice Miriam (d 1959), yst da of Ellis Abraham Franklin; *b* 23 Dec 1900; *Educ* Westminster, Trinity Coll Cambridge; *Career* Hong Kong Vol Defence Corps (prisoner) 1939-45; *Clubs* Royal Institution, Royal Overseas League, Victory Services; *Style—* The Hon Philip Samuel; c/o Royal Institution, Albemarle St, London W1X 4BS

SAMUELS, Hon Mrs (Ann); eld da of Baron Bruce of Donington (Life Peer); *b* 1942; *m* T Samuels; *Style—* The Hon Mrs Samuels

SAMUELS, John Edward Anthony; QC (1981); s of Albert Edward Samuels (d 1982), of The Chantry Relgate Surrey; *b* 15 August 1940; *Educ* Charterhouse, Queens' Coll Cambridge (MA); *m* 1967, Maxine, da of Lt Col F D Robertson, MC, of Oakville, Ontario, Canada; 2 s (David b 1970, Adam b 1973); *Career* barrister, recorder Crown Court 1985; chm jt Regulations Ctee of the Inns' Cncl and the Bar Cncl 1987-; *Clubs* Athenaeum; *Style—* John Samuels, Esq, QC; Spring House, Sheen Road, Richmond, Surrey TW9 1AJ; 22 Old Buildings, Lincoln's Inn, London WC2A 3UJ (☎ 01 831 0222, telex 883500 CICERO G)

SAMUELS, Dr John Richard; s of Richard Arthur Samuels, of Istead-Rise, Kent, and Iris Molene Phylis, *née* Jenkins; *b* 13 Sept 1952; *Educ* Gravesend Tech HS, Univ Coll Cardiff (BA), Univ of Nottingham (PhD); *m* 1, 7 Sept 1979 (m dis 1985), (Frances) Naomi Field, da of Dr Gerard Field, of Dundas, Ontario, Canada; 1 da (Jenny b 1984); m 2, 10 Sept 1986, Harriet Annabel, da of Stephen Leslie Richard of Newark, Nottinghamshire; 1 s (William b 1986); *Career* archaeologist, writer, lectr and publisher; archaeological field offr Humberside Archaeological Ctee 1975-76, res asst dept of archaeology unit Liverpool Univ 1980-81, tutor organiser for Notts in local history & archaeology Workers' Educnl Assoc 1981-, fndr The Cromwell Pres 1986-, ed East Midlands Archaeology (BA Gp 14 Jl); memb: N Lincs Archaeological Unit Ctee 1976-81, Tst for Lincs Archaeology 1982- (exec ctee 1984-87) Trent & Peak Archaeological Tst 1984-, Cncl for British Archaeology (Gp 14 exec ctee) 1984-, Thoroton Soc 1987-; MIFA (1983); *Books* Figure Brasses in N Lincs (1976), Aspects of Local History in Aslochton, Whatton & Scarrington Notts (1987), Excavation & Survey of Lydiate Hall, Merseyside (1982), Roman Pottery Production in the E Midlands (1983), Green Fields Beyond (1984), Life & Landscape in E Bridgford 1600-1900 (1985), Discovering Newark-on-Trent (1989); *Recreations* squash, horse-riding, walking; *Style—* Dr John Samuels; 6 Old North Rd, Cromwell, Newark, Notts NG23 6JE (☎ 0636 821727)

SAMUELS, Prof Michael Louis; s of Harry Samuels OBE (d 1976), of London, and Céline, *née* Aronowitz (d 1983); *b* 14 Sept 1920; *Educ* St Paul's, Balliol Coll Oxford (MA); *m* 21 Dec 1950, Hilary Miriam, da of Julius Marcus Samuel, of Glasgow (d 1942); 1 da (Vivien b 1953); *Career* lectr in English language Univ of Edinburgh 1949-59 (asst 1948-49), prof of English language Univ of Glasgow 1959-; chm Scottish Studentships Selection Ctee Scottish Educn Dept 1975-88; *Books* Linguistic Evolution (1972), A Linguistic Atlas of Late Mediaeval English (jt ed 1986); *Style—* Prof Michael Samuels; 4 Queen's Gate, Dowanhill, Glasgow G12 9DN (☎ 041 334 4999); Dept of English Language, The University, Glasgow G12 8QQ (☎ 041 339 8855, telex 777070 UNIGLA)

SAMUELSON, David Wylie; s of George Berthold Samuelson (d 1947), and Marjorie Emma Elizabeth, *née* Vint; bro of Sydney Wylie Samuelson, CBE, and Michael Edward Wylie Samuelson; *m* 1, 1949 (m dis 1973), Joan da of Philip Woolf; 2 s (Paul, Adam), 2 da (Gail, Zoe); m 2, 1978 Elaine Witz; *Career* served RAF 1944-47; with Br Movietone News 1941-60, fndr dir Samuelson Gp plc 1958-84, dir Sam Ltd 1984-, as cameraman filmed in over 40 countries and 4 Olympic games; original inventions incl: through-the-lens camera crane, Samcine inclining prism; winner many awards incl: SMPTE Special Commendation Award 1978, SMPTG Presidential Proclamation Award 1984, AMPAS Scientific and Engineering Award 1980, Academy Tech Achievement Award 1987; govr London Int Film Sch 1981- (chm 1984-86), vice pres Int Union of Film Tech Assocs 1974-80; FRPS, FBKSTS (pres 1970-72, memb cncl 1966-78 and 1984-), memb ACTT; *Books* Motion Picture Camera and Lighting Equipment, Motion Picture Camera Techiques, Motion Picture Camera Date, The Samuelson Manuel,ed American Cinematographer magazine (contrib ed, 1973-83); *Recreations* skiing, jogging, work; *Style—* DW Samuelson, Esq; 7 Montagu Mews West, London W1H 1TF, fax 01 724 4025

SAMUELSON, James Francis; s and h of Sir Michael Samuelson, 5 Bt; *b* 20 Dec 1956; *Educ* Hailsham; *Style—* James Samuelson Esq; c/o Hollingwood, Stunts Green, Herstmonceux, Hailsham, East Sussex

SAMUELSON, Michael Edward Wylie; s of George Berthold Samuelson (d 1947), pioneer film producer making first film 1908, and Margorie Emma Elizabeth, *née* Vint; bro of Sydney Wylie Samuelson, CBE, *qv*; *b* 25 Jan 1931; *Educ* Shoreham GS; *m* Madeleine; 3 s (James d 1970, Richard b 1964, Benjamin b 1972), 2 da (Louise b 1959, Emma b 1960, actress Emma Samms); *Career* photographer RAF 1949-51, stage dir 1952-56, Br Movietone News cameraman 1957-61; joined Samuelson Gp plc 1957- (dep chm 1984-); credits as dir or producer or cinematographer on Offl Films to Olympic Games 1968, 1972, 1974, 1976 and 1984 and World Cup Soccer 1966, 1970, 1974, 1982, Tstee Adopt-a-Student Scheme 1985-; exec crew Variety Club of GB 1967-74, chief Barker 1974, exec bd 1974-; chm Sunshine Coach Scheme GB 1979-85, tstee Young Variety Club of GB 1980-; Worldwide Sunshine Coach chm 1983-87; cncl memb Sick Childrens Tst 1983-), vice chm and tstee Hospital for Sick Children Great Ormond St redevelopment appeal 1984-; vice pres Nat Asson for Maternal & Child Welfare 1979, pres Variety Clubs International 1987-89; *Recreations* canal boating enthusiast, skiing, opera, shooting; *Clubs* MCC; *Style—* Michael Samuelson, Esq; 9 Hillsleigh Rd, London W8 7LE (☎ 01 727 8701/0882); Samuelson Gp plc, Dudden Hill Lane, London NW10 1DS (☎ 01 452 6400, fax 01 450 1530, car ☎ 0836 203273)

SAMUELSON, Sir (Bernard) Michael Francis; 5 Bt (UK 1884), of Bodicote, Banbury, Oxfordshire; s of Sir Francis Samuelson, 4 Bt (d 1981), and Margaret (d 1980), da of H Kendal Barnes; *b* 17 Jan 1917; *Educ* Eton; *m* 1952, Janet Amy, da of Lt-Cdre Laurence Garrett Elkington; 2 s, 2 da; *Heir* s, James Francis Samuelson; *Career* Lt RA, Burma 1939-45 (despatches); *Style—* Sir Michael Samuelson, Bt; Hollingwood, Stunts Green, Herstmonceux, Hailsham, East Sussex

SAMUELSON, Sydney Wylie; CBE (1978); s of George Berthold Samuelson (d 1947), and Marjorie Emma Elizabeth, *née* Vint; bro of Michael Edward Wylie Samuelson, *qv*; *b* 7 Dec 1925; *Educ* Lancing Cncl Sch; *m* 7 Sept 1947, Doris Cicely, da of Jack Magen, d 1956; 3 s (Peter b 1951, Jonathan b 1955, Marc b 1961); *Career* served RAF 1943-47; from age 14 career devoted to Br film ind; cinema projectionist, 1939-42, asst film ed 1943, cameraman and dir documentry films 1947-59, founded co to service film and TV prodn orgns, chm Samuelson Gp plc 1966-; perm tstee and currently chm of mgmnt BAFTA; memb: exec ctee Cinema and TV Veterans (pres 1980-81), exec ctee Cinema and TV Benevolent Fund (tstee 1982-, pres 1983-86), Brit Soc of Cinematographers (Govr 1969-79, 1 vice-pres 1976-77, award outstanding contrib to film indust 1967), assoc memb Amer Soc of Cinematographers, hon tech adv RN Film Corp, Guild of Film Prod Exec Award of Merit 1986, Miche Balcon award 1985, pres UK Friends of Akim, vice-pres Muscular Dystrophy Assoc of GB; *Recreations* vintage motoring, veteran, jogging; *Style—* Mr Sydney Samuelson; 303-315 Cricklewood Broadway, London NW2 6PQ (☎ 01 452 8090, telex 21430, fax 01 450 3881, car tel 225061)

SAMWELL, Stanley David; s of David Arthur Samwell (d 1981), of Harrow, Middx, and Ergentine Ellen, *née* Evans (d 1981); *b* 12 June 1927; *Educ* Harrow Co GS; *m* 23

Aug 1974, Diana Mary, da of Capt Harry Lovibond Windsor (d 1946), of Johannesburg, SA; *Career* CA; ptnr Arthur Young (and predecessor firm) 1969-83; Dept of Trade inspr: affairs of Kuehne & Nagel Ltd 1974-75, Peachey Property Corpn 1977-78; pres Insolvency Practitioners Assoc 1980-81; memb Worshipful Co of CAs 1978; FCA 1954, MIPA 1970; *Books* Corporate Receiverships (second edn 1988); *Recreations* skiing, travel, theatre, photography; *Clubs* Ski Club of GB; *Style*— Stanley Samwell, Esq; 5 Old Manor Yard, London SW5 9AB (☎ 01 373 4067)

SAMWORTH, David Chetwode; CBE (1985), DL (1984); s of Frank Samworth; *b* 25 June 1935; *Educ* Uppingham; *m* 1969, Rosemary Grace, *née* Hobbs; 1 s (Mark b 1970), 3 da (Mary b 1972, Susannah b 1975, Victoria b 1977); *Career* Lt Sudan and Cyprus, chm Meat and Livestock Cmmn 1980-84, chm Pork Farms Ltd 1968-81, dir Northern Foods Ltd 1978-81, vice-chm Leics 33 Hosp Management Ctee 1970-74, memb Cncl of Nottingham Univ 1975-76, vice-chm governing body Uppingham Sch 1980-, non-exec dir Imperial Gp 1983-85, chm Samworth Bro Ltd 1984-; *Recreations* tennis, hunting; *Style*— David Samworth Esq, CBE, DL; Markham House, Thorpe Satchville, Melton Mowbray, Leics

SANCROFT-BAKER, Raymond Samuel; s of Anthony Sancroft-Baker (d 1985), and Jean Norah, *née* Heron-Maxwell (d 1981); *b* 30 July 1950; *Educ* Bromsgrove Sch; *m* 29 Jan 1983, (Daphne) Caroline, da of Gp Capt Maurice Admas, OBE, AFC (d 1976); 2 s (Robert b 1985, Hugh b 1987); *Career* Christie's: head of coin and metal dept 1973, dir 1981, dir of jewellery dept 1988, vice-chm Bayswater Ward Conservatives, govr Essendine Sch London 1976-; Freeman City of London 1972; Liveryman: Worshipful Co of Wax Chandlers 1973, Worshipful Co of Patternmakers 1972, (asst 1987); FRNS 1971; *Recreations* tennis, squash, visiting antique shops; *Clubs* RAC; *Style*— Raymond Sancroft-Baker, Esq; 4 Westbourne Pk Rd, London W2 5PH (☎ 01 727 9600); Christie's, 8 King St, St James's, London SW1Y 6QT (☎ 01 839 9060)

SANDBACH, Richard Stainton Edward; s of Frank Stainton Sandbach (d 1917), and Beatrice Emmeline, *née* Clifton (d 1963); *b* 13 June 1915; *Educ* Manchester GS, St John's Coll Cambridge (MA, LLM); *m* 10 Sept 1949, (Brenda Mary) Wendy, da of Charles Lionel Osborn Cleminson (d 1958), of the White House, Ickleford, Herts; 2 s (John Christopher Stainton b 1950, (Richard Paul Stainton Dickon b 1956); *Career* Private VR Suffolk Reg 1939, OCTV 1940, 22 Cheshire Regt 1940-46, Jr Staff Coll 1941, Gen Staff GS03 Capt 12 Corps 1942-43, 21 Army Gp 1943, GS02 Maj 1 Canadian Army 1943-44, Airborne Corps 1944-46, Lucknow Dist 1946; admitted slr 1946, sr ptnr Greenwoods Peterborough 1970-79 (ptnr 1951-79), clerk Huntingdon Freeman 1968-76; chm: DHSS Local Appeals Tribunal Peterborough 1980-88, Paten & Co Ltd 1988-; past pres Peterborough & Dist Law Soc, fndr chm Minister Gen Housing Assoc Ltd; past chm: City & Cos Club Peterborough, Burgh Soc Peterborough; tstee: Peterborough Assoc of Boys' Club, Nat Deaf-Blind Helpers' League, Peterborough Cathedral Appeal, Mark Masons' Fund of Benevolence; chm Peterborough Diocesan Bd of Fin 1974-84, provincial grand master for Northamptonshire & Huntingdonshire, Ancient Free & Accepted Masons of England 1984-; memb Law Soc 1947; *Books* Introduction to The Book of the Lodge (G Oliver 1986); Priest and Freemason (1988); *Recreations* hill walking, photography, historic research; *Clubs* United Oxford and Cambridge, City & Counties Peterborough; *Style*— Richard Sandbach, Esq; 91 Lincoln Rd, Peterborough PE1 2SH; (☎ 0733 43012); The Moorings, Fairbourne, Gwynedd; Drumnagarrachan, Kiltarlity, by Beauly, Inverness

SANDBERG, Sir Michael Graham Ruddock; CBE (1982, OBE 1977); s of Gerald Arthur Clifford and Ethel Marion Sandberg; *b* 31 May 1927; *Educ* St Edward's Sch Oxford; *m* 1954, Carmel Mary Roseleen, *née* Donnelly; 2 s, 2 da; *Career* served 6 Lancers (Indian Army) and King's Dragoon Gds 1945; joined Hong Kong and Shanghai Banking Corpn 1949, chm 1977-86; chm Br Bank of the Middle East 1980-86; tres University of Hong Kong 1977-86, memb Exec Cncl of Hong Kong 1978-86; dir: Marine Midland Bank 1980-87, The Interpublic Gp of Cos (USA) 1981, Int Re-Insurance Inc, Int Totalizer Systems Inc, Global Yield Inc, New World Development Ltd, Winsor Industrial Corporation, North Kalquile Gold Mines, Pioneer Concrete Cornwall Resource Corpn Ltd; chm bd of stewards Royal Hong Kong Jockey Club 1981-, vice-pres The Inst of Bankers 1984-87 (Fellow 1977), JP Hong Kong 1972-86; Hon Steward Royal Hong Kong Jockey Club 1986; kt 1986; *Recreations* racing, horology, cricket, bridge; *Clubs* Cavalry and Guards, Carlton, MCC, Surrey CCC (vice-pres), Portland, Hong Kong; *Style*— Sir Michael Sandberg, CBE; The Hongkong and Shanghai Banking Corporation, 1 Queen's Rd Central, Hong Kong (☎ 5-8221111; telex HKBG HX)

SANDELL, Kenneth Edwin; s of Ernest Arthur Sandell (d 1980); *b* 28 April 1929; *Educ* Tollington Sch; *m* 1960, Lillian Rose, *née* Buckingham; 1 s (Mark b 1966), 1 da (Joanne b 1970); *Career* served Suez 1948-49, insurance broker; dir: Fenchurch Marine Brokers Ltd 1971-85, Samson Menzies Ltd 1972-85, dir Well Marine Reinsurance Brokers Ltd 1985, memb Lloyds; *Recreations* reading, youth work; *Style*— Kenneth Sandell, Esq; 4 Cranley Rd, Westcliff-on-Sea, Essex (☎ 0702 342906)

SANDELSON, Neville Devonshire; s of David Sandelson, OBE; *b* 27 Nov 1923; *Educ* Westminster, Trinity Coll Cambridge; *m* 1959, Nana Karlinski, of Neuilly sur Seine; 1 s, 2 da; *Career* barr Inner Temple 1946, MP (Lab) Hayes and Harlington 1971-74, Hillingdon, Hayes and Harlington (SDP 1981-84) 1974-83, having fought previous elections in other constituencies; fndr memb and tres Manifesto Gp 1975-80, fndr memb SDP 1981; former memb: European Cmmn Lab Ctee for Europe, European Cmmn Wider Share Ownership Cncl, National Ctee Electoral Reform Cncl; jt sec British-Greek Parly Gp, vice-chm SDP Friends of Israel (resigned over Israeli bombardment of Beirut 1982); SDP spokesman on NI and Arts to 1983; vice-chm Afghanistan Support Ctee; *Clubs* Reform; *Style*— Neville Sandelson Esq; 1 Hare Court, Temple, London EC4 (☎ 01 353 0691); Woodside, Horsegate Ride, Ascot, Berks (☎ 0990 22721)

SANDEMAN, Hon Mrs (Sylvia Margaret); yr da of Baron Maclehose of Beoch; *b* 29 July 1949; *Educ* Downe House; *m* 1970, Ronald Leighton, s of Cargil Leighton Sandeman; 1 da (b 1975); *Recreations* sailing; *Clubs* Royal Northern and Clyde Yacht; *Style*— The Hon Mrs Sandeman; Oakdene, Armadale Rd, Rhu, Dunbartons (☎ 0436 820867)

SANDEMAN, Timothy Walter; s of Maj Patrick Walter Sandeman, MC (d 1959), and Olive Eva, *née* Wootton; *b* 6 April 1928; *Educ* Eton; *m* 14 Dec 1951, Selma Anna Elizabeth, yst da of late Carl Dines Dreyer, of Copenhagen, Denmark; 2 s (John Carl Patrick b 1953, Michael Walter b 1962), 1 da (Susanne b 1956); *Career* chm Seagram UK Ltd Nov 1981-; *Style*— Timothy Sandeman Esq; c/o Seagram UK Ltd, Seagram Distillers House, Dacre St, SW1 (T 01 222 4343)

SANDERS, Colin Derek; s of Joseph Sanders (d 1988), and Josephine May, *née* Bryer; *b* 2 Jan 1944; *Educ* Cheltenham; *m* 7 Sept 1968, Marlene Elizabeth, da of Reginald Frank Webb; 2 s (Paul Edward, Timothy Colin), 1 da (Phillippa Jane); *Career* fndr and non exec dir Brewmaker plc (formerly chm), underwriting memb Lloyds of London; *Recreations* travel, old cars, gardening; *Style*— Colin Sanders, Esq; Webb's Land, Wickham, Hants PO17 5N5 (fax 0329 832756)

SANDERS, (June) Deidre; s of Philip Ronald Heaton, of Scotland, and Audrey Minton, *née* Harvey (d 1972); *b* 9 June 1945; *Educ* Harrow County GS for Girls, Sheffield Univ (BA); *m* 12 Dec 1949, Richard James, 1 da (Susan b 1976); *Career* journalist, author, broadcaster; problem-page ed The Sun; Jubilee Medal 1977; *Books* Kitchen Sink or Swim? (Penguin 1982), Women and Depression (Sheldon Press 1984), Woman Book of Love and Sex (Michael Joseph 1985), Woman Report on Men (Sphere 1987); *Recreations* horse-riding; *Style*— Mrs Deidre Sanders; PO Box 488, The Sun, Virginia Street, London E1 9BZ (☎ 01-481 4100, telex 925 088)

SANDERS, Donald Neil; CB (1983); s of Lorenzo George Sander (d 1965), and Rosina May Marsh; *b* 21 June 1927; *Educ* Wollongong HS NSW Australia, Univ of Sydney (B Ec); *m* 1952, Betty Elaine, da of William Bertie Constance (d 1955); 4 s (Michael, Robert, Jonathan, Martin), 1 da (Jennifer); *Career* cwlth Bank of Australia 1943-60, Aust Treasy 1956, Bank of England 1960; Reserve Bank of Australia 1960: supt credit policy, banking dept 1964-66, dep mangr banking dept 1966-67, dep mangr res dept 1967-70; Aust Embassy Washington 1968: chief mangr securities markets dept 1970-72, chief mangr banking & finance dept 1972-74; dep govr and dep chm Reserve Bank of Australia 1975-87; md Commonwealth Banking Corporation 1987-; *Recreations* opera, music, golf; *Clubs* Killara Golf; *Style*— D N Sanders, Esq; Commonwealth Banking Corporation, Cnr Pitt St & Martin Place, Sydney NSW 2000

SANDERS, Sir Robert Tait; KBE (1980), CMG (1974); s of Alexander Scott Wilson Sanders (d 1934), of Dunfermline, Fife, and Charlotte McCulloch; *b* 2 Feb 1925,Dunfermline,; *Educ* Canmore Public Sch Dunfermline, Dunfermline HS, Fettes Coll Edinburgh, Pembroke Coll Cambridge (MA), LSE; *m* 1951, Barbara, da of George Sutcliffe (d 1983); 3 s; *Career* served Lt 1 Bn Royal Scots 1943-46, dist offr Fiji 1950, sec to govt Tonga 1956-58, sec to Coconut Industry Inquiry 1963, MLC Fiji 1963-64, sec for Natural Resources 1965-67, acting sec Fijian Affrs 1967 (acting chm Native Lands and Fisheries Cmmn, memb MEC 1967-; sec: chief min and cncl of mins 1967-70, Cabinet 1970-79, Foreign Affrs 1970-74, Home Affrs 1972-74, Info 1975-76; Treaties advsr to Govt of Fiji 1985-87, Fiji Independence Medal 1970; *Books* Interlude in Fiji (1963), Fiji Treaties (1987), newspaper and magazine articles; *Recreations* golf, music; *Clubs* Royal Scots (Edinburgh), Nausori Golf (Fiji); *Style*— Sir Robert Sanders, KBE, CMG; Greystones Lodge, Broich Terrace, Crieff

SANDERS, Roger Benedict; JP; s of Maurice Sanders JP, FRIBA, of 24 Boydell Court, St Johns Wood Park, London NW8, and Lilian *née* Stone; *b* 1 Oct 1940; *Educ* Highgate Sch; *m* 5 Jan 1969, Susan Rachel, da of Simon Brenner, md Windsmoor plc, of 14 Fitzroy Court, 57 Shepherds Hill, London N6; 2 s (Matthew b 1973, Thomas b 1980), 1 da (Grace b 1971, d 1976); *Career* barr Inner Temple 1965, chm Inner London Juvenile Cts 1980-87; metropolitan Stipendiary magistrate 1986-, rec Crown Ct 1986-; *Recreations* gardening, french, travel, model railways; *Clubs* Players Theatre; *Style*— Roger Sanders, JP; Old Street, Magistrates Court, London EC1V 9LJ (☎ 01 488 5221)

SANDERS, Ronald; *b* 26 Jan 1948; *Educ* Sacred Heart RC Sch Guyana, Westminster Sch (London), Boston Univ; *m* 1975, Susan Ramphal; *Career* high cmmr to UK 1984-87, ambass extraordinary and plenipotentiary, accredited to UNESCO 1983-87; dep perm rep to UN in New York 1982-83, special advsr to Min of Foreign Affairs of Antigua and Barbuda 1978-82, conslt to Pres of Carribean Devpt Bank in Barbados 1977-78; md Guyana Broadcasting Serv 1973-76, public affairs advsr to PM of Guyana 1973-76; memb Bd of Dir Carribean News Agency 1976-77, pres Carribean Broadcasting Union 1975-76, lectr in communications Univ of Guyana 1975-76; Memb Exec Bd of UNESCO 1985-87; memb of delgn: Non Aligned Heads of Govt Conference 1976, Cwlth Heads of Govt 1975 and 1983, 1985; fell Queen Elizabeth House Oxford Univ 1988; *Publications* Broadcasting in Guyana (1978), Antigua and Barbuda: Transition, Trial, Triumph (1984); Is Britain Indispensable to the Commonwealth (1987); *Style*— Ronald Sanders, Esq; 24 Chelmsford Sq, London NW10 3AR

SANDERS, Roy; s of Leslie John Sanders, and Marguerite Alice, *née* Knight; *b* 20 August 1937; *Educ* Hertford GS, Univ of London (BSc, MBBS); *m* 1, 25 July 1961 (m dis 1977), Ann Ruth, da of William Costar; 2 s (Andrew St John William b 1965, Charles St John David b 1966), 1 da (Lyvia Ann b 1963); m 2, 6 Jan 1984, Fleur Annette, da of Brian Chandler, of St Gallen, Austria; *Career* HAC Gunner 1957-62, Regt MO 1963-75, HAC Co of Pikemen and Musketeers 1982-; conslt plastic surgn The Mount Vernon Centre for Plastic Maxillofacial and Oral Surgery; hon sr lectr Univ of London; sec: Br Assoc of Plastic Surgns 1986-88, Br Assoc of Aesthetic Plastic Surgns 1985-87; chm Medical Equestrian Assoc 1985-86, pres Plastic Surgery Section RSM of London 1989-90, memb Medical Artists' Assoc; Freeman City of London, Liveryman Soc of Apothecaries of London; LRCP, MRCS 1962, FRCS 1967; *Recreations* equestrian activities, painting in watercolour; *Clubs* Athenaeum; *Style*— Roy Sanders, Esq; 77 Harley St, London WIN 1DE (☎ 01 935 7417); Upper Rye Farm, Moreton in Marsh, Glos (☎ 0608 50542); Suite 1, 82 Portland Place, London W1 (☎ 01 580 3541, fax 01 436 2954)

SANDERS-CROOK, William Stanley; MBE (1972); s of William Charles Herbert Crook (d 1966), of Roseview, Rosebine Gardens, Twickenham, Middx, and Mary Amelia, *née* Green (d 1986); *b* 2 Nov 1933; *Educ* Latymer Upper Sch, RMA Sandhurst; *m* 1, 5 May 1962; 1 s (William b 1963), 1 da (Deborah b 1972); m 2, 20 Dec 1982, Jean Rosemary, da of Eric Walker (d 1966), of Beaconside, Barstaple, N Devon; *Career* Regular Army Offr 1953-77: Maj BAOR, Suez, Malaya, Borneo, Singapore, Miny of Def, Brunei; equestrian journalist, dir: John Roberts Consultants 1977-79, Jean Kittermaster Public Relations 1981; *novels* Four Days (1979), Death Run (1980), Triple Seven (1981); *Recreations* journalism, travel, scuba diving (PADI instructor), riding (BHSAI), narrowboating, sport, racing canoeing, (Cross Channel Record (Guinness Book of Records) 1961-80, Devizes to Westminster Record 1961), judo (Army Class One Finalist 1961); *Style*— William Sanders-Crook, MBE; Jean Kittermaster Public Relations, 239 Kings Rd, London SW3 5EL (☎ 01 352 6811, fax 01 351 9215)

SANDERSON, Dr Alan Lindsay; s (twin) of 1 Baron Sanderson of Ayot, MC (UK 1960); suc father 15 Aug 1971 and disclaimed his peerage for life 28 Sept 1971; *b* 12 Jan 1931; *Educ* Uppingham; *m* 1959, Gertrud, da of Herman Boschler; 1 s (Michael), 4 da (Evelyn, Frances, Andrea, Stephanie b 1970); *Career* MB, BS London, MRCP London; *Style*— Dr Alan Sanderson; 2 Caroline Close, W2 (☎ 01 229 8533)

SANDERSON, Col (Thomas) Allan; s of James Brown Sanderson (d 1932), and Margaret Robertson, *née* Neil (d 1950); *b* 7 May 1927; *Educ* George Watson's Boys Coll, Univ of Edinburgh (MB, ChB); *m* 1 1954, (m dis) Winifred Brown; 2 da (Sarah b 1955, Janey b 1957); m 2, 2 Sept 1963, Anne Patricia, da of Walter Roland Haresign, of Durban; 1 da (Tracy b 1964); *Career* Col Cdr: Med Army in Scotland 1985, Med Br Forces Hong Kong 1982-85, Med Army in Scotland 1980-82; Maj 1 Bn 1 Kings African rifles Nyasaland 1962-64; *Recreations* golf, curling, reading; *Clubs* Murrayfield Golf Edinburgh; *Style*— Col Allan Sanderson; Kellerstain Lodge, By Gogar, Edinburgh EH12 9BS (☎ 031 339 5347); Army Headquarters, Scotland, Edinburgh EG1 2YX (☎ 031 336 1761)

SANDERSON, Hon Andrea; da of Dr Alan Sanderson, *qv*; *b* 1964; *Style*— The Hon Andrea Sanderson

SANDERSON, Annie Helena (Nan); *née* McDonagh; da of James McDonagh (d 1962), and Elizabeth, *née* McGeough (d 1935); *b* 8 Oct 1919; *Educ* St Clare's Convent, Sacred Heart, Newry Co Down NI; *m* 1, 14 Feb 1942 (m dis 1942), Pilot Offr Edward Frederick Lloyd (d 1942), m 2, 26 April 1947, Rupert Anthony, s of late Herbert James Walter Sanderson; 2 s (Colin b 26 June 1948, Stephen b 5 Dec 1953); *Career* dir and co sec Sanderson Marine Craft Ltd Norwich; parish cncllr 1960-88, dist cncllr Blofield & Flegg RDC 1961-74, Broadland DC 1976-; memb: Gt Yarmouth & Waveney Co Health Cncl, Gt Yarmouth & Waveney Dist Health Authy 1976-, Norfolk Valuation Panel 1976-; *Recreations* sailing, reading, music; *Style*— Mrs Nan Sanderson; The Warren, Riverside, Reedham, Norwich NR13 3TE (☎ 0493 700 242);

SANDERSON, Sir (Frank Philip) Bryan; 2 Bt (UK 1920) of Malling Deanery, South Malling, Co Sussex; s of Sir Frank Bernard Sanderson, 1 Bt (d 1965); *b* 18 Feb 1910; *Educ* Stowe, Pembroke Coll Oxford; *m* 1933, Annette Irene Caroline (d 1967), da of late Col Korab Laskowski of Warsaw and gda of Gen Count Edouard de Castellaz; 2 s, 1 da; *Heir* s, Frank Sanderson; *Career* memb Lloyd's, chm Humber Fish Manure Co Ltd, Hull; *Style*— Sir Bryan Sanderson, Bt; Lychgate Cottage, Scaynes Hill, Haywards Heath, W Sussex

SANDERSON, Charles James; s of J C Sanderson, of 19 Ansell Terrace, London W8, and E K Sanderson; *b* 18 August 1949; *Educ* Millfield, Byam Shaw Sch of Drawing and Painting; *Career* painter; exhibited: Royal Academy, Paris Salon, Camden Arts Centre, Westminster Cathedral, New Arts Centre, John Neville Gallery Canterbury; *Recreations* jogging, music, gardening, cooking, travel; *Style*— Charles Sanderson, Esq; 7 Gordon Place, London W8 4JD (☎ 01 937 4922)

SANDERSON, Hon Evelyn; da of Dr Alan Sanderson, *qv*; *b* 1961; *Style*— The Hon Evelyn Sanderson

SANDERSON, Hon Frances; da of Dr Alan Sanderson, *qv*

SANDERSON, Frank Linton; s and h of Sir Bryan Sanderson, 2 Bt, by Annette Irene Caroline (d 1967), da of late Col Korab Laskowski, of Warsaw, and gda of Gen Count Edouard de Castellaz; *b* 21 Nov 1933; *Educ* Stowe, Salamanca Univ; *m* 1961, Margaret Ann, da of John C Maxwell (d 1976), of New York USA; 2 s (David b 1962, Michael b 1965), 3 da (Caroline b 1966, Nina b 1968, Katherine b 1968 (twins)); *Career* RNVR 1950-65; *Style*— Frank Sanderson Esq; Grandturzel Farm, Burwash, E Sussex

SANDERSON, Hon Michael; s and h of Dr Alan Sanderson, *qv* (Baron Sanderson of Ayot, who disclamed his peerage for life); *b* 6 Dec 1959; *Style*— The Hon Michael Sanderson

SANDERSON, Hon Murray Lee; s (twin) of 1 Baron Sanderson of Ayot, MC (d 1971), and bro of Dr Alan Sanderson, *qv*; *b* 1931; *Educ* Rugby, Trinity Coll Oxford, King's Cambridge; *m* 1, 1966 (m dis 1972), Muriel, da of late George Williams; m 2, 1973, Eva, da of Rev David Simfukwe; 1 s, 1 da; *Career* company dir; admin offr Kenya 1956-63; *Style*— The Hon Murray Sanderson; PO Box 2253, Kitwe, Zambia

SANDERSON, Very Rev Peter Oliver; s of Harold Beckwith Carling Sanderson (d 1978), and Doris Amelia, *née* Oliver (d 1981); *b* 26 Jan 1929; *Educ* South Shields HS, St Chad's Coll Durham Univ (BA, DipTh); *m* 4 April 1956, Doreen da of Robert Kay Gibson (d 1968); 2 s (Michael b 1958, Richard b 1968, d 1985), 1 da (Jane b 1959); *Career* Nat Serv RAF 1947-49, chaplains' branch, RAF 1963-67; ordained: deacon 1954, priest 1955; asst Curate Houghton-le-Spring Durham Diocese 1954-59, rector St Thomas-ye-Vale Diocese of Jamaica 1959-63; vicar: Winksley-cum-Grantley and Aldfield with Studley Ripon Diocese 1967-74, St Aidan's Leeds Diocese of Ripon 1974-84; provost St Paul's Cathedral Dundee Diocese of Brechin 1984-; *Recreations* reading, walking, listening to music; *Style*— The Very Rev the Provost of St Paul's Cathedral Dundee; Cathedral Rectory, 4 Richmond Terrace, Dundee DD2 1BQ (☎ 0382 68 548); Cathedral Office, Castlehill, Dundee DD1 1TD (☎ 0382 24 486)

SANDERSON, Roy; OBE (1983); s of George Sanderson (d 1938), and Lillian, *née* Charlesworth (d 1939); *b* 15 Feb 1931; *Educ* Leicester, Kings Richards Royal GS; *m* 25 Aug 1951, Jean Lillian, s of James Booth; 3 s (Roy James, Alan (d 1973), Kevin); *Career* Nat Serv lance-corpl REME 1949-51; convenor of shop stewards Lucos Aerospace Hemel Hempstead 1952-67, nat sec EETPU 1987- (asst educn offr 1967-69, nat offr 1969-87); non exec dir UKAEA 1987-; memb: exec ctee The Industrial Soc, Armed Forces Pay Review Body, NEDO innovation ctee, exec cncl Confedn of Shipbuilding and Engrg Unions; *Recreations* golf, snooker, supporter of Watford FC; *Clubs* Shendish (Hemel Hempstead); *Style*— Roy Sanderson, Esqn; 162 Belswains Lane, Hemel Hempstead, Hertfordshire (☎ 0442 42033); Hayes Court, West Common Rd, Hayes, Bromley, Kent (☎ 01 462 7755)

SANDERSON OF AYOT, Barony of (UK 1960); *see*: Sanderson, Dr Alan

SANDERSON OF BOWDEN, Baron (Life Peer UK 1985); Sir (Charles) Russell Sanderson; Kt (1981); s of Charles Plummer Sanderson (d 1976), of Melrose, Roxburghshire, and (Martha) Evelyn (d 1954), da of Joseph Gardiner, of Glasgow; *b* 30 April 1933; *Educ* St Mary's Sch Melrose, Trin Coll Glenalmond, Bradford Technical Coll, Scottish Coll of Textiles Galashiels; *m* 5 July 1958, (Frances) Elizabeth, da of Donald Alfred Ramsden Macaulay (d 1982), of Rylstone, Skipton, Yorks; 2 s (Hon (Charles) David Russell b 1960, Hon Andrew b 1968), 2 da (Hon Claire (Hon Mrs Walker) b 1961, Hon Georgina b 1963); *Career* cmmnd Royal Signals 1952, served 51 (Highland) Inf Div Signal Regt (TA) 1953-56, KOSB (TA) 1956-58; chm Central & Southern Area, Scottish Cons Unionist Assoc, 1974-75 (vice-pres 1975-77, pres 1977-79), ptnr Chas P Sanderson, Wool and Yarn Merchants Melrose 1978-, vice-chm Nat Union of Cons Assocs 1979-81 (memb exec ctee 1977-, chm 1981-86); govr: St Mary's Sch Melrose, Scottish Coll of Textiles 1980-87; memb Cncl Trin Coll, Glenalmond 1982-; chm: Edinburgh Fin Tst 1983-87, Shires Investmt Tst 1984-87, Clydesdale Bank 1985-87; memb: Scottish Cncl Independent Schls 1984-87, Ctee Governing Bodies 1984-87; Minister of State Scottish Office 1987-; cmmr Gen Assembly Church of Scotland 1972; kt 1981; *Recreations* golf; *Clubs* Caledonian, Hon Co of Edinburgh Golfers; *Style*— The Rt Hon Lord Sanderson of Bowden; Becketts Field, Bowden, Melrose, Roxburgh TD6 0ST (☎ 0835 22736); Scottish Office, St Andrew's House, Edinburgh

SANDFORD, Arthur; s of Arthur and Lilian Sandford; *b* 12 May 1941; *Educ* Queen Elizabeth's GS Blackburn, UC London (LLB); *m* 1963, Kathleen, da of James Entwistle (d 1976); 2 da (Allison b 1967, Janet b 1969); *Career* asst slr Preston County Borough Cncl 1965-66, sr asst slr Preston CBC 1966-68, asst slr Hampshire CC 1968-70; Nottinghamshire CC: 2 asst clerk 1970-72, first asst clerk 1972-74, dep dir of admin 1974-75, dir of admin 1975-77, dep clerk of CC and county sec, clerk of the CC and chief exec 1978-; *Recreations* half marathons, gardening; *Clubs* Royal Overseas League; *Style*— Arthur Sandford, Esq; Fairford House, 66 Loughborough Road, Bunny, Nottingham NG11 6QD (☎ 0602 212440); Nottinghamshire County Council, County Hall, West Bridgford, Nottinghamshire (☎ 0602 823823, fax (0602) 817945)

SANDFORD, Prof Cedric Thomas; s of Thomas Sandford (d 1951), of Bristol, and Louisa Kate, *née* Hodge (d 1971); *b* 21 Nov 1924; *Educ* Manchester Univ (BA, MA), London Univ (BA); *m* 1, 1 Dec 1945, Evelyn (d 1982), da of Horace Belch, of Leigh, 1 s (John b 1955) 1 da (Gillian b 1956); m 2, 21 July 1984, Christina Katarin Privett; *Career* WWII Pilot RAF 1943-46; prof political economy Bath Univ 1965-87, pres Econs Assoc 1983-86, memb Meade Ctee; memb SW Electricity consultative ctee; consultancies incl: UN, World Bank, IMF, EEC, OECD, Irish Tax Cmmn; active in local and nat affairs of Methodist Church, memb Bath DHA; memb Econs Assoc (1948); *Books* author, many pubns in field of public fin; *Recreations* fishing, gardening, walking; *Style*— Prof Cedric Sandford; Old Coach House, Fersfield, Perrymead, Bath BA2 5AR (☎ 0225 832 683)

SANDFORD, Humphrey; o s of Maj Humphrey Sandford, TD (d 1988), and Marjorie Travers, *née* Pickmere (d 1970); descended from Thomas de Saundford, a Norman recorded in Domesday Book as holding the manor of Sandford, Shropshire; Richard Sandford (d 1588) was the first to move to the Isle of Rossall, which has remained in the possession of the family ever since (*see* Burke's Landed Gentry, 18 edn, vol III, 1972); *b* 12 June 1922; *Educ* Shrewsbury, St John's Coll Camb (MA 1953); *m* 1, 22 Aug 1953 (m dis 1975), Mary Evelyn (Eve), da of Maj William Blackwood Michael, of 6 Stormont Ct, Belfast; m 2, Sheila Ann Tate (d 1987); m 3, 19 March 1988, Joan Margaret Michael; *Career* served in WW II as Maj 2/3 Gurkha Rifles; agricultural offr in HM Colonial Serv: Sarawak 1949-52, Tanganyika 1952-57; agronomist with Shell 1957-81; farmer and landowner; MFH South Shropshire Hounds; ex-pres Fertilizer Soc; *Recreations* hunting, fishing, golf; *Style*— Humphrey Sandford, Esq; The Isle, Bicton, Shrewsbury, Shropshire (☎ 0743 850912)

SANDFORD, 2 Baron (UK 1945); Rev John Cyril Edmondson; DSC (1942); s of 1 Baron Sandford, DL, sometime MP Banbury, lord cmmr treasy and vice-chamberlain HM's Household 1939-42 (d 1959), by his w Edith, *née* Freeman; *b* 22 Dec 1920; *Educ* Eton, RNC Dartmouth; *m* 4 Jan 1947, Catharine Mary, da of late Rev Oswald Andrew Hunt; 2 s, 2 da; *Heir* s, Hon James Edmondson; *Career* takes Cons Whip in House of Lords; RN: midshipman 1940, Med Fleet 1940-41, N African and Sicily Invasions 1942, Normandy Invasions 1944, Signal Offr 1945, House Offr RNC Dartmouth 1947, Flag Lt to Flag Offr cmdg 3 Aircraft Sqdn 1949, Flag Lt to flag offr air (Home) 1951, on Staff C-in-C Far East Station 1953, Cdr 1953, ret 1956; ordained 1958, curate Parish of St Nicholas Harpenden 1958-63, exec chaplain to Bishop of St Albans 1965-68, oppn whip House of Lords 1966-70, parly under-sec of state Dept of Environment 1970-73 and of Dept of Educn and Sci 1973-74; bd memb Ecclesiastical Insurance Office 1978-; pres: Anglo-Swiss Soc 1976-84, pres Assoc of Dist Cncls 1980-86; Church Cmmr 1982-; hon fell Inst of Landscape Architects 1971; *Style*— The Rev the Rt Hon the Lord Sandford, DSC; 6 Smith Sq, London SW1 (☎ 01 222 5715)

SANDFORD, Rear Adm Sefton Ronald; CB (1976); *b* 23 July 1925; *Educ* RNC Dartmouth; *m* 1, 1950, Mary Ann Prins (d 1972); 1 s; m 2, 1972, Jennifer Rachel Newell; 2 da; *Career* served WW II; cmd HMS Protector 1965-67, naval attaché Moscow 1968-70, cmd HMS Devonshire 1971-73, ADC to HM The Queen 1974, Flag Offr Gibralter 1974-76; a yr brother Trinity House 1968; *Recreations* sailing, photography; *Clubs* Royal Yacht Sqdn, MCC; *Style*— Rear Adm Sefton Sandford, CB; Dolphins, Rue de St Jean, St Lawrence, Jersey, CI

SANDHURST, 5 Baron (UK 1871); (John Edward) Terence Mansfield; DFC (1944); s of 4 Baron, OBE (d 1964); *b* 4 Sept 1920; *Educ* Harrow; *m* 1, 1942 (m dis 1946), Priscilla Ann (d 1970), da of late J Fielder Johnson; m 2, 1947, Janet Mary, eldest da of late John Edward Lloyd of Long Island, New York; 1 s, 1 da; *Heir* s, Hon Guy Mansfield; *Career* served RAFVR WW II; md Leslie Rankin Ltd Jersey, Hon ADC to Lt-Govr of Jersey 1969-74; *Recreations* golf; *Clubs* RAF, MCC, United (Jersey); *Style*— The Rt Hon The Lord Sandhurst, DFC; Les Sapins, St Mary, Jersey, CI

SANDIFORD, Noel Buckley; s of Jack Sandiford (d 1950), and Doris Kate, *née* Wild; *b* 7 Nov 1927; *Educ* Manchester Univ (CChem FRSC); *m* 26 March 1942, Kathleen, da of George Hardie Currie (d 1978), of Edinburgh; *Career* served RA and RAEC Lt 1946-48; chief exec Quaker Chemical Ltd 1964-84, chm Designate, md Masspec (analytical) 1975-80, sr ptnr Elberton Associates 1984-; *Recreations* walking in hill country, environmental protection; *Style*— Noel B Sandiford, Esq; Elberton Manor, Elberton, Bristol BS12 3AA (☎ Thornbury 412371)

SANDILANDS, Sir Francis Edwin Prescott; CBE (1967); s of late Lt-Col Prescott Sandilands, DSO, and late Gladys Baird Murton; cadet branch of the Sandilands of Calder (Lords Torphichen, *see* 15 Lord Torphichen); *b* 11 Dec 1913; *Educ* Eton, Corpus Christi Cambridge (MA); *m* 1939, (Susan) Gillian, da of Bramwell Jackson (d 1920), of Bury St Edmunds, Suffolk; 2 s; *Career* served WW II, Lt-Col, Royal Scots Fus and Gen Staff (despatches); chm Commercial Union Assurance Co 1972-83 (dir 1965-83, vice-chm 1968-72), chm: Royal Tst Co of Canada 1974-84; dir: Plessey Co, Lewis and Peat 1983-, chm Ctee on Invisible Exports 1975-83; memb Royal Opera House Bd 1975-85; chm Royal Opera House Trust 1974-86; tstee British Museum 1977-85; memb Royal Fine Art Cmmn 1980-84; hon fell: Univ Coll London, Corpus

Christi Cambridge; Cdr Ordre de la Couronne (Belgium) 1974; kt 1976; *Recreations* music, mediaeval studies; *Style*— Sir Francis Sandilands, CBE; 53 Cadogan Sq, London SW1X 0HY (☎ 01 235 6384)

SANDILANDS, Lt Col Patrick Stanley; DSO (1945); s of Lt Col Prescott Sandilands (d 1956), and Gladys Baird, *née* Murton (d 1964); family, cadet branch of the Sandilands of Calder (now Lords Torphichen); *b* 30 Nov 1911; *Educ* Wellington Coll Berks, RM Coll Sandhurst; *m* 12 March 1949, Madeoline Mary, da of Lt Col Sir Hugh Stephenson Turnbull, KCVO, KBE, of Moray; 1 s (Andrew b 1960), 1 da (Mary b 1956); *Career* cmmnd 1931 Royal Scots Fusiliers: served UK, Palestine, Egypt, 5 Ba Kings Africa Rifles Kenya 1935-58, BEF & Staff Coll 1939-40, Staff in UK & HQ 1 Army 1941-43, ATSH Sicily, 2 RSF Italy & NW Europe 1943-45; Col: 11 RSF Instr Sch of Inf, 5 Scottish Ba The Parachute Regt 1945-53); CO 15 Scottish Ba The Parachute Regt TA 1953-56, HQ Allied Forces Central Europe 1956-59; ret 1959; landowner Laggonmore; memb of the Royal Co of Archers (Queen's Bodyguard for Scotland) 1956; OStJ; elder of the Church of Scotland; *Recreations* fishing, gardening, family history; *Style*— Lt Col Patrick S Sandilands, DSO; Lagganmore, Ilninver, by Oban, Argyll PA34 4UU

SANDISON, Francis Gunn; s of Capt Dr Andrew Tawse Sandison (d 1982), of Glasgow, and Dr Ann Brougham, *née* Austin; *b* 25 May 1949; *Educ* Glasgow Acad Charterhouse, Magdalen Coll Oxford (BCL, MA); *m* 5 Sept 1981, Milva Lou, da of Prof John Emory McCaw, of Des Moines, Iowa; 1 s (Gavin b 1985); *Career* slr 1974; ptnr Freshfields 1980- (asst slr 1974-80); memb Law Soc 1974 (London Law Soc 1980); *Books* Profit Sharing and Other Share Acquisition Shemes (1979), Whiteman on Income Tax (co author 3 ed 1988); *Recreations* fishing, wine, photography; *Style*— Francis Sandison, Esq; 2 The Chase, Churt, Farnham, Surrey GU10 2PU (☎ 025 125 2556); 3 Earl's Court Sq, London SW5 9BY (☎ 01 373 8811); Freshfields, Grindall Ho, 25 Newgate St, London EC1A 7LH (☎ 01 606 6677, fax 01 248 3487, telex 889292 FRSLDN G)

SANDLAND, Eric Michael (Mike); s of Eric Darnley Sandland, and Mary Cairns, *née* Blyth (d 1956); *b* 29 April 1938; *Educ* Edinburgh Acad, Trinity Coll Cambridge (MA); *m* 1, 1961 (m dis 1965), Susan, *née* Wright; m 2, 15 Aug 1969, Jacqueline Marie-Therese, da of Pierre Gauthier, fo Broue, France; 3 s (James Alexander b 9 Jan 1980, Peter Michael (twin) 9 Jan 1980, Thomas William 2 Feb 1982); *Career* Norwich Union Life Insur Soc: actuarial student 1961-64, actuarial asst 1964-66, asst sec for Fr (subsequently sec) 1966-69, gp statistician 1969-72, investment mangr 1972-86, chief investmt mangr 1986; chief investmt mangr Norwich Union Fund Mangrs 1988; chm investmt ctee Assoc Br Insurers 1988-; FIA 1964, ASIA 1972; *Recreations* golf, DIY, snooker, bridge, music; *Style*— Eric Sandland, Esq; 35 Mount Pleasant, Norwich, Norfolk NR2 2DH (☎ 0603 54212); Norwich Union Fund Managers Ltd, PO Box No 4, Surrey Street, Norwich, Norfolk NR1 2NG (☎ 0603 682226, fax 0603 681747, car 0860 347394, telex 97388)

SANDLER, Prof Merton; s of Frank Sandler, of Salford, Lancs, and the late Edith, *née* Stein; *b* 28 Mar 1926; *Educ* Manchester GS, Manchester Univ (MB, ChB, MD); *m* 1961, Lorna Rosemary, da of late Ian Michael, of Colindale, London; 2 s, 2 da; *Career* Capt RAMC; jr specialist in pathology 1951-53, res fell in clinical pathology Brompton Hosp 1953-54, lectr in chem pathology Royal Free Hosp Sch of Med 1955-58; prof of chem pathology Royal Postgrad Med Sch Inst of Obstetrics and Gynaecology Univ of London 1973-, conslt chem pathologist Queen Charlotte's Maternity Hosp 1958-, visiting prof: Univ of New Mexico 1983, Chicago Med Sch 1984, Univ of S Florida 1988; recognised teacher in chem pathology 1960 (examiner various Br and foreign univs and Royal Colls); memb standing advsy ctee Bd of Studies in Pathology Univ of London 1972-76 (chem pathology sub ctee 1973-); Inst of Obstetrics and Gynaecology: chm academic bd 1972-73, chm bd of mgmnt 1975-; govr: Br Postgrad Med Fedn 1976-78, Queen Charlotte's Hosp for Women; cncl memb and meetings sec Assoc of Clinical Pathologists 1959-70, cncl memb Collegium Int Neuro-Psychopharmacologicum 1982-, hon librarian RSM 1977-; pres: section Med Experimental Med and Therapeutics 1979-80, Br Assoc for Psychopharmacology 1980, Br Assoc for Postnatal Illness 1980-; chm tstees Nat Soc for Res into Mental Health 1983-; memb: Med Advsy Cncls of Migraine Tst 1975-80 (chm Scientific Advsy Ctee 1985), Schizophrenia Assoc of GB 1975-78, Parkinson's Disease Soc 1981; chm and sec Biol Cncl Symposium on Drug Action 1979, sec memb bd of mgmnt and chm awards sub ctee Biol Cncl 1983; memb exec ctee: Marcé Soc 1983-86, Med Cncl on Alcoholism 1957-, sec and memb of cncl Harveian Soc of London 1979-, memb of cncl of mgmnt and patron Helping Hand Organisation 1981-87, for corres memb American Coll of Neuropsychoparmacology 1975; hon memb: Indian Acad of Neurosis 1982, Hungarian Pharmacological Soc 1985; jt ed: Br Jl of Pharmacology 1974-80, Clinical Science 1975-77, Jl of Neural Transmission 1979-82; jt ed in chief Jl of Psychiatric Res 1982, present or past ed bd memb of 17 other sci jls; lectr to various learned socs incl: 1 Cummings Meml 1976, James E Beall II Meml 1980, Biol Cncl Lecture Medal 1984; Anna Monika int prize for res on Biol Aspects of Depression 1973, Gold Medal Brit Migraine Assoc 1974, Senator Dr Franz Burda int prize for res on Parkinsons disease 1988; FRCP, FRCPath, FRCPsych, CBiol, FIBiol; *Books* Mental Illness in Pregnancy and the Puerperium (1978), The Pschopharmacology of Aggression (1979), Enzyme Inhibitors as Drugs (1980), Amniotic Fluid and its Clinical Significance (1980), The Psychopharmacology of Alcohol (1980), The Psychopathology of Anticonvulsants (1981); jtly: The Adrenal Cortex (1961), The Thyroid Gland (1967), Advances in Pharmacology (1968), Monoamine Oxidases (1972), Serotonin - New Vistas (1974), Sexual Behaviour: Pharmacology and Biochemistry (1975), Trace Amines and the Brain (1976), Phenotsulphotransferase in Mental Health Research (1981), Tetrahydroisoquindrines and B-Carbolines (1982), Progress towards a Male Contraceptive (1982), Neurobiology of the Trace Amines (1984), Psychopharmacology and Food (1985), Neurotransmitter Interactions (1986), Design of Enzyme Inhibitors as Drugs (1987), Progress in Catechdamine Research (1988); *Recreations* reading, listening to music, lying in the sun; *Clubs* Athenaeum; *Style*— Prof Merton Sandler; 27 St Peters Rd, Twickenham, Middx TW1 1QY (☎ 01 892 8433)

SANDLER, Michael Stephen; s of Carl Bernard Sandler, of Leeds and London, and Taube Irene Barash (d 1980); *b* 17 Oct 1947; *Educ* Leeds GS, Boston Univ (BA); *m* 1973, Gail Michele, da of Dr David Granet, JP, of Scotland; 2 s (Andrew b 1975, Jonathan b 1978); *Career* chartered surveyor, conrad Ritblat & Co 1971-78, dir Streets Fin Ltd 1979-86, md Kingsway Fin Public Relations (Saatchi & Saatchi Co) 1986-; ARICS; *Recreations* tennis, theatre, cinema, spiral staircases; *Style*— Michael Sandler, Esq; 2 Marston Close, London NW6 4EU (☎ 01 328 7510); 5 Giltspur Street, London EC1 (☎ 01 248 1999)

SANDON, Viscount; (Dudley Adrian) Conroy Ryder; o s of 7 Earl of Harrowby, TD, *qv*; *b* 18 Mar 1951; *Educ* Eton, Univ of Newcastle-upon-Tyne, Magdalene Coll Cambridge (MA); *m* 1977, Sarah Nicola Hobhouse, o da of Capt Anthony Dennis Phillpotts Payne, of Great Down Farm, Marnhull, Dorset; 3 s (Hon Dudley Anthony Hugo Coventry b 5 Sept 1981, Hon Frederick Whitmore Dudley b 6 Feb 1984, Hon Henry Mansell Dudley b 13 July 1985); *Career* ARICS; *Style*— Viscount Sandon; The Old Rectory, Fifield, Oxford OX7 6HF

SANDON, Raoul Peter Gauvain; s of Edward Gauvain Sandon MIMM (d 1979), of Bilbao Spain, and Jeanne Emilie, *née* Cottens (d 1979); *b* 2 May 1915; *Educ* Arcachon France, Kings Coll Hosp, London Univ (MB, BS); *m* 20 July 1940, Natalie Naomi, da of Alfred Ewing (d 1950); 2 s (Peter b 1942, Ian b 1951); *Career* capt RAMC 1942-46 (despatches), served in Italy and Middle East; conslt Plastic Surgeon: Hosps for Sick Children London 1956-80, NE Thames Region 1958-80, hon civilian advsr British Army, past pres British Assoc of Plastic Surgeons (BAPS) (also elected to French, Belgium, Spanish and Italian assocs), UK Rep Union of Europ de Medecins Specialistes (UEMS), hon life pres Plastic Surg Sect; author of various chapters in surgical textbooks; MRCS, LCRP 1941, FRCS 1951; *Style*— Raoul P G Sandon, Esq; 17 Langley Ave, Surbiton, Surrey KT6 6QN (☎ 01 399 1487), 152 Harley Street, London W1N 1HH (☎ 01 935 1858)

SANDS, Charles Francis; s of Arthur Landgale Snads (d 1954), and Margaret Soames (d 1978); *b* 3 Mar 1938; *Educ* Marlborough Coll, Lincoln Coll Oxford (MA); *m* 19 Nov 1965, (m dis 1988), Carolyn Clare Barbadee, da of Sir Anthony Ashley Meyer Bt, MP; 2 s (Robert b 1970, David b 1973); *Career* Nat Serv 1956-58, 2 Lt 2 RTR; ptnr Herbert Smith (solicitors) 1972; memb: Law Soc, City of London Solicitors Co; *Recreations* fishing, shooting, golf, tennis, riding; *Clubs* RAC; *Style*— Charles Sands, Esq; Forge Hse, 1c Ravensdon St, London SE11 4AQ (☎ 01 735 7010); Herbert Smith, Watling Hse, 35 Cannon St, London EC4M 5SD (☎ 01 489 8000, fax 01 236 5733, telex 886633)

SANDWICH, Earldom of;; *see*: Montagu, (Alexander) Victor Edward

SANDY, Martyn Graeme; s of Albert Henry Sandy, and Victoria Margaret, *née* Squires; *b* 21 May 1949; *Educ* Plymouth Coll, North East London Poly (BA); *m* 23 Oct 1977, Gillian Evelyn, da of John Aird; 2 s (Daniel b 1982, James b 1984); *Career* dir Boase Massioni Pollitt Advertising 1982-; *Recreations* family, reading; *Style*— Martyn Sandy, Esq; 35 Wingston Lane, Teddington, Middx; Boase Massimi, Pollitt, 12 Bishopsbridge Road, London W2 (☎ 258 3979)

SANDYS, Cynthia, Baroness; Cynthia Mary; da of late Col Frederic Richard Thomas Trench-Gascoigne, DSO (gs of Charles Trench, bro of 1 Baron Ashtown); *b* 1898; *m* 1924, 6 Baron Sandys (d 1961); 1 s, 1 da; *Style*— The Rt Hon Cynthia, Lady Sandys; Himbleton Manor, nr Droitwich, Worcs

SANDYS, Hon Mrs Edwina; *née* Sandys; da (by 1 m) of Baron Duncan-Sandys, CH, PC; *b* 1938; *m* 1960 (m dis 1973), Pierson John Shirley Dixon, MP, s of late Sir Pierson John Dixon, GCMG, CB; 2 s; has assumed her former surname of Sandys; *Style*— The Hon Mrs Kaplan; 210 E 46th St, NY 10017, USA

SANDYS, Julian George Winston; QC (1983); s (by 1 m) of Baron Duncan-Sandys, CH, PC; does not use Hon title; *b* 1936; *m* 1970, Elisabeth Jane, only da of John Besley Martin, CBE, of Kenton; 3 s, 1 da; *Career* barrister Inner Temple 1959 and Gray's Inn 1970; *Recreations* flying small aeroplanes; *Clubs* Pratts, Tiger; *Style*— Julian Sandys, QC; Charnwood, Shackleford, Godalming, Surrey (☎ 0483 22167)

SANDYS, 7 Baron (UK 1802); Richard Michael Oliver Hill; DL (Worcs 1968); s of 6 Baron Sandys, DL (d 1961), and Cynthia; *b* 21 July 1931; *Educ* RNC Dartmouth; *m* 1961, Patricia Simpson, da of late Capt Lionel Hall, MC; *Heir* cous, Marcus Hill; *Career* sits as a Cons peer in the House of Lords; late Lt Royal Scots Greys; patron of one living; a lord-in-waiting to HM Jan to March 1974, oppn whip House of Lords 1974-79, Capt HM Bodyguard of the Yeomen of the Guard (govt dep chief whip in House of Lords) 1979-82; FRGS; *Clubs* Cavalry & Guards; *Style*— The Rt Hon the Lord Sandys, DL; Ombersley Court, Droitwich, Worcs (☎ 0905 620220)

SANDYS-LUMSDAINE OF THAT ILK AND BLANERNE, Patrick (Gillem); s of Colin Cren Sandys-Lumsdaine (d 1967), of Scotland, and Joyce Dorothy, *née* Leeson; *b* 15 Oct 1938; *Educ* Charterhouse; *m* 1966, Beverley June, da of Capt Ralph Ernest Shorter (d 1982); 2 s (Cren b 1968, James b 1976), 1 da (Amy b 1969); *Career* East India merchant; dir: George Williamson & Co Ltd 1977, George Williamson (Assam) Ltd 1978, Macneill & Magor Ltd 1982; *Recreations* golf; *Clubs* Oriental, Tollygunge, Harewood Downs; *Style*— Lumsdaine of that Ilk and Blanerne; Kinderslegh, Bois Avenue, Chesham Bois, Amersham, Bucks HP6 5NS (☎ 02403 21466); George Williamson & Co Ltd, Sir John Lyon House, 5 High Timber Street, London EC4V 3LD (☎ 248-0471, fax 248-3150, telex 887865)

SANDYS-RENTON, Major James Stapleton Sandys; s of Major Mervyn John Renton (d 1941), and Barbara Frances, *née* Sandys (d 1975); *b* 13 Mar 1926; *Educ* Sherborne, Queens Coll Oxford; *m* 24 April 1957, Elizabeth Anne, da of Major Astley Thomas Terry (d 1971); 2 s (Richard b 1959, William b 1964), 2 da (Jane b 1966, Lucia b 1967); *Career* cmmnd RA 1945, Palestine 1946-48 (despatches), ret 1965 with rank of Maj; memb Stock Exchange 1975, ptnr Cawood Smithie & Co Harrogate 1980; *Recreations* conjuring; *Style*— Major James Sandsy-Renton; Laurel House, Dishfork, Thirsk, N Yorkshire YO7 3LP

SANFORD, Henry Ayshford; o s of Lt-Col Stephen Ayshford Sanford (d 1975), and Princess Olga Mickeladze (d 1955); *b* 26 May 1926; *Educ* Radley, Trinity Coll Cambridge (MA 1949), St Thomas's Hospital Medical Sch (MB, BCh 1951); *m* m 1 16 June 1959, Marcelle Martha Maria, da of late Jean Louis Joseph Ghislain Van Caille, of Prevote St Christophe, Damme, Belgium; 1 s (Anthony Louis Ayshford b 21 March 1960); m 2 1978, Akiko, da of Wakiji Nishida (d 1979), of Japan; 1 da (Marietta Sophia b 1981); *Career* Capt RAMC; assoc conslt Rheumatology Dept St Thomas's Hosp SE1; vice-chm and princ lecturer Cyriax Fndn; *Recreations* shooting, field sports; *Clubs* Savile; *Style*— Henry A Sanford, Esq; Weatherham Farm, Brompton Regis, Somerset TA22 9LG; 59 Harley Street W1 N1AF (☎ 01 935 2414)

SANFORD, (Edward) William Ayshford; s of William Charles Ayshford Sanford (d 1974), of Chipley Park, Somerset, and his 1 w, Rosemary Jean Aileen (d 1968), yr da of Maj Hon Robert Hamilton Lindsay, Royal Scots Grays (s of 26 Earl of Crawford); descended from Henry Sanford (d 1644), of Nynehead, Somerset (of a family traceable since the reign of Richard II), who m Mary, da of Henry Ayshford, of Ayshford,

Devon, where the Ayshfords had been seated since the reign of Henry III (*see* Burke's Landed Gentry, 18 edn, Vol III, 1972); *b* 3 June 1929; *Educ* Summer Fields Oxford, Geelong GS Australia; *m* 21 Jan 1977, Judy Ann, da of Samuel Anthony Parkington Vickery (d 1976), of The Quadrant, Glasgow; 1 s (Edward b 1978), 1 da (Susanna b 1980); *Career* served RHG 1947-49; in business 1950-60; Govt Service: Bahamas 1961-63, Central Office of Information 1964-85; hon tres Taunton Constituency Conservative Assoc; Lord of the Manors of Nynehead and Burlescombe; *Recreations* travel, history, country pursuits; *Clubs* Lansdowne, Old Somerset Dining; *Style—* E W A Sanford, Esq; Chipley Park, Wellington, Somerset (☎ 0823 400 270)

SANGER, Dr Frederick; OM (1986), CH (1981), CBE (1963); s of Frederick Sanger, MD, and Cicely, *née* Crewdson; *b* 13 August 1918; *Educ* Bryanston, St John's Coll Cambridge; *m* 1940, M Joan, da of Alfred Howe; 2 s, 1 da; *Career* res scientist Laboratory of Molecular Biol MRC Cambridge 1951-83 (ret); winner Nobel Prize for Chemisty 1958 and jt 1980; Hon DSc Cambridge 1983; FRS; *Style—* Dr Frederick Sanger, OM, CH, CBE; Far Leys, Fen Lane, Swaffham Bulbeck, Cambridge CB5 0NJ (☎ Cambridge (0223) 811610)

SANGSTER, John Alexander; s of Alexander Findlay Sangster (d 1986), of Watton Norfolk and Doreen Magaret, *née* Bridgeford; *b* 4 July 1936; *Educ* Powis Sch Aberdeen, Twickenham Tech Coll; *m* 1, 1960 (m dis 1963), Violet Taylor; 1 s (Tony Allison b 1963), 1 da (Claire b 1961); m 2, 1964 (m dis 1975), Helen Swatman; 1 s (Alexander John b 1964); *Career* Pilot Offr Zambian Air Force 1967-69; structural engr designer AA Thornton Ltd 1953-58, design draughtsman Br Euro Airways 1958-61, sales exec Liebherr Tower Cranes Germany 1961-63, conslt and md family engrg co Scotland 1963-66, md Lourho Cos Zambia 1966-72 (md/mangr 1972-84, sold 1984), md Silcom Ltd Export Buyers and Business Conslts 1984-; memb N London Rent Assessment Tribunal 1987; memb Rotary Club Lusaka Zambia 1966, currently memb Rotary Club Maidenhead; radio broadcaster Hosp Broadcasting Network 1981-; AMBIM 1970, FInstD 1971; *Recreations* gliding, sporting aircraft, collector and restorer of Rolls Royce vintage automobiles; *Clubs* Rolls Royce Enthusiasts, Bentley Drivers, Wig and Pen; *Style—* John Sangster, Esq; Bix House, Cannon Hill, Bray, Berkshire SL6 2EW (☎ 0628 26833); Silcom Limited, 1 Curfew Yard, Thames St, Windsor, Berkshire SL4 1SN (☎ 0753 855 553, fax 0753 831 320, telex 225710)

SANGSTER, John Laing; s of Albert James Laing Sangster (d 1967), of London and Aberdeen, and Ottile Elizabeth *née* Ritzdorff; *b* 21 Nov 1922; *Educ* Emanuel Sch and Emmanuel Coll, Cambridge, MA (Cantab); *m* 18 Jan 1952, Mary Louise Fitz-Alan, da of Dr George Stuart, OBE, and Dr Elizabeth Gray Stuart; 2 s (Timothy b 1953, Christopher b 1958); *Career* central banker, served in Bank for Int Settlements Basle, and Bank of England 1949-82 becoming asst dir i/c for exchange div; dep chm and chm 1982-86, chm London Forfeiting Co Ltd 1984-86; *Style—* John Sangster

SANKEY, John Anthony; CMG (1983); o s of Henry and Ivy Sankey, of Plumstead Common; *b* 8 June 1930; *Educ* Cardinal Vaughan Sch, Peterhouse Cambridge (MA); *m* 1958, Gwendoline, da of Stanley and Winifred Putman, of Croxley Green; 2s, 2 da; *Career* Lt RA serv Singapore and Malaya 1951-53; FCO: UK Mission to UN New York 1961, dep high cmmr Guyana 1968, cnsllr Singapore 1971, NATO Def Coll Rome 1973, dep high cmmr Malta 1973-75, cnsllr The Hague 1975-79, special cnsllr African Affrs FCO 1979-82, high cmmr to Tanzania 1982-85; perm rep with personal rank of ambass to: UN, GATT, other int orgns at Geneva 1985-; *Clubs* Athenaeum; *Style—* John Sankey, Esq, CMG; United Kingdom Mission, 37/9 Rue de Vermont, Geneva; c/ o Foreign and Commonwealth Office, London SW1

SANSEVERINO, Hon Mrs (Julia Collbran); *née* Cokayne; da (by 1 m) of 2 Baron Cullen; *b* 1943; *m* 1968, Don Francesco Costa Sanseverino; 2 s; *Style—* The Hon Mrs Sanseverino; 75 Cadogan Gdns, SW3

SANT, William Howard; s of Stanley Sant (d 1967), of London, and Mary Sant (d 1976); *b* 22 Mar 1925; *Educ* BEC Secondary Sch, Regent St Poly Sch of Architecture (Dip Arch); *m* 1, 1950, Audrey Elizabeth (m dis 1972); 2 s (David b 1963, Paul b 1965), 3 da (Georgina b 1952, Claire b 1954, Louise b 1957); m 2 4 July 1974, Lesley Anne; 2 s (Dominich b 1976, Adam b 1978); *Career* architect and retail consultant; ptnr J P Bennet and Son 1957-69; snr ptnr Howard Saint Partnership 1969-85; md Saint Design 1985-; ptnr Saint Associates 1984-; princ Howard Sant 1987-; conslt Harrods Ltd 1984-86; AciARB, FRSA, FCSD; *Recreations* walking, yachting; *Clubs* Royal Harwich Yacht; *Style—* Howard Sant, Esq; Royal House, Dedham, Essex CO7 6HD (☎ (0206) 322107, fax (0206) 322930)

SANTER, Rt Rev Mark; s of the Revd Canon Eric Arthur Robert Santer (d 1979), of The Chaplain's Lodge, St Cross, Winchester, Hants, and Phyllis Clare, *née* Barlow (d 1978); *b* 29 Dec 1936; *Educ* Marlborough Coll, Queens Coll Cantab (MA); *m* 3 Oct 1964, Henriette Cornelia, *née* Westrate; 2 da (Hendrika b 1966, Miriam b 1967), 1 s (Diederick b 1969); *Career* curate of Cuddesdon, tutor of Cuddesdon Coll, Oxford 1963-67; fellow and dean Clare Coll Cambridge 1967-72; asst lectr in Divinity Univ Cambridge 1968-72; principal of Westcott House Cambridge 1973-81; bishop of Kensington 1981-87; bishop of Birmingham 1987-88; co-chm Anglican-Roman Catholic Int Cmmn 1983-; hon fell Clare Coll Cambridge 1988; *Style—* The Rt Rev Mark Santer; Bishop's Croft, Old Church Rd, Harborne, Birmingham B17 0BG (☎ (021) 427 1163)

SANTS, (Hector) John; s of Maj Edwin Vincent Sants, MC (d 1954), of Norton St Philip, Som, and Gertrude Rose, *née* Collins (d 1975); descendant of Don Joseph Antonia Dos Santos who sailed from Oporto to Gloucester 1803, where he founded a clay-pipe factory and subsequently in Bath; *b* 26 May 1923; *Educ* Haberdashers' Aske's, Brasenose Coll Oxford (MA); *m* 1952, Elsie Ann, da of William Watt Hepburn (d 1953), of Aberdeen; 1 s (Hector b 1955), 1 da (Harriet b 1953); *Career* MN 1940-47 (ret as 2 Offr); educnl psychologist Kent and Birmingham LEAs 1952-60, lectr in educl psychology Univ Coll of N Wales Bangor 1960-65, lectr and reader in developmental psychology Sussex Univ 1965-86; co-ed (with H J Butcher) of Developmental Psychology: Selected Readings (1974), ed and contrib Developmental Psychology and Society (1980); *Recreations* books, writing; *Style—* John Sants, Esq; Finlarig, Killin, Perthshire (☎ 056 72 259)

SAPHIR, Nicholas Peter George; s of Emanuel Saphir, MBE, and Anne; *b* 30 Nov 1944; *Educ* City of London, Manchester Univ (LLB); *m* 1971, Ena, da of Raphael Bodin; 1 s; *Career* barr; chm Hunter Saphir plc; former chm Food From Britain; memb Food & Drinks EDC; *Recreations* horses, modern art; *Clubs* Farmers'; *Style—* Nicholas Saphir, Esq; Hunter Saphir plc, Whitstable Rd, Faversham, Kent ME13 8BQ

SAPSTEAD, Gordon John; s of Herbert John Sapstead (d 1976), and Dora Lancaster, *née* Jemmett (d 1987); *b* 16 April 1923; *Educ* Hertford GS; *m* 1, 17 July 1947 (m dis); 2 s (Christopher Jolyon b and d 1948, Christopher Hugh b 17 July 1949), 1 da (Rosemary (Mrs Finch) b 12 July 1952); m 2, Jill, da of William Mcconnell, of Rhyl, N Wales; 1 s (Mark Richard b 28 Oct 1977), 2 da (Kathryn b 3 Feb 1973, Nicole b 18 April 1974); *Career* enlisted RAF Aircrew 1941, called up 1942, Pilot Offr 1943, Flying Offr 1944, Fl Lt 1945, Sqdn Ldr 1946; Westminster Bank 1939-42 and 1946-47, exec and managerial appts (India, Pakistan, Bahrain, Qatar) with Eastern Bank and Chartered Bank 1947-65; First Nat Bank of Chicago 1965-: mangr AVP London 1966, mangr VP London 1969, area head Asia Pacific (based Hong Kong) SVP 1975, head of treasy Chicago 1979, head int treasy Geneva 1981, seconded as md and chief exec offr Int Commercial Bank plc 1984; patron and memb Chicago Cncl For Relations; ACIB, MInstD; *Recreations* gardening, walking, golf; *Clubs* RAC, Overseas Bankers; *Style—* Gordon Sapstead, Esq

SARELL, Sir Roderick Francis Gisbert; KCMG (1968, CMG 1958), KCVO (1971); 4 s of Philip Sarell (d 1942), of Braeside, Ashurstwood, E Grinstead; *b* 23 Jan 1913; *Educ* Radley, Magdalen Coll Oxford; *m* 1946, Pamela Muriel, da of Vivian Crowther-Smith; 3 s; *Career* entered Consular Service 1936, cnsllr and consul-gen Rangoon 1953-56, consul-gen Algiers 1956-59, cnsllr FO 1960, ambass: Libya 1964-69, Turkey 1969-73; Coronation medal 1953; *Clubs* Oriental, Leander; *Style—* Sir Roderick Sarell, KCMG, KCVO; The Litten, Hampstead Norreys, Newbury, Berks (☎ 0635 201274)

SARGAN, Prof John Denis; s of Harry Sargan (d 1981), of Humberston, S Humberside, and Gertrude Amy, *née* Porter (d 1984); *b* 23 August 1924; *Educ* Doncaster GS, Cambridge Univ (BA, BA); *m* 4 July 1953, Phyllis Mary, da of Walter Malcolm Millard (d 1969), of Pinner, Middx; 2 s (John b 1954, David b 1955), 1 da (Barbara b 1952); *Career* lectr of econs Univ of Leeds 1948-63; LSE: reader econs 1963-64, prof econs 1964-84, emeritus prof 1984; pres of econometrics Soc 1979-80; FBA 1981, memb American Acad Arts and Scis 1987; *Books* contributions to Econometrics vols 1 and II (1988), Advanced Econometric Theory (1988); *Recreations* painting, bridge, playing the piano, gardening; *Style—* Prof John D Sargan; 49 Dukes Ave, Theydon Bois, Epping, Essex CM16 7HQ (☎ 037 881 2222)

SARGANT, Sir (Henry) Edmund; s of Rt Hon Sir Charles Sargant, Ld Justice of Appeal; *b* 24 May 1906; *Educ* Rugby, Trin Cambridge; *m* 1930, Mary Kathleen (d 1979), da of Tom Lemmey; 1 s; m 2, 1981, Evelyn Noel, *née* Arnold-Wallinger; *Career* served WWII RAF; slr 1930, ptnr Radcliffes & Co 1930-71, pres Law Soc 1968-69; *Style—* Sir Edmund Sargant; 902 Keyes House, Dolphin Square, London SW1V 3NB

SARGANT, Prof Naomi Ellen; *see*: McIntosh of Haringey, Baroness

SARGEANT, Col (William) Anthony Franks; TD 91965); s of Rev William Sargeant (d 1969), of Lichfield Staffs, and Gertrude Eveline, *née* Franks (d 1972); *b* 5 Oct 1929; *Educ* Lancing Coll, Nat Foundry Coll (Dip); *m* 5 Sept 1953, Mary Elizabeth, da of Philip Burns (d 1977), of Tettenhall, Wolverhampton; 1 s (Christopher Peter William b 1956), 1 da (Carolyn Mary b 1961); *Career* 2 Lt RA 1948-50, cmmnd Staff Yeo 1953, Lt-Col cmdg offr 1968-69, appointed TA Col W Mid District 1971-73; dir Baelz Equipment Ltd 1966-75, chm (non exec) Hope Works Ltd 1979; memb Public Sch Exploring Soc; asst ldr of Br Schs Exploring Soc 1952; Br Inst of Mgmnt Dip in Mgmnt Studies 1960, City & Guilds Cert Farm Business Mgmnt 1978 (Silver Medal); DL Staffs 1973; High Sheriff Staffs 1980-81; *Recreations* skiing, sailing, nature conservation; *Style—* Col Anthony Sargeant; Bromesberrow Court, Bromesberrow, nr Ledbury, Herefordshire HR8J 1RU; (☎ 053 181 214)

SARGEAUNT, Lt-Col Henry Anthony (Tony); CB (1961, OBE 1948); s of Lt-Col Henry Sargeaunt (d 1951), and Nora Ierne, *née* Carden Bart (d 1969); *b* 11 June 1907; *Educ* Clfton Coll, Reading Univ, Emanuel Coll Cambridge (BA); *m* 13 July 1937, Winifred Doris, da of John Parkinson (d 1921); 2 s (Anthony John b 1941, David b 1942), 1 da (Julia b 1946); *Career* WWII, Maj HQ 21 Army Gp 1941-47, Lt-Col Supt Army Operational Gp 1947-52, IDC 1952-53; scientific advsr: WO Army Cncl 1953-56, Defence Res Policy Ctee 1953-56, SHAPE and NATO 1959, Palais de Chaillot 1960; chief scientist Home Office 1960-67, ret 1967, conslt to UNO NY 1967-68; memb Operational Res Soc 1947, fndr memb Br Soc of the History of Sci; *Books* Grand Strategy (1941); *Recreations* fly fishing, horse racing, beagling, sailing, golf; *Clubs* Brokenhurst Fly Fishing, Bibury HR RLYC, Brockenhurst; *Style—* Lt-Col Tony Sargeaunt, CB, OBE; 7 Bond Close, SWay, Lyminton, Hants (☎ 0590 683112)

SARGENT, Hon Dr (Caroline Mary); *née* McLaren; does not use husband's surname; yr da of 3 Baron Aberconway by his 1 wi, Deirdre, *née* Knewstub; *b* 24 Oct 1944; *Educ* Imperial Coll London (BSc, DIC, PhD, FLS); *m* 1, 1962, Raimund Guernsey Sargent, of Massachusetts; 2 s (Dominic b 1963; Orlando b 1964); m 2, 1978, Graham Charles Steele, BSc, PhD; *Career* botanist, scientific Civil Service; holder of the Ness Award for Exploration 1986, of the Royal Geographical Soc; *Style—* The Hon Dr Sargent; Beaulieu Hall, Hemington, Oundle, Northants; work: Inst of Terrestrial Ecology, Monks Wood, Abbots Ripon, Cambs (☎ (048 73) 381)

SARGENT, (John Richard) Dick; s of Sir John Philip Sargent, CIE (d 1972), and Ruth Taunton (d 1932); *b* 22 Mar 1925; *Educ* Dragon Sch, Rugby, Christ Church Oxford (BA, MA);; *m* 1, July 16 1949 (m dis 1980), Anne Elizabeth, da of Lt Col John F Haigh, MBE (d 1976); 1 s (Simon b 1953), 2 da (Sally b 1950, Vicky b 1957); m 2, Oct 1980, Hester Mary, wid of Dr J D E Campbell, 3 step s (Francis, Laurence, Nicholas); *Career* RN 1943-46, Sub Lt RNVR 1945; lectr in econs and fell Worcester Coll Oxford 1951-62, econ conslt HM Treasy 1963-65; prof and fndr memb dept of econs Univ of Warwick 1964-73 (pro vice-chllr 1970-72); gp econ advsr Midland Bank 1974-84 (ex-officio ed Midland Bank Review), economic advsr Miny of Technol 1969-71, memb Doctors and Dentists Pay Review Body 1972-75, memb Armed Forces Pay Review Body 1972-86, cncl memb Royal Econ Soc 1969-74, govr Nat Inst for Econ Res 1969-, pres Societé de Recherches Financiéres 1985-88 (cncl memb 1976-); tres comforts and amenities fund Burford Hosp 1986-, former memb educn ctee City of Oxford; author of numerous articles in econ jnls;; *Books* British Transport Policy (1958); *Recreations* gardening; *Clubs* Reform; *Style—* Dick Sargent, Esq; Trentham House, Fulbrook, Burford, Oxon OX8 4BL (☎ 099 382 3525)

SARGENT, Prof Roger William Herbert; s of Herbert Alfred Sargent (d 1959), and May Elizabeth, *née* Gill (d 1933); *b* 14 Oct 1926; *Educ* Bedford Sch, Imperial Coll (BSc PhD DIC, DSc); *m* 11 Aug 1951, Shirley Jane Levesque, da of Archer Wilfrid Spooner (d 1973); 2 s (Philip Michael b 1 Aug 1954, Anthony John b 26 Dec 1955); *Career* asst lectr Imperial Coll London 1950-51, design engr Air Liquide Paris 1951-58, Imperial Coll London 1958-: sr lectr 1958-62, prof of chem engrg 1962-66, Courtaulds prof of chem engrg 1966-, dean City and Guilds Coll 1973-76, head dept of chem engrg and chem technol 1975-88, memb governing body 1967-77 and 1979-87, memb bd of studies chem engrg Univ of London 1966-69; pres Inst of Chem Engrs 1973-74 (vice pres 1969-71 and 1972-73), chm chem engrg and technol ctee SRC 1971-73 (memb 1969-73), chm process pland ctee DTI 1981-87 (memb 1980-81), chm engrg and technol advsy ctee Br Cncl 1984- (memb 1976-); memb: technol sub ctee UGC 1984-, Br-French Mixed Cultural Cmmn 1985-, Br nat ctee for Int Engrg Affairs 1987-, ed advsy bd of Computers and Chem Engrg; ed of various learned jls and prolific contrib to scientific literature; Hon FCGI 1976, Docteur Honoris Causa Institut National Polytechnique De Lorraine 1987; ACGI, FIChemE 1964, FIMA 1972, FEng 1976 ACGI; *Style—* Prof Roger Sargent; Mulberry cottage, 291A Sheen Rd, Richmond upon Thames, Surrey TW10 5AW (☎ 01 876 9623); Imperial college, London SW7 2BY (☎ 01 589 5111 ext 4301, fax 01 584 7596, telex 929 484 IMPCOL G)

SARGINSON, David Richard; s of Richard Herbert Sarginson (d 1984), and Ursula Rose, *née* Brown (d 1950); *b* 9 May 1936; *Educ* Wrekin Coll Shropshire; *m* 28 Sept 1961, Pamela Ann, da of Stephen James Clifford (d 1967); 1 s (Mark Richard b 1964); 1 da (Jane Elizabeth b 1962); *Career* slr; HM coroner for City of Coventry 1985; fndr of Sarginson & Co Slrs in Coventry and Leamington Spa; chm West Midlands Rent Assessment Panel 1985; chm and md Sarginson Bros Ltd; manufacturers of foundry equipment and aluminium fndrs automotive industry; *Recreations* france, its life and good food, music; *Clubs* Drapers Coventry; *Style—* David Sarginson, Esq; Abbeyfield Lodge, Castle Road, Kenilworth, Warwickshire (☎ 0926 55272); 11 Warwick Row Coventry (☎ 0203 553181, fax 0203 58573)

SARKANY, Imrich; s of Dr Edmund Sarkany (d 1938), and Maria *née* Pollitzer; *b* 7 Jan 1923; *Educ* St Thomas' Hosp Medical Sch; *m* 12 Dec 1956, Helen Ruth Veronica, da of Israel Pomerance, of St Albans; 1 da (Elizabeth b 1960), 2 s (Robert b 1962, Andrew b 1965); *Career* Czechoslovak Armoured brigade Gt Britain 1944-45; physician (diseases of the skin); consultant dermatologist Royal Free Hosp 1960-; pres: British Assoc of Dermatologists 1987-88, dermatology section RSM 1981-82, monosection for dermato-venereology of European Union of Medical Specialists 1987-, St Johns' Dermatological Society 1976-77, Dermatological Bowling Club; memb: Bd of Gov Royal Free Hosp, cncl RSM; fndr chm British Soc for Investigative Dermatology; *Style—* Imrich Sarkany, Esq; 2 Romney Close, London NW11 7JD; 132 Harley St, W1 (☎ (01) 935 3678)

SAROOP, Narindar; CBE (1982); s of Chief Ram Saroop (d 1988), of Lahore and Chandigarh, and Shyam *née* Devi (d 1981); *b* 14 August 1929; *Educ* Aitchison Coll for Punjab Chiefs Lahore, Indian Mil Acad Dehra Dun, India; *m* 1, Oct 1952 (m dis 1967), Ravi Gill, da of the Sardar of Premgarh (d 1968), of Goodwood, Simla, Punjab, India; 1 s (Vijayendra b 1953), 2 da (Vaneeta b 1954, Kavita b 1961); m 2, Feb 1968, Stephanie Denise (d 1983), da of Alexander Panyotis Cronopulo (d 1977), of Zakynthos, Greece; *Career* 2 Royal Lancers (Gardner's Horse), Queen Victoria's Own The Poona Horse, served as Sqdn Offr, Regtl Signals Offr, Regtl Gunnery Offr, Actg Sqdn Ldr; mgmnt trainee Yule Catto & Co Ltd 1954-55, sr exec Andrew Yule & Co Ltd 1955-61; subsidiary bd dir: Davy Ashmore Gp 1961-64, Turner & Newall Gp 1965-71, mgmnt consultancy 1972-76; devpt advsr H Clarkson Gp 1976-87, conslt Banque Belge 1987-; pres India Welfare Soc 1984-; cncl memb: The Freedom Assoc 1980-88, Inst of Dirs 1983-; memb: BBC Advsy Panel 1977-80, Charity Organs Review Royal Borough of Kensington and Chelsea 1974-; contested (Cons) Greenwich general election 1979 (first Asian Tory Party candidate this century), cncllr Royal Borough of Kensington and Chelsea 1974-82; fndr and chm: Anglo Asian Cons Soc 1976-79 and 1985-86, The Durbar Club 1981-;; *Books* In Defence of Feedom (jtly, 1978), A Squire of Hindustan (1985); *Style—* Narindar Saroop, Esq, CBE; 25 de Vere Gdns, London W8

SARSON, Hon Mrs; Hon Gillian Isolda Josephine; *née* Pollock; o da of 2 Viscount Hanworth; *b* 1 April 1944; *m* 24 Aug 1963, Timothy von Weber Sarson; 2 s, 2 da; *Style—* Hon Mrs Sarson; 8 Gatcombe Rd, N19

SARTIN, John Henry; s of Arthur Henry Sartin, of Hertford, and Mona, *née* Weston; *b* 2 Mar 1945; *Educ* Hertford GS; *m* 7 Sept 1974, Mary Stewart, da of George Newlands (d 1986), of Welwyn Garden City; 1 s (David b 1978), 1 da (Jane b 1976); *Career* self employed shopkeeper; Cons memb Hertford Borough Cncl 1970-73, ldr East Herts DC 1986- (memb 1973), chm Herts Assoc Dist Cncls 1986-87, chaired various ctees incl housing 1979-81; memb Hertford CAB mgmt cmmn, govr Richard Hale Sch Hertford; *Recreations* family, some DIY, the box in the corner; *Clubs* Hertford; *Style—* John Sartin, Esq; 2 Park Rd, Hertford (☎ 0992 553 335); 15 Market Place, Hertford (☎ 0992 584 889)

SARUM, Archdeacon of; *see*: Hopkinson, Ven Barnabas John (Barney)

SAS, Tadeusz Robert; JP (Inner London 1977); s of Tadeusz Julian Sas, of London (d 1974), and Zofia T Sas; *b* 13 Dec 1941; *Educ* Harrow; *m* 1967, Irena Eugenia; 2 s, 2 da; *Career* chm and md: Sas Gp of Cos Ltd, Sas Admin Services Ltd, Sas Devpts Ltd, Sas Chemicals Ltd, Sas Pharmaceuticals Ltd, Sas R & D Services Ltd, Sas of America Inc, Sas (Jersey) Ltd, Elektromodul Ltd, Varimex Ltd; vice chm Anglo Polish Conservative Assoc (APCS) 1967; memb Westminster City Council 1964-71 (also served on various ctees); ctee memb Assoc of Br Chemical Manufacturers 1972-75; ctee memb Defence Manufacturers Assoc 1978-82; memb Int Assoc of Bomb Technicians and Investigators 1974-; FBIM, FInstM, MNDEA; kt Cdr Order of Polonia Restituta 1980; *Recreations* sleeping, work; *Clubs* Carlton, Surf (Miami), Les Ambassadeurs (London); *Style—* Tadeusz Sas, Esq, JP; Craven House, Hamstead Marshall, Newbury, Berks RG15 0JG (radiophone (0039) 222521); 10350 Old Cutler Road, South Miami, Florida 33156, USA (☎ (305) 667 8494); Villa Annabell, Atalaya Park, Estepona, Malaga, Spain (☎ 78 13 98); Sas Group of Companies, Sas Gp House, Wycombe End, Beaconsfield, Bucks HP9 1LZ (☎ 04946-78181, telex 24508)

SASSOON, David; s of George Sassoon, and Victoria, *née* Gurgi; *b* 5 Oct 1932; *Educ* Chelsea Coll of Art, RCA; *Career* fashion designer, joined Belinda Belville 1958, first Ready to Wear Collection 1963, dir 1964, co became Belville Sassoon 1970, sole shareholder 1983; licencee: Vogue Butterick USA 1966, Japan 1988; *Recreations* theatre, ballet; *Style—* David Sassoon, Esq; Bellville Sassoon, 73 Pavilion Road, London SW1 (☎ 01 235 3087)

SATCHELL, Keith; s of Dennis Joseph Satchell, of Hemel Hempstead, and Joan Betty, *née* Elms; *b* 3 June 1951; *Educ* Hemel Hempstead GS, Univ of Aston (BSc); *m* 1 July 1972, Hazel Dorothy, da of Douglas Burston, of Birmingham; 2 s (Paul b 1978, Richard b 1980), 1 da (Olivia b 1984); *Career* gen mangr (Products) Friends Provident Life Office 1987-; govr of Middle Sch Verwood; FIA 1976; *Recreations* sport, reading; *Style—* Keith Satchell, Esq; Oakfield, 63 Moorlands Road, Verwood, Dorset BH21 6PD (☎ 0202 824 118); Friends Provident, 72/122 Castle St, Salisbury, Wilts (☎ 0722 336 242)

SATTERTHWAITE, Rt Rev John Richard; *see*: Gibraltar in Europe, Bishop of

SAUGMAN, Per Gotfred; s of Emanuel A G Saugman (d 1962), and Esther, *née* Lehmann (d 1986); *b* 26 June 1925; *Educ* Gentofte GS, Commercial Coll Copenhagen; *m* 28 Dec 1950, Patricia, da of William Henry Fulford (d 1982); 3 s (Peter b 1951, Philip b 1955), and 1 s decd, 1 da (Penelope b 1959); *Career* bookselling and publishing try in Denmark, Switzerland, England 1941-49, sales mangr Blackwell Scientific Pubns Ltd 1952, dir Univ Bookshops (Oxford) Ltd 1963; chm: Wm George's Sons Ltd 1965, Blackwell N America Inc 1973, Einar Munksgaard Publishers Copenhagen 1967, Kooyker Boehandel Leiden 1973; chm Blackwell Scientific Pubns Ltd 1972- (md 1954-87); memb: Int Publishers Assoc 1976-79, Publishers Assoc of GB and Ireland 1977-82; hon memb Br Ecological Soc 1960-; govr: Oxford Poly 1972-82, Dragon Sch 1975; Hon MA (Oxon) 1978, fell Green Coll, Oxford 1981; *Recreations* reading, art, English, watercolours, golf; *Clubs* Athenaeum, RAC, Frilford Golf (Oxford); *Style—* Per Saugman, Esq; Sunningwood House, Lincombe Lane, Boars Hill, Oxford OX1 5DZ (☎ 735503); Blackwell Scientific Publications Ltd, Osney Mead, Oxford OX2 0EL (☎ 240201, telex 83355 MEDBOK G, fax 721205)

SAUL, Philip Bycroft; s of Maj John Bycroft Saul, MC (d 1946), and Juliana Margaret, *née* Watson (d 1987); *b* 19 Feb 1933; *Educ* Dover Coll, St Edmund Hall Oxford (MA); *m* 31 July 1956, Jane, da of Maj Gerald William Gostwyck May (d 1963); 2 s (George, Thomas), 3 da (Dorothy, Frances, Lucy); *Career* slr 1959, sr ptnr Stringer Saul; *Recreations* rifle shooting, skiing; *Style—* Philip Saul, Esq; 6 Wyndham Mews, London W1 (☎ 01 262 4013); Valbonne, Alpes-Maritimes, France; Marcol House, 293 Regent St, London W1 (☎ 01 631 4048, fax 01 636 2306, telex 267427)

SAUL, Roger John; s of (Frederick) Michael Saul, of Chilcompton, Somerset, and Joan *née* Legg; *b* 25 July 1950; *Educ* Kingswood Sch Bath, Westminster Coll London; *m* 23 July 1977, Marion Joan, da of Clifford Cameron; 3 s (William Michale, Cameron Robert, Frederick Jakes); *Career* fndr, creator, designer and md of Mulberry Co 1971-, awarded Queen's Award for Export 1979, BKCEC Exporter of the Year 1987-88, brand label in British contemporary classic fashion worldwide; memb Bd BKCEC; *Recreations* tennis, historic car racing, skiing, shooting, garden design; *Style—* Roger Saul, Esq; Mulberry Company, Chilcompton, Bath, Somerset (☎ 0761 237855, fax 0761 232876, telex 444305)

SAUMAREZ; *see*: de Saumarez

SAUMAREZ, Hon Eric Douglas; er twin s and h of 6 Baron de Saumarez, *qv*; *b* 13 August 1956; *Educ* Milton Abbey, Nottingham Univ, RAC Cirencester; *m* 14 July 1982, Christine Elizabeth, yr da of Bernard Neil Halliday, OBE, of Woodford Green, Essex; 2 da (Claire b 1984, Emily b 1985); *Career* farmer; *Recreations* shooting, fishing, flying, driving, sailing; *Style—* The Hon Eric Saumarez; Vicarage Farm, Coddenham, Suffolk (☎ 044 979 573)

SAUMAREZ, Hon Victor Thomas; s (yr twin) of 6 Baron de Saumarez; *b* 13 August 1956; *Educ* Milton Abbey, Exeter Univ (BA); *Style—* The Hon Victor Saumarez; c/o Shrubland Hall, Coddenham, Suffolk IP6 9QH (☎ Ipswich (0473) 830404/832202)

SAUNDERS, Basil; s of Cdr John Edward Saunders, RN (missing presumed dead 1941), and Marjorie Saunders, *née* Purdon (d 1983); *b* 12 August 1925; *Educ* Merchant Taylors' Sch, Wadham Coll Oxford (MA); *m* 1957, Betty, da of Victor Smith (d 1957); 2 s (William, Edward), 4 da (Kate, Louisa, Etta, Charlotte); *Career* Sub Lt RNVR 1943-46; asst D'Anglais College De Tarascon 1951-52, writer General Electric (USA) 1953-54, pub rels offr BIM 1954-57, consultant Pritchard Wood (later Infoplan) 1958-63), head of pub rels The Wellcome Fndn 1963-78, dir gen ASLIB 1978-80, conslt Traverse-Healy Ltd 1981-84, dir Traverse-Healy & Regester Ltd 1984-87, dir Charles Barker Traverse Healy 1987-; FIPR; *Books* Crackle of Thorns (1968); *Clubs* Savile; *Style—* Basil Saunders Esq; 18 Dartmouth Park Ave, London NW5 1JN (☎ 01 485 4672); Charles Barker Traverse-Healy Ltd, 30 Farringdon St, London EC4A 4EA (☎ 01 634 1000)

SAUNDERS, Christopher John; s of Rupert Henry Saunders (d 1977), of Guildford, Surrey, and Gladys Susan, *née* Harris (d 1975); *b* 7 May 1940; *Educ* Lancing, Fitwilliam Coll Cambridge (MA), Wadham Coll Oxford (Cert Ed); *m* 27 Oct 1973, Cynthia Elizabeth J P, da of Harold Deverell Stiles, TD, JP, of Hove, Sussex; 1 s (Jonathan b 31 March 1975), 1 da (Lucy b 29 Aug 1976); *Career* Housemaster Bradfield 1972-80 (asst master 1964-80), headmaster Eastbourne Coll 1981-; Oxford Blue: Soccer 1963, Cricket 1964; memb MCC cricket tour 1967, chm Independant Sch FA 1981-; govr: St Andrews Schy Eastbourne E Sussex, Ashdown House Forest Row E Sussex, Stoke Brunswick Sch Ashurst Wood E Sussex, Holmewood House Langton Green kent, Harris Hill Newbury Berks; FA (cncl memb 1982-); *Recreations* cricket, soccer, gardening, theatre, listening to music, meeting people; *Clubs* Hawks (Cambridge), MCC; *Style—* Christopher Saunders, Esq; Headmaster House, Eastbourne College, Eastbourne, East Sussex, BN21 4JX (☎ 0323 37655)

SAUNDERS, Christopher Thomas; CMG (1953); s of Thomas Beckenn Avening Saunders (d 1950), and Mary Theodora Slater (d 1928); *b* 5 Nov 1907; *Educ* St Edwards Oxford, ChCh Oxford (BA); *m* 1947, Cornelia Jacomijntje, da of Tjisse Gielstra (d 1957), of The Netherlands; 1 s (John); *Career* economist Liverpool and Manchester Univs 1930-35; jt ctee Cotton Trade 1935-40, govr Cotton Control 1940-45; civil servant Miny of Labour and Central Statistical Off 1945-57, dir Nat Inst for Econ and Social Research London 1957-65, research dir UN Econ Cmmn for Europe Geneva 1965-73, prof Sussex Euro Research Centre Sussex Univ 1973-84, visiting fell (part-time) Science Policy Research Unit Sussex Univ 1984-; *Books* Seasonal Variations in Employment (1936), Pay Inequalities in EEC (1981), many anonymous contributions to official national and international reports, numerous journal articles and editing of conference transactions; *Recreations* walking, travel, painting; *Clubs* Reform; *Style—* Christopher Thomas Saunders, Esq, CMG; 73 Wick Hall, Furze Hill, Hove, E Sussex BN3 1NG (☎ (0273) 24219)

SAUNDERS, Dame Cicely Mary Strode; DBE (1980, OBE 1967); da of Philip Gordon Saunders (d 1961), of The Chase, Hadley Common, Barnet and Mary Christian Knight (d 1968); *b* 22 June 1918; *Educ* Roedean, St Anne's Coll Oxford, St Thomas's Hosp Med Sch; *m* 1980, Prof Marian Bohusz-Szyszko, s of Antoni Bohusz-Szyszko, of Wilno, Poland; *Career* fndr and medical dir St Christopher's Hospice, London SE26; dep chm Attendance Allowance Bd; Hon DSc Yale 1969, DUniv Open Univ 1978, DHL Jewish Theol Seminary of America 1982, Gold Medal Soc of

Apothecaries of London 1979, Templeton Fndn Award 1981, Hon LLD Leicester 1983, Hon DUniv Essex 1983, Hon DSc London 1983, Hon LLD Oxford 1986; Hon LLD Cambridge 1986, awarded British Medical Assocn Gold Medal, 1987; *Recreations* home; *Style*— Dame Cicely Saunders, DBE; St Christopher's Hospice, 51-59 Lawrie Park Rd, Sydenham, SE26 6DZ (☎ 01 778 9252); 50 Lawrie Park Gdns, Sydenham, SE26 (T 01 778 9252)

SAUNDERS, Cynthia Anne; *née* Llewellyn; da of Frank Horace Llewellyn (d 1961), of Walsall, and Ivy Evelyn, *née* Gwinnutt (d 1968); *b* 27 June 1939; *Educ* Joseph Leckie Comprehensive, Walsall Coll of Technol, Wenesbury Coll of Commerce; *m* 17 Sept 1960, Kenneth Thomas Saunders, s of Thomas Samuel Spencer Saunders, of Willenhall; 2 s (Mark Ryan b 1964, Jared Llewellyn b 1967); *Career* gp co sec Blue Ribbon Equestrian Gp 1972-79, co sec and dir Qualis Gp of Cos 1979-; Girl Guide Assoc: PR advsr Midlands, PR advsr W Mercia County; pres Soroptimist Int (Walsall Club) 1989-90 (sr vice pres 1988-89); FFA 1976; *Recreations* swimming, reading; *Style*— Mrs Kenneth Saunders; 16 Riding Way, Huntlands, Willenhall, West Midlands WV12 5PH (☎ 0922 476 058); Qualis Gp, Noose Lane, Willenhall, West Midland WV13 3LW (☎ 0902 366 789, fax 0902 368 844)

SAUNDERS, Brigadier (Arthur) David (Rich); MBE (1947); s of Maj Harold Cecil Rich Saunders DSO (ka 1918); and Dorothy May, *née* Triscott (d 1974); *b* 5 July 1917; *Educ* Clifton, RMC Sandhurst; *m* 3 July 1948, Margaret Mitchell, da of Robert Bell (ka 1914), of Dumfrieshire; 1 s (Christopher b 10 October 1940); *Career* cmmnd 2 Lt E Yorks Regt 1937, Dunkirk evacuation 1940, Staff Coll Camberly 1941, Bde Maj 198 Inf Bde 1942, GS02 WO (SD) 1942, Bde Maj 197 Inf Bde NW Europe 1944-45, RAF Staff Coll 1945, Bde Maj 161 Ind Inf Bde 1945-46 Burma (Burma Star 1945), Netherlands, E Indies, India) (despatches 1946); GS02 WO 1947-48, seconded to Jamaica Regt 1948-51, dep asst mily sec WO 1952-54, OC E York Regtl Depot 1955-56, 2 Cmmd 1 Bn E York Regt BAOR 1957-58, Lt-Col GS01 Allied Forces S Europe Naples 1958, OC 1 Bn Yorks & Lancs Regt Berlin BAOR 1959-62, Col (Milr Trg) WO 1963, Cdr (Brig) 47 Inf Bde TA, 1964-66 Brig i/c Admin HQ Southern Cmmd and later HQ Army Strategic Cmmd, 1966-68, ret 1968; sr inspector: DoE 1974 (main grade housing & planning inspector DoE 1969), Welsh Office 1975, ret 1986; hon sec (planning) Cncl for Protection of Rural Wales (Pembrokeshire Branch) 1988-; *Recreations* gardening, walking; *Clubs* Army and Navy; *Style*— Brig David Saunders, MBE; Castle House, Castlefield, Narberth, Pembrokeshire, Dyfed SA67 8SW (☎ 0834 860979)

SAUNDERS, David Martin St George; s of Hilary Aidan St George Saunders CBE, MC, of, Broadway, Sussex (d Nassau 1951), and Helen Foley (d Geneva 1937); f was a professional author (under the pseudonyms of Francis Beeding and David Pilgrim), offical historial for the RAF in WWII, and librarian of the House of Commons for some years; *b* 23 July 1930; *Educ* Marlborough; RMA Sandhurst; Staff Coll Quetta, Pakistan; *m* 23 July 1960, Patricia Sybil, da of J H Methold, CBE (d 1984); 1 s (Rupert b 1965), 1 da (Camilla b 1968); *Career* cmmnd Welsh Gds 1950; Staff Capt 1 Gds Bde, Egypt 1954-56; Asst Adj RMA Sandhurst 1956-58; Adj 1 Battalion Welsh Gds, Pirbright 1958-60; GSO III The War Off 1960-62; Staff Coll Quetta 1963; Co Cdr 1 Bn Welsh Gds 1964; GSO II Br Def Liaison Staff, Canberra 1965-67; Co Cdr Gds Depot Pirbright 1967-68; joined the Foreign & Cwlth Off 1968; FCO London 1968-70; consul econ Johannesburg 1970-72; first sec: FCO London 1973-74, Dakar 1974-76, FCO 1976-77, Pretoria 1977-79, The Hague 1979-83; cncllr FCO London 1983-; *Recreations* cinema, skiing, military history, wines of Burgundy, shooting; *Style*— David M Saunders, Esq; c/o National Westminster Bank, 246 Westminster Bridge Rd, London SE7

SAUNDERS, Sandy - David Michael; RD; s of Aubrey Saunders, of High Mount, London NW4, and Rosie Leonie Finestone; *b* 23 June 1935; *Educ* Highgate Sch, Stafford Coll of Technology; *m* 1958, Rosemary Ann, da of Trevor Smith, of Surrey Rd, Bournemouth; 4 da; *Career* Lt Cdr Royal Naval Reserve; chm: Howmac plc, Mellerware Int plc, Eagle Electro Optic, Boston Investmt Mgmnt Gp Ltd; dir and former chm Eagle Tst plc and Evered Hldgs plc; *Recreations* squash, sailing, bridge; *Clubs* RNVR; *Style*— Sandy Saunders, Esq, RD; 1 Riding House Street, London W1P 7PA

SAUNDERS, David William; s of William Ernest Saunders, of 5 Ernest Rd, Horchurch, Essex, and Lilian Grace, *née* Ward (d 1987); *b* 4 Nov 1936; *Educ* Hornchurch GS, Worcester Coll Oxford (BA, MA); *m* 15 April 1963, Margaret Susan Rose, da of William Colin Bartholomew (d 1980), of 7C Friese Greene House, Chelsea Manor St, London; *Career* Nat Serv RAF 1955-57 (Russian Linguist), articled clerk later slr private pratice 1960-69; Parly Counsel: asst counsel 1970-75, on loan to Law Cmmn 1972-74, sr asst counsel 1975-78, dep counsel 1978-80, counsel 1980-, on loan to Law Cmmn as sr draftsman 1986-87; memb Law Soc 1964-; *Recreations* bridge, golf; *Style*— David Saunders, Esq; 104A Belgrave Rd, London SW1V 2BJ (☎ 01 834 4403); Office of the Parliamentary Counsel, 36 Whitehall, London SW1 (☎ 01 210 6602)

SAUNDERS, Emma Elizabeth (Mrs Peter Earl); da of Peter Saunders, of London, and Patricia Mabel, *née* Annesley; *b* 14 May 1955; *Educ* Godolphin and Latymer, Oxford (BA, MA); *m* 19 Jan 1980, Peter Richard Stephen Earl, s of Peter Richard Walter Earl; 1 s (Richard b 10 March 1987), 1 da (Amelia-Rose b 8 July 1985); *Career* Layard Bros & Co Ltd 1977-80, vice pres Bear Stearns Int 1980-84, dir and fndr memb Tranwood Earl 1985-, chm and fndr memb Analysis Corpn plc 1988-; FIMBRA; *Recreations* riding, skiing, picture restoration and framing; *Style*— Ms Emma Saunders; 41 Moore Street, London SW3 (☎ 01 589 2560); Tranwood Earl & Company Ltd, 125 Sloane St, London SW1 9BW (☎ 01 730 3412, fax 01 730 5770, telex 932016 SLOANE G)

SAUNDERS, Jeremy Martin; s of Lt-Col John Grant Saunders (d 1973), of New Barn Farm, Seer Green, Beaconsfield, Bucks, and Helen, *née* McNeill; *b* 7 May 1933; *Educ* Repton; *m* 4 April 1959 (m dis 1968), Alaine Caroline Winnifred, da of Alan Paul Joell; *Career* Nat Serv Lt 16/5 Queen's Royal Lancers 1951-53, Capt Staff Yeo (TA) 1954-62; film and tv prodr 1956-; asst dir and film ed for Br and American Corpns, recent work incl exec prodr The Shooting Party; memb: Br Acad Film and TV Arts, Br Film and TV Prodrs Assoc; *Recreations* off shore sailing, travel, the media; *Clubs* Garrick; *Style*— Jeremy Saunders, Esq; 4 Embankment Gdns, London SW3 4LJ (☎ 01 352 1683)

SAUNDERS, Joanna Christina; da of Col John Offley Crewe-Read, OBE, of Aston Tirrold, Didcot, Oxon, and Hon Diana Mary, *née* Robins; *b* 13 Dec 1941; *Educ* Rye St Anthony, Oxford; *m* 1, 28 April 1962 (m dis 1969), Capt John A F Morton, late RHA; m 2, 1 March 1974, Alasdair James Hew Saunders, s of Capt L S Saunders, RN, DSO, of Rockington, Market Harborough, Leics; 2 s (Dominic b 1964, Tom b 1977), 2 da (Serena b 1966, Alice b 1975); *Career* interior designer, previously researcher for Lady Antonia Pinter Kenneth Tynan, worked in theatre, reader to lit agents; design works incl: American banks, city offices, company flats, houses for prominent Greek families, many private house in London, etc; *Recreations* books, opera, music, art, travel; *Clubs* Hurlingham; *Style*— Mrs Alasdair Saunders; 17 The Little Boltons, London SW10 9LJ; Pastures House, Pockingham, Leics (☎ 01 373 5314)

SAUNDERS, Sir John Anthony Holt; CBE (1970), DSO (1945), MC (1944); s of E B Saunders of Kidderminster; *b* 29 July 1917; *Educ* Bromsgrove Sch; *m* 1942, Enid Mary Durant, da of C D Cassidy of London; 2 da; *Career* former chm International Commercial Bank London, chm Hong Kong and Shanghai Banking Corpn and of London Ctee 1964-72; JP 1955-72 Hong Kong, MEC 1966-72; kt 1972; *Style*— Sir John Saunders, CBE, DSO, MC; The Dairy House, Maresfield Park, Uckfield, East Sussex

SAUNDERS, Prof Sir Owen Alfred; s of Alfred George Saunders and Margaret Ellen Jones; *b* 24 Sept 1904; *Educ* Emanuel Sch, Birkbeck Coll London, Trin Coll Cambridge (MA, DSc); *m* 1, 1935, Marion McKechney (d 1981); 1 s, 2 da; m 2, 1981, Mrs Daphne Holmes; *Career* emeritus prof mechanical engrg Imperial Coll London (actg rector 1966-67, pro-rector 1964-67, head dept 1946-65, prof 1946), vice-chllr London Univ 1967-69; past pres IMechE, pres Br Flame Research Ctee, chm cncl Royal Holloway Coll 1971-; hon memb: Yugoslav Acad 1959-, Japan Soc Mech Engrs 1960-, Mark Twain Soc 1976-; Hon FIMechE, Hon FCGI, Hon DSc Strathclyde; FRS, FEng, FInstP, FInstF, FRAeS, life memb ASME; kt 1965; *Clubs* Athenaeum; *Style*— Prof Sir Owen Saunders; Oak Bank, 19 Sea Lane, Middleton-on-Sea, West Sussex PO22 7RX (☎ (0243) 692966)

SAUNDERS, Sir Peter; s of Ernest and Aletta Saunders; *b* 23 Nov 1911; *Educ* Oundle, Lausanne; *m* 1, 1959, Ann Stewart (d 1976); m 2, 1979, Catherine Imperiali di Francavilla (Katie Boyle, *qv*); *Career* impresario (profns incl Agatha Christie's The Mousetrap); chm & md Peter Saunders Ltd, Volcano Productions; dir Theatre Investmnt Finance Ltd, West End Theatre Managers Ltd, Dominfast Investmnts, Duke of York's Theatre Ltd; former film dir and journalist; former dir Yorkshire TV; vice-pres Actors' Benevolent Fund, memb exec cncl Soc of West End Theatre (pres 1961-62 and 1967-69); kt 1981; *Style*— Sir Peter Saunders; Vaudeville Theatre Offices, 10 Maiden Lane, London WC2E 7NA (T 01 240 3177)

SAUNDERS, Richard; s of Richard Edward Saunders (d 1971), of Henley-on-Thames, and Betty, *née* Belsey; *b* 4 July 1937; *Educ* St Edmund's Sch Hindhead, Uppingham; *m* 1, 21 Sept 1961, Suzannah, da of Thomas Rhodes-Cooke (d 1985), of Chiswick; 1 s (Andrew b 1964); m 2, 12 June 1970, Alison, da of Maj J A Fiddes (d 1964) of Wimbledon; *Career* 2 Lt LG 1958-60, served in Germany; govr Royal Star and Garter Home 1984-; chartered surveyor; chm: Baker Harris Saunders Gp plc 1986-, CityBranch RICS 1979-80, Metropolitan Public Gdns Assoc 1984-; dep for Ward of Chandlewick 1983-; Sheriff City of London 1987-88; bd Gen Practice Finance Corp 1985; govr and almoner Christ's Hosp 1980-, govr Bridewell Royal Hosp and King Edward's Sch Witley 1976-; dir: Baker Harris Saunders Ltd, Br Property Fedn St Edmunds Sch Tst Ltd, Gen Practice Finance Corp, Star and Garter Trading and Promotions Ltd; memb: Cncl Br Property Fedn 1974 (hon tres 1974-85), Ct of Common Cncl Corpn of London 1975-; pres Associated Owners of City Properties 1984-86; Liveryman Worshipful Co of: Clothworkers' 1960, Chartered Surveyors 1979; FRICS; *Recreations* golf, tennis (lawn and real), music; *Clubs* Cavalry and Guards, MCC, City Livery; *Style*— Richard Saunders, Esq; 13 Caroline Place, London W2 4AW (☎ 01 727 1630); The Old Rectory, Bagendon, Cirencester (North Cerney 352); Blackwell House, Guildhall Yard, London EC2 (☎ 01 726 2711, telex 8953966, fax 01 606 9828)

SAUNDERS, Stephen Frederick; s of Stanley Charles, of Southsea, Hampshire, and Joan Marianne Barnet, *née* Clarke; *b* 26 July 1942; *Educ* Sherborne; *m* 15 Oct 1966, (Jean) Lindsay, da of Stanley MacEwan (d 1975), of Southampton; 1 s (Craig Philip b 1973), 1 da (Nicola Gail Saunders b 1970); *Career* co sec and fin controller Liberty plc 1977-81; fin dir and co sec: Liberty Retail Ltd 1981, Liberty of London Prints Ltd 1981; dir Hampshire Building Soc 1981-88; Waddington Galleries Ltd: co sec and fin controller 1982-85, fin dir and co sec 1985-; Friend of Kent Opera, Friend of Royal Acad, NACF, FCA 1966; *Recreations* tennis, cricket, opera; *Clubs* Hampshire CCC; *Style*— Stephen Saunders, Esq; Bybrook House, Canterbury Rd, Kennington, Ashford, Kent (☎ 0233 33916); Waddington Galleries Ltd, 11 Cork St, London W1 (☎ 01 437 8611, fax 01 734 4146, telex 266772)

SAUNDERS, Prof Wilfred Leonard; CBE (1982); s of Leonard Saunders (d 1962), of Birmingham, and Annie, *née* Vine (d 1973); *b* 18 April 1920; *Educ* King Edward's GS Birmingham, Fitzwilliam House Cambridge (BA, MA); *m* 15 June 1946, Joan Mary, da of Maj W E Rider, TD (d 1949), of Birmingham; 2 s (John b 11 Jan 1948, Peter b 24 Nov 1952); *Career* enlisted Signalman 48 Div Signals TA; served BEF France and Belgium 1940 (evacuated Dunkirk), cmmnd RCS 1942, 1 Army N Africa 1942-43, CMF Italy 1943-46, Capt and Adj 1945, Staff Capt Q at GHQ Caserta; dep librarian Inst of Bankers 1948-49, founding librarian Univ of Birmingham Inst of Educn 1949-56, dep librarian Univ of Sheffield 1956-63, seconded UNESCO Uganda 1962, founding dir postgrad sch of librarianship (now dept of info studies) Univ of Sheffield 1963, prof of librarianship and info sci Univ of Sheffield 1968-82 (dean faculty of educn studies 1974-77, emeritus prof 1982-), pres Library Assoc 1980, library and info advsy work and consultancy UNESCO and Br Cncl 1981-, chm Library and Info Servs Cncl 1981-84, visiting prof Univ of California Los Angeles 1985; chm Br Cncl's Libraries Advsy Panel 1975-81 (memb 1970-87), memb Lord Chllr's Advsy Cncl on Public Records; author of numerous pubns on librarianship and info work; FLA 1952, hon FIInfSci 1977, hon FCP 1983; *Recreations* gardening, listening to music, book collecting, walking, dancing; *Clubs* Royal Cwlth Soc; *Style*— Prof Wilfred Saunders, CBE; 15 Princess Drive, Sawston, Cambridge CB2 4DL

SAUNDERS WATSON, Cdr (Leslie) Michael Macdonald; DL (Northants 1979); s of Capt Leslie Swain Saunders, DSO, JP, RN, and Elizabeth, da of Vice Adm Sir Michael Culme-Seymour, 4 Bt, KCB, MVO; *b* 9 Oct 1934; *Educ* Eton, RNC Dartmouth; *m* 1958, Georgina Elizabeth Laetitia, da of Adm Sir William Davis, *qv*; 2 s, 1 da; *Career* served RN 1951-71 (Cdr 1969); High Sheriff Northants 1978-79, vice-chm Northants Small Industs Ctee 1974-79; chm: Northants Assoc Youth Clubs 1977-, Heritage Educn Year 1977, Corby Community advsy gp 1979-86, Ironstone Royalty

Owners Assoc 1979 (Northamptons Hire Tourism advsy panel); memb: taxation and legal ctees CLA 1975-, exec ctees CLA 1975-80 and 1987-, British Heritage Ctee 1978-, Northants branch CLA 1981- (chm 1981-84); dir: Lamport Hall Preservation Tst 1978-, English Sinfonia 1980, Northants Enterprise Agency 1986-; chm govrs Lodge Pk Comprehensive 1977-83, tstee Oakham Sch 1975-77 (dep pres 1978-82, chm Tax and Parly Ctee 1975-82), pres Historic Houses Assoc 1982-88; tstee: Royal Botanic Gardens Kew 1983-, Nat Heritage Memorial Fund 1987-, chm Heritage Educn Tst; *Recreations* sailing, music, gardening; *Clubs* Brook's; *Style*— Commander L M M Saunders Watson, DL; Rockingham Castle, Market Harborough, Leics LE16 8TH (☎ (0536) 770326, office 770240)

SAUNDERSON, (Edward) John Hardress; DSO (1944), DFC (1944); s of Capt John Vernon Saunderson, RFA (d 1960), and Hon Eva Norah, *née* Mulholland (d 1972), da of 2 Baron Dunleath; *b* 10 April 1918; *Educ* Eton; *m* 1, 30 June 1954, Diana Elizabeth, da of Maj Thomas Sydney d'Arcy Hankey (d 1977); 3 s (David John b 1956, Richard Michael b 1957, Thomas Alexander b 1961), 1 da (Joan Angela b 1958); m 2, 25 July 1980, Elisabeth Adelheid Rita Ingeborg Clara, da of Baron Philip von Behr, Cdr German Navy (d 1986), of Güttingen, Germany; *Career* RAF Gd Branch 1938-45, bomber cmd 1940-44 (despatches twice), CO Middle East Flight Harwell 1943, tactics staff offr 91 Gp 1944, Empire Test Pilots Sch 1945, Sqdn Ldr, Test Pilot Percival Aircraft 1946-47; former Engineering Co 1948; chm/man dir: Farrow Eng Ltd 1956, Crotall Eng Ltd (chm) 1959, and chm Saunderson & Costin (cemented carbides) Ltd 1965-; *Recreations* gliding, music, gardening; *Style*— John Saunderson, Esq, DSO, DFC; Honeybottom, Newbury, Berks RG11 8AL (☎ Newbury (0635) 43754); Saunderson & Costin Ltd, Arnhem Road, Newbury, Berks RG14 5RU (☎ (0635) 524524, telex 849382 SAVCO G)

SAUZIER, Sir (André) Guy; CBE (1959), ED; s of J Adrian Sauzier of Mauritius; *b* 20 Oct 1910; *Educ* Royal Coll Mauritius; *m* 1936, Thérèse, da of Henri Mallac; 6 s, 2 da; *Career* served WW II, Maj Mauritius TF; MLC Mauritius 1949-57, Mauritius rep at Coronation 1953, memb Mauritius political delegn to UK 1955, min Works and Communications 1957-59, gen overseas rep Mauritius Chamber of Agric 1959-79, min plen to EEC 1972-79; FRSA; kt 1973; *Clubs* Athenaeum, Cercle Royal Gaulois (Brussels); *Style*— Sir Guy Sauzier, CBE, ED; 15 Marloes Rd, London W8 6LQ

SAVAGE, David Jack; s of Arthur Jack Savage (d 1953), of Farnborough, and Sylvia Maude, *née* Bacon (descendant of Sir Nicholas Bacon Lord Keeper of the Great Seal to Queen Elizabeth I); *b* 7 August 1939; *Educ* Hurstpierpoint Coll, London Univ (LLB), Coll of Law; *m* 16 May 1981, Elizabeth Mary, da of late Dr Edmond Louis Ives; 2 s (Nicholas David St John b 1982, Louis Arthur Ives b 1983); *Career* slr 1963-; ptnr Foster, Savage & Gordon of Farnborough (sr ptnr 1984-); pres Hampshire Inc Law Soc 1983-84, dir Slrs Benevolent Assoc 1984-; cmmr of income tax 1969-, memb N Hants Local Valuation Tribunal 1976- (vice-chm 1984-); chm of Govrs Farnborough GS 1970-72, dir Aldershot FC 1971; cncllr Farnborough UDC 1964-73 (vice-chm 1972-73), cncllr Rushmore Borough Cncl 1973-80; Cons parly candidate: Birmingham Sparkbrook 1974, Birmingham Smallheath 1979; *Recreations* travel (preferably by train), browsing, bricklaying; *Clubs* Royal Aldershot Offrs, Law Soc; *Style*— David Savage, Esq; Ridgeway, 16 Clockhouse Rd, Farnborough, Hants; Phillack, Hayle, Cornwall; 269 Farnborough Rd, Farnborough, Hants (☎ (0252) 54140, telex 858770 FOSTER G, fax (0252) 373428)

SAVAGE, Donald William John; s of George William Savage (d 1980), of the Firs, Mattishall, Norfolk, and Kate Ethel, *née* Logsdaile (d 1978); *b* 20 August 1922; *Educ* The Grove Sch London, Regent St Poly, Battersea Poly (external BSc); *m* 15 June 1962, Dorothy Clarissa, da of Stanley J Titterton (d 1977) of Gymea, NSW, Aust; 1 s (Adrian b 1963), 1 da (Lisa b 1965); *Career* WWII RAFVR 1941-46, cmmnd 1943 capt flying boats 1943-46; coastal cmd: 204 Sqdn W Africa, 209 Sqdn E Africa, SEAC Ceylon, Hong Kong, Seletar, Singapore; demob Flt Lt 1946; pupil civil engr 1938-41, asst engr and agent for contractors Concrete Piling Ltd (London and Belfast) 1946-50; Gammon Pakistan Ltd (Karachi) 1950-58: civil engr, agent, divnl engr, chief engr, dir; res dir Gammon Pakistan Ltd Bahrain, md Gammon Gulf Ltd Bahrain 1958-62 Tilbury Contracting Gp 1962-79: gp asst md, gp md, gp dep chm; non exec dir various cos; hon sec and ctee memb Radlett Soc; memb: Green Belt Assoc, Probus Club of Radlett; Freeman Worshipful Co of Paviors 1967; FICE; *Recreations* travel, game shooting, walking, gardening; *Style*— Donald Savage, Esq

SAVAGE, Sir Ernest Walter; s of late Walter Edwin Savage; *b* 24 August 1912; *Educ* Brisbane GS, Scots Coll Warwick Qld; *m* 1938, Dorothy Winifred, da of A W Nicholls; 1 s, 1 da; *Career* CA in public practice 1940-76, hon consul for Norway in Brisbane 1950-76, memb: bd of govrs Cromwell Univ 1950-77, Queensland State Cncl of CA 1951-76 (chm 1958-60 and 1966); chm Bank of Qld 1960; Knight (1 class) of Order of St Olaf; FCA; kt 1979; *Style*— Sir Ernest Savage; 12 Mount Ommaney Drive, Jindalee, Brisbane, Qld 4074, Australia

SAVAGE, Paul Stephen Gladstone; s of Edward Stephen Savage (d 1980), of Southwick, Sussex, and Gladys Vera, *née* Turrell (d 1934); *b* 21 Jan 1934; *Educ* Steyning GS Sussex; *m* 16 March 1957, Patricia Polly, da of Alan Spencer Gill (d 1966), of Brighton; 1 da (Susan Carol (Mrs Pearson) b 1960); *Career* sr ptnr Hilton Sharp & Clarke; dir Findhorn Finance plc; FCA 1957; *Recreations* wine, theatre, walking; *Style*— Paul Savage, Esq; 3 Lesser Foxholes, Shoreham-by-Sea, W Sussex BN4 5NT (☎ 0273 464246); 30 New Road, Brighton, E Sussex BN1 1BN (☎ 0273 24163, telex 878380, fax 0273 23983)

SAVAGE, Wendy Dianne; da of William George Edwards (d 1984), and Anne, *née* Smith (d 1943); *b* 12 April 1935; *Educ* Croydon HS, Girton Coll Cambridge (BA), London Hosp Med Coll (MB BCH); *m* 27 July 1960 (m dis 1973), (Miguel) Mike Babatunde Richard Savage, s of Richard Gabriel Akiwande Savage FRCS, of 35 Moray Place, Edinburgh; 2 s (Nicholas Richard b 10 June 1964, Jonathan Chukuma b 18 April 1969), 2 da (Yewande Patricia b 9 April 1961, Wendy Claire b 28 May 1962); *Career* res fell Harvard Univ 1962-64, md Awo-omama and Enugu Nigeria 1964 -67; registrar: Kenyatta Hosp Nairobi 1967-69, Royal Free Hosp London 1969-71, various posts Tower Hamlets, Islington Borough and Pregnancy Advsy Serv 1971-73, specialist in obstetrics Cook Hosp NZ 1973-76, lectr London Hosp 1976-77, sr lectr in obstetrics and gynaecology London Hosp Med Coll and hon conslt London Hosp 1977-; PR Doctors For Women's Choice on Abortion; tstee: Pregnancy Advsy Serv Simon Population Tst, Birth Control Campaign; advsr Maternity Alliance; fdr memb: Women in Medicine, Women in Gynaecology and Obstetrics; chair Forum on Maternity and the Newborn RSM; MRCOG 1971 FRCOG 1985; *Books* Hysterectomy (1982), Coping with Caesarian Section and Other Difficult Births (with Fran Reader 1983) A Savage Enquiry (1986); *Recreations* reading novels, playing piano duets, travel; *Style*— Mrs Wendy Savage; 19 Vincent Terrace, London N1 (☎ 01 837 7635); London Hospital, Whitechapel, London E1 (☎ 01 377 7240)

SAVERNAKE, Visc Thomas James Brudenell-Bruce; only s, and h of Earl of Cardigan; gs of 8 Marquess of Ailesbury; *b* 11 Feb 1982; *Style*— Viscount Savernake

SAVERY, Thomas Edward James; s of Tom Edward Mark Savery (d 1967), and May, *née* Young; *b* 2 Nov 1932; *Educ* Plymouth Coll, Hertford Coll Oxford (MA) London (LLB); *m* 8 Aug 1958, Margaret Elsie, da of Herbert Maurice Rogers (d 1986); 1 s (Christopher John b 1960); 3 da (Catherine Louise b 1962, Gillian Rachel b 1965, Elizabeth Anne b 1967); *Career* slr, private practice (Plymouth); elected Plymouth City Cncl 1966, deputy leader of Cncl and Chm; Finance Ctee 1981-87; leader of City Cncl and chm Policy and Resources Ctee 1987; *Recreations* gardening, moor walking, travel; *Style*— Thomas Savery, Esq; Furkry, 122 Mannamead Rd, Plymouth PL3 5QH (☎ (0752) 662535); Saverys, 5 The Crescent, Plymouth PL1 3AJ (☎ (0752) 660066)

SAVILE, Lady Alethea Frances Clare; *née* Savile; da of 8 Earl of Mexborough; *b* 1963; *Style*— Lady Alethea Savile; c/o Arden Hall, Hawnby, York YO6 SLS

SAVILE, Hon Charles Anthony; yr s of 7 Earl of Mexborough (d 1980); *b* 28 June 1934; *Educ* Eton; *m* 5 Nov 1966, Zita Loretta, da of Leslie White; 2 s (Henry b 1970, Andrew b 1973); *Career* Lt Grenadier Guards; *Style*— The Hon Charles Savile; Youngsbury, Ware, Herts

SAVILE, 3 Baron (UK 1888); George Halifax Lumley-Savile; JP (Borough of Dewsbury 1955), DL (W Yorks 1954); patron of two livings; s of 2 Baron (d 1931) of Rufford Abbey, Ollerton, Notts, and Esmé Grace Virginia (d 1958), da of John Wolton; *b* 24 Jan 1919; *Educ* Eton; *Heir* bro, Hon Henry Lumley-Savile; *Career* formerly Capt Duke of Wellington's Regt, attached 1 Bn Lincs Regt, Burma 1943-44; chm St John Cncl S and W Yorks 1980, landowner (18,000 acres); CStJ 1983; *Recreations* shooting, listening to classical music; *Clubs* Brooks's, Huddersfield, Sloane; *Style*— The Rt Hon the Lord Savile, JP, DL; Gryce Hall, Shelley, Huddersfield, W Yorks (☎ Huddersfield 602774); Savile Estate Office, Thornhill, Dewsbury, W Yorks (☎ Dewsbury 462341)

SAVILE, James Wilson Vincent (Jimmy); OBE (1971); s of Vincent Savile, and Agnes, *née* Kelly; *b* 31 Oct 1926; *Educ* St Annes Elementary Sch Leeds; *Career* 'Bevin Boy' Coal Mines 1942-48; TV and radio personality; presenter: Radio 1 Show, Jim'll Fix it, Mind How You Go, Top of The Pops; regular Sunday People Columnist; voluntary helper: Leeds Infirmary, Stoke Mandeville Hosp, Broadmoor Hosp; major fundraiser for various national charities; Hon LLD Leeds Univ 1986; memb MENSA; KCSG (Holy See) 1982; *Books* As It Happens/Love is an Uphill Thing (autobiography 1975), God'll Fix It (1979); *Recreations* running, cycling, wrestling; *Clubs* Athenaeum; *Style*— Jimmy Savile, Esq; National Spinal Injuries Centre, Stoke Mandeville Hospital, Aylesbury, Bucks

SAVILL, His Hon David Malcolm; QC (1969); s of Lionel H Savill (d 1972), of East Guinstedd, and Lisbeth, *née* de Saumarez Brock; *b* 18 Sept 1930; *Educ* Marlborough, Clare Coll Cambridge (BA); *m* 2 April 1955, Mary, JP, da of Hon Sir Raymond Kuichcliffe (d 1973); 1 s (Richard b 1956), 2 da (Caroline b 1957, Jenny b 1963); *Career* Nat Serv 2 Lt Cmmn Grendier Gds 1950; barr Middle Temple 1954, memb Senate Inns of Ct and Bar 1976, 1980-83, ldr North Eastern circuit; circuit judge 1984, chm advsy ctee on Conscientius Objectives 1976-; Diocese Bradford 1976, Diocese Ripon 1987-; *Recreations* golf, gardening; *Clubs* MCC; *Style*— His Hon Judge David Savill, QC; Leeds Crown Court, Oxford Peace, Leeds 1 (☎ 0532 451 616)

SAVILL, Timothy Lydall; s of Edwin Lydall Savill (d 1940), (gs of Alfred Savill, fndr Alfred Savill & Sons, Chartered Surveyors, in 1859) and Margaret H K Thorne (d 1976); uncle Sir Eric Savill, KCVO, MBE, MC, FRICS, fndr the Savill Gardens in Windsor Great Park when dep ranger, also chm Royal Forests, and Keeper of Gardens at Windsor; *b* 25 Mar 1940; *Educ* Haileybury & Imperial Services Coll Windsor, Radley, Coll of Estate Mgmnt London Univ; *m* 1, 14 June 1963 (m dis 1973), Sonia Mary Barradale; 1 s (Nicholas b 1966), 1 da (Caroline b 1968); m 2, 1 June 1982 (m dis 1986), Ann Rosemary Stone; *Career* chartered surveyor; fndr dir Timothy Savill & Co; FRICS; ARVA; Freeman: City of London, Worshipful Co of Skinners; *Recreations* fly fishing, shooting, gardening, swimming; *Clubs* RAC, Pall Mall London; *Style*— Timothy L Savill, Esq; Pikes Farm, House, Forest Road, Bill Hill, Wokingham, Surrey RG11 5QR (☎ 0734 783280); PO Box 7, Forest Rd, Bill Hill, Wokingham, Surrey RG11 5NZ (☎ 0734 783280, fax 0734 783280)

SAVILLE, John David; JP; s of Bertie Edward Saville, of Barrie, and Catherine, *née* Taysum (d 1965); *b* 5 Jan 1932; *Educ* Aston Commercial Coll; *m* 19 June 1954, Moira Angela (d 1983), da of Maurice Goggin (d 1946), of Birmingham; 1 s (David John b 4 April 1964), 2 da (Sharon Ann (Mrs Wilson-Gunn) b 15 Jan 1958, Amanda Theresa (Mrs Cazalet) b 17 Feb 1960); *Career* Nat Serv Royal Warwicks 1950-52; chm and md J Saville Gordon Gp plc 1955-; dir: Duport plc 1983-86, Wolverhampton Racecourse plc 1983-, Dunstall Park Securities Ltd, Leigh Interests plc 1989-; ctee memb Solihull Inst for Med Trg and Res; scout co cmmr Birmingham Co; chm The Stonehouse Gang; dir: Task Undertakings, Birmingham Gang Show Ltd, Silhill Tst Ltd; *Recreations* horse riding, skiing, tennis, swimming; *Clubs* Midlands Sporting; *Style*— John Saville, Esq, JP; Barrells park, Ullenhall, Nr Henley in Arden, Warwicks B95 5NQ; J Saville Gordon Gp plc, Savill Gordon House, 4 Wharfdale Rd, Tyselsey, Birmingham B11 2SB (☎ 021 707 3530, fax 021 707 5903, telex 339184)

SAVILLE, Hon Mrs (Yvonne Catherine); da of Baron Schon (Life Peer); *b* 12 June 1944; *Educ* Badminton Sch Bristol, St Godric's Secretarial Coll, Montessori Coll London Dyslexia Institute; *m* 1979, Norman Saville, s of Mark Sville, of Hampstead; 1 s (Daniel), 2 step s; *Career* Montessori teacher 1970-72, dyslexia teacher 1987-; *Recreations* theatre, tennis, music, cooking; *Style*— The Hon Mrs Saville; 21 Hillview Road, Mill Hill Village, London NW7

SAVOURS; *see*: Campbell-Savours

SAWBRIDGE, Edward Henry Ewen; s of Henry Raywood Sawbridge, CBE, of The Moorings, Kiwgsgate, kent, and Lilian, *née* Wood; *b* 14 August 1953; *Educ* Radley, Balliol Coll (MA); *m* 23 July 1983, Angela Rose Louisa, da of Maj Anthony James MacDonald Watt, of Longwood, Sunning Hill, Berks; 2 s (Jack William Hugo b 1986, Hugh Anthony b 1988); *Career* Peat Marwick Mitchell & Co 1976-83, ACLI Metals (London) Ltd 1983- 85, fin dir Shearson Lehman Hutton Commodities Ltd 1985; *Recreations* bridge, fishing, cooking; *Clubs* United Oxford & Cambridge; *Style*— Edward Sawbridge, Esq; 1 Broadgate, London EC2 M7HA (☎ 01 260 2177, fax 01

260 2516, telex 917273 SLMETLG)

SAWKO, Prof Felicjan; s of Czeslaw Sawko (d 1985), and Franciszka, *née* Nawrot; *b* 17 May 1937; *Educ* Lilford Hall, Leeds University (BSc, MSc); *m* 18 April 1960, Genowefa Stefania, da of Wladyslaw Bak (d 1973); 4 s (Andrew Martin b 1961, Peter Ian b 1963, Richard Felicjan b 1965, Paul b 1968), 1 da (Barbara Maria b 1962); *Career* asst engr Rendel Palmer & Tritton 1959-62, reader in civil engrg Leeds Univ 1967 (lectr 1962-67), prof Liverpool Univ 1967-1988, prof of civil engrg Sultan Qaboos Univ 1986-; Hon DSc Leeds Univ 1973; FICE 1986, FIStructE 1986, FASCE 1986; *Books* Developments in Prestressed Concrete (1982), Computer Methods for Civil Engineers (1984); *Recreations* bridge, numismatics, travel; *Style—* Prof Felicjan Sawko; 9 Harthill Road, Liverpool L18 6HU (☎ 051 724 2726)

SAWREY-COOKSON, Maj (John) Henry Crackan Thorpe; s of John Clement Basil Sawrey-Cookson (d 1987), of Ashbrook, Winsford, nr Minehead, Somerset, and Joan, *née* Luxmoore; *b* 17 Sept 1913; *Educ* Upingham, Royal Agric Coll Cirencester; *m* 16 Dec 1967, Merrilyn Patricia, da of Maj R Thomas (ka 1944); 1 s (Rawlinson b 1977), 1 da (Emma b 1973); *Career* Nat Serv 1959, cmmnd Lifeguards attended MONS OLS; cmmnd RA: 8/60 short-serv cmmn, 2/66 reg cmmn; served: Sierra Leonean Army 1960-63, Nigerian & Army UN Congo 1961-62, 18/39 Regt RA BAOR Hong Kong and NI, US 8 Army S Korea 1966, Canadian Army 1969, Sultan's Forces Oman Dhofur War 1972, Nat Army Zimbabwe 1981-83; OC light gun roles USA 1985, ldr Op Raleigh Expedition Patagonia, Chile 1988; Lord of Manor: Newbiggin and Hale, Ousby and Bank; patron of living parishes Newbiggin, Kirby Thore, Temple Sowerby; MRAC, FRGS; *Recreations* game shooting, gardening, exploration; *Style—* Maj Henry Sawrey-Cookson

SAX, George Hans; s of Oscar Sax (d 1974), of 37 Manor Way, Beckenham, Kent, and Margaret, *née* Bohm (d 1977); *b* 11 Feb 1913; *Educ* Dulwich, Leeds Univ, Imperial Coll of Sci & Technol; *m* 19 Feb 1938, Yvonne Anna Marcelle, da of Leopold Joseph Trausel (d 1971), of IOW; 2 s (Richard Noel b 26 Dec 1938, John Paul b 3 Aug 1944); *Career* Territorial Serv Sharpshooters 3 Co of London Yeomanry 1932-37, cmmnd RASC 1939 served in France 1940, transferred RAOC served in France, Belgium, Germany 1944-46, GSO1 HQ 21 Army Gp Lt-Col 1944, demob 1946; md Martin Rice Ltd, dir GR Hldgs, underwriter Lloyds 1965; pres Br Fur Trade Assoc; hon local rep Offrs Assoc Br Legion 1968-; Freeman City of London 1937, Liveryman Worshipful Co of Skinners 1937; *Recreations* travel, fly fishing, gardening; *Style—* George Sax, Esq

SAX, Richard Noel; s of Lt-Col George Hans Sax, of Leeford Oaks, Whatlington, Nr Battle, E Sussex, and Yvonne Anna Marcelle Sax; *b* 26 Dec 1938; *Educ* Tonbridge, St Johns Coll Oxford (MA); *m* 8 April 1967, Margaret, da of Ronald Frank Penny (d 1988); 3 da (Catherine b 1968, Josephine b 1971, Charlotte b 1974); *Career* Nat Serv: cmmnd 2 Lt RASC 1957, attatched 1 Gds Bde Irish Gds Cyprus (GSM Cyprus clasp), Lt 1959; admitted slr 1967, equity ptnr Rubinstein Callingham 1968-84, managing ptnr Rubinstein Callingham 1984-; memb Law Cmmns Working Party on Family Property 1974, chm Solicitors Family Law Assoc 1987-; Liveryman Worshipful Co of Skinners; memb Law Soc 1967; *Recreations* current affairs, gardening, history and archeology, travel, art; *Clubs* MCC; *Style—* 29 Kelsey Way, Beckenham, Kent BR3 3LP; 2 Raymond Buildings, Grays Inn, London WCIR 5BZ (☎ 01 650 8272, fax 01 831 7413, tlx 894 100 RUBCAL G)

SAXBY, John Christopher Leslie; s of Leslie Eric Saxby (d 1958), and Florence Mildred, *née* Gallimore (d 1983); *b* 2 April 1933; *Educ* Caterham Sch; *m* 19 Oct 1968, Heather Peel, da of Eric Peel Yates (d 1987); 1 s (Robin b 1975), 1 da (Fiona b 1972); *Career* chartered accountant, articled West Wake Price and Co 1951-58, qualified clerk Ceepers and Lybrand 1959-65, chief accountant London Merchant Securities plc 1965-70 (gp accountant) co sec Carlton Industs plc 1970-81, sr ptnr Saxby and Sinden (previously Saxby and Marner) 1981-; FCA 1957; *Recreations* golf; *Clubs* Worlebury Golf, Winscombe Cricket (pres); *Style—* John Saxby, Esq; Orchard House, Main Road Cleeve, Bristol BS19 4PN (☎ 0934 832 262); 61 Park St, Bristol BS1 5NU (☎ 0272 221 751); 18 High St, Budleigh, Salterton, Devon EX9 6LQ

SAXBY, John James; s of James Samuel Saxby (d 1967, Sqdn Ldr RAuxAf 1938-45), of Ovingdean, Sussex, and Florence Evelyn, *née* Wilson (d 1965); *b* 16 June 1925; *Educ* Bradfield, Magdalene Coll Cambridge; *m* 1, 1952 (m dis 1964), Thelma Winifred Whitehouse; 1 s (Peter b 1955), 1 da (Judith b 1954); m 2, 1984, Susan Josephine Gabriel Scott, *née* White; *Career* RAFVR 1943-47, cmmnd Pilot Offr 1944, physical trg instr and staff parachute instr RAF Upper Heyford 1945, OC ME Parachute Sch (Aqir, Palestine) 1946-47, parachute advsr to OC 6 Airborne Div 1946-47 (Flt-Lt); Hecht Levis & Khan Gp 1947-54 (China, Hong Kong, Singapore, Dutch, East Indies and latterly London), md main commodity subsid of W M Brandts Sons & Co Ltd 1954-64; barr Gray's Inn 1962; legal advsr Revertex Ltd 1964-72, UK legal advsr int mktg div of Kuwait Nat Petroleum Co (later Kuwait Petroleum Corpn) 1972-84; former: cncllr Met Borough Cncl Paddington South, gen cmmr Inland Revenue, memb arbitration panel Rubber Trade Assoc of London; panels chm Diary Produce Quota Tbnls 1984-85; Freeman: City of London, Worshipful Co of Fruiterers 1973; FCIArb; *Recreations* fly fishing, falconry, fencing, oil painting; *Clubs* Flyfishers, Carlton, Br Falconers; *Style—* John Saxby, Esq; Freshfields, Grindall House, 25 Newgate St, London EC1A 7LH (☎ 01 606 6677)

SAXENA, Dr Sideshwar Raj; s of late Rai Bhim Raj Saxena, and late Mrs Gunna Bee Bee; *b* 6 Feb 1933; *Educ* MB; BS (OSM), MD (Ped), DCH, RGCP (London); *m* 8 May 1960, Prahba Devi Saxena, da of late Rai Jadubans Chandra; *Career* formerly asst prof Paediatries Niloufer Hosp, Nuffield Fndn fell and hon sr registrar at Queen Elizabeth Hosp for Children; presently principal in gen practise, hon tutor and clerical asst Kings Coll Hosp, conslt Harley St; past pres Indian Med Assoc, ed Mediscene (Journal for overseas doctors in UK), memb eur assoc of Sci Eds; panel doctor of Indian High Cmmn; FRSM; *Books* Life of Ghandi 'Badu' (1948), Jokes Jokes Jokes (1986), A Prescription for Laughter (1988); *Style—* Dr Sidehwar Raj Saxena; Prasidh, 12 A Alleyn Rd, W Dulwich SE21 8AL; 142 Harley St, London W1 (☎ (01) 935 5790)

SAXTON, Patrick Vincent; s of Patrick Cyril Saxton (d 1979), and Zara Pearl, *née* Moore; *b* 6 Sept 1929; *Educ* High Oakham Sch Mansfield; *m* 19 July 1980, Vera (Vee) Margaret, da of Alexander John Temple (d 1958), of Sanderstead, Surrey; *Career* Nat Serv RA; Willis Faber and Dumas 1950-53, clerk to agency supt Caledonian Insur Co 1953-63; Chartered Insur Inst: careers advsy off 1964-, asst sec 1965-, admin sec 1979-, sec gen 1983-; lay asst St Georges Church Beckenham; sec Insur Indust Trg Cncl 1972-80; chm: Br Insur Law Assoc 1981-83, Insur Trg Ctee of Comité Européen des Assurances, All Saints Educational Tst, Inst Trg and Devpt 1984-86; memb London Univ Careers Advsy Bd; Freedom City of London 1973; Liveryman: Worshipful Co of Gold and Silver Wyre Drawers 1973, Worshipful Co Insurers 1984; assoc memb Inst of Insur Sci for services to Anglo-German insur educn, Hon FICO 1977; FCII 1956, FITD 1978, FBIM 1982; *Books* Allured to Adventure (1974); *Recreations* chess, music, photography, watching sport; *Clubs* MCC, Cripplegate Ward; *Style—* Patrick Saxton, Esq; 24 Lakeside, Wickham Road, Beckenham, Kent (☎ 01 658 6298); Chartered Insurance Institute, 20 Aldermanbury, London EC2V 7HY (☎ 01 606 3835, fax (group 2 + 3) 01 726 0131, telex 957017)

SAY, Rt Rev (Richard) David; KCVO (1988); *see*: Rochester, Bishop of; s of Cdr Richard Say, OBE, RNVR (d 1958), and Kathleen Mary, *née* Wildy (d 1968); *b* 4 Oct 1914; *Educ* Univ Coll Sch, Christ's Coll Camb (BA 1938, MA 1941), Ridley Hall Camb; *m* 16 Oct 1943, Irene Frances, OBE, JP, da of Seaburne Rayner (d 1952), of Exeter; 2 s (Richard William Gurney b and d 1950, William David b 1952), 2 da (Mary Penelope b 1945, Anne Caroline b 1948); 1943, Irene, OBE, JP, da of Seaburne Rayner, of Exeter; 1 s, 2 da (and 1 s decd); *Career* ordained deacon 1939, priest 1940; gen sec Br Cncl of Churches 1947-55; rector of Hatfield and domestic chaplain to Marquess of Salisbury 1955-61; chaplain to Pilgrims of GB 1968-; Lord High Almoner to HM The Queen 1970-88; dep-pro-chllr Kent Univ 1977-83, pro-chllr 1983-; chm ctee on State Aid for Churches in Use 1971-; sub-prelate and chaplain Order of St John of Jerusalem; 104 Bishop of Rochester 1961-88; memb House of Lords 1969-88; asst Bishop of Canterbury 1988-; memb Court of Ecclesiastical Causes Reserved 1984-; vice-pres UN Assoc of GB 1986, chm Age Concern England 1986-89; hon memb Inst of RE 1987; Hon Freeman: Borough of Tonbridge and Malling 1987, City of Rochester upon Medway 1988; DD Lambeth 1961; Hon DCL Univ of Kent at Canterbury 1987; *Recreations* walking, travel; *Clubs* United Oxford and Cambridge; *Style—* The Rt Rev Dr David Say, KCVO; 23 Chequers Park, Wye, Ashford, Kent TN25 5BB (☎ 0233 812720)

SAYE AND SELE, 21 Baron (E 1447 and 1603); Nathaniel Thomas Allen Fiennes; DL (Oxon 1979); s of 20 Baron, OBE, MC (Ivo Murray Twisleton-Wykeham-Fiennes, d 1968) and Hersey, da of late Capt Sir Thomas Dacres Butler, KCVO; relinquished by deed poll 1965 the additional surnames of Twisleton and Wykeham; *b* 22 Sept 1920; *Educ* Eton, New Coll Oxford; *m* 1958, Mariette Helena, da of Maj-Gen Sir (Arthur) Guy Salisbury-Jones, GCVO, CMG, CBE, MC (d 1985), and Hilda, da of Rt Hon Sir Maurice de Bunsen, 1 and last Bt, GCMG, GCVO, CB; 3 s, 1 da; *Heir* s, Hon Richard Fiennes; *Career* Rifle Bde (despatches twice) 1939-45; chartered surveyor; *Style—* The Rt Hon the Lord Saye and Sele, DL; Broughton Castle, Banbury, Oxon (☎ 62624)

SAYEED, Dr (Abul Fatah) Akram; OBE (1976); s of Mokhles Ahmed (d 1967), of Pirwalistan, Jessore, Bangladesh, and Noor Jehan Begum, *née* Munshi (d 1987); *b* 23 Nov 1935; *Educ* St Joseph's Sch Khulna, Univ of Dhaka (MB, BS); *m* 11 Oct 1959, Hosen-ara, da of Al-Haj M Sabet Ali; 2 s (Rana Ahmed b 10 March 1967, Reza Abu b 15 April 1972), 1 da (Dina Jesmin b 17 June 1963); *Career* sr house offr (opthalmology) Dhaka Univ Hosp 1950-60 (house offr 1958-59), rotating internship Monmouth Med Centre Long Branch New Jersey 1960-61, sr house offr (opthalmology) Leicester Royal Infirmary 1961-63, GP 1964- (asst in practice 1963), pt/t med offr Leicester Royal Infirmary; advsr NCCI 1965-68, fndr memb Leicester Cncl for Community Relations 1965-, memb CRC 1968-77, chm Standing Conference Asian Orgns in UK 1973-77 (vice-chm 1970-73); memb: BBC Asian Programme Advsy Ctee 1972-77, Leics Med Ctee 1977, Leics Family Practitioners Ctee 1977, Univ Mgmnt Team 1977; vice-pres Fedn Bangladeshi Orgns in UK and Europe 1984, memb Home Sec's Advsy Cncl on Community Relations 1983, sec Inst of Transcultural Health Care 1985, UK del First World Conference on Muslim Educn King Abdul Aziz Univ Mecca 1977, memb DHSS Working Gps (Asian Health, treatment of overseas visitors), chm Stop Rickets Campaign Leics; overseas Doctors Assoc: fndr chm 1975, gen sec 1975-77, vice-pres 1979-84, vice-chm 1984, chm S Trent Div 1981; memb Bangladesh Med Assoc UK 1972- (CEC memb 1982-), EC memb BMA Leics & Rutland Div 1975-, life memb Opthalmological Soc of Bangladesh, ed Bangladesh Medical Directory (three edns); FRSM 1981, fell Overseas Doctors' Assoc 1985; memb: BMA 1961, MJA; *Books* Caring for Asians in General Practice (contrib 1989), numerous articles on medico politics; *Recreations* reading, oriental music, photography, gardening; *Clubs* Rotary (Leicester City); *Style—* Dr Akram Sayeed, OBE; RAMNA, 2 Mickelton Drive, Leicester LE5 6GD (☎ 0533 416703); 352 East Pk Rd, Leicester LE5 5AY (☎ 0533 737569, 730388)

SAYEED, Jonathan; MP (C) Bristol East 1983-; *b* 20 Mar 1948; *Educ* RN Coll Dartmouth, RN Engineering Coll; *Career* unsuccessfully fought (C) E Lewisham and N Islington GLC elections; shipping consultant, chm insurance service co; defeated Rt Hon Tony Benn in 1983 election; memb Select Ctee on Environment 1987, memb Select Ctee on Defence 1987-; vice chm Shipping and Shipbuilding Ctee; dep chm Maritime Ctee; *Style—* Jonathan Sayeed, Esq, MP; House of Commons, London SW1A 0AA (☎ 01 219 6389)

SAYER, Maj Douglas James William; MBE (1941), TD; lord of the manor of Sparham; er s of Capt James Arthur Sayer, JP (d 1960), of Sparham Hall, Norfolk, and Georganna Margaret, *née* Garrod (d 1951); descends from John Sawyer, of Cambrydges in Swanton Morley, Norfolk 'assessed there for subsidy 1543'; *b* 8 May 1906; *Educ* Aldenham; *m* 24 April 1946, Mary Elisabeth, 4 da and co-heiress of Rev Edward Croxton Weddall, MA (d 1961; formerly rector of Lyng, Norfolk) and gda of Rev William Charles Weddall, rector of Linby, Notts, by his w Susan, da of James Sutton, JP, DL, of Shardlow Hall, Derbys; 2 s (Michael *qv*, Charles); *Career* Lt Reserve of Offrs King's African Rifles 1934, Capt 5 Bn (TA) Royal Norfolk Regt 1937, served 1939-45, Maj 1941; cmmr of Taxes (Norfolk) 1945-76; JP Norfolk 1945-81; lord of manor of Sparham; *Recreations* arboriculture; *Clubs* Naval & Military, Norfolk (Norwich); *Style—* Maj Douglas Sayer, MBE, TD; Sparham Hall, Norwich, Norfolk NR9 5QY (☎ Norwich (0603) 872226)

SAYER, Guy Mowbray; CBE (1977); s of late Geoffrey Robley Sayer; *b* 18 June 1924; *Educ* Shrewsbury; *m* 1951, Marie Anne Sophie, da of the late Arnold Henri-Marie Mertens of Brussels, 1 s, 2 da; *Career* banker; chm Hong Kong and Shanghai Banking Corpn 1972-77 (joined 1946, dir 1969-); tres Hong Kong Univ 1971-77, memb Legislative and Executive Councils of Hong Kong 1972-77; dir of various shipping and ship finance cos: Hong Kong, Bermuda, Bahamas; govr Sutton's Hosp Charterhouse; *Recreations* golf, walking; *Clubs* Hong Kong, Royal Hong Kong Jockey, Royal Hong

Kong Golf, MCC, Royal Wimbledon Golf, Oriental; *Style—* Guy Sayer, Esq; Hong Kong and Shanghai Banking Corporation, 99 Bishopsgate, London EC2 (☎ 01 638 2300)

SAYER, Michael John; s of Maj Douglas James William Sayer, MBE, TD *qv*, of Sparham Hall, Norfolk, and Mary Elizabeth, *née* Weddall; *b* 11 Oct 1947; *Educ* Repton, Pembroke Coll Oxford (BA, MA, BLitt); *Career* landowner, author; chm Norfolk Churches Tst 1984-86, Country Landowners' Assoc; memb Norfolk Branch Ctee 1972, Water Sub Ctee 1980-84; memb Norwich Diocesan Synod 1973-82 (pastoral ctee 1974-82), tax cmmr 1979-; FSA 1982; *Books* English Nobility: The Gentry, The Heralds and The Continental Context (1979), Norfolk section of Burkes and Savill's Guide to Country Houses vol III, East Anglia (1981); *Recreations* history, architecture, shooting; *Clubs* Norfolk; *Style—* Michael J Sayer, Esq; Sparham House, Norwich NR9 5PJ (☎ Norwich 872268)

SAYER, Stephen Thomas; s of Charles Martin Sayer, of Epping, Essex, and Justina, *née* Marsden Jones; *b* 8 July 1945; *Educ* Framlingham Coll Suffolk, Coll of Law; *m* 1, 20 July 1968 (m dis 1987), Gillian Susan, da of John Talbot Warwick, of Rustington, Sussex; 2 s (Edward b 1971, Timothy b and d 1973), 1 da (Harriet b 1976); m 2, 30 Jan 1988, Aileen, da of Roy Victor Wegener, of Toowoomba, Queensland, Australia; *Career* Richards Butler Slrs: asst slr 1968, admitted slr 1969, ptnr 1974; Freeman City of London 1978; Liveryman Worshipful Co of Slrs 1975; memb: Law Soc 1968, Lawyers Club 1980; *Books* contributor to: Longmans Practical Commercial Precedents (1987), International Joint Ventures (1989); *Recreations* real tennis, rackets, theatre, reading; *Clubs* Reform, City of London, Queens; *Style—* Stephen Sayer, Esq; 1 Friston St, Fulham, London SW6 3AS (☎ 01 731 7135); 5 Clifton St, London EC2A 4DQ (☎ 01 247 6555, fax 01 247 5091, telex 949494 RBLAW G)

SAYERS, Arnold Lewis; CBE (1986); s of Maj Lorne Douglas Watson Sayers (d 1940), of Alston Hall, Holbeton, Plymouth, and Dame Lucile Newell, JP, *née* Schiff (d 1959); *b* 24 April 1923; *Educ* Wellington Coll, Corpus Christie Coll Cambridge (BA); *m* 10 July 1954, Sylvia Penelope, da of late Brig Gen Spencer Vaughan Percy Weston, DSO, MC, of Sevenoaks, Kent; 1 s (Geoffrey b 1965), 3 da (Charlotte b 1956, Priscilla b 1958, Catherine b 1961); *Career* farmer; ldr Devon Co Cncl 1981-85, govr Seale-Hayne Coll, memb Exeter Univ Cncl, chm Assoc Co Cncls Planning and Transformation Ctee 1981-84, chm Dartmoor Cattle Breeding Centre 1986-; *Recreations* walking, music; *Clubs* Farmers; *Style—* Arnold L Sayers, CBE; Carswell, Holbeton, nr Plymouth (☎ 075 530 282)

SAYERS, Prof Bruce McArther; s of John William McArthur Sayers (d 1980) of Melbourne, Aust, and Mabel Florence, *née* Howe (d 1980); *b* 6 Feb 1928; *Educ* Melbourne HS Aust, Univ of Melbourne (BSc MSc), Univ of London (PhD, DIC, DSc); *Career* professional biophysicist Baker Med Res Inst and Alfred Hosp Melbourne 1949-54; Imperial Coll London: res asst 1954-56, Philips electrical res fell 1956-58, lectr in electronics engrg applied to med electronics 1963-65, reader 1965-68, prof of electronic engrg applied to med 1968-84, head dept of electronic engrg 1979-84, prof of computing applied to med and head dept of computing 1984-, dean City & Guilds Coll 1984-88; hon conslt Royal Nat Throat Nose and Ear Hosp 1974-; univ visiting prof: McGill, Melbourne Rio de Janiero, Torento; travelling lectr Nuffields Fndn and Nat Res Cncl Canada 1971; advsr: Advent Eurofund Ltd 1981-, Shinan Investmt Serv SA 1984-87, Advent Capital Ltd 1985-, Nevroscience Ltd 1985-, Transatlantic Capital (BioSci) Fund Ltd 1985-; dir: Imperial Software Technol Ltd 1984-, Imperial Info Technol Ltd 1986-; pres section of measurement in med Royal Soc of Med 1971-72, memb Global advsy ctee on health res WHO 1988-; Freeman City of London 1986, Liveryman Worshipful Co of Scientific Instrument Makers' 1985; Hon for memb Societa Medioca Chirurgica du Bologna 1965; Hon memb: Med Soc WHO 1974, Eta Kappa Na 1980; FRSA 1975, CEng, FIEE 1980, FCGI 1983; *Recreations* composing comic doggerel, pottering around France and Switzerland; *Clubs* Athenaeum; *Style—* Prof Bruce Sayers; 40 Queen's Gate, London SW7 5HR (☎ 01 584 3742); Department of Computing, Imperial College, 180 Queen's Gate, London SW7 2BZ (☎ 01 589 5111, fax 01 584 7596, telex 929484 G)

SAYERS, Michael Bernard; s of Joseph David Sayers (d 1981), of London, and Miriam May, *née* Konskier; *b* 23 April 1934; *Educ* Winchester, Magdalen Oxford (MA); *m* 17 Dec 1958, Peta Ann, da of David Levi, of London; 1 s (Nicholas b 1959), 2 da (Catherine b 1961, Ruth b 1963); *Career* Nat Serv 1952-54: Midshipman 1953, Sub Lt 1954; slr 1960, asst slr 1960-62 Macfarlanes (articled clerk 1957-60), ptnr Norton Rose 1965- (asst slr 1962-64); *Style—* Michael Sayers, Esq; 9 Burgess Hill, London NW2 2BY (☎ 01 435 4348); The Old School House, Holwell, Nr Burford, Oxfordshire OX8 4JS (☎ 099 382 3084); Norton Rose, Kempson House, PO Box 570, Camomile St, London EC3A 7AN (☎ 01 283 2434, fax 01 588 1181, telex 883652)

SAYERS, Michael Patrick; QC (1988); s of Maj (Herbert James) Michael Sayers RA (ka 1943) and Sheilah De Courey Holroyd *née* Stephenson (d 1969); *b* 28 Mar 1940; *Educ* Harrow, Fitzwilliam Coll Cambridge (MA); *m* 12 Mar 1976, Moussie Brougham *née* Hallstrom 1 s (Frederick b 3 Dec 1981), 1 da (Nicola b 27 Dec 1980) 1 step s (Henry Brougham b 12 Nov 1971); *Career* barr Inner Temple 1970; recorder of the Crown Ct 1986-; *Recreations* shooting, stalking, theatre, sweden; *Clubs* Garrick, Pratts, Queen's, Swinley Forest Golf; *Style—* Michael Sayers, Esq, QC; 2 Harcourt Buildings, Temple, London, EC4Y 9DB, (☎ 01 353 2112 fax 01 353 8339)

SAYWELL, (John Anthony) Telfer; JP (Richmond 1985); s of Maj John Rupert Saywell (d 1948), of Kensington, and Winifred, *née* Green (d 1980); *b* 19 August 1939; *Educ* Abingdon Sch; *m* 8 June 1968, June Mary, da of Maurice Thomas Hunnable (d 1972), of Rivenhall, Essex; 2 s (Thomas b 1971, Henry b 1977), 1 da (Polly b 1969); *Career* CA; Fincham Vallance & Co 1958-63, Tansley Witt & Co 1963-69; Layton Fern & Co Ltd (coffee and tea specialists): joined 1969, md 1970, chm 1975-; underwriting memb of Lloyds 1983-; pres UK Coffee Trade Benevolent Soc 1985-86, govr RSC 1982-; tres: Harlequin FC 1971-78 Union Soc City of Westminster 1985-, St Lukes Educnl Centre 1989-; hon auditor Richmond Upon Thames Handicapped Soc 1973-; master Billingsgate Ward Club 1987-88; Freeman City of London 1981, memb Ct Assts Worshipful Co of Carmen 1986; FCA 1964; *Recreations* sailing, studying, skiing; *Clubs* Harlequins FC, Stewards Enclosure Henley RA; *Style—* Telfer Saywell, Esq, JP; 2 Cumberland Rd, Kew Gardens, Richmond, Surrey TW9 3HQ (☎ 01 940 0298); Layton Fern & Co Ltd, 27 Rathbone Place, London WIP 2EP (☎ 01 636 2237, fax 01 785 4191)

SCADDING, Prof John Guyett (Guy); Prof; s of John William Scadding (d 1960), of London, and Jessima Alice, *née* Guyett (d 1959); *b* 30 August 1907; *Educ* Mercers' Sch, Middx Hosp Med Sch Univ of London (MB, BS, MD); *m* 30 Aug 1940, Mabel, da of John Pennington (d 1962), of Cheshire; 1 s (John b 1948), 2 da (Jane (Mrs Jarvis) b 1949, Sarah (Mrs Fielder) b 1950); *Career* WWII serv in RAMC 1940-45: M East 1941-45, Maj 1940, Lt-Col 1942; hon conslt in diseases of the chest Army 1952-72 (awarded Guthrie Medal 1973); jr hosp appts 1930-33, res med offr Brompton Hosp 1931-35; Royal (formerly Br) Postgrad Med Sch and Hammersmith Hosp: first asst Dept of Med 1935-45, sr lect 1945-62; hon conslt physician Hammersmith Hosp 1935-, conslt physician Brompton Hosp 1939-; Inst for Diseases of the Chest Univ of London: dean 1946-60, dir of studies 1950-62, prof of med 1962-72 (emeritus 1972-); Royal College of Physicians: censor 1968-69, second vice pres 1971, Moxon Medal 1974; visiting prof: Stanford Univ of Colorado 1965, McMaster Univ 1973, Manitoba Univ 1974, Chicago 1976, Dalhousie Univ 1977; pres Br TB Assoc 1959-61, section med RSM 1969-71, memb Thoracic Soc 1970-76, ed Thorax 1946-60; memb standing med advsy ctee and central health servs cncl Miny of Health 1954-66 (chm standing TB advsy ctee), conslt advsr in diseases of the chest DHSS 1960-72, memb clinical res bd MRC 1969-65, chm industl med panel NCB 1962-72; hon memb: Société Francaise de la Tuberculose et des Maladies Respiratoires, Sociedad Espanola de Anatomia Patologica, Canadian Thoracic Soc; Freeman City of London 1950, Liveryman Worshipful Soc of Apothecaries 1950; Doctor honoris causa Univ Reims 1978; FRCP; *Books* Sarcoidosis (first ed 1967, second ed 1985); *Recreations* music, walking preferably in hills; *Clubs* Athenaeum; *Style—* Prof Guy Scadding; 18 Seagrave Rd, Beaconsfield, Bucks HP9 15U (☎ 0494 676033)

SCALES, Prof John Tracey; OBE (1986); s of Walter Laurence Scales (d 1972), of Heathfield, Wierfields, Totnes, and Ethel Margaret, *née* Tracey (d 1949); *b* 2 July 1920; *Educ* Haberdasher's Askes Sch, King's Coll Univ London, Charing Cross Hosp Med Sch (MRCS, LRCP); *m* 22 May 1945, Cecilia May, da of Albert Wesley Sparrow (d 1960), of 67 Newport Rd, Barnstaple, Devon; 2 da (Sally (Mrs Miller) b 1949, Helen (Mrs Hargreaves) b 1955); *Career* Capt RAMC 1945-47; casualty and res anaesthetist Charing Cross Hosp 1944, Royal Nat Orthopaedic Hosp 1947-87 (hon conslt 1958-); Inst of Orthopaedics Univ of London 1951-87 (prof biomedical engrg 1974-); hon conslt: Mt Vernon Hosp 1969-85, Royal Orthopaedic Hosp Birmingham 1978-87; emeritus prof Univ of London 1985-; hon conslt and hon dir dept of res in plastic surgery Mt Vernon Hosp 1988-; memb: Cncl Friends of the RNO Hosp, Action Ctee RNOH; tstee restoration of appearance and function tst Mt Vernon Hosp, memb advsy panel on med engrg Nat Fund for Res into Crippling Diseases; FRCS (1969), CIMechE (1966), RSM, BSI, ISO, fndr memb Euro Soc of Biomechanics; *Recreations* walking dogs, collecting Goss china; *Clubs* Army and Navy; *Style—* Prof John Scales, OBE; 17 Brockley Avenue, Stanmore, Middx HA7 4LX (☎ 01 958 8773); Dept of Research in Plastic Surgery, Mount Vernon Hospital, Northwood, Middx HA6 2RN (☎ 09274 26111 extn 4350)

SCALES, Prunella Margaret Rumney; *née* Illingworth; da of John Richardson Illingworth (d 1977), and Catherine, *née* Scales (d 1982); *b* 22 June 1932; *Educ* Moira House Eastborune, Old Vic Theatre Sch London; *m* 1963, Timothy Lancaster West, s of H Lockwood West, of Brighton, Sussex; 2 s (Samuel b 1966, Joseph b 1969); *Career* actress, dir and teacher; seasons at Stratford-on-Avon and Chichester Festival Theatre 1967-68; plays on London stage include: The Promise 1967, Hay Fever 1968, It's a Two-Foot-Six-Inches-Above-The-Ground-World 1970, The Wolf 1975, Breezeblock Park 1978, Make and Break 1980, An Evening with Queen Victoria 1980, The Merchant of Venice 1981, Quartermaine's Terms 1981, Big in Brazil 1984; television: Fawlty Towers 1975-79, Grand Duo, The Merry Wives of Windsor 1982, Mapp and Lucia 1985; films include: The Wicked Lady 1982; frequent broadcasts, readings, poetry recitals and fringe productions, has directed plays at: Bristol Old Vic, Arts Theatre Cambridge, Billingham Forum, Almost Free Theatre London, Nottingham Playhouse, Nat Theatre of WA Perth; taught at several drama schools; memb Accreditation Panel NCDT; *Recreations* gardening, canal boat; *Clubs* BBC; *Style—* Prunella Scales; c/o Jeremy Conway Ltd, 109 Jermyn Street, London W1 (☎ 01 839 2121)

SCAMMELL, Jean Margaret; da of Capt Charles Edgar Elders (d 1963), and Caroline Mary, *née* Tetley (d 1978); *b* 25 Jan 1930; *Educ* Harrogate GS, Durham Univ (BA), Cambridge (MA); *m* 3 Oct 1953, Geoffrey Vaughan Scammell, s of Edwin Scammell (d 1934); 1 s (Peter Geoffrey b 1959); *Career* Durham Colls Res Scholarship 1951-53, lectr Durham Univ 1959-65; lectr sev Colls, author, broadcaster and critic 1965-; written many articles on medical history; *Recreations* sailing, walking, music; *Style—* Jean Scammell; 137 Huntingdon Rd, Cambridge CB3 0DQ (☎ 356250)

SCANLAN, Charles John; s of Michael Herbert Scanlan (d 1963), of London, and Mary Ann, *née* Inglis (d 1963); *b* 4 Sept 1920; *Educ* Robert Browning Sch, Archbishop Tenison's Sch; *m* 1, 24 Dec 1949 (m dis 1973), Doris Elsie, da of Dr Thomas; 2 s (Phillip b 4 Feb 1951, Michael b 1 Dec 196), 1 da (Christine b 6 Jan 1954); m 2, Jennifer Jane, 1973; 1 da (Camilla b 13 Nov 1976); *Career* Essex Regt 1939-41, Middx Regt 1941-47: 2 Lt 1941, Lt 1943, Capt 1943, Maj 1944, Lt Col 1947; demob 1947; export mangr Coty Ltd 1948-69, export dir and gen sales mangr Fizer Ltd 1948-69, chief exec Revlon Ltd 1976 (gen sales dir 1969, gen mangr 1973), exec vice-pres Revlon Int 1979, chief exec Revlon UK 1986-; dir: Vagabond Ltd 1987, Austin Morgan Ltd; memb ctee friends of Perse School (Cambridge); MIEX 1970, FBIM 1980, Fell IOD 1986; *Clubs* Les Ambassadors, Henry's Bar; *Style—* Charles Scanlan, Esq; Wheel Hall, Cole End Lane, Sewards Lbd, Saffron Walden, Essex (☎ 0799 27477); 86 Brook St, London W1 (☎ 01 629 7400)

SCANLON, Baron (Life Peer UK 1979); Hugh Parr Scanlon; s of Hugh Scanlon; *b* 26 Oct 1913, in Australia; *Educ* Stretford Elementary Sch, Nat Council of Labour Colls; *m* 1943, Nora, da of James Markey; 2 da; *Career* apprentice instrument maker; chm Engrg Industry Training Bd to 1982; memb British Gas Corpn 1976-, pres AEUW 1968-78 (formerly div organiser and memb Londn Exec Cncl); *Style—* The Rt Hon the Lord Scanlon; 23 Seven Stones Drive, Broadstairs, Kent

SCANNELL, Vernon; *b* 23 Jan 1922; *Educ* Leeds Univ; *m* 1 Oct 1954, Josephine da of Lt-Col Claude Higson, of Edenbridge, Kent; 3 s (Toby b 1959, John b 1961, Jacob b 1967), 2 da (Jane b 1955, Nancy b 1957); *Career* 70 Bn Argyll & Sutherland Highlanders 1940-42, 5/7 Bn Gordon Highlanders 1942-45; poet in res: Berinsfield Oxfordshire 1975-76, King's Sch Canterbury 1979, Wakefield Dist Coll 1987, Mount Sch York 1987, awards: Heinemann Award for Lit 1961, Cholmondoley Peotry Prize 1974, Travelling Scholarship Soc of Authors 1987; FRSL 1961; *Books* A Sense of Danger (1962), Walking Wounded (1965), Epithets of War (1968), New & Collected

Poems (1980), The Tiger and the Rose, An Autobiography (1971), Argument of Kings (1987); *Style*— Vernon Scannell, Esq; 51 North Street, Otley, W Yorks LSL1 1AH (☎ 0943 467 176)

SCARBROUGH, Countess of; Lady Elizabeth; *née* Ramsay; da of 16 Earl of Dalhousie, KT, GCVO, GBE, MC; *b* 16 Sept 1941; *m* 1970, 12 Earl of Scarbrough, *qv*; *Style*— The Rt Hon the Countess of Scarbrough; Sandbeck Park, Maltby, Rotherham, Yorks

SCARBROUGH, 12 Earl of (E 1690); Richard Aldred Lumley; DL (S Yorks 1974); also Viscount Lumley of Waterford (I 1628), Baron Lumley of Lumley Castle (E 1681), and Viscount Lumley of Lumley Castle (E 1690); s of 11 Earl, KG, GCSI, GCIE, GCVO (d 1969); *b* 5 Dec 1932; *Educ* Eton, Magdalen Oxford; *m* 1970, Lady Elizabeth, *née* Ramsay, da of 16 Earl of Dalhousie, KT, GCVO, GBE, MC; 2 s (Robert, Thomas Henry Lumley b 6 Feb 1980), 1 da (Rose Frederica Lily b 6 Aug 1981); *Heir* s, Viscount Lumley; *Career* Lt Queen's Own Yorks Dragoons and 2 Lt 11 Hussars, ADC to Govr and CIC Cyprus 1956, Hon Col 1 Bn Yorks Volunteers 1975-; *Style*— The Rt Hon The Earl of Scarbrough, DL; Sandbeck Park, Maltby, Rotherham, S Yorks (☎ Doncaster 742210)

SCARFE, Christopher Edward; s of Edward James Scarfe, and Leah Florence, *née* Stracey (d 1983); *b* 2 July 1953; *Educ* Highgate, Middlesex Poly (Business Studies Dipl); *Career* chm and md Robert Deards Ltd, Deards Gp Ltd, Deards Services Ltd, Beacon Mimms Ltd, South Mimms Services Ltd, W Freeborn & Son Ltd 1981-; *Recreations* football, tennis, squash, golf, swimming; *Clubs* South Herts Golf, Southgate Roundtable; *Style*— Christopher E Scarfe, Esq; 14 Oakleigh Park North, Whetstone, London N20 9AR (☎ (01) 445 4000); Robert Deards Ltd, North Circulr Road, Finchley, London N12 0AJ

SCARFE, Gerald Anthony; s of Reginald Thomas Scarfe, and Dorothy Edna, *née* Garuner; *b* 1 June 1936; *m* Jane, da of Dr Richard Asher (d 1968), of 57 Wimpole St, London W1; 2 s (Alexander David b 16 Dec 1981, Rory Christopher b 10 Dec 1983), 1 da (Katie Geraldine b 11 April 1974); *Career* political cartoonist of the Sunday Times 1967-88; designer of theatre scenery and costumes: Orpheus in the Underworld London Coliseum, What a Lucky Boy Manchester Royal Exchange, Ubu Roi Traverse Theatre, and many others; designer and dir of animation Pink Floyd the Wall MGM; dir of films for the BBC: Hogarth 1970, Scarfe by Scarfe 1986, Scarfes Follies 1987; *Books* Scarfe by Scarfe (1986), Scarfes Seaven Deadly Sins (1987), Scarfes Line of Attack (1988); *Recreations* skiing; *Clubs* Brooks's; *Style*— Gerald Scarfe, Esq

SCARLETT, Albert James Morton; s of Albert James Scarlet (d 1975), of Fife, and Janet Dall, *née* Venters; *b* 25 August 1946; *Educ* The Royal HS Edinburgh, Edinburgh Sch of Architecture, Heriot Watt Univ (BArch); *m* 24 Aug 1968, Jean Bell, da of James Stenhouse (d 1969); 1s (Euan 6 1972), 1 da (Victoria b 1975); *Career* architect; city of Dundee DC 1972-79; area tech offr The Housing Corp (Glasgow) 1979-82; chartered architect in private practice 1982; ARIBA; ARIAS; *Recreations* reading, social, charitable activities, building; *Style*— Albert J M Scarlett, Esq; Elleraybank, 22 Alexandra Street, Kirkintilloch, Glasgow G66 1HE (☎ 041 7764677); Albert T M Scarlett Chartered Architect, 91 Townhead, Kirkintilloch, Glasgow G66 1NX (☎ 041 776 0731)

SCARLETT, Hon James Harry; s and h of 8 Baron Abinger, DL, *qv*; *b* 28 May 1959; *Style*— The Hon James Scarlett

SCARLETT, His Hon Judge; James Harvey Anglin Scarlett; s of Lt-Col James Alexander Scarlett, DSO, RA (d 1925) and Muriel Blease (d 1945); *b* 27 Jan 1924; *Educ* Shrewsbury, Ch Ch Oxford (MA); *Career* Lt RA 1944-47; barrister Inner Temple 1950, Malayan Civil Service 1955-58, recorder of the Crown Court 1972-74, circuit judge 1974-; *Recreations* walking; *Clubs* Athenaeum; *Style*— His Hon Judge Scarlett; Chilmington Green, Great Chart, nr Ashford, Kent

SCARLETT, The Hon John Leopold Campbell; CBE (1973); s of 7 Baron Abinger, DSO (d 1943); *b* 18 Dec 1916; *Educ* Eton, Magdalene Coll Cambridge; *m* 26 April 1947, Bridget, da of late H B Crook, of Kensington; 2 s, 1 da; *Career* formerly Maj RA; *Style*— The Hon John Scarlett, CBE; Bramblewood, Castle Walk, Wadhurst, Sussex TN5 6DB

SCARLETT, Hon Peter Richard; s of 8 Baron Abinger, DL; *b* 21 Mar 1961; *Educ* Cheltenham Coll; *Style*— The Hon Peter Scarlett; 26 Lupus Street, London SW1V 3DZ

SCARLETT-STREATFEILD, Cdr Norman John; DSC (1940); s of Air Vice-Marshal Francis Rowland Scarlett, CB, DSO (d 1934 (*see* Burke's LG 18th Edn, vol ii), and yr bro of AVM James Rowland Scarlett-Streatfeild, CBE (d 1945), who assumed the latter surname upon inheriting the The Rocks, Uckfield, Sussex (sold 1979); and Dora, *née* Blakiston-Houston (d 1954) (*see* Burke's Irish family Records, 1976); *b* 4 August 1910; *Educ* RNC Dartmouth; *m* 14 Dec 1938, Pamela Susan, da of Lt Col Richard Oakley, DSO, JP; 1 s (John b 1949), 3 da (Sarah Penelope b 1940, Anne b 1946, Rosemary b 1951 d 1952, Caroline b 1953); *Career* Naval Offr WWII; served: HMS Glorious 1938-40, HMS Illustrious 1940; took part in Fleet Air Arm attack on Taranto 1940 (POW 1940-45) (despatches 1945), subsequently various naval appts, ret 1958; *Recreations* sailing, fishing, gardening; *Clubs* The Farmers, Whitehall; *Style*— Cdr Norman J Scarlett-Streatfeild, DSC; The Field House, East Tytherton, nr Chippenham, Wilts (☎ Kellaways 268)

SCARMAN, Baron (Life Peer UK 1977); Leslie George Scarman; OBE (1944), PC (1973); s of late George Charles Scarman; *b* 29 July 1911; *Educ* Radley, BNC Oxford; *m* 1947, Ruth Clement, da of late Clement Wright, ICS; 1 s; *Career* sits as Independent peer in House of Lords; Hon DCL Oxford 1982, hon fellow BNC, visitor St Hilda's; author of report into Brixton Riots 1981; pres Roy Inst of Public Administration 1981-; barr 1936, QC 1957, judge of the High Court 1961-73, lord justice of appeal 1973-77, lord of appeal in ordinary 1977-; chllr Univ of Warwick 1977-, former memb Arts Council, chm Law Cmmn 1965-72; kt 1961; *Style*— The Rt Hon the Lord Scarman, OBE, PC; House of Lords, London SW1

SCARSDALE, 3 Viscount (UK 1911); Sir Francis John Nathaniel Curzon; 11 Bt (S 1636) and 11 Bt (E 1641); also 7 Baron Scarsdale (GB 1761); 30 Lord (territorial lordship) of Kedleston; s of late Hon Francis Nathaniel Curzon (yr bro of 1 & last Marquess Curzon of Kedleston and s of 4 Baron Scarsdale) and Phyllis, da of Capt Christian Combe, by his w, Lady Jane Seymour, da of 3 Marquess Conyngham; *b* 28 July 1924; *Educ* Eton; *m* 1, 1948 (m dis 1967), Solange Yvonne Palmyre Ghislaine (d 1974), da of late Oscar Hanse, of Mont-sur-Marchienne, Belgium; 2 s, 1 da; m 2, 1968, Helene Gladys Frances, da of late Maj William Ferguson Thomson, of Kinellar, Aberdeenshire; 2 s; *Heir* s, Hon Peter Curzon; *Career* late Capt Scots Gds; *Recreations* piping, photography, shooting; *Clubs* County, Derby; *Style*— The Rt Hon the Viscount Scarsdale; Kedleston Hall, Derby (☎ (0332) 840386)

SCARSDALE, Ottilie, Viscountess; Ottilie Margarete Julie; da of late Charles Pretzlik, of Lowfield Park, Crawley, and Ottilie Hennig; *b* 19 Nov 1905; *Educ* North Foreland Lodge, Finishing School Berchtesacabden Bavaria and Munich; *m* 1, 1925, James Henry Harris; 2 s; m 2, 1946, as his 2 w, 2 Viscount Scarsdale (d 1977); *Career* ensign FANY; *Recreations* fishing, gardening, travel; *Style*— The Rt Hon Ottilie, Viscountess Scarsdale; The Dower House, Rowler Manor, Croughton, Brackley, Northants (T Croughton 810438)

SCHAAFSMA, Hubert Alle; s of Hubert Alle Schaafsma (d 1930), of Holland, and Elisabeth Cornelia Boerlage (d 1934); *b* 5 Mar 1920; *Educ* Eindhoven Holland (Dipl Ing ME London); *m* 1, 12 Nov 1942 (m dis), Vera Palmer, da of George Shaw (d 1930); 2 s (Hubert Alle b 1944, Michael George b 1946), 1 da (Elizabeth Irene b 1947); 29 Oct 1971, Maria, da of Alphons Frans de Vilder (d 1954); *Career* RMA Sandhurst 1942, served in Br and Dutch Forces -1945; engrg and logistic advsy capacity Shell Int Petroleum Co 1945-70; *Recreations* golf; *Clubs* Royal Ashdown Forest Golf, Tandridge Golf, Mougins/Cannes Country Golf; *Style*— Hubert A Schaafsma, Esq; Residence le Clerfayts, 37 Av Jean de Hoailles, 06400 Cannes, France; High Stables, Roodlands Lane, Four Elms, Edenbridge, Kent TN8 6PG (☎ 0732-70293)

SCHAEFER, Prof Stephen Martin; s of Gerhardt Martin Schaefer, OBE (d 1986), of Bramhall, Cheshire, and Helga Maria Schaefer; *b* 18 Nov 1946; *Educ* Manchester GS, Univ of Cambridge (BA, MA), Univ of London (PhD); *m* 26 July 1969, Teresa Evelyn; 2 s (Maximilian b 1974, Joshua b 1977); *Career* London Business Sch: res offr, sr res offr, lectr 1970-79; Stanford Univ asst prof 1979-80; visting asst prof: Univ of Chicago, Univ of California (Berkeley) 1977; sr res fell Prof of Finance London Business Sch 1981-; memb American Fin Assoc; *Style*— Prof Stephen Schaefer; London Business Sch, Sussex Place, Regents Park, London NW1 4SA (☎ 01 262 5050)

SCHAFFER, Louis Isaac; s of Harry Schaffer (d 1963), and Harriet, *née* Burman (d 1965); *b* 22 April 1930; *Educ* Luton GS, Trinity Coll Cambridge (MA, LLB); *m* 1 Jan 1961, Nina Valerie, da of Raymond Richard Thomas; 2 s (Daniel) b 13 Oct 1963, Benjamim b 5 May 1965), 1 da (Rachel b 8 April 1967); *Career* RAOC: 1949-62, Capt 1954; called to the Bar Middle Temple 1955; memb Brent Police Liason Gp 1985-, Bd of Deps of Br Jews 1985-; *Recreations* walking the dog; *Style*— Louis Schaffer, Esq; 3 Barn Rise, Wembley Park, Middlesex HA9 9NA; 10 King's Bench Walk, Temple, London EC4Y 7EB (☎ 01 353 2501

SCHANSCHIEFF, Simon George; JP (1971-); s of Brian Alexander Schanschieff, and Nina, *née* Robinson; *b* 22 Oct 1938; *Educ* Oakham Sch Rutland; *m* 27 June 1964, Arman Philippa (Pip), da of Charles Henry Arman (d 1970); 3 s (Guy b 1966, Christopher b 1968, Nicholas b 1978); *Career* qualified CA 1961, ptnr Grant Thornton Northampton 1966-, gp managing ptnr 1985; chm Northampton Health Authy 1978-; chm Trustees Oakham Sch 1980-, memb Northamptonshire CCC Ctee 1969-; FCA 1971; *Style*— Simon Schanschieff, Esq, JP; Old Rectory, Great Billing, Northampton (☎ 0604 407842); Elgin Hse, Billing Rd, Northampton (☎ 0604 27811)

SCHARF, Gilbert D; *Educ* Duke Univ (BA); *m* 13 April 1986, Ruth *née* Calvin; *Career* managing ptnr Mendez Scharf & Co USA 1983-85; md: Morgan Stanley & Co Inc USA 1978-83, Lazard Brothers & Co Ltd UK 1986-; *Recreations* art, antiques, athletics; *Clubs* Annabel's, RAC, Queens, Crawley & Horsham Hunt; USA: Milbrook Golf & Tennis, Mashomack Hunting & Fishing, NY Athletics, Sawgrass, Rombout Hunt; *Style*— Gilbert Scharf, Esq; Lazard Bros & Co Ltd, 21 Moorfields, London EC2P 2HT (☎ 01 588 2721, fax 01 374 0906, telex 947030)

SCHAUFUSS, Peter; *b* 26 April 1950; *Educ* Royal Danish Ballet Sch; *Career* apprenticeship Royal Danish Ballet Co 1965-67 and 1969; Soloist Nat Ballet of Canada 1967-68, princ London Festival Ballet 1970-78, numerous guest appearances incl: Royal Ballet, Nat Ballet of Canada, Ballet of Canada, Ballet National de Marseille, La Scala Milan, Vienna State Opera, Tokyo Ballet Co, American Ballet Theatre, Royal Danish Ballet, Deutsche Oper Berlin, Scottish Ballet, Bavarian State Opera, Paris Opera, Teatro dell'Opera (Rome), Teatro Comunale (Florence); prodns incl: La Sylphide London Festival Ballet 1979, Ballet National de Marseille 1980, Deutsche Oper Berlin 1982, Stuttgart Ballet 1982, Teatro Comunale Firenze 1983, Napoli Nat Ballet of Canada 1981, Folktale Deutsche Oper Berlin 1983, Dances from Napoli London Festival Ballet 1983, Bournonville Aterballetto 1984, The Nutcracker, London Festival Ballet 1986; created roles: George Balanchine The Steadfast Tin Soldier 1975, Rhapsodie Espagnole 1975, Roland Petit Phantom of the Opera 1980, Sir Kenneth MacMillan Verdi Variations 1982, Orphens 1982; BBC TV ballet series: Dancer 1984, Phantom of the Opera 1980, documentary Great Dancers of the World French television; present profession: dancer, choreographer, producer; artistic dir London Festival Ballet 1984-; Solo Award 2nd Int Ballet Competition Moscow 1973, Stern des jahres (Star of the year) Fed Rep of Germany 1979, Soc of W End Theatres Award for ballet 1979, Evening Standard Award for most outstanding achievement in dance 1979; *Recreations* boxing; *Style*— Peter Schaufuss, Esq; c/o Papoutsis Representation Ltd, 18 Sundial Ave, London SE25 4BX

SCHEER, Cherrill Shiela; *née* Hille; da of Maurice Hille (d 1968), and Ray Hille (d 1986); *b* 29 Mar 1939; *Educ* Copthall Co GS, Architectural Assoc London, Architectural Dept Kingston Sch of Art; *m* 3 Dec 1961, Ian Scheer, s of Oscar Scheer (d 1988); 1 s (Ivan), 1 da (Danielle Ann (Mrs Benson)); *Career* mktg dir Hille Int Ltd 1970-83 (mktg mangr 1961-70), dir Print Forum Ltd 1965-, dir gp mktg Hille Ergonom plc 1983-; vice pres Design & Indust Assoc (chm 1976-78); memb: advsy panel London Coll of Furniture, cncl Business Equipment and Info Technol Assoc (chm Furniture Div); Assoc Chartered Soc of Designers; *Style*— Mrs Ian Scheer; 16 Kerry Ave, Stanmore, Middx HA7 4NN (☎ 01 954 3839); Hille Ergonom plc, 365/369 Euston Rd, London NW1 3AR (☎ 01 380 1513, fax 01 387 4276, telex 27679)

SCHEFFERS, Peter Anthony; s of Jean Maurice Scheffers (d 1950), and Vera Veronica Whately (d 1949); *b* 9 June 1924; *Educ* Downside, St Georges, Ch Ch Oxford, (BSc); *m* 17 Dec 1954, Josephine Jean, da of Charles Johnson (d 1965), of Weybridge; 1 da (Sally Louise b 1960); *Career* Capt cmmnd RCS 1942; served Cairo joined SOE, captured in Yugoslavia 1944 (POW in Germany), invalided out of army 1945; joined fathers textile importing business (took control 1950), ret; farmer 128 acres; Freeman City of London 1954, memb Worshipful Co of Horners (memb Court of Assistance 1977-87); Goldene Ehrenzeichen (Austria) 1984; *Clubs* Special Forces (fndr memb 1945-46); *Style*— Peter A Scheffers, Esq; Punch Bowl Farm, Thursley,

Godalming, Surrey SU8 6DJ

SCHETRUMPF, John Robert; s of Leslie John Schetrumpf (d 1956), of Aust, and Dorothy Linda, *née* Rose (d 1957); *b* 2 Jan 1939; *Educ* Sydney Univ (MB BS); *Career* cosmetic surgn; FRCS (Edinburgh) 1969; *Books* on subjects of dermabrasion, prominent ear deformity, artificial finger joints, spinal surgery; *Recreations* sailing; *Clubs* RAF Yacht, Hamble; *Style*— John Schetrumpf, Esq; 17 Harley St, London W1 (☎ 01 637 5005)

SCHIEMANN, Hon Mr Justice; Hon Sir Konrad Hermann Theodor; s of Dr Helmuth Schiemann (d 1945), and Beate Schiemann, *née* von Simson (d 1946); *b* 15 Sept 1937; *Educ* King Edwards Sch Birmingham, Pembroke Coll Cambridge (MA, LLB); *m* 1965, Elisabeth Hanna Eleonore, da of late John Holroyd-Reece; 1 da (Juliet b 1966); *Career* jr cnsl to the Crown (Common Law) 1978-80; QC 1980, rec Crown Court 1985, bencher Inner Temple 1985, High Court judge (Queen's Bench Div) 1986-; Kt 1986; *Recreations* music, reading, walking; *Style*— Hon Mr Justice Schiemann; Royal Courts of Justice, Strand, London WC2

SCHIFF, Andras; s of Odon Schiff, and Klara, *née* Osengeri; *b* 21 Dec 1953; *Educ* Franz Liszt Acad of Music Budapest, Private Study with George Malcolm; *m* Oct 1987, Yuuko, *née* Shikawa; *Career* concert pianist; regular orchestral engagements: NY Philharmonic, Chicago Symphony, Vienna Philharmonic, Concertgebown Orchestra, Paris Philharmonic, London Philharmonic, London Symphony, Royal Philharmonic, Israel Philharmonic, Washington Nat Symphony; festivals include: Salzburg, Edinburgh, Aldeburgh, Tanglewood; *Recreations* literature, languages, soccer; *Style*— Andras Schiff, Esq; Terry Harrison Artists Mmgnt, 9A Penzance Place, London W11 4PE (☎ 01 221 7741, fax 01 221 2610, telex 25872)

SCHILIZZI, Maj John Stephen; s of Stephen Schilizzi (descended from a family prominent in Byzantium under the Emperors Nicephorus III and Isaac Comnenus II - *ca* 1080 - and until the 14th century; the first Schilizzis to settle in England did so after the massacre of Chios 1822); unc of Edmund Brudenell, the proprietor of Deene Park; *b* 15 Dec 1896; *Educ* Eton; *m* 20 Dec 1935, Lady Sophia Waldegrave; 1 s, 2 da; *Career* served WWI Capt Northants Yeo & WWII as Maj RASC; *Clubs* Jockey; *Style*— Maj John Schilizzi; Chacombe House, Banbury, Oxon

SCHILIZZI, Lady (Gabrielle) Sophia Annette; Waldegrave; *b* 7 June 1908; *m* 20 Dec 1935, Maj John Schilizzi, *qv*; 1 s, 2 da; *Style*— Lady Sophia Schilizzi; Chacombe House, Banbury, Oxon

SCHOFIELD, Jack William Lionel; s of Capt Leslie Schofield (d 1971), and Edna Morris (d 1975); da of Ethel Lumley, undefeated Lady Champion Puntist on the Thames; *b* 29 April 1927; *Educ* Merchant Taylor's, Imperial Coll, London Univ; *m* 12 Sept 1954, Sonia Fay, da of Dr E G Copeland (d 1977); 1 s (Colin b 1960), 1 da (Rosalyn b 1956); *Career* served RE 1946-48, Germany, N Italy (Trieste); dir S I Gp plc (jt md), Ambressey Engrs Ltd, S G L Sheet Metal Ltd, chm Schofield and Samson Ltd, chm and mangr Hibbert and Richards Ltd, chm Southern Industries Ltd, Cellar and Bar Serv Ltd; *Recreations* golf, tennis, rugby football; *Clubs* IOD, Finchley Golf, OMT Rugby; *Style*— Jack Schofield, Esq; Willowmead, Oakleigh Park North, London N20 9AU (☎ 01 445 8255); 4B Orsmam Road, London N1 (☎ 01 739 6817, telex 261640)

SCHOFIELD, John Michael; s of James William Schofield (d 1982), and Donaldina McKay McMichael; *b* 11 April 1926; *Educ* St Georges Sch Harpenden, Middx Hosp Med Sch and London Univ (MB BS); *m* 3 June 1952, Arlette Marie-Elvire Julie, da of Francois van Calck; 2 s (Philip, James), 1 da (Olivia (Mrs Walker)); *Career* surgn Lt RNVR 1950-53; conslt ENT surgn Warwick Hosp 1962-; gen sec Br Academic Conf in Otology 1979-83 (chm 1983- 87), pres section of laryngology RSM 1986-87; parish cncllr Kineton Parish Cncl; FRCS (Ed), FRCS; *Recreations* golf, real tennis, reading, travel; *Clubs* MCC, Anglo - Belgian; *Style*— John Schofield, Esq; Brookhampton Farm, Kineton, Warwick (☎ 0926 640 330); Warwick Hospital, Wakin Rd, Warwick

SCHOFIELD, Michael George; s of Snowden Schofield, JP (d 1949), and Ella, *née* Dawson (d *ca* 1968); *b* 24 June 1919; *Educ* Clare Coll Cambridge, Harvard; *Career* social res conslt; res dir: Central Cncl for Health Educn London 1961-65, Govt advsy ctee on Drug Dependence 1967, Wootton Ctee on Cannabis 1969, Police Powers of Arrest and Search 1970; many TV and radio programmes, ret; *Books* The Sexual Behaviour of Young People (1965), The Sociological Aspects of Homosexuality (1965), Society and the Young School Leaver (1967), Drugs and Civil Liberties (1968); co-author: Behind the Drug Scene (1970), The Strange Case of Pot (1971), The Rights of Children (1972); author: The Sexual Behaviour of Young Adults (1973), Promiscuity (1976), The Sexual Containment Act (1978); *Recreations* theatre, arts, consumer affairs, civil rights, environment; *Style*— Michael Schofield, Esq; 28 Lyndhurst Gardens, London NW3 5NW (☎ 01-794-5125)

SCHOFIELD, Phillip Bryan; s of Brian Homer Schofield, and Patricia, *née* Parry; *b* 1 April 1962; *Educ* Newquay GS; *Career* first invision anchorman BBC Childrens TV 1985-87, main presenter BBC TV's marathon magazine programme Going Live, voted Top Man on TV 1987-88, voted no 1 TV personality in all maj teenage magazines 1987-88; involved in: Children's Royal Variety performance 1987-88, Stars Orgn for Spastics, NSPCC, Br Heart Fndn; *Style*— Phillip Schofield, Esq; James Grant Group of Cos, PO Box 676, London W4 3UT (☎ 01 994 8579, fax 01 995 6667, car 0836 719001)

SCHOLAR, Dr Michael Charles; s of Richard Herbert Scholar, of Truro, Cornwall, and Mary Blodwen, *née* Jones (d 1985); *b* 3 Jan 1942; *Educ* St Olave's and St Saviour's GS, St John's Coll Cambridge (MA, PhD), Univ of Calif at Berkeley, Harvard Univ; *m* 26 Aug 1984, Angela Mary, da of William Whinfield Sweet (d 1984), of Wylam, Northumberland; 3 s (Thomas b 1968, Richard b 1973, John b 1980), 1 da (Jane b 1976, d 1977); *Career* asst lectr philosophy Leicester Univ 1968, fell St Johns Coll Cambridge 1969, asst princ HM Treasy 1970, private sec to Chief Sec HM Treasy 1974-76, sr int mangr Barclays Bank plc 1979-81, private sec to PM 1981-83, dep sec HM Treasy 1987 (under sec 1983); ARCO 1965; *Recreations* music, opera, walking, gardening; *Style*— Dr Michael Scholar; HM Treasy, Parliament St, London SW1 (☎ 01 270 4389)

SCHOLES, Alwyn Denton; s of Denton Scholes (d 1928), of Bournemouth, and Violet Penelope Hill, *née* Birch (d 1970); *b* 16 Dec 1910; *Educ* Cheltenham, Cambridge Univ (MA); *m* 16 Dec 1939, Juliet Angela Ierne, da of Maj Frederick Sparke Pyne, DSO, RA; 1 s (Richard), 4 da (Sarah, Juliet, Petrina, Jill); *Career* Gold Coast Voluntary Army Force 1939-45, Hong Kong RNVR 1950-58; barr Inner Temple 1934, practised London and Midlands circuit 1934-38, appt dist magistrate Gold Coast 1938 (actg crown counsel and slr gen 1941), magistrate Hong Kong 1948; first magistrate: Kowloon 1949, Hong Kong 1949, dist judge Hong Kong 1953, puisne judge Hong Kong 1958, cmmr Supreme Ct of Brunei 1964-67 and 1968-71, pres memb Hong Kong Full Ct of Appeal 1949-71, sr puisne judge Hong Kong 1970, actg chief justice of Hong Kong 1971, ret 1971; memb: Sidmouth PCC 1972-82, Ottery Deanery Synod 1973-82; govr St Nicholas Sch Sidmouth 1984-; *Recreations* walking, gardening; *Clubs* Royal Cwlth Soc (life memb); *Style*— Alwyn Scholes, Esq; West Hayes, Convent Rd, Sidmouth, Devon EX10 8RL; Gentle Jane, St Minver, Wadebridge, Cornwall PL27 6RN (☎ 0395 512 970)

SCHOLES, Bryan Richard; s of Richard Scholes (d 1968), and Ellen Maud, *née* Heywood (d 1958); *b* 8 July 1914; *Educ* Ackworth Sch; *m* 29 April 1939, Joan Hilda Reeve; 4 da; *Career* chm W H Heywood & Co Ltd 1955-76 (joined 1930, dir 1957, md 1950); chm: W M Oddy & Co Ltd 1955-60, Neaversons Ltd 1940-87; former pres Huddersfield C of C, vice-pres Assoc Br C of C, past chm NE BIM; fndr pres: Aluminium Window Assoc, Suspended Ceilings Assoc; former pres Fedn of Euro Metal Window Mfrs Assocs, fndr tstee Huddersfield Common Good Tst; *Recreations* farming, walking, gardening, beagling; *Clubs* Huddersfield, RAC, farmers, IOD; *Style*— Bryan Scholes, Esq; Folly Hall, Thornthwaite, Harrogate HG3 2QU (☎ Harrogate 780228)

SCHOLES, John Francis Millar; s of Frank Victor Gordon Scholes, CMG (d 1954), and Annie (Nancie) Noble, *née* Millar (d 1958); *b* 7 April 1919; *Educ* Scotch Coll Melbourne, Melbourne Univ (BEng Sc), Sydney Univ (BE); *m* 1947, Joyce Bartlett, da of Sidney Frank Henry Laws (d 1973), of Sydney; *Career* engr: Aeronautical Res Laboratory Melbourne 1943-49, Royal Aircraft Establishment 1950-58, Int Computers and Tabulators Ltd 1958-65, National Research Devpt Corpn 1965-81 (memb and chief exec engrg 1977-81); Hon FInst MC (pres 1966-67); CEng, FIEE, MRAeS, MIEAust; *Recreations* genealogy, stamp collecting; *Style*— John Scholes, Esq; 22 Outlook Drive, Burwood, Victoria 3125, Australia (☎ 03 29 1923)

SCHOLES, Rodney James; QC (1987); s of Henry Scholes (d 1971), of Widnes, and Margaret Bower, *née* Aldred; *b* 26 Sept 1945; *Educ* Wade Deacon GS Widnes, St Catherinés Coll Oxford (BA, BCL); *m* 13 Aug 1977, Katherin Elizabeth (Kate), da of Dermot Keogh, of Heaton Mersey; 3 s (Michael b 7 June 1978, Jonathan b 7 Oct 1980, Nicholas b 15 Dec 1982); *Career* barr Lincolns Inn 1968, memb Northern circuit 1968-, recorder Crown Ct 1986-; *Recreations* watching rugby league football; *Style*— Rodney Scholes, Esq, QC; 5 Essex Ct, Temple London EC4Y 9AH (☎ 01 353 4363, fax 01 583 1491); 25 Byrom St, Manchester M3 4PF (☎ 061 834 5238, fax 061 834 0394)

SCHOLEY, Sir David Gerald; CBE; s of Dudley and Lois Scholey; *b* 28 June 1935; *Educ* Wellington, Ch Ch Oxford; *m* 1960, Alexandra Beatrix, da of Hon George Drew, of Canada; 1 s, 1 da; *Career* joined S G Warburg & Co Ltd 1965 (dir 1967, dep chm 1977), chm S G Warburg Group plc 1984; dir: Mercury Securities plc 1969 (chm 1984-86), Orion Insurance Co Ltd 1963, Stewart Wrightson Holdings Ltd 1972-81, Union Discount Co of London Ltd 1976-87, British Telecom plc 1985-; memb Export Guarantees Advsy Cncl 1970-75 (dep chm 1974-75); chm Construction Exports Advsy Bd 1975-78; memb ctee on Finance for Industry NEDO 1980-, hon tres IISS 1984-; govr Wellington Coll 1977-; NIESR 1984-; FRSA 1987; kt 1987; *Style*— Sir David Scholey, CBE; c/o S G Warburg Group plc, 33 King William Street, London EC4R 9AS (☎ 01 280 2222)

SCHOLTENS, Sir James Henry; KCVO (1977, CVO 1963); s of late Theo F J Scholtens; *b* 12 June 1920; *Educ* St Patrick's Marist Brothers Coll Sale Vic; *m* 1945, Mary, da of C D Maguire (decd); 1 s, 5 da; *Career* dir Office of Govt Ceremonial Hospitality Dept of PM and Cabinet 1973-80; dir of visits to Australia by HM The Queen, HRH The Duke of Edinburgh and members of The Royal Family, Heads of State, Monarchs and Presidents; extra gentleman usher to HM The Queen 1981-; *see Debrett's Handbook of Australia and New Zealand for further details*; *Style*— Sir James Scholtens, KCVO; 74 Boldrewood St, Turner, Canberra, ACT 2601, Australia (T 48 6639)

SCHON, Baron (Life Peer UK 1976); Frank Schon; s of late Dr Frederick Schon, of Vienna, and Henriette, *née* Nettel; *b* 18 May 1912; *Educ* Rainer Gymnasium Vienna, Prague Univ, Vienna Univ; *m* 1936, Gertrude, da of late Abraham Secher; 2 da; *Career* co-fndr Marchon Products Ltd 1939, Solway Chemicals Ltd 1943, chm and md of both until 1967; chm National Research Devpt Corpn 1969-79 (memb 1967-79), dir Blue Circle Industries 1967-82; memb cncl King's Coll Durham 1959-63; Univ of Newcastle upon Tyne: memb cncl 1963-66, memb court 1963-78; chm Cumberland Devpt Cncl 1964-68; memb: Northern Economic Planning Cncl 1965-68, Industrial Reorganisation Corpn 1966-71, Advsy Cncl of Technology 1968-70; pt/t memb Northern Gas Bd 1963-66; Hon Freeman of Whitehaven 1961; Hon DCL Durham 1961; kt 1966; *Recreations* golf, reading; *Style*— The Rt Hon the Lord Schon; Flat 82, Prince Albert Court, 33 Prince Albert Rd, London NW8 7LU (☎ 01 586 1461)

SCHOOLAR, James Hardie; s of John Schoolar (d 1951), of Stirling, and Jessie, *née* Hardie; *b* 2 June 1936; *Educ* Stirling HS, Univ of Glasgow (BDS); *m* 28 Sept 1985, Linda Ann, da of Stanley Edward Quinn, of 97 Ashley Drive, Bramhall, Cheshire; *Career* Nat Serv RN 1954-56; Royal Bank of Scotland 1956-58 (apprentice 1952), Univ of Glasgow Faculty of Medicine 1958-64, asst in Stirling Dental practice 1964-65, started own practice in Stirling 1965, in practice in Jersey CI 1980-84; returned to Stirling 1985; *Recreations* gardening, stamp collecting, animals, walking, tennis; *Clubs* Travel, The Church; *Style*— James Schoolar, Esq; Brunnen, Birkhill Rd, Stirling (☎ 0786 72446)

SCHOOLING, John Duprey; TD (1945), DL (Hereford and Worcester 1972); s of Arthur John Schooling (d 1971), and Eva Winifred, *née* Duprey (d 1983); *b* 8 July 1911; *Educ* Dean Close Sch, Sheffield Univ (LLB); *m* 1939, Ursula Mary (d 1985), da of Harold Taylor (d 1971), of Barnsley; 1 s (Christopher); *Career* TA 1931-61, War Service in Burma with rank of Maj RA (TA); solicitor 1934, asst solicitor Worcs CC 1945-63, asst clerk and dep clerk of the peace Worcs CC 1963-71, dep clerk of WCC 1971-74, dep county sec Hereford and Worcs CC 1974-75; private practice 1975-; *Recreations* local history; *Clubs* Naval and Military; *Style*— John Schooling, Esq, TD, DL; The Walhatch, Forest Row Sussex RH18 5AW

SCHOUVALOFF, Alexander; s of Paul Schouvaloff (d 1961), and Anna, *née* Raevsky, MBE; *b* 4 May 1934; *Educ* Harrow, Jesus Coll Oxford (MA); *m* 1, 18 Feb 1959 (m dis), Gillian Baker; 1 s (Alexander b 1959); *m* 2, 18 Nov 1971, Daria Chorley, *née* de Méndol; *Career* Nat Serv 2 Lt RMP Shape Paris 1957-59, Award of Merit Eaton Hall OCS; asst dir Edinburgh Festival 1965-67; dir: NW Arts Assoc 1967-74, Rochdale

Festival 1971, Chester Festival 1973; curator Theatre Museum 1974-; radio plays Radio Four: Summer of the Bullshine Boys 1981, No Saleable Value 1982; sec gen Société Internationale des Bibliotheques et des Musees des Arts du Spectacle; FRSA; Polonia Restituta Poland 1971; *Books* Summer of the Bullshine Boys (1979), Stravinsky on Stage (with Victor Borovsky, 1982), Catalogue of Set and Costume Designs in Thyssen-Bornemisza Collection (1987), The Theatre Museum (1987); *Clubs* Garrick; *Style—* Alexander Schouvaloff, Esq; 59 Lyndhurst Grove, London SE15 5QN (☎ 01 703 3671); Theatre Museum, 1E Tavistock St, London WC2E 7PA (☎ 01 836 7891)

SCHREIBER, Mark Shuldham; s of John Shuldham Schreiber (d 1968), of Marlesford Hall, Woodbridge, Suffolk, and Constance Maureen Schreiber (d 1980); *b* 11 Sept 1931; *Educ* Eton, Trinity Coll Cambridge (MA); *m* 1969, Gabriella Federica, da of Conte Teodoro Veglio Di Castelletto Uzonne; 2 da (Nicola Charlotte (b 1971), Sophie Louisa (b 1973); *Career* Nat Service Coldstream Gds, 2 Lt; Fisons Ltd 1957-63, Conservative Research Dept 1963-67, dir Conservative Party Public Sector Research Unit 1967-70, special adviser HM Govt 1970-74, special adviser to leader of the Opposition 1974-75, editorial staff The Economist 1974- (parly lobby correspondent); memb: Countryside Cmmn 1980-, Devpt Cmmn for Rural England 1985-; *Clubs* Pratt's; *Style—* Mark Schreiber, Esq; Marlesford Hall, Woodbridge, Suffolk; 5 Kersley St, London SW11; The Economist, 25 St James's St, London SW1 (☎ 01 839 7000)

SCHRODER, Baron Bruno Lionel; s of Baron Helmut William Bruno Schroder (d 1969) s of Baron Bruno Schroder or von Schröder, chief of the London branch of the Banking House of J Henry Schroder & Co, cr Freiherr by Kaiser Wilhelm II aboard the yacht 'Hohenzollern' on 27 July 1904; the Baron's er bro Rudolph was cr Freiherr eight months later), and Margaret Eleanor Phyllis, eld da of Sir Lionel Darell, 6 Bt, DSO, JP, DL; *b* 17 Jan 1933; *Educ* Eton, Univ Coll Oxford (MA), Harvard Business School (MBA); *m* 30 May 1969, Patricia Leonie Mary (Piffa), da of Maj Adrian Holt (d 1984); 1 da (Leonie b 1974); *Career* 2 Lt The Life Gds 1951-53; dir: Schroders plc 1963-, J Henry Schroder Wagg & Co Ltd 1966-, Schroders Inc 1984-; memb exec ctee The Air Sqdn; memb ct of assts The Goldsmiths' Co; has Queen Beatrix of the Netherlands Wedding Medal; *Recreations* shooting, stalking, flying; *Clubs* Brooks's; *Style—* Baron Schroder; 42 Lansdowne Road, London W11 4LU (☎ 01 229 1433); 120 Cheapside, London EC2V 6DS (☎ 01 382 6000, fax 01 382 6878, telex 885029)

SCHROEDER, Hon Mrs; Hon Sheila Kathleen; *née* Atkins; eld da of Baron Colnbrook (Life Peer), *qv*; *b* 26 Oct 1944; *m* 1, 15 Feb 1964 (m dis 1974), Peter Thornycroft Romer-Lee, er s of Charles Romer-Lee; 2 s; m 2, 1975 (m dis 1978), Keith Allen Manners; m 3, 1982, Royston Joseph Schroeder; *Style—* The Hon Mrs Schroeder; Ellimore Farm, Lustleigh, Devon

SCHÜFFEL, Hon Mrs; Hon Sh`an; da of Baron Edmund-Davies, PC (Life Peer); *b* 1940; *m* 1964, Wolfram Schüffel, MD; *Style—* The Hon Mrs Schüffel; 3550 Marburg/Lahn, Kaffweg 17A, W Germany

SCHUIL-BREWER, Graham; s of Lt A E Schuil, RNVR (d 1943), and M E Brewer, *née* Hepple; *b* 20 Feb 1942; *Educ* Harrow Sch; *m* 22 June 1968, Josephine Diana, da of David L Ellis (d 1969); 1 s (Justin b 6 June 1971), 1 da (Sophie b 25 April 1976); *Career* corporate fin controller Br Shipbuilders 1982-85; non-exec dir: Scott Lithgow Ltd 1982-85, Br Shipbuilders Offshore Div 1982-85; dir: Austin and Pickersgill Ltd 1985-87, Sunderland Shipbuilders Ltd 1986-87, NE Shipbuilders Ltd 1986-87, Courtaulds Engrg Ltd 1988-; *Recreations* golf, squash, rugby union; *Style—* Graham Schuil-Brewer, Esq; 65 Newbold Road, Barlestone, nr Nuneaton, Warwickshire CV13 0DY (☎ 0455 290 412); P O Box 11, Foleshill Road, Conventry CV6 5AB (☎ 0203 688 771, fax 0203 687 325, telex 312 171)

SCHUSTER, Sir (Felix) James Moncrieff; 3 Bt (UK 1906), of Collingham Rd, Royal Borough of Kensington, OBE (Mil 1955), TD; s of Sir (Felix) Victor Schuster, 2 Bt (d 1962); *b* 8 Jan 1913; *Educ* Winchester; *m* 1937, Ragna, da of late Direktor Sundøoe of Copenhagen; 2 da; *Heir* none; *Career* served WWII with The Rifle Bde in Middle East and Combined Operations attaining rank of Maj 1939-45; Hon Col 5 Bn Royal Green Jackets T & AVR 1970-75; *Clubs* Naval and Military, Lansdowne; *Style—* Sir James Schuster, Bt, OBE, TD; Piltdown Cottage, Piltdown, Uckfield, E Sussex TN22 3XB

SCHUSTER, Hon Mrs (Lorna Frances); *née* Hermon-Hodge; da of 2 Baron Wyfold, DSO, MVO; *b* 25 Feb 1911; *m* 1941, John Schuster, TD, DL, eld s of Sir George Schuster, KCSI, KCMG, CBE, MC; 2 s, 1 da (all adopted); *Style—* The Hon Mrs Schuster; The Manor Farm, Nether Worton, Oxon (☎ Great Tew 254)

SCHWABE, Prof Walter Wolfgang; s of Dr Walter Schwabe (d 1962), of Wimbledon, and Anne, *née* Lagershausen (d 1954); *b* 1 June 1920; *Educ* Regent St Poly, Imperial Coll London Univ (BSc, ARCS, PhD, DIC, DSc, DAghc); *m* 15 Nov 1958 (m dis); 1 s (John b 1965), 2 da (Fiona b 1960, Ruth b 1962); *Career* plant physiologist and prof of horticulture London Univ and Wye Coll 1965-85, princ scientific offr Agric Research Cncl 1958-65, memb governing body (exec ctee) East Malling Research Station; memb: Nat Vegetable Research Station, Glasshouse Crops Research Station; ed in chief Journal of Experimental Botany, assoc ed jl Hort Sci and Physiologia Plantarum (Scandinavia); *Recreations* hill walking, skiing; *Style—* Prof Walter W Schwabe; Audlea, Bilting, nr Ashford, Kent (☎ 0233 812 482); Dept Horticulture, Wye Coll, London Univ, Wye, nr Ashford, Kent (☎ 0233 812 401)

SCHWARZ, Prof Kurt Karl; s of Benno Schwarz (d 1965), of Norwich, Norfolk, and Margaretha Emilia Julia, *née* Petz (d 1985); *b* 24 May 1926; *Educ* Leys Sch Cambridge, Univ of Cambridge (MA); *m* 6 Aug 1949, Brenda Patricia, da of Fred Pilling, CBE, of Lytham St Annes; 1 s (David Roger Charles b 31 May 1950), 2 da (Jennifer Patricia (Mrs Orton) b 15 Sept 1952, Mary Brenda Margaret b 7 May 1958); *Career* tech dir Laurence Scott and Electromotors Ltd 1965-86 (dir 1968-86), visiting indust prof Univ of Southampton 1987; memb Norfolk Engrg Soc, Norfolk and Norwich Music Club; ctee memb: BSI, BEAMA, EIC; memb Inst M and C 1957, memb BNES 1960, FIEE 1961, FIMechE 1961; *Recreations* music, walking, swimming, gardening; *Style—* Prof Kurt Schwarz; Threshfield, Bullockshed Lane, Bramerton, Norwich NR14 7HG (☎ 050 88 446)

SCIAMA, Prof Dennis William; s of Abraham Sciama (d 1969), and Nellie, *née* Ades (1974); *b* 18 Nov 1926; *Educ* Malvern, Trinity Coll Cambridge (BA, PhD); *m* 26 Nov 1959, Lidia, da of Guido Dina (d 1975), of Venice; 2 da (Susan b 26 Oct 1962, Sonia b 30 Oct 1964); *Career* Private REME 1947-49; jr res fell Trinity Coll Cambridge 1952-56, lectr mathematics Univ of Cambridge 1961-70, sr res fell All Souls Coll Oxford 1970-85, prof astrophysics Int Sch Advanced Studies Trieste 1983-; FRS 1983; foreign memb: American Philosophical Soc 1982, American Acad Arts and Scis 1983, Accademia Dei Lincei 1984; *Books* The Unity of the Universe (1959), The Physical Foundations of General Relativity (1969), Modern Cosmology (1971); *Style—* Prof Dennis Sciama; 7 Park Town, Oxford (☎ 0865 59441); Sissa, Strada Costiera 11, 34014, Trieste, Italy (☎ 040 224 9330)

SCICLUNA, Martin Anthony; s of William L Scicluna, of Malta, and Miriam, *née* Gouder; *b* 20 Nov 1950; *Educ* Berkhamstead Sch Herts, Leeds Univ (BCom); *m* 28 July 1979, (Kathrine) Fenella, da of Rev Canon Norman Haddock, of Cheltenham, Gloucs; 1 s (Mark William b 26 April 1984), 2 da (Claire Alexandra b 11 Aug 1987); *Career* CA; ptnr Touche Ross & Co 1982- (articled 1973-76); chm London Soc of CAs (ICEAW) 1988-89; ACA 1976, FCA 1980, MBIM 1976; *Books* Money for Microchips (1983), High on Tech/Low on Cash (1986); *Recreations* gardening, wine appreciation; *Style—* Martin A Scicluna, Esq; Carnforth, The Warren, Radlett, Herts, WD7 7DU (☎ 0923 857 390); Touceh Ross & Co, Hill House, 1 Little New St, London, EC4A 3TR (☎ 01 353 8011, fax 01 583 8517, telex 884739)

SCLATER, John Richard; s of Arthur William Sclater and Alice, *née* Collett; *b* 14 July 1940; *Educ* Charterhouse, Gonville and Caius Coll Cambridge, Yale, Harvard; *m* 1, 1967 (m dis), Nicola Mary Gloria Cropper; 1 s, 1 da; 2, 1985, Grizel Elizabeth Catherine, o da of Lt-Col H V Dawson; *Career* chm: Guinness Mahon & Co Ltd 1987-, Guinness Mahon Hldgs Ltd, Sclater Farming Ltd, Foreign and Colonial Investment Tst plc, F&C Enterprise Tst plc; dep chm: Guinness Peat Gp plc 1987-, The Union Discount Co of London plc 1985-; dir: S&W Berisford plc, Berner Nicol & Co Ltd, Billingsgate City Securities plc, The Equitable Life Assurance Soc, Foreign and Colonial Mgmnt Ltd, GMBH Ltd, Halifax Building Soc (London Bd), Holker Estates Co Ltd, The Union Discount Superannuation Fund Tst Ltd, Yamaichi International (Europe) Ltd; govr International Students Tst Ltd; *Recreations* field sports, gardening, forestry, running; *Clubs* Brooks's, The Univ Pitt (Cambridge); *Style—* John Sclater, Esq; Sutton Hall, Barcombe, Lewes, Sussex (☎ 0273 400 450); Yamaichi International (Europe) Ltd, Finsbury Court, 111-117 Finsbury Pavement, London EC2A 1EQ (☎ 01 623 6222, telex 893065)

SCLATER, Patrick Henry; s of Henry Nicolai Sclater, of Stockbridge, Hants, and Suzanna Mary, *née* Agnew; *b* 9 Jan 1944; *Educ* Charterhouse, RAC Cirencester; *m* 8 July 1968, Rosalyn Heather, da of Urban George Eric Stephenson, of Frith House, Stalbridge, Dorset; 3 s (William b 1969, Alastair b 1971, Peter b 1976), 1 da (Heather b 1978); *Career* estate agent; sole princ Sclater Real Estate Dorchester 1974-83, Symonds, Sampson & Sclater 1983-87, local dir Fulljames & Still Dorchester 1987; relocation agent; princ Sclater Property Search 1988-; *Recreations* shooting, sailing, walking, gardening, reading, travel; *Style—* Patrick H Sclater, Esq; Old Farmhouse, Frith, Stalbridge, Sturminster Newton, Dorset; 55 High West Street, Dorchester (☎ 0963 251363)

SCOFIELD, (David) Paul; CBE (1956); s of Edward Henry Scofield (d 1976), of Hurstpierpoint, Sussex, and Mary, *née* Wild; *b* 21 Jan 1922; *Educ* Hurstpierpoint, Varndean Sch for Boys Brighton; *m* 15 May 1943, Joy Mary, da of Edward Henry Parker (d 1947); 1 s (Martin Paul b 6 March 1945); 1 da (Sarah b 22 Aug 1951); *Career* actor; Birmingham Repertory Theatre 1942-45; Stratford-upon-Avon 1946, 1947, 1948; London theatres: Adventure Story and The Seagull St James's 1949, Ring Round the Moon Globe 1950-52, Much Ado About Nothing Phoenix 1952, The River Line Edinburgh Festival, Lyric (Hammersmith) Strand 1952, Richard II, The Way of the World, Venice Preserved, Lyric (Hammersmith) 1952-53; A Question of Fact Piccadilly 1953-54, Time Remembered New Theatre 1954-55, Hamlet Moscow 1955; Paul Scofield-Peter Brook Season 1956, The Power and the Glory, Hamet and Family Reunion Phoenix, A Dead Secret Piccadilly 1957, Expresso Bongo Saville 1958, The Complaisant Lover Globe 1959, A Man for All Seasons Globe 1960, and Anta Theatre New York 1961-62, Coriolanus, Love's Labours Lost, Shakespeare Festival Theatre Stratford Ontario, King Lear, Stratford on Avon, Aldwych 1962-63, and Moscow, W Berlin, Prague, Warsaw, Budapest, Bucharest, Belgrade and New York 1964, Timon of Athens Stratford on Avon 1965, The Government Inspector, Staircase, Aldwych 1966, Macbeth, Stratford on Avon, Russia, Finland 1967, A Hotel in Amsterdam, Royal Court and New 1968, Uncle Vanya Royal Court 1970, Savages Royal Court and Comedy 1973; The Tempest Wyndham's 1975; National Theatre: Captain of Köpenick, The Rules of the Game, Volpone, Amadeus, Othello, Don Quixote, 1971-83; I'm Not Rappaport Apollo 1986-87; *Films* That Lady, Carve Her Name with Pride, The Train, A Man for All Seasons, Bartleby, King Lear, Scorpio, A Delicate Balance, Anna Karenina, Nineteen Nineteen, The Attic, When the Whales Came, Henry V and numerous television plays *Awards* Evening Standard 1956 and 1963, New York Tony 1962, Oscar and Br Film Academy 1966, Danish Film Academy 1971, Hamburg Shakespeare Prize 1972; Hon LLD Glasgow 1968; Variety Club 1956, 1963 and 1987; Hon DLitt: Kent 1973, Sussex 1985; *Recreations* walking, reading; *Clubs* Athenaeum; *Style—* Paul Scofield, Esq, CBE

SCOON, HE Sir Paul; GCMG (1979), GCVO (1985), OBE (1970); *b* 1935; *Career* taught in Grenada 1953-67, former Cabinet sec, govr-gen Grenada 1978-; *Style—* HE Sir Paul Scoon, GCMG, OBE, Governor-General of Grenada; Governor-General's House, St George's, Grenada (☎ 2401)

SCOONES, Maj-Gen Sir Reginald Laurence; KBE (1955, OBE 1941), CB (1951), DSO (1945); s of late Maj Fitzmaurice Scoones, Royal Fusiliers; *b* 18 Dec 1900; *Educ* Wellington, RMC Sandhurst; *m* 1933, Isabella Bowie, da of John Nisbet, of Cumbrae Isles, Scotland; 1 da; *Career* late RAC; 2 Lt Royal Fusiliers 1920, transferred Royal Tank Corps 1923, attached Sudan Defence Force 1926-34, 1939-45 War Middle East and Burma; Lt-Col 1941, Brig 1942, Maj-Gen 1950, Maj-Gen Commanding British Troops Sudan and Cmdt Sudan Defence Force 1950-54; dir The Brewers' Soc 1957-69; *Style—* Maj-Gen Sir Reginald Scoones, KBE, CB, DSO; Flat 51, 50 Sloane St, London SW1X 9SN (☎ 01 235 4680)

SCOPES, Prof Jon Wilfred; s of Rev Wilfred Scopes (d 1986), missionary in India, and Edith Annie, *née* Hacker (d 1947); *b* 20 Nov 1930; *Educ* Eltham Coll, St Mary's Hosp Sch and London Univ (MB BS, PhD, MRCS, LRCS); *m* 5 Sept 1959, Evelyn Kathleen, da of Cdr Frederick Gordon Wynne, MBE, RN (d 1971), of Lymington, Hants (d 1971); 2 da (Heather b 1960, Jennifer b 1963); *Career* jr med posts 1953-60: St Mary's Ealing Hosp, ships surgn Orient Line, Rochford Hosp, Gt Ormond St, Guys; Nuffield res fell Oxford 1960-61, lectr in paediatrics Royal Postgrad Med Sch (RPMS) Hammersmith, visiting lectr Columbia Univ NY USA 1965-66; RPMS: sr lectr in paediatrics 1966-70, hon conslt paediatrician 1966-70, reader 1970-73; visiting lectr Makere Univ Uganda 1970, St Thomas's Hosp Med Sch: reader in paediatrics 1973-

76, prof in paediatrics 1976-; memb: BMA 1953, BPA 1966; Freeman City of London, Liveryman Worshipful Soc of Apothecaries; FRCP 1968, FRSM 1960 (pres paediatrics section 1988); hon memb Burmese Med Assoc 1988, examiner in Med finals (paediatrics) Nigeria and Burma; *Books* Medical Care of Newborn Babies (co author 1972); *Recreations* gardening, walking, DIY, pres St Thomas' Hosp rugby football club; *Clubs* Savile; *Style*— Prof Jon Scopes; 3 Chestnut Ave, Hampton, Middx (☎ 01 979 6933); Dept Paediatrics St Thomas Hospital London SE1 7EH

SCOPES, Sir Leonard Arthur; KCVO (1961), CMG (1957), OBE (1946); s of late Arthur Edward Scopes (d 1968), of Monifieth, Angus, by his w Jessie Russell Hendry; *b* 19 Mar 1912; *Educ* St Dunstan's Coll, Gonville and Caius Coll Cambridge; *m* 21 Dec 1938, Brunhilde Slater, da of late Victor Emmanuel Rolfe, of Worthing; 2 s, 2 da; *Career* memb British Consular Foreign and Diplomatic Services 1933-67; vice-consul: Antwerp 1933, Saigon 1935, Canton 1937; acting consul Surabaya 1941, vice-consul Lourenço Marques 1942, consul Skoplje and Ljubljana 1945, commercial sec Bogota 1947, asst in UN (econ and social) Dept of Foreign Office 1950, cnsllr Djakarta 1952, FO inspr 1954; ambass: Nepal 1957-62, Paraguay 1962-67; memb jt inspection unit of UN and Specialised Agencies 1968-71; *Style*— Sir Leonard Scopes, KCVO, CMG, OBE; 2 Whaddon Hall Mews, Whaddon, Bucks

SCOPES, Richard Henry; s of Eric Henry Scopes, of Funtington, W Sussex, and Ida Lucy Mary, *née* Hare; *b* 6 June 1944; *Educ* Univ Coll Sch, Magdalene Coll Cambridge (LLB); *m* 29 March 1969, Jacqueline Elizabeth Mary, da of Maj Ronald Walter Monk (d 1973), of Blackheath; 1 da (Katie b 1972); *Career* admitted slr, Ashhurst Morris Crisp & Co 1963-69, dir Scopes & Sons 1970-75, Wilde Sapte 1976- (ptnr 1980); memb City of London Slrs Co 1981; memb Law Soc; *Recreations* gardening, painting; *Style*— Richard Scopes, Esq; Westfield House, River Hill, Flamstead, Herts AL3 8DA; Wilde Sapte, Queensbridge House, 60 Upper Thames St, London EC4V 3BD (☎ 01 236 3050, fax 01 236 9624, telex 887793)

SCORAH, Kay Lesley; da of Allan Scorah, of Valley House, Great Longstone, Bakewell, Derbys, and Joyce, *née* Siddons; *b* 4 Sept 1954; *Educ* Christ's Hosp Hertford, Lady Manners Sch Bakewell, Univ of London (BSc); *Career* md Holder and Scorah Ltd 1982-84, planning dir BBDO (UK) Ltd 1984-86, exec devpt dir Ted Bates London 1986-87; fndr and md: Warbaby Prodns Ltd, Warbaby Marketing Ltd; contributor to The Independent, appearances on BBC Radio Leeds and BBC TV; *Recreations* skiing, running, cinema; *Style*— Ms Kay Scorah; 9 Ladbroke Grove House, 77 Ladbroke Grove, London W11 2DF (☎ 01 727 5534); Hillgate House, 13 Hillgate St, London W8 (☎ 01 229 3162)

SCOREY, Dr John; s of Edward William Scorey (d 1976), of New Zealand, and Nancy Houston, *née* Glasgow; *b* 5 August 1928; *Educ* Portsmouth, Guy's Hosp Univ of London (MB BS); *m* 11 May 1955, (Julia) Diana da of John Morris Wolley (d 1950), of Rowton Grange, Aston on Clun, Craven Arms, Shropshire; 1 s (Jeremy b 1957), 1 da (Phillipa b 1959); *Career* RAMC Capt Surgical dept Cambridge Mil Hosp Aldershot 1952-54; princ Gen Practice 1956-86, hosp practitoner in surgery 1966-86, tresmo 1958-86, mo Equity & Law Life Assur Soc 1970-86, mo Wiggins Teape Ltd 1978-86; fund raising for London Fedn of Boys Clubs; Freeman City of London 1970, Master Worshipful Co of Woolmen 1989- (asst 1983, Liveryman 1970); *Recreations* fly fishing, walking, gardening; *Clubs* City Livery, Royal Soc of St George, Sloane; *Style*— Dr John Scorey; Griffin Cottage, Woodrow, near Amersham, Bucks HP7 0QQ (☎ 0494 725 851)

SCOTT; *see*: Maxwell-Scott, Montagu Douglas Scott, Morrison-Scott

SCOTT, Rev Adam; TD (1978); s of Brig Fraser Scott, of Wonersh, and Bridget Penelope, *née* Williams; *b* 6 May 1947; *Educ* Marlborough, Christ Coll Oxford (BA, MA), City Univ Business Sch (MSc); *m* 30 Sept 1978, Oona MacDonald, da of Prof R J D Graham, (d 1950), of St Andrews; *Career* OUOTC 1965-68, CVHQ RA, 94 Regt, cmd Reserve Meteorologists, Capt 1968-81; reader Oxford 1970-75; ordained: deacon 1975, priest 1976 in Southwark; asst curate St Michael and All Angels Blackheath Park London SE3 1975-; trained as intellectual property lawyer 1970-74; called to the Bar Inner Temple 1972; with: ITT 1974-77, The Post Office 1977-81; British Telecom: corporate planner 1981-86, dir office of Iain Vallance (chm of BT) 1986-88; dir Int Affairs BT Int 1988-; CEng, MIEE 1981; *Recreations* gardening, walking; *Style*— The Rev Adam Scott, TD; British Telecom International, 918 Holborn Centre, 120 Holborn, London EC1N 2TE (☎ 01 492 2060, fax 01 492 3001, telex 21601 BTI G)

SCOTT, Hon Lady; (Anna Drusilla); *née* Lindsay; da of 1 Baron Lindsay of Birker, CBE (d 1952); *b* 1911; *m* 1937, Sir Ian Dixon Scott, KCMG, KCVO, CIE; 1 s, 4 da; *Books* A D Lindsay, a Biography (1971), Everyman Revived: the Common Sense of Michael Polanyi (1985); *Style*— The Hon Lady Scott; Ash House, Alde Lane, Aldeburgh, Suffolk

SCOTT, Anthony Douglas; TD (1972); s of late Douglas Ernest Scott; *b* 6 Nov 1933; *Educ* Gateshead GS; *m* 1962, Irene, nee Robson; 1 s, 1 da; *Career* Maj TA; chartered accountant; chief exec and dir Council for Small Industries in Rural Areas 1981-, dir Consumer Credit Office of Fair Trading 1975-80, dir-gen Internal Audit MOD 1972-74; *Recreations* antique collecting, mountaineering; *Clubs* Army and Navy; *Style*— Anthony Scott, Esq; 33 Barlings Rd, Harpenden, Herts (☎ 058 27 63067)

SCOTT, Sir Anthony Percy; 3 Bt (UK 1913) of Witley, Surrey; s of Col Sir Douglas Scott, 2 Bt (d 1984), and Elizabeth Joyce, née Glanley (d 1983); *b* 1 May 1937; *Educ* Harrow, Ch Ch Oxford; *m* 1962, Caroline Teresa Anne, da of Edward Bacon; 2 s, (Henry Douglas, Simon b 1965), 1 da (Miranda b 1968); *Heir* Henry Douglas Edward, *qv*; *Career* barr 1960; ptnr in stockbroking firm Laurie Milbank & Co 1974-; chm and md LM (Moneybrokers) Ltd 1986-; *Style*— Sir Anthony Scott, Bt; North Park Farm, Fernhurst, Haslemere, Surrey (☎ 0428 52826, office 01 929 3171)

SCOTT, Hon Mrs; (Cecilia Anne); *née* Hawke; da of 9 Baron Hawke (d 1985); *b* 1943; *m* 1, 1963 (m dis 1971), Peter Hannay Bailey Tapsell, MP (later Sir Peter Tapsell); 1 s (James Hawke b 1966, d 1985); m 2, 1979, as his 2 w, Nicholas Paul Scott, MBE, JP, MP, *qv*; 1 s (Patrick Martin Iain b 1982), 1 da (Amber b 1987); *Recreations* tennis, golf; *Clubs* Hurlingham, Royal Mid Surrey Golf; *Style*— The Hon Mrs Scott

SCOTT, Charles Clive; s of Lt Col Sir James Walter Scott, 2 Bt, *qv*, of Rotherfield Park, Alton, Hants, and Anne Constantia, *née* Austin; *b* 31 July 1954; *Educ* Eton, Trinity Coll Cambridge (MA), Insead (MBA); *m* 6 Oct 1979, Caroline Frances, da of (Hugh Graham) Jago; 3 da (Eleanor, Rose, Alice); *Career* dir de Zoete & Bevan Ltd 1988; memb The Stock Exchange; Freeman City of London 1977, Liveryman Worshipful Co of Mercers 1980; memb Law Soc; *Recreations* usual fun and games; *Clubs* Leander; *Style*— Charles Scott, Esq; Ebbgate Hse, 2 Swan Lane, London EC4 (☎ 01 623 2323)

SCOTT, Christopher James Anderson; s and h of Sir Oliver Scott, 3 Bt; *b* 16 Jan 1955; *Educ* Bryanston, Trinity Coll Cambridge; *Clubs* Brooks's; *Style*— Christopher Scott, Esq

SCOTT, Sir David Aubrey; GCMG (1979, KCMG 1974, CMG 1966); s of Hugh Sumner Scott (d 1960), and Barbara Easton Scott, JP; *b* 3 August 1919; *Educ* Charterhouse, Birmingham Univ; *m* 1941, Vera Kathleen, da of Maj G H Ibbitson, MBE, RA (d 1958); 2 s, 1 da; *Career* served WWII RA (Maj); Foreign Serv: high cmmr Uganda 1967-70, asst under-sec of state FCO 1970-72, high cmmr NZ and govr Pitcairn Islands 1973-75, ambass S Africa 1976-79; chm: Nuclear Resources Ltd, Ellerman Lines 1982-83 (vice-chm 1981-82), Royal Overseas League 1981-86 (vice-chm to 1981); dir: Barclays Bank International 1979-85, Mitchell Cotts Gp 1980-86, Bradbury-Wilkinson plc 1984-86; vice-pres UK-South Africa Trade Assoc 1981-85; *Books* Ambassador in Black and White (1981); *Recreations* music, birdwatching; *Clubs* Royal Overseas League; *Style*— Sir David Scott, GCMG; Wayside, Moushill Lane, Milford, Surrey GU8 5BQ (☎ 048 68 21935)

SCOTT, David Gidley; s of Bernard Wardlaw Habershon Scott (d 1978), of Little Almshoe, St Ippolyts, Hitchin, Herts, and Florence May, *née* Wheeler; *b* 3 Jan 1924; *Educ* Sutton Valence Sch, St John's Coll Cambridge (MA, LLM); *m* 10 April 1948, (Elinor) Anne, da of Maj Alan Garthwaite, DSO, MC (d 1964), of Penny Bridge, Ulveston; 2 s (Antony b 1956, Robin b 1959), 2 da (Judith b 1952, Dinah b 1961); *Career* WWII RE 1942-47, cmmnd 1944, Trp Cdr assault sqdn (wounded Rhine Crossing 1945), Temp Capt (later Actg Maj) cmdg 4 BESD Haifa 1947; barr Middle Temple 1952, practised Chancery Bar 1952-84, registrar bankruptcy High Ct 1984-; vice chm Parish Cncl, former churchwarden and memb PCC; *Recreations* sailing, choral singing; *Clubs* Bar Yacht, Parkstone Yacht; *Style*— David Scott, Esq; Little Almshoe House, St Ippolyts, Hitchin, Herts (☎ 0462 34391); Thomas More Bldg, Royal Cts of Justice, Strand, London WC2

SCOTT, David Griffiths; s of Wilfred Emberton Scott (d 1967), and Gwenith, *née* Griffiths; *b* 15 Feb 1942; *Educ* Adams GS Newport Shropshire, Christs Coll Camb (MA), London Business School (MSC); *m* 1969, Alison Jane Fraser; 1 s (James b 1974), 2 da (Helen b 1971, Katherine b 1976); *Career* md: ISC Alloy Ltd 1975-84, Impalloy Ltd 1978-84, Kleen-e-ze Hldgs plc 1984-; *Recreations* golf, sailing, cricket; *Style*— David Scott, Esq; Meadow Bank, Coventry Rd, Berkswell, nr Coventry (☎ 0676 32836); Kleen-e-ze Holdings plc, Martins Road, Hanham, Bristol BS15 3DY (☎ 0272 670861, telex 449950)

SCOTT, David Morris Fitzgerald; s of Rev Canon William Morris Fitzgerald Scott (d 1959), of St Aidan's Coll, Birkenhead, Cheshire, and Nora Compigne, *née* Shaw; *b* 7 June 1946; *Educ* St Lawrence Coll Ramsgate, The Hotchkiss Sch Lakeville Connecticut USA, Corpus Christi Coll Oxford (MA); *m* 10 June 1972, Jacqueline Mary, da of Kenneth Percy Pool; 1 s (Michael b 1981), 2 da (Elizabeth b 1976, Sarah b 1978); *Career* ptnr Kitcat & Aitken 1974-80 (investmt analyst 1967-74), vice-pres Bank of NY 1980-83; dir: Warburg Investmt Mgmnt Int 1983-85, Mercury Warburg Investmt Mgmnt 1985-87, Mercury Rowan Mullens 1987-; tres Wadhurst PCC, govr Corp of St Lawrence Coll; Freeman City of London, Liveryman Worshipful Co Scriveners; FInstPet 1974, Assoc Soc of Investmt Analysts; *Recreations* reading; *Clubs* Brooks's, Turf, City of London; *Style*— David Scott, Esq; Windmill Hse, Windmill Lane, Wadhurst, East Sussex TN5 6HX (☎ 089 288 2683), Mercury Rowan Mullens, 33 King William St, London EC4 (☎ 01 280 2900, fax 01 280 2820, telex 888478)

SCOTT, Rear Adm Sir (William) David Stewart; KBE (1977), CB (1974); yst s of Brig Henry St George Stewart Scott, CB, DSO (d 1940), and Ida Christabel Trower, *née* Hogg; *b* 5 April 1921; *Educ* Tonbridge; *m* 1952, Pamela Dorothy Whitlock; 1 s, 2 da; *Career* Capt RN 1962, Rear Adm 1971, Cdr British Naval Staff Washington 1971-73, Dep Controller Polaris 1973, Chief Polaris exec 1976-80; *Style*— Rear Adm Sir David Scott, KBE, CB; c/o Lloyds Bank, 6 Pall Mall, London SW1

SCOTT, Donald Dundas; JP (1967), DL (1972); s of James Douglas Slott (d 1973), of Harsfold Farm House, Wisborough Green, W Sussex, and Bridget Violet Penfold-Wyatt (d 1968); *b* 1 June 1924; *Educ* Winchester, Christ Church Oxford (BA); *m* 3 Oct 1953, Fiona Mary, da of The Hon Angus Dudley Campbell, CBE, JP, of Doddington Cottage, Nantwich, Cheshire; 2 s (Roderick b 16 Feb 1958, Angus b 15 Feb 1964), 2 da (Henrietta (Mrs Drake), b 18 Jan 1957, Rosanna b 23 Feb 1962); *Career* Capt Scots Gds 1944-47; underwriter Lloyds, ret 1972; dep chm King Edward VII Hosp Midhurst, lay chm Deanery Synod; ctee memb: Chichester Diocesan Housing Assoc, CLA; gen cmmr of revenue; High Sheriff 1975; *Recreations* shooting, gardening, music; *Clubs* Pratts; *Style*— Donald Slott, Esq, JP, DL; Harsfold Manor, Wisborough Green, Billingshurst, West Sussex (☎ 0403 700285)

SCOTT, Douglas Gordon; s of Herbert Scott (d 1956), of Liverpool, and Emily, *née* Smith (d 1955); *b* 23 Dec 1928; *Educ* Liverpool Collegiate Sch; *m* 12 June 1948, Barbara Joyce, da of Reginald Arthur Cyril Rayner (d 1960), of Coulsdon, Surrey; 1 s (Ian Gordon); *Career* Scots Gds 1946-48; asst accountant Hambros Bank Gp 1950-53, area mangr Lombard Banking 1953-67; dir: Lyon Gp 1970-74, John Finlan 1974-77, Trust Securities 1977-80; chm Urban & City Properties 1980-; chm Purley Sports Club, sec Purley Bowls Club; Freeman City of London, Liveryman Worshipful Co of Carmen 1984; *Recreations* cricket; *Clubs* KMCC, Forty; *Style*— Douglas Scott, Esq; Caprice, Hillcroft Ave, Purley, Surrey; Appt Phenicia, Passeig Maritim, L'Escala, Costa Brava, Spain; Greenfield House, 69-73, Manor rd, Wallington, Surrey (☎ 01 773 1429, fax 01 647 0321)

SCOTT, Douglas Keith; s of George Douglas Scott, of Nottingham, and Edith Joyce Scott; *b* 29 May 1941; *Educ* Cottesmore Sch, Mundella Sch, Loughborough Coll; *m* 1962 (m dis), Janice Elaine, da of Thomas Arthur Brook, of Notts; 1 s (Michael b 1963), 2 da (Martha b 1973, Rosie b 1978); *Career* began climbing 12 years old, visited Alps 16 years old and every year thereafter; first ascent: Tarso Teiroko Tibest Mountains Sahara 1965, Cilo Dag Mountains SE Turkey 1966, S face Koh-i-Bandaka (22500 feet) Hindu Kush Afghanistan 1967; first Br ascent Salathé Wall El Capitain Yosemite 1971; memb: Euro Mt Everest Expedition to SW face 1972, Br Mt Everest Expedition to SW face 1974 (first ascent: Changabang, SE Spur, Pic Lenin, reached summit of Mt Everest via SW Face 1975); first ascent: E face Direct Mount Kenya 1976, Ogre (23900 feet) Karakoram Mountains 1977, N Ridge route Kangchenjunga (28146 feet) without oxygen 1979, N Summit Kussum Kanggurn 1979, Pungpa Ridge

(7445m) 1982, Xixabangma South Face (26291 feet) 1982, Broad Peak 1983, Baruntse Chamlang 1984, Diran 1985; FRGS; *Publications* Big Wall Climbing (1974), Shishapangma Tibet (1984); contributor to Alpine Journal, American Alpine Journal and Mountain Magazine; *Clubs* Alpine, Nottingham Climbers; *Style*— Douglas Scott, Esq; Oaklands, Laversdale Lane End, Irthington, Cumbria CA6 4PS

SCOTT, Lady Elizabeth Louise Margaret; *née* Meade; da of 5 Earl of Clanwilliam; *b* 18 April 1911; *m* 1933, Lt-Col Charles Rankin Scott, KRRC (d 1965); 2 s; *Style*— Lady Elizabeth Scott; Culkerton, Tetbury, Glos

SCOTT, (John) Fenwick Easton; JP; s of Dr (John) Alwyn Easton Scott (d 1955), of Midhurst, and Eveleen Dorothy, *née* Purcell (d 1984); *b* 30 May 1942; *Educ* Cranleigh; *m* 9 Sept 1966, Jayne Anne, da of Douglas Craven Hodgson, of Lincs; 1 s (Simon b 11 Oct 1969), 2 da (Clarissa b 24 Nov 1971, Kirstie b 7 July 1974); *Career* dir Nationwide Anglia Estate Agencies, chm and md King & Chasemore; gen cmmr for tax; Freeman City of London, Liveryman Worshipful Co of Armourers and Brasiers; FRICS; *Recreations* golf; *Clubs* West Sussex Golf; *Style*— Fenwick Scott, Esq, JP; Amblehurst Manor Farm, Wisborough Green, Billinghurst, W Sussex RH14 OEP (☎ 0403 700231); Richmond House, Carfax, Horsham, W Sussex RH12 1AQ (☎ 0403 64441)

SCOTT, (Celia) Gay; da of Ivor Norman Bailey (d 1986), and Enid Alice, *née* Sherwood; *b* 25 Mar 1944; *Educ* St Angela's Providence Convent London, NW London Poly Brighton Coll Of Librarianship; *m* 18 May 1967, Michael James Frederick Scott, s of Capt John Bristol Irwin Scott, of 20 De Parys Ave, Bedford; 1 s (Charles b 1982); *Career* membs' info serv House of Commons 1973-74, head of euro unit Gtr London Cncl 1976-80, fndr and dir Euro Information Ltd (acquired by Eurofi 1982) 1980-, dir public affrs and info Eurofi 1982-; assoc Library Assoc 1967, MIInf Sci 1977; *Books* The European Economic Community (1979), A Guide to European Community Grants and Loans (annual 1980-), Money for Research and Development (jtly 1986), Eurobrief (monthly 1981-83); *Recreations* riding, walking, skiing, theatre going, gardening; *Style*— Mrs Michael Scott; The Old Rectory, Northill, Beds SG18 9AH (☎ 076727 680); Guildgate House, Pelican Lane, Newbury, Berks (☎ 0635 31900, fax 0635 37370/076727 580)

SCOTT, Sir George Edward; CBE (1963, OBE 1941), KPM (1949); s of late Frederick William Scott, of Norwich; *b* 6 June 1903; *Educ* City of Norwich Sch; *m* 1926, Lilian, da of Mathew Brown, of Norwich; 1 s, 1 da; *Career* cadet Norwich City Police 1918, dep chief constable Norwich 1933-36; chief constable: Luton 1936-44, Newcastle-upon-Tyne 1944-48, Sheffield 1948-59, West Riding 1959-68, West Yorkshire 1968-69; former pres Northern Police Charities, vice pres Royal Soc for Prevention of Accidents; KStJ 1966; kt 1967; *Style*— Sir George Scott, CBE, KPM; White Lodge, Barham Close, Weybridge, Surrey

SCOTT, Graham Robert; s of Robert Alexander Scott, of Alness, Ross-shire, and Helen, *née* Tawse (d 1987); *b* 8 Dec 1944; *Educ* Bryanston Sch, Nottingham Univ (BSc); *m* 19 Aug 1967, Wendy Jean, da of Harry Mumford (d 1983); 1 s (Andrew), 1 da (Harriet); *Career* gen mangr Unitrition Int Ltd 1984-86, md BP Nutrition (UK) Ltd 1987-, chm BP Nutrition (Ireland) Ltd 1988-; CEng 1971, MIChemE 1971; *Style*— Graham Scott, Esq; BP Nutrition (UK) Ltd, Wincham, Northwich, Ches, (☎ 0606 41133, fax 0606 41963, telex 668994)

SCOTT, Guy Baliol; s of Reginald Benjamin Scott (d 1950), of Alan Rd, Wimbledon, and Eileen Ann, *née* Brownlow (d 1978); *b* 26 July 1919; *Educ* Charterhouse; *m* 1, 17 July 1948, Elizabeth Winifred (d 1982), da of Charles Hendry (d 1952), of Parkside, Wimbledon; m 2, Gale Stirling, da of James Athelstane Stedman (d 1985), of Boxford, Suffolk; 1 s (Benjamin Brownlow b 15 Sept 1984); *Career* enlisted RA 1939, cmmnd 2 Lt RA 1940 (Lt 1941, Capt 1943), attached Indian Artillery 1940, Maharajah Rao Scindia Field Battery 1943, demobbed Larkhill 1946; memb London Stock Exchange 1946, sr ptnr Benjamin J Scott & Co 1951, jt sr ptnr Penney Easton & Co 1985; *Recreations* shooting, fishing, historical, reading, travel; *Clubs* Army & Navy, Pall Mall London; *Style*— Guy Scott, Esq

SCOTT, Henry Douglas Edward; s and h of Sir Anthony Percy Scott, 3 Bt, and Caroline Teresa Anne, er da of (William Charles) Edward Bacon; *b* 26 Mar 1964; *Educ* Harrow; *Career* Anglo Chemical Commodities, a div of Philipp Brothers Ltd; *Style*— Henry Scott, Esq

SCOTT, Sir (Charles) Hilary; s of Lt-Col Charles Edward Scott (ka 1916), of Heaton, Bradford, Yorks, and Margaret Elizabeth Mary Ackroyd (d 1972); *b* 27 Mar 1906; *Educ* Sedbergh; *m* 16 July 1932, Beatrice Margery, da of late Rev Canon Robert Garrad, of Bentham, Yorks; 1 s, 2 da; *Career* articled Wade & Co Bradford Slr 1930; ptnr Slaughter and May 1937-74, RNVR 1940-45; memb: Cncl of Law Soc 1948-71 (vice-pres 1965-66, pres 1966-67), Nat Film Finance Corpn 1948-70 (chm 1964-70), Jenkins Ctee on Co Law 1959-62; trustee Glyndebourne Arts Trust 1963-76; dir: Tarmac Ltd 1968-76, Equity and Law Life Assurance Soc Ltd 1955-82; chm Ctee on Property Bonds and Equity Linked Life Assurance 1971-73; memb: London Local Bd of Bank of Scotland 1966-76, Panel of Judges of the Accounts Awards for Company Accounts 1961-69, London advsy bd of Salvation Army 1966-81, cncl of Royal Sch of Church Music 1975-85, Noise Advsy Cncl 1971-74; FRSA; kt 1967; *Style*— Sir Hilary Scott; Knowle House, Bishop's Walk, Addington, Surrey CR0 5BA (☎ 01 654 3638)

SCOTT, Iain William St Clair; s of Lt-Col Joseph William St Clair Scott, and Margaret Brown, *née* Rodger (d 1977); *b* 14 May 1946; *Educ* George Watsons Coll Edinburgh; *m* 1 Oct 1971, Noelle Margaret Gilmour (Jill), da of Archibald Gilmour Young, of 61 Newhailes Cresent, Musselburgh, Edinburgh; 1 s (Ruaridh b 1976), 1 da (Susan b 1973); *Career* Bank of Scotland: accountant 1973, asst chief accountant 1981, mangr corporate planning 1983, asst gen mangr corporate planning 1985, div gen mangr accounting and fin 1986-; memb Scottish consultative ctee on the Curriculum; AIB (Scot) 1988; *Recreations* golf, curling, squash; *Clubs* Hon Co of Edinburgh Golfers, Bruntsfield Links GS; *Style*— Iain Scott, Esq; 22 Bramdean Rise, Edinburgh EH10 6JR (☎ 031 447 2453); 13 Woodlands Road, Lundin Links, Fife; Bank of Scotland, Head Office, The Mound, Edinburgh EH1 1Y2 (☎ 031 243 5541, fax 031 243 5437, telex 72275)

SCOTT, Sir Ian Dixon; KCMG (1962, CMG 1959), KCVO (1965), CIE (1947); s of Thomas Henderson Scott, OBE, of Selkirk, and Mary Agnes, *née* Dixon; *b* 6 Mar 1909; *Educ* Queen's Royal Coll Trinidad, Balliol Coll Oxford, LSE; *m* 1937, Hon Anna Drusilla, o da of 1 Baron Lindsay of Birker, CBE (d 1952); 1 s, 4 da; *Career* entered ICS 1932, transferred Political Service 1935, dep private sec to Viceroy 1945-47, first sec UK High Cmmr's Office Pakistan 1947-48, dep dir personnel John Lewis & Co Ltd London 1948-50, entered FO 1950; first sec: British Legation Helsinki 1952-53, British Embassy Beirut 1954; cnsllr 1956-58, IDC 1959, consul-gen Leopoldville 1960; ambass: Republic of Congo 1960-61, Sudan 1961-65, Norway 1965-68; dir Clarkson's Holidays Ltd 1969-72, chm 1972-73; chm Suffolk Area Health Authority 1973-77; memb cncl Dr Barnardo's 1970-84 (chm 1972-78); memb bd of govrs Felixstowe Coll 1971-84 (chm 1972-80); pres Indian Civil Service (ret) Association 1977-; *Books* Tumbled House, The Congo At Independence; *Recreations* yachting; *Style*— Sir Ian Scott, KCMG, KCVO, CIE; Ash House, Alde Lane, Aldeburgh, Suffolk

SCOTT, Prof Ian Richard; s of Ernest Richard Scott (d 1971), of Geelong, Aust, and Edith Miriam Scott (d 1976); *b* 8 Jan 1940; *Educ* Geelong Coll, Queen's Coll, Univ of Melbourne (LLB), King's Coll Univ of London (PhD); *m* 31 Oct 1971, Ecce Scott, da of Prof Boris Norman Cole, of Leeds; 2 da (Anneke b 1 Jan 1978, Kaatye b 3 Jan 1981); *Career* barr and slr Supreme Ct of Victoria 1964-, reader judicial admin Univ of Birmingham 1976-78, dir Inst of Judicial Admin Univ of Birmingham 1976-82, visiting res prof Whittier Coll California 1978-79, Barber prof of law Univ of Birmingham 1978-, exec dir Victoria Law Fndn 1982-84, dean Faculty of Law Univ of Birmingham 1985-, memb Ld Chllrs Review Body on Civil Justice 1985-88; hon master of the Bench Gray's Inn 1988; *Books* The Crown Court (1971), English Criminal Justice (jtly with E C Friesen 1976); *Style*— Prof Ian Richard; Faculty of Law, University of Birmingham, Birmingham B15 2TT (☎ 021 414 6291)

SCOTT, Ian Russell; s of William Russell Scott (d 1974), of Weymouth, and Winifred Mabel, *née* Morgan; *b* 12 Sept 1942; *Educ* Sherborne, London Univ (LLB); *m* 3 May 1969, Mary Peverell, da of Robert Riggs Wright, TD, of Piddletrenthide, Dorchester, Dorset; 1 s (William b 1975), 2 da (Katharine b 1971, Louise b 1973); *Career* asst slr: Sharp Pritchand & Co 1967-68, Ashurst Morris Crisp 1968-72 (ptnr 1972-); memb Law Soc 1965; *Recreations* theatre, tennis, hockey, golf, sailing; *Clubs* City of London, Roehampton; *Style*— Ian Scott, Esq; 15 Briar Walk, London SW15; Moonfleet, Ringstead Bay, Dorchester (☎ 01 788 1588); Ashurst Morris Crisp, Broadgate House, 7 Eldon Street, London EC2M 7HD (☎ 01 247 7666, fax 377 5659, telex 887067)

SCOTT, James Archibald; CB (1988), LVO (1961); s of James Scott, MBE (d 1983), of Beechhurst, Hawick, Roxburghshire, and Agnes Bone, *née* Howie (d 1985); *b* 5 Mar 1932; *Educ* Dollar Acad, Univ of St Andrew's, Queen's Univ of Ontario (MA); *m* 27 Aug 1957, Elizabeth Agnes Joyce, da of John Trant Buchan-Hepburn (d 1953), of Chagford, St Andrews, Fife; 3 s (Buchan b 1962, Robert b 1964, Hector b 1969), 1 da (Frances (Mrs Rive) b 1960); *Career* RAF Aircrew 1954-56, Flying Offr XI Sqdn 1956; joined CRO 1956; first sec: UK High Cmmn New Delhi 1958-62, UK Mission to UN NY 1962-65; transferred Scottish Off 1965, PPS to Sec of State for Scotland 1969-71, asst sec Scottish Devpt Dept 1971, under sec Industl Dept for Scotland 1976-84, sec Scottish Educn Dept 1984-87, sec Industl Dept for Scotland 1987-; *Recreations* music, golf; *Clubs* Travellers'; *Style*— James Scott, Esq, CB, LVO; Scottish Education Dept, New St Andrew's House, Edinburgh EH1 3SY (☎ 031 244 4593)

SCOTT, James Jervoise; s and h of Sir James Scott, 2 Bt, DL; *b* 12 Oct 1952; *m* 13 Oct 1982, Judy Evelyn, da of Brian Trafford, of Tismans, Rudgwick, Sussex; 1 s (Arthur Jervoise Trafford b 1984); *Style*— James Scott, Esq; 36 Endlesham Rd, London SW12 8JU

SCOTT, Sir James Walter; 2 Bt (UK 1962), of Rotherfield Park, Alton, Hants; s of Col Sir Jervoise Bolitho Scott, 1 Bt (d 1965); *b* 26 Oct 1924; *Educ* Eton; *m* 8 Dec 1951, Anne Constantia, da of late Lt-Col Clive Grantham Austin, DL, and Lady Lilian Mary Theodora Lumley, sis of 11 Earl of Scarbrough; 3 s, 1 da; *Heir* s, James Jervoise Scott; *Career* Lt-Col (ret) Life Gds formerly Gren Gds; served WWII, NW Europe 1944-45, Palestine 1945-46; ADC to viceroy and govr-gen of India 1946-48, Malaya 1948-49, Cyprus 1958, 1960 and 1964, Malaysia 1966, ret 1969; memb Lloyd's; Master of Mercers' Co 1976; HM Body Guard of Hon Corps of Gentlemen-at-Arms 1977-; High Sheriff Hants 1981-82, Lord-Lieut of Hants 1982- (DL 1978-82); JP 1982; hon Col 2 Bn The Wessex Regt; KStJ 1984; *Recreations* countryside activities; *Clubs* Cavalry and Guards', Farmers, IOD; *Style*— Sir James Scott, Bt, HM Lord-Lieut of Hants; Rotherfield Park, Alton, Hants (☎ 042058 204)

SCOTT, (Katharine) Joan; da of Charles Ernest Cater (d 1934), and Katharine Theodora, *née* Horley (d 1970); *b* 16 May 1902; *Educ* Highfield Sch; *m* 28 April 1926, Leonard Winstone Scott (d 1975), s of Francis Winstone Scott; 3 s (Charles Leonard Masson b 1927, (Edward) John b 1928, Andrew Henry Rowe b 1930); *Career* commercial bloodstock breeder, leading breeder in Br Isles 1969; horses bred inc: Park Top (Racehorse of the Year 1969, winner of 13 races incl Coronation Cup and King George VI and Queen Elizabeth Stakes at Ascot), Precipice Wood (winner Ascot Gold Cup), Luciano (German Derby Winner), Spartan General (champion NH sire); memb Thoroughbred Breed Assoc; *Style*— Mrs K J Scott; Buttermilk Farm, Barford St Michael, Banbury, Oxon (☎ 0295 720 221)

SCOTT, Dr John James; s of Lt-Col John Creagh Scott, DSO, OBE, of Langhill, Moretonhampstead, Devon (d 1959), and Mary Elizabeth Marjory, *née* Murray of Polmaise (d 1981), da of Maj Alastair Bruce Murray 13th of Touchadam and Polmaise, co Stirling (d 1924) (*see* Burke's LG 19379 edn); *b* 4 Sept 1924; *Educ* Radley, Corpus Christi Coll Cambridge (BA, MA), London Univ (PhD); *m* 1, 1948, Katherine Mary, da of Robert Bruce, of London (d 1955); 2 da (Caroline b 1950, Katherine b 1950 (twins)); m 2, 1956, Heather Marguerite, da of Lt-Col Ivor Douglas-Browne, of Venice, Alpes Maritimes, France (d 1948); m 3, 1963, June Rose, da of Arthur Ernest Mackie, of London; 2 s (James b 1966, John b 1966 (twins)); *Career* Capt Argyll & Sutherland Highlanders 1944-47, Palestine; Staff of Nat Inst for Med Research 1950-55, sr lectr Chemical Pathology St Mary's Hosp 1955-61, Editorial Bd Biochemical Journal 1956-61; memb ctee Biochemical Soc 1961; visiting scientist Nat Institutes of Health, Bethesda, Md, 1961; entered Dip Serv 1961; Off of Cmmr Gen for SE Asia, Singapore 1962; Off of Political Advsr to C-in-C Far East 1963; FO 1966; cncllr Rio de Janeiro and Brasilia 1971; seconded to NI Off as asst sec Stormont 1974; asst under-sec of State FCO 1978-80; commercial dir Industrial Engines (Sales) Ltd, Elbar Gp 1980; fin planning conslt and md Dudmass Ltd 1983-; Francis Bacon Prize, Cambridge 1950; *Publications* in Biochem Journal, Proceedings Royal Soc and other learned journals 1951-61; rowed for Cambridge in Oxford Cambridge Boat Race 1944; *Recreations* botany, music, wine; *Clubs* Institute of Directors, Leander, Hawks, Ski (of GB); *Style*— Dr John J Scott; The Cottage, South Rauceby, Sleaford, Lincs NG34 7QG (☎ 05298 254)

SCOTT, John Newton; OBE (1971), TD (1945); s of Newton Livingstone Scott, (d 1955), of Bournemouth, and Dora, *née* Greenhill (d 1965); *b* 26 June 1917; *Educ* Marlborough; *m* 22 Dec 1949, Suzanne Louise, da of Frederick George Deane (d

1960), of Sydney, Aust; 2 s (James Antony b 1950, David b 1961), 1 da (Sarah Jane b 1954); *Career* WWII Capt Hampshire Regt, Maj RWAFF 1942; admitted slr 1947, sr ptnr Scott Bailey & Co Lymington 1950-82; dir Dukes Hotel London 1976-; clerk to New Forest Ct of Verderers 1955-73; memb Law Soc; *Recreations* boating, fishing, unskilled carpentry; *Clubs* Lymington Town Sailing; *Style—* John Scott, Esq, OBE, TD; The Old School House, Melbury Abbas, Shaftsbury, Dorset (☎ 0747 53408)

SCOTT, John William; s of Donald Alan Scott (d 1960), memb London Stock Exchange, and Minnie Gertrude Scott, *née* Watts (d 1968); *b* 6 April 1930; *Educ* Marlborough, Worcester Coll Oxford (MA); *m* 1957, Rhoda Janet, da of Robert Cecil Mayall, CMG, DSO, MC (d 1962); 3 s; *Career* Nat and TA Serv, Middx Regt, Capt; slr; ptnr Clifford-Turner 1961-86, conslt Clifford Chance 1987-; *Publications* Legibus, a history of Clifford-Turner; *Recreations* cricket, golf, family history; *Clubs* City Univ, MCC, Lord's Taverners; *Style—* John Scott, Esq; Bemerton, Lingfield Rd, East Grinstead, West Sussex; Clifford Chance, Blackfriars House, New Bridge St, London EC4V 6BY (☎ 01 353 0211, telex 887847)

SCOTT, (Ian) Jonathan; s of Col Alexander Brassey Jonathan Scott, DSO, MC (d 1978), of Lasborough Manor, Tetbury, and Rhona Margaret, *née* Stewart; *b* 7 Feb 1940; *Educ* Harrow, Balliol Coll Oxford (BA); *m* 12 June 1970, Annabella Constance, da of Francis William Hope Loudon (d 1985), of Olantigh, Kent, and his w Lady Prudence, *née* Jellicoe, da of 1 Earl Jellicoe; 2 s (Alexander b 1966, Justin b 1970), 1 da (Julia b 1969); *Career* dir: Charterhouse Japhet Ltd 1973-80, Barclays Merchant Bank Ltd 1980-85, Barclays de Zoete Wedd Ltd 1985-; chm Reviewing Ctee on the Export of Works of Art 1985-; tstee Imp War Museum 1984-; FSA 1980; *Books* Piranesi (1975); *Clubs* Brooks's; *Style—* Jonathan Scott, Esq; Lasborough Manor, Tetbury, Glos; 18 Abingdon Villas, London W8; Barclays de Zoete Wedd Ltd, Ebbgate House, Swan Lane London EC4

SCOTT, Dr (Edward) Keith; s of Dr Frank Sholl Scott (d 1952), of Veryan, Cornwall, and Ethel Emmeline Ham (d 1967); *b* 16 June 1918; *Educ* Clifton, Oxford Univ, St Mary's Hosp Paddington; *m* 12 Sept 1944, Una Mary (d 1977), da of Alex Coulson Bond (d 1963), of Forest Row; 1 s (Lawrence Keith b 1947), 1 da (Penelope b 1946); m 2, 7 Dec 1977, Georgiana Jane, da of Wing Cdr George Francis Hales (d 1952); *Career* general practitioner 1947-81; MRCS, MRCP; Rugby: capt Oxford Univ 1940, played for England in all Victory Internationals 1947, captained England 1947-48, also played for Barbarians, London Counties, Harlequins, St Marys Hosp (capt), Redruth, capt Cornwall from 1938-50; cricket: Gloucestershire CC 1937, capt Oxford Univ 1940, played for All England XI and was 12th man in first Victory Test, MCC Tour to Canada 1951, capt Cornwall from 1935-52; *Recreations* shooting, fishing; *Clubs* Vincents, Oxford; *Style—* Dr Keith Scott; Beacon Ridge, Portscatho, Cornwall TR2 5EN (☎ 087258 468)

SCOTT, (Norman) Keith; CBE (1989); s of Norman Scott (d 1986), and Dora Scott (d 1979); *b* 10 Feb 1927; *Educ* Preston GS, Liverpool Univ Sch of Architecture (BArch, MA), Liverpool Univ Sch of Planning (DipCD), Massachusetts Inst of Technol Boston USA (MArch); *Career* chm North Lancs Soc Architects 1966-67, architect Dean and Chapter Liverpool Cathedral 1979-; chm: awards panel RIBA 1982-84, BDP 1984 (ptnr 1963-); bd memb Lake Dist Summer Music 1984-, govr Lancs Poly 1988-; life memb Victorian Soc, chm BDP Music Soc; FRIBA, MRTPI; *Books* Shopping Centre Design (1989); *Recreations* music, fell walking, sketching; *Clubs* Oriental London; *Style—* N Keith Scott, Esq, CBE; Overleigh House, East Cliff, Preston PR1 3JE (☎ 0772 53545); Building Design Partnership, Vernon St, Moor Lane, Preston PR1 3PQ (☎ 0772 59383, fax 0772 201378 Gp 3, car tel 0836 601 170, telex 677160)

SCOTT, Laurence Keith; s of Dr Edward Keith Scott, of Beacon Ridge, Portscatho, Truro, Cornwall, and Mary, *née* Bond (d 1977); *b* 7 Nov 1947; *Educ* Downside; *m* 22 Aug 1981, Lucinda Jane, da of Lt Cdr HV Bruce, RN, JP, DL; 4 s (Edward b 1982, Toby b 1984, Oliver b 1987, Barbeby b 1989); *Career* RAF 1967-72, cmmnd 1967, pilots wings 1969; commercial pilot 1972; co pilot Vickers Ltd 1972-73, with JH Minet Lloyds 1973-76, dir Robt Arnold Lloyds 1979- 80 (joined 1977), vice pres Greig Fester (N America), 1980-83, with Jardine Thompson Graham 1983-88; dir: Heath Carroll Ltd 1988-, The Wilcox Gp (USA) 1988-; chm Grimston Scott Ltd 1988-; *Recreations* fishing, shooting, sailing, gardening, philately; *Clubs* MCC; *Style—* Laurence Scott, Esq; Roe Green, Martyr Worthy, Winchester, Hampshire (☎ 096 278 278)

SCOTT, Dame (Catherine) Margaret Mary (Mrs Denton); DBE (1981, OBE 1977); da of John Douglas Scott (d 1985), of Swaziland, and Marjorie Heath, *née* Bagley; *b* 26 April 1922; *Educ* Parktown Convent Johannesburg S Africa; *m* 1953, Prof Derek Ashworth Denton; 2 s (Matthew, Angus); *Career* founding dir Australian Ballet Sch 1964-; awarded DBE for service to ballet; *Recreations* swimming, walking, garden; *Clubs* Alexander, Melbourne; *Style—* Dame Margaret Scott, DBE; 816 Orrong Rd, Toorak, Melbourne, Vic 3142, Australia (☎ 03 241 2640); Aust Ballet Centre, 11 Mount Alexander Road, Flemington, Vic 3031, Australia (☎ 03 376 1400)

SCOTT, Maurice Fitzgerald; s of Col Gerald Chaplin Scott, OBE (d 1953), of Ramsey, Isle of Man, and Harriet Mary Geraldine, *née* Fitzgerald (d 1983); *b* 6 Dec 1924; *Educ* Campbell Coll Belfast, Wadham Coll Oxford (BA, MA), Nuffield Coll Oxford (BLitt); *m* 30 March 1953, Eleanor Warren, da of Norman Dawson (d 1971), of Aberdeen; 3 da (Alison b 1955, Sheila b 1957, Jean b 1960); *Career* RE 1943-46 (Temp Capt); OEEC Paris 1949-51, PM's statistical section under Lord Cherwell 1951-53, econ section Cabinet off 1953-54, NIESR 1954-57, tutor in econs Christ Church Oxford (fell) 1957-68, NEDO 1962-63, Devpt Centre of OECD Paris, official fell in econs Nuffield Coll Oxford 1968-; *Books* A Study of UK Imports (1963), Industry and Trade in some Developing Countries (with I M D Little and T Scitovsky, 1970), Project Appraisal in Practice (with J D MacArthur and D M G Newbery, 1976), Can We Get Back to Full Employment? (with R A Loslett, 1978), A New View of Economic Growth (1989); *Recreations* walking; *Clubs* Political Economy (Oxford); *Style—* Maurice Scott, Esq; 11 Blandford Ave, Oxford, OX2 8EA (☎ 0865 59115); Nuffield College, Oxford OX1 1NF (☎ 0865 278 566)

SCOTT, Sir Michael; KCVO (1979, MVO 1961), CMG (1977); s of John Scott (d 1957), and Kathleen Scott (d 1983), of Newcastle upon Tyne; *b* 19 May 1923; *Educ* Dame Allan's Sch, Durham Univ; *m* 1, 1944 (m dis 1967), Vivienne Sylvia Vincent-Barwood (d 1985); 3 s; m 2, 1971, Jennifer Cameron Smith; *Career* served 1942-47 with 1 Gurkha Rifles; 1949-57 Colonial Office; Dip Serv: dep high cmmr Peshawar, Pakistan 1959-62, cnsllr British High Cmmn New Delhi 1963-65 and Nicosia 1968-72, RCDS 1973, ambass to Nepal 1974-77, high cmmr Malawi 1977-79, Bangladesh 1980-81, ret; sec-gen Royal Cwlth Soc 1983-; cncl Overseas Devpt Inst 1983-; *Clubs* Oriental; Royal Commonwealth Society; *Style—* Sir Michael Scott, KCVO, CMG; 87A Cornwall Gdns, London SW7 4AY (☎ 01 589 6794)

SCOTT, Nicholas Paul; MBE (1964), JP (London 1961), MP (C) Chelsea 1974-; s of Percival John Scott; *b* 5 August 1933; *Educ* Clapham Coll, City of London Coll; *m* 1, 1964 (m dis 1976), Elizabeth, da of Robert Robinson, of Thornborough, Bucks; 1 s, 2 da; m 2, 1979, Hon Mrs Tapsell (Hon Cecilia, *qv*, da of 9 Baron Hawke); 1 s, 1 da; *Career* Parly candidate Islington (C) SW 1959 and 1964; MP (C): Paddington S 1966-Feb 1974, Kensington and Chelsea 1974-; PPS to Rt Hon Iain Macleod as Chllr Exchequer 1970 and to Rt Hon Robert Carr as Home Sec 1972-74, parly under-sec Dept of Employment 1974, oppn spokesman Housing 1974-75; parly under-sec Northern Ireland Office Sept 1981-; exec memb 1922 Ctee 1978-1981; dir: A S Kerswill 1970-81, Eastbourne Printers 1970-81, Juniper Studios 1970-81, Bonusbond Hldgs 1980-81, Bonusplan Ltd 1977-81, Cleveland Offshore Fund Inc 1970-81, Learplan 1978-81; consultant Hill & Knowlton UK Ltd 1981; former chm Creative Consultants and md E Allom & Co; govr British Inst Human Rights, memb cncl Community Serv Volunteers, dep chm Br Caribbean Assoc, nat pres Tory Reform Gp; former chm Conservative Parly Employment Ctee; nat chm YCs 1963; dir London Office Euro Cons Gp in Euro Parl 1974; memb Guild Air Pilots & Air Navigators; *Clubs* Buck's, Pratt's, MCC; *Style—* Nicholas Scott Esq, MBE, JP, MP; House of Commons, SW1A 0AA

SCOTT, Sir Oliver Christopher Anderson; 3 Bt (UK 1909) of Yews, Undermilbeck, Westmorland; Sir Samuel Haslam Scott, 2 Bt (d 1960), and his 2 wife, Nancy Lilian, *née* Anderson (d 1935); *b* 6 Nov 1922; *Educ* Charterhouse, King's Coll Cambridge; *m* 1951, Phoebe Anne, er da of Desmond O'Neill Tolhurst; 1 s, 2 da; *Heir* s, Christopher James Scott b 16 Jan 1955; *Career* High Sheriff of Westmorland 1966; dir of res unit of radiobiology British Empire Cancer Campaign 1966-69, conslt Inst of Cancer Res 1974-82, radiobiologist St Thomas's Hosp London; *Clubs* Brooks's; *Style—* Sir Oliver Scott, Bt; 31 Kensington Sq, London W8

SCOTT, Dr Oliver Lester Schreiner; s of Ralph Lester Scott (d 1952), of Cape Town, and Ursula Hester (d 1965); *b* 16 June 1919; *Educ* Diocesan Coll Cape Town, Trinity Coll Cambridge, St Thomas's Hosp London; *m* 17 July 1943, Katherine Ogle, da of Hugh Shimwell Branfoot (d 1945); 2 da (Oenone b 1945, Lyndall b 1948); *Career* Sqdn Ldr Med Branch RAFVR, served NW Europe; conslt dermatologist: physician i/c skin dept Charing Cross Hosp & Med Sch 1956-84, St Luke's Hosp & Royal Surrey Co Hosp Guildford 1953-84; hon conslt: dermatologist L'Hôpital Française et Dispensaire Français 1960-, King Edward VII Hospital 1977-; hon memb and former pres (1982) British Assoc of Dermatologists; hon tres Royal Med Fndn of Epsom Coll, former dir Med Insur Agency; author of articles on dermatology in med jls; Chevalier de l'Ordre Merité (France) 1979; *Recreations* gardening, fishing; *Style—* Dr Oliver Scott; 114 Harley Street, London W1 (☎ 01 935 0621)

SCOTT, Sir (Charles) Peter; KBE (1978, OBE 1948), CMG (1964); s of Rev John Joseph Scott (d 1947), and Hannah Dorothea, *née* Senior (d 1953); *b* 30 Dec 1917; *Educ* Weymouth Coll, Pembroke Coll Cambridge; *m* 1954, Rachael, yr da of late Cyril Walter Lloyd-Jones, CIE, of Guildford; 1 s (Harry), 2 da (Katherine, Maria); *Career* ICS 1940-47, entered FO 1947, second sec Toyko 1948 (first sec 1949); FO 1950-52; private sec to Gen Lord Ismay at NATO Paris 1952-54; first sec: Vienna 1954, British Info Services (New York) 1956; cnsllr and consul-gen Washington 1959-61, IDC 1962, head of UK perm mission to Euro Office of UN Geneva 1963-66, min Rome 1966-69, seconded to Centre for Contemporary European Studies Sussex Univ 1969, asst under-sec state FCO 1970-75, ambass Norway 1975-77; private sec to HRH Prince Michael of Kent 1978-79 (tres 1979-81); *Recreations* walking, skiing; *Clubs* Utd Oxford and Cambridge Univ, Norfolk (Norwich); *Style—* Sir Peter Scott, KBE, CMG; Bisley Farmhouse, Irstead, nr Norwich, Norfolk NR12 8XT (☎ Horning 630413)

SCOTT, Peter Denys John; QC (1978); s of John Ernest Dudley Scott, and Joan Steinberg, *née* Clayton-Cooper; *b* 19 April 1935; *Educ* Monroe HS Rochester New York USA, Balliol Coll Oxford (MA); *Career* Nat Serv Lt RHA; barr; chm General Cncl of the Bar 1987 (vice-chm 1985-86); *Style—* Peter D J Scott, Esq, QC; 4 Eldon Rd, London W8 5PU (☎ 01 937 3301); Fountain Court Temple, London EC4 (☎ 01 353 7356, fax 353 0329, telex 8813408 FON LEG G)

SCOTT, Sir Peter Markham; CBE (1953, MBE 1942), DSC (1943 and bar); s of Capt Robert Falcon Scott, CVO, RN (Scott of the Antarctic), by his w Kathhleen, who m subsequently 1 Baron Kennet; *b* 14 Sept 1909; *Educ* Oundle, Trinity Coll Cambridge, Munich State Acad, Royal Acad Schs London; *m* 1, 1942 (m dis 1951), Elizabeth Jane, da of David Howard; 1 da; m 2, 1951, Philippa, da of Cdr F Talbot-Ponsonby, RN; 1 s, 1 da; *Career* former Lt Cdr RNVR; artist, naturalist; chllr Birmingham Univ 1974-83; chm of cncl World Wildlife Fund Int; hon dir: Wildfowl Tst, Survival Anglia Ltd; pres: Flora & Fauna Preservation Soc 1981-, pres Glos Assoc Youth Clubs; vice-pres: Br Gliding Assoc, Inland Waterways Assoc, Camping Club of GB, Bristol Gliding Club; memb cncl Boy Scout Assoc and Winston Churchill Memorial Tst; pres British Butterfly Conservation Soc; chm Falkland Islands Fndn 1979-; RGS Founder's Medal 1983, Philadelphia Acad of Natural Sciences Gold Medal 1983; kt 1973; *Style—* Lt-Cdr Sir Peter Scott, CBE, DSC; New Grounds, Slimbridge, Glos (☎ 045 389 333)

SCOTT, Philip Edward Hannay; s of Edward Beattie Scott, MBE, and Mary, *née* Potter; *b* 6 April 1957; *Educ* Millfield, Cricklade Coll Andover; *Career* formerly in films indust Tor Films Ltd (Tarka the Otter), paralysed in motor racing accident 1977, illustrator 1978-; work incl Poly series of childrens books; freelance journalist and broadcaster (BBC) 1979-: Radio 4, World series, Local Radio; work with the disabled to encourage movement tran res into the community 1979-; achievements incl: Indr memb project 81, Indr memb Hampshire Centre for Indp living 1982, became one of first people to be completely supported in the community by a health authy; promotor of interests of the disabled through aviation achievements incl: indr Operation ability 1984, first tetraplegic to pass a Civil Aviation Authy med to gain Private Pilots licence, involved First G tests for tetraplegic person 1985; "Man of the Year" award for serv to disabled community 1988; Freeman: City of London, Worshipful Co of Habderdashers 1978; FRAeS 1985; *Recreations* art, engineering, travel, calligraphy, aviation; *Clubs* Chess; *Style—* Philip Scott, Esq; The Meadows, Firgrove Rd, Whitehill, Nr Bordon, Hampshire GU35 9DY, (☎ 042 03 5062)

SCOTT, Sheriff Richard John Dinwoodie; s of Prof Richard Scott (d 1983), and Mary Ellen Maclachlan (d 1987); *b* 28 May 1939; *Educ* Edinburgh Acad, Univ of Edinburgh (MA, LLB); *m* 1969, Josephine Moretta, da of Allan Holland Blake, (d 1954), of Edinburgh; 2 da (Victoria b 1970, Joanna b 1972); *Career* advocate 1965;

Scottish bar 1965-77, Sheriff of Grampian Highland and Islands at Aberdeen and Stonehaven 1977-86; Sheriff of Lothian and Borders at Edinburgh 1986-; *Style—* Sheriff Richard Scott; Sheriff's Chambers, Edinburgh EH1 2NS

SCOTT, Hon Mr Justice; Richard Rashleigh Folliott Scott; *Career* barr Inner Temple 1959 (bencher 1981), QC 1975, attorney-gen Duchy of Lancaster 1980-, High Court judge 1983-; *Style—* The Hon Mr Justice Scott; 11 Old Sq, Lincoln's Inn, London WC2

SCOTT, Hon Mrs (Rita); *née* Blyton; yst da of Baron Blyton (Life Peer; d 1987); *b* 1930; *m* 1954, Andrew Scott; children; *Style—* The Hon Mrs Scott; 67 Australia Grove, S Shields, Tyne & Wear

SCOTT, Wing Cdr Robert Dunlop Irwin; MBE (1946); s of John Irwin Scott (d 1943), late headmaster Kettering GS, and Maud Jane Margaret, *née* Dunlop (d 1976); *b* 7 Jan 1913; *Educ* Framlingham Coll Suffolk; *m* 6 July 1946, Kathleen Edith Annie, da of Maj Robert Smith (d 1956), of Greystones, Co Wicklow; 2 s (John b 1949, Patrick b 1957), 1 da (Caroline b 1953); *Career* RAF Pilot Offr 1938, served in Iraq, Singapore, Malaya, Kuala Lumpar, Java, Australia, India, W Africa 1939-47 UK 1948, Wing Cdr 1956 (ret); CA Hereford and Powys 1956-; *Recreations* golf, preservation steam rlways; *Clubs* RAF, Royal Porthcawl Golf, Nairn Golf; *Style—* Wing Cdr Robert Scott, MBE; The Friars House, Barton Rd, Hereford (☎ Hfd 263776); 61 Edgar St, Hereford; 4A China St, Llanidloes, Powys

SCOTT, Robin Hugh; *see*: Scutt, Robin Hugh

SCOTT, Sarah Caroline; *née* Gordon; yr adopted da of 4 Marquess of Aberdeen and Temair (d 1974); *b* 25 Mar 1948; *m* 1969, Patrick John Raleigh Scott, er son of late R S G Scott, of The Hermitage, Peasmarsh, Sussex; *Style—* Mrs Patrick Scott

SCOTT, Hon Simon Peter; 2 s of 4 Earl of Eldon, GCVO (d 1976); *b* 13 Sept 1939; *Educ* Ampleforth, Salamanca and Madrid Univs, Sorbonne; *m* 28 Oct 1966, Mary Isabel, 2 da of late Andrew Ramon Dalzell de Bertodano; 3 s, 1 da; *Career* page of honour to HM The Queen 1953-56; Lt Scots Gds Army Emergency Reserve; *Clubs* White's; *Style—* The Hon Simon Scott; Frogden, Kelso, Roxburghshire TD5 8AB

SCOTT, Sir Walter; 4 Bt (UK 1907), of Beauclere, Bywell St Andrews, Co Northumberland, DL (E Sussex 1975); s of Sir Walter Scott, 3 Bt (d 1967), and his 1 w, Nancy Margaret (Margot), *née* March (d 1944); *b* 29 July 1918; *Educ* Eton, Jesus Coll Cambridge; *m* 15 Jan 1944, Diana Mary, da of James Owen; 1 s, 1 da (Sarah Jane, now Duchess of Hamilton and Brandon); *Heir* s, (Walter) John Scott; *Career* Maj 1 Royal Dragoons; JP (E Sussex 1963); *Style—* Sir Walter Scott, Bt, DL; Newhouse Farm, Chalvington, Hailsham, Sussex

SCOTT, Walter Grant; s of Thomas Scott (d 1979), and Marion Urie Roberts; *b* 13 May 1947; *Educ* Eastwood HS, Edinburgh Univ (BSc), Trin Hall Cambridge (PhD); *m* 1973, Rosemary Ann Clark, da of Alfred W C Lobban, of Bedfordshire; 1 s (Matthew), 2 da (Rachel, Diana); *Career* dir Ivory & Sime Ltd 1972-82; Ind Investment Co nominee dir Systems Designers International 1981-, dir Integrated Micro Applications Ltd 1981-; sr ptnr Walter Scott & Ptnrs 1982-, portfolio management (circa 500m), chm Walter Scott International 1983-, joint venture First Interstate Bank; *Recreations* rowing, running, gardening; *Clubs* Leander, New (Edinburgh); *Style—* Walter Scott, Esq; Hillwood, Loanhead, Midlothian EH20 (☎ 031 440 0587); 9 Great Stuart St, Edinburgh EH3 7TP (☎ 031 225 9211, telex 727613)

SCOTT, Walter John; s and h of Sir Walter Scott, 4 Bt; *b* 24 Feb 1948; *Educ* privately; *m* 1, 5 July 1969 (m dis 1971), Lowell Patria, da of late Pat Vaughan Goddard, of Auckland, NZ; 1 da (Rebecca b 1970); m 2, 1977, Mary Gavin Anderson, 1 s (Walter Samuel b 1984), 1 da (Diana Helen Rose b 1977); *Career* Farmer; *Recreations* field sports; *Style—* Walter Scott, Esq

SCOTT, William Patrick; OBE (1970), TD (1945), DL (1967); *b* 1 Dec 1910; *Educ* Sedbergh; *m* 1938, Philippa, 1 s 3 da; *Career* Capt Lanarks Yeo; dir Highland Distilleries 1928-78, chairman LEC Orkney 1948-78, RSPB Orkney 1950-64; member Highland TA&VR Assoc 1950-78; Hon Sheriff Grampian, Highlands and Islands 1972-; memb Royal Co of Archers, (Queen's Body Guard for Scotland), memb Snr Golfers' Soc; *Recreations* golf, shooting, fishing; *Clubs* New, R & A, Western Meeting, Ayr, Prestwick Golf; *Style—* William Scott, Esq, OBE, TD, DL; Kierfiold House, Sandwick, Stromness, Orkney (☎ Sandwick 503)

SCOTT, Hon Lady; Winifred Kathleen; *née* Brodrick; *m* 1941, Hon Sir Ernest Stowell Scott, KCMG, MVO (s of 3 Earl of Eldon and who d 1953); 1 da; *Style—* The Hon Lady Scott; The Manor House, Bradford, Peverell, Dorchester, Dorset

SCOTT FOX, Sir (Robert) David John; KCMG (1963, CMG 1956); s of late Judge John Scott Fox, KC; *b* 20 June 1910; *Educ* Eton, Ch Ch Oxford; *m* 1951, Brigitte, da of Pierre Taton; 3 da; *Career* entered Foreign Office 1934, served Rio de Janiero 1940-44, counsellor Jeddah and Ankara 1951-54, min to UK Delegation to UN 1955-58, min to Rumania 1959-61, ambass to Chile 1961-66, ambass to Finland 1966-1969, ret; special rep of the Sec of State for Foreign and Commonwealth Affairs 1970-75; Grand Cross Chilean Order of Merit 1965, Order of the Finnish Lion 1969; author of: Mediterranean Heritage (1978), St George (1983); *Style—* Sir David Scott Fox, KCMG; 47 Eaton Terrace, London SW1 (☎ 01 730 5505)

SCOTT McIVER, Fiona; da of Major Dougal Campbell McIver, and Jessica Smith, *née* Castellano; *b* 13 Sept 1944; *Educ* St Martin's Covent; *Career* proprietor Images Health Studio; dir: Corporate Images Ltd, Outlines Ltd, Silhouettes Ltd, Profiles Ltd; features ed The Marylebone Times; chm ASTO; *Recreations* tennis, squash; *Style—* Miss Fiona Scott McIver; 19 Paddington St, London W1 (☎ 01 935 3166, fax 01 935 4131, telex 94012662 IMAG G)

SCOTT MONCRIEFF, David Charles; CVO (1960), TD, WS (1946); s of John Irving Scott Moncrieff (d 1920), and nephew of Charles Scott Moncrieff, the translator of Proust; gggs of John Philp (*sic*) Wood, editor of the Douglas Peerage (in which his name is incorrectly spelt *Philip*); *b* 2 July 1915; *Educ* Sedbergh, Edinburgh Univ (BL); *m* 1948, Ann Pamela, da of Sir Kenneth Murray of Geanies (d 1979); 2 s, 1 da; *Career* slr, ret, Bailie of Holyrood 1957-79, purse-bearer to Lord High Cmmr to Gen Assembly of Church of Scotland (Earl of Wemyss and March) 1959 and 1960; memb Royal Co of Archers (Queen's Body Guard for Scotland); *Recreations* hill walking; *Style—* David Scott Moncrieff, Esq, CVO, TD, WS; 23 Cluny Drive, Edinburgh (☎ 031 447 2578)

SCOTT OF WEEDON, Baron (Life Peer UK 1988), of Newcastle-under-Lyme, Co Staffs Robert Scott Alexander; QC (1973); s of late Samuel James and Hannah May Alexander; *b* 5 Sept 1936; *Educ* Brighton Coll, King's Coll Cambridge; *m* 1, 1963 (m dis 1973), Frances Rosemary Heveningham Pughe; 2 s, 1 da; m 2, 1978, Elizabeth, da of Col C Norman; 1 s; *Career* barr Middle Temple 1961, bencher 1979; pres King's Coll Assoc 1980-81; chm of the Bar 1985-86; *Style—* Robert Alexander, Esq, QC; 1 Brick Court, Temple, London EC4 (☎ 01 353 0777)

SCOTT PLUMMER, (Patrick) Joseph; s of Charles Humphrey Scott Plummer, of Mainhouse, Kelso, Roxburghshire, and The Hon Pamela Lilias, *née* Balfour; *b* 24 August 1943; *Educ* Radley, Magdalene Coll Cambridge (MA); *m* 1, 12 March 1970 (m dis 1977), Elizabeth-Anne, da of Col Anthony Way, MC, of Kincairney, Murthly, Perthshire; 1 s (Charles b 18 Aug 1971), 1 da (Annabel b 26 June 1973); m 2, 15 Sept 1977, Christine Hermione Roberts, da of The Hon Anthony Gerard Bampfylde (d 1968), of Boyton Ho, Woodbridge, Suffolk 1 s (Guy b 13 Aug 1978); *Career* ptnr Cazenove and Co 1974-80; dir: Martin Currie Ltd 1981-, Candover Invs plc 1987-, Life Assoc of Scotland 1988-; FCA 1967; *Recreations* tennis; *Clubs* New (Edinburgh), Pratt's; *Style—* Joseph Scott Plummer, Esq; Mainhouse, Kelso, Roxburghshire (☎ 0573 23 327); 20 Keith Rd, Edinburgh; Martin Currie Ltd, 29 Charlotte Sq, Edinburgh (☎ 031 225 3811)

SCOTT WARREN, Dr David Noël Martin; s of Rev Percival Scott Warren (d 1949), and Ione Mason, *née* Wilkinson (d 1941); *b* 8 Jan 1924; *Educ* St John's Sch Leatherhead, London Hosp Med Coll; *m* 8 Jan 1949, June Mary, da of Howard John Raymond Feeny (d 1978), of The Little House, Feckenham, Worcs; 3 s (Anthony David b 1949, Jonathan Michael b 1952, Timothy Nicholas b 1954), 2 da (Amanda Frances Ione b 1957, Fiona Mary b 1959); *Career* med practitioner; CStJ; memb BMA Jersey Med Soc, MRCS, LRCP; *Recreations* motoring, photography; *Clubs* Jersey Old Motor, London Hosp Med, Jersey Motor Cycl & Light Car; *Style—* Dr D N M Scott Warren; Mont du Ouaisne, St Brelade, Jersey CI (☎ 0534 42939 43590); 41 David Place, St Helier, Jersey CI (☎ 0534 23318)

SCOTT-BARRETT, Lt-Gen Sir David William; KBE (1976, MBE 1956), MC (1945); s of late Brig Rev H Scott-Barrett, CB, CBE; *b* 16 Dec 1922; *Educ* Westminster Sch; *m* 1948, Marie Elise, *née* Morris (d 1985); 3 s; *Career* cmmnd Scots Guard 1942, served NW Europe WWII, GOC Eastern Dist 1971-73, GOC Berlin 1973-75, Col Cmdt Scottish Div and GOC Scotland 1976-79, govr Edinburgh Castle 1976-79; former dir Arbuthnot Securities; chm Army Cadet Force Assoc 1981-, dir Haven Project for Mental Health Provision 1983-84; *Style—* Lt-Gen Sir David Scott-Barrett, KBE, MC; Hall House, Kersey, Ipswich, Suffolk IP7 6DZ (☎ 0473 822 365)

SCOTT-DEMPSTER, Lt-Col Ronald; WS (1974); s of Thomas Dempster, DL (d 1937), Lord Provost of Perth, and Constance Elizabeth Georgina, *née* Greig (d 1954); *b* 8 May 1898; *Educ* Perth Acad, Edinburgh Univ (BL); *m* 5 Sept 1933, Ann, da of Rt Rev Edward Thomas Scott Reid, DD (d 1938), Bishop of St Andrew's, Dunkeld and Dunblane; 1 s (Colin b 1937), 2 da (Fiona b 1935, Jane b 1950); *Career* Lt RFA 1916-19, wounded Paschendale 1917, Lt-Col Army Welfare Offr Perthshire 1943-50; ptnr Robertson Dempster & Co WS Perth 1924-74, conslt Condie, Mackenzie & Co WC Perth 1974-87; sec TA Assoc 1939-48; registrar Dioc of St Andrews, Dunkeld and Dunblane 1928-74 (chllr 1974-86), tstee Scottish Episcopal Church 1960-87 (convenor exec ctee 1959-67), dir/ships inc: Grampian Properties Ltd 1967-77, Eng Life Assur Co plc 1962-77, jt legal advsr Br Deer soc 1968-72, deer conslt Grampian Properties 1977-83; *Recreations* golf, tennis, deer stalking, piping, gardening; *Clubs* Lansdowne, Royal Perth Golfing and County; *Style—* Lt-Col Ronald Scott-Dempster; Tayhill, Brae Street, Dunkeld, Perthshire PH8 0BA (☎ 03502 277); 2 Tay Street, Perth (☎ 0738 33171, telex 76557 PERSOL G, fax 0738 43425)

SCOTT-ELLIOT, Aydua Helen; CVO (1969, MVO 1958); da of Lewis Alexander Scott-Elliot (d 1916); *b* 11 Dec 1909; *Educ* St Paul's Girls' Sch, and abroad; *Career* keeper of Prints and Drawings Royal Collection Windsor Castle 1946-69, ret 1970, temp assist civilian officer Admiralty 1941-45; FSA; *Clubs* Univ Women's; *Style—* Miss Scott-Elliot, CVO; Shaldon, Station Rd, Mayfield, East Sussex

SCOTT-HARDEN, Anthony Walter; s of Dr Walter Geoffrey Scott-Harden (d 1984), of Orchard House, Scotby, Carlisle, and Mary, *née* Connell; *b* 4 July 1940; *Educ* St Edwards Oxford, Cumberland, and Westmorland Farm Sch, Newton Rigg, Penrith (DipiAgric); *m* July 1965, Daphne Elizabeth, da of Maj Laurence Wilfred Anrett (d 1966), of Pond House, Hurworth on Tees, Darlington; 1 s (James b 1969), 1 da (Lucy b 1966); *Career* Lt Cumberland and Westmorland Yeo (TA) 1960-66; dir: Lowther Scott-Harden Ltd (and chm), chartered surveyors, New Cavendish Estates plc (Property Investmt and Devpt), Metrorural Properties Ltd, West Hall Youngstock plc (bloodstock dealing), Simonside Farms Ltd (farming and consulting); FRICS 1963; *Recreations* shooting, foxhunting, scubadiving, travel, horse racing; *Clubs* Turf, Farmers, Northern Counties; *Style—* Anthony Scott-Harden, Esq; West Hall, Middleton Tyas, Richmond, N Yorks (☎ 0325 772 65); Monkend Estate Off, Croft, Darlington, Co Durham (☎ 0325 720 614, fax 0325 721 249, car phone 0860 814 517, telex 58657 ANSHG)

SCOTT-HOPKINS, Maj Sir James Sidney Rawdon; MEP (EDG) Hereford & Worcester 1979-; s of Lt-Col Rawdon Scott-Hopkins, DSO, MC (d 1974), of Phyllis Court Club, Henley-on-Thames, formerly of Wadeford House, Chard, Somerset; *b* 29 Nov 1921; *Educ* Eton, Oxford, Cambridge; *m* 1946, Geraldine Elizabeth, CBE, o da of Lt-Col John Carne Hargreaves, of Drinkstone Park, Suffolk, by his former w Hon Angela, *née* Goschen (sis of 3 Viscount Goschen); 3 s, 1 da (*see* Timothy Smith, MP); *Career* served King's Own Yorks Ll of & QAO Gurkha Rfles 1939-50; farmer and memb NFU 1950-59; MP (C) Cornwall N 1959-66, W Derbyshire 1967-79; PPS to: Jt Parly Sec State CRO 1961-62, Jt Parly Sec Min Agric Fish & Food 1962-64; dep ldr Cons Gp & spokesman Agric 1973-79 (vice-pres 1976-79), chm Euro Democratic Gp 1979-81 (nominated memb Euro Parl); *Style—* Maj Sir James Scott-Hopkins, MEP; 602 Nelson House, Dolphin Sq, SW1

SCOTT-NOBLE, Lt-Col James Robert; MC (1940), TD (1943), JP (Roxburghshire 1961), DL (1962); s of Robert Scott-Noble (d 1968), of Hawick, and Edith Alice Hutton (d 1978); *b* 23 Feb 1915; *Educ* Loretto, Musselburgh; *m* 18 June 1941, Diana Mabean, da of Lt-Col William Geddes Borran Dickson (d 1945); 1 s (Anthony William b 1952), 2 da (Sarnia Anne b 1942, Diana Vanessa b 1945); *Career* Lt-Col France 1942, Egypt, Italy 1943-44, Instr Staff Coll 1945; Woollen Manufacturer 1934-65, farmer 1965-81 (ret); *Recreations* shooting, walking; *Clubs* RAC; *Style—* Lt-Col James Scott-Noble, MC, TD, JP, DL; Ravenslea, Hawick TD9 7HS (☎ 0450 72175)

SCOTT-SMITH, Catharine Mary; da of Edward Montagu Scott-Smith (d 1951), and Catharine Lorance, *née* Garland (d 1949); *b* 4 April 1912; *Educ* Wycombe Abbey Sch High Wycombe Bucks, Girton Coll Cambridge (BA, MA); *Career* asst mistress: St Katharine's Sch Wantage 1933-37, Godolphin Sch Salisbury 1937-41; Headington Sch

Oxford 1941-47: house mistress, sr mistress; sr mistress Wycombe Abbey Sch Bucks 1951-54 (house mistress 1947-55), headmistress Weston Birt Sch Gloucs 1955-65, princ Beachlawn Tutorial Coll Oxford 1966-71; AAM 1933-35 and 1955-65, AHMBS 1955-65 (memb ctee); *Recreations* gardening, travel, reading, crosswords; *Clubs* University Women's; *Style*— Miss Catharine Scott-Smith

SCOTT-WHITE, Raymond; s of Lawson Scott-White, OBE (d 1967), and Muriel Annie, *née* Ward; *b* 22 August 1934; *Educ* Whitgift Sch Croydon, Imp Coll London Univ (BSc, ACGI); *m* 6 July 1967, Patricia Anne, da of Ronald John Elmes (d 1981), of Hayes, Kent; 1 s (David Andrew b 9 Nov 1958, d 11 June 1976), 1 da Sally Anne (b 2 Nov 1959); *Career* fndr Scott-White and Hookins conslt engrs 1963; memb Croydon 41 Club, chm Croydon Round Table 1973; Freeman City of London, Warden of Worshipful Co of Fan Makers; CEng, FIStructE, MICE, MIHT, MConsE; *Recreations* golf; *Clubs* Livery, Kingswood Golf (Capt); *Style*— Raymond Scott-White, Esq; London House, 42 West St, Carshalton, Surrey SM5 2PU (☎ 01 773 3131, fax 01 773 2605)

SCOULLER, (John) Alan; s of Charles James Scouller (d 1974), of Banstead, Surrey, and Mary Helena, *née* Pyne (d 1972); *b* 23 Sept 1929; *Educ* John Fisher Sch Purley Surrey; *m* 29 May 1954, Angela Gemeste, da of Harry Ambrose (d 1937), of Maidstone, Kent; 2 s (James Paul b 1955, Edward John b 1964), 5 da (Catherine Mary b 1956, Frances Elizabeth b 1958, Sarah Margaret b 1961, Helen Louise b 1966, Joanna Clare b 1968); *Career* Nat Serv 1948, cmmnd 2 Lt Queen's Own Royal West Kent Regt 1949, reg cmmn Lt 1951, 1 Bn Malaya 1953-54, Germany 1954, Capt Instructor Sch of Inf (Signals) 1955-56, 1 Bn Cyprus 1957-58, resigned cmmn 1958; Unilever Ltd: personnel mangr Walls Ice Cream Gloucester 1958-62, asst to trg mangr Rotterdam 1962, personnel mangr Domestos Ltd Newcastle Upon Tyne 1962-66, personnel mangr Commercial Plastics & Holpak 1966-69; head industl rels Midland Bank Gp 1975-88, visiting prof in industl rels Kingston Poly 1988-; chm of govrs John Henry Newman Sch Stevenage Herts; cmmr Cmmn on Industl Rels 1973 (1969-74), pt/t memb Employment Appeal Tribunal 1976-; FIPM; *Recreations* music, reading, walking, travel, studying employment law; *Style*— Alan Scouller, Esq; 32 Sollershott West, Letchworth, Herts SG6 3PX (☎ 0462 682781)

SCOWEN, Sir Eric Frank; s of Frank Edward Scowen; *b* 1910; *Educ* City of London Sch, St Bartholomew's Hosp Med Coll London Univ (MD, DSc); *Career* physician to St Bartholomew's Hosp 1946-75, dir of Medical Professorial Unit 1955-75, prof of Medicine London Univ 1961-75, chm British Pharmacopoeia Cmmn 1963-69; chm: Cncl of Imperial Cancer Research Fund 1967-82 (vice-pres 1982), Ctee of Safety of Medicines 1970-81, Ctee on Review of Medicines 1975-78, Poisons Bd 1976-83, cncl sch of pharmacy Univ of London 1979-, clinical trials ethical ctee Royal Coll of Gen Practitioners 1981-; FRCP, FRCS, FRCPE, FRCPath; Hon LLD Nottingham, Hon FPS 1984, Hon Fell Sch of Pharmacy 1986; kt 1973; *Clubs* Athenaeum; *Style*— Sir Eric Scowen; Flat 77, 6/9 Charterhouse Sq, London EC1M 6EX (☎ 01 251 3212)

SCREECH, Dr Michael Andrew; s of Richard John Screech, MM (d 1986), of Pomphlet, Plymstock, Plymouth, and Nellie Ernestine, *née* Maunder (d 1977); *b* 2 May 1926; *Educ* Sutton HS Plymouth, UCL (BA), Univ of Birmingham (DLitt), Univ of London (DLit), Univ of Oxford (MA); *m* 3 April 1956, (Ursula) Anne Grace, John William Reeve (d 1960); 3 s (Matthew b 13 Jan 1960, Timothy b 28 Sept 1961, Toby b 3 Oct 1963); *Career* Staff Sgt Intelligence Corps Far East 1944-48; asst lectr, lectr, sr lectr Univ of Birmingham 1951-56, reader, prof of french Univ of London 1961-71, Fielden prof of french language and lit 1971-84, Johnson prof Inst for Res in the Humanities Madison Wisconsin 1978, Campion lectr Regina Saskatchewan 1983, Dorothy Ford Wiley prof of renaissance culture N Carolina 1986, Zaharoff lectr Oxford 1988, sr res fell All Soul's Coll Oxford 1984-; memb comité d'Humanisme et Renaissance 1958-; formerly: memb Whitchurch Parish Cncl, Whitchurch St Mary's PCC, chm of mangrs Whitchurch Primary Sch; Freeman Ville de Tours 1984; Fell UCL 1981; FBA 1958; Chevalier dans l'Ordre National du Mérite France; *Books* The Rabelaisian Marriage (1958), L'Evangélisme de Rabelais (1959), Marot Evangélique (1967); trans Rabelais edns: Tiers Livre (1964), Gargantua (1970), Prognostication (1975); Regrets (by Dubellay, trans 1964), Rabelais (1979), Ecstasy and the Praise of Folly (by Erasmus, trans 1980), Montaigne and Melancholy (1983), Apology for Raymond Sebond (by Montaigne, trans 1987); *Recreations* walking; *Style*— Dr Michael Screech; 5 Swanston Field, Whitchurch, Reading RG9 7HP; All Souls College, Oxford OX1 4AL

SCRIMGEOUR, Angus Muire Edington; s of Dr David Muir Scrimgeour (d 1977), and May Burton Clair, *née* Edington (d 1988); *b* 19 Feb 1945; *Educ* Westminster, New Coll Oxford (MA), Univ Coll London; *m* 21 Dec 1968, Clare Christian Gauvain, da of Dr Ronald Ormiston Murray, MBE; 1 s (Alexander b 1971); *Career* vice pres Citibank NA 1974-84, fndr and chief exec Eddington Plc merchant bank 1986-, jt chief exec Henry Cooke Gp 1988-; *Recreations* farming, design, chess, music; *Clubs* Inst of Dirs, Berkshire Golf, Manchester Racquet; *Style*— Angus Scrimgeour, Esq; 29 Eaton Mews South, London SW1W 9HR; Paddock House Farm, Alstonefield, Nr Ashbourne, Derbyshire DE6 2FT (☎ 033527 284); 1 King St, Manchester M2 6AW (☎ 061 834 2535, fax 061 834 8650)

SCRIVEN, Richard Gordon; JP (W Sussex 1963); s of Charles Douglas Scriven (d 1966), of The Dower House, Walberton, Arundel, Sussex, and Jane Sheila, *née* Gordon (d 1985); *b* 6 June 1928; *Educ* Winchester; *m* 5 April 1954, Gillian Elizabeth, da of Llewelyn Wynn Riley, of Hollycrift, Hebers Ghyll Drive, Ilkley, W Yorks; 1 s (David John Gordon b 1960), 2 da (Hilary Elizabeth b 1955, Clare Jane b 1958); *Career* mil service, regular cmmn in Scots Gds Lt; merchant banker; dir: Morgan Grenfell Finance Ltd, Morgan Grenfell (Local Authy Services) Ltd, Morgan Grenfell (Local Authy Finance) Ltd (ret 1984); conslt to Phillips and Drew on local authy finance 1985-87; dir London Court of Int Arbitration Ltd; fin dir Citicare St Clements Ltd; chm Talbot Ct Design Ltd; Freeman City of London, past Master Worshipful Co of Slaters and Memb of Court of Assistants 1982, Master Worshipful Co of Leather Sellers and Memb Court of Assistants 1987-88; past chm Bd of Govrs of Queenswood Sch, vice-chm Bd of Govrs of Colfe's Sch; Govr: Christs Hosp, City of London Freemans' Sch, Central Fndn Boys' Sch; tstee of Central Fndn Schs of London; gen cmmr of Income Tax; memb of Court of Common Cncl of Corp of London 1984 (elected for Ward of Candlewick); past chm E Grinstead UDC, ctee memb Friends of Ashdown Forset; MIEx; *Recreations* sailing, golf; *Clubs* Overseas Bankers, Third Guards, Guildhall, HAC; *Style*— Richard Scriven, Esq, JP; Shepherds Bank, Forset Row, E Sussex RH18 5BG (☎ 034282 4506)

SCRIVENER, Ronald Stratford; CMG (1965); s of Sir Patrick Stratford Scrivener, KCMG (d 1966), of Gt Bedwyn, Wiltshire, and Margaret Morris, *née* Dorling (d 1972); *b* 29 Dec 1919; *Educ* Westminster, St Catharine's Convent Cambridge; *m* 1, 1947 (m dis 1952), Elizabeth Drake-Brockman; m 2, 1962, Mary Alice Olga Sofia Jane, da of Robert Charlton Lane, and formerly w of Christopher Hohler; 2 step s, 2 step da; *Career* ambass to Panama 1969-70, ambass to Czechoslovakia 1971-74, asst under-sec of State Foreign and Cwlth Off 1974-76; *Recreations* travel, fishing; *Clubs* White's, Beefsteak; *Style*— Ronald Scrivener, Esq, CMG; 38 Lysia St, London SW6 6NG

SCRIVENOR, Sir Thomas Vaisey; CMG (1956); eld s of John Brooke Scrivenor, ISO (d 1950), of Horncastle, Lincs, and Violet, *née* Vaisey; *b* 28 August 1908; *Educ* King's Sch Canterbury, Oriel Coll Oxford (MA); *m* 4 June 1934, Mary Elizabeth, da of late Albert Augustine Neatby, of Court House, Chiselborough, Somerset; 1 s, 3 da; *Career* entered Colonial Office 1930, served in Tanganyika, Palestine and Malta; civil service cmmr Nigeria 1948-53, dep high cmmr Basutoland, Bechuanaland, and Swaziland 1953-60; sec Cwlth Agric Bureaux 1961-73; kt 1960; *Style*— Sir Thomas Scrivenor, CMG; Vine Cottage, Minster Lovell, Oxon

SCROGGIE, Alan Ure Reith; CBE (1973, OBE 1961), QPM (1968); s of Col William Reith John Scroggie, CIE, IMS (d 1953), and Florence Marjorie, *née* Ure (d 1974); *b* 10 Mar 1912; *Educ* Cargilfield Prep Sch, Fettes Coll, Edinburgh Univ (BL); *m* 1940, Sheila Catherine, da of Finlay Mackenzie, of Elgin (d 1957); 2 s; *Career* Edinburgh Police 1930-47, asst chief constable Bucks 1947-53, chief constable Northumberland 1953-63, HM inspector of Constabulary 1963-75; OStJ 1954; *Recreations* golf, fishing; *Clubs* Royal and Ancient (St Andrews), Golf House (Elie); *Style*— Alan Scroggie, Esq, CBE, QPM; Fowler's Cottage, Abercrombie, by St Monans, Fife (☎ 033 37 595)

SCROPE, Richard Ladislas; s of Henry Aloysius Scrope and Maria Mercedes (da of Alexander de Laski and Joaquina, Marquesa de Souza Lisboa); *b* 22 August 1901; *Educ* Oratory Sch Edgbaston, Gonville and Caius Cambridge; *m* 1934, Lady Jane Egerton (d 1978), da of 4 Earl of Ellesmere; 1 s (Simon, *qv*), 1 da (Elizabeth Jane); *Career* Maj Coldstream Gds, served M East and Europe; landowner; *Recreations* shooting, hunting, fishing; *Clubs* Brooks's; *Style*— Richard Scrope, Esq; Danby House, Middleham, N Yorks (☎ 0969 23225)

SCROPE, Simon Egerton; s of Richard Ladislas Scrope, *qv*; *b* 23 Dec 1934; *Educ* Ampleforth, Trin Coll Cambridge; *m* 1970, Jennifer Jane, da of Sir Kenneth Wade Parkinson, DL (d 1981); 1 s, 1 da; *Career* insurance broker, memb Lloyd's 1956, chm Richards Longstaff Gp 1974; farmer and landowner; *Recreations* racing, shooting, gardening, fishing; *Clubs* Brooks's; *Style*— Simon Scrope, Esq; Danby on Yore, Leyburn, N Yorks DL8 4PX (☎ 0969 23297)

SCRUTON, Prof Roger; s of John Scruton, of High Wycombe, Bucks, and Beryl Clarys, *née* Haines (d 1967); *b* 27 Feb 1944; *Educ* Royal GS High Wycombe, Jesus Coll Cambridge (BA, MA, PhD); *m* 1975 (m dis 1979), (Marie Genevieve) Danielle, da of Robert Laffitte, of Orthez, France; *Career* called to the Bar Inner Temple 1974, fell Peterhouse Coll Cambridge 1969-71, prof of aesthetics Dept of Philosophy Birkbeck Coll London (formerly lectr and reader); ed Salisbury Review; *Books* Art and Imagination (1974), The Aesthetics of Architecture (1979), The Meaning of Conservatism (1980), Fortnight's Anger (1981), A Dictionary of Political Thought (1983), Sexual Desire (1986), Thinkers of the New Left (1986), A Land Held Hostage (1987); *Recreations* music, hunting; *Clubs* Athenaeum; *Style*— Prof Roger Scruton; Birkbeck College, Malet St, London WC1 (☎ 01 631 6549)

SCRYMGEOUR, Lord; Henry David; s and h of 12 Earl of Dundee; *b* 20 June 1982; *Style*— Lord Scrymgeour

SCRYMGEOUR-WEDDERBURN, Hon Mrs William; Joyce; *née* Norman Jennings; da of late Col Robert Henry Jennings, CSI, RE; *b* 25 June 1899; *Educ* Cheltenham Coll; *m* 1921, Capt the Hon William Ogilvy Scrymgeour-Wedderburn, DSC, RN (s of de jure 9 Earl of Dundee) who d 1958; 1 s, 1 da; *Style*— The Hon Mrs William Scrymgeour-; c/o Cmmdr I A Scrymgeour-Wedderburn, Dunlichity Lodge, Farr, Inverness 1VI 2AN

SCRYMSOURE STEUART FOTHRINGHAM, Robert; DL (Angus 1985); eld s of Maj Thomas Scrymsoure Steuart Fothringham (d 1979, 2 s of Lt-Col Walter Thomas James Scrymsoure Steuart Fothringham, of Pourie-Fothringham and Tealing Angus, and of Grantully and Murthly Castle, Perthshire, who took the name Steuart on succeeding Sir Archibald Douglas Stewart, 8 and last Bt, in the lands of Grantully and Murthly in 1890; *b* 5 August 1937; *Educ* Fort Augustus Abbey, Trinity Coll Cambridge, RAC Cirencester; *m* 16 Feb 1962, Elizabeth Mary Charlotte, da of Thomas Hope Brendan Lawther, of Earl's Court, London SW5; 2 s (Thomas b 1971, Lionel b 1973), 2 da (Mariana b 1966, Ilona b 1969); *Career* chartered accountant; memb Royal Co Archers; *Recreations* shooting, fishing, archery, music; *Clubs* Puffin's, Turf, New (Edinburgh); *Style*— Robert Scrymsoure Steuart Fothringham, Esq, DL; Fothringham, Forfar, Angus DD8 2JP (☎ 030 782 231); Murthly Castle, Murthly, Perthshire PH1 4HP (☎ 073871 397)

SCUDAMORE, Paul Henry; s of James Henry Scudamore, JP (d 1973), of Ross-on-Wye, Herefords, and Mildred, *née* Davies; said to descend from a collateral branch of Lucas-Scudamore, of Kentchurch, Herefordshire; *b* 14 Nov 1941; *Educ* St Edward's Sch Oxford, Harper Adams Agric Coll; *m* 24 April 1965, Elizabeth Margaret, da of Capt Alfred Eric Crockatt, of Hereford; 1 s (Jeremy Paul Henry b 1969), 1 da (Nicola Jane Elizabeth b 1967); *Career* chm Farmplan gp of cos; dir: Farmplan Constructions, Farmplan Products, Farmplan Computer Systems, Farmplan Int 1972-, Aberfoyle Holdings plc 1984-; CMA Farm Mgmt Award; *Recreations* golf; *Clubs* BIM, Farmers, Ross-on-Wye Golf; *Style*— Paul H Scudamore, Esq; Brampton Lodge, Brampton Abbots, Ross-on-Wye, Herefords; Farmplan Gp, Netherton, Ross-on-Wye, Herefords (☎ 0989 64324, telex 35407)

SCULLY, (Marie Elizabeth) Ann; da of Charles Francis Lyons, and Mary Elizabeth, *née* Godfrey; *b* 21 Nov 1943; *Educ* Notre Dame Prep and HS Sheffield, Lanchester Coll Coventry, London Univ; *m* 21 Aug 1965, Michael Joseph Scully, of Horsforth, Leeds; 2 s (Nicholas Michael b 15 Sept 1972, Peter b 9 Jan 1983), 1 da (Clare b 16 April 1967); *Career* ptnr Regency Conslts Chester 1980-; parish cncllr 1975-87, sch govr 1977-; memb: Nat Fedn of Self Employed and Small Businesses Chester, Small Business Bureau Chester, C of C Chester; chm Domestic Coal Consumers Cncl London, memb Nat Consumer Cncl London; MBIM (1982), FICM (1986); *Recreations* membership chester music soc choir, badminton; *Clubs* Chester Music Soc; *Style*— Mrs Ann Scully; Hockenhull House, Hockenhull Lane, Tarvin, Chester (☎ 0829 40 561); The Grange, 1 Hoole Rd, Chester (☎ 0244 319 912, fax 0244 314 635, telex

61556)

SCULLY, Prof Crispian; s of Patrick Scully, and Rosaleen Scully; *b* 24 May 1945; *Educ* Univ of London (BDS, MBBS, BSc, PhD), Univ of Bristol (MD); *m* 5 Oct 1977, Zoitsa; 1 da (Frances b 31 Jan 1982); *Career* sr lectr Univ of Glasgow 1982 (lectr 1979), prof of stomatology Univ of Bristol 1982-; memb: Gen Dental Cncl, Med Res Cncl, Advsy Cncl on Drug Misuse; MRCS, LRCP, LDS RCS, MRCPath, FDS RCPS, MD; *Books* Medical Problems in Dentistry (1982, 1987), Multiple Choice Questions in Dentistry (jtly 1985), Handbook for Hospital Dental Surgeons (1985), Slide Interpretation in Oral Disease (jtly 1986), Colour Aids in Oral Medicine (1988), The Dental Patient (1988), The Mouth and Peri-oral Tissues (1988), Dental Surgery Assistant's Handbook (jtly 1988); *Style*— Prof Crispian Scully; Univ Dept of Oral Medicine, Surgery and Pathology, Bristol Dental Hosp and School, Lower Maudlin St, Bristol BS1 2LY (☎ 0272 276201)

SCURFIELD, Hugh Hedley; s of William Russell Scurfield (d 1981), of Worcestershire, and Elizabeth, *née* Morton; *b* 9 Dec 1935; *Educ* King's Sch Worcester, Hertford Coll Oxford (MA); *m* 1, 11 July 1959, Ann Beverley; 1 s (Bryan b 1960), 3 da (Jane b 1962, Mary b 1964, Clare b 1967); m 2, 8 Dec 1978, Gillian Myfannwy (Jill), da of Rt Rev Mervyn Charles-Edwards, Bishop of Worcester (d 1983); 1 step-s (Timothy b 1958), 3 step-da (Anne b 1955, Emma b 1958, Suki b 1973); *Career* gen mangr actuary and dir Norwich Union Insurance Gp; FIA; rowing: winner at Henley Royal Regatta, rowed for GB and a national selector; *Recreations* large family, home, walking; *Style*— Hugh Scurfield, Esq; Norwich Union Life Insurance Society, Surrey St, Norwich, Norfolk NR1 3NG (☎ 0603 622200, telex 97388, fax 0603 684659)

SCURR, Dr Cyril Frederick; CBE (1979), LVO (1952); s of Cyril Albert Scurr (d 1961), of Barnet, and Mabel Rose, *née* Magrath; *b* 14 July 1920; *Educ* Kings Coll London (MB BS), Westminster Hosp (MRCS, LRCP); *m* 25 Aug 1947, Isobel Jean, da of Leonard Spiller (d 1978); 3 s (Martin John b 1950, David Antony b 1955, Andrew James b 1963), 1 da (Judith Ann b 1948); *Career* Maj (specialist anaesthetist) RAMC served N Africa, Italy, Greece 1942-47; conslt anaesthetist: Westminster Hosp 1949-85, Hosp of St John & St Elizabeth 1950-; dean faculty of anaesthetists 1970-73; pres Assoc of Anaesthetics 1973-76, memb Health Servs Bd 1976-79, Frederick Hewitt lectr RCS 1971, Dudley Buxton Prize 1977, Faculty Gold Medal RCS 1983, John Snow Medal 1984, Magill Centenary Oration 1988; Hon FFARCS (Ireland) 1977, FFARCS 1953, FRCS 1974, FRSM; *Books* Scientific Foundations of Anaesthesia, Drugs in Anaesthesia; *Recreations* photography, gardening; *Style*— Dr Cyril Scurr, CBE, LVO; 16 Grange Ave, Totteridge Common, London N20 8AD (☎ 01 445 7188)

SCUSE, Dennis George; MBE (1957), TD (1946); s of Charles Henry Scuse (d 1945), of Ilford, Essex, and Kate, *née* Hooder (d 1976, aged 98); *b* 19 May 1921; *Educ* Park Sch Ilford, Mercers' High Holborn London; *m* 23 April 1948, Joyce Evelyn, da of Frank Burt (d 1931), of Cheltenham, Glos; 1 s (Jeremy b 1953); *Career* WWII 1939-46, cmmnd RA (HAA) 1940, air def GB 1940-41, cmmd Entertainments Offr Ceylon 1941-42, served MELF & CMF 1942-44, Army Broadcasting Serv (Bari, Rome and Athens) 1945-46; BBC Overseas Serv (seconded WO for Forces Broadcasting Serv in Benghazi and Canal Zone) 1947, asst dir Br Forces Network Germany 1949-50, dir 1950-57; introduced Two Way Family Favourites with Jean Metcalfe 1952-57, sr planning asst BBC TV 1958-59, chief asst (light entertainment) BBC TV 1960, chief asst (TV) BBC NY Office and BBC rep N America 1962; md: Trident TV Enterprises 1972-76, Dennis Scuse Ltd PR Radio and TV Conslts 1976-; *Books* contributed many articles to numerous publications; *Recreations* writing, reading, watching television; *Clubs* Royal Green Jackets London; *Style*— Dennis G Scuse, Esq, MBE, TD; 2 York House, Courtlands, Sheen Rd, Richmond, Surrey (☎ 01 948 4737); 1 Grosvenor Place, London SW1X 7JH (☎ 01 245 1245, telex 917698, fax 01 235 1270)

SCUTT, Robin Hugh, (known professionally as Scott); CBE (1976); s of late Rev Arthur Octavius Scutt, MA; *b* 24 Oct 1920; *Educ* Bryanston, British Institute Sorbonne Paris, Jesus Coll Cambridge; *m* 1, 1943 (m dis 1960), Judy, *née* Watson, 2 s; m 2, 1961, Patricia Anne Marie, *née* Pilkington-Smith; *Career* BBC radio prodr and exec (European Service) 1942-54, BBC TV prodr 1955-58, BBC Paris rep 1958-62, BBC prodr 1963-66, controller BBC Radio 1 and 2 1967-68, BBC2 TV 1969-74, controller Devpt BBC TV 1974-77, dep md BBC TV 1977-80, dir of productions Nat Video Corpn; chm United Media Ltd, dir London Weekend Television, chm Saxon Radio, dir Suffolk Radio Gp; fell and Gold Medallist Royal TV Soc; Officie de la Légion d'Honneur 1983; FRSA 1985; *Recreations* gardening, theatre, travel; *Clubs* Garrick; *Style*— Robin Scott, Esq, CBE; The Abbey Cottage, Cockfield, Suffolk

SEABRIGHT, John Walter (Jack); s of Walter Alexander Seabright, of Henley-on-Thames, Oxon, and Emily Gladys, *née* Onion; *b* 2 May 1929; *Educ* Brentwood Sch Essex, Downing Coll Cambridge (MA); *m* 23 Oct 1954, Diana Bartlett, da of George Forrester Fairbairn (d 1966), of Torquay; 2 s (Paul b 1958, Alistair b 1961), 2 da (Theresa b 1960, Lucy b 1963); *Career* dir Coats Patons (UK) 1969-73, md MFI Furniture Gp 1974-81, chief exec Henley Distance Learning Ltd 1981-85; dir: Church & Co plc 1982-, Clydesdale Gp Ltd 1982-85; chm: Midlands Convenience Stores plc 1986-, Compular Ltd 1987-, Teamband Ltd 1981-; *Recreations* walking, travel; *Style*— Jack W Seabright, Esq; Wanwood, Park Corner, Nettlebed, Oxon (☎ 0491 641184); Teamband Ltd, Park Corner, Nettlebed, Oxon

SEABROOK, Air Vice-Marshal Geoffrey Leonard; CB (1965); s of Robert Leonard Seabrook (d 1946); *b* 25 August 1909; *Educ* King's Sch Canterbury; *m* 1949, Beryl Mary, *née* Hughes; 1 s, 1 da; *Career* CA 1931, RAF 1933 (Iraq & Far East), Air Vice-Marshal, dir of Personnel (G) Air Ministry 1961-63, AOA Tech Trg Cmd 1963-66 (ret); *Recreations* golf, sailing; *Clubs* RAF, Piltdown Golf; *Style*— Air Vice-Marshal Geoffrey Seabrook, CB; Long Pightle, Piltdown, Uckfield, Sussex (☎ 082 572 2322)

SEABROOK, Michael Richard; s of Robert Henry Seabrook (d 1983), of Solihull, and Clara, *née* Berry; *b* 24 Mar 1952; *Educ* King Edwards Sch Birmingham, Exeter Univ (LLB); *m* 1 Sept 1979, Hilary Margaret, da of Anthony John Pettitt, of Bromley; 2 s (Nicholas b 1983, William b 1986); *Career* articled clerk Lovell White & King 1974-76, asst slr Clifford-Turner 1976-79; ptnr: Needham & James 1981-86 (asst slr 1980), Evershed & Tomkinson 1986-, memb Law Soc 1976; *Recreations* sporting; *Clubs* Copt Heath Golf, Warwicks Pilgrims CC, Knowie & Dorridge CC; *Style*— Michael R Seabrook, Esq; 2 Granville Rd, Dorridge, Solihull, West Midlands, B93 8BY (☎ 0564 773 732); Evershed & Tomkinson, 10 Newhall St, Birmingham, B3 3LX (☎ 021 233 2001, fax 021 236 1583, telex 336688)

SEABROOK, Peter John; s of Robert Henry Seabrook (d 1987), of Galleywood, Essex, and Emma Mary, *née* Cottey (d 1989); *b* 2 Nov 1935; *Educ* King Edward VI GS Chelmsford, Essex Inst of Agric Writtle (MHort, Dip Hort); *m* 14 May 1960, Margaret Ruth, da of Arthur Wilfred Risbey, of Churchdown, Glos; 1 s (Roger b 9 Feb 1962), 1 da (Alison b 13 May 1964); *Career* Nat Serv RASC 1956-58; TV presenter; horticultural advsr and dir Cramphom Ltd 1958-66, tech rep Bord na Mona 1966-70, horticultural conslt 1971; dir: William Strike Ltd 1972-, Roger Harvey Ltd 1981-; Radio: In Your Garden 1965-70, Gardeners Question Time 1981-82; garden presenter: Pebble Mill at One BBC1 1975-86 (Gardeners Direct Line 1982-), WGBH TV Boston USA 1975-, Chelsea Flower Show 1976-, Gardeners World BBC2 1976-81; gardening corr: The Sun 1977-, The Yorkshire Post 1981-; FIHort; *Books* Shrubs For Your Garden (1973), Complete Vegetable Gardener (1976), Book of the Garden (1979), Good Plant Guide (1981), Good Food Gardening (1983); *Recreations* gardening; *Style*— Peter Seabrook, Esq; Great Baddow Rd, Chelmsford, Essex

SEABROOK, Robert John; QC (1983); s of Alan Thomas Pertwee Seabrook, MBE, of Hindhead, Surrey, and Mary Seabrook, *née* Parker (d 1977); *b* 6 Oct 1941; *Educ* St George's Coll Salisbury Southern Rhodesia, UCL (LLB); *m* 19 Oct 1965, Liv Karin, da of Rev Bjarne Djupvik (d 1983), of Bergen, Norway; 2 s (Justin b 20 Dec 1969, Magnus b 23 April 1975), 1 da (Marianne b 23 Oct 1971); *Career* barr Middle Temple 1964, recorder 1984; memb of court Univ of Sussex 1988; Liveryman Worshipful Co of Curriers 1972; *Recreations* wine, listening to music, travel; *Style*— Robert Seabrook, Esq, QC; 41 Surrenden Rd, Brighton, E Sussex (☎ 0273 505491); 1 Crown Office Row, Temple, London EC4Y 7HH (☎ 01 353 1801, fax 01 583 1700, telex 24988 ICOR G)

SEABROOK, Timothy James; s of Frederick James Seabrook (d 1979), of The Walnuts, Ashton Keynes, Swindon, Wilts, and Ethel Mary Seabrook; *b* 20 May 1940; *Educ* Wellington; *m* 1967, Catherine Marion-Jean, da of Cdr Herbert Geoffrey St John Bury, of Mead Cottage, Grayshott, Hindhead, Surrey; 1 da; *Career* mangr industl subsids div Investors in Industry plc 1975-82, dep chm Triangle International Ltd 1980-, dir Wayne Kerr plc 1984-; chm: Dynamic Logic Ltd 1984-87, Imatronic Ltd 1987-; independent dir; FCA; *Recreations* golf, gardening; *Clubs* MCC; *Style*— Timothy Seabrook, Esq; Church Cottage, Greywell, Basingstoke, Hants RG25 1DA (☎ 025 671 2108)

SEAFIELD, 13 Earl of (S 1701); Ian Derek Francis Ogilvie-Grant; Lord Ogilvy of Cullen and Viscount Seafield (S 1698), Lord Ogilvy of Deskford and Cullen and Viscount Reidhaven (S 1701); s of Countess of Seafield (12 in line, d 1969) and Derek Studley-Herbert (who assumed by deed poll 1939 the additional surnames of Ogilvie-Grant, the present Peer being recognised in those surnames by warrant of Lord Lyon 1971); *b* 20 Mar 1939; *Educ* Eton; *m* 1, 1960 (m dis 1971), Mary Dawn Mackenzie, da of Henry Illingworth; 2 s (Viscount Reidhaven, Hon Alexander b 1966); m 2, 1971, Leila, da of Mahmoud Refaat of Cairo; *Heir* s, Viscount Reidhaven, *qv*; *Clubs* Whites; *Style*— The Rt Hon The Earl of Seafield; Old Cullen, Cullen, Banffshire

SEAGA, Rt Hon Edward Philip George; PC (1981); s of Philip Seaga; *b* 28 May 1930; *Educ* Wolmers Boys' Sch Kingston Jamaica, Harvard Univ; *m* 1965, Marie Elizabeth, *née* Constantine (Miss Jamaica 1964); 2 s, 1 da; *Career* MP Western Kingston (Jamaica) 1962-, leader Jamaican Labour Pty 1974- (asst sec 1960-62, sec 1962), oppn leader 1974-80, PM Jamaica 1980-; *Style*— The Rt Hon Edward Seaga; Vale Royal, Kingston, Jamaica (☎ 927 7854)

SEAGER, Hon Carole Mary Leighton; da of 2 Baron Leighton of St Mellons

SEAGER, Hon Douglas Leighton; s of 1 Baron Leighton of St Mellons, CBE (d 1963); *b* 1925; *m* 1960, Gillian Claire, da of Leonard Warwick Greenwood, of Pound Piece, Astley, Stourport, Worcs; 3 da; *Style*— The Hon Douglas Seager; Leighton House, 5929 Hudson St, Vancouver, British Columbia V6M 2Z4, Canada

SEAGER, Gerald Elliot; s of Capt John Elliot, MC (d 1955), and Dorothy Irene Seager, *née* Jones (d 1986); gs of Sir William Seager (d 1941) shipowner and MP (Lib) Cardiff East 1918-22; *b* 29 June 1924; *Educ* Charterhouse; *m* 17 April 1948, Margaret Elizabeth, da of William Jones Morgan (d 1971), of Aberbran Fawr, Brecon; *Career* WWII Lt Welsh Gds 1943-46, served Italy, POW 1944; dir: Stalco Aden 1966-67, Newport Stevedoring Co Ltd and Newport Screw Towing Co Ltd 1967-69, Cory Bros Shipping Ltd 1968-77, Stephenson Clarke Shipping Ltd 1970-77, Newport Stevedoring Co Ltd 1970-77, Transcontinental Air Ltd, Powell Duffryn Shipping Services Ltd 1976-77; chief exec: Rais Hassan Saadi & Co Dubai (UAE) 1977-78, Rais Shipping Co Dubai (UAE) 1977-78; dir Thabet Int Ltd 1987- (chief exec 1978-86); vice chm Aden Shipping Conf 1967, life govr Royal Hosp and Home for Incurables Putney 1967; chm: Newport Shipowners Assoc 1972-77, Newport Harbour Cmmrs 1974-75, S Wales Coal Exporters Assoc 1970-71; memb Baltic Exchange 1964; *Recreations* gardening, football, welsh affairs; *Style*— Gerald E Seager, Esq; Ty Mawr, Llyswen, Powys, Wales (☎ 087 485 208)

SEAGER, Hon Robert William Henry Leighton; s and h of 2 Baron Leighton of St Mellons

SEAGER, Hon Simon John Leighton; s of 2 Baron Leighton of St Mellons

SEAL, Dr Barry Herbert; MEP (Lab) W Yorks 1979-; s of Herbert and Rose Ann Seal; *b* 28 Oct 1937; *Educ* Bradford Univ, Harvard Business Sch; *m* 1963, Frances Catherine Wilkinson; 1 s (Robert), 1 da (Catherine); *Career* chemical engr, control engr, univ lectr; former ldr Bradford Cncl Labour Gp; vice-chm Economic and Monetary ctee of European Parliament; *Books* Dissertations on Computer Control; *Recreations* running, flying; *Clubs* Dudley Hill and Tong Socialist; *Style*— Dr Barry Seal, MEP; Brookfields Farm, Wyke, Bradford, W Yorks BD12 9LU

SEAL, David Herbert; s of Maj Jefferson Seal, TD (d 1977), and Florence Eileen, *née* Herbert (d 1980); *b* 7 April 1935; *Educ* Marlborough, Pembroke Coll Cambridge (MA); *m* 19 Nov 1958, Juliet Rose, da of John Perrot (d 1940); 1 s (John b 1964), 2 da (Kate b 1959, Sarah b 1962); *Career* ptnr: Jefferson Seal and Co 1956, Seal Arnold 1968, D Q Henriques and Co 1973; dir: Charlton Seal 1978, Jefferson Seal Ltd 1987, Cavendish Securities (Jersey) Ltd 1970; memb Stock Exchange 1956; *Recreations* riding, boating, farming; *Clubs* Jersey Riding (vice pres); *Style*— David Seal, Esq; Holmbury, Augres, Trinity, Jersey, CI (☎ 0534 61614); office: Channel House, Green St, St Helier, Jersey, CI (☎ 0534 74725, telex 4192354)

SEAL, Raymond; s of Clifford Seal (d 1978), and Hannah, *née* Woodcock; *b* 23 Dec 1932; *Educ* Bingley GS; *m* 1, 14 Feb 1956, Mary; 2 s (Andrew David b 1957, Jeremy Charles b 1960); m 2, 10 May 1985, Gisela; *Career* Textile Speciality Fibre specialist; md: Seal Int Ltd, Morton Fibres Ltd, Bradford Mohair Ltd, Ladywell Fibres Ltd, Spencer & Rae Ltd; *Recreations* golf, rugby, cricket; *Clubs* Shipley Golf, Yorkshire

Cricket, Bingley Cricket, Headingley Taverners, Lloyds Bradford; *Style*— Raymond Seal, Esq; East Beck Farm, Askwith, Otley, Yorkshire (☎ 0943 462635); Seal Int Ltd, Ladywell Mills, Hall Lane, Bradford, Yorkshire (☎ 0274 726744, fax 0274 735522, telex 517471)

SEALE, Sir John Henry; 5 Bt (UK 1838), of Mount Boone, Devonshire; patron of one living; s of Sir John Carteret Hyde Seale, 4 Bt (d 1964); *b* 3 Mar 1921; *Educ* Eton, Ch Ch Oxford; *m* 1953, Ray Josephine, da of late R G Charters, MC, of Christchurch, New Zealand; 1 s, 1 da; *Heir* s, John Robert Charters Seale; *Career* Capt RA; architect, sr lectr Plymouth Sch of Architecture; RIBA; *Style*— Sir John Seale, Bt; Slade, nr Kingsbridge, Devon

SEALE, John Robert Charters; s and h of Sir John Seale, 5 Bt; *b* 17 August 1954; *Style*— John Seale Esq

SEALES, Peter Clinton; s of James M Seales (d 1940), of Dublin, and Angela, *née* O'Doherty; *b* 1 Nov 1929; *Educ* Dublin Univ; *m* May 1955, Bernadette Rogers; 1 da (Elizabeth Devereaux b 1962), and 1 da dec'd; *Career* called to bar 1953, chief exec Operation Raleigh 1984-; conslt to Saatchi & Saatchi Compton plc 1984-, commercial dir Wassen Int Ltd 1985-; Hon Cncl Memb Operation Innovator 1987-; Fell Inst of Dirs 1972; *Recreations* sailing, music; *Clubs* White Elephant, Wig and Pen, IOD, Real Tennis; *Style*— Peter Seales, Esq; 78 Northumberland Rd, Leamington Spa, Warwicks (☎ 0926 31562, office tel 0372 379828)

SEALY, Hon Mrs (Lavinia Caroline); twin da of 2 Baron Piercy; *b* 24 May 1947; *Educ* Badminton Sch, St Hugh's Coll Oxford (MA); *m* 1971, Nicholas John Elliot Sealy; 1 s, 1 da; *Style*— The Hon Mrs Sealy; Timber Hill, Chobham, Surrey (☎ Ottershaw 3875)

SEAMAN, Sir Keith Douglas; KCVO (1981), OBE (1976); s of Eli Semmens Seaman (d 1955), and Ethel Maud Seaman (d 1930); *b* 11 June 1920; *Educ* Unley HS, Adelaide Univ (BA, LLB), Flinders Univ (MA, Dip Hum); *m* 1946, Joan Isabel, da of late Fred Birbeck; 1 s, 1 da; *Career* memb exec World Assoc of Christian Broadcasting Cos 1960, chm 5KA, 5AU and 5RM Broadcasting Cos 1971-77 (dir 1960), memb Aust Govt Social Welfare Cmmn 1973-76, govr South Australia 1977-82; KStJ 1978; *see Debrett's Handbook of Australia and New Zealand for further details*; *Style*— Sir Keith Seaman, KCVO, OBE; 31 Heggerton St, Victor Harbor, South Australia 5211

SEAMAN, Marvin Roy; s of Charles Seaman, of Haleston, Norfolk, and Mary Elizabeth, *née* Goldsmith; *b* 11 Sept 1945; *Educ* Stradbrooke Secdy Sch, RAF Tech Trg Sch; *m* 19 Oct 1976, Judy Ragobar, da of Joseph Ragobar, of Marbella, Trinidad; 2 s (Christian b 1978, Jonathan b 1982), 1 da (Michelle Anne b 1981); *Career* with RAF for 6 yrs; chm and md Franchise Devpt Services Ltd 1971-; visiting lectr seminars and colls on franchise and licensing laws; memb CBI, FInstD (memb Inst exec), MInstEx, MInstM; *Recreations* running, hunting, walking, fishing; *Clubs* The Millionaires, The Caribbean; *Style*— Marvin R Seaman, Esq; The Cedars Farm, Cedar Lodge, Norwich Rd, Tasburgh, Norfolk (☎ 0508 470686); Franchise Development Services Ltd, Castle House, Norwich NA2 1PJ (☎ 0603 620301, fax 0603 630174)

SEARBY, Dr Norman Halifax; CBE (1961); s of Albert Searby (d 1940), and Mary Evelyn, *née* Wood; *b* 12 Mar 1910; *Educ* Bishop Vesey's Sutton Coldfield, Birmingham Univ (BSch, PhD); *m* 1934, Violet Olive, da of Joseph Leonard Monk; 1 s, 3 da; *Career* elec engr Ferranti Ltd 1932-75, chief engr Radio Dept 1940, mangr Guided Weapons Dept 1951, dir Ferranti 1963-75; FIEE; *Recreations* organ building, carpentry, gardening, church activities, painting, snooker; *Style*— Dr Norman Searby, Esq, CBE; Bryancliffe, Wilmslow Park, Wilmslow, Cheshire

SEARBY, Lt-Col Robin Vincent; s of Air-Cdre John Henry Searby, DSO, DFC (d 1986), and Eva, *née* Rowland (d 1976); *b* 20 July 1947; *Educ* Leasam House Sch; *m* 8 May 1976, Caroline Angela, da of late Maj John Beamish, MC; 1 s (Henry b 6 June 1977), 2 da (Louisa b 19 Jan 1979, Alice b 31 March 1981); *Career* RMA Sandhurst 1966-68, 2 Lt 9/12 Royal Lancers (POW) 1968, regtl duty Berlin, BAOR, NI 1968-73, loan serv Dhofar (Sultanate of Oman) 1973-75, regtl duty NI and UK 1976-79, Maj 1979, Army Staff Coll Camberley 1980, GSO II Ops 2 Armd Div BAOR 1981-83, regtl duty 1983-85, Lt-Col dir staff Army Staff Coll 1985-87, CO 9/12 Royal Lancers 1987-; Distinguished Service Medal (Gallantry) Sultanate of Oman 1975; *Recreations* reading, equitation; *Clubs* Cavalry; *Style*— Lt-Col Robin Searby; c/o 9/12 Royal Lancers, Carver Barracks, Wimbish, Saffron Walden, Essex CB10 2YA (☎ 0799 231 64)

SEARL, Peter John; s of Edward George Charles Searl (d 1947), and Emma, *née* Carlisle (d 1949); *b* 1 April 1939; *Educ* Woking GS, Kingstone & Brighton Schs of Architecture (RIBA); *m* 1 Sept 1962, Carolyn Ann, da of Geoffrey William Ede, of Hove, E Sussex; 2 s (Nicholas b 1964, Timothy b 1965), 2 da Emma b 1971, Susanna b 1978); *Career* architect; ptnr David A P Brookbank & Ptnrs 1969-76; sole princ Peter Searl Assocs 1976-; W Sussex Co Historic Buildings Award and Civic Trust commendation for restoratioon of Cuckfield House, W Sussex (1983); *Recreations* drama, sport, charity work; *Style*— Peter J Searl, Esq; Old Inn House, London Rd, Balcombe, W Sussex RH17 6JQ (☎ 0444 811303); Old Inn Studio, London Rd, Balcombe, W Sussex RH17 6JQ (☎ 0444 811223)

SEARLE, Geoffrey William; CBE (1972), DSC (1943); s of William Arthur Searle (d 1957); *b* 11 April 1914; *m* 1940, Constance, da of Charles Tyrrell; 1 s, 1 da; *Career* CA 1936; Lt Cdr RNVR; joined BP 1946: dir of Finance & Planning and chm of exec ctee BP Trading Ltd, ret 1974; chm: London & Scottish Marine Oil plc 1978-85 (md 1974-78, non-exec dir 1985-86), Assoc of British Independent Oil Exploration Cos (Brindex) 1982, Belden & Blake Int Ltd 1986-; *Recreations* tennis, golf, music, gardening; *Clubs* Naval, RAC, City of London; *Style*— Geoffrey Searle, Esq, CBE, DSC; 20 Beech Rd, Reigate, Surrey RH2 9LR (☎ 0737 245803); Belden & Blake International Ltd, Thirty Cedar Avenue, Hamilton HM09, Bermuda

SEARLE, Norman Percy Walter; JP (Inner London); s of William Cecil Searle (d 1972), and Ada Gladys, *née* Page; *b* 7 June 1930; *Educ* Battersea GS, West Ham Coll of Technol; *m* 1, 1953 (m dis 1976), Dorothy Sylvia, da of Frederick Jackson; 1 s (Matthew b 1961), 2 da (Helen b 1959, Laura b 1966); m 2, 1977, Christine Joyce, da of Norman Frederick Jackson ; 1 s (Caspar b 1982), 1 da (Martha b 1978); *Career* Nat Serv RAMC 1948-49; md Mosford Joinery Ltd 1966, dir Eight Force Ltd 1982-; memb: Conservation Area Advsy Ctee City of London, Nat Cncl Prison Visitors; chm Wood St Crime Prevention Assoc, vice-chm City Heritage Soc, chm West London Liq Lic Ctee; Freeman City of London, Liveryman Worshipful Co of Painter-Stainers, Memb Worshipful Co of Parish Clerks; memb IWSc 1960; *Clubs* Royal Thames Yacht, Nat Lib; *Style*— Norman Searle, Esq, JP; 166 Defoe House, Barbican, London EC2Y 8DN (☎ 01 638 5233); 105 Mount Pleasant Rd, London NW10 4EH (☎ 01 459 6241, fax 01 451 1499, telex 888941 LCCI MOSFORD)

SEARLE, Ronald William Fordham; s of William James Searle (d 1967), and Nellie, *née* Hunt; *b* 3 Mar 1920; *Educ* Cambridge Sch of Art; *m* 1, (m dis 1967), Kay Webb *qv*; 1 s (John b 1949), 1 da (Kate b 1947); m 2, 1967, Monica Iise Koenig; *Career* Sapper 287 Field Co RE 1939-46 (Japanese POW) Siam and Malaya 1942-45), dept psychological warfare Allied Force HQ Port Said Ops 1956; contrib Punch 1947-61, special features artist Life Magazine 1955-62, contrib New Yorker Magazine 1966-, designer commemorative medals to the French Mint 1975- and BAMS 1984-; film designer: John Gilpin, On the Twelfth Day, Energetically Yours, Germany 1960, Toulouse-Lautrec, Dick Deadeye; designer of animation sequences: Those Magnificent Men in their Flying Machines 1965, Monte Carlo or Bust! 1969, Scrooge 1970; one-man exhibitions 1950-88 incl: Leicester Galleries London, Imperial War Museum, Kraushaar Gallery NY, Bianchini Gallery NY, Kunsthalle Bremen, Bibliotéque Nationale Paris, Munich, Neue Galerie Vienna; Awards: LA Art Dirs Club Medal 1959, Philadelphia Art Dirs Club Medal 1959, Nat Cartoonists Soc Award 1959 and 1960, Gold Medal III Biennale Tolentino Italy 1965, Prix de la Critique Belge 1968, Grand Prix de l'Humour Noir (France) 1971, Prix d'Humour Festival d'Avignon 1971, Medal of French Circus 1971, Prix Internationale 'Charles Huard' 1972, La Monnaie de Paris Medal 1974; RDI, AGI; *Books* Forty Drawings (1946), John Gilpin (1952), Souls in Torment (1953), Rake's Progress (1955), Merry England (1956), Paris Sketchbook (1957), The St Trinian's Story (with Kaye Webb 1959); with Alex Atkinson: The Big City (1958), USA for Beginners (1959), Russia for Beginners (1960); Refugees (1960), Which Way did He Go? (1961), Escape from the Amazon (1963), From Frozen North to Filthy Lucre (1964), Those Magnificent Men in their Flying Machines (1965), Havn't We Met Before Somewhere? (with Heinz Huber 1966), Searle's Cats (1967), The Square Egg (1968), Hello - Where did all the People Go? (1969), Secret Sketchbook (1970), The Second Coming of Toulouse - Lautrec (1970), The Addict (1971), More Cats (1975), Designs for Gilbert and Sullivan (1975), Paris! Paris! (with Irwin Shaw 1977), Searle's Zoodiac (1977), Ronald Searle (monograph 1978), The King of Beasts (1980), The Big Fat Cat Book (1982), Illustrated Winespeak (1983), Ronald Searle in Perspective (monograph 1984), Ronald Searle's Golden Oldies 1941-1961 (1985), Something in the Cellar (1986), To the Kwai - and Back (1986), Ah Yes, I Remember It Well...: Paris 1961-75 (1987), Non-Sexist Dictionary (1988); *Clubs* Garrick; *Style*— Ronald Searle, Esq; c/o Tessa Sayle Agency, 11 Jubilee Place, Chelsea, London SW3 3TE (☎ 01 823 3883, fax 01 823 3363); John Locke Studios, 15 East 76th St, New York City, NY 10021 (☎ 212 288 8010)

SEARS, Dr Charles Alistair Newton; s of Dr Harold Trevor Newton Sears, *qv*, and Dr Janet Sorley, *née* Conn; *b* 30 Dec 1952; *Educ* Sandbach Sch, Middx Hosp, Univ of London (MB BS); *m* 6 May 1978, Judith Lesley, da of Dr Leslie Victor Martin, of Oxbridge, Dorset; 3 s (James b 1979, Robert b 1982, Nicholas b 1986); *Career* house offr Middx Hosp 1978; sr house offr: neurosurgery Royal Free Hosp 1978-79, medicine Queen Elizabeth Hosp Birmingham 1979-82; ptnr in gen practice Salisbury 1983-, clinical asst rheumatology dept and community mental handicap unit Salisbury DHA; trainer in gen practice Salisbury Dist Vocational Trg Scheme, tres Salisbury Med Soc, vice pres Salisbury branch Chartered Soc of Physiotherapists; MRCGP 1988; *Clubs* Inst of Orthopoedic Medicine, CGA; *Style*— Dr Charles Sears; Close House, The Green, Pitton, Salisbury, Wilts SP5 1DZ (☎ 0722 72 745); Grove House, 18 Wilton Rd, Salisbury, Wilts SP2 7EE (☎ 0722 333034)

SEARS, Dr (Harold) Trevor Newton; s of Dr Charles Newton Sears, MD (d 1944), of London SE12, and Annie Florence, *née* Dew (d 1961); *b* 29 Dec 1919; *Educ* Westminster, London Univ, St Thomas's Hosp London (MD, MB BS, MRCS, LRCP); *m* 4 Sept 1948, Janet Sorley, da of Rev Dr James Charles Conn, MA, PhD, BD (d 1969), of Edinburgh; 2 s (Charles b 1952, Andrew b 1954), 1 da (Elizabeth b 1950); *Career* served RAMC in the CMF, RMO to the Kent Yeomanry and subsequently Maj Med Specialist 1943-44; House Appts at St Thomas's Hosp London 1943-44, sr med registrar Prince of Wales' Hosp Plymouth 1948-50, med registrar St Thomas's Hosp 1950-53, gen practitioner Holmes Chapel Cheshire 1954-82, clinical asst Professorial Unit Manchester Univ, i/c the Hypertension Follow-Up Clinic at the Manchester Royal Infirmary 1954-79, Upjohn Travelling Fellowship (1960), Nuffield Fndn Travelling Fellowship (1962); FRCP; *Books* Hypertension, Encyclopaedia of General Practice (1960), Cardiovascular Disease: A Textbook of Medical Practice (1976), Do Something About Those Arteries (1968 and 1969); *Recreations* opera, photography, travel, gardening; *Clubs* British Med Assoc, Mid-Cheshire Pitt; *Style*— Trevor Sears, Esq; Parish School, Swettenham, nr Congleton, Cheshire CW12 2PX

SEATH, Derrick Stephen; s of Bertram Harrison Seath (d 1920); *b* 16 Sept 1918; *Educ* Trawalla Victoria Australia, Shillelagh Wicklow Ireland; *m* 1948, Mildred Lilian Kathleen, *née* Browning; 1 s, 1 da; *Career* dir: Carters (Merchants) Ltd, Rolls & Son (Produce) Ltd, Skins Hides & Leather Trades Assoc Ltd; ret 1982, cnllr Cotswold DC; *Recreations* Cirencester Park Polo; *Style*— Derrick Seath, Esq; 75 Chesterton Park, Cirencester, Glos GL7 1XS (☎ 0285 66245)

SEATON, Colin Robert; s of Arthur William Robert Seaton (d 1959), and Helen Amelia, *née* Stone (d 1985); *b* 21 Nov 1928; *Educ* Wallington County GS, Worcester Coll Oxford (BA, MA); *m* 24 Dec 1952, Betty, da of James Oliver Gosling (d 1959); 2 s (Paul b 10 March 1961, David b 3 June 1966); *Career* RAF 1947-49, air wireless mechanic Berlin Airlift; schoolmaster with LCC 1953-57; barr Inner Temple 1956; entered govt legal service 1957, served in Ministries of Health, Housing, and Local Govt 1957-71; Master Nat Industrial Relations Court 1971-74; circuit administrator Lord Chancellor's Dept: Northern Circuit 1974-82, South Eastern Circuit 1982-83; under-sec Lord Chancellor's Dept, head of Legislation Gp 1983-88; sec: Lord Chancellor's Law Reform Ctee 1983-88, Univ Cmmrs 1988-; part time chm Med Appeal Tribunals 1989-; *Books* Aspects of the National Health Service Acts (1966); *Publications* Aspects of the National Health Service Acts 1966; *Recreations* golf, photography; *Clubs* Civil Service; *Style*— Colin R Seaton, Esq; Treetops, The Drive, Coulsdon, Surrey CR3 2BL (☎ 01 668 5538); Office of The University Commissioners, 19-29 Woburn Place, London WC1 (☎ 01 278 4042)

SEAWARD, Colin Hugh; CBE (1987); s of Sydney Widmer Seaward (d 1967), and Molly Wendela, *née* Darwen (d 1985); *b* 16 Sept 1926; *Educ* RNC Dartmouth, Cambridge Univ; *m* 1, 1 Sept 1949, Jean, *née* Bugler (d 1949); 3 s (Jonathan Louis b 1952, Nicholas William b 1956, Thomas Edward b 1967), 1 da (Petronella Jane (Mrs Seccombe) b 1950); m 2, Judith Margaret, da of Canon W T Hinkley, of Alnwick, Northumberland; 2 da (Candida b 1974, Jessica Lucy b 1976); *Career* War Serv HMS

Ajax 1944-45, served Far East 1946-48, Med 1951-52, Admty 1953-55, cmd HMS Aberford 1956-58, Asst Naval Attaché Moscow and Naval Attaché Warsaw 1958-60, HMS Centaur 1960-62, MOD 1962-64, ret; joined HM Dip Serv 1965, dep high cmmr The Gambia 1966-68, FCO 1968-71, Rio de Janeiro 1971, Prague 1972-73, FCO 1973-76; Sr Offrs War Course RNC Greenwich 1976, cnsllr (econ and commercial) Islamabad 1977-80, HM consul-gen Rio de Janiero 1980-86, ret 1986, re-employed Protocol Dept FCO 1987-; hon sec Anglo-Brazilian Soc 1986; memb: Parochial Church Cncl St Martin's Brasted, Brasted Parish Cncl; Freeman City of London 1987; Hon Citizen State of Rio de Janiero 1985; *Recreations* country life; *Style*— Colin Seaward, Esq; Brasted House, Brasted, Westerham, Kent, TN16 1JA (☎ 0959 63736); Honours Section, Protocol Department, FCO, Old Admiralty Building, London SW1A 2AZ (☎ 01 210 6396)

SEBAG-MONTEFIORE, Charles Adam Laurie; s of Denzil Charles Sebag-Montefiore, of Highfield House, Forcombe, Kent, and Ruth Emily *née* Magnus; *b* 25 Oct 1949; *Educ* Eton, St Andrews Univ (MA); *m* 5 Oct 1979, Pamela Mary Diana, da of Archibald Tennant, of 12 Victoria Square, London SW1 (d 1955); 1 s (Archibald Edward Charles b 1987), 2 da (Elizabeth Anne b 1982, Laura Rose b 1984); *Career* Touche Ross & Co Chartered Accountants, ptnr Grieveson Grant & Co 1981, dir Kleinwort Benson Securities Ltd 1986; chm projects ctee Nat Art Collections Fund 1977-86, tstee London Historic House Museums Tst 1987-; Liveryman of the Worshipful Co of Spectacle Makers 1973; FCA 1974, FRSA; *Recreations* visiting pictures galleries, collecting books; *Clubs* Brooks's; *Style*— Charles Sebag-Montefiore, Esq; 21 Hazlewell Rd, London SW15 6LT (☎ 01 789 5999), Kleinwort Benson Securities Ltd, 20 Fenchurch St, London EC3P 3DB (☎ 01 623 8000, fax 01 929 2657, telex 887348)

SEBAG-MONTEFIORE, Harold Henry; eldest s of late John Sebag-Montefiore (5 s of Arthur Sebag-Montefiore, himself s of Sir Joseph Sebag-Montefiore and gs of Sarah, sis of the philanthropist Sir Moses Montefiore, 1 and last Bt), and Violet Maud, *née* Solomon; *b* 5 Dec 1924; *Educ* Stowe, Lower Canada Coll Montreal, Pembroke Coll Cambridge; *m* 1968, Harriet, o da of Benjamin Harrison Paley, of New York; 1 step da (Jennifer Tess); *Career* served WW II with RAF; barr Lincoln's Inn 1951, dep circuit judge; contested (C) N Paddington 1959; trustee National Theatre Fndn; freeman City of London; Chevalier de la Legion d'Honneur 1973; *Recreations* broadcasting, polo; *Clubs* Carlton, Hurlingham; *Style*— Harold Sebag-Montefiore Esq; 2 Paper Buildings, Temple, London EC4 (☎ 01 353 5835)

SEBASTIAN, Timothy (Tim); s of Peter Sebastian, of Hove, E Sussex, and Pegitha, *née* Saunders; *b* 13 Mar 1952; *Educ* Westminster, New Coll Oxford (BA), Univ Coll Cardiff (DipJournalism); *m* 4 June 1977, Diane, da of John Buscombe, of Frensham, Surrey; 1 s (Peter b 1981), 2 da (Clare b 1983, Caroline b 1986); *Career* BBC TV: eastern Euro corr 1979-82, Moscow corr 1984-85, Washington corr 1986-; *Books* Nice Promises (1984), I Spy in Russia (1985), The Spy in Question (1987); *Style*— Timothy Sebastian, Esq; c/o BBC, 2030 M St M W, Washington DC 20036, USA (☎ 202 223 2050)

SEBLEY, (Frances) Rae; *née* Holt; da of Frederick Appleby Holt, OBE (d 1980), of The Red House, Muster Green, Haywards Heath, Sussex, and Rae Vera Franz, *née* Hutchinson; *b* 9 May 1921; *Educ* Oxford & Cambridge Jt Bd Sch; *m* 1, 28 Aug 1942 (m dis 1946), (Francis) Russel Jeffs, s of Harold Jeffs, of Twickenham, Middx; 1 da (Diane Rae b 8 Aug 1943); m 2, 5 June 1970, Peter Arnold Sebley; *Career* PA to Dir of Bombing Ops Air Miny Whitehall 1940-42; copywriter Lambe & Robinson 1949-50, ad mangr Hutchinson Assoc Cos 1950-57, publicity mangr Hutchinson Gp 1957-62, freelance writer 1962-70; contrib: TLS, Encounter, Spectator and others; ed for Heron Books; advsr and participant in the film documentary, A Hungry Feeling: The Life and Death of Brendan Behan New York USA; memb ctee Nat Whippet Assoc; involved with: Sussex Youth Assoc, Brighton Festival; hon memb: Mark Twain Soc, Soc of Authors; *Books* Brendan Behan: Man and Showman (1966), Brendan Behan's Island (with Brendan Behan, 1962), Brendan Behan's New York (1964), Confessions of an Irish Rebel (1965), Hold Your Hour & Have Another (ed, 1963), The Scarperer (ed, 1966); *Recreations* breeding and showing whippets, walking, needlepoint; *Style*— Mrs Peter Sebley; Rotherfield Farmhouse, Newick, Lewes, Sussex BN8 4JH (☎ 082572 2676)

SEBRIGHT, Sir Peter Giles Vivian; 15 Bt (E 1626) of Besford, Worcs; s of Sir Hugo Giles Edmund Sebright, 14 Bt (d 1984), and his 1 w, Deirdre Ann, née Slingsby Bethell, gggda of 1 Baron Westbury; *b* 2 August 1953; *m* 1977, Regina Maria, da of Francis Steven Clarebrough, of Melbourne, Australia; 1 s; *Heir* s, Rufus Hugo Giles Sebright b 1978; *Style*— Sir Peter Sebright, Bt

SECCOMBE, Hugh Digorie; CBE (1976); s of Lawrence Henry Seccombe, CBE (d 1954), and Norah, *née* Wood (d 1959); ggf Sir Thomas Lawrence Seccombe, GCSI, GCIE, was head of the Fin Dept of the E India Co and later Fin Sec for India; *b* 3 June 1917; *Educ* Stowe, Sidney Sussex Coll, Cambridge Univ (MA); *m* 24 July 1947, Eirene Rosemary, da of Richard Whittow (d 1953), of Muryn, Brockenhurst, Hants, and wid of Lieut P C McC Banister, DSC, RN; 1 s (Geoffrey b 1949), 1 da (Celia b 1948); *Career* served RN 1939-46; Lt Cdr RNVR Destroyers in Home Fleet and Med; chm Seccombe Marshall & Campion Ltd 1962-77 (dir 1947, ret 1977); chm YWCA Central Club 1971-86; *Recreations* gardening, fishing, study of wildlife; *Clubs* Army and Navy; *Style*— Hugh Seccombe, Esq, CBE; Sparkes Place, Wonersh, Guildford, Surrey GU5 0PH (☎ 0483 893296); Benmore Lodge, Salen/Aros, Isle of Mull, Argyll PA71 6HU (☎ 068 03 351)

SECCOMBE, Dame Joan Anna Dalziel; DBE (1984), JP (Solihull 1968); da of Robert John Owen (d 1941), of Solihull, W Midlands, and Olive Barlow; *b* 3 May 1930; *Educ* St Martin's Sch Solihull; *m* 1950, Henry Lawrence Seccombe, s of Herbert Stanley Seccombe (d 1951), of Lapworth, Warwickshire; 2 s (Philip, Murray); *Career* West Mids CC 1977-81, chm Trading Standards 1979-81, Mids Elec Consultative Cncl 1981-, magistrate 1968-; chm: Cons Womens Nat Ctee 1981-84, Nat Union of Cons & Unionists Assoc 1987- (vice-chm 1984-87); memb West Mids Police Ctee 1977-81 and 1985-; vice-chm Cons Party 1987-; *Recreations* skiing, golf; *Style*— Dame Joan Seccombe, DBE, JP; Tythe Barn, Walsal End Lane, Hampton-in-Arden, Solihull, W Midlands B92 0HX (☎ 067 55 3252)

SECCOMBE, Sir (William) Vernon Stephen; s of Stephen Seccombe (d 1964), and Edith-Violet, *née* Henbry-Smith (d 1980); *b* 14 Jan 1928; *Educ* Saltash GS, Plymouth and Devon Tech Coll; *m* 2 Sept 1950, Margaret Vern, da of Joseph Edgar Profit (d 1988); 4 s (Michael b 1952, Paul b 1953, Tony b 1958, Patrick b 1960); *Career* Nat Serv XII Royal Lancers 1947-49; ret electrical engr; memb: Saltash Borough Cncl 1953-74, E Cornwall Water Co 1960-74, Caradon DC 1973-79; traffic cmmr Western Area 1977-81 (dep traffic cmmr 1970-77), govr Saltash Sch 1970-81, magistrate Co of Cornwall 1970-; chm Health Authy: Cornwall and Isles of Scilly 1981-83, South Western Regnl 1983-; Queens Silver Jubilee Medal 1977, Club Keystone Gold Award 1984; kt 1988; *Recreations* gardening, walking; *Style*— Sir Vernon Seccombe; King Sq House, 26/27 King Sq, Bristol BS2 8EF (☎ 0272 423271, fax 0272 425398)

SECKER, Prof Philip Edward; s of Cyril Edward Secker (d 1980); *b* 28 April 1936; *Educ* Haberdashers' Aske's Hampstead Sch, London Univ; *m* 1968, Judith Andrea, da of Douglas Eric Lee (d 1981); 2 s; *Career* chartered engr; lectr London Univ 1961-64, visiting asst prof Massachusetts Inst of Tech 1964-65; Univ Coll of N Wales: lectr 1965-69, sr lectr 1969-73, reader 1973-75, prof 1975-80; md of IDB (UCNW) Ltd 1971-80, engrg dir Royal Doulton Ltd 1980-, visiting prof Dept of physics and electronics Univ of Keele 1985-; *Recreations* flying light aircraft, gardening; *Style*— Prof Philip Secker; Gwel-Y-Don, Awel Menai, Beaumaris, Gwynedd (☎ 0248 810771)

SECOMBE, Sir Harry Donald; CBE (1963); *b* 8 Sept 1921; *Educ* Dynevor Sch Swansea; *m* 1948, Myra Joan Atherton, of Swansea; 2 s, 2 da; *Career* entertainer, actor, singer, comedian, author; served WWII in North Africa and Italy; films incl: Song of Norway, Oliver and others; radio: Educating Archie, The Goon Show; pres: Lord's Taverners 1980-81, Barker Variety Club of GB; past chm Stars Organisation for Spastics, pres Panda (World Wildlife) Fund Club; kt 1981; *Books* Twice Brightly, Goon For Lunch, Katy and The Nurgla, Welsh Fargo, Goon Abroad, The Harry Secombe Diet Book, Harry Secombe's Highway, The Highway Companion; *Recreations* photography, cricket, golf; *Clubs* Savage, RAC; *Style*— Sir Harry Secombe, CBE; 46 St James's Place, London SW1

SECONDÉ, Sir Reginald Louis; KCMG (1981, CMG 1972), CVO (1968, MVO 1957); s of Lt-Col Emile Charles Secondé (d 1952); *b* 28 July 1922; *Educ* Beaumont, King's Coll Cambridge; *m* 1951, Catherine Penelope, da of Thomas Ralph Sneyd-Kynnersley, OBE, MC; 1 s, 2 da; *Career* Major WWII Coldstream Gds in N Africa and Italy (despatches); served Dip Corps 1949-82: UK Delgn to United Nations and British Embassies in Portugal, Cambodia, Poland and Brazil 1949-69, head S European Dept FCO 1969-72, Royal Coll Def Studies 1972-73; ambassador: Chile 1973-76, Romania 1977-79, Venezuela 1979-82, ret 1982; *Recreations* gardening, shooting; *Clubs* Cavalry and Guards; *Style*— Sir Reginald Secondé, KCMG, CVO; Wamil Hall, nr Mildenhall, Suffolk (☎ 0638 714160)

SEDCOLE, (Cecil) Frazer; *b* 15 Mar 1927; *Educ* Uppingham; *m* 1962, Jennifer B Riggall; 1 s, 1 da; *Career* RAF 1945-48; joined Unilever 1952; dir: Birds Eye Food Ltd 1960-66, Unilever plc and NV 1984 (vice chm 1982-85), Tate and Lyle 1982-; dep chm Reed Int 1985-87; memb: Overseas Ctee CBI 1979-, Br Overseas Trade Bd 1982-86, Bd of Cwlth Devpt Corpn 1984-; tstee Leverhulme Tst 1982-; *Recreations* golf; *Style*— Frazer Sedcole, Esq; Beeches, Tyrrells Wood, Leatherhead, Surrey KT22 8QH

SEDDON, Arthur William; s of William Seddon, MC (d 1946), of 274 Shobnall Rd, Burton-upon-Trent, Staffs, and Charlotte Annie, *née* Martin (d 1973); *b* 15 Dec 1934; *Educ* Denstone Coll, Manchester Coll of Tech; *m* 27 June 1959, Beryl, da of Arthur Bentley Crompton, of Robin Hill, Deganwy Rd, Llandudno; 2 da (Jane Helen (Mrs Woodward) b 21 May 1961, Anne Elizaeth b 30 July 1974); *Career* plant dir Bass Burton upon Trent 1967-74 (head brewer 1963-66, asst brewer 1956-62), md Bass Runcorn 1976-82 (plant dir 1975), regnl md Charrington & Co 1983-; memb Barton-under-Needwood Parish Cncl 1970-75; chm Burton upon Trent Jr C of C 1971-72, Halton C of C 1978-79; memb: Inst of Brewers, Inc Brewers Guild, Master Brewers of America; MBII; *Recreations* cricket, rugby, athletics, hockey, fly fishing; *Style*— Arthur Seddon, Esq; Charrington West, Charrington & Co, 36-39 Cumberland Ave, Park Royal London NW10 7RF (☎ 01 965 0688, car tel 0860 419 530)

SEDDON, (Edward) Jeremy; s of Col Roland Nelson Seddon, OBE, of Stourton Caundle, Dorset, and Dorothy Ida Kathleen, *née* Canning (d 1982); *b* 14 April 1941; *Educ* Kings Sch Bruton, Southampton Univ (BSc); *m* 20 Sept 1975, Prudence Mary, da of Arthur William George Clarke (d 1955); 1 s (Thomas b 1985), 2 da (Serena b 1979, Alexandra b 1980); *Career* with Assoc Electrical Industs Ltd 1958-68, Dalgety Ltd 1968-73, dir Barclays de Zoete Wedd Ltd 1973- (head of public sector unit), hon exec dir Victaulic plc 1983-; Freeman City of London 1976; *Recreations* sailing, music, gardening; *Clubs* Royal Thames Yacht, Special Forces; *Style*— Jeremy Seddon, Esq; Jesters, Oak Lane, Sevenoaks, Kent TN13 1UF (☎ 0732 461 180); Barclays de Zoete Wedd Ltd, Ebbgate House, 2 Swan Lane, London EC4R 3TS (☎ 01 623 2323)

SEDDON, Dr Richard Harding; s of Cyril Harding Seddon (d 1974), of Bury St Edmunds, and Mary Seddon, *née* Booth (d 1983); *b* 1 May 1915; *Educ* King Edward VII Sch Sheffield, Sheffield Coll of Arts & Crafts, Univ of Reading (PhD); *m* 1946, Audrey Madeline, da of Albert Edward Wareham (d 1973), of Sussex; *Career* Vol Lance-Corpl RAOC 1939-40 (invalided after Dunkirk, on pension; King's Badge 1940), Co Intelligence Offr Home Guard 1941-43, Instr (Lieut) Reading Univ Sr Training Corps 1943-45; staff tutor in fine art Birmingham Univ 1947-47; dir Sheffield City Art Galleries 1948-64, head of art history & liberal studies Buckinghamshire Coll of Technology & Art 1964-80; co-fndr and pres Ludlow Art Soc 1948-64, pres Yorkshire Fedn of Museums of Art Galleries 1954-55, sec of Yorkshire Fact-Finding Ctee of Regionalisation of Art Galleries 1959, Nat Art Collections Fund rep for Yorkshire 1954-64, dep chm Sheffield Cncl for Gold, Silver and Jewellry Trades 1960 (also memb), memb BBC '51 Soc 1960; exhibitor at RA, RI and leading London Galleries 1947-; London Art Critic Yorkshire Post 1972-, hon memb Mark Twain Soc (USA) 1976, memb Royal Soc of Painters in Water Colours 1972 (tres 1974-84, tstee 1984-85); Civic Medal Neuchatel France 1978; *Books* A Hand Uplifted (1963), The Academic Technique of Painting (1960), Illustrated Dictionary of Art Terms (1984), The Artist's Studio Book (1983); *Recreations* gardening, photography; *Clubs* Royal Society of Painters in Water Colours; *Style*— Dr Richard Seddon; 6 Arlesey Close, London SW15 (☎ 01 788 5899)

SEDGEMORE, Brian Charles John; MP (Lab) Hackney South and Shoreditch 1983-; *b* 17 Mar 1937; *Educ* Heles Sch Exeter, Oxford Univ; *m* 1964, Mary Reece; 1 s; *Career* civil servant 1962-66, barr Middle Temple 1966; Wandsworth Boro cncllr 1971-74, MP (Lab) Luton West Feb 1974-79, PPS to Tony Benn 1977-78; researcher for Granada TV 1980-84; memb: NUJ, ACTT, Writers Guild of GB; *Style*— Brian Sedgemore, Esq, MP; c/o House of Commons, London SW1

SEDGHI, Bijan Martin; s of Mahmood Sedghi, of Sutton Colfield, W Mids, and Jefin, *née* Martin; *b* 3 Jan 1953; *Educ* King Edward VI Camp Hill Sch Birmingham, Durham

Univ (BA), Coll of Law Chester; *m* 18 Oct 1975, Carole Ann, da of Michael Ernest Colson, of Bispham, Blackpool, Lancashire; 3 s (Dominic Guy b 1980, Marcus Edward b 1982, James Jack b 1984); *Career* slr: Supreme Ct, Wragge and Co Birmingham 1977-78, Edge and Ellison 1978-81 (ptnr 1981-88, conslt 1988-), chm Bluemel Bros plc 1985, exec chm Bromsgrove Industries plc 1987-, chm Neville Gp Ltd 1988-; memb Law Soc 1975-; *Recreations* association football, rugby football, cricket, walking; *Clubs* The Priory (Edgbaston); *Style—* Bijan Sedghi, Esq; Harborne Ct, 67-69 Harborne Rd, Birmingham, W Mids B15 3BU (☎ 021 456 1088, fax 021 456 1407, car tel 0836 599212)

SEDGWICK, Lady Henrietta Laura; *née* Phipps; 4 da of 4 Marquess of Normanby, CBE, JP, DL; *b* 29 Nov 1962; *m* 1982, Adam C Sedgwick (d 1985), eldest s of John Sedgwick, *qv*, of 49 Novello St, London SW6; *Style—* Lady Henrietta Sedgwick; Burtree House, York Rd, Hutton Sessay, Thirsk, N Yorks

SEDGWICK, John Humphrey Gerrie; s of Dr Charles Humphrey Sedgwick (d 1963), and Anne Jane, *née* Gerrie (d 1959); *b* 5 Jan 1923; *Educ* Eastbourne Coll, RMA Sandhurst; *m* 1 Jan 1949, Ursula Mary Thomason, da of Maj-Gen Clifford Thomason Beckett, CB, CBE, MC, DL (d 1972), of Templecombe, Somerset; 3 s (Adam Charles b 13 June 1952, d 1985, Toby John b 6 Dec 1954, Tom Oliver b 12 Aug 1956); *Career* Coldstream Guards 1942-46 serving N W Europe Campaign (Capt 1945); md: R E Thomas & Newman Ltd 1959-69, Wiltshier Contract Furnishing Ltd 1969-82, chm Bosham Yacht Serv Ltd 1972-; *Recreations* sailing (yacht "Mistral of Var"), painting, travel; *Clubs* Cavalry & Guards, Hurlingham, Royal Southern Yacht, Household Div Yacht; *Style—* John Sedgwick, Esq; 49 Novello St, London SW6 4JB (☎ 01 736 7326); 21 Rue des Aires, La Garde-Freinet, 83310 Cogolin, France (☎ 94 436 550)

SEDGWICK, Dr John Philip; s of Philip Giles Sedgwick (d 1940), and Vera Constance, *née* Everard; *b* 6 Dec 1938; *Educ* Dean Close, Guy's, Univ of London (MBBS, DA); *m* 1, 23 March 1963 (m dis 1978), Judith Ann, da of Edgar Nelson, of Upper Shirley, Southhampton; 1 s (Philip Giles), 2 da (Nicola Jane, Helen Louise); m 2, 7 April 1982, Anne Louise Warren, da of Arthur Henry Dickinson, of Dinnington, nr Doncaster, Yorks; *Career* house surgn Guy's Hosp 1964, house physician Lewisham Hosp 1964-65, sr house offr Royal Sussex Co Hosp 1965-66; med advsr: John Wyeth 1966, Servier Laboratories 1967; GP 1968-75, private practitioner 1975-77, dir health servs Brunel Univ 1978, sr clincial occupational health physician Hillingdon Borough; MO: Pioneer, Milupa, Kabi Virtnum, Fiat, Coca-cola; Memb Worshipful Co of Feltmakers 1970; Hon Fell RSM; *Recreations* golf, riding; *Style—* Dr John Sedgwick; 13 The Pagoda, Boulters Lock, Maidenhead, Berks SL6 8EU (☎ 0628 328 13); The Medical Centre, Univ of Brunel, Uxbridge, Middx UB8 3P (☎ 0895 34 426)

SEEAR, Baroness (Life Peer UK 1971), of Paddington in the City of Westminster; Beatrice Nancy Seear; PC (1985); da of late Herbert Charles Seear, of Croydon; *b* 7 August 1913; *Educ* Croydon HS, Newnham Coll Cambridge, LSE; *Career* ldr of Liberal peers in House of Lords 1984; personnel mangr C J Clark Ltd 1936-46, reader in Personnel Mgmnt LSE 1946-78; Liberal Pty Orgn 1965-66; author of books on working women; Hon Dr of Laws Leeds 1979, Hon DLitt Bath 1982; *Recreations* gardening, reading, travelling; *Clubs* Royal Commonwealth Soc, Nat Lib; *Style—* The Rt Hon the Lady Seear, PC; The Garden Flat, 44 Blomfield Rd, London W9 (☎ 01 286 5701)

SEEBOHM, Baron (Life Peer UK 1972), of Hertford; Frederic Seebohm; TD (1949); 2 s of Hugh Exton Seebohm, JP (d 1946), of Poynder's End, Hitchin, Herts, and his 1 w, Leslie, *née* Gribble (d 1913); *b* 18 Jan 1909; *Educ* Leighton Park Sch, Trinity Coll Cambridge; *m* 9 April 1932, Evangeline, da of late Sir Gerald Berkeley Hurst, TD, QC; 1 s, 2 da; *Career* Lt-Col RA; dir: Barclays Bank Ltd 1947-79 (dep chm 1968-74), Barclays Bank Int Ltd 1951-79 (chm 1965-72), ICFC (later Finance for Industry) 1967-80 (chm 1974-79); High Sheriff of Herts 1970-71; former vice-chm Barclays Bank SA, former pres Inst of Bankers, pres Age Concern, jt-pres Policy Studies Inst; US Bronze Star 1948; kt 1970; *Recreations* gardening, painting, golf; *Clubs* Carlton, Hurlingham, Royal Commonwealth Soc; *Style—* The Rt Hon the Lord Seebohm, TD; 28 Marsham Court, Marsham St, London SW1 (☎ 01 828 2168)

SEEBOHM, Hon Richard Hugh; s of Baron Seebohm; *b* 1933; *m* 1966, Margaret Evelyne Hok; *Style—* The Hon Richard Seebohm; Stable Cottage, Flatford Lane, East Bergholt, Colchester, Essex CO7 6UN

SEELY, Michael James; s of Frank James Wriothesly Seely (d 1956), and Vera Lilian, *née* Birkin (d 1970); *b* 20 August 1926; *Educ* Eton; *m* 1, 1952 (m dis 1964), Barbara Callahan; m 2, 1966, Patricia Ann Auchterlonie, da of George Wright (d 1940); 1 da (Rachel b 1967); *Career* racing correspondant The Times 1975-; *Recreations* shooting, windsurfing; *Style—* Michael Seely, Esq; Ramsdale Farm, Arnold, Nottingham (☎ 0602 653872); The Times (☎ 01 481 4100)

SEELY, Sir Nigel Edward; 5 Bt (UK 1896) of Sherwood Lodge, Arnold, Notts and Brooke House, Brooke, Isle of Wight; s of Sir Victor Seely, 4 Bt (d 1980), by 1 w, Sybil, *née* Gibbons, widow of Sir John Bridger Shiffner, 6 Bt; *b* 28 July 1923; *Educ* Stowe; *m* 1, 1949, Loraine, da of late Wilfred W Lindley-Travis; 3 da; m 2, 1984, Trudi, da of Sydney Pacter; *Heir* half-bro, Victor Seely; *Career* with Dorland International; *Clubs* Bucks, Royal Solent Yacht; *Style—* Sir Nigel Seely, Bt; 3 Craven Hill Mews, London W2; Dorland International, 121-141 Westbourne Terrace, London W2 6JR (☎ 01 262 5077, telex 27778)

SEELY, Hon Patrick Michael; s of 4 Baron Mottistone; *b* 12 Oct 1960; *Educ* Harrow, Trinity Coll Cambridge; *m* 1984, Susannah Shelley, da of Cdr J C Q Johnson, RN (ret), of Bradfield, Berks; *Style—* The Hon Patrick Seely; 65 Castletown Road, London W14 9HG (☎ 01 385 7382)

SEELY, Hon Peter John Philip; s and h of 4 Baron Mottistone; *b* 29 Oct 1949; *Educ* Uppingham; *m* 1, 1972 (m dis 1975), Joyce, da of Mrs Ellen Cairns, of St Ninians, Stirling; 1 s (Christopher David Peter b 1 Oct 1974); m 2, 1982, Lynda, da of W Swain, of Judds Farm, Bulphan Fen, Upminster, Essex; 1 da (Penelope Jane b 1984); *Style—* The Hon Peter Seely; 99 Bow Lane, Finchley, London N12

SEELY, Maj Victor Ronald; s of late Sir Victor Seely, 4 Bt (d 1980), by his 3 w, Mary, da of late Ronald Collins; hp of half-bro, Sir Nigel Seely, 5 Bt; *b* 1 August 1941; *Educ* Eton, RMAS, Staff Coll Camberley; *m* 1972, Annette Bruce, da of late Lt-Col J A D McEwen; 1 s (William b 1983), 1 da (Natasha b 1979); *Career* Maj The Royal Hussars (PWO), served on secondment to Sultan of Oman's Armed Forces 1970-71; *Recreations* hunting, event riding; *Clubs* Army & Navy; *Style—* Maj Victor Seely; Church Farm, Siddington, Cirencester, Glos

SEENEY, Leslie Elon Sidney; OBE (1978); s of Sidney Leonard Seeney (d 1950), of Forest Hill, London SE23, and Daisy Florence Alice, *née* Norman (d 1975); *b* 19 Jan 1922; *Educ* St Matthews Camberwell, London Borough Poly (pre RAF Serv); *m* 4 Jan 1947, Marjory Doreen, da of Arthur William Greenwood (d 1946), of Spalding, Lincs; 1 s (Michael b 1951); *Career* RAF (Volunteer Reserve), War Serv, Flt Lt (pilot), coastal cmd; dir gen Nat Chamber of Trade 1971-87; dir: Retail Consortium (fndr dir) 1987, Assoc for Prevention of Theft in Shops 1987; memb: Home Sec Standing Conference on Crime Prevention 1971-86, Retail Prices Index Advsy Ctee 1984-; Fell Soc of Assoc Executives 1976-86 (memb 1970-); *Recreations* reading, writing, travel, photography, grandchildren; *Style—* Leslie Seeney, Esq, OBE

SEFTON OF GARSTON, Baron (Life Peer UK 1978); William Henry Sefton; s of George Sefton; *b* 5 August 1915; *Educ* Duncombe Rd Sch Liverpool; *m* 1940, Phyllis, *née* Kerr; *Career* sits as Labour peer in House of Lords; leader Liverpool CC 1964-78, oppn leader Merseyside CC 1977-79 (formerly leader); chm: Runcorn Devpt Corpn 1974-81, North West Planning Corpn 1975-80; *Style—* The Rt Hon The Lord Sefton of Garston; 88 Tramway Rd, Liverpool L17 7AZ

SEFTON-FORBES, Bernard Norman; s of Gerald Sefton (d 1937), and Emily Rose, *née* Wischhusen (d 1964); *b* 8 April 1929; *Educ* Norwood Orphanage, Hackney Tech Coll, Swinton Coll; *m* 1, 15 Oct 1949 (m dis 1968), Hazel Helen, da of George Davies, of Anglesey; 1 s (Philip b 1954),1 da (Hazel b 1950); m 2, 1973; 1 step-da (Maxine b 1968); *Career* Nat Serv RAF WO/DF Air Sea Rescue 1947-49; divnl dir BSA Motor Cycles 1968-71, dir of personnel Dawson & Barfos 1971-73, md Aish & Co 1985-86, dir business devpt Hortsmann Gp 1986- (gp exec 1973- 75); non-exec dir: Apex New Enterprises Ltd, Hortsmann Timers & Controls, Notedale Ltd, Hortsmann Gauge & Metrology; dir Dorset Employers' Network, various indust and advsy and charitable ctees; town cncllr Solihull 1953-55, pres Bath C of C 1981; FIPM, FITO, FInstD; *Recreations* after dinner speaking, literature, writing, various charities; *Style—* Bernard Forbes, Esq; Fairfield Lodge, Blandford, Dorset DT11 7HL (☎ 0258 51768); Hortsmann Gp Ltd, 6 Princes Ct, Princes Rd, Ferndown, Dorset BH22 9JG (☎ 0202 861644, fax 0202 86145, telex 41586 HGG UK G)

SEGAL, Michael John; s of Abraham Charles Segal, of 18 Greenhill, London NW3 (d 1981), and Iris Muriel, *née* Parsons (d 1971); *b* 20 Sept 1937; *Educ* Strode's Sch Surrey; *m* 1 March 1963, Barbara Gina, da of Dr Joseph Leon Fluxman, of Johannesburg, S Africa (d 1954); 1 da (Leila b 10 Sept 1966); *Career* registrar family div High Court of Justice 1985, called to bar Middle Temple 1962, practiced on Midland and Oxford circuit 1963-84; memb Queen's Bench Procedure Ctee 1975-80; dep stipendiary magistrate 1980-84; memb Medico - Legal Soc, fndr memb Trollope Soc; *Recreations* reading, music, watching cricket; *Style—* Michael Segal, Esq; 28 Grange Rd, London N6 (☎ 01 348 0680); Principal Registry, Family Division, Somerset House, London, WC2

SEGAL, Baroness; Molly; *née* Rolo; da of Robert J Rolo, OBE, of Alexandria, Egypt; *m* 1934, Baron Segal, MRCS, LRCP (Life Peer) (d 1985); 2 da; *Style—* The Rt Hon Lady Segal; 2 Park Town, Oxford OX2 6TB

SEGAWA, Takao; s of Hideo Segawa, of Nara, Japan (d 1982), and Ayako, *née* Nishikawa; *b* 26 May 1948; *Educ* Unebi HS, Keio Univ (BA); *m* 1 Aug 1975, Chieko, da of Chikara Takiuchi, of Tokyo; 2 s (Hiroyoshi b 1976, Kohei b 1980), 1 da (Junko b 1978); *Career* Nomura Securities Co Tokyo 1971-73, asst sales mangr Nomura Int (HK) Ltd 1973-76, portfolio mangr Jardine Fleming Hong Kong 1976-77, asst mangr Nomura Securities Co Tokyo 1977-80, vice pres Nomura Securities Int Inc 1980-84, sr vice pres Singapore Nomura Merchant Banking Ltd 1984-87, dep gen mangr Nomura Bank Int Plc London 1987-; *Recreations* golf, tennis, swimming; *Style—* Takao Segawa, Esq; 3 Tilligham Way, London N12; Nomura Bank International plc, Nomura House, 24 Monument Street, London EC3 8AJ (☎ 01 929 2366, ext 2003, fax 01 626 0851, telex 9413062/4/5/6)

SEIFERT, John Michael; s of Lt-Col Richard Seifert, and Josephine Jeanette, *née* Harding; *b* 17 Feb 1949; *Educ* Mill Hill Sch, Bartlett Sch of Architecture, UCL (BSc; Dip Arch); *m* 1 Feb 1985, Johanna Marion, da of Elias Hofmann; 2 s (James, Edward), 1 da (Elizabeth), 1 step s (Marlon); *Career* architect, chm Seiferts Ltd; major projects incl: Cutlers Gdns 1983, Mermaid Theatre 1983, Bank of Chicago House 1984, Sheraton Hotel Lagos 1985, Bishops Bridge 1985, MISR Bank Tower 1986, South Quay Plaza 1987, Swiss Banking Corpn 1988, Hambros Bank 1988, Sceptre Ct 1988, Greenwich View 1989, Glengall Bridge 1989; major competitions won: Surrey Docks Shopping Centre 1983, Limehouse Basin 1985, Heathrow Hotel 1988, Sandwell Mall; Liveryman Worshipful Co of Glaziers and Painters of Glass 1967; RIBA 1976, CROAIF (France) 1981, NCARB (USA) 1983; *Recreations* painting, sculpture, numismatics; *Clubs* Carlton, Arts, Army and Navy; *Style—* John Seifert, Esq; 164 Shaftesbury Ave, London WC2 (☎ 01 242 1644)

SEIRADHAKIS, Hon Mrs (Mercy Burdett); *née* Money-Coutts; da of 6 Baron Money-Coutts, TD (d 1949); *b* 1910; *Educ* Lady Margaret Hall, Oxford (BA); *m* 1947, Michael Seiradhakis; 1 s, 1 da; *Career* served with British Red Cross Mission in Greece and Central Mediterranean and with UN Relief and Rehabilitation Administration in Crete; *Style—* The Hon Mrs Seiradhakis; 19 Odos Seirenon, Byrona, Athens

SEKACZ, Ilona Anna; da of Aleksander Sekacz, and Olive, *née* Swithenbank; *b* 6 April 1948; *Educ* Arnold HS Blackpool, Univ of Birmingham; *Career* composer works for Royal Shakespeare Theatre: King Lear (1982), Twelfth Night (1983), Henry VIII (1983), Measure for Measure (1983) Les Liaisons Dangeureuses (1985), Cymbeline (1987), The Jew of Malta (1987), The Man of Mode (1988), Across Oka (1988), The Love of the Nightingale (1988), A Midsummer Night's Dream (1989), Dr Faustus (1989), Cymbeline (1989), As You Like It (1989); music composed for The Nat Theatre: Major Barbara (1982), The Cherry Orchard (1986), The Wandering Jew (1987), Countrymania (1987), Cat on a Hot Tin Roof (1987), The Secret Rapture (1988), Bartholomew Fair (1988); opera A Small Green Space ENO (1989); ballet The Queue English Dance Theatre 1989; many scores for TV and radio prodns 1982-; work for WWF for nature: music composed for WWF's 25 anniversary celebration in Assisi 1986, music composed for WWF's harvest festival at Winchester Cathedral 1987 and advent serv at St George's Chapel Windsor 1988, music composed for WWF's multi- religious celebration at Canterbury Cathedral 1989; *Recreations* seeing friends, ecology, cinema; *Style—* Miss Ilona Sekacz; 40 Earlham St, London WC2H 9LA (☎ 01 240 9360)

SELBORNE, 4 Earl of (UK 1882); John Roundell Palmer; KBE (1987), DL (Hants 1982); s of Viscount Wolmer (k on active service 1942; s of 3 Earl) and

Priscilla (*see* Baron Newton); suc gf 1971. Lord Selborne's gggf, the 1 Earl, was Lord Chllr 1872-74 and 1880-85 and his ggf was First Lord of the Admiralty 1900-05 and helped establish the RNVR, the RFR, Osborne & Dartmouth Naval Colleges and the Designs Committee which resulted in the Royal Navy being equipped with Dreadnoughts; *b* 24 Mar 1940; *Educ* Eton, Ch Ch Oxford; *m* 1969, Joanna Van Antwerp, da of Evan James, of Upwood Park, Abingdon (and sis of Countess Baldwin of Bewdley); 3 s (Viscount Wolmer, Hon George b 1974, Hon Luke (twin) b 1974), 1 da (Lady Emily b 1978); *Heir* s, Viscount Wolmer; *Career* sits as Conservative in House of Lords; chm Hops Marketing Bd 1978-82, former vice-chm The Apple and Pear Devpt Cncl, tres Bridewell Royal Hosp (King Edward's Sch Witley) 1972-83; memb Agric & Food Research Cncl 1975-, dep chm 1982, chm 1983-; *Clubs* Brooks's, Farmers'; *Style—* The Rt Hon the Earl of Selborne, KBE, DL; Temple Manor, Selborne, Alton, Hants (☎ Bordon 042 03 3646)

SELBY, Bishop of 1983; Rt Rev Clifford Conder Barker; TD (1971); s of Rev Sidney Barker (d 1979), and Kathleen Alice, *née* Conder (d 1973); *b* 22 April 1926; *Educ* Middlesbrough HS, Oriel Coll Oxford (BA, MA), St Chad's Coll Durham (Dip Theol); *m* 1, 14 Aug 1952, Marie (d 1982), da of Richard Edwards (d 1958); 1 s (Richard b 1960), 2 da (Helena b 1954, Catherine b 1962); m 2, 23 July 1983, Audrey Vera Gregron, da of Charles Ernest Fisher (d 1961); 2 step s (Timothy b 1954, Simon b 1955), 1 step da (Louise b 1959); *Career* Nat Serv Green Howard 1944-48 (cmmnd 1946), Chaplain TA 1958-74; ordained: deacon 1952, priest 1953; curate: All Saints Scarborough 1952-55, Redcar 1955-57; vicar: Sculcoates Hull 1957-63, Rudby in Cleveland with Middleton 1963-70, St Olave York 1970-76; rural dean: Stokesley 1965-70, City of York 1971-76; canon and prebendary York Minster 1973-76, consecrated bishop 1976, bishop of Whitby 1976-83; *Recreations* most sports, gardening, music, travel, crosswords, natural history; *Clubs* Yorkshire; *Style—* The Rt Rev the Bishop of Selby, TD; 8 Bankside Close, Upper Poppleton, York YO2 6LH (☎ 0904 795342)

SELBY, Sir Kenneth; s of Thomas William Selby (d 1963), and Ruth Selby (d 1919); *b* 16 Feb 1914; *Educ* HS for Boys Worthing; *m* 1937, Elma Gertrude, da of Johnstone Sleator, of Roscrea, Co Tipperary; 2 s; *Career* chm Bath & Portland Gp 1969-82, pres 1982-; pro-chllr Bath Univ 1974-; kt 1970; *Clubs* Reform, Savages (Bristol); *Style—* Sir Kenneth Selby; Hartham Park, Corsham, Wilts SN13 0PZ (☎ 0249 713176)

SELBY, 4 Viscount (UK 1905); Michael Guy John Gully; s of 3 Viscount (d 1959); *b* 15 August 1942; *Educ* Harrow; *m* 1965, Mary Theresa, da of Capt Thomas F Powell; 1 s, 1 da (Hon Catherine Mary Albinia b 1971); *Heir* s, Hon Edward Gully; *Career* chartered accountant; tribology consultant, fish farm advsr, banking systems computer conslt; FCA; *Recreations* shooting, sailing; *Style—* The Rt Hon The Viscount Selby; Ardfern House, by Lochgilphead, Argyll; Island of Shuna, Arduaine, by Oban, Argyll

SELBY, Ralph Walford; CMG (1961); s of Sir Walford Selby, KCMG, CB, CVO (d 1965), and Dorothy Orme, *née* Carter (d 1981); *b* 20 Mar 1915; *Educ* Eton, Ch Ch Oxford; *m* 8 Dec 1945, Julianna da Capt Ivan Edward Snell, MC (d 1958), by his w, Marjorie Villiers (d 1981), gda of 4 Earl of Clarendon; 3 da (Virginia, Pamela, Cynthia); *Career* entered HM Dip Service 1938, Capt Grenadier Guards 1939-45, served in Delhi, The Hague, FO, Tokyo, Copenhagen, Djarkarta, Warsaw 1965-66; consul-gen Boston 1966, min Rome 1969, ambass Oslo 1972-75; *Recreations* sailing (yacht Jandar), tennis, beagling, lumberjack; *Clubs* Royal Yacht Squadron, MCC; *Style—* Ralph Selby Esq, CMG; Mengeham House, Hayling Island, Hants PO11 9JX (☎ 0705 463833)

SELBY, Hon Mrs (Susan Lorna); *née* Pennock; da of Baron Pennock (Life Peer), *qv*; *b* 1948; *m* 1970, David Frederick McLaren Selby; 2 s, 1 da; *Style—* The Hon Mrs Selby; Goodchilds Hill, Stratfield Saye, nr Reading, Berks

SELBY, Dowager Viscountess; Veronica Catherine Briscoe; da of late J George; *m* 1933, 3 Viscount Selby (d 1959); 2 s, 1 da; *Style—* The Rt Hon The Dowager Viscountess Selby; c/o The Rt Hon the Viscount Selby, Shuna Castle, Island of Shuna, Argyll

SELBY BENNETT, James Sebastian; TD (1987); s of Cdr Harry Selby Bennett RN, of Slepe Green, Slepe, nr Poole, Dorset, and Dolores, *née* Lees; *b* 14 June 1954; *Educ* Eton, Coll of Law; *m* 22 April 1978, Priscilla Mary, da of Charles Murray MacFarlane Barrow, of Mourne Cottage, Piddlehinton, Dorchester, Dorset; 2 s (Andrew b 1982, Nicholas b 1986); *Career* joined TA 1973; slr, farmer; Theodore Goddard & Co (London and Madrid), ptnr Humphries Kirk and Miller; slr Dorset Nat Farmers Union; The Law Soc; *Style—* James S Selby Bennett, Esq, TD; Slepe Farm, Slepe, nr Poole, Dorset (☎ 0202 622 737); Humphries Kirk and Miller, Glebe House, North St, Wareham, Dorset, BH20 4AN (☎ 09295 2141, fax 09295 6701)

SELF, Hugh Michael; QC (1973); s of Sir Henry Self, KCMG, KCB, KBE (d 1975), and Rosalind Audrey (d 1987); *b* 19 Mar 1921; *Educ* Lancing, Worcester Coll Oxford (BA); *m* 1950, Penelope Ann, da of John Drinkwater (d 1936, poet and playwright), and Daisy Kennedy (violinist); 2 da (Susannah, Melanie); *Career* served RN 1941-46, Lt RNVR 1946; barr Lincoln's Inn 1951, recorder 1975, bencher Lincoln's Inn 1980; *Recreations* golf, walking, wine; *Clubs* Savile; *Style—* Michael Self, Esq, QC; 59 Maresfield Gardens, Hampstead, London NW3 (☎ 01 435 8311); Christmas Cottage, Ingram's Green, Midhurst, Sussex

SELF, Hon Mrs (Ruth Kathleen); *née* Napier; twin da of 5 Baron Napier of Magdala, OBE; *b* 1947; *m* 1972, John Arthur Self, PhD; *Style—* The Hon Mrs Self; 70 Victoria Rd, Hawthorn East, Melbourne, Vic 3123, Australia

SELIGMAN, (Richard) Madron; MEP (EDG) W Sussex 1979-; 4 s of Dr Richard Joseph Simon Seligman, FCGI, FIM (d 1972), and Hilda Mary, *née* MacDowell (d 1966); bro of Sir Peter Seligman, *qv*; *b* 10 Nov 1918; *Educ* Harrow, Balliol Coll Oxford (BA), Sch of Slavonic Studies London Univ; *m* 1947, Nancy-Joan, da of Julian Marks (d 1950); 3 s, 1 da; *Career* Maj 1945, 6 Armd Divl Signals, North Africa, Italy 1940-46; dir: ARV Holdings plc, Fluor GB 1966-83, St Regis Int 1983-85, chm Incinerator Co 1950-; pres: Oxford Union Soc 1940, Oxford Univ Ski-Team 1938-39, Harrow cricket and rugby teams; *Recreations* skiing, tennis, travel, piano, gardening; *Clubs* Royal Thames Yacht, Royal Inst of International Affairs, MCC; *Style—* Madron Seligman, Esq, MEP; Micklepage House, Nuthurst, Horsham, West Sussex (☎ 040376 259)

SELIGMAN, Sir Peter Wendel; CBE (1969); s of Dr Richard Joseph Simon Seligman, FCGI, FIM (d 1972), and Hilda Mary, *née* McDowell (d 1966); bro of Madron Seligman, *qv*; *b* 16 Jan 1913; *Educ* King's Coll Sch, Harrow, Kantonschule Zürich, Gonville and Caius Coll Cambridge (BA); *m* 1937, Elizabeth Lavinia Mary, da of Prof John Laviers Wheatley, ARA, RWS (d 1955); 2 s (Peter, Bruce), 4 da (Hildagnace, Lavinia, Johanna, Gabrielle); *Career* engineer; md APV Hldgs Ltd 1942-65; chm: APV Hldgs Ltd 1965-77, British Chemical Plant Manufacturers Assoc 1965-67; dir: St Regis International Ltd 1973-83, Eibis Int Ltd 1980-; chm: Kandahar Ski Club 1972-76, National Ski Fedn of GB 1977-81; FIMechE; kt 1978; *Recreations* skiing, carpentry, travel, boating (yacht 'Thornele II'); *Clubs* Hawks', Kandahar Ski (invitation life memb), Ski of Great Britain (hon life memb), Royal Lymington Yacht, Royal Overseas League; *Style—* Sir Peter Seligman, CBE; King's Lea, King's Saltern Rd, Lymington, Hants SO41 9QF (☎ 0590 76569)

SELKIRK, Master of; Alasdair Malcolm Douglas-Hamilton; s of late Lord Malcolm Douglas-Hamilton, OBE, DFC (3 s of 13 Duke of Hamilton), by 1 w, (Clodagh) Pamela, da of late Lt-Col the Hon Malcom Bowes-Lyon (s of 13 Earl of Strathmore); *b* 10 Sept 1939; *Educ* Gordonstoun, Edinburgh Univ; *m* 1965, Angela Kathleen, da of John Molony Longley; 2 s, 2 da; *Career* with Morgan Guaranty Tst Co of New York 1964-68, Bank of Scotland 1969-; *Recreations* mountaineering, skiing, photography; *Clubs* New (Edinburgh); *Style—* The Master of Selkirk; Lessudden, St Boswells, Roxburghshire

SELKIRK, Hon Nadia Mickey; *née* Lucas; er da of 1 Baron Lucas of Chilworth (d 1967); *b* 19 Jan 1923; *m* 4 March 1944 (m dis 1980), Flt Lt Hamish Rattray Selkirk, DFC, RAF, s of late James Logie Selkirk; 1 s (other twin s decd), 1 da; *Style—* The Hon Nadia M Selkirk; Saffron Cottage, Northfield End, Henley-on-Thames, Oxon

SELKIRK, 10 Earl of (S 1646); (George) Nigel Douglas-Hamilton; KT (1976), GCMG (1959), GBE (1963, OBE 1941), AFC, AE, PC (1955), QC (Scot 1959); s of 13 Duke of Hamilton (d 1940); yr bro of 14 Duke of Hamilton; suc to Earldom under terms of special remainder 1940, the Earldom having been held by the Duke of Hamilton in fiduciary fee until that date; *b* 4 Jan 1906; *Educ* Eton, Balliol Coll Oxford (MA), Edinburgh Univ (LLB); *m* 6 Aug 1949, Audrey Durell, da of late Maurice Drummond-Sale-Barker; *Heir* uncertain; *Career* takes Conservative whip in Lords; served AAF and RAF 1932-45, Gp Capt; chm House of Lords Branch RAF Assoc; pres: Building Socs Assoc to 1982, Caledonian Club to 1986; advocate Scotland 1934, memb Royal Co of Archers (Queen's Body Guard for Scotland), chllr Duchy of Lancaster 1955-57, First Lord of Admiralty 1957-1959, UK cmmr for Singapore and cmmr-gen S E Asia 1959-63, Scottish rep peer 1945-63; hon chief Saulteaux Indians 1967, hon citizen of Winnipeg (Manitoba), freeman of Hamilton; *Clubs* Athenaeum, New (Edinburgh), Caledonian; *Style—* The Rt Hon the Earl of Selkirk, KT, GCMG, GBE, AC, AE, PC, QC; 60 Eaton Place, London SW1X 8AT (☎ 01 235 6926); Rose Lawn Coppice, Wimborne, Dorset BH21 3DB (☎ 0202 883160)

SELLAR, (Alexander) John Patrick; s of Lt-Col Thomas Byrne Sellar, CMG, DSO, KOSB (d 1924), and Evelyn, *née* Pugh (d 1952); *b* 16 April 1905; *Educ* Winchester, Balliol Coll Oxford (MA); *m* 20 Jan 1934, Mary Penelope, yr da of Ronald Collet Norman (d 1963), of Moor Place, Much Hadham, Herts; 2 da (Dione Isobel b 1935, Christina Mary b 1937); *Career* Res of Offrs 1938, KOSB 1939-45, Capt Intelligence Corps, serv 10 Army, Iran, 14 Army Far E, SEAC; sr ptnr Halsey Lightly & Co, chm Western Merthyr Tydfil Colliery, literary exec John Galsworthy Estate; legal advsr: King George's Tst, Arab Horse, Welsh Pony and Cob Soc; jt owner Lanhill Stud, winner, owner, rider point to point; memb: RSPB, RGS, Royal Soc Asian Affairs; *Recreations* ornithology, natural history, hunting, stalking, fishing, travel, mountaineering, photography, archaeology, showing; *Clubs* United Univ, Lowtonian Soc, MCC (playing memb), Vincents; *Style—* John Sellar, Esq; Sparrow Farm, Lanhill, Chippenham, Wiltshire SN14 6LX

SELLARS, John Ernest; s of Ernest Buttle Sellar, of Grimsby, and Edna Grace Mordaunt; *b* 5 Feb 1936; *Educ* Wintringham GS Grimsby, Manchester Univ (BSc, MSc); *m* 20 Dec 1958, Dorothy Beatrice, da of Maj Douglas Norman Morrison, of Humberston, Cleethorpes; 3 da (Karen b 1961, Fiona b 1962, Ann b 1964); *Career* research engr English Electric (GW) Ltd 1958-61; lectr Royal Coll of Advanced Technol (now Univ of Salford) 1961-67, head of mathematics Lanchester Coll of Technol 1967-71, head of computer science Lanchester Poly 1971-74; chief offr Business Educn Cncl 1974-83, dir and chief exec Business and Technician Educn Cncl 1983-, dir Higher Educn Info Services Unit; *Recreations* walking, aspiring broadcaster; *Clubs* Reform, IOD, Middlesex CCC; *Style—* John Sellars, Esq; 306 Cassiobury Drive, Watford, Herts WD1 3AW (☎ 0923 33055); BTEC Central House, Upper Woburn Place, London WC1H 0HH (☎ 01 388 3288)

SELLERS, His Honour Judge; Norman William Malin; VRD, DL (Lancs 1986); s of Rt Hon Sir Frederic Aked Sellers, Lord Justice of Appeal (d 1979), and Grace Lilian, *née* Malin (d 1987); *b* 29 August 1919; *Educ* Merchant Taylors' Crosby, Silcoates Sch, Hertford Coll Oxford (MA); *m* 30 March 1946, Angela Laurie, da of Sydney Clapham Jukes; 4 da (Wendy b 1947, Elizabeth b 1950, Julia b 1952, Helena b 1956); *Career* served RNVR 1940-65 (despatches HMS Nelson 1942), Lt Cdr 1953, cmd HMS Mersey; contested Liberal Crosby Div 1964; barr Grays Inn 1947; recorder Crown Court 1972,circuit judge Northern Circuit 1974-; *Recreations* sailing, walking; *Clubs* Ribble Cruising, BHR Yacht; *Style—* His Honour Judge Sellers, VRD, DL; Hillside, Lower Road, Loncridge, Preston PR3 2YN (☎ 077 478 3222)

SELLICK, James Alan; s of Alan Edwin Sellick (d 1975), of Burwash, E Sussex, and Constance Leonora, *née* Quilter (d 1986); *b* 25 Jan 1934; *Educ* Eastbourne Coll; *m* 15 Sept 1962, Angela Louise, da of Capt Alan Scott Webb, RN (d 1974), of Etchingham, E Sussex; 2 s (James b 1966, Nicholas b 1966), 2 da (Amelia b 1964, Harriet b 1973); *Career* Lieut Royal Sussex Regt 1954-56; co dir Diploma plc and subsids 1957-83; *Recreations* gardening, fishing, shooting, skiing; *Style—* James A Sellick, Esq; Pashley Manor, Ticehurst, Sussex TN5 7HE (☎ 0580 200692)

SELLIER, Robert Hugh; s of Maj Philip Joseph Sellier (d 1963), and Lorna Geraldine Luxton (d 1983); *b* 15 Nov 1933; *Educ* St Joseph's Coll Oxford, Kings Coll Durham (BSc); *m* 1 16 Aug 1963, Cynthia Ann (decd), da of Lt-Col F W Dwelly (d 1984); 1 da (Nicola Jane b 1968); m 2, 15 April 1987, Gillian, da of late J Clark; *Career* md: New Ideal Houses 1972-74, Cementation Construction 1979-83; dep md Cementation International 1974-79, chm Cementation Group of Companies 1983-86, group md George Wimpey plc 1986-; *Recreations* skiing, squash; *Style—* Robert H Sellier, Esq; "Heatherlands", Glenmore Road, Crowborough, E Sussex TN6 1TN (☎ Crowborough 63413); George Wimpey plc, Hammersmith Grove, London W6 7EN (☎ 01 748 2000)

SELLS, (Edward) Andrew Perronet; s of Sir David Sells, of Royston, Herts (*qv*); *b* 30 Nov 1948; *Educ* St Peters Seaford, Wellington Coll, London Business Sch; *Career* chartered accountant 1971; J Henry Schroder Wagg & Co Ltd 1972-82, Thompson

Clive & Partners 1982-87; md Albany Venture Ltd; dir: Micrelec plc, Normond Instruments plc, Ditec Ltd, Drew Scientific Ltd; *Recreations* reading, cricket, hunting; *Style*— Andrew Sells, Esq; 10 Kensington Place, London W8 7PT (☎ 01 727 5080); Cambridge House, 375 Evston Road, London NW1 3AR (☎ 01 380 0838, fax 01 388 0777)

SELLS, Sir David Perronet; s of late Edward Perronet Sells, and late Margaret Mary de Grave Sells; *b* 23 June 1918; *Educ* Repton, Ch Ch Oxford (MA); *m* 1948, Beryl Cecilia, da of late Cecil Ernest Wells Charrington, MC; 3 s (incl Andrew Sells, *qv*); *Career* chm Conservative Central Council 1977-78, holder of numerous other offices in National Union of Cons and Unionist Assocs; kt 1980; *Recreations* fishing, shooting; *Clubs* Savile, Carlton; *Style*— Sir David Sells; Tadlow House, Tadlow, Royston, Herts SG8 0EL (☎ 076 723 228)

SELSDON, 3 Baron (UK 1932); Sir Malcolm McEacharn Mitchell-Thomson; 4th Bt (UK 1900); s of 2 Baron Selsdon, DSC (d 1963), and his 1 w, Phoebette Sitwell, da of Crossley Swithinbank; *b* 27 Oct 1937; *Educ* Winchester; *m* 1965, Patricia Anne, da of Donald Smith; 1 s; *Heir* s, Hon Callum Malcolm McEacharn Mitchell-Thomson b 7 Nov 1969; *Career* Sub-Lt RNVR; banker with Midland Bank Gp, British del to Cncl of Europe and Western European Union 1972-78, chm Ctee of Middle East Trade (Comet) 1979-86, memb British Overseas Trade Bd 1983-86; chm: Greater London and S E Cncl for Sport and Recreation 1978-83, London Docklands Arena Tst 1984-; *Recreations* tennis, lawn tennis, skiing, sailing; *Clubs* MCC; *Style*— The Rt Hon the Lord Selsdon; Walker House, 87 Queen Victoria Street, London EC4V 4AP

SELWOOD, Brig David Henry Deering; s of Cdr George Deering Selwood, RN (d 1972), and Enid Marguerite, *née* Rowlinson; *b* 27 June 1934; *Educ* Kelly Coll, Univ Coll of South-West, Law Soc's Sch of Law; *m* 1, 17 March 1962 (m dis), Joanne Christine, da of Capt R F Pink, of Saltash, Cornwall; 1 s (Stephen b 1963), 1 da (Suzanne b 1966); m 2, 3 Nov 1973, Barbara Dorothea, da of late Dr Kurt Franz Richard Hütter; 2 step-s (Andreas b 1967, Dominic b 1970); *Career* cmmnd (nat serv list) RASC 1958; TA (4 Devons) 1959-61, regular cmmn Army Legal Serv Staff List 1961, served on staff of WO MOD, HQ BAOR, HQ MELF, HQ FARELF; admitted slr 1957; Brig Legal HQ BAOR, recorder SE Circuit 1985-, hon attorney and counsellor US Court of Military Appeals; *Books* Criminal Law and Psychiatry (co-author) (1987); *Recreations* reading, writing, gardening; *Clubs* Lansdowne, London House Fellowship; *Style*— Brig David Selwood; c/o Barclays Bank plc, 7 North Street, Wilton, Salisbury SP2 0HA

SELWYN, Jeffrey Michael; s of Arthur Selwyn and Vera, *née* Schuchman (d 1984); *b* 2 Dec 1936; *Educ* Mill Hill; *m* 5 March 1961, June Margaret, da of Leonard Koetser (d 1979); 2 s (Richard Leonard b 17 Nov 1961, Anthony David b 14 May 1966), 1 da (Karina Margaret b 5 March 1964); *Career* chartered accountant; md Allied Dunbar Provident plc 1973-, chm Assoc of Br Insur Housing Working Pty 1985; FCA 1965; *Recreations* golf; *Style*— Jeffrey Selwyn, Esq; The Pines, Totteridge Village, London N20 (☎ 01 446 2206); 9/15 Sackville Street, London W1 (☎ 01 434 3894, fax 01 437 9527)

SELWYN, Maj John Jasper; MC (1942); s of Rev Stephen John Selwyn (d 1960), of Henley-on-Thames,and Phyllis Graeme, *née* Hickling (d 1967); *b* 11 August 1918; *Educ* Eton, Trinity Coll Cambridge (BA, MA); *m* 1, 1943, Margaret Evelyn Whittingham (d 1980), da of late George Gee, of Ely Grange, Frant, Sussex; 2 s (Nicholas Jasper b 1946, William Henry b 1947), 1 da (Albina Victoria b 1950); m 2, 16 Mar 1983, Mary Mitchell, wid of Capt Michael Radcliffe (d 1975), and da of Leonard Brooke-Edwards (d 1988), of Philadelphia, USA; *Career* cmmnd 13/18 Queen Mary's Own Royal Hussars 1939; served: Dunkirk, Dieppe, D-Day (Normandy) 1940-44; cmd Sqdn in 6 Airborne RECCE in the Ardennes campaign 1944-45, Staff Coll Camberley 1948, cmd Sqdn 13/18 Hussars Malaya 1951-53 (despatches), Regtl 2 i/c 13/18 Hussars 1957-58, ret 1959; barr Lincolns Inn 1963, practised S E Circuit and Kent Sessions, dep circuit judge 1974/78, ret from practise 1978; memb Br Legion (formerly Pres Cookham and Pinkneys Green Branch), Nat Tst, Museum Ctee 13/18 Hussars, Berks CC (C) 1962-68; *Recreations* field sports, sailing; *Clubs* Cavalry & Guards, Leander; *Style*— Maj John Selwyn, MC; The Orchards, Pinkneys Green, Maidenhead, Berks SL6 6PA (☎ 0628 30537)

SELWYN GUMMER; *see*: Gummer

SELWYN SHARPE, Richard Charles; s of Rev Roger Sharpe,*qv*, and Mary Gordon, *née* Selwyn; *b* 14 Dec 1962; *Educ* Marlborough, Bristol Univ (LLB); *Career* called to the Bar Lincoln's Inn 1985, practice NE Circuit 1987-; Freeman City of London, Liveryman Worshipful Co of Broderers; Whipper-in New Forest Hounds 1984-86; contrib of articles on hunting to: Horse and Hound, Harpers and Queen; *Recreations* hunting, fishing, music, portraiture; *Clubs* Northern Counties (Newcastle), Old Raby Hunt, New Forest Hunt; *Style*— Richard Selwyn Sharpe, Esq; 1 Harcourt Buildings, Third Floor, Temple, London EC4 (☎ 01 353 2214); Gowtons Cottage, Manfield, nr Richmond, N Yorks; 73 Westgate Road, Newcastle NE1 (☎ 091 262 4407, fax 091 222 1845)

SEMKEN, John Douglas; CB (1980), MC (1944); s of William Richard Semken (d 1970), and Beatrice Rose, *née* Craymer (d 1964); *b* 9 Jan 1921; *Educ* St Albans Sch Pembroke Coll Oxford (BCL, MA); *m* 4 Sept 1952, (Edna) Margaret, da of Thomas Robert Poole (d 1978); 3 s (Christopher b 1955, David b 1956, Robert b 1962); *Career* cmmnd Sherwood Rangers Yeo 1940, Lt 1941, Capt 1942, Maj 1944, tank commander N Africa and NW Europe 1942-44; barr at the Chancery Bar 1949-53, joined office of the Legal Advsr to the HO 1953, dep under sec of state and legal advsr to the HO 1977-83; Silver Star USA 1944; *Style*— John Semken, Esq, CB, MC; 2 The Ridgeway, London NW7 1RS (☎ 01 346 3092)

SEMMENCE, Dr Adrian Murdoch; CB (1986); s of Adrian George Semmence (d 1962), of Schoolhouse, Cults, Aberdeenshire, and Henrietta Scorgie, *née* Murdoch; *b* 5 April 1926; *Educ* Robert Gordon's Coll, Univ of Aberdeen (MB, ChB, MD), Univ of London (MSc); *m* 24 Sept 1949, Joan, da of Hugh McAskill Wood (d 1963), of Crown St, Aberdeen; 4 s (Adrian b 1950, Jonathan b 1953, Timothy b 1959, Peter b 1961), 1 da (Joanna b 1964); *Career* Pilot Observer trg FAA 1943-44, Able Seaman (torpedo man) RN 1944-47; house posts Aberdeen Royal Infirmary and Aberdeen Maternity Hosp 1953-54, gen practice Berks and Oxon 1961-76, princ med offr Civil Serv Dept 1976-7, med advsr Civil Serv 1979-86, conslt Cabinet Office of Miny for Civil Serv 1987-; Oxford Med Soc 1961, FRSM 1976; former pres Occupational Med Section; *Recreations* reading, gardening; *Clubs* Athenaeum; *Style*— Dr Adrian Semmence, CB; Stone Cottage, Steventon, Abingdon, Oxon OX13 6RZ (☎ 0235 831 527); Tilbury House, Petty France, Westminster SW1H 9EU (☎ 01 273 6314/6324)

SEMPILL, Lady (20 in line, S 1489); Ann Moira Sempill; *née* Forbes-Sempill; da of Lord Sempill (19 in line, d 1965) by his 1 w, Eileen, da of Sir John Lavery, RA; niece of Hon Sir Ewan Forbes of Craigievar, 11th Bt, *qv*; half-sis of Hon Mrs Menuhin, *qv*; *b* 19 Mar 1920; *Educ* convents in Austria and Germany, Poles Convent Ware; *m* 1, 1942 (m dis 1945), Capt Eric Holt, Manchester Regt; 1 da; m 2, 1948, Lt-Col Stuart Whitemore Chant-Sempill, OBE, MC, late Gordon Highlanders (who assumed by decree of Lyon Court 1966 the additional name of Sempill); 2 s, 1 da; *Heir* s, Master of Sempill, *qv*; *Career* Petty Offr WRNS, ctee memb House of Lords, Cons Peer 1966-; *Style*— The Rt Hon the Lady Sempill; East Lodge, Druminnor, Rhynie, Aberdeenshire (☎ 046 46 663); 15 Onslow Ct, Drayton Gdns, London SW10

SEMPILL, Master of; Hon James William Stuart Whitemore Sempill; s (by 2 m) of Lady Sempill, *qv*; *b* 25 Feb 1949; *Educ* Oratory Sch, St Clare's Hall and Hertford Coll Oxford; *m* 1977, Josephine Ann Edith, da of Joseph Norman Rees, of Johannesburg; 1 s (Francis b 1979), 1 da (Cosima b 1983); *Career* with Argus of Ayr Ltd; *Style*— The Master of Sempill; Pibworth House, Aldworth, Berks (☎ Compton 202)

SEMPLE, Andrew Greenlees; s of William Hugh Semple (d 1981), of Manchester, and Hilda Madeline, *née* Wood (d 1978); *b* 16 Jan 1934; *Educ* Winchester, St John's Coll Cambridge (BA, MA); *m* 27 May 1961, Janet Elizabeth, da of Harold Richard Grant Whates (d 1961), of Ludlow; 1 s (Robert b 1965), 1 da (Susanna b 1969); *Career* Nat Serv RN 1952-54 (Russian interpreter), Acting Sub Lt (special) RNVR; princ Miny of Tport 1962-69 (joined 1957), asst sec 1969-75, princ private sec to Sec of State for the Environment 1972-75, under sec DOE 1976-83, sec Water Authy Assoc 1983-87; md Anglian Water 1987-; Hon Memb AWO 1988; companion IWEM 1985; *Recreations* walking, travel, reading, occasional golf; *Style*— Andrew Semple, Esq; 83 Burbage Rd, London SE24 9HB (☎ 01 274 6550); 3 Church Lane, Covington, Cambs PE18 0RT (☎ 0480 860 497); Anglian Water, Ambury Rd, Huntingdon, Cambs PE18 6NZ (☎ 0480 56181)

SEMPLE, (William) David Crowe; s of George Crowe Semple (d 1985), of 3 Athol Crescent, Laurieston, Falkirk, and Helen Davidson, *née* Paterson (d 1975); *b* 11 June 1933; *Educ* Grangemouth HS, Falkirk HS, Glasgow Univ (BSc), Jordanhill Coll of Educn, London Univ (Dip Ed); *m* 9 July 1958, Margaret Bain, da of Andrew Kerr Donald (d 1972), of 2 Sharp Terrace, Grangemouth; 1 s (Richard b 1961), 1 da (Lynn b 1962); *Career* educn offr Northern Rhodesia 1958-61, educn offr and offr i/c educn TV Northern Rhodesia 1961-63, chief educn offr Zambia 1966-67 (dep chief educn offr 1964-66), actg dir of tech educn Zambia 1967-68, dep dir of educn Edinburgh 1972-74 (asst dir 1968-72), dir of educn Lothian Region 1974-; memb Edinburgh Rotary Club, gen sec Assoc of Dirs of Educn in Scotland 1985-; memb: UK advsy ctee on UNESCO 1981-86, UGC 1983-, memb Sec of States Working Party on Educn Catering 1971-73, Scottish Cncl for Tertiary Educn 1979-83 (chm educn ctee 1979-85); FBIM 1985, ADES 1968; *Recreations* gardening, reading; *Style*— David Semple, Esq; 15 Essex Park, Edinburgh, Lothian (☎ 031 339 6157); Dept of Education, 40 Torphichen St, Edinburgh, Lothian EH3 8JJ (☎ 031 229 9166)

SENIOR, Sir Edward Walters; CMG (1955); s of late Albert Senior, CBE, of Sheffield; *b* 29 Mar 1902; *Educ* Repton, Sheffield Univ; *m* 1928, Stephanie Vera, da of Basil M Heald, of Torquay; 1 s, 1 da; *Career* RA (TA) 1920-52, Maj 1938; JP Sheffield 1937-50; memb Iron and Steel Control 1940-44, controller of Ball and Roller Bearings 1944-45, dir British Iron and Steel Fedn 1949-62, dir-gen 1962-66; chm George Senior & Sons Ltd; kt 1970; *Clubs* Naval & Military; *Style*— Sir Edward Senior, CMG; Hollies, Church Close, Brenchley, Tonbridge, Kent (☎ 089 272 2359)

SENIOR, (Alan) Gordon; CBE (1981); s of Oscar Senior (d 1973), of Ash Vale, Surrey, and Helen, *née* Cooper (d 1964); *b* 1 Jan 1928; *Educ* Normanton GS, Leeds Univ (BSc, MSc); *m* 1, Dec 1954 (m dis 1960), Sheila Mary, da of Ernest Lockyer (d 1959), of Normanton, Yorks; m 2, 29 Nov 1968 (m dis 1978), Lawmary Mitchell, da of Lawrence Champion (d 1981), of Cape Town, SA; 1 s (John b 12 Feb 1970); *Career* served UTC and TA 1945-49; engr; with: J B Edwards (Whyteleafe) Ltd 1949-51, Oscar Faber & Ptnrs Consltg Engrs 1951-54, W S Atkins Gp 1954-80 (tech dir 1967); md Atkins Res and Devpt 1971; dir: W S Atkins and Ptnrs 1975, Atkins Franlab Ltd 1977; fndr Gordon Senior Assocs Consltg Engrs 1980; dir: ANSEN Ltd 1981-83, McMillan Sloan and Ptnrs 1981-83, Armstrong Technol Servs ltd 1986-87; chm: Surface Engrg and Inspection Ltd (subsid of Yarrow plc) 1983-86, Masta Corpn Ltd 1987-, Aptech Ltd 1988-; FICE, FIStructE, FRICS, FSUT; *Books* Brittle Fracture of Steel Structures (co-author, 1970); author of various papers on welding, fatigue, brittle fracture and future devpts offshore and in the oceans; *Recreations* food, wine, travel, conversation, skiing; *Clubs* Athenaeum; *Style*— Gordon Senior, Esq, CBE; Deanlands, Normandy, Surrey GU3 2AR (☎ 0483 235 496/235 066)

SENIOR, Michael; DL (Gwynedd 1989); s of Geoffrey Senior (d 1957), of Glan Conwy, N Wales, and Julia Elaine, *née* Cotterell (d 1984); *b* 14 April 1940; *Educ* Uppingham, Open Univ (BA); *Career* writer and farmer; radio play The Coffee Table (1964); *Books* Portrait of North Wales (1973), Portrait of South Wales (1974), Greece and its Myths (1978), Myths of Britain (1979), The Age of Myth and Legend in Heroes and Heroines (1980), Sir Thomas Malory's Tales of King Arthur (ed 1980), The Life and Times of Richard II (1981), Who's Who in Mythology (1985), Conway, The Town's Story (1977), additional local history booklets; *Recreations* hill walking, painting, croquet; *Style*— Michael Senior, Esq, DL; Bryn Eisteddfod, Glan Conwy, Colwyn Bay, N Wales LL28 5LF; c/o David Higham Associates Ltd, 5-8 Lower John Street, London W1R 4HA

SENIOR, Hon Mrs (Rosemary); da of Baron Hunt of Fawley, CBE (Life Peer); *b* 1943; *Educ* St Andrews Univ (MA); *m* 1974, Dr Clive Malcolm Senior; 1 s, 1 da; *Style*— The Hon Mrs Senior; 20 Derby St, Swanbourne, Perth, W Australia

SENTANCE, David Geoffrey; *b* 17 Jan 1930; *Educ* Newark and Grantham Colls, Huddersfield Poly; *m* 1955, Joan Margaret; 2 c; *Career* chartered engr; dir Sutcliffe Engrg Holdings Ltd, md Neils Larson & Son Ltd, dir Recticel Sutcliffe Ltd and Sutcliffe Impact Ltd; MIMechE, MIProdE, CDipAF; *Recreations* music, gardening; *Style*— David Sentance Esq; 21 Far View Crescent, Almondbury, Huddersfield (☎ 0484 27651)

SERGEANT, Sir Patrick John Rushton; s of George and Rene Sergeant; *b* 17 Mar 1924; *Educ* Beaumont Coll; *m* 1952, Gillian, *née* Wilks; 2 da (Harriet, Emma); *Career* Lt RNVR 1945; asst city ed News Chronicle 1948; dep city ed, Daily Mail, 1953; city ed, Daily Mail 1960-84, fndr and md Euromoney Publications 1969-85; chm

Euromoney Publications 1985-; dir, Assoc Newspapers Gp 1971-83; dir, Daily Mail and General Tst 1983- Winner of Wincott Award as Financial Journalist of the Year, 1979; Freeman of the City of London; kt 1984; *Books* Another Road to Samarkand 1955, Money Matters 1967, Inflation Fighters Handbook 1976; *Recreations* tennis, skiing, swimming, talking; *Clubs* RAC, Annabel's, Mark's, Cumberland Lawn Tennis; *Style—* Sir Patrick Sergeant; No 1 The Grove, Highgate Village, London N6; Euromoney Publications Ltd, Nestor House, Playhouse Yard, London EC4V 5EX (☎ (01) 236 3288)

SERGISON-BROOKE, Hon Mrs (Mary Anne); *née* Hare; er da of 1 Viscount Blakenham, OBE, PC (d 1982); *b* 9 April 1936; *m* 1964, Timothy Mark Sergison-Brooke, s late Gen Sir Bertram Norman Sergison-Brooke, KCB, KCVO, CMG, DSO; 1 s, 1 da; *Style—* Hon Mrs Sergison-Brooke; Chipping Warden Manor, Banbury, Oxon

SERIES, Sir (Joseph Michel) Emile; CBE (1974); *b* 29 Sept 1918; *Career* chm and gen mangr Flacq United Estates Ltd 1968-; kt 1978; *Style—* Sir Emile Series, CBE; Flacq United Estates Ltd, Union Flacq, Mauritius

SERLE, Christopher Richard; s of Frank Raymond Serle (d 1988), of Bristol, and Winifred Mary, *née* Pugsley; *b* 13 July 1943; *Educ* Clifton, Trinity Coll Dublin; *m* 22 Jan 983, Anna Catharine, da of Stephen Readhead Southall, of Clifford, Hereford and Worcester; 2 s (Harry b 1983, Jack b 1987); *Career* actor 1964-68, prodr BBC radio and TV 1968-78, TV journalist and presenter; programmes incl: That's Life, In At The Deep End, People; *Recreations* gliding, jazz drumming; *Style—* Christopher Serle, Esq; c/o Curtis Brown, 162-168 Regent St, London W1R 5TB (☎ 01 872 0331)

SERMON, (Thomas) Richard; s of Eric Thomas Sermon (d 1978), of Nottingham, and Marjorie Hilda, *née* Parsons (d 1969); *b* 25 Feb 1947; *Educ* Nottingham HS; *m* 10 Oct 1970, Rosemary Diane, da of Thomas Smith (d 1971), of Sheffield; 1 s (Thomas Christopher b 1971), 1 da (Catherine Marjorie b 1975); *Career* co sec Crest Hotels Ltd 1969-74, dep chm Good Relations Ltd 1974-79; md: Shandwick Conslts Ltd 1979-87, Shandwick Conslt Gp plc 1987-88; chief exec Shandwick Europe plc 1988-; vice pres RADAR; Freeman City of London 1968; Liveryman: Worshipful Co of Wheelwrights 1968, Worshipful Co of Chartered Secs and Administrators 1974; FCIS 1972; *Clubs* City of London, City Livery, Marks; *Style—* Richard Sermon, Esq; 95 Park Lane, London W1, (☎ 01 353 1908, fax 01 355 3244, car tel 0836 240766)

SEROCOLD, Lt-Col Walter Pearce; DSO (1945, TD and Bar 1945); s of Col Oswald Pearce Serocold, CMG, DL (d 1951), of Bucks, and Gwendolyn Pearce Serocold, *née* Combe (d 1966); *b* 11 Oct 1907; *Educ* Eton, Trinity Coll Cambridge; *m* 1, 1937, Ann, da of James Whitehouse; 1 s (Edward b 1938); m 2, 24 Oct 1957, Monica Elizabeth Gibbs, da of Sir Edmund Wyldbore-Smith (d 1938); *Career* Royal Berkshire Regt (TA) 1926-41, reconnaissance corps 1941-44, i/c 2 Derbyshire Yeomanry 1944-45 NW Europe; dir: Whitney Combe Reid & Co Ltd 1937-59, Watney Mann Ltd 1959-68; master of the Brewers Co 1953, chm Governing Body, Aldenham Sch 1964-68; *Recreations* fishing, gardening, travel; *Style—* Lt-Col Walter P Serocold, DSO, TD; Ridge House, Highclere, Newbury, Berks (☎ 0635 253-523)

SEROTA, Baroness (Life Peeress UK 1967); Beatrice; JP (Inner London); da of Alexander Katz; *b* 15 Oct 1919; *Educ* LSE; *m* 1942, Stanley Serota, FICE; 1 s, 1 da; *Career* chm Commission for Local Administration to 1982; memb LCC 1954-65 (chm Children's Ctee 1958-65) and of GLC (Lambeth) 1964-67, memb Advisory Cncl in Child Care and Central Training Cncl in Child Care 1958-68, min of state DHSS 1969-70, Govr BBC 1977-82, pres Nat Cncl for Unmarried Mother and Her Child 1971-; *Style—* The Rt Hon The Lady Serota, JP; The Coach House, 15 Lyndhurst Terrace, London NW3

SEROTA, Hon Nicholas Andrew; o s of Baroness Serota, *qv*; *b* 27 April 1946; *Educ* Haberdashers' Aske's Sch, Christ's Coll Camb, Courtauld Inst (MA); *Career* dir The Tate Gallery; *Style—* The Hon Nicholas Serota; c/o The Tate Gallery, Millbank, London SW1P 4RG

SERPELL, Sir David Radford; KCB (1968, CB 1962), CMG (1952), OBE (1944); s of Charles Robert Serpell (d 1949), of Plymouth, and Elsie Leila Serpell (d 1958); *b* 10 Nov 1911; *Educ* Plymouth Coll, Exeter Coll Oxford, Toulouse Univ, Syracuse Univ NY, Fletcher Sch of Law and Diplomacy USA; *m* 1 (m dis), Ann Dooley; 3 s; m 2, Doris Farr; *Career* entered Civil Service 1939, Minys of Food, Fuel and Power; under-sec Treasy 1954-60, dep sec Miny of Transport 1960-63, second sec BOT 1963-66, second perm sec 1966-68, second sec Tres 1968, perm sec Miny of Transport 1968-70, perm sec Dept of Environment 1970-72; former chm: Nature Conservancy Cncl, Ordnance Survey Review Ctee; former memb Cncl National Trust; memb British Railways Bd 1974-82, memb NERC 1973-76, chm of independent ctee to review BR's finances 1982; *Recreations* golf, walking; *Clubs* Utd Oxford and Cambridge Univ; *Style—* Sir David Serpell, KCB, CMG, OBE; 25 Crossparks, Dartmouth, Devon TQ6 9HP (☎ 080 43 2073)

SERRELL-WATTS, D'Arcy John; s of John Serrell-Watts, CBE, JP (d 1975), of Marlow Place, Bucks, and Cynthia Mary, *née* Mason (d 1969); *b* 12 May 1939; *Educ* Harrow, Lincoln Coll Oxford; *m* 1, 1962 (m dis 1972), Lyn, *née* Tippetts; 1 s (Sebastian John b 1965), 1 da (Arabella Alice b 1968); m 2, 1977 (m dis), Linda, *née* Berry; m 3, 30 June 1987, Slyvaine, da of Comte Bernard de Robinet de Plas; *Career* md HTS Mgmnt Conslts Ltd 1964, vice pres Golightly Int NY 1974, md London Car Telephones Ltd 1982; underwriting memb of Lloyds 1977; Freeman City of London 1960, Warden Worshipful Co of Saddlers 1988; *Recreations* shooting, skiing; *Clubs* Turf; *Style—* D'Arcy Serrell-Watts, Esq; Bacons Farm, Bradwell-on-Sea, Essex; 9 Bedford Gardens House, London W8 7EE (☎ 01 727 2918, fax 01 221 5949)

SERVAES, William Reginald; s of Vice Adm Reginald Maxwell Servaes, CB, CBE (d 1978), and Hilda Edith Anna, *née* Johnson (d 1956); *b* 30 June 1989; *Educ* RNC Dartmouth; *m* 16 Jan 1945, Patricia, da of Percy Charles Vestey (d 1939); 3 s (Michael b 1947 d 1986, James b 1949, Mark b 1963), 2 da (Diana b 1951, Elizabeth b 1953); *Career* Lt RN 1939-46, destroyers, combined ops (despatches 1943); dir: Anderson Green & Co Ltd, (shipowners and brokers, Orient Line) 1952-61, P & O Orient Mgmnt Ltd 1961-63; administrator George Trew Dunn 1963-72; gen mangr Aldeburgh Festival of Music and the Arts 1972-81; *Clubs* Garrick, Lansdowne; *Style—* William Servaes, Esq; Barclays Bank plc, Aldeburgh, Suffolk

SERVATIUS, Hon Mrs (Prunella Jane Alice); da of 9 Baron Hawke (d 1985); *b* 1951; *Educ* Heathfield Sch; *m* 1976, Albert Hendrik Servatius; 2 s (Timothy b 1979, Julian b 1982); *Style—* The Hon Mrs Servatius; Van Alkemadelaan 354, 2597 AS The Hague, Netherlands

SERVICE, Alastair Stanley Douglas; s of Lt-Cdr Douglas Service (d 1976), and Evelyn Caroline, *née* Sharp (d 1986); *b* 8 May 1933; *Educ* Westminster, Queen's Coll Oxford; *m* 1959 (m dis 1984), Louisa Anne, *qv*, da of Lt-Col Henry Hemming; 1 s, 1 da; *Career* writer and publisher; chm: Birth Control Campaign 1970-74, Family Planning Assoc 1975-79, vice-chm Health Educn Cncl 1979-87, gen sec Family Planning Assoc 1980-89, dep-chm Health Education Auth 1987-89; *Books Incl:* A Birth Control Plan for Britain (jt-author, 1972), Edwardian Architecture and its Origins (1975), The Architects of London, 1066-Today (1979), Lost Worlds (1981), A Guide to the Megaliths of Europe (1981), Anglo-Saxon and Norman Buildings of Britain (1982), Edwardian Interiors (1982); *Recreations* cycling, the pursuit of stone circles, mounds and historic buildings; *Clubs* Garrick; *Style—* Alastair Service Esq; Swan House, Avebury, Wilts, (☎ 067 23 312)

SERVICE, Graham Andrew; s of Malcolm James Service, of Highcliffe, Dorset, and Janette Sophia, *née* McAdam; *b* 3 June 1947; *Educ* Kingston GS, Trinity Coll Oxford (BA); *m* 28 June 1974, Susan Elizabeth, da of John Ernest Brooke, of Woking, Surrey; 2 s (Timothy b 1980, Jonathan b 1984); *Career* CA Longcrofts 1969-73, dir corporate fin Hill Samuel Bank Ltd 1973-; FCA 1973; *Style—* Graham Service, Esq; Eagle Lodge, Mile Path, Hook Heath, Woking, Surrey GU22 OJX; 100 Wood St, London EC2P 2AJ (☎ 01 628 8011)

SERVICE, Hon Mrs Hon Helen; da of 2 Baron Loch, CB, CMG, MVO, DSO (d 1942); *b* 1919; *m* 1947, G Ronald Service (d 1961); 1 s; *Style—* The Hon Mrs Service; Kinfauns House, Kinfauns, by Perth

SERVICE, Ms Louisa Anne; JP (1969); da of Lt-Col Henry Hemming, OBE, MC (d 1976), of 35 Elsworthy Rd, London NW3, and Alice Louisa, *née* Weaver, OBE; *b* 13 Dec 1931; *Educ* St Hilda's Coll Oxford (BA, MA) ; *m* 28 Feb 1959 (m dis 1984), Alastair Stanley Douglas, s of Lt-Cdr Douglas Service (d 1976), of 16 Reddington Rd, London NW3; 1 s (Nicholas Alistair McFee Douglas b 9 May 1961), 1 da (Sophia Alice Louisa Douglas b 20 April 1963); *Career* export dir Ladybird Electric 1955-59; jt chm: Municipal Gp of Cos 1976- (fin dir 1966-76), Hemming Publishing 1985-; chm Glass's Guide Serv Ltd 1981- (dir 1971-, dep chm 1976-81); memb mgmnt ctee Friends of Covent Garden 1982-, chm Mayer-Lissman Opera Workshop 1976-, cncl memb Youth and Music 1987-, hon sec Womans India Assoc 1967-74, dep chm Paddington Probation Hostel 1976-86; chm Hackney Juvenile Ct 1975-82, memb ctee of magistrates Westminster Juvenile Ct 1982-88, chm Hammersmith and Fulham Juvenile Ct; memb Dept of Trade's Consumer Credit Appeals Panel 1981-; FRGS; *Recreations* music, travel, reading; *Clubs* Arts; *Style—* Ms Louisa A Service, JP; c/o Hemming Publishing Ltd, 178-202 Great Portland Street, London, W1N 6NH (☎ 01 637 2400, fax 01 631 0360)

SESSFORD, George Minshull; *see*: Moray Ross and Caithness, Bishop of

SETCHELL, David Lloyd; s of Raymond Setchell (d 1967), and Phyllis Jane, *née* Lloyd (d 1952); *b* 16 April 1937; *Educ* Woodhouse GS, Jesus Coll Cambridge (MA); *m* 11 Aug 1962, Muriel Mary; 1 s (Andrew b 1970); 1 da (Justine b 1967); *Career* CA, Peat Marwick London 1960-64, Shawinigan Ltd 1964-71, mktg mangr Gulf Oil Chemicals (Europe) 1971-77, vice-pres Gulf Oil Chemicals (Europe) 1978-82, md Gulf Oil (GB) Ltd 1982-, dir UK Petroleum Industl Assoc; FCA; *Recreations* golf, tennis, theatre; *Clubs* Oriental, MCC, Cotswold Hills Golf; *Style—* David Setchell, Esq; South Hayes, Sandy Lane Rd, Cheltenham, Glos GL53 9DE (☎ 0242 571390); Gulf Oil (GB) Ltd, The Quadrangle, Imperial Square, Cheltenham GL50 1TF (☎ 0242 225300, telex 43542, fax 0242 225365)

SETCHELL, Marcus Edward; s of Eric Hedley Setchell (d 1980), of Cambridge, and Barbara Mary, *née* Whitworth; *b* 4 Oct 1943; *Educ* Felsted Sch, Cambridge Univ, St Bartholomew's Hosp Med Coll (MA, MB, BChir); *m* 1973, Sarah Loveday, da of Vernon Alfred Robert French (d 1967), of Middlesex; 2 s (Thomas b 1976, David b 1984), 2 da (Anna b 1974, Catherine b 1980); *Career* conslt gynaecologist and obstetrician: St Bartholomew's Hosp, King Edward VII Hosp for Offrs, St Luke's Hospital for the Clergy; dir Fertility Unit Portland Hosp; contributor: Ten Teachers Gynaecology (1985), Ten Teachers Obstetrics (1985), Progress in Obstetrics and Gynaecology (1987), General Surgical Operations (1982); FRCS, FRCSEd, FRCOG; *Recreations* tennis, skiing, travel, gardening; *Clubs* Royal Soc of Medicine, Fountain, St Albans Medical; *Style—* Marcus Setchell, Esq; 64 Wood Vale, London N10 3DN (☎ 01 444 5266); 137 Harley Street, London W1 (☎ 01 935 6122)

SETCHIM, Hon Mrs Hon Marjorie Elizabeth; *née* Yerburgh; da (by 1 m) of 1 Baron Alvingham (d 1955); *b* 1916; *m* 1, 1938, Abdul Hamid Mustafa Risk; 1 da; m 2, 1952, Leon Setchim; 1 s; *Style—* The Hon Mrs Setchim; 134 Lynton Rd, London W3

SETH-SMITH, Hon Mrs Hon Gabrielle Mary; *née* Sclater-Booth; yst da of 3 Baron Basing, TD (d 1969); *b* 18 Jan 1929; *m* 1953, Cdr Martin Parnell Seth-Smith, RN, s of Brig Hugh Garden Seth-Smith, DSO; 1 s (Nicholas John b 1961), 1 da (Imogen Gabrielle b 1963); *Career* LTCL; *Style—* The Hon Mrs Seth-Smith; The Triangle, Wildhern, Andover, Hants

SETH-SMITH, Hon Mrs (Moana Elizabeth Jean); *née* McGowan; da of 2 Baron McGowan (d 1966); *b* 1948; *m* 1978, John David Vaughan Seth-Smith; *Style—* The Hon Mrs Seth-Smith

SETON, Sir Iain Bruce; 13 Bt (NS 1663), of Abercorn, Linlithgowshire; s of Sir (Christopher) Bruce Seton, 12 Bt (d 1988) ; *b* 27 August 1942; *Educ* Colchester, Chadacre Agric Inst; *m* 1963, Margaret Ann, o da of Walter Charles Faulkner, of Barlee Road, W Australia: 1 s (Laurence Bruce), 1 da (Amanda Jane b 1971); *Heir* s, Laurence Bruce Seton b 1 July 1968; *Style—* Sir Iain Seton, Bt; PO Box 253, Bridgetown 6255, W Australia

SETON, James Christall; s of late Christall Seton, gs of 7 Bt; hp of kinsman, Sir Robert Seton, 11 Bt; *b* 21 Jan 1913; *m* 1939, Evelyn, da of Ray Hafer; *Career* Private US Army; *Style—* James Seton, Esq; 814 Buckeye St, Miamisburg, Ohio, USA

SETON, Joyce, Lady; Joyce Vivien; *née* Barnard; er da of late Oliver George Barnard, of Lockington House, Stowmarket, Suffolk; *m* 1939, Sir Christopher Bruce Seton, 12 Bt (d 1988); 2 s (Sir Iain Bruce, 13 Bt, *qv*, Michael Charles b 1944), 2 da (Sarah Ann (Mrs Good) (twin) b 1944, Joanna Mary (Mrs Gillespie) b 1946); *Style—* Joyce, Lady Seton; Flat 1B, Papillon House, Balkerne Gdns, Colchester CO1 1PR (☎ 0206 43364)

SETON, Lady Julia; OBE; da of late Frank Clements; *m* 1962, as his 3 w, Sir Alexander Hay Seton, 10 Bt (d 1963); *Career* VMH; *Style—* Lady Julia Seton, OBE; 122 Swan Court, Chelsea Manor St, London SW3 5RU

SETON, Sir Robert James; 11 Bt (NS 1683) of Pitmedden, Aberdeenshire; s of Capt Sir John Hastings Seton, 10 Bt (d 1956); *b* 20 April 1926; *Educ* HMS Worcester

(Thames Nautical Training Coll) 1940-43; *Heir* kinsman, James Seton, *qv*; *Career* midshipman RNVR 1943-45; banker The Hong Kong and Shanghai Bank, ret 1961; *Recreations* philately; *Style*— Sir Robert Seton, Bt; c/o Hong Kong and Shanghai Banking Corporation, 99 Bishopsgate, London EC2

SETTRINGTON, Lord; Charles Henry Gordon-Lennox; s and h of Earl of March and Kinrara, DL; *b* 8 Jan 1955; *Educ* Eton; *m* 1976 (m dis 1989), Sally, da of late Maurice Clayton, and Mrs Dennis Irwin; 1 da (Hon Alexandra b 1985); *Style*— Lord Settrington; Goodwood, Chichester, Sussex

SEVERIN, Prof Dorothy Sherman; s of Wilbur B Sherman, of Dallas, USA, and Virginia, *née* Tucker; *b* 24 Mar 1942; *Educ* Harvard Univ (AB, AM, PhD); *m* 24 March 1966 (m dis 1979), Giles Timothy Severin; 1 da (Ida); *Career* tutor Harvard Univ 1964-66, visiting lectr Univ of West Indies 1967-68, asst prof Vassar Coll NY 1968-69, lectr Westfield Coll London 1969-82, prof of Spanish and head of dept of Hispanic studies Liverpool Univ 1982- (ed Bulletin of Hispanic Studies 1982-); visting assoc prof: Harvard Univ 1982, Columbia Univ NY 1985, Yale Univ 1985); memb Int Courtly Literature Soc (pres Br branch), ctee memb Modern Humanities Res Assoc, memb Assoc of Hispanists of GB and NI; *Books* Memory in La Celestina (1970), Diego de San Pedro, La pasión trobada (1973), La Lengua de Erasmo romancada por muy elegante estilo (ed 1975), Diego de San Pedro, Poesía (ed with Keith Whinnom 1979), cosas sacadas de lab crónica del rey Juan II (ed with Angus Mackay, 1982), Celestina (edns 1969, 1987), Tragicomedy and Novelistic Discourse in Celestina (1989); *Style*— Prof Dorothy Severin; Department of Hispanic Studies, University of Liverpool, PO Box 147, Liverpool L69 3BX (☎ 051 794 2773, fax 051 708 6502, telex 627095 UNILPL G)

SEVERIS, Nicolas Constantine; s of Constantine Demosthenes Severis, of Nicosia Cyprus; *b* 12 Oct 1943; *Educ* Giggleswick Sch, St John's Coll Cambridge (MA); *m* 1967, Michele Louise, da of Frederick Francois, of Antwerp; 2 children; *Career* banker; md Bank of Cyprus (London) Ltd 1969-75, gen mangr American Express Bank Belgium 1978-79, administratore delegato and direttore generale American Express Bank SPA 1979-81; gen mangr: Amex Bank Ltd 1981-82, FVP Europe, M East and Africa Private Banking 1982; centl mangr Trade Devpt Bank Geneva, gen mangr Franck & Cie SA Bankers 1987; *Recreations* golf, tennis, squash; *Clubs* Travellers', RAC, Bonmont (Switzerland); *Style*— Nicolas Severis, Esq; 42 Rue De L'Athenee, 1206 Geneva

SEVERN, Prof Roy Thomas; s of Ernest Severn (d 1988), of Gt Yarmouth, Norfolk, and Muriel, *née* Woollatt (d 1975); *b* 6 Sept 1929; *Educ* Deacon's Sch Peterborough, Gt Yarmouth GS, Imperial Coll London; *m* 12 Sept 1957, Hilary Irene, da of Harold Batty Saxton; 2 da (Fiona Rae b 1960, Elizabeth Louise b 1962); *Career* 2 Lt RE (Survey) 1954-56; lectr Imperial Coll London 1952-54; Bristol Univ: lectr 1956-65, reader 1965-68, prof 1968-, pro vice-chllr 1981-84; memb: UGC tech sub-ctee 1982-, Engrg Bd SERC 1986-, vice pres Inst of Civil Engrs 1987-; FEng 1982; *Style*— Prof Roy Severn; Institution of Civil Engineers, Great George St, London, SW1 (☎ 01 222 7722)

SEVERNE, Air Vice-Marshal John de Milt; LVO (1961), OBE (1968), AFC (1955); s of Dr Alfred de Milt Severne (d 1967), and Joane Mary Margaret, *née* Haydon; *b* 15 August 1925; *Educ* Marlborough; *m* 1951, Katharine Veronica, da of Capt Vero Elliot Kemball, RN (1963); 3 da (Veronica, Amanda, Christina); *Career* joined RAF 1944, flying instr RAF Coll Cranwell 1948, staff instr Central Flying Sch 1950, flt cdr 98 Sqn 1954, sqdn cdr 26 Sqdn 1956, Air Miny 1958, Equerry to HRH The Duke of Edinburgh 1958, Staff Coll 1962, Chief Instr 226 OCU 1963, JSSC 1965, Jt HQ Middle East Cmd Aden and air advsr to S Arabian Govt 1966, directing staff JSSC 1968, Gp Capt ORG HQ STC 1968, stn cdr RAF Kinloss 1971, Royal Coll of Def Studies 1973, Cmdt CFS 1974, Air Cdre Flying Trg HQRAFSC 1976, cdr Southern Maritime Air Region 1978, ret RAF 1980; Capt of The Queen's Flight 1982-89; ADC to HM The Queen 1972-73; pres SW area RAFA 1981, won Kings Cup Air Race and Br Air Racing Champion 1960, pres RAF Equitation Assoc 1976-79 (chm 1973); *Style*— Air Vice-Marshal John de Milt Severne, LVO, OBE, AFC; c/o National Westminster Bank plc, PO Box 20, 91 High St, Maidstone, Kent, ME14 1XT

SEVERNE, Michael Meysey Wigley; s of Capt Edmund Charles Wigley Severne (d 1935), of Thenford House, Banbury, Oxon, and Cecily Mary, *née* Burden-Muller (d 1981); *b* 15 Feb 1922; *Educ* Eton, Jesus Coll Cambridge; *m* 15 April 1952, (Giralda) Rachel, da of Desmond Fitz-Gerald, 28 Knight of Glin (d 1949), of Glin Castle, Co Limerick; 1 da (Amanda Caroline b 1954); *Career* RMA Sandhurst 1940-41, Capt Coldstream Guards 1942-47, dir Damancy Co Ltd (now Aspro Nicholas) 1948-65; md: Technacryl Ltd 1967-, Aluminium and Plastics Ltd 1967-, Argo Plastics Ltd 1980-; *Recreations* shooting, fishing; *Style*— Michael Severne, Esq; Shakenhurst Hall, Cleobury Mortimer, Nr Kidderminster, Worcs (☎ 029922 300); 44 Cheyne Ct, Royal Hospital Rd, London SW3 5TS (☎ 352 1270, car tel 0836 260 953)

SEWARD, Desmond; s of Maj W E L Seward, MC (d 1975); *b* 22 May 1935; *Educ* Ampleforth, St Catharine's Coll Cambridge (BA); *Career* author; Knight SMO Malta 1978; *Books* The First Bourbon (1971), The Monks of War (1972), Prince of the Renaissance (1973), The Bourbon Kings of France (1976), Eleanor of Aquitane (1978), The Hundred Years War (1978), Monks and Wine (1979), Marie Antoinette (1981), Richard III (1983), Naples (1984), Italy's Knights of St George (1986), Napoleon's Family (1986), Henry V (1987), Napoleon and Hitler (1988), Byzantium (with Susan Monntgarret, 1988); *Recreations* walking, France, Italy; *Clubs* Brooks's, Pratt's, Puffin's (Edinburgh); *Style*— Desmond Seward, Esq; 53/54 Regency Square, Brighton BN1 2FF (☎ 0273 23914)

SEWARD, Lady; Ella Maud; da of Frederick L'Estrange Wallace by his w Gwendoline, *née* Gilling-Lax; *m* 1924, Sir Eric Seward, KBE, sometime chm British Chamber of Commerce in The Argentine (d 1981); 3 s; *Style*— Lady Seward; Dr G Rawson 2420, 1636 Olivos, Provincia de Buenos Aires, Argentina

SEWARD, John Richard Gowing; s of Henry Thomas Seward (d 1980), of Bramhall, and Helen Margaret, *née* Gowing (d 1974); *b* 6 Jan 1929; *Educ* Uppingham, Manchester Univ (Dip Arch); *m* 28 July 1955, (Anne) Hilary, da of George Reginald Davies (d 1978), of Marford; 1 s (Charles b 1963), 3 da (Nicola b 1961, Deborah b 1970, Anna b 1973); *Career* Nat Serv 2 Lt 7 Armd Div Engr Regt 1953-55; architect, sr ptnr Crickshank of Seward; princ buildings: HQ Royal London Mutual Insur Soc, Colchester Church and Chaplaincy Manchester Univ, Queen's Elms Halls of Residence Queen's Univ Belfast, Res and Devpt Bldgs ICL West Gorton; pres Manchester Soc Architects 1975-76; RIBA: chm Northwest Region 1977-78, chm practice ctee 1980-81, vice-pres 1980-81; pres: Manchester FC, Gentleman of Cheshire CC; tstee, Uppingham Sch, Broughton House Old Soldiers Home, dep chm of Cncl UMIST FRIBA 1968, FRSA 1982; *Recreations* sport, painting; *Clubs* St James (Manchester), MCC, Free Foresters Cricket; *Style*— John Seward, Esq; The Garden Wood, Henshaw Lane, Siddington, Macclesfield, Cheshire SK11 9JW (☎ 02604 383); Cruickshank & Seward, Architects, Planners, Designers, Royal London Ho, 196 Deansgate, Manchester M3 3WP (☎ 061 832 6161, fax 061 832 0820)

SEWELL, Sir (John) Allan; ISO (1968); s of late George Allan Sewell; *b* 23 July 1915; *Educ* Enoggera State Sch, Brisbane GS; *m* 1939, Thelma (d 1965), da of H S Buchholz; 1 s, 1 da; *Career* dir Local Govt Qld 1948-61, under-tres of Qld 1961-69, former auditor-gen of Qld; chm State Electricty Cmmn, dir Qld Alumina Ltd, Crusader Oil; dep chllr Griffiths Univ; AASA, ACIS, FIMA; kt 1977; *Style*— Sir Allan Sewell, ISO

SEWELL, (Edward Rainforth) Andrew; MC (1942); s of E O Sewell, OBE, MC (d 1979), and Lucy Theodora, *née* Walker (d 1934); *b* 23 Feb 1921; *Educ* Marlborough Coll; *m* 11 Sept 1953, Ishbel, da of Dr J Milne, MC (d 1943); 1 s (John b 1958), 3 da (Anne b 1954, Rosemary b 1956 (d 1982), Elspeth b 1961); *Career* Regular Army 1939-73; war serv Lanarkshire Yeo RA, Malaya; MOD R&D: HM Civil Serv 1973-81, princ DOE /Dept Tport, chief admin offr Countryside Cmmn SW Regnl Off; chm Wilts Archaeological and Natural History Soc; *Recreations* archaeology, local history; *Style*— Andrew Sewell, Esq, MC; Bay House, Aldbourne, Wiltshire

SEWELL, Maj David Nigel Wynn; eld s of Maj Geoffrey Richard Michael Sewell (d 1983), of Tysoe Manor, Tysoe, Warwick, and Joan, yst da of Sir Watkin Williams-Wynn, 8 Bt; *b* 4 April 1953; *Educ* Harrow; *m* 17 April 1982, Julia Anne; 2 s (Percy b 1984, Herbert b 1986); *Career* cmmnd Gren Gds 1974, served BAOR, N Ireland, Berlin, London; *Recreations* shooting, fishing, woodwork; *Style*— Maj David Sewell; Midland Bank plc, Shipston-on-Stour, Warwick; 2 Crew Gos The Barrack Caterham, Surrey CR3 5YB

SEWELL, Col John Walter (Toby); s of Lt-Col Edward Owen Sewell, OBE, MC (d 1978), of Radlett, Herts, and Lucy Theodora, *née* Walker (d 1934); *b* 13 Jan 1923; *Educ* Marlborough, Staff Coll Camberley; *m* 29 Jan 1948, Muriel Maureen, da of Leonard Hyde, of Lincoln; 1 s (Nicholas b 1951), 1 da (Sarah (Mrs Wadham) b 1949); *Career* enlisted Grenadier Gds 1941, cmmnd Queen's Royal Regt 1942, Italy 1943-45 (wounded, despatches twice), India 1946-47, seconded Para Regt 1947-53, active serv Palestine 1948, Staff Coll Camberley 1954, Egypt 1955, active serv Cyprus 1955-56, Aden and Hong Kong 1962-63, active serv Borneo 1965, cmd 1 Bn Queens Royal Surrey Regt/Queen's Regt Germany and Bahrein 1965-68, Col 1969, sr army liaison offr RAF 1972-74, ret 1978; re-employed (RO 1) as schs liaison offr 1978-83; pres The Queen's Royal Surrey Regt Assoc 1983, chm diocesan advsy ctee Guildford Diocese 1987; Freeman: City of London 1953, Worshipful Co of Merchant Taylors 1953; FBIM 1979; *Clubs* Army & Navy; *Style*— Col J W Sewell; Uplands, Grayswood Road, Haslemere, Surrey GU27 2BS (☎ 0428 4543)

SEWELL, Robert Henry; s of Dr James Scott Sewell (d 1952), and Emily, *née* Patton (d 1960); *b* 21 Sept 1920; *Educ* Bolton Sch, Manchester Univ, Manchester Royal Infirmary (BSc, MB, ChB, MRCS, LRCP, ChM); *m* 20 July 1945, (Peggy) Joan Kearton, da of Albert Chandler (d 1970), of The Gables, Kingswood Way, Selsdon, Sanderstead, Surrey; 2 da (Gay Whittaker b 1949, Cherry Sewell b 1951); *Career* RAMC: cmmnd Lt 1946, Capt 1947, surgn to N and S Caribbean Cmds 1946-48; house appts Manchester Royal Infirmary 1943-46, registrar and sr registrar Royal Nat Orthopaedic Hosp London 1948-52, conslt orthopaedic surgn Greenwich 1952-83; memb Greenwich Dist Health Authy 1970; Freeman City of London, Liveryman Worshipful Co of Apothecaries; FRCS, FRCS (Edin), FRSM; *Recreations* travel, gardening, bridge; *Style*— Robert Sewell, Esq; 4 Bayards, Warlingham, Surrey CR3 9BP (☎ 08832 4343)

SEWELL-RUTTER, John Stuart; s of Albert Alfred Sewell-Rutter (d 1983), and Edith, *née* Greeno; *b* 28 August 1943; *Educ* Harrow Co GS, London Poly Sch of Commerce, Brunel Univ (BSc, MTech); *m* 15 Sept 1973, Jean Joseanne, da of Ronald Norman Wood (d 1989), of Battenhall, Worcester; 1 s (Neil b 2 June 1976); *Career* mkt res asst Nabisco Ltd 1963-64, mktg servs mangr Leo Burnett Co Ltd 1964-68, brand mangr Cadbury-Schweppes Ltd 1968-71, mktg mangr Tower Housewares Ltd 1971-73; md: Whitecroft-Scovill Ltd 1982-87 (mktg dir 1973-82), J & J Cash Ltd 1987-; former: chm and pres Tewkesbury Round Table, chm Tewkesbury Carnival Ctee; fndr memb Bredon Hill Rotary Club, life memb Nat Tst, life fell Wild Fowl Tst; MBIM, MInstM; *Recreations* golf, donkeys, country life; *Clubs* Tewkesbury Park Golf and Country; *Style*— John Sewell-Rutter, Esq; J & J Cash Ltd, Torrington Ave, Coventry CV4 9UZ (☎ 0203 466 466, fax 0203 462 525, telex 31397 Cash CVG)

SEXTON, Maj Gen Francis Michael; CB (1980), OBE (1966); s of Timothy Sexton and Catherine Regan; *b* 15 July 1923; *Educ* Oxford Univ (MA); *m* 1947, Naomi, da of Bertram Alonzo Middleton; 1 s (Christopher), 1 da (Deborah); *Career* Maj Gen; dir Military Survey 1980, inspr Panel of Independant Insprs 1980, bursar St Peters Coll Oxford 1980-85 (fell); *Clubs* MCC, Army and Navy, Geographical Soc; *Style*— Maj Gen Michael Sexton, CB, OBE; Pipers Croft, Elsenwood Cres, Camberley, Surrey

SEXTON, Jean Margaret; da of Alistair George Charles Robertson (d 1959), of Barnet SW13, and Eileen Margaret, *née* Henman (d 1973); *b* 1 May 1937; *Educ* Putney HS, Nat Coll of Domestic Subjects; *m* 2 Sept 1959, Reginald Clair Sexton, s of Reginald A W Sexton (d 1985); *Career* Int Lawn Tennis Referee (MIPTC), asst referee at Wimbledon Championships 1983-; cncl memb Lawn Tennis Assoc (LTA), vice-pres Br Womens Tennis Assoc (BWTA), chm Nat Assoc for Gifted Children 1984-; *Recreations* playing tennis, needlepoint; *Clubs* Sheen LTS (chm); *Style*— Mrs Jean Sexton; Parkview, 24 Fife Rd, East Sheen, London SW14 7EL (☎ 01 876 3695)

SEYMOUR, Lady Anne Frances Mary; only da of 18 Duke of Somerset, DL (d 1984); *b* 1954; *Style*— Lady Anne Seymour

SEYMOUR, Lady Anne Katherine; da of 8 Marquess of Hertford; *b* 1966; *Style*— Lady Anne Seymour; Ragley Hall, Alcester, Warwicks

SEYMOUR, Lady Carolyn Mary; da of 8 Marquess of Hertford; *b* 1960; *Style*— Lady Carolyn Seymour; Ragley Hall, Alcester, Warwicks

SEYMOUR, Christopher Mark; s of Christopher George Seymour (d 1982), of Pamphius Bentley, Farnham, and Honor Catherine, *née* Leatham; *b* 10 Sept 1942; *Educ* Eton, Dartmouth RNC; *m* Carol Daphne, da of Peter Reginald Crawford Pitman, of Pelts Cottage, Swanmore, Bishops Waltham, Hants; 2 s (Thomas Mark Middleton b 1972, Peter Christopher James b 1977), 1 da (Katherine Louise b 1970); *Career* RN

1960-70, Submarine Service, Lieut; assoc dir Christie & Co 1978-82, principal Mark Seymour Specialist Estate Agency 1982; *Recreations* skiing, outdoor activities; *Clubs* RN Ski; *Style—* Christopher Seymour, Esq; The Mill House, Fintry, Stirlingshire G63 0YD (☎ 0360 86342/86581, fax 0360 86348, car tell 0860 614724)

SEYMOUR, Lady Diana Helen; da of 8 Marquess of Hertford; *b* 1963; *Style—* Lady Diana Seymour; Ragley Hall, Alcester, Warwicks

SEYMOUR, Lord Francis Charles Edward; yr s of 18 Duke of Somerset, DL (d 1984); bro of 19 Duke of Somerset, *qv*; *b* 10 August 1956; *Educ* Eton; *m* 1982, Paddy, yr da of Col Anthony John Irvine Poynder, MC, RE, of Gassons, Slindon, W Sussex; 1 da (b 25 Sept 1988); *Career* slr, memb HAC, dir Guinness Flight Global Asset Mgmnt; *Recreations* shooting, eating, collecting military vehicles; *Clubs* MCC; *Style—* Lord Francis Seymour; 27 Palliser Road, London W14

SEYMOUR, George FitzRoy; JP (Nottinghamshire 1960-), DL (Nottinghamshire 1973-); s of Richard Sturgis Seymour, MVO (d 1959, himself gggs of 1 Marquess of Hertford), of 108 Swan Court, Chelsea SW3, and Lady Victoria Alexandrina Mabel FitzRoy (d 1969, sis of 10 Duke of Grafton); *b* 8 Feb 1923; *Educ* Winchester; *m* 1 June 1946, Hon Rosemary, *née* Scott-Ellis, *qv* da of 8 Baron Howard de Walden; *qv* 1 s (Thomas b 1952), 1 da (Miranda b 1948); *Career* War Service: 60 Rifles 1941-42 (invalided out); landowner; Lord of the Manor of Thrumpton (and Patron of the Living); High Sheriff of Nottinghamshire 1966; *Recreations* shooting, stalking; *Clubs* White's, Pratts', MCC; *Style—* George Seymour, Esq, JP, DL; Thrumpton Hall, Notts (☎ 0602 830333); 38 Molyneux St, London W1 (☎ 01 262 7684)

SEYMOUR, Jane; da of John Frankenberg, of Hillingdon, Middx, and Mieke, *née* van Tricht; *b* 15 Feb 1951; *Educ* Wimbledon HS, Arts Educnl Tst; *m* 1, (m dis), Michael Attenborough; m 2, (m dis), Geoffrey Planer; m 3, 18 July 1981, David Flynn, s of Lloyd Flynn, of Santa Barbara, California; 1 s (Sean Michael b 31 July 1985), 1 da (Katherine Jane b 7 Jan 1982); *Career* actress; films incl: Live and Let Die 1971, Somewhere in Time 1980, The French Revolution 1989; tv incl: The Onedin Line 1973, East of Eden (Golden Globe Award) 1981, Oh, Heavenly Dog 1981, Lassiter 1984, The Woman He Loved 1987, Onassis (Emmy Award) 1988, War and Remembrance 1988; theatre work incl: Amadeus Broadway 1981; hon chm RP Fndn USA (fighting blindness); hon citizen Illinois USA 1977; *Books* Jane Seymour's Guide to Romantic Living (1987); *Style—* Miss Jane Seymour; c/o James Sharkey & Assoc, 3rd Floor Suite, 15 Golden Sq, London W1R 3AG (☎ 01 434 3801); CAA USA (☎ 213 277 3000)

SEYMOUR, Hon Mrs Mary Quenelda; da of 1 Baron Ismay (d 1965); *b* 1929; *m* 1, 1952, Robert Mervyn Fitz Finnis (d 1955); 2 da; m 2, 1957, Maj George Raymond Seymour, LVO, *qv*; 1 da; *Style—* The Hon Mrs Seymour; The Old Vicarage, Bucklebury, Reading, Berks (☎ 0734 712504); Appletrees, Swains Rd, Bembridge, Isle of Wight (☎ 0983 872760)

SEYMOUR, Maj (George) Raymond; LVO (1972); s of Sir Reginald Seymour, KCVO (gs of Rt Hon Sir George Seymour, GCB, GCH, PC, and Hon Gertrude, da of 21 Baron Dacre; Sir George was gs of 1 Marquess of Hertford, KG); *b* 5 May 1923; *Educ* Eton; *m* 1957, Hon Mary Quenelda Stanley, *qv*, da of Gen 1 Baron Ismay (extinct 1965); 1 da, 2 step da; *Career* Maj KRRC, served Palestine, Germany; dir: J R Phillips & Co, chm W H Brakspear & Sons; *Recreations* sailing, fishing, shooting; *Clubs* Boodle's; *Style—* Maj Raymond Seymour, LVO; The Old Vicarage, Bucklebury, Reading, Berks (☎ 0734 712504) Appletrees, Swains Rd, Bembridge, Isle of Wight (☎ 0983 872760)

SEYMOUR, Hon Mrs Rosemary Nest; *née* Scott-Ellis; da of 8 Baron Howard de Walden and 4 Baron Seaford (d 1946), and Margherita, CBE, er da of late Charles Van Raalte, JP; *b* 28 Oct 1922; *m* 1946, George FitzRoy Seymour, *qv*, yr s of Richard Sturgis Seymour, MVO (d 1959); 1 s, 1 da; *Style—* The Hon Mrs Seymour; Thrumpton Hall, Nottingham (☎ 0602 830333); 38 Molyneux St, London W1 (☎ 01 262 7684)

SEYMOUR, Lord; Sebastian Edward Seymour; s and h of 19 Duke of Somerset; *b* 3 Feb 1982; *Style—* Lord Seymour

SEYMOUR, Lady Susan Mary; da of late 17 Duke of Somerset, DSO, OBE; *b* 26 April 1913; *Career* Cdt Wilts 36 Red Cross Detachment 1939-45, late Div Pres; Red Cross Long Service Medal; *Style—* Lady Susan Seymour; Sunnyside, Maiden Bradley, Wilts

SEYMOUR, Maj William Napier; s of Lt-Col Charles Hugh Napier Seymour, DSO (d 1933), and Mary Adelaide; *b* 8 Sept 1914; *Educ* Eton; *m* 28 April 1945, Rachel Mary, da of Angus Hambro (d 1957); 3 da (Carolyn b 1946, Sarah b 1947, Arabella b 1952); *Career* cmmnd Scots Gds 1934; served: Palestine, Western Desert, Burma (despatches), Malaya (left Army 1949); land agent to Crichel Estate for 30 years; author of eight books incl Ordeal by Ambition, a biography of ancestor Edward Seymour, Duke of Somerset and Protector of the Realm; *Recreations* shooting, golf, racing; *Clubs* Army and Navy, Pratts; *Style—* Maj William Seymour; Park House, Shaftesbury, Dorset

SEYMOUR-NEWTON, Cyril Terence; s of Maj Cyril Frank Newton (d 1978), of Guersey, CI, and Mary Jane Frances Fermoix de Chantal Newton, *née* Gallagher (d 1976); *b* 8 Sept 1927; *Educ* Ampleforth, Trinity Coll, Cambridge; *m* 31 Jan 1964, Carol, da of Lt-Col Ivor Watkins Birts (ka 1944); 1 s (Rupert Edward Cyril 3 Nov 1968); *Career* elected underwriting memb Lloyds 1954 (joined Lloyds 1949); dir (at Lloyds): Seymour-Newton Ltd 1964-89 (fndr and chm), Shead Gray Ltd 1966-72, Halford Shead Underwriting Agencies Ltd 1968-72, Crump & Johnson Underwriting Agencies Ltd 1980-, Crump & Cackett Agencies Ltd 1983-, RK Harrison Underwriting Agencies Ltd 1986-89, Wendover Underwriting Agency Ltd 1987-; dir : London & Provincial Insurances Ltd 1962-72, Merritt Houthwaite Ltd 1962-64, Seton Wines Ltd 1964-72 (fndr and chm), Halford Shead Life & Pensions Ltd 1968-72; hon tres 1900 Club 1978- (memb ctee 1970-, hon sec 1973-78), cncl of the PDSA 1968-82 (dep chm 1971-82); Freeman City of London 1955, Liveryman Worshipful Co Coachmakers and Coach Harness Makers 1955; *Recreations* reading, music, big game fishing; *Clubs* Brooks's, MCC, 1900; *Style—* T Seymour-Newton, Esq; 21 Ennismore Gdns, London SW7 1AB (☎ 01 584 3143); La Canova, Nr Pollensa, Mallorca; Wendover Underwriting Agency Ltd, 3 St Helen's Place, London EC3A 6AU (☎ 01 628 1317, fax 01 628 1713)

SEYS LLEWELLYN, His Hon Judge John Desmond; s of Charles Ernest Llewellyn (d 1957), and Hannah Margretta Llewellyn (d 1961); *b* 3 May 1912; *Educ* Cardiff HS, Jesus Coll Oxford (MA); *m* 1, 1939, Elaine (d 1984), da of Henry Leonard Procher (d 1961); m 2, 1986, Joan, da of Reginald Holmes-Cuming, JP, of Plymouth; 3 s; *Career* serv RTR 1940-46 (Capt); barr Inner Temple 1945, practising Wales and Chester circuit 1947-71, dep chm Cheshire QS 1968-71, county ct judge 1971, circuit judge 1972; contested Chester (Lib) 1955 and 1956; Profumo - Prizeman 1947; *Recreations* travel, art, archaeology, English Setters; *Clubs* Athenaeum (Liverpool); *Style—* His Hon Judge John Seys Llewellyn; Little Chetwyn, Gresford, Clwyd (☎ 097 883 2419)

SHACKLES, (Derek George) Guy; s of Derek Holmes Shackles, CBE (d 1973), of Argyll, and Lella Dalglish Shackles (d 1980); *b* 19 Oct 1936; *Educ* Edinburgh Acad; *Career* slr, qualified 1959; clerk to Gen Cmmrs of Taxes, sr ptnr Shackles Slrs; *Recreations* yacht racing, yacht cruising, youth seamanship trg; *Clubs* Royal Ocean Racing, Royal Yorkshire Yacht; *Style—* Guy Shackles, Esq; Chequers, 64 A South Marine Drive, Bridlington, E Yorkshire (☎ 0262 676781); Merrs Shackles, 7 Land of Green Ginger, Hull, Humberside (☎ 0482 26404)

SHACKLETON, Lady Caroline Harriet; *née* Hastings; da of 15 Earl of Huntingdon and his 2 w, Margaret, *née* Lane; *b* 12 June 1946; *Educ* St Paul's Girls' Sch, Edinburgh Univ (MA), Oxford Univ (BA), London Univ (MPhil, PhD); *m* 1970, Hon Charles Edward Ernest Shackleton (d 1979), s of Baron Shackleton, KG, OBE, PC (Life Peer); *Career* lectr in clinical psychology London Univ 1977-82; clinical and research psychologist 1982-; *Style—* Lady Caroline Shackleton

SHACKLETON, Baron (Life Peer UK 1958); Edward Arthur Alexander Shackleton; KG (1974), OBE (1945), PC (1966); s of late Sir Ernest Shackleton, CVO, OBE, the explorer of the Antarctic; *b* 15 July 1911; *Educ* Radley, Magdalen Coll Oxford (MA); *m* 1938, Betty, da of Capt Charles E Homan, Elder Bro of Trinity House; (1 s decd), 1 da; *Career* accompanied expeditions: Borneo and Sarawak 1932, Ellesmere Land 1934-35; author, lectr, broadcaster; lecture tours in Europe and America; served WW II RAF, Naval and Military Intelligence Air Miny, Wing Cdr (despatches 2); MP (Lab) Preston 1946-50, Preston S 1950-55, min Defence for RAF 1964-67, min without portfolio and dep leader House of Lords 1967-68, PMG 1968, Lord Privy Seal 1968-70, leader House of Lords 1968-70, min in charge CSD 1968-70, oppn leader House of Lords 1970-74; chm: advsy cncl on Oil Pollution 1962-64, Political Honours Scrutiny Ctee 1976-, Economic Survey of Falkland Islands 1976 (updated 1982), report on Anti-Terrorist Legislation 1978, East European Trade Cncl 1977-86; chm Lords select ctee Sci and Technol; sr exec and dir J Lewis Partnership 1955-64, chm RTZ Devpt Enterprises 1973-83, dep chm RTZ Corpn 1975-82 (exec dir 1973-82), chm Anglesey Aluminium Ltd 1981-85; pres: RGS 1971-74, Parly & Scientific Ctee 1976-80, Br Standards Inst 1977-80; hon elder brother Trinity House 1980, Hon LLD Newfoundland 1970, Hon DSc Warwick 1978, Hon DSc Southampton Univ, Hon fell Magdalen Coll and St Hugh's Coll Oxford; Freedom of Stanley (Falkland Islands) 1988; FBIM; *Publications* Arctic Journeys, Nansen the Explorer, Borneo Jungle (pt-author); *Style—* The Rt Hon the Lord Shackleton, KG, OBE, PC; Cleveland House, 19 St James's Square, London SW1Y 4JG (☎ 01 930 1752/01 930 8697)

SHAFFER, Peter Levin; CBE (1987); s of Jack Shaffer (d 1987), of London, and Reka, *née* Fredman; *b* 15 May 1926; *Educ* St Pauls London; Trinity Coll Cambridge; *Career* playwright: Five Finger Exercise (1958), The Private Ear, The Public Eye (1961), The Royal Hunt of the Sun (1964), Black Comedy (1965), The Battle of Shrivings (1967), Equus (1973), Amadeus (1979), Yonadab (1986), Lettice and Lovage (1987); screeplays: Equus (1977), Amadeus (1984); *Recreations* walking; *Clubs* Garrick, Arts London; *Style—* Peter L Shaffer, Esq, CBE; Lloyds Bank, Kensington, London

SHAFTO, Robert James; s of George Oliver Holt Shafto (d 1980), and Kathleen Mary, *née* Offer; *b* 4 Dec 1938; *Educ* Epsom Coll; *Career* audit ptnr Smith & Williamson 1969-81, sr ptnr Stainton & Shafto 1982-; dir Bavington Mgmnt Ltd 1983-; Methodist local preacher 1980-; FCA 1961; *Books* Tax Aspects of Personal Investments (1984), Investments Other Than Land (1987); *Recreations* genealogy, mountain walking; *Style—* Robert Shafto, Esq; 7 Walkerscroft Mead, Dulwich, London SE21 8LJ (☎ 01 670 6350); 21 Wigmore St, London W1H 9LA (☎ 01 491 7355, fax 01 493 7177)

SHAKERLEY, Lady; Barbara Storrs; JP (Glos 1962); da of J Howard, JP, of Kidderminster; *m* 1932, Lt-Col Sir Geoffrey Shakerley, CBE, MC, TD (d 1982), sometime vice-Lt Glos, chm Glos CC; 2 s, 2 da; *Style—* Lady Shakerley, JP; The Old Barn, Sevenhampton, nr Cheltenham, Glos GL54 5SW (☎ Andoversford 402)

SHAKERLEY, Charles Frederick Eardley; s of late Maj Sir Cyril Shakerley, 5 Bt and bro of Sir Geoffrey Shakerley, 6 Bt, *qv*; *b* 14 June 1934; *Educ* Harrow, Ch Ch Oxford, Univ of Pennsylvania; *m* 1962, Lucy Carolyn, da of Francis St G Fisher of Cragg, Cockermouth, Cumbria; 3 da; *Career* chm Provincial Insurance Co Ltd 1977-, dir Williams and Glyn's 1980-5, Royal Bank of Scotland Gp 1985; former memb Stock Exchange, sr ptnr Roger Mortimer & Co 1970-75; *Recreations* forestry, shooting, fishing; *Clubs* Brooks's; *Style—* Charles Shakerley, Esq; Cudworth Manor, Newdigate, Surrey (☎ 030 677 275)

SHAKERLEY, Lady Elizabeth Georgiana; *née* Anson; granted style, rank and precedence of an Earl's da 1961; da of Lt-Col Thomas William Arnold, Viscount Anson (d 1958), and late Princess Anne of Denmark, *née* Anne Bowes-Lyon; sis of 5 Earl of Lichfield; *b* 7 June 1941, (HM King George VI stood sponsor); *m* 1972, as his 2 wife, Sir Geoffrey Adam Shakerley, 6 Bt, *qv*; 1 da; *Career* proprietress Party Planners, dir Kanga, dir Mosimann's (a memb's only dining club); *Books* Lady Elizabeth Anson's Party Planners Book (1986); *Style—* Lady Elizabeth Shakerley; 56 Ladbroke Grove, London W11 2PB

SHAKERLEY, Sir Geoffrey Adam; 6 Bt (UK 1838) of Somerford Park, Cheshire; s of Maj Sir Cyril Holland Shakerley, 5 Bt (d 1970) and Elizabeth, MBE, da of late Edward Gwynne Eardley-Wilmot, gggda of Sir John Eardley Eardley-Wilmot, 1 Bt; *b* 9 Dec 1932; *Educ* Harrow, Trinity Coll Oxford; *m* 1, 1962, Virginia Elizabeth (d 1968), da of W E Maskell; 2 s; m 2, 1972, Lady Elizabeth, *née* Anson, *qv*; 1 da; *Heir* s, Nicholas Shakerley; *Career* 2 Lt KRRC; dir Phonographic Records Ltd 1970-; *Style—* Sir Geoffrey Shakerley, Bt; 57 Artesian Rd, London W2 5DB

SHAKERLEY, Nicholas Simon Adam; s (by 1 m) and h of Sir Geoffrey Shakerley, 6 Bt; *b* 20 Dec 1963; *Style—* Nicholas Shakerley Esq

SHAKESPEARE, Elizabeth, Lady; Elizabeth; da of Brig-Gen Robert Hare, CMG, DSO, DL (d 1953; great nephew of 2 Earl of Listowel), and Helen Mary, *née* Atkinson (d 1972); *b* 4 May 1914; *m* 29 Feb 1952, as his 2 w, Rt Hon Sir Geoffrey Shakespeare, 1 Bt, PC (d 1980); *Career* serv WWII, Section Offr WAAF (despatches); Bronze Star (USA); Freeman City of London 1974; *Recreations* gardening, travel;

Style— Elizabeth, Lady Shakespeare; Flat 6, Great Ash, Lubbock Rd, Chislehurst, Kent BR7 5JZ

SHAKESPEARE, John William Richmond; CMG (1985), LVO (1968); s of Dr William Goodman Shakespeare (d 1975), and Ruth, *née* Etty; *b* 11 June 1930; *Educ* Winchester, Trinity Coll Oxford (MA); *m* 1955, Lalage Ann, da of S P B Mais (d 1975), of Lindfield, Sussex; 3 s, 1 da; *Career* served Irish Gds 1949-50, 2 Lt; lectr Ecole Normale Supérieure Paris 1953-54, on editorial staff The Times 1955-59; Dip Serv; FCO 1959, served Paris, Phnom Penh, Singapore, Rio de Janeiro, FCO 1969-73, cnsllr Buenos Aires 1973-75, chargé d'affaires Buenos Aires 1976-77, head Mexico and Caribbean Dept FCO 1977-79, cnsllr Lisbon 1979-83, ambass to Peru 1983-87, ambass to Morocco 1987-; *Recreations* swimming, tennis, walking, gardening; *Style—* HE Mr John Shakespeare, CMG, LVO; British Embassy, Rabat, Morocco; Foreign and Commonwealth Office, King Charles St, London SW1

SHAKESPEARE, Sir William Geoffrey; 2 Bt (UK 1942) of Lakenham, City of Norwich; s of Rt Hon Sir Geoffrey Hithersay Shakespeare, 1 Bt, PC (d 1980), by his 1 w, Aimée (d 1950), da of Walter Loveridge and widow of Cdr Sir Thomas Fisher, RN; half-bro of Sir Nigel Fisher, KCB, MC, *qv*; *b* 12 Oct 1927; *Educ* Radley, Clare Coll Cambridge (MA), St George's Hosp Cambridge (MB, BChir), DCH England; *m* 1964, Susan Mary, da of A Douglas Raffel (d 1965), of Colombo, Ceylon; 2 s; *Heir* s, Thomas William Shakespeare b 11 May 1966; *Career* GP 1968-; clinical asst Manor House Hosp Aylesbury 1972-; registrar: St George's Hosp 1961-63, Stoke Mandeville Hosp 1964-66; memb Snowdon working party into Integration of Handicapped; vice-pres: Physically Handicapped and Able-Bodied 1977-, Assoc for Research into Restricted Growth (ARRG) 1982; *Recreations* gardening, reading; *Clubs* MCC, Leander, Stewards' Enclosure Henley Regatta; *Style—* Sir William Shakespeare, Bt

SHALE, Christopher Michael Henry; s of Michael Thomas Shale, of Edinburgh, and Norma Clementine, *née* Swan; *b* 23 August 1954; *Educ* Oakham Sch, RMA Sandhurst; *Career* cmmnd 17/21 Lancers 1975, ADC to Field Marshal Sir Richard Hull for Queens Silver Jubilee Parade 1977; dir Bede Securities Ltd 1983-85, md SGL Ltd 1983-85; chm: SGL Communications plc 1985-, SGL Corporate Ltd 1985-, SGL Consumer Ltd 1986-, SGL Property Ltd 1987-, Kingsgate Communications Ltd 1987-; SGL Leisure Ltd 1988-, Air Call Med Servs Ltd 1988-; *Recreations* shooting, fishing; *Clubs* Cavalry and Guards, Annabels; *Style—* Christopher Shale, Esq; c/o Cavalry and Guards Club, London W1; SGL Communications plc, Kingsgate House, 536 King's Rd, London SW10 0UH (☎ 01 351 2377, fax 01 351 4207)

SHALLOW, Col (John) David; MC (1951); s of George Shallow (d 1971), of Wraxall, Somerset, and Phyllis Margaret, *née* Dawson (d 1988); *b* 4 June 1927; *Educ* Allhallows Sch Rousdon Devon; *m* 9 Sept 1952, Sally Robertson, da of Eric James Gordon Gibb, MC (d 1977), of S Africa; 2 s (Christopher Patrick b 9 Sept 1953, Andrew John Robertson b 7 May 1957), 1 da (Rosalind b 23 March 1961); *Career* RM; cmmd Jan 1945, HMS Leander 1946-47, 40 Commando 1948-51, Royal Naval Coll Dartmouth 1953-55, HMS Newfoundland 1958-59, mil asst to Cdt Gen 1959-60, RAF Staff Coll psa 1961, 40 Commando 1963-65, Jt Servs Staff Coll Latimer 1967, asst sec Chiefs of Staff Ctee 1968-70, GSO1 HQ Commando Forces 1970-71, exchange appt US Marine Corps 1971-72, CO RM Eastney and CSO 1973-75, CO RM Deal and Cmdt Sch of Music 1976-77, ret 1978; entered Civil Serv; Civil Def Coll: tutor 1978, gp dir 1984, vice princ and dir of studies 1986; churchwarden; Freeman City of London 1976; FBIM 1977; *Style—* Col David Shallow, MC

SHAMAH, Shani Beverly; da of Ellis Pruchine, of Cardiff, and Mamie, *née* Stross; *b* 12 Feb 1957; *Educ* Cardiff High for Girls, Univ of Wales, Inst of Science and Technol (BSc); *m* 5 April 1981, Ellis Jonathan Shamah, s of Menahem Zion Shamah (d 1979); 2 da (Samantha Michal b 1984, Gemma Stefannie Laya b 1987); *Career* consultant of Treasury; *Recreations* tennis, squash; *Clubs* RAC, Network, Lawn Tennis Assoc; *Style—* Mrs Shani Shamah; Normura Bank International plc, Nomura House, 24 Monument St, London EC3R 8AJ (☎ 01 623 9553, fax 626 0951, telex 9413065)

SHAMMAS, Claude Jean; *b* 29 April 1941; *Educ* Seaford Coll, Loughborough Univ; *Career* dir Cole Gp plc; chm Plastic Prods Ltd (subsidiary of Cole Gp); *Clubs* Roehampton; *Style—* Claude Shammas, Esq; 9 St Mary's Rd, London SW19 7DF (☎ 01 947 3016); Cole Group plc, Whitecliff House, 852 Brighton Rd, Purley, Surrey CR2 2UY (☎ 01 686 4411)

SHAND, Alexander Thomas Basil; CBE (1984); s of Lt-Col T Shand (d 1953); *b* 26 Oct 1925; *Educ* Oundle School, Nottingham Univ; *Career* civil engineer; dir Charter Consolidated Ltd, chm Alexander Shand (Holdings) Ltd, pres Federation of Civil Engrg Contractors; *Recreations* music, opera, old houses; *Clubs* Hurlingham; *Style—* Alexander Shand, Esq, CBE; Horham Hall, Thaxted, Essex (☎ 0371 830 389)

SHAND, Maj Bruce Middleton Hope; MC (1940) and bar (1942), DL (1962); s of Philip Morton Shand (d 1960); *b* 22 Jan 1917; *Educ* Rugby, RMC Sandhurst; *m* 1946, Hon Rosalind Maud Cubitt, *qv*; 1 s (Mark Roland b 1951), 2 da (Camilla Parker-Bowles, *qv*; Sonia Annabel b 1949, m 1972 Simon, s of late Air Ch Marshal Sir William Elliot, GCVO, KCB, KBE, DFC; 1 s, 2 da); *Career* Maj 12 Royal Lancers, ret 1947, Clerk of the Cheque and Adj Queen's Bodyguard of the Yeomen of the Guard 1985 (Ensign 1978, Exon 1971), ret 1987; vice-Lord-Lt E Sussex 1974-; *Recreations* hunting, gardening; *Clubs* Cavalry and Guards; *Style—* Maj Bruce Shand, MC; The Laines, Plumpton, nr Lewes, E Sussex (☎ 0273 890248)

SHAND, His Honour Judge; John Alexander Ogilvie Shand; s of Alexander Shand, MBE, QPM (d 1968; of West Bridgeford, Notts, and Marguerite Marie, *née* Farcy; *b* 6 Nov 1942; *Educ* Nottingham HS, Queens' Coll Cambridge (MA, LLB, Chancellor's Medal for Law 1965); *m* 18 Dec 1965 (m dis 1988), Patricia Margaret, da of Frederick Toynbee, Nottingham (d 1958); 2 s (James b 1967, Simon b 1972), 1 da (Juliet b 1969); *Career* barr Middle Temple 1965; Midland and Oxford circuit 1965-70 and 1973-81, asst lectr fell and tutor Queens' Coll Cambridge 1970-73, chm Industl Tribunals 1981-88, recorder 1981-88; chllr Diocese of Southwell 1981-; Circuit Judge 1988; *Books* Legal Values in Western Society (1974, co-author); *Style—* His Honour Judge Shand; c/o Courts Administrator's Office, Greyfriars House, Greyfriars, Stafford ST16 2SE (☎ 0785 41643)

SHAND, Hon Mrs (Rosalind Maud); *née* Cubitt; only da of 3 Baron Ashcombe (d 1962); *b* 11 August 1921; *m* 1946, Maj Bruce Shand, MC, late 12 Royal Lancers; 1 s, 2 da; *Style—* The Hon Mrs Shand; The Laines, Plumpton, Lewes, E Sussex (☎ 0273 890248)

SHAND, Terence Richard; s of Terence James Shand, and Dorothy Joyce, *née* Shackell; *b* 27 Oct 1954; *Educ* Borehamwood GS; *m* 1, (m dis 1985) Maureen; 1 s (Elliot James b 1977); m 2, 22 March 1986, Arja, da of Paavo Saren; 1 s (Terence Elias b 1984), 1 da (Natalia Sirka b 1988); *Career* dir Stage One Records Ltd 1978-83, chm Castle Communications plc 1983-; *Recreations* tennis, shooting, reading; *Style—* Terence Shand, Esq; 15/16 Northfield Prospect, Putney Bridge Rd, London SW18 1PE (☎ 01 877 0922, fax 01 871 0470, telex 911515)

SHAND KYDD, Hon Mrs; Hon Frances Ruth Burke; *née* Roche; yr da of 4 Baron Fermoy (d 1955), and Ruth, Lady Fermoy, DCVO, OBE, JP, *qv*; *b* 20 Jan 1936; *m* 1, 1 June 1954 (m dis 1969), 8 Earl Spencer, MVO, DL; 1 s (Viscount Althorp, and 1 s decd), 3 da (Lady Sarah McCorquodale, Lady Jane Fellowes, HRH The Princess of Wales); m 2, 2 May 1969, Peter Shand Kydd; *Style—* The Hon Mrs Shand Kydd; 5 Warwick Sq, London SW1; Ardencaple, Isle of Seil, by Oban, Argyll

SHANK, Hon Mrs (Fiona Marilyn); *née* Monckton; 2 da of 12 Viscount Galway; *b* 1947; *m* 1974, Robert Wilford Shank; 1 s (Kevin William), 1 da (Adriane Leigh); *Style—* The Hon Mrs Shank; 9770 SW Buckskin Terr, Beaverton, Oregon, USA

SHANKS, Prof Ian Alexander; s of Alexander Shanks, of Maryville, 44 Victoria St, Dumbarton, Dunbartonshire, and Isabella Affleck Shanks (*née* Beaton); *b* 22 June 1948; *Educ* Dumbarton Acad, Glasgow Univ, (BSc Hons in Electrical Eng, PhD); *m* 14 May 1971, Janice Smillie, da of J Coulter, of 3 Aitkenbar Circle, Bellsmyre, Dumbarton, Dunbartonshire; 1 da (Emma b 1977); *Career* projects mangr Scottish Colorfoto Labs Alexandria 1970-72, princ sci offr RSRE Malvern 1973-82, princ sci Unilever Res 1982-86, visiting prof of Electrical and Electronic Engrg Univ of Glasgow 1985-, chief sci Thorn EMI plc 1986-; CEng, MIEE; FRS; *Recreations* music; *Style—* Prof Ian Shanks; Flintwood Cottage, Channer Drive, Penn, Bucks HP10 8AQ (☎ 049 481 6941); Thorn EMI, Central Research Labs, Dawley Rd, Hayes, Middx UB3 1HH (☎ 01 848 6602)

SHANKS, Philip David; s of Frank Ernest Shanks; *b* 6 Nov 1934; *Educ* Uppingham, Coventry Coll of Art; *m* 1, July 1960 (m dis), Mary Christine, da of John Davis of Stratford-on-Avon; 1 s (Jonathan David b 1961), 1 da (Katherine Mary b 1962); m 2, Aug 1970 (m dis), Susan Elizabeth, da of Walter Burnhill (decd); 1 s (Hugo Christian b 1976); *Career* Nat Serv Lt RE 1953-55; designer and co dir; design mangr Reckitt & Colman (Overseas) Ltd 1962-68, md Philip Shanks Assoc Ltd 1968-75, ptnr Consortium Design 1968-72, dir Philip Shanks Design 1972-78, chief exec New Forest Show Soc 1978-, dir Agric Show Promotions 1985-86 (md 1986-); MSIAD; *Recreations* sailing, walking; *Clubs* Lymington Town SC; *Style—* Philip Shanks, Esq; 11 River court, Gosport St, Lymington SO41 9BB (☎ 0590 71602)

SHANNON, Dr (Michael) Colin; CBE (1988); s of Victor Charles Shannon, of Sandling House, Hollesley, Suffolk, and Ruth, *née* Fenton (d 1958); *b* 25 Dec 1929; *Educ* Whitgift Sch, Guys Hosp London Univ (MB, BS); *m* 31 Oct 1959, Patricia Anne, da of Rev Heber Goldsworthy (d 1938), of China; 2 s (Samuel Richard, George Russell), 2 da (Clare Margaret, Alexandra Jane); *Career* RAC 1948-50: 2 Lt 1949, Garrison Def Egypt Canal Zone 1949-50; GP Hollesley Suffolk 1959; MO 1966-: HMYCC Hollesley Bay, RAF Bawdsey; memb: Deben RDC 1964-74 (chm 1971-74), Suffolk Coastal DC 1973- (chm 1973-75, chm policy ctee 1979-89, ldr cncl 1979-89), Assoc DC 1977-, Health and Safety Cmmn 1981-; MRCGP 1966; *Style—* Dr Colin Shannon, CBE; Sandling House, Hollesley, Woodbridge, Suffolk (☎ 0394 411214)

SHANNON, John; s of John Shannon (d 1951), and Sarah, *née* McHenry (d 1968); *b* 29 Mar 1917; *Educ* Belfast Public Elementary Sch; *m* 15 June 1946, Isobel May Smith; 1 s (Thomas b 1957), 1 da (Moira b 1956); *Career* internal auditor Electricty Bd N Ireland 1940-45, asst budget offr Fisons plc 1945-51, chief accountant Vitamins Ltd 1951-57, accounting mangr Du Pont UK 1959-62; dir and sec: Truscon Ltd 1964-74, Tileman Ltd 1975-82; ret 1982; active private investor 1982-; memb: Richmond and Garnes Cons Assoc, investmt and fin servs gp Inst of Chartered Secretaries; Freeman City of London, Worshipful Co of Chartered Secretaries; FCIS 1945, FCMA 1950; *Clubs* City Livery, IOD; *Style—* John Shannon, Esq; Silver Birches, 2 Temple Sheen, E Sheen, London SW14 7RP (☎ 01 876 1701)

SHANNON, 9 Earl of (I 1756); Richard Bentinck Boyle; sits as Baron Carleton (GB 1786); also Viscount Boyle and Baron Castle-Martyr (both I 1756); s of 8 Earl (d 1963); *b* 23 Oct 1924; *Educ* Eton; *m* 1, 1947 (m dis 1955), Donna Catherine Irene Helen, da of Marchese Demetrio Imperiali di Francavilla (created by of King Victor Amadeus III of Piedmont 1779); m 2, 1957 (m dis 1979), Susan Margaret, da of late John Russell Hogg; 1 s, 2 da; *Heir* s, Viscount Boyle; *Career* Capt Irish Gds and RWAFF 1942-54; sec Fedn of Euro Indust Co-op Res Orgns 1975-86, chm Fndn Sci and Technol 1977-83, dir Ctee Dirs Res Assoc 1969-85; vice-pres Inland Waterways Assoc, dep speaker and dep chm Ctees House of Lords 1968-78; FRSA, FBIM, MBHI; *Recreations* horology, inland waterways; *Clubs* White's; *Style—* The Rt Hon the Earl of Shannon; Pimm's Cottage, Man's Hill, Burghfield Common, Berkshire RG7 3BD

SHAPCOTT, Sidney Edward; s of Percy Thomas Shapcott (d 1966), of Torquay, and Beatrice, *née* Hobbs (d 1968); *b* 20 June 1920; *Educ* Hele's Sch Exeter, King's Coll London (BSc); *m* 4 Sept 1943, Betty Jean, *née* Richens; 2 s (Christopher b 1955, William b 1961), 1 da (Susan b 1951); *Career* Miny of Supply and Miny of Aviation 1941-65 (DSCO 1963), dir of projects Euro Space Res Orgn Delft Netherlands 1963-65, Navy Dept MOD 1965-75 (CSO 1968), dep dir Admty Surface Weapons Estab Portsmouth 1968-72, dir under water weapon projects Admty Under Water Weapons Estab Portland 1972-75, dir gen Airborne Weapons and Electronic Systems MOD Procurement Exec 1976-80; engrg conslt in private practice 1981-85; memb Devonshire Assoc; FInstP 1971, FIEE 1974; *Recreations* motoring, English churches; *Style—* Sidney Shapcott, Esq; 23 Upper Churston Rise, Seaton, Devon EX12 2HD (☎ 0297 21545)

SHAPIRO, Erin Patria Margaret; *née* Carney; da of Cyril Carney, MBE (d 1980), and Ruth Patricia Last; *b* 19 Feb 1939; *Educ* Leweston Manor Sherborne Dorset; *m* 1, 1961 (m dis 1979), John Leo Pizzey; 1 s (Amos b 1967), 1 da (Cleo b 1961); m 2, 1980, Jeffrey Scott Shapiro; 5 stepchildren (Francis, Trevor, Annie, Richard, Daren); *Career* author, journalist, social reformer; fndr Shelter Movement for Battered Men, Women and Children; Int Order of Volunteers for Peace Diploma of Honour (1981), Nancy Astor Award for Journalism (1983), Distinguished Leadership Award (World Congress of Victimology, 1987); *Books* Scream Quietly or the Neighbours Will Hear, Infernal Child, Sluts Cookbook, Erin Pizzey Collects, Prone To Violence, All In The Name of Love; fiction: The Watershed, In the Shadow of the Castle, The Pleasure Palace, First Lady, The Consul General's Daughter (1988) The Snow Leopard of Shanghai (1989); short stories: The Man in the Blue Van, The Frangipani Tree,

Addiction, Dancing; articles: Choosing a Non-Violent Relationship, Sexual Abuse Within the Family; has contributed to many leading newspapers and journals; TV documentaries incl: Scream Quietly (1975), Chiswick Womens Aid (1977), That Awful Woman (1987); *Recreations* reading, cooking, antiques, violin, wine, travel; *Style*— Mrs Shapiro; c/o Christopher Little 236-5881, 49 Queen Consultant, Victoria St, London, EC4N 4SA Christopher Little 236-5881

SHAPIRO, Hon Mrs; Hon (Virginia); *née* Makins; da of 1 Baron Sherfield, GCB, GCMG; *b* 1939; *Educ* LMH Oxford; *m* 1972, David Michael Shapiro; *Style*— The Hon Mrs Shapiro; 14 Woodstock Rd, London W4

SHAPLAND, Edward (Eddie); s of Fred Shapland Burnley (d 1957), and Emily Shapland Burnley; *b* 3 April 1946; *Educ* Burnley GS, Associate of Chartered Building Societies Inst (Dip Mgmnt Studies 1978); *m* 23 March 1968, Janet Mary, da of Eric Williamson (d 1979); 1 s (Mark b 1970), 2 da (Kay b 1972); *Career* accounting mangr 1962-79, Burnley Bldg Soc, asst gen mangr Marsden Bldg Soc 1980-84, dep asst gen mangr 1984-86, gen mangr 1986-; *Recreations* house renovations, watching sport (football); *Style*— Eddie Shapland, Esq; The Barn, Little Tom's Farm, Burnley, Lancs BB10 2BY (☎ 21978); Marsden Building Society, Russell Street, Nelson, Lancs BB9 7NJ (☎ 692821, fax 0282 698110)

SHAPLAND, Maj-Gen Peter Charles; CB (1977), MBE (1960); s of Frederick Charles Shapland (d 1960), of Merton Park, Surrey, and Annie Frances, *née* Carr (d 1970); *b* 14 July 1923; *Educ* Rutlish Sch Merton Park, St Catharine's Coll Cambridge (MA); *m* 1 April 1954, Joyce Barbara, da of Fraser Leopold Peradon (d 1973), of India, Jersey and Chichester; 2 s (Michael b 1958, Timothy b 1962); *Career* served WW II with RE in UK and India, Lt-Col 1965, Brig 1968, Cdr Engr Bde TA & VR 1968, RCDS 1971, dep cdr and COS HQ SE Dist 1972-74; dir Volunteers, Territorials and Cadets MOD 1974-78, Hon Col 73 Engr Regt TA 1979-, sr planning inspector DOE 1980-, Col Cmdt RE 1981-86, pres Instr of Royal Engrs 1982-87, chm Combined Cadet Force Assoc 1982-; Freeman City of London 1983, Liveryman Worshipful Co of Painter-Stainers 1983; *Clubs* Royal Ocean Racing, Royal Engineer Yacht, Lansdowne; *Style*— Maj-Gen Peter Shapland, CB, MBE; c/o Holts Branch, Royal Bank of Scotland, Kirkland House, Whitehall, London SW1A 2EB

SHAPLAND, Richard Guy; s of Thomas John Shapland; *b* 7 August 1932; *Educ* Wellington Sch Somerset; *m* 1956, Dorothy, née Carter; 1 da (Sarah Jane b 1961); *Career* chartered accountant, pres South Western Soc of Chartered Accountants 1981-82; *Recreations* sailing (yacht owned 'Resurrection'); *Clubs* Royal Cornwall Yacht Club, Royal Overseas League; *Style*— Richard Shapland, Esq; Nauron, Tregenver Rd, Falmouth, Cornwall (☎ 0326 313 634)

SHAPLAND, Sydney Ivor; s of Arthur William Shapland (d 1941), and Alice Maud, *née* Jackson (d 1975); *b* 9 Feb 1929; *Educ* Tollington GS London, Northern Poly London; *m* 29 May 1954, Margaret Elizabeth, da of Francis Edward Lynden (d 1980), of Seaford, Sussex; 2 s (Jonathan b 1957, Anthony b 1960); *Career* RN 1947-49; ptnr Cluttons Chartered Surveyors 1972, agent and receiver to Church Cmmnrs 1976; life memb Royal Soc of St George; Freeman City of London 1979, Liveryman Worshipful Co of Paviors 1979; FRICS 1954; *Recreations* bridge, gardening, swimming; *Clubs* City Livery; *Style*— Sydney Shapland, Esq; 38 Kingsley Way, Hampstead, London N2 (☎ 01 458 1010, fax 01 629 3263, telex 23620)

SHAPLAND, Sir William Arthur; s of Arthur Frederick Shapland and Alice Maud, *née* Jackson; *b* 20 Oct 1912; *Educ* Tollington Sch Muswell Hill; *m* 1943, Madeline Annie, da of James Amiss; 2 da (Janet, Anne); *Career* Allan Charlesworth & Co CAs 1929-55 (ptnr 1946-55, FCA 1936); Blackwood Hodge plc 1946-83 (dir 1946-55, exec dir 1955-64, exec chm 1964-83); Bernard Sunley Charitable Fndn (tstee dir 1960-); govr Utd World Coll of the Atlantic, Irene Coll; tstee: Charing Cross Sunley Res Centre Tst, Monks Ferry Trg Tst; memb: Cncl Charing Cross Westminster Med Sch, Ct of Leicester Univ; vice-pres: London Fedn of Boys' Clubs, S London Scouts Cncl, Wildfowl Tst; Hon FRCS 1978; memb Master Paviors Co 1980-81; Wayneflete Fell Magdalen Coll Oxford 1981; OStJ 1981; Hon Fell St Catherine's Coll Oxford 1982, Hon DSc Buckingham 1986, Hon DLitt Leicester 1983; kt 1982; *Recreations* golf, fishing, travel; *Clubs* City Livery; *Style*— Sir William Shapland; 44 Beech Drive, London N2 9NY (☎ 01 883 5073); office: 25 Berkeley Sq, London W1A 4AX (☎ 01 493 1873)

SHARLAND, (Edward) John; s of William Rex Sharland (d 1987), and Phyllis Eileen, *née* Pitts; *b* 25 Dec 1937; *Educ* Monmouth, Jesus Coll Oxford (BA, MA); *m* 14 Feb 1970, Susan Mary Rodway, da of Douglas Rodway Millard, of Mill Ford House, Long Melford, Sudbury, Suffolk; 4 da (Nicola b 1971, Sandy b 1972, Philippa b 1974, Rebecca b 1975); *Career* FCO: London 1961-62, 2 sec (commercial) Bangkok 1962-67, Far E Dept London 1967-69, 1 sec Vienna 1969-72, 1 sec and head of chancery Bangkok 1972-76, 1 sec (commercial) and consul Montevideo 1976-79, asst Cultural Rels Dept London 1979-82; consul gen: Perth 1982-87, Cleveland 1987-; *Recreations* tennis, bridge, gardening; *Style*— John Sharland, Esq; c/o FCO, King Charles St, London SW1A 2AH

SHARMAN, Charles Algernon; s of Algernon Sharman (d 1975), of Cambridgeshire, and Ida Margaret Ling (d 1972); *b* 9 Mar 1907; *Educ* Aldenham Sch Herts; *m* 9 June 1932, Roll, da of Sir Frederick James Roll (d 1927), of Surrey; 4 s (James b 1934, John b 1936, Patrick b 1939, Nicholas b 1945), 1 da (Briony b 1942); *Career* Lt Cambridgeshire Regt 1931, Lt RNVR 1945; Newspaper Proprietor, Sharman & Co Ltd (founded 1910) 1931-87; tstee Boston Savings Bank 1952-75 (chm 1974), memb regnl bd Tstee Savings Bank of Eastern England 1975-80 (custodian tstee 1977-80), fell eastern div Woodard Corpn; govr Westwood House Sch Peterborough 1968-81 (chm 1977-); *Recreations* game shooting; *Clubs* Peterborough City & Counties; *Style*— Charles A Sharman, Esq; Front Park, 110 Thorpe Park, Peterborough

SHARMAN, Peter William; CBE (1984); s of William Charles Sharman (d 1971), and Olive Mabel, *née* Burl (d 1961); *b* 1 June 1924; *Educ* Northgate GS Ipswich, Edinburgh Univ (MA); *m* 1946, Eileen Barbara, *née* Crix; 1 s, 2 da; *Career* chief gen mangr Norwich Union Insurance Gp 1975-84 (dir 1974-); chm Life Offices Assoc 1977-79, chm British Insurance Association 1982-1983 (dep chm 1981-82); dir: A P Bank Ltd 1976-; Norwich and Peterborough Building Soc 1985-; FIA; *Recreations* golf, tennis, badminton; *Style*— Peter Sharman, Esq, CBE; 28B Eaton Rd, Norwich NR4 6PZ; Norwich Union Insurance Group, P O Box 4, Norwich (☎ 0603 622200)

SHARP, Sir Adrian; 4 Bt (UK 1922), of Warden Court, Maidstone, Kent; s of Sir Edward Herbert Sharp, 3 Bt (d 1985), and Beryl, Lady Sharp, *qv*; *b* 17 Sept 1951; *m* 1976, Hazel Patricia, only da of James Trevor Wallace, of Pietersburg, S Africa, and former w of William Ian Barrett Bothwell; *Heir* br, Owen Sharp, *qv*; *Career* exec sales mangr Ford Motor Co; *Style*— Sir Adrian Sharp, Bt; 119 Nirvana Road, Brighton Beach, Durban, S Africa

SHARP, His Hon Alastair George; MBE (1945), QC (1961), DL (1973); s of Alexander Sharp (d 1923), of Aberdeen, and Isabella, *née* Lyall, OBE (d 1962); *b* 25 May 1911; *Educ* Aberdeen GS, Fettes Sch, Clare Coll Cambridge (BA); *m* 10 Sept 1940, Daphne Sybil, da of Maj Harold Smithers (ka 1916), of Plymouth; 1 s (Alastair b 13 April 1944), 2 da (Lindsay b 1 Oct 1942, Clare b 12 Jan 1950); *Career* cmmnd The Gordon Highlanders 1939, served 1939-45, 2 Bn The London Scottish 1943, WO Gen Staff 1944-45; called to the Bar Middle Temple 1936, in practice 1936-62, rec Rotherham 1960-62, county ct judge 1962-70, chm Durham County Quarter Sessions 1970-72, circuit judge 1972-84; chm Washington New Town Licenced Premises Ctee 1966-78, Faculty of Law Durham Univ 1971-84, ctee memb Durham County Magistrates Cts 1972-84, liaison judge Durham County Magistrates 1972-84, govr Sherburn Hosp 1978-81; *Recreations* golf, gardening, hillwalking, music, fishing; *Clubs* Durham County, Brancepeth GC; *Style*— His Hon Alastair Sharp, MBE, QC, DL; High Point, Western Hill, Durham DH1 4RG; The Old Kennels, Tomintoul, Banffshire AB3 9EN

SHARP, Anthony Arthur Vivian; s of Vivian Arthur Sharp (d 1978), of Violet Elizabeth, *née* Johnson (d 1981); *b* 5 Nov 1938; *Educ* Repton; *m* 17 Sept 1966, Jill Treharne, da of Hugh Treharne Morgan, OBE, of Alchornes, Lordswell Lane, Crowborough, Sussex; 2 da (Antionette b 1969, Fiona b 1970); *Career* Nat Serv 1957-59, cmmnd Midshipman 1958; RNR 1958-66, Sub Lt 1959, Lt 1962; dir: H Clarkson Ltd 1978-86 (asst dir 1975-78), Clarkson Puckle Ltd 1978-86, Horace Holman Ltd 1986-88, Nelson Hurst and Marsh Agencies Ltd 1988-; underwriting memb Lloyd's 1972; tres Wivelsfield Cons Assoc 1979-82 (ctee memb 1978-82); memb London ctee Sail Trg Assoc 1968-81; memb Insur Brokers' Registration Cncl 1983-88; *Recreations* tennis, shooting, sailing, skiing; *Clubs* City Univ, Lloyd's YC, Lloyd's Lawn Tennis; *Style*— Anthony Sharp, Esq; Nelson Hurst & Marsh Agencies Ltd, No 1 Seething Lane, London EC3N 4NH (☎ 01 481 9090, fax 01 481 9450, telex 883756 NHURST G)

SHARP, Beryl, Lady; Beryl Kathleen; *née* Simmons-Green; da of Leonard Simmons-Green, of 273 Langmore Road, Shirley, Warwickshire; *m* 1949, Sir Edward Herbert Sharp, 3 Bt (d 1985); 2 s, 1 da; *Style*— Beryl, Lady Sharp; 5 Raynham Gardens, 28 Howick Road, Pietermaritzburg 3201, Natal, S Africa

SHARP, Dr David Henry; OBE (1982); s of Rev Douglas Simmonds Sharp (d 1938), and late Gwendoline Helen, *née* Roberts; *b* 24 Feb 1917; *Educ* Tynemouth HS, Queen Elixabeth's GS Blackburn, Univ Coll Southampton, Univ of London (BSc, PhD); *m* 18 July 1942, Enid Catherine, da of Rev Emlyn Maurice William (d 1953), of Caernarfon; 2 s (Roger b 28 Jan 1946, Richard b 24 Aug 1952), 1 da (Lalage b 11 Nov 1956); *Career* sci offr Chemical Def Res Dept 1937-44, head of res Sutcliffe Speakman & Co Ltd 1944-48, section head Br Ceramic Res Assoc 1948-51, works mangr asst to md Fisons Ltd 1951-61; tech dir: FBI, CBI 1961-67; gen sec: Inst Chemical Engrs, Soc of Chemical Indust 1967-82; assoc ed Ellis Horwood Ltd Chichester 1982-, served on various govt ctees including Key Ctee on Disposal of Solid Toxic Waste; active memb and off holder Methodist Church; FRSC 1943, FIChemE 1968, FRSH 1972; Das Grosse Verdienstkreuz, Federal Republic of Germany 1981; *Books* The Chemical Industry (jt ed 1981), Bioprotein Manufacture (1989); *Recreations* swimming, colour photography, model railways; *Clubs* Anglo-Belgian, Probus (Sevenoaks); *Style*— Dr David Sharp, OBE; Greenhill House, Shoreham Rd, Otford, Sevenoaks, Kent TN14 5RN (☎ 095 92 3332)

SHARP, Prof Dennis Charles; s of Walter Charles Henry Sharp (d 1976), of Bedford, and Elsie, *née* Evans; *Educ* Bedford Mod Sch, Architectural Assoc London (AA Dipl), Univ of Liverpool (MA); *m* 1, 1963 (m dis 1973), Joanna Leighton, da of William Scales (d 1986); 1 da (Melanie Clare); m 2, 8 Dec 1983, Yasmin, da of C Amirali Shariff; 1 s (Deen b 1984); *Career* architect, writer; ARIBA 1959, lectr in architecture Manchester Univ 1964-68, Leverhulme Fell in Architecture Liverpool Univ 1960-63, sr lectr i/c history course AA Sch 1968-72, sr tutor & lectr Gen Studies Unit AA Sch 1973-81, gen ed AA 1968-82 (AA Quarterly, AA Papers Res Series, etc), visiting prof Columbia Univ of NY 1981, distinguished visiting critic Finnish Assoc of Architects 1980-81, dist visiting scholar Adelaide Univ SA 1984; visiting lectr: Imperial Coll Univ of London 1969-70, Royal Univ of Malta (1971, 1972, 1974), PNL London 1977-78, Univ of Sheffield 1988-89; Graham Fnd Lectures Chicago 1974 and 1986; John Player Lectr on 'Film & Environment' NFT 1977; external examiner: Bartlett Sch, UCL 1971-78, Univs of Oxford, Sheffield, Bristol, Liverpool etc, Kingston Poly, Lanchester & Trent Polys (CNAA); dir CICA 1979-; prof Int Acad of Architecture, Sofia; Dennis Sharp Architects London 1964-; *Books* Modern Architecture & Expressionism (1966), Sources of modern Architecture (1967, 1981), A Visual History of 20th Century Architecture (1972), The Picture Palace (1969), Glass Architecture (ed 1972), From Schinkel to the Bauhaus (1970), Van de Velde: Theatres 1904-14 (1974), The Rationilists (1978), Muthesius H: The English House (ed 1979, and 1987); *Recreations* photography, investigating towns & buildings; *Clubs* Arts; *Style*— Prof Dennis Sharp; Dennis Sharp Architects, 4 All Saints Street, London N1 9RL (☎ 01 278 8924/0707 875253)

SHARP, (William) Drummond; s of William Sharp (d 1977), of Clackmannanshire, and Margaret, *née* Hutton; *b* 3 June 1932; *Educ* Dunfermline HS; *m* 1957, Kathleen Margaret Maxwell, da of Robert Alexander (d 1974), of Alloa; 2 da (Carol b 1961, Heather b 1964); *Career* merchant banker; dir Arbuthnot Latham Bank Ltd 1978-84, jt md Burns-Anderson plc 1982-87, alternate memb Bank of England Deposit Protection Bd 1986-87, chm Dial-A-Phone plc, non-exec dir Carbo plc; FIB (Scotland); *Recreations* golf; *Clubs* St James (Manchester), Hale GC; *Style*— Drummond Sharp, Esq; Norwood, 12A Harrop Road, Hale, Altrincham WA15 9BX (☎ 061 941 2260); Dial-A-Phone plc, Dial-A-Phone House, Newton St, Hyde SK14 4RY (☎ 061 367 8044)

SHARP, Sir Eric; CBE (1980); s of Isaac and Martha Sharp; *b* 17 August 1916; *Educ* LSE; *m* 1950, Marion, *née* Freedman; 1 s, 2 da; *Career* chm Cable & Wireless 1981-, Monsanto 1975- (dep chm 1973-74), Polyamide Intermediates 1975-; memb Econ Devpt Ctee Chem Indust 1980-, CEGB 1980-; previously with Miny Fuel & Power; kt 1984; *Style*— Sir Eric Sharp, CBE; c/o Monsanto Ltd, Monsanto House, Victoria St, SW1 (☎ 01 222 5678)

SHARP, Sir George; OBE (1969), JP (Fife 1975), DL (Fife 1978); s of Angus Sharp and Mary, *née* McNee; *b* 8 April 1919; *m* 1948, Elsie May, da of David Porter Rodger;

1 s; *Career* vice-chm: Tay Rd Bridge Jt Bd 1942-48, Forth Bridge Ctee 1972-78, dir Grampian TV 1975-; memb: Scottish Devpt Agency 1975-80, Royal Cmmn on Legal Services in Scotland 1978-80; chm: Fife and Kinross Water Bd 1967-75, Fife CC (convenor) 1973-75, Fife Regnl Cncl 1974-78 (convenor), Glenrothes Devpt Corpn 1978-86, Scottish Tourist Bd Consultative Cncl 1979-83; pres: Assoc of CCs 1971-73, Convention Scottish Local Authys 1975-78; managing tstee Municipal Mutual Insur 1979-; memb Nat Girobank (Scottish Bd) 1984-; memb econ and social ctee EEC 1982-86; kt 1976; *Style—* Sir George Sharp, OBE, JP, DL; Strathlea, 56 Station Rd, Thornton, Fife (☎ 0592 774347)

SHARP, James Christopher; s of Stanley Sharp (d 1962), of 429 Gorton Rd, Reddish Stockport, Cheshire, and Annie, *née* Owrid; *b* 24 Dec 1939; *Educ* Stockport GS, Pembroke Coll Oxford (MA); *m* 20 July 1963, Mary, da of Roland Bromfield (d 1983), of 4 Quarry Place, Shrewsbury; 1 s (Jeremy b 1964), 2 da (Catherine b 1968, Rosemary b 1978); *Career* slrs articled clerk and asst slr 1963-68, asst slr G H Morgan and Co Shrewsbury 1968-70, md Northern Rock Building Soc; dir: Northern Rock Housing Tst Ltd, Northern Rock Property Servs Ltd, Nat House-Bldg Cncl, NHBC Bldg Control Servs Ltd, North Housing Assoc Ltd, North Housing Ltd, North Housing Tst Ltd, Building Socs Ombudsman Co Ltd (chm), The Coll for Fin Planning in the UK Ltd; *Style—* James Sharp, Esq; 5 Richmond Way, Ponteland, Newcastle upon Tyne (☎ 0661 24519); Northern Rock Building Society, Northern Rock House, Gosforth, Newcastle upon Tyne (☎ 091 285 7191)

SHARP, John; s of Alfred Sharp (d 1968), and May Sharp, *née* Gillibrand (d 1966); *b* 18 Dec 1927; *Educ* Keighley GS, BNC Oxford; *m* 1950, Jean, *née* Prosser; 1 s, 2 da; *Career* asst master Marlborough Coll 1954-62, sr sci master Marlborough Coll 1959-62, headmaster Christ Coll Brecon 1962-72, headmaster Rossall 1973-87; *Recreations* fishing, photography, roses, local history, genealogy; *Clubs* East India; *Style—* John Sharp, Esq; Wood End Cottage, St Michael's, Tenbury Wells, Worcs WR15 8TG

SHARP, Sir Kenneth Johnston; TD (1960); *b* 1926; *Career* former ptnr Armstrong, Watson & Co; former head Govt Accountancy Serv (DTI), ptnr Howard Tilly & Co; pres Inst of CAs 1974-75, master Co of CAs in England and Wales 1979-80; ACA, FCA; kt 1984; *Style—* Sir Kenneth Sharp, TD; Flat 1, Coker House, East Coker, Yeovil BA22 9HS

SHARP, (Thomas) Michael Budworth; CBE (1971, OBE 1966); s of John Sharp (d 1943); *b* 29 Sept 1923; *Educ* Tonbridge, Aberdeen Univ, Queens' Coll Cambridge, London Univ; *m* 1966, Ellen Jane Luke, *née* McCartney; 1 child; *Career* WWII, Capt RA Burma; Indian Civil Serv 1946; Colonial Admin Serv: dep perm sec Miny for Local Govt N Nigeria 1963-68, sec Interim Common Serv Agency 1968-70, princ admin offr Skelmersdale Devpt Corpn 1973-85, ret; *Books* Plain Beauty (1987); *Clubs* Army & Navy; *Style—* Michael Sharp, Esq, CBE; 36 Dunbar Cres, Southport, Merseyside

SHARP, Sir Milton Reginald; 3 Bt (UK 120) of Heckmondwike, W Riding, Co York; s of Sir Milton Sharp, 2 Bt (d 1941); *b* 21 Nov 1909; *Educ* Shrewsbury, Trinity Hall Cambridge; *m* 1, 1935, Dorothy Mary, nee McCarrick; m 2, 1951, Marie-Louise de Vignon of Paris; *Heir* cous, Samuel Sharp; *Career* Capt REME (TA); *Style—* Sir Milton Sharp, Bt; c/o Messrs Redfearns, Midland Bank Chambers, Heckmondwike, Yorks

SHARP, Neil Muir; MBE (1976), TD (1966 and 2 bars), O St J 1982); s of Col (John) Stuart Caden Head Sharp, OBE, TD, DL (d 1986), of Bruce Court, Carnoustie, Angus, and Dorothy Kate, *née* Muir (d 1988), Bruce Court, Carnoustie, Angus; *b* 18 May 1934; *Educ* Trinity Coll Glenalmond; *m* 1, 1960 (m dis 1970), Jean Katherine, *née* Woodruff; 2 da (Sarah b 1961, Heather 1963); m 2, 18 May 1974, Muriel Anne, da of Victor Slack, of Ormshirk, Lancs; 1 da (Sally b 1975); *Career* Nat Serv 2 Lt RA 1952-54, 2 Lt then Col RA TA 1954-82; CA 1954; ptnr: RC Thomson and Murdoch 1961-69 (student 1954-60), Arthur Young 1969 (current managing ptnr); chm, ctee memb, and tres of a number of local charities; former chm Tayside Branch IOD; OStJ; CA 1960, MIPA 1988; *Recreations* shooting, golf; *Clubs* Royal and Ancient GC (St Andrews), Caledonian; *Style—* Neil Sharp, Esq, MBE, TD; Hilloch Wood, Letham Grange, By Arbroath, Angus (☎ 0241 892345); Arthur Young, City House, 16 Overgate, Dundee (☎ 0382 202561, fax 0382 27177, telex 76356 AYDU)

SHARP, Owen; yr s of Sir Edward Herbert Sharp, 3 Bt (d 1985), and Beryl, Lady Sharp, *qv*; br and hp of Sir Adrian Sharp, 4 Bt; *b* 17 Sept 1956; *m* Caroline; 1 s (Declan b 1980); *Style—* Owen Sharp Esq; c/o Beryl, Lady Sharp, 5 Raynham Gardens, 28 Howick Road, Pietermaritzburg 3201, Natal, S Africa

SHARP, Richard Adrian William; OBE (1986); s of Frederick George Sharp (d 1964), and Kathleen Muriel, *née* Chandler; *b* 9 Sept 1938; *Educ* Blundells Sch, Balliol Coll Oxford (MA); *m* 1963, Esther Marian, da of Sir Frederick Johnson Pedler, of Moor Park; 2 s (Quentin b 1965, Jeremy b 1967), 1 da (Rachel b 1970); *Career* Nat Serv 1957-59, 2 Lt RM Commandos; asst master Sherborne Sch 1963-68, joined Eng China Clays 1968, distribution servs mangr ECC Int 1986-, dir Treneglos Co Ltd 1977, tstee and tres Maitland Tst, pres Nanpean AFC 1969-; chm SW Cncl for Sport and Recreation 1984- (vice-chm 1982-84), rugby corr Sunday Telegraph 1976-85; played rugby for: Redruth, Wasps, Bristol, Barbarians, Oxford Univ 1959-62, Cornwall 1957-67 (Capt 1963-65), England 1960-67 (Capt 1963), Br Isles Touring Team 1962; played cricket for Cornwall 1956-69; fell Inst of Logistics and Distribution Mgmnt 1981; *Recreations* tennis, gardening, walking, bird watching; *Clubs* British Sportsman's; *Style—* Richard Sharp, Esq; Rosenannon, Carlyon Road, St Austell, Cornwall PL25 4LE; ECC International, John Keay House, St Austell, Cornwall PL25 4DJ

SHARP, Sir Richard Lyall; KCVO (1982), CB (1977); s of late Alexander Sharp, Advocate of Aberdeen, by his late w Isabella, OBE; bro of His Honour Alastair George Sharp, *qv*, and of late Lady Mackie of Benshie; *b* 27 Mar 1915; *Educ* Fettes, Aberdeen Univ, Clare Coll Cambridge; *m* 1950, Jean Helen, eld da of Sir James Crombie, KCB, KBE, CMG; 2 s, 2 da (1 da decd); *Career* served WWII Royal Northumberland Fusiliers (POW Singapore and Siam); joined Treasy 1946, IDC 1961, under-sec Prices and Incomes Bd 1966-68, with Treasy 1968-77, ceremonial offr CSD 1977-82; *Style—* Sir Richard Sharp, KCVO, CB; Home Farm House, Briston, Norfolk NR24 2HN (☎ 0263 860445)

SHARP, Richard Simon; s of Sir Eric Sharp, CBE, of London, and Marion, *née* Freeman; *b* 8 Feb 1956; *Educ* Merchant Taylors', Christ Church Oxford (MA); *m* 29 Aug 1988, Victoria Susan, da of Lloyd Nelson Hull; *Career* Morgan Guaranty Tst Co 1978-84, exec dir investment banking dir Goldman Sachs Int Ltd 1984-; *Recreations* eating, tennis, reading; *Style—* Richard Sharp, Esq; 8-10 New Fetter Lane, London EC4A 1DB (☎ 01 459 5094, fax 01 459 5432)

SHARP, Ronald Landels; s of Charles Sharp (d 1955); *b* 18 May 1916; *Educ* Daniel Stewart's Coll Edinburgh; *m* 1951, Marian Pinkerton, da of John Burns (d 1956); 1 s, 1 da; *Career* dir Bruce Lindsay Bros Ltd 1956-85 (co sec 1950-82); FSCA; *Recreations* golf, hill-walking; *Clubs* Royal Overseas, Bruntsfield Links Golfing Soc; *Style—* Ronald Sharp, Esq; Holmcroft, 1 Maybury Rd, Edinburgh EH4 8DX (☎ 031 339 1924)

SHARP, William Johnstone; CB (1983); s of Frederick Matthew Sharp (d 1931), and Gladys Evelyn; *b* 30 May 1926; *Educ* Queen Elizabeth G S Hexham, Emmanuel Coll Cambridge (MA); *m* 1952, Joan Alice, MBE, da of Arnold Gardner Clark (d 1965); *Career* Capt Durham LI (Malaya); govt official; controller and chief exec Her Majesty's Stationery Off 1981-86; *Recreations* the turf; *Style—* William Sharp, Esq, CB; 43 Friars Quay, Norwich NR3 1ES (☎ 0603 624258)

SHARPE, Hon Sir John Henry; CBE (1972), JP, MP (UBP) Warwick West Bermuda 1963-; s of late Harry Sharpe, and late Jessie, *née* White; *b* 8 Nov 1921; *Educ* Warwick Academy, Mt Allison Commercial Coll Canada; *m* 1948, Eileen Margaret Morrow of Vancouver Canada; 1 s (John), 1 da (Kathleen); *Career* served WWII, Bermuda Rifles 1939-42, Royal Canadian AF 1942-45 (qualified as navigator in Canada, posted UK and served with RAF Bomber Cmd in operations over Europe); chm Purvis Ltd (joined 1938) Ltd 1938-: elected Parliament 1963, dep premier of Bermuda 1972-75, premier 1975-77; min: finance 1968-75, tport 1980, marine and air services 1980-81, lab and home affairs 1981-88, delegated external affairs 1989; dir Bank of Bermuda Ltd 1978-87; hon vice-patron RAF Assoc, hon vice-pres Bermuda Football Assoc; chm Bermuda Nat Olympic Cncl; former memb Synod C of E, church warden St Mary's Church Warwick; chm Bd of Inquiry into various Tax matters 1980; kt 1977; *Recreations* reading, bridge, gardening, tennis, formerly soccer and rugby; *Clubs* Royal Hamilton Amateur Dinghy, Royal Bermuda Yacht, Coral Beach and Tennis; *Style—* The Hon Sir John Sharpe, CBE, JP, MP; Uplands, 26 Harbour Rd, Warwick West, Bermuda; Purvis Ltd, PO Box 461, Hamilton 5

SHARPE, Rev Canon Kenneth Henry; s of William Kenneth Sharpe (d 1974), of Portslade, Sussex, and Florence Annie, *née* Holmes (d 1976); *b* 29 Mar 1920; *Educ* Varndean Brighton, Rochester Theol Coll; *m* 27 July 1957, Mary, *née* Swabey; 1 s (Simon b 1961, 1 da (Jacqueline b 1966); *Career* Banking 1937-48, hon tres Cranleigh Village Hosp 1942-48, admin Diocese of the Upper Nile 1949-54, sec and tres Mbale Cathedral Bldg Appeal 1949-60, diocesan sec and tres Diocese of the Upper Nile 1953-60, prov tres Church of Uganda, Rwanda and Burundi 1962-69; chm: Uganda Bookshop 1962-69; memb: Canon Law and Constitution Cmmn Church of Uganda 1965-69, Prov Liturgical Ctee Church of Uganda 1967-69; commissary to the Bishop of the Sudan 1963-69, hon correspondent for Uganda Royal Cwlth Soc 1962-69, vicar of the Mau Kenya 1969-78, canon of Nakuru Kenya 1973, canon emeritus 1978, hon tres of the Diocese of Nakuru Kenya 1971-78, vicar of Coley Diocese of Wakefield 1978; AIB 1942; *Recreations* wine-making, dog walking; *Clubs* Alcuin, Anglican Soc, Uganda Kobs; *Style—* The Rev Canon Kenneth Sharpe; Coley Vicarage, Coley Rd, Halifax HX3 7SA (☎ 0422 202292)

SHARPE, Sir Reginald Taaffe; QC; only s of Herbert Sharpe (d 1956), of Lindfield, Sussex; *b* 20 Nov 1898; *Educ* Westminster; *m* 1, 1922 (m dis 1929), Phyllis Maude, da of late Major Edward Whinney of Haywards Heath, 2 da; m 2, 1930, Eileen Kate (d 1946), yr da of Thomas Howarth Usherwood of Christ's Hosp, Horsham; m 3, 1947, Vivien Travers (d 1971), da of late Rev Herbert Rowley of Wretham Norfolk; m 4, 1976, Mary Millicent, da of late Maj-Gen Patrick Barclay Sangster, CB, CMG, DSO, of Roehampton; *Career* 2 Lt Grenadier Gds 1917, Lt 1918, served with 2 Bn (Fr, wounded); barr Gray's Inn 1920, judge of High Court Rangoon 1937-48, dir of supply Burma (at Calcutta) 1942-44, JP Sussex 1949, dep chm E Sussex QS 1949-69, memb E Sussex Standing Jt Ctee 1958-65, chm Hailsham petty sessions 1957-58, asst chm W Sussex QS 1950-70, memb W Sussex Standing Jt Ctee 1953-65, dep chm W Kent QS 1949-62 and Kent 1962-69, asst chm Middlesex QS 1951-63, dep-chm 1963-65 and Middlesex Area of Greater London 1965-71; cmmr of assize 1949, 1950, 1952, 1954 and 1960; special divorce cmmr 1948-67, chm Nat health Service Tbnl for Eng and Wales 1948-71, memb Nat Arbitration Tribunal and Industl Disputes Tbnl 1951, sole cmmr for Br Honduras Inquiry (at Belize) 1954, chm Departmental Ctee on Summary Trial of Minor Offences in Magistrates' Courts 1954-55; memb governing body Westminster Sch 1955-83; kt 1947; *Style—* Sir Reginald Sharpe, QC; The Old Post Office, Rushlake Green, Sussex

SHARPE, Rev Roger; s of Rev Gilbert Harry Sharpe, MA (d 1971), late of Stottesdon Vicarage, Salop, and Margaret, *née* Edwards (d 1987); *b* 15 Mar 1935; *Educ* Lancing, Trinity Coll Dublin (MA), Queen's Coll Birmingham; *m* 2 April 1959, Mary Gordon, da of Rev Herbert Gordon Selwyn, MA (d 1975), of S Perrott Rectory, Dorset; 1 s (Richard Charles Selwyn b 1962), 2 da (Rachel Mary b 1961 (Mrs Geoffrey Ramsey), Sarah Brigid b 1965); *Career* clerk-in-Holy-Orders, vicar Redlynch and Morgan's Vale Wilts 1968-86, rural dean of Alderbury 1982-86; rector: St Denys Warminster, Upton Scudamore; priest-in-charge Horningsham 1986; *Recreations* sailing, gardening, beagling; *Style—* The Rev Roger Sharpe; The Rectory, Church St, Warminster, Wilts BA12 8PG (☎ 0985 213456)

SHARPE, Hon Mrs (Sheena MacIntosh); *née* Carmichael; da of Baron Carmichael of Kelvingrove (Life Peer); *b* 1949; *m* 1974, Thomas Anthony Edward Sharpe, 1 s (Christopher b 1977), 1 da (Victoria b 1979); *Style—* The Hon Mrs Sharpe; 7 Lathbury Road, Oxford OX2 7AT

SHARPE, Thomas Ridley; s of Rev George Coverdale Sharpe (d 1944), and Grace Egerton Sharpe, *née* Brown (d 1975); *b* 30 Mar 1928; *Educ* Lancing Coll, Pembroke Coll Cambridge (MA); *m* 1969, Nancy Anne Looper; 3 da (Melanie, Grace, Jemima); *Career* RM 1946-48; social worker Johannesburg SA 1951-52, teacher Natal SA 1952-56, photographer SA 1956-61, deported from SA on political grounds 1961, teacher trg Cambridge 1962-63, lectr in history Cambridge Coll of Arts & Technology 1963-71, novelist 1971-; *Books* Riotous Assembly (1971), Indecent Exposure (1973), Porterhouse Blue (1974), Blott on the Landscape (1975), Wilt (1976), The Great Pursuit (1977), The Throwback (1978), The Wilt Alternative (1979), Ancestral Vices (1980), Vintage Stuff (1982), Wilt on High (1984); *Recreations* photography, old typewriters, gardening, reading, cats, talking; *Style—* Tom Sharpe, Esq; 38 Tunwells Lane, Great Shelford, Cambridge CB2 5LJ

SHARPE NEWTON, Geraldine; da of Jesse J Sharpe, of New York City, and Adrienne Rosaire; *Educ* Univ of Illinois (BA), Univ of Pittsburgh (MLS Hons); *m* June 1962 (m dis 1972), Thomas Alan, s of Frank Newton of Florida; 1 s (Matthew Ross Newton b 1968), 1 da (Jennifer Jesse Newton b 1965); *Career* associate dir special projects Burston Marsteller Public Relations 1974-77, vice pres Niki Singer Inc 1977-79, vice pres dir of Pulic Relations Simon and Schuster 1979-80; dir Information Servs CBS News 1980-83, head of Press and Public Affairs ITN 1983-; *Recreations* riding, hiking, rock collecting; *Clubs* Reform; *Style*— Ms Geraldine Sharpe Newton; 29 Albert Mansions, Albert Bridge Road, London SW11 (☎ 01 228 1151); ITN, ITN House, 48 Wells Street, London W1P 4DE (☎ 01 637 2424)

SHARPLES, Anthony Frederick Gillett; *b* 19 Jan 1936; *Educ* Ratcliffe Coll, Queens' Coll Cambridge; *m* 1969, Anne Elizabeth, da of George Tallentire Blair; 1 da; *Career* md CTP Investmts Ltd; chm CTP Gp Ltd; *Recreations* sailing; *Style*— Anthony Sharples, Esq; Three Elms, Grosvenor Rd, Gloucester, Glos (☎ 0452 23077)

SHARPLES, Hon Christopher John; s of Baroness Sharples, *qv*, and Sir Richard Sharples, KCMG, OBE, MC, (d 1973); *b* 24 May 1947; *Educ* Eton; *m* 1975, Sharon, da of late Robert Sweeny, DFC; 3 children; *Career* C Czarnikow Ltd (sugar brokers) 1968-72, co-fndr and dir Inter Commodities Ltd (brokers in futures and options) 1972-, subsequently renamed GNI Ltd in 1984 following partial acquisition by Gerrard & National plc, dir Internat Petroleum Exchange 1981-87 (vice chm 1986-); served on ctees of: London Commodity Exchange (PR), London Internat Financial Futures Exchange (Clearing), Br Fedn of Commodity Assocs (Taxation), London Commodity Exchange Regulatory Advsy Gp, Internat Petroleum Exchange (PR), Advsy Panel to the Securities and Investmts Bd (1986), Assoc of Futures Brokers and Dealers (Rules Ctee, Membership Ctee, Fin and Gen Purposes Ctee); chm: ICV Information Systems Ltd 1981- (electronic publishers of internat financial data; joint-venture ptnrs Br Telecom), Intercom Data Systems Ltd 1982- (software and systems house), Assoc of Futures Brokers and Dealers 1987- (self regulatory body designated under Financial Services Act 1986); *Recreations* sailing; *Clubs* Royal Yacht Sqdn, White; *Style*— The Hon Christopher Sharples; 72 Elm Park Rd, London SW3 (☎ 01 352 3791, 01 378 7171)

SHARPLES, Hon David Richard; s of Sir Richard Christopher Sharples, KCMG, OBE, MC (assass 1973) Baroness Sharples, *qv*; *b* 14 April 1955; *Educ* Eton; *m* 1981, Annabel, da of Col Thomas Argyle Hall, OBE; *Career* company dir; *Recreations* skiing, sailing, surfing; *Clubs* Windermere Island; *Style*— The Hon David Sharples; 8721 Sunset Plaza Terrace, Los Angeles, Ca 90069, USA (☎ 213 854 1819); office: 5818 W Third St, Los Angeles, CA 90036, USA (☎ 213 934 6000)

SHARPLES, Baroness (Life Peer UK 1973); Pamela; da of Keith William Newall (d 1938), and Lady Claud Hamilton, (d 1984); *b* 11 Feb 1923; *Educ* Southover Manor Lewes; *m* 1, 1946, Sir Richard Christopher Sharples, KCMG, OBE, MC, govr of Bermuda (assas in Bermuda 1973), s of Richard William Sharples, OBE; 2 s, 2 da; m 2, 1977, Patrick de Laszlo (d 1980); m 3, 1983, Robert Douglas Swan; *Career* served WAAF 1941-46, Armed Forces Pay Review Bd 1979-81; sits as Cons peer in House of Lords; dir TVS 1981; *Recreations* walking, tennis, golf, gardening; *Clubs* Mid Ocean, Bermuda; *Style*— The Rt Hon the Lady Sharples; 60 Westminster Gdns, Marsham St, London SW1P 4JG (☎ 01 821 1875) Nunswell, Higher Coombe, Shaftesbury, Dorset SP7 9LR (☎ 0747 2971)

SHARPLEY, Mark Alistair; s of Dr John Edward Sharpley, of Field House, Fulbrook, Burford, Oxon, and Elizabeth Sharpley; da of Maj-Gen Sir Colin Arthur Jardine, 3 Bt, CB, DSO, MC (d 1957); *b* 15 August 1947; *Educ* Marlborough; *m* 6 April 1974, Mhairi, da of Dr John Anderson, of Meikle Hill, Woodlands Ave, Kirkudbright; 1 s (James b 14 June 1976), 1 da (Clare b 3 Oct 1978); *Career* dir Amalgamated Metal Trading Ltd 1980-; *Recreations* fishing, rare pheasants, shooting; *Style*— Mark Sharpley, Esq; The Old Sun House, Pednor, Chesham, Bucks HP5 2SZ (☎ (0494) 782870); Amalgamated Metal Trading Ltd, Ground Floor, Adelaide House, London EC4R 9DT (☎ 01 626 4521)

SHARPLEY, Ven Roger Ernest Dion; s of Frederick Charles Sharpley, OBE (d 1966), and Doris Irene, *née* Wills; *b* 19 Dec 1928; *Educ* Dulwich, Christ Church Oxford (MA); *Career* vicar All Saints' Middlesbrough 1960-81, rural dean Middlesbrough 1970-81, canon of York Minster 1974-81, archdeacon Hackney and vicar Guild Church of Saint Andrew Holborn 1981-; *Style*— The Ven the Archdeacon of Hackney; St Andrew's Vicarage, 5 St Andrew St, London EC4A 3AB (☎ 01 353 3544)

SHARROCK, Ivan; s of William Arthur Sharrock, and Gladys Muriel, *née* Roberts; *b* 17 July 1941; *Educ* Newquay GS, Cornwall Tech Coll; *m* 5 Oct 1974, Suzanne Jacqueline Clare, da of Jack Cecil Edward Haig, of Sutton Coldfield; 1 s (Sky Kelly Ivan b 1975); *Career* joined BBC 1961, trained in film sound techniques at Ealing Film Studios 1961-64, BBC TV outside broadcasts 1964-65, freelance sound mixer with Alan King Assocs 1965-81; has recorded over 40 feature films including: The French Lieutenant's Woman 1981 (Br Acad Award), Greystoke 1984 (Br Acad Nomination), The Last Emperor 1987 (US Acad Award); memb Acad of Motion Picture Arts and Sciences, Cinema Audio Soc (USA), BAFTA, ACTT, BKSTS; *Recreations* sailing, skiing, windsurfing, music, reading; *Style*— Ivan Sharrock, Esq; 9 Burghley Road, London NW5 1UG (☎ 01 267 3170, 01 722 1572, car tel 0836 254983)

SHARWOOD-SMITH, Lady; (Winifred) Joan; da of late Thomas Mitchell; *Educ* Berkhamstead Sch; *m* 1939, as his 2 w, Sir Bryan Evers, KCMG, KCVO, KBE, ED (d 1983, govr Northern Nigeria 1954-57); 2 s, 1 da; *Clubs* RAF; *Style*— Lady Sharwood-Smith; 34 Redford Road, Edinburgh EH13 0AA

SHATTOCK, Sir Gordon; s of Frederick Thomas Shattock (d 1974), of Exeter, Devon, and Rose May Irene, *née* James (d 1988); *b* 12 May 1928; *Educ* Hele's Sch Exeter, RVC London; *m* 17 July 1952, Jeanne Mary (d 1984), da of Austin Edwin Watkins (d 1970), of Exeter; 1 s (Simon John b 1954), 1 da (Clare Lucinda b 1956); m 2, 17 Sept 1988, Mrs David Sale (wid); *Career* sr ptnr St David Veterinary Hosp Exeter 1951-84, dir Veterinary Drug Co plc 1982-, divnl bursar Westron Area Woodard Sch's 1988-; fndr chm (now pres) Devon Euro Constituency Cons Cncl, memb TV SW Political Advsy Bd, chm Local Cancer Res Campaign 1972-88, fell Woodward Corpn of Sch's 1973-88, chm Grenville Coll and memb sch cncl 1973-88, pres Br Veterinary Hosps Assoc 1974, memb exec cncl Animal Health Tst 1974-, chm Western Area Cons Pty (Avon, Somerset, Devon, Cornwall) 1982-85, chm Exeter Cathedral Music Fndn 1985-, memb Exeter Health Authy 1985-, exec cncl memb Guide Dogs for the Blind; Freeman City of London 1978, memb Ct and Liveryman Worshipful Co of Farriers; MRCVS 1951; *Recreations* gardening, restoration of old houses; *Clubs* RSM; *Style*— Sir Gordon Shattock; Glasshayes, Higher Shapter St, Topsham, Exeter EX3 0AW (☎ 0392 877434)

SHAUGHNESSY, Alfred James; s of Capt the Hon Alfred T Shaughnessy (ka France 1916), of 905 Dorchester St, Montreal, and the late Sarah Polk, *née* Bradford (later Lady Legh), of Nashville, Tennesee; *b* 19 May 1916; *Educ* Eton, RMC Sandhurst; *m* 18 Sept 1948, Jean Margaret, da of George Lodge (d 1951), of Kirkella, Hull, Yorks; 2 s (Charles George Patrick b 9 Feb 1955, David James Bradford b 3 March 1957); *Career* WWII cmmnd Capt Grenadier Gds; served 1940-46: Normandy, Belgium, Holland, Germany, demob Maj 1946; playwright and screenwriter; author of 14 stage plays incl: Release, Holiday for Simon. Breaking Point, The Heat of the Moment, Old Herbaceous, Love Affair, Double Cut; author of numerous screenplays for films, tv plays, West End revues and radio plays; US Emmy nominee 1974 and 1975 (tv series Upstairs, Downstairs); memb exec cncl Writers Guild of GB 1982-88; *Books* Both Ends of the Candle (autobiography, 1978); *Recreations* music, golf, walking; *Clubs* Garrick; *Style*— Alfred Shaughnessy, Esq; 25 Lyndhurst Way, London SE15 (☎ 01 701 1035)

SHAUGHNESSY, Hon Brigid Mary; da of 3 Baron Shaughnessy; *b* 1948; *Style*— The Hon Brigid Shaughnessy

SHAUGHNESSY, Hon Marion Kathleen; da of 3 Baron Shaughnessy; *b* 1951; *Style*— The Hon Marion Shaughnessy

SHAUGHNESSY, Hon Michael James; 2 s and h of 3 Baron Shaughnessy, *qv*; *b* 12 Nov 1946; *Style*— The Hon Michael Shaughnessy

SHAUGHNESSY, 3 Baron (UK 1916); William Graham Shaughnessy; CD; s of 2 Baron (d 1938); 1 Baron Shaughnessy was pres of Canadian Pacific Railway 1899-1918 and chm 1918-23; *b* 28 Mar 1922; *Educ* Bishop's Coll Sch, Bishop's Univ Lennoxville Canada (BA), Columbia Univ (MSc); *m* 1944, Mary, da of John Whitley (d 1953), of Letchworth, Herts; 1 s (and 1 s decd), 2 da; *Heir* s, Hon Michael Shaughnessy, *qv*; *Career* WWII Canadian Grenadier Gds, Canadian Army 1941-46 served UK and NW Europe (despatches), ret Maj; co dir; exec asst Canadian Miny Fin 1945-51, dir Canada NW Energy Ltd 1955-83 (vice-pres 1969-82); dir: Arbor Capital Inc (Toronto), 1973-, Corona Corpn (Toronto) 1987-; tstee Last Post Fund of Canada, pres Royal Cwlth Soc Montreal 1959-61; *Recreations* history, fishing; *Clubs* Cavalry & Guards, University (Montreal), Montreal Racket; *Style*— The Rt Hon the Lord Shaughnessy; House of Lords, London SW1

SHAW, Hon Alexander Joseph Ranald; yst s of 3 Baron Craigmyle; *b* 20 Nov 1971; *Style*— The Hon Alexander Shaw

SHAW, Hon Alison Margaret; da of 3 Baron Craigmyle; *b* 8 August 1956; *Educ* Harvard Univ (BA 1979); *Career* psychologist; *Clubs* Harvard (NYC); *Style*— The Hon Alison Shaw; 6/6 Collingham Gdns, London SW5 OHW

SHAW, Sir (Charles) Barry; CB (1974), QC (1964); *b* 12 April 1923; *Career* dir of Public Prosecutions for NI 1972-; kt 1980; *Style*— Sir Barry Shaw, CB, QC; Royal Courts of Justice, Belfast, Northern Ireland

SHAW, Prof Bernard Leslie; s of Tom Shaw (d 1971), and Vera, *née* Dale; *b* 28 Mar 1930; *Educ* Hulme GS Oldham, Univ of Manchester (BSc, PhD); *m* 2 June 1951, Mary Elizabeth, da of William Birdsall Neild, 3 s (John Ewart Hardern b 1953, Andrew b 1956, d 1956, Jonathan Bernard b 1980); *Career* sci offr Civil Serv 1953-56, res sci ICI 1956-61, prof Univ of Leeds 1971- (lectr 1962, reader 1966); FRS 1978; *Recreations* tennis, pottery; *Style*— Prof Bernard Shaw; 14 Monkbridge Rd, Leeds LS6 4DX (☎ 0532 755 895); School of Chemistry, Univ of Leeds, Leeds LS2 9JT (☎ 0532 336 402, fax 0532 336 017, telex 556473 UNILDS G)

SHAW, Sir Brian Piers; s of Percy Augustus Shaw; *b* 21 Mar 1933; *Educ* Wrekin Coll, Corpus Christi Coll Cambridge; *m* 1962, Penelope Gay, *née* Reece; 3 s; *Career* chm Furness Withy & Co 1979- (md 1977-87), chm Cncl of Euro and Japanese Nat Shipowners' Assocs 1979-84, pres Gen Cncl of Br Shipping 1985-86, chm Int Chamber of Shipping 1987-; kt 1986; *Recreations* golf, theatre, music; *Clubs* MCC, Denham GC; *Style*— Sir Brian Shaw; 42 Norland Square, London W11 (☎ 01 221 4066);

SHAW, Maj Charles de Vere; s of late Capt John Frederick de Vere Shaw, yr s of 6 Bt; hp of unc, Sir Robert Shaw, 7 Bt; *b* 1 Mar 1957; *Educ* Michaelhouse S Africa; *m* 1985, Sonia, *née* Eden; 1 s (Robert b 1988), 1 da (Alexandra b 1986); *Career* co dir; associate memb: Lloyd's, BIM; *Recreations* sport; *Style*— Charles de Vere Shaw, Esq; West View, Nunnington, Hereford HR1 3NJ

SHAW, Prof Charles Thurstan; CBE (1972); s of Rev John Herbert Shaw, CF 1914-18 (d 1945), of Nethercott, Silverton, nr Exeter, Devon, and Grace Irene Woollatt (d 1964); *b* 27 June 1914; *Educ* Blundell's, Sidney Sussex Coll Cambridge (BA, MA, PhD) London Univ Inst of Educn (Post Grad teachers Dip); *m* 21 Jan 1939, Gilian Ione Maud, da of Edward John Penberthy Magor (d 1941), of Lamellan St Tudy, Bodmin, Cornwall; 2 s (Timothy, Jonathan), 3 da (Rosanne, Gilian, Joanna); *Career* Achimota Coll Gold Coast 1937-45, Cambridgeshire Educn Ctee 1945-51, Cambridge Inst of Educn 1951-63, prof of archaeology Univ of Ibadan Nigeria 1963-74, dir of studies archaeology and anthropology Magdalene Coll Cambridge 1975-80; memb Cambridge Cncl for Racial Equality 1980-, fndr and chm Ichnield Way Assoc, pres Prehistoric Soc 1986-90; Hon DSc Univ of Nigeria 1983; FRAI, FSA; Onunu-Ekwulu Ora of Igbo-Ukwa Nigeria; *Books* Excavation at Dawu (1961), Archaeology and Nigeria (1963), Igbo- Ukwu: An account of Archaeological Discoveries in Eastern Nigeria (2 Vols, 1970), Africa and The Origins of Man (1973), Why 'Darkest' Africa? (1975), Unearthing Igbo-Ukwu (1977), Nigeria: Its Archaeology and Early History (1978); *Recreations* walking; *Clubs* Athenaeum; *Style*— Prof Thurstan Shaw, CBE; 37 Hawthorne Rd, Stapleford, Cambridge CB2 5DU (☎ 0223 842283)

SHAW, Prof Charles Timothy (Tim); s of Charles John Shaw (d 1985), and Constance Olive, *née* Scotton (d 1961) ; *b* 10 Oct 1934; *Educ* Diocesan Coll Rondebosch Cape SA, Witwatersrand Univ (BSc), McGill Univ Montreal Canada (MSc); *m* 1 Sept 1962, Tuulike Raili, da of Dr Artur Aleksander Linari-Linholm (d 1984); 1 s (Jeffrey Charles b 15 Sept 1973), 2 da (Karen b 1 Sept 1963, Nicolette b 29 Jan 1966); *Career* Johannesburg Consolidated Investmt Co Gp: employed variously 1960-65, head of computing 1966-69, mangr 1969-71, consulting engr (Randfontein Estates, GM Co Ltd, Consolidated Murchison Ltd) 1971-73, consulting engr and dir Rustenburg Platinum Mines Ltd 1973-75, chief consulting engr and alternative dir JCI 1975-77, md Western Areas Gold Mining Co Ltd 1975-77; assoc prof Virginia Poly Inst and State Univ Blacksburg Virginia USA 1977-80, prof of mining Royal Sch of Mines Imperial Coll London 1980-; chm special sub-ctee on engrg qualifications Mining Qualifications Bd 1986-87, assessor for Inquiry Kinoulton Notts 1985; memb: Professional Engrs 1977, scientific ctee Inst for Archaeo-Metallurgical Studies 1982-, Safety in Mines Res Advsy Bd UK 1985-88, res advsy ctee Mining Indust Res Orgn UK 1983-, ctee of mgmnt Inst of Archaeology 1985-87, advsy ctee Inst of Archaeology 1987-, cncl Royal Sch of Mines Assoc 1982 (pres 1988-89); govr Camborne Sch of

Mines 1982-; fell: South African Inst of Mining and Metallurgy 1961, Inst of Mining and Metallurgy 1980 (memb cncl 1981-88), Inst of Mining Engrs 1981 (pres Southern Counties Branch 1988-89), Inst of Quarrying 1981; CEng 1980; *Style*— Prof Tim Shaw; Imperial Coll of Sci, Technol and Med, S Kensington, London (☎ 01 883 5111 x 6401, fax 01 589 6806)

SHAW, Dr (James) Charlton Haliday; s of James Henry Shaw (d 1932), of Annamount, Kingstown, Co Dublin, and Eva Susanna, *née* Exshaw (d 1961); *b* 6 Mar 1921; *Educ* Kingstown Sch Dun Laoghaire Co Dublin, Trinity Coll, Univ College Dublin (BA, MB BCh, BAO, DCH, RCP, RCS); *m* (Violet) Elizabeth, da of Ernest Joseph Cotter (d 1964); 1 s (Robert Charlton O'Molloy); *Career* Surgn Lt RNVR 1945-48, PMO 1 Submarine Flotilla Med Station, PMO 3 Destroyer Flotilla; sr ptnr Drs Shaw & Veale Fairford 1950-82; MO child welfare clinics: Cirencester, Fairford & Kempstord 1951-72; chm and fndr Fairford Preservaton Tst, hon sec benevolent ctee Royal Br Legion Fairford branch; *Books* The Molloy Family of Kells (1961), The Waters of Waterstown Co Carlow (1965), The Charltons of Mount Charlton alias Curraghstown (1969); *Recreations* fishing, shooting, beagling, botany, fly tying, washing up; *Style*— Dr Charlton Shaw; Waynes Cottage, Fairford, Glos (☎ 0285 712456)

SHAW, Christopher John; s of William Shaw, of Marple, Cheshire, and Magdalen Dolores Shaw (d 1985); *b* 28 Nov 1940; *Educ* Stockport GS, Manchester Univ (BSc); *Career* gen mangr Dunlop Ltd 1973-77, md J Halstead Ltd 1977-83, gp md Br Syphon plc 1983; *Style*— Christopher Shaw, Esq; British Syphon Industries plc, Emerson Court, Alderley Rd, Wilmslow, Cheshire SK9 1NX (☎ 0625 535 353)

SHAW, Colin Don; s of Rupert Morris Shaw (d 1980), and Enid Fryer, *née* Smith (d 1955); *b* 2 Nov 1928; *Educ* Liverpool Coll, St Peters Hall Oxford (BA, MA); *m* 1955, Elizabeth Ann, da of Paul Alan Bower, 1 s (Giles), 2 da (Tessa, Susan); *Career* barr Inner Temple 1960; chief sec BBC 1972-76, dir: TV IBA 1977-83, Programme Planning Secretariat ITCA 1953-, memb Arts Cncl 1975-80, govr ESU 1977-83, author of radio plays and a stage play for children; *Clubs* Reform; *Style*— Colin Shaw, Esq; Lesters, Little Ickford, Aylesbury, Bucks HP18 9HZ (☎ (084 47) 225); Independent TV Cos Assoc (ITCA), 56 Mortimer Street, London W1N 6AN (☎ 01 636 0749)

SHAW, Prof David Aitken; CBE (1989); s of Col John James McIntosh Shaw, MC, RAMC (d 1940), and Mina, *née* Draper (d 1979); *b* 11 April 1924; *Educ* Edinburgh Acad, Edinburgh Univ (MB ChB); *m* 22 Oct 1960, Jill, da of Eric Parry, CBE, of Lydiate; 1 s (Andrew b 1965), 2 da (Alison b 1963, Katriona b 1969); *Career* WWII RNVR; Ordinary Seaman 1943, Sub Lt 1944, Lt 1946; lectr in clinical neurology Inst of Neurology Univ of London 1957; Univ of Newcastle upon Tyne: sr lectr in neurology 1964- 76, prof of clinical neurology 1976-89, dean of med 1981-89; FRCP 1976, FRCP 1968, Hon FCST 1988; *Clubs* Athenaeum; *Style*— Prof David Shaw, CBE; The Coach House, Moor Rd North, Gosforth, Newcastle Upon Tyne NE3 1AB (☎ 091 285 2029)

SHAW, David Lawrence; MP (Cons) Dover 1987-; *b* 14 Nov 1950; *Educ* King's Sch Wimbledon, City of London Poly; *m* 1986, Dr Lesley Brown; *Career* CA; Coppers & Lybrand 1971-79, Co Bank 1979-83; dir: Invicta Sound plc, Adscene Gp plc, City Gate Estates plc, Palladian Estates plc; fndr and md Sabrelance Ltd; chm Bow Gp 1983-84, fndr Transatlantic Conf; cncllr Royal Borough of Kingston upon Thames Cncl 1974-78, contested Leigh 1979, vice-chm Kingston and Malden Cons Assoc 1979-86; FCA 1974; *Style*— David Shaw, Esq, MP; House of Commons, London SW1A OAA

SHAW, Dennis Frederick; CBE (1974); s of Albert Shaw (d 1957), of Kenton, Middx, and Lily Florence, *née* Hill (d 1968); *b* 20 April 1944; *Educ* Harrow Co Sch, Christ Church Oxford, (BA, MA, DPhil); *m* 25 June 1949, Joan Irene, da of Sydney Chandler; 1 s (Peter James b 1951), 3 da (Margaret b 1953, Katherine b 1956, Deborah b 1959); *Career* memb Civil Def Corps 1942-45, jr sci offr MAP 1944-46; Oxford Univ: demonstrator in physics 1946-49, res offr 1950-57, lectr in physics 1957-75, keeper of sci books 1975-, professorial fell Keble Coll 1977- (fell and tutor in physics 1957-75); visiting prof of physics Univ of S Tennessee USA 1974, pres Int Assoc of Technol Univ Libraries 1986-, chm sci and technol libraries section IFLA 1987-; memb Oxford City Cncl 1963-67; Home Off: memb sci advsy cncl 1966-78, chm police sci devpt ctee 1970-74, memb def sci advsy ctee 1968-; Almoner Christs Hosp 1980; memb: APS 1957, NYAS 1981; FZS 1970, FInst P 1971, CPhys 1984; *Books* Introduction to Electronics (second edn, 1970), Oxford University Science Libraries (second edn, 1981), Information Sources in Physics (1985); *Recreations* enjoying music; *Clubs* Utd Oxford and Cambridge; *Style*— Dr Dennis Shaw, CBE; Keble College, Oxford (☎ 0 865 272 768, fax 0 865 272 821)

SHAW, Fiona Mary; da of Dr Denis Joseph Wilson, of Cork, Ireland, and Mary Teresa, *née* Flynn; *b* 10 July 1958; *Educ* Scoil Mhuire Cork, Univ Coll Cork, RADA; *Career* actress; Julia in the Rivals Nat Theatre 1983, Mary Shelley in Bloody Poetry Leicester and Hampstead 1984; RSC 1985-88: Tatyana Vasilyenia in Philistines, Celia in As You Like It, Madame de Volange in Les Liasons Dangereuses, Erika Brckner in Mephisto, Beatrice in Much Ado About Nothing, Portia in The Merchant of Venice, Mistress Carol in Hyde Park, Katherine in The Taming of the Shrew, Lady Frampul in New Inn, title role in Electra; title role in Mary Stuart Greenwich Theatre 1988, Elspeth in Fireworks for Elspeth Granada TV 1983; films: Christy Brown 1988, The Mountains of the Moon 1988; *Books* Players of Shakespeare (1987), Clamerous Voices' (contrib 1988); *Recreations* tennis, hoping; *Style*— Miss Fiona Shaw; 28A Bellefields Rd, London SW9 9UE (☎ 01 733 0712); Eglantine, Montenotte, Cork, Ireland; c/o Jeremy Conway, Eagle House, 109 Jermyn St, London SW1 6HB

SHAW, Gavin Edmund; s of Alan Linsley Shaw, of Edinburgh, and Marjory Morton, *née* Brown; *b* 9 July 1946; *Educ* Altrincham GS, St John's Coll Cambridge (MA); *m* 19 Jan 1974, Gail, da of Ernest Thomas Inglis Wooderson, of Hertfordshire; 1 da (Georgina Kate b 1979); *Career* advtg mktg consultancy, video prodn; mktg dir Burton Menswear 1975-76, bd dir McCormicks Advtg Agency 1976-81, dir i/c J Walter Thompson (London) 1981-85, dir of devpt and mktg Burger King Europe 1985; prodr, dir and marketer of Transatlantic with Street (an instructional video for yachtsmen on ocean sailing) 1985-87, mktg conslt advertising agencies and retailers 1986-87; *Recreations* yachting, skiing, cycling; *Style*— Gavin Shaw, Esq; 54 Bolingbroke Grove, London SW11 6HR (☎ 01 223 7587); 47 Berners Street, London W1 (☎ 01 436 3355, fax 01 637 1296)

SHAW, George Gavin; s of George Bernard James Shaw, and Audry June Rose, *née* Markwick; *b* 18 June 1957; *Educ* Sir Walter St Johns Sch, Bristol Univ (BA); *Career* md: Joslin Shaw Ltd 1984, Shaw PR Co Ltd 1988; memb ctee Sinjuns Club, Capt Old Sinjuns AFC; *Recreations* horse racing, shooting, fishing, assoc football, skiing; *Clubs* Whites', Sinjuns; *Style*— George Shaw, Esq; 241 Upper St, Islington, London N1 1RU (☎ 01 226 9177, fax 01 359 6351, car tel 0860 383 368)

SHAW, Sir (John) Giles Dunkerley; MP (C) Pudsey Feb 1974-; s of Hugh Dunkerley Shaw; *b* 16 Nov 1931; *Educ* Sedbergh, St John's Coll Cambridge; *m* 1962, Dione Patricia Crosthwaite, da of Prof Mervyn Ellison, of Dublin; 1 s, 2 da; *Career* former pres Cambridge Union; parly candidate (C) Kingston-on-Hull W 1966, mktg dir confectionary div Rowntree Mackintosh Ltd 1969-74; Parly under-sec state: NI Off 1979-81, DOE 1981-83, Energy 1983-84; min of state: Home Off 1984-86, Indust 1986-87; elected tres 1922 Ctee 1988, apptionted to Speaker's panel of chm 1989; kt 1987; *Recreations* ornithology, fishing; *Style*— Sir Giles Shaw, MP; House of Commons, London SW1

SHAW, Henry Jagoe; VRD (1968); s of Dr Benjamin Henry Shaw (d 1955), and Adelaide, JP (d 1965); *b* 16 Mar 1922; *Educ* Eton, Oxford Univ (BM BCh, MA); *m* 1, 10 March 1967 (m dis 1988), Susan Patricia, da of A D Ramsay (d 1952); m 2, 30 Dec 1988, Daphne Joan Hayes, da of H Charney (d 1978); *Career* conslt ENT surgn Royal Nat Throat Nose and Ear Hosp London, civilian conslt ENT surgn RN, conslt ENT surgn St Mary's Hosp Praed St London; conslt head and neck surgn Royal Marsden Hosp London, Hunterian prof RCS 1957, sr lectr Univ of London 1984, Ernest Miles lectr Royal Marsden Hosp 1985; memb: Assoc of Head and Neck Surgns of GB, Br Assoc of surgical Oncology; corresponding memb Assoc of Head and Neck Surgns of USA, British Assoc of Otolaryngologists; hon memb: American Laryngological Assoc and Otolaryngological Assoc of Aust, Sociéte Francaise d'Otorhinolaryngologie; FRCS 1950; *Books* Partial Laryngectomy after Irradiation (1978), Malignant Diseases of the Oropharynx (1980), Conservation and Repair in Cancer Surgery of the Head and Neck (1980), Head and Neck Oncology (jt ed 1987); *Recreations* walking, sailing, swimming; *Clubs* Hurlingham, Army and Navy, RSM; *Style*— Henry Shaw, Esq, VRD; Lislee Hse, Tredenham Rd, St Mawes, Cornwall TR2 5AN

SHAW, James Thomas Durrant; s of Lt-Col Geoffrey Devereux Shaw (d 1960); *b* 14 June 1927; *Educ* Eton, King's Coll Cambridge; *m* 1956, Jennifer June, da of the late Christopher Birkbeck, of Hevingham, Norfolk; 1 s, 1 da; *Career* chm and md Scottow Farms Ltd, dir Scottow Mgmnt Servs, chm of Sywelll Airport & Sywell Motel Ltd, MFH of North Norfolk Harriers 1973-78; *Recreations* hunting, shooting, horse breeding; *Clubs* RAC; *Style*— James Durrant Shaw Esq; Scottow Hall, Norwich, Norfolk (☎ Swanton Abbott 601)

SHAW, John Arthur (Jack); s of Arthur Shaw (d 1981), of Windridge, Guiseley, Leeds, and Genevieve, *née* Fattorini (d 1977); *b* 7 April 1925; *Educ* Stonyhurst, Leeds Univ; *m* 1, 10 Dec 1948, Nan (d 1983), da of Herbert Armitage; 6 s (John b 1949, Michael b 1951, David b 1953, Brian b 1955, Richard b 1957, Patrick b 1961); m 2, Helgard Sofie Greth; *Career* RE 1944-47; Bradford Steel Pin Co Ltd: co sec 1948-60, dir 1960-67, asst md 1967-71, jt md 1971-74, md 1974-, chm 1978-; Cons Assoc: dep chm Pudsey constituency (chm, pres, election agent Aireborough m Ward), former pres Rawdon branch; jt winner Cons Nat Speaking Competition 1967; FBIM; *Recreations* pistol shooting, sea angling, trout fishing, photography; *Clubs* Shark Angling Club of GS, Irish Shark; *Style*— Jack Shaw, Esq; Larkfield Grange, Rawdon, Leeds LS19 6DZ (☎ 0532 506 128); Bradford Steel Pin Co Ltd, Dick Lane, Laisterdyke, Bradford BD4 8JE (☎ 0274 665 780, telex 51249)

SHAW, Josephine; da of James Henry Shaw, and Gwendoline Mabel, *née* Baker; *b* 15 August 1930; *Educ* Barr Hill GS Coventry, Birmingham Secretarial Coll; *Career* commercial trg advsr ILO Geneva 1965-76 (long-term assignments Sierra Leone and Ghana, short-term Africa), md Teaching Aids Ltd 1976- (chm 1988); MInstAM, FBIM, FIOD; *Books* Teach Yourself Office Practice (1972), Secretarial Work Experience (jtly, 1978), Office Organisation for Managers (1978), West African Office Practice (adaption of British edn, 1978), Administration in Business (1981), Caribbean Office Procedures (jtly, 1984), Word Processing and Computer Training Techniques (1988); *Recreations* needlework, tapestry, photography, classical music; *Style*— Miss Josephine Shaw; Teaching Aids Ltd, Denestead House, Station Rd, New Milton, Hants BH25 6LD (☎ 0425 612 911, car tel 0836 589 629)

SHAW, Hon Justin Edward Magnus; s of 3 Baron Thomas Donald Macay, Lord Craigmyle, and Anthea Esther Cristine, *née* Rich; *b* 1 April 1965; *Educ* Eton, Gonville and Caius Coll Cambridge; *Style*— The Hon Justin Shaw; 18 The Boltons, SW10 9SY (☎ 01 373 3533)

SHAW, Hon Madeleine Claire; da of 3 Baron Craigmyle; *b* 23 Oct 1963; *Style*— The Hon Madeleine Shaw

SHAW, Dr Mark Robert; s of William Shaw, of Willowbeck, Drayton St Leonard, Oxon, and Mabel Courtenay, *née* Bower; *b* 11 May 1945; *Educ* Dartington Hall Sch, Oriel Coll Oxford (BA, MA, DPhil); *m* 11 July 1970, Francesca Dennis, da of Rev Dennis Wilkinson (d 1971); 2 da (Zerynthia b 23 Dec 1972, Melitaea b 19 April 1978); *Career* res asst dept zoology Univ of Manchester 1973-76, univ res fell Univ of Reading 1977-80; Nat Museums of Scotland (formerly Royal Scottish Museum): asst keeper dept of natural history 1980-83, keeper of natural history 1983-; frequent contrib to various pubns on entomology and chemistry; FRES 1974; *Style*— Dr Mark Shaw

SHAW, Martin; s of Albert Cyril Shaw (d 1967), of Leeds, and Letitia Whitehead (d 1978); *b* 31 Oct 1944; *Educ* Leeds GS, UCL (LLB); *m* 19 Aug 1967, Christine Helen, da of Maurice Grenville Whitwam (d 1986), of Leeds; 2 s (Simon b 17 March 1973, Jonathan b 4 Aug 1978), 1 da (Sarah b 25 Nov 1970); *Career* Simpson Curtis: articled clerk 1966-69, slr 1969-71, ptnr 1971-, head corporate dept 1980-88; chm: Minstergate plc 1985-, ABI Caravans Ltd 1986-88, Legal Resources Gp 1988-, Minster Corpn plc 1988-, govr: Richmond House Sch (and chm), Gateways Sch; memb: econ and trade ctee Leeds C of C and Indust, Headingley Rotary Club, Yorks & Humberside Devpt Assoc, Leeds Business Venture (dir 1982), Variety Club of GB; memb: Slrs Euro Gp 1975, Law Soc 1969, Leeds Law Soc 1969, ABA 1985, IBA 1985; *Recreations* running, golf, squash, tennis; *Clubs* The Leeds, Alwoodley GC, Chapel Allerton Lawn Tennis & Squash; *Style*— Martin Shaw, Esq; Sycamore Lodge, Harrowby Rd, West Park, Leeds LS16 5HN (☎ 0532 785350); Simpson Curtis, 41 Park Square, Leeds LS1 2NS (☎ 0532 433433, fax 0532 445598, car tel 0836 253898, telex 55376)

SHAW, Gp Capt Mary Michal; RRC (1982); da of Ven Archdeacon Herbert Thorndike Shaw, and Violet Rosario, *née* Hobbs; *b* 7 April 1933; *Educ* Wokingham Co Girls Sch; *Career* SRN Royal Berks Hosp 1955, state registered midwife Battle Hosp Reading 1957, cmmr Princess Marys RAF Nursing Serv 1963-; sr matron RAF Hosp:

Wegberg Germany 1981-83, Ely Cambs 1983-84; Gp Capt MOD 1984, appt Matron in Chief PMRAFNS, dir Nursing Serv RAF and dep dir Def Nursing Servs 1985-88, ret 1988; involved with St Edmundsbury Cathedral; OStJ 1975; *Recreations* gardening, cake decorating, handicrafts; *Clubs* RAF; *Style—* Gp Capt Mary Michal Shaw, RRC; 5 William Barnaby Yard, College St, Bury St Edmunds, Suffolk IP33 1PQ (☎ 0284 705 836)

SHAW, (Francis) Michael; s of Joseph Stanley Shaw (d 1959), of Yorks, and Irene Shaw, *née* Weldrake; *b* 12 August 1936; *Educ* Rotherham GS; *m* 1960, Margaret Elinor, da of Ralph William Russum (d 1986); 2 da (Caroline b 1963, Juliet b 1964); *Career* chief accountant: Eastern Counties Bldg Soc 1967-74, Britannia Bldg Soc 1974-75 (md 1985-); FICA; *Recreations* golf, photography, travel; *Clubs* Leek GC, British Pottery Mfrs Fedn; *Style—* Michael Shaw, Esq; Rock House, Cheadle Road, Wetley Rocks, Stoke-on-Trent (☎ (0782) 550655); Britannia Building Soc, Newton House, Leek, Staffs (☎ (0538) 399399, fax (0538) 399261)

SHAW, Hon Michael Frank; s of Baron Kilbrandon, PC (Life Peer); *b* 1944; *m* 1978, Catherine Ballantine; 1 s (Torquil b 1981), 1 da (Tamara b 1980); *Recreations* sailing, shooting, skiing, fishing; *Clubs* New (Edinburgh), Royal Highland YC; *Style—* The Hon Michael Shaw; Kilbrandon House, Balvicar, By Oban, Argyll

SHAW, Michael Gordon (Mike); s of Leslie Shaw, of Buckhurst Hill, and Pauline, *née* Gordon (d 1971); *b* 8 July 1931; *Educ* Epsom Co GS; *m* 23 Nov 1957 (m dis 1981), Ann, da of Henry Newbury; 3 s (Kevin b 1958, Simon b 1959, Adam b 1962), 2 da (Zoe b 1963, Melanie b 1969); *Career* Nat Serv RAF 1949-51; advtg copywriter and creative dir; Cunningham Hurst 1979, Progress Advtg 1981; numerous advtg campaigns incl: Honeywell, Calorgas, Wella, Honda, Pilkington Glass, Mountfield Psion; memb Mensa 1975; *Recreations* writing, computing, photography (video); *Style—* Mike Shaw, Esq; 45 Beechfield Rd, Bromley, Kent BR1 3BT (☎ 01 464 0853); No 2 Parkwest Place, Kendal Street, London W2 2QZ (☎ 01 402 9361)

SHAW, Michael Hewitt; s of Donald Smethurst Shaw (d 1982), and Marian Clarissa, *née* Hewitt; *b* 5 Jan 1935; *Educ* Sedbergh, Clare Coll Cambridge (BA, MA); *m* 10 Aug 1963, Elizabeth Monica, da of Maj-Gen Sir Hubert Elvin Rance, GCB, GBE (d 1974); 4 da (Melanie b 1964, Sarah b 1968, Lucy b 1970, d 1973, Suzanna b 1973); *Career* Nat Serv 2 Lt RA 1953-55; dist offr and ADC to govr of Tanganyika HMOCS 1959-62; FCO 1963-: London 1963 and 1965, second sec The Hague 1964, second sec Vientiane 1966, first sec Valletta 1972, first sec and cnsllr Brussels 1982, cnsllr London 1987; *Recreations* cricket, theatre, walking; *Clubs* MCC, Army and Navy; *Style—* Michael Shaw, Esq; Foreign and Cwlth Off, King Charles St, London SW1A 2AH

SHAW, Sir Michael Norman; JP (Dewsbury 1953), DL (W Yorks 1977), MP (C) Scarborough 1974-; eld s of late Norman Shaw; *b* 9 Oct 1920; *Educ* Sedbergh; *m* 1951, Joan Mary Louise, da of late Sir Alfred Mowat, 2 and last Bt, DSO, OBE, MC; 3 s; *Career* MP: (Lib and C) Brighouse and Spenborough 1960-64, (C) Scarborough and Whitby 1966-74; PPS: Min of Lab and Nat Serv 1962-63, sec of state DTI 1970-72; Chllr Duchy of Lancaster 1973-74; memb UK Delgn Euro Parl 1974-79; FCA; kt 1982; *Style—* Sir Michael Shaw, JP, DL, MP; Duxbury Hall, Liversedge, W Yorks WF15 7NR (☎ (0924) 402270)

SHAW, Hon Patrick James; s of Baron Kilbrandon, PC (Life Peer); *b* 1938; *m* 1964, Elisabeth Campbell-Gibson; *Style—* The Hon Patrick Shaw; Highfield, Taynuilt, Argyll

SHAW, Capt Peter Jack; s of Jack Shaw (d 1968), of London, and Gladys Elizabeth Shaw *née* Knight (d 1981); *b* 27 Oct 1924; *Educ* Watford GS, RN Coll Dartmouth, RN Staff Coll Greenwich, NATO Def Coll Paris; *m* 18 Aug 1951, Pauline da of Sir Frank William Madge, 2 Bt (d 1962); 1 s (Christopher John b 1957), 1 da (Carol Anne (Mrs Livett) b 1952); *Career* WWII 1942-45; serv: Russian, Atlantic, Malta convoys, Normandy Invasion (on HM Ships: Kenya, Quadrant, Resolution, London, Kelvin), cmd HM LCI (L) 377 1945, staff of Flag Offr Germany 1951-53 and 1946-48, HMS Corunna 1949-51, exec offr HMS Chevron and HMS Whirlwind 1953-55, naval instr RAF Coll Cranwell 1956-58, cmd HMS Venus and HMS Carron 1958, HMS Vigilant 1960, staff of C-in-C Portsmouth 1961-63, MOD 1963-65, SHAPE 1966-68, Cdr RN Coll Greenwich 1968-70, def and naval attache The Hague 1971-73, Capt of the Port and Queen's Harbourmaster Plymouth 1973-76, Capt of the Port and Queen's Harbourmaster Chatham, and chief of staff to Flag Offr Medway 1976-79; gen sec Interparl Union (Br Gp) 1979-; FIL 1956, MBIM 1975; *Recreations* international affairs, foreign languages, domestic pursuits; *Style—* Capt Peter Shaw; Woodside Rogate, Petersfield, Hants, GU31 5DJ (☎ 073 080 344); Interparliamentary Union, Palace of Westminster, London SW1 (☎ 01 219 3013)

SHAW, Richard John Gildroy; s of Edward Philip Shaw (d 1970), and Mary Elizabeth Shaw; *b* 7 June 1936; *Educ* Dragon Sch, Eton; *m* 1973, Yvonne Kathleen, da of Henry Percival Maskell (d 1978); 1 s (Rupert Henry Gildroy b 1974); *Career* dir Hill Samuel Group Ltd, chief exec and dep chm Lowndes Lambert Group Ltd (insur brokers); *Recreations* golf, cricket, yachting (MY Moonmaiden II), reading, horseracing; *Clubs* Royal Thames YC, Sunningdale GC, Portland, Clermont, Lloyd's YC; *Style—* Richard Shaw, Esq; 18 Phillimore Gdns, London W8 7QE (☎ 01 937 2942); Lowndes Lambert Group Ltd, Lowndes Lambert House, PO Box 431, 53 Eastcheap, London EC3P 3HL (☎ 01 283 2000, telex 8814631)

SHAW, Sir Robert; 7 Bt (UK 1821), of Bushy Park, Dublin; s of Lt-Col Sir Robert de Vere Shaw, 6 Bt, MC (d 1969); *b* 31 Jan 1925; *Educ* Harrow, Iklahome Univ, Missouri Univ; *m* 1954, Jocelyn Mary, da of Andrew McGuffie (decd), of Mbabane, Swaziland; 2 da; *Heir* n, Charles de Vere Shaw; *Career* Lt RN (ret); professional engr (Alberta); *Style—* Sir Robert Shaw, Bt; 234 40 Avenue SW, Calgary, Alberta, Canada

SHAW, Sir Roy; s of late Frederick Shaw, and Elsie, *née* Odgen; *b* 8 July 1918; *Educ* Firth Park GS Sheffield, Manchester Univ; *m* 1946, Gwenyth Baron; 5 s, 2 da; *Career* writer and lectr, lectr in adult educn Leeds Univ, prof and dir adult educn Keele Univ 1962-75, sec gen Arts Cncl 1975-83; Hon DLitt: City Univ, Southampton Univ; D Univ Open Univ, patron Artists' Campaign against Tobacco Sponsorship; kt 1979; *Books* The Arts and the People (1987); *Recreations* arts, walking, swimming; *Clubs* Arts; *Style—* Sir Roy Shaw; 48 Farrer Rd, London N8 8LB (☎ 01 348 1857)

SHAW, Roy Edwin; *née* Reilly; s of Edwin Victor Shaw (d 1938), and Edith Lily, *née* Clarke (d 1987); *b* 21 July 1925; *Educ* William Ellis Sch London; *Career* tank crew 5 RIDG 1943-45, CSM intelligence corps 1945-47; mktg conslt and lectr; cncl memb: Hampstead 1956-62, St Pancras 1962-65; memb Camden cncl 1964-: chm planning ctee 1967-68, memb fin ctee 1971-74, chief whip and dep ldr 1965-75, ldr 1975-82; vice chm Assoc of Metro Authorities 1980-83, dep chm and ldr Lab Pty London Boroughs Assoc 1978-83; memb: Consultative Cncl of Local Govt Fin 1978-83, advsy ctee on Local govt Audit 1979-82, Audit Cmmn for Eng and Wales 1983-, pt/t London Electricity Bd 1977-83, Tport Users Consultative Ctee for London 1974-80; *Recreations* listening to music; *Style—* Roy Shaw, Esq; Town Hall, Euston Rd, London NW1 2RU (☎ 01 278 4444)

SHAW, Sir Run Run; CBE (1974); *b* 14 Oct 1907; *m* 1932, Wong Mee Chun, 4 children; *Career* pres: Shaw Orgn 1963-, Hong Kong Red Cross Soc 1972-; chm Hong Kong Arts Festival 1974-, bd of govrs Hong Kong Arts Centre 1978-, Hong Kong TV Ltd (TVB) 1980-, Bd of Tstees Utd Coll Hong Kong 1983-; memb cncl Chinese Univ of Hong Kong 1977- (fndr Shaw Coll Chinese Univ of Hong Kong 1986-); kt 1977; *Style—* Sir Run Run Shaw, CBE; Shaw House, Lot 220 Clearwater Bay Rd, Kowloon, Hong Kong (☎ 3 7191551, telex 43514 SHAWS HX)

SHAW, Sebastian Lewis; s of Geoffrey Turton Shaw (d 1943), and Mary Grace Shaw (d 1954); *b* 29 May 1905; *Educ* Gresham's, Slade Sch of Fine Art, RADA; *m* 9 June 1929, Margaret Kate, *née* Wellesley-Lynn (decd); 1 da (Drusilla b 9 Sept 1932, m 1961, John Macleod of Macleod, 29th Chief); *Career* WWII RAF 1940-44; actor, author; first stage appearance as one of the Juvenile Band in Me Cockyolly Bird Court Theatre 1914; distinguished career in theatre, radio, films, TV 1925- incl: first London appearance as Archangel in The Sign of the Sun (Regent Theatre) 1925, Wyndham Brandon in Rope (Strand Theatre) 1929 (also Masque Theatre New York), title-role in first English prodn of Everyman Ludlow Festival 1956, Sir George Crofts in Mrs Warren's Profession and Morell in Candida (Dublin Festival) 1961 (also European tour); Royal Court Theatre 1965-66: General Conrad von Hotzendorf in A Patriot for Me, Sir Francis Harker in The Cresta Run, Private Attercliffe in Serjeant Musgrave's Dance, Sir Walter Whorehound in A Chaste Maid in Cheapside, Mr Voysey in The Voysey Inheritance, Jack Latham and Reginald Maitland in Their Very Own and Golden City; joined RSC 1966 performances incl: Sir Gerald Catesley in Belchers Luck, Sir Oblong Fitz Oblong in The Thwarting of Baron Bollingrew, Friar Laurence in Romeo and Juliet, King of France in All's Well that Ends Well, Duncan in Macbeth (toured Finland and Russia), Gloucester in King Lear, Ulysses in Troilus and Cressida, Leonato in Much Ado About Nothing (towed USA), Justice Adam Ouerdo in Bartholomew Fair, Vincentio in Measure for Measure, Polonius in Hamlet, Sir Eglalmour in The Two Gentlemen of Verona; artist RSC; *Books plays*: The Cliff Walk, Take a Life, The Glass Maze; *novel* The Christening (1975); *Recreations* chess, music; *Style—* Sebastian Shaw, Esq; c/o Royal Shakespeare Co, The Barbican Theatre, London EC2

SHAW, Sydney Herbert; OBE (1958) CMG (1963); s of late John Beaumont Shaw; *b* 6 Nov 1903; *Educ* Kings Coll Sch Wimbledon, Imperial Coll London (BSc, PhD), Birmingham Univ (MSc); *m* 1930, Mary Louise, *née* Chapman; 1 s 1 da; *Career* dir Overseas Geological Surveys and geological advsr to Sec State for the Colonies 1959-68; *Style—* Sydney Shaw Esq; Bisham Edge, Stoney Ware, Marlow, Bucks SL7 1RN (☎ (062 84) 4951)

SHAW, Hon Thomas Columba; s and h of 3 Baron Craigmyle; *b* 19 Oct 1960; *m* 25 April 1987, Alice, 2 da of David Floyd, of Combe Down, Bath; *Style—* The Hon Thomas Shaw; c/o Rt Hon Lord Craigmyle, 18 The Boltons, London, SW10 9SY

SHAW OF TORDARROCH, John; 22 Chief of the Highland Clan of Shaw; s of late Maj Charles John Shaw of Tordarroch, MBE, TD, DL, JP; *b* 1937; *Educ* Eton, Magdalene Coll Cambridge (MA); *m* 1960, Silvia Margaret, da of late Rev David John Silian Jones; 1 s; *Heir* s, Iain b 1968; *Career* late 2 Lt Seaforth Highlanders 1955-57; memb Royal Co of Archers (Queen's Body Guard for Scotland); hon vice-pres Clan Chattan Assoc (UK); memb standing Cncl of Scottish Chiefs, Convenor of the Northern Meeting 1984-; *Books* A History of Clan Shaw (ed); *Clubs* New, Turf, Puffins; *Style—* John Shaw of Tordarroch; Tordarroch, Farr, Inverness IV1 2XF; Newhall, Balblair, by Dingwall, Ross-shire IV7 8lQ

SHAW-STEWART, Sir Houston Mark; 11 Bt (NS 1667) of Greenock and Blackhall, Renfrewshire, MC (1950), TD (1968); s of Lt-Col Sir (Walter) Guy Shaw-Stewart, 9 Bt, MC (d 1976); suc bro, Sir Euan Guy Shaw-Stewart, 10 Bt, 1980; *b* 24 April 1931; *Educ* Eton; *m* 1982, Lucinda Victoria, yr da of Alexander Fletcher, of The Old Vicarage, Wighill, nr Tadcaster; 1 s (Ludovic Houston); *Heir* s, Ludovic Houston b 1986; *Career* 2 Lt RUR Korea 1950, Ayrshire Yeo 1952, ret Maj 1969; jt MFH Lanarkshire and Renfrewshire 1974-78, Vice Lord-Lieut Strathclyde Region 1980-; memb Royal Co Archers; *Recreations* shooting and racing; *Clubs* White's, Turf, Pratt's; *Style—* Sir Houston Shaw-Stewart, Bt, MC, TD,; Ardgowan, Inverkip, Renfrewshire (☎ (0475) 521226)

SHAWCROSS, Baron (Life Peer UK 1959); Hartley William Shawcross; GBE (1974), PC (1946), QC (KC 1939); s of John Shawcross (d 1968), and Hilda (d 1942); *b* 4 Feb 1902; *Educ* Dulwich, London Univ, Geneva Univ; *m* 1, 1924, Rosita Alberta (d 1943), da of William Shyvers (d 1944); m 2, 1945, Joan Winifred (d riding accident 1974), da of Hume Mather (d 1968), of Carlton Lodge, Tunbridge Wells; 2 s, 1 da; *Career* barr Gray's Inn 1925, chief UK prosecutor Nuremburg Trials, asst chm Sussex QS 1941; rec: Salford 1941-45, Kingston-upon-Thames 1946-61; JP Sussex 1948-61; former dir: EMI Ltd, Rank Hovis McDougall Ltd, Hawker Siddeley Gp, (and chm) Upjohn & Co Ltd, Times Newspapers; former chm Morgan Guaranty Tst Co's int advsy cncl; MP (Lab) St Helens 1945-58, attorney-gen 1945-51, pres BOT 1951, UK memb Perm Ct Arbitration The Hague 1950-67; chllr Sussex Univ 1965-86, chm Int C of C Cmmn on Unethical Practices 1976; dir: Caffyns Motors Ltd, Morgan et Cie SA, TVB (Hong Kong) Ltd, Shaw Bros (Hong Kong) Ltd, Observer Newspapers 1982-; a dir of public cos and a conslt on foreign business to Morgan Guaranty Trust of NY and other cos; Hon FRCS, Hon FRCOG; Kt Grand Cross of Imperial Iranian Order of Homayoon 1965; kt 1945; *Recreations* yachting (yacht, 'Talisker'); *Clubs* Bucks, White's, RAC, Royal Cornwall YC, Royal Yacht Squadron, New York YC, Travellers' (Paris); *Style—* The Rt Hon the Lord Shawcross, GBE, PC, QC; 12 Gray's Inn Sq, London WC1 (☎ 01 242 5500); Friston Place, Sussex BN30 0AH (☎ (032 15) 2206); Anchorage St Mawes, Cornwall: Morgan Bank, 1 Angel Court, London EC2 (☎ 01 600 2300)

SHAWCROSS, Hon Hume; s (by 2 m) of Baron Shawcross (Life Peer); *b* 18 Mar 1953; *Educ* Eton; *Style—* The Hon Hume Shawcross

SHAWCROSS, Dr Hon Joanna (The Hon Mrs Peck); da (by 2 m) of Baron Shawcross (Life Peer); *b* 20 Sept 1948,V-; *Educ* Benenden, London Univ (MB BS); *m* 11 Oct 1986, Charles Russell Peck, s of Russell Hastings Peck, of Cambridge, Mass, USA; 1 s (Henry Russell Hartley b 6 Aug 1988); *Career* med practitioner; *Style—* Dr

The Hon Joanna Shawcross; 105 Mayola Rd, London E5 0RG

SHAWCROSS, Roger Michael; s of Michael Campbell Shawcross (d 1945), of London, and Friedel Marie Partington, *née* Freund (d 1983); *b* 27 Mar 1941; *Educ* Radley, Christ Church Oxford (MA); *m* 15 Feb 1969, Sarah, da of Maurice Henry Peter Broom (d 1987), of Farnham, Surrey; 1 s (Philip b 1974), 1 da (Miranda b 1972); *Career* barr Grays Inn 1967, rec Western circuit 1985; *Recreations* tennis, music, literature, travel; *Style*— Roger Shawcross, Esq; Oakleigh, Sarum Road, Winchester; Francis Taylor Building, Temple, London EC4Y 7BY (☎ 01 353 2182, fax 01 583 1727, telex 25182)

SHAWCROSS, Hon William Hartley Hume; s (by 2 m) Baron Shawcross (Life Peer); *b* 28 May 1946; *Educ* Eton, Univ Coll Oxford; *m* 1, 1972, Marina Warner; m 2, 1981, Michal, da of late A J Levin by his w Leah; *Style*— The Hon William Shawcross; 40 Estelle Rd, NW3 (☎ 01 267 1852)

SHAWE-TAYLOR, Desmond Christopher; CBE (1965); s of Francis Manley Shawe-Taylor (d 1920), of Moor Park, Athenry, Co Galway, by his w, Agnes Mary Eleanor (d 1939), elder da of Christopher Ussher, of Eastwell, Loughrea, Co Galway; *b* 29 May 1907; *Educ* Shrewsbury, Oriel Coll Oxford; *Career* WWII served Capt RA (AA); literary and occasional musical criticism New Statesman and Spectator until 1939; music critic New Statesman and Nation 1945-58, Sunday Times 1958-, New Yorker (guest critic) 1973-74; *Books* Covent Garden (1948), The Record Guide (with Edward Sackville-West, later Lord Sackville, with supplements 1951-56); *Recreations* travel, croquet, gramophone; *Clubs* Brooks's; *Style*— Desmond Shawe-Taylor, Esq, CBE; Long Crichel House, Wimborne, Dorset BH21 5JU (☎ 0258 89250); 15 Furlong Rd, London N7 8LS (☎ 01 607 4854)

SHAWYER, Peter Michael; s of Edward William Francis Shawyer (d 1986), of Brookmans Park Herts, and Majorie Josephine Shawyer; *b* 11 Sept 1950; *Educ* Enfield GS, Sheffield Univ (BA); *m* 23 June 1979, Margot Anne, da of Wing Cdr Norman Edwin Bishop (d 1975), of Sidmouth, Devon; 1 s (Richard b 14 March 1984), 1 da (Emily b 3 Dec 1980); *Career* CA; joined Touche Ross & Co 1972 (ptnr 1982-), specialist in taxation and writer of numerous tax articles in specialist literature; ACA 1975; *Recreations* golf, squash; *Clubs* Enfield GC, Broxbourne Sports; *Style*— Peter Shawyer, Esq; Touche Ross & Co, Hill House, 1 Little New St, London EC4A 3TR (☎ 01 353 8011, fax 01 583 8517, telex 884739 TRLNDN G)

SHAWYER, Robert Cort; eld s of Arthur Frederic Shawyer, and Elizabeth Mary, *née* Park; *b* 9 Oct 1913; *Educ* Charterhouse, Corpus Christi Coll Oxford (MA), Birkbeck Coll London (PhD); *m* 1939, Isabel Jessie, *née* Rogers (d 1986); 2 da; *Career* cmmnd RAEC 1938 (Lt-Col 1945); Bank of England 1935-37, princ Miny of Nat Insur 1948, Admty 1951, asst sec 1957, seconded NATO 1960, Nat Def Coll Canada 1961-62, Cwlth Off 1967, consul-gen Buenos Aires 1967-70, cultural rels dept FCO 1970-72, ret; FRGS; *Recreations* mediaeval history, astronomy; *Clubs* Army and Navy; *Style*— R C Shawyer, Esq; Southfield, 3 South Road, Taunton, Somerset (☎ 0823 333061)

SHEA, Michael Sinclair MacAuslan; CVO (1987, LVO 1985); s of James Michael Shea, of Lenzie; *b* 10 May 1938; *Educ* Gordonstoun, Edinburgh Univ (MA, PhD); *m* 1968, Mona Grec Stensen, da of Egil Stensen, of Oslo; 2 da; *Career* FO 1963, former first sec Bonn, head of chancery Bucharest 1973, dep dir-gen Br Info Servs NY 1976, Press sec to HM The Queen 1978-87; dir of public affairs for Hanson plc 1987-; govr Gordonstown Sch; author; *Books* Britain's Offshore Islands (1981), Tomorrow's Men (1982), Influence (1988), and six other novels under the name Michael Sinclair; *Recreations* writing, sailing; *Style*— Michael Shea, Esq, CVO; c/o Hanson plc, 1 Grosvenor Place, London SW1X 7JH

SHEARD, (John) Neville; s of Edgar Sheard (d 1982), of Huddersfield, and Kathleen, *née* Frobisher; *b* 7 July 1935; *Educ* Rossall, Exeter Coll Oxford (MA); *m* 1, 26 Feb 1962, Glenys Mary (d 1970), da of Eric Jebson, of Huddersfield; 2 s (Charles b 1962, James b 1965); m 2, 20 July 1973, Elizabeth Mary, da of Eustace Lloyd Howell-Jones (d 1976), of Leamington Spa; 1 s (Jonathan b 1975); *Career* Nat Serv 2 Lt RCS TA; slr 1962, sr ptnr Armitage Sykes & Hinchcliffe Huddersfield 1980 (ptnr 1963-80); chm Kirkwood Hospice Huddersfield, tstee Huddersfield YMCA, ctee memb Huddersfield Parish Church Appeal Fund; hon slr: Huddersfield Scouts, Colne Valley Beagles; memb Law Soc 1962-; *Recreations* cricket, fell walking; *Style*— Neville Sheard, Esq; 4 Butternab Rd, Beaumont Park, Huddersfield, W Yorks HD4 7AH (☎ 0484 652 996); 72 New North Rd, Huddersfield, W Yorks HD1 5NW (☎ 0484 538 121, fax 0484 518968, telex 518123 ASHUD G)

SHEARER, Anthony Patrick (Tony); s of James Francis Shearer, of London, and Judith Margaret, *née* Bowman; *b* 24 Oct 1948; *Educ* Rugby; *m* 1 Dec 1972, Jennifer, da of Alfred Dixon (d 1981); 2 da (Juliet b 19 Aug 1980, Lauretta b 30 March 1982); *Career* ptnr Deloitte Haskins & Sells 1980-88 (joined 1967), dir M & Gp plc 1988-; FCA; *Recreations* tennis, garden, family, rock 'n' roll; *Clubs* Brooks'; *Style*— Tony Shearer, Esq; Gaston House, East Bergholt, Suffolk (☎ 0206 298 525); 3 Quays, Tower Hill, London EC3R 6BQ (☎ 01 626 4588, fax 01 623 8615, telex 887196)

SHEARER, (Edgar) Donald Reid; CBE (1974, OBE 1945), TD (1950); s of Edgar Walter Shearer (d 1926); *b* 6 June 1909; *Educ* Aldenham; *m* 1935, Hester Helena, *née* Cooke; 3 da; *Career* Col TA Middle East Forces; dir Sir Alfred McAlpine Son Ltd (N Ireland) 1959-85, chm Lindsay Bros (Belfast) Ltd and associated cos 1970-73; memb Londonderry Devpt Cmmn 1968-73; chm: NI Territorial Assoc 1971-74, Sports Cncl for N Ireland 1974-77, Ulster Sports and Recreation Trust 1976-79; Hon ADC to HM The Queen 1960-69, High Sheriff Co Down 1979; DL Co Down 1959-86; *Recreations* shooting, golf, spectator sports; *Clubs* Friendly Brothers (Dublin), MCC; *Style*— Donald Shearer, Esq, CBE, TD; Saltwater Cottage, Finnebrogue, Downpatrick, Co Down, N Ireland (☎ 0396 2081)

SHEARER, Rt Hon Hugh Lawson; PC (1969); *b* 18 May 1923; *Educ* St Simons Coll Jamaica; *Career* former journalist & trade unionist; PM of Jamaica and min Def and External Affrs 1967-72, MP SE Clarendon 1976- (S Clarendon 1967-76), oppn ldr 1972-74, dep leader Jamaican Labour Party 1967-74, dep PM and min Foreign Affairs & Foreign Trade Jamaica 1980-; Order of Francisco de Miranda (Venezuela); Hon LLD Harvard Univ; *Style*— The Rt Hon Hugh Shearer; House of Representatives, Kingston, Jamaica

SHEARER, John Charles Johnston; s of Brig Eric James Shearer, CB, CBE, MC (d 1980), and Phyllis Muriel, *née* Mules (d 1981); *b* 10 Nov 1924; *Educ* Eton, RMA Sandhurst; *m* 1, 1952 (m dis), Sylvia Elizabeth, da of Wilfrid F Coombs (d 1977), of Surrey; 2 s (Charles b 1952, d 1984, Michael b 1961); m 2, 10 April 1975, Ellen Ingeborg, da of Cdr Edward Nennecke, of Hamburg (d 1952); 2 s (Philip b 1974, Edward b 1976); *Career* served Scots Gds 1943-49: 2 Lt 1944, Lt 1944, Capt 1946 (despatches), 24 and 4 Gds Bde 1946-48, ret 1949; joined Thomas R Miller & Son 1952 (ptnr 1962-85), ptnr T R Miller & Son (Bermuda) 1968-87; dir: Turks Caicos Islands, Hanseatic Conslt Ltd 1974-, Blue Hills Aviation Ltd 1977-, Hanseatic Investmt 1977-, Pelican Hldgs 1985-, Grand Turk Petroleum Ltd 1987-; *Recreations* skiing, fishing, tennis, music, boating; *Clubs* MCC, Mid Ocean Bermuda, Royal Hamilton Amateur Dinghy; *Style*— John C Shearer, Esq; c/o S C Warburg & Co Ltd, 33 King William St, London EC4R 9AS; P O Box 665, Hamilton, Bermuda (☎ 809 292 4724, telex 3317 MUTUAL BA)

SHEARER, Capt Magnus Macdonald; JP (Shetland 1969), DL (Shetland 1973); s of Col Magnus Shearer, OBE, TD, JP (d 1960), and Flora, *née* Stephen (d 1987); *b* 27 Feb 1924; *Educ* Anderson Educnl Inst Shetland, George Watson's Coll Edinburgh; *m* 1949, Martha Nicholson, da of John Henderson, DSM, Master Mariner (d 1957); 1 s; *Career* served RN 1942-46, 2 Lt RA (TA) 1949, Capt TARO 1959; md J & M Shearer Ltd 1960-85; hon consul in Shetland: Sweden 1958-, West Germany 1972-88; hon sec Lerwick Life Boat Station (RNLI) 1968-; Lord-Lieut for Shetland 1982-; Kt first class Royal Order of Vasa (Sweden), Offr first class Order of Merit Federal Republic of Germany 1983, Offr first class Order of Polar Star Sweden 1983; *Recreations* reading, bird watching, ships; *Style*— Captain Magnus Shearer, JP, DL; Birka, Cruester, Bressay, Shetland ZE2 9EL (☎ 0595 82 363)

SHEARLOCK, Very Rev David John; s of Arthur John Shearlock (d 1947), and Honora Frances Baker, *née* Hawkins; *b* 1 July 1932; *Educ* Surbiton CGS, Univ of Birmingham (BA), Westcott House Cambridge; *m* 30 May 1959, Jean Margaret, da of John Marr, Sandlands, Sidbury, Devon; 1 s (Timothy b 1963), 1 da (Ann b 1961); *Career* RA 1950-52, HAC 1952-56; curate: Guisborough Yorkshire 1957-60; Christchurch Priory Hants 1960-64, vicar L Kingsclere Hants 1964-71, Romsey Abbey Hants 1971-82; diocesan dir of ordinands Winchester 1977-82, Hon Canon of Winchester Cathedral 1978-82, dean of Truro 1982-; Cornwall area chm Royal Sch of Church Music 1983-; chm Truro Victims Support Scheme 1985-; pres: Cornwall Rural Music Sch Friends and Concerts Soc, Truro Cancer Relief; vice-pres Truro RA Assoc; *Recreations* railways, music, walking, wine making; *Style*— The Very Rev the Dean of Truro; The Deanery, Lemon St, Truro TR1 2PE (☎ 0872 72661); Maxfield Cottage, Netherbury, Bridport, Dorset; Truro Cathedral Office, 21 Old Bridge St, Truro TR1 2AH (☎ 0872 76782)

SHEASBY, (Herbert) Basil; OBE (1957, MBE 1947); s of Herbert James Sheasby (d 1957), and Kate Helen, *née* Worwood (d 1947); *b* 1 August 1905; *Educ* Lawrence Sheriff Sch, Rugby; *m* 5 Sept 1934, (Edith) Barbara, OBE, da of William Norman Parker (d 1970) of Ecclesfield, Sheffield; 2 s (Michael b 1936, David b 1939), 1 da (Margaret b 1943); *Career* qualified CA 1929, in practice 1934-75; JP 1948; memb Maidenhead and District Civic Soc, Ellington Lodge, Windsor and Maidenhead Cons Assoc; Freeman: City of London 1963, Worshipful Co of Tobacco Pipe Makers and Tobacco Blenders 1960; FCA 1929; *Books* Design of Accounts (1944); *Clubs* Royal Cwlth Soc, Maidenhead Cons; *Style*— Basil Sheasby, Esq, OBE, MBE; 2 Clarfield Dr, Pinknetts Gn, Maidenhead, Berks SL6 5DP (☎ 0628 20726)

SHEDDEN, Prof (William) Ian Hamilton; s of George Shedden (d 1966), of Bathgate, Scotland, and Agnes Hamilton, *née* Heigh (d 1979); *b* 21 Mar 1934; *Educ* The Acad Bathgate, Univ of Edinburgh (BSc, MB ChB), Univ of Birmingham (MD), City Univ London (Dip Law); *m* 21 March 1960, Elma Joyce, da of Lewis M Jobson (d 1985), of Edinburgh; 3 s (Malcolm b 1960, Andrew b 1962, Colin b 1971), 1 da (Clare b 1968); *Career* cmmnd Capt RAMC 1961-67, regtl MO Hallamshire Bn York and Lancaster Regt 1961-67; lectr Univ of Sheffield 1960-64, sr res fell MRC 1964-67, dir R & O Lilly Industs Ltd 1968-77, vice-pres Eli Lilly & Co USA 1977-83, prof of med Indiana Univ USA 1979-, md Glaxo Gp RCs Ltd 1983-86; underwriting memb Lloyds of London 1987-, dir Porton Devpts Ltd 1988-, asst dep coroner St Pancras London 1987-; ed Vinca Alkaloids in the Chemotherapy of Malignant Disease vol 1-3 (1968-70); Freeman City of London 1975, Liveryman Worshipful Soc of Apothecaries 1974; MRCP 1976, FRCP 1983, FACP 1981; *Style*— Prof Ian Shedden; Brook House, Park Rd, Stoke Poges, Bucks SL2 4PG (☎ 0 2814 5773); Porton Int plc, 100 Piccadilly, London W1V 9EN (☎ 01 629 0220, fax 01 499 6486, telex 946162 HITECH G, car tel 0836 318910)

SHEDDEN, Hon Mrs (Joan Frances); MBE (1946); s of 2 Baron Vestey (d 1954); *b* 1914; *m* 1, 1934 (m dis 1944), Maj John Hammon Paine, formerly KRAC; 1 s; m 2, 1954, John Lindesay Compton Shedden; *Career* sometime Lt First Aid Nursing Yeo; *Style*— The Hon Mrs Shedden, MBE; The Manor, Fossebridge, Glos; Greenhill Farm, Chedworth, Glos

SHEEHAN, Sheriff Albert Vincent; s of Richard Greig Sheehan, of Bo'ness, and Mary, *née* Moffat; *b* 23 August 1936; *Educ* Bo'ness Acad, Edinburgh Univ (MA, LLB); *m* 1965, Edna Georgina Scott, da of Andrew Hastings, of Coatbridge; 2 da (Wendy b 1968, Susan b 1971); *Career* Capt Royal Scots (The Royal Regt) 1959-61; slr; depute procurator fiscal 1961-71; Leverhulme fell 1971-72; dep crown agent for Scotland 1974-79, Scottish Law Cmmn 1979-81, sheriff: Edinburgh 1981, Falkirk 1983; *Recreations* curling, naval history, gardening; *Style*— Sheriff Albert Sheehan; 63 Murrayfield Gdns, Edinburgh EH12 6DL; Falkirk Sheriff Ct, Falkirk (☎ 0324 20822)

SHEEHY, Hon Mrs (Mary Anne); *née* Lyon-Dalberg-Acton; 5 da of 3 Baron Acton, CMG, MBE, TD (d 1989); *b* 30 Mar 1951; *m* 1972, Timothy John Sheehy; 2 da; *Style*— The Hon Mrs Sheehy; 8 St Margarets Road, Oxford

SHEEN, Hon Mr Justice; Hon Sir Barry Cross Sheen; s of Ronald Cross Sheen (d 1973), and Ethel May, *née* Powell (d 1980); *b* 31 August 1918; *Educ* Haileybury, Trinity Hall Cambridge (MA); *m* 1, 27 July 1946, Diane (d 1986), da of Cecil Lucas Donne (d 1957); 3 s (Christopher b 1948, Adrian b 1952, Roderick b 1959); m 2, 5 Nov 1988, Helen Ursula, *née* Woodmansey, wid of Philip Spink; *Career* RNVR 1939-46, CO HMS Kilkenzie 1943-45; barr Middle Temple 1947, wreck commr, Lloyd's arbitrator in salvage claims, memb Gen Cncl of the Bar 1960-64, jr counsel to Admty 1961-66, QC 1966, bencher 1971, rec of the Crown Ct 1971-78, judge of the High Ct of Justice Queen's Bench Div 1978-; pres Haileybury Soc 1982, chm assoc of Average Adjustees 1986-7; Liveryman of Worshipful Shipwrights 1983; kt 1978; *Recreations* golf; *Clubs* Royal Wimbledon GC, Hurlingham; *Style*— The Hon Mr Justice Sheen; Royal Courts of Justice, London WC2

SHEENE, Barry Stephen Frank; MBE (1978); s of Frank Sheene and Iris Sheene; *b* 11 Sept 1950; *Educ* St Martins in the Field; *m* 1984, Stephanie, da of Frederick Harrison; 1 da (Sidonie b 1984); *Career* motor cycle racer 1969-84, World Champion

1976-77, more Int Race wins than any other UK rider 1974-84, winner Foreign Sportsman award Italy, Spain, France; dir: Spectra Automotive Products plc Ltd 1983, Barry Sheene Racing Ltd 1972; presenter ITV Just Amazing 1983-85; helicopter licence 1980; survived 2 accidents at high speed 1975 (175 mph), 1982 (165 mph), most satisfying achievement regaining 100 per cent fitness; landowner (22 acres); *Recreations* Hughes 500 Helicopter GSTEF; *Style*— Barry Sheene, MBE; The Manor House, Charlwood, Surrey (☎ 0293 862319); The Manor House, 2 Riverbend Avenue, Carrara, Gold Coast, Queensland 4211, Australia

SHEEPSHANKS, David Richard; s of Capt Robin J Sheepshanks, DL, of the Rookery, Eyke, Woodbridge, Suffolk, and Lilias, *née* Noble; *b* 30 Oct 1952; *Educ* Eton; *m* 26 Aug 1978, Mona Gunilla, da of Nils Rickard Ullbin, of Bragevagen 12, Stockholm, Sweden; 1 da (Sophie Anna Lisa Kirsty b 16 Feb 1987); *Career* mangr Arabian Fish and Canning Co 1974, md Interoccan Seafoods Co Ltd 1975-79, fndr and md Starfish Ltd Ipswich 1980-, co-fndr and chm Suffolk Foods Ltd 1988-; dir: Radio Orwell 1985-, Ipswich Town FC 1987-; memb of Shellfish Ctee Sea Fish Indust Authy; *Recreations* football, shooting, tennis, music, fishing, cricket; *Clubs* Turf; *Style*— David Sheepshanks, Esq; Hasketon Old Rectory, Woodbridge, Suffolk IP13 6HR (☎ 039 43 7917); Starfish Ltd, Reker Hse, 17 Betts Ave, Martlesham, Ipswich, Suffolk (☎ 0473 626 662, fax 0473 625 991, telex 988821); Suffolk Foods Ltd, 2 Betts Ave, Martlesham, Ipswich, Suffolk (☎ 0473 623 459, fax 039 43 2686, car tel 0860 353 139)

SHEEPSHANKS, Robin John; DL (Suffolk 1979); s of Maj Richard Sheepshanks, DSO, MVO (d 1951), by his w Hon Bridget, Thesiger (d 1983), da of 1 Viscount Chelmsford; *b* 4 August 1925; *Educ* Eton; *m* 1951, Lilias Mulgrave, da of Maj Sir Humphrey Noble, 4 Bt, MBE, MC (d 1968), of Walwick Hall; 4 s (David b 1952, Richard b 1955, Andrew b 1960, Christopher b 1964); *Career* Capt 1 King's Dragoon Gds 1943-52; farmer 1952-; chm ADFAM (Suffolk) 1987-, memb E Suffolk CC 1963-74, chm Suffolk CC 1982-84 (memb 1974-); High Sheriff Suffolk 1981; chm: Suffolk Police Authy, Agric Ctee Assoc of CCs 1986-88, Standing Conf of E Anglian Local Authys 1987-; *Recreations* shooting, golf, gardening; *Clubs* Cavalry and Guards', Pratt's; *Style*— Robin Sheepshanks, Esq, DL; The Rookery, Eyke, Woodbridge, Suffolk (☎ 0394 460226)

SHEERIN, His Hon Judge John Declan; s of John Patrick Sheerin (d 1969), and Agnes Mary Josephine Sheerin, *née* Keane (d 1975); *b* 29 Nov 1932; *Educ* Wimbledon Coll, LSE (LLB); *m* 1958, Helen Suzanne, da of Philippus Lodewicus le Roux (d 1964); 2 s (Paul, James), 2 da (Sarah, Nicola); *Career* RAF 1958-60, MEAF Nicosia Flying Offr; slr 1957, ptnr Greene & Greene 1962, ret 1982; rec 1979, circuit judge 1982; *Recreations* Golf; *Clubs* Flempton Golf; *Style*— His Honour Judge Sheerin; c/o The County Ct, Arcade St, Ipswich

SHEERMAN, Barry John; MP (Lab) Huddersfield 1983-; s of Albert Sheerman; *b* 17 August 1940; *Educ* Hampton GS, Kingston Tech Coll, LSE, London U; *m* 1965, Pamela Elizabeth, *née* Brenchley; 1 s, 3 da; *Career* former lectr; MP (Lab) Huddersfield E 1979-1983, memb Public Accounts Ctee 1980-83; chm: Parly Advsy Cncl for Tport Safety, Parly Lab Pty Trade Ctee 1981-83; oppn front bench spokesman on Employment and Educn with special responsibility for devpt of educn policy and trg for over-16s 1983-87, spokesman on employment 1987-; *Style*— Barry Sheerman, Esq, MP; House of Commons, SW1A 0AA (☎ 01 219 4553/5037, home 0484 710 687, office 0924 495277)

SHEFF, Sylvia Claire; JP (1976); da of Isaac Glickman (d 1981), of Flat 2, Bristol Court, Bury Old Road, Prestwich, Manchester, and Rita, *née* Bor (d 1976); *b* 9 Nov 1935; *Educ* Stand GS for Girls, Univ of Manchester (BA); *m* 28 Dec 1958, Alan Frederick Sheff (d 1986), s of Lewis Sheff (d 1975), of 1 Stanley Rd, Broughton Park, Salford; 1 s (Marcus Jeremy b 1963), 1 da (Janine Rachel b 1960); *Career* teacher 1958-77; asst nat dir Cons Friends of Israel 1985- (nat project dir 1974-85), fndr and dir Friendship with Israel Gp (in Euro Parl) 1979-, fndr Soviet Jewry 1972- (pres 1980-), fndr and chm Manchester 35 Gp Women's Campaign for Soviet Jewry, hon sec Nat Cncl for Soviet Jewry 1987- (cncl memb 1975-87), del Bd of Deps of Br Jews 1987-; memb: exec ctee Jewish Rep Cncl of Gtr Manchester 1974-81, Bury Family Conciliation Serv Mgmnt Ctee 1985-87; memb Magistrates Assoc; *Recreations* bridge, theatre, opera, travel, antiques; *Clubs* Last Drop; *Style*— Mrs Sylvia Sheff, JP; 6 The Meadows, Old Hall Lane, Whitefield, Manchester M25 7RZ (☎ 061 766 4391); 45B Westbourne Terrace, Paddington, London W2 3UR (☎ 01 262 2493)

SHEFFIELD, Bishop of 1980-; Rt Rev David Ramsay Lunn; patron of seventy livings and the Rural Deaneries of Attercliffe, Doncaster, Ecclesfield, Ecclesall, Hallam, Laughton, Rotherham, Tankersley, Wath and Snaith; the see was founded in 1914; *b* 1930; *Educ* King's Cambridge (MA), Cuddesdon Coll Oxford; *Career* deacon 1955, priest 1956, chaplain Lincoln Theol Coll 1963-66, sub-warden 1966-70, vicar St George Cullercoats 1970-75, rector 1975-80 and rural dean of Tynemouth 1975-80; *Style*— The Rt Rev the Lord Bishop of Sheffield; Bishopscroft, Snaithing Lane, Sheffield, S Yorks S10 3LG (☎ 0742 302170)

SHEFFIELD, John Julian Lionel George; s of John Vincent Sheffield, CBE (himself 4 s of Sir Berkeley Sheffield, 6 Bt, JP, DL), *qv*; *b* 28 August 1938; *Educ* Eton, Christ's Coll Cambridge Univ; *m* 1961, Carolyn Alexandra, er da of the late Brig Sir Alexander Abel Smith, TD, by his 1 w, Elizabeth (da of David B Morgan, of N Carolina); 3 s (John b 1963, Simon b 1964, Lionel b 1969), 1 da (Nicola b 1973); *Career* industrialist; chm Portals Hldgs plc (water treatment & papermaking, Queen's Award for Export 1966, 1977, 1982); dep chm: Norcros Ltd 1974-, Guardian Royal Exchange 1981-; dir: Edward Le Bas Ltd 1971-, North Foreland Lodge Ltd 1987-, Tex Hldgs plc, dep chm Br Water and Effluent Treatment Assoc 1979-83 (chm 1981); chm Basingstoke Sports Tst 1975-84; *Recreations* outdoor sports, collecting; *Clubs* White's, MCC; *Style*— John Sheffield, Esq; Laverstoke House, Whitchurch, Basingstoke, Hants (☎ 0256 770 245); Portals Holdings plc, Laverstoke Mill Hse, Whitchurch, Hants RG28 7NR (☎ 0256 89 2360)

SHEFFIELD, John Vincent; CBE; s of late Sir Berkeley Sheffield, 6 Bt; *b* 11 Nov 1913; *Educ* Eton, Magdalene Coll Cambridge (MA); *m* 1, 1936, Anne Margaret (d 1969), da of Sir Lionel Lawson Faudel Faudel-Phillips, 3 Bt; 1 s, 3 da; m 2, 1971, Frances Mary Agnes, da of Brig-Gen Goland Clarke; *Career* former private sec Miny of Works, chm: Norcros Ltd 1956-81, Portals Hldgs 1968-78, Atlantic Assets Tst Ltd 1972-83, Business Educn Cncl 1980-83; (High Sheriff Lincs 1944-45); OStJ; *Clubs* Whites; *Style*— John Sheffield, Esq, CBE; New Barn House, Laverstoke, Whitchurch, Hants (☎ 0256 893187)

SHEFFIELD, Michael Joseph Forster; TD, DL (1975); s of Brig Thomas Tredwell Jackson Sheffield, CBE, TD, DL; *b* 11 April 1930; *Educ* Denstone College Staffs, London Univ (LLB); *m* 1958, Joan Margaret, *née* Ridley; 2 children; *Career* HM coroner Cleveland 1973-; dir Solicitors' Benevolent Assoc 1973- (chm 1986); sec Teesside Cheshire Home 1973-81 (chm 1988), vice-pres Middlesbrough Rugby Club 1965- (chm 1977-80); Cmdt Durham and South Tyne Army Cadet Force 1977; govr Middlesbrough HS 1965-67; chm: Med Appeal Tbnl 1986-, Social Security Appeal Tbnl 1985; *Recreations* tennis, rugby, theatre, mil affairs, gardening; *Clubs* Lansdowne, Cleveland Middlesbrough; *Style*— Michael Sheffield Esq, TD, DL; Ayton House, Easby Lane, Great Ayton, North Yorkshire; office: 9-13 Bedford St, Middlesbrough, Cleveland (☎ 0642 241311)

SHEFFIELD, Sir Reginald Adrian Berkeley; 8 Bt (GB 1755), of Normanby, Lincolns; DL (Humberside); s of Maj Edmund Sheffield, JP, DL (d 1977), of Sutton Park, Sutton on Forest, York; (s of 6 Bt), and Nancie Miriel Denise, wid of Lt-Cdr Glen Kidston, RN, and yst da of Edward Roland Soames, of Framland House, Melton Mowbray; suc unc, Sir Robert Sheffield, 7 Bt 1977; *b* 9 May 1946; *Educ* Eton; *m* 1, 1969 (m dis 1975), Annabel Lucy Veronica, da of late Timothy Angus Jones, and late Hon Mrs Pandora Astor; 2 da (Samantha b 1971, Emily b 1973); m 2, 1977, Victoria Penelope, da of late Ronald Walker, DFC; 1 s (Robert b 1984), 2 da (Alice b 1980, Lucy Mary b 1981); *Heir* s, Robert Charles Berkeley; *Career* chm: Alpwood Hldgs plc, Aylesford Hldgs Ltd; dir Normandy Estate Hldgs and Subsidiaries; memb Lloyd's; county cncllr Humberside, vice-chm S Humberside Business Advice Centre Ltd; landowner (6,000 acres); pres: S Humberside CPRE, Scunthorpe FC Ltd; *Recreations* shooting, stalking; *Clubs* Whites; *Style*— Sir Reginald Sheffield, Bt, DL; Thealby Hall, Thealby, Scunthorpe, S Humberside DN15 9AB; Estate Office, Normanby, Scunthorpe, South Humberside DN15 9HS (☎ 0724 720618)

SHEHADIE, Sir Nicholas Michael; OBE (1971); s of Michael Shehadie (decd), and Hannah Shehadie; *b* 15 Nov 1926; *Educ* Crown St & Cleveland St Schs Sydney; *m* 1957, Dr Marie Roslyn, *née* Bashir; 1 s, 1 da; *Career* md Nicholas Shehadie Pty Ltd 1959-, alderman City of Sydney 1962, dep lord mayor 1969-73, lord mayor of Sydney 1973-75; dir Rothmans Pall Mall (Australia) Ltd; capt Aust Rugby teams toured Br, Canada, USA, Africa, NZ, pres Aust Rugby Union, mangr Wallabies Rugby Team Br Tour 1981-82; kt 1976; *see Debrett's Handbook of Australia and New Zealand for further details*; *Style*— Sir Nicholas Shehadie, OBE; c/o Nicholas Shehadie Pty Ltd, 118 Old Canterbury Rd, Lewisham, NSW 2049, Australia

SHELBOURNE, Sir Philip; s of late Leslie John Shelbourne; *b* 15 June 1924; *Educ* Radley Coll, CCC Oxford, Harvard Law Sch; *Career* barr Inner Temple, taxation barr 1951-62, ptnr N M Rothschild & Sons 1962-70, chief exec Drayton Corpn 1971-72 (chm 1973-74), chm and chief exec Samuel Montagu & Co 1974-80, Br Nat Oil Corpn 1980- (Britoil 1982-88), chm Henry Ansbacher Hldgs plc; kt 1984; *Recreations* music; *Clubs* Brooks's; *Style*— Sir Philip Shelbourne; One Mitre Square London EC3A 5AN

SHELBURNE, Earl of; Charles Maurice Petty-Fitzmaurice; s (by 1 m) and h of 8 Marquess of Lansdowne, *qv*, and Barbara Stuart Chase (d 1965); *b* 21 Feb 1941; *Educ* Eton; *m* 1, 1965 (m dis 1987), Lady Frances Eliot, da of 9 Earl of St Germans; 2 s (Simon b 1970, William b 1973), 2 da (Arabella b 1966, Rachel b 1968); m 2, 1987, Fiona Mary, da of Donald Merritt ; *Heir* s, Viscount Calne and Calstone, *qv*; *Career* Page of Honour to HM The Queen 1956-57; served: Kenya Regt 1960-61, Wiltshire Yeomanry (TA), amalgamated with Royal Yeomanry Regt 1963-73; pres Wiltshire Playing Fields Assoc 1965-75, Wilts Co cncllr 1970-85, memb SW Econ Planning Cncl 1972-77; chm: Working Ctee Population & Settlement Pattern (SWEPC) 1972-77, N Wilts DC 1973-76; memb Calne and Chippenham RDC 1964-73, memb Historic Bldgs and Monuments Cmmn 1983-; pres: Wilts Assoc of Boy's Clubs and Youth Clubs 1976-, NW Wilts Dist Scout Cncl 1977-; contested (C) Coventry NE 1979; dep pres HHA 1986-88, pres 1988-; *Clubs* Turf, Whites; *Style*— Earl of Shelburne; Bowood House, Calne, Wiltshire SN11 0LZ (☎ 0249 812102)

SHELBURNE, Countess of; Lady Frances Helen Mary; *née* Eliot; da (by 1 m) of 9 Earl of St Germans, *qv*; *b* 1943; *m* 1965 (m dis 1987), Earl of Shelburne, *qv*; *Style*— Francis Countess of Shelburne; 60 Abingdon Rd, London W8 6AP

SHELDON, Hon Sir (John) Gervase Kensington Sheldon; s of Dr John Henry Sheldon (d 1960), of Hopton, Churt, Surrey, and Dr Eleanor Gladys, *née* Kensington (d 1966); *b* 4 Oct 1913; *Educ* Winchester, Trinity Coll Cambridge (MA); *m* 1, 10 Jan 1940, Patricia Mary, da of Lt-Col Arthur Claude Mardon, DSO (d 1950), of Willingdon, Sussex; 1 s (Robin b 1942); m 2, 10 Aug 1960, Janet Marguerite, da of George Wilfrid Seager (d 1979), of Sevenoaks, Kent; 2 s (Jeremy b 1961, Timothy b 1962), 1 da (Sophie b 1964); *Career* served RA (TA) 1939-45 (despatches twice) Egypt, N Africa, Italy, Maj 1943; barr Lincoln's Inn 1939, county court judge 1968-72, circuit judge 1972-78, bencher 1978, judge of High Court of Justice (family div) 1978-88, presiding judge Western circuit 1980-84; kt 1978; *Recreations* shooting, stalking, cricket; *Clubs* Oxford and Cambridge; *Style*— The Hon Sir Gervase Sheldon; Hopton, Churt, Surrey GU10 2LD (☎ 025 125 2035); Royal Courts of Justice, Strand, London WC2A 2LL

SHELDON, Mark Hebberton; s of George Hebberton Sheldon (d 1971), and Marie, *née* Hazlitt (d 1974); *b* 6 Feb 1931; *Educ* Stand GS, Wycliffe Coll, Corpus Christi Coll Oxford (BA, MA); *m* 16 June 1971, Catherine Eve, da of Edwin Charles James Ashwort (d 1968), of USA; 1s (Edward b 1976), 1 da (Alice b 1972); *Career* Nat Serv Lt RCS 1949-50, TA 1950-54; admitted slr 1957; Linklaters & Paines: articled 1953-56, asst slr 1957-59, ptnr 1959-, resident ptnr New York 1972-74, sr ptnr 1988-; tres cncl Law Soc 1981-86 (cncl memb 1978-), pres City of London Law Soc 1987-88, memb cncl Corp of Lloyd's 1989-; Freeman City of London Slrs Co (Master 1987-88); *Recreations* music, english, watercolours, wine/food, swimming; *Clubs* Travellers, City of London; *Style*— Mark Sheldon, Esq; 5 St Albans Grove, London W8 5PN; Barrington Hse, 59-67 Gresham St, London EC2V 7JA (☎ 01 606 7080, fax 01 606 5113, telex 884349/888167)

SHELDON, Rt Hon Robert Edward; PC (1977), MP (Lab Ashton-under-Lyne 1964-); *b* 13 Sept 1923; *m* 1, 1945, Eileen Shamash (d 1969); 1 s, 1 da; m 2, 1971, Mary Shield; *Career* trained as engr; parly candidate (Lab) Manchester Withington 1959, dir Manchester C of C 1964-74 (DAD 1979); chm: Lab Parly econ affrs and fin gp 1967-68, NW Gp Lab MPs 1970-74; oppn spokesman Treasy matters, civil service, machinery of govt 1970-74, memb Public Expenditure Ctee 1972-74 (chm gen sub-ctee); min state: CSD 1974, Treasy 1974-75; fin sec to Treasy 1975-79, oppn front bench spokesman Treasy and econ affrs 1981-83, memb select ctee on Treasury and Civil Service until 1981 (and chm sub-ctee), chm Public Accounts Ctee 1983- (memb

1965-70 and 1975-79); *Style*— The Rt Hon Robert Sheldon, PC, MP; 2 Ryder St, London SW1 (☎ 01 839 4533, 930 1528); 27 Darley Ave, Manchester M20 8ZD (☎ 061 445 3489)

SHELDON, Thomas Clifford; s of John Rodney Clifford Sheldon, and Pamela, *née* Watney, JP; *b* 6 Nov 1952; *Educ* Marlborough, Poly of Central London; *m* 20 Oct 1979, Julie Gay, da of Rev (Michael) David Mumford, of The Rectory, Ewhurst Green, Sussex; 2 da (Amelia b 1982, Georgina b 1985); *Career* assoc: Donaldsons 1979-81, Savills plc 1984-88; dir Sheldon Scammell (property devpt co) 1988-; Freeman City of London, Liveryman Worshipful Co of Mercers; ARICS 1978; *Recreations* sailing, skiing, walking, theatre; *Clubs* Medway YC; *Style*— Thomas Sheldon, Esq; 86 Kings Rd, Wimbledon, London SW19 8QW (☎ 01 542 8034); Hammond House, 117 Piccadilly, London W1V 9PJ (☎ 01 629 2484, fax 01 491 2367, telex 0836 723575)

SHELDON, Timothy James Ralph (Jamie); s of Anthony John Sheldon, and Elizabeth Mary, *née* Ferguson; *b* 9 July 1956; *Educ* Eton, Exeter Univ (BA); *m* 25 Feb 1984, Susan Jean (Susie), da of John Ridell Best; 1 s (Charles b 14 Oct 1985), 1 da (Sophie b 23 Nov 1987); *Career* CA; Armitage & Norton 1978-82, Robert Fleming & Co Ltd 1982-87, dir GNI Ltd 1987-; non-exec dir Harry Ferguson Ltd 1983-; memb ICAEW; *Recreations* sailing, skiing, farming, tennis, squash, piano, shooting; *Clubs* Royal Yacht Squadron, Queens; *Style*— Jamie Sheldon, Esq; Colechurch House, 1 London Bridge Walk, London SE1 2SX (☎ 01 378 7171, fax 01 403 1635)

SHELFORD, (William) Bill (Thomas Cornelius); s of C W Shelford DL, and Huelen Beatrice Hilda *née* Schuster; *b* 27 Jan 1943; *Educ* Eton, Christ Church Oxford (MA Jurisprudence); *m* 30 March 1971, Annette Betty, *née* Heap Holt; 2 s (Henry b 1973, Thomas b 1980), 1 da (Laura b 1975); *Career* ptnr Cameron Markby, slrs, 1970-; *Recreations* skiing, gardening, garden design; *Clubs* Brooks's, City of London; *Style*— Bill Shelford, Esq; Freshfields, Scaynes Hill, Haywards Heath, Sussex RH17 7NS (☎ 0825 790335); Cameron Markby, Moor House, London Wall, London EC2Y 5HE (☎ 01 374 2377)

SHELLEY, Alan John; s of Stanley Arnold Shelley (d 1983), and Ivy May Shelley; *b* 7 August 1931; *Educ* People's Coll Nottingham; *m* 20 Sept 1958, Josephine Flintoft, da of James Flood (d 1981); 1 s (Matthew b 1965), 1 da (Joanna b 1962); *Career* sr ptnr: Knight Frank & Rutley 1983-, Knight Frank & Rutley (Nigeria) 1965-1979; dir John Holt Investmt Co 1981-; chm West Africa Ctee 1985-, gen cmmr income tax 1983-; *Recreations* squash, theatre; *Clubs* Oriental, MCC; *Style*— Alan Shelley, Esq; 20 Hanover Square, London W12 0AH (☎ 01 629 8171, fax 01 493 4114)

SHELLEY, Andrew Colin; s of Charles Andrew Shelley (Chief Inspr Essex Constabulary, d 1944), of Chelmsford, and Elizabeth Annie Constance, *née* Harper (d 1985); *b* 17 Jan 1937; *Educ* Royal Masonic Sch, Harvard Business Sch; *m* 22 Aug 1963, Susan, da of Jack Trevor Mills (d 1987); 2 s (Gerald Robin b 1964, Robert Andrew b 1967); *Career* CA; joined Crittall Mfrg 1965, chief accountant Munton and Fison Ltd 1965 (co sec 1968), fin dir Munton and Fison plc 1972, dir Munton and Fison (Hldgs) plc 1979 (gp chief exec 1982), chm Edward Fison Ltd; dir: Eling Tport Ltd, Bridlington Farms Ltd, Munton and Fison (Exports) Ltd, Newnham Hldgs (Beford) Ltd, Luzcampo Sociedade Agricola Intensiva do Algarve LDA (Portugal); ptnr Shelley and Co Chartered Accountants Stowmarket; pres: E Anglian Dist Soc of Chartered Accountants 1989-, Ipswich and Colchester soc of CA's 1978-, vice chm ICA's Industl and Commercial Membs ctee 1982-84, chm CA's Working Party re Revolution of Fraud in Industry; memb: ICA's Res Bd 1982, CA's Tech Advsy Ctee E Anglia, CA's Nat TAC, ICA's Parly and Law Ctee 1987, Cncl ICA 1981-84, Cncl CBI 1988-; tres Malsterers' Assoc of GB 1986-; examiner Suffolk Coll DMS 1983-88; memb Isnt of Brewing 1983; FID 1982, FCA 1959, AMP Harvard 1981; *Recreations* gardening, swimming, estate maintenance; *Clubs* Harvard Club of London, Chartered Accountants Dining; *Style*— Andrew Shelley, Esq; Munton and Fison plc, Cedars Factory, Stowmarket, Suffolk IP14 2AG (☎ 0449 612401, fax 0449 677800, telex 98205)

SHELLEY, Howard Gordon; s of Frederick Gordon Shelley (d 1979), and Katharine Anne, *née* Taylor; *b* 9 Mar 1950; *Educ* Highgate Sch, RCM; *m* 7 June 1975, Hilary Mary Pauline, *née* Macnamara; 1 s (Alexander Gordon b 1979), 1 step s (Peter Cullivan b 1962); *Career* concert pianist and conductor; London debut Wigmore Hall 1971, Henry Wood Prom debut (TV) 1972, conducting debut London Symphony Orch Barbican 1985, solo career extends over five continents, piano concertos written for him by Cowie Chapple and Dickinson, performed first cycle of the complete solo piano works of Rachmaninov at Wigmore Hall 1983; recordings include: complete solo piano works of Rachmaninov, Mozart Piano Concertos 21 and 24, several Br works for EMI incl Piano Concertos by Vaughan Williams Howard Ferguson and Peter Dickinson; memb Worshipful Co of Musicians 1971; *Style*— Howard Shelley, Esq; 38 Cholmeley Park, Highgate, London N6 5ER (☎ 01 341 2811); c/o Intermusica Artists Management, 16 Duncan Terrace, London N1 8BZ (☎ 01 278 5455, fax 01 278 8434, telex 931 210 2058 sl g)

SHELLEY, James Edward; s of Vice Adm Richard Benyon, CB, CBE, DL (d 1968) named changed by Deed Poll 1968, and Eve Alice, *née* Cecil Cecil; *b* 18 June 1932; *Educ* Eton, Univ Coll Oxford (MA); *m* 16 June 1938, Judith, da of George Grubb (d 1970); 2 s (Timothy b 1966, Philip b 1966), 2 da (Alison b 1959, Penelope b 1960); *Career* memb Church Cmmrs Staff 1954-: under sec gen 1976-81, assets sec 1981-85, sec 1985-; *Recreations* country pursuits; *Clubs* Naval and Military; *Style*— James Shelley, Esq; Mays Farm Hse, Ramsdell, Basingstoke, Hants RG26 5RE (☎ 0256 850 770); Church Commissioners, 1 Millbank, London SW1P 3JZ (☎ 01 222 7010, fax 01 233 0171)

SHELLEY, Dr (Sir) John Richard; 11 Bt (E 1611) of Michelgrove, Sussex; does not use title; s of John Shelley (d 1974); suc gf, Maj Sir John Frederick Shelley, 10 Bt (d 1976); *b* 18 Jan 1943; *Educ* King's Sch Bruton, Trinity Coll Cambridge (MA), St Mary's Hosp London Univ (MB, BChir); *m* 1965, Clare, da of Claud Bicknell, OBE; 2 da; *Heir* bro, Thomas Shelley; *Career* general practitioner; ptnr Drs Shelley, Newth and Doddington (med practitioners); farmer; DObstRCOG, MRCGP; *Style*— Dr John Shelley; Shobrooke Park, Credition, Devon; Molford House, 27 South St, South Molton, Devon EX36 4AA (☎ 076 95 3101)

SHELLEY, Ruth (Mrs Michael Silverman); da of Jack Shelley, of London, and Mildred, *née* Schama, of London; *b* 19 July 1942; *Educ* S Hampstead HS for Girls; *m* 20 March 1966, Michael Anthony Silverman, s of Ernest Silverman, of London; 1 s (Paul Conrad Alexander b 1969), 1 da (Katie Mimi b 1971); *Career* accountant and prodn mangr Libertas Film Prodns Ltd 1960-63, accountant PA Mgmnt (Conslts) SA 1963-65, gen mangr Drake Personnel Ltd 1965-66, fin dir and divnl dir Lloyds Gp of Co's 1966-75, fin dir Merton Assocs (Conslts) Ltd 1976-; AMIPM 1971; *Recreations* tennis, swimming, yachting; *Clubs* Club Nauticol (Santa Ponsa); *Style*— Miss Ruth Shelley; Merton House, 70 Grafton Way, London W1P 5LE (☎ 01 388 2051, fax 01 387 5324, telex 8953742 MERTON G)

SHELLEY, Thomas Henry; s of late John Shelley and hp of bro, Sir John Shelley, 11 Bt; *b* 3 Feb 1945; *Educ* King's Sch Bruton, Trinity Coll Cambridge; *m* 1970, Katharine Mary Holton; 3 da (Kirsten Rachel Irvine b 1973, Victoria Juliet b 1974, Benita Mary 1978); *Style*— Thomas Shelley, Esq

SHELTON, Hon Mrs; Hon Sarah; *née* Fellowes; da of 3 Baron De Ramsey, KBE; *b* 1938; *m* 1972, Peter Shelton; 1 s, 1 da; *Style*— The Hon Mrs Shelton; Es Moli Nou de Canet, Es Glayeta, Mallorca

SHELTON, Shirley Megan; da of Lt-Col T F Goodwin, DSO, TD (d 1965), of SA, and Lucia Vera May, *née* Pike (d 1983); *b* 8 Mar 1934; *m* 21 July 1960, (William) Timothy Shelton, s of Stephen Shelton (d 1956); 1 s (Edward b 1964), 2 da (Alice b 1961, Laura b 1965); *Career* journalist; ed: Woman and Home 1978-82, Home and Freezer Digest 1988-; *Recreations* open university, music; *Style*— Mrs Shirley Shelton

SHELTON, Sir William Jeremy Masefield; MP (C) Streatham 1974-; s of late Lt-Col Richard Charles Masefield Shelton, MBE, of St Saviour's, Guernsey, and (Ruth Eevelyn) Penelope, *née* Coode; *b* 30 Oct 1929; *Educ* Radley, Tabor Acad (Massachusetts), Worcester Coll Oxford (MA), Univ of Texas (Austin); *m* 24 Sept 1960, Anne Patricia, da of John Arthur Warder, CBE, of Guernsey; 1 s (Charles b 17 Dec 1972), 1 da (Victoria b 14 Dec 1968); *Career* with the advertising agency Colman Prentis & Varley 1952-55, Corpa (Caracas) 1955-60; md: CPV (Int) Bogotà 1960-64, CPV (Int) 1967-74, Grosvenor Advertising 1969-74; chm: Fletcher Shelton Delaney & Reynolds 1974-81, GGK London 1984-; memb Wandsworth GLC 1967-70, chief whip ILEA 1968-70; pps to: Min of Posts and Telecommunications 1972-74, Rt Hon Margaret Thatcher 1975; parly under-sec DES 1981-83; memb Cncl of Europe and Western Euro Union 1987-; kt 1989; *Clubs* Carlton, Huntercombe Golf; *Style*— Sir William Shelton, MP; The Manor House, Long Crendon, Bucks (☎ 0844 208748); 27 Ponsonby Terrace, London SW1 (☎ 01 821 8204)

SHENNAN, Capt David Bowes; s of Major Kenneth Gordon Woodbine Shennan (d 1971), of London, and Lilah Maude, *née* Daly; *b* 1 Oct 1931; *Educ* Eton, RMA Sandhurst; *m* 1, 25 May 1976, Fiona Mary Daughne, da of Gavin Thomas Fairfax (d 1987), of Berks; m 2, 6 April 1985, Jennifer Ann, da of Major Peter Guy Ormrod (d 1954), of Hants; *Career* Capt Royal Scots Greys 1952-61; *Recreations* shooting, fishing; *Clubs* Cavalry, Northern Counties; *Style*— Capt David B Shennan; Quarry Farm, Farnham, Knaresborough, North Yorkshire HG5 9JS (☎ Boroughbridge 340425)

SHENNAN, (Francis Frank) Gerard; s of Thomas Gerard Shennan, of Tadley, Hants, and Cecelia, *née* Strype; *b* 14 Sept 1949; *Educ* Preston Catholic Coll, St Joseph's Coll, Dumfries, Univ of Edinburgh (LLB); *Career* writer and journalist; news sub ed: Daily Mirror Manchester 1975-76, Scottish Daily Record 1976-88, recruitment columnist the Scotsman 1988-, fndr Francis Shennan Agency 1988-; law examiner for Scotland Nat Cncl for the Trg of Journalists 1981-84, external examiner media law Napier Poly Edinburgh 1984-; guest lectr and speaker: Napier Poly, NW Writers Assoc, SE Writers Assoc; contrib to: Scottish Field, Woman, Woman's Own Television Weekly; *Books* The Life, Passions, and Legacies of John Napier (1989); *Recreations* travelling, walking; *Clubs* Country Gentlemen's Assoc; *Style*— Francis Shennan, Esq; Francis Shennan Agency, 134 Wilton Street, Glasgow G20 6DG (☎ 041 946 9030)

SHENSTONE, Gerald Guy; TD (1946); s of Brig Gerald Shenstone, CBE, TD, JP, DL (d 1976), and Muriel Berna, *née* Johnson (d 1977); *b* 3 May 1918; *Educ* Tonbridge, Cambridge Univ (MA); *m* 22 Nov 1947, Pamela Patricia, da of Reginald Hugh Poole (d 1949); 1 s (Simon), 1 da (Clare); *Career* chartered architect, ptnr Gerald Shenstone & Ptnrs; architect: Chelmsford Cathedral 1977-84, numerous Churches and Historic Buildings; FRIBA, AADip, FCIArb; *Recreations* golf; *Clubs* Surveyors; *Style*— Gerald G Shenstone, Esq, TD; 25 Kings Court, Kings Road, Westcliff-on-Sea SS0 8LL (☎ 0702 352722); 26 Bloomsbury Square, London WC1A 2PN (☎ 01 636 8595)

SHENTON, David William; s of Sir William Leonard Shenton, KB (d 1967), and Erica Lucy, *née* Denison (d 1978); *b* 1 Dec 1924; *Educ* Westminster Sch, Magdalen Coll Oxford (BA); *m* 1, 1972 (m dis 1987), Della, da of F G Marshall (d 1977), of Sutton, Surrey; m 2, 12 May 1988, Charmian Nancy, LVO, da of Christopher William Lacey (d 1966), of Walmer, Kent; *Career* WWII Lt Coldstream Gds 1943-46 served Italy (despatches); admitted slr 1951; ptnr Lovell White and King 1955, conslt Lovell White and Durrant 1988-; chm: Slrs Euro Gp of Law Soc 1980-81, Ctee D of Int Bar Assoc 1983-87 (chm emeritus 1987-); memb: editorial ctee International Business Lawyer 1986-88, chms advsy ctee Int Bar Assoc 1988-; Freeman City of London 1950, Liveryman: Grocers Company 1954, Solicitors Co 1970; FCIA; *Recreations* sailing, visiting ancient sites and buildings, photography; *Clubs* RYS; *Style*— David Shenton, Esq; 16 Eldix Grove, Hampstead, London NW3 (☎ 01 794 8002); Moons Hill House, Moons Hill, Totland Bay, IoW (☎ 0983 752255); 21 Holborn Viaduct, London EC1A 2DY (☎ 01 236 0066, fax 01 248 4212, telex 887122 LWD G)

SHEPARD, Giles Richard Carless; s of Richard Stanley Howard Shepard, MC, TD, and Kathleen Carless (d 1977); *b* 1 April 1937; *Educ* Eton, Harvard Business Sch; *m* 1966, Peter Carolyn Fern, da of Geoffrey Keighley (d 1966); 1 s, 1 da; *Career* Coldstream Guards 1955-60; dir: Charrington & Co Ltd 1962-64, H P Bulmer & Co Ltd 1964-70; md: Westminster & Country Properties Ltd 1970-76, Savoy Hotel plc 1976-; govr Gresham's Sch Holt, memb exec ctee Cystic Fibrosis Research Tst; Cncl of Hotel and Catering Benevolent Assoc; High Sheriff of Greater London 1986-87; prime warden of Fishmongers Co 1987-88; *Recreations* gardening, shooting, tennis; *Clubs* White's, Pratt's; *Style*— Giles Shepard, Esq; 1 Savoy Hill, London WC2R 0BP (☎ 01 836 1533)

SHEPHARD, Hon Mrs (Belinda Anne); *née* Renwick; da of 1 Baron Renwick, KBE, by his 1 w, Dorothy; *b* 6 Mar 1934; *m* 1959, John Horatio Gordon Shephard; 1 s, 1 da; *Style*— The Hon Mrs Shephard; 26 Ecclestone Square Mews, London SW1V 1QN

SHEPHARD, Air Cdre Harold Montague; CBE (1974), OBE (1959); s of Rev Leonard Benjamin Shephard (d 1961), of Wareham, Dorset, and Lilian Shephard (d 1982); *b* 15 August 1918; *Educ* St John's Leatherhead; *m* 20 May 1939, Margaret Isobel, da of Frederick Girdlestone, of Ewell; 1 s (David Harold Andrew Shephard, 1 da (Angela Margaret (Mrs Colgate)); *Career* RAF 1941-74, Air Cdre, provost marshal and dir RAF Security 1971-74; Met Police (CID) 1937-41; MBIM 1970-74; *Recreations* sport, reading; *Clubs* RAF; *Style—* Air Cdre Harold Shephard, CBE, OBE; 6 Bennetts Mews, West Cross, Tenterden, Kent TN30 6JN (☎ 05806 4945)

SHEPHARD, Hon Mrs (Harriet Olivia); *née* Davies; da of Baron Davies of Leek, PC (Life Peer, d 1985); *b* 1930; *Educ* London (BSc); *m* 1950, Derek Shephard; 1 da (Sue); *Style—* The Hon Mrs Shephard; 36 Clevenden Mansions, Lissenden Gdns, NW5

SHEPHARD, (John) Horatio Gordon; s of Harold Shephard (d 1946), and Grace Winifred, *née* Birbeck (d 1942); *b* 12 August 1921; *Educ* Summer Fields Oxford, Eton, New Coll Oxford (BA); *m* 1, 29 June 1948 (m dis), Carola, da of Cdr Sir Geoffrey Congreve, 1 Bt (ka 1941); 2 s (Thomas b 1949, Henry b 1955); m2, Belinda Anne, da of 1 Baron Renwick of Coombe, KBE, of Berks (d 1973); 1 s (William b 1962), 1 da (Sarah b 1959); *Career* Capt Grenadier Gds 1941-46, served in N Africa and Italy; ptnr Thicknesse and Hull Slrs, Westminster 1951-80, sr ptnr Goddens and Thicknesse 1980-87; *Recreations* travelling, golf; *Clubs* Boodles, Swinley Forest GC, Berkshire GC, Inst of Directors; *Style—* Horatio Shephard, Esq; The Barn, Elcot Park, nr Newbury, Berks RG16 8NJ (☎ 0488 57049); William Sturges and Co, Alliance House, 12 Caxton St, SW1 (☎ 01 222 1391)

SHEPHARD, Hon Mrs (Mary Anna); *née* Shaw; 2nd da of Baron Kilbrandon, PC (Life Peer), *qv*; *b* 1946; *m* 1971, Thomas H C Shephard; 4 s (Samuel b 1973, Edward b 1975, Francis b 1977, Christien b 1985), 2 da (Josephine b 1981); *Style—* The Hon Mrs Shephard; The Keeper's Cottage, Dunvegan Castle, Isle of Skye

SHEPHARD, Prof Ronald William; s of William Joseph Shephard (d 1975), of Leicester, and Nellie, *née* Simmonds (d 1964); *b* 25 April 1923; *Educ* Manchester GS, Stockport Sch, Wyggeston Sch Leicester, Queens' Coll Cambridge (BA, MA); *m* 2 May 1949, Betty Mabel Shephard; 1 s (Michael Clive Anthony), 1 da (Gillian Elizabeth); *Career* operational res sci MOD Army Dept 1943-, supt weapons and tactics Army Operational Res Estab 1961-64, supt land ops Def Operational Analysis Estab 1964-68, prof operational res RMCS 1969-83, advsr to hd of new projects Royal Ordnance plc 1983-, conslt Centre for Operational Res and Def Analysis London, conslt with BDM Corp Mclean VA USA; memb: CNAA, NATO Advsy Panel on Operational Res; FOR 1970 (chm), memb Wiltshire Assoc of Magicians, Assoc Inner Magic Circle F; *Books* Applied Operations Research: Examples from Defense Assessment (jtly, 1988); *Recreations* magic, military archival res; *Clubs* Magic Circle; *Style—* Prof Ronald Shephard; Old Westmill Farmhouse, Watchfield, Swindon, Wilts SN6 8TH (☎ 0793 782 321); Royal Ordnance Future Systems Gp, P O Box 243, Shrivenham, Swindon, Wilts SN6 8QD (☎ 0793 783 610, fax 0793 783 616, telex 444112)

SHEPHEARD, Sir Peter Faulkner; CBE (1972); s of Thomas Faulkner Shepheard; *b* 1913; *Educ* Birkenhead Sch, Liverpool Sch of Arch; *m* 1943, Mary, da of Charles James Bailey; 1 s, 1 da; *Career* architect, town planner and landscape architect; ptnr Shepheard, Epstein & Hunter 1948-; dean Graduate Sch of Fine Arts Pennsylvania Univ (USA) 1971-; kt 1980; *Clubs* Savile, Athenaeum; *Style—* Sir Peter Shepheard, CBE; 14-22 Ganton St, London W1

SHEPHEARD, Sir Victor George; KCB (1954), CB (1950); s of V G Shepheard (d 1958), of Shortlands, Kent; *b* 1893; *Educ* H M Dockyard Sch Devonport, RN Coll Greenwich; *m* 1924, Florence (d 1984), da of Capt James Wood of Bridgwater, Somerset; *Career* WW I Constructor Lt in Grand Fleet (present at Battle of Jutland), prof naval architecture RN Coll Greenwich 1934-39, chief constructor Admiralty 1939-42, asst dir Naval Construction 1942-47, dep dir Naval Construction Admiralty 1947-51, dir and head Royal Corps of Naval Constructors 1951-58, dir of res British Ship Research Assoc 1959-63; dir: Marinite Ltd, William Denny & Brothers Ltd 1959-63; memb Admiralty advsy ctee on structural steel, awarded William Froude Gold Medal for services to naval architecture 1965, Chev de la Légion d'Honneur (Fr); *Style—* Sir Victor Shepheard, KCB, CB; Manor Place, Manor Park, Chislehurst, Kent (☎ 01 467 5455)

SHEPHERD, Colin Ryley; MP (C) Hereford Oct 1974-; *b* 13 Jan 1938; *Educ* Oundle, Caius Coll Cambridge, McGill Univ Montreal; *Career* marketing dir and parly advsr Haigh Engineering Co Ltd 1963-; jt v-chm Cons parly ctee Agric 1979-, memb select ctee House of Commons Services 1979, chm Library Sub-Ctee 1983-, pps to sec of State for Wales 1987-; fell Indus & Parliament Tst; *Style—* Colin Shepherd Esq, MP; Manor House, Ganarew, Nr Monmouth, Gwent (☎ 0600 890220)

SHEPHERD, (Richard) David; OBE (1979); s of Raymond Oxley Shepherd (d 1960), and Margaret Joyce, *née* Williamson (d 1978); *b* 25 April 1931; *Educ* Stowe; *m* 2 Feb 1957, Avril Shirley, da of Hugh Dowling-Gaywood (d 1940); 4 da (Melinda b 1958, Mandy b 1960, Melanie b 1962, Wendy b 1964); *Career* trained under Robin Goodwin 1950-53, exhibited RA Summer Exhibition 1956, first one man exhibition 1962, painted religious painting of Christ for Army Garrison Church Bordan Hants 1964; one man shows: London 1966, Johannesburg 1966, London 1978, NY 1979; London 1984; portraits: HE Dr K Kaunda Pres of Zambia 1967, HM The Queen Mother 1969, Sheikh Zaid of Abu Dhabi 1970; lifestory World About Us BBC TV 1971 (The Man Who Loves Giants), BBC documentary Last Train to Mulobezi 1974, series for Thames TV in Search of Wildlife 1988; memb of hon World Wild Fund for Nature, fndr David Shepherd Conservation Fndn for the Enviroment and Wildlife, fndr and chm E Somerset Railway; Hon Doctorate Fine Arts Pratt Inst of NY 1971; FRSA 1987; FRGS 1989; Order of Distinguished Service First Div Rep of Zambia; *Books* A Man Who Loves Giants - Autobiography (1975), An Artist in Africa (1967), A Brush with Steam (1983), Painting of Africa and India (1978), David Shepherd The Man and His Paintings (1986); *Recreations* raising funds for wildlife conservation and driving steam locamotives; *Style—* David Shepherd, Esq, OBE; Winkworth Farm, Hascombe, Godalming, Surrey GU8 4JW (☎ 048 632 220)

SHEPHERD, Hon Douglas Newton; s of 2 Baron Shepherd, PC; *b* 1952; *Style—* The Hon Douglas Shepherd

SHEPHERD, Freda Margaret; da of John Edward Gresley (d 1958), of 252 Calais Hill, Burton upon Trent, Staffs, and Sarah Margaret Gresley, *née* Harden (d 1979); *b* 29 Nov 1930; *Educ* Burton upon Trent Girls' HS; *m* 31 Aug 1957, Richard John Shepherd, s of Arthur John Shepherd (d 1971), of 176 Rollestson Rd, Burton upon Trent, Staffs; *Career* audit clerk and PA Thomas Bourne & Co 1946-67, chief exec and sec Burton upon Trent & Dist C of C and Indust 1986- (co sec 1969); memb PCC St John's Horninglow, sec Burton upon Trent Girls' HS Assoc; memb Br C of C Execs; *Recreations* music, gardening, travel, cookery; *Style—* Mrs Richard Shepherd; 158 Derby St, Burton upon Trent, Staffs DE14 2NZ (☎ 0283 63761, fax 0283 510 753)

SHEPHERD, Hon Graeme George; s and h of 2 Baron Shepherd, PC; *b* 6 Jan 1949; *m* 1971, Eleanor; 1 s (Patrick Malcolm); *Style—* The Hon Graeme Shepherd; Suite 72, Wheelock House, 20 Pedder st C, Hong Kong

SHEPHERD, Lt Col Ian; s of Edward Basil Branch Shepherd (d 1980), and Una, *née* Sadler (d 1987); *b* 6 April 1939; *Educ* Queen's Coll of British Guiana, Dollar Acad, RMA Sandhurst; *m* 19 June 1965, Belinda, da of Brig Archibald Ian Buchanan-Dunlop, CBE, DSO, of Broughton Place, Broughton, Peebles-Shire; 2 s (Rupert Graham b 1968, Christian James b 1971), 1 da (Josephine Mary b 1975); *Career* cmmnd into Royal Highland Fusiliers 1960, Assist Mil Attaché (Tech) Moscow 1981-82, cmmdg offr: Scottish Infantry Depot (Bridge of Don) 1984-86, Aberdeen Univ OTC 1986-88; *Recreations* history, mil costume, photography, Russian-Soviet empire; *Clubs* Army and Navy; *Style—* Lt Col Ian Shepherd; c/o Bank of Scotland, 426 Morningside Road, Edinburgh EH10 5QF

SHEPHERD, John Dodson; CBE (1979); s of Norman Shepherd (d 1970), of Gawthwaite, nr Ulverston, and Elizabeth Ellen, *née* Dodson (d 1970); *b* 24 Dec 1920; *Educ* Barrow GS; *m* 21 Aug 1948, Marjorie, da of Albert James Nettleton (d 1983), of Lancaster; 1 s (David b 1949), 2 da (Margaret (Mrs Chadwick) b 1952, Elizabeth (Mrs Adkinson) b 1952; *Career* WWII RAF 1940-46; sec Newcastle Gen Hosp 1958-62, gp sec E Cumberland Hosp Mgmnt Ctee 1962-67, sec Liverpool Regnl Hosp Bd 1967-74; regnl administrator: Mersey RHA 1974-77, Yorks RHA 1977-82; tstee The Leonard Cheshire Fndn, vice pres Rotary Club of Harrogate 1988-89; pres Inst of Health Serv Administrators 1974-75; *Recreations* golf, caravanning, music; *Style—* John Shepherd, Esq, CBE; 14 Leconfield Garth, Follifoot, Harrogate, North Yorks HG3 1NF (☎ 0423 870520)

SHEPHERD, 2 Baron (UK 1946); Malcolm Newton Shepherd; PC (1965); s of 1 Baron Shepherd, PC, sometime Chief Labour Whip Lords, Capt Yeomen of the Gd & Hon Corps Gentlemen at Arms, also Nat Agent Lab Pty (d 1954); *b* 27 Sept 1918; *Educ* Friends' Sch Saffron Walden; *m* 1941, Allison, JP, da of Patrick Redmond; 2 s; *Heir* s, Hon Graeme Shepherd; *Career* chm: Nat Bus Co 1979-, Packaging Cncl 1978-, Civil Ser Pay Res Unit Bd 1978-82, Sterling Gp of Cos 1976-, MRC to 1982; dep ldr House of Lords 1968-70, lord privy seal and leader of the House of Lords 1974-76, min of state Cwlth Off 1967-70; *Style—* The Rt Hon the Lord Shepherd, PC; 29 Kennington Palace Court, Sancroft St, London SE11 (☎ 01 582 6772)

SHEPHERD, Dame Margaret Alice; DBE (1964), CBE (1962); da of Percy S Turner; *b* 1910; *Educ* Wimbledon, London Univ; *m* 1935, Thomas Cropper Ryley Shepherd (d 1975); 3 s, 1 da; *Career* chm Conservative and Unionist Women's Nat Advsy Ctee 1960-63, chm Nat Union of Conservative and Unionist Assocs 1963-64, pres 72-73; memb: House of Laity, Gen Synod of C of E 1980-, chm Haigh Engrg Co Ltd; *Recreations* swimming; *Style—* Dame Margaret Shepherd, DBE, CBE; Moraston House, Bridstow, Ross-on-Wye, Herefordshire (☎ Ross-on-Wye 62370)

SHEPHERD, Sir Peter; CBE (1967), DL (N Yorks 1982); s of Alderman Frederick Welton Shepherd, and Martha Eleanor; *b* 18 Oct 1916; *Educ* Nunthorpe GS York, Rossall; *m* 1940, Patricia Mary, da of Frank Edward Welton; 4 s; *Career* dir Shepherd Bldg Gp Ltd (chm 1958-86), chm Shepherd Construction Ltd; memb President's Consultative Ctee Bldg Employers Confedn 1956- (formerly Nat Fedn Bldg Trades Employers), pres Chartered Inst of Building 1964-65 (memb Nat Cncl 1956-87), chm Bd of Bldg Educn 1965-68 (memb 1957-75), cncl memb CBI 1976-; BIM; memb nat cncl 1965-71, memb bd fellows 1969-73, fndr chm Yorks and N Lincs Advsy Bd 1969-71; fndr memb Technician Educn Cncl 1973-79, vice-chm CIOB Professional Practice Bd 1975- (chm 1964-75), former chm Construction Indust Trg Bd and Wool Jute and Flax Indust Trg Bd, govr St Peter's Sch York; memb: Co of Merchant Adventurers of City of York (govr 1984-85), Court of the Univ of York; DSc Heriot Watt 1979, Hon DUniv York; Hon Life memb: BEC Yorkshire Region 1986, BEC York Assoc 1986; Hon Fellowship of Leeds Poly 1987; FCIOB (Hon Fell 1987-), CBIM, FInstD; kt 1976; *Recreations* sailing; *Clubs* Yorkshire; *Style—* Sir Peter Shepherd, CBE, DL; Galtres House, Rawcliffe Lane, York Y03 6NP (☎ 0904 24250); office: Blue Bridge Lane, York Y01 4AS (☎ 0904 53040, telex 57402)

SHEPHERD, Peter Geoffrey; CBE (1988); s of Raymond Oxley Shepherd (d 1960), of Farnham, Surrey, and Margaret Joyce, *née* Williamson (d 1977); *b* 13 April 1927; *Educ* Stowe, Trinity Coll Cambridge (BA); *m* 12 Jan 1951, da of Thomas Llewelyn Roberts (d 1948), of Hinderton Cheshire, High Sheriff of Merionmeth; 2 s (Robert b 1953, Jonathan b 1959); *Career* chm: Brighton & Storrington Investmts Ltd 1965-, Business Fin (Sussex) Ltd 1970-; memb: W Sussex CC 1969- (chm 1985-89), Assoc of CCs 1974-, Local Authorities Mgmnt Servs 1982- (chm 1986-88), Schools Cncl 1976-82; *Recreations* horse racing (steward at Fontwell, Plumpton, Brighton); *Style—* Peter Shepherd, Esq, CBE

SHEPHERD, Richard Charles Scrimgeour; MP (C) Aldridge-Brownhills 1979-; s of Alfred Shepherd; *b* 6 Dec 1942; *Educ* LSE, Johns Hopkins Univ; *Career* dir: Partridges of Sloane St Ltd, Shepherd Foods Ltd; memb SE econ planning cncl 1970-74, contested (C) Nottingham E Feb 1974; Lloyds underwriting memb 1974-; memb select ctee on Treasy and CS 1979-, sec Euro affairs and indust C ctees 1980-81; *Style—* Richard Shepherd Esq, MP; 14 Addison Rd, London W14 (☎ 01 603 7108)

SHEPHERD, Richard James; s of late William James Affleck Shepherd (d 1970), of Stratton End, Cirencester, Glos, and Katharine Flora, *née* MacAndrew; *b* 8 Mar 1947; *Educ* Marlborough, St Catherine's Coll Oxford (BA); *m* 10 January 1974, Clare Harriet Faviell, da of Sir Charles Ian Russell, of Hidden House, Sandwich, Kent; 3 s (Edward b 1977, Andrew b 1979, Thomas b 1982); *Career* CA, ptnr Shepherd Smail & Co Cirencester 1973-; amateur rider: winner 118 point to points and steeplechases; tstee Cirencester Benefit Soc; FCA 1979, ACA 1971; *Recreations* hunting, racing; *Style—* Richard J Shepherd, Esq; Stratton End, Cirencester, Glos (☎ 0285 653 686); Northway Hse, Cirencester, Glos (☎ 0285 655 955)

SHEPHERD, Robert Priestley; JP (1979, Lancs); s of Harry Priestley Shepherd (d 1956), of Rossendale, and Marion Scott, *née* Neill; *b* 1 Dec 1931; *Educ* Rossall Sch, Leicester Coll of Art and Technol; *m* 30 June 1954, Anne, da of Donald Robert Heyworth (d 1980), of Rossendale; 2 s (Philip b 22 June 1955, Henry b 3 Jan 1960), 1 da (Joy (Mrs Allsop) b 19 Nov 1956); *Career* dep chm Pentland Industs plc, chm Priestley Footwear Ltd govr and tstee Rossall Sch, tstee Richard Whittaker Charity Tst, area dep chm Rossendale Br Heart Fndn; pres: Otters Swimming Assoc Lancs, Rossendale Museum; High Sheriff Lancs 1987-88; Freeman City of London, memb

Worshipful Co of Patternmakers 1983; ACFI 1974, FIOD 1986; *Recreations* sailing, travel; *Clubs* South Caern YC, Royal Windermere YC; *Style—* Robert Shepherd, Esq, JP; Woodcliffe, Horncliffe, Rossendale, Lancs (☎ 0706 213096); Pentland Ind (Northern) plc, Albion Mill, Gt Harwood, Lancs (☎ 0254 886241)

SHEPHERD, Roland Walter; s of Walter James Shepherd,of Old Hearne Farm, Gospel Green, Haselmere, Surrey, and Marjorie Dorothy Shepherd; *b* 26 Nov 1933; *Educ* Bryanston, Merrist Wood Surrey Farm Inst (NCA), Worshipful Co of Farmers (Advanced Farm Business Mgmnt) Nuffield Travelling Scholarship; *m* 1, 15 Sept 1956 (m dis 1972), Christine Barbara Fenwick Smith, da of Stanley Fermor, of Surrey, 1 s (Ben b 2 Sept 1964), 3 da (Arabella b 19 July 1958, Camilla b 13 Dec 1959, Thomasin b 16 March 1963); m 2, 10 March 1972, Elizabeth Marian, da of Dr G W Ayres, TD, of Wilts; 2 s (Robert b 9 Oct 1974, Oliver b 31 May 1976); *Career* nat 2 Lt RA Troop Cdr 75 Heavy (antiaircraft) Regt Gravesend Kent 1952-54; clerk Lloyd's Broker's, farmer 1050 acres with 640 milking cows 1954-, fndr pig mktg gp 1957, co fndr Central Southern Cereal Growers 1964 (now part of SEGRAIN), invited to join Bd of Scats (Southern Counties Agricultural Trading Soc Ltd) 1967 (chm 1979), pres FAC (Fed of Agricultural Cooperatives) 1987-88 (joined cncl 1984), name at Lloyds 1958-; chm Wispers Sch 1981-87 (govr 1977-87), chm local Cons Assoc 1976-, County branch chm NFU 1976, chm parliamentary ctee NFU 1984-86; Freeman City of London, memb Worshipful Co of Barber Surgns; FBIM 1981-85; *Recreations* reading, antiques, photography, tennis, skiing; *Clubs* Farmers, Ski Club GB; *Style—* Roland W Shepherd, Esq; Boxalland Farm, Gospel Green, Haslemere, Surrey GU27 3BH (☎ 0428 2280)

SHEPHERD, William Stanley; s of William Donald Shepherd; *b* 12 Mar 1912; *Educ* Edleston Rd Elementary Sch Cheshire; *m* 12 Sept 1943, Betty, da of T F Howard; 2 s; *Career* Army 1939-45; md firms engaged in the bldg and devpt of property; MP (C) Cheshire 1945-66; *Recreations* skiing, repairing motor cars, dancing, eating out; *Clubs* Savile; *Style—* William S Shepherd, Esq; 33 Queens Grove, St Johns Wood, London NW8 (☎ 01 722 7526); 77 George Street, London W1 (☎ 01 935 0753)

SHEPHERD-BARRON, John Adrian; s of Wilfred Phillip Shepherd-Barron, MC, TD, LLD, (d 1979), and Dorothy Cunliffe Shepherd (d 1953), Wimbledon Ladies Doubles Champion (1931) and Wightman Cup Capt (1950-53); *b* 23 June 1925; *Educ* Stowe Cambridge; *m* 21 April 1954, Caroline, da of Sir Kenneth Murray, Kt (d 1979); 3 s (Nickolas b 1955, James b 1957, Andrew b 1959); *Career* Capt RA; served India, Egypt, Palestine 1945-47; chm: Security Express 1963-79, De La Rue Instruments 1967-79; regnl dir De La Rue Co plc 1979-85; chm Atlantic Freshwater plc 1987-; panel memb Scottish Ventures Fund; *Recreations* fishing, shooting, tennis; *Clubs* Army and Navy, All England LTC, New York Univ; *Style—* John A Shepherd-Barron, Esq; 14 Onslow Square, London SW7; Mains of Geanies, Fearn, Ross-shire (☎ 01 581 2491 and 086 287 443)

SHEPLEY, Richard Seymour Duart; s of Seymour Beadle Shepley (d 1987), and Marion Lea, *née* Jolly (d 1969); *b* 30 April 1950; *Educ* Oundle, Reading Univ (BSc Agric); *m* 23 Sept 1978, Sarah Susan Raisbeck, da of Sqdn-Ldr Douglas Raisbeck Gelling, of Buxton; 1 s (Timothy b 1983), 1 da (Rosanna b 1983); *Career* estate mgmnt, farming and forestry; memb: Historic Commercial Vehicle Soc, Mil Vehicle Conservation Gp; *Recreations* restoration of a variety of human artefacts; *Style—* Richard Shepley, Esq; Woodthorpe Hall, Holmesfield, Sheffield (☎ 0742 361997)

SHEPPARD, Allen John George; s of John Sheppard (d 1985), and Lily Sheppard, *née* Palmer; *b* 25 Dec 1932; *Educ* Ilford Co HS; London Sch of Economics (BSc Econ); *m* 1, 1958 (m dis 1980) Damaris, da of David Jones (d 1964); m 2, 1980, Mary, da of Harry Stewart, of London; *Career* Ford UK and Ford Eur 1958-68, dir Rootes 1968, mktg dir Br Leyland Int, md BL Euro, chief exec Watney Mann & Truman Brewers of Grand Metropolition, gp md Grand Met 1982 (dp chief exec 1986); non exec dir: UBM 1981-83 (non exec chm 1985, gp chm), Mallinson Denny Gp Ltd 1985-87; pt-time memb Br Railways Bd 1985-, vice-pres Brewers Soc 1987-, memb CBI Econ and Fin Policy Ctee; *Recreations* gardening, reading, red-setter dogs; *Style—* Allan Sheppard, Esq; 11-12 Hanover Square, London W1A 1DP (☎ 01 629 7488, telex 299606)

SHEPPARD, Hon Mrs Angela; *née* Spring Rice; twin da of 6 Baron Monteagle of Brandon and Anne, *née* Browncow, The Lady Monteagle of Brandon; *b* 23 April 1950; *m* 1973 (m dis 1982), Christopher Richard Seton Sheppard; 1 da (Catherine b 1976); *Recreations* bridge, tennis, gardening; *Clubs* Hurlingham; *Style—* The Hon Mrs Sheppard

SHEPPARD, (Richard David) Anthony; s of Daniel Gurney Sheppard (d 1988), of Bennetts, Ashwell, Baldock, Herts, and Cinthia, *née* Hill; *b* 17 Feb 1950; *Educ* Milton Abbey, Royal Agric Coll Cirencester; *m* 27 Sept 1975 (m dis 1989), Angela Marion, da of Col Arther Clerke Brown, MBE; 1 s (Harry 8 Aug 1984), 1 da (Amanda b 16 June 1982); *Career* farmer; memb: Oxfordshire Ctee Co Landowners Assoc, Oxfordshire Ctee Game Conservancy; *Recreations* shooting, riding the cresta; *Clubs* Saint Moritz Toboggan, Raffles; *Style—* Anthony Sheppard, Esq; Red House Farm, Murcott, Islip, Oxon OX5 2BJ (☎ 0869 244 886, car tel 0860 824 563)

SHEPPARD, Rt Rev David Stuart; *see*: Liverpool, Bishop of

SHEPPARD, James Lancelot; s of George Sheppard (d 1939); *b* 13 Sept 1926; *Educ* St Julian's HS Newport; *m* 1951, Margaret Mary, da of late Alfred Harris; 1 s, 1 da; *Career* asst md IMI Santon Ltd 1975-86 (CA 1950, co sec 1965, fin dir 1970), also dir of various subsidiaries & assoc cos UK and overseas, ret 1986, non exec dir Monmouthshire Bldg Soc; chm fin ctee of Gwent branch Br Red Cross Soc, gen cmmr Income Tax Newport Gwent; *Recreations* hill walking, charity work; *Clubs* Rotary, 41; *Style—* Lance Sheppard, Esq; The Croft, Ridgeway Grove, Newport, Gwent NP9 5AN (☎ 0633 66744)

SHEPPERD, Sir Alfred Joseph; s of Alfred Charles Shepperd (d 1939); *b* 19 June 1925; *Educ* Archbp Tenison's Sch, Univ Coll London; *m* 1950, Gabrielle Marie Yvette, da of late France Bouloux, MRCS, LRCP, ENT; 2 da; *Career* Sub-Lt RNVR UK and Canada; chm & chief exec (fin dir 1972-) The Wellcome Fndn Ltd 1977-, chm Wellcome plc 1986-; dir: Anglia Maltings (Hldgs) Ltd 1972-, Mercury Asset Mgmnt Gp plc 1987-; kt 1989; *Clubs* Athenaeum, Oriental, Naval; *Style—* Sir Alfred Shepperd; 183 Euston Rd, London NW1 2BP

SHER, Antony; s of Emanuel Sher, and Margery, *née* Abramowitz; *b* 14 June 1949; *Educ* Sea Point Boys HS Cape Town SA, Webber-Douglas Acad of Dramatic Art London, Post Grad drama course Manchester Univ drama dept and Manchester Poly Sch of Theatre; *Career* actor; roles incl: Howard Kirk in The History Man (BBC TV) 1980, Austin in True West (Nat Theatre) 1981; assoc artist RSC 1982-88 roles incl: Richard III (Drama magazine Best Actor Award 1984, London Standard Best Actor Award 1985, Laurence Olivier Best Actor Award 1985), Shylock in Merchant of Venice, The Fool in King Lear, Vindice in The Revenger's Tragedy, Tartuffe, Johnnie in Hello and Goodbye; Arnold in Torch Song Trilogy 1985 (Albery Theatre, Laurence Olivier Best Actor Award 1985); RSC 1985; *Books* Year of the King (actor's diary and sketchbook, 1985), Middlepost (1988); *Style—* Antony Sher, Esq; c/o Hope & Lyne, 108 Leonard St, London EC2 4RT (☎ 01 739 6200)

SHER, (Samuel) Julius; QC (1981); s of Philip Sher (d 1985), and Isa Phyllis, *née* Hesselson; *b* 22 Oct 1941; *Educ* Athlone HS, Witwatersrand Univ SA (BCom, LLB), Oxford Univ (BCL); *m* 29 Aug 1965, Sandra, da of Michael Maris, of Johannesburg, SA; 1 s (Brian b 10 July 67), 2 da (Joanne b 8 Aug 69, Debby b 6 May 74); *Career* called to the Bar Inner Temple 1968, rec 1987, master of the bench of the Hon Soc of the Inner Temple 1988-; *Recreations* tennis; *Style—* Jules Sher, Esq, QC; 12 Constable Close, London NW11 (☎ 01 455 2753); 3 New Square, Lincoln's Inn, London WC2 (☎ 01 405 5296, fax 01 831 6803, telex 267 699 EQUITY)

SHERBORNE, Archdeacon of; *see*: Oliver, Ven John

SHEREK, Hon Mrs (Kathleen Pamela Mary Corona); *née* Boscawen; da of late 7 Viscount Falmouth, KCVO, CB; *b* 1902; *m* 1937, Maj Henry Sherek, Rifle Bde (d 1967); *Style—* The Hon Mrs Sherek; 89A Route de Florissant, 1206 Geneva, Switzerland

SHERFIELD, 1 Baron (UK 1964), of Sherfield-on-Loddon, Co Southampton; Roger Mellor Makins; GCB (1960), KCB (1953, GCMG 1955, KCMG 1949, CMG 1944, DL (Hants 1978); s of Brig-Gen Sir Ernest Makins, KBE, CB, DSO (d 1959, n of Sir William Makins, 1 Bt), and Maria Florence, *née* Mellor; *b* 3 Feb 1904; *Educ* Winchester, Christ Church Oxford; *m* 30 April 1934, Alice (d 1985), da of Hon Dwight Filley Davis (d 1945), of Washington DC, USA; 2 s, 4 da; *Heir* s, Hon Christopher Makins; *Career* sits as Ind peer in House of Lords; chm House of Lords Select Ctee on Sci and Technol 1984-87; fell All Souls Coll Oxford, chllr of Reading Univ, hon student Christ Church Oxford, memb Cncl of Royal Albert Hall 1962-87; barr 1927, joined FO 1928, ambass to USA 1953-56, jt perm sec of Treasy 1956-60, chm UKAEA 1960-64; former chm of Industl and Commercial Fin Corpn, Fin for Industry Ltd, Hill Samuel & Co Ltd, A C Cossor Ltd, Raytheon Europe Int Co, Wells Fargo Ltd Parly and Scientific Ctee; dir Times Newspapers Ltd 1964-67; fell Winchester Coll 1962-79 (warden 1974-79), chm governing body mperial Coll of Science and Technol 1962-72, pres BSI 1970-73; Hon DCL Oxford, Hon LLD London and Sheffield, Hon DL Reading, Hon FICE; awarded RSA's Benjamin Franklin Medal 1982; FRS 1986; *Clubs* Boodle's, Pratt's MCC; *Style—* The Rt Hon the Lord Sherfield, GCB, KCB, GCMG, KCMG, CMG, DL; 81 Onslow Sq, London SW7 (☎ 01 589 6295); Ham Farm House, Ramsdell, nr Basingstoke, Hants RG2G 5SD (☎ 073 56 3526)

SHERIDAN, Cecil Majella; CMG (1961); s of John Peter Sheridan (d 1959), of Liverpool, and Teresa, *née* Myerscough (d 1970); *b* 9 Feb 1911; *Educ* Ampleforth, Univ of Liverpool (BA); *m* 19 Dec 1949, Monica, da of late Herbert Frank Eipeaut, MBE, of St Helier, Jersey; 2 s (Richard b 1952, Michael b 1956), 1 da (Paualine b 1980); *Career* WWII 1940-46, pilot trg RAFVR 1940-41, cmmnd Pilot Offr 1941, instr Rhodesian Air Trg Gp 1941-42, RAF Tport Cmd 1943-45, Br Mil Admin Malaya 1945-46, demobbed Sqdn Ldr 1946; admitted slr 1952, slr 1934-39; attached Colonial Off 1946, state legal advsr and dep public procecutor Malayian Union and Fedn of Malaya 1946-55; Fedn of Malaya: legal draughtsman 1955-57, solicitor-general 1957-59, attorney-general 1959-63; attorney-general Malaysia 1963; barr Inner Temple 1952-63, slr in private practice 1963-; dir Michael Sheridon & Co Ltd 1983-, Project in Prodn Co Ltd 1989-; chm of traffic Cmmrs E Midlands 1965-81, memb Licensing Authy for Goods Vehicles E Midlands 1965-83, memb Nottingham Mechanics Inst; PMM Fedn of Malaya 1962; *Style—* Cecil Sheridan, Esq, CMG; 18 Private Rd, Sherwood, Nottingham MG5 4DB

SHERIDAN, Dinah Nadyejda (Mrs John Merivale); da of Fernard Archer Sheridan (d 1958), and Lisa Charlotte, *née* Everth (d 1966, both photographers by appt to HM The Queen and Queen Elizabeth The Queen Mother); *b* 17 Sept 1920; *Educ* Sherrards Wood Sch Welwyn Garden City Italia Conti Stage Sch; *m* 1, 8 May 1942 (m dis 1952), Jimmy Hanley (d 1970); 1 s (Jeremy James Hanley Mp *qv* b 17 Nov 1945), 2 da (Carol Ann b and d 1944, Jenny b 15 Aug 1947); m 2, 3 March 1954 (m dis 1965) Sir John Davis *qv* ; m 3, 29 May 1986, John Herman Merivale *qv*; *Career* actress; numerous stage, tv and film appearances since 1932; offr St John's Ambulance Bde; *Recreations* gardening, knitting, cooking; *Style—* Miss Dinah Sheridan; 7A Berkeley Gardens, London W8

SHERIDAN, John Phillip; s of John David Hatton Sheridan (d 1987), of Beckenham, Kent and Marjorie Eleanor *née* Rich; *b* 18 Feb 1936; *Educ* Dulwich, Royal Veterinary Coll London Univ (BVet Med) ; *m* 6 June 1960, Maureen Dorothy, da of William Alfred Sullivan (d 1984), of Hildenborough Kent; 1 s (Gavin b 1963), 2 da (Corinne b 1961, Bridie b 1966); *Career* gen veterinary practice: Fakenham Norfolk 1960-61, Reigate Surrey 1961-64, Southwick Sussex 1964; partnership then practice princ 1971-86; md Anicare Gp Servs (mgmnt servs to veterinary profession) 1976-, pres Br Small Animal Veterinary Assoc 1974-75; branch tres Horsham Cons Assoc; memb: W Sussex Co Cncl 1976- (ldr 1984-), Sussex Police Authy 1985-, Arundel Castle Tstees 1988-; MRCVS 1960; *Recreations* skiing, sub aqua; *Style—* John Sheridan, Esq; High Banks, Bracken Lane, Storrington, Pulborough, W Sussex RH20 3HR (☎ 09066 5341); Anicare Group Services (Veterinary) Ltd, 23 Buckingham Rd, Shoreham by Sea, W Sussex BN4 5UA (☎ 0273 463 022, fax 0273 463 431)

SHERIDAN, Dr (Lionel Astor) Lee; s of Stanley Frederic Sheridan (d 1949), and Anne Agnes, *née* Quednau (d 1980); *b* 21 July 1927; *Educ* Whitgift Sch, London Univ (LLB, LLD), Queens Univ Belfast (PhD); *m* 1 June 1948, Margaret Helen, da of Louis Charles Béghin (d 1961); 1 s (Peter b 1958), 1 da (Linda b 1955, d 1975); *Career* barr Lincoln's Inn 1948, prof of law Univ of Malaya Singapore 1956-63, prof of comparative law Queens Univ Belfast 1963-71, dep princ Univ Coll Cardiff 1977-80 (prof of law 1971-88, actg princ 1980 and 87); chm NI Off of Law Reform Land Law working Pty 1967-70; LLD Univ of Singapore 1963; *Books* Fraud in Equity (1957), Federation of Malaya Constitution (1961), Constitutional Protection: Expropriation and Restrictions on Property Rights (with V T H Delany 1963), The British Commonwealth: Malaya, Singapore, The Borneo Territories: The Development of their Laws and constitutions (1961), The Constitution of Malaysia (with H E Groves 1987), Equity (with G W Keeton 1969), The Modern Law of Charities (with G W Keeton 1971), The Law of Trusts (1983), The Comparative Law of Trusts in the Commonwealth and the Irish Republic (1976), Digest of the English of Trusts (1979); *Recreations* walking, theatre-going; *Clubs* Athenaeum; *Style*— Dr Lee Sheridan; Cherry Trees, Broadway Green, Vale of Glamorgan CF5 6SR (☎ 0446 760 403)

SHERIDAN, Paul Richard; TD 1982; s of Patrick William Sheridan, of Grimsby, and Claire, JP, *née* Marklew; *b* 19 July 1951; *Educ* Havelock Sch Grimsby, Grimsby Coll of Tech, Univ of Kent (BA); *m* 30 Jun 1985, Beverley; *Career* served RCT, TA, Maj 1985 (Cadet 1969, Lt 1972, Capt 1977); admitted slr 1976; ptnr Wilkins & Chapman 1982-; NP 1985; chm League of Friends of Grimsby Hosps 1985-88; Lord of the Manor of Aspenden Herts 1985, Freeman City of London 1985, Liveryman Co of Carmen 1986; memb: Law Soc 1979 , Notaries Soc 1985; *Recreations* heraldry; *Clubs* Victory Services, London; *Style*— Paul Sheridan, Esq, TD; Vernon Holme, 130 Grimsby Road, Cleethorpes, South Humberside DN35 7DN (☎ 0472 698 124); Wilkin & Chapman, The Hollies, 46 St Peter's Avenue, Cleethorpes, South Humberside DN35 8HR (☎ 0472 691 285, fax 0472 695 872)

SHERIDAN, Peter Warner Alexander; QC (1977); s of Hugo Sheridan (d 1973), of Park Rd, Regents Park, London, and Marie Sheridan (d 1927); *b* 29 May 1927; *Educ* Lincoln Coll Oxford (BA); *Career* called to the Bar Middle Temple 1954 (master of the bench 1988); *Recreations* sports cars, archery, radio, astronomy; *Style*— Peter Sheridan, Esq, QC; 17 Brompton Sq, London SW3 (☎ 01 584 7250); Pile Oak Lodge, Donhead-St-Andrew, Dorset; 2 Crown Office Row, The Temple, London EC4Y 7HJ (☎ 01 583 2681, fax 01 583 2850, telex 8955733 INLAWS)

SHERIDAN, Richard Jonathan; s of Dr Morris (Roger) Sheridan, of 15 The Brookdales, Bridge Lane, London NW11, and Yvonne, *née* Brook; *b* 20 Dec 1956; *Educ* City of London Sch, Guy's Hosp Med Sch London Univ; *Career* sr registrar obstetrics and gynaecology Central Middx Hosp and St Mary's Hosp 1988-; Freeman City of London, Liveryman Worshipful Soc of Apothecaries; MRCOG 1985, FRCS 1985; *Publications* incl: Fertility in a Male with Trisomy 21 (1989); *Recreations* squash, skiing, riding; *Style*— Richard Sheridan, Esq; 15 Belgrave Court, Wellesley Road, Chiswick, London W4 4LG (☎ 01 995 0489); Central Middlesex Hospital, Acton Lane, London NW10 (☎ 01 965 5733)

SHERIDAN, Dr (Morris) Roger; JP; s of William Sheridan (d 1964), of London, and Rebecca Sheridan (d 1982); *b* 11 Nov 1923; *Educ* Central Fndn Sch, UCL, UCH Med Sch; *m* 3 July 1947, Yvonne Leila, da of Abraham Brook (d 1957), of London; 1 s (Richard Jonathan b 1956), 1 da (Amanda Jane b 1959); *Career* substantive Capt RAMC 1947-49, (ENT Surgn F East Land Forces, staff surgn Br Troops Austria); gen cmmr Taxes, dep chm Haringey Petty Sessional Area; div mo Br Boxing Bd of Control, former chm Local Med Ctee; former memb: Haringey DMT, NE Thames Med Advsy Ctee; Freeman City of London, Liveryman Worshipful Soc of Apothecaries of London; MRCS, LRCP, fell BMA, fell Hunterian and Harveian Soc; VMSP 1962; *Books* Really Nurse (1959), Wake up Nurse (1962); *Recreations* cricket, bridge; *Clubs* Bluc del Sol Calahonda; *Style*— Dr Roger Sheridan, JP; 15 The Brookdales, Bridge Lane, London NW11 9JU (☎ 01 455 8848)

SHERLAW-JOHNSON, Dr Robert; s of Robert Johnson (d 1980), and Helen Smith (d 1976); *b* 21 May 1932; *Educ* Gosforth GS Newcastle upon Tyne, Univ of Durham (BA, BMUS), DMUS (Leeds), MA (Oxon), FRAM; *m* 28 July 1959, Rachael Maria, da of Cyril Clarke (d 1974); 3 s (Christopher b 1962, Austin b 1964, Oliver b 1976) 2 da (Rebecca b 1960, Griselda b 1966); *Career* univ lectr in music (Oxford), author of Messiaen (Dent, 1975); recordings (as pianist) of Catalosue D'Oiseaux, Br Messiaen (and other works), and later works by Liszt; composer of: 3 piano sonatas, piano concerto, ciprinot concerto, Opera The Lambton Worm, Carmina ver Nalia, 2 string quartets, Ruintey; various songs and other chamber works; *Recreations* collecting playing cards, croquet; *Style*— Dr Robert Sherlaw-Johnson; Malton Croft, Woodlands Rise, Stonesfield, Oxon (☎ Stonesfield 318); Worcestor College, Oxford (☎ Oxford 278360); Faculty of Music, St Aldates, Oxford (☎ Oxford 276132)

SHERLOCK, Dr Alexander; CBE (1989), MEP (EDG) SW Essex 1979-; s of Thomas Sherlock, MM (d 1971), of Bognor Regis, Sussex, and Evelyn Mary, *née* Alexander; *b* 14 Feb 1922; *Educ* Magdalen Coll Sch Oxford, Stowmarket GS, London Hosp (MB, BS 1945); *m* 1, 24 March 1945, Clarice Constance (Peggy) (d 1975), da of Edward G Scarff (d 1976), of Stowmarket, Suffolk; 1 s (Jim b 18 Feb 1951), 2 da (Penny b 10 March 1946, Sandra b 18 Aug 1948); m 2, 1976, Eileen, da of Leslie Hall (d 1976), of Bawtry; 1 step da (Clare b 6 March 1960); *Career* Fl Lt RAF 1946-48; med practitioner and conslt 1948-79; barr Gray's Inn 1961; asst dep coroner St Pancras 1971-72; memb: Felixstone UDC 1960-74, E Suffolk CC 1966-74, Suffolk CC 1974-; chm Fire and Public Protection Ctee 1977-; vice-pres: Assoc of Dist Cncls, Inst of Environmental Health Offrs, Trading Standards Inst; OStJ 1974; FRSA 1987; *Recreations* walking, gardening; *Clubs* RAF, Royal Belgian Automobile; *Style*— Dr Alexander Sherlock, CBE, MEP; 58 Orwell Road, Felixstowe, Suffolk IP11 7PS (☎ 0394 284503); 13 rue du Grand Duc, Bruxelles 1040, Belgium (☎ 02 640 49 30)

SHERLOCK, (Edward) Barry Orton; s of Victor Edward Sherlock (d 1973); *b* 10 Feb 1932; *Educ* Merchant Taylors' Sch, Pembroke Coll Cambridge; *m* 1955, Lucy Trerice, da of Professor Basil Willey (d 1978); 2 da; *Career* dir, gen mangr and actuary The Equitable Life Assurance Society, chm Lantro 1986-; FIA; *Recreations* music; *Style*— Barry Sherlock, Esq; 63 Sunnyfield, London NW7 4RE (☎ 01 959 5193)

SHERLOCK, Nigel; s of Horace Sherlock (d 1967), and Dorothea, *née* Robinson (d 1980); *b* 12 Jan 1940; *Educ* Barnard Castle Sch, Univ of Nottingham (BA); *m* 3 Sept 1966, Helen Diana Frances, da of M Sigmund; 2 s (Andrew b July 1968, Mark b 7 July 1976), 1 da (Emma b 5 Sept 1970); *Career* stockbroker; dir Wise Speke Ltd; memb: cncl Univ of Newcastle, cncl St John's Coll Univ of Durham, Bishops cncl Diocese of Newcastle; chm: Northern Sinfonia Orchestra, Northumberland Co Scout Assoc; Freeman City of Newcastle Upon Tyne; AMSIA (1972), FBIM (1985); *Recreations* the countryside; *Clubs* New (assoc memb, Edinburgh), Northern Counties, Newcastle; *Style*— Nigel Sherlock, Esq; 14 North Ave, Gosforth, Newcastle-Upon-Tyne NE3 4DS (☎ 091 2854379); Commercial Union Hse, 39 Pilgrim St, Newcastle-Upon-Tyne NE1 6RQ (☎ 091 2611266)

SHERLOCK, Sir Philip Manderson; KBE (1967, CBE 1953); s of Rev Terence Manderson Sherlock, Methodist minister; *b* 25 Feb 1902; *Educ* Calabar HS; *m* 1942, Grace Marjorie, da of late Douglas James Verity, OBE; 2 s, 1 da; *Career* headmaster Wolmer's Boy's Sch Jamaica 1933-38, dir of extra-mural studies Univ of WI 1947-60, pro-vice-chllr 1960-63, vice-chllr 1963-69; MLC Jamaica 1952-59, vice-pres Caribbean Resources Dvpt Fndn 1983-; *Clubs* Nat Liberal; *Style*— Sir Philip Sherlock, KBE; Caribbean Resources Development Foundation Inc, 7855 NW 12 Street, Suite 217, Miami, FLA 33126, USA

SHERLOCK, Prof Dame Sheila Patricia Violet; DBE (1978); da of Samuel Philip Sherlock (d 1979), and Violet Mary Catherine Beckett (d 1969); *b* 31 Mar 1918; *Educ* Folkestone Co Sch, Edinburgh Univ (MD), Yale Univ (Rockefeller fellow); *m* 1951, David Geraint James; 2 da (Amanda, Auriole); *Career* physician and lectr in medicine Post-Graduate Medical Sch of London 1948-59, prof medicine London Univ Royal Free Hosp Sch Medicine 1959-83; memb Senate London Univ 1976-81; sr censor and vice-pres Royal Coll of Physicians of London 1976-77; Hon MD: Lisbon, Oslo, Leuven 1985; Hon LLD Aberdeen 1982; Hon DSc City Univ (NY), Yale Univ 1983, Edinburgh 1985; FRCP, FRCPEd, FRACP, Hon FACP, Hon FRCP (C), Hon FRCP (I), Hon FRCP (Glasgow); *Books* Diseases of the Liver and Biliary System (7 Ed 1985); *Recreations* cricket, travel; *Style*— Prof Dame Sheila Sherlock, DBE; 41 York Terrace East, London NW1 4PT (☎ 01 486 4560); Royal Free Hospital, London NW3 (☎ 01 794 0500 ext 3934)

SHERMAN, Sir Alfred; s of Jacob Vladimir Sherman, and Eva, *née* Goldental; *b* 10 Nov 1919; *Educ* Hackney Downs Co Secdy Sch, LSE (BScEcon); *m* 1958, Zahava, *née* Levin; 1 s; *Career* journalist and public affairs advsr; leader writer Daily Telegraph; conslt: Nat Bus Co, Booz, Allen & Hamilton (UK); kt 1983; *Clubs* Reform, Hurlingham; *Style*— Sir Alfred Sherman; 10 Gerald Rd, London SW1 (☎ 01 730 2838, office 01 730 3453/930 8144)

SHERMAN, Sir Lou (Louis); OBE (1967), JP (Inner London); *m* Sally, CBE, JP; *Career* chm Housing Corpn 1977-80, dep chm Harlow Dvpt Corpn, initiator Lea Valley Regnl Park Authy; kt 1975; *Style*— Sir Lou Sherman, OBE, JP

SHERRARD, Michael David; QC (1968); s of Morris Sherrard (d 1965), and Ethel, *née* Werbner (d 1983); *b* 23 June 1928; *Educ* Kings Coll London (LLB 1949); *m* 6 April 1952, Shirley, da of Maurice Bagrit (d 1973); 2 s (Nicholas b 9 June 1953, Jonathan b 5 Aug 1957); *Career* barr Middle Temple 1949, memb Winn Ctee on Personal Injury Litigation 1966-68, rec of the Crown Court 1974-, master of the Bench Middle Temple 1977, bench rep on Senate 1978-80, inspr Dept of Trade under Companies Act(s) (London Capital Gp) 1975-77; chm Normansfield Hosp Public Inquiry 1977-78; contributor to British Accounting Standards - the first 10 years (1981); *Recreations* travel, listening to opera, oriental art; *Clubs* Oriental; *Style*— Michael Sherrard Esq, QC; Flat 15, 55 Portland Place, London W1N 3AH (☎ 01 255 1513); Crooked Beams, 4 Church Road, Alderton, Glos; 2 Crown Office Row, Temple, London EC4Y 7HJ (☎ 01 583 2681, fax 01 583 2850, telex 8955733 INLAWS G)

SHERRARD, Simon Patrick; s of Patrick Sherrard, and Angela Beatrice Sherrard, *née* Stacey; *b* 22 Sept 1947; *Educ* Eton; *m* 23 Aug 1975, Sara Anne, da of Major Peter Pain St Ancliffe, MBE; 1 s (James b 1984), 3 da (Emma b 1977, Kate b 1978, Polly b 1983); *Career* Samuel Montaru & Co Ltd 1968-74, Jardine Matheson & Co Ltd 1974-84, md Bibby Line Ltd 1985-; *Books* tennis, shooting; *Recreations* White's; *Style*— Simon Sherrard, Esq; Norwich House, Water Street, Liverpool LE8 (☎ 051 236 0492, telex 629241, fax 051 236 1163)

SHERRIN, Ned (Edward George); s of Thomas Adam Sherrin, of Kingweston, Somerset (d 1965), and Dorothy Finch, *née* Drewett, of Kingweston, Somerset (d 1974); *b* 18 Feb 1931; *Educ* Sexey's Bruton, Exeter Coll, Oxford (MA); Gray's Inn, Barr of Law; *Career* prod, dir presenter, writer, films, theatre radio and tv; TW3 (TV), Loose Ends (radio), Side by Side by Sondheim (theatre); *Books* A Small Thing Like an Earthquake (autobiog); *Style*— Ned Sherrin, Esq; 4 Cornwall Mansions, Ashburnham Rd, SW10 0PE

SHERRY, Prof Norman; s of Michael Sherry, and Sarah, *née* Taylor; *b* 6 July 1935; *Educ* Univ of Durham (BA), Univ of Singapore (PhD 1963); *m* June 1960 Dulcie Sylvia, da of Samuel William Brunt; *Career* lectr in english lit, Univ of Singapore 1961-66, lectr and sr lectr Univ of Liverpool 1966-70, prof of english Univ of Lancaster 1970-82, Mitchell Distinguished prof of literature Trinity Univ San Antonia Texas 1983-; fell Humanities Res Center N Carolina 1982; FRSL 1986; *Books* Conrad's Eastern World (1966), Jane Austen (1966), Charlotte and Emily Bronte (1969), Conrad's Western World (1971), Conrad and His World (1972), Conrad; The Critical Heritage (1973), Conrad in Conference (1976), The Life of Graham Green Vol One 1904-39 (1989); ed Conrad Edns: Lord Jim (1967, 1974), An Outpost of Progress, Heart of Darkness (1973), Nostromo (1974), The Secret Agent (1974), The Nigger of The Narcissus, Typhoon, Falk and Other Stories (1975); contrib: The Academic American Encyclopedia, Guardian, Daily Telegraph, Oxford Magazine, Modern Language Review, Review of English Studies, Notes and Queries; BBC book contrib: Kenneth Muir Festschrift (1987), Creativity (1989); TV and radios; Conrad and His Critics BBC Radio 3 1981, film on Graham Greene Arena BBC TV 1989; *Recreations* talking, writing, reading, public speaking, jogging, weight training, table tennis; *Clubs* Savile; *Style*— Prof Norman Sherry

SHERSBY, (Julian) Michael; MP (C) Uxbridge 1983-; s of William Henry and Elinor Shersby; *b* 17 Feb 1933; *Educ* John Lyon Sch Harrow-on-the-Hill; *m* 1958, Barbara Joan, da of John Henry Barrow; 1 s, 1 da; *Career* MP (C): Uxbridge 1972-74, Hillingdon Uxbridge 1974-1983; pps to min for Aerospace and Shipping 1974; memb: panel of dep chairmen of House of Commons and temp chm of standing ctees, ctee on Public Accounts 1983-; memb: Paddington Borough Cncl 1959-64, Westminster City Cncl 1964-71 (dep Lord Mayor 1967-68); dir-gen The Sugar Bureau, sec UK Sugar Indust Assoc, hon tres World Sugar Res Orgn; memb Food and Drink Indust Cncl; *Recreations* theatre and travel; *Clubs* Conservative (Uxbridge); *Style*— Michael Shersby, Esq, MP; House of Commons, London SW1A 0AA (☎ 01 219 3000); constituency office: 36 Harefield Rd, Uxbridge, Middx (☎ Uxbridge 39465)

SHERSTON, Felicity Mary Forster; da of late Essex Loftus Digby, and Violet Muriel Louise Digby (Jane Baird, actress d 1953); *b* 8 May 1923; *Educ* Moira House Eastbourne, Licenciate Coll of Speech Therapists, Inchbald Sch of Design (Dip Fine and Decorative Arts); *m* 16 Aug 1948, Arthur Timothy, s of Charles Talbot Sherston, of W Sussex; 2 s (Timothy James b 1954, Nicholas Christopher (twin) b 1954, 4 da (Clarissa Ann b 1949, Sarah Felicity b 1951, Miranda Sophia b 1958, Cressida Rose b 1967); *Career* tutor: Extra-Mural Dept Univ of Surrey, continuing Educn Dept Univ of Sussex; lectr: NADFAS, WEA, Nat Tst, Thesis Children in Art 1974; *Recreations* all aspects of fine and decorating arts; *Style*— Mrs Felicity Sherston; Dove Cottage, Tillington, Petworth, W Sussex (☎ 0798 42834)

SHERSTON-BAKER, Sir Humphrey Dodington Benedict; 6 Bt (GB 1796) of Dunstable House, Richmond, Surrey; s of Lt-Col Sir Dodington Sherston-Baker, 5 Bt (d 1944), and Irene, da of Sir Roper Parkington; *b* 13 Oct 1907; *Educ* Downside, Christ's Cambridge; *m* 1938 (m dis 1952), Margaret Alice, only da of H W Binns; 1 s,

3 da; *Heir* s, Robert George Humphrey Sherston-Baker b 3 April 1951; *Style*— Sir Humphrey Sherston-Baker, Bt; 22 Frognal Ct, NW3

SHERSTON-BAKER, Robert George Humphrey; s and h of Sir Humphrey Sherston-Baker, 6 Bt; *b* 3 April 1951; *Style*— Robert Sherston-Baker, Esq

SHERWEN, J Timothy R; s of A R Sherwen, of Correnden, Dry Hill Park Rd, Tonbridge, Kent, and Catherine Joyce Sherwen (d 1982); *b* 21 Nov 1937; *Educ* Tonbridge Sch, Selwyn Coll Cambridge (BA); *m* 1969, Mary Christiane, da of Gerald Charles Stokes (d 1980); 1 s; *Career* md Linguaphone Gp 1986, md Thomas Nelson & Sons Ltd 1982-; parly candidate Faversham 1979; *Recreations* sailing, music (eighteenth century wind music); *Style*— Timothy Sherwen, Esq; Linguaphone Group, Linguaphone House, Beavor Lane, London W6 9AR (☎ 01 741 1655, telex 266181); Ward House, North St, Winkfield, Berks (☎ 0344 882393)

SHERWOOD, (Robert) Antony (Frank); CMG (1981); s of Franil Henry Sherwood (d 1964), and Mollie, *née* Moore (d 1952); *b* 29 May 1923; *Educ* Christs Hosp, St Johns Coll Oxford (MA); *m* 21 Nov 1953, Margaret Elizabeth, da of Frank Ratcliffe Simpson (d 1979); 2 s (Simon b 1956, Jeremy b 1957), 2 da (Deborah b 1954, Harriet b 1958); *Career* RAF 1942-46; Br Cncl 1949-81; serv Turkey, Nigeria (twice), Syria, Uganda, Somalia, UK, ret as asst dir gen 1981; Help The Aged: chm Overseas Ctee 1988- (memb 1982-), tstee 1988; ed Directory of Statutory and Voluntary Health Social and Welfare Servs in Surrey 1986 and 1987; Guildford Inst Univ of Surrey: memb mgmnt ctee, chm fin ctee; *Recreations* reading, travel, genealogy; *Style*— Antony Sherwood, Esq; 18 Rivermount Gardens, Guildford, Surrey GU2 5DN (☎ 0483 382 77)

SHERWOOD, The Bishop of, The Rt Rev Harold Richard Darby; s of William Darby (d 1978), and Miriam, *née* Jephcott (d 1936); *b* 28 Feb 1919; *Educ* Cathedral Sch Shanghai, St John's Coll Durham (BA); *m* 3 Sept 1949, Audrey Elizabeth Lesley, da of Charles Leslie (d 1968); 2 s (John b 1953, Mark b 1964), 3 da (Jane b 1950, Anne b 1955, Mary b 1959); *Career* WWII 1939-45 Army, serv Far East (POW) 1941-45, Thomson & Co chartered accountants Shanghai and Hong Kong 1936-39; Hong Kong Govt revenue dept 1939; deacon, priest 1951; curate of: Leyton 1950-52, Harlow 1952-53; vicar of: Shrub End Colchester 1953-59, Waltham Abbey Essex 1959-70, dean of Battle 1970-75, consecrated bishop of Sherwood in York Minster 1975; *Recreations* vintage motoring; *Style*— The Rt Rev Harold Sherwood; Applegarth, Halam, Newark, Notts NG22 8AN (☎ 0636 814041)

SHERWOOD, James Blair; s of William Earl and Florence Balph Sherwood; *b* 8 August 1933; *Educ* Yale Univ (BA); *m* 31 Dec 1977, Shirley Angela, da of Geoffrey Masser Briggs, of The Garden House, Hinton Manor, Hinton Waldrist, Oxon; 2 step s (Charles Nigel Cross b 1959, Simon Michael Cross b 1960); *Career* Lt US Naval Reserve 1955-58; pres Sea Containers Ltd; chm: Br Ferries Ltd, Orient-Express Hotels Ltd; proprietor Illustrated London News; *Recreations* tennis, skiing, sailing; *Clubs* Pilgrims, Mory's, Hurlingham, Mark's; *Style*— James Sherwood, Esq; (☎ 01 928 6969)

SHERWOOD, Kenneth Alan; s of Frederick Sherwood (d 1950), of Pinner, and Winifred Edith Maud, *née* White (d 1987); *b* 20 May 1935; *Educ* Merchant Taylors; *m* 18 Feb 1961, Jennifer Edith, da of Geoffrey Higginson Allard (d 1986), of Herts; 1 s (Graham b 1961), 2 da (Heather b 1964, Frances b 1966); *Career* ptnr Hodgson Impey (formerly Chalmers Impey & Co) chartered accountants 1968- (nat tech ptnr 1978-); cncl memb ICAEW 1977-83, vice pres AAT 1987 (cncl memb 1983-), chm ICAEW Ctee on Housing Assocs 1976-, vice chm Hightown Housing Assoc 1983- (ctee memb 1980-), vice chm Berkhamsted Town Hall Tst 1986-, chm Berkhamsted Citizens Assoc 1974-76; *Recreations* gardening, walking, reading, theatre, local community gps; *Clubs* Chartered Accountant Dining, Old Merchant Taylors' Soc; *Style*— Kenneth Sherwood, Esq; Rhenigidale, Ivy House Lane, Berkhamsted, Herts HP4 2PP (☎ (04427) 5158); Hodgson Impey, Spectrum House, 20-26 Cursitor Street, London EC4A 1HY (☎ 01 405 2088, telex 8814562, fax 01-831-2206)

SHETH, Pranlal; s of Purashotam Virji Sheth (d 1936), and Sakarben Sheth (d 1985); *b* 20 Dec 1924; *m* 1951, Indumati, da of Dr Chaganlal Druva (d 1958); 1 s (Sunil), 1 da (Vandna); *Career* journalist Kenya 1943-52, chm Nyanza Farmers Coop Soc 1954-60, barr Lincoln's Inn 1962, memb: Central Agric Bd Kenya 1963-66, Econ Planning and Devpt Cncl Kenya 1964-66; dep chm Asian Hosp Authy 1964-66; memb: N Metropolitan Conciliation Ctee, Race Rels Bd 1973-77, chief ed Gujar Samacher Weekly 1972-73; dir: Abbey Life Assur Co Ltd 1974-, Ambassador Life Assurance Co Ltd 1980-, Abbey Life Assurance (Ireland) Ltd 1981-85; legal dir Hartford Europe Gp of cos 1977-86, gp sec ITT gp cos in UK 1983-86, dep chm CRE 1977-80; sec Abbey Life Gp plc (dir 23 companies within the gp); dir Roundhouse Arts Centres (1986-; memb: BBC Consultative Gp on Indust and Business Affairs 1986-, BBC Asian Programmes Advsy Ctee 1986-, ct of govrs Poly of N London 1979-; tstee: Project Fullemploy (Charitable Tst) 1977-, Runnymede Tst 1987-, Urban Tst 1987-; vice patron UK Assoc Int Year of the Child 1978-80; FIOD, FBIM; *Recreations* music, theatre, sports, literature; *Clubs* Royal Overseas League, Scribes; *Style*— P Sheth, Esq; 70 Howberry Rd, Edgware, Middx (☎ 01 952 2413); Abbey Life Assurance Co Ltd, 80 Holdenhurst Rd, Bournemouth BH8 8AL (☎ 0202 292373, telex 417247)

SHEWAN, Henry Alexander; CB (1974), OBE (Mil 1946), QC (1949); s of James Smith Shewan (d 1939); *b* 7 Nov 1906; *Educ* Robert Gordon's Coll Aberdeen, Aberdeen Univ, Emmanuel Coll Cambridge; *m* 1937, Ann Fraser, *née* Thomson; 2 s; *Career* Sqdn Ldr RAFVR; advocate 1933, Nat Insur cmmr (full-time) 1955-79, Nat Insurance cmmr (pt/t) 1979-87, red; *Style*— Henry Shewan, Esq, CB, OBE, QC; St Raphael's Nursing Home, 6 Blackford Avenue, Edinburgh

SHEWEN, Lt-Col Antony Gordon Mansel; s of Lt-Col Douglas Gordon Mansel Shewen (d 1982), of Ipplepen, Devon, and Margaret Evelyn, *née* Walker (d 1979); *b* 7 Oct 1927; *Educ* Sherborne, Ch Ch Oxford, RMA Sandhurst; *m* 17 May 1958, Rosemary Margaret, da of Dudley Frederick Oliphant Dangar, of Dittisham; 1 s (Christopher b 1959), 2 da (Celia b 1963, Laura b 1967); *Career* serv in RHA The Queen's Bays, Queen's Dragoon Guards, Malaya 1964, Aden 1967; seconded Cabinet Off 1969-71; memb Trg ctee The Pony Club; sec Taunton Race Course; *Recreations* horses, hunting, racing, farming; *Style*— Lt-Col Antony G M Shewen; Myrtle Farm, Bickenhall, Taunton, Somerset (☎ 0823 480656); Taunton Racecourse (☎ 0823 337172)

SHIACH, Allan George; s of Maj Gordon Leslie Shiach, WS (d 1948), and Lucie Sybil, *née* de Freitas ; *b* 16 Sept 1941; *Educ* Gordonstoun, McGill Univ (BA); *m* 12 Nov 1966, Kathleen Beaumont, da of Richard B Swarbreck (d 1977), of Rhodesia; (Dominic Leslie b 1967, Luke Allan b 1974), 1 da (Philippa Lucie b 1969); *Career* chm Macallan-Glenlivet plc 1980- (dep chm 1978-80); dir: Rafford Films Ltd 1984-, Whitegate Leisure plc 1988-; screenwriter/producer 1970-; writer/co-writer: Don't Look Now 1975, Castaway 1985, The Girl from Petrovka 1978, DARYL 1984, Tenebrae 1982, Joseph Andrews 1979, The Witches 1988, and others; memb: BBC Broadcasting Cncl (Scotland), Cncl of Scotch Whisky Assoc, Exec Cncl Writers Guild of GB; Freeman City of London 1988, Liveryman Worshipful Co of Distillers; BAFTA, WGA, AIP; *Clubs* Savile; *Style*— Allan Shiach, Esq; 1 Hereford Square, London SW7 4TT (☎ 01 370 2694, fax 01 373 4044)

SHIACH, Sheriff Gordon Iain Wilson; s of John Crawford Shiach (d 1978), and Florence Bygott Shiach, *née* Wilson; *b* 15 Oct 1935; *Educ* Gordonstoun, Edinburgh Univ (MA, LLB); *m* 1962, Margaret Grant, da of Donald Duff Smith, of Grantown-on-Spey; 2 da (Katherine, Alison); *Career* advocate 1960-72 (Edinburgh); Sheriff: Fife and Kinross at Dunfermline 1972-79, Lothian and Borders at Linlithgow 1979-84, Lothian and Borders at Edinburgh 1984-; *Recreations* orienteering, music, theatre; *Clubs* New (Edinburgh); *Style*— Sheriff Gordon Shiach; Sheriffs' Chambers, Sheriff Ct House, Lawnmarket, Edinburgh EH1 2NS (☎ 031 226 7181)

SHIATIS, Michael; s of Avraam Constantine (d 1974), and Kalliopi Avraam; *b* 18 May 1934; *Educ* Pancyprian Gymneseum Cyprus, Inst of Chartered Accountants; *m* 31 March 1964, Helena Joyce, da of Symeon Michael Pittas, of London; 2 s (Constantine Michael b 1965, Andreas Michael b 1966), 1 da (Christina Helena b 1970); *Career* CA; dir: M A S Enterprises Ltd, Skilful Finance Ltd, Europafrica Ltd, Ion Finance (London) Ltd, Earnison Hldgs plc, Guestguard Ltd, Guestlock Ltd, Guestcare Ltd, Free Trade Warf Ltd, Feiser Ltd, Corintia Court Properties Ltd; FCA, ATII, AM, BIM, IOD; *Recreations* jogging, shooting, walking; *Style*— Michael Shiatis, Esq; 23 Craven Terrace, Lancaster Gate W2 3QH (☎ 01 262 9324); work: (☎ 01 402 2223, telex LONDON 22359)

SHIELD, Dr Michael James; s of Joseph Wishart Shield, DSC, and Phyllis Mabel Rosemary Lyphin, *née* Bullivant; *b* 17 Oct 1949; *Educ* Cheltenham, Univ of London, Middx Hosp Med Sch (MB BS, MRCPath); *m* 27 March 1976, Amelia Joan, da of Leyshon Edward Thomas (d 1952); 1 s (James b 1981), 1 da (Zabrina b 1983); *Career* sr lectr and hon conslt microbiologist St Mary's Hosp 1980-81; dir: G D Searle & Co Ltd UK 1986-, European Clinical Res; *Recreations* golf, photography, travel, house renovation; *Style*— Dr Michael Shield, Esq; G D Searle & Co, PO Box 53, Lane End Rd, High Wycombe, Bucks HP12 4HL (☎ 0494 21124)

SHIELDS, Elizabeth Lois; da of Thomas Henry Teare (d 1977), and Dorothy Emma Elizabeth, *née* Roberts-Lawrence (d 1977); *b* 27 Feb 1928; *Educ* Whyteleafe Girls' GS Surrey, UCL (BA), Univ of York (MA); *m* 12 Aug 1961, David Cathro Shields, s of Arthur William Strachan Shields; *Career* teacher: classics at St Philomena's Carshalton, Jersey Coll for Girls, St Swithun's Winchester, Trowbridge HS, Queen Ethelburga', Harrogate, Malton Sch; lectr Hull Univ 1989-; memb SLDP, cncllr Ryedale DC May 1980, MP (SLDP) Ryedale May 1986-June 1987, re-selected prospective Parly candidate Ryedale; chm: Malton Sch PTA, govrs Langton CP Sch; govrs memb Norton Sch, patron Malton and Norton Boys' Club; *Clubs* Nat Lib, Ryedale House; *Style*— Mrs Elizabeth Shields; Firby Hall, Kirkham Abbey, Westow, York TO6 7LH (☎ 0653 81 474)

SHIELDS, Frank Cox; s of Joseph F Shields (d 1973), of Dublin, and Alice, *née* Cox (d 1972); *b* 10 Sept 1944; *Educ* Harvard Coll (AB), Wharton Sch of Fin and Commerce (MBA); *m* 9 Oct 1971, Elizabeth Jean, da of John Blythe Kinross, CBE, of London; 2 s (Oliver b 1975, Alexander b 1980), 1 da (Henrietta b 1973); *Career* res staff LSE 1969-71; stockbroker: Cazenove & Co 1971-73, Grieveson Grant & Co 1973-78; exec dir: Euro Banking Co Ltd 1978-85, EBC AMRO Bank Ltd 1985-86; sr rep Maruman Securities Co Ltd London 1987, dir and gen mangr Maruman Securities (Europe) Ltd 1987-; *Recreations* architecture, reading, travel; *Clubs* Buck's; *Style*— Frank Shields, Esq; 24 Church Ros, Hampstead, London NW3 6UP (☎ 01 435 1175); Maruman Securities (Europe) Ltd, 1 Liverpool St, London EC2M 7NH (☎ 01 374 4000, fax 01 382 9143, telex 929347 MSEL G)

SHIELDS, Sir Neil Stanley; MC (1946); s of Archie Shields (d 1958), and Hannah Shields (d 1976); *b* 7 Sept 1919; *m* 1970, (Gloria) Dawn, *née* Wilson; *Career* Maj NW Europe 1940 and 1944-46; dir Continental and Sheerwood plc 1969-83; chm: Holcombe Hldgs plc 1978-83, Standard Catalogue Co Ltd 1976-83, Anglo Continental Investment & Finance Co Ltd 1965-74, Trianco Redfyre Ltd 1979-83, London Regnl Tport Property Bd 1986-, md Chesham Amalagamations & Investmts Ltd 1968-78 (dir 1964-83), London Area Nat Union of Conservative and Unionist Assocs 1961-63; chm: Cmmn for the New Towns 1982-, memb LRT Bd 1986 (chm 1988-); memb cncl of Aims of Indust 1975-; govr Bedford Coll 1983-85; kt 1964; *Recreations* reading, music, wining and dining; *Clubs* Carlton, HAC; *Style*— Sir Neil Shields, MC; 12 London House, Avenue Rd, London NW8 (☎ 01 586 4155); office: Glen House, Stag Place, London SW1 (☎ 01 828 7722)

SHIELDS, Prof Robert; s of Robert Alexander Shields (d 1947), of Paisley, Scotland, and Isobel MacDougall, *née* Ried (d 1982); *b* 8 Nov 1930; *Educ* John Neilson Inst Paisley, Univ of Glasgow (MB ChB); *m* 19 Jan 1957, (Grace) Marianne, da of George Swinburn (d 1953), of London; 1 s (Andrew Duncan Robert b 1966), 2 da (Gillian Elizabeth b 1959, Jennifer Anne b 1962); *Career* RAMC: Nat Serv 1954-56, Lieut 1954, Capt 1955, Maj (TA) 1956-61; Regtl MO: 1 Bn Argyll and Sutherland Highlanders 1954-56, 7 Bn Argyll and Sutherland Highlanders (TA) 1965-61; Western Infirmary Glasgow: house offr 1953-54, sr house offr 1956-57, registrar in surgery 1958-59; Glasgow Univ: Hall tutorial fell 1957-58, lectr in surgery 1959-62; res asst Dept of Surgical Res Mayo Clinic USA 1959-60, sr lectr then reader in surgery Welsh Nat Sch of Med 1962-69, prof of surgery Univ of Liverpool 1969-, hon conslt surgn Royal Liverpool Hosp and Broadgreen Hosp 1969-, dean faculty of med Univ of Liverpool 1982-85; memb Liverpool Health Authy 1974-78, chm Mill Educn Ctee Univ of Liverpool 1987-, vice chm Mersey RHA 1983-85 (memb res ctee 1976-), pres Liverpool Med Inst 1988 regnl advsr RCS 1986-; memb: Gen Med Cncl 1984-, MRC 1987, cncl RCS Ed, Assoc of Surgns of GB and Ireland (pres 1986-87), Surgical Res Soc (pres 1983-85), cncl Br Soc of Gastroenterology; FRCS, FRCSEd; *Books* Surgical Emergencies II (1979), Surgical Management (1983); *Recreations* sailing, horse riding, reading; *Clubs* Army and Navy, Racquets (Liverpool); *Style*— Prof Robert Shields; Strathmore, 81 Meols Drive, West Kirby, Wirral L48 5DF (☎ 051 632 3588); Dept of Surgery, Univ of Liverpool, P O Box 147, Liverpool L69 3BX (☎ 051 708 7139, fax 051 708 6502, telex 67095 UNILPL)

SHIELDS, Tom; s of Charles Shields (d 1982), of 36 Brockburn Rd, Glasgow, and Annie Shields (d 1988); *b* 8 Feb 1948; *Educ* St Bernard's Comprehensive Sch, Bellarmine Comprehensive Sch, Strathclyde Univ; *m* 21 June 1969, Mhairi Couper, da of Robert Graham; 1 s (Graham b 19 July 1971), 1 da (Anna b 1 Nov 1969); *Career* journalist; Sunday Post 1969-73, diary ed Glasgow Herald 1986- (reporter 1978-86, joined 1983), publisher and chm Culture City Magazine; *Books* Celtic/Rangers Joke Book (1976); *Recreations* culture, viniculture; *Clubs* Hamilton Accies Supporters; *Style*— Tom Shields, Esq; Torrance House, East Kilbride, Glasgow (☎ 03552 369 11); 195 Albion St, Glasgow (☎ 041 552 6255, fax 041 552 2288)

SHIER, Jonathan Fraser; s of Frank Eric Shier, of 25 Bede House, Manor Fields, Putney, London, and Margery Mary, *née* Dutton; *b* 18 Oct 1947; *Educ* Geelong C of E GS Australia, Monash Univ Melbourne (LLB, BEC); *Career* private sec to dep senate ldr and attorney gen of Australia 1973-76, mktg-controller and dir of sales and mktg Scottish TV 1977-85, dir of sales and mktg Thames TV plc 1985-; dir London Telethon Tst; MInstM; *Recreations* travel, theatre, music, skiing, beachcombing; *Clubs* East India, Annabels, IOD; *Style*— Jonathan Shier, Esq; 14 Bowerdean St, Fulham, London SW6; Thames Television plc, 149 Tottenham Court Rd, London W1P 9LL, (☎ 01 387 9494, fax 01 3835534)

SHIFFNER, George Frederick; s of late Capt Edward Shiffner (gs of 4 Bt); hp of kinsman, Sir Henry Shiffner, 8 Bt; *b* 3 August 1936; *Educ* Wellington; *m* 1961, Dorothea Helena Cynthia, da of late T H McLean; 1 s, 1 da; *Career* photographer, ABIPP; *Style*— George Shiffner, Esq; 14 Coggeshall Rd, Braintree, Essex (☎ 0376 22524); Searles, Alderford Street, Sible Hedingham, Essex (☎ 0787 60486)

SHIFFNER, Sir Henry David; 8 Bt (UK 1818) of Coombe, Sussex; s of Maj Sir Henry Burrows Shiffner, 7 Bt, OBE (d 1941); *b* 2 Feb 1930; *Educ* Rugby, Trinity Hall Cambridge; *m* 1, 1951 (m dis 1956), Dorothy, da of W G Jackson; 1 da; m 2, 1957 (m dis 1970), Beryl, da of George Milburn; 1 da; m 3, 1971, Joaquina Rames Lopez of Madrid; *Heir* kinsman, George Shiffner; *Career* company dir; *Style*— Sir Henry Shiffner, Bt

SHILLAKER, (George) Graham; s of George Edward Shillaker, and Kathleen Eva, *née* Pridgton; *b* 12 July 1939; *Educ* St Paul's; *m* 4 April 1973, Mary Jennifer, da of Tom Thomas (d 1964), of 22 Trafalgar Rd, Strawberry Hill, Middx; *Career* shipping accountant Matheson & Co Ltd 1961-64; dir: Howe Robinson & Co Ltd 1978 (shipbroker 1964-), Matheson (Chartering) Ltd 1979, Howe Robinson (Hldgs) Ltd 1984; md Howe Robinson Investmts Ltd 1988; memb Baltic Exchange 1964-; FCIS 1975; *Recreations* cricket, golf; *Clubs* MCC, Royal Mid-Surrey Golf; *Style*— Graham Shillaker, Esq; 130-138 Minories, London EC3N 1NS (☎ 01 488 3444, fax 01 488 4679, car 0860 306095, telex 8811461)

SHILLING, David; s of Ronald Shilling, and Gertrude Shilling; *b* 27 June 1953; *Educ* Colet Ct, St Paul's London; *Career* designer; important shows incl: Ulster Museum Exhibition 'D5 The Hats' exhibited at Worthing, Plymouth, Salisbury, Durham, Leeds and Exeter museums 1981-; other exhibitions incl: Angela Flowers London, Tino Ghelfi Vicenza Italy, Rendezvous Gallery Aberdeen, Phillip Francis Sheffield; in other museum collections: V & A London, Metropolitan NY, Los Angeles County, Mappin Gallery Sheffield; designs include: menswear, womens wear, lingerie, furs, jewellry, fine china and limited edition pieces and ceramic tiles, wallpapers, upholstery fabrics and designs for film and theatre; *Books* Thinking Rich (1986); *Recreations* listening and/or looking, swimming, jet-skiing, driving, antique collecting; *Style*— David Shilling, Esq; 44 Chiltern St, London W1 (☎ 01-935 8473)

SHILLINGFORD, James Hugh; *b* 18 August 1953; *Educ* Westminster, Christ Church Oxford (MA), London Business Sch (MSc); *Career* Coopers & Lybrand 1975-79, md M & G Investmt Mgmnt Ltd 1987-, dir M & G Gp plc 1988-; ACA; *Style*— James Shillingford, Esq; Three Quays, Tower Hill, London EC3 (☎ 01 229 0443)

SHILLINGTON, Sir (Robert Edward) Graham; CBE (1970, OBE 1959, MBE 1951), DL (Co Down 1975); s of Maj D Graham Shillington, DL, MP (d 1944); *b* 2 April 1911; *Educ* Sedbergh, Clare Coll Cambridge; *m* 1935, Mary E R Bulloch (d 1977); 2 s, 1 da; *Career* dep chief constable RUC (chief constable 1970-73); kt 1972; *Recreations* golf, gardening; *Clubs* Royal overseas, Royal Co Down Golf; *Style*— Sir Graham Shillington, CBE, DL; Ardeevin, 184 Bangor Road, Holywood, Co Down, NI

SHILLITOE, Peter Christie Mauldon; LVO (1974), MBE (1984); s of Cyril Arthur Shillitoe (d 1931), and Margaret Anna Mauldon (d 1974); *b* 21 Oct 1917; *Educ* Dickson's Sch, BEC (Abbey) Sch; *m* 19 Jan 1945, Frederica Lilian, da of David Templeton (d 1942), of Oxford; *Career* trainee Imperial Airways Ltd 1937-40, various appts BOAC in M East, Africa, India 1940-46; BEA: operations mangr 1946-62, gen mangr (Operations) and dep to Dir of Flight Operations 1962-66; dir: Cyprus Airways Ltd 1967-76, Gibralter Airways Ltd 1972-76; freelance aviation conslt 1976-; chm Chawton Parish Cncl; Freeman Sudbury Suffolk 1955 (Freedom by Patrimony - Family Freemen for over 200 years); FCIT 1970; *Recreations* squash, gardening; *Clubs* Royal Aero, Royal Ascot Squash; *Style*— Peter Shillitoe, Esq, LVO, MBE; White Gates, Chawton, Alton, Hants (☎ 0420 82142); 227 Dedworth Road, Windsor (☎ 0753 855860)

SHINDLER, Alfred Burnett; s of Louis Shindler (d 1957), of London, and Celia, *née* Garfinkle (d 1940); *b* 31 August 1912; *Educ* Highbury Co Sch London, Law Soc Coll of Law; *m* 25 June 1939, Phyllis Netta, da of Louis Myers (d 1930), of London; 3 da (Hilary Louise, Karolyn Celia, Barbara Elise); *Career* WWII RAF; slr 1935; hon slr: The United Wards Club, Metro Parks and Gardens Assoc, The Hon Ir Soc, The Royal Soc of St George; chm London Ct of Int Arbitration Inc; master Billingsgate Ward Club 1955, memb Ct of Common Cncl (London) 1966, dep for the Ward of Billingsgate 1982, life govr Imp Conclr Res; memb: Hon Irish Soc (dep govr 1979), City Lands and Bridge House Estates, Establishment (chm 1984-87), Coal Corn and Rates Fin, Central Markets (chm 1974-78), Working Party concerned with the future of Central Markets; chm Gresham Ctee, memb Ctee of Mgmnt W Ham Park (chm 1972), former chm of the Med Servs Ctee of the FPC for City and E London Arca Health Authy 1974-86; memb Hampstead Health Ctee; Freeman of the City of London 1947; memb Worshipful Co of: Slrs 1948-, Gardeners 1973-, Arbitrators 1976- (Master 1987-88); Order of the Ghurkas (Nepal 1979); *Recreations* gardening (past chm Orchid Soc of GB), skiing; *Clubs* Guildhall, City Livery (currently vice pres), RAC, Billingsgate Ward, United Wards (life govr), Royal Soc of St George (vice pres, City of London branch); *Style*— Alfred Schindler, Esq; 10 North End Road, London NW11 7PW; 37-39 Eastcheap, London EC3M 1AY (☎ 01 455 9925, 01 283 6376, fax 01 458 8523, telex 924404 SHNDLR G)

SHINDLER, Dr Colin; s of Israel Shindler, of Prestwich, Manchester, and Florence, *née* Weidberg; *b* 28 June 1949; *Educ* Bury GS Lancs, Gonville and Caius Coll Cambridge (BA, MA, PhD); *m* 23 Sept 1972, (Nancy) Lynn, da of Prof Robert Stephen White, of Riverside, Californa, USA; 1 s (David b 1977), 1 da (Amy b 1975); *Career* res fell American Film Inst Beverley Hills 1972; film and TV writer/prodr; prodr: Love Story, series BBC TV 1981-, East Lynne, BBC TV 1982-, The Worst Witch, Central TV (winner American Cable Emmy) 1985-, A Little Princess, LWT (BAFTA winner) 1986-; Screenplay author; Buster feature film 1988; publications: Hollywood Goes to War: Cinema and Society 1939-52, Routledge and Kegan Paul, 1979, Buster, Sphere Books 1988; memb: BAFTA; *Books* Hollywood Goes to War (1979), Buster (1988); *Recreations* cricket, soccer, badminton, theatre, music, walking in the Lake District; *Style*— Dr Colin Shindler; c/o Duncan Heath Associates Ltd, 162 Wardour St, London W1 (☎ 01 439 1471)

SHINDLER, His Hon Judge; George John; QC (1970); s of Bruno Schindler; Dr Phil (d 1964); and Alma Schindler (d 1958); *b* 21 Oct 1922; *Educ* Regents Park Sch, Univ Coll Sch Hampstead; *m* 16 Oct 1955, Eve, da of Ott Muller (d 1961); 3 s (David b 1958, Daniel b 1961, William b 1969); *Career* served RTR NW Europe 1942-47; called to Bar Inner Temple 1952, QC 1970, Master of Bench, Inner Temple 1976, circuit judge 1980; Mental Health Review Tbnls 1983-87; sr resident judge Inner London Crown Ct 1987-; *Recreations* theatre, music, watching cricket, reading, travel, swimming; *Clubs* MCC; *Style*— His Hon Judge George Shindler, QC; Inner London Sessions House, Newington Causeway SE1 (☎ 01 407 7111)

SHINER, Brendan Elias John; s of G L O Shiner (d 1969), and N K Shiner (d 1942); *b* 23 June 1928; *Educ* Stonyhurst, Pembroke Coll Oxford (MA); *m* 27 May 1954, Mary Gwyneth, da of J C T Thornton (d 1960); 3 s (Brendan Niall b 18 April 1959, Charles Graham b 7 Jan 1963, Timothy John b 30 Dec 1968), 1 da (Ceridwen Mary (Mrs Scott) b 24 Sept 1960); *Career* 2 Lt RTR 1948-49; called to the Bar Middle Temple 1955; ldr Cons gp Stroud DC 1983-88, vice chm planning ctee Lambeth Borough Cncl 1968-70 (vice chm highways ctee 1970-71); *Recreations* farming, racing; *Style*— Brendan Shiner, Esq; The Culver House, Culver Hill, Amberley, Glos GL5 5BA (☎ 045 387 3337); All Saints Chambers, Bristol (☎ 0272 211 966, fax 0272 276 493)

SHINGLES, Maj Raymond Edward Laws; MBE (1945); s of Charles Edward Shingles (d 1948), and Lillie Waldock (d 1957); *b* 11 Mar 1913; *Educ* Cranleigh Sch; *m* 1952, Phyllis Willan, da of Lt Col Charles Edward Jefferis, of Cookham House Hotel (d 1963); 2 s (Justin, Rupert); *Career* Lt Col 9 JAT Regt Indian Army, served in forces 1939-46, passed Staff Coll Quetta, served in India; slr Supreme Ct, ptnr Linklaters & Paines 1950-74; dir: Air Products Ltd 1957-80, Brown Shipley Hldgs plc 1969-74, Brown Shipley & Co Ltd 1969-74, Bowthorpe Hldgs Ltd 1970-76, Hongkong & Shanghai Banking Corpn (Jersey) Ltd 1975-84, Albany Dollar Fund Ltd 1978-, Brown Shipley (Jersey) Ltd 1977-87, Brown Shipley (Guernsey) Ltd 1977-87, Brown Shipley Sterling Bond Fund Ltd 1978-, Brown Shipley Int Currency Fund Ltd 1982-, Brown Shipley Int Bond Fund Ltd 1983-, Brown Shipley Sterling Capital Fund Ltd 1979-, Robert Fleming (Jersey) Ltd, Robert Fleming Investmt Mgmnt (Jersey) Ltd 1985-, Credit Int Bancshares Ltd; *Recreations* horse racing, golf; *Clubs* Victoria, Channel Islands Race and Hunt, La Moye Golf; *Style*— Raymond Shingles, Esq, MBE; Domaine de Maitland, Mont-au-Prêtre, Jersey (☎ 0534 37435)

SHINGLETON, Andrew Philip; s of Wilfrid James Shingleton (d 1984), of Suffolk, and Grace Bernadina Shingleton, *née* Pole; m direct descendent of Cardinal Reginald Pole, Archbp of Canterbury under Tudors; *b* 28 June 1943; *Educ* Douai Sch; *m* 1, 1967, Vanessa Jane (d 1977), da of Capt John Liley, of Marbella; 3 s (Toby John-James b 1972, Alexander William (b 1975), Barnaby Andrew (twin) b 1975); m 2, 1982, Wendy Elizabeth, da of Alec Barnes, of S Lancing; *Career* advertising dir McCann Erickson 1987; MIPA 1972; memb CAM 1973; *Recreations* walking the Cornish cliffs, golf, 18 century French history; *Style*— Andrew P Shingleton, Esq; Bossiney, Orchehill Avenue, Gerrards Cross SL9 8QH (☎ 0753 887985); McCann Erickson Advertising, 36 Howland Street, London W1A 1AT (☎ 01 580 6690)

SHIPLEY, (Norman) Graham (de Mattos); s of Capt Norman Douglas Holbrook Shipley (d 1979), of Bromborough, Wirral, Merseyside, and Lesley Cynthia, *née* Stott; *b* 10 Jan 1948; *Educ* Kings Sch Chester, Trinity Coll Cambridge (BA, Dip Computer Sci, MA) Inns of Ct Sch of Law; *m* 11 Sept 1982, Helen Rhian, da of David Christopher De Mattos, of Witchampton, Wimborne, Dorset; 2 da (Jemima, Kate); *Career* called to the Bar Lincoln's Inn 1973; currently specialising in: patent, copyright, trade mark law, confidential information, computer law; memb Senate of Inns of Ct and the Bar 1973-; *Recreations* electronics, motor cycling, DIY, charity, children; *Clubs* Wig & Pen; *Style*— Graham Shipley, Esq; Crumble Cottage, Stanbrook, Thaxed, Dunmow, Essex CM6 2NG (☎ 0371 830531); 3 Pump Ct, Temple, London EC4Y 7AJ (☎ 01 583 5110, fax 01 583 1130)

SHIPMAN, John Jeffrey; s of late H Shipman, and late R Horwich; *b* 20 Sept 1917; *Educ* UC and Hosp (MB BS); *m* 18 April 1942, Elizabeth Mary, da of late W R Corlett, of Cumberland; 1 s (Dr John Anthony b 1952); *Career* served 2 Army 5 Bn DLI (RMO, Capt RAMC) 1942-46, Normandy, Caen, Seine, Somme, Ardennes, Norway; asst lectr Post-Grad Sch 1947-51, sr registrar St Mark's Hosp and Southend Gen Hosp 1951-52, surgeon Lister Hosp 1952-83; memb Cntl Conslts and Specialist Ctee, chm Hitchin Hosp, chm Medical Staffing (HCSA); *Books* Operative Surgical Revision (4 edn, 1987), Mnemonics & Tactics in Surgery & Medicine (2 edn, 1987); MRCS (FRCS 1947), LRCP 1941, Queen's Silver Jubilee Medal 1977; *Recreations* golf, game fishing, gardening; *Style*— John J Shipman, Esq; Conoleigh, 505 Broadway, Letchworth, Herts (☎ 0462 683248)

SHIPSTER, Col John Neville; CBE (1973), DSO (1944); s of Col G C Shipster, MC (d 1941); *b* 31 Jan 1922; *Educ* Marlborough; *m* 1948, Cornelia Margarethe, nee Arends; 2 s, 1 da; *Career* WWII served 2 Punjab Regt Indian Army, CO 1 Bn Middlesex Regt 1965-67, Cdr Br Forces Belize 1970-73, Cmdt Def NBC Sch 1974; Dep Col Queen's Regt 1975; *Recreations* golf, sailing; *Clubs* Army and Navy; *Style*— Col John Shipster, CBE, DSO; Deben House, 41 Cumberland St, Woodbridge, Suffolk (☎ 039 43 3957)

SHIPTON, (Lady) Janet Helen; *née* Attlee; da of late 1 Earl Attlee; does not use courtesy title; *b* 1923; *m* 1947, Harold William Shipton; 1 da; *Style*— Mrs Harold Shipton; 820 Woodside Drive, Iowa City, Iowa, USA

SHIPWAY, Frank; s of Alfred Edwin Shipway (d 1986), and Edith Doris Owen; *b* 9 July 1935; *Educ* RCM; *m* 17 July 1986, Imogen Vanessa (distinguished int oboeist), da of David Alan Triner; 1 da (Eugene); *Career* symphonic opera conductor; studied with:

Igor Markevitch, Sir John Barbirolii, Herbert von Karajan; worked with: Eng Nat Opera, Glyndebourne Fest Opera, Deutche Opera Berlin (at personal invitation of Lorin Maazel; conducted orchestras in: Germany, Italy, France, Belgium, Denmark, Sweden, Norway, Iceland, Finland; in GB has given concerts for: BBC, Royal Philharmonic, London Philharmonic, Philharmonica, Royal Liverpool Philharmonic, City of Birmingham Symphony Orchestra; conducts works of: Strauss, Mahler, Rachmaninar, Wagner, Verdi; also worked in field of 20 century music; gave first Euro performance of Polish composer Andrzej Panufriks 8 Symphony, was first conductor Boulez' Livre pour Cordes; received Gold Disc for recordings with Royal Philharmonic Orchestra; *Recreations* antiques, gardening, riding, painting, vintage cars; *Style*— Frank Shipway, Esq; Corner Cottage, Friars, Stile Place, Richmond Hill, Richmond, Surrey TW10 6NL

SHIPWRIGHT, Adrian John; s of Jack Shipwright, and Jennie, *née* Eastman; *b* 2 July 1950; *Educ* King Edward VI Sch Southampton, Ch Ch Oxford (BA, BCL, MA); *m* 17 Aug 1974, Diana Evelyn, da of Percival Denys Treseder (d 1971); 1 s (Henry b 1983) 1 da (Fiona b 1985); *Career* asst slr Linklaters & Paines 1977, lectr and tutor in law Oxford Univ 1977-82, ptnr Denton Hall Burgin & Warrens 1984-87 (asst slr 1982-84), hon lectr in laws Kings Coll London 1986-, ptnr S J Berwin & Co 1987-; govr King Edward VI Sch Southampton, memb Law Soc; *Books* CCH British Tax Reporter Vol 5 (1986) Tax Planning and UK Land Development (1988); *Recreations* music; *Style*— Adrian Shipwright, Esq; 55 Homesdale Rd, Teddington, Middx TW11 9LJ; c/o S J Berwin & Co, 236 Grays Inn Rd, London WC1X 8HB (☎ 01 278 0444, fax 01 833 2860, telex 8814928 WINLAW G)

SHIRLEY, Agnes; *née* Kerr; da of William Shaw Kerr, of Ayrshire, Scotland, and Helen, *née* Collins; *b* 28 Sept 1934; *Educ* St Joseph's HS Kilmarnock, Int Graphoanalysis Soc Chicago (MGA); *m* 22 April 1957, Robert Gerald, s of Robert Shirley, of Normoss, Blackpool; 1 s (Martin b 1963), 2 da (Helen b 1958, Mairi b 1959); *Career* handwriting analyst and cnsllr; co-fndr and dir Ross Shirley & Assocs 1972-76 (md Ross Int SA Brussels 1976-80), dir PACE Assessments Ltd 1982- (researcher how to assess business women from significant traits in their handwriting); Cert Cnslling (RCA Lond); memb Exec Res Assoc; FIOD; *Books* Characteristics of High Achieving Business Women (1976, 1988), feature in Personnel Today (1988); *Recreations* swimming, golf, reading; *Clubs* RAC, Network; *Style*— Mrs Agnes Shirley; 10 Groom Place, Belgravia, London SW1X 7BA; PACE Assessments Ltd, 46/47 Pall Mall, London, SW1Y 5GG (☎ 01 839 1512)

SHIRLEY, Hon Andrew John Carr Sewallis; yr s of 13 Earl Ferrers, PC, DL, *qv*; *b* 24 June 1965; *Educ* Ampleforth, RAC Cirencester; *Style*— The Hon Andrew Shirley; c/o Ditchingham Hall, Bungay, Suffolk NR35 2LE

SHIRLEY, Gerald Ferrers; MBE (Mil); s of John Lawrence Shirley (d 1932), and Ellen Mary, *née* Jefferies (d 1969); *b* 3 April 1911; *Educ* Dauntsey's Sch; *m* 14 July 1945, Evelyn Bridget, da of Murray Newton Phelps (d 1952); 1 s (Martin b 1946); *Career* CO RN Mine and Bomb disposal Unit in Med and Black Sea 1941-46; dir: Br Oil and Cake Mills Ltd 1960-70, Utd Agric Merchants 1965-70; pres Nat Seed Crushers of Scotland 1970; *Recreations* cricket, rugby, tennis; *Style*— Gerald Shirley, Esq, MBE; Knowle House, Knowle Street, Giles, Chard, Somerset

SHIRLEY, Maj John Evelyn; s of Lt Col Evelyn Charles Shirley (d 1956), and Kathleen Mary, *née* Cardew (d 1977); *b* 11 Nov 1922; *Educ* Eton; *m* 17 Jan 1952, Judith Margaret, da of Sir William Francis Stratford Dugdale, 1 Bt, of Merevale Hall, Atherstone, Warwicks; 2 s (Philip Evelyn b 1955, Hugh Sewallis b 1961), 1 da (Emily Margaret b 1957); *Career* Army, served 60 Rifles 1941-55; landowner;; *Recreations* field sports; *Clubs* Kildare Street (Dublin), Army and Navy; *Style*— Maj John Shirley; Ormly Hall, Ramsey, Isle of Man; Ettington Park, Stratford on Avon, Warwickshire; Lough Lea, Carrickmacross, Co Monaghan

SHIRLEY, Capt Malcolm Christopher; s of Lt Cdr Leonard Noel Shirley, RN (1988), of Burford, Oxon, and Edith Florence, *née* Bullen; *b* 10 April 1945; *Educ* Churchers Coll Petersfield, RN Engrg Coll (BSc); *m* 18 April 1970, Lucilla Rose Geary, da of Cdr Thomas Geary Dyer, RN, of Axminster, Devon; 3 s (Guy b 1 March 1975, Ben b 1 March 1977, Hugo b 2 Jan 1979); *Career* Midshipman 1964, Sub Lt 1965-69, Lt 1969, dep Marine engr offr HMS Zulu 1970-73, trg offr HMS Eastbourne 1973-75, sr engr offr HM Yacht Britannia 1975-77, Lt Cdr 1976, RN Staff Coll 1977-78, Ship Design Authy MOD Bath 1978-79, marine engr off HMS Coventry 1980-81, asst naval attaché Paris (1982-84), manning and trg policy desk offr MOD Whitehall 1984-86, OC Machinery Trials Unit 1987-, Capt 1989; FIMarE, CEng; *Recreations* sailing, skiing, house restoration, wine; *Clubs* RNSA, Royal Naval and Royal Albert Yacht; *Style*— Capt Malcolm Shirley

SHIRLEY, Lady Sallyanne Margaret; da of 13 Earl Ferrers, PC, DL; *b* 1957; *Style*— Lady Sallyanne Shirley; c/o The Rt Hon The Earl Ferrers, PC, DL, Ditchingham Hall, Bungay, Suffolk

SHIRLEY, Lady; Vera Kathleen; *née* Overton; da of George Overton, of The Grange, Navenby, Lincs; *b* 27 Jan 1911; *Educ* Lincoln HS; *m* 1935, Air Vice-Marshal Sir Thomas Shirley, KBE, CB (d 1982), sometime Air Offr C-in-C Signals Cmd; 1 s (Simon), 1 da (Susan); *Clubs* RAF; *Style*— Lady Shirley; 3 Raglan House, Kilfillan Gdns, Graemesdyke Rd, Berkhamsted, Herts (☎ 044 27 73262)

SHIRLEY, Vera Stephanie (Steve); OBE (1980); da of Arnold Buchthal (d 1970), and Margaret, *née* Schick (d 1987); arrived in UK with two suitcases as child refugee in 1939; f moved from being friendly enemy alien (one of the Dunera boys) prior to UK Army, to US Army (serving at Nuremberg trials) later German equivalent of High Ct Judge, changed name on naturalisation to Brook to honour Rupert Brooke; *b* 16 Sept 1933; *Educ* motley schooling, Sir John Cass Coll London (BSc); *m* 14 Nov 1959, Derek George Millington Shirley, s of George Millington Shirley (d 1970); 1 s (Giles Millington); *Career* PO Res Station Dollis Hill 1951-59; CDL 1959-62; fin dir F Int Gp plc 1962; vice pres Br Computer Soc 1979-82; memb: Computer, Systems and Electronics Requirements Bd 1979-81, Electronics and Avionics Requirements Bd 1981-83; cncl memb Industl Soc 1984-; memb Nat Cncl for Vocational Qualifications 1986-, ct company of Info Technologists 1986-, tstee Help The Aged 1987-, pres British Computer Soc 1989; Freeman City of London 1987, memb ct of assts Co of Information Technologists; FBCS 1971, CBIM 1984; *Publications* articles in prof journals, reviews; *Recreations* sleep; *Clubs* Reform; *Style*— Mrs Steve Shirley; F International Group plc, The Bury, Church Street, Chesham, Buckinghamshire HP5 1HW (☎ 0494 791234, telex 0494 791381)

SHIRLEY-BEAVAN, Mary Sevasty; *née* Hamilton; da of Capt George Hamilton, RD, RNR, and Lilian Ellen, *née* Jackson; *b* 19 Oct 1917; *Educ* Chelsea Poly, Hammersmith Sch of Art; *m* 17 June (m dis 1972), Michael Shirley-Beavan, s of Lt-Col FW Shirley-Beavan, DSO, DL; 4 s (David b 1951, Mark b 1952, Simon b 1954, Jack b 1956), 2 da (Boo b 1959, Buff b 1963); *Career* WWII CPO WRNS 1940-45; equine and wild life artist in oils and watercolours, painting under maiden name of Mary Hamilton; JP 1960-86; *Recreations* hunting, racing; *Style*— Mrs Mary Shirley-Beavan; The Piggery, Stockham, Dulverton, Somerset

SHIVAS, Mark; s of James Dallas Shivas (d 1986), of Banstead, Surrey, and Winifred Alice, *née* Lighton (d 1978); *b* 24 April 1938; *Educ* Whitgift Sch, Merton Coll Oxford (MA); *Career* asst ed Movie Magazine 1961-64, dir/prodr/presenter Granada TV 1964-68; drama prodr BBC TV 1969-79 prodns incl: The Six Wives of Henry VIII, Casanova, To Encourage the Others, The Evacuees, 84 Charing Cross Road, Abide with Me, The Glittering Prizes, Rogue Male, She Fell Among Thieves, Professional Foul, On Giants Shoulders, Telford's Change; dir Southern Pictures 1979-81, (exec prodr: Winston Churchill the Wilderness Years, Bad Blood); prodr Channel 4: The Price 1985, What if it's Raining? 1986, The Storyteller 1987; film prodr: Moonlighting 1982, A Private Function 1985, The Witches 1989; head of drama BBC TV 1988-; BAFTA 1970-88, BFTPA 1984-88; *Recreations* swimming, gardening, windsurfing; *Clubs* Groucho's; *Style*— Mark Shivas, Esq; BBC TV, Wood Lane, London W12 (☎ 01 743 8000)

SHIVELY, William Jerome; s of Robert Shively; *b* 3 Jan 1929; *Educ* Hamilton HS Hamilton New York, Deerfield Acad Mass, Colgate Univ Hamilton New York, Harvard Business Sch; *m* 1953, Eleanor, da of Dr William Jackson; 4 children; *Career* served USAF 2 Lt; advertising and marketing executive; chm and md McCann & Co London 1981-; regnl dir McCann-Erickson Int 1980-; formerly exec vice-pres Johnson Wax; exec vice-pres McCann-Erickson 1980-; *Recreations* scuba diving, skiing, flying, shooting, fishing; *Clubs* American, Philippics, Hindhead Golf; *Style*— William Shively, Esq; 1 The Vale, SW3 (☎ 01 351 4850); Avalon, Old Barn Lane, Churt, Surrey (☎ Hindhead 4686)

SHOAT, Michael Edward; s of Thomas Edward Short, of Blackheath, and Anne Elizabeth, *née* Roffe; *b* 16 Sept 1941; *Educ* Greenwich Boys Tech Coll; *m* 12 May 1962, Maureen, da of Christoher Thorington (d 1984); 1 s (Ian Michael Edward b 1973), 1 da (Joanne Maureen (twin) b 1973); *Career* gp md Pearce Gp Holdings Ltd, dep chm Pearce Maintenance Ltd; chm: Pearce Southern Ltd, Pearce Northern Ltd, Pearce Gowshall Ltd, Davand Palstics Ltd; FIOD 1974; *Recreations* golf, badminton, music; *Clubs* RAC, Pall Mall; *Style*— Michael Shoat, Esq; Rowans, High Halstow, Kent ME3 8SF; Pearce Group Holdings, Insignia House, New Cross, London SE14 6AB (☎ 01 692 6611, fax 01 692 1753, car 0860 517513, telex 965683 PESIGN G)

SHODA, Toshio; s of Atsushi Shoda, of Japan and Ayako, *née* Saito; *b* 12 Mar 1938; *Educ* Meiji Univ Tokyo Japan (BEcon); *m* 11 Nov 1964, Keiko da of Takeshi Abe, of Japan; 1 s (Ken-Ichi b 1966), 1 da (Kanako b 1972); *Career* Nikko Securities Co Ltd: chief rep Singapore Off 1979-84, jt gen mangr Int Fin div 984-85, jt gen mangr Int Underwriting Div 1985- 87, md corporate fin (Europe) Ltd 1987-; *Recreations* music, skiing; *Clubs* Tanglin; *Style*— Toshio Shoda, Esq; 55 Victoria Street, London SW1H OEU (☎ 01 799 2222, fax 01 222 3642, telex 884717)

SHOLL, Hon Sir Reginald Richard; QC; s of Reginald Frank Sholl (d 1948), and Alice Maud, *née* Mumby (d 1928); *b* 8 Oct 1902; *Educ* Melbourne GS, Trinity Coll Melbourne Univ (MA), New Coll Oxford Univ (MA, BCL); *m* 1, 1927, Hazel Ethel (d 1962), da of Alfred Leonard Bradshaw (d 1910); 2 s, 2 da; m 2, 1964, Anna Campbell, da of Campbell Colin Carpenter (d 1936), wid of Alister Bruce McLean; *Career* official law fell Brasenose Coll Oxford 1927, barr and slr Victoria 1928, lectr in law Melbourne Univ 1928-38, barr Melbourne 1929-49, KC Victoria and Tasmania 1947, NSW 1948, judge Supreme Ct of Victoria 1950-66; Aust consul-gen in NY 1966-69, chm WA Parly Salaries Tbnl 1971-77, chm Royal Cmmn WA Enquiry into Airline System 1974-75; fell Trinity Coll Melbourne Univ 1981; kt 1962; *see Debrett's Handbook of Australia and New Zealand for further details*; *Style*— The Hon Sir Reginald Sholl, QC; Apt 6, Chelsea, 7 Britannia Ave, Broadbeach, Qld 4218, Australia

SHONE, Sir Robert Minshull; CBE (1949); s of Robert Harold Shone of Liverpool; *b* 1906; *Educ* Sedbergh, Liverpool Univ, Chicago Univ; *Career* Cwlth fell USA 1932-34, lectr LSE 1935-36, Br Iron and Steel Fedn 1936-39 and 1945-53 (dir 1950-53); dir Iron and Steel Control 1940-45, jt chm UK and European Coal and Steel Community Steel Ctee 1954-62, exec memb Iron and Steel Bd 1953-62, dir-gen of staff and memb NEDC 1962-66; dir: M & G Group Ltd 1966-84, Rank Organisation 1969-78, APV Holdings Ltd 1970-76; visiting prof City Univ London 1967-84, special prof Nottingham Univ 1972-74; kt 1955; *Style*— Sir Robert Shone, CBE; 7 Windmill Hill, London NW3 (☎ 01 435 1930)

SHOOTER, Prof Reginald Arthur; CBE (1980); s of Rev Arthur Edwin Shooter, TD, and Mabel Kate, *née* Pinniger; *b* 4 April 1916; *Educ* Cambridge Univ (MA, MD); *m* 4 Dec 1946, Jean, da of Prof T W Wallace, CBE, MC, of Long Ashton Res Station; 1 s (Adrian), 3 da (Joanna, Felicity, Anthea); *Career* surgn Lt RNVR 1943-46; Rockefeller travelling fell 1950-51, prof of med microbiology Univ of London 1961-81, bacteriologist to St Bart's Hosp 1961-81, dean med coll of St Bart's Hosp 1972-81; memb: Public Health Lab Servs Bd 1970-82, City and E London Area Health Authy 1974-81, scientific advsy cncl Stress Fndn 1980-88; chm Dangerous Pathogens advsy gp 1975-81; govr: St Bart's Hosp 1972-74, Queen Mary Coll 1972-81; tstee Mitchell City of London Tst 1958-82; Pybus Medal N of Eng Surgical Soc 1979; FRCP, FRCS, FRCPath; *Recreations* fishing, gardening; *Style*— Prof Reginald Shooter, CBE; Eastlea, Back Edge Lane, Edge, Stoud, Glos GL6 6PE; Painswick (☎ 812408)

SHORE, David Teignmouth; OBE (1982); s of Geoffrey Teignmouth Shore (d 1963), of Morden, Surrey, and Cecilia Mary, *née* Proctor; *b* 15 Nov 1928; *Educ* Tiffin Boys' Sch, Imperial Coll of Sci London (BSc, MSc); *m* 15 April 1950, Pamela Rose, da of Arthur Henry Goodge (d 1964); 1 s (Timothy b 1954), 2 da (Hilary b 1956, Sarah b 1963); *Career* APC Co Ltd: process design engr 1950-52, chief process engr 1954-64, res dir 1964-77 (md 1977-82); heat transfer engr Foster Wheeler Ltd 1953-54, dir food div APV Hldgs plc 1982-84, tech dir APV plc 1984-88; chm: Food Res Assoc 1983-87, Engrg Bd Serv 1985-89; memb ct and cncl Univ of Reading; FIMechE 1967, FIChemE 1970, FIFST 1970, FCGI 1979, FEng 1979; *Recreations* walking, astronomy, wine making; *Clubs* Nat Lib; *Style*— David Shore, Esq, OBE; Hembury, Garratts Lane, Banstead, Surrey SM7 2BA (☎ 0737 353 721)

SHORE, Dr Elizabeth Catherine; *née* Wrong; CB (1978); da of Edward Murray Wrong (d 1928), and Rosalind Grace Smith (d 1983); *b* 19 August 1927; *Educ*

Newnham Coll Cambridge, St Bart's Hosp; *m* 1948, Peter David Shore, s of Robert Norman Shore (d 1942); 2 s (Piers (d 1977), Crispin), 2 da (Thomasina, Tracy); *Career* dep chief med offr DHSS, postgrad med dean NW Thames Region 1984-; *Recreations* swimming, reading; *Style*— Dr Elizabeth Shore, CB; 23 Dryburgh Rd, London SW15; British Postgraduate Medical Federation, 33 Millman St, London WC1 (☎ 01 831 6222)

SHORE, Rt Hon Peter David; PC (1967), MP (Lab) Bethnal Green and Stepney 1983-; *b* 20 May 1924; *Educ* Quarry Bank HS Liverpool, King's Coll Cambridge; *m* 1948, Dr Elizabeth Catherine, *née* Wrong, CB (dep chief med offr DHSS 1977-); 1 s, 2 da (and 1 s decd); *Career* Parly candidate (Lab): St Ives (Cornwall) 1950, Halifax 1959; MP (Lab): Stepney 1964-74, Tower Hamlets, Stepney and Poplar 1974-83; head Lab Res Dept 1959-64; PPS to Harold Wilson as PM 1965-66; jt parly sec Miny Technol 1966-67 and Dept Econ Affrs 1967, sec state Econ Affrs 1967-69, min without portfolio and dep ldr House of Commons 1969-70, oppn spokesman on Europe 1971-74, trade sec 1974-76, environment sec 1976-79; memb Shadow Cabinet and chief oppn spokesman on: Foreign Affrs 1979-80, Treasy and Econ Affairs 1981-Nov 1983, Trade and Indust and shadow ldr of The House Nov 1983-; *Recreations* swimming; *Style*— The Rt Hon Peter Shore, MP; 23 Dryburgh Rd, London SW15

SHORE, Sydney Frederick; s of Sydney George Gordon Shore (d 1951), and Beatrice Maud, *née* Turner; *b* 13 Mar 1933; *Educ* Wanstead Co HS; *m* 28 May 1955, Joyce Margaret Lucy, da of Albert Edward English (d 1983); 1 s (Graeme Edward b 1966), 1 da (Elizabeth Jane b 1963); *Career* Nat Serv RCS 1951-53; Lloyds Bank plc: branch mangrs appts City of London 1966-78, mangr Colmore Row Birmingham 1978-81, regnl dir and gen mangr West Midlands 1981-83, asst gen mangr corporate banking div 1983-87, gen mangr corporate banking 1987-; elder and chm of ctees Utd Reformed Church; FCIB; *Recreations* theatre, opera, music; *Style*— Sydney Shore, Esq; 17 Robin Hill Dr, Camberley, Surrey GU15 1EC (☎ 0276 29830); 71 Lombard EC3B 3BS (☎ 01 356 1191, fax 01 929 1669, telex 8813742,

SHORROCK, Dr Stanley; s of Arthur Shorrock (d 1977), of Blackpool, and Emily Ann, *née* Aspin; *b* 14 June 1926; *Educ* RNC Dartmouth, Leeds Univ; *m* 2 March 1954, Marjorie, JP, da of Festus Kenyon (d 1956), of Blackburn; 1 da (Alison b 1957); *Career* md: British Tufting Machinery Ltd Blackburn 1954-61, Shorrock Developments Ltd 1962-87, Shorrock Security Systems 1862-87, Shorrock plc 1983-87; dir BET; Hon DSc Lancaster Univ; *Recreations* field sports, flying; *Style*— Dr Stanley Shorrock; Higher Feniscowles Hall, Peasington, Blackburn (☎ 0254 29058); Shorrock Security Systems, Shadsworth Road, Blackburn (☎ 0254 63644)

SHORT, (Charles) Alan; s of Charles Ronald Short, of Hillingdon, Middx, and Dorothea Henrietta Winterfeldt; *b* 23 Mar 1955; *Educ* Lower Sch of John Lyon Harrow, Trinity Coll Cambridge (MA), Harvard Univ Graduate Sch of Design; *m* 12 April 1985, The Noble Romina Scicluna Patrizia Corinne Desirée, da of Alan Edward Marshall (d 1983), and the Noble Mignon Scicluna-Marshall, sister of the Baron of Tabria and the Marquis Scicluna; *Career* architect; ptnr Edward Cullinan Architects 1981-86, founded Peake Short & Ptnrs 1986; visiting lectr and critic at Edinburgh Univ, Leicester Poly, Cambridge Univ, Univ of Bath, RCA, Washington Univ USA; fndr int summer sch for architects Malta (with UNESCO); Dip Arch RIBA; *Recreations* collecting drawings, restoration of family home (Palazzo Parisio Malta); *Clubs* Groucho; *Style*— Charles Short, Esq; 212 Old Brompton Rd, London SW5 (☎ 01 370 1759); Peake Short and Ptnrs, Prescott Studios, 15 Prescott Place, London SW4 (☎ 01 720 9994)

SHORT, Clare; MP (Lab) Birmingham Ladywood 1983-; da of Frank and Joan Short; *b* 15 Feb 1946; *Educ* Keele Univ, Leeds Univ; *m* Alexander Lyon, former MP (Lab) York; *Career* dir Youthaid and the Unemployment Unit; *Style*— Ms Clare Short, MP; House of Commons, London SW1

SHORT, (Bernard) David; s of Bernard Charles Short (d 1970), and Ethel Florence, *née* Matthews; *b* 9 June 1935; *Educ* St Edmund Hall, Oxford (MA); *m* 3 Sept 1960, Susan Yvonne, da of Charles Henry Taylor; 2 s (Nicholas b 1970, Timothy b 1973), 1 da (Katherine b 1972); *Career* cmmnd 2 Lt 1954 (Lt 1955) Royal Scots 1953-56; teacher Ingliz Erkek Lisesi Istanbul 1960-65, lectr Univ of Fukjova Kyushu Japan 1963-65, asst lectr Garretts Green Tech Coll Birmingham 1966-67, sr lectr Henley Coll of Further Education Coventry 1971-73, head dept gen studies Bournville Coll Further Educn Birmingham 1973-76 (lectr 1967-71); HM inspr schs 1976- (staff inspr 1984, chief inspr further educn 1986-); *Books* A Guide to Stress in English (1967), Humour (1971); *Recreations* music, boats, gardening; *Style*— David Short, Esq; Department of Education and Science, Elizabeth House, York Rd, London

SHORT, Prof David Somerset; s of Latimer James Short (d 1976), of Weston-Super-Mare, and Mabel Annie, *née* Wood (d 1974); *b* 6 August 1918; *Educ* Bristol GS, Cambridge Univ (MA, MD, BChir), London Univ (PhD); *m* 30 Dec 1948, Joan Anne, da of Cyril Evans McLay (d 1981), of Cardiff; 1 s (Peter b 1954), 4 da (Elizabeth b 1949, Margaret b 1951, Jane b 1959, Hazel b 1961); *Career* RAMC 1944-47, Lt 1944, Capt 1945, graded specialist in medicine 1946; registrar Southmead Hosp Bristol 1947-49, sr registrar Nat Heart Hosp and London Hosp 1950-54, lectr in medicine Middx Hosp 1955-59, conslt physician Aberdeen Royal Infirmary 1960-83, physician to The Queen in Scotland 1977-83, emeritus prof in clinical medicine Univ of Aberdeen 1983; FRCP 1964, FRCPE 1966; *Books* Medicine as a Vocation (1972); *Recreations* walking, music; *Clubs* Aberdeen, Medico-Chirurgical Soc; *Style*— Prof David Short; 48 Victoria St, Aberdeen AB9 2PL (☎ 0224 645853)

SHORT, (Andrew) Gregor; s of Dr Ian Alexander Short (d 1976), of Glasgow, and Dr Margaret Alberta Elder Smith; *b* 9 Nov 1955; *Educ* Glasgow Acad, Christchurch Oxford (MA); *m* 18 Aug 1984, Jane Anne, da of Robert Geoffrey Lunn, of Marbella, Spain; *Career* Citibank NA London: corp fin exec 1977, vice pres 1982; fndr new fin co Sleipner UK Ltd 1985-; *Recreations* downhill skiing, tennis, golf; *Style*— Gregor Short, Esq; Sleipner UK Ltd, 6 Mount Row, Mayfair, London W1Y 5TA (☎ 01 409 0380, fax 01 491 7563, telex 266771 SLEIP)

SHORT, Ian Gradon; *b* 24 June 1927; *Educ* Nottingham HS, Hertford GS; *m* 1953, Sheila Ann; 1 s; *Career* underwriting memb Lloyd's 1979-, Lloyd's broker 1955-, md Cayzer Steel Bowater Holdings Ltd, chm Cayzer Steel Bowater Ltd, chm Cayzer Steel Reinsurance Brokers Ltd; *Clubs* Oriental; *Style*— Ian Short Esq; 12A Calverley Park, Tunbridge Wells, Kent (☎ 0892 30586)

SHORT, Hon Michael Christian; s of Baron Glenamara (Life Peer); *b* 1943; *Educ* Durham Sch, Durham Univ; *m* 1968, Ann, da of Joseph Gibbon, of Whickham, Tyne and Wear; *Career* slr; *Recreations* theatre; *Clubs* Reform; *Style*— The Hon Michael Short; Holly House, Whickham Park, Whickham, Newcastle upon Tyne (☎ 4887617)

SHORT, Sir Noel; MBE (1951), MC (1945); *b* 19 Jan 1916; *Educ* Radley, RMA Sandhurst; *Career* 6 Gurkha Rifles 1937-, Col 6 Queen Elizabeth's Own Gurkha Rifles 1978; Speaker's sec House of Commons 1970-82; kt 1977; *Style*— Brig Sir Noel Short, MBE, MC

SHORT, (Orville) Peter; s of Francis Augustus Short (d 1970), and Lucy Minnie Edwards (d 1968); *b* 23 Nov 1927; *Educ* Priory Sch for Boys, Shrewsbury Sch of Architecture, Univ of Liverpool; *m* 2 April 1961, Fiona Mary, da of George Francis McConnell (d 1978); 1 s (Stephen b 1962), 1 da (Rachel b 1963); *Career* Nat Serv, KOYLI Berlin, SCLI Jamaica; chartered architect; Salop Co Architects, Sir Percy Thomas & Son, IDC & Turriff Tech Servs, sr ptnr Peter Short & Ptnrs (Architectural and Planning Conslts) 1971-87, princ Peter Short architect 1987-; memb Worcester Festival Choral Soc 1968- (ctee 1985-); memb church choirs: St Giles Shrewsbury 1939-45, Abbey Shrewsbury 1955-64, St Nicholas Alcester 1964-; memb Alcester: War Memorial Restoration Ctee, Civic Soc (public footpath sub ctee for Heart of England Way, produced footpath booklets), Rotary Club 1981- (sec); ARIBA; *Recreations* tennis, badminton, walking, watching cricket, singing, water colour painting; *Clubs* Rotary Alcester, Alcester: Tennis, Unionist, Civic Soc; Worcestershire CCC; *Style*— Peter Short, Esq; 46 Birmingham Road, Alcester, Warwickshire B49 5EP (☎ 0789 762731); Peter Short, Chartered Architect, 9c High Street, Alcester, Warwickshire B49 5AE (☎ 0789 764250)

SHORT, Renee; *Educ* Manchester Univ; *m* 2 da; *Career* freelance journalist, memb Watford RDC 1952-64, cncllr Herts CC 1952-67; contested St Albans 1955 and Watford 1959; MP (Lab) Wolverhampton NE 1964-87; chm: Parly and Scientific Ctee 1982-, Parly Select Ctee Social Servs 1979-87; memb Lab NEC 1970-81 and 1983-; *Books* The Care of Long Term Prisoners (1979); *Recreations* theatre, music; *Style*— Mrs Renée Short; House of Commons, London SW1

SHORT, Rodney Neil Terry; s of Flt Lt Cyril Herbert Terry Short, AFC, of Edgarley, Allandale Rd, Burnham-on-Sea, Somerset, and Deborah Allen, *née* Hobbs; *b* 4 August 1946; *Educ* Sherborne, Coll of Law, Insead (MBA); *m* 16 April 1977, Penelope Anne, da of Capt Emile William Goodman, OBE; 1 s (Jonathan b 1980), 1 da (Anna b 1983); *Career* admitted slr 1970, asst slr Freshfields 1970-73 and 1974-77, corp fin dept Kleinwort Benson 1974-75; Clifford Chance (formerly Coward Chance) 1977-: Dubai off 1978-81, Bahrain off 1981-83, ptnr 1982-; Freeman City of London Solicitors Co 1983; memb: Law Soc 1970, IBA 1982; *Recreations* tennis, golf, shooting, skiing; *Clubs* Roehampton; *Style*— Rodney Short, Esq; 18 Langside Ave, London SW15 (☎ 01 876 1859); Clifford Chance, Royex House, Aldermanbury Sq, London EC2V 7LD (☎ 01 600 0808, fax 01 726 8561, telex 8959991)

SHORTALL, Michael Patrick; s of John Shortall (d 1967), Mary Shortall (d 1967); *b* 16 Mar 1934; *Educ* Medway Coll, RMA Sandhurst, Staff Coll Camberley; *m* 7 June 1969, Patricia Hastings, da of Cdr John Manwaring Parker, RN (d 1979); 1 d (Clare b 1979); *Career* Maj cmd Sqdn, Europe, N Ireland, Far East; ADC to COS N Army Gp DAAO QMG; logistic opr MOD, ret 1972; fine art auctioneer and valuer; dir: Phillips SE, Histohold Property Co; territorial lordship (Irish) The Lord of Ballylorcan; *Recreations* shooting, sailing, music; *Clubs* MCC; *Style*— Michael Shortall, Esq; 120 Marina, St Leonards on Sea, E Sussex (☎ 0424 434 854); Phillips, Fine Art Auctioneers, Blenstock House, 7 Blenhom St, New Bond St, London W1Y 0AD (☎ 01 629 6602)

SHORTIS, Maj-Gen Colin; CBE (1980, OBE 1977, MBE 1972); *b* 18 Jan 1934; *Educ* Bedford Sch; *m* 1955, Sylvia Mary Jenkinson; 2 s, 2 da; *Career* Cdr 8 Inf Bde 1978-80, RCDS 1981, Cdr Br Mil Advsy and Trg Team Zimbabwe 1982-83, Dir of Infantry 1983-86, GOC NW District 1986-, Col Cmdt Prince of Wales Divn 1983-, Col Devonshire and Dorset Regt 1984-; *Recreations* sailing; *Clubs* Army and Navy; *Style*— Maj-Gen Colin Shortis, CBE; c/o Bank of Scotland, 57/60 Haymarket, London SW1Y 4QY

SHOULER, Hon Mrs (Margaret Fiona); *née* Eden; er da of 9 Baron Auckland and Dorothy Margaret, JP, yr da of Henry Joseph Manser, of Beechwood, Friday St, Eastbourne, Sussex; *b* 12 Dec 1955; *m* 1979, Michael Shouler, yr s of J R Shouler, of Bramcote, Nottingham; 1 s (Benjamin b 1987), 2 das (Elizabeth b 1982, Katherine b 1983); *Style*— The Hon Mrs Shouler; 137 Appledore Ave, Wollaton, Nottingham NG8 2RW

SHOVELTON, Prof David Scott; s of Leslie Shovelton (d 1967), of Kirkee, Croft Road, Evesham, Worcs, and Marion, *née* de Winton Scott (d 1948); *b* 12 Sept 1925; *Educ* King's Sch Worcester, Univ of Birmingham (BSc, LDS, BDS); *m* 20 April 1949, (Dorothy) Pearl, da of Sam Herbert Holland (d 1955); 2 s (Christoher John b 1950, Michael Paul b 1956); *Career* RAF Dental Branch: Flying Offr 1951-52, Flt Lt 1952-53; lectr in operative dental surgery Univ of Birmingham 1953-60, visiting asst prof clinical dentistry Univ of Alabama 1959-60, sr lectr operative dentist Surgery Univ of Birmingham 1960-64, conslt dental surgn Utd Birminghams Hosps (now Centl Birmingham Health Authy), dir of dental sch Univ of Birmingham 1974-78 (prof of conservative dentistry 1964-); pres Br Soc for Restorative Dentistry 1970-71, conslt Cmmn on Dental Practice Fedn Dentaire Int 1972-79; memb: Birmingham Area Health Authy (teaching) 1973-79, Gen Dental Ctee, Jt Ctee for Higher Trg in Dentistry 1979-84, Standing Dental Advsy Ctee 1982-88, bd of faculty of Dental Surgery RCS 1983-, ctee of Enquiry into Unnecessary Dental Treatment 1984-85, Jt Dental Ctee of MRC Health Depts and SERC 1984-87; conslt advsr in restorative dentistry DHSS 1983-; memb: Br Dental Assoc, Br Soc for Dental Res; *Books* Inlays, Crowns and Bridges (jtly 1963, 4 ed 1985); *Recreations* gardening, caravanning, learning about wine; *Clubs* RAF; *Style*— Prof David Shovelton; 86 Broad Oaks Rd, Solihull, W Midlands B91 1HZ (☎ 021 705 3026); The Dental Sch, St Chad's Queensway, Birmingham B4 6NN (☎ 021 236 8611 ext 5762)

SHOVELTON, Walter Patrick; CB (1976), CMG (1972); s of Sydney Taverner Shovelton, CBE (d 1968), and May Catherine Kelly (d 1958); *b* 18 August 1919; *Educ* Charterhouse, Keble Coll Oxford (MA); *m* 1968, Helena, da of Denis George Richards; *Career* WWII 1940-46, Maj; Civil Serv; dep sec 1946-78, dir gen Gen Cncl of Br Shipping 1978-85; dir: Br Airports Authy 1982-5, The Maersk Co Ltd 1985-87 (vice chm 1987-); advsr: House of Lords Ctee on Euro Communities 1985-86, House of Commons Select Ctee on Tport 1986; chm Maritime Ctee William & Mary Tercentenary Tst 1985-; *Recreations* golf; *Clubs* Royal Ashdown Forest Golf, Rye Golf, Hampstead Golf, Seniors Golf; *Style*— W P Shovelton, Esq, CB, CMG; 63 London Road, Tunbridge Wells, TN1 1DT (☎ 0892 27885); Maersk Co Ltd, Black

Swan House, Kennet Wharf Lane, Upper Thames St, EC4V 3ET (☎ 01 248 9666)

SHRAGER, Robert Neil; s of Benjamin, of London, and Rose Ruth, *née* Kempner; *b* 21 May 1948; *Educ* Charterhouse, St John Coll Oxford (MA), City Univ (MSc); *m* 1982, Elizabeth Fiona, da of Mortimer Stuart Bogod (d 1964); 2 s (James b 1985, Edward b 1987); *Career* merchant banker; dir Morgan Grenfell & Co Ltd 1985-; *Recreations* golf, arts, walking; *Clubs* RAC; *Style*— Robert Shrager, Esq; Woodstock, 5 Hollycroft Avenue, London NW3 7QG (☎ 01 435 4367); Morgan Grenfell & Co Ltd, 23 Great Winchester Street, London EC2P 2AX (☎ 01 588 4545)

SHREEVE, Rev Christopher John; s of Isaac John Shreeve (d 1975), of 428 Hall Rd, Norwich, Norfolk, and Joan Kathleen Shreeve (*née* Chapman); *b* 18 May 1948; *Educ* City of Norwich GS, RAF: Sch of Tech Trg, OCTU Coll; Wesley House Cambridge; *m* 26 July 1986, Esther Frances Mary Hilderbrandt, da of Franz Hilderbrtandt; Rev Dr Prof (d 1985), of 6 Comiston Springs Ave, Edinburgh, EH10 6LY; 1 da (Sarah b 1987); *Career* RAF engr offr, Flt/Lt 1964-77; methodist min 1977-84; supt min The Joijoima/Pendembu Circuit, The Methodist Church Sierra Leone 1984-86; *Recreations* cartooning, photography, model making; *Style*— Rev Christopher Shreeve; Wesley House, Hawes, Wensleydale, N Yorks DL8 3NT (☎ Hawes 268)

SHREEVE, The Ven David Herbert; s of Hubert Ernest Shreeve (d 1965), of Oxford, and Ivy Eleanor, *née* Whiting; *b* 18 Jan 1934; *Educ* Southfield Sch Oxford, St Peter's Coll Oxford (MA), Ridley Hall Cambridge; *m* 12 Dec 1957, Barbara, da of Arthur Thomas Fogden (d 1964), of Oxford; 1 da (Gillian Barbara b 1960); 1 s (Ian David b 1962); *Career* ordained deacon Exeter 1959, priest 1960, asst curate St Andrew's (Plymouth) 1959-64, vicar St Anne (Bermondsey) 1964-71, vicar St Luke (Eccleshill) 1971-84, rural dean Calverley 1978-84; hon canon Bradford Cathedral 1983-84, archdeacon Bradford 1984-; *Recreations* walking, camping, jogging, photography; *Style*— The Ven the Archdeacon of Bradford; Rowan House, 11 The Rowans, Baildon, Shipley, W Yorks BD17 5DB (☎ 0274 583735)

SHREWSBURY, Bishop Suffragan of, 1987-; Rt Rev John Dudley Davies; s of Charles Edward Steedman Davies (d 1960); *b* 12 August 1927; *Educ* Trinity Coll Cambridge (MA), Lincoln Theological Coll; *m* 1956, Shirley Dorothy, da of late Alfred Gough; 1 s, 2 da; *Career* deacon 1953, priest 1954, curate off Halton, Leeds 1953-56, Yeoville, Johannesburg 1957, priest-in-charge Evander, diocese of Johannesburg 1957-61, rector and dir of missions Empangeni, diocese of Zululand and Swaziland 1961-63, Anglican chaplain Univ of Witwatersrand and Johannesburg Coll of Educn 1963-70, sec for Chaplaincies of Higher Educn, Church of England Bd of Educn 1970-74, vicar of Keele and Anglican chaplain Keele Univ 1974-76, princ Coll of Ascension, Selly Oak 1976-81, preb of Sandiacre in Lichfield Cathedral 1976-87, diocesan missioner St Asaph 1982, canon residentiary and Hellins lect, diocese of St Asaph 1982-85, vicar/rector Llanrhaeadr-yn-Mochnant, Llanarmon MM, Pennant, Hirnant and Llangynog 1985-87; *Books* Crisis, Free to Be, Beginning Now, Good News in Galatians, Greed and Conflict, The Faith Abroad, Seeing our Faith, His and Ours, Agenda for Apostles, Mark at Work; *Style*— The Rt Rev the Bishop of Shrewsbury; Athlone House, 68 London Road, Shrewsbury, Shropshire SY2 6PG (☎ 0743 235867, tel 0743 56410)

SHREWSBURY, Bishop of (RC, cr 1851) 1980-; Rt Rev Joseph Gray; s of late Terence Gray, and Mary, *née* Alwill; *b* 20 Oct 1919; *Educ* St Patrick's Cavan, Oscott Coll Sutton Coldfield, Maynooth Coll, Pontifical Univ Rome (DCL); *Career* ordained priest 1943, vicar gen of Birmingham 1960-69, aux bishop of Liverpool 1969-80, bishop of Shrewsbury (RC) 1980-; *Recreations* music, reading, travel; *Style*— The Rt Rev the Bishop of Shrewsbury; The Bishop's House, Eleanor Rd, Birkenhead L43 7QW (☎ 051 653 3600)

SHREWSBURY, Nadine, Countess of; Nadine Muriel; da of late Brig-Gen Cyril Randell Crofton, CBE; *m* 1936 (m dis 1963), 21 Earl (d 1980); 2 s, 4 da; *Style*— Nadine, Countess of Shrewsbury; The Annexe, Upper Bolney, Henley-on-Thames, Oxon

SHREWSBURY AND WATERFORD, 22 Earl of (E 1442, I 1446 respectively); Charles Henry John Benedict Crofton Chetwynd Chetwynd-Talbot; Premier Earl (on the Roll) in peerages both of England and Ireland; Baron Talbot (GB 1723), Earl Talbot and Viscount Ingestre (GB 1784); Hereditary Lord High Steward of Ireland; patron of 11 livings; s of 21 Earl (d 1980) by 1 w, Nadine, Countess of Shrewsbury, *qv*; *b* 18 Dec 1952; *Educ* Harrow; *m* 1974, Deborah Jane, da of Noel Staughton Hutchinson, of Ellerton House, Sambrook, Salop; 2 s (Viscount Ingestre b 11 Jan 1978, Hon Edward William Henry Alexander b 18 Sept 1981), 1 da (Lady Victoria Jane b 7 Sept 1975); *Heir* s, Viscount Ingestre; dep chm Britannia Building Soc; chm Sporting Pursuits Ltd; *Recreations* fishing, shooting, hunting; *Style*— The Rt Hon the Earl of Shrewsbury and Waterford; Wanfield Hall, Kingstone, Uttoxeter, Staffs ST14 8QT

SHRIMPLIN, John Steven; s of John Reginald Shrimplin (d 1977), of Chelmsford, Essex, and Kathleen Mary, *née* Stevens; *b* 9 May 1934; *Educ* Colchester Royal Gs, Kings Coll London (BSc); *m* 17 August 1957, Hazel, da of Frederick Baughen (d 1969), of Coventry, Warwickshire; 2 s (Peter b 1960, Russell b 1963); *Career* Guided Weapons Dept Royal Aircraft Est Farnborough 1956-66, Def Operational Est W Byfleet 1966-71, attended Jt Servs Staff Coll 1971, Def Res and Devpt Staff Br Embassy Washington USA 1972-73, asst dir (Future Aircraft System) MOD Procurement Exec 1974-79, asst chief scientist RAF MOD 1979-83, head Weapons Dept Royal Aircraft Est Farnborough 1983-85, minister/cncllr Def Equipment 1985-88, dep head Br Dep Staff Br Embassy Washington 1985-88, dir Sci Studies MOD 1988-; *Recreations* walking, gardening, travel; *Style*— John Shrimplin, Esq; MOD, Whitehall, London (☎ 01 218 3534)

SHRIMPLIN, Roger Clifford; s of Clifford Walter Shrimplin (d 1987), and Grace Florence, *née* Davies; *b* 9 Sept 1948; *Educ* St Albans Sch, Jesus Coll Cambridge (MA, DipArch); *m* 21 Sept 1974, Catalina Maria Eugenia, da of L Alomar - Josa (d 1982); 3 s (Robert b 1977, Richard b 1980, Edward b 1985); *Career* architect; ptnr princ CW & RC Shrimplin (Chartered Architects and Chartered Town Planners) 1975-; cncl memb ARCUK 1985-88, memb various ctees RIBA, ARCUK; Lord of the Manor Shimpling Norfolk 1987; Freeman and Liveryman: City of London, Worshipful Co of Glaziers Painters of Glass 1974; RIBA 1974, FRIPI 1985, FCI Arb 1986; *Style*— Roger Shrimplin, Esq; 11 Cardiff Road, Luton, Bedforshire LU1 1PP

SHRIMPTON, Col George Henry Thomas; CBE (1962), TD (1948 and 4 bars); s of Henry David Shrimpton (d 1956), and Louisa Mary, *née* Burt (d 1950); *b* 12 Oct 1914; *Educ* Christ's Hosp; *m* 1940, Joyce Margaret, da of William Frederick Little (d 1963), of Grand Falls, Newfoundland; 2 s; *Career* raised and commanded 11 Signal Regt TA 1947-51, raised and cmd London Dist Signal Regt, Supplementary Res (latterly renamed Army Emergency Reserve, AER) 1952-59, Col AER 1959-62, Col TA 1962-69, ADC (TA) to HM The Queen 1964-69; *Style*— Col George Shrimpton, CBE, TD; 24 Walkerscroft Mead, W Dulwich, London SE21 (☎ 01 670 5346)

SHRIMSLEY, Bernard; s of John Shrimsley (d 1975), and Alice Shrimsley (d 1942); *b* 13 Jan 1931; *Educ* Kilburn GS; *m* 1952, Norma Jessie Alexandra, da of Albert Porter (d 1959), of Southport; 1 da; *Career* RAF 1949-51; journalist and author; dep northern ed Sunday Express 1958, northern ed Daly Mirror 1962; ed: Liverpool Daily Post 1968-69, The Sun 1972-75, News of the World 1975-80, The Mail on Sunday 1982; dir News Gp Newspapers Ltd 1975-80 (later vice-chm) Mail on Sunday Ltd 1981-82; assoc ed Daily Express 1986-; *Books* The Candidates (1968), Lion Rampant (1984); *Clubs* Garrick; *Style*— Bernard Shrimsley, Esq; 121 Fleet Street, London, EC4P 4JT

SHRUBSALL, Brian Thomas Edward; s of Thomas Bertie Charles, and Eva Allen; *b* 23 Sept 1940; *Educ* Westlands Sch, Sittingbourne & Medway Coll; *m* 14 March 1964, Dawn, da of Norman Marcus Bassart Camp (d 1986), of Faversham, Kent; 2 s (Ian b 1967, David b 1970); *Career* chm: Tellings Ltd, Speyhawk Devpt Mgmnt Ltd and other Gp directorships; FFB, FCIOB; *Recreations* golf, horse racing owner, sport, theatre; *Clubs* West Hertfordshire and Harpenden Golf; *Style*— Brian Shrubsall, Esq; 26 St Michaels Avenue, Hemel Hempstead, Hertfordshire (☎ 0442 53416); Speyhawk plc, Osprey House, Lower Square, Old Isleworth, Middlesex TW7 6BN (☎ 01 560 2161, fax 01 847 2704, telex 8954569, car tel 0860 311383)

SHRUBSOLE, Dr Alison Cheveley; CBE (1981); da of Rev Stanley Smith (d 1959), and Margaret Castelfranc Cheveley (d 1984); *b* 7 April 1925; *Educ* Milton Mount Coll, London Univ (BA), Cambridge Univ (MA), (Open, Hon Decorate); *Career* posts held in schs and colls 1946-57; princ: Machakos Trg Coll Kenya 1957-63, Philippa Fawcett Coll London 1963-71, Homerton Coll Cambridge 1971-85; *Recreations* books, music, gardening, cooking, mountain walking; *Style*— Dr Alison Shrubsole, CBE; Cortijo Abulagar, Rubite, Granada, Spain

SHUCKBURGH, Sir (Charles Arthur) Evelyn; GCMG (1967), KCMG (1959, CMG 1949, CB 1954); eld s of Sir John Evelyn Shuckburgh, KCMG, CB (d 1953); *b* 1909; *Educ* Winchester, King's Coll Cambridge; *m* 1937, Hon Nancy Mildred Gladys Brett *qv*, 2 da of 3 Visc Esher, GBE (d 1963); 2 s, 1 da; *Career* cnsllr HM Diplomatic Service 1947, Buenos Aires 1942-45, Prague 1945-47, principal private sec to sec state Foreign Affrs 1951-54, asst under-sec state FO 1954-56, civilian instr IDC 1956-57, asst sec gen (political) NATO 1958-60, dep under-sec state FO 1960-62, perm UK rep NATO 1962-66, ambass Italy 1966-69; chm: exec ctee Br Red Cross Soc 1970-80, Standing Cmmn Int Red Cross 1976-80; *Style*— Sir Evelyn Shuckburgh, GCMG, KCMG, CMG, CB; High Wood, Watlington, Oxon

SHUCKBURGH, Hon Lady; Hon Nancy Mildred Gladys; *née* Brett; da of late 3 Viscount Esher, GBE; *b* 1918; *m* 1937, Sir (Charles Arthur) Evelyn Shuckburgh, GCMG, CB, *qv*; *Style*— The Hon Lady Shuckburgh; High Wood House, Watlington, Oxon

SHUCKBURGH, Sir Rupert Charles Gerald; 13 Bt (E 1660), of Shuckburgh, Warwickshire; s of Sir Charles Gerald Stewkley Shuckburgh, 12 Bt, TD, JP, DL (d 1988), and his 2 w Nancy Diana Mary, OBE (d 1984), da of late Capt R Egerton Lubbock, RN, bro of 1 Baron Avebury; *b* 12 Feb 1949; *Educ* Worksop Coll; *m* 1, 1976 (m dis 1987), Judith, da of William Gordon Mackaness, of Paddock Lodge, Everdon, Daventry; 2 s (James Rupert Charles, Peter Gerald William b 1982); m 2, 5 Sept 1987, Margaret Ida, da of late William Evans, of Middleton, Derbyshire; *Heir* s, James Rupert Charles Shuckburgh b 4 Jan 1978; *Style*— Sir Rupert Shuckburgh

SHUFFREY, Ralph Frederick Dendy; CB (1983), CVO (1981); s of Frederick Arthur Shuffrey, MC (d 1982), of Windmill House, Uppingham, Rutland, and Mary, *née* Dendy (d 1951); *b* 9 Dec 1925; *Educ* Shrewsbury, Balliol Coll Oxford; *m* 1953, Sheila, da of Brig John Lingham, CB, DSO, MC (d 1976); 1 s, 1 da; *Career* served Army 1944-47, Capt (occupation of Greece); joined Home Office 1951, dep under-sec state and princ estab offr 1980-84; hon sec Soc for Individual Freedom 1985; *Recreations* riding, squash; *Clubs* Reform; *Style*— Ralph Shuffrey, Esq, CB, CVO; Bridge House, 21 Claremont Rd, Claygate, Surrey (☎ Esher 65123)

SHULMAN, Keith John; s of Leonard Shulman, of Northampton, and Sylvia, *née* Samuels; *b* 23 Feb 1944; *Educ* St Giles VP Sch, Trinity HS Northampton; *Career* fin dir co sec: The Equine and Livestock Insur Co Ltd 1979-, Equine Underwriting Agencies Ltd 1976-, Oriden Ltd 1983-; FCA, FINSTD; *Recreations* bridge, reading; *Style*— Keith Shulman, Esq; 11 Harley Court, High Road, Whetstone, London N20 0QD (☎ 01 446 4072, 01 563 3431, fax 568 1269); Grove House, 551 London Road, Isleworth, Middlesex TW7 4EP (☎ 01 563 3431, fax 568 1269)

SHULMAN, Milton; s of Samuel Shulman and Ethel Rice; *Educ* Univ of Toronto (BA), Osgood Hall Ontario Canada (barr); *m* 1956, Drusilla, da of Norman Bry, FVS; 1 s (Jason), 2 da (Alexandra, Nicola); *Career* Maj Canadian Armoured Corps 1940-46 (despatches); writer; film critic Standard 1948-53; theatre critic Standard 1953; TV Critil Standard 1966-72; TV exec Granada 1958-62, Rediffusion 1962-64; film critic Vogue 1975-87, political and social columnist Standard and Daily Express 1973-87; regular memb Radio 4 Stop The Week 1972, memb advisory cncl Br Theatre Museum 1983-86; *Books* Defeat in West (1948), How to be a Celebrity (1950), Kill Three (1967), Ravenous Eye (1973), Least Worst Television in World (1973); *Clubs* Hurlingham, Garrick; *Style*— Milton Shulman, Esq; 51 Easton Square, London SW1 (☎ 01 235 7162)

SHULMAN, Neville; s of J W Shulman (d 1971), and A Shulman; *b* 2 Dec 1939; *m* 8 Jan 1970, Emma, *née* Broide; 2 s (Alon Hamilton b 9 Sept 1970, Lee Hamilton b 23 June 1973), 1 da (Lauren Hamilton b 8 Aug 1984); *Career* chartered accountant in private practice 1961-; ed magazine Industry 1967 and 1968; mangr actors and film dirs 1973-, producer theatrical productions, documentaries and short films; chm: Int Theatre Inst 1985-, Land and City Families Tst 1967-, Friends of Camden Arts Centre 1988-; sec Fedn of Industrial Devpt Assocs 1965- 68; memb Theatres Advsry Cncl 1985-; prison visitor Pentonville 1966; Hon Col Tennessee Army 1977; memb NUJ 1967; FCA 1961; *Books* Exit of a Dragonfly (1985), Triple Destiny (1989); *Recreations* contemporary art, archaeology, theatre; *Style*— Neville Shulman, Esq; 52 Redington Rd, Hampstead, London NW3 7RS; 15 Hanover Square, London W1R 9AJ (☎ 01 486 6363, fax 01 408 1388, telex 27689)

SHURMAN, Laurence Paul Lyons; s of Joseph Shurman (d 1964), and Sarah, *née* Lyons; *b* 25 Nov 1930; *Educ* Newcastle Upon Tyne Roy GS, Magdalen Coll Oxford (MA); *m* 22 Nov 1963, Mary Seamans, da of the late Orin McMullan; 2 s (Daniel b

1965, Morley b 1966), 1 da (Ruth b 1970); *Career* admitted slr 1957; fndr: Shurman and Bindman 1961, Shurman and Co 1964 (amalgamated with Kingsley Napley 1967), managing ptnr Kingsley Napley 1975, banking ombudsman 1989; govr (vice-chm) Channing Sch, legal memb Mental Health Review Tbnl 1976-, cncl memb Justice 1973-, pres City of Westminster Law Soc 1980-81; memb Law Soc 1957; *Books* The Practical Skills of the Solicitor (1981, 1985), Atkins Encyclopaedia of Court Forms, Vol 26- (contributor on mental health review tbnls); *Recreations* law reform, literature, fell walking, jogging, swimming; *Clubs* Leander; *Style—* Laurence Shurman, Esq; 14 Southwood Avenue, London N6 5RZ (☎ 01 348 5409); 107-115 Long Acre, London WC2E 9PT (☎ 01 240 2411, fax GP-2/3 01 836 5357, car 0836 591 243, telex 28756 KINNAP G)

SHUTLER, Ronald Barry (Rex); s of Ronald Edgar Coggin Shutler, and Helen Emile, *née* Lawes; *b* 27 June 1933; *Educ* Hardye's Sch Dorchester; *m* 6 Dec 1958, Patricia Elizabeth, da of Henry George Longman; 2 s (Mark Richard Scott b 1962, Lee Howard Lawes b 1965); *Career* chartered surveyor HY Duke & Son Dorchester 1952-59; Inland Revenue valuation off 1959-: dist valuer Hereford 1972-75, superintending valuer Wales 1975-85, dep chief valuer 1985-88, chief valuer 1988-; FRICS 1975; *Recreations* golf, county pursuits; *Style—* Rex Shutler, Esq; Chief Valuers Office, New Court, Carey St, London WC2A 2JE (☎ 01 324 1155, fax 01 324 1190)

SHUTTLE, Penelope Diane; da of Jack Frederick Shuttle, of Middlesex, and Joan Shepherdess Lipscombe; *b* 12 May 1947; *m* Peter William Redgrove, s of G J Redgrove, of Hampstead; 1 da (Zoe b 1976); *Career* writer and poet; radio plays: The Girl who Lost her Glove (1975, jt 3rd Prize Winner Radio Times Drama Bursaries Comp 1974), The Dauntless Girl (1978); poetry recorded for Poetry Room Harvard U Arts Cncl Award 1969 and 1972, Greenwwod Poetry Prize 1972, EC Gregory Award for Poetry 1974; *Books* novels: An Excusable Vengeance (1967), All the Usual Hours of Sleeping (1969), Wailing Monkey Embracing a Tree (1974), Rainsplitter in the Zodiac Garden (1976), Mirror of the Giant (1979); poetry: Nostalgia Neurosis (1968), Midwinter Mandala (1973), Photographs of Persephone (1973), Autumn Piano (1973), Songbook of the Snow (1973), Webson Fire (1977), The Orchard Upstairs (1981), The child-stealer (1983), The Lion from Rio (1986), with Peter Redgrove: The Hermaphrodite Album (poems, 1973), The Terrors of Dr Treviles (novel, 1974), The Wise Wound (psychology, 1978), (re-issued 1986); *Recreations* gardening, walking, re-learning the piano; *Style—* Ms Penelope Shuttle; c/o David Higham Associates, 5-8 Lower John Street, Golden Sq, London W1R 4HA

SHUTTLEWORTH, Dowager Baroness; Anne Elizabeth; *née* Phillips; JP, DL; da of late Col Geoffrey Francis Phillips, CBE, DSO; *b* 17 Mar 1922; *m* 1947, 4 Baron (d 1975); 3 s, 1 da; *Style—* The Rt Hon The Dowager Lady Shuttleworth, JP, DL; Heber House, Leck, Carnforth, Lancs

SHUTTLEWORTH, 5 Baron (UK 1902); Sir Charles Geoffrey Nicholas Kay-Shuttleworth; 6 Bt (UK 1850); s of 4 Baron, MC (d 1975), and Anne, da of late Col Geoffrey Phillips, CBE, DSO; *b* 2 August 1948; *Educ* Eton; *m* 1975, Ann Mary, da of James Whatman and former w of late Daniel Henry Barclay; 3 s; *Heir* s, Hon Thomas Kay-Shuttleworth; *Career* dir Burnley Bldg Soc 1978-82, dir and dep chm Nat and Prov Bldg Soc 1983-; chartered surveyor, ptnr Burton Barnes and Vigers 1977-; bd memb Skelmersdale Devpt Corpn 1982-85, govr Giggleswick Sch N Yorks 1982- (chm of govrs 1984-); DL Lancashire; FRICS; *Recreations* Brooks's; *Style—* The Rt Hon the Lord Shuttleworth; Leck Hall, Carnforth, Lancs; 14 Sloane Ave, London SW3 (☎ 01 589 8374)

SHUTTLEWORTH, Hon Mrs (Idonea Mary Ellice); da of 2 Viscount Cross, of Eccle Riggs, Broughton-in-Furness (d 1932), and Maud Evelyn; da of late Maj Gen Inigo Richmund Jones, CVO, CB; *b* 30 Nov 1918; *m* 1946, Lt-Col William Preston Ashton Shuttleworth, RCT, late Royal Norfolk Regt (gggs of 1 Bt (Preston)); 2 s (Hugh Ashton John b 4 May 1948, William Richard Ashton b 1 March 1958), 2 da (Celia Mary Ashton b 16 Feb 1951, Rosamond Ashton b 30 Dec 1953); *Style—* The Hon Mrs Shuttleworth; Stoke Lodge, Clee Downton, Ludlow, Shropshire

SHUTTLEWORTH, Maj Noel Charles; s of Rev Richard Charles Shuttleworth (d 1955), and Doris Marian, *née* Sims (d 1978); *b* 4 Jan 1933; *Educ* Haileybury, ISC, RMA Sandhurst; *Career* Scots Guards 1953-63 served Germany, Canada, Kenya, UK, ret Maj 1963; fnd and chm The English Courtyard Assoc 1979- (winners: 3 Civic Tst Commendations, 5 Housing Design Awards from DOE, RIBA, NHBC for excellence in housing design), dir Les Blancs Bois Ltd Guernsey 1987-; govr The Elderly Accomodation Cncl 1987-, vice pres Devizes Constituency Cons Assoc 1980- (chm 1977-80); *Recreations* cricket, tennis; *Clubs* Cavalry and Guards; *Style—* Maj Noel Shuttleworth; 38 St Johns Rd, Hampton Wick, Middx; Crabtree, Savernake Forest, Marlborough, Wiltshire; The English Courtyard Assoc, 8 Holland St, London W8 4LT (☎ 01 937 4511, fax 01 937 3890)

SHUTTLEWORTH, Lt-Col William Preston Ashton (Bill); s of Capt William Gabbett Ashton Shutteworth RN (d 1968), of Oak Lodge, Aylsham, Norfolk, and Constance Esther Sophia, *née*, Preston (d 1951); *b* 22 May 1915; *Educ* Nautical Coll Pangbourne, Royal Military Coll Sandhurst; *m* 19 Nov 1946, Hon Donea Mary Ellice, da of 2 Viscount Cross, of Eccle Riggs, Broughton-in-Furness, N Lancashire; 2 s (Hugh b 1948, William b 1958), 2 da (Celia b 1951, Rosamond b 1953); *Career* served WWII in France and Belgium 1939-40, Gibraltar 1942, India and Burma 1942-46, cmmnd R Norfolk Regt 1935, served with King's own Royal Regt 1940-43, cmmnd Column with Chindits 1943-44, cmmnd 1 Bn Lancashire Fusiliers 1944-46, Brigade Maj 4 Infantry Bde 1948-52, AA-QMG 1 Br Corps 1962-65, ret 1965; in business in London 1966-76; farming in Shropshire 1976-; *Recreations* shooting, farming, reading; *Clubs* Army and Navy, English Speaking Union; *Style—* Lt-Col William Shuttleworth, Esq; Stoke Lodge, Chec Downton, Ludow, Shropshire (☎ 058 475 212); 8 Culford Mansions, Culford Gardens SW3 (☎ 01 589 3708)

SHUTZ, Roy Martin; s of Joseph Shutz (d 1969), of Birmingham, and Alice, *née* Susz; *b* 23 Jan 1943; *Educ* King Edwards Five Ways Sch Birmingham, Univ of Birmingham (LLB), Coll of Law; *Career* teacher Longsands Sch Cambridge 1966-68, admin asst Univ of Warwick 1968-69, asst to Academic and Fin Secs LSE 1969-74, barr 1974, London Borough of Barnet (cllr 1982-, chm Educn ctee 1985-), govr Middlesex Poly, memb: Middex Area Probation Ctee, London Electricity Consultative Cncl; *Recreations* golf, rugby union, theatre; *Style—* Roy Shutz, Esq; 41 Denman Drive, North, Hampstead, Garden Suburb, London NW11 (☎ 01 455 2248); 19 Old Buildings, Lincolns Inn, London WC2 (☎ 01 831 6381, fax 01 831 2575)

SIBBALD, Maj Gen Peter Frank Aubrey; CB (1982), OBE (1972); s of Maj P V Sibbald, MBE, MM, BEM (d 1957), and Alice Emma, *née* Hawking (d 1971); *b* 24 Mar 1928; *Educ* Haileybury; *m* 27 July 1957, (Margaret) Maureen, da of W E Entwistle (d 1972); 1 s (Paul Edward b 9 Jan 1965), 1 da (Joanna Bonney b 23 Feb 1963); *Career* enlisted 1946, RMA Sandhurst 1947-48, cmmnd Kings Own Yorks LI 1948, Malayan Emergency (despatches) 1948-51, Capt Korea 1953-54, Kenya 1954-55, Staff Coll 1961, JSSC 1964, Aden 1965, Lt-Col Cmdg 1968-71, Col BAOR 1972, Brig Hong Kong 1972, Maj-Gen 1977, dir of Inf 1979-83, ret 1983; conslt to: def indust co's 1982-, Def Mfrs Assoc 1982-; memb local Cons Ctees; FBIM 1973-84; *Recreations* shooting, fishing; *Clubs* Army and Navy; *Style—* Maj-Gen Peter Sibbald, CB, OBE; c/o Lloyds Bank plc, 8 Royal Parade, Plymouth PL1 1HB (☎ 0252 332 482)

SIBBERING, George Seymour Leslie Ewart; s of John Cyril Pritchard Sibbering (d 1983), of Charmouth, Dorset, and late Florence, *née* Ewart; *b* 13 Dec 1920; *Educ* Pangbourne Coll Berks; *m* 13 June 1942, Vivien, da of Sir Horace Perkins Hamilton, GCB (d 1971); 2 s (Michael John b 1945, Anthony Paul b 1947); *Career* RNVR 1940-45, Lt Coastal Forces Home fleet; incorporated surveyor and estate agent; jt sr ptnr Hampton and Sons St James's 1964-69, dir Whitbread Trafalgar Properties 1969-73; dir Trollope and Colls Devpts 1969-73; underwriting memb of Lloyds 1973-; Freeman City of London 1950, Liveryman Co of Horners 1950; FSVA; *Recreations* gardening, golf; *Clubs* The City Livery, Piltdown Golf; *Style—* George Sibbering, Esq; Oak Hatch, Cowbeech, Hailsham, E Sussex

SIBLEY, Antoinette; CBE (1973); da of Edward George Sibley, of Kent, and Winifred Maude, *née* Smith; *b* 27 Feb 1939; *Educ* Arts Educnl Sch Tring Herts, Royal Ballet Sch; *m* 1974, Richard Panton, s of William Corbett, of Salop; 1 s (Isambard b 1980), 1 da (Eloise b 1975); *Career* graduated into the Royal Ballet 1956, promoted to Soloist 1959 and to princ dancer 1960, achieved outstanding success at Covent Garden when she took over the role of Odette/Odile in Swan Lake at short notice 1959; noted for interpretation of Aurora in Sleeping Beauty, the title role in Giselle, the title role in Ashton's Cinderella, and Juliet in Macmillans Romeo & Juliet, Titania in Ashton's The Dream, Manon in the ballet of that name created for her by Macmillan, Dorabella created for her by Ashton for his Enigma Variations, Chloe in Ashton's Daphnis & Chloe, Ashtons A Month in the Country and many other roles; toured N and S America, USSR, Aust, Europe; prima ballerina role film Turning Point; *Publications* Sibley and Dowell (1976), Antoinette Sibley (1981), Antoinette Sibley - Reflections of a Ballerina (1986); *Recreations* opera going, reading, music; *Style—* Miss Antoinette Sibley, CBE; c/o The Royal Opera House, Covent Garden, London WC2

SIBLEY, Richard Edmonde Miles Phillippe; s of William Alfred Sibley, JP, of Street Farm, Crowfield, Suffolk, and Florence May, *née* Marsh; *b* 23 May 1949; *Educ* Clark's Coll London, Anglican Regnl Coll; *m* 5 June 1976, Hannelore, da of Hans Njammasch, of W Germany; 1 s (Alexander b 21 March 1979); *Career* co sec Caldenwood Housing Assoc 1970-75, chief exec Ogilby Housing Soc Ltd 1987-; dir: Sibley Property Co Ltd, Libra Fin Co Ltd (co sec 1971-80); dep chm NE London Valuation Ct (rating) 1981- (memb 1976); Rotarian 1982-; Freeman City of London 1980, Liveryman Worshipful Co of Coopers 1980 (sec of the Soc of the Livery 1986-); *Recreations* painting, politics, english vinyard owner; *Style—* R E M P Sibley, Esq; 60 Parkstone Ave, Emerson Park, Hornchurch, Essex RM11 3LS (☎ 04024 71320); Ogilby Housing Society, Estate Office, Greenways Court, Butts Green Rd, Hornchurch, Essex RM11 2JL (☎ 04024 75 115/6)

SIBTHORP, Mary Margaret; OBE; da of Shumer Llewellyn Wilfrid Sibthorp, and Midred Amelie, *née* Lane (d 1909); *b* 24 Dec 1905; *Educ* Henrietta Barnet Sch, Hampstead Garden Suburb; *Career* hon sec Nat Ctee for Resue from Nazi Terror (formerly Refugee Aliens Protection Ctee) 1939-45; The David Davies Inst of Int Studies (formerly The New Cwlth): asst sec, asst sec and ed, dir and ed 1969-84; *Books* Oceanic Pollution, A Survey and Some Suggestions for Control (1966), Study Groups on Draft Rules Concerning Changes in the Enviroment of the Earth (1962), Draft Treaty on Outer Space The Moon and Other Celestial Bodies (1966), Principels Governing Certain Changes in the Enviroment of Natural Resources (1969), Aid to Developing Countries: Improving its Effectiveness (with G R Edwards, 1984); *Style—* Miss Mary Sibthorp, OBE; David Davies Memorial Institute, Thorney House, 34 Smith Square, London SW1

SICH, Sir Rupert Leigh; CB (1953); s of Alexander Ernest Sich (d 1926); *b* 3 August 1908; *Educ* Radley, Merton Coll Oxford; *m* 1933, Elizabeth Mary, *née* Hutchison; 1 s, 2 da; *Career* barr 1930; Bd of Trade 1932-48, princl asst Treasury Slr 1948-56, registrar Restrictive Trading Agreements 1956-73; kt 1968; *Recreations* music, gardening, golf; *Clubs* United Oxford and Cambridge, MCC; *Style—* Sir Rupert Sich, CB; Norfolk House, The Mall, Chiswick, London W4 (☎ 01 994 2133)

SIDAWAY, Ronald; OBE; *b* 19 Mar 1916; *Educ* Wolverhampton GS; *m* 1969, Irene Mary Catherine; 1 s, 3 da; *Career* chm: Ironbridge Gorge Museum Dvpt Trust, Advisory Ctee Wolverhampton Nuffield Hospital; *Recreations* golf, skiing, gardening, Wolverhampton Wanderers Football Club; *Style—* Ronald Sidaway Esq, OBE; Meadow House, Oldbury, Bridgnorth, Salop (☎ Bridgnorth 3331)

SIDDALL, Sir Norman; CBE (1975); *b* 4 May 1918; *Educ* Sheffield U; *m* 1943; 2 s, 1 da; *Career* National Coal Bd: ch mining engr 1966-67, dir-gen of prodn 1967-71, bd memb 1971-, dep chm 1973-82, chm July 1982-; FEng, FRSA, FIMinE, FBIM; kt 1983; *Style—* Sir Norman Siddall, CBE; c/o National Coal Board, Hobart House, Grosvenor Place, SW1 (☎ 01 235 2020)

SIDDELEY, Hon Mrs; Pamela; da of late G A Williams, of Gorey, Jersey; *m* 1953, as his 2 wife, Hon Norman Goodier Siddeley (d 1971, 3 s of 1 Baron Kenilworth); *Style—* The Hon Mrs Siddeley; 1 Belle Vue Court, Longueville, St Saviour, Jersey (☎ 0534 52031)

SIDEY, Air Marshal Sir Ernest Shaw; KBE (1972), CB (1965); s of Thomas Sidey (d 1943), of Alyth, Perthshire; *b* 2 Jan 1913; *Educ* Morgan Acad Dundee, St Andrews Univ; *m* 1946, Doreen Florence, da of Cecil Ronald Lurring, of Dublin, Eire; 1 da (and 1 da decd); *Career* RAF (UK and Burma) WW II, Air Cdre 1961, PMO Tport Cmd 1965-66, dep dir-gen RAF Medical Services 1966-68, Air Vice-Marshal 1966-71, PMO Strike Cmd 1968-70, dir-gen RAF Med Services 1971-74 (ret), Air Marshal 1971; QHS 1966-74, dir-gen Chest, Heart and Stroke Assoc 1974-85; govr Royal Star and Garter Home 1974-86; MD, FFCM, DPH; *Recreations* racing, golf, bridge; *Clubs* RAF; *Style—* Air Marshal Sir Ernest Sidey, KBE, CB; Callums, Tugwood Common, Cookham Dean, Berks SL6 9TU

SIDEY, Lt-Col John Macnaughton; DSO (1945); s of John Sidey (d 1968); *b* 11 July

1914; *Educ* Exeter Sch; *m* 1941, Eileen, da of Sir George Wilkinson 1 Bt, KCVO (d 1967); 1 s, 1 da (decd); *Career* served WWII Royal Tank Regt and Westminster Dragoons, Lt-Col cmd 22 Dragoons, served in Europe 1940 and 1944-45; dir P & O Steam Navigation Co 1970-77, divisional chief exec 1972-77; Br Railways Bd 1962-68, chm Southern Region Bd BRB 1962, bd memb 1955-61, chm Eastern Region Bd BRB 1963-65; *Recreations* golf, gardening, fishing; *Style—* Lt-Col John Sidey, DSO; Brook Furlong, Station Rd, Chipping Campden, Glos GL55 6HY

SIDMOUTH, 7 Viscount; John Tonge Anthony Pellew Addington; s of 6 Viscount Sidmouth (d 1976, himself fourth in descent from 1 Viscount, PM 1801-04), and Gladys Mary Dever (d 1983); *b* 3 Oct 1914; *Educ* Downside, BNC Oxford; *m* 1940, Barbara Mary Angela (d 1989), da of Bernard Rochford, OBE; 2 s, 5 da; *Heir* s, Hon Christopher Addington; *Career* Colonial Serv E Africa 1938-54, dir John Rochford & Sons Ltd, pres St Gregory's Soc (old boys of Downside); kt of Malta 1962; *Style—* The Rt Hon The Viscount Sidmouth; 16 Westminster Palace Gardens, Artillery Row, London SW1P 1RL; Highnay Manor, Calne, Wilts SN11 8SR

SIDNEY, Elizabeth Anne; JP (1964); da of James Frank William Mudford (d 1954), and Charlotte Mary Henrietta, *née* Hawes (d 1975); *b* 14 June 1924; *Educ* Sherborne Sch for Girls, Oxford Univ (BA), London Univ (MA); *m* 1952 (m dis 1972), Deryck Malcolm Sidney, s of John Barham Sidney (d 1939); 1 s (David b 1956), 3 da (Francesca b 1954, Rebecca b 1959 (decd), Madeleine b 1962); *Career* ed Nat Inst of Industrial Psychology 1946-49, lectr Mgmnt Studies Poly of Central London 1949-55, psychologist (pt-time), civil service cmmn 1957-72, trg dir (pt-time) Family Planning Assoc 1970-74, managing ptnr Mantra Consults and Trainers in Public & Private Sectors UK, Europe, USA, Far East, md Centre 257 Ltd Trg Centre; pres Women's Lib Fedn 1982-84, chm Lib Pty Policy Panel on Employment 1980-83, dep chm Candidates Ctee Lib Pty 1986-, chm The Green Alliance 1984-; *Books* The Skills of Interviewing (1961), Case Studies of Management Initiative (1967), Skills with People: A Guide for Managers (1973), The Industrial Society (1970), Future Woman: How to Survive Life (1982); *Recreations* political work, environment, travel; *Clubs* Reform, Royal Society of Arts; *Style—* Ms Elizabeth Sidney, JP; 25 Ellington Street, London N7 8PN (☎ 01 607 6592); Mantra, Centre 257, Liverpool Road N1 1LX (☎ 01 609 9055, telex 265871 MONREF-G)

SIDNEY, Maj Hon Philip John Algernon; MBE (1977); s and h of 1 Viscount De L'Isle, VC, KG, GCMG, GCVO, PC, *qv*, and his 1 w, Hon Jacqueline Corinne Yvonne, *née* Vereker (d 1962) ; *b* 21 April 1945; *Educ* Tabley House Cheshire; *m* 15 Nov 1980, Isobel Tresyllian, da of Sir Edmund Gerald Compton, GCB, KBE; 1 s (Philip William Edmund b 2 April 1985), 1 da (Sophia Jacqueline Mary b 25 March 1983); *Career* cmmnd Grenadier Gds 1966, served BAOR, NI, Belize, GSO3 Ops/SD HQ 3 Inf Bde NI 1974-76, ret 1979; farmer and landowner; dir and chm Wood Products of Westerham 1984-; memb: ctee CLA Kent (chm 1983-85), Kent Archives Office advsry ctee; Freeman of City of London, Liveryman of Worshipful Co of Goldsmiths; *Clubs* White's, Pratt's, The Brook (New York); *Style—* Major The Hon Philip Sidney, MBE; Estate Office, Place Barn Farm, Penshurst, Tonbridge, Kent TN11 8BH (☎ 0892 870304)

SIDNEY-WILMOT, Air Vice-Marshal Aubrey; CB (1977), OBE (1948); s of Alfred Robert Sidney-Wilmot (d 1935), of The Grove, Great Horkesley, Colchester, Essex, and Harriet, *née* Strong (d 1957); *b* 4 Jan 1915; *Educ* Framlingham Coll Suffolk; *m* 1, 1 Oct 1938 (m dis 1968), Wendy Elizabeth Vyvian, *née* Wellings; 1 s (Colin Michael Anthony b 2 June 1940); m 2, 28 Sept 1968, Ursula, da of Johann Josef Wirz (d 1968), of Düsseldorf, W Germany; *Career* admitted slr 1938, practised with Metcalf, Copeman & Pettifer, Wisbech, Cambs 1938-40; joined RAFVR in rank of Pilot Offr May 1940, Flying Offr June 1940, Fl Lt Sept 1940; posted to office of Judge Advocate Gen 1942, Sqdn-Ldr 1943; sr legal staff offr HQ MAAF, La Marsa, Tunisia and Italy 1944; posted to office of dir of Legal Services, Air Miny 1945, Wing-Cdr 1946, Gp Capt 1948, Dep Judge Advocate Gen (Army and RAF) Far East, Singapore 1948-50, Dep Dir of Legal Services HQ RAF Aden and E Africa 1957-58, HQ RAF Cyprus 1959-60, HQ RAF Far East, Singapore 1960-63, Air Miny London 1963-65; Dep Dir of Legal Services HQ RAF Germany 1965-69; Air-Cdre 1969, Dep Dir Legal Services (RAF) MOD (Air) 1969-70, Air Vice-Marshal 1970; Dir of Legal Services (RAF) MOD (Air) 1970-79, ret 1979; chm industl tbnls London and Bury St Edmunds 1979-88; *Recreations* gardening, travel; *Clubs* RAF; *Style—* Air Vice-Marshal Aubrey Sidney-Wilmot, CB, OBE; Grove House, Great Horkesley, Colchester, Essex CO6 4AG (☎ 0206 271335)

SIDWELL, Prof (John William) Martindale; s of John William Sidwell, of Glastonbury, Somerset, and Mary, *née* Martindale; *b* 23 Feb 1916; *Educ* Wells Cathedral Sch; *m* 5 Sept 1944, Barbara Anne, da of Edwin Hill; 2 s (Peter, Timothy); *Career* N Somerset Yeo TA 1937, acting Lance Corpl 1939-42 (boarded out); sub-organist Wells Cathedral, dir music Warwick Sch 1943-46, organist Holy Trinity Church Leamington Spa 1943-46; organist and dir of music: Hampstead Parish Church 1946, St Clement Danes Church (centl church of RAF) 1957; prof: Royal Sch of Church Music 1958- 63, Trinity Coll of Music 1955-63, RAM 1963-82; fndr and conductor: Hampstead Choral Soc 1946-81, London Bach Orchestra, Martindale Sidwell Choir, St Clement Danes Music Soc, St Clement Danes Chorale; guest conductor: BBC Symphony Orchestra, BBC Singers, LSO; conductor for numerous broadcastings and recordings; Harriet Cohen Bach Medal; FRAM, FRCO; *Clubs* Savage, Wig & Pen; *Style—* Prof Martindale Sidwell; 1 Frognal Gardens, Hampstead NW3 6UY (☎ 01 435 92100

SIE *see also*: Tejan-Sie

SIEFF, Hon Amanda Jane; da (by 3 m) of Baron Sieff of Brimpton (Life Peer), *qv*; *b* 1958; *Style—* The Hon Amanda Sieff

SIEFF, Hon Daniela Frederica; da of Baron Sieff of Brimpton (Life Peer), *qv*; *b* 1965; *Style—* The Hon Daniela Sieff

SIEFF, Hon David Daniel; s (by 1 m) of Baron Sieff of Brimpton (Life Peer), *qv*; *b* 1939; *Educ* Repton; *m* 1962, Jennifer, da of H Walton; *Style—* The Hon David Sieff

SIEFF, Jonathan; s of Hon Michael Sieff (himself eld s of late Baron Sieff, a Life Peer); *b* 21 Dec 1933; *Educ* Marlborough; *m* 1, 1959 (m dis 1966), Nicole, da of Francis Moschietto, of Monte Carlo; 2 s (Mark b 1959, Patrick b 1963); m 2, 1966 (m dis), Angela, da of Brig Douglas Pringle, of Canterbury; 1 da (Rebecca b 1967); m 3, 1986, Candy Seymour-Smith; *Career* chm The Cooper Gp 1982-; *Style—* Jonathan Sieff, Esq

SIEFF OF BRIMPTON, Baron (Life Peer UK 1980); Hon Marcus Joseph Sieff; OBE (1944); 2 s of Baron Sieff (Life Peer, d 1972), and Rebecca Doro, *née* Marks, OBE (d 1966); *b* 2 July 1913; *Educ* Manchester GS, St Paul's, CCC Cambridge (MA); *m* 1, 1937 (m dis 1947), Rosalie Fromson; 1 s (Hon David b 1939); m 2, 1951 (m dis 1953), Elsie Florence Gosen; m 3, 1956 (m dis 1962), Brenda Mary Beith; 1 da (Hon Amanda b 1958); m 4, 1963 (as her 2 husb), Mrs (Pauline) Lily Moretzki, da of Friedrich Spatz; 1 da (Hon Daniela b 1965); *Career* WWII 1939-45, Col RA; memb BNEC 1965-71; joined Marks and Spencer Ltd 1935-85 (pres 1984-85), hon pres Marks & Spencer 1983-84 (chm and md 1972-84, asst md 1963, vice-chm 1965, jt md 1967, dep chm 1971); chm First Inst Bank of Israel 1983, dir of N M Rothschild 1983-; hon pres Joint Israel Appeal 1984, vice-pres Policy Studies Inst Exec 1975; pres Anglo-Israel C of C 1975, tstee Nat Portrait Gallery 1986; Hon FRCS 1984, Hon LLD St Andrew's 1983, Hon Dr Babson Coll 1984, Hon DLitt Reading Univ 1986; D Univ Stirling 1986; fell CCC Camb 1975; Hambro Award Businessman of the Year 1977, Aims Nat Free Enterprise Award 1978, B'nai B'rith Int gold medal 1982, Retailer of the Year Award USA 1982, BIM Gold Medal 1983, Presidents Medal 1982 (Ist Public Relations); kt 1971; *Books* Don't Ask the Price (1987); *Style—* The Rt Hon The Lord Sieff of Brimpton, OBE; Michael House, Baker St, London W1 (☎ 01 935 4422)

SIEGEL, Jeffrey; s of Harold Siegel, and Ruth Berman (d 1972); *b* 18 Nov 1942; *Educ* Chicago Musical Coll, Royal Acad of Music London, Juilliard Sch of Music (Dr of Musical Arts 1971); *m* 20 May 1973, Laura, da of Edmund Mizel; 1 s (Noah b 1988), 1 da (Rachel b 1983); *Career* piano soloist with Worlds leading orchestra's including: LSO, London Philharmonic, Royal Philharmonic, Philharmonia, Hallé Orchestra, Birmingham Symphony, New York, Chicago, Boston, Philadelphia, Cleveland; solo concerts at: Carnegie Hall, Queen Elizabeth Hall, Festival Hall; *Style—* Jeffrey Siegel, Esq; Inspell and Williams Concert Agents, 14 Kensington Court, London W8 5DN; (☎ 01 937 5158)

SIEGER, Joshua; CBE (1981), OBE (1970); s of Maurice Sieger (d 1950); *b* 5 Jan 1907; *Educ* Latymer Sch, London Poly Sch Engrg; *m* 1935, Sylvia Doreen de Wilton, *née* Tabbernor; 2 da; *Career* technical staff Amateur Wireless, Wireless Magazine 1920-29, chief engr Lotus Radio Liverpool 1929-30, design engr Scophony TV Ltd, responsible for large screen high definition TV pictures in London theatres 1930-40, princ tech offr TRE Malvern 1940-44, dir Hamworthy Engrg Ltd Poole 1944-46, engr Servo Corp Long Island USA 1946-47, vice-pres and dir of engrg and research Freed Radio Corpn (NY) 1947-51, pres JH Bunnell & Co Ltd Communication Engrs (NY) 1952-53, chm and md J & S Sieger Ltd (Poole) 1954-80, dir Sieger Ltd 1980-, chm and md Sieger Dvpts Ltd (Poole) 1982-86, chm UK Export Clubs Steering Ctee 1980-85; FInstD (chm Wessex branch 1975-82), FRTS; *Recreations* yachting (TSDY 'Environist'), motoring; *Clubs* Wessex Export (pres and chm 1968-85, pres 1985-); *Style—* Joshua Sieger Esq, CBE, OBE; Tinkers Revel, 8 Crichel Mount Rd, Parkstone, Poole, Dorset (T Canford Cliffs 700353); Castel du Cap, Avenue Marechal Juin, Cap D'Antibes 06600, France

SIEMENS, Herman Werner; s of Prof Dr Hermann Werner Siemens (d 1969), of Leiden, The Netherlands, and Berta Luise von Müller (d 1985); *b* 21 May 1925; *Educ* Leiden Gymnasium Sch, Delft Technol Univ (MSc, Nuclear Physics), Universidad Del Valle (MBA); *m* 7 June 1955, Cornélie, da of Herman Constantyn, Count Schimmelpenninck (d 1948), of The Hague; 1 s (Herman Werner b 1963), 4 da (Louise b 1956 m Dr Ignazio Savona, Clara b 1957 m Richard Charles Furse, Sabine b 1959 m Maurits, Baron Van Hövell tot Westerflier, Julie b 1961); *Career* research engr Centre à l'Energie Atomique, Paris 1953, former exec with aluminium companies in Colombia, Denmark, Nigeria and UK, pres and chief exec Aluminio Alcan de Colombia SA Cali Colombia 1961-69, md and chief exec Aluminord AS Copenhagen Denmark 1969-75, chm and chief exec Alcan Aluminum of Nigeria Ltd and Alcan Aluminum Products Ltd (both in Lagos) 1978-83, chm and chief exec Siemens Mgmnt Conslts Ltd London, sr conslt for ILO Geneva; *Recreations* music, riding, sailing, squash; *Clubs* Lansdowne, Royal Overseas League, IOD, Metropolitan (Lagos); *Style—* Herman Siemens, Esq; Kendal Lodge, 19 Garrad's Road, London SW16 1JX (☎ 01 677 2585); 108 Riouwstraat, The Hague, The Netherlands (☎ 070 504 018)

SILBER, (Rudolf) Martin; s of Paul Silber (d 1931), and Vally, *née* Schlochauer (d 1944); *b* 22 Sept 1918; *Educ* Univ of London, London Sch of Building (HND); *m* 1, 9 Jan 1938 (m dis 1948), Irene, da of Thomas Arnold White (d 1936), of Australia; 1 s (Paul Dorian b 1939); m 2, 10 Sept 1949, Ila MacNeill, da of Dr William Fraser (d 1977); 1 s (Andrew Ernest b 1954), 1 da (Lucy Anne b 1950); *Career* WWII cmmnd RE 1940-46, serv Egypt, Persia and Iraq, SO WO ctee (Fortification and Works Europe); dist surveyor: Lambeth (responsible for Nat Theatre) 1965-75, City of London (responsible for Barbican Devpt and Nat West Tower) 1975-79; ptnr Silber & James 1979-; former pres: Dist Surveyors Assoc 1966, Assoc of Architects & Surveyors 1963, Faculty of Bldg 1970; Freeman City of London, Liveryman Worshipful Co of Fan Makers; CEng, FIStructE, FIAS, ACIArb; *Recreations* music theatre, gourmet; *Clubs* Royal Cwlth; *Style—* Martin Silber, Esq; Crittle's Ct, Wadhurst, East Sussex TN5 6BY (☎ 0892 88 3743)

SILBERSTON, Prof (Zangwill) Aubrey; CBE (1987); s of Louis Silberston (d 1975), of London, and Polly, *née* Kern (d 1976); *b* 26 Jan 1922; *Educ* Hackney Downs Sch London, Jesus Coll Cambridge (BA, MA), Oxford Univ (MA); *m* 1, 1945 (m dis 1985), Dorothy Marion, da of A S Nicholls (d 1965), of London; 1 s (Jeremy b 1950), 1 da (Katharine b 1948, d 1982); m 2, 1985, Michèle, da of Vitomir Ledić, of Zagreb, Yugoslavia; *Career* OCTU Heysham Lancs 1941-42, Lt (formerly 2 Lt) Royal Fusiliers 1942-45; serv: Iraq, Egypt, N Africa, Italy (POW Anzio 1944-45); economist Courtaulds Ltd 1946-50; Univ of Cambridge: res fell St Cathrines Coll 1950-53, lectr in econ 1951-71, fell St John's Coll 1958-71; official fell Nuffield Coll Oxford 1971-78, prof of econ Imp Coll London 1978-87, prof emeritus of econs Univ of London 1987-, sr res fell Imperial Coll 1987-; memb: M & MC bd Br Steel Corpn, Royal Cmmn on Envirnomental Pollution, Royal Cmmn on Pres, Restrictive Practices Ct; sec gen Royal Econ Soc 1979-(memb 1946), involved with Nat Tst, Nat Schizophrenia Fellowship; *Books* The Motor Industry (jtly 1959), Economic Impact of the Patent System (jtly 1973), The Steel Industry (jtly 1974), The Multi-Fibre Arangement and the UK Economy (1984); *Recreations* opera, ballet; *Clubs* Travellers; *Style—* Prof Aubrey Silberston, CBE; Imperial College, 53 Princes Gate, London SW7 2PG, (☎ 01 589 5111, fax 01 823 7685, telex 261503)

SILK; *see*: Kilroy-Silk

SILK, Dennis Raoul Whitehall; JP (Oxon 1973); s of Rev Dr Claude Whitehall Silk (d

1974), and Louise Enicita, *née* Dumoret (d 1936); *b* 8 Oct 1931; *Educ* Christ's Hosp Horsham, Sidney Sussex Coll Cambridge (MA 1958); *m* 6 April 1963, Diana Merilyn, da of William Frank Milton (d 1970), of Taunton, Somerset; 2 s (Thomas b 1967, William b 1969), 2 da (Katharine b 1964, Alexandra b 1966); *Career* asst master Marlborough Coll 1955-68 (housemaster 1957-68), warden of Radley Coll 1968-; memb: MCC Ctee 1965-89, TCCB 1984-89; *Books* Cricket for Schools (1964), Attacking Cricket (1965), Blues in Cricket (1955), Rugby Football, Rugby Fives; *Recreations* gardening, reading; *Clubs* Hawks, E India Sports and Devonshire; *Style—* Warden Dennis Silk, JP; The Warden's House, Radley Coll, Abingdon, Oxon OX14 2HR (☎ 0235 20585)

SILK, Dr Nicholas; s of Colin Edward Bailey Silk, of 13 Highdown Rd, Lewes, Sussex, and Beryl Mary, *née* Greenslade; *b* 26 May 1941; *Educ* Lewes Co GS, Merton Coll Oxford (MA, BSc, BM Bch), St Thomas' Hosp London (DObst, Dch); *m* 2 March 1968, Beverley-Anne, da of Norman James Bazell (d 1953); 3 s (William b 1973, Edward b 1977, Jonanthan b 1979), 1 da (Harriet b 1971); *Career* mo Bedales Sch 1972-84, sr ptnr Dr Silk & Ptnrs Petersfield; rugby football, capt Oxford Univ RFC 1963, Blue 1961-63, 4 England Caps against Wales, Ireland, France, Scotland, capt Br Univs 1966, Harlequins FC 1959-66, chm Petersfield Mini Jr Rugby 1988-89; Freeman City of London, memb Worshipful Soc of Apothecaries of London; MRCS, LRCP, RCOG; *Recreations* golf, tennis, bee-keeping; *Style—* Dr Nicholas Silk; Brownfields, Westmark, Petersfield, Hants GU31 5AT (☎ 0730 638 22); 18 Heath Rd, Petersfield, Hants GU31 4DU (☎ 0730 640 11)

SILK, Peter George; s of Herbert Silk (d 1955), and Edith, *née* Silvester; *b* 20 June 1927; *Educ* Churcher's Coll Petersfield; *m* 30 March 1956, Felicity May; 2 da (Clare b 1957, Jessica b 1964); *Career* farming; *Recreations* shooting; *Style—* Peter Silk, Esq; Stoney Dene Farm, West Meon, nr Petersfield, Hants (☎ West MKeon 273)

SILK, The Ven Robert David; s of Robert Reeve Silk, of 105 Sturdee Avenue, Gillingham, Kent, and Winifred Patience Silk (d 1985); *b* 23 August 1936; *Educ* Gillingham GS, Univ of Exeter (BA), St Stephen's House Oxford; *m* 21 Sept 1957, Joyce Irene, da of Richard Bracey (d 1981; Brig Salvation Army); 1 s (Richard b 1967), 1 da (Mary b 1970); *Career* deacon 1959, priest 1960; curate: St Barnabas, Gillingham 1959-63, Holy Redeemer, Lamorbey 1963-69; priest-in-charge of The Good Shepherd Blackfen 1967-69; rector: of Swanscombe 1969-75, Beckenham St George 1975-80; proctor in Convocation 1970-, memb of the Liturgical Cmmn 1976-, archdeacon of Leicester 1980-, prolocutor of the Convocation of Canterbury 1980-, team rector of the Holy Spirit Leicester 1982-; chm Leicester Cncl of Faiths 1986-; *Publications* Prays for use at the Alternative Services (1980), Compline- An Alternative Order (1980), In Penitence and Faith (1988); *Recreations* tennis, Richard the third; *Clubs* Leics; *Style—* The Ven the Archdeacon of Leicester; 13 Stoneygate Avenue, Leicester LE2 3HE (☎ 0533 704441)

SILKIN, Hon Christopher Lewis; er s of Baron Silkin of Dulwich (Life Peer, d 1988); *b* 12 Sept 1947; *Educ* Dulwich, Mid-Essex Tech Coll (LLB); *Career* slr 1977; *Style—* Hon Christopher Silkin

SILKIN, Jon; s of Joseph Silkin, and Doris, *née* Rubenstein; *b* 2 Dec 1930; *Educ* Wycliffe Coll, Dulwich; *m* 4 March 1974, Lorna, *née* Tracy; 3 s (Adam (decd), David, Richard), 1 da (Rachel); *Career* Nat Serv Sgt Instr Educn Corps 1948-50; journalist 1947-48, manual labourer 1950-56, teacher of English to foreign students in language sch 1956-58; poet: awarded Gregory Fellowship in Poetry Univ of Leeds 1958-60, undertook res on poets of WWI 1962, Beck visiting lectr Denison Univ Ohio 1965, teacher Writers Workshop Univ of Iowa 1968-69, visiting lectr Aust Arts Cncl and Univ of Sydney 1974-, C Day Lewis Fellowship London 1976-77, teacher creative writing Coll of Idaho 1978, visiting poet Mishkenot Sh'ananim Jerusalem 1980, Bingham poet Univ of Louisville 1981, Elliston poet Univ Cincinnati 1983, visiting poet at yearly fest of Univ of Notre Dame 1985, visiting poet Writers Conf of Univ of N Alabama, visiting poet The American Univ 1989; FRSL 1987; *Books* The Peacable Kingdom (1954), The Two Freedoms (1958), The Re- ordering of the Stones (1961), Nature with Man (1965), Poems New and Selected (1966), Amana Grass (1971), Out of Battle (Criticism of poets of WWI 1972/1987), Poetry of the Committed Individual (anthology of poetry from Stand 1973), The Principle of Water (1974), The Little Time-keeper (1976), The Penguin Book of First World War Poetry (ed 1979), The Psalms with their Spoils (1980), Selected Poems (1980, 1988), Gurney: A Play in Verse (1985), The War Poems of Wilfred Owen (ed 1985), The Penguin Book of First World War Prose (ed with Jon Glover 1989), The Ship's Pasture (poems 1986), The first twenty-four years (1987); *Style—* Jon Silkin, Esq; 19 Haldane Terrace, Newcastle on Tyne, Tyne and Wear NE2 3AN (☎ 091 281 2614)

SILKIN, Hon Patricia Jane; *née* Silkin (to which she has reverted); yr da of Baron Silkin of Dulwich (Life Peer, d 1988); *b* 12 Sept 1947, (twin); *Educ* James Allen's Girls' Sch, Sussex Univ (BA); *m* 1970, Michael Johnson, BA, PhD; *Style—* Hon Patricia Silkin

SILKIN, Hon Peter David Arthur; yr s of Baron Silkin of Dulwich (Life Peer, d 1988); *b* 28 Dec 1952; *Educ* Dulwich, Sussex Univ (MA); *m* 1974 (m dis 1982), Frances, da of Dr Patrick Kemp, of Woking; *Style—* Hon Peter Silkin

SILLARS, Derek Gordon; TD (1961); s of Ralph Gordon Sillars (d 1959), of Middlesbrough, and Annie (Nan Clifford, *née* MacFarlane (d 1976); *b* 4 May 1918; *Educ* Oundle; *m* 22 June 1942, Patricia Dora, da of Henry Chandler Lovell (d 1953), of Middx; 4 s (Michael Gordon b 1943, Timothy John b 1945, Anthony Geoffrey b 1950, Duncan Henry Clifford b 1953); *Career* co dir; mil serv; TA cmmn 1939 (RA), France 1939-40, Brig Gunnery Offr UK 1941-42, Battery Cdr E Africa 1945-46, Maj 1948; emigrated S Africa 1951, fndr and md Sillars Constructions (pty) Ltd, Cape Town, Sillars, SW Pty Ltd Windhoek, SW Africa (non Namibia); dir and gm Tarmac Roadstone Ltd N England 1961); fndr & md Sillars Road Construction Ltd 1965, dir Sillars Building & Civil Engrg Ltd 1981, Norman Jevons Ltd (Insurance), chm & dir Sillars Hldgs Ltd 1985, Sillars Life Pensions Ltd 1985; *Recreations* fishing, shooting, tennis, golf, gardening; *Clubs* Kelvin Grove (Capt Town), Cleveland; *Style—* Derek G Sillars, TD; Greendales, Nether Silton, Thirsk, North Yorkshire YO7 2JZ (☎ 060983 355); Sillars Hldgs Ltd, Sillcon House, Graythorp Industrial Estate, Hartlepool, Cleveland TS25 2DJ (☎ 30429 268125)

SILLEY, Jonathan Henry; s of Henry Arthur John Silley, CBE (d 1972), and Betty Stewart, *née* Cotton (d 1981); *b* 2 May 1937; *Educ* Winchester; *m* 17 June 1961, Alison Mary, da of Richard Kenneth May (d 1965), of Purley, Surrey; 3 da (Jennifer Mary b 1964, Jane Elizabeth b 1965, Nichola Anne b 1969); *Career* Nat Serv 1955-57, 2 Lt Queens Royal Regt; joined Samuel Hodge Gp 1959; dir: Surface Protection 1959- (chm 1971-84), E Wood Ltd 1963- (chm 1971-84), S Hodge Ltd 1965- (chm and md 1971-), Hodge Clemco Ltd 1965- (chm 1971-), Victor Pyrate Ltd 1965- (chm 1971-), Hodge Separators Ltd 1976- (chm), Autoclude Ltd 1984- (chm), Stetfield Ltd 1987- (chm), Western Selection plc 1988-; memb HAC 1988; *Recreations* golf, tennis, racquets; *Clubs* City of London; *Style—* Jonathan Silley, Esq; Oudle House, Much Hadham, Herts SG10 6BT (☎ 027 984 2359); Samuel Hodge Ltd, Prince of Wales House, 3 Bluecoats Avenue, Hertford SG14 1PB (☎ 0992 558675)

SILLITOE, Alan; s of Christopher Archibald (d 1959), and Sylvina Burton (d 1986); *b* 4 Mar 1928; *Educ* Radford Boulevard Sch Nottingham, Manchester Poly (Hon Degree 1976); *m* 19 Nov 1959, Ruth Fainlight, da of Leslie Alexander Jonas Fainlight, of Sussex; 1 s (David Nimrod b 1962), 1 da (Susan Dawn b 1961); *Career* air traffic control 1945-46, RAF wireless operator 1946-49; writer since 1948; *Books* Saturday Night and Sunday Morning (1958, Authors Club Award 1958, film 1960, play 1964), The Loneliness of the Long Distance Runner (1959), Key to the Door (1961), Raw Material (1972), The Widower's Son (1976), The Storyteller (1979, Hawthornden Prize, film 1962), Her Victory (1982), The Lost Flying Boat (1983), The Open Door (1989); *Poems* include: The Rats and Other Poems (1960), A Falling Out of Love (1964), Show on the N side of Lucifer (1979), Tides and Stone Walls (1986); creator of Childrens Character Marmalade Jim: City Adventures (1967), At The Form (1980), And The Fox (1985); *Recreations* short wave w/t listening, travel; *Clubs* Savage; *Style—* Alan Sillitoe, Esq; 14 Ladbroke Terrace, London W11

SILLITOE, Leslie Richard; OBE (1977), JP (1963); s of Leonard Richard Sillitoe (d 1926), and Ellen, *née* Sutton (d 1933); *b* 30 August 1915; *Educ* St George's, St Giles Sch, Stoke-on-Trent Sch of Art, Stoke-on-Trent Tech Coll; *m* 1939, Lucy, da of Arthur Goulding (d 1923); 2 da (Christine, Margaret); *Career* served 1939-45 war with N Staffs Regt, RE, and RA, served with Br Liberation Army and BAOR (Normandy to Hartz Mountains), Sr NCO 30th Corps (France, Belgium, Holland, Luxembourg and Germany); modler ceramics ind 1931-63, gen pres Ceramic and Allied Trade Union 1961-63 (organiser 1963-67, asst gen sec 1967-75, gen sec 1975-80), dep chm Ceramic Glass Mineral Products Training Bd 1977-83; chm: Nat Jt Cncl for Ceramic Ind 1975-80, N Staffs Manpower Ctee 1975-83; pres N Staffs Trades Cncl 1963-81, memb Stoke on Trent City Cncl 1953-83, vice-chm Museums Ctee; lord mayor of Stoke-on-Trent 1981-82 (dep lord mayor 1982-83); memb: W Midland TAURA 1979-83, Staffs War Pensions Ctee 1980-; chm Friends of the Staffs Regt 1982-, vice pres Pottery and Glass Benevolent Inst 1980-; re-elected to Stoke-on-Trent City Cncl 1986-; *Recreations* walking, photography, swimming, history; *Clubs* Rotary, Gideons Int, Longton Rotary (pres 1987-88); *Style—* Leslie Sillitoe, Esq, OBE, JP; 19 Sillitoe Place, Penkhull, Stoke-on-Trent ST4 5DQ (☎ 47866)

SILLS, Thomas Herbert; MBE (1946), TD (1958, DL 1976); s of Walter Sills (d 1950); *b* 5 August 1915; *Educ* Bradfield; *m* 1939, Eileen Mary, *née* Yeadon; 1 s, 1 da; *Career* Maj WWII 1939-45; slr 1938; dir Sidney C Banks Ltd 1951-80, sec Sandy Building Soc 1939-73, md Sandy Bldg Soc 1973-79; *Recreations* shooting, fishing; *Clubs* Army & Navy; *Style—* Thomas Sills Esq, MBE, TD, DL; Broadlands, Sandy, Bedfordshire (☎ 0767 80229)

SILSOE, 2 Baron (UK 1963); Sir David Malcom Trustram Eve; 2 Bt (UK 1943), QC (1972); s of late 1 Baron Silsoe, GBE, MC, TD, QC (d 1976), by 1 w, Marguerite, da of Sir Augustus Meredith Nanton; *b* 2 May 1930; *Educ* Winchester, Ch Ch Oxford; *m* 1963, Bridget Min, da of Sir Rupert Hart-Davis, *qv*; 1 s, 1 da (Hon Amy b 1964); *Heir* s, Hon Simon Rupert b 1966; *Career* barr 1955, bar auditor Inner Temple 1965-70, bencher 1970; *Style—* The Rt Hon The Lord Silsoe, QC; Neals Farm, Wyfold, Reading, Berks

SILVER, Prof Ian Adair; s of Capt George James Silver (d 1937), and Nora Adair, *née* Seckham (d 1979); *b* 28 Dec 1927; *Educ* Rugby Sch, Corpus Christi Coll Cambridge (BA, MA), Royal Veterinary Coll London (MRCVS); *m* 30 June 1950, Marian, da of Dr Frederick John Scrase, DSc (d 1981); 2 s (Alastair b 1960, Angus b 1963), 2 da (Alison b 1956, Fiona b 1959); *Career* RN 'Y' Scheme 1945; seconded Cambridge Univ; trans to Tech & Scientific Reg 1948; demonstrator in Zoology, Cambridge 1952-57 (lecturer anatomy 1957-70), prof comparative pathology Bristol 1970-81, prof & chm dept of pathology Univ of Bristol 1981- (dean Faculty of Medicine 1987-); prof: of Neurology Univ of Pennsylvania USA 1977-, (visiting) Cayetana Heredia Univ, Lima Peru 1976, (Royal Soc) Federal Univ Rio de Janeiro Brazil 1977, (visiting) Louisiana Tech Univ USA 1973; pres: RCVS 1985-86 and 1987, Int Soc for Study of O_2 transport to tissue 1977 and 1986; fell and sr tutor Churchill Coll Cambridge 1965-70; memb research cncl ctees: MRC, SERC, AFRC; MRCVS; *Books* edited 6 scientific books, published over 200 learned papers; *Recreations* exploration, DIY, fishing; *Style—* Prof Ian Silver; c/o Dept of Pathology, Medical School, Bristol Univ, Bristol BS8 1TD (☎ 0272 303446)

SILVER, Leslie Howard; OBE (1982); s of Harry Silver, and Bessie, *née* Hoffman; *b* 22 Jan 1925; *m* 1, Anita (d 1983); 1 s (Mark b 1960), 2 da (Hilary b 1948, Jane b 1950); m 2, 29 April 1984, Sheila Estelle; *Career* WWII Warrent Offr RAF 1943-46; pres: Paintmakers Assoc of GB, Oil Colour Chemists Assoc, Paint Res Assoc, Paint Indust Club; chm Leeds Utd AFC; MBIM; *Style—* Leslie Silver, Esq, OBE

SILVER, Max Joseph; s of Benjamin Silver (d 1981), of Cardiff, and Rose, *née* Spira (d 1941); *b* 14 April 1925; *Educ* City of Cardiff HS, Univ of Wales (BSc), Poly Croydon (Dip Telecoms); *m* 9 Feb 1964, Muriel, da of Jack Grasin (d 1960), of Palmers Green London; 1 s (Jonathan b 1970), 1 da (Rochelle b 1965); *Career* electronics res worker GEC Wembley 1947-50, res and predn mgmnt with assoc co of GEC and on airbourne def projects 1950-59 with Elliot Automation and md Assoc Automation Ltd 1960-70, co doctor Philips Gp and Pye of Cambridge Sub gp 1971-80, own consultancy with contract to PA Conslts (acquisitions mergers and investments), advsr on ctee Brent Cncl, vice chm govrs Kilburn Poly 1982-86; CEng, FIEE, FIERE, FIProdE, FBIM, FSCA, FMS, FFA; *Recreations* reading, gardening, travel; *Style—* Max Silver, Esq; 34 Pangbourne Drive, Stanmoor, Middx HA7 4Q7 (☎ 01 958 7885); c/o PA Developments, Dowater House East, 68 Knightsbridge, London SW1X 7LS (☎ 01 584 2863, fax 589/2498)

SILVER, Prof Robert Simpson; CBE (1967); s of Alexander Clark Silver (d 1962), of Montrose, Angus, and Isabella Simpson (d 1950); *b* 13 Mar 1913; *Educ* Montrose Acad, Glasgow Univ (MA, DSc); *m* 1937, Jean McIntyre, da of Alexander Bruce, and Elizabeth, *née* Livingstone (d 1950); 2 s; *Career* consultant engrg scientist, consultant, James Watt prof of mechanical engrg Glas Univ 1967-79, prof emeritus 1979-, prof of mechanical engrg Heriot-Watt Coll Edinburgh 1962-66, dir G & J Weir Ltd 1958- (head of res 1939-46, chief of R & D 1956-62); UNESCO Science Prize 1968, foreign assoc of US Acad of Engrg 1979; FInstP (1942), FIMechE (1953), FRSE (1963); Hon DSc Strathclyde 1948; *Books* Introduction to Thermodynamics (1971), The Bruce (A Play in 3 acts, 1986); *Recreations* fly-fishing, poetry; *Style*— Prof Robert Silver, CBE; Oakbank, Breadalbane St, Tobermory, Isle of Mull, Scotland (☎ Tobermory 0688 2024)

SILVERMAN, Julius; s of Nathan Silverman, of Leeds; *b* 8 Dec 1905; *Educ* Central HS Leeds; *m* 1959, Eva, *née* Price; *Career* barr 1931; contested Moseley Div 1935; MP (Lab): Birmingham Erdington 1945-55, Birmingham Aston 1955-74, Birmingham Erdington 1974-83; chm (apptd by Birmingham City Cncl) of Hanworth Inquiry 1985, India League 1971; Freeman City of Birmingham 1982, Hon Fell City of Birmingham Poly 1987; *Books* A Centenary History of the Indian National Congress (chap XII, 1987); *Style*— Julius Silverman, Esq; 132A Croxted Road, London SE21 8NR

SILVERMAN, Michael Anthony; s of Ernest Silverman, of London, and Anne, *née* Taylor; *b* 12 August 1940; *Educ* Dulwich; *m* 1966, Ruth, da of Jack Shelley, of London; 1 s (Paul b 1969), 1 da (Katie b 1971); *Career* chm and md: Merton Assoc (conslts) 1977-87, Lloyd Gp of Cos 1968-76; pres Transearch Internat 1981-87; hon librarian Carlton Club 1979-87; memb: Ward of Cheap City of London, Worshipful Company of Marketors; FIMC, FIPM, MBIM, memb Market Research Soc; *Recreations* horse riding, sailing, rugby; *Clubs* Carlton (London), Club Nautico (Mallorca) Crouch Yacht; *Style*— Michael Silverman, Esq; 181 Adelaide Road, Hampstead, London NW3 3NN (☎ 01 722 7425); Merton House, 70 Grafton Way, London W1P 5LE (☎ 01 388 2051, fax 01 387 5324, telex 8953742)

SILVERWOOD, Albert William; s of Joseph Silverwood (d 1962), of Ty Bryn, Waddington, Clitheroe, Lancs, and Annie Jane, *née* Herd (d 1957); *b* 11 April 1920; *Educ* Clitheroe Royal GS, Polytechnic of N London; *m* 21 Aug 1950, Joan Mary, da of Frederick James Joseph Palmer (d 1972), of Northfield Farm, Clophill, Beds; 2 da (Lilian Margaret b 1952, Alison Anne b 1956); *Career* serv Royal Corps of Signals 1940-45: Br W Africa 1942-43, Europe 1944-45 (despatches 1945); RIBA 1955; chartered architect Silverwood and Southworth 1936-40; consulting architect, Country Gentlemen's Assoc plc, Letchworth 1959-85; *Recreations* fishing, photography; *Style*— Albert Silverwood, Esq; 38 Hitchin Rd, Stotfold, Hitchin, Herts SG5 4HP (☎ (0462) 730333)

SILVESTER, Frederick John; MP (C) Manchester, Withington Feb 1974-; s of William Silvester and Kathleen Gertrude, *née* Jones; *b* 20 Sept 1933; *Educ* Sir George Monoux GS, Sidney Sussex Coll Cambridge; *m* 1971, Victoria Ann, da of James Harold Lloyd Davies; 2 da; *Career* former teacher Wolstanton GS 1955-57; political educn offr Cons Political Centre 1957-60; memb Walthamstow Borough Cncl 1961-64; chm Walthamstow W Cons Assoc 1961-64; MP Walthamstow W 1967-70, oppn whip 1974-76, PPS to Sec State of Employment 1979-81; Sec of State NI 1981-83; memb: Public Accounts Ctee 1983-87, Procedure Ctee 1983-87; Exec 1922 Ctee 1985-87; vice-chm Cons Employment Ctee 1976-79; sr assoc dir J Walter Thompson; *Style*— Frederick Silvester, Esq, MP; House of Commons, London SW1

SILVESTER, Peter; s of Eric William James Silvester, and Dorothy May, *née* Collier; *b* 21 Jan 1936; *Educ* Godalming GS; *m* 8 Feb 1964, Christine Catherine; *Career* Nat Serv RAF sac; Friends Provident Life Off: asst gen mangr 1981-87, gen mangr (Investmt) 1987-88, exec dir and gen mangr Investmt 1988-; dir of various subsid cos; non exec dir Presidio Oil Co, Esprit and Maindrive; formerly vice pres The Pensions Mgmnt Inst, pres Insur Lawn Tennis Assoc; memb RSPB; FIA 1971, FPMI 1979, MInstD; *Recreations* skiing, fishing, golf, tennis; *Style*— Peter Silvester, Esq; Friends Provident Life Off, Pixham End, Dorking, Surrey (☎ 01 329 4454)

SIM, John Mackay; MBE (Mil 1944); s of William Aberdeen Mackay Sim (d 1982), of Dunragit House, Dunragit, Wigtownshire, and Zoë, *née* Jenner (d 1963); *b* 4 Oct 1917; *Educ* Glenalmond, Pembroke Coll Cambridge (MA); *m* 1, 1944, Dora Cecilia Plumridge (d 1951), da of Sir Cecil Levita, KCVO, CBE; 2 da (Amanda Baird, Alexandra Baird); m 2, 1963, Muriel Harvard Harris; *Career* WWII RA 2 Lt 1941, Lt 1942, Capt 1943; dir Inchcape and Co Ltd, dep chm Inchcape plc; *Style*— John Sim, Esq, MBE; 6 Bryanston Mews West, London W1H 7FR (☎ 01 262 7073)

SIM, Peter Anderson; s of Stewart Anderson Sim (d 1970), and Bertha Roberts (d 1980); *b* 16 July 1939; *Educ* High Wycombe Royal GS, Coll of Estate Mgmnt; *m* 8 Oct 1966, Gilliam Margaret Ann, da of Thomas Cedric Nicholson (d 1960); 2 s (Andrew b 1968, David b 1970), 1 da (Christina b 1976); *Career* dir Taylor Woodrow Property Co 1974, md Property Legal & Gen 1974-; dir: Legal & Gen Investmt Mgmnt (Hldgs) Ltd, Legal & Gen Assur (Pensions Mgmnt) Ltd, Legal & Gen Property Ltd, Cavendish Land Co Ltd, Watling Street Properties Ltd, Paramount Reality Hldgs Ltd, Bridge End Properties Ltd, Glanfield Securities Ltd, Investmt Property Databank Ltd; FRICS; *Recreations* gardening, swimming, squash; *Style*— Peter Sim, Esq; Little Mount, Church Road, Cookham Dean, Berks SL6 9PR (☎ Marlow 4196); Fitzroy House, 355 Euston Rd, London NW1 3AG (☎ 01 388 3211)

SIMCOX, Richard Alfred; CBE (1975, MBE 1956); s of late Alfred William and Alice Simcox; *b* 29 Mar 1915; *Educ* Wolverhampton, Gonville and Caius Coll Cambridge; *m* 1951, Patricia Elisabeth, *née* Gutteridge; 1 s, 2 da; *Career* Br Cncl 1943-75, rep Jordan 1957-60, Libya 1960, Cultural Attaché Br Embassy Cairo 1968-71, rep Iran 1971-75, currently govr Gabbitas-Thring Edcl Tst; *Style*— Richard Simcox, Esq, CBE; Little Brockhurst, Lye Green Rd, Chesham, Bucks (☎ (0494) 783797)

SIME, Peter Ernest Miller; s of Ian Falkner Sime, and Marjorie Joan Thompson, *née* Miller; *b* 18 Nov 1954; *Educ* Crewe Co GS, Jesus Coll Oxford (MA), Birbeck Coll London (MSc); *Career* CA, Deloitte Hoskins & Sells 1976-83, fin dir and co sec Gardner Lohmann ltd 1983-85, head of enforcement Assoc of Futures Brokers & Dealers Ltd 1988-(compliance mangr 1985-88); memb ICEAN 1979; *Recreations* flying, mountaineering; *Style*— Peter Sime, Esq; Assoc of Futures Brokers & Dealers Ltd, B Sect, 5th Floor, Plantation Hse, 5-8 Mincing La, London, EC3H 3DX (☎ 01 626 9763, fax 01 626 9760)

SIMEON, Sir John Edmund Barrington; 7 Bt (UK 1815) of Grazeley, Berks; s of Sir John Walter Barrington Simeon, 6 Bt (d 1957); 1 Bt m da and heir of Sir FitzWilliam Barrington 10 Bt, extinct 1833; *b* 1 Mar 1911; *Educ* Eton, Christ Church Oxford; *m* 10 July 1937, Anne Robina Mary, er da of Hamilton Dean; 1 s, 2 da; *Heir* s, Richard Edmund Barrington Simeon, *qv*; *Career* serv WWII RAF 1939-43, invalided rank of Flt Lt, emigrated to Canada 1951, civil servant in Dept of Social Welfare Govt Br Columbia 1951-75; *Style*— Sir John Simeon, Bt; 987 Wavertree Road, North Vancouver, BC V7R 1S6, Canada

SIMEON, John Power Barrington; OBE (1978); s of Cornwall Barrington Simeon, of Jersey (d 1957; himself ggs of Sir Richard Simeon, 2 Bt), and Ellaline Margery Mary, *née* Le Poer Power (d 1966), of Co Tipperary; *b* 15 Nov 1929; *Educ* Beaumont Coll, RMA Sandhurst; *m* 1970, Carina Renate Elisabeth, da of Michael Schüller (ka 1945), of Bonn; 1 s (Charles); *Career* entered HM Dip Serv 1965, first sec (commercial) Colombo 1967, Bonn 1968-70, first sec and sometime actg high cmmr Port of Spain 1970-73, FCO 1973-75, dep high cmmr and head of Post Ibadan, Nigeria 1975-79, consul-gen W Berlin 1979-81, consul-gen Hamburg 1981-84, ret; *Recreations* travel, photography, shooting, books; *Style*— John Simeon Esq, OBE; 4 Cliff Road, Dovercourt, Harwich, Essex CO12 3PP (☎ Harwich 552820)

SIMEON, Prof Richard Edmund Barrington; s and h of Sir John Simeon, 7 Bt, by his w, Anne Mary Dean; *b* 2 Mar 1943; *Educ* St George's Sch Vancouver, Br Columbia Univ (BA), Yale Univ (MA, PhD); *m* 6 Aug 1966, Agnes Joan, o da of George Frederick Weld; 1 s (Stephen b 1970), 1 da (Rachel b 1973); *Career* prof dept of political studies, Queen's Univ Kingston Canada; dir: Inst of Intergovernmental Relations Queen's Univ 1976-83, Sch of Pub Admin Queen's Univ Kingston 1986-; res co-ordinator (Royal Commn on the Economic Union and Canada's Dvpt Prospects Canada) 1983-85; *Books* Federal-Provincial Diplomacy (1972), Federalism and the Economic Union with K Novine and M Knosnick (1985), Federal Society, Federal State: A History with Ian Robinson (1987), Politics of Constitutional Change, ed with Keith Bonting (1984), and others; *Style*— Prof Richard Simeon; 95 Mack St, Kingston, Ontario, Canada (☎ 613 544 5667); Queen's Univ, Kingston, Ontario K7L 3N6, Canada (☎ 613 545 2159)

SIMEONE, Reginald (Reggie) Nicola; CBE (1985); s of Nicola Francisco Simeone (d 1985), of Inglenook, Fay Rd, Horsham, Sussex, and Phyllis Simeone, *née* Iles (d 1985); *b* 12 July 1927; *Educ* Raynes Park GS, St John's Coll Cambridge (MA); *m* 2 April 1954, Josephine Frances, da of Robert Hope, of Minister Moorgate, Beverley, Yorks (d 1979); 2 s (Nigel b 1956, Robert b 1961); *Career* RN 1947-50, instr Lt RN (Meteorologist) UK, Admty 1955-59; princ (asst 1950-55); bd memd for Fin and Admin 1987; comptroller of Fin and Admin 1984-87; authy personnel offr 1976-84; princ estab offr 1970-76; chief personnel offr: Awre Aldermaston 1965-69, Economics and Programmes Branch 1961-65, Finance Branch 1959-61; *Recreations* travel, music; *Clubs* Utd Oxford and Cambridge Univs; *Style*— Reginald N Simenoe, Esq, CBE; UK Atomic Energy Authy, HQ, 11 Charles II Street, London SW1 (☎ 01 930 5454)

SIMEONS, Charles Fitzmaurice Creighton; s of Charles Albert Simeons (d 1957), and Vera Hildegarde, *née* Creighton (d 1982); *b* 22 Sept 1921; *Educ* Oundle, Queens' Coll Cambridge (MA); *m* 10 March 1945, Rosemary Margaret, da of Ashley Tabrum, OBE; 1 s (Peter), 1 da (Jennifer (Mrs Bishop)); *Career* cmmnd RA 1942, 52 Field Regt, serv 8 Indian Div Middle East and Italy, Maj; md Br Gelatine Works 1957, Croda Gelatins 1968-70, environmental control conslt 1974-, health and safety advsr Control of Toxic Substances 1980-, int mkt res studies, communication with govt covering Europe, Japan and the US; pres: Rotary Club Luton 1960-61, Luton and Dunstable Chamber of Commerce 1967-68; dist govr Rotary Int Dist 109 1967-68, chm: Luton Cons Assoc 1960-64, Ampthill Cheshire Home 1963-72, Cancer Res Campaign Luton 1963-80, Nat Childrens Home Luton 1976-; hon sec Union of Ind Companies 1978-80, memb Small Firms Panel Assoc 1985-; JP Luton 1959-74, MP Luton 1970-74, dep lt Beds 1987-, memb Customer Consultative Ctee Anglia and Thames Water; Freeman City of London 1969, Master Worshipful Co of Feltmakers 1987-88 (Liveryman 1969); FIIM 1975; *Books* Coal: Its Role in Tomorrows Technology (1978), Water As An Alternative Source of Energy (1980); *Recreations* charitable activities, watching most sports, walking; *Clubs* City Livery, Clover (8th Indian affrs, hon sec); *Style*— Charles Simeons, Esq; 21 Ludlow Ave, Luton LU1 3RW (☎ 0582 30965)

SIMEY, Baroness; Margaret Bayne; *née* Todd; da of John Alton Todd, sometime clerk of the Ct Gorbals, Glasgow; *m* 1935, Baron Simey (Life Peer, d 1969); 1 s (Hon Thomas b 1938); hus Thomas Simey cr Life peer 1965; *Career* chm of Br Sociological Assoc and Pres Nat Fedn of Community Assoc; *Books* Government By Consent (1985); *Style*— The Rt Hon The Lady Simey; 3 Blackburne Terrace, Blackburne Place, Liverpool 8

SIMISTER, Graham Richard; s of Andrew Gordon Simister MBE, of Manchester, and Winifred *née* Thompson; *b* 13 April 1956; *Educ* Trinity Coll Cambridge (BA, MA), Harvard Business Sch Boston Mass USA (MBA); *m* 26 May 1984, Ceiri, da of Norman Roberts, of New Brighton, Wirral; 1 s (Paul Richard b 1987); *Career* banker Citibank London 1977-82, Midland Bank London 1984-86 (head of foreign exchange, head of futures and options); gen mangr treasy dir Nomura Bank London 1986-; *Recreations* squash, travel, fine wine; *Clubs* Cottons, Mosimanns; *Style*— Graham Simister, Esq; Nomura Bank Int Ltd, 24 Monument St, London EC3R 8AJ (☎ 929 2366)

SIMKINS, (Charles) Anthony Goodall; CB (1969, CBE 1963); s of Charles Wickens Simkins (d 1942), and Helen, *née* Sillem (d 1955); *b* 2 Mar 1912; *Educ* Marlborough, New Coll Oxford (MA Mod Hist); *m* 2 June 1938, Sylvia Evelyn, da of Thomas Milham Hartley (d 1966), of Silchester House, nr Reading; 2 s (Charles b 1946, John b 1948), 1 da (Joanna b 1940); *Career* serv WWII Capt Rifle Bde, POW N Africa 1941; barr Lincoln's Inn 1937; WO 1945-71, historial section Cabinet Off 1971-87; *Clubs* Naval and Military, MCC; *Style*— Anthony Simkins, CB, CBE; The Cottage, 94 Broad Street, nr Guildford (☎ 0483 572456)

SIMM, Ralph Octavian; s of Eric Simm (d 1935); *b* 6 May 1921; *Educ* City of London Coll, Southampton Univ (BCom); *m* 1963, Ursula, da of George Sornowski (d 1977); *Career* dir Hoechst UK Ltd; chm: Harlow chemical Co Ltd 1975-, Hoechst Fibre Indust 1980-, TR Oil Servs 1982-, ret 1985; *Recreations* music, painting; *Style*— Ralph Simm, Esq; Bamford Cottage, South Hill Ave, Harrow on the Hill, Middlesex

SIMMERS, Graeme Maxwell; OBE (1982); s of William Maxwell Simmers (d 1972), the Scottish Rugby Int, and Gwenyth Reinagle, *née* Sterry, Tennis Champion (Wightman Cup); gm Mrs C R Sterry, *née* Cooper, Tennis Champion, won Wimbledon (5 times); *b* 2 May 1935; *Educ* Galsgow Acad, Larchfield Prep Sch, Loretto Sch; *m* 10 Sept 1966, Jennifer Margaret Hunter, da of William Roxburgh, OBE, of Fife; 2 s (Mark William b 1967, Peter Hunter Maxwell b 1973), 2 da (Corinne Charlotte b 1969, Kirstin Margaret b 1970); *Career* Nat Serv Lt RM 1959-61; FCA (1959), ptnr Kidson Simmers 1959, chm Scottish Highland Gp Ltd 1972, memb: bd of mgmnt Br Hotels Restaurants and Caterers Assoc 1987, Hotel and Catering Benevolent Assoc

(Scotland) 1984-87, championship ctee Royal and Ancient Golf Club 1988, Scottish Tourist Bd 1979-86; vice-chm of Gov of Loretto Sch, elder and tres of Killearn Kirk; *Recreations* golf, tennis, skiing; *Clubs* Royal and Ancient Golf (St Andrews); *Style—* Graeme M Simmers, Esq; Kincaple, Boquhan, Balfron, Glasgow G63 0RW (☎ 0360 40375); 98 West George Street, Glasgow G2 1PW (☎ 041 332 6538)

SIMMONDS, Lady Caroline; *née* Knox; o da of 6 Earl of Ranfurly, KCMG (d 1988); *b* 11 Dec 1948; *m* 1975, John Edward Simmonds; 2 da; *Style—* Lady Caroline Simmonds; Great Pednor, Chesham, Bucks

SIMMONDS, David Anthony Kenward; JP (Hertfordshire 1980-); s of Maurice Alan Charles Simmonds (d 1983), and Florence Mary, *née* Kenward, of Orchard End, Nan Clarks Lane, Mill Hill NW7; *b* 8 Sept 1939; *Educ* Stowe, Univ of London (BSc); *m* 1, 23 Sept 1963 (m dis 1974), Carole Anne, da of Geoffrey Charles Thomas Parkes (d 1987); 2 da (Jane b 1965, Lucy b 1968); m 2, 27 March 1975, Valerie, da of John Barsley (d 1972); 2 s (Matthew b 1975, Mark b 1978); *Career* chartered surveyor Hendon; chm Hendon Round Table 1974-75, dep chm Juvenile Panel Barnet PSA 1988; Freeman City of London 1963, Liveryman Worshipful Co of Tallow Chandlers 1963; ARICS 1963, FRICS 1972; *Recreations* travel, gardening, wine, philately, railways; *Clubs* MCC; *Style—* David Simmonds, Esq, JP; Little Orchard, Barnet Lane, Elstree, Herts WD6 3QX (☎ 01 207 1232); Burroughs House, The Burroughs, Hendon NW4 4AP (☎ 01 202 8181, fax 01 202 3383)

SIMMONDS, Jeremy Basil Canter; RD (1979); s of Reginald Arthur Canter Simmonds (d 1974), of Woodlands Farm, Cookham Dean, Berkshire, and Enid Marian, *née* Cahusac; *b* 2 July 1941; *Educ* Trinity Coll Glenalmond, Keble Coll Oxford (BA); *m* 4 March 1967, Sally, da of John Bertrand Aust (Capt RA, d 1979), of Green Meadows, Pound Lane, Marlow; 2 s (Timothy b 1967, Michael 1970), 2 da (Anne b 1973, Clare b 1973); *Career* Ordinary Seaman London Div RNR 1963, Actg Sub Lt 1965, Sub Lt 1966, Actg Lt 1968, Lt 1969, Lt Cdr 1976, ret 1982; Radcliffes & Co: articled 1965-67, admitted slr 1967, asst slr 1967-69, ptnr 1969-73; ptnr Glovers (formerly Glover & Co) 1973-; chm E Berks Branch Asthma Res Soc; Freeman City of London 1980, Liveryman Worshipful Co of Fishmongers 1980; memb Law Soc 1967; *Recreations* walking, photography; *Clubs* Naval; *Style—* Jeremy Simmonds, Esq; Woodmancutts Church Rd, Cookham Dean, Maidenhead, Berks SL6 9PJ (☎ 06284 74991); Glovers, 115 Park St, London W1Y 4DY (☎ 01 629 5121, fax 01 491 0930, telex 261648 VERGLO G)

SIMMONDS, Jeremy Peter; s of John Armstrong Simmonds, of 12 Chestnut Close, Uppingham, Rutland, and Elizabeth, *née* Buckley; *b* 3 June 1944; *Educ* Bolton Sch, Oakham Sch, Cambridge Univ (MA); *m* 20 September 1969, Patricia Mary, da of George Charles Gray, of 4 Hannah's Field, Ridlington, Rutland; 1 s (Jeremy b 1972), 1 da (Lucy b 1975); *Career* Cambridge Athletics Blue; slr 1971- in private practice; *Recreations* cricket, golf, gardening, fell-walking; *Clubs* MCC, Cambridge Univ Hawks, Gentlemen of Leics Cricket, Burghley Park Cricket, Luffenham Heath Cricket, Achilles; *Style—* Jeremy Simmonds, Esq; The Old Hall, Morcott, nr Oakham, Rutland LE15 9DN (☎ 0572 87408); 4 Mill St, Oakham, Rutland, LE15 6EA (☎ 0572 56866)

SIMMONDS, Kenneth Willison; CMG (1956); s of William Henry Simmonds (d 1958), Home Civil Serv, and Ida (d 1956), yr da of John Willison of Acharn, Killin, Perthshire; *b* 13 May 1912; *Educ* Bedford Sch, Humberstone Sch, St Catharine's Coll Cambridge (MA); *m* 1, 1939 (m dis 1974), Ruth Constance, er da of Thomas Howard Sargant (d 1958), of Leatherhead; 2 s; m 2, 1974, Mrs Catherine Clare Lewis, yst da of Col Francis Brakenridge, CMG, MRCS, LRCP, RAMC (d 1955); *Career* Colonial Admin Serv (HMOCS), dist admin and secretariat Kenya 1935-48, dep fin sec Uganda 1948-51, fin sec Nyasaland (now Malawi) 1951-57, chief sec Aden 1957-63; FRSA; painter: exhibited RA, Royal W of England Acad, Southern Arts Open, Westward Open, Royal Bath & West, Bladon Andover (one-man); *Recreations* angling, gardening; *Style—* Kenneth Simmonds, Esq, CMG; 1 Fons George Rd, Taunton, Somerset TA1 3JU (☎ 0823 333128)

SIMMONDS, Richard James; MEP (EDG) Wight and Hamps E 1984- (Midlands West 1979-84); s of Reginald A C Simmonds and Elisabeth, *née* Cahusac; sis Posy Simmonds the illustrator and cartoonist; *b* 1944,Aug; *Career* vice-chm Young Cons 1973-75; Founding Chm Young European Democrats 1974; PA to Rt Hon Edward Heath, MBE, MP 1973-75; PPS to Sir James Scott-Hopkins ldr EDG 1979-82 spokesman on Youth and Education 1982-84; on Budget Control 1984-87; Br Whip 1987-; chm Govrs Berks Coll of Agric 1979; *Publications* The Common Agric Policy, a sad misnomer (1979), A to Z of Myths and Misunderstandings of EEC (1981), European Parl report on farm animal welfare (1985); *Clubs* Carlton, Tamworth, Ancient Britons; *Style—* Richard Simmonds, Esq, MEP; Woodlands Farm, Cookham Dean, Berkshire

SIMMONDS, Lady; Sheila; *née* Kingham; *m* 1979, as his 2 w, Sir Oliver Edwin Simmonds (fndr Simmonds Aircraft Ltd and Simmonds Aerocessories Ltd, sometime MP (C) Duddleston Birmingham; d 1985), s of Rev F T Simmonds (decd); 1 step s, 2 step da; *Style—* Lady Simmonds; PO Box 1480, Nassau, Bahamas

SIMMONDS, Stefan Marshall; s of Paul Benjamin and Edna Margaret Simmonds , of Bradford; *b* 16 August 1945; *Educ* Bradford Tech Coll; *m* 1970, Shahnaz, da of late Col Ambass Sadeghian, of Tehran, Iran; 3 da (Shaeda, Samantha, Sara); *Career* chm Drummond Gp plc; chm: Simco Supermarkets Ltd, Discount Tobacco Concessions Ltd, Tavirno Property Gp; *Style—* Stefan Simmonds, Esq; Drummond Group plc, Drummond House, PO Box 18, Lumb Lane Mills, Bradford, W Yorks BD8 7RP (☎ 0274 721435)

SIMMONS, David; s of Charles Simmons, and Margaret Elizabeth, *née* Fixter; *b* 23 Dec 1937; *Educ* Haberdashers' Askes' GS; *m* 3 Jan 1963 (m dis) Christine, *née* Plowman; 1 s (Dale Stuart b 12 Jan 1964), 1 da (Lynn Michelle b 7 Aug 1967); *Career* Nat Serv RAF 1956-58; accounts supervisor Harris & Graham Ltd Lloyds brokers 1954-60, off mangr Leonard Davis Assocs Washington DC 1961-64, vice-pres admin Int Gp Plans Inc Washington DC 1964-72; fndr and md: Gp Plans Mktg Ltd London 1972-78, Intelmark Gp Ltd 1978-; fndr chm MER Singles Club 1973-; memb cncl Br Direct Mktg Assoc, chm of Judges for Br Direct Mktg Assoc Awards, ctee memb Insur Direct Mktg Practitioners Gp, insur broker; Cert in Data Processing by Inst for Certification of Computer Professionals USA; *Books* chapter on direct mktg in Insurance Markets (1987 and 88); *Recreations* badminton, computers, skiing, theatre, music; *Style—* David Simmons, Esq; 18 Seven Dials Ct, Shotts Saldens, Covent Garden, London WCZH 9DP; 2 Regents Place, Blackheath, London SE3 OLX (☎ 01 240 9499, 01 853 1525); Direct Mktg, 28-32 Shelton St, Covent Gdn, London WC2H 9HP (☎ 01 836 0055, fax 379 5076)

SIMMONS, Prof Jack; s of Seymour Francis Simmons, and Katharine Lillias, *née* French;; *b* 30 August 1915; *Educ* Westminster, Christ Church Oxford (BA, MA); *Career* Beit lectr in the history of Br empire Univ of Oxford 1943-47; Univ of Leicester: prof of history 1947-75, pro-vice chllr 1960-63, public orator 1965-68, emeritus prof 1975-; chm Leicester Local Bdcasting Cncl 1967-70, pres Leics Archaeological & Historical Soc 1966-77, memb advsy cncl Sci Museum London 1969-84, chm advsy ctee Nat Railway Museum York 1981-84; FSA 1975; *Books* Southey (1945), Parish & Empire (1952), New University (1958), The Railways of Britain (1961, 3 edn 1986), Britain and the World (1965), St Pancras Station (1968), Transport Museums (1970), Leicester Past and Present (1974), The Railway in England and Wales 1830-1914 (1978), A Selective Guide to England (1979), The Railway in Town and Country (1986); *Clubs* Utd Oxford and Cambridge; *Style—* Prof Jack Simmons; Flat 6, 36 Victoria Pk Rd, Leicester LE2 1XB

SIMMONS, John Harry Walrond; MBE (1960); s of John Thomas Simmons (d 1966), and Maud, *née* Wolverson (d 1967); *b* 25 July 1916; *Educ* Hereford HS for Boys, Birmingham Univ (BSc); *m* 29 June 1946, Mary Edith Barrard, da of Sydney Lewis Dashwood, MBE (d 1966); 3 s (Geoffrey Philip b 1952, Julian Charles b 1955 (d aged 11 days), Roland Paul b 1957), 2 da (Rosemary Jane b 1949, Pamela Anne b 1959); *Career* Royal Aircraft Estab 1941-46; scientific offr UKAEA 1946-81; banded offr; *Style—* John H W Simmons, MBE; Selva, Lincombe Lane, Boars Hill, Oxford (☎ 0865 735879)

SIMMONS, (Osmond) Paul; MBE (1979); s of Archibald Guy Simmons, MC (d 1974), of Godalming, Surrey, and Sybil Valpy, *née* Hensley (d 1965); *b* 30 August 1917; *Educ* Charterhouse, Hertford Coll Oxford (MA); *m* 22 June 1946, Mary Rosanne, da of Maj Alan Robert Charles Johnston (d 1970), of Lightwater, Surrey; 4 da (Nicola Mary (Jack) b 1948, Judith Hilary (Brennan) b 1950, Bettiwe Jane (Sunderland) 1956, Philippa Beatrice (Insken) b 1956); *Career* serv WWII 1940-46, Capt HAC RA and So III Educn HQ 5 INF Div, Normandy Campaign from 6 June 1944 (despatches); Divisional or Dist Educn Offr Hertfordshire 1949-52, Lancashire 1952-61, Hampshire Havant 1961-74, Sehants 1974-78; *Recreations* hockey, walking the countryside; *Style—* Osmond Simmons, MBE; Melin-y-Grogue, Llanfair Waterdine, Knighton, Powys (☎ 05477 222)

SIMMONS, Richard John; s of John Eric Simmons, and Joy Mary, *née* Foat; *b* 2 June 1947; *Educ* Moseley GS Birmingham, LSE (BSc), Univ of California Berkeley Business Sch; *m* 23 April 1983, Veronica, da of Richard Sinkins; 1 s (Oliver b 1986), 1 da (Alexandra b 1988); *Career* CA, asst sec to IASC 1973-75, ptnr Arthur Andersen & Co 1979-; non-exec dir Cranfield Info Techno Inst; memb: advsy bd Royal Acad of Arts, political ctee Carlton Club; chm Bow Gp 1980-81; FCA 1971; *Recreations* horse racing, tennis, gardening; *Style—* Richard Simmons, Esq; 1 Hurst Avenue, Highgate, London N6 5TX; 1 Surrey St , London WC2R 2PS (☎ 438 3302)

SIMMS, Alan John Gordon; s of Edward Gordon Clark, formerly Januskiewiscz (d 1981), of 12 Lucian Rd, Aigburth, Liverpool, and Hilda Mary, *née* Gordon; *b* 3 April 1954; *Educ* Liverpool Collegiate GS, London Univ (LLB); *m* 2 Aug 1980, Julia Jane, da of Paul Ferguson, of Leintwardine, Shropshire; *Career* called to the Bar Lincoln's Inn 1976, practising Northern Circuit 1980-; sec Inst of Advanced Motorists 1986-88, chm Royal Soc for Prevention of Accidents Chester; memb: Br Motor Racing Marshals Club, Br Automobile Racing Club (Oulton Park), Hon Soc of Lincoln's Inn 1976, Br Acad of Forensic Sci 1978, Bar Assoc of Commerce Fin and Indust 1980; *Recreations* reading, motor racing, motor racing marshalling, road safety, blues and jazz music, guitar playing, crime (theory only); *Style—* Alan Simms, Esq; Fruit Exchange, Victoria St, Liverpool (☎ 051 236 5107)

SIMMS, Most Rev George Otto; 3 s of John Francis Arthur Simms (crown slr, d 1941), of Combermore, Lifford, Co Donegal, Ireland, and Ottilie Sophie Simms (d 1960); *b* 4 July 1910; *Educ* Cheltenham, Trinity Coll Dublin (BA, MA, BD, PhD, DD); *m* 1941, Mercy Felicia, da of Brian James Gwynn (d 1973), of Temple Hill, Terenure, Dublin; 3 s, 2 da; *Career* ordained deacon 1935, priest 1936, curate asst St Bartholomew's Dublin 1935-38, chaplain and lectr Lincoln Theol Coll 1938-39, dean of residence and lectr Trinity Coll Dublin 1940-52, dean of Cork 1952, bishop of Cork, Cloyne and Ross 1952-56, pres: The Leprosy Mission from 1964, archbishop of Dublin and primate of Ireland 1956-69, archbishop of Armagh and primate of All Ireland 1969-80; hon fellow Trinity Coll Dublin, Hon DD Huron 1963, Hon DCL Kent 1978, Hon DLitt New Univ of Ulster 1981, hon life memb The Royal Dublin Soc 1984-; MRIA; *Publications* Books of Kells (short description 1949), The Psalms in the Days of St Columba (1963), Christ within Me (1974), In My Understanding (1982); contributor to facsimile editions of The Book of Kells (1950), and The Book of Durrow (1960), Irish Illuminated Manuscripts (1980), Tullow's Story (1983), Pioneers and Partners (with R G F Jenkins 1985), contributor to Treasures of the Library of Trinity Coll Dublin (1986); *Recreations* walking; *Clubs* Royal Irish Acad, Trinity Coll Common Room; *Style—* The Most Rev George Simms; 62 Cypress Grove Rd, Dublin 6, Ireland (☎ 0001 905594)

SIMON, Hon Brian; 2 s of 1 Baron Simon of Wythenshawe (d 1960); *b* 1915; *Educ* Gresham's, Trinity Coll Cambridge; *m* 1941, Joan Home, da of late Capt Home Peel, DSO, MC and Hon Mary Gwendolen, *née* Emmott, da of 1 and last Baron Emmott (extinct 1926); 2 s (Alan b 1943, Martin b 1944); *Style—* The Hon Brian Simon; 11 Pendene Rd, Leicester

SIMON, Hon (Dominic) Crispin Adam; s (by 2 m) of Baron Simon of Glaisdale (Life Peer); *b* 1958; *m* 1983, Georgina, da of R G Brown, of Albrighton, Shrops; *Style—* The Hon Crispin Simon

SIMON, David Alec Gwyn; s of Roger and Barbara, *née* Hudd; *Educ* Christ's Hosp, Gonville and Caius Coll Camb (MA); *m* 1964, Hann, *née* Mohn; 2 s; *Career* mktg dir BP Oil UK 1980-82, dep md BP Oil Int 1982, md BP Oil Int 1982, md The BP Co plc 1986-; dir Plessey Co plc; memb Int Cncl and UK Advsy Bd INSEAD; *Recreations* music, golf, reading, tennis; *Style—* David Simon, Esq; The Br Petroleum Co plc, Britannic House, Moor Lane, London EC2Y 9BU (☎ 01 920 8000, 01 821 2600)

SIMON, Hon Jan David; s and h of 2 Viscount Simon, CMG; *b* 20 July 1940; *Educ* Westminster; *m* 1969, Mary Elizabeth, da of John Joseph Burns, of Sydney, NSW; 1 da (Fiona Elizabeth b 1971); *Style—* The Hon Jan Simon; Northfield House, Southery, Downham Market, Norfolk PE38 0HT

SIMON, 2 Viscount (UK 1940); John Gilbert Simon; CMG (1947); s (by 1 m) of 1 Viscount, GCSI, GCVO, OBE, QC, PC (d 1954); *b* 2 Sept 1902; *Educ* Winchester, Balliol Coll Oxford; *m* 1930, Christie, da of William Stanley Hunt; 1 s, 1 da; *Heir* s,

Hon Jan Simon, *qv*; *Career* with Miny of War Tport 1940-47, md P & O Steam Navigation Co 1947-58 (dep chm 1951-58), chm Port of London Authy 1958-71; pres: Chamber of Shipping UK 1957-58, Inst of Marine Engrs 1960-61, RINA 1961-71, Br Hydromechanics Res Assoc 1968-80; Offr O of Orange Nassau; *Style*— The Rt Hon the Viscount Simon, CMG; 2 Church Cottages, Abbotskerswell, Newton Abbot, Devon TQ12 5NY (☎ 0626 65573)

SIMON, Hon Margaret; o da of 2 Baron Simon of Wythenshawe (who does not use his title, *see Roger Simon*); *b* 1953; *Style*— The Hon Margaret Simon

SIMON, Hon (Benedict) Mark Leycester; s (by 2 m) of Baron Simon of Glaisdale (Life Peer); *b* 1953; *m* 1980, Patricia, da of Ricardo Hernandez y Perez of Mexico City; 1 da; *Style*— The Hon Mark Simon

SIMON, Hon Matthew; s and h of 2 Baron Simon of Wythenshawe (who does not use his title, *see Roger Simon*); *b* 10 April 1955; *Educ* St Paul's; *Style*— The Hon Matthew Simon

SIMON, Hon Peregrine Charles Hugo; s (by 2 m) of Baron Simon of Glaisdale (Life Peer); *b* 1950; *Educ* Ashdown House; *m* Francesca, da of Maj T W E Fortescue Hitchins; 1 s (Alexander b 1986), 2 da (Polly b 1982, Lucy Persephone Frances b 1984); *Clubs* Coningsby; *Style*— The Hon Peregrine Simon

SIMON, Peter Walter; s of Prof Walter Simon (d 1981), and Kate, *née* Jungmann (d 1984); *b* 25 Nov 1929; *Educ* Thames Valley Sch, LSE (BSc, PhD), ACII; *m* 1960, Sheila Rose, da of James Brimacombe (d 1985); 1 s (Nicholas b 1961; 1 da (Susannah b 1964); *Career* vice-chm Export Fin Co Ltd 1984-; dir Legal and Gen Gp plc and subsidiaries, Lion Hldgs 1974-87, Victory Insur Hldgs 1984-87; chm: Cogent Ltd 1984-88; Dir - Concord Fin Advisers UK Ltd 1987-; *Recreations* cricket, hockey, golf, bridge; *Clubs* MCC, East India Sports, Teddington Cricket, Teddington Hockey, Lord's Taverners; *Style*— Peter W Simon, Esq, BSc, PhD; 54 Ormond Ave, Hampton, Middlesex TW12 2RX (☎ 01 979 2538)

SIMON, Roger; 2 Baron Simon of Wythenshawe (UK 1947), but does not use title; s of 1 Baron (d 1960); *b* 16 Oct 1913; *Educ* Gresham's, Gonville and Caius Cambridge; *m* 1951, (Anthea) Daphne, da of Sidney May; 1 s, 1 da (Hon Margaret, *qv*); *Heir* s, Hon Matthew Simon, *qv*; *Style*— Roger Simon Esq; Oakhill, Chester Av, Richmond, Surrey

SIMON OF GLAISDALE, Baron (Life Peer UK 1971); Jocelyn Edward Salis; PC (1961), DL (N Yorks 1973); s of Frank Simon; *b* 15 Jan 1911; *Educ* Gresham's, Trinity Hall Cambridge; *m* 1, 1934, Gwendolen Helen (d 1937), da of E J Evans; m 2, 1948, Fay Elizabeth Leicester, JP, da of Brig H Guy A Pearson, of Jersey; 3 s; *Career* barr 1934, KC 1951, MP (C) Middlesborough W 1951-62, jt parly under-sec of state Home Off 1957-58, fin sec to the Treasy 1958-59, slr-gen 1959-62, pres Probate Divorce and Admtly Div High Ct of Justice 1962-71, a lord of appeal in Ordinary 1971-77, el bro Trinity House; kt 1959; *Style*— The Rt Hon The Lord Simon of Glaisdale, PC, DL; Midge Hall, Glaisdale Head, Whitby, N Yorks

SIMON OF WYTHENSHAWE, Barony of; *see* Roger Simon

SIMONIAN, Lady (Imelda) Clare; *née* Feilding; da of late 10 Earl of Denbigh and Desmond; *b* 1941; *m* 1, 1966 (m dis 1979), David Rodney Doig; 1 s (Andrew b 1969), 2 da (Rowena b 1967, Zoe b 1971); m 2, 1984, Jack Levon Simonian, of Harrogate; *Style*— Lady Clare Simonian

SIMONIS, Peter George; *b* 3 June 1926; *Educ* Cranleigh; *m* 1956, Erica, da of Eric Marsden; 1 s, 1 da; *Career* Lt RNVR; dir Burmah Oil Co Ltd 1970-79, chm Haden plc 1979-87; dir: Ellerman Lines Ltd 1979-83, The Morgan Crucible Co plc 1983-, Rowan Cos Inc (USA) 1985-, Gibralter Shiprepair Ltd 1985-, Haden Machellan Hldgs plc, Whessoe plc; chm: Br American Offshore Ltd, Beans Engrg Ltd; *Clubs* Naval, Oriental; *Style*— Peter Simonis, Esq; British American Offshore Ltd, 43 Upper Grosvenor St, London W1X 9PG

SIMONS, Allan Barry; s of late Douglas David Simons, and Anne Bessie Simons, and late Anne Bessie Simons; *b* 3 Jan 1936; *Educ* Manchester Univ, London Univ; *m* 1961, Shirley; 1 s (Keith Michael b 1968); *Career* slr, cmmnr for Oaths, former law lectr, former FBSC, life memb Slrs Benevolent Assoc, memb The Law Soc; *Recreations* violin, involved in evangelistic & divine healing crusades; *Clubs* Gospel Businessmens Fellowship Int; *Style*— Allan Simons, Esq; Solicitor, Cheadle, Cheshire

SIMONS, Elkan; CBE (1968); s of David Simons (d 1935); *b* 21 Mar 1902; *Educ* King Edward's; *m* 1927, Coralie Ann, da of Montague Hart (d 1932); 1 s, 1 da; *Career* entered Simons Brothers (London) Ltd 1922, chm 1947-; fndr and jt chm Int Spring Fair; chm: Hallmarking Conference 1954-62, Trade Promotion Servs Ltd 1956-, John Edgington (Exhibitions) Ltd 1972-; memb: Industl Art Bursaries Bd of Royal Soc of Arts 1956-, grand cncl Fedn of Br Industs 1957-62, Cncl of Industl Design 1957-64, BOTB European Ctee 1975-; pres Export Cncl for Jewellery and Gift Indust 1964-; FRSA, FICD Freeman City of London, Liveryman Worshipful Co of Clockmakers; *Recreations* golf, walking; *Clubs* City Livery, Bushey Hall Golf; *Style*— Elkan Simons, Esq, CBE; 10 Park Way, Temple Fortune, London NW11 0EX (☎ 01 455 7448); Exhibition House, 6 Warren Lane, Woolwich, London SE18 6BW (☎ 01 955 9201, telex 896152)

SIMONS, (Alfred) Murray; CMG (1983); s of Louis Simons (d 1950), and Fay Simons; *b* 9 August 1927; *Educ* City of London Sch, Magdalen Coll Oxford (MA); *m* 1975, Patricia Jill, da of David Murray Barclay (d 1959); 2 s (Julian b 1977, Jonathan b 1978); *Career* HM Dip Serv 1951-85; 1 sec: Off of Commr-Gen for SE Asia and Singapore 1958-61, Br High Cmmn New Delhi 1964-68; head of SE Asia Dept FCO 1975-79, consul-gen Montreal 1980-82, ambass & head of UK Delgn (negotiations on mutual reduction of forces and armaments and assoc measures in Central Europe, at Vienna) 1982-85; memb Int Inst of Strategic Studies; *Recreations* theatre, tennis; *Style*— Murray Simons, Esq; 128 Longland Drive, Totteridge, London N20 8HL (☎ 01 445 0896)

SIMONS, Sidney; s of Woolf Simons (d 1967), of London N16, and Deborah, *née* Kosatsky; *b* 6 Dec 1930; *Educ* St Marylebone GS; *m* 1, 31 Aug 1958, Valerie Marion, da of Harry Davis (d 1961), of Ilford, Essex; 2 s (David Russell b 1963, Adrian Mark b 1966); m 2, 21 Aug 1971, Sophie Ann, da of Eliezar Isaac Reynolds Tomlinson (d 1986), of Ilford, Essex; *Career* Corpl RAPC Reading and Devizes; CA; divnl fin controller BP Nutrition (UK) Ltd 1980-82; dir: Kevin Mayhew Ltd 1982-88, Palm Tree Press Ltd 1982-88; accountant Moledene Gp of Cos 1988-; *Recreations* reading newspapers, gardening; *Style*— Sidney Simons, Esq; 52 Leasway, Westcliff-on-Sea, Essex SSO 8PB (☎ 0702 78959); 54/56 Euston Street, London NW1 2ES (☎ 01 387 0155)

SIMPKIN, Andrew Gordon; s of Ronald William Simpkin, of Menorca, and Garry, *née* Braidwood; *b* 31 Mar 1947; *Educ* Chethams Hosp Sch Manchester; *m* 09 Sept 1972, Gail Yvonne, da of John Hartley Turner, of Knutsford, Cheshire; 2 s (Robert Gordon b 1974, James William b 1976); *Career* slr; ptnr: Ogden & Simpkin 1973-78, Pannone Blackburn (formerly Goldberg Blackburn & Howards) 1978-; non-exec dir Trafford Park Estates plc 1986-; memb of the Equal Opportunities Cmmn 1986-; memb young slrs gp Law Soc 1972-82; *Recreations* fell walking, sailing, gardening; *Clubs* Law Soc, St James's; *Style*— Andrew G Simpkin, Esq; Chapel Lane House, Mere, Cheshire WA16 6PP; 123 Deansgate, Manchester M3 2BU (☎ 061 832 3000, telex 668172, fax 061 834 2067)

SIMPKISS, Michael John; s of Percival Frederick Simpkiss (d 1985), of Stourbridge, Worcs, and Mary Adeline, *née* Jones; *b* 1 Oct 1924; *Educ* King Edward VI Sch Stourbridge, Univ of Birmingham (MB, ChB); *m* 3 Feb 1949, Eileen Edna, da of Enoch Bartlett (d 1978), of Stourton, Worcs; 1 s (Jonathon b 1951), 1 da (Alison b 1954); *Career* sr conslt paediatrician E Dorset (Wessex Regnl Health Authy), Hon conslt paediatrician Hosp of Sick Children, Gt Ormond St, London; Hon sr lectr Inst of Child Health Univ of London, clinical teacher Univ of Southampton, rendent asst physician The Hosp of Sick Children ·Gt Ormond St 1959-61; seconded Kampala, Uganda 1956-58; RAF Med Branch 1948-50, Sqdn Ldr; dep dir Med Servs Fighter Cmd; memb Cncl Br Paediatric Assoc 1977-80; author of Numerous papers on metabolic and genetic deseases of childhood; *Recreations* flyfishing, shooting, stalking, gardening, music; *Style*— Michael John, Esq; 41 Western Rd, Branksome Park, Poole, Dorset BH13 6EP (☎ 0202 765877); Poole General Hospital, Poole, Dorset (☎ 0202 675100)

SIMPSON, Alan Francis; s of Francis Simpson (d 1947), and Lilian, *née* Ellwood; *b* 27 Nov 1929; *Educ* Mitcham GS; *m* 1958, Kathleen (d 1978), da of George Phillips (d 1975); *Career* author and scripwriter 1951- (in collaboration with Ray Galton, *qv*); works incl: TV: Hancock's Half Hour 1954-61, Comedy Playhouse 1962-63, Steptoe and Son 1962-, Galton-Simpson Comedy 1969, Clochmerle 1971, Casanova 1974, Dawson's Weekly 1975, The Galton and Simpson Playhouse 1976; *films*: The Rebel 1960, The Bargee 1963, The Wrong Arm of the Law 1963, The Spy with a Cold Nose 1966, Loot 1969, Steptoe and Son 1971, Den Siste Fleksnes (Norway) 1974; theatre: Way out in Piccadilly 1966, The Wind in the Sassafras Trees 1968, Albert och Herbert (Sweden) 1981; *awards*: Scriptwriters of the Year (Guild of TV Prodrs and Dirs) 1959, Best TV Comedy Series (Steptoe and Son 1962/3/4/5 (Screenwriters Guild), John Logie Baird Award 1964, Best Comedy Series (Steptoe and Son (Dutch TV)) 1966, Best Comedy Screenplay (Screenwriters Guild) 1972; *Books* (jointly with Ray Galton) Hancock (1961), Steptoe and Son (1963), The Reunion and Other Plays (1966), Hancock Scripts (1974), The Best of Hancock (1986), Hancock - The Classic Years (1987); *Recreations* gastronomy, football, travelling; *Clubs* Hampton Football (pres); *Style*— Alan Simpson, Esq; c/o Tessa Le Bars Management, 18 Queen Anne Street, London W1 (☎ 01 636 3191)

SIMPSON, Alasdair John; s of James White Simpson (d 1987), and Joan Margaret, *née* Ebsworth; *b* 10 Mar 1943; *Educ* Queen Elizabeth GS Carmarthen, London Univ (LLB); *m* 11 March 1966, (Judith) Jane, da of Sidney Zebulin Manches, of St John's Wood, London; 1 s (Thomas), 2 da (Emily, Sarah); *Career* slr 1967, sr ptnr Manches & Co 1981- (asst slr 1967, ptnr 1968); govr Christ Church Sch Hampstead; memb The Law Soc 1967-; *Recreations* tennis, thoroughbreds, claret and Provence; *Clubs* RAC, Turf; *Style*— Alasdair Simpson, Esq; Cannon Hall, 14 Cannon Place, London NW3 1EJ (☎ 01 435 0763, 01 794 9053); Villa Chapman, 19 Chemin du Bois d Opio, Residences du Golf, 06650, Le Rouret, South of France (☎ 010 33 93 774183); Messrs Manches & Co, 10 Duke St, London, W1M 6BH (☎ 01 486 6050, fax 01 935 1276, car tel 0836 271 586, telex 266174)

SIMPSON, Alastair Derek McLean; s of John McLean Simpson (d 1968), and Edith Simpson, *née* Alexander; *b* 25 Mar 1938; *m* 11 July 1963, Morag, da of William Frederick McDonald; 1 s (Gavin Alexander b 1972), 3 da (Elidh Jane b 1965, Morna Anne b 1968, Kirstine McDonald (twin) b 1972); *Career* architect and planning cnslt, qualified 1966; work inc: housing for Univ of Zambia 1970-71, oil related offs, electronics factory, housing; *Recreations* swimming, shooting, travelling; *Clubs* Western Glasgow; *Style*— Alastair Simpson, Esq; Dunstan House, Buchltvie, by Stirling FK8 3LS (☎ 036 085 271); Simpson Associates, Chartered Architects, 2 Stewart St, Milngate

SIMPSON, Anthony Maurice Herbert; TD (1973), MEP (EDG Northants and South Leics 1979-); s of Lt-Col M R Simpson, OBE, TD, DL (d 1981), and Renée Claire Lafitte (d 1973), of Leicester; *b* 28 Oct 1935; *Educ* Rugby, Magdalene Coll Cambridge (MA, LLM); *m* 1961, Penelope Gillian, da of Howard Dixon Spackman (d 1965), of Swindon; 1 s, 2 da; *Career* serv TA 1960-73, Maj 1968; barr Inner Temple 1961; memb Euro Cmmn's Legal Serv 1975-79, quaestor of Euro Parly 1979-87; *Recreations* walking, travelling; *Clubs* Special Forces; *Style*— Anthony Simpson, Esq, TD, MEP; Bassets, Great Glen, Leics (☎ 053 759 2386); Avenue Michel-Ange 57, 1040 Brussels, Belgium (☎ 02 736 4219)

SIMPSON, Anthony Victor Joseph (Tony); s of Vincent Joseph Simpson (d 1972), of Doncaster, Yorks, and Lily Winifred, *née* Chantrey; *b* 6 May 1931; *Educ* Harron Weald GS, Hendon Coll of Technol (Business Mgmnt Dip), St Albans Coll; *m* 15 March 1956, Joan Sheila, da of Horace James Broughton (d 1980); 2 s (Gary Keith b 31 Jan 1957, Dean Kevin b 19 Dec 1958), 1 da (Claire Karla b 11 March 1971); *Career* Hoover Ltd: controller 1967-73, divnl exec 1973-74, assoc dir admin 1974-81, main bd dir 1981-86; md Hoover Europe 1986-, pres Hoover Trading Co 1988-, jt md Hoover plc 1986-; chm: Hoover Apparete Switzerland, Hoover Oy Finland; pres supervisory bd SA Hoover France, dir Hoover Etab Belgium; hon tres Middx Assoc of Boys' Clubs, chm Hoover Fdn (charitable tst), memb French C of C in London; FCMA, FBIM; *Recreations* golf, soccer supporter Watford AFC; *Clubs* Crockfords, Confrerie Des Chevaliers Du Tastevin; *Style*— Tony Simpson, Esq; Rothlea Lodge, Flaunden Lane, Bovingdon, Herts (☎ 0442 833 898); Hoover plc, Hayes Gate Ho, 27 Uxbridge Rd, Hayes, Middx (☎ 01 848 8228, fax 01 848 2440, telex 915245 HOOVER G)

SIMPSON, Air Cdre Charles Hunting; CBE (1961); s of John Andrew Simpson (d 1936, Maj Calcutta Light Horse), of Elmdon, IOW, and Winifred Elizabeth Louise, *née* Hunting (d 1952); *b* 11 Feb 1915; *Educ* Oundle, Pembroke Coll Cambridge (MA); *m* 1945, Beatrice Gillian Patricia, da of Capt Arthur Noel Vernon Hill-Lowe (d 1964), of Court Hill, Shrops; 2 da; *Career* joined RAF 1937, Bomber and Flying Trg Cmds 1939-45, Air Attaché Stockholm 1946-48, Cdr Cambridge Univ Air Sqdn 1948-50, Staff Coll 1951, Air Staff Policy 1951-53, dep dir Air Intelligence 1953-54, Asst Cmdt RAF

Staff Coll Andover 1954-58, Gp Capt 1954, Cdr RAF E Africa 1958-61, ret 1961 with rank of Air Cdre; memb Lloyd's; Freeman City of London, Liveryman Worshipful Co of Gunmakers; FRMets, FBIS; *Recreations* yachting, racing; *Clubs* Royal Yacht Squadron, Boodle's, RAF; *Style—* Air Cdre Charles Simpson, CBE; Fugelmere Grange, Fulmer, Bucks SL3 6HN (☎ 02816 2051)

SIMPSON, Christopher Robert; s of Lt-Col Maurice Rowton Simpson, OBE, TD, DL (d 1981), of Leics, and Renée Claire, *née* Laffitte (d 1973); *b* 7 Dec 1929; *Educ* Rugby, Magdalene Coll Cambridge (MA, LLM); *m* 2 July 1955, Jane, da of Ernest Gustav Byng (d 1944), of Northants; 1 s (David b 1957), 1 da (Charlotte b 1959); *Career* Nat Serv RA 1955-57, TA 1957-61, Capt 1961, ret; slr 1955; ptnr: Herbert Simpson Son & Bennett 1957-77, Stone & Simpson 1978-87; FAI Diamond Badge for gliding, Royal Aero Club Silver Medal 1976, chm Br Gliding Assoc 1972-76 (vice-pres 1976-), vice-chm Royal Aero Club 1988-, chm IOD Leics branch 1977-79; vice-chm E Midlands Regnl Cncl for Sport & Recreation 1981-; *Recreations* gliding, mountaineering; *Clubs* Army & Navy, Alpine; *Style—* Christopher Simpson, Esq; The Clock House, Roman Rd, Birstall, Leics LE4 4BF (☎ 0533 674173)

SIMPSON, David Martin Wynn; s of William Wynn Simpson, OBE, (d 1987), of Northwood, and Winifred Marjorie, *née* Povey, of Bristol; *b* 31 Jan 1938; *Educ* Queens Coll Taunton, Christ's Coll Cambridge (MA); *m* 6 Dec 1968, Susan Katherine, da of Robert Windsor, of Steyning; 2 da (Vanessa b 1970, Fiona b 1971); *Career* slr, ptnr Trump & ptnrs 1968, chm Legal Aid Ctee 1987, vice pres Bristol Law Soc 1988, vice chm govnrs Queens Coll Taunton; chm Gen Cmmrs of Taxes Wrington div 1986; MBIM, ACIArb, FFB;; *Recreations* flying, gardening, swimming; *Style—* David Simpson, Esq; The Post House, Burrington, Bristol BS18 7AA, (☎ 0761 62664); 34 Gt Nicholas St, Bristol BS1 1TS, (☎ 0272 299901, fax 0272 298232)

SIMPSON, David Richard Salisbury; s of Richard Salisbury Simpson and Joan Margaret, *née* Braund; *b* 1 Oct 1945; *Educ* Merchiston Castle Sch Edinburgh; *Career* VSO Teacher in W Pakistan 1963-64, CA, joined Peat, Marwick, Mitchell & Co 1964-72, Scottish dir Shelter Campaign for the Homeless 1972-74; dir: Amnesty Int (Br Section) 1974-79, Action on Smoking and Health 1979-; conslt: Int Union against Cancer, Special Project on Smoking and Cancer (responsibility for Indian Sub-Continent) 1980-; sundry journalism, broadcasting and public lectures; *Recreations* reading, music, hill-walking, Orkney; *Style—* David Simpson, Esq; 5-11 Mortimer St, London W1 (☎ 01 637 9843)

SIMPSON, Douglas Arthur Reginald Norman; s of Joseph Norman Simpson (d 1932), of Gormyre, Kurunegala, Ceylon, and Alice Dorothy, *née* Peake (d 1966); *b* 28 Dec 1920; *Educ* Ashburton GS, Ellesmere Coll Shrops, Univ Coll Cardiff (BSc); *m* 9 Oct 1941, Tryfana Jenny, da of John Woodford-Williams (d 1941), of Park Grove, Cardiff; 1 s (James b 24 July 1959), 2 da (Mary b 28 May 1953, Angela b 18 June 1958); *Career* mangr Abercynon Colliery 1947-49, mangr (later agent) Nantgarw Colliery 1949-53, chief mining engr Abernant Colliery 1953-58, dep area prodn mangr NCB Area 3 (Rhondda) S Wales 1958-63; NCB London: head of mining (gen) prodn dept 1963-67, head of reconstruction and capital projects 1967-72, chief maj projects engr 1972-84, ret 1984; pres: Nat Assoc of Colliery Mangrs S Wales 1961, S Wales Inst of Engrs 1966-67, Inst of Mining Engrs 1983-84; chm nat advsy ctee on mining City & Guilds of London Inst 1980-; chm Meath Green Protection Soc Horley Surrey 1974-, vice chm Reigate & Dist Crime Prevention Panel 1986-, ctee memb Gatwick Area Conservation Campaign 1984-; chm Horley branch Cons Assoc 1988 (dep chm Reigate); memb: Surrey CC 1987-, E Surrey Health Authy 1987-; awarded Inst Medal by Inst Mining Engrs 1985; Freeman City of London 1984, Liveryman Worshipful Co of Engrs 1984; hon fell Univ Coll Cardiff 1983; CEng, fell Inst of Mining Engrs; *Recreations* beekeeping, vintage cars; *Style—* Douglas Simpson, Esq; Meath Green House, Meath Green Lane, Horley, Surrey RH6 8HZ (☎ 0293 784 990)

SIMPSON, Air Vice-Marshal (Charles) Ednam; QHS (1984); s of Charles Walker Clark Simpson (d 1970) , of Stirling, and Margaret Gourlay, *née* Doig (d 1970); *b* 24 Sept 1929; *Educ* Stirling HS, Falkirk HS, Univ of Glasgow (BM, ChB), London Univ (MSc); *m* 2 May 1955, Margaret Riddell, da of (Robert) Wallace Hunter (d 1981), of Glasgow; 2 s (David b 1956, Ian b 1957), 1 da (Fiona b 1960); *Career* joined RAF 1955, staff offr (aviation med) Br def staff Washington DC 1975, dep dir health and res RAF 1979; offr cmdg RAF hosps: Wegberg 1981, Princess Alexandra Hosp Wroughton 1982; dir health and res RAF 1984, ass surgn gen (environmental health and res) 1985, princ MO RAF strike command 1986-88; MFCM, FFOM; *Recreations* golf, bird-watching; *Clubs* RAF; *Style—* Air Vice-Marshal Simpson, QHS; Am Bruach, Kippen, Stirling FK8 3DT (☎ 078687 281)

SIMPSON, Ffreebairn Liddon; CMG (1967); s of James Liddon Simpson (d 1969), of Uckfield, Sussex; *b* 11 July 1967; *Educ* Westminster Sch, Trinity Coll Cambridge (BA); *m* 1947, Dorina Laura Magda, da of Nencho Ilie (d 1944), of Sofia, Bulgaria; 1 s (Christopher Liddon b 5 Aug 1952); *Career* FO & Dip Serv Tokyo and Sofia 1939-48, Overseas Fin Div HM Tresy 1948-50, Colonial Serv Gold Coast 1950-55, dep colonial sec Mauritius 1955; permanent sec: Miny of Works and Internal Communications Mauritius 1961-66, Premier's Off Mauritius 1966-78, sec to Cncl of Ministers Mauritius 1967-68 (Mauritius became independent 1968), sec to Cabinet and hd of Civil Serv Mauritius 1968-76, ret 1976, gen mangr Central Water Authy Mauritius 1976-78; *Recreations* reading, philately; *Clubs* Utd Oxford and Cambridge; *Style—* Ffreebairn Simpson, Esq, CMG; c/o Lloyds Bank, 6 Pall Mall, London SW1Y 5NH

SIMPSON, Gordon Russell; DSO (1944 and Bar 1945), LVO (1979), TD (1945 and 2 bars, DL (Central Region - Stirling and Falkirk 1981); s of Alexander Russell Simpson, WS (d 1928); *b* 2 Jan 1917; *Educ* Rugby; *m* 1943, Marion Elizabeth, *née* King (d 1976); 2 s; *Career* 2 Lothians and Border Horse 1938-50, Col (TA) UK 1950; stockbroker 1938; sr ptnr Bell Cowan & Co (now Bell Lawrie Macgregor) 1955-82; chm Gen Accident Fire & Life Assur Co 1979-87 (dir 1967-87), former chm Edinburgh then Scottish Stock Exchange, former dep chm The Stock Exchange; Brig Royal Co of Archers (Queen's Body Guard for Scotland), (tres 1959-79); cmmr Queen Victoria Sch, memb of ct Stirling Univ 1980-88; *Recreations* skiing, archery, music; *Clubs* New (Edinburgh); *Style—* Gordon R Simpson, Esq, DSO, LVO, TD, DL; Arntomie, Port of Menteith, Perthshire FK8 3RD

SIMPSON, Harry Arthur; AE; s of Cyril Simpson (d 1950), of Ferndown, Dorset, and Nellie, *née* Buckley (d 1967); *b* 16 Dec 1914; *Educ* Moseley GS Warwickshire; *m* 1, 10 July 1943 (m dis 1983), Lilian Jackson, *née* Macdonald; 1 s (Roger Graham b 13 Feb 1948, killed 1974), 2 da (Dianne Gail b 13 March 1945, Julie Jackson b 11 Dec 1956); m 2, 9 May 1984, Deborah Jane, da of Philip J Camp, of Bookham, Surrey; *Career* serv WWII RAF, specialist 'N' Symbol Award 1942, Pilot, Sqdn Ldr; chemist Bakelite Ltd 1936-39; dir: Flexible Abrasives Ltd 1947-65, chm and chief exec Arrow Abrasives Ltd 1966-; FRMetS, Fell Royal Inst Directors; *Recreations* yachting, golf, fishing; *Clubs* Royal Thames Yacht, RAC, RAF; *Style—* Harry Simpson, Esq, AE; Little Langley Farm, Rake, nr Liss, Hampshire (☎ 0730 892 142); Arrow Abrasives Ltd, Rodney Rd, Portsmouth, Hampshire PO4 8TH (☎ 0705 750 836, fax 0705 826 323, car tel 0836 227 869, telex 86787 ARROWA G)

SIMPSON, Ian; s of Herbert William Simpson (d 1972), of Sunderland, Co Durham, and Elsie, *née* Jagger; *b* 12 Nov 1933; *Educ* Bede GS Sunderland, Sunderland Coll of Art, RCA; *m* 26 July 1958 (m dis 1982), Joan, da of Donald Charlton (d 1958), of Sunderland; 2 s (Robert b 2 Sept 1962, Howard b 13 Feb 1964), 1 da (Katharine b 8 March 1967); m 2, 26 March 1982, Birgitta, da of Yngve Brädde (d 1976), of Björketorp, Sweden; *Career* Nat Serv RAF 1953-55; head dept co-ordinated studies Hornsey Coll of Art 1969-72 (head dept visual res 1967-69), visiting prof Syracuse Univ NY 1977, head of sch St Martin's Sch of Art 1986-88 (princ 1972-86), asst rector London Inst 1986-88, freelance artsit and writer 1988-; One Man Exhibitions: Cambridge 1975, Durham 1977, Hambledom Gallery Blandford 1985; broadcast wrote and presented: Eyeline 1968, Picture Making 1973, Reading the Signs 1976; chm fine art bd (CNAA 1976-81 memb cncl 1974-80), conslt Leisure Study Gp 1986-87; ARCA 1958, FSAE 1976, FRSA 1983; *Books* Eyeline (1968), Drawing Seeing and Observation (1973), Picture Making (1973), Guide to Painting and Composition (1979), Painters Progress (1983), An Encyclopaedia of Drawing Techniques (1987), A Course in Painting (1988); *Recreations* reading, music; *Style—* Ian Simpson, Esq; Motts Farm House, Chilton St, Clare, Sudbury, Suffolk CO10 8QS (☎ 0787 277835)

SIMPSON, Jack William; CBE (1976); s of John Sandall Simpson (d 1950); *b* 30 Mar 1915; *Educ* Leyton Tech Coll, Woolwich Poly; *m* 1939, Winifred Doris, nee Mitchell; 2 da; *Career* chartered mech engr, exec MOD 1967-76, special advsr to md ROF, visiting prof RMC 1978-84, engrg assessor SE Area 1977-85, chm Young Enterprise W Kent Area Bd 1978-83; *Recreations* golf, gardening; *Clubs* Nevill Golf; *Style—* Jack Simpson Esq, CBE; 59 The Ridgeway, Tonbridge, Kent (☎ Tonbridge 357376)

SIMPSON, James; s of William Watson Simpson, of N Baddesley, Southampton, Hants, and Beatrice Hilda, *née* Dixon; *b* 16 April 1944; *Educ* Barlton Peveril GS Eastleigh Hants, Univ of London (LLB), Coll of Law London; *m* 28 Dec 1968 (m dis 19821), Patricia Viviaen (Tricia), da of Michael Joseph Sheridan, of Southampton; 1 s (Toby b 1973), 1 da (Charlotte b 1975); *Career* RNR 1965, cmmnd Sub Lt 1966, Lt 1969, resigned cmmn 1974; slr 1969; asst Litigation slr Coffin Mew & Clover Southampton 1969-70; prosecuting slr Hants CC Portsmouth 1970-72; asst slr Brutton & Co Fareham 1972-73, ptnr 1973-87, sr ptnr 1987-; Dep High/Co ct registrar 1978-; hon sec Hants Inc Law Soc 1987-; fndr chm Hamble Valley Round Table 1975-76, (chm Area I 1981-82); ward cnllr Fareham BC 1978-82; memb Law Soc; *Recreations* foreign travel, photography, golf; *Clubs* Hamble Valley Stick, Meon Valley GC, Grenelefe FL GC; *Style—* James Simpson, Esq; West End Ho, 288 West St, Fareham, Hants PO16 0AJ, (☎ 0329 236171, fax 0329 289915, telex 86875 BRUFAR G)

SIMPSON, (Cortlandt) James Woore; CBE (1956), DSC (1945); s of Rear Adm C H Simpson, CBE (d 1943), of Old Vicarage House, Stoke-by-Nayland, Suffolk, and Edith Octavia, *née* Busby (d 1954); *b* 2 Sept 1911; *Educ* St Ronans Sch, RNC Dartmouth, London Univ (BSc); *m* 1, Lettice Mary, *née* Johnstone; m 2, Ann Margaret, *née* Tooth; m 3, Joan Mary, *née* Cooke; 1 da (Bonella Mary b 1971); m 4, 13 April 1985, (Vanessa) Ann, *née* Heald; *Career* RN: Midshipman 1929, Lt 1934, WWII serv Home and Med Fleets, Cdr 1948, ret 1961; summer expeditions to Greenland 1950 and 1951, ldr Br N Greenland Expedition 1952-54; Polar Medal 1954, RGS Founder's Medal 1955; *Publications* Northice (1957); *Recreations* mountaineering, sailing, fishing; *Clubs* Alpine; *Style—* Cdr James Simpson, CBE, DSC; Lower Lambie, Luxborough, Watchet, Somerset

SIMPSON, Jeremy Miles; s of Gordon Simpson (d 1984), of Glastonbury, and Barbara, *née* Wilkes (d 1976); *b* 25 Nov 1933; *Educ* Malvern, Clare Coll Cambridge (MA); *m* 21 July 1956, Penelope Ann Mary, da of Harvey James (d 1979), of Hayle, Cornwall; 1 s (Mark b 1962), 4 da (Clare b 1957, Rebecca b 1961, Miranda b 1962, Catherine b 1964); *Career* Lt RN 1955-58; md Tan Sad Chair Co 1967-69, chm Giroflex Ltd 1972-86, md Papropack Ltd 1972-86, chm Gordon Russell plc; Freeman City of London 1988, memb Worshipful Co of Furniture Makers; Order of the Finnish Lion (First Class) Finland 1986; *Recreations* family, reading, walking, travel; *Clubs* Utd Oxford and Cambridge; *Style—* Jeremy Simpson, Esq; Gordon Russell plc, Broadway, Worcs WR12 7AD (☎ 0386 858483, fax 0386 852975, telex 338918)

SIMPSON, Very Rev John Arthur; s of Arthur Simpson (d 1958), and Mary Esther, *née* Price (d 1982); *b* 7 June 1933; *Educ* Cathays HS Cardiff, Keble Coll Oxford (BA, MA), Clifton Theol Coll; *m* 15 Aug 1968, Ruth Marian, da of Leo Dibbens (d 1966); 1 s (Damian b 1972), 2 da (Rebecca b 1970, Helen b 1974); *Career* curate: Leyton 1958-59, Christ Church Oprington 1959-62; tutor Oak Hill Coll London 1962-72, vicar Ridge Herts 1972-79, dir Ordinands and Post-Ordination Trg Diocese of St Albans 1975-81, hon canon St Albans Cathedral 1977-79, residentiary canon St Albans and priest i-c of Ridge 1979-81, archdeacon of Canterbury and residentiary canon of Canterbury Cathedral 1981-86, dean of Canterbury 1986-, dir Ecclesiastical Insur Off plc 1983-; chm (Canterbury) Cathedral Gifts Ltd 1986-, govrs Kings Sch Canterbury 1986-; *Recreations* travel, theatre, opera; *Clubs* Athenaeum; *Style—* The Very Rev the Dean of Canterbury; The Deanery, Caterbury, Kent CT1 2EP(☎ 0227 65983); Cathedral House, 11 The Precincts, Caterbury CT1 2EH (☎ 0227 762862)

SIMPSON, (Robert) John Blantyre; MBE (1954), TD (1947, and three clasps), WS; Alexander Russell Simpson (d 1928), of Edinburgh, and Dorothy, *née* Lowe (d 1974); *b* 28 August 1914; *Educ* Rugby,Magdalene Coll Oxford (MA), Edinburgh Univ (LLB); *m* 1, 7 Oct 1939, Helen Mary Radmore, da of William Personal Miller (d 1966), of Warwicks; m 2, 2 April 1962, Barbara Helen, da of John Macrobert (d 1949), of Paisley; 1 s (Michael John Russell b 1941), 1 da (Elizabeth Mary Darley b 1948); *Career* Lt-Col Royal Scots (TA) 1935-60; writer to HM Signet (ret): sec Highlands and Islands Educn Tst 1958-; sec Soc in Scotland for Propagating Christian Knowledge 1958; gov and hon sec St Columba's Hospice 1971, chm The Royal Scots Museum Tst 1959; dir The Royal Scots Regtl Shop, chm Scottish Veterans Garden City Assoc 1965; dir and hon sec Gem and Jar Ltd; Belgian Croix Militaire; *Recreations* fishing, gardening; *Clubs* New (Edinburgh), The Royal Scots, Hon Co of Edinburgh Golfers; *Style—* R J B Simson,Esq, MBE, TD, WS; 6 Belgrave Crescent, Edinburgh EH4 3AL (☎ 031 332 5722); Reef, Glenfinnan, Invernesshire PH37 4LT (☎ 039 783 291)

SIMPSON, Lt-Col John Rowton; TD (1963), DL (1972); s of Lt Col Maurice Rowton Simpson, OBE, TD, DL (d 1981), of Leicester, and Renee Claire, *née* Lafitte; *b* 19 Sept 1926; *Educ* Rugby, Magdelene Coll Cambridge (MA, LLM); *m* 8 Oct 1959, Roxane Eveline, da of William Pickford (d 1984), of Leicester; 2 s (Jeremy b 17 Nov 1963, Matthew b 29 Sept 1966) 1 da (Lucy b 28 Dec 1970); *Career* Coldstream Guards 1944, cmmnd 2 Lt Gordon Highlanders 1945, Lt Sierra Leone Regt 1946 (Capt 1947), transferred to reserve 1948, Maj RA TA 1958 (Lt 1951, Capt 1954), RE TA 1961 (Lt Col 1965), Sherwood Foresters 1966, reserve RE 1968; slr 1953, ptnr Herbert Simpson & Co 1960; sr ptnr: Stone & Simpson 1978, Harvey Ingram Stone & Simpson 1988-; memb TAVR Assoc E Mids 1958-; hon sec Westleigh RFC 1954-59, Leicestershire Rugby Union 1959-78 (pres 1979, 1980, 1985); memb RFU ctee 1968- (pres 1988), capt Leicestershire GC 1972, vice chm Leicestershire Sports & Recreation Advsy Cncl 1976-, chm Cadet Ctee TAVR Assoc 1985-, chm City of Leicester Sport and Recreation Advsy Cncl 1976-88; Freeman of The City of London, memb Worshipful Co of Framework Knitters; memb Law Soc; *Recreations* rugby football, golf; *Clubs* E India; *Style*— Lt-Col John R Simpson, TD, DL; 16 Knighton Grange Rd, Leics, LE2 2LE (☎ 0533 705753); 20 New Walk, Leics, LE1 6TX (☎ 0533 545454, fax 0533 554559)

SIMPSON, Lady Juliet; da of late 4 Earl of Cranbrook by 2 w, Fidelity (*see Dowager Countess of Cranbrook*); *b* 1934; *m* 1958 (m dis 1970), Charles Colin Simpson, TD; 2 s (Charles b 1962, Edward b 1965), 2 da (Fidelity b 1960, Amanda b 1964); *Style*— Lady Juliet Simpson; The White House, Rooks Hill, Underriver, Sevenoaks, Kent

SIMPSON, Keppel Moore; s of George William Simpson (d 1983), of Liverpool, and Ethel Annie, *née* Moore (d 1975); *b* 10 August 1933; *Educ* Abergele GS, Univ of Liverpool (B Eng); *m* 7 April 1956, Barbara Pauline, da of Lt-Col Wesley Thomas Lee, of Chesham Bois, Buck; 1 s (Mark b 1958), 3 da (Philippa (Mrs Soundy) b 1960, Caroline (Mrs Baines) b 1962, Amanda (Mrs Myatt) b 1965); *Career* Sub Lt RN 1953-55; dir PA Int Mgmnt Conslts Ltd 1976-84, chm PA Int Mgmnt Conslts Inc 1980-84; dir: Sundridge Park Mgmnt Centre Ltd 1979-84, PA Int Hldgs Ltd 1982-84, Yeoward Bros Ltd 1983-, Reginald Watts Assoc Ltd 1985-, Hedsor Ltd 1988; chm: Karran Prods Ltd 1987-, Central Land Charges Co Ltd; dep chm Chesham Prep Sch Tst Ltd, fndr memb Workaid; CEng, MIEE, FIMC; *Clubs* Naval, Flyfishers; *Style*— Keppel Simpson, Esq; Galloway House, High St, Amersham, Bucks HP7 0ED (☎ 0494 724 984, 0494 728 659, fax 0494 721 785, car tel 0860 511 180)

SIMPSON, Lady; Maria Teresa; da of late Captain John Sutherland Harvey, of Romerillo, Biarritz; *m* 1945, as his 2 w, Sir Cyril Simpson, 3 and last Bt, stockbroker (d 1981); *Style*— Lady Simpson; Corchester Towers, Corbridge, Northumberland, (☎ 066 14 2246)

SIMPSON, Rear Adm Michael Frank; CB (1985); s of Robert Michael Simpson and Florence Mabel Simpson; *b* 27 Sept 1928; *Educ* King Edward VI Sch Bath, RNEC Manadon (CEng); *m* 1973, Sandra, *née* Cliff; 2 s, 1 da; *Career* joined RN 1944; Air Engr Offr 1956; serv: FAA Sqdns, cruisers and carriers; US Navy 1964-66; Ark Royal 1970-72; supt RN Aircraft Yard Fleetlands 1978-80; Cdre RN Barracks Portsmouth 1981-83; dir-gen Aircraft (Navy) 1983-85; dir Field Aircraft of Croydon 1985-, md Field Airmotive Ltd 1988-, chm Field Somet Ltd 1988-, dir Field Aviation Ltd 1988-; *Style*— Rear-Adm Michael F Simpson; Keppel, Blackhills, Esher, Surrey KT10 9JW

SIMPSON, Norman; s of James Robert Simpson (d 1942), of Warsop Notts, and Alice May Lody *née* Eaton (d 1982); *b* 22 Sept 1933; *Educ* Warsop Infants Secondary Sch, Mansfield Technical Sch, Mansfield Sch of Art, Notts Sch of Architects (External RIBA); *m* 2 Sept 1958, Margaret Audry, da of Frederick Israel Woodhouse (d 1969), of Sutton in Ashfield, Notts; *Career* Assoc Royal Inst Br Architects 1964; Dip in landscape design (Trent) 1971; Assoc landscape Inst 1976; ARCUK 1964; Hon conslt Architect to The Amatuer Swimming Assoc; Civic Tst Award 1968 and Countryside Award 1970 for West Burton 'A' Power Station; Sports Cncl Mgmnt award 1973 and 1978; (Nat Water Sports Centre Holme Pier Pony); Bldg for Disabled Awards 1976, Altrincham Leisure Centre; has won various other awards; Assoc of the Inst of Baths and recreationi mgmnt 1972; memb: The Assoc of Consulting Architects 1980, The Assoc for the Studies in Conservation of historic Bldgs 1981, fellow RIBA 1968; FBIM 1982; *Recreations* photography, rotary club work; *Clubs* Rotary (Nottingham North) (past pres); *Style*— Norman Simpson, Esq; 68A Front St, Arnold, Nottingham (☎ 0602 670107)

SIMPSON, Ven Rennie; LVO (1974); o s of Doctor Taylor Simpson (d 1966), and May Simpson (d 1962); *b* 13 Jan 1920; *Educ* Lambeth (MA), Kelham Theol Coll; *m* 30 April 1949, Margaret, da of Herbert Hardy (d 1957), of Yorks; 1 s (Jonathan Michael b 1961), 1 da (Katherine Mary b 1957); *Career* chaplain RNVR 1953-55; curate S Elmsall Yorks 1945-49; succentor: Blackburn Cathedral 1949-52, St Paul's Cathedral London 1952-58 (jr cardinal 1954-55, sr 1955-58); vicar John Keble Church Mill Hill 1958-63, precentor Westminster Abbey 1963-74, vice dean Chester Cathedral 1974-78, archdeacon of Macclesfield and rector of Gawsworth 1978-85; dep priest to HM the Queen 1956-67, priest in ordinary to HM the Queen 1967-74, chaplain to HM the Queen 1982-; life govr Imperial Cancer Research Fndn 1963; sub-prelate OStJ 1973-; Freeman City of London 1955, Liveryman Worshipful Co of Wax Chandlers; Hon Chaplain Worshipful Soc of Apothecaries 1934-85; Jt Hon Tres Corpn of Sons of the Clergy 1967-74; *Style*— The Ven Rennie Simpson, LVO; Gawsworth Cottage, 18 Roseberry Green, North Stainley, nr Ripon, North Yorks HG4 3HZ (☎ 0765 85286)

SIMPSON, Robin Muschamp Garry; QC (1971); s of Ronald Simpson (d 1957), of Aldeburgh, Suffolk, and Lila, *née* Muschamp (d 1951); *b* 19 June 1927; *Educ* Charterhouse, Peterhouse Cambridge (MA); *m* 1, 13 Oct 1956 (m dis 1968), Avril Carolyn, da of Dr J E M Harrisson, of Bovey Tracey, S Devon; 1 s (Charles b 17 Oct 1961); m 2, 23 March 1968, Faith Mary, da of Dr F G Laughton-Scott, of 25 Upper Wimpole St, London W1; 1 s (Hugo b 14 March 1972), 2 da (Anna b 13 Aug 1963, Kate b 14 Oct 1968); *Career* barr Middle Temple 1951; memb Central Criminal Ct Bar Mess, practising SE circuit, rec Crown Ct 1976-86, master bench Middle Temple 1979, appeal steward Br Boxing Bd of Control; *Recreations* real tennis, sailing; *Clubs* MCC, Garrick, Aldeburgh Yacht; *Style*— Robin Simpson, Esq, QC; 9 Drayton Gdns, London SW10 9RY (☎ 01 373 3284); 3 Raymond Bldgs, Grays Inn, London WC1

SIMPSON, Roderick Wykeham; s of Dr John Emerson Simpson of 23 Knebworth Rd, Bexhill-on-Sea, Sussex, and Margot Cobbett, *née* Hughes; *b* 3 Feb 1941; *Educ* The Edinburgh Acad; *m* 4 June 1966, Valerie Patricia Jean, da of Frederick John Taylor Huggett of Shaftesbury, Dorset; 2 s (Jeremy John Cobbett b 1971, Michael Giles Cobbett b 1976); *Career* Peat Marwick Mitchell & Co London 1959-69, dir and vice-pres Operations & Aviation Data Serv Inc Kansas USA 1969-71, asst md Gardner Merchant Ltd Surrey 1971-; dir: Kelvin Int Servs Ltd, SNSA France, Lockhart Catering Equipment Ltd, Vendability Ltd, Servosnax Inc USA, Superior Restaurant Equipment Inc USA, CERES France, Interserve SA Belgium, Personal Restaurant Systems GmbH Germany, Grooms Coffee House Ltd, Gardner Merchant Keyline Travel Ltd; princ ptnr Aeroplan Servs; MICAS 1965; *Books* The General Aviation Handbook (3 vols 1981, 1982, 1984), numerous papers published on aviation historical and technical subjects; *Recreations* photography, private flying, aviation histrical res; *Style*— Roderick Simpson, Esq; The Haven, South Close Green, Merstham, Surrey RH1 3DU (☎ 0737 42 527); Kenley House, Kenley Lane, Kenley, Surrey CR2 5YR (☎ 01 763 1212, fax 01 763 1044, car tel 0836 526 478, telex 926717)

SIMPSON, Stanhope Rowton; CBE (1953); s of Herbert Simpson DL (d 1932); *b* 7 May 1903; *Educ* Rossall Sch, Magdalene Coll Cambridge; *m* 1930, Evelyn Constance, nee Adams; 1 s, 3 da; *Career* barr 1933, Sudan Political Serv 1925-42, registrar-gen and cmmr of Lands Sudan 1943-53, Land Tenure Adv Colonial Off and Miny of Overseas Devpt 1953-69; *Style*— Stanhope Simpson Esq, CBE; 065 Collington Ave, Bexhill-on-Sea, E Sussex (☎ 0424 211858)

SIMPSON, Sir William James; s of William Simpson, and Margaret, *née* Nimmo; *b* 1920; *Educ* Victoria Sch, Falkirk Tech Sch; *m* 1942, Catherine McEwan Nichol; 1 s; *Career* WWII 1939-45, Sgt Argyll and Sutherland Highlanders; gen sec AUEW (foundry section) 1967-75, memb Race Relations Bd 1967-74, chm Labs Pty 1972-73, memb Flixborough Inquiry 1973-74, chm Advsy Ctee on Asbestos 1976-79, former chm Health and Safety Cmmn; kt 1984; *Books* Labour - The Unions and The Party (1973); *Style*— Sir William Simpson; 11 Strude Howe, Alva, Clacks, Scotland (☎ 0259 60859)

SIMPSON-ORLEBAR, Michael Keith Orlebar; CMG (1982); s of Aubrey Orlebar Simpson (d 1933), and Laura Violet, *née* Keith-Jones; *b* 5 Feb 1932; *Educ* Eton, Christ Church Oxford (MA); *m* 19 April 1964, Rosita, da of Ignacio Duarte (d 1959); 2 s (Aubrey b 1965, Edward b 1966), 1 da (Charlotte b 1972); *Career* Nat Serv Lt KRRC 1950-51; Dip Serv 1954-: Tehran 1955-57, FO 1957- 62, Bogota 1962-65, FCO 1966-68, Paris 1969-72, Tehran 1972-76, FCO 1977-80, min Rome 1980-83, head Br interest section Tehran 1983-85, ambassador Lisbon 1985-; *Recreations* gardening, fishing; *Clubs* Travellers'; *Style*— HE Michael Simpson-Orlebar, CMG; British Embassy, Lisbon, Portugal (☎ 010 351 661191)

SIMS, Bernard John; s of John Sims (d 1949), of London, and Minnie, *née* Everitt (d 1962); *b* 13 May 1915; *Educ* Wimbledon Coll London, LSE (LLB); *m* 27 April 1963, Elizabeth Margaret Eileen, da of Philip Edward Filbee (d 1960), of St Leonards on Sea, Sussex; *Career* WWII: RA 1940-42, RAOC 1942-45, SO HQ AA Cmd 1943-45, Capt 1944, SO Northumbrian Dist Northern Cmd 1945; slr 1938; lectr Law Soc's Sch of Law 1945-47, sr legal asst Bd of Inland Revenue 1947-53, legal advsr Indust & Commercial Fin Corpn 1953-61, chief examiner and moderator Law Soc 1953-81; consulted Encyclopaedia of Forms and Precedents 1965-; chm editorial bd: Simon's Taxes 1970-, Capital Taxes Encyclopeadia 1976-; hon tres Church of Holy Redeemer and St Thomas More Chelsea; Freeman City of London 1951, memb Worshipful Co of Slrs; memb Law Soc 1938, FIT 1965; Knight Cdr of the Equestrian Order of the Holy Sepulchre 1967; *Books* Controls on Company Finance (1958), Estate Duty Changes (1969), Capital Duty (1975), Halsbury's Laws of England (contrib, fourth edn 1983), UK Tax Guide 1988 (ed of chapter on stamp duties), Sergeant and Sims on Stamp Duties (1988); *Recreations* music; *Clubs* City Livery, Lansdowne; *Style*— Bernard Sims, Esq; 89 Dovehouse St, Chelsea, London SW3 6JZ (☎ 01 352 1798)

SIMS, Frank; s of Frank Sims (d 1986), and Doris Elizabeth, *née* Hayes; *b* 21 July 1943; *Educ* Hitchen GS, Sheffield Univ (BA); *m* 29 Oct 1966, Jean Caroline, da of Edward Francis Whitworth; 1 s (Richard b 1974), 1 da (Claire b 1972); *Career* CA BDO Binder Hamlyn; Freeman City of London 1977, memb Worshipful Co of Glovers; FCA 1970; *Recreations* golf; *Clubs* Wig and Pen; *Style*— Frank Sims, Esq; 52 Russell Rd, Buckhurst Hill, Essex IG9 5QE (☎ 01 505 0019); BDO Binder Hamlyn, 8 St Bride St, London EC4A 4DA (☎ 01 353 3020, fax 01 583 0031, telex 24276)

SIMS, Geoffrey Donald; OBE (1971); s of Albert Edward Hope Sims, and Jessie Elizabeth Sims; *b* 13 Dec 1926; *Educ* Wembley Co GS, Imperial Coll of Sci and Technol (BSc, MSc, PhD, DIC); *m* 9 April 1949, Pamela Audrey, da of Thomas Edwin Richings; 1 s (Graham b 12 Jan 1950), 2 da (Patricia b 7 Feb 1953, Anne b 16 Sept 1960); *Career* res physicist GEC Wembley 1948-54, seconded to work with Prof D Gabor (Nobel Laureate) Imperial Coll 1950-54, sr sci offr UKAEA Harwell, lectr (later sr lectr) dept electrical engrg UCL 1956-63; Univ of Southampton: prof and head dept electronics 1963-74, dean faculty of engrg and applied sci 1967-70, sr dep vice-chllr 1970-72; vice-chllr Univ of Sheffield 1974-; memb: Br Library Organising Ctee 1971-73, Annan Ctee on the Future of Broadcasting 1974-77; chm engrg advsy ctee BBC 1981-, vice-chm Br Cncl ctee Int Cooperation Higher Educn 1985- (memb 1981-), hon dep tres Assoc Commonwealth Univs 1984-, memb Conf Euro Rectors Perm Ctee 1981, pres liaison ctee Rectors Confs of Memb States of Euro Communities 1987-; fell Midland Chapter Woodard Sch 1977-, Custos Worksop Coll 1984-, Guardian of the Standard of Wrought Plate within the Town of Sheffield 1984-, Capital Burgess Sheffield Church Burgesses Tst 1988-89 (memb 1984-); Hon DSc Univ of Southampton 1980, Hon LLD Univ of Dundee 1987; ARCS (physics) 1947, ARCS (mathematics) 1948, FIEE 1963, FEng 1980, FCGI 1980; *Books* Microwave Tubes and Semiconductor Devices (with I M Stephenson, 1963), Variational Techniques in Electromagnetism (1965); *Recreations* golf, travel, music; *Clubs* Athenaeum; *Style*— Prof Geoffrey Sims, OBE; Vice-Chllr's Lodge, 408 Fulwood Rd, Sheffield S10 3GG (☎ 0742 301 400); Vice-Chllr's Off, Univ of Sheffield, Western Bank, Sheffield S10 2TN (☎ 0742 768 555, fax 0742 768 496, telex 547216 UGSHEF G)

SIMS, John Haesaert Mancel; s of Capt Harold Mancel Sims (d 1958), of London, and Jeanie Emilie Anne, *née* Haesaert, (d 1965); *b* 16 Dec 1929; *Educ* Highfield Sch Wandsworth, Brixton Sch of Bldg; *Career* Nat Serv RE 1948-50; various appts with quantity surveyors firms in private practice 1950-73, sole princ in private practice as bldg contracts conslt, lectr writer and arbitrator 1973-, author of numerous articles on bldg contacts for Building 1975-; Freeman City of London 1981, Liveryman Worshipful Co of Arbitrators 1982; ARICS 1954, FRICS 1967, FCIArb 1970; *Books* with Vincent Powell-Smith: Building Contract Claims (1983, second edn 1988), Contract Documentation for Contractors (1985), Determination and Suspension of Contruction Contracts (1985), The JCT Management Contract: A Practical Guide (1988), Construction Arbitrations (1989); *Recreations* classical music, choral singing, reading;

Clubs Wig and Pen; *Style*— John H M Sims, Esq; 15 Cheyne Place, London SW3 4HH (☎ 01 353 0643); 7 Gray's Inn Sq, London WC1R 5BG (☎ 01 242 0572, fax 01 405 2853, telex 261 524 BHB G)

SIMS, Neville William; MBE (1974); s of William Ellis Sims (d 1954), of Whitchurch, Cardiff, and Ethel Stacey Colley, *née* Inman (d 1980); *b* 15 June 1933; *Educ* Penarth Co Sch; *m* 2 April 1964, Jennifer Ann, da of Horace George Warwick, of Rhiwbina, Cardiff; 2 s (Jeremy b 1971, Matthew b 1981), 2 da (Heather b 1973, Caroline b 1980); *Career* articles with T H Trump, qualified CA 1957, ptnr Ernst & Whinney 1960-85 (managing ptnr Cardiff off 1974-84, ret 1985), conslt Watts Gregory & Daniel 1986-, dir Compact Cases Ltd Caerphilly 1986-; pres S Wales Soc of CAs 1977-78, cncl memb ICAEW 1981-, memb Welsh regnl bd memb Homeowners Friendly Soc 1984-88; chm: Wales area Young Cons 1960-63, Barry Cons Assoc 1962-72; hon tres: Cardiff Central Cons Assoc 1987-, YWCA Centre Cardiff 1963-70; chm govrs Howell's Sch Llandaff Cardiff 1981-; FICA; *Recreations* theatre, music, gardening, walking; *Clubs* Cardiff Business, Cardiff and County; *Style*— Neville Sims, Esq, MBE; The Chimes, 15 Westminster Cres, Cyncoed, Cardiff CF2 6SE (☎ 0222 753424, fax 0222 383022)

SIMS, Roger Edward; MP (C) Chislehurst 1974-; s of Herbert William Sims (d 1981), of London, and Annie Amy, *née* Savidge (d 1987); *b* 27 Jan 1930; *Educ* City Boys' GS Leicester, St Olave's GS Tower Bridge London; *m* 1956, Angela, da of John Robert Mathews (d 1951); 2 s (Matthew, Toby), 1 da (Virginia); *Career* advsr(formerly dept mangr) Dodwell & Co Ltd 1962-, dir Inchcape Int; parly priv sec to Home Sec 1979-83, vice-chm Health and Social Services Ctee; chm 1912 Club; JP Bromley 1960-72; *Recreations* swimming, singing (Royal Choral Soc); *Clubs* Bromley Cons; *Style*— Roger Sims Esq, MP; House of Commons, London SW1 (☎ 01 219 5000); 68 Towncourt Crescent, Petts Wood, Oprington, Kent BR5 1PJ (☎ 0689 25676)

SIMSON, Peregrine Anthony Litton; s of Brig Ernest Clive Litton Simson, of Aston Rowant, Oxon, and Daphne Camilla Marian, *née* Todhunter (d 1985); *b* 10 April 1944; *Educ* Charterhouse, Worcester Coll Oxford (BA); *m* 6 May 1967 (m dis 1979), Caroline Basina, da of Frank Hosier (d 1965), of Wexcombe Manor, Marlborough, Wilts; 1 s (Christian Edward Litton b 9 April 1970), 1 da (Camilla Basina Litton b 12 July 1972); *Career* slr; ptnr: Clifford-Turner 1972-87, Clifford Chance (merged firm of Clifford Turner and Coward Chance) 1987-; Liveryman Worshipful Co of Slrs 1974; memb Law Soc 1970; *Recreations* shooting, tennis, travel; *Clubs* Annabel's, Hurlingham; *Style*— Peregrine Simson, Esq; Corn Hall, Bures St Mary, Suffolk; 59 Waterford Rd, London SW6; Clifford Chance, Blackfriars House, 19 New Bridge St, London EC4V 6BY (☎ 01 353 0211)

SINCLAIR; *see*: Alexander-Sinclair

SINCLAIR, Lady (Margaret) Alison; raised to the rank of an Earl's da 1948; 3 da of Rev Canon the Hon Charles Augustus Sinclair (d 1944, s of 16 Earl of Caithness), and Mary Ann, *née* Harman (d 1938); *b* 29 Nov 1910; *Style*— Lady Alison Sinclair; Wych Elm, Kennington, Oxford (☎ 0865 735856)

SINCLAIR, Dr Andrew Annandale; s of Stanley Charles Sinclair, CBE, (d 1973), and Kathleen, *née* Nash-Webber; *b* 21 Jan 1935; *Educ* Eton, Trinity Coll Cambridge, Harvard Univ, Columbia Univ; *m* 1, (m dis 1971), Marianne Alexandre; 2 s (Timon Alexandre, Merlin George); m 2, (m dis 1984), Miranda Seymour; m 3, 25 July 1984, Sonia, Lady Melchett; *Career* Ensign Coldstream Gds 1953-55; ed and publisher Lorrimer Publishing 1968-87, md Timon Films 1968-; FRSL 1970, FSAH 1970; *Books* novels: The Breaking of Bumbo (1957), My Friend Judas (1958), The Project (1960), The Hallelujah Bum (1963), The Raker (1964), Gog (1967), Magog (1972), A Patriot for Hire (1978), The Facts in the Case of E A Poe (1980), Beau Bumbo (1985), King Ludd (1988); non-fiction: Prohibition The Era of Excess (1962), The Available Man The Life Behind the Mask of Warren Gamaliel Harding (1965), The Better Half The Emancipation of the American Woman (1965), A Concise History of the United States (1967), The Last of the Best The Aristocracy of Europe in the Twentieth Century (1969), Che Guevara (1970), Dylan Thomas Poet of His People (1975), The Savage A History of Misunderstanding (1977), Jack A Biography of Jack London (1977), John Ford (1979), Corsair The Life of J Pierpoint Morgan (1981), The Other Victoria The Princess Royal and the Great Game of Europe (1981), The Red and the Blue (1986), Speigel (1987), War Like a Wasp (1989), The War Decade (1989); *Recreations* visiting ruins; *Clubs* Groucho's; *Style*— Dr Andrew Sinclair; 16 Tite St, London SW3 4HZ (☎ 01 352 7645)

SINCLAIR, Hon Angus John; s of 1 Viscount Thurso, KT, CMG, PC (d 1970); *b* 1925; *Educ* Eton, New Coll Oxford; *m* 1, 1955 (m dis 1967), Pamela Karen, da of Dallas Bower; m 2, 1968, Judith Anne Percy; 1 s; *Career* WWII Lt Scots Gds 1944-47, NW Europe 1945; BBC 1950-54, Nigerian Broadcasting Corpn 1954-58; Central Off of Info 1959-85; author: Poetry, radio features; *Clubs* Pratt's; *Style*— The Hon Angus Sinclair

SINCLAIR, Lady Bridget Ellinor; da (by 1 m) of late 6 Earl Fortescue; *b* 1927; *m* 1952, Wing Cdr Gordon Leonard Sinclair, DFC; 2 s (Alan b 1956, Robert b 1965), 2 da (Fiona (Mrs Julian Smith) b 1958, Joanna b 1963); *Style*— Lady Bridget Sinclair; Fairwood House, Great Durnford, Salisbury, Wiltshire SP4 6BD (☎ 0980 23372)

SINCLAIR, Charles James Francis; s of Sir George Evelyn Sinclair, CMG, OBE, of Carlton Rookery, Saxmundham, Suffolk, and Katharine Jane, *née* Burdekin (d 1971); *b* 4 April 1948; *Educ* Winchester, Magdalen Coll Oxford (BA); *m* 15 June 1974, Nicola, da of Maj W R Bayliss, RM; 2 s (Jeremy b 1977, Robert b 1979); *Career* CA 1974, Dearden Farrow CAs London 1970-75, fin accountant Assoc Newspaper Gp 1975; Assoc Newspapers Hldgs plc: asst md 1986, dep md 1987, md 1988, gp md Daily Mail and Gen Tst plc 1989; chm tstees Minack Theatre Tst (Porthcurno Cornwall); FCA 1980; *Recreations* opera, fishing, skiing; *Clubs* The Athenaeum, Vincents; *Style*— Charles Sinclair, Esq; New Carmelite House, Carmelite St, London EC4Y OJA (☎ 01 353 5941, fax 01 583 3920)

SINCLAIR, 17 Lord (**S** *c* 1449, confirmed 1488-9); **Charles Murray Kennedy St Clair**; LVO (1953); s of 16 Lord Sinclair, MVO, JP (d 1957); 1 Lord resigned the Earldoms of Orkney and Caithness to the crown 1470, 10 Lord obtained Charter under Gt Seal 1677 confirming his honours with remainders to male heirs whatsoever; *b* 21 June 1914; *Educ* Eton, Magdalene Coll Cambridge; *m* 1968, Anne Lettice, da of Sir Richard Cotterell, 5 Bt, CBE, TD; 1 s, 2 da (Hon Laura b 1972, Hon Annabel b 1973); *Heir* s, Master of Sinclair; *Career* Maj Coldstream Gds; memb Queen's Body Guard for Scotland (Royal Co of Archers), Portcullis Pursuivant of Arms 1949-57, York Herald 1957-68, hon genealogist to Royal Victorian Order 1960-68, an extra equerry to HM Queen Elizabeth The Queen Mother 1953-; Lord-Lieut Dumfries and Galloway (Dist of Stewartry) 1982- (Vice Lord-Lieut 1977-82, DL Kirkcudbrights 1969), rep peer for Scotland 1959-63; *Clubs* New (Edinburgh); *Style*— The Rt Hon the Lord Sinclair, LVO; Knocknalling, St John's Town of Dalry, Castle Douglas, Kirkcudbrightshire DG7 3ST (☎ (064 43) 221)

SINCLAIR, Sir Clive Marles; s of George William Carter Sinclair, and Thora Edith Ella, *née* Marles; *b* 30 July 1940; *Educ* Highgate Sch, St George's Coll Weybridge; *m* 1962 (m dis 1985) Ann, *née* Trevor Briscoe; 2 s, 1 da; *Career* ed Bernards (publishers) 1958-61, chm Sinclair Res Ltd 1979- (Sinclair Radionics 1962-79, produced pocket TV), fndr Sinclair Browne (publishers) 1981 (annual Sinclair Prize for fiction); chm: Br MENSA, Cambridge Computer Ltd 1986-; visiting fell Robinson Coll Cambridge; Hon DSc Bath 1983, Hon DSc Warwick 1983, Hon DSc Heriot Watt 1983, hon fell Imperial Coll of Sci and Technol 1984, hon fell UMIST 1984, Mullard Award Royal Soc 1984; kt 1983; *Publications* Practical Transistor Receivers (1959), Br Semiconductor Survey (1963); *Recreations* music, poetry, mathematics, science; *Clubs* Carlton; *Style*— Sir Clive Sinclair; 18 Shepherd House, 5 Shepherd St, London W1Y 7LD (☎ 01 408 0199)

SINCLAIR, David Grant; s of Leslie Sinclair (d 1978), of London, and Beatrice Zena, *née* Samuel (d 1979); *b* 12 Feb 1948; *Educ* Latymer Upper Sch; *m* 7 June 1970, Susan Carol, da of Alexander Merkin (d 1963), of London; 2 s (Alexander James b 1972, Julian Lloyd b 1974); 1 da (Olivia Lesley b 1982); *Career* fndr and sr ptnr Sinclair & Co 1972-, exec chm Summer Int plc; non-exec chm: Lifehomes plc, Master Fin Servs Ltd; conslt City and Westminster Fin plc; recognised expert in forensic accounting; FCA 1972; *Recreations* charity work, international causes, travel, swimming; *Style*— David G Sinclair, Esq; Orchard Close, Beechwood Avenue, London N3 3AU (☎ 01 346 2524); 1 Great Cumberland Place, London W1 (☎ 01 723 0093, fax 01 706 3719); car ☎ 0836 261691

SINCLAIR, Eldon McCuaig; s of Maj Charles Eldon Sinclair, MC (d 1956), of Toronto, Canada, and Margaret, *née* McCuaig (d 1929); *b* 13 Mar 1928; *Educ* Upper Canada Coll, Trinity Coll Sch, Univ of Toronto (BASC); *m* 13 Feb 1970, Judith Ellen, da of Albert Rule (d 1965), of Toronto, Canada; 1 s (Joseph McCuaig b 1974); *Career* Unilever: int mgmnt trainee UK and Canada 1950-52, brand mangr Canada 1952-54; Leo Burnett Co Inc (advtg): account exec Canada 1954-56, vice pres account supervisor USA 1956-58, pres in Canada 1958-65, chm and md UK 1965-70, exec vice pres int 1970-73; EM Sinclair Conslts Ltd 1974-86; chm and md UK Storwal Int Inc 1986-; memb bd govrs: Lockers Park Sch Herts, Trinity Coll Sch; chm Dunford Novelists Assoc, memb exec ctee Southern Writers Assoc; *Recreations* field sports, writing; *Clubs* Denham GC; *Style*— Eldon Sinclair, Esq; 16 Chester St, London SW1 (☎ 01 235 4177); Storwal International Home Park, Kings Langley, Herts WD4 8LZ (☎ 092 776 0411, fax 092 776 7136), telex 923273 ELMAR G)

SINCLAIR, Sir George Evelyn; CMG (1956), OBE (1950); s of Francis Sinclair (d 1953), of Chynance, St Buryan, Cornwall; *b* 6 Nov 1912; *Educ* Abingdon Sch, Pembroke Coll Oxford (MA); *m* 1, 1941, Katharine Jane (d 1971), da of Beauford Burdekin (d 1963) of Sydney, NSW, and Mrs K P Burdekin (d 1964), of The Firs, Marlesford, Suffolk; 1 s, 3 da; m 2, Mary Violet, wid of G L Sawday; *Career* WWII RWAFF (W Africa), Temp Maj; entered Colonial Serv 1936, Colonial Off 1943-45, sec Elliot Cmmn on Higher Educn in W Africa 1943-45, Gold Coast 1945-55, regnl offr Trans-Volta Togoland 1952-55, dep govr Cyprus 1955-60, ret 1961; political work in UK and overseas 1960-, memb Wimbledon Borough Cncl 1962-65; MP (C) Dorking 1964-1979; vice-pres Intermediate Technol Devpt Gp 1966-79 (dir 1979-82), fndr tstee Physically Handicapped & Able Bodied; memb: bd Christian Aid 1973-78, cncl Oxford Soc 1982-, cncl Overseas Servs Resettlement Bureau; fndr memb Human Rights Tst 1971-74; memb Assoc of Governing Bodies of Public Schs (chm 1979-84); memb bd of govrs: Abingdon Sch 1971-88 (chm 1973-80), Felixstowe Coll 1980-87, Campian Sch Athens 1983-; chm Independent Schs Jt Cncl 1980-83; tstee Runnymede Trust 1969-75; conslt: UN Fund for Population Affrs, Int Planned Parenthood Fedn; special advsr Global Ctee of Parliamentarians on Population and Devpt; chm 1988-89 UK consultative ctee for Oxford Conf 1988 of Global Forum of Spiritual and Parly Ldrs on Human Survival; Hon fell Pembroke Coll Oxford; kt 1960; *Recreations* golf, fishing; *Clubs* Athenaeum, Royal Cwlth Soc; *Style*— Sir George Sinclair, CMG, OBE; Carlton Rookery, Saxmundham, Suffolk IP17 2NN (☎ 0728 2217)

SINCLAIR, Hugh Macdonald; s of Col Hugh Montogomerie Sinclair, CB, CMG, CBE, and Rosalie, da of Sir John Jackson, CVO; *b* 4 Feb 1910; *Educ* Winchester, Oriel Coll Oxford (DM, DSc); *Career* hon nutrition conslt Control Cmmn for Germany 1945-47 (Brig), dir Laboratory of Human Nutrition Oxford Univ and reader in human nutrition 1947-57; dir Int Inst of Human Nutrition 1972-, visiting prof of food sci Reading Univ 1970-80; fell Magdalen Coll Oxford 1937-80 (emeritus fell 1980-), ed-in-chief Int Encyclopaedia of Food and Nutrition (24 vols, 1969), author of numerous papers on nutrition and brain metabolism; Gotch Prize 1933; Rolleston Prize 1938; FRCP, FRSC; US Medal of Freedom with Silver Palm, Offr Order of Orange Nassau; *Recreations* medical history, horticulture; *Clubs* Athenaeum, MCC; *Style*— Dr Hugh Sinclair; Lady Place, Sutton Courtenay, Abingdon, Oxon (☎ 0235 848 246)

SINCLAIR, Sir Ian McTaggart; KCMG (1977, CMG 1972), QC (1979); s of John Sinclair (d 1950), of Whitecraigs, Renfrewshire, and Margaret Wilson Gardner, *née* Love (d 1965); *b* 14 Jan 1926; *Educ* Merchiston Castle Sch, King's Coll Cambridge (BA, LLB); *m* 24 April 1954, Barbara Elizabeth, da of Stanley Lenton (d 1982), of Grimsby; 2 s (Andrew b 1958, Philip b 1962), 1 da (Jane b 1956); *Career* Intelligence Corps 1944-47; called to the Bar Middle Temple 1952 (bencher 1980); entered Dip Serv 1950; legal cnsllr: NY and Washington 1964-67, FCO 1967-71; dep legal advsr FCO 1971-72, second legal advsr 1973-75, legal advsr 1976-84; barr 1984-; memb Int Law Cmmn 1981-86; assoc memb Institut de Droit Int 1983-87 (memb 1987-); FRGS 1987; *Books* Vienna Convention on the Law of Treaties (1973, second edn 1984), International Law Commission (1987); *Recreations* golf, bird-watching, reading; *Clubs* Athenaeum; *Style*— Sir Ian Sinclair, KCMG, QC; 2 Hare Court, Temple, London EC4Y 7BH (☎ 01 583 1770, telex 27193 LINLAW)

SINCLAIR, Sir John Rollo Norman Blair; 9 Bt (NS 1704), of Dunbeath, Caithness; s of Sir Ronald Sinclair, 8 Bt, TD, JP, DL (d 1952), and Reba Blair, *née* Inglis (later Hildreth) (d 1985); sis cr Life Peeress 1970, Baroness Masham, of Ilton (*qv* Countess of Swinton); *b* 4 Nov 1928; *Educ* Wellington; *Heir* cous, Patrick Sinclair; *Career* Lt Intelligence Corps BA in Austria; actor, author, lectr; tstee: Lucis Tst 1957-61, The Human Devpt Tst 1970-, The Natural Health Fndn 1980-, The Lynwood Fellowship

1983-; landowner (2,000 acres); *Books* Mystical Ladder (1968), The Other Universe (1973), The Alice Bailey Heritage (1984); *Recreations* answering correspondence; *Style—* Sir John Sinclair, Bt; Barrock House, Lyth, by Wick, Caithness, Scotland; c/o Messrs Coutts & Co, 440 Strand, WC2R 0QS

SINCLAIR, Kenneth Brian; s of Joseph Frederick Sinclair, and May,*née née* Hadden; *b* 14 Mar 1931; *Educ* Heath Clark Sch Croydon,; *m* 5 Jan 1957, Yvonne Joan, da of Walter Henry Tucker; 1 s (Keith Andrew Brian b 1 May 1960); *Career* assgilt edged portfolio Eagle Star Insur 1949-54, investmt offr NCB 1954, managing ptnr David A Bevan Simpson 1960-70 (joined 1954), exec ptnr de Zoete and Bevan 1974 (ptnr 1963, managing ptnr 1969), dep chm Barclays de Zoete Wedd Securities Ltd 1988-; *Recreations* bridge, chess, football; *Clubs* City of London, Gresham; *Style—* Kenneth Sinclair, Esq; Hedley, High Drive, Woldingham, Surrey (☎ 0883 8503240); Barclays de Zoete Wedd Ltd, Ebbgate House, 2 Swan Lane, London EC4R 3TS (☎ 01 623 2323, fax 01 895 1525, telex 917102 BZWGLT G)

SINCLAIR, Air Vice-Marshal Sir Laurence Frank; GC (1941), KCB (1957, CB 1946), CBE (1943), DSO (1940) and bar (1943); s of late Frank Sinclair, Nigerian Political Serv; *b* 1908; *Educ* ISC, RAF Coll Cranwell; *m* 1941, Valeria, da of Col Joseph Dalton White; 1 s, 1 da; *Career* Sqdn Ldr 1938, Gp Capt 1943-44, ADC to the King 1943-49, CO No 110 (Blenheim) Sqdn 1940, CO RAF Watton 1941, CO No 324 Wing, N Africa 1943, AOC Tactical Bomber Force, MAAF, SASO, Balkan Air Force, MEAF 1944, AOC No 2 Gp BAFO 1949-50, asst cmdt RAF Staff Coll Bracknell 1950; cmdt: RAF Coll Cranwell 1950-52, Sch of Land-Air Warfare Old Sarum 1952-53; Air Vice-Marshal 1952, asst chief of air staff (ops) 1953-55, AOC Br Forces Arabian Peninsula 1955-57, cmdt Jt Servs Staff Coll 1958, ret 1960; controller: Ground Servs Miny Aviation 1960-61, Nat Air Traffic Control Servs 1962-66; Legion of Merit USA 1943, Légion d'Honneur France 1944, Partisan Star with gold leaves (Yugoslavia); *Recreations* fishing; *Clubs* RAF; *Style—* Air Vice-Marshal Sir Laurence Sinclair, GC, KCB, CBE, DSO; Haines Land, Great Brickhill, Bucks

SINCLAIR, Master of; Hon Matthew Murray Kennedy St Clair; s and h of 17 Lord Sinclair, MVO; *b* 9 Dec 1968; *Style—* The Master of Sinclair

SINCLAIR, Lady (Euphemia) Meredith; raised to the rank of an Earl's da 1948; da of Rev the Hon Charles Augustus Sinclair (d 1943; s of 16 Earl of Caithness), and Marianne Sinclair (d 1938); *b* 22 Oct 1915; *Career* SRN; *Style—* Lady Meredith Sinclair; The Old Exchange, 13 Station Road, Wheatley, Oxon OX9 1ST (☎ 08677 3876)

SINCLAIR, Hon Patrick James; s of 2 Viscount Thurso; *b* 1954; *m* Carol North; 2 s; *Style—* The Hon Patrick Sinclair; Archway Cottage, Thurso East, Thurso, Caithness KW14 8HW

SINCLAIR, Patrick Robert Richard; s of late Alexander Sinclair, bro of 8 Bt; hp of cous, Sir John Sinclair, 9 Bt; *b* 21 May 1936; *Educ* Winchester, Oriel Coll Oxford; *m* 1974, Susan Catherine Beresford, da of Geoffrey Davies, OBE; 1 s (William b 1979), 1 da (Helen b 1984); *Career* Sub Lt RNVR; barr Lincoln's Inn 1961; *Style—* Patrick Sinclair, Esq; 1 New Sq, Lincoln's Inn, London WC2 (☎ 01 242 7427); 5 New Sq, Lincoln's Inn, London WC2 (☎ 01 404 0404)

SINCLAIR, Sonia Elizabeth; *née* Graham; da of late Col Roland Harris Graham, RAMC (ret), and Kathleen Graham (d 1983), of the Lodge, Bridge, Kent; *m* 1, 1947, 3 Baron Melchett (d 1973); 1 s, 2 da; m 2, 1984, Dr Andrew Annandale Sinclair, historian and writer; 2 step s; *Career* novelist and travel writer; JP for 10 years; memb: exec NSPCC for 7 years, cncl Royal Ct Theatre, Nat Theatre 1983-; *Recreations* travelling, reading; *Style—* Mrs Andrew Sinclair; 16 Tite St, Chelsea, London SW3 (☎ 01 352 7645)

SINCLAIR, Thomas Humphrey; s of William Sinclair Boston (d 1972), and Jean, *née* Matthews; *b* 17 August 1938; *Educ* Oundle, RAC Cirencester; *m* 1, (m dis 1970), Sheila Kyle, *née* Davies; m 2, 30 May 1970 Ann Pauline, da of Flt Lt Harold Rowson (d 1983); 2 s (Michael John); *Career* Nat Serv 1958-60; chm William Sinclair Hdlgs plc 1984- (md 1978); FInstD, FNIAB; *Recreations* golf, tennis; *Style—* Thomas Sinclair, Esq; Wyberton, Boston, Lincs (☎ 0205 56003); Vale-Do-Lobo, Algarve, Portugal; WM Sinclair Holdings plc, Firth Rd, Lincoln (☎ 0522 537 561, fax 0522 513 609, telex 56367)

SINCLAIR OF CLEVE, 3 Baron (UK 1957); John Lawrence Robert Sinclair; o s 2 Baron (d 1985), and Lady Sinclair of Cleve, *née* Patricia Hellyer; *b* 6 Jan 1953; *Educ* Winchester Coll, Bath Univ, Manchester Univ; *Career* craft, design and technol; workshop technician in an Inner London Comprehensive Sch; teaching support staff rep on sch bd of govrs 1985-; *Recreations* mime, motorcycling, music; *Clubs* Scala Cinema; *Style—* Rt Hon Lord Sinclair of Cleve; c/o The Royal Bank of Scotland, Holt's Branch, Kirkland Ho, Whitehall SW1

SINCLAIR, YOUNGER OF ULBSTER, Hon John Archibald; s and h of 2 Viscount Thurso; *b* 10 Sept 1953; *Educ* Eton; *m* 1976, Marion Ticknor, da of Louis D Sage, of Connecticut, USA; 1 s (James, b Jan 1984), 1 da (Louisa b 1980); *Career* mangr Lancaster Hotel (Paris, part of the Savoy Gp) 1981-85, dir SA Lancaster 1983-85, vice-chm Prestige Hotels 1984-, gen mangr Cliveden Bucks for Blakeney Hotels 1985-; landowner (20,000 acres); *Style—* The Hon John Sinclair, younger of Ulbster; Cliveden, Taplow, Berks SL6 0JF

SINCLAIR-LOCKHART, Sir Simon John Edward Francis; 15 Bt (NS 1636), of Murkle Co Caithness, and Stevenson, Co Haddington;; s of Sir Muir Edward Sinclair-Lockhart, 14 Bt (d 1985); *b* 22 July 1941; *m* 1973, Felicity Edith, da of late Ivan Lachlan Campbell Stewart, of Havelock North, NZ; 2 s (Robert Muir b 1973, James Lachlan (twin) b 1973), 1 da (Fiona Mary b 1979); *Heir* s, Robert Muir Sinclair-Lockhart; *Style—* Sir Simon Sinclair-Lockhart, Bt; 54 Duart Rd, Havelock North, New Zealand

SINCLAIR-LOCKHART, Winifred, Lady; Winifred Ray (Graham); da of late Tom Ray Cavaghan, of Aglionby Grange, Carlisle; *m* 1949, Sir John Beresford Sinclair-Lockhart, 13 Bt (d 1970); *Style—* Winifred, Lady Sinclair-Lockhart; 22 Winton Court, Petersfield, Hants GU32 3HB

SINDEN, Donald Alfred; CBE (1979); s of Alfred Edward Sinden (d 1972), and Mabel Agnes, *née* Fuller (d 1959); *b* 9 Oct 1923; *Educ* Webber-Douglas Sch of Dramatic Art; *m* 3 May 1948, Diana, da of Daniel Mahony (d 1981); 2 s (Jeremy b, 14 June 1950, Marcus b 9 May 1954); *Career* TV, film and stage actor; first stage performance 1942; 1952-60 Rank Orgn appearing in 23 films incl: Doctor in the House, The Cruel Sea; RSC 1963- (Variety Club of GB Best Stage Actor 1976, Evening Standard Drama Award 1977, for King Lear); assoc artist RSC 1967-; Drama Desk Award (for Sir Harcourt Courtly 1974) TV series include: Two's Company, Never the Twain, Discovering English Churches; pres: Fedn of Playgoers Socs 1968-, Royal Gen Theatrical Fund 1983-, Theatre Museum Assoc 1985-; tstee Br Actors Equity Assoc; FRSA; *Books* A Touch of the Memoirs (autobiog, 1982), Laughter in the Second Act (autobiog, 1985), The Everyman Book of Theatrical Anecdotes (ed 1987), The English Country Church (1988); *Recreations* serendipity; *Clubs* Garrick (tstee), Beefsteak, MCC; *Style—* Donald Sinden, Esq, CBE; 60 Temple Fortune Lane, London NW11

SINDEN, Jeremy Mahony; s of Donald Sinden, CBE, of London, and Diana, *née* Mahony; *b* 14 June 1950; *Educ* Lancing, LAMDA; *m* 1 July 1978, Delia Ann Patricia, da of P A R Lindsay, of West Orchard, Dorset; 2 da (Kezia b 18 Dec 1979, Harriet b 1 July 1984); *Career* actor; TV incl: The Expert, Brideshead Revisited, Danger UXB, The Far Pavillions, Fairly Secret Army, Have His Carcase (Dorothy L Sayers), After The War, Square Deal, Virtuoso; theatre incl: RSC 1969-72, Lady Harry (Savoy Theatre), Spin of the Wheel (Comedy Theatre), Bless the Bride (Sadler's Wells Theatre), The Chiltern Hundreds (on tour), Conduct Unbecoming (on tour), French Without Tears (Greenwich Theatre and tour), The Winslow Boy (on tour, also dir), The Jungle Book (Adelphi Theatre), The Philanthropist (Chichester), John Bull's Other Island (Cambridge Theatre Co, on tour), Mother Goose (Leatherhead), Semi Monde (Royalty Theatre); films incl: Star Wars, Chariots of Fire, Madame Sousatzka; formed Catchfavour prodn co, prodr An Ideal Husband (for nat tour): cncllr: Br Actor's Equity Assoc 1980-84, Actors Benevolent Fund 1984-; tstee Evelyn Norris Tst 1984-; Freeman City of London 1977, Liveryman Worshipful Co of Innholders; *Recreations* walking, photography, cinema, opera; *Clubs* Garrick; *Style—* Jeremy Sinden, Esq; C/O ICM, 388/396 Oxford St, London WC1 (☎ 01 629 8080)

SINDEN, Marcus Andrew (Marc); s of Donald Alfred Sinden, CBE, *qv*, of London, and Diana, *née* Mahony; *b* 9 May 1954; *Educ* Hall Sch Hampstead, Edgeborough Surrey, Stanbridge Earls Hampshire, Bristol Old Vic Theatre Sch; *m* 20 Aug 1977, Joanne Lesley, da of Geoffrey Gilbert, of Dorset; 1 s (Henry b 1980); *Career* jeweller and goldsmith H Knowles-Brown Ltd Hampstead 1973-78; actor 1978-; West End: Enjoy, Her Royal Highness, Underground, School for Scandal, Two into One, Ross, Over My Dead Body; G B Shaw's: John Bulls Other Island (Dublin), Major Barbara (Chichester Festival Theatre); films: The Wicked Lady, Clash of Loyalties, White Nights, Manges D'Homme; TV: Crossroads, Home Front, Magnum PI, Country Boy; Freeman City of London, Liveryman Worshipful Co of Innholders; FZS London; *Recreations* theatrical history, zoology, ethology, cricket, motor racing, history of stunt-work; *Clubs* Garrick; *Style—* Marc Sinden, Esq; 1 Hogarth Hill, London NW11 6AY (☎ 01 458 8087); Smallhythe Productions Ltd, 1 Hogarth Hill, London NW11 6AY (☎ 01 455 2323)

SINGER, Aubrey Edward; CBE (1984); s of Louis Henry Singer, and, Elizabeth, *née* Walton; *b* 21 Jan 1927; *Educ* Bradford GS; *m* 1949, Cynthia Adams; 1 s, 3 da; *Career* joined BBC TV 1949, asst head outside broadcasts 1956-59, head sci features 1959-61, head features gp 1967-74, controller BBC2 1974-78, md BBC Radio 1978-82, dep dir gen BBC 1982-84, md BBC TV 1982-84; chm White City Films 1984-; vice pres Royal TV Soc 1982-88 (fell 1978), chm Screen Sport 1984-88; ctee memb Nat Museum of Photography Film and TV Bradford 1985-, dir Goldcrest Films and TV 1988-; Hon DLitt Bradford Univ 1984; fell Royal Aslatic Soc; *Recreations* walking; *Clubs* Savile; *Style—* Aubrey Singer, Esq, CBE; White City Films Ltd, 79 Sutton Court Rd, Chiswick, London W4 3EQ (☎ 01 994 6795, 01 994 4856, fax 01 995 9379, telex 9312102353 AS G)

SINGER, Hon Mrs (Evelyn Anne); da of Baron Kissin (Life Peer); *b* 1944; *Educ* BA (1966); *m* 1972, Jack Donald Singer, MD, FAAPaed; 1 s (Jeremy b 1974), 1 da (Juliet d 1978); *Style—* The Hon Mrs Singer; 45 Campden Hill Court, Campden Hill Rd, London W8 (☎ 01 937 9382)

SINGER, His Hon Judge Harold Samuel; s of Ellis Singer, and Minnie, *née* Coffman (d 1964); *b* 17 July 1935; *Educ* Salford GS, Fitzwilliam House Cambridge (BA); *m* 1966, Adele Berenice, da of Julius Emanuel; 1 s (Andrew b 1967), 2 da (Rachel b 1970, Victoria b 1974); *Career* barr Gray's Inn 1957, rec Crown Ct 1981-84, circuit judge 1984; *Recreations* golf, music, reading, painting, photography; *Style—* His Hon Judge Singer

SINGER, Dr Norbert; s of Salomon Singer (d 1970), and Mina, *née* Korn (d 1976); *b* 3 May 1931; *Educ* Highbury Co Sch, QMC London (BSc, PhD); *m* 23 May 1980, Dr Brenda Margaret, da of Richard Walter, of Tunbridge Wells; *Career* project ldr Morgan Crucible Co Ltd 1954-58; N London Poly 1958-70: lectr, sr lectr, princ lectr, dep head of dept of chemistry; prof and head of life sci dept Poly of Central London 1971-74, asst (later dept dir) Poly of N London 1974-78, dir Thames Poly 1978-; cncl memb CNAA 1982-88; CChem, FRSC 1954; *Recreations* reading, walking; *Style—* Dr Norbert Singer; Croft Lodge, Bayhall Road, Tunbridge Wells, Kent TN2 4TD (☎ 0892 23821); Thames Polytechnic, Wellington St, Woolwich, London SE18 6PF (☎ 01 854 2030)

SINGER, Very Rev Samuel Stanfield; s of William Haus Singer (d 1944); *b* 2 May 1920; *Educ* Acad Baubridge Dublin, Trinity Coll Dublin (BA, MA); *m* 1942, Helen Audrey, *née* Naughton; 3 s, 1 da; *Career* vicar of Middleton-by-Wirksworth 1949-52, rector St George's Maryhill Glasgow 1952-62, rector All Saints' Glasgow 1962-75, synod clerk and canon St Mary's Cath Glasgow 1966-74, dean of Diocese of Glasgow and Galloway 1974-, rector Holy Trinity Ayr with St Oswald's Maybole 1975-87; *Recreations* fishing; *Style—* The Very Rev the Dean of Glasgow and Galloway; 12 Barns Terrace, Ayr, Scotland (☎ 0292 62382)

SINGH, His Hon Judge; Mota; QC; s of Dalip Singh (stabbed to death 1946 while protecting a woman from attack in Nairobi), and Harnam Kaur; *b* 26 July 1930; *Educ* Duke of Gloucester Sch Nairobi; *m* 9 Nov 1950, Swaran, da of Gurcharan Singh Matharu, BEM (d 1987); 2 s (Satinder b 1956, Jaswinder b 1958), 2 da (Paramjeet b 1951, Kiranjit b 1955); *Career* barr Lincoln's Inn 1956; late city cncllr and alderman of Nairobi, sec Law Soc of Kenya, vice-chm Kenya Justice, memb (and chm) London Rent Assessment Ctee, memb Race Relations Bd, UK; QC 1978, recorder 1979, circuit judge 1982; Hon LLD Guru Nanak Dev Univ 1981; *Recreations* reading; *Clubs* MCC; *Style—* His Hon Judge Mota Singh; 3 Somerset Rd, Wimbledon, London SW19 5JU; (☎ office 01 403 4141 ext 279)

SINGLETON, Lady Amelia Myfanwy Polly; da of 7 Marquess of Anglesey, DL; *b* 12 Sept 1963; *m* 1984, Andrew Michael, 2 s of Sir Edward H S Singleton, *qv*; *Style—* Lady Amelia Singleton

SINGLETON, (William) Brian; CBE (1974); s of William Max Singleton (d 1977), and Blanche May Singleton (d 1975); *b* 23 Feb 1923; *Educ* Queen Elizabeth GS Darlington,

Royal (Dick) Sch of Veterinary Med Edinburgh Univ; *m* 1947, Hilda, da of Herbert A Stott (d 1974); 2 s (Neil, Mark, and 1 s decd), 1 da (Maxine); *Career* vet advsr IBA 1968-, first pres Royal Coll of Vet Surgn 1969-70; served govt ctee of inquiry into the Future Role of the Vet Profession in GB under the chmnship of Sir Michael Swann 1971-75; visiting prof surgery Ontario Vet Coll Guelph Canada 1973-74; hon vet advsr Jockey Club 1977-88; pres: Br Small Animal Vet Assoc 1960-61, World Small Animal Vet Assoc 1975-77; pres Br Equine Vet Assoc 1987-88, dir Animal Health Tst 1977-88; memb UGC working Pty on Veterinary Educn into the 21 Century; FRCVS 1976;; *Recreations* gardening, sailing, bird watching, horse riding; *Clubs* Farmers; *Style—* Brian Singleton, Esq, CBE; Vine Cottage, Blakeney, Norfolk, NR25 7BE (☎ 0263 740246)

SINGLETON, Sir Edward Henry Sibbald; s of William Parkinson Singleton, JP (d 1960), by Florence Octavia, da of Sir Francis Sibbald-Scott, 5 Bt; *b* 7 April 1921; *Educ* Shrewsbury, BNC Oxford (MA); *m* 1943, Margaret Vere, *née* Hutton; 3 s (*see* Singleton, Lady Amelia), 1 da; *Career* Lt RNVR 1941-45, Pilot Fleet Air Arm; slr; former ptnr Macfarlanes (conslt 1977-86); memb: Cncl of the Law Soc 1961-80 (pres 1974), Slrs' Law Stationery Soc plc 1980-85, Companion Inst Civil Engrs 1982; tstee Fleet Air Arm Museum and Temple Bar Tst 1976-; memb Cncl Securities Indust 1979-84; dir Abbey Nat Bldg Soc and various cos; FCIArb; kt 1975; *Recreations* relaxing; *Clubs* City of London, Vincent's (Oxford); *Style—* Sir Edward Singleton; Flat 7, 62 Queen's Gate, London SW7 (☎ office: 01 581 4151)

SINGLETON, Michael John Houghton; s of Clifford Houghton Singleton, OBE, of 55 Lammack Rd, Blackburn, Lancs, and Kathleen, *née* Slater; *b* 28 Mar 1951; *Educ* Baines GS Poulton-le-Flyde, Sheffield Univ (LLB); *m* 2 Oct 1976, Carolyn Anne, da of Geoffrey Ewart Lawrence, of 46A Wrottesley Rd, Tettenhall, Wolverhampton; 1 s (Matthew b 1983), 1 da (Jennifer b 1985); *Career* slr; ptnr Fieldings; *Style—* Michael Singleton, Esq; 34 Somerset Ave, Wilpshire, Blackburn, Lancs (☎ 0254 46191); Royal Chambers, Richmond Terrace, Blackburn, Lancs (☎ 0254 679321)

SINGLETON, Valerie; da of Wing Cdr Denis Gordon Singleton, OBE, and Catherine Eileen Singleton; *b* 9 April 1937; *Educ* Arts Educnl Sch London, RADA; *Career* Bromley Rep 1956-57, No 1 tours Cambridge Arts Theatre 1957-62, TV appearances in Compact and Emergency Ward 10, top voice-over commentator for TV commercials 1957-62; BBC1: continuity announcer 1962-64, Blue Peter 1962-72, Nationwide 1972-78, Val Meets the VIPs (3 series), Blue Peter Special Assignment (4 series), Blue Peter Royal Safari with HRH Princess Anne, Tonight and Tonight in Town 1978-79, Blue Peter Special Assignments Rivers Yukon and Niagara; BBC 2: Echoes of Holocaust, The Migrant Workers of Europe, The Money Programme 1980-88; Radio 4 pm 1981-; numerous appearances in TV advertising; NUJ, Equity; *Recreations* travelling, photography, exploring London, sailing, walking, visiting salesrooms, museums; *Style—* Miss Valerie Singleton; c/o Onlington Enterprises, 1-3 Charlotte St, London W1

SINHA, Hon A K; s (by 2 m) of 2 Baron Sinha (d 1967); *b* 1930; *Style—* The Hon A K Sinha

SINHA, Hon Anjana; da of 3 Baron Sinha; *b* 1950; *Style—* The Hon Anjana Sinha

SINHA, Hon Bina; da (by 1 m) of late 2 Baron Sinha; *b* 1917; *Style—* The Hon Bina Sinha

SINHA, Hon Gita; da (by 1 m) of late 2 Baron Sinha; *b* 1918; *Style—* The Hon Gita Sinha

SINHA, Hon Manjula; da of 3 Baron Sinha; *b* 1947; *Style—* The Hon Manjula Sinha

SINHA, Nirupama, Baroness; Nirupama; da of Rai Bahadur Lalit Mohan Chatterjee; *m* 1919, 2 Baron (d 1967); 2 s, 1 da; *Style—* The Rt Hon Nirupama, Lady Sinha; 7 Lord Sinha Rd, Calcutta, India

SINHA, Hon Sheila; da (by 2 m) of late 2 Baron Sinha; *b* 1923; *Style—* The Hon Sheila Sinha

SINHA, 3 Baron (UK 1919); Sudhindro Prasanna Sinha; s (by 2 m) of 2 Baron Sinha (d 1967, s in his turn of 1 Baron, the first Indian raised to the Peerage and the first memb of the Viceroy's Exec Cncl in the wake of the Morley-Minto Reforms under the Raj); *b* 29 Oct 1920; *Educ* Bryanston; *m* 1945, Madhabi, da of late Monoranjan Chatterjee, of Calcutta; 1 s, 2 da; *Heir* s, Hon Susanta Prasanna Sinha *qv*; *Career* chm and md McNeill and Barry Ltd Calcutta; *Style—* The Rt Hon The Lord Sinha; 7 Lord Sinha Rd, Calcutta, India

SINHA, Hon Susanta Prasanna; only s and h of 3 Baron Sinha, *qv*; *b* 1953; *m* 1972, Patricia Orchard; 1 da (Caroline b 1973), 1 s and 1 da (decd); *Career* tea broker; *Style—* Hon Susanta Sinha; 7 Lord Sinha Rd, Calcutta, India

SINKER, David Tennant; JP; s of Philip Tennant Sinker (d 1986), of Merton Cottage, Queens' Rd, Cambridge, and Mary Louisa, *née* Pearson; *b* 12 May 1938; *Educ* Winchester, Trinity Coll Cambridge (MA); *m* 6 Aug 1966, (Alice) Selina Marjorie, da of Charles Evelyn Townley (d 1983), of Fulbourn Manor, Cambridge; 1 s (Andrew b 9 July 1968); *Career* Nat Serv 1 Royal Dragoons 1957-58; 2 Lt Kent and London Yeo Sharpshooters TA 1961-64; articled clerk Peat Marwick Mitchell & Co 1961-64, chief economist Hunting Tech Servs Ltd 1969-71 (conslt economist 1964-69), md Hunting Survey & Conslts 1978-86 (fin dir 1971-76, dep md 1976-78); dir: Leach Gp 1971- (chm 1978-88), Hunting Survey & Photographic 1984-, BUT 1987- (chm), City Technol 1988-; seconded to Nat Bd for Prices and Incomes 1967-69; memb: Ctee of Enquiry into Handling of Geographical Info 1985-87, Legal Aid Bd 1988-; Freeman City of London, Liveryman Worshipful Co of Broderers 1981; FCA 1964, FBIM 1987, FInstD 1987; *Recreations* gardening, walking, golf, tennis, skiing; *Clubs* IOD; *Style—* David Sinker, Esq, JP; Tare Close, Benington, Herts (☎ 0438 85 238, fax 0438 85 601)

SINKER, Patrick Andrew Charles Chisholm; s of Capt Leonard Chisholm Sinker, RN (d 1970), and Nancy, *née* Johnston; *b* 14 Jan 1939; *Educ* Pangbourne Nautical Coll; *m* 3 April 1964, Letitia Ann, da of Robert King Anderson, of Whitstable, Kent; 2 da (Kate Letitia b 1967, Polly Anna b 1969); *Career* co dir; FCA; *Recreations* sailing, golf; *Clubs* Chestfield GC; *Style—* Patrick Sinker, Esq; The Orchard, Alexandra Rd, Whitstable, Kent; Brent's Boatyard, Brents, Faversham, Kent (☎ 0795 537 809)

SINNATT, Maj-Gen Martin Henry; CB (1984); s of Capt Oliver Sturdy Sinnatt (d 1965), and Marjorie Helen, *née* Randall (d 1964); *b* 28 Jan 1928; *Educ* Hitchin GS, Hertford Coll Oxford, RMA Sandhurst; *m* 20 July 1957, Susan Rosemary, da of Capt Sydney Landor Clarke (d 1966); 4 da (Jacqueline Margaret b 22 April 1959, Katherine Susan b 30 March 1961, Nicola Jane b 16 Aug 1963, Victoria Helen b 1 Oct 1965); *Career* RTR 1948-; served: W Germany, Korea, Hong Kong, Aden, Norway; CO 4 RTR BAOR 1969-71, cdr RAC 1 Corps BAOR 1972-74, dir operational requirements MOD 1974-77, dir combat devpt 1979-81, COS and head UK Delgn 'Live Oak' SHAPE 1982-84; sr exec and sec Kennel Club 1984-; Freeman of City of London 1981; *Recreations* golf, skiing, gardening, travel, medieval history; *Clubs* Army and Navy, Kennel; *Style—* Maj-Gen Martin Sinnatt, CB; c/o Barclays Bank, 92 Church Rd, Hove, E Sussex BN3 2ED

SIRA, Gurmit Singh; s of Nirmal Singh Sira (d 1982), and Bhagwanti Sira, *née* Paddi; *b* 19 July 1938; *Educ* Duke of Gloucester (Nairobi), Nairobi Univ (Kenya), Leeds Univ (BA); *m* 16 Sept 1972, Jaswant Kaur, da of Ronak Singh Sagoo, of Ealing; 2 da Amrita b 1982, Shateen b 1975, 1 s (Manoreet b 1974); *Career* slr and Notary Public dir: Tanglewood Properties (Lichfield) Ltd, Masu Properties Ltd; *Recreations* walking, badminton, reading, theatre; *Style—* Gurmit S Sira, Esq; 16 Woodfields Drive, Lichfield WS14 9HH; Permanent House, 6A Conduit St, Lichfield (☎ 254382/3, fax 253713)

SIRS, William (Bill); JP; s of Fredrick Sirs (d 1972), and Margaret Sirs, *née* Powell; *b* 6 Jan 1920; *Educ* Middleton St Johns; *m* 1941, Joan, da of Harry Clark (d 1944); 1 s (John), 1 da (Margaret); *Career* gen sec Iron & Steel Trades Confedn 1975-85, TUC gen cncl 1975-85, employment appeals tbnl 1976; Freeman City of London 1983; Winston Chruchill Meml Tst 1984; *Recreations* squash, weight training, running, golf; *Style—* Bill Sirs Esq, JP; 11 Sunnyfield, The Ryde Hatfield, Herts

SISLEY, Francis Barton; s of John Barton Sisley (d 1940), of SE London, and Elsie May, *née* Hawkins (d 1963); *b* 28 Nov 1921; *Educ* Woolwich Poly, Woolwich Poly Sch of Art; *m* 1, 29 Nov 1941 (m dis 1953), May Victoria, da of James Mortimer (d 1950); 1 da (Janet Irene b 23 Feb 1944); m 2, 24 Nov 1962, Joan Patricia, da of William Patrick Veness (d 1963); *Career* artist; group exhibitions incl: Young Contemporaries RBA Galleries, AIA Gallery London, Redfern Gallery, Havant Art Centre, Free Painters and Sculptors, Ford Exhibition Dearborn USA and Lisbon Portugal; one-man exhibitions incl: Loggia Galleries London 1974 (also 1976 and 1979), Assembly Rooms Chichester 1975, Gallery 20 Brighton 1977, Christ's Hosp Arts Fair 1977 and 79, Bognor Regis Centre 1984 (twice); work in private collections in: USA, Canada, Australia, Spain, UK; large acrylic painting Celtic Cross acquired for Catholic Educn Centre Canterbury 1977; memb Free Painters and Sculptors 1963; *Recreations* chess, wine making, DIY, gardening, reading, walking, travel; *Style—* Francis Sisley, Esq; Shelley House, 59 Nyewood lane, Bognor Regis, W. Sussex PO21 2SQ, (☎ 0243 828 539)

SISMEY, Lt-Col Oliver North Deane; DL (Hunts 1952-74, Cambs 1974); s of George Herbert Sismey (d 1958), of Offord Cluny Manor, Huntingdon, and Catherine Edith, *née* Buckmaster (d 1953) ; *b* 25 Oct 1900; *Educ* Cheam Sch, Eton, Sandhurst; *m* 1, 1931, Anne Laetitia, da of Brig-Gen Lewis Francis Philips, CB, CMG, CBE, DSO (d 1935); 1 da (Islay Anne); m 2, 1956, Pauline Vincent, *née* Turner (d 1980); *Career* cmmnd 2 Lt KRRC 1920, Adj 1 Bn KRRC 1926-29, instr RMC Sandhurst 1935-38, AMS to Govr and C-in-C Malta 1939-40, CO 2 Bn KRRC 1941 (with 1 Armd Div and 7 Armd Div in Middle East and took part in actions in Libya and Egypt 1941-42), GSO1 No 2 Dist 1942-45, Tripolitania, Sicily, Italy (despatches); dep pres Regular Cmmns Bd 1947, dep pres Sandhurst Selection Bd 1947, ret Lt-Col 1948; chm Police Authy 1954-64; co alderman: Huntingdonshire 1960-65, Huntingdon and Peterborough 1965-74; *Recreations* formerly hunting, shooting, polo, rackets, now gardening; *Clubs* Naval and Military; *Style—* Lt-Col Oliver Sismey, DL; Offord Cluny Manor, nr Huntingdon, Cambridgeshire (☎ 0480 810 259)

SISSON, Brig Arthur Alexander; MBE (1968), CBE (1978); s of Prof Geoffrey Roy Sisson, OBE (d 1964), and Lucy Cameron, *née* Ward (d 1982); *b* 30 May 1924; *Educ* Highgate Sch, Edinburgh Univ; *m* 1 Oct 1951, Audrey Pamela, da of Maj John Cyril Joseph Chadwick (d 1981); 2 s (Richard b 1957, Peter b 1962), 2 da (Jennifer b 1954, Sarah Jane b 1965); *Career* Brig; serv: SE Asia, India, Palestine, Malaya, Cyprus, Aden; intro Army bulk refuelling system 1970-79, initiated DROPS (demountable rack system), dir logistic orgn and devpt MOD (Army) 1976-79; mgmnt and def conslt; FMS; *Studies* Logistic Concept 1985-2005 (1979), Vulnerability of the British LOC in Europe (1985); *Recreations* butterfly photography, racehorse owner; *Clubs* Naval; *Style—* Brig Arthur A Sisson, CBE; Ferranti International Dynamics Ltd, Signal House, Swan Road, Hanworth, Middx TW13 6LL (☎ 01 894 5533)

SISSON, Dr Charles Hubert; s of Richard Percy Sisson 9d 1958), of and Ellen Minnie, *née* Worlock (d 1955); *b* 2 April 1914; *Educ* Fairfield Secdy Sch Bristol, Univ of Bristol (BA), Univ of Berlin and Freiburg, The Sorbonne; *m* 19 Aug 1937, Nora, da of Anthony Huddleston Gilbertson (d 1954), of Bristol;; 2 da (Janet, Hilary); *Career* WWII Sgt Intelligence Corps 1942-45 served India; asst princ Miny of Lab 1936, under sec Miny of Lab Dept of Employment 1962-72, Simon sr res fell Univ of Manchester 1956-57; author; Hon DLitt Bristol 1980; FRSL 1972; *Books* The Spirit of British Administration, with some European comparisons (1959), Christopher Homm (novel 1965), English Poetry 1900-1950 (1971), In the Trojan Ditch (collected poems and selected translations 1974), The Avoidance of Literature (1978), Collected Poems (1984), God Bless Karl Marx (poems 1987); translations incl: Dante, Virgil, Lucretius; *Recreations* gardening, washing up; *Style—* Dr Charles Sisson; Moorfield Cottage, The Hill, Langport, Somerset TA10 9PU (☎ 0458 250845)

SISSON, Douglas; s of Harry Sisson (d 1970), of Huddersfield, and Ivy, *née* Peace (d 1987); family descended from the Huguenot Counts of Sissonne in Picardy; *b* 12 Nov 1921; *Educ* Huddersfield Coll, Leeds Univ; *m* 17 April 1954, Victoria, da of Harry Brown-Leslie (d 1964), of Huddersfield; *Career* Lt Royal Signals 1941-46, serv home and NW Europe; slr in private practice; chm Social Security Appeals Tbnls 1976-; Huddersfield CB Cncl: cncllr 1960-67, alderman 1967-74, chm educn ctee, dep ldr and whip Cons Gp; memb cncls Leeds and Bradford Univs 1974; first pres Huddersfield Poly 1970-74 and first fell of the Poly, conferred by Margaret Thatcher 1971; appointed to Literary Advsy Cncl for England 1971-75, Parly Candidate (C): Goole 1959, Bolton W 1964; nat chm Cons candidates 1963-64 (during Premiership of Sir Alec Douglas-Home); life memb: Nat Tst, Royal Signals Assoc; vice-pres Coldstreamers Assoc, Owns Easley Abbey (Ancient Monument) memb of Historic House Assoc; FRSA, FPH, FSA (Scot), FBIM; *Recreations* history, travel, art and architecture, heraldry; *Clubs* Naval and Military, Huddersfield and Co Cons (pres); *Style—* Douglas Sisson, Esq; The Mount, Edgerton, Huddersfield, W Yorkshire (☎ 0484 26726); Abbey House, Easby, Richmond, N Yorkshire; Lion Chambers, St George's Square, Huddersfield (☎ 0484 27291)

SISSON, Lady Emma Bridget; da of 12 Earl of Carlisle, MC, *qv*; *b* 20 July 1952; *m* 1,

1974 (m dis 1981), John Philip Charles Langton-Lockton; 1 s (Maximilian b 1980), 1 da (Tabitha b 1978); m 2, 1983 (m dis 1988), Robie Patrick Maxwell Uniacke, s of Capt Robie David Corbett Uniacke, of Challons Yarde, Midhurst, Sussex; 1 s (Robie Jonjo b 12 Oct 1984); m 3, 16 July 1988, Guy Mark Sisson, yst s of late John Hamilton Sisson; *Style—* Lady Emma Sisson; c/o Rt Hon Earl of Carlisle, MC, Naworth Castle, Brampton, Cumbria

SISSON, Rosemary Anne; da of Prof Charles Jasper Sisson (d 1965), and Vera Kathleen Ginn; *b* 13 Oct 1923; *Educ* Cheltenham Ladies Coll, UCL (BA), Newham Coll Cambridge (MLit); *Career* WWII with Royal Observer Corps 1943-45; lectr in english: Univ of Wisconsin 1949-50, UCL 1950-55, Univ of Birmingham 1956-58; co-chm The Writers Guild of GB 1979 and 1980; tstee Ray Cooney's Theatre of Comedy; stage plays incl: The Queen and the Welshman (1957), Fear Came to Supper (1958), The Splendid Outcasts (1958), Home and the Heart, The Royal Captivity (1960), Bitter Sanctuary (1963), I Married a Clever Girl, A Ghost on Tiptoe (with Robert Morley), The Dark Horse (1979); *Books* novels incl: The Exciseman (1972), The Killer of Horseman's Flats (1973), The Stratford Story (1975), The Queen and the Welshman (1979), Escape from the Dark (1976), The Manions of America (1981), Bury Love Deep (1985), Beneath the Visiting Moon (1986), The Bretts (1987, televised 1987); has also published six children's books, contrib to TV series: Upstairs, Downstairs, The Duchess of Duke Street, and made adaptations for TV and radio; *Recreations* riding, travel; *Clubs* BAFTA; *Style—* Miss R A Sisson; Andrew Mann Ltd, 1 Old Compton St, W1 (☎ 01 734 4751)

SISSON, Sir (Eric) Roy; *b* 1914,June; *m* 1943, Constance Mary (*née* Cutchey); 2 s, 2 da; *Career* joined Smiths Industs Ltd 1955 from BOAC rising to chm 1976-85; kt 1980; *Recreations* gardening, golf; *Clubs* RAF, Royal Dartmouth YC; *Style—* Sir Roy Sisson; Gustard Wood House, Gustard Wood, Wheathampstead, Herts

SISSONS, (Thomas) Michael Beswick; s of Capt T E B Sissons (ka 1940), and Marjorie, *née* Shepherd; *b* 13 Oct 1934; *Educ* Winchester, Exeter Coll Oxford (BA, MA); *m* 1, 1960 (m dis), Nicola Ann, *née* Fowler; 1 s, 1 da; m 2, 1974, Ilze, *née* Kadegis; 2 da; *Career* Nat Serv 2 Lt Royal Hussars 1953-55; lectr in history Tulane Univ New Orleans 1958-59, freelance writer and journalist 1958-60, chm and md AD Peters & Co Ltd 1973-88 (joined 1959, dir 1965); jt chm and md The Peters Fraser & Dunlop Gp Ltd 1988-; pres Assoc of Authors' Agents 1978-81, dir London Broadcasting Co 1973-75; *Books* Age of Austerity (ed with Philip French, second edn 1986); *Recreations* riding, gardening, cricket, music; *Clubs* Garrick, Groucho, MCC (memb ctee 1984-87, chm arts and library sub ctee 1985-); *Style—* Michael Sissons, Esq; Flinty, Clanville, Andover, Hants SP11 9HZ (☎ 026 477 2197); Peter Fraser & Dunlop, Fifth Floor, The Chambers, Chelsea Harbour, Lots Rd, London SW10 0XF (☎ 01 376 7676, fax 01 352 7356)

SITWELL, Francis Trajan Sacheverell; yr s of Sir Sacheverell Sitwell, 6 Bt (d 1988); bro and h of Sir Reresby Sitwell, 7 Bt, *qv*; *b* 17 Sept 1935; *Educ* Eton; *m* 21 June 1966, Susanna Carolyn, 3 da of late Rt Hon Sir Ronald Hibbert Cross, 1 Bt, KCMG, KCVO; 2 s (George Reresby Sacheverell b 22 April 1967, William Ronald Sacheverell b 1969), 1 da (Henrietta Louise Vereker b 1973); *Career* late Sub Lt RN; assoc dir Charles Barker City Ltd 1969; memb Cncl London Philharmonic Orch 1965; MIPR 1969; *Clubs* Brooks's; *Style—* Francis Sitwell, Esq; 20 Ladbroke Grove, London W11

SITWELL, Sir (Sacheverell) Reresby; 7 Bt (UK 1808), of Renishaw, Derbyshire; DL (Derbyshire 1984); s of Sir Sacheverell Sitwell, 6 Bt (d 1988), by his w, Georgia Louise, *née* Doble (d 1980); *b* 15 April 1927; *Educ* Eton, King's Coll Cambridge; *m* 1952, Penelope, da of Col the Hon Donald Forbes, DSO, MVO (d 1938), s of 7 Earl of Granard; 1 da (Alexandra b 1958); *Heir* br, Francis Trajan Sacheverell Sitwell b 17 Sept 1935; *Career* former Lt 2 Bn Grenadier Gds, BAOR Germany 1946-48; advtg and PR exec 1948-60, vending machines operator 1960-70, wine merchant 1960-75; landowner 1965-; lord of the manors of Eckington and Barlborough in Derbyshire and of Whiston and Brampton-en-le-Morthen in South Yorks; High Sheriff Derbyshire 1983; Freeman of City of London 1984; *Recreations* travel, music, architecture, racing; *Clubs* White's, Brooks's, Pratt's, Pitt (Cambridge), Soc of Dilettanti; *Style—* Sir Reresby Sitwell; Renishaw Hall, Renishaw, nr Sheffield S31 9WB (☎ 0246 432042); 4 Southwick Place, London W2 2TN (☎ 01 262 3939)

SIVEWRIGHT, Bt-Col (Robert) Charles Townsend; CB (1983), MC (1945), DL (Glos 1965); s of Capt R H V Sivewright DSC, RN (d 1981), and Sylvia Townsend, *née* Cobbold (d 1988); *b* 7 Sept 1923; *Educ* Repton, RAC Glos; *m* 1951, Pamela Molly, da of Dr J C Ryder-Richardson (d 1961), of Whitchurch, Bucks; 3 da (Pamela, Amanda, Sarah); *Career* Bt-Col, cmmnd 11 Hussars 1943, served Italy and NW Europe (despatches), ADC to FM Lord Harding of Petherton 1948-50; CO Royal Gloucestershire Hussars TA 1964-67, farmer; jt princ The Talland Sch of Equitation (Glos); chm W Wessex TA & VRA 1970-83, vice-chm cncl TA & VRA 1970-83; High Sheriff Glos 1977;; *Recreations* racing; *Clubs* Cavalry and Guards; *Style—* Bt-Col Robert Sivewright, CB, MC, DL; Church Farm, Siddington, Cirencester, Glos GL7 6EZ (☎ 0285 652318)

SKAE, John Robin; s of Reginald John Skae (d 1988), and Gwendoline Catharine Bleakley Skae (d 1981); *b* 11 July 1936; *Educ* Oundle Sch; *m* 1 Sept 1961, Cynthia Fay, da of Norman Louis Forrest (d 1988), of Stoke-On-Trent; 1 s (Christopher b 13 Sept 1962), 2 da (Jennifer b 18 March 1965, Joanna b 16 Dec 1968); *Career* dir and co sec Bamfords Ltd Uttoxeter Staffs 1964-74, gp sec Dowty Gp plc Cheltenham 1974-85, gp co sec Midland Bank plc London 1985-; FCA 1962; *Recreations* sport, music, countryside, gardening; *Clubs* New (Cheltenham); *Style—* John Skae, Esq; Midland Bank Plc, Head Office, 27-32 Poultry, London EC2P 2BX (☎ 01 260 8180, fax 01 260 8463)

SKEET, Muriel Hilda Henrietta; da of Col Frederick William Claude (d 1974), of Colchester, Essex, and Mabel Constance, *née* Pitt-King (d 1976); *b* 12 July 1926; *Educ* Endsleigh House, London Univ (MPH, DipH and TM), Yale Univ; *Career* trg Middx Hosp and London Sch of Hygiene and Tropical Med 1949-40 (SRN), ward and admin sister Middx Hosp 1949-60, field work organiser operational res unit Nuffield Provincial Hosps Tst 1961-64, res organiser Dan Mason Nursing Ctee of Nat Florence Nightingale Meml Ctee of GB and NI 1965-70, chief nursing offr and nursing advsr BRCS and St John of Jerusalem and BRCS Jt Ctee 1970-78, res conslt WHO SE Asia 1970, euro del and first chm bd of Cwlth Nurses' Fedn 1971, Leverhume Fellowship 1974-75, health servs advsr and conslt WHO and other int agencies and orgns 1978-; memb: Hosp and Med Servs Ctee 1970, Ex-Servs War Disabled Help Ctee 1970, Br Cwlth Nurses War Meml Fund 1970 ctee and cncl, Br Cwlth Nurses War Meml Fund 1970, mgmnt cncl Nat Florence Nightingale Meml Ctee 1970, cncl Queen's Inst of Dist Nursing 1970, cncl of nurses Royal Coll of Nursing; MRsH, FRSN, FRCN 1977, memb RSM 1980; *Books* Waiting in Outpatients Departments (1965), Marriage and Nursing (1968), Home from Hospital (1970), Home Nursing (1975), Health Needs Help (1977), Health Auxiliaries in the Health Team (jtly, 1978), Self Care for the People of Developing Countries (1979), Discharge Procedures (1980), Notes on Nursing 1860 and 1980 (1980), Emergency Procedures and First Aid for Nurses (1981), The Third Age (1982), Providing Continuing Care for Elderly People (1983), First Aid for Developing Countries (1983), various articles for professional jls; *Recreations* music, opera, painting, reading; *Clubs* Arts, Royal Overseas League; *Style—* Miss Muriel Skeet; World Health Organisation, Geneva, Switzerland

SKEET, Sir Trevor Herbert Harry; MP (C) N Bedfordshire 1983-; s of Harry May Skeet; *b* 28 Jan 1918; *Educ* King's Coll Auckland NZ, Univ of NZ (LLB); *m* 1957, Elizabeth (decd), da of Montague Gilling, of Bedford; 2 s, 1 da; m 2, 1985, Valerie A E Benson; *Career* Lt RNZNVR; barr and slr NZ, barr UK; MP (C): Willesden E 1959-64, Bedford 1970-83; chm Parly and Scientific Ctee 1983-; kt 1986; *Recreations* walking, travel, gardening; *Clubs* Royal Cwlth Soc, Army & Navy; *Style—* Sir Trevor Skeet, MP; The Gables, Milton Ernest, Beds MK44 1RS (☎ 02302 2307)

SKEFFINGTON, Hon John David Clotworthy Whyte-Melville Foster; s and h of 13 Viscount Massereene and Ferrard; *b* 3 June 1940; *Educ* Millfield, Inst Monte Rosa; *m* 1970, Anne Denise, da of Norman Rowlandson (d 1966); 2 s, 1 da; *Career* served Grenadier Gds 1959-61; dir: Shirlstar Container Tport Ltd, Wingspan Travel Ltd; chm: Atkin Grant & Lang (Gunmakers), Ambrit Oil plc; stockbroker with Russell Wood & Co; *Recreations* shooting, vintage cars; *Clubs* Turf, Pratt's; *Style—* The Hon John Skeffington; Scarisdale House, New Rd, Esher, Surrey (☎ office: 01 638 8871)

SKEGGS, Dr David Bartholomew Lyndon; s of Dr Basil Lyndon Skeggs (d 1956), of Herts, and Gladys Jessie, *née* Tucker (d 1978); *b* 26 August 1928; *Educ* Winchester Coll, Oriel Coll Oxford, St Bart's Hosp London; *m* 16 Nov 1957, Anita Violet, da of Horace Norman Hughes, of Worcs; 2 da (Lucinda b 1960, Imogen b 1963); *Career* RN 1954-56; Surgn Lt Cdr RNR 1956-70; dir of Radiotherapy Royal Free Hosp London 1966-86, hon conslt Royal N Hosp London and Lister Hosp Stevenage; chm bd of examiners Part 1 FRCR, sr examiner DMRI 1970-75; use of computerised radiotherapy and devpt of computerised 3 D radiotherapy treatment planning; memb bd of visitors for prisons; memb Cncl Wycombe Abbey Sch; *Books* contribs: Maingot's Textbook of Surgery, Shaw's Textbook of Gynaecology, Scott Brown's Textbook of ENT Surgery; *Recreations* gardening, music, travel, viniculture, competitive games; *Style—* Dr David Skeggs; The Coach House, Barnes Common, London SW13 (☎ 01 876 7929); 152 Harley St, London W1N 1HH (☎ 01 935 0444)

SKELLEY, Dr Eva; *née* Kosek; da of Dr Francis Kosek, of Brno, Czechoslovakia, and Blazena Koskova (d 1982); *b* 7 Oct 1932; *Educ* Charles Univ Prague Czechoslovakia (MA, PhD, Dip); *m* 26 July 1957, Jeff, s of Francis Skelley; 1 da (Danielle Barbara); *Career* translator, reporter and broadcaster Radio Prague, md Collets Hldgs 1981-; *Books* Soviet Satire (gen ed, 1968), Soviet Scene (co-ed 1987), Perestroika in Action (1988); *Recreations* skiing, gardening, music, travel; *Style—* Dr Eva Skelley; Collets Hldgs, Denington Estate, Wellingborough, Northants (☎ 0933 22 4351, fax 0933 76402, telex 317 320 Collet G)

SKELMERSDALE, 7 Baron (UK 1828); Roger Bootle-Wilbraham; s of Brig 6 Baron Skelmersdale, DSO, MC (d 1973), and Ann (d 1974), da of Percy Quilter and gda of Sir Cuthbert Quilter, 1 Bt; *b* 2 April 1945; *Educ* Eton, Lord Wandsworth Coll; *m* 1972, Christine, da of Roy Morgan, of Hamel Evercreech Somerset; 1 s, 1 da (Hon Carolyn Ann b 1974); *Heir* s, Hon Andrew Bootle-Wilbraham b 9 Aug 1977; *Career* horticulturist; md Broadleigh Nurseries 1973-81; pres Somerset Tst for Nature Conservation 1980-, pres Br Watercolourists Tst 1980-; a Lord in waiting to HM 1981-86; Parly under sec of state: DOE 1986-87, DHSS 1987-88, DSS 1988-; *Recreations* gardening, reading, bridge; *Style—* The Lord Skelmersdale; c/o House of Lords

SKELTON, John Martin; s of Martin Oliver Skelton, and Marie Lillian, *née* Bartlett; *b* 22 May 1952; *Educ* Westminster, BNC Oxford (BA); *m* 3 Sept 1982, Clare Louise; 1 s (Simon Martin Sheridan), 1 da (Georgina Louise); *Career* admitted slr 1977, ptnr Withers 1980-87 (asst slr 1977-79), ptnr Macfarlanes 1987-; *Style—* John Skelton, Esq; 46 Blackheath Park, London SE3 9SJ (☎ 01 852 6077); 10 Norwich St, London EC4A 1BD (☎ 831 9222, fax 831 9607)

SKELTON, Joseph Osmotherley; s of Matthew Skelton; *b* 10 May 1929; *Educ* Cockermouth GS, Durham Univ (BCom); *m* 1953, Sheila Daphne Trimble, da of Laurence Trimble Carruthers (d 1976); 2 s; *Career* md The Wagon Fin Corpn plc 1967-, chm Fin Houses Assoc 1978-80, dir: HP Info Ltd 1979-, Frilford Heath G C Ltd; cncl memb European Fedn of Fin Houses Assoc 1978-; memb Bank of England Deposit Protection Bd 1982-; ACA, FCA; *Recreations* golf, gardening, swimming; *Clubs* Frilford Heath GC; *Style—* Joseph Skelton, Esq; Kinloss, Woodside, Abingdon, Oxon (☎ 0865 390500)

SKELTON, Rt Rev Kenneth John Fraser; CBE (1972); s of Henry Edmund Skelton (d 1957); *b* 16 May 1918; *Educ* Dulwich, Corpus Christi Coll Cambridge; *m* 1945, Phyllis Barbara, da of James Emerton; 2 s, 1 da; *Career* ordained 1941, rector of Walton-on-the-Hill Liverpool 1955-62, bishop of Matabeleland 1962-70, asst bishop of Durham, rural dean of Wearmouth and rector of Bishopwearmouth 1970-75, ninety-sixth bishop of Lichfield 1975-84, asst bishop in Dioceses of Sheffield and Derby 1984-; *Books* Bishop in Smith's Rhodesia (1985); *Style—* The Rt Rev Kenneth Skelton, CBE; 65 Crescent Road, Sheffield S7 1HN (☎ 0742 551260)

SKEPPER, (Herbert) Gordon; MBE (1962); s of Herbert Amos Skepper (d 1958), and Ethel, *née* Grundy (d 1982); *b* 2 May 1923; *Educ* UMIST (BSc); *m* 23 June 1951, Ann Rosemary, da of Arthur Gilbert Hewlett, MM (d 1968); 2 s (John Gordon b 1953, Michael David b 1955), 1 da (Helen Catherine b 1958); *Career* civil engr; Colonial Serv (later-HMOCS) asst dir public works Malaya 1953-65, conslt (former exec ptnr and regnl dir) Ove Arup & Ptnrs 1966-; CEng, FICE, FIHT; *Recreations* music, reading, travel; *Style—* Herbert Skepper, Esq, MBE; 57 Bullimore Grove, Kenilworth, Warwickshire LV8 2QF (☎ 0926 53092); Ove Arup and Ptnrs, Barrack St, Warwick CB34 4TH (☎ 0926 493053, telex 312635 OVARPART G, fax 0926 400187)

SKEWIS, Dr (William) Iain; s of John Jamieson Skewis, and Margaret Jack; *b* 1 May 1936; *Educ* Hamilton Acad, Univ of Glasgow (BSc, PhD); *m* 1963, Jessie Frame, da of John Weir (d 1982); 2 s (Alan b 1971, Guy b 1980), 1 da (Jan b 1968); *Career* dir of tourism Highlands and Islands Devpt Bd 1966-72; dir: industl devpt and Mktg Highlands and Islands Devpt Bd 1966-72, Yorks and Humberside Devpt Assoc 1972-77, chief exec Mid Wales Devpt 1977-; vice chm Regnl Stuies Assoc; MCIT, FIT; *Recreations* assoc football; *Style—* Dr Iain Skewis; Rock House, The Square, Montgomery, Powys SY15 6RA (☎ 0686 81276); Ladywell House, Newtown, Powys SY16 1JB (☎ 0686 626965, telex 35387)

SKIDELSKY, Prof Robert Jacob Alexander; s of Boris J Skidelsky (d 1982), and Galia V, *née* Sapelkin (d 1987); *b* 25 April 1939; *Educ* Brighton Coll, Jesus Coll Oxford (BA, MA, PPhil); *m* 2 Sept 1970, Augusta Mary Clarissa, da of John Humphrey Hope (d 1974); 2 s (Edward b 1973, William b 1976), 1 da Juliet (b 1981); *Career* res fell Nuffield Coll Oxford 1965, assoc prof John Hopkins Univ USA 1970, prof int studies Univ of Warwick 1978; memb Lord Chllr's Advsy Cncl on Public Records, policy ctee SDP, Bd of the Socl Market Fndn; FR Hist S 1973, FRSL 1978; *Books* Politicians and the Slump (1967), English Progressive Schools (1970), Oswald Mosley (1975), John Maynard Keynes (1983); *Recreations* tennis, opera; *Clubs* Utd Oxford and Cambridge; *Style—* Prof Robert Skidelsky; Tilton House, Firle, E Sussex BN8 6LL (☎ 032 183 570)

SKIDMORE, Hon Mrs (Felicity Margaret); *née* Hall; da of Baron Roberthall, KCMG, CB; *b* 30 June 1936; *Educ* Oxford HS For Girls, LMH Oxford; *m* 1957, Thomas Skidmore; 3 s; *Style—* The Hon Mrs Skidmore; 2025 Chadbourne Av, Madison, Wisconsin, 53705 USA

SKILLINGTON, William Patrick Denny; CB (1964); s of S J Skillington (d 1967); *b* 13 Feb 1913; *Educ* Malvern, Exeter Coll Oxford; *m* 1941, Dorin, nee Kahn; 2 da; *Career* Lt-Col WWII, civil servant 1946-73, under sec Min of Public Bldg and Works 1956-64, asst under sec of State Home Off 1964-66, dep sec Min of Public Bldg and Works 1966-70, dep sec Dept of the Environment 1970-73; *Clubs* Utd Oxford and Cambridge; *Style—* Patrick Skillington Esq, CB; 95A Saint Mark's rd, Henley-on-Thames, Oxon (☎ 0491 573756)

SKILTON, Charles Philip; *b* 6 Mar 1921; *Educ* Alleyn's Sch Dulwich; *m* 1 June 1946 (m dis), Isabella Hoy Gloag; 1 da (Virginia, (Mrs Kennedy)); *Career* former vice chm Abortion Law Reform Assoc, former vice chm Divorce Law Reform Union, sec Cancer Support; fndr memb and former chm Ind Publishers' Guild, former pres Postcard Assoc, hon memb ctee Wind and Watermill Section SPAB; hon RWS, FSA (Scot), memb Art Workers Guild; *Books* British Windmills and Watermills (1947), Old London Postcard Album (ed 1980); *Recreations* book collecting; *Clubs* Scottish Arts (Edinburgh); *Style—* Charles Skilton, Esq

SKINGSLEY, Air Marshal Sir Anthony Gerald; KCB (1986, CB 1983); *b* 19 Oct 1933; *Educ* Cambridge Univ (MA); *m* 1957 Lilwen Dixon; 2 s, 1 da; *Career* joined RAF 1955, HQ 2 ATAF (ACOS offensive ops) 1977-78, Hon ADC to HM The Queen 1976-77; RCDS course 1978, dir air plans MOD 1979-80, ACOS plans and policy SHAPE 1980-83, cmdt RAF Staff Coll Bracknell 1983-84, Asst Chief of Air Staff 1985-86, air memb for personnel 1986-87, CIC RAF Germany, cdr 2 Allied Tactical Air Force 1987-, Dep C-in-C Allied Forces Central Europe 1989-; *Recreations* golf, sailing, skiing; *Clubs* RAF; *Style—* Air Marshal Sir Anthony Skingsley, KCB, RAF; c/o National Westminster Bank plc, 43 Swan St, West Malling, Maidstone, Kent ME19 6LE

SKINNER, Alexander Morrison (Sandy); s of Lt-Col James Beattie Skinner, OBE, TD, of 50 Liberton Dr, Edinburgh, and Gertrude, *née* Morrison; *b* 23 Sept 1942; *Educ* Daniel Stewart's Coll Edinburgh, Forres Acad, Univ of Aberdeen (MA); *m* 16 July 1966, Gay Henderson, da of William Brown (d 1979); 2 s (Alastair Neil b 16 Sept 1972, Ian Malcolm b 20 Feb 1975), 1 da (Alison Jane b 6 Feb 1970); *Career* Standard Life Assur Co: asst pensions actuary head off Edinburgh 1963-70, asst actuary head off Montreal 1970-72, head off Edinburgh 1972- (asst pensions mangr, pension sales mangr, asst gen mangr, dep gen mangr admin); FFA, FPMI; *Recreations* swimming, gardening, theatre, occasional golf; *Clubs* Royal Scots, Scottish Actuaries (hon sec), Univ of Edinburgh staff; *Style—* Sandy Skinner, Esq; 20 Hallhead Road, Edinburgh (☎ 031 667 6254); Standard Life Assurance Company, 3 George Street, Edinburgh EH2 2XZ (☎ 031 225 2552)

SKINNER, Prof Andrew Stewart; s of Andrew Paterson Skinner (d 1975), of Cardross, Dunbartonshire, and Isabella Bateman, *née* Stewart (d 1986); *b* 11 Jan 1935; *Educ* Kiel Sch Dumbarton, Cornell Univ, Univ of Glasgow (MA, BLitt); *m* 29 Aug 1966, Margaret Mary Dorothy, da of William Robertson (d 1986), of Alloway, Ayrshire; *Career* Queens Univ Belfast 1960-62, Queens Coll Dundee 1962-64; Univ of Glasgow: lectr 1964, reader 1976, Daniel Jack chair of political economy 1985, head dept of political economy 1979-86, dean faculty of social scis 1980-83, clerk of senate 1983-; govr: Mankinnon MacKiel Tst 1976-86, Jordanhill Coll of Educn 1986-; FRSE 1988; *Books* Principles of Political Economy (ed Sir James Stewart, 1966), Adam Smith - The Wealth of Nations (ed with RH Campbell and WB Todd, 1976), A System of Social Science - papers relating to Adam Smith (1979); *Recreations* gardening; *Clubs* The University, Caledonian; *Style—* Prof Andrew Skinner; Glen House, Cardross, Dunbartonshire G82 5ES (☎ 038 984 1603); Senate Office, Univ of Glasgow, Glasgow G12 8QQ (☎ 041 339 8855 ext 4242, fax 041 330 4920, telex 777070 UNIGLA)

SKINNER, David Michael Benson; s of Michael Owen Skinner, of Chichester, W Sussex, and Patricia Alma, *née* Benson-Young; *b* 1 Feb 1942; *Educ* Rugby, Christ Coll Cambridge (MA); *m* 5 June 1965, Judith Diana, da of John Kennedy Cater, of Chichester, W Sussex; 1 da (Mary Diana b 1 May 1966); *Career* dir JT Davies and Sons Ltd 1968- (joined 1964); Freeman City of London, Liveryman Worshipful Co of Cordwainers; *Recreations* tennis, squash, gardening, golf; *Style—* David Skinner, Esq; 7 Aberdeen Rd, Croydon, Surrey CRO 1EQ (☎ 01 681 3222, fax 01 760 0390, telex Davson G 8955142)

SKINNER, Dennis Edward; MP (Lab) Bolsover 1970-; *b* 1932; *Educ* Tupton Hall GS, Ruskin Coll Oxford; *m* 1960, Mary, da of James Parker; 1 s, 2 da; *Career* former miner; joined Lab Pty 1950; memb: NEC 1978-, Campaign Gp Labour MPs 1982-, Lab Pty Youth Ctee until 1982, Tribune Gp until 1982, chm Lab Pty 1988-89; *Style—* Dennis Skinner, Esq, MP; House of Commons, London SW1

SKINNER, (Thomas) James Hewitt; s and h of Sir (Thomas) Keith Hewitt Skinner, 4 Bt, *qv*; *b* 10 Sept 1962; *Style—* Thomas Skinner, Esq; Wood Farm, Reydon, nr Southwold IP18 6SL

SKINNER, Jennifer Dingly; da of John Corbett, and Hilary Dingley Corgett (Dingley); *b* 12 June 1939; *Educ* Howells Sch, Birmingham Coll of Art (NDD); *m* 4 June 1966, Peter Girling Hewitt Skinner, s of Sir Thomas Gordon Hewitt Skinner, 2 Bt (d 1969); 2 s (Justin b 1968, Dominic b 1970), 1 da (Gemma b 1977); *Career* children's book illustrator (Alice Uttley) 1962-67; *Recreations* swimming, tennis; *Clubs* Chris Lawn Tennis Centre; *Style—* Mrs Jennifer Skinner; Highway Farm, Downside, Cobham, Surrey

SKINNER, Jeremy John Banks; s of R Banks Skinner (d 19780, of Moor Park Herts, and Betty, *née* Short; *b* 15 Nov 1936; *Educ* Rugby, Clare Coll Cambridge (BA); *m* 31 Aug 1963, Judith Anne, da of Jack William Austin (d 1986), of Letchworth, Herts; 1 s (Spencer b 13 July 1966), 2 da (Sophie (Mrs Payne) b 24 Nov 1964, Sasha b 9 July 1968); *Career* Nat Serv 2 Lt 16/5 The Queen's Royal Lancers 1956/57; ptnr Linklaters & Paines 1967-; memb cncl and exec ctee Inst of Fiscal Studies, Int Bar Assoc; memb governing body Rugby; Freeman Worshipful Co of Cordwainers; *Recreations* hunting; *Style—* Jeremy Skinner, Esq; Stocking Farm, Stocking Pelham, nr Buntingford, Herts (☎ 027 878556); Barrington House, 59/67 Gresham St, London EC2 (☎ 01 606 7080)

SKINNER, Sir (Thomas) Keith Hewitt; 4 Bt (UK 1912) of Pont Street, Borough of Chelsea; s of Sir (Thomas) Gordon Skinner, 3 Bt (d 1972), and his 1 w, Mollie Barbara, *née* Girling (d 1965); *b* 6 Dec 1927; *Educ* Charterhouse; *m* 29 April 1959, Jill, da of late Cedric Ivor Tuckett, of Tonbridge, Kent; 2 s; *Heir* s, (Thomas) James Hewitt Skinner; *Career* chm and chief exec Reed Publishing, dir Reed Int; *Style—* Sir Keith Skinner, Bt; Wood Farm, Reydon, nr Southwold IP18 4SL

SKINNER, Nicholas James Sylvester; s of Ian William Sylvester Skinner (d 1973), of Holt Lodge, Kintbury, Newbury, Berks, and Cecily Joan Burns, *née* Dumbell; *b* 9 Jan 1948; *Educ* Marlborough, RAC (MRAC); *m* 24 Nov 1984, Jacqueline Irene Kaye, da of Jack Woolly, of Rowan Dr, Wolverton, Milton Keynes; *Career* farmer and sport horse breeder; *Recreations* riding, travel; *Style—* Nicholas Skinner, Esq; Clere House, Ecchinswell, Newbury, Berks (☎ 0635 298 341)

SKINNER, Prof Quentin Robert Duthie; s of Alexander Skinner, CBE (d 1979), and Winifred Rose Margaret, *née* Duthie; *b* 26 Nov 1940; *Educ* Bedford Sch, Gonville and Caius Coll Cambridge (BA, MA); *m* 31 Aug 1979, Dr Susan Deborah Thorpe, da of Prof Derrick James, of London; 1 s (Marcus b 13 July 1982), 1 da (Olivia b 7 Dec 1979); *Career* Cambridge Univ: fell Christ's Coll 1962-, prof of political sci 1978-; FRHS 1970, FBA 1980; *Books* The Foundations of Modern Political Thought (1978), Machiavelli (1981), Meaning & Context (1988); *Style—* Prof Quentin Skinner; Christ's College, Cambridge, Cambs, CB2 3BU

SKINNER, Robin Charles Owen; s of Michael Owen Skinner, of Meadow Cottage, Sandy Lane, East Ashling, Chichester, West Sussex, and Patricia Alma, *née* Benson-Young; *b* 20 Sept 1949; *Educ* Rugby, FitzWilliam Coll Cambridge (MA), Coll of Law Guildford; *m* 21 July 1973, Jillian Mary, da of Benjamin Ian Gilmour Mantle, of 62 Storeys Way, Cambridge; 2 s (Charles b 30 May 1974, Toby b 24 June 1976), 1 da (Emily b 20 Oct 1982); *Career* articled Linklaters & Paines 1974, admitted slr 1975, sr ptnr Rawlinson & Butler 1984-; memb Worshipful Co of Cordwainers (Steward Warden 1988); Rugby Blue 1970-71, Rugby Fives Blue 1971 ; *Recreations* squash, tennis, family; *Clubs* Hawks and City Livery; *Style—* Robin Skinner, Esq; Beacon Platt, Dormansland, Lingfield, Surrey RH7 6RB; Rawlison & Butler, Griffin House, 135 High St, Crawley, West Sussex RH10 1DQ (☎ 0293 27 744, fax 0293 20 202, telex 877 751 RAWLEX)

SKINNER, Hon Mrs (Rose Marian); da of Maj Geoffrey Seymour Rowley-Conwy, and sis of 9 Baron Langford, OBE; *b* 6 June 1915; *m* 1938, Ralph Becher Skinner; 1 s, 2 da; *Career* raised to the rank of a Baron's da 1955; *Style—* The Hon Mrs Skinner; The Fold, Cwm, Nr Rhyl, Clwyd

SKINNER, Thomas Monier; CMG (1956), MBE (1941); s of Lt-Col Thomas Burrell Skinner, of Devon, and Mrs Mona Isobel Skinner, *née* Brown (d 1967); ancestors founded: RE 1 Newfoundland Fencibles, Skinner's Horse; *b* 2 Feb 1913; *Educ* Cheltenham, Lincoln Coll Oxford; *m* 1935, Margaret Adeline, *née* Pope (d 1969), da of Frederick Robert Pope (d 1934), of Sussex; 2 s (Anthony, Keith); m 2, 1981, Elizabeth Jane, da of Phillip Leicester Hardie (d 1977), of Cumbria; *Career* asst dist offr (cadet) 1935, asst dist offr 1937, dist offr Tanganyika 1947, sr asst sec E Africa High Cmmn 1952, dir of estabs Kenya 1955-62, ret; memb Civil Serv Cmmn E Caribbean Territories 1962-63, chm Nyasaland Local Civil Serv Cmmn 1963, salaries cmmr Basutoland The Bechuanaland Protectorate and Swaziland 1964; reports on localisation of Civil Serv, Gilbert and Ellice Islands Colony, Br Nat Serv New Hebrides 1968; chm and md: Bear Securities Ltd 19623-73, Exeter Tst plc 1973-78; chm: The Glassmaster Co Ltd 1979-87, Edinburgh Bond and Mortgage Corpn 1988-; dir Business Mortgages Tst plc 1979-87; *Recreations* fishing; *Clubs* Army and Navy; *Style—* Thomas Skinner, Esq, CMG, MBE; Innerpeffray Lodge, by Crieff, Perthshire PH7 3QW

SKIPPER, David John; s of Herbert George Skipper (d 1962), and Edna Skipper; *b* 14 April 1931; *Educ* Watford GS, Oxford Univ (MA); *m* 1955, Brenda Ann, da of late Alfred George Williams; 3 s, 1 da; *Career* served RAF 1954-57; asst master: Radley Coll 1957-63, Rugby Sch 1963-69; headmaster: Ellesmere Coll Salop 1969-81, Merchant Taylors' Sch 1981-; chm: special needs ctee ISJC, Soc of Sch Masters; *Recreations* golf, hill walking, painting, fungi, herbs; *Clubs* East India Devonshire and Public Schools; *Style—* David Skipper, Esq; Headmaster's House, Merchant Taylors' School, Northwood, Middx (☎ home 09274 27980, office 09274 1850)

SKIPWITH, Alexander Sebastian Grey d'Estoteville; s (by 1 m) and h of Sir Patrick Skipwith, 12 Bt; *b* 9 April 1969; *Educ* Harrow; *Style—* Alexander Skipwith, Esq; 27H Bramham Gdns, London SW5

SKIPWITH, Sir Patrick Alexander d'Estoteville; 12 Bt (E 1622), of Prestwould, Leicestershire; s of Grey d'Estoteville Townsend Skipwith (ka 1942), and Sofka, da of Prince Peter Alexandrovitch Dolgorouky; suc gf, Sir Grey Humberston d'Estoteville Skipwith 1950; *b* 1 Sept 1938; *Educ* Harrow, Trinity Coll Dublin (MA), Imperial Coll London (PhD); *m* 1, 24 June 1964 (m dis 1970), Gillian Patricia, adopted da of late Charles Frederick Harwood; 1 s, 1 da; m 2, 1972, Ashkhain, da of Bedros Atikian, of Calgary, Alberta, Canada; *Heir* s, Alexander Sebastian Grey d'Estoteville Skipwith b 9 April 1969; *Career* marine geologist: Ocean Mining Inc 1966-70, Directorate-Gen of Mineral Resources Jeddah 1970-73; geological ed Bureau de Recherches Géologiques et Minières Jeddah Saudi Arabia 1973-86, md Immel Publishing Ltd 1988-; freelance editing and public relations 1986-; *Recreations* riding, deep sea fishing, hill walking; *Clubs* Chelsea Arts, Dover Street Arts; *Style—* Sir Patrick Skipwith, Bt; c/o Lloyds Bank plc, 164 Kings Rd, Chelsea, London SW3 4UR

SKYRME, Hon Mrs (Barbara Suzanne); *née* Lyle; da of 1 Baron Lyle of Westbourne (d 1954); *b* 1915; *m* 1938 (m dis 1953), William Thomas Charles Skyrme, KCVO, CB

CBE, TD, JP, *qv*; 1 s, 2 da (*see* Sir Gerard Waterlow, Bt); *Style*— The Hon Mrs Skyrme; River House, Remenham, Henley-on-Thames, Oxon; 1 Sloane Court East, London SW3

SKYRME, Sir (William) Thomas Charles; KCVO (1974), CB (1966), CBE (1953), TD (1949), JP (Oxon 1948), DL (Glos 1983); s of C G Skyrme of Monmouth; *b* 1913; *Educ* Rugby, New Coll Oxford, Dresden Univ, Paris Univ; *m* 1, 1938 (m dis 1953), Hon Barbara Suzanne, *qv*, yr da of 1 Baron Lyle of Westbourne (d 1954); 1 s, 2 da (*see* Sir Gerard Waterlow, Bt); m 2, 1957, Mary, da of Dr R C Leaning; *Career* WWII RA (wounded twice), Lt-Col; called to the bar Inner Temple 1935, (Master of the Bench 1988), Western circuit, sec to Lord Chllr 1944-48, sec of Cmmns 1948-77; pres Cwlth Magistrates' and Judges' Assoc 1970-79, (life vice-pres 1979), chm Magistrates' Assoc of Eng and Wales 1979-81, (vice-pres 1981-), income tax gen cmmr 1977-88, cmmr Broadcasting Complaints Cmmn 1981- (chm 1985-87), memb Top Salaries Review Bd 1981-, chm Judicial Salaries Ctee 1984-; Freeman City of London 1970, HM lt City of London 1977-; FRGS; *Books* The Changing Image of the Magistracy (1979); *Clubs* Army and Navy, Hurlingham; *Style*— Sir Thomas Skyrme, KCVO, CB, CBE, TD, JP, DL; Casa Larissa, Klosters, Switzerland; Elm Barns, Blockley, Moreton-in-Marsh, Glos

SLACK, Timothy Willatt; s of Cecil Moorhouse Slack, MC (d 1986), and Dora, *née* Willatt (d 1978); *b* 18 April 1928; *Educ* Winchester, New Coll Oxford (MA); *m* 31 Aug 1957, Katharine, da of Norman Hughes (d 1982); 1 s (Henry b 1962), 3 da (Caroline b 1960, Louisa b 1966, Rebecca b 1969); *Career* Nat Serv RN; asst master: Lycée de Garcons Rennes France 1951-52, Schule Schloss Salem W Germany 1952-53, Repton Derbys 1953-59; headmaster: Kambawsa Coll Burma 1959-62, Bedales Sch Hants 1962-74; dir FCO Wiston House Conf Centre 1977-83 (asst dir 1975-77), headmaster Hellenic Coll London 1983-84, princ St Catharine's Fndn Cumberland Lodge Windsor 1985-; Parly candidate: (Lib) Petersfield Feb and Oct 1974, (Alliance) Enfield Southgate 1984 (Alliance) Fareham 1987; memb Soc of Headmasters of Independent Schs (chm 1965-67); *Style*— Timothy Slack, Esq; Hamlet House, Hambledon, Hants PO7 6RY (☎ 070132 358); Cumberland Lodge, The Great Park, Windsor, Berks SL4 2HP (☎ 0784 32316/34893, fax 0784 38507)

SLADE, Adrian Carnegie; CBE (1988); s of George Penkivil Slade, KC (d 1942), and Mary Albinia Alice, *née* Slade (d 1988); *b* 25 May 1936; *Educ* Eton, Trinity Coll Cambridge (BA); *m* 22 June 1960, Susan Elizabeth, da of Edward Forsyth (d 1978); 1 s (Rupert b 15 Jan 1965), 1 da (Nicola b 28 March 1962); *Career* Nat Serv: 2 Lt 9 Lancers 1955-56, Lt Emergency Res 1956-60; dir S H Benson (advertising) 1969-71, co-fndr and md Slade Hamilton Fenech 1986- (prev Slade Bluff & Bigg 1975-85, Slade Monica Bluff 1971-74); memb mgmnt ctee Wandsworth Cncl for Community Relations 1967-81, dir Orange Tree Theatre Ltd (Richmond) 1966 and 1974; Parly Candidate: (Lib) Putney 1966 and 1974, Wimbledon (Alliance) 1987; memb GLC and Alliance Gp Ldr 1981-86; pres London Lib Pty 1982-85, pres Lib Pty 1987-88, joint interim pres SLD 1984, (Eng vice pres 1988-); *Recreations* theatre, music, photography, piano playing; *Style*— Adrian Slade, Esq, CBE

SLADE, (Sir) (Julian) Benjamin Alfred; 7 Bt (UK 1831), of Maunsel House, Somersetshire; does not use title; s of Capt Sir Michael Niall Slade, 6 Bt (d 1962), and Angela (d 1959), da of Capt Orlando Chichester; *b* 22 May 1946; *Educ* Millfield; *m* 1977, Pauline Carol, da of Maj Claude Myburgh; *Career* chm and md Shirlstar Container Transport Ltd, dir Pyman Bell Ltd; Freeman City of London 1979, memb Worshipful Co of Ironmongers; *Recreations* hunting, shooting, racing, polo, bridge; *Clubs* Turf, Old Somerset Dining, Bucks; *Style*— Benjamin Slade, Esq; 164 Ashley Gdns, Emery Hill St, London SW1 (☎ 01 828 2809); Maunsel, North Newton, Bridgwater, Somerset (☎ 0278 663413; estate office ☎ 0278 662387); office: Shirlstar House, 37 St John's Road, Uxbridge, Middx (☎ 0895 72929, telex 885635)

SLADE, Brian John; s of Albert Edward Victor Slade, of Portsmouth, Hants, and Florence Elizabeth, *née* Eveleigh; *b* 28 April 1931; *Educ* Portsmouth Northern GS, London Univ; *m* 5 March 1955, Grace, da of William McKerrow Murray, (d 1943), of Ayr; 1 s (Ian Murray b 1962), 1 da (Maureen Grace b 1959); *Career* joined Miny of Supply 1951, private sec to permanent sec Miny of Aviation 1962-64, head industl personnel branch Miny of Technol 1968-73; MOD: head of contracts policy branch 1978-82, princ dir of contracts (air) 1982-86, dir gen of def contracts 1986-; memb Synod London SW Dist Methodist Church 1981-, sec to church cncl Epsom Methodist Church 1981-; FInstPS 1986; *Recreations* downs walking, cricket; *Style*— Brian Slade, Esq; Doonbank, 16 Greenway, Gt Bookham, Surrey (☎ 0372 54359); St George's Ct, 14 New Oxford St, London WC1A 1EJ (☎ 01 632 3600)

SLADE, Rt Hon Lord Justice; Rt Hon Sir Christopher John Slade; PC (1982); s of George Penkivil Slade, KC (d 1942), and Mary Albinia Alice Slade; *b* 2 June 1927; *Educ* Eton, New Coll Oxford; *m* 1958, Jane Gwenllian Armstrong, da of Rt Hon Sir Denys Buckley, MBE; 1 s, 3 da; *Career* barr 1951, QC 1965, attorney-general Duchy of Lancaster 1972-75, bencher Lincoln's Inn 1973, judge of High Ct of Justice (Chancery Div) 1975-82, judge of Restrictive Practices Ct 1980-82 and pres 1981-1982, lord justice of appeal 1982-; kt 1975; *Clubs* Garrick; *Style*— The Rt Hon Lord Justice Slade; 12 Harley Gdns, London SW10 (☎ 01 373 7695)

SLADE, Hon Mrs; Hon Constance; *née* Montague; da of 2 Baron Amwell; *b* 2 Mar 1915; *Educ* N London Collegiate Sch; *m* 1938, Albert Slade; 1 s, 2 da; *Style*— The Hon Mrs Slade; 27 Howitt Rd, NW3

SLADE, Julian Penkivil; s of George, Penkivil Slade, KC (d 1942), of London and Mary Albina Alice, *née* Carnegie (d 1988); *b* 28 May 1930; *Educ* Eton, Trinity Coll Cambridge (BA); *Career* composer/author; musical plays incl: Bang Goes the Meringue! Lady May (1951), Christmas in King Street (with Dorothy Reynolds, 1952), The Duenna (1953), The Merry Gentleman (1953), Salad Days (1954-60), Free as Air (1957), Hooray for Daisy (1959), Follow that Girl (1960), Wildest Dreams (1961); other musicals: Vanity Fair (1962), Nutmeg and Ginger (1963), Sixty Thousand Nights (1966), The Pursuit of Love (1967), Winnie the Pooh (1970), Trelawny (1972), Out of Bounds (1975), Love in a Cold Climate (Thames TV, 1981), Now We Are Sixty; (1986) published scripts incl: Salad Days, Free as Air, Follow that Girl, The Duenna, The Merry Gentleman, Trelawny; Nibble The Squirrel (1946); *Recreations* going to theatre and cinema, drawing, listening to music; *Style*— Julian Slade, Esq; 86 Beaufort Street, London SW3 6BU (☎ 01 376 4480)

SLADEN, Angus Murray; s of Sqdn Ldr Algernon Ivan Sladen, DSO (d 1976), and Dorviegelda Malvina, *née* MacGregor; *b* 17 Dec 1950; *Educ* Stowe, Univ of Texas; *Career* insur broker 1974-; dir: Wendover Underwriting Agency Ltd (Lloyd's underwriting agencies); *Recreations* shooting, stalking, fishing; *Clubs* Buck's, City of London; *Style*— Angus Sladen, Esq; Glencarron Lodge, Achnashellach, Ross-shire; 14 Shafto Mews, London SW1; 3 St Helens Place, Bishopsgate, London EC3 (☎ 01 628 1317)

SLANE, Viscount; Alexander Burton Conyngham; s and h of Earl of Mount Charles, *qv*; *b* 30 Jan 1975; *Style*— Viscount Slane

SLANEY, Prof Sir Geoffrey; KBE (1984); s of Richard and Gladys Lois Slaney; *b* 19 Sept 1922; *Educ* Brewood GS, Univs of Birmingham, London and Illinois USA; *m* 1956, Josephine Mary Davy; 1 s, 2 da; *Career* Barling prof head of dept of surgery Queen Elizabeth Hosp Birmingham 1971-; hon conslt surgn: Utd Birmingham Hosps and Regnl Hosp Bd 1959-, Royal Prince Alfred Hosp Sydney 1981-; pres Royal Coll of Surgeons; *Style*— Prof Sir Geoffrey Slaney, KBE; 23 Aston Bury, Edgbaston, Birmingham B15 3QB (☎ 021 454 0261)

SLATER, Hon Mrs Alexandra Janet; eld da of Dr Geoffrey Tyndale Young, and Baroness Young (Life Peer); *b* 1951; *m* 1974, John Douglas Slater; 1 s, 1 da; *Style*— The Hon Mrs Slater; 12 Edgar Road, Winchester, Hants

SLATER, Arnold; s of Arnold Slater, of Holmfirth, Yorks, and Pauline Margaret, *née* Shaw-Parker; *b* 26 Mar 1948; *Educ* Hadham Hall Sch, Regent St Poly; *m* 21 Oct 1972, Judith Helen, da of Philip Ellison, of Bishops Stortford, Herts; 1 s (Ross Adrian b 24 Sept 1973), 1 da (Anthea Helen b 15 Feb 1978); *Career* chief photographer Herts and Essex Observer 1973-78; photographer: Press Assoc 1978-87, London Daily News Jan 1987 - June 1987, Sunday People 1987-88, Daily Mirror 1988-; winner: Simeon Edmunds Award Best Young Press Photographer, Ilford Press Photographer of the Year 1987; *Recreations* squash, skiing, fly tying, fly fishing; *Style*— Arnold Slater, Esq; Shingle Sand, Copthall Lane, Thaxted, Essex, CM5 2LG (☎ 0371 830452); Mirror Group Newspapers, Holborn Circus, London, EC1P 1DQ (☎ 01 822 3851)

SLATER, Hon Brian; s of Baron Slater (Life Peer, d 1977); *b* 1948; *Style*— The Hon Brian Slater

SLATER, Duncan; CMG (1982); *b* 15 July 1934; *m* 1972, Candida Coralie Anne Wheatley; 1 s, 2 da; *Career* joined FO 1958; served: Abu Dhabi, Islamabad, New Delhi; head of chancery Aden 1968-69, FO 1969, special asst to Sir William Luce 1970-71, first sec UK Representation to EEC Brussels 1973-75, UK rep to Int Atomic Energy Authy and UN Industl Devpt Orgn 1975-78, cnsllr and head of chancery Lagos 1978-81 and on staff of Govt House Salisbury 1979-80, ambass to Muscat 1981-86, asst leader Sec of State FCO 1986-; *Style*— Duncan Slater, Esq, CMG; c/o Foreign and Commonwealth Office, London SW1

SLATER, Gordon Charles Henry; CMG (1964), CBE (1956); s of Matthew Slater (d 1922); *b* 14 Dec 1903; *Educ* Croydon Poly, London Univ; *m* 1928, Doris Primrose, *née* Hammond; 1 s, 1 da; *Career* Miny of Labour 1928-64, (asst sec 1945, under sec 1958-64); dir London branch office ILO 1964-70; memb Berks CC 1970-81 (vice chm 1977-79; *Recreations* gardening, civic affairs mainly concerning environment; *Style*— Gordon Slater, Esq, CMG, CBE; White House, 66 Altwood Rd, Maidenhead, Berks (☎ 0628 27 463)

SLATER, Vice Adm Sir (John Cunningham Kirkwood) Jock; KCB (1988), LVO (1971); s of Dr James K Slater, OBE (d 1965), of Edinburgh, and Margaret Claire Byrom, *née* Bramwell; *b* 27 Mar 1938; *Educ* Edinburgh Acad, Sedbergh; *m* 1972, Ann Frances, da of William Patrick Scott, OBE, DL, of Orkney Islands; 2 s (Charles b 1974, Rory b 1977); *Career* RN; Equerry to HM The Queen 1968-71; CO: HMS Jupiter (frigate) 1972-73, HMS Kent (guided missile destroyer) 1976-77; Royal Coll of Defence Studies 1978; CO: HMS Illustrious (aircraft carrier) 1981-83, HMS Dryad & Capt Sch of Maritime Ops 1983-85; ACODS (Policy & Nuclear) 1985-87; Flag Offr Scotland & N Ireland, Naval Base Cdr Rosyth, NATO Cdr N sub area E Atlantic, Cdr Nore sub-area Channel 1987-89, Chief of Fleet Support 1989-; *Recreations* outdoor; *Clubs* Army and Navy; *Style*— Vice Adm Sir Jock Slater, KCB, LVO; c/o Royal Bank of Scotland, West End Office, Princes Street, Edinburgh; MOD, Whitehall, London SW1A 2HB

SLATER, Kenneth Frederick; s of Charles Frederick Slater (d 1929), and Emily Gertrude, *née* Rodmell (d 1959); *b* 31 July 1925; *Educ* Hull GS, Manchester Univ (BSc); *m* 1965, Marjorie Gladys, da of Horace Beadsworth (d 1942); *Career* leader UK team of nat experts for definition of NATO Air Defence Ground Environment Malvern 1964, head of Ground Radar and Air Traffic Control Gp 1971, head of applied physics dept and dep dir Royal Signals and Radar Establishment (RSRE) Malvern 1976, head of Civil and Military Systems Dept and dep dir RSRE 1977; dir: Admty Surface Weapons Establishment Portsmouth 1978, engrg at Marconi Underwater Systems Ltd Waterlooville 1984; FIEE, FEng; *Publications* articles for Scientific journals and conferences including articles in the Dictionary of Applied Physics and the Encyclopaedia Britannica; *Recreations* (yacht 'Ripples'), music, photography, walking; *Clubs* Royal Corinthian Yacht (Isle of Wight), Royal Naval & Royal Albert Yacht (Portsmouth), RN Sailing Assoc; *Style*— Kenneth Slater, Esq; 'Wessenden', Biddenfield Lane, Wickham, Hants; Marconi Underwater Systems Ltd, Waterlooville, Hants (☎ 0705 260009)

SLATER, Peter; s of Harry Slater (d 1984), of Yorks, and Vivian, *née* Buckle (d 1987); *b* 22 Jan 1934; *Educ* Cockburn HS Leeds; *m* 1957, June Marlene; 1 da (Linda Anne b 1958); *Career* dir: IMI Valves Int Ltd 1978, IMI Fluid Power Int Ltd 1983, Norgren Martonair Pty Ltd (Hong Kong) 1984, Norgren Martonair Hong Kong Ltd 1984, Shavo Norgren (India) Pvt Ltd 1986, IMI Control and Instrumentation Ltd 1988, Control Components (UK) Ltd 1988, fin dir IMI Fluid Control Gp 1988; memb Assoc Inst of CA (1962), FCA (1972); *Recreations* clay pigeon shooting, motoring, reading; *Style*— Peter Slater, Esq; Springfield, Appletree Lane, Inkberrow, Worcs (☎ 0386 792934); 21 Storry Hills Park, Limestone Rd, Burniston, nr Scarborough, Yorks; IMI plc, PO Box 216, Witton, Birmingham B6 7BA (☎ 021 356 4848)

SLATER, Richard Mercer Keene; CMG (1962); s of Samuel Henry Slater CMG, CIE (d 1968); *b* 27 May 1915; *Educ* Eton, Cambridge; *m* 1939, Barbara Janet, da of Lt-Col Clive Murdoch, DSO (d 1942); 4 s; *Career* asst under-sec state FCO 1973, high cmmr Uganda 1970-72, ambass to Cuba 1966-70; *Style*— Richard Slater, Esq, CMG; Vicary's, Odiham, Hants (☎ 025 671 2648)

SLATER, William Bell; CBE (1982), VRD (1959); s of William Bell Slater (d 1985), of 15 King's Walk, W Kirby, Wirral, Cheshire, by his w May; *b* 7 Jan 1925; *Educ* Lancaster Royal GS; *m* 1950, Jean Mary, da of George William Kiernan (d 1964); 2 s; *Career* war serv RM Commando Capt (Far East), RM Reserve 1949-63, Lt-Col and CO Mersyside Unit 1959-63, Hon Col 1986; chm: Thos & Jno Brocklebank 1972-85 (dir 1966-85, joined as trainee 1947), Cunard Brocklebank Ltd 1975-85 (dir 1967-85), Cunard Ship Mgmnt Servs Ltd 1970-85, Cunard Int Servs Ltd 1972-85, Albion & Overseas Shipping Agency Ltd 1972-85, Charles Howson & Co Ltd 1972-85, Moss Tankers Ltd 1972-85, Port Line Ltd 1975-85 (dir 1972-85), Cunard Shipping Servs Ltd 1972-85, Cunard Int Technical Servs Ltd 1974-85, Transworld Leasing Ltd 1977-85, Heavy Lift Cargo Airlines Ltd 1978-85; dir: Cunard Steam-Ship Co plc 1972-85 and 1986-88 (md Cargo Shipping and Aviation Div 1974-85), Cunard Gp Pension Tstees Ltd 1972-88, Osmarine Int Ltd 1972-85, Trafalgar House Tstees Ltd 1978-88 (Port Line Assoc cos) ACTA/ANL Assets Ltd 1975-85, ACT(A) Leasing Ltd 1975-85, Blueport ACT(N-Z) Ltd 1976-85 Blue Star Port Lines Mgmnt 1974-85, ACT(A) Investmts (Australia) Ltd 1978-85; chm Assoc Container Transportation (Australia) Ltd 1982-85 (dir 1974-85); chm: (Cunard Assoc cos): Assoc Containers Tportation 1982-85 (dir 1974-85), Atlantic Container Line Ltd 1977-78 and 1983-84 (dir 1968-85), Mersey Docks & Harbour Co 1987- (dep chm 1985-87, dir 1980-); dir Trafalgar House plc 1975-88; memb Gen Cncl of Br Shipping 1975-85, pres Inst of Freight Forwarders Ltd 1987-88, FCIT (vice-pres 1984-87), Order of El Istiglal (2nd Class) Jordan 1972; *Recreations* swimming, gardening, walking, (previously rugby, cricket); *Clubs* Naval; *Style—* William Slater, Esq, CBE, VRD; Gayton Ct, 419 Woodham Lane, Woodham, Weybridge, Surrey KT15 3PP (☎ 09323 49389)

SLATTERY, Rear Adm Sir Matthew Sausse; KBE (1960), CB (1946); s of Henry Francis Slattery (d 1911), sometime chm National Bank Ltd; *b* 12 May 1902; *Educ* Stonyhurst, RNCs Osborne and Dartmouth; *m* 1925, Mica Mary, da of Lt-Col George Swain, CMG (d 1924); 2 s, 1 da; *Career* Admiral served RN 1916-48 (ret), vice-controller (Air) and chief Naval Air Equipment Admty, and chief naval rep Supply Cncl (Miny Supply) 1945-48; Short Bros & Harland: md 1948-52, chm and md 1952-60; special advsr to PM on Tport of Middle East Oil 1957-59, dir National Bank Ltd 1959-60 and 1964-70, chm BOAC-Cunard Ltd 1962-63 and chm BOAC 1960-63, chm R & W Hawthorn Leslie & Co Ltd 1965-75; kt 1955; *Recreations* country pursuits; *Clubs* Naval & Military; *Style—* Rear Admiral Sir Matthew Slattery; Harvey's Farm, Warninglid, W Sussex (☎ 044 485 291)

SLATTERY, Peter Anthony; s of Rear Adm Sir Matthew Sausse Slattery, KBE, CB, *qv*; *b* 21 Mar 1926; *Educ* Ampleforth; *m* 1, 1951 (m dis 1979) Joanella Elizabeth Agnes, *née* Scrymsour-Nichol; 1 s, 2 da; m 2, 1979, Judith Mary, *née* Gilbert; *Career* studied law at Middle Temple; md: Hobbs Savill & Bradford Ltd 1967-71 (asst md 1967-71), H S Tstees Ltd 1961-71, Williams & Glyn's Insur Conslts Ltd 1971-75, dep dir Williams & Glyn's Bank 1972-75, dir and gen mangr Marine and Gen Mutual Life Assur Soc 1975-85, (non-exec dir 1985-86), dir MGM Assur (Tstees) Ltd 1976-85 (chm 1985-86), chm and md MGM Unit Mangrs Ltd 1982-85 (non-exec chm 1985-86), dir Shield Assur Ltd 1986-, dir and sec Unicorn Heritage plc 1987-; *Recreations* photography, gardening; *Style—* Peter Slattery, Esq; 18 Holmwood Rd, Cheam, Sutton, Surrey (☎ 01 393 6018)

SLAUGHTER, Giles David; s of Gerald Slaughter (d 1945), of Harpenden, Herts, and Enid Lilian, *née* Crane (d 1987); *b* 11 July 1937; *Educ* Royal Masonic Sch Bushey Herts, King's Coll Cambridge (BA, MA); *m* 14 Aug 1965, Gillian Rothwell, da of Philip Rothwell Shepherd (d 1981); 3 da (Miranda b 1966, Victoria b 1967, Imogen b 1976); *Career* Nat Serv 2 Lt 1 Bn Suffolk Regt 1955-57; housemaster Ormiston House Campbell Coll Belfast; headmaster: Solihull Sch West Midlands 1973-82, Univ Coll Sch Hampstead 1983-; memb HMC 1973-; memb mgmnt cncl Assoc Prevention of Addiction; JP Solihull 1977-82; FRSA; ; *Recreations* theatre, gardening, cricket, golf; *Clubs* East India Devonshire Sports and Public Schs; *Style—* Giles Slaughter, Esq; 5 Redington Rd, Hampstead, London NW3 7QX; 6 Church Lane, Lower Ufford, Woodbridge, Suffolk (☎ 0394 461 281); Univ Coll, Frognal, London NW3 6XH (☎ 01 435 2215)

SLAYMAKER, Paul Ellis; s of Ellis Hamilton Slaymaker, of Surrey, and Barbara Joan, *née* Langfield; *b* 10 Mar 1945; *Educ* Sunbury GS (BA), Ealing Tech Coll; *m* 1968, Ann Elizabeth, da of Edward Michael Frederick Piercey (d 1982), of Isle of Wight; 1 s (Nicholas b 1978), 1 da (Emma b 1975); *Career* advertising; mgmnt conslt McKinsey & Co Inc 1975-76, head of mktg CPC (UK) Ltd 1977-80, dep md Leo Burnett Ltd 1980-86; md Slaymaker Cowley White 1986-; *Recreations* photography, badminton, running, gardening; *Style—* Paul Slaymaker, Esq; 10 Beaufort Close, Lynden Gate, London SW15 3TL (☎ 01 788 0578); Slaymaker Cowley White, 8 Henrietta Street, London WC2E 8PS (☎ 01 836 3474)

SLEDGE, The Ven Richard Kitson; s of Sidney Kitson Sledge (d 1968), and Mary Sylvia Sledge, *née* Harland, of Sandal, Wakefield; *b* 13 April 1930; *Educ* Epsom Coll, Peterhouse Cambridge (MA); *m* 12 April 1958, Patricia Henley, da of Gordon Sear of Dunstable (d 1985); 2 s (Timothy b 1964, Nicholas (decd)), 2 da (Elizabeth b 1959, Hilary b 1966); *Career* ordained deacon 1954, priest 1955; curate of: Compton Gifford Devon 1954-57, St Martin, St Stephen, St Laurence, Exeter 1957-63; rector of Dronfield Derbyshire 1963-78; rural dean of Chesterfield 1972-78; rector of Hemingford Abbots Cambs 1978-; hon canon of Ely 1978-; archdeacon of Huntingdon 1978-; *Style—* The Ven R K Sledge MA; The Rectory, Hemingford Abbots, Huntingdon, Cambs PE18 9AN (☎ 0480 69856)

SLEEMAN, John Henry; s of Herbert Sleeman (d 1950); *b* 4 May 1922; *Educ* Thorpe Sch; *m* 1945, Elsie; 2 s; *Career* chartered sec; chm Charterhouse Japhet Bank & Tst Int Ltd (Nassau) until 1982, dir Charterhouse Japhet plc until 1982; chm: Industl Finance & Investmt Corpn plc, Personal Assurance plc; dir: Personal Assurance plc, Refuge Gp plc, Refuge Assurance plc, Canterbury Life Assurance Co Ltd, chm Nat Children's Charities Fund; *Style—* John Sleeman Esq; 1 Paternoster Row, St Paul's, London EC4M 7DH (☎ 01 248 3999)

SLEEMAN, His Hon Stuart Colin; s of Stuart Bertram Sleeman (d 1970), of Alton, Parry's Lane, Bristol, and Phyllis Grace, *née* Pitt (d 1976); *b* 10 Mar 1914; *Educ* Clifton, Merton Coll Oxford (MA); *m* 1944, Margaret Emily, yst da of William Joseph Farmer (d 1939), of Minehead, Somerset; 2 s (Stuart, Jeremy), 1 da (Jenifer); *Career* WWII Lt-Col 16/5 Lancers; barr Gray's Inn 1938, Western circuit 1938-49, admin offr prize dept Miny of Economic Warfare 1939-40, asst-judge advocate-gen HQ Allied Land Forces SE Asia 1945-46, Midland circuit 1949, London corr Scottish Law Review 1949-54, bencher Gray's Inn 1974, rec 1975, circuit judge 1976-86; *Books* The Trial of Gozawa Sadaichi and Nine Others (1948), The Double Tenth Trial (with S C Silkin, 1951); *Recreations* travel, genealogy; *Style—* His Hon Colin Sleeman; West Walls, Cotmandene, Dorking, Surrey RH4 2BL (☎ 0306 883616); 1 Gray's Inn Sq, London WC1R 5AA (☎ 01 404 0763)

SLEIGHT, Sir John Frederick; 3 Bt (UK 1920) of Weelsby Hall, Clee, Co Lincoln; s of Sir Ernest Sleight, 2 Bt, OBE, TD (d 1946), and Margaret, *née* Carter; *b* 13 April 1909; *m* 1942, Jacqueline Margaret, eld da of Maj H R Carter, of Brisbane, and wid of Ronald Mundell; 1 s; *Heir* s, Richard Sleight; *Style—* Sir John Sleight, Bt; 4 Plumosa Ct, Broadbeach Waters, Queensland, 4218, Australia

SLEIGHT, Michael Marcus; s of George Frederick Sleight (d 1954), 4 s of Sir George Frederick Sleight, Bt, of Binbrook Hall, Binbrook, Lincoln, and Edith Mary, *née* Brockway (d 1963); *b* 12 August 1924; *Educ* private tutor Cambridge; *Career* WWII ROC 1942-45; landowner; jt patron of 21 parishes, lord of 3 manors, churchwarden, cncl memb Lincoln Record Soc; memb: Royal Archaeological Inst, Br Archaeological Assoc; *Recreations* visiting old churches; *Style—* Michael Sleight, Esq; Binbrook Hall, Binbrook, Lincoln LN3 6BW (☎ 047283 209)

SLEIGHT, Richard; s and h of Sir John Sleight, 3 Bt; *b* 27 May 1946; *m* 1978, Marie-Thérèse, da of O M Stepan; *Style—* Richard Sleight, Esq

SLESSOR, Gp Capt John Arthur Guinness; s of Marshal of the RAF Sir John Slessor, GCB, DSO, MC (d 1979), and Hermione Grace, *née* Guinness (d 1970); *b* 14 August 1925; *Educ* Eton, Ch Ch Oxford; *m* 6 Oct 1951, Ann Dorothea, da of late George Gibson; 1 s (Anthony b 1954), 1 da (Catherine b 1955); *Career* joined RAF 1943, served N France 1944, cmmnd 1945, various flying appts 1946-59 (inc: Germany and Rhodesia), Staff Coll 1959-60 , USAF Acad Colorado 1960-62, OC 83 Sqdn (V-Force) 1962-65, Jt Servs Staff Coll 1965, MOD 1966-68, Air Attaché Madrid 1968-70, OC RAF Odiham 1971-73, Chief Intelligence Offr RAF Germany 1973-75, MOD 1976-77, ret 1978; sec overseas relations HQ St John Ambulance 1978-, pres Alton div St John Ambulance 1988-; Gentleman Usher to HM The Queen 1978-; OStJ 1981; *Recreations* country pursuits; *Clubs* RAF; *Style—* Gp Capt J A G Slessor, RAF (ret); Honeywell, Birkham, Alton, Hants GU34 5RT (☎ 025 683 325); 1 Grosvenor Crescent, London SW1X 7EF (☎ 01 235 5231)

SLEVIN, Brian Francis Patrick; CMG (1975), OBE (1973), CPM (1965), QPM (1968); s of Thomas Francis Slevin, and Helen, *née* Murray (d 1954); *b* 13 August 1926; *Educ* Blackrock Coll Ireland; *m* 15 July 1972, (Constance) Gay, da of Maj Ronald Moody (d 1988); 1 s (Simon b 1973); *Career* Palestine Police 1946-48; Royal Hong Kong Police 1949-79: ADC to HE Govr of Hong Kong 1952, directing staff overseas police courses Met Police Coll Hendon London 1955-57, dir Special Branch 1966-69, sr asst cmmr of police (cmdg Kowloon Dist) 1969-70, dir CID 1971, dep cmmr of police 1971 (cmmr of police 1974-79); recently in Hong Kong: vice pres Hong Kong RFU, vice pres Hong Kong Boy Scouts Assoc, govr Hong Kong Life Gd Club; *Recreations* walking, golf, tennis, gardening, reading, painting; *Clubs* Royal Hong Kong Golf, Royal Jockey (Hong Kong), The Hong Kong; *Style—* Brian Slevin, Esq, CMG, OBE, CPM, QPM; Lantau Lodge, 152 Coonanbarra Rd, Wahrounga, Sydney, NSW 2076, Australia (☎ 02 4896671)

SLIGO, 10 Marquess of (I 1800); Denis Edward Browne; sits as Baron Monteagle (UK 1806); Baron Mount Eagle (I 1760), Viscount Westport (I 1768), Earl of Altamont (I 1771), Earl of Clanricarde (I 1543 and 1800, with special remainder); s of late Lt-Col Lord Alfred Eden Browne, DSO (s of 5 Marquess of Sligo); suc unc, 9 Marquess of Sligo 1952; *b* 13 Dec 1908; *Educ* Eton; *m* 1930, José Gauche; 1 s; *Heir* s, Earl of Altamont; *Style—* The Most Hon The Marquess of Sligo; c/o Messrs Trower, Still and Keeling, 5 New sq, Lincoln's Inn (☎ WC2)

SLIM, Aileen, Viscountess; Aileen; da of Rev J A Robertson of Edinburgh; *m* 1926, 1 Viscount Slim, KG, GCB, GCMG, GCVO, GBE, DSO, MC (d 1970); 1 s, 1 da; *Career* DStJ, has Kaisar-i-Hind Medal; *Style—* The Rt Hon Aileen, Viscountess Slim; 18 STack House, Cundy St Flats, Ebury St, London SW1W 9JS

SLIM, Hon Hugo John Robertson; s of 2 Viscount Slim, OBE; *b* 1961; *Educ* MA (Oxon); *Career* field admin Save The Children Fund Morocco 1983, Sudan 1985, Ethiopia E 1986; *Clubs* Bucks, Special Forces; *Style—* The Hon Hugo Slim

SLIM, 2 Viscount (UK 1960); John Douglas Slim; OBE (1973), DL (Greater London 1988); s of Field Marshal 1 Viscount (Sir William Joseph) Slim, KG, GCB, GCMG, GCVO, GBE, DSO, MC, sometime GOC Allied Land Forces SE Asia, govr-gen Australia and govr and constable Windsor Castle (d 1970); *b* 20 July 1927; *Educ* Prince of Wales Royal Indian Military Coll Dehra Dun; *m* 1958, Elisabeth, da of Arthur Rawdon Spinney, CBE (decd); 2 s, 1 da; *Heir* s, Hon Mark Slim; *Career* cmmnd Indian Army 6 Gurkha Rifles 1945-48, Lt Argyll and Sutherland Highlanders 1948, Staff Coll 1961, Jt Service Staff Coll 1964, Cdr 22 SAS Regt 1967-70, GSO1 (Special Forces) HQ UK Land Forces 1970-72, ret 1972; chm Peek plc; dir of other cos; pres Burma Star Assoc; vice-pres Britain-Australia Soc; vice-chm Arab-British C of C and Indust; FRGS 1983; *Clubs* White's, Special Forces; *Style—* The Rt Hon the Viscount Slim, OBE, DL; c/o Lloyds Bank plc, 6 Pall Mall, SW1

SLIM, Hon Mark William Rawdon; s and h of 2 Viscount Slim, OBE; *b* 13 Feb 1960; *Career* mktg dir Stavling Projects Inc Dallas Texas USA; *Clubs* Bucks, Special Forces; *Style—* The Hon Mark Slim

SLIM, Hon Mary Ann; da of 2 Viscount Slim, OBE

SLIMMINGS, Sir William Kenneth MacLeod; CBE (1960); s of George Slimmings (d 1952), of Dunfermline, Fife; *b* 15 Dec 1912; *Educ* Dunfermline HS; *m* 1943, Lilian Ellen, da of Walter Edward Willis, of Hornchurch, Essex; 1 s, 1 da; *Career* CA; ptnr Thomson McLintock & Co 1946-78, chm Bd of Trade Advsy Ctee 1957-66; memb: ctee of inquiry on cost of housebuilding 1947-53, ctee on Tax-paid Stocks 1952-53, ctee on Cheque Endorsement 1955-56, Performing Right Tbnl 1963-72, cncl Scottish Inst of CAs 1962-66 (pres 1969-70), Scottish Tourist Bd 1969-76, Review Body on Doctors and Dentists Remuneration 1976-83, Crown Agents' Tbnl 1978-82; chm review body for Govt Contracts 1971-81; kt 1966; *Style—* Sir William Slimmings, CBE; 62 The Avenue, Worcester Park, Surrey (☎ 01 337 2579)

SLINGER, Alexander (Michael) Foulds; s of Milton Slinger (d 1957), of Colne, Lancs, and Edith, JP, *née* Foulds; *b* 8 Feb 1939; *Educ* Giggleswick, Clare Coll Cambridge (BA, MA); *m* 15 April 1967, Felicity Margaret, da of Sir William Rowley, Bt (d 1971), of Widdington, Saffron Walden, Essex; 2 da (Arabella b 1972, Katharine b 1977); *Career* Nat Serv 2 Lt Loyals, Malaya 1959, Germany 1960; Allied Breweries 1964-73, sales dir Hatch Mansfield & Co 1970-73, nat accounts dir Saccone & Speed 1975-78, md John E Fells & Sons 1978-81, estab own businesses fine wine merchants and shippers: Chesterford Vintners 1981, Tempest Slinger & Co 1981, Town & Country Vintners 1981; capt Cambridge Univ Ski Club 1962-63, memb Br Univs Ski Team 1963; Freeman City of London 1982, Liveryman Worshipful Co of Distillers 1982; *Recreations* travel, skiing, photography, wine, food, golf; *Clubs* Hawks

Cambridge, Univ Pitt Cambridge, Ski Club of GB, Kandahar Ski Club; *Style—* Michael Slinger, Esq; Slaters House, Widdington, Saffron Walden, Essex CB11 3SN (☎ 0799 40066); 34 Hornton St, London W8 7NR (☎ 01 937 0303); business: The Old Greyhound, Great Chesterford, Saffron Walden, Essex CB10 1NY (☎ 0799 30088)

SLINGER, Edward; s of Thomas Slinger (d 1957), of Lancs, and Rhoda, *née* Bradshaw (d 1987); *b* 2 Feb 1938; *Educ* Accrington GS, Balliol Coll Oxford (BA); *m* 31 July 1965, Rosalind Margaret, da of Stanley Albert Jewitt, of Chiddingfield, Surrey; 2 s (Giles b 1969, Fergus b 1975), 2 da (Nicola b 1967, Emma b 1971); *Career* admitted slr 1961; dep dist registrar High Ct 1981-88, asst rec Crown Ct 1988-; memb TCCB disciplinary ctee 1987-, vice chm Lancs CCC 1987-; *Clubs* Lancashire CCC, MCC; *Style—* Edward Slinger, Esq; 25/29 Victoria Street, Blackburn, Lancs (☎ 0254 672222)

SLIPMAN, Sue; da of Max Slipman (d 1971), of London, and Doris *née* Barham (d 1972); *b* 3 August 1949; *Educ* Stockwell Manor Sch, Univ of Wales (BA), Univ of London (PGCE); 1 s (Gideon Max b 1988); *Career* pres NUS 1977-78, vice chm Br Youth Cncl 1977-78, cncl memb the Open Univ 1978-81, memb City and Guilds Numeracy Examination Bd 1984, chair of ctee of mgmnt workbase 1981-86; memb: exec ctee 300 Group 1985, advsy cncl for Adult and continuing Educ 1978-, Nat Union of Public Employees 1970-85, dir nat cncl for one parent families 1985-; author of chapters in: The Re - Birth of Britain 1983, Public Issues, Private Pain 1988;; *Books* Helping Ourselves to Power: A Training Manual for Women in Public Life Skills 1986, Helping one Parent Families to Work 1988; *Recreations* swimming; *Style—* Ms Sue Slipman; National Council for One Parent Families, 255 Kentish Town Road, London, NW5 (☎ 267 1361, fax 482 4851)

SLOAM, Nigel Spencer; s of Maurice Sloam, of London, and Ruth, *née* Davis, of London; *b* 17 Dec 1950; *Educ* Haberdasher's Aske's, Corpus Christi Coll Oxford (BA, MA); *m* 3 Sept 1978, Elizabeth Augusta, da of Arnold Hertzberg; 1 s (Oliver Julian Richard b 1983), 1 da (Natalia Sylvia Caroline b 1979); *Career* trainee actuary Messrs Bacon & Woodrow 1972-76, actuary Sahar Insur Co of Israel 1976-77, mangr actuarial dept Charterhouse Magna Assur Co 1977-78, dir Messrs Bevington Lowndes Ltd 1978-79, princ and ptnr Nigel Sloam & Co 1979-; Freeman City of London, Liveryman Worshipful Co of Basketmakers; FIA 1977, AFIMA 1979, ASA 1987; *Clubs* Utd Oxford and Cambridge, City Livery, PHIATUS; *Style—* Nigel Sloam, Esq; Nigel Sloam & Co, Annandale, West Heath Ave, London NW11 7QU (☎ 01 209 1222, fax 01 4555 3973, telex 261507 (ref 2921))

SLOAN, Andrew Kirkpatrick; QPM; s of Andrew Kirkpatrick Sloan, of Kirkcudbright, and Amelia Sarah, *née* Vernon; *b* 27 Feb 1931; *Educ* Kirkcubright and Dumfries Acad, Open Univ (BA), Storvik; *m* 1953, Agnes Sofie, da of Nils Jaeger Aleksander, of Norway (d 1975); 3 da (Ann-Soffi, Dorothy, Janet); *Career* RN 1947-53, served in cruisers and submarines in Home Waters, Mediterranean and Caribbean, Petty Offr; West Yorks Police (reaching rank of Chief Supt) 1955-66, asst chief constable Lincs Police 1976-79, nat co-ordinator Regnl Crime Sqads England & Wales 1979-81, dep chief constable Lincs Police 1981-83; chief constable: Beds Police 1983-85, Strathclyde; *Recreations* walking, travel, conversation; *Style—* Andrew Sloan Esq; 173 Pitt St, Glasgow (☎ 041 204 2626); Strathclyde Police HQ, 173 Pitt St, Glasgow (☎ 041 204 2626)

SLOAN, Gordon McMillan; s of Samuel Sloan, of Muirkirk, Ayrshire, Scotland, and Christine McMillan, *née* Turner; *b* 30 Dec 1934; *Educ* Muirkirk Sch, Kilmarnock Acad, Glasgow Royal Tech Coll; *m* 5 Aug 1961, Patricia Mary, da of William Stewart McKim (d 1979); 1 s (John), 4 da (Christine, Elizabeth, Mary, Rachel); *Career* dir: Parsons Brown & Newton Consulting Engrs 1973-81, McMillan Sloan & Ptnrs Consulting Engrs 1981-; notable works incl: studies master plans reports and detailed plans for major new ports at Dammam (Saudi Arabia), and Muara (Brunei), study and re-devpt plan with designs for Cardiff Port, design of floating port Aqaba (Jordan), detailed study of abandonment and removal of major N Sea prodn platform; Freeman City of London 1967, Liveryman Worshipful Co of Turners 1968 (memb ct of assts 1987); CEng 1967, FInstPet 1974, FIMechE 1978, MSocIS (France) 1978, FInstPW 1988; *Recreations* music appreciation, property renovation and restoration; *Style—* Gordon Sloan, Esq; 32 Murray Rd, Wimbledon, London SW19 4PE (☎ 01 947 0767, fax 01 947 7801)

SLOAN, Ronald Kenneth (Ronnie); s of D Kenneth G Sloan (d 1958), of Edinburgh, and Elfriede, *née* Stapf; *b* 21 July 1943; *Educ* Edinburgh Acad; *m* 29 May 1965, Sandra, da of Alexander Cochran (d 1984), of Edinburgh; 2 s (Elliot b 1969, Moray b 1971), 1 da (Hazel b 1978); *Career* dir: Antony Gibbs Pensions Ltd 1971, Martin Paterson Assocs Ltd 1972-87; divnl dir and actuary Buck Paterson Conslts Ltd 1987-; capt Edinburgh Academicals RFC 1973-74; fund raiser for RSSPCC running 15 marathons dressed as Superman (in Edinburgh, Glasgow, Aberdeen, Dublin, London, NY, Boston, Athens) raising over £60,000 to date; govr Scottish Sports Aid Fndn; FFA 1967, FPMI 1977, FIOD 1980; *Recreations* tennis, rugby, marathons, Scottish country dancing; *Clubs* New (Edinburgh); *Style—* Ronnie Sloan, Esq; Buck Paterson Conslts, 12 Alva St, Edinburgh EH2 4QG (☎ 031 225 3324, fax 031 225 2192)

SLOANE, Prof Peter James; s of John Joseph Sloane, of Cheadle, Cheshire, and Elizabeth, *née* Clarke; *b* 6 August 1942; *Educ* Cheadle Hulme Sch, Univ of Sheffield (BA), Univ of Strathclyde; *m* 30 July 1969, Avril Mary, da of Kenneth Urquhart (d 1984); 1 s (Christopher b 1971); *Career* asst lectr/ lectr in political economy Univ of Aberdeen 1966-69, lectr in industl econs Univ of Nottingham 1969-75, econ advsr Unit for Manpower Studies Dept of Employment 1973-74, prof of econs and mgmnt Paisley Coll 1975-84, visiting prof McMaster Univ Hamilton Ontario Canada 1978 (Cwlth Fell), prof of political econ Univ of Aberdeen 1984- (Jaffrey prof of political econ 1985-); memb: Sec of State for Scotland's panel of econ conslts 1981-, cncl Scottish Econ Soc 1983-, ct Univ of Aberdeen 1987-; cncl memb Econ and Socl Res Cncl 1979-85; *Books* Changing Patterns of Working Hours (1975), Sex Discrimination in the Labour market (with B Chiplin, 1975), Sport in the Market? (1980), Women and Low Pay (ed 1980), The Earnings Gap Between Men and Women in Great Britain (1981), Equal Employment Issues (with H C Jain, 1981), Tackling Discrimination in the Workplace (with B Chiplin, 1982), Labour Economics (with D Carline, et al 1985), Sec at Work: Equal Pay and the Comparable Worth Controversy (1985); plus contributions to various academic jls; *Recreations* golf; *Clubs* Royal Cwlth Soc; *Style—* Prof Peter Sloane; The Eaves, Kwcardine Road, Torphins, Aberdeenshire AB3 4HH (☎ 033 982 553); Department of Economics, University of Aberdeen, Edward Wright Building, Dunbar Street, Old Aberdeen (☎ 0224 272166, fax 0224 487048, telex 73458 UNIABN G)

SLOCOCK, (David) Michael; s of Maj Arthur Anthony Slocock, of Budleigh Salterton, Devon and Elizabeth Anthea, *née* Sturdy; *b* 1 Feb 1945; *Educ* Radley Coll, Lincoln Coll Oxford (BA); *m* 1969, Theresa Mary, da of Maj Anthony Clyde-Smith, of Trinity, Jersey; 2 s (Julian b 1973, Mark b 1976), 1 da (Lucinda b 1971); *Career* chm and chief exec Normans Gp plc 1973-; landowner (100 acres Dorset, 4000 acres Zimbabwe); *Recreations* gardening, golf, tennis, sailing; *Clubs* IOD, Royal Southern Dorset Yacht; *Style—* Michael Slocock, Esq; Southover House, Tolpuddle, Dorchester, Dorset DT2 7HF (☎ 030 584 220); Normans Group plc, 123 Kennington Rd, London SE11 6SF (☎ 01 582 4030)

SLOGGETT, Jolyon Edward; s of Edward Cornelius Sloggett (d 1974), of Harrow, Middx, and Lena May, *née* Norton; *b* 30 May 1933; *Educ* John Lyon Sch, Univ of Glasgow (BSc); *m* 4 July 1970, Patricia Marjorie Iverson, da of Leonard Artemus Ward, of Steyning, W Sussex; 2 da (Alexandra, Clementine); *Career* joined RNVR 1955, Nat Serv 1957-58, commnd temporary Actg Sub Lt(E) 1957, RNEC 1957, HMS Camperdown 1958, sr engrg offr 51 minesweeping sqdn 1958, resigned as Lt(E) from RNR 1964; ship designer WM Denny & Bros Ltd 1956-57 and 1959-60; Houlder Bros & Co Ltd: Naval architect 1965-68, mangr new projects 1968-72, exec dir fin and devpt 1972-78, exec dep chm Houlder Offshore; md Br Shipbuilders: mktg and product devpt 1978-79, offshore 1979-81; chm Vickers Offshore (P & D) Ltd 1979-80, conslt Jolyon Soggett Assocs 1981-86; vice pres Old Lyonian Assoc; Liveryman Worshipful Co of Shipwrights; FIMarE (sec 1986-), FRINA 1972, FICS 1967; *Books* Shipping Finance (1984); *Recreations* gardening, woodwork, sailing; *Style—* Jolyon Sloggett, Esq; Annington Ho, Steyning, W Sussex BN44 3WA (☎ 0903 812 259); Inst of Marine Engineers, 76 Mark Lane, London EC3R 7JN (☎ 01 481 8493, fax 01 488 1854, telex 886841)

SLOMAN, Sir Albert Edward; CBE (1980); s of Albert Sloman (d 1969), of Launceston, Cornwall, and Lillie Brewer (d 1973); *b* 14 Feb 1921; *Educ* Launceston Coll, Cornwall; Wadham Coll, Oxford (MA, DPhil); *m* 4 Aug 1948, Marie Bernadette, da of Leo Bergeron (d 1976); 3 da (Anne Veronique b 1949, Isabel Patricia b 1952,d Bernadette Jeanne b 1955); *Career* night-fighter pilot with 219, 68 squadrons, served UK, N Africa, Malta, Sicily (despatches) Flt Lt 1939-45; vice-chllr Univ of Essex 1962-87; lectr in spanish Univ of California Berkeley USA 1946-47, reader in spanish Univ of Dublin 1947-53, fell Trinity Coll Dublin 1950-53, Gilmour prof of spanish Univ of Liverpool 1955-62, dean Faculty of Arts 1960-62; chm: ctee of Vice-Chllr Princs 1981-83, Br Acad Studentship Ctee 1965-87, bd of govrs Centre for Inf on Lang teaching in Res 1979-87, Overseas Res Students Fees Support Scheme 1980-87, univs cncl for Adult Continuing Educn 1984-87, Inter Univ and Polytechnic Cncl 1985-, ctee for Int Coop in Higher Education 1985-, selection ctee of Cwlth Scholarship Cmmn 1986-, int bd Utd World Coll 1988; vice-chm Assoc of Cwlth Univ 1985-; vice-pres Int Assoc of Univs 1970-75; memb: bd Br Cncl 1985, Reith lectr 1963; Guildhall Granada lectr 1969; kt 1987; *Recreations* travel; *Clubs* Savile; *Style—* Sir Albert E Sloman; 19 Inglis Rd, Colchester, Essex CO3 3HU (☎ 0206 47270)

SLOMAN, Kenneth Thomas; s of Arthur Thomas Sloman (d 1980), and Nina Elizabeth Emma, *née* Davis; *b* 3 June 1925; *Educ* Hillcroft Coll; *m* 10 Nov 1956, Elaine, da of Elie Jean Tournoud (d 1960); 1 s (Gregory Thomas Boyd b 26 May 1961), 1 da (Gillian Michele b 22 March 1966); *Career* WWII forces 1944-47; dir Starline Paints Ltd 1963-; chm: Logis Ltd 1955, Aviation Marine & Auto Ltd 1968, Starline Decorating Centres Ltd 1973-; Freeman City of London 1976, Liveryman Worshipful Co of Upholders 1976; *Recreations* yachting, shooting; *Clubs* Burnham Sailing, BASC; *Style—* Kenneth Sloman, Esq

SLOWEY, Brian Aodh; *b* 1933; *Educ* Castleknock Coll, Univ Coll Dublin; *m* Marie; 4 children; *Career* vice chm Guiness Brewing Worldwide Ltd London; chm: Guiness Ireland Ltd, Aer Lingus plc, Aerlinte Eireann plc; dir Cantrell and Cochrane Gp Ltd; memb: nat exec ctee and cncl Confedn of Irish Indust, Irish Mgmnt Inst Cncl; fell Irish Mgmnt Inst; *Style—* Brian Slowey, Esq; Guinness Ireland Ltd, St James's Gate, Dublin 8, Eire (☎ 0001 753645)

SLYNN, Hon Sir Gordon; QC (1974); s of John and Edith Slynn; *b* 17 Feb 1930; *Educ* Sandbach Sch, Goldsmiths' Coll, Trinity Coll Cambridge; *m* 1962, Odile Marie Henriette Boutin; *Career* barr Gray's Inn 1956, vice lectr 1987, lectr Air Law LSE 1958-61, jr counsel Miny Labour 1967-68, jr counsel Treasy 1968-74, rec 1971 (hon rec Hereford 1972-76), leading counsel Treasy 1974-76, High Court judge Queen's Bench 1976-81, pres Employment Appeal Tbnl 1978-81, visiting prof law Durham Univ 1981-, advocate-gen Court of Justice European Communities 1981-; dep chief steward Hereford 1977-78, chief steward 1978-; govr Int Students Tst 1979-85; hon vice-pres Union Internationale des Avocats 1976-, chm exec cncl Int Law Assoc 1988-; memb Ct Broderers' Co; hon fell Univ Coll Buckingham 1982; Hon LLD: Birmingham 1983, Buckingham 1983, Exeter 1985; kt 1976; Hon Decanus Juris Mercer USA; *Clubs* Beefsteak, Garrick; *Style—* The Hon Sir Gordon Slynn, QC; Court of Justice, Kirchberg, Luxembourg

SMAIL, Col James Ingram Miles; OBE (1963), MC (1944), TD (1962), DL (Northumberland 1971); s of James Ingram Smail (d 1947), of Christchurch New Zealand, and Jane Louise (d 1974); seventh generation in family newspaper business; The Tweeddale Press Group, which produces six papers, including NZ, News UK; *b* 21 August 1921,New Zealand,; *Educ* Christ's Coll NZ, Canterbury Univ New Zealand, Heriot Watt Coll Edinburgh; *m* 1948, Dorothy Margaret, da of Daniel Reese (d 1954), of Cashmere Hills, Christchurch, NZ; 2 s, 2 da; *Career* served WWII with 1 Canterbury Regt, then 2 NZEF in Africa, Tunisia and Italy, cmd 7 Bn RNF TA 1963, 149 Inf Bde TA 1967, Territorial Col 4 Bns 1968-69; newspaper proprietor; dir Border TV, chm Northumberland County Planning Ctee 1973-83; pres: Scottish Newspaper Proprietors' Assoc 1962-64, NZ Soc 1977; memb CPU Cncl 1977-; Berwick upon Tweed: memb Borough Cncl for 18 years, Sheriff 1964-65 and 1975-76, Mayor 1971, alderman 1983, alderman CC 1985; OStJ 1985; *Recreations* shooting, gardening; *Clubs* Northern Counties, Newcastle, Lansdowne, Press; *Style—* Col James Smail, OBE, MC, TD, DL; Kiwi Cottage, Scremerston, Berwick upon Tweed, Northumberland TD15 2RB (☎ 0289 306219); Tweeddale Press Group, 90 Marygate, Berwick upon Tweed, Northumberland TD15 1BW (☎ 0289 306677)

SMAIL, William Prophet; s of William Galbraith Smail (d 1962), and Jean Prophet Ramsay (d 1963); *b* 8 Mar 1925; *Educ* Perth Acad, Dundee Coll of Art (DipArch); *m* 4 Aug 1951, Joyce, da of Peter Scott Whyte (d 1955); 1 s (Roderick b 1960), 2 da (Deborah b 1954, Julie b 1957); *Career* War Serv 1943-46; chartered architect, ptnr Wilson Mason & Ptners London and Middle East 1960-76, sr ptnr Wilson Mason &

Partners 1976-87 (conslt to the practise 1990); ARIBA; *Recreations* shooting, gardening; *Clubs* Caledonian (London); *Style*— William Smail, Esq; Southend House, High Ham, Langport, Somerset (☎ 0458 250436); 30 Ashley Court, Morpeth Terrace, London (☎ 01 834 0809); 3 Chandos Street, London W1 (☎ 01 637 1501, telex 262597, fax 01 631 0325)

SMALE-ADAMS, Kenneth Barry; s of Douglas William Smale-Adams; *b* 30 June 1932; *Educ* St John's Coll Johannesburg, Camborne Sch of Mines; *m* 1953, Marion June, *née* Hosken; 2 s (Mark, Jeremy), 1 da (Deborah); *Career* mining engr, The Rio Tinto Zinc Corpn 1967-87 (exec dir Con Zinc Rio Tinto Malaysia Ltd and Rio Tinto Bethlehem Indonesia 1967-72), gen mangr and dir Rio Tinto Fin and Exploration Ltd 1973-80, md RTZ Deep Sea Mining Enterprises Ltd 1974-87, chm Riofinex Ltd 1976-83 (dep chm 1983-), consulting engr to mining dir 1983-87; non exec dir Robertson Gp plc, chm Robertson Mining Fin; FEng; *Recreations* fishing, reading, music, theatre, sports (generally now as spectator); *Clubs* RAC; *Style*— Kenneth Smale-Adams, Esq; Cedar Lawn, 15 Queen's Drive, Thames Ditton, Surrey KT7 0TJ (☎ 01 398 3163); office: 11/12 Buckingham Gate, London SW1Y 6LB (☎ 01 828 2226, telex 914001)

SMALE-SAUNDERS, Colin Michael; s of James Richard Aubry Smale-Saunders, and Eva Smale-Saunders, *née* Sackley; *b* 12 July 1944; *Educ* Private Educn, Bexley Univ Sch, 5 year Electronic Apprenticeship Min of Tech; *m* 1 1969, (m dis) Linda, da of William Baines; 3 s (Nicholas b 1973, Alun b 1976, Daniel b 1979), 1 da (Shelley b 1971); m 2, 1985, Dilys, da of Louis Charles Solomon (d 1949); *Career* md Rendar Ltd 1984-86, pres Wayne Kerr Inc 1986-87 (gp md 1987-); *Recreations* photography, travelling, shooting, fishing; *Clubs* IOD; *Style*— Colin M Smale-Saunders, Esq; The Coach House, Arundel Rd, Fontwell, W Sussex; Durban Rd, Bognor Regis, West Sussex

SMALES, Paul Fletcher; s of Bernard Fletcher Smales, of Falmouth, Cornwall, and Eileen Isabel, *née* Prior; *b* 23 July 1946; *Educ* Falmouth GS, Fitzwilliam Coll Cambridge (MA); *Career* barr Inner Temple 1970; Bard of the Cornish Gorseddy 1978-; chm: Assoc of Cornish Barrs 1982-, Conf on Cornwall 1983-, London Cornish Assoc 1987-, The Charitable Soc of St George Vilangad India; vice pres Cornish Music Guild; chm: Chelsea Lib Assoc 1985-88, Assoc of Lib Lawyers 1986-88; vice-chm Assoc SLD Lawyers 1988-; *Books* The Prosecutorial Process in England and Wales (1979), An Lyver Kevarwedha Kernewek (A Directory of Cornish Institutions and People) (1984); *Recreations* opera, tennis, travel, bridge; *Clubs* Nat Liberal; *Style*— Paul Smales, Esq; Fortunes, Flushing, Falmouth, Cornwall; 33A Barkston Gardens, London SW5 (☎ 01 244 9758); Goldsmith Building, Temple, London EC4Y 7BL (☎ 01 353 6802, fax 01 583 5255)

SMALL, David Purvis; CMG (1988), MBE (1966); s of Joseph Small (d 1958), of Wishaw, Scotland, and Ann Purvis (d 1985); *b* 17 Oct 1930; *Educ* Our Lady's HS Motherwell; *m* 12 Oct 1957, Patricia, da of John Kennedy (d 1979); 3 s (Joseph b 25 March 1959, John b 10 Aug 1960, David b 30 June 1965); *Career* Nat Serv RAF, serv Egypt Sudan Eritrea and Kenya 1949-51; clerical offr Admty (Civil Serv) 1953, asst sec 1955-60, CRO 1961, Madras 1962-64, FCO Madras 1962-64, second sec Ibanian 1964-68, first sec Ecuador 1968-73 (former second sec), first sec FCO 1973-76, first sec and head of chancery Dacca 1976-80, first sec Stockholm 1980-82, cnsllr commercial and econ Copenhagen 1982-87, high commr and ambass George Town Guyana 1987-; *Recreations* golf, soccer, gardening; *Clubs* Rotary, (Georgetown), The Georgetown, Georgetown GC; *Style*— David Small, Esq, CMG, MBE; Ashbank, Strachur, Argyll, Scotland, (☎ 036986 282); The British high Commission, 44 Main St, Georgetown, Guyana, (☎ 02 65881 4, telex 2221)

SMALL, Gladstone Cleophas; s of Chelston Cleophas Small, of Birmingham, and Gladys, *née* Carter; *b* 18 Oct 1961; *Educ* Combermere GS Barbados, Hall Green Tech Coll Birmingham; *m* 19 Sept 1987, Lois Christine, da of Peter Bernhardt Friedlander, of Mandurah, W Australia; *Career* cricketer Warwickshire CCC 1979-; test debut v NZ 1986, career best 5 wickets for 42 runs v Australia 1986; supporter many charitable organisations; *Recreations* golf, tennis; *Clubs* Kings Norton Golf; *Style*— Gladstone Small, Esq; Warwickshire CCC, County Ground, Edgbaston, Birmingham B5 7QV (☎ 021 440 4292)

SMALL, Dr Ramsay George; s of Robert Small (d 1974), of Dundee, and Ann Stewart, *née* Ramsay (d 1967); *b* 5 Feb 1930; *Educ* Harris Acad Dundee, Univ of St Andrew's (MB, ChB, DPH); *m* 29 Sept 1951, Aileen Stiven, da of Anson Stiven Masterton (d 1959), of Dundee; 4 s (Ronald b 1954, Douglas b 1955, Kenneth b 1958, Iain b 1961); *Career* Nat Serv RAMC 1955-57, Lt 1955, Capt 1956, RAMC TA 1957-61; asst med offr of health Ayr CC 1958-61, princ med offr Corpn of Dundee 1968-74 (sr med offr 1961-68), hon sr lectr Univ of Dundee 1974-, chief admin med offr Tayside Health Bd 1986- (community med specialist 1974-86); chm Eastern Regnl PostGrad Med Educn Ctee 1980-83, memb Jt Ctee on Vaccination and Immunisation 1978-86, convenor Scottish Affrs Ctee Faculty of Community Med 1983-86 (memb bd 1983-), cncl memb RCPE 1987-; sec Broughty Ferry Baptist Church 1969-, pres Baptist Union of Scotland 1972-73; FFCM 1978, FRCPE 1987; *Recreations* music, bird watching, medieval churches; *Style*— Dr Ramsay Small; 46 Monifieth Rd, Broughty Ferry, Dundee DD5 2RX (☎ 0382 78408); Tayside Health Board, PO Box 75, Vernonholme, Riverside Drive, Dundee DD1 9NL (☎ 0382 645151, fax 0382 69734)

SMALLEY, Very Rev Dr Stephen Stewart; s of Arthur Thomas Smalley, OBE, of Banstead, Surrey (d 1975), and May Elizabeth Selina Smalley, *née* Kimm (d 1986); *b* 11 May 1931; *Educ* Battersea GS, Jesus Coll Cambridge (MA, PhD), Eden Theol Seminary USA (BD); *m* 13 July 1974, Susan Jane, da of Wing Cdr Arthur James Paterson, of Banstead, Surrey (d 1987); 1 s (Jovian b 1977), 1 da (Evelyn b 1983); *Career* asst curate St Paul's Church Portman Square 1958-60 chaplain Peterhouse Cambridge 1960-63, acting dean 1962-63; lectr and sr lectr: Univ of Ibadan Nigeria 1963-69, Univ of Manchester 1970-77; canon residentiary and precentor Coventry Cathedral 1977-86, vice provost 1986, dean of Chester Cathedral 1987-; *Books* Christ and Spirit in the New Testament (ed with B Lindars, 1973), John: Evangelist and Interpreter (1978), 1, 2, 3, John (1984); *Recreations* music, drama, literature, travel; *Style*— The Very Rev Dr Stephen Smalley; The Deanery, 7 Abbey St, Chester CH1 2JF (☎ 0224 351380); Hadrians, Bourton-on-the-Hill, Moreton-in-Marsh, Glos (☎ 0386 700564); Cathedral Office, 1 Abbey Square, Chester CH1 2HU (☎ 0224 324756)

SMALLMAN, Barry Granger; CMG, CVO (1972); s of Charles Stanley Smallman CBE, ARMC (d 1981), of Worthing, Sussex, and Ruby Marian, *née* Granger (d 1949); *b* 22 Feb 1924; *Educ* St Paul's, Trinity Coll Cambridge (MA); *m* 6 Sept 1952, Sheila Maxine, da of William Henry Knight, of Sissinghurst, Kent; 2 s (Mark b 1955, Robin b 1957), 1 da (Joy b 1953); *Career* served 1939-45, Lt Intelligence Corps; br dep high cmmr Sierra Leone 1963-64 and NZ 1964-67, IDC 1968, consul-gen Br Embassy Thailand 1971-74, br high cmmr Bangladesh 1975-78, Dip Serv resident chm, Civil Service Selection Bd 1978-81, Br high cmmr Jamaica and ambass Haiti 1982-84; chm cncl Benenden Sch 1986-; memb cncl St Lawrence Coll Ramsgate 1984-, The Leprosy Mission 1984-, The Soc for Promoting Christian Knowledge 1984-; fndr and dir Granger Consultancies 1984-; *Recreations* reading, writing, short stories and verse, singing, piano, bird watching, tennis, golf; *Clubs* Royal Cwlth Soc; Beacon Shaw, Benenden, Kent TN17 4BU (☎ 0580 240 625)

SMALLMAN, Prof (Edward) Raymond; s of David Smallman, and Edith, *née* French; *b* 4 August 1929; *Educ* Rugeley GS, Univ of Birmingham (BSc, PhD, DSc); *m* 6 Sept 1952, Joan Doreen, da of George Faulkner, of Wolverhampton; 1 s (Robert Ian b 1959), 1 da (Lesley Ann (Mrs Grimer) b 1955); *Career* sr scientific offr AERE Harwell 1953-58; Univ of Birmingham: lectr dept of physical metallurgy 1958-63 (sr lectr 1963-64), prof of physical metallurgy 1964-69, head of physical metallurgy and sci of materials 1969-81, head of dept metallurgy and materials 1981-88, dean of Faculty of Sci and Engrg 1984-85 Faculty of Engrg 1985-87, vice-princ 1987-; Sir George Beilby Gold Metal 1969, Rosenhain Medal 1972; pres Birmingham Metallurgical Assoc 1972; FRS 1986, FIM 1965, CEng, ASM; *Books* Modern Physical Metallurgy (1962), Modern Metallography (1966), Structure of Metals and Alloys, The Metals and Metallurgy Trust (1969), Defect Analysis in Electron Microscopy (1975), Vacancies 76 (1976); *Recreations* golf, bridge, travel; *Clubs* Athenaeum, South Staffs Golf; *Style*— Prof Raymond Smallman; 59 Woodthorne Rd Sth, Tettenhall, Wolverhampton WV6 8SN (☎ 021 414 5223, fax 021 414 5232, telex SPAPHYG 338938)

SMALLMAN, Timothy Gilpin; s of Stanley Cottrell Smallman (d 1965), of Sedgemere, Fen End, Kenilworth, Warwicks, and Grace Mary Louise, *née* Wilson; *b* 6 Nov 1938; *Educ* Stowe; *m* 18 April 1964, Jane, da of Edward Holloway (d 1988), of Acocks Green, Birmingham 27; 2 s (Guy b 1965, Simon b 1967); *Career* chm and md: W F Smallman & Son Ltd (md 1965 chm 1978), Smallman Lubricants Ltd 1978, chm Smallman Lubricants (Hereford) Ltd 1972, Coronet Oil Refineries Ltd 1979, Needwood Oils and Solvents Ltd 1984; dir: Br Lubricants Fedn Ltd 1977- (nat pres 1983-85); FIOD (1965), FInstPet (1968); *Recreations* golf, bridge, ornithology, nature and wildlife conservation; *Clubs* Copt Heath Golf, Rugby Club of London; *Style*— Timothy Smallman, Esq; 74 Lovelace Ave, Solihull, W Midlands B91 3JR (☎ 021 705 0499); W F Smallman & Son Ltd, 216 Great Bridge St, W Bromwich, W Midlands (☎ 021 557 3372)

SMALLPEICE, Sir Basil; KCVO (1961); s of Herbert Charles Smallpeice (d 1927), and Georgina Ruth, *née* Rust (d 1970); *b* 18 Sept 1906; *Educ* Shrewsbury; *m* 1, 1931, Kathleen Ivey Singleton (d 1973), da of Edwin Singleton Brame; m 2, 1973, Rita, yr da of late Maj W Burns; *Career* chartered accountant 1930, Hoover Ltd 1930-37, chief accountant and then sec Doulton and Co Ltd 1937-48, dir Costs and Statistics British Transport Cmmn 1948-50; BOAC: fin comptroller 1950, memb bd 1953, dep chief exec 1954, md 1956-63; dir BOAC-Cunard Ltd 1962-63, admin advsr HM Household 1964-80; chm: Nat Jt Cncl for Civil Air Tport 1960-61, Cunard Steam-Ship Co Ltd 1965-71, Eng Speaking Union of the Cwlth 1965-68, Offshore Marine Ltd 1968-70, ACT(A) Australian Nat Line Co-ordinating Bd 1969-79, cncl BIM 1970-72 (memb 1959-75, vice-pres 1972-), Assoc Container Transportation (Australia) Ltd 1971-79, The Air League 1971-74 (vice-pres 1975), Cavendish Med Centre Ltd 1973-79; dep chm Lonrho Ltd 1972-73; memb: cncl Inst of Chartered Accountants 1948-57, cncl Inst of Tport 1958-61, Ctee for Exports to USA 1964-66, Martins Bank 1965-69, Barclays Bank London Local Bd 1969-74; OStJ, Order of the Cedar Lebanon (1955); *Books* Of Comets and Queens (1981); *Clubs* Athenaeum, Boodle's, Melbourne (Australia); *Style*— Sir Basil Smallpeice, KCVO; Bridge House, 45 Leigh Hill Rd, Cobham, Surrey KT11 2HU (☎ 0932 65425)

SMALLWOOD, Christopher Marten; s of Canon Graham Marten, of Worcs, and Jean, *née* Calderwood; *b* 8 Mar 1945; *Educ* Ellesmere Coll Shropshire, Warwick Sch, The Architectural Assoc; *m* 1975, Hon Kirsty Jane Aitken, da of Sir Max Aitken, Bt, DSO, DFC (d 1985); 1 da (Eleanor b 1982); *Career* architect, RIBA; *Style*— Christopher Smallwood, Esq; The Vineyard, Hurlingham Road, London SW6 3NR (☎ 01 736 3240); 79/89 Lots Road, London SW10 (☎ 01 376 5744, fax 376 34714)

SMALLWOOD, Air Chief Marshal Sir Denis Graham; GBE (1975), CBE (1961), MBE (1951), KCB (1969), CB (1966), DSO (1944), DFC (1942); s of Frederick William Smallwood, of Moseley, Birmingham; *b* 13 August 1918; *Educ* King Edward's Sch Birmingham; *m* 1940, Frances Jeanne, da of Walter Needham, of Birmingham; 1 s, 1 da; *Career* RAF 1938, served WWII as fighter pilot Fighter Cmd, RAF Staff Coll Haifa 1945-46; asst Sec, Chiefs of Staff Ctee 1947-49; dir staff, Joint Servs Staff Coll 1950-53; Cdr RAF Biggin Hill, 1953-55; dir staff, IDC, 1955-56; Gp Capt Plans Air Task Force Suez Campaign 1956, Cdr RAF Guided Missiles Station Lincs 1959-61, AOC and Cmdt RAF Coll of Air Warfare, Manby 1961, Air Cdre 1961, asst chief of staff (Ops) 1963-65, AOC 3 Gp Bomber Cmd 1965-67, SASO Bomber Cmd 1967-68, COS Strike Cmd 1969, Air Marshal 1969, Cdr British Forces Near East and AOC-in-C NEAF and Admin of Sovereign Base Areas of Akrotiri and Dhekelia, Cyprus 1969-70, Vice-Chief of Air Staff 1970-73, AOC-in-C Strike Cmd 1974, Air Chief Marshal 1973, C-in-C UK Air Forces 1975-76; ADC to HM The Queen 1954-59; mil advsr British Aerospace 1977-83; pres Air League 1981-84; FRSA, FRAeS; Freeman City of London; Liveryman Guild of Air Pilots and Navigators; *Books* RAF Biggin Hill; *Recreations* Equitation, gardening, swimming, wild life; *Clubs* RAF, Les Ambassadeu; *Style*— Air Chief Marshal Sir Denis Smallwood; The Flint House, Owlswick, Aylesbury, Bucks HP17 9RH

SMALLWOOD, Hon Mrs (Kirsty Jane); *née* Aitken; da (by 2 w) of Sir Max Aitken, Bt (d 1985; 2 Baron Beaverbrook who disclaimed his title 1964), and Ursula Jane Kenyon-Slaney; *b* 22 June 1947; *m* 1, 1966 (m dis 1973), Jonathan Derek Morley, yr s of Brig Michael Frederick Morley, MBE; 2 s (Dominic b 1967, Sebastian b 1969); m 2, 1975, Christopher Marten Smallwood, s of Canon Graham Marten Smallwood; 1 da (Eleanor b 1982); *Style*— The Hon Mrs Smallwood; The Vineyard, Hurlingham Road, London SW6 3NR (☎ 01 736 3240)

SMART, Andrew; CB (1980); s of William Somerville Smart (d 1957), and Janet Smart, *née* Russell (d 1976); *b* 12 Feb 1924; *Educ* Denny Public Sch, HS of Stirling, Glasgow Univ (MA); *m* 1949, Pamela Kathleen, da of Alan Charles Stephens, of Worcs; 2 s (James, Jeremy), 2 da (Sheila, Frances); *Career* Scientific Civil Service - TRE 1943;

Air Min 1950; TRE/RRE 1953 (head GW 1968); DOAE dep dir 1970; RAE 1972; dep dir 1974; RSRE dir 1978-84; conslt to the Marconi Co Ltd 1985; *Recreations* gardening, caravanning; *Style*— Andrew Smart Esq, CB; 'Hill Orchard', Shelsley Drive, Colwall, Malvern, Worcs WR13 6PS (☎ Colwall 40664)

SMART, Geoffrey John Neville; s of John Frederick Smart (d 1979), of Lincoln, and Elsie, *née* Blunt; *b* 19 Sept 1946; *Educ* Lincoln Sch, Emmanuel Coll Cambridge (MA); *m* 5 Nov 1970, Karen Martha Margareta, da of Maj August Wilhelm Cordes; 3 da (Katherine b 1974, Harriet b 1976, Clare b 1978); *Career* analyst Mgmnt Dynamics Ltd 1967-70, ptnr Deloitte Haskins & Sells 1980 - (mgmnt consIt 1970-74, mangr 1974-80); *Recreations* golf, theatre, music; *Clubs* RAC; *Style*— Geoffrey Smart, Esq; Deloitte Haskins & Sells, 128 Queen Victoria St, London EC4P 4JX (☎ 01 248 3913, fax 01 248 3623, telex 894941)

SMART, Prof Sir George Algernon; s of Algernon Smart (d 1952), and Mary Ann Smart (d 1984); *b* 16 Dec 1913; *Educ* Uppingham, Durham Univ (BSc, MD); *m* 1939, Monica Helen, da of Joseph Ernest Carrick; 2 s, 1 da; *Career* prof of med Univ of Durham and Newcastle upon Tyne 1956-72; dir British Postgraduate Medical Fedn and prof of med London Univ 1971-78; vice-pres and sr censor RCP 1972; kt 1978; *Books* Fundamentals of Clinical Endocrinology (co-author); *Style*— Prof Sir George Smart; Taffrail, Crede Lane, Old Bosham, Chichester, Sussex PO18 8NX

SMART, Prof (Arthur David) Gerald; s of Arthur Herbert John Smart (d 1979), of Seaton, Devon, and Amelia Olwen Mona, *née* Evans (d 1967); *b* 19 Mar 1925; *Educ* Rugby, Kings Coll Cambridge (MA), Regent St Poly (DipTP); *m* 18 June 1955, Anne Patience, da of Charles William Baxter, CMG, MC (d 1969), of Storrington, Sussex; 2 da (Amelia b 1 May 1959, Susan b 9 July 1960); *Career* planner in local govt 1950-75, co planning offr Hants CC 1963-75, head of Bartlett Sch of Architecture and Planning UCL 1975-80, prof of urban planning London Univ 1975-85 (now emeritus); memb: Milford-on-Sea Parish Cncl, cncl Solent Protection Soc, various govt ctees on planning 1963-77; chm structure plan examinations in pub DOE, cncl memb RSPB 1985-90, memb governing body GB E Europe Centre; ARICS 1953, FRTPI 1964; *Recreations* ornithology, sailing, walking, music; *Clubs* Royal Lymington YC; *Style*— Prof Gerald Smart; 10 Harewood Green, Keyhaven, Lymington, Hants SO41 0TZ (☎ 0590 454 75)

SMART, Sir Jack; CBE (1976), JP (Castleford 1960), DL (West Yorkshire 1987); s of James William Smart (d 1968), and Emily Smart, *née* Greenanay (d 1955); *b* 25 April 1920; *Educ* Altofts Colliery Sch; *m* 1941, Ethel, da of Henry King, (d 1963), of Gutsyke, Castleford; 1 da (Joan); *Career* miner 1934-59; mayor Castleford 1962-63; memb Wakefield Metropolitan Dist Cncl 1973- (leader 1973-); chm Wakefield DHA 1977-; Hon Freeman City of Wakefield Metropolitan Dist Cncl 1985; hon fellow Bretton Coll; FRSA; *Recreations* golf, swimming; *Style*— Sir Jack Smart, CBE, JP; Churchside, Weetworth, Pontefract Rd, Castleford, W Yorks (☎ 0977 554880)

SMART, (Raymond) Jack; s of Frank Smart; *b* 1 August 1917; *Educ* Redhill Tech; *m* 1942, Jessie Tyrrell; 1 s, 1 da; *Career* served with Aeronautical Inspection Directorate of Air Miny 1939-40, Rotol Airscrews/Dowty Rotol 1940-59, former md British Light Steel Pressings, gp exec dir and dep md BL 1976-79 (gp manufacturing dir 1972-76, md Truck Div 1966-72), md Aveling Barford Hldgs 1979-; *Style*— Jack Smart, Esq; 17 Whitecroft Park, Northfield Road, Nailsworth, Glos GL6 0NS (☎ 045 383 5634)

SMART, John Dalziel Beveridge; s of George late Beveridge Smart; *b* 12 August 1932; *Educ* Harrow; *m* 1960, Valerie Bigelow, da of late Col Hugh Kenneth Blaber, CBE; 2 s; *Career* Lt Black Watch Korea; dir: J & J Smart (Brechin) Ltd 1954, Don Brothers Buist plc 1964 (md 1985, ret 1987); chm Br Polyolefin Textiles Assoc; *Recreations* skiing, shooting; *Style*— John Smart, Esq; Woodmyre, Edzell, Angus (☎ 035 64 416)

SMART, Richard; s of Horace Alfred (David) Smart (d 1985), and Vera Mary Naomi, *née* Latham; *b* 9 Oct 1942; *Educ* The Sorbonne (Diplome d'Etudes), Bristol Univ (BA), London Univ (MA); *m* 21 Feb 1976, Margaret Mary, da of Richard Gregory, of 26 Kineton Road, Sutton Coldfield; *Career* headmaster Hampden House Sch 1978-80, princ Milestone Tutorial Coll 1981-; chm conf for Ind Further Educ 1983-85; cncl memb Assoc of Tutors 1984-; cmmnd RAFVR(T) 1966; FBIM, FCollP; *Recreations* chamber music, tennis, travel; *Clubs* Reform, Leander, Athenaeum; *Style*— Richard Smart, Esq; 170 Sloane Street, London SW1 (☎ 01 235 1736); Whistler Court, Preston Park Avenue, Brighton (☎ 0273 506 818); Milestone Tutorial College, 85 Cromwell Road, London SW7 (☎ 01 3734956)

SMEDLEY, His Hon Judge (Frank) Brian; QC (1977); s of Leslie Smedley (d 1970); *b* 28 Nov 1934; *Educ* West Bridgford GS, London Univ (LLB); *Career* barr Gray's Inn 1960, rec of Crown Ct 1971-84, memb Senate of Inns of Ct and the Bar 1973-77; Circuit Judge July 1987; *Recreations* travel, gardening; *Clubs* Garrick; *Style*— His Hon Judge Brian Smedley, QC; c/o Central Criminal Court, Old Bailey, London EC4

SMEDLEY, (Roscoe Relph) George (Boleyne); s of Lt Charles Boleyne Smedley (d 1920), and Aimie Blaine, *née* Relph (d 1948); *b* 3 Sept 1919; *Educ* King's Sch Ely, King's Coll London (LLB); *m* 1, 27 Sept 1947, Muriel Hallaway (d 1975), da of Arthur Stanley Murray (d 1945); 1 s (Robert Charles b 1948); m 2, 11 July 1979, Margaret Gerrard Gourlay, da of Augustus Thorburn Hallaway (d 1939), and wid of Dr John Stewart Gourlay; *Career* WWII Artists Rifles TA 1939-40, Lt S Lancs Lancs Regt 1940-42, Capt Indian Army 1942-46; FO 1937 and 1946; Dip Serv (formerly Foreign Serv): Rangoon 1947, Maymo 1950, Brussels 1952, Baghdad 1954, FO 1958, Beirut 1963, Kuwait 1965, FCO 1969, consul gen Lubumbashi 1972-74, Br Mil Govt Berlin 1974-76, FCO 1976, head nationality and treaty dept 1977-79; pt/t appts since ret: legal memb Mental Health Review Tbnl, chm Rent Assessment Ctee, adjudicator under Immigration Act 1971, inspr planning inspectorate Depts of Environment and Tport, dep traffic cmmr NE Traffic Area, memb No 2 Dip Serv Appeal Bd; *Clubs* RAC, Royal Overseas League; *Style*— George Smedley, Esq; Garden Ho, Whorlton, Barnard Castle, Co Durham DL12 8XQ (☎ 0833 27 381)

SMEDLEY, Sir Harold; KCMG (1978, CMG 1965), MBE (1946); s of Ralph Davies Smedley (d 1954), of Worthing; *b* 19 June 1920; *Educ* Aldenham, Pembroke Coll Cambridge; *m* 1950, Beryl, da of Harold Brown, of Wellington, NZ; 2 s, 2 da; *Career* WWII RM served UK, Med, W Europe; entered Dominions Off 1946, private sec to sec of state Cwlth Relations Off 1954-57, Br high cmmr Ghana 1964-67, ambass Laos 1968-70, asst under sec FCO 1970, sec gen Cmmn on Rhodesian Opinion 1971-72, high cmmr Republic of Sri Lanka and ambass to Maldives Republic 1973-75, high cmmr in NZ and govr of Pitcairn 1976-80; chm Bank of NZ (London) 1983- (dep chm 1981-83); pres Hakluyt Soc 1987-; vice chm Victoria League 1981-; *Clubs* Utd Oxford and Cambridge, Royal Cwlth Soc; *Style*— Sir Harold Smedley, KCMG, MBE; Beehive Lane, Ferring, West Sussex BN12 5NN

SMEDLEY, Roger William; s of Thomas Smedley (d 1947), and Marguerite Esther, *née* Taylor; *b* 21 April 1935; *Educ* Colston's Boys Sch Bristol; *m* 19 Aug 1961, Suzanne, da of Ian Murray Robertson; 2 s (Christopher b 1963, Tobias b 1965); *Career* chm and md SAC Int plc 1961-; CEng, MIMechE; *Recreations* motor cycling; *Clubs* Rotary of Clifton (Bristol), Clifton (Bristol); *Style*— Roger Smedley, Esq; Savernake, 5 Stoke Paddock Rd, Stoke Bishop, Bristol BS9 2DJ (☎ 0272 683673); SAC International plc, Brunswick House, Upper York St, Bristol (☎ 0272 232162)

SMEE, Clive Harrod; s of Victor Woolley Smee, of Kingsbridge, Devon, and Leila Olive, *née* Harrod (d 1956); *b* 29 April 1942; *Educ* Royal GS Guildford, LSE (BSc), Business Sch Indiana Univ (MBA), Inst of Cwlth Studies Oxford; *m* 5 April 1975, Denise Eileen, da of Edward Ernest Sell (d 1968), of Shafton, Yorks; 1 s (David b 1981), 2 da (Anna b 1978, Elizabeth b 1985); *Career* Br Cncl Nigeria 1966-68, econ advsr ODM 1969-75, sr econ advsr DHSS 1975-82, Nuffield and Leverhulme Travelling fell USA and Canada 1978-79, advsr Centl Policy Review Staff 1982-83, sr econ advsr HM Treasy 1983-84, chief econ advsr DHSS 1984-, conslt NZ Treasy 1988; chm Social policy working pty OECD 1987-; *Recreations* running, gardening, family; *Style*— Clive Smee, Esq; c/o Dept of Health and Dept of Social Security, Friars House, Blackfriars Road, London SE1 (☎ 01 703 6380)

SMEE, John Michael Alan; s of Edward Albert Smee (d 1975), of Wentworth, Surrey, and Hilda Florence, *née* Smith; *b* 29 Dec 1927; *Educ* Ealing Coll, Taunton and Ealing Art Coll; *m* 12 July 1952, Daphne Violet Joan, da of Albert Edward Mallandain (d 1982); 1 s (Anthony Edward b 1954), 1 da (Susan Pamela b 1960); *Career* chm and md: Smee's Advertising Ltd 1975, Smee's Estates (London) Ltd 1975; chm Taylor Advertising Ltd 1975; *Recreations* rugby, golf; *Clubs* IOD, Wentworth, Wellington; *Style*— John M A Smee, Esq; c/o Smee's Advertising Ltd, 3/5 Duke St, London W1 (fax 01 935 8588, telex 27719 SMET AY)

SMEETON, Vice Admiral Sir Richard Michael; KCB (1964), CB (1961, MBE 1942, DL (Surrey 1976)); s of Edward Leaf Smeeton (d 1935), and Charlotte Mildred, *née* Leighton (s 1934), of Triangle, Halifax, Yorks; *b* 24 Sept 1912; *Educ* RNC Dartmouth; *m* 1940, Mary Elizabeth, da of Cecil Horlock Hawkins, of London; *Career* joined RN 1926, served in HMS: Ark Royal, Furious and Br Pacific Fleet WW II, Capt 1950, IDC 1955; dir of Plans, Admty 1957-59; Rear Adm 1959, Flag Offr Aircraft Carriers 1960-62, Vice Adm 1962, Dep Supreme Allied Cdr Atlantic 1962-64, Flag Offr Naval Air Cmd 1964-65, ret at own request 1965; dir and chief exec Soc of Br Aerospace Cos 1966-79, sec Def Industs Cncl 1970-79; *Clubs* Army and Navy; *Style*— Vice Admiral Sir Richard Smeeton, KCB, MBE, DL; St Mary's Cottage, Woodhill Lane, Shamley Green, Guildford, Surrey (☎ 0483 893478)

SMETHURST, John Michael; s of Albert Smethurst (d 1973), of 20 Cliffe Lane, Barrow-in-Furness, and Nelly, *née* Kitchin (d 1985); *b* 25 April 1934; *Educ* William Hulme's GS Manchester, Manchester Univ (BA); *m* 2 Jan 1960, Mary, da of Ernest Edwin Clayworth (d 1986), of Manchester; 1 s (Matthew b 1966), 1 da (Laura b 1964); *Career* sch master 1956-60, lectr and coll librarian Lancaster Coll of Art 1960-63, tutor librarian Bede Coll Univ of Durham 1963-66, librarian Inst of Educn Newcastle Univ 1966-69, dep librarian Glasgow Univ 1969-72, univ librarian Aberdeen Univ 1972-86, dir gen Humanities and Social Sciences Br Library 1986-; former chm: Friends of Aberdeen Art Gallery, Aberdeen Maritime Museum Appeal; pres: Friends of Aberdeen Univ Library 1986-, Scottish Library Assoc 1983, Liber Ligue Int Des Bibliotheques Européens de Researches 1989-; chm: Standing Conf of Nat and Univ Libraries 1983-85 (vice-chm 1988-89, memb cncl 1981-), Library and Info Servs Ctee Scotland 1980-86, Tstees of the Brotherton Collection Univ of Leeds 1987-; tstee Nat Library of Scotland 1975-86, memb Br Librarian Bd 1986-; ALA, FRSA; hon memb SLA, hon res fell UCL 1986-; *Books* various articles in professional jls and other pubns; *Recreations* music, gardening, art, travel; *Clubs* Athenaeum; *Style*— Michael Smethurst, Esq; Romney, 72 Grove Rd, Tring, Herts HP23 (☎ 044 282 5465); British Library, Gt Russell St, London WC1B 3DG (☎ 01 323 7530, telex 21462)

SMIDDY, (Francis) Paul; s of Francis Geoffrey Smiddy, Leeds, West Yorks, and Thelma Vivenne Smiddy, JP; *b* 13 Nov 1953; *Educ* Winchester, Manchester Univ; *m* 2 Sept 1978, Kathleen (Katy) Maude, da of Stewart MacDougall Watson, Newport, Gwent; 2 s (Oliver b 1980, Alexander b 1982); *Career* mangr Price Waterhouse 1978-82, fin analyst J Sainsbury 1982-84, res analyst Capel-Cure Myers 1984-85, assoc dir Wood Mackenzie 1985-88, dir retail res Kleinwort Benson Securities 1988-; ACA 1978, FCA 1988; *Recreations* flying, motor sport, squash, theatre, walking; *Clubs* Air Touring, BARC, Dulwich Sports; *Style*— Paul Smiddy, Esq; West Hall, 54 Wood Vale, London SE23 3ED (☎ 01 693 4927); Kleinwort Benson Securities Ltd, PO Box 560, 20 Fenchurch Street, London EC3P 3DB (☎ 01 623 8000, fax 01 623 4572, telex 922241)

SMIETON, Dame Mary Guillan; DBE (1949); da of John Guillan Smieton and Maria Judith, *née* Toop; *b* 5 Dec 1902; *Educ* Perse Sch Cambridge, Wimbledon HS, Bedford Coll London, Lady Margaret Hall Oxford (MA); *Career* asst keeper PRO 1925-28, Miny of Labour and Nat Serv 1928-59, gen sec Women's Vol Servs 1938-40, on loan to UN as dir of personnel 1946-48, perm sec Miny of Educn 1959-63, UK rep UNESCO Exec Bd 1962-68; tstee Br Museum 1963-73; cncl chm: Bedford Coll 1963-70; memb: Advsy Cncl on Public Records 1965-73, Standing Cmmn on Museums and Galleries 1970-73, vice-pres Museums Assoc 1974-77; hon fell: Lady Margaret Hall Oxford 1959, Bedford Coll 1971, Royal Holloway Bedford New Coll 1985; *Clubs* United Oxford and Cambridge University; *Style*— Dame Mary Smieton, DBE; 14 St George's Rd, St Margaret's on Thames, Middlesex TW1 1QR (☎ 01 892 9279)

SMILEY, Col David de Crespigny; LVO (1952), OBE (1945, MC 1943 and bar 1944); s of Maj Sir John Smiley, 2 Bt (d 1930), and Valerie, *née* Champion de Crespigny (d 1978); *b* 11 April 1916; *Educ* Nautical Coll Pangbourne, RMC Sandhurst; *m* 28 April 1947, Moyra Eileen, da of Lt-Col Lord Francis George Montagu Douglas Scott, KCMG, DSO (d 1952; yst s of 6 Duke of Buccleuch), and widow of Maj Hugo Douglas Tweedie, Scots Gds (ka 1945); 2 s (Xan, *qv*, Philip b 1951); *Career* cmmnd Royal Horse Gds (The Blues) 1936; served WWII with 1 Houshold Cav Regt in M East (despatches) 1940-42, SOE 1943-45, with Special Forces in Balkans 1943-44, Far East 1945; Staff Coll 1946, asst mil attaché Warsaw 1947, cmd RHG 1952-54, mil attaché Stockholm 1955-58 (Kt Cdr of Order of Sword of Sweden 1957), Cdr Armed Forces of Sultan of Oman 1958-61, mil advsr to Imam of Yemen 1963-68; memb HM Bodyguard of Hon Corps of Gentlemen-at-Arms 1966-68; Order of Skanderbeg

(Albania); *Books* Arabian Assignment (1975), Albanian Assignment (1984); *Recreations* shooting, cooking, gardening; *Clubs* White's, Special Forces, MCC; *Style*— Col David Smiley, LVO, OBE, MC; Well Farm, Lower Ansford, Castle Cary, Somerset BA7 7JZ (☎ 0963 50619)

SMILEY, Sir Hugh Houston; 3 Bt (UK 1903), of Drumalis, Larne, Co Antrim, and Gallowhill, Paisley, Co Renfrew, JP (Hants 1952), DL (1962); s of Sir John Smiley, 2 Bt (d 1930), and Valerie, da of Sir Claude Champion de Crespigny, 4 Bt; *b* 14 Nov 1905; *Educ* Eton, RMC Sandhurst; *m* 18 Jan 1933, Nancy Elizabeth Louise Hardy, er da of late Ernest Walter Hardy Beaton; 1 s; *Heir* s, Lt-Col John Philip Smiley; *Career* Capt Grenadier Guards NW Europe 1944-45; High Sheriff Hants 1959-60, vice Lord-Lt Hants 1973-82; *Clubs* Cavalry and Guards'; *Style*— Sir Hugh Smiley, Bt, JP, DL; Ivalls, Bentworth, Alton, Hants (☎ 0420 63193)

SMILEY, Hon Mrs (Jane); *née* Lyon-Dalberg-Acton; 6 and yst da of 3 Baron Acton, CMG, MBE, TD (d 1989); *b* 25 Jan 1954; *m* 1, 1975 (m dis 1982), Charles Thomas Pugh; 2 da; m 2, 1983, Xan Smiley, *qv*; 2 s (Ben b 1985, Adam b 1988); *Style*— The Hon Mrs Smiley; 36 Rectory Grove, London SW4 (☎ 01 720 8811)

SMILEY, Lt-Col John Philip; s and h of Sir Hugh Smiley, 3 Bt, JP, DL, and Nancy Elizabeth Louise Hardy Beaton; *b* 24 Feb 1934; *Educ* Eton, RMA Sandhurst; *m* 2 Nov 1963, Davina Elizabeth, da of Denis Charles Griffiths (d 1949), of Orlingbury Hall, nr Kettering, Northants; 2 s (Christopher b 1968, William b 1972), 1 da (Melinda b 1965); *Career* cmmnd Gren Guards 1954, served in Cyprus 1958, ADC to Govr of Bermuda 1961-62, Regtl Adj 1970-73, ret Lt-Col 1986; Liveryman Worshipful Co of Grocers 1972; *Clubs* Army and Navy; *Style*— Lt-Col John Smiley; Cornerway House, Chobham, nr Woking, Surrey GU24 8SW (☎ 09905 8992); c/o Russell Reynolds Associates Inc, 24 St James's Square, London SW1Y 4HZ (☎ 01 839 7788, fax 01 839 9395)

SMILEY, Major (Charles) Michael; CVO (1980); s of Capt Hubert Stewart Smiley, and Elsie, *née* Gill; *b* 25 June 1910; *Educ* Eton, RMC Sandhurst; *m* 15 Sept 1939, Lavinia, da of Hon Clive Pearson, of Sussex; 2 s (James b 1947, Andrew b 1951), 1 da (Miranda b 1940); *Career* serv WWII Rifle Bde until 1947 (Calais 1940); farmer; *Recreations* cricket, shooting; *Clubs* Whites; *Style*— Maj Michael Smiley, CVO; Castle Fraser, Inverurie, Aberdeenshire AB3 7LD

SMILEY, Xan de Crespigny; s of Col David Smiley, LVO, OBE, MC, *qv* (3 s of Sir John Smiley, 2 Bt), and Moyra, widow of Maj Hugo Tweedie, and da of Lt-Col Lord Francis Montagu Douglas Scott, KCMG, DSO (6 s of 6 Duke of Buccleuch); *b* 1 May 1949; *Educ* Eton, New Coll Oxford (MA); *m* 1983, Hon Jane, *qv*; 2 s (Ben Richard Philip de Crespigny b 1985, Adam David Emerich b 1988), 2 step da; *Career* journalist and broadcaster; commentator BBC Radio External Serv current affrs 1974-75, corr Spectator and Observer in Africa 1975-77, dir African Confidential Newsletter 1981- (ed 1977-81); Noel Buxton lectr in African politics 1980; ldr writer The Times 1982-83; The Economist 1983-86: foreign affrs, staff writer, Middle East ed; Moscow corr, Daily Telegraph 1986-; *Recreations* food, sport (memb Br ski team 1969), travel, genealogy; *Clubs* White's, Beefsteak, Polish Hearth; *Style*— Xan Smiley, Esq; 36 Rectory Grove, London SW4 (☎ 01 720 8811); 12/24 Sadovo-Samotechnaya, Kv-51, Moscow, USSR (☎ 200 0261, 200 2261 and 200 2707)

SMILLIE, Prof Ian Scott; OBE (1944); s of John Smillie (d 1959), of Dunbartonshire, and Catherine McNidder (d 1950); *b* 5 April 1907; *Educ* St Andrew's Coll Dublin, Merchiston Castle Sch Edinburgh, Univ of Edinburgh (MB, ChB); *m* 1, 16 Aug 1941, Gertrude Delicia, da of John Brian Wilson Ash (d 1965); 2 da (Catherine Anne b 1945, Dorothy Clair b 1951); m 2, 11 July 1956, Janet Nichol, da of James Andrew Sloan (d 1948), of Roxburghshire; *Career* prof of Orthopaedic Surgery, i/c Orthopaedic Hosp Emergency Med Serv Larbert Stirlingshire 1939-46, surgn-in-charge Orthopaedic Serv Eastern Region of Scotland 1948-67, prof Orthopaedic Surgery: Univ of St Andrews 1967, Univ of Dundee 1968-73; emeritus prof and hon res fell of the Univ of Dundee 1974-; Swedish Surgical Soc 1971, McKeown Medal of the Royal Coll of Surgns Edinburgh 1980; FRCS (Edinburgh), FRCS (Glasgow), ChM (Gold Medal) Univ of Edinburgh, Chiene Medal 1948; *Books* Injuries of the Knee Joint (first edn 1946, fifth edn 1978), Diseases of the Knee Joint (first edn 1974, second edn 1980, translated into Spanish, Italian, Portuguese, German), Osteochondritis Dissecans (1960), A Colour Atlas of Traditional Meniscectomy (1983), A Guide to the Stalking of Red Deer in Scotland (1983); *Recreations* stalking, shooting, fishing; *Clubs* RAC; *Style*— Prof Ian S Smillie; Milton of Drimmie, Bridge of Cally, Blairgowrie, Perthshire (☎ 025 086 245); Dalnessie, by Lairg, Sutherland (☎ 0549 2287)

SMILLIE, James; s of Maj Robert Smillie (d 1977), of Stanmore, Middx, and Jean Young, *née* Burnside (d 1970); *b* 7 June 1929; *Educ* Merchant Taylors; *m* 1, 19 June 1949 (m dis 1978), Brenda, da of Herbert Lionel Kelsey, of Harrow, Middx; 4 da (Anne Patricia (Mrs Palmer) b 22 Jan 1958, Sheena Jane (Mrs Owen) b 26 July 1959, Elizabeth Dawn b 10 Dec 1963, Susan Carole b 14 Dec 1965); m 2, 7 March 1981, Chloë Ann, *née* Rich; *Career* Nat Serv 2 Lt/Actg Capt RASC 1953-55; CA; Ramsay Brown & Co 1947-53, Rootes Gp Coventry 1955-56; Stratstone Ltd (subsideary Thomas Tilling Ltd) 1956-: co sec, dir, md (mgmnt buy-out 1981), chm and md 1981-; chm Stratsons Leasing Ltd 1981-, sr ptnr Rover Tport Co 1968-84, non exec dir Great Southern Gp plc 1987-, chm Jaguar Dealer Cncl 1982-; pres Motor Agents Assoc 1988-89 (dep pres 1987-88), vice-pres Motor Trade Benevolent Soc 1988-89; memb: Stanmore (later Beaconsfield) Cons Assoc 1961-84, Chesham and Amersham Cons Assoc 1984-; life govr Imp Cancer Res Fund 1987-; Liveryman Worshipful Co of Coachmakers and Coach Harness Makers 1975 (memb ct 1983); CA (Scot) 1953, FIMI 1978, FInstD; *Recreations* golf, theatre, Glyndebourne; *Clubs* Carlton, RAC, Denham GC; *Style*— James Smillie, Esq; Whyteposts, 66 High St, Old Amersham, Bucks (☎ 0494 727181); Stratstone Ltd, 40 Berkeley St, London W1 (☎ 01 629 4404, telex 01 499 0881)

SMILLIE, (William) John Jones; s of John Smillie (d 1978), and Emily Mary Caroline, *née* Jones (d 1981); *b* 18 Feb 1940; *Educ* Lauriston Sch Falkirk, Territorial Sch Stirling, Stirling H S; *Career* personnel mangr House of Commons Catering Dept 1967, asst to catering mangr 1970, gen mangr 1971, head of dept 1980-; fndr memb Wine Guild of UK 1984; memb: Brit Inst of Cleaning Science 1976, Health Soc 1979, Restaurateurs Assoc of GB 1983, Br Epilepsy Assoc 1981, League Against Cruel Sports 1983; FUCIMA 1979, ACF 1972, FCFA 1967; contrib articles to catering trade papers; *Recreations* theatre, ballet, music, piano, motoring, boating, disc jockey, travel, gourmandising, rock music, intervals at the opera; *Style*— John Smillie, Esq; The Gatehouse, 90 Wimbledon Parkside, Wimbledon Common, London SW19 5LT (☎ 01 788 7456); House of Commons, London SW1 (☎ 01 219 3686, fax 01 219 6696)

SMITH; *see*: Abel Smith, Alec-Smith, Austen-Smith, Babington Smith, Bracewell Smith, Buchanan-Smith, Harrison-Smith, Humphrey-Smith, Johnson Smith, Law-Smith, Montagu-Smith, Newson-Smith, Seth-Smith, Sharwood-Smith, Walker-Smith, Wyldbore-Smith

SMITH, Agnes, Lady; Agnes; o da of Bernard Page, of Wellington, NZ; *m* 20 July 1935, Sir Thomas Turner Smith, 3 Bt (d 1961); 2 s, 2 da; *Style*— Agnes, Lady Smith; 118 Liverpool Street, Wanganui, New Zealand

SMITH, Sir Alan; CBE (1976), DFC (1941) and bar (1942), DL (Kinross 1967); s of Capt Alfred Smith, Merchant Navy (d 1931), of Sunderland, and Lilian, *née* Robinson (d 1956); *b* 14 Mar 1917; *Educ* Bede Coll Sunderland; *m* 1, 10 July 1943, Margaret Stewart (d 1971), da of Herbert Charles Todd (d 1954), of St Ronans, Kinross; 3 s (Michael Charles b 1948, Bruce Alan b 1948, Stuart Duncan b 1956), 2 da (Susan Janet (Mrs Anstead) b 1945, Ailsa Hilda b 1959); m 2, 1977, Alice Elizabeth, da of Robert Stewart Moncur (d 1961); *Career* served as pilot RAF WW II 1939-45; chief exec Todd & Duncan Ltd 1946-60; chm and chief exec Dawson Int 1960-82, pres (life) 1982-; chm: Quayle Munro Ltd 1983-, Gleneagles Hotels 1982-84, Scottish Cashmere Assoc 1964-; dir Global Recovery Investmt Tst 1981-86; bd memb: Scottish Devpt Agency 1981-86, Scottish Tourist Bd 1982-85; Kinross Burgh Cncllr 1952-65, Provost of Kinross 1959-65; Tayside Region Cncllr 1979-; CTI; kt 1982; *Recreations* sailing, swimming; *Clubs* Lansdowne; *Style*— Sir Alan Smith, CBE, DFC, DL; Ardgairney House, Cleish, by Kinross (☎ 0577 5265); Dawson International plc, Lochleven Mills, Kinross, Scotland (☎ 0577 63521, telex 76168)

SMITH, Alan Christopher; s of Herbert Sidney Smith (d 1986), of Birmingham, and Elsie Blanche, *née* Ward; *b* 25 Oct 1936; *Educ* King Edward's Sch, Birmingham, Bransenose Coll Oxford (BA); *m* 12 Oct 1963, Anne Elizabeth, da of John Gill Boddy, of Braunston, nr Rugby; 1 s (Mark b 1965), 1 da (Lara b 1969); *Career* Nat Serv 2 Lt RCS 1956; capt Oxford Univ CC 1959-60, Warwicks CCC 1958-78 (capt 1968-74), 6 tests for England, England selector 1969-73 and 1982-86; England mangr: W Indies test 1981, NZ test 1984; gen sec Warwicks CCC 1976-86, chief exec TCCB 1987-; dir: Aston Villa FC 1972-78, Royds Advertising and Mktg 1970-86; *Recreations* cricket, both football codes, golf, motoring, bridge; *Clubs* MCC, I Zingari, Vincents; *Style*— Alan Smith, Esq; The Bridge house, Oversley Green, Alcester, Warwicks B49 6LE (☎ 0789 762847); TCCB, Lord's Cricket Ground, London NW8 (☎ 01 286 4405, fax 01 289 5619, car 0860 533313, telex 24462 TCCB G)

SMITH, Alec Quinton; JP (Herts); s of Thomas Quinton Smith (d 1953), of London Colney, Herts, and Irene Ethel, *née* Eames (d 1958); *b* 15 Dec 1927; *Educ* St Albans GS for Boys, Sch of Architecture and Surveying Northern Poly London, Brunel Univ (MA); *m* 19 July 1952, Monica Joan, da of Thomas William Hill (d 1965), of London Colney, Herts; 1 s (Graham b 1956), 1 da (Andrea b 1954); *Career* 5002 Sqdn RAF 1946-48; ptnr and sr ptnr VB Johnson and ptnrs 1952-, panel memb CIArb 1972-, chm Beds and Herts Chartered Surveyors 1973, chm Masterbill Micro Systems Ltd 1981-, dir Fencing Contractors Assoc 1983-, managing ed Laxtons Bldg Price Book 1984-; tstee Lucy Kemp-Welch Meml Tst; dep chm Watford Bench of Magistrates, memb Herts Magistrates Cts Ctee; Freeman City of London 1981, Liveryman Worshipful Co of Arbitrators 1981; FRICS 1960, FBIM 1971, FCIArb 1972, Memb Soc of Construction Law 1987; *Recreations* photography, light gardening, after dinner speaking; *Style*— Alec Smith, Esq, JP; The Corners, 23 Finch Lane, Bushey, Herts (☎ 01 950 3811); St John's House, 23 St John's Rd, Watford, Herts WD1 1PY (☎ 0923 227236, fax 0923 31134)

SMITH, Sir Alexander (Alex) Mair; s of John Smith; *b* 15 Oct 1922; *Educ* Aberdeen Univ (PhD); *m* 1, 1956, Doris, *née* Patrick (d 1980); 3 da; m 2, 1984, Jennifer, *née* Pearce; *Career* co dir, physicist with UKAEA 1952-56, dir and chief scientist Rolls Royce & Assocs Ltd 1967-69 (head of advanced res 1956-67), dir Manchester Poly 1969-81; chm: Ctee of Dirs of Polytechnics 1974-76, Schls Cncls 1975-78; memb: Univ Grants Ctee 1974-76, BBC Gen Advsy Cncl 1978-81, RSA Cncl 1979-84; vice-pres City & Guilds of London Inst 1981-; FInstP; kt 1975; *Recreations* golf; *Clubs* Athenaeum; *Style*— Sir Alex Smith; 33 Parkway, Wilmslow, Cheshire SK9 1LS (☎ 0625 522011)

SMITH, Hon Alexander David; s of 4 Visc Hambleden; *b* 11 Mar 1959; *Style*— The Hon Alexander Smith

SMITH, Dr (Edward) Alistair; CBE (1982); s of Archibald Smith (d 1977), of 14 Maryfield Cres, Inverurie, Aberdeenshire, and Jean Milne, *née* Johnston; *b* 16 Jan 1939; *Educ* Aberdeen GS, Univ of Aberdeen (MA, PhD); *Career* lectr in geography 1963-1988, dir Univ of Aberdeen Devpt Tst 1982-, assoc dir overseas off Univ of Aberdeen 1988-; memb: Grampian Health Bd 1983-, NE Cncl on Disability, exec ctee Grampian Ash, pres Scottish Cons and Unionist Assoc 1979-81, dep chm Scottish Cons Pty 1981-85; *Books* Europe: A Geographical Survey of the Continent (with REM Mellor, 1979); *Recreations* photography, travel, music; *Style*— Dr Alistair Smith, CBE; 68A Beaconsfield Place, Aberdeen AB2 4AJ (☎ 0224 642932); University of Aberdeen, Regent Walk, Aberdeen, AB9 1FX (☎ 0224 272096, 0224273 503, fax 0224 487048, telex 73458 UNIABN G

SMITH, Allen Donald Warren; OBE (1984); s of Donald Charles Wesley Smith (d 1983), of Olive Kathleen Smith (d 1979); *b* 20 Oct 1922; *Educ* Ipswich Sch, London Univ (BSc); *m* 12 Aug 1949, June Mary, da of Kenneth Pearce (d 1946); 3 s (Andrew b 1951, Christopher b 1953, Nicholas b 1958); *Career* RAF Airfield Construction Serv 1944-47, Flt Lt, serv France, Belgium, Holland, Germany and Singapore; various engrg appts 1948-62: E Suffolk CC, Surrey CC, W Riding of Yorks CC, Somerset CC, Sir Alexander Gibbs Ptnrs Conslt Engrs; dep county surveyor; E Sussex CC 1962-68, Kent CC 1968-71; county surveyor Kent 1972-84, conslt transportation planning and highways; pres County Surveyor's Soc 1978-79; parish cncllr Fritlenden Kent, chm Engrg Cncl Regnl Orgn Kent and Sussex; Freeman City of London 1984, Liveryman Worshipful Co of Engrs 1984; FEng, FICE, FIHT, MIWM, FRSA; *Books* A History of the County Surveyors' Society 1885-1985 (1985); *Recreations* music, gardening, reading; *Clubs* RAC; *Style*— Allen Smith, Esq, OBE; Kippens', Frittenden, Cranbrook, Kent TN17 2DD (☎ 058 080 358)

SMITH, Prof Alwyn; CBE (1986); s of Ernest Smith (d 1976); *b* 9 Nov 1925; *Educ* Queen Mary's Sch Walsall, Birmingham Univ (PhD); *m* 1950, Doreen, *née* Preston; 1 s, 1 da; *Career* Prof: community med Manchester 1967-79, epidemiology and social oncology Manchester 1979-; pres Faculty Community Med Royal Coll of Physicians 1981-; FRCP, FFCM, FRCGP; *Recreations* sailing, music, watching football; *Style*—

Prof Alwyn Smith, CBE; 66 Kingston Rd, Didsbury, Manchester M20; University of Manchester & University Hospital of South Manchester, Dept of Epidemiology and Social Oncology, Kinnaird Rd, Manchester M20 9QL (☎ 061 434 7721)

SMITH, Andrew David; MP (Lab) Oxford East 1987-; s of late David E C Smith, and Georgina H J Smith; *b* 1 Feb 1951; *Educ* Reading Sch, St John's Coll Oxford (MA, BPhil); *m* 26 March 1976, Valerie, da of William Labert; 1 s; *Career* Oxford City cncllr 1976-; chm: Recreation & Amenities Ctee 1980-83, planning Ctee 1985-87, Race & Community Relations Ctee 1985-87; Relations Off Oxford & Swindon Co-Op Soc 1979-87, memb parly Panel Union of Shop Distributive & Allied Workers 1986, memb social servs select ctee 1988-, Labour front bench educn spokesman (higher educn) 1988-; chm Govrs of Oxford Polytechnic 1987;; *Clubs* Headington Labour, Blackbird Leys Community Assoc; *Style—* Andrew Smith, Esq, MP; 4 Flaxfield Road, Blackbird Leys, Oxford OX4 5QD; Constituency (☎ 0865 772893); c/o House of Commons, London SW1 (☎ 01-219-5102)

SMITH, Hon Andrew Edward Rodney; s (by 1 m) of Baron Smith, KBE (Life Peer); *b* 1948; *Style—* The Hon Andrew Smith; Dower Cottage, Marlow Common, Bucks

SMITH, Andrew James; s of Clifford John Smith, of Leatherhead, Surrey, and Ella Smith; *b* 9 Oct 1958; *Educ* Malvern, Magdalene Coll Cambridge (MA); *Career* Peat Marwick McLintock 1980-88, fin controller Foreign & Colonial Ventures Ltd 1989-; ACA 1986; *Recreations* sailing, horseriding; *Clubs* RAC; *Style—* Andrew J Smith, Esq; 16 Claremont Rd, Highgate, London N6 (☎ 01 340 0063); 6 Laurence Pountney Hill, London EC4R 0BL (☎ 01 782 9829, fax 01 782 9834 telex 886197 Forcol G)

SMITH, Andrew Thomas; s and h of Sir Gilbert Smith, 4 Bt; *b* 17 Oct 1965; *Style—* Andrew Smith Esq

SMITH, Dame (Katharine) Annis Calder; DBE; *see*: Gillie, Dame A C

SMITH, Anthony David; CBE (1987); s of Henry Smith (d 1951), and Esther, *née* Berdiowsky (d 1967); *b* 14 Mar 1938; *Educ* Harrow Co Sch, Brasenose Coll Oxford (BA); *Career* BBC TV current affairs producer 1960-71; dir: Br Film Inst 1979-88, Channel Four TV 1980-84; fell St Antony's Coll Oxford 1971-76, pres Magdalen Coll Oxford; *Books* The Shadow in the Cave, Goodbye Gutenberg, The Geopolitics of Information, and numerous other titles; *Style—* Anthony Smith, Esq, CBE; (☎ 0865 276102)

SMITH, Anthony Howard Leslie; s of Wing Cdr Arthur Leslie Smith (d 1983), of Thames Ditton, Surrey, and Marjorie Jean, *née* Dodridge; *b* 26 Nov 1943; *Educ* Allhollows Sch; *m* 1, Rosemary Smith (m dis); m 2 18 April 1981, Heather, da of John Beattie, of Harrow, Middx; 1 da (Lucy Jeannine Antonia); *Career* admitted slr 1967, memb Law Soc Child Care Panel; former chm and pres Brackhell Round Table; memb Law Soc; *Recreations* sailing and skiing; *Style—* Anthony Smith, Esq; 3 The Brambles, Crowthorne, Berks (☎ 0344 776352); Coppid Hall, Warfield Rd, Bracknell, Berks (☎ 0344 420555, fax 0344 860486)

SMITH, Anthony John Francis; s of Hubert J F Smith (d 1984), of Dorset, and Diana, *née* Watkin; *b* 30 Mar 1926; *Educ* Dragon, Blundell's Sch Devon, Balliol Coll Oxford (MA); *m* 1, 1 Sept 1956 (m dis 1983), Barbara Dorothy, da of Maj-Gen Charles Richard Newman CB, CMG, DSO (d 1954), of Ottery St Mary, Devon; 1 s (Adam b 1963), 2 da (Polly b 1968, Laura b 1969); m 2, 1984, Margaret Ann (formerly Mrs Holloway), da of George Hounsom (d 1987); 1 s (Quintin b 1986); *Career* RAF 1944-48; reporter Manchester Guardian 1953-57, sci corr Daily Telegraph 1957-63; freelance: broadcaster, author, journalist 1964-; FRGS 1966, FZS 1969; *Books* Blind White Fish in Persia (1953), High Street Africa (1961), Throw Out Two Hands (1963), The Body (1968), The Dangerous Sort (1970), Mato Grosso (1971), The Human Pedigree (1975), Wilderness (1978), A Persian Quarter Century (1979), The Mind (1984), Smith & Son (1984), The Great Rift (1988), Explorers of the Amazon (1989); *Recreations* ballooning; *Clubs* Explorers (NY); *Style—* Anthony Smith, Esq; 10 Aldbourne Rd, London W12 (☎ 01 743 6935); St Aidan's, Bamburgh, Northumberland

SMITH, Ven Anthony Michael Percival; s of Canon Kenneth Smith (d 1951), and Audrey Mary, *née* Clarke (d 1972); *b* 5 Sept 1924; *Educ* Shrewsbury, Gonville and Caius Coll Cambridge (MA), Westcott House Cambridge; *m* 16 July 1950, Mildred Elizabeth, da of William Brown, OBE (d 1978), of Covington, Huntingdon, Cambridgeshire; 2 da (Susan Percival b 1951, Claire Percival b 1954); *Career* Lt Rifle Bde 1943-46 N Euro; domestic chaplain to Archbishop of Canterbury 1953-58; vicar: All Saints' Upper Norwood S London 1958-66, Yeovil 1966-72; rural dean of Murston 1968-72, prebendary of Wells Cathedral 1970-72, vicar St Mildred's Addiscombe Croydon 1972-80, archdeacon of Maidstone 1980-; diocesan dir Ordinands 1980-, hon canon Canterbury Cathedral 1980; *Recreations* reading; *Style—* The Ven the Archdeacon of Maidstone; Archdeacon's House, the Hill, Charing, Ashford, Kent (☎ 023 371 2294)

SMITH, Antony Gervase; s of Gervase Gorst Smith (d 1963), and Gladys Alford (d 1968); *b* 31 July 1927; *Educ* Haileybury; *m* 4 Nov 1955, Penelope Faux, da of Pearson Faux, of Durban Natal (d 1964); 1 s (Julian Gervase b 21 Feb 1958); 2 da (Miranda b 9 Mar 1962, Philippa b 30 Apr 1963); *Career* served KRRC 1945-48, Capt Queen Victoria's Rifles 1948-52; dir Long Till & Colvin 1960-68; md Astley & Pearce (Sterling) 1980; chm MH Cockell Ltd 1987; Liveryman Worshipful Co of Turners 1969; *Recreations* shooting; *Clubs* City of London, Royal Green Jackets; *Style—* Antony Smith, Esq; Cozen's House, Ocherston, Salisbury, Wilts SP3 4RW (☎ 0980 620 257)

SMITH, Ven Arthur Cyril; VRD (1955); s of Arthur Smith (d 1916); *b* 26 Jan 1909; *Educ* St John's Coll Winnipeg, Sheffield Univ, Westcott Coll Cambridge; *m* 1940, Patricia Marion, da of late Col Ranolf Greenwood, MC; 2 s, 2 da; *Career* ordained 1934, canon and prebendary of Centum Solidorum, archdeacon of Lincoln 1960-76 & (now emeritus), dir Ecclesiastical Insurance Office Ltd 1967-77, church cmmr 1970-76, conslt Inter-Church Travel; *Recreations* Tennyson Soc, travel; *Clubs* Army and Navy; *Style—* The Ven Arthur Smith, VRD; 2 Cavendish Court, 14 Blackwater Road, Eastbourne BN21 4JD (☎ 0323 36204)

SMITH, Sir Arthur Henry; s of Frederick Smith of Bolton; *b* 18 Jan 1905; *Educ* Bolton Sch; *m* 1930, Dorothy, da of Henry Percy of Southport; 2 s; *Career* dir Unilever Ltd 1948-69, chm United Africa Co Ltd 1955-69; Offr Légion d'Honneur 1957; kt 1968,; *Style—* Sir Arthur Smith; 102 Kingway Court, Queens Gardens, Hove

SMITH, Hon Bernardo James; s of 4 Viscount Hambleden; *b* 17 May 1957; *Style—* The Hon Bernardo Smith

SMITH, Ven Brian Arthur; s of Arthur Smith, of 224 Telford Rd, Edinburgh, and Doris Marion, *née* Henderson; *b* 15 August 1943; *Educ* George Heriot's Sch Edinburgh, Edinburgh Univ (MA), Cambridge Univ (MA, MLitt); *m* 1 Aug 1970, Elizabeth Berring, da of Lt-Col Charles Francis Hutchinson (d 1980), of Moor Farm, Longframlington, Northumberland; 2 da (Tessa b 1974, Alice b 1978); *Career* ordained: deacon 1972, priest 1973; curate of Cuddesdon 1972-79, tutor in doctrine Cuddesdon Coll Oxford 1972-75, dir of studies Ripon Coll Oxford 1975-78 (sr tutor 1978-79), dir of ministerial training Diocese of Wakefield 1979-87, priest i/c Cragg Vale 1978-86, warden of readers Diocese of Wakefield 1981-87, hon canon Wakefield Cathedral 1981-87, archdeacon of Craven 1987-; vice-chm Northern Ordination Course 1986-; *Recreations* reading, music, walking, browsing in junk shops, short-wave radio listening; *Clubs* National Liberal; *Style—* The Ven the Archdeacon of Craven; Brooklands, Bridge End, Long Preston, Skipton, N Yorks BD23 4RA (☎ 07294 334)

SMITH, (Howard) Brian; *b* 11 Dec 1931; *Educ* Kettering GS; *m* 1958, Joy Elizabeth; 2 s (Adrian b 1959, Philip b 1962), 1 da (Julia b 1965); *Career* Nat Serv cmmnd RAPC 1954-56; CA; sr ptnr Smith Starmer Hart Kettering 1954-86, Moore Stephens E Midlands 1985-86; chm: Midland Bd Eagle Star Insurance Co Ltd 1986-88, Grangetime Ltd, Pink & Jones Ltd, Bardate Ltd, Haynes & Cann Ltd, Cheney-Spiro Engrg Ltd; vice chm Britannia Movers Int Ltd, Britannia Movers Int (London) Ltd; dir: William Levene Ltd, Manna Ltd, P B Truck Centre Ltd; Liveryman Worshipful Co of CAs; *Recreations* golf, travel; *Clubs* Luffenham Heath Golf; *Style—* Brian Smith, Esq; Northfield House, Pytchley, Kettering, Northants NN14 1EX (☎ 0536 790243); 2 Baron Avenue, Telford Way, Kettering, Northants NN16 8UN (☎ 0536 512019, fax 0536 410585)

SMITH, (John) Brian; s of Sydney John Smith (d 1979), of Beaconsfield, and Florence May Dean Smith; *b* 5 June 1928; *Educ* Bradford GS, Sidney Sussex Coll Cambridge (MA); *m* 23 July 1953, Joan Margaret, da of Horace Newton Jennings (d 1951), of Bradford; 2 s (Timothy b 1954, Nicholas b 1962), 2 da (Penelope b 1956, Joanna b 1963); *Career* dir: The Rank Orgn 1976-83, Eley & Warren Ltd 1984-, Manganese Bronze Hldgs plc 1984-, Gerald Gobert Hldgs Ltd 1985-; chm: J B Smith Conslts Ltd 1983, City Jeroboam plc 1988; business cnclir DTI 1985; memb: Bucks CC 1985-, exec ctee Beaconsfield Constituency Cons Assoc; Freeman: City of London, Worshipful Co of Scientific Instrument Makers; IOD, CBIM 1981; *Recreations* golf, tennis, bridge; *Style—* Brian Smith, Esq; Hebden House, Eghams Close, Beaconsfield, Bucks HP9 1XN (☎ 0494 673063); 1 The Highway, Beaconsfield, Bucks (☎ 0494 677794, fax 0494 672556, car tel 0836 229819)

SMITH, Brian Roy; s of Arthur Roy Smith (d 1971), and Phyllis Edith Smith; *b* 18 August 1937; *Educ* Sir George Monoux GS; *m* 4 July 1959, Barbara Gladys, da of James Richard Beasley (d 1980); 1 s (Stewart Spencer 26 Jan 1963), 1 da (Justine Caroline b 10 April 1967); *Career* RAF 1956-58; BR Smith and Others (Lloyds Syndicate) 1969-; dir: Garwyn Ltd 1972-, Bankside Syndicates Ltd 1985-, Bankside Members Agency Ltd 1985-, Bankside Underwriting Agencies Ltd 1985-, Cotesworth and Co Ltd 1985-, Reed Stenhouse Syndicates Ltd 1976-85; memb Lloyds 1972-: Non Marine Assoc Ctee 1985-; *Recreations* squash, tennis, theatre, opera, boating; *Clubs* Old Chigwellians; *Style—* Brian Smith, Esq; Bishops Hall, Lambourne End, Essex (☎ 01 500 6510); B R Smith and Others, 120 Middlesex Street, London EC1 (☎ 01 247 0304)

SMITH, Brian Stanley; s of Ernest Stanley Smith (ka 1943), of Leeds, and Dorothy Maud Smith; *b* 15 May 1932; *Educ* Bloxham, Keble Coll Oxford (BA, MA); *m* 28 Sept 1963, Alison Margaret, da of Robert George Alexander Hemming, of Cardross, Dumbarton; 2 da (Frances b 1964, Jennifer b) 1966); *Career* asst archivist: Worcs 1956-58, Essex 1958-60, Glos 1961-68 (co archivist 1968-79); sec Royal Cmmn Historical MSS 1982- (asst sec 1980-81); memb ctee of mgmnt Inst Hist Res London Univ 1982-87; pt/t ed Victoria Co Mist Glos 1968-70; Bristol and Glos Archaeological Soc (ed 1971-79, pres 1986-87, vice pres 1987-; lay memb Glos Diocesan Synod; FSA 1972, FR Hist S 1980, memb Soc of Archivists (chm 1979-80); *Books* The Cotswolds (1976), History of Bloxham School (1978), History of Malvern (second edn 1987), History of Bristol and Gloucestershire (second edn 1982); *Recreations* mountaineering, gardening; *Style—* Brian Smith, Esq; Midwoods, Shire Lane, Cholesbury Tring, Herts HP23 6NA; Royal Commission on Historical Manuscripts, Quality House, Quality Court, Chancery Lane, London WC2A 1HP (☎ 01 242 1198)

SMITH, Brian William; JP (1972); s of Lambert Smith, of Glos, and Lily Anne, *née* Hobbs-Savoury (d 1969); *b* 12 July 1925; *Educ* Marling Sch Stroud, St Catharine's Coll Cambridge (MA); *m* 10 Oct 1953, Hilary Heslop, da of Sidney Gordon Griffin, of Weston-super-Mare; 2 s (Clive b 1955, Russell b 1959), 2 da (Clare b 1957 d 1965, April b 1966); *Career* Sub Lt RNVR, served 1943-46 Far East; co dir and chm; Sutcliffe Catering Gp 1952, dir Sutcliffe Midlands 1958, md 1962-73, chm and fndr Brian Smith Catering Services (industrial caterers); *Recreations* rugby, cricket, hockey, tennis, golf; *Style—* Brian W Smith, Esq; 26 Buddon Lane, Quorn, Leics LE12 8AA; 106 New Walk, Leicester (☎ Leicester 544727)

SMITH, Sheriff Charles; s of Charles Smith (d 1973), of Perth, and Mary, *née* Allan (d 1988); *b* 15 August 1930; *Educ* Perth Acad, St Andrews Univ (MA, LLB); *m* 1959, Janet Elizabeth, da of James Hurst (d 1942); 1 s (Charles), 1 da (Jennifer); *Career* slr 1956, practiced in Perth 1956-62 (princ 1961-82); hon tutor dept of law Dundee Univ; memb Perth Town Cncl 1966-68, temp Sheriff 1977-82, memb cncl of Law Soc of Scotland (convenor various ctees) 1977-82; Sheriff of: Glasgow and Strahtkelvin 1982-86, Tayside Central and Fife at Perth 1986-; *Recreations* tennis, golf, croquet; *Style—* Sheriff Charles Smith; c/o Sheriff Ct, Perth (☎ 0738 205416)

SMITH, Sir Charles Bracewell; 5 Bt, (UK 1947), of Keighley, Co York; suc bro Sir Guy Bracewell Smith, 4 Bt, (d 1983); *b* 13 Oct 1955; *Educ* Harrow; *m* 1977, Carol Vivien, da of Norman Hough, of Cookham, Berks; *Style—* Sir Charles Smith, Bt; Park Lane Hotel, Piccadilly, London W1

SMITH, Christopher (Chris) Robert; MP (Lab) Islington S and Finsbury 1983-; s of Colin Smith and Gladys, *née* Luscombe; *b* 24 July 1951; *Educ* George Watson's Coll Edinburgh, Pembroke Coll Cambridge (PhD), Harvard Univ; *Career* contested (Lab) Epsom and Ewell 1979; cncllr London Borough of Islington 1978-83, chief whip 1978-79, chm of housing 1981-83; ASTMS branch: sec 1978-80, chm 1980-83; memb Cncl for National Parks; housing dvpt worker; memb of Environment Select Ctee 1983-87, sec of Tribune Gp of MPs 1984-, chm of Labour Campaign for Criminal Justice 1985-; Labour spokesman of Treasury and Economic affairs 1987-; memb bd of Shelter 1987-; exec ctee memb NCCL 1986-; *Style—* Chris Smith, Esq, MP; House of Commons, London SW1 (☎ 01 219 5119)

SMITH, Christopher Gordon; s of Maj (Joseph) Cordon Smith, of St Aster, Duras

47120, France, and Sheila Mary, *née* Gleeson (d 1982); *b* 3 Sept 1952; *Educ* The Abbey Sch Fort Augustus; *m* 16 Aug 1980, Jean Helen, da of (James Craufuird) Roger Inglis, of Gifford, E Lothian, Scotland; 1 s (Jeremy b 14 June 1983), 1 da (Camilla b 4 June 1985); *Career* co sec: C R McRithcie & Co Ltd 1977-84, Norloch Ltd 1977-84; dir: C R McRitchie & Co Ltd, Norloch Ltd; asst dir Noble Grossart Ltd 1987 (dir 1989, tres 1985); *Recreations* squash, running; *Clubs* Edinburgh Sports; *Style*— Christopher Smith, Esq; 1 Wester Coates Terr, Edinburgh EH12 5LR; Noble Crossart Ltd, 48 Queen St, Edinburgh (☎ 031 226 7011, fax 031 226 6032)

SMITH, Sir Christopher Sydney Winwood; 5 Bt (UK 1809) of Eardiston, Worcestershire; s of Sir William Sydney Winwood Smith, 4 Bt (d 1953); *b* 20 Sept 1906; *m* 1932, Phyllis Berenice, da of late Thomas Robert O'Grady; 3 s, 2 da; *Heir* s, Robert Sydney Winwood Smith; *Style*— Sir Christopher Smith, Bt; Junction Rd, via Grafton, NSW, 2460, Australia

SMITH, Colin; s of Henry Edmund Smith (d 1976), and A Estelle, *née* Pearson (d 1979); *b* 4 July 1941; *Educ* Upton House Sch; *Career* sec gen Int Assoc Against Painful Experiments on Animals 1969-, dir American Fund for Alternatives to Animal Res 1977-, gen sec Nat Anti-Vivisection Soc 1971-81, ed Animals' Defender and Anti-Vivisection News 1982-86; *Style*— Colin Smith, Esq; PO Box 215, St Albans, Herts AL3 4RD

SMITH, Prof (Christopher) Colin; s of Alfred Edward Smith (d 1969), of Brighton, Sussex, and Dorothy May, *née* Berry (d 1984); *b* 17 Sept 1927; *Educ* Varndean Sch for Boys Brighton, Univ of Cambridge (BA, MA, PhD, LittD); *m* 14 Aug 1954, Ruth Margaret, da of Harry James Barnes (d 1987), of Brighton, Sussex; 1 s (Roderick b 1958, d 1960), 3 da (Jennifer b 1960, Rebecca b 1961, Jocelyn b 1964); *Career* asst lectr dept of Spanish Univ of Leeds 1953-56 (lectr 1956-64, sr lectr 1964-68, sub-dean of arts 1963-67), univ lectr in spanish Univ of Cambridge 1968-75 (prof of spanish 1975-, fell St Catharine's Coll Cambridge 1968-), visiting prof Univ of Virginia USA 1981; memb Assoc of Hispanists of GB and Ireland (pres 1977-79); comendador de numero de la Orden de Isabel la Catdica (Spain) 1988; *Books* Spanish Ballads (1964), Collins English/Spanish, Spanish/English Dictionary (1971, 2 ed, 1988), The Poema de mio Cid (1972, 2 ed, 1985), Estudios cidianos (1977), Place-names of Roman Britain (with ALF Rivet, 1979), The Making of the Poema de mio cid (1983); *Recreations* natural history (especially entomology), archaeology, squash; *Style*— Prof Colin Smith; 56 Girton Rd, Cambridge CB3 0LL (☎ 0223 276 214); St Catharine's Coll, Cambridge CB2 1RL (☎ 0223 338 351)

SMITH, Colin Ferguson; s of Henry Ferguson Smith, of Sillgrove Farm, Kinlet, Salop, and Barbara Catharine, *née* Tangye; *b* 12 Oct 1932; *Educ* Leighton Park Sch reading, Gonvill and Caius Coll Cambridge (MA, LLB); *Career* prodn controller Tangyes Ltd 1960-62 (chief buyer 1962-64, co sec and accounts mangr 1964-67), asst co sec Central Wagon Co Ltd 1967-69, dir Smith Keen Cutler Ltd 1986- (ptnr and res mangr 1971-86); memb Stock Exchange FCIS 1971; *Clubs* Carlton; *Style*— Colin Smith, Esq; 55 Warwick Crest, Arthur Road, Birmingham, West Midlands; The Clos Mill, St Clears, Dyfed, Wales (☎ 021 454 4698); Smith Keen Cutler Ltd, Exchange Buildings Stephensom Place, Birmingham, West Midlands B2 4NN (☎ 021 643 9977, fax 021 643 0345, telex 336730)

SMITH, Colin Milner; s of Alan Milner Smith, OBE, of Russets, Hillydeal Road, Otford, Kent, and Vera Ivy, *née* Cannon (d 1973); *b* 2 Nov 1936; *Educ* Tonbridge, Brasenose Coll Oxford (BA), Univ of Chicago (JD); *m* 14 Dec 1979, Moira Soraya, da of Charles Reginald Braybrooke of Crofts, Lower Layham, Suffolk; 1 s (Alexander b 1982), 1 da (Camilla b 1987); *Career* Nat Serv Lt RM (3 Commando Brig) 1955-57; called to the Bar Gray's Inn 1962, QC 1985, rec 1987-; *Recreations* cricket, skiing, reading; *Clubs* MCC; *Style*— Colin Smith, Esq, QC; 3 Gray's Inn Place, Gray's Inn, London WC 1R5 EA (☎ 01 831 8441)

SMITH, Lady Corisande; *née* Bennet; da of 8 Earl of Tankerville (d 1971), and his 2 w, Violet, *qv*; *b* 1938; *m* 1963, Lt Cdr Timothy Bain Smith, RN; 2 s; *Style*— Lady Corisande Smith; Wickens Manor, Charing, Kent

SMITH, Sir Cyril; MBE (1966), MP (Lib) Rochdale 1972-; *b* 28 June 1928; *Educ* Rochdale GS for Boys; *Career* cncllr Rochdale 1952-66, alderman 1966-74, memb Rochdale Metropolitan Dist Cncl 1974-75, chief Lib Whip 1975-76; dir; kt 1988; *Recreations* listening to music, reading, TV; *Clubs* National Liberal (chm 1987-88); *Style*— Sir Cyril Smith, Esq, MBE, MP; 14 Emma St, Rochdale, Lancs (☎ 0706 48840)

SMITH, Dr Cyril Stanley; CBE (1985); s of Walter Charles Smith (d 1932), of London, and Beatrice May Smith (d 1978); *b* 21 July 1925; *Educ* Plaistow Municipal Secdy Sch, LSE (MSc), Univ of London (PhD); *m* 1, 1949 (m dis 1968), Helena Ursula; 2 da (Vanessa (Mrs Hallam) b 1952, Emma Josephine b 1956, d 1978); m 2, 8 May 1968, Eileen Cameron, da of Samuel Dentith (d 1976), of Salford; *Career* Dorset Regt 1943-47; dir dept of youth work Univ of Manchester 1961- 70, dir socl policy studies Civil Serv Coll 1971-75, sec SSRC 1975-85, md Restart 1985-; chm Br Sociological Assoc 1972-74, memb sec of state's ctee on Inequalities in Health (DHSS) 1977-80; author of various books and articles on adolescence, leisure, socl sciences; chm Br Assoc for Servs to the Elderly 1988-; *Books* Adolescence (1968), The Wincroft Youth Project (1972), Society of Leisure in Britain (jt ed 1973); *Recreations* football; *Clubs* West Ham FC; *Style*— Dr Cyril Smith, CBE; Cornwall House, Cornwall Gardens, London SW7 4AE

SMITH, David; s of Walter Horace Smith (d 1960), and Annie, *née* Matthews (d 1971); *b* 18 July 1927; *Educ* Burton GS, Sheffield Univ (BSc, PhD); *m* 1951, Nancy Elizabeth, da of Harold Hawley (d 1968); 2 s, 3 da; *Career* vice-pres Exxon Chemical Co 1971-78, chm and md Esso Chemical Ltd 1979-86; petroleum and chemical conslt 1987- ;memb cncl Chemical Indust Assoc 1982-86;; *Recreations* golf, cricket; *Clubs* MCC, Royal Winchester GC; *Style*— David Smith, Esq; Meadowlands, Stockbridge Rd, Winchester, Hants (☎ 0962 64880)

SMITH, His Hon Judge David Arthur; QC (1982); s of Arthur Heber Smith (d 1983), of Kent, and Marjorie Edith Pounds Smith, *née* Broome; *b* 7 May 1938; *Educ* Lancing, Merton Coll Oxford (MA); *m* 1967, Clementine, da of William Taylor Gordon Urquhart (d 1977); 2 s (Rupert b 1969, Julian b 1970); *Career* official princ Archdeaconry of Hackney 1973-, rec Crown Ct 1978-86, circuit judge 1986-; wine tres Western Circuit 1980-86; *Recreations* sec Int Bee Res Assoc; *Style*— His Hon Judge David Smith, QC; Bristol Crown Court, The Guildhall, Bristol

SMITH, David Arthur George; JP (Bradford, 1975); s of Stanley George Smith (d 1967), of Bath, and Winifred May Francis (d 1985); *b* 17 Dec 1934; *Educ* City of Bath Boys' Sch, Balliol Coll Oxford (BA, Dip Ed, MA); *m* 31 Aug 1957, Jennifer, da of John Ronald Anning (d 1963), of Launceston; 1 s (John b 1962), 2 da (Sarah b 1961, Charlotte b 1967); *Career* asst master Manchester GS 1957-62, head of history Rossall Sch 1963-70; headmaster: Kings Sch Peterborough 1970-74, Bradford GS 1974-; JP Peterborough 1972-74; chm HMC 1988; FRSA 1985; Left and Right in Twentieth Century Europe (1970), Russia of the Tsars (1970); *Recreations* walking, writing; *Clubs* Athenaeum (Bradford); *Style*— David Smith, Esq, JP; Bradford Grammar School, Bradford, W Yorks BD9 43P (☎ 0274 545 461)

SMITH, David Bruce Boyter; s of Bruce A Smith, of Dunfermline, and Helen, *née* Boyter; *b* 11 Mar 1942; *Educ* HS Dunfermline, Edinburgh Univ (MA, LLB); *m* 7 Aug 1965, Christine Anne, da of Robert McKenzie (d 1971); 1 s (Andrew b 1 Aug 1969), 1 da (Caroline b 1 July 1974); *Career* admitted slr 1968, NP 1969, slr Standard Life Assur Co 1969-73; Dunfermline Bldg Soc: sec 1974, gen mangr 1981, dep chief exec 1986, chief exec 1987, dir 1987; chm BSA Scottish Liaison Ctee 1988-, cncl memb NHBC 1987-, vice-chm Care & Repair Nat Ctee 1988-, dir South Fife Enterprise Tst 1988-, bd memb Glenrothes New Town Devpt Corpn 1989-, gen cmmr Inland Revenue 1975-; memb Law Soc of Scotland 1968-; *Recreations* golf, sailing, the arts; *Clubs* New (Edinburgh), Dunfermline GC; *Style*— David Smith, Esq; 4 Garvock Hill, Dunfermline (☎ 0383 723863); 12 East Port, Dunfermline (☎ 0383 721621, fax 0383 738845, car 0836 707080)

SMITH, Sheriff David Buchanan; s of William Adam Smith (d 1955), of Elderslie, Renfrewshire, and Irene Mary Calderwood, *née* Hogarth (d 1976); *b* 31 Oct 1936; *Educ* Paisley GS (MA), Glasgow Univ (MA), Edinburgh Univ (LLB); *m* 1 April 1961, Hazel Mary, da of James Alexander Walker Sinclair, MBE (d 1960); 2 s (David Ewan b 1962, Patrick Sinclair b 1965), 1 da (Alison Mary b 1963); *Career* admited advocate 1961; Sheriff of N Strathclyde at Kilmarnock 1975; *Books* Curling an illustrated history (1981), The Sheriff Court in the Laws of Scotland, Stair Memorial Encyclopedia vol 6 (1988); *Recreations* curling, history, music, Scotland; *Style*— Sheriff David B Smith; 72 South Beach, Troon, Ayrshire KA10 6EG (☎ 0292 312130); Sheriff Court House, Kilmarnock, Ayrshire KA1 1ED (☎ 0563 20211)

SMITH, Sir David Cecil; s of William John Smith, and Elva Emily, *née* Deeble; *b* 21 May 1930; *Educ* St Paul's, Queen's Coll Oxford (MA, DPhil); *m* 1965, Lesley Margaret, s of Henry John Mollison Mutch (d 1946); 2 s (Adam, Cameron), 1 da (Bryony); *Career* 2 Lt RA 1955-56; Swedish Inst scholar Uppsala Univ 1951-52, Brown res fell Queen's Coll Oxford 1956-59, Harkness fell Berkeley Univ California 1959-60, lectr dept of agric Oxford Univ 1960-74, tutorial fell and tutor for admissions Wadham Coll Oxford 1971-74 (Roy Soc res fell 1964-71), Melville Wills prof of botany Bristol Univ 1974-80 (dir of biological studies 1977-80), Sibthorpian prof of rural economy Oxford Univ 1980-87, princ and vice-chllr Univ of Edinburgh 1987-; Hon DSc: Liverpool 1986, Exeter 1986, Hull 1987; FRS 1975, FRSE 1988; *Books* The Biology of Symbiosis (with A Douglas, 1987); *Clubs* Farmers'; *Style*— Sir David Smith; 14 Heriot Row, Edinburgh EH3 6HP (☎ 031 556 6959); University of Edinburgh, Old College, South Bridge, Edinburgh EH8 9YL (☎ 031 667 1011, fax 031 667 7938, telex 727442 UNIVED G)

SMITH, Rt Rev David James; *see*: Maidstone, Bishop of

SMITH, Dr David John Leslie; s of Arthur George Smith (d 1975), and Gertrude Mary Duce, *née* Buck; *b* 8 Oct 1938; *Educ* North Gloucs Tech Coll (HND), Coll of Aeronautics (MSc), Univ of London (PhD), RCDS; *m* 14 April 1962, Wendy Lavinia, da of Frederick James Smith (d 1955); 2 da (Andrea, Penelope); *Career* Nat Gas Turbine Estab: scientific offr 1961, head turbomachinery dept 1979; student RCDS, dir aircraft mechanical and electrical equipment controllerate of aircraft MOD (PE) 1980, head aerodynamics dept Royal Aircraft Estab 1981; dep dir: Marine Technol Admty Res Estab 1984, planning Admiralty Res Estab 1986; head of def res study team and asst under sec state civilian mgmnt specialists MOD 1988; CEng 1972, FRAes 1986; *Recreations* gardening; *Style*— Dr David Smith; MOD, Northumberland House, Northumberland Ave, London WC2N 5BP (☎ 01 218 5662)

SMITH, (Cecil) David Lorimer; s of Wilfrid Smith (d 1977), and Lillian Hunter, *née* Smith; *b* 18 Oct 1924; *Educ* Mill Hill; *m* 10 Oct 1953, Anne Jeanette, da of John Priestley Greenwood (d 1979); 2 s (Michael b 1954, Ian b 1964); *Career* chm Wilfrid Smith Hldgs Ltd 1972; govr Mill Hill Sch 1970, Master Worshipful Co of Turners 1975-76; *Recreations* fell-walking, crosswords, reading; *Clubs* Old Millhillians, MCC, City Livery; *Style*— David Smith, Esq; Fairways, 98 Wise Lane, Mill Hill, London NW7 2RD (☎ 01 959 1094); Gemini House, High St, Edgware, Middx HA8 7ET (☎ 01 952 6655, telex 261259, fax 01 952 6694)

SMITH, Very Rev Dr David Macintyure Bell Armour; s of Rev Frederick Smith (d 1977), and Matilda Shearer (d 1958); *b* 5 April 1923; *Educ* Monkton Combe, Peebles HS, St Andrews Univ (MA, BD), Stirling Univ (DUniv); *m* 1, 1951, Margaret (d 1958), da of Charles Alexander Piper and Margaret Harcus; 2 s (David, Donald); m 2, 1960, Mary Kulvear, da of William Baxter Cumming (d 1939); 1 s (Alasdair); *Career* min Logie Kirk Stirling 1965-, moderator of the Gen Assembly of the Church of Scotland 1985-86; *Style*— The Very Rev Dr David Smith; 28 Millar Place, Stirling FK9 1XD

SMITH, Maj-Gen (James) Desmond Blaise; CBE (1944, OBE 1943), DSO (1944), CD (1948); s of William George Smith, of Bronson Ave, Ottawa, Canada; *b* 7 Oct 1911; *Educ* Ottawa Univ, RMC Canada, IDC London, Nat Def Coll Canada; *m* 1, 1937, Miriam Irene (d 1969), da of Walter Juxton Blackburn, of London, Ontario; 2 s; m 2, 1979, Mrs Belle Shenkman, CM, of Ottawa; *Career* joined Canadian Army 1933, served WW II in Italy and NW Europe (despatches twice), mil sec Canadian Cabinet Def Ctee 1948-50, QMG Canadian Army 1951, chm Canadian Jt Staff London 1951-54, Cmdt Nat Def Coll of Canada 1954-58, Adj-Gen 1958-62, resigned 1962; Col HM Regt of Canadian Guards 1961-66; chm and chief exec Pillar Engrg Ltd 1964-82; chm: Blaise Investmts, Desmond Smith Investmts, Dashabel Properties & Interiors Ltd; dir: Meco Hldgs Hong Kong, Indal Technologies Ltd Canada 1980-85, Teron Croix de Guerre 1944, Chev Legion of Honour 1944, Cmdr Mil Order of Italy 1944, Offr Legion of Merit (USA) 1944, Order of Valour of Greece 1945, KStJ 1961,CStJ; *Clubs* Annabels, Marks, Harry's Bar, Carlton; *Style*— Maj-Gen Desmond Smith, CBE, DSO, CD; 50 Albert Court, Prince Consort Rd, London SW7 2BH (☎ 01 584 6817)

SMITH, Prof (Stanley) Desmond; s of Henry George Stanley Smith (d 1969), and Sarah Emily Ruth Weare; *b* 3 Mar 1931; *Educ* Cotham Bristol, Univ of Bristol (BSc, DSc), Univ of Reading (PhD); *m* 1 July 1956, Gillian Anne, da of Howard Stanley Parish; 1 s (David), 1 da (Nicola); *Career* SSO RAE Farnborough 1956-59; res asst

Imperial Coll (Met Dept) 1959-60, reader Reading Univ 1966-70 (lectr 1960-66), prof of Physics and dept head Heriot-Watt Univ Edinburgh 1970-; chm and dir: Edinburgh Instruments Ltd 1971-, Edinburgh Sensors Ltd 1988; dir Edinburgh C of C 1981-84; memb: cabinet ACOST 1987-88 (formerly ACARD 1985-87), Def Sci Advsy Cncl MOD 1985-; Inst P, FR Met S 1962, FRS 1976, FRSE 1973; *Recreations* mountaineering, skiing, tennis, golf; *Clubs* Royal Soc; *Style—* Prof Desmond Smith; Tree Tops, 29D Gillespie Rd, Colinton, Lothian EH13 0NW (☎ 031 441 7225); Physics Department, Heriot-Watt University, Riccarton, Edinburgh EH14 4AS (☎ 031 449 5542, fax 031 451 3088, telex 72553 EDINST G)

SMITH, Lady; Diana May Violet Peel; da of Warwick Goodchild; *m* 1, George Ian Young; m 2, 1958 (as his 2 w), Lt-Cdr Sir (William) Gordon Smith, 2 Bt, VRD (d 1983); 2 s; *Style—* Lady Smith; Crowmallie House, Pitcaple, Inverurie, Aberdeenshire AB5 9HR

SMITH, Ven Donald John; *b* 10 April 1926; *Educ* Clifton Theol Coll Bristol; *m* 1 Jan 1948, Violet Olive Goss; 2 s (Timothy b 1951, Michael b 1954), 1 da (Alison b 1956, d 1986); *Career* ordained St Paul's Cathedral 1953; asst curate: St Margaret's Edgeware 1953-56, St Margaret's Ipswich 1956-58; vicar St Mary's Hornsey Rise London 1958-62, rector Whitton Suffolk 1962-75, canon St Edmundsbury 1973-, rector Redgrave cum Botesdale and The Rickinghalls 1975-79, archdeacon of Suffolk 1975-84, archdeacon of Sudbury Suffolk 1984-; memb Nat Tst, tstee Pro-Corda Music Sch Leiston ; *Books* A Confirmation Course (1974), Covenanting for Disunity (1981), Thank You Lord for Alison (1986); *Recreations* caravanning, foreign travel, dining out, collecting; *Style—* The Ven the Archdeacon of Sudbury; 84 Southgate St, Bury St Edmunds IP33 2BJ (☎ 0284 66796); St Peter's Cottage, Stretton-on-Fosse, Moreton-in-Marsh, Glos GL56 9SE (☎ 0608 62790)

SMITH, Douglas; TD, DL (Tyne and Wear); s of Douglas Smith (d 1972), of Newcastle upon Tyne, and Maggie Annie Jane, *née* Symon (d 1956); *b* 23 Nov 1924; *Educ* FETTES; *m* 4 Aug 1949, Freda, da of George Frederick Thompson (d 1957), of Newcastle Upon Tyne; 3 da (Christine b 19 Sept 1951, Julia b 15 April 1954, Fiona b 19 April 1958); *Career* serv WWII: 2 Lt Sandhurst 1943, 5 RTR 1944, demob 1947; 324 HAA Regt RA TA 1949, Lt-Col Cmd Offr; 101 Northumbria Field regt RA TA (Hon Col); chm (formerly dir) Ringtons ltd 1953-; involved in Boy Scouts Newcastle and St John Ambulance; memb Worshipful Co of CA's in England and Wales; ACA 1951; *Recreations* golf, rugby; *Clubs* RA, Gosforth, Army and Navy; *Style—* Douglas Smith, Esq, TD, DL; Dene Grange, Lindisfarne Rd, Newcastle Upon Tyne NE2 2HE (☎ 091 281 5096); Ringtons, Algernon Rd, Newcastle Upon Tyne NE6 2YN (☎ 091 265 6181, fax 01 276 3500, tlx 53120)

SMITH, (Fraser) Drew; s of Frank and Beatrice; *b* 30 Mar 1950; *Educ* Westminster Sch; *Career* editor Good Food Guide; *Style—* Drew Smith Esq; 14 Buckingham St, London WC2 (☎ 01 839 1222)

SMITH, Sir Dudley Gordon; MP (C) Warwick and Leamington 1968-, DL (Warwickshire 1988-); s of Hugh William Smith (d 1977), of Cambridge, and Florence Elizabeth Smith (d 1967); *b* 14 Nov 1926; *Educ* Chichester HS; *m* 1, 1958 (m dis 1974), Anthea Maureen, o da of Robert Higgins, of Kingsbury, Middx; 1 s, 2 da; m 2, 1976, Catherine, o da of late Thomas Amos, of Liverpool;; *Career* mgmnt consultant and former journalist; asst news editor Sunday Express 1953-59, divnl dir Beecham Gp 1966-70; contested (C) Peckham, Camberwell 1955; MP (C) Brentford and Chiswick 1959-66, oppn whip 1964-66; Parly under-sec of state: Dept of Employment 1970-74, (Army) MOD 1974; vice-chm Parly Select Ctee on Race Relations and Immigration 1974-79, UK delegate to Cncl of Europe and WEU 1979-, sec-gen European Democratic Gp of both 1983-; chm United and Cecil Club 1975-80; Freeman City of London, memb Livery Horners Co; kt 1983; *Books* Harold Wilson: A Critical Biography (1963); *Recreations* travel, books, music, preservation of Wild Life; *Style—* Sir Dudley Smith, MP, DL; Church Farm, Weston-under-Wetherley, nr Leamington Spa, Warwicks (☎ 0926 632352); House of Commons, Westminster, London SW1A 0AA (☎ 01 219 4517)

SMITH, Edward (Ted) Richard; s of Albert Edward Smith (d 1961), of Finchley, London N12, and Elsie Florence, *née* Turner; *b* 19 Mar 1936; *Educ* Highgate Sch; *m* 10 Sept 1960, Pamela Margaret, da of Alfred Montague Mundy (d 1976), of Gidea Pk; 2 s (Donald E P b 1966, Philip R J b 1969); *Career* Nat Serv RAOC 1954-56; Martins Bank 1954-68; dir: Hill Samuel Bank Ltd 1974-, Gross Hill Properties Ltd 1983-, London & Cambridge Investmts Ltd 1987, Control Securities plc 1988-, European Equity Corpn Ltd 1988-; Freedom City of London, Liveryman Worshipful Co of Pattenmakers; FCIB 1982; *Recreations* old books, gardening; *Clubs* City Livery, RAC, MCC; *Style—* Edward R Smith, Esq; Phildon Lodge, Seal Hollow Road, Sevenoaks, Kent TN13 3SL (☎ 0732 456928); Hill Samuel Bank Ltd, 100 Wood St, London EC2P 2AJ (☎ 01 628 8011, fax 01 606 3319)

SMITH, Edward John Gregg; CB (1982); s of Maj James William Smith, MBE, and Violet Harriet Eudora, *née* Mildred; *b* 1 Oct 1930; *Educ* Churcher's Coll Petersfield, Queens' Coll Cambridge (MA); *m* 1956, Jean Margaret, da of Reginald Clayton (d 1949); 1 s (Nicholas), 2 da (Katharine, Elizabeth); *Career* princ private sec to Lord Pres of Cncl and ldr House of Commons 1968-70, under sec Cabinet Off 1974-76, memb Agric and Food Res Cncl 1979-, dep sec MAFF 1979-, chm House of Laity Guildford Diocesan Synod 1985-88, memb Archbishops Cmmn on Rural Area 1988-; FRGS, FRSA; *Recreations* choral music, christian activities; *Clubs* Reform; *Style—* Edward Smith, Esq, CB; The Holme, Oakfield Rd, Ashtead, Surrey (☎ 037 22 72311); Min of Agric, Fisheries & Food, Whitehall Place, London SW1

SMITH, Hon Elinor; da (by 1 m) of Baron Smith, KBE (Life Peer); *b* 1950; *Style—* The Hon Elinor Smith

SMITH, Hon Mrs (Elissa); *née* Haden-Guest; o da of 4 Baron Haden-Guest; *b* 10 Jan 1953; *m* 1981, Nicholas Carey Smith, s of Corlies Morgan Smith; 1 s (Nathanael Haden b 1988), 1 da (Gena Haden b 1984); *Style—* Hon Mrs Smith; 824 Nowita Place, Los Angeles, California 90291, USA

SMITH, Brig Eric David; CBE (1975), DSO (1945), MBE (1951); s of Christopher Smith (d 1958), and Jessica Lucy, *née* Bartram (d 1965); *b* 19 August 1923; *Educ* Allhallows Sch Devon; *m* 5 Jan 1957, Jill Helene, da of Brig J C Way Cott, OBE (d 1981); 2 da (Joanna Davis b 1959, Beverly b 1962); *Career* cmmnd 7 Gurkha Rifles 1942, active service Italy and Greece 1944-45 (wounded), operational serv Malaya 1950-54, student Staff Coll Camberley 1956, operational serv Borneo 1963-64 (badly injured in helicopter 1964), operational serv Sabah 1965, Co 1/2 Gurkha Rifles 1965-68, Col Bde of Gurkhas 1970-71, Brig cmdg Br Gurkhas Nepal 1971-74, Hon Col 7 Gurkha Rifles 1975-83, ret active list 1978; special advsr to Commons Def Ctee on Bde of Gurkhas Report 1988-89; author; chm Sidmouth Town Cncl 1988-; *Books* Britain's Brigade of Gurkhas (1973), Battles For Cassino (1975), East of Kathmandu (1976), Even the Brave Falter (1978), Battle for Burma (1979), Malaya and Borneo (counter-insurgency) 1985, Johnny Gurkha Victory of a Sort 1988; *Recreations* keen on all sport until loss of right arm (now a spectator), walking; *Style—* Brig Eric Smith, CBE, DSO, MBE; 2 Balfour Mews, Sidmouth, Devon

SMITH, Sir (Frank) Ewart; s of Richard Sidney Smith (d 1938), and Laura, *née* East (d 1952); *b* 31 May 1897; *Educ* Christ's Hosp Cambridge Univ (MA); *m* 1924, Kathleen Winifred, da of Herbert Rudd Dawes (d 1950); 1 s (d 1976), 1 da; *Career* Lt RGA Flanders 1916-19; chartered engr; joined ICI Ltd 1923, dep chm 1954-59; past chm Br Productivity Cncl, chief engr and supt armament design dept Min of Supply 1942-45; former memb: Scientific Advsy Cncl Miny of Fuel and Power, Advsy Cncl of Scientific Policy; former chm Nat Health Service Advsy Cncl for Mgnt Efficiency; hon fell Sidney Sussex Coll Cambridge; kt 1946; *Recreations* gardening, cabinet making; *Style—* Sir Ewart Smith; Park Hill Cottage, Sandy Lane, Watersfield, W Sussex RH20 1NF

SMITH, Rev Francis Taylor Smith (Frank); s of James William Smith (d 1977), of Aberdeen, and Jeannie Moir Catto, *née* Cockburn (d 1970); *b* 22 Jan 1933; *Educ* Aberdeen GS, Aberdeen Univ (MA), Christ's Coll Aberdeen; *m* 22 July 1957, Jean Millar, da of William Wallace (d 1973), of IOM; 3 s (Mark, Philip, Barry), 1 da (Naomi); *Career* sr asst minister Govan Old Parish Church Glasgow 1957-58; parish minister: Aberlour Banffshire 1958-64, St Paul's Dunfermline 1964-; chaplain Dunfermline and W Fife Maternity Hosps 1964-; ccncllr Banff 1964, chm W Fife Local Health Cncl 1975-84, pres Assoc of Scottish Local Health Cncls 1979-81 (vice pres 1978), memb GMC 1979-; *Recreations* reading, fishing, music; *Clubs* Caledonian; *Style—* The Rev Frank T Smith; 6 Park Avenue, Dunfermline, Fife KY12 7HX (☎ 0383 721124)

SMITH, Prof Frank Thomas; s of Leslie Maxwell Smith, of Havant, Hants, and Catherine Matilda, *née* Wilken; *b* 24 Feb 1948; *Educ* Kinson CP Sch, Bournemouth GS, Jesus Coll Oxford (BA D Phil); *m* 16 Sept 1972, Valerie Sheila, da of Albert Alfred Hearn; 3 da (Helen b 1976, Natalie b 1978, Amy b 1987); *Career* res fell Theoretical Aerodynamics Unit Southampton 1972-73, lectr Imperial Coll London 1973-78, visiting prof Univ of W Ontario 1978-79, reader and prof Imperial Coll 1979-84; Goldsmid prof in applied maths UCL 1984-, FRS 1984; *Books* Boundary - Layer Separation (with Prof Susan Brown 1987); *Recreations* sports, reading, family; *Style—* Prof F T Smith; Mathematics Dept, Univ Coll, Gower St, London WC1E 6BT (☎ 01 387 7050 ext 2837)

SMITH, Geoffrey Edwin; OBE (1981); s of Curtis Edwin Smith, of Hertford, Herts, and Mabel Alice, *née* Bacon (d 1971); *b* 9 Nov 1930; *Educ* Hertford GS; *m* 5 April 1958, (Jeanette) Jan Mary, da of Rex Saynor (d 1976), of Mirfield; 1 s (Jeremy Redington b 12 March 1969), 1 da (Charlotte Victoria b 2 Oct 1964); *Career* RAF 1949; sr asst co librarian Herts CC, dep Co librarian Hants Co Library 1959-63, co librarian Leicestershire CC 1963-73, dir libraries and information serv Leicestershire CC 1973-, hon res fell Loughborough Univ of Technol 1987; memb: Library Assoc Cncl 1962-79, Library Advsy Cncl 1972-78, Library and Information Servs Cncl 1985-88; Soc Co Librarians: memb exec ctee 1963-, vice-pres 1982-88, pres 1989-; memb: Leicestershire Rural Community Cncl, Exec Bd Age Concern Leicester; FLA 1956; *Recreations* swimming, cinema; *Clubs* Book Trust; *Style—* Geoffrey Smith, Esq, OBE; 16 Soar Rd, Quorn, Loughborough, Leics LE12 8BW (☎ 0509 412 655); Leicestershire Libraries and Information Serv, Thames Tower, 2 Navigation St, Burleys Way, Leicestershire LE1 3TZ (☎ 0533 538 921, fax 0533 514 483)

SMITH, Geoffrey Herbert; s of Herbert Samuel Smith (d 1975), of Colchester, Essex, and Constance Madeline Hatcher (d 1983); *b* 10 June 1925; *Educ* Felsted, Trinity Coll Cambridge (MA); *m* 18 April 1953, Patricia, da of Capt William Thrift (d 1939), (David b 1966); *Career* serv WWII Sub Lt RNVR Atlantic and Coastal Forces Ghm G H Smith & Ptnrs Ltd and subsidiaries 1956-; *Recreations* fishing; *Style—* Geoffrey H Smith, Esq; The Barn, Brook Road, Great Tey, Colchester, Essex CO6 1JF (☎ 0206 210471); Berechurch Rd, Colchester CO2 7QH (☎ 0206 760760, telex 987801, fax 0206 762626)

SMITH, Wing Cdr Geoffrey Wilfred Tracey; s of Claude Smith (d 1974), of Upper Poppleton, York, and Doris Lilian Tracey Smith (d 1977); *b* 18 Mar 1927; *Educ* West Hartlepool GS, Downing Coll Cambridge (MA, MB BChir), St Bartholomews Hosp; *m* 22 Dec 1954 (m dis 1977), (Barbara) Megan, da of William Ashley, DSM (d 1946), of Cairo; 1 s (Nigel b 1963); m 2, 16 Feb 1978, Teresa Jeanne, da of Robert Audley Furtado, CB, of Langton Herring, Dorset; *Career* Lt HLI 1945-48, RAF 1959-75 (ret Wing Cdr); conslt ophthalmology RAF 1971-75, asst opthalmic surgn Guys Hosp 1976-78, sr conslt Miny of Public Health QATAR 1978-85; pty candidate (Lab) Fylde constituency 1987, currently prospective euro candidate (Lab) for Lancs Central; chm Monks Orchard branch (Croydon NE) Lab Pty; FRCSE 1971; *Recreations* organist; *Clubs* The Golfers; *Style—* Wing Cdr Geoffrey Smith; 77 Groome Ct, Regency Walk, Orchard Way, Shirley, Croydon, Surrey CR0 7UT (☎ 01 776 0553)

SMITH, Prof Gerald Stanton; s of Thomas Arthur Smith (d 1974), of Manchester, and Ruth Annie, *née* Stanton; *b* 17 April 1938; *Educ* Stretford GS, Sch of Slavonic and E Euro Studies Univ of London (BA, PhD); *m* 2 Aug 1961 (m dis 1981), Frances, da of Percy Wetherill, of Deganwy, N Wales; 1 s (Ian b 1964), 1 da (Gillian b 1963); m 2, 16 Feb 1982, Barbara, da of Maj John Henry Heldt (d 1986, US Army), of Sarasota, Florida; 1 step s (Gus b 1969), 1 step da (Elizabeth b 1971); *Career* RAF 1957-60, Cpl 1959 Jt Servs Sch for Linguists 1958, RAF Gatow, Berlin 1959-60; lectr in Russian: Univ of Nottingham 1964-71, Univ of Birmingham 1971-79; res fell Univ of Liverpool 1979-82; visiting prof: Indiana Univ 1984, Univ of California Berkeley 1984; private scholar Social Scis and Humanities Res Cncl of Canada 1985, John Simon Guggenheim Meml Fell 1986, prof of Russian and fell New Coll Oxford Univ 1986-; jazz musician London 1961-64; fndr Jazz Orchestra: Nottingham 1968, Birmingham 1970; memb: Br Assoc for Slavonic Soviet and E Euro Studies, American Assoc for Advancement of Slavic Studies; *Books* Songs to Seven Strings (1985); *Recreations* jazz music, watching water; *Style—* Prof Gerald Stanton; Taylor Institution, Oxford University, St Giles, Oxford OX1 3NA (☎ 0865 270476)

SMITH, Sir (Thomas) Gilbert; 4 Bt (UK 1897) of Stratford Place, St Marylebone, Co London; s of Sir Thomas Turner, 3 Bt (1961); *b* 2 July 1937; *Educ* Huntley Sch, Nelson Coll; *m* 1962, Patricia Christine, da of David Cooper, of Paraparaumu, New

Zealand; 2 s, 1 da; *Heir* s, Andrew Thomas Smith; *Career* engr; *Style*— Sir Gilbert Smith, Bt; PO Box 654, 50 Titoki St, Masterton, New Zealand

SMITH, Dr (Charles) Gordon; s (by 2 m) of Sir (William) Gordon Smith, 2 Bt, VRD (d 1983); hp of bro Sir Robert Hill Smith, 3 Bt; *b* 21 April 1959; *Educ* Merchant Taylors', St Andrew's Univ (BSc), Oregon Univ, Trinity Hall Cambridge (PhD); *Career* res sci; *Recreations* windsurfing, drinking; *Clubs* Grafham Water Sailing; *Style*— Dr Gordon Smith; c/o Cavendish Laboratory, Madingley Road, Cambridge

SMITH, Dr (Charles Edward) Gordon; CB (1970); s of John Alexander Smith (d 1966), of Fife, and Margaret Inglis, *née* Fletcher; *b* 12 May 1924; *Educ* Forfar Acad, St Andrew's Univ (MD, DSc); *m* 1948, Elsie, da of Samuel Sydney McClellan (d 1971), of Cockermouth; 1 s (Alastair), 2 da (Elizabeth, Sally); *Career* HM Colonial Med Serv Malaysia 1948-57, sr lectr and reader London Sch of Hygiene and Tropical Med 1957-64, dir Microbiological Res Estab MOD 1964-70, dean London Sch of Hygiene and Tropical Med 1971-89, chm Public Health Lab Serv 1972-, A Wellcome tstee 1972- (dep chm 1983-); *Recreations* golf, gardening; *Clubs* Savile, Bramshaw Golf, New Zealand Golf; *Style*— Dr Gordon Smith, Esq, CB; Flat A, Guilford Ct, 51 Guilford St, London WC1; Wild Close, Woodgreen, Fordingbridge, Hants SP6 2QX; London Sch of Hygiene and Tropical Medicine, Keppel St, London WC1E 7HT (☎ 01 636 8636, telex 8952474)

SMITH, Gordon Walkerley; JP (1977); s of George Arthur Smith (d 1976), and Elsie, *née* Johnson; *b* 20 Mar 1933; *Educ* St James Sch Grimsby, Hull Coll of Architecture; *m* 15 Sept 1956, Anne, da of George Adam Young (d 1978); 1 s (David b 1957), 1 da (Diane b 1961); *Career* architect; princ Sir Charles Nicholson Gp; diocesan surveyor: Lincoln 1970, Southwell 1974; fell of Woodard Corpn 1976, Custos St James Sch Grimsby 1985, Liveryman Worshipful Co of Paviors; FRIBA; *Recreations* reading, gardening, walking, music; *Clubs* City Livery; *Style*— Gordon W Smith, JP; Walkerley House, Barnoldby le Beck, nr Grimsby DN37 0AS (☎ 0472 827665); The Old Rectory, Bargate, Grimsby DN3L 2AL (☎ 0472 355 288)

SMITH, Graham Frederick; s of Archibald Frederick Smith, of High Wycombe, Bucks, and Janet Mearing, *née* Hall; *b* 17 Feb 1943; *Educ* Royal GS High Wycombe; *m* 8 Oct 1966, Wendy Elizabeth, da of John Maltby (d 1982), of Oxford; 1 s (Andrew b 1968), 2 da (Lucy b 1972, Melanie b 1976); *Career* ptnr Ernst & Whinney (CAs) 1975-; former chm High Wycombe Lawn Tennis Club, Bucks County Tennis Colour 1967; FCA 1964; *Recreations* golf, garden, music; *Style*— Graham F Smith, Esq; Crabtrees, Nairdwood Lane, Prestwood, Great Missenden, Bucks HP16 0QH (☎ 02406 5128); Ernst & Whinney, Becket House, 1 Lambeth Palace Rd, London SE1 7EU (☎ 01 928 2000, fax 01 928 1345)

SMITH, Graham Paul; s of James Alfred Smith (d 1985), and Elsie Winifred, *née* Cleathero; *b* 25 Dec 1949; *Educ* Royal GS High Wycombe, Univ of Durham (BA), Osgoode Hall Law School Toronto (LLM); *Career* slr Supreme Ct 1975; ptnr: Clifford-Turner 1981-87, Clifford Chance 1987-; memb: Law Soc 1975, Computer Law Assoc; Liveryman Worshipful Co of Slrs; *Recreations* opera, cricket; *Clubs* MCC; *Style*— Graham Smith, Esq; Clifford Chance, Bow Bells House, Bread St, London EC4 (☎ 01 600 0808, fax 956 0199, telex 887847)

SMITH, Lady Helen; *née* Pleydell-Bouverie; OBE (1946), DL (Berkshire); 5 and youngest da of 6 Earl of Radnor; *b* 2 Jan 1908; *m* 1931, Lt-Col Hon David Smith, CBE, JP, Lord Lt of Berks 1960-74, sometime chm W H Smith & Son Hldgs (d 1976), 3 s of 2 Viscount Hambleden; 4 s (Julian b 1932, m 1966 Eleanor Blyth: 1 s, 1 da; Antony b 1937, m 1962 Alison Pyper: 2 s, 2 da; Peter b 1939, m 1967 Scilla Ann Bennett: 1 s, 2 da; David b 1947, m 1970 Caroline Ardill; 1 s, 1 da), 1 da (Esther Joanna b 1934); *Style*— Lady Helen Smith; King's Copse House, Bradfield-Southend, Reading, Berks RG7 6JR (☎ 0734 744366)

SMITH, Lady Helen Dorothy; *née* Primrose; da of 6 Earl of Rosebery, KT, DSO, MC, PC, by his 1 w, Lady Dorothy Grosvenor, sis of 3 Duke of Westminster; half-sis of 7 Earl of Rosebery; *b* 1913; *m* 1933, Hon Hugh Vivian Smith (d 1978), 3 s of 1 Baron Bicester; 1 s, 1 da; *Style*— Lady Helen Smith; The Old Rectory, Souldern, Bicester, Oxon OX6 9HU

SMITH, Lt-Col Henry (Martin) Lockhart; s of Col Henry Brockton Lockhart Smith, MC, of Ellingham Hall, nr Bungay, Suffolk, and Dorothy Helen, *née* Douglas; *b* 23 Dec 1936; *Educ* Royal Nautical Coll Pangbourne, RMA Sandhurst, NDC Latimer; *m* 31 March 1962, Margaret Louise, da of Sydney Wilfred Eaton (d 1977); 2 s (Vaughan b 1963, Charles b 1965); *Career* joined Army 1955, cmmnd Grenadier Gds 1957, Staff Coll Camberly 1969, NDC Latimer 1978, cmd 2 Bn Grenadier Gds 1978-80; served: Cyprus, Malta, Ireland, Br Guiana, W Germany (despatches 1974), ret 1983; joined Corps of Queens Messengers 1984;; *Recreations* shooting, skiing, conservation; *Style*— Lt-Col Martin Smith; Ellingham Hall, Bungay, Suffolk NR35 2EN (☎ 050845 314)

SMITH, Hon (William) Henry Bernard; s and h of 4 Viscount Hambleden; *b* 18 Nov 1955; *m* 1983, Sara, da of Joseph Anlauf, of Palos Verdes Estates, California; *Style*— The Hon Henry Smith; 109 Eccleston Mews, London SW1X 8AQ (☎ 01 235 4785)

SMITH, Horace Anthony; s of Osbourne Smith (d 1975), and Gertrude Mabel, *née* Reason; *b* 17 Jan 1941; *Educ* De Aston Sch Market Rasen; *m* 1, 4 June 1959 (m dis 1981), Catherine Mary, da of Flt Lt J A Tindall, DFC, of E Yorks; 2 s (David b 1960, Richard b 1962); m 2, 30 Aug 1984, Imelda, da of Jesus Paez, of Manila; 2 da (Annalisa b 1985, Emma Jade b 1987); *Career* sr exec offr Dept of Employment 1965-73, overseas dir Professional and Exec Recruitment 1973-85, md Int Trg and Recruitment Link 1985-; chm Maidstone Cavaliers CC; MRGS 1974; *Books* Guide to Working Abroad (1983, 1985, 1986, 1987, 1988); *Recreations* cricket, horseracing, bridge, oriental studies; *Clubs* Lions Int; *Style*— Horace Smith, Esq; 21 Tilton Rd, Borough Green, Kent TN15 8RS; ITRL, 51A Bryanston St, London W1H 7DN (☎ 01 706 3646, fax 01 724 3948, telex 928079 TRL G

SMITH, Sir Howard Frank Trayton; GCMG (1981, KCMG 1976, CMG 1966); s of Frank Howard Smith (d 1975), of Brighton; *b* 15 Oct 1919; *Educ* Sidney Sussex Coll Cambridge; *m* 1, 1943, Winifred Mary (d 1982), da of Edward Cropper, of London; 1 da; m 2, 1983, Mary Penney; *Career* HM Diplomatic Service: Caracas 1953, Washington (1950-53), FO 1964-68, ambass to Czechoslovakia 1968-71, dep sec Cabinet Office (secondment) 1972-75, ambass to Moscow 1976-78 (cnsllr 1961-63), ret; *Style*— Sir Howard Smith, GCMG; Coromandel, Cross in Hand, Heathfield, E Sussex TN21 0TN (☎ 043 52 4420)

SMITH, Ian Newell; s of Harry Smith (d 1985), of Ashthorn, Southbank Rd, Kenilworth, and Edith Mary, *née* Newell; *b* 27 July 1933; *Educ* Malvern; *m* 3 Oct 1964, (José) Jillian, da of Fl Lt John Foster Drake, DFC, BEM (d 1959); 1 da (Anna Louise b 9 Sept 1965); *Career* Pilot Offr RAF 1 July 1958; admitted slr 1957, ptnr Seymour Smith & Co Coventry 1960, dir Coventry Bldg Soc 1973- (chm 1985-87); trustee: Edwards Charity 1962, Coventry Nursing Tst 1972- (chm 1984-), The Helen Ley House 1975-, Warwicks Boys Tst 1977-, Samuel Smiths Charity 1987-; sec: Milverton Lawn Tennis 1960-62, Leamington and Dist Round Table (chm 1967-68); Freeman City of Coventry 1960, memb Drapers Guild (Coventry) 1986, clerk Broadweavers and Clothiers Co (Coventry) 1988; memb Law Soc 1957; *Recreations* golf, sailing, skiing, choral singing, gardening; *Clubs* Drapers (Coventry); *Style*— Ian Smith, Esq; Hexworthy, Birches Lane, Kenilworth (☎ 0926 53238); Queens House, Queens Rd, Coventry (☎ 0203 553961, fax 0203 251634)

SMITH, Ivo; s of Guy Sydney Smith (d 1972), of Market Rasen, Lincs, and Florence Maud, *née* Titmarsh (d 1981); *b* 31 May 1931; *Educ* De Aston GS, Market Rasen Lincs, Jesus Coll Cambridge (MA, MChir), Saint Mary's Hosp Med Sch Univ of London; *m* 17 Feb 1962, Janet, da of George James Twyman (d 1936), of Deal, Kent; 2 s (Robin b 1966, Simon b 1969), 1 da (Mary b 1965); *Career* Nat Serv RAF (Educn Branch) 1950-51; consult surgn, lectr and author on surgery of the breast and the breast in art; Freeman City of London 1965, Liveryman Worshipful Co of Apothecaries 1964; FRCS (Eng); *Recreations* my family, fishing, farming; *Style*— Ivo Smith, Esq; 100 Harley St, London W1N 1AF (☎ 01 935 0721)

SMITH, Jack; s of John Edward Smith (d 1984), and Laura Amanda, *née* Booth (d 1949); *b* 18 June 1928; *Educ* Netheredge GS Sheffield, Sheffield Coll of Art, St Martins Sch of Art, RCA (ARCA); *m* 23 June 1956, Susan, da of Brig Gen Hugh Marjoribanks Craigie Halkett (d 1951); *Career* Nat Serv RAF 1946-48; artist; exhibitions: Beaux Arts Gall London 1952-58, Catherine Vivian Gall NY 1958, 1962, 1963, Whitechapel Gall 1959, Matthiesen Gall 1960, 1963, Grosvenor Gall 1965, Marlborough Fine Art 1981, 1983; work shown: Venice Biennale 1956, Br Painting Madrid 1983 et al; work in permanent collections inc: Tate Gallery, Arts Cncl, Contemporary Art Soc, Br Cncl; *Style*— Jack Smith, Esq; 29 Seafield Rd, Hove, Sussex BN23 2TP (☎ 0273 738 312)

SMITH, Hon Sir James Alfred; CBE (1964), TD; s of late Charles Silas Smith; *b* 1913,May; *Career* serv WWII Maj (on staff of Supreme Allied Cdr SE Asia 1944-45); RA barr Lincoln's Inn 1949; entered Colonial Legal Service Nigeria 1946, Puisne judge 1955, Northern Nigeria: High Ct judge 1955, Sr Puisne High Ct judge 1960-65; Bahamas: Supreme Ct Puisne judge 1965-75, sr justice 1975-78, chief justice 1978-80, memb Ct of Appeal 1980- (and Cts of Appeal for Bahamas and Belize 1981-); kt 1979; *Style*— The Hon Sir James Smith, CBE, TD; Court of Appeal for the Bahamas, Nassau, Bahamas

SMITH, Dr James Andrew Buchan; CBE (1959); s of James Fleming Smith, JP, MA, MB, CM (d 1919), of Whithorn, Scotland, and Emma Jane Adelaide Lawrence, *née* Buchan (d 1949); *b* 26 May 1906; *Educ* Leamington Coll, Univ of Birmingham (BSc, PhD), Univ of London (DSc); *m* 29 July 1933, (Elizabeth) Marion, da of James Kerr, (d 1929), of Wallasey, Ches; 3 da (Margaret b 1936, Sheila b 1940, Brenda b 1947, and 1 da dec'd (Alison b 1943, d 1966); *Career* graduate res asst: UCL 1929-30, Imperial Coll London 1930-32; lectr Univ of Liverpool 1932-36, biochemist Hannah Res Inst Ayr 1936-46, lectr Univ of Glasgow 1946-47, dir Hannah Res Inst 1951-70 (acting dir 1948-51); pres: Soc of Dairy Tech 1951-52, Nutrition Soc 1968-71; tres Int Union of Nutritional Sciences 1969-75; FRSC, FRSE; memb: Biochemical Soc, Nutrition Soc; *Recreations* gardening, walking; *Clubs* Farmers London; *Style*— Dr James Smith; Flaxton House, 1 St Leonard's Rd, Ayr KA7 2PR (☎ 0292 264 865)

SMITH, James Boyd; GM (1943); s of James Hughes Smith (d 1950); *b* 9 Feb 1920; *Educ* George Heriot's Sch Edinburgh, Edinburgh Univ; *m* 1946, May, *née* Campbell; 1 s (Peter), 1 da (Pamela); *Career* serv WWII Capt RE; chartered electrical engr; joined Ferranti plc 1947, dir of various subsidiary cos: Ferranti Offshore Systems 1974-85, Ferranti Cetec Graphics 1977-85, TRW Ferranti Subsea 1977-85, asst gen mangr Ferranti Edinburgh 1980-83, pt/t advsr 1983-85; dir Wolfson Microelectronics Ltd 1984-; memb Edinburgh Univ Ct 1975-84; FRSE; *Recreations* organ playing, orchid growing, gardening; *Clubs* New (Edinburgh); *Style*— James Smith, Esq, GM; Brunstane Bank House, 120 Milton Rd East, Edinburgh EH15 2NZ (☎ 031 669 5791)

SMITH, Mrs Janet Hilary (Mrs R E A Mathieson); QC (1986); da of Alexander Roe Holt (d 1970), and Margaret Holt, *née* Birchall; *b* 29 Nov 1940; *Educ* Bolton Sch; *m* 1, 6 June 1959 (m dis 1984), (Ednard) Stuart, s of Edward Austin Carruthers Smith; 2 s (Richard b 1959, Alasdair b 1963), 1 da (Rachel b 1962); m 2, 12 Oct 1984, Robin Edward Alexander, s of Alexander John Mathieson, MC (d 1974), of Yoxall, Staffs; *Career* barr Lincoln's Inn 1972, rec Crown Ct 1988, memb Criminal Injuries Compensation Bd 1988; *Style*— Mrs Janet Smith, QC; 5 Essex Ct, Temple, London (☎ 01 353 4363, fax 01 583 1491); 25 Byrom St, Manchester (☎ 061 834 5238, fax 061 834 0394)

SMITH, Jeffrey Bernard; s of Edwin Frederick Smith, and Gladys Valerie Smith, *née* Burridge; *b* 28 Dec 1949; *Educ* Eton Coll Choir Sch, High Wycombe GS, Leeds Univ (BSc (Hons)); *Career* CA, ptnr Eacott Worrall & Co 1979, FCA, ATII; *Recreations* clarinet, walking, playing; *Clubs* Mortons, Berkeley; *Style*— Jeffrey Smith, Esq; 6 Drews Park, Knotty Green, Beaconsfield, Bucks HP9 2TT; Eacott Worrall & Co, Park House, Park St, Maidenhead, Berks SL6 1SL (☎ fax (0628) 74117)

SMITH, Jeremy Fox Eric; DL; s of Capt Evan Cadogan Eric Smith, MC (d 1950), and B H Smith, *née* Williams (d 1988); *b* 17 Nov 1928; *Educ* Eton, New Coll Oxford; *m* 1953, Julia Mary Rona, yr da of Sir Walter Burrell, 8 Bt, CBE, TD, DL (d 1985); 2 s (Julian b 1956, Hugo b 1957), 2 da (Diane b 1954, m 1976, Earl of Verulam, Sarah b 1962, m 1987, Ashley Preston); *Career* 2 Lt 9 QR Lancers; dir: Transparent Paper Ltd 1958-76 and 1980-83 (chm 1965-76), BARD Discount House Ltd 1959-86, Discount House of S Africa Ltd 1961-86, Techn Devpt Capital Ltd 1962-66, Ship Mortgage Fin Co 1963-78; chm: Smith St Aubyn & Co Ltd 1973-86 (joined 1951, dir 1955), London Discount Market Assoc 1978-80 (dep chm 1976-78); tstee Henry Smith's Charity 1971-; *Recreations* hunting, shooting, stalking, skiing; *Clubs* Cavalry and Guards', Beefsteak, Leander; *Style*— Jeremy Smith, Esq, DL; Balcombe House, Balcombe, Sussex (☎ 0444 811267); Flat 11 Tarnbrook Court, 9 Holbein Place SW1

SMITH, Rt Hon John; PC (1978), QC (Scot, 1983), MP (Lab) Monklands E 1983-; s of late Archibald Leitch Smith, of Dunoon, Argyll; *b* 13 Sept 1938; *Educ* Dunoon GS, Glasgow Univ (MA, LLB); *m* 1967, Elizabeth Margaret, da of late Frederick William Moncrieff Bennett; 3 da; *Career* advocate 1967, MP (Lab) N Lanarkshire 1970-1983, Parly under-sec of state Energy 1974-75, min state Energy 1975-76, min of state

Privy Cncl Off 1976-78, sec of state for Trade 1978-79; memb shadow cabinet and oppn front bench spokesman on: Trade, Prices and Consumer Protection 1979-82, Energy 1982-83, Employment 1983-84, Trade and Indust 1984-87, Treasy and Econ Affrs 1987-; *Recreations* tennis, hill walking; *Style*— The Rt Hon John Smith, PC, QC, MP; 21 Cluny Dr, Edinburgh EH10 6DW (☎ 031 447 3667)

SMITH, Dr John Derek; s of Richard Ernest Smith (d 1933), of Mayfield, Wetherby, Yorks, and Winifred Strickland, *née* Davis (d 1932); *b* 8 Dec 1924; *Educ* King James' GS Knaresborough, Clare Coll Cambridge (MA, PhD); *Career* scientific staff ARC virus res unit ARC Cambridge 1945-59, res fell Clare Coll Cambridge 1949-52, visiting scientist Inst Pasteur Paris 1952-53, Rockefeller Fndn fell Univ of California Berkeley 1955-57 sr res fell California Inst of Technol 1959-62, memb scientific staff MRC lab of molecular biology Cambridge 1962-88, ret; Sherman Fairchild Distinguished Scholar California Inst of Technol 1974-75; FRS 1976; *Recreations* travel, cuisine; *Style*— Dr John Smith; 12 Stansgate Avenue, Cambridge CB2 2QZ (☎ 0223 247 841)

SMITH, John Ernest; s of Ernest Theodore Smith of Chigwell, and Sybil Margaret, *née* Jones; *b* 30 Mar 1949; *Educ* Chigwell Sch; *m* 2 Sep 1971, Jill Kathleen, da of Leonard Victor George Dennis, of Wanstead, London; 1 s (Richard b 1979), 1 da (Sarah); *Career* qualified CA 1971; regnl managing ptnr Arthur Young 1986- (nat dir bus servs 1982-85, ptnr since 1978); pres CA Students Soc London 1983-85; chm: London Soc CA, res bd 1 CAEW 1988-(memb cncl 1987-); ind memb Agric Wages Bd Eng and Wales 1987-; FCA 1971; *Recreations* golf, cricket, football, food and drink; *Clubs* MCC, Wig & Pen; *Style*— John E Smith, Esq; St Kenelms Hall, St Kenelms Road, Romsley, West Midlands, B62 0NF (☎ 0562 710 810); Arthur Young, PO Box No 1, 3 Colmore Row, Birmingham, B3 2DB (☎ 021 233 4030, fax 021 236 0236, telex 337904 AYB1)

SMITH, Sir John Lindsay Eric; CBE (1975), JP (1964, Berks), DL (1978); s of Capt E C E Smith, MC, of Ashfold, Handcross, Sussex; *b* 3 April 1923; *Educ* Eton, New Coll Oxford; *m* 1952, Christian, da of late Col Ughtred Elliott Carnegy, DSO, MC and bar, of Lour, Forfar, Angus; 2 s, 2 da (and 1 da decd 1983); *Career* served RNVR 1942-46; dir: Coutts & Co 1950-, Rolls Royce 1955-75, Financial Times 1959-68; dep govr Royal Exchange Assurance 1961-66; MP (C) Cities of London and Westminster 1965-70; memb: Historic Buildings Cncl 1971-78, Redundant Churches Fund 1972-74, Nat Heritage Memorial Fund 1980-82; dep chm Nat Tst 1980-85 (memb Exec Ctee 1961-85); high steward Maidenhead 1966-75; Lord-Lt Berks 1975-78; chm: Cumulus Systems Ltd, Manifold Tstee Co Ltd (and fndr); dir: Fleming American Tst plc, Greycoat Gp plc London, gen ctee Ottoman Bank; fell Eton 1974-; hon fell New Coll Oxford 1979, hon FRIBA; KStJ; Kt 1988; *Style*— Sir John Smith, CBE, JP, DL; Shottesbrooke Park, Maidenhead, Berks; 21 Dean's Yard, Westminster, London SW1P 3PA (☎ 01 222 6581)

SMITH, John Patrick; s of Col Neville Frederick Smith (d 1979); *b* 25 August 1932; *Educ* St Edward's Sch, Brasenose Coll Oxford; *m* 1961, Ann Felicity, *née* Hawker; 2 s, 1 da; *Career* actuary; chief investment mangr Equity and Law Life Assurance Society Ltd 1977- (dir 1984-); *Recreations* golf; *Clubs* Dale Hill Golf; *Style*— John Smith Esq; Hadlow Lodge, Burgh Hill, Etchingham, Sussex (☎ 058 086 282)

SMITH, John Wilson; CBE, JP, DL; s of Robert Henry Smith, JP (d 1956), and Edith, *née* Wilson; *b* 6 Nov 1920; *Educ* Oulton HS Liverpool; *m* 22 Nov 1946, Doris Mabel, da of Percy Albert Parfitt; 1 s (Colin Parfitt b 25 May 1951); *Career* serv WWII RAF 1940-46; chm Sports Cncl 1985-89; chm: BLESMA Merseyside 1975-80, appeals ctee SSAFA 1980-86; *Recreations* association football, golf; *Clubs* Reform; *Style*— John Smith, Esq, CBE, JP, DL; Pine Close, Mill Lane, Gayton, Wirral, Merseyside (☎ 051 342 5362); Brunswick Business Park, 212 Tower St, Liverpool L3 4BS (☎ 051 709 3949, fax 051 709 3824)

SMITH, Dr Joseph William Grenville; s of Douglas Ralph Smith (d 1987), of Cardiff and Hannah Leticia Margaret, *née* Leonard (d 1968); *b* 14 Nov 1930; *Educ* Cathays HS for Boys Cardiff 1941-48, Welsh Nat Sch of Med 1948-53 (MB BCh), Univ of London, Univ of Wales (MD); *m* 3 Aug 1954, Nira Jean da of Oliver Davies (d 1964), of Burry Port Carms; 1 s (Jonathan b 1955); *Career* Nat Serv RAF 1954-56, Flying Offr Med Branch (later Flt Lt), MO RAF SYLT, 2 TAF BAOR; lectr (later sr lectr) bacteriology and immunology London Sch of Hygiene and Tropical Medicine 1960-65, conslt clinical bacteriologist Radcliffe Infirmary Oxford 1965-69, head of bacteriology Wellcome Res Laboratories 1969, princ in gen practice Islington 1970-71, dep dir epidemiological res lab Public Health Laboratory Serv 1971-76; dir: Nat Inst for Biological Standards and Control 1976-85, dir Public Health Laboratory Serv of England and Wales 1985-; cncl memb RC Path 1988, memb MRC 1988; FRCPath 1975, FFCM 1976, FRCP 1987; *Books* Tetanus (jtly, 1969); *Style*— Dr Joseph Smith; Public Health Laboratory Service Board, 61 Colindale Ave, London NW9 (☎ 01 200 1295, fax 01 200 8130)

SMITH, Joye Powlett; DL (S Yorks 1988); assumed additional name of Powlett by deed poll of 1980; da of Hubert Cecil Nicholson, and Helen Marjorie, *née* Ayliffe; *b* 18 Oct 1925; *Educ* Hawnes Sch Haynes Park Beds; *m* 1946, Sydney Powlett Smith, s of Godfrey Scott Smith (d 1944, 6 s of Francis Patrick Smith of Barnes Hall who d 1919), formerly Archdeacon of Furness; 1 s, 1 da; *Career* JP: Hallamshire 1961-68, Rotherham 1968; High Sheriff of S Yorks 1981-82; *Recreations* gardening, fishing; *Style*— Mrs Powlett Smith, DL; Strafford Lodge, 97A Sunderland St, Tickhill, nr Doncaster DN11 9QH

SMITH, Julian Martin; MC (1943); s of Everard Martin Smith (d 1938), of Hitchin, and Violet Hambro (d 1965); *b* 7 June 1916; *Educ* Eton; *m* 1 Nov 1939, Susan, da of Major Pearson Gregory, MC (d 1952), of Windsor; 2 s (Andrew b 1952, Jonathan b 1957); *Career* Major Welsh Gds; BEF N Africa, Italy; dir: Rowe and Pitman, Smith St Awlyn 1951-86, The London Tst, Ashdown Investmt Tst 1951-86, Hambros plc 1979-86, The Pacific Fund 1968; *Recreations* golf, shooting; *Clubs* White's, Pratt's

SMITH, Karl Wingett; s of Ernest Walter Smith (d 1979), of Wheathampstead, Herts (form of Croydon Surrey), and Muriel Mary Wingett; *b* 16 Dec 1932; *Educ* Pontypridd Intermediate Sch S Wales, John Ruskin GS Croydon, Battersea Coll of Technol Univ of London; *m* 17 Sept 1962, Patricia Grace Smith (Pat), da of James David Franklin, of Plympton, Plymouth, Devon; 6 s (Andrew b 1965, Ian b 1969, Gavin b 1972, Neil b 1974, Alastair b 1975, Duncan b 1977); *Career* aircraft fluid systems designing engr Handley Page Ltd 1952-60, design and devpt engr Hawker Aircraft Ltd 1960-62, liaison engr/asst tech sales mangr Teddington Aircraft Controls Ltd 1962-68, project mgmnt & tech sales Hawker Siddeley Dynamics Ltd 1968-72, airliner sales exec Hawker Siddeley Aviation Ltd 1974-75, aviation conslt 1975-78; lectr RAF Halton 1978-82, RAF Coll Cranwell 1982-; cncllr Wheathampstead Herts 1972-75; former Scout asst dist cmmr: S Croydon, Abergavenny; dist cmmr Sleaford 1985-87; CEng 1983, MRAes; *Recreations* aviation (private pilot), res: into breathing aparatus (for aircraft passengers & others), into fire resistance of a breakdown emissions of composite materials; *Style*— Karl Smith, Esq; Heckington House, Heckington, Lincs NG34 9JD (☎ 0529 60502)

SMITH, Kenneth David; s of Percival Smith (d 1986), and Doris Lillian, *née* Townsend; *b* 27 Feb 1944; *Educ* Beckenham Tech Sch, Beckenham Art Sch, S E London Tech Coll; *m* 28 Aug 1964, Pamela Jean Smith; 1 s (Ivan David b 26 Feb 1969), 2 da (Julia Hazel b 4 Dec 1966, Michelle Christine b 18 Aug 1970); *Career* designer; Elsom PackRoberts (chartered architects, and town planners) 1978-86, ptnr EPR Design Partnership 1985-89, md EPR Design Ltd 1988, Freeman: City of London 1981, Worshipful Co of Paviors (ctee memb 1988-); FCSD; *Recreations* art, theatre, music; *Clubs* Travellers'; *Style*— Kenneth Smith, Esq; Hartfield Cottage, 91 Harvest Bank Rd, West Wickham, Kent; 90 Meddon St, Bideford, North Devon, (☎ 01 462 1797); EPR Design Ltd, 21 Douglas St, London, (☎ 01 834 4411 fax 01 630 0356 telex 917940 PRLON G)

SMITH, Kenneth Graeme Stewart; CMG (1958), AE (1944, JP Dorset 1967); 3 s of Prof Herbert Arthur Smith, DCL (1961); *b* 26 July 1918; *Educ* Bradfield, Magdalen Coll Oxford; *Career* Flt Lt RAFVR 1940-46, admin cadet Colonial Serv 1940, dist cmmr Zanzibar 1946, govt sec Seychelles 1949, asst chief sec Aden 1952, colonial sec Gambia 1956, (ret 1962); *Style*— Kenneth Smith, Esq, CMG, JP; The Old House, 64 Newland, Sherborne, Dorset DT9 3AQ (☎ 0935 812754)

SMITH, Lawrence George Albert; s of Lawrence Cyril Smith (d 1966), of 150 St John's Ave, Kidderminster, Worcs, and Ida Mildred Smith, *née* Moule (d 1970); *b* 17 Dec 1930; *Educ* King Charles I Sch Kidderminster, Birmingham Univ (LLB); *m* 12 Nov 1955, Tess, da of Bertram Bishop (d 1957), of Worcs; 3 da (Sally b 1960, Rachel b 1963, Rebecca b 1968); *Career* Nat Serv Lt S Staffs Regt BAOR 1955; slr, ptnr Thursfield Adams & Westons 1964-, notary public 1977-, clerk Clare Witnell & Blount Charity 1973-; dep chm Kidderminster Cons Assoc 1971-73, pres Kidderminster and Dist C of C 1984-86; *Recreations* rugby football, sailing, politics; *Style*— Lawrence Smith, Esq; Bracton House, 5 Westville Ave, Kidderminster, Worcs DY11 6BZ (☎ 0562 824806); Thursfield Adams & Westons, 14 Church St, Kidderminster (☎ 0562 820575, fax 0562 66783, telex 337837)

SMITH, Sir Leonard Herbert; CBE (1977, MBE 1963); s of Herbert Thomas Smith, and Harriett Smith; *b* 28 May 1907; *Educ* King's Sch Chester; *m* 1943, (Ruth) Pauline, *née* Lees; 2 da; *Career* memb Lib Pty 1922-; kt 1981; *Style*— Sir Leonard Smith, CBE

SMITH, Sir Leslie Edward George; *b* 15 April 1919; *Educ* Christ's Hosp; *m* 1, 1943, Lorna Pickworth; 2 da; m 2, 1964, Cynthia Holmes; 1 s, 1 da; *Career* chm The BOC Group 1979- (chm and chief exec 1972-79, gp md 1969-72, joined 1956), dir Cadbury Schweppes 1977-; Exec Ctee King Edward VII Hosp for Offrs 1978-, NEB 1979; part-time memb British Gas Corpn 1982-; FCA; kt 1977; *Style*— Sir Leslie Smith; Cookley House, Cookley Green, Swyncombe, Henley-on-Thames, Oxon (☎ 0491 641258); The BOC Group, Hammersmith House, London W6 9DX (☎ 01 748 2020)

SMITH, Hon Mrs (Lois Jean); da of Baron Pearson, CBE, PC (Life Peer) (d 1980); *b* 1938; *m* 1961, the Rev Robin Jonathan Norman Smith; *Style*— The Hon Mrs Smith; St Mary's Vicarage, Chesham, Bucks

SMITH, Hon Lorenzo Patrick Harold; s of 4 Visc Hambleden; *b* 1962; *Style*— The Hon Lorenzo Smith

SMITH, Hon Mrs (Margaret Bertha Meriel); *née* Ward; da of late 6 Viscount Bangor, OBE, PC; *b* 1914; *m* 1, 1938, Maj Desmond Charles Forde, Coldstream Gds (mdis 1947), 1 s, 1 da; m 2, 1947 (m dis 1962), Gavin Robert Sligh; m 3, 1967, Maj Dennis Eric Smith; *Style*— The Hon Mrs Smith; Flat 6, 17/21 Sloane Court West, London, SW3 4TD (☎ 01 730 4153)

SMITH, Dame Margôt; DBE (1974); da of Leonard Graham-Brown, MC, FRCS (d 1950); *b* 5 Sept 1918; *Educ* Hilders, Hindhead, Westonbirt Glos; *m* 1947, Roy Smith, MC, TD, (d 1983); 2 s, 1 da; *Career* chm: Yorks Cons Women's Ctee 1963-66, Nat Cons Women's Ctee 1969-72, Nat Assoc of Cons & Unionist Assocs 1973-74; memb NSPCC Central Exec Ctee 1969-85; *Recreations* foxhunting, riding, gardening; *Style*— Dame Margot Smith, DBE; Howden Lodge, Spennithorne, Leyburn, N Yorks (☎ 0969 23621)

SMITH, Mark Aynsley; s of Frank Sidney Smith (d 1987), and Sheila Gertrude, *née* Cowin (d 1987); *b* 24 May 1939; *Educ* Kings Coll Sch Wimbledon; *m* 10 Oct 1964, Carol Ann, da of Harold Jones (d 1983); 1 s (Jeremy b 1973), 1 da (Melissa b 1975); *Career* Peat Marwick Mitchell & co London 1958-66, SG Warburg & Co Ltd 1966-, (dir 1971, dep hd of corporate finance div 1986); govr Milbourne Lodge jr sch, Esher Surrey; ACA 1971, FCA 1976; *Recreations* tennis, walking, collecting; *Style*— Mark Smith, Esq; S G Warburg & Co Ltd, 2 Finsbury Avenue, London, EC2M 2PA, (☎ 01 860 1090, fax 01 860 0901, telex 920301)

SMITH, His Hon Judge; Mark Barnet; s of David Smith (d 1933), by his w, Sophie Abrahams (d 1960); *b* 11 Feb 1917; *Educ* Manchester GS, Sidney Sussex Coll Cambridge; *m* 1943, Edith Winifred, *née* Harrison; 2 da; *Career* serv WWII RA 1940-46, asst examiner HM Patent Off 1939, promoted to examiner 1944; barr Middle Temple 1948, temp rec of Folkstone 1971, rec 1972, circuit judge 1972-; *Recreations* gardening, spectator sports; *Style*— His Hon Judge Smith; 6 Pump Court, Temple, London EC4

SMITH, Martin Gregory; s of Archibald Gregory Smith, OBE (d 1981), of St Albans, and Mary Eleanor Smith (d 1975); *Educ* St Albans Sch, St Edmund Hall Oxford (BA, MA), Stanford Univ Californa (MBA, AM); *m* 2 Oct 1971, Elise Becket, da of George Campbell Beckett, of Lakeville, Conn, USA; 1 s (Jeremy b 28 Jan 1974), 1 da (Katie b 5 Aug 1975); *Career* asst brewer Arthur Guinness Son and Co Dublin Ltd 1964-69, engagement mangr McKinsey and Co Inc 1971-74, vice pres and dir hd of corp fin Citicorp Int Bank Ltd 1974-80, sr vice pres and chm Bankers Tst Int Ltd 1980-85, dir Phoenix Securities Ltd 1983-, dir Becket Pubns Ltd; dir Orchestra of the Age of Enlightment; *Recreations* hunting, sailing, skiing, tennis; *Clubs* Royal St George Yacht (Dublin); *Style*— Martin Smith, Esq; 4 Essex Villas, London W8 7BN; The Old Rectory, Shipton Oliffe, Glos GL54 6HU; Phoenix Securities Ltd, 99 Bishopsgate, London EC2 (☎ 01 638 2191, fax 01 6387 0707)

SMITH, Hon Martin Rodney; s (by 1 m) of Baron Smith, KBE (Life Peer); *b* 1942; *Style*— The Hon Martin Smith; Dower Cottage, Marlow Common, Bucks

SMITH, Maureen; *b* 30 July 1947; *m* 8 Nov 1978, Alan Lewis Sutherland; 1 da (Natasha b 1980); *Career* md: BBDO PR Ltd 1972, (dir 1971), Good Relations Ltd

1973; chief exec: Good Relations Gp Ltd 1975, Good Relations Gp plc; chm The Communication Gp plc (PR consultancy); *Style*— Ms Maureen Smith; The Communication Gp plc, 19 Buckingham plc, London SW1E 6LB (☎ 01 630 1411)

SMITH, Maxwell; TD (1967); s of Maj (William Henry) Harold Smith (d 1957), of Romford, Essex, and Norah Newman, *née* Taylor; *b* 19 Dec 1929; *Educ* Royal Liberty Sch Romford, London Univ (BSc, DipEd); *m* 29 Sept 1956, Anne, da of John Frederick Kendall (d 1967), of Sheffield, Essex; 1 s (Duncan b 1970), 2 da (Helen b 1962, Isobel b 1965); *Career* RE 1951-67 (Maj i/c Essex Field Sqdn 54 Div Engrs 1964-67); South Bank Poly: head dept of Estate Mgmnt 1970-77, dean of faculty 1972-77, asst dir 1977-86, conslt 1986-; chm SERC Building sub-Ctee 1980-86, memb gen cncl RICS 1975-86 (divnl pres 1977-78); memb Worshipful Co of Chartered Surveyors 1977; hon fell South Bank Poly 1988, ARICS 1951, FRICS 1965, MBIM 1969; *Books* Manual of British Standards in Buliding Construction & Specification (second edn 1987); *Recreations* walking, music, painting; *Style*— Maxwell Smith, Esq, TD; 50 Pickwick Rd, Dulwich Village, London SE21 7JW (☎ 01 274 9041)

SMITH, Michael John; s of late Reginald Charles George Smith, of Ashford, Kent, and late Kate, *née* Godden; *b* 9 Mar 1943; *Educ* Ashford GS; *m* 15 Sept 1965 (m dis 1978), Anne; 1 s (Ian Michael Sommerfield b 1969), 1 da (Samantha Jane b 1967); *Career* joined CAP Gp 1963 (md 1981-88), jt md Sema Gp plc 1988-; tstee Leadership Tst; memb Worshipful Co of Information Technologists 1988; FBIM 1986; Lord of the Manor: Hawridge and Cholesbury 1987; *Style*— Michael Smith, Esq; Hawridge Ct, Hawridge, Bucks HP5 2UG (☎ 024 029240); SEMA Group plc, 22 Long Acre, London WC2E 9LY (☎ 01 379 4711, fax 01 240 6778, telex 263498)

SMITH, Dr The Hon Mildred Vivian; OBE (1962); da of late 1 Baron Bicester; *b* 1908; *Educ* London Univ (BSc, BS, MD), Oxford Univ (MA); *Career* MRCS, LRCP, MRCP, FRCP; *Style*— Dr The Hon Smith, OBE; Croft Lodge, Yarpole, Leominster, Herefordshire HR6 0BN

SMITH, Hon Lady; Hon Monica Victoria; *née* Crossley; da of late 1 Baron Somerleyton, MP, and Phyllis, CBE, da of Gen Sir Henry Percival de Bathe, 4 Bt, KCB; *b* 1897; *m* 1918, Lt-Gen Sir Arthur Francis Smith, KCB, KBE, DSO, MC, late Coldstream Gds (d 1977; gs of 8 Earl of Kintore); 1 s, 3 da; *Style*— The Hon Lady Smith; Birklands, Kithurst Lane, Storrington, W Sussex (☎ 090 66 5082)

SMITH, Hon Mrs (Myfanwy Ann); *née* Philipps; da (by 1 m) of 2 Viscount St Davids, *qv*; *b* 1944; *m* 1968, Anthony John Frederick Smith; 2 s; *Style*— The Hon Mrs Smith; 23 Pyrland Rd, London N5

SMITH, (George) Neil; CMS (1987); s of George William Smith (d 1982), of Sheffield, and Ena Hill; *b* 12 July 1936; *Educ* King Edward VII Sch, Sheffield; *m* 5 May 1956, Elvi Vappus, da of Johannes Hämäläinen, of Finland (d 1962); 1 s (Kim b 1959), 1 da (Helen b 1957); *Career* joined Dip Serv 1953, RAF (Nat Serv) 1954-56; commercial attaché Br Embassy Rangoon 1958-61; second sec (commercial) Br Embassy Berne 1961-65; Dip Serv Admin 1965-66, first sec Cwlth Off 1966-68, Br Mil Govt Berlin 1969-73, FCO (European Integrations and N America Depts) 1973-77; counsellor (commercial) Br Embassy, Helsinki 1977-80, HM Consul-General Zurich and Principality of Liechtenstein 1980-85, head of Trade Relations and Exports Dept FCO; *Recreations* music; *Clubs* Travellers; *Style*— Neil Smith, Esq, CMS; Foreign and Commonwealth Office, Whitehall, London SW1 (☎ 01 270 2568)

SMITH, Hon Nicolas Robin Bartolomeo; s of 4 Visc Hambleden; *b* 17 August 1960; *Style*— The Hon Nicolas Smith

SMITH, Nigel Fearn Clive; MBE; s of Bernard Clive Smith (d 1970); *b* 24 Jan 1928; *Educ* Stowe; *m* 1962, Audrey Geraldine, *née* Catto; 1 s, 1 da; *Career* underwriter; *Recreations* skiing, sailing; *Clubs* Special Forces; *Style*— Nigel Smith, Esq, MBE; Vynes Farmhouse, Staunton, Gloucester GL19 3NZ

SMITH, Norman Jack; s of Maurice Leslie Smith, formerly of Newton Abbot, Devon (d 1967), and Ellen Dorothy, *née* Solly; *b* 14 April 1936; *Educ* Henley GS, Oriel Coll Oxford (MA), City Univ (MPhil); *m* 4 March 1967, Valerie Ann, da of Capt Arthur Ernest Frost, formerly of Ramsgate, Kent (d 1978); 1 s (Malcolm b 1970); 1 da (Gail b 1974); *Career* mkt analyst Dexion Ltd 1957-60, comm evaluation mangr Vickers Ltd 1960-69, business devpt mangr Baring Bros and Co Ltd 1969-80; dir: Burnstisland Engrs and Fabricators Ltd 1974-76, Zenith Reed Ltd 1975-76, Int Economic Services Ltd 1975-76, SAI Tubular Services Ltd 1983-88, Atkins Oil and Gs Engrg Ltd 1984-86, Smith Rea Energy Analysts Ltd 1985-; md Smith Rea Energy Assocs 1983-, dir gen Offshire Supplies Office 1978-80, chm Br Underwater Engrg Ltd 1981-83, Mentor Engrg Consits Ltd 1988-; *Recreations* archaeology, walking, swimming, gardening; *Clubs* United Oxford and Cambridge; *Style*— Norman Jack Smith, Esq; Smith Rea Energy Associates Ltd, 3 Beer Cart Lane, Canterbury, Kent CT1 2NJ (☎ 0227 763 456)

SMITH, Paul Ronald; s of Ronald Edward Smith (d 1980), of Bristol, and Doreen Alice, *née* Young; *b* 4 July 1948; *Educ* Glasgow Acad, Weston-Super-Mare Tech Coll; *m* 20 July 1974, Sarah, da of Horace William (Digger) Knight (d 1985), of Bristol; 1 s (Adam b 1981), 1 da (Georgina b 1979); *Career* CA; trainee W O & H O Wills 1967-69, asst chief accountant May & Hassell plc 1969-72, commercial dir Carlton JCB Ltd 1972-75, PA to sr ptnr Watkins Gray Woodgate Architects 1975-76; J A Devenish plc: admin dir gp mgmnt bd 1979, md Devenish Redruth Brewery Ltd 1985 (chief accountant 1976-79), gp md 1987; FCCA 1972; *Recreations* squash, sailing, rugby football; *Clubs* Redruth RC, Clifton RC; *Style*— Paul Smith, Esq; Carclew, Perranarworthal, Truro, Cornwall TR3 7PB (☎ 0872 865045); J A Devenish plc, Trinity House, 15 Trinity St, Weymouth, Dorset DT4 8TP (☎ 0305 761111, fax 0305 782397, car 0836 243683)

SMITH, Paul William Cliburn; s of Alfred Edward Smith (d 1985), professional golfer and world record holder, and Georgina, *née* Cliburn; *b* 28 August 1949; *Educ* St Lawrence Coll Ramsgate, Queen's Univ Belfast (BA); *m* 7 Sept 1974, Elizabeth Anne, da of William Arthur Smitton, of High Rigg, Heathwaite, Windermere, Cumbria; 2 da (Rebecca Emily Louise b 1979, Catherine Lauren Elizabeth b 1984); *Career* slr; ptnr Pearson & Pearson; chm Herdwick Historical Reprints (specialist book publishers) 1987-; dir Herdwick Investmts Ltd 1984-; *Recreations* local history, fell walking, golf; *Style*— Paul Smith, Esq; The Croft, 18 Kentrigg, Kendal, Cumbria (☎ 0539 28 763); Pearson & Pearson, 98A Stricklandgate, Kendal, Cumbria (☎ 0539 29 555)

SMITH, Peter; s of Walter Smith (d 1984), of Brotton, Cleveland, and Mary Elizabeth, *née* Welham; *b* 14 Mar 1941; *Educ* St Mary's Coll Middlesbrough; *m* 20 Feb 1965, Maureen, da of Maurice O'Brien, (d 1957); 3 da (Katherine b 4 March 1966, Josephine b 16 Sept 1967, Clare b 31 Aug 1980); *Career* CA; sr ptnr Calvert Smith and Co 1969-; Chllr Worshipful Co of Merchant Taylors in the City of York, former pres and sec York Catenian Assoc, tres Lawrence Sterne Tst; Pro Ecclesia et Pontifice (Papal Decoration) 1983; FCA 1965; *Recreations* walking, cricket; *Style*— Peter Smith, Esq; The Hollies, Bonneycroft Lane, Easingwold, York YO6 3AR (☎ 0347 21570); Calvert Smith and Co, Chartered Accountants, 104-106 The Mount, York YO2 2AR (☎ 0904 655626)

SMITH, Peter; s of Lt Laurence Willis Smith (d 1983), of Aberystwyth, and Hilda, *née* Halsted (d 1980); *b* 15 June 1926; *Educ* Royal GS Newcastle, King Edward VI Sch Southampton, Peter Symond's Sch Winchester, Oriel Coll Oxford, Lincoln Coll Oxford (MA), Hammersmith Sch of Arts and Crafts; *m* 29 March 1954, Joyce Evelyn, da of John William Abbot (d 1963), of Brynford, Clwyd; 2 s (Stephen Lloyd b 1954, Charles Kenyon b 1957), 1 da (Sarah Caroline b 1960); *Career* Royal Cmmn Ancient Monuments Wales: jr investigator 1949-54, sr investigator 1954-63, investigator i/c of Nat Monuments Record 1963-73, sec of the cmmn 1973-; pres: Cambrian Archaeological Assoc 1979, Vernacular Architecture Gp 1984-87; Alice Davis Hitchcock Medallion (Soc of Architectural Historians) 1978; ARIBA 1950; *Books* Houses of the Welsh Countryside (1975, 2 ed 1988), The Cambridge Agricultural History (contributor); *Recreations* reading, drawing, learning Welsh, bricklaying; *Style*— Peter Smith, Esq; Tŷ-cock, Lluest, Llanbadarn Fawr, Aberystwyth, Dyfed (☎ 0970 623 556); RCAM (Wales), Edleston Ho, Queens Rd, Aberystwyth, Dyfed (☎ 0970 624 381)

SMITH, Peter; s of Ernest Sidney Smith (d 1950), of Yotes Cottage, St Mary's Platt, Sevenoaks, Kent, and Ellen Smith (d 1967); *Educ* Sevenoaks Sch; *m* 1, (m dis), Christina De Vries; m 2, 17 Oct 1953, Pamela Mary, da of Cyril Leigh Francis, MM (d 1972), of 33 Goldington Ave, Bedford; 1 s (Richard Peter b 26 May 1954), 3 da (Jane Alexander b 28 July 1945, Susan Christina b 27 Oct 1947, Sally Ann b 1 May 1956); *Career* 2 Lt Royal West Kent 1955; chm Borough Green Sawmills Ltd 1967-89 (md 1962), pres Full Gospel Business Mens Fellowship Maidstone Chapter 1989; memb: Boughton Monchelsea Parish Cncl 1972-89, Baughton Monchelsea PCC 1973-89, Rochester Deanery Synod 1982-87; *Recreations* walking, racing; *Clubs* Lingfield Park, Folkestone Racing; *Style*— Peter Smith, Esq; (☎ 0622 43555); Borough Green Sawmills Ltd, Borough Green, Kent (☎ 0732 882 012)

SMITH, Peter Alan; s of Dudley Vaughan Smith (d 1983), and Beatrice Ellen, *née* Sketcher; *b* 5 August 1946; *Educ* Mill Hill, Univ of Southampton (BSc); *m* 2 Oct 1971, Cherry, da of Thomas A Blandford (d 1986); 2 s (Nicholas David b 1975, Richard James b 1977); *Career* RAFVR 1964-67, cmmnd actg PO 1967; Coopers and Lybrand CAs 1967- (ptnr 1975-, chm Int banking indust ctee 1988-); vice pres Beaconsfield Cons Assoc, former hon tres UK Housing Tst; FCA; *Books* Housing Association Accounts and their Audit (1980); *Recreations* golf, gardening; *Clubs* Carlton, Beaconsfield golf; *Style*— Peter Smith, Esq; Littleworth House, Common Lane, Littleworth Common, Bucks (☎ 06286 5018); 208 Bunyan Ct, Barbican, London EC2; Coopers & Lybrand, Plumtree Court, London EC4A 4HT (☎ 01 822 4586, fax 01 822 4652, telex 884730)

SMITH, Peter Alexander Charles; OBE (1981); s of Alexander Smith and Gwendoline, *née* Beer; *b* 18 August 1920; *Educ* St Paul's; *m* 1945, Marjorie May (d 1988), *née* Humphrey; 1 s; *Career* served WWII RA; slr 1948-; chm Securicor Gp plc 1974- (chief exec 1974-85), dir Fitch Lovell 1982-, non-exec chm Metal Closures Gp plc 1983-87 (dir 1972-87, dep chm 1981-83), chm Br Security Indust Assoc 1977-81; pres Royal Warrant Holders Assoc 1982-83 (memb cncl 1976-, vice-pres 1981-82); FRSA; CBIM; *Recreations* golf, music, photography; *Clubs* British Racing Drivers'; *Style*— Peter Smith, Esq, OBE; Securicor Gp plc, Sutton Park Hse, 15 Carshalton Rd, Sutton, Surrey SM1 4LE (☎ 01 770 7000)

SMITH, Peter Angus; s of Edward Angus Smith, JP (d 1970), of Southerndown, Highworth, Wilts and Mary Glenn, *née* Wallis; *b* 28 Mar 1936; *Educ* Winchester; *m* 30 May 1964, Bridget Rosemary, da of Maj Ernest Oscar Yates (d 1955), of Haywards, Woodmancote, nr Cheltenham; 2 da (Nicola b 8 Oct 1966, Annabel b 1 July 1969); *Career* Nat Serv 1954-56, cmmnd 15/19 Royal Hussars served Malaya; sales dir Wilts Carpets Ltd 1963-70, md Humphries & Taplings Ltd 1970-72; dir: Richard Bondy Ltd 1970-71, Dorville Fashions Ltd 1970; chm: Peter Smith Associates Ltd 1972-87, Threshold Floorings Ltd 1974-87; md Alvescot Int Ltd 1987-, ptnr Prime Designs 1987-; memb Bampton Parish Cncl 1970-73; pres: London Floorcovering Assoc 1980-, Bampton CC 1987-; *Recreations* cricket, tennis, fishing, shooting; *Clubs* Cavalry and Guard's; *Style*— Peter Smith, Esq; Churchgate House, Bampton, Oxford OX8 2LZ (☎ 0993 850 251);

SMITH, Peter James Mead; s of Douglas William Mead Smith (d 1985), of Port Talbot, and Doris Maud, *née* Duchien; *b* 25 August 1948; *Educ* St Clares Convent Porthcawl Mid Glam, Dyffryn GS Port Talbot, Coll of Law Guildford Surrey; *m* 3 Oct 1972, Sarah Madeline Anita, da of William Thomas Richards, of Swansea; 1 s (Richard b 1976); *Career* slr, sr ptnr Smith Spring and Co 1972-; hon sec Aberavon Green Stars RFC, fndn govr St Josephs Primary Sch Neath W Glam 1985-; memb Br Legal Assoc; *Recreations* rugby union and other sports; *Style*— Peter Smith, Esq; Hendre, 1 Westernmoor Rd, Neath, W Glam SA11 1BJ (☎ 0639 56635); 18 Princess Way, Swansea SA1 3LW (☎ 0792 464444, fax 0792 464726); 2 Forge Rd, Port Talbot (☎ 0639 897075)

SMITH, Peter Vivian Henworth; CB 1989; s of Vivian Smith (d 1973), of Craig, 22 Victoria Rd, Clacton-on-Sea, Essex, and Dorothea, *née* Ovende (d 1941); *b* 5 Dec 1928; *Educ* Clacton Co HS, Brasenose Coll Oxford (MA, BCL); *m* 19 Feb 1955, Mary Marjorie, da of Frank John Willsher (d 1947), of Babbocombe, Holland Rd, Clacton-on-Sea; 5 da (Kathleen b 1955, Jacqueline b 1958, Susan b 1961, Linda b 1962, Johanna b 1967); *Career* called to the Bar Lincoln's inn, HM Overseas Legal Serv 1955-70, ret puisne judge Malawi 1970, legal asst HM Customs and Excise 1970-72 (sr legal asst 1972-76, asst slr 1976-82, princ asst slr, legal sec 1982-85), slr dep sec HM Customs and Excise 1986-; *Recreations* classical music, walking; *Style*— Peter Smith, Esq; Likabula, 14 St Albans Rd, Clacton-on-Sea, Essex CO15 6BA (☎ 0255 422053); The Solicitor, HM Customs and Excise, New Kings Beam House, 22 Upper Ground, London SE1 9PJ (☎ 01 382 5121)

SMITH, Philip Henry; s of Alfred Henry Smith (d 1977), of Leicester, and Georgina May, *née* Ives (d 1969); *b* 24 Nov 1946; *Educ* Loughborough Coll GS, Leicester Regnl Coll of Technol, Nottingham Poly; *m* 27 Dec 1968, Sonia Idena, da of Ivan Garnet Moody (d 19640, of Leicester; 2 s (Christian Philip b 13 June 1972, Philip Raouol b 28 Feb 1975), 1 da (Melissa b 21 June 1969); *Career* sr audit asst Leics CC 1964-69, gp accountant Lusaka City Cncl Zambia 1969-72, branch accountant Dairy Produce Bd Zambia 1972-74, divnl dir and sec Dorada Hldgs plc 1974-81, divnl fin dir Brook Tool Engrg Hldgs, plc 1981-83, gp tres Asda Gp plc 1983-; chm Padbury United Football, life memb Clifton Rangers Youth Football; memb IPFA 1971, CIMA 1974; MBIM 1974; *Recreations* sports, gardening, political and Econ affairs; *Style*— Philip Smith, Esq; The Old White Horse, Main St, Padbury, Buckingham, Bucks MK18 2AY (☎ 0280 814848); Asda Group plc, Asda House, Southbank Great Wilson St, Leeds, W Yorks (☎ 0532 418908, fax 0532 418018, car tel 0836 277988, telex 556623 ASDAHO G)

SMITH, Philip John Mytton; s of Herbert George Smith (d 1988), of Northleach, Gloucestershire, and Margery Eleanor, *née* Haynes (d 1983); *b* 6 Jan 1936; *Educ* Uppingham, Aston Univ Birmingham (BSc); *m* 1974, Sarah Anne Ruth, da of David Hugh Stafford Forsyth, of Stanton, Gloucestershire; 2 da (Heather b 1976, Philippa b 1978); *Career* mfr: Gen Electric Co plc 1954-64 Ian Heath Ltd Birmingham 1964-67, P-E Consulting Gp 1968-72; dir Brass Turned Parts Ltd Birmingham 1972-; CEng, MIEE, MIMC; *Recreations* hunting; *Style*— Philip Smith, Esq; Garretts Farm, Buckland, Broadway, Worcs; Brass Turned Parts Ltd, Fallows Rd, Sparkbrook, Birmingham B11 1PL

SMITH, Hon Philip Reginald; s of 3 Visc Hambleden (d 1948); *b* 7 Sept 1945; *Educ* Eton; *m* 1973, Mary, da of John Roberts, of Checkendon, Oxon; 2 s, 2 da; *Career* farmer; *Style*— The Hon Philip Smith; Campden House, Chipping Campden, Glos

SMITH, Sir Raymond Horace; KBE (1967, CBE 1960), AFC (1968); s of Horace P Smith (d 1965), of London, and Mabelle E, *née* Couzens (d 1960); *b* 18 Mar 1917; *Educ* Salesian Coll London, Barcelona Univ Spain; *m* 1943, Dorothy, da of Robert Cheney Hart (d 1946), of London; 3 s; *Career* serv WWII with Br Security Co-ordination W Hemisphere (USA, Canada, Caribbean and S America), civil attaché Br Embassy Caracas 1941, negotiator for sale of British owned railway cos to S American Govts 1946-53; pres British Cwlth Assoc of Venezuela 1955-57; consultant to: Rolls Royce, Fairey Engineering, Hawker Siddeley, Brackett; CRAeS; *Recreations* Cresta Run, tennis, skiing, water skiing; *Clubs* White's, Naval and Military, Country, Jockey (C~racas); *Style*— Sir Raymond Smith, KBE; Quinta San Antonio, Calla El Samancito, Caracas Country Club, Caracas, Venezuela (☎ 32 92 18/33 36 96); 37 Lowndes St, London SW1 (☎ 01 235 6249); Calle Real de Sabana Grande, Edificio Las Américas, Chacaito, Caracas, Venezuela (☎ 71 40 18/ 72 92 29; telex 21644)

SMITH, Sir Reginald Beaumont; *Career* chm George Wimpey plc (to retire Dec 1983: *see* C J Chetwood); dir: Grove Charity Management, Oldham Estate Co, Wimpey Pension Fund, Wimpey Pension Trustees; FCIOB; kt; *Style*— Sir Reginald Smith; c/o George Wimpey plc, 27 Hammersmith Grove, W6 (☎ 01 748 2000)

SMITH, Hon Richard Edward; s of 3 Viscount Hambleden (d 1948); *b* 1937; *m* 1973, Christine Hickey; 1 s; *Style*— The Hon Richard Smith; c/o 19 Warwick Square, London SW1

SMITH, Dr Robert Carr; CBE (1988); s of Mr Edward Albert Smith, of Herts, and Olive Winifred, *née* Carstairs; *b* 19 Nov 1935; *Educ* Queen Elizabeth's Sch Barnet, Southampton Univ (BSc), London Univ (PhD); *m* 1960, Rosalie Mary, da of Mr Talbot Victor Spencer, of Sussex; 1 s (James b 1965), 1 da (Georgina b 1968); *Career* dir Kingston Poly 1982-; previously prof of physical electronics Southmpton Univ; memb: cncl for Industry and Higher Educn, cncl of Inst of Manpower Studies, Polys and Colls Funding Cncl; *Recreations* visual arts; *Style*— Dr Robert Smith, CBE; Mayberry Cottage, Raleigh Drive, Claygate, Surrey KT10 9DE (☎ 0372 63352); Kingston Polytechnic, Penrhyn Road, Kingston Upon Thames, Surrey KT1 2EE (☎ 01 549 1366 ext 2000)

SMITH, Sir Robert Courtney; CBE (1980); s of John Smith, JP, DL (d 1954), of Glasgow and Symington, and Agnes, *née* Brown (d 1969); *b* 29 Mar 1989; *Educ* Kelvinside Acad Glasgow, Sedbergh, Trinity Coll Cambambridge (BA,MA); *m* 6 March 1954, Moira Rose, da of Wilfred Hugh MacDougall, CA (d 1948), of Glasgow; 2 s (Nigel b 1956 d 1971, Christopher b 1961), 2 da (Lorna (Mrs Bromley-Martin) b 1958, Rosalind b 1964); *Career* RM 1945-47, RMFVR 1951-57; CA 1953; ptnr Arthur Young McLlelland Marcus 1957-78; chm: Alliance Tst plc, Second Alliance Tst plc, Bank of Scotland, Br Alcan Aluminium Ltd, Edinburgh Investmt Tst plc, Sidlaw Gp plc, Standard Life Assur Co, Volvo Trucks (GB) Ltd; vice-chm William Collins plc; Chllr's assessor Glasgow Univ, pres Business Archives Cncl Scotland, tstee Carnegie Tst for Univs of Scotland, memb Scottish Industs Devpt Bd 1972-88 (chm 1981-88); Hon LLD Glasgow 1978; FRSE 1988; kt 1987; chm Scottish Industrial Develop Advisory Board; Chancellor's assessor Glasgow Univ; President Business Archives, Council, Scotland Trustee Carnege Trust for Universities of Scotland; Dir Natioinal Register of Archives, Scotland; kt 1987; *Recreations* gardening, racing; *Clubs* East India, Western (Glasgow), Hawks (Cambridge); *Style*— Sir Robert Smith, CBE; North Lodge, Dunkeld, Perthshire PH8 OAR (☎ Dunkeld 035 02 574); 64 Reform Street, Dundee DD1 1JJ (☎ 0382 201700, fax 0382 25133, telex 76195)

SMITH, Sir Robert Hill; 3 Bt (UK 1945), of Crowmallie, Co Aberdeen; s (by 2 m) of Sir Gordon Smith, 2 Bt, VRD (d 1983); *b* 15 April 1958; *Educ* Merchant Taylors', Aberdeen Univ; *Heir* bro, Charles Gordon Smith, b 21 April 1959; *Recreations* sailing; *Clubs* Royal Thames Yacht; *Style*— Sir Robert Smith, Bt; Crowmallie, Pitcaple, Aberdeenshire

SMITH, Robert Sydney Winwood; s and h of Sir Christopher Smith, 5 Bt; *b* 1939; *Style*— Robert Smith, Esq

SMITH, Robin Barker; s of Arthur Smith of Clandown, Somerset, and Mary, *née* Thompson; *b* 22 August 1946; *Educ* Ulverston GS, Univ of Leeds (MB, ChB, ChM), Univ of Oxford (MA), Univ of Chicago; *m* 4 Dec 1971 (m dis 1987), Judith Mary, da of Robert Walton Anderson (d 1986); 1 s (Matthew Robert b 18 Feb 1978), 1 da (Victoria Clare b 5 Feb 1975); *Career* surgical tutor Radcliffe Infirmary Oxford 1975-81 (registrar 1973-75), res fell Univ of Chicago 1979-80; conslt surgeon Royal Utd Hosp Bath 1981-; FRCS (1975); *Books* chapters in various surgical texts 1980-88; *Recreations* skiing, tennis, music, reading; *Style*— Robin Barker Smith, Esq; Homefield, Widcombe Hill, Bath BA2 6EA (☎ 0225 64718); Longwood House, The Bath Clinic, Claverton Down Rd, Bath (☎ 0225 835 555)

SMITH, Baron (Life Peer UK 1978); (Edwin) Rodney; KBE (1975); s of Dr Edwin Smith; *b* 10 May 1914; *Educ* Westminster Sch, London Univ (MS, BS, MRCS, LRCP, FRCS, MS); *m* 1, 1938 (m dis 1971), Mary Rodwell; 3 s, 1 da; m 2, 1971, Susan, da of Dr Rowdon Marrian Fry; *Career* pres RSC 1973-77, chm Conference of Royal Colls (UK) 1976-78, pres Royal Soc of Med 1978; examiner in surgery London Univ; consulting surgn: St George's Hosp (surgn 1946), Wimbledon Hosp, Royal Prince Alfred Hosp Sydney NSW: memb House of Lords Bridge Team in match against Commons 1982; *Style*— The Rt Hon The Lord Smith, KBE; 135 Harley St, W1

SMITH, Roland Hedley; s of Alan Hedley Smith, of Sheffield, and Elizabeth Louise, *née* Froggatt; *b* 11 April 1943; *Educ* King Edward VII Sch Sheffield, Keble Coll Oxford (BA, MA); *m* 27 Feb 1971, Katherine Jane, da of Philip Graham Lawrence, (d 1975), of Brighton; 2 da (Rebecca b 1972, Ursula b 1975); *Career* HM Dip Serv: third sec FO 1967, second sec Moscow 1969, second later first sec UK Delegation to NATO Brussels 1971, first sec FCO 1974, first sec and cultural attaché Moscow 1978, FCO 1980, attached to Int Inst for Strategic Studies 1983, political advsr and head of Chancery, Berlin 1984, Sci Energy and Nuclear Dept FCO 1988; *Books* Soviet Policy Towards West Germany (1985); *Recreations* music, choral singing; *Clubs* Royal Cwlth Soc; *Style*— Roland Smith, Esq; c/o Foreign & Commonwealth Office, London SW1A 2AH (☎ 01 270 2258)

SMITH, Ronald (Frederick); s of Norman Fred Smith (d 1959), and Alice Blanch, *née* Wright (d 1980); *b* 9 August 1930; *Educ* Sch of Architecture Birmingham, Tech Coll (Dip Arch); *m* 1, 1955, Joan Dorothy, da of Fred Snape (d 1970); 1 s (Martyn b 1965), 1 da (Tracy b 1961); m 2, Eunice Gillian, da of Walter Hooley; 1 s (Adam b 1975), 1 da (Claire b 1978); *Career* architect; The Ronald Smith Partnership: ptnr 1958-69, assoc 1969-79, ptnr 1979-; dir Fred Smith Walsall Ltd 1980-; *Recreations* clasic cars, motor racing, photography; *Style*— Ronald Smith, Esq; 5 Heathfield Drive, Bloxwich, Walsall, W Midlands WS3 3NN (☎ 0922 475046)

SMITH, (George) Ronald; MBE (1984); s of George Cran Smith (d 1979), and Hilda Jane, *née* Jack; *b* 14 July 1939; *Educ* George Watson's Coll Edinburgh, Univ of Edinburgh (MA, LLB); *m* 1 April 1966, Frances Margaret, da of John Leete Paterson (d 1943); 1 s (Ronald Michael b 1968), 1 da (Susan Frances b 1970); *Career* ptnr Wallace & Somerville Edinburgh 1965-69 (merged with Whinney Murray & Co, now Ernst & Whinney); Ernst & Whinney 1969-86: ptnr UK firm 1969-71, ptnr in charge Hamburg, managing ptnr Netherlands, managing ptnr Scandinavia, chm and sr ptnr Continental firm, memb Int Exec Ctee; dir compliance Investmt Mgmnt Regulatory Orgn Ltd (IMRO) 1987-; govr The Br Sch in the Netherlands 1977-85; MInstCAs of Scotland, MICAEW 1976; *Books* De Vierde Richtlijn - Kluwer - Deventer (contrib 1978); *Recreations* gardening, fishing, occasional golf; *Style*— G Ronald Smith, Esq, MBE; IMRO, Centre Point, 193 New Oxford St, London WC1A 1PT (☎ 01 379 0601, fax 01 379 4121)

SMITH, Sheriff Ronald Good; s of Adam Smith (d 1961), and Selina Spence, *née* Wotherspoon (d 1969); *b* 24 July 1933; *Educ* King's Park Sr Secondary Sch, Glasgow Univ (BL); *m* 16 Feb 1962, Joan Robertson Beharrie (d 1984), of Perth (d 2 Oct 1984); 2 s (Douglas Adam b 1964, Andrew John b 1967); *Career* Nat Serv 1952-54, served in Korea and Keyna (Corpl); slr 1962-84; Sheriff 1984-85; *Style*— Sheriff Ronald Smith; 369 Mearns Rd, Newton Mearns, Glasgow G77 5LZ (☎ 041 639 3904); The Sheriff Court, St James St, Paisley, Strathclyde (☎ 041 887 5291)

SMITH, Rowland Austin; TD, JP (S Humberside); s of Frank Smith (d 1968), of Heck House, Grimsby, and late Florence Elizabeth, *née* Frusher; *b* 30 June 1914; *Educ* Worksop Coll; *m* 21 June 1946, Joan, da of Hugh Halmshaw, of Riby Grove, Grimsby; *Career* Maj RA TA 1937; chm: The Expanded Piling Co Ltd, Expanded Driven Piling Co Ltd, F Smith & Son (Grimsby) Ltd; underwriter memb Lloyds 1983, dep chm Grimsby and Cleethorpes Bench; Freeman Worshipful Co of Paviors 1985; FGS 1950; *Recreations* shooting, racing; *Style*— Rowland Smith, Esq, JP, TD; Old Rectory, Swinhope, Lincoln LN3 6HT (☎ 0472 83258); Cheapside Works, Waltham Grimsby, S Humberside DN37 OJD (☎ 0472 822522, fax 0472 220675, telex 527118)

SMITH, Maj Roy Alfred; s of Alfred Philip Smith (d 1962), of Dartford, and Jane Smith (d 1966); *b* 16 Mar 1919; *Educ* Dartford GS, King's Coll London; *m* 30 April 1948, Zeline Monrad, da of Wilhelm Frederik Holst (d 1981), of Oslo; 1 s (Paul b 1953), 1 da (Christine (Mrs Hunter) b 1949); *Career* cmmnd Middx Regt 1939, Platoon Cdr 1/8 Middx France and Belguim 1940, instr Machine Gun Trg Centre Middx Regt 1940-41, Intelligence Offr No 5 Army Air Support Control 1941, serv Iraq Lebanon and Western Desert 1942, GSO3 (Air) Main HQ Eighth Army in Desert and Sicily 1942-43, seconded to HQ Fifth US Army for Salerno landings 1943, GSO2 Fifth US Army and 2 i/c 7 Army Air Support Control 1943, OC No 9 AASC 1944, dir of studies and GSO2 (Air) Tactical Sch Central Mediterranean Trg Centre 1944, GSO2 (Air) HQ Palestine & Trans-Jordan and OC 21 AASC 1945, dir of studies (Air Support) Sch of Land/Air Warfare 1946, ret 1946; Dunlop Rubber Co: overseas div 1946, resident rep Norway & Finland 1947, sr asst Latin America Dept 1951, sr asst Europe dept 1951, sales mangr Sweden 1954-57, strategic studies Europe (Head Off) 1958, gen mangr Euro sales div 1963, Euro coordinator 1968; dir mktg coordination Dunlop Euro Tyre Gp, ret 1960; chm overseas trade ctee Fndn of Br Rubber Manufacturers' Assocs 1968-72; memb: business advsy gp Sch of Euro Studies Univ of Sussex 1970-79, bd and exec ctee Int Road Fedn Geneva 1972-79; tstee Dormans Park Roads Tst 1977-, chm Abbeyfield Lingfield Soc 1986; *Books* Air Support in the Desert (1988); *Clubs* Army and Navy; *Style*— Maj Roy Smith

SMITH, Hon Mrs (Sheila Marguerite Evelyn); *née* de Montmorency; da of 7 Viscount Mountmorres (d 1951), and Katherine Sofia Clay, *née* Warrand (d 1971); *b* 8 May 1918; *Educ* Brentwood Sch Southport, Princess Christian Nursery Coll; *m* 1950, Robert Vernon, s of William Smith (d 1961); 2 s (Alastair b 1951, Robert b 1953); *Career* served WW II as London Ambulance Driver; a Princess Christian Nursery Nurse; *Style*— The Hon Mrs Smith; 34 Dorset Lake Ave, Lilliput, Poole, Dorset BH14 8JD (☎ 0202 709185)

SMITH, Stewart Ranson; CBE (1987); s of John Smith (d 1980), of Ashington, Northumberland, and Elizabeth Atkinson, *née* Barnes; *b* 16 Feb 1931; *Educ* Bedlington GS, Univ of Nottingham (BA, MA), Yale Univ USA (MA); *m* 2 Jan 1960, (Lee) Tjam Mui Smith; *Career* Nat Serv RAEC 1955-57; Br Cncl: asst rep Singapore 1957-59, HQ London 1959-61, dir Br Inst Curitiba Brazil 1961-65, asst rep Sri Lanka 1965-69, seconded to ODA London 1970-73, rep Kenya 1973-76, controller overseas B HQ 1976-80, rep Spain 1980-87, controller Higher Educn Div 1988, controller Europe Div 1989-; *Recreations* cricket, music; *Style*— Stewart Smith, Esq, CBE; British Council, 10 Spring Gardens, London SW1A 2BN (☎ 01 389 4310, telex 8952201 BRICON Cr)

SMITH, Hon Mrs (Susanna Mary); *née* Arbuthnott; only da of 16 Viscount of Arbuthnott, DSC; *b* 1 May 1954; *Educ* Overstone Sch Northants, Dorset House Sch of Occupational Therapy; *m* 1978, Hugh T B Smith; 1 s (Andrew b 1981), 1 da (Emma b 1983); *Style*— The Hon Mrs Smith; 52 King's Rd, Wimbledon, London SW19 8QW

SMITH, Terence Denby; s of Sydney Smith (d 1986), of Wakefield, Yorkshire, and Forence Evelyn, *née* Lister; *b* 28 Jan 1934; *Educ* Wheelwright GS Densbury Yorks; *m* 1, 1957 (m dis 1980), Audrey Booth; 2 s (Howard Michael b 1965, David Mathew b 1968); m 2, 1983, Pamela Elaine Leather; *Career* professional journalist 1951-60, fndr Mercury Press Agency Ltd1960, fndr and md Radio City plc 1973 to present, chm Broadcast Mktg Servs Ltd, dir Ind Radio News Ltd, dir Satellite Media Servs Ltd; dir Liverpool Empire Theatre Tst Ltd; *Recreations* football, golf, winter sports; *Clubs* Royal Liverpool Golf, Liverpool Artists, Liverpool Raquet; *Style*— Terence Smith, Esq; PO Box 194, Liverpool L69 ILD (☎ 051 227 5100)

SMITH, Hon Timothy Hamilton; s of late 2 Baron Colwyn; *b* 1944; *Educ* Cheltenham, Oxford Univ (MA); *m* 1967, Carolyn, da of Bernulf Llewelyn Hodge, MRCS, LRCP, of The Old Cottage, Jac-na-Pare, Polperro, S Cornwall; 2 da; *Style*— The Hon Timothy Smith; 45 Third Ave, Claremont 7700, S Africa

SMITH, Timothy John; MP (C) Beaconsfield 1982-; s of late Capt Norman Wesley Smith, CBE (sometime Cdre Orient Steam Navigation Co), and Nancy Phyllis, da of Engr Capt F J Pedrick, RN; *b* 5 Oct 1947; *Educ* Harrow, St Peter's Coll Oxford (MA, pres Oxford Univ Cons Assoc 1968); *m* 1980, Jennifer Jane, da of Maj Sir James Scott-Hopkins, MEP, *qv*; 2 s (Henry b 1982, Charles b 1984); *Career* articled Gibson Harris & Turnbull 1969-71, sr auditor Peat Marwick Mitchell 1971-73, co sec Coubro and Scrutton Hldgs 1973-79, sec Parly and Law Ctee Inst of CAs 1979-82, MP Ashfield April 1977-79, pps to Rt Hon Leon Brittan 1983-85; memb Public Accounts ctee 1987-; FCA; *Style*— Timothy Smith, Esq, MP; 27 Rosenau Cres, London SW11; House of Commons, London SW1 (☎ 01 219 3000)

SMITH, Prof Trevor Arthur; s of Arthur James Smith, of Newnham-on-Severn, Gloucs, and Vera Gladys, *née* Cross; *b* 14 June 1937; *Educ* LSE (BSc); *m* 1, 14 Feb 1960 (m dis 1973), Brenda Susan, da of George William Francis Eustace; 2 s (Adam James William b 6 June 1964, Gideon Matthew Kingsley b 14 May 1966); m 2, 9 Aug 1979, Julia Dannithorne, *née* Bullock; 1 da (Naomi Thérése b 8 June 1981);; *Career* schoolteacher LCC 1958-59, temp asst lectr Exeter Univ 1959-60, res offr Acton Soc Tst 1960-62, lectr in politics Hull Univ 1962-67; QMC London: lectr (later sr lectr) in political studies 1967-83, head of dept 1972-85, dean of social studies 1979-82, prof 1983-, pro-princ 1985-87, sr pro-princ 1987-; visiting assoc prof California State Univ Los Angeles 1969; dir: Job Ownership Ltd 1978-85, New Society Ltd 1986-, Statesman and Nation Publishing Co Ltd 1988-; chm: Joseph Rowntree Social Serv Tst 1987-, Political Studies Assoc of UK 1988-; govr: Sir John Cass and Redcoats Sch 1979-84, Univ of Haifa 1985-, Bell Educn Tst 1988-; memb Tower Hamlets DHA 1987-; vice pres Patients Assoc 1988-, Parly Candidate (Lib) Lewisham West 1959; FRHistS; *Clubs* Reform; *Style*— Prof Trevor Smith; Queen Mary College, University of London, Mile End Rd, London E1 4NS, (☎ 01 980 4811, fax 01 981 7517, telex 893750)

SMITH, Hon Mrs (Vera Lesley Meryl); *née* West; da of Baron Granville-West (Life Peer); *b* 1937; *m* 1959, William Smith; children; *Style*— The Hon Mrs Smith; Hollycroft, Sunnybank Rd, Griffithstown, Monmouthshire

SMITH, Adm Sir Victor Alfred Trumper; AC (1975), KBE (1969, CBE 1963), CB (1968), DSC (1941); s of George Smith (d 1959), and Una Margaret, *née* Trumper (d 1971); *b* 9 May 1913; *Educ* Chatswood Sch, RAN Coll; *m* 1944, Nanette Suzanne, da of Charles Reginald Harrison (d 1925); 3 s; *Career* joined RAN 1927, Chief of Naval Personnel 1962-64, Chief of Naval Supply 1964-66, Flag Offr Cmdg HM Aust Fleet 1966, dep Chief of Naval Staff 1967, Vice Adm 1968, chief of Naval Staff 1968-70, Adm 1970, Chm Chiefs of Naval Staff Ctee 1970-75, ret; *see Debrett's Handbook of Australia and New Zealand for further details*; *Style*— Adm Sir Victor Smith, AC, KBE, CB, DS; 15 Fishburn St, Red Hill, ACT 2603, Australia (☎ 062 95 8942)

SMITH, William Finch; s of William Frederich Smith (d 1968), of 50 Stoey Lane, Winchester, Hants, and Mary Janet, *née* Melton (d 1971); *b* 16 April 1916; *Educ* Borough Poly, Croydon Poly; *m* 30 June 1941, Edith Theresa (d 1982), da of Charles Charlwood (d 1970), of Leeford Place, Whatlington, E Sussex; 2 s (Peter b 1946, Alan b 1950); *Career* WWII memb HG, res occupation instrument mfrs; ptnr (ret) F J Samuely 19560 (engr 1946-53, chief engr 1953-56); maj projects incl: Hatfield Tech Coll maj precast bldg, Slough Hosp, Battle Hosp, St Thomas' stage 1 and residential blocks, St Thomas Stage 1 residential blocks and Stage 2 library Trinity Coll Dublin, Kuwait housing, Newcastle shopping centre, Wakefield shopping centre, banks for Saudi Arabian Monetary Banks of Damman Rehad and Jeddah; Fell Inst Welding 1959, FIStructE 1964, memb Assoc Conslt Engrs 1964, memb Civil Engrs 1968; *Style*— William Smith, Esq; Beech House, Stonestile Lane, Hastings, E Sussex (☎ 0424 752 168)

SMITH, Dr William Leggat; CBE (1988), MC (1944), TD (1945),; s of Rev Dr William James Smith (d 1953), and Isabella, *née* Leggat (d 1969); *b* 30 Jan 1918; *Educ* Glasgow Acad, Queen's Coll Oxford (BA), Glasgow Univ (LLB); *m* 10 Oct 1941, Yvonne Menna, da of Arthur Williams, JP, High Sheriff of Carmarthenshire; 1 s, 2 da (Lindsay, Deborah (Mrs Walker), Alison (Mrs Ferguson)); *Career* WWII 1939-46, cmmnd TA The Cameronians served France, USA, Holland, Germany, demobbed as Maj 1946; admitted slr 1948, ptnr Carruthers Gemmill 1948-87; dean Royal Faculty of Procurators 1977-79; Deacon Convenor Glasgow 1964-65; govr: Glasgow Acad War Memorial Tst 1962-80 (chm 1972-80), Glasgow Sch of Art 1967-88 (chm 1975-88); chm: Trades Hall of Glasgow Tst 1977-87, The Charles Rennie Macintosh Soc, Cumbernauld New Town Licensing Planning Ctee 1979, Royal Soc for the Relief of Indigent Gentlewomen of Scotland; LLD Glasgow 1987, OStJ 1965; *Clubs* Western (Glasgow), RSAC; *Style*— Dr W Leggat Smith, CBE, MC, DL; Clachan of Campsie, Glasgow

SMITH-BINGHAM, Col Jeremy David; s of Col Oswald Cyril Smith-Bingham (d 1979), of Glos, and Vera Mabel Johnson; *b* 29 July 1939; *Educ* Eton, Sandhurst; *m* 22 July 1969, Priscilla Mary, da of Lt-Col Godfrey Sturdy Incledon-Webber TD (d 1985); 3 s (Richard David b 1970, Alexander John b 1973, Guy Jeremy b 1978); *Career* cmmnd Royal Horse Gds (The Blues) 1959, served England, Cyprus, N Ireland, Germany, CO The Blues and Royals 1982-85; *Recreations* skiing, tennis, squash, water sports, riding; *Clubs* Whites, Cavalry; *Style*— Col Jeremy Smith-Bingham; St Brannocks House, Braunton, Devon EX33 1HN (☎ 0271 812 270); HQ Northern Army Group, BFPO460, (☎ 01049 2161 47 5472)

SMITH-CARINGTON, Wing Cdr John Hanbury; AFC (1953), DL (Leics 1972); s of Hamo Folville Smith-Carington (d 1946); *b* 26 Oct 1921; *Educ* Harrow, Oriel Coll Oxford; *m* 1951, Noreen, *née* Magee; 1 da; *Career* RAF 1941-71 (ret Wing Cdr), asst Air Attache Poland 1957-59, Mil and Air Attache Denmark 1965-68, Insp Serv Attaches 1970-71, chm Parish Cncl and District Cncllr 1972-, memb Borough Cncl 1972-79, dir Leics Red Cross 1972-, E Leics Community Health Cncl 1973-79, memb Leics Ctee Country Landowners 1973- (centl cncl 1985-), high sheriff Leics 1982-83; chm E Midlands Heraldic Soc 1982-; pres Leics Assoc of Parish Cncls 1985-; chm local Cons Branch 1985-; patron Leics History Soc 1985-; vice-pres Leics Record Off; memb Exec ctee Leics Rural Community Cncl 1985-; *Recreations* country pursuits; *Clubs* RAF, Leics, Far and Near; *Style*— Wing Cdr John Smith-Carington, AFC, DL; Ashby Folville Lodge, nr Melton Mowbray, Leics (☎ 066 64 840293); office: Red Cross House, 244 London Rd, Leicester (☎ 0533 705087)

SMITH-COX, (Sidney) Clifton; CBE (1963), TD (1947), JP (1955); s of Sidney Cox, JP (d 1949), of Bristol, and Ada Beatrice, *née* Smith (d 1939); *b* 8 Feb 1911; *Educ* Clifton; *m* 1, Margot, *née* Randal; 1 s (Geoffrey Randal b 7 April 1933); m 2, 10 May 1943, Marjorie Joyce, da of Frank Lawrence Playford (d 1976), of Newmarket; 1 s (Peter b 15 Aug 1947); *Career* WWII Lt Col areas of operation Malaya and Normandy; CA; chm Mount Charlotte Investmts plc and subsidiary companies (head office) Leeds (dir 1944 of one company, now part of Mount Charlotte and subsequently varying other companies at different dates through the years; pres: Bristol Zoological Soc, Dudley Zoological Soc; FCA, FHC, IMI, CBIM; *Recreations* swimming, walking, golf; *Style*— Sidney Smith-Cox, Esq, CBE, TD, JP; Westward Ho, 27 Edgehill Road, Walton St Mary, Clevedon BS21 7BZ (☎ 0272 8724550); 2 The Calls, Leeds LS2 2JU (☎ 0532 439111, fax 0532 465008, telex 557934)

SMITH-DODSWORTH, David John; s and h of Sir John Smith-Dodsworth, 8 Bt; *b* 23 Oct 1963; *Educ* Ampleforth; *Career* farmer; *Style*— David Smith-Dodsworth, Esq; Thornton Watlass Hall, Ripon, Yorkshire

SMITH-DODSWORTH, Sir John (Christopher); 8 Bt (GB 1784) of Newland Park, Yorks; s of Sir Claude Matthew Smith-Dodsworth, 7 Bt (d 1940); *b* 4 Mar 1935; *Educ* Ampleforth; *m* 1961, Margaret Anne, da of Alfred Jones, of Pludds, Glos; 1 s, 1 da; *Heir* s, David Smith-Dodsworth; *Style*— Sir John Smith-Dodsworth, Bt; Thornton Watlass Hall, Ripon, Yorks

SMITH-DORRIEN-SMITH, Lady Emma; *see*: Dorrien-Smith

SMITH-GORDON, Sir (Lionel) Eldred Peter; 5 Bt (UK 1838); s of Sir Lionel Eldred Pottinger Smith-Gordon, 4 Bt (d 1976); *b* 7 May 1935; *Educ* Eton, Trinity Coll Oxford; *m* 1962, Sandra Rosamund Ann, da of late Wing Cdr Walter Farley, DFC; 1 s, 1 da; *Heir* s, Lionel Smith-Gordon; *Style*— Sir Eldred Smith-Gordon, Bt; 13 Shalcomb St, London SW10 (☎ 01 352 8506)

SMITH-GORDON, Lionel George Eldred; s and h of Sir Eldred Smith-Gordon, 5 Bt; *b* 1 July 1964; *Educ* Eton, Westfield Coll and King's Coll Univ of London; *Career* with J P Morgan 1986-; *Clubs* Hurlingham; *Style*— Lionel Smith-Gordon, Esq; Flat 4, 48/50 Harrington Gardens, London SW7 4LT (☎ 01 373 6206)

SMITH-MARRIOTT, Sir Hugh Cavendish; 11 Bt (GB 1774), of Sydling, St Nicholas, Dorset; s (by 1 m) of Sir Ralph Smith-Marriott, 10 Bt; *b* 22 Mar 1925; *Educ* Bristol Cathedral Sch; *m* 1953, Pauline Anne (d 1985), da of Frank Fawcett Holt of Bristol; 1 da (d 1985); *Heir* bro, Peter Francis b 1927; *Clubs* Gloucetterphir CCC, MCC; *Style*— Sir Hugh Smith-Marriott, Bt; 26 Shipley Rd, Westbury-on-Trym, Bristol BS9 3HS

SMITH-RYLAND, Charles Mortimer Tollemache; DL (Warwicks 1955), JP; s of Charles Ivor Philipson Smith-Ryland (d 1929), of Barford Hill Warwick by his w Leila Mary (d 1971), da of late Capt Hon Mortimer Granville Tollemache; *b* 24 May 1927; *Educ* Eton; *m* 1952, Hon Jeryl Marcia Sarah, only da of Hon Robert Brampton Gurdon (decd), of Grundisburgh Hall Suffolk, and sister of 3 Baron Cranworth; 2 s (Robin, David), 3 da (Sarah, Joanna, Petra); *Career* landowner and farmer; Lt Coldstream Gds 1945-48; Warwick CC 1949-74; vice-chm Warwichshire Police Ctee 1963-69, chm Warwichshire and Coventry Police Authority 1969-74, chm Cncl RASE 1976-, High Sheriff Warwicks 1967-68 (Lord-Lt 1967-); *Recreations* shooting, golf; *Clubs* White's; *Style*— Charles Smith-Ryland, JP; Sherbourne, Warwick (☎ 0926 624 255); 50E Cornwall Gardens (☎ 937 6276); Estate Office, Sherbourne, Warwick (☎ 0926 624215)

SMITH-RYLAND, Hon Mrs (Jeryl Marcia Sarah); *née* Gurdon; raised to rank of a Baron's da 1964; da of late Hon Robert Brampton Gurdon (s of 2 Baron Cranworth) and Hon Daisy, *née* Pearson, da of 2 Viscount Cowdray and subsequently w of (1) Lt-Col Alistair Gibb and (2) 1 Baron McCorquodale of Newton; sis of 3 Baron Cranworth; *b* 1932; *m* 1952, Charles Mortimer Tollemache Smith-Ryland; 2 s, 3 da; *Career* CStJ 1981; *Style*— The Hon Mrs Smith-Ryland; Sherbourne Park, Warwick CV35 8AP

SMITHERS, Andrew Reeve Waldron; s of Prof Sir David Smithers, MD, FRCP, FRCS, FRCR, of Ringfield, Knockholt, Kent, and Gwladys Margaret Smithers, *née* Angel: gs of Sir Waldron Smithers MP for 30 yrs Chiselhurst and Orpington; *b* 21 Sept 1937; *Educ* Winchester, Clare Coll Cambridge (MA); *m* 8 June 1963, Amanda Jill, da of E G Kennedy, Esq, of Chirton Wilts; 2 s (Matthew Pelham b 10 Oct 1964, Jonathan Kit b 6 Dec 1967); *Career* chm Whatman Reeve Angel plc 1967-, (dir 1961-); dir S G Warburg, Akroyd, Rowe & Pitman, Mullens Securities Ltd (1965); chm Mercury Common Mkt Tst Ltd (dir 1972-); dept chm Mercury Transatlantic Tst; *Recreations* reading, conversation, cricket; *Clubs* Brooks's, Yokohama Cricket; *Style*— Mr Andrew Smithers; c/o S G Warburg Securities (Japan) Inc, New Edobashi Bldg, 1-7-2 Nihonbashi-Honcho, Tokyo

SMITHERS, David Leonard O'Meara; MBE (1945); s of Brig Leonard Sueton Smithers, CB (d 1954), and Grace Margaret, *née* O'Meara (d 1966); *b* 9 May 1917; *Educ* Downside, Pembroke Coll Oxford (MA, BPhil); *Career* WWII 1939-46, Maj RCS, served SOE and Germany; barr Lincoln's Inn 1955; chm Castle Cary and dist branch Royal Br Legion; legal advsr Depts of Tport and the environment, asst treasy slr ret 1982; City of London Livery of Worshipful Co of Turners 1953 (Ct of Assistants 1969, Renter Warden 1974, Upper Warden 1975, Master 1976); memb Royal Dublin Soc; Medaille d'Argent Assoc Nationale des Anciens combattants SR 1985; *Recreations* golf, snooker, rowing, Greek and Roman Lit (Ancient); *Clubs* Woking Golf, Royal Dublin Golf, Lahinch Golf, Special Forces, Naval and Military, Leander, and Kildare Street and University; *Style*— David Smithers, Esq, MBE; Little Sark, Ansford, Castle Cary, Somerset (☎ 0963 507 58)

SMITHERS, Prof Sir David Waldron; s of Sir Waldron Smithers, JP, MP (d 1954); *b* 17 Jan 1908; *Educ* Charterhouse, Clare Coll Cambridge; *m* 1933, Gwladys Margaret, *née* Angel; 1 s, 1 da; *Career* prof radiotherapy Inst of Cancer Res and Royal Marsden Hosp 1943-72, hon conslt radiotherapist Brompton Hosp Diseases of the Chest and to the RN; Kt Cdr SMOM 1972; Kt 1969; *Books* Jane Austen in Kent (1982), Dickens's

Doctors (1979); *Recreations* book collecting, growing roses, arts; *Style*— Prof Sir David Smithers; Ringfield, Knockholt, Kent (☎ 0959 32122)

SMITHERS, Sir Peter Henry Berry Otway; VRD and clasp; s of Lt-Col H O Smithers, JP, of Itchen Stoke House; *b* 9 Dec 1913; *Educ* Harrow, Magdalen Coll Oxford (MA, DPhil); *m* 1943, Dojean, da of T M Sayman of St Louis, USA; 2 da; *Career* RNVR WWII (Lt Cdr; naval staff France, Br Embassy Washington, Mexico, Central American Republics, Panama); barr Inner Temple 1946, memb Winchester RDC 1946-49; MP (C) Winchester 1950-64, PPS to: Min state Colonial Affrs 1952, sec state Colonies 1956-59, vice-chm Cons Parly Foreign Affrs Ctee 1959-61, Parly under-sec state FO 1962-64; del Consultative Assembly Cncl of Europe 1952-56, UK del to UN Gen Assembly 1960-62, sec-gen Cncl of Europe 1964-69; Master Worshipful Co of Turners 1955, sr fell UN Inst for Trg and Res 1969-72; hon DJur Zurich 1969, Alexander von Humboldt Gold Medal 1970, chev de la Légion Honneur, Aguila Azteca Mexicana, Medal of the Parly Assembly of the Cncl of Europe 1984; Royal Hort Soc's Gold Medal (3) and Grenfell Medal for Photography Sixteen one man shows of photography in Museums and Galleries in the US and Europe; kt 1970 Galleries in the US and Europe; kt 1970; *Books* Life of Joseph Addison; *Recreations* gardening; *Clubs* Carlton, Everglades (Palm Beach), Bath & Tennis (Palm Beach); *Style*— Sir Peter Smithers, VRD; CH-6911, Vico Morcote, Switzerland

SMITHERS, Sir Reginald Allfree; s of F Smithers; *b* 3 Feb 1903; *Educ* Melbourne GS, Melbourne Univ (LLB); *m* 1932, Dorothy, da of J Smalley; 2 s, 1 da; *Career* served RAAF Australia, New Guinea, Philippines 1942-45, Sqdn Ldr; liaison offr Gen MacArthur's Publicity Section; QC 1951, judge of Supreme Ct Papua New Guinea 1962-64, additional judge Supreme Ct of ACT and Supreme Ct of NT 1964-, judge Aust Indust Ct 1965-, dep pres Admin Appeals Tribunal 1977-80, judge of Fed Ct of Australia 1977-86; chm Victorian Bar Cncl 1959-60, pres Young Nationalists Orgn of Victoria 1959-, chllr La Trove Univ Melbourne 1972-80; kt 1980; *see Debrett's Handbook of Australia and New Zealand for further details*; *Style*— Sir Reginald Smithers; 11 Florence Ave, Kew, Vic 3101, Australia

SMITHIE, Jonathan Maxwell Stanley; *b* 26 Sept 1936; *Educ* Lancing, Brasenose Coll Oxford; *Career* sr ptnr Cawood Smithie & Co; *Style*— J M S Smithie, Esq; Cawood Smithie & Co, Stockbrokers, 22 East Parade, Harrogate, N Yorks HG1 5LT (☎ 0423 66781)

SMITHIES, Frederick Albert; s of Frederick Albert (d 1981), of Lancashire, and Lilian, *née* Pate; *b* 12 May 1929; *Educ* St Mary's Coll Lancashire, St Mary's Coll Twickenham; *m* 1960, Olga Margaret, da of Frederick Yates (d 1960); *Career* sch teacher: Lancashire 1948-60, Northampton 1960-76; gen sec Nat Assoc of Schoolmasters and Union of Women Teachers 1983 (asst gen sec 1976-80, dep gen sec 1980-83); *Recreations* walking, reading, music and theatre; *Style*— Frederick Smithies, Esq; 22 Upper Brook St, London W1 (☎ 01 629 3916)

SMITHIES, Jeremy Charles Stewart Fulford; s of Harry Fulford (names changed by deed poll), and Nancy Barbara, *née* Smithies (d 1970); *b* 10 May 1947; *Educ* Giggleswick, Poly of Central London (BSc), Open Univ (BA); *m* 8 May 1971, Mary Helen, da of Xavier Philip Mary Spruyt de Bay (d 1983), of Bath; 1 s (Roland b 1973), 1 da (Frances b 1976); *Career* fndr memb & vice chm Channel Islands MENSA 1974; Engrg Medal 1982; AMIMechE; *Recreations* croquet, theatre; *Clubs* Bath Croquet; *Style*— Jeremy Smithies, Esq; 20 Longfellow Ave, Bath BA2 4SJ; Rolls-Royce plc, PO Box 3, Filton Bristol BS12 7QE (☎ 0272 791234, telex 44185, fax 0272 798005)

SMITHSON, Peter Denham; s of William Blenkiron Smithson (d 1974), and Elizabeth, *née* Denham (d 1978); *b* 18 Sept 1923; *Educ* The Gs Stock-on-Tees, The Sch of Architecture Univ of Durham Newcastle-upon-Tyne, Royal Acad Schs London; *m* 18 Aug 1949, Alison Margaret, da of Ernest Gill (d 1980); 1 s (Simon), 2 da (Samantha Target, Soraya Wilson); *Career* RE 1942-45; architect in private practice; maj projects incl: Hunstanton Secdy Modern Sch 1950-54, The Economist Bldg St James St 1959-64, Robin Hood Gdns Tower Hamlets 1963-72, Garden Bldg St Hildas Coll Oxford 1967-70, Second Arts Bldg 1978-81 and Amenity Bldg 1978-85 Univ of Bath, Sch of Architecture and Bldg Engrg Univ of Bath 1982-87; visiting prof: Delft, Munich, Harvard; currently at Univ of Bath; memb The Boltons Assoc; *Books* The Shift (1982), The 30's (1985), Upper Lawn (1986); with Alison Smithson: Ordinariness and Light (1970), Without Rhetoric (1973); *Style*— Peter Smithson, Esq; The Limes, Off Priory Walk, London SW10 9SP; Cato Lodge, 24 Gilston Rd, London SW10 9SR (☎ 01 373 7423)

SMITHWICK, Lt Cdr Robert Standish; s of Canon Frederick Standish Smithwick (Chaplain to the Forces, d 1962), of Youghal House, Nenagh, Ireland, and Violet, *née* Odlum (d 1922); *b* 17 August 1918; *Educ* Haileybury, RN; *m* 12 April 1947, Rosemary, da of George Sherriff, CBE (d 1949), of Stirling; 1 s (Michael b 1949), 1 da (Belinda b 1960); *Career* RN 1936-58, WWII destroyers: Atlantic, North Sea, Indian Ocean; cmd Loch Veyatie and Wrangler 1946-50, Staff Course 1950, Br Naval Mission to Greece, 1 Lt HMS Vanguard's last sea-going cmmn 1953-55, ret 1958; fndr Crookham Ct Sch Newbury 1961, ret 1977; *Recreations* golf, painting, cooking; *Style*— Lt Cdr Robert Smithwick, RN; 18 Canal Walk, Hungerford, Berks RG17 0EQ (☎ 0488 83363)

SMITS, Benjamin Arthur; s of Arthur Charles Smits, of 5 Woodlands Way, St Ives, nr Ringwood, Hants, and Laurance Maria, *née* Panjoul; *b* 21 Sept 1934; *Educ* Watford GS, Watford Coll of FE; *m* 1, 14 Feb 1958 (m dis 1986), Ann,*née* Jarvis; 2 s (David Charles b 30 June 1959, Jeremy Paul b 19 Nov 1960), 1 da (Joanna Louise b 3 July 1965); m 2, 16 April 1988, Monica Mary, da of Thomas Dempsey (d 1970), of Dublin; *Career* Nat Serv RAF 1952-54; sales and mktg dir Courtaulds hosiery div (Hinckley Gp) 1964-73, sales dir Pretty Polly Ltd 1973-84, jt md GT Mktg Ltd 1984-87, (sales and mktg dir 1987-88), md Bear Brand Hosiery Ltd 1988-; represented Herts CC Athletics 1956-57; MInstM 1965; *Recreations* reading, gardening, music; *Style*— Benjamin Smits, Esq; 27 Grasmere Drive, Linton Croft, Wetherby, W Yorks LS11 4GP, (☎ 0937 65745); Bear Brand Hosiery Ltd, Allerton Rd, Woolton, Liverpool L25 7SF, (☎ 051 428 1291, fax 051 428 7320, car phone 0860 828801, telex 627209)

SMOLLETT OF BONHILL; *see*: Telfer-Smollett of Bonhill

SMYLY, Hon Mrs (Harriet Lucy); *née* Beckett; da of 4 Baron Grimthorpe, OBE; *b* 18 Feb 1961; *Educ* Heathfield; *m* 1985, Capt Mark Smyly; *Career* interior decorator; *Recreations* skiing, racing; *Style*— The Hon Mrs Smyly; Kingwood House, Lambourne, nr Newbury, Berks RG16 7RS

SMYLY, (Cecil) William; s of Philip Austin Smyly (d 1968); *b* 29 April 1928; *Educ* Aldenham; *m* 1955, Fiona Daphne, *née* Wilson; 4 children; *Career* sales consultant OUP, town and dist cncllr govr and coll govr; *Recreations* sports generally, tennis particularly (Wimbledon umpire); *Clubs* National, Victory; *Style*— William Smyly Esq; Pathways, Grenofen, Tavistock, Devon (☎ 0822 61239)

SMYTH, Christopher Jackson; s of Col Edward Hugh Jackson Smyth, of 29 Castle Street, Farnham, Surrey, and Ursula Helen Lucy, *née* Ross (d 1984); *b* 9 August 1946; *Educ* St Lawrence Coll, Trinity Hall Cambridge (MA); *m* 9 Dec 1972, Jane Elizabeth, da of Dr Robert Alexander Porter (d 1981); 3 s (Debbie b 1976, Sophie b 1979, Amanda b 1982); *Career* Lt RN 1966-76; Lt Cdr Sussex Div RNR 1978-82; barr Inner Temple 1972, practice SE circuit; *Recreations* sailing; *Clubs* Army and Navy; *Style*— Christopher Smyth, Esq; Ridge House, Kingston, Lewes, East Sussex BN7 3JX (☎ 0273 480 075); 1 Crown Office Row, Temple, London EC4Y 7HH (☎ 01 353 1801, fax 01 583 1700, telex 24988 ICOR G)

SMYTH, Frances, Lady; Frances Mary Blair; da of Lt-Col Robert Alexander Chambers, OBE, IMS (decd), and Elsie Blair Saunders (decd); *b* 30 Jan 1908; *Educ* St Georges Harpenden; *m* 1, Lt-Col J E Read, IA (dec'd), 1 s (Charles), 1 da (Mary); m 2, 1940, as his 2 w, Brig Rt Hon Sir John George Smyth, Bt, VC, MC (d 1983); *Style*— Frances, Lady Smyth; 603 Grenville House, Dolphin Sq, London SW1V 3LR

SMYTH, His Hon Judge James Robert Staples; s of Maj Robert Smyth, of Gaybrook, Mullingar, Co Westmeath (d 1952); and Mabel Anne Georgiana, *née* MacGeough-Bond (d 1985); *b* 11 July 1926; *Educ* St Columba's Coll Dublin, Merton Coll Oxford (BA, MA); *m* 3 April 1971, Fenella Joan, da of Ian Blair Mowat of Bridge of Weir, Renfrewshire; 1 s (Ralph b 1976); *Career* serv WWII RAF; barr Inner Temple 1949; resident Magistrate Northern Rhodesia 1951-55; dep chm Agric Land Tribunal, 1974; Stipendiary Magistrate West Midlands 1978; rec of the Crown Court 1983; appt circuit Judge 1986; *Recreations* shooting, fishing; *Style*— His Hon Judge Robert Smyth; Leys, Shelsley Beauchamp, Worcester WR6 6RB (☎ 088 65 291)

SMYTH, John Clifford; TD; s of Harold Smyth, of Liverpool, and Alice, *née* Halsall; *b* 22 August 1920; *Educ* Liverpool Collegiate; *m* 29 Nov 1944, Norah Myfanwy, da of Percival J Powell, of Caslte Donington, Leics; 1 s ((John) Rodney b 23 Aug 1953); *Career* RA (TA) 1939-56:87 (1 West Lancs) FD Regt, 136 (1 West Lancs) FD Regt, 287 (1 West Lancs) Medium Regt (despatches 1946); slr; ptnr: Weightman Pedder & Co 1949-70, Weightmans 1970-88, Weightman Rutherfords 1988-; chm Wirral UDC 1973-74 (cncllr 1963-74), co cncllr Merseyside CC 1976-86; pres and chm Royal Sch For Blind Liverpool 1955- (memb ctee 1951-); former: chm Abbeyfield Heswall, vice-pres Heswall cncl voluntary Serv; memb ctee Heswall Soc 1960-; memb Law Soc; *Clubs* Racquet (Liverpool); *Style*— John Smyth, Esq; Chestnut Cottage, 67 Thurstaton Rd, Heswall, Wirral, Merseyside L60 6SA (☎ 051 342 3475); Weightman Rutherfords, Richmond House, Rumford Place, Liverpool L3 9QW (☎ 051 227 2601, fax 051 227 3223, telex 627538)

SMYTH, Maj John Montagu (Monty); MBE (1983); s of Capt John Robert Henry Smyth (d 1938), of The Manor House, Fladbury, Pershore, Worcestershire, and Elizabeth, *née* Stone (d 1945); *b* 18 Feb 1905; *Educ* Charterhouse, RMC; *m* 22 April 1936, Rosamund May, da of Maj William Harker (d 1950), of Blofield Hall, Norwich, Norfolk; 1 da (Margaret Ann (Mrs Humphries)); *Career* joined Norfolk Regt 1924, Adj Depot 1935-36, Adj and QM The Royal Militia Island of Jersey 1936-40, Maj 1941, POW Malaya 1942-45, ret 1946; vice-chm and vice pres S Worcs Cons Assoc 1946-; memb: Fladbury PC 1946-50 (and chm), Pershore RDC 1946-50 (vice-chm 1948-50), Hawley Castle PCC 1951-65, Upton on Severn RDC 1967-73, Worcs CC 1967-71, for Upton on Severn, Hereford and Worcester CC 1973-85; govr of three sch's, chm Guarlford PC, Lasletts Tstee, memb CLA Co Ctee; High Sheriff Worcestershire 1966; memb Three Co's Agric Soc, life govr RASE; *Recreations* shooting, travel; *Clubs* Army and Navy; *Style*— Maj J M Smyth, MBE; 19 Upton Gdns, Upton on Severn, Worcester WR8 0NU (☎ 06846 4488)

SMYTH, The Rev (William) Martin; MP (UU) Belfast South, March 1982-; s of James Smyth, JP, of 40 Ardenlee Ave, Belfast (d 1982), and Minnie Kane; *b* 15 June 1931; *Educ* Methodist Coll Belfast, Magee Univ Coll Londonderry, Trinity Coll Dublin (BA, BD), Presbyterian Coll Belfast; *m* 1957, Kathleen Jean, da of David Johnston (d 1978), of Ballymatoskerty, Toomebridge; 2 da (and 1 da decd); *Career* ordained Presbyterian Church 1957, installed Alexandra (Belfast) 1963-82, minister without charge April 1982; grand master: Grand Orange Lodge of Ireland 1972-, World Orange Cncl 1973-82; hon dep grand master Orange Order: USA, New Zealand, New South Wales; hon past grand master Canada; elected NI Assembly Oct 1982-86, chm of Assembly Health and Social Services Ctee; UU Pty spokesman on health, social services; vice-chm All Party Ctee on Soviet Jewry; memb: British Executive IPU 1985-, Social Servs Select Ctee; *Recreations* reading, photography, travel; *Style*— The Rev Martin Smyth, MP; 6 Mornington, Annadale Ave, Belfast BT7 3JS, N Ireland; office: 117 Cregagh Rd, Belfast BT6 0LA, N Ireland (☎ 0232 457009); House of Commons, London SW1 (☎ 01 219 4198)

SMYTH, Hon Mrs (Patricia Margaret); da of Baron Black (Life Peer) (d 1984), and his w Margaret Patricia (d 1976), da of James Dallas, of Dundee; *b* 26 June 1919; *m* 1942, Leslie John Smyth 1 s (Timothy), 2 da (Tessa, Lesley-Anne); *Style*— The Hon Mrs Smyth; Goudie's Farm, Lower Hamswell, Bath, Avon BA1 9DE

SMYTH, (John) Rodney; s of John Clifford Smyth, of Heswall, Merseyside, and Norah Myfannwy, *née* Powell; *b* 23 August 1953; *Educ* Shrewsbury, Magdalene Coll Cambridge (MA); *Career* barr 1975-79; asst slr: Holman Fenwick & Willan 1980-82, Lovell White Durrant (formerly Durrant Piesse) 1982-85 (ptnr 1985-); memb Law Soc; *Recreations* birdwatching, paintings; *Style*— Rodney Smyth, Esq; Dingley Dell, Stoke, Rochester, Kent ME3 9SE (☎ 0634 270 326); Lovell White Durrant, 73 Cheapside, London EC2V 6ER (☎ 01 236 0066, fax 01 236 0084, telex 919014 LWD G)

SMYTH, Sir Timothy John; 2 Bt (UK 1956), of Teignmouth, Co Devon; s of Julian Smyth (d 1974, himself 2 s of Brig Rt Hon Sir John Smyth, 1 Bt, VC, MC, PC (d 1983)), and his 1 w Margaret; *b* 16 April 1953; *Educ* Univ of NSW (MB BS, LLB, MBA); *m* 1981, Bernadette Mary, da of Leo Askew; 2 s, 2 da; *Heir* s, Brendan Julian Smyth (b 1981); *Career* hosp mangr; *Style*— Dr Sir Timothy Smyth, Bt; 21 King St, Sydney, NSW 2031, Australia

SMYTH-TYRRELL, Anthony James; *Career* chm Baxter Fell Northfleet Ltd (mfr of modular shopfitting equipment, supplied in kit form for easy assembly by local unskilled labour; Queen's Award for Export 1982); *Style*— Anthony Smyth-Tyrrell, Esq; Baxter Fell Northfleet Ltd, Tower Works, Lower Rd, Gravesend, Kent DA11 9BE (☎ 01 828 5656)

SNAGGE, Maj Carron Edward Mordaunt; s of Maj Ralph Mordaunt Snagge, MBE,

TD, of Folly Hill, 10 Baring Rd, Cowes, IOW PO31 8DA, and Pamela Mordaunt, *née* Scrimgeour; *b* 23 June 1951; *Educ* Eton; *m* 15 Dec 1973, Jennifer Anne, da of (John) Dugald Thomson, of 11/107 Darling Point Rd, Darling Point, Sydney 2027, New South Wales, Australia; 1 s ((Thomas) Henry Dugald b 15 April 1984), 2 da (Emily Jane b 20 Aug 1977, Jemima Alice b 8 May 1979); *Career* Cadet Mons OCS 1970, 2 Lt 1 Bn Royal Creek Jackets (IRGJ) Germany and NI 1971, Platoon Cdr Jr Infantrymen's Bn Shorncliffe 1972, Lt Reg Careers Course Sandhurst 1974, Capt IRGJ Dover, NI, Cyprus, Hong Kong 1975, Adj Rifle Depot Winchester 1979, Maj Co Cdr Rifle Depot 1980, student Australian Cmd and Staff Coll 1983, Co Cdr IRGJ Falkland Islands Tidworth 1984, Co's Br Forces Belize 1986, 2 i/c IRGJ Germany; Freeman City of London 1972, Liveryman Worshipful Co of Skinners 1978; *Recreations* sailing, sub aqua diving, hill walking; *Clubs* Royal Yacht Sqdn, Pratt's, Army and Navy; *Style*— Maj Carron Snagge; 1 Bn Royal Green Jackets, Mercer Barracks, BFPO 36

SNAGGE, John Derrick Mordaunt; OBE (1945); s of His Hon Sir Mordaunt Snagge (d 1956), and Gwendaline Rose Emily Colomb (d 1968); ancestor Sir Thomas Snagge (d 1593), Serjeant-at-Law and Speaker of the House of Commons 1588, Lord of the Manor of Marston Morteyne which came to Mr John Snagge upon the death of his brother in 1984; *b* 8 May 1904; *Educ* Winchester, Pembroke Coll Oxford; *m* 1, 1936, Eileen Mary Joscelyne (d 1980); m 2, 1983, Joan Mary, da of William Wilson (d 1961), of Greenisland, Co Antrim; *Career* broadcaster; asst station dir BBC Stoke-on-Trent 1924, announcer London (Savoy Hill) 1928, asst Outside Broadcast Dept 1933, commentator: Oxford and Cambridge Boat Race 1931-80, Westminster Abbey for Coronation of Queen Elizabeth II 1953 (Radio); asst dir Outside Broadcasts 1939, presentation dir BBC 1939-45, head of Presentation; Home Service 1945-57, and BBC (sound) 1957-63; special duties BBC 1963-65, ret BBC 1965; chm Lord's Taverners 1956-1961 (pres 1952-1964, sec 1965-67, tstee 1970-76); *Books* Those Vintage Years of Radio (with Michael Barsley, 1972); *Recreations* fishing; *Clubs* MCC, Leander, Lord's Taverners; *Style*— John Snagge, Esq; Delgaty, Village Rd, Dorney, nr Windsor SL4 6QJ (☎ 06286 61303)

SNAGGE, Air Cmdt Dame Nancy Marion; DBE (1955), OBE (1945); da of late Henry Thomas Salmon; *b* 2 May 1906; *Educ* Notting Hill High Sch; *m* 1962, Thomas Geoffrey Mordaunt Snagge, DSC (d 1984); *Career* joined WAAF 1939, offr in the WAAF and WRAF 1939-, ADC to HM King George VI 1950-52, ADC to HM The Queen 1952-56, dir WRAF 1950-56; *Style*— Air Cmdt Dame Nancy Snagge, DBE; Test Lodge, Longstock, Stockbridge, Hampshire (☎ 0264 810558)

SNAILHAM, (George) Richard; s of Capt William Rushton Snailham (d 1942), and Mabel, *née* Wilson; *b* 18 May 1930; *Educ* Oakham Sch, Keble Coll Oxford; *Career* Nat Serv 1948-50, Duke of Wellingtons Regt, Intelligence Corps M18; schoolmaster: Alleyn Ct Sch Westcliff 1954-55, Clayesmore Sch Iwerne Minster Dorset 1955-57, Exeter Sch Devon 1957-65; sr lectr RMA Sandhurst 1965-; semi finalist Mastermind 1973, semi finalist Brain of Britain 1976, twice winner Busmans Holiday 1987; fndr memb Scientific Exploration Soc 1969 (memb cncl), pres Globetrotters Club 1977-, sec Young Explorers Trust 1984- (memb cncl), Winston Churchill Fellowship Surrey and West Sussex 1984- (memb cncl); expeditions to Ethiopia: 1966, (Blue Nile) 1968, (Dahlak Islands) 1970-71, 1972; expeditions to: Zaire River 1974-75, Ecuador 1976, Kenya (op Drake) 1980, Kenya (Op Raleigh) 1988; Mrs Patrick Ness Award RGS 1980; FRGS 1973 (memb cncl 1986-88); *Books* The Blue Nile Revealed (1970), A Giant Among Rivers (1976), Sangay Survived (1978), Normandy and Brittany (1986); *Recreations* reviewing books, giving travel and expedition talks; *Clubs* Globetrotters, Mastermind; *Style*— Richard Snailham, Esq; 4 Belmont News, Camberley, Surrey GU15 2PH (☎ 0276 63344, ext 2502)

SNAPE, Peter Charles; MP (Lab) West Bromwich E Feb 1974-; s of Thomas & Kathleen Snape; *b* 12 Feb 1942; *Educ* St Joseph's Stockport, St Winifred's Stockport; *m* 1963, Winifred Grimshaw; 2 da; *Career* former railway signalman then guard, soldier (RE & RCT), British Rail clerk; memb Cncl Europe & WEU 1975, asst govt whip 1975-77, Lord Cmmr Treasury 1977-79, oppn front bench spokesman: Def and Disarmament 1981-82, Home Affrs 1982-83, Transport Nov 1983-; *Style*— Peter Snape, Esq, MP; Dane House, Buglawton, Congleton, Cheshire (☎ 026 02 3934)

SNAPE, (Thomas) Peter; OBE (1988); s of Charles Snape (d 1961), of Leeds, and Jane Middleton (d 1956); *b* 4 June 1925; *Educ* Cockburn Sch Leeds, Exeter Coll Oxford (MA); *m* 1951, Anne Christina, da of Dr H E McColl (d 1964), of Shropshire; 1 s (Adam), 3 da (Penelope, Sarah, Virginia); *Career* gen sec Secondary Heads' Assoc and Headmasters' Conference 1983-88; formerly headmaster: King Edward VI Sch Totnes Devon 1964-83, Settle HS Yorks 1960-64; Leverhulme res fell (USA) 1970, memb of Consultative Ctee of Assessment of Performance Unit 1975-83, chm Mulberry Press Ltd; FRSA 1989; *Style*— Peter Snape, Esq, OBE; 10 Chalcot Square, London NW1 (☎ 01 722 9478)

SNAPE, Royden Eric; s of John Robert Snape (d 1961), and Gwladys Constance, *née* Jones (d 971); *b* 20 April 1922; *Educ* Bromsgrove Sch; *m* 4 June 1949, Unity Frances (Jo), da of George Chester Tancred Money (d 1938); 1 s (Peter b 1950); 1 da (Sarah b 1952); *Career* RA Field 1940-46; Adj 80 Field Regt 1945, Major (DAAG); slr 1949-, recorder 1979-; chm Med Appeal Tbnl 1985-; govr St Johns Sch Porthcawl 1971-88; *Recreations* golf, rugby union football, cricket, swimming; *Clubs* Royal Porthcawl Golf, Cardiff Athletic, Glamorgan CCC; *Style*— Roy Snape, Esq; West Winds, Llanblethian Cowbridge, S Glamorgan CF7 7JQ (☎ 044 63 2362); Wyndham House, Bridgend, Mid Glamorgan (☎ 0656 61115)

SNEATH, Christopher Gilbert; s of Colin Frank Sneath, of Brookmans Park,; *b* 25 June 1938; *Educ* Framlingham Coll Suffolk; *m* 25 May 1963, Elizabeth Mary, da of Bernard Stephen Copson, Little Heath, Potters Bar, Herts; 2 da (Lucy Jane b 1965, Julia Elizabeth b 1967); *Career* Nat Serv RCS 1957-59; gp md dir Barrett & Wright Gp Ltd 1982- (md 1971-); vice-pres Heating & Ventilating Contractors Assoc 1988; capt Brookmans Park golf 1980-81, chm London Area Clubs Physically Handicapped Able Bodied 1987; companion memb Chartered Inst of Bldg Servs Engrs 1983; *Recreations* golf, marathon running; *Clubs* Brookmans Park golf, RAC; *Style*— Christopher Sneath, Esq; 31 Brookmans Ave, Brookmans Pk, Hatfield, Herts AL9 7QH (☎ 0707 58709); Barrett & Wright Gp Ltd, 200 Hornsey Rd, London N7 7LG (☎ 01 607 6700, fax 01 700 4683)

SNEDDEN, David King; s of David Snedden; *b* 23 Feb 1933; *Educ* Daniel Stewart's Coll Edinburgh; *m* 1958, Jean, da of Edward Goldie Smith; 2 s (Keith b 1961, Stuart b 1963), 1 da (Ann); *Career* formerly: investmt advsr Guinness Mahon Ltd, dir Radio Forth Ltd, memb Press Cncl; md: Belfast Telegraph Newspapers 1966-70 (dir 1979-82), Scotsman Publications 1970-79; jt md Thomson Regnl Newspapers Ltd 1980-82 (dir 1974-, gp asst md 1979-80); md and chief exec Trinity Int Hldgs plc; vice-chm Press Assoc; dir Reuters Hldgs plc; *Recreations* golf, shooting, fishing; *Clubs* Caledonian, Bruntisfield Links Golfing Soc; *Style*— David Snedden, Esq; Apartment 223, The Colonnades, Albert Dock Village, Liverpool L3 4AA, Merseyside

SNEDDON, Hutchison Burt; CBE (1983, OBE 1968, JP); s of Robert Cleland Sneddon, of 261 Bonkle Road, Newmains, Wishaw, Lanarkshire, and Catherine McDade, *née* McComisky (d 1978); *b* 17 April 1929; *Educ* Wishaw HS, Burnbank Tech Coll; *m* 3 Oct 1960, Elizabeth Ross, da of Allan Jardine (d 1963); 1 s (Cleland b 1967), 2 da (Joanne b 1961, Irene b 1964); *Career* Nat Serv NCO RE 1950-52; serv: Sch of Survey Newbury, II Armd Div HQ Hereford, W Germany 1951-52; air photo graphic interpreter; construction engr 1943-64, Br gas: tech sales mangr 1964-71, area mangr 1971-79, sales mangr (special projects) 1983-88; memb: W regnl Hosp Bd 1968-70, Motherwell and Wishaw Borough Cncl 1958-75 (provost 1971-75); chm Motherwell Dist Cncl 1974-77, JP 1964-, memb: Scottish Tourist Bd 1969-83; Scottish chm: Nat Bldg Agency 1977-82 (dir 1974-82), The Housing Corpn 1980-83 (memb 1977-83); chm Cumbernauld Devpt Corpn 1979-83, vice pres Confedn of Scottish Local Authys 1974-76; sec Nat Bible Soc of Scotland Wishaw Branch 1986-, vice pres World Fedn of Burns Clubs 1988-89, chm Gas Higher Mangrs Assoc 1986; City of Schweinfurt Gold Medal of Freedom 1975; *Recreations* watching football, philately; *Style*— Hutchison Sneddon, Esq, CBE; 36 Shand St, Wishaw M62 8HN (☎ 0698 73685)

SNEDDON, Robert; CMG (1976), MBE (1945); s of John Sneddon (d 1928), and Jean McLachlan (d 1969); *b* 8 June 1920; *Educ* Dalziel HS, Kettering GS, Univ Coll Nottingham; *m* 1945, Kathleen Margaret, da of Thomas Malcolm Cambray Smith (d 1971); 2 da (Heather, Fiona); *Career* WWII Maj 8 Army (N Africa, Italy and 30 Corps Germany) 1940-46; Foreign (later Diplomatic) Serv 1946-: 3 sec Warsaw 1946-50, 2 sec Stockholm 1950-54, FO 1954-56, 1 sec Oslo 1956-61, 1 sec Berlin 1961-63, Foreign and Cwlth Office 1963-69 and 1971-77, cnsllr Bonn 1969-71, ret 1977; *Recreations* golf; *Clubs* Westhill Golf; *Style*— Robert Sneddon, Esq, CMG, MBE; Windrose, Church Rd, Horsell, Woking, Surrey (☎ 048 62 4335)

SNELGROVE, Rt Rev Donald George; *see*: Hull, Bishop of

SNELL, John Bernard; s of Harold Emley Snell (d 1966); *b* 28 Mar 1932; *Educ* Bryanston, Balliol Coll Oxford; *Career* author; barr Lincoln's Inn, md Romney Hythe and Dymchurch Railway Co 1972-; *Recreations* music, literature and photography; *Style*— John Snell, Esq; 15 Tudor Avenue, Dymchurch, Kent (☎ 0303 872789)

SNELLING, Sir Arthur Wendell; KCMG (1960, CMG 1954), KCVO (1962); s of Arthur Snelling; *b* 7 May 1914; *Educ* Ackworth Sch Yorks, UCL; *m* 1939, Frieda, da of Lt-Col F Barnes; 1 s; *Career* Royal Inst of Int Affrs 1934-36; entered Dominions Office 1936, jt sec to UK Delegn to Int Monetary Conf Bretton Woods USA 1944; UK dep high cmmr in: NZ 1947-50, S Africa 1953-55; asst under-sec CRO 1956-59, high cmmr Ghana 1959-61, dep under-sec state FCO 1961-69, ambass to S Africa 1970-72; dir Gordon & Gotch Holdings 1973-81; fellow UCL 1970 and memb Cncl 1976, vice-pres UK-South Africa Trade Assoc 1974-80, memb Ciskei Cmmn 1978-80; *Style*— Sir Arthur Snelling, KCMG, KCVO; 19 Albany Park Rd, Kingston-upon-Thames, Surrey KT2 5SW (☎ 01 549 4160)

SNELLING-COLYER, Nigel John; s of John Edward Snelling-Colyer, of Wadhurst, Sussex, and Miriam Annette, *née* Edbrooke; *b* 21 Sept 1954; *Educ* The Skinners' Sch Tunbridge Wells, RMA Sandhurst; *Career* Lt RE served UK, BAOR, Cyprus with UN Forces, Belize 1978-83; asst to md Pauling plc 1983-85, London residential off Chestertons 1985-86; London residential off Cluttons 1986-, property devpt 1988-; *Recreations* riding, hunting, shooting, cars; *Clubs* Army and Navy; *Style*— Nigel Snelling-Colyer, Esq; Nat West Bank, 1 St James' Square, Wadhurst, Sussex

SNELSON, Sir Edward Alec Abbott; KBE (1954), OBE (1946); er s of Thomas Edward Snelson (d 1965), of Chester; *b* 1904; *Educ* St Olave's, Gonville and Caius Coll Cambridge, SOAS London; *m* 1956, Prof Jean Johnston, da of Donald Mackay, of Craigendorran; 2 s; *Career* barr Gray's Inn 1929, entered ICS 1929, dist judge Central Provinces 1936, legal sec 1946, jt sec govt of India 1947, sec Pakistan Minys of Law and Parly Affrs 1951-61; Justice Supreme Restitution Court Herford (FDR) 1962-81, memb Arbitral Tribunal for Agreement on German External Debts and the Mixed Cmmn 1969-77; *Clubs* Utd Oxford and Cambridge; *Style*— Sir Edward Snelson, KBE; The Forge House, Binsted, Alton, Hants

SNELUS, Alan Roe; CMG (1960); s of John Ernest Snelus (d 1933); *b* 19 May 1911; *Educ* Haileybury, Cambridge Univ; *m* 1947, Margaret Bird, *née* Elliott; 1 s, 1 da; *Career* Sarawak Civil Serv 1934, barr Gray's Inn 1934, Colonial Serv 1946, sec of def 1951, dep chief sec 1955-64, ret 1964; *Recreations* gardening and contemplation; *Style*— Alan Snelus, Esq, CMG; 115A Hansford Square, Combe Down, Bath, Avon

SNOAD, Harold Edward; s of Sidney Edward Snoad, of "Bankside", Silverdale Rd, Eastbourne, Sussex, and Irene Dora, *née* Janes; *b* 28 August 1935; *Educ* Eastbourne Coll; *m* 1, 21 Sept 1957 (m dis 18 June 1963) Anne Christine, *née* Cadwallader; m 2, 6 July 1963, Jean, da of James Green (d 1968), of 46 Pemberton Gardens, London; 2 da (Helen Julie b 1969, Jeanette Claire b 1975); *Career* Nat Serv RAF 1954-56; with BBC 1957-: prodr and dir 1970-83, exec prodr and dir 1983-; produced and directed many successful comedy series incl: The Dick Emery Show, Rings on their Fingers, The Further Adventures of Lucky Jim, Tears Before Bedtime, Hilary Don't Wait Up, Ever Decreasing Circles, Brush Strokes; dir feature film Not Now Comrade, re-wrote Dad's Army for radio; scripted original comedy series: Share and Share and Alike and It Sticks Out Half a Mile (radio), High and Dry (TV); *Books* Directing Situation Comedy (1988); *Recreations* swimming, gardening, theatre going, DIY, motoring; *Style*— Harold Snoad, Esq; Fir Tree Cottage, 43 Hawkewood Rd, Sunbury-on-Thames, Middx TW16 6HL (☎ 0932 785887); Room 4138 BBC Television Centre, Wood Lane London W12 7RJ (☎ 01 743 8000 exts 4816/1817/8490, telex 265 781)

SNODGRASS, John Michael Owen; CMG (1981); s of Maj William McElrea Snodgrass (d 1934), and Mrs Kathleen Mabel Snodgrass, *née* Owen (d 1988); *b* 12 August 1928; *Educ* Marlborough, Cambridge Univ (MA); *m* 1957, Jennifer, da of Robert James (d 1970), of S Rhodesia; 3 s (Andrew, Peter, James); *Career* HM Dip Serv (ret): consul gen Jerusalem 1970-74, cnsllr British Embassy S Africa 1974-77, head of S Pacific Dept FCO 1977-80, ambassador to: Zaire 1980-83, Bulgaria 1983-86; *Recreations* skiing, travel; *Style*— John Snodgrass, Esq, CMG; The Barn House, North Warnborough, Hants RG25 1ET (☎ 0256 702816)

SNOW, Adrian John; s of Edward Percy John Snow, of Middleton-on-Sea, W Sussex, and Marjory Ellen, *née* Nicholls; *b* 20 Mar 1939; *Educ* Hurstpierpoint Coll, Trinity Coll

Dublin (BA, MA, H Dip, Ed), Reading Univ (M Ed); *m* 1963, (Alessina) Teresa, da of Charles Arthur Kilkelly, ARICS, of Far Field, Killiney Hill Rd, Killiney, Co Dublin; 1 s (Robin Edward Charles b 1965), 1 da (Susan Alessina b 1963); *Career* Pilot Offr RAF 1962; asst master: New Beacon Prep Sch 1958-59, Kings Sch Sherborne 1963-64, Dublin HS (pt/t) 1964-65, Brighton Coll 1965-66; The Oratory: head of economic and political studies 1966-73, head of history 1967-73, housemaster 1967-73, actg headmaster 1972-73, headmaster 1973-88; Warden to the govrs, The Oratory Sch Assoc 1989-, govr: St Mary's Ascot 1986-, St Edward's Reading 1985-, Highlands Reading 1985-, Moreton Hall 1984-, Prior Park Coll 1980-87; *Recreations* bridge, farming, squash, golf, real tennis; *Clubs* Leander; *Style—* Adrian Snow, Esq; Ward's Farmhouse, Greenmore, Woodcote, nr Reading; The Oratory Construction Ltd, The Oratory Sch, Woodcote, nr Reading

SNOW, Antony Edmund; s of Thomas Maitland Snow, CMG, of Vevy, Switzerland, and Phyllis Annette Hopkins, *née* Malcolmson; *b* 5 Dec 1932; *Educ* Sherborne, New Coll Oxford; *m* 8 April 1961, Caroline, da of Comar Wilson, of Oakley Manor, nr Basingstoke, Hants (d 1961); 1 s (Lucian b 1965), 2 da (Arabella b 1964, Henrietta b 1970); *Career* 10 Roy Hussars, cmmnd 1952-53; dep chm Charles Barker & Sons 1971-76, vice pres Mkt Planning Stueben Glass NY 1976-78, dep dir Corning Museum of Glass USA 1978-79, dir Rockwell Museum USA 1979-83, chm Charles Barker plc 1983-87; tstee: Arnott Museum USA 1980-, Corning Museum of Glass USA; memb: ctee of mgmnt Courtauld Inst of Art, exec ctee Nat Art Collections Fund MIPA, FIPR, CBIM; *Recreations* windsurfing, skiing, tennis, English watercolours; *Clubs* Cavalry and Guard's, City of London;; *Style—* Antony Snow, Esq; 16 Rumbold Rd, London SW6 2JA (☎ 01 731 2881)

SNOW, Hon Harriet Flavia Hazlitt; only child of Baron Burntwood (Life Peer d 1982); *b* 1950; *Educ* Lycèe Français de Londres, London Coll of Printing; *Career* Illustrator; *Style—* The Hon Harriet Snow; The Thatched Cottage, Walberswick, Southwold, Suffolk; Flat 2, 37 Chester Way, London SE11 (☎ 01 735 6770)

SNOW, Jonathan George (Jon); s of Rt Rev George D'Oyly Snow, Bishop of Whitby (d 1977), and Joan Monica *née* Way; *b* 28 Sept 1947; *Educ* St Edward's Sch Oxford, Liverpool Univ; 2 da (Leila Snow Colvin b 1982, Freya Snow Colvin b 1986); *Career* dir New Horrizon Youth Centre Covent Garden 1970-73; Journalist: LBC and IRN 1973-76, ITN 1976- (Washington corr 1983-86, dip ed 1986-; NUJ; *Books* Atlas of Today (1987); *Style—* Jon Snow, Esq; 9 Torriano Cottages, Torriano Ave, London NWS ZTA (☎ 01 485 3513); ITN, ITN House, 48 Wells St, London W1 (☎ 01 637 5454, fax 01 636 0349, telex 22101)

SNOW, Peter John; s of Brig John Fitzgerald Snow (d 1973), and Peggy Mary, *née* Pringle (d 1970); *b* 20 April 1938; *Educ* Wellington, Balliol Coll Oxford (BA); *m* 1, 30 Sept 1964 (m dis), Alison, da of George Carter, of Uckfield, Sussex; 1 s (Shane Fitzgerald b 1966), 1 da (Shuna b 1968); m 2, 15 May 1976,l Ann MacMillan, da of Dr Robert MacMillan, of Toronto, Canada; 1 s (Daniel b 1978), 2 da (Rebecca b 1980, Katherine b 1983); *Career* Nat Serv 2 Lt Somerset LI 1956-58; reporter and newscaster ITN 1962-79 (dep and def corr 1966-79), presenter BBC TV Newsnight and election progs 1979-; *Books* Hussein: A Biography (1972), Leila's Hijack War (1970); *Recreations* sailing, skiing, model railways; *Style—* Peter Snow, Esq; BBC TV, BBC TV Centre, Wood Lane, London W12 (☎ 01 743 8000)

SNOW, Philip Albert; OBE (1985, MBE 1979), JP (Warwicks 1967-76, W Sussex 1976-); s of William Edward Snow, FRCO (d 1954), and Ada Sophia, *née* Robinson; bro of late Baron Show, CBE (Life Peer, better known as C P Snow, the novelist); *b* 7 August 1915; *Educ* Alderman Newton's Scho Leicester, Christ's Coll Cambridge (MA; played table tennis and chess for Cambridge Univ and Cambs); *m* 1940, (Mary) Anne, da of Henry Harris (d 1970), of Leicester; 1 da (Stefanie Dale Vivien Vuikaba, AIL, b 1947, m 1973, Peter Edward Waine, BSc, FBIM; 1 da (Philippa b 1981)); *Career* author, bibliographer, administrator; served Colonial Admin Service as admin offr, magistrate, provincial cmmr and asst colonial sec in Fiji and Western Pacific 1937-52 (ADC to Govr and C-in-C Fiji 1939, liaison offr with US and NZ forces WWII); vice-pres Fiji Soc 1944-52; bursar (1952-76) and clerk (1967-76) to Governing Body Rugby Scho; chm Independent Schs Bursars' Assoc 1962-65 (vice-chm 1959-62, memb ctee 1956-69); memb jt ctee Governing Bodies of Schs' Assoc 1959-64; foreign specialist ward USA 1964; fndr Fiji Cricket Assoc 1946 (vice-patron 1952-), perm Fiji rep on Int Cricket Conference 1955-; memb first Cricket World Cup Ctee 1970-75; chm Assoc Memb Countries of Int Cricket Conference 1982-; first pres The Worthing Soc 1983- (vice-chm 1977-83); literary executor and executor of Lord Show; FRSA, FRAI; elected Special Hon Life Memb MCC for services to int cricket; *Books* Civil Defence Services, Fiji (1942), Cricket in the Fiji Islands (1949), Report on the Visit of Three Bursars to the United States of America in 1964 (1965); Best Stories of the South Seas (1967), Bibliography of Fiji, Tonga and Rotuma (1969), The People from the Horizon; an illustrated history of the Europeans among the South Sea Islanders (1979; co-author with daugher Stefanie Waine; Stranger and Brother: a Portrait of C P Snow (1982); *Recreations* formerly cricket (Cap Leics 2nd XI 1936-38, played for Cambridge Crusaders 1934-45, Leics 1946, and Authors 1952-58, Capt MCC teams 1951-65, Capt Fiji Nat first class team touring NZ 1948), deck-tennis, tennis; *Clubs* MCC, Hawks (Cambridge), Mastermine; *Style—* Philip Snow, Esq, OBE, JP; Gables, Station Rd, Angmering, W Sussex BN16 4HY (☎ 0903 773594)

SNOW, Hon Philip Charles Hansford; s of Baron Snow, CBE (C P Snow, the author, d 1980), and Pamela Hansford-Johnson (d 1981; novelist); *b* 26 August 1952; *Educ* Eton, Balliol Coll Oxford; *m* 19 Sept 1987, Amanda C, er da of Sir Clive Anthony Whitmore, *qv*; *Style—* The Hon Philip Snow

SNOW, Surgn Rear Adm Ronald Edward; LVO (1972), OBE (1977), QHP (1984); s of Arthur Chandos Pole Snow (formerly Soppitt, name changed by deed pole, d 1984), of Cape Town, S Africa, and Evelyn Dorothea, *née* Joyce (d 1956); *b* 17 May 1933; *Educ* St Andrew's Coll Grahamstown S Africa, Trinity Coll Dublin (MA, MB BCh, BAO), RCS Ireland (DA), RCP Ireland (MFOM) Licentiate of Medical Council of Canada - LMCC; *m* 16 Dec 1959, Valerie Melian, da of Raymond Arthur French (d 1981), of Dublin, Ireland; 2 da (Suzanne Lynn, Nicola Jane); *Career* MO HMS Victorious 1966; MO Submarine Escape Trg Tank 1967, HMS Dolphin 1967; princ MO HM Yacht Britannia 1970; asst to SMO (Admin) RN Hosp Haslar 1972; duties with MDG(N) as Naval Health 2 MOD (Navy) 1973; dir of Studies Inst Naval Med 1975; duties with MDG(N) as dep dir of med personnel (Naval) 1977; Staff MO to Surgn Rear Adm (Naval Hosps) 1980; Fleet MO to CINCFLEET and med advsr to CINCHAN and CINCEASTLANT 1982; MO i/c Inst of Naval Med 1984; Asst Surgn Gen (Serv Hosps) and Dep Med Dir-Gen (Naval) 1985; Rear Adm (Support Med Servs) 1987; Surgn Rear Adm (operational med servs) 1989; RSM (fell of cncl of Utd Servs Section) 1987, memb Soc of Occupational Med 1977, O St J 1986; *Recreations* Nat Hunt racing, cruising; *Clubs* Army & Navy, RN Sailing Assoc (Portsmouth); *Style—* Surgn Rear Adm Ronald Snow, LVO, OBE, QHP; c/o Naval Secretary, Ministry of Defence, Ripley Block, Old Admiralty Building, Spring Gardens, London SW1A 2BE (☎ 01 218 7600)

SNOW, Thomas Maitland; CMG (1934); s of Thomas Snow (d 1927, Mayor of Exeter 1890), of Cleve and Hurston nr Exeter, and Edith, *née* Banbury (d 1917); *b* 21 May 1890; *Educ* Winchester, New Coll Oxford (BA); *m* 1, 1927 (m dis), Phyllis Annette, da of Ivor Forbes Malcolmson (d 1927), of Callum Lodge St Albans; 3 s (Thomas, Antony, Richard); m 2, 1949, Sylvia, da of Walter Delmar, of Budapest; *Career* entered FO 1914; third sec: Christiania, Athens; second sec Berne; first sec: Madrid, Warsaw; cnsllr: Tokyo Embassy, Madrid Embassy; HM min: Cuba 1935-37, Finland 1937-39, Colombia 1941-44; ambass 1944-45, min Switzerland 1946-50; *Style—* Thomas Maitland Snow, Esq, CMG; 35 Rue de Vuarennes, 1820 Montreux, Switzerland

SNOWBALL, Hon Mrs; Clarinda Susan; da of 3 Viscount Knollys; *b* 1960; *m* 4 Feb 1988, Andrew M B Snowball, yr s of late Brig E J D Snowball, of Ballochneck, Thornhill, Perthshire; *Style—* The Hon Mrs Snowball

SNOWBALL, Hon Mrs; Clarinda Susan; da of 3 Viscount Knollys; *b* 1960; *m* 4 Feb 1988, Andrew M B Snowball, yr s of late Brig E J D Snowball, of Ballochneck, Thornhill, Perthshire; *Style—* The Hon Mrs Snowball

SNOWDON, 1 Earl of (UK 1961); Antony Charles Robert Armstrong-Jones; GCVO (1969); also Viscount Linley (UK 1961); s of Ronald Owen Lloyd Armstrong-Jones, MBE, QC, DL (d 1966) of Plas Dinas, Caernarvonshire and Anne, Countess of Rosse, *qv*; *b* 7 Mar 1930; *Educ* Eton, Jesus Coll Cambridge; *m* 1, 6 May 1960 (m dis 1978), HRH The Princess Margaret Rose (*see* Royal Family), yr da of HM the late King George VI; 1 s, 1 da; m 2, 15 Dec 1978, Lucy Mary, da of Donald Brook Davies, of Enniskerry, Co Wicklow, and formerly w of Michael Lindsay-Hogg (film dir, s of Edward Lindsay-Hogg, gs of Sir Lindsay Lindsay-Hogg, 1 Bt, JP); 1 da (Lady Frances b 17 July 1979); *Heir* s, Viscount Linley, *qv*; *Career* Constable of Caernarvon Castle 1963-; photographer; artistic advsr Sunday Times and Sunday Times Publications 1962-, consultative advsr to Design Cncl London 1962-87, ed advsr Design Magazine 1962-87; *Exhibitions* Photocall (London 1958), Assignments (Photokina 1972), London (1973), Brussels (1974), Los Angeles, St Louis, Kansas, New York, Tokyo (1975), Sydney and Melbourne (1976), Copenhagen (1976), Paris (1977), Amsterdam (1977); *TV films* Don't Count the Candles (CBS 1968; 2 Hollywood Emmys, St George Prix, Venice Dip, Prague and Barcelona Film Festival Award), Love of a Kind (BBC 1969), Born to be Small (ATV 1971, Chicago Hugo Award), Happy being Happy (ATV 1973), Mary Kingsley (BBC 1975), Burke and Wills (1975), Peter, Tina and Steve (ATV 1977), Snowdon on Camera (BBC 1981); pres: Contemporary Art Soc for Wales, Civic Tst for Wales, Welsh Theatre Co, Gtr London Arts Assoc, Int Year of Disabled People (1981) England; vice-pres Bristol Univ Photographic Soc; memb: Cncl of Nat Fund for Research into Crippling Diseases, Faculty of Designers for Industry; patron: Metropolitan Union of YMCAs, British Water Ski Fedn, Welsh Nat Rowing Club, Physically Handicapped and Able-Bodied, Circle of Guide Dog Owners, Demand; designer: Snowdown Aviary for London Zoo 1965, electric chair for disabled people (Chairmobile) 1972; fndr Snowdon Award Scheme for Disabled Students 1980; Arts Dirs Club of NY Certificate of Merit 1969; Soc of Publication Designers: Cert of Merit 1970, Designers Award of Excellence 1973; Wilson Hicks Cert of Merit for Photocommunication 1971, Design and Art Directors 1978, Royal Photographic Soc Hood Award 1979; RDI, FRSA, FSIAD, FRPS, sr fell Royal Coll of Arts 1986, fell Manchester Coll of Art and Design; *Publications* Malta (collab with Sacheverell Sitwell 1958), London (1958), Private View (collab with John Russell and Bryan Robertson 1965), Assignments (1972), A View of Venice (1972), The Sack of Bath (1972), Inchcape Review (1977), Pride of the Shire (collab with John Oaksey 1979), Personal View (1979), Tasmania Essay (1981), Sittings (1983), My Wales (collab with Lord Tony Pandy 1986), Israel: a first view (1986), Stills 1984-87 (1987); *Style—* The Rt Hon the Earl of Snowdon, GCVO; 22 Launceston Place, London W8 (☎ 01 937 1524)

SNYDER, Michael John; s of Percy Elsworth Snyder (d 1953), and Pauline Edith, *née* Davenport; *b* 30 July 1950; *Educ* Brentwood Sch, City of London Coll; *m* 14 Dec 1974, Mary Barbara, da of Rev Wilfrid Edgar Dickinson; 2 da (Julia Caroline b 10 Nov 1976, Susanna Jane b 9 Sept 1978); *Career* CA, Kingston Smith 1968-: ptnr 1974, managing ptnr 1979-; dep chm JR Gp plc; dir: Jade Interiors LTd, Jade Interiors Int Ltd, Quodeck Ltd, Skewfell Ltd, Cheviot Asset Mgmnt Ltd, Gp Consultancy (computer servs) Ltd, Kingston Smith Fin Servs Ltd; ICAEW: chm City Dist Trg Bd, memb Parly and Law Ctee, fndr memb and sec Assoc of Practising Accountants, common councilman City of London; memb: housing ctee, music ctee, Port and City of London Health and Soc Servs Ctee, bd of govrs City of London Sch for Girls; hon tres Hoddeston area victims support scheme; Freeman of the City of London 1980, Liveryman Worshipful Co of Needlemakers; ACA 1973, FCA 1978, FInstD; *Recreations* narrowboat and inland waterways, music, squash; *Clubs* City Livery, Cordwainer Ward, Bishopgate Ward; *Style—* Michael Snyder, Esq; Devonshire House, 146 Bishopsgate, London EC2H 4JX (☎ 01 377 8888, fax 01 247 7048, car tel 0836 733 761, telex 894477)

SOAMES, Hon (Emma Mary); *née* Soames; da of Baron Soames, GCMG, GCVO, CH, CBE, PC, *qv*; *b* 6 Sept 1949; *m* 4 July 1981 (m dis 1989), James MacManus feature ed for The Sunday Telegraph), s of Dr Niall MacManus, of Warwick Sq, London SW1; 1 da (Emily b 1983); *Career* journalist Evening Standard, ed Literary Review, Features ed Vogue, ed Tatler; *Clubs* Groucho; *Style—* The Hon Emma Soames; Vogue House, Hanover Square, London W1R 0AD (☎ 01 499 9080)

SOAMES, Hon Jeremy Bernard; s of Baron Soames, GCMG, GCVO, CH, CBE, PC, *qv*; *b* 1952; *Educ* Eton; *m* 1978, Susanna, da of (James) David Agar Keith; 1 s (b 1988), 2 da; *Style—* The Hon Jeremy Soames; c/o West Barsham Hall, Fakenham, Norfolk

SOAMES, Baroness; Hon Mary; *née* Spencer Churchill; DBE (1980, MBE Mil 1945); da of late Rt Hon Sir Winston Leonard Spencer Churchill, KG, OM, CH, TD, PC, FRS (gs of 7 Duke of Marlborough and who d 1965) and Baroness Spencer Churchill (Dame Clementine Ogilvy, GBE, cr Life Peeress 1965, da of late Col Sir Henry

Montague Hozier, KCB, bro of 1 Baron Newlands, and Lady (Henrietta) Blanche Ogilvy, da of 5 (10 but for attainder) Earl of Airlie, KT); *b* 1922; *m* 1947, Capt Christopher Soames (later Baron Soames, GCMG, GCVO, CH, CBE, PC, d 1987); 3 s, 2 da; *Career* formerly Jr Cdr ATS; memb Cncl Winston Churchill Memorial Tst 1978-, chm Royal Nat Theatre Bd 1989-; pres Nat Benvt Fund for the Aged 1978-; govr Harrow Sch 1981-; hon fellow Churchill College, Cambridge; *Books* Clementine Churchill by Her Daughter Mary Soames (1979), A Churchill Family Album (1982), The Profligate Duke: George Spencer Churchill 5th Duke of Marlborough and his Duchess (1987); *Style*— The Rt Hon The Lady Soames, DBE

SOAMES, Hon (Arthur) Nicholas Winston; MP (C) Crawley 1983-; s of Baron Soames, *qv*, and Hon Mary, *née* Spencer-Churchill, da of late Sir Winston Churchill and Baroness Spencer-Churchill; *b* 12 Feb 1948; *Educ* Eton; *m* 1981 (at which wedding HRH The Prince of Wales was best man), Catherine, da of Capt Tony Weatherall, of Dumfries; 1 s (Arthur b 1985); *Career* served 11 Hussars, extra equerry to HRH The Prince of Wales, Lloyd's insurance broker; *Clubs* White's, Turf, Carlton; *Style*— The Hon Nicholas Soames, MP; The House of Commons, London SW1 0AA

SOAMES, Hon Rupert Christopher; s of Baron Soames, GCMG, GCVO, CH, CBE, PC, *qv*, and The Hon Lady Soames DBE, *née* Churchill; *b* 18 May 1959; *Educ* Eton, Worcester Coll Oxford (BA); *Career* pres The Oxford Union 1980; employed by GEC plc 1981-; *Clubs* Turf; *Style*— The Hon Rupert Soames

SOBELL, Sir Michael; s of Lewis Sobell (d 1945), and Esther Sobell (d 1952); *b* 1 Nov 1892; *Educ* Central London Foundation Sch; *m* 1917, Anne, da of Samuel Rakusen (d 1933), of London; 2 da; *Career* chm GEC (Radio and TV) Ltd; hon dir Technion Israel; hon doctorate Bar Ilan Univ Israel; hon fell: Jews Coll London, Royal Coll of Pathologists; kt 1972; *Recreations* racing (racehorse owner, Charity); *Clubs* Jockey (Newmarket); *Style*— Sir Michael Sobell; Bakeham House, Englefield Green, Surrey TW20 9TX

SOBER, Phillip; *b* 1 April 1931; *Educ* Haberdasher Aske's; *m* 20 Nov 1957, Vivien Louise, *née* Oppenheimer; 3 da (Belinda Clare b 20 July 1961, Juliet Anne b 28 June 1963, Georgina Jane b 9 July 1966); *Career* CA; Stoy Hayward: ptnr 1958, int ptnr 1975, sr ptnr 1985; non exec dir: Stoy Hayward Assocs 1985, Transatlantic Hldgs plc 1983, Horwath & Horwath UK Ltd 1986; advsr Br Property Fedn, tstee Royal Opera House, Crown Estate Cmmr; memb Worshipful Co of CAs; FCA 1963; *Recreations* interested in all the arts (particularly opera), golf; *Clubs* Savile, RAC; *Style*— Phillip Sober, Esq; 10 Longwood Drive, Roehampton, London SW15 5DL (☎ 01 789 0437); Stoy Hayward, 8 Baker St, London W1M 1DA (☎ 01 486 5888, fax 01 487 3686, telex 267716 HORWAT)

SOBERS, Sir Garry (Garfield) St Auburn; *b* 28 July 1936,Bridgetown, Barbados; *Educ* Bay St Sch Barbados; *m* 1969, Prudence Kirby; 2 s, 1 da; *Career* cricketer; played in 93 test matches for WI (39 as capt) 1953-74, capt WI and Barbados teams 1964-74, capt Notts CCC 1968-74, ret; held world records in test cricket: 365 not out, 26 centuries, 235 wickets, 110 catches; memb Appeal Panel Immigrations Dept 1982; kt 1975; *Books* Cricket Advance (1965), Cricket Crusader (1966), Cricket in the Sun (1967); *Style*— Sir Garry Sobers; Melbourne, Victoria, Australia

SOFER, Hon Mrs (Anne Hallowell); da of Baron Crowther (Life Peer, d 1972); *b* 1937; *Educ* St Paul's Sch, Swarthmore Coll USA, Somerville Coll Oxford (MA); *m* 1958, Jonathan Sofer, barrister-at-law; 2 s, 1 da; *Career* sec Nat Assoc of Govrs and Mangrs 1972-75, additional memb ILEA Educn Cte 1974-77, chm ILEA Schs Sub-Ctee 1978-81; dir Channel 4 1981-83; columnist The Times 1983-87; memb GLC St Pancreas N (Lab 1977-81, SDP 1981-86); *Books* The School Govenors Handbook (with Tyrrell Buyess) (1978 and 1986), The London Left Takeover (1987); *Style*— The Hon Mrs Sofer; 46 Regent's Park Rd, London NW1 (☎ 01 722 8970)

SOFIER, Jacob (Jack); s of Abraham Sofier (d 1986), of London, and Renee Sarah, *née* Shine (d 1983); *b* 2 July 1932; *Educ* Quintin Sch, Regent St Poly; *m* 3 July 1955, Maureen Barbara, da of Emanuel Lyttleston (d 1962), of London; 2 da (Rochelle Katrina (Shelley) b 3 Sept 1956, Hilary Deborah b 27 Oct 1958); *Career* S London rep Raelbrook Ltd 1955-68; sales dir Mr Harry Menswear 1968-70, ptnr Jacob Bernard 1970-73, fndr and chm Gabicci plc 1973-; chm business div JIA; *Recreations* golf, bridge and gin rummy; *Clubs* Potters Bar, Herts and Las Brisas Marbella Spain; *Style*— Jack Sofier, Esq; 54 Highpoint, North Hill, Highgate, London N6 4AZ (☎ 01 340 3491); 9B Molambo Residencia, Neuva Andalucia, Marbella, Malaga, Spain (☎ 52 81 15 84); Gabicci plc, Gabicci House, Humber Road, London NW2 6HN (☎ 01 208 1111, fax 01 208 2809, car 0860 626499, telex 299177)

SOKOLNICKI, Count Juliusz (Nowina-); s of Count Antoni (Nowina-)Sokolnicki (d 1946; proprietor of the manors of Siedlemin (district of Jarocin) and Izabelin (district of Biala Podlaska), Poland; descendant of old Polish nobility dating from 1284), and Irena, *née* Skirmunt (d 1981; heiress of Albrechtow, nr Pinsk; descendant of old Lithuanian nobility and niece of Constantin Skirmunt, Polish Ambass to London 1926-35); *b* 16 Dec 1920; *Educ* Joseph Pilsudski Coll Pinsk, Warsaw Univ; *m* 1, Elizabeth Mary Krokowski, *née* Mayal (d 1982); m 2, 29 July 1983, Margaret Thornburn, da of Francis Docherty (d 1947); *Career* Cadet Offr 84 Bn Polish Armed Forces during campaign in Poland Sept 1939, captured by Russians escaped, active Polish underground, arrested by Gestapo Aug 1940, released 1942 and rejoined underground in Lublin, Capt 1943, escaped to Italy after Warsaw Rising, Lt-Col 1945; active in Polish political organisations in Britain since 1947; chm Polish Nat Revival Movement 1954; memb Cncl of Republic of Poland in exile 1954-72 (vice-chm 1963-67); ed fortnightly 'Rzeczpospolita Polska' 1967-71; Min of Information Govt in Exile 1967-71, and Home Affairs 1970-71; Pres of the Republic of Poland in Exile 1972-; a fndr Central Euro Cncl New York 1986 (membership comprising seven govts or monarchs in exile: Albania, Bulgaria, Croatia, Czechoslovakia, Estonia, Poland and Roumania); vice-pres London Appreciation Soc 1981; memb: Royal Soc of St George, Club des Intellectuels Français 1979, Polish Nobility Assoc in USA 1982; delegtate for England of Inst Héraldique, Historique et Généalogique de France 1971; hon Life Memb Augustan Soc (USA) 1982; hon Citizen: State of Texas 1982, State of Nebraska 1982, city of Minneapolis 1982, city of Baltimore 1985; Hon Lt-Col State of Alabama Militia 1981; Recteur Hon de l'Institut de Documentation et d'Etudes Européannes Bruxelles 1981, Hon Prof of Political Science Institut St Irène France, Dr of Art and Philosophy Academia Int Americana Mexico 1981; Sen Int Parliament for Safety and Peace 1982; orders and decorations include: Order of Besa (Albania) 1988, Order of the White Eagle (Poland), Order of Polonia Restituta (Poland), Cdr Merito Commercial (Mexico) 1979, Order of Masaryk (Czechoslovakia) 1987, Gd Collar Equitem Crucis Hierosolimae (Patriarchate of Antioch) 1982, Gd Croix Etoile de la Paix (France) 1948, Etoile Civique Medaille d'Or (France) 1980, Gd Croix Encouragement Public (France) 1982, Medaille de Vermeil Grand Prix Humanitaire (France) 1980; *Recreations* travelling, painting; *Clubs* Special Forces; *Style*— Count Juliusz Sokolnicki; 19 The Croft, Marton, Middlesbrough, Cleveland TS7 8DZ (☎ 0642 319181)

SOLANDT, Jean Bernard; s of Solandt, Alfred Ernest (d 1977), Solandt, Mathilde *née* Braun; *b* 23 Dec 1936; *Educ* Lycee Pasteur Strasbourg France; *m* 6 Aug 1966 Sheila, da of Hammill William OBE (d 1974); 2 da (Nathalie, Claire), 1 s (Jean-Luc); *Career* dir Schroder plc 1982, jt vice-chm J Henry Schrode Wagg & Co Ltd 1984; md Treasy & Secuirites; chm Schroder Securities London, Hong Kong, Tokyo 1986; *Recreations* golf, skiing, reading, music; *Style*— Jean Solandt, Esq; 120 Cheapside, London EC 2 (☎ 01 382 6363)

SOLANKI, Ramniklal Chhaganlal; s of Chhaganlal Kalidas Solanki (d 1963), and Ichchhaben Chhaganlal Solanki; *b* 12 July 1931; *Educ* Irish Presbyterian Mission Sch Surat, MTB Coll Gujarat Univ (BA), Sarvajanik Law Coll Surat (LLB); *m* 16 June 1955, Parvatiben Ramniklal, da of Makanji Dullabhji Chavda (d 1979); 2 s (Kalpesh b 9 Nov 1960, Shailesh b 3 June 1964), 2 da (Sadhana (Mrs Ravindra Karia) b 18 May 1956, Smita (Mrs Mukesh Thakkar) b 5 July 1958); *Career* sub ed Nutan Bharat and Lok Vani Dailies Surat 1954-56, freelance columnist for several newspapers while serving State Govt in India 1956-63, London corr Gujarat Mitra Surat 1964-68, Euro corr Janmabhoomi Gp of Newspapers 1968-; ed and md: Garavi Gujarat Newspapers 1968-, Asian Trader 1985-; md Garavi Gujarat Property Ltd 1982; Reporter of the Year Award 1970; memb: Asian Advsy Ctee BBC 1976-80, Nat Centre for Indian Language Trg Steering Gp 1978, exec ctee Gujarati Arya Kshtriya Maha Sabha UK 1979-84, exec ctee Gujarati Arya Assoc 1974-84 (vice-pres 1980-83), CPU 1964-, Foreign Press Assoc 1984-, Parly Press Gallery House of Commons; sec Indian Journalists Assoc of Europe 1978-79; memb Guild Br Newspaper Eds 1976; *Recreations* reading, writing, meeting people, politics, travelling; *Style*— Ramniklal Solanki, Esq; 74 Harrowdene Rd, Wembley, Middlesex HA0 (☎ 01 902 2879); Garavi Gujarat Publications, Garavai Gujarat House, 1/2 Silex St, London SE1 0DW (☎ 01 928 1234, fax 01 261 0055, telex 8955335 GUJARAT G)

SOLE, Brig Denis Story; CVO (1971), OBE (1964); s of Brig Denis Mavesyn Anslow Sole, DSO (d 1962), and Lilian May, *née* Story (d 1974); *b* 26 July 1917; *Educ* Cheltenham, Sandhurst Staff Coll Quetta; *m* 5 March 1957, Susan Margaret, da of Maj Cecil Arnold Williams (d 1951); 1 s (Simon John b 1960), 1 da (Sarah Elizabeth b 1958); *Career* served in The Border Regt 1937, Palestine 1937-39, India, Burma 1939-48, AAG Royal Nigerian Mil Forces 1959-62; def advsr to Br High Cmmn Zambia 1964-66, Defence and Mil Attache Turkey 1968-72; *Recreations* sailing, shooting, fishing, tennis; *Clubs* Army and Navy; *Style*— Brig Denis Sole, CVO, OBE

SOLEY, Clive Stafford; MP (Lab) Hammersmith 1983-; *b* 7 May 1939; *Educ* Downhill Secondary Modern, Newbattle Abbey Adult Educ Coll, Strathclyde Univ, Southampton Univ; *Career* probation offr 1970-75, sr probation offr 1975-79, MP (Lab) Hammersmith N 1979-83, oppn front bench spokesman: NI 1981-82 and Nov 1983-, NI 1983-84, Home Affrs 1984-87, Housing 1987-; *Style*— Clive Soley, Esq, MP; House of Commons, London SW1 (☎ 01 219 5118/5490; home: 01 740 7585)

SOLIMAN, Dr John Iskandar; s of Iskandar Soliman, and Ines, *née* Abdallah; *b* 24 Sept 1926; *Educ* Alexandria Univ (BSc, MSc), Univ of London (PhD); *m* 17 July 1953 (m dis 1981), Gabrielle, da of John Zammit; 1 s (Andre b 1955), 1 da (Monette b 1956); *Career* lectr Alexandria Univ Egypt 1948-61, sr scientific offr Br Iron and Steel Res Assoc London 1961-62, lectr QMC 1962-87, dir Allied Automation Ltd Croydon, chm Int Cmmns Europe, organizer Int Conferences Europe, prof Univ of Rome 1981-, visiting prof to Univs in USA and Europe, conslt to multinational cos; numerous articles in jls; MIMechE, memb: Soc of Automotive Engrs USA; *Clubs* Annabel's; *Style*— Dr John Soliman; 42 Lloyd Park Avenue, Croydon, CR0 5SB (☎ 01 688 2719); Allied Automation Ltd, 62 High St, Croydon CR0 1NA (☎ 01 681 3069/686 1329, fax 01 686 1490)

SOLMAN, Robert Frederick; s of Edward Vickery Solman (d 1977), of Spire House, Comberton, Kidderminster, and Marjorie Anne Watts,*née* Styles; *b* 27 Jan 1934; *Educ* Sebright Sch, Birmingham Univ (LLB); *Career* called to the Bar Middle Temple 1958, MO circuit, Rec 1985; *Style*— Robert Solman, Esq; Roydfield, Blakedown, nr Kidderminster, Worcs (☎ 0562 700 275); 5 Fountain Ct, Steelhouse Lane, Birmingham (☎ 021 236 5771)

SOLOMON, David; s of Leslie Ezekiel Solomon, of London, and Peggy, *née* Shatzman; *b* 6 August 1948; *Educ* Clarks Coll, City of London Coll; *m* 15 July 1973 (m dis 1986), Sarah-Lou Reekie; 1 s (Tony Daniel b 1980); *Career* began career in advtg with Garland-Compton, fndr Pink-Soda Fashion Co 1983-; winner Queen's Award for Export Achievement 1987; BKCEC Award for Export Achievement (awarded by The Princess Royal); *Recreations* running, tennis; *Style*— David Solomon, Esq; 22 Eastcastle St, London W1N 7PA (☎ 01 636 9001, fax 01 637 1641, telex 22827 PK SODA G)

SOLOMON, David Joseph; s of Sydney Solomon (d 1963), of Bournemouth, Hants, and Rosie *née* Joseph (d 1978); *b* 31 Dec 1930; *Educ* Torquay GS, Manchester Univ (LLB); *m* 5 April 1959, Hazel, da of Joseph Boam, of London; 1 s (Jonathan b 1961), 2 da (Ruth b 1963, Joanne b 1966); *Career* Sgt Royal Hants Regt 1955-57; slr; ptnr: Nabarro Nathanson 1961-68, head of property dept D J Freeman & Co 1976-; memb cncl: Br Shopping Centres, Oriental Ceramic Soc; Freeman Worshipful Co Solicitors; memb: Law Soc, Int Bar Assoc; *Recreations* chinese ceramics, music, architecture, modern art, wine, tai chi; *Style*— David Solomon, Esq; Russell House, 9 South Grove, London N6 6BS (☎ 01 341 6151); Longecourt Les Culetre, 21230 Arnay le Duc, Cote d'or, France; D J Freeman & Co, 43 Fetter Lane, London EC4A 1NA (☎ 01 583 4055, fax 01 353 7377, telex 894 579)

SOLOMON, Gerald Oliver; s of Thomas Oliver Solomon (d 1987), of Barnard Castle, Co Durham, and Florence, *née* Towers (d 1978); *b* 18 June 1935; *Educ* King James I GS Bishop Auckland, UCL (LLB); *m* 4 May 1957, Norma, da of Harold Crofton Barron, BEM (d 1965), of Barnard Castle, Co Durham; 1 s (Jeremy b 1959, d 1981), 1 da (Amanda b 1963); *Career* Lloyds Bank 1958-: asst tres 1976-79, dep chief accountant 1979-80, regnl dir S Wales 1980-82, gen mangr UK Retail Banking 1982-; dir Jt Credit Card Co Ltd (Access) 1984-; memb Cncl of Banking Ombudsman 1987; Freeman City of London 1970; FCIB 1983; *Recreations* golf, fell walking; *Clubs* Royal Overseas League, United (Jersey); *Style*— Gerald Solomon, Esq; Littlegarth, Churchfields Ave, Weybridge, Surrey KT13 9YA (☎ 0932 847 337); Lloyd's Bank plc, 71 Lombard St, London EC3P 3BS (☎ 01 626 1500)

SOLOMON, Rev Gerald Tankerville Norris; s of Charles Edwin Solomon (d 1952), and Gertrude Ellen, *née* Norris (d 1948); *b* 14 Feb 1912; *Educ* St Edward's Sch Oxford, London Univ (BA); *m* 11 May 1950, Betty Helene, da of Robert Brooke Clarke (d 1972); 2 s (Charles b 1952, Robert b 1952), 1 da (Jane b 1951); *Career* ordained C of E 1939; curate Broadstone Dorset 1939-42; CF 1942-63; WWII Tunisian and Italian campaigns, BAOR 1950-54, sr chaplain Blackdowns 1954-57, Nigerian Mil Force 1957-60, York Garrison 1960-63; rector of Corsley with Chapmanslade Wilts 1963-78; *Recreations* golf, beagling; *Style—* Rev Gerald T N Solomon; The Old Forge, Hindon, Wilts (☎ 074 789 255)

SOLOMON, Jonathan; s of Samuel Solomon, ICS (d 1988), of London, and Moselle Solomon ; *b* 3 Mar 1939; *Educ* Clifton, King's Coll Cambridge (MA); *m* 6 Oct 1966, Hester Madeline, da of Orrin McFarland, of Florida, USA; 1 s (Gabriel b 27 April 1967); *Career* supervisor Sidney Sussex Coll Cambridge 1960-72, lectr Extra-Mural Dept Univ of London 1963-70; princ 1967-72: Bd of Trade (asst princ 1963-67), DTI, Treasury; asst sec 1973-80: Dept of Prices and Consumer Protection, Dept of Indust; under sec Dept of Indust 1980-85; Cable and Wireless plc: dir Special Projects 1985-87, dir Corporate Strategy 1987-; dir Int Digital Communications 1987-; *Recreations* sport, research, futurology, writing; *Clubs* English Speaking Union; *Style—* Jonathan Solomon, Esq; 12 Kidderpore Gardens, London NW3 (☎ 01 794 6230); Mercury House, Theobalds Road, London WC1 (☎ 01 315 4611)

SOLOMON, Nathaniel; s of Leopold Solomon and Fanny, *née* Hertz; *b* 20 Nov 1925; *Educ* Owen's Sch London, Emmanuel Coll Cambridge (MA); *m* 1951, Patricia, da of Arthur Creak; 2 s, 1 da; *Career* dir: United Africa Co Ltd 1964-72, William Baird plc 1972-74; md Assoc Leisure plc 1974-84, chm Pleasurama plc 1984-88; *Recreations* bridge, tennis, opera, theatre, watching soccer; *Clubs* Reform, The Wimbledon, Harvard Business Sch of London; *Style—* Nathaniel Solomon, Esq; 4 Pembroke Walk, London W8 6PQ; 3 Berkeley Square, London W1X 5HG

SOLOMONS, Hon Sir (Louis) Adrian; s of G A Solomons (decd); *b* 9 June 1922; *Educ* Tamworth HS, New England Univ Coll, Sydney Univ (BA, LLB); *m* 1944, Olwyn, da of F J Bishop; 2 s; *Career* sr ptnr Everingham Solomons & Co, memb NCP 1949-, chm Tamworth Electorate Cncl 1960-69, state vice-chm 1967-69, state chm 1969-74 Fedn pres 1974-79; chm of Ctees NSW Legislative Cncl 1985; kt 1982; *Recreations* Deep Sea Fishing; *Clubs* Tattersall (Sydney), Lansdowne (London); MLC (NSW) Nat Party 1969; *Style—* The Hon Sir Adrian Solomons, MLC; 17 Campbell Rd, Calala, Tamworth, NSW 2340, Australia

SOLOMONS, Anthony Nathan; s of Lesly Emmanuel Solomons (d 1938), and Susy, *née* Schneiders; *b* 26 Jan 1930; *Educ* Oundle; *m* 16 Dec 1958, Jean, da of Dr Jack Joseph Golding; 2 da (Nicola Jane b 2 June 1960, Jennifer Anne b 30 June 1963); *Career* Nat Serv cmmnd Dorset Regt 1953-54; chm Singer & Friedlander Ltd 1976- (joined 1958, chief exec 1973); dir Britannia Arrow Hldgs 1984-; dir: Bullough plc, Milton Keynes Devpt Corpn; FCA, FBIM; *Clubs* Carlton; *Style—* Anthony Solomons Esq; 10 Constable Close, London NW11 6TY (☎ 01 458 6716); 21 New St, London EC2M 4HR (☎ 01 623 3000, fax 01 623 2122, telex 886977)

SOLTI, Sir Georg; KBE (1971, Hon CBE 1968); *b* 21 Oct 1912, Budapest; *Educ* Budapest HS of Music; *m* 1, 1946, Hedwig Oeschli; m 2, 1967, Anne Valerie Pitts; 2 da (Gabrielle b 1970, Claudia b 1973); *Career* studied under Kodály, Bartók, Dohnányi; won First Prize as pianist Concours Int Geneva 1942; former conductor and pianist Budapest State Opera; musical dir: Bavarian State Opera 1946-52, Frankfurt Opera 1952-61, Covent Garden Opera 1961-71, Chicago Symphony Orchestra 1969-, Orchestre de Paris 1971-75; princ conductor and artistic dir LPO 1979-83 (conductor emeritus 1983-); Hon FRCM 1980; Hon DMus: Leeds (1971), Oxon (1972), Yale (1974), De Paul (1975), Harvard (1979), Furman (1983), Surrey (1983) London (1986), Rochester (1987); prof (Honoris Causa) Baden-Württemberg (1985); Knight Commander's Cross with Badge and Star, Fed Republic of Germany (1986), 26 Grammy Awards (1987); adopted UK citizenship 1972; *Style—* Sir Georg Solti, KBE; Chalet Haut Près, Villars sur Ollon, Vaud, Switzerland

SOMERLEYTON, 3 Baron (UK 1916); Sir Savile William Francis Crossley; 4 Bt (UK 1863), JP (Lowestoft), DL (Suffolk 1964); s of 2 Baron, MC, DL (d 1959), and Bridget, Baroness Somerleyton (d 1983); *b* 17 Sept 1928; *Educ* Eton; *m* 1963, Belinda Maris, da of late Vivian Lloyd, of Kingsmoor, Ascot; 1 s (Hugh b 1974), 4 da (Isabel, Camilla b 1967, Alicia b 1969, Louisa b 1974); *Heir* s, Hon Hugh Francis Savile Crossley b 27 Sept 1971; page of honour to HM 1983-; *Career* cmmnd Coldstream Gds 1948, Capt 1956; former ccllr E Suffolk, non-political lord-in-waiting to HM The Queen (permanent) 1978-; farmer; patron of one living; dir E Anglian Water Co; landowner (5,000 acres); *Recreations* hunting, shooting; *Clubs* Pratt's, White's; *Style—* The Rt Hon the Lord Somerleyton, JP, DL; Somerleyton Hall, nr Lowestoft, Suffolk NR32 5QQ (☎ 0502 730308, 0502 730224)

SOMERS, 8 Baron (GB 1784); Sir John Patrick Somers Cocks; 8 Bt (GB 1772); s of 7 Baron Somers (d 1953, fifth in descent from the sis of the 1 and last Baron Somers of a previous creation. The latter was the celebrated Lord High Chllr, who was a memb of the Whig Junta in Queen Anne's reign and architect of the Union with Scotland); *b* 30 April 1907; *Educ* privately, RCM (BMus, ARCM); *m* 1, 15 Aug 1935, Barbara Marianne (d 1959), da of late Charles Henry Southall, of Norwich; m 2, 28 July 1961, Dora Helen, da of late John Mountfort, of Sydney, NSW; *Heir* kinsman, Philip Sebastian Somers Cocks b 4 Jan 1948; *Career* sits as independent in House of Lords; organist and professional musician; organist and choirmaster Westonbirt Sch 1935-38, dir of music Epsom Coll 1949-53, prof of theory and composition RCM 1967-77; *Recreations* carpentry; *Style—* The Rt Hon the Lord Somers; 35 Links Rd, Epsom, Surrey KT17 3PP (☎ 03727 26514)

SOMERS, Hon Mrs (Sara Margaret); *née* Byers; da of Baron Byers (Life Peer, d Feb 1984), and Baroness Byers, *qv*; *b* 1952; *m* 1979 (m dis), Simon John Somers; 2 da (Laura Sian b 1982, Amy Rowena b 1984); *Style—* The Hon Mrs Somers

SOMERSET, David Henry FitzRoy; s of Brig Hon Nigel FitzRoy Somerset, CBE, DSO, MC, (s of 3 Baron Raglan), and Phyllis Marion Offley, *née* Irwin (d 1979); *b* 19 June 1930; *Educ* Wellington, Peterhouse Cambridge (MA); *m* 1955, Ruth Ivy, da of Wilfred Robert Wildbur (d 1978), of King's Lynn, Norfolk; 1 s (Henry b 1961), 1 da (Louise b 1956); *Career* joined Bank of England 1952, personal asst to md of Int Monetary Fund (IMF) Washington DC 1959-62, priv sec to Govr of Bank of England 1962-63, Chief Cashier and Chief of Banking Dept Bank of England 1980-88 (ret 1988); chm EBS Investmts Ltd 1977-; dir: Prolific Gp plc 1988-, Yamaichi Bank (UK) plc 1988-; Peterhouse Cambridge Univ: memb cncl Friends of Peterhouse 1981-, fell and fin advsr 1988-; chm Old Wellingtonian Soc 1988-, cmmr English Heritage 1988-; FCIB, FICT, CBIM; *Recreations* gardening, shooting, racing; *Style—* D H F Somerset, Esq; White Wickets, Boars Head, Crowborough, Sussex TN6 3HE (☎ 0892 661111)

SOMERSET, Lord Edward Alexander; s of 11 Duke of Beaufort; *b* 1 May 1958; *m* 1982, Hon (Georgina) Caroline Davidson, *qv*, 2 da of 2 Viscount Davidson; 1 da (Francesca b 1984); *Style—* Lord Edward Somerset

SOMERSET, Hon Geoffrey; 2 surv s of 4 Baron Raglan, JP (d 1964); bro and hp of 5 Baron Raglan, JP, DL; *b* 29 August 1932; *Educ* Westminster, RAC Cirencester; *m* 6 Oct 1956, Caroline Rachel, o da of Col Edward Roderick Hill, DSO, JP, DL, of Manor Farm Cottage, Stanford-in-the-Vale, Oxon; 1 s (Arthur b 27 April 1960), 2 da (Belinda (Mrs Nicholas Boyd) b 9 Feb 1958, Lucy b 8 Feb 1963); *Career* Nat Serv with Gren Guards 1952-54; instr Standard Motor Co Ltd Coventry 1958-60; gp marketing mangr Lambourn Engrg Gp 1960-71; dir Trenchermans Ltd 1971-79; underwriting memb of Lloyd's 1981; chm Stanford Area Branch Conservatives; memb Berks CC 1966-75 (chm: children's ctee, mental welfare sub-ctee; memb Newbury Dist Cncl 1979-83 (chm recreation and amenities ctee); memb: Oxfordshire Valuation Court 1988-, Oxfordshire CC 1988-; Freeman City of London, Liveryman Worshipful Co of Skinners 1968; *Recreations* shooting, gardening, conservation; *Clubs* City Univ; *Style—* The Hon Geoffrey Somerset; Manor Farm, Stanford-in-the-Vale, Faringdon, Oxon SN7 8NN (☎ 036 77 558); 3 Market Place, Cirencester, Glos GL7 2PE (☎ 0285 657807)

SOMERSET, Jane, Duchess of; Gwendoline Collette (Jane); *née* Thomas; 2 da of late Maj John Cyril Collette Thomas, N Staffordshire Regt, of Burn Cottage, Bude, Cornwall; *m* 18 Dec 1951, 18 Duke of Somerset (d 1984); 2 s (19 Duke, Lord Francis Seymour), 1 da (Lady Anne Seymour); *Style—* Her Grace Jane, Duchess of Somerset; Bradley Cottage, Maiden Bradley, Warminster, Wilts

SOMERSET, Sir Henry Beaufort; CBE (1961); s of Henry St John Somerset (d 1952), and Jessie Bowie, *née* Wilson (d 1957); *b* 21 May 1906; *Educ* St Peter's Coll Adelaide, Melbourne Univ (BSc, MSc); *m* 1930, Patricia Agnes, da of Tom Percival Strickland (d 1955); 2 da (Susan, Diana); *Career* industrial chemist; company dir: Goliath Cement Hldgs Ltd 1948-82 (chm 1967-82), ICI Australia Ltd 1963-76, chllr Univ of Tasmania 1964-72; The Perpetual Executors & Tstees Assoc of Australia Ltd 1971-81 (chm 1973-81); pres Aust Inst of Mining and Metallurgy 1958 and 1966 (cncllr 1956-82), memb exec CSIRO 1965-74; chm Australian Mineral Fndn 1970-83; Cncl Nat Museum 1968-78; dir: Nioxide Australia Pty 1949-82, (chm 1953-76); Humes Ltd 1957-82, (chm 1961-82); Assoc Pulp & Paper Mills Ltd 1945-81, (md 1948-69, dep chm 1969-81); EZ Industs Ltd 1953-78; Aust Fertilisers Ltd 1961-78; Central Norsemon Gold Ltd 1977-82; Hon DSc Univ of Tasmania 1973-; FRACI; FATS; kt 1966; *see Debrett's Handbook of Australia and New Zealand for further details*; *Clubs* Melbourne, Australian; *Style—* Sir Henry Somerset, CBE; Flat 10/1, 193 Domain Rd, South Yarra, Vic 3141, Australia; 360 Collins St, Melbourne, Vic 3000

SOMERSET, 19 Duke of (E 1547); Sir John Michael Edward Seymour; 17 Bt (E 1611); also Baron Seymour (E 1547); s of 18 Duke of Somerset, DL (d 1984), and Gwendoline Collette (Jane), née Thomas; *b* 30 Dec 1952; *Educ* Eton; *m* 20 May 1978, Judith-Rose, da of John Hull; 1 s, 2 da (Lady Sophia b 1987, Lady Henrietta Charlotte b 1989); *Heir* s, Sebastian Edward, Lord Seymour, b 3 Feb 1982; *Style—* His Grace the Duke of Somerset; Maiden Bradley, Warminster, Wilts

SOMERSET, Lord John Robert; s of 11 Duke of Beaufort; *b* 5 Nov 1964; *Style—* Lord John Somerset

SOMERSET, Brig Hon Nigel FitzRoy; CBE (1945), DSO (1918), MC (1918); s of 3 Baron Raglan, GBE (d 1920); *b* 27 July 1893; *Educ* King William's Coll Isle of Man, RMC; *m* 16 March 1922, Phyllis Marion Offley (d 1979), da of Dr Henry Offley Irwin, of Western Australia; 1 s, 1 da; *Career* joined Gloucs regt 1913, served WW I (wounded 2, despatches 3), Afghan War 1919; ADC to govr of S Australia 1920-22, AMS Southern Cmd India 1926-30, Lt-Col 1938, cmdg 2 Bn Gloucs Regt, served 1940-45 (despatches), Actg Brig cmdg 145 Inf Bde 1940 (POW 1940-45), Temp Brig 1947; *Style—* Brig the Hon Nigel Somerset, CBE, DSO, MC; 8 Regency Close, Uckfield, Sussex

SOMERSET FRY, Peter (George Robin) Plantagenet; s of Cdr (E) Peter Kenneth Llewellyn Fry, OBE, FIMechE, RN (d 1977), of Chagford Cross, Moretonhampstead, Devon, and Ruth Emily, *née* Marriott (d 1978); *b* 3 Jan 1931; *Educ* Lancing, St Thomas's Hosp Med Sch, London Univ, St Catherine's Coll Oxford; *m* 1, 29 March 1952 (m dis 1957), Audrey Anne, *née* Russell; m 2, 29 May 1958, Daphne Diana Elizabeth Caroline (d 1961), o da of Lt-Col Frederick Reginald Yorke; m 3, 17 Nov 1961 (m dis 1973), Leri (d 1985), eldest da of Dr Gruffydd Llywelyn-Jones (d 1952), of Bryn Glas, Llangefni, Anglesey, and formerly w of Hon Pierce Alan Somerset David Butler, TD (s of 7 Earl of Carrick); m 4, 5 March 1974, (Pamela) Fiona Ileene, eldest da of Col Henry Maurice Whitcombe, MBE (d 1984); *Career* asst master Wallop Preparatory Sch Weybridge Surrey 1952-54 and 1958-60; account exec TAF Int Ltd (public relations conslts) 1960- 63; dir and head of public relations Maxwell Public Relations 1963- 64; Information Offr: Incorporated Assoc of Architects and Surveyors 1965-67, Miny of Public Building and Works 1967-70; Head of Information Cncl for Small Industries in Rural Areas (COSIRA) 1970-74; ed with HMSO 1975-80; sr memb Wolfson Coll Cambridge 1980-; mangr (part-time) Eastern Region Charities Aid Fndn 1987-; parish cncllr and clerk Little Bardfield Parish Cncl Essex 1973-74; fndr and hon sec: Little Bardfield Community Tst 1973, Burgh Soc Norfolk 1977-80; antique furniture conslt Christ Church Mansion (Ipswich Museums) Ipswich 1987-; FRSA 1966; *Books* The Cankered Rose (1959), Antique Furniture (1971), Children's History of the World (1972), Great Caesar (1974), 1000 Great Lives (1975), 2000 Years of British Life (1976), Chequers, the Country Home of Britain's Prime Ministers (1977), The Book of Castles (1980), Fountains Abbey (official guide 1981), Revolt against Rome (1982), A History of Scotland (with Fiona Somerset Fry 1982); Battle Abbey (official guide 1984), Roman Britain: History and Sites (1984), Rievaulx Abbey (official guide 1986), A History of Ireland (with Fiona Somerset Fry 1988); *Recreations* visiting castles, studying 18th century French furniture, campaigning for Freedom of Information; *Style—* Peter Plantagenet Somerset Fry, Esq; Wood Cottage, Wattisfield, Bury St Edmunds, Suffolk (☎ 0359 51324)

SOMERSET JONES, Eric; QC (1978); s of late Daniel Jones and Florence Somerset Jones, of Birkenhead; *b* 21 Nov 1925; *Educ* Birkenhead Inst, Lincoln Coll Oxford (MA); *m* 1966, Brenda Marion, da of late Hedley Shimmin; 2 da (Wendy b 1967, Felicity b 1970); *Career* served RAF Coll Cranwell, link trainer instr SE Asia Cmd 1944-47; barr Middle Temple 1952, bencher 1988, memb Lord Chllr's County Cts

Rule Ctee 1975-78, Crown Ct rec 1975-, bencher 1988; *Recreations* family pursuits, travel, listening to music, photography; *Clubs* Oxford and Cambridge, Royal Chester Rowing; *Style*— Eric Somerset Jones, Esq; Goldsmith Building, Temple, London EC4Y 7BL (☎ 01 353 7881); Southmead, Mill Lane, Willaston Wirral, Cheshire (☎ 051 327 5138)

SOMERSET-WARD, Richard Adrian; s of Rev Canon A D Somerset-Ward (d 1976); *b* 29 May 1942; *Educ* Charterhouse, CCC Cambridge; *Career* joined BBC 1963, seconded to HM Diplomatic Service 1964-65, BBC dir in USA 1976-78, head of Music and Arts Programming BBC-TV 1981-; *Recreations* opera, music, tennis, golf; *Clubs* Savile; *Style*— Richard Somerset-Ward Esq; 47 Welsby Court, Eaton Rise, London W5 (☎ 01 998 5789)

SOMERTON, Viscount; James Shaun Christian Welbore Ellis Agar; s and h of 6 Earl of Normanton; *b* 7 Sept 1982; *Style*— Viscount Somerton

SOMERVILLE, Edgar William; s of Dr Edgar Somerville (d 1949), of Leek, Staffs, and Muriel Helen, *née* Watson (d 1973); *b* 4 Nov 1913; *Educ* Shrewsbury, Cambridge Univ (MA, MB); *m* 25 March 1941, Margaret, da of Lt Cdr George Forbes Esson, RNR; 1 da (Judith Margaret); *Career* Dr orthopaedic surgn (developed orthopaedic servs worldwide), conslt Nuffield Othopaedic Centre Oxford 1948-77; pres: Orthopaedic Res Soc 1967, orthopaedic section RSM 1973-73, vice-pres Br Orthopaedic Assoc 1976 (ed sec 1957-59); Cambridge hockey blue; FRCS, FRCSE (d); *Books* Bone and Joint Tuberculosis (1952, 1965), Displacement of the Hip in Childhood (1981); *Recreations* golf, tennis, gardening, sailing; *Clubs* Hawk's (Cambridge), Royal Cruising, Hunter Combe GC; *Style*— Edgar W Somerville, Esq; Stone House, South End, Garsington, Oxford OX9 9DH (☎ 086 736 388)

SOMERVILLE, Ian Christopher; *b* 2 Oct 1948; *Educ* St Edwards Coll Liverpool, Imperial Coll London Univ (BSc); *m* 11 July 1970, Felicity Ann; *Career* taxation mangr Arthur Andersen & Co (London and Manchester) 1976-82, nat VAT ptnr Deloitte Haskins & Sells 1985- (sr taxation mangr 1982- 85); sometime chm Stockport Family Practitioner Ctee, memb ctee Family Welfare Assoc Manchester 1980-85, chm N Cheshire branch BIM 1984-85; ACA 1973, FCA 1978, FBIM 1984; *Books* contrib to: Tolley's VAT Planning (1986-89), ICAEW Taxation Service (1988); *Recreations* music, gardening, cats; *Style*— Ian Somerville, Esq; Deloitte Haskins & Sells, PO Box 207, 128 Queen Victoria St, London EC4P 4JX (☎ 01 248 3913, fax 01 248 3623, telex 894941)

SOMERVILLE, John Arthur Fownes; CB (1977), CBE (1964), DL (1985); s of Admiral Sir James Fownes Somerville, GCB, GBE, DSO (d 1949), and Mary Kerr, *née* Main (d 1945);; *b* 5 Dec 1917; *Educ* RNC Dartmouth; *m* 16 June 1945, (Julia) Elizabeth, da of Vice Adm Christopher Russell Payne (d 1952); 1 s (Christopher b 1949), 2 da (Julia b 1947, Louisa b 1956); *Career* served RN 1931-50; GCHQ Cheltenham 1950-78 (ret as undersec); chm Friends of Wells Cathedral;; *Recreations* walking; *Clubs* Army & Navy; *Style*— JAF Somerville; The Old Rectory, Dinder, Wells, Somerset BA5 3PL (☎ 0749 74900)

SOMERVILLE, Brig Sir (John) Nicholas; CBE (1978); e; s of Brig Desmond Henry Sykes Somerville, CBE, MC (d 1976), of Drishane House, Castletownshend, Skibbereen, Co Cork, and Moira Burke, *née* Roche (d 1976); *b* 16 Jan 1924; *Educ* Winchester; *m* 6 Aug 1951, Jenifer Dorothea, da of Capt W M Nash, OBE, of The Point House, Castletownshend, Skibbereen, Co Cork; 1 s (Robin b 1959), 2 da (Philippa b 1953, Penelope b 1954); *Career* enlisted 1942, cmmnd 2 Lt 24 Regt SWB 1943, active serv D Day to VE Day intelligence offr (later Adj and co cdr) 1944-45, signal offr (later Adj) 1 SWB Palestine and Cyprus 1945-48, instr RMA Sandhurst 1949-52, Staff Coll Camberley 1954, DA & QMG (ops and plans) BAOR 1955-57, co cdr 1 SWB Malayan Emergency 1958-63, Brevet Lt-Col 1963, JSSC 1963, GSO1 (plans) HQ FARELF 1964-66, CO 1 SWB Hong Kong and Aden 1966-68, instr Jt Servs Staff Coll 1969, cmdt Jr Div Staff Coll 1970-73, Brig dir army recruiting 1973-76, Regular Cmmns Bd 1978-79; devpt co-ordinator Royal Cwlth Soc 1980-81, md Saladin Security Ltd 1981-86, self-employed conslt personnel selection 1986-, voluntary conslt Parly selection bd procedure Cons Pty; kt 1985; *Recreations* sailing; *Clubs* Landsdowne; *Style*— Brig Sir Nicholas Somerville, CBE; Deptford Cottage, Greywell, Basingstoke, Hants RG25 1BS (☎ 0256 702796)

SOMERVILLE, Sir Robert; KCVO (1961, CVO 1953); s of Robert Somerville, FRSE, of Dunfermline; *b* 5 June 1906; *Educ* Fettes, St John's Coll Cambridge, Edinburgh Univ; *m* 1, 1932, Marie-Louise Cornelia (d 1976), da of Heinrich Bergené, of Aachen; 1 da; m 2, 1981, Mrs Jessie B Warburton, of Sydney; *Career* served in Miny of Shipping (later War Transport) 1940-44; entered Duchy of Lancaster Office 1930, chief clerk 1945, clerk of the Cncl 1952-70; memb Royal Cmmn on Historical Manuscripts 1966-88; FSA, FRHistS; *Style*— Sir Robert Somerville, KCVO; 3 Hunt's Close, Morden Rd, London SE3

SOMERVILLE, Maj-Gen Ronald Macaulay; CB (1974), OBE (1963); s of Rev David Somerville (d 1923); *b* 2 July 1919; *Educ* George Watson's Coll, Heriot-Watt Coll; *m* 1947, Jean McEwen, da of John Balderston (d 1951), of Glasgow; *Career* cmmnd RA 1940; World War II in UK, NW Europe and Far East (MBE, despatches), psc 1944, jssc 1956, Cdr Maiwand Battery in Cyprus Emergency 1957-59, Brevet Lt-Col 1960, Cdr 4 Light Regt in Hong Kong 1963-65 and in 1965 for Borneo Confrontation Campaign, Brig 1965, CRA 51 (Highland) Div 1965-66, idc 1967, DQMG, BAOR 1968-70, Maj Gen 1970, GOC Yorkshire Dist 1970-72, VQMG MOD 1972-74, Hon Col 3 Bn Yorkshire Vol 1972-77, Col Cmdt RA 1974-79; pres: RA Assoc Scotland 1978-, Scottish Union Jack Assoc 1982-; chm Offrs Assoc Scotland; gen mangr Scottish Special Housing Assoc 1975-84; chm Buildings Investigation Centre Ltd 1985-; CBIM, Hon MIH, Kt offr Order of Orange Nassau with Swords 1946; *Recreations* golf, gardening, painting; *Clubs* New (Edinburgh); *Style*— Maj Gen Ronald Somerville, CB, OBE; 6 Magdala Mews, Edinburgh EH12 5BX (☎ 031 346 0371); Bynack Mhor Boat of Garten, Invernessshire PH24 3BP (☎ 047 983 245)

SOMMERVILLE, William; s of William Sommerville, of Bay Trees, Church St, Blagdon, nr Bristol, and Mary Salome, *née* Whiskard (d 1988); *b* 28 April 1939; *Educ* Marlborough, Clare Coll Cambridge (MA), Imperial Coll London (MSc); *m* 21 Nov 1964, Mary, da of James Westhead, of 27 Lyndrick Rd, Mannamead, Plymouth; 1 s (John b 12 Jan 1970), 2 da (Katherine (Kate) b 13 Aug 1965, Rachel b 12 Feb 1967); *Career* ptnr MRM Partnership (consulting engrs); FICE 1984; *Style*— William Sommerville, Esq; Kilncroft, Limekiln Lane, Countess Wear, Exeter EX2 6LW (☎ 0392 52 301); MRM Partnership, 11-15 Dix's Field, Exeter EX1 1QA (☎ 0392 50 211)

SONDES, 5 Earl (UK 1880); Henry George Herbert Milles-Lade; also Baron Sondes (GB 1760) and Viscount Throwley (UK 1880); s of 4 Earl Sondes (d 1970, descended from 1 Baron Monson through the latter's 2 s, who was cr Baron Sondes) and Pamela, da of Lt-Col Herbert McDougall, of Cawston Manor, Norfolk; *b* 1 May 1940; *Educ* Eton; *m* 1, 1968 (m dis 1969), Primrose Anne, da of late Lawrence Stopford Llewellyn Cotter (s of 5 Bt); m 2 1976 (m dis 1980), Altgräfin Sissy, da of Altgraf Niklas zu Salm-Reifferscheidt-Raitz; *Heir* none; *Style*— The Rt Hon The Earl Sondes; Stringman's Farm, Faversham, Kent

SONDHEIMER, Prof Ernst Helmut; s of Max Sondheimer (d 1982), and Ida, *née* Oppenheimer; *b* 8 Sept 1923; *Educ* Univ Coll Sch, Trinity Coll Cambridge (MA, PhD, ScD); *m* 18 Aug 1950, Janet Harrington, da of Edgar Harrington Matthews (d 1968); 1 s (Julian b 1952), 1 da (Judith (Mrs Robertson) b 1956); *Career* WWII Cavendish Laboratory Cambridge 1944-45; fell Trinity Coll Cambridge 1948-52, Univ of London lectr mathematics Imperial Coll of Science and Technol 1951-54; reader in applied maths Queen Mary Coll 1954-60 prof of maths Westfield Coll 1960-82, prof emeritus 1982-; ed Alpine Journal 1986-; memb Highgate Literary and Scientific Inst; fell: King's Coll London 1985-, Westfield Coll London 1987-; memb London Mathematical Soc 1963-; *Books* Green's Functions for Solid State Physicists (with S Doniach 1974), Numbers and Infinity (with A Rogerson 1981), papers on the electron theory of metals; *Recreations* mountaineering, growing alpines, reading history; *Clubs* Alpine; *Style*— Prof Ernst Sondheimer; 51 Cholmeley Crescent, London N6 5EX (☎ 01 340 6607)

SOOKE, Thomas Peter; s of Dr Paul Joseph Sooke, of London, and Gertrude, *née* Klinger (d 1969); *b* 8 Jan 1945; *Educ* Westminster, Pembroke Coll Cambridge (MA), Columbia Univ New York (MBA); *m* 8 June 1975, Ceridwen Leeuwke Bathhurst, da of Derek Howard Matthews, of Amersham, Bucks; 1 s (Alastair b 1981), 1 da (Leonie b 1985); *Career* Price Waterhouse & Co 1968-70, mangr corpn fin Wallace Bros Bank Ltd 1972-76, dir corpn fin Granville & Co Ltd 1976-87, dir Lovat Enterprise Fund Ltd 1981-87, fndr memb Br Venture Capital Assoc 1983; bd memb: Granville Business Expansion Fund 1983-87, Wessex Business Expansion Fund 1983-87, Granville Modern Mgmnt Tst 1985-88; non exec dir: Granville Tst 1986-87, Franchise Investors Ltd 1985-; corp fin ptnr Touche Ross & Co 1988-; FCA 1979; *Recreations* tennis, golf, old english watercolours; *Clubs* Utd Oxford and Cambridge, Isle of Purbeck Golf; *Style*— Thomas Sooke, Esq; Touche Ross & Co, Hill House, 1 Little New St, London EC4A 3TR (☎ 01 936 3000, fax 01 583 8517, telex 884 739 TRLNDNG)

SOOLE, Michael Alexander; s of Brian Alfred Seymour Soole (d 1974), and Rosemary Una, *née* Salt; *b* 18 July 1954; *Educ* Berkhamsted Sch, Univ Coll Oxford (MA); *Career* called to Bar Inner Temple 1977, practising barrister 1978-; contested Aylesbury (SDP/Liberal Alliance) general elections 1983 and 1987; *Recreations* conversation; *Clubs* National Liberal; *Style*— Michael Soole, Esq; 36 Calabria Rd, London N5 1JA (☎ 01 359 0759); 1 Harcourt Buildings, 3rd Floor, Temple, London EC4Y 9DA (☎ 01 353 2214, fax 01 583 1656)

SOPER, Baron (Life Peer UK 1965); Rev Donald Oliver Soper; s of Ernest Frankham and Caroline Soper; *b* 31 Jan 1903; *Educ* Aske's Sch Hatcham, St Catharine's Coll Cambridge, Wesley House Cambridge, LSE (PhD); *m* 1929, Marie Gertrude, da of Arthur Dean; 4 da; *Career* sits as Labour Peer in House of Lords; min: South London Mission 1926-29, Central London Mission 1929-36; supt min W London Mission 1936-78, chm Shelter 1974-78; pres: League Against Cruel Sports, Christian Socialist Movement, Fellowship of Reconciliation, Methodist Conference (1953); World Methodist Peace Prize 1982; open-air speaker - Tower Hill every Wednesday for last 60 years, Hyde Park every Sunday; Hon DD Cambridge; *Books* Aflame with Faith, It is hard to work for God, The Advocacy of the Gospel, All His Grace, Christianity and Politics, Calling for Action (Autobiography); Practical Christianity Today, Will Christianity Work?; *Style*— The Rev Rt Hon The Lord Soper; 19 Thayer Street, London W1M 5LJ

SOPER, Michael Henry Ray; OBE (1963); s of John Philpott Henry Soper (d 1946), of Woodlands, Theydon Bois, Essex, and Edith Munro (d 1942); *b* 30 Sept 1913; *Educ* Tonbridge, Pembroke Coll Cambridge (MA, Dip Agric); *Career* lectr in Agric, Reading Univ 1936-38; inspector of Agric Sudan Govt 1938-40, deputy exec offr Surrey WAEC 1940-46; lectr in Agric Oxford Univ 1946-81; dir Oxford Univ Farm 1950-81; Student of Christ Church (tutorial fell) Oxford 1976-81; chief assessor Nat Certificate in Agric Examinations Bd 1962-87, organiser Oxford Farming Conf 1950-80; chm: Assoc of Agric 1982-, Oxfordshire Agric Soc Tst 1983-, City and Guilds Advsy Ctee for Agric 1963-76, English Panel Cncl for Awards of Royal Agric Soc 1984-87, author (with E S Carter) Modern Farming and the Countryside 1985, FRAgS, hon FCGI, hon fell City and Guilds of London Inst, MIBiol; *Recreations* golf, gardening; *Style*— Michael Soper, OBE; Larksmead, Brightwell cum Sotwell, Wallingford, Oxon OX10 0QF (☎ 0491 37416)

SOPHER, Ivan; s of James Joseph Sopher, of 22 Manor Hall Ave, London NW4, and Sophie Sopher; *b* 27 August 1949; *m* 1973, Helen; 1 s, 2 da; *Career* sole proprietor Ivan Sopher & Co CAs; jt md EWS Entertainments Ltd (jt venture with Ernst & Whinney); dir: Professional Pubns Ltd, Delta Financial Mgmnt Ltd; FCA, FCCA, ATII, MBIM; *Recreations* travel, sport; *Style*— Ivan Sopher, Esq; Studio House, Elstree Studios, Boreham Wood, Herts WD6 1JG

SOPWITH, Sir Charles Ronald; s of Alfred Sopwith (d 1946), of S Shields, Co Durham; *b* 12 Nov 1905; *Educ* S Shields HS; *m* 1946, Ivy Violet (d 1968), da of Frederick Leonard Yeates, of Gidea Park, Essex; *Career* CA 1928, slr 1938, asst dir Press Censorship 1943-45, princ asst slr Bd of Inland Revenue 1956-61, public tstee 1961-63, slr Inland Revenue 1963-70, dep sec Cabinet Off 1970-72, dir Royal Acad of Music 1973-87, (hon fell 1984), second counsel to chm of ctees House of Lords 1974-82; kt 1966; *Recreations* music; *Clubs* Reform; *Style*— Sir Charles Sopwith; 18 Moor Lane, Rickmansworth, Herts

SOPWITH, Thomas Edward Brodie; s of Sir Thomas Octave Murdoch Sopwith, CBE (d 1989, aged 101), and his 2 w, Phyllis, *née* Brodie (d 1978); *b* 15 Nov 1932; *Educ* Stowe; *m* 1977, Gina Melissa, *née* Hathorn; 2 da; *Career* Lt Coldstream Gds, company chm; *Recreations* yachting, flying, skiing; *Clubs* Royal Yacht Sqdn, Corviglia Ski, BRDC; *Style*— Thomas Sopwith, Esq; 67 Clabon Mews, London SW1 (☎ 01 589 3305); Axford House, Axord, nr Basingstoke, Hants (☎ 025 687 221)

SOREL-CAMERON, Air Cdre Robert; CBE (1945), AFC (1943); s of Lt-Col George Cecil Minett Sorel-Cameron, CBE (d 1947), and Marguerite Emily, er da of Hon Hamilton James Tollemache (4 s of 1 Baron Tollemache); *b* 27 Nov 1911; *Educ*

Wellington, Edinburgh Univ; *m* 1939, Henrietta Grace, *née* Radford-Norcop; 2 s, 1 da; *Career* joined RAF 1931 (served UK, Burma, India, Netherlands, East Indies), Air Cdre 1960, air attaché Athens 1960-62 (ret 1962); *Recreations* fishing, flat racing, wildlife; *Clubs* RAF; *Style—* Air Cdre Robert Sorel-Cameron, CBE, AFC; The White House, Whitwell, Norfolk NR10 4RF (☎ 0603 872394)

SORENSEN, (Nils Jorgen) Philip; s of Erik Philip Sorensen, consul-gen, of Lillon, Skane, Sweden, and Brita Hjordis Bendix, *née* Lundgren (d 1984); *b* 23 Sept 1938; *Educ* Herlufsholm Kostskole Naerstved Denmark, Niels Brock Commercial Sch Copenhagen; *m* 1962, Ingrid, da of Eigil Baltzer-Anderson (d 1965); 1 s (Mark b 13 March 1973), 3 da (Annette b 27 Aug 1963, Christina b 29 June 1965, Louisa b 18 Feb 1968); *Career* chm fndr Gp 4 Securitas cos: UK, Ireland, Belgium, Denmark, Luxembourg, Malta, Netherlands, Greece, Spain, Portugal; bd menb var security cos: Sweden, Norway, Australia, France, Japan, Thailand; pres Ligue Internationale des Societes de Surveillance, memb cncl Br Security Industl Assoc; owner of two small select hotels: Dormy House Hotel, Broadway and Strandhotellet, Skagen Denmark; Soldier of the Year Award, Sweden; hon citizen Cork 1985; *Recreations* sailing (fishing vessel 'Oke'), photography, travelling, book collecting; *Clubs* Buck's, Eccentric, Hurlingham, Mosimanns; *Style—* Philip Sorensen, Esq; Prinsevinkenpark 2, PO Box 85911, 2508 Den Haag, The Netherlands (☎ 010 31 70 519191); Group 4 Securitas Ltd, Farncombe House, Broadway, Worcs WR12 7LJ (☎ 0386 858585, fax 0386 858254, telex 338571)

SORKIN, (Alexander) Michael; s of Joseph Sorking, of London (d 1984), and Hilda Ruth, *née* Fiebusch; *b* 2 Mar 1943; *Educ* St Paul's; Manchester Univ (BA); *m* 27 Nov 1977, Angela Lucille, da of Leon Berman (MC), of London; 1 s (Jacob b 1983), 2 da (Zoe b 1979, Kim b 1980); *Career* joined Hambro Bank 1968 (dir 1973, exec dir 1983, vice chm 1987); dirships for A M Sorkin: dir: DBS UK Ltd 1986-, Fleet Street Properties Ltd 1986, Hambros Bank Ltd (vice-chm) 1973-, Hambros plc 1986-, Strauss Turnbull & Co Ltd 1986-, TNT (UK) Ltd 1979-, Hambro America Inc (USA) 1986-, Hambro Pacific Ltd (Hong Kong) 1978; *Recreations* opera, golf, tennis; *Style—* Michael Sorkin, Esq; 3 Robin Grove, London N6 (☎ 01 348 7111); Boxhall, Shottisham, Suffolk (☎ (0394) 411097); Hambros Bank, 41 Bishopsgate, London EC2 (☎ 01 588 2851, car ☎ (0836) 202 119)

SORRELL, Alec Dudley Mott; s of Dudley Sorrell (d 1972), of Theydon Bois, Essex, and Mary Dorothy Sybil, *née* Motts d 1947); *b* 17 April 1925; *Educ* Forest Sch, Downing Coll Cambridge (MA, LLB); *m* 3 Feb 1951, Elisabeth Ffolliot, da of Dr Albert Malcolm Barlow (d 1957), of Porthcurno, Cornwall; 2 s (Jeremy b 1951, Robin b 1955); *Career* Lt Royal Marines Far East and Malta 1943-47; snr ptnr Craigen Wilders & Sorrell, slrs; clerk: Parmiter's Governor's Fndn and Sch 1959-; dir: Spurstowe's Charity Tstees 1959-, Queen Adelaide's Charity Tstees 1963-, other London Charities; general commr of Income Tax 1962; JP: Inner London 1968-69, City of London 1969-; Royal Nat Throat, Nose and Ear Hosp: govr 1972-74 and 1980-82, special tstee 1982-; govr Forest Sch 1985-; Liveryman Worshipful Co of Basketmakers 1954- (prime warden 1986-87); *Recreations* fresh air, walking; *Clubs* Naval, City Livery; *Style—* Alec D M Sorrell, Esq; Clunes House, Toot Hill, nr Ongar, Essex CM5 9SF (☎ North Weald 2281); 81/83 High Road, London N22 6BE (☎ 01 888 2255, fax 01 881 5080)

SORRELL, Martin Stuart; s of Jack Sorrell of Mill Hill, London NW7; *b* 14 Feb 1945; *Educ* Haberdashers' Aske's, Christ's Coll Cambridge, Harvard Business Sch; *m* 1971, Sandra Carol Ann, *née* Finestone; 3 s; *Career* gp fin dir Saatchi & Saatchi Co plc (business services) 1977-86; Gp chief exec WPP gp plc (marketing services) 1986-; *Recreations* skiing; *Clubs* Reform, Harvard; *Style—* Martin Sorrell, Esq; Courtlands, Winnington Road, London N2 OTP; WPP Gp plc; 27 Farm St, London W1X 6RD (☎ 01 408 2204)

SOSKICE, Hon David William; s of Baron Stow Hill, PC, QC (Life Peer, d 1979), and Baroness Stow Hill, *qv*; *b* 1941; *Educ* Winchester, Trinity Oxford; *m* 1966, Alison, da of Walter Black, of Nateley Scures House, Hook, Hants; 1 s, 1 da; *Career* economist HM Treasury 1965-66, fell and praelector in economics Univ Coll Oxford 1966-; *Style—* The Hon David Soskice; 10 Staverton Rd, Oxford

SOSKICE, Hon Oliver Cloudesley Hunter; s of Baron Stow Hill (Life Peer, d 1979), and Baroness Stow Hill, *qv*; *b* 1947; *Educ* Winchester, Trinity Hall Cambridge; *m* 1982, Janet, eldest da of A M Martin, of St Louis, Mo; 2 da (Catherine b 1984, Isabelle b 1987); *Style—* The Hon Oliver Soskice

SOUGHTON, John Edward; s of Lt Edward Charles Soughton, RN (ka 1945), and Emily May, *née* Austen; *b* 22 August 1939; *Educ* John Lyon Sch, Harrow-on-the-Hill Middx; *Career* CA; sr ptnr Hill Wooldridge and Co Harrow Middx; FCA (1968); *Recreations* travel, the arts; *Clubs* St James's, London and Antigua; *Style—* John E Soughton, Esq; Herries, 4 Amberley Close, Moss Lane, Pinner, Middx HA5 3BH (☎ 01 868 0944); Hill Wooldridge & Co, 107 Hindes Road, Harrow, Middx HA1 1RU (☎ 01 427 1944)

SOUHAMI, Mark J; s of John F and Freda Souhami; *b* 25 Sept 1935; *Educ* St Marylebone GS; *m* 1964, Margaret, da of Joseph Austin; 2 da (Emma b.1966, Charlotte b 1968); *Career* gp mktg dir Dixons Gp plc 1970, jt md Retail Div 1973, chm and md Dixons Ltd 1976, dir Dixons Gp plc 1978, md Dixons Gp plc 1986; chm Currys Gp plc, Dixons Colour Laboratories Ltd, Dixons Gp USA inc, Supa Snaps Ltd, Wallace Heaton Ltd; *Clubs* Savile, RAC; *Style—* Mark Souhami, Esq; 29 Farm St, London W1

SOUKUP, Lady (Constance) Ann; *née* Butler; da of 7 Marquess of Ormonde, MBE; *b* 13 Dec 1940; *m* 1965, Henry Lea Soukup; 1 s (Andrew), 1 da (Meghan); *Style—* Lady Ann Soukup; 618 North Washington, Hinsdale, Illinois, USA

SOULBURY, 2 Viscount (UK 1954); James Herwald Ramsbotham; also Baron Soulbury (UK 1941); s of 1 Viscount, GCMG, GCVO, OBE, MC, PC (d 1971); *b* 21 Mar 1915; *Educ* Eton, Magdalen Oxford; *m* 1949, Anthea Margaret (d 1950), da of late David Wilton; *Heir* bro, Hon Sir Peter Edward Ramsbotham, GCMG, GCVO; *Style—* The Rt Hon the Viscount Soulbury; East Lane, Ovington, Alresford, Hants SO24 0RA

SOUNDY, Andrew John; s of Maj Harold Cecil Soundy, MBE, MC, TD (d 1969), and Adele Monica Templeton, *née* Westley; *b* 29 Mar 1940; *Educ* Boxgrove Sch Guildford, Shrewsbury Sch Salop, Trinity Coll Cambridge (Law Tripos, BA, MA); *m* 12 Oct 1963, Jill Marion, da of Frank Nathaniel Steiner (d 1977), of Gerrards Cross, Bucks; 1 s (Mark b 1964), 2 da (Emma b 1967, Victoria b 1969); *Career* admitted slr 1966; ptnr Ashurst Morris Crisp slrs, farmer and breeder of pedigree cattle; *Recreations* opera, tennis, good living; *Clubs* Cavalry and Guards; *Style—* Andrew J Soundy, Esq; Bartletts Farm, Mattingley, nr Basingstoke, Hampshire RG27 8JU; Broadgate House, 7 Feldon St, London EC2M 7HD (☎ 01 247 7666, telex 887067, fax 01 377 5659)

SOUNESS, James McGill; *m* 2 s, 1 da; *Career* md Life Assoc of Scotland; chm (2 year term) Associated Scottish Life Offices 1982-, dir: Hibernian Life Assur, LAS Pensions Mgmnt Ltd, Dunedin Property Devpt Co, Dunedin Property Investmt Co, Merchant Investors Assur Co Ltd, Chamber Devpt Ltd, Edinburgh's Capital Ltd, Scottish Fin Enterprise; chm: Crescent Life Assur Co Ltd, LAS Investmt Mgmnt Ltd, LAS Unit Tst Managers; fin convener Royal Scottish Soc for Prevention of Cruelty to Children; hon consul to Netherlands (Edinburgh); memb Music Ctee Scottish Arts Cncl; FFA 1956; *Recreations* hill and mountain climbing, golf, music, gardening, tennis, badminton, jogging; *Style—* James Souness Esq; c/o The Life Association of Scotland Ltd, 10 George St, Edinburgh EH2 (☎ (031 225) 8494)

SOUTAR, Air Marshal Sir Charles John Williamson; KBE (1978), MBE (1958); s of Charles A Soutar, and Mary H Watson; *b* 1920 June; *Educ* Brentwood Sch, London Hosp; *m* 1944, Joy Dorée Upton; 1 s, 2 da; *Career* RAF 1946, QHS 1974-81, PMO Strike Cmd 1975-78, Dir-Gen RAF Med Services 1978-81; CStJ 1972; *Clubs* RAF; *Style—* Air Marshal Sir Charles Soutar, KBE; Oak Cottage, High St, Aldeburgh, Suffolk

SOUTER, Hon Amanda Elizabeth; da and co-heiress presumptive of 25 Baron Audley; *b* 5 May 1958; *Style—* The Hon Amanda Souter; c/o Friendly Green, Cowden, nr Edenbridge, Kent TN8 7DU

SOUTER, Christopher David William; s of David Cowley Souter, VRD, of Belford, Northumberland, and Joan Margaret, *née* Wear; *b* 9 Mar 1941; *Educ* Fettes Coll Edinburgh; *m* 14 Nov 1964, Erica Sibbald, da of Geoffrey Balfour Stenhouse (d 1975); 2 s (Rory b 1967, Justin b 1970), 1 da (Zoë b 1965); *Career* dir WA Souter & Co Ltd Sheaf Steam Shipping Co Ltd 1970, owner Souter Ship Spares 1980; dir: James Marine Servs Ltd 1987-, James Industl Servs Ltd; dir Brandling Lawn Tennis Club Hldgs Ltd; former chm N of Eng Shipowners Assoç 1974, Offr First Class Royal Order of Polar Star (Sweden) 1986, hon consul of Sweden Newcastle upon Tyne; MICS; *Recreations* tennis, ornithology, victorian art; *Clubs* Northern Counties; *Style—* Christopher Souter, Esq; c/o James Marine Services Ltd, 3-10, Broad Chare, Newcastle upon Tyne 1 (☎ 091 232 4145, fax 091 261 4543, telex 537812 JAMAR G)

SOUTER, David Cowley; s of Sir William Alfred Souter, KB (d 1968), and Madalene, *née* Robson (d 1972); *b* 25 Nov 1939; *Educ* Fettes; *m* 25 Aug 1939, Joan Margaret, da of Lt-Col Dr Arthur Taylor Wear (d 1932), of Newcastle Upon Tyne; 3 s (Christopher, Julian, Nigel), 1 da (Diana); *Career* RNVR Tyne div HMS Calliope 1936, mobilised Munich Crisis, HMS Carlisle 1938, MTB 22 HMS Vernon 1939, HMS Hornet 1940, in cmd MTB 100, 68 and 268 Br Waters and Mediterranian 1941-44, HMS Windsor, HMS Montrose Harwich, HMS Arbella 1945, ret RNVR Lt Cdr 1951; William Dickinson & Co Ltd Newcastle Upon Tyne 1934-39, WA Souter & Co Ltd 1945-80 (later years jt md and chm); past pres: Gosforth Unit Sea Cadets, Northumberland Lawn Tennis Assoc, Mission to Seamen South Sheilds, Blyth Harbour Cmmn; gen cmmr of taxes 1953-, High Sheriff Tyne & Wear 1984-85, vice-pres Royal Merchant Navy Sch; FICS, fell NE Coast Inst of Engrs and Shipbuilders; VRD (1951); *Recreations* golf, tennis, bee-keeping, ornithology, shooting, forestry, gardening; *Clubs* Army & Navy; *Style—* David Souter, Esq; Chatsworth, Moor Crescent, Gosforth, Newcastle Upon Tyne NE3 4AQ (☎ 091 2852412); Detchant Park, Belford, Northumberland NE70 7PQ (☎ 06683 353)

SOUTH, Sir Arthur; JP (Norwich 1949); s of Arthur South; *b* 29 Oct 1914; *Educ* City of Norwich Sch; *m* 1, 1937 (m dis 1976), May Adamson; 2 s; m 2, 1976, Mary June (d 1982), widow of Robert Carter, JP, DL; *Career* former Lord Mayor Norwich and former chm Norwich Lowestoft, and Gt Yarmouth Hosp Mgmnt Ctee; chm Norfolk AHA 1974-78 and E Anglian RHA 1978-87; former chm Labour Party Gp Norwich City Cncl; kt 1974; *Style—* Sir Arthur South, JP; The Lowlands, Drayton, Norfolk (☎ 0603 867 355)

SOUTH, Edward Clark; s of Edward South (d 1967), of Whitchurch, Shropshire, and Lydia, *née* Williams (d 1984); *b* 10 May 1936; *Educ* Queens Coll Taunton; *m* 12 Dec 1959, Helen Mary, da of Guilherme Romano Favacho (d 1962), of Shanghai; 3 s (Edward b 1962 (d 1986), Antony b 1964, Richard b 1965), 1 da (Alison b 1966); *Career* CA; ptnr Stubbs, Parkin, South & Phillips; magistrate 1980-87; assoc memb Inst of Taxation; *Recreations* sailing, cookery, travel; *Clubs* Royal Overseas League; *Style—* Edward South, Esq; The Old Smithy, Burlton, nr Shrewsbury, Shropshire SY4 5TB; Stubbs, Parkin, South & Phillips, 4 High St, Wem, Shropshire and Branch Offices

SOUTHAM, Kenneth (Hubert); s of Hubert Basil Southam, MBE (d 1978), and Millicent Edith, *née* Johnson (d 1982); *b* 24 Feb 1927; *Educ* Harborne Collegiate Birmingham; *m* 29 Aug 1953, Marjorie, da of Herbert Lever (d 1985); *Career* served RA 1944-48; qualified CA 1955; chief acct Atomic Power Constructions Ltd 1957-76; own practice Southam & Co 1977-; Freeman City of London, Liveryman Worshipful Co of Woolmen 1969-; *Recreations* photography, philately, reading, charitable work; *Clubs* City Livery; *Style—* Kenneth Southam, Esq; 23 Penshurst Rd, Potters Bar, Herts (☎ (0707) 56129); Southam & Co, Suite 33, 93/94 Chancery Lane, London WC2 1DT (☎ 01 831 0401)

SOUTHAMPTON, Barony of (GB 1780); *see*: FitzRoy, Charles

SOUTHAMPTON, Bishop Suffragan of 1984-; Rt Rev (Edward) David Cartwright; o s of John Edward Cartwright (d 1957), of Grimsby, and Gertrude, *née* Lusby (d 1957); *b* 15 July 1920; *Educ* St James's Choir Sch Grimsby, Lincoln Sch, Selwyn Coll and Westcott House Cambridge (BA 1941, MA 1945); *m* 12 June 1946, Elsie Irene, o da of Walter Rogers (d 1930), of Grimsby; 1 s (Roger Edward Henry b 1948), 2 da (Sarah Elizabeth (Mrs Thornton) b 1952, Rachel Mary b 1958); *Career* curate of Boston, Lincs 1943-48; mayor's chaplain 1945-48; vicar of St Leonard's, Redfield, Bristol 1948-52, of Olveston with Aust 1952-60, and of Bishopston 1960-73; hon canon of Bristol 1970, of Winchester 1973; archdeacon of Winchester 1973-84; vicar of Sparsholt 1973-84; memb: Church Assembly and General Synod 1956-83; Church of England Pensions Bd 1980-84; Church Cmmr 1973-84; *Recreations* books, music; *Style—* The Rt Rev the Bishop of Southampton; Jollers, Sparsholt, Winchester, Hants SO21 2MS (☎ 096 272 265)

SOUTHAN, His Hon Judge Robert Joseph; s of Thomas Southan (d 1962), of Warwicks, and Kathleen Annie, *née* Beck (d 1987); *b* 13 July 1928; *Educ* Rugby, St Edmund Hall Oxford (MA), UCL (LLM); *m* 1960, Elizabeth Andreas, da of Clive

Raleigh Evatt, QC (d 1984), of Australia; 1 s (Richard b 1962, d 1984), 1 da (Anne b 1969); *Career* barr: England and Wales 1953, New South Wales 1974; rec Crown Ct 1982, circuit judge 1986; *Recreations* sailing, skiing, tennis, squash, theatre, opera; *Clubs* Royal Corinthian Yacht, Bar Yacht, Cumberland LT; *Style*— His Hon Judge Robert Southan; Snaresbrook Crown Court, Hollybush Hill, London E11 1QW (☎ 01 989 6666)

SOUTHBOROUGH, Audrey, Baroness; Audrey Evelyn Dorothy; yr da of Edgar George Money; *m* 1918, 3 Baron Southborough (d 1982), sometime md Shell Transport and Trading; 1 s (4 Baron), 1 da (Hon Mrs Rank); *Style*— The Rt Hon Audrey, Lady Southborough; The Dower House, Landhurst, Hartfield, E Sussex (☎ 089 277 835)

SOUTHBOROUGH, 4 Baron (UK 1917); (Francis) Michael Hopwood; only s of 3 Baron Southborough (d 1982), and Audrey, Baroness Southborough, *qv*; *b* 3 May 1922; *Educ* Wellington, Ch Ch Oxford; *m* 1945, Moyna Kemp (d 1987), da of Robert John Kemp Chattey; 1 da (adopted); *Heir* none; *Career* serv Lt Rifle Bde WWII; Lloyd's underwriter 1949-; dir Glanvill, Enthoven & Co Ltd 1954, dep chm 1977-80; dir Robert Woodson Ltd 1950 and chm 1970-72; *Clubs* Brooks's, City of London; *Style*— The Rt Hon the Lord Southborough; 50a Eaton Sq, London SW1W 9BE (☎ 01 235 3181)

SOUTHBY, Iris, Lady; Iris Mackay; *née* Heriot; da of late Lt-Col Granville Mackay Heriot, DSO, RM, and Marta Luisa, da of William Paynter; *m* 1, Brig Ian Charles Alexander Robertson; m 2, 1979, as his 4 w, Lt-Col Sir (Archibald) Richard Charles Southby, 2 Bt, OBE (d 1988); Greystone House, Stone, Tenterden, Kent; No 7 Bolur Avenue, Kenilworth 7700, Cape, S Africa

SOUTHBY, Sir John Richard Bilbe; 3 Bt (UK 1937); s of Sir (Archibald) Richard Charles Southby, 2 Bt, OBE (d 1988) and his 2 w Olive, da of late Sir Thomas Bilbe-Robinson, GBE, KCMG; *b* 2 April 1948; *Educ* Peterhouse Rhodesia, Loughborough Univ (BSc); *m* 1971, Victoria, da of John Wilfred Sturrock, of Tettenhall, Wolverhampton; 2 s (Peter John, James William b 1984), 1 da (Sarah Jane b 1975); *Heir* s, Peter John Southby b 20 Aug 1973; *Style*— Sir John Southby, Bt; 20 Harrowby Lane, Grantham, Lincs NG31 9HX

SOUTHBY, Noreen, Lady Noreen Vera; da of late Bernard Compton Simm; *m* 28 March 1962, as his 2 w, Cdr Sir Archibald Richard James Southby, RN, 1 Bt (d 1969); *Style*— Noreen, Lady Southby; 18 Harbour View Rd, Parkstone, Poole, Dorset

SOUTHERN, Richard; s of Harry Southern (d 1963), of Beckenham, and Edith, *née* Hockney (d 1963); *b* 5 Oct 1903; *Educ* St Dunstan's Coll Catford, Goldsmith's Art Sch, Royal Acad; *m* 8 April 1933, Grace Kathleen, da of Ernest John Loosemore (d 1933), of Ladywell; 2 da (Jane b 1934, Catharine b 1943); *Career* NFS 1931-45; theatre conslt designer and historian 1928-; tech lectr: Goldsmiths Coll 1932, London Theatre Studio 1937, RADA 1945, Old Vic Theatre Centre 1947, also in France Norway Sweden Japan USA; theatre planning advsr Arts Cncl 1947; advsr on Univ theatres at: Bristol 1951, RCA 1952, Glasgow 1953, Reading 1957, Nottingham 1959, Southampton 1961, Manchester 1965, UCL 1967; reconstruction of historic theatres at: Richmond Yorks 1950, King's Lynn 1951, Williamsburg Va 1953; lectr in drama dept Univ of Bristol 1959-69, dir Nuffield Theatre Univ of Southampton 1964-66; hon life memb Assoc of Br Theatre Technicians 1974-; Hon DLitt Bristol 1956; *Books* Stage Setting (1937), Proscenium and Sightlines (1939), The Georgian Playhouse (1948), Changeable Scenery (1952), The Open Stage (1953), The Medieval Theatre in the Round (1957), The Seven Ages of the Theatre (1961), The Victorian Theatre (1970), The Staging of Plays before Shakespeare (1973); *Recreations* figure drawing; *Style*— Dr Richard Southern; 37 Langham Rd, Teddington TW11 9HF (☎ 01 943 1979)

SOUTHERN, Sir Richard William; s of Matthew Southern; *b* 8 Feb 1912; *Educ* Newcastle-upon-Tyne Royal GS, Balliol Coll Oxford; *m* 1944, Sheila, *née* Cobley, widow of Sqdn Ldr C Crichton-Miller; 2 s; *Career* served WWII: Oxford and Bucks LI, Durham LI, RAC, Political Intelligence Dept FO; historian: fell and tutor Balliol Coll Oxford 1937-61, jr proctor Oxford Univ 1948-49, Birkbeck lectr Ecclesiastical History Trinity Coll Cambridge 1959-60, Chichele Prof Modern History Oxford 1961-69; pres: St John's Coll Oxford 1969-81 (hon fell 1981-), Royal Historical Soc 1968-72, Selden Soc 1973-76; FBA; hon fell: Sidney Sussex Coll Cambridge, Balliol Coll Oxford; Hon DLitt: Glasgow, Durham, Cantab, Bristol, Newcastle, Warwick; Hon LLD Harvard; kt 1974; *Style*— Sir Richard Southern; 40 St John St, Oxford (☎ 0865 57778)

SOUTHERN, Sir Robert; CBE (1953); s of Job Southern of Parkview, Park Lane, Whitefield; *b* 17 Mar 1907; *Educ* Stand GS, Co-op Coll Manchester Univ; *m* 1933, Lena, da of George Henry Chapman, of Whitefield; 1 s, 1 da; *Career* gen-sec Co-operative Union Ltd 1948-72; kt 1970; *Style*— Sir Robert Southern, CBE; 22 Glebelands Rd, Prestwich, Nr Manchester (☎ 061 773 2699)

SOUTHESK, 11 Earl of (S 1633); Sir Charles Alexander Carnegie; 8 Bt (NS 1663), KCVO (1926), DL (Angus); also Lord Carnegie (S 1616), Baron Balinhard (UK 1869); s of 10 Earl (d 1941, whose f, the 9 Earl, was a poet, antiquary and author of Herminius, described as a romance) and Ethel, da of Sir Alexander Bannerman, 9 Bt; *b* 23 Sept 1893; *Educ* Eton; *m* 1, 1923, HH Princess Alexandra Victoria Georgina Bertha Maud (d 1945), yr da of HRH the late Princess Royal and the 1 Duke of Fife; 1 s, 1 da; m 2, 1952, Evelyn Julia, da of Lt-Col Arthur Peere Williams-Freeman, DSO, OBE, and widow of Major Ion Edward FitzGerald Campbell, Duke of Cornwall's LI (gs of 2 Bt, cr UK 1815); *Heir* s, Duke of Fife; *Career* Maj (ret) Scots Gds; ADC to The Viceroy of India 1917-1919; *Style*— The Rt Hon the Earl of Southesk, KCVO, DL; Kinnaird Castle, Brechin, Angus (☎ 067 481 209)

SOUTHEY, Sir Robert John; CMG (1970); s of late Allen Hope Southey, and late Ethel Thorpe McComas, MBE; *b* 20 Mar 1922; *Educ* Geelong GS, Magdalen Coll Oxford Univ (MA); *m* 1, 1946, Valerie Janet Cotton (d 1977), da of Hon Sir Francis Grenville Clarke, KBE, MLC (d 1955); 5 s; m 2, 1982, Marigold Merlyn Baillieu, da of Sidney Myer (d 1934) and Dame (Margery) Merlyn Myer, DBE (d 1982); *Career* WWII Coldstream Gds 1941-46, served N Africa and Italy, Capt 1944; dir: Buckley & Nunn 1958-78, BP Co of Aust Ltd, Int Computers (Aust) Pty Ltd, Nat West Fin Aust Ltd 1983-85, Natwest Australia Bank Ltd 1985-87, General Accident Fire & Life Assur Corpn plc (chm Aust advsy cncl), Wm Haughton & Co Ltd 1953-80, Kawasaki (Aust) Pty Ltd 1986-; memb fedn exec Lib Party 1966-82, pres Lib Pty Victoria 1966-70, fed pres Lib Party 1970-75; chm Aust Ballet Fndn 1980-; kt 1976; *See Debrett's Handbook of Australia and New Zealand for further details*; *Recreations* music, fishing, golf; *Clubs* Cavalry and Guards, MCC, Leander, Melbourne and Australian (Melbourne), Union (Sydney); *Style*— Sir Robert Southey, CMG; 3 Denistoun Ave, Mt Eliza, Vic 3930, Australia

SOUTHGATE, Crispin John; s of Brig John Terence Southgate, OBE, and Stancia Lillian, *née* Collins; *b* 16 Feb 1955; *Educ* Christ's Hosp Horsham, Merton Coll Oxford (MA); *m* 15 Sept 1979, Joanna Mary, da of Gerald Norman Donaldson, TD; 1 s (William b 1987), 1 da (Eleanor b 1985); *Career* Price Waterhouse & Co 1977-82; dir Charterhouse Bank Ltd 1987- (joined 1982); tres The Rainer Fndn 1984-; ACA 1980; *Style*— Crispin Southgate, Esq; Charter House Bank Ltd, 1 Paternoster Row, St Pauls London EC4M 7DH (☎ 01 248 4000, fax 01 248 6522, telex 884276)

SOUTHGATE, Very Rev John Eliot; s of Reginald Henry Southgate; *b* 2 Sept 1926; *Educ* City of Norwich, Durham Univ; *m* 1958, Patricia Mary, *née* Plumb; 2 s, 1 da; *Career* ordained 1955 (Leicester), vicar of Plumstead Southwark 1962, rector of Charlton Southwark 1966, dean of Greenwich 1968, archdeacon of Cleveland York 1974, dean of York 1984-; *Recreations* music; *Clubs* Yorkshire; *Style*— The Very Rev The Dean of York; The Deanery, York YO1 2JD

SOUTHGATE-SAYERS, John Edward; s of Edward Herbert Charles Southgate-Sayers (d 1956), and Lilian Florence, *née* Trevett (d 1980); *b* 17 June 1961; *Educ* Bishops Stortford Coll, Arch Assoc Sch of Arch; *m* 27 Aug 1960, Susan Mary, da of Sir John B Greaves, CBE (d 1967); 1 s (Jonathan b 1967), 2 da (Susannah b 1961, Celina b 1968); *Career* chartered architect and surveyor, ptnr Sir John Brown Henson & Ptnrs London 1956-64; princ Speakman Sayers & Ptnrs Jersey & Guernsey 1969-; *Recreations* painting; *Style*— John Southgate-Sayers, Esq; La Cotte, Fort Road, St Peter Port, Guernsey C1 (☎ 0481 21952); Estate House, Mansell Street, St Peter Port, Guernsey (☎ 0481 24022, fax 0481 27359); Anley House, Anley St, St Helier, Jersey (☎ 0534 74637, fax 0534 36940)

SOUTHWARD, Dr Nigel Ralph; LVO (1985); s of Sir Ralph Southward, KCVO, FRCP, of 9 Devonshire Place, London W1N 1PB, and Evelyn, *née* Tassell; *b* 8 Feb 1941; *Educ* Rugby, Trinity Hall Cambridge (MA, MB, BChir); *m* 24 July 1965, Annette, da of Johan Heinrich Hoffmann, of Strandvesen, Skodsborg, Denmark; 1 s (Nicholas b 1966), 2 da (Karen b 1968, Emma b 1970); *Career* apothecary to HM The Queen, apothecary to the household and to the households of: HM Queen Elizabeth the Queen Mother, the Princess Margaret Countess of Snowdon, Princess Alice, Duchess of Gloucester, the Duke and Duchess of Gloucester and the Duke and Duchess of Kent 1975-; *Recreations* sailing, golf, skiing; *Clubs* RYS; *Style*— Dr Nigel R Southward, LVO; 56 Primrose Gardens, London NW3 4TP (☎ 01 935 8425); 9 Devonshire Place, London W1N 1PB (☎ 01 935 8425); car (☎ (0836) 255 900)

SOUTHWARD, Sir Ralph; KCVO (1975); s of Henry Stalker Southward, of Cumberland; *b* 2 Jan 1908,Glasgow; *Educ* Glasgow HS, Glasgow Univ (MB, ChB); *m* 1935, Evelyn, da of J G Tassell, of Harrogate; 4 s; *Career* Col RAMC (N Africa, India, Ceylon) 1940-45; apothecary to: Royal Household 1964-74, HM Queen Elizabeth the Queen Mother 1966-, TRH the Duke and Duchess of Gloucester 1966-75, HM The Queen 1972-74; Hon Freeman Worshipful Soc of Apothecaries 1975; FRCP; *Recreations* fishing (trout, salmon), golf, travel; *Style*— Sir Ralph Southward, KCVO; 9 Devonshire Place, London W1N 1PB (☎ 01 935 7969); Amerden Priory, Taplow, Bucks (☎ (0628) 23525)

SOUTHWARK, 7 Bishop of, 1980-; Rt Rev Ronald Oliver Bowlby; patron of one hundred and sixty-three livings, of the Archdeaconries of Southwark, Lewisham, Lambeth, Wandsworth, Croydon and Reigate, and of the Provostship and six Residentiary Canonries in Southwark Cathedral; the See was founded by Act of Parliament 1905; s of Oliver Bowlby; *b* 16 August 1926; *Educ* Eton, Trinity Coll Oxford, Westcott House Cambridge; *m* 1956, Elizabeth Trevelyan Monro; 3 s, 2 da; *Career* curate 1952-57, vicar of St Aidan Billingham 1957-66, vicar of Croydon 1966-72, bishop of Newcastle 1973-80; chm: Hosp Chaplaincies Cncl 1975-82, Social Policy Ctee C of E Bd for Social Responsibility; memb: Anglican Consultative Cncl 1978-85, Duke of Edinburgh's Nat Housing Inquiry 1984-85; Hon Fell Newcastle-upon-Tyne Poly; *Books* contributor to: Church without Walls (1969, 1 edn), Church and Politics Today (1985, 2 edn); *Recreations* gardening, walking, music, family history; *Style*— The Rt Rev the Bishop of Southwark; Bishop's House, 38 Tooting Bec Gardens, Streatham, London SW16 1QZ (☎ 01 769 3256)

SOUTHWELL, Hon Charles Anthony John; yr s of 7th Viscount Southwell; *b* 27 Sept 1962; *Style*— The Hon Charles Southwell

SOUTHWELL, Hon Mrs John; Daphne Lewin; da of Sir Geoffrey Lewin Watson, 3 and last Bt (cr 1918, extinct 1959); *m* 1932, Lt-Cdr Hon John Michael Southwell, RN (ka 1944, 3 s of 5 Viscount Southwell); *Style*— The Hon Mrs John Southwell; Buckclose, Longparish, nr Andover, Hants

SOUTHWELL, Bishop of 1988-, Rt Rev Patrick Burnet Harris; s of Edward James Burnet Harris, and Astrid, *née* Kendall; *b* 30 Sept 1934; *Educ* St Albans Sch, Keble Coll Oxford (MA); *m* 1968, Valerie Margaret Pilbrow; 1 s, 2 da; *Career* asst curate St Ebbe's Oxford 1960-63, missionary with S American Missionary Soc 1963-73, archdeacon of Salta Argentina 1969-73, diocesan bishop Northern Argentina 1973-80, rector Kirdheaton and asst bishop Diocese of Wakefield 1981-85, sec Ptnrship for World Mission 1986-88, asst bishop Diocese of Oxford 1986-88; *Recreations* ornithology, S American Indian culture, music; *Style*— The Rt Rev the Bishop of Southwell; Bishop's Manor, Southwell, Notts NG25 0JR

SOUTHWELL, 7 Viscount (I 1776); Sir Pyers Anthony Joseph Southwell; 10 Bt (I 1662); also Baron Southwell (I 1717); s of late Hon Francis Joseph Southwell, 2 s of 5 Viscount; suc unc 1960; *b* 14 Sept 1930; *Educ* Beaumont Coll, RMA Sandhurst; *m* 1955, Barbara Jacqueline, da of A Raynes; 2 s; *Heir* s, Hon Richard Southwell; *Career* Capt (ret) 8 Hussars; company dir; *Clubs* MCC, Woburn Golf and Country, Diners; *Style*— The Rt Hon the Viscount Southwell; 4 Roseberry Av, Harpenden, Herts (☎ 05827 5831)

SOUTHWELL, Hon Richard Andrew Pyers; s and h of 7 Viscount Southwell; *b* 15 June 1956; *Style*— The Hon Richard Southwell

SOUTHWICK, Douglas Arthur; OBE (1988); s of Norman Arthur Fitton, and Hilda, *née* Schofield (d 1988); *b* 2 Oct 1924; *Educ* Thirsk GS N Yorks; *m* 4 June 1949, Enid Lillian, da of William Howard Screeton (d 1959), of Willowfield House, Keyingham, N Humberside; *Career* NFS 1939-45; owner and occupier farmer Village Farm Skipsea Driffield N Humberside 1948-87, publican Bd Inn Skipsea 1964-73, turf accountant Skipsea and other offs 1961-; memb: Bridlington RDC, Skipsea Parish Cncl, E Riding of Yorks CC (until reorganisation 1973); Humberside CC 1973-: chm and shadow chm public protection ctee 1974-88, dep ldr 1979-81, chm 1988-89; 40 years serv to local

Cons Party; constituency chm: to Lord Holderness 1970-77, to John Townend MP Bridlington 1977-80; chm local Parish Cncl; memb Soc of Industl and Emergency Safety Offrs; *Style*— Douglas A Southwick, Esq, OBE; The Finishing Post, Skipsea, Driffield, N Humberside YO25 8SW (☎ 026 286 217/367/607/716)

SOUTHWOOD, Prof Sir (Thomas) Richard Edmund; s of Edmund William Southwood (d 1984), of Parrock Manor, Gravesend, and Ada Mary, *née* Regg (d 1949), da of Ven Archdeacon Thos R Regg, of Newcastle, NSW; *b* 20 June 1931; *Educ* Gravesend GS, Imperial Coll London (BSc, PhD, DSc), Oxford Univ (MA, DSc); *m* 1955, Alison Langley, da of Arthur Langley Harden (d 1983), of Fallows Green, Harpenden, Herts; 2 s (Richard, Charles); *Career* prof of zoology and applied entomology Univ of London 1967-79; head of dept of zoology Imperial Coll London; Linacre prof of zoology and head of dept Univ of Oxford 1979-, vice-chllr Univ of Oxford (1989-93); chm bd of tstees Br Museum (Nat Hist) 1980-84 (memb 1973), chm Royal Cmmn on Environmental Pollution 1981-86 (memb 1974-), vice-pres Royal Soc of London 1982-84, pres Royal Entomological Soc of London 1983-85, prof at large Cornell Univ USA 1985-91, chm Nat Radiological Protection Bd 1985 (memb 1981-), fell Merton Coll Oxford 1979-; foreign memb: American Acad of Arts and Scis 1980, Norwegian Acad of Sci and Letters 1987, US Nat Acad of Scis 1988; Hon DSc: Griffith, East-Anglia, McGill, Warwick; Hon Doctorate Lund; kt 1984; *Books* Land and water Bugs of the British Isles (with D Leston, 1959), Life of the Wayside and Woodland (1963), Ecological Methods (1966, 2 ed 1978), Insects on Plants (jtly, 1984), Insects & The Plant Surface (jtly, 1986), Radiation and Health (jtly, 1987); *Recreations* gardening, natural history; *Clubs* Athenaeum, Oxford and Cambridge; *Style*— Prof Sir Richard Southwood; Merton College, Oxford; Zoology Dept, South Parks Rd, Oxford (☎ 0865 271277); University Offices, Wellington Square, Oxford (☎ 0865 270242)

SOUTHWOOD, William Frederick Walter; s of Stuart Walter, Southwood, MC (d 1982), of London, and Mildred Mary, *née* Southwood (d 1988); *b* 8 June 1925; *Educ* Charterhouse, Cambridge (MB BChir, MA, MChir, MD); *m* 1 May 1965, Margaret Carleton, da of Sir Ernest William Holderness, 2 Bt, CBE (d 1968); 2 s (Robert b 1966, John b 1967); *Career* Nat Serv Capt RAMC 1949-51; conslt surgn Bath Health Dist 1966-, Hunterian prof RCS 1961, memb Professional and Linguistic Assessment Bd 1976-87 (chm 1984-87), visiting prof of surgery Univ of Cape Town 1987; Memb of Court Worshipful Soc of Apothecaries 1975-, (Liveryman 1953, Master 1986-87); FRSM 1952; *Books* Progress in Proctology (chp on carcinoid tumours, 1969); *Recreations* fishing, shooting, snooker; *Clubs* East India, Bath and County; *Style*— William Southwood, Esq; Upton Hse, Bathwick Hill, Bath BA2 6EX (☎ 0225 465 152); The Bath Clinic, Claverton Down, Bath BA2 7BR (☎ 0225 835 555)

SOUTHWORTH, Sir Frederick; QC (Bahamas 1952); s of late Harper Southworth, of Blackburn, Lancs; *b* 9 May 1910; *Educ* Queen Elizabeth's GS Blackburn, Exeter Coll Oxford (MA, BCL); *m* 1942, Margaret, da of James Rice, of Monaghan, Ireland; 3 da; *Career* S Lancs Regt, Lancs Fus, JAG Dept India 1939-46, Hon Col; barr Gray's Inn 1936; crown counsel: Palestine 1946-47, Tanganyika 1947-51; attorney-gen Bahamas 1951-55 (sometime act govr-gen and CJ), CJ Malawi 1964-70 (sometime act govr-gen); kt 1965; *Style*— Sir Frederick Southworth, QC; c/o Barclays Bank, Darwen Street, Blackburn, Lancs

SOUYAVE, His Honour Judge; Sir (Louis) Georges Souyave; *b* 29 May 1926; *Educ* St Louis Coll Seychelles; *m* 1953, Mona de Chermont; 2 s, 4 da; *Career* barr Gray's Inn 1949; Seychelles: asst attorney-gen 1956-62, additional Judge Supreme Ct 1962-64, Puisne Judge 1964-70, chief justice 1970-76; High Ct res judge and Br judge of Supreme Ct of Condominium, New Hebrides 1976-80, district judge Hong Kong 1980-; kt 1971; *Style*— His Honour Judge Souyave; District Court, Victoria, Hong Kong

SOUZA E SILVA, His Excellency Ambassador Celso de; s of Oswaldo de Souza e Silva and Silvia de Souza e Silva; *b* 28 Sept 1924; *Educ* Catholic Univ Rio de Janeiro, Rio Branco Inst, Inst des Hautes Etudes Int, Geneva Univ; *m* Maria Alice; 2 s (Antonio, Jorge); *Career* entered Brazilian Diplomatic Service 1948; sec Embassy: Geneva, Caracas, El Salvador, Paris; dep rep UN 1966-73; ambass Moscow 1974-79; special rep for Disarmament 1979-86; ambass London 1986-; chm: Disarmament Ctee Geneva 1979, Disarmament Cmmn of UN New York 1983, first ctee General Assembly 1984; pres Disarmament Conference Geneva 1986; Brazil: Order of Rio Branco (Grand Cross), Order of Military Merit (Grand Offr), Order of Aeronautical Merit (Grand Offr); Argentina Order of San Martin (Cdr); Belgium Order of the Crown (Cdr); Colombia Order of Boyaca (Cdr); Ecuador Order of National Merit (Grand Offr); Federal Republic of Germany Order of Merit (Cdr); Portugal Order of Prince Henry of Portugal (Cdr); *Style*— His Excellency Ambassador Souza e Silva; Brazilian Embassy, 54 Mount Street, London W1 (☎ 01 629 0507); Brazilian Embassy, 32 Green Street, London W1Y 4AT (☎ 01 499 0877)

SOWDEN, Harold Thomas (Harry); s of Frank Thomas Sowden (d 1982), of Minehead, Somerset, and Gladys Panton, *née* Harrison (d 1970); *b* 3 Jan 1924; *Educ* Kings Coll Sch Wimbledon, Merton Coll Oxford; *m* 25 May 1949, (Eiyred) Margaret, da of Rev Canon Frederick James Meyrick (d 1945), of Hove, Sussex; *Career* various appts Exchequer and Audit Dept (now the Nat Audit Off) 1946-72, dir Off of the Health Serv Cmmrs 1973-83; churchwarden St Michael's Church Mickleham Surrey 1976-82; memb Royal Soc of Med 1974-77; *Recreations* reading, writing, travel; *Style*— H T Sowden, Esq

SOWDEN, John Percival; s of Percival Sowden (d 1956), of Todmorden, Yorks, and Gertrude, *née* Moss (d 1953); *b* 6 Jan 1917; *Educ* Hebden Bridge GS, Silcoates Sch Wakefield, Imperial Coll of Science and Technology (BSc (Eng), ACGI); *m* 1, 29 March 1940 (m dis 1969), Ruth Dorothy, da of Gustave Keane (d 1967), of Canon's Park, London; 1 s (Christopher b 26 Aug 1948); m 2, 11 July 1969, Joyce Diana Mary Timpson, da of Charalambos Hji-Ioannou (d 1947), of Nicosia, Cyprus; *Career* cmmnd RE 1939, served in UK, Middle East and Italy (despatches), demobilised with rank of Capt; joined Richard Costain Ltd 1947; site project mangr on various projects including Festival of Britain, Apapa Wharf, Nigeria and Bridgetown Harbour, Barbados 1948-60; jt md Richard Costain (Associates) Ltd 1960-62; md Costain-Blankevoort Int Dredging Co Ltd 1962-65; mangr Civil Engrg Divn Richard Costain Ltd 1965-69, bd memb 1967; chief exec Int Area Richard Costain Ltd 1969-70, group chief exec 1970-75, chm Costain Gp 1972-80; memb governing body Imperial Coll of Science Technol and Medicine 1971; FCGI 1972, FIC 1979, FBIM 1972, FRSA 1983; *Recreations* reading, joinery, cabinet making; *Clubs* RAC; *Style*— John Sowden Esq; Below Star Cottage, East Tytherley Road, Lockerley, Romsey, Hants (☎ 0794 41172)

SOWREY, Air Marshal Sir Frederick Beresford; KCB (1978, CB 1968), CBE (1965), AFC (1954); s of Gp Capt F Sowrey, DSO, MC, AFC (d 1968), of Eastbourne and Warsash; *b* 14 Sept 1922; *Educ* Charterhouse; *m* 1946, Anne Margaret, da of Capt C T A Bunbury, OBE, RN (d 1951), of Crowborough; 1 s, 1 da; *Career* RAF 1940, served War 1939-45 in Fighter Reconnaissance Units in European Theatre, Gp Capt 1962, Air Cdre 1965, SASO Air Forces, Mid E, Aden 1966, dir Overseas Def Policy MOD 1968-70, SASO RAF Trg Cmd with rank of Air Vice-Marshal 1970-72, Cmdt Nat Def Coll 1972-75, Dir-Gen RAF Trg 1975-77, UK Rep Perm Mil Deputies Gp CENTO 1977-79, Research fellow Int Inst of Strategic Studies 1980-81; chm Victory Servs Assoc 1985-; chm RAF Historical Society 1986-; *Books* Articles, contributions, and reviews in military and defence journals; *Recreations* early motoring, industrial archaeology; *Clubs* RAF; *Style*— Air Marshal Sir Frederick Sowrey, KCB, CB, CBE, AFC; 40 Adam and Eve Mews, London W8

SPACIE, Maj-Gen Keith; CB (1987), OBE (1974); s of Frederick Percy Spacie (d 1981), and Kathleen, *née* Wrench; *b* 21 June 1935; *m* 16 Sept 1961, Valerie Elise, da of Lt-Col Harry William Wallace Rich (d 1971); 1s (Dominic b 1964); *Career* RMA Sandhurst 1954-55, cmmnd Royal Lincolnshire Regt 1955, transferred Para Regt 1959, cdr Ind Para Co 1964-65, Army Staff Coll 1965-66, DAA & QMG Para Bde 1968-70 instr RMA Sandhurst 1970-72, Nat Def Coll 1972-73, cdr 3 Bn Para Regt 1973-75, NATO staff SHAPE, 1976-78, instr Nat Def Coll 178-79, cdr 7 Field Force 1979-81, RCDS 1982, Mil Cdr and Cdr Br Forces Falkland Islands 1983-84, dir Army Trg 1984-87; md Cranfield Edn and Trng Ltd 1987-; MIOD; *Recreations* cross country running, military history, country pursuits; *Clubs* Army and Navy, Thames Hare and Hounds; *Style*— Maj-Gen Keith Spacie, CB, OBE; c/o Lloyds Bank, Obelisk Way, Camberley, Surrey; business address: Sudbury House, London Rd, Farringdon, Oxon SN7 8AA (☎ 0367 22297)

SPACKMAN, Brig John William Charles; s of Robert Thomas Spackman, MBE (d 1982), and Ann, *née* Samuel (d 1982); *b* 12 May 1932; *Educ* Cyfarthfa Castle GS Merthyr Tydfil, Wellington GS, Royal Mil Coll of Sci, London Univ (external BSc, PhD), UMIST (MSc); *m* Jeanette Vera, da of George Samuel (d 1953); 2 s (Michael, David), 1 da (Sarah); *Career* Nat Sev 1950-52; cmmnd RAOC 1952, regtl appts 1952-72, Lt-Col Project Wavell 1969-72, Lt-Col GSO1 RARDE 1972-75, Col sr mil offr Chemical Dif and Microbiological Def Estab Porton Down 1975-78, branch chief info systems div SHAPE 1978-80, dir supply computer servs 1980-83, ret Brig 1983; dir (under sec) operational strategy DHSS 1983-86, dir computing and info servs Br Telecom 1986-; Freeman City of London, Asst at Ct Worshipful Co of Info Technologists; MBCS 1970, FBCS 1987, MBIM, MIOD; *Recreations* hillwalking, opera, gardening; *Clubs* Naval & Military; *Style*— Brig John Spackman; 4 The Green, Evenley, Brackley, Northants (☎ 0280 703317); 3 Kennington Palace Ct, Sancroft St, Kennington, London; British Telecom Centre, 81 Newgate St, London (☎ 01 356 5136, fax 01 356 6007, telex 418847)

SPACKMAN, Michael Kenneth Maurice; s of Harry Maurice Spackman (d 1984), of Godalming, and Mary Madeline (Molly) Pinson (d 1959); *b* 2 Feb 1926; *Educ* Marlborough; *m* 9 Jan 1960, Ann Veronica, da of Francis Mervyn Cook (d 1979), of Burford; 2 da (Henrietta b 1960, Catriona b 1962); *Career* Lt attached Indian RA: merchant banker, dir Singer & Friedlander Investmt Mgmnt Ltd 1986, First Spanish Investmt Tst 1987; *Recreations* horse trials, tennis; *Style*— Michael Spackman, Esq; c/o Singer and Friedlander plc, 21 New Street, Bishopsgate, London EC2M 4HR (☎ 01 623 3000, telex 886977, fax CG37 623 2122)

SPACKMAN, Susan Jane; da of William John Wotton, of Devon, and Dorothy Wotton, *née* Cooper; *b* 14 Mar 1947; *Educ* St Dunstan's Abbey Plymouth, Tavistock Comprehensive, Plymouth Poly Sch of Architecture (Dip Arch); *m* 28 Aug 1970, Richard Benjamin James, s of Arthur James Spackman, of Tavistock; 1 s (Edward b 1979), 1 da (Clair b 1974); *Career* chartered architect; principal Crookes & Spackman; ARIBA (chm Plymouth Branch 1987-89), nat jt vice chm The Assoc of Conslt Architects 1987-89 (representing the Assoc of Conslt Architects with The Campaign for the Bar, investigating Law Reform for all professionals with respect to liability); *Recreations* equestrianism; *Style*— Mrs Susan J Spackman; Briar House, 243 Whitchurch Road, Tavistock, Devon (☎ Tavistock 615221); Crookes & Spackman, The Old Stables, Paddons Row, Tavistock, Devon (☎ (0822) 614222)

SPAFFORD, Very Rev Christopher Garnett Howsin; s of Douglas Norman Spafford, and Frances Alison, *née* Garnett; *Educ* Marlborough Coll, Edinburgh Univ, St John's Coll Oxford, Wells Theol Coll; *m* 20 June 1953, Stephanie, da of Lionel George Peel (d 1964), of 24 Stokewood Rd, Bournemouth; 3 s (Martin Christopher Peter b 1954, Timothy Lionel b 1956, (Stephen) Jeremy b 1959); *Career* served RA 1943-46, Capt 1 Indian Medium Regt; asst curate: Brighouse 1950-53, Huddersfield 1953-55; vicar Hebden Bridge 1955-61, rector Thornhill 1961-69, vicar St Chad's Shrewbury 1969-76, provost Newcastle Cathedral and vicar of Newcastle 1976-89; chm: Bd of Social Responsibility Newcastle Diocese 1977-82, Bd of Mission and Unity Newcastle Diocese 1987-88, Inter-Faith Panel CRC 1987-89, Cleveland Steering Ctee for Community Relations 1987-88; memb Community Relations Cncl Tyne and Wear 1978-89; *Recreations* reading, walking, gardening; *Style*— The Very Rev the Provost of Newcastle Cathedral Vicarage, 23 Montagu Ave, Newcastle upon Tyne NE3 4HY (☎ 091 285 3472); St Nicholas Cathedral, Newcastle upon Tyne NE1 1PF (☎ 091 232 1939)

SPALDING, Prof (Dudley) Brian; s of Harold Andrew Spalding, and Kathleen Constance Spalding; *b* 9 Jan 1923; *Educ* Kings Coll Sch Wimbledon, Oxford Univ (BA, MA), Cambridge Univ (PhD, ScD); *m* 1, Eda Isle-Lotte, *née* Goericke; 2 s, 2 da; m 2, Colleen, *née* King; 2 s; *Career* professor of heat transfer Imp Coll 1958-88, emeritus prof 1988-; md Concentration Heat & Momentum Ltd 1970-, chm and dir CHAM of N America Inc 1977-; Reilly prof Purdue Univ Indiana 1978-79; awards incl; Medaille d'Or (Inst Francais de l'Energic) 1980, Bernard Lewis Medal 1982, Luikov Medal 1986; hon prof USTC Hefei China 1988; FRS 1983, FIMechE, FInstE, FIChemE, ASME; *Books* incl: Some Fundamentals of Combustion (1955), Convective Mass Transfer (1963), Heat and Mass Transfer in Recirculating Flows (with Gosman, Pun, Runchal and Wolfstein, 1969), Engineering Thermodynamics (with Cole, 1974), Genmix (1978), Combustion and Mass Transfer (1974); *Recreations* computing, jogging; *Style*— Prof Brian Spaulding; CHAM Ltd, Bakery House, 40 High St, London SW19 5AU (☎ 01 947 7651, fax 01 879 3497, telex 928517)

SPALDING, William Liddell; s of William Liddell Spalding (d 1953), of Balconnel, Brechin, Angus Scotland; *b* 20 Dec 1911; *Educ* Brechin HS, London Univ (BSc Econ);

m 1946, Margaret Laing, da of William Thomson, BD, MB, CHB, (d 1935); 2 da; *Career* CA; sec and chief accountant Richards Ltd Aberdeen 1935-48; Aquascutum Assoc Cos Ltd 1949-54; exec Decca Ltd 1954, sec and gp comptroller 1967-81, dir 1976-; FCMA (pres 1966-67), FCIS; *Recreations* reading, walking; *Style—* William Spalding, Esq; Bankside, 71 Frognal, Hampstead, London NW3 6XY (☎ 01 435 1688)

SPANNER, John Hedley; TD (1981); s of Maj Sydney Spanner, of Gatcombe Cottage, Streatley-on-Thames, Berks, and Una *née* Brown; *b* 21 Feb 1945; *Educ* Reading Sch; *m* 19 Aug 1967 (m dis 1984); 2 da (Annabel b 1968, Rebecca b 1970); *Career* cmmnd Royal Berks Regt (TA) 1966, currently Co Cdr and PMC Offrs Mess 2 Wessex (V); support servs mangr Standard Chartered Bank; former chm Broad St Ward Club; common cncllr Ward of Broad St in City of London 1984-; Freeman City of London 1975, Liveryman Worshipful Co of Glovers; *Recreations* TA, gardening; *Clubs* Cavalry and Guards; *Style—* John Spanner, Esq TD; Weighbridge Cottage, Merstham, Surrey RH1 3BN (☎ 07374 2094); Standard Chartered Bank, 38 Bishopsgate, London EC2N 4DE (☎ 01 280 7777

SPANTON, (Harry) Merrik; OBE (1975); s of Henry Broadley Spanton (d 1947), of Canterbury and Edith Jane, *née* Castle; *b* 27 Nov 1924; *Educ* Eastbourne Coll, Royal Sch of Mines London (BSc Min Eng);; *m* 3 Feb 1945, Mary Margaret, da of George Westcombe Hawkins (d 1958), of Bournemouth; 1 s (Graham Leslie b 1949); *Career* colliery mangr 1950, agent 1954, gp mangr 1956, dep area prodn mangr 1958, dep prodn dir Yorkshire 1960, asst area gen mangr 1962, gen mangr Kent 1964, area dir N Notts 1967-80, memb NCB 1980-85; dir: J H Sankey & Son (chm 1982-83), Br Mining Conslts 1980-87 (chm 1981-83), Canpower 1981-85 (chm 1984-85), NCB (Coal Products) Ltd 1981-83, Br Fuel Co Ltd 1983-87; chm Br Coal Enterprise Ltd 1984-, jt sec Coal Indust Social Welfare Orgn 1983-85; memb: W European Coal Prodrs Assoc 1980-85, CBI Overseas Ctee 1981-85, vice-pres Coal Trade Benevolent Assoc 1979- (chm 1978), ARSM 1945, CEng, CBIM 1979. Hon FIMinE 1986; *Recreations* travel, shooting; *Style—* Merrik Spanton, Esq; 4 Roselands, Canterbury, Kent CT2 7LP (☎ 0227 69356); 14/15 Lower Grosvenor Place, London SW1W 0EX (☎ 01 630 5304)

SPARK, Muriel Sarah; OBE (1967); da of Bernard Camberg, and Sarah Elizabeth Maud, *née* Vezzell; *Educ* James Gillespiés Sch for Girls Edinburgh, Heriot Watt Coll Edinburgh; *m* 1937 (m Dis), 1 s; *Career* gen sec The Poetry Soc, ed The Poetry review 1947-49; non memb American Acad of Arts and Letters 1978, Hon D Litt Strathclyde 1971; FRSL 1963; *Books* critical and Biographical: Tribute to Wordsworth (ed jtly 1950), Selected Poems of Emily Brontë (ed 1952), Child of Light: Reassessment of Mary Shelley (1951), My Best Mary: The letters of Mary Shelley (ed jtly 1953), John Masefield (1953), Emily Brontë: Her Life and Work (jtly 1953), The Brontë Letters (ed 1954), Letters of John Henry Newman (ed jtly 1957), Mary Shelley (1987); poems: The Fanfarlo and other Verse (1952), Collected poems 1 (1967), Going Up to Sotheby's and other Poems (1982); fiction: The Comforters (1957), Robinson (1958), The Go-Away Bird (1958), Memento Mori (1959 adapted for stage 1964), The Ballad of Peckham Rye (1960 Italia prize for dramatic radio 1962), The Bachelors (1960), Voices at Play (1961), The Prime of Miss Jean Brodie (1961 adapted for stage 1966, filmed 1969, BBC TV 1978), Doctors of Philosophy (play 1963), The Girls of Slender Means (1963, adapted for radio 1964, BBC TV 1975), The Mandelbaum Gate (1965, James Tait Black Memorial Prize), Collected Stories 1 (1967), The Public Image (1968), The Very Fine Clock (1969), The Drivers Seat (1970, filmed 1974), Not to Disturb (1971), The Hothouse by the East River (1973), The Abbess of Crewe (1974, filmed 1977), The Takeover (1976), Territorial Rights (1979), Loitering with Intent (1981), Bang-Bang You're Dead and other Stories (1982), The Only Problem (1984), The Stories of Muriel Spark (1987); *Recreations* reading, travel; *Style—* Mrs Muriel Spark; Mucmillan & Co Ltd, Little Essex St, London WC2

SPARKES, Kenneth Henry Norman; s of Henry Arthur Sparkes (d 1963), of Ilford, Essex, and Hilda Agnes Sparkes; *b* 27 Nov 1932; *Educ* Bancroft's Sch Essex; *m* 1959, Pamela Jean, da of William Bernard Woods (d 1968), of Oxted, Surrey; 3 s, 1 da (decd); *Career* farmer; slr; sr ptnr Constant & Constant (slrs); *Recreations* sailing (yacht 'Keramos' Ocean 75) gardening, farming and forestry; *Clubs* RAC, Little Ship; *Style—* Kenneth Sparkes Esq; 21 Alleyn Park, Dulwich, London SE21 8AU (☎ 01 670 3922)

SPARKES, Sir Robert Lyndley; s of Sir James Sparkes (d 1974), and Alice, *née* Goongarry; *b* 30 May 1929; *Educ* Southport Sch Qld; *m* 1953, June M, da of Methuen Young Morgan (d 1969); 2 s; *Career* memb Wambo Shire Cncl 1952-55 and 1964-67 (chm 1967-); state pres Nat Party of Australia (Qld) 1970-; pastoralist; kt 1979; *Style—* Sir Robert Sparkes; Dundonald, PO Box 117, Jandowae, Qld 4410, Australia

SPARKS, Alexander Pratt; s of Capt Cedric Harold Sparks (d 1973), of Surrey, and Lilian Margaret, *née* Johnson (d 1982); *b* 28 Jan 1931; *Educ* Repton, St John's Coll Cambridge (MA) ; *m* 2 July 1976, Serena Evelyn, da of Gavin Thomas Fairfax (d 1987), of Shurlock Row, Berks; 1 s (Hugo b 20 Feb 1981), 1 da (Emma b 1 Jan 1978); *Career* Bateson & Payne (Lloyds Insur Brokers) 1953-56, James Howden 1956-60, Stewarts & Lloyds 1960-63, Air Prods 1963-66, Coopers & Lybrand (mgmnt conslt) 1966-75, CT Bowring (Lloyds Insur Brokers) 1975, dir Bowring UK, dir RICS Insur Servs; chm: Bowring Financial Servs Ltd, Bowring Accountants Insur Servs Ltd; BIIBA: memb cncl and gen purposes ctee; memb the Ct of Worshipful Co of Grocers (Master 1985-86); *Recreations* tennis, horse racing, gardening, golf; *Style—* Alexander Sparks, Esq; 35 Cornwall Gdns, London SW7 4AP; C T Bowring, Tower Place, London EC3 (☎ 01 283 3100)

SPARKS, Hon Mrs (Juliet Jane Margaretta); *née* Moynihan; da of 2 Baron Moynihan, OBE, TD (d 1965); *b* 1934; *m* 1, 1958, Thomas Edwin Bidwell Abraham (d 1976); 2 s; m 2, 1978, Harry Hougham Sparks; *Style—* The Hon Mrs Sparks; Uplands, Bonnington, W Ashford, Kent

SPARKS, Hon Mrs (Rosemary); *née* Monslow; da of Baron Monslow (Life Peer, d 1966) and Mary, *née* Rogers (d 1959); *b* 12 Oct 1921; *Educ* convent; *m* 1948, William Harold Sparks (d 1985); *Style—* The Hon Mrs Sparks; 41 Trinity St, Rhostyllen, Wrexham, Denbighshire

SPARROW, Basil Henry George; MC (1944); s of Guy Sparrow, of Ball Copse Hall Brent Knoll Somerset (d 1955); *b* 16 April 1921; *Educ* Stowe, CCC Oxford (MA); *m* 1945, Patricia Ina, da of Lt-Col Sir Henry Cox, KCMG (d 1958); 1 s (Oliver); *Career* Capt Coldstream Guards, served in Northern Europe; dir: Wavin Plastics Ltd, Wavin Overseas Ltd, Wavin Overseas B U (Netherlands), ret 1985; *Recreations* gardening, shooting; *Style—* Basil Sparrow, Esq, MC; Bottle Lane Cottage, Shottesbrooke, Maidenhead, Berks ☎ 062 882 2827)

SPARROW, Bryan; *b* 8 June 1933; *Educ* Hemel Hempstead GS, Pembroke Oxford; *m* 1958, Fiona Mylechreest; 1 s, 1 da; *Career* Dip Serv; served: Belgrade, Moscow, Tunis, Casablanca, Kinshasa, Prague, Belgrade; ambassador Cameroon 1981-84, non-res ambassador Central African Republic and Equatorial Guinea 1982-84, Canadian Nat Def Coll 1984-85, consul gen Toronto 1985; *Style—* Bryan Sparrow, Esq; British Consultate General, Suite 1910, College Park, 777 Bay St, Toronto, Ontario, Canada; Foreign and Commonwealth Office, King Charles St, London SW1

SPARROW, Sir John; s of Richard Albert and Winifred Sparrow; *b* 4 June 1933; *Educ* Stationers' Company's Sch, LSE (BSc Econ); *m* 1967, Cynthia Naomi Whitehouse; *Career* with Rawlinson & Hunter chartered accountants 1954-59, Ford Motor Co 1960, AEI Hotpoint Ltd 1960-63, United Leasing Corp 1963-64, Morgan Grenfell 1964-88; dir: Federated Chemicals (formerly Greeff Chemicals) 1969-78 (chm 1974-78), Morgan Grenfell & Co Ltd 1970-82 and 1983-85, Harris Lebus 1973-79, United Gas Industs 1974-82 (dep chm 1981-82), Gas and oil Acreage 1975-78, Tioxide Gp 1977-78; chm Wormald Int Hldgs (formerly Mather & Platt) 1979-81, Head of Central Policy Review Staff 1982-83; dir Morgan Grenfell Gp plc (formerly Morgan Grenfell Hldgs Ltd) 1971-82 and 1983-88; chm: Morgan Grenfell Asset Mgmnt Ltd 1985-88, Morgan Grenfell Laurie Hldgs Ltd 1985-88; dir: Coalite Gp plc 1974-82 and 1984-, Short Bros plc 1984- (dep chm 1985-), ASW Hldgs plc 1987-; Cons cllr in Enfield 1961-62; memb: Peterborough Devpt Corp 1981-88, London Advsy Panel Nat and Provincial Building Soc 1986-; chm: Process Plant EDC 1984-85, Ctee of Enquiry into the Future of the National Stud 1985; vice-chm of govrs LSE 1984-; chm Univs Superannuation Scheme 1988-, Nat Stud 1988-; FCA; kt 1984; *Recreations* reading, walking, racing, cricket, crosswords; *Clubs* MCC, Buck's; *Style—* Sir John Sparrow; 46 New Broad Street, London EC2M 1NB

SPARROW, (Albert) Ronald; *Career* chm: Blagden Industries PLC 1981- (formerly Blagden & Noakes (Hldgs)), B & N Chemicals, Blagden Campbell Chemicals, Chemical Supply Co, Martindale Electric Co, R B Blowmoulders Ltd, Rex Campbell & Co, Rheem Blagden Ltd, Willamot Industrial Mouldings, W W Ball & Sons; FCA; *Style—* Ronald Sparrow Esq; Meads, Beechcroft Avenue, Kenley, Surrey (☎ 01 668 3355); Blagden Industries PLC, 16-18 Hatton Garden, London EC1 (☎ 01 242 6571)

SPAWFORTH, David Meredith; s of Lawrence Spawforth (d 1965), and Gwendoline, *née* Meredith; *b* 2 Jan 1938; *Educ* Silcoaten Sch, Hertford Coll Oxford (MA); *m* 17 Aug 1963, Yvonne Mary, da of Roy Gude (d 1987); 1 s (Graham David b 22 Dec 1964), 1 da (Fiona Jane b 20 Sept 1968); *Career* asst master Winchester Coll 1961-64, house master Wellington Coll 1967-80 (asst master 1964-), headmaster Merchiston Castle Sch Edinburgh 1981-; govr various schs, memb Br Atlantic Educn Ctee; memb HMC; *Recreations* walking, theatre, France; *Clubs* East India; *Style—* David Spawforth, Esq; Headmaster's House, Merihiston Castle Sch, Colimton, Edinburgh (☎ 031 441 3468, 031 441 1722)

SPEAIGHT, Anthony Hugh; s of George Victor Speaight, of Kew Gardens, Surrey, and Mary Olive, *née* Mudd; *b* 31 July 1948; *Educ* St Benedict's Sch Ealing, Lincoln Coll Oxford (MA); *Career* barr (Middle Temple) 1973, elected memb Gen Cncl of the Bar 1987-, memb Bar Cncl Working Pty on televising cts 1988-; nat chm Fedn of Cons Students 1972-73, chm Youth Bd of the Euro Movement (UK) 1974-75, dep chm Cons Gp for Europe 1977; Freeman City of London; Schuman Silver Medal (awarded by FVS Fndn of the FDR 1976); *Books* The Law of Defective Premises (with G Stone, 1982), The Architects Journal Legal Handbook (jtly 1985); *Recreations* fox-hunting, acting in and writing revues; *Clubs* Carlton, Hurlingham; *Style—* Anthony Speaight, Esq; 83 Napier Ct, Ranelagh Gdns, London SW6 (☎ 01 736 1842); Cliff Cottage, Gutch Common, Semley, Shaftesbury, Dorset; 12 King's Bench Walk, Temple, London EC4 (☎ 01 353 5892, fax 01 583 3026)

SPEAIGHT, George Victor; s of Frederick William Speaight (d 1942), and Emily Isabella, *née* Elliott (d 1947); *b* 6 Sept 1914; *Educ* Haileybury; *m* 9 July 1946, Mary Olive, da of John Reginald Mudd (d 1918); 1 s (Anthony b 1948), 1 da (Margaret b 1951); *Career* Sub Lt RNVR 1943; mangr Pollock's Toy Theatres 1946-51; ed Odhams Press 1955-60, George Rainbird Ltd 1960-70, editorial dir 1970-74; *Books* Juvenile Drama (1947), The History of the English Puppet Theatre (1955), The History of the English Toy Theatre (1969), Punch and Judy: A History (1970), The Book of Clowns (1980), A History of the Circus (1980), Collecting Theatre Memorabilia (1988); ed Bawdy Songs of the Early Music Hall, etc; *Recreations* walking, canal cruising, travelling; *Style—* George V Speaight, Esq; 6 Maze Rd, Kew Gardens, Richmond, Surrey TW9 3DA (☎ 01 940 3757)

SPEAR, Prof Walter Eric; s of David Spear (d 1945), of London, and Eva, *née* Reineck (d 1978); *b* 20 Jan 1921; *Educ* Musterschule Frankfurt/Main, Univ of London (BSc, PhD, DSc); *m* 15 Dec 1952, Hilda Doris, da of John Charles King (d 1985), of London; 2 da (Gillian b 1961, Kathryn b 1963); *Career* lectr (later reader) in physics Univs of Leicester 1953, Harris prof of physics Univ of Dundee 1968; numerous res papers on electronic and tport properties in crystalline solids, liquids and amorphous semi conductors; prizes: Europhysics Prize of Europ Physical Soc 1977, Max Born Medal and Prize of Inst of Physics and German Physical Soc 1977, Makdougall-Brisbane Medal of RSE 1981, Maxwell Premium of IEE 1981 and 1982, Rank Prize for Optoelectronics 1988; FInstP 1962, FRSE 1972, FRS 1980; *Recreations* music, literature; *Style—* Prof Walter Spear; 323 Blackness Rd, Dundee DD2 1SH (☎ 0382 67649); Carnegie Lab of Physics, The Univ of Dundee, Dundee DD1 4HN (☎ 0382 23181 ext 4563, fax 0382 201604, telex 76293 ULDUND G)

SPEARING, (David) Nicholas; s of George David Spearing, of Caterham, Surrey, and Josephine Mary, *née* Newbould); *b* 4 May 1954; *Educ* Caterham Sch, Hertford Coll Oxford (BA, MA); *m* 20 Sept 1980, Annemarie, da of Ernest Thomas John Gatford (d 1989), of Smallfield, Surrey; 2 da (Laura b 1982, Elizabeth b 1987); *Career* articled clerk Gordon Dadds & Co 1976-78, ptnr Freshfields 1984 (admitted slr 1978); ctee memb Law Soc Slrs Euro Gp; memb: JT Law Soc, Bar Competition Law Working Pty; memb City of London Slrs Co; *Books* Encyclopedia of Forms and Precedents (1985), Articles in Professional Journals; *Recreations* reading, tennis, snooker; *Style—* Nicholas Spearing, Esq; The Coach House, St Mary's Abbey, Woolmer Hill, Haslemere, Surrey GU27 1QA (☎ 0428 53 210, fax 0428 61 570); Grindall House, 25 Newgate St, London EC1A 7LH (☎ 01 606 6677, fax 01 248 3487/8/9, telex 889292)

SPEARING, Nigel John; MP (Lab) Newham S 1974-; L; s of T A E Spearing, of Hammersmith; *b* 8 Oct 1930; *Educ* Latymer Upper Sch, St Catharine's Coll Cambridge; *m* 1956, Wendy, da of Percy Newman, of Newport; 1 s, 2 da; *Career* RCS ranks and cmmn 1950-52, teacher Wandsworth Sch 1956-68, dir Thameside R & D Gp

1968-69, housemaster Elliott Sch Putney 1969-70, parly cand (Lab) Warwick and Leamington 1964, co-opted GLC Planning Ctee, regained Acton for Lab 1970 (MP until 1974); pres Socialist Environment and Resources Assoc 1977-86, chm Anti-Common Market Campaign 1977-83; memb Select Ctees on: Procedure 1975-79, Overseas Devpt 1972-74 and 1977-79, Sound Broadcasting 1978-83, Foreign Affairs 1979-87, European Legislation 1979- (chm 1983-); *Style*— Nigel Spearing, Esq, MP; House of Commons, London SW1

SPEARMAN, Sir Alexander Young Richard Mainwaring Spearman; 5 Bt (UK 1840) of Hanwell, Middlesex; s of Sir Alexander Bowyer Spearman, 4 Bt (d 1977); *b* 3 Feb 1969; *Heir* unc, Dr Richard Spearman; *Style*— Sir Alexander Spearman, Bt; Windwards, Klein Constantia Rd, Constantia, Cape Town, 7800, S Africa

SPEARMAN, Lady (Diana Josephine); da of Col Sir (Albert) Lambert Ward, 1 Bt, CVO, DSO, TD (d 1956); *b* 1921; *m* 1951, as his 2 w, Sir Alexander Cadwaller Mainwaring Spearman (s of late Com Alexander Young Crawshay Mainwaring Spearman, RN, himself half-bro of 2 Bt; d 1982); 4 s, 1 da; *Style*— Lady Spearman; The Old Rectory, Sarratt, Herts

SPEARMAN, Richard; s of Clement Spearman, CBE, of 56 Riverview Gardens, Barnes, London SW13 9QZ, and Olwen Regina, *née* Morgan; *b* 19 Jan 1953; *Educ* Bedales Sch, King's Coll Cambridge (BA, MA), Coll of Law ; *m* 30 April 1983, Alexandra Elizabeth, da of Bryan A Harris, of Churchills, Sidmouth, Devon; 2 da (Olivia b 6 July 1985, Annabel b 11 Oct 1987); *Career* called to Bar Middle Temple 1977; *Books* Sale of Goods Litigation (with FA Philpott, 1983); *Recreations* tennis, skiing; *Clubs* Hurlingham; *Style*— Richard Spearman, Esq; 62 Clonmel Rd, London SW6 5BJ; 10 South Square, Gray's Inn, London WC1R 5EU (☎ 01 242 2902, fax 01 831 2686)

SPEARMAN, Dr Richard Ian Campbell; s of Sir Alexander Young Spearman, 3 Bt (d 1959), and Dorothy Catherine (d 1982); hp of nephew, Sir Alexander Spearman, 5 Bt; *b* 14 August 1926; *Educ* Clayesmore Sch, Birkbeck Coll London (BSc), UCL (PhD, DSc); *Career* biologist; MRC staff 1957-70, res conslt 1970-, hon sr lectr UCL 1970-; memb: Soc of Experimental Biology, Int Cmmn for Avian Anatomical Nomenclature 1971-, chm Integument Sub-Ctee 1985; fndr memb European Soc for Dermatological Res 1971-, memb mgmnt ctee London Skin Club 1977-81, pres Euro Soc for Comparative Skin Biology 1978-1982, chm Int Cmmn on Skin Biology of Int Union for Biological Sciences 1979-82, memb mgmnt ctee Biological Cncl 1980-, memb Royal Soc and Inst of Biology Jt Ctee on Biological Educn 1980-, ed Biological Cncl Conference Guide 1981- (and Handbook 1989-); FIBiol, scientific FZS, FRSM, FLS (vice-pres 1977-79); author of over 80 research papers, reviews and books, mainly on skin biology (especially keratinization) and ornithology; *Books* Birds Ecology and World Distribution, The Integument, Comparative Biology of Skin, The Skin of Vertebrates, The Biochemistry of Skin Disease; *Recreations* bird watching, appreciation of ballet, music; *Style*— Dr Richard Spearman; Oaks Bungalow, Oaks Avenue, London SE19 1QY (☎ 01 670 5488)

SPEDDING, Charles; s of Joseph Bryce Spedding, of Durham, and Mabel, *née* Todd; *b* 19 May 1952; *Educ* Durham Sch, Sunderland Poly (BSc); *m* 9 Aug 1986, Jane Elizabeth, da of James Halliwell, of Orrell, Wigan; 1 s (Joseph James b 25 May 1988); *Career* athlete; winner London Marathon 1984, Bronze Medallist marathon Olympic Games 1984, sixth marathon Olympics Games 1988, English record holder marathon since 1985; life memb Gateshead Harriers pres Valley Striders Leeds; *Style*— Charles Spedding, Esq; Nike (UK) Ltd, Coniston Hse, Washington NE38 7RN (☎ 091 417 9062, fax 091 716 7526, telex 537976 NIKEUK G)

SPEDDING, Prof Colin Raymond William; CBE (1988); s of late Rev Robert K Spedding, and Ilynn *née* Bannister; *b* 16 June 1894; *Educ* Univ of London (BSc, MSc, PhD, DSc); *m* 6 Sept 1952, Betty Noreen (d 1988), da of the late A H George; 2 s (Peter George b 1954, d 1958, Geoffrey Robert b 1957), 1 da (Lucilla Mary (Mrs Weston) b 1960); *Career* Sub Lt RNVR 1943-46; Grassland Res Inst 1949-75 (dep dir 1972-75); Reading Univ: prof of agric systems 1970-, head of dept of agric and hort 1975-83, dean faculty of agric and food 1983-86, pro vice-chllr 1986-; chm: UKROFS, Farm Animal Welfare Cncl; special advsr House of Commons Select Ctee on Agric 1980-83; Hort 1986, FRAgS 1986, FRSA 1988, FZS 1955, FIBioe 1967, CBiol 1984, FRASE 1984, FI; *Books* Sheep Production and Grazing Management (2 edn 1970), Grassland Ecology (1971), Grasses and Legumes in British Agriculture (ed with E C Diekmatins 1972) The Biology of Agricultural Systems (1975), Vegetable Productivity (with JM Warsingham and AM Hoxey 1981), Biological Efficiency in Agriculture (1981), Fream's Agriculture (1983), An Introduction to Agriculture Systems (2 edn 1988); *Clubs* Athenaeum, Farmers; *Style*— Prof Colin Spedding; Vine Cottage, Orchard Rd, Hurst, Berks, RG10 0SD (☎ 0734 341 771); Dept of Agric, Univ of Reading, Earley Gate, Reading RG6 2AT (☎ 0734 875 123 ext 8474)

SPEDDING, David Rolland; CVO (1984), OBE (1980); s of Lt Col Carlisle Montague Rodney Spedding, OBE, TD (d 1977), and Gwynfydd Joan Llewellyn; *b* 7 Mar 1943; *Educ* Sherborne, Hertford Coll Oxford (MA); *m* 7 March 1970, Gillian Leslie, da of Charles Blackadder Kinnear (d 1958); 2 s (Richard b 1971, Christopher b 1975); *Career* HM Diplomatic Service; third sec FO 1967; second sec 1969: Mecas 1968, Beirut 1970, Santiago 1972; first sec FCO 1974: Abu Dhabi 1978, FCO 1981; cnsllr: Amman 1983, FCO 1987-; *Recreations* golf, tennis, reading, walking; *Clubs* Huntercombe Golf; *Style*— David R Spedding, CVO, OBE; c/o FCO, King Charles Street, London SW1A 2AH

SPEED, George Raymond (Mac); s of William George Hamilton Speed (d 19750, of Ravensdale, Long Eaton, Nottingham, and Dorothy Amelia, *née* Sutton (d 1964); *b* 15 April 1925; *Educ* Long Eaton County Secdy Sch, London Univ; *m* 15 May 1954, Helena (Helen) Christina, da of Joseph Fallowfield (d 1948), of 2 Bearton Rd, Hitchin, Herts; 1 s (Martin b 1958), 1 da (Madeleine b 1961); *Career* TA, REME 1943-47; Midland Bank Gp 1941-85 (supervisory credit controller 1978-85); dir: Richmond Fin Ltd 1977-80, Tririding Fin Ltd 1977-80, Forward Tst Car Leasing Ltd 1977-84, Roadmaster Fin Ltd 1977-84; underwriting memb Lloyds; district memb TOC H, auditor and memb exec ctee Int Camellia Soc, hon divnl sec SSAFA; memb: cncl Royal Nat Rose Soc, ctee Cyclamen Soc, Royal Soc of St George, Int Shakespeare Soc, RHS, Nat Tst for Scotland, Econ Res Cncl, CABE; involved locally with: Nat Tst, RSPB; Freeman City of London 1977, Liveryman Worshipful Co of Feltmakers 1977; MIL (c 1945), FBSC 1949, FCIB 1965, FBIM 1975, FLS 1984; *Recreations* horticulture, photography, music; *Style*— George Speed, Esq; High Trees, Oldhill Wood, Studham, Bedfordshire (☎ 0582 872 293)

SPEED, Hugh David McConnachie; s of Hugh Neill Speed (d 1982), of Newcastle upon Tyne, and Mary Bell McConnachie (d 1975); *b* 28 Sept 1936; *Educ* George Watson's Boys Coll Edinburgh, Edinburgh Univ (BSc), Glasgow Univ (MEng); *m* 14 July 1960, Joan, da of Robert Walker Forsyth (d 1987), of Edinburgh; 3 s (Neil b 28 Sep 1963, Mark b 25 Aug 1965, Paul b 23 Dec 1969); *Career* RAF 1960-63: Flt Lt airfield construction branch, serv Cyprus; sr engr (later assoc ptnr) Crouch & Hogg (conslt engrs) Glasgow 1963-71, md Newcastle & Gateshead Water Co 1986- (chief engr 1971-86); chm NSPCC Newcastle Branch 1986-, memb ctee CBI Northern Region; former chm: BIM Northumbria, BIM NE Branches Area Ctee; govr Newcastle Prep Sch; FICE 1972, FIWEM, CBIM 1988; *Recreations* sailing, hill walking, gardening; *Clubs* Northern Counties, Northumberland Golf; *Style*— Hugh Speed, Esq; Montana, 86 Moorside North, Newcastle upon Tyne, NE4 9DU; 5 Sciennes House Place, Edinburgh; 52 Hameau de Coriolan, Plan da la Tour, Ste Maxime, France (☎ 091 273 3870); Newcastle and Gateshead Water Company, PO Box 10, Allendale Road, Newcastle upon Tyne, NE6 2SW (☎ 091 265 4144, fax 091 276 6612, telex 537681/2 (NGWC)

SPEED, (Herbert) Keith; RD (1967), MP (C) Ashford Oct 1974-; s of Herbert Speed; *b* 11 Mar 1934; *Educ* Bedford Modern, RNC Dartmouth, RNC Greenwich; *m* 1961, Peggy Voss Clarke; 2 s (and 1 s decd), 1 da; *Career* served RN 1947-56, Lt Cdr RNR; sales mangr Amos (Electronics) 1957-60, marketing mangr Plysu Products 1960-65, with CRD 1965-68, MP (C) Meriden 1968-74, asst govt whip 1970-71, lord cmmr Treasury 1971-72; parly under-sec: Environment 1972-74, Defence (RN) 1979-81; memb: Parly Select Ctee on Defence 1983-, Council of Europe, Western European Univ Parlimentry Assemblies 1987-; oppn spokesman: Home Affrs 1977-79, Local Govt 1976-77, parly conslt to Professional Assoc Teachers 1982-, chm Westminster Communications Ltd 1982-, Machine Tool Trades Assoc 1984-; *Books* Sea Change (1982); *Style*— Keith Speed, Esq, RD, MP; Strood House, Rolvenden, Cranbrook, Kent

SPEED, Sir Robert William Arney; CB (1946), QC (1963); s of Sir Edwin Arney Speed (d 1941), of Remenham House, Henley-on-Thames, and Ada Frances, *née* Ross (d 1953); *b* 18 July 1905; *Educ* Rugby, Trinity Coll Cambridge (LLB); *m* 25 April 1929, Phyllis, da of Rev Philip Armitage (d 1960), of Farne, Nettlebed, Oxon; 1 s (John b 30 March 1934), 1 da (Sarah b 5 April 1931, d 24 Aug 1976); *Career* barr Inner Temple 1928, princ asst slr HM Procurator Gen and Treasy slr1945-48, slr BOT 1948-60; bencher 1961, counsel to the speaker 1960-80; kt 1954; *Recreations* golf; *Clubs* Utd Oxford and Cambridge, Hon Co of Edinburgh Golfers, Huntercombe Golf; *Style*— Sir Robert Speed, CB, QC; Upper Culham, Wargrave, Reading, Berks RG10 8NR (☎ 0491 574271)

SPEELMAN, Jonkheer Sir Cornelius Jacob; 8 Bt (E 1686); s of Jonkheer Sir Cornelius Speelman, 7 Bt (d 1949); *b* 17 Mar 1917; *Educ* Perth Univ Western Australia; *m* 1972, Julia Mona Le Besque (d 1978); *Heir* none; *Career* formerly in Education Dept Royal Dutch Army, former master of Geelong GS and Clifton Coll, tutor Exeter Tutorial Coll; British subject; *Style*— Jonkheer Sir Cornelius Speelman, Bt; The Nab House, Flat 5, Beach House Road, Bembridge, 1OW

SPEIGHT, Stanley Lester; OBE (1976); s of Clifford Speight (d 1945), and Elizabeth Winifred, *née* Raynes (d 1974); *b* 20 Dec 1920; *Educ* Firth Park GS, Sheffield Tech Coll; *m* 1947, Barbara Joan, da of John Robert Alborough (d 1958); 1 s, 1 da; *Career* Capt RA serv Europe and SE Asia 1939-46; chm Neepsend plc (engrg gp) 1972-; chm Sheffield Health Authy; *Recreations* golf, football; *Clubs* Army and Navy, Sickleholms Golf; *Style*— Stanley Lester Speight, Esq, OBE; The Limes, Froggatt Lane, Froggatt, Derbys S30 1ZA (☎ 0433 31023); Neepsend plc, Lancaster St, Sheffield S3 8AQ (☎ 0742 23231)

SPEIR, Sir Rupert Malise; 3 s of Lt-Col Guy Speir (whose mother was Hon Emily Gifford, 3 da of 2nd Baron Gifford) by his w Mary (6 da of John Fletcher of Saltoun, JP, DL, whose w Bertha was a member of the Talbot family of Lacock Abbey & hence a connection of William Henry Fox Talbot, the pioneer of photography); *b* 10 Sept 1910; *Educ* Eton, Pembroke Coll Cambridge; *Career* serv WWII Intelligence Corps (Lt-Col 1945); chm Matthew Hall & Co to 1982 (remains as non-exec dir), Common Bros; dir J Henry Schroder Wagg, Lloyds Bank N Regnl Bd; slr 1936; MP (C) Hexham 1951-66, PPS to: Min State FO & Parly Sec CRO 1956-59, Parly & Financial Sec Admiralty & Civil Lord of the Admiralty 1952-56, fought Linlithgow 1945, Leek 1950; vice-pres Keep Britain Tidy Gp; kt 1964; *Style*— Sir Rupert Speir; Birtley Hall, Hexham, Northumberland (☎ 0660 30275); 240 Cranmer Court, Sloane Ave, SW3 (☎ 01 589 2057)

SPEKE, (Ian) Benjamin; s of Col Neil Hanning Reed Speke, MC, TD, of Aydon White House, Corbridge, Northumberland, and Averil Allgood, *née* Straker; *b* 12 Mar 1950; *Educ* Eton; *m* 30 July 1983, Ailsa Elizabeth, da of Matthew Hall Fenwick, of New Onstead, Gt Bavingon, Capheaton, Newcastle upon Tyne; 1 da (Zara b 1988); *Career* 9/12 Royal Lancers (Prince of Wales) 1968-72, Northumberland Hussars (Queens Own Yeo) 1974-87; Pinchin Denny 1974-77, Hoare Govett Equity sales 1977-80, ptnr Wise Speke & Co 1980-87, dir Wise Speke Ltd 1987-; memb Int Stock Exchange 1980; *Recreations* field sports; *Clubs* Pratts, Cavalry & Guards, Northern Cos; *Style*— Benjamin Speke, Esq; Thornbrough High House, Corbridge, Northumberland NE45 5PR (☎ 043 471 3080); Wise Speke Ltd, Commercial Union House, 39 Pilgrim St, Newcastle upon Tyne NE1 6RQ (☎ 091 261 1266, telex 53429)

SPEKE, Lt-Col Neil Hanning Reed; MC & bar (1942, 1945), DL (Northumberland 1971); only s of Capt Herber Speke, OBE, JP (himself n of John Speke, the African explorer, who discovered Lake Victoria and (with Sir Richard Burton) Lake Tanganyika); *b* 11 May 1917; *Educ* Eton, Magdalene Coll Cambridge; *m* 1948, Averil Allgood, da of Maj John Straker; 2 s (Ian b 1950, Charles b 1960), 2 da (Rosalind b 1951, Clayre b 1955); *Career* cmmnd into 12 Royal Lancers 1937, serv WWII: NW Europe, M East, N Africa, Italy; Maj 1942, resigned 1948, Northumberland Hussars 1950, Lt-Col 1955; one of HM's Body Guard of Hon Corps of Gentlemen-at-Arms 1967-87; High Sheriff Northumberland 1959; Hon Col Northumberland Hussars Sqdn Queen's Own Yeo 1974; *Style*— Lt-Col Neil Speke, MC, DL; Aydon White House, Corbridge, Northumberland (☎ 043 471 2248)

SPELLAR, John Francis; *b* 1947; *Educ* Oxford Univ; *m* ; 1 da (Judith b 1979); *Career* EETU official, former researcher; MP (Lab) Birmingham Northfield 1982-83; *Style*— John Spellar, Esq; 115 London Lane, Bromley, Kent

SPELLER, Antony; MP (C) N Devon 1979-; s of late John and Ethel Speller; *b* 12 June 1929; *Educ* Exeter Sch, London Univ (BSc), Exeter Univ (BA); *m* 1960,

Maureen R McLellan; 1 s, 1 da; *Career* Maj TA, Devonshire & Dorset Regt Regular Serv 1951-53; worked in Nigeria 1953-62; dir Copyshops of SW England 1963-; cncllr Exeter CC 1963-74, contested (C) N Devon Oct 1974, vice-chm E Devon Water Bd; memb Energy Select Ctee 1982-, vice-chm Cons backbench Energy Ctee 1983-86; chm: Parly Alternative Energy Liaison Ctee 1983-, West County Cons MP's 1983-87, Cons W Africa Ctee; pres Catering Industs Liaison Ctee, fell Hotel Catering Institutional Mgmnt Assoc, hon fell Ind Caterers Assoc; *Clubs* Carlton, North Devon Yacht; *Style*— Antony Speller Esq, MP; House of Commons, London SW1 0AA (☎ 01 219 4589, constituency office: Barnstaple 0271 45617)

SPELMAN, Kenneth John; s of Patrick Joseph Spelman, of Lantern Court, Christchurch Rd, Winchester, and Madge Spelman, *née* Simmons; *b* 25 April 1934; *Educ* Brighton Tech Coll (Dip Eng Civil and Structural), Birmingham Coll of Art and Design (Dip TP); *Career* planning offr/borough devpt offr Epsom & Ewell BC 1971-75; city planning offr and engr Gloucester CC 1975-78; principal KJ Spelman & Assoc, Town Planning & Property Devpt Consultants 1979-; dir Pauntley Properties Ltd 1985-; ptnr The Naturmed Ptnrship 1985-; chm Natural Health Network 1986-; memb: Business Network, Financial Initiative, Br Soc of Dowsers, Anthroposophical Soc, Theosophical Soc, IOD, Medicina Alternativa, Royal Archaeological Inst, Radionic Assoc; FRTPI; FICE; FBIM; FIAS; MIHT; *Recreations* archaeology, walking, reading; *Style*— Kenneth Spelman, Esq; Silver Birches, Private Rd, Rodborough Common, Stroud, Gloucestershire GL5 5BT (☎ 045 387 2618/383 3446, telex 045 383 437105, fax 045 383 4004)

SPENCE, Christopher John; s of Brig Ian Fleming Morris Spence, OBE, MC, TD, ADC (d 1966), of London, and Ruth Spence, *née* Peacock (d 1961); *b* 4 June 1937; *Educ* Marlborough; *m* 1, 1960, (m dis 1968) Merle Aurelia, er da of Sir Leonard Ropner, 1 Bt, MC, TD (d 1977); 1 s (Jeremy b 1964 (d 1982)), 1 da (Miranda b 1963); m 2, 1970, Susan, da of Brig Michael Morley, MBE, of Wiltshire; 1 s (Jonathan b 1975), 1 da (Lara b 1972); *Career* 2 Lt 10 Royal Hussars (PWO) 1955-57, Royal Wilts Yeo 1957-66; memb of London Stock Exchange 1959-78, PK English Tst Gp plc, (md 1978-86, dep chm 1986-, merchant banker); chm: Tyndall Hldgs plc, Australia Investmt Tst plc, Wills Gp plc; *Recreations* racing, shooting, golf; *Clubs* Jockey, Cavalry and Guards', City of London, Swinley Forest Golf; *Style*— Christopher Spence, Esq; Chieveley Manor, Newbury, Berks (☎ 0635 248208); 18A Maunsel Street, London SW1 (☎ 01 828 1484); 4 Fore Street, London EC2 (☎ 01 920 9120)

SPENCE, David Lane; s of Dr AS Spence, and Edith F, *née* Lane; *b* 5 Oct 1943; *Educ* Fettes; *m* 1966, Beverley Esther, da of Gp Capt Jasper Cardale (d 1981); 1 s (William b 1978), 2 da (Sally b 1976, Sarah b 1980); *Career* CA; C F Middleton & Co 1962-67; Grant Thornton (formerly Thornton Baker) 1967-; ptnr 1970, ptnr euro practice 1974-79, chm corp fin 1975-84, exec ptnr 1984-89; memb: ICAS (Parly and Law Ctee), ICA; Liveryman Worshipful Co of Glaziers; *Recreations* golf, skiing, opera; *Clubs* Caledonian, Royal Mid Surrey Golf, Sunningdale Golf; *Style*— David Spence, Esq; Grant Thornton House, Melton St, Euston Square, London NW1 2EP (☎ 01 383 5100, fax 01 383 4715)

SPENCE, James William (Bill); DL (1988); s of James William Spence, of Stromness, Orkney, and Margaret Duncan, *née* Peace; *b* 19 Jan 1945; *Educ* Firth Jr Secdy Sch Orkney, Leith Nautical Coll Edinburgh, Robert Gordon's Inst Science and Technol Aberdeen, Univ of Wales Inst Science and Technol Cardiff (BSc); *m* 31 July 1971, Margaret Paplay, da of Henry Stevenson (d 1983, of Stromness, Orkney; 3 s (James b 1976, Steven b 1978, Thomas b 1980); *Career* Merchant Navy 1961-74: apprentice; deck offr Watts Watts & Co Ltd 1961-65, certificated deck offr P & O Steam Navigation Co Ltd 1965-74; temp asst site co-ordinator Scapa Flow Project, Micoperi SPA 1974-75; John Jolly: Mangr 1975, jr ptnr 1976-77, md and proprietor 1977-; vice consul: Norway 1976-78 (consul 1978), The Netherlands 1978; DL Orkney 1988; dep Launching Authy RNLI Kirkwall Lifeboat 1976-87 (hon sec 1987), memb Kirkwell Community Cncl 1978-82, memb Orkney Pilotage Ctee 1979-88, chm Kirkwell Port Employers Assoc 1979-87, tstee Pier Arts Centre Tst Orkney 1980, chm Br Horse Soc Orkney Riding Club 1985; MNI 1972, AICS 1979, MRIN 1971, Cdr Royal Norwegian Order of Merit 1987; *Recreations* oenophilist, equestrian matters, orcadian history; *Clubs* Caledonian; *Style*— J William Spence, Esq, DL; Alton House, Kirkwall, Orkney KW15 1NA; John Jolly, PO Box 2, 21 Bridge St, Kirkwall, Orkney KW15 1HR (☎ 0856 2268, fax 0856 5002, car tel 0035 240 618, telex 75253)

SPENCE, John Francis Gordon; s of Patrick Walter Gordon Spence (d 1974), and Helen Winifred, *née* Fincham; *b* 4 April 1934; *Educ* Douai Sch, RMA Sandhurst; *m* 1962, Sheila Veronica, da of Charles Henry Thomas, of Essex; 1 s (Nicholas b 1963), 2 da (Clare b 1965, Cathryn b 1971); *Career* Royal Tank Regt Germany 1955-59; dir personnel services Hill Samuel Investmt Services Gp Ltd; dir: Hill Samuel Life Assur Co Ltd 1981-, Hill Samuel Life Facilities Ltd, Gisborne Life Assur Co Ltd, NLA Tower Mgmnt Ltd; personnel dir Williams Lea Gp Ltd 1970-74; FPIM; *Recreations* painting, walking, theatre; *Style*— John Spence, Esq; 45 Epsom Road, Guildford, Surrey GU1 3LA; Hill Samuel Investment Services Group, NLA Tower, 12-16 Addiscombe Road, Croydon CR9 2DR (☎ 01 686 4355, telex 946929)

SPENCE, Malcolm Hugh; QC (1979); s of Dr Allan William Spence, and Martha Lena, *née* Hutchison (d 1981), clan McDuff; *b* 23 Mar 1934; *Educ* Stowe, Gonville and Caius Coll Cambridge (MA, LLM); *m* 18 March 1967, (Jennifer) Jane, da of Lt-Gen Sir George Sinclair Cole, KCB, CBE (d 1973); 1 s (Robert William b 1971), 1 da (Annabelle Irene b 1969); *Career* Nat Serv 1 Lt Worcestershire Regt 1952-54; barr Gray's Inn 1958, entered Chambers of John Widgery, QC 1958, pupil to Nigel Bridge (now Lord Bridge of Harwich) 1958; chm of Panel Examination in Public of Hartlepool and Cleveland Structure Plans 1979; asst rec 1982, rec 1985, bencher Gray's Inn 1988; landowner (1100 acres); *Books* Rating Law and Valuation (jtly 1961); *Recreations* trout fishing, golf; *Clubs* Hawks (Cambridge); *Style*— Malcolm Spence, Esq, QC; 23 Ennerdale Rd, Kew, Richmond, Surrey (☎ 01 940 9884); Scamadale, Arisaig, Inverness-shire (☎ 06875 698); 8 New Square, Lincoln's Inn, London WC2 (☎ 01 242 4986, fax 01 405 1166, telex 21785 ADVICE G)

SPENCE, Margaret; *née* Ferguson; da of Robert Ferguson (d 1937), of Longlands, Comber, Co Down, N Ireland, and Sarah Ann, *née* Phillips (d 1981); *b* 17 Sept 1937; *Educ* Bangor Collegiate Sch; *m* 22 Sept 1956, William Herbert (d 1969), s of Herbert Spence (d 1959), of 5 Glenbroom Park, Jordanstown, Co Antrim, N Ireland; *Career* dir Nat West Ulster Bank Ltd 1985, awarded Business Woman of the Year 1984; memb: Local Enterprise Unit LEDU 1980-82, N Ireland Econ Cncl 1981-85; dep chm Newtownards Devpt Cncl 1987, chm Ards Small Business Centre 1988; FIMI 1984, memb IOD 1977; *Recreations* squash; *Clubs* Kiltonga Squash Club; *Style*— Mrs Margaret Spence; M Ferguson - Newtownards, Regent House, Regent St, Newtownards, Co Down, N Ireland (☎ 0247 812626, fax 0247 818845, car tel 0836 509573, telex 747923)

SPENCE, Saxon May; *née* Fairbairn; da of George Frederick Fairbairn (d 1981), and Ann May, *née* Northcott; *b* 25 Feb 1929; *Educ* Ealing Girls GS, UCL (BA), Sch of Educn; *m* 12 May 1952, John George Spence, s of Jack Spence (d 1953); 1 s (Ian b 1961), 1 da (Catherine b 1956); *Career* city cncllr Exeter 1972-74, co cncllr Devon 1973-77 and 1981-, ldr (former dep ldr 1973-77 and 1981-85) Devon Lab Gp 1985-, memb ACC 1985-, dep ldr ACC Lab Gp 1987-, vice-chm ACC Policy Ctee 1989; memb: nat jt ctee Working Womens Organisations 1973-85, Nat Lab Womens Ctee 1973-85 (chm 1979-80), Womens Nat Cmmn 1982-85; memb bd SWEB 1978-81, vice chm Western Regnl Tport Users Consultative Ctee 1985-88 (memb 1975-88), govr Exeter Coll 1972-(chm govrs 1985-), vice-chm govrs Rolle Coll 1981-88; memb: Devon regnl ctee Co-op Retail Servs 1978-, Devon and Cornwall Area Manpower Bd 1983-88; *Recreations* reading, travelling, theatre, music; *Clubs* Pinmoe & Whipton Labour; *Style*— Mrs Saxon Spence; 5 Regent's Park, Exeter, Devon EX1 2NT ☎0392 71 785); Devon CC, County Hall, Exeter, Devon ☎0392 272 501, fax 0392 51 096)

SPENCER, Alan Douglas; s of Thomas Spencer, of Dumbleton, Gloucs, and Laura Spencer (d 1977); *b* 22 August 1920; *Educ* Prince Henry's GS Evesham; *m* 18 March 1944, Dorothy Joan; 2 da (Sally b 1946, Jocelyn b 1956); *Career* cmmnd Gloster Regt 1940, Green Howards 1940-45, Sch of Inf 1945-47; chm Boots The Chemist 1977-80, vice-chm The Boots Co 1978-80, dir Johnson Wax Ltd 1980-; CBIM 1975; *Recreations* shooting; *Style*— Alan Spencer, Esq; Oakwood, Grange Rd, Edwalton, Notts NG12 4BT (☎ 0602 231722)

SPENCER, Prof Anthony James Merrill; s of James Lawrence Spencer (d 1961), of Streetly, Staffs, and Gladys, *née* Merrill; *b* 23 August 1929; *Educ* Queen Mary's GS Walsall, Queens Coll Cambridge (BA, MA ScD), Univ of Birmingham (PhD); *m* 1 Jan 1955, Margaret, da of Ernest Albert Bosker (d 1949), of Walmley, Sutton Coldfield; 3 s (John b 1957, Timothy b 1960, Richard b 1963); *Career* Private 1 Bn West Yorks Regt 1948-49, res assoc Brown univ USA 1955-57, sr scientific offr UKAEA 1957-60, prof and head of dept of theoretical mechanics Univ of Nottingham 1965- (lectr 1960-63, reader 1963-65); visiting prof: Brown Univ 1966 and 1971, Lehigh Univ 1978, Univ of Queensland Aust 1982; memb: mathematics ctee SRC 1978-81, mathematical scis sub-ctee UGC 1983-87; FRS 1987; *Books* Deformations of Fibre-Reinforced Materials (1972), Engineering Mathematics (2 vols, 1977), Continuum Mechanics (1980); *Style*— Prof Anthony Spencer; 43 Stanton Lane, Stanton-on-the-Wolds, Keyworth, Nottingham NG12 5BE, (☎ 06077 3134); Dept of Theoretical Mechanics, University of Nottingham, University Park, Nottingham NG7 2RD, (☎ 0602 484848, fax 0602 420825, telex 373 UNINOT G)

SPENCER, Aubrey Raymond; s of Isaac Spencer (d 1977), and Leah, *née* Cohen (d 1959); *b* 31 August 1924; *Educ* Christ's Coll Finchley, Maidenhead County Boys Sch, Reading Univ (BSc) ; *m* 13 Sept 1948, Ruth, da of Jack Broder, of 39 Berwyn Rd, Richmond, Surrey; 3 s (Steven Mark Broder b 14 Oct 1949, Daniel Leigh b 19 Oct 1965, Andrew James b 15 July 1967), 1 da (Janine Anne b 12 Feb 1953); *Career* dir: Richmonhd Metal CoLtd 1950 (md 1970), Broder Bros Metals Hldg Co Ltd 1952; chm and chief exec Richmond Metal Gp 1988; cncl memb: Br Secdy Metals Assoc 1959- (pres 1980-81), CBI (Smaller Firms); pres Richmond & Barnes Cons Assoc; memb Lloyd's; Freeman City of London 1980, memb Worshipful Co of Fletchers 1980; *Recreations* gardening, tennis, swimming, theatre, opera, reading, music; *Clubs* City Livery, MCC; *Style*— Aubrey Spencer, Esq; Richmond Metal Gp, Feltham, Middx TW13 0SQ (☎ 01 890 0981, fax 01 751 6452, telex 934 857)

SPENCER, Hon Mrs (Catherine Anne); *née* Blades; da of 2 Baron Ebbisham, of St Ann's Mere, Warminster, Wilts, and Flavia Mary, *née* Meade; *b* 3 Dec 1955; *Educ* St Mary's Sch Calne, Prior's Field, Wye Coll London Univ (BSc); *m* 1981, Charles James, s of Kenneth Clarke Spencer of St Martin's Farm, Zeals, Warminster, Wilts; 1 s (Thomas James b 1985), 1 da (Flora Antonia Blades b 1987); *Career* agric tech advsr; farmer's wife; *Recreations* farming; *Style*— The Hon Mrs Spencer; Search Farm, Stourton, Warminster, Wilts

SPENCER, Christopher Paul; s of Anthony John Spencer, of Cornerstones, Beachwood Ave, Weybridge, Surrey, and Elizabeth, *née* Carruthers; *b* 7 July 1950; *Educ* St Georges Coll Weybridge; *m* 28 June 1975, Margaret Elizabeth, da of Lt-Col Cyril Meredith Battye Howard, OBE, of Rowan Cottage, Rydens Ave, Walton-On-Thames, Surrey; 2 da (Katharine b 13 Aug 1978, Anna Lisa b 24 July 1981); *Career* CA; ptnr: Midgley Snelling Spencer & Co 1978-83, Pannell Kerr Forster (CI) 1984-; hon sec Guernsey Branch IOD, memb Guernsey: C of C, Soc of Chartered and Certified Accountants, Int Business Assoc; FCA; *Recreations* sailing, skiing, tennis; *Clubs* Utd, Guernsey Yacht, The Ski of GB; *Style*— Christopher Spencer, Esq; La Chimere, George Rd, St Peter Port, Guernsey (☎ 0481 711 040); Pannell Kerr Forster, 1 Queens Rd, St Peter Port, Guernsey (☎ 0481 27927, fax 0481 710 511, telex 4191177 Panker G)

SPENCER, Derek Harold; QC (1980), MP (C); s of Thomas and Gladys Spencer; *b* 31 Mar 1936; *Educ* Clitheroe Royal GS, Keble Coll Oxford, (MA, BCL); *m* 1, 1960, Joan *née* Nutter; 2 s, 1 da; m 2, 26 Nov 1988, Caroline A, *née* Parn; *Career* barr Gray's Inn 1961; cncllr London Borough of Camden 1978-, dep ldr Cons Pty 1979-81; rec Crown Ct 1979; Leicester South 1983-87; *Recreations* reading, swimming; *Style*— Derek Spencer Esq, QC; 5 King's Bench Walk, Temple, London EC4 (☎ 01 353 4713)

SPENCER, Gp Capt Desmond Gerard Heath; CBE (1965, MBE); s of late Arthur Spencer; *b* 18 Mar 1912; *Educ* Harrow; *m* 1939, Ellen Catherine da Maj Capel Adye (d 1940); 1 s, 1 da; *Career* 2 Lt Duke of Cornwall's LI 1932-33, RAF 1933, NW Frontier 1935-39, Gp Capt (Ops) Air HQ Eastern Mediterranean 1942-44, Sr Air Staff Off Air HQ Levant Jerusalem, serv Cyprus 1954-56; ret 1967; *Recreations* cruising; *Clubs* Army and Navy, R Fowey Yacht; *Style*— Gp Capt Desmond Spencer, CBE; c/o Gp Capt Chichester, Hayne Manor, Lewdown, Okehampton, Devon (☎ Lewdown 216)

SPENCER, Geoffrey Thomas; s of James W Spencer, and Doris W,*née* Gillingham; *b* 16 May 1946; *Educ* Chestnut GS, City of London Coll; *m* June 1974, Barbara; 1 s (Alexander b Oct 1983), 1 da (Hilary b Sept 1978); *Career* Coutts & Co Ltd: asst mangr business devpt div 1972-74, account mangr Cavendish Sq branch 1974-78, mangr Kensington branch 1978-82, mangr mktg and planning dept branch banking div

1982-83, head int banking div 1986-88 (sr mangr 1983-84, dep head 1984-86), full bd dir (Nassau) 1985, assoc dir 1986, head commercial banking gp 1988, memb bd of fin 1989; ACIB 1970, FCIB 1988; *Recreations* badmington, gardening, travel; *Clubs* Overseas Bankers; *Style*— Geoffrey Spencer, Esq; Coutts & Co, 27 Bush Lane, Cannon St, London EC4R OAA

SPENCER, (Richard) Harry Ramsay; s of Col Richard Augustus Spencer, DSO, OBE (d 1956), and Maud Evelyn, *née* Ramsay; hp (to Barony only), of 3 Viscount Churchill; *b* 11 Oct 1926; *Educ* Wellington, Architectural Assoc (AADip); *m* 1958, Antoinette Rose-Marie, da of Godefroy de Charrière, of Préverenges, Lausanne, Switzerland; 2 s (Michael b 1960, David b 1970); *Career* former Lt Coldstream Gds; ret architect; painter of house portraits; ARIBA; *Recreations* the arts; *Style*— Harry Spencer, Esq; The Old Vicarage, Vernham Dean, Hants (☎ 026 487 386)

SPENCER, Herbert; s of Harold Spencer, and Sarah Ellen, *née* Tagg; *b* 22 June 1924; *m* 23 Sept 1954, Marianne Mols, *née* Dordrecht; 1 da 9Mafalda Saskia b 1958); *Career* RAF 1942-45; dir Lund Humphries Publishers 1970-88, prof of graphic arts Royal Coll of Art 1978-85; Royal Designer for Indust 1965, memb Stamp advsy ctee PO 1968-, int pres Alaince Graphique Int 1971-73, Master Royal Designers for Indust and vice pres Royal Soc of Arts 1979-81, conslt: W H Smith Ltd 1973-, Tate Gallery 1981-; one man exhibitions of paintings: Bleddfa Tst 1986, Gallery 202 London 1988-89; photographs in permanent collection of V & A Museum; ed: Typographica 1949-67, Penrose Annual 1964-73; RDI 1965, FRSA 1965, DrRCA 1970, hon fell RCA 1985; *Books* Traces of Man (photographs 1967), The Visible Word (1968), London's Canal (second edn 1976), Pioneers of Modern Typography (second edn 1982), The Liberated Page (1987); *Clubs* Chelsea Arts; *Style*— Herbert Spencer, Esq; 75 Deodar Rd, Putney, London SW15 2NU (☎ 01 874 6352); Runnis Chapel, Dutlas, Knighton, Powys (☎ 054 77 648)

SPENCER, Ivor; DL (London 1985); s of Barnett Isaacs (d 1962), of London, and Dora Pokrasse (d 1963); *b* 20 Nov 1924; *m* 1948, Estella, da of Israel Mogilever (d 1962), of London; 1 s (Nigel), 1 da (Philippa); *Career* pres Guild of Professional Toastmasters 1963-; princ Ivor Spencer Int Sch for Butler Administrators 1981-; chm and md Ivor Spencer Enterprises Ltd; *Recreations* after dinner speaking; *Clubs* IOD; *Style*— Ivor Spencer, Esq; 12 & 14 Little Bornes, Alleyn Park, Dulwich, London SE21 8SE (☎ 01 670 5585, 01 670 8424); Ivor Spencer Int Sch, The Queen's Hotel, Church Rd, Norwood, London SE19 (☎ 01 670 5585, 01 670 8424)

SPENCER, John Loraine; TD (1960); s of Arthur Loraine Spencer, OBE (d 1958), of Woodford Gn, Essex, and Emily Maude Spencer, OBE (d 1985); *b* 19 Jan 1923; *Educ* Bancrofts Sch, Gonville and Caius Coll Cambridge (MA); *m* 3 April 1954, Brenda Elizabeth, da of Percy Frederick Loft (d 1949), of Woodford Gn, Essex; 2 s (Christopher Loraine b 1955, Nicholas John b 1960), 1 da (Elizabeth Mary b 1957); *Career* Essex Regt 1942-45: serv Normandy landings 1944, Capt (despatches); Offr Haileybury CCF (TA) 1948-61 (Maj); asst master (later housemaster and head of classics) Haileybury 1947-61; headmaster: Royal GS Lancaster 1961-72, Berkhamsted Sch 1972-83; asst dir GAP Activity Projects 1985-; pres Soc of Schoolmasters, memb Bd of Visitors HM YCC Aylesbury; *Clubs* Royal Cwlth; *Style*— John Spencer, Esq, TD; Crofts Close, 7 Aston Rd, Haddenham, Bucks HP17 8AF (☎ 0844 291235)

SPENCER, John Southern; s of Robert Southern Spencer, of Benson Cottage, Hetton, Skipton, N Yorks, and Marjorie Turner, *née* Frankland; *b* 10 August 1947; *Educ* Sedbergh, Queens' Coll Cambridge (MA); *m* 8 Dec 1984, Alison, da of Anthony Heap, of Pk Grange Cottage, Threshfield, Skipton, N Yorks; 1 s (David b 1971), 3 da (Suzanne b 1972, Hazel b 1975, Emily b 1988); *Career* slr, ptnr Sugden & Spencer 1975; Rugby Union, formerly: Capt Yorkshire, Capt Cambridge Univ (3 Blues), Capt Barbarians, Capt England (16 Capt), British Lions Tour 1971; pres Wharfedale RUFC, sec Grassington Angling Club, trustee Upper Wharfedale Immediate Care Scheme, govr Netherside Special School, vice-chm govrs Ermysted's GS, Skipton; memb Law Soc; *Recreations* rugby, squash, cricket; *Clubs* The Sportmans, Wig & Pen, The Rugby; *Style*— John Spencer, Esq; High Pasture, Moor Lane, Threshfield, Skipton, N Yorks BD23 5NS (☎ 0756 752456); 6A Station Rd, Grassington, Skipton, N Yorks BD23 5NQ (☎ 0756 753015)

SPENCER, 8 Earl (GB 1765); (Edward) John Spencer; LVO (1954), JP (Norfolk 1970), DL (Northants 1961); also Viscount Spencer, Baron Spencer (both GB 1761), and Viscount Althorp (GB 1765 & UK 1905); s of 7 Earl Spencer, TD (d 1975) and Lady Cynthia, *née* Hamilton, DCVO, OBE, da of 3 Duke of Abercorn; *b* 24 Jan 1924; *Educ* Eton, RAC Cirencester; *m* 1, 1954 (m dis 1969), Hon Frances Ruth Roche (now Hon Mrs Shand Kydd, *qv*), da of 4 Baron Fermoy, and Ruth, Lady Fermoy, DCVO, OBE, JP, *qv*); 1 s (and 1 s decd), 3 da (Lady Sarah McCorquodale, Lady Jane Fellowes, HRH The Princess of Wales); m 2, 1976, Raine (memb British Tourist Authority 1982-, chm BTA's Spas Ctee 1982-), da of Alexander McCorquodale and his 1 w, Barbara Cartland, *qv*; *Heir* s, Viscount Althorp; *Career* late Capt Royal Scots Greys, cllr Northants (High Sheriff 1959); patron of 12 livings; temp Equerry to HM King George VI 1950-52 and to HM The Queen 1952-54; ADC to Govr S Australia 1947-50; Dep Hon Col Royal Anglian Regt (TA) 1972-; chm Nene Fndn; memb UK Cncl European Architectural Heritage Year 1975; *Books* Japan and the East (1986); *Recreations* farming, tourism, cricket, music, art, family life; *Clubs* Turf, Brooks's (tstee), MCC, Royal Overseas League, Pratt's; *Style*— The Rt Hon Earl Spencer, JP, DL; Althorp, Northampton NN7 4HG (☎ 060 4770 760)

SPENCER, Sir Kelvin Tallent; CBE (1950), MC (1918); s of Charles Tallent Spencer (d 1948), of The Hall, Harmondsworth, Middx, and Edith AElfrida, *née* Swithinbank (d 1946); *b* 7 July 1898; *Educ* UCS, London Univ (BSc); *m* June 1927, Phoebe Mary, da of Henry Wills; 1 s (Geoffrey Tallent b 1929); *Career* 2 Lt RE 1918-19; scientist Royal Aeronautical Establishment Farnborough 1923-35; joined Civil Service 1923; seconded to help start airworthiness div of Provisional Int Civil Aviation Orgn (now ICAO) Canada 1946-47, seconded to start Air registration Bd's tecnical responsibilities London 1945-46, fndr memb The Scientific and Med Network, FCGI 1959; lay memb cncl Univ of Exeter 1961-75; Hon LLD Exeter 1975; FICE, FRAeS; *Recreations* keeping abreast of progress in relationship between subatomic physics and metaphysics; *Clubs* Farmers'; *Style*— Sir Kelvin Spencer, CBE, MC; Wootans, Branscombe, Devon EX12 3DN; Honeyditches House, Seaton Down Road, Seaton, Devon EX12 2JD

SPENCER, Maj (Richard) Peter Michael; s of Richard Percy Spencer (d 1960); *b* 23 Sept 1920; *Educ* Sedbergh; *m* 1951, Bettyne Ione, da of late Sir Lindsay Everard; 1 s, 1 da; *Career* Maj 1 King's Dragoon Gds; serv: Italy, Greece, Palestine, Middle East; farmer; High Sheriff Leics 1968-69; *Recreations* fishing, shooting; *Style*— Maj Peter Spencer; Rotherby Grange, Melton Mowbray, Leics (☎ 066 475 206)

SPENCER, Countess Raine; da of Alexander McCorquodale (1 cous of 1 Baron McCorquodale of Newton, PC) by his 1 w Barbara Cartland, *qv*; *b* 9 Sept 1929; *m* 1, 1948 (m dis 1976), as his 1 w, 9 Earl of Dartmouth; 3 s (Viscount Lewisham, Hon Rupert and Henry Legge), 1 da (Lady Charlotte Legge); m 2, 1976, as his 2 w, 8 Earl Spencer; *Career* formerly a LCC Voluntary Care Ctee worker in Wandsworth and Vauxhall, and actively involved in the welfare of the elderly in other areas; Lewisham W memb of LCC 1958-65; memb: GLC (Richmond) 1967-73, GLC Gen Purposes Ctee 1971-73; former memb BBC Nat Agric Advsy Ctee; chm Govt Working Pty on the Human Habitat for UN Conference on the Environment (which produced The Dartmouth Report, How Do You Want To Live?), and a UK delegate at the Conf in Stockholm 1972; chm: GLC Historic Bldgs Bd 1968-71, Covent Gdn Devpt Ctee 1971-75, UK Exec Ctee of European Architectural Heritage Year 1975; memb: English Tourist Bd 1971-75, BTA Infrastructure Ctee 1972-, Advsy Cncl V & A 1980-, BTA 1982-; chm: BTA Spas Ctee 1981-83, BTA Hotels and Restaurants Ctee 1983-; memb Min of Arts Ctee for Business Sponsorship of the Arts; awarded a Gold Medal for public speaking, and a former guest speaker at Oxford Univ and Cambridge Univ debates, lectr at: Holloway, Maidstone and Wandsworth Prisons; - and a lectr at Holloway, Maidstone and Wandsworth Prisons; *Books* The Spencers on Spas (with photographs by Earl Spencer); *Style*— The Rt Hon the Countess Spencer; Althorp, Northampton NN7 4HG

SPENCER, Ritchie Lloyd; s of Capt P Lloyd Spencer; *b* 27 Sept 1942; *Educ* St Bees Sch, Manchester Univ (BA), LSE; *m* 1965, Catherine Dilys, MA, da of Dr John Naish; 3 s (Hal b 1968, Patrick b 1969, James b 1972); *Career* dir Sunderland Shipbuilders Ltd 1972-76, md Reliant Motor plc Tamworth Staffs 1977-87; dir Nash Industries plc 1980-87; cncl memb Soc Motor Manufacturers & Traders 1978-87; chm Motor Indust Res Assoc 1984-; chief exec GKN Powder Metallgy Div 1987-; chm: Bound Brook Lichfield Ltd 1987-, Firth Cleveland Sintered Products Ltd 1987-, Sheepbridge Sintered Products Ltd 1987-; pres: Bound Brook Italia SpA, Brunico 1987-, Saini SpA, Milan 1987-; dir: Mahindra Sintered Products Pune Ltd India 1987-, Sintered SA de CV Mexico 1987-; MIPM; *Recreations* theatre, gardening, squash, tennis, skiing; *Style*— Ritchie Spencer, Esq; 16 London Rd, Lichfield, Staffs (☎ 0543 262507); Dorlinn View, Argyll Terrace, Tobermory, Isle of Mull

SPENCER, Rosemary Jane; da of Air Vice-Marshal Geoffrey Roger Cole Spencer, CB, CBE (d 1969), and Juliet Mary, *née* Warwick; *b* 1 April 1941; *Educ* Upper Chine Sch, Shanklin IOW, St Hilda's Coll Oxford (BA); *Career* FO 1962-65, Br High Cmmn Nairobi 1965-67, FCO 1967-70, 2 sec and private sec to Hon Sir Con O'Neill EC negotiating team Brussels 1970-71; 1 sec UK rep to EC Brussels 1972-73, Br High Cmmn Lagos 1974-77, asst head of Rhodesia Dept FCO 1977-79, RCDS 1980, cnsllr: Br Embassy Paris 1980-84, external relations VK rep to EC Brussels 1984-87, head of Euro community Dept External FCO 1987-; govr Upper Chine Sch IOW 1984-; *Recreations* country walking, domestic arts, reading; *Clubs* Royal Commonwealth Society; *Style*— Miss Rosemary Spencer; Foreign and Commonwealth Office, King Charles St, London SW11

SPENCER, Ms Sarah Ann; da of Dr Ian Osborne Bradford Spencer (d 1978), Consultant Physician, and Dr Elspeth Wilkinson, Consultant Psychiatrist; *b* 11 Dec 1952; *Educ* Mount Sch York, King's Sch Tynemouth, Nottingham Univ (BA Hons), Univ Coll London (MPhil); *m* 1978, Brian Anthony, s of Alan Keith Hackland; 1 s (James b 1986); *Career* gen sec Nat Cncl for Civil Liberties 1985; formerly dir The Cobden Tst; *Books* Called to Account: Police Accountability in England and Wales (1985), The New Prevention of Terrorism Act: The Case for Repeal (co-author 1985); *Style*— Ms Sarah Spencer; 21 Tabard St, London SE1

SPENCER, Thomas Newnham Bayley; MEP (EDG) Derbyshire 1979-; s of Thomas Henry Newnham Spencer (d 1979); *b* 10 April 1948; *Educ* Nautical Coll Pangbourne, Southampton Univ; *m* 1979, Elizabeth Nan, nee Bath; 1 da (step); *Recreations* fencing, opera; *Clubs* Carlton; *Style*— Thomas Spencer Esq, MEP; 13 Goulton Rd, London E5 (☎ 01 985 5839); 1 Sant Lane, Doveridge, Derbys

SPENCER, (John) William James; s of Capt John Lawrence Spencer, DSO, MC (d 1967), and Jane Lilian Spencer, *née* Duff; *b* 26 Dec 1957; *Educ* Sedbergh, Magdalene Coll Cambridge (MA); *m* 2 Oct 1987, Jane Elizabeth, da of Andrew Young (d 1974); *Career* dir: Dewey Warren & Co Ltd, Lloyd's Brokers 1986-88, PWS N America (Lloyd's brokers) 1988-; *Style*— William Spencer, Esq; Ghyllas, Sedbergh, Cumbria; 9 Defoe Avenue, Kew, Surrey (☎ 01 876 0255); Lloyds Brokers, 10 St Mary at Hill, London EC3 (☎ 01 626 9833)

SPENCER, William Randolph; s of Randolph Churchill Spencer (d 1941), of Liverpool, and Elizabeth, *née* Parington; *b* 17 Jan 1907; *Educ* Liverpool Colligate Sch; *m* 2 April 1938, Olive, da of Dr Arthur William Latham; 2 da (Mary Elizabeth, Susan Margaret); *Career* Harmood Banner and Son CA's 1924-34, asst accountant Primitive Hldgs Ltd 1934-36, sec Hobart Mfrg Co Ltd 1937-39, asst gen mangr of subsid to Yorks Electric Power Co 1939-40, conslt dir Urwick Orr and Ptnrs 1940-61, dir of several public co's 1961-82, chm Allied Investmts Ltd 1972-77, lectr on mgmnt thoughout Europe; memb Mgmnt Res Gps Ctee, memb Wilmslow GC Ctee 1953; memb Lloyds of London 1977, Master Worshipful Co of Glovers 1979-80, memb City of London Livery Consultative ctee 1981-87; FCA (1934), JDipMA (1954), FCMA (1954), FBIM; *Recreations* golf, walking, reading, charity work; *Clubs* RAC, Guards Polo, Ascot Boxholder; *Style*— William Spencer, Esq; Belmont, Blackpond Lane, Farnham Common, Bucks SL2 3FL (☎ 0281412829)

SPENCER LEE, Fred George; TD (1964); s of Fred Lee (d 1964), and Georgina, *née* Sparrow (d 1959); *b* 25 August 1929; *Educ* Oundle; *m* 11 June 1955, Joan Elizabeth, *née* Botwood; 1 s (Christopher b 1961), 2 da (Sarah b 1956, Karen b 1959); *Career* Nat Serv The Royal Scots Regt 1947-49; TA 1953-70: Royal Warwicks Regt, SAS Regt 1966; joined family business Johnson and Mason Ltd 1947, Grants of St James's Ltd 1955, Ind Coope Ltd 1969, Wm Grant and Sons 1982; retired 1988; *Recreations* shooting, hill walking; *Clubs* Special Forces, Drapers (Coventry); *Style*— F G Spencer Lee, TD; The Stone House, Braunston, Northamptonshire NN11 7HS (☎ 0788 890343)

SPENCER ROBERTS, Arthur; s of Arthur Meyrick Roberts (d 1967), and Catherine, *née* Spencer (d 1961); *b* 8 Jan 1920; *Educ* Hastings GS, Hastings Sch of Art, Scholarship RCA (Hons Degree in Fine Art); *m* 18 Sept 1946, Mavis Ethel Wynne, da of Capt Cyril Hubert Board (d 1978); *Career* served fighter pilot & artillery 1939-46

Far East, Actg/Capt Mountbattens Staff; artist (wildlife), one man shows in Tokyo, Bonn 1982, museum Konig/Hammer Gallery NY 1978-79, Dallas; one man shows in London and Bristol, other exhibitions in Las Vegas, Houston, mural Port Lympne Kent 1985, 1986, 1987 for John Aspinall; Aspinal Collection; Exhibition Guildhall London; olympic trialist, 100 metres freestyle swimming 1938-39, selected for Olympic team to swim at Helsinki, war interfered; paintings in Collections of HRH Duke of Edinburgh, Museum Konig, Bonn, John Aspinall; *Recreations* fishing, swimming, wild life conservation; *Clubs* Gam Conservation Int (USA), 20's; *Style*— Arthur Spencer Roberts, Esq; The Boat House, Pet Level, nr Hastings, E Sussex (☎ 0404 813209)

SPENCER-CHURCHILL, Lord Charles George William Colin; s of 10 Duke of Marlborough (d 1972); *b* 1940; *Educ* Eton; *m* 1, 1965 (m dis 1968), Gillian, da of Andrew Fuller; m 2, 1970, Elizabeth Jane, da of Capt the Hon Mark Hugh Wyndham, MC; 2 s; *Style*— Lord Charles Spencer-Churchill; 4 Ormond Place, London SW1

SPENCER-CHURCHILL, Lady Ivor; Elizabeth; *née* Cunningham; er da of late James Cyril Cunningham, of 27 Culross St, London W1; *m* 15 Nov 1947, Lord Ivor Charles Spencer-Churchill (d 1956), yr s of 9 Duke of Marlborough, KG, PC, and his 1 w, Consuelo, *née* Vanderbilt; 1 s (Robert b 1954); *Style*— Lady Ivor Spencer-Churchill

SPENCER-CHURCHILL, John George Spencer; s of John Strange Spencer Churchill, DSO, TD, (yr bro of Sir Winston and 2 s of Lord Randolph Churchill) and Lady Gwendeline Bertie (da of 7 Earl of Abingdon); 2 cous of 10 Duke of Marlborough; bro of Countess of Avon, *qv*; *b* 31 May 1909; *Educ* Harrow, RCA, Central Sch Art, Pembroke Coll Oxford, Ruskin Sch of Art; *m* 1, 1934 (m dis 1938), Angela (*see* Rauf, Bayan), da of Capt George Culme-Seymour (3 s of Sir Michael Culme-Seymour, 3 Bt, GCB, GCVO, and Mary, gda of 2 Baron Sondes); 1 da (Sarah m Colin, bro of Quentin Crewe, *qv*); m 2, 1941 (m dis 1953), Mary, da of Kenneth Cookson (now Mrs Jacob Huizinga); m 3, 1953, Mrs Kathlyn Tandy (d 1957), da of Maj-Gen Walter Beddall, CB, OBE; m 4, 1958, Anna, da of John Janson, of Kristianstad, Sweden, and widow of Granger Boston; *Career* serv WWII Maj RE, GSO2; artist, sculptor, lectr, author; *Recreations* music, travel; *Style*— John Spencer-Churchill Esq; Place du Cros, Grimaud 83360, France (☎ 94 43 21); 15 Cheyne Walk, London SW3 5RB (☎ 01 352 2352)

SPENCER-COOPER, Peter Henry Harvey; TD (1961); s of Capt Henry Edmund Harvey Spencer-Cooper, MVO, RN, 21 St Petersburgh Place, London W2 (d 1968), s of Col Charles Lacon Harvey of Exmouth, name changed by Royal Licence 1906 to Spencer-Cooper), and Norah Isabel, *née* Sherston (d 1932, g-niece of FM Earl Roberts of Kandahar, YC, KG); *b* 26 Nov 1923; *Educ* Stowe, Wadham Coll Oxford; *m* 27 Sept 1952, Penelope Holdsworth, da of Basil Holdsworth Hunt, of Manor Fields, London SW15 (d 1960); 1 s (Jeremy Peter Harvey b 1954), 1 da (Victoria Louise Harvey b 1957); *Career* Lt Rifle Bde 1942-47, NW Europe and Palestine; Joseph Barber & Co Ltd Bonded Warehousemen 1955-76 (dir 1959, md 1963) ret 1976; *Recreations* gardening, walking, reading, social work; *Clubs* Army and Navy, Sea View Yacht; *Style*— Peter Spencer-Cooper, Esq; The Gables, Upton Grey, Basingstoke, Hants RG25 2RA (☎ 0256 862425); 6 Seaview House, Seaview, IoW (☎ 0983 613221)

SPENCER-JONES, John Franklin; s of Sir Harold Spencer-Jones, KBE (d 1962), and Mary, *née* Owers (d 1970); *b* 17 Jan 1934; *Educ* Gresham Sch Holt Norfolk, Jesus Coll Cambridge (BA, MA); *m* 27 Sept 1956, Ruth Muriel, da of John Edward Arnott Betts, JP, of The Manor Hse, Hampstead, Norreys, Berks; 3 s (Robert b 17 Feb 1957, Charles b 20 Sept 1959, James b 21 Aug 1968), 1 da (Jane b 12 Nov 1965); *Career* Nat Serv RAF, cmmnd gen duties branch, substantive Pilot Offr 1953-55, RAFVR pilot with CU Air Sqnd (substantive Flying Offr); Aspro Nicholas Ltd 1958-70: export mangr Advance Industs Ltd 1961, gen mangr ME 1963, md Pakistan Gp 1965-70; self employed mgmnt conslt 1970-88 (internat assignments in engrg, aviation, energy, pharmaceuticals and hotels industs, especially in ME), dir and co secs The Heritage Gp 1988-; Freeman City of London, Liveryman Worshipful Co of Clockmakers 1962; memb Inst of Export MIEX 1985, ARAeS 1986; *Recreations* collecting, antiques, aviation, history, DIY, travel and exploration; *Style*— John Spencer-Jones, Esq; Merriedene, Dean Lane, Cookham Dean, Maidenhead, Berks SL6 9BG (☎ 062 84 2082); The Heritage Gp, 235 Old Marylebone Rd, London NW1 5QT (☎ 01 706 1051/2, fax 01 724 5856)

SPENCER-NAIRN, Angus; s of Michael Alastair Spencer-Nairn, of Baltilly House, Ceres, Fife, and Ursula Helen, *née* Devitt; *b* 23 Jan 1947; *Educ* Eton, RAC (MRAC); *m* 6 July 1968, Christina Janet, da of Col Hugh Gillies, of Kindar House, New Abbey, Dumfriess-shire; 1 s (Michael b 1975), 1 da (Fiona b 1974); *Career* CA; sr ptnr Rawlinson and Hunter, CA, St Helier, Jersey, CI; *Recreations* motor racing, tennis, deer stalking, golf; *Clubs* Royal and Ancient Golf (St Andrews) New (Edinburgh); *Style*— Angus Spencer-Nairn, Esq; La Fontaine, Rue Du Pont, St John, Jersey, CI (☎ 0534 61716); Ordnance House, Box 83, 31 Pier Rd, St Helier, Jersey, CI (☎ 0534 75141, telex 4192075, fax 0534 32876)

SPENCER-NAIRN, Sir Robert Arnold; 3 Bt (UK 1933) of Monimail, Co Fife; s of Lt-Col Sir Douglas Leslie Spencer Spencer-Nairn, TD, 2 Bt (d 1970); *b* 11 Oct 1933; *Educ* Eton, Trinity Hall Cambridge; *m* 1963, Joanna Elizabeth, da of late Lt Cdr George Stevenson Salt, RN, s of 2 Bt (cr 1899); 2 s, 1 da; *Heir* s, James Robert Spencer-Nairn b 7 Dec 1966; *Career* late Lt Scots Gds; *Style*— Sir Robert Spencer-Nairn, Bt; Barham, Cupar, Fife

SPENCER-SMITH, Sir John Hamilton; 7 Bt (UK 1804) of Tring Park, Hertfordshire; s of Capt Sir Thomas Cospatric Spencer-Smith, 6 Bt (d 1959), and Lucy Ashton, *née* Ingram; *b* 18 Mar 1947; *Educ* Milton Abbey, Lackham Coll of Agric; *m* 1980, Mrs Christine Sandra Parris, da of late John T C Osborne, of Durrington, Worthing, Sussex ; 1 da (Jessica b 1985); *Heir* kinsman, Peter Spencer-Smith; *Career* owner Hazel House Quarantine Kennels, Midhurst; *Recreations* watching polo; *Clubs* Cowdray Park Polo; *Style*— Sir John Spencer-Smith, Bt; Hazel House Quarantine Kennels, Midhurst, W Sussex

SPENCER-SMITH, Lucy, Lady; Lucy Ashton; da of late Thomas Ashton Ingram; *m* 1944, Sir Thomas Cospatric Hamilton Spencer-Smith, 6 Bt (d 1959); 1 s (7 Bt); *Style*— Lucy, Lady Spencer-Smith; 2 Heathfield Gate, Bepton Rd, Midhurst, Sussex

SPENCER-SMITH, Peter Compton; s of late Lt-Col Michael Seymour Hamilton-Spencer-Smith, DSO, MC (gs of bro of 2 Bt and who did not use surname Hamilton); hp of kinsman, Sir John Spencer-Smith, 7 Bt; *b* 12 Nov 1912; *Educ* Eton, New Coll Oxford; *m* 1950, Philippa Mary, da of late Capt Richard Ford, Rifle Bde; 2 s; *Career* formerly Maj 79 Herts Yeo (Heavy Anti-Aircraft Regt), RA (TA); chm Charles Barker Gp plc 1961-72, High Sheriff Hertfordshire 1976; *Style*— Peter Spencer-Smith, Esq; High Down House, Hitchin, Herts

SPENDER, Lady; Eileen Beryl; *née* Congreve; da of Philip Wells Congreve and Elizabeth Graham; *b* 3 Oct 1916; *Educ* Wellington Coll (NZ), Istituto Britannico Florence; *m* 1983, as his 3 w, Hon Sir Percy Claude Spender, KCVO, KBE, QC (d 1985), Australian statesman and lawyer, Australian Ambass to USA 1951-58, Pres Int Ct of Justice, The Hague 1964-67, etc; *Career* art, journalism, interior decoration; patron Australian Opera (NSW); travel offr Australian Govt Bd; memb Black and White Ctee for Royal Blind Soc; *Recreations* skiing, reading, world travel, historical architectural interests, gardening; *Clubs* St James's, Lord's, Taverners'; *Style*— Lady Spender; 105A Darling Point Road, Darling Point, NSW 2027, Australia

SPENDER, Prof Sir Stephen Harold; CBE (1962); s of Edward Harold Spender and Violet Hilda, *née* Schuster; *b* 28 Feb 1909; *Educ* University Coll Sch Oxford; *m* 1, 1936, Agnes Marie, da of late W H Pearn; m 2, 1941, Natasha Litvin; 1 s, 1 da; *Career* poet and critic; prof of English Univ Coll London 1970-77, now Emeritus; FRSL; kt 1983; *Publications include* Poems for Spain (1939), The Still Centre (1939), Ruins and Visions (1941), World Within World (autobiography, 1951), Collected Poems (1954), Selected Poems (1965), The Generous Days (1971), Love-Hate Relations (1974), T S Eliot (1975), The Thirties and After (with David Hockney, 1978), Chinese Journal (1980); editor: D H Lawrence: novelist, poet, prophet (1973), W H Auden: a tribute (1975); *Style*— Prof Sir Stephen Spender, CBE; 15 Loudoun Rd, London NW8 (☎ 01 624 7194)

SPENS, Colin Hope; CB (1962); s of Archibald Hope Spens (d 1943), and Hilda Constance, *née* Hooper (d 1952); Spens of Lathallan, in unbroken line of succession from Henry de Spens, first Spens of Lathallan (d 1300); *b* 22 May 1906; *Educ* Lancing, City & Guilds Eng Coll; *m* 1941, Thyrza Josephine, da of Septimus Duncan Simond (d 1916); 2 s (David, John), 1 da (Joanna); *Career* chief engr Miny of Housing & Local Govt 1960-67, dep chm & dir of Sutton Dist Water Co 1971-83; CEng; *Style*— Colin Spens, Esq, CB; 10 Ashbourne Ct, Burlington Place, Eastbourne BN21 4AX (☎ 0323 638742)

SPENS, Hon (William) David Ralph; s of 2 Baron Spens (d 1984), and Joan Elizabeth, da of late Reginald Goodall; *b* 23 Nov 1943; *Educ* Rugby, Corpus Christ: Coll Cambridge; *m* 1967, Gillian, da of Albert Jowett, OBE, MD, FRCS; 1 s (James), 1 da (Tamsin); *Career* barr 1972; *Style*— The Hon David Spens; Marsh Mills Cottage, Over Stowey, Somerset

SPENS, John Alexander; RD (1970), WS; s of T P Spens; *b* 1933; *Educ* BA, LLB; *m* Finella Jane Gilroy; 2 s, 1 da; *Career* Carrick Pursuivant of Arms 1974-85; Albany Herald of Arms 1985-; ptnr Maclay Murray & Spens (Slrs); dir Scottish Amicable; *Style*— John Spens, Esq, RD, WS, Albany Herald of Arms; c/o Lyon Ct, HM New Register House, Edinburgh

SPENS, Dowager Baroness; Kathleen Annie Fedden; da of Roger Dodds, of Bath and Northumberland; *m* 1963, as his 2 w, 1 Baron Spens, KBE, PC (d 1973); *Style*— The Rt Hon the Dowager Lady Spens; Gould, Frittenden, Kent

SPENS, Hon Mallowry Ann; da of 2 Baron Spens; *b* 30 Sept 1949; *Career* int show jumper; *Recreations* hunting; *Style*— The Hon Mallowry Spens; Lambden, Pluckley, Ashford, Kent (☎ 023 384 373)

SPENS, 3 Baron (UK 1959); Patrick Michael Rex; s of 2 Baron Spens (d 1984), and Joan Elizabeth, da of late Reginald Goodall; *b* 22 July 1942; *Educ* Rugby, CCC Cambridge (MA); *m* 1966, Barbara, da of Rear-Adm Ralph Fisher, CB, DSO, OBE, DSC; 1 s, 1 da (Hon Sarah b 1970); *Heir* s, Hon Patrick Nathaniel George Spens b 1968; *Career* md Henry Ansbacher & Co 1982-; FCA; *Style*— The Rt Hon Patrick Spens; Gould, Frittenden, Kent

SPENS, Hon (Emily) Susan; MBE (1970); da of William Patrick, 1 Baron Spens, KBE, PC (d 1973), and Hilda Mary Spens, *née* Bowyer (d 1962); William Patrick Spens, KBE, PC, created Baron Spens 1957; *b* 25 April 1924; *Educ* Heathfield Sch Ascot, Birkbeck Coll London (MA); *Career* Serv WWII WRNS 1941-46; secretarial career in BA (formerly BOAC) 1948-53; FCO 1954-72; Int Atomic Energy Agency (IAEA) Vienna Austria 1972-80; *Recreations* classical music, the countryside; *Style*— The Hon E Susan Spens, MBE; Flat 6, 47 The Drive, Hove, E Sussex, BN3 3JE

SPENSLEY, Dr Philip Calvert; s of (John Hackett) Kent Spensley (d 1963), of Ealing, London W5, and Mary, *née* Schofield (d 1951); *b* 7 May 1920; *Educ* St Paul's, Keble Coll Oxford (MA, BSc, DPhil); *m* 24 Aug 1957, Sheila Ross, da of Alexander Lillingston Fraser (d 1977), of Forres, Morayshire, Scotland; 1 s (Colin b 1958), 3 da (Fiona b 1959, Charis b 1962, Tanya b 1966); *Career* tech offr Royal Ordnance Factories Miny of Supply 1940-45, res chemist Nat Inst for Med Res (MRC) 1950-54, scientific sec colonial prods cncl Colonial Off 1954-58, asst dir Tropical Prods Inst DSIR 1958-61 (dep dir 1961-66, dir overseas devpt admin 1966-81), memb panel of chm of scientific selection bds Civil Serv Cmmn 1982-86, ed Tropical Science 1984-; memb: protein advsy gp FAO/WHO/Unicef 1968-71, ctee on needs of developed countries Int Union of Food Sci of Technol 1970-78, CENTO Cncl for Scientific Educn and Res 1970-78, int ctee Royal Soc of Chemistry 1982-86, Br nat ctee for chemistry Royal Soc 1986-, cncl Royal Inst 1985-88, hon tres Keble Assoc Oxford 1987-; Freeman City of London 1951; CChem, FRSC; *Recreations* house and garden development, travel; *Clubs* Athenaeum, RAC, Island Cruising (Salcombe); *Style*— Dr Philip Spensley; 96 Laurel Way, Totteridge, London N20 8HU (☎ 01 445 7895); Pool Ho, Frogmore, Kingsbridge, S Devon TQ7 2NU; Cole & Whurr, 19B Compton Terr, London N1 2UN (☎ 01 359 5979, fax 01 226 3652)

SPERRING, Donald James; s of John Roland Sperring, of Sussex, and Edna Joan, *née* Ashton; *b* 5 Mar 1951; *Educ* Ravensbourne Kent; *m* 18 April 1981, Laura Jane, da of Desmond Champ; 3 s (Ben b 1983, Sam b 1985, Thomas b 1987); *Career* dir Grandfield Rork Collins (Ad Agency) 1981-86, exec dir Young & Rubicam (Ad Agency) 1986-; *Recreations* golf, squash; *Clubs* RAC; *Style*— Donald Sperring, Esq; 3 Maywood Close, Beckenham Place Park, Beckenham, Kent (☎ 01 650 9807); Young & Rubicam, Greater London House, Hampstead Road NW1

SPERRYN, Simon George; s of George Roland Neville Sperryn, Hampton Lucy, Warwickshire, and Wendy, *née* King; *b* 7 April 1946; *Educ* Royal Sch Clwydd, Pembroke Coll Cambridge (MA), Cranfield Sch of Mgmnt (MBA); *Career* Chamber of Industry and Commerce: Birmingham 1967-77, chief exec Northants 1979-85, chief exec Manchester 1986-, regnl sec NW 1986-; with Joseph Gillott & Sons Ltd 1977-78; FBIM; *Recreations* singing, drawing; *Clubs* St James's (Manchester); *Style*— Simon Sperryn; Lilac Cottage, Wincle, Macclesfield, Cheshire SK11 0QE (☎ 0260 227 620); Manchester Chamber of Commerce and Industry, 56 Oxford St, Manchester M60 7HJ

(☎ 061 236 3210, fax 061 236 4160, telex 667822 CHACON G)

SPEYER, Hon Mrs (Beatrice Sophie); *née* Liddell; yr da of 6 Baron Ravensworth, JP, DL (d 1932), and Isolda Blance, *née* Prideaux-Brune (d 1938); *b* 23 Sept 1906; *m* 16 Dec 1931, Edward Richard Speyer, yst s of Edward Speyer, of Ridgehurst, Shenley, Herts; 2 da; *Style*— The Hon Mrs Speyer

SPICER, Cdr Bruce Evan; s of Dr Gerald Evan Spicer, MC (d 1976), of Appin, Argyll, and Mary Cecilia, *née* Bethune (d 1983); gs of Sir Evan Spicer and Lt Gen Sir Edward Bethune 'father' of the Territorial Army; *b* 24 Mar 1927; *Educ* Ludgrove, Britannia RNC Dartmouth; *m* 5 Aug 1954, Susan, da of Maj James Dance, MP, TD (d 1971), of Moreton Morrell, Warwick; *Career* Royal Naval Offr 1940-82; md GB Marine Ltd 1984-; memb of Ctee Royal Humane Soc 1977-; memb Cncls: Hawkley Parish, Hawkley Parochial Church; Freeman City of London, Liveryman of the Co of Fishmongers; memb of Lloyds; OStJ; *Recreations* cricket, golf, shooting, photography, gardening; *Clubs* Royal Scottish Automobile, MCC, Liphook Golf, Free Foresters CC; *Style*— Cdr Bruce E Spicer, RN; Champlers Cottage, Hawkley, Liss, Hampshire GU33 6NG (☎ 073 084 391, fax (M) 073 084 391)

SPICER, Christopher James Evan; s of Adrian Evan Spicer (d 1975), and Martha Esther Kingsley, *née* Mason (d 1988); *b* 26 April 1940; *Educ* Eton; *m* 13 Dec 1975, Joanna Grizelda, da of Ven E J G Ward, LVO, Chaplain to HM The Queen and formerly Archdeacon of Sherborne; 2 da (Rachel b 1977, Annabel b 1980); *Career* resident estate mangr Euston Estate (Duke of Grafton, KG); *Style*— Christopher J E Spicer, Esq; Blackbourne House, Euston, Thetford (☎ 0842 763504); Estate Office, Euston, Thetford, Norfolk (☎ 0842 766366)

SPICER, James Wilton; MP (C) Dorset West Feb 1974-; s of James and Florence Clara Spicer; *b* 4 Oct 1925; *Educ* Latymer Sch; *m* 1954, Winifred Douglas Shanks; 2 da; *Career* Regular Army 1943-57; contested (C) Southampton, Itchen by-election 1971, UK memb Euro Parl 1975-78, MEP (EDG) Wessex 1979-84; chm Cons Political Centre 1969-72, chm Cons Gp for Europe 1975-78, chief whip of Cons Gp in Euro Parl 1976-80, memb Select Ctee Agric 1984-85, appointed vice-chm Cons Party and chm Int Office 1984-; chm British-Turkish Parly Gp, chm British Maltese Parly Gp, dep chm South Africa Club; chm Fitness for Industry, dir Thames and Kennett Marina Co; *Style*— James Spicer, Esq, MP; Whatley, Beaminster, Dorset (☎ (0308) 862337); House of Commons, London SW1A 0AA

SPICER, John Vincent; s of Herbert Gordon Spicer, of Billericay, Essex, and Doreen Mary, *née* Collings; *b* 2 Mar 1951; *Educ* Billericay Comp Sch, Univ of Sheffield (BA); *m* 23 June 1973, Patricia Ann, da of Raymond Sidney Bracher (d 1986), of Harlow, Essex; *Career* business planner Kodak 1975-77, strategic planner Whitbread & Co plc 1978-82, brewery analyst Grenfell & Colegrave 1982-84, dir Kleinwort Benson Securities Ltd 1986-; memb Stock Exchange; *Recreations* golf, squash, hill walking; *Style*— John Spicer, Esq; Flat 9, 56 Holland Park, London W11 3RS (☎ 01 229 0316); Kleinwort Benson Securities Ltd, 20 Fenchurch St, London (☎ 01 623 8000, telex 922 241)

SPICER, (William) Michael Hardy; MP (C) Worcestershire S Feb 1974-; s of Brig Leslie Hardy Spicer (d 1981), of Whitley Bay, Northumberland, and Muriel Winifred Alice Spicer; *b* 22 Jan 1943; *Educ* Wellington, Emmanuel Coll Cambridge (MA); *m* 1967, Patricia Ann, da of Patrick Sinclair Hunter (d 1981); 1 s, 2 da; *Career* former asst to ed of The Statist; dir Cons Systems Res Centre 1968-70, md Economic Models Ltd 1970-80, pps to Trade mins 1979-81, vice-chm Cons Pty 1981-83, dep chm Cons Pty 1983-84; Parly under sec of state Dept of Transport 1985-86, Min for Aviation 1986-87; Parly under sec of State Dept of Energy 1987-; *Books* Final Act (1983), Prime Minister, Spy (1986); *Recreations* painting, writing, tennis, squash; *Style*— Michael Spicer, Esq, MP; House of Commons, London SW1 (☎ 01 219 3000)

SPICER, Dr Nicholas Adrian Albert; s and h of (Sir) Peter Spicer, 4 Bt, *qv*; *b* 28 Oct 1953; *Educ* Eton; *Career* medical practioner; *Style*— Dr Nicholas Spicer; 6 Linton Lane, Bromyard, Herefordshire HR7 4DQ

SPICER, Paul George Bullen; s of Col Roy Godfrey Bullen Spicer, CMG, MC (d 1946), and Margaret Ina Frances, *née* Money; *b* 6 Feb 1928; *Educ* Eton; *m* 10 Sep 1954, June Elizabeth Cadogan, da of Antony Fenwick (d 1954), of Kiambu, Kenya, and Brinkburn Priory, Northumberland; 1 s (Rupert b 1955); 1 da (Venetia, b 1959); *Career* Lt Coldstream Gds 1945-49; md Overseas with Shell Int Petroleum, (served 1949-70); joined Lonrho 1970; (dir Main Bd 1978); *Recreations* books, music, horses; *Clubs* Brooks's; *Style*— Paul Spicer, Esq; Cheapside House, 138 Cheapside, London EC2V 6BL

SPICER, Sir Peter James; 4 Bt (UK 1906), of Lancaster Gate, Borough of Paddington, but does not use title; s of Sir Stewart Dykes Spicer, 3 Bt (d 1968); *b* 20 May 1921; *Educ* Winchester, Trinity Coll Cambridge, Ch Ch Oxford; *m* 1949, Margaret, da of late Sir (James) Steuart Wilson; 1 s, 3 da (and 1 da decd); *Heir* s, Dr Nicholas Spicer; *Career* serv WWII Lt RNVR (despatches), on publishing staff Oxford Univ Press 1947-81, chm Educational Publishers Cncl 1974-76, appeal dir Mansfield Coll Oxford 1981-85; *Recreations* sailing, walking, gardening, reading, music; *Style*— Peter Spicer, Esq; Salt Mill House, Fishbourne, Chichester, W Sussex PO19 3JN (☎ 0243 782825)

SPICER, Hon Mrs; (Sarah Margaret); *née* Watkinson; da of 1 Viscount Watkinson, CH, PC; *b* 17 April 1944; *m* 1965, David Bethune Spicer; 4 da; *Style*— The Hon Mrs Spicer; Shortacre, Park Rd, Winchester

SPICKERNELL, Rear Admiral Derek Garland; CB (1974); s of Cdr Sydney Garland Spickernell, RN (ka 1940), and Florence Elizabeth Curtis, *née* March (d 1980); *b* 1 June 1921; *Educ* RNEC Keyham; *m* 1946, Ursula Rosemary Sheila, da of Frederick Cowslade Money (d 1953), of Newbury; 2 s (Richard, John (decd)), 1 da (Susan); *Career* Rear Adm MOD Whitehall 1971-75, dir gen Br Standards Instn 1981-86, vice-pres Int Standards Orgn Geneva 1985-; *Recreations* Golf; *Clubs* Naval & Military, English Speaking Union, Royal Fowey Yacht; *Style*— Rear Admiral Spickernell, CB; Ridgefield, Shawford, Hants (☎ (0962) 712157); BSI, 2 Park St, London W1 (☎ 01 629 9000)

SPICKOVA, Hon Mrs (Victoria Wentworth); *née* Reilly; da of Baron Reilly, of Alexander Place, London SW7, and Pamela Wentworth Martin, *née* Foster; *b* 30 July 1941; *Educ* Francis Holland London, Trinity Coll Toronto Univ (BA) (English); *m* 1973, Daniel, s of Dr Hilar Spicka, of Prague; 2 da (Katherine b 1974, Lucie b 1977); *Career* former journalist: Illustrated London News, The Sunday Telegraph; *Recreations* music, travel, reading; *Style*— The Hon Mrs Spickova; U Mrázovky 7, Prague 5, Czechoslovakia 150 00

SPIEGELBERG, Richard George; s of Francis Edward Frederick Spiegelberg (d 1979), and Margaret Neville, *née* Clegg; *b* 21 Jan 1944; *Educ* Marlborough, Hotchkiss Sch USA, New Coll Oxford (MA); *m* 1, 1970 (m dis 1979), Coralie Eve, *née* Dreyfus; 2 s (Rupert b 1971, Maximilian b 1974); m 2, 1980, Suzanne Louise; 1 s (Assheton b 1981), 1 da (Henrietta b 1984); *Career* Economist Intelligence Unit 1965-67, business journalist and mgmnt ed The Times 1964-74, princ Dept of Indust 1974-75, Nat Econ Devpt Off 1975-76; assoc dir: J Walter Thompson & Co 1976-80, Coopers & Lybrand 1980-84; dir and jt md Streets Fin 1984-87, exec dir corporate communications Merrill Lynch Europe Ltd 1987-; tstee and cncl memb Invalid Childrens Aid Nationwide; *Books* The City (1973); *Recreations* walking, golf, opera; *Clubs* Brooks's; *Style*— Richard Spiegelberg, Esq

SPIERS, (John) Anthony; *b* 19 Sept 1944; *Educ* Bishop Vesey's GS, Sutton Coldfield, Warwickshire; *m* 1971, Catherine Anne; 3 s (Jonathan (by first w), Benjamin b 1972, Gerald b 1973), 2 da (Catherine b 1975, Hannah-May b 1981); *Career* slr, ptnr Peter Peter & Wright 1970; clerk to Blanchminster Charity 1976-84; memb Cornwall CC 1981-88; FRSA; *Recreations* fishing, reading, walking; *Style*— Anthony Spiers, Esq; 8 Fore St, Holsworthy, Devon (☎ 0409 253262), fax 0409 254 091);

SPIERS, Donald Maurice; CB (1987), TD (1966); s of Harold Herbert Spurs (d 1968), and Emma *née* Fost4er (d 1978); *b* 27 Jan 1934; *Educ* Trinity Coll Cambridge MA; *m* 13 Dec 1958, Sylvia Mary, da of Sammuel Lowman (d 1963); 2 s (Simon b 1965, Philip b 1969); *Career* 2nd Lt RE 1952-54, Devpt Engr de Havillend 1957-60, Operational Research Air Miny 1961-66, Scientific advsr Far East AF 1987-70, Asst Chief Scientist RAF 1971-78, MOD PE 1978-84, dep controller Aircraft 1984-86; controller Estabs Res & Nucl 1987-; *Style*— Donald Spiers, Esq; MOD, Whitehall, London SW1 (☎ 01 218 3502)

SPIERS, Ven Graeme Hendry Gordon; s of Charles Gordon Spiers (d 1974), of London, and Mary McArthur, *née* Hendry (d 1980); *b* 15 Jan 1925; *Educ* Mercers Sch, Univ of London (ALCD); *m* 17 May 1958, (Patricia) Ann May, da of late Harold Chadwick, of Bournemouth; 2 s (Andrew b 1959, Peter b 1961); *Career* RNVR Sub-Lt 1944, demobbed 1946; ordained: deacon 1952, priest 1953 (Canterbury Cathedral); curate Addiscombe Parish Church Croydon 1952-56, succentor Bradford Cathedral 1956-58; vicar: Speke Liverpool 1958-66, Aigburth Liverpool 1966-80, rural dean Childwall 1976-79, hon canon Liverpool Cathedral 1977-, archdeacon of Liverpool 1979-; chm: Tstees William Edmonds Fund, Josephine Butler Tst; govr St Margarets C of E Sch Liverpool; *Recreations* reading, gardening, wine making; *Clubs* Liverpool Athenaeum; *Style*— The Ven the Archdeacon of Liverpool; 40 Sinclair Drive, Liverpool L18 3H10 (☎ 051 722 6675); Church House, 1 Hanover St, Liverpool L1 3DW (☎ 051 709 9722)

SPIERS, Michael David; s of Montague, of Middx, and Doris Pruim; *b* 20 Dec 1949; *Educ* John Lyon Sch Harrow-on-the-Hill; *m* 6 June 1971 (m dis), Carole, da of David Fortuyn (d 1956); 1 s (Daniel b 1979), 2 da (Lisa b 1973, Tanya b 1975); *Career* CA 1973, licensed insolvency practitioner 1986; dir: Teampace Hldgs Ltd, Burmans Ltd, Dando Drilling Systems, GMS Computers Ltd; *Recreations* squash, bridge, horse-riding; *Style*— Michael D Spiers, Esq; Highgate Hill, London N19 5NL (☎ 01 281 4474, fax 01 281 3691)

SPIERS, Air Cdre Reginald James; OBE (1972); s of Alfred James Oscar Spiers (d 1963), and Rose Emma Alice, *née* Watson (d 1975); *b* 8 Nov 1928; *Educ* Haberdashers' Askes', RAF coll Cranwell; *m* 1 Dec 1956, Cynthia Jeanette, da of Arnold S Williams; 2 da ((Sally) Linda b 11 April 1958, Carolyn Deirdre b 30 Sept 1959); *Career* RAF: cmmnd 1949, Pilot 247 (Fighter) Sqdn 1950-52, Day Fighter Ldrs Course 1952, Fl Cdr 64 (Fighter) Sqdn 1952-54 (RAF Aerobatics Team 1953-54), Empire Test Pilots Course RAE Farnborough 1955, Fighter Test Sqdn A & AEE 1955-59, OC 4 (Fighter) Sqdn 1959-61, PSO to C in C RAF Germany 1961-63, RAF Staff Coll 1964, FCO 1965-67, OC RAF Masirah 1967-68, chief test flying instr ETPS 1968-71, Air Warfare Course 1972, air secs dept MOD 1972-73, MA to Govr Gibraltar 1973-75, co-experimental flying dept RAE Farnborough 1975-78, Staff MOD 1978-79, Cmdt A & AEE Boscombe Down 1979-83; mktg exec GEC Avionics 1984-; FRAeS 1975; *Recreations* aviation, shooting; *Clubs* RAF; *Style*— Air Cdre Reginald Spiers, OBE; Barnside, Penton Mewsey, nr Andover, Hampshire SP11 0RQ (☎ 026 477 2376); GEC Avionics, 132/135 Long Acre, London EC2 9AH (☎ 01 836 3444)

SPILLANE, Mary C; *b* 7 May 1950; *Educ* Harvard Univ (MPA), Simmons Coll (MLIS), Merrimack Coll (BA); *m* 15 Sept 1979, Roger C H Luscombe; 2 da (Anna b 1983, Lucinda b 1985); *Career* started Color Me Beautiful (image consltg firm 1983), formerly in journalism and public affrs, crisis mangr in Carter Admin; active in human and refugee rights, political lobbyist in America & Geneva; *Recreations* running, music, 19 century novels; *Clubs* Network, Metropolitan, IOD; *Style*— Ms Mary Spillane; 45 Abbey Business Centre, Ingate Place, London SW8 3NS

SPILLER, Brian Frederick; s of Robert Frederick Spiller (d 1938), of Belfast, and Norah Allan Spiller (d 1963); *b* 27 May 1917; *Educ* Royal Belfast Academical Inst, UCL (BA); *m* 20 Aug 1958, Millicent, da of Col Charles Albert Wood, MC (and Bar, d 1961), of Bloxham, Oxon; 1 da (Shira b 1960, d 1962); *Career* served 1939-46 with Royal Ulster Rifles, Durham Light Inf, 1st KGVO Gurkha Rifles and Gen Staff Intelligence, in India, Middle East, N Africa and NW Europe, latterly as Maj (despatches); Br Cncl programme organiser 1947-48, ed a monthly bulletin published by the Brewing Indust 1948-60, dep public rels offr The Distillers Co 1960-74, head Public Relations Ltd 1974-82; *Publications* Victorian Public Houses (1972), The Chameleon's Eye: James Buchanan & Co Ltd 1884-1984 (1984), Cardhu: The World of Malt Whisky (1985), Innkeeping: A Manual for Licensed Victuallers (ed, 1952), Cowper: Poetry and Prose, Reynard Library (1968); *Recreations* reading, running, swimming, natural history; *Style*— Brian Spiller, Esq; 3 Wolvercote Ct, Wolvercote Green, Oxford OX2 8AB (☎ 0865 59979)

SPILLER, Richard John; s of Capt Michael Macnaughton Spiller, of Belfast, and Agnes Gall, *née* Algie; *b* 31 Dec 1953; *Educ* Royal Belfast Academical Inst, Univ of Exeter (LLB), City of London Poly (MA); *m* 17 Sept 1982, Hilary Phyllis, da of William Wright, of Kingston-on-Thames, Surrey; 1 s (James b 1984), 1 da (Emily b 1987); *Career* admitted slr 1980; asst slr: Hedleys 1978-81, Norton Rose 1981-83; ptnr D J Freeman and Co 1983-; Freeman: City of London 1986, Worshipful Co of Slrs 1986 (dep chm commercial law sub-ctee); memb Law Soc; *Recreations* squash, dining out; *Style*— Richard Spiller, Esq; D J Freeman and Co, 43 Fetter Lane, London EC4A 1HN (☎ 01 583 4055, fax 01 353 7377, telex 894579)

SPILMAN, John Ellerker; JP (1984); s of Maj Harry Spilman, MC, DL, JP (d 1980), and Phyllis Emily, *née* Hind; *b* 9 Mar 1940; *Educ* Sedbergh Sch, Royal Agric Coll Cirencester; *m* 25 Oct 1975, Patricia Mary, da of Gilbert Sutcliffe, of Cleethorpes; 1 s (David b 1984), 1 da (Joanna b 1980); *Career* md Farming Co; dir Aylesby Manor Farms Ltd; church warden, tstee Stanford Charity; *Recreations* fishing, shooting, tennis, music; *Style—* John E Spilman, Esq; Aylesby Manor, Grimsby, S Humberside (☎ 0472 71800); Manor Farm, Aylesby, Grimsby (☎ 0472 72550)

SPINKS, Mrs Mary; da of William White (d 1952), and Mary White (d 1987); *b* 21 Feb 1947; *m* 1968, Henry Spinks; 1 s (Michael b 1975), 1 da (Susanna 1972); *Career* memb Asthma Res Cncl, sponsor of King's Med Res Tst, fndr and hon organiser of The Starlight Ball 1985-88 in aid of the Asthma Research Cncl; *Recreations* family life, voluntary fund raising, armchair politics; *Style—* Mrs Henry Spinks; Tantons, Leesons Hill, Chislehurst, Kent BR7 6QH (☎ 0689 38388)

SPIRA, Peter John Ralph; s of Dr Jean-Jacques Spira (d 1970); *b* 2 Mar 1930; *Educ* Eton, King's Coll Cambridge; *m* 1, 1957, Meriel, *née* Gold; m 2, 1969, Anne Marie Marguerite Renée, *née* Landon; 6 children; *Career* SG Waeburg & Co Ltd 1957-74 (vice chm 1971-74, non exec dir until 1982), fin dir Sotheby Parke Bernet Gp plc 1974-82, vice chm Goldman Sachs Int Corpn London 1982-87, dir Société Génèale de Surveillance Hldg SA Geneva 1987-, dep chm Co NatWest Ltd 1988-; Nat Film Fin Corpn 1981-86; FCA; *Recreations* music, reading, photography; *Clubs* Buck's; *Style—* Peter Spira, Esq; 63 Bedford Gardens, London W8 7EF (☎ 01 727 5295)

SPITTALL, Lt-Col Peter Arthur; s of Capt Arthur Millward Spittall (d 1941), of Injebreck, IOM, and Jocelyn Mary, *née* Devas (d 1956); *b* 5 May 1916; *Educ* King William Coll IOM; *m* 1, 19 Nov 1939, Margaret Keith, da of Edwin Lionel Sim (d 1956), of Ashfield, Douglas, IOM; 1 s, 3 da; m 2, 30 Jan 1965, Pamela Honor, da of Surgn Cdr William Edgar Roberts, RAN (d 1948), of Sydney, NSW; *Career* Lt-Col RM 1934-56 serv Atlantic, Pacific, Mid East; farmer 1957-89; JP 1970; *Recreations* gardening, shooting; *Style—* Lt-Col Peter Spittall; Injebreck, Braddan, IOM (☎ 0624 851254)

SPITTLE, Leslie; s of Samuel Spittle (d 1942), and Irene, *née* Smith; *b* 14 Nov 1940; *Educ* Acklam Hall GTS, Constantine Coll of Technol, Univ of Hull (LLB); *m* 7 Sept 1963, Brenda, da of Charles Alexander Clayton (d 1961); 3 s (Nicholas b 21 June 1968, Jonathan b 23 Sept 1971, Matthew b 14 Dec 1981); *Career* Univ of Hull Air Sqdn RAFVR; mgmnt trainee 1956-62, lectr and sr lectr Teeside Poly 1965-70; barr Grays Inn 1970, asst rec 1985; former: chm Round Table, chm Yarm Sch Assoc, vice-chm govrs Kirklevington Sch, master Lodge of Freedom; ACIS 1960; *Recreations* amateur dramatics, golf, various charitable bodies; *Clubs* Eaglescliffe GC, Lodge of Freedom, Lodge of Jurists; *Style—* Leslie Spittle, Esq; 83 Forest Lane, Kirklevington, Cleveland TS15 9NG (☎ 0642 780195); 4 Paper Bldg, Temple, London; Park Ct Chambers, 40 Pd Cross St, Leeds, W Yorks (☎ 0532 433277)

SPITTLE, (Anthony) Trevor; s of Stanley Spittle (d 1958); *b* 25 Dec 1929; *Educ* Lindisfarne Coll, Univ of Southampton (BCom); *m* 1955, Jennifer Mae, *née* Emery; 2 s (Graham b 1957, Robert b 1962), 2 da (Frances b 1958, Laura b 1964); *Career* ptnr Deloitte Haskins & Sells 1963-76, dep chm Great Universal Stores plc 1976-; FCA; *Recreations* gardening, sport as a spectator particularly rugby union; *Style—* Trevor Spittle Esq; Croft House, Cole Hill, S Hanningfield Rd, Rettendon Common, Chelmsford, Essex

SPOKES, John Arthur Clayton; QC (1973); s of Peter Spencer Spokes (d 1976), of Oxford, and Lilla Jane, *née* Clayton (d 1979); *b* 6 Feb 1931; *Educ* Westminster, Brasenose Coll Oxford (MA); *m* 30 Dec 1961 Jean, da of Dr Robert McLean (d 1972) of Carluke; 1 s (Andrew), 1 da (Gillian); *Career* barr Gray's Inn 1955; bencher 1985, recorder of Crown Ct 1972-; chllr Diocese of Winchester 1985-; chm Data Protection Tribunal 1985-; *Clubs* Utd Oxford and Cambridge Univ; *Style—* J A C Spokes, QC; 3 Pump Court, Temple, London EC4Y 7AJ (☎ 01 353 0711, fax 01 353 3319)

SPOKES SYMONDS, Ann; da of Peter Spencer Spokes (d 1976), and Lilla Jane, *née* Clayton (d 1979); *b* 10 Nov 1925; *Educ* The Masters Sch Dobbs Ferry NY, St Anne's Coll Oxford (MA); *m* 1980, (John) Richard Symonds, s of Sir Charles Symonds, KBE, CB (d 1978); twin step s (Jeremy, Peter); *Career* memb Oxford City Cncl 1957-, parly candidate gen elections of 1959, 1966 and 1970, lord mayor of Oxford 1976-77; memb W Midlands bd Central Independent TV (formerly ATV) 1978- (dir 1978-81), Sucial Servs admin until 1980; chm: ACCs social servs ctee 1978-82, Prince of Wales advsy gp on disability 1983-, Hearing Aid cncl 1987-, Bd of Anchor Housing Assn 1976-83 (1985-) Oxon CC 1981-83, organising sec Age Concern Oxford 1968-80, chm Age Concern England 1983-86; *Books* Celebrating Age An Authology (1987); *Recreations* photography, travel, lawn tennis, swimming; *Clubs* Royal Overseas League; *Style—* Mrs Ann Spokes Symonds; 43 Davenant Rd, Oxford OX2 8BU

SPON; *see*: de Spon

SPOONER, Prof Frank Clyffurde; s of Harry Gordon Morrison Spooner (d 1967), and Ethel Beatrice, *née* Walden (d 1985); *b* 5 Mar 1924; *Educ* Christ's Coll Cambridge (BA, MA, PhD, LittD); *Career* RNVR 1942-46, Sub Lt (S); serv: HMS Shippigan, HMS Swiftsure, HMS Newfoundland, HMS Rome Head; bachelor scholar Christ's Coll Cambridge 1947 (bachelor res scholar 1948), Chargé de Recherches Centre Nat de la Recherche Scièntifique Paris 1949-50, Allen scholar Univ of Cambridge 1951, fell Christ's Coll 1951-57; Cwlth Fund fell: Univ of Chicago 1955-56, Univs of NY, Columbia and Harvard 1956-57; Ecole Pratique des Hautes Etudes Paris 1957-63; lectr: ctee for advanced studies Univ of Oxford 1958-59, econs Harvard Univ 1961-62; Irving Fisher res prof of econs Yale Univ 1962-63; Univ of Durham: lectr 1963, reader 1964, prof 1966, emeritus prof of econ history 1985, Leverhulme fell 1977-79 and 1985-86; FRHistS 1970, FSA 1983; Prix Limantour, Lauréat de l'Académie des Sciences Morales et Politiques (1957); *Books* L'économie mondiale et les frappes monétaires en France, 1493-1680 (1956), The International Economy and Monetary Movements in France, 1493-1725 (1972), Risks at sea: Amsterdam insurance and maritime Europe, 1766-1780 (1983); *Recreations* music, walking, photography; *Clubs* United Oxford and Cambridge Univ; *Style—* Prof Frank Spooner; 31 Chatsworth Ave, Bromley, Kent BR1 5DP (☎ 01 857 7040); Dept of Economics, 23 Old Elvet, Durham DH1 3HY (☎ 091 374 2272)

SPOONER, Graham Michael; s of Ronald Sidney Spooner (d 1968), of Westcliff-on-Sea, Essex, and Kitty Margaret, *née* Cole (d 1985); *b* 23 August 1953; *Educ* Westcliff HS, St John's Coll Cambridge (MA); *Career* joined ICFC (now part of 3i Gp plc) 1974: area mangr Nottingham 1983, local dir in London 1986, dir 3i plc 1987- ; *Recreations* sports (playing and watching), reading, theatre, travel; *Clubs* United Oxford and Cambridge University; *Style—* Graham Spooner, Esq; 4 Hope Close, Canonbury, London N1 (☎ 01 226 6780); 20 Cavendish Rd East, The Park, Nottingham (☎ 0602 472 118); 3i plc, 91 Waterloo Rd, London SE1 8XP (☎ 01 928 7822, fax 01 928 0058, telex 917844)

SPOONER, Sir James Douglas; o s of Vice Adm Ernest John Spooner, DSO (d 1942), and Megan, *née* Foster (d 1987); *b* 11 July 1932; *Educ* Eton, Christ Church Oxford; *m* 1958, Jane Alison, da of Sir Gerald Glover (d 1986); 2 s, 1 da; *Career* former ptnr Dixon Wilson & Co CAs; chm: Coats Viyella 1969- (Navy, Army and Air Force Inst 1973-86), Morgan Crucible 1983-; dir: John Swire & Sons 1970-, J Sainsbury 1981-, Barclays Bank 1983-; pres KIDS (handicapped children's charity); fell and chm Cncl King's Coll London 1986-, dir Royal Opera House, Covent Gdn 1987-; FCA; kt 1981; *Recreations* history, music, shooting; *Clubs* White's, Beefsteak; *Style—* Sir James Spooner; Swire House, 59 Buckingham Gate, London SW1E 6AJ

SPOONER, Philip Rutland; s of Basil Spooner (d 1963), of Gainsborough, and Phyllis Mary, *née* Shephard (d 1979); *b* 11 July 1922; *Educ* The Leys Sch Cambridge; *m* 19 July 1952, Mary Bryce, da of Alfred John Maltby (d 1978), of Gainsborough; 2 s (John Michael, Simon), 2 da (Marion (Mrs Law), Jill); *Career* Sgt (intelligence section) 11 Lindsey Bn Home Gd; CA; Spooners Gainsborough: ptnr 1946-63, sole princ 1963-74, sr ptnr 1974-88, conslt 1988-; dir Gainsborough Bldg Soc 1988-; govr: Queen Elizabeth HS Gainsborough 1981-88 (vice-chm 1981-85); chm: Lincoln and 5 Lincs branch CAs 1969-70, Gainsborough Town Tennis Club 1973-84, Gainsborough and Dist Cncl of Churches 1984-85; ACA 1946, FCA 1960; *Recreations* tennis, walking, reading; *Style—* Philip Spooner, Esq; 1 The Ave, Gainsborough DN21 1EP (☎ 0427 2826); 7 Spring Gdns, Gainsborough DN21 2AZ (☎ 04271 4742)

SPOONER, Raymond Philip; s of Henry James Spooner, and Ethel, *née* Phillips (d 1986); *b* 31 August 1934; *Educ* Addey and Stanhope Sch London, City Univ London (MSc); *m* 23 Oct 1954, Beryl Jean, da of Percy Charles Bratton (d 1973); 1 s (Kevin Paul b 2 Oct 1956, d 1985), 1 da (Yvette Kay Dawn b 14 Oct 1958); *Career* Sgt Intelligence Corps 1952-54, TA 1954-62; sr lectr accountancy and audit Southbank Poly 1982-, co sec lectr 1967-, (conslt in internal auditing and mgmnt control); author of Spooner report (brought about the creation of UK professional qualification for internal auditors); past govr: Inst of Internal Auditors UK 1976-78, SW London Coll 1970-81; past pres Soc Co and Commercial Accountants 1987-88; Freeman: City of London 1978, Worshipful Co of Secs and Admins 1978; FSCA 1968, MBIM 1967, ACIS 1971, FIIA 1986; *Recreations* bridge, DIY; *Style—* Raymond Spooner, Esq; Conifers, Orestan Lane, Effingham, Surrey KT24 5SN (☎ 0372 57248); South Bank Poly, Borough Rd, London SE1 0AA (☎ 01 928 8989)

SPOONER, Richard Hamilton; s of Derek Richard Spooner(d 1978), and Patricia Sackville, *née* Hamilton; *b* 17 Feb 1952; *Educ* Kings Sch Ely, Lanchester Sch of Business Studies (BA); *m* 8 April 1978, Susan Elizabeth Ann, da of Anthony John Rowntree; 2 da (Victoria, Catherine); *Career* audit mangr Howard Tilly 1976-79, chief accountant Yeoman Aggregates Ltd 1979-83; dir: Yeoman Heavy Haulage Ltd 1980-83, Buckingham Computers Ltd 1981-84, Howard Tilly Assocs 1983-88; md Howard Tilly Assocs Ltd 1984-88, Howard Tilly Assocs Property Systems Ltd 1987-, Baker Tilly Mgmnt Conslts 1988-; ptnr: Howard Tilly & Co 1986-, Baker Tilly & co 1988-; ACA; memb: ICEAW, IOD, BIM; *Recreations* tennis, bridge, good food; *Style—* Richard Spooner, Esq; 3 Green Hill, High Wycombe, Bucks (☎ 0494 446 083); Baker Tilly, Cwlth Ho, 1 New Oxford St, London WC1A 1PF (☎ 01 404 5541, fax 01 405 2836, car tel 0836 774 351, telex 21594)

SPORBORG, Christopher Henry; s of Henry Nathan Sporborg, CMG (d 1985), of Upwick Hall, Upwick, Albury, Ware, Herts, and Mary, *née* Rowlands; *b* 17 April 1939; *Educ* Rugby Sch, Emmanuel Coll Cambridge; *m* 1961, Lucinda Jane, da of Brig Richard Nigel Hanbury (d 1971), of Hay Lodge, Braughing, Herts; 2 s (William b 1965, Simon b 1972), 2 da (Sarah b 1964, Eliza b 1967); *Career* Nat Serv Lt Coldstream Gds; dep chm Hambros Bank Ltd 1962- (dir 1970, exec dir 1975, currently dep chm); dep chm: Hambros plc (bd memb 1983), Hambro Pacific; chm: Hambro Countrywide plc 1986-, Hambros Australia Ltd 1978-, Hambro America Inc 1985-, Atlas Copco Gp in GB 1984-, BFSS Investmts Ltd 1980-, Hambro Aust Ltd 1978-; tres BFSS; jt master Puckeridge and Thurlow Foxhounds; landowner; *Recreations* racing, hunting, master of foxhounds; *Clubs* Boodles, Jockey; *Style—* Christopher Sporborg, Esq; Walkers Farm House, Farnham, nr Bishop's Stortford, Herts (☎ 027 974 444); Hambros Bank Ltd, 41 Towerhill, London EC3N 4HA (☎ 01 480 5000, telex 883851)

SPOTSWOOD, Marshal of the Royal Air Force Sir Denis Frank; GCB (1970, KCB 1966, CB 1961), CBE (1946), DSO (1943), DFC (1942); s of Frank Henry Spotswood (d 1957), of Elstead, Surrey, and Caroline Spotswood (d 1984); *b* 26 Sept 1916; *m* 1942, Ann, da of Solomon Child (d 1968); 1 s; *Career* joined RAF 1936, served WW II in Europe, N Africa and SE Asia (despatches twice), Gp Capt 1954, ADC to HM The Queen 1957-61, Actg Air Cdre 1958, Cdr RAF Coll Cranwell 1958-61, Air Cdre 1960, AVM 1961, Asst COS air def div SHAPE 1961-63, AOC 3 Gp Bomber Cmd 1964-65, C-in-C RAF Germany 1965-68, Cdr 2 Allied TAF 1966-68, Air Marshal 1965, Air Chief Marshal 1968, AOC-in-C RAF Strike Cmd 1968-71, Air ADC to HM The Queen 1970-74, chief of Air Staff 1971-74, Marshal of the RAF 1974; vice-chm Rolls Royce 1974-80, chm Smith's Industs Aerospace Cos 1980-83 (dir 1983-), dir Dowty Gp 1980-, chm Royal Star and Garter Home 1980- (govr 1975-); FRAeS; Offr Legion of Merit (USA); *Recreations* golf, bridge, rugby (spectator), rowing (spectator); *Clubs* RAF, Royal Aeronautical Soc, Phyllis Court, Huntercombe Golf; *Style—* Marshal of the Royal Air Force, Sir Denis Spotswood, GCB, CBE, DSO, DFC; Coombe Cottage, Hambleden, Henley-on-Thames, Oxon

SPOTTISWOOD, Air Vice-Marshal James Donald; CB (1988), CVO (1977), AFC (1971); s of James Thomas Spottiswood (d 1981), of Hartlepool, and Caroline Margaret, *née* Taylor; *b* 27 May 1934; *Educ* West Hartlepool GS, Univ of Boston (MA); *m* 3 April 1957, Margaret Maxwell, da of John James Harrison (d 1939), of Wingate; 2 s (Ian b 1960, David b 1963), 1 da (Lynne b 1958); *Career* RAF: joined 1951, with 139 Sqdn 1954, CFS 1956 Fl-Cdr RAF Halton 1959, Fl Cdr 617 Sqdn 1963, RNSC 1965, Personal SO C-in-C Middle East 1966, Sqdn-Cdr 53 Sqdn 1968, JSSC 1970, Station Cdr RAF Thorney Is 1971, Station Cdr and Dep Capt Queens F1 1974, DSD RAF Staff Coll Bracknell 1977, RCDS 1978, Int Mil Staff NATO HQ 1979, dir gen of Trg 1983, AO Trg/ AO Cmdg Trg Units 1985; chm RAF Gliding and Soaring Assoc, dep chm Br Gliding Assoc; FBIM; *Recreations* gliding, sailing, golf; *Clubs* RAF; *Style—* Air Vice-Marshal Donald Spottiswood, CB, CVO, AFC; c/o Royal Bank of Scotland, Oxford; Headquarters Royal Air Force Support Command, Royal Air Force Brampton, Huntingdon, Cambridgeshire PE18 8QL (☎ 0480 5251 ext 6218)

SPRAGGS, Rear Adm Trevor Owen Keith; CB (1982); s of Cecil James Spraggs (d 1979), and Gladys Maud, *née* Morey (d 1949); *b* 17 June 1926; *Educ* Portsmouth GS, St John's Coll Southsea, Imperial Coll London (BSc); *m* 1, 1955, Mary Patricia (d 1983), da of Bernard Leslie Light (d 1980); 2 s; m 2, 1986 Gwynedd Kate, da of Augustus Stephen George Adams; *Career* joined RN 1945, dean RNC Greenwich 1975-77, dir Naval Educn and Trg Support 1977-79, ADC to HM The Queen 1979, dean RNEC 1979-80, chief naval instr MOD 1981-83, Rear Adm 1981, COS to C-in-C Naval Home Cmd 1981-83; memb ctee of mgmnt Royal Hosp Sch Holbrook 1981-83; ACGI, CEng, FIEE; *Recreations* golf, sailing; *Clubs* Royal Naval Sailing Assoc, Hayling Island Golf; *Style*— Rear Adm Trevor Spraggs, CB; c/o Lloyds Bank, 46 Station Rd, Hayling Island, Hants PO11 0EJ

SPRAGUE, Christopher William; s of Coulam Alfred Joseph Sprague, of New Malden, Surrey, and Joan Gertrude, *née* Jackson (d 1986); *b* 19 August 1943; *Educ* St Edwards Sch Oxford, Christ Church Oxford (MA); *m* 24 April 1971, Clare, da of Dr John Russell Bradshaw, (d 1968), of Topsham, Devon; 4 da (Katharine b 1972, Alison b 1974, Hannah b 1979, Alexandra b 1981); *Career* articled Simmons & Simmons, admitted slr 1970, ptnr Ince & Co 1975-, specialist in insur and maritime law, lectr on maritime law and assoc subjects; supporting memb London Maritime Arbitrators Assoc; tres Thames regnl Rowing Cncl, memb Thames Regnl Umpires Cmmn; Liveryman Worshipful Co of Barbers; *Recreations* reading, rowing, bellringing; *Clubs* Oxford and Cambridge, London Rowing, Leander; *Style*— C W Sprague, Esq; Pasturewood, Woodhill Lane, Shamley Green, Guildford, Surrey GU5 0SP

SPRATT, Sir Greville Douglas; GBE (1987), TD (1962, and bar 1968), JP (City Bench 1978), DL (Gtr London 1986); er s of Hugh Douglas Spratt, of Henley-on-Thames, and Sheelah Ivy, *née* Stace; *b* 1 May 1927; *Educ* Leighton Park Sch, Charterhouse; *m* 1954, Sheila Farrow, yst da of late Joseph Wade, of the Old Mill, Langstone, Hants; 3 da; *Career* Coldstream Gds 1945-46, cmmnd 1946, seconded to Arab Legion, served Palestine, Jordan and Egypt 1946-48, GSO III (Ops and Intelligence) 1948; joined HAC as Private 1950, re-cmmnd 1950, Capt 1952, Maj 1954, CO (Lt-Col) 1962-65, Regtl Col 1966-70, memb Ct of Assts HAC 1960-70 and 1978- ; underwriting memb of Lloyd's 1951-; joined J & N Wade Gp of Cos 1961, dir 1969-76, md 1972-76 (when gp sold), ADC to HM The Queen 1973-78, Alderman of City of London (Castle Baynard Ward) 1978-, Sheriff of City of London 1984-85, Lord Mayor of London 1987-88; Freeman City of London 1977, Liveryman Worshipful Co of Ironmongers 1977; FRSA, OStJ; Chevalier de la Légion d'Honneur 1961, Commandeur de l'Ordre Nationale du Mérite 1984, Cdr Order of the Lion (Malawi) 1985, memb Nat Order of Aztec Eagle (Mexico) 1985; FRSA; *Recreations* tennis, music, military history, forestry, stamp, coin and bank note collecting; *Clubs* Cowdray park Golf and Polo, United Wards, City Livery, Guildhall, City Pickwick; *Style*— Sir Greville Spratt, GBE, TD, JP, DL; Grayswood Place, Haslemere, Surrey GU27 2ET (☎ 0428 4367)

SPRECKLEY, (John) Nicholas Teague; CMG (1983); s of Air Marshal Sir Herbert Spreckley, KBE, CB (d 1963), and Winifred Emery, *née* Teague; *b* 6 Dec 1934; *Educ* Winchester, Magdalene Coll Cambridge (BA); *m* 1958, Margaret Paula Jane, da of Prof William McCausland Stewart; 1 s (Robin), 1 da (Bridget); *Career* For Off: head of Euro community dept (Internal) FCO 1979-83, ambass to Rep of Korea 1983-86, High Cmmr to Malaysia 1986-; *Clubs* Army and Navy; *Style*— HE Mr Nicholas Spreckley, CMG; British High Commission, Wisma Damansara, Jalan Semantan, Kuala Lumpur 50490; c/o Foreign and Commonwealth Office, King Charles Street, London SW1

SPRIGGE, Prof Timothy Lauro Squire; s of Cecil Jackson Squire Sprigge (d 1959), of Rome and London, and Katriona, *née* Gordon Brown (d 1965); *b* 14 Jan 1932; *Educ* Gonville and Caius Coll Cambridge (MA, PhD); *m* 4 April 1959, Giglia, da of Gavin Gordon (d 1965); 1 s (Samuel Felix b 1961), 2 da (Georgina Nessie b 1960, Lucy Cecilia b 1960); *Career* lectr in philosophy UCL 1961-63, reader in philosophy Univ of Sussex 1963-69 (lectr 1963-70), prof of logic and metaphysics Univ of Edinburgh 1979-; ctee memb Scottish Soc for the Prevention of Vivisection; memb: Aristotelian Soc, Mind Assoc, Scots Philosophical Club; *Books* The Correspondence of Jeremy Bentham Vols 1 and 2 (ed 1968), Facts, Words and Beliefs (1970), Santayana: An Examination of his Philosophy (1974), The Vindication of Absolute Idealism (1983), Theories of Existence (1984), The Rational Foundations of Ethics (1987); *Recreations* backgammon; *Style*— Prof Timothy Sprigge; 14 Great Stuart St, Edinburgh EH4 7TN (☎ 031 225 7735); Sherkin Island, County Cork, Rep of Ireland; David Hume Tower, Univ of Edinburgh, George Square, Edinburgh (☎ 031 667 1011 ext 6212)

SPRING, Hon Mrs; Hon Jane Elizabeth; *née* Henniker-Major; da of 8 Baron Henniker, KCMG, CVO, MC, of Red House, Thornham, Suffolk, and Margaret Osla, *née* Benning (d 1974); *b* 6 July 1954; *Educ* Benenden, Durham Univ, UCL (BA); *m* 1979, Richard John Grenville, s of Herbert John Arthur Spring, of Cape Town; 1 s (Frederick b 1987), 1 da (b 1983); *Career* Magistrate Inner London 1984-87; sec gen Int Federation of Settlements; tstee; Housing the Homeless Central Fund, OSLA Henniker Charitable Tst; *Recreations* opera, riding, tennis; *Clubs* Boodle's (lady memb); *Style*— The Hon Mrs Spring; 124 Cambridge St, London SW1V 4QF (☎ 01 834 1820); Valley Farm, Yaxley, Eye, Suffolk (☎ (037 983) 288)

SPRING RICE, Hon Charles James; s and h of 6 Baron Monteagle of Brandon; *b* 24 Feb 1953; *Educ* Harrow; *Style*— The Hon Charles Spring Rice

SPRING RICE, Hon Michael; s of 5 Baron Monteagle of Brandon (d 1946); *b* 1935; *Educ* Harrow; *m* 1959, Fiona, da of James Edward Kenneth Sprot; 1 s, 1 da; *Career* late Lt Irish Gds; Bowmaker Ltd (now Lloyds Bowmaker Fin Gp) 1956-86, Compagnie Bancaire Group 1986-; *Recreations* golf, shooting; *Clubs* Boodle's, Pratt's, Royal Ashdown Forest Golf, Swinley Forest Golf, Royal and Ancient Golf of St Andrews; *Style*— The Hon Michael Spring Rice; Fosseway House, Nettleton Shrub, Chippenham, Wilts SN14 7NL (☎ 0249 782875); UFB Asset Finance Limited, 54 Jermyn St, London SW1Y 6LX (☎ 01 491 3637, telex 22884, fax 01 493 0008)

SPRINGBETT, David John; *b* 2 May 1938; *Educ* Dulwich Coll London; *m* ; 3 s (Bruce b 1965, Duncan b 1967, d 1977, Jack b 1985), 4 da (Sally b 1963, Lucy b 1964, Zoe b 1980, Josie b 1981); *Career* reinsurance broker; chm PWS Gp London (fndr memb 1964); underwriting memb Lloyd's; Britain's Salesman of the Year (1981); 3 records in Guinness Book of Records; *Style*— David Springbett, Esq; 52 Minories, London EC3N 1JJ

SPRINGER, Sir Hugh Worrell; GCMG (1984, KCMG 1971), GCVO (1985), KA (1984), CBE (1961, OBE 1954); s of Charles Wilkinson Springer (d 1914), and Florence Nightingale, *née* Barrow (d 1977); *b* 22 June 1913; *Educ* Harrison Coll Barbados, Hertford Coll Oxford; *m* 1942, Dorothy Drinan, 3 da of late Lionel Gittenns; 3 s, 1 da; *Career* barr Inner Temple 1938, Barbados 1938-47, former memb Colonial Parliament and MEC Barbados 1938-47, former memb Colonial Parliament and MEC Barbados, gen sec Barbados Lab Pty 1940-47, dir Univ of WI Inst of Educn 1963-66, acting govr Barbados 1964; chm Cwlth Caribbean Med Res Cncl 1965-84; Cwlth asst sec gen 1966-70, sec gen Assoc of Cwlth Universities 1970-80, chm Cwlth Human Ecology Cncl 1971-84 (hon pres 1984-), vice-pres British Caribbean Assoc 1974-80; memb Ct of Govrs: LSE 1970-80, Exeter Univ 1970-80, Hull Univ 1970-80, London Sch of Hygiene and Tropical Med 1974-77, Inst of Cwlth Studies 1974-80; memb: Advsy Ctee Science Policy Fndn 1977-, bd dirs United World Colls 1978-; govr-gen Barbados 1984-; sr visiting fell All Souls Coll Oxford 1962-63 (hon fell 1988-), hon fell Hertford Coll Oxford 1974-, Hon DSC Soc Laval; Hon LLD: Victoria (BC), Univ of West Indies, City Univ, Manchester, York, Ontario, Zimbabwe, Bristol 1982, Birmingham 1983; Hon DLitt: Warwick, Ulster, Heriot-Watt, Hong Kong, St Andrews; Hon DCL: New Brunswick, Oxford, E Anglia; Knight of St Andrew (Order of Barbados); *Clubs* Athenaeum, Royal Cwlth Soc; *Style*— Sir Hugh Springer, GCMG, GCVO, KA, CBE; Barclays Bank International, Oceanic House, 1 Cockspur St, London SW1; Gibbes, St Peter, Barbados (☎ 4222591); Government House, Barbados

SPRINGMAN, Nicholas Michael Eyre; s of Paul Michael Eyre Springman, of Little Horsted, E Sussex, and Dame Ann Marcella, *née* Mulloy, DBE (d 1987); *b* 6 Dec 1960; *Educ* Eton, Kingston Poly, Inchbald Sch of Design and Decoration; *Career* Sarah Thomson Designs Ltd 1986-88, dir Michael Springman Assocs 1987-, freelance interior designer 1988-; jt jr chm The Rose Ball (Alexandra Rose Day) 1987-, jt vice-chm The Cinderella Ball (NSPCC) 1988; Freeman City of London 1983, Liveryman Worshipful Co Upholders 1983; *Recreations* literature, tennis, music, travel; *Style*— Nicholas Springman, Esq; 51 Powerscroft Rd, London E5 0PU (☎ 01 985 0539)

SPROAT, Iain MacDonald; s of William and Lydia Sproat; *b* 8 Nov 1938; *Educ* Melrose, Winchester, Magdalen Coll Oxford; *m* 1979, Judith Kernot, *née* King; 1 step s (Charles); *Career* MP (C) Aberdeen S 1970-83, pps to sec of State for Scotland 1973-74; chm Soviet & East Euro Gp of Cons Foreign Affairs ctee 1975-81; leader, Cons Gp on Scottish Select ctee 1979-81; leader Br Parly Delgn to Austria 1980; parly under-sec Trade 1981-83; conslt N M Rothschild & Sons Merchant Bankers Ltd 1983-; chm: Milner and Co Ltd, Cricketers' Who's Who Ltd; dir D'Arcy, Marvis Benton & Bowler Ltd; Min: Aviation and Shipping, Tourism; Min responsible for Govt Statistics; distributive retail trader for cinema, film, video; and Board of African Medical and research Fndn 1987-; special advisr to PM Gen Election 1987; *Books* Wodehouse at War (1981), Cricketers' Who's Who (ed, 1980); *Clubs* Oxford and Cambridge; *Style*— Iain Sproat, Esq; Hedenham Hall, Hedenham, Norfolk NR35 2LE

SPROT, Lt-Col Aidan Mark; MC (1944), JP (Peeblesshire 1966); yr s of Maj Mark Sprot of Riddell, JP, DL (d 1946), of Riddell, Roxburghshire, and Meliora (d 1979), er da of Sir John Adam Hay, 9 Bt, of Haystoun and Smithfield; *b* 17 June 1919; *Educ* Stowe; *Career* landowner, farmer; Ld-Lt of Tweeddale (formerly Peeblesshire, DL 1966-80) 1980-; Lt-Col served Royal Scots Greys 1940-62; pres Lowlands of Scotland TA & VRA; memb: Royal Company of Archers (Queen's Body Guard for Scotland), Peeblesshire CC 1963-75; hon sec Royal Caledonian Hunt 1964-74; dir Peeblesshire Branch Red Cross 1966-74 (now Patron); County Cmmnr, Peeblesshire Scout Assoc 1968-73 (now Pres); *Recreations* country pursuits, motor-cycle touring; *Clubs* New (Edinburgh); *Style*— Lt-Col Aidan Sprot, MC, JP; Crookston, by Peebles EH45 9JQ (☎ 07214 209)

SPROXTON, Rev (Charles) Vernon; s of Alan Sproxton (d 1977), of Hull, and Eleanor *née* Swales (d 1970); *b* 8 May 1920; *Educ* Riley HS Hull, Edinburgh Univ, The United Independent (Theol) Coll Bradford; *m* 27 July 1944, Margaret Joan, da of William Ireland (d 1957), of Edinburgh; 1 s (David b 1954), 1 s decd (Andrew b 1948, d 1977), 1 da (Ruth b 1951); *Career* sec of Student Christian Mvmnt Leeds Sheffield Univ 1944-47, Christian Educn Mvmnt 1947-53; min Waterloo-with-Seaforth Congregational Church 1953-57; radio and TV producer BBC 1957-77, freelance writer and broadcaster 1977-; writer and producer of TV biographies on: Pope Paul VI, Saint Augustine, Luther, Erasmus, Jan Hus, Pascal, Kierkegaard, Simone Weil, Dietrich Bonhoeffer; filmed inverviews ;with great theologians: Karl Barth, Martin Buber, Emil Brunner, Rudolph Bultman, Paul Tillich, Yves Congar; writer of radio features on: C S Lewis, Dorothy Sayers, Reinhold Niebuhr, William Temple, J H Oldham, R H Tawney, Florence Allshorn, H J S Guntrip; occasional contributor to: The Times, The Listener, The Guardian, The New Statesman; film critic: The New Christian; chm Impressions Gallery of Photography, York; *Books* Love and Marriage (1970), Teilhard de Chardin (1971), Revelation (1976); *Recreations* photography, metal and woodwork; *Style*— The Rev Vernon Sproxton; The Old Smithy, Tunstall, Richmond, North Yorkshire (☎ 0748 818436)

SPRY, Brig Sir Charles Chambers Fowell; CBE (1956), DSO (1943); s of Augustus Frederick Spry (d 1960), and Firenze Josephine Eglington Spry (d 1941); *b* 26 June 1910; *Educ* Brisbane GS, RMC Duntroon (psc); *m* 1939, Kathleen Edith Hull, da of Rev Godfrey Smith (d 1939); 1 s, 2 da; *Career* dep dir Staff Duties Land Forces HQ (Aust) 1943-45, Col Gen Staff Aust Mission (SEAC) 1945-46, dir Military Intelligence 1946-50, hon ADC govr-gen 1946, dir-gen Aust Security Serv 1950-70, ret; tstee Aust War Meml Canberra 1967-73; kt 1964; *see Debrett's Handbook of Australia and New Zealand for further details*; *Clubs* Melbourne, Royal Melbourne GC; *Style*— Brig Sir Charles Spry, CBE, DSO; 2 Mandeville Crescent, Toorak, Vic 3142, Australia (☎ 241 8595)

SPRY, Maj-Gen Daniel Charles; CBE (1945), DSO (1944), CD; s of Maj-Gen Daniel William Bigelow Spry (d 1939), and Ethelyn Alma Rich (d 1955); *b* 4 Feb 1913; *m* 1939, Jessie Elizabeth, da of late Roy Fletcher Forbes; 1 s (Daniel), 1 da (Margot); *Career* with Canadian Militia, 2 Lt Princess Louise Fus 1932, Royal Canadian Regt (permanent force) 1934, World War II 1939-46, Capt 1939, Maj 1940, Lt-Col 1943, Brig 1943, Maj-Gen 1944; GOC 3 Canadian Inf Div 1944-45; ret as vice-chief of Gen Staff 1946; Col The Royal Canadian Regt 1965-78; chief exec cmmr The Boy Scouts' Assoc of Canada 1946-51, dep dir Boy Scouts World Bureau 1951-53, dir 1953-65; Cdr Order of Crown of Belgium 1945, Belgian Croix de Guerre 1945; *Recreations* gardening, fishing; *Clubs* Rideau, Ottawa; *Style*— Maj Gen Daniel Spry, CBE, DSO, CD; 4 Rock Ave, Ottawa, Ontario, K1M 1A6

SPRY, Sir John Farley; s of Joseph Farley Spry (d 1923); *b* 11 Mar 1910; *Educ* Perse Sch, Peterhouse Cambridge; *m* 1 (m dis 1940); 1 s, 1 da; m 2, 1953, Stella Marie, da of Sydney Carlisle Fichat; *Career* solicitor; asst registrar of Titles and Conveyance

Uganda 1936-44, asst dir Land Registration Palestine 1944-48, puisne judge Tanganyika 1961-64, justice of appeal Ct of Appeal East Africa 1964-70 (vice-pres 1970-75), chm Pensions Appeal Tribunal 1975-76; Gibraltar: chief justice 1976-80, cmmr for Revision of Laws 1981-85, pres court of appeal 1983-, chief justice British Indian Ocean Territory 1981-88, chief justice St Helena 1983-; kt 1975; *Books* Sea Shells of Dar es Salaam (Parts: 1 1961, 2 1964, 3 1968), Civil Procedure in East Africa (1969), Civil Law of Defamation in East Africa (1976); *Recreations* conchology; *Style*— Sir John Spry; 15 de Vere Gardens, London W8

SPURGEON, Maj-Gen Peter Lester; CB (1980); s of Harold Sidney Spurgeon (d 1959), of Suffolk, and Mrs Emily Anne Spurgeon, *née* Bolton; *b* 27 August 1927; *Educ* Merchant Taylors Sch Northwood; *m* 1959, da of Cyril Bland Aylward, of Bournemouth (d 1972); 1 s (Simon), 1 da (Nicola); *Career* RM 1946-80; Col Commandant Royal Marines 1987-; Maj-Gen cmdg Tning and Res Forces RM 1977-80, chief exec Royal Agric Benevolent Inst 1982-; pres RM Assocn 1986; *Recreations* gardening, golf; *Clubs* Army & Navy; *Style*— Maj-Gen P L Spurgeon, CB; Shaw House, 27 Westway, Oxford OX2 0QH (☎ (0865) 724931)

SPURLING, Lady (Marian Taylor); *née* Gurr; *m* 1940, Hon Sir Dudley Spurling, CBE, JP (d 1986); 3 s (1 decd), 1 da; *Style*— Lady Spurling; Three Chimneys, 5 Speaker's Drive, Wellington, St George's 1-12, Bermuda

SPURR, Margaret Anne (Mrs John Spurr); *née* Spurr; da of John William Spurr, and Anne Spurr; *b* 7 Oct 1933; *Educ* Abbeydale Girls' GS Sheffield, Univ of Keele (BA, PGCE); *m* 7 Nov 1953, John Spurr; 1 s (David b 2 Nov 1959), 1 da (Jane b 26 Aug 1961); *Career* tutor English literature: Univ of Glasgow 1971, Univ of Keele 1972-73; sr examiner Univ of London 1971-80; memb: advsy ctee american studies res centre PCL 1977-, scholarship selection ctee English Speaking Union 1983-, CBI Schs' Panel 1985-, nat ctee Women in Indust Year 1986-; chm: PR ctee Girls' Schs Assoc 1986- (pres 1985-86), Nat Isis Ctee 1987; *Recreations* gardening, theatre, poetry; *Clubs* Univ Womens, Royal Overseas; *Style*— Mrs John Spurr; The Old Vicarage, Croxden, Uttoxeter ST14 5JQ (☎ 088 926 214); Bolton School Girls' Division, Chorley New Rd, Bolton, Lancs BL1 4PB (☎ 0204 40201)

SPURRIER, Hon Mrs (Elizabeth Jane); *née* Maude; da of Baron Maude of Stratford-upon-Avon (Life Peer); *b* 1946; *Educ* St Mary's Wantage; *m* 1973, Peter Brotherton Spurrier, *qv*; 2 s (Benedict b 1979, Thomas b 1982); *Career* researcher BBC Radio 4, freelance broadcaster and writer, Southside Magazine 1988; *Style*— The Hon Mrs Spurrier; 15 Morella Rd, Wandsworth Common, London SW12 (☎ 01 675 1431)

SPURRIER, Peter Brotherton; s of Eric Jack Spurrier, MBE, of Storrington Sussex, and Frances Mary, *née* Brotherton; *b* 9 August 1942; *Educ* Gayhurst Prep Sch Gerrards Cross, Chetham's Hosp Sch, Manchester Coll of Art and Design (NDD) 1964; *m* 1973, Hon Elizabeth Jane, *qv*, da of Baron Maude of Stratford-upon-Avon; 2 s (Benedict, Thomas), 1 da (Lucinda b 1985); *Career* Portcullis Pursuivant of Arms 1981-; cncl memb The Heraldry Soc; FRSA; Freeman City of London; Freeman and Liveryman Worshipful Co of Painter-Stainers 1985; memb Chartered Soc of Designers; Esquire in the Venerable Order of St John; *Recreations* beagling, fishing, painting; *Clubs* City Livery; *Style*— Peter Spurrier, Esq, Portcullis Pursuivant of Arms; 15 Morella Rd, Wandsworth Common, London SW12 (☎ 01 675 1431); College of Arms, Queen Victoria St, London EC4 (☎ 01 248 5214)

SPURRIER, Roger Hawley; s of Rev Henry Cecil Marriott Spurrier, MA (d 1954), of Roughton, Lincs, and Olive Victoria, *née* Hawley (d 1981); *b* 15 Feb 1928; *Educ* Marlborough; *m* 1955, Margaret Judith Briony (d 1987), da of John Otto Richards, of NZ; 2 s (Timothy John b 1957, Roger Dermot 1958); *Career* land agent (FRICS), sr ptnr in the firm of Jas Martin XX, 8 Bank St, Lincoln; *Style*— Roger Spurrier, Esq; The Old Rectory, Blankney, Lincoln (☎ (0526) 20483); Jas Martin XX, 8 Bank St, Lincoln (☎ (0522) 510234)

SPURRIER-KIMBELL, David Henry; s of Norman Kenneth Bernard Kimbell, FRCOG (d 1982), of Warmington, N'hants, and Mary Pamela, da of Sir Henry Spurrier; *b* 24 Sept 1944; *Educ* Oundle, Heidelberg Univ; *m* 25 July 1970, Maureen Patricia, da of Dr Eric Charles Elliot Golden; 1 s (Henry b 1986), 2 da (Antonia b 1977, Deborah b 1979); *Career* Br Leyland Motor Corp Ltd 1966-78, overseas dir Leyland Vehicles Ltd 1978, joined Spencer Stuart & Assocs Ltd London 1979 (1983 int ptnr, 1985 md UK, 1987 int chm); *Recreations* golf, tennis; *Clubs* Oriental Wentworth; *Style*— David Spurrier-Kimbell, Esq; Chalkpit House, Ecchinswell, Hants (☎ 0635 298269); 113 Park Lane Lane, London W1 (☎ 01 493 1238)

SPURWAY, (Marcus) John; s of Marcus Humphrey Spurway, of Goudhurst, Kent, and Eva, *née* Mann (d 1980); *b* 28 Oct 1938; *Educ* Archbishop Tenison's Sch Croydon; *m* 23 Oct 1963, Christine Kate, da of Robert Charles Townshend (d 1981), of Canterbury; 2 s (Marcus b 1967, Edward b 1969); *Career* Nat Serv; 4 Regt RHA; insur broker; dir insur brokers div of B & C Aviation Insur and Reinsurance Brokers Ltd 1988, specialist in aviation insur; *Style*— John Spurway, Esq; Lomeer, Common Rd, Sissinghurst, Kent; 32-38 Dukes Place, London EC3A 7LX (☎ 01 626 4393, fax 01 621 1532, telex 886191 CSBLDN G)

SPYER, David Oswald; s of Samuel Michael Spyer (d 1969); *b* 1 August 1927; *Educ* West Ham Secdy Sch, Bournemouth Sch, Woodhouse Sch; *m* 1957, Janice Ruth; 1 s, 1 da; *Career* Corpl RAF 1945-48; dir: Hill Samuel Securities 1972-80, Lynn Regis Finance 1973-80; chm (dir 1975-79) PHH Leasing Ltd 1977-79; md C E Coates & Co 1980-82, mangr Bank Hapoalim B M 1982-; hon gen sec The London Soc of Rugby Football Union Referees, vice-pres Middlx County Rugby Football Union, chm Lensbury RFC; *Recreations* dramatics, philately, rugby football, cricket, squash, table tennis, quizzes; *Clubs* MCC, Lensbury; *Style*— David Spyer, Esq; 36 The Avenue, Hatch End, Middx HA5 4EY

SQUIBB, George Drewry; LVO (1982), QC (1956); s of Reginald Augustus Hodder Squibb (d 1946); *b* 1 Dec 1906; *Educ* King's Sch Chester, Queen's Coll Oxford (BCL, MA); *m* 1, 1936, Bessie, *née* Whittaker (d 1954); 1 da; m 2, 1955, Evelyn May, *née* Higgins; *Career* barr Inner Temple 1930, bencher 1951, tres 1976, chm Dorset QS 1953-71; jr counsel to Crown in Peerage and Baronetcy Cases 1954-56, hon historical advsr in peerage cases to the Attorney-Gen 1965-, pres Tport Tbnl 1962-81, chief Commons cmmr 1971-85; Norfolk Herald Extraordinary 1959-, Earl Marshal's Lieut, assessor and surrogate in the Court of Chivalry 1976-; Master Worshipful Co Scriveners 1980-81; *Recreations* heraldic and genealogical research; *Clubs* Athenaeum, United Oxford and Cambridge; *Style*— George Squibb, Esq, LVO, QC; The Old House, Cerne Abbas, Dorset (☎ 030 03 272)

SQUIRE, Clifford William; CMG (1978), LVO (1972); s of Clifford John Squire (d 1938), of Gt Yarmouth; *b* 7 Oct 1928; *Educ* Royal Masonic Sch, St John's Coll Oxford (MA), Univ of London (PhD), Coll of Europe Bruges; *m* 1, 6 July 1959, Marie José (d 1973), da of René Paul Carlier (d 1978), of Paris; 2 s (Stephen b 1961, Christophe b 1963, decd), 2 da (Catherine b 1960, Anne Louise b 1965); m 2, 22 May 1976, Sara Laetitia, da of Michael David Hutchison, of Richmond, Surrey; 1 s (James b 1977), 1 da (Emma b 1979); *Career* Br Army 2 Lt, Palestine and Greece 1947-49; HM Overseas Civil Service Assist District Offr Nigeria 1953-59; HM Diplomatic Serv Foreign Off, Bucharest, United Nations NY; Ambassador to Gen 1979, Bankok, Washington 1959-79; Ambass to Israel 1984-; *Clubs* Travellers (London); *Style*— Clifford Squire, Esq, CMG, LVO; Royal Bank of Scotland, Holts, Whitehall, London SW1A 2EB; HM Embassy, Tel Aviv

SQUIRE, David Michael; s of Denis Arthur Squire, of Esher, Surrey, and (Patricia) Mary Joyce, *née* Davie; *b* 26 Feb 1949; *Educ* St Edward's Sch Oxford, Univ Coll Oxford (MA); *m* 1 June 1974, Karen StClair, da of Peter Edward Hook (d 1982); 3 da (Isabelle b 1976, Eleanor b 1980, Madeline b 1982); *Career* CA 1973; joined Price Waterhouse London Off 1970, ptnr 1981-; FCA 1979; *Recreations* sailing, local history, nautical archaeology; *Style*— David Squire, Esq; 2 St Stephens Ave, London W13 8ES (☎ 01 977 5906); Southwark Towers, 32 London Bridge St, London SE1 9SY (☎ 01 407 8989, 01 334 2255, fax 01 403 5265, telex 931709, 934716)

SQUIRE, Robin Clifford; MP (C) Hornchurch 1979-; *b* 12 July 1944; *Educ* Tiffin Sch Kingston-upon-Thames; *m* Susan Fey, *née* Branch; 1 step s, 1 step da; *Career* cllr London Borough of Sutton 1968-82 (ldr 1976-79), asst chief accountant Lombard Central Ltd 1972-79, chm Gtr London Young Cons 1973, vice-chm Nat Young Cons 1974-75; contested (C) Havering, Hornchurch 1974, PPS to Min of State Dept of Tport 1983-85; sec Cons Parly European Affrs Ctee 1979-80; memb: Select Ctee on Environment 1979-83 (Tory ldr 1982-83) and 1987, Select Ctee on European Legislation 1985-88, vice-chm: Cons Parly Trade Ctee 1981-83, Cons Parly Environment Ctee 1985-; chm Cons Action on Electoral Reform 1983-86, memb bd of mgmnt Shelter 1982-; successful sponsor of Local Govt (Access to Information) Act 1985; Freedom of Information award as individual who had most advanced freedom of information in 1985; FCA (ACA 1966); *Books* Set the Party Free (Jtly, 1969); *Recreations* bridge, modern music, films; *Style*— Robin Squire, Esq, MP; House of Commons, London SW1A 0AA (☎ 01 219 4526)

SQUIRES, Richard John; s of Richard George Squires (d 1982), of Dulwich, and Lilian Florence, *née* Fuller (d 1987); *b* 9 Dec 1937; *Educ* Alleyns Sch Dulwich; *m* 19 August 1961, Valerie Jean, da of Richard Wotton Wood, of Southfields, Wimbledon; 1 s (Paul Julian b 1970), 1 da (Fiona Jane b 1967); *Career* asst Actuary Imperial Life Assur of Canada 1963-65, Canada Life Co 1965-68; dir Save & Prosper Gp Ltd 1981- (gp actuary 1969-); Freeman of the City of London, Liveryman of the Worshipful Co of Actuaries; FIA 1962, ASA 1963; *Recreations* golf, gardening, painting; *Clubs* Cuddington GC (Banstead); *Style*— Richard Squires, Esq; 6 the Highway, Sutton, Surrey SM2 5QT (☎ 01 642 7532); Save & Prosper Group Ltd, 1 Finsbury Ave, London EC2M 2QY (☎ 01 588 1717, fax 01 247 5006, telex 883838 SAVPROG)

SQUIRRELL, John Gordon; s of Percy Lee Squirrell (d 1968); *b* 30 April 1925; *Educ* Woodbridge Sch, St Edmund Hall Oxford; *m* 1948, Sheila Anne, *née* Holliday; 2 da; *Career* Fl Lt; dir Harveys of Bristol 1969-85 (ret) (dep md 1978, UK sales and marketing dir 1976-78, UK sales dir 1969-76), dir: Grants of St James's Ltd 1978-85, A Delor & Cie Bordeaux 1977; md John Harvey & Sons Ltd 1981-85, ret; *Recreations* tennis, squash, music, art; *Clubs* East India Devonshire Sports and Public Schools; *Style*— John Squirrell, Esq; Pagans Hill House, Chew Stoke, near Bristol (☎ (0272) 332793)

STABB, His Honour Sir William Walter; QC (1968); 2 s of Sir Newton John Stabb, OBE (d 1931), and Ethel Mary, *née* Townsend, DBE (d 1961); *b* 6 Oct 1913; *Educ* Rugby, Univ Coll Oxford; *m* 1940, Dorothy Margaret,*née* Leckie; 4 da; *Career* RAF 1940-46; barr 1936; bencher Inner Temple 1964- (tres 1985), official referee of the Supreme Court 1969-, circuit judge sr official referee 1978-85, ret; kt 1981; *Style*— His Honour Sir William Stabb, QC; The Pale Farm, Chipperfield, Kings Langley, Herts (☎ 092 77 63124)

STABLE, Maj-Gen Hugh Huntington; CB (1947), CIE (1938); s of Alfred Henry Stable (d 1907); *b* 30 April 1896; *Educ* Malvern; *m* 1934, Cyrille Helen Dorothy, *née* Bayfield (d 1979); *Career* cmmnd 2/4 Dorset Regt 1914, served Palestine 1917-18 (despatches), Central India Horse 1919, NW Frontier; Army HQ India, staff offr to Maj-Gen Cavalry 1932, asst mil sec to Cdr-in-Chief India 1933-36, mil sec to Viceroy of India 1936-38, Cmdt 8 King George's Own Cav 1939-40, Bde Cdr 1941-43, DQMG GHQ India Dec 1943-44, Cdr Lucknow Sub Area 1945-46, Bihar and Orissa Area 1947, QMG India 1947, ret 1950; govr Malvern Coll; emeritus cmmr Boy Scouts of S Africa; *Clubs* Army and Navy, City and Civil Service (Cape Town); *Style*— Maj-Gen Hugh Stable, CB, CIE; 810 Rapallo, Sea Point, Cape Town, S Africa (☎ 447981)

STABLE, His Hon Judge (Rondle) Owen (Charles); QC (1963); s of Rt Hon Sir Wintringham Stable, MC (d 1977), of Plas Llwyn Owen, Llanbrynmair, Powis, and Lucie Haden, *née* Freeman; *b* 28 Jan 1923; *Educ* Winchester; *m* 6 April 1949, Yvonne Brook, da of Lionel Brook Holliday, OBE (d 1965), of Copgrove Hall, Boroughbridge, Yorkshire; 2 da (Emma (Mrs Hay), Victoria); *Career* WWII Capt RB 1940-46; barr Middle Temple 1948, bencher 1969, dep chm Herts Quarter Sessions 1963-71, recorder of Crown Cts 1972-79, circuit judge 1979; res judge: Wood Green Crown Ct 1980-81, Snaresbrook Crown Ct 1982-; sr circuit judge 1982-, bd of trade isnpector Cadco Gp of Cos 1963-64, HS Whiteside and Co Ltd 1965-67, Int Learning Systems Corpn Ltd 1969-71, Pergamon Press 1969-73; memb: Gen Cncl of the Bar 1962-64, Senate of 4 Inns of Ct 1971-74, Senate of Inns of Ct and the Bar 1974-75; chllr Dio of Bangor 1959-88, memb Governing Body of Church in Wales 1960-, layreader Dio of St Albans 1961-; chm Horserace Betting Levy Appeal Tbnl 1969-74; *Books* A Review of Coursing (with R M Stuttard, 1971); *Recreations* shooting, listening to music; *Clubs* Boodles, Pratts; *Style*— His Hon Judge Owen Stable, QC; The Crown Court at Snaresbrook, Holly Bush Hill, London E11

STABLER, Arthur Fletcher; s of Edward Stabler (d 1934), of 29 Richard St, Elswick, Newcastle-upon-Tyne, and Maggie, *née* Churnside (d 1965); *b* 7 Nov 1919; *Educ* Cruddas Park Sch; *m* 30 Oct 1948, Margaret, da of John McIntosh (d 1936), of Newcastle upon Tyne; 2 s (Roy b 13 May 1949, David b 5 March 1960); *Career* WWII serv Royal Northumberland Fusilers 1939-46; engr Vickers Armstrong Engrg Works 1933-82; memb Supplementary Benefits Commn 1976-79, involved in many residents' assocs; cncllr Newcastle-upon-Tyne (dep Lord Mayor 1982-83, Lord Mayor 1983-84); *Books* Gannin Along the Scotswood Road (1976); *Recreations* social work, local history; *Clubs* Polish White Eagle, Tyneside Irish, Royal Br Legion; *Style*— Councillor A F Stabler; 10 Whitebeam Place, Elswick, Newcastle-upon-Tyne NE4 7EJ (☎ 091 273 2362)

STACEY, Hon Mrs; (Anne Caroline Mary); *née* Bridgeman; e da of 2 Viscount Bridgeman; *b* 30 July 1932; *Educ* Reading Univ (BSc); *m* 1955, Rev Nicolas David Stacey, er s of David Stacey, of Knaphill Manor, nr Woking (whose mother was Beatrice, sister of 1 Baron Brassey of Apethorpe); 1 s (David Robert b 1958), 2 da (Caroline Jill b 1956, Mary Elizabeth b 1961); *Career* memb Nat Tst Regnl Ctee Kent and E Sussex 1984-, ptnr Eng Homes and Country Tours; *Style*— The Hon Mrs Stacey; The Old Vicarage, Selling, Faversham, Kent (☎ 022 785 833)

STACEY, Air Vice-Marshal John Nichol; CBE (1972), DSO (1945), DFC (1943); s of Capt Herbert Chambers Stacey (d 1966), of Rhydyfantwn, Moylegrove, nr Cardigan, S Wales, and Britrannia May, *née* Davies (d 1972); *b* 14 Sept 1920; *Educ* Whitgift Middle Sch; *m* 29 April 1950, Veronica, da of Air Vice-Marshal Harry Vivian Satterly, CB, CBE, DFC (d 1982); 2 da (Amanda (Mrs Reuter) b 1953, Caroline (Mrs Russell) b 1956); *Career* WWII govr operational tours incl co 160 Liberator sqdn Ceylon as Wing Cdr 1944-45 (despatches 3 times), asst air attaché Washington DC 1947-48, RAF Staff Coll Bracknell 1949, instructional staff Bracknell 1958-60, CO Royal Malayan Air Force 1960-63, CO RAF Station Laarbruch Germany 1963-66, Air Offr Commanding the ATC and RAF Air Cadets 1968-71, AOA Air Support Command 1974-75, ret RAF 1975; dir Stanham Housing Assoc 1976-82; memb: Tunbridge Wells Health Authy 1981-85, RAF Housing ASSOC 1982-86; tstee: Housing Assoc Charitable Tst 1978-86, Bedgebury Sch governing cncl 1983-, Tunbridge Wells Cancer Help Centre 1983-; MBIM 1966-82; Johan Mangku Negara Malaya 1963; *Recreations* golf, DIY; *Clubs* RAF, Dale Hill GC, Lamberhurst GC; *Style*— Air Vice-Marshal John Stacey, CBE, DSO, DFC; Riseden Cottage, Riseden, Goodhurst, Kent TN17 1HJ (☎ 0580 211 239)

STACEY, Prof Maurice; CBE (1968); s of John Henry Stacey (d 1938), of Bromstead, nr Newport, Shropshire, and Ellen, *née* Titley (d 1955); *b* 8 April 1907; *Educ* Moreton C of E Sch, Adams GS Newport Shropshire, Birmingham Univ (BSc, PhD, DSc); *m* 29 Jan 1937, Constance Mary (d 1985), da of William Ernest Pugh (d 1961), of Selly Oak, Birmingham; 2 s (Michael John b 21 April 1942, David William b 20 Jan 1951, d 18 Dec 1980) 2 da (Marion Joan b 18 June 1938, Diana Mary b 30 Oct 1946); *Career* Univ OTC 1926-29, Capt Warwicks Regt HG 1942-44; demonstrator Birmingham Univ 1929-33, Beit Meml fell London Univ 1933-36, lectr in chem Birmingham Univ 1936-44, res fell Columbia Univ NY 1937; Birmingham Univ: reader in chem 1944-46, prof of chem 1946-56, Mason prof and head of dept 1956-74, hon sr res fell 1974-76, emeritus prof 1975-; industl conslt 1976-82; memb Weobley Hill Village Cncl and Gardeners Clubs, chief scientific advsr Civil Def (Midlands) 1957-78, originator and organiser Sch Sci Fairs 1959-64, hon memb Assoc for Sci Educn 1972-, chm Jt Recruiting Bd (Midlands) 1954-62, memb: Home Office Sci Cncl 1967-75, Sci Res Cncls; vice pres Edgbaston HS 1984-; former memb ct of govrs Univs: Warwick, Loughborough, Keele; memb missions for Royal Soc Br Lit Cncl: Egypt, Rhodesia, S America; hon DSc Keele 1977, Grand Award USA Nat Acad Sci 1950, hon fell Mark Twain Soc, emeritus memb American Chem Soc, Bronze Medal Univ of Helsinki 1966, Virtanen Medal Biochem Soc Finland 1964, John Scott Medal City of Philadelphia USA 1969, Medaille d'Honneur Biol Soc France 1974, Catedratico Honor and Medal St Marcus Univ Lima Peru 1962; former vice-pres Royal Soc Chem & Meldola, Tilden & Haworth, lectr and medals Royals Soc Chem; FRS 1950, C Chem, FRSC; *Books* Polysaccarides of Microorganisam (with SA Barker 1961), Carbohydrates of Living Tissues (with Barker 1962); *Recreations* athletics (life memb AAA), antique collecting, horticulture, foreign travel; *Clubs* Athenaeum; *Style*— Prof Maurice Stacey, CBE; 12 Bryony Rd, Weoley Hill, Birmingham B29 4BU (☎ 021 475 2065)

STACEY, Rear Adm Michael Lawrence; CB (1979), ADC (1975); s of Maurice Stacey (d 1971), and Dorice Evelyn, *née* Bulling (d 1967); *b* 6 July 1924; *Educ* Epsom Coll; *m* 1955, Penelope Leana, da of Alister Riddoch (d 1968); 2 s (Hugo, Mark); *Career* various sea appts and cmds 1942-70; dep dir Naval Warfare 1970-72; in cmd HMS Tiger 1973-75; asst chief of naval staff (policy) 1975-76; flag offr Gibraltar 1976-79; dir Marine Pollution Control Unit Dept of Tport 1979-88, UK vice pres Advsy Ctee on Pollution of the Sea; *Recreations* fly-fishing, sailing; *Clubs* Army and Navy; *Style*— Rear Adm Michael Stacey, CB, ADC; 'Little Hintock', 40 Lynch Rd, Farnham, Surrey (☎ 0252 613032)

STACEY, Nicholas Anthony Howard; s of Maurus Stacey (d 1945), and Lily, *née* Balkanyi; *Educ* Pietist Gymnasium, Commercial Acad, Univ of Birmingham, Univ of London; *m* 1 (m dis 1986), Gloria Rose Cooklin; m 2, 10 March 1987, Marianne Louise; *Career* editorial staff Financial Times 1945-46, asst sec Assoc of Certified and Corporate Accountants 1947-51, asst ed The Director (jl of IOD) 1953-54, econ and mktg advsr GEC plc 1955-62; chm: Nicholas Stacey Assocs 1960-, Cel-Sci Corpn Washington DC, Chesham Amalgamations & Investmts Ltd 1963-83, Integrated Asset Mgmnt 1984; dir Asset Mgmnt Fin & Settlement Ltd (NY); Karbotek St Louis USA; chm tstees Soc for the Promotion of New Music 1969-86; memb: consultative ctee for Indust Bd of Trade 1958-62, US-UK Educnl (Fulbright) Cmmn 1983-, governing ctee Br Fulbright Scholars Assoc 1982-; fell Chartered Inst of Secretaries and Administrators; *Books* English Accountancy, A Study in Social and Economic History (1954), Changing Pattern of Distribution (1988), Industrial Market Research (1963), Mergers In Modern Business (1976), Living in an Alibi Society (1988); *Recreations* skiing, walking, swimming; *Clubs* Reform; *Style*— Nicholas Stacey, Esq; c/o Reform Club, Pall Mall, London FN1

STACEY, Rev Nicolas David; s of David Henry Stacey (d 1986), and Isobel Ewem *née* Part; *b* 27 Nov 1927; *Educ* RNC Dartmouth, St Edmund Hall Oxford (BA), Cuddesdon Theol Coll Oxford; *m* 19 July 1955, Anne Caroline Mary, eld da of 2 Viscount Bridgeman, KBE, CB, DSO, MC, JP (d 1982); 1 s (David Robert b 10 May 1958), 2 da (Caroline Jill b 28 Aug 1956, Mary Elizabeth b 15 May 1961); *Career* Midshipman RN 1945-46, Sub-Lt 1946-48; asst curate St Marks Portsmouth 1953-58, domestic chaplain to Bishop of Birmingham 1958-60, rector of Woolwich 1960-68, dean London Borough of Greenwich 1965-68, dep dir Oxfam 1968-70; dir social services: London Borough of Ealing 1971-74, Kent CC 1974-85; social services conslt 1985-88, dir Aids Policy Unit 1988-, ptnr English Homes and Country Tours, govr Reeds Sch Cobham, dir Faversham Oyster Co, patron Terrence Higgins Tst, hon sr memb Darwin Coll Univ of Kent, chm Youth Call 1981, dep chm Television South Charitable Tst 1988, six preacher Canterbury Cathedral 1984-; int sprinter 1948-52, Br Empire Games 1949, Olympic Games 1952, pres Oxford Univ Athletic Club 1951, capt Combined Oxford and Cambridge Athletics Team 1951; *Books* Who Cares (autobiography, 1971); *Recreations* skiing, golf; *Clubs* Beefsteak, Vincents (Oxford), Royal St Georges Golf (Sandwich); *Style*— The Rev Nicolas Stacey; The Old Vicarage, Selling, Faversham, Kent E13 9RS (☎ 0227 752 833) 53 Queen Anne St, London W1M 0LJ (☎ 01 486 7100, fax 01 935 0277)

STACEY, Maj Nigel William; s of William Percival Stacey (d 1972), and Pamela Iris Gledhill, *née* Prudent; *b* 22 Dec 1946; *Educ* Truro Cathedral Sch, Mons Offr Cadet Sch, RMA Sandhurst; *m* 16 March 1973, Pauline Joyce, da of Charles Hallet Taylor (d 1970); 2 s (Simon Nigel James b 1975, Richard Charles George b 1979); *Career* Army Offr Regular Army Cmmnd The Light Infantry 1972; Industrial Banking 1964-69; *Recreations* golf, squash, photography; *Clubs* The Lansdowne, The Light Infantry; *Style*— Maj Nigel Stacey; Coutts & Co, 1 Old Park Lane, London W1Y 4BS; 5 Battalion The Light Infantry, Drill Hall, Coleham, Shrewsbury SY3 7DF (☎ 0743 236 060, ext 2455)

STACEY, Tom Charles Gerard (Thomas); s of David Henry Stacey (d 1986), and Gwen Isobel, *née* Part; *b* 11 Jan 1930; *Educ* Eton, Worcester Coll Oxford; *m* 5 Jan 1952, Caroline Susan, da of Charles Nightingale Clay (d 1961); 1 s (Sam b 1966), 4 da (Emma b 1952, Mathilda b 1954, Isabella b 1957, Tomasina b 1967); *Career* formerly chief roving correspondent The Sunday Times; author and screenwriter; works inc: The Hostile Sun (1953), The Brothers M (1960), Summons to Ruwenzori (1963), To-day's World (1970), The Living and The Dying (1976), The Pandemonium (1980), The Worm in the Rose (1985), Deadline (1988, the novel and the film screenplay), Bodies and Souls (1989); chm: Stacey Int 1974, The Kensington Film Co; fndr and dir The Offender's Tag Assoc; awarded John Llewellyn Rhys Memorial Prize 1953, Granada Award (as foreign correspondent) 1961; FRSL 1977 (memb of cncl 1987); *Recreations* trees, music; *Clubs* White's, Beefsteak, Pratt's; *Style*— Thomas Stacey, Esq; 128 Kensington Church St, London W8 4BH (☎ 01 221 7166, telex 298768)

STACK, (Maurice) Neville; s of Maurice Stack (d 1970); *b* 2 Sept 1928; *Educ* Arnold Sch; *m* 1953, Molly, *née* Rowe; 1 s, 1 da; *Career* Express and Star 1950, Sheffield Telegraph and Kemsley Nat Newspapers 1955, Northern news ed IPC Nat Newspapers 1971, sub-ed Daily Express 1973, ed Stockport Advertiser 1974, ed-in-chief Leicester Mercury 1974-87, dir F Hewitt & Co Ltd Leicester 1985-88, editorial conslt Straits Times Singapore 1988-; Hon MA Univ of Leicester 1988; press fell Wolfson Coll Cambridge 1987-88; *Books* The Empty Palace (1977), Editing for the Nineties (1988); *Recreations* sailing (boat Jo-Jo), writing, flying, riding; *Clubs* Leicestershire, Rutland Sailing, Leicestershire Aero; *Style*— Neville Stack, Esq; 34 Main St, Belton-in-Rutland, Leics LE15 9LB (☎ 057 286 645)

STACK, Air Chief Marshal Sir (Thomas) Neville; KCB (1972, CB 1969), CVO (1963), CBE (1965), AFC (1957); s of Thomas Neville Stack, AFC, pioneer airman (d 1949); *b* 19 Oct 1919; *Educ* St Edmund's Coll, RAF Coll Cranwell; *m* 1955, Diana Virginia, da of late Oliver Stuart Todd, MBE; 1 s, 1 da; *Career* joined RAF 1939, served WW II, flying boats 1939-45, Coastal Cmd 1945-52, Tport Support Far East and UK 1954-59, Dep Capt The Queen's Flight 1960-62, Transport Cmd Far East 1962-64, Cmdt RAF Coll Cranwell 1967-70, UK perm mil dep CENTO Ankara 1970-72, AOC-in-C RAF Trg Cmd 1973-75, Air Chief Marshal, Air Sec MOD (Air) 1976-78, Air ADC to HM The Queen 1976-78; Gentleman Usher to HM The Queen 1978-89; FRMetS; dir gen Asbestos Int Assoc 1978-; memb Cncl of Cancer Res Campaign 1979-; govr Wellington Coll 1980-89; pres Old Cranwellian Assoc 1985-; *Recreations* under-gardening, various outdoor sports; *Clubs* RAF, Boodle's; *Style*— Air Chief Marshal Sir Neville Stack, KCB, CVO, CBE, AFC; 4 Perrymead St, London SW6 (☎ 01 736 4410)

STACY, Reginald Joseph William; CB (1955); s of Frank Dixon Stacy (d 1972); *b* 1 Jan 1904; *Educ* Sir Walter St John's London, Trinity Coll Cambridge; *m* 1932, Nina Grace, *née* Holder; 1 s, 1 da; *Career* under sec BOT 1949-64, French and Latin master Parkside Prep Sch Surrey 1967-69; *Recreations* any foreign language; *Style*— Reginald Stacy, Esq, CB; 2 Beech Ct, Easington Place, Guildford, Surrey (☎ Guildford 60761)

STAËL VON HOLSTEIN, Baron (Sweden 1675); Robert Alexander Karl Constantin; s of Baron Constantin Staël von Holstein (d 1964 in Dawlish) by his w Countess Sylvia von der Recke von Volmerstein, da of (Karl) 4 Count von der Recke von Volmerstein (of a Prussian cr of 1817 by King Frederick William III, though the family originally hailed from Westphalia); the Baron is *chef de famille* and a direct descendant of Madame de Staël, the French authoress; *b* 20 Feb 1928; *Educ* Prebendal Sch Chichester; *m* 15 Sept 1978, (as her 2 husb) Carol, da of Hon Douglas Westwood (2 s of 1 Baron Westwood) and formerly w of Maj John Ralli (whose f John was 3 cous of Sir Godfrey Ralli, 3 Bt); 1 s (Jeremy John Alexander b 1957), 1 da (Victoria Anne b 1962) and 1 step s (Charles Douglas Stephen Ralli b 1968); *Career* exec in construction indust in Africa, S America, M East; consultant in W African economic affairs and planning advsr; *Recreations* tennis, golf; *Clubs* Travellers', Lansdowne; *Style*— Baron Staël von Holstein; 77 Ashworth Mansions, Maida Vale, London W9 1LN (☎ 01 286 7495, telex 296927)

STAFFORD, Hon Mrs; Hon Elizabeth Anne; *née* Richardson; da of Baron Richardson, MVO; *b* 24 July 1937; *m* 1, 1960 (m dis 1970), Angus Jack, s of Brig-Gen James Jack, DSO, DL, by his w, Jeanette, da of Thomas Watson (3 s of Sir John Watson, 1 Bt, JP, DL); 1 s; m 2, 1971, Gregory Stafford; 1 s; *Style*— The Hon Mrs Stafford; 49 Deodar Rd, London SW15

STAFFORD, 15 Baron (E 1640) Francis Melfort William Fitzherbert; s of 14 Baron (d 1986), and Morag Nada, da of late Lt-Col Alastair Campbell, of Altries, Milltimber, Aberdeenshire; *b* 13 Mar 1954; *Educ* Ampleforth, Reading Univ, RAC Cirencester; *m* 1980, Katharine M, 3 da of John Codrington, of Barnes, London SW14; 2 s (Hon Benjamin John Basil b 1983, Hon Toby Francis b 1985), 1 da (Hon Teresa Emily b 1987); *Heir* s, Hon Benjamin Fitzherbert b 8 Nov 1983; *Career* patron Stoke-on-Trent Amateur Operatic Soc; pres: North Staffs Sporting Club, Staffordshire Assoc Boys' Clubs, Stone Cricket Club, Stafford Rugby Club; non-exec dir Tarmac Ind Products Div; *Recreations* cricket, shooting, golf; *Clubs* Farmers, Lord's Taverners; *Style*— The Rt Hon Lord Stafford

STAFFORD, (Thomas Henry) Michael; s of John Richard Stafford (d 1985), of Atherstone, Warwicks, and Henrietta, *née* Allen; *b* 15 July 1926; *Educ* Oakham Sch,

Oxford Univ (MA); *m* 15 July 1950, Lorna Beatrice, da of Douglas James Vero (d 1937), of Atherstone; 2 s (Andrew b 1955, Rupert b 1971), 3 da (Judith b 1951, Alison b 1953, Charlotte b 1959); *Career* aircrew cadet ACI RAF 1945-47; hat mfr: chm Wilson & Stafford Ltd 1985 (dir 1952-); pres Br Felt Hat Manufacturers' Fedn 1959; freemason; *Recreations* gardening, motoring, fishing, singing light opera, reading; *Style*— Michael Stafford, Esq; Limes, 67 South St, Atherstone (☎ 0827 713370); Wilson and Stafford Ltd, Station St, Atherstone, Warwicks (☎ 0827 717941)

STAFFORD, Baroness; Morag Nada; *née* Campbell; yr da of late Lt-Col Alastair Campbell, of Aberdeenshire; *m* 1952, 14 Baron Stafford (d 1986); 3 s (15 Baron, Hon Thomas, Hon Philip), 3 da (Hon Aileen, Hon Caroline, Hon Wendy); *Style*— The Rt Hon Morag, Lady Stafford; Beech Farm House, Beech, Stoke-on-Trent, Staffordshire ST4 8SJ

STAINE, Sir Albert Llewellyn; CBE (1979); s of Robert George Staine and Beatrice Elizabeth Jeffries; *b* 4 July 1928; *Educ* St Michael's Coll Belize, Hull Univ (LLB); *m* 1959, Laura Jean, da of Donald Osman Hope, of Belize City; 1 s (David b 1976); *Career* barr, chief justice 1979-82, chief scout 1980, justice of appeal 1982; kt 1984 for service to the law; *Recreations* photography, reading, music, tape recording; *Clubs* Soc of Midd; *Style*— Sir Albert Staine; 17 Princess Margaret Drive, Belize City (☎ Belize City 02-44385); Court of Appeal (☎ 02-2079)

STAINER, Michael; s of Peter Stainer (agent to the Duke of Bedford's Estates 1951-67), of The Grand, Folkestone, and Gretl Ilse Emmi Ruth, *née* Gosewisch; *b* 20 Dec 1947; *Educ* Bedford Sch; *Career* CA; Touche Ross & Co 1966-73; own practice 1973-; chm and md The Grand Hotel Ltd 1976-; Freeman City of London 1983, Worshipful Co of CAs; *Style*— Michael Stainer, Esq; The Grand, Folkestone, Kent CT20 2LR (☎ 0303 56789)

STAINTON, Sir (John) Ross; CBE (1971); s of George Stainton, and Helen, *née* Ross; *b* 27 May 1914; *Educ* Malvern; *m* 1939, Doreen Werner; 3 da; *Career* served WWII, RAF; Imperial Airways 1933-40, chm BA 1979-80 (dep chm and chief exec 1977-79, dir 1971-, chm and chief exec BOAC 1972 prior to merger into BA 1974, dir 1968-74, md 1971-72, dep md 1968-71, commercial dir 1964-68, joined 1942); vice pres Private Patients Plan plc; dir Direct Mail Servs Standards Bd; FBIM, FCIT (pres 1970-71); kt 1981; *Style*— Sir Ross Stainton, CBE; c/o Private Patients Plan plc, Tavistock House South, Tavistock Sq, WC1 (☎ 01 388 2468)

STAIR, 13 Earl of (S 1703); Sir John Aymer Dalrymple; 14 Bt of Stair (S 1664) and 10 of Killock (S 1698), KCVO (1978, CVO 1964), MBE (1941); also Viscount Stair, and Lord Glenluce and Stranraer (S 1690); Viscount Dalrymple and Lord Newliston (S 1703), Baron Oxenfoord (UK 1841); s of 12 Earl of Stair (d 1961); *b* 9 Oct 1906; *Educ* Eton; *m* 1960, Davina Katharine, da of late Hon Sir David Bowes-Lyon, KCVO, s of 14 Earl of Strathmore and Kinghorne; 3 s; *Heir* s, Viscount Dalrymple; *Career* Col late Scots Gds, Capt Gen Queen's Body Guard for Scotland (Royal Co of Archers), Gold Stick for Scotland, Lord-Lt for Wigtownshire 1961-81; *Style*— The Rt Hon the Earl of Stair, KCVO, MBE; Lochinch Castle, Stranraer, Wigtownshire

STALKER, John Lawson; s of Percy Stalker (d 1958), late of Windermere, Cumbria, and Dorothy, *née* Pickles; *b* 7 Oct 1951; *Educ* Royal Masonic Inst for Boys, Newcastle Univ (BSc); *m* 20 July 1973, Marie, da of Charles Richard Matterson (d 1980), late of Sunderland; 2 da (Rachel Rose b 1983, Naomi Dorothy Ruth b 1987); *Career* ptnr Clark Whitehill CAs; chm Thames Valley Branch Inst of Taxation, lay memb Bucks Family Practitioner Ctee; *Recreations* fishing; *Style*— John Stalker, Esq;; 143 Beech Lane, Earley, Reading, Berks (☎ 0734 862352); Clark Whitehill, 4 Easton St, High Wycombe, Bucks HP11 1NJ (☎ (0494) 444088)

STALLARD, Baron (Life Peer UK 1983), of St Pancras in the London Borough of Camden; Albert William Stallard; s of Frederick Stallard, of Tottenham; *b* 5 Nov 1921; *Educ* Low Waters Public Sch, Hamilton Acad Scotland; *m* 1944, Julie, da of William Cornelius Murphy, of Co Kerry; 1 s, 1 da; *Career* engr 1937-65, tech trg offr 1965-70; memb St Pancras Borough Cncl 1953-59 (alderman 1962-65); chm: Pub Health Ctee 1956-59 and 1962-65, Housing and Planning Dept 1956-59; memb Camden Borough Cncl 1965-70 (alderman 1971-); MP (Lab): St Pancras North 1970-74, Camden Div of St Pancras North 1974-83; PPS: Min of Agric 1973-74, min of Housing and Construction 1974-76; govt whip 1978-79 (asst 1976-78), Lords Cmmr Treasy; memb and chm Camden Town Disablement Advsy Ctee 1951-83, vice pres Camden Assoc of Mental Health; memb AEU Order of Merit (1968), former memb Inst of Trg & Devpt; *Style*— The Rt Hon the Lord Stallard; 2 Belmont St, Chalk Farm, London NW1

STALLARD, Sir Peter Hyla Gawne; KCMG (1961, CMG 1960), CVO (1956), MBE (1945); s of Rev Leonard B Stallard (d 1945), of Ottery St Mary, Devon; *b* 6 Mar 1915; *Educ* Bromsgrove Sch, CCC Oxford (MA); *m* 1941, Mary Elizabeth, CStJ, da of Rev H A Kirke of Burnham-on-Sea, Somerset; 1 s, 1 da; *Career* entered Colonial Serv Nigeria 1937, RWAFF (Artillery) W Africa and Burma 1939-45, Lt-Col 1945; sec to PM of Fedn of Nigeria 1957-61, govr and C-in-C Br Honduras 1961-66, Lt-Govr Isle of Man 1966-73, pres Devon and Cornwall Rent Assessment Panel 1976-85; KStJ 1961, Chapter-Gen Order of St John 1976-; *Style*— Sir Peter Stallard, KCMG, CVO, MBE; 18 Henley Road, Taunton, Somerset (☎ 0823 331505)

STALLARD, Hon Richard; s of Baron Stallard (Life Peer); *b* 1945; *Educ* Richard Acland Sch London; *m* 1969, Carol, da of William Packman, of Swanley, Kent; 1 s, 1 da; *Style*— The Hon Richard Stallard

STALLWORTHY, Sir John Arthur; s of Arthur John Stallworthy, of NZ; *b* 26 July 1906; *Educ* Auckland GS, Auckland and Otago Univs (NZ); *m* 1934, Margaret Wright, da of John Howie, of Scotland; 1 s, 2 da; *Career* pres: Cancer Information Assoc; Royal Soc of Medicine, Medical Protection Soc, BMA 1975; emeritus prof obstetrics and gynaecology Oxford (prof 1967-73), hon fell Oriel Oxford; MRCOG, FRCS, ERCOG; kt 1972; *Style*— Sir John Stallworthy; 8a College Green, Gloucester GL1 2LX (☎ (0452) 421243)

STALLWORTHY, Jon Howie; s of Sir John Arthur Stallworthy, of 8A College Green, Glouc GL1 2LX, and Lady Margaret Wright, *née* Howie (d 1980); *b* 18 Jan 1935; *Educ* Rugby Sch, Oxford Univ (BA, MA, BLitt); *m* 25 June 1960, Gillian (Jill), da of Sir Claude Humphrey Meredith Waldock, CMG, OBE, QC (d 1981); 2 s (Jonathan b 1965, Nicolas b 1970), 1 da (Pippa b 1967); *Career* Nat Serv 1954-55, 2 Lt Oxfordshire and Buckinghamshire LI, seconded Royal West African Frontier Force; visiting fell All Souls Coll Oxford 1971-72, dep academic publisher Oxford Univ Press 1972-77, Anderson prof eng Lit Cornell Univ 1977-86, Professional fell Wolfson Coll and reader eng lit Oxford Univ-; FRSH; *Books* Wilfred Owen (winner Duff Cooper Meml Prize, W H Smith & Son Literary Award, E M Forster Award, 1974), The Anzac Sonata: New and Selected Poems (1986), The Penguin Book of Love Poetry (ed 1973), The Osford Book of War Poetry (ed 1984); *Style*— Jon Stallworthy, Esq; Long Farm, Elsfield Rd, Old Marston, Oxford OX3 OPR; Wolfson Coll, Oxford OX2 6UD

STALLYBRASS, Hon Mrs; Hon Agnes Mary; *née* Clifford; o da of 11 Baron Clifford of Chudleigh (d 1962), and his 1 w Dorothy, *née* Hornyold (d 1918); *b* 26 Nov 1918; *m* 1944, Robert Weatherhead Stallybrass, 2 s of late Greville Stallybrass; 1 s, 2 da; *Style*— The Hon Mrs Stallybrass; The Old Laundry, Oakhill, nr Bath

STAMER, Sir (Lovelace) Anthony; 5 Bt (UK 1809) of Beauchamp, Dublin; s of Sir Lovelace Stamer, 4 Bt (d 1941), and Mary, *née* Otter (d 1974; her mother Marianne was seventh in descent from 4 Baron North); *b* 28 Feb 1917; *Educ* Harrow, Trinity Coll Cambridge (MA); *m* 1, 1948 (m dis 1953), Stella Huguette, da of Paul Burnell Binnie; 1 s, 1 da; m 2, 1955 (m dis 1959), Margaret Lucy, da of late Maj Belben; m 3, 1960 (m dis 1968), Marjorie June, da of T C Noakes; m 4, 1983, Elizabeth Graham Smith, da of late C J R Magrath and wid of G P H Smith; *Heir* s, Flt Lt Peter Tomlinson Stamer, RAF; *Career* PO RAF 1939-41, 1 Offr Air Tport Aux 1941-45; exec dir: Bentley Drivers Club Ltd 1969-73, Bugatti and Ferrari Owners Clubs 1973-74; hon tres Ferrari Owners Club 1976-81; *Style*— Sir Anthony Stamer, Bt; White Farm Cottage, White Farm Lane, West Hill, Ottery St Mary, Devon EX11 1XF (☎ 040 481 2706)

STAMER, Flt Lt Peter Tomlinson; s and h of Sir Anthony Stamer, 5 Bt; *b* 19 Nov 1951; *m* 1979, Dinah Louise, da of Thomas Selwyn Berry, of Apple Cross, Stoke Bliss, Tenbury Wells, Worcs; 1 s (William b 1983), 1 da (Antonia b 1981); *Career* Flt-Lt RAF; *Style*— Flt Lt Peter Stamer, RAF; c/o Lloyds Bank, Sloane Square, London SW1

STAMLER, Samuel Aaron; QC (1971); s of Herman Stamler (d 1962), and Bronia, *née* Rosshandler (d 1973); *b* 3 Dec 1925; *Educ* Berkhamsted, King's Coll Cambridge (MA, LLB); *m* 3 Aug 1953, (Vivienne) Honor, da of Adolph Brotman (d 1970); 2 s (Martin Stephen b 1958, Robin Jacob b 1961), 1 da (Anne Elizabeth b 1957); *Career* barr Middle Temple 1949; recorder of Crown Court 1974; master of the Bench Middle Temple 1979; *Recreations* tennis, walking; *Clubs* Athenaeum; *Style*— Samuel Stamler, Esq, QC; 47 Forty Avenue, Wembley, Middlesex (☎ 01 904 1714)

STAMMERS, Lionel John; s of Frederick Arthur Stammers, and Dorothy Irene, *née* Heales (d 1987); *b* 11 May 1933; *Educ* Harlow Coll, London (BSc Econ); *m* 5 Aug 1957, Sybil Ann, da of William James Wescott; (2 da (Jane Emma b 1963, Susan Fiona b 1965); *Career* dir: BTR plc, Dunlop Hldgs plc, Thomas Tilling plc, Serck plc, Silvertown Rubber Co Ltd, BTR Industries Ltd, Dunlop Armaline Ltd, Unidev Ltd; *Style*— Lionel Stammers, Esq; BTR plc, Silvertown House, Vincent Square, London SW1P 2PL (☎ 01 834 3848, fax 01 834 1841)

STAMP, David Paul; s of Thomas George Stamp, of Tiptree, Essex, and Betty Caroline, *née* Parnum; *b* 23 June 1955; *Educ* Royal Liberty Sch; *m* 21 July 1979, Helen Mary, da of Harold William Balls (d 1966), of Maldon, Essex; 3 s (James b 1975, Benjamin b 1980, Alastair b 1981); *Career* financier; Euro leasing mangr The Greyhound Gp 1980-85; md Finlease Hldgs Ltd (hldg co of The Finlease Gp) 1985: (UK) Ltd, EFL Ltd, Finance Ltd, Insurance Servs Ltd, Specialised Insurance Servs Ltd; md 1989: United Financial Servs Ltd, Leasepack Ltd, Finlease Travel Ltd, Maple Devpt Ltd; *Recreations* golf, ten-pin bowling; *Style*— David P Stamp; 1 Campbell Drive, Gunthorpe, Peterborough, PE 2RJ (☎ 0733 555855, fax 0733 310227, car telephone 0860 743666)

STAMP, Hon (Nancy) Elizabeth; da of 2 Baron Stamp (d 1941, as a result of enemy action); *b* 1931; *Educ* St Andrews Univ (MA); *Career* info offr, Oxfam; *Recreations* skiing, boating; *Style*— The Hon Elizabeth Stamp; 11 Harpes Rd, Oxford

STAMP, Gavin Mark; s of Barry Hartnell Stamp, of Hereford, and Norah Clare, *née* Rich; *b* 15 Mar 1948; *Educ* Dulwich Coll, Gonville and Caius Coll Cambridge (MA, PhD); *m* 12 Feb 1982, Alexandra Frances, da of Frank Artley, of Redcar; 2 da (Agnes Mary b 1984, Cecilia Jane b 1986); *Career* architectural historian, author; contrib: The Spectator, Daily Telegraph, Independent, Architects Jl, Private Eye; chm Thirties Soc; *Books* The Architects Calendar (1974), The Victorian Buildings of London (with C Amery 1980), Temples of Power (text only 1979), Robert Weir Schultz and His Work for The Marquesses of Bute (1981), The Great Perspectivists (1982), The Changing Metropolis (1984), The English House 1860-1914 (1986); *Style*— Gavin Stamp, Esq; 1 St Chads St, London WC1 (☎ 01 837 9646)

STAMP, Dr John Trevor; CBE (1973); s of Harold Stamp (d 1966); *b* 3 Dec 1915; *Educ* Orme Boys' Sch and County GS Newcastle, Edinburgh Univ; *m* 1941, Margaret May, *née* Scott; 2 s, 1 da; *Career* vet surgn; sr lectr Edinburgh Univ 1942-47 (hon lectr 1947-77), vet investigator offr East of Scotland 1947-53, dir Moredun Res Inst Edinburgh 1953-77, pres RCVS 1970-71; conslt FAO UN; ed Journal of Comparative Pathology; *Books* Sheep Husbandry - Diseases (6 edns 1949-87); *Recreations* caravaning at home and abroad; *Style*— Dr John Stamp, CBE; Valebank, N Berwick, E Lothian (☎ 0620 2595)

STAMP, Hon Jos Colin; s of 1 Baron Stamp, GCB, GBE (d 1941, as a result of enemy action); *b* 22 Dec 1917; *Educ* Leys Sch, Queens' Coll Cambridge; *m* 1, 26 June 1940 (m dis 1956), Althea da of late Mrs William Dawes, of Evanston, Illinois, USA; 4 da; m 2, 27 Dec 1958, Gillian Penelope, da of late Guy St John Tatham, of Johannesburg, SA; 2 s; *Career* late Lt RNVR; former dir of mktg servs for Europe of American Express Int; ptnr Martlet (audiovisual conslts) and filter Stamp Assocs (mgmnt conslts); *Productions include* Best Course to Windward (1982; BISFA Silver Award), A Gift from Doctor Schweitzer (1983); *Recreations* sailing, music, photography, lecturing; *Style*— The Hon Colin Stamp; 12 Ullswater Rd, London SW13 (☎ 01 748 2782)

STAMP, Hon Mrs Maxwell; (Alice) Mary; er da of Walter Richards, of Hereford; *m* 28 Jan 1944, as his 2 w, Hon (Arthur) Maxwell Stamp (d 1984), 3 s of 1 Baron Stamp, GCB, GBE (d 1941); 1 s, 2 da; *Style*— The Hon Mrs Maxwell Stamp; 1 Hollyoaks, Wormingford, Essex CO6 3BD (☎ Bures 228067)

STAMP, Hon (Josiah) Richard; s of 3 Baron Stamp (d 1987); *b* 15 Dec 1943; *Educ* Winchester, Queens' Coll Cambridge; *Style*— The Hon Richard Stamp; Flat B, 11 Lymington Road, London NW6 1HX

STAMP, 4 Baron (UK 1938) Trevor Charles Bosworth Stamp; s of 3 Baron Stamp (d 1987); *Educ* Leys Sch, Gonville and Caius Cambridge (BA), St Mary's Hosp Med Sch (MB, BCh); *m* 1, 1963 (m dis 1971), Anne Carolynn, da of John Kenneth

Churchill, of Tunbridge Wells; 2 da; m 2, 1975, Carol Anne, da of Robert Keith Russell, of Farnham, Surrey; 1 s, 1 da; *Heir* s, Hon Nicholas Charles Trevor Stamp b 1978; *Career* consultant physician 1974-; FRCP, MD; *Style*— The Rt Hon the Lord Stamp; Pennyroyal, Village Lane, Hedgerley, Bucks, SL2 3UY; Royal National Orthopaedic Hospital, Stanmore, Middx

STANBRIDGE, Andrew Morrisroe; s of Arthur George Stanbridge, and Monica Patricia, *née* Morrisroe; *b* 24 May 1951; *Educ* St Michaels Coll Herts; *m* 1982, Helen Maya, da of Vivian Graham Beardsell (d 1982), of Sussex; 1 da (Alexandra b 1986) and 1 step da (Christina b 1978); *Career* advertiser; dir Saatchi & Saatchi Compton Ltd; *Style*— Andrew Stanbridge, Esq; 381 Wimbledon Park Road, London SW19 (☎ 01 788 1378); 80 Charlotte Street W1 (☎ 01 636 5060)

STANBRIDGE, Air Vice-Marshal Sir Brian Gerald Tivy; KCVO (1979, MVO 1958), CBE (1974), AFC (1952); s of Gerald Edward Stanbridge (d 1966); *b* 6 July 1924; *Educ* Thurlestone Coll Dartmouth; *m* 1949 (m dis 1984), (Kathleen) Diana, *née* Hayes; 2 da; *Career* Air Vice-Marshal; Burma Campaign 1944-45, personal pilot and flying instr to HRH the Duke of Edinburgh 1954-58, sec to COS Ctee 1971-73, defence serv sec to the Queen 1975-79 (ret); dir-gen Air Transport Users Ctee 1979-; *Recreations* house maintenance, gardening; *Clubs* RAF; *Style*— Air Vice-Marshal Sir Brian Stanbridge KCVO, CBE, AFC; 9 Paines Lane, Pinner, Middx (☎ 01 866 6643)

STANBRIDGE, Ven Leslie Cyril; *b* 19 May 1920; *Educ* Bromley GS Kent, St John's Coll Durham, Durham Univ (BA, Dip Theol, MA); *Career* local govt offr 1936-46; served RAPC (Pte) 1940-45; curate of Erith, Kent 1949-51, tutor and chaplain St John's Coll Durham 1951-55, vicar of St Martin Hull 1955-64, rector of Cottingham 1964-72, archdeacon of York 1972-88, canon of York 1968-, succentor canonicorum 1988-; *Recreations* fell walking, cycling; *Style*— The Ven Leslie C Stanbridge; 1 Deangate, York YO1 2JB (☎ 0904 621174)

STANBRIDGE, Dr Raymond John; s of Sidney John Stanbridge, of Herts, and Dora Margaret Stanbridge; *b* 19 Feb 1947; *Educ* Hemel Hempstead GS, Leeds Univ (BCom), Nottingham Univ (MSc), Victoria Univ of Wellington New Zealand (PhD); *m* 1970, Rosemary, da of William Norris, OBE (d 1987); 1 s (Timothy Jonathan b 1974), 2 da (Nicola Josephine b 1976, Felicity Juliet b 1980); *Career* mgmnt conslt Peat Marwick Mitchell & Co 1972-75, head of business planning Nickerson Gp 1975-80; md: Stanbridge Mumby and Moore Ltd 1981-, Exchequergate Hldgs plc 1987-; *Recreations* cricket, travel; *Style*— Dr Raymond Stanbridge; The Old Vicarage, Nettleham, Lincoln LN2 2RH (☎ 0522 752467); 2A Exchequergate, Lincoln LN2 1PZ (☎ 0522 538081, fax 0522 40940, telex 37688)

STANBROOK, Clive St George Clement; OBE (1988); s of Ivor Robert Stanbrook, MP, and Joan, *née* Clement; *b* 10 April 1948; *Educ* Dragon Sch Oxford, Westminster, UCL (LLB); *m* 3 April 1971, Julia Suzanne, da of Victor Hillary; 1 s (Ivor Victor Hillary), 3 da (Fleur Elizabeth, Sophie Noelette, Isabella Grace); *Career* barr 1972; bd memb World Trade Center Assoc 1977-83 (London), fndr and sr ptnr Stanbrook & Hooper (int lawyers) Brussels 1977, pres Br CofC for Belgium and Luxembourg 1985-87; *Books* Extradition the Law and Practice (jtly 1980), Dumping Manual on the EEC Anti Dumping Law (1980), International Trade Law and Practice (co ed 1984); *Recreations* tennis, sailing; *Style*— Clive Stanbrook, Esq; Stanbrook & Hooper, 42 Rue du Taciturne, Brussels 1040, Belgium (☎ 230 5059, fax 230 5713, telex 61975 STALAW)

STANBROOK, Ivor Robert; MP (Cons) Orpington 1970-; yst s of Arthur William, and Lilian Stanbrook; *b* 13 Jan 1924; *Educ* London Univ, Oxford Univ; *m* 1946, Joan Clement; 2 s; *Career* RAF 1943-46, colonial dist offr Nigeria 1950-60, asst sec Cncl of Ministers Lagos 1954, barr 1960, contested (C) East Ham S 1966, chm Cons Backbench Constitutional Ctee, former sec and jt vice-chm of Cons Backbench Home Affairs Ctee, jt vice-chm Cons NI Ctee 1982-85; chm: Br-Nigerian All Pty Gp, Br-Zambian All Pty Gp; memb Ct of Referees, memb select ctee on Home Affairs; partner Stanbrook & Hooper European Law Office Brussels; *Publications* Extradition, the Law and Practice (1980), British Nationality, the New Law (1982), A Year in Politics (1987); *Style*— Ivor Stanbrook, Esq, MP; 6 Sevenoaks Rd, Orpington, Kent (☎ 0689 20347); 42 rue du Taciturne, Brussels 1040, Belgium (☎ 010 322 230 5059)

STANCLIFFE, Very Rev David Staffurth; s of Very Rev Michael S Stancliffe (d 1987 formerly Dean of Winchester), and Barbara Elizabeth, da of Rev Canon Tissington Tatlow; *b* 1 Oct 1942; *Educ* Westminster, Trinity Coll Oxford, Cuddesdon Theological Coll (MA); *m* 17 July 1965, Sarah Loveday, da of Philip Sascha Smith, of Mead House, Great Ayton; 1 s (Benjamin b 1972), 2 da (Rachel b 1968, Hannah b 1969); *Career* asst curate St Bartholomew's, Armley 1967-70; chaplain to Clifton Coll Bristol 1970-77; residentiary canon Portsmouth Cathedral 1977-82, diocesan dir of ordinands and lay ministry advsr Portsmouth 1977-82, provost of Portsmouth 1982-; memb: cncl of Chichester Theological Coll 1977-, governing body of the Southern Dioceses Ministerial Training Sch 1977-84; chm: Southern Regional Inst 1979-81 and 1984-89, Diocesan Advsy Ctee 1982-; memb: C of E Liturgical Cmmn 1985-, Gen Synod 1985-, vice-pres Assoc European Cathedrals 1986-; *Recreations* old music, Italy; *Style*— The Very Rev the Provost of Portsmouth; Provost's House, Pembroke Rd, Portsmouth PO1 2NS (☎ 0705 824 400); Portsmouth Cathedral, St Thomas' St, Portsmouth PO1 2HH (☎ 0705 823300)

STANDARD, Prof Sir Kenneth Livingstone; CD (1976); *b* 8 Dec 1920; *Educ* UC of W Indies (MB, BS), Univ of Pittsburgh (MPH), Univ of London (MD); *m* 1955, Evelyn Francis; 1 da; *Career* head dept social and preventive med Univ of West Indies 1966-, prof 1968-; FFCM 1972; kt 1982; *Style*— Prof Sir Kenneth Standard, CD; Dept Social & Preventive Medicine, University of West Indies, Kingston, Jamaica

STANDEN, John Francis; s of Dr Edward Peter Standen (d 1976), and Margaret, *née* O'Shea; *b* 14 Oct 1948; *Educ* St James' Sch Burnt Oak, Durham Univ (BA); *m* 9 Aug 1975, Kathleen Mary, da of Joseph Quilty of Co Galway, Ireland; 2 s (Luke b 1981, Owen b 1984), 1 da (Aine b 1979); *Career* dir: Barclays Merchant Bank Ltd 1986-, Barclays de Zoete Wedd Ltd 1986 (dir property Equity Fund Mgmnt Ltd 1987, head fin advsy unit 1988); ACIB 1974; *Recreations* relaxing, walking, family fun, theatre opera; *Style*— John Standen, Esq; The Blue House, Thorley St, Nr Bishops Stortford, Herts CM23 4AL (☎ 0279 508 413); Barclays de Zoete Wedd, Ebbgate House, 2 Swan Lane, London EC4 (☎ 01 623 2323, fax 01 895 1523, telex 923141)

STANDEVEN, (Susan) Marjorie; da of Edward Cambridge Ffooks (d 1965), of Tanganyika, and Eileen Catharine, *née* Gordon; *b* 29 Oct 1934; *Educ* Queen Bertha's Sch Kent, Durham Sch for Girls; *m* 1, 1953, Peter Sheridan-Patterson; 1 da (Alexandra b 1957); m 2, 1963, John Melville-Smith; m 3, 1978, Trevor Crossley Standeven, s of Harry Crossley Standeven (d 1934), of Nottingham; *Career* housewife; sec to dirs Consolidated African Selection Tst, Diamond Mines Ghana 1953-57; *Recreations* tennis, gardening, bridge, painting; *Style*— Mrs Trevor Standeven; The Old Vicarage, Chardstock, Axminster, Devon (☎ 0460 20424)

STANDING; *see*: Leon, Sir John, Bt

STANDING, Norman Roy; s of Capt Norman Ebenezer Standing (ka 1943), and Joan Mabel, *née* Cambridge (d 1969); *b* 27 Oct 1938; *Educ* The George Spicer Sch Enfield; *m* 1, 29 Oct 1960 (m dis), Brenda Constance, da of Charles Pickering, of Essex; 1 s (David b 1964), 1 da (Deborah b 1961); m 2, 16 June 1981, Gillian Mary, da of Leonard Richard Wallace, of Cambs; *Career* mktg servs conslt; *Recreations* collecting, travel, walking; *Style*— Norman R Standing, Esq; 8 Burlington Way, Hemingford Grey, Huntingdon, Cambs PE18 9BS (☎ 0480 62654, fax 0480 67563, car phone 0836 204960)

STANDISH, John Victor; s of Albert Victor Standish (d 1981), of Littlehampton, Sussex, and Ethel Alice, *née* Salmon (d 1985); *b* 14 Jan 1930; *Educ* Ilfracombe GS, City of London Coll; *m* 15 Sept 1955, Vivienne Judith, da of Kenneth Lloyd Martin (d 1983), of Wimbledon; 1 s (Miles b 1965), 3 da (Martine b 1956, Amanda b 1957, Jennifer b 1960); *Career* Industl res and media conslt 1988-; memb: ABC Cncl IPA media panel, Industl Mkt Res Assoc; dir: Ad Group Services Ltd 1978-82, Parker Research Ltd 1978-86, Roles & Parker Ltd 1982-84, Ayer Barker Barker Ltd 1984-86 Internat Communications Ltd 1986-87; urban district and town cncllr Chesham Bucks 1971-79; MIPA, DipCAM; *Recreations* archaeology, conservation, war gaming; *Clubs* RAC, Wig and Pen, '41'; *Style*— John V Standish, Esq; The Boat House, Lyminster Road, Littlehampton, W Sussex (☎ 0903 883587); 90 Trinity Court, Gray's Inn Road, London WC1 (☎ 01 837 9804)

STANDISH, Tony; s of Elias Stern (d 1961), and Gertrud Agnes Alwine Hullebrandt (d 1971); *b* 11 April 1922; *Educ* RG II Gymnasium, Vienna; *m* 12 Jan 1958, Verna Ella, da of Malcolm John Tomlinson, Chief Inspector, Shanghai Police; 3 s (Troy b 1970, Tristan b 1965, Tracy b 1959), 2 da (Tiffany b 1963, Talita b 1970); *Career* Army service 1939-42 Royal Navy German Branch Intelligence; Raymond Gp: 28 dirships 1957-86, incl: Goldmount Houses 1985-87, Goldmount Construction 1982-87, Goldmount Properties 1980-87, M & S T's Supper Room 1972-87, T S Properties 1965-87; chm The Wessex Gp plc 1987; *Recreations* skiing; *Style*— Tony Standish, Esq; Newguards, 30 Western Ave, Branksome Park, Poole, Dorset BH13 7AV; Wessex Bowl, Poole Rd, Bury (☎ 02020 762253)

STANESBY, Rev Canon Derek Malcolm; s of Laurence John Charles Stanesby, of Congleton, Cheshire, and Elsie Lilian, *née* Stean (d 1959); *b* 28 Mar 1931; *Educ* Orange Hill Sch Edgware, Northampton Poly London, Leeds Univ (BA), Coll of the Resurrection Mirfield, Manchester Univ (M Ed, PhD); *m* 29 July 1958, Christine Adela, da of David Payne (d 1985), of Tamworth, Staffs; 3 s (Michael b 1961, Mark b 1963, Peter b 1966), 1 da (Helen b 1959); *Career* RAF ;1951-53, PO, Navigator; ordained Norwich Cathedral 1958; curate: Norwich 1958-61, Southwark 1961-63, vicar St Mark Bury 1963-67, rector St Chad Ladybarn 1967-85, canon of Windsor 1985-; memb Archbishops Cmmn on Christian Doctrine; author of various articles; *Books* Science, Reason and Religion (1985); *Recreations* hill walking, sailing, woodwork, idling; *Style*— The Rev Canon Derek Stanesby; 4 The Cloisters, Windsor Castle, Berks SL4 1NJ (☎ 0753 864142)

STANFIELD, Brian John; *b* 12 July 1934; *Educ* LLB (London); *m* 1956, Janet Margery Mary; 1 s, 1 da; *Career* slr 1959; legal dir UK Grand Met plc 1986-; dir Business in the Cities; pres City of Westminster Law Soc 1979; *Recreations* theatre, music; *Clubs* Savile and Landsdowne; *Style*— Brian Stanfield, Esq; Cheriton, 35 Worple Rd, Epsom, Surrey (☎ 03727 20715); Grand Metropolitan plc; 11/12 Hanover Square, London W1 (☎ 01 629 7488)

STANFORD, Adrian Timothy James; s of Ven Leonard John Stanford (d 1967), formerly Archdeacon of Coventry, and Dora Kathleen, *née* Timms (d 1939); *b* 19 July 1935; *Educ* Rugby, Merton Coll Oxford (MA); *Career* Nat Serv 2 Lt The Sherwood Foresters 1954-55; dir Samuel Montagu & Co Ltd 1972 (joined 1958); *Recreations* gardening, architecture, opera; *Clubs* Boodle's, Brooks's; *Style*— Adrian Stanford, Esq; The Old Rectory, Preston Capes, nr Daventry, Northamptonshire NN11 6TE; 27 Charles St, London W1X 7HD; Samuel Montagu & Co Ltd, 10 Lower Thames Street, London EC3R 6AE (☎ 01 260 9000)

STANFORD, Julian George; s of Ven Leonard John Stanford (d 1967, formerly Archdeacon of Coventry), and Dora Kathleen, *née* Timms (d 1939); *b* 15 Jan 1933; *Educ* Rugby, Worcester Coll Oxford (MA); *m* 20 April 1963, Elizabeth Constance Julia, da of Francis Basil Aglionby (d 1962), of Tonbridge; 2 s (Henry b 1965, Geoffrey b 1971), 1 da (Lucy b 1967); *Career* Nat Serv trained RB cmmnd in Sherwood Foresters 1951-53; merchant banker; dir Morgan Grenfell & Co Ltd and of other Gp Cos 1977-86; *Clubs* Brooks's; *Style*— Julian G Stanford, Esq; The Old Rectory, Tendring, Essex (☎ 0255 830287)

STANFORD, Adm Sir Peter Maxwell; GCB (1986, KCB 1983), LVO (1970); s of Brig Henry Morrant Stanford, CBE, MC (d 1957), of The Stone House, Aldringham, Leiston, Suffolk, and Edith Hamilton, *née* Warren (d 1980); *b* 11 July 1929; *Educ* RNC Britannia; *m* 1957, (Helen) Ann, da of Henry Lingard (d 1935), of Chiengmai, Thailand; 1 s, 2 da; *Career* RN: Flag Offr Second Flotilla 1978-80, Asst Chief of Naval Staff 1980-82, Vice-Chief 1982-84, C-in-C Naval Home Cmd 1985-87; *Recreations* field sports, ornithology; *Clubs* Flyfishers'; *Style*— Adm Sir Peter Stanford, GCB, LVO; c/o Lloyd's Bank Ltd, Cox's and King's Branch, 6 Pall Mall, London SW1Y 5NH

STANGER, David Harry; OBE (1987); s of Charles Harry Stanger, CBE (d 1987), of Mill Cottage, Knole, Long Sutton, Somerset, and Florence Bessie Hepworth, *née* Bowden; *b* 14 Feb 1939; *Educ* Oundle, Millfield; *m* 20 July 1963, Jill Patricia, da of Reginald Arthur Barnes, of Chessbord, Troutstream Way, Loudwater, Chorley Wood, Herts; 1 s (Edward b 1972); 2 da (Vanessa b 1966, Miranda b 1967); *Career* served RE 1960-66, seconded Malaysian Engineers 1963-66, operational serv Kenya, Nothern Malaysia and Sarawak, Capt RE; joined R H Harry Stanger 1966, ptnr Al Hoty Stanger Ltd 1975; chm Harry Stanger Ltd 1972-; memb: steering ctee NATLAS 1981-85, advsy cncl for Calibration/Measurement 1982-87; chm: Assoc of Consulting Scientists 1981-83, NAMAS advsy ctee 1985-87, Standards Quality Measurement advsy ctee 1987-; vice-pres IQA 1986, sec-gen Union Int des Laboratoires 1984-, memb Guild of Water Conservators 1989-; *Recreations* collecting vintage wines; *Clubs* Carlton, St Stephen's Constitutional; *Style*— D H Stanger, Esq, OBE; Summerfield House, Barnet Lane, Elstree, Herts WD6 3HQ (☎ 01 953 0022); Harry Stanger Ltd, Fortune Lane,

Elstree, Herts WD6 3HQ (☎ 01 207 3191, telex 922262 TESLAB G, fax 01 207 4706)

STANGER, Keith Burroughs; s of Eric Alfred (d 1971), d Gildersome, Yorks, and Mary, *née* Burroughs; *b* 17 Sept 1939; *Educ* Leeds G, St Andrews Univ (MA), Harvard Business Sch (PHD); *m* 29 April 1967, Susan Margaret, da of Reginald Arthur Banham d (1969), of Buenos Aires; 2 s (Julian Patrick b 1971, Edward Alexander b 1974); *Career* Bank of London and South America (Argentina, Paraguay, Columbia) 1964-72, chief accountant Bank of London and Montreal 1972-76; Lloyds Bank: (Int) USA 1976-80, Uruguay and Brazil 1980-86, gen mangr strategic planning 1985-88, gen mangr corporate planning and treasy 1988-; memb Putney Soc, Basset Hound Club, Albany Bassets club; *Recreations* tennis, climbing, walking; *Clubs* Montevideo CC; *Style*— Keith Stanger, Esq; 9 Spencer Walk, London SW15 (☎ 01 789 1866; Faryners House, 25 Monument St, London EC3R 8BQ (☎ 01 283 1000 fax 623 7560

STANGROOM SPRINTHALL, Sonya Mary; da of Samuel Frederick Coates-Sprinthall (d 1973) and Dorothy Mary, *née* Philipson-Atkinson; *b* 19 August 1940; *Educ* Lancaster Coll of Art (NDD); *m* 3 Aug 1963 (m dis 1984), James Edward Stangroom, s of Alfred William Stangroom (d 1986); *Career* one woman exhibitions: Holland Park Galleries 1964, Sheffield Indust Exhibition Centre (1965, 1967, 1968), Sheffield Univ 1965, Philip Frances Gallery Sheffield (1972, 1974), Sheffield Univ Library Gallery 1980, Saint Edmund's Church Castleton 1980, Edward Mayor Gallery Sheffield (1980, 1982) Abbot Hall Art Gallery Kendal 1987; gp exhibitions incl: Young Contemporaries London 1961, Mansard Gallery London 1969-1975, Richard Bradley Gallery Billingford, Graves Open Exhibition Sheffield, Philip Frances Gallery (8 Sheffield artists) Sheffield Univ Fine Arts Soc, Mappin Art Gallery (artists Christmas cards), Tate Gallery London (artists Christmas cards); mural commissions: Sheffield Corpn Dept Education, two murals for Richmond Coll of educn; portrait cmmns, incl: Prof WR Robinson, Prof Sir William Empson, Mrs Hildegard Hertzog; former pres Sheffield Soc for the Encouragement of Art; memb: Br Inst of Persian Studies, Soc for the Promotion of Byzantine Studies, Hawk Tst; *Recreations* archaeology (draughtsman Siraf Persian Gulf 1968), travel, music, Islamic architecture and art, the study of Russian ikons; *Style*— Sonya Stangroom Sprinthall

STANHOPE, Lady Isabella Rachel; da of 11 Earl of Harrington, of Co Limerick, and his 3 w, Priscilla Margaret, *née* Cubitt; *b* 11 Oct 1966; *Educ* Heathfield, American Coll; *Style*— Lady Isabella Stanhope; Greenmount, Patrickswell, Co Limerick, Ireland

STANHOPE, Hon John Fitzroy; s of 11 Earl of Harrington, and his 3 w, Priscilla Margaret, *née* Cubitt; *b* 20 August 1965; *Style*— The Hon John Stanhope; Greenmount, Patrickswell, Co Limerick, Ireland

STANHOPE, Hon Steven Francis Lincoln; s of 11 Earl of Harrington, of Co Limerick, and his 2 w, Anne Theodora, *née* Chute (d 1970); *b* 12 Dec 1951; *Educ* Eton; *m* 1978, Maureen Elizabeth Irvine, da of Maj Harold William Cole, of Poundbury, Dorset; 1 s (Ben b 1978), 1 da (Tara b 1979); *Career* stud farmer, landowner (150 acres); *Recreations* racing, antiques; *Style*— The Hon Steven Stanhope; Dooneen Stud, Patrickswell, Co Limerick, Ireland (☎ Limerick 355106)

STANHOPE, Lady Trina Maria; da of 11 Earl of Harrington, and his 2 w, Anne Theodora, *née* Chute (d 1970); *b* 1947; *Style*— Lady Trina Stanhope; Greenmount, Patrickswell, Co Limerick, Ireland

STANHOPE, Hon William Henry Leicester; s and h of Viscount Petersham; *b* 14 Oct 1967; *Educ* Aysgarth School, Aiglon College; *Recreations* skiing, fishing, shooting; *Style*— The Hon William Stanhope; Baynton House, Coulston, westbury, Wiltshire

STANIER, Brig Sir Alexander Beville Gibbons; 2 Bt (UK 1917), of Peplow Hall, Hodnet, Shropshire; DSO (1940) and bar (1945), MC (1918), JP (Shropshire 1949), DL (1951); patron of two livings; s of Sir Beville Stanier, 1 Bt, JP, DL (d 1921), sometime MP Newport (Shropshire) then Ludlow, and Sarah Constance (d 1948), da of Rev Benjamin Gibbons, MA, of Waresley House, Worcester; *b* 31 Jan 1899; *Educ* Eton, RMC Sandhurst; *m* 1927, Dorothy Gladys (d 1973), da of late Brig-Gen Alfred Douglas Miller, CBE, DSO; 1 s, 1 da; *Heir* s, Beville Douglas Stanier; *Career* serv WWI (France 1918); serv WWII in France (despatches, American Silver Star, Cdr Order of Leopold of Belgium with palms, Belgian Croix de Guerre with palms); Brig (ret) late Welsh Gds (cmding 1945-48); High Sheriff Shropshire 1951; CC for Salop 1950-58, Cdr Order Legion of Honour (France); CStJ; *Style*— Brigadier Sir Alexander Stanier, Bt, DSO, MC, JP, DL; Park Cottage, Ludford, Ludlow, Shropshire SY8 1PP (☎ 0584 2675); Hill House, Shotover Park, Wheatley, Oxford 0X9 1QN (☎ 086 77 2996)

STANIER, Capt Beville Douglas; s and h of Brig Sir Alexander Beville Gibbons Stanier, 2 Bt, DSO, MC, JP, DL, and Dorothy Gladys, *née* Miller (d 1973); *b* 20 April 1934; *Educ* Eton; *m* 23 Feb 1963, (Violet) Shelagh, da of Maj James Stockley Sinnott (ka 1942), of Tetbury, Glos; 1 s (Alexander b 1970), 2 da (Henrietta b 1965, Lucinda b 1967); *Career* serv Welsh Gds 1952-60 (2 Lt 1953, Lt 1955, Capt 1958), UK, Egypt, Aust; ADC to Govr-Gen of Aust (Field Marshal Viscount Slim) 1959-60; stockbroker, ptnr Kitcat & Aitken 1960-76; farmer 1974-; conslt Hales Snails Ltd 1976-88; chm Whaddon Parish Cncl; *Recreations* shooting, cricket; *Clubs* MCC; *Style*— Capt Beville Stanier; Kings Close House, Whaddon, Bucks MK17 0NG (☎ 0908 501738); Home Farm, Shotover Park, Wheatley, Oxford OX9 1QP (☎ 08677 2996)

STANIER, Field Marshal Sir John Wilfred; GCB (1982, KCB 1978), MBE (1961), DL (Hampshire 1986); s of Harold Allan Stanier (d 1932), and Penelope Rose, *née* Price (d 1974); *b* 6 Oct 1925; *Educ* Marlborough, Merton Coll Oxford; *m* 1955, Cicely Constance, da of Cmdr Denis Malet Lambert, DSC; 4 da (Emma, Harriet, Miranda, Candia); *Career* cmmnd QOH 1946, served in N Italy, Germany, Hong Kong; cmd: Royal Scots Greys 1966-68, 20 Armoured Bde 1969-71; GOC1 Div 1973-75, Cmdt Staff Coll Camberley 1975-78, Vice CGS 1978-80, Col Royal Scots Dragoon Guards 1979-84, ADC Gen to HM The Queen 1981-85, Col Cmdt RAC 1982-85, C-in-C UKLF 1981-82, CGS 1981-85; chm of Cncl Royal United Services Inst for Defence Studies; *Recreations* hunting, fishing; *Clubs* Cavalry and Guards, Pratts; *Style*— Field Marshal Sir John Stanier, GCB, MBE, DL; c/o Messrs Coutts & Co, 440 Strand, London WC2R 0QS

STANIFORTH, John Arthur Reginald; CBE (1969); s of Capt Reginald Staniforth, MC (d 1939), of Anston House, Anston, Yorks, and Anne (d 1975), da of Sir John Duncan; *b* 19 Sept 1912; *Educ* Marlborough; *m* 25 April 1936, Penelope Cecile, da of Maj-Gen Sir Henry Francis Edward Freeland, KCIE, CB, DSO, MVO, 1 S (decd), 1 da; *Career* John Brown Gp 1929-: dir John Brown & Co Ltd, dir Constructors John Brown Engrg Clydebank Ltd; memb Expolrt Guarantees Advsy Cncl 1971-76 (dep chm 1975-76), fndr and chm Br Chemical Engrg Contractors Assoc 1965-68; govr Bryanston Sch, St Wilfrid's Hospice (South Coast) Ltd; *Recreations* golf, fishing, sailing; *Clubs* MCC, Goodwood Golf; *Style*— John Staniforth, Esq, CBE; 11 The Holdens, Bosham Lane, Old Bosham, Chichester, W Sussex PO18 8LN (☎ 0243 572401)

STANISZEWSKI, His Excellency Monsieur Stefan; *b* 11 Feb 1931; *Career* Polish ambass to UK 1981- (joined Polish Dip Serv 1960), formerly ambass to Sweden, has also served in Paris; previously chief ed Iskry (Polish publishers); *Style*— HE Monsieur Stefan Staniszewski; Embassy of the Polish People's Republic, 47 Portland Place, W1N 3AG (☎ 01 580 4324/9)

STANLEY, Brian Robert; s of William Augustus Stanley (d 1964), and Elsa Maria Stanley (d 1987); *b* 26 Dec 1935; *Educ* Christ's Hosp; *m* 1 April 1961, Marion, da of Joseph Thacker 1961; 1 da (Clair b 1967), 1 s (Sean b 1968); *Career* CA; dir: Harrison-Sons Ltd, Printers 1965-76, Papla Ltd 1976-; Liveryman Worshipful Co of Stationers; authority on silicone coating; *Recreations* music, sports; *Style*— Brian Stanley, Esq; Zlatorog, Bryants Bottom, Great Missenden, Bucks HP16 0JU; Papla Ltd, York House, Oxford Rd, Beaconsfield, Bucks HP9 1XA (telex 837978)

STANLEY, Hon Charles Ernest; 2 s of 8 Baron Stanley of Alderley; *b* 30 June 1960; *Educ* St Edwards Sch Oxford, Nottingham Univ (BA); *Career* area sales mangr Plessey; *Recreations* sailing, skiing; *Style*— The Hon Charles Stanley; Plessey, 9 Dallington Street, London EC1 (☎ 01 251 6251)

STANLEY, David John; s of Vincent Arthur Stanley (d 1978), of Ruislip, Middlesex, and Joy Harriet Kendall; *b* 15 June 1947; *Educ* Merchant Taylors', Pembroke Coll Cambridge (BA, MA, PhD); *m* 29 July 1972, Meryl Ruth, da of Derwent Mark Atkinson Mercer, of Chandler's Ford, Hampshire; 1 s (Joel b 1985), 3 da (Lydia b 1976, Miriam b 1978, Bethany b 1983); *Career* dir Logica UK Ltd 1982-84; tech dir Logica Space & Def Systems Ltd 1984-86; md Logica Cambridge Ltd; tech dir Logica plc 1985-86; innovation dir Organisation & System Innovations Ltd 1986-; *Recreations* christian activities, music, gardening; *Style*— Dr David Stanley; 25 Sedley Taylor Rd, Cambridge CB2 2PN (☎ 0223 210468); Oasis, Tectonic Place, Holyport Rd, Maidenhead (☎ 0628 770600, car ☎ 0836 200264)

STANLEY, Edward Richard William; s of Hon Hugh Henry Montagu Stanley (d 1971, gs of 17 Earl of Derby), and Mary Rose (who m 2, A William A Spiegelberg) da of late Charles Francis Birch, of Rhodesia; hp of kinsman, 18 Earl of Derby; *b* 10 Oct 1962; *Educ* Eton, RAC Cirencester; *Career* cmmnd Grenadier Gds 1982-85; stockbroker, Fleming Montagu Stanley and Co Ltd (formerly Montagu Loebl Stanley and Co Ltd); *Clubs* Cavalry and Guards, Turf; *Style*— Edward Stanley, Esq; 90 Old Church Street, Chelsea, London SW3; New England Stud, Bottisham, Newmarket, Suffolk

STANLEY, Hon Harry John; s of 8 Baron Stanley of Alderley; *b* 20 August 1963; *Educ* St Edwards Sch, London Univ (LLB), Cambridge Univ (LLM); *Style*— The Hon Harry Stanley; c/o The Rt Hon The Lord Stanley of Alderley, Rectory Farm, Stanton St John, Oxford

STANLEY, James Andrew; s of John Gilbert Stanley, of Fox Bank Farm, Sutton Cheshire, and Sally Ann Hammond, *née* Gibson; *b* 11 May 1966; *Educ* The King's Sch Macclesfield; *Career* Sub Lt RN; served warships: HMS Nurton, HMS Apollo, HMS Illustrious, HMS Bristol; represented RN flying Chipmunk aircraft in nat and int air races, led two man RN diving expedition to Praia da Luz Portugal 1987 (previously unchartered waters); *Recreations* air racing, full bore shooting, mountaineering, vintage cars; *Clubs* Brathay Expeditionary Soc, Br Field Sports Soc, Old Boys and Park Green Gentlemans, East India; *Style*— James Stanley, Esq; Greycot, 15 Mayfield rd, Bramhall, Stockport, Cheshire SK7 1JU

STANLEY, Rt Hon Sir John Paul; PC (1984), MP (C) Tonbridge and Malling Feb 1974-; s of Harry Stanley (d 1956), and Maud Stanley; *b* 19 Jan 1942; *Educ* Repton, Lincoln Coll Oxford; *m* 1968, Susan Elizabeth Giles; 2 s, 1 da; *Career* Cons Research Dept (Housing) 1967-68; res assoc Int Inst Strategic Studies 1968-69, fin exec RTZ Corpn 1969-74; memb parly select ctee Nationalised Industs 1974-76, pps to Rt Hon Margaret Thatcher 1976-79, min for Housing and Construction with rank of min of state (DOE) 1979-83, min of state for the Armed Forces MOD 1983-87, min of State for Northern Ireland 1987-88; kt 1988; *Recreations* music, arts, sailing; *Style*— The Rt Hon Sir John Stanley, MP; House of Commons, London SW1

STANLEY, Louis Thomas; s of Louis Stanley, of Stanley House, Stanley Rd, Hoylake, and Mary Ann, *née* Appelby; *b* 6 Jan 1912; *Educ* Emmanuel Coll Cambridge (MA); *m* 25 May 1955, (Helen) Jean Beech, da of Sir Alfred Owen, of New Hall, Sutton Coldfield; 2 s (Thomas b 1957, Edward b 1961), 2 da (Caroline Jane b 1959, Roberta Marigold b 1963); *Career* economist; dir gen Int Grand Prix Med Servs, chm and jt md BRM; chm Siffert Cncl, hon sec and tres Grand Prix Drivers Assoc, tstee Jim Clark Fndn, memb Royal Inst of Int Affrs; *Books* author of over 70 titles incl: In Search of Genius, Cambridge City of Dreams, Germany After The War, People Places and Pleasures, St Andrews, Public Masks and Private Faces, Newmarket; *Recreations* golf; *Style*— Louis Stanley, Esq; Old Mill House, Trumpington, Cambridge (☎ 0223 840107, 841337)

STANLEY, Michael Charles; MBE (1945), DL (Cumbria 1974); s of Col Rt Hon Oliver Frederick George Stanley, MC, MP (d 1950), 2 s of 17 Earl of Derby, and Lady Maureen Vane-Tempest-Stewart, eldest da of 7 Marquess of Londonderry; *b* 11 August 1921; *Educ* Eton, Trinity Coll Cambridge; *m* 1951, (Ailleen) Fortune, eldest da of Owen Hugh Smith, of Old Hall, Langham, Oakham, Rutland; 2 s; *Career* served WW II with Royal Signals (N Africa and Italy), Capt 1943; chartered electrical engineer, DL Westmorland 1964-74, Vice-Lieut Westmorland 1965-74; High Sheriff: Westmorland 1959-60, Cumbria 1975-76; Hon Col 33 Signal Regt 1981-87; *Recreations* wine, walking, idleness; *Clubs* White's, Brook's; *Style*— Michael Stanley Esq, MBE, DL; Halecat, Witherslack, Grange-over-Sands, Cumbria LA11 6RU (☎ 044 852 229); 46 Bedford Court Mansions, London W1

STANLEY, Oliver Duncan; s of late Bernard Stanley, and Mabel *née* Best; *b* 5 June 1925; *Educ* Rityl GS, Ch Ch Oxford (MA), Harvard Univ, Middletemple MA (Oxon) Barr; *m* 7 Sept 1954, Ruth Leah; 1 s (Julian b 1958); 3 da (Nicola b 1955, Katherine b 1960, Sarah b 1963); *Career* served 8 Hussars 1943-47; barr Middle Temple; HM inspr of Taxes 1952-65, dir Gray Dawes Bank 1966-72; chm Comprehensive Financial Services plc 1987- (dir 1972-87); *Books* Guide to Taxation (1967), Creation and Protection of Capital (1974), Taxology (1971), Taxation Farmers and Landowners (3 edn 1987); *Recreations* music, tennis, French; *Clubs* Travellers'; *Style*— Oliver

Stanley, Esq; University House, London SW1 W0EX

STANLEY, Hon Richard Morgan Oliver; s of Hon Oliver Stanley, DSO, and Lady Kathleen Thynne, da of 5 Marquess of Bath; raised to rank of Barons s 1973 and yr bro of 8 Baron Stanley pf Alderley; *b* 30 April 1931; *Educ* Winchester, New Coll Oxford; *m* 27 July 1956, Phyllida Mary Katharine, 3 da of Lt-Col Clive Grantham Austin, JP, DL, of Micheldever, and Lady Lilian Lumley, sis of 11 Earl of Scarbrough; 2 s, 2 da; *Career* late Lt Coldstream Gds; dir: Friends' Provident Instn, Drawlane Ltd, Gt Ventup Investmnt plc, GA Securities Ltd; memb Lloyd's, govr Bradfield, chm Carr Gomm Soc, tstee Disabled Living Fndn; *Style*— The Hon Richard Stanley; Wood End House, Ridgeway Lane, Lymington, Hants (☎ 0590 74019)

STANLEY, Hon Richard Oliver; s and h of 8 Baron Stanley of Alderley; *b* 24 April 1956; *Educ* St Edward's Sch Oxford, Univ Coll London (BSc); *m* 1983, Carla, er da of Dr K T C McKenzie, of Solihull, 1 s (Oliver Richard Hugh b 1986), 1 da (Maria Elizabeth Jane b 1988); *Style*— The Hon Richard Stanley

STANLEY, Hon Mrs (Susan Elizabeth Josephine Gabrielle Haden); da of 3 Baron Haden-Guest, and his 1 w, Hilda, *née* Russell-Cruise (d 1980); *b* 12 April 1930; *Educ* St Mary's Convent Ascot; *m* 1953, John Orr Stanley; 4 s (Nicholas Charles b 1954, Martin b 1956, Shaun b 1958, Philip b 1962); *Style*— The Hon Mrs Stanley; Granary House, Holly Hill, London NW3

STANLEY OF ALDERLEY, Kathleen, Baroness; Kathleen Margaret; da of late Cecil Murray Wright, of Malden, Surrey, and wid of Sir Edmund Frank Crane; *m* 1961, as his 4 w, 6 Baron (d 1971); *Style*— The Rt Hon Kathleen, Lady Stanley of Alderley; 1 Links Court, Grouville, Jersey

STANLEY OF ALDERLEY, 8 Baron (UK 1839); Sir Thomas Henry Oliver Stanley; DL (Gwynedd) 14 Bt (E 1660); also Baron Sheffield (I 1783) and Baron Eddisbury of Winnington (UK 1848); s of Lt-Col the Hon Oliver Hugh Stanley, DSO, JP, DL (d 1952, s of 4 Baron; descended from Sir John Stanley of Weever, yr bro of 1 Earl of Derby), and Lady Kathleen, *née* Thynne (d 1977), da of 5 Marquess of Bath; suc cous, 7 Baron (who preferred to be known as Lord Sheffield) 1971; *b* 28 Sept 1927; *Educ* Wellington Coll; *m* 30 April 1955, Jane Barrett, da of late Ernest George Hartley; 3 s (Richard, Charles, Harry), 1 da (Lucinda); *Heir* s, Hon Richard Stanley; *Career* Capt (ret) Coldstream Gds and Gds Ind Parachute Co; farmer in Anglesey and Oxfordshire; chm Thames Valley Cereals Ltd 1979-81; govr St Edwards Sch Oxford 1979-, RNLI Ctee of Mgmnt 1981- (chm Fund Raising Ctee 1986-); sits as Cons in House of Lords; *Recreations* sailing, fishing, skiing; *Clubs* Farmers'; *Style*— The Rt Hon the Lord Stanley of Alderley; Trysglwyn Fawr, Rhosybol, Amlwch, Anglesey (☎ 0407 830 364); Rectory Farm, Stanton St John, Oxford (☎ 086 735 214)

STANLEY PRICE, His Hon Peter; QC (1956); s of Herbert Stanley Price (d 1957); *b* 27 Nov 1911; *Educ* Cheltenham, Exeter Coll Oxford; *m* 1, 1946, Harriett Ella Theresa, *née* Pownall (d 1948); 2 s (twins); m 2, 1950, Margaret Jane, wid of William Hebditch (d 1941); 1 da; *Career* barr Inner Temple 1936, recorder Pontefract 1954, York 1955, Kingston-upon-Hull 1958, chm N Riding of Yorks QS 1958-70, bencher Inner Temple 1963, judge of appeal Jersey and Guernsey 1964-69, recorder Sheffield 1965-69, judge of the Chancery Ct of York 1967-, circuit judge (formerly judge of Central Criminal Ct) 1969-84; pres Nat Reference Tbnl: Conciliation Scheme for Deputies employed in Coal-Mining Industry 1967-79, Conciliation Scheme for Coal-Mining Industry 1979-83; *Recreations* birds and trees, gardening, shooting; *Clubs* Brooks's, Yorkshire; *Style*— His Honour Peter Stanley Price, QC; Church Hill, Great Ouseburn, York (☎ 0901 30252)

STANNARD, Timothy John (Tim); s of Henry John Edward Stannard (d 1974), and Betty Pauline Stannard; *b* 29 Oct 1942; *Educ* Cheltenham; *m* 29 Sept 1973, Doreen Ann, da of James Mathias Goff; 2 da Nicola Zoe, Olivia Ann); *Career* slr; entered in Guinness Book of Records as having the largest collection of British beermats (over 37,500); *Recreations* beermat collecting, science fiction, hi-fi, golf; *Clubs* British Beermat Collectors' Soc, Birmingham Science Fiction Gp, Moseley GC; *Style*— Tim Stannard, Esq; Lombard House, Gt Charles St, Birmingham B3 3LP (☎ 021 236 1174)

STANNING, Capt John Gordon; CBE (1957, OBE 1945); s of Rev John Stanning (d 1953), Rector of Meonstoke, Hants, and Sybil May, *née* Jolliffe (d 1963); *b* 9 May 1915; *Educ* Marlborough; *m* 23 Aug 1941, Kathleen Mary (d 1986), da of Bernard George Gillett (d 1956), of Hordle and Milford-on-Sea, Hants; 3 s (Lt-Cdr Timothy, RN b 1943, David b 1945, Julian b 1949), 1 da (Jill b 1951); *Career* supply and secretariat branch of RN 1932-68, dep sec First Sea Lord 1940-44, sec to late Adm of the Fleet Sir George Creasy (in his appts as COS to Allied Naval C-in-C XF 1944-45), Flag Offr S/M 1945-47; FO Air Far East 1947, fifth Sea Lord 1949-50, vice-chief Naval Staff 1950-52, C-in-C Home Fleet 1952-54, C-in-C Portsmouth 1954-57, supply offr 1 S/M Sqdn Med Fleet 1957-59, sec to First Sea Lord 1959-60, memb Admty Interview Bd 1960-62, chief staff offr (admin) Flag Offr S/M's 1962-63, CO HMS Terror (Singapore) 1963-66, dir Naval Admin Planning 1966-67, chief staff offr admin CINC HF, E Atlantic and Channel, ret with rank of Capt 1968; sec and chm Abbeyfield Lymington Soc 1969-81, church warden of All Saints Milford-on-Sea 1974-81; *Recreations* walking, cycling (in the past golf and tennis); *Style*— Capt John Stanning, CBE, RN; Sun Cottage, Barnes Lane, Milford-on-Sea, Lymington, Hants SO41 0RR (☎ 0590 42064)

STANSBY, John; s of Dumon Stansby (d 1980), and Vera Margaret, *née* Main (d 1972); *b* 2 July 1930; *Educ* Oundle, Jesus Coll Cambridge (MA); *m* 22 July 1966, Anna-Maria, da of Dr Harald Kruschewsky; 1 da (Daniela b 1967), 1 step s (Oliver b 1957), 1 step da (Veronica b 1960); *Career* Nat Serv cmmnd Queens Royal Regt with Somaliland Scouts Br Somaliland 1949-50, Essex Regt TA 1950-55; domestic fuels mktg mangr Shell Mex & BP Ltd 1955-62, sr mktg conslt AIC Ltd 1962-66, dir Rank Leisure Servs Ltd 1966-70, dir energy div POSN Co 1970-74; chm: Dumon Stansby & Co Ltd 1974-, UIE (UK) Ltd 1974-, SAUR (UK) Ltd 1986-, Cementation-SAUR Water Servs Ltd 1987-, SAUR Water Servs plc 1988-; dep chm London Tport Exec 1978-80, chief exec Bouygues (UK) Exec 1986-; FInstPet, FCIT, FRSA, MInstM; *Books* Privatisation and Management - the UK experience, Privatisation of UK Water and Electricity, The Business Prospect - Privatisation and Management; *Recreations* music, theatre, swimming, tennis; *Clubs* Travellers; *Style*— John Stansby, Esq; 19 Brook Green, London W6 7BL (☎ 01 603 0886); 14 Curzon St, London W1Y 7FH (☎ 01 629 8155, fax 01 493 2443, car tel 0836 662738, telex 935677)

STANSFELD, John Raoul Wilmot; JP (Angus), DL (Angus); s of Capt John de Bourbel Stansfeld, MC, JP, DL (d 1975), of Dunninald, Montrose (*see* Burke's Landed Gentry, 18 edn, vol 3), and Mary Marow, *née* Eardley-Wilmot; *b* 15 Jan 1935; *Educ* Eton, Ch Ch Oxford (MA); *m* 20 Jan 1965, Rosalinde Rachel, da of Desmond Gurney Buxton, DL (d 1987), of Norfolk; 3 s (Edward b 1966, Robert b 1967, Nicholas b 1972); *Career* Lt Gordon Highlanders 1954-58; Salmon Fisheries mangr; chm: North Esk District Salmon Fishery Bd 1967-80, Esk Fishery Bd Ctee 1980-85; vice-chm Assoc of Scottish District Salmon Fishery Bds 1970-75; memb Inst of Fisheries Mgmnt; dir: Joseph Johnston & Sons Ltd 1962-, Atlantic Salmon Tst 1967-77, Seaboard Supplies Ltd 1972-84, Dunninald Investmts Ltd 1975-; dir and chm Montrose Chamber of Commerce 1984-; ed Salmon Net Magazine 1978-85; chm Scottish Fish Farmers Assoc 1970-73; sec Diocese of Brechin 1968-76; *Recreations* reading, jigsaw puzzles, working in the woods; *Style*— John R W Stansfeld, Esq, JP, DL; Dunninald, Montrose, Angus DD10 (☎ 0674 74842); 3 America St, Montrose, Angus DD10 (☎ 0674 72666, telex 76332)

STANSFIELD, George Norman; CBE 1985 (OBE 1980); s of George Stansfield (d 1975), of Cheadle Hulme, and Martha Alice, *née* Leadbetter; *b* 28 Feb 1926; *Educ* Liscard HS; *m* 1947, Elizabeth Margaret, da of Hugh Williams, of Colwyn Bay Clwyd, and Mary B Williams; *Career* RAF 1944-47; Min of Food and Supply 1948-58; personal asst to: Dir-Gen of Armaments Prod War Off 1958-61, Cwlth Rel Off 1961-62; HM Diplomatic Serv 1965: second sec: Calcutta 1962-66, Port of Spain 1966-68; first sec: FCO 1968-71, (Commercial) Singapore 1971-74; special aide to Earl Mountbatten of Burma on visits to Singapore in 1972 and 1974; HM consul: Durban 1974-78, FCO 1978; cnsllr 1980, head Overseas Estate Dept FCO 1980-82; cnslt Training Dept FCO 1986-; Br high cmmr Solomon Islands 1982-86, cncl memb Pacific Islands Soc; *Recreations* sailing (yacht 'Tikopia'), cine photography, wild life; *Clubs* Royal Cwlth Soc, Royal Southampton YC, Salcombe YC; *Style*— George Stansfield, Esq; Deryns Wood, Westfield Rd, Woking, Surrey (☎ 04862 28678)

STANSFIELD SMITH, Colin; CBE (1988); s of Mr Stansfield Smith, and Mary, *née* Simpson; *b* 1 Oct 1932; *Educ* William Hulmes GS, Univ of Cambridge (BA, Dip Arch); *m* 17 Feb 1961, Angela Jean Earnshaw, da of Eric Maw (d 1970), of Rustington, Sussex; 1 s (Oliver b 1970), 1 da (Sophie b 1967); *Career* Nat Serv Intelligence Corps 1951-53; ptnr Emberton Tardrew & Ptnrs 1965-, dep co architect Cheshire CC 1971, co architect Hants 1973; vice-pres RIBA 1983-86; chm estates sub ctee MCC; ARIBA; *Recreations* painting, golf; *Clubs* MCC, Hockley GC; *Style*— Colin Stansfield Smith, Esq, CBE; (☎ 0962 51970); Three Minsters House, High St, Winchester, Hants

STANSGATE, Viscountcy of, *see* Benn, Rt Hon Tony (Neil) Wedgwood, MP

STANSGATE, Viscountess; Margaret Eadie; da of Daniel Turner Holmes, late MP for Govan; *m* 1920, 1 Viscount Stansgate (d 1960); 2 s (*see* Rt Hon Tony Benn, MP) and 1 s (decd); *Career* first pres Congregational Fedn of England 1972-73, (now pres emeritus); vice pres Cncl of Christians and Jews; hon fell Hebrew Univ of Jerusalem 1982; *Style*— The Rt Hon Viscountess Stansgate; Stansgate Abbey House, nr Southminster, Essex; 10 North Court, Great Peter St, London SW1P 3LL (☎ 01 222 1988)

STANTON, Alan William; *b* 19 April 1944; *Educ* Architectural Assoc Sch (Dip Arch), Univ of California (MArch); *m* 8 July 1985, Wendy Robin; *Career* architect; medallist, Societé des Architectes, Diplome Par Le Gouvernment Paris; projects: Centre Pompidou Paris 1971-77 (team architect), La Villette Sci Museum Paris 1984-86 Jt, as Stanton, Williams, Age of Chivalry Exhibition RA, Shop Issey Miyake; currently: New Gallery Bldg for RIBA London, Winchester Cathedral Museum, Design Museum, London, Birmingham City Museum; *Style*— Alan Stanton, Esq; Studio 9A, 17 Heneage St, London E1 (☎ (247) 3171/2)

STANTON, Arthur Holbrow; MBE (1944), TD (1945); s of Arthur William Stanton, JP (d 1944), of Field Place, Stroud, Gloucs, and Violet Fairfax, *née* Taylor (d 1957); *b* 20 Jan 1910; *Educ* Marlborough, Staff Coll Haifa; *m* 30 April 1938, Joan Constance, da of Col Edwin Henry Ethelbert Collen, CMG, DSO, RA (d 1943), of Brakeys, Hatfield Peverel, Essex; 3 da (Anne Catharine b 1941, Juliet Mary b 1945, Elizabeth Holbrow b 1948); *Career* cmmnd 2 LT Royal Gloucs Hussars 1939, WWII, Staff Capt 1 Armd Div 1940-42, serv France 1940, Maj DAQMG 7 Armd Div 1942-43, Lt-Col AA and QMG 50 Northumbrian Div 1944, Maj DAA and QMG 4 Ind Armd Bde 1944-45, serv Western Desert Tripolitania, Tunisia, Italy, France, Belgium, Holland, Germany (despatches twice 1944); md of Nation Discount Co 1962-70, chm Discount Mkt Assoc 1967-69; church warden St Andrew's Hatfield Peverel Essex 1948-80, chm Hatfield Peverel Soc 1970-80; Freeman City of London 1932, Liveryman Worshipful Co of Vintners (Master 1970 and 1974); *Recreations* shooting, painting, travelling, things historical; *Clubs* Naval and Military, 7 Armd Div, Dining, Blackwater SC; *Style*— Arthur Stanton, Esq, MBE, TD; Brakeys, Hatfield Peverel, Chelmsford, Essex CM3 2NY

STANTON, Lt-Col John Richard Guy; MBE (1953), DL (Derbyshire 1973); s of Cdr Henry Guy Stanton, RN (d 1960); *b* 28 Nov 1919; *Educ* Hon Co of Skinners Sch, RMC Sandhurst; *m* 1941, Margaret Frances, *née* Harries (OBE 1986); 2 s, 3 da; *Career* Lt-Col Royal Sussex Regt 1939-67, Queen's Regt 1967-72; High Sheriff Derbyshire 1974-75 (Vice Lord Lieut 1987), chm E Midland Region Nat Tst 1975-85, Derbyshire branch CLA 1983-85; *Recreations* country pursuits, shooting; *Clubs* Army and Navy; *Style*— Lt-Col J R G Stanton, MBE, DL; Snelston Hall, Ashbourne, Derbyshire (☎ 0335 42064)

STANTON-JONES, Dr Richard; s of Brig John C Stanton-Jones (d 1976), and Katharine, *née* Stanton; *b* 25 Sept 1926; *Educ* King Edward VI Sch Stourbridge, King's Coll Cambridge (MA), Cranfield Coll of Aeronautics (MSc); *m* 8 Sept 1949, Dorine Mary, da of Lt Charles Watkins, RFC (d 1989); 1 s (Richard b Nov 1950); *Career* aerodynamicist at DeHavilland, Saunders-Roe and Lockheed (USA) 1949-56; chief aerodynamicist Saunders-Roe 1956-59; chief designer Br Hovercraft Corp (SRN series hovercraft) 1959-66; Royal Aero Soc Silver Medal (Black Knight/Hovercraft Devpt) 1965; tech dir Br Hovercraft corp 1966-68; Elmer A Sperry Award USA (Hovercraft Devpt) 1968; md BHC 1968-82, dep chm 1982-84; dir: RSJ Engrg Ltd 1984-, Slingsby Aviation Ltd 1985-; tech conslt US Dept of Justice 1988-; FEng 1984, hon DSc Exeter Univ 1987; FRINA, FBIM, FRAeS; *Recreations* sailing, carpentry; *Clubs* Naval and Military, Island Sailing Cowes; *Style*— Dr Richard Stanton-Jones; Doubloon, Springvale, Seaview, IOW (☎ 0983 613363)

STAPLE, George Warren; s of Kenneth Harry Staple, OBE (d 1978), of Paramour Grange, Ash, Kent, and Betty Mary, *née* Lemon; *b* 13 Sept 1940; *Educ* Haileybury; *m* Jan 1968, Olivia Deirdre, da of William James Lowry (d 1952), of Mtoko, Southern

Rhodesia; 2 s (Harry b 1976, Edward b 1978), 2 da (Alice b 1969, Polly b 1970); *Career* slr 1964, ptnr Clifford Chance (formerly Clifford-Turner) 1967-; DTI inspr Consolidated Gold Fields plc 1986 and Aldermanbury Tst plc 1988; chm of tbnls The Securities Assoc; memb: Commercial Ct Ctee 1978-, ct of govrs City of London Poly 1982, cncl Law Soc 1986; FCIArb 1985; *Recreations* cricket, hill walking; *Clubs* Brooks's, City of London, MCC; *Style*— George Staple, Esq; Clifford Chance, 19 New Bridge St, London EC4 (☎ 01 353 0211, fax 01 489 0046, telex 887847 LEGIS G)

STAPLE, William Philip; s of Kenneth Harry Staple, OBE (d 1978), and Betty Mary, *née* Lemon; *b* 28 Sept 1947; *Educ* Haileybury, Law Soc Coll of Law; *m* 14 May 1977 (m dis 1986), Jennifer Frances, da of Brig James Douglas Walker, OBE, of Farnham; 1 s (Oliver b 1980), 1 da (Sophia b 1982); *Career* barr Inner Temple 1970-82, exec Casenove and Co 1972-81, dir NM Rothschild and Sons Ltd 1986- (asst dir from 1982), non exec dir Grampian Hldgs plc 1984-; *Recreations* fishing, theatre; *Clubs* Whites; *Style*— William Staple, Esq; NM Rothschild & Sons Ltd, New Court, St Swithins Lane, London EC4P 4DU (☎ 01 280 5000)

STAPLES, (Hubert Anthony) Justin; CMG (1981); s of Francis Hammond (d 1970), of Sussex, and Catherine Margaret Mary, *née* Pownall (d 1981); *b* 14 Nov 1929; *Educ* Downside, Oriel Coll Oxford (BA); *m* 1962, Susan Angela, da of William Langston Collingwood Carter (d 1976), of Oxford; 1 s (Roderick), 1 da (Antonia); *Career* Dip Serv (formerly Foreign Serv) 1954- served in: Bangkok, Berlin, Vientiane, Brussels (UK Delgn NATO), Dublin; HM ambass: Bangkok 1981-86, Helsinki 1986-89;; *Recreations* skiing, riding, golf; *Clubs* Travellers', Kildare St and Univ (Dublin); *Style*— Justin Staples, Esq, CMG; British Embassy, Helsinki, Finland

STAPLES, Kenneth Derek; s of Stanley Holt Staples (d 1967), of Rayleigh, Essex, and Catherinee Emma Annie (Nan), *née* Walding (d 1982); *b* 10 Oct 1930; *Educ* Northampton GS, Battersea Poly; *m* 2 April 1955, Jean Mary, da of Walter Henry Creek (d 1981), of Tenterden, Kent; 1 s (Martin William b 2 Oct 1957), 2 da (Jennifer Anne b 8 Aug 1959, Katherine Mary b 10 Jan 1962); *Career* sr civil engr Corpn of London 1957-60, princ civil engr Kershaw & Kaufman 1960-63, sewerage planning engr pub works dept Govt of Singapore 1963-69, engr i/c NE JD & JM Watson 1969-72; ptnr: JD & JM Watson 1972-78, Watson Hawksley Consulting Engrs 1978-; memb ctee on underground construction for Construction Ind Res Info Assoc; FICE 1973 (assoc memb 1956), FIWEM (memb Inst WPC 1970), MConsE; *Recreations* reading photography, gardening; *Style*— Kenneth Staples, Esq; 15 Middle Rd, Aylesbury, Bucks HP21 7AD (☎ 0296 86 488), Watson Hawksley, Terriers House, Amersham Rd, High Wycombe Bucks (☎ 0494 26 240, fax 0494 22 074, telex 83 439 Watson G)

STAPLETON, Sir (Henry) Alfred; 10 Bt (E 1679) of The Leeward Islands; s of Brig Francis Harry Stapleton, CMG (d 1956), and Maud Ellen (d 1960), da of Maj Alfred Wrottesley, gs of 1 Baron Wrottesley; Sir Alfred succeeded his f's 1 cous Sir Miles Talbot Stapleton, 9 Bt, in 1977. Sir Alfred's ggf, Rev Hon Sir Francis Stapleton, 7 Bt, was 4 (but only surviving) s of Sir Thomas Stapleton, 6 Bt, in whose favour the abeyance of the Barony of Le Despencer was terminated 1788. The latter dignity descended to Sir Thomas's eldest son's da Mary, and through her marriage with 6 Viscount Falmouth to the present Viscount; *b* 2 May 1913; *Educ* Marlborough, Ch Ch Oxford; *m* 1961, Rosslyne Murray, da of Capt Harold Stanley Warren, RN (d 1960), of Parkstone, Dorset; *Heir* none; *Career* served 1939-45 War as Lt Oxfordshire and Bucks LI; *Recreations* cricket umpiring, gardening; *Clubs* Garrick, MCC; *Style*— Sir Alfred Stapleton, Bt; 7 Ridgeway, Horsecastles Lane, Sherborne, Dorset DT9 6BZ (☎ 093 581 2295)

STAPLETON, David Eric Cramer; s of Edward Eric Stapleton (d 1957); *b* 7 Nov 1933; *Educ* Ampleforth, RAC Cirencester; *m* 1960, Annabel Alison, da of Sir Gerald Gordon Ley, 3 Bt, TD, of Epperstone Manor; 4 da; *Career* former ptnr W I Carr and memb Stock Exchange, ret; chm: Pinneys of Scotland (formerly Pinneys Smokehouses Ltd), Gressingham Ducks plc; dir Border Financial Servs; farmer; *Recreations* shooting, fishing; *Clubs* Buck's; *Style*— David Stapleton, Esq; Armathwaite Place, Armathwaite, Carlisle, Cumbria (☎ 069 92 225); 25 Parthenia Rd, London SW6 (☎ 01 736 3581); Pinneys of Scotland, Annan, Dumfries (☎ 057 63 401); The Estate Office, Castlerigg Farm, Armathwaite, Carlisle, Cumbria CA4 9TS (☎ 076 885 331, telex 779151)

STAPLETON, Air Vice-Marshal Deryck Cameron; CB (1960), CBE (1948), DFC (1941), AFC (1939); s of John Rouse Stapleton, OBE, of Sarnia, Natal; *Educ* King Edward VI Sch Totnes; *m* 1942, Ethleen Joan Clifford, da of Sir Cuthbert William Whiteside (d 1969); 3 s; *Career* joined RAF 1936; served in Transjordan and Palestine 1937-39; WW II 1939-45 in Middle East, N Africa and Italy; Asst Sec (Air) War Cabinet Offices 1945-46; sec Chiefs of Staff Ctee, Min of Defence 1947-49; OC: RAF Odiham 1949-51, RAF Oldenburg 1955-57; dir Joint Plans, Air Ministry 1961-62; dir Defence Plans, Min of Defence 1963-64; Air Vice-Marshal 1963; AOC No 1 Gp, Bomber Cmd 1964-66; Cmdt RAF Staff Coll Bracknell 1966-68; ret 1968; BAC Area Mangr Libya 1969-70; BAC Rep Iran 1970-79; BAe Rep China and chm British Cos Assoc Peking 1979-83; Assoc Fell British Interplanetary Soc 1960; *Clubs* White's; *Style*— Air Vice-Marshal Deryck Stapleton, CB, CBE, DFC, AFC; c/o National Westminster Bank, Haymarket, London SW1

STAPLETON, Guy; s of William Algernon Swann Stapleton (d 1981), of Moreton in Marsh, and Joan Denise, *née* Wilson; *b* 10 Nov 1935; *Educ* Malvern; *Career* Govt Serv: with Miny of Tport and Civil Aviation 1954-59, Off of Dir Gen of Navigational Servs 1956-58, Miny of Aviation 1959-65, Civil Aviation Asst Br Embassy Rome 1960-63, private sec to Controller of NATCS 1963-65, MAFF 1965-74 (private sec and jt parly sec 1967-68), Dept of Prices and Consumer Protection 1974-76, MAFF 1976-82, Cabinet Off 1982-85 dir of estabs MAFF 1985-86, chief exec Intervention Bd 1986-; *Books* A Walk of Verse (1961), Poets England (ed), Gloucestershire (1977), Avon and Somerset (1981), Devon (1986), Hertfordshire (with Margaret Tims 1988); *Recreations* local history, genealogy, topographical verse; *Clubs* Civil Service, Royal Cwlth Soc; *Style*— Guy Stapleton, Esq; Fountain House, 2 Queen's Walk, Reading RG1 7QW (☎ 0734 583626, fax 0734 583626 ext 2370, telex 848302)

STAPLETON, Lt Cdr Nicholas Bryan John; RD (1943); s of Capt Nicholas Stapleton (d 1918), and Mary Jane, *née* Abraham (d 1939); *b* 4 Jan 1909; *Educ* Christ's Hosp, HMS Conway (School Ship) Birkenhead; *m* 3 June 1940, Laetitia Frances Mary, da of Lt-Col Charles à Court Repington, CMG; *Career* serv Midshipman Home Fleet RNR 1926, Navigating Offr (formerly cadet) Canadian Pacific Steamships Ltd 1926-37, marine airport offr Imperial Airways Ltd Southampton 1938; WWII cmd: HMS Brimness, HMS Southern Pride, HMS Amaranthus, HMS Betony, HMS Dere; serv Royal Fleet Aux Serv 1947-69: Master 1957, sr Master of Fleet 1968, ret 1969; publicity offr RNLI Brighton & Hove 1973-85; Freeman City of London 1961, Liveryman Hon Co of Master Mariners 1961; *Books* Steam Picket Boats of the Royal Navy (1980); *Recreations* bird watching, watching county cricket; *Style*— Lt Cdr Nicholas Stapleton, RNR; 38 Wilbury Crescent, Hove, E Sussex BN3 6FJ (☎ 0273 733627)

STAPLETON, Nigel John; s of Capt Frederick Ernest John Stapleton, of Winchmore Hill, London N21, and Katie Margaret, *née* Tyson; *b* 1 Nov 1946; *Educ* City of London Sch, Fitzwilliam Coll Cambridge (BA, MA); *m* 21 Dec 1982, Johanna Augusta, da of Johan Molhoek, of Vienna, Austria; 1 s (Henry James 1988); *Career* Unilever plc: various commerical appts 1968-75, devpt dir BOCM Silcock Ltd 1977-80 (corp planning mangr 1975-77), commercial advsr to regnl dir for N America Unilever plc 1980-83, vice pres fin Unilever US Inc 1983-86; fin dir Reed Int plc 1986-; memb NEDO Ctee on Industry and Fin; ACMA 1972, FCMA 1986; *Recreations* music, travel, tennis, opera; *Clubs* Oxford & Cambridge, Naval & Military; *Style*— Nigel Stapleton, Esq; Reed Int plc, 6 Chesterfield Gardens, London W1A 1EJ (☎ 01 491 8269, fax 01 491 8273, car tel 0836 597 589)

STAPLETON, William Sidney; s of William Henry Stapleton, and Winifred Grace, *née* Lee; *b* 5 July 1923; *Educ* Christ Church Sch London; *m* 5 July 1947, Doris Lilian (Dot), da of Frederick Granger; 1 da (Kay (Mrs Alcina) b 13 Aug 1950); *Career* WWII RN (visual signals) 1942-46; legal exec: Shaen Roscoe & Co 1938-42 and 1946-53, W H Thompson 1953-65; slr 1965, ptnr and sr ptnr Lawford & Co 1965-88 (conslt ptnr 1988-); memb: Lloyds Holborn Law Soc, Legal Aid Area Ctee, Soc of Labour Lawyers; life memb Apex Union; rep player: Surrey Cricket Assoc, Amateur Football Alliance (memb cncl); chm and rep player South Amateur Football League; vice-pres: Southbank Poly Football Club, Southbank Poly Cricket Club; memb Law Soc 1965, FInstLEx; *Recreations* work, cricket, golf, chess, watching and administrating soccer; *Clubs* MCC, Southbank Poly Football, Southbank Poly Cricket, West Kent GC; *Style*— William Stapleton, Esq; 33 Valleyfield Rd, Streatham, London S3W1G 2H5 (☎ 01 769 0899); 15 Devereux Court, Strand, London WC2R 3JJ (☎ 01 353 5099, fax 01 353 5355, telex 892303 FORLAW G)

STAPLETON-COTTON, Hon David Peter Dudley; s of late 4 Viscount Combermere; *b* 6 Mar 1932; *Educ* Eton; *m* 1955, Susan Nomakepu, da of Sir George Werner Albu, 2 Bt; 2 s (Simon b 1959, Toby James b 1966), 2 da (Nicola Caroline Louisa b 1957, Polly b 1961); *Career* Lt LG (Res); *Clubs* Royal Cape Yacht; *Style*— The Hon David Stapleton-Cotton; Sherwood House, 19 Sherwood Ave, Kenilworth, Cape Town, S Africa

STAPLETON-COTTON, Hon Sophia Mary; da of 5 Viscount Combermere; *b* 1963; *Style*— The Hon Sophia Stapleton-Cotton

STAPLETON-COTTON, Hon Tara Christabel; da of 5 Viscount Combermere; *b* 1961; *Style*— The Hon Tara Stapleton-Cotton

STARK, Sir Andrew Alexander Steel; KCMG (1975, CMG 1964), CVO 1965, DL (Essex 1982)); s of Thomas Bow Stark (d 1917) and Barbara Black, *née* Steel (d 1954), of Fauldhouse, W Lothian; *b* 30 Dec 1916; *Educ* Bathgate Acad, Edinburgh Univ; *m* 1944, (Helen) Rosemary, da of Lt-Col John Oxley Parker, TD (d 1980), of Faulkbourne, Essex; 2 s (& 1 s decd); *Career* served WW II Green Howards and staff appointments, Maj 1945; entered Foreign Off 1948; served Vienna, Belgrade, Rome, Bonn; ambass attached to UK mission UN 1968, under-sec gen UN 1968, ambass Denmark 1971-76, dep under sec FCO 1976; dir The Maersk Co (chm 1978-87), Scandinavian Bank 1978-88, Carlsberg Brewery 1980-87; advsr on European affrs to Soc Motor Mfrs and Traders 1977-; chm: Anglo-Danish Soc 1983-, Anglo-Danish Trade Advsy Bd 1983-; chm cncl and pro-chllr Essex Univ 1983-; *Recreations* shooting, skiing, tennis; *Clubs* Travellers', MCC; *Style*— Sir Andrew Stark, KCMG, CVO, DL; Fambridge Hall, White Notley, Essex (☎ 0376 83117)

STARK, Dame Freya Madeline; DBE (1972, CBE 1953); da of Robert Stark; *Educ* privately, Bedford Coll London, Sch Oriental Studies; *m* 1947, Stewart Perowne, OBE; *Career* traveller and writer; CStJ 1981 (OStJ 1949); LLD Glasgow, DLitt Durham; *Style*— Dame Freya Stark, DBE; c/o John Murray, 50 Albemarle St, W1

STARK, Ian David; s of late Ross Stark, and Margaret Barrie, *née* Grubb; *b* 22 Feb 1954; *Educ* Galashiels Acad; *m* 30 Nov 1979, Janet Dixon, da of Dr George Ballantyne McAulay; 1 s (Timothy b 8 Aug 1981), 1 da (Stephanie b 3 June 1980); *Career* equestrian; Team Silver Medallist LA Olympics 1984, Team Gold and Invividual Bronze Medallist Euro Championships 1985, Team Gold Medallist World Championships 1986, Champion Badminton Horse Trials 1986, Team Gold and Individual Silver Medallist Euro Championships 1987, 1 and 2 place Badminton 1988, team Silver and Individual Silver Medallist Seoul Olympics 1988; *Books* Flying Scott (with Janet Stark 1988); *Clubs* British Horse Soc; *Style*— Ian Stark, Esq; Haugh Head, Ashkirk, Selkirk, Scotland (☎ 0750 32238, car tel 0860 522 289, Horsebox tel 0860 522 290)

STARKE, Hon Mr Justice; Sir John Erskine; s of late Hon Sir Hayden Starke, KCMG; *b* 1 Dec 1913; *Educ* Melbourne C of E G S, Melbourne Univ; *m* Elizabeth, da of late Colin Campbell; *Career* Artillery 2 AIF, Mid East and New Guinea WW II; barr Vic 1939, QC 1955, judge of the Supreme Court of Vic 1964-; kt 1976; *Style*— Hon Mr Justice Starke; Supreme Court, Melbourne, Vic 3000, Australia

STARKEY, Hon Mrs (Alleyne Evelyn Maureen Louisa); da of 5 Viscount Templetown (d 1981, when the title became ext); *b* 1921; *m* 1, 1947, Maj John Hackett, late RAOC; 1 s; m 2, 1961, Michael Starkey; *Career* late ATS; *Style*— The Hon Mrs Starkey; Backstreet, Dalry, Castle Douglas

STARKEY, Sir John Philip; 3 Bt (UK 1935) of Norwood Park, Parish of Southwell and Co of Nottingham, JP (1982), DL (1981); s of Lt-Col Sir William Randle Starkey, 2 Bt (d 1977); *b* 8 May 1938; *Educ* Eton, Ch Ch Oxford; *m* 1966, Victoria Henrietta Fleetwood, da of the late Lt-Col Christopher Herbert Fleetwood Fuller, TD; 1 s, 3 da; *Heir* s, Henry John Starkey b 13 Oct 1973; *Recreations* cricket; *Style*— Sir John Starkey, Bt, JP, DL; Norwood Park, Southwell, Notts (☎ 0636 812762)

STARKIE, James Hugh Nicholas Le Gendre; s of Piers Cecil Le Gendre Starkie (d 1947), and Cicely, *née* de Hoghton (d 1972); *b* 13 August 1921; *Educ* Eton, RAC Cirencester; *m* 26 Oct 1963, (Margaret) Jean, da of Francis Graham Grant-Mackintosh; *Career* Lt RNVR 1940-46; farmer; *Recreations* sailing, shooting; *Style*— James Starkie, Esq; Gaulden Manor, Tolland, nr Taunton, Somerset (☎ 09847 213)

STARKIN, Ivan; s of Julian Starkin (d 1972), and Anne Mary, *née* Lewis (d 1978); *b* 3 Dec 1935; *Educ* Northern Poly of Architecture (Dip Arch); *m* 1, 27 March 1960,

Lucille Maureen; m 2, 1 Sept 1976, Jacqueline Susan Wills; 3 s (Stewart b 17 July 1961, Jeremy b 11 April 1964, Ben b 23 July 1982), 3 da (Emma b 31 March 1966, Caroline b 22 Oct 1970, Samantha b 5 July 1980); *Career* architect, md ICSA Ltd 1982 (specialise in office devpts and private hosps); ARIBA; *Recreations* painting and sketching, theatre; *Style—* Ivan Starkin, Esq; 36 King St, Covent Garden, London WC2E 8JS (telex 22726, fax 01 379 0852), car (☎ (0836) 235950)

START, Philip Grant; s of Eric Start, of Norfolk, and Beatrice May; *b* 12 June 1946; *Educ* William Grimshaw Sch London; *m* 9 Nov 1974, Jackie, da of William Albery (d 1982); 2 s (Matthew Dunstone b 1970, Rocky William b 1982); *Career* dir Village Gate 1967-74, chm md Woodhouse 1975-; *Recreations* reading, sports, family; *Style—* Philip Start, Esq ; 103A Oxford Street, London W11 (☎ 01 439 6785)

STARY, Erica Frances Margaret; da of Eric Halstead Smith (d 1987), and Barbara Maud, *née* Creeke (d 1947); *b* 20 Jan 1943; *Educ* Hunmanby Hall, LSE; *m* 1, 1966; m 2, 1971, Michael McKirdy Anthony Stary, s of John Henry Stary (presumed dead 1939); 1 da (Philippa b 1977); *Career* slr 1965; lectr (later sr lectr) Coll of Law 1966-73, slr of Inland Revenue 1974-75, asst ed (later ed) Br Tax Review 1976-; tech offr Inst of Taxation 1981-86, ptnr Speechly Bircham 1988-; chm London Young Slrs Gp 1972; memb Nat Ctee of Young Slrs 1969-77, dir Slrs Benevolent Assoc 1973-77, dir and tstee London Suzuki Gp and Tst 1984-, asst clerk second East Brixton Gen Cmmrs of Income Tax 1987-, frequent lectr and author on taxation matters; FTII 1984; *Recreations* sailing, music, theatre; *Style—* Mrs Michael Stary; 19 Keystone Crescent, London N1 9DS

STASSINOPOULOS, Mary; da of John Stassinopolous (d 1975), of Athens, and Pauline, *née* Kalliadis; *b* 9 Jan 1943; *Educ* Greece, Geneva Univ; *m* 1, 1963 (m dis 1977), Michael E Xilas; 1 s (Elias b 1965), 1 da (Irene b 1967); m 2, 1985, John G Carras; *Career* fell Imp Soc of Teachers of Dancing; dir Vacani Sch of Dancing (sch under patronage of HM Queen Elizabeth the Queen Mother); *Recreations* theatre, classical music, reading; *Clubs* Harry's Bar; *Style—* Miss Mary Stassinopoulos; 20 Norfolk Rd, London NW8 6HG (☎ 01 586 3691); Vacani Sch of Dancing, 38-42 Harrington Rd, London SW7 (☎ 01 589 6100)

STATHAM, Sir Norman; KCMG (1977, CMG 1967), CVO (1968); s of Frederick Statham, and Maud, *née* Lynes; *b* 15 August 1922; *Educ* Seymour Park Cncl Sch, Manchester GS, Gonville and Caius Coll Cambridge; *m* 1948, Hedwig Gerlich; 1 s (and 1 s decd), 1 da; *Career* served WWII and to 1947, Intelligence Corps; with Manchester Oil Refinery Ltd and Petrochemicals Ltd 1948-50; FO (later FCO) 1951-79, head european economic integration dept FCO (rank of cnsllr) 1965-68 and 1970-71, consul-gen São Paulo 1968-70, min (econ) Bonn 1971-75, dep under-sec FCO 1975-77, ambass Brazil 1977-79; vice-pres British C of C in Germany 1981-, pres COBCOE 1982-84; *Recreations* gardening, reading, birdwatching; *Clubs* Travellers'; *Style—* Sir Norman Statham, KCMG, CVO; 11 Underhill Park Rd, Reigate, Surrey RH2 9LU

STAUGHTON, Rt Hon Lord Justice; Rt Hon Sir Christopher Stephen Thomas Jonathan Thayer Staughton; PC (1988); yr s of Simon Thomas Samuel Staughton and Edith Madeline, *née* Jones; *b* 24 May 1933; *Educ* Eton, Magdalene Coll Cambridge; *m* 1960, Joanna Susan Elizabeth, er da of George Frederick Arthur Burgess; 2 da; *Career* served 2Lt 11 Hussars; barr 1957, QC 1970, Crown Court recorder 1972-81, High Court judge (Queen's Bench) 1981-87, Lord Justice of Appeal 1987-; kt 1981; *Style—* The Rt Hon Lord Justice Staughton; Royal Courts of Justice, Strand, London WC2A 2LL (☎ 01 936 6000)

STAUGHTON, Simon David Howard Ladd; s of Simon Staughton (d 1967), and Madeline Somers-Cox, *née* Jones (d 1974); *b* 24 Jan 1931; *Educ* Eton; *m* 12 oct 1957, Olivia Katharine , da of Egbert Cecil Barnes (d 1987); 1 s (James b 1959), 2 da (Julia b 1960, Fiona b 1963); *Career* 2 Lt 10 Royal Hussars (PWO); sr ptnr Lee & Pembertons slrs, chm St Austell Brewery Co Ltd; *Clubs* Cavalry and Guards; *Style—* David Staughton, Esq; The Old Rectory, Latimer, Bucks HP5 1UA (☎ 024 04 4567); 45 Pont St, London Sw1X 0BX (☎ 01 589 1114)

STAUNTON, Edmund George; s of Maj Reginald Evelyn Boothby (d 1976), of Burwell Hall, Louth Lincs, and Frances Katherine, *née* Staunton; assumed the name of Staunton by deed poll 1956; *b* 25 April 1943; *Educ* Eton, Royal Agric Coll; *m* 7 March 1970, Elizabeth Anne, da of John Peter Foster, of Harcourt, Hemingford Grey, Hintingdon; 2 s (William B 1972, Robert b 1974); *Career* farming and estate mgmnt; Nottinghamshire: chm Farming and Wildlife Advsy Gp 1981-86, chm Country Landowners Assoc 1984-86, pres Ramblers Assoc 1987-, pres elect Fed of Young Farmers Clubs 1987-, chm ctee Celebration of British Food and Farming 1989; ARICS (1970); *Style—* Edmund Staunton, Esq; Staunton Hall, Near Orston, Nottingham

STAUNTON, Marie; da of Austin Staunton, of Grange-over-Sands, Cumbria, and Ann, *née* McAuley; *b* 28 May 1952; *Educ* Larkhill House Sch Preston, Lancs, Lancaster Univ (BA Hons), Coll of Law; *m* 15 March 1986, James Albert Provan, s of William Provan, of Wallaceton, Bridge of Erne, Perthshire; 1 da (Lucy Mary Anne b 1987); *Career* slr; dir Amnesty Int Br Section; *Recreations* walking, gardening, children, dancing; *Style—* Ms Marie Staunton; 18 Grove Lane, SE5 (☎ 01 701 919); 5 Roberts Place, off Bowling Green Lane, London EC1R 0ES (fax 01 251 1558, telex 97621 AIB)

STAVELEY, Adm Sir William Doveton Minet; GCB (1984, KCB 1981), ADC (1985); s of Adm Cecil Minet Staveley, CB, CMG (d 1934), and Margaret Adela, *née* Sturdee (d 1960); gs of Gen Sir Charles Staveley and of Adm of the Fleet Sir Doveton Sturdee Bt, of First World War Battle of the Falkland Islands fame; *b* 10 Nov 1928; *Educ* West Downs Winchester, RNC Dartmouth, RNC Greenwich; *m* 1954, Bettina Kirstine, da of L R A Shuter (d 1960); 1 s (Richard), 1 da (Juliet); *Career* joined RN 1942, served HM Yacht Britannia 1957, subsequently in Far East and Mediterranean, Dir Naval Plans Naval Staff 1974-76, Flag Offr 2 Flotilla 1976-77, Flag Offr Carriers and Amphibious Ships and NATO Cdr Carrier Striking Gp 2 1977-78, Chief Staff to C-in-C Fleet 1978-80, Vice-Chief of Naval Staff 1980-82, Allied CINC Channel, CINC Eastern Atlantic Area and CINC Fleet 1982-85; Freeman City of London, Liveryman Worshipful Co of Shipwrights, yr bro Trinity House, CBIM; *Recreations* gardening, shooting, tennis, riding, sailing, restoring antiques, fishing; *Clubs* Boodle's, RNSA; *Style—* Admiral Sir William Staveley, GCB, ADC; Ministry of Defence, Main Building, Whitehall, London SW1

STAVERT OF HOSCOTE, Lt-Col Adam William; o s of Ralph Alan Stavert of Hoscote (d 1978), and (Edna) Pearl, *née* Gallagher (d 1985); the Stavert family acquired Hoscote through the marriage (1744) of Thomas Stavert to Elizabeth Pott, whose family had purchased it *ca* 1728 from the Scotts of Harden, who in their turn had purchased it from 4 Lord Home 1535 (*see* Burke's Landed Gentry, 18 edn, vol III, 1972); *b* 12 Oct 1939; *Educ* Stowe, RMA Sandhurst; *m* 12 Dec 1964, Shuna Nancy, da of Andrew Denis McNab (d 1981), of Tor Bracken, Howwood, Renfrewshire; 2 da (Sarah Vanessa b 30 March 1967, Victoria Gillian b 8 May 1970); *Career* cmmnd 2 Lt KOSB 1959; Platoon Cdr 1960-61, Berlin, Edinburgh; ADC to Govr of Aden 1961-62; CO 2 i/c 1965-68, Malaysia, Borneo, UK, W Germany; Adjt Scottish Inf Depot 1969-70; Army Staff Coll 1971; DAAG MI (A) MOD (Army) 1972-73; Co Cdr 1973-75, Berlin, Belfast; GSO2 HQ 52 Lowland Bde 1976-78 (despatches 1976); Lt-Col and Cdr 2 Bn 52 Lowland Vols 1982-85 (ret); regnl appeals dir for Barnardo's (Scotland) 1978-; memb Lowland TAVRA (vice convener Borders Ctee); pres SSAFA Roxburgh branch 1988-; MBIM, MICFM; *Recreations* tree planting, sailing, shooting; *Clubs* New (Edinburgh), Lansdowne; *Style—* Lt-Col Adam Stavert of Hoscote; Hoscote, Hawick, Roxburghshire TD9 7PN (☎ 045088 217); Barnardo's, 235 Corstorphine Road, Edinburgh EH12 7AR (☎ 031 334 8765)

STEAD, David; s of Albert Edward Stead (d 1982), and Barbara Valerie Vyall (d 1972); *b* 15 June 1946; *Educ* St Bartholomew's GS Berks, Paston Sch Norfolk, NE London Poly Sch of Architecture (Dip Arch); *m* 1, 27 Dec 1969, Gillian; 1 s (Thomas b 1978), 2 da (Ruth b 1973, Esther b 1975); m 2, 14 Jun 1986, Lynnette Elizabeth; 1 s (Daniel b 1987); *Career* architect; sole princ in own practice; RIBA; FSAI; *Recreations* golf, swimming, work; *Style—* David Stead, Esq; The Dutch House, 18 Austins Grove, Sheringham, Norfolk; Malvern House, 26 Church St, Sheringham, Norfolk

STEADMAN, Howard Ian; s of Maurice Steadman, and Gertrude Steadman; *b* 17 Dec 1939; *Educ* Kilburn GS, Jesus Coll Oxford (MA); *m* 30 March 1969, Joy Elaine, da of Harry Fisher; 1 s (Richard b 1970), 2 da (Elizabeth b 1973, Victoria b 1980); *Career* McAnally Montogomery and Co Stockbrokers 1966-74 (ptnr 1971-74), The Br Petroleum Pension Tst Ltd 1974- (portfolio mangr 1982-); memb Stock Exchange 1971-74, AMSIA 1966; *Recreations* bridge, badminton, tennis; *Style—* Howard Steadman, Esq; The British Petroleum Pension Tst Ltd, Britannic House, Moor Lane, London EC2Y 9BU (☎ 01 920 4280, fax 01 920 3836, telex 888811)

STEAFEL, Sheila; da of Harold Steafel, of S Africa, and Eda, *née* Cohen; *b* 26 May 1935; *Educ* Barnato Park Johannesburg Girls' HS, Univ of the Witwatersrand (BA), Webber Douglas Sch of Drama; *m* 1958 (m dis 1964), Harry H Corbett; *Career* actress; stage rôles incl: Billy Liar (1960), How the Other Half Loves (1972), as Harpo in A Day in Hollywood; A Night in the Ukraine (1979), with Players Theatre Old Time Music Hall (1979), revival of Salad Days (1976), Twelfth Night (1983), The Duenna (1983), as the witch in Humperdinck's Hansel and Gretel (1983), with Royal Shakespeare Co as Mistress Quickly in Merry Wives of Windsor (1985), Barbican season (1986), Ivanov (1989), Much Ado About Nothing (1989), Façade with Mozart Players (1988-89); films incl: Baby Love (1969), Some Will Some Won't (1969), Tropic of Cancer (1970), Percy (1971), SWALK (1971), The Waiting Room (1976), Bloodbath in the House of Death (1983); has also appeared in TV series, one woman shows and on radio; *Style—* Ms Sheila Steafel; 6 James Ave, London, NW2 4AJ; Agent: Ken McReddie, 91 Regent St, London W1 (☎ 01 439 1456)

STEARS, Michael John; s of Frank Albert Stears (d 1984), of Hastings, E Sussex, and Elsie Ellis, *née* Munns (d 1985); *b* 25 August 1934; *Educ* Harrow Art Coll, Southall Tech Coll; *m* 15 Sept 1960, Brenda Doreen, da of William Albert George Livy, of Stoke Poges, Bucks; 2 da (Jacqueline Anne b 2 March 1961, Janet Madeline b 6 July 1962); *Career* Nat Serv, served RMP (Signals) 1952-54; designer and creator of special effects for films; md Special Effects (World Wide Ltd) 1970-; films incl: Reach for the Sky (1956), Carve Her Name with Pride (1958), Operation Amsterdam (1960), The Guns of Navarone (1961), Dr No (1962), Call Me Bwana (1963), From Russia With Love (1963), Goldfinger (1964), Thunderball (Oscar, 1965), You Only Live Twice (1967), Chitty Chitty Bang Bang (1968), OHMS (1969), Fiddler on the Roof (1971), The Pied Piper (1972), Theatre of Blood (1973), The Black Windmill (1974), That Lucky Touch (1975), One of Our Dinosaurs is Missing (1976), Star Wars (Oscar, 1977) The Martian Chronicles (1979), Outland (1980), Megaforce (1982), Sahara (1984), Haunted Honeymoon (1985), Murder by Illusion (1987); ACTT 1954, BKSTS 1979; *Recreations* breeding, showing & luring Russian wolf hounds, model aircraft; *Clubs* The Borzoi, The Northern Borzoi Assoc, Soc of Model Aeronautical Engrs; *Style—* Michael Stears, Esq; Welders House, Welders Lane (Jordans), Chalfont St Peter, Bucks (☎ 024 075 505)

STEBBING, John Reynolds; OBE (1953, MBE 1949); s of Rev Charles Ferdinand Stebbing (d 1957), and Cicely Mary Stebbing (d 1965); *b* 19 May 1910; *Educ* Christ's Hosp and Brasenose Coll Oxford (MLitt, Oxon); *m* 27 Feb 1937, Margaret Florence, da of Cdr Robert Seed RN (ret) (d 1971); 2 da (Judith b 1939, Angela b 1942); *Career* Flying Offr (pilot) RAF 1928-33 and 1940-46, Sqdn Ldr UK; Col Admin Serv: Nigeria 1934-46, (released to RAF 1940), Swaziland 1946-55, dep resident cmmr; Somaliland, chief sec 1955-59; actg resident cmmr Swaziland on various occasions, actg govr and C-in-C Somaliland in 1955 and 1957 (ret 1959); appointed to admin posts in UK Atomic Energy Authy Harwell and Culham Lab (ret 1971); sr assoc memb St Antony's Coll Oxford, Leverhulme Tst res award, published nine papers in journal of David Davies Memorial Inst of Int Studies (Int Relations) on Arab-Israeli conflict; *Recreations* gardening; *Clubs* Royal Cwlth Soc; *Style—* John Stebbing, Esq, MBE, OBE; Fair Beeches, Burcot, Abingdon OX14 3DJ (☎ 086 730 7859)

STEDALL, Robert Henry; s of Lt Col M B P Stedall, OBE, TD (d 1982), of Hurstgate, Milford, Godalming, Surrey, and Audrey Wishart, *née* Cottam; *b* 6 August 1942; *Educ* Marlborough, McGill Univ Montreal (BCom); *m* 24 June 1972, Elizabeth (Liz) Jane, da of C J J Clay (d 1988), of Lamberts, Hascombe, Godalming, Surrey; 2 s (Oliver Marcus b 1976, James Robert b and d 1978), 1 da (Victoria Patricia b 1979); *Career* CA 1967, articled McClelland Moores & Co 1964-68, Bowater Corpn Ltd 1968-82: cash controller 1968-72, fin dir Far E 1972-75, fin dir Ralli Bros Ltd 1975-82, md Engelhard Metals 1982-84, dir of fin designate Greenwell Montagu 1984-85; fin dir Gartmore Investmt Mgmnt 1985-88, dir of admin Nat Employers Life Assur Co Ltd 1989-; memb Dunsfold PC; Liveryman Worshipful Co of Ironmongers (Sr Warden 1988); FCA; *Recreations* gardening, tennis, golf, bridge; *Clubs* Boodles; *Style—* Robert Stedall, Esq; Knightons, Dunsfold, Godalming, Surrey GU8 4NU (☎ 048 649 245); National Employers Life Assurance Co Ltd, Milton Court, Dorking, Surrey RH4 3LZ (☎ 0306 887766, fax 0306 881394)

STEDMAN, Baroness (Life Peeress UK 1974); Phyllis Stedman; OBE (1965); da of Percy Adams; *b* 14 July 1916; *Educ* County GS Peterborough; *m* 1941, Henry William Stedman, OBE (d 1988); *Career* branch librarian Peterborough 1932-41, gp offr

NFS 1941-44, memb bd Peterborough Devpt Corpn 1972-75, vice-chm Cambs CC 1973-75 (cllr 1946-75); baroness-in-waiting to HM (govt whip) 1975-79; govt spokesman in: House of Lords on Tport, Environment and Trade 1975-79; parly under-sec Dept of Environment 1979; joined SDP 1981; SDP whip House of Lords 1981-88, SDP Leader in House of Lord 1988-, SDP spokesman House of Lords on local govt, new towns, Tport, facilities for disabled, environmental protection; memb Cncl of Fire Servs Nat Benevolent Fund 1976-; vice-pres: Nat PHAB 1979-, Assoc of Dist cncls 1980-, Nat Assoc of Local Cncls 1983-, Assoc of County Cncls 1986-, Nat PHAB 1979-; *Recreations* reading, countryside; *Style—* The Rt Hon the Lady Stedman, OBE; 1 Grovelands, Thorpe Road, Peterborough, Northants PE3 6AQ (☎ 0733 61109); House of Lords, London SW1 (☎ 01 219 3229)

STEED, Mark Wickham; s of Richard David Wickham Steed and Jennifer Mary, *née* Hugh-Jones; gf Henry Wickham Steed, editor of the Times; *b* 31 Oct 1952; *Educ* Downside; *Career* chartered accountant; dir: Oxford Investmts Ltd 1981-86, Beckdest Ltd 1981-88, Colt Securities Ltd 1983-; *Recreations* shooting; *Clubs* Naval and Military; *Style—* Mark Steed, Esq; Grenville Cottage, Gawcott, Buckingham (☎ 0280 813236); 605 Nelson House, Dolphin Square, London SW1 (☎ 01 821 8172)

STEED, Nigel Harry Campbell; s of Cyril Frederick Steed (d 1978), of Great Bealings Suffolk, and Mary Gertrude Millicent, *née* Pausch; *b* 11 Oct 1945; *Educ* Felsted Essex; *m* 19 June 1975, Priscilla, da of Eric Geoffrey Pawsey (d 1978), of Braintree, Essex; 1 s (Ian b 1978), 2 da (Susannah b 1976, Nicola b 1980); *Career* slr; lord of the manor of Lavenham, Suffolk; *Recreations* hockey, golf, gardening; *Clubs* Ipswich and Suffolk; *Style—* Nigel Steed, Esq; Drumbeg, 4 Constitution Hill, Ipswich, Suffolk (☎ 0473 54479); Neale House, Neale St, Ipswich, Suffolk (☎ 0473 55556)

STEEDMAN, Air Chief Marshal Sir Alasdair; GCB (1980, KCB 1976, CB 1973), CBE (1965), DFC (1944); s of James Steedman (d 1953); *b* 29 Jan 1922; *Educ* Hampton GS; *m* 1945, Dorothy Isobel (d 1983), da of Col Walter Frederick Todd, late Cameronians; 1 s, 2 da; *Career* RAF 1941, Station Cdr RAF Lyneham 1962-65, CAS Royal Malaysian Air Force 1965-67, ACAS (Policy) RAF 1969-71, sr Air Staff Offr RAF Strike Cmd 1971-72, Cmdt RAF Staff Coll 1972-75, air memb of Air Force Bd for Supply and Orgn 1976-77, UK mil rep NATO 1977-80, controller RAF Benevolent Fund 1981-88, memb Security Cmmn 1982-; govr Hampton Sch 1976- (chm 1988-), memb fndn ctee and govr Gordons Sch 1981-; FRAeS, CBIM; *Recreations* sport, reading, DIY, motoring; *Clubs* RAF; *Style—* Air Chief Marshal Sir Alasdair Steedman, GCB, CBE, DFC; Rutherford, St Chloe, Amberley, near Stroud, Glos GL5 5AS (☎ 045387 2769)

STEEDMAN, Robert Russell; s of Robert Smith Steedman (d 1950), of Sevenoaks, Kent, and Helen Hope, *née* Brazier; *b* 3 Jan 1929; *Educ* Loretto Sch, School of Architecture, Edinburgh Coll of Art (DA), Univ of Pennsylvania (MLA); *m* 1, July 1956 (m dis 1974), Susan Elizabeth, da of Sir Robert Scott, GCMG, CBE (d 1982), of Peebles, Scotland; 1 s (Robert Scott b 1958), 2 da (Helena Elizabeth b 1960, Sarah Aeliz b 1962); m 2, 23 July 1977, Martha, da of Rev John Edmund Hamilton; *Career* Nat Serv Lt RWAFF 1947-48; ptnr Morris and Steedman Edinburgh 1959-; memb: Countryside Cmmn for Scotland 1980-88, Royal Fine Art Cmmn for Scotland 1984-; sec Royal Scottish Acad 1983- (memb cncl 1981-, dep pres 1982-83), govr Edinburgh Coll of Art 1974-88, memb Edinburgh Festival Soc 1978-; former cncl memb: Royal Incorporation of Architects in Scotland, Soc of Scottish Artists, Scottish Museums 1984-; chm Central Scotland Woodlands Tst 1984-87; awards: Civic Tst ten times 1963-88, Br Steel 1971, Saltire 1971, RIBA (Scotland) 1974, Euro Architectural Heritage Medal 1975, Assoc for the Preservation of Rural Scotland 1983 (1977); elected Academician Royal Scottish Acad 1979, RIBA, FRIAS, ALI; *Clubs* New (Edinburgh), Royal and Ancient (St Andrews); *Style—* Robert Steedman, Esq; Muir of Blebo, Bledocraigs, Cupar, Fife (☎ 0334 85 781), 11B Belford Mews, Edinburgh, Lothian; Morris & Steedman, 38 Young St Lane, North, Edinburgh (☎ 031 226 6563, fax 031 220 0224)

STEEL, Her Hon Judge Anne Heather; da of His Hon Edward Steel (d 1976), of Cheshire, and Mary Evelyn Griffith, *née* Roberts (d 1987); *b* 3 July 1940; *Educ* Howell's Sch Denbigh North Wales, Liverpool Univ (LLB); *m* 1967, David Kerr-Muir Beattie, s of Harold Beattie (d 1957), of Manchester; 1 s (Andrew b 1972), 1 da (Elinor b 1970); *Career* barr Gray's Inn 1963, practised Northern circuit, prosecuting counsel for DHSS 1984-86; recorder of the Crown Court 1984-86, circuit judge 1986; *Recreations* theatre, art, antiques, gardening; *Style—* Her Hon Judge Heather Steel; The Sessions House, Lancaster Road, Preston

STEEL, Brig Charles Deane; CMG (1957), OBE (1941); s of Dr Gerard Steel, JP (d 1937), of Leominster, and Margaret Sarah, *née* Masterson (d 1913); *b* 29 May 1901; *Educ* Bedford, RMA Woolwich; *m* 1932, Elizabeth (d 1973), da of Col Lawrence Chenevix Trench, CMG, DSO (d 1957); 2 s; *Career* 2 Lt Royal Engrs 1921, Bengal Sappers and Miners (India) 1924-29, Staff Coll Camberley 1936-37, East Africa and Abyssinia 1941, Western Desert 1942 (POW 1942), Switzerland 1943, dep head of Br Mil Mission to Greece 1945-49, Brig 1946, dep mil sec 1949-52, head of Conference and Supply Dept FO 1952-64, head of Accommodation Dept FCO 1964-67; *Recreations* golf, gardening; *Clubs* Naval and Military, Shikar; *Style—* Brig Charles Steel, CMG, OBE; Little Hill, Nettlebed, Oxon (☎ 0491 641287)

STEEL, Charlotte Elizabeth; da of Lt Cdr David Alan Robert Malcolm Ramsay, OBE, DSC, DSO, RN (d 1981), and Christine Elizabeth Warwick; *b* 29 June 1948; *Educ* St Mary's Sch Wantage; *m* 12 Sept 1970, David William Steel, s of Sir Lincoln Steel (d 1985); 2 s (Jonathan b 1971, Timothy b 1974); *Career* horse trainer and event rider representing England as individual European Championships 1977; dressage judge; previously voluntary worker, ctee memb Stoke Mandeville Hosp, fund raiser Br Paraplegic Sports Soc, SOS Poland helper;; *Recreations* theatre, reading, music; *Style—* Mrs David Steel; Chinnor Manor, Chinnor, Oxon OX9 4BG (☎ 0844 51469)

STEEL, (Antony) David; s of Sir James Steel, CBE, JP; *b* 1 May 1938; *Educ* Rugby, Queen's Coll Oxford; *m* 1968, Jane Harriet, da of N C Macpherson, CBE, WS; 1 s, 1 da; *Career* md Grove Coles Ltd, dir Grove Coles France SA; *Recreations* field sports; *Style—* David Steel, Esq; The Old Vicarage, Hillesden, Bucks (☎ (029 673) 350)

STEEL, Sir David Edward Charles; DSO (1940), MC (1945), TD; s of Gerald Arthur Steel, CB; *b* 29 Nov 1916; *Educ* Rugby, Oxford Univ (BA); *m* 3 Nov 1956, Ann Wynne, da of Maj-Gen Charles Basil Price, CB, DSO, DCM, VD, CD (d 1975); 1 s (Richard), 2 da (Nicola, Caroline); *Career* WWII 9 Queen's Royal Lancers Serv: France, M East, N Africa, Italy; slr Linklaters & Paines 1948, legal asst BP 1950, pres BP N America 1959-61; md: Kuwait Oil 1962-65, BP 1965-75 (dep chm 1972-75, chm 1975-81); dir Bank of England 1978-85; tstee The Economist 1979-, chm Wellcome Trust 1982-89 (tstee 1981-89), pres London Chamber of Commerce and Indust 1982-85; chm govrs Rugby Sch 1984-88; hon fell Univ Coll Oxford, hon DCL City Univ; kt 1977; *Recreations* golf, gardening; *Clubs* Cavalry and Guards', Royal and Ancient St Andrews; *Style—* Sir David Steel, DSO, MC, TD

STEEL, Rt Hon David Martin Scott; PC (1977), MP (SLD) Tweeddale, Ettrick and Lauderdale 1983-; s of Very Rev Dr David Steel; *b* 31 Mar 1938; *Educ* Prince of Wales Sch Nairobi, George Watson's Coll Edinburgh, Edinburgh Univ (MA, LLB); *m* 1962, Judith Mary, da of W D MacGregor, CBE; 2 s (and 1 s adopted), 1 da; *Career* sometime journalist, asst sec Scottish Lib Pty 1962-64, BBC TV interviewer in Scotland 1965-65 and later presenter of religious programmes for STV, Granada and BBC; MP (Lib) Roxburgh, Selkirk and Peebles 1965-83 (gained from Cons in by-election, first contested 1964); pres Anti-Apartheid Movement of GB 1966-69, memb parly delegation to UN 1967, sponsored Abortion Act 1967, trustee of Shelter 1970- (former chm Shelter Scotland), memb Br Cncl of Churches 1971-74, Lib chief whip 1970-75, spokesman on Foreign Affrs 1975-76, ldr of Lib Pty 1976-88, memb Select Ctee on Privileges 1979-86; rector Edinburgh Univ 1982-85; Chubb Fell Yale Univ 1987; *Books* Boost for the Borders (1964), Out of Control (1968), No Entry (1969), The Liberal Way Forward (1975), A New Political Agenda (1976), Militant for the Reasonable Man (1977), Border Country (1985), The Time Has Come (1987), Mary Stuart's Scotland (1987); *Recreations* vintage cars, fishing; *Style—* The Rt Hon David Steel, MP; House of Commons, London SW1A 0AA

STEEL, David William; QC (1981); s of Sir Lincoln Steel (d 1985), and Bucks, and Barbara, *née* Goldschmidt; *b* 7 May 1943; *Educ* Eton, Keble Coll Oxford (MA); *m* 1970, Charlotte Elizabeth, da of Lt Cdr David A R M Ramsay, DSM (d 1981); 2 s (Jonathan b 1971, Timothy b 1974); *Career* barr Inner Temple 1966; junior counsel to Treasy (Admiralty), (Common Law) 1978-81; memb: Panel Wreck Cmmrs 1982-, panel of Lloyd's Savage Arbitraters 1981-; ed; Temperley, Merchant Shipping Acts 1975, Kennedy on Salvage 1985; *Recreations* shooting, fishing; *Clubs* Turf, Beefsteak; *Style—* David Steel, Esq, QC; The Bell House, Askett, nr Aylesbury, Bucks (☎ Princes Risborough 3453); 2 Essex Court, Temple, London EC4 (☎ 01 583 8381, telex 881 2528)

STEEL, Elizabeth Anne; da of William Frederick Steel (d 1961), and Amy Winifred Steel (d 1975); *b* 3 July 1936; *Educ* Saint Bernard's Convent Slough, Univ of Reading (BSc, MSc); *Career* behavioural endocrinologist: Univ of Cambridge 1960-65, MRC 1985; *Recreations* riding, walking, taking the lid off things; *Style—* Miss Elizabeth Steel; Department of Zoology, Downing St, Cambridge (☎ 0223 336600)

STEEL, Sir James; CBE (1964), JP (1964), DL (Durham Co 1969); s of Alfred Steel (d 1920), of Thornhill Park, Sunderland, and Katharine, *née* Meikle (d 1943); *b* 19 May 1909; *Educ* Trent Coll; *m* 1935, Margaret Jean, da of Robert Sangster MacLauchlan; 2 s, 2 da; *Career* chm: Steel & Co Ltd 1956-67, CBI Northern Regnl Cncl 1963-66, Washington Devpt Corpn 1964-77, Br Productivity Cncl 1966-67, Textile Cncl of GB 1968-72, Natural History Soc of Northumbria 1970-85, Furness Withy & Co Ltd 1975-79, N of England Bldg Soc 1977-85; vice-chm: Rea Bros plc 1973-81, Durham Univ Cncl 1978-1983; dir Newcastle bd Barclays Bank 1975-82; memb: Nat Res Devpt Corpn 1963-73, Northern Econss Planning Cncl 1965-68, Royal Cmmn on the Constitution 1969-73; jt pres Cncl of Order of St John 1974-84; pres: Northumbria Assoc of Youth Clubs 1976-84, TA & VRA for North of England 1979-84; vice-pres: Durham Co Scout Assoc 1975-, Wildfowl Tst 1982-; vice-pres nat cncl YMCA's NE div 1984-; govr: St Aidan's Coll Durham 1967-, Chad's Coll Durham 1977-83, Trent Coll 1979-83; High Sheriff Co Durham 1972-73, HM Lord-Liet in the Metropolitan Co of Tyne and Wear 1974-84; Queens Silver Jubilee Medal 1977; Freeman Worshipful Co of Founders; Hon DCL Univ of Durham; KJStJ 1981, CBIM; kt 1967; *Recreations* ornithology; *Style—* Sir James Steel, CBE, JP, DL; Fawnlees Hall, Wolsingham, Co Durham DL13 3LW (☎ 0388 527307)

STEEL, (Rupert) Oliver; s of Joseph Steel (d 1959), of Kirkwood, Lockerbie, and Beatrice Elizabeth, *née* Courage (d 1965); *b* 30 April 1922; *Educ* Eton; *m* 1, 1944, Marigold Katharine, da of Percy Roycroft Lowe (d 1952); 2 s (Rupert Michael b 1947, Jonathan Robin b 1949); m 2, 1967, Lucinda Evelyn, da of Arthur Walter James (d 1982); 1 s (James Oliver b 1971), 1 da (Emily Jane b 1970); *Career* Pilot Fleet Air Arm RNVR Lt, Atlantic, Pacific 1941-46; Courage & Co Ltd 1946-78; Imperial Gp 1975-78; Everards Brewery 1978-84, South Uist Estates Ltd 1980-, Umeco Hldgs Ltd 1979-, Lloyds Bank & Subsidiaries 1977-; *Clubs* Brooks's; *Style—* Oliver Steel, Esq; Winterbourne Holt, Newbury RG16 8AP

STEEL, Patricia Ann; da of Thomas Norman Steel (d 1970), of Huddersfield Yorks, and Winifred, *née* Pearson (d 1974); *b* 30 Oct 1941; *Educ* Hunmanby Hall nr Filey, Exeter Univ (BA); *Career* sec Inst of Highways and Transportation (formerly Inst of Highway Engrs) 1973-; non exec dir LRT 1984-, chm Docklands Light Railway 1988- (dir 1986), memb Occupational Pensions Bd 1981-84; *Recreations* politics, music, travel; *Style—* Miss Patricia Steel; 27 Petersham Rd, Richmond, Surrey; 3 Lygon Place, London SW1 (☎ 01 730 5245, fax 01 730 1628)

STEEL, Richard Hugh Jordan; eldest s of Sir Christopher Eden Steel, GCMG, MVO (d 1973), of Southrop Lodge, Lechlade, and Catherine, er da of Lt-Gen Sir Sidney Clive, GCVO, KCB, CMG, DSO (d 1959); *b* 5 Dec 1932; *Educ* Eton; *m* 1959, Lady Rosemary, *née* Villiers, *qv*, sis of 7 Earl of Clarendon; 2 s (James Thomas Jordan b 1960, Oliver George Nigel b 1962), 1 da (Arabella Rosemary Louise b 1966); *Career* late 2 Lt RHG The Blues; md Lazard Bros 1953-73, asst sec HM Treasury 1969-70, corp fin dir Barclays Bank 1973-; *Recreations* gardening, shooting, fishing; *Clubs* Boodle's; *Style—* Richard Steel, Esq; The Glebe House, Notgrove, Cheltenham, Glos (☎ 045 15 347); Flat 15, Rupert House, Nevern Sq, London SW5 (☎ 01 373 5366)

STEEL, Robert King; s of Charles Leighton Steel III, and Elizabeth Deaton Steel; *b* 3 August 1951; *Educ* Duke Univ Durham N Carolina USA (BA), Univ of Chicago (MBA); *m* 30 Aug 1980, Gillian V, da of Alexander Hettmeyer; *Career* md Goldman Sachs Int 1988- (vice pres 1976-88); *Style—* Robert Steel, Esq

STEEL, Prof Robert Walter; CBE (1983); s of Frederick Grabham Steel (d 1948), and Winifred Barry, *née* Harrison (d 1974); *b* 31 July 1915; *Educ* Great Yarmouth GS, Cambridge and Co HS, Jesus Coll Oxford (BA, BSc, MA); *m* 9 Jan 1940, Eileen Margaret, da of Arthur Ernest Page (d 1941), of Bournemouth; 1 s (David Robert b 1948), 2 da (Alison Margaret b 1942, Elizabeth Mary b 1945); *Career* WWII Naval Intelligence 1940-45; geographer Ashanti Social Survey Gold Coast 1945-46, lectr (later sr lectr) in cwlth geography Univ of Oxford 1947-56 (fell Jesus Coll 1954-56, hon fell 1981); Univ of Liverpool: John Rankin prof of geography 1957-74, dean faculty of arts 1965-68, pro vice-chllr 1971-73; princ Univ Coll Swansea 1974-82, vice chllr Univ of Wales 1979-81; hon dir Cwlth Geographical Bureau 1972-81; chm: Univs' Cncl for Adult and Continuing Educn 1976-80, Lower Swansea Valley Devpt Gp 1979-88, govrs Westhill Coll Birmingham 1981 (vice chm cncl of church and assoc colls 1988-), Wales Advsy Body for Local Authy Higher Educn 1982-86, (with Human Ecology Cncl 1988-), Swansea Festival of Music and the Arts 1982-, Swansea Civic Gp 1988-; Hon DSc Salford Univ 1977, Hon LLD Wales 1983, Hon LLD Liverpool 1985, Hon DUniv Open Open Univ 1987; FRGS 1939, hon memb Inst of Br Geographers 1939- (pres 1969 added 1950-61), hon memb Geographical Assoc 1946- (pres 1973), memb African Studies Assoc UK 1963- (pres 1973), memb Royal African Soc 1939 (vice pres 1977-); *Recreations* walking, gardening, reading, music; *Clubs* Royal Cwlth Soc; *Style—* Prof Robert Steel; 12 Cambridge Rd, Langland, Swansea SA3 4PE (☎ 0792 369 087)

STEEL, Lady Rosemary Verena Edith; *née* Villiers; posthumous da of late George Herbert Arthur Edward, Lord Hyde (s of 6 Earl of Clarendon, KG, GCMG, GCVO, PC), and Hon Marion Feodorovna Louise Glyn, DCVO (d 1970), er da of 4 Baron Wolverton; raised to the rank of an Earl's da 1956; *b* 29 June 1935,(posthumous); *m* 1959, Richard Hugh Jordan Steel, *qv*, s of Sir Christopher Steel, GCMG, MVO; 2 s (James b 1960, Oliver b 1962), 1 da (Arabella b 1966); *Style—* Lady Rosemary Steel; The Glebe House, Notgrove, Cheltenham, Glos (☎ (045 15) 347)

STEEL, Hon Mrs; Hon Sophia Rose Eileen; *née* Maude; only da of 8 Viscount Hawarden; *b* 20 Jan 1959; *m* 26 June 1982, Timothy Michael Steel, only s of Anthony Steel, of Rock House Farm, Lower Froyle, Alton, Hants; 1 s (Anthony b 1988), 1 da (Isabella b 1984); *Recreations* riding, reading, singing, tennis; *Clubs* Millbrook Golf and Tennis Club NY; *Style—* The Hon Mrs Steel; 43B Museum Tower, 15 West 53rd St, New York, NY 10019, USA

STEEL, Maj Sir (Fiennes) William Strang; 2 Bt (UK 1938) of Philiphaugh, Co Selkirk, JP (Selkirkshire 1965), DL (1955); eld s of Maj Sir Samuel Strang Steel, 1st Bt (d 1961), by his w Hon Vere Mabel (d 1964), da of 1st Baron Cornwallis; *b* 24 July 1912; *Educ* Eton, RMC Sandhurst; *m* 1941, Joan (d 1982), o da of late Brig-Gen Sir Brodie Haldane Henderson, KCMG, CB; 2 s (1 da decd); *Heir* s, (Fiennes) Michael Strang Steel b 22 Feb 1943; *Career* Maj (ret) 17/21 Lancers (serv 1933-47); convenor Selkirk CC 1967-75; forestry cmmn 1958-73; *Style—* Maj Sir William Strang Steel, Bt, JP, DL; Philiphaugh, Selkirk (☎ 0750 21216)

STEELE, Hon Mrs (Caroline Mary); *see*: Sargent, Hon Dr

STEELE, Frank Fenwick; OBE (1969); late Capt Frank Robert Steele, and Mary, *née* Fenwick; *b* 11 Dec 1923; *Educ* St Peter's Sch York, Cambridge Univ; *m* 1944, Evelyn Angela, da of late Col Henry C Scott; 1 s (Frank b 1950), 1 da (Venetia b 1954); *Career* served Army 1943-47, Capt Uganda Colonial serv 1948-50; HM Diplomatic Serv 1951-75, chm Network Television Ltd 1981-87; dir: Kleinwort Benson Ltd 1985-87 (advsr 1975-85), Cluff gp of companies 1979-87, Arab-British Chamber of Commerce 1978-87; memb: cncls of Royal Soc for Asian Affairs (vice-pres), Royal Asiatic Soc and Anglo-Indonesian Soc; RGS Finance and Gen Purposes Ctee; *Recreations* travel; *Clubs* Beefsteak, Shikar, Travellers; *Style—* Frank Fenwick, Esq, OBE; 9 Ashley Gardens, London SW1P 1QD (☎ 01 834 7596)

STEELE, John Roderic; CB (1978); s of Harold G Steele (d 1968), of Wakefield, and Doris, *née* Hall (d 1986); *b* 22 Feb 1929; *Educ* Queen Elizabeth GS Wakefield, Queen's Coll Oxford (MA); *m* 22 Sept 1956, (Margaret) Marie, da of Joseph Stevens (d 1984), of Ingleton, Yorks; 2 s (Richard b 1957, David b 1963), 2 da (Alison b 1959, Elisabeth b 1965); *Career* civil serv; asst princ Miny of Civil Aviation 1951-54, private sec to Parly sec 1954-57; princ: road tport div 1957-60, sea tport 1960-62, shipping policy 1962-64; asst sec shipping policy Bd of Trade 1964-67, cnsllr (shipping) Br Embassy Washington 1967-71, asst sec (civil aviation div) DTI 1971-73; under sec: (space div) 1973-74, shipping policy 1974-75; gen div Bd of Trade 1975-76 (dep sec 1976-80), dep sec Dept Indust 1980-81, dir gen tport Cmmn of Euro Communities 1981-86; tport conslt 1986-; FCIT; *Recreations* cricket, tennis, opera; *Clubs* Utd Oxford and Cambridge, Philippics; *Style—* John Steele, Esq, CB; 7 Kemerton Rd, Beckenham, Kent; Sq Ambiorix 30, BTE 30, 1040 Bruxelles, Belgium; c/o Prisma Transport Consultants, 4 Rue Charles Bennet Case 269, 1211 Geneve 12, Switzerland

STEELE, Maj Gen Michael Chandos Merrett; MBE (1972); s of William Chandos Steele (d 1969), of Kingswood, Surrey, and Daisy Rhoda, *née* Merrett (d 1956); *b* 1 Dec 1931; *Educ* Westminster Sch, RMA Sandhurst; *m* 1961, Judith Ann, da of Edward James Huxford, of Grimsby; 2 s (Timothy, Jeremy), 1 da (Elizabeth); *Career* BMRA Welsh Div 1965-67, BM 8 Inf Bde Londonderry 1970-72, CO 22 AD Regt RA 1972-74, GI HQDRA 1974-76, Cmd Artillery Bde 1976-78, BGS Def Sales Organization MOD London 1979-82; Chief Jt Services Liaison Orgn Bonn 1983-86; *Recreations* tennis, gardening, walking; *Style—* Maj-Gen Michael Steele, MBE; Elders, Masons Bridge Rd, Redhill, Surrey RH1 5LE (☎ 0737 763982)

STEELE, Richard Charles; s of Maj Richard Orson Steele, MBE (d 1984), of Gloucester, and Helen Curtis, *née* Robertson; *b* 26 May 1928; *Educ* Ashburton Coll Devon, Univ Coll of N Wales (BSc), Univ of Oxford; *m* 12 Dec 1956, Anne Freda, da of Hugh White Nelson (d 1978), of New Milton, Hants; 2 s (Richard Hugh b 21 June 1958, John David b 9 Aug 1964), 1 da ((Anne) Mary b 18 Jan 1960); *Career* Gunner 66 Airborne Anti-Tank Regt 1946-48; asst conservator of forests Tanganyika 1951-63, head Woodland mgmnt section Nature Conservancy 1963-72, head terrestrial and freshwater life sciences NERC 1972-78, head div of scientific servs Inst of Terrestrial Ecology 1978-80, dir gen Nature Conservancy Cncl 1980-88; regnl cncllr and tres ICUN, memb cncl Fauna and Flora Preservation Soc, memb cncl Nat Tst, former pres Inst of Chartered Foresters, memb conservation ctee Surrey Wildlife Tst; FICFor 1968, FIBiol 1974, FBIM 1980; *Books* Monks Wood: A Nature Reserve Relord (ed 1972); *Recreations* gardening, hill-walking; *Clubs* Athenaeum; *Style—* Richard Steele, Esq; Treetops, 20 Deepdene Wood, Dorking, Surrey RH5 4BQ (☎ 0306 883 106)

STEELE, Lt-Col Robert; MBE (1955); s of Robert Steele (d 1969), and Norah Esmé Steele (d 1967); *b* 31 July 1920; *Educ* Marlborough, Freiburg Univ, Sandhurst; *m* 1946, Gyllian Diane, da of Lt-Col Kenneth Greville Williams, OBE (d 1974); 2 s, 1 da; *Career* Grenadier Gds 1939-60, dir Staff Coll Camberley 1956-57, cmd 1 Bn 1957-60, Gentleman-at-Arms HM Body Guard 1969- (appointed Harbinger 1987); chm: Boat Showrooms of London 1961-64, Boat Showrooms of Birmingham 1962-66, Speedy Tport (Belgravia) Ltd 1973-82; memb cncl of E Children's Soc 1966- (chm 1982-83, vice-chm 1983-84); JP (Hants) 1971-79; *Recreations* shooting, kite flying, collecting Treen; *Clubs* White's, Pratts; *Style—* Lt-Col Robert Steele, MBE; Church Bottom, Broad Chalke, Salisbury, Wilts SP5 5DS (☎ 0722 780364)

STEELE, Sir (Philip John) Rupert; s of late C Steele; *b* 3 Nov 1920; *Educ* Melbourne CEGS; *m* 1946, Judith, da of Dr Clifford Sharp; 1 s, 2 da; *Career* RAAF 115 Sqdn (Lancaster), RAF (POW 1944); dir Steele & Co 1949-59, chm ctee Vic Racing Club 1977-82 (memb 1958-85, hon tres 1971-73, vice-chm 1973-77); dir: Carlton Brewery Ltd 1964-73, Carlton and Utd Breweries 1973-84, Trust Co of Australia Ltd (formerly Union-Fidelity Trustee Co Ltd) 1984; memb Racecourses Licences Bd 1975-81; pres Prahran Football Club 1980-84 (ctee memb 1979-88); kt 1980; *Style—* Sir Rupert Steele; 2/64 Irving Rd, Toorak, Vic 3142, Australia

STEELE, Tommy; OBE (1979); s of Thomas Walter Hicks (d 1980), and Elizabeth Ellen Bennett (d 1982); *b* 17 Dec 1936; *Educ* Bacon's Sch for Boys Bermondsey; *m* 1960, Ann, *née* Donoughue; 1 da (Emma b 1969); *Career* actor, stage debut Sunderland 1956, London stage debut 1957, New York stage debut 1965; Arthur Kipps in Half a Sixpence (London 1963/New York 1965/film 1967), Hans Andersen in Hans Anderson (London 1974), Don Lockwood in Singin' in the Rain (London 1983); *Books* Quincy (1981), The Final Run (1983); *Recreations* squash, painting; *Style—* Tommy Steele, Esq, 28573; c/o Isobel Davie Ltd, 37 Hill St, London W1X 8JY (☎ 01 629 3252, telex 28573 (Artist G))

STEELE-BODGER, Prof Alasdair; CBE (1980); s of Henry William Steele-Bodger, MRCVS (d 1952), of Lichfield St, Tamworth, Staffs, and Katherine, *née* Macdonald (1983); *b* 1 Jan 1924; *Educ* Shrewsbury, Gonville and Caius Coll Cambridge (BA, MA), Royal 'Dick' Veterinary Coll, Univ of Edinburgh (BSc) RCVS; *m* 4 Sept 1948, Anne Chisholm, da of Capt Alfred William John Finlayson, RNI (d 1957), of Berry Knoll, Burley, Ringwood, Hants; 3 da (Catherine b 1954, Fiona b1956, Gillie b 1957); *Career* veterinary surgn, gen practice 1948-77, conslt practice 1977-79; prof of veterinary clinical studies Univ of Cambridge 1979-, pres Br Veterinary Assoc 1966, pres RCVS 1972, EEC official veterinary expert 1974-; Cncl Royal Agricultural Soc of Eng 1967-, memb bd of advsrs Univ of London 1984-, memb Home Off Panel of Assessors under Animal (Scientific Producers) Act 1986-, dir Bantin & Kingman Ltd 1980; Cambridge triple blue; MRCVS, FRCVS; *Recreations* walking, fishing, travel; *Clubs* Farmers, Hawks (Cambridge); *Style—* Prof Alasdair Steele-Bodger, CBE; The Miller's House, Mill Causeway, Chrishall, Royston, Herts SG8 8QH; Dep of Clinical Veterinary Medicine, Madingley Rd, Cambridge CB3 0ES

STEELE-PERKINS, Surgn Vice Adm Sir Derek Duncombe; KCB (1966, CB 1963), KCVO (1964, CVO 1954); s of Dr Duncombe Steele-Perkins (d 1958), of Honiton, Devon, and Sybil Mary Hill-Jones (d 1953); *b* 19 June 1908; *Educ* Allhallows Sch Rousdon, Royal Coll of Surgeons Edinburgh and Univ of Edinburgh; *m* 1937, Joan (d 1985), da of John Boddan (d 1935), of Heaton Mersey, Lancs; 3 da (Deryn b 1939, Margaret b 1942, Gale b 1944); *Career* joined RN 1932, MO RN 1932-66, sr surgical specialist RN Hosp Haslar 1939-40, Chatham 1940-44, Sydney 1944-46, Malta 1946-50, MO Royal Commonwealth Tours 1951-66, Cmd MO on Staff of C-in-C Portsmouth and medical offr-in-chief RN Hosp Haslar 1961-63, QHS 1961-66, medical dir-gen of the Navy 1963-66, ret as Surg Vice-Adm; FRCSEng, FRACS, LRCP; *Recreations* sailing, fishing, rugby football; *Clubs* Royal Lymington Yacht (Cdre 1968-71); *Style—* Surg Vice Adm Sir Derek Steele-Perkins, KCB, KCVO; c/o National Westminster Bank, Lymington, Hants SO4 8ER

STEELE-WILLIAMS, Kevin; s of Robertus Williams, of Dukinfield, Cheshire (d 1948), and Irene Steele, *née* Budds (d 1983); *b* 18 July 1938; *Educ* St John's C of E Sch, Dukinfield, William Hulme's Manchester, Fitzwilliam House Cambridge (BA, MA); *m* 29 Aug 1964, Cicely, da of Edward Twentyman (d 1945); 1 s (Simon Timothy b 1966), 2 da (Nichola Charlotte b 1967, Sophie Louise b 1973); *Career* admitted slr 1966, cmmr for oaths 1972, clerk cmmrs Inland Revenue Altrincham Cheshire and Wythenshawe Manchester 1978 -, former ptnr March Pearson & Skelton, currently sr ptnr Sedgley Caldecutt & Co Knutsford & Macclesfield; Cambridge blue lacrosse 1959-61 (toured USA combined Oxford/Cambridge team 1961); tstee (former chm) Ollerton village hall ctee, govr Knutsford County High School; *Recreations* philately, cricket, golf, travel, wine and English cookery; *Clubs* Cambridge Soc; *Style—* Kevin Steele-Williams, Esq; Marble Arch, King St, Knutsford, Cheshire (☎ 0565 4234, fax 0565 52711)

STEEN, Anthony David; MP (C) South Hams 1983-; s of Stephen N Steen, of London; *b* 22 July 1939; *Educ* Westminster Sch, London Univ; *m* Carolyn Padfield; 1 s, 1 da; *Career* social worker, youth ldr, barr Gray's Inn 1962; fndr dir: Task Force 1964-68, YVF 1968-74; MP Liverpool Wavertree 1974-83; memb Select Ctee Race Relations 1975-79, chm Cons Urban Affrs Ctee 1979-83; vice-chm: Social Services Ctee 1979-81, Environment Ctee 1983-86, chm Conservative Urban and New Town Affairs Ctee 1987-; vice-chm, West Country members 1987-; Task Force Trust; advsy tutor Sch of Environment Central London Poly 1982-83, chm Outlandos Trust, jt chm Impact '80s Cons Central Office, vice-chm British Caribbean Group, pres Int Centre for Child Studies, vice-pres Ecology Building Soc, bd memb Community Transport; cncl memb: Anglo-Jewish Assoc, Reference Int Cncl for Christian Relief, Voluntary Services Overseas, Nat Playing Fields Assoc; chm Commons and Lord's Cycle Club; *Books* New Life for Old Cities (1981), Tested Ideas for Political Success (1983-87); *Style—* Anthony Steen Esq, MP; House of Commons, London SW1A 0AA

STEEN, (David) Michael Cochrane Elsworth; s of Prof Robert Elsworth Steen, MD (d 1981), and Elizabeth Margaret, *née* Cochrane; *b* 5 Mar 1945; *Educ* Eton, Oriel Coll Oxford (Organ Scholar), (MA); *m* 18 Dec 1971, Rosemary Florence, da of Maj William Bellingham Denis Dobbs; 1 s (Peter b 1977), 3 da (Jane b 1973, Lucy b 1975, Rosalie b 1977); *Career* Peat Marwick McLintock (formerly Peat Marwick Mitchell & Co) 1968-81 (ptnr 1982-, head audit servs 1987-); FCA, ARCM; *Books* Guide to Directors Transactions (1983); *Recreations* music (organ playing), riding, reading; *Clubs* Carlton, Leander; *Style—* Michael Steen, Esq; Nevilles, Mattingley, Hants RG27 8JU (☎ 025 672 2144_; 5 Vicarage Gate, London W8 (☎ 01 937 6558); 1 Puddle Dock, London EC4V 3PD (☎ 01 236 8000, fax 01 248 6552, telex 8811541 PMM LON G)

STEENGRACHT VAN MOYLAND, Mevrouw Jan; Hon Cecily; *née* Somerset; da of 4 Baron Raglan, JP; *b* 10 August 1938; *m* 1961, Jonkheer Jan Tewdyr Patrick Steengracht van Moyland, Capt Irish Gds (ret; b 12 March 1933, educ Bradfield; portraitist; memb Cavalry and Guards' Club), yr s of Baron Steengracht van Moyland, of Pant-y-Goitre, Abergavenny; 1 s (Jonkheer Henry Jan Berrington S v M, b 18 Dec 1963), 1 da (Jonkvrouwe Suzanna Cecily S v M, b 3 Nov 1968); *Style—* Mevrouw Jan Steengracht van Moyland; Lanwecha, Llandenny, Usk, Gwent; 14 Addison Ave,

London W11 (T 01 603 3522)

STEER, Lt-Col Peter Frank; s of Alfred Albert (Peter) Steer, of Heathfield, Bovey Tracey, Devon, and Gertrude Elizabeth, *née* Murrin; *b* 1 May 1933; *Educ* Newton Abbot GS; *m* 21 Aug 1956, Rosina, da of late George William Ethelston, MSM, of Oswestry, Salop; 1 s (Martin b 1957), 1 da (Susan b 1960); *Career* cmmnd RA (2 Lt short serv cmmn) Mons OCS 1952, regular cmmn 1956; Troop Offr 31 Trg Regt RA Rhyl, 61 Light Regt RA Korea 1953-54, Adventure Trg instr 64 Trg Regt RA Oswestry 1954-57, 12 LAA Regt (Adj) BAOR, Regimental Serv 33 Para Light Regt RA and 7 Para Regt RHA in Cyprus, Libya, Bahrein and Gulf 1959-83, student Canadian Army Staff Coll 1963-65, GS02 (Intelligence) HQ 1Div BAOR 1965-68, cmd 39 (Roberts) Battery of Jr Ldrs Regt RA Nuneaton 1968-69, 7 Para Regt RHA cmdg I (Bull's Troop) Battery in Malaya and N Ireland 1969-71, Instr Jr Div Staff Coll Warminster 1971-73, Lt-Col and Chief Special Projects HQ Afnorth, Oslo 1973, GSOI Review Study Ammunition Rates and Scales MOD 1976, Head African Sectn D14, Def Int Staff MoD 1976 (ret Nov 1979), recalled to serv Dec 1979 as int coordinator mil advrs staff to Gov of Rhodesia Zimbabwe during cease fire and election supervision; ret 1980; conslt Resources and Engrg, gen mgr Securiguard, exec dir Br Schs Exploring Soc 1981- (expdns incl: Greenland 1982-83, Arctic, Norway 1984, Alaska 1985, Papua New Guinea 1987); chm Govs Greenfields Primary Sch Hartley Wintney 1976-89; *Recreations* riding, hill walking, cross country skiing, expeditioning; *Clubs* Special Forces; *Style—* Lt-Col Peter Steer, Esq, RA (ret); Nightingales, West Green Rd, Hartley, Wintney, Hants RG27 8RE (☎ 025 126 3688); British Schools Exploring Society, RGS, 1 Kensington Gore SW7 2AR (☎ 01 584 0710)

STEER, William Reed Hornby; DL (1950); s of Rev William Henry Hornby Steer, TD, JP (d 1938); *b* 5 April 1899; *Educ* Eton, Trinity Coll Cambridge (MA, LLM); *Career* RA 1917-19; called to the bar 1922, recorder South Molton 1936-51, DJAG Malta 1941-43, (Lt-Col 1943), dep chm LCC 1948-49; Master Worshipful Co of Turners 1949; KStJ 1951; *Clubs* Royal Corinthian Yacht, Oxford and Cambridge Univ, Carlton, Pratt's, MCC; *Style—* W R Hornby Steer, Esq, DL; 71A Whitehall Court, London SW1 (☎ 01 930 3160)

STEERS, Ian Sydney; s of Sydney Charles Steers (d 1956), and Rosalie Lilian Emily Steers; *b* 11 Sept 1928; *m* 1955, Barbara Joan; 3 s (Austen b 1957, Nigel b 1961, Jeremy b 1964), 1 da (Nicola b 1958); *Career* dir: Tribune Securities, Euro-Clear Clearance Systems plc, United Corporations Ltd, Heronsgate Investmts Ltd; vice-chm Wood Gundy Inc, memb bd of dir of Exec ctee of Int Primary Mkt Assoc; *Recreations* golf, reading, swimming; *Clubs* National Liberal, City of London, Denham Golf; *Style—* Ian Steers, Esq; Ladywalk, Long Lane, Heronsgate, Rickmansworth, Herts; Wood Gundy Inc, 30 Finsbury Square, London EC2A 1SB (☎ 886752, fax 01 638 0953); (☎ 01 628 4030, telex: 886752)

STEFFENS, Guenter Zeno; OBE; s of Dr jur Guenter Steffens (d 1937), of Berlin, and Ursula Margarete, *née* Lilge (d 1963); *b* 26 Oct 1937; *Educ* Gymnasium Essen W Germany, Hermann Lietz Sch Isle of Spiekeroog W Germany; *m* 1, (m dis 1977); 1 s (Christian b 16 July 1965), 1 da (Ursula b 11 May 1964); m 2, 4 Nov 1977, Dorothee Fey Louisa, da of Baron Herbert von Stackelberg (d 1975), of Bonn; *Career* Lt Res W German Luftwaffe 1958-59; Canadian Imperial Bank of Commerce Montreal 1961-62, Swiss Bank Corpn Zurich 1963-64, Credit Commercial de France Paris 1964, Dresdner Bank AG Cologne W Germany 1965-68, gen mangr Dresdner Bank AG London branch 1968-; chm: German Chamber Indust and Commerce UK 1974-, For Banks Assoc 1978-79 Lombard Assoc 1982-83, Officer's Cross of the Order of Merit of the Federal Repub of Germany 1984; *Clubs* Brook's, Mid-Atlantic; *Style—* Guenter Z Steffens, Esq, OBE; 30 Thurloe Sq, London SW7 2SD (☎ 01 589 5996; Dresdner Bank AG, Dresdner Bank House, 125 Wood St, London EC2 7AQ (☎ 01 606 7030)

STEIN, Cyril; s of late Jack Stein, and late Rebecca, *née* Selner; *b* 20 Feb 1928; *m* 1949, Betty, *née* Young, 2 s, 1 da; *Career* chm and chief exec Ladbroke Gp plc; FIOD; *Style—* Cyril Stein, Esq; c/o The Ladbroke Group plc, 87 Wimpole St, London W1M 7DB (☎ 01 935 2853, telex 291268)

STEIN, Keith Peter Sydney; s of Victor Stein (d 1984), and Pearl Stein; *b* 27 July 1945; *Educ* Preston Manor GS, Leeds Univ (BA), LSE (MSc); *m* 13 Dec 1970, Linda, da of Michael Collins (d 1976); 1 s (JonathAn), 1 da (Nicole); *Career* sr operational res Int Wool Secretariat 1968-70; Unigate Mgmnt Servs Div and Foods Div 1971-76: sr conslt, ops mangr, div planning mangr, special projects dir, commercial accountant; ptnr and nat dir: mgmnt consultancy 1977-86, strategic mgmnt Arthur Young 1986-; FCMA 1976, MIMC 1981; *Recreations* sports co schs and univ cricket, soccer, table tennis, golf, skiing, bridge; *Style—* Keith Stein, Esq; Valley View, Rasehill Close, Rickmansworth, Herts WD3 4EW (☎ 0923 779134); Rolls House, 7 Rolls Buildings, Fetter Lane, London EC4A 1NH (☎ 01 831 7130, fax 01 405 2147 & 4610, Telex 888604 & 262973 AYLO)

STEIN, Prof Peter Gonville; JP (1970); s of Walter Oscar Stein (d 1967), of London and Montreux, and Effie Drummond, *née* Walker (d 1969); *b* 29 May 1926; *Educ* Liverpool Coll, Gonville and Caius Coll Cambridge (MA, LLB), Collegio Borromeo Pavia, Univ of Aberdeen (PhD); *m* 1, 22 July 1953 (m dis 1978), Janet Mary, da of Clifford Chamberlain (d 1969), of Manor House, Desborough, Northants; 3 da (Barbara b 1956, Penelope b 1959, Dorothy b 1960); m2, 16 Aug 1978, Anne Mary Howard, da of Harrison Sayer (d 1980), of Seven Dials, Saffron Walden, Essex; *Career* joined RN 1944, Japanese translator 1945, Sub-Lt (sp) RNVR 1945-47; slr of the Supreme Ct 1951; dean faculty of law Univ of Aberdeen 1961-64 (prof of jurisprudence 1956-68); Univ of Cambridge: regius prof of civil law and fell of Queens' Coll 1968- (vice pres 1974-81), chm faculty bd of law 1973-76, fell Winchester Coll 1978-; memb bd of mgmnt Royal Cornhill and Assoc (Mental) Hosps 1963-68 (chm 1967-68), sec of state for Scotlands's Working Pty on Hosp Endowments 1966-69, memb Univ Grants Ctee 1971-75, pres Soc of Pub Teachers of Law 1980-81, memb US-UK Educnl Cmmn (Fulbright) 1985-; Hon Dr Juris Göttingen 1980; FBA 1974; For Fell Accademia di Scienze Morali e Politiche (Naples) 1982, For Fell Accademia Nazionale dei Lincei (Rome) 1987, Corresponding Fell Accademia degli Intronati (Siena) 1988; *Books* Fault in the Formation of Contract in Roman Law and Scots Law (1958), Regulae Iuris: From Juristic Rules to Legal Maxims (1966), Legal Values in Western Society (with J Shand, 1974), Adam Smith's Lectures on Jurisprudence (jt ed, 1978), Legal Evolution (1980), Legal Institutions, the Development of Dispute Settlement (1984), The Character & Influence of the Roman Civil Law: Historical Essays (1988); *Style—* Prof Peter Stein, JP; Wimpole Cottage, Wimpole Rd, Great Eversden, Cambridge CB3 7HR (☎ 0223 262349); Queens' Coll, Cambridge CB3 9ET (☎ 0223 335569)

STEINBERG, Prof Hannah; da of late Michael Steinberg, and Marie, *née* Wein; *Educ* Putney HS, Queen Anne's Sch Caversham, Univ of Reading, Denton Secretarial Coll, UCL (BA, PhD); *Career* sec to md Omes Ltd; UCL 1954-: lectr in pharmacology (formerly asst lectr), reader in psychopharmacology, prof in psychopharmacology (first in Western Europe) and head of psychopharmacology gp 1970; hon consulting clinical psychologist dept of psychological med Royal Free Hosp 1970, visiting prof in psychiatry McMaster Univ Ontario 1971; vice pres: Collegium International Neuro-Psychopharmacologicum 1968-74, Br Assoc for Psychopharmacology 1974-76; convener Academic Women's Achievement Gp 1979-, special tstee Middx Hosp 1988-; memb editorial bd psychopharmacologia 1965-80 and Pharmacopsychoecologia 1987-; memb: MRC working parties, Experimental Psychological Soc, Br Pharmacological Soc, Assoc for Study of Animal Behaviour, Soc for Study of Addiction, Euro Behavioural Pharmacology Soc (fndr memb 1986), Euro Coll of Neuro-Psychopharmacology (fndr memb 1987);; *Books* Animals and Men (trans and jt ed, 1951), Animal Behaviour and Drug Action (ed 1963), Scientific Basis of Drug Dependence (1968), Psychopharmacology: Sexual Disorders and Drug Abuse (jt ed 1972); *Style—* Prof Hannah Steinberg; University College London, Kathleen Lonsdale Building, Gower Street, London WC1E 6BT (☎ 01 387 7050, 01 380 7232)

STEINBERG, Jack; s of Alexander Steinberg (d 1957) and Sophie Steinberg; *b* 23 May 1913; *Educ* privately, London; *m* 1938, Hannah Anne, da of Solomon Wolfson, JP (d 1941); 2 da; *Career* underwriting memb of Lloyds, chm Steinberg Gp 1966-81; memb Nat Econ Devpt Ctee 1966-78, vice-pres British Knitting and Clothing Export Cncl 1984- (chm 1970-78), chm King's Med Res Tst; Freeman City of London, memb Worshipful Co of Plumbers; *Clubs* Brooks's, Portland, Carlton; *Style—* Jack Steinberg, Esq; 74 Portland Place, London W1 (☎ 01 580 5908)

STEINBERG, Dr (Victor) Leonard; s of Nathan Steinberg (d 1947), of London, and Sarah, *née* Bardiger; *b* 26 August 1926; *Educ* Shoreham GS, Regent St Poly, St Bart's Hosp (MB BS, DPhysMed); *m* 25 Jan 1953, Leni, da of Max Ackerman (d 1964), of London; 3 s (Nathan Anthony b 28 Nov 1953, Michael John b 8 Feb 1955, Stephen David b 30 Jan 1960); *Career* conslt rheumatologist: Enfield Gp of Hosps 1959-67, Central Middx Hosp 1960-, Wembley Hosp 1967-; former pres section of rheumatology RSM, pres London Jewish Med Soc; memb: Br Soc of Rheumatology, Harveian Soc of London, Br Med Acupuncture Soc: Freeman City of London, Liveryman Worshipful Soc of Apothecaries of London, BMA, FRCP (London), FRCP (Edinburgh); *Recreations* swimming, walking, opera, theatre; *Clubs* RAC; *Style—* Dr Leonard Steinberg; 22 Holne Chase, London N2 (☎ 01 458 27264); 39 Devonshire Pl, London W1 (☎ 01 935 9365)

STEINER, Jeffrey Josef; s of Beno Steiner, and Paula Borstein; *b* 3 April 1937; *Educ* Bradford Inst of Technol London, London Univ City and Guild; *m* 1, 1958 (m dis 1970), Claud; 1 s (Eric 25 Oct 1961), 2 da (Natalia b 14 Sept 1965, Thierry Tama Tama (foster) b 31 Dec 1970); m 2, 6 March 1976 (m dis 1983), Linda, *née* Schaller; 1 s (Benjamin b 3 April 1978), 1 da (Alexandra b 1980); m 3, 19 March 1987, Irja, *née* Bonnier; *Career* mangr metals and controls div Texas Instruments 1959-60 (mgmnt trainee 1958-59), pres Texas Instruments 1960-66 (Argentina, Brazil, Mexico, Switzerland, France), pres Burlington Tapis 1967-72, chm and pres Cedec SA Engrg Co 1973-84, chm, pres and chief exec offr Banner Industs Inc 1985- (a NY Stock Exchange Co); hon consul gen of Costa Rica; chm bd of govrs Haifa Univ; memb: Anti-Defamation League, Boys Town of Italy, Montefiore Med Centre; *Recreations* tennis, sailing, art collectng; *Clubs* Annabel's, Cavaliere, St James's, Mark's; *Style—* Jeffrey Steiner, Esq; 6 Cheyne Walk, London SW3; Banner Industries Inc, 110 East 59th St, NY, NY 10022 USA (☎ 212 3066 700, fax 212 888 5674, telex 971 391 BNR

STEINER, Rear Adm O(ttakar Harold Mojmir) St John; CB (1967); s of Ferdinand Steiner (d 1961), and Alice Mary Dorothea, *née* Whittington (d 1964); *b* 8 July 1916; *Educ* St Pauls; *m* 1, 1940 (m dis 1974), Evelyn Mary, da of Henry Thomas Young; 1 s (Anthony St John b 1942), 1 da (Angela St John b 1948); m 2, Edith Eleanor Powell, wid of Sqdn Ldr J A F Powell; 1 step s (Jonathan Powell b 1955); *Career* joined RN 1934; served 1935-41: HMS Frobisher, HMS Orion, HMS Southampton, HMS Electra, HMS Courageous, HMS Ilex, HMS Havelock; sqdn torpedo offr HMS Superb 1945-47, staff of C-in-C Far East 1948-50, naval staff Admty 1950-52, exec offr HMS Ceylon 1953-54, exec offr HMS Daedalus 1955-56, naval staff Admty 1956-57, Capt 3 Destroyer Sqdn and CO HMS Saintes 1958-59, NA to UK High Cmmr Canada 1960-62, Capt HMS Centaur 1963-65, asst chief def staff 1966-68; ADC to HM The Queen 1965; chm: Whitbread Round the World Races 1972-78, Transglobe Expedition 1979-80, Shipwrecked Fisherman and Mariners Royal Benevolent Soc; cdre RNSA 1974-76 (life vice-cdre 1978); Freeman City of London 1966, memb Worshipful Co of Coachmakers and Coach Harness Makers 1966; *Recreations* sailing, golf, bowls, garden; *Style—* Rear Adm O St John Steiner, CB

STEINER, Prof Robert Emil; CBE (1979); s of Rudolf Steiner (d 1958), of Vienna, and Clary, *née* Nördlinger (d 1921); *b* 1 Feb 1918; *Educ* Theresiamische Academie and Franz Josephs Redlgymnasium Vienna, Univ of Vienna, Univ of Vienna, Univ Coll Dublin (MB, DMR, MD); *m* 17 March 1945, Gertrude Margaret, da of Fritz Konirsch (d 1943), of Castlebar, Co Mayo, Ireland; 2 da (Hilary Clare b 1950, Ann Elizabeth b 1953); *Career* WWII; MO Emergency Med Serv: Guys Hosp 1941, Macclesfield Infirmary 1941-42, Winwick Emergency Hosp 1942-44; trainee Sheffield Royal Infirmary 1944; dir dept of diagnostic radiology Hammersmith Hosp 1957-60 (dep dir 1950-57); prof diagnostic radiology: dept of diagnostic radiology Hammersmith Hosp, London Univ, Royal Postgrad Med Sch 1960-83 (emeritus prof 1984-); pres: Br Inst of Radiology 1972-73, Royal Coll of Radiologists 1977-79; formerly: dep chm Nat Radiological Protection Bd, civilian conslt radiology to med dir gen (Naval), conslt advsr radiology to Dept of Health; hon: FACR 1965, FCRA 1971, FFR, RCSI 1972; FRCR 1945, FRCP 1965, FRCS 1982; author of over 250 scientific pubns and 5 books; *Recreations* gardening, swimming, walking, music; *Clubs* Hurlingham; *Style—* Prof Robert Steiner, CBE; 12 Stonehill Rd, East Sheen, London SW14 8RW (☎ 01 876 4038); NMR Unit, Univ of London, Hammersmith Hosp, Du Cane Rd, London W12 OHS (☎ 01 740 3298, 01 743 2030)

STEINFELD, Alan Geoffrey; QC (1986); s of Henry C Steinfeld (d 1967), of London, and Deborah, *née* Brickman; *b* 13 July 1946; *Educ* City of London Sch, Downing Coll Cambridge (BA, LLB); *m* 19 Feb 1976, Josephine Nicole, da of Eugene Gros, of London; 2 s (Martin b 28 Jan 1980, Sebastian b 1 Jan 1981); *Career* barr Lincoln's Inn 1968; *Recreations* lawn tennis, skiing, opera, cinema, lying in turkish baths; *Clubs* RAC, Cumberland Lawn Tennis; *Style—* Alan Steinfeld, Esq, QC; 29 Boundary Road,

St John's Wood, London NW8 OJE (☎ 01 624 8995); Jardin des Hesperides, Antibes, France; 24 Old Buildings, Lincoln's Inn, London WC2 (☎ 01 404 0946, fax 01 405 1360, telex 94014909 BROD G)

STENHAM, Cob - Anthony William Paul; s of Bernard Basil Stenham (d 1972); *b* 28 Jan 1932; *Educ* Eton, Trinity Coll Cambridge (MA); *m* 1, 1966 (m dis), Hon Sheila Marion, *qv*, da of 1 Baron Poole, CBE, TD, PC; m 2, 1983, Anne Martha Mary O'Rawe; 1 da (Polly Elizabeth Josephine b 1986); *Career* accountant, memb Inner Temple 1954, md Bankers Tst Co Ltd (NY); exec-chm Europe, Middle East and Africa Bankers Tst Co (London) 1986-, fin dir Unilever plc and Unilever NV 1970-86, chm ICA 1977-; underwriting memb of Lloyd's 1978-; dir: Equity Capital for Industry 1976-81, William Baird & Co 1964-69, Philip Hill Higginson Erlanger 1962-64, Price Waterhouse 1955-61, Capital Radio 1982-, Virgin Gp plc 1986-, The Rank Orgn plc 1987-, VSEL Consortium plc 1986-, Colonial Mutual Life Assur Gp 1987-; memb cncl Architectural Assoc 1982-, chm cncl and pro-provost Royal Coll of Art 1979-81 (memb court 1978-, hon fell 1980), bd of govrs Museum of London 1986-; FCA 1958, FRSA; *Recreations* cinema, contemporary art; *Clubs* Turf, Whites; *Style*— Cob Stenham Esq; 4 The Grove, Highgate, N6 (☎ 01 340 2266, office 01 382 2000)

STENHOUSE, Sir Nicol; s of late John Stenhouse; *b* 14 Feb 1911; *Educ* Repton; *m* 1951, Barbara Heath Wilson; 2 s, 1 da; *Career* chm and md Andrew Yule & Co Ltd Calcutta 1959-62; pres Bengal Chamber of Commerce and Industry (Calcutta) and Associated Chambers of Commerce of India 1961-62; kt 1962; *Style*— Sir Nicol Stenhouse; 3 St Mary's Court, Sixpenny Handley, nr Salisbury, Wilts SP5 5PH

STENING, Sir George Grafton Lees; ED; s of George Smith Stening (d 1941) and Muriel Grafton, *née* Lees (d 1960); *b* 16 Feb 1904; *Educ* Sydney HS, Sydney Univ (MB BS); *m* 1935, Kathleen Mary, da of Robert Clyde Packer (d 1934); 1 s, 1 da; *Career* visiting specialist Concord Repatriation Hosp 1945, chllr Priory Order of St John in Australia 1961, hon conslt gynaecological surgn Royal Prince Alfred Hosp 1964-; GCStJ, kt 1968; *see Debrett's Handbook of Australia and New Zealand for further details*; *Style*— Sir George Stening, ED; 229 Macquarie St, Sydney, NSW 2000, Australia

STENNING, Christopher John William (Kit); s of Col Philip Dives Stenning, of Sunnyside, Elie, Fife, and Cynthia Margaret, *née* Rycroft; *b* 16 Oct 1950; *Educ* Marlborough; *m* 19 Sept 1982, Ruth Marian, da of George Thomas Chenery Draper; 1 s (Jonathan b 1985), 1 da (Rachel b 1983); *Career* slr 1970-82, slr to Prudential Corpn 1982-88, dir corporate fin David Garrick 1988-; Freeman: City of London 1971, Worshipful Co of Haberdashers 1971; *Books* The Takeover Guide (1988); *Recreations* sport; *Clubs* Hurlingham; *Style*— Kit Stenning, Esq; 1 de Walden Ct, 85 New Cavendish St, London W1 (☎ 01 631 0659, fax 01 436 4311)

STENSON, Roger; s of Frederick Stenson (d 1982), of Nottingham, and Mary Agnes, *née* Bagshaw (d 1987); *b* 6 Feb 1936; *Educ* Mundella GS Nottingham, Keble Coll Oxford (MA); *m* 22 July 1960, Janet Elisabeth, da of John Collins McCall (d 1962), of Bookham, Surrey; 2 s (Benjamin James b 1963, Jules Angus b 1966), 1 da (Kate b 1962); *Career* Nat Serv sr aircraftsman RAF 1955-57; md BSG Computer Servs 1977-83, dir mgmnt serv Boots Co plc 1983-87, AGM servs - Norwich Union 1987-; FBCS; *Recreations* orienteering, choral singing, running; *Style*— Roger Stenson, Esq; 2 Albermarle Rd, Norwich NR2 2DR (☎ 0603 507 442); Norwich Union Insurance Gp, 8 Surrey St, Norwich NR1 (☎ 0603 682 886)

STEPHEN, Alexander Moncrieff Mitchell; s of Sir Alexander Murray Stephen (d 1974), whose family were shipbuilders 1750-1968, and Katherene Paton, *née* Mitchell (d 1978); *b* 5 Mar 1927; *Educ* Rugby, Cambridge (BA); *m* 24 Sept 1954, Susan Mary, *née* Orr, da of James George Orr Thomson (d 1950); 1 s (Graham b 1956); 3 da (Alice d 1959, Susannah b 1960, Alexandra d 1985); *Career* served RN 1945-8 (Petty Offr); shipbuilder 1951-68 mainly with Alexander Stephen & Sons Ltd (md 1968), chm Polymer Scotland 1973-; dir: Murray Income Tst plc, Murray Ventures plc, Murray Mgmnt Ltd, Murray Johnstone Hldgs Ltd, Murray Johnstone Ltd, Murray Johnstone Unit Tst Mgmnt Ltd, Murray Smaller Mkt Tst plc, Murray Technol Investments plc, Murray Int Tst plc, Scottish Technical Devpts Ltd, Scottish Widows' Fund and Life Assurance Soc, Pensions Mgmnt (SWF) Ltd; *Recreations* sailing, shooting, skiing; *Clubs* Western, Royal Northern and Clyde Yacht, Mudhook Yacht (Adm 1984-); *Style*— Alexander Stephen, Esq; Ballindalloch, Balfron, Stirlingshire (☎ (0360) 40202)

STEPHEN, (John) David; s of John Stephen (d 1968), and Anne Eileen Stephen; *b* 3 April 1942; *Educ* Luton GS, King's Coll Cambridge (BA, MA), Univ of Essex (MA); *m* 28 Dec 1968, Susan Dorothy, da of W C G Harris of Barnstaple, Devon; 3 s (John b 1972, Edward b 1977, Alexander b 1982), 1 da (Sophy b 1974); *Career* Runnymede Tst 1970-75 (dir 1973-75), Latin American regnl rep Int Univ Exchange Fund 1975-77, special advsr to Sec of State for Foreign and Cwlth Affairs 1977-79, freelance writer and conslt 1979-84, memb gen mgmnt bd and dir of corporate relations Cwlth Devpt Corpn 1984-; contested (Alliance) N Luton 1983 and 1987; *Style*— David Stephen, Esq; 123 Sundon Rd, Harlington, Beds LU5 6LW (☎ 05255 4799); CDC 1 Bessborough Gardens, London SW1 (☎ 01 828 4488, fax 01 828 6505)

STEPHEN, Harbourne Mackay; CBE (1985), DSO (1941), DFC (and bar 1940), AE (1943); s of Thomas M Stephen, JP; *b* 18 April 1916; *Educ* Shrewsbury; *m* 1947, Sybil Palmer; 2 da; *Career* RAF WWII served, RAuxAF 1950-52; joined Allied Newspapers 1931, Evening Standard 1936-39, md Daily Telegraph and Sunday Telegraph 1963-86; previously: dir Int Newspaper Colour Assoc (Darmstadt), gen mangr Thomson Newspapers London, Sunday Graphic, Sunday Express; also has worked on: Scottish Daily Express, Scottish Sunday Express, Evening Citizen (Glasgow); *Recreations* golf, fishing, shooting; *Clubs* RAF, Naval and Military; *Style*— Harbourne Stephen, Esq, CBE, DSO, DFC, AE; Donnington Fields, Newbury, Berks RG16 9BA (☎ 0635 40105)

STEPHEN, Dr (George) Martin; s of Sir Andrew Stephen, KB (d 1980), of Sheffield, and Frances, *née* Barker; *b* 18 July 1949; *Educ* Uppingham, Univ of Leeds (BA), Univ of Sheffield (DipEd, DPhil); *m* 21 Aug 1971, Jennifer Elaine, da of George Fisher, of Polloch Lodge, Polloch, Invernesshire; 3 s (Neill b 26 July 1976, Simon b 31 Aug 1978, Henry b 20 March 1981); *Career* various posts in remand homes 1966-71, teacher of english Uppingham 1971-72, housemaster and teacher of Eng Halleybury and ISC 1972-83, second master Sedbergh Sch 1983-87, headmaster The Perse Sch 1987-; memb Cambridge Rotary Club; memb HMC 1987-; *Books* An Introductory Guide to English Literature (1982), Studying Shakespeare (1982), British Warship Designs Since 1906 (1984), English Literature (1986), Sea Battles in Close Up (1987), Never Such Innocence (1988); *Recreations* sailing, fishing, rough shooting, writing, theatre; *Clubs* East India Devonshire Sports & Public School (hon memb); *Style*— Dr Martin Stephen; 80 Glebe Rd, Cambridge CB1 (☎ 0223 247 964); The Perse Sch, Hils Rd, Cambridge CB2 2QF (☎ 0223 248 127)

STEPHEN, HE Rt Hon Sir Ninian Martin; AK (1982), GCMG (1982), GCVO (1982), KBE (1972), PC (1979); s of late Frederick Stephen; *b* 15 June 1923; *Educ* George Watson's Edinburgh, Edinburgh Acad, St Paul's, Melbourne Univ; *m* 1949, Valery, da of A Q Sinclair; 5 da; *Career* Lt 2 AIF; barr and slr 1949, barr Vic 1952, QC 1966, judge Supreme Ct of Vic 1970-72, justice of High Court of Australia 1972-82, hon bencher Gray's Inn 1981, govr gen of Australia 1982-; AK (1982); KStJ 1982; *Style*— HE The Rt Hon Sir Ninian Stephen, AK, GCM; Government House, Yarralumla, Canberra, ACT 2600, Australia

STEPHENS, Air Cmdt Dame Anne; DBE (1961, MBE 1946); da of late Gen Sir Reginald Byng Stephens, KCB, CMG; *b* 4 Nov 1912; *Educ* privately; *Career* joined WAAF 1939, inspr WRAF 1952-54, dep dir 1954-57, dir WRAF 1960-63; Hon ADC to HM The Queen 1960-63; *Style*— Air Cmdt Dame Anne Stephens, DBE; The Forge, Sibford Ferris, Banbury, Oxfordshire (☎ 029 578 452)

STEPHENS, Cedric John; s of Col James Edward Stephens (d 1974), of Truro, Cornwall, and Hilda Emily Stephens (d 1972); *b* 13 Feb 1921; *Educ* London Univ (BSc); *Career* transmission devpt engr STC 1945-57, defenece res ADE IOM Halsted and RAE Farnborough 1951-60, dir (space) Miny of Aviatoin 1961-64, memb cncl (chm tech ctee) Euro Launcher Devpt Organisation 1962-64, chm tech Euro Organisation on Satellite Communications 1964, Imperial Defence Coll 1965, dir Signals Res and Devpt Estab MOD 1966-67, chief scientific advsr Home Office 1967-69, chief scientist and dir gen res Home Office 1969-73, memb Defence Scientific Advsy Cncl, chm Civil Serv Engrg Graduate Selection Bds 1973-75, memb Electronics Divnl Bd IEE 1973-, dir Exford (Highcliffe) Ltd 1987-; called to the Bar Gray's Inn 1971; CEng, FIEE, FRAeS, memb Forensic Sci Soc, memb Hon Soc Grays Inn; *Recreations* playing voila; *Style*— Cedric Stephens, Esq; 6 Newlyn Rd, Welling, Kent DA16 3LH; 7 Exeter Ct, Wharncliffe Rd, Christchurch, Dorset BH23 5DF (☎ 01 856 1750)

STEPHENS, Lt-Col Charles (Frederick Byng); s of Brig Frederick Stephens, CBE, DSO (d 1967), of Ivy Farm, Farringdon, Hants, and Esme Mackenzie, *née* Churchill (d 1987); *b* 12 Nov 1940; *Educ* Haileybury, RMA Sandhurst; *m* 3 Aug 1971, Helen Anne, da of Lt Cdr Sir Geoffrey Style, CBE, DSC, RN; 2 da (Alexandra b 1973, Georgina b 1976); *Career* cmmnd Welsh Gds 1961; served: Germany, Aden, Hong Kong; Lt-Col 1983; *Recreations* fishing, hunting, music; *Clubs* Cavalry and Guards'; *Style*— Lt-Col Charles Stephens; Brook House, Amport Andover, Hants (☎ 026477 2635); Horse Guards, Whitehall, London SW1A 2AX (☎ 01 930 4466 X2297)

STEPHENS, Sir David; KCB (1964), CVO (1960); s of Berkeley John Byng Stephens, CIE (d 1950), of Coxwell Street, Cirencester, and Gwendolen Elizabeth, *née* Cripps (d 1969); *b* 25 April 1910; *Educ* Winchester, Christ Chruch Oxford, Queen's Coll Oxford (Laming travelling fell 1932-034); *m* 1, 1941, Mary Clemency (d 1966), da of Sir Eric Gore Browne DSO, OBE, TD (d 1964); 3 s (Mark b 1942, John b 1944, Christopher b 1948), 1 da (Caroline b 1946, MBE; (*see* Richard Ryder, OBE, MP); m 2, 1967, Charlotte Evelyn, widow of Henry Manisty and da of Rev Alexander McEwen Baird-Smith (d 1944); *Career* clerk in Parliament Office House of Lords 1935-38, memb Runciman Mission to Czechoslovakia 1938, transferred HM Treasury 1938, Political Warfare Exec 1941-43, principal private sec to Lord Pres of the Cncl (Mr Herbert Morrison) 1947-49, asst sec Treasury 1949; sec for appointments to PMs Sir Anthony Eden and Mr Harold Macmillan 1955-61, reading clerk House of Lords 1961-63, clerk of the Parliaments (House of Lords) 1963-74; chm Redundant Churches Fund 1976-81, memb Cotswold Dist Cncl 1976-83, pres Friends of Cirencester Parish Church 1976-; *Recreations* gardening, tennis, country life; *Clubs* Brooks's, MCC; *Style*— Sir David Stephens, KCB, CVO; The Old Rectory, Coates, nr Cirencester, Glos GL7 6NS (☎ (0285) 770 258)

STEPHENS, Maj-Gen Keith Fielding; CB (1970), OBE (1957); s of Edgar Percy Stephens (d 1953), and Mary Louise Stephens; *b* 28 July 1910; *Educ* Eastbourne Coll, London Univ (MB BS); *m* 1937, Margaret Ann, da of late Alexander MacGregor; 2 s; *Career* cmmnd RAMC 1937, MO 1936-70, consult advsr in anaesthetics 1957-66, hon surgeon to HM The Queen 1964-70, cmdt RA Medical Coll London 1966-68, dep dir Medical Serv South Cmd UK 1968-70, ret; MO DHSS 1970-85; QHS 1964-70; Mitchiner Medal 1962, CStJ 1966; FFARCS; *Clubs* Naval and Military; *Style*— Maj-Gen Keith Stephens, CB, OBE; 3 Carnegie place, Wimbledon, London SW19 (☎ 01 946 0911)

STEPHENS, Prof Kenneth Gilbert; s of George Harry Stephens (d 1972), and Christiana, *née* Jackson (d 1986); *b* 3 May 1931; *Educ* Bablake Sch Coventry, Univ of Birmingham (BSc, PhD); *m* 7 Dec 1957 (m dis 1980), Miriam Anne, da of Tom Sim, of Newbury, Berks; 1 s (Ian b 1963), 1 da (Jane b 1961); m 2, Elizabeth Carolynn, da of Howard Jones, of Oxted, Surrey; *Career* res physicist AEI Aldermaston 1955-62, chief physicist Pye Laboratories Cambridge 1963-66; Univ of Surrey: lectr 1966-67, reader 1967-78, prof 1978-, head of Dept of electronic and electrical engrg 1983-; govr Royal GS 1977-, chm Blackheath CC; author varius pubns on ion implantation of materials in scientific jls; FInstP 1972, FIEE 1979; *Recreations* cricket, gardening, music, reading; *Clubs* MCC; *Style*— Prof Kenneth Stephens; 10 Brockway Close, Merrow, Guildford, Surrey GU1 2LW (☎ 0483 575 087); Dept of Electronic and Electrical Eng, Univ of Surrey, Guildford GU2 5XH (☎ 0483 509 135, fax 0483 34 139, telex 859331)

STEPHENS, Malcolm George; s of Frank Ernest, and Annie Mary Janet Macqueen; *b* 14 July 1937; *Educ* St Michael and All Angels and Shooters Hill GS, St John's Coll Oxford (BA); *m* 5 Dec 1975, Lynette Marie, da of John Patrick Caffery (d 1972); *Career* Dip Serv 19534-65; Shara 1959-62, Kenya 1963-65, exports credits guarantee dept 1965-82, principal 1970, seconded to Civil Service Staff Coll as dir of economics and social admin courses 1971-72, asst sec 1974, establishments offr 1977, under sec 1978, head project gp 1978-79, principal fin offr 1979-82; int fin dir Barclays Bank Int 1982, export fin dir and dir Barclays Export Services with Barclays Bank 1983-87; memb: Overseas Projects Bd 1985-87, British Overseas Trade Bd 1987; FIB, fell Inst of Export; *Recreations* gardening, reading; *Clubs* Overseas Bankers, Travellers'; *Style*— Malcolm Stephens, Esq; 111 Woolwich Road, Bexleyheath, Kent DA7 4LP (☎ 01 303 6782); ECGD, PO Box 272, Export house, 50 Ludgate Hill, London EC4M 7AY (☎ 01 382 7004)

STEPHENS, His Honour Judge (Stephen) Martin; QC (1982); s of Abraham Stephens (d 1977), of Swansea, and Freda, *née* Ruck; *b* 26 June 1939; *Educ* Swansea GS, Wadham Coll Oxford (MA); *m* 1965, Patricia Alison, da of Joseph Morris (d 1981), of Nottingham; 2 s (Richard b 1966, Anthony b 1968), 1 da (Marianne b 1971); *Career* barr 1963-86, circuit judge 1986-; *Recreations* theatre, cricket; *Style—* His Honour Judge Stephens, QC; c/o The Law Courts, Cathays Park, Cardiff

STEPHENS, Dr William Henry; s of William Henry Stephens, MBE (d 1967), and Helena Reid, *née* Cantley (d 1961); *b* 18 Mar 1913; *Educ* Methodist Coll Belfast, Queen's Univ Belfast (BSc, MSc); *m* 1938, Elizabeth Margaret, da of James Robert Brown (d 1960), of Belfast; 1 s (William b 1946), 1 da (Elizbeth b 1941, decd); *Career* scientific civil servant; aerodynamic and ballistics res 1936-43, asst dir UK Scientific Mission Washington 1943-47, dep dir RAE Farnborough 1957-59, dir gen ballistic missiles Min of Aviation 1959-62, tech dir European Space Launcher Devpt Orgn 1962-69, min for Def R & D Br Embassy Washington 1969-72, exec dir general Technol Systems 1973-87; Hon DSc Quuens Univ Belfast; memb Int Acad of Astronautics 1972; FBIS (bronze medal) 1972, FRAes;; *Recreations* travel, music; *Clubs* Athenaeum; *Style—* Dr William Stephens; Rosebrook House, Oriel Hill, Camberley, Surrey GU15 2JW (☎ (0276 24398)

STEPHENSON, (Robert) Ashley Shute; MVO (1979); s of James Stephenson (d 1960), and Agnes Maud, *née* Shute (d 1983); *b* 1 Sept 1927; *Educ* Heddon-on-the-Wall Sch, Walbottle Secdy Sch; *m* 21 May 1955, Isabel, da of Edward Dunn (d 1960); 1 s (Ian Ashley b 1964), 1 da (Carol b 1959); *Career* bailiff The Royal Parks 1980-; freelance gardening corr; some radio and TV appearances; ctee memb: The London Children's Flower Soc, The Royal Gardeners Benevolent Fund, Rotten Row 300'; vice-chm London in Bloom, judge Britain in Bloom; *Books* The Garden Planner (1981); *Recreations* golf, walking, reading, gardening; *Clubs* Arts; *Style—* Ashley Stephenson, Esq, MVO; Ranger's Lodge, Hyde Park, London W2 2OH (☎ 01 402 7994); 17 Sandore Rd, Seaford, East Sussex (☎ 0323 891050); Bailiff of Royal Parks Office, Room C11/11, 2 Marsham St, London SW1P 3EB (☎ 01 276 3757)

STEPHENSON, Maj Charles Lyon; TD; s of Col Charles E K Stephenson (d 1971), and Nancy Barbara, *née* Lyon; *b* 15 August 1935; *Educ* Eton; *m* 1, 1 March 1960, Margot Jane, da of J Tinker (d 1941); 2 s (George b 1962, Rupert b 1964); 1 da (Belinda b 1963); m 2, 17 Sept 1974, Sarah Merryweather, da of Lt-Gen The Lord Norrie (d 1977), of Berks; *Career* 9 Queens Lancers 1954-55, TA The Yorks Yeo (Maj 1956-68), Maj The Royal Yeomanry 1969-72 (Sherwood Ranger Sqdn); co dir MD Stephenson Blake (Hldgs) Ltd, non-exec dir: Lyon & Lyon plc, Carlton main Brickworks Ltd; High Sheriff Derbyshire 1984-85; pres Bakewell Agric Show 1980; *Recreations* shooting, fishing, gardening; *Clubs* Cavalry and Guards, MCC, The Sheffield; *Style—* Maj Charles Stephenson, TD; The Cottage, Great Longstone, Derbyshire DE4 1UA (☎ 062987 213); Sheaf House, Sheffield S4 7YL (☎ 0742 738531)

STEPHENSON, (Robert Noel) David; s of Capt Arthur Charles Robert Stephenson, MC (d 1965), and Margaret, *née* Smyth (d 1975); *b* 10 June 1932; *Educ* Loretto Sch; *m* 19 Nov 1966, Heather June, da of George Weatherston, of Gosforth, Newcastle upon Tyne; 2 s (Mark b 8 June 1968, John b 3 Oct 1972), 1 da (Julia b 27 July 1969); *Career* CA 1955, Peat Marwick Mitchell Canada 1956-60, Scottish & Newcastle Breweries plc 1960-, currently md Newcastle Breweries Ltd; bd memb: Tyne & Wear Enterprise Tst, Theatre Royal Tst; chm Area Manpower Bd N Tyne 1984-88; govr: Loretto Sch, Newcastle-upon-Tyne Poly; memb cncl Newcastle-upon-Tyne Univ; FCA 1960; *Recreations* golf, fishing, gardening; *Clubs* Hon Co of Edinburgh Golfers; *Style—* David Stephenson, Esq; Newton Low Hall, Felton, Northumberland NE65 9LD (☎ 066 575 617); The Newcastle Breweries Ltd, The Tyne Brewery, Gallowgate, Newcastle upon Tyne NE99 1RA (☎ 091 2325091, fax 091 2612301)

STEPHENSON, Sir Henry Upton; 3 Bt (UK 1936), of Hassop Hall, Co Derby, TD; s of Lt-Col Sir (Henry) Francis Stephenson, 2nd Bt, OBE, TD, JP, DL; *b* 26 Nov 1926; *Educ* Eton; *m* 1962, Susan, da of Maj J E Clowes; 4 da; *Heir* 1 cous, Timothy Stephenson; *Career* high sheriff Derbyshire 1975; late Capt Yorkshire Yeo; dir Stephenson Blake (Hldgs) Ltd and Thos Thurton & Sons Ltd; *Style—* Sir Henry Stephenson, Bt, TD; Tissington Cottage, Rowland, Bakewell, Derbyshire

STEPHENSON, (James) Ian (Love); s of James Stephenson (d 1979), of Hunwick, Bishop Auckland and May, *née* Emery (d 1966); *b* 11 Jan 1934; *Educ* Blyth GS, Univ of Durham (BA); *m* 3 Jan 1959, Kate da of James Robert Brown (d 1987), of Ponteland; 1 s (Stephen b 1964), 1 da (Stella b 1970); *Career* studio demonstrator Kings Coll Newcastle upon Tyne 1957-58, Boise Sch Italy 1959, visiting lectr Poly Sch of Art London 1959-62, visiting painter Chelsea Sch of Art 1959-66, dir foundation studies dept of fine art Newcastle Univ 1966-70, dir postgrad painting Chelsea Sch of Art 1970-, int course ldr voss Summer Sch 1979, vice-pres Sunderland Arts Centre 1982-, first specialist advsr CNAA 1980-83, fine art advsr Canterbury Art Coll 1974-79, RA Steward Artists Gen Benevolent Inst 1979-80; memb: visual arts panel Northern Arts Assoc Newcastle 1967-70, fine art panel NCDAD 1972-74, perm ctee New Contemporaries Assoc 1973-75, fine art bd CNAA 1974-75, advsy ctee Nat Exhibition of Childrens' Art Manchester 1975-, working pty RA Jubilee Exhibition 1976-77, selection ctee Arts Cncl Awards 1977-78, painting faculty Rome and Abbey Major Scholarships 1978-82, recommending ctee Chantrey Bequest 1979-80, Boise Scholarship ctee UCL 1983, former examiner at various polytechnics; exhibitions include: Br Painting in the Sixties London 1963, Mostra di Pittura Contemporanea Amsterdam and Europe 1964-65, 9o Biennio Lugano 1966, 5e Biennale and 18e Salon Paris 1967, Recent Br Painting London and world tour 1967-75, Junge Generation Grossbritannien Berlin 1968, Retrospective Newcastle 1970, La Peinture Anglaise Aujourd'hui Paris 1973, Elf Englische Zeichner Baden Baden and Bremen 1973, Recente Britse Tekenkunst Antwerp 1973, 13a Bienal Sao Paulo and Latin America 1975, Arte Inglese Oggi Milan 1976, Retrospective London and Bristol 1977, Englische Kunst der Gegenwart Bregenz 1977, Br Painting 1952-77 London 1977, Color en la Pintura Britanica Rio de Janeiro and Latin America 1977-79, Abstract Paintings from UK Washington 1978, Retrospective Birmingham and Cardiff 1978, Royal Acad of Arts Edinburgh 1979-80, Art Anglais d'Aujourd'hui Geneva 1980, Br Art 1940-80 London 1980, Colour in Br Painting Hong Kong and Far East 1980-81, Contemporary Br Drawing Tel Aviv and Near East 1980-82, The Deck of Cards Athens and Arabia 1980-82, A Taste of Br Art Today Brussels 1982, Arteder Muestra Internacional Bilbao 1982, La Couleur en la Peinture Britannique Luxembourg and Bucharest 1982-83, Int Print Biennales Bradford 1982 (1984, 1986), 15a Bienale Ljubljana 1983; illustrations: Cubism and After (BBC film) 1962, Comtemporary Br Art 1965, Private View 1965, Blow Up (MGM) film 1966, Art of Our Time 1967, Recent Br Painting 1968, Adventure in Art 1969, In Vogue 1975, Painting in Britain (1525-1975) 1976, Br Painting 1976, Contemporary Artists 1977 (1982), Contemporary Br Artists 1979, Tendenze e Testimoniaze 1983; work in collections including: Leeds City Art Gallery, Tate Gallery, Gulbenkian Foundation, Madison Art Center, V & A Museum; ARA 1975-86, RA 1986; memb: Mark Twain Soc 1978-, Accademia Italia 1980-, CAS 1980-81; *Style—* Ian Stephenson, Esq; Chelsea School of Art, Manresa Rd, London SW3 6LS (☎ 01 351 3844)

STEPHENSON, His Hon Judge; Jim; s of Alexander Stephenson (d 1958), of Heworth, Co Durham, and Norah Stephenson; *b* 17 July 1932; *Educ* Royal GS Newcastle upon Tyne, Exeter Coll Oxford (BA); *m* 1964, Jill Christine, da of Dr Edward William Lindeck, of Yew Tree Cottage, Fairwarp, Sussex; 3 s; *Career* barr; rec Crown Ct 1974, circuit judge North-Eastern circuit 1983-; *Recreations* history, walking, music; *Clubs* Durham Co; *Style—* His Hon Judge Stephenson; Kenton Bar Crown Court, Ponteland Rd, Newcastle upon Tyne NE1 2YH (☎ 091 2868901)

STEPHENSON, Joan, Lady; Joan; 2 da of Maj John Herbert Upton, JP, Lord of the Manor of Flamborough, by his 1 w Hilda (3 da of Horace Trelawny, of Shotwick Park, Chester); *b* 20 April 1901; *m* 1925, Lt-Col Sir Francis Stephenson, 2 Bt, OBE, TD, JP, DL (d 1982); 1 s (Sir Henry Stephenson, 3 Bt, *qv*); *Style—* Joan, Lady Upton; Hassop Green, Bakewell, Derbyshire

STEPHENSON, Maj-Gen John Aubrey; CB (1982), OBE (1971),; s of Reginald Jack Stephenson (d 1976), of 3 Russell Ave, Weymouth, Dorset, and Florence, *née* Pick (d 1947); *b* 15 May 1929; *Educ* Dorchester GS, RMA Sandhurst, RMCS Shrivenham, Staff Coll Camberley, RCDS London; *m* 29 July 1953, Sheila, da of Henry Douglas Colbeck (d 1978), of 5 Northumberland Ave, Newcastle-on-Tyne; 2 s (Guy b 1957, Peter b 1963), 1 da (Susan b 1955); *Career* Forces (despatches) 1951; pilot 652 Air Op Sqdn RAF 1954-56, Capt 1 Regt RHA 1956-58, Capt 39 Missile Regt 1960-61, Maj combat devpt MOD London 1963-64, battery cdr (Maj) 25 Field Regt RA 1965-67, CO 16 Light Air Def Regt RA 1969-71, Col project mangr 155 MM Systems 1971-73, Brig cdr 1 Artillery Bde 1975-77, Brig SMO RARDE 1977-78; Maj Gen: DGW/A MOD London 1978-80, VMGO MOD London 1980-81; md Weapon Systems Ltd 1982-, dir ATX Ltd 1984-86; pres Royal Br Legion Houghton 1987; govr Hardye's Sch Dorchester 1984-, chm Stockbridge Cons (vice chm Area 7 Cons), PCC St Peters Stockbridge; FBIM 1977; *Recreations* fishing, sailing, walking, reading, history, travel; *Clubs* IOD, Royal Cwlth Soc; *Style—* Maj Gen John Stephenson, CB, OBE; Collingwood 27 Trafalgar Way, Stockbridge, Hants SO20 6ET (☎ 0264 810 458, telex 477379 WINSER G)

STEPHENSON, Rt Hon Sir John Frederick Eustace Stephenson; PC (1971); 2 s of Sir Guy Stephenson, CB (er s of Sir Augustus Keppel Stephenson, KCB, KC), by his w Gwendolen, da of Rt Hon John Gilbert Talbot, PC, JP, DL, MP, sometime Parly sec BOT and s in his turn of Hon John Chetwynd Talbot (4 s of 2 Earl Talbot); *b* 28 Mar 1910; *Educ* Winchester, New Coll Oxford (MA, hon fell); *m* 1951, Hon (Frances) Rose, yr da of Baron Asquith of Bishopstone, PC (*see* Stephenson, Hon Lady); 2 s (David b 1954, Daniel b 1960), 2 da (Mary b 1952, Laura b 1958); *Career* WWII RE and Intelligence Corps served Middle East and NW Europe, Lt-Col 1946; barr Inner Temple 1934, QC 1960; recorder: Bridgwater 1954-59, Winchester 1959-62; chllr Diocese: Peterborough 1956-62, Winchester 1958-62; High Court judge (Queen's Bench) 1962-71, dep chm Dorset QS 1962-71, Lord Justice of Appeal 1971-85; kt 1962; *Books* A Royal Correspondence (1938); *Recreations* reading, music, golf; *Clubs* MCC, Hurlingham; *Style—* The Rt Hon Sir John Stephenson; 26 Doneraile Street, London SW6 (☎ 01 736 6782)

STEPHENSON, Lt-Col John Robin; OBE (1976); s of John Stewart Stephenson (d 1975), and Edith Gerda Greenwell Stephenson (d 1975); *b* 25 Feb 1931; *Educ* Christ's Hosp, RMA Sandhurst; *m* 27 Jan 1962, Karen Margrethe, da of August Hansen Koppang (d 1973); 1 s (Robin b 1967), 2 da (Celia b 1963, Kristina b 1964); *Career* cmmnd Royal Sussex Regt 1951, platoon cdr Egypt 1951-53, Lt 1953, instr regtl depot 1953-54, ADC and co 2 i/c Korea 1955-56, company 2 i/c Gibraltar 1956-57, Capt 1957, instr Mons Offr Cadet Sch 1958-60, company cdr NI 1960-61, company cdr regtl depot 1962-64, Maj 1963, GSO3 Libya 1964-65, company cdr Germany 1966-67, infantry rep Sch of Signals 1968-70, bn 2 i/c NI 1970-72, Lt-Col 1972, sr offrs war course 1972-73, CO 5 Bn Queen's Regt 1973-76, dep pres Regular Cmmns Bd 1976, SO UK C in C's Ctee 1977-79, ret 1979; asst sec MCC 1979-86, sec MCC and Int Cricket Conf 1987-; Order of Orange-Nassau 1972; *Recreations* cricket, rugby, squash, golf, boating and gardening; *Clubs* MCC, IZ, Free Foresters; *Style—* Lt-Col Stephenson, OBE; Plum Tree Cottage, Barford St Martin, nr Salisbury, Wiltshire SP3 4BL; Flat 3, 58 Aberdare Gardens, London NW6; Marylebone Cricket Club, Lord's Ground, London NW8 8QN (☎ 01 289 1611-5, fax 289 9100, telex 297329 MCCG G)

STEPHENSON, Hon Lady; (Frances) Rose; *née* Asquith; yr da of Baron Asquith of Bishopstone (4 s of 1 Earl of Oxford and Asquith, otherwise H H Asquith, the Liberal PM), and Anne Stephanie, *née* Pollock (d 1964); *b* 4 Oct 1925; *Educ* private; *m* 1951, Rt Hon Sir John Stephenson, *qv*; 2 s, 2 da; *Career* sec War Graves Cmmn; FO 1943-51; chm London Cncl for Welfare of Women & Girls 1959-71; *Style—* The Hon Lady Stephenson

STEPHENSON, Hon Mrs (Sarah Merryweather); *née* Norrie; da of 1 Baron Norrie, GCMG, GCVO, CB, DSO, MC (d 1977); *b* 1943; *Educ* The Guildhall School of Music; *m* 1974, Charles Lyon Stephenson, TD; *Career* Music teacher; *Style—* The Hon Mrs Stephenson; The Cottage, Great Longstone, Bakewell, Derbys DE4 1UA

STEPHENSON, Timothy Congreve; s of Augustus William Stephenson, of Saxbys Mead, Cowden, nr Eden Bridge, Kent, and Mary Gloria (only and posthumous child of Maj William La T Congreve VC, DSO, MC); *b* 7 Mar 1940; *Educ* Harrow, London Business Sch; *m* 1, 14 April 1966 (m dis 1980), Nerena Anne, d of Maj the Hon William Nicholas Somers Laurence Hyde Villiers; 2 s (Guy b 1969, Frederick b 1978), 2 da (Lucinda b 1967, Henrietta b 1975); m 2, 16 June 1980, Diana-Margaret, da of HE Dr Otto Soltmann, of Coblenz, W Germany; 2 s (Christopher b 1983, William b 1986); *Career* Welsh Gds 1959-65; Gallaher Ltd 1965-79, md Grafton Ltd and chm Grafton Off Products Inc 1980-86, dir TED Assocs Ltd 1985-, md Stephenson Cobbold Ltd 1987-; former memb Indust Tbnls and fndr memb Bd of Lab Relations (ACAS) NI; IOD; *Recreations* bridge, shooting, gardening; *Clubs* Brook's, Beefsteak, Pratts; *Style—* T C Stephenson, Esq; c/o Stephenson Cobbold Limited, 84 Palace Court, London W2 4JE (☎ 01 727 5335, 01 243 1383, fax 01 221 2628)

STEPHENSON, Timothy Hugh; JP (Sheffield); only s of Wiliam Raymond Shirecliffe Stephenson, himself 2 s of Sir Henry Stephenson, 1 Bt; hp to 1 cous, Sir Henry Stephenson, 3 Bt, TD; *b* 5 Jan 1930; *Educ* Eton; *m* 1959, Susan Lesley, yr da of

George Harris, of Sheffiedl; 2 s (Matthew b 1960, Oliver b 1962); *Clubs* Cavalry and Guards, The Sheffield; *Style*— Timothy Stephenson Esq, JP; Lomberdale Hall, Bakewell, Derbyshire

STEPHENSON, (Augustus) William; s of Sir Guy Stephenson, CB (d 1930), and Gwendolen, *née* Talbot (d 1961); *b* 1 Mar 1909; *Educ* Harrow; *m* 1, 18 April 1939 (m dis 1952), (Mary) Gloria, da of Maj William La Touche Congreve, VC, DSO, MC (ka 1917); 3 s (Tim b 1940, Martin b 1942, Ben b 1948); m 2, 21 Sept 1961, Elizabeth, da of Arthur James Whittall (d 1971); *Career* RE (TA) 1938, WWII Capt Welsh Gds in N Africa and Italy 1943-45; joined Whitbread & Co 1930 (mangr for Belgium 1935-38), ptnr James Capel & Co 1946-74; memb London Stock Exchange; *Clubs* Army and Navy, MCC; *Style*— William Stephenson, Esq; Saxbys Mead, Cowden, Edenbridge, Kent (☎ 034 286 520)

STERLING, (John) Adrian Lawrence; s of Francis Thomas Sterling (d 1942), of Melbourne, Aust, and Millicent Lloyd, *née* Pitt; *b* 17 April 1927; *Educ* Scotch Coll Melbourne, CEPS Mosman NSW, Barker Coll NSW, Univ of Sydney (LLB); *m* 6 Nov 1976, Caroline Snow, da of Octavius Samuel Wallace (d 1984), of Strabane, Co Tyrone; *Career* admitted to the Bar NSW Aust 1949, called to the Bar Middle Temple 1953, dep dir gen Int Fedn of Phonogram and Videogram Prodrs 1961-73; *Books* various pubns incl: The Data Protection Act (1984), Copyright Law in the UK and the Rights of Performers Authors and Composers in Europe (1986); *Recreations* reading, music; *Style*— JAL Sterling, Esq; Lamb Building, The Temple, London EC4Y 7AS (☎ 01 353 6701, fax 01 353 4686, telex 261 511 Jurist G)

STERLING, Sir Jeffrey Maurice; CBE (1977); s of Harry Sterling, and Alice Sterling; *b* 27 Dec 1934; *Educ* Reigate GS, Preston Manor County Sch, Guildhall Sch of Music; *m* 1985, Dorothy Ann, *née* Smith, 1 da; *Career* advsr Paul Schweder & Co (Stock Exchange) 1957-63, fin dir Gen Guarantee Corpn 1963-64, md Gula Investmts Ltd 1964-69, chm Sterling Guarantee Tst 1969- (merging with P & O 1985), memb British Airways Bd 1979-82; special advsr to Sec of State for Indust 1982-83 (to Sec of State for Trade and Indust 1983-), chm P & O Steam Navigation Co 1983-; chm: orgn ctee 1969-73 World chm ORT Union, ORT Tech Servs 1974; vice-pres Br ORT 1978-; dep chm and hon tres London celebrations ctee Queen's Silver Jubilee 1975-83; chm: Young Vic Co 1975-83; govrs Royal Ballet Sch 1983- (govr 1986-); vice-chm (later chm) of exec Motability 1977-; kt 1985; *Recreations* music, swimming, tennis; *Clubs* Garrick, Carlton, Hurlingham; *Style*— Sir Jeffrey Sterling, CBE; The Peninsular & Oriental Steam Navigation Company, Peninsular House, 79 Pall Mall, London SW1Y 5EJ (☎ 01 930 4343, telex 885551)

STERN, Dr Gerald Malcolm; s of Aaron Nathan Stern (d 1975), of London, and Rebecca, *née* Marks (d 1981); *b* 9 Oct 1930; *Educ* Thomas Parmiters Sch, London Hosp Med Coll (MB BS, MD); *m* 28 Sep 1962, Jennifer Rosemary, da of Maj Alfred Charles Pritchard (d 1974); 2 s (Robert Max James b 24 April 1965, Edward Gerald Matthew b 7 April 1972), 1 da (Melanie Rosemary b 6 July 1963); *Career* temp cmmn Surgn Lt RNVR 1956-58; sr conslt neurologist: UCH, Middlesex Hosp; hon conslt neurologist: Nat Hosp Nervous Diseases, St Luke's Hosp for the Clergy; memb: Assoc Br Neurologists 1964-, Assoc Physicians GB and Ireland, bd govrs Nat Hosp Nervous Diseases 1982-, exec bd Parkinson's Disease Soc; FRCP 1970 (memb cncl 1982); Ehrenmitgleid Osterreichishe Parkinson Gesellschaft (1986); *Books* Parkinson's Disease (1989); *Recreations* music, squash; *Clubs* Athenaeum; *Style*— Dr Gerald Stern; 17 Park Village West, Regent's Park, London NW1 (☎ 01 387 7514); 48 Wimpole St, London W1 (☎ 01 388 0640)

STERN, Michael Charles; MP (C) Bristol NW 1983-; s of Maurice Leonard Stern (d 1967), of Finchley, and Rose, *née* Dzialosinski; *b* 3 August 1942; *Educ* Christ's Coll GS Finchley; *m* 1976, Jillian Denise, da of Raymond Denis Aldridge, of York; 1 da (Katharine b 1980); *Career* ptnr: Halpern & Woolf 1980-; Percy Phillips & Co 1964-80; chm Bow Gp 1977-78; co-opted memb London Borough of Ealing Educn Ctee 1980-83; ACA FCA; *Recreations* fellwalking, bridge, chess; *Clubs* United & Cecil, Millbank, London Mountaineering; *Style*— Michael Stern Esq, MP; House of Commons, London SW1

STERN, Prof Nicholas Herbert; s of Adalbert Stern, and Marion Fatima, *née* Swann; *b* 22 April 1946; *Educ* Latymer Upper Sch, Cambridge Univ (BA), Oxford Univ (D Phil); *m* 7 Sept 1968, Susan Ruth, da of Albert Edward Chesterton (d 1978), of Pinner, Middx; 2 s (Daniel b 1979, Michael b 1980), 1 da (Helen b 1976); *Career* fell and tutor in econs St Catherine's Coll Oxford, lectr in industl maths Oxford Univ 1970-77, prof of econs Warwick Univ 1978-85, prof econs LSE 1986-; memb ctee Oxfam Africa 1974-79, memb Asia Ctee 1979, ed Jl of Public Econs 1981; Fell of Econometric Soc 1978; *Books* Crime, the Police and Criminal Statistics (with R Carr-Hill, 1979), Palanpur The Economy of an Indian Village (with C Bliss, 1982), The Theory of Taxation for Developing Countries (with D Newbery, 1987); *Recreations* walking, reading, watching football; *Style*— Prof Nicholas Stern; LSE, Houghton St, London WC2A 2AE (☎ 01 405 7686 ext 3037, fax 01 242 2357, telex 24655 BLPES G)

STERNBERG, Hon Francesca Nicola; da of Baron Plurenden (Life Peer; d 1978), and Baroness Plurenden, *qv*; *b* 1962; *Style*— The Hon Francesca Sternberg; Plurenden Manor, High Halden, Kent

STERNBERG, Michael Vivian; s of Sir Sigmund Sternberg, JP, *qv*, and Beartrice Ruth, *née* Schiff; *b* 12 Sept 1951; *Educ* Carmel Coll Wallingford, Queens' Coll Cambridge (MA, LLM); *m* 20 July 1975, Janine Lois, da of Harold Levinson; 1 s (Daniel Isaiah b 24 Sept 1982), 2 da (Rachel Serena b 2 Feb 1980, Sarah Jessica b 4 Jan 1988); *Career* called to the Bar Grays Inn 1975; asst sec Family Law Bar Assoc 1986-88; tstee: London Jewish East End Museum, Sternberg Charitable Settlement; Lloyds Underwriter 1978-, Freeman City of London Liverymans Horner's Co 1987; *Recreations* walking, reading, wine, theatre, amusing children; *Clubs* Reform, City Livery; *Style*— Michael Sternberg, Esq; 3 Dr Johnsons Bldgs, Temple, London EC4Y 7BA (☎ 01 353 4854, fax 01 583 8784)

STERNBERG, Hon Rosanne Monica Michelle; da of Baron Plurenden (Life Peer; d 1978), and Baroness Plurenden, *qv*; *b* 1960; *m* 21 June 1986, Robert William Kenneth Harris; *Career* farmer, co dir; *Recreations* horse breeding; *Style*— The Hon Rosanne Sternberg; Court Lodge Oast, Bodiam, Robertsbridge, East Sussex TN32 5UJ

STERNBERG, Sir Sigmund; JP (Middx 1965); s of Abraham Sternberg (d 1935), of Hungary; *b* 2 June 1921; *m* 1970, Hazel, da of Albert Everett-Jones; 1 s, 1 da, 1 step s, 1 step da; *Career* served WWII; chm: Martin Slowe Estates Ltd 1971-, ISYS plc 1973-; Lloyds underwriter 1969-; chm exec ctee Int Cncl of Christians and Jews, memb Bd of Deps of Br Jews, govr Hebrew Univ of Jerusalem, jt hon tres Cncl of Christians and Jews, co-chm Friends of Keston Coll; chm: Function Ctee Inst of Jewish Affairs, Friends of Oxford Centre of Post-Grad Hewbrew Studies; Judge Templeton Prize Fndn, speaker chm Rotary Club of London 1980-83; Freeman City of London, Liveryman Worshipful Co of London; Hon FRSM 1981, Brotherhood Award Nat Conf of Christians and Jews Inc 1980, Silver Pontifical Medal 1986; KCSG 1985, OStJ 1989; kt 1976; *Recreations* golf, swimming; *Clubs* Reform, Rotary, Livery; *Style*— Sir Sigmund Sternberg; The Steinbery Centre for Jerusalem, 80 East End Rd, London N 25Y (☎ 01 485 2538, fax, 01 485 4512)

STEVEN, Stewart Gustav; s of Rudolph Steven and Trude Steven; *b* 30 Sept 1938; *Educ* Mayfield Coll Sussex; *m* 1965, Inka; 1 s (Jack); *Career* political reporter, central press features 1961-63, political corr Western Daily Press 1963-64, Daily Express political reporter 1964-65, dip corr 1965-67, foreign ed 1967-72; Daily Mail: asst ed 1972-74 associate ed 1974-82; ed Mail on Sunday 1982; *Books* Operation Splinter Factor (1974), The Spymasters of Israel (1976), The Poles (1982); *Recreations* travel, skiing, writing; *Style*— Stewart Steven Esq; Northcliffe House, Tudor Street, London EC4Y 0JA (☎ 01 353 6000)

STEVENS, Alan Michael; s of Raymond Alfred George Stevens, of Bournemouth, and Joan Patricia, *née* Drury; *b* 8 April 1955; *Educ* Malvern, Selwyn Coll Cambridge (MA); *m* 2 May 1987, Lynn Sarah, da of Henry B Hopfinger, of Coventry; 1 da (Eloise b 1988); *Career* slr 1980, ptnr Linklaters and Paines 1987 (joined 1978); memb Law Soc, Freeman Worshipful Co of Slrs; *Recreations* tennis, skiing, water sports; *Clubs* David Lloyd Slazenger Racquet; *Style*— Alan Stevens, Esq; Putney, London; Linklaters and Paines, Barrington House, 59-67 Gresham St, London EC2V 7JA (☎ 01 606 7080, fax 01 606 5113, telex 884349/888167)

STEVENS, Anne Eileen; da of Wilfred Willett (d 1961), and Eileen Estelle Josephine, *née* Stenhouse (d 1961); *b* 6 May 1923; *Educ* St Clair Tunbridge Wells; *m* 1, Jan 1973, Roger Finney; 1 da (Elizabeth Anne); m 2, Sept 1947, James Palmer; m 3, Jan 1978, Ronald Stevens; *Career* fndr and md Consultus Servs Agency 1962-; *Recreations* gardening; *Style*— Mrs Anne Stevens; The Oast Cottage, Uckfield, E Sussex; Consultus Services Agency, 17 London Rd, Tonbridge, Kent (☎ 0732 355231)

STEVENS, Lady; (Frances) Anne; only child of Capt Christopher Hely-Hutchinson, MC (d 1958; himself 2 s of Rt Hon Sir Walter Hely-Hutchinson, GCMG, 2 s of 4 Earl of Donoughmore), and Gladys Beachy-Head (d 1974); *b* 20 May 1917; *Educ* Southover Manor, Lausanne; *m* 1940, Sir John Stevens, KCMG, DSO, OBE (d 1973), sometime exec dir Bank of England and md Morgan Grenfell; 1 s (John), 2 da (Jane, Mary Anne); *Career* Devon rep Nat Art Collection Fund 1977-88, memb Devon Ctee; *Recreations* music, gardening, poetry; *Clubs* Special Forces, Devon and Exeter Inst; *Style*— Lady Stevens; East Worlington House, Crediton, Devon (☎ 0884 860332)

STEVENS, Hon Corinne; da of Baron Mulley (Life Baron); *b* 1953; *m* 1983, Nicholas Stevens of Stafford; *Style*— The Hon Corinne Stevens

STEVENS, Derek George; s of George William Stevens (d 1967), of London, and Georgina, *née* Crisp (d 1987); *b* 28 Jan 1928; *Educ* Southall Co Sch, Coll of Estate Mgmnt; *m* 5 July 1952, Sheelah Kathleen, da of Frederick Roy Llewelyn Bishop (d 1988); 1 s (Neil Andrew b 1959), 1 da (Susan Elizabeth b 1965); *Career* Corpl RCS 1946-48; surveyor; pupil Frank & Rutley 1944 (various appts until 1969), sr ptnr Stickley & Kent 1969-87, conslt 1987-; London Borough of Harrow: cncllr 1967-72 (1978-86), alderman 1976-78, former chm Housing Ctee; memb NW Valuation Panel, chm and govr of three schs; FRICS; *Recreations* golf, swimming, reading, music; *Style*— Derek Stevens, Esq; 41 Bellfield Ave, Harrow, London (☎ 01 428 4048); Casa Caracus, Campo, Mijas, Spain; Stickley & Kent, Wells House, 80 Upper St, London N1 (☎ 01 226 1120, fax 01 226 5365, car tel 0836 227 470)

STEVENS, Eric Randolph; s of George Randolph Stevens, of Great Bookham, Surrey, and Olive Joyce, *née* Wordley; *b* 31 Dec 1939; *Educ* Dorking Co GS, Guildford Tech Coll; *m* 6 June 1964 (m dis 1979), Linda Kathleen, da of Arthur J Bentley; 1 s (Russel George b 1969), 1 da (Emma Rachel b 1967); *Career* chief engrg advsr Nat Petrochemical Co of Iran 1975-79, project engr Upper Zakum Oilfield Devpt Abu-Dhabi UAE 1979-84, sr mangr London Underground Ltd 1984-; former co chess player Durham & Surrey, capt Bandar Mahshar Cricket Team, winner All Iran Cricket Tournament 1978, Gulf Windsurfing Champion 1982, RYA windsurfing instr; MIStructE 1967; *Recreations* sailing, flying; *Clubs* Surrey CCC, Bewl Valley SC; *Style*— Eric Stevens, Esq; Burwash, E Sussex; Kingston-on-Thames, Surrey; London Underground Ltd, 55 Broadway, London SW1 OBD (☎ 01 724 5600, ext 56253)

STEVENS, Handley Michael Gambrell; s of Dr Ernest Norman Stevens, of Highcliffe, Dorset, and Dr Kathleen Emily Gambrell (d 1986); *b* 29 June 1941; *Educ* The Leys Sch, Phillips Acad Andover Mass, King's Coll Cambridge (MA); *m* 5 March 1966, Anne Frances, da of Robert Ross, of Evesbatch, Hereford, Worcester; 3 da (Hilary b 1970, Lucy b 1971, Mary b 1980); *Career* Dip Serv 1964-70 (Kuala Lumpur 1966-69); asst private sec Lord Privy Seal 1970-71; civil service 1970-73; DTI 1973-83, under-sec int aviation Dept of Tport 1983-; *Recreations* music, walking; *Style*— Handley M G Stevens, Esq; Dept of Transport, 2 Marsham St, London SW1 (☎ (01) 212 7668)

STEVENS, Hon Mrs (Henrietta Maria); *née* Hughes-Young; da of 1 Baron St Helens, MC (d 1980); *b* 1940; *m* 1970, Brian Turnbull Julius Stevens; *Style*— The Hon Mrs Stevens

STEVENS, Jocelyn Edward Greville; s of Maj (Charles) Greville Bartlett Stewart-Stevens, *née* Stevens, JP (d 1972, having m subsequently (1936) Muriel Athelstan Hood, *née* Stewart, 10 Lady of Balnakeilly, Perthshire. They adopted (1937) the name Stewart-Stevens). Jocelyn is maternal gs of Sir Edward Hulton (who owned the Evening Standard till 1923, when he sold it to 1 Baron Beaverbrook); *b* 14 Feb 1932; *Educ* Eton, Trinity Cambridge; *m* 1956 (m dis 1979), Jane Armyne, da of John Vincent Sheffield; 2 s, 2 da (*see* Delevingne, Charles); *Career* journalist, chm and md Stevens Press Ltd and ed of Queen Magazine 1957-68, dir Beaverbrook Newspapers 1971-77 (md 1974-77), md Evening Standard Co Ltd 1969-72, md Daily Express 1972-74, dep chm and md Express Newspapers 1977-81, dir Centaur Communications Ltd 1982-85, publisher and ed The Magazine 1982-84; govr: ICST 1985-, Winchester Sch of Art 1986-; rector and vice-provost RCA 1984-; FRSA; *Recreations* ski-ing; *Clubs* White's, Buck's, Beefsteak; *Style*— Jocelyn Stevens, Esq; Testbourne, Longparish, nr Andover, Hants SP11 6QT (☎ (026 472) 232); 14 Cheyne Walk, London SW3 5RA (☎ home 01 351 1141, work 01 584 5020)

STEVENS, Vice-Adm Sir John Felgate; KBE (1955, CBE 1945), CB 1951; s of

Henry Marshall Stevens (d 1953), of Droveway Corner, Hove, Sussex; *b* 1900; *m* 1928, Mary, da of J Harry Gilkes, JP of Wychote, Patcham, Sussex; 1 s, 2 da; *Career* Midshipman RN 1918, WWI and WWII (despatches), Capt 1940, cmd HMS Cleopatra 1942-43, Capt Coastal Forces Med 1943-45, dir of plans Admty 1945-47, Rear Adm 1949, COS to head of Br Jt Services Mission Washington 1950-52, Vice Adm 1952, flag offr Home Fleet Trg Sqdn 1952-53, C-in-C American and WI Station and Dep Supreme Allied Cdr Atlantic 1953-55, ret 1956; *Clubs* Naval and Military; *Style*— Vice-Adm Sir John Stevens, KBE, CB; Withy Springs, Petworth Road, Haslemere, Surrey (☎ (0428) 2970)

STEVENS, Lewis David; MBE (1982), MP (C) Nuneaton 1983-; *b* 13 April 1936; *Educ* Oldbury GS Worcestershire, Liverpool Univ, Lanchester Coll Coventry; *m* ;2 s, 1 da; *Career* mgmnt conslt; memb Nuneaton Borough Cncl 1966-72, Parly candidate (C) Nuneaton 1979; *Style*— Lewis Stevens, Esq, MBE, MP; 151 Sherbourne Avenue, Nuneaton CV10 9JN (☎ 0203 396105)

STEVENS, Patrick Tom; s of Tom Stevens, of Norfolk, and Gwendoline, *née* Nurse; *b* 21 August 1949; *Educ* Paston GS Norfolk; *m* 24 Aug 1973, Agnes; *Career* tax specialist Coopers & Lybrand 1975-79 (audit specialist 1972-75), sr tax ptnr Finnie & Co 1986- (tax ptnr 1979-86); sec Kytes Theatre Gp; FCA 1972, ATII 1975; *Recreations* theatre; *Style*— Patrick Stevens, Esq; 19 Risebridge Road, Gidea Park, Essex; Finnies & Co, Kreston House, 8 Gate St, London WC2A 3HJ (☎ 01 831 9100, fax 01 831 2666)

STEVENS, Peter Rupert; s of Surgn Capt R W Stevens RN; *b* 14 May 1938; *Educ* Winchester, Taft Sch (USA); *m* 1963, Sarah Venetia Mary, da of Air Vice-Marshal H A V Hogan, CB, DSO, DFC; 3 children; *Career* 2 Lt KRRC; stockbroker; sr ptnr Laurie Milbank 1981-86 (ptnr 1969-81), Head Sterling Fixed Interest and Int Chase Manhattan Gilts Ltd; memb Stock Exchange Cncl: memb 1974-87 and 1988-, dep chm 1988-, memb Bd of The Securities Assoc 1987-; *Recreations* cricket, tennis, gardening, country pursuits; *Style*— Peter Stevens, Esq; Highmead House, Alton, Hants GU34 4BN (☎ 0420 83945)

STEVENS, Richard; s of C E Stevens (d 1976), of Magdalen Coll, Oxford, and Leila, *née* Porter; *b* 9 Dec 1943; *Educ* Winchester, Univ of Cambridge (MA); *Career* investmt mangr; exec dir: Certa Investmt Mgmnt Ltd 1985-, Multitrust plc 1986-; ACIB; *Recreations* supporting Sunderland FC, railways, music, Georgian architecture; *Clubs* Carlton, Special Forces, IOD; *Style*— Richard Stevens, Esq; The Sheepcote, Bartestree, Hereford HR1 4DE (☎ 0432 850236); 30 Finsbury Circus, London EC2M 7QQ (☎ 01 489 0131, fax 01 256 7178, telex 945065)

STEVENS, William David; s of Walter G Stevens, of Corpus Christi, Texas, USA; *b* 18 Sept 1934; *Educ* Texas A & I Univ; *m* 1954, Barbara Ann, *née* Duncan; 4 children; *Career* mgmnt Exxon Co USA 1958-73, asst to pres Exxon 1974-75, dep mangr Producing 1976-78, vice-pres: Esso Gas 1978, Europe 1982; md Esso Petroleum Co Ltd 1978-82; *Recreations* golf, shooting, hiking; *Style*— William Stevens Esq; 24 Harley House, Marylebone Rd, London NW1 (☎ 01 935 6003)

STEVENSON, (William) Bristow; DL (1977); s of James Stevenson, JP, DL (d 1956), of Knockan, Feeny, Co Londonderry, and Kathleen Mary, *née* Young (d 1945); *b* 1 Nov 1924; *Educ* St Edward's Sch Oxford, Trinity Coll Oxford (MA); *m* 1, 25 Nov 1949 (m dis 1958), Barbara Stephanie Boyd, da of Sir William Angus Boyd Iliff, CMG, MBE (d 1974); 2 s (Adrian b 1950, Peter b 1952); m 2, 15 Nov 1958, Julia Heather Margaret , da of Lt-Col Gualter Hugh Rodger Bellingham Somerville, MC; 2 s (James b 1963, Henry b 1970), 1 da (Diana b 1961); *Career* WWII Lt RNVR: Atlantic and Russian Convoys, D Day; slr 1950; farmer; chllr Diocese of Derry and Raphoe 1975-; lay hon sec gen Synod of Church of Ireland; pres: Ulster Ram Breeders Assoc, City of Londonderry Slrs Assoc; chm Londonderry Feis; High Sheriff Co Londonderry 1971; pres Mental Health Review Tbnl (NI); formerly NI rep on Hill Farming Advsy Ctee; assessor Gen Synod of the Church of Ireland; underwriting memb of Lloyds 1980; vice chm of govrs Foyle & Londonderry Coll; *Recreations* golf, shooting; *Clubs* Northern Counties Londonderry, Naval; *Style*— Bristow Stevenson, Esq, DL; Knockan, Feeny, Co Londonderry (☎ 0504 781265); Court Chambers, 25D Bishop St, Londonderry (☎ 0504 363131/362858)

STEVENSON, Vice Adm Sir (Hugh) David; AC (1976), KBE (1977, CBE 1970); s of Rt Rev William Henry Webster Stevenson (d 1945), and Katherine Saumarez Stevenson (d 1955); *b* 24 August 1918; *Educ* Southport Sch Qld, RAN Coll, HM Navigation Sch, RN Staff Coll, IDC; *m* 1, 1944, Myra Joyce Clarke (d 1978), da of Marie Clarke; 1 s, 1 da; m 2, 1979, Margaret Lorraine, da of Lila Wheeler; *Career* served WWII; naval offr i/c WA 1967-68, chief of Naval Staff 1973-76, ret; dir Queen Elizabeth Silver Jubilee Tst for Young Australians 1977, conslt Aust Bicentennial Authy, dir Canberra YMCA; *see Debrett's Handbook of Australia and New Zealand for further details*; *Style*— Vice Adm Sir David Stevenson, AC, KBE; 4 Charlotte St, Red Hill, ACT 2603, Australia (☎ (062) 95 6172)

STEVENSON, (Henry) Dennistoun; CBE (1981); s of the Alexander James Stevenson, of Scotland, and Sylvia Florence, *née* Inglby; *b* 19 July 1945; *Educ* Edinburgh Acad, Glenalmond, Kings Coll Cambridge; *m* 15 Feb 1972, Charlotte Susan, da of Air Cdre Hon Sir Peter Beckford Rutgers Vanneck, GBE, CB, AFC, 4 s (Alexander, Heneage, Charles, William); *Career* chm: SRU Gp (founded 1972), Aycliffe & Peterlee Corpn 1972-81, Nat Assoc of Youth Clubs 1972-80; dir: Br Technol Gp 1979-, London Docklands Devpt Corpn 1981-88, Tyne Tees TV 1982-87; chm Intermediate Technol Devpt Gp 1984-; dir: Pearson plc 1988-, Blue Arrow plc 1988-; chm Tstees of Tate Gallery 1989-; *Recreations* tennis, violin, reading; *Clubs* MCC, Brooks's; SRU Ltd, 78/80 St John St, London EC1M 4HR (☎ 01 250 1131, fax 01 608 0089)

STEVENSON, Dr Derek Paul; CBE (1972); s of Frederick Paul Stevenson (d 1949), and Blanch Maud, *née* Coucher (d 1948); *b* 11 July 1911; *Educ* Epsom Coll, Univ of London and Guys Hosp; *m* 10 May 1941, Pamela Mary, da of Lt-Col Charles Jervelund, OBE (d 1962); 2 s (John b 1944, Timothy b 1948), 1 da (Wendy b 1942); *Career* regular offr RAMC, MO Sandhurst, overseas serv: Malaya, Singpore, China; Capt 1937, WWII served BEF 1939-40, Adj RAMC depot 1940-42, WO 1942-46, Maj 1942, Lt-Col 1943, asst dir gen Army Med Servs WO 1943; sec BMA 1958-76, chm cncl World Med Assoc 1969-71, vice-pres Private Patients Plan, conslt Med Insur Agency; ccncllr West Sussex CC 1980- 85, Chichester Local Health Authy 1983-85, Med Servs Bd 1977-79, Hon LLD Univ of Manchester 1964; MRCS, LRCP, BMA; *Recreations* golf, gardening; *Clubs* Athenaeum; *Style*— Dr Derek Stevenson, CBE; Bodrigy, Hollycombe, Liphook, Hants GU30 4LR (☎ 0428 724205)

STEVENSON, (Donald) Maylin; s of Donald Robert Louis Stevenson (d 1962), of Doncaster, S Yorks, and Idonea Maylin, *née* Vipan (d 1982); *b* 19 Nov 1932; *Educ* Oundle, St Johns Coll Cambridge (MA); *m* 6 June 1981, Veronica Jane, da of Reginald Stephen Loaring (d 1983), of St Peter Port, Guernsey; *Career* Nat Serv 2 Lt E Yorks Regt, Capt W Yorks Regt TA; slr 1959, ptnr Williams Thompson & Co Slrs Christchurch 1975-87 (conslt 1987-); *Recreations* sailing, history; *Clubs* Christchurch Sailing; *Style*— Maylin Stevenson, Esq; Laurel Bank, Croft Rd, Bransgore, Christchurch, Dorset (☎ 0425 725 46); Bridge Ho, Castle St, Christchurch, Dorset (☎ 0202 484 242)

STEVENSON, Robert Wilfrid (Wilf); s of James Alexander Stevenson, and Elizabeth Anne, *née* Macrae; *b* 19 April 1947; *Educ* Edinburgh Acad, Univ Coll Oxford (BA), Napier Poly pt/t (ACCA); *m* 15 April 1972 (m dis 1979), Jennifer Grace, da of David Grace Antonio (d 1986), of Edinburgh; *Career* res offr Edinburgh Univ Students Assoc 1970-74, sec Napier Poly Edinburgh 1974-87, dir Br Film Inst 1988- (dep dir 1987-88); *Recreations* cinema, hill walking, bridge; *Style*— Wilf Stevenson, Esq; 21 Stephen St, London W1P 1PL (☎ 01 255 1444, fax 01 436 7950, telex 27624 BFILDNG)

STEVENSON, Samuel; s of Samuel Stevenson, of Castle Donington, Derby, and Gladys, *née* Daniel; *b* 14 Mar 1933; *Educ* Charterhouse; *m* 18 Dec 1986, Christine Rosemary Nessa, da of Sidney Galkin, of Ruislip, Middx; *Career* Nat Serv Sub Lt RN; ptnr Arthur Young 1962-69; md: Gartmore Investmt Ltd 1969-83, C S Investmt 1983; Freeman City of Glasgow 1935, memb Inc Wrights and Grand Antiquities Soc; MICAS; *Recreations* golf; *Clubs* Brooks's, City of London, MCC; *Style*— Samuel Stevenson, Esq; 149 Pavilion Rd, London SW1X 0BJ (☎ 01 235 6238); C S Investments, 125 High Holborn, London WC1V 6PY (☎ 01 242 1148, fax 01 831 7187, telex 291986)

STEVENSON, Cdr Shannan; s of Ronald Cochran Stevenson (d 1934); *b* 9 Mar 1903; *Educ* RNC Osborne and Dartmouth; *m* 1929, Daphne Evelyn da Capt Albert Edward House (d 1957); 4 s; *Career* joined RN 1916, Cdr RN WWII; md North of England Newspaper Co Ltd 1950-68, dir Westminster Press Provincial Newspapers Ltd 1953-68, pres The Newspaper Soc 1964, High Sheriff Co Durham 1963; *Style*— Cdr Shannan Stevenson; Bolton Old Hall, Bolton-on-Swale, Richmond, N Yorks (☎ 0748 811315)

STEVENSON, Sir Simpson; s of Thomas Henry Stevenson of Greenock; *b* 18 August 1921,, Greenock; *Educ* Greenock HS; *m* 1945, Jean Holmes, da of George Henry; *Career* chm Western Regnl Hosp Bd 1968-74, memb Inverclyde DC 1974-; chm: Scottish Health Servs Common Agency 1973-77, Gt Glasgow Health Bd 1973-, Consortium of Local Authorities Special Programme 1974; memb Royal Cmmn on NHS 1976-79; Hon LLD Glasgow 1982; kt 1976; *Style*— Sir Simpson Stevenson; The Gables, 64a Reservoir Road, Gourock, Renfrewshire (☎ 0475 31774)

STEVENSON, Hon Mrs; Hon Susan Mary; *née* Blades; da of 2 Baron Ebbisham, TD; *b* 1951; *m* 1980, Peter D Stevenson, 1 s (George b 1987), 1 da (Mary b 1984); *Style*— The Hon Mrs Stevenson; 29 Warriston Crescent, Edinburgh EH3 5LB

STEWARD, Rear Adm Cedric John; CB (1984); s of Ethelbert Harold Steward (d 1977), and Anne Isabelle, *née* West (d 1986); *b* 31 Jan 1931; *Educ* Northcote Coll Auckland, Britannia RNC Dartmouth, Greenwich Naval Coll, JSSC, RCDS; *m* 1952, Marie Antoinette, da of Arthur Gordon Gurr (d 1951), of Sydney, NSW; 3 s (Mark, Bretton, John); *Career* staff Royal Aust Naval Coll Jervis Bay 1959-62, dep head NZ Defence Liaison Staff Canberra 1969-73, Capt 11 Frigate Sqdn 1974-75, dep chief of naval staff 1979-81, Cdre Auckland 1981-83, chief of naval staff 1983-86; proprietor: Fontainebleau Int 1986-, Antric Park Horse Stud 1986-; *Recreations* philately, boating, golf, tennis, equestrian, fishing; *Clubs* Helensville Golf, Auckland RC (Ellerslie); *Style*— Rear Adm Cedric Steward

STEWARD, Maj Charles Anthony (Tony); s of Capt Charles Knowles Steward, DSO, MC (d 1929), and Cunitia Charlotte Atwood, *née* Morris, JP (d 1957); *b* 22 June 1919; *Educ* Rugby, RMC Sandhurst; *m* 16 Aug 1941, Feridah Lucretia Mary, da of Lt-Col Edward Francis Jenico Joseph Farrell, JP, DL (d 1951), of Walterstown, Moynalty Kells, Co Meath, Ireland; 1 s (Charles b 26 May 1951), 1 da (Valerie b 8 May 1942); *Career* cmmnd 9 Queens Royal Lancers 1939; WWII served: France 1940, Western Desert 1941, Persia and Iraq 1942-43, India and Burma 1944-45; Staff Coll Camberley 1949, Bde Maj 7 Armd Bde 1950-51, Regtl serv 1952-53, MOD 1954-55, US Cmd and Gen Staff Coll 1956-57, HQ BAOR 1957-59, MOD 1959-60, HQ 1 (Br) Corps 1961-63, ret 1963; cncllr Wintney RDC 1969-73; Hart DC 1969-73: chm planning 1973-75, vice chm 1976-77, chm 1978-79; fndr and chm Crondall Soc, memb local ctee cncl for the Protection of Rural Eng, community advsr Crondall Parish; *Recreations* shooting, game fishing; *Style*— Maj Tony Steward; The Platt, Crondall, Farnham, Surrey GU10 5NY (☎ 0252 850288)

STEWARD, Stanley Feargus; CBE (1947); s of Arthur Robert Steward (d 1964), of Mundesley, Norfolk, and Minnie Elizabeth; *b* 9 July 1904; *Educ* The Paston Sch Norfolk; *m* 1929, Phyllis Winifred, da of late J Thurlow, of Stowmarket, Suffolk; 1 s, 1 da; *Career* chartered engr; dir-gen machine tools Miny of Supply 1941-45, dir Bull Motors Ltd 1937-47; chm: South Western Electricity Bd 1948-55, Lancashire Dynamo Gp 1956-59; md Br Electrical and Allied Mfrs Assoc 1959-71; chm: William Steward & Co Ltd, George Thurlow & Sons Ltd, Thurlow Nunn & Sons Ltd; dir: ERA Technol Ltd, Bull Motors Ltd; pres: Organisation de Liaison des Industries Metalliques Européennes 1963-66, Electrical Industs Benevolent Assoc and Assoc of Supervisory and Exec Engrs 1971-73, Inst of Engr-in-Charge 1982-84; Master Worshipful Co of Glaziers & Painters of Glass 1964; CEng, FIProdE; master, Worshipful Co of Glaziers & Painters of Glass (1964); CEng, FIProdE; *Books* Electricity Manufacture in the National Economy (1961), Electricity and Food Production (1965), Twenty Five Years of South Western Electricity (1973), The Story of Electrex (1983), The Dynamicables (1983); *Recreations* books, music, watching cricket; *Clubs* Athenaeum, MCC; *Style*— Stanley Steward, Esq, CBE; 41 Fairacres, Roehampton Lane, London SW15 (☎ 01 876 2457)

STEWART; *see*: Shaw-Stewart

STEWART, Sir Alan D'Arcy; 13 Bt (I 1623), of Ramelton, Co Donegal; s (by 1 m) of Sir Jocelyn Harry Stewart, 12 Bt (d 1982); *b* 29 Nov 1932; *Educ* All Saints, Bathurst NSW; *m* 1952, Patricia, da of Lawrence Turner; 2 s, 2 da; *Heir* s, Nicholas Courtney D'Arcy Stewart b 1953; *Career* yacht builder, marine engr; *Style*— Sir Alan Stewart, Bt; One Acre House, Church st, Ramelton, Co Donegal

STEWART, Sheriff Alastair Lindsay; s of Alexander Lindsay Stewart (d 1977); *b* 28 Nov 1938; *Educ* Edinburgh Acad, St Edmund Hall Oxford, Edinburgh Univ; *m* 1968,

Annabel Claire, da of Prof William McCausland Stewart; 2 s; *Career* tutor faculty law Edinburgh Univ 1963-73, standing jr cncl Registrar of Restrictive Trading Agreements 1968-70, advocate depute 1970-73; Sheriff: South Strathclyde, Dumfries and Galloway at Airdrie 1973-79, Grampian, Highland and Islands at Aberdeen 1979-; govr Robert Gordon's Inst of Technol 1982-; chm: Grampian Family Conciliation Serv 1984-87, Scottish Assoc of Family Conciliation Servs 1986-; *Recreations* reading, music; *Style—* Sheriff Alastair Stewart; 131 Desswood Place, Aberdeen (☎ 0224 644683); Sheriff's Chambers, Sheriff Court House, Aberdeen (☎ 0224 572780))

STEWART, Alexander Donald; DL (Perthshire 1988); s of John Alexander McLaren Stewart TD, JP, DL (d 1985), of Ardvorlich, Lochearnhead, Perthshire, and Violet Hermione, *née* Cameron (d 1979); *b* 18 June 1933; *Educ* Wellington, Oxford Univ (BA), Edinburgh Univ (LLB); *m* 4 Dec 1970, Virginia Mary, da of Capt Peter Washington (d 1983), of Pine Farm, Wokingham, Berks; 1 s (James b 1980) 5 da (Sophie b 1972, Emily b 1974, Theresa b 1976, Catrina b 1978, Petra b 1982); *Career* admitted slr (WS) 1961; ptnr McGrigor Donald Glasgow 1965-; dir: Clyde Cablevision Ltd 1984-, Scottish Amicable Life Assur Soc 1986-; *Recreations* field sports, winter sports, music; *Clubs* Puffin's; *Style—* Alexander Stewart, Esq, DL WS; Ardvorlich, Lochearnhead, Perthshire (☎ 05673 218); c/o McGrigor Donald, Pacific House, 70 Wellington Street, Glasgow G2 6SB (☎ 041 248 6677, fax 041 221 1390)

STEWART, (John) Allan; MP (C) Eastwood 1983-; s of Edward MacPherson Stewart by his w Eadie Barrie; *b* 1 June 1942; *Educ* Bell Baxter HS (Cupar), St Andrews Univ, Harvard; *m* 1973, Susie (Marjorie Sally), *née* Gourlay; 1 s, 1 da; *Career* lectr political economy St Andrews Univ 1965-70; with CBI 1971-78: head regnl devpt dept 1971-73, dep dir econs 1974, Scottish sec 1974, Scottish dir 1978; cncllr Bromley 1975-76; Parly candidate (C) Dundee East 1970, MP (C) Renfrewshire E 1979-1983; memb select ctee Scottish Affrs, parly under-sec Scottish Off 1981-86 (responsibility for home affrs and environment in Scottish Office April 1982), Scottish min Industry and Educn 1983-86; *Recreations* golf, bridge; *Style—* Allan Stewart, Esq, MP; 34 Rowan Rd, Dumbreck, Glasgow G41 5BZ (☎ (041) 427 2178)

STEWART, Andrew Struthers; MP (C) Sherwood 1983-; *b* 1937; *Educ* Strathaven Acad Lanark, West of Scotland Agric Coll; *Career* memb Nottinghamshire CC 1974-; memb: Parly select ctee for Agric 1985-, all pty ctee on Textiles; memb Cons Pty ctees on Energy and Agric; PPS to Min of Agric John MacGregor; *Style—* Andrew Stewart, Esq, MP; House of Commons, London SW1

STEWART, Dowager Lady; Avril Veronica; *née* Gibb; o da of late Andrew Adamson Gibb, of Glasgow; *m* 1980, as his 2 w, Sir James Watson Stewart, 4 Bt (d 1988); *Career* FRSA, Hon FBID, Hon MASC; *Clubs* Royal Scottish Automobile; *Style—* The Dowager Lady Stewart; Undercliff Court, Wemyss Bay, Renfrewshire PA18 6AL (☎ 0475 521019)

STEWART, Dr (George) Barry; s of Robert Temple Stewart, of 319 Ryhope Road, Sunderland, Tyne and Wear, and Sarah Alice, *née* Robson; *b* 3 Sept 1943; *Educ* Robert Richardson GS, Nottingham Univ (LLB), Fitzwilliam Coll and Inst of Criminology, Cambridge Univ (Dip Crim, JD); *Career* barr Grays Inn 1968, attorney and cnsllr at Law Federal Cts USA, memb of Bar of NY 1987; head of chambers, sr memb of Cleveland Bar; Methodist preacher, Danby circuit N Yorks accredited 1964;; *Recreations* reading, foreign travel; *Style—* G Barry Stewart, Esq; Ridge Hall, Ridge Lane, Staithes, Saltburn-by-the-Sea, Cleveland TS13 5DX (☎ 0947 840511); 71A Borough Rd, Middlesbrough, Cleveland TS1 3AA (☎ 0642 226036)

STEWART, Brian Alexander; s of Alexander Bellamy Stewart (d 1977), of West Ridge, Walpole Ave, Chipstead, Coulsdon, Surrey, and Jessie, *née* Hopkins; *b* 7 May 1926; *Educ* Stowe, Trinity Coll Cambridge; *Career* Nat Serv REME 1947-50 (cmmnd Capt, WRS i/c basic section electronics wing REME Trg Centre); memb Lloyds 1949, dir Stewart & Hughman Ltd 1955-87 (joined 1950); dir until 1987: Stewart Grays Inn, Rockall Underwriting Agency, Peninsula Underwriting Agency, Walrond Scarman, Trojan Underwriting Agency; chm River Clyde Hldgs plc until 1988; cdre Lloyds YC, dep chm In Sail Trg Assoc 1974- (chm schooner ctee 1966-85); *Recreations* sailing; *Clubs* Lloyds YC, Royal Thames YC, Royal Ocean Racing; *Style—* Brian Stewart, Esq; (☎ 0836 251706, fax 0737 557759)

STEWART, Callum John Tyndale; s of Air Vice-Marshal William K Stewart CB, CBE, AFC, QHP (d 1967), of Farnborough, Hants, and Audrey Wentworth, *née* Tyndale (who m2 1970, Sir Bryan Harold Cabot Matthews, CBE (d 1986); *b* 2 Feb 1945; *Educ* Wellington Coll; *m* 18 July 1975 (m dis 1982), Elaine Alison, da of Francies Bairstow (d 1979); *Career* exec dir Bland Welch & Co Ltd 1963-72; dir; CE Heath (Int) Ltd 1972-75, Fielding & Ptnrs 1975-86 (dep chm 1984-86), CE Heath plc 1986-; *Recreations* tennis, jogging, antiques; *Style—* Callum Stewart, Esq; Flat 5, 8 Chelsea Embankment, London SW3 (☎ 01 488 1488); La Petite Tourraque, Bastide Blanche, Ramatuelle, France; c/o CE Heath plc, Cuthbert Heath House, 150 Minories, London EC3M 1NR

STEWART, Prof (William Alexander) Campbell; DL (1972); s of Thomas Stewart (d 1921); *b* 17 Dec 1915; *Educ* Colfe's GS, London Univ; *m* 1947, Ella Elizabeth, *née* Burnett; 1 s, 1 da; *Career* schoolmaster 1938-44, univ lectr (Nottingham and Wales) 1944-50, univ prof Keele 1950-67, vice-chllr Keele Univ 1967-79 (emeritus prof 1979-); fell UCL 1974; *Books* Quakers and Education (1953), Progressives and Radicals in English Education 1750-1970 (1972), Higher Education in Postwar Britain (1989); *Recreations* music, theatre; *Clubs* Oriental; *Style—* Prof Campbell Stewart, DL; Flat 4, 74 Westgate, Chichester, West Sussex PO19 3HH

STEWART, Colin MacDonald; CB (1983); s of John Stewart, of Glasgow, and Lillias Cecilia MacDonald Fraser; *b* 26 Dec 1922; *Educ* Queens Park Secdy Sch; *m* 1948, Gladys Edith, da of Ernest Alfred Thwaites, of Barnet, Herts; 3 da; *Career* WWII clerical offr Admty Rosyth Dockyard 1939-42, Fleet Air Arm 1942-46, med serv with 809 Sqdn followed by staff posts in Scotland, Lt (A) RNVR; directing actuary Govt Actuary's Dept 1974-84 (joined 1946); assoc dir (actuarial res) Godwins Ltd 1985-88; FIA 1953; *Books* The Students' Socy Log 1960-85; *Recreations* genealogical research; *Style—* Colin Stewart, Esq, CB; 8 The Chase, Coulsdon, Surrey CR3 2EG (☎ 01 660 3966)

STEWART, Air Vice-Marshal Colin Murray; CB (1962), CBE (1952, OBE 1945); s of Archie Stewart, of Sherborne, Dorset; *b* 17 June 1910; *Educ* Wycliffe Coll Stonehouse Glos; *m* 1940, Anthea, da of Maynard Loveless, of Stockbridge, Hants; 4 s; *Career* joined RAF 1932, served 5 Sqdn NWF India and 16 Sqdn at home, specialised in signals 1937, served WWII (despatches), CSO various formations at home and in Europe; chm: Br Jt Communications Bd 1952-55, Communications Electronics Ctee of Standing Gp Washington 1955-57; AOC 27 Gp 1957-58, cmd electronics offr Fighter Cmd 1958-61, dir-gen of signals Air Miny 1961-64, STSO Fighter Cmd 1964-67, SASO Tech Trg Cmd 1967-68, ret 1968; controller computing servs Univ of London 1968-73; *Recreations* fishing, gardening; *Style—* Air Vice-Marshal Colin Stewart, CB, CBE; Byelanes, Moult Rd, Salcombe, S Devon TQ8 8LG (☎ 054 884 2042)

STEWART, Lady (Christine) Daphne; *née* Hay; da of 11 Marquess of Tweeddale (d 1967), and Marguerite Christine (d 1946), da of Alexander Ralli and step da of Lewis Einstein; *b* 29 Mar 1919; *Educ* at home; *m* 1, 1939 (m dis 1947), Lt-Col David Morley-Fletcher, OBE, TD, yr s of Bernard Morley Morley-Fletcher; 1 s, 1 da; m 2, 1957, Lt-Col Francis Robert Cameron Stewart, late Indian Army, s of late Sir Francis Hugh Stewart, CIE; *Recreations* breeding ponies; *Style—* Lady Daphne Stewart; Middle Blainslie, by Galashiels, Selkirkshire (☎ (089 686) 217)

STEWART, Sir David Brodribb; 2 Bt (UK 1960) of Strathgarry, Co Perth; TD (1948); s of Sir Kenneth Dugald Stewart, 1 Bt, GBE (d 1972), and Noel, *née* Brodribb (d 1946); *b* 20 Dec 1913; *Educ* Marlborough, Manchester Coll of Technol (BSc); *m* 14 Sept 1963, Barbara Dykes, da of late Harry Dykes Lloyd, and wid of Donald Ian Stewart; *Heir* bro, Robin Alastair Stewart, *qv*; *Career* cmmd into TA 1934, served WWII France and Belgium 1940 and Italy, cmd Duke of Lancaster's Own Yeo 1952-56, ret as Bt-Col 1956; md Francis Price (Fabrics) Ltd, ret 1981; *Recreations* gardening; *Style—* Sir David Stewart, Bt, TD; Delamere, Heyes Lane, Alderley Edge, Cheshire SK9 7JY (☎ 0625 582312)

STEWART, David Charles; s of Andrew Graham Stewart (d 1964), of Corsliehill, Houston, Renfrewshire, and Barabel Ethel, *née* Greig (d 1985); *b* 23 June 1936; *Educ* Winchester, Trinity Coll Cambridge (BA); *m* 16 Nov 1978, Wendy Ann, da of John McMillan (d 1951), of Kingswood, Surrey; 1 s (Jonathan b 1979), 3 da (Tara b 1981, Serena b 1983, Fleur (twin) b 1983); *Career* Nat Serv 2 Lt Royal Scots Greys 1956-57; dir: The Victaulic Co Ltd 1965, Stewarts and Lloyds Plastics Ltd 1965; md Victaulic plc 1983-; *Style—* David Stewart, Esq; The Brewery House, Old, Northamptonshire (☎ 0604 781 577); Victaulic plc, 382 Silbury Boulevard, Milton Keynes, Bucks (☎ 0908 691 000)

STEWART, David Howat; s of William Gray Stewart (d 1980), and Helen Dorothy, *née* Howat (d 1986); *b* 27 Oct 1945; *Educ* Grangefield GS Stockton-on-Teas; *m* 1, 14 Sept 1968 (m dis 1985), Gillian; 2 da (Caroline b 1977, Sarah b 1982); m 2, 19 Aug 1985, Susan Andrea, da of Brig George Laing, CBE (ADC to HM th Queen 1962, d 1986); 1 s (Harry b 1985); *Career* National Westminister Bank Gp 1963-70, exec dir County Natwest Ltd 1970-87, gen mangr and chief exec Creditanstalt-Bankverein 1987-; ACIB 1967; *Recreations* music; *Style—* David Stewart, Esq; 29 Gresham St, London EC2V 7AH (☎ 01 822 2600, fax 01 822 2663, telex 894 612)

STEWART, Capt David John Christopher; s (by 1 m) and h of Sir Hugh Charlie Godfray Stewart, 6 Bt of Athenree; *b* 19 June 1935; *Educ* Bradfield, RMA Sandhurst; *m* 7 Nov 1959, Bridget Anne, er da of late Patrick Wood Sim; 3 da; *Career* Capt (ret) Royal Inniskilling Fus (seconded Trucial Oman Scouts); sometime dir Maurice James (Hldgs) Ltd, currently fundraiser Taunton Constituency Cons Assoc; *Clubs* MCC; *Style—* Capt David Stewart; Tower View, 8 Silver St, Wilveliscombe, Somerset

STEWART, David Purcell; s of Maurice Edward Stewart (d 1967), of Epsom, Surrey, and Joyce Ethel, of Worthing, Sussex; *b* 8 Sept 1941; *Educ* Rutlish Sch Merton Park; *m* 14 Sept 1968, Judith Esther, da of Charles Owen (d 1983), of Bexleyheath; 1 da (Susannah Celia b 23 April 1977); *Career* Deloitte Haskins & Sells (formerly Harmood Banner) 1958-: ptnr 1967-, ptnr for nat tax 1982-, ptnr for corp strategy 1986-; Freeman City of London 1982; FCA 1963, FCCA 1981, FIOD 1982; *Recreations* numismatics, theatre, opera; *Clubs* RAC, MCC; *Style—* David Stewart, Esq; The Oast House, Best Beech, Wadhurst, Sussex TN5 6JH; Deloitte Haskins & Sells, 128 Queen Victoria St, London EC4 (☎ 01 248 3913)

STEWART, Rt Hon Donald James; PC (1977), MP (SNP) Western Isles 1970-87; *b* 17 Oct 1920; *Educ* Nicolson Inst Stornoway; *m* 1955, Christina Macaulay; *Career* provost of Stornoway 1958-64 and 1968-70; Hon Sheriff 1960; memb cncl Get Britain Out (EEC), ldr Parly SNP 1974-87; *Style—* The Rt Hon Donald Stewart; Hillcrest, 41 Goathill Rd, Stornoway, Isle of Lewis (☎ 0851 2672)

STEWART, Sir Edward Jackson; s of Charles Jackson Stewart (d 1954), and Jessie, *née* Dobbie (d 1976); *b* 10 Dec 1923; *Educ* St Joseph's Coll Brisbane; *m* 1956, Shirley Patricia, da of James Harvy Holmes (d 1956); 4 s; *Career* company dir; chm and dir Stewarts Hotels Pty Ltd 1956-, nat pres Aust Hotels Assoc 1965-67, memb Totalisator Admin Bd of Qld 1977-81, cncllr Qld Inst Med Res 1979-, chm Qld Inst of Med Res Tst 1980-, dir Besser (Qld) Ltd 1981-87; kt 1980; *see Debrett's Handbook of Australia and New Zealand for further details*; *Style—* Sir Edward Stewart; 34 Charlton St, Ascot, Qld 4007, Australia

STEWART, Ewen; s of late Duncan Stewart, of Kinlocheil, and Kate, *née* Blunt; *b* 22 April 1926; *Educ* Edinburgh (BSc, MA, LLB); *m* 1959, Norma Porteous, da of late William Charteris Hollands, of Earlston; 1 da; *Career* agric economist E of Scotland Coll of Agric 1946-49, practised at Scottish Bar 1952-62, lectr on agric law Edinburgh Univ 1957-62, former standing jr counsel Miny of Fuel and Power; Parly candidate (Lab) 1962; Sheriff: Wick Caithness 1962-, Dornoch 1977-, Sutherland, and Tain Ross and Cromarty 1977-; *Style—* Ewen Stewart, Esq; Rose Cottage, Swiney, Lybster, Caithness, Highlands KW3 6BT

STEWART, Hon Mrs (Frances Julia); da of Baron Kaldor (Life Peer); *b* 1940; *m* 1962, Michael John Stewart; *Style—* The Hon Mrs Stewart; 39 Upper Park Rd, NW3

STEWART, Prof Sir Frederick Henry; s of Frederick Stewart and Hester, *née* Alexander; *b* 16 Jan 1916; *Educ* Fettes, Aberdeen Univ (BSc), Emmanuel Coll Cambridge (PhD); *m* 1945, Mary Rainbow (the writer Mary Stewart); *Career* former chm: NERC, advsy bd for the Res Cncls; regius prof geology Edinburgh Univ 1956-82; tstee Br Museum (Natural History) 1983-87; Hon DSc: Aberdeen, Leicester, Heriot Watt, Durham, Glasgow; FRS, FRSE, FGS; kt 1974; *Style—* Prof Sir Frederick Stewart; 79 Morningside Park, Edinburgh (☎ 031 447 2620); House of Letterawe, Lochawe, Argyll (☎ 083 82 329)

STEWART, George Girdwood; CB (1979), MC (1945), TD (1954); s of Herbert Alexander Stewart (d 1966), and Janetta Dunlop, *née* Girdwood; *b* 12 Dec 1919; *Educ* Kelvinside Academy Glasgow, Glasgow Univ, Edinburgh Univ (BSc); *m* 1950, Shelagh Jean Morven, da of Dr R R Murray; 1 s (Alan b 1955), 1 da (Sarah b 1953); *Career* Cmd Offr 278 (L) Field Regt RA (TA) 1957-60; forestry cmmr 1969-79; pres Scottish Ski Club 1971-75, vice-pres Nat Ski Fedn of GB 1975-78; rep Nat Tst for Scotland

Perth 1980-; memb: environment panel BR Bd 1980, Countryside Cmmn for Scotland 1981-; chm Scottish Wildlife Tst 1981-87, memb Cairngorm Recreation Tst 1986; FICFor, Hon FLI; *Recreations* skiing, tennis, studying Scottish painting; *Clubs* Ski Club of Great Britain, Royal Perth Golfing Soc; *Style—* George Stewart, Esq, CB, MC, TD; Branklyn House, Dundee Rd, Perth PH2 7BB (☎ 0738 25535)

STEWART, George Rex; s of John Stewart (d 1931); *b* 8 May 1912; *Educ* Macdonalds, Rutherglen Acad; *m* 1939, Margaret Elizabeth, *née* Murray; *Career* chm: Rex Stewart & Associates Ltd UK, Int Markets Advertising Assoc Inc (New York); *Recreations* golf, opera; *Clubs* Caledonian, RSA, 21 Walton Heath, Gullane Golf; *Style—* George Stewart, Esq; Breezes, Bear Hill, Oxshott, Surrey (☎ 037 284 2848)

STEWART, Gordon; s of Archibald Leitch Stewart, of Luton, Beds, and Christina Macpherson, *née* Taylor (d 1976); *b* 18 April 1953; *Educ* Luton GS, Univ of Durham (BA); *m* 2 Oct 1982, Teresa Violet, da of Sir James Holmes Henry, Bt, CMG, MC, TD, QC, of Hampton, Middx; 2 s (Edmund James b 24 May 1985, Roland Valentine b 16 Jan 1988); *Career* asst slr Slaughter and May 1978-83 (articled 1976), ptnr Simmons & Simmons 1985- (asst slr 1983-85); memb Law Soc; *Style—* Gordon Stewart, Esq; 7 Vanbrugh Fields, Blackheath, London SE3 7TZ (☎ 01 858 9417); 14 Dominion St, London EC2M 2RJ (☎ 01 628 2020, fax 01 588 4129, telex 888562 SIMMON G)

STEWART, (George Robert) Gordon; OBE (1983), WS (1949); s of Capt David Gordon Stewart, MC (d 1967), of Edinburgh, and Mary Grant, *née* Thompson (d 1954); *b* 13 Oct 1924; *Educ* George Watson's Coll Edinburgh, Univ of Edinburgh (MA, LLB); *m* 11 Oct 1952, Rachel Jean, da of Maj John Baxter Morrison (d 1960), of Edinburgh; 2 s (Robert Ian David b 1956, John Douglas b 1961), 1 da (Gillian Mary Jean b 1954); *Career* volunteered Royal Scots 1942, transferred RCS 1944, WWII Burma India Sumatra SEAC, Capt 1946; slr 1951, ptnr Melville & Lindesay WS Edinburgh 1951-56 (legal asst 1949-50), Notary Puclib 1952; sec and personnel dir Ideal Standard Ltd Yorks 1975-76 (asst sec 1956-75), legal advsr Inst of CA of Scotland 1985- (sec 1976-85); memb Law Soc; *Recreations* pot gardening, music, walking; *Clubs* Royal Scots (Edinburgh); *Style—* Gordon Stewart, Esq, OBE, WS; 15 Hillpark Loan, Edinburgh EH4 7BH (☎ 031 312 7079)

STEWART, Gordon William; CVO (1964); s of James Edward Stewart (d 1913); *b* 13 April 1906; *Educ* Daniel Stewart's Coll, George Heriot's Sch Edinburgh; *m* 1935, Dorothy Swan, *née* Taylor; *Career* asst gen mangr BR Scotland 1956, chm and gen mangr BR 1967-71, chm and md Br Tport Ship Mgmnt 1967-71, dir Br Tport Hotels Ltd 1968-71; *Recreations* golf, gardening; *Style—* Gordon Stewart, Esq, CVO

STEWART, Prof Harold Charles; CBE (1975), DL (Greater London 1967); s of Dr Bernard Halley Stewart (d 1958); s of Sir Halley Stewart, and Mabel Florence Wyatt (d 1968); *b* 23 Nov 1906; *Educ* Mill Hill, Cambridge, Univ Coll Hosp; *m* 1, 1929, Dorothy Irene, *née* Löwen (d 1969); 1 s (Ian Halley Stewart, MP, *qv*), 1 da; m 2, 1970, Audrey Patricia Nicolle, da of Edward le Vavasour dit Durell Nicolle (d 1981), of Jersey; *Career* head pharmacology dept St Mary's Hosp Med Sch 1950-74, emeritus prof of pharmacology 1974-; conslt MOD 1961-74, Gresham prof in physic City of London 1968-70; dir gen St John Ambulance 1976-78, KStJ 1969; chm: Sir Halley Stewart Tst for Res 1978-, Buttle Tst for Children 1979-; vice-chm Med Cncl Alcoholism and St Christopher's Hosp for Terminal Cases; Guthrie Memorial Medal for distinguished services to MOD (Army) 1974; *Recreations* genealogy, heraldry, voluntary work; *Clubs* Athenaeum, St John House; *Style—* Prof Harold Stewart, CBE, DL; 41 The Glen, Green Lane, Northwood, Middx (☎ 65 248 93)

STEWART, Sir Hugh Charlie Godfray; 6 Bt (UK 1803) of Athenree, Tyrone; DL (Tyrone 1971); s of Sir George Powell Stewart, 5 Bt (d 1945), and Florence Georgina, *née* Godfray (d 1957); *b* 13 April 1897; *Educ* Bradfield Coll Berkshire, RMC Sandhurst; *m* 1, 1929 (m dis 1942) Rosemary Elinor Dorothy, da of late Maj George Peacocke; 1 s, 1 da; m 2, 1948, Diana Margaret, da of late Capt J E Hibbert, MC, DFC; 1 s Hugh b 1955), 1 da (Jane b 1949); *Heir* s by 1 m, Capt David Stewart; *Career* 1914-18 war in France (wounded, first battle Arras 1917), 1939-45 war in France, and as Asst Cmdt Imperial Forces Transhipment Camp, Durban and in Syria; Maj Royal Inniskilling Fusiliers, ret 1945; High Sheriff Tyrone 1955; *Clubs* Tyrone County; *Style—* Sir Hugh Stewart, Bt, DL; Cottesbrook, Sandy Pluck Lane, Bentham, Cheltenham

STEWART, Rt Hon (Bernard Harold) Ian Halley; RD (1972), PC (1989), MP (C) North Hertfordshire 1983-; s of Prof Harold Stewart, CBE, DL, *qv*, and his 1 w Dorothy, *née* Löwen (d 1969); *b* 10 August 1935; *Educ* Haileybury, Jesus Coll Cambridge (MA); *m* 1966, Deborah Charlotte, JP, da of Hon William Buchan (2 s of 1 Baron Tweedsmuir, otherwise known as John Buchan, the author); 1 s, 2 da; *Career* served RNVR 1954-56, Lt-Cdr RNR; with Seccombe Marshall & Campion (bill brokers) 1959-60; dir: Brown Shipley & Co (merchant bankers) 1971-83 (joined 1960, asst mangr 1963, mangr 1966), Brown Shipley Hldgs 1981-83, Victory Insur 1976-83; MP (C) Hitchin Feb 1974-83; oppn spokesman Banking Bill 1978-79, PPS to Geoffrey Howe (as Chllr Exchequer) 1979-83, under-sec MOD (Def Procurement) Jan-Oct 1983, econ sec Treasury with special responsibility for monetary policy and fin insts 1983-87, min of State for the Armed Forces 1987-88, min of state NI 1988-; former jt-sec Cons Parly Fin Ctee and memb Public Expenditure Ctee; FBA 1981, FRSE 1986, FSA, FSA Scotland, CStJ (and v-pres St John Ambulance Herts 1978-); memb Br Acad Ctee Sylloge Coins of Br Isles 1967-, vice-chm Westminster Ctee Protection Children 1975-, vice-pres Herts Soc 1974-; memb cncl Haileybury 1980- (life govr 1977); tstee Sir Halley Stewart Tst 1978-; LittD 1978; *Recreations* history, tennis; *Clubs* MCC, Hawks; *Style—* The Rt Hon Ian Stewart, RD, MP; House of Commons, London SW1

STEWART, Ian William; s of late Rev William Stewart; *b* 24 Mar 1923; *Educ* Merchiston Castle; *m* 1953, Jane Alison, *née* Cunningham; 2 c; *Career* Flt Offr Italy; dir William Low & Co Ltd 1952-88, dep chm William Low & Co plc 1982-88; pres Dundee & Tayside C of C 1983-84; *Recreations* shooting, golf, music; *Clubs* New (Edinburgh), Panmure Golf; *Style—* Ian Stewart, Esq; Greenbank, Barry, Carnoustie, Angus (☎ 0241 53043)

STEWART, James Cecil Campbell; CBE (1960); s of late James Stewart, and Mary Stewart; *b* 25 July 1916; *Educ* Armstrong Coll, King's Coll Durham Univ; *m* 1946, Pamela Rouselle, da of William King-Smith; 1 da; *Career* Telecommunication Res Estab 1939-45, AERE Harwell 1946-49, Industl Gp Risley 1949-63, bd memb of UKAEA and CEGB 1963-69, dir of Nat Nuclear Corpn Ltd 1969-82, conslt chm Br Nuclear Forum 1974-, chm NNC Pension Tstee Ltd 1979-; *Recreations* tending a garden; *Clubs* East India, Les Ambassadeurs; *Style—* James Stewart, Esq, CBE; Whitethorns, Higher Whitley, Warrington, Cheshire WA4 4QJ (☎ 0925 73377)

STEWART, James Harvey; s of Harvey Stewart, of Fochabers, Moray, and Annie, *née* Gray; *b* 15 August 1939; *Educ* Peterhead Acad, Univ of Aberdeen (MA), Univ of Manchester (Dip Soc Admin); *m* 24 April 1965, Fiona Maria Maclay, da of John Reid (d 1973), of Peterhead; 3 s (Iain b 1969, Alasdair b 1972, Gordon b 1974), 1 da (Marie b 1966); *Career* hosp sec Princess' Margaret Rose Orthopaedic Hosp Edinburgh 1965-67, princ admin asst York A Hosp Mgmnt Ctee 1967-68, dep gp sec York A HMC 1968-73, area admin Northumberland AHA 1973-83, dist admin Northumberland Health Authy 1982-83, regnl admin E Anglian RHA 1983-85, dist gen mangr Barking Havering and Brentwood Health Authy 1985-; sr vice-pres York Jr Chamber 1973 (jr vice-pres 1972); AHSM; *Recreations* music, reading, squash, rugby, food, wine; *Clubs* Rotary, Cambridge RUFC, Cambridge Univ RUFC; *Style—* James Stewart, Esq; The Grange, Harold Wood Hosp, Gubbins Lane, Romford RM3 0BE (☎ 04023 495 11, fax 04023 813 68)

STEWART, James Simeon Hamilton; QC (1982); s of Henry Hamilton Stewart (d 1970), and Edna Mary, *née* Pulman; *b* 2 May 1943; *Educ* Cheltenham, Leeds Univ (LLB); *m* 19 April 1972, Helen Margaret, da of (Thomas) Kenneth Whiteley; 2 da (Alexandra b 18 Jan 1974, Georgina b 27 Nov 1975); *Career* barr Inner Temple 1966, practising N Eastern circuit and London, rec of Crown Ct 1982-; *Recreations* cricket, gardening, tennis; *Clubs* Bradford, Leeds Taverners; *Style—* James Stewart, Esq, QC; Park Court Chambers, 40 Park Cross St, Leeds S1 2QH (☎ 0532 433277, fax 0532 421285, telex 666135)

STEWART, John Anthony Benedict; CMG (1979), OBE (1973); s of Edward Vincent Stewart (d 1974), and Emily Veronica, *née* Jones (d 1988); *b* 24 May 1927; *Educ* St Illtyd's Coll, Univ of Wales, Univ of Cambridge, Imp Coll of Science and Technol (MA, BSc, DIC); *m* 1960, Geraldine Margaret, o da of Captain G C Clifton (d 1975); 2 s (Anthony, 1 s decd), 1 da (Drusilla); *Career* RNVR Midshipman 1944-47; geologist Somaliland Protectorate 1952-56, Anglo Ethiopian Liaison serv 1957-60, (sr liaison offr 1960), dist offr N Rhodesia 1960 (dist cmmnr 1962-64), resident local govt offr Barotseland 1964-67; HM Dip Serv 1968, served FCO Barbodas, Uganda, RCDS 1974, HM ambass to Democratic Rep of Vietnam 1975-76, head of Hong Kong dept FCO 1976-78; HM ambass: Laos 1978-80, Mozambique 1980-84; high cmmnr to Sri Lanka 1984-87; ret 1987; *Publications* The Geology of the Mait Area (1955), papers in geological journals; *Recreations* shooting, fishing, flying light aeroplanes; *Clubs* Royal Cwlth, Flyfishers, Guildford County; *Style—* J A B Stewart, Esq, CMG, OBE; c/o Westminster Bank, Guildford, Surrey GU13 3AB; FCO, London SW1A 2AH

STEWART, Dr John Simon Watson; s and h of Sir (John) Keith Watson Stewart, 5 Bt; *b* 5 July 1955; *Educ* Uppingham, Charing Cross Hosp Med Sch (MRCP, FRCP); *m* 1978, Catherine Stewart, da of Gordon Bond, of Shiplake, Oxon; 1 s (John Hamish Watson b 12 Dec 1983), 1 da (Anna Rebecca Watson b 1 May 1987); *Style—* Dr John Stewart; 52 Grosvenor Road, London W4

STEWART, Capt John Stephen; OBE; s of William Stewart, JP (d 1987), of Weston Underwood, Bucks, and Theresa, *née* Daniels (d 1948); *b* 14 July 1922; *Educ* Clifton Coll Bristol, Univ of London Med Sch; *m* 15 July 1954, Eileen Mary, da of John Ryan Lahiff (d 1966), of Preston, Lancs; 3 s (Hugh b 1955, Mark b 1956, Kevin b 1959), 1 da (Isabel b 1958); *Career* RM: 2 Lt 1941, Commando Ser Europe 1942-48 (twice wounded), Adj RMB Chatham and Estney 1948-51, SRMO HMS Implacable Home Fleet Trg Sqdn 1951-53, 45 RM Commando serv Malta and Cyprus (invalided blast injuries), ret 1956; farmer Weston Underwood Bucks 1956-80, dir Nuffield Farming Scholarships Tst 1969-89; chm: Milton Keynes Gen Cmmn of Tax, Arthritis & Rheumatisim Cncl Olney and Dist; Life memb Int Wine and Food Soc (chm and sec Northampton, chm Strasbourg Conf); Nuffield Scholars Beef Prodn Europe 1964, Winston Churchill fell Liveryman Husbandry NZ 1974; Freeman City of London, Liveryman Worshipful Co Farmers 1974; FRAgS 1986; *Recreations* travel by car and caravan, wine and food, reading, watching sport; *Clubs* Farmers'; *Style—* Capt John Stewart, OBE; The Mill House, Olney, Bucks MK46 4AD (☎ 0234 711 381, fax 0234 712 095)

STEWART, John Young (Jackie); OBE (1972); s of Robert Paul Stewart (d 1972), and Jean Clark Young; *b* 11 June 1939; *Educ* Dumbarton Acad; *m* 1962, Helen McGregor; 2 s (Paul b 1965, Mark b 1968); *Career* memb Scottish and Br Team for Clay Pigeon Shooting; former Scottish, English, Irish, Welsh and Br Champion, won Coupe des Nations 1959 and 1960; first raced 1961, competed in 4 meetings driving for Barry Filer Glasgow 1961-62, drove for Ecurie Ecosse and Barry Filer winning 14 out of 23 starts 1963, 28 wins out of 53 starts 1964, drove Formula 1 for Br Racing Motors (BRM) 1965-67, for Ken Tyrrell 1968-73, has won Australian, NZ, Swedish, Mediterranean, Japanese and many other non-championship maj int motor races; set new world record by winning his 26 World Championship Grand Prix (Zandvoort) 1973, 27 (Nürburgring) 1973, third in World Championship 1965, second in 1968 and 1972, World Champion 1969, 1971, 1973; Br Automobile Racing Club Gold Medal 1971 and 1973, Daily Express Sportsman of the Year 1971 and 1973; BBC Sports Personality of the Year 1973, Segrave Trophy 1973; Scottish Sportsman of the Year 1973, USA Sportsman of the Year 1973; film: Weekend of a Champion 1972; *Books* World Champion (with Eric Dymock 1970), Faster! (with Peter Manso, 1971), On the Road (1983), Jackie Stewart's Principles of Performance Driving (with Alan Henry, 1986); *Recreations* tennis, shooting; *Clubs* RAC, RSAC, Br Racing Drivers', Royal and Ancient Golf (St Andrews), Scottish Motor Racing; *Style—* Jackie Stewart, Esq; 24 Rte de Divonne, 1260 Nyon, Switzerland (☎ GVA (022) 61 01 52, telex 419922)

STEWART, Sir (John) Keith Watson; 5 Bt (UK 1920), of Balgownie, Bearsden, Co Dumbarton; yr s of Sir James Watson Stewart, 3 Bt (d 1955); suc bro Sir James Watson Stewart, 4 Bt (d 1988); *b* 25 Feb 1929; *Educ* Uppingham, RMA Sandhurst; *m* 7 May 1954, Mary Elizabeth, er da of John Francis Moxon, of Horton Hall, Leek, Staffs; 2 s (John Simon Watson, James Watson b 1960), 1 da (Caroline Felicity Watson (Mrs Niel Barry Solomons) b 1958); *Heir* s, John Simon Watson Stewart, *qv*; *Career* Capt Scottish Horse TA (ret); memb Stock Exchange; *Clubs* Cavalry and Guards; *Style—* Keith Stewart, Esq; 10 Foster Road, Chiswick, London W4 4NY

STEWART, Malcolm; s (by 2 m) of Sir (Percy) Malcolm Stewart, Bt, OBE (d 1951) and hp of half-bro Sir Ronald Compton Stewart, 2 Bt; *b* 20 Dec 1909; *Educ* Harrow, Brasenose Coll Oxford; *m* 1935 (m dis 1957), Mary Stephanie, da of Frederick Ramon de Bertodano, 8 Marquis del Moral (Spain); *Career* European War 1942-45 as Lt RNVR; *Style—* Malcolm Stewart, Esq; Hoy Lodge, Orkney

STEWART, Lady Mary Florence Elinor; da of Frederick Albert Rainbow (d 1967), and Mary Edith, *née* Matthews (d 1963); *b* 17 Sept 1916; *Educ* Eden Hall Sch Penrith Cumberland, Skellfield Sch Topcliffe Yorks, Univ of Durham (BA, MA); *m* 24 Sept 1945, Sir Frederick Henry Stewart, *qv*, s of Frederick Robert Stewart (d 1974); *Career* pt/t ROC 1941-45; lectr in english Univ of Durham 1941-45 (pt/t lectr 1945-56), novelist 1954-, hon fell Newnham Coll Cambridge 1986; *Books* Madam Will You Talk? (1954), Wildfire at Midnight (1956), Thunder on the Right (1957), Nine Coahes Waiting (1958), My Brother Michael (1959), The Ivy Tree (1961), The Moonspinners (1962), This Rough Magic (1964), Airs Above the Ground (1965), The Gabriel Hounds (1967), The Wind off the Small Isles (1968), The Crystal Cave (1970, Frederick Niven Award), The Little Broomstick (1971), The Hollow Hills (1973), Ludo and the Star Horse (1974, Scottish Arts Cncl Award), Touch Not the Cat (1976), The Last Enchantment (1979), A Walk in Wolf Wood (1980), The Wicked Day (1983), Thornyhold (1988); *Recreations* gardening, painting, music; *Clubs* New (Edinburgh); *Style*— Lady Stewart; c/o Hodder and Stoughton Ltd, 47 Bedford Sq, London WC1B 3DD

STEWART, Michael James; s of John Innes MacIntosh Stewart, of Huddersfield, Yorks, and Margaret, *née* Hardwick (d 1979); *b* 6 Feb 1933; *Educ* St Edward's Sch Oxford, Magdalen Coll Oxford (BA, MA); *m* 23 June 1962, Hon Frances Julia, da of Baron Kaldor, FBA (Life Peer d 1986); 1 s (David b 1974), 3 da (Lucy b 1964, Anna b 1966, d 1978, Kitty b 1970); *Career* econ advsr HM Treasy 1961-62 (econ asst 1957-60), sr econ advsr Cabinet Off 1967 (econ advsr 1964-67), econ advsr Kenya Treasy 1967-69, reader in political econ UCL 1969-, special advsr to Foreign Sec 1977-78; *Books* Keynes and After (1967), The Jekyll and Hyde Years (1977), Controlling the Economic Future (1983), Apocalypse 2000 (with Peter Jay, 1987); *Recreations* looking at paintings, eating in restaurants; *Clubs* United Oxford and Cambridge Univ; *Style*— Michael Stewart, Esq; 79 South Hill Park, London NW3 2SS (☎ 01 435 3686); University Coll London, Gower St, London WC1E 6BT (☎ 01 387 7050 ext 2287)

STEWART, Sir Michael Norman Francis; KCMG (1966, CMG 1957), OBE (1948); s of Sir Francis Hugh Stewart, CIE (d 1921); *b* 18 Jan 1911; *Educ* Shrewsbury, Trinity Coll Cambridge; *m* 1951, Katharine Damaris, da of late Capt C H du Boulay, RN; 1 s, 2 da; *Career* asst keeper V & A 1935-39, seconded Miny of Info 1939-41, transferred FO 1941, cnsllr Ankara 1954-59, chargé d'affaires Peking 1959-62, chief civilian instr IDC 1962-64, min Br Embassy Washington 1964-67, ambass Greece 1967-71, dir Ditchley Fndn 1971-76, dir Sotheby's 1977-; *Style*— Sir Michael Stewart, KCMG, OBE; Combe, Nr Newbury, Berks

STEWART, Dame Muriel Acadia; DBE (1968); da of late James Edmund Stewart; *b* 22 Oct 1905; *Educ* Gateshead GS, Durham Univ (BA); *Career* teacher: Newcastle-upon-Tyne 1927-29, Northumberland 1929-70; nat pres Nat Union of Teachers 1964-65, headmistress Shiremoor Middle Sch 1969-70; chm Schools Cncl 1969-72, vice-chm Bullock Ctee 1972-74; Hon MEd Newcastle Univ; *Style*— Dame Muriel Stewart, DBE; 44 Caldwell Rd, Gosforth, Newcastle upon Tyne, NE3 2AX

STEWART, Norman Macleod; s of George Stewart (d 1965), and Elspeth, *née* Stewart (d 1982); *b* 2 Dec 1934; *Educ* Elgin Acad, Univ of Edinburgh (BL); *m* 17 July 1959, Mary Slater, da of William Campbell (d 1977); 4 da (Gillian b 1961, Alison b 1964, Carol b 1967, Morag b 1969); *Career* asst slr Alex Monison and Co Edinburgh 1957-58; Allen Black and McCaskie Elgin: asst slr 1959-61, ptnr 1961-, now sr ptnr; pres Edinburgh Univ Rotary Club of Moray, former pres Elgin Rotary Club, former chm Moray Crime Prevention Panel, former sec Lossimouth and Hensbruck (Barania) Twin Town Assoc, former tres Moray GC; The Law Soc of Scot: cncl memb 1976-89, convenor public rels cmmn 1979-81, convenor professional practice cmmn 1981-84, vice pres 1984-85, pres 1985-86; hon memb American Bar Assoc (1985); memb: Law Soc of Scot, Int Bar Assoc, Cwlth Lawyers Assoc, cncl Soc of Slrs in the Supreme Ct (Scot); *Recreations* travel, music, golf, Spain and its culture; *Clubs* New (Edinburgh); *Style*— Norman Stewart, Esq; Argyll Lodge, Lossiemouth, Moray (☎ 0343 813150); 151 High St, Elgin, Moray (☎ 0343 3355, fax 0343 49667)

STEWART, Richard; CBE (1976), JP; s of Richard Stewart (d 1964), and Agnes, *née* Cunningham (d 1945); *b* 27 May 1920; *Educ* Harthill Sch, Strathclyde Univ; *m* 1942, Elizabeth, da of George Dryborough Peat (d 1983); 1 da (Agnes Ann); *Career* former memb Lanark CC for (chm several ctees finally chm social work ctee); full-time sec and organiser Lab Pty 1950-84; former agent for: Rt Hon Miss Margaret Herbison, Rt Hon John Smith MP 1970-85; memb bd of dirs Scottish Tport Gp 1975-88; ldr of admin Strathclyde Regnl Cncl 1974-86; vice-pres Convention of Scottish Local Authys 1982-84 (pres 1984-86); former chm: Scottish Cncl of Lab Party, Nat Union of Lab Organisers; Hon LLD Strathclyde Univ; *Recreations* music, chess; *Style*— Richard Stewart, Esq, CBE, JP; 28 Hawthorn Drive, Harthill, Lanarkshire ML7 5SG; (☎ 0501 51303)

STEWART, Col Robert Christie; CBE (1983), TD (1962); s of Maj Alexander C Stewart, MC (d 1927), of Arndean, by Dollar, Scotland, and Florence Hamilton, *née* Lighton (d 1982); *b* 3 August 1926; *Educ* Eton, Oxford Univ (BA, MA); *m* 21 May 1953, Ann Grizel, da of Air Chief Marshal Hon Sir Ralph Alexander Cochrane, GBE, KCB, AFC (d 1977); 3 s (Alexander, John, David), 2 da (Catriona (Mrs Marsham), Sara); *Career* Lt Scots Guards 1944-49, 7 Bn Argyll and Sutherland Highlanders TA 1951-65, Lt Col 1963-66, Hon Col 1/51 Highland Volunteers 1972-75; landowner; memb Palin and Kinross CC 1953-75 (chm 1963-73), chm and pres bd of govrs East of Scotland Coll of Agric 1970-83; Lord Lt of Kinross-shire 1966-74; *Recreations* shooting, golf, the country; *Clubs* Royal Perth Golfing Soc; *Style*— Col Robert Stewart, CBE, TD; Arndean, Dollar, Scotland (☎ 025 942 527)

STEWART, Robin Milton; QC (1978); s of Brig Guy Milton Stewart (d 1943), and Dr Elaine Oenone Stewart, MD, *née* Earengey; *b* 5 August 1938; *Educ* Winchester, New Coll Oxford (MA); *m* 8 Sept 1962, Lynda Grace, da of Arthur Thomas Albert Medhurst (d 1976); 3 s (Andrew Douglas Lorn b 1964, James Milton b 1966, Sholto Robert Douglas b 1969); *Career* barr Middle Temple 1963, Kings Inns Dublin 1975; prosecuting counsel to Inland Revenue (NE circuit) 1976-78, rec Crown Ct 1978-, bencher Middle Temple 1988; former memb Hexham UDC and Tynedale DC; Parly candidate (C) Newcastle-upon-Tyne West 1974; Freeman City of London, Liveryman Worshipful Co of Glaziers 1986; *Recreations* gardens, silver, pictures, opera, Scottish family history; *Clubs* Oriental; *Style*— R M Stewart, Esq, QC; South Garth, Tockwith, York YO5 8PY (☎ 0423 358754); 13 Denbigh Rd, London W11 2SJ (☎ 01 221 5179); 2 Harcourt Bldgs, Temple, London EC4Y 9DB (☎ 01 353 1394, fax 01 353 4134)

STEWART, Sir Ronald Compton; 2 Bt (UK 1937) of Stewartby, Co Bedford; DL (1974); s of Sir (Percy) Malcolm Stewart, 1 Bt, OBE (d 1951); *b* 14 August 1903; *Educ* Rugby, Jesus Coll Cambridge; *m* 1936, Cynthia Alexandra, OBE, JP (d 1987), da of Harold Farmiloe (d 1987); *Heir* half-bro, Malcolm Stewart; *Career* High Sheriff Bedfordshire 1954; *Style*— Sir Ronald Stewart, Bt, DL; Maulden Grange, Maulden, Bedfordshire

STEWART, Sinclair Shepherd; s of Harold Sinclair Stewart (d 1960), of Dolphin Rd, Glasgow, and Frances Marjorie Stewart, of Melville St, Glasgow; *b* 10 Mar 1938; *Educ* Glasgow HS; *m* 1961, Avril Marjorie, da of John William Gillott; 2 s, 1 da; *Career* 2 Lt RA; dep md Foote Cone & Belding Ltd 1977-82; md Richard Heath Ltd 1971-74, chm Underline Ltd 1977-82; dep chm Bounty Services Ltd 1982-84, dir Waveney Catering Ltd 1982-, chm Bounty Services Ltd 1984-; *Recreations* trout fishing, gardening; *Clubs* Flyfishers'; *Style*— Sinclair Stewart, Esq; 2 Mornington, New Rd, Digswell, Welwyn (☎ 043 871 6509); Bounty Services Ltd, 140A Gloucester Mansions, Cambridge Circus, London WC2

STEWART, Victor Colvin; s of Victor Colvin Stewart (d 1963), of Selkirk, and Jean Cameron Stewart (d 1969); *b* 12 April 1921; *Educ* Selkirk HS, Edinburgh Univ (BCom); *m* 1949, Aileen, da of Walter Laurie (d 1953), of Edinburgh; 1 s (Laurie); *Career* RAF (FO) Africa & ME 1942-46; joined Scottish Off 1938: chief exec offr 1959, princ 1963, asst sec 1971, dep registrar gen for Scotland 1976, registrar gen for Scotland 1978-82; FCA; *Recreations* golf, walking; *Clubs* Royal Cwlth Soc; *Style*— V Colvin Stewart, Esq; Tynet, Lodgehill Road, Nairn IV12 4QL (☎ 0667 52050)

STEWART, Hon Mrs; Hon Virginia; *née* Galpern; da of Baron Galpern (Life Peer); *b* 1941; *m* 1968, Alan John Stewart; *Style*— The Hon Mrs Stewart; The Dower House, Shillinglee Park, Chiddingfold, Surrey

STEWART, Hon Mrs (Zoë Leighton); *née* Seager; da of 1 Baron Leighton of St Mellons, CBE (d 1963); *b* 28 April 1928; *m* 1, 1955, Malcolm James Peniston (d 1981); 1 s (Douglas), 2 da (Angela, Rosemary); m 2, 1984, Alan Carnegie Stewart; *Style*— The Hon Mrs Stewart; Westwood, Hardgate, Castle Douglas, Kirkcudbrightshire DG7 3LD (☎ 055 666 215)

STEWART LOCKHART, Christopher Hallimond; s of Cdr Charles Stewart Lockhart, DSC, RN (d 1963), and Eileen Norton Hallimond (d 1976); *b* 14 July 1922; *Educ* Marlborough; *m* 1951, Kermode, da of Rev Sir William Kermode Derwent, KCMG; 1 s, 1 da; *Career* chm Br-American Tobacco Co Ltd until 1983; dir: BAT Industries plc until 1983, Mardons Packaging Int Ltd, G Percy Trentham Ltd 1983-; *Clubs* MCC; *Style*— Christopher Stewart Lockhart Esq; 108 Oakwood Ct, London W14 8JZ (☎ 01 602 2279); Hop Garden Cottage, Church Rd, Didcot, Oxon (☎ 0235 850513); G Percy Trentham Ltd, Pangbourne, Reading, Berks (☎ 073 57 3333)

STEWART OF DALBUIE, George Prince McKean; s of George Stewart (d 1942), of Bothwell, Lanarkshire, and Eileen Eva, *née* Atkinson (d 1942); *b* 2 Nov 1925; *Educ* Glenalmond, Glasgow Univ (MA); *m* 17 July 1952, Jean Thomson, da of John McNaught (d 1971); 2 s (George b 1953, Roderick b 1961), Ann (b 1956); *Career* served in RNAS 1943-47; dir: Alexander Dunn Ltd 1958-70, Airdun Ltd 1970-; gen mangr Creda Ltd (Glasgow) 1987-, dir Midscot Trg Servs Ltd 1987-; *Recreations* gardening, watercolours, antiquities; *Style*— George Stewart of Dalbuie; Dalbuie, Southend, Argyll; Creda Ltd, Airdun Works, Bothwell Road, Uddington, Glasgow G71 7EX (☎ 0698 816331, fax 0698 818032, telex 776429)

STEWART OF FULHAM, Baron (Life Peer UK 1979); (Robert) Michael Maitland Stewart; CH (1969), PC (1964); s of Robert Wallace Stewart, DSc (d 1910); *b* 6 Nov 1906; *Educ* Christ's Hosp, St John's Coll Oxford (hon fellow 1965); *m* 1941, Baroness Stewart of Alvechurch (d 1984); *Career* MP (Lab): East Fulham 1945-55, Fulham 1955-79; sec state: Educn and Science 1964-65, Foreign Affrs 1965-66, Econ Affrs 1966-67; first sec state 1967-68, sec state Foreign and Cwlth Affrs 1968-70; MEP 1975-76; Freeman London Borough of Hammersmith and Fulham 1967; Hon LLD Leeds 1966, Hon DSc Benin 1972; *Books* British Approach to Politics (1938), Modern Forms of Government (1959), Life and Labour (autobiography) 1980; *Recreations* painting; *Style*— The Rt Hon the Lord Stewart of Fulham, CH, PC; 11 Felden St, London SW6 (☎ 01 736 5194)

STEWART-CLARK, Alexander Dudley; s and h of Sir John Stewart-Clark, 3 Bt, MEP, *qv*; *b* 21 Nov 1960; *Educ* Worth Abbey; *Career* dir Douglas Timber Ltd; *Books* Hydroscopics of Oak (1987); *Recreations* rugby, tennis; *Style*— Alexander Stewart-Clark, Esq; Puckstye House, nr Cowden, Kent TN8 7ED; 28 Edgeley Road, London SW4 6ES

STEWART-CLARK, Jane, Lady; Jane Pamela; da of Maj Arundell Clarke, of Fremington House, N Devon; *m* 1927, Sir Stewart Stewart-Clark, 2 Bt (d 1971); 1 s (Sir John, 3 Bt), 1 da (Mrs Patrick Bowlby); *Style*— Jane, Lady Stewart-Clark; Dundas Castle, S Queensferry, W Lothian

STEWART-CLARK, Sir John (Jack); 3 Bt (UK 1918), of Dundas, W Lothian; MEP (EDG) E Sussex 1979-; s of Sir Stewart Stewart-Clark, 2 Bt (d 1971); *b* 17 Sept 1929; *Educ* Eton, Balliol Coll Oxford, Harvard Business Sch; *m* 1958, Jonkvrouwe Lydia Fredericke, da of Jonkheer James William Loudon, of The Netherlands; 1 s, 4 da; *Heir* s, Alexander Stewart-Clark; *Career* late Coldstream Gds; Parly candidate (C & U) Aberdeen N 1959; tres EDG 1979-, memb Economic and Monetary Ctee, chm EP Delgn to Canada 1979-82, vice-chm EP Delgn to Japan 1986-, spokesman Int Affairs 1983-85; dir: Oppenheimer Int Ltd until 1984, Low & Bonar 1982-, Cope Allman Int Ltd until 1983; AT Kearney Mgmnt Conslts 1985-; memb bd Tstee Savings Bank Scotland 1986-; Reditronics Ltd 1985; md J & P Coats (Pakistan) Ltd 1961-67, J A Carp's Garenfabrieken (Helmond) Holland 1967-70, Philips Electrical Ltd London 1971-75, Pye of Cambridge Ltd 1975-79; memb Royal Co of Archers (Queen's Bodyguard for Scotland), former cncl memb Royal Utd Servs Inst, chm Supervisory Bd Euro Inst for Security 1984-86, tstee dir Euro Centre for Work and Soc 1983-, vice-chm EPIC (Euro Parliamentarians & Industrialists Cncl) 1984-; pres CRONWE CRONWE (Conference Regnl Organisations of NW Europe) 1987-; *Recreations* golf, tennis, squash, skiing, music, travel, vintage cars; *Clubs* White's, Royal Ashdown Forest Golf; *Style*— Sir Jack Stewart-Clark, Bt, MEP; Puckstye House, Holtye Common, nr Cowden, Kent (☎ 034 286 541)

STEWART-FITZROY, Capt (William) Wentworth; s of Capt Frederick Henry Fitzroy (d 1937), and Eleanor Lawson Allan (d 1969); *b* 28 Sept 1907; *Educ* NC HMS Worcester, RNC Greenwich; *m* 26 April 1934, Margaret Patricia, da of Douglas Stewart Grant (d 1921), of USA; 3 s (Allen b 1935, James b 1943, Roderick b 1947), 1 da (Anne b 1936); *Career* serv WWII HMS Warspite 1939-41 (arctic Patrol 1940, Narvik 1940, Med 1941, Matapan and Crete 1941); cmd destroyers: HMS Buxton (N Atlantic 1941), HMS Valorous (North Sea 1942-43), HMS Arrow (force Z Med 1943 &

Sicily landings), HMS King Alfred (1944, trg), HMS Comet (BR Pacific Fleet 1945-47); naval attaché HM Embassy Belgrade 1947-49, served Korea as Cdr (exec offr) Fleet Flagship HMS Belfast 1950-51, Cdr RN Air Station HMS Seahawk 1951-52; Capt in Policy Plans & Operations Div SHAPE 1952-54; asst dir of Naval Equipment Admty 1954-56, Capt of Dockyard and Queen's harbourmaster Rosyth 1957-58, Cdre HM Dockyard Singapore 1959-61, naval ADC to HM The Queen 1961-62, naval regnl offr MOD for Scotland & NI 1962-72; Hon Sheriff for Sutherland 1974-; pres Stewart Soc of Clan Stewart 1971-74 (hon vice-pres 1974-); *Recreations* sailing, fishing, golf, amateur petrologist; *Style—* Capt Wentworth Stewart-Fitzroy; 1137 Westmoreland Road, Alexandria, Virginia 22308, USA

STEWART-LIBERTY, Arthur Ivor; MC (1944), TD (1946); s of Ivor Stewart-Liberty, MC, DL (d 1952), and Evelyn Catharine Phipps (d 1966); *b* 11 Jan 1916; *Educ* Winchester, Ch Ch Oxford; *m* 1, 1942 (m dis 1953), Rosabel Fremantle, *née* Fynn; 2 s, 1 da; m 2, 1955, Elizabeth Cicely, *née* Stuart; 1 da; *Career* Maj served in France 1940, Assam/Burma 1943-45, chm Liberty & Co Ltd 1953-81, dir Liberty & Co Ltd 1981-; *Style—* Arthur Stewart-Liberty Esq, MC, TD; Pipers, The Lee, Great Missenden, Bucks

STEWART-LIBERTY, Oliver James; s of Arthur Ivor Stewart-Liberty, of Buckinghamshire, Rosabel Fremantle; *b* 8 Oct 1947; *Educ* Bryanston Sch; *m* 16 Sept 1972, Anne Catherine, da of Frank Arthur Bicknell, of London; 1 s (Charles b 1978), 1 da (Alexandra b 1980); *Career* dir Liberty plc 1977-; *Recreations* shooting, cricket, tennis, boules; *Style—* Oliver Stewart-Liberty, Esq; Regent Street, London W1R 6AH (☎ 01 734 1234, telex 295850, fax 734 8323)

STEWART-PATTERSON, Lady Alison Margaret Katherine Antoinette; *née* Bruce; da of late 10 Earl of Elgin and (14 of) Kincardine, KT, CMG, TD, CD, and Hon Dame Katherine Cochrane, DBE, da of late 1 Baron Cochrane of Cults and Lady Gertrude Boyle, OBE, da of 6 Earl of Glasgow; *b* 1931; *Educ* McGill Univ (BTh, STM), Presbyterian Coll Montreal (Dip); *m* 1957, Cleveland Stewart-Patterson; 2 s, 1 da; *Career* LRAM; ordained min Presbyterian Church in Canada 1977, asst min Church of St Andrew and St Paul Montreal 1977-79, pasteur Eglise Presbytérienne St-Luc Montréal 1980-; *Style—* Lady Alison Stewart-Patterson; Drishane Farm, 251 Senneville Rd, Senneville, Québec H9X 3L2, Canada

STEWART-RICHARDSON, Alastair Lucas Graham; s of Lt-Col Neil Graham Stewart-Richardson, DSO (d 1934), and Alexandra, *née* Ralli (d 1972); *b* 29 Nov 1927; *Educ* Eton, Magdalene Coll Cambridge (MA); *m* 29 May 1969, (Diana) Claire, da of Brig George Streynsham Rawstone, CBE, MC (d 1962); 2 s (James George b 1971, Hugh Neil b 1977), 1 da (Sarah Alexandra b 1974); *Career* called to the Bar Inner Temple 1952, bencher 1978; *Style—* Alastair Stewart-Richardson, Esq; 120 Woodsford Sq, London W14 8DT; 7 King's Bench Walk, Temple, London EC4Y 7DS

STEWART-RICHARDSON, Ninian Rorie; s of Sir Ian Stewart Richardson (d 1969), and Audrey Meryl Odlum (who m 2, 1975, Patrick Robertson, CMG); hp of bro Sir Simon Stewart-Richardson, 17 Bt; *b* 20 Jan 1949; *Educ* Dannoch Sch Perthshire, Commercial Pilot Training; *m* 21 Oct 1983, Joan Kristina, da of Howard Smee, of Rio de Janeiro; *Career* late commercial air pilot; industrialist Brazil Ultra Violet Application to Industry; *Recreations* sailing, skiing; *Style—* Ninian Stewart-Richardson, Esq; c/o Mrs P A P Robertson, Lynedale, Long Cross, Chertsey, Surrey KT16 0DP; Rua Dr Julio Otoni 451 Santa Teresa Rio de Janeiro, Brazil; Germetec, Rua Matinore 227 Jacare, Rio de Janeiro (☎ 261 9244)

STEWART-RICHARDSON, Sir Simon Alaisdair (Ian Neile); 17 Bt (NS 1630), of Pencaitland, Haddingtonshire; s of Sir Ian Rorie Hay Stewart-Richardson, 16 Bt (d 1969), by his 2 w, Audrey Meryl Odlum (who m 2, 1975, Patrick Robertson, CMG); *b* 9 June 1947; *Educ* Trinity Coll Glenalmond; *Heir* bro, Ninian Rorie Stewart-Richardson, *qv*; *Recreations* music, theatre, sailing; *Style—* Sir Simon Stewart-Richardson, Bt; Lynedale, Longcross, nr Chertsey, Surrey KT16 0DP (☎ 093287 2329)

STEWART-SMITH, Christopher Dudley; s of Ean Kendal Stewart-Smith (d 1964); *b* 21 Jan 1941; *Educ* Winchester, King's Coll Cambridge, Massachusetts Inst of Tech; *m* 1964, Olivia, da of Col John Barstow, DSO; 1 s, 2 da; *Career* chm: Earls Court and Olympia Ltd 1974-85, McKinsey and Co Inc 1967-71; dir: P&O Steam Navigation Co plc 1985-86, Sterling Guarantee Tst plc 1971-85, Williamson Tea Hldgs 1986-, Phicom plc 1987-, Nat Westminster Bank plc (outer London Region) 1984-; chm Conder Gp plc 1987-; *Clubs* Travellers'; *Style—* Christopher Stewart-Smith, Esq; Kingsworthy Court, Kings Worthy, Winchester SO23 7QA (☎ 0962 882222)

STEWART-SMITH, John Ronald; s of Maj James Geoffrey Stewart-Smith (d 1938), of Falcon Hill Kinver, nr Stourbridge, Worcs, and Bertha Mabel Milner, *née* Roberts; *b* 23 Feb 1932; *Educ* Marlborough, Waitaki (NZ); *m* 22 Oct 1955, Catherine May, da of Walter Douglas Montgomery Clarke, JP (d 1948), of Bombay, India; 1 s (Geoffrey b 1958), 2 da (Joanna b 1960, Nicola b 1962); *Career* gp mktg dir Glover Gp Ltd 1976-79, projects dir and co sec Dashwood Finance Co Ltd 1983-, dir Kowloon Shipyard Co Ltd 1983-; CEng, MIMechE 1967, MIMarE 1969, MInst Export 1974; *Recreations* tennis, skiing; *Style—* John Stewart-Smith, Esq; Dashwood Finance Co Ltd, Georgian House, 63 Coleman St, London EC2R 5BB (☎ 01 588 3215, fax 01 588 4818, telex 885624)

STEWART-WALLACE, (Helen) Mary; da of Edward Schooling (d 1928), of Christchurch Park, Sutton, Surrey (*see* Burke's Landed Gentry, 18 edn, vol II, 1969), and Nellie Vera, *née* Price (d 1959); the firm of Schooling, Lawrence and Schooling were goldsmiths and merchant bankers in the 18th century; *b* 7 Mar 1914; *Educ* Sutton HS, GPDST and The Central Sch of Speech Trg and Dramatic Art, Univ London (Dip Dramatic Art); *m* 4 Nov 1939, Dr Arthur Maurice Stewart-Wallace, s of Sir John Stewart-Wallace, CB (d 1963), of The Paddock House, Gerrards Cross, Bucks (*see* Burke's Landed Gentry, 18 edn, vol II, 1969); 1 s (John b 1943), 2 da (Jane b 1940, Elizabeth b 1950); *Career* official speaker for Britain in Europe Referendum Campaign 1974, speaker Cons Nat Womens' Conf; memb: Cons Women's Consultative Ctee, SE Panel of Cons Speakers, monthly House of Lords meeting on educn issues; assoc memb Bruges Gp 1989, former memb Educn Cmmn of Euro Union of Women; writer of genealogical articles and occasional reviews, author of res into secdy educn in cmparable western democracies 1978; Freeman City of London, memb Worshipful Co of Goldsmiths; *Books* Research into Secondary Education in Comparable Western Democracies (1978); *Recreations* genealogy and family research, educational research, foreign travel; *Clubs* Soc of Genealogists; *Style—* Mrs A M Stewart-Wallace; The Moot House, Ditchling, Sussex

STEWART-WILSON, Lt-Col Blair Aubyn; CVO (1989, LVO 1983); s of Aubyn Harold Raymond Wilson (d 1934), and Muriel Athelstan Hood Stewart-Stevens, *née* Stewart (d 1982); *b* 17 July 1929; *Educ* Eton, RMA Sandhurst; *m* 1962, Helen Mary, da of Maj Wilfred Michael Fox (d 1974), of Taunton; 3 da (Alice b 1963, Sophia b 1966, Belinda b 1970); *Career* dep master of HM Household and Equerry to HM The Queen 1976-; cmmnd Scots Gds 1949, served UK, Germany and Far East, Lt-Col 1969; def mil and air attaché Vienna 1975-76; Capt Atholl Highlanders; *Recreations* shooting, fishing; *Clubs* Pratt's and White's; *Style—* Lt-Col Blair Stewart-Wilson, CVO; 3 Browning Close, London W9 1BW (☎ 01 286 9891); The Old Brewery, N Curry, Somerset TA3 6JS (☎ 0823 490111); office: Buckingham Palace, London SW1 (☎ 01 930 4832)

STEWART-WILSON, Col Ralph Stewart; MC (1944); s of Aubyn Harold Raymond Wilson (d 1934), of Aust, and Muriel Athelstane Hood Stewart-Stevens, *née* Stewart (d 1982); 11 Laird of Balnakeilly; ggs of Charls Wilson pioneer grazier in NSW and Victoria; *b* 26 Jan 1923; *Educ* Eton; *m* 4 Oct 1949, Rosalind, da of Col H S O P Stedall, OBE, of Oxon; 1 s (Aubyn b 1963), 2 da (Maria b 1952, Lorna b 1954); *Career* soldier and farmer; served Rifle Bde, 60 Rifles, Staffordshire Regt 1941-68; theatres of ops incl: Tunisia 1942-43, Italy and Austria 1944-45, Kenya 1956, Malaya 1956-57; appts incl: BM7 Armd Bde 1954-56, jt planning and defense policy staff, 2 i/c 60 Rifles 1963-64, CO 1 Bn The Staffordshire Regt 1964-66; memb Queen's Body Guard for Scotland (Royal Co of Archers), Capt in Atholl Highlanders, former pres Atholl NFU for Scotland, pres The Stewart Soc, memb Br Onithologists Union; *Recreations* ornithology, shooting; *Clubs* Royal and Ancient Golf (St Andrews); *Style—* Col Ralph S Stewart-Wilson of Balnakeilly, MC; Pitlochry, Perthshire PH16 5JJ (☎ 0796 2059)

STIBBON, Gen Sir John James; KCB (1988), OBE (1977); s of Jack Stibbon (d 1939), and Elizabeth Matilda, *née* Dixon (d 1968); *b* 5 Jan 1935; *Educ* Portsmouth Southern GS, RMA, RMCS (BSc Eng); *m* 10 Aug 1957, Jean Fergusson, da of John Robert Skeggs, of Newquay, Cornwall; 2 da (Jane b 1958, Emma b 1962); *Career* cmmnd RE 1954, Staff Capt MOD 1962-64, Adj 32 Armd Engr Regt 1964-66, instr RAC centre 1967-68, OC 2 Armd Engr sqdn 1968-70, DAA md QMG 12 Mech Bde 1971-72, GSO1 (DS) Staff Coll 1973-75, CO 28 Amphibious Engr Regt 1975-77, asst mil sec MOD 1977-79, Cmd 20 Armd Bde 1979-81, Royal Coll of Def Studies 1982, Cmdt RMCS 1983-85, asst chief of def staff (operational requirements) MOD 1985-87, Master Gen of the Ordnance 1987-; Col Cmdt: RAPC 1985, RPC 1986, RE 1988; hon vice pres FA; *Recreations* watercolour painting, association football, paleantology; *Clubs* Lansdowne; *Style—* Gen Sir John Stibbon, KCB, OBE; MOD, Whitehall, London (☎ 01 218 6908)

STIBBS, Prof (Douglas) Walter Noble; s of Edward John Stibbs (d 1922), of Sydney, Aust, and Jane, *née* Monro (d 1963); *b* 17 Feb 1919; *Educ* Sydney Boys' HS, Univ of Sydney (BSc, MSc), New Coll Oxford Univ (D Phil); *m* 8 Jan 1949, Margaret Lilian Calvert, da of Rev John Calvert (1949), of Sydney, Aust; 2 da (Helen b 1956, Elizabeth b 1959); *Career* lectr dept of mathematics and physics New England Univ Coll Armidale NSW 1942-45, sr sci offr Cwlth Solar Observatory Canberra 1945-51 (res asst 1940-42), Radcliffe travelling fell Radcliffe Observatory Pretoria SA and Univ observatory Oxford 1951-54, princ sci offr UKAEA Aldermaston 1955-59, sr prof Senatus Academicus Univ of St Andrews 1987- (Napier prof of astronomy and dir of univ observatory 1959-), visiting prof of astrophysics Yale Univ observatory 1966-67, Br Cncl visiting prof Univ of Utrecht 1968-69, prof Collège de France Paris 1975-76; memb: Int Astronomical Union 1951- (pres fin ctee 1964-67, 1973-76 and 1976-79), Nat Ctee for Astronomy 1964-76, advsy ctee for Meteorology in Scotland 1960-69 (also 1972-75 and 1978-80), Science Research Cncl 1972-76, Royal Greenwich Observatory Ctee 1966-70 (memb bd of visitors 1963-65), Royal Observatory Edinburgh ctee 1966-76 (chm 1970-76), Astronomy Space and Radio Bd 1970-76, SA Astronomical advsy ctee 1972-76; chm: Astronomy Policy and Grants Ctee 1972-74, N Hemisphere Observatory Planning Ctee 1970-76; FRAS 1942 (memb cncl 1964-67 and 1970-73, vice pres 1972-73), FRSE 1960 (memb cncl 1970-72); *Books* The Outer Layers of a Star (with Sir Richard Woolley, 1953); *Recreations* music (organ), ornithology, photography, golf, long distance running (medals for 17 marathons during 1983-87 incl: Athens, Berlin, Boston, Edinburgh 3h 59m 23s, Honolulu, London, Paris); *Clubs* Royal and Ancient Golf (St Andrews), Br Marathon RC; *Style—* Prof D W N Stibbs; 10 Lawhead Road East, St Andrews Fife, Scotland; University Observatory, Buchanan Gardens, St Andrews Fife

STIBY, Robert Andrew; JP (1976); s of Arthur Robert Charles Stiby, TD, JP, and Peggy Stiby, *née* Hartley (d 1974); *b* 25 May 1937; *Educ* Marlborough, London Coll of Printing; *m* 1; 1 s (Jonathon b 1963), 1 da (Emma b 1965); m 2, 1980, Heather; m 3, 1986, Julia; *Career* md Croydon Advertiser Gp of Newspapers 1969-74, chm 1974-83; dir: Capital Radio 1972-, Chiltern Radio 1981-; Radio Mercury 1983, dir Portsmouth & Sunderland Newspapers 1983, chm of govrs London Coll of Printing 1980; pres Newspaper Soc 1983; chm Local News of London Ltd 1972-; *Recreations* sailing, gliding, golf; *Clubs* MCC, Reigate Heath Golf; *Style—* Robert Stiby Esq, JP; The White House, Reigate Heath, Surrey RH2 8QR (☎ 242 781)

STIDDARD, Timothy John Wentworth; s of Capt Jack William Stiddard, MC (d 1986), of Lodewell Farm, Hutton, nr Weston-Super-Mare, Avon, and Joline Olive Wentworth Stiddard, *née* Alexander; *b* 7 April 1957; *Educ* Cheltenham, Lanchester Poly (LLB); *m* 3 April 1982, Joanne Jeanette, da of John Edward White, of 7 Dickenson Rd, Weston-super-Mare, Avon; 1 da (Heather Shona); *Career* slr: Supreme Ct of England and Wales 1981, Weston Super Mare Hoteliers Assoc 1981, Int Audiology Soc 1985; vice-pres Weston Super Mare Operative Soc 1983; tres Weston Super Mare Sea Cadet Corps 1979-; memb: The Law Soc, Bristol Law Soc; *Recreations* golf, rugby, fishing, philately, freemasonry; *Clubs* Western Golf; *Style—* Timothy Stiddard, Esq; 23 Hillcroft Close, Worlebury, Weston-super-Mare, Avon (☎ 0934 419 504); 64 Orchard St, Weston-super-Mare, Avon (☎ 0934 24102, fax 0934 636 076)

STIGWOOD, Robert Colin; s of late Gordon Stigwood, of Beaumont, Adelaide, and Gwendolyn Burrows; *b* 1932, Adelaide Aust,; *Educ* Sacred Heart Coll; *Career* theatre, movie, TV and record prodr; came to Eng 1956, held a variety of jobs incl mangr prov theatre and halfway house for delinquents in Cambridge; opened talent agency in London 1962, first ind record prodr in Eng with release of single Johnny Remember Me (liquidated firm 1965); business mangr Graham Bond Org; co-md NEMS Enterprises 1967, fndr Robert Stigwood Orgn 1967, formed RSO Records 1973, dir

Polygram 1976; prodr; films incl: Jesus Christ Superstar, Bugsy Malone, Tommy, Saturday Night Fever, Grease, Sgt Pepper's Lonely Hearts Club Band, Moment by Moment, The Fan, Times Square, Grease 2, Staying Alive, Gallipoli; prodr, stage musicals in Eng and US incl: Oh! Calcutta, The Dirtiest Show in Town, Pippin, Jesus Christ Superstar, Evita, Sweeney Todd; TV producer in Eng and US; prodns incl: The Entertainer, The Prime of Miss Jean Brodie (series); Int Producer of Year, ABC Interstate Theatres Inc 1976; *Recreations* sailing (Jezebel), tennis; *Style—* Robert Stigwood Esq; Robert Stigwood Organisation, 118-120 Wardour St, London W1V 4BT (☎ 01 437 2512; telex 264267)

STILL, Brig Nigel Maxwell; CBE (1983); s of Brig George Bingham Still, OBE (d 1965), of London, and Violet Winifred, *née* Maxwell (d 1980); *b* 27 Mar 1936; *Educ* Marlborough, Clare Coll Cambridge (BA); *m* 3 April 1965, Mary Richenda, da of Maj P J D Macfarlane, of 79 Bramley Grange, Guildford, Surrey; 1 s (George b 1973), 1 da (Caroline b 1967); *Career* cmmnd 17/21 Lancers 1958 (Adj 1960), instr RMA Sandhurst 1962, Sqdn Ldr 17/21 Lancers 1965, Army Staff Course 1966, GSO 2 (Armd) HQ Army Strategic Cmd 1968, DAMS Mil Sec's Dept MOD 1972, CO 17/21 Lancers 1975, GSO 1 (Directing Staff) Aust Army Staff Coll 1977, Col GS (OR) 17 MOD 1979, Coll Cdr RMA Sandhurst 1982, Cdr 43 Inf Bde 1984, ret 1987; dir of admin Lyddon (Stockbrokers) Cardiff 1987-88; *Recreations* golf, cricket, rugby football, music; *Clubs* I Zingari (cricket); *Style—* Brig Nigel M Still, CBE; c/o Midland Bank plc, Wellington Square, Minehead, Somerset

STILL, Robert Flisher; s of Robert Herbert Still, and Mabel Caroline, *née* Brown; *b* 5 Mar 1923; *Educ* Hove Co Sch Sussex; *m* 22 Aug 1944, Gwendoline Jessie, da of Douglas Gordon Everard Barrie (d 1967); 1 s (Christopher Michael b 23 July 1946), 1 da (Lindsay Ann (Mrs Cook) b 10 Oct 1951); *Career* WWII RN: Ordinary Seaman HMS Howe 1941, Midshipman 1942, underwater def HMS Osprey and HMS Curlew 1942, Sub Lt 1943, cable laying ops HMS Curlew 1943-46 (N Africa, Sicily, Italy, Belguim, Holland, Germany), Lt 1944, demob 1946; clerk Westminster Bank 1940-41; Metway Electrical Industs Ltd Brighton: sales clerk 1946, dir 1947, jt md 1961, md 1967, chm 1987-; life vice pres Sussex Radio and Electrical Industs Golfing Soc, memb Hove branch Lions Int 1962-, memb Electrical Commercial Travellers Assoc; memb: IOD, Assoc of Supervisory and Exec Engrs; *Recreations* gardening, swimming, walking; *Style—* Robert Still, Esq; 16 Woodruff Ave, Hove, E Sussex BN3 6PG (☎ 0273 556678); 55 Canning St, Brighton, BN2 2ES (☎ 0273 606433, fax 0273 6677473, telex 877166)

STILLWELL, Peter Frederic Thomas Cryer; s of late Samuel Stillwell, OBE; *b* 13 Mar 1924; *Educ* Uppingham, Clare Coll Cambridge; *Career* physicist, electronics engr, dir Rank Res Laboratories 1970-82, dir Rank Precision Industries Ltd 1975-82, ret; scientific consultancy work; CEng, FIEE; *Recreations* gardening and growing species cyclamen, the pursuit of trout; *Style—* Peter Stillwell Esq; The Cedars, Hillside Close, Crookham Village, Aldershot, Hants (☎ 025 14 617167)

STILLWELL, Richard Leon Mortimer; s of Sydney Walter Stillwell, of The Limes, Clewer, Windsor, Berks (d 1947), and Anne Lucille (d 1961), da of Silas Manville Burroughs (fndr Burroughs Wellcome); *b* 5 Jan 1921; *Educ* Stafferton Lodge, Maidenhead; *m* 19 June 1950, Joan Mary, da of Charles Lampard Bundy (d 1933); 1 da (Julia Anne b 1952); *Career* int trainer of horses; memb: exec ctee Br Show Jumping Assocn, Br Horse Soc and BSJA Ctees, Horse of the Year Show; former memb: Int Horse Show Ctee, Rules Ctee BSJA, Finance Ctee BSJA, and mgmnt Ctee of Nat Equestrian Centre, Stoneleigh; winner: Daily Telegraph Cup (1960), Daily Telegraph Horse and Hound Cup (Horse of the Year Show) (1961), Olympic Trial at Lavant (1954); trained riders for Olympics; sr instr for BSJA; Dip Br Horse Soc (1977), BHS Trainer Award (1984), Br Equestrian Fedn Medal of Honour (1986); *Recreations* hunting, racing; *Style—* Richard Stillwell, Esq; Handpost Farm, Barkham, nr Wokingham, Berkshire, Arborfield (☎ 0734 760 267)

STIMPSON, Peter; s of Victor George Stimpson (d 1958), of Ashington, and Eva, *née* Warne (d 1985); *b* 19 Oct 1935; *Educ* Denstone Coll, Durham Univ (LLB); *m* 14 Oct 1960, Susan Winifred, da of Dr Thomas Young Muir (d 1977), of Gosforth; 2 s (Philip b 1961, Andrew b 1964), 2 da (Jane b 1962, Elizabeth b 1978); *Career* slr; *Recreations* sailing, skiing; *Style—* Peter Stimpson, Esq; Heugh Mill, Stamfordham, Northumberland (☎ 378); 5 Marden Road, Whitley Bay, Tyne and Wear (☎ 091 2530424)

STINSON, Sir Charles Alexander; KBE (1979, OBE 1962); s of W J B Stinson; *b* 1919,June; *Educ* Levuka Public Sch, Suva GS; *m* 1946, Mollie Dean; 2 s, 1 da; *Career* mayor of Suva 1959-66; Fiji min: Communications, Works and Tourism 1970-72, Finance 1972-79; *Style—* Sir Charles Stinson; PO Box 798, Suva, Fiji

STINSON, His Hon David John; s of Henry John Edwin Stinson, MC (d 1969), of Beckenham, Kent, and Margaret, *née* Little (d 1969); *b* 22 Feb 1921; *Educ* Eastbourne Coll, Emmanuel Coll Cambridge (MA); *m* 11 Aug 1950, (Eleanor) Judith, da of Kenneth Miles Chance, DSO, DL (d 1980), of Wreay, Carlisle, Cumbria; 3 s (Adam b 13 Dec 1953, Rupert b 21 March 1955 d 25 March 1955, Daniel b 14 Feb 1959), 2 da (Sarah (Mrs Nevill) b 6 March 1952, Emma (Mrs Nash) b 8 July 1956); *Career* 2 Lt 147 Essex Yeo Field Regt RHA 1941, Lt 191 Herts & Essex Yeo Field Regt RA 1942, Actg Capt (despatches) 1944, Actg Capt Air Op Pilot RA 1945-46; barr Middle Temple 1947, dep chm Herts QS 1965, county ct judge 1969, circuit judge 1972-86 (appt to co Cts of Suffolk 1973-86); chllr Diocese of Carlisle 1971-, chm Ipswich & Dist Family Conciliation Serv 1982-89, pres Parents Conciliation Tst (PACT) in Suffolk 1988-; *Recreations* gardening, sailing, birdwatching; *Clubs* Army and Navy, Waldringfield Sailing; *Style—* His Hon David Stinson; Barrack Row, Waldringfield, Woodbridge, Suffolk IP12 4QX (☎ 0473 36 280)

STINTON, Sqdn Ldr (ret) Darrol; MBE (Mil) 1964; s of Ernest Thomas Stinton (d 1980), and Vera Stinton, *née* Hall; *b* 9 Dec 1927; *Educ* Beverley GS; *m* 1, March 1952, Barbara, *née* Chapman; 1 s (Julian b 1957), 1 da (Caroline b 1959); m 2, June 1971, Christine Diane, da of Frederick Miller Roehampton; 1 s (Matthew b 1973); m 3, July 1976, Ann Jacqueline Frances, da of Robert Spence Adair (d 1978), 1 step s (Terence Gent Eggett b 1971), 1 da (Penelope b 1977); *Career* served RAF 1953-69; Empire Test Pilot Sch 1959, RAF Staff Coll 1964, Ship's Diving Offr RN 1965, qualified test pilot Air Registration Bd 1969-, Air Worthiness Div of CAA, Far East Air Force and MOD until 1969; md Darrol Stinton Ltd, Int Aero-Marine Conslts 1982-; fndr: Historic Aircraft Assoc, Subaqua Assoc; CEng, FRAeS, MRINA, MIMechE; *Books* numerous textbooks and papers on aircraft design (John Britten Meml Prize RAes 1986, George Taylor Prize RAes 1987); *Recreations* subaqua, sailing, writing; *Clubs* RAF, The Tiger; *Style—* Darrol Stinton, Esq, MBE; 40 Castle St, Farnham, Surrey GU9 7JB (☎ 0252 713120); Civil Aviation Authy, Aviation House, Gatwick, West Sussex RH6 0YR

STIRK, James Richard; s of Edward Thomas Stirk, TD, of Clochfaen, Llangurig, Powys SY18 6RP, and Peggy Isobel Phyllis Stirk, *née* Soper; *b* 29 Oct 1959; *Educ* Shrewsbury, Trinity Coll Cambridge (MA); *Career* commercial slr; dir Samuel Parker & Co Ltd 1981-; tstee The Curig Charity 1986-; cncl memb: The Powyrland Club, The Radnorshire Soc 1987-; *Publications* Works in the 'Montgomeryshire Collections' and the 'Radnorshire Transactions', Current work: 'Biography of Chevalier J Y W Lloyd'; *Recreations* writing on historical and legal subjects; *Clubs* Powysland, Radnorshire Soc; *Style—* James Stirk, Esq; Mount Severn, 17 Hunter St, Shrewsbury SY3 8QN (☎ 0743 247 734); Clochfaen, Llangurig, Powys SY18 6RP (☎ 05515 687); Tarmac Quarry Products Ltd, Ettingshall, Wolverthampton WV4 6JP (☎ 0902 41101, fax 0902 402032, telex 338544)

STIRLING, Angus Duncan Aeneas; s of Duncan Alexander Stirling, and Lady Marjorie Stirling, *qv*; *b* 1933; *Educ* Eton, Trinity Coll Cambridge; *m* 1959, Armyne Morar Helen Schofield, er da of Mr and Hon Mrs William Schofield of Masham Yorks; 1 s, 2 da; *Career* former dep sec-gen Arts Cncl of GB; dep-dir Nat Tst 1979-83 (dir-gen 1983-); dir Royal Opera House Covent Garden, chm Friends of Covent Garden 1981-; memb exec ctee London Symphony Orchestra 1979-; *Clubs* Garrick, Brooks; *Style—* Angus Stirling, Esq; 25 Ladbroke Grove, London W11

STIRLING, Dr (Thomas) Boyd; s of John Stirling, JP (d 1967), of Aldridge, W Midlands, and Christina Buntin, *née* McNaught (d 1981); *b* 28 Nov 1923; *Educ* Queen Mary's GS, Walsall, Birmingham Univ Med Sch (MB ChB); *m* 11 Nov 1950, Marjory Sarah Glen, da of Alexander Glen McDougall (d 1959), of Bonhill, Dunbartonshire; 2 s (Alistair b 1953, Iain b 1956), 1 da (Fionna b 1959); *Career* Maj RAMC 1947-49; GP 1950-, industl med offr GEC 1959-79, anaesthetist 1951-80, police surgn 1952-83; memb: fndr chm Walsall Hosp GP Ward 1970-83, Soc of Occupational Health; BMA; *Recreations* family, walking, reading, golf; *Clubs* Royal Scottish Automobile; *Style—* Thomas Stirling, Esq; 15 Northgate, Aldridge, Walsall, W Midlands WS9 8QD (☎ 0922 52201)

STIRLING, Prof Charles James Matthew; s of Brig Alexander Dickson Stirling, DSO (d 1961), and Isobel Millicent, *née* Matthew (d 1984); *b* 8 Dec 1930; *Educ* Edinburgh Acad, St Andrew Univ (BSc), Kings Coll London (PhD, DSc); *m* 1 Sept 1956, Eileen Gibson, da of William Leslie Powell (d 1974), of Bournemouth; 3 da (Catherine, Julie, Alexandra); *Career* res fell: civil service Porton 1955-57, ICI Edinburgh 1957-59; lectr chemistry Queens Univ Belfast 1959-65, reader organic chemistry Kings Coll London 1965-69, head dept Univ Coll North Wales 1981- (prof organic chemistry 1969-); pres Perkin div Royal Soc of Chemistry 1989-; memb: Menai Bridge Cncl of Churches 1982-83, Bangor Monteverdi singers 1974-79; FRS 1986, FRSC 1967; *Books* Radicals in Organic Chemistry (1965), Organosulphur Chemistry (ed 1975), Chemistry of the Sulphonium Group (ed 1982); *Recreations* choral music, travel, furniture restoration; *Style—* Prof Charles Stirling; Cae Maen, Druid Road, Menai Bridge, Gwynedd; Department of Chemistry, University College of North Wales, Bangor, Gwynedd LL57 2UW (☎ 0248 351151), telex 61100)

STIRLING, (Archibald) David; DSO (1942), OBE (1946); 3 s of Brig-Gen Archibald Stirling of Keir, DL, sometime MP Perthshire W (himself 2 s of Sir William Stirling-Maxwell, 9 Bt, KT, DL, by his 1 w, Lady Anna Maria, *née* Leslie, she being da of 8 Earl of Leven); David's mother was Hon Margaret, *née* Fraser, da of 13 Lord Lovat; yr bro of late William Stirling of Keir; *b* 15 Nov 1915; *Educ* Ampleforth, Cambridge Univ; *Career* serv WWII Scots Gds, 3 Commando Bde of Gds, 1 SAS Regt; chm Television Int Enterprises; Officier Légion d'Honneur; *Clubs* White's; *Style—* David Stirling Esq, DSO, OBE; Television International Enterprises Ltd, 22 South Audley St, London W1Y 6ES (☎ 01 499 9252)

STIRLING, Duncan Alexander; s of William Stirling, JP, DL, of Fairburn (d 1914); *b* 6 Oct 1899; *Educ* Harrow, New Coll Oxford; *m* 1926, Lady Marjorie Murray, da of 8 Earl of Dunmore VC DSO MVO (d 1962); 2 s; *Career* Coldstream Gds 1918 and 1940-43, ptnr H S Lefersne & Co, (Merchant Bankers) 1929-49, dir Westminster Bank (later National Westminster) 1935-74 (chm 1962-69), dir London Life Assoc 1935-80 (pres 1951-65); prime warden Fishmongers Co 1954-55; *Clubs* Brooks's; *Style—* Duncan Stirling, Esq; 20 Kingston House South, Ennismore Gardens, London SW7

STIRLING, Lady; Frances Marguerite Wedderburn; the Stirlings descend from Thoraldus, Vicecomes de Striveling, who is mentioned under that name in a charter of David I of Scotland dated 1147; da of John Wedderburn Wilson (d 1960), of Whitehall Court, London and Elisabeth May, *née* Stephens, of Montreal, Canada; *b* 24 July 1906; *Educ* St James's West Malvern; *m* 1941, Gen Sir William Gurdon Stirling, GCB, CBE, DSO (decd, sometime C-in-C BAOR and gentleman usher to the Sword of State), s of Maj Charles Stirling, RHA (d 1914), and Hon Amy Gurdon, JP, er da of 1 Baron Cranworth; 3 da (Elizabeth, Patricia, Mary); *Career* OStJ; *Style—* Lady Stirling; Great Saxham Hall, Great Saxham, Bury St Edmunds, Suffolk IP29 5JW (☎ 0284 810259)

STIRLING, Hugh Gerald; s of Surgn Lt Cdr Hugh Stirling of Chipping Campden, Glos, and Hilda Irene, *née* Harris; *b* 16 April 1947; *Educ* Glenalmond, Silsoe Coll, West of Scotland Agric Coll (NDAgrE); *m* 24 February 1973, Sheila Janet, da of Lt-Col Patrick Alpin, OBE (d 1974), of Jersey, CI; 1 da (Charlotte b 1973); *Career* RN Aux Serv 1979-; served inshore minesweeper/fast patrol boat, agric engr, Coffee Bd of Kenya 1971-75, tech mktg mangr Gunsons Sortex 1975-79, PR exec Br Technol Gp (promoting agric innovation) 1979-; FIAgricE 1987, RAS; *Recreations* sailing, shooting, fishing; *Clubs* Farmer's, Muthaiga, Kenya Fly Fishers, RNSA; *Style—* Hugh Stirling, Esq; 67D Shooters Hill Rd, Blackheath, London SE3 (☎ 01 853 2292); British Technolsogy Group, 101 Newington Causeway, London SE1 6BU (☎ 01 403 6666, telex 894397, fax 01 403 7586)

STIRLING, Malcolm Douglas; s of Douglas Windebank Stirling (d 1984), of Solihull, W Midlands, and Katharine Anne, *née* Folland; *b* 29 May 1933; *Educ* King Edward's Sch Birmingham; *m* 4 July 1959, Shirley, da of William Clayton Pilkington (d 1980), of Liverpool; 1 s (Alistair b 1960), 2 da (Sian b 1961, Elizabeth b 1966); *Career* Nat Serv cmmnd RA 1957-59; qualified CA 1957, Coopers & Lybrand 1959-61, ptnr Spicer & Oppenheim Birmingham 1961- (managing ptnr 1981, sr ptnr 1986); hon sec Birmingham CAs Students Soc 1955-56; memb: Midlands advsy bd of Legal and Gen Assur Soc 1970-86, ctee of Birmingham & W Midlands Soc of CAs 1967-78 (pres 1977-78), Midlands advsy bd Williams & Glyn Bank 1972-78; dir numerous cos incl

Dowding & Mills plc 1974-; memb Worshipful Co of CAs; *Recreations* squash, dinghy sailing; *Clubs* Birmingham, The Royal Overseas League; *Style*— Malcolm Stirling, Esq; Exhall Crt, Exhall, nr Alcester, Warwicks; Spicer & Oppenheim, Newater House, 11 Newhall St, Birmingham B3 3NY (☎ 021 200 2211, fax 021 236 1515, 021 233 4503, telex 335 517 ESANO G

STIRLING, Lady Marjorie Hilda; *née* Murray; da of late 8 Earl of Dunmore, VC, DSO, MVO; *b* 1904; *m* 1926, Duncan Alexander Stirling (former chm Westminster, later Nat Westminster Bank); 2 s (*see* Stirling, Angus); *Career* Order of Mercy; *Style*— Lady Marjorie Stirling; 20 Kingston House South, Ennismore Gardens, London SW7

STIRLING, Nicholas Charles; s of Hugh Patrick, of Witney House Leafield, and Anne Marietta Patience; gf Sir Charles Mander Bt, chm Manders' Hldgs plc; *b* 3 Oct 1947; *Educ* Eton Coll; *m* 29 April 1975, Elizabeth Emma, da of Brig V W Barlow DSO, OBE; 1 s (William b 1978), 2 da (Frances b 1980, Patience b 1983); *Career* sr ptnr N C Stirling & Co; jt master North Pennine and S Notts Hunts; previously master Cattistock and Braes of Derwent Hunts in Dorset and Northumberland respectively; *Recreations* foxhunting, sailing; *Clubs* Northern Counties, Farmers, White Hall; *Style*— Nicholas Stirling, Esq; Dipton Cottage, Corbridge, Northumberland; 53 Stowell St, Newcastle upon Tyne 1

STIRLING OF FAIRBURN, Capt Roderick William Kenneth; TD (1965), JP (Ross and Cromarty 1975), DL (Ross and Cromarty 1971); s of Maj Sir John Stirling of Fairburn, KT, MBE (d 1975), of Fairburn, Muir of Ord, Ross-shire, and Marjorie Kythé, *née* Mackenzie of Gairloch; *b* 17 June 1932; *Educ* Harrow, Aberdeen Univ Sch of Agric; *m* 26 Oct 1963, Penelope Jane, da of Lt-Col Charles Henry Wright, TD, DL (d 1978), of The Cottage, Shadforth, Co Durham, formerly of Tuthill, Haswell, Co Durham; 4 da (Charlotte b 1965, Katharine b 1967, Jane b 1968, Fiona b 1971); *Career* Nat Serv Scots Gds 1950-52, cmmnd 1951, Seaforth Highlands and Queen's Own Highlanders 1953-69, ret Capt; dir: Scottish Salmon and White Fish Co Ltd 1972- (chm 1980-), Moray Firth Salmon Fishing Co Ltd 1973-; vice chm Red Deer Cmmn 1975- (memb 1964-); chm: highland ctee Scottish Landowners Fedn 1974-79, Scatwell and Strathcoanon Community Cncl 1975-88; gen cmmr for income tax 1975-; memb Ross and and Cromarty Dist Cncl 1984-; Lord Lieut Ross and Skye and Lachalsh 1988; *Recreations* field sports, gardening, curling; *Clubs* New (Edinburgh); *Style*— Capt Roderick Stirling of Fairburn, TD, JP; Arcan, Muir of Ord, Ross and Cromarty IVG 7UL (☎ 099 73 207); Fairburn Estate Office, Urray, Muir of Ord, Ross and Cromarty IV6 7UT (☎ 099 73 273)

STIRLING OF GARDEN, Col James; CBE, TD; s of Col Archibald Stirling of Garden, OBE, DL, JP (d 1947); *b* 8 Sept 1930; *Educ* Rugby, Trinity Coll Cambridge; *m* 1958, Fiona Janetta Sophia, da of Lt-Col D A C Wood Parker, OBE, TD, DL (d 1967), of Keithick, Coupar, Angus; 2 s, 2 da; *Career* cmmnd 1 Bn Argyll and Sutherland Highlanders 1950, served Korea (wounded), transferred 7 Bn (TA) 1951, Lt-Col cmdg 1966; CO 3 Bn 1968; Scottish dir Woolwich Building Soc, ptnr Kenneth Ryden and Ptnrs (chartered surveyors), dir Scottish Widows Soc 1976, chm Highland TAVRA 1982-; DL Stirlingshire 1969, HM Lord-Lt of Central Region (dists of Stirling and Falkirk) 1983-; FRICS; *Clubs* New (Edinburgh); *Style*— Lt-Col James Stirling of Garden, CBE, TD, HM Lord-Lieut of Central Region; Garden, Buchlyvie, Stirling (☎ 036 085 212)

STIRLING-AIRD, Lady Margaret Dorothea; *née* Boyle; yst da of Patrick James Boyle, 8 Earl of Glasgow, DSO, DL (d 1963), Capt RN, and Hyacinthe Mary, Countess of Glasgow (d 1977); *b* 20 Nov 1920; *m* 1, 1944 (m dis 1962), Capt Oliver Payan Dawnay, CVO, Coldstream Gds; 2 s, 1 da; m 2, 1973, Peter Douglas Miller Stirling-Aird of Kippendavie, TD; *Style*— Lady Margaret Stirling-Aird; 9 Lansdowne Road, London W11 3AG

STIRLING-HAMILTON, Sir Bruce; 13 Bt (NS 1673), of Preston, Haddingtonshire; yr but only surviving s of Capt Sir Robert William Stirling-Hamilton, 12 Bt, RN, DL (d 1982); himself descended from Sir John Hamilton of Fingaltoun, yr bro of Sir David Hamilton, 3 of Cadzow (died *ante* 1392), from whom descend the Dukes of Abercorn, while the uncle of Sir David and Sir John, John Hamilton of Ballencrieff, was ancestor of the Earls of Haddington); *b* 5 August 1940; *Educ* Pangbourne NC, RMA Sandhurst; *m* 1968, Stephanie, eld da of Dr William Campbell, of Alloway, Ayrshire; 1 s, 2 da (Georgina b 1970, Iona b 1985); *Heir* s, Malcolm William Bruce Stirling-Hamilton b 6 Aug 1979; *Career* cmmnd Queen's Own Highlanders 1961 (ADC to GOC 51 Highland Div 1964-65, Capt 1967, resigned cmmn 1971); Kimberly-Clark Ltd 1971-74, Seismograph Serv Ltd 1974-83; mgmnt conslt (MAST Scotland) 1983-85; md Glasgow Business Services Ltd; *Style*— Sir Bruce Stirling-Hamilton, Bt; 16 Bath Place, Ayr, Ayrshire KA7 1DP

STIRLING-HAMILTON, Eileen, Lady; Eileen Augusta Baden; da of Rt Rev Henry Kemble Southwell, CMG, DD, sometime Bishop of Lewes (himself s of Thomas Southwell, JP, who in his turn was ggs of Hon John Southwell, 4 s of 1 Baron Southwell; The 1 Baron's eldest son's only surviving son was cr Viscount Southwell 1776, *see* Southwell, 7 Viscount); *b* 1905; *m* 1930, Capt Sir Robert Stirling-Hamilton, 12 Bt, RN (d 1982); 1 s (13 Bt), 2 da (Mrs Ian MacKinnon, Mrs George Walker); *Style*— Eileen, Lady Stirling-Hamilton; Nyton House, Westergate, W Sussex

STISTED, Brig (Joseph) Nigel; OBE (1978); o s of Joseph Laurence Heathcote Stisted (d 1975), of Fordlands, Catsfield, Sussex, and Katherine Dorothea, *née* Sayer; *b* 23 July 1931; *Educ* Winchester, RMA Sandhurst; *m* 11 Aug 1962, Judith Ann, da of Col Duncan Arthur Davidson Eykyn, DSO, DL (d 1986), of Howgatemouth, Howgate, Penicuik, Midlothian, Scotland; 2 s (Charles b 21 July 1963, William b 12 April 1965); *Career* cmmnd The Royal Scots 1952; served 1 Bn in Berlin, Korea, Egypt, Cyprus, Scotland, Suez Operations; Adjt Depot The Royal Scots 1957-58; ADC to Cmdt British Sector Berlin 1959-60; instructor RMA Sandhurst 1960-61; Staff Coll Camberley 1962; BM 155 (Lowland) Bde 1963-65; Co Cdr 1 Bn The Royal Scots 1965-67; Jt Services Staff Coll 1967; asst military advsr British High Cmmn Ottawa 1968-70; 2 IC 1 Bn The Royal Scots 1970-71, CO 1 Bn 1971-73 (despatches 1972); AAG Scottish Div Edinburgh 1974-76; cmd New Coll (SMC) RMA Sandhurst 1976-79; Brig Inf HQ UKLF 1980; cmd 52 Lowland Bde 1980-83, medically ret 1983; memb Seagull Tst; guide at the Georgian House Edinburgh (Nat Tst); vol gardener St Columba's Hospice Edinburgh; elected memb Queen's Body Guard for Scotland (Royal Co of Archers) 1966; *Recreations* shooting, stamp collecting; *Clubs* The Royal Scots (Edinburgh); *Style*— Brig Nigel Stisted, OBE; c/o The Bank of Scotland, New Town Branch, 103 George Street, Edinburgh EH2 3HR

STITCHER, Gerald Maurice; CBE (1979); s of David Stitcher, OStJ (d 1947), and Eva, *née* Ruda; *b* 25 June 1915; *Educ* St George Monoux GS; *m* 22 Dec 1940, Marie; 1 s (Malcolm David b 1949), 1 da (Carole Linda b 1944); *Career* WWII served RAMC, RAOC and REME 1940-46; dir: Gerimar Ltd, Centl Meat Supply Ltd, George Waller Meat Products; former chm Fin Corpn of London, chm Lidstone Ltd; asst chm joint conciliation bd Smithfield Market; cncllr Corpn of London 1967- (chief commoner 1979-80); Freeman City of London, memb Worshipful Co of Butchers; *Recreations* debating; *Clubs* City Livery, Guildhall; *Style*— Gerald Stitcher, Esq; 7 South Lodge, Grove End Road, St John's Wood, London NW8 9ER (☎ 01 286 2462)

STITT, Iain Paul Anderson; s of John Anderson Stitt, of Harrogate, and Elise Marie, *née* Dias; *b* 21 Dec 1939; *Educ* Ampleforth, RNC Dartmouth; *m* 1 July 1961, Barbara Mary, da of Richard Bertram George, of Carlisle (d 1986); 2 s (Jonathan b 1964, Paul b 1965), 3 da (Philippa b 1962, Kristina b 1966, Francesca b 1968); *Career* divnl midshipman RNC Dartmouth 1960, HMS Wotton (Fishery Protection Sqdn) 1960-61, HMS Alert (Far East Despatch Vessel) 1961-63, HMS Yarmouth (Londonderry Sqdn) 1963-64, Lt HMS Fiskerton (Singapore Minesweeping Sqdn) 1964-66; Arthur Andersen & Co 1966-: tax ptnr 1974, off managing ptnr Leeds Off 1975-81, UK dir of tax competence 1981-88, Euro dir of tax competence 1992 office in Brussels; cncl memb Inst of Taxation 1969- (pres 1982-84); memb tax ctee: CBI 1980-86, Inst of CA in Eng and Wales 1984-; involved with diocesian fin bd Leeds RC Diocese 1987-; memb Hon Co of CA in Eng and Wales; ATII 1964, FTII 1969, ACA 1970, FCA 1975; *Books* Deferred Tax Accounting (1986), Chapters Contributed to Development Land Tax (1976), Tolley's Tax Planning (1980-88) ; *Recreations* skiing, classical music; *Clubs* Royal Automobile, Royal Oversea League; *Style*— Iain Stitt, Esq ; 2 Hereford Rd, Harrogate HG1 2NP, North Yorkshire (☎ 0423 63 846); Avenue Moliere 204, 1060 Bruxelles, Belgium (☎ 32 2 344 96 26); Arthur Andersen & Co, 1992 Off, Avenue Des Arts 56, 1040 Bruxelles, Belgium (☎ 32 2 510 42 73, fax 32 2 510 43 08, telex 21678)

STOCK, Dr Anthony Frederick (Tony); s of Raymond Gilbert Stock (d 1982), of Plymouth, and Lilian; *b* 2 Jan 1947; *Educ* Sutton HS for Boys Plymouth, Univ of Nottingham (PhD), Univ of Surrey (BSc, MPhil); *m* 1, 11 April 1968, Jennifer Mary, da of James Thomas Parcell, of Weston Super Mare; 1 s (Jonathan b 1971), 2 da (Maria b 1970, Rebecca b 1973); m 2, Anne Caroline, da of James Thomas Tynan, of Hartlepool; 1 s (Nathaniel James b 1985); *Career* civil engr; res assoc Br Petroleum Co plc BP Res Centre, lectr Civil Engrg Univ of Dundee, sr res asst Univ of Nottingham, published tech papers with the princ topics of pavement design and recycling bituminous materials, major contrib to the tech of recycling bituminous materials within the UK; visiting researcher at Texas Tport Inst 1984-85; *Books* Concrete Pavements (1988); *Recreations* sailing, hill walking, squash; *Clubs* Royal Ocean Racing; *Style*— Dr Tony Stock; The Clydesdale Bank, Chief Off, 96 High Street, Dundee DD1 9DD; BP Research Centre, Chertsey Rd, Sunbury-on-Thames, Middlesex TW16 7LN

STOCK, Keith Lievesley; CB (1957); s of late Cyril Lievesley Stock, of Surrey, and Irene Mary, *née* Tomkins (decd); *b* 23 Oct 1911; *Educ* Charterhouse, New Coll Oxford (MA); *m* 1937, Joan Katherine, da of John Rothwell Milne (d 1935); 2 s (Andrew, David), 1 da (Juliet); *Career* Petroleum Dept BOT 1935, Miny of Fuel and Power 1942, IDC 1951, Cabinet Office 1954, Miny of Fuel and Power 1955, Miny of Technol 1964, under sec Dept of Economic Affrs 1965-68, ret; *Books* Rose Books 1550-1975 (1984); *Style*— Keith Stock, Esq, CB; c/o Barclays Bank Ltd, 12 Millbank, London SW1P 3JH

STOCKDALE, His Hon Judge Frank Alleyne; s of Sir Frank Arthur Stockdale, GCMG, CBE (d 1959), and Annie Dora, *née* Packer; *b* 16 Oct 1910; *Educ* Repton, Magdalene Coll Cambridge (MA); *m* 14 Sept 1942, (Frances) Jean, da of late Sir Fitzroy Anstruther Gough Calthorpe, Bt, of Elvesham Hall, Hartley Wintney, Hants; 1 s (James Arther Fitzroy), 2 da ((Sarah) Victoria (Mrs Castleman) d 1979, (Frances) Jane (Mrs Deacon); *Career* serv WWII 1939-45, Lt-Col Inniskilling Dragoon Gds BEF 1939-40, N Africa 1942-43 (despatches); barr Gray's Inn 1934, bencher 1964, dep chm Hampshire QS 1954-66, dep chm London QS 1966-71, circuit judge (formerly county ct judge Ilford and Westminster cts) 1964-79; memb Inter-Departmental Ctee on Adoption Law 1969-72 (chm 1971-72); chm Hampshire County Br Legion; *Clubs* Garrick; *Style*— His Hon Frank Stockdale; Victoria Place, Monmouth, Gwent NP5 3BR (☎ 0600 5039)

STOCKDALE, Gp Capt George William; s of William Stockdale (d 1980), and Lilian Mabel, *née* Clubley (d 1966); *b* 17 Dec 1932; *Educ* Coll of Commerce Hull, RMA Sandhurst (MITD, FSAE); *m* 14 Sept 1957, Ann, da of John James Caldon (d 1981); 2 s (Michael b 19 Oct 1960, Robert b 9 Oct 1962), 2 da (Anna b 4 Sept 1959, Elizabeth b 15 Jan 1965); *Career* RAF 1951-81, served in Egypt, Aden, Oman, Germany, Singapore, Malaysia, Hong Kong; Staff Coll Bracknell 1967; Policy and Planning Div 1976-79; cmd Regt Offr Germany 1979-81; sec-gen Plastics and Rubber Inst 1985- (dep sec-gen 1982-85); FBIM 1978, MITD 1978, FSAE 1986; *Recreations* fell walking, painting, music; *Clubs* RAF; *Style*— Gp Capt George W Stockdale; The Plastics and Rubber Institute, 11 Hobart Place, London SW1W 0HL (☎ 01 245 9555, fax 01 823 1379, telex 915719 PRIUK G)

STOCKDALE, Hon Lady (Louise); *née* Fermor-Hesketh; da of 1 Baron Hesketh, JP (d 1944); *b* 15 Dec 1911; *m* 1937, Sir Edmund Villiers Minshull Stockdale, 1 Bt, JP (d 1989); 2 s, 1 da (d 1970); *Style*— The Hon Lady Stockdale; Hoddington House, Upton Grey, Basingstoke, Hants (☎ Basingstoke 862 437)

STOCKDALE, (Arthur) Noel; DFM; *Career* chm Associated Dairies Ltd; dir: Adel Investmt Tst, Anzo Hldgs, A R McIndoe Ltd, Austragrades Chemists, Bramhams Foods, Burnley Dairies, Calder Vale Creamery, Club Life Ltd, Craven Dairies Ltd, Farm Stores Ltd, G E M Super Centres Ltd, Gazeley Properties, Grimshawe Hldgs, Halifax Bldg Soc, J Bradbury & Sons, Northern Provincial Dairies, Parkside General Estate, Robert Hardman Ltd, Sandmartin Foods, Steeton Investments Ltd, Valu Petroleum, Wades Departmental Stores, Wharfedale Creamery Co; regional dir Nat West Bank (Eastern bd); kt 1986; *Style*— Sir Noel Stockdale, DFM; c/o Associated Dairies Ltd, Craven House, Kirkstall Rd, Leeds 3, W Yorks (☎ 0532 440141)

STOCKDALE, Sir Thomas Minshull; 2 Bt (UK), of Hoddington, Co Southampton; er s of Sir Edmund Villiers Minshull Stockdale, 1 Bt, JP (d 1989); *b* 7 Jan 1940; *Educ* Eton, Worcester Coll Oxford; *m* 1965, Jacqueline, da of Ha-Van-Vuong, of Saigon (now Ho Chi Minh City); 1 s, 1 da; *Heir* s, John Minshull Stockdale b 13 Dec 1967; *Career* barr 1966; *Recreations* shooting, travel; *Clubs* Turf, MCC; *Style*— Sir Thomas Stockdale, Bt; Conington Hall, Cambridge (☎ Elsworth 252)

STOCKEN, (George Hubert) Anthony; s of George Walter Stocken (d 1974), of Wilts, and Olga Germaine, *née* Helson; *b* 30 June 1929; *Educ* Kings Coll Taunton, Royal West of England Acad Faculty of Arch, Bristol Univ (RIBA); *m* 7 Sept 1956, Pauline Denise Cruse, da of Arthur Ford (d 1987), of Hampshire; 1 s (Michael George Anthony b 1957), 1 da (Sarah Ann b 1958); *Career* chartered architect; princ in private arch practice, Architectural Heritage Year Award 1975, Times RICS Conservation Award 1976, Civic Tst Commendation Award 1986; Liveryman and memb of the Ct of Assts of Coach Makers and Coach Harness Makers of London (chm of Livery Ctee 1983-85); Salisbury ccncllr 1968-74 (dist cncllr 1974-83, chm dist Cncl 1976-77), mayor of City of Salisbury 1975-76; chm Salisbury Round Table 1966-67, vice chm Nat Assoc of Chartered Tstees; chm: Sarum 76 Salisbury Recreation Centre, Salisbury Branch Nat Fed of Old Age Pensioners Assoc 1975-82 (pres 1982); chm Salisbury Dist Queen's Silver Jubilee Appeal Fund, tstee Salisbury Almshouse and Welfare Charities; fndr memb Sarum Housing Assoc; fndr chm Rehabilitation Engrg Movement Advsy Panel in Salisbury Dist; chm Workface Community Serv Scheme; memb: Salisbury DHA 1981-83, Salisbury Dist Health Cncl 1983-87; chm govrs Salisbury Coll of Technol 1979-81; vice chm of govrs Bishop Wordsworth GS 1980-83; govr: Exeter House Sch for Disabled Children, St Martin's CE Junior Aided Sch; fndr chm Cncl for Sport and Recreation in Salisbury Dist, chm Westwood Sports Centre, memb of Salisbury Festival Cncl; patron: Salisbury Playhouse, St Edmunds Art Centre; chm of Wilts Assoc of Boys Clubs and Youth Clubs, fndr chm Salisbury Boys Club 1974-76 (pres 1977); memb of Nat Cncl of Boys Club 1974-76, chm Nat Devpt of Boys Club 1983-86, ARIBA, FFAS, FRSA, FFB; *Recreations* horse riding, hunting, swimming, walking; *Clubs* Naval, Royal Soc of Arts, RIBA; *Style*— Anthony Stocken, Esq; St Andrew's House, West Street, Wilton, Salisbury, Wilts (☎ 0722 744222); Wilts and Bodrigy, The Lizard, Helston, Cornwall

STOCKEN, Oliver Henry James; s of Henry Edmund West Stocken (d 1980); *b* 22 Dec 1941; *Educ* Felsted, Univ Coll Oxford; *m* 1967, Sally Forbes, da of James Dishon of Aust; 2 s, 1 da; *Career* md Barclays Aust 1982-; dir: N M Rothschild & Sons 1972-77, Esperanza Ltd 1977-79, Barclays Merchant Bank Ltd 1979-1986, Barclays de Zoete Wedd 1986-; ACA 1967; *Style*— Oliver Stocken Esq; Barclays de Zoete Wedd Ltd, Ebbgate House, 2 Swan Lane, London EC4

STOCKER, Lt-Col Edward Llewellyn; MC; s of Rear Adm Percy Stocker, OBE (d 1960), and Phillis Edith Llewellyn, *née* Wathen (d 1932); *b* 10 July 1916; *Educ* Marlborough, RMA Woolwich; *m* 1 Feb 1966, Philippa Ruth, da of George Alexander Holmden; *Career* army offr; RMA Woolwich 1935, cmmnd RA 1936; 23 Field Bde RA UK 1936; Mountain Artillery IA served NW Frontier, India, Burma 1938-44; staff coll Camberley 1944; Italy HQ BAOR cmd 25 Field Regt RA 1958-60; UK and Cyprus HQ BAOR 1960-62; ret 1962; *Recreations* hunting, sailing, skiing; *Clubs* Army and Navy, ROR, Ski Club of GB; *Style*— Lt-Col Edward L Stocker, MC; Woodrow Farm, Stourton Caundie, Sturminster Newton, Dorset (☎ Bishops Caundle 265)

STOCKER, Rt Hon Lord Justice; Sir John Dexter; MC (1943), TD; s of late John Augustus Stocker, of Carshalton Surrey; *b* 7 Oct 1918; *Educ* Westminster Sch, London Univ (LLB); *m* 1956, Margaret Mary, da of Alexander Patrick Hegarty, of Wimbledon; *Career* 2 Lt Queen's Own Royal West Kent Regt (TA) 1939, served in France 1940, ME 1942-43, Italy 1943-46, DAAG mil mission to Italian Army 1946; barr Middle Temple 1948, QC 1965, master of the Bench 1971, recorder of Crown Ct 1972-73, a judge of High Ct of Justice (Queen's Bench div) 1973-86, presiding judge SE circuit 1976-79; Lord Justice of Appeal 1986-; kt 1973; *Clubs* MCC, Naval and Military; *Style*— Sir John Dexter Stocker, MC, TD; Royal Courts of Justice, Strand, London WC2

STOCKER, Col Simon Robin Alonzo; OBE (1982); s of Lt-Col A J Stocker, DSO (d 1950), of Northlands, Chichester, Sussex, and Margaret Aileen, *née* Slane (d 1978); *b* 17 May 1939; *Educ* Wellington Coll, RMA Sandhurst; *m* 25 Sept 1965, Rosemary Victoria, da of Maj Gen George Robert Turner-Cain, CB, CBE, DSO, of Norfolk; 2 s (James b 1967, William b 1969), 1 da (Victoria b 1974); *Career* Col; served in Borneo, Aden, N Ireland; instr RMA Sandhurst 1975-77, CO IRRW 1980-82, Chief G2 HQ N Ireland 1982-84, ADC GOC Berlin 1964-, currently Branch Chief SHAPE; chm Army Hockey 1982-83, rep army at: cricket 1969 and 1971, hockey 1964 and 1969-70; *Recreations* cricket, hockey, tennis, shooting, singing; *Clubs* MCC; *Style*— Col Simon Stocker, OBE; Grindlays Bank plc, 13 St James's Square, London SW1Y 4LF

STOCKS, Alan George Hubert; TD (1971 and clasp 1977); s of Hubert Sydney Stocks, and Phyllis Margaret Mary, *née* Knight (d 1972); *b* 22 Sept 1940; *Educ* St John's Leatherhead; *m* 23 March 1974, Marie Georgina, da of George Leander Lowe (d 1956); *Career* Maj: King's Regt (TA) 1959-64, Royal Sussex Regt (TA) 1964-67, Queen's Regt (TA) 1967-; Freeman City of London 1980; memb SE TA&VRA; tstee of Marshall's Charity; dir: G A Turner & Co 1967-87, Sussex Prints 1987-; *Recreations* theatre, shooting; *Style*— Alan Stocks, Esq, TD; Old Meadows, Randalls Rd, Leatherhead, Surrey

STOCKS, Hon Helen Jane; JP (Inner London); da of Baroness Stocks (Life Peeress, d 1975), and Prof John Leofric Stocks, DSO (d 1937); *b* 1920; *Style*— The Hon Helen Stocks, JP; 44 Regents Park Rd, London NW1 (☎ 01 586 2431)

STOCKTON, 2 Earl of (1984); Alexander Daniel Alan Macmillan; also Viscount Macmillan of Ovenden; s of Rt Hon Maurice Victor Macmillan, PC, MP (Viscount Macmillan of Ovenden, d 1984), and Katharine, Viscountess Macmillan of Ovenden, DBE, *qv*, gs of 1 Earl of Stockton (d 1986); *b* 10 Oct 1943; *Educ* Eton, Ecole Politique Université de Paris, Strathclyde Univ; *m* 1970, Hélène Birgitte (Bitta), da of late Alan Douglas Christie Hamilton, of Stable Green, Mitford, Northumberland; 1 s (Daniel Maurice Alan b 1974), 2 da (Rebecca b 1980, Louisa b 1982); *Heir* s, Viscount Macmillan of Ovenden; *Career* book and magazine publisher; journalist Glasgow Herald 1965-66, reporter Daily Telegraph 1967, foreign corr Daily Telegraph 1968-69, chief Euro corr Sunday Telegraph 1969-70, dep chm Macmillan Ltd 1972-80, chm Macmillan Publishers 1980-; English Speaking Union 1978-84 and 1986-; FBIM, FRSA; *Recreations* shooting, fishing, photography, conversation; *Clubs* Beefsteak, Buck's, Carlton, Garrick, Pratts, White's; *Style*— The Rt Hon the Earl of Stockton; Macmillan Publishers Ltd, 4 Little Essex St, London WC2R 3LF (☎ 01 836 6633)

STOCKTON, Fay (Mrs Millett); da of Capt Albert Reginald Stockton, TD, of Sale, Ches, and Maureen, *née* May; *b* 12 Nov 1953; *Educ* Withington Girl Sch, Manchester Univ (LLB); *m* 25 April 1983, Lawrence Randolph Elijah Millett, s of Elijah Millett, of Manchester (d 1984); 1 s (Mitchell b 25 Jan 1984); *Career* called to the Bar Lincoln's Inn 1976, practises London and N circuit; *Style*— Miss Fay Stockton; 24 Old Buildings, Lincoln's Inn, London WC2 (☎ 01 242 2744, fax 01 831 8095); 40 King St, Manchester M2 6BA (☎ 061 832 9082, fax 061 835 2139); (portable tel: 0860 812098, home fax 061 434 5094)

STODART OF LEASTON, Baron (Life Peer UK 1981); (James) Anthony Stodart; PC (1974); s of late Col Thomas Stodart, CIE, and Mary Alice Coullie; *b* 6 June 1916; *Educ* Wellington; *m* 1940, Hazel Jean, da of late Lt Ronald James Usher, RN; *Career* sits as Cons peer in House of Lords; farmer; MP (C) Edinburgh W 1959-74 (stood as Lib Berwick & E Lothian 1950, C Midlothian and Peebles 1951, Midlothian 1955), under-sec of state for Scotland 1963-64, min Agric and Fish 1972-74 (parly sec 1970-72); chm: Agric Credit Corpn 1975-87, Ctee Inquiry Local Govt Scotland 1980-, Manpower Review of Vet Profession in UK 1984-85; dir FMC 1980-82; *Recreations* playing golf and preserving a sense of humour; *Clubs* New (Edinburgh), Hon Co of Edinburgh Golfers, Caledonian; *Style*— The Rt Hon the Lord Stodart of Leaston, PC; Lorimers, N Berwick, E Lothian (☎ 0620 2457); Leaston, Humbie, E Lothian (☎ 087 533 213)

STODDART, John Maurice; s of Gordon Stoddart (d 1983), of Wallasey, and May, *née* Ledder (d 1970); *b* 18 Sept 1938; *Educ* Wallasey GS, Reading Univ (BA); *Career* head dept econ and business studies Sheffield Poly 1970-72, asst dir NE London Poly 1972-76, dir Humberside Coll 1976-83, princ Sheffield City Poly 1983-; memb: Cncl for Nat Academic Awards 1982-88, cncl for Mgmnt Educn and Devpt 1987-, Ct Univ of Sheffield 1983-; dir Sheffield Sci Park 1988-, memb bd mgmnt Crucible Theatre; hon fell Humberside Coll 1983, companion Br Business Graduates Soc 1984; FBIM 1978, FRSA 1980; *Books* various articles on business and mgmnt educn; *Recreations* hill walking, squash, rowing, biography; *Clubs* Reform; *Style*— John Stoddart, Esq; 58 Riverdale Rd, Sheffield S10 3FB (☎ 0742 683 636); Sheffield City Polytechnic, Pond St, Sheffield (☎ 0742 738 626, telex 54 680 SH POLY G)

STODDART, Wing Cdr Sir Kenneth Maxwell; KCVO (1989), AE (1942), JP (Liverpool 1952); s of Wilfrid Bowring Stoddart (d 1935), of Liverpool, and Mary Hyslop, *née* Maxwell; *b* 26 May 1914; *Educ* Sedbergh, Clare Coll Cambridge; *m* 5 Sept 1940, Jean Roberta Benson, da of late Dr John Benson Young; 2 da (Jennifer Jean Maxwell (Mrs Jackson) b 1941, Charlotte Maxwell b 1949); *Career* served RAuxAF 1936-45 (vice-chm (Air) W Lancs T&AFA 1954-64); Ld-Lt Merseyside 1979-89 (DL 1974-79, Lancs 1958), High Sheriff Merseyside 1974; chm Cearns & Brown 1973-84, United Mersey Supply Co 1978-81; chm Liverpool Child Welfare Assoc 1965-81; Hon LLD Liverpool; KStJ 1979; *Clubs* Liverpool Racquet; *Style*— Wing Cdr Kenneth Stoddart, AE, JP, HM Ld-Lt for Merseyside; The Spinney, Overdale Rd, Willaston, S Wirral L64 1SY (☎ 051 327 5183)

STODDART, Michael Craig; s of Frank Ogle Boyd Stoddart, of Westbourne, Hants, and Barbara Vincent, *née* Craig; *b* 27 Mar 1932; *Educ* Marlborough; *m* 15 April 1961, (Susan) Brigid, da of late Capt Denis North-East O'Halloran, RA, of IOW; 2 s (James b 1965, Edward b 1973), 2 da (Philippa b 1963, Lucinda b 1970); *Career* jt chief exec Singer & Friedlander Ltd 1955-73; chm Electra Investment Tst plc 1986 (dep chm and chief exec 1974-86); memb: cncl of Aims of Industry, London cncl Ironbridge Gorge Museum Tst; tstee All Hallows Church; memb Worshipful Co of Chartered Accountants in England and Wales; FCA 1955; *Recreations* country pursuits, shooting, golf, tennis, theatre, travel; *Clubs* Boodle's; *Style*— Michael Stoddart Esq; Compton House, Kinver, Worcs DY7 5LY; Warwick Lodge, 42 St George's Drive, London SW1V 4BT; Electra Investment Trust plc, 65 Kingsway, London WC2B 6QT (☎ 01 831 6464, telex 265525 ELECG, fax 01 404 5388, car tel 0836 510649/0860 371399)

STODDART, Peter Laurence Bowring; s of Laurence Bowring Stoddart JP (d 1973), of Cheddington Manor, Leighton Buzzard Beds, and Gwendolen Mary, *née* Russell; *b* 24 June 1934; *Educ* Sandroyd Sch, Eton Trinity Coll Oxford; *m* 29 May 1957, Joanna, da of Thomas Adams; 1 s (Clive Laurence Bowring), 2 da (Fiona Gwendolen Jane, Belinda May); *Career* Nat Serv 2 Lt 14/20 Kings Hussars 1952-54; with C T Bowring Gp 1955- 80; dir: C T Bowring & Co Ltd 1967-80, Singer & Friedlander, Crusader Insur Co Ltd 1967-80, English & American Insur Co Ltd 1967- 80; Fleming Mercantile Investmt Tst plc 1976-80; chm: Robert Fleming Insur Brokers 1980-89, Greenfriar Investmt Co Ltd 1977-89; Capt Bucks CCC 1957-66; master: Whaddon Chase Hunt 1969-83 Heythrop Hunt 1988-; former Master Worshipful Co of Salters 1986-87; memb Lloyds; *Recreations* field sports & countryside, travel; *Clubs* Whites, Cavalry and Guards, MCC; *Style*— Peter Stoddart, Esq; North Rye House, Moreton-in-Marsh, Glos GL56 0XU (☎ 0451 30 636); Robert Fleming Insurance Brokers Ltd, Staple Hall, Stone House Ct, London EC3A 7AX (☎ 01 621 1263, fax 01 623 6175, telex 883 735/6)

STODDART OF SWINDON, Baron (Life Peer UK 1983), of Reading in the Royal Co of Berkshire; David Leonard Stoddart; s of late Arthur Stoddart and Queenie, *née* Price; *b* 4 May 1926; *Educ* St Clement Danes GS, Henley GS; *m* 1, 1946 (m dis 1960), Doreen M Maynard; 1 da; m 2, 1961, Jennifer, adopted da of late Mrs Lois Percival-Alwyn, of Battle, Sussex; 2 s (Hon Howard b 1966, Hon Mathwyn b 1969); *Career* former clerical worker: PO telephones, railways, power station and hosp; former ldr Lab Gp Reading Cncl (memb Reading County Borough Cncl 1954-72); Parly candidate (Lab): Newbury 1959 and 1964, Swindon by-election 1969; MP (Lab) Swindon 1970-83; PPS to Min of Housing and Construction 1974-75, asst govt whip 1975, lord cmmr Treasury 1976-77, oppn spokesman Industry 1982-83; oppn energy spokesman (Lords) 1983-88, oppn whip (Lords) 1983-88, Trade Unions EETPU 1953-, NALGO 1951-70, memb of nat jt cncl Electricity Supply Ind 1967-70; *Style*— The Rt Hon the Lord Stoddart of Swindon; Sintra, 37a Bath Rd, Reading, Berks (☎ 0734 576726); House of Lords, London SW1

STODDARY, David Russell; s of Laurence Bowring Stoddary (d 1972), of Cheddineton Manor, Leighton Buzzard, Beds, and Gwendoline Mary Russell; *b* 25 Dec 1937; *Educ* Eton Coll; *m* 27 Nov 1968, Eleanor Mary, da of Samuel Soames; 2 s (Edward Laurence, Jonathan William); *Career* Lt 14/20 Kings Hussars, cmmnd 1956, served BAOR Germany 1956-59; joined Wedd Jefferson 1959 (ptnr 1961-), joined Tattersalls Ltd 1980 (dir 1983-86); memb Stock Exchange 1961-80; *Recreations* horse racing and breeding, cricket; *Style*— David Stoddary, Esq

STOFFBERG, Leon Dutoit; s of William Dutoit Stoffberg, and Yvonne Mei, *née* Robinson; *b* 11 Feb 1951; *Educ* Rondesbosch Boys Sch, Cape Town Univ (CTA); *m* 17 July 1979, Pauline Jean; 1 da (Lisa); *Career* fin dir: fin div Great Universal Stores Gp plc 1983-85, Gibbs Hartley Cooper Ltd 1985-; memb Inst of South African CAs; *Style*— Leon Stoffberg, Esq; Bishops Court, Artillery Lane, London E1 7LP (☎ 01 2477 5433)

STOKE, Gordon Alexander; MBE (1942), DSC (1941); s of Stephen Stoke (d 1980), and Barbara Stoke (d 1966); *b* 28 June 1921; *Educ* Westcliff HS; *m* 1944, Doreen, da of Engr Capt H E Le Poidevin, RN (d 1982); 3 s; *Career* served RN WWII (despatches 1941), invalided 1947; dir: Tower Works Property Co Ltd, Lewis Electric Gp Ltd GS Managerial Services Ltd, Vasayr Ltd, Success Through Ptnrship Ltd, fndr Preformations Gp; ret 1983; *Recreations* sailing (yacht 'Arbella'), theatre, opera; *Clubs* RNSA, Hornet, Warsash; *Style*— Gordon Stoke, Esq, MBE, DSC; Ashwick House, Holly Hill Lane, Sarisbury Green, nr Southampton, Hants SO3 6AH (☎ 048 95 84248)

STOKELY, Guy Robert; *b* 30 Oct 1943; *Educ* Forest Sch, Oxford Univ (MA); *m* 4 Oct 1968, Wendy Anne; 3 s (Robert b 1970, Tom b 1979, Tim b 1983), 1 da (Sarah b 1973); *Career* fin vice-pres Manufacturers Life Insur Co 1966-78, gen mangr Saudi Int Bank 1978-; *Recreations* golf, water sports, gardening; *Clubs* RAC; *Style*— Guy Stokely, Esq; The Parsonage, Great Dunmow, Essex CM6 2AT (☎ 0371 2430); 99 Bishopsgate, London EC2M 3TB (☎ 01 638 2323, fax 01 628 8633, telex 8812261/2)

STOKER, Dr Dennis James; s of Dr George Morris Stoker (d 1949), of Mitcham, Surrey, and Elsie Margaret, *née* Macqueen (d 1986); *b* 22 Mar 1928; *Educ* Oundle, Guy's Hosp Med Sch Univ of London (BM, BS); *m* 22 Sept 1951, Anne Sylvia Nelson, da of Norman Forster (d 1962), of Haywards Heath, Sussex; 2 s (Philip b 1954, Neil b 1956), 2 da (Claire b 1952, Catherine b 1958); *Career* cmmnd med branch RAF 1952, RAF Brompton 1952-53, RAF Bridgnorth 1953-55, RAF Hosp West Kirby 1955-56, med div RAF Hosp Wroughton 1956-58, i/c med div RAF Hosp Akrotiri Cyprus 1958-61, physician i/c chest unit RAF Hosp Wroughton 1961-64, metabolic unit St Mary's Hosp London 1964-65 (sabbatical), i/c med div RAF Hosp Steamer Point Aden 1965-67, i/c med div RAF Hosp Cosford Staffs 1967-68, ret Wing Cdr 1968; conslt radiologist: St George's Hosp 1972-87, Royal Nat Orthopaedic Hosp 1972-; dir of radiologist studies Inst of Orthopaedics 1975 (dean 1987-), ed Skeletal Radiology 1984-, vice pres Royal Coll of Radiologists 1989- (memb of faculty bd 1983-85, cncl memb 1985-88, cncl memb 1985-88); DMRD, FRCP 1976, FRCR 1976, FRSM 1958; *Books* Knee Arthrography (1980), Orthopaedics; self assessment in radiology (jtly, 1988), Radiology of Skeletal Disorders (jtly, third ed 1989); *Recreations* medical history, patio gardening, dinghy sailing in warm climates; *Clubs* RAF; *Style*— Dr Dennis Stoker; 4 Waterloo Terrace, Islington, London N1 1TQ (☎ 01 359 0617); 25 Wimpole St, London W1M 7AD (☎ 01 935 4747); Dept of Radiology, Royal Nat Orthopaedic Hosp, 45-51 Bolsover St, London W1P 8AQ (☎ 01 387 5070, ext 269)

STOKER, Linda Beryl; da of Bernard Alistar Dow, and Beryl Georgina Edith, *née* Taylor; *b* 10 July 1954; *Educ* Goffs GS, NE London Poly, memb of Inst of Personnel Mgmnt; *m* 28 Sept 1974, Martin John, s of Albert James Stoker; *Career* publicity offr The Rank Orgn; trg mangr EMI Leisure 1977, trg advsr Hotel and Catering Indust Trg Bd 1979, field organiser Manpower Servs Cmmn 1981, md Dow-Stoker Trg Assocs 1983-; *Recreations* sailing, netball; *Style*— Mrs Linda Stoker; Dow-Stoker, The Mill, Stortford Rd, Hatfield Heath, Nr Bishop's Stortford, Herts (☎ 0279 730056)

STOKER, Sir Michael George Parke; CBE (1974); *b* 1918,July; *Career* former lectr in pathology Cambridge Univ, fell and dir med studies Clare Coll Cambridge and prof of virology Glasgow Univ, dir Imperial Cancer Research Fund Laboratories 1968-79; former foreign sec and vice-pres Royal Soc 1976-81, former pres Clare Hall Cambridge 1980-87; FRSE, FRS, FRCP; kt 1980; *Style*— Sir Michael Stoker, CBE; Clare Hall, Cambridge

STOKER, Robert Burdon; s of Kenneth Stoker, JP (d 1979); *b* 12 July 1914; *Educ* Marlborough; *m* 1941, Mildred, da of Rev Prof Allan Cameron; 1 s, 2 da; *Career* dep Miny War Tport rep in Gourock Bougie, S Tunisia, Sicily, N Adriatic; former chm: Br Engine Insurance Co, Manchester Liners 1968-79; former pres: Manchester C of C 1967-68, Cheadle Cons Assoc; pres Outward Bound (Manchester); Jubilee Medal; Hon MA Manchester Univ; *Books* The Legacy of Arthur's Chester (1966), The Saga of Manchester Liners (1985); *Recreations* golf; *Clubs* St James's (Manchester), Royal Liverpool Golf; *Style*— Robert Stoker, Esq; 23 Carrwood Rd, Wilmslow, Cheshire SK9 5DJ (☎ 0625 524916)

STOKES, Dr Adrian Victor; OBE (1983); s of Alfred Samuel Stokes, of 23 Hale Grove Gardens, Mill Hill, London, and Edna, *née* Kerrison; *b* 25 June 1945; *Educ* Orange Hill GS, UCL (BSc, PhD); *m* 3 Oct 1970 (m dis 1978), Caroline Therese, da of Arthur Campbell Miles, of London; *Career* chm Disabled Drivers' Motor Club 1972-82, vice pres Disabled Drivers' Motor Club 1982-, chm exec ctee Royal Assoc for Disability and Rehabilitation 1985-, govr and memb cncl of Mgmnt Motability 1977-, memb fin and gen purposes ctee Assoc for Spina Bifida and Hydrocephalus 1983-, tstee and memb cncl of mgmnt PHAB 1982-; memb: DHSS Working Party on Mobility Allowance 1975, DHSS Working Party on the Invalid Tricycle Repair Serv 1976-80, DHSS Silver Jubilee Ctee On Improving Access for Disabled People 1977-78, DHSS Ctee on Restricions Against Disabled People 1979-81, Social Security Advsy Ctee 1980-, Dept of Tport Panel of Advsrs on Disability 1983-85, Disabled Person's Advsy Ctee 1986-; pres Hendon North Lib Assoc, 1981-83, candidate for London Borough of Barnet Cncl Mill Hill Ward 1968, 1971, 1974 and 1978; Freeman: City of London 1988, Co of Info Technologists 1988; FBCS 1979, FIOD 1986, CChem 1976, MRSC 1976, MBIM 1986; res programmer GEC Computers Ltd 1969-71, res asst/res fell Inst Computer Sci/Dept stats and Computer Sci Univ Coll London 1971-77, sr res fell and sr lectr Sch of Info Sci The Hatfie ld Poly 1977-81, dir computing St Thomas' Hosp 1981-88, princ conslt NHS Info Mgmnt Centre 1988; *Books* An Introduction to Data Processing Networks (1978), Viewdata: A Public Information Utility (2 edn 1980), The Concise Encyclopaedia of Computer Terminology (1981), Networks (1981), What to Read in Microcomputing (with C Saiady, 1982), A Concise Encyclopaedia of Information Technology (3 edn 1986), Integrated Office Systems (1982), Computer Networks: Fundamentals and Practice (with M D and J M Bacon, 1984), Overview of Data Communications (1985), Communications Standards (1986), The A-Z of Business Computing (1986), OSI Standards and Acronyms (2 edn 1988); *Recreations* philately, computer programming; *Style*— Dr Adrian V Stokes, OBE; 97 Millway, Mill Hill, London NW7 3JL (☎ 01 959 6665); NHS Info Mgmnt Centre, 19 Calthorpe Road, Birmingham B15 1RP (☎ 021 454 1112, car tel 0860 549 584)

STOKES, Dr Alistair; *b* 22 July 1948; *Educ* Univ of Wales (BSc, PhD), Univ of Oxford (SRC res fellowship); *m* 22 Aug 1970, Stephanie Mary, da of B H Garland, of Fordingbridge, Hants; 2 da (Charlotte, Samantha); *Career* commercial dir Monsato Co St Louis Missouri USA 1980-82 (joined 1976); Glaxo Pharmaceuticals Ltd: int prod mangr 1982-83, mktg and sales dir Duncan Flockhart Ltd 1983-85; gen mangr Yorks Regnl Authy 1985-87; Glaxo Pharaceuticals Ltd; dir business devpt 1987-88, md Glaxo Labs Ltd 1988-; memb community advsy bd Clementine Churchill Hosps, memb East Berks Health Authy; *Books* Plasma Proteins (1977); *Recreations* reading, walking, music; *Style*— Dr Alistair Stokes; Glaxo Pharmaceuticals Ltd, Greenford, Middx UB6 OHE (☎ 01 422 3434, fax 01 423 4232, car tel 0836 207451, telex 946442 GLXEPT G)

STOKES, David Mayhew Allen; s of Henry Pauntley Allen Stokes (d 1965), and Marjorie Joan, *née* Mollison; *b* 12 Feb 1944; *Educ* Radley, Inst de Touraine (Tours), Churchill Coll Cambridge (MA); *m* 1970, Ruth Elizabeth, da of Charles Tunstall Evans, CMG, of Sussex; 1 s (Harry b 1974), 1 da (Jennifer b 1978); *Career* barr, rec of the Crown Ct 1985-; memb Gen Cncl of the Bar 1984-, guest Instr/Team Ldr Nat Inst of Trial Advocacy York Univ Toronto Canada 1986-, tstee London Suzuki Gp 1988-; *Recreations* amateur dramatics, madrigals; *Clubs* Norfolk (Norwich); *Style*— David M A Stokes, Esq; 30 Carmalt Gdns, London SW15 6NE (☎ 01 788 0913); 5 Paper Buildings Temple EC4Y 7HB (☎ 01 583 6117)

STOKES, Baron (Life Peer UK 1969); Donald Gresham Stokes; TD, DL (Lancs 1968); s of Harry Potts Stokes (d 1954), of Looe, Cornwall, and Mary Emma Gresham Stokes (d 1969); *b* 22 Mar 1914; *Educ* Blundell's, Harris Inst of Technol Preston; *m* 1939, Laura Elizabeth Courteney, da of Frederick C Lamb; 1 s; *Career* WWII Lt-Col REME, N Africa and Italy; gen sales mangr Leyland Motors Ltd 1950 (dir 1954), chm and md Leyland Motor Corpn 1968-75 (chief exec 1973-75), pres Br Leyland Ltd 1975-79 (conslt 1979-81); chm: Dutton-Forshaw Motor Gp Ltd, Jack Barclay Ltd; dir: Nat West Bank 1969-81, KBH Communications 1985-, Scottish Universal Investmts Ltd 1980-, Beherman Auto-Tports SA 1982-; chm: Two Counties Radio Ltd 1979-84, Br Arabian Advsy Co Ltd 1977-85, Dovercourt Motor Co Ltd 1982-; FEng 1976, FIMechE (pres 1972); fell Keble Coll Oxford; kt 1965; *Recreations* yachting ('Speedwell of Leyland'); *Clubs* Royal Motor Yacht (Cdre 1979-81), Beefsteak, Army & Navy; *Style*— The Rt Hon the Lord Stokes, TD, DL; Branksome Cliff, Westminster Rd, Poole, Dorset BH13 6JW (☎ 0202 763088); Jack Barclay Ltd, 18 Berkeley Sq, London W1X 6AE (☎ 01 629 7444)

STOKES, Dr John Fisher; s of Dr Kenneth Henry Stokes (d 1962), of Bexhill-on-Sea, and Mary Fisher (d 1973); *b* 19 Sept 1912; *Educ* Haileybury, Gonville and Caius Coll Cambridge (MB, BCh, MA, MD), Univ Coll Hosp Med Sch; *m* 21 Sept 1940, (Elizabeth) Joan, da of Thomas Rooke (d 1956); 1 s (Adrian b 1947), 1 da (Jennifer (Mrs Harrison) b 1942); *Career* WWII RAMC 1942-46, 14 Army in Far E, attached to Gen Orde Wingate's 2 Chindit Operation (despatches), demobbed Lt-Col; conslt physician UCH 1947-77; visiting physician: Mass Gen Hosp Boston 1958, Royal Victoria Hosp Montreal 1966; conslt in postgrad med educn in India and Sri Lanka WHO 1967 and 1979, chm common examining bd MRCP (UK) 1968-77, sr censor and vice pres RCP London 1969, pres section of med RSM London 1972, annual med educn visits to Thailand MOD FCO Colombo Pln 1969-75; squash racquets: runner up Br Is Amateur Championship 1937, Br Int 1938; chm Jesters Club 1953-59; Harveian Orator RCP London 1981; hon med advsr Leeds Castle Fndn 1977 (tstee 1984); FRCP 1947, FRCPE 1976; *Books* Examinations in Medicine (jtly, 1976 and 1977), MCQ on Lecture Notes on General Surgery (jtly, 1977, 1980, 1987), MCQ on Clinical Pharmacology (jtly, 1983 and 1988); *Recreations* piano-playing, chamber music, cooking, painting; *Clubs* Athenaeum, Savile; *Style*— Dr John Stokes; Ossicles, Newnham Hill, nr Henley-on-Thames, Oxon RG9 5TL (☎ 0491 641526)

STOKES, Sir John Heydon Romaine; MP (C) Halesowen and Stourbridge 1974-; s of late Victor Romaine Stokes, of Hitchin, Herts; *b* 23 July 1917; *Educ* Haileybury Coll, Queen's Coll Oxford; *m* 1, 1939, Barbara Esmée (d 1988), da of late R E Yorke, of Wellingborough, Northants; 1 s, 2 da; m 2, 21 Jan 1989, Mrs E F Plowman, wid of John Plowman; *Career* army 1939-46: Dakar expedition 1940, wounded N Africa 1943, mil asst to HM Min Beirut and Damascus 1944-46, Maj; personnel offr ICI 1946-51, personnel mangr Br Celanese 1951-59, dep personnel mangr Courtaulds 1957-59, ptnr Clive and Stokes Personnel Conslts 1959-80; Parly candidate (C): Gloucester 1964, Hitchin 1966; MP (C) Oldbury and Halesowen 1970-74, delegate to Cncl of Europe and WEU 1983-; elected to House of Laity gen Synod of Church of England 1985, chm General Purposes Ctee Primrose League 1971-85, vice-pres Royal Stuart Soc; kt 1988; *Clubs* Carlton, Buck's; *Style*— Sir John Stokes, MP; Down Hse, Steeple Claydon, nr Buckingham MK18 2PR

STOKES, Hon Michael Donald Gresham; s of Baron Stokes, TD (Life Peer); *b* 1947; *Educ* Southampton Univ (BSc); *m* 1970 (m dis 1982), Inger Anita, da of Douglas Percy; 1 s, 1 da; *Style*— The Hon Michael Stokes; 6 Boulters Crt, Maidenhead, Berks

STOKES, Michael George Thomas; s of Michael Philip Stokes (d 1988), and Elsie, *née* Brown (d 1980); *b* 30 May 1948; *Educ* Preston Catholic Coll, Univ of Leeds (LLB); *Career* called to the Bar Gray's Inn 1971, asst lectr Univ of Nottingham 1970-72, in practice MO ciruit 1973-, asst rec Crown Ct 1986-; *Recreations* skiing, theatre, racing, reading; *Clubs* Northampton and County (Northampton); *Style*— Michael Stokes, Esq; Alpha House, The Marsh, Crick, Northants NN6 7TN (☎ 0788 823 484); 7 Fountain Ct, Steelhouse Lane, Birmingham B4 6DR (☎ 021 236 8531, fax 021 236 4408)

STOKES, Dr Wilfred James; s of Alfred Stokes, JP (d 1943), and Frances Beatrice (Maeve) Stokes (d 1960); *b* 15 Dec 1911; *Educ* Bancrofts Sch, London Hosp (London); *m* 24 Aug 1939, Dorothy Kathleen, da of Lawrence Pillans Waddell, RNR (d 1932); 1 s (Ian b 1940), 1 da (Ann b 1943); *Career* WWII Maj RAMC; Paterson Scholar and chief asst cardiac dept London Hosp, tutor in postgraduate medicine Stoke Mandeville Hosp 1949-76; former conslt physician and cardiologist Stoke Mandeville Hosp, extraordinary memb Br Cardiac Soc 1977-; Liveryman Soc of Apothecaries, Freeman City of London; FRCP, DRCOG; *Publications* in leading med journals inc (in Br Heart Journal): Nicotinic Acid in Angina Pectoris (1944), Effect of Nitrates and exerciseon the inverted T wave (1946), Complete Heart Block and Bundle Branch Block (1947), The Heart in Scleroderma (1960); *Recreations* Wilfred Stokes library, Duke of Edinburgh hall; *Style*— Dr Wilfred Stokes; 25 Wellington Ave, Princes Risborough, Aylesbury, Bucks (☎ 08444 6000)

STONE, Dr Alexander; OBE (1988); s of Morris Stone (d 1945), and Rebecca Levi (d 1954); *b* 21 April 1907; *Educ* Hutcheson Boys GS Glasgow, Univ of Glasgow; *m* 26 May 1988, (Phyllis) Bette; *Career* lawyer and banker; chm Combined Capital Ltd; memb: investmt advsy ctee Univ of Glasgow, Scottish Business Gp; vice-pres Scottish Cncl for Spastics; settlor The Alexander Stone Fndn; Hon LLD Univ of Glasgow 1986; Hon memb Royal Glasgow Inst of the Fine Arts; *Style*— Dr Alexander Stone, OBE; 62 Sherbrooke Ave, Pollokshields, Glasgow G2 4RY (☎ 041 427 1567); 36 Renfield St,

Glasgow G2 1LU (☎ 041 226 4431, fax 041 332 5482, telex 7790570)

STONE, Brig Anthony Charles Peter; s of Maj (ret) Charles Cecil Stone, of The Coach House, Castle Rd, Salisbury, Wilts, and Kathleen Mons, *née* Grogan; *b* 25 Mar 1939; *Educ* St Joseph's Coll, RMA Sandhurst, Staff Coll Camberley; *m* 29 July 1967, (Elizabeth) Mary Eirlys Stone, da of Rev Canon Gideon Davies (d 1987), of Little Comberton, Worcs; 2 s (Guy b 1972, Mark b 1979); *Career* RA: cmmnd 1960, serv in Far and M East, BAOR and UK (light field, medium, locating and air def artillery), Battery Cdr Q (Sanna's Post) Battery and 2 i/c 5 Regt RA 1974-75, GSO 2 DAD MOD 1976, DS RMCS 1977, CO 5 Regt RA 1980, Col GS Def Progs Staff MOD 1983, mil dir of studies RMCS 1985, dir of operational requirements (Land) MOD 1986, dir light weapons projects MOD 1989-; *Recreations* shooting, country pursuits, family; *Clubs* Army & Navy; *Style*— Brig Anthony Stone

STONE, Carole; da of Harry A Stone (d 1976), and Kathleen Jacques (re-m 1979), *née* Conroy; *b* 30 May 1942; *Educ* Ashford County GS for Girls, Southampton Tech Coll; *Career* joined BBC in 1963 as Copytypist in Newsroom BBC South, asst prodr Radio Brighton 1967-70, gen talks prodr Radio FM 1970, prodr Radio 4's Any Questions? programme 1977-; *Clubs* Reform; *Style*— Miss Carole Stone; Flat 1, 39 Rutland Gate, London SW7 1PD (☎ 01 584 9430); BBC, Bristol, BS8 2LR (☎ 0272 732211, telex 265781 BSA, fax 0272 744114)

STONE, Clive Graham; s of Charles Thomas Stone and Frances Lilian Stone; *b* 7 July 1936; *Educ* Farnborough Hants, Northampton Coll of Advanced Technol, City Univ London; *m* 1957, Pamela Mary; 3 s; *Career* fell Br Coll of Optometrists; chm Dollond & Aitchison Group plc 1980- (gen mgmnt 1968, md 1973, dep chm 1978); dir Gallaher Ltd 1981-, dir Gallaher Pensions Ltd 1984-; dir Br Retailers Assoc Ltd 1985-; Freeman City of London; Memb Court Worshipful Co of Spectacle Makers; govr Royal Nat Coll for the Blind; tstee Fight for Sight; *Recreations* sailing, real tennis; *Clubs* Leamington Tennis Court Club; *Style*— C G Stone, Esq; c/o Dollond & Aitchison Gp plc, 1323 Coventry Rd, Yardley, Birmingham B25 8LP (☎ 021 706 6133, fax 021 7062741, telex 339435); Abbey Meads, Forrest Rd, Kenilworth, Warwicks CV8 1LT (☎ 0926 54553)

STONE, David; s of Joseph Stone (d 1972), and Zena, *née* Mindel (d 1987); *b* 27 May 1953; *Educ* Hasmonean Sch; *Career* CA in private practice (sole practitioner); personal asst to Norman Tebbit gen elections 1974 and 1979, cncllr London Borough of Camden 1982-86 (opposition spokesman on leisure servs 1983-86), Parly candidate (Cons) Stoke-on-Trent Central 1987, memb Cons Pty Nat Union Exec Ctee and Gen Purpose Ctees, nat chm Cons Political Centre 1987- (vice-chm 1984-87); *Recreations* cricket; *Clubs* MCC; *Style*— David Stone, Esq; 16 Goldhurst Terrace, London NW6 (☎ 01 328 4578, car tel 0836 213413)

STONE, Geoffrey Charles; s of Robert Stone, of London, and Olive Stone; *b* 27 Mar 1939; *Educ* Leyton Co HS, St David's Coll Lampeter (BA), St Catherines Coll Oxford (MA), Bristol Univ (PACE), Liverpool Univ (DASE); *m* 30 July 1965, Valerie Anne, da of William Jones (d 1985), of Liverpool; 1 s (Matthew b 1972), 1 da (Rachel b 1975); *Career* asst teacher Ruffwood Sch Kirkby Liverpool 1963-70, dep head teacher Grange Sch Halewood Liverpool 1970-72, warden and head teacher Arthur Mellows Village Coll Glinton Peterborough, headteacher Parrs Wood HS Didsbury Manchester 1978-; chm Manchester HS Head's Gp, memb ct Univ of Manchester; memb Jt Assoc of Classics Teachers, memb SHA; *Recreations* horticulture, ancient history; *Style*— Geoffrey Stone, Esq; 15 Fog Lane, Didsbury, Manchester; Parrs Wood High Sch, Wilmstow Rd, Didsbury, Manchester M20 1UU (☎ 061 445 8786)

STONE, Georgina Mary (Gina); da of George Leslie De Lacherois, DL, JP (d 1948), and (Catherine Charlotte) Sheila, *née* Blizard (d 1922); *b* 13 Feb 1921; *Educ* Hayes Ct Kent; *m* 19 July 1945, Johan Stone (d 1974); *Career* WWII 1940-45, 3 Offr WRNS 1943-45; farmer & estate owner; fndr and present co chm Abbeyfield Donaghadee Soc; memb Donaghadee JOC 1955-73 (chm 1963-65), chm N Down Area Plan steering ctee 1967-73; *Recreations* gardening, swimming; *Style*— Mrs Gina Stone; The Manor House, Donaghadee, Co Down BT21 OHA

STONE, Howard Victor; s of Harold Montague Stone, of 83 Avenue Rd, London NW8, and Niki, *née* Winsor; *b* 9 May 1945; *Educ* Highgate Sch, Coll of Law London; *m* 17 March 1968, Hilary Louise, da of Alfred Burnett Shindler, of 16 West Heath Ave, London NW11; 1 da (Victoria b 10 Sept 1971); *Career* trainee slr 1964-65 and 1975-78, retail motor indust 1965-75, admitted slr 1978, ptnr Shindler & Co 1981- (asst 1978-81); freelance TV and radio broadcaster on legal matters incl: Moneyspinner, You and Yours, TV AM, Breakfast Time, BBC TV News, LBC, Captial Radio; master Billingsgate Ward Club 1988-89; Freeman City of London; Liveryman Worshipful Cos of: Glovers, Arbitrators, Slrs; ACIArb 1979, memb IBA 1985; *Recreations* reading, travel, theatre; *Clubs* Gresham, City Livery; *Style*— Howard Stone, Esq; Shindler & Co, 37/39 Eastcheap, London EC3M 1AY (☎ 01 283 6376, fax 01 626 5735, car tel 0836 213 117, telex 924404)

STONE, John Michael; s of Robert Alfred Stone (d 1983), and Josephine Margery, *née* Sheen; *b* 26 April 1941; *Educ* Framlingham Coll; *m* 2 May 1964, Maxine Campbell, da of John Campbell-Lemon, of The Grange, Aylesbury Rd, Wendover, Bucks; 1 s (Timothy b 1974), 3 da (Karen b 1965, Paula b 1966, Nicola b 1970); *Career* dir E Russell Ltd 1962 (chm 1983), md E Russell (W Country) Ltd 1971; chm: Russell Meats Ltd 1984, Donald Russell Ltd 1984; md Russard Kitchen Ltd 1987, jt chm Sims Food Gp plc 1989 (chief exec 1988); Freeman: City of London 1964, Worshipful Co of Butchers 1965; memb Inst of Meat; *Books* Meat Buyers Guide for Caterers (1983); *Recreations* shooting, golf, cricket; *Clubs* MCC; *Style*— John Stone, Esq; Bramleys, Little Kingshill, Great Missenden, Bucks HP16 0EB (☎ 0240 66220); Sims Food Group plc, Douglas House, 32-34 Simpson Rd, Fenny Stratford, Milton Keynes MK1 1BA (☎ 0908 270 061, fax 0908 270 260, car tel 0860 362 746, telex 27568 DONRUS)

STONE, Sheriff Marcus; s of Morris (d 1945), of Glasgow, and Reva (d 1954); *b* 22 Mar 1921; *Educ* HS of Glasgow, Univ of Glasgow (MA, LLB); *m* 1956, Jacqueline, da of Paul Barnoin (d 1967), of France; 3 s (Patrick, William, Donald), 2 da (Cynthia, Martine); *Career* served war 1939-45, RASC W Africa; advocate 1965; Sheriff: Dumbarton 1971-76, Glasgow 1976-84, Lothian & Borders at Linlithgow 1984-; *Books* Proof of Fact in Criminal Trials (1984), Cross-examination in Criminal Trials (1988), Fact-finding for Magistrates (1989); *Recreations* music, swimming; *Style*— Sheriff Marcus Stone; Sheriffs' Chambers, Sheriff Ct House, Ct Square, Linlithgow EH49 7EQ (☎ 050 684 2922)

STONE, Martin Howard; s of Dr Jacob Stone (d 1972) of London, and Gloria Lucille, *née* Supper; *b* 26 May 1949; *Educ* Wanstead Sch; *m* 27 July 1975, Melanie Yvette, da of Joseph Owide, of London; 2 s (Jeremy b 22 Oct 1976, Michael b 23 Nov 1978), 1 da (Emily b 14 Oct 1981); *Career* ptnr Freeda Milston Cedar Baker; currently dir: Wonderworld plc, Bricolpar Ltd, Owide Properties Ltd, Upshire Investmts Ltd, The Colquhoun Gp of Co's; hon tres Ravenswood (in aid of mentally handicapped children); FCA 1976; *Recreations* tennis, hockey, reading; *Clubs* Connaught Tennis, Las Brisas, White Elephant; *Style*— Martin Stone, Esq; 22 Upper Grosvenor St, London W1X ODP (☎ 01 491 4864, fax 01 409 3505, car telephone 0860 397 352, telex 21179)

STONE, Michael John Christopher; s of Henry Frederick Stone (d 1979), and Joan Barbara, *née* Da Silva; *b* 10 May 1936; *Educ* Bradfield, Hamburg (Language Course); *m* 8 Jan 1966, Louisa, da of Robert Dyson, of Hawaii; 2 s (Charles b 9 Oct 1966, Andrew b 21 Nov 1970), 1 da (Nicola b 11 Jan 1968); *Career* cmmnd RHA 1955-57, served Germany, cmmnd HAC 1957-63; commodity broker E D & F Man 1957 (gp chm 1983-), chm London Sugar Futures Mkt 1981-84; dir: Farr Man Inc (New York), London Fox (formerly London Commodity Exchange), Holco Trading Co; former dir The English Assoc plc; *Recreations* shooting, fishing, skiing, farming, gardening; *Clubs* Brooks's, HAC; *Style*— Michael Stone, Esq; Little Mynthurst Farm, Norwood Hill, Nr Horley, Surrey (☎ 0293 862314); E D & F Man Ltd, Sugar Quay, Lower Thames St, London EC3R 6DU (☎ 01 626 8788)

STONE, Prof Norman; s of Flt Lt Norman Stone, RAF (ka 1942), and Mary Robertson, *née* Pettigrew; *b* 8 Mar 1941; *Educ* Glasgow Acad, Gonville and Caius Coll Cambridge (BA, MA); *m* 1, 2 July 1966 (m dis 1977), Marie Nicole Aubry; 2 s (Nicholas b 1966, Sebastian b 1972); m 2, 11 Aug 1982, Christine Margaret Booker, *née* Verity; 1 s (Rupert b 1983); *Career* Univ of Cambridge: fell Gonville and Caius Coll 1965-71, lectr russian history 1968-84, fell Jesus Coll 1971-79, fell Trinity Coll 1979-84; Univ of Oxford: prof modern history 1984-, fell Worcester Coll 1984-; *Books* The Eastern Front 1914-1917 (1975, Wolfson Prize 1976), Hitler (1980), Europe Transformed 1878-1919 (1983); *Recreations* journalism, eastern europe, music; *Clubs* Garrick, Beefsteak; *Style*— Prof Norman Stone; 18 Thorncliffe Rd, Oxford OX2 7BB (☎ 0865 511 334); The Grey Barn, Queen St, Bampton, Oxon; Worcester Coll Oxford

STONE, Peter John; s of Dr Thomas Scott Stone; *b* 24 June 1946; *Educ* King's Sch Canterbury, Christ's Coll Cambridge; *m* 1972, Alison, da of Robert Smith Moffett; 1 s, 1 da; *Career* slr, ptnr Clintons 1972-75; banker Close Brothers Ltd 1975-; dir: Close Brothers Gp plc, Close Brothers Hldgs Ltd, Close Brothers Ltd, Close Registrars Ltd, Century Factors Ltd, Close Brothers Tst Ltd, Close Brothers Securities Ltd, Close Brothers Merchant Securities Ltd, Close Nominees Ltd, Clearbook Tst Ltd, Close Investmt Mgmnt Ltd, Air & General Finance Ltd, Safeguard Investmts Ltd, Close Asset Finance Ltd; *Recreations* hot-air ballooning, cricket, tennis, real tennis, choral singing, travel; *Style*— Peter Stone, Esq; c/o Close Brothers, 36 Great St Helen's, London EC3A 6AP

STONE, Philippa (Jane); da of Vivian Harry (Harold) George Stubbs, of Duston, Northampton, and Merle Josephine Muir Mckerrell, *née* Carver; *b* 6 Mar 1946; *Educ* Notre Dame HS Northampton, St Andrews and Oxford Univs (BSc); *m* 1978, (as his second wife), David Robert Stone, s of Robert Charles Stone; 1 da; *Career* business conslt; land agent; memb Local Authorities Mgmnt Servs & Computer ctee 1969-70, Wm Cory & Son 1970, City Chile 1983-86 (chm 1985-86); dir: Sharepoint Ltd 1984-88, P J Stone Ltd 1984-; FMS; *Recreations* arts, tennis, sailing, skiing; *Clubs* ICA, Essex Sailboard, Drummond tennis; *Style*— Philippa Stone; 26 The Drive, London E18 2BL (☎ 01 989 5561)

STONE, Rex; s of Hiram Stone, of Belper, Derbyshire, and Elsie Lorraine, *née* Taylor; *b* 13 August 1938; *Educ* Herbert Strutt GS; *m* 16 Oct 1965, Anita Kay, da of Albert Arthur Hammond (d 1974), of London; 1 s (Alistair D b 7 May 1976), 1 da (Rachel C b 23 March 1969); *Career* CA; audit mngr Peat Marwich Mitchell & Co 1961-65, co sec RB MacMillan Ltd 1965-69, chm Alida Hldgs 1974- (fin dir 1969-72, jt md 1972-74), non exec dir Derbyshire Bldg Soc 1985-; FCA 1961; *Recreations* travel, game shooting, golf; *Style*— Rex Stone, Esq; Alida Holdings plc, Heanor, Derby DE7 7RG (☎ 0773 530530 fax 0773 530429, telex 377163)

STONE, Hon Richard Malcolm Ellis; s of Baron Stone (Life Peer) (d 1986), and Beryl Florence, *née* Bernstein (d 1989); *b* 1937; *Educ* Univ of Oxford (MA); *m* 1970, Ruth Perry, 1 s (Toby), 2 da (Rebecca, Hannah); *Career* BM, BCh, MRCGP; *Style*— The Hon Richard Stone; 15 Blenheim Rd, London NW8

STONE, Sir (John) Richard Nicholas; CBE (1946); *b* 1913,Aug; *Career* fell King's Coll Cambridge 1945-, P D Leake prof of fin and accounting Cambridge Univ 1955-80; FBA; Nobel Prize for Economics 1984; kt 1980; *Style*— Sir Richard Stone, CBE; 13 Millington Road, Cambridge

STONE, Terence Reginald Stewart; s of Harry Victor Stone, of Grey Stones, Dawlish, Devon, and Hilda Mary, *née* Western; *b* 18 August 1928; *Educ* Willesden Tech Coll, Coll of Arch, Regent St Poly; *m* 1952, Beryl Joan, da of Douglas Bramwell Stewart; 4 s, 2 da; *Career* chm Terence Stone Gp of Companies 1970-; md: Terence Stone (Devpt) Ltd 1962-, Terence Stone (Construction) Ltd 1975-; chief architect Costain (West Africa) Ltd 1956-60; sr architect RAF Air Works Sqdn Air Miny 1947-49; FIAS, FRSH, FFB, FBIM; *Recreations* swimming, tennis, badminton, running, motor rallying, skiing, sponsorship and promotion of sport, travel, arts; *Clubs* Rolls Royce Enthusiasts, RAC; *Style*— Terence Stone, Esq; Treston House, Earlstone Place, Dawlish, Devon (☎ 0626 863160); Treston Court, Dawlish, Devon (☎ 0626 862732); Terence Stone Group, Company House, Dawlish, Devon (☎ 0626 863543)

STONEFROST, Maurice Frank; CBE (1983), DL (1986); s of Arthur Stonefrost (d 1980), of Bristol, and Anne, *née* Williams; *b* 1 Sept 1927; *Educ* Merrywood GS Bristol; *m* June 1953, Audrey Jean, da of Charles Fishlock (d 1986); 1 s (Mark), 1 da (Hilary); *Career* Nat Serv RAF 1948-51; local govt: Bristol 1951-54, Slough 1954-56, Coventry 1956-61, W Sussex 1961-64; sec Chartered Inst of Public Fin and Accountancy 1964-73, controller of fin GLC 1973-84, dir gen and clerk GLC and ILEA 1984-85, dir and chief exec BR Pension Fund 1986-; centenary pres Chartered Inst of Public Fin 1984-85, pres Soc of Co Treasurers 1982-83, memb Layfield Ctee on Local Govt Fin 1974-76, memb ctee on the Future of the Legal Profession 1987-88, chm Public Sector Liaison Ctee of the Accountancy Profession 1987-, managing tstee Municipal Mutual Insur Co 1987-, chm Speakers Cmmn of Citizenship 1988-; DSc City Univ 1987; DPA 1953, CIPIA 1955; *Books* Capital Accounting (1958); *Recreations* walking, gardening; *Style*— Maurice Stonefrost, Esq, CBE, DL; British Rail Pension Fund Company, Broad St House, 55 Old Broad St, London EC3M 1RX (☎ 01 374 0242, fax 01 588 0217)

STONEHAM, Roger Antony; s of Derrick William Stoneham, and Clara Marjorie, *née* Ryan; *b* 24 May 1944; *Educ* Luton GS, Bedford Modern Sch, Univ of Hull (BSc); *m* 26 Sept 1970, Carole Christine, da of Frank Fosbrook; 1 s (Stephen b 1966), 3 da (Sharon b 1972, Sonja b 1975, Sara b 1981); *Career* CA; Whitbread & Co plc 1975-87; IPFA, FCCA; *Recreations* caravanning, traction engines, philately, photography, tiddley winks; *Style*— Roger Stoneham, Esq; The Poplars, 8 Spinney Field, Ellington, Huntingdon, Cambs; The Brewery, Chiswell St, London (☎ 01 606 4455)

STONELEY, Dr Robert; s of Dr Robert Stoneley (d 1976), of Cambridge, and Dorothy, *née* Minn (d 1988); *b* 22 July 1929; *Educ* The Leys Sch Cambridge, Pembroke Coll Cambridge (BA, MA, PhD); *m* 22 Oct 1953, Hilda Mary Margaret, da of Dr L R Cox (d 1964); 1 s (Robert Leslie Gayford b 1966), 1 da (Elizabeth Mary Margaret b 1964); *Career* geologist: Falkland Islands Dependencies Survey 1951-53, BP The Br Petroleum Co Ltd 1953-78; prof Imperial Coll of Science & Technol Med Dept Univ of London 1978-; Polar Medal; *Recreations* walking, gardening; *Style*— Dr Robert Stoneley; Harestone, Red Cross Lane, Cambridge CB2 2QU; Dept of Geology, Imperial Coll of Science & Technology, Prince Consort Rd, London SW7 2BP

STONER, Roy Frederick; s of Albert Edward Stoner, and Lily, *née* Dowson; *b* 29 Jan 1930; *Educ* Cheltenham GS, Univ of Durham (BSc,); *m* 29 Oct 1952, Alice, da of Mr Dyson; 2 s (Timothy b 1958, Jeremy b 1962), 1 da (Christine b 1954); *Career* RAF Airfield Construction Branch, Flying Offr Detachment Cdr RAF Fassberg Germany 1954-56; chartered civil engr; Sir M Macdonald & Ptnrs: joined 1956, assoc 1969-76, ptnr 1976-87, sr ptnr 1987, gp chm 1987-; chm Groundwater Devpt Consultants Ltd 1984-; FICE 1969 (memb 1956); *Recreations* boating, gardening; *Style*— Roy Stoner, Esq; 10 West St, Comberton, Cambs (☎ 0223 262 455); Demeter House, Station Rd, Cambridge CB1 2RS (☎ 0223 460 660, fax 0223 461 007, telex 817260)

STONHOUSE, Rev Michael Philip; s and h of Sir Philip Allan Stonhouse, 18 Bt; *b* 4 Sept 1948; *Educ* Medicine Hat Coll, Univ of Alberta (BA) [Edmonton], Wycliffe Coll (LTh) [Toronto]; *m* 1977, Colleen Eleanor, da of James Albert Coucill (d 1968), of Toronto, Canada; 2 s (Allan b 1981, David b 1983); *Career* ordained deacon 1977; ordained priest 1978 (both Diocese of Calgary, Canada); asst curate St Peter's, Calgary 1977-80; rector and incumbent Parkland Parish 1980-; *Style*— Rev Michael Stonhouse; Box 539, Elnora, Alberta TOM OYO, Canada (☎ (403) 773 3594)

STONHOUSE, Sir Philip Allan; 18 & 15 Bt (E 1628 & 1670), of Radley, Berkshire; s of Sir Arthur Stonhouse, 17 & 14 Bt (d 1967); *b* 24 Oct 1916; *Educ* W Canada Coll, Queen's Univ, Alberta Univ; *m* 1946, Winnifred, da of John Shield; 2 s; *Heir* s, Michael Stonhouse; *Career* admin mangr; *Recreations* golf, skiing, travel, shooting; *Clubs* Medicine Hat Ski, Connaught Golf; *Style*— Sir Phillip Stonhouse, Bt; 521, 12 St SW, Medicine Hat, Alberta, Canada (☎ 403 526 5832)

STONOR, Hon Georgina Mary Hope; da of late 6 Baron Camoys; *b* 8 Nov 1941; *Educ* St Mary's Convent Ascot; *Style*— The Hon Georgina Stonor; 108 West Street, Henley-on-Thames, Oxon RG9 2EA

STONOR, Hon John Edmund Robert; s of late 6 Baron Camoys; *b* 1946; *Educ* Beaumont and Oscott Coll; *Style*— The Hon John Stonor

STONOR, Hon Mrs Julia Maria Cristina Mildred; *née* Stonor; eldest da of 6 Baron Camoys (d 1976); resumed her maiden name of Stonor by Deed Poll 1978; *b* 19 April 1939; *Educ* St Mary's Convent Ascot, Reading Tech Coll; *m* 4 May 1963 (m dis 1977 and annulled by Sacred Rota, Rome 1978), Donald Robin Slomnicki Saunders; 1 s (Alexander William Joseph Stonor Saunders b 1964), 1 da (Frances Hélène Jeanne Stonor Saunders b 1966); *Career* traveller and courier, article and short story writer, garden patio designer, public relations and social worker, prison after care, race relations and age concern; FRGS; *Recreations* travel, classical music, literature, theatre, fine arts, gardening, continental cookery and catering internationally; *Style*— The Hon Julia Stonor; 90 Burnthwaite Rd, Fulham, London SW6 5BG (☎ 01 385 8528)

STOPFORD, Hon Edward Richard Barrington; s of late 7 Earl of Courtown; *b* 1914; *Educ* Stowe; *m* 1, 1946, Ann Marie Elizabeth Douglas (d 1976), da of late Brig Harold Gordon Henderson, CBE; 2 s, 1 da; m 2, 1978, Mrs Millicent Davies, previously wife of late Trevor Waterson; *Career* formerly Capt Royal Norfolk Regt; *Style*— The Hon Edward Stopford; Long Hedge, 8 Turners Lane, Humberside

STOPFORD, Capt Hon Jeremy Neville; LVO (1984); yr s of 8 Earl of Courtown, OBE, TD (d 1975); *b* 22 June 1958; *Educ* Eton, RMA Sandhurst; *m* 1984, Bronwen MacDonald, da of Lt-Col David MacDonald Milner, of Hollycroft, Ashford Hill, Newbury, Berks; 2 da (Clementine Lucy Patricia b 1986, Matilda Rose Philippa b 1988); *Career* Capt Irish Gds; Equerry (temp) to HM Queen Elizabeth The Queen Mother 1982-84; stockbroker 1984-; *Recreations* shooting, photography, squash; *Clubs* Buck's, Annabels; *Style*— Captain The Hon Jeremy Stopford, LVO

STOPFORD, Lady Marjorie Gertrude; da of late 6 Earl of Courtown; *b* 1904; *Style*— Lady Marjorie Stopford; 40 Herkomer Rd, Bushey, Herts WD2 3LU

STOPFORD, Lady Rosemary Katharine; da of late 7 Earl of Courtown; *b* 23 Oct 1911; *Career* served 2 offr WRNS 1942-46; welfare organiser 1936-71; *Style*— Lady Rosemary Stopford; 8 Stanford Rise, Sway, Lymington SO41 6DW

STOPFORD, Maj-Gen Stephen Robert Anthony; CB (1989), MBE (1971); s of Cdr Robert Stopford, DSC, RN (d 1977), and Elsie, *née* Lawson (d 1967); *b* 1 April 1934; *Educ* Downside, Millfield, RMA Sandhurst; *m* 8 Feb 1963, Vanessa, da of Theodore Baron (d 1982); *Career* cmmnd Scots Greys 1955 (Regtl Serv 1955-70), OC D Sqdn Scots DG 1970-72, MOD Central Staff 1972-75, CO Scots DG 1975-77, project mangr MBT 80 1977-80, Col OR 1/10 1980-83, mil attaché Washington 1983-85, dir gen Fighting Vehicles and Engr Equipment (DGFVE) 1985-89; AIMEE; *Recreations* electronics, shooting, scuba diving; *Clubs* Cavalry and Guards; *Style*— Maj-Gen Stephen Stopford, CB, MBE; 18 Thornton Ave, London SW2 4HG (☎ 01 674 1416)

STOPFORD, Capt the Hon Terence Victor; s of 7 Earl of Courtown (d 1957), and Cicely Mary Birch (d 1973); *b* 3 Oct 1918; *Educ* Eton; *m* 1951, Sheila Adèle, da of Philip Henry Walter Page (d 1959); 3 s (Henry b 1953, Robert b 1958, James b 1961), 1 da (Catherine b 1965); *Career* RN 1936, HMS Dorsetshire China Sationa 1937-39, WW II HMS Valiant, HMS Scylla, 1945-51 HMS Grenville, HMS Saumarez, HMS Devonshire, Cdr Admty Underwater Weapons and Ops Div 1952, HMS Forth (CO at Suez Ops 1956), naval advsr to UK High Cmmr Ottawa 1959-60, Capt 1960, asst dir Underwater Weapons Admty 1961-63, CO HMS Manxman and Capt Inshore Flotilla Far East Fleet 1963-64, cos to C-in-C Naval Home Cmmd 1965-67, cos offr to Flag Offr Gibraltar 1967-69, Naval ADC to HM 1969, ret; *Recreations* cricket; *Style*— Capt the Hon Terence Stopford, RN; Lake End House, Dorney, Windsor, Berks

STOPFORD, Hon Thomas; s of Baron Stopford of Fallowfield (Life Peer, d 1961); *b* 28 June 1921; *Educ* Manchester GS, Univ of Manchester; *m* 6 July 1943, Mary Howard, da of late Alfred James Small, of Manchester; 1 s; *Career* Capt RA WWII; *Style*— The Hon Thomas Stopford; Mylor, 12 Bazley Rd, Ansdell, Lytham St Annes, Lancs FY8 1AJ (☎ 0253 736844)

STOPFORD SACKVILLE, Lionel Geoffrey; only s of Lt-Col Nigel Stopford Sackville, CBE, TD, JP, DL, by his 1 w, Beatrix, da of Col Hercules Pakenham, CMG (gn of 2 Earl of Longford), Col Stopford Sackville was gs of William Bruce Stopford (whose f Richard was 4 s of 2 Earl of Courtown), by William's wife Caroline, da of Hon George Germain and niece and heir of 5 and last Duke of Dorset; *b* 4 Nov 1932; *Educ* Eton; *m* 1, 1960, Susan, da of Jenkin Coles, of the Abbey, Knaresborough; 2 s (Charles b 1961, Thomas b 1968), 1 da (Lucinda b 1963); m 2, 1980, Hon Teresa, *née* Pearson, *qv*; 1 da (Camilla b 1981); *Career* late Lt Northants Yeo, former Lt 14/20 Hussars served Libya; chm: Lowick Manor Farms Ltd, Union Jack Oil plc, Goedhuis & Co Ltd; dir: Anglo American Gold Investmt Co Ltd, GT Venture Investmt Co plc, Japan Ventures Ltd, The Lynton Gp Ltd, New Goliath Minerals Ltd; former dir Charter Consolidated; High Sheriff Northants 1976-77; FCA; *Clubs* White's, Pratt's, MCC; *Style*— Lionel Stopford Sackville, Esq; Drayton House, Lowick, Kettering, Northants NN14 3BB; Ranger House, 69/71 Great Peter St, London SW1P 2BN (☎ 01 222 4363, fax 01 222 5480)

STOPFORD SACKVILLE, Hon Mrs; Hon (Mary) Teresa; *née* Pearson; er da of 3 Viscount Cowdray, TD, by his 1 w, Lady Anne Pamela, *née* Bridgeman; *b* 3 June 1940, (HRH The Princess Royal stood sponsor); *m* 1980, Lionel Geoffrey Stopford Sackville, *qv*; 1 da (Camilla Anne b 1981); *Recreations* racing, hunting, skiing; *Style*— The Hon Mrs Stopford Sackville; Drayton House, Lowick, Kettering, Northants NN14 3BB; 21 Greville House, Kinnerton St, London SW1X 8EY

STOPS, Leigh Warwick; s of Dr Denis Warwick Stops, of Kingston, Surrey, and Patricia, *née* Hill; *b* 29 May 1946; *Educ* Latymer Upper Sch, Univ of Sussex (BSc), Univ of Lancaster (MA); *m* 3 Dec 1976, Patricia Jane, da of F J Terry; 2 s (Caspar b 1986, Galen b 1988); *Career* advertiser; dir: Colman RSCG & Ptnrs 1984-85, res and planning Allen Brady & Marsh Ltd 1985-; *Recreations* sailing, theatre, media, advertisements; *Style*— Leigh W Stops, Esq; 5 Foster Road, Chiswick, London W4 4NY (☎ 01 388 1100, fax 01 387 1155); Allen Brady & Marsh Ltd, 7-12 Tavistock Square, London WC1H 9SX

STORER, Prof Roy; s of Harry Storer (d 1980), of Wallasey, and Jessie, *née* Tophan (d 1978); *b* 21 Feb 1928; *Educ* Wallasey GS, Univ of Liverpool (LDS, MSc, FDS, DRD); *m* 16 May 1953, Kathleen Mary Frances Pitman, da of Francis Charles Green; 1 s (Michael b 10 March 1961), 2 da (Sheila b 26 Feb 1956, Carolyn b 6 May 1958); *Career* Capt RADC 1951-52 (Lt 1950-51); sr lectr in dental prosthetics Univ of Liverpool 1962-67 (lectr 1954-61), visiting assoc prof Northwestern Univ Chicago 1961-62, hon conslt dental surgn Utd Liverpool Hosps 1962-67; Univ of Newcastle upon Tyne: prof of prosthodontics 1968-, clinical sub-dean dental sch 1970-77, dean of dentistry 1977-; sec and cncl memb of Br Soc for the Study of Prosthetic Dentistry 1960-69; memb: Gen Dental Cncl 1977- (chm educn ctee 1986-), Dental Educn Advsy Cncl (UK) 1978-, Bd of Faculty of Dental Surgery RCS 1982-, dental sub-ctee of Univ Grants Ctee 1982-, EEC Dental Cncl Trg of Dental Practioners 1986-; Univ of Newcastle upon Tyne: memb of Senate, Cncl and Court, chm physical recreation ctee; memb Northern Sports Cncl; memb Br Dental Assoc 1950; *Recreations* rugby football, cricket, gardening; *Clubs* East India, Athenaeum, MCC; *Style*— Prof Roy Storer; 164 Eastern Way, Darras Hall, Ponteland, Newcastle Upon Tyne NE20 9RH; The Dental Sch, Univ of Newcastle Upon Tyne, Framlington Place, Newcastle Upon Tyne NE2 4BW (☎ 091 2328511)

STOREY, Graham; s of Stanley Runton Storey (d 1971), of Meldreth, Cambs, and Winifred Graham (d 1975); *b* 8 Nov 1920; *Educ* St Edwards Oxford, Trinity Hall Cambridge (MA); *Career* WWII 1941-45 served UK France and Germany, Lt 1942 (despatches); called to Bar Middle Temple 1950, Trinity Hall Cambridge fell 1949-88, sr tutor 1958-68, vice-master 1970-74 emeritus fell 1988-; reader in English 1981-88 (lectur 1965-81, chm faculty bd 1972-74), visiting fell All Souls Coll Oxford 1968; lectr for Br Cncl overseas, Warton lectr Br Acad 1984, Leverhulme Emeritus fellowship, syndic CUP 1983, gen ed Cambridge English Prose Texts 1980-; vice pres G M Hopkins Soc 1971, pres Dickens Soc of America 1983-84; govr: St Edwards Oxford 1959-69, Eastbourne Coll 1965-69; *Books* Reuters' Century(1951), Journals and Papers of G M Hopkins (1959), Angel with Horns (1961), Selected Verse and Prose of G M Hopkins (ed 1966), Letters of Dickens (jt ed 1965-), A Preface to Hopkins (1981), Revolutionary Prose of the English Civil War (jt ed 1983), Bleak House A Critical Study (1987); *Recreations* tennis, gardening, theatre, travel; *Style*— Graham Storey, Esq; Crown House, Caxton, Cambs (☎ 09544 316); Trinity Hall, Cambridge (☎ 0223 332538)

STOREY, Jeremy Brian; *née* Fisher; s of Capt James Mackie Storey (d 1976), of Harrogate, N Yorks, and Veronica, *née* Walmsley (d 1978); *b* 21 Oct 1952; *Educ* Uppingham, Downing Coll Cambridge (MA); *m* 19 September 1981, Carolyn Margaret, da of Eric Raymond Ansell, of Edenbridge, Kent; *Career* barr Inner Temple 1974; *Recreations* travel, theatre, cricket; *Style*— Jeremy Storey, Esq; 56 Westbere Rd, London NW2 3RU (☎ 01 435 4227, 4 Pump Ct Temple, London EC4Y 7AN (☎ 01 353 2656, fax 01 583 2036, telex 8813250)

STOREY, Kenelm; s and h of Sir Richard Storey, 2 Bt, and Virginia Anne, *née* Cayley; *b* 4 Jan 1963; *Educ* Winchester, George Washington Univ USA; *Career* Euro sales mangr (distribution, mktg, circulation sales) The Guardian Newspaper; *Recreations* football, cricket, tennis, golf, squash; *Clubs* IZ, MCC, Yorkshire Gents CC, Butterflies CC, Old Wykehamists CC; *Style*— Kenelm Storey, Esq; Settrington House, Malton, Yorkshire; 7 Douro Place, London W8 5PH (☎ 01 937 8823); 300 E 75th St, Apt 33L, NY, NY 10021, USA

STOREY, Leonard Charles; s of Herbert James Storey (d 1944); *b* 12 August 1910; *Educ* LCC Cent Sch; *m* 1952, Emily, *née* Hodgson; *Career* RAF 1940-46; CA; dir: Collateral Securities Ltd, Dwelling Devpt Ltd, Linit Flyte Ltd, Silvermoor Property Ltd; dir Kensington Perm Bldg Soc 1954-69; chm St Stephen's Bldg Soc; MRSH, MPCS, FInstD; *Recreations* reading, swimming; *Style*— Leonard Storey Esq; Kensington, 82 Malvern Ave, South Harrow, Middlesex (☎ 422 6008)

STOREY, Maude; CBE (1987); da of Henry Storey (d 1971), and Sarah Farrimond, *née* Davies (d 1981); *b* 30 Mar 1930; *Educ* Wigan and Dist Mining and Tech Coll, St Mary's Hosp Manchester, Lancaster Royal Infirmary, Paddington Gen Hosp, Royal

Coll of Nursing Edinburgh (SRN, SCM, RCI), Queen Elizabeth Coll Univ of London (STD); *Career* domicillary midwife Wigan Co Borough 1953-56, midwifery sister St Mary's Hosp Manchester 1956-59, head nurse intensive therapy unit Mayo Clinic USA 1957-59, theatre sister (clinical instr and nurse tutor) Royal Albert Edward Infirmary Wigan 1959-68, lectr in community nursing Univ of Manchester 1968-71, asst and subsequently princ reg nursing offr Liverpool Regnl Hosp Bd 1971-73, reg nursing offr Mersey RHA 1973-77, registrar Gen Nursing Cncl for England and Wales 1977-81, chief exec UK Centl Cncl for Nursing Midwifery and Health Visiting (UKCC) 1981-87; memb: W Berks Health Authy, Standing Nursing and Midwifery Advsy Ctee; elected pres Royal Coll of Nursing of the UK 1986; *Recreations* theatre, travel; *Style*— Miss Maude Storey, CBE; 14 Conifer Drive, Tilehurst, Reading, Berks RG3 6YU (☎ 0734 412082); 20 Cavendish Sq, London W1M 0AB (☎ 01 409 3333)

STOREY, Michael John William; s of Jack Storey, and Pamela Jessamine, *née* Helmore; *b* 30 Dec 1927; *Educ* Wells Cathedral Sch, Centl Sch of Speech and Drama; *m* 3 Sept 1976, Virginia, da of Havelock Clive-Smith (d 1964); 2 s (Daniel b 1 Feb 1978, d 30 Sept 1985, Alec b 26 April 1983), 1 da (Florence b 8 March 1987); *Career* composer of music for numerous films including: Gertler, Another Country, Every Picture tells a Story, The Dress, Coming Up Roses, Hidden City, A Perfect Spy; active memb Greenpeace; *Recreations* tennis, squash, snooker; *Style*— Michael Storey, Esq; Walnut Tree Farm, Bylford, Halesworth, Suffolk IP19 9JX (☎ 050 270 660)

STOREY, Hon Sir Richard; 2 Bt (UK 1960) of Settrington, Co York; s of Baron Buckton (Life Peer d 1978), and Elisabeth (d 1951), da of late Brig-Gen W J Woodcock, DSO; *b* 23 Jan 1937; *Educ* Winchester, Trinity Coll Cambridge (BA, LLB); *m* 1961, Virginia Anne, da of late Sir Kenelm Henry Ernest Cayley, 10 Bt; 1 s, 2 da; *Heir* s, Kenelm Storey, *qv*; *Career* barr Inner Temple 1962; chm, Portsmouth & Sunderland Newspapers plc 1973 - (chief exec 1973-86); memb: Newspaper Soc Cncl and ctees, Press Cncl 1980-86, nat cncl and exec ctee CLA 1980-84 (Yorkshire exec, chm 1974-76); cncl memb INCA-FIEJ Research Assoc 1983-, memb CBI Employment Policy Ctee 1984 -88-; farms and administers land in Yorkshire; dir: United Cable (South London) Ltd, The Press Assoc Ltd, Reuters Hldgs plc, Portsmouth News Shops Ltd; *Recreations* sport, silviculture; *Style*— Hon Sir Richard Storey; 7 Douro Place, London W8 5PH (☎ 01 937 8823); Settrington House, Malton, N Yorks; Portsmouth & Sunderland Newspapers plc, Buckton House, 39 Abingdon Rd, London W8 (☎ 01 938 1066, telex 261091)

STOREY, Richard Alec; s of Edwin Alexander Storey, of Mundesley-on-Sea, and Minnie Florence, *née* Trundle (d 1988); *b* 2 June 1937; *Educ* Hertford GS, Downing Coll Cambridge; *m* 14 Jan 1961, Jennifer, da of James Clare, of Ware; 2 s (Daniel b 1966, Lawrence b 1968), 1 da (Emma b 1969); *Career* archivist Historical Manuscripts Cmmn 1963-73, sr archivist Modern Records Centre Univ of Warwick Library 1973-; ed Business Archives 1969-73 and 1975-78; formerly chm Kenilworth History and Archeology Soc, co-proprietor Odibourne Press; *Books* Primary Sources for Victorian Studies (1977), Ambit (contrib poetry); *Recreations* literature, cinema, local and transport history; *Style*— Richard Storey, Esq; 9 New Street, Kenilworth, Warwicks CV8 2EY (☎ 0926 57 409); Modern Records Centre, University of Warwick Library, Coventry CV4 7AL (☎ 0203 523 523 ext 2014)

STORIE-PUGH, Col Peter David; CBE (1981, MBE 1945), MC, (1940), TD (1945), DL (1963); s of late Prof Leslie Pugh, CBE, and Paula Storie; *b* 1 Nov 1919; *Educ* Malvern Coll, Queens' Coll Cambridge, Royal Veterinary Coll Univ of London (MA, PhD); *m* 1, 1946 (m dis 1971), Alison, da of late Sir Oliver Lyle, OBE; 1 s, 2 da; m 2, 1971, Leslie Helen, da of Earl Striegel; 3 s, 1 da; *Career* served WWII, Queen's Own Royal W Kent Regt (escaped from Spangenberg and Colditz), cmd 1 Bn Cambs Regt, Suffolk and Cambs Regt, Col Dep Cdr 161 Inf Bde, ACF County Cmdt; lectr Univ of Cambridge 1953-82, UK del EEC Vet Liaison Ctee 1962-75 (pres 1973-75), UK rep Fedn of Veterinarians of EEC 1975-83 (pres 1975-79); chm: Nat Sheepbreeders Assoc 1964-68, Eurovet 1971-73; pres: Cambridge Soc for Study of Comparative Medicine 1966-67, Int Pig Vet Soc 1967-69 (life pres 1969), Br Vet Assoc 1968-69 and 1970-71, 1 Euro Vet congress Wiesbaden 1972, pres RCVS 1977-78; memb: Econ and Social Consultative Assembly of the Euro Communities 1982-, Parly and Scientific Ctee 1962-67, Home Sec's Advsy Ctee 1963-80, Nat Agric Centre Advsy Bd 1966-69, Min of Agric Farm Animal Advsy Ctee 1970-73; fell Wolfson Coll Cambridge; CChem, FRCVS, FRSC; *Books* Eurovet: an Anatomy of Veterinary Europe (1972), Eurovet 2 (1975); *Clubs* United Oxford and Cambridge University; *Style*— Col Peter Storie-Pugh, CBE, MC, TD, DL; Duxford Grange, Duxford, Cambridge CB2 4QF (☎ 076 382 403)

STORMONT, Viscount; Alexander David Mungo; s and h of 8 Earl of Mansfield and Mansfield; *b* 17 Oct 1956; *Educ* Eton; *m* 1985, Sophia Mary Veronica, only da of Philip Biden Derwent Ashbrooke, of La Grande Maison, St John, Jersey, CI; 1 s (William Philip David Mungo b 1 Nov 1988), 1 da (Hon Isabella Mary Alexandra Murray b 1987); *Clubs* White's, Turf, Pratt's; *Style*— Viscount Stormont; 56 Drakefield Rd, London SW17 8RP

STORMONTH DARLING, Sir James Carlisle (Jamie); CBE (1972), MC (1945), TD, WS (1949); s of Robert Stormonth Darling, WS (d 1956) and Beryl Madeleine, *née* Sayer (d 1955); *b* 18 July 1918; *Educ* Winchester, Ch Ch Oxford (MA), Univ of Edinburgh (LLB); *m* 1948, Mary Finella, BEM (1945), DL (East Lothian), da of Lt-Gen Sir James Gammell, KCB, DSO, MC (d 1975); 1 s (Angus), 2 da (Caroline, Priscilla); *Career* served WWII KOSB and 52 (Lowland) Div Reconnaissance Regt RAC, Lt-Col 1945; memb Royal Co of Archers (Queen's Bodyguard for Scotland) 1958-; dir: Scottish Widows' Fund and Life Assur Soc 1981-89, Nat Tst for Scotland 1971-83 (chief exec and dir 1949-83, vice pres emeritus 1985), memb Ancient Monuments Bd for Scotland 1983-; a vice pres Scottish Conservation Projects Tst (former pres), chm Edinburgh Old Town Tst 1987, tstee Holyrood Brewery Fndn Tst 1987; DSc Stirling 1983, Hon FRIAS 1982. Hon LLD Aberdeen 1984; kt 1982; *Recreations* hill walking, gardening, countryside pursuits; *Clubs* New (Edinburgh), Hon Co of Edinburgh Golfers; *Style*— Sir Jamie Stormonth Darling, CBE, MC, TD, WS; Chapelhill House, Dirleton, N Berwick, East Lothian EH39 5HG (☎ 062 085 296)

STORMONTH DARLING, Peter; s of Patrick Stormonth Darling (d 1961), and Edith, *née* Lamb (d 1980); *b* 29 Sept 1932; *Educ* Winchester, New Coll Oxford (MA); *m* 1, 1958 (m dis), Candis Hitzig; 3 da (Candis Christa b 1959, Elizabeth Iona b 1960, Arabella b 1962); m 2, 1970, Maureen O'Leary; *Career* 2 Lt Black Watch 1950-53, served Korean War, Fl Lt RAFVR 1953-56; chm Mercury Asset Mgmnt Gp plc; dir: S G Warburg Gp plc, Orion Ins plc; *Recreations* stone circles, biographies, photography, watching cricket; *Clubs* MCC, Swinley, New York Racquet and Tennis, Toronto; *Style*— Peter Stormonth Darling, Esq; 33 King William St, London EC4

STORMONTH-DARLING, Robin Andrew; s of Patrick Stormonth-Darling (d 1960); *b* 1 Oct 1926; *Educ* Abberley Hall, Winchester; *m* 1, 1956 (m dis 1974), Susan, *née* Clifford-Turner; 3 s, 1 da; m 2, 1974 (m dis 1979), Harriet, da of Lt-Gen Sir Archibald Nye, GCSI, GCIE, GCMG, KCB, KBE, MC (d 1967); m 3, 1981, Carola Marion, da of Sir Robert Erskine-Hill, 2 Bt, *qv*, and formerly w of (Richard) David Brooke, *qv*; *Career* Capt 9 Queen's Royal Lancers 1947-54; stockbroker; sr ptnr Laing of Cruickshank 1980-87 (joined 1954, ptnr 1956); memb London Stock Exchange 1955-87, chm Disciplinary Appeals Ctee 1983-, memb cncl of Stock Exchange 1978-87, chm Quotations Ctee 1981-85, dep chm Panel on Takeovers of Mergers 1985-87; dir: Br Motor Corpn 1960-68, BL Motor Corpn 1968-75, Mercantile House Hldgs plc 1984-87 (dep chm 1987), London Scottish Bank plc 1984-, Securities of Investmts Bd 1985-87, GPI, Leisure Corpn 1986-; chm Tranwood plc 1987-; *Recreations* shooting, skiing, flying, swimming; *Clubs* White's, City of London, MCC, Hurlingham; *Style*— Robin Stormonth-Darling, Esq; Balvarran, Enochdhu, Blairgowrie, Perthshire, Scotland (☎ 025 081 248); 21 Paradise Walk, London SW3 (☎ 01 352 4161)

STORR, Dr Charles Anthony; s of The Rev Vernon Faithfull Storr (d 1940), of Westminster, and Katherine Cecilia Storr (d 1954); gggf Paul Storr (1771-1844) was the Regency Silversmith and also gggf to Laurence & Rex Whistler; *b* 18 May 1920; *Educ* Winchester, Christ's Coll Cambridge (MB, BChir, MA); *m* 1, 1942, Catherine, da of late Arthur Cole, of Lincoln's Inn; 3 da (Sophia, Polly, Emma); m 2, 1970, Catherine, da of late A D Peters; *Career* hon conslt psychiatrist Oxford Health Authy, formerly clinical lectr in psychiatry Univ of Oxford, fell Green Coll Oxford 1979 (emeritus fell 1984); FRCPsych, FRCP; *Books* The Integrity of the Personality (1960), Sexual Deviation (1964), Human Aggression (1968), Human Destructiveness (1972), The Dynamics of Creation (1972), Jung (1973), The Art of Psychotherapy (1979), Jung: Selected writings (ed 1983), Solitude: A Return to the Self (1988), Churchill's Black Dog & Other Phenomena of the Human Mind (1989), Freud (1989); *Recreations* music, journalism, broadcasting; *Clubs* Savile; *Style*— Dr Anthony Storr; 45 Chalfont Rd, Oxford, OX2 6TJ (☎ 0865 53348)

STORRAR, Wing Cdr James Eric; DFC (1940, bar 1943), AFC (1953) AE (1956); s of James Storrar (d 1973), of Chester, and Margaret, *née* Taylor (d 1974); longest established qualified vet surgns in UK, James Storrar established in Chester 1853; *b* 24 June 1921; *Educ* Chester GS, Univ of Edinburgh (BSc); *m* 6 Nov 1946, Winifrede, da of Bertram J Bridgeman (d 1939), of Weymouth, Dorset; 3 s (James Andrew b 1947, Christopher John b 1949, Simon James b 1952), 1 da (Penelope Jane b 1953); *Career* cmmnd RAF 1938 Fighter Cmd 1939, 11 Gp 1939-40, youngest pilot in Battle of Britain, Western Desert 1941-42, UK based 2 JA Force Sqdn Cdr 1943, Cdr Air Delivery Serv Normandy 1944, Cdr 239 Wing Italy 1945-46, Sqdn-Ldr aged 20 1942, Wing Cdr aged 23 1944, (despatches twice), Polish Cross of Valour Croix de Guerre; resigned serv 1947; veterinary surgeon; joined Royal Aux AF 1948 603 (City of Edinburgh Sqdn), Cdr 610 (County of Chester Sqdn) disbanded 1957; MRCVS 1952, vet surgn Cncl RSPCA 1979-85, FRSH 1978; *Recreations* motoring, off shore sailing; *Clubs* RAF, Chester City; *Style*— Wing Cdr James Storrar, DFC, AFC, AE; Tower House, Curzon Park North, Chester CH4 8AR (☎ 0244 677638); Park Cottage, Duke St, Chester CH1 1RP (☎ 0244 311106)

STORRY, Kenneth Charles; *b* 11 July 1923; *Educ* Hull GS; *m* 1959, Patricia Irene Frances, *née* McLaughlin; 1 s; *Career* Sub Lt RNVR; dir and md Barclays Unicorn Group Ltd 1977-82, gen mangr Barclays Unicorn Ltd 1974-, district mangr Barclays Bank London (SW dist) 1970-; *Recreations* golf, reading, travel, sailing; *Clubs* Royal Western Yacht, Royal Plymouth, Corinthian Yacht, Yelverton Golf, St Mellion Country; *Style*— Kenneth Storry Esq; 1 Haddington Rd, Stoke, Plymouth, Devon (☎ 0752 569528)

STOTE, Alan Edward Charles; s of Horace Albert, and Frances May, *née* Webb; *b* 16 Sept 1948; *Educ* Lordswood Tech Birmingham; *m* 24 July 1976, Susan Annette Sheila, da of Michael Joseph Carding, of Wolverhampton; 1 s (Richard b 1977), 1 da (Hannah b 1985); *Career* chm and chief exec BTS Gp plc; chm CBI Smaller Firms Cncl 1984-86; memb: NEDC 1985-87, Midland CBI Regnl Cncl 1987-; *Recreations* rowing, vintage cars; *Clubs* Bewdley Rowing; *Style*— Alan E C Stote, Esq; Yarhampton House, Yarhampton, Stourport-on-Severn, Worcestershire DY13 0XA (☎ 0299 21 401); The BTS Group plc, Maybrook House, Queensway, Halesowen B63 4AH (☎ 021 550 1832)

STOTHART, William; *b* 29 Sept 1926; *Educ* Quarry Bank HS Liverpool, Downing Coll Cambridge; *m* 1958, Margaret Elizabeth, *née* Bowden; 1 s, 1 da; *Career* co sec and dir Owen Owen plc, ret; tres Univ of Liverpool; *Recreations* golf, fell walking, photography; *Style*— William Stothart, Esq; 6 Croome Drive, West Kirby, Wirral, Merseyside

STOTHERS, Michael Anthony; CBE (1988); s of Stanley Holdsworth Stothers (d 1984), of Wyke, Bradford, W Yorks, and Phyllis, *née* Priestley; *b* 10 August 1933; *Educ* Belle Vue GS for Boys Bradford Yorks, Bradford Tech Coll; *m* 20 Aug 1955, Margaret, da of Maurice Horner (d 1976), of Scholes, Cleckheaton, Yorks; 2 da (Anne Kathryne (Mrs McEwen) b 1957, Sally Margaret (Mrs Skegg) b 1960); *Career* Nat Serv RN radio electrical artificer 1955-57; electrical engrg apprenticeship and post apprenticeship as estimating and contracts engr Southern and Redfern Ltd Bradford 1949-55; NG Bailey and Co Ltd: contracts engr Sheffield 1959-60, branch mangr Cardiff 1960-64; chm William Steward and Co Ltd London 1964- (formerly branch mangr, div md); chm High Wycombe and Dist branch Br Diabetic Assoc (cncl memb), pres Electrical Contractors Assoc 1974-75, chief negotiator for Employers in Electrical Contracting; Freeman: City of London, Worshipful Co of Glaziers and Painters of Glass; FIEE; *Recreations* horse riding, amateur farming; *Style*— Michael Stothers, Esq, CBE; Pens Place, Pound Lane, Marlow, Bucks (☎ 06284 2766); Nash House, Old Oak Lane, London NW10 6DH (☎ 01 965 9888, fax 01 961 5595, car tel 0860 743713, telex 299030)

STOTHERS, Thomas; s of Robert James Stothers (d 1966), and Elizabeth Charlotte Gibson; *b* 24 July 1926; *Educ* Belfast Tech Coll; *m* 1952, Florence Elizabeth, da of Capt William S Simms (d 1960); 2 s (James b 1954, John b 1957); *Career* md H & J Martin Ltd (bldg and civil engrg contracting firm); quantity surveyor; dir: R J Stothers & Sons Ltd 1947, D W Stothers & Co Ltd 1958; FCIOB, FCSI, FInstD; *Recreations* golf, boating, rugby; *Clubs* Royal Belfast Golf, Malone Rugby, Down Cruising; *Style*— Thomas Stothers, Esq; Cloverlinks, 22 Quarter Road, Cloughy, Co Down; R J

Stothers & Sons Ltd, 68 Orby Road, Belfast (☎ 702626)

STOTT, Sir Adrian George Ellingham; 4 Bt (UK 1920), of Stanton, Co Gloucester; s of Sir Philip Sidney Stott, 3 Bt (d 1979), and Lady Stott, *qv*; *b* 7 Oct 1948; *Educ* Univ of British Columbia (BSc, MSc), Univ of Waterloo Ontario (MMaths); *Heir* bro, Vyvyan Philip Stott; *Career* dir of planning (county) 1974-77, town planning conslt 1977-80, real estate portfolio mangr 1980-85, mangr of conservation agency 1985, md of marketing co 1986-88; mgmnt conslt 1989; *Recreations* music, inland waterways, politics; *Clubs* MENSA, Inland Waterways Assoc; *Style—* Sir Adrian Stott, Bt; RR3 Site 320 C65, Parksville, British Columbia V0R 2S0, Canada (☎ 604 7525774)

STOTT, Alan Edward; JP (Staffordshire 1957), DL (1969); s of Charles Ernest Stott (d 1935); *b* 6 June 1910; *Educ* Repton; *m* 1, 1935, Marguerite Marie Maye, *née* Knowles (d 1957); 3 da (1 s decd); m 2, 1973, Marion Morrow, wid of Russell Harriman; *Career* dir (1933) and dep chm (1965) Armitage Shanks Gp Ltd of England and Overseas; High Sheriff Staffordshire 1968, pres British Ceramic Mfrs Fedn 1969, ret 1972; *Clubs* Leander, Phyllis Court; *Style—* Alan Stott Esq, JP, DL; 8 Rupert Close, Henley-on-Thames, Oxon RG9 2JD (☎ Henley 575732); The White Lodge, Milford, Stafford (☎ 0785 661000)

STOTT, Lady; Cicely Florence; da of Bertram Ellingham, of Ely House, Hertford; *m* 1947, Sir Philip Sidney Stott, 3 Bt, ARIBA (d 1979); 2 s; *Style—* Lady Stott; 1104 Esquimalt Towers, 1552 Esquimalt Ave, West Vancouver, BC, Canada

STOTT, Rt Hon Lord; George Gordon Stott; PC (1964); s of late Rev Dr G Gordon Stott, and late Flora Corsar Stott; *b* 22 Dec 1909; *Educ* Cramond Sch, Edinburgh Acad, Univ of Edinburgh (MA, LLB, DipEd); *m* 1947, Nancy Deverell, da of late A D Braggins; 1 s, 1 da; *Career* Scottish advocate 1936, advocate-depute 1947-51, KC 1950, sheriff of Roxburgh, Berwick and Selkirk 1961-64, lord advocate 1964-67; a Lord of Session 1967-84; *Style—* The Rt Hon Lord Stott; 12 Midmar Gdns, Edinburgh (☎ 031 447 4251)

STOTT, James Howard; s of Selwyn Stott (d 1962), and Helena, *née* Heap (d 1966); *b* 26 June 1920; *Educ* Barkisland Sch, Sowerby Bridge Secdry Sch, Univ of Manchester (LLB); *m* 23 April 1943, Margery, da of John William Collis (d 1950); 2 s (Richard b 1950, Peter b 1954); *Career* RN 1941, Lt RNVR 1942-45, CO 1943-45; textile dir 1976-84, slr 1949-; *Recreations* singing, gardening; *Style—* James Stott, Esq; 10A Trenance Gdns, Greetland, Halifax (☎ 0422 72166); 13 Harrison Rd, Halifax (☎ 0422 362011)

STOTT, Prof Peter Frank; CBE; s of Clarence Stott, MC, OBE (d 1981), of London, and Mabel, *née* Sutcliffe; *b* 8 August 1927; *Educ* Bradford GS, Clare Coll Cambridge (MA); *m* 5 Sept 1953, Vera, da of Henry Watkins (d 1982), of Norwich; 2 s (Andrew b 1955, Richard b 1958); *Career* ptnr G Maunsell & Ptnrs 1957-63, chief engr London CC 1963-65; dir highways and transportation and controller planning and transportation GLC 1965-73; dir gen Nat Water Cncl 1973-83, Nash prof of civil engrg 1987-89; FEng, FICE, FCIT. FIHT; *Recreations* pottery; *Clubs* Athenaeum; *Style—* Prof Peter Stott, CBE; 7 Frank Dixon Way, Dulwich, London SE21 7BB (☎ 01 693 5121)

STOTT, Richard Keith; s of Fred Brookes Stott (d 1964), and Bertha, *née* Pickford, of Oxford; *b* 17 August 1943; *Educ* Clifton; *m* 1970, Penelope Anne, yr da of Air Vice-Marshal Sir Colin Scragg, KBE, CB, AFC and bar *qv*; 1 s (Christopher b 1978), 2 da (Emily b 1972, Hannah b 1975); *Career* jr reporter Bucks Herald (Aylesbury) 1963-65, Ferrari News Agency Dartford 1965-68, reporter Daily Mirror 1968-79, (features ed 1979-81, asst ed 1981-84), ed: Sunday People 1984-85, editor Daily Mirror 1985-; Br Press Award for Reporter of the Year 1977; *Recreations* theatre, reading; *Style—* Richard Stott; c/o Daily Mirror, 33 Holborn, London EC1P 1DQ

STOTT, Roger; CBE (1979), MP (Lab) Wigan 1983-; s of Richard Stott; *b* 7 August 1943; *Educ* Rochdale Tech Coll, Ruskin Coll; *m* 1969 (m dis 1982), Irene Mills; 2 s; *Career* former merchant seaman and PO telephone engr; Rochdale cllr 1970-74 (chm housing ctee), contested (Lab) Cheadle 1970, MP (Lab) Westhoughton May 1973-1983, sponsored by POEU; PPS to: Indust Sec 1975-76, Rt Hon James Callaghan as PM 1976-79 and as ldr of oppn 1979-1980; vice-chm NW area PLP, memb select ctee Agric 1980-; oppn front bench spokesman: Tport 1981-1983, Trade and Indust 1983-; *Style—* Roger Stott, Esq, CBE, MP; 24 Highgate Crescent, Appley Bridge, Wigan

STOTT, Vyvyan Philip; s of Sir Philip Sidney Stott, 3 Bt (d 1979), and Lady Stott, *qv*; hp of bro, Sir Adrian Stott, 4 Bt; *b* 5 August 1952; *Style—* Vyvyan Stott, Esq; c/o Knoll Wood, Victoria, British Columbia V9B 1E4, Canada

STOUGHTON-HARRIS, Anthony (Tony) Geoffrey; s of Geoffrey Stoughton-Harris (d 1966), and Kathleen Mary, *née* Baker Brown; *b* 5 June 1932; *Educ* Sherborne; *m* 1959, Elizabeth Thackery, da of Joseph Brian White, of Ramsgate; 1 s (Peter), 2 da (Sarah, Helen); *Career* RTR 1956-58; pt/t tres W Herts Main Drainage Authy 1964-70, exec vice chm Nationwide Anglia Bldg Soc 1987-, dir Maidenhead and Berkshire Bldg Soc 1967, (md 1975, renamed South of England Bldg Soc 1980, Anglia Bldg Soc in 1983 and Nationwide Anglia Bldg Soc 1987); chm Met Assoc of Bldg Socs 1979-80; gen cmmr Inland Revenue 1982-; memb: cncl Bldg Socs Assoc 1979- (chm 1987-), pt/t memb Southern Electricity Bd 1981-; dir and chm Electronic Funds Transfer Ltd 1984-; FCA; *Recreations* sport, gardening, DIY; *Style—* Tony Stoughton-Harris, Esq; Old Farm House, Blackmile Lane, Grendon, Northants NN7 1JR (☎ Wellingborough 664235); Nationwide Anglia Building Society, New Oxford House, High Holborn, London WC1V 6PW (☎ 01 242 8822 telex 264549)

STOURTON, Hon Charlotte Mary; da of 24 Baron Mowbray, (25) Segrave and (21) Stourton (d 1936); *b* 20 Jan 1904; *Recreations* motoring, walking, dancing; *Clubs* Anglo-Blegium; *Style—* The Hon Charlotte Stourton; 2 Arthington Ave, Harrogate, North Yorkshire

STOURTON, Hon Edward William Stephen; s and h of 26 Baron Mowbray, 27 Segrave and 23 Stourton; *b* 17 April 1953; *Educ* Ampleforth; *m* 1980, Penelope (Nell) Lucy, da of Dr Peter Brunet, of 4 Rawlinson Rd, Oxford; 3 da (Sarah Louise b 1982, Isabel b 1983, Camilla b 1987); *Style—* The Hon Edward Stourton; 23 Warwick Sq, SW1

STOURTON, Hon James Alastair; s of 26 Baron Mowbray, 27 Segrave and 23 Stourton (CBE), and Jane Faith, *née* de Yarburgh-Bateson da of Stephen 5 Baron Deramore; *b* 3 July 1956; *Educ* Ampleforth, Magdalene Coll Cambridge (MA); *Career* joined Sotheby's picture Dept since 1979, dir Sotheby's London 1987- (dep dir 1986); proprietor The Stourton Press; dir: Crawley-Wilson Investmts Ltd (Restaurants); Knight in Honour and Devotion SMO Malta; *Clubs* Pratt's, Beefsteak; *Style—* The Hon James Stourton; 21 Moreton Place, London SW1V 2NL (☎ 01 821 1101); Sotheby's, 34-35 New Bond St, London W1 (☎ 01 493 8080)

STOURTON, Lady Joanna; *née* Lambart; da of Field Marshal 10 Earl of Cavan (d 1946), by his 2 w Hester Joan, Countess of Cavan (d 1976); *b* 8 Dec 1929; *m* 1955, Maj Michael Godwin Plantagenet, s of Hon John Joseph Stourton, s of 24 Baron Mowbray; 2 s (Thomas b 1965, Henry b 1971), 2 da (Julia b 1958, Clare b 1962); *Style—* Lady Joanna Stourton; The Old Rectory, Great Rollright, Chipping Norton, Oxon (☎ 0608 737385)

STOURTON, Hon John Joseph; TD; 2 s of 24, 25 & 21 Baron Mowbray, Segrave and Stourton (who made a claim, which was rejected, to the Earldom of Norfolk in 1906) by his w Mary, *née* Constable; *b* 5 Mar 1899; *Educ* Downside; *m* 1, 1923 (m dis 1933), Kathleen, da of Robert Gunther; 2 s, 2 da (one of whom m the 5 Earl of Gainsborough); m 2, 1934 (m dis 1947), Gladys (d 1953), da of Col Sir William Waldron; *Career* Lt 18 Queen Mary's Own Hussars, Yorks Hussars Yeo, 10 Royal Prince of Wales Own Hussars, Maj Royal Norfolk Regt (TA), ret; served with N Russia relief force 1919 and WW II; MP (U) Salford S 1931-45; sec Cons Foreign Affrs Ctee 1944-45; *Style—* Maj The Hon John Stourton, TD; 3 Rosebery Ave, Hampden Pk, nr Eastbourne, E Sussex (☎ 0323 503631)

STOUT, (John) Bernard; s of John Mitchell Stout (d 1955), of Inkerman Terr, Whitehaven, Cumbria, and Kate Stout (d 1974); *b* 11 Jan 1929; *Educ* Worksop Coll, Pembroke Coll Cambridge (MA); *m* 31 Jan 1959, Elizabeth Clayton, da of David Thomson (d 1954), of Alstonby Hall, Westlinton, Carlisle; 1 s (David Edward b 1960), 2 da (Susan Claire (Mrs Tolson) b 1962, Jennifer Elizabeth b 1969); *Career* Nat Serv RN; admitted slr 1955; ptnr: Blackburn & Main Carlisle 1956-71, Cartmell Mawson & Main Carlisle 1971-88 (latterly sr ptnr); ret 1988; pres Carlisle and Dist Law Soc 1982; chm Carlisle and N Cumbria NSPCC 1986 - (pres 1981-85, chm appeal ctee 1984); pres Boys Bde Carlisle Dist 1971-76; memb Law Soc; *Recreations* golf, fishing, shooting, fell-walking; *Clubs* Border & County (Carlisle); *Style—* Bernard Stout, Esq; Croft Head, Scotby, Carlisle CA4 8BX (☎ 0228 513 325); Viaduct House, The Viaduct, Carlisle CA3 8EZ (☎ 0228 31561, fax 0228 401 490, telex 64106)

STOUT, Prof David Ker; 31 July 1956, Margaret, da of William Sugden (d 1951); 2 s (Nigel b 1957, Rowland b 1959), 2 da (Lucy b 1961, Eleanor b 1963); *b* 27 Jan 1932; *Educ* Sydney HS Sydney NSW, Univ of Sydney (BA), Rhodes scholar, Magdalene Coll Oxford (BA); *m* 31 July 1956, Margaret, da of William Sugden (d 1951); 2 s (Nigel b 1957, Rowland b 1959), 2 da (Lucy b 1961, Eleanor b 1963); *Career* Mynors fell and lectr in econs Univ Coll Oxford 1959-76, econ advsr to various govts 1965-76 (Syria, New Hebrides, Aust, Canada), econ dir NEDO 1970-72 and 1976-80, visiting prof of econs Univ of Leicester 1982-(Tyler prof of econs 1980-82), head econs dept Unilever 1982; author of various papers in books and jls on taxation, growth, inflation, balance of payments and other topics; memb bd of tstees: Strategic Planning Inst Cambridge Man, Centre for Economic Policy Res, Inst of Fiscal Studies; memb exec ctee and govr Nat Inst for Economic and Social Res 1972; *Style—* Prof David Stout; Unilever plc, Blackfriars, PO Box 68, London EC4 (☎ 01 822 6557)

STOUTE, Michael Ronald; s of Maj Ronald Audley Stoute, OBE, of Barbados, West Indies, and Mildred Dorothy, *née* Bowen; *b* 22 Oct 1945; *Educ* Harrison Coll Barbados; *m* 14 June 1969, Joan Patricia, *née* Baker; 1 s (James Robert Michael b 6 June 1974), 1 da (Caroline Elizabeth b 23 Jan 1972); *Career* race horse trainer 1972-, reading flat racing trainer 1981 and 1986; trained Derby winners: Shergar 1981, Shahrastani 1986; Irish Derby winners: Shergar 1981, Shareef Dancer 1983, Shahrastani 1986; *Recreations* cricket, hunting, skiing; *Style—* Michael Stoute, Esq; Freemason Lodge, Bury Road, Newmarket, Suffolk (☎ 0638 663 801); work ☎ 0638 667 276, telex 817 811)

STOUTZKER, Ian; s of Aron Stoutzker (d 1968), and Dora Stoutzker (d 1968); *b* 21 Jan 1929; *Educ* Berkhamstead Sch, RCM (ARCM), LSE (BSc); *m* 3 Sept 1958, Mercedes; 1 s (Robert b 1962), 1 da (Riquita (Mrs Wade Newmark) b 1960); *Career* Samuel Montagu 1952-56, A Keyser and Co (tutor Keyser Ullmann Ltd) 1956-75, chm London Interstate Bank 1971-75; chm Dawnay Day Int 1985-; pres Philharmonia Orch 1976-79 (chm 1972-76); memb: exec ctee RCM 1968-, Musicians Benevolent Fund 1980-; chm Live Music Now 1980-; FRCM; *Recreations* music, cross country walking; *Clubs* Carlton; *Style—* Ian Stoutzker, Esq; 33 Wilton Crescent, London SW1X 8RX; 15 Grosvenor Gardens, London SW1 WOBD (☎ 01 834 8060, fax 828 1984, telex 8955547)

STOVIN-BRADFORD, Frank Randolph; s of William Stovin-Bradford (d 1940), of Golders Green, and Rose Amelia, *née* Phillips (d 1960); *b* 31 Dec 1923; *Educ* Univ Coll Sch London; *m* 20 July 1944, Jacqueline, da of Frank Brown (d 1940), of Temple Fortune; 2 s (Nigel b 1946, Richard Noel b 1957); *Career* Sub Lt (A) RNVR pilot 857 Sqdn RN (Grumman Avengers), HMS Indomitable, South Indian Ocean Fleet and Br Pacific Fleet 1941-45; chartered architect private practice 1957; in 1970 was first architect to bring a successful action in the High Court for breach of copyright since 1934 and the Law affecting copyright was decisively amended as a direct result of this action defining clearly the protection of an architect's drawings; *Recreations* travelling, painting; *Clubs* City Livery, Fleet Air Arm Officers' Assoc; *Style—* Frank R Stovin-Bradford, Esq; 20 Crail View, Northleach, Cheltenham, Gloucestershire GL54 3QH (☎ 0451 60153)

STOW, Sir John Montague; GCMG (1966, KCMG 1959, CMG 1950), KCVO (1966); s of Sir Alexander Stow, KCIE, OBE (d 1936), of Netherwood, Newbury, Berks; *b* 1911; *Educ* Harrow, Pembroke Coll Cambridge; *m* 1939, Beatrice, da of late Capt Tryhorne; *Career* entered Colonial Serv (Nigeria) 1934, asst colonial sec Gambia 1938, chief sec Windward Is 1944, admin St Lucia 1947, dir of estab Kenya 1952-55, colonial sec Jamaica 1955-59, govr and C-in-C Barbados 1959-66, govr-gen Barbados 1966-67, ret; KStJ 1959; *Clubs* Caledonian, MCC; *Style—* Sir John Stow, GCMG, KCVO; 26a Tregunter Rd, London SW10 9LH

STOW, Ralph Conyers; CBE (1981); s of late Albert Conyers Stow, and Mabel Louise, *née* Boulet; *b* 19 Dec 1916; *Educ* Woodhouse Sch; *m* 1943, Eleanor Joyce Appleby; 1 s, 1 da; *Career* Cheltenham & Gloucester Bldg Soc: md 1962-82, pres and chm 1982-87; chm Bldg Socs Assoc 1977-79, past pres Chartered Bldg Socs Inst; chm Cheltenham DHA 1982-88; *Clubs* Rotary; *Style—* Ralph Stow, Esq, CBE; Shepherds Fold, Charlton Hill, Charlton Kings, Cheltenham, Glos (☎ 0242 87305)

STOW HILL, Susan, Baroness; Susan Isabella Cloudesley; da of William Auchterlony Hunter, of Spean Bridge, Inverness-shire; *m* 1940, Baron Stow Hill (Life Peer, d 1979); 2 s; *Style—* The Rt Hon Susan, Lady Stow Hill; 19 Church Row, Hampstead, NW3

STOWASSER, Hon Dr (Helen Margaret); *née* Platt; yr da of Baron Platt (Life Peer and 1 Bt) (d 1978), and Margaret Irene, *née* Cannon; *b* 16 Mar 1933; *Educ* Manchester HS for Girls, Newnham Coll Cambridge, Univ of QLD (PhD); *m* 10 July 1954, Cecil Henry Stowasser, s of late Marian Stowasser, of Karlsbad, Czechoslovakia; 3 s; *Career* sr lectr Qld Conservatorium of Music 1987, assoc prof of music educn Univ of Western Australia 1989; *Books* Discover Music 1-3 (1978 and 1983), Discover Music-making (1989); *Style*— The Hon Dr Stowasser; 1-9 Park Rd, Nedlands, Western Australia, 6009, Australia

STOWE, Grahame Conway; s of Harry Stowe (d 1968), and Evelyn, *née* Pester; *b* 22 May 1949; *Educ* Allerton Grange Sch Leeds, Univ of Leeds (LLB); *m* 27 Dec 1981, Marilyn Joyce, da of Arnold Morris; 1 s (Benjamin Harry George b 21 May 1988); *Career* admitted slr 1974, commenced own practice 1981; chm Benefit Appeal Tbnl 1985, pres Mental Health Tbnl 1987; memb Law Soc, FCI Arb 1979; *Recreations* squash; *Style*— Grahame Stowe, Esq; Two Willows, 4 Sandmoor Drive, Leeds LS17 7DG; Flat 6, 45 Warrington Cresc, Little Venice, London W9 (☎ 0532 692902); Portland House, 7 Portland Street, Leeds LS1 3DR (☎ 0532 468163, fax 0532 426682)

STOWE, Sir Kenneth Ronald; GCB (1986, KCB 1980, CB 1977), CVO (1979); s of Arthur Stowe (d 1965), and Emily Stowe; *b* 17 July 1927; *Educ* Dagenham County HS, Exeter Coll Oxford; *m* 1949, Joan Cullen; 2 s (Timothy, Richard), 1 da (Janet); *Career* formerly DHSS Off, UNO, Cabinet princ private sec to PM 1975-79, PUS NI Off 1979-81, perm sec DHSS 1981-87, perm sec Cabinet Off 1987; chm Inst of Cancer Res 1987, memb Pres Mugabe's Cmmn to review Zimbabwe Police Serv, life tstee Carnegie UK Tst; *Clubs* Athenaeum; *Style*— Sir Kenneth Stowe, GCB, CVO; c/o Athenaeum Club, Pall Mall, London SW1

STRABOLGI, 11 Baron (E 1318); David Montague de Burgh Kenworthy; s of 10 Baron (d 1953), by his 1 w, Doris Whitley (d 1988), da of Sir Frederick Whitley-Thomson, JP, MP; co-heir to Baronies of Cobham and Burgh; *b* 1 Nov 1914; *Educ* Gresham's, Chelsea Sch of Art; *m* 1, 1939 (m dis 1946), Denise, da of Jocelyn William Godefroi, MVO; m 2, 1947 (m dis 1951), Angela, da of George Street; m 3, 1955 (m dis 1961), Myra Sheila Litewka; m 4, 1961, Doreen Margaret, er da of late Alexander Morgan, of Ashton-under-Lyne, Lancs; *Heir* bro, Rev the Hon Jonathan Malcolm Kenworthy; *Career* Maj and actg Lt-Col RAOC WW II, Capt Queen's Bodyguard of Yeomen of the Guard; dep chief govt whip 1974-79, pps to ldr of House of Lords and Lord Privy Seal 1969-70, asst oppn whip House of Lords 1970-74; oppn spokesman: on Energy 1979-83, on Arts and Libraries 1979-86; dep speaker House of Lords 1986-; memb Br Section Franco-British Cncl 1981; chm Bolton Bldg Soc 1986-87 (dep chm 1983-86, chm 1986-87); Offr de la Légion d'Honneur 1981; *Style*— The Rt Hon The Lord Strabolgi; House of Lords, London SW1A 0PW

STRACEY, Sir John Simon; 9 Bt (UK 1818), of Rackheath, Norfolk; s of Capt Algernon Augustus Henry Stracey (d 1940), and Olive Beryl Stracey (d 1972); Sir John Stracey, 1 Bt, was a recorder of City of London; suc cous, Sir Michael George Motely Stracey, 8 Bt, 1971; *b* 30 Nov 1938; *Educ* Wellington, McGill Univ Montreal; *m* 1968, Martha Maria, da of Johann Egger (d 1936), of Innsbruck, Austria; 2 da; *Heir* cous, Henry Mounteney Stracey; *Career* conslt and designer; specialised in wine trade; own co Vinexperts-Rackheath Inc; *Recreations* yachting (yacht Miss Muffet); *Clubs* Royal St Lawrence Yacht; *Style*— Sir John Stracey, Bt; 652 Belmont Ave, Montréal, PQ H3Y 2W2, Canada (☎ 514 482 9668)

STRACHAN, Maj Benjamin Leckie (Ben); CMG (1978); s of Charles Gordon Strachan, MC (d 1957), of Crieff, Perthshire, and Annie Primrose, *née* Leckie (d 1972); *b* 4 Jan 1924; *Educ* Rossall Sch Fleetwood Lancs; *m* 1, 5 Dec 1946 (m dis 1957), Ellen, *née* Braasch; 1 s (Christian b 1949); m 2, 29 Nov 1958, Lize, da of Tage Lund (d 1985), of Copenhagen; 2 s (Robert b 1960, James b 1963); *Career* enlisted 1942, Durham Univ 1942-43, OCTU Sandhurst 1943-44, 2 Lt Royal Dragoons 1944: Lt serv France and Germany (despatches, wounded, POW) 1944-45, Capt instr OCTU 1946-48, Lt 4 QOH serv Malaya (wounded) 1948-51, Capt MECAS 1951-53, Maj GSO2 (int) HQ BT Egypt 1954-55, Capt Sqdn 2 i/c 4 QOH Germany 1955-56 RMSC Shrivenham 1956-58, Maj Sqdn Ldr 10 Royal Hussars 1958-60, GSO2 (int) WO 1960-61, ret to join HM foreign Serv; FO: first sec info res dept 1961-62, info advsr to Govt of Aden 1962-63, asst head of dept Scientific Relations Dept 1964-66, commercial sec Kuwait 1966-69, cnsllr and charge d'affaires of Amman (Jordan) 1969-71, trade cmmr Toronto 1971-74, consul gen Vancouver 1974-76, HM ambass Sana'a and Djibouti 1977-78, HM ambass Beirut 1978-81, HM ambass Algiers 1981-84; vice chm Banchory Branch LSD; Citoyen D'Honneur Grimaud France 1987; *Recreations* sailing, crofting, writing; *Clubs* Lansdowne; *Style*— Maj Ben Strachan, CMG; Mill of Strachan, Strachan, Banchory, Kincardineshire AB3 3NS (☎ 033 045 663)

STRACHAN, Graham Robert; CBE (1977), DL (Co Dunbartonshire 1979); s of George Strachan, of Kenmore, Castlegate, W Chiltington, nr Pulborough, Sussex, and Lily Elizabeth, *née* Ayres; third generation of Clydeside engineers since 1872; *b* 1 Nov 1931; *Educ* Trinity Coll Glenalmond, Trinity Coll Cambridge (MA); *m* 1960, Catherine Nicol Liston, da of John Vivian (d 1978); 2 s; *Career* Nat Serv 1955-57, actg Sub-Lt RNVR Far East and Suez 1963-66; engrg dir John Brown Engrg (Clydebank) Ltd 1966-68, dir and gen mangr John Brown Engrg Ltd 1968-83 (md 1983-, dep chm); FEng, FIMechE, FIMarE; *Recreations* skiing, golf, jogging; *Clubs* Caledonian, Buchanan Castle Golf; *Style*— Graham Strachan, Esq, CBE, DL; The Mill House, Mildavie Rd, Strathblane, Stirlingshire G63 9EP (☎ 0360 70220); John Brown Engineering Ltd, Clydebank, Dunbartonshire G81 1YA (☎ 041 952 2030; telex 778395)

STRACHAN, Ian Charles; s of Dr Charles Strachan, of Wilmslow, Cheshire, and Margaret, *née* Craig; *b* 7 April 1943; *Educ* Fettes, Christ's Coll Cambridge (BA, MA), Princeton Univ (MPA), Harvard Univ; *m* 1, 29 July 1967 (m dis 1987), Diane Shafer, da of Govr Raymond P Shafer, of Washington DC, USA; 1 da (Shona Elizabeth b 15 Feb 1970); m 2, 28 Nov 1987, Margaret, da of Dr Hugh Auchincloss, of New Jersey, USA; *Career* VSO Grand Cayman Island BWI 1961-62, assoc The Ford Fndn Malaysia 1967-69, various positions Exxon Corpn 1970-77, fin mangr Esso Eastern Houston 1977-79, fin dir Gen Sekiyu Tokyo Japan 1979-82, chm and chief exec Esso Hong Kong and Esso China 1982-83, mangr corp strategy Exxon Corpn NY 1984-86 (exec asst to chm 1983-84), chief fin offr and sr vice pres Johnson and Higgins NY 1986-87, fin dir The RTZ Corpn plc London 1987-; *Recreations* tennis, reading, oriental antiques; *Clubs* Harvard (NY), Hong Kong; *Style*— Ian Strachan, Esq; The RTZ Corporation plc, 6 St James's Sq, London SW1Y 4LD (☎ 01 930 2399, fax 01 930 3249, telex 24639)

STRACHAN, James Murray; s of Eric Alexander Howieson Strachan, and Jacqueline Georgina; *b* 10 Nov 1953; *Educ* King's Sch Canterbury, Christ Coll Cambridge (BA); *Career* Chase Manhattan Bank 1976-77, md Merrill Lynch Capital Mkts (joined 1977); *Recreations* photography, squash, opera; *Clubs* United Oxford and Cambridge; *Style*— James Strachan, Esq; 10B Wedderburn Rd, Hampstead, London NW3 (☎ 01 794 9687); Merrill Lynch Int & Co, 25 Ropemaker St, London EC2 (☎ 01 867 2431, fax 01 867 2040/01 867 4040, telex 8811047 MERLYN G)

STRACHAN, John; JP; s of John Strachan (d 1950), of Craigewan, Fraserburgh, and Annie Isabella, *née* Sutherland (d 1983); *b* 9 August 1929; *Educ* Fraserburgh Acad, Univ of Aberdeen; 21 March 1957, Margaret (d 1986), da of William Cheyne (d 1963), of Sheildarroch, Cults, Aberdeen; 1s (Neil b 1962), 2 da (Pamela b 1965, Caroline b 1966); *Career* Sub Lt RNVR 1954-56; advocate in Aberdeen, sr ptnr Davidson and Garden 1972-; dir: William Wilson Hldgs Ltd 1973, William McKinnon & Co Ltd 1979-, Osprey Communications plc 1982; chm Hunter Construction (Aberdeen) Ltd 1987 (dir since inception); *Recreations* salmon fishing, shooting, golf (minor); *Clubs* East India, St James; Royal Northern (Aberdeen), Aberdeen Petroleum; *Style*— John Strachan, Esq; 2 Queen's Rd, Aberdeen (☎ 0224 644276, tel 313906)

STRACHAN, John Charles Haggart; s of late Charles George Strachan, and Elsie Strachan; *b* 2 Oct 1936; *Educ* Univ of London, St Mary's Hosp (MB BS); *m* Caroline Mary, da of John William Parks, MBE, of London; 1 s (James b 1971), 3 da (Alexandra b 1969, Elisabeth b 1972, Cressida b 1983); *Career* conslt orthopaedic surgn New Charing Cross Hosp 1971; surgn to Royal Ballet 1971; FBOA, FRSM, FRCS (Eng). FRCS (Ed); *Recreations* fishing, sailing, stalking; *Clubs* Royal Thames YC, Royal Southern YC, Flyfisher's; *Style*— John Strachan, Esq; 28 Chalcot Square, London NW1 (☎ 01 586 1278); 126 Harley Street, London W1N 1AH (☎ 01 935 0142)

STRACHAN, (Douglas) Mark Arthur; QC (1987); s of Fl-Lt William Arthur Watkin Strachan, of 51 Blockley Rd, Wembley, Middx, and Joyce, *née* Smith; *b* 25 Sept 1946; *Educ* Orange Hill GS Edgware, St Catherine's Coll Oxford (BCL, MA), Nancy Univ France; *Career* called to the Bar Inner Temple 1969, asst rec 1987; contrib to legal jls: Modern Law Review, New Law Journal, Slrs' Journal; *Recreations* France, food, antiques; *Style*— Mark Strachan, Esq, QC; 38 Bedford Gdns, Kensington, London W8 (☎ 01 727 4725); 1 Crown Office Row, Temple, London EC4 (☎ 01 583 9292)

STRACHAN, Walter John; s of Bertram Lionel Strachan, and Edith Annie, *née* Gale; *b* 25 Jan 1903; *Educ* Hymers Coll Hull, St Catharine's Coll Cambridge (MA); *m* 7 Aug 1929, Margaret Jason, da of Dr Thomas Jason Wood; 1 s (Geoffrey b 1935), 1 da (Jean b 1932); *Career* poet, author and translator; head modern language dept Bishop's Stortford Coll 1928-68, (second master 1958-68); lectr: Cambridge Co of Art & Technol 1974-84, Nat Assoc of Fine & Decorative Arts 1975-; Chevalier des Arts et des Lettres 1968, Commandeur des Palmes Academiques 1970; *Books* Moments of Times (poetry, 1947), The Artist and the Book in France (1969), Open Air Sculpture in Britain (1984), Towards the Lost Domain, Alan-Fournier's Letters (1986), A Relationship with Henry Moore 1942-86 (1988), translations incl works of Herman Hesse (Demian, The Prodigy, Peter Camenzind); *Recreations* drawings in pen and wash of medieval bridges; *Style*— Walter Strachan, Esq; 10 Pleasant Rd, Bishop's Stortford, Herts (☎ 0279 54493)

STRACHEY, Charles; 6 Bt (UK 1801), of Sutton Court, Somerset; s of Rt Hon Evelyn John St Loe Strachey (d 1963), and cous of 2 Baron Strachie (d 1973); *b* 20 June 1934; *Educ* Westminster, Magdalen Coll Oxford; *m* 1973, Janet Megan, da of Alexander Miller; 1 da; *Heir* kinsman, Richard Philip Farquhar Strachey, b 10 Aug 1902; *Career* district dealer, representative mangr Ford Motor Co Ltd 1972-75, local govt offr; *Style*— Charles Strachey, Esq; 31 Northchurch Terrace, London N1 4EB

STRACHEY, Hon (Jane Towneley); *née* Strachey; da of late Hon (Thomas) Anthony Edward Towneley Strachey, by his w Mary Sophia, *see* Lady Mary Gore; sis of 4 Baron O'Hagan; *b* 1953; *m* 1972, William Stone; *Style*— The Hon Jane Strachey

STRADBROKE, 6 Earl of (UK 1821); Sir (Robert) Keith Rous; 11 Bt (E 1660); also Viscount Dunwich (UK 1821) and Baron Rous (GB 1796); s of 5 Earl of Stradbroke (d 1983, shortly after his brother, 4 Earl) and (1 w) Pamela Catherine Mabell (who d 1972, having obtained a divorce 1941), da of late Capt the Hon Edward James Kay-Shuttleworth (s of 1 Baron Shuttleworth); *b* 25 Mar 1937; *Educ* Harrow; *m* 1, 1960 (m dis 1976), Dawn Antoinette, da of Thomas Edward Beverley, of Brisbane; 2 s (Viscount Dunwich, Hon Wesley b 1972), 5 da (Lady Ingrid b 1963, Lady Rayner b 1964, Lady Heidi b 1966, Lady Pamela b 1968, Lady Brigitte-Alana b 1970); m 2, 1977, Roseanna Mary Blanche, da of Francis Reitman (d 1955), and Susan, née Vernon; 4 s, 1 da; *Heir* s, Viscount Dunwich, *qv*; *Career* grazier, land developer and commercial investigator; dir: Rewitu Pty Ltd, Sutuse Pty Ltd, Thorroldtown Pty Ltd, Thorroldtown (Hong Kong) Pty Ltd, Keith Rous (No 2) Pty Ltd; landowner (7500 acres); *Recreations* making babies; *Style*— The Rt Hon the Earl of Stradbroke; Thorroldtown Pty Ltd, 286 Moore Pk Rd, Paddington, NSW 2021, Aust (☎ 02 332 1804); The Old Borralon Rdd, Armidale, NSW 2350, Australia; work: Second Floor, 630 George St, Sydney, NSW 2000, Australia (☎ 02 267 2011)

STRADLING, Donald George; s of George Frederick Stradling, of Somerset, and Olive Emily, *née* Simper; *b* 7 Sept 1929; *Educ* Clifton, Magdalen Coll Oxford (MA); *m* 1955, Mary Anne, da of Oscar Cecil Hartridge (d 1983); 2 da(Annette, Marguerite); *Career* master St Albans Sch 1954-55, gp trg and educn offr John Laing & Son Ltd 1955 (gp personnel dir 1969), cmmr Manpower Servs Cmmn 1980-82, dir Bldg and Civil Engrg Holidays Scheme Mgmnt 1984, vice-pres Inst of Personnel Mgmnt 1974-76; visiting prof Univ of Salford 1989; vice chm of govrs St Albans HS 1977; memb cncl: Inst of Manpower Studies 1975-81, CBI 1982, Tyndale House 1977, Fedn of Civil Engrg Contractors 1956; memb: Fedn of Civil Engrg Contractors Wages and Industl Ctee 1978, nat steering gp New Technical & Vocational Educn Initiative 1983, NHS Trg Authy 1986; Liveryman Worshipful Co of Glaziers' and Painters of Glass 1983; Hon DPhil; *Publications* contribs on music and musical instruments to New Bible Dictionary 1962; *Recreations* singing (choral music), listening to music (opera), walking; *Clubs* IOD, English-Speaking Union; *Style*— Donald Stradling, Esq; Courts Edge, 12 The Warren, Harpenden, Herts AL5 2NH (☎ 05827 2744); Page Street, Mill Hill, London NW7 2ER (☎ 959 3636, telex 263271)

STRADLING THOMAS, Sir John; MP (C) Monmouth 1970-; s of Thomas Roger Thomas, of Carmarthen; *b* 10 June 1925; *Educ* Rugby, Univ of London; *m* 1957 (m dis), Freda Rhys, da of Simon Rhys Evans, of Carmarthen; 1 s, 2 da; *Career* farmer; memb HQ Cncl NFU 1963-70; memb Carmarthen Cncl 1961-64; fought (C) Aberavon 1964 and Cardigan 1966; asst govt whip 1971-73, lord cmmr Treasury (govt whip)

1973-74, oppn whip 1974-79, tres of HM Household and dep chief whip 1979-83, min of State Welsh Off 1983-1985; kt 1985; *Style—* John Stradling Thomas, Esq, MP; House of Commons, SW1

STRAETFEILD-JAMES, Capt RN John Jocelyn; s of Cdr Rev E C Streatfeild-James, OBE, and Elizabeth Ann, *née* Kirby (d 1937); *b* 14 April 1929; *Educ* RNC Dartmouth; *m* 11 Aug 1962, Sally Madeline, da of R D Stewart (d 1970); 3 s (David b 22 Oct 1963, Douglas b 13 June 1967, Dominic b 21 April 1969); *Career* Naval Cadet 1943-47, Midshipman 1947-49, Sub Lt Minesweeping, Diving Anti-Bandit Ops Far East 1949-51, Lt Rating Trg, qualified in Undersea Warfare, ship and staff duties Far East 1952-59, Lt Cdr Offr Trg, Nat and NATO Undersea Warfare appts 1960-67, Cdr at Staff Coll (JSSC) 1968-73, Capt Computer Project Mgmnt, War Coll 1974-77, Cdre Head Br Def Liaison Staff Canada in cmd HMS Howard 1978-80, Capt HMS Excellent 1981-82; clerk to bd of govrs RNS Haslemere; vice chm local political pty; FBIM, MNI; *Recreations* painting, carpentry; *Style—* Capt Jo Streatfeild-James, RN; South Lodge, Tower Rd, Hindhead, Surrey GU26 6SP (☎ 042 873 6064); Royal Naval Sch, Haslemere, Surrey GU27 1HQ (☎ 042 873 6636)

STRAFFORD, 8 Earl of (UK 1847); Thomas Edmund Byng; also Baron Strafford (UK 1835), Viscount Enfield (UK 1847); s of 7 Earl of Strafford (d 1984) and his 1 w, Maria Magdalena Elizabeth, da of late Henry Cloete, CMG, of Alpha, S Africa; *b* 26 Sept 1936; *Educ* Eton, Clare Coll Cambridge; *m* 1, 1963 (m dis), Jennifer Mary Denise (she m, 1982, Christopher Bland), da of late Rt Hon William Morrison May, MP; 2 s (Viscount Enfield, Hon James b 1969), 2 da (Lady Georgia b 1965, Lady Harriet b 1967); m 2, 1981, Mrs Judy (Julia Mary) Howard, yr da of Sir Dennis Pilcher, CBE, *qv*; *Heir* s, Viscount Enfield; *Style—* The Rt Hon the Earl of Strafford; 11 St James Terrace, Winchester, Hants (☎ 0962 53905)

STRAIGHT, Lady Daphne Margarita; *née* Finch Hatton; da of 14 (& 9) Earl of Winchilsea and Nottingham by Margaretta, only surviving da of Anthony Joseph Drexel, s of the Anthony Drexel who founded the banks of Drexel, Morgan & Co, New York, and Drexel, Harjes & Co, Paris, also the Drexel Inst of Art, Science & Industry in Philadelphia with an endowment of two million dollars in 1891; *b* 1913; *m* 1935, Air Cdre Whitney Straight (d 1979, a memb of the celebrated American family of Whitney); 2 da; *Style—* Lady Daphne Straight; 3 Aubrey Rd, W8 7JJ (01 727 7822)

STRAKER, Hon Mrs (Ann Geraldine); *née* Milne; da of 2 Baron Milne; *b* 1946; *Educ* Queens Gate Sch London; *m* 1969, Ian Frederick Lawrence Straker; 1 s (Ross b 1977), 1 da (Frances b 1980); *Career* home and publishing; dir Bishopsgate Press London; Liveryman Worshipful Co of Grocers; *Recreations* tennis, skiing, gardening, art, Birman cats; *Style—* The Hon Mrs Straker; Hever Warren, Hever, Kent

STRAKER, Maj Ivan; s of Maj Arthur Coppin Straker (d 1961), of Pawston, Mindrum, Northumberland, and Cicely Longueville, *née* Hayward-Jones (d 1981); *b* 17 June 1928; *Educ* Harrow; *m* 1954, Gillian Elizabeth, da of Lewis Russell Harley Grant (d 1947); 2 s (Hugo b 1955, Simon b 1957), 1 da (Clare b 1960); m 2, Sally Jane, da of Maj William Hastings of Tod-le-Moor, Whittingham, Northumberland; 1 s (Tom b 1977); *Career* RMA Sandhurst, cmmnd 11 Hussars (PAO) 1948, served Germany, NI, M East and Mil Intelligence Staff WO, ret as Maj 1962; chm and chief exec Seagram Distillers plc 1984-, chm: The Glenlivet Distillers Ltd, Hill Thomson and Co Ltd; dir Lothians Racing Syndicate Ltd 1986-; *Recreations* horse racing, shooting, fishing, golf; *Clubs* Cavalry and Guards; *Style—* Maj Ivan Straker; 33 Cluny Drive, Edinburgh EH10 6DT (☎ 031 447 6621); Seagram Distillers House, Dacre Street, London SW1 (☎ 01 222 4343)

STRAKER, Karen Elizabeth; da of Hugh Charles Straker, and Elaine, *née* Peat; *b* 17 Sept 1964; *Educ* St Annes HS, St Godrics Coll Hampstead; *Career* int 3-day-event rider; jr Euro Champion 1982, Most Outstanding Young Rider of the Year 1982, Young Riders Euro Silver Medalist 1983, int competition Badminton and Burghley 1984-87, memb Br Equestrian 3 Day Event team Seoul Olympics (silver medallist) 1988; helper Riding for the Disabled, public speaker, instr and demonstrator; *Recreations* swimming, tennis, skiing; *Style—* Miss Karen Straker; Wycliffe Grange, Barnard Castle, Co Durham (☎ 0833 27500)

STRAKER, Sir Michael Ian Bowstead; CBE (1973), JP (Northumberland 1962); yr and only surv s of Edward Charles Straker (d 1943), of High Warden, Hexham, Northumberland, and Margaret Alice Bridget Straker; *b* 10 Mar 1928; *Educ* Eton; *Career* Coldstream Gds 1946-49; farmer; former chm Newcastle and Gateshead Water Co, chm Newcastle-upon-Tyne AHA (Teaching) 1973-81; chm: Aycliffe and Peterlee Devpt Corpn 1980-, Northumbrian Water Authy 1980-; chm: Northern Area Cons Assoc 1969-72; bd of Port of Tyne Authy; High Sheriff Northumberland 1977; DCL Newcastle Univ 1987; kt 1984; *Style—* Sir Michael Straker, CBE, JP; High Warden, Hexham, Northumberland

STRAKER, Hon Mrs (Sophie Henrietta); *née* Kimball; da of Baron Kimball (Life Peer); *b* 30 Nov 1960; *m* 1982, Reuben Thomas Coppin Straker, 4 and yst son of Hugh Charles Straker, of Spain; 1 da (Camilla Sophie, b 1985); *Style—* Hon Mrs Straker; Stonecroft, Fourstones, Hexham, Northumberland

STRANG, Christopher Forrest; s of John Strang (d 1971); *b* 31 May 1926; *Educ* Glasgow Acad, Univ of Glasgow; *m* 1956, Kathleen Mayfield, *née* Fetherston; 1 s, 2 da; *Career* CA; chm Ault & Wiborg Gp Ltd; *Recreations* social charity works, golf; *Clubs* Caledonian, RAC; *Style—* Christopher Strang Esq; Lyncourt, 4 Clifton Rd, SW19 (☎ 01 946 5765)

STRANG, 2 Baron (UK 1954); Colin Strang; s of 1st Baron, GCB, GCMG, MBE (d 1978), and Elsie Wynne Jones (d 1974); mother's ancestor Col John Jones, signed Charles I death warrant; *b* 12 June 1922; *Educ* Merchant Taylors', St John's Coll Oxford (MA, BPhil); *m* 1, 1948, Patricia Marie, da of Meiert C Avis, of Johannesburg, S Africa; m 2, 1955, Barbara Mary Hope (d 1982), da of Frederick Albert Carr, of Wimbledon; 1 da (Caroline b 1957); m 3, 1984, Mary Shewell, da of Richard Miles, of Thornaby-on-Tees; *Heir* none; *Career* prof of philosophy Univ of Newcastle, ret 1982; *Style—* The Rt Hon The Lord Strang; The Manse, Heptonstall Slack, Hebden Bridge, W Yorks HX7 76Z

STRANG, Gavin Steel; MP (Lab) Edinburgh E 1970-; s of James Steel Strang, of Perthshire; *b* 10 July 1943; *Educ* Morrison's Acad Crieff, Univ of Edinburgh (PhD), Univ of Cambridge (Dip Agric Sci); married, 1 s; *Career* oppn front bench spokesman Agric Fish and Food 1981-82, resigning over Labour policy on Falklands crisis (parly sec 1974-79), parly under-sec Energy March-Oct 1974; former scientist with ARC and memb Tayside Econ Planning Consultative Gp; *Style—* Gavin Strang, Esq, MP; 80 Argyle Crescent, Edinburgh EH15 2QD (☎ 031 669 5999; constituency office: 031 669 6002)

STRANG, Richard William; s of Gordon William Strang, of Lymedale, Milford-on-Sea, Hants, and Elizabeth Piercy, *née* Bernard (d 1981); *b* 19 June 1950; *Educ* Radley, CCC Oxford (MA); *Career* CA with Peat Marwick Mitchell London 1971-78, dir Morgan Grenfell & Co Ltd 1986- (joined 1978), non exec dir Morgan Grenfell Aust (Hldgs) Ltd 1987-; FCA 1974; *Recreations* opera, skiing, sailing, tennis, bridge; *Style—* Richard Strang, Esq; 19 Rosary Gardens, London SW7 (☎ 01 373 445); Morgan Grenfell & Co Limited, 23 Great Winchester Street, London EC2P 2AX (☎ 01 826 6827)

STRANG STEEL, Colin Brodie; yr s of Maj Sir William Strang Steel, 2 Bt, of Philiphaugh, Selkirk, (*qv*), and Joan Ella Brodie, *née* Henderson (d 1982); *b* 2 June 1945; *Educ* Eton, RAC Cirencester; *m* 24 Oct 1970, April Eileen, da of Aubrey Fairfax Studd, of Cahoo House, Ramsey, IoM; 3 s (James b 1973, Alistair b 1975, Peter b 1977); *Career* chartered surveyor; ptnr Knight Frank & Rutley 1974-; dir Field & Lawn (Marquees) Ltd 1986-; FRICS; *Recreations* cricket, football, squash, tennis, wildlife; *Clubs* MCC, Scottish Cricket Union, New (Edinburgh); *Style—* Colin Strang Steel, Esq; Newlandburn House, Newlandrig, Gorebridge, Midlothian (☎ 031 225 7105); 2 North Charlotte St, Edinburgh EH2 4HR (☎ 031 225 7105, fax 031 220 1403)

STRANG STEEL, Jock Wykeham; s of Sir Samuel Strang Steel, 1 Bt (d 1961), of Selkirk, and Hon Vere Mabel (d 1964), da of 1 Baron Cornwallis; *b* 23 April 1914; *Educ* Eton; *m* 14 Nov 1945, Lesley, da of Lt-Col Sir John Reginald Noble Graham, 3 Bt, VC, OBE (d 1980); 1 s (Malcolm Graham b 1946), 2 da (Celia Jane b 1948, Susan Rachel b 1952); *Career* farmer; *Recreations* cricket, shooting; *Style—* Jock W Strang Steel, Esq; Logie, Kirriemuir, Angus (☎ 0575 72249)

STRANG STEEL, Malcolm Graham; WS; s of Jock Wykeham Strang Steel, of Kirriemuir Angus, and Lesley Strang Steel, *née* Graham; *b* 24 Nov 1946; *Educ* Eton, Trinity Coll Cambridge, Univ of Edinburgh; *m* 21 Oct 1972, Margaret Philippa, da of William Patrick Scott, OBE, DL, of Stromness, Orkney; 1 s (Patrick Reginald b 1975), 1 da (Laura b 1977); *Career* slr 1973-; ptnr W & J Burness WS; memb of cncl Law Soc of Scotland 1984-; *Recreations* shooting, fishing, skiing, tennis, reading; *Clubs* New (Edinburgh), MCC; *Style—* Malcolm G Strang Steel, Esq, WS; Barrowmore, Mawcarse, Kinross KY13 7SL (☎ 0577 63225); 16 Hope St, Edinburgh EH2 4DD (☎ 031 226 2561, telex 72405, fax 031 225 2964)

STRANG STEEL, Maj (Fiennes) Michael; s and h of Sir William Strang Steel, 2 Bt, JP, DL; *b* 22 Feb 1943; *m* 1977, Sarah Jane, da of late J A S Russell; 2 s, 1 da; *Career* Maj 17/21 Lancers, ret; *Style—* Maj Michael Strang Steel; Ravensheugh, Selkirk

STRANGE, Lady (16 Holder of Title, E 1628) (Jean) Cherry Drummond of Megginch; eldest da of 15 Baron Strange (d 1982), and Violet Margaret Florence (d 1975), o da of Sir Robert William Buchanan-Jardine, 2 Bt; suc as 16 holder of the peerage when the abeyance between her and her two sisters was terminated after petition to HM The Queen 1986; *b* 17 Dec 1928; *Educ* Univ of St Andrew's (MA), Univ of Cambridge; *m* 2 June 1952, Capt Humphrey ap Evans, MC, who assumed the name of Drummond of Megginch by decree of Lord Lyon 1966, s of Maj James John Pugh Evans, MBE, MC, JP, DL, of Lovegrove, Aberystwyth; 3 s (Hon Adam Humphrey, Hon Humphrey John Jardine b 11 March 1961, Hon John Humphrey Hugo b 26 June 1966), 3 da (Hon Charlotte Cherry b 14 May 1955, Hon Amélie Margaret Mary b 2 July 1963, Hon Catherine Star Violetta b 15 Dec 1967); *Heir* s, Hon Adam Humphrey Drummond of Megginch b 20 April 1953; *Style—* The Rt Hon Lady Strange; Megginch Castle, Errol, Perthshire; 160 Kennington Road, London SE11

STRANGE, Frederick Griffiths St Clair; s of Dr Charles Frederick Strange (d 1927), of 5 Rosslyn Hill, Hampstead, and Olive Cecelia Harrison (d 1970); *b* 22 July 1911; *Educ* Rugby, London Hosp Med Coll, Univ of London; *m* 17 June 1939, Joyce Elsie, da of A Percy Kimber (d 1944), of South Croxted Road, Dulwich; 1 s (Richard b 1942), 2 da (Diana b 1941, Angela b 1944); *Career* consulting orthopaedic surgeon: Kent, Canterbury and Ramsgate Hosps 1947-48, Canterbury and Thanet HMC (later dist) areas 1948-75 (hon 1975-); vice pres British Orthopaedic Assoc 1971-72, pres orthopaedic section RSM 1965-66 (hon memb 1975-), vice pres RSM 1965-66, Hunterian prof RCS 1947, hon civilian conslt orthopaedics to the Army at The Royal Herbert Hosp 1967-76; former pres combined services orthopaedic soc; Robert Jones Gold Medallist Brit Orthopaedic Assoc 1943; Nuffield travelling fell 1948; MRCS, LRCP, FRCS; *Publications* The Hip (1965), many contributions to orthopaedic literature; *Recreations* photography, philately, travel; *Style—* F G St Clair Strange, Esq

STRANGE, Raymond Charles; s of Harry Charles Strange (1974); *b* 4 Mar 1922; *Educ* Raine's Sch; *m* 1950, Margaret Helen, nee Gummer; 1 da; *Career* Lt RE; chm: A R Stenhouse and Ptnrs Ltd, Stenhouse Reed Shaw Ltd; dir: Stenhouse Hldgs Ltd, Reed Stenhouse Co Ltd (Canada); vice pres Societe Generale de Courtage d'Assurances Paris; *Recreations* golf, riding, driving, fishing; *Clubs* Army and Navy; *Style—* Raymond C Strange, Esq; Lower Farm House, Broadwell, Moreton-i-March, Glos (☎ 0451 30250)

STRANGE, Prof Susan (Mrs Clifford Selly); da of Lt Col Louis Arbon Strange, DSO, OBE, MC, DFC (d 1966), and Marjorie, *née* Beath (d 1968); *b* 9 June 1923; *Educ* Royal Sch Bath, LSE (BSc); *m* 1 Sept 1945 (m dis 1955), Denis McVicar Merritt, s of Sidney Merritt (d 1967); 1 s (Giles b 20 Nov 1943), 1 da (Jane (Mrs Streatfield) b 5 March 1948); m 2, 14 Dec 1955, Clifford Selly; 3 s (Mark b 28 July 1957, Roger b 21 April 1960, Adam b 22 Oct 1963), 1 da (Kate b 24 Oct 1961); *Career* Washington UN and econ corr: The Economist 1944-46, The Observer 1946-57; lectr in int relations UCL 1949-64, res fell RIIA 1965-76, German Marshall Fund fell 1976-78, visiting prof Univ of S California 1978, Montague Burton prof of int relations LSE 1978-88, prof of int relations Euro Univ Inst Florence 1989-; *Books* Sterling and British Policy (1971), International Monetary Relations (1976), The International Politics of Surplus Capacity (co ed with R Tooze 1981), Paths to International Political Economy (ed 1984), Casino Capitalism (1986); States and Markets (1988); *Recreations* cooking, gardening, tennis, canoeing; *Style—* Prof Susan Strange; Weedon Hill House, Aylesbury, Bucks HP22 YDP (☎ 0296 27772); European University Institute 50016, S Domenico Di Fiesole (FI), Italy (☎ Italy 55 50921)

STRANGER-JONES, Anthony John; s of Leonard Ivan Stranger-Jones (d 1983), and Iris Christine, *née* Truscott; *b* 30 Dec 1944; *Educ* Westminster, Christ Church Oxford (MA); *m* 19 June 1976, Kazumi, da of Kazuo Matsuo, of 4500-97 Fukuma-Machi, Munakata-Gun, Fukuoka Pref 811-32, Japan; 1 s (David b 1983), 2 da (Amiko b 1977, Yukiko b 1980); *Career* md Rib Fin (Hong Kong) Ltd 1974-76; dir Amex Bank Ltd 1977-79, Korea Merchant Banking Corpn 1979-82, Barclays Merchant Bank Ltd 1979-

86; dir Barclays de Zoete Wedd Ltd 1986-; *Clubs* MCC, Hong Kong; *Style*— Anthony Stranger-Jones, Esq; 33 Randolph Crescent, London W9 1DP (☎ 01 286 7342); Barclays de Zoete Wedd Ltd, Ebbgate House, 2 Swan Lane, London EC4R 3TS (☎ 01 623 2323, telex 8950851, fax 01 623 6075)

STRATFORD, Dr Martin Gould; VRD (1943); s of late Dr Howard Martin Blenheim Stratford, and late Sybil Kathleen Lucy, *née* Gould; *b* 20 Feb 1908; *Educ* Westminster, UCH (MB, BS); *m* 15 Sept 1934, da of late Herbert Muir Beddall; 2 s (Muir b 1936, Neil b 1938); *Career* Surgn Lt Cmdr RNVR, served HMS Hermes and RN Hosp Chatham; former physician Charterhouse Rheumatism Clinic, physician St Lukes Hosp for Clergy,asst med offr Br Coal; MRCS, LRCP; *Recreations* cricket, football, golf; *Clubs* MCC, Royal Soc of Medicine; *Style*— Dr Martin Stratford; 27 Bryanston Square, London W1H 7LS; 42 Harley Street, London W1M 1AB

STRATFORD, (Howard) Muir; JP (1978); s of Dr Martin Gould Stratford, of London, and Dr Mavis Winifred Muir Stratford; *b* 6 June 1936; *Educ* Marlborough; *m* 8 July 1961, Margaret Reid, da of Robert Linton Roderick Ballantine (d 1957); 1 s (Duncan b 1971), 2 da (Gail b 1964, Fiona b 1967); *Career* insur broker; dir Bowring London Ltd 1980-85 and 1986-, chief exec Bowring M K Ltd 1985-86; dir Watford FC 1971-; *Recreations* golf, watching football and cricket; *Clubs* MCC, Moor Park GC, City Livery; *Style*— Muir Stratford, Esq, JP; Nobles, Church Lane, Sarratt, Herts (☎ 09277 60475); Bowring London Ltd, The Bowring Building, Tower Place, London EC3 (☎ 01 283 3100, telex 882191, car ☎ 0836 219412)

STRATHALLAN, Viscount; John Eric Drummond; s and h of 17 Earl of Perth, PC; *b* 7 July 1935; *m* 1, 1963 (m dis 1972), Margaret Ann, da of Robert Gordon; 2 s (Hon James, Hon Robert b 7 May 1967); m 2, 6 Oct 1988, Mrs Marion Elliot; *Heir* s, Hon James Drummond; *Style*— Viscount Strathallan; Stobhall, by Perth

STRATHALMOND, Letitia, Baroness; Letitia; da of late Walter Martin Krementz, of Morristown, New Jersey, USA; *m* 1945, 2 Baron, CMG, OBE, TD (d 1976); 1 s, 2 da; *Style*— The Rt Hon Letitia, Lady Strathalmond; 155 Fawn Lane, Portola Valley, California 94125, USA

STRATHALMOND, 3 Baron (UK 1955); William Roberton Fraser; o s of 2 Baron Strathalmond, CMG, OBE, TD (d 1976), and Letitia, *née* Krementz; *b* 22 July 1947; *Educ* Loretto; *m* 1973, Amanda Rose, da of Rev Gordon Clifford Taylor, of St Giles-in-the-Fields Rectory, Gower St, London; 2 s (Hon William, Hon George b 1979), 1 da (Hon Virginia b 22 Dec 1982); *Heir* s, Hon William Gordon Fraser b 24 Sept 1976; *Career* md London Wall Members Agency Ltd 1986- (formerly Bain Dawes Underwriting Agency), dir London Wall Hldgs plc 1986; MICAS 1972; *Style*— The Rt Hon The Lord Strathalmond; Holt House, Elstead, Godalming, Surrey GU8 6LF

STRATHAVON AND GLENLIVET, Lord; Alistair Granville Gordon; s and h of Earl of Aboyne, *qv*; gs of 12 Marquess of Huntly; *b* 26 July 1973; *Style*— Lord Strathavon and Glenlivet

STRATHCARRON, 2 Baron (UK 1936); Sir David William Anthony Blyth Macpherson; 2 Bt (UK 1933); s of 1 Baron, KC, PC (d 1937), and Jill, da of Sir George Wood Rhodes, 1 Bt, JP; *b* 23 Jan 1924; *Educ* Eton, Jesus Coll Cambridge; *m* 1, 1947 (m dis 1947), Valerie Cole; m 2, 1948, Diana Hawtry (d 1973), da of late Cdr R H Deane and formerly w of J N O Curle; 2 s; m 3, 1974, Mary Eve, da of late John Comyn Higgins, CIE, and formerly w of Hon Anthony Gerald Samuel, *qv*; *Heir* s, Hon Ian Macpherson; *Career* formerly Fl-Lt RAFVR, motoring correspondent of The Field, ptnr Strathcarron & Co; dir: Kirchoffs (London) Ltd, Seabourne Express Co Ltd, Kent Int Airport Ltd; pres: Driving Instrs Assoc, Nat Breakdown Recovery Club, Guild of Motor Writers; chm: The Order of the Road; *Books* Motoring for Pleasure; *Style*— The Rt Hon The Lord Strathcarron; 22 Rutland Gate, London SW7 1BB (☎ 01 584 1240); Otterwood, Beaulieu, Hants (☎ 0590 612334)

STRATHCLYDE, 2 Baron (UK 1955); Thomas Galloway Dunlop du Roy de Blicquy Galbraith; er s of Hon Sir Thomas Galbraith, KBE, MP (C & Unionist) Glasgow Hillhead 1948-82 (d 1982), by his w, Simone Clothilde Fernande Marie Ghislaine (eldest da of late Jean du Roy de Blicquy, of Bois d'Hautmont, Brabant), whose marriage with Sir Thomas was dissolved 1974; suc gf, 1 Baron Strathclyde, PC, JP (d 1985); *b* 22 Feb 1960; *Educ* Sussex House London, Wellington, Univ of East Anglia (BA), Université d'Aix-en-Provence; *Career* insurance broker Bain Clarkson Ltd (formerly Bain Dawes) 1982-88; Lord in Waiting (Govt Whip House of Lords) 1988-; spokesman for DTI: Cons candidate Euro Election Merseyside East 1984; *Style*— The Rt Hon Lord Strathclyde; Old Barskimming, Mauchline, Ayrshire KA5 5HB; 2 Cowley St, London SW1 (☎ 01 222 2966)

STRATHCONA AND MOUNT ROYAL, 4 Baron (UK 1900); Donald Euan Palmer Howard; s of 3 Baron Strathcona and Mount Royal (d 1959), and Hon Diana, *née* Loder (d 1985), da of 1 Baron Wakehurst; *b* 26 Nov 1923; *Educ* Eton, Trinity Coll Cambridge, McGill Univ Montreal; *m* 1, 1954 (m dis 1977), Lady Jane Mary, da of 12 Earl Waldegrave, KG, GCVO, TD (*see* Howard, Lady Jane); 2 s, 4 da; m 2, 1978, Patricia, da of late Harvey Evelyn Thomas and wid of John Middleton; *Heir* s, Hon Donald Howard; *Career* sits as Cons in Lords; late Lt RNVR, vice chm Maritime Tst, pres UK Pilots Assoc and Steamboat Assoc of GB, a Lord in Waiting to HM (Govt Whip) 1973-74, parly under-sec of state for RAF 1974, jt dep leader of oppn House of Lords 1976-79, min of state MOD 1979-81; dir: Computing Servs Co Ltd, Warrior Preservation Tst ; *Recreations* gardening, sailing; *Clubs* Brooks's, Pratt's, RYS, Air Squadron; *Style*— The Rt Hon The Lord Strathcona and Mount Royal; 5 Ridgway Gardens, Wimbledon, London SW19 (☎ 01 947 8157); House of Lords, London SW1; Kiloran, Isle of Colonsay, Scotland (☎ 095 21 301)

STRATHEDEN AND CAMPBELL, 6 Baron (UK 1836 and 1841 respectively); Donald Campbell; o s of 5 Baron Stratheden and Campbell (d 1987), and Evelyn Mary Austen, *née* Smith; *b* 4 April 1934; *Educ* Eton; *m* 8 Nov 1957, Hilary Ann Holland, da of Lt-Col William Derington Turner, of Simonstown, S Africa; 1 s (Hon David Anthony), 3 da (Hon Tania Ann b 19 Sept 1960, Hon Wendy Meriel b 27 Jan 1969, Hon Joyce Margaret b 1971); *Heir* s, Hon David Anthony Campbell, *qv*; *Style*— Christopher Chaitow, Esq; Ridgewood, MS 1064, Cooroy, Queensland 4563, Australia

STRATHEDEN AND CAMPBELL, Evelyn, Baroness; Evelyn Mary Austen; yr da of Col Herbert Austen Smith, CIE, IMS (d 1949), of Springfield, Hawkhurst, Kent, and Harriet Emma, *née* Shewell; *m* 26 April 1933, 5 Baron Stratheden and Campbell (d 1987); 1 s (6 Baron, *qv*); *Style*— The Rt Hon Evelyn, Lady Stratheden and Campbell

STRATHEDEN AND CAMPBELL, Noël, Baroness; Noël Christabel; da of late Capt Conrad Viner; *m* 1, George Vincent; m 2, 21 Dec 1964, as his 2 w, 4 Baron Stratheden and Campbell, CBE (d 1981); *Style*— The Rt Hon Noël, Lady Stratheden and Campbell; 4 Bannisters Field, Church Road, Newick, East Sussex BN8 4JS

STRATHMORE AND KINGHORNE, 18 Earl of (S 1606 and 1677) Michael Fergus Bowes Lyon; also Lord Glamis (S 1445), Earl of Kinghorne (S 1606), Lord Glamis, Tannadyce, Sidlaw and Strathdichtie, Viscount Lyon and Earl of Strathmore and Kinghorne by special charter (S 1677), Baron Bowes (UK 1887), Earl of Strathmore and Kinghorne (UK 1937); s of 17 Earl of Strathmore and Kinghorne (d 1987), and Mary Pamela, *née* McCorquodale; *b* 7 June 1957; *Educ* Univ of Aberdeen (B Land Econ); *m* 14 Nov 1984, Isobel Charlotte, da of Capt Anthony Weatherall, of Cowhill, Dumfries; 2 s (Simon Patrick (Lord Glamis) b 1986, Hon John Fergus b 1988); *Heir* s, Lord Glamis; *Career* a Page of Honour to HM Queen Elizabeth the Queen Mother (his great aunt) 1971-73; Capt Scots Gds; *Clubs* Turf, Buck's, Pratt's, Perth; *Style*— The Rt Hon the Earl of Strathmore and Kinghorne; Glamis Castle, Forfar, Angus (☎ 030 784 244)

STRATHNAVER, Lord; Alistair Charles St Clair Sutherland; also Master of Sutherland; s (twin) and h of Countess of Sutherland, *qv*; *b* 7 Jan 1947; *Educ* Eton, Christ Church Oxford (BA); *m* 1, 1968, Eileen Elizabeth, o da of Richard Wheeler Baker, of Princeton, USA; 2 da (Hon Rachel b 1970, Hon Rosemary b 1972); m 2, 1980, Gillian Margaret St Clair, da of Robert Murray, of Gourock, Renfrewshire; 1 s, 1 da (Hon Elizabeth b 1984); *Heir* s, Hon Alexander Charles Robert Sutherland b 1 Oct 1981; *Career* constable Met Police 1969-74, IBM UK Ltd 1975-78, Sutherland Estates 1979-; *Style*— Lord Strathnaver; Sutherland Estates Office, Golspie, Sutherland (☎ 040 83 3268)

STRATHSPEY, 5 Baron (UK 1884); Sir Donald Patrick Trevor Grant of Grant; 17 Bt (NS 1625); 32 Chief of the Clan Grant, recognised in the surname of Grant of Grant by decree of Lord Lyon 1950; s of 4 Baron Strathspey (d 1948); *b* 18 Mar 1912; *Educ* Stowe, SE Agric Coll; *m* 1, 24 Sept 1938 (m dis 1951), Alice, o da of late Francis Bowe, of NZ; 1 s, 2 da; m 2, 1 Sept 1951, Olive, o da of late Wallace Henry Grant, of Norwich; 1 s, 1 da; *Heir* s, Hon James Grant of Grant; *Career* late Lt-Col Gen List; asst chief land agent Def Land Servs, ret; memb: standing cncl Scottish Chiefs, Highland Soc London, Clan Grant Socs in USA, Canada, NZ, Australia; pres Civil Serv Motoring Assoc; FRICS; *Books* A History of Clan Grant (1983); *Recreations* sailing, gardening; *Style*— The Rt Hon The Lord Strathspey; Elms Ride, W Wittering, Sussex

STRATON, Dr Thomas; s of Dr Alexander Walter Kieth Straton (d 1947), of West Lodge, Wilton, nr Salisbury, and Hilda Grace, *née* Garrett (d 1973); an ancestor boiled up a tax collector in a Scottish glen; *b* 2 Oct 1920; *Educ* Claysemore Monkton Combe, Univ of Bristol (MB, ChB); *m* 29 Jan 1946, Rae Hervey, da of Maj Frank Pilkington Scott (d 1974), of Stoke Green House, nr Slough; 3 s (David b 1949, Kieth b and d 1954), Peter b 1956), 1 da (Nicola b 1951); *Career* Surgn Lt RNVR 1946-48; gen medical practitioner; medical offr Fordingbridge Branch of Salisbury Hosp Gp, hon med advsr to Salisbury Rehabilitation Dept 1949-85, ret; memb: BMA, Nat Tst, New Forest Med Soc; *Recreations* sailing, fishing, shooting, carpentry, gardening, general boat and estate maintainance; *Clubs* Royal Cruising, RAC, RSPB, WWF, Shoreline, Lymington Town Yacht; *Style*— Dr Thomas Straton; The Paddocks, Provost St, Fordingbridge, Hants SP6 1AY (☎ 0425 52391, boat ☎ 2.GMM)

STRATTON, (John) Mark; s of Capt Charles Michael Stratton, of Brackley, Northants, and Anne Windsor-Lewis, *née* Drummond (d 1985); *b* 27 April 1931; *Educ* Eton, Univ of Lausanne; *m* 1 June 1961, Diana Miranda, da of Eric Martin Smith, MP (d 1951), of Codicote Lodge, Hitchin, Herts; 2 s (James b 1963, Andrew b 1968), 1 da (Kate b 1965); *Career* Army 1949-51, Capt; md: H E Taylor & Co Ltd 1967, Triconfort Ltd 1970-; *Recreations* shooting, fishing, swimming, gardening; *Clubs* Boodles; *Style*— Mark Stratton, Esq; Witton Old Rectory, Norwich, Norfolk NR13 5DS (☎ 0603 712425); Triconfort Ltd, Oak St, Norwich NR3 3BP (☎ 0603 625287)

STRATTON, Vernon Gordon-Lennox; s of Undecimus Stratton (d 1929), and Muriel Dorothy Phipps, of Boldre, Hants; *b* 26 Oct 1927; *Educ* Eton; *m* 1952, Penelope Anne, da of Sir Geoffrey Lowles; 3 s (James, Charles, Richard), 1 da (Sarah); *Career* 2 Lt 11 Hussars; advertisement mangr Sunday Times Advertisement 1954-56, retail dir Jaeger 1956-64, chm and md Vernon Stratton Ltd 1964-, chm Wilkins Campbell Ltd 1979-86; chm and mangr RYA Olympic Ctee 1977-80, mangr Olympic Sailing 1968, 1972, 1980, Olympic Team (Finn Class) 1960; *Recreations* sailing, skiing, photography; *Clubs* Royal Thames Yacht, Bembridge Sailing; *Style*— Vernon Stratton, Esq; St Helens Station, IOW (☎ 0983 872865); 15 Donne Place, London SW3 (☎ 01 584 5284); business: 21 Ives St, London SW3 (☎ 01 584 4211)

STRATTON, Lt-Gen Sir William Henry; KCB (1957, CB 1948), CVO 1944, CBE 1943, DS0 1945; s of late Lt-Col H W Stratton, OBE; *b* 1903; *Educ* Dulwich, RMA; *m* 1930, Noreen Mabel Brabazon, da of late Dr F H B Noble of Sittingbourne, Kent; *Career* 2 Lt RE 1924, seconded to the Colonial Off for serv on the Gold Coast 1927-31, Lt-Col 1940, served UK 1939-43, CRE 11 Armoured Div, CRE 61 Div, Brig GHQ Home Forces 1941; served Italy 1944-45, Brig-Gen Staff HQ British 8 Army 1944 (despatches), Cdr 169 Infantry Bde 1944-45, Maj-Gen 1946, cos BAOR 1947-49, cmdt Jt Servs Staff Coll 1949-51,; Cdr Br Army Staff and mil memb Br Jt Services Mission Washington 1952-53, GOC 42 (Lancs) Inf Div (TA) and North West Dist 1953-55, Lt-Gen 1955, Cdr Br Forces Hong Kong 1955-57, vice-CIGS 1957-60, inspr-Gen Civil Def Home Off 1960-62, Col Cmdt RE 1960-68; chm: Edwin Danks & Co Ltd, Penman & Co Ltd 1961-71, Babcock-Moxey Ltd 1965-71; *Style*— Lt-Gen Sir William Stratton, KCB, CVO, CBE, DSO; Stable Cottage, Carron Lane, Midhurst, Sussex (☎ 073 081 3964)

STRAUGHAN, Dr John (Kenmore); s of Albert Straughan (d 1975), of Goody Hills, Cumbria, and Mary, *née* Martin (d 1987); *b* 31 Oct 1934; *Educ* Keswick Sch, Univ of Durham (MB BS); *m* 1, 5 Jan 1963 (m dis 1972), Corol (Felicity), da of Geoffrey Hoyles (d 1965), of Jesmond, Newcastle-upon-Tyne; 1 s (Anthony John b 26 March 1965), 1 da (Justina Jane b 31 Oct 1963); m 2, 27 Aug 1975, Patricia Cunningham, da of Maj Arthur (Colin) Bell (d 1942), of Gosforth, Northumbria; *Career* chief MO: Ever Ready Battery Co 1978-82, Occidental Oil 1982-86; med dir Br Rubber Mfrg Assoc 1986-; memb: Nat Rubber Indust Advsy Ctee, Soc Occupational Medicine 1972, MFOM 1982; *Recreations* fly fishing; *Clubs* Northern Counties; *Style*— Dr John K Straughan; Cleobury Ct, Cleobury North, nr Bridgenorth, Shrops WV16 6QQ (☎ 074 633 420); British Rubber Manufacturers' Assoc Ltd, Health Res Unit, Scala House, Holloway Circus, Birmingham B1 1EQ (☎ 021 643 9269, fax 021 631 3297)

STRAUGHAN, Jonathan Nicholson; s of William Christopher Straughan, and Caroline, *née* Nicholson; *b* 29 Dec 1923; *m* 6 Aug 1955, Elizabeth Ruby, da of William

Charlton Mason; 1 s (Brian Jonathan), 1 da (Judith Elizabeth); *Career* served Army WWII; fndr ptnr JN Straughan & Co CAS 1953- (conslt 1988-), ptnr Rainbow Straughan & Elliot CAs Sunderland; vice chm NE Bd Bradford & Bingley Bldg Soc, former vice chm Stanley Bldg Soc, chm ERESKO Ltd (fin advsy co), fndr Provincial Ind CA Gp; lay preacher Methodist Church, past pres Rotary Club Chester-le-Street, fndr sec Chester-le-Street CAB, past pres Northern Soc of CAS; FICA, memb Inst of Taxation; *Recreations* golf, tennis, cricket, badminton; *Clubs* Lansdowne; *Style*— Jonathan Straughan, Esq; J N Straughan & Co, Hadrian House, Front St, Chester-le-Street, Co Durham (☎ 091 388 3186)

STRAUSS, Hon Brian Timothy; s of Baron Strauss, PC (Life Peer); *b* 1935; *Style*— The Hon Brian Strauss

STRAUSS, Lt-Cdr Derek Ronald; s of Ronald Strauss; *b* 16 May 1939; *Educ* Eton; *m* 1967, Nicola Mary, da of Gp-Capt William Blackwood, OBE, DFC; 2 children; *Career* Lt-Cdr RNR; dep chm SGST Securities Ltd; *Recreations* fishing, shooting, skiing; *Clubs* White's, City of London, Pratts; *Style*— Lt-Cdr Derek Strauss, RNR; Stonehurst, Ardingly, West Sussex; SGST Securities Ltd, 3 Moorgate Place, London EC2R 6HR (☎ 01 638 5699; telex 883201)

STRAUSS, Baron (Life Peer UK 1979); George Russell Strauss; PC (1947); s of late Arthur Strauss, MP; *b* 18 July 1901; *Educ* Rugby; *m* 1932, Patricia Francis (d 1987), da of F O'Flynn; 2 s, 1 da; m 2, 11 Aug 1987, Benita Armstrong; *Career* MP (L) Vauxhall Div of Lambeth 1929-31, 1934-50 and 1950-79, pps to Min of Tport 1929-31, parly sec Min of Tport 1945-47, and Min of Supply 1947-51; *Style*— The Rt Hon The Lord Strauss, PC; 1 Palace Green, W8 (☎ 01 937 1630)

STRAUSS, Hon Hilary Jane; da of Baron Strauss, PC (Life Peer); *b* 1937; *Style*— The Hon Hilary Strauss

STRAUSS, Hon Roger Anthony; s of Baron Strauss, PC; *b* 1934; *Style*— The Hon Roger Strauss

STRAW, Jack - John Whitaker; MP (Lab) Blackburn 1979-; s of Walter Straw, and Joan Straw; *b* 3 August 1946; *Educ* Brentwood Sch Essex, Univ of Leeds; *m* 1, 1968 (m dis 1978), Anthea Weston; (1 da decd); m 2, 1978, Alice Elizabeth Perkins; 1 s, 1 da; *Career* barr 1972; pres NUS 1969-71, memb Islington Cncl 1971-78, dep ldr ILEA 1973-74, memb Lab Nat Exec Sub-Ctee Educn and Science 1970, contested (Lab) Tonbridge and Malling 1974; political advsr to: Social Servs sec 1974-76, Environment sec 1976-77; with Granada TV (World in Action) 1977-79; oppn front bench spokesman: Treasy and Econ Affrs 1981-83, Environment 1983-87; elected as Shadow Cabinet 1987, shadow educn sec 1987-; *Style*— Jack Straw, Esq, MP; House of Commons, London SW1A 0AA

STRAWSON, Maj-Gen John Michael; CB (1975), OBE (1964); s of Cyril Walter Strawson (d 1937), of London, and Nellie Dora, *née* Jewell (d 1975); *b* 1 Jan 1921; *Educ* Christs Coll Finchley; *m* 29 Dec 1960, Baroness Wilfried Marie, da of Baron Harold von Schellersheim (d 1986), of Rittergut Eisbergen, Germany; 2 da (Viola b 1961, Carolin b 1963); *Career* cmmnd 1941, 4 Queens Own Hussars 1942; served: Middle East, Italy, Germany, Malaya; Staff Coll Camberley 1950, Bde Maj 1951-52, directing staff Camberley 1958-60 (master of Staff Coll Drag Hounds), GSO1 and Col GS WO (later MOD) 1961-62 and 1965-66, cmd The Queens Royal Irish Hussars 1963-65, cmd 39 Inf Bde 1967-68, Imperial Def Coll 1969; chief of staff: SHAPE 1970-72, HQ UKLF 1972-76; ret 1976; Col The Queens Royal Irish Hussars 1975-85; mil advsr Westland plc 1976-85; chm The Friends of Boyton Church, vice pres The Royal Br Legion (Codford); US Bronze Star 1945; *Books* The Battle for North Africa (1969), Hitler as Military Commander (1971), The Battle for the Ardennes (1972), The Battle for Berlin (1974), El Alamein (1981), A History of the SAS Regiment (1984), The Italian Campaign (1987), The Third World War (jtly, 2 vols 1978 and 1982); *Recreations* equitation, shooting, tennis, reading; *Clubs* Cavalry and Guards (chm 1984-87); *Style*— Maj-Gen John Strawson, CB, OBE; The Old Rectory, Boyton, Warminster, Wilts BA12 0SS, (☎ 0985 50218)

STRAWSON, Sir Peter Frederick; s of late Cyril Walter and Nellie Dora Strawson; *Educ* Christ's Coll Finchley, St John's Coll Oxford; *m* 1945, Grace Hall Martin; 2 s, 2 da; *Career* Waynflete prof metaphysical philosophy Oxford Univ 1968-87, fell Magdalen Coll; FBA; kt 1977; *Style*— Sir Peter Strawson; 25 Farndon Rd, Oxford

STREATFEILD, Lady Moyra Charlotte; *née* Stopford; BEM (1984); da of 7 Earl of Courtown (d 1957); *b* 7 Sept 1917; *m* 1943, Lt-Cdr David Henry Champion Streatfield, RN, s of Rev Claude Arthur Cecil Streatfield (d 1951); 3 s (Anthony b 1945, Timothy b 1947, Peter b 1954), 1 da (Mary b 1950); *Style*— Lady Moyra Streatfeild, BEM; Redberry House, Bierton, Aylesbury, Bucks (☎ 0296 82126)

STREATHER, Bruce Godfrey; s of William Godfrey Streather, of Lakeside, Little Aston Hall, Staffs, and Pamela Mary, *née* Revell; *b* 3 June 1946; *Educ* Malvern, Oxford Univ (MA); *m* 15 Dec 1973, Geraldine Susan, da of Colin Herbert Clout, of San Franciso, California, USA; 3 da (Charlotte, Annabel, Miranda); *Career* sr ptnr: Streather & Co, Streather & Thomson, Streather Thomson & Hauser, Baines & Baines, GA Fry & Co; dir Aid Call plc; memb Law Soc; *Recreations* family, golf; *Clubs* Royal and Ancient GC of St Andrews, Sunningdale GC, Vincents, Little Aston GC, Littlestone GC; *Style*— Bruce Streather, Esq; 16 Clifford St, London W11 (☎ 01 734 4363, fax 01 734 7539)

STREET, Alan Thomas; s of late Thomas Albert Street; *b* 22 Jan 1928; *Educ* Uddingston and Stockport GS; *m* 1953, Betty Diamond, *née* Shaw; 3 da; *Career* dir: J D Williams Gp 1970, Oxendale & Co Ltd 1968, Heather Valley (Woollens) Ltd 1972, Hilton Mailing Services Ltd 1980; MInstM, MCAM; *Recreations* sailing (yacht 'Milady of Ollerton'), skiing; *Clubs* Royal Welsh Yacht, Manchester Cruising Assoc; *Style*— Alan Street, Esq; Ollerton Hall, Knutsford, Cheshire (☎ 0565 50222); J D Williams Group Ltd, 53 Dale St, Manchester M60 6EU (☎ 061 236 3764, telex 667610 BYPOST)

STREET, Brian Frederick; s of Frederick Street, and Ellen, *née* Hollis; *b* 2 June 1927; *Educ* St Phillip's GS Edgbaston, Birmingham Univ (BSc), Harvard (AMP); *m* 1951, Margaret Patricia, da of Ald John William Carleton, JP (d 1951); 1 s (decd), 5 da (Teresa b 1952, Veronica b 1954, Amanda b 1957, Rebecca b 1959, Francesca b 1965); *Career* chartered engr; chief technologist Shell Chemicals UK Ltd 1964-68, dir British Cellophane Ltd 1972-75, md Air Prods Ltd 1975-80 (chm 1981-), dir Stearns Catalytic Int 1983-86, dep chm and chief exec Apcel Ltd 1984-86, non exec chm NMC Mgmnt Conslts 1989-; visiting prof: Dept of Chemical and Process Engrg Univ of Surrey 1985-, Univ of Bath 1988-; pres IChemE 1983-84; memb: CBI Cncl 1983-, Univ of Surrey Cncl 1985- (vice-chm 1988-), Engrg Bd SERC 1985-87; chm CBI SE Regnl Cncl 1987-; Hon D Surrey 1988; FEng, FIChemE, CBIM, FRSA; *Recreations* sailing, golf, oil painting; *Style*— Brian Street, Esq; Jubilee House, Square Drive, Kingsley Green, Haslemere, Surrey GU27 3LW (☎ 0428 51726); Air Products plc, Hersham Place, Molesey Rd, Walton on Thames, Surrey KT12 4RZ (☎ 0932 249771)

STREET, Hon Sir Laurence Whistler; KCMG (1976); s of Hon Sir Kenneth Whistler Street, KCMG (d 1972), Lt-Gov of NSW 1950-72, and Jessie Mary Grey, *née* Lillingston (d 1970); *b* 3 July 1926; *Educ* Cranbrook, Sydney Univ (LLB); *m* 1952, Susan Gai, da of E A S Watt; 2 s, 2 da; *Career* barr NSW 1951, QC 1963, judge Supreme Ct NSW 1965, chief judge in equity 1972, judge Ct of Appeal 1972, chief justice 1974-88; Lt-Govr of NSW 1974-; cdr and sr offr RAN Reserve Legal Branch 1964-65, pres Cts Martial Appeal Tbnl 1971-74; KStJ 1976, Grand Offr of Merit SMO Malta 1977; Hon DL Sydney Univ 1984, Hon Col 1/15 Royal NSW Lancers; memb London Ct of Int Arbitration 1988-; *Style*— The Hon Sir Laurence Street, KCMG; Box 5341 GPO, Sydney, NSW 2001, Australia (☎ 02 228 5987, fax 02 228 5968)

STREETER, John Stuart; DL (1986 Kent); yr s of Wilfrid Alberto Streeter (d 1962), of Park St, London, and Margaret Law, *née* Stuart (d 1982); *b* 20 May 1920; *Educ* Sherborne; *m* 1956, (Margaret) Nancy, da of Arthur Maurice Richardson (d 1980), of Nutfield, Surrey; 1 s (Graham), 2 da (Coralie, Jacqueline); *Career* WWII Capt Royal Scots Fusiliers (despatches); called to the bar Gray's Inn 1947, counsel to PO SE Circuit 1959, tres counsel London Sessions 1961, dep chm Kent QS 1963 (permanent 1967, chm 1971), circuit judge 1972, resident judge Kent 1972-85; ret 1986; *Style*— His Honour John Stuart Streeter, DL; Playstole, Sissinghurst, Cranbrook, Kent TN17 2JN (☎ 0580 712847); Law Courts, Barker Rd, Maidstone, Kent ME16 8EQ (☎ 0622 54966)

STREETER, Patrick Thomas; s of Thomas Thornton Streeter (d 1960), and Nesta, *née* Mavrojani; *b* 1 August 1946; *Educ* Harrow; *m* 28 June 1979, Judith Mary, da of Roland Percy Turk; 2 s (George Roland b 1982, Frederick Leopold b 1987), 1 da (Tania Sarah b 1980); *Career* CA, ptnr Streeter Gomme & Co; underwriting memb of Lloyds; contested Croydon NW (Lib) 1974-79; cllr London Borough of Tower Hamlets 1982-, (ldr opposition 1984-85); chair Bethnal Green Ctee 1986-88; *Recreations* tennis, skiing, reading; *Clubs* RAC; *Style*— Patrick Streeter, Esq; 89 Cressy House, Hannibal Rd, London E1 3JF (☎ 01 790 5965); 1 Waterman's End, Matching, Harlow, Essex CM17 0RQ (☎ 0279 730076)

STREETON, Terence George; CMG (1981), MBE (1969); s of Alfred Victor Streeton, of Northampton, and Edith, *née* Deiton; *b* 12 Jan 1930; *Educ* Wellingborough GS; *m* 1962, Molly, da of Oliver Garley (d 1967), of Leicester; 2 s (Matthew, Simon), 2 da (Sarah, Catherine); *Career* HM Diplomatic Serv: British High Cmmn to Bangladesh 1983-, first sec Bonn 1966, FCO 1970, first sec and head of chancery Bombay 1972, cncllr Brussels 1975, FCO 1979, asst under sec of state 1982; *Recreations* walking, golf; *Clubs* Oriental; *Style*— Terence Streeton, Esq, CMG, MBE; c/o Foreign Cwlth Office, London SW1A 2AH; British High Cmmn, Dhaka, Bangladesh

STRETCH, James Lionel; s of Edwin Frederick Stretch; *b* 16 Feb 1935; *Educ* Tottenham G S; *m* 1961, Pamela Helen, *née* Minos; 1 s, 1 da; *Career* md Century Power & Light Ltd 1980-87, dir of oil operations Imperial Continental Gas Assoc 1980-87, asst md Agip (UK) Ltd 1987; FCA; *Recreations* squash, walking; *Clubs* City of London; *Style*— James Stretch, Esq; Clibbons, Bulls Green, Datchworth, Herts; Agip (UK) Ltd, 105 Victoria St, London SW1E 6QU (☎ 01 630 1400, telex 8813547)

STREVENS, Frederick Albert John; s of Frank Strevens (d 1968), of Sussex, and Ruby Louise Eliza, *née* Pointing; *b* 24 Oct 1935; *Educ* Steyning GS, Brighton Tech Coll, Harlow Tech Coll; *m* 3 April 1961, Margaret, da of Sidney Walter Westoby (d 1972), of Hertfordshire; 3 s (Andrew b 1963 decd, David b 1964, Richard b 1968), 1 da (Elizabeth b 1970 decd); *Career* mgmnt servs offr, electrical and industl engr NW Thames RHA and Barnet Health Authy 1983-; dir F A Strevens (Industl Engrg) Ltd 1972-83; memb Inst of Mgmnt Services; Queens Scout 1953, Benemerenti Medal 1986, Medal of Merit for services to Scouting 1988; memb Scout Movement (Gp Scout Ldr, dist advisor for D of E Award); Kt of St Columba (Past Grand Kt of Cncl 565 Bishop's Stortford); *Recreations* scouting, sailing, mountaineering, drama, reading, DIY; *Style*— Frederick A J Strevens, Esq; 21 Maze Green Road, Bishop's Stortford, Hertfordshire CM23 2PG (☎ 0279 52999); Barnet Health Authy, Management Services Dept, Napsbury Hospital, London Colney, nr St Albans, Herts AL2 1AA (☎ 0727 23333 ext 213)

STREVENS, Peter; s of Stanley Dawson Strevens (d 1966), and Dorothy Victoria, *née* Compson (d 1987); *b* 18 April 1938; *Educ* Eltham Coll Mottingham London; *m* April 1969, Janet Hyde, da of Lees Hyde Marland (d 1974); 2 s (Nigel Jeremy b 1971, Timothy Maxwell b 1974); *Career* franchise mangr Hertz Int Ltd NY 1963-67; md: United Serv Tport Co Ltd (Hertz Truck Rental) 1969-72 (operations mangr 1967-69), Chatfields-Martin Walter Ltd 1972-; MInstM, MIMI; *Recreations* tennis, golf, gardening; *Clubs* RAC; *Style*— Peter Strevens, Esq; Chatfields-Martin Walter Ltd, Clough St, Hanley, Stoke-on-Trent ST1 4AR (☎ 0782 202591, fax 0782 202171, car telephone 0836 291065, telex 36253)

STREVENS, Peter Jeffrey; s of Alfred John Strevens (d 1980), of London, and Lilian Ellen, *née* Wiggins (d 1970); *b* 3 Dec 1945; *Educ* Barnsbury Sch; *m* 27 April 1968, Janet Linda, da of George Daniels (d 1982) of Hereford; 1 s (Richard b 1971), 1 da (Emma b 1970); *Career* qualified CA 1968; ptnr: Sydenham & Co 1974, Hodgson Harris 1980, Hodgson Impey 1985; reader Hereford Diocese, govr Bishop of Herefords Bluecoat Sch; memb: Centre for Mgmnt in Agric, Ramblers Assoc; FCA 1968, ACIArb 1989; *Recreations* hill walking, music, wildlife & conservation; *Style*— Peter Strevens, Esq; 7 Admirals Close, Hereford HR1 1BU (☎ 0432 268 585); Hodgson Impey, Elgar House, Holmer Rd, Hereford HR4 9SF (☎ 0432 352 222, fax 0432 269 367, telex 35850)

STRICK, Robert Charles Gordon; s of Charles Gordon Strick (d 1981), of Guildford, and Doris Gwendoline, *née* Bench (d 1981); *b* 23 Mar 1931; *Educ* Royal GS Guildford, Sidney Sussex Coll Cambridge (MA); *m* 30 May 1960, Jennifer Mary, da of Alec John Hathway, of Dorchester on Thames; 1 s (Charles), 1 da (Catherine); *Career* 2 Lt RA 1950, Lt RA (TA) 1951-55; admin offr HMOCS 1955, sec cmmn Natural Resources & Population Trends Fiji 1959-60, sec to govt Kingdom of Tonga 1961-63, devpt offr and divnl cmmr Fiji 1963-67 (sec for Natural Resources 1967-71), under sec Inst of Chartered Accountants 1971-72, asst sec gen Royal Inst of Chartered Surveyors 1972-80; govr Queen Mary Coll London 1980-(chm estates ctee 1984-); Freeman City of London 1977, clerk to Worshipful Co of Chartered Surveyors 1977-80, former clerk Worshipful Co of Drapers (Freeman 1986, Liveryman 1987); *Recreations* walking, cycling, gardening, DIY; *Style*— Robert Strick, Esq; Drapers Hall, Throgmorton St, London EC2N 2DQ (☎ 01 588 5001)

STRICKLAND, Benjamin Vincent Michael; s of Maj-Gen Eugene Vincent Michael Strickland, CMG, DSO, OBE, MM, Gd Offr of Al-Kawkab of Jordan (d 1982), and Barbara Mary Farquharson Meares, da of Maj Benjamin Lamb and gda of Sir John Lamb; *b* 20 Sept 1939; *Educ* Mayfield Coll, Univ Coll Oxford (MA), Harvard Business Sch (Dip AMP 1978); *m* 1965, Tessa Mary Edwina Grant, da of Rear-Adm John Grant, CB, DSO, of Rivermead Court; 1 s (Benjamin Michael John b 1968), 1 da (Columbine Mary Grizel b 1971); *Career* Lt 17/21 Lancers BAOR 1959-60; jr mangr Price Waterhouse & Co 1963-68, dir corporate fin J Henry Schroder Wagg & Co 1974-, chm and chief exec Schroders Australia 1978-82, gp md Schroders plc 1983-; FCA; *Recreations* travel, military and general history, shooting, theatre; *Clubs* Cavalry and Guards, Hurlingham; *Style*— Benjamin Strickland, Esq; 6 Queens Elm Square, Chelsea, London SW3 6ED (☎ 01-351-0372); 120 Cheapside, London EC2V 6DS (☎ 01-382-6000)

STRICKLAND, Frank; OBE (1986); s of Robert Strickland (d 1972), of Chorley, Lancashire, and Esther, *née* Jackson (d 1974); *b* 4 Feb 1928; *Educ* Harris Inst Preston; *m* 24 Jan 1953, Marian, da of Horace Holt (d 1953), of Chorley, Lancs; 1 da (Barbara b 1954); *Career* Nat Serv RE 1946-48; asst sec Chorley and Dist Bldg Soc, branch mangr Hastings and Thanet Bldg Soc; sec: Corpn Bldg Soc 1962-69, Sunderland and Shields Bldg Soc 1969-75; dir and chief exec North of Eng Bldg Soc 1975-; pres Sunderland & Dist Centre Chartered Bldg Socs Inst, chm Sunderland & Co Durham Royal Inst for Blind, tstee Hudson Charity; cncl memb Bldg Socs Assoc 1971- (chm 1989-), vice pres Euro Fedn of Bldg Socs; FCBSI 1973; *Clubs* Royal Overseas League, MCC Sunderland; *Style*— Frank Strickland, Esq, OBE; 383 Sunderland Rd, South Shields, Tyne & Wear NE34 8DG (☎ 091 4561216); North of England Building Society, Fancett St, Sunderland SR1 1SA, (☎ 091 5141431)

STRICKLAND, John; s of Thomas Gill Strickland (d 1951), of Westcott, Lodge Lane, Brompton, Northallerton, and Ellen May, *née* Hodgson (d 1958); *b* 2 July 1927; *Educ* Northallerton GS; *m* 2 April 1955, Alice, da of Robert Vincent Hogg (d 1964), of 59 Ainderby Rd, Romanby, Northallerton; 2 s (Thomas Graham b 1959, Paul Juliam b 1961); *Career* chartered surveyor; asst surveyor District Bank Ltd 1955-69, property investmt mangr National Westminster Bank Gp 1969-85; Freeman City of London, Liveryman Worshipful Co of Chartered Surveyors; FRICS, FCIArb, FRVA; *Recreations* beekeeping, gardening; *Style*— John Strickland, Esq; Tamarind, Church Lane, Flyingthorpe, Whitby, Yorks YO22 4PN (☎ 0947 880188)

STRICKLAND-CONSTABLE, Edina, Lady; Countess (Ernestine) Edina; da of late (4) Count von Rex (cr of HRE by Francis I 1764, recognised by Elector Frederick Augustus III of Saxony 1765; the family was from Upper Silesia), former Saxon Min in Vienna; *b* 27 Sept 1905,, Vienna; *m* 1929, Sir Henry Marmaduke Strickland-Constable, 10 Bt (d 1975); *Style*— Edina, Lady Strickland-Constable; Wassland Hall, nr Hull, Yorks

STRICKLAND-CONSTABLE, Frederic; s (by 2 m) and h of Sir Robert Strickland-Constable, 11 Bt; *b* 21 Oct 1943; *Educ* Westminster, CCC Cambridge (BA); *Style*— Frederic Strickland-Constable, Esq; Elm Tree Cottage, Rowdow Lane, Otford Hills, Sevenoaks TN16 6XN

STRICKLAND-CONSTABLE, Sir Robert Frederick; 11 Bt (E 1641), of Boynton, Yorkshire; s of Lt-Col Frederick Charles Strickland-Constable (d 1916) (ggs of 7 Bt), and Margaret (d 1959), da of late Rear-Adm Hon Thomas Pakenham, s of 2 Earl of Longford, KP, and bro of 3 and 4 Earls; suc bro, Sir Henry Marmaduke Strickland-Constable, 10 Bt, 1975; *b* 22 Oct 1903; *Educ* Eton, Magdalen Coll Oxford (MA, DPhil); *m* 1, 1929 (m annulled 1931), Rosalind Mary, da of Arthur Webster; m 2, 1936, Lettice, da of late Maj Frederic Strickland (d 1934), (2 s of 8 Bt), and Mary, da of late Sir John Isaac Thornycroft; 2 s (Frederick b 1944, J R F b 1949), 2 da (Miranda b 1938, Elizabeth b 1940); memb Royal Soc of Chem; *Heir* s, Frederick Strickland-Constable; *Career* Lt-Cdr RNVR 1940-44; Imperial Coll London Chem Engrg Dept 1948-71 (reader 1963-71); memb Royal Soc of Chemistry; *Books* Kinetics of Crystallisation (1968), contributed to numerous scientific journals; *Recreations* mountaineering, music; *Style*— Dr Robert Strickland-Constable, Bt; c/o Barclays Bank, The Green, Westerham, Kent

STRICKLAND-EALES, David Ian; s of Harry Eales, of 84 Brockley Crescent, Bleadon Hill, Weston-Super-Mare, Avon, and Edith Emily, *née* Smith; *b* 16 Dec 1948; *Educ* Stratton Sch Beds; *m* 1, 22 May 1971 (m dis 1981); 1 s (Oliver b 1976); m 2, 29 July 1983, Gillian Lesley, da of Ernest Washbourne, of Drummonie, Bowring Rd, Ramsey, IOM; 1 da (Chloe b 1984); *Career* Borg Warner Ltd 1965-70, ICL plc 1970-72, IMC Consultancy Gp 1972-74, Ladbroke Gp plc 1974-80, Chapter One Direct plc 1980-; memb: Tewkesbury Evangelical Baptist Church, Cheltenham Everyman Theatre Devpt Bd; ICFM; *Recreations* tennis, shooting, carriage driving, gardening; *Clubs* Naval & Military; *Style*— David Strickland-Eales, Esq; Hillfield House, Eldersfield, Gloucester (☎ 045 284 250); Chapter One Direct plc, Green Lane, Tewkesbury, Glos GL20 8EZ (☎ 0684 850 040, fax 0684 850 113)

STRIDE, Rev Desmond William Adair (Dick); s of Cdr Desmond Adair Stride RN (d 1968), and Dorothea Rangeley Hensley (d 1976); *b* 10 Mar 1915; *Educ* Imperial Service Coll, Christ's Coll Cambridge (MA), Ridley Hall Cambridge; *m* 4 Sept 1941, Mary Pleasant Lowry, da of Ernest Henry Lamb, 1 Baron Rochester (d 1955); *Career* chaplain Dover Coll 1945-56 (housemaster 1951-56); warden and headmaster St Michael's Coll Tenbury 1957-65, chaplain Heathfield Sch Ascot 1967-80; *Recreations* European travel, looking at paintings, listening to music; *Style*— The Rev Desmond Stride; 5 Oakmede Way, Ringmer, Lewes, E Sussex BN8 5JL (☎ 0273 813 561)

STRIDE, James Tarver; s of George Tarver Stride, and Ivy May Finch; *b* 18 Mar 1955; *Educ* Dulwich, LSE (B Econ); *m* 1 June 1985, Alexandra Evelyn, da of Luc Louis Clement Smets; 1 s (Sebastian b 1986); *Career* investment mangr; dep chm Selsdon Gp; dir: Trumab Ltd, Jamavik International Ltd; cncllr Buckinghamshire CC 1985-; govr of five schs; author political pamphlets; *Recreations* bridge, gardening; *Clubs* Old Alleynian, Peel; *Style*— James T Stride, Esq; 98 High Street South, Stewkley, nr Leighton Buzzard, Bedfordshire LU7 0HR; 107 Cheapside, London EC2V 6DU (☎ 01-606-7788)

STRIDE, Hon Mrs; Hon Mary Pleasant Lowry; *née* Lamb; 2 da of 1 Baron Rochester, CMG, JP (d 1955), and Rosa Dorothea (d 1979), yr da of late William John Hurst, JP, CC, of Drumaness, Co Down; *b* 13 Oct 1919; *m* 4 Sept 1941, Rev Desmond William Adair Stride (chaplain Heathfield Sch 1967-80, ret), er s of late Cdr Desmond Adair Stride, RN; *Career* LRAM 1939; *Style*— The Hon Mrs Stride; 5 Oakmede Way, Ringmer, Lewes, East Sussex BN8 5JL (☎ 0273 813561)

STRIDE, Hon Mrs; Hon Susan; *née* Macdonald; da of 2 Baron Macdonald of Gwaenysgor; *b* 1947; *m* 1968 (sep 1983), David Hensley Adair Stride; 1 s, 1 da (decd); *Career* dir Terry Walsby PR; *Style*— The Hon Mrs Stride; 73 Swinburne Rd, London SW15

STRIGNER, Andrew Ernest; s of Andrew Strigner (d 1952), and Olimpia Tasselli (d 1964); *b* 5 June 1921; *Educ* St Aloysius Coll Highgate, Guy's Hosp (MB BS), Royal London Homoeopathic Hosp (MFHom); *m* 15 April 1950, Constance, da of George Hackett, submariner (ka 1940); 2 s (Andrew b 1951, Peter b 1952), 1 da (Miriam b 1953); *Career* Army Serv: Capt/Fl Cdr Air Op, RA Europe, India 1941-46; lectr materia medica Royal London Homoeopathic Hosp; asst physician paediatric & cardiological depts Royal London Homoeopathic Hosp (now physician specialist in hypnosis, nutrition and homoeopathy); cncl memb Inst for the Study and Treatment of Delinquency; chm (now vice pres) The McGarrison Soc (for the study of the relationship between nutrition and health); *Clubs* RSM; *Style*— Andrew Strigner, Esq; Chipley Manor, Bickington, nr Newton Abbot, Devonshire TQ12 6NT; 17 Harley Street, London W1N 1DA (☎ 01 935 4543)

STRINGER, Donald Arthur; OBE (1975); s of Harry William George (d 1963), and Ellen Emily Isted (d 1983); *b* 15 June 1922; *Educ* Bordon GS Sittingbourne Kent; *m* 1945, Hazel, da of William Handley (d 1964); 1 s (David), 1 da (Christine); *Career* Col Engr and Tport Corps RE (TA) 1974; memb Nat Dock Labour Bd 1972-85, chm Nat Assoc of Port Employers 1981-85, dep chm and jt md Assoc British Ports 1985; *Clubs* Army & Navy, Royal Southampton YC; *Style*— Donald Stringer, Esq, OBE; Hillcrest, Pinehurst Rd, Bassett, Southampton (☎ 0703 768887)

STRINGER, Frederick Charles; s of late John Stringer; *b* 24 June 1904; *Educ* Taunton Sch; *m* 1, 1966, Elsie, *née* Warrington; 1 s, 1 da; m 2, 1973, Joan, *née* Trigg; *Career* chm Wadham Stringer Ltd 1969-; fell Inst of Motor Indust 1928-, MInstD; *Recreations* fishing, swimming, bridge; *Clubs* Royal Naval (Portsmouth); *Style*— Frederick Stringer, Esq; Meonpool, Tanfield Park, Wickham, Hants (☎ 0323 833115)

STRIPLING, William Henry; s of Anthony Edwin (d 1975), of Green Tye, Herts, and Maud Jane, *née* Walsby (d 1974); *b* 31 August 1930; *Educ* Penzance Co Sch, Chingford Co HS; *m* 15 June 1957, Doreen, da of William Raymond Duce (d 1982); 3 da (Beverley Ann (Mrs Binney) b 1958, Jacqueline Mary (Mrs Smith) b 1960, Stephanie Jane b 1964); *Career* RAF 1950-52; elected memb: East Herts Dist Cncl (chm 1975-78), Sawbridgeworth Town Cncl (Mayor 1979); *Recreations* golf, travel; *Style*— William Stripling, Esq; 19 Hoestock Rd, Sawbridgeworth, Herts CM21 ODZ (☎ 0279 722395); Marshgate Dr, Hertford SG13 7JY (☎ 0992 589491)

STROLOGO, Eric Reginald Charles Alexander; s of Lt-Col Reginald Charles Strologo, OBE (d 1958), and Xenia (d 1936), da of Gen Alexander Spiridovitch, Chief of Russian Imperial Gd and sometime Govr of the Crimea ; *b* 4 August 1920; *Educ* Wellington, RMA Woolwich; *m* 22 July 1946, Marianne Elizabeth, da of Dr Jan Savicki (d 1940), of Czechoslovakia; 1 s (Mark b 1951), 1 da (Jacqueline b 1947); *Career* regular offr RA 1939-58, served Middle East, 8 Army, RHA, Staff Coll, Europe, Gen Montgomery's HQ 21 Army Gp, ret as Maj; exec dir Royal Automobile Club 1958-82, special conslt Fédération Internationale de L'automobile Paris 1982-; inventor and patentee of the Carbridge temporary flyover; creator and chm Worldwide Information Service (WISE) Data Base (the world's first int tourism data base); hon citizen of New Orleans USA 1972, hon memb Le Jurat de St Emilion France 1973; *Recreations* golf, antiques, travel, skiing, foxhunting, private pilot's licence ; *Clubs* RAC; *Style*— Eric Strologo, Esq; Ravenswood, Mayes Green, Ockley, Surrey RH5 5PN (☎ 0306 70227); Riocaud, Ste Foy-la-Grande, Gironde 33220, France (☎ 57412305); Electronic Mailbox, Microlink, MAG 10066

STRONG, Air Cdre David Malcolm; CB (1964), AFC (1941); s of Theophilus Edgar Strong (d 1952), of Llanishen, Glam, and Margaret, *née* McGregor (d 1955); *b* 30 Sept 1913; *Educ* Cardiff HS; *m* 29 March 1941, Daphne Irene, da of Frederick Arthur Brown (d 1922), of Dover Ct; 2 s (Simon David McGregor b 3 March 1946, Christopher Richard b 14 Aug 1947), 1 da (Carolyn Irene Jane b 7 July 1949); *Career* under trg as pilot 1936, No 166 (B) Sqdn 1936-39, No 10 Operation Trg Unit Abingdon 1940-41, No 104 (B) Sqdn 1941 (POW Germany 1941-45), Co No 5 Air Nav Sch Jurby 1945-46, Co No 10 Air Nav Sch Driffield 1946-47, Air Miny P Staff 1947-48, RAF Staff Coll Drachne Brachnell (psa) 1948-49, Air HQ Rhodesian Air Trg Gp 1949-51, staff dir RAF Staff Coll 1952-55, Flying Coll Manby 1956, Co RAF Coningsby 1957-58, Air Miny D of P (A) 1959-61, SASO RAF Germany 1961-63, Cmdt RAF Halton 1963-66; chm RAF RFU 1954-55, chm RAF Golf Soc 1962-63; *Recreations* golf, walking; *Clubs* RAF, Ashridge GC; *Style*— Air Cdre David Strong, CB, AFC; Old Coach Ho, Wendover, Bucks HP22 6EB (☎ 0296 624 724)

STRONG, John Clifford; CBE (1980); s of Clifford Maurice Strong (d 1967); *b* 14 Jan 1922; *Educ* Beckenham GS, London Univ; *m* 1942, Janet Doris, *née* Browning; 3 da; *Career* Lt RNVR; HM Overseas Civil Service Tanzania 1946-63, Commonwealth Relations Office 1963, first sec Nairobi 1964-68, FCO 1968-73, cnsllr and head Chancery Dar-es-Salaam 1973-78, govr Turks and Caicos Islands 1978-82; *Clubs* Royal Overseas League; *Style*— John Strong, Esq, CBE

STRONG, Michael John; s of Frank James Strong (d 1987), and Ivy Rose, *née* Fruin (d 1964); *b* 27 Dec 1947; *Educ* Rutlish Sch Merton, Coll of Estate Mgmnt; *m* 25 April 1970, Anne Mary, da of Rev William Hurst Nightingale, of Wimbledon, London; 1 s (Jonathan Alexander b 1977); *Career* chartered surveyor, ptnr Richard Ellis; Freeman City of London 1981, memb Worshipful Co Plumbers 1982; FRICS; memb: Royal Acad, Royal Hort Soc; *Recreations* golf, tennis, music, travel, gardens; *Style*— Michael Strong, Esq; The Coolins, Manor House Lane, Little Bookham, Surrey (☎ 0372 52 196); La Borna, SaTuna, Begur, Spain; Richard Ellis, Berkeley Square House, Berkeley Square, London W1 (☎ 01 629 6290, fax 01 493 3734)

STRONG, Oswald Brian; s of James Beaver Strong; *b* 3 August 1909; *Educ* Cranleigh, National Leathersellers Coll London; *m* 1948, Margaret Mary, *née* Smee; 1 s, 1 da (1 child decd); *Career* tanner, consultant Strong & Fisher (Holdings) Ltd and subsidiary companies 1949-81, London Heatsave Ltd 1979-81; *Recreations* tennis, golf, gardening; *Style*— Oswald Strong, Esq; Southbrook, 115 Sussex Rd, Petersfield, Hants (☎ 0730 63616)

STRONG, Richard James; s of John Paterson Strong, OBE, of Tilford, Tilbrook, Huntingdon, and Margaret St Claire, *née* Ford (d 1981); *b* 5 July 1936; *Educ* Sherborne, Nat Leather Sellers Coll; *m* 1 May 1963, Camilla Lucretia, da of Maj

William Walter Dowding (d 1981); 1 s (James b 30 May 1977), 3 da (Melissa b 30 Dec 1965, Amanda b 13 Nov 1968, Samantha b 28 March 1972); *Career* Nat Serv cmmnd 10 Royal Hussars (PWO); Tanner Strong & Fisher Ltd 1960, md Strong & Fisher (Hldgs) plc 1972; govr Bilton Grange Sch Tst, memb E Midlands Industl Cncl; hon tres Oakley Hunt, memb Bletsoe Church PCC; Liveryman Worshipful Co of Grocers; *Recreations* fox hunting, farming, sailing, tennis; *Clubs* Cavalry, Royal Thames YC; *Style*— Richard Strong, Esq; Bletsoe Castle, Bletsoe, Beds MK44 1QE; Strong & Fisher (Hldgs) plc, 100 Irchester Rd, Rushden, Northants NN10 9XQ (☎ 0933 410 300, fax 0933 410800, telex 31522 AQATAN)

STRONG, Richard Martin; s of Theodore Martin William Strong (d 1978), and Alice Louisa Jean, *née* Spearman, of 8 Woodside Rd, Burton Joyce, Nottingham; the Strongs were originally Sjogrens from Sweden; name changed by Deed Poll on naturalisation in New Zealand 1900; *b* 3 Oct 1929; *Educ* Bedford Sch, Trinity Coll Cambridge (MA); *m* 1, 1956, Ann Georgina; 1 s (Simon Alexander b 1959); m 2, 1971, Venetia Mary, da of Ian Thomson Henderson, CBE (d 1987), of Pond House, Crawley, nr Winchester, Hants; 2 step da; *Career* National Service 2 Lt, Capt TA; CA 1955; dir: Rees Gp Ltd 1961-, Charterhouse Devpt Ltd 1965-, Rees Gp Pension Tstees Ltd 1974-, SEMA Gp plc 1977-, RH Gp Ltd 1977-, Charterhouse Devpt Capital Ltd 1983-, New English Ltd 1983-, Resort Hotels Ltd 1984-, ROCC Corpn Ltd and subsidiaries 1984-, Crawford Services Ltd 1985-; *Recreations* golf, photography; *Clubs* Royal Wimbledon Golf; *Style*— Richard Strong, Esq; 25 Newstead Way, Somerset Rd, London SW19 5HR (☎ 01 946 0285); Charterhouse Development Capital Ltd, 7 Ludgate Broadway, London EC4V 6DX (☎ 01 248 4000)

STRONG, Sir Roy Colin; s of G E C Strong; *b* 23 August 1935; *Educ* Edmonton Co GS, Queen Mary Coll London (fell 1975), Warburg Inst (PhD); *m* 1971, Julia Trevelyan Oman, *qv*; *Career* writer and historian, critic (radio, TV and lectures Eng and America); asst keeper Nat Portrait Gallery 1959 (dir, keeper and sec 1967-73); dir (and sec) V & A 1974-87, Ferens prof of Fine Art Hull Univ 1972, Walls lectures Pierpont Morgan Library 1974, Shakespeare Prize FVS Fndn Hamburg 1980, vice chm South Bank Bd 1986-; memb: Arts Cncl of GB 1983-87 (chm Arts Panel), St Paul's Cathedral Ct of Advsrs, former memb Br Cncl Fine Arts advsy ctee, Craft Advsy Cncl, RCA Cncl, Br Film Inst Archive advsy ctee, Westminster Abbey Architectural Panel, Historic Bldgs Cncl Historic Houses Ctee; former tstee: Arundel Castle, Chevening; Hon DLitt: Leeds 1983, Keele 1984; sr fell RCA 1983; FSA; kt 1981; *Publications* Portraits of Queen Elizabeth I, Leicester's Triumph (with J A van Dorsten), Holbein and Henry VIII, Tudor and Jacobean Portraits (1969), The English Icon: Elizabethan and Jacobean Portraiture, Elizabeth R (with Julia Trevelyan Oman), Van Dyck - Charles I on Horseback (1972), Mary Queen of Scots (with Julia Trevelyan Oman 1972), Inigo Jones - The Theatre of the Stuart Cout (with Stephen Orgel 1973), Splendour at Court - Renaissance Spectacle and Illusion (1973), An Early Victorian Album; The Hill/Adamson Collection (with Colin Ford 1974), Nicholas Hilliard (1975), The Cult of Elizabeth: Elizabethan Portraiture and Pageantry (1977), And When Did You Last See Your Father? The Victorian Painter and the British Past (1978), The Renaissance Garden in England (1979), Britannia Triumphans: Inigo Jones, Rubens and Whitehall Palace (1980), The English Year (with Julia Trevelyan Oman 1982), The Renaissance Miniature in England (1983); *contrib* Designing for the Dancer (1981), The English Miniature (1981), The New Pelican Guide to English Literature (1982), Artists of the Tudor Court (catalogue 1983), Art and Power (1984), Glyndebourne - A Celebration (1984), Strong Points (1985), Henry Prince of Wales (1986), contrib For Vienna Wedgewood These (1986), Creating Small Gardens (1986), Gloriana (1987), A Small Garden Designer's Handbook (1987), Cecil Beaton The Royal Portraits (1988), Creating Formal Gardens, Designs for Small Gardens (1989); *Recreations* gardening, weight training; *Clubs* Garrick, Beefsteak; *Style*— Sir Roy Strong; 3cc Morpeth Terrace, London SW1P 1EW

STRONGE, Sir James Anselan Maxwell; 10 Bt (UK 1803), of Tynan, Co Armagh; s of late Maxwell Du Pre James Stronge, and 2 cousin of Capt Sir James Matthew Stronge, 9 Bt (assas 1981); *b* 17 July 1946; *Educ* privately; *Style*— Sir James Stronge, Bt; c/o Helen Allen-Morgan, Mnaor South, Bishopstone, Sussex BN25 2UD

STROUD, Prof Sir (Charles) Eric; s of Frank Edmund Stroud (d 1973), of 7 Green Verges, Marlow on Thames, Bucks, and Lavinia May, *née* Noakes (d 1988); *b* 15 May 1924; *Educ* Cardiff HS, Welsh Nat Sch of Med (BSc, MB, BCH 1948, DCH 1955); *m* 15 April 1950, June Mary, da of Harold Dockerill Neep (d 1984), of 55 Merthyr Mawa Rd, Bridgend, Mid Glamorgan; 1 s (David b 1961), 2 da (Diana b 1956, Amanda b 1958); *Career* RAF Med Br, Flying Offr 1950-51, Sqdn Ldr 1951-52; sr registrar Hosp for Sick Children Gt Ormond St 1956-61, paediatrician Uganda Govt 1958-60, asst to dir paediatric Dept Guys Hosp 1961-62, conslt paediatrician Kings Coll Hosp 1962-68, prof and dir Paediatric Dept Kings 1968-88; dir Variety Club Childrens Hosp Kings 1984-88, emeritus prof of Paediatrics Univ of London and Kings Coll Hosp 1989; hon med dir Children Nationwide Medical Research Fund; chm standing Medical Advsy Ctee to sec of State 1986-89; civil conslt in paediatrics RAF; MRCP 1955, FRCP 1968; kt 1988; *Recreations* fishing, golf, cricket; *Style*— Prof Sir Eric Stroud; Children Nationwide Medical Research Fund, Nicholas House, 181 Union St, London SE1 0LN; Dept of Haematology, Kings Coll Hosp, London SE5 (☎ 01 928 2425)

STROUD, Ven Ernest Charles Frederick; s of Charles Henry Stroud (d 1975), of Bristol, and Irene Doris, *née* Venn (d 1975); *b* 20 May 1931; *Educ* Merrywood GS Bristol, Merchant Venturers Tech Coll, Univ of Durham (BA, Dip Theol), Luton Industl Coll (Dip in Rural Studies & Rural Ministry); *m* 15 Aug 1959, Jeanne Marquerite, da of Alfred Henry Evans (d 1966), of Bristol; 2 da (Teresa b 1961, Bridget b 1963); *Career* ordained: deacon 1960, priest 1961; curate All Saints S Kirkby Pontefract 1960-63, priest i-c St Ninian Whitby 1963-66; incumbent of: All Saints Chelmsford 1966-75, St Margaret Leigh on Sea 1975-83; rural dean Hadleigh 1979-83, hon canon Chelmsford 1982-83, archdeacon of Colchester 1983-; proctor Gen Synod 1980-88; chm: Additional Curates Soc, Church Union; memb: C of E Pensions Bd, Essex CC Libraries and Museums Ctee; *Recreations* travel, theatre, gardening; *Style*— The Ven the Archdeacon of Colchester; Archdeacon's House, 63 Powers Hall End, Witham, Essex CM8 1NH (☎ 0376 513 130)

STROUD, Roy Vivian; OBE (1982), JP (Bradford 1972), DL (W Yorks 1983); *Career* chm Stroud Riley Drummond Gp Ltd, and various related cos; dir Commerical Union (Bradford Bd); *Style*— Roy V Stroud, Esq, OBE, JP, DL; Ryden House, Esholt Ave, Guiseley, W Yorks LS20 8AX (☎ 0943 73020)

STROYAN, His Hon Judge (Ronald) Angus Ropner; QC; s of Ronald Strathearn Stroyan (d 1957), of Boreland, and Mary Enid, *née* Ropner (d 1985); *b* 27 Nov 1924; *Educ* Harrow, Trinity Coll Cambridge (BA); *m* 1, 2 June 1952(m dis 1965), Elisabeth Anna, da of Col J P Grant, MC (d 1964), of Rothiemurchus; 2 da (Victoria b 1953, Julia b 1958), 1 s (John b 1955); m 2, 22 Sept 1967, Jill Annette Johnston, da of Sir Douglas Marshall, of Hatt House, Saltash; 1 s (Mark b 1969), 2 step s (Robert b 1952, William b 1963), 2 step da (Lucy b 1954, Henrietta b 1959); *Career* Black Watch (RHR) NW Europe 1943-45, Argyll and Sutherland Highlanders Palestine 1945-47, Capt (despatches), serv TA; barr Inner Temple 1950; dep chm N Riding of Yorks QS 1962-70, chm 1970-71, recorder of Crown Court 1972-75; memb Gen Cncl of Bar 1963-67, 1969-73 and 1975; circuit judge 1957-; *Recreations* shooting, fishing, stalking; *Clubs* Caledonian, Yorkshire (York); *Style*— His Hon Judge Stroyan, QC; Boreland, Killin, Perthshire (☎ 05672 252); Chapel Cottage, Whashton, Richmond, North Yorks

STRUTT, Clifford Robert; s of Robert Henry Joslin Strutt (d 1975), of London, and Millicent May, *née* Reynolds (d 1942); *b* 29 Dec 1911; *Educ* Colfe's GS London, Univ of London, Leathersellers Coll London, City and Guilds of London Inst; *m* 13 July 1937, (Mary) Josephine, da of Alexander Heskin, of Lismore, Co Waterford, Ireland; 1 da (Ann Josephine b 1 July 1938); *Career* Dickens Leather Co Ltd: mangr 1936-42, dir 1942-46, jt md 1946-48; chm Carr Tanning Co Ltd 1960- (md 1948-60); assoc Leathersellers Coll 1931, cncl memb Br Leather Fedn 1970, memb Pelman Inst 1942, underwriting memb Lloyd's 1976; FInstD 1963, FBIM 1968, FFA 1988, life memb Soc of Leather Technologists and Chemists 1980; *Style*— Clifford Strutt, Esq; Carr Tanning Co Ltd, Woodchester, Stroud, Glos (☎ 045387 2252, fax 045387 2799, car tel 0836 597830, telex 43230)

STRUTT, Hon Guy Robert; s of 4 Baron Rayleigh, FRS, JP, DL, by his 2 w, Kathleen, OBE; *b* 16 April 1921; *Educ* Eton, Trinity Coll Cambridge; *Style*— The Hon Guy Strutt; The Old Rectory, Terling, Chelmsford, Essex

STRUTT, Hon Hedley Vicars; s of 4 Baron Rayleigh, JP, DL, by his 1 w, Lady Mary Clements (da of 4 Earl of Leitrim); *b* 19 Feb 1915; *Educ* Eton, Trinity Coll Cambridge; *Career* Capt Scots Gds (ret), served WW II; *Clubs* Brooks'; *Style*— The Hon Hedley Strutt; Mulroy, Co Donegal, Ireland

STRUTT, Hon Mrs Charles; (Jean Elizabeth); *née* Davidson; yr da of 1 Viscount Davidson, GCVO, CH, CB, PC; *b* 19 June 1924; *m* 17 Dec 1952, Hon Charles Richard Strutt (d 1981; s of late 4 Baron Rayleigh); 1 s (6 Baron Rayleigh, *qv*), 2 da (Anne Caroline b 1955, Mary Jean b 1957); *Career* late Capt WRAC (TA); *Style*— The Hon Mrs Charles Strutt; Berwick Place, Hatfield Peverel, Chelmsford, Essex CM3 2EY (☎ 0245 380321)

STRUTT, Sir Nigel Edward; TD, DL (Essex 1954); s of Edward Jolliffe Strutt (d 1964); *b* 18 Jan 1916; *Educ* Winchester, Wye Agric Coll (fell 1970); *Career* Essex Yeo (Maj) 1937-56, serv WWII as Capt 104 (Essex) Yeo RHA (TA) ME 1939-45; former chm and md Strutt & Parker (Farms) Ltd, md Lord Rayleigh's Farms Inc, memb Eastern Electricity Bd 1964-76, chm Advsy Cncl for Agric and Hort 1973-80; pres CLA 1967-69; High Sheriff of Essex 1966; Hon FRASE 1971 (pres 1983); Master Worshipful Co of Farmers 1976; Johann Heinrich von Thunen Gold Medal (Kiel Univ) 1974, Massey-Ferguson Nat Award for Servs to UK Agric 1976; Hon DSc Cranfield 1979, Hon DUniv Essex 1981; kt 1972; *Recreations* shooting, skiing; *Clubs* Brooks's, Farmers'; *Style*— Sir Nigel Strutt, TD, DL; Sparrows, Terling, Chelmsford, Essex (☎ 024 533 213); office: Whitelands, Hatfield Peverel, Chelmsford, Essex (☎ 0245 380372)

STRUTT, Hon Peter Algernon; MC; s of late 3 Baron Belper by his 2 w; *b* 1924; *Educ* Eton; *m* 1953, Gay Margaret, da of Sir (Frank Guy) Clavering Fison, of Crepping Hall, Sutton, Suffolk; 2 s, 2 da; *Career* serv WWII Lt Coldstream Gds; chm Tollemache & Cobbold Brewerie Ltd; dir: Britannia Building Soc, Ellerman Lines; *Style*— The Hon Peter Strutt, MC; Tollemache & Cobbold Breweries, PO Box 5, Cliff Brewery, Ipswich, Suffolk IP3 0AZ (☎ 0473 56751, telex 987994 Barjon G); Stutton Hall, Ipswich

STRUTT, Hon Richard Henry; s and h of 4 Baron Belper; *b* 24 Oct 1941; *Educ* Harrow; *m* 1, 1966 (m dis), Jennifer Vivian, da of late Capt Peter Winser; 1 s, 1 da; m 2, 1980, Mrs Judith Mary de Jonge, da of James Twynam, of Kitemore House, Faringdon, Oxon; *Style*— The Hon Richard Strutt; Slaughter Farm, Bourton-on-the-Water, Glos

STRUTT, Hon (Desmond) Rupert; s of late 3 Baron Belper by his 2 w; *b* 1926; *Educ* Eton; *m* 1, 1951 (m dis 1961), Jean Felicity (d 1984), da of Hon Francis Walter Erskine; 2 s; m 2, 1964, Lucy Gwendolen, da of Maj James William Stirling Home Drummond Moray, Scots Gds, of Abercairny, Crieff, Perthshire; 2 s; *Style*— The Hon Rupert Strutt; Rockleys, Goldhanger, Maldon, Essex

STUART; *see*: Burnett-Stuart

STUART, Hon Mrs (Alicia St George); *née* Caulfeild; da of late 12 Visc Charlemont; *b* 1918; *Educ* St George's Sch Montreux Switzerland; *m* 1939, Gp Capt Gordon Hackworth Stuart, MD, RAF; 1 s; *Books* theatre, travel; *Recreations* RAF; *Style*— The Hon Mrs Stuart; 3 Lovel hill, Windsor Forest, Berks

STUART, Andrew Christopher; CMG (1979), CPM (1961); s of Rt Rev Cyril Stuart, Bishop of Uganda, (d 1981); and Mary *née* Summerhayes, OBE; *b* 30 Nov 1928; *Educ* Bryanston, Clare Coll Cambridge (MA); *m* 18 July 1959, Patricia Moira, da of Robert Douglas Kelly (d 1953), of Uganda; 2 s (James b 11 March 1962, Charles b 17 May 1962), 1 da (Fiona Mary (Mrs Frarrelly) b 12 Nov 1960); *Career* barr Middle Temple; HMOCS Uganda 1952-64 (ret Judicial Advsr); FCO: Head of Chancery Helsinki 1968-71, asst S Asian Dept 1971-72, cncllr and head of chancery Hong Kong and India Ocean Dept 1972-75, head of chancery Jakarta 1975-78, Br resident cmmr New Hebrides 1978-80, HM ambass Finland 1980-83; princ World Coll of the Atlantic 1983-; *Recreations* sailing, gliding, moutaineering; *Clubs* Utd Oxford and Cambridge, Alpine, Jesters; *Style*— Andrew Stuart, Esq, CMG, CPM; St Donat's Castle, Llantwit Major, South Glamorgan CF6 9WF (☎ 04465 2615); Atlantic College, St Donat's Castle, Llantwit Major, South Glamorgan, CF6 9NF (☎ 04465 2530, fax 04465 4163, telex 265871 MONREF G ref IBO 17)

STUART, Hon Andrew Moray; s (by 2 m) of 2 Viscount Stuart of Findhorn; *b* 1957; *Style*— The Hon Andrew Stuart

STUART, Viscount; Andrew Richard Charles Stuart; s and h of 8 Earl Castle Stewart; *b* 7 Oct 1953; *Educ* Millfield, Bicton Agric Coll; *m* 1973, Annie Yvette, da of Robert le Poulain, of Paris; 1 da (Hon Celia b 1976); *Career* farmer; *Recreations* flying; *Clubs* Ebury Ct; *Style*— Viscount Stuart; Combehaues Farm, Buckerell, Honiton, Devon (☎ 0404 850345)

STUART, Lady Arabella; *née* Stuart; da of 18 Earl of Moray (d 1943); *b* 11 July 1934; *m* 1956 (m dis), (Charles) Mark Edward Boxer (Marc the cartoonist, d 1988); 1 s, 1 da; *Career* author, professional name Arabella Boxer; food en Vogue; fndr memb Guild of Food Writers; Glenfiddich Food Writer of the Year; *Books* First Slice Your Cookbook, Arabella Boxer's Garden Cookbook, Mediterranean Cookbook, The Sunday Times Complete Cookbook; *Style*— Lady Arabella Stuart; 44 Elm Park Rd, London SW3 6AX

STUART, Charles Murray; *b* 28 July 1933; *Educ* Glasgow Univ; *m* 1963, Netta Caroline, *née* Thomson; 1 s, 1 da; *Career* fin dir Int Computers Ltd 1974-81, memb bd ICL 1976-81, dep md ICL 1978-81; fin dir Metal Box plc 1981-; *Recreations* golf, reading, theatre; *Style*— Charles Stuart, Esq; Greenaway House, Forest Rd, Pyrford, Woking (☎ 093 23 40245); Metal Box plc, Queens House, Forbury Rd, Reading RG1 3JH (☎ 0734 581177, telex 849561 MBRDG)

STUART, Hon Charles Rodney Stanford; s of 19 Earl of Moray (d 1974); *b* 1933; *Educ* Stowe, McGill Univ Montreal; *m* 1, 1961 (m dis 1987), Sasha A, da of Lt-Col R G Lewis, of Stow on the Wold; 3 s; m 2, 1987, Frauke Norman, da of Hans Stender of Marne, Schleswig Holstein; *Career* late 2 Lt The Queen's Bays; *Style*— The Hon Charles Stuart

STUART, Charles Rowell; s of Charles Rowell Stuart, MBE (d 1957); *b* 20 May 1928; *Educ* St Olave's and St Saviours GS, LSE (BScEcon); *m* 1951, Anne Grace, da of Rayond Plimsoll Mingo, of Sidbury, Devon (d 1971); 1 s (Duncan), 2 da (Sheridan, Lindsey b 1962); *Career* serv as Lt in HM Armed Forces in Europe; head of Commercial Devept Br Airways; dir; Cyprus Airways Ltd, Br Airtours Ltd, BA Assoc Co Ltd, BA Helicopters Ltd, IAL Ltd; FRAeS, FCIT; *Recreations* marathon running; *Clubs* Oriental, RAC, Rd Runner Clubs of UK and New York, Ranelagh; *Style*— Charles Stuart Esq; Hawthorn Hill Cottage, Warfield, Bracknell, Berks (☎ 03447 2362)

STUART, Hon Chloe Anne-Marie; da (by 2 m) of 2 Viscount Stuart of Findhorn; *b* 1952; *Style*— The Hon Chloe Stuart

STUART, Cristina Mary; da of Javier Jesus (d 1985), and Eileen Gertrude, *née* Dunn; *b* 11 August 1941; *Educ* St Francis Coll Letherwork, Sorbonne Paris, Univ of Barcelona; *m* 1 May 1965, John Arthur, s of Oscar John Stuart (d 1966); 1 s (John Frederick Douglas b 1966); *Career* md and fndr Speakeasy Trg Ltd; *Books* Effective Speaking (1988); *Recreations* avoiding chocolate; *Clubs* Network, Internat Training in Communications, Inst of Training and Devpt, Assoc of Mgmnt and Educn Devpt; *Style*— Mrs Cristina Stuart; Speakeasy Training Ltd, 17 Clifton Rd, London N3 2AS

STUART, Hon (James) Dominic; s (by 1 m) and h of 2 Viscount Stuart of Findhorn; *b* 25 Mar 1948; *Educ* Eton, Thames Poly (Dip in Estate Mgmnt); *m* 1979, Yvonne Lucienne, da of Edgar Després, of Ottawa; *Career* ARICS; CDIPAF; *Recreations* walking, gardening, humanistic psychology; *Style*— The Hon Dominic Stuart; 15 Stowe Rd, W12

STUART, Helen Winifred; *née* Lynden-Bell; da of Col Charles Perceval Lynden-Bell (d 1934); holder: of the Commendatore Crown (Italy), Legion d'Honeur (France), Order of St Vladimir (Russia), Sudan Campaign Medal; of Fairlawn House, Tadley, Basingstoke, and Helen Ceraldine, *née* Rate (d 1955); *Educ* St George's Asoct; *m* 18 Nov 1937, Col John Ochiltree Stuart, s of Maj Godfrey Walter Conyngham Stuart, CB; *Career* actress with Minack Theatre Cornwall and the Old Benson (Skaespeare) Co 1926-30; obtained pilot's A licence 1929, discovered live volcano Congo 1936; *Style*— Mrs John Stuart

STUART, Ian; s of Eric Mansfield Stuart (d 1983), and Phyllis Audrey Stuart; *b* 10 Feb 1929; *Educ* Rossall Sch; *m* 1957, Jennifer Mary, da of Philip Montague Lloyd (d 1971); 1 s, 1 da; *Career* chm Stuart Crystal; *Recreations* golf; *Style*— Ian Stuart, Esq; c/o Stuart & Sons Ltd, Red House Glass Works, Stourbridge, W Midlands DY8 4AA (☎ 0384 71161; telex STUART G 335204); Lower House, The Paddock, Pedmore, Stourbridge, W Midlands

STUART, Hon James Wallace Wilson; twin s of 19 Earl of Moray (d 1974), of Darnaway Castle, Forres, Moray, and Mable Nelson Maude (d 1969); *b* 30 May 1933; *Educ* Stowe, McGill Univ Montreal; *m* 1958, Jane-Scott, da of Gp Capt Henry Gordon Richards, of Louisville, Kentucky, USA; 1 da (Elizabeth, b 1967); *Career* late 2 Lt, 13/18 Hussars; co dir; *Clubs* Atlantic Cavalry (Montreal), Highland Inverness; *Style*— The Hon James Stuart; Dunphail, Moray IV36 0QG (☎ 030 96 237)

STUART, Hon John Douglas; s of 1 Viscount Stuart of Findhorn, CH, MVO, MC (d 1970) and Lady Rachel, *née* Cavendish (d 1977), da of 9 Duke of Devonshire; *b* 11 June 1925; *Educ* RNC Dartmouth; *m* 1, 1957 (m dis 1958), Mrs Cecile Margaret Tonge, da of G H Barr; m 2, 1969 (m dis 1972), Lady Caroline, *née* Child-Villiers, da of 9 Earl of Jersey and formerly w of Gilbert Edward George Lariston, Viscount Melgund, MBE, now 6 Earl of Minto, *qv*; *Career* Lt RN (ret); *Recreations* golf; *Clubs* White's; *Style*— The Hon John Stuart; 57 Shawfield St, SW3 (☎ 01 351 3000)

STUART, Prof Sir Kenneth Lamonte; *b* 16 June 1920; *Educ* Harrison Coll Barbados, McGill Univ Montreal (BA), Queen's Univ Belfast (MB, BCh, BAO); *m* 1958, Barbara Cecille; 1 s, 2 da; *Career* Univ of the WI: dean med faculty 1969-71, head dept of med 1972-76; med advsr Cwlth Secretariat 1976-85; chm ct of govrs London Sch of Hygiene and Tropical Med 1983; conslt advsr The Wellcome Tst 1984-; memb bd of govrs Int Devpt Res Centre of Canada 1985; Hon DSc' Gresham prof of phsic Gresham Coll London 1988-; FRCP, FRCPE, FACP, DTM; kt 1977; *Recreations* tennis; *Clubs* St Georges Hill Tennis, Royal Cwlth Soc, RSM; *Style*— Prof Sir Kenneth Stuart; Red Oak, Fairmaile Ave, Cobham, Surrey (☎ 09326 3826); Wellcome Trust, 1 Park Square West, London NW1 (☎ 01 486 4902)

STUART, Lady Louisa Helena; da of 20 Earl of Moray; *b* 18 August 1968; *Style*— Lady Louisa Stuart

STUART, Malcolm Moncrieff; CIE (1947), OBE (1944); s of George Malcolm Stuart (d 1952); *b* 21 May 1903; *Educ* Sedbergh, St John's Coll Cambridge, Queen's Coll Oxford; *m* 1928, Grizel, da of Arthur Balfour Paul; 1 s, 1 da; *Career* Indian Civil Serv 1927-50, rec to Cncl of Lord High Commrs to Gen Assembly of Church of Scotland; *Recreations* golf, bridge; *Clubs* New (Edinburgh), Hon Co Edinburgh Golfers; *Style*— Malcolm Stuart, Esq, CIE, OBE; Old Manse, Pilmuir, Haddington, E Lothian (☎ 0875 340263)

STUART, (Charles) Murray; s of Charles Maitland Stuart (d 1984), and Grace Forrester, *née* Kerr; *b* 28 July 1933; *Educ* Glasgow Acad, Glasgow Univ (MA, LLB); *m* 10 April 1963, Netta Caroline, da of Robert Thomson (d 1981); 1 s (David Charles Thomson b 19 Oct 1970), 1 da (Caroline Alison b 29 Dec 1972); *Career* CA 1961, dep md ICL plc 1977-81 (fin dir 1974-77); Metal Box plc: fin dir 1981-85, gp md 1985-86, gp chief exec 1987-; memb Audit Cmmn; memb Law Soc Scotland 1957, FCT 1984, CBIM 1986, FRSA 1988; *Recreations* sailing, tennis; *Style*— Murray Stuart, Esq; Longacre, Guildford Rd, Chobham, Surrey GU24 8EA (☎ 09905 7144); MB Group plc, Caversham Bridge House, Waterman Place, Reading RG1 8DN (☎ 0734 581 177, fax 0724 587 078, car tel 0836 606 428, telex 846445)

STUART, Nicholas Willoughby; s of Douglas Willoughby Stuart, of Gt Henny, nr Sudbury, Suffolk, and Margaret Eileen, *née* Holms; *b* 2 Oct 1942; *Educ* Harrow, Christ Church Oxford (MA); *m* 1, July 1963 (m dis 1974), Sarah, *née* Mustard; 1 s (Sebastian b 26 Dec 1963, d 8 Dec 1976), 1 da (Henrietta b 21 March 1965); m 2, 29 Dec 1975, Susan Jane, *née* Fletcher; 1 s (Alexander b 1 Feb 1989), 1 da (Emily b 12 Sept 1983); *Career* asst princ DES 1964-68, private sec to Min of Arts 1968-69, princ DES 1969-73, private sec to: Head of CS 1973, PM 1973-76; asst sec DES 1976-79, memb cabinet of Pres of Euro Cmmn 1979-81, under sec DES 1981-87 (dep sec 1987-); *Style*— Nicholas Stuart, Esq; Dept of Educn and Science, Elizabeth Hse, York Rd, London SE1 (☎ 01 934 9955)

STUART, Sir Phillip Luttrell Stuart; 9 Bt (E 1660), of Hartley Mauduit, Hants; s of late Luttrell Hamilton Stuart and nephew of 8 Bt (d 1959); *b* 7 Sept 1937; *m* 1, 1962 (m dis 1968), Marlene Rose, da of Otto Muth; 2 da; m 2, 1969, Beverley Claire Pieri; 1 s, 1 da; *Heir* s, Geoffrey Phillip Stuart, b 5 July 1973; *Career* Flying Offr RCAF 1957-62; pres Agassiz Industs Ltd; *Style*— Sir Phillip Stuart, Bt; 604-1770 Barclay St, Vancouver, BC, Canada V6G 1K5

STUART, Hon Rosalie Jane; da (by 2 m) of 2 Viscount Stuart of Findhorn; *b* 1954; *Style*— The Hon Rosalie Stuart

STUART, Lady Sarah Gray; 2 da of 18 Earl of Moray, MC (d 1943); *b* 23 Sept 1928; *m* 9 Aug 1947 (m dis 1977), 4 Baron Hillingdon (d 1978); 1 s, 3 da; *Style*— Lady Sarah Stuart

STUART, Hon Simon Walter Erskine; s of late 7 Earl Castle Stewart; *b* 22 August 1930; *Educ* Eton, Trinity Coll Cambridge; *m* 1973, Deborah Jane, *née* Mounsey; 3 s (Thomas b 1974, Corin b 1975, Tristram b 1977); *Career* former 2 Lt Scots Gds, serv Malaya 1949-50; asst english master Haberdashers' Aske's Sch 1961-78 (formerly King's Canterbury and Stowe); writer 1978-; *Clubs* Beafsteak; *Style*— The Hon Simon Stuart; 16 Neville Drive, London N2 (☎ 01 458 4149); Windyridge, Wych Cross, Forest Row, Sussex (☎ 034 282 2333)

STUART, Sir (James) Keith; s of James Stuart; *b* 1940; *Educ* Cambridge (MA); *m* Kathleen Anne Pinder; 3 s, 1 da; *Career* chm Associated British Ports Hldgs plc 1983-; *Style*— Sir Keith Stuart; Associated British Ports Holdings plc, 150 Holborn, London EC1N 2LR

STUART, Hon Vanessa Mary; da (by 2 m) of 2 Viscount Stuart of Findhorn; *b* 1960; *Style*— The Hon Vanessa Stuart

STUART OF FINDHORN, 2 Viscount (UK 1959); David Randolph Moray Stuart; s of 1 Viscount, CH, MVO, MC, PC (d 1971), and Lady Rachel, nee Cavendish, OBE, da of 9 Duke of Devonshire; through his mother Lord S of F is 1 cous of Rt Hon Maurice Macmillan, PC, MP; *b* 20 June 1924; *Educ* Eton; *m* 1, 1945, Grizel Mary Wilfreda (d 1948), da of late Theodore Fyfe and widow of Michael Gillilan; 1 s; m 2, 1951 (m dis 1979), Marian, da of late Gerald Wilson; 1 s, 3 da; m 3, 1979, Margaret Anne, da of Cdr Peter Du Cane, CBE, RN, and Victoria, sis of Sir John Gawen Carew Pole, 12 Bt, DSO, TD; *Heir* s, Hon (James) Dominic Stuart; *Career* late Lt KRRC, Maj 6/7 Royal Welch Fus (TA), FRICS, Page of Honour to HM 1938-40, DL of Caerns 1963-68, land agent; *Style*— The Rt Hon The Viscount Stuart of Findhorn; 38 Findhorn, nr Forres, Morayshire

STUART OF FINDHORN, Viscountess; Margaret Anne; da of Cdr Peter Du Cane, CBE, RN and Victoria, sis of Sir John Gawen Carew Pole, 12 Bt, DSO, TD; *b* 1932; *m* 1979, 2 Viscount Stuart of Findhorn; *Career* interior designer; *Style*— The Rt Hon the Viscountess Stuart of Findhorn; 63 Winchenden Rd, London SW6

STUART TAYLOR, Hope, Lady; (Ada) Hope; da of Forrest Bertram Leeder, MRCS, FRCP, BC, and widow of Norman Alfred Yarrow; *m* 1959, as his 3 w, Sir Eric Stuart Taylor, 2 Bt, OBE, MD, MRCP (d 1977); *Style*— Hope, Lady Stuart Taylor

STUART TAYLOR, Lady; Iris Mary; da of Rev Edwin John Gargery and Marjorie Grace, *née* Clapp; *b* 8 Oct 1923; *Educ* Micklefield Sch Seaford, Barnett House Oxford (Dip Social Sci), LSE (Dip Mental Health); *m* 1950, Sir Richard Laurence Stuart Taylor, 3 Bt (d 1978); 1 s (Sir Nicholas Richard Stuart Taylor, 4 Bt, *qv*), 1 da (Anne Caroline b 1955); *Career* subaltern ATS; psychiatric social worker 1949-52; *Clubs* Ski Club of Great Britain; *Style*— Iris, Lady Stuart Taylor; White Lodge, Hambrook, Chichester, Sussex PO18 8RG

STUART TAYLOR, Sir Nicholas Richard; 4 Bt (UK 1917), of Kennington, Co London; s of Sir Richard Laurence Stuart Taylor, 3 Bt (d 1978) and Iris Mary Stuart Taylor; Sir Frederick Taylor, 1 Bt was pres of RCP; *b* 14 Jan 1952; *Educ* Bradfield; *m* 1984, Malvena Elizabeth, da of Daniel David Charles Sullivan; *Heir* none; *Career* slr 1977; ptnr Christopher Green & Ptnrs; *Recreations* skiing and other sports; *Style*— Sir Nicholas Stuart Taylor, Bt; 3 Horseshoe Drive, Romsey, Hants; Christopher Green & Ptnrs, 35 Carlton Crescent, Southampton, Hants

STUART-FORBES, Sir Charles Edward; 12 Bt (NS 1626), of Pitsligo and Monymusk; s of late Sir Charles Hay Hepburn Stuart-Forbes, 10 Bt; suc bro, Sir Hugh Stuart-Forbes, 11 Bt (d 1937); *b* 6 August 1903; *Educ* Ocean Bay Coll; *m* 1966, Ijah Leah MacCabe (d 1974), of Wellington, NZ; *Heir* kinsman, William Daniel Stuart-Forbes; *Career* former co mangr building indust; *Style*— Sir Charles Stuart-Forbes, Bt; 33 Dillons Point Rd, Blenheim, S Island, NZ

STUART-FORBES, William Daniel; s of late William Kenneth Stuart-Forbes, 3 s of 10 Bt; hp of kinsman, Sir Charles Stuart-Forbes, 12 Bt; *b* 21 August 1935; *m* 1956, Jannette MacDonald; 3 s, 2 da; *Style*— William Stuart-Forbes, Esq; Omaka Valley, Marlborough, NZ

STUART-HARRIS, Sir Charles Herbert; CBE (1961); s of late Dr Charles Herbert Harris; *b* 12 July 1909; *Educ* King Edward's HS Birmingham, St Bartholomew's Hosp; *m* 1937, Marjorie Robinson; 2 s, 1 da; *Career* physician Utd Sheffield Hosps 1946-72; Sheffield Univ: prof of med 1946-72, emeritus prof 1972-, postgraduate dean of Med 1972-77; Fogarty scholar-in-residence Nat Insts of Health Bethesda Maryland USA 1979 and 1980; MD, FRCP; kt 1970; *Style*— Sir Charles Stuart-Harris, CBE; 28 Whitworth Rd, Sheffield S10 3HD (☎ 0740 301200)

STUART-MENTETH, Charles Grieves; s and h of Sir James Wallace Stuart-Menteth, 6 Bt, by his w, Dorothy Patricia, *née* Warburton; *b* 25 Nov 1950; *m* 1976, Nicola Mary Jane, da of Vincent Charles Raleigh St Lawrence; 3 da; *Style*— Charles Stuart-Menteth

Esq; Hillend House, Dalry, Ayrshire (☎ 029 483 3871); work: 75 Durham St, Glasgow (☎ 041 427 6991)

STUART-MENTETH, Sir James Wallace; 6 Bt (UK 1838), of Closeburn, Dumfrieshire, and Mansfield, Ayrshire; s of Sir William Frederick Stuart-Menteth, 5 Bt (d 1952); *b* 13 Nov 1922; *Educ* Fettes, St Andrews Univ, Trinity Coll Oxford (MA); *m* 23 April 1949, (Dorothy) Patricia, da of late Frank Greaves Warburton, of Thorrington, Stirling; 2 s; *Heir* s, Charles Stuart-Menteth; *Career* serv WWII Lt Scots Gds; and alkali & paints div ICI Ltd; *Style*— Sir James Stuart-Menteth, Bt; Nutwood, Auchencairn, Castle Douglas, Kirkcudbrightshire DG7 1QZ

STUART-MOORE, Michael; s of Kenneth Basil Moore (d 1987), and Marjorie Elizabeth, *née* Hodges; *b* 7 July 1944; *Educ* Cranleigh Sch; *m* 8 Dec 1973, Katherine Ann, da of Kenneth William Scott; 1 s (James), 1 da (Zoe-Olivia); *Career* barr Middle Temple 1966, rec of the Crown Ct 1985-; *Recreations* cine-photography, flute, tennis, travel off the beaten track; *Style*— Michael Stuart-Moore, Esq; 1 Hare Ct, Temple, London EC4Y 7BE (☎ 01 353 5324, fax 353 0667)

STUART-MOSS, Harold; s of A H Moss (d 1953), of Clevelands, Stoney Lane, Bovingdon, Herts, and Mary *née* O'Hanlon; *b* 3 Feb 1910; *Educ* Berkhamsted Sch, St Catharine's Coll, Cambridge (MA); *m* 25 July 1946, Gretchen; *Career* head of modern language dept: Mercers Sch Holborn London 1936-59, Royal Masonic Sch Bushey (dep headmaster 1971, headmaster when sch closed 1977); memb Gray's Inn Holborn 1933; *Recreations* piano playing, gardening, travelling, mainly in Scandinavia and Europe; *Style*— Harold Stuart-Moss, Esq; Clevelands, Stoney Lane, Bovingdon, Herts HP3 0DP (☎ 0442 833266)

STUART-SMITH, Hon Mrs (Arabella Clare); *née* Montgomery; only da of 2 Viscount Montgomery of Alamein, CBE; *m* 1982, Jeremy Hugh, eld s of The Rt Hon Lord Justice (Rt Hon Sir Murray) Stuart-Smith; 1 s (Edward b 1988), 1 da (Emma b 1984); *Style*— The Hon Mrs Stuart-Smith

STUART-SMITH, James; CB (1986), QC (1988); s of James Stuart-Smith (d 1937), of Brighton, Sussex, and Florence Emma, *née* Armfield (d 1952); *b* 13 Sept 1919; *Educ* Brighton Coll, London Hosp Med Sch; *m* 28 Dec 1957, Jean Marie Therese, da of Hubert Young Groundsell, of Newport, IOW; 1 s (James b 24 Nov 1959), 1 da (Mary b 11 Nov 1958); *Career* Serv WWII 1939-47, cmmnd 2 Lt KRRC 1940, serv Middle E and Italy 1940-45, staff appts UK 1945-47, demobbed as Actg Lt-Col 1947; called to the Bar Middle Temple 1948, in practice London 1948-55, legal asst to off of Judge Adv-Gen 1955, dep judge adv 1957, asst judge adv-gen 1968, vice-judge adv-gen 1979, judge adv-gen 1984; serv: Germany 1959-62, 1971-74 and 1976-79 (as dep judge adv-gen), ME Cmd Aden 1964-65 (as dep judge adv); rec Crown Ct 1985-; pres Int Soc for Mil Law and the Law of War 1985- (vice-pres 1979-85); *Recreations* lawn tennis, writing letters, mowing lawns; *Clubs* RAF; *Style*— James Stuart-Smith, Esq, CB, QC; Office of the Judge Advocate General, 22 Kingsway, London WC2B 6LE (☎ 01 430 5153)

STUART-SMITH, Lady; Joan Elizabeth Mary; *née* Motion; JP, DL (Herefords 1987); da of Maj T A Motion and Lady Elizabeth Grimston; *b* 14 Feb 1929; *Educ* Oxford Univ (BA); *m* Rt Hon Lord Justice Stuart-Smith, *qv*; 3 s, 3 da; *Career* High Sheriff (and first woman sheriff) Hertfords 1983; *Recreations* book-binding, music, propagating plants, building; *Style*— Lady Stuart-Smith, JP

STUART-SMITH, Rt Hon Lord Justice; Rt Hon Sir Murray Stuart-Smith; PC (1988), QC (1970); s of Edward Stuart-Smith and Doris Laughland; *b* 18 Nov 1927; *Educ* Radley, Corpus Christi Coll Cambridge; *m* 1953, Joan, *qv*; 3 s, 3 da; *Career* barr 1952, rec Crown Ct 1972-81, master of Bench Gray's Inn 1978, High Ct judge (Queen's Bench) 1981-87, Lord Justice of Appeal 1987; memb Criminal Injuries Compensation Bd 1979-81; presiding judge Western circuit 1982-86; kt 1981; *Recreations* playing cello, shooting, building, playing bridge; *Style*— The Rt Hon Lord Justice Stuart-Smith; Royal Courts of Justice, Strand, London

STUBBLEFIELD, Sir (Cyril) James; s of James Stubblefield (d 1926), of Cambridge; *b* 6 Sept 1901; *Educ* Perse Sch Cambridge, Chelsea Poly, RCS London Univ; *m* 1932, Emily Muriel Elizabeth, da of late L R Yakchee, of Calcutta and Jersey, CI; 2 s; *Career* geology demonstrator Imperial Coll London 1923-28; memb Geological Survey of GB 1928, chief palaeontologist 1947-53, asst dir 1953-60, dir 1960-66; dir: Geological Survey of NI 1960-66, Museum of Practical Geology 1960-66; pres Geological Soc London 1958-60, Palaeontographical Soc 1966-71, 8 Int Congress Carboniferous Stratigraphy & Geology 1968 and ed 4 vol CR; DSc, FRS, FGS, FZS, ARCS; kt 1965; *Style*— Sir James Stubblefield; 35 Kent Ave, Ealing, London W13 8BE (☎ 01 997 5051)

STUBBS, Antony Furneaux (Toby); MC (1941); s of Phillip Stanley Fewston Stubbs (d 1949), and Marjorie Furneaux (d 1940); *b* 20 Feb 1915; *Educ* Repton, King's Coll Cambridge; *m* 17 March 1945, Lilian, da of Rev W S Pakenham-Walsh, of Peterborough; 1 s (Tony Stubbs b 1946), 1 da (Gillian Murdoch b 1947); *Career* serv WWII Sudan Def Force, Rank Kaimakan, serv Sudan, Eritrea, N Africa (despatches 1940); Sudan Agric 1938-51; *Recreations* squash, polo, gardening; *Clubs* Phyllis Ct, Henley-on-Thames Royal Overseas League London; *Style*— Toby Stubbs, MC; Badgers, Fawley Court, Henley-on-Thames (☎ 0491 574615); Toad Hall Garden Centre, Marlow Rd, Henley-on-Thames

STUBBS, Sir James Wilfrid; KCVO (1979), TD (1946); s of Rev Wilfrid Thomas Stubbs (d 1968), and Muriel Elizabeth, *née* Pope (d 1966); *b* 13 August 1910; *Educ* Charterhouse, Brasenose Coll Oxford (MA); *m* 1938, Richenda Katherine Theodora, da of Rt Rev William Champion Streatfeild, Bishop of Lewes (d 1929); 1 s, 1 da (decd); *Career* serv WWII, Royal Signals, Lt-Col 1946; asst master St Paul's Sch 1934-46; Utd Grand Lodge of England: asst grand sec 1948-54, dep grand sec 1954-58, grand sec 1958-80; *Books* The Four Corners (1983), Freemasons' Hall, The Home and Heritage of The Craft (co-author 1984), Freemasonry in my Life (1985); *Recreations* travel, family history; *Clubs* Athenaeum; *Style*— Sir James Stubbs, KCVO, TD; 5 Pensioners Court, The Charterhouse, London EC1M 6AU (☎ 01 253 1982)

STUBBS, William Hamilton; s of Joseph Stubbs, and Mary, *née* McNicol; *b* 5 Nov 1937; *Educ* Workington GS Cumberland, St Aloysius Coll Glasgow, Univ of Glasgow (BSc, PhD), Univ of Arizona; *m* 19 Sept 1963, Marie Margaret, da of Joseph Pierce; 3 da (Nadine Ann b 1964, Hilary Jo b 1966, Fiona Mairi b 1967); *Career* Shell Oil Co California 1964-67, teacher in Glasgow 1967-72, asst dir of educn Carlisle 1972-73 and Cumbria 1973-76, dep dir of educn 1976-77, dep educn offr ILEA 1977-82, educn offr and chief exec ILEA 1982-88, chief exec Poly and Colls Funding Cncl; *Style*— William Stubbs, Esq; 122 Cromwell Tower, Barbican, London EC2Y 8DD

STUCKEN, Norah Kathleen Sara; da of Maj Edward Herbert Alexander (d 1958), and Sara Jane, *née* Moore (d 1942); *b* 10 Nov 1912; *Educ* Private in Harrogate, Germany and France; *m* 1, 1943, Lionel Sidney Francis Condon (d 1955); 2 s (David b 1949, twin br Jonathan (d 1984)), 1 da (Avril b 1947); m 2, 1957, George Stucken (d 1985); *Career* as Norah Alexander asst literary ed Everybodys Weekly 1934-35, opened Time's first London Off 1935, on Life (Paris and NY) 1935-39, reporter and columnist Sunday Pictorial 1939-45, columnist Daily Mail 1945-48; life pres Grower Publications Ltd 1988- (chm 1955-87); *Recreations* reading, languages, travel; *Style*— Ms Norah Stucken; 3 South Grove House, London N6 6LP (☎ 01 340 1472)

STUCLEY, Sir Hugh George Copleston Bampfylde; 6 Bt (UK 1859), of Affeton Castle, Devon; s of Sir Dennis Frederic Bankes Stucley, 5 Bt (d 1983), and Hon Lady Stucley, *qv*; *b* 8 Jan 1945; *Educ* RAC Cirencester; *m* 1969, Angela Caroline, er da of Richard Toller, of Theale, Berks; 2 s, 2 da; *Heir* s, George Dennis Bampfylde Stucley b 26 Dec 1970; *Career* Lt RHG; *Clubs* Cavalry and Guards, Sloane; *Style*— Sir Hugh Stucley, Bt; Affeton Castle, Worlington, Crediton, Devon

STUCLEY, Hon Lady (Sheila Margaret Warwick); *née* Bampfylde; patron of two livings, landowner; da of 4 Baron Poltimore (d 1965), and Cynthia Rachel (d 1961), o da of Hon Gerald Lascelles, CB; *b* 26 Oct 1912; *Educ* privately; *m* 5 Jan 1932, Maj Sir Dennis Frederic Bankes Stucley, 5 Bt, JP, DL (d 1983), s of Sir Hugh Nicholas Granville Stucley 4 Bt (d 1956); 2 s (John b and d 30 July 1933, (Sir) Hugh George Coplestone Bampfylde (6 Bt), *qv*), 4 da (Margaret Cynthia b 3 Sept 1934, Rosemary Anne b 8 Jan 1936, Christine Elizabeth b 25 April 1940, Sarah Susan b 6 Aug 1942); *Career* landowner; Mayoress of Bideford 1954-55; memb: Hartland Church Cncl, Hartland Paris Cncl; pres Garden Show; govr Bideford GS and Bideford Comprehensive Sch (pre-amalgamation); *Recreations* music, gardening; *Style*— The Hon Lady Stucley; Hartland Abbey, Bideford, N Devon EX39 6DT (☎ 02374 234)

STUDD, Anastasia, Lady; Anastasia; da of Lt-Col Harold Leveson-Gower (d 1972), (6 in descent from 1 Earl Gower and 5 cous of 5 Duke of Sutherland) and Kathleen, JP, OBE (d 1984), (da of Sir Murrough Wilson, KBE, JP, DL, by his 1 w, Sybil, 2 da of Sir Powlett Milbank, 2 Bt); *b* 26 Nov 1931; *m* 1958, Capt Sir Kynaston Studd, 3 Bt (d 1977), s of Sir Eric Studd 2 Bt (d 1975); 3 da (Sara, Jane, Anne); *Style*— Anastasia, Lady Studd; Manor Farm, Rockbourne, Fordingbridge, Hants (☎ 072 53 214)

STUDD, Sir Edward Fairfax; 4 Bt (UK 1929), of Netheravon, Wilts; s of Sir Eric Studd, 2 Bt, OBE, and Kathleen Stephana, da of Lydstone Joseph Langmead; suc bro, Sir (Robert) Kynaston Studd, 3 Bt, 1977; *b* 3 May 1929; *Educ* Winchester; *m* 1960, Prudence Janet, da of Alastair Douglas Fyfe, OBE, of Grey Court, Riding Mill, Northumberland; 2 s, 1 da; *Heir* s, Philip Alastair Fairfax (b 1961); *Career* Subaltern Coldstream Gds, serv Malaya 1948-49; chm Gray Davies Travel Agency Ltd; memb ct of assts Worshipful Co of Merchant Taylors; *Recreations* rural activities; *Clubs* Boodle's, Pratt's; *Style*— Sir Edward Studd, Bt; Danceys, Clavering, Saffron Walden, Essex

STUDD, Sir Peter Malden; GBE (1971), KCVO (1979), DL (Wilts 1983); s of late Brig Malden Studd, DSO, MC, and late Netta *née* Cramsie; *b* 15 Sept 1916,Dublin; *Educ* Harrow, Clare Coll Cambridge (MA); *m* 1943, Angela, *née* Garnier; 2 s; *Career* RA 1939-45, serv Middle E and Euro Campaigns; De La Rue Co plc 1939-74, dir Lloyds of Scottish plc 1973-84; UK pres Chiropractic Advancement Assoc; tstee: Royal Jubilee Tsts 1980-, Arts Educnl Schs 1984-; capt cricket Harrow and Cambridge Univ; Lord Mayor London 1970-71 (alderman 1959, Sheriff 1967); KstJ; former and past master Worshipful Co Merchant Taylors, Liveryman Worshipful Co Fruiterers and Plaisterers; Hon Dsc City Univ; kt 1969; *Recreations* fishing, shooting, gardening, saving St Pauls, lighting the Thames; *Clubs* I Zingari, MCC; *Style*— Sir Peter Studd, GBE, KCVO, DL; c/o Hoare & Co, 37 Fleet St, London EC4

STUDER, Keith Ronald; s of Ronald Walter Studer, of River Lodge, Coole, Co Cork; *b* 15 Sept 1945; *Educ* Ampleford, Queen's Coll Oxford, Univ of Br Columbia; *m* 1971, Jane Margaret; 1 s, 1 da; *Career* int freight forwarder; md LEP Int Ltd (dir 1975-); chm Birmingham Exhibition Freight Ltd 1980-; dir LEP Int Mgmnt Ltd 1986-; *Style*— Keith Studer, Esq; Dorne House, Chichester Rd, Dorking, Surrey RH4 1LR (☎ 0306 884305); LEP International Ltd, LEP House, 87 East Street, Epsom, Surrey KT14 1DT

STUDHOLME, Henry William; er s and h of Sir Paul Studholme, 2 Bt, DL, *qv*; *b* 31 Jan 1958; *Educ* Eton, Trinity Hall Cambridge (MA); *m* 1 Oct 1988, S Lucy R Deans-Chrystall, o da of Richard S Deans, of Christchurch, NZ, and the late Jane R M Deans, of West Wellow, Hants; *Career* ACA, ATII; *Style*— H W Studholme, Esq; Perry's Cottage, Ribston Hall, nr Wetherby, N Yorks LS22 4EZ

STUDHOLME, Joseph Gilfred; s of Sir Henry Gray Studholme, 1 Bt, CVO (d 1987), of Wembury Hse, Wembury, Plymouth, Devon, and Judith, *née* Whitbread; *b* 14 Jan 1936; *Educ* Eton, Magdalen Coll Oxford (BA, MA); *m* 5 Sept 1959, Rachel, da of Sir William Albemarle Fellowes, KCVO (d 1986), of Flitcham Hse, Kings Lynn, Norfolk; 3 s (Andrew b 1962, Alexander b 1967, Hugo b 1968); *Career* Nat Serv cmmnd 2Lt 60 Rifles (KRRC) 1954-56; md King & Shaxson Ltd 1961-63, chm and md Editions Alecto Ltd and subsid cos; cncl of mgmnt Byam Shaw Soc of Art 1988- (memb 1963-); FRSA; *Clubs* Garrick, MCC; *Style*— Joseph Studholme, Esq; Foundry hse, Stratfield Mortimer, Reading, Berks RG7 3NR (☎ 0734 333 000); 46 Kelso Place, London W8 5QG (☎ 01 937 6611, fax 01 937 5795, telex 94012669)

STUDHOLME, Lady Judith Joan Mary; *née* Whitbread; o da of Henry William Whitbread (d 1947), of Warminster, Wilts, and Mary, *née* Raymond (d 1926); *b* 15 Nov 1898; *m* 10 April 1929, Sir Henry Gray Studholme, 1 Bt, CVO (d 1987); 2 s, 1 da; *Style*— Lady Studholme; 30 Abbey Mews, Amesbury Abbey, Amesbury, Wilts SPA 7EX (☎ 0980 24812)

STUDHOLME, Sir Paul Henry William; 2 Bt (UK 1956), of Perridge, Co Devon; DL (Devon 1981); er s of Sir Henry Studholme, 1 Bt, CVO, DL (d 1987), by his w Judith Joan Mary, *née* Whitbread; *b* 16 Jan 1930; *Educ* Eton, RMA Sandhurst; *m* 2 March 1957, Virginia Katherine, yr da of Sir (Herbert) Richmond Palmer, KCMG, CBE (d 1958); 2 s (Henry William b 1958, James Paul Gilfred b 1960), 1 da (Anna Katherine b 1965); *Heir* s, Henry William Studholme, *qv*; *Career* Capt Coldstream Gds; farmer, landowner; tstee Devon and Exeer Savings Bank 1971, custodian tstee SW TSB 1978, memb SW regnl bd TSB 1983, dir TSB Gp plc (chm SW Regnl Bd 1987); pres Devon Branch of Country Landowners Assoc 1981-83, vice-pres Timber Growers England and Wales 1983, dep chm Timber Growers UK 1983-85; chm Gen Cmmrs of Income Tax (Crediton div) 1972; *Recreations* shooting, family and local history, travel, forestry; *Clubs* Cavalry and Guard's; *Style*— Sir Paul Studholme, Bt,

DL; Perridge House, Longdown, Exeter, Devon EX6 7RU (☎ 0392 81 237)

STUNELL, (Robert) Andrew; s of Robert George Stunell, of Powick, nr Worcester, and Trixie Stunell; *b* 24 Nov 1942; *Educ* Surbiton GS, Univ of Manchester, Liverpool Poly; *m* 29 July 1967, Gillian Mary Stunell; 3 s (Peter b 1973, Mark b 1974, Daniel b 1979), 2 da (Judith b 1969, Kari b 1970); *Career* architectural asst: various posts 1965-81, freelance 1981-85; cncllrs offr Assoc of Liberal Cncllrs 1985-88, devpt offr Assoc of SLD Cncllrs 1988-, Chester City Co 1979, Cheshire CC 1981, Assoc of CC's 1985, ldr SLD GP 1985, vice-chm ACC, parly card chester (1979, 1983 and 1987); *Books* Guide to Local Government Finance (1985), Success on Balanced Councils (1985), Parish Finance (1986), Success on the Council (1988); *Style—* Andrew Stunell, Esq; 18 Halkyn Rd, Chester CH2 3QE; Assoc of Social & Liberal Democrat Cncllrs, Birchcliffe Centre, Hebden Bridge, W Yorks HX7 8DG (☎ 0422 843 785, fax 0422 843 036)

STUNT, Stewart Robert; s of David James Stunt, of Chichester, Sussex, and Irene Rosina Stunt; *b* 13 Feb 1949; *Educ* Reigate GS, Kingston Poly; *m* 21 April 1971, Celia Mary, da of Dr Andrew Skarbek; 1 da (Sophie Victoria b 1981); *Career* Ogilvy & Mather 1971-72, fndr ptnr The Stewart Stunt Ptnrship 1979; MInstM; *Recreations* golf, squash, sub-aqua; *Clubs* Long Ashton Golf; *Style—* Stewart Stunt, Esq; The Stewart Stunt Partnership, 10 Saville Place, Bristol BS8 4EJ (☎ 0272 237 877, fax 0272 237 839)

STURDEE, Rear Adm (Arthur) Rodney Barry; CB (1971), DSC (1944); s of Cdr Barry Victor Sturdee (d 1951), of London, and Barbara, *née*, Sturdee (d 1972); *b* 6 Dec 1919; *Educ* Canford Sch, RN Staff Coll, Jt Serv Staff Coll, NATO Def Coll; *m* 1953, Marie-Claire, da of Pierre Amstoutz (d 1976), of France; 1 s (Christopher), 1 da (Dominique (Mrs Christopher Pearce)); *Career* entered RN as Special Entry Cadet 1937, specialized as Navigating Offr 1944, Cdr 1952, Capt 1960, Chief of Staff to C-in-C Portsmouth 1967-69 (in rank of Cdre), Rear-Adm 1969, Flag Offr Gibraltar 1969-72, ret 1972; ADC to HM The Queen 1969, bursar Malvern Girls' Coll 1972-85; *Recreations* playing with words; *Style—* Rear Adm Rodney Sturdee, CB, DSC; 3 Tibberton Mews, Tibberton Rd, Malvern, Worcs WR14 3AS (☎ 0684 57 5402)

STURGE, Maj Gen (Henry Arthur) John; CB (1978); s of Henry George Arthur Sturge (d 1955), and Lilian Beatrice (*née* Goodale) (d 1978); *b* 27 April 1925; *Educ* Wilsons GS Camberwell, QMC, London; *m* 18 July 1953, Jean Ailsa, da of John Alfred Mountain (d 1969); 2 s (Simon John b 1959, James Henry b 1962), 1 da (Susan Jean b 1954); *Career* RS 1945-80; serv in UK, Egypt, Malaya, Hong Kong, BAOR; Army Staff Coll 1955; Jt Servs Staff Coll 1962; regt cmd BAOR 1967-69; Brig cmd UK 1971-73; chief Signal Offr BAOR 1975-77; ACSD (signals) MoD 1977-80; asst dir Marconi Space and Def Systems 1980; gen mangr 1981-84; md Marconi Secure Radio Systems 1984-86; princ conslt Logica Space and Def systems 1986-; *Clubs* Army and Navy; *Style—* Maj Gen John Sturge, CB; Logica Space and Defence Systems Ltd, Cobham Park, Downside Rd, Cobham, Surrey KT11 3LY (☎ (01) 637 9111)

STURGES, James Aldersey Dicken; s of Gp Capt J A D Sturges, RAF (d 1974), and Dorothy Joan Norman; *b* 17 August 1945; *Educ* The Prep Sch Sherborne of Sherborne, Durham Univ (BA); *Career* md Past and Present Antiques; Totnes Devon; chm Narrows Traders Assoc; area organiser Disabled Ski Club; *Style—* James Sturges, Esq; Bow Cottage, Tuckenhay, Totnes, Devon

STURGESS-SMITH, Ian Charles; s of Charles Alfred Smith (d 1981), and Doris Ivy, *née* Sturgess; *b* 3 Sept 1937; *Educ* City of Leicester Boy; GS, Univ Coll Hosp Dental Sch (BDS Univ of London, LDS RCS England); *Career* dental surgn in gen practice; memb: Br Dental Assoc, Gen Dental Practioners Assoc; *Recreations* gardening; *Style—* Ian Sturgess-Smith, Esq; 19 Markfield Rd, Groby, Leicester LE6 2FL (☎ 0533 876724); 34 Leicester Rd, Oadby, Leicester LE2 5BA (☎ 0533 714792)

STURGIS, Ann Elisabeth; da of Maj Peter Sturgis, of Dauntsey Park, Chippenham, Wilts (d 1986), and Rachel Sybil, *née* Borthwick; *b* 23 Oct 1945; *Educ* N Forcland Lodge; *Career* estate agent; chm and md Malvern Estate Agents; FCEA 1988; *Recreations* gardening, riding; *Style—* Miss Ann Sturgis; 6 Hyde Park Gdns, London W2 (☎ 01 262 9552); Garden Cottage, Dauntsey Park, Chippenham, Wilts; Malverns, Malvern Ct, Onslow Sq, London SW7 3HU (☎ 01 589 8122, fax 01 589 4403)

STURRIDGE, Marvin Francis; s of Frank Alexander Leslie Sturridge (d 1978), of Hampstead, London, and Helen Marie, *née* Tucker (d 1980); *b* 12 Sept 1926; *Educ* Ladycross, Univ Coll Sch, Middx Hosp Med Sch, London Univ (MB, BS, MS); *m* 8 Feb 1958, June Pamela Linda, da of John Frederick Desmond Rowley (d 1970); 2 s (Paul b 1960, Jonathan b 1966), 2 da (Jacquelin b 1958, Nicola b 1963); *Career* surgn London Chest Hosp 1967-, hon cardiothoracic surgn Nat Hosp for Nervous Diseases 1970-; cardiothoracic surgn The Middx Hosp 1987; FRCS 1958; memb: Soc Thoracic and Cardiovascular Surgns of GB and Ireland, memb Br Cardiac Soc; *Recreations* restoration; *Style—* Marvin Sturridge, Esq; 41 Arden Rd, London N3 3AD (☎ 01 346 6394); 6 Upper Wimpole St, London W1 (☎ 01 486 1412)

STURROCK, Dr Ford Gibson; *b* 30 July 1910; *Educ* Glasgow Acad (BSc), Cambridge (PhD, MA); *m* 12 Sept 1978, Nancy, da of Frank Quentery Farmer, architect (farmer and Darke); *Career* dir Agric Economics Unit Cambridge 1950-77; memb Br Econ Mission to Malawi 1965, Royal Cmmn on Sugar Indus (for Govt of Jamaica) 1966, Planning Unit min of Agric Ghana 1973-74; *Recreations* shooting, foreign, travel; *Clubs* Farmers; *Style—* Dr Ford Sturrock; The Manor, Madingley, Cambridge CB3 8AL

STURROCK, Susan Jean; da of William Horace Haycock, of W Midlands, and Vera Haycock, *née* Garbett; *b* 10 April 1950; *Educ* Queen Mary's HS Walsall, Royal Coll of Music (ARCM), London Univ (BMus, MTC); *m* 5 Aug 1972, Philip James Sturrock, s of James Cars Sturrock, of Yorkshire; 1 s (Hugh b 1981), 2 da (Anna b 1977, Jane b 1983); *Career* music journalist; regular columnist for Review Newspaper Gp; contrib BBC Radio Bedforshire's Arts Magazine programme; co-author and ed of several books; *Books* Musical Instruments of the World (1976), The Book of Music (1978); *Recreations* music, cookery, reading, theatre; *Style—* Mrs Susan Sturrock; 52 Hill St, St Albans, Herts AL3 4QT; Home office (☎ 0727 58849)

STURT, Hon Mrs (Penelope Ann); *née* Mills; da of 3 Baron Hillingdon (d 1952); *b* 1917; *m* 1940, Evelyn Lennox Napier Sturt (d 1945); 1 s, 2 da; *Style—* The Hon Mrs Sturt; Thorn Croft, Chawleigh, Chumleigh, Devon

STUTTAFORD, Dr (Irving) Thomas; s of Dr William Joseph Edward Stuttaford, MC, (d 1956), of Horning, Norfolk, and Mary Marjorie Dean, *née* Royden (d 1976); *b* 4 May 1931; *Educ* Greshams Sch, Brasenose Coll Oxford, W London Hosp (MRCS, LRCP, DObstRCOG); *m* 1 June 1957, Pamela Christine, da of Lt-Col Richard Ropner, TD (d 1975), of Aldie, Tain, Rossshire; 3 s (Andrew b 1958, Thomas b 1961, Hugo b 1964); *Career* 2 Lt 10 Royal Hussars (PWO) 1953-55, Lt Scottish Horse TA 1955-59;jr hosp appts 1959-60, gen practice 1960-70, visiting physician BUPA 1970- (asst clincial dir 1979-81); clinical asst venereology: The London Hosp 1974-, Queen Mary's Hosp for the East End 1974-79, Moorfields Eye Hosp 1975-79; sr med advsr The Rank Orgn 1980-85, med corr The Times 1982-, private practice occupational health 1986-; memb: Blofield and flegg RDC 1964-66, Norwich City Cncl 1969-71; MP (C) Norwich S 1970-74, Parly candidate (C) Isle of Ely 1974 and 1979 sec, Cons Health and Social Servs Ctee; memb: Cncl Res Def Soc 1970-79, Built Control Campaign 1970-79, Select Ctee on Sci and Technol; *Books* A Birth Control Plan for Britain (with Mr Alistair Service and Dr John Dunwoody, 1972); *Recreations* living in the country, conservation of old buildings; *Clubs* Athenaeum, Reform, Cavalry and Guard's, Norfolk (Norwich); *Style—* Dr Thomas Stuttaford; The Grange, Bressingham, Diss, Norfolk IP22 2AT (☎ 037 988 245); 8 Devonshire Place, London W1

STUTTAFORD, William Royden; OBE (1983); s of Dr William Joseph Edward Stuttaford (d 1956), of Horning, Norfolk, and Mary Marjorie *née* Dean (d 1975); *b* 21 Nov 1928; *Educ* Gresham's Sch Holt, Trinity Coll Oxford (MA); *m* 1, 1958 (m dis), Sarah Jane, da of Philip Legge; 2 s, 2 da; m 2, 1974 Susan d'Esterre, da of Capt Sir Gerald Curteis, KCVO, RN (d 1972), Broomwood, Sevenoaks, Kent; *Career* memb Stock Exchange 1959-, chm Framlington Gp plc 1983-, sr ptnr Laurence Prust & Co (stockbrokers) 1983-86; chm: Cons Political Centre 1978-81, Unit Tst Assocn 1987-; *Clubs* Cavalry and Guard's; *Style—* William Stuttaford, Esq, OBE; Moulshams Manor, Great Wigborough, Colchester, Essex CO5 7RL (☎ 020 635 330); Framlington Investmt Mgmnt, 22-25 Finsbury Sq, London EC2A 1PJ (☎ 01 374 2931, telex 915619)

STUTTARD, Arthur Rupert Davies; s of Harold Stuttard, and Annie Constance, *née* Davies (d 1966); *b* 16 July 1943; *Educ* Accrington GS, Ch Ch Oxford (MA); *m* 10 Aug 1972, Margaret Evelyn, da of Reginald Wall Sykes; *Career* barr Middle Temple 1967, practises Northern circuit, dep stipendiary magistrate Liverpool; *Books* English Law Notebook (1969), author various articles on Lancashire Witchcraft trials; *Recreations* local history, Egyptian and Minoan archaeology; *Style—* Arthur Stuttard, Esq; Acre House, Fence, Near Burnley, Lancs; St James Chambers, 68 Quay St, Manchester 3 (☎ 061 834 7000)

STUTTARD, John Boothman; s of Thomas Boothman Stuttard (d 1969), of Helena, *née* Teasdale (d 1969); *b* 6 Feb 1945; *Educ* Shrewbury, Churchill Coll Cambridge Univ (MA); *m* 26 Sept 1970, Lesley Sylvia, da of Thomas Geoffrey Daish, of Kenilworth; 2 s (Thomas Henry Boothman (Tom) b 20 Jan 1975, James Midgley (Jamie) b 21 Aug 1976); *Career* VSO teacher SOAS Brunei 1966-67, trainee accountant Coopers & Lybrand (formerly Cooper Bros & Co) 1967-70: CA 1970-75, ptnr 1975-, currently dir of planning and mktg and head of Scandinavian mkt gp; accounting advsr to CPRS Cabinet Off Whitehall 1982-83; memb Cambridge Univ Appts Bd 1977-81, tres Totteridge Manor Assoc; FCA; *Recreations* travel, squash, tennis, theatre; *Clubs* Naval and Military; *Style—* John B Stuttard, Esq; West End House, 56 Totteridge Common, London N20 8LZ (☎ 01 959 1692); Coopers & Lybrand, Plumtree Ct, London EC4A 4HT (☎ 01 583 5000, fax 01 822 8362)

STYCH, Dorothy Elsie; da of Benjamin Stych (d 1940), and Maud Dugmore (d 1965); *b* 2 July 1912; *Educ* King Edward Sch Camp Hill; *Career* md B Stych & Co Ltd for over 20 yrs, ret 1988; tres: Unitarian New Meeting, Solihull Residents Assoc; exhibitions at: The Solihull Library Exhibition Hall, The Staff House at Birmingham Univ, Edgbaston Botanical Gdns, Royal Birmingham Soc of Artists; *Recreations* painting, growing orchids, gardening, travelling abroad, photography; *Clubs* Midland Assoc of Mountaineers, Solihull Photography Soc, Catherine de Barnes Art Soc, Memb Solihull Literary Soc, Solihull Art Soc; *Style—* Miss Dorothy Stych; 21 Whitefield Rd, Solihull, W Midlands

STYLE, Christopher John David; s of Maj David Carlyle Willoughby Style, MC, TD (d 1978), of Loweswater, Cumbria, and Dr Anne Marion, *née* Phillips; *b* 13 April 1955; *Educ* St Bees Sch Cumbria, Trinity Hall Cambridge (MA), City of London Poly; *Career* Linklaters & Paines 1977-: articles 1977-79, slr 1979, asst slr 1979-85, ptnr 1985-; seconded to Sullivan & Cromwell NY 1983; memb London Slrs Litigation Assoc; Freeman City of London 1985, memb City of London Slrs Co ; *Books* Documentary Evidence (co-author, 2 edn 1987); *Recreations* fell walking, rock climbing; *Style—* Christopher Style, Esq; 2 Village Close, Belsize Lane, London NW3 5AH (☎ 01 435 5711); Linklaters & Paines, Barrington House, 59-67 Gresham St, London EC2V 7JA (☎ 01 606 7080, fax 01 606 5113, telex 884349)

STYLE, Frederick Montague; s of Sir William Style, 12 Bt (d 1981), and La Verne, Lady Style, *qv*; *b* 5 Nov 1947; *Educ* De Sales Seminary, Marquette Univ; *m* 1971, Sharon, da of William H Kurz, of Menomonee Falls, Wisconsin USA; 2 da (Jennifer b 1977, Christina b 1979); *Style—* Frederick Style, Esq; 745 N 115 St, Milwaukee, WI 53226, USA (☎ 414 476-4541)

STYLE, Col (Rodney) Gerald; s of Brig-Gen Rodney Charles Style (d 1957), and Helene Pauline, *née* Kleinwort (d 1974); see Debretts Peerage and Baronetage 1 Bt cr 1627; *b* 28 Oct 1920; *Educ* Eton, Staff Coll Camberley (psc); *m* 18 Oct 1952, Barbara, da of John Austin Hill (d 1950), of Natick, Massachussetts; 3 s (William b 1954, Rodney b 1956, John b 1957), 1 da (Caroline b 1964); *Career* RA, Capt Coldstream Gds 5 Bn and Gds Armd Div, NW Europe 1940-46, Royal Northumberland Fus (Mau Mau Campaign Kenya) 1953-55, Maj 29 Inf Bde (Suez Expdn) 1956; CO 1 Bn Royal Northumberland Fus 1962-65; Col Cmdt Royal Mil Sch of Music, Kneller Hall 1973-75; ret 1975; professional photographer 1975-; memb Nat Cncl BIPP (twice vice-pres 1984-86); Licentiate Br Inst of Professional Photography 1978; *Clubs* Lansdowne; *Style—* Col Gerald Style; 19 Crooksbury Rd, Farnham, Surrey GU10 1QD (☎ 025 18 2558)

STYLE, Lt Cdr Sir Godfrey William; CBE (1961), DSC (1942); er s of Brig-Gen Rodney Style (4 s of Sir William Style, 9 Bt), of Wierton Grange, Boughton-Monchelsea, Kent, and Hélène, 2 da of Herman Kleinwort; *b* 3 April 1915; *Educ* Eton; *m* 1, 1942 (m dis 1951), Jill Elizabeth, da of George Bellis Caruth, of Ballymena; 1 s (Montague), 2 da (Helen, Marieka); m 2, 1951, Sigrid Elisabeth Julin (d 1985), da of Per Stellan Carlberg, of Jönköping, Sweden; 1 s (Charles); m 3, 1986, Valerie Beauclerk, da of Cdr Cecil Henry Hulton-Sams; *Career* joined RN 1933, serv HM Yacht Victoria & Albert 1938, Flag Lt to C-in-C Home Fleet 1939-41, Med 1941-42 (Malta convoys), (wounded 1942, despatches 1940 and 1943), thereafter HQ 4 Gp Bomber Cmd and Admty, invalided from RN 1946; Lloyd's underwriter 1944-; chm Nat Advsy Cncl Employment Disabled People 1963-74, govr Queen Elizabeth's Fndn, memb Cncl Sir Oswald Stoll Fndn 1975-84; dir Star Centre for Youth, Cheltenham; kt 1973; *Recreations* field sports, horticulture, lapidary work; *Clubs* Naval and Military; *Style*— Lt Cdr Sir Godfrey Style, CBE, DSC, RN; 30 Carlyle Court, Chelsea Harbour, London SW10 0UQ (☎ 01 352 6512)

STYLE, La Verne, Lady; La Verne; da of Theron Comstock, (d 1985), of Palm Springs, California, and La Verne Comstock (*née* Nehrbas) (d 1983); *b* 17 Feb 1917; *Educ* Marquette U; *m* 1941, Sir William Montague Style, 12 Bt (d 1981), s of 11 Bt (d 1942); 2 s (William, Frederick, *qqv*); *Style*— La Verne, Lady Style; 619 Elm St, Hartford, WI 53027, USA (☎ 414 673-5611)

STYLE, Rodney Hill; s of Col (Rodney) Gerald Style, of Runfold, Farnham, Surrey, and Barbara Hill Style; *b* 25 Mar 1956; *Educ* Eton; *m* 24 April 1982, Georgina Eve, da of John Kinloch Kerr, of Abbottrule, Frocester, Glos; 2 s (George b 1985, Hugo b 1985); *Career* Spicer and Pegler (CAs) 1976-85, ptnr Haines Watts 1985-, md Haines Watts Fin Servs Ltd 1987-; Freeman Worshipful Co of Grocers 1981; ACA 1981, ATII 1983; *Recreations* skiing; *Style*— Rodney Style, Esq; Greenacre, Steeple Aston, Oxfordshire; Sterling House, 19/23 High St, Kidlington, Oxon OX5 2DH (☎ 08675 78282, fax 08675 77518)

STYLE, Sir William Frederick; 13 Bt (E 1627), of Wateringbury, Kent; s of Sir William Montague Style, 12 Bt (d 1981), and La Verne, Lady Style, *qv*; *b* 13 May 1945; *Educ* (BSc, MEd); *m* 1, 1968, Wendy Gay, da of Gene and Marjory Wittenberger, of Hartford, Wisconsin, USA; 2 da (Shannon b 1969, Erin b 1973); m 2, 1986, Linnea L, da of Donn and Elizabeth Erickson, of Sussex, Wisconsin, USA; 1 da (McKenna b 1987); *Heir* bro, Frederick Montague Style; *Career* public sch teacher; *Recreations* yacht (Summer Style); *Clubs* Fond du Lac Yacht; *Style*— Sir William Style, Bt; 2430 N 3rd Lane, Oconomowoc, WI 53066, USA

SUDBURY, John Charles; *b* 7 Mar 1944; *Educ* E Ham GS, NE London Poly; *m* 1965, Carol Ann, *née* Auker; 1 s, 2 da; *Career* chartered engr, dir Lex Motor Co Ltd; *Recreations* golf, travel, work; *Style*— John Sudbury, Esq; Sycamore, Fishery Rd, Bray, Berks

SUDDABY, Dr Arthur; CBE (1980); s of George Suddaby, of Kingston upon Hull (d 1950), and Alice May, *née* Holmes (d 1970); *b* 26 Feb 1919; *Educ* Riley HS Hull, Hull Tech Coll (BSc), Chelsea Coll (BSc, MSc), QMC London (PhD); *m* 23 Dec 1944, Elizabeth Bullin (d 1965), da of the late Charles Vyse, of Cheyne Row, Chelsea; 2 s (John b 1946, Anthony b 1947); *Career* chem engr 1937-47, sr lectr in chem engng Westham Coll of Technol 1947-50; Sir John Cass Coll: sr lectr in physics 1950-61, head of dept 1961-66, princ 1966-70, provost City of London Poly 1970-81; on various CNAA ctees 1969-81; memb: London and Home Cos Regnl Advsy Ctee on Higher Educn 1971-81, Ct of City Univ 1967-81; chm: Ctee of Dirs of Polys 1976-78, Assoc of Navigation Schs 1972; MIChemE 1944, FRSC 1980; *Recreations* fishing, hunting; *Clubs* Athenaeum; *Style*— Dr Arthur Suddaby, CBE; Castle Hill House, Godshill Wood, Fordingbridge, Hants (☎ 0425 52234); Flat 3, 16 Elm Park Gardens, Chelsea, London SW10 9NY (☎ 01 352 9164)

SUDDABY, Dominic; *b* 27 Oct 1939; *Educ* St Edwards Sch Oxford; *m* 1964, Sheelagh Maureen, nee Minns; 5 children; *Career* md PHH Servs Ltd and PHH Leasing Ltd, md Autolease Ltd 1972-74; MInstD; *Recreations* shooting, reading, cricket; *Style*— Dominic Suddaby Esq; PHH International Ltd, PO Box 31, Princes House, Princes St, Swindon SN1 2HL

SUDDARDS, Roger Whitley; CBE (1987); s pf John Whitley Suddards, OBE (d 1978), and Jean, *née* Rollitt; *b* 5 June 1930; *Educ* Bradford GS; *m* 1 Aug 1963, Elizabeth Anne, da of Donald Stuart Rayner; 2 da (Jane Elizabeth b 21 June 1965, Helen Victoria b 1 Aug 1967); *Career* RASC 1952-54; dir 1952; slr and sr ptnr Last Suddards 1952-88, conslt Hammond Suddards 1988-, visiting lectr Leeds Sch of Town Planning 1964-74, memb planning law ctee Law Soc 1964-81, planning law conslt to UN 1974-77, memb bye-laws revision ctee Law Soc 1984-87, legal memb Royal Town Planning Inst; chm of advsy ctee for Land Cmmn for Yorkshire & Humberside, pro chllr and chm of cncl Univ of Bradford 1987-, chm Yorks Building Soc; tstee Friends of Bradford Art Galleries 1962-, pres Bradford Law Soc 1969, tstee Bradford Playhouse of Film Theatre 1962-87, chm working pty on Future of Bradford Churches 1978-79, former chm examinations bd ISVA; Hon Fell Soc of Valuers of Auctioneers; Liveryman City of London Slrs Co 1988-; *Books* Towm Planning Law of West Indies (1974), History of Bradford Law Society (1975), A Lawyer's Peregrination (1984, 2 Edn 1987), Bradford Disaster Appeal (1986), Listed Buildings: the Law and Practise (2 edn 1982 and 1988); *Recreations* theatre, music, reading, travel; *Clubs* Arts, Bradford Club (Bradford); *Style*— Roger Suddards, Esq, CBE; Low House, High Eldwick, Bingley, W Yorks BD16 3AZ (☎ 0274 564 832); Empire House, 10 Piccadilly, Bradford BD1 3LR (☎ 0274 734 700, fax 0274 737 547, telex 517201)

SUDELEY, 7 Baron (UK 1838); Merlin Charles Sainthill Hanbury-Tracy; s of Capt David Hanbury-Tracy (gs of 4 Baron) and Colline, da of Lt-Col Collis St Hill; the 1 Baron was chm of the Cmmn for the Rebuilding of the new Houses of Parliament 1835; suc kinsman (6 Baron) 1941; *b* 17 June 1939; *Educ* Eton, Worcester Coll Oxford; *m* 1980 (m dis 1988), Hon Mrs Elizabeth Villiers, da of late Viscount Bury (s of 9 Earl of Albemarle) and formerly w of Alastair John Hanbury-Tracy, *qv*; *Heir* kinsman, (Desmond) Andrew John Hanbury-Tracy, *qv*; *Career* former chm Human Rights Soc (founded by Lord St John of Fawsley to oppose legalisation of euthanasia); introduced debates in the House of Lords on the export of manuscripts 1973, the English Tourist Bd's report "Cathedral & Tourism" 1980, and the teaching & use of the Prayer Bk in Theological colls 1987; patron: Anglican Assoc, St Peter's (Petersham); patron Prayer Book Soc (introduced Prayer Book (Protection) Bill 1981), memb Ctee Manorial Soc; past pres The Montgomeryshire Soc; has contributed to Contemporary Review, London Magazine, Quarterly Review, Vogue, The Universe, Pick of Today's Short Stories, Montgomeryshire Collections, Salisbury Review, Transactions of the Bristol and Gloucs Archaeological Soc, Die Waage (Zeifschrift der Chemie Grünenal), author (with others) The Sudeleys - Lords of Toddlington (1987); *Recreations* conversation; *Clubs* Brooks's; *Style*— The Rt Hon The Lord Sudeley; 25 Melcombe Court, Dorset Sq, NW1 (☎ 01 723 7502); c/o Williams & Glyn's Bank, 21 Grosvenor Gdns, SW1

SUENSON-TAYLOR, Hon Christopher John; s and h of 2 Baron Grantchester, QC; *b* 8 April 1951; *Educ* Winchester, LSE (BSc); *m* 1973, Jacqueline, da of Dr Leo Jaffé; 2 s, 2 da; *Career* dairy farmer and cattle breeder; memb Holstein Soc Exec Cncl, memb Cheshire Agric Soc Cncl; champion Holstein Cow RASE 1983; 2 All- Britain and 3 Reserve Awards; *Recreations* music; *Style*— The Hon Christopher Suenson-Taylor; Lower House Farm, Back Coole Lane, Audlem, Crewe, Cheshire (☎ 0270 811363)

SUENSON-TAYLOR, Hon James Gunnar; 3 and yst s of 2 Baron Grantchester, QC; *b* 30 Sept 1955; *Educ* Eton, Kingston Poly; *m* 1981, Gillian Susan, yr da of Peter Ayling, of Worcester Park, Surrey; 1 s (Andrew James b 1985), 1 da (Katherine Joyce b 1988); *Career* co dir; *Recreations* rowing, shooting, fishing; *Style*— The Hon James Suenson-Taylor; Mole House, 63 Pelhams Walk, Esher, Surrey (☎ Esher 65207)

SUENSON-TAYLOR, Hon Jeremy Kenneth; 2 (twin) s of 2 Baron Grantchester, CBE, QC; *b* 8 April 1951; *Educ* Winchester; *m* Lindsay Anne Kirby, of Leicester; 2 s (Rowan b 1974, Daniel b 1983), 2 da (Laurel b 1979, Zoë b 1982); *Style*— The Hon Jeremy Suenson-Taylor; Hillside Farm, Clutton, nr Bristol, Avon

SUENSON-TAYLOR, Hon Kirsten Victoria Mary; 3 da of 2 Baron Grantchester, QC; *b* 25 Sept 1961; *Style*— The Hon Kirsten Suenson-Taylor; The Gate House, Coombe Wood Rd, Kingston Hill, Surrey

SUESS, Nigel Marcus; *b* 13 Dec 1945; *Educ* Chigwell Sch, Cambridge Univ; *m* 1978, Maureen, nee Ferguson; 1 da; *Career* banker; dir The Br Linen Bank Ltd; *Recreations* mountaineering, chess, ornithology; *Style*— Nigel Suess, Esq; Drumornie, 35 Woodhall Rd, Edinburgh

SUFFIELD, 11 Baron (GB 1786); Sir Anthony Philip Harbord-Hamond; 12 Bt (GB 1745), MC (1950); s of 10 Baron (d 1951), and Nina Annette Mary Crawfuird (d 1955), da of John William Hutchison, of Lauriston Hall, and Edlingham, Kirkcudbrightshire; *b* 19 June 1922; *Educ* Eton; *m* 1952, Elizabeth Eve, da of late Judge (Samuel Richard) Edgedale, QC, of Field Lodge, Crowthorne, Berks; 3 s, 1 da; *Heir* s, Hon Charles Harbord-Hamond; *Career* Maj Coldstream Gds (ret); serv: WWII N Africa and Italy, Malaya 1948-50; appt one of HM Bodyguard of Hon Corps of Gentlemen-at-Arms 1973; *Clubs* Army and Navy, Pratt's; *Style*— The Rt Hon the Lord Suffield, MC; Wood Norton Grange, Dereham, Norfolk (☎ 036 284 235)

SUFFIELD, Sir Henry John Lester; *b* 28 April 1911; *Educ* Camberwell Central Sch; *m* 1940, Elizabeth Mary White; 1 s, 1 da; *Career* serv WWII Maj RASC, with LNER 1926-35, Morris Motor Corpn Canada and USA 1952-64, dep manager and dir Br Motor Corpn Birmingham 1964-68, sales dir BL Motor Corpn 1968-69, head of def sales MOD 1969-76; kt 1973; *Clubs* RAC; *Style*— Sir Henry Suffield; 16 Glebe Court, Fleet, Hants

SUFFOLK, Archdeacon of; *see*: Robinson, Ven Neil

SUFFOLK AND BERKSHIRE, Earl of, 21 of Suffolk (E 1603), 14 of Berkshire (E 1626); Michael John James George Robert Howard; also Viscount Andover and Baron Howard of Charlton (E 1622); s of 20 Earl (k on active serv 1941); the 1 Earl was 2 s of 4 Duke of Norfolk; the 9 Earl's w was mistress of George II, who built Marble Hill House, on the Thames between Twickenham and Richmond, for her (the style is Palladian, designed by Lord Pembroke); *b* 27 Mar 1935; *Educ* Winchester; *m* 1, 1960 (m dis 1967), Mme Simone Paulmier, da of Georges Litman, of Paris; m 2, 1973 (m dis 1980), Anita Robsham, da of Robin Fuglesang, of Cuckfield, Sussex; 1 s, 1 da (Lady Katharine b 9 April 1976); m 3, 1983, Linda Jacqueline, da of Col Vincent Paravicini and former w of 4 Viscount Bridport; 2 da (Lady Philippa b 1985, Lady Natasha b 1987); *Heir* s, Viscount Andover; *Style*— The Rt Hon The Earl of Suffolk and Berks; Charlton Park, Malmesbury, Wilts (☎ 0666 82206/823200)

SUGDEN, Sir Arthur; s of Arthur Sugden (d 1940), of Manchester, and Elizabeth Ann Sugden (d 1952); *b* 12 Sept 1918; *Educ* Thomas St Sch W Gorton, HS of Commerce Manchester; *m* 1946, Agnes, da of Francis Grayston (d 1930); 2 s; *Career* serv WWII Maj RA, UK and India; certified accountant and chartered sec; chief exec Coop Wholesale Soc Ltd 1973-80, chm Coop Bank 1973-80; FIB, kt 1978; *Recreations* reading, walking, travel; *Style*— Sir Arthur Sugden; 56 Old Wool Lane, Cheadle Hulme, Cheadle, Cheshire SK8 5JA

SUGDEN, John Christopher; TD (1966); s of Howard Davy Sugden (d 1965), of 3 Prince Arthur Rd, Hampstead, London NW3, and Olive Mary, *née* Brayfield (d 1973); *b* 10 Jan 1933; *Educ* Aldenham; *m* 23 May 1959, Jennifer Jean, da of Ronald George Hilder, of 5 St Christophers Green, Haslemere, Surrey; 1 s (Oliver Davy b 1963), 1 da (Philippa Ann b 1961); *Career* joined Army 1951, cmmnd RASC 1952, serv Germany, Capt 1953, 56 London Armd Div TA 1954-67, Duke of Yorks HQ Chelsea BRASCO 1954; export mangr Sharp Perrin & Co 1958-60, self employed retailer 1960-; md: Three Counties Toys Ltd 1983-, Concorde Toys Ltd 1984-; memb: Haslemere Town Cncl 1976-84, Waverley Dist Cncl 1978-82; chm: Dolmetsch Fndn of Early Music, Tstees of Haslemere Hall 1983-; Mayor of Haslemere 1979-80; *Recreations* music, languages; *Style*— John Sugden, Esq, TD; Little Orchard, Kingsley Green, Haslemere, Surrey (☎ 0428 2162) Clotamar, L'Escala, Girona, Spain; 2-4 Petworth Rd, Haslemere, Surrey (☎ 0428 4165, fax 0428 58420)

SUGGETT, Gavin Robert; s of Kenneth Frederick Suggett (d 1984), of Weybridge, Surrey, and Nancy, *née* Voss-Bark; *b* 11 May 1944; *Educ* Felsted Sch, Christ's Coll Cambridge (MA), London Business Sch (MSc); *m* 11 Sept 1971, Louise, da of Hon Lord Migdale (d 1983), of Edinburgh and Sutherland; 1 s (Gordon b 1977), 2 da (Clare b 1975, Katie b 1980); *Career* CA; articled clerk Deloittes 1962-66, fin mangr Weir Gp Ltd 1971-73, dir Alliance Tst plc 1987- (co sec 1973-); pt/t lectr law faculty and MBA course Univ of Dundee; FCA 1971; *Recreations* skiing, gardening, hill walking; *Clubs* New (Edinburgh), Royal Perth Golf; *Style*— Gavin Suggett, Esq; The Alliance Tst, 64 Reform St, Dundee DD1 1TJ (☎ 0382 201700, fax 0382 25133, telex 76195)

SUIRDALE, Viscount; John Michael James Hely-Hutchinson; er s and h of 8 Earl of Donoughmore; *b* 7 August 1952; *Educ* Harrow; *m* 1977, Marie-Claire, da of Gerard van den Driessche (d 1985); 1 s (Hon Richard Gregory b 1980), 2 da (Hon Marie-Pierre Joanna b 1978, Hon Tatiana Louise b 1985); *Heir* s, Hon Richard Gregory Hely-Hutchinson b 1980; *Career* dir; *Recreations* shooting, fishing, skiing; *Style*— Viscount Suirdale; 8 Kensington Palace Gdns, London W8

SULLIVAN, Edmund Wendell; s of Thomas James Llewellyn Sullivan (d 1965), of Portadown, and Letitia, *née* Holmes (d 1968); *b* 21 Mar 1925; *Educ* Portadown Coll, Queen's Univ Belfast, Royal Veterinary Coll; *m* 1957, Elinor, da of John Wilson Melville (d 1975), of Fife; 2 s (Kenneth, Colin), 1 da (Morna); *Career* veterinary surgn, gen vet practice 1947-, joined State Veterinary Serv in NI 1948, chief veterinary offr Dept of Agric for NI; MRCVS; *Recreations* hill walking, woodcraft, following rugby & cricket; *Style*— Edmund W Sullivan, Esq; 26 Dillon's Ave, Newtownabbey, Co Antrim (☎ 0232 862323); Dept of Agric for NI, Dundonald House, Upper Newtownards Rd, Belfast (☎ 0232 650111, telex 74578 DEPAGR G)

SULLIVAN, Hon Mrs; Hon Jennifer; *née* Lowther; raised to rank of Viscounts da 1950; 3 da (but 2 surviving) of Maj Hon Christopher Lowther (d 1935; er s of 1

Viscount Ullswater & f by his 1 w of 2nd Viscount), sometime MP Cumberland N, by his 2 w, Dorothy (da of Arthur Bromley Davenport and who had m 1 late Captain Samuel Loveridge; she subsequently m, as her 3 husb, 1936 (m dis 1951), Capt Hugh Cullen, MC, and m 4, 1958, Charles de Rougemont (d 1964)); *b* 11 June 1932; *m* 1, 1954 (m dis 1962), her 1 cous twice removed, 7 Earl of Lonsdale (she being his 2 w); 1 s (Hon William Lowther), 2 da (Ladies Caroline & Miranda Lowther, *qqv*); m 2, 1962 (m dis 1972), Flt Lt William Edward Clayfield, DFC, RAF; m 3, 1976 (m dis), Rev Oswald Dickin Carter (d 1986); m 4, 1981 (having previously reverted to the name Hon Mrs Jennifer Lowther), James Cornelius Sullivan; *Style—* The Hon Mrs Sullivan; The Cottage, Timberland Fen, Lincoln

SULLIVAN, Jeremy Mirth; QC (1982); s of Arthur Brian Sullivan and Pamela Jean, *née* Kendall; *b* 17 Sept 1945; *Educ* Framlingham Coll, King's Coll London (LLB, LLM); *m* 1970, Ursula Klara Marie, da of late Benno August Friederich Hildenbrock; 2 s (Richard b 1974, Geoffrey b 1976); *Career* 2 Lt Suffolk & Cambs Regt (TA) 1963-65; barr Inner Temple 1968, lectr in law City of London Poly 1968-71; in practice Planning & Local Govt Bar 1971-, LAMRTPI 1970, LMRTPI 1976, memb of cncl RTPI 1983-87, memb Exec Ctee Georgian Gp 1985-, recorder 1989-; *Recreations* walking, railways, canals, reading history; *Style—* Jeremy Sullivan, Esq, QC; 4-5 Grays Inn Square, London WC1R 5JA (☎ 01 404 5252, telex 895 3743 GRAYLAW)

SULLIVAN, Michael Francis; s of Sir Richard Benjamin Magniac Sullivan, 8 Bt (d 1977), and Muriel Mary Paget Pineo (d 1988); *b* 4 April 1936; *Educ* St Andrew Coll SA, Clare Coll Cambridge (MA, MB Chir), St Mary's Hosp Univ of London; *m* 1, 22 Aug 1957 (m dis 1978), Inger, da of Arne Mathieson (d 1984); 1 s (Richard b 9 Jan 1961), 1 da (Nicola b 20 Aug 1965); m 2, 22 Dec 1978, Caroline Mary, da of Maj Christopher Griffin, of Oxborough, Norfolk; 1 da (Lucy b 22 Nov 1980); *Career* conslt orthopaedic surgn Royal Nat Orthopaedic Hosp London 1971-, sr clerical lectr Univ of London; FRCS 1967; *Recreations* cricket, sailing, shooting; *Clubs* MCC, Royal Harwich Yacht; *Style—* Michael Sullivan, Esq; 12 Gloucester Crescent, London NW1 7DS (☎ 01 485 4473); High Lodge Farm, Mildenhall, Suffolk (☎ 0638 716664); 95 Harley St, London W1N 1DF (☎ 01 486 4970)

SULLIVAN, (Sir) Richard Arthur; 9 Bt (UK 1804); does not use title; s of Sir Richard Benjamin Magniac Sullivan, 8 Bt (d 1977), and Muriel Mary Paget; *b* 9 August 1931; *Educ* Univ of Cape Town (BSc), MIT (MS); *m* 1962, Elenor Mary, da of Kenneth Merson Thorpe, of Somerset W, S Africa; 1 s, 3 da; *Heir* s, Charles Merson Sullivan, b 15 Dec 1962; *Career* civil engr; mangr Woodward Clyde Oceaneering; *Recreations* tennis; *Clubs* Houston Racquet; *Style—* Richard Sullivan, Esq; 1060 Royal York Rd, Toronto, Ontario M8X 2G7, Canada (☎: 416 232 9750); Geocon Inc, 3210 American Drive, Mississanga, Ontario L4V 1B3, Canada (☎: 416 673 1664

SULTOON, Jeffrey Alan; s of Maurice Joseph Sultoon, of London, and Babette Doreen, *née* Braun; *b* 8 Oct 1953; *Educ* Haberdashers' Aske's, St Edmund Hall Oxford; *m* 11 May 1985, Vivien Caryl, da of Peter Woodbridge, of Guildford, Surrey; *Career* admitted slr 1978, slr Freshfields 1978-81, ptnr Ashurst Morris Crisp 1986- (slr 1981-86); *Books* Tolley's Company Law (1988); *Style—* Jeffrey Sultoon, Esq; Ashurst, Morris, Crisp, Broadgate House, 7 Eldon St, London EC2M 7HD (☎ 01 247 7666, fax 01 377 5659, telex 887067)

SULTZBERGER, John Peter; VRD (1955); s of Albert Sultzberger (d 1954), of Lynton Grange, Croydon, Surrey, and Alice Emilie, *née* Tobler (d 1972); ggs of Jonas Furrer the first pres of Switzerland under the present constitution 1855; *b* 21 August 1920; *Educ* Malvern, Ecole Superior de Commerce Neuchatel Switzerland; *Career* Capt RM 1941-46, 41 Commando Landings Sicily and Salerno 1943, 2 Bn RM Engrs Far E 1945-46, RMFVR 1948-61; Lloyds Insur broker 1946-62; memb Lloyds 1946; *Style—* John Sultzberger, VRD; The Dower House, Gesting Thorpe, Halstead, Essex

SULYAK, Hon Mrs (Rosamund Sybil); *née* Allen; o da of Baron Croham, GCB (Life Peer), *qv*; *b* 1942; *m* 1974, Stephan Sulyák; *Heir* Veronica; *Career* lectr (as R S Allen) QMC London; *Books* editions and translations of Medieval texts; *Recreations* riding; *Style—* The Hon Mrs Sulyák; 8A Harewood Road, S Croydon, Surrey CR2 7AL

SUMBERG, David Anthony Gerald; MP (C) Bury S 1983-; s of late Joshua Sumberg and Lorna Sumberg; *b* 2 June 1941; *Educ* Tettenhall Coll Wolverhampton; Coll of Law London; *m* 1972, Carolyn Franks; 1 s, 1 da; *Career* slr; PPS to Attorney-Gen Sir Patrick Mayhew, QC, MP; memb Manchester CC; contested (C) Manchester, Wythenshawe 1979; *Recreations* family and friends; *Style—* David Sumberg, Esq, MP; House of Commons, London SW1A 0AA (☎ 01 219 4459)

SUMMERFIELD, Hon Mr Justice; Hon Sir John Crampton Summerfield; CBE (1966, OBE 1961), QC (Bermuda 1963); s of Arthur Frederick Summerfield (d 1941), and Lilian Winifred, *née* Staas (d 1958); *b* 20 Sept 1920; *Educ* Lucton Sch Herefordshire; *m* 11 Aug 1945, Patricia Sandra, da of John Geoffrey Musgrave (d 1926), of Salisbury, Rhodesia; 2 s (John b 1946, Michael b 1948), 2 da (Rosemary b 1955, Margaret b 1960); *Career* serv WWII, Ethiopia and Madagascar, Capt Royal Signals; barr Gray's Inn 1949; Tanganyika Crown Coubnsel/Legal Draftsman 1949-58; dep legal sec E Africa High Cmmn 1958-62; attorney-gen Bermuda 1962-72; chief justice Bermuda 1972-77; chief justice Cayman Islands 1977-87; justice of appeal (Ct of Appeal) Bermuda 1980-, pres Ct of Appeal Belize 1981-82; memb exec cncl and MLC Bermuda until 1966; kt 1973; *Recreations* photography, chess; *Clubs* Royal Cwlth Soc; *Style—* The Hon Mr Justice Summerfield, CBE, QC; 3 The Corniche, Sandgate, Folkestone, Kent CT20 3TA (☎ 0303 39479)

SUMMERHAYES, David Michael; CMG (1974); s of Sir Christopher Summerhayes, KBE, CMG, *qv*; *b* 29 Sept 1922; *Educ* Marlborough, Emmanuel Coll Cambridge; *m* 1959, June, da of late Lt-Col H A G van der Hardt Aberson; 2 s, 1 da; *Career* HM Dip Serv: ldr UK Delegn to Ctee on Disarmament Geneva with rank of ambass 1979-82, disarmament advsr FCO 1982-; *Recreations* walking, sailing, golf; *Clubs* Utd Oxford and Cambridge, Hurlingham, Royal Wimbledon Golf; *Style—* David Summerhayes, Esq, CMG; 6 Kingsmere Rd, Wimbledon, London SW19 6PX (☎ 01 788 7026); Foreign and Commonwealth Office, London SW1 (☎ 01 270 2259)

SUMMERHAYES, Gerald Victor; CMG (1979), OBE (1969); s of Victor Samuel Summerhayes, OBE (d 1977), and Florence Ann Victoria Summerhayes (d 1978); *b* 28 Jan 1928; *Educ* Kings' Sch Ely, Brasenose Coll Oxford; *Career* admin offr Col Serv 1952-60, Overseas Civil Serv 1960-83, permenant sec Sokoto State Nigeria 1970-81, various ministries including Cabinet Off, Health and Local Govt, ret 1983; *Style—* Gerald Summerhayes Esq, CMG, OBE; Bridge Cottage, Bridge St, Sidbury, Devon (☎ 037 57 311), PO Box 172, Sokoto, Nigeria

SUMMERS, Eric William; *b* 10 Dec 1914; *Educ* Dartford Tech Coll; *m* 1939, Janet; 2 children; *Career* CIBS; chm Courtney, Pope (Hldgs) Ltd; fell Inst of Plant Engrg, companion CIBS; FRSA; *Clubs* RAC, Livery; *Style—* Eric Summers, Esq; Muskoday, 29 The Meadow, Chislehurst, Kent BR7 6AA (☎ 01 467 8047); Courtney, Pope (Hldgs) Ltd, Amhurst Park Works, South Tottenham, London N15 6RB (☎ 01 800 1270)

SUMMERS, Felix Roland Brattan; 2 Bt (UK 1952), of Shotton, Co Flint; s of Sir Geoffrey Summers, 1 Bt, CBE, JP, DL (d 1972); *b* 1 Oct 1918; *Educ* Shrewsbury; *m* 1945, Anna Marie Louise, da of late Gustave Demaegd of Brussels; 1 da; *Heir* none; *Career* serv 8 Army (Middle E, N Africa, France and Belgium) 1937-45; *Style—* Felix Summers, Esq; Warren House, 16 Warren Lane, Friston, Eastbourne, Sussex

SUMMERS, Dr Maxwell Hamilton; DSO (1946), OBE (1962), TD (1941) and 3 bars; s of Gilbert Hamilton Summers (d 1955), and Fanny Joyce, *née* New (d 1941); *b* 12 Sept 1899; *Educ* St Paul's, Middx Hosp, London Univ (MRCS, LRCP); *m* 1927, Evelyne Elizabeth, da of Rev William Baird (d 1936); 2 s (William, Alastair), 1 da (Elizabeth); *Career* 2 Lt Middx Regt (TA) 1922, transfered RAMC (TA) 1923, Col 1950; med practitioner; house surgn Middx Hosp 1923, hon anaesthetist King Edward VII Hosp Windsor 1928-48; area conslt smallpox 1958-85; lectr on Indust First Aid for Order of St John and BRCS, pres Burnham Bucks branch RBL; DL: Middx 1948-65, Gtr London 1965-76; OStJ 1978; *Recreations* bridge, territorials; *Clubs* RSM; *Style—* Dr Maxwell Summers, DSO, OBE, TD; 58 Bulstrode Court, Gerrards Cross, Bucks SL9 7RU (☎ 0753 889963)

SUMMERS, (Robert) Michael; s of Leslie Summers, and Sophie Summers; *b* 4 May 1940; *Educ* Haberdashers' Aske's Hampstead Sch; *m* Cilla; 1 s (Raphael b 1979), 3 da (Gaye b 1966, Dawn b 1969, Coral b 1984); *Career* fin dir London City & Westcliff Properties Ltd 1966-77; md: The Sterling Publishing Gp plc 1978-, Debrett's Peerage Ltd 1988-; FCA; *Recreations* family, music, literature, scrabble; *Clubs* Old Haberdashers' Assoc; *Style—* Michael Summers, Esq; 6 Woodtree Close, Hendon, London NW4 1HQ (☎ 01 203 3351); The Sterling Publishing Gp plc, Garfield House, 86/88 Edgware Road, London W2 2YW (☎ 01 258 0066, fax 01 723 5766)

SUMMERS, Nicholas; s of Henry Forbes Summers, CB, of Tunbridge Wells, and Rosemary, *née* Roberts; *b* 11 July 1939; *Educ* Tonbridge, Corpus Christi Coll Oxford (BA, MA); *m* 3 April 1965, Marian Elizabeth (Mandy), da of Stanley George Ottley, of Fairlight; 4 s (Timothy b 1966, William b 1968, Michael b 1973, Stephen b 1977); *Career* Civil Serv; Dept of Educn and Sci (formerly Miny of Educn): asst princ 1961-66, princ 1966-74, asst sec 1976-81, under sec 1981-; asst sec Cabinet Off 1975-76 (princ 1974-75); *Recreations* music; *Style—* Nicholas Summers, Esq; Dept of Education and Science, Elizabeth House, York Rd, London SE1 7PH (☎ 01 934 9928)

SUMMERS, William Hamilton; MVO (1974); s of Dr Maxwell Hamilton Summers, DSO, OBE, and Evelyne Elizabeth Baird, MA, MB, ChB, Ed; *b* 4 Oct 1930; *Educ* King's Sch Bruton Somerset; *m* 1959, Rosemarie Jean, da of Thomas Norman Hutchison (d 1982), of Chile; 1 s (John b 1964), 2 da (Alison Jane b 1961, Catherine b 1969); *Career* jeweller, fell the Gemologists Assoc, dir Garrard and Co 1972; FGA; *Recreations* walking, reading; *Style—* William Summers, Esq, MVO; National Westminster Bank, 1 New Bond St, London W1Y 0HU; Garrard & Co Ltd, 112 Regent St, London W1 2JJ (☎ 01 734 7020, fax 01-439 9197, telex 8952365 REGENT G)

SUMMERSCALE, (Jack) John Nelson; s of Sir John Percival Sumerscale, KBE (d 1980), and Nelle Blossom, *née* Stogsdall (d 1977); *b* 27 July 1944; *Educ* Bryanston Sch, Pembroke Coll Cambridge (BA); *m* 1, 15 March 1969, Cordelia Isobel, da of Sir Alexander Lees Mayall, KCVO, GCMG, of Sturford Mead, Walminster, Wilts; 2 s (Aaron b 26 Aug 1969, Gideon b 24 Dec 1970); m 2, 25 July 1981, Lynda Susan, da of Eric Stewart, of 36 Allbrook House, Roehampton, London; *Career* AC, Coopers & Lybrand 1965-69, Market Investigations Ltd 1969-70, ptnr deZoete & Bevan 1970-86, dir Barclays deZoete Wedd Securities 1986-; tres Fulham Parents and Children; FCA 1968; *Style—* Jack Summerscale, Esq; 23 Chelverton Rd, London SW15; Barclays De Zoete Wedd, Ebbgate House, 2 Swan Lane, London EC4 (☎ 01 623 2323, fax 01 626 1753)

SUMMERSKILL, Hon Michael Brynmor; s of Baroness Summerskill, CH, PC, MRCS, LRCP (Life Peeress, d 1980), and Dr Edward Jeffrey Samuel, MB, BS (d 1983); *b* 28 Nov 1927; *Educ* St Paul's, Merton Coll Oxford (BCL, MA); *m* June 1951, Florence Marion Johnston, da of Sydney Robert Elliott, of Glasgow; 1 s (Ben b 1961), 2 da (Anna b 1959, Clare (twin) b 1961); m 2, 1972, Audrey Alexandra Brontë Blemings; m 3, 1983, Maryly Blew LaFollette, da of Erle Blew; *Career* barr Middle Temple 1952; former dir Thomas Miller & Co and ptnr Thos R Miller & Son, former pres London Maritime Arbitrators' Assoc 1983-85; FCIArb, ACII; *Books* Penguin Dictionary of Politics (with Florence Elliott), Laytime; Oil Rigs; China on the Western Front; *Clubs* Chelsea Arts, Colony Room, Reform; *Style—* The Hon Michael Summerskill; 4 Millfield Lane, London N6 (☎ 01 341 7531)

SUMMERSKILL, Dr the Hon Shirley Catherine Wynne; da of Baroness Summerskill, CH, PC (Life Peeress, d 1980), and Dr Edward Jeffrey Samuel, MB, BS (d 1983); *b* 9 Sept 1931; *Educ* St Paul's Girls' Sch, Somerville Coll Oxford, St Thomas' Hosp; *m* 1957 (m dis 1971), John Ryman, barr; *Career* MP (L) Halifax 1964-83, parly under-sec of state Home Off 1974-79, oppn spokesman on: Home Affairs 1979-83, Health 1970-74; UK del UN Status of Women Cmmn 1968 & 1969, memb Br Delgn Cncl Europe & WEU 1968 & 1969; chm PLP Health Gp 1969-70 (vice-chm 1964-69), memb Lab Orgn Ctee 1982-83; Dr 1960- (MA, BM, BCh, resident house surgn, subsequently house physician St Helier Hosp Carshalton 1959); fought Blackpool N (by-election) 1962; med offr Nat Blood Transfusion Serv; *Style—* Dr The Hon Shirley Summerskill, MP; House of Commons, SW1

SUMMERSON, Sir John Newenham; CH (1987), CBE (1952); s of Samuel James Summerson (d 1907) of Darlington; *b* 25 Nov 1904; *Educ* Harrow, UCL; *m* 1938, Elizabeth Alison, da of late Herbert Raikes Hepworth, CBE, of Leeds; 3 s; *Career* dep dir Nat Bldgs Record 1941-45, curator Sir John Soane's Museum 1945-84, Slade prof of fine art: Oxford 1958-59, Cambridge 1966-67; lectr history of architecture Birkbeck Coll London 1950-67, chm Nat Cncl for Diplomas in Art and Design 1961-70, tstee Nat Portrait Gallery 1966-73; FBA, FSA, ARIBA; kt 1958; *Clubs* Athenaeum; *Style—* Sir John Summerson, CH, CBE; 1 Eton Villas, London NW3 (☎ 01 722 6247)

SUMNER, His Hon Judge Christopher John; s of His Hon William Donald Massey Sumner, OBE, QC, of High Halden, Kent, and Muriel Kathleen, *née* Wilson; *b* 28 August 1939; *Educ* Charterhouse, Sidney Sussex Coll Cambridge (MA); *m* 24 Sept 1970, Carole Ashley, da of John Ashley Mann (d 1985); 1 s (William Mark b 30 Nov

1978), 2 da (Claire Louise b 6 Sept 1972, Emma Jane b 29 Oct 1974); *Career* called to the Bar Inner Temple 1961, asst rec 1983, rec 1986, circuit judge 1987; *Recreations* reading, theatre, sport; *Clubs* Hurlingham; *Style—* His Hon Judge Christopher Sumner

SUMNER, Christopher Kent; s of George Tomlinson Sumner (d 1979), and Mary Bettley, *née* Brown; *b* 28 Sept 1943; *Educ* The King's Sch, Chester Univ of Durham (BA, MA); *m* 2 Aug 1967, Marjorie, da of George Prince, of 12B Derwent Court, Troutbeck Rd, Liverpool 18; 2 s (Stuart b 1970, Edward b 1974); *Career* slr; chm Social Security Appeal Tbnls 1984-; Parly candidate (Lib) Runcorn 1970; *Recreations* squash, scouting; *Style—* Christopher K Sumner, Esq; 4 Mossgiel Ave, Ainsdale, Southport (☎ 0704 73153); Christopher Sumner & Co, 15 Hoghton St, Southport (☎ 0704 47247)

SUMNER-FERGUSSON, William Howard David; s of William Graham Sumner-Fergusson (d 1945), and Catharine Mary, *née* Sumner (d 1984); *b* 11 Mar 1946; *Educ* Elston Hall Newark, Oratory Sch Reading; *m* 1979, Lucienne Gay Elizabeth, da of William Hilder (d 1986), of Valentines, Hurstbourne, Tarrant, and of Chiswick; 1 s (William Rupert Giles b 1982), 1 da (Rebecca b 1980); *Career* dir: Everards Brewery Ltd, John Sarson Ltd, John Sarson Wines Ltd, Anglesey Rd Devpt Ltd 1974-85, Quality Hire, Quality Fare 1987, Salmon Charles (London & Home Counties) Ltd 1986-87, dir Gibbs Mew plc Salisbury Wilts; *Recreations* gardening, shooting, bridge; *Style—* Howard Sumner-Fergusson, Esq; Tinwell House, Tinwell, Stamford, Lincolnshire PE9 3UD (☎ 0780 51222)

SUMPTION, Jonathan Philip Chadwick; QC (1986); s of Anthony James Sumption, DSC, and Hedy, *née* Hedigan; *b* 9 Dec 1948; *Educ* Eton, Magdalen Coll Oxford (MA); *m* 26 June 1971, Teresa Mary, da of Jerome Bernard Whelan; 1 s (Bernard b 1981), 2 da (Frederique b 1979, Madeleine b 1983); *Career* fell Magdalen Coll Oxford 1971-75, barr Middle Temple 1975; *Books* Pilgrimage An Image of Medieval Religion (1975), The Albigensian Crusade (1978); *Recreations* music, history; *Style—* Jonathan Sumption, Esq, QC; 34 Crooms Hill, London SE14 (☎ 858 4444); 1 Brick Court, Temple, London EC4 (☎ 01 583 0777, fax 01 583 9401 (Group 3), telex 892687 IBRICK G)

SUMSION, John Walbridge; s of Dr Herbert Sumsion, CBE; *b* 16 August 1928; *Educ* Rendcomb Coll, Clare Coll Cambridge (BA), Yale Univ (MA), Cornell Univ; *m* 1, 1961 (m dis 1979), Annette Dorothea, *née* Wilson; 2 s (Christopher b 1965, Michael b 1968), 2 da (Bridget b 1963, Kate b 1970); m 2, 1979, Hazel Mary, *née* English; *Career* dir K Shoemakers Ltd 1962-81, registrar of Public Lending Right 1981-; *Recreations* music (singing, flute), tennis; *Clubs* Utd Oxford and Cambridge; *Style—* John Sumsion, Esq; Appleton Wiske, Northallerton, N Yorks (☎ 060 981 408); office: Bayheath House, Prince Regent St, Stockton-on-Tees, Cleveland

SUNDERLAND, Prof Eric; s of Leonard Sunderland, of Ammanford Dyfed, and Mary Agnes, *née* Davies; *b* 18 Mar 1930; *Educ* Amman Valley GS, Univ Coll Wales Aberystwyth (BA, MA), UCL (PhD); *m* 19 Oct 1957, (Jean) Patricia, da of George Albert Watson (d 1972), of Cardiff; 2 da (Rowena, Frances); *Career* res asst NCB 1957-58; Univ of Durham: lectr in anthropology 1958-66, sr lectr 1966-71, prof 1971-84, pro vice-chllr 1979-84; princ Univ Coll of N Wales Bangor 1984-; patron Schizophrenia Assoc GB 1985-, hon memb Gorsedd of Bards Rhyl Eisteddfod, dir Gregynog Press 1986, chm Welsh Language Educn Devpt Ctee 1987, memb Welsh Language Bd 1988, vice-pres Gwynedd branch Gt Ormond St Hosp Appeal 1988; FIBiol 1975, RAI (hon tres 1985-89, pres designate 1989-91), SSHB, Biosocial Soc, Int Union of Anthropological and Ethnological Scis 1978; Hrdlicka Medal for Anthropological Res 1976, hon fell Croatian Anthropological Soc Gorjanovic-Krambergeri Medal; *Books* Genetic Variation in Britain (1973), The Operation of Intelligence: Biological Preconditions for Operation of Intelligence (1980), Genetic and Population Studies in Wales (1986); *Recreations* book collecting, watercolours, gardening, music, travelling; *Clubs* Athenaeum; *Style—* Prof Eric Sunderland; Bryn, Ffriddoedd Rd, Bangor, Gwynedd LL57 2EH; Principal's Office, Univ College of North Wales, Bangor, Gwynedd LL57 2DG (☎ 0248 351 151 ext 2000, fax 0258 361 429, telex 61100 UCNWSL G)

SUNDERLAND, Eric Edgar; JP (1978); s of Edgar Sunderland (d 1928), and Ida Evelyn (d 1985); *b* 16 Nov 1927; *Educ* Queen Elizabeth GS Horncastle, Bradford Inst Technol; *m* 1958, Irene Mary, *née* Beecroft; *Career* gp md Hamfray & Co Textile Divn 1972-76, md Henry Mason Ltd 1976-80, gp md E & T Wall Ltd 1980-, chm and chief exec Contessa Cars & Electro-Acoustic Devpts Ltd 1976-, vice-chm Bradford Hosp Fund 1974-, dir Nottingham Wine Buying Gp 1983-; chm Bradford S Constituency Cons Assoc 1988, fell Inst of Plant Engrs; *Recreations* music, cars, chess, railway preservation; *Clubs* Cons (Bradford); *Style—* Eric Sunderland, Esq, JP; Sundial House, 5 Manscombe Rd, Allerton, Bradford, West Yorks BD15 7AQ (☎ 0274 546 568, office 0535 602738)

SUNDERLAND, (Arthur) John; s of His Honour Judge George Frederick Irvon Sunderland (d 1984), and Mary Katherine, *née* Bowen (d 1983); *b* 24 Feb 1932; *Educ* Marlborough, London Coll of Printing; *m* 6 Sept 1958, Audrey Ann, da of George Henry Thompson (d 1980); 3 s (Andrew John, Timothy James, Richard Mark); *Career* Nat Serv 2 Lt RE 1953-55; dir: James Upton Ltd 1963-69, Surrey Fine Art Press Ltd 1963-69, Sunderland Print Ltd 1969-84, Alday Green & Welburn Ltd 1978-84, Randall Bross Ltd 1970-84, Foxplan Ltd 1984-87, Rapidflow Ltd 1985-; chm Ladypool Rd Neighbourhood Centre Birmingham 1970-76, govr W House Sch Birmingham 1973-; St John Ambulance Bde W Midlands: dep co cmmr 1976-78, co cmmr/cdr 1978-86, cmmr-in-chief 1986-; KStJ (1986, OStJ 1978, CStJ 1982); memb Field Survey Assoc 1955-; *Recreations* walking, sport; *Clubs* Army and Navy; *Style—* John Sunderland, Esq; Cherry Hill House, Cherry Hill Rd, Barnt Gn, Birmingham B45 8LJ (☎ 021 445 1232)

SUNDERLAND, John Michael; s of Harry Sunderland, and Joyce Eileen, *née* Farnish; *b* 24 August 1945; *Educ* King Edward VII Lytham, St Andrews (MA); *m* Sept 1965, Jean Margaret, da of Col Alexander Grieve (d 1975); 3 s (Jonothan b 1969, Robin b 1972, Ben Alexander b 1978), 1 da (Corianne b 1966); *Career* commercial dir Coca-Cola and Schweppes Beverages Ltd; *Style—* John Sunderland, Esq; Woodlands, Penn St, Bucks (☎ 0494 713235); Charter Place, Uxbridge, Middlesex (☎ 0895 31313)

SUNDERLAND, Prof Sir Sydney; CMG (1961); s of Harry Sunderland (d 1964), and Anne, *née* Smith (d 1967); *b* 31 Dec 1910; *Educ* Brisbane H S, Scotch Coll, Melbourne Univ (BM, BS, DSc, DMed); *m* 1939, Nina Gwendoline, da of Arthur Harry Johnston (d 1980); 1 s; *Career* dean faculty of med Melbourne Univ 1953-71; memb Def Res and Devpt Policy Ctee 1957-75, prof of experimental neurology Melbourne Univ 1961-75 (emeritus prof 1976), memb Bd Walter & Eliza Hall Inst of Med Res 1968-75; hon memb: American Neurological Assoc, Neurosurgical Soc of Australiasia, vice-pres Int Soc for the Study of Pain 1975-78; kt 1971; *see Debrett's Handbook of Australia and New Zealand for further details*; *Style—* Prof Sir Sydney Sunderland, CMG; 72 Kingstoun, 461 St Kilda Rd, Melbourne, Vic 3004, Australia (☎ 266 5858)

SUNDIUS-HILL, Lady Helen (Maglona); *née* Vane-Tempest-Stewart; da of 7 Marquess of Londonderry, KG, MVO, TD, PC (d 1949); *b* 1911; *m* 1, 1935 (m dis 1960), 2 Baron Jessel; m 2, 1960, Dennis Cecil Whittington Walsh, s of late Sir Cecil Henry Walsh, KC; m 3, 1978, Nigel Sundius-Hill; *Style—* Lady Helen Sundius-Hill; 25 Redington Gdns, Hampstead, NW3

SUNNUCKS, James Horrace George; s of Stanley Lloyd Sunnucks (d 1953), and Edith Vera Constance, *née* Sendell (d 1979); *b* 20 Sept 1925; *Educ* Wellington, Trinity Hall Cambridge (MA); *m* 1 Oct 1955, Rosemary Ann (Tessa), da of Col J W Borradaile (d 1946); 4 s (William b 2 Aug 1956, John b 4 March 1959, David b 4 April 1961, Andrew b 3 May 1965); *Career* RNVR 1943-46; barr Lincoln's Inn 1950, bencher 1980, memb senate of the Inn's of Ct and the Bar, pres Inst of Conveyancers 1988-89 (memb 1974-); licensed reader diocese of Chelmsford 1954, memb Parole Review Ctee Chelmsford Prison (later chm) 1970-82; asst parly boundary cmmnr (Wandsworth, Camden, Wilts) 1975-85; Freeman: City of London 1986, Worshipful Co of Gardeners 1986; *Books* Williams and Mortimer on Executors (ed), Halsbury's Laws of England (ed); *Recreations* gardening, local history, sailing; *Clubs* United Oxford and Cambridge, Norfolk; *Style—* James Sunnucks, Esq; East Mersea Hall, Colchester, Essex CO5 8TJ (☎ 0206 383 215); 5 Hale Ct, Lincoln's Inn, London WC2 (☎ 01 242 4764); 5 New Sq, Lincoln's Inn WC2A 3RJ (☎ 01 404 0404, fax 01 831 6016); Octagon House, Colegate, Norwich

SURATGAR, Prof David; s of Prof Lotfali Suratgar (d 1969), of Tehran, and Prof Edith Olive, *née* Hepburn; *b* 23 Oct 1938; *Educ* Silcoates Sch Yorks, New Coll Oxford (BA, MA), Columbia Univ NY (MIA); *m* 6 Aug 1962, Barbara Lita, da of Donald Telfer Low, of Wytham Abbey, Wytham, Oxford; 1 s (Karim Donald Hepburn b 4 Aug 1966), 1 da (Roxanne Christina Noelle b 25 Dec 1964); *Career* legal dept UN Secretariat 1961-62, Sullivan & Cromwell (lawyers) NYC 1963-64, legal counsel World Bank 1964-73, adjunct prof of law, Georgetown Univ 1966-73, dir Morgan Grenfell & Co Ltd 1973-88 (gp dir 1988-), legal counsel Bank of England and Nat Water Cncl 1976, legal conslt Miny of Mines Argentina 1985-86, conslt Jones Day Reavis & Pogue (international lawyers) 1988-; dir: Societe Internationale Financiere Pour Investissements et le Developpement en Anfrique 1981, Oxford Playhouse Tst 1989, Northern Ballet Theatre 1981-83; chm West India Ctee (Royal Charter) 1987-89; memb: bd Major Projects Assoc Templeton Coll Oxford, Oxford Univ bd of mgmnt Oxford Playhouse, Bodleian Library Appeal 1987-; sr res fell Int Law Inst Washington DC; memb: Gray's Inn, Int Bar Assoc, Br Inst of nt and Comparative Law; *Books* Default and Rescheduling - Sovereign and Corporate Borrowers in Difficulty (1984), International Financial Law (jlty, 1980); *Recreations* shooting, book collecting, theatre, travelling; *Clubs* Travellers; Chelsea Arts; *Style—* David Suratgar, Esq; 265 Woodstock Road, Oxford OX2 7AE; Morgen Grenfell & Co Ltd, 23 Gt Winchester St, London EC2P 2AX (☎ 01 588 4545, fax 01 826 6155, telex 893511)

SURRELL, Hon Mrs (Maureen Dawn); *née* Vernon; da of 5 Baron Lyveden (d 1973); *b* 1926; *m* 1946, Noel Surrell; 1 s; *Style—* The Hon Mrs Surrell; 17 Duncan St, Taupo, NZ

SURRIDGE, Sir (Ernest) Rex Edward; CMG (1946); s of E E Surridge (d 1945), of Coggeshall, Essex; *b* 1899; *Educ* Felsted, St John's Coll Oxford; *m* 1926, Roy, da of Maj F E Bradstock, DSO, MC (d 1982) of Tanganyika; 2 s; *Career* 7 Bn DCLI WWI, entered Colonial Admin Serv Tanganyika 1924, dep chief sec Kenya 1940-46, chief sec Tanganyika 1946-52, ret 1952; kt 1951; *Style—* Sir Rex Surridge; 10 Park Manor, St Aldhelm's Rd, Branksome Park, Poole, Dorset

SURTEES, Maj John Freville Henry; OBE (1975), MC (1940); s of Maj Robert Lambton Surtees,OBE, JP (d 1968), of Littlestone-on-Sea Kent, and Anne Olive Marguerite, *née* Beck (d 1944); *b* 26 Jan 1919; *Educ* Eton, RMC Sandhurst; *m* 1, 1946 (m dis 1967) Audrey, da of Maj Basil Baillie Falkner (d 1964); 2 da (Anna, Christian); m 2, 1969 (m dis 1985) Anne, da of Sir Edward Denham, GCVO, KBE (d 1938); *Career* 2 Lt 1 Bn The Rifle Bde 1939, (POW wounded) Calais 1940-45, 2 Bn Rifle Bde 1945-46, GSO 2 Allied Liaison Branch BAOR 1946-47, ret 1948 md: Percy Fox & Co (Wine Importers) 1962 (chm 1970-73); Garvey (London) Ltd 1973-84 govr Oundle Sch, memb Inst of Masters of Wine 1956;Master Worshipful Co Grocers 1966-67; *Recreations* fishing, racing, music; *Clubs* Boodle's, Green Jackets, White's; *Style—* Maj John Surtees, OBE, MC; Down Ho, Wylye, Warminster, Wilt

SURTEES, Richard Vere Norman; s of Maj Vere Nathaniel Faber Surtees, of The Old Farm House, Hopesay, Craven Arms, Shropshire, and Mary Petronella, *née* Comper (d 1957); *b* 9 April 1924; *Educ* Shrewsbury, Pembroke Coll Cambridge (BA); *m* 8 Dec 1951 Elizabeth Vivienne, da of Capt F C Ainley, MBE (ka 1938 The Green Howards); 2 s (Nicholas Vere b 28 June 1953, Jonathan Michael b 9 Feb 1957), 1 da (Frances Mary b 28 Feb 1956, d 19 March 1956); *Career* serv WWII Lt Grenadier Gds, cmmnd 1943, (wounded 1945), serv NW Germany 1 Bn (Gds Armd Div), asst sec Burt Boulton & Haywood Ltd 1952-61, staff and off mangr Antony Gibbs & Sons Ltd (merchant bankers) 1961-69, Nat Farmers Union (Agric House, Knightsbridge) 1969-84, exec Fed of Agric Co Ops (UK) Ltd (UK Euro rep body) sec Br Agric Cncl, sec Nat Fedn of Pest Control Socs Ltd, sec Fedn of Syndicate Credit Soc, ret 1984; vice-chm Plunkett Fndn for Co-op Studies in Oxford 1984-, sec Land Tsts Assoc; Hon BA (Law) Cambridge; *Recreations* gardening, collecting things, music, travel; *Clubs* Brooks's, Farmer's; *Style—* Richard Surtees, Esq; Grove End, Byfleet Rd, Cobham, Surrey KT11 1DS (☎ 0932 62575)

SURTEES, Col William Francis; OBE (1963), TD (1960), DL (1970); *b* 12 Sept 1920; *Educ* Ashville Coll Harrogate; *m* 1945, Gwendoline, *née* Plews; 1 s, 1 da; *Career* branch mangr Barclays Bank Ltd, ret 1978; CStJ 1983; *Recreations* fishing, fell walking; *Style—* Col William Surtees, OBE, TD, DL; Heth House, Gallowlaw, Wooler, Northumberland NE71 6ST (☎ 0668 81219)

SUSCHITZKY, (John) Peter; s of Wolfgang Suschitzky, and Ilona, *née* Donath; *b* 6 April 1940; *Educ* Mountgrace Sch, Inst des Hautes Etudes Cinématographiques, Paris; *m* June 1964 (m dis 1982), Johanna Roeber; 1 s (Adam b 1972), 2 da (Anya b 1969, Rebecca b 1974); *Career* dir of photography films incl: Charlie Bubbles 1966, Leo The Last 1967, The Rocky Horror Picture Show 1974, The Empire Strikes Back 1978, Falling in Love 1984, Dead Ringers 1988; Br Soc of Cinematographers, Dirs Guild of

America; *Recreations* music, playing the transverse flute, history, cooking; *Style—* Peter Suschitzky, Esq; 13 Priory Rd, London NW6 4NN (☎ 01 624 3734)

SUSMAN, Peter Joseph; s of Albert Leonard Susman, of London, and Sybil Rebecca, *née* Joseph; *b* 20 Feb 1943; *Educ* Dulwich, Lincoln Coll Oxford (MA), Law Sch Univ of Chicago (JD); *m* 5 June 1966, Peggy Judith, da of Harvey Stone, of New Jersey, USA; 1 s (Daniel b 13 Feb 1979), 1 da (Deborah b 16 Nov 1976); *Career* barr 1967-70, 1972-; assoc New York City Law Firm 1970-72; *Style—* Peter Susman, Esq; New Court, Temple, London EC4Y 9BE (☎ 01 583 6166, fax 01 583 2827)

SUTCH, Andrew Lang; s of Rev Canon Christopher Lang Sutch, of 18 Linden Rd, Bristol, and Gladys Ethelwyn, *née* Larrington; *b* 10 July 1952; *Educ* Haileybury Coll, Oriel Coll Oxford (MA); *m* 22 May 1982, Shirley Anne, da of Gordon Alger Teichmann, of 47 Lexden Rd, Colchester; 2 s (James b 12 Dec 1983, Francis b 24 Aug 1986); *Career* Lt Intelligence Corps TA 1976-86; admitted slr 1979, ptnr Stephenson Harwood 1984- (employed 1977-); memb Law Soc 1979; *Recreations* theatre, running; *Style—* Andrew Sutch, Esq; Stephenson Harwood, One, St Paul's Churchyard, London EC4M 8SH (☎ 01 329 4422, fax 01 606 0822)

SUTCLIFF, Cdr (Archibald) Edward; OBE (1958), DSC (1944); s of Capt Archibald Alfred Sutcliff, RAMC (d 1915), and Mary Natalie Vaughan (d 1967); *b* 12 June 1911; *Educ* RNC Dartmouth; *m* 11 Aug 1944, Dinah Sarah Joanna, da of Lawrence Metelerkamp (d 1961), of Johannesburg; 1 s (Edward b 1946), 1 da (Sarah b 1949); *Career* regular RN offr 1928-58, navigation specialist; serv WWII continuously at sea: Atlantic, Arctic, Antarctic, Indian & Pacific Oceans; ret cmdr RN 1958; mangr (then gen mangr) Middle E Navigation Aids Serv; *Recreations* fly fishing, birdwatching, hill walking, listening to music; *Clubs* Naval & Military; *Style—* Cdr Edward Sutcliff, OBE, DSC; Creach, Aros, Isle of Mull, Argyll PA72 6JZ (☎ 068 85 242)

SUTCLIFFE, (Charles Wilfred) David; s of Max Sutcliffe (d 1976), of Shipley, W Yorks, and Mary Doreen Sutcliffe (d 1977); *b* 21 June 1936; *Educ* Uppingham, Leeds Univ (BA); *m* 6 May 1960, Hanne, da of Carl Olaf Carlsen (d 1967), of Copenhagen, Denmark; 2 s (Charles Peter David b 1961, John Mark Benson b 1963); *Career* Lt 4 Royal Tank Regt; chm and jt md Benson Turner Ltd 1978- (jt md from 1968), chm Benson Turner (Dyers) Ltd 1976-78; dir: Bradford Microfirms Ltd 1981-88, Enterflow Ltd 1983-; pres Bradford C of C 1983-85, memb High Steward's ctee York Minster 1980- (tstee York Minster 1987-), fndr and chm Bradford Enterprise Agency 1983-89, pres Bradford Textile Soc 1987-88; memb Co Merchants of the Staple of Englandd 1979, Freeman City of London, Liveryman Guild of Framework Knitters 1983; hon fell Bradford & likely community Coll 1985; C Text, FTI; *Recreations* golf, shooting, sailing; *Clubs* Brooks's, (Bradford); *Style—* David Sutcliffe, Esq; Ivy House Farm, Kettlesing, nr Harrogate, N Yorks HG3 2LR (☎ 0423 770561); 133 New Kings Road, London SW6 4SL (☎ 01 731 8417); Benson Turner Ltd, Station Mills, Wyke, Bradford, West Yorkshire BD12 8LA (☎ 0274 601122, fax 0274 691170, telex 517683 BENTUR G)

SUTCLIFFE, Hon Mrs; Helen; *née* Rhodes; da of Baron Rhodes, KG, DFC*, PC, DL; *b* 15 August 1929; *m* 1954, John, JP, s of Herbert Sutcliffe, of Colwyn Bay; 2 s, 1 da; *Style—* The Hon Mrs Sutcliffe; Lower Carr, Diggle, Dobcross, Oldham, Lancs

SUTCLIFFE, Ian Sharp; s of Harold Nelson Sutcliffe (d 1962), of Houghton Hall, Houghton, Carlisle, and Isabella Fox, *née* Jerdan; *b* 30 Jan 1931; *Educ* Marlborough, Emmanuel Coll Cambridge (MA, LLB); *m* 10 June 1960, Anne Lyon, da of Robert Lyon Wyllie, CBE, JP, DL, of Cockermouth, Cumbria; 3 s (Andrew Robert Nelson b 6 May 1962, (Ian) Jonathan Wyllie b 11 Feb 1967, Nicholas Richard b 27 Nov 1968); *Career* 2 Lt RASC (water tport div) 1950-51, RARO 1952-60; admitted slr 1958; notary public 1958, ptnr Mounseys (formerly Mounsey Bowman & Sutcliffe) 1960, sr ptnr 1964-; dir: Sekers Inc Ltd 1963-, Metrorural Ltd 1987-, registrar and legal sec to Bishopric of Carlisle 1963-, clerk to Dean and Chapter of Carlisle Cathedral 1963-; Cambridge hockey blue 1954-55; Cumbria Squash 1955-60, Northumberland Hockey 1955-64; memb: Law Soc, Soc of Notaries Public; *Recreations* golf, tennis; *Clubs* County and Border (Carlisle); *Style—* Ian S Sutcliffe, Esq; Mulcaster House, Stanwix, Carlisle, Cumbria (☎ 0228 26314); 19 Castle St, Carlisle, Cumbria (☎ 0228 25195)

SUTCLIFFE, Col Patrick Malcolm Brogden; CBE (1983, MBE 1966), TD, DL (Hants 1973); s of William Francis Sutcliffe, MRCS, LRCP (d 1959) and Edna Mary, *née* Brogden (d 1978); *b* 21 Oct 1922; *Educ* Marlborough Coll, Pembroke Coll Cambridge (MA); *m* 1950, Dorothy Anne Daly, da of Arnold Daly Briscoe, TD, MB, BChir, of Woodbridge, Suffolk; 2 s, 1 da; *Career* Berks Yeo 1942-60, Berks & Westminster Dragoons 1961-67, Lt-Col Royal Berks Territorials 1967-69, Col TA & VR E and S E District 1969-74, vice-chm (Hants) Eastern Wessex TA & VRA 1974, chm 1975-84, vice-chm cncl 1981-84; ADC to HM The Queen 1970; conslt Smiths Gore, Chartered Surveyors; FRICS; *Clubs* Army and Navy; *Style—* Col Patrick Sutcliffe, CBE, TD, DL; Burntwood Farm, Winchester, Hants (☎ 0962 882384)

SUTCLIFFE, Hon Mrs; Hon (Dora) Valerie Patricia; *née* Canning; elder da of 4 Baron Garvagh (d 1956); *b* 31 Oct 1919; *m* 1, 13 Jan 1942, Philip Anthony Wellesley Colley, Lt RA (ka 1944); 2 da; m 2, 28 Aug 1950, Peter Stocks Sutcliffe, o s of Ernest Sutcliffe, of Stewton House, Louth, Lincs; 1 s; *Style—* The Hon Mrs Sutcliffe; c/o Mrs D C Anderson, 14 Lauriston Rd, Wimbledon, London SW19

SUTHERLAND, Clare, Duchess of; Clare Josephine; 2 da of late Herbert O'Brien, of Calcutta; *m* 1, 1922 (m dis), Alexander Blake Shakespear, CIE (d 1949), of Cawnpore, India; m 2 (m dis), Col Vincent Blundell Dunkerly (decd); m 3, 1944, as his 2 w, 5 Duke of Sutherland, KT, PC (d 1963); *Style—* Her Grace Clare, Duchess of Sutherland; 14 Hyde Park Gdns, W2 (☎ 01 262 3305); ES Carregedur, Capdedera, Mallorca, Spain

SUTHERLAND, David George Carr; CBE (1974), MC (1942, and bar 1943), TD, DL (Tweeddale 1974); s of Lt-Col Arthur Henry Carr Sutherland, OBE, MC (d 1962), of Cringletie, Peebles, Scotland, and Ruby, *née* Miller (d 1982); *b* 28 Oct 1920; *Educ* Eton, Sandhurst RMA; *m* 1, Sept 1945, Jean Beatrice (d 1963), s of Evelyn Henderson, of Sedgwick Park, Nr Horsham, Sussex; 1 s (Michael b 1946), 2 da (Sarah (Twin) b 1946, Fiona b 1953); m2, May 1964, Christine; *Career* serv WWII Black Watch and SAS: Dunkirk, W Desert, Aegean, Adriatic (wounded, despatches); various cmd and staff appts 1945-55 incl: Br Mil Mission to Greece, instr Sandhurst, Gold Staff Offr at HM The Queen's Coronation; ret 1955, Cmdr 21 SAS Regt (Artists Rifles) TA 1956-60; MOD 1955-80, landowner and farmer 1962-, non-exec dir Asset Protection Int Ltd 1981-85, conslt Control Risks Gp Ltd 1985-; memb Queen's Bodyguard for Scotland Royal Co of Archers 1949-; FRGS; Greek War Cross 1945 and 1946; *Recreations* fishing, shooting, walking; *Clubs* Brook's, Special Forces; *Style—* David Sutherland, Esq, CBE, MC, TD, DL; 51 Victoria Rd, London W8; Ferniehaugh, Dolphinton, Tweeddale

SUTHERLAND, Countess of (24 in line, S circa 1235); Elizabeth Millicent Sutherland Janson; also Lady Strathnaver (strictly speaking a territorial style, but treated as a Lordship for purposes of use as courtesy title for heir to Earldom since the end of the sixteenth century); adopted surname of Sutherland under Scots law 1963; Chief of the Clan Sutherland; o da of Lord Alastair St Clair Sutherland-Leveson-Gower, MC (d 1921, s of 4 Duke of Sutherland, KG, and Lady Millicent St Clair-Erskine, da of 4 Earl of Rosslyn), and Elizabeth Hélène, *née* Demarest (d 1931); suc to Earldom of Sutherland held by unc, 5 Duke of Sutherland, KT, PC, 1963 (thus came about precisely the contingency that might have caused objection to be made when the Dukedom was so named on its creation 130 years earlier in 1833, *viz* that because the latter was heritable in tail male while the Earldom not only could be held by a female but actually was (by the 1 Duke's wife) at the time of the cr, the two might become separated; the then Countess of Sutherland in her own right (gggg mother of present Countess) was known as the 'Duchess-Countess' in a style analogous to that of the Spanish Count-Duke Olivares of the seventeenth century; *b* 30 Mar 1921; *Educ* Queen's Coll Harley St, abroad; *m* 5 Jan 1946, Charles Noel Janson, DL, eldest s of late Charles Wilfrid Janson, of 16 Wilton Crescent, London SW1; 2 s (Alistair, Martin (twins)), 1 s (Matthew decd), 1 da (Annabel); *Heir* s, Lord Strathnaver; *Career* serv Land Army 1939-41; hosp lab technician Raigmore Hosp Inverness, St Thomas's Hosp London; chm: Northern Times 1963-88 (dir 1988-), Dunrobin Sch Ltd 1965-72, Dunrobin Castle Ltd 1972-; *Recreations* reading, swimming; *Style—* The Rt Hon the Countess of Sutherland; 39 Edwardes Sq, London W8 (☎ 01 603 0659); Dunrobin Castle, Golspie, Sutherland; House of Tongue, by Lairg, Sutherland

SUTHERLAND, Ian Douglas; s of Col Francis Ian Sinclair Sutherland, OBE, MC, ED (d 1962), of Moffat and Ceylon, and Helen Myrtle Sutherland (d 1988); *b* 23 Oct 1945; *Educ* St Bees Sch Cumberland; *m* 11 Oct 1975, Kathyrn, da of John Henry Wallace, of Haltwhistle, Northumberland; 1 s (Jonathan b 6 Nov 1976), 1 da (Iseabail b 13 July 1972); *Career* D M Hall & Son 1965-: trainee surveyor, ptnr 1975; memb Co of Merchants of the City of Edinburgh; FRICS 1980; *Clubs* New Edinburgh, Royal Scots Edinburgh; *Style—* Douglas Sutherland, Esq; 2 Ormidale Terr, Edinburgh EH12 6EQ (☎ 031 337 5584); D M Hall & Son, Chartered Surveyors, Gogar Park, 167 Glasgow Rd, Edinburgh EH12 9DJ (☎ 031 339 5345, fax 031 339 7280, car tel 0836 705 000, telex 727264)

SUTHERLAND, (Robert) James Mackay; s of James Fleming Sutherland (d 1932), of Knockbrex, Kirkcudbright, Scotland, and Edith Mary, *née* Meredith (d 1964); *b* 3 Nov 1922; *Educ* Stowe, Trinity Coll Cambridge (BA); *m* 7 June 1947, Anthea, da of John Christopher Hyland (d 1961), of Donegal, Ireland; 2 da (Chloe Helena Meredith b 15 Sept 1952, Sabina Rachel b 20 Nov 1954); *Career* RNVR 1943-46, Lt, demob 1946; asst civil engr: Sir William Halcrow & Ptnrs 1946-56, AJ Harris 1956-58; Harris & Sutherland: ptnr 1958-87, active conslt 1987-; memb Royal Fine Art Cmmn, pres Newcome Soc for the Study of Hist Sci and Technol 1987-89; various many ctees incl: Br Standards Inst, English Heritage; FEng, FICE, FIStructE (vice-pres 1980-82); *Recreations* engrg history, architectural travel; *Clubs* Travellers'; *Style—* James Sutherland, Esq; 4 Pitt St, London W8 4NX (☎ 01 937 7961); Harris & Sutherland, 82-83 Blackfriars Rd, London SE1

SUTHERLAND, Lady Jeanne Edith; *née* Nutt; da of Thomas Dixon Nutt, of Linden House, Gazeley, nr Newmarket, Suffolk; *b* 9 Dec 1927; *Educ* London Univ (MA); *m* 1955, Sir Iain Johnstone Macbeth Sutherland, KCMG (d 1986); 1 s, 2 da; *Career* formerly attaché Br Embasy Moscow, lectr Poly N London, chm Greek Animal Welfare Fund (GAWF-UK). ctee memb and tres UK Study Gp on Soviet Educn; *Recreations* travel, theatre, literature, tennis; *Style—* Lady Sutherland; 24 Cholmeley Park, Highgate, London N6 5EU

SUTHERLAND, Dame Joan; AC (1975), DBE (1979, CBE 1961); da of William Sutherland, of Sydney; *b* 7 Nov 1926; *Educ* St Catherine's Waverley; *m* 1954, Richard Bonynge; 1 s; *Career* opera singer; debut Sydney 1947, Royal Opera House Covent Garden 1952, performed in operas at: Glyndebourne, La Scala Milan, Vienna State Opera, Metropolitan Opera NY; has made numerous recordings; *Style—* Dame Joan Sutherland, AC, DBE; c/o Ingpen & Williams, 14 Kensington Court, London, W8 5DN

SUTHERLAND, 6 Duke of (UK 1833); Sir John Sutherland Egerton; 13 Bt (E 1620), TD, DL (Berwicks); also 5 Earl of Ellesmere (UK 1846), which known as 1944-63 (when he inherited the Dukedom); also Baron Gower (GB 1703), Earl Gower and Viscount Trentham (GB 1746), Marquess of Stafford (GB 1786), Viscount Brackley (UK 1846); s of 4 Earl of Ellesmere (d 1944), and Lady Violet Lambton, da of 4 Earl of Durham; *b* 10 May 1915; *Educ* Eton, Trinity Coll Cambridge; *m* 1, 1939, Lady Diana Percy (d 1978), da of 8 Duke of Northumberland; m 2, 1979, Evelyn, da of late Maj Robert Moubray (whose w Claire was gda of Sir Charles Morrison-Bell, 1 Bt); *Heir* Cyril Egerton, *qv*; *Career* late Capt RAC (TA), serv WWII (POW); *Style—* His Grace The Duke of Sutherland, TD DL; Mertoun, St Boswell's, Roxburghshire; Lingay Cottage, Hall Farm, Newmarket, Suffolk

SUTHERLAND, Margaret, Lady; Margaret; JP; da of Albert Owen (d 1965), of Chalfont St Giles Bucks, and Elsie Owen, *née* Wright (d 1964); *b* 3 June 1916; *Educ* Ilford GS Essex; *m* 1944, as his 2 w, Sir Ivan Sutherland, 2 Bt (d 1980), of Thurso House, Newcastle upon Tyne; 3 s (William, Owen, Ben); *Career* magistrate 1966, Northumberland CC 1961-74, cncllr Embleton Parish 1964-74; Alnwick dist cncllr 1960-74; pres: Northumberland Assoc of Local Cncls, Seahouses Lifeboat Guild, Seahouses Harbour Cmmrs; vice-pres Community Cncl of Northumberland, chm govrs Seahouses Middle Sch; *Recreations* handbell ringing, embroidery, yoga; *Style—* Margaret, Lady Sutherland, JP; The Smithy, Embleton, Alnwick, Northumberland (☎ 066 576 467)

SUTHERLAND, Sir Maurice; s of Thomas Daniel Sutherland (d 1953); *b* 12 July 1915; *Educ* Stockton Secdy Sch; *m* 1, 1941, Beatrice Skinner, 1 s; m 2, 1960, Jane Ellen; 1 step da; m 3, 1984, Ellen Margaret, 1 step s; *Career* slr; ldr Teesside County Boro Cncl 1968-74, mayor 1972-73, ldr Cleveland CC 1974-77 (ldr of oppn 1977-81, ldr 1981); kt 1976; *Style—* Sir Maurice Sutherland; 8 Manor Close, Low Worsall, Yarm, Cleveland; work: PO Box 100A, Municipal Buildings, Middlesbrough, Cleveland TS1 2QH (☎ 0642 248155)

SUTHERLAND, (David) Michael; s of Sir Benjamin Ivan Sutherland Bt, (d 1980), of Embleton, Alnwick, and Marjorie Constance Daniel Bousfield, *née* Brewer (d 1980); *b*

14 June 1940; *Educ* Sedbergh Sch, St Catharine's Coll Cambridge (MA); *m* 11 Aug 1966, Caroline Mary, da of Robert S Hogan (d 1944); 3 da (Julia Ruth b 1967, Serena Louise b 1971, Polly Anne b 1975); *Career* farmer; *Recreations* tennis, curling; *Style*— Michael Sutherland, Esq

SUTHERLAND, Sir (Frederick) Neil; CBE (1955); s of late Neil Hugh Sutherland; *b* 4 Mar 1900; *Educ* St Catherine's Coll Cambridge; *m* 1, 1931, Naruna d'Amorim Jordan (d 1970), 1 s; m 2, 1973, Gladys Jackman (d 1986); *Career* former chm Marconi Co Ltd, ret 1969; kt 1969; *Style*— Sir Neil Sutherland, CBE; Conifers, 45 High St, Wickham Market, Woodbridge, Suffolk IP13 0HE

SUTHERLAND, Peter Berkeley Douglas; s of late Douglas Sutherland, and late Ethel, *née* Page; *b* 13 Feb 1925; *Educ* Shrewsbury Sch, St Catharine's Coll Cambridge (MA), Univ Coll London (Dipl Arch (UCL)), Royal Acad; *m* 16 March 1962, Diane Marie, da of Charles Joseph Wyatt (d 1986), of Somers Road, Reigate; 1 s (Justin Charles Berkeley b 1966), 1 da (Belinda Marie b 1968); *Career* Royal Devon Yeo RA 1943-47, Capt (India/Malaya); architect; chm Henley Cons Assoc 1967, pres 1971; Henley Cmmrs of Taxes 1974- (chm 1983); coach Oxford Univ Olympic VIII 1960; Desborough Medal; RIBA 1954; *Recreations* rowing, punting; *Clubs* Leander (past capt and life memb), MCC, Upper Thames Rowing (pres and founder), Phyllis Court; *Style*— Peter Sutherland, Esq; Bird Place, Henley-on-Thames (☎ Henley 572033); Saragossa House, New Street, Henley-on-Thames (☎ Henley 573003)

SUTHERLAND, Peter Denis William; s of William George Sutherland, and Barbara, *née* Neahon; *b* 25 April 1946; *Edvc* Gonzaga Coll, Univ Coll Dublin (BCL); *m* 1971, Mariz Pilar, da of Paulino Cabria of Reinosa, Sentander, Spain; 2 s (Shane b 1972, Ian b 1974); 1 da (Natalia b 1979); *Career* barr: Kings Inns 1968, Middle Temple 1976, attorney of New York Bar, admitted to practice before the Supreme Ct of the US, practising memb of Irish Bar 1968-81 (Sen Cncl 1980); tutor in law Univ Coll Dublin 1969-71, memb cncl of State of Ireland and attorney-gen of Ireland 1981-Aug 1982 and Dec 1982-1984; Cmmr of EC for Competition and Relations with Euro Parl 1985-; Hon LLD St Louis Univ (1985); *Recreations* reading, sport; *Clubs* Hibernian Utd Service (Dublin); Fitz William (Dublin); Lansdowne FC; *Style*— Peter Sutherland, Esq; c/o Berlaymont, Rue de la Loi 200, Brussels, Belgium (☎ Brussels 235 11 11)

SUTHERLAND, Prof Stewart Ross; s of George Arthur Caswell Sutherland (d 1974), of Aberdeen, and Ethel, *née* Masson; *b* 25 Feb 1941; *Educ* Robert Gordons Coll Aberdeen, Univ of Aberdeen (MA), Corpus Christi Coll Cambridge (MA); *m* 1 Aug 1964, Sheena, da of John Robertson (d 1975), of Fraserburgh; 1 s (Duncan Stewart b 9 March 1970), 2 da (Fiona Mair b 11 Dec 1966, Kirsten Ann b 20 Aug 1968); *Career* asst lectr Univ of North Wales Bangor 1965-68; Univ of Stirling: lectr 1968, sr lectr 1972, reader 1976-77; Kings Coll London: prof of history and philosophy of religion 1977-85, vice-princ 1981-85, princ 1985-; lectures: Hope (Stirling) 1979, Wilde (Oxford) 1981-84, Ferguson (Manchester) 1984, Boutwood (Corpus Christi Cambridge) 1989-; CoE Bd of Educn 1980-84; chm: Br Academy Postgrad Studentships Ctee 1987-, cncl of Royal Inst of Philosophy 1988-; memb Worhipful Co Goldsmiths 1986; Hon LHO Wooster Shio USA; *Books* Atheism and Rejection of God (1977), God, Jesus and Belief (1984), Faith and Ambiguity (1984), The World's Religions (ed 1988); *Recreations* tassie medallions, jazz, theatre; *Clubs* Athenaeum; *Style*— Prof Stewart Sutherland; Kings College, Strand, London WC2R 2LS (☎ 01 873 2027)

SUTHERLAND, Veronica Evelyn; CMG (1988); da of Lt-Col M G Beckett KOYLI (d 1949), and Constance Mary, *née* Cavanagh-Mainwaring; *b* 25 April 1939; *Educ* Royal Sch Bath, London Univ (BA), Southampton Univ (MA); *m* 29 Dec 1981, Alex James, s of James Sutherland (d 1969); *Career* third later second sec FCO 1965, second sec Copenhagen 1967, first sec FCO 1970, first sec Devpt New Delhi 1975, FCO 1978; cnsllr and perm UK del UNESCO Pans 1981, cnsllr FCO 1984, HM Ambassador Abidjan 1987; *Recreations* painting; *Style*— Mrs Veronica E Sutherland, CMG; c/o FCO, London SW1

SUTHERLAND, William George MacKenzie; QPM; *b* 12 Nov 1933; *Educ* Inverness Technical HS; *m* Jennie; 2 da; *Career* Cheshire Police 1954-73, Surrey Police 1973-75, Hertfords Police 1975-79, chief constable Bedfords Police (1979-83), Lothian and Borders Police 1983; *Recreations* squash, hill-walking; *Style*— Sir William Sutherland, QPM; Chief Constable, Lothian and Borders Police, Police Headquarters, Fettes Avenue, Edinburgh EH4 1RB (☎ 031 311 3131)

SUTHERLAND JANSON, Hon Martin Dearman; s (yr twin) of Countess of Sutherland; *Educ* Eton; *m* 1974, Hon Mary Ann, *qv*; 5 s; *Style*— The Hon Martin Sutherland Janson; Meadow Cottage, Christmas Common, Watlington, Oxon OX9 5HR

SUTHERLAND JANSON, Hon Mrs (Mary Ann); *née* Balfour; da of 1 Baron Balfour of Inchrye, MC, PC (d 1988), and Mary, Baroness Balfour of Inchrye, *qv*; *m* 1974, Hon Martin Sutherland Janson *qv*; 5 s; *Style*— The Hon Mrs Sutherland Janson; Meadow Cottage, Christmas Common, Watlington, Oxon OX9 5HR

SUTRO, Joan Maud; da of Arthur Bertram Colyer (d 1976), and Florence Maud, *née* Maycroft (d 1982); *Educ* Farnborough Hill Convent, Bedford HS, Coll De Jeunes Filles, Dreux; *m* 29 March 1941, Edward Leopold, MC, s of Leopold Sutro (d 1943); 2 da (Caroline Alexandra b 1943, Rosemary Jane b 1945), 1 s (decd); *Career* WWII served Balkans 1939-41; memb Godstone Rural Dist Cncl 1948-52, chm Int Spring Fair 1974-79, chm Women's Cncl 1981-87, memb Roy Inst Int Affairs 1944-; govr: Oxted Co Sch 150-71, Central Sch of Speech & Drama 1956-; vice-pres Anglo-Turkish Soc 1983-; *Recreations* travel to remote places, theatre; *Style*— Mrs Edward Sutro; c/o Barclay's Bank, Sloane Square, London SW1W 8AF

SUTTIE; *see*: Grant-Suttie

SUTTIE, Ian Alexander; s of John Alexander Suttie, of Aberdeen, and Christina Mary, *née* Mackie; *b* 8 June 1945; *Educ* Robert Gordons Coll Aberdeen, Aberdeen Univ (CA); *m* 1 Dec 1971, Dorothy Elizabeth, da of Charles John George Small; 1 s (Martin b 1978), 2 da (Julia b 1974, Fiona b 1976); *Career* dir: Petrocon Gp plc, Petrocon Flotec Ltd, Petrocon Tech Services Ltd, Petrocon Prod Services Ltd, Petrocon Norge A/S, Petrocon Drilling Tools BV, Petrocon Drilling Tools plc; md: Petrocon Well services Ltd, Petrocon Wood Oilfield Rentals Ltd; *Recreations* golf, curling, swimming; *Clubs* Aberdeen Petroleum; *Style*— Ian A Suttie, Esq; 18 Earlswells Drive, Cults, Aberdeen AB1 9NW (☎ 0224 861389); Souterhead Road, Altens, Aberdeen

SUTTILL, Bernard Roy (Rab); *b* 17 June 1919; *Educ* Univ Coll Sch, Royal Coll of Science (DIC, BSc, ARCS); *m* 1947, Ruth, 2 s, 3 da; *Career* served WW II RAF 1941-46 Fl Lt; oil exec Shell 1947-74, md Shell Co of Quatar, ret; Thompson North Sea Ltd 1974-; *Clubs* RAF; *Style*— Rab Suttill Esq; c/o Thomson North Sea Ltd, 75 Davies Street, London W1Y 1FA (☎ 01 493 7541); Stoke Park Farm, Abbotswood, Guildford GU1 1UT

SUTTON; *see*: Foster-Sutton

SUTTON, Alan John; s of William Clifford Sutton (d 1964), of Abertillery, and Emily, *née* Batten; *b* 16 Mar 1936; *Educ* Hafod-Y-Ddôl GS, Bristol Univ (BSc); *m* 7 Sept 1957, Glenis, da of George Henry (d 1986), of Ebbw Vale; 1 s (Andrew Jonathan b 1964), 1 da (Lisa Jayne b 1963); *Career* chief engr Eng Electric 1957-62, sales mangr Solartron 1962-69, md AB Connectors 1969-76, chm and chief exec Anglolink Ltd 1988-, industl dir Welsh off 1976-79, exec dir Welsh Devpt Agency 1979-88; MIEE 1962; *Recreations* golf, walking; *Style*— Alan Sutton, Esq; Brockton House Heol-y-Delyn, Lisvane, Cardiff CF4 5SR (☎ 0222 753 194, fax 0222 747 037)

SUTTON, Andrew; s of William Stanley Sutton, of Birkenhead, Merseyside, and Evelyn Margaret, *née* Kitchin; *b* 27 August 1947; *Educ* Jesus Coll Cambridge (MA); *Career* ptnr Price Waterhouse London 1978-; vice pres Opportunities for the Disabled, cncl chm Bede House Assoc; Freeman City of London 1988; ACA 1971, FCA 1979; *Recreations* walking, opera, music, reading; *Clubs* Oxford and Cambridge; *Style*— Andrew Sutton, Esq; 53 Fitzjames Ave, London W14 0RR (☎ 01 603 5881); Southwark Towers, 32 London Bridge St, London SE1 9SY (☎ 01 407 8989, fax 01 378 0647, telex 884657)

SUTTON, Andrew William; *b* 4 Oct 1939; *Educ* Brentwood Sch, Univ of Birmingham, Univ of Aston; *m* 13 July 1964, Kay, da of Lionel Edge, of Birmingham; 1 s (Benjamin b 21 Feb 1969), 1 da (Rebecca b 6 April 1967); *Career* psychologist: Newport (Mon) 1965-67, Birmingham 1968-84; Univ of Birmingham: hon lectr in educn psychology 1970-84, assoc Centre for Russian & East Euro Studies 1980-, hon res fell dept of psychology 1984-; dir Fndn for Conductive Educn 1986-; *Books* Home, School and Leisure in the Soviet Union (1980), Reconstructing Psychological Practice (1981), Conductive Education (1985); *Recreations* gardening, garden-railways; *Style*— Andrew Sutton, Esq; 78 Clarendon St, Leamington Spa, Warks CV32 4PE (☎ 0926 311966); The Foundation For Conductive Education, The University, Birmingham B15 2TT (☎ 021 414 4947, fax 021 414 3971, telex 333 762)

SUTTON, Barry Bridge; s of Albert Sutton (d 1976), of Taunton, and Ethel Ada, *née* Bridge; *b* 21 Jan 1937; *Educ* Eltham Coll, Peterhouse Coll Cambridge (MA), Univ of Bristol (Dip Ed); *m* 12 Aug 1961, Margaret Helen, da of (Edward) Thomas Palmer (d 1986); 1 s (Mark b 1964), 2 da (Clare b 1965, Jane b 1968); *Career* housemaster and sr history master Wycliffe Coll Stonehouse Glos 1961-75; headmaster: Hereford Cathedral Sch 1975-87, Taunton Sch 1987-; memb gen purpose sub-ctee of Scout Cncl (by nat appt), tres Somerset Scout Cncl; former JP Hereford; memb: HMC, Historical Assoc; *Recreations* mountain walking; *Clubs* E India, Devonshire, Sports, Pub Sch; *Style*— Barry Sutton, Esq; Headmaster's House, Private Rd, Staplegrove, Taunton TA2 6AJ (☎ 0823 272 588); Taunton Sch, Taunton TA2 6AD (☎ 0823 284 596)

SUTTON, Colin Bertie John; QPM (1985); s of Bertie Sydney Russel Sutton (d 1978), and Phyllis May, *née* Edkins, of Warwickshire; *b* 6 Dec 1938; *Educ* King Edward VI GS, UCL (LLB); *m* 1960, Anne Margaret, da of Henry Edward Davis, of Warwickshire; *Career* asst chief constable Leics Constabulary 1977-81, asst cmmr Metropolitan Police 1984-87 (dep asst cmmr 1981-84); FBIM; *Recreations* golf, fishing, music, reading, conservation, fellow of RSPB; *Clubs* RAC; *Style*— Colin Sutton, Esq, QPM; Police Requirements for Sci & Technol, Home Off, Horseferry House, Dean Ryle St, London SW1P 2AW

SUTTON, Denys Miller; CBE (1985); s of Edmund Miller Sutton, and Dulcie Laura, *née* Wheeler; *b* 10 August 1917; *Educ* Uppingham, Exeter Coll Oxford (BA, BLitt); *m* 1, Sonja Klibansky (m dis); m 2, Gertrude Kbke Knudsen (m dis); 1 s (Caspar b 1956), 1 da (Madeleine O'Broin b 1941); m 3, 1960, Cynthia Leah Sassoon; *Career* FO 1940-45, sec Ctee for Restitution of Looted Works of Art, Visual art specialist UNESCO Paris, visiting lectr Yale Univ; sale room corr Daily Telegraph; art critic: Country Life, Financial Times; ed Apollo 1962-87; corr memb Institut de France; *Books* French Drawings of the 18th Century (1949), American Painting (1949) Derain (1959), Whistler (1964), Rodin (1966), Letters of Roger Fry (1972), Walker Sickert (1976), Robert Langton Douglas (1979), Fads and Fancies (1979), Edgar Degar (1986); *Clubs* Traveller; *Style*— Denys Sutton, Esq, CBE; 22 Chelsea Park Gardens, London SW3 6AA (☎ 01 352 5141)

SUTTON, Sir Frederick Walter; OBE (1971); s of William W Sutton (decd); *b* 1 Feb 1915; *Educ* Sydney Tech Coll; *m* 1, 1934, Adriene Marie Gardner; 3 s; m 2, 1977, Morna Smyth; *Career* fndr and chm Sutton Gp of Cos; life govr Royal NSW Inst for Deaf and Blind Children, chm Art Union Ctee; kt 1974; *Style*— Sir Frederick Sutton, OBE; c/o Sutton's Motors Pty Ltd, 114 Bourke St, E Sydney, NSW 2000, Australia

SUTTON, Graham Charles; s of Charles James Sutton (d 1975), and Ruby Ethel, *née* Moorecroft (d 1984); *b* 29 August 1942; *Educ* Brentwood Sch, Coll of Estate Mgmnt; *m* 12 March 1966, Elizabeth Anne, da of Robert Woodman, of 21 Reed Pond Walk, Gidea Pk, Essex; 2 s (Matthew b 1968, Christopher b 1971); *Career* articled pupil asst Stanley Hicks & Son 1959-66, asst surveyor Debenham Tewson & Chinnocks 1966-68, sr ptnr Taylor & Melhuish 1982- (asst surveyor 1969-72, ptnr 1972-82); Freeman City of London 1982, Liveryman Worshipful Co of Coopers; FRICS 1965, FRVA 1971; *Recreations* shooting, golf, skiing, windsurfing; *Clubs* Harpenden Common GC, Surveyors 1894, Soc of Old Brentwoods; *Style*— Graham Sutton, Esq; 32 Milton Rd, Harpenden, Herts AL5 5LS (☎ 05827 3489); 24 Holywell Hill, St Albans, Herts AL1 1BZ (☎ 0727 66646, fax 0727 51745)

SUTTON, James; s of Thomas Alfred Victor Sutton (d 1982), of Poynton, Cheshire, and Emily, *née* Firth (d 1967); *b* 12 Jan 1923; *Educ* Kingswood Sch Bath; *m* 21 June 1950, Joan, da of Ezra Wainwright (d 1956); 1 s (Michael b 5 July 1955), 1 da (Angela (Mrs Fendall) b 5 May 1959); *Career* WW II RAF meteorologist 1942-47; meteorologist Air Miny 1941-42, asst gen mangr Vernon Building Soc 1948; qualified CA 1953, ptnr TAV Sutton & Co 1953-, dir and chief exec Vernon Building Soc 1971 (gen mangr 1970), dir Deanwater Hotel (Cheshire) Ltd; chm NW Building Socs Assoc 1986; chm Poyntonf Sports Club 1962-83 (memb 1948-83); FCA 1953; *Recreations* travel, gardening; *Style*— James Sutton, Esq; 26 St Petersgate, Stockport, Cheshire SK1 1HD (☎ 061 477 9797, fax 061 480 3414)

SUTTON, Prof John; s of Gerald John Sutton (d 1958), and Kathleen Alice, *née* Richard, MBE; *b* 8 July 1919; *Educ* King's Sch Worcester, Imperial Coll London (DSc, PhD, BSc); *m* 1, 13 June 1949, Janet Vida Watson (d 1985), da of Prof David Meredith Seares Watson; m2, 21 Aug 1985, Betty Middleton-Sandford, da of James Middleton

Honeychurch; *Career* cmmnd 2 Lt RAOC 1941, transferred to REME 1942, capt 1944, served AA cmd UK 1941-46; Imperial Coll: lectr in geology 1948-58, prof of geology 1958-64, head of geology dept 1964-74; dean Royal Sch of Mines 1965-68 and 1974-77, Centre for Enviromental Technol 1976-83, prorector 1980-83; fell Imperial Coll; FRS 1966; *Recreations* gardening; *Style—* Prof John Sutton; The Manor House, Martinstown, Dorchester, Dorset DT2 9JN

SUTTON, Air Marshal Sir John Matthias Dobson; CB (1980), KBC (1986); s of Harry Rowston Sutton, of Alford, Lincs, and Gertrude, *née* Dobson; *b* 9 July 1932; *Educ* Queens Elizabeth GS Alford Lincs; *m* 1, (m dis 1968), 1 s (Shaun b 1961), 1 da (Shenagh b 1957); m 2, 23 May 1969, Angela Faith, da of Wing Cdr GJ Gray, DFC, of Fowey, Cornwall; 2 s (Mark b 1971, Stephen 1972); *Career* joined RAF 1950, pilot tning cmmnd 1951, fighter sqdns UK and Germany 1952-61, staff coll 1963, CO 249 sqdn 1964-66, asst sec Chief of Staff's Ctee 1966-69, OC 14 sqdn 1970-71, asst chief of state (plans and policy) HQ 2ATAF 1971-73, staff Chief of Defence Staff 1973-74, RCDS 1975, cmdt Central Flying Sch 1976-77, asst chief of air staff (policy) 1977-79, dep cdr RAf Germany 1980-82, asst chief of defence staff (commitments) 1982-85, asst chief of defence staff (overseas) 1985, AOC-in-C RAf Support Cmmnd 1986-89 ; *Recreations* golf, skiing; *Clubs* RAF, Luffenham Heath Golf; *Style—* Air Marshal Sir John Sutton CB, KCB; HQ RAF Support Command RAF Brampton, Huntingdon, Cambs PE18 8QL (☎ 0480 52151 ext 6200)

SUTTON, Kirby (Washington); OBE (1973); s of late Eugene John Sutton, and Lilian Eugenie, *née* Kilburn (d 1950); *b* 4 Oct 1918; *Educ* Newent GS; *m* 23 Jan 1948, Mary, da of George Stuart (d 1960); 1 s (Kevan Kirby b 1952), 1 da (Rosamond Mary b 1949); *Career* WWII 1939-46, Maj Royal Signals, served Euro theatre and Burma; journalist and writer Northcliffe Press 1938-39, chief ed Pan-Malayan Broadcasting 1948-50, COI London 1958-79 (asst controller and controller overseas service 1973-77); memb of official which team negotiated Br entry to EEC; *Recreations* oil painting; *Clubs* Wig and Pen; *Style—* Kirby Sutton, Esq, OBE; 225 Whyke Rd, Chichester, W Sussex

SUTTON, Leslie Ernest; s of Edgar William Sutton (d 1972), and Margaret Lilian Winifred, *née* Heard (d 1965); *b* 22 June 1906; *Educ* Watford GS, Oxford (MA, DPhil), Leipzig Univ; *m* 1, 1932, Catharine Virginia (d 1962), da of Wallace Teall Stock (d 1944); 2 s (Stephen b 1938, Richard b 1945), 1 da (Virginia b 1936); m 2, 1963, Rachel Ann Long (d 1987), da of Lt-Col John Forbes Batten, OBE (d 1978); 2 s (Geoffrey b 1964, Martin b 1967); *Career* fell and lectr Magdalen Coll Oxford 1936-73, fell emeritus 1973, vice-pres 1947-48, vice pres Chem Soc 1957-60, reader in physical chem Oxford Univ 1962-73, Rockefeller fell Cal Inst of Tech 1933-34, visiting prof Heidelberg Univ 1960, 1964, 1967; chm: Lawes Agric Tst Ctee 1982-89 (tres 1978-82), Dielectrics Soc 1975-86; Meldola Medal 1932, Harrison prize 1935, hon DSc (Salford) 1973, FRS; published numerous papers in scientific journals; *Recreations* music, photography; *Style—* Leslie E Sutton, Esq; 62 Osler Rd, Old Headington, Oxford OX3 9BN (☎ 0865 66456)

SUTTON, Michael Antony (Tony); MC (1944); s of Brig William Moxhay Sutton, DSO, MC (d 1949), of Bath, and Barbara Marie *née* Corballis; *b* 29 Mar 1921; *Educ* Ampleforth, Worcester Coll Oxford (MA); *m* 12 April 1958, Bridget Gillian Mary, da of Brig Walter Lindley Fawcett, MC (missing presumed killed 1942) of Yorks and India; 2 s (Philip b 8 Dec 1966, Michael b 9 Feb 1968), 3 da (Veronica Ford b 3 March 1959, Bridget b 3 Sept 1960, Teresa b 24 Jan 1962); *Career* Lance Corpl Royal Warwicks Regt 1940, Capt Westminster Dragoons 1941-45, Normandy to Germany via Belgium and Holland 1944-45; Capt North Somerset Yeo 1948-53; admitted slr 1951, ptnr Tozers 1952-; Oxford blue rugby 1945-46 and cricket 1946, Barbarians 1946, rugby referee Devon Soc; memb Law Soc 1951; KCSG Papal 1969; *Recreations* member Magic Circle, keeping fit, Times crossword; *Clubs* Vincent's (Oxford), MCC; *Style—* MA Sutton, Esq, MC; Duncombe, Landscore Rd, Teignmouth, Devon TQ14 9JS (☎ 0626 774 453); 2 Orchard Gdns, Teignmouth, Devon TQ14 8DR (☎ 0626 772 376)

SUTTON, Michael Phillip; s of Charles Phillip Sutton, of Worksop, Notts, and Maisie Sutton, *née* Kelsey; *b* 25 Feb 1946; *Educ* Haileybury and Imperial Serv Coll; *m* 24 July 1971, Susan Margaret, da of John Turner, JP, DL, of Lound, Notts; *Career* CA 1970, Old Broad St Securities Ltd 1970-71, md Singer and Fridlander Ltd 1983 (joined 1971); Freeman City of London 1978, Freeman Worshipful Co of Pipe Tobacco Makers and Blenders, memb Ct of Assts 1982; ACA 1971, FCA 1976; *Recreations* shooting, fishing, horse racing, gardening; *Style—* Michael Sutton, Esq; West Bank, Gamston, Retford, Notts (☎ 077 783 387); 123 Hagley Rd, Birmingham B16 8LP (☎ 021 456 3311, car tel 0860 207 998/0860 334 293)

SUTTON, Philip John; s of Louis Sutton (d 1976), and Ann, *née* Lazarus (d 1980); *b* 20 Oct 1928; *Educ* Slade Sch of Fine Art UCL (Dip Fine Art); *m* 11 July 1953, Heather Minifie Ellis, da of Arthur Owen Ellis Cooke; 1 s (Jacob b 11 may 1954), 3 da (Imogen b 21 Beb 1956, Saskia b 19 Jan 1958, Rebekah b 30 Sept 1960); *Career* aircraftsman RAF 1947-49; artist, designer and painter; designed poster and flag for RA summer show 1979, exhibition of painted ceramics at Odette Gilbert Gallery 1987, painting of William Shakespeare for Int Shakespeare Globe Centre 1988, exhibition of paintings at RA summer show 1988; ARA 1977; RA 1988; *Recreations* running, swimming; *Style—* Philip Sutton, Esq; 10 Soudan Rd, London SW11 4HH (☎ 01 622 2647); 4 Morfa Terr Manorbier, Tenby, Dyfed

SUTTON, Dr Richard; s of Dick Brasnett Sutton (d 1981), of Newport, Gwent, and Greta Mary, *née* Leadbeter; *b* 1 Sept 1940; *Educ* Gresham's Sch Holt Norfolk, King's Coll London Univ, King's Coll Hosp London Univ (MB, BS); *m* 28 Nov 1969, (Anna) Gunilla, da of Carl-Axel Cassö (d 1976), of Stockholm, Sweden; 1 s (Edmund b 24 April 1967); *Career* house offr: Plymouth Gen Hosp 1964-65, Kings Coll Hosp 1965, St Stephens Hosp 1966, London Chest Hosp 1966-67; registrar St George's Hosp 1967-68, fell in cardiology Univ N Carolina USA 1968-69, registrar (later sr registrar and temporary conslt) Nat Heart Hosp 1970-76, conslt cardiologist Westminster and St Stephens Hosps 1976-; DSc (Med) London Univ 1988; hon conslt cardiologist: Italian Hosp 1977-, SW Thames RHA 1979-, St Luke's Hosp for the Clergy 1980-; govr's award American Coll of Cardiology 1979 and 1982; co fndr and former sec Br Pacing and Electrophysiology Gp; MRCP 1967, FRCP 1982, BMA, RSM; memb: Br Cardiac Soc, American Coll of Cardiology, American Heart Assoc; *Books* Pacemakers: chapter in Oxford textbook of Medicine (1987); *Recreations* opera, tennis, cross-country skiing; *Style—* Dr Richard Sutton; 149 Harley St, London W1N 1HG (☎ 01 935 4444, fax 01 486 3782, telex 263250)

SUTTON, Sir Richard Lexington; 9 Bt (GB 1772), of Norwood Park, Nottinghamshire; s of Sir Robert Lexington Sutton, 8 Bt (d 1981); *b* 27 April 1937; *Educ* Stowe; *m* 1959, Fiamma, da of G M Ferrari, of Rome; 1 s, 1 da; *Heir* s, David Robert Sutton, b 26 Feb 1960; *Style—* Sir Richard Sutton, Bt; Moor Hill, Langham, Gillingham, Dorset

SUTTON, Robert Hiles; s of John Ormerod Sutton, of The Old School House Tichborne, Hants, and Margaret Patricia, *née* Buckland; *b* 19 Jan 1954; *Educ* Winchester, Magdalen Coll Oxford (BA); *m* 8 Aug 1981, Carola Jane, da of Sir Anthony Dewey, 3 Bt, of The Rag, Galhampton, Yeovil, Somerset; 1 s (Patrick b 1984), 1 da (Joanna b 1987); *Career* Macfarlanes Slrs 1976-83 (ptnr 1983-); memb Law Soc; *Recreations* rackets, poker; *Clubs* Queens; *Style—* Robert Sutton, Esq; Macfarlanes, 10 Norwich St, London EC4 A1BD (☎ 01 831 9222, fax 01 831 9607)

SUTTON, Thomas Francis (Tom); *b* 9 Feb 1923; *Educ* King's Sch Worcester, St Peter's Coll Oxford (MA 1953); *m* 1, 23 June 1950 (m dis 1974), Anne, *née* Fleming; 1 s (Jonathan b 1951), 2 da (Nicola b 1954, Alison b 1959); m 2, 1 Sept 1982, Maki, *née* Watanabe; *Career* res offr BR Mkt Res Bureau Ltd 1949-51, advertising mangr Pasolds Ltd 1951-52, md J Walter Thompson GmbH Frankfurt 1952-59; dir: J Walter Thompson Co Ltd 1960-73 (md 1960-66), J Walter Thompson Co (New York) 1965-83 (exec vice-pres Int Operations 1966-72), md J Walter Thompson Co (Japan) 1972-80; pres J Walter Thompson (Asia/Pacific) 1980-81, chm E A Int New York 1981-, chm LansdownEuro Advertising Ltd 1983; pt/t lectr in advertising and mktg: Rutger's Univ New Jersey 1968-71, Columbia Univ New York 1971-73, Sophia Univ Tokyo 1974-81; Int Advertising Man of the Year Award 1970; *Recreations* chess, riding, reading; *Clubs* Princeton (New York), Walton Hall (Warks), Pudding (Mickleton); *Style—* Tom Sutton, Esq; Rushway House, Willington, Shipston-on-Stour, Warwickshire

SUZMAN, Janet; da of Saul Peter Suzman, of Johannesburg, SA, and Betty Sonnenberg; *b* 9 Feb 1939; *Educ* Kingsmead Coll Johannesburg, Univ of the Witwatersrand (BA); *m* 1969 (m dis 1986), Trevor Robert Nunn; 1 s (Joshua b 1980); *Career* actor; performances incl: The Wars of the Roses 1964, The Relapse 1967, The Taming of the Shrew 1967, A Day in the Death of Joe Egg 1970, Nicholas and Alexandra (Acad Award nomination 1971), Antony and Cleopatra 1972, Hello and Goodbye (Evening Standard Award 1973), Three Sisters (Standard Award 1976), Hedda Gabler 1978, The Greeks 1980, The Draughtsmans Contract 1981, Vassa 1985, Mountbatten Viceroy of India 1986, The Singing Detective 1987, Andrumache 1988, A Dry White Season 1989; directed Othello Market Theatre, Johannesburg 1987, and for TV 1988; *Recreations* yacht 'Chicken Sloop'; *Style—* Miss Janet Suzman; William Morris, 31/32 Soho Square, London W1 (☎ 01 434 2191)

SVENNINGSON, Hon Mrs (Daphne Rose); *née* Canning; da of 4 Baron Garvagh (d 1956); *b* 1922; *m* 1950, Bancroft Svenningson; 1 s, 2 da; *Style—* The Hon Mrs Svenningson; 53 Ferdon Ave, Westmount, Montreal, Canada

SWAAB, Roger Henry; s of Cyril Henry Swaab, of Shrewsbury, and Betty Joan Swaab, *née* Moore; *b* 6 June 1944; *Educ* Brewood GS, Birmingham Sch of Arch (Dip Arch); *m* 12 July 1968, Elizabeth Kay, da of William Edward Smith Penlon, of Staffs; 1 s (Christian b 1973), 1 da (Beth b 1973); *Career* architect; snr ptnr Hickton Madeley & Ptnrs; dir: Hickton Madeley Interiors Ltd 1986, Hickton Madeley Landscape Ltd 1989-, Hickton Madeley Project Management Ltd 1988-; ACIArb; *Recreations* golf; *Clubs* Shrewsbury Golf, Nefyn & Dist Golf; *Style—* Roger H Swaab, Esq; 24 Hatherton Rd, Walsall WS1 1XP (☎ 0922 645400, fax 0922 647359 HMP)

SWAEBE, Barry James; s of Albert Victor Swaebe (d 1967), and Sophy Estlin Hancock, *née* Grundy (d 1982); *b* 12 May 1923; *m* 28 May 1966, Miriam Isobel, da of Robert Owen Morgans; 2 da (Sophy Anna b 1 Jan 1967, Clare Isobel b 9 Jan 1968); *Career* WWII RAF; social/portrait photographer AV Swaebe Ltd 1946-; photographs in numerous pubns incl: Tatler, Harpers and Queen; exhibition photographs of Barbados Harrods 1965; *Style—* Barry Swaebe, Esq; 16 Southwood Lane, Highgate Village, London N6 5EE (☎ 01 348 6010)

SWAFFIELD, Sir James Chesebrough; CBE (1971), RD (1967, DL (Greater London 1978)); s of Frederick Swaffield (d 1970); *b* 1924; *Educ* Cheltenham GS, Haberdashers' Aske's Sch, London Univ; *m* 1950, Elizabeth Margaret Ellen, da of Albert Victor Maunder (d 1965); 2 s, 2 da; *Career* Atlantic and NW Europe WWII, Lt-Cdr RNVR; asst slr: Norwich Corpn 1949-52, Cheltenham Corpn 1952-53, Southend on Sea Corpn 1953-56; dep town clerk Blackpool 1956-61, town clerk 1961-62; sec Assoc of Municipal Corpns 1962-72, dir-gen and clerk GLC 1973-84, clerk to ILEA 1973-84, clerk of Lieutenancy for Gtr London 1973-84; chm BR Property Bd 1984-; Distinguished Service Award (Int City Mgmnt Assoc) 1984; hon fell Inst Local Govt Studies Birmingham Univ; OStJ; FRSG; kt 1976; *Clubs* Reform, Naval; *Style—* Sir James Swaffield, CBE, RD, DL; 10 Kelsey Way, Beckenham, Kent

SWAINE, Anthony Wells; s of Albert Victor Alexander Swaine (d 1972), of Cornwall, and Hilda May Allen (d 1983); *b* 25 August 1913; *Educ* Chatham House, Ramsgate; *Career* architect, private practice historic bldgs, architectural advsr: Faversham oldown and (wrote Faversham Conserved), Thanet Dist Cncl of Old Margate, to Historic Churches Preservation Tst (on panel of hon conslt architects); taught architecture pt/t at Canterbury Coll of Art; was clerk of works to Dean and Chapter of Canterbury (responsible for Cathedral and precincts); memb of cncl and tech panel Ancient Monuments Soc (reps the Soc on Int Cncl), patron Venice in Peril, wrote report on conservation I1 Problema di Venezia which went to UNESCO, served on Int Confer for Stone Conservation Athens; memb SPAB, FRIBA, FSA; *Recreations* travelling, languages, lecturing (as memb of panel of speakers of Civic Tst), history as applied to architecture, drawing, painting, photography; *Style—* Anthony Swaine, Esq; 19 Farrier St, Deal, Kent (☎ 0304 366369); Latchmere House, Watling St, Canterbury, Kent (☎ 0277 462680)

SWAINE, Richard Carter; s of Charles Frederick Swaine (d 1980), of Cottingham, Hull, and Kathleen Mary Swaine, *née* Battye (d 1987); *b* 2 July 1933; *Educ* Oakham Sch Rutland, Hull Sch of Architect, RIBA; *Career* RAF (Nat Sev) navigator; architect, own business 1969-; awards: Save Commendation, Civic Tst Commendation 1978, Euro Heritage Team Commendation 1974, E Yorkshire Planning Award 1982; *Recreations* sculpture, photography, all sport, town planning; *Clubs* Brough Golf, Welton Hockey and Cricket; *Style—* Richard Swaine, Esq; 1 Creyle Lane, Welton, Brough, N Humberside HU15 1NQ

SWAINSON, Eric; CBE (1981); *b* 5 Dec 1926; *Educ* Sheffield Univ (BMet); *m* 1953, Betty Irene; 2 da; *Career* md IMI plc (metals fabricating and gen engrg) 1974-86, dir Birmingham Broadcasting Ltd 1973-, dir Midlands Radio Hldgs plc 1988-, memb review bd for govt contracts 1978-, chm Lloyds Bank (Birmingham & W Mids Regnl

Bd) 1985- (memb 1979-); dir: Lloyds Bank plc 1986-, Fairey Gp 1987-, Amec plc 1987-; chm W Mids Indust Devpt Bd; pro-chllr Aston Univ 1981-86; Hon DSc (Aston) 1986; *Style—* Eric Swainson Esq, CBE; Paddox Hollow, Norton Lindsey, Warwick CV35 8JA (☎ 092 684 3190)

SWAINSON, Richard Gellienne; TD (1946); s of John Gallienne Swainson (d 1958), of Marshrange, Lancs, and Edith, *née* Barrett (d 1954); *b* 16 Oct 1911; *Educ* Lancaster Royal GS, Cambridge Univ (MA); *m* Aug 1950, Stella Margaret, da of Edwin Charles Colborn, of Spalding, Lincs; 1 s (William), 3 da (Margaret, Caroline, Sarah), 1 step da (Diana); *Career* 88 FD Regt RA (TA) 1939-46, Capt, France 1939-40, (POW Malaya 1941-45); slr 1936-88, conslt slr Swainson Son & Reynolds; govr LRGS; NP 1946-; memb Law Soc; *Recreations* golf; *Style—* Richard G Swainson, Esq, TD; Marshrange, Lancaster LA1 1YQ (☎ 0524 65347)

SWALES, Peter Brian; s of Ernest Wilfed Swales (d 1956), of Leamington Spa, and Gladys Mildred, *née* Wright (d 1962); *b* 25 July 1929; *Educ* Warwick Sch, St Catharine's Coll Cambridge (BSc); *m* 9 April 1960, Jean Brenda, da of Rowell Vines (d 1962), of Leamington Spa; 2 s (David b 1963, Peter b 1969), 3 da (Catharine b 1961, Alison b 1965, Nicola b 1967); *Career* Nat Serv RAF 1948-49; dir: Irvin GB 1970-73, Chiswell Wire Co Ltd 1977-; md Swales Mgmnt Consultancy 1973-77; memb Letchworth Cons Pty; MICE 1956, MIMechE 1960, CEng 1960; *Recreations* golf, fishing, hill walking; *Style—* Peter Swales, Esq; 302 Norton Way South, Letchworth, Herts (☎ 0462 685 971); Garthlwyd, Landderfel, Bala, Gwynedd; Chiswell Wire Co Ltd, Sandown Rd, Watford, Herts (☎ 0923 35412, fax 0923 54754, telex 924588)

SWALLOW, Charles John; s of John Cuthbert Swallow (d 1968), and Irene Dupont, *née* Rée; *b* 29 July 1938; *Educ* Charterhouse, Lincoln Coll Oxford (MA), Wolfson Coll Oxford (MSc); *m* 28 July 1961, Susanna Janet, da of Maj Kenneth Arnold Gibbs (d 1988), of Crawley; 1 s (Mark b 18 Sept 1963), 1 da (Amanda b 28 Feb 1967); *Career* Ensign Scots Guards 1956-58; asst master Harrow Sch 1961-73, history teacher Bicester Sch 1973-76, headmaster Mount Grace School 1976-84; dir Vanderbilt Racquet Club 1974-; Open Racquets Champion of British Isles 1970, Open Real Tennis Doubles Champion of British Isles 1971, 1972 and 1973; High Sheriff Oxfordshire 1986-87; memb: gen advsy cncl IBA 1977-83, educn for capability ctee; RSA, FRSA; *Books* The Sick Man of Europe, The Decline of The Ottoman Empire 1789-1923 (1972); *Recreations* music, theatre, travel, ball games; *Clubs* All England LTC, MCC, Izingari, Whites, Pratts; *Style—* Charles Swallow, Esq; Manor Barn House, Wendlebury, Bicester, Oxon OX6 8PP (☎ 0869 253179); Vanderbilt Racquet Club, 31 Sterne St, London W12 8AB (☎ 01 743 9822)

SWALLOW, Sir William; s of late W T Swallow; *b* 2 Jan 1905; *m* 1929, Kathleen Lucy, *née* Smith; *Career* chm and md: General Motors Ltd 1953-61, Vauxhall Motors Ltd 1961-66; kt 1967; *Recreations* golf; *Style—* Sir William Swallow; Alderton Lodge, Ashridge Park, Berkhamsted, Herts (☎ 044 284 2284)

SWALWELL, (John) Anthony; s of Anthony Swalwell, MM (d 1967), and Ann Winifred, *née* Unsworth (d 1985); *b* 5 Dec 1931; *Educ* Wigan GS, Victoria Univ of Manchester (LLB); *m* 2 April 1956, Sylvia Mary, da of Albert George Mount; 1 s (William b 1957), 1 da (Alison b 1960); *Career* asst slr Manchester Corpn 1956-69, ptnr Rhodes & Swalwell 1969-, dep coroner Greater Manchester (W Dist) 1974-, acting stipendiary magistrate Liverpool 1986-; pres Wigan Law Soc 1982-83; hon slr: Royal Br Legion (Wigan Town Branch), Bellingham (Wigan) Bowling Green Ltd; memb Law Soc; *Recreations* cricket, crown green bowling; *Clubs* Bellingham Bowling (Wigan), Lancs CCC; *Style—* John Swalwell, Esq; 1 Kingsmede, Wigan Lane, Wigan, Lancashire (☎ 0942 42118); Rhodes & Swalwell, 30 Market Place, Wigan WN1 1PJ (☎ 0942 491227, fax 0942 820083)

SWAN, Conrad Marshall John Fisher; CVO (1986); s of Dr Henry Swan (*née* Swenciski or Swiecicki), of Vancouver (whose f, Paul, emigrated from Poland, where the family had long been landed proprietors and from time to time represented in the Senate of pre-Partition Poland); *b* 13 May 1924; *Educ* St George's Coll Weybridge, Sch of Oriental and African studies London Univ, Univ of Western Ontario, Peterhouse Cambridge; *m* 1957, Lady Hilda Susan Mary, *qv*, da of 3 Earl of Iddesleigh; 1 s, 4 da; *Career* Rouge Dragon Pursuivant 1962-68, York Herald of Arms 1968-, sr herald and registrar Coll of Arms 1982-; genealogist of Order of Bath 1972-; KStJ (genealogist of Grand Priory, Order of St John 1976-); Kt of Honour & Devotion SMO Malta 1979; FSA; lectr; *Books* Canada: Symbols of Sovereignty (1977), The Chapel of the Order of the Bath (1978); *Style—* Conrad Swan Esq, CVO, York Herald of Arms; Boxford House, Boxford, Colchester, Essex (☎ 0787 210208)

SWAN, Lady Hilda Susan Mary; *née* Northcote; da of 3 Earl of Iddesleigh (d 1970), and Elizabeth, Dowager Countess of Iddesleigh, *qv*; *b* 1937; *m* 1957, Conrad Swan, CVO, *qv*, York Herald; 1 s (Andrew), 4 da (Elizabeth Magdalen b 1959, (Hilda) Juliana b 1961, Catherine b 1962, Anastasia b 1966); *Career* Dame of Honour and Devotion Sov Mil Order of Malta 1979; *Style—* Lady Hilda Swan; Boxford House, Boxford, Colchester (☎ 0787 210208)

SWAN, Richard Roland Seymour; s of Capt Seymour Lankester Swan, RM (d 1988), and Ethel Hayward, *née* Drew; *b* 21 April 1937; *Educ* Cranleigh, Sidney Sussex Coll Cambridge (MA); *m* 1, 16 Sept 1961 (m dis 1967), Penelope Ann, da of Anthony Urling Clark, of Gwelhale, Rock, nr Wadebridge, Cornwall; 2 s (Mark b 1963, Rupert b 1965); m 2, 14 Oct 1967, Hedwig Erna Lydia, da of Dr Franz Pesendorfer (d 1944), of Vienna, Austria; 1 s (Michael b 1969), 2 da (Caroline b 1968, Olivia b 1970); *Career* Nat Serv Royal Sussex Regt, 2 Lt 1956, Lt 1959 East Surrey Regt; slr 1963; managing ptnr (former ptnr Heald Johnson & Co 1963) Heald Nickinson 1985; memb youth and community sub ctee Bucks CC, pres (former chm 1984-86) Milton Keynes and Dist C of C and Indust 1986-88, memb Norman Hawes Educnl Tst; Notary Public; chm: Buckinghamshire Assoc Boys Clubs 1986-, City Gallery Arts Tst 1987-; memb cncl Nat Assoc Boys Clubs; memb Law Soc 1963; *Recreations* book collecting, reading, walking; *Clubs* Naval and Military, Woburn Golf and Country; *Style—* Richard Swan, Esq; Five Pines, Wood Lane, Aspley Guise, Milton Keynes MK17 8EL (☎ 0908 583 495); Chancery House, 199 Silbury Boulevard, Grafton Gate East, Central Milton Keynes MK9 1LN (☎ 0908 662 277, fax 0908 675 667 car tel 0836 742 932, telex 826480); 48 Bedford Sq, London WC1B 3DS

SWAN, Lt Col Sir William Bertram; KCVO(1988), CBE (1968, TD 1955, JP 1964); s of Nichol Allan Swan (d 1924), of West Blanerne Duns, and Anne Gardiner Swan, *née* Keir (d 1959); *b* 19 Sept 1914; *Educ* St Mary's Sch Melrose, Edinburgh Acad; *m* 1948, Ann, da of George Gilroy (d 1961), of Hogarth, Spring Valley, Kirk Yetholm; 4 s (Allan, Richard and Charles (twins), John); *Career* served 1939-42 4 Bn KDSB (UK and France) IA 1942-45; farmer; pres: Nat Farmers' Union of Scotland 1961-62, Scottish Agric Orgn Soc Ltd 1966-68; memb Devpt Cmmn 1964-76; chm Rural Forum Scotland 1982-88;Co Cmdt Roxburgh Berwick and Selkirk ACF 1959-73; pres: Lowlands TA and VRA 1983-86, Scottish Cricket Union 1972-73; Lord Lt Berks 1969-; pres: Borders Scout Assoc 1973-, Borders Assoc of Youth Clubs 1974-, Berwickshire Naturalists Club 1987-88; *Recreations* sport; *Style—* Lt-Col Sir William Bertram Swan, KCVO, CBE, TD, JP; Blackhouse, Eyemouth, Berwickshire (☎ 0361 82842)

SWANN, Sir Anthony Charles Christopher; 3 Bt (UK 1906), of Prince's Gardens, Royal Borough of Kensington, CMG (1958), OBE (1950); s of Sir Duncan Swann, 2 Bt (d 1962), Dorothy Margaret, *née* Johnson; *b* 29 June 1913; *Educ* Eton, New Coll Oxford (MA); *m* 28 Nov 1940, Jean, da of John Herbert Niblock-Stuart, of Nairobi; 1 s; *Heir* s, Michael Swann; *Career* Maj KAR, served E Africa, Abyssinia; formerly min of Def and Home Security Kenya; *Recreations* fishing, racing, reading, music; *Clubs* Army and Navy, Pratt's; *Style—* Sir Anthony Swann Bt, CMG, OBE; 23 Montpelier Sq, SW7 (☎ 01 589 5546)

SWANN, Hon Mrs (Lydia Mary); *née* Hewitt; eldest da of 8 Viscount Lifford; *b* 10 May 1938; *m* 24 April 1965, Michael Christopher Swann, o s of Sir Anthony Charles Christopher Swann, 3 Bt, CMG, OBE; 2 s, 1 da; *Style—* The Hon Mrs Swann; Snail House, Brightling, Robertsbridge, Sussex

SWANN, Michael Christopher; TD; s and h of Sir Anthony Swann, 3 Bt, CMG, OBE; *b* 23 Sept 1941; *Educ* Eton; *m* 1965, Hon Lydia Hewitt, da of 8 Viscount Lifford; 2 s (Jonathan b 1966, Toby b 1971), 1 da (Tessa b 1969); *Career* late 60 Rifles; *Style—* Michael Swann Esq TD; Snail House, Brightling, Robertsbridge, Sussex

SWANN, Baron (Life Peer UK 1980); Michael Meredith; s of Meredith Blake Robson Swann, MD; *b* 1 Mar 1920; *Educ* Winchester, Gonville and Caius Cambridge (MA, PhD); *m* 1942, Teresa Ann, da of Reginald Gleadowe, CVO; 2 s, 2 da; *Career* Lt-Col served Iceland, NW Europe WW II; fell of Gonville and Caius Coll Cambridge 1946-52, prof of natural history Edinburgh Univ 1952-65, princ and vice-chllr Edinburgh Univ 1965-73; chm BBC 1973-80, chllr York Univ 1980-, tstee Wellcome Tst 1973-, chm: Company Pensions Information Ctee 1984-, RAM 1982-; Hon DUniv Edinburgh 1983; FRS, FRSE; kt 1972; *Recreations* gardening, sailing; *Clubs* Athenaeum, New (Edinburgh); *Style—* The Rt Hon The Lord Swann; Tallat Steps, Coln St Denys, nr Cheltenham, Glos (☎ 0285 72 533)

SWANN, Hon Peter; s of Baron Swann (Life Peer); *b* 25 April 1955; *Educ* Edinburgh Academy, St Andrews Univ (MA), Bristol Univ, LSE; *Career* lectr Brunel Univ; *Recreations* sailing; *Style—* The Hon Peter Swann; 23 Sheffield Terrace, London W8

SWANN, Hon Richard Meredith; s of Baron Swann (Life Peer); *b* 31 August 1944; *Educ* Edin Acad, Trin Cambridge, UCL; *m* 1969, Julia Coke-Steel; 1 s; *Career* architect; *Recreations* sailing; *Style—* The Hon Richard Swann; 1 Carmel Court, Holland St, London W8

SWANNELL, Robert William Ashburnham; s of Maj David William Ashburnham Swannell, MBE, and Pamela Mary, *née* Woods; *b* 28 Dec 1924; *Educ* Rugby; *m* Jan 1982, Patricia Ann, da of John, *née* Ward; 1 s (William), 1 da (Alicia); *Career* CA 1973 with Peat Marwick Mitchell & Co 1969-73, Inns of Ct Sch of Law 1973-76, barr Lincolns Inn 1976; dir: United Gulf Ltd 1983-84, J Henry Schroder Wagg & Co 1985-; *Style—* Robert Swannell, Esq; 120 Cheapside, London EC2 (☎ 01 382 6000, fax 01 382 6459)

SWANSEA, 4 Baron (UK 1893); Sir John Hussey Hamilton; 4 Bt (UK 1882), DL (Powys 1962); s of 3 Baron Swansea, DSO, MVO, TD (d 1934), and Hon Winifred Hamilton, da of 1 Baron Holmpatrick; *b* 24 Jan 1957; *Educ* Eton, Trinity Coll Cambridge; *m* 1, 1956 (m dis 1973), Miriam (d 1975), da of Anthony Caccia-Birch, MC; 1 s, 2 da; m 2, 1982, Mrs Lucy Temple-Richards, da of Rt Rev Hugh Gough and Hon Mrs (M E) Gough, *qqv*; *Heir* s, Hon Richard Vivian; *Career* vice-pres and vice-chm of cncl of Nat Rifle Assoc; pres: Shooting Sports Tst, Welsh Rifle Assoc; chm Br Shooting Sports cncl; *Recreations* shooting, fishing, rifle shooting; *Style—* The Rt Hon the Lord Swansea, DL; Chapel House Cottage, Alltmawr, Builth Wells, Powys (☎ 098 23 662)

SWANTON, Ernest William (Jim); OBE (1965); s of William Swanton (d 1966), of Malvern, Worcs, and Lillian Emily, *née* Walters (d 1953); *b* 11 Feb 1907; *Educ* Cranleigh Sch; *m* 11 Feb 1958, Ann Marion Carbutt, da of R H de Montmorency (d 1938), of Wentworth, Surrey; *Career* WWII 1939-45, Acta Maj 148 FD Regt Bedfords Yeo RA (Captured Singapore POW 1942-45); journalist, author and bdcaster 1924-; journalist Evening Standard 1927-39; Daily Telegraph: cricket corr 1946-75, rugby corr 1948-64; played cricket for Middx 1937-38, managed own X1: W Indies 1956 and 1961, Malaya and far East 1964; pres: Cricket Soc 1976-83, Sandwich Town CC 1977-, Forty Club 1983-86, The Cricketer 1988-; ctee memb MCC 1975-85 and Kent CCC 1971-89; *Books* A History of Cricket (with HS Altham 1938), Denis Compton a Cricket Sketch (1948), Elusive Victory (1951), Cricket and the Clock (1952), Best Cricket Stories (1953), West Indian Adventure (1954), Victory in Australia 1954/55 (1955), Reports from South Africa (1957), West Indies Revisited (1960), The Ashes in Suspense (1963), World of Cricket (ed 1966, 1980, 1986), Cricket from All Angles (1968), Sort of a Cricket Person (1972), Swanton in Australia (1975), Follow On (1985), As I Said at the Time (anthology 1984), Kent Cricket a Photographic History 1744-1984 (with CH Taylor 1985), Back Page Cricket (1987); *Recreations* golf, watching cricket; *Clubs* MCC, Vincent's (Oxford), Naval and Military, 1 Zingari; *Style—* Jim Swanton, Esq, OBE; Delfs House, Sandwich, Kent CT13 9HB

SWANWICK, Sir Graham Russell; MBE (1944); s of Eric Drayton Swanwick (d 1955), of Whittington House, Chesterfield, and Margery Eleanor, *née* Norton (d 1959); *b* 24 August 1906; *Educ* Winchester, Univ Coll Oxford; *m* 1, 1933 (m dis 1945), Helen Barbara Reid (d 1970); 2 s (Richard, Anthony); m 2, 1952, Mrs Audrey Celia Parkinson (d 1987), da of H C Hextall of Ford, Ashurst, Steyning, Sussex (d 1987); 1 step s (Richard) (and 1 step s (Dale) decd); *Career* WWII Wing Cdr RAFUR 1040-45 (despatches); barr Inner Temple 1930, QC 1956, bencher 1962; rec of: Lincoln 1957-59, Leicester 1959-66; dep chm Lincs QS (parts of Kesteven) 1960-63, chm Derbyshire QS 1963-66, dep chm 1966-71; judge Jersey and Guernsey Cts of Appeal 1964-66, judge of High Ct of Justice (Queen's Bench Div) 1966-80, presiding judge Midland and Oxford Circuit 1975-78; kt 1966; *Recreations* shooting; *Clubs* RAF; *Style—* Sir Graham Swanwick, MBE; Burnett's Ashurst, Steyning, West Sussex (☎ 0403 710241)

SWARTZ, Col Hon Sir Reginald William Colin; KBE (1972), MBE ((Mil) 1948,

ED); s of J Swartz (decd); *b* 14 April 1911; *Educ* Toowoomba GS, Brisbane GS,; *m* 1936, Hilda, *née* Robinson; 2 s, 1 da; *Career* MHR (Lib) for Darling Downs Qld 1949-72, dep Govt whip 1950-51, parly sec for: Commerce and Agric 1951-61, Trade 1961-72; min of state for Repatriation, Health, Social Services, Civil Aviation, Nat Devpt; ldr of House of Reps Canberra 1971-72; ldr of many delegations incl Aust Delegation to India 1957, Aust Delegation to Cwlth Health Mins' Conference Edinburgh 1965; life memb Lib Party; former co dir; FBIM, FAIM; *see Debrett's Handbook of Australia and New Zealand for further details*; *Recreations* bowls; *Clubs* United Service (Brisbane), Roy Automobile and Australian (Melbourne), Twin Towns Services (Tweed Heads), Templestowe Bowls, Darling Downs Aero (Toowoomba); *Style*— Col the Hon Sir Reginald Swartz, KBE, MBE, ED, JP; 32 Leawarra Crescent, Doncaster East, Vic 3109, Australia (☎ 03 842 1439)

SWAYNE, Sir Ronald Oliver Carless; MC (1945); s of Col Oswald Rocke Swayne, DSO (d 1948) of Tillington Court, nr Hereford, by his w, Brenda (d 1956), yr da of Arthur Butler, of Brooklyn, Chislehurst; *b* 11 May 1918; *Educ* Bromsgrove Sch Worcester, Oxford Univ; *m* 1941, Charmian (d 1984), da of Maj W E P Cairnes (d 1953), of Eardsley, Herefords; 1 s (Giles b 1946);1 da (Amanda b 1951); *Career* served WW II Herefs Regt and 1 Commando; chm Overseas Containers 1973-82 (md 1978-82); dir Ocean Tport & Trading, Nat Freight Co 1973-85; pres: Inst of Freight Forwarders 1980, Gen Cncl Br Shipping 1978-79; vice-chm Br Shipping Fedn 1976; former pres Ctee des Assocs d'Armateurs EEC; kt 1979; *Clubs* Flyfishers (London), Houghton (Stockbridge); *Style*— Sir Ronald Swayne, MC; Puddle House, Chicksgrove, Tisbury, Salisbury, Wilts SP3 6NA (☎ 072 276 454)

SWAYTHLING, 3 Baron (UK 1907); Sir Stuart Albert Samuel Montagu; 3 Bt (UK 1894), OBE (1947); s of 2 Baron (d 1927), and Gladys, OBE, da of late Col Albert Goldsmid, MVO (d 1965); *b* 19 Dec 1898; *Educ* Clifton Coll, Westminster Sch, Trin Cambridge; *m* 1, 1925 (m dis 1942), Mary Violet, da of late Maj Walter Levy, DSO; 2 s, 1 da; m 2, 1945, Mrs Jean Marcia Knox, CBE (chief controller and dir of ATS 1941-43), da of late G G Leith Marshall; *Heir* s, Hon David Montagu; *Career* WW 1 Lt Gren Guards 1917-20, WW II Capt Home Guard; dir Samuel Montagu & Co Ltd 1951-54 (ptnr from 1925); JP: County of Southampton 1928-48, Surrey 1948-80; chm Woking Bench 1967-70, hon tres Franco-Br Parly Relations Ctee 1970-77, master of Farmers' Co 1962-63 (memb of ct 1950-), pres Royal Assoc of Br Dairy Farmers 1972-73 (dep pres 1970-72, 1973-74, cncl memb 1935-), memb Cncl RASE 1961; judged cattle at many events inc: The Royal Show, The Royal Dairy Show, Royal Show Kenya, Royal Show Wester Australia, The Royal Guernsey Agric and The Nat Dairy Herds Show; vice pres Hampshire CCC, tres Spitfire Mitchell Meml Fund 1944-52, pres and hon cmdt Jewish Lads' and Girls' Bd 1972- (cmdt 1963-72), memb: Bd of Deputies of Br Jews 1929-49 (hon auditor 1941-47), Anglo-Jewish Assoc Cncl 1926-45; *Style*— The Rt Hon Lord Swaythling; Crocker Hill House, Crocker Hill, Chichester, West Sussex PO18 0LH (☎ 0243 532406)

SWEENEY, Dr Thomas Kevin; s of John Francis Sweeney (d 1975), of Clontarf, Dublin, and Mildred, *née* Forbes (d 1987); *b* 10 August 1923; *Educ* O'Connell Sch Dublin, Nat Univ Coll Dublin (MB Bchir, BAO, FFCM, DTM&H, TDD); *m* 25 Jan 1950, Eveleen Moira, da of Driryan (d 1959), of 27 Fitzwilliam Sq, Dublin; 2 s (Niall b 1950, Paul b 1962), 2 da (Geainne (Mrs Hedges) b 1956, Maedb (Mrs Newman) b 1958); *Career* princ med offr Colonial Med Serv 1950-65, asst sr med offr Welsh Hosp Bd 1965-68; Dept of Health: med offr 1968-88, sr princ med offr 1979-83, sr med offr 1983-88; QHP 1984-87; memb BR Med Assoc; *Recreations* golf, cathedrals, gardening, reading; *Style*— Dr Thomas Sweeney; The White House, Sheerwater Ave, Woodham, Weybridge, Surrey KT15 3DD (☎ 093 234 3559)

SWEET, Lt-Col Peter Leo; s of Leo Parke Sweet (d 1966), and Betty Vera Myer (second husband), *née* Cowell' (d 1976), Cowells descended from margaret Tudor da of Henry VII, via Spencers & Spencer-Cowell; *b* 6 Mar 1920; *Educ* Dean Close Sch Cheltenham, RMA Woolwich; *m* 1, 29 March 1944, Elizabeth Joan, da of Denis Evans (d 1982); 1 s (Nicholas b 1953), 3 da (Sally Joan b 1946, Caroline b 1948, Jane b 1950); m 2, 29 April 1977, Mathilde-Noelle Marie, da of Vicomte Gaston Boula De Mareüil (d 1937); 2 s (Jean Loup b 1948, Francois b 1949 (Formé-Becherèt)); *Career* Lt-Col, RA; served in: France 1939-40, Iceland 1941-42, Europe 1944 Burma and IndoChina 1945-47 (despatches 1944), Staff Offr Lt-Col 1966-68, ret 1968; master of hounds 1956-58, race course steward France; LeFroy Gold Medal 1964, offr of the Order of Merit of Cambodgia 1946; *Recreations* hunting, fishing, shooting, sailing, racing (horse); *Clubs* Royal Lymington Yacht, Société de Venerie (France); *Style*— Lt-Col Peter Sweet; Les Robineaux, Oizoix, 18700 Aubighy Sur Nére, France

SWEETEN, Anthony Ricardo; s of Benjamin Arthur Sweeten (d 1975); *b* 24 Oct 1941; *Educ* Clare Hall Coll Halifax, Tech Coll Halifax, Bradford Univ; *m* 1966, Marion Brenda Mary, nee Hayter; 2 s, 1 da; *Career* dir TS Harrison & Sons Ltd 1975-; *Recreations* golf, shooting, fishing; *Clubs* Lightcliffe Golf, Leeds Serv Rifle; *Style*— Anthony Sweeten, Esq; Green Acre, Bramley Lane, Lightcliffe, Halifax, W Yorkshire (☎ Halifax 201467)

SWEETING, Lt Col Henry Kennett; s of Henry Carol Sweeting, OBE, JP (d 1956); *b* 13 August 1919; *Educ* Eton, Sandhurst; *m* 1945, Aileen, da Capt Keith Seth-Smith, OBE (d 1959); 2 da (1 s decd); *Career* Lt Col Coldstream Gds 1939-61, Gen Staff Offr (2) HQ London Dist 1950-53, mil asst to Cmdt Berlin (Br Sector) 1956-58, Cdr 2 Bn Coldstream Gds 1958-60, ret 1961; memb Lloyd's; MInstD; *Clubs* Cavalry & Guards'; *Style*— Lt Col Henry Sweeting; Ballashamrock House, Port Soderick, Isle of Man (☎ Douglas 4670)

SWEETMAN, Mrs Ronald; Jennifer Joan; *see*: Jennifer Dickson

SWEETNAM, (David) Rodney; s of Dr William Sweetnam (d 1970), and Irene, *née* Black (d 1967); *b* 5 Feb 1927; *Educ* Clayesmore Sch, Cambridge Univ & Middlesex Hosp Med Sch, London Univ (MA, MB BChir, FRCS); *m* 1959, Patricia, da of A Staveley Gough, OBE, FRCS; 1 s (David), 1 d (Sarah); *Career* Surgn-Lt RN VR 1950-52; orthapaedic surgn to HM the Queen, conslt orthopaedic surgn to the Middx Hosp and King Edward VII Hosp for Offrs; hon Civil conslt in orthopaedic surgery to the Army; conslt advsr in orthopaedic surgery to Dept of Health and Social Security; hon conslt surgn Royal Nat Orthopaedic Hosp; memb cncl RCS; pres Combined Services Orthopaedic Soc; div, sec and tres Br Editorial Soc of Bone and Jt Surgery; hon conslt orthopaedic surgn Royal Hosp Chelsea, dir Med Sickness Annaity and Life Assur Soc Ltd, pres Br Orthopaedic Assoc 1985-86, chm Med Res Cncls Working Pty on Bone Sarcoma 1981-86; *Publications* The Basis and Practise of Orthopaedics (jtly 1980), 'Osteosarcoma' Br Medical Journal (1979), papers on bone tumours and gen orthopaedic surgery and fractures; *Style*— Rodney Sweetnam, Esq; 33 Harley Street, London W1N 1DA (☎ 01 580 5409)

SWEETNAM, (Robert) William; s of George William Sweetnam, of Chardstock, Devon, and Elisabeth Ann, *née* Randolph; *b* 25 Nov 1954; *Educ* Clifton Coll Bristol (LLB); *m* 26 April 1980, Philippa Mary, da of John Eastell, of Ingatestone, Essex; 1 s (James William b 1982), 1 da (Jeniffer Susan b 1985); *Career* slr 1978-; dir Dryfield Finance Ltd 1983; ptnr Battern & Co Slrs 1983-; *Recreations* skiing, sailing, classic cars, carpentry; *Style*— William Sweetnam, Esq; 33 Glenavon Park, Sneyd Park, Bristol; 2 St Pauls Road, Clifton, Bristol (☎ 0272 737848, fax 272 237040)

SWETENHAM, John Foster; s of Brig John Edmund Swetenham, DSO (d 1982), and Alison Ann, yst da of Col the Hon Guy Greville Wilson, CMG, DSO; descended from Elias de Swetenham living in the reigns of Richard I, John and Henry III. Family received land at the Somerford Booths 1298, land sold 1930's; *b* 16 Jan 1939; *Educ* Eton, Sandhurst; *m* 1964, Marion Sylvia, yr da of George Alfred Parker (d 1982); 1 s, 1 da; *Career* served 1956-70, adjutant Royal Scots Greys 1965-67, Capt, ret 1970; memb Stock Exchange 1973-; *Recreations* sailing, shooting, fishing, skiing; *Clubs* Royal Yacht Sqadron, Royal Ocean Racing, Cavalry and Guards', Pratt's; *Style*— Foster Swetenham, Esq; Pound Farmhouse, Rayne, Braintree, Essex CM7 5DJ (☎ 0376 26738); 84 Campden St, London W8 (☎ 01 727 5176); office: William de Broe Hill Chaplin & Company Ltd, Pinners Hall, Austin Friars, London EC2 (☎ 01 588 7511)

SWIFT, Lionel; s of Harris Swift (d 1971), and Bassie Swift; *b* 3 Oct 1931; *Educ* UC London (LLB), Brasenose Coll Oxford (BCL), Univ of Chicago Law Sch (JD); *m* 1966, Elizabeth, da of Max Herzig, of Montreal; 1 da (Allison b 1968); *Career* jr counsel to treasy in probate 1974; barr, QC 1975, rec 1979; bencher (Inner Temple) 1984; chm Institute of Laryngology and Otology 1985; *Style*— Lionel Swift, QC; 4 Paper Buildings, Temple, London EC4Y 7EX (☎ 01 353 3420)

SWIFT, Malcolm Robin; QC (1988); s of Willie Swift, Huddersfield, W Yorks, and Heather May Farquhar Swift, OBE, *née* Nield; *b* 19 Jan 1948; *Educ* Colne Valley HS W Yorks, Kings Coll London (LLB); *m* 20 Sept 1969, (Anne) Rachael, da of Ernest Rothery Ayre, of Bolton-by-Bowland, Lancs; 1 s (Daniel b 1977), 2 da (Joanna b 1972, Catherine b 1975); *Career* barr Grays Inn 1970, practice NE circuit, recorder Crown Ct 1987, co-opted memb remuneration ctee of Bar Cncl 1978-, vice chm Brighouse Civic Tst; *Recreations* squash, cycling, music, theatre; *Style*— Malcolm Swift, Esq, QC; Park Court Chambers, 40 Park Cross St, Leeds LS1 2QH (☎ 0532 433277, fax 0532 421285, telex 666135 DX Leeds 26401)

SWIFT, Ronald Cephas; s of James Swift (d 1981), and Maud Mary, *née* Coleman (d 1981); *b* 4 August 1920; *Educ* Haberdasher's Aske's; *m* 16 Oct 1943, Constance Maude (Connie), da of Frederick William Edwards (d 1970); 2 s (Peter Michael b 12 Dec 1944, Brian Paul b 19 Feb 1947); *Career* RNVR 1938-39, RN 1939-46; mktg mangr Foil-James Booth Aluminium Ltd 1963-65 (sales promotion mangr 1962-63), gen mangr Foil div Foil-Alcan Booth Industries Ltd 1965-77, dir Alcan Foils Ltd 1971-77, commercial dir and gen mangr Foil-Alcan Booth Sheet Ltd 1977-82 (co name changed to Alcan Plate Ltd 1978), chm promotion ctee Euro Aluminium Foil Assoc 1978-82; former pres Past Rotariam Club Eastbourne and dist; memb: Probus Club Eastbourne, Post Office and Telephone Advsy Ctees Eastbourne, Glyndebourne Festival Soc, Friends of Devonshire Park Theatre Eastbourne, Friends of Eastbourne Hosps; *Clubs* Wig and Pen, City Livery; *Style*— Ronald Swift Esq; 15 Tavistock, Devonshire Place, Eastbourne, E Sussex BN21 4AG (☎ 0323 35282)

SWIFT, Timothy John; s of Kenneth Alan Swift, of Great Glen, Leicestershire, and Olive Mary, *née* Brown; *b* 1 July 1957; *Educ* Beauchamp Coll Oadby, Univ of Leicester (BSc); *m* 10 Feb 1979, Diane Elizabeth, da of David Bryant, of Stafford; 1 s (Owen b 1987); *Career* sr analyst GEC Gas Turbines 1978-85, res technologist GEC ERC Whetstone 1985-; ccncllr Leics 1981- (gp ldr 1981-88), Oadby and Wigston Borough cncllr 1983-, Parly candidate Harborough 1983 and 1987, memb ACC 1985-, chm social servs ctee ACC 1988-; *Recreations* squash, badminton, country walking; *Style*— Timothy Swift, Esq; 31 Cheshire Drive, South Wigton, Leicester LE8 2WA (☎ 0533 786844)

SWIFT, William James; CVO (1961); s of late James Swift; *b* 3 Nov 1915; *Educ* Park High Sch Birkenhead, Liverpool Univ; *m* 1939, Elspeth Madeleine, *née* Bruyn; 2 da; *Career* Gp Capt RAF Euro theatre 1943-45, cmd 216 Sqdn Middle East 1953-56, Suez operation 1956, air attaché Tehran 1958-61, CO RAF Station Manston 1961-64, NATO Int Mil Staff Washington and Brussels 1966-69, ret 1970; dir Br Red Cross Soc, Berkshire Branch 1971-80, Red Cross Badge of Honour for Distinguished Service 1980; *Recreations* golf, swimming, gardening; *Clubs* Calcot Park Golf; *Style*— William Swift Esq, CVO; Clompers, Broadlands Close, Calcot Park, Reading (☎ 0734 27696)

SWINBURNE, Prof Richard Granville; s of William Henry Swinburne, of Colchester, and Gladys Edith Swinburne (d 1988); *b* 26 Dec 1934; *Educ* Exeter Coll Oxford (BA, MA, BPhil); *m* 1960, Monica; 2 da (Caroline b 1961, Nicola b 1962); *Career* Fereday fell St Johns Coll Oxford 1958-61, Leverhulme res fell Leeds Univ 1961-63, lectr Hull Univ 1963-69 (sr lectr 1969-72), visiting assoc prof of philosophy Maryland Univ 1969-70, prof of philosophy Keele Univ 1972-84, Nolloth prof of the philosophy of the Christian religion Oxford Univ 1985-; visiting lectureships: Wilde lectr Oxford Univ 1975-78, Marrett Memorial lectr Exeter Coll Oxford 1980, Gifford lectr Aberdeen Univ 1982-83 and 1983-84, Edward Cadbury lectr Birmingham University 1987, distinguished visiting scholar Univ of Adelaide, visiting prof of philosophy Syracuse Univ 1987; *Books* Space and Time (1968), The Concept of Miracle (1971), An Introduction to Confirmation Theory (1973), The Coherence of Theism (1977), The Existence of God (1979), Faith and Reason (1981), Personal Identity (with Sydney Shoemaker 1984), The Evolution of the Soul (1986); ed: The Justification of Induction (1974), Space, Time and Causality (1983), Miracles (1988); *Style*— Prof Richard Swinburne; Oriel College, Oxford OX1 4EW (☎ 0865 276 589)

SWINBURNE, Prof Terence Reginald; s of Reginald Swinburne, of Gravesend, Kent, and Gladys Hannah, *née* Shrusbsall; *b* 17 July 1936; *Educ* Kent Co GS for Boys Gravesend, Imp Coll of Sci and Technol Univ of London (BSc, PhD, DSc); *m* 23 Aug 1958, Valerie Mary, da of Daniel Parkes; 2 s (Julian Edward b 25 Sept 1965, Nigel David b 17 Jan 1968); *Career* reader faculty of agric Queens Univ of Belfast 1977 (joined 1960), sr princ sci offr Plant Pathology Res Div Dept of Agric NI 1979-80, head of crop protection div E Malling Reo Station 1980-85, dir AFRC Inst of Hort Res 1985-; memb Br Mycological Soc, Assoc of Applied Biologists, Inst of Biol; FIHort; *Books* Iron, Siderophores and Plant Diseases; *Recreations* sailing; *Clubs* Farmers; *Style*— Prof Terence Swinburne; Tan House, Frog lane, West Malling, Kent (☎ 0732

846 090); AFRC Institute of Horticultural Research, Bradbourne House, East Malling, Kent (☎ 0732 843 833)

SWINDELLS, Maj-Gen (George) Michael Geoffrey; CB (1985); s of George Martyn Swindells (d 1960), and Marjorie, *née* Leigh; *b* 15 Jan 1930; *Educ* Rugby; *m* 8 July 1955, Prudence Bridget Barbara, da of William Scarth Carlisle Tully, CBE (d 1987); 1 s (Adam b 1975), 2 da (Diana Harris b 1956, Georgina b 1961); *Career* cmmnd 5 Royal Inniskilling Dragoon Guards 1949, cmmd 9/12 Royal Lancers 1968-71, cdr 11 Armd Bde 1975-76, Royal Coll Defence Studies 1977, chief jt servs Liason Organisation Bonn 1980-83, dir mgmnt and support of intelligence 1983-85; head admin Smith and Williamson 1985-87, controller Army Benevolent Fund 1987-; chm governing body Royal Sch Hampstead, servs liason Variety Club of GB; *Recreations* country life; *Clubs* Cavalry and Guards, Army & Navy; *Style—* Maj-Gen Michael Swindells, CB; Wilcot Lodge, Pewsey, Wilts; 41 Queen's Gate, London SW7 5HR (☎ 01 584 5232)

SWINDELLS, Robert; JP (Ashton-upon-Lyne 1977); s of William Swindells (d 1962), and Mary Alice Swindells; *b* 27 May 1928; *Educ* Glossop GS Derbys, John Dalton Coll of Technol Manchester; *m* 2 July 1965, Annette, da of Harold Greenwood, of Audenshaw, Manchester; 3 s (Jonathan b 13 March 1966, David b 12 June 1968, Christopher b 2 May 1970); *Career* fndr dir Berwin Rubber Co Ltd 1953, chm and md Berwin Polymer Processing Gp Ltd 1958-83; HM gen cmmr for income tax Oldham dist 1981; memb: Longdendale Footpath Preservation Soc, Masonic Club Ashton-upon-Lyne; FPRI 1979; *Recreations* music, wildlife, charities, travelling; *Clubs* Lancs CC, North Cheshire Cruising; *Style—* Robert Swindells, Esq, JP; Minorca House, Hollingworth via Hyde, Cheshire SK14 8HY (☎ 0457 62396)

SWINDEN, (Thomas) Alan; CBE (1971); s of Dr Thomas Swinden (d 1944), of Sheffield, and Ethel Taylor, *née* Thomp-son (d 1978); *b* 27 August 1915; *Educ* Rydal Sch, Univ of Sheffield (BEng); *m* 21 June 1941, Brenda Elise, da of Frederick John Roe (d 1961), of Epsom; 1 da (Gail b 1950); *Career* Rolls Royce Ltd 1937-55 (seconded armd fighting vehicle div Miny of Supply 1941-45); dir: Engrg Employers Fedn 1964-65 (joined 1955), Engrg Indust Trg Bd 1965-70, dep dir-gen Confedn Br Indust 1970-78, chm Inst Manpower Studies 1977-86, dir Kingston Regnl Mgmnt Centre 1980-84; memb cncl ACAS 1974-84, memb consultative gp on industl and business affrs BBC 1977-83; chm Derby No 1 Hosp Mgmnt ctee 1953-55, chm govrs N E Surrey Coll Technol 1986- (govr 1973-); *Recreations* gardening, golf, reading; *Clubs* RAC; *Style—* Alan Swinden, Esq, CBE; 85 College Rd, Epsom, Surrey KT17 4HH (☎ 03727 20848)

SWINDON, Archdeacon of; *see*: Clark, Ven Kenneth James

SWINEY, Col David Alexander; s of Maj Gen Sir Neville Swiney KBE, CB, MC, ADC (d 1970), of Bourton-on-the-Water, Glos, and Ena Margery Le Poer, *née* Power (d 1975); *b* 22 Jan 1924; *Educ* Cheltenham Coll, ASC Camberley, Joint Services Staff Coll Latimer; *m* 9 Sept 1950, Hazel Anne Elisabeth, da of Col Arthur Joynes, MC (d 1978), of Frinton-on-Sea; 1 s (Michael b 1951), 2 da (Amanda b 1954, Tessa b 1958); *Career* WWII cmmnd RA, Lt 75 Anti-Tank Regt NW Europe 1944-45, 8 Field Regt India 1945-46 (despatches 1945), pilot trg UK 1946-47, Capt 651 AOP Sqdn RAF (Palestine, Jordan, Tripoli, Egypt) 1947-50, Instr Mons OCS 1951-54, Adj 37 Regt Malta 1956-58, Maj staff of Dir Ops Cyprus 1958-60, 2 i/c 36 Guided Weapons Regt 1960-62 Germany, planning staff HQ BAOR Germany 1963-65, Lt-Col CO Lovat Scouts Scotland 1965-67, staff naval C in C Plymouth 1967-69, Col ops plans and logistics HQ FARELF Singapore 1969-71, trng staff UKLF 1972-74, MOD 1975-78; admin Glos Red Cross, co-ordinator Glos Co Jt Emergency Exec Ctee, chm Bourton Hosp Friends; pres Bourton Vale CC; MBIM; *Recreations* shooting, fishing, history, Cotswold churches; *Clubs* MCC, Lansdowne; *Style—* Col David Swiney; Nethercote House, Bourton-on-the-Water, Glos GL54 2DT (☎ 0451 20354)

SWINFEN, Averil, Baroness Swinfen; Averil Kathleen Suzanne; da of late Maj William Marshall Hickman Humphreys and formerly w of Lt-Col Andrew Knowles, TD; *m* 1950, as his 2 w, 2 Baron (d 1977); *Style—* The Rt Hon Averil, Lady Swinfen; Keentlea, Clifden, Corofin, Co Clare, Ireland

SWINFEN, 3 Baron (UK 1919); Roger Mynors Swinfen Eady; JP (Kent 1983-86); s of 2 Baron (d 1977), and Mary Aline, da of late Col Harold Mynors Farmar, CMG, DSO; *b* 14 Dec 1938; *Educ* Westminster, RMA Sandhurst; *m* 24 Oct 1962, Patricia Anne, o da of Frank D Blackmore (d 1968), of Dublin; 1 s, 3 da (Hon Georgina b 1964, Hon Katherine b 1966, Hon Arabella b 1969); *Heir* s, Hon Charles Roger Peregrine Swinfen Eady b 8 March 1971; *Career* Lt Royal Scots; memb Direct Mail Services Standard Bd 1983-; ARICS 1970-; chm Parly Gp Video Enquiry Working Party 1983-85; Fell Indust and Parly Tst 1983; pres SE Region - Br Sports Assoc for the Disabled 1986-; *Style—* The Rt Hon the Lord Swinfen; House of Lords, London SW1

SWINGLAND, Owen Merlin Webb; QC (1974); s of Charles Swingland (d 1941), of Kent, and Maggie Eveline , *née* Webb (d 1961); family moved from Worcestershire circa 1680 to parish of St Margaret Pattens, Eastcheap London, lived in Kent about 200 Years; *b* 26 Sept 1919; *Educ* Haberdashers' Aske's, Kings Coll London; *m* 1941, Kathleen Joan Eason, *née* Parry, da of late Frederick William Parry; 1 s (Charles), 2 da (Diana, Carole); *Career* barr; bencher of Gray's Inn, gen cmmr of income tax; a church cmmr for England; Master of Haberdashers' Co 1987; Lincoln's Inn 1978; *Recreations* reading, music, theatre, heavy work in woodland and grounds; *Style—* Owen Swingland, Esq, QC; Redwings House, Weald, Sevenoaks, Kent (☎ 0732 451667)

SWINGLEHURST, John James Hutton; s of Hutton Swinglehurst (d 1986), Broadwell House, Market Lavington, Wilts, and Margaret Lascelles, *née* Reynolds; *b* 27 Dec 1931; *Educ* St Bees Sch; *m* 1 (m dis), Hazel Anne, *née* Godfrey-Faussett; 2 s (Anthony b 25 Nov 1958, Richard b 21 Aug 1960); m 2, 4 Dec 1964, Patricia Maureen, da of Daniel John Bowen, of Bolnore, Cuckfield, Sussex; 1 s (Hutton b 28 July 1970); *Career* insur broker; dir: Sedgwick Gp plc 1979-, Sedgwick Overseas Investmts 1975-, Sedgwick Gp Africa Property Ltd 1982-, Sedgwick Ltd 1986-, Sedgwick Hldgs RV 1987-; *Recreations* skiing, tennis, swimming, music; *Style—* John Swinglehurst, Esq; 26 Holland St, London W8 (☎ 01 937 1995); Sedgwick Gp plc, Sedgwick House, The Sedgwick Centre, London E1 8DX (☎ 01 377 3138, fax 01 377 3292, car 0836 224 043, telex 882131)

SWINGLER, Raymond John Peter; s of Raymond Joseph Swingler (d 1942), of Christ Church, NZ, and Mary Elizabeth Swingler (d 1974); *b* 8 Oct 1933; *Educ* St Bede's Coll NZ, Univ of Kent; *m* 30 June 1960, Shirley (d 1980), da of Frederick Wilkinson (d 1958), of Plymouth; 2 da (Elizabeth-Jane b 1961, Claire-Louise b 1963); *Career* journalist: The Press (NZ) 1956-57, Marlborough Express 1957-59, Nelson Mail 1959-61, freelance Middle East 1961-62, Cambridge Evening News 1962-79; memb: Press Cncl 1975-78, Press Cncl Complaints Ctee 1976-78, Nat Exec Cncl NUJ 1973-75 and 1978-79, Prov Newspapers Indust Cncl 1976-79; chm Gen Purposes Ctee 1974-75, sec Press Cncl 1980-89 (asst dir 1989); *Recreations* nursing an old rolls; *Style—* Raymond Swingler, Esq; 147 Hemingford Rd, London N1 (☎ 01 704 7879); no 1 Salisbury Square, London EC4Y 8AE

SWINLEY, Margaret Albinia Joanna; OBE (1980); da of Capt Casper Silas Balfour Swinley DSO, DSC, RN (d 1983), and Sylvia Jocosa, *née* Carnegie; *b* 30 Sept 1935; *Educ* Southover Manor Sch Lewes Sussex, Univ of Edinburgh (MA) ; *Career* English teacher/sec United Paper Mills Ltd Jämsänkoski Finland 1958-60; joined British Cncl 1960: Birmingham Area Office 1960-63, Tel Aviv 1963, Lagos 1963-66; seconded to London HQ of VSO 1966-67, New Delhi 1967-70, dep rep Lagos 1970-73, dir Tech Cooperation Trg Dept 1973-76, rep Israel 1976-80, asst (then dep) controller Educn, Medicine & Science Divn 1980-82; controller: Africa and Middle East Divn 1982-86, Home Divn 1986-89; ret 1989; memb Soroptimist Int of Greater London (pres 1988-89); tstee Lloyd Fndn; govr Int Students House London; advsr Overseas Projects and memb Overseas Ctee Help the Aged;govr Westbury-on-Severn Church of England Primary Sch; *Recreations* theatre going, country life, keeping dogs; *Clubs* Royal Cwlth, Soroptimist Int of Greater London; *Style—* Miss Margaret Swinley, OBE; Broughtons Lodge, Flaxley, nr Newnham, Gloucestershire GL14 1JW

SWINNERTON, Col Iain Spencer; TD, JP, DL (W Midlands 1976); s of James Percy Swinnerton (d 1977), and Lilian, *née* Spencer (d 1935); *b* 23 April 1932; *Educ* King Edward VI Sch Stourbridge, RMA Sandhurst; *m* 1958, Angela, da of Maurice Bent Sellers; 1 s, 2 da; *Career* proprietor The Swinford Press; magistrate Worcs 1972-; sr vice pres and chm of cncl Birmingham & Midland Inst 1987-; govr: King Edwards Sch 1976-88, The Royal Sch Wolverhampton 1987-; div pres St John Ambulance 1977-85; pres Birmingham & Midland Soc for genealogy and Heraldry 1972-, chm Br Fedn of Family History Socs 1974-77 (pres 1978-), tstee Inst of Heraldic and Geneological Studies 1977-88 (Gold Medal 1977), fell Soc of Genealogists 1975; *Publications* A History of the Worcestershire Artillery, Heraldry can be Fun, also many papers on genealogy and heraldry; *Recreations* genealogy, heraldry, travel; *Clubs* Army and Navy, Old Edwardian; *Style—* Col Iain Swinnerton, TD, JP, DL; Owls Barn, Bridgnorth Rd, Stourton, nr Stourbridge, W Midlands DY7 6RS (☎ 0384 872717)

SWINNERTON-DYER; *see*: Dyer

SWINSON, Christopher; s of Arthur Ontagu Swinson, of 52 Green Moor Link, Winchmore Hill, London, and Jean, *née* Dudley; *b* 27 Jan 1948; *Educ* Wadham Coll Oxford (BA, MA); *m* 9 Sept 1972, Christine Margaret, da of Walter Yeats Hallam (d 1973); 1 s (Timothy b 1987); *Career* mangr Price Waterhouse 1970-78, ptnr Binder Hamlyn 1981- (sr mangr 1978-81); memb cncl and chm Euro Ctee ICEAW, hon tres Naval Records Soc; Freeman City of London 1985, memb Worshipful Co of CAs; RCA 1974; *Clubs* Athenaeum; *Style—* Christopher Swinson, Esq; 2 Seymour Close, Hatch End, Pinner, Middx; BDO Binder Hamlyn, 8 St Bride St, London EC4A 4DA (☎ 01 353 3020, fax 01 583 0031, telex 24276)

SWINSON, Sir John Henry Alan; OBE (1973); s of Edward Alexander Swinson (d 1944), of Knock Belfast, and Mary Margaret, *née* McLeod (d 1966); *b* 12 July 1922; *Educ* Royal Belfast Acad Inst; *m* 1944, Gallagher, da of John Gallagher (d 1958), of Castlereach, Belfast; 2 s (Alan, Peter); *Career* commercial dir for Ireland Trusthouse Forte plc 1962-; chm: NI Tourist Bd 1980-88 (memb 1970-80), Livestock Mktg Cmmn 1970-85, Catering Industry Trg Bd (NI) 1966-75, NI Trg Exec 1975-83; dir of various subsid cos; kt 1984; *Recreations* sailing (schooner 'Vanique'); *Clubs* Royal NI Yacht; *Style—* Sir John H A Swinson, OBE; 10 Circular Road East, Cultra, Co Down BT18 0HA, N Ireland (☎ (Holywood 2494); c/o Trusthouse Forte plc, Conway Hotel, Dunmurry, Belfast BT17 9ES (☎ Belfast 612101)

SWINTON, 2 Earl of (UK 1955); David Yarburgh Cunliffe-Lister; JP (N Yorks 1971), DL (1978); also Viscount Swinton (UK 1935), Baron Masham (UK 1955); s of late Maj the Hon John Yarburgh Cunliffe-Lister, eldest s of 1 Earl, GBE, CH, MC, MP; suc gf 1972; *b* 21 Mar 1937; *Educ* Winchester, RAC Cirencester; *m* 1959, Susan Lilian Primrose (Baroness Masham of Ilton, *qv*), da of late Sir Ronald Norman John Charles Udny Sinclair, 8 Bt (cr 1704); 1 s, 1 da (both adopted); *Heir* bro, Hon Nicholas Cunliffe-Lister; *Career* sits as Cons in House of Lords, Capt HM's Body Guard of Yeomen of the Guard (dep govt chief whip in Lords) 1982-86; cllr: N Riding Yorks 1961-74, N Yorks 1973-77; countryside cmmr 1987-; *Clubs* Whites's, Leyburn Market; *Style—* The Rt Hon the Earl of Swinton, JP DL; Dykes Hill House, Masham, N Yorks (☎ 0765 89241); 46 Westminster Gdns, Marsham St, London SW1 (☎ 01 834 0700)

SWINTON, Maj-Gen Sir John; KCVO (1979), OBE (1969), DL (Berwicks 1980); the family of Swinton of that Ilk, now represented by the Kimmerghame branch, has owned land in the Swinton area of Berwickshire since the eleventh century; s of Brig A H C Swinton, MC (d 1972), of Kimmerghame, Duns, Berwicks, and Mrs I D Erskine, of Swinton, Berwickshire; *b* 21 April 1925; *Educ* Harrow; *m* 1954, Judith Balfour, da of Harold Killen, of Merribee, NSW; 3 s, 1 da; *Career* served Scots Gds 1943-71; Lt-Col cmdg 1970-71, cmd 4 Gds Armd Bde 1972-73, Brig Lowlands 1975-76, GOC London Dist and Maj-Gen cmdg The Household Div 1976-79, ret 1979; Brig (Royal Co of Archers) Queen's Body Guard for Scotland; Hon Col 2 Bn 52 Lowland Volunteers 1983-, nat chm Royal Br Legion Scotland 1986-89 (vice chm 1984-86); chm: Berwickshire Civic Soc 1982-, Scottish Ex-Serv Charitable Orgns SESCO 1988-; tstee: Scottish Nat War Meml 1984-, Army Museums Ogilby Tst 1978-; memb centl advsy on War Pensions 1986-; chm Thirlestane Castle Tst 1984-; *Clubs* New (Edinburgh), Pratt's; *Style—* Maj-Gen Sir John Swinton, KCVO, OBE, DL; Kimmerghame, Duns, Berwicks TD11 3LU (☎ 0361 83277)

SWINTON OF THAT ILK, John Walter (Jack); s of Liulf Swinton of that Ilk (d 1977), of Henderson, Nevada, USA, and Alice Gertrude Kidney (d 1977); suc f as Chief of the Name of Swinton 1977; *b* 6 Oct 1934; *Educ* Montana State Univ (BArch); *m* 1956, Marlene Louise, da of Charles Herbert Wakelen (d 1976), of Lethbridge, Alberta; 1 s (Rolfe b 1971); *Heir* s, Rolfe William Swinton, b 1970; *Career* princ and pres Swinton Architects Ltd; *Recreations* skiing, fishing, tennis; *Clubs* Rotary West Calgary, Calgary Burns; *Style—* John Swinton of that Ilk; 123 Superior Ave SW, Calgary, Alberta T3C 2H8, Canada (☎ 403 245 3631); 5917 - 1A Street SW, Calgary, Alberta, Canada T2H 0G4 (☎ AC 403 255 1125)

SWIRE, Sir Adrian Christopher; yr s of John Kidston Swire, DL (d 1983), of

Hubbards Hall, Old Harlow, Essex, by his w Juliet Richenda (d 1981), da of Charles Barclay, bro of John A Swire, CBE, *qv*; *b* 15 Feb 1932; *Educ* Eton, Univ Coll Oxford (MA); *m* 1970, Lady Judith, *qv*; 2 s, 1 da; *Career* served Nat Service Coldstream Gds 1950-52, RAFVR and Royal Hong Kong AAF 1953-61; joined Butterfield & Swire in Far East 1956, dir John Swire & Son Ltd 1961, dep chm 1966, (chm 1987); chm China Navigation Co Ltd 1968-88; dir: Swire Pacific, Cathay Pacific Airways; dep chm: Overseas Containers (Pacific) Ltd, NAAFI 1972-86; pres Gen Cncl of Br Shipping 1980-81, chm Int Chamber of Shipping 1982-87; memb Gen Ctee Lloyd's Register; visiting fell Nuffield Coll Oxford 1981-; Hon Air Cdre RAuxAF; *Clubs* White's, Brooks's, Pratts; *Style*— Sir Adrian Swire; Sparsholt Manor, nr Wantage, Oxon; John Swire & Sons Ltd, Swire House, 59 Buckingham Gate, London SW1E 6AJ (☎ 01 834 7717)

SWIRE, John Anthony; CBE (1977); s of John Kidston Swire (d 1983); bro of Sir Adrian Swire, *qv*; *b* 1927; *Educ* Eton, Univ Coll Oxford; *m* 1961, Moira Ducharne; 2 s, 1 da; *Career* served Irish Gds (UK and Palestine) 1945-48; joined Butterfield & Swire Hong Kong 1950, dir John Swire & Sons Ltd 1955 (chm 1966-); former dir: Royal Insur Co, Br Bank of the Middle East, Ocean Tport & Trading Ltd; dir James Finlay & Co plc 1976-; memb: London Advsy Ctee Hongkong and Shanghai Banking Corpn 1969-, Euro-Asia Centre Advsy Bd 1980-, Advsy Cncl Sch of Business Stanford Univ 1981-; hon fell St Antony's Coll Oxford, Hon DL Hong Kong 1989;; *Style*— John Swire Esq, CBE; Luton House, Selling, nr Faversham, Kent; John Swire & Sons Ltd, Swire House, 59 Buckingham Gate, London SW1E 6AJ (☎ 01 834 7717)

SWIRE, Lady Judith; *née* Compton; er da of 6 Marquess of Northampton, DSO (d 1978), and his 2 w, Virginia, da of Col David Heaton, DSO; *b* 26 Sept 1943; *Educ* RCM, London Univ; *m* 1970, Sir Adrian Swire, *qv*; 2 s (Merlin b 1973, Samuel b 1980), 1 da (Martha b 1972); *Style*— The Lady Judith Swire; Sparsholt Manor, nr Wantage, Oxfordshire OX12 9PT

SWIRE, Rhoderick Martin; s of Patrick Douglas Swire, (d 1960), of Shropshire, and Joan Mary, *née* Allison (d 1970); *b* 27 Mar 1951; *Educ* Eton, Birmingham Univ (BSc) 1975 ACA 1980 FCA; *m* 11 June 1977, Georgina Mary, da of Christopher Ronald Thompson, qv, of Shropshire; 1 s (Hugh b 1979), 2 da (Henrietta b 1981, Camilla b 1985); *Career* Peat Marwick Mitchell 1972-76; John Swire & Sons Ltd 1976-81: gp accountant Hong Kong 1976-79, Aust 1979-81, asst to chm London 1981; GT Mgmnt plc: mangr unquoted investmt 1981-88, dir main bd 1987; md GT Venture Mgmnt; ACA 1975, FCC 1975, FCA 1980; *Recreations* shooting, tennis, gardening; *Clubs* Boodles; *Style*— Rhoderick Swire, Esq; Aldenham Park, Bridgnorth, Shropshire; Stafford House, 5 Stafford St, London W1X 3PD (☎ 01 493 5685, fax 01 629 0844)

SWISS, Sir Rodney Geoffrey; OBE (1964), JP (Middlesex 1949); s of Henry Herbert Swiss (d 1958) of Devonport, Devon; *b* 4 August 1904,Devonport,; *Educ* Plymouth Coll, Dean Close Sch Cheltenham, Guy's Hosp; *m* 1928, Muriel Alberta Gledhill (d 1985); *Career* dental surgn, pres Br Dental Assoc 1971-, pres Gen Dental Cncl 1974-79, FDSRCS; kt 1975; *Style*— Sir Rodney Swiss, OBE, JP; Shrublands, 23 West Way, Pinner, Middx (01 866 0621)

SWORD, Robert Arthur Hallifax; s of James Michael Sword JP, and Diana Dominica Sword; *b* 16 May 1952; *Educ* Southern Highlands Sch Tanzania, St Edmunds Sch, Hindhead Surrey, Bradfield Coll Reading Berks, RAC Cirencester Glos; *m* 22 July 1978, Rosemary, da of Richard Arthur Bedford-Payne, of Grassington, N Yorks; 2 s (Edmund James Bedford b 1984, Sam Richard b 1986); *Career* chartered surveyor/land agent 1977, ptnr Yorks off Humberts 1983- (joined as agent at Badminto Estate and Hatfield Park Estate; memb Co of the Merchants of the Staple of Eng; FRICS; *Recreations* shooting, gardening; *Clubs* Yorks, Farmers; *Style*— Robert Sword, Esq; Wood Cottage, Scackleton, Hovingham, York YO6 4NB (☎ 0653-82 304); Humberts, 37 Mickelgate, York YO1 1JH (☎ 0904 611828)

SWYNNERTON, Sir Roger John Massy; CMG (1959), OBE (1951), MC (1941); s of Charles Francis Massy Swynnerton, CMG (d 1938), and Norah Aimee Geraldine Smyth (d 1963); *b* 16 Jan 1911; *Educ* Lancing, Gonville & Caius Cambridge (BA, Dip Agric), Imperial Coll of Tropical Agric Trinidad (AICTA); *m* 1943, Grizel Beryl, da of Ralph William Richardson Miller, CMG (d 1958) of Lushoto, Tanganyika; 2 s (John, Charles); *Career* 2 Lt OC CUOTC Artillery Battery 1932-33, TARO 1933-60, served with 1/6 KAR (Kenya, Italian Somaliland, Abyssinia) 1939-42, temp Capt Colonial Agric Service Tanganyika 1934-51, seconded to agric duties Malta 1942-43, Kenya 1951-63 (asst dir of Agric 1951, dep 1954, dir 1956-60, perm sec Miny of Agric 1960-62, temp min 1961, MLC 1956-61, ret 1963); memb Advsy Ctee on Devpt of Economic Resources of Southern Rhodesia 1961-62, agric advsr and memb Exec Mgmnt Bd Cwlth Devpt Corpn 1962-76, self-employed conslt in tropical agric and devpt 1976-85, dir Booker Agric Int Ltd 1976-; pres Swinnerton Family Soc 1982-, Tropical Agric Assoc 1983-88; kt 1976; *Publications* All about KNCU Coffee (1948), A Plan to Intensify the Development of African Agriculture in Kenya (1954); *Clubs* Royal Overseas League, Royal Cwlth Soc; *Style*— Sir Roger Swynnerton, CMG, OBE, MC; Cherry House, 2 Vincent Rd, Stoke D'Abernon, Cobham, Surrey KT11 3JB

SYBORN, Victor Jack; s of Arthur Robert Syborn (d 1974), and Alice, *née* Coles (d 1979); *b* 28 June 1920; *Educ* Ealing Coll; *m* 1 April 1950, Patricia Eveleen, da of Harold Blomeley (d 1972); 1 s (Philip Charles b 12 Aug 1954), 1 da (Veronica Frances (Mrs Carbone) b 22 Aug 1956); *Career* RA 1941-47: cmmnd 5 Regt 1943, seconded RM 1944 (Normandy Landing), serv 5 Regt RHA and 7 Armd Div 1944-46, Air Liaison Offr 2 Gp RAF 1946-47; TA 1947-54; princ Syborn & Atkinson Chartered Architects 1951-; Freeman City of London 1975, Liveryman Worshipful Co of Gardeners 1975; FRIBA 1954; *Recreations* travel, sailing; *Clubs* RAC, RLym YC; *Style*— Victor Syborn, Esq; The Shepherd's House, The Sands, Farnham, Surrey GU10 1JN (☎ 02518 2080); Syborn & Atkinson, 4 Pratt Walk, London SE11 6AR (☎ 01 735 2071, fax 01 735 9799)

SYCAMORE, Phillip; s of Frank Sycamore, of Lancaster, Lancs, and Evelyn Martin, *née* Burley; *b* 9 Mar 1951; *Educ* Lancaster Royal GS, London Univ (LLB); *m* 22 June 1974, Sandra, da of Peter Frederick Cooper (d 1986), of Morecambe, Lancs; 2 s (Thomas b 1980, Jonathan b 1983), 1 da (Hannah b 1978); *Career* slr; ptnr with Lonsdale slrs Blackpool Lancs; memb The Law Soc Remuneration and Practice Devpt Ctee; *Clubs* Royal Lytham and St Annes Golf; *Style*— Phillip Sycamore, Esq; 213 Clifton Drive South, Lytham St Annes (☎ 0253 728532); 342 Lytham Road, South Shore, Blackpool, Lancs (☎ 0253 45258, fax 0253 48943)

SYDNEY, His Eminence the Cardinal Archbishop (RC) of James Darcy Freeman; KBE (1977); s of Robert Freeman (decd), and Margaret, *née* Smith; *b* 19 Nov 1907; *Educ* Christian Brothers' Coll, St Mary's Cathedral Sydney, St Columba's Springwood NSW, St Patrick's Manly; *Career* Hon DD 1957; priest 1930, private sec to Archbishop fo Sydney 1941-46, ordained Bishop 1957, bishop of Armidale 1968, Archbishop of Sydney 1971-83, cardinal 1973; Knight of the Holy Sepulchre; *see Debrett's Handbook of Australia and New Zealand for further details*; *Recreations* reading, history and biography; *Style*— His Eminence the Cardinal Archbishop of Sydney, KBE; St Mary's Cathedral, Sydney, NSW 2000, Australia (☎ 232 3788, office: 264 7211)

SYERS, Lady; Yvonne Amy Inglis; da of Inglis Allen, of Rottingdean; *m* Sir Cecil Syers, KCMG, CVO, JP (d 1981), sometime UK High Cmmr Ceylon; 1 s; *Style*— Lady Syers; 25 One Grand Avenue, Hove, E Sussex BN3 2LA (☎ 0273 732545)

SYKES, Allen; s of Jack Sykes, of Slaithewaite, Yorks, and Dorothy, *née* Main (d 1956); *b* 26 Dec 1931; *Educ* Texas Country Day Sch Dallas, Selhurst GS, LSE (BSc); *m* 17 Jan 1959, Dorothy June, da of Wilfred Hugh Moore (d 1982), of Sutton, Surrey; 1 s (Jeremy Jonathan Nicholas b 1961), 1 da (Caroline Emma Jane b 1964); *Career* cmmnd Sub Lt exec branch and Lt RNVR 1951-65, Nat Serv 1953-55; economist and mgmnt trainee econs dept Unilever 1955-60, head project evaluation RTZ 1960-70, md RTZ Devpt Enterprises (in charge of Channel Tunnel Project for RTZ and Br Channel Tunnel Co) 1970-72; dir Willis Faber plc 1972-86: advsr to govts, banks, utilities, mining and oil cos on major int projects; md Consolidated Gold Fields plc 1986- (responsible for devpt Br and part of N America, advsr later non-exec dir 1972-86); fndr and memb cncl Br Major Projects Assoc 1981- (fndr Canadian Assoc 1984); *Publications* Finance & Analysis of Capital Projects (with A J Merrett 1963 and 1972), Housing Finance 1965 (with A J Merrett), Successful Accomplishment of Giant Projects (1979), Privatise Coal (with Colin Robinson 1987), Current Choices - Ways to Privatise Electricity (with Colin Robinson 1987); *Recreations* tennis, chess, opera; *Clubs* ESU, Gresham, RAC; *Style*— Allen Sykes, Esq; Mallington, 29 The Mount, Leatherhead, Surrey KT22 9EB (☎ 0372 375851); 31 Charles II St, St James's Sq, London SW1Y 4AG (☎ 01 930 6200, fax 01 930 9677, telex 883071)

SYKES, Audrey, Lady; Audrey Winifred; da of Frederick Thompson, of Cricklewood; *m* 1935, Sir Hugh Sykes, 2 Bt (d 1974); *Style*— Audrey, Lady Sykes; 19 Bouverie Gdns, Harrow, Middx

SYKES, Bonar Hugh Charles; s of Maj-Gen Rt Hon Sir Frederick Sykes, GCSI, GCIE, KCB, CMG (d 1954), and Isabel Harrington, *née* Law (d 1969), da of Rt Hon Andrew Bonar Law; *b* 20 Dec 1922; *Educ* Eton, Queen's Coll Oxford (MA); *m* 28 Sept 1949, Mary, da of Rt Hon Sir Eric Phiipps, GCB, GCMG, GCV (d 1945); 4 s (Hugh b 1950, David b 1953, James b 1956, Alan b 1960); *Career* Lt RNVR 1942-46; trainee Tractor Div Ford Motor Co 1948-49; Dip Serv 1949-69: second sec Prague 1953, second sec (later first sec) Bonn 1953-57, first sec (later Cnsllr) Tehran 1961-65, cnsllr Ottawa 1966-68; farming in Wilts 1969-; tstee Wilts Archaeological & Nat History Soc (pres 1975-85); cncl memb: Area Museums cncl for SW 1975-86, Museums Assoc 1981-84, memb Bd of Visitors Erlestoke Prison 1977-87 (chm 1983-85); High Sheriff Wiltshire 1988-89; FSA 1985; *Style*— Bonar Sykes, Esq; Conock Manor, Devizes, Wiltshire (☎ 0380 84 227)

SYKES, David Michael; s of Michael le Gallais Sykes (d 1981; yr s of Capt Stanley Edgar Sykes, who was yr s of Sir Charles Sykes, 1 Bt, KBE), and his 1 w, Joan, *née* Groome; hp of unc, Sir John Charles Anthony le Gallais Sykes, 3 Bt; *b* 10 June 1954; *m* 1974 (m dis 1987), Susan Elizabeth, 3 da of G W Hall; 1 s (Stephen David b 1978); m 2, 1987, Margaret Lynne, da of JT McGreavy; 1 da (Joanna Lauren b 1986); *Style*— David Sykes Esq; c/o Sir John Sykes, Bt, The Chestnuts, Middle Lane, Nether Broughton, Leics LE14 3HD

SYKES, Eric; OBE; s of Vernon Sykes, and Harriet Sykes; *b* 4 May 1923; *m* 14 Feb 1952, Edith Eleanore, da of Bruno Milbradt; 1 s (David Kurt b 2 June 1959), 3 da (Katherine Lee b 6 Sept 1952, Susan Jane b 20 Sep 1953, Julie Louise b 2 July 1958); *Career* wireless operator mobile signals unit RAF 1941-47; comic actor, writer and dir; varied TV and film career (20 feature films); numerous TV appearances incl writing and lead role Sykes Show for 20 years; silent film writer and dir: The Plank (V), Rhubarb, Mr H is Late; Freeman City of London; *Recreations* golf; *Clubs* Royal and Ancient GC; *Style*— Eric Sykes, OBE, Esq; 9 Orme Court, Bayswater, London W2 (☎ 01 727 1544)

SYKES, Sir Francis Godfrey; 9 Bt (GB 1781), of Basildon, Berks; s of Francis William Sykes (d 1944), and Beatrice Agnes, *née* Webb (d 1953); suc f's 1 cous, Rev Sir Frederick John Sykes, 8 Bt, 1956; *b* 27 August 1907; *Educ* Blundell's, Nelson Coll NZ; *m* 1, 1934, Eira Betty (d 1970), da of George Wallace Badcock, of Hove and Nether Maudlin, Steyning, Sussex; 1 s, 1 da; m 2, 1972, Nesta Mabel (d 1982), da of late Col Harold Sykes; m 3, 1985, Ethel Florence Ogden, w of B G MacCartney-Filgate and W G Ogden, da of Lt-Col J S Liddell (decd); *Heir* s, Francis John Badcock Sykes b 1942; *Career* teaplanter 1930-39; Air Miny 1939-45; fruit farmer & estate mangr 1945-57; regnl sec Country landowners Assoc 1957-72; *Style*— Sir Francis Sykes, Bt; 7 Linney, Ludlow, Shropshire SY8 1EF (☎ 0584 4336)

SYKES, Francis John Badcock; only s and h of Sir Francis Sykes, 9 Bt (by his 1 w); *b* 7 June 1942; *Educ* Shrewsbury, Worcester Coll Oxford; *m* 1966, Susan Alexandra, da of Adm of the Fleet Sir Edward Ashmore, GCB, DSC, by his w Elizabeth (da of Sir Lionel Sturdee, 2 and last Bt, CBE); 3 s (Francis Charles b 1968, Edward b 1970, Alexander b 1974); *Career* slr 1968, ptnr in legal firm of Townsends, Swindon and Newbury; *Style*— Francis Sykes, Esq; Kingsbury Croft, Kingsbury St, Marlborough, Wilts; 42 Cricklade St, Swindon (☎ 0793 35421, telex 44712)

SYKES, Jeremy John; s of Lt-Col Sir (Mark Tatton) Richard Tatton-Sykes, 7 Bt (d 1978); hp of bro Sir Tatton Christopher Mark Sykes, 8 Bt; *b* 8 Mar 1946; *Educ* Ampleforth; *Style*— Jeremy Sykes Esq; c/o Sledmere, Driffield, Yorkshire

SYKES, Dr John Bradbury; s of Stanley William Sykes (d 1961), of Margate, and Eleanor, *née* Bradbury (d 1967); *b* 26 Jan 1929; *Educ* Wallasey GS, Rochdale HS, St Lawrence Coll, Oxford Univ (MA, DPhil); *m* 1955 (m dis 1988), Avril Barbara, da of Ernest Hart (d 1938), of Lei (Steven); *Career* lexicographer, translator; head of translations off AERE Harwell 1958-71; ed Concise and Pocket Oxford Dictionaries 1971-81, head German Dictionaries OUP 1981-; memb Translators' Guild, 1960-68 (chm 1984-88); fell Inst of Linguists 1960-86; fell Inst of Translation and Interpreting (chm 1986-); Hon DLitt City Univ 1984; *Recreations* crosswords (Times national champion 1972-75, 1977, 1980, 1983, 1985); *Clubs* Pen; *Style*— Dr John Sykes; 19 Walton Manor Court, Adelaide St, Oxford OX2 6EL (☎ 0865 57532); Oxford University Press, Walton Street, Oxford OX2 6DP (☎ 0865 56767)

SYKES, Sir John Charles Anthony le Gallais; 3 Bt (UK 1921), of Kingsknowes, Galashiels, Co Selkirk; s of Capt Stanley Sykes (yr s of Sir Charles Sykes, 1 Bt, KBE, JP, sometime MP Huddersfield) and Florence Anaïse, da of François le Gallais, of Jersey; suc unc, Sir Hugh Sykes, 2 Bt, 1974; *b* 19 April 1928; *Educ* Churchers Coll; *m* 1954 (m dis 1969), Aitha Isobel, da of Lionel Dean, of Huddersfield; *Heir* nephew, David Sykes; *Career* export merchant (textile business); *Recreations* wine, food, travel, bridge; *Clubs* Br Epicure Soc; *Style*— Sir John Sykes, Bt; 58 Alders View Drive, E Grinstead, W Sussex (☎ 0342 322027); Sir John Sykes & Co Ltd, P O Box 200, East Grinstead, W Sussex RH19 2YN

SYKES, (John) Keith; *b* 5 Feb 1933; *Educ* Wrekin Coll, Leeds Univ, Grays Inn; *m* 1958, Undine, *née* Hodgetts; 1 s, 4 da; *Career* chm: Keith Ceramic Materials Ltd; dir Television South West plc, CPA Hldgs Ltd; *Recreations* fishing; *Style*— J Keith Sykes, Esq; Keith Ceramic Materials Ltd, Fishers Way, Crabtree Manor Way, Belvedere, Kent

SYKES, Hon Mrs (Laura Catherine); *née* James; da (by 1 m) of Baron Saint Brides (Life Peer); *b* 1948; *m* 1981, Robert Lacy Tatton Sykes, s of Geoffrey Sykes of Kirribilli, NSW; *Style*— The Hon Mrs Sykes; 6 Hans Cres, London SW1X OLJ (☎ 01 589 6463)

SYKES, Prof Malcolm Keith; s of Prof Joseph Sykes, OBE, (d 1967), and Phyllis Mary Sykes (d 1972); *b* 13 Sept 1925; *Educ* Magdalene Coll Cambridge (MA, MB, BChir) Univ Coll Hosp London (DA; FFARCS); *m* 14 Jan 1956, Michelle June, da of William Ewart Ratcliffe (d 1951); 1 s (Jonathan b 1964), 3 da (Karen b 1957, Virginia b 1958, Susan b 1967); *Career* cmmnd RAMC 1950-52, Capt, served BAOR; prof of clinical anaesthesia Royal Post Graduate Med Sch London 1970-80 (lectr, sr lectr then reader 1958-70); Nuffield prof of anaesthetics and fell Pembroke Coll Oxford 1980-; Rickman Godlee travelling scholar and fell in anaesthetics Massachusetts Gen Hosp Boston USA 1954-55, past vice pres and senator Euro Acad of Anaesthesiology; hon FFARACS (1978), hon FFA (SA) (1989) BMA, RSM; *Books* Respiratory Failure (1965, 1976), Principles of Measurement for Anaesthetics (1970), Principles of Clinical Measurement (1981); *Recreations* walking, sailing, birdwatching, gardening; *Style*— Prof MK Sykes; 10 Fitzherbert Close, Iffley, Oxford OX4 4EN (☎ 0865 771152); Radcliffe Infirmary, Woodstock Rd, Oxford OX2 6HE 0865 249891)

SYKES, Hon Mrs Nicola Mary Caroline; *née* Buxton; el da of Baron Buxton of Alsa, and Pamela Mary Birkin (d 1983); *b* 7 July 1947; *Educ* New Hall Chelmsford Essex; *m* 1970, Adrian William Guy, s of Peter Henry Sykes; 1 s (Samuel b 1974), 4 da (Eleanor b 1972, Miranda b 1982, Pandora b 1987), 1 da decd (Daisy b and d 1985); *Style*— The Hon Mrs Sykes; Cook's Mill, Fordham Heath, Colchester, Essex (☎ 0206 240242); Kinloch Lodge, Tongue, Sutherland (☎ 084 755 226)

SYKES, Lt-Col Nigel Stanley; s of Maj Samuel Stanley Sykes (d 1950), and Sibyl Westrope, *née* Green (d 1977); *b* 2 June 1910; *Educ* Charterhouse; *m* 12 July 1947, Marjorie Jean Tripp, da of Lt-Col Charles Hector Congdon (d 1958); 3 s (Nigel Peter Samuel b 1948, Colin Roland b 1952, William George b 1954), 1 da (Daphne Hilda b 1950); *Career* cmmnd York & Lancaster Regt 1931, Adj Depot 1937, Adj 1 Bn 1940, 2 i/c 7 Bn 1941, CO 2 Bn 1945, DAAG HQ AA Cmd 1947, CO 1 Bn 1948, AAG HQ Land Forces Hong Kong 1951, AA QMG RMA Sandhurst 1954, ret 1957; *Style*— Lt-Col Nigel Sykes; Llyndu, Nantmor, Caernarfon, Gwynedd LL55 4YN

SYKES, Lady; Norah; da of J E Staton, of Clowne; *m* 1930, Sir Charles Sykes, CBE, FRS, FInstP, DSc, PhD, DMe, sometime chm Firth Brown Ltd and pro-chllr Sheffield Univ (d 1982); 1 s (Howard), 1 da (Patricia); *Style*— Lady Sykes; Upholme, Blackamoor Crescent, Dore, Sheffield

SYKES, Lady Pauline Anne; *née* Ogilvie-Grant; da of Countess of Seafield (12 in line), and Derek Studley-Herbert (who assumed by deed poll additional surnames of Ogilvie-Grant); *b* 1944; *m* 1, 1964 (m dis 1970), James Henry Harcourt Illingworth (whose sis m 1, Earl of Seafield, *qv*); m 2, 1972 (m dis 1976), Sir William Gordon Cumming, 6 Bt; m 3, 1976, Hugh Richard Sykes; 1 s; *Style*— Lady Pauline Sykes; Revack Lodge, Grantown-on-Spey, Morayshire

SYKES, Phillip Rodney; s of Sir Richard Adam Sykes, KCMG, MC (d 1979), and Lady Ann Georgina, *née* Fisher; *b* 17 Mar 1955; *Educ* Winchester Coll, Ch Ch Oxford (MA); *m* 26 June 1982, Caroline Frances Gordon Sykes, da of Michael Dawson Miller, of 52 Scarsdale Villas, London W8; 2 s (Richard b 1985, Christopher b 1988); *Career* ptnr BDO Binder Hamlyn 1986- (joined 1976), seconded fin services section Nat West Bank plc 1985-86; ACA 1986; *Recreations* field sports, tennis, reading, theatre; *Style*— Phillip Sykes, Esq; BDO Binder Hamlyn, 8 St Bride St, London EC4A 4DA (☎ 01 353 3020, fax 01 583 0031, telex 24276)

SYKES, Maj Roy Forester; TD (1950 and clasp), DL (Northants 1983); s of Lt-Col Vincent Harold Sykes (d 1976), and Olive Annie Louise, *née* Webb (d 1966); *b* 29 July 1916; *Educ* The Leys Sch, Emmanuel Coll Cambridge (MA, LLM); *m* 1947, Pamela Anne Mary, da of Wing-Cdr Arthur Leslie Horrell (d 1981); 3 da (Carolyn, Diana, Judith); *Career* cmmnd 5 Bn Northamptonshire Regt TA 1934, served WW II Maj UK & NI, TARO 1948-66; slr 1946-; clerk to the Justices of Oundle-Thrapston Courts 1957-74; diocesan reader C of E 1949-, Archbishop's diploma 1958; Northants co pres Royal Br Legion 1976-; E Midlands area pres Royal Br Legion 1982-83 and 1987-88; *Recreations* game shooting, history, gardening; *Style*— Maj Roy Sykes, TD, DL; Tavern Cottage, Aldwincle, Kettering, Northants

SYKES, Sir Tatton Christopher Mark; 8 Bt (GB 1783), of Sledmere, Yorkshire; s of Lt-Col Sir (Mark Tatton) Richard Tatton-Sykes, 7 Bt (d 1978; assumed additional surname of Tatton by deed poll 1977, discontinued at his demise); *b* 24 Dec 1943; *Educ* Eton, Université d'Aix Marseilles, RAC Cirencester; *Heir* bro, Jeremy John Sykes; *Style*— Sir Tatton Sykes, Bt; Sledmere, Driffield, Yorkshire

SYLVESTER BRADLEY, Hon Mrs (Elizabeth Mary Jean); *née* Annesley; eldest da of 14 Viscount Valentia, MC; *b* 6 May 1926; *m* 1948, Maj James Terence Ralphe Sylvester Bradley (d 1987), s of late Lt-Col Charles Reginald Sylvester Bradley, of the Manor House, Langton Herring, Dorset; 1 s (Charles b 1959), 3 da (Fiona b 1949, Heather b 1951, Catherine b 1957); *Style*— The Hon Mrs Sylvester Bradley; Knighton Manor, Durweston, Blandford, Dorset

SYME, Sir Ronald; OM (1976); s of David Syme, of Eltham, NZ; *b* 11 Mar 1903; *Educ* New Plymouth Boys' HS, Victoria Univ Wellington, Auckland Univ (BA), Oriel Coll Oxford (BA, MA); *Career* dean of Trinity Coll 1938; press attaché Br Legation Belgrade 1940-41, Br Embassy Ankara 1941-42, prof of classical philology Istanbul Univ 1942-45, Camden prof of ancient history Oxford Univ 1949-70 (ret), pres Int Ctee for Philosophy and Humanistic Studies (Paris) 1971-75 (sec 1952-71), prof of ancient history Royal Acad of Arts 1976-; hon fell Oriel Coll Oxford 1958, membre Associé Institut de France 1967; memb Order pour le Merite for Science and the Arts 1975, Cdr de l'Ordre des Arts et des Lettres 1975; kt 1959; *Books* The Roman Revolution (1939), Tacitus (1958), Colonial Elites (1958), Sallust (1964), Ammianus and The Historia Augusta (1968), Ten Studies in Tacitus (1970), Emperors and Biography (1970), History in Ovid (1978), Roman Papers (1979), Some Arval Brethren (1980), Historia Augusta Papers (1983), Roman Papers III (1984), The Augustan Aristocracy (1986), Roman Papers IV and V (1988); *Clubs* Athenaeum; *Style*— Sir Ronald Syme, OM; Wolfson Coll, Oxford, England

SYMES, John Dudley; s of Capt John Roy Symes (d 1974), of Oxshott; *b* 15 April 1920; *Educ* Merchant Taylors'; *m* 1947, Mary Magdelen, da of Prof Albert Bernard, CBE, MD, DFH, DTM&H, Malta; 2 children; *Career* Capt (ret); *Recreations* golf; *Clubs* Carlton, Royal Mid-Surrey Golf; *Style*— John Symes, Esq; 9/121 Haverstock Hill, London NW3

SYMINGTON, Prof Sir Thomas; s of James Symington (d 1919), of Muirkirk, Ayrshire, and Margaret Steven Symington (d 1967); *b* 1 April 1915; *Educ* Cumnock Acad, Glasgow Univ (BSc, MB ChB, MD); *m* 1943, Esther Margaret, da of John Forsyth, of Viewfield Farm, Bellshill (d 1951); 1 s (and 1 s decd), 1 da; *Career* Maj RAMC, served Malaya 1947-49; prof of Pathology Univ of Glasgow 1954-70, prof of Pathology Univ of London 1971-77, dir Inst of Cancer Res Royal Cancer Hosp London 1970-77; visiting prof of Pathology Stanford Univ 1965-67; Hon Dr of Med Szeged Univ Hungary (1971), Hon DSc McGill Univ Canada 1983; kt 1978; *Recreations* golf, gardening; *Clubs* Roy Troon Golf; *Style*— Prof Sir Thomas Symington; Greenbriar, 2 Lady Margaret Drive, Troon KA10 7AL (☎ 315 707)

SYMONDS, Kenneth Thomas; s of Percival Harold Symonds (d 1980), and Gladys Symonds (d 1942); *b* 11 Mar 1928; *Educ* Queen Elizabeth's GS Barnet; *m* 11 March 1958, Gunvor, da of Rudolf Orre (d 1976); *Career* chm Gradus Ltd 1986- (md 1966-86); *Recreations* travel, cinema, theatre; *Style*— Kenneth Symonds, Esq; 27 Chapel Side, Moscow Rd, London W2 4LE (☎ 01 727 9296); Gradus Ltd, 298 Westbourne Grove, London W11 2PS (☎ 01 229 4352, fax 01 221 4466)

SYMONDS, Richard; *see*: Spokes, Ann

SYMONS, Ernest Vize; CB (1975); s of Ernest William Symons (d 1924); *b* 19 June 1913; *Educ* Stationers' Company's Sch, Univ Coll London; *m* 1938, Elizabeth Megan, nee Jenkins; 1 s, 2 da; *Career* chief insp of Taxes 1973-75, dir gen Bd of Inland Revenue 1975-77, dep chm The English Speaking Union, hon tres NACRO; memb: Cncl Univ Coll London, Lord Keith's Ctee on Enforcement Powers; *Recreations* chess, bridge; *Clubs* Athenaeum; *Style*— Ernest Symons Esq, CB; 1 Terrace House, 128 Richmond Hill, Richmond, Surrey

SYMONS, Dr John Charles; s of Dr Percy Symons (d 1969), of Reading, Berks, and Constance Mary, *née* Dyer (d 1982); *b* 13 May 1938; *Educ* Oratory Sch, Trinity Coll Cambridge (BA, MA), St Thomas Med Sch (MB, BChir); *m* 3 Aug 1968, Louisa Beverley McKenzie, da of Dr S G M Francis, of Sudbury, Suffolk; 1 s (James b 1977), 2 da (Emma b 1970, Rebecca b 1973); *Career* house offr: surgery (later medicine) Burton on Trent 1962-63, obstetrics St Thomas' Hosp 1963-64; sr house offr (later registrar) paediatrics Royal Berks Hosp 1964-67, paediatric specialist Corner Brook Newfoundland 1967-68, princ gen practice Wonersh Guildford 1968-69, med registrar Prospect Park Hosp Reading 1969-71; sr registrar: Jenny Lind Hosp Norwich 1971-73, Brompton Hosp 1973-75; conslt paediatrician Colchester 1975-, hon clinical tutor Guys Hosp Med Sch 1985-; memb Colchester Med Soc 1975; chm: Colchester Action for Epilepsy, Colchester branch Liver Fndn; med advsr local branches Asthma Soc & Diabetic Assoc, aeromedical advsr St Johns, church warden Colchester, parish Cncllr Colchester; DObrl RCOG 1964, DCH 1967; memb: BMA 1962, Br Paediatric Assoc 1968; FRCP 1987 (MRCP 1971); *Recreations* game fishing, cricket; *Style*— Dr John Symons; Moors Farm, Assington, Suffolk CO6 5NE (☎ 0787 227 379); Colchester Gen Hosp, Turner Rd, Colchester, Essex (☎ 0206 853 853 535); Rooms: 29 Oaks Drive, Colchester

SYMONS, Prof Martyn Christian Raymond; s of Stephen White Symons (d 1972), and Marjorie, *née* Le Brassuer (d 1958); *b* 12 Nov 1925; *Educ* John Fisher Sch Purley Surrey, Battersea Poly London (BSc, PhD, DSc); *m* 1, Joy, *née* Lendon (d 1963); 1 s (Richard b 1957), 1 da (Susan b 1954); m 2, 12 Jan 1972, Janice (Jan) Olive, da of George O'Connor; *Career* Army 1946-49 (actg Capt 1948); lectr in chemistry Battersea Poly 1949-53, lectr in organic chemistry Southampton Univ 1953-60, prof of physical chemistry Leicester Univ 1960-; author of 2 books and over 850 original scientific papers; FRSC 1949, FRSA 1965, FRS 1985; *Recreations* water colour painting, piano playing; *Style*— Professor Martyn Symons; 144 Victoria Park Rd, Leicester LE2 1XD (☎ 0533 700 314); Dept of Chemistry, The University, Leicester (☎ 0533 522 141, fax 0533 522 200, telex LIECWL 341198)

SYMONS, Michael John; s of Kenneth Francis Symons, and Aileen Joyce, *née* Winship (d 1972); *b* 23 Nov 1947; *Educ* Sir William Borlase's Sch Marlow Bucks, Trinity Coll Cambridge (MA); *m* 10 Dec 1974, Gwendoline Winifred Symons; *Career* gp fin dir Ridgeon Gp; FCA, MCT; *Recreations* athletics, making money; *Style*— Michael Symons, Esq; Cyril Ridgeon & Son Ltd, Tenison Rd, Cambridge CB1 2DS (☎ 0223 61177)

SYNGE, Sir Robert Carson; 8 Bt (UK 1801), of Kiltrough; s of late Neale Hutchinson Synge and n of 7 Bt (d 1942); *b* 4 May 1922; *m* 1944, Dorothy Jean, da of Theodore Johnson, of Cloverdale, BC, Canada; 2 da; *Heir* cousin, Neale Francis Synge, b 28 Feb 1917; *Style*— Sir Robert Synge, Bt; 19364 Fraser Valley Highway, RR4 Langley, BC, Canada

SYNNOT, Admiral Sir Anthony Monckton; KBE (1979), AO (1976); s of Monckton Synnot, JP (d 1954) and Mary Constance, *née* Hay (d 1965); *b* 5 Jan 1922; *Educ* Geelong GS; *m* 1, 1959, M Virginia (d 1965), da of Dr W K Davenport (d 1965); 2 da; m 2, 1968, E Anne, da of E W Manifold, MC (d 1961); *Career* RAN 1939, served in WW II; Cdr 1954, Capt 1960, Rear-Admiral 1970, Vice-Adm 1976, Admiral 1979; Administrative Staff Coll Mt Eliza 1965, IDC London 1968, dir Joint Staff 1974-76, chief of Naval Staff 1976-78, chief of Def Force Staff 1979-82 (ret); Hon JMN 1965, Hon PSM 1982; *see Debrett's Handbook of Australia and New Zealand for further details*; *Style*— Admiral Sir Anthony Synnot, KBE, AO; Wanna Wanna, Box 33, Queanbeyan, NSW 2620, Australia

SYSON, William Watson Cockburn (Bill); s of William Cockburn Syson (d 1939), of Edinburgh, and Mary Jane, *née* Watson (d 1983); *b* 12 Sept 1930; *Educ* Broughton; *Career* Nat Serv Army 1949-51; TA 1951-58; Bank of Scotland: joined 1947;

Greenside Edinburgh: mangr 1966-69,sr managerial positions Edinburgh 1969-81, chief mangr Head Off 1981-87, asst gen mangr 1987-; chm Bank of Scotland Edinburgh & District Mangrs and Officials Circle 1978; former lectr, examiner and moderator Heriot Watt Coll and Univ; memb Jr C of C 1962-73 (bd memb 1968-73, world senator 1970); sr vice-pres Edinburgh and Midlothian Bn Boys' Bde 1970- (actg pres 1987-88); chm City Centre Christian Outreach 1981-82; hon tres: East of Scotland branch Br Red Cross 1974-82 (memb Scottish Finance Committee 1976-81), Scottish branch Soldiers Sailors and Airmen's Families Assoc 1974-82, Victoria League Scotland 1969-75, Scottish Churches Architectural Heritage Tst 1980-84; tres and cncl memb The Prince Tst East of Scotland and Borders Area 1978-84; FIB Scot 1979 (memb 1954); *Books* Interpretation of Balance Sheets (1957), Sources of Finance (1973), Forestry (1985);; *Recreations* art, music, reading, hill walking, sport; *Clubs* New (Edinburgh), Cronies, Edinburgh Academicals Sports ; *Style*— Bill Syson, Esq; 27 Succoth Park, Edinburgh EH12 6BX (☎ 031 337 1321) Bank of Scotland, The Mound, Edinburgh (☎ 031 243 5571, fax 031 243 5517, car telephone 0836 7313 44, telex 031 243 5517)

SYSONBY, 3 Baron (UK 1935); John Frederick Ponsonby; s of 2 Baron, DSO (d 1956); *b* 5 August 1945; *Heir* none; *Style*— The Rt Hon the Lord Sysonby; c/o Friars, Whitefriars, Chester

SZPIRO, Richard David; s of George Szpiro of Belgrave Place, London, and Halina Szpiro; *b* 11 August 1944; *Educ* St Paul's Sch, Churchill Coll Cambridge (MA); *m* annulled; 2 s (Toby b 1971, Jamie b 1973); *Career* merchant banker; md: Wintrust plc 1969-, Wintrust Securities plc; *Recreations* golf, tennis; *Clubs* Mark's, Hurlingham; *Style*— Richard Szpiro, Esq; 15 Holland Park Avenue, London W11 (☎ 01 236 2360)

T

TABERNER, Michael John; s of Ernest Taberner, and Una, *née* Dean; *b* 5 June 1950; *Educ* King Henry VIII Sch Coventry, Oxford Univ (MA); *m* 9 Oct 1976, Siobain Mary, da of Donald Gillespie Macnab; 1 s (Richard James Philip b 1983), 1 da (Sarah Alexandra b 1987); *Career* slr; admitted to Law Soc 1974, ptnr Angel & Co Coventry 1980; govr St Thomas More's Sch Coventry, tstee Coventry and Warwicks Cancer Treatment Fund; *Recreations* rugby football, theatre, hill-walking; *Clubs* Old Coventrians Assoc, Old Coventrians RFC; *Style*— Michael Taberner, Esq; Leamount, 74 St Martins Rd, Finham, Coventry (☎ 0203 419171); Angel & Co, 117 New Union St, Coventry (☎ 0203 252211)

TABOR, Charles James; er s of Robert Charles Tabor (d 1985), of Great Codham Hall, Shalford, nr Braintree, Essex, and Beryl Nora, *née* Lewis; *b* 15 Mar 1946; *Educ* Summer Fields Oxford, Cokethorpe Sch Witney Oxon, RAC Cirencester (NCA); *m* 23 Oct 1968, Gillian, da of John Buckley (d 1966), of Hartsmead, Ashdon Keynes, Wilts; 2 s (Christopher Charles Robert b 26 Sept 1970, Oliver Charles John b 7 Oct 1978), 1 da ((Sarah) Claire Buckley b 26 Jan 1973); *Career* dir Tabor Farms Ltd, Rochford; memb: Essex Farming and Wildlife Advsy Gp, Essex Farmers' Union, Essex Country Landowners' Assoc; dir The Rolls Royce Enthusiasts' Club; tstee The Sir Henry Royce Memorial Foundation; *Clubs* Farmers', Essex; *Style*— Charles Tabour, Esq; Sutton Hall, Rochford, Essex SS4 1LQ (☎ 0702 545730)

TABOR, Maj-Gen David St John Maur; CB (1977), MC (1944); yst s of Harry Ernest Tabor; *b* 5 Oct 1922; *Educ* Eton, RMA Sandhurst; *m* 27 July 1955, Hon Pamela Roxane Nivison (d 1987), 2 da of 2 Baron Glendyne (d 1967); 2 s; *Career* 2 Lt RHG 1942, served NW Europe WW II (wounded), Lt-Col cmdg Household Cavalry and Silver Stick in Waiting 1964, Brig 1966, Cdr Berlin Inf Bde 1966, Cd Br Army Staff and mil attaché Washington 1968, RCDS 1971, Maj-Gen 1972, defence attaché Paris 1972-74, GOC Eastern Dist 1975-77; v-chm ACFA 1979; *Recreations* Shooting, Fishing, Gardening; *Clubs* MCC, Turf, RAC; *Style*— Maj-Gen David Tabor, CB, MC; Lower Farm, Compton Abdale, Glos GL54 4 DS

TABOR, John Edward; OBE (1944), DL (Essex 1972); s of Edward Henry Tabor; *b* 31 Mar 1911; *Educ* Westminster, Felsted, Emmanuel Coll Cambridge (MA); *m* 1, 1945, Marjorie Lorenzen (d 1953); 1 s, 3 da; *m* 2 1960, Margaret Anne Turner, *née* Benson; *Career* civil service 1932-45, farmer, landowner, pro chancellor (and chm to 1983) Cncl Univ of Essex, memb Essex CC 1952-77, High Sheriff Essex 1980; hon degree Univ of Essex 1984; *Recreations* hunting, travel; *Clubs* Farmers'; *Style*— John Tabor Esq, OBE, DL; Bovingdon Hall, Braintree, Essex (☎ 0371 850205)

TABOR, Mark Sydney; s of Maj John Bentley Sydney Tabor, TD (d 1967), and Jane, *née* Pauling; *b* 6 August 1939; *Educ* Stonyhurst, London Graduate Sch of Business Studies; *m* 26 Jan 1972, Jane Louise, da Brig Sir (Robert) Louis Hargroves, CBE, DL, *qv*; 1 s (John b 1973), 1 da (Camilla b 1979); *Career* Lt RHG 1960-62; entered Whitbread & Co Ltd 1962-; dir: Whitbread (London) Ltd 1974-77, W H Brakspear & Sons Ltd 1975-77, regnl dir Whitbread Flowers Ltd 1977-81, md Whitbread W Country 1982-87; community affairs dir Whitbread & Co plc 1988-; Liveryman Worshipful Co of Brewers 1970; *Recreations* hunting; *Clubs* Cavalry and Guards'; *Style*— Mark Tabor, Esq; Whitbread & Co plc, Chiswell St, London EC1Y 4SD (☎ 01 606 4455); The Old Rectory, Skilgate, Taunton, Somerset (☎ 0398 31357)

TACKABERRY, John Antony; QC (1982); Thomas Raphael Tackaberry (d 1971), and Mary Catherine, *née* Geoghegan (d 1985); *b* 13 Nov 1939; *Educ* Downside, Trinity Coll Dublin, Downing Coll Cambridge (MA, LLM); *m* Penelope, da of Seth Holt (d 1971); 2 s (Christopher b 1966, Antony b 1968); *Career* lectr: Chinese Min of Further Educn 1963-64, Poly of Centl London 1965-67; called to the bar 1967 (Republic of Ireland bar 1987, Californian Bar 1988); rec 1988; pres: Soc of Construction Law 1987-85, Euro Soc of Construction Law 1985-87; memb arbitral panels of Los Angeles Center for Commercial Arbitration 1987; vice pres Chartered Inst of Arbitrators 1988; author of numerous articles; FCIArb, FFB; *Recreations* good food, good wine, good company, windsurfing, photography; *Clubs* Athenaeum; *Style*— John Tackaberry, Esq, QC; 22 Willes Road, London NW5 (☎ 01 267 2137, fax 01 482 1018); Atkin Building, Grays Inn, London WC1R 34J (☎ 01 404 0102, fax 01 405 7456, telex 298623 - HUDSON)

TADDEI, Hon Mrs (Charlotte Mary); da of 2 Baron Piercy (d 1981), and Oonagh Lavinia Baylay; *b* 24 May 1947; *Educ* Badminton Sch, Univ of Florence; *m* 1966, Paolo Emilio, s of Enrico Taddei; 1 s, 1 da; *Career* teacher; *Style*— The Hon Mrs Taddei; Via Lorenzo il Magnifico 70, Florence, Italy

TADIÉ, Prof Jean-Yves; s of Henri Tadié (d 1980) of Paris, and Marie *née* Forester (d 1988); *b* 7 Oct 1936; *Educ* Coll St Louis de Gougagne (Jesuits) Paris, Lic à lettres Sorbonne des Agrégation de Lettres Ecole Normale Supérieure Docteur ès Lettres Sorbonne; *m* 13 June 1962, Arlette-Gabrielle, da of H Khoury (d 1964) of Cairo; 3 s (Alexis b 27 March 1963, Bendit b 13 Feb 1968, Jerome b 28 April 1972); *Career* French Mily Serv 1963-64; lectr Alexandria Univ 1962, asst prof Fac Lettres de Paris 1967-68, prof Université de Caen 1968, (de Tours 1972), prof of French Lit Université de Sorbonne Nouvelle (Paris III) 1970- and Cairo Univ 1972-78, dir French Inst London 1976-81, Marshall Foch Prof of French Lit and fell All Souls Coll 1988; Ordre National du Mérite (Chevalier), Palais Académiques (offr) 1975, Grand Prix de l'Académie Francaise 1988 Belgium, Ordre de la Courenne de Belgique (offr) 1979; *Books* Proust et le Roman (1971), Introd à la Vie Litt XIX siècle (1970), Le Recit Poëtique 91978), Le Roman D'Adventures (1982), Proust (1983), La Critique Literataire Au XX siècle (1987), Proust (ed), A La Recherche du Temps Perdu, Bibl de la Pléiade (4 vol Paris 1987-89); *Recreations* tennis, golf, cinema, opera, music; *Style*— Prof Jean-Yves Tadié; All Souls College, Oxford OX1 4AL (☎ 0865 279 289)

TADMAN, Colonel John; s of George Ronald Tadman, of Hampton-on-Thames, and Phyllis Selena, *née* Laker; *b* 1 April 1933; *Educ* Hampton Sch, RMA Sandhurst, Staff Coll, Nat Def Coll; *m* 8 April 1961, Corinna Mary, da of Cdr Charles William Medlicott Vereker, RN (ret) of Wylye, Wiltshire; 1 s (Miles William Vereker b 1966), 2 da (Carey Joanna b 1962, Fenella Jane b 1964); *Career* professional soldier 1951-84, Cdr 5 Bn Royal Anglian Regt, head of Secretariat to UK C in C's Ctee; md Dyas (Marquees) Ltd 1984; dir Julianas Leisure div 1987-; *Recreations* sailing, shooting; *Clubs* Hampshire CCC; *Style*— Col John Tadman; West End Mill, Donhead St Andrew, Shaftesbury, Dorset SP7 9YY (☎ Donhead 346); Dyas (Marquees) Ltd, Unit 3, Nursling Ind Estate, Southampton

TAGER, Romie; s of Osias Tager, of London, and Minnie Tager (d 1974); *b* 19 July 1947; *Educ* Hasmonean GS Hendon London, UCL (LLB); *m* 29 Aug 1971, Esther Marianne, da of Rev Leo Sichel, of London; 2 s (twins Joseph b 23 Oct 1980, Simon (twin)); *Career* barr Middle Temple 1970, head of own Chambers in Inner Temple 1987-; memb: Hon Socs of Middle and Inner Temples, Int Bar Assoc; *Recreations* opera, theatre, travel; *Clubs* Peak; *Style*— Romie Tager, Esq; 5 The Leys, London N2 0HE (☎ 01 455 2827); 13 Kings Bench Walk, Temple, London EC4Y 7EN (☎ 01 353 7571, fax 01 353 5966)

TAHANY, Lady Caroline Ann; da (by 1 m) of 7 Earl Cadogan; *b* 1946; *m* 1965, Euan Woodroffe Foster; assumed name Tahnay in lieu of Foster 1981; 2 s; *Style*— Lady Caroline Tahany; 57 Cadogan Sq, London SW1

TAIT, Andrew Wilson; OBE (1967); s of Dr Adam Tait (d 1934), of Fife, and Jenny Tait (d 1925); *b* 25 Sept 1922; *Educ* George Watson's Coll Edinburgh, Edinburgh Univ; *m* 1954, Betty Isobel, da of Finlay Maclennan (d 1960); 2 da (Jane, Susan); *Career* ldr writer The Scotsman 1947-48, Scottish Off 1948-64, fndr Int Home Warranty 1979 (dir-gen 1964-85); chm: Nat Housebuilding Cncl 1984-87, New Homes Enviromental Gp, Johnson Fry Property; dir Barratts plc; conslt in: USA, Canada, Aust; *Recreations* golf, tennis; *Clubs* Caledonian; *Style*— Andrew Tait, Esq, OBE; Orchard Croft, Grimmshill, Great Missenden, Bucks

TAIT, Brian Sharland; s of Ernest Waldegrave Tait (d 1953), of 'Vaila', Killara, NSW, Aust, and Florence Eva, *née* Sharland (d 1975); *b* 13 Jan 1918; *Educ* Sydney C of E GS, Sydney Tech Coll (Univ of NSW) Assoc in Arch 1940; *m* 16 March 1944, Marjorie Joan, da of Tom Lewis Lawrence (d 1970), of Court House, Kenilworth Ave, Gloucester; 1 s (James b 1948), 2 da (Amanda (Chamberlayne) b 1947, Joannah b 1952); *Career* Mil Serv 1940 with Aut Light Horse Regt awaiting call up to RAAF; 1940-45 RAAF, Sqdn Ldr, two operational tours as pilot and Flt Cdr 202 Sqdn, RAF Coastal Cmd (flying boats) Gibraltar, W Africa, Shetlands and N Ireland; architect: ptnr Moore & Ward, Sydney Aust 1946-48, asst County Arch Glos 1948-49, own practice 1950-65, ptnr ASTAM Design Partnership 1965-72, own practice 1972-, conslt to Dyer Assocs 1982-; memb cncl RIBA 1971; pres Glos Arch Assoc 1971; 1962-64: founder chm Gloucester Civic Design Gp 1957, chm Gloucester Civic Tst 1978-81; dir Gloucester Historic Bldgs Ltd, Gloucestershire Historic Churches Preservation Tst, tstee Gloucestershire Heritage Tst; clerk to Tirley Parish Cncl 1985-; FRIBA; *Recreations* painting (watercolours), golf; *Clubs* Rotary (Gloucester), Conservative (Gloucester), Tewkesbury Park and Country; *Style*— Brian Tait, Esq; Prince's Plume Cottage, Tirley, Gloucester GL19 4ET (☎ 045 278 335); Old Pitch, Tirley, Gloucester GL19 4ET (☎ 045 278

TAIT, Eric; MBE (Mil 1980); s of William Johnston Tait (d 1959), and Sarah, *née* Jones; *b* 10 Jan 1945; *Educ* George Heriots Sch, RMA Sandhurst, London Univ BSc(Eng), Cambridge Univ (MPhil); *m* 29 March 1967, Agnes Jane Boag, da of Capt Henry George Anderson (d 1958); 1 s (Michael b 1969), 1 da (Eva b 1973); *Career* Lt Col RE, served BAOR, Mid East, Caribbean, N Ireland (despatches 1976); ed in chief The Accountants Magazine; sec Inst of CA of Scotland 1984-; memb of exec Scottish Cncl Dvpt and Indust; *Recreations* hillwalking, swimming, reading, writing; *Style*— Eric Tait, Esq, MBE; Inst of Chartered Accountants of Scotland, 27 Queen St, Edinburgh EH1 2LA (☎ 031 225 5673, telex 727530, fax 031 225 3813

TAIT, Admiral Sir (Allan) Gordon; KCB (1977), DSC (1943); s of Allan G Tait, of Timaru, NZ (d 1970); *b* 30 Oct 1921; *Educ* Timaru Boys' HS, RN Coll Dartmouth; *m* 1952, Philippa, da of Sir Bryan Todd; 2 s, 2 da; *Career* HMS Nigeria 1940-42, HMS/M Taurus 1943 (awarded DSC), HMS/M Tudor 1945 (despatches), cmd HMS/M Teredo 1947, Solent 1948, ADC to Govr-Gen of NZ, Lt Gen Lord Preyberg VC 1949-51; cmd Ambush 1951, Aurochs 1951-53, Tally Ho 1955, Sanguine 1955-56, HMS Caprice 1960-62, Ajax and 2 Destroyer Sqdn Far East 1965-66, HMS Maidstone and 3 Submarine Sqdn 1967-69, COS Submarine Cmd 1969-70, cmd Britannia RNC 1970-72, naval ADC to HM the Queen 1972; Capt RN 1963, Rear Adm 1972, Naval Sec 1972-74, Vice Adm 1974, Flag Offr Plymouth, Port Adm, Devonport; NATO cdr Central Atlantic Sub Area and Plymouth Channel Area 1975-77, Second Sea Lord and Chief of Naval Personnel 1977-79, Adm 1978; pres and chm of Tstees NZ Sports Fndn 1981-86, chm: NZ Family Tst 1982-, NZ Int Yachting Tst 1988-, Lion Breweries 1984-, Lion Corp 1985-, Mount Cook Northland 1982-84, Regl TV Networks News 1985-88; dir: NZ Bd West Pac Banking Corp 1982-, Mt Cook Gp 1982-84, Todd Bros Ltd 1982-, Todd Motors Corpn 1982-87; dep chm: Todd Corpn 1987-, Owens Gp Ltd 1985; AGC (NZ) Ltd 1988-; *Clubs* White's, Royal Yacht Sqdn; *Style*— Admiral Sir Gordon Tait, KCB, DSC; 22 Orakei Road, Auckland 5, New Zealand; Hiwiroa Farm, PO Box 2, Tokaanu, New Zealand

TAIT, Sir James Sharp; s of William Blyth Tait; *b* 13 June 1912; *Educ* Royal Tech

Coll Glasgow, Glasgow Univ (BSc, PhD, LLD); *m* 1939, Mary Cassidy, da of Archibald Linton of Kilmaurs, Ayrshire; 2 s, 1 da; *Career* princ: Woolwich Poly 1951-56, Northampton Coll of Advanced Technol London 1956-66; vice-chllr and princ The City Univ 1966-74; Hon DSc Glasgow Univ; kt 1969; *Style*— Sir James Tait; 23 Trowlock Avenue, Teddington, Middx

TAIT, Lady Katharine Jane; *née* Russell; da of 3 Earl Russell (Bertrand Russell) by his 2 w, Dora; *b* 29 Dec 1923; *m* 1948, Rev Charles Tait; 4 s, 1 da; *Style*— Lady Katharine Tait; Falls Village, Conn 06031, USA

TAIT, Marion Hooper (Mrs Marion Morse); da of Charles Arnold Browell Tait, OBE (d 1962), of London, and Betty Maude, *née* Hooper; *b* 7 Oct 1950; *Educ* Royal Acad of Dancing, Royal Ballet Sch; *m* 9 Oct 1971, David Thomas Morse, s of Thomas Walter Morse (d 1984); *Career* princ dancer with Sadler's Wells Royal Ballet-, worked with leading choreographers and had roles created by: Sir Kenneth MacMillan, Sir Frederick Ashton, David Bintley, Christopher Bruce, Joe Layton; danced all the major classical repetoire; *Recreations* singing, tap dancing, producing 'Company Cabarets'; *Style*— Ms Marion Tait (Mrs Marion Morse); c/o Sadlers Wells Royal Ballet, Sadlers Wells Theatre, Rosbery Avenue, London EC1

TAIT, Sir Peter; KBE (1975, OBE 1967); s of John Oliver Tait (d 1947), and Barbara Ann Isbister (d 1976); *b* 5 Sept 1915; *Educ* Wellington Coll; *m* 1946, Lilian Jean, da of James Dunn; 1 s (David), 1 da (Judith); *Career* stockbroker 1960-76, conslt 1976-; chm: Tait Assoc Ltd, Princess Alex Community Hosp, Advisorcorp Ltd; *Recreations* Bowls, gardening; *Clubs* Napier Lions and Cosmopolitan; *Style*— Sir Peter Tait, KBE; 1 Avon Terrace, Taradale, Napier, New Zeland, (☎ 445266); 4th Floor Manchester Unity Building, 100 Emerson Street, Napier, New Zealand (☎ 355555)

TALBOT, Hon Mrs (Cynthia Edith); *née* Guest; da of 1 Viscount Wimborne, JP, and Hon Alice Grosvenor, da of 2 Baron Ebury; *b* 24 Oct 1908; *m* 1933, Capt Thomas Talbot, CB, QC, *qv*; 1 s, 3 da; *Style*— The Hon Mrs Talbot; Falconhurst, Edenbridge, Kent (☎ Cowden 641)

TALBOT, Vice Adm Sir (Arthur Allison) FitzRoy; KBE (1964), CB (1961), DSO (1940) and bar (1942), DL (Somerset 1973); s of Capt Henry FitzRoy George Talbot, DSO, RN (gs of Rev Henry Talbot by his w Mary, da of Maj-Gen Hon Sir William Ponsonby, KCB (ka Waterloo 1815, 2 s of 1 Baron Ponsonby of Imokilly, cr 1806 & extinct 1866) by his w Georgiana, da of 1 Baron Southampton. The Rev Henry Talbot was eldest s of Very Rev Charles Talbot, Dean of Salisbury, by his w Lady Elizabeth Somerset, da of 5 Duke of Beaufort. The Dean was 2 s of Rev and Hon George Talbot, 3 s of 1 Baron Talbot (cr 1833) and unc of 1 Earl Talbot (of the 1784 cr); *b* 22 Oct 1909; *Educ* RNC Dartmouth; *m* 1, 1940, Joyce Gertrude, er da of late Frank Edwin Linley, of Fowey; 2 da (Anthea Jane, b 1944, m 1969 James Charrington; Elizabeth Ann, b 1945, m 1969 Michel Shuttleworth); m 2, 1983, Elizabeth Mary, da of Rupert Charles Ensor, of Co Armagh, and formerly w of (1) Capt Richard Steele, RN (m dis 1951), (2) Sir Esmond Otho Durlacher (d 1982), stockbroker; *Career* served RN 1922-67: Channel, East Coast UK, Mediterranean, Western Isles during WWII, Staff Offr Ops to C-in-C Br Pacific Fleet & Far East Station 1947-48, Capt 1950, Naval Attaché Moscow & Helsinki 1951-53, IDC 1954, Cdre RN Barracks Portsmouth 1957-59, Rear-Adm 1960, Flag Offr Arabian Seas & Persian Gulf 1960-61, ME 1961-62, Vice-Adml 1962, C-in-C S Atlantic & S America 1963-65, C-in-C Plymouth 1965-67; *Style*— Vice Admiral Sir FitzRoy Talbot, KB CB, DSO*, DL

TALBOT, Frank Heyworth; QC (KC 1949); s of Edward John Talbot (d 1940), and Susan, *née* Heyworth (d 1952); *b* 4 June 1895; *Educ* Tottenham GS, Univ of London (LLB); *m* 1, 6 Feb 1922, Mabel Jane (d 1956), da of John Williams (d 1915), of Brecon; 2 s (Clifford b 22 April 1925, John b 19 Oct 1930); m 2, 18 April 1969, Heather, da of J F Williams of Truro, Cornwall; *Career* Inns of Ct Regt 1918-19; Civil Serv 1912-31; barr Middle Temple 1931 (ad eundem Lincoln's Inn), practice at Bar 1931-84, bencher Middle Temple 1958; *Recreations* music; *Style*— F Heyworth Talbot, Esq, QC; 9 West Field, Little Abington, Cambridge CB1 6BE (☎ 0223 891 330)

TALBOT, Godfrey Walker; LVO (1986, MVO 1960), OBE (1946); s of Frank Talbot (d 1931), and Kate Bertha, *née* Walker (d 1938); *b* 8 Oct 1908; *Educ* Leeds GS; *m* 1933, Bess, da of Robert Owen (d 1953), of Anglesey; 2 s (David, Richard (decd)); *Career* author, broadcaster, journalist, lectr, news commentator; editorial staff The Yorkshire Post 1928, ed Manchester City News 1932-34, editorial staff Daily Dispatch 1934-37, joined BBC 1937, BBC war corr overseas 1941-45 (despatches), organised BBC reporting unit as sr reporter after war, BBC's first ct corr accredited to Buckingham Palace 1947-69, BBC chief commentator Royal Tours 1948-69, pres Queen's English Soc; *Books* Speaking from the Desert (1944), The Queen Mother (1973), Ten Seconds from Now (1973), Permission to Speak (1976) Our Royal Heritage (1978), The Country Life Book of The Royal Family (1980), The Royal Family (1983), The Country Life Book of Queen Elizabeth The Queen Mother (new and revised edn 1983), Royalty Annual (1952-56); *Recreations* lone pedestrianism, keeping quiet; *Clubs* Royal Overseas League (deputy-chm); *Style*— Godfrey Talbot, Esq, LVO, OBE; Holmwell, Hook Hill, Sanderstead, Surrey CR2 0LA (☎ 01 657 3476)

TALBOT, Sir Hilary Gwynne; s of Rev Prebendary A Talbot, RD; *b* 22 Jan 1912; *Educ* Haileybury, Worcester Coll Oxford; *m* 1963, Jean Whitworth, JP, da of Kenneth Fisher; *Career* served WWII RA; called to the Bar 1935, dep chm Northants Quarter Sessions 1948-62, chm Derbyshire Quarter Sessions 1958-63, judge of County Cts 1962-68, dep chm Hants Quarter Sessions 1964-71, high court judge Queen's Bench 1968-83, judge Employment Appeals Tbnl 1978-81, memb Parole Bd 1980-83, dep chm Boundary Cmmn Wales 1980-83, memb rule ctee Supreme Ct until Nov 1981; kt 1968; *Style*— Sir Hilary Talbot; Old Chapel House, Little Ashley, Bradford on Avon, Wilts BA15 2PN (☎ 022 16 2182)

TALBOT, John Bentley; MC (1946); s of Charles White Talbot (d 1965), of Rowledge, nr Farnham, Surrey, Mary Rhoda, *née* Flux (d 1940) ; *b* 30 April 1917; *Educ* Highgate; *m* 17 Dec 1942, Marguerite Maxwell, da of Col Herbert Townley (d 1970), of Little Stretton, Shropshire; 2 s (Patrick John b 28 July 1946, Nigel Charles b 25 April 1951), 1 da (Sheenagh Elizabeth (Mrs Kent) b 18 Nov 1948); *Career* Maj RA NW Europe (despatches); admitted slr 1946; joined Williams & James 1946, sr ptnr 1970, conslt 1985-88; conslt Charles Russell Williams & James 1989-; hon slr Alexandra Rose Day 1956-85; govr Dorset House Sch of Occupational Therapy Oxford 1958-88; memb Law Soc; *Recreations* travel, swimming, tennis; *Clubs* Army and Navy, HAC; *Style*— John Talbot, Esq, MC; Hall Court, Lincoln's Inn, London WC2A 3UL (☎ 01 242 1031, fax 01 430 0388, telex 23521 LAWYER G)

TALBOT, John Michael Arthur; s of John Edward Lightfoot Talbot (Capt WWI and WWII, d 1974), of 22 Chepstow Place, London, and Muriel Emily Mary, *née* Horsley; *b* 29 Dec 1934; *Educ* Sherborne, Trinity Hall Cambridge (MA); *m* 9 Sept 1961, Adrienne Mary, da of Capt R F T Stannard, CBE, DSC, RN (d 1969), of Little Barley Mow, Headley, Hants; 1 s (Michael b 1962), 1 da (Claire b 1964); *Career* Nat Serv 2 Lt Middx Regt; sr ptnr Bower Cotton & Bower 1982- (ptnr 1964-); clerk to govrs Highgate Sch; vice pres Blackheath FC; memb Law Soc; *Recreations* swimming, walking, wine, history; *Clubs* Blackheath FC, Teddington CC; *Style*— John Talbot, Esq; 51 Culmington Rd, Ealing, London W13 9NJ (☎ 01 567 4905); 36 Whitefriars St, London EC4Y 8BH (☎ 01 353 3040)

TALBOT, Hon Rose Maud; da of late Col the Hon Milo George Talbot, CB (4 s of late 4 Baron Talbot de Malahide) and sis of 7 Baron Talbot de Malahide (d 1973, when the UK Barony became ext); *b* 1915; *Style*— The Hon Rose Talbot; Malahide, Fingal, Tasmania, Australia 7214

TALBOT, Thomas George; CB (1960), QC (1954); s of Rt Hon Sir George Talbot, PC (gs of Hon John Talbot, QC, 4 s of 2 Earl Talbot, which title is now merged with Earldom of Shrewsbury), and Gertrude, *née* Cator; *b* 21 Dec 1904; *Educ* Winchester, New Coll Oxford; *m* 1933, Hon Cynthia Guest (*see* Hon Mrs Talbot); 1 s, 3 da; *Career* served WW II RE (TA) and Scots Gds; barr Inner Temple 1929, bencher 1960; asst, subsequently dep parly counsel to Treasury 1944-53; counsel chm ctees House of Lords 1953-77; asst counsel chm ctees House of Lords 1977-82; *Clubs* Brooks's; *Style*— Thomas Talbot, Esq, CB, QC; Falconhurst, Edenbridge, Kent (☎ 034286 641)

TALBOT OF MALAHIDE, 10 Baron (I 1831); Reginald John Richard Arundell; DL (Wilts); also Hereditary Lord Adm of Malahide and the Adjacent Seas (a distinction dating, by charter, from 5 March in the 15 year of the reign of Edward IV). The mother of the 2 and 3 Barons, who was the first holder of the title, was, to use the full designation, cr Baroness Talbot of Malahide and Lady Malahide of Malahide; s of Reginald John Arthur Arundell (changed his surname to Arundell 1945, s of Reginald Aloysius Talbot, ggs of Baroness Talbot of Malahide), and Mabile Arundell, gda of 9 Baron Arundell of Wardour; suc kinsman 9 Baron Talbot of Malahide (d 1987); *b* 9 Jan 1931; *Educ* Stonyhurst, RMA Sandhurst; *m* 1955, Laura Duff, yr da of Gp Capt Edward Tennant, DSO, MC, JP (n of 1 Baron Glenconner), and his 2 w, Victoria, MBE, o da of Sir Robert Duff, 2 Bt; 1 s (Richard), 4 da (Juliet, Catherine, Rose, Lucy); *Heir* s, Hon Richard John Tennant Arundell b 1957; *Career* chm St John Cncl for Wilts; KStJ 1988 (CStJ 1983, OStJ 1978); Kt of Honour and Devotion SMOM 1977; hon citizen of State of Maryland; *Style*— The Rt Hon Lord Talbot of Malahide, DL; Hook Manor, Donhead St Andrew, Shaftesbury, Dorset (☎ 074 788 270)

TALBOT WILLCOX, Peter Desmond Ropner; s of George Talbot Willcox, MC (d 1968), and Constance Winsome, *née* Ropner (d 1988); *b* 17 Mar 1927; *Educ* Eton; *m* 31 March 1950, Jennifer April, da of Lt Col E Holt, OBE, MC (d 1969), of Little Tew, Oxon; 1 s (Paul b 1952), 3 da (Jane b 1955, Lucy b 1957, Henrietta b 1964); *Career* Lt Irish Gds 1946-48; chm: Wilts Shipping Co Ltd 1962-, Eggar Forrester Gp 1966 (dir Eggar Forrester and Verner Ltd 1955-66); dir Gallic Mgmnt Co Ltd 1979-, chm Douglas and Gordon Ltd 1979-; pres Inst of Chartered Shipbrokers 1986-88, chm of Centre for Spiritual and Psychological Studies 1987-; *Recreations* meditation, painting, walking, gardening, reading, practising Tai Chi, listening to music; *Clubs* City of London; *Style*— Peter Talbot Willcox, Esq; Thanescroft, Shamely Green, Guildford, Surrey GU5 0TJ; Eggar Forrester Holdings Ltd, Rodwell House, Middlesex Street, London E17 7HJ (☎ 01 377 9366, telex 8811671)

TALBOT-PONSONBY, Michael Clement; s of Col J A Talbot-Ponsonby, of Todenham Manor, Moreton-in-Marsh (d 1969), and Elizabeth Frances, *née* Fraser (d 1980); *b* 3 Jan 1932; *Educ* Eton; *m* 28 Jan 1956, Judith Katherine (d 1985), da of Bishop T S Gibson, of, Kimberley, S Africa (d 1953); 4 da (Caroline Frances b 1958, Charlotte Jane b 1963, Lucy Elizabeth b 1965, Katherine Louisa b 1967); *Career* dir Ogilvy & Mather 1968-78; chm: Mather's Advertising Foster Turner & Benson 1978-83, Alexander Fraser Parva Properties; non exec dir Phoenix Advertising 1984-86; memb various charity ctees; *Recreations* riding, hunting, racing, gardening; *Clubs* The Turf; *Style*— Michael Talbot-Ponsonby, Esq; 10 Westmoreland Place, London SW1V 4AD (☎ 01 834 5218); Hinton Manor, Hinton Parua, nr Swindon (☎ 0793 790507)

TALBOT-PONSONBY, Nigel Edward Charles; s of Edward Fitzroy Talbot-Ponsonby (ggs of Adm Sir Charles Talbot, KCB, who was s of Very Rev Charles Talbot, Dean of Salisbury, by Lady Elizabeth Somerset, da of 5 Duke of Beaufort; the Dean was n of 3 Baron and 1 Earl Talbot, which two dignities are now held by the Earl of Shrewsbury); *b* 24 Sept 1946; *Educ* Harrow; *m* 1977, Robina, da of Lt Cdr Henry Bruce, JP, DL, RN ret (gs of 9 Earl of Elgin & 13 ofX Kincardine), of Barley Down House, Alresford; 3 s (Henry b 1981, James b 1986, Alexander b 1987); *Career* chartered surveyor; ptnr Humberts (chartered surveyors) and managing ptnr Humberts Int Leisure Divn (the firm which handled the sale of Highgrove to HRH The Prince of Wales (Duchy of Cornwall) 1981 and the purchase of Lands End for Peter de Savary 1987); dir Singleton Open Air Museum Sussex; memb recreation and leisure mgmnt ctee Royal Inst of Chartered Surveyors; memb Land Decade Cncl; FRICS; *Recreations* sailing, field sports; *Clubs* Royal Thames Yacht, Lloyds; *Style*— Nigel Talbot-Ponsonby, Esq; Langrish Lodge, Langrish, Petersfield, Hants GU32 1RB (T 0730 63374); 25 Grosvenor Street, London W1X 9FE (☎ 01 629 6700, telex 27444)

TALBOT-RICE, Nigel; s of Mervyn Gurney Talbot-Rice (d 1979), and Eleanor Butler Adair, *née* Williamson (d 1965); *b* 14 May 1938; *Educ* Charterhouse, Christ Church Oxford (MA, Dip Ed); *m* 20 July 1968, (Rosfrith) Joanna Sarah, da of Air-Cdr F J Manning, CB, CBE, RAF ret (d 1988); 1 s (Samuel b 17 March 1982), 4 da (Sarah b 24 Oct 1969, Caroline b 26 Sept 1971, Rebecca b 2 Sept 1973, Helena b 28 Jan 1977); *Career* Nat Serv Coldstream Gds 1957-58; asst master Papplewick Sch Ascot 1961-64, headmaster Summer Fields Sch Oxford 1975- (asst master 1965-71, asst headmaster 1971-75); memb IAPS 1971; *Books* Survey of Religion in Preparatory Schools (1965); *Recreations* golf, gardening; *Style*— Nigel Talbot-Rice, Esq; Beech House, Mayfield Rd, Oxford; Cool Bawn, Thurlestone, Devon; Summer Fields, Oxford OX2 7EN (☎ 0865 54433)

TALBOYS, Rt Hon Brian Edward; CH (1981), PC (1977), MP (Nat) Wallace, NZ 1957-; *b* 1921; *Educ* Wanganui Collegiate Sch, Manitoba Univ, Victoria Univ Wellington; married; 2 s; *Career* dep ldr Nat Pty 1974-, min For Affrs & Overseas Trade 1975-, late dep pm NZ; landowner; *Style*— The Rt Hon Brian Talboys, CH, PC, MP; Parliament House, Wellington, New Zealand

TALINTYRE, Douglas George; s of Henry Matthew Talintyre (d 1962), and Gladys, *née* Gould; *b* 26 July 1932; *Educ* Harrow Co GS for Boys, LSE (BSc, MSc); *m* 29 Dec 1956, Maureen Diana, da of Edward Lyons (d 1978); 1 s (John b 1963), 1 da (April b 1965); *Career* NCB 1956-66, princ Navy Dept MOD 1966-69; Cmmn on Industl Rels: sr industl rels offr (princ) 1969-71, dir of industl rels (asst sec) 1971-74; asst sec Trg Servs Agency 1974-75, cnsllr (Lab) HM Embassy Washington DC 1975-77, head of policy and planning MSC 1977-80; Dept of Employment: asst sec 1980-86, dir of fin and res mgmnt and princ fin offr (undersec) 1986-; Freeman Worshipful Co of Cordwainers Newcastle upon Tyne, 1952; *Clubs* Reform; *Style—* D G Talintyre, Esq; Department of Employment, Caxton House, Tothill St, London SW1H 9NF (☎ 01 273 5763)

TALLBOYS, Richard Gilbert; CMG, OBE; s of Harry Tallboys (d 1963), and Doris Gilbert (d 1967); *b* 25 April 1931; *Educ* Palmers Sch (LLB, London), (BCOM, Tasmania); *m* 1954, Margaret Evelyn, da of Brig Horace William Strutt DSO, ED (d 1985), of Tasmania; 2 s (Roger, Peter), 2 da (Prudence, Sarah); *Career* Merchant Navy Lt Cdr RANR 1947-55; accountant in Aust 1955-62 with Aust Govt Trade Cmmn 1962-68, serving in Johannesburg Singapore Jakarta; HM Dip Serv 1968-87 serving in: Brasilia, Phnom Penh, commercial cnsllr Seoul 1976-80, HM consul-gen Houston 1980-85, HM ambass Hanoi 1985-87; chief exec World Coal Inst 1988-; Freeman City of London 1985; FCA, FCIS, FASA, CPA; *Books* Doing Business with Indonesia (1968); *Recreations* skiing; *Clubs* Travellers, Naval, Tasmanian; *Style—* Richard Tallboys, Esq

TAMBLIN, Air Cdre Pamela Joy; CB (1980); *b* 1926; *Career* RAF 1951; dir Women's RAF 1976-80; *Style—* Air Cdre Pamela Tamblin, CB; 2 Carlton Court, Eastbury Rd, Watford, Herts

TAMM, Mary; da of Endel Tamm, of Surrey, and Raissa, *née* Kisseliev; *b* 22 Mar 1950; *Educ* Bradford, Rada; *m* 14 Jan 1978, Marcus Jonathan Hardman Ringrose, s of Wing Cdr Richard Ringrose, DFC (d 1973) of London; 1 da (Lauren Zoe b 18 Nov 1979); *Career* actress; theatre appearances incl: Mother Earth, The Bitter Tears of Petra Von Kant, Cards on the Table, Good Morning Bill, Swimming Pools at War, Present Laughter; films incl: Witness Madness, Odessa File, The Likely Lads, The Doubt, Rampage, Three Kinds of Heat; tv appearances incl: Donati Conspiracy, Warship, Girls of Slender Means, Not the Nine O'Clock News, The Assassination Run, The Treachery Game, Hunter's Walk, Jane Eyre, Bergerac, The Hello Goodbye Man, Coronation Street, A Raging Calm, Public Eye, Whodunnit, The Inheritors, Only When I Laugh, Quest for Love, Return of the Saint, World's Beyond, Hercule Poirot, Casualty, assoc of RADA; *Recreations* riding, piano, reading, theatre, opera, art; *Style—* Ms Mary Tamm; London Management, 235/241 Regent St, London W1A 2JT

TAMWORTH, Viscount; Robert William Saswalo Shirley; s and h of 13 Earl Ferrers; *b* 29 Dec 1952; *Educ* Ampleforth; *m* 21 June 1980, Susannah Mary, da of Charles Edward William Sheepshanks, of Arthington Hall, Otley, W Yorks; 1 s (Hon William Robert Charles b 10 Dec 1984), 1 da (Hon Hermione Mary Annabel b 11 Dec 1982); *Heir* s, Hon William Shirley; *Career* Ernst & Whinney, Chartered Accountants 1972-82, gp auditor and sr treasy analyst with BICC plc 1982-86, gp fin controller Viking Property Gp Ltd 1986, dir Viking Property Gp Ltd 1987-88, dir Norseman Holdings Ltd (formerly Ashby Securities Ltd) and assoc cos 1988-; FCA; *Recreations* country pursuits; *Clubs* Boodle's; *Style—* Viscount Tamworth; The Old Vicarage, Shirley, Derby DE6 3AZ (☎ 0335 60815)

TANG, Charles Michael Whitton; s of Peter Whitton Tang (d 1977), and Ruby Winifred, *née* Woon-Sam; *b* 17 April 1940; *Educ* Queen's Coll Guyana, UCL (LLB), The Queens Coll Oxford (BCL); *m* 13 Sept 1975, Denise Margaret, da of John Hall (d 1970); 3 s (Peter Whitton b 4 Nov 1980, Edward James Whitton b 4 Sept 1985, Charles Michael Whitton b 4 May 1988), 1 da (Bethany Louise b 6 Sept 1978); *Career* slr 1970, sr ptnr Michael Tang and Co Slrs; Oxford blue at tennis 1964 and 1965, played int lawn tennis tournament circuit 1965-66, played Davis Cup 1965; memb Law Soc; *Books* Matrimonial Law - The Financial Aspects (1989); *Recreations* golf, tennis; *Clubs* RAC, Hurlingham, Vincents, Gerrards Cross GC; *Style—* Michael Tang, Esq; Purbeck, Martinsend Lane, Great Missenden, Bucks; Michael Tang & Co, 66-70 Shaftesbury Ave, London W1V 7DG (☎ 01 437 6154)

TANGE, Sir Arthur Harold; AC (1977), CBE (1955); s of Charles Louis Tange (d 1931), and Evelyn Maud Kingsmill (d 1971); *b* 18 August 1914; *Educ* Gosford HS, Univ of W Aust (BA); *m* 1940, Marjorie, da of Prof Edward Shann (d 1935); 1 s, 1 da; *Career* dip serv; first sec Aust Mission to UN 1946-49, cllr UN Div Canberra 1948-50, asst sec Canberra 1950-53, min Washington 1953-54, sec Aust Dept of External Affrs 1954-65, high cmmr to India 1965-70, sec to Aust Dept of Def 1970-79; delegate to various int and cwlth conferences 1944-79; ret; *Recreations* stream fishing; *Clubs* Cwlth (Canberra); *Style—* Sir Arthur Tange, AC, CBE; 32 La Perouse St, Griffith, ACT 2603, Australia (☎ 958879)

TANGLEY, Hon Peter Meldrum; s of Baron Tangley (Life Peer, d 1973); *b* 1936; *m* 1961, Annabel Binnie; *Style—* The Hon Peter Tangley; Byways, Little London, Witley, Surrey

TANGNEY, Dame Dorothy Margaret; DBE (1968); da of E Tangney, of Claremont WA; *b* 13 Mar 1911; *Educ* St Joseph's Convent Fremantle, Univ of WA; *Career* first woman to be elected to Cwlth Senate; senator for WA 1943-68, teaching staff Educn Dept WA; memb standing Ctee of Convocation Univ of WA; *Recreations* tennis, motoring; *Style—* Dame Dorothy Tangney, DBE; 12 Mary St, Claremont, W Australia 6010 (☎ 31 2631)

TANGYE, Lady; Clarisse Renée Elisabeth; da of Baron Victor Schosberger de Tornya, of Tura, Hungary; *m* 1924, Sir Basil Tangye, 2 & last Bt (d 1969); 1 da; *Style—* Lady Tangye; Flat 15, High Point, Richmon Hill Rd, Edgbaston, Birmingham 15

TANGYE, Derek Alan Trevithick; s of Lt-Col Richard Trevithick Gilbertson Tangye (d 1944), and Sophie Elizabeth Frieda, *née* Kidman (d 1954); *b* 29 Feb 1912; *Educ* Harrow; *m* 20 Feb 1943, Jean Everald (d 1986), da of Frank Nicol (d 1952); *Career* enlisted Duke of Cornwall's Light Inf 1939, transferred MI (Capt) 1940-50; *Books* Time Was Mine (1941), One King (1944), The Minack Chronicles: A Gull on the Roof (1961), Jeannie (1988); *Recreations* contemplation; *Style—* Derek Tangye, Esq; Dorminack, nr Lamorna, Penzance, Cornwall

TANGYE, Lady Marguerite Rose; *née* Bligh; da of 9 Earl of Darnley (d 1955), and Daphne Rachel (d 1948), da of Hon Alfred John Mulholland (yst s of 1 Baron Dunleath); *b* 24 April 1913; *m* 1, 3 Aug 1934 (m dis 1941), Claud Dobrée Strickland (ka 1941); m 2, 30 April 1942 (m dis 1951), Wing-Cdr Gordon Stanley Keith Haywood, RAF; 1 s, 1 da (twins); m 3, 5 May 1951 (m dis 1963), as his 2 w, Nigel Trevithick Tangye (d 1988); *Style—* Lady Marguerite Tangye; 52 Redcliffe Gardens, London SW10 (☎ 01 351 4875)

TANKERVILLE, Countess of; Georgiana Lilian Maude; *née* Wilson; da of late Gilbert Wilson, DD, PhD of Vancouver, BC,; *Educ* Univ of Br Columbia (BA), BLS Univ of Toronto; *m* 1954, as his 2 w, 9 Earl of Tankerville (d 1980); *Career* WRCNS, 1944-46; Librarian: BC Provincial Library, Victoria Public Library, The Hamlin School San Francisco, UNICEF, San Francisco; *Style—* The Rt Hon the Countess of Tankerville; 139 Olympia Way, San Francisco, Calif, USA, 94131

TANKERVILLE, 10 Earl of (GB 1714); Peter Grey Bennet; also Baron Ossulston (E 1682); s of 9 Earl of Tankerville (d 1980), and Georgiana Lilian Maude, *née* Wilson; *b* 18 Oct 1956; *Educ* Grace Cathedral Sch (Chorister) San Francisco, Oberlin Conservatory, Ohio (BMus); *Heir* uncle, Rev the Hon George Arthur Grey Bennet; *Career* musician, San Francisco; *Style—* The Rt Hon the Earl of Tankerville; 139 Olympia Way, San Francisco, Calif 94131, USA (☎ 415 826 6639)

TANKERVILLE, Dowager Countess of; Violet; da of Erik Pallin, of Stockholm; *m* 1930, as his 2 w, 8 Earl of Tankerville (d 1971); 1 s, 1 da; *Career* Order of Vasa of Sweden; JP (Northumberland) 1942-, pres Chillingham Wild Cattle Assoc Ltd 1972-; *Style—* The Rt Hon the Dowager Countess of Tankerville; Estate House, Chillingham, Alnwick, Northumberland NE66 5NW

TANLAW, Baron (Life Peer UK 1971); Hon Simon Brooke Mackay; yst s of 2 Earl of Inchcape (d 1939), and Leonora Margaret Brooke, da of HH the 3 Rajah of Sarawak (Sir Charles Vyner Brooke (d 1963)); *b* 30 Mar 1934; *Educ* Eton, Trinity Coll Cambridge (MA); *m* 1, 1959, Joanna Susan, only da of Maj John Henry Hirsch (d 1983); 1 s (and 1 s decd), 2 da; m 2, 1976, Rina Siew Yong, da of late Tiong Cha Tan, of Kuala Lumpur, Malaysia; 1 s (Brooke b 1982), 1 da (Asia b 1980); *Career* sits as Ind (formerly Lib) in House of Lords; 2 Lt 12 Royal Lancers 1952-54; chm and md Fandstan Gp of private cos, dir Inchcape plc, pres Sarawak Assoc 1972-75; memb of govrs LSE 1980-; hon fell Univ of Buckingham 1981, Hon DUniv Buckingham 1983; nat appeal chm of the Elizabeth FitzRoy Homes for the Mentally Handicapped 1985-; *Clubs* White's, Oriental, Buck's, Puffin's; *Style—* The Rt Hon the Lord Tanlaw; Tanlawhill, Eskadalemuir, By Langholm, Dumfriesshire; 31 Brompton Sq, London SW3; work: 36 Ennismore Gardens, London SW7

TANNER, Adrian Christopher; s of Alfred Charles Tanner, and Betty Margaret Tanner; *b* 13 Oct 1946; *Educ* Skinners Sch Tunbridge Wells; *m* 1969, Anna Margaret, *née* Shepherd; 2 da; *Career* marine insur broker; dir Alexander Howden Insur Brokers Ltd 1978-81, Robert Fleming Marine Ltd 1982-; memb of Lloyd's; *Style—* Adrian Tanner Esq; Wallington House, Smarden, Kent

TANNER, Amoret Frances Venables; da of Col Thomas Venables Scudamore (d 1951), and Joyce Carr, *née* Shields (d 1977); Rev James Venables, Vicar of Buckland Newton, Dorset, received Horticultural Soc's silver medal for first treatise on making compost 1816; *b* 27 Mar 1930; *Educ* Uplands Sch Dorset; *m* 1, 4 April 1953, Christopher Scott; m 2, 13 Aug 1985, Ralph Esmond Selby Tanner; *Career* fndr memb The Ephemera Soc, tstee Fndn for Ephemera Studies; *Books* Hedgerow Harvest (1979), Murmur of Bees (1980), with Christopher Scott: Dummy Board Figures (1966), Antiques as an Investment (1967), Treasures in Your Attic (1971), Discovering Stately Homes (1973, 1975, 1981, 1988); *Recreations* collecting printed ephemera pre-1920, garden history, plant collecting; *Clubs* Royal Cwlth Soc; *Style—* Mrs Ralph Tanner; The Footprint, Padworth Common, Reading RG7 4QG (☎ 0734 701190)

TANNER, Bruce Winton; s of Lt Denis Frank Winton Tanner, MC, and Gladys, *née* Colegrove; *b* 21 Feb 1931; *Educ* King Edward's Sch Birmingham, St Catherine's Coll Oxford (BA); *m* 4 April 1960, Alma, da of Harold Athur Stoddard; 3 da (Jane b 1963, Ruth b 1965, Judith b 1968); *Career* 2 Lt RASC 1950; md Horizon Midlands Ltd 1965-74, chm and chief exec Horizon Travel Ltd 1974-85, chm Horizon Travel plc 1985-87, chm Chimes Restuarants (UK) plc 1987-, dir Birmingham Cable Corpn 1988-; pres Int Fedn of Tour Operators 1980-83; chm Birmingham Hippodrome Theatre devpt tst 1982-, memb cncl Birmingham C of Indust and C 1984-, dep chm Birmingham Cons Assoc 1987-; *Recreations* theatre, tennis; *Style—* Bruce Tanner, Esq; 37 St Agnes Rd, Moseley, Birmingham B13 9PJ (☎ 021 449 3953, car tel 0836 529 019); Flat 10, 4 Hans Place, London SW1X 0EY

TANNER, Dr John Ian; CBE (1979); s of R A Tanner, and I D M Tanner; *b* 2 Jan 1927; *Educ* City of London Library Sch, Univ of London (MA), Univ of Nottingham (PhD), Univ of Oxford (MA); *m* 1953, April, *née* Rothery; *Career* Reading Public Library 1950, archivist and librarian Kensington Library 1950-51, Leighton House Art Gallery and Museum 1951-53, curator, librarian and tutor RAF Coll 1953-63, extra mural lectr in history of art Univ of Nottingham 1959-63; founding dir: RAF Museum 1963-87, Battle of Britain Museum 1978-87, Cosford Aero-Space Museum 1978-87, Bomber Cmd Museum 1982-87; sr res fell Pembroke Coll Oxford 1982- (hon archivist 1980-); Walmsley lectr City Univ 1980, visiting fell Wolfson Coll Cambridge 1983-; chm Int Air Museum Ctee; pres: Anglo-American Ecumenical Assoc, bd of advsrs Battle Harbour Fndn's Anglican Serv, Trg and Religious Orgn, USAF Euro Meml Fndn; tstee Manchester Air and Space Museum, memb founding ctee All England Lawn Tennis Museum, memb advsy cncl Inst of Heraldic and Genealogical Studies, hon sec Old Cranwellian Assoc 1956-64; Hon DLitt City Univ; Freeman City of London 1966; Liveryman: Worshipful Co of Gold and Silver Wyre Drawers 1966, Worshipful Co of Scriveners 1978; Freeman Guild of Air Pilots and Air Navigators 1979; FLA, FMA, FRHistS, FRAeS, FSA; hon memb Collegio Araldico of Rome 1963, Tissandier Award Fedn Aeronautique Int 1977; Ost J 1964, KStJ 1978 (St John Serv Medal 1985), KCSG 1977 (star 1985), Order of Malta 1978, Grand Cdr OM Holy Sepulchre Vatican; *Books* List of Cranwell Graduates (ed, second edn 1963), Encyclopaedic Dictionary of Heraldry (jtly, 1968), How to Trace Your Ancestors (1971), Man in Flight (1973), The Royal Air Force Museum: one hundred years of aviation history (1973), Badges and Insignia of the Britsh Armed Forces (with W E May and W Y Carmen, 1974), Charles I (1974), Who's Famous in Your Family (second edn 1979), Wings of the Eagle (exhibiton catalogue, 1976), The Fell in the Battle (1980), Sir William Rothenstein (exhibtion catalogue, 1985), RAF Museum - a combined guide (1987); gen ed: Museums and Librarians, Studies in Air History; *Recreations* cricket, opera, reading; *Clubs* Athenaeum, Beefsteak, Reform, MCC, RAF; *Style—* Dr John Tanner, CBE; Flat One, 57 Drayton gardens, London SW10 9RU

TANQUERAY, David Andrew; s of David Yeo Bartholemew Tanqueray (d 1944), and Majorie Edith, *née* MacDonald; *b* 23 May 1939; *Educ* Rugby Sch, Clare Coll

Cambridge (MA), Univ of California Berkeley; *m* 20 Aug 1966, Tamsin Mary, da of Air Cdre Cyril Montague Heard; 1 s (David b 1981), 2 da (Venetiz b 1974, Tabitha b 1977); *Career* conslt Control Data Ltd 1969-84, Floating Point Systems UK Ltd 1985-; awarded Harkeneo Fellowship; *Recreations* music; *Style—* David Tanqueray, Esq; 27 Cheriton Ave, Twyford, Berks RG10 9DB (☎ 0734 341544); Floating Point Systems UK Ltd, Apex House, London Rd, Bracknell, Berks RG12 2TE (☎ 0344 56921)

TANSLEY, Sir Eric Crawford; CMG (1946); s of William Tansley; *b* 1901; *Educ* Mercer's Sch; *m* 1931, Iris, da of Thomas Richards, of Eltham; 1 s, 1 da; *Career* entered Civil Serv 1939, dir mktg W African Produce Control Bd Colonial Off 1940-47, ret 1947; dir Cwlth (formerly Colonial) Devpt Corpn 1948-51 and 1961-68, md Ghana Cocoa Mktg Co 1961, advsr to Nigerian Produce Mktg Co to 1961, dir: Standard Bank, Bank of W Africa, Standard and Chartered Banking Gp 1972, chm Plantation and Colonial Products to 1972, (ret) kt; 1953; *Style—* Sir Eric Tansley, CMG; 11 Cadogan Sq, London SW1 (☎ 01 235 2752)

TAPNER, John Walter; s of Walter Frederick Searle Tapner (d 1977), and Margot Elizabeth, *née* Pellant (d 1979); *b* 12 June 1929; *Educ* King's Coll Taunton, London Univ (LLB); *m* 26 Jan 1957, Cherry, da of Capt Ralph Joseph Moreton (d 1957); 2 s (Rory b 1959, Paul b 1963), 1 da (Michelle b 1961); *Career* slr; ptnr Slaughter and May 1964-, (dep sr ptnr 1986-); *Recreations* music, various spectator sports; *Style—* John W Tapner, Esq; Hornbeams, Harmer Green, Welwyn, Herts AL6 0ET; 35 Basinghall Street, London EC2V 5DB (☎ 01 600 1200, telex 883486)

TAPP, David Redvers; s of Horace Redvers Tapp (d 1965), of Chelmsford, Essex, and Jessie Margaret, *née* Davis (d 1978); *b* 26 Feb 1930; *Educ* King Edward VI GS Chelmsford Essex, Chelmsford Sch of Arch; *m* 10 July 1954, Irene Theodosia, da of Charles Smith (d 1982), of Essex; 1 s (Christopher b 1961), 1 da (Alison b 1958); *Career* RE Cyprus 1956-57; chartered architect, princ in own architect's practice 1969-, broadcaster on Timber Frame Housing on BBC; ARIBA; *Recreations* tennis, cricket, gardening, wine; *Clubs* Phyllis Court Henley, Rotary, Jaguar Drivers; *Style—* David R Tapp, Esq; Shandi, Hop Gardens, Henley on Thames, Oxon (☎ 0491 575730); 13 Fair Mile, Henley on Thames (☎ 0491 576336)

TAPP, Maj-Gen Sir Nigel Prior Hanson; KBE (1960, CBE 1954), CB (1956), DSO (1945); s of Lt-Col James Hanson Tapp, DSO, RA (d 1951), and Winefred Grace, *née* Molesworth (d 1958); *b* 11 June 1904; *Educ* Cheltenham, RMA Woolwich; *m* 22 Jan 1948, Dorothy (d 1978), da of late Alexander Harvey, formerly Mrs Macintosh; *Career* joined RA 1924, served Sudan, CO 7 Field Regt RA UK Normandy Belgium 1942-45, 25 Div SEAC 1945, Dist Cdr Eritrea 1946-47; dep dir: Land/Air Warfare 1948, RA 1949; Cdr 1 Corps BAOR 1951-53, GOC 2 AA Gp 1954, dir Mil Trg WO 1955-57, Cmdt GOC E Africa 1957-60, ret, Col Cmmdt RA 1963-68; Lt Govr and sec Royal Hosp Chelsea 1967-73; DL Greater London 1973-82, pres Assoc of Serv Newspapers 1974-86; Hon Freeman City of London 1978; *Style—* Maj Gen Sir Nigel Tapp, KBE, CB, DSO; 9 Cadogan Sq, London SW1

TAPPS-GERVIS-MEYRICK, Ann, Lady; Ann; *née* Miller; yr da of Edward Clive Miller (d 1956), of Melbourne, Aust; *m* 20 March 1940, Sir George David Eliott Tapps-Gervis-Meyrick, 6 Bt, MC (d 1988); 1 s (Sir George, 7 Bt, *qv*), 1 da (Caroline Susan Joan (Mrs Hulse) b 30 April 1942); *Style—* Ann, Lady Tapps-Gervis-Meyrick; Hinton Admiral, Christchurch, Hants

TAPPS-GERVIS-MEYRICK, Sir George Christopher Cadafael; 7 Bt (GB 1791), of Hinton Admiral, Hampshire; o s of Sir George David Eliott Tapps-Gervis-Meyrick, 6 Bt, MC (d 1988); *b* 10 Mar 1941; *Educ* Eton, Trinity Coll Cambridge; *m* 14 March 1968, Jean Louise, yst da of Lord William Walter Montagu Douglas Scott, MC (d 1958), 2 s of 7 Duke of Buccleuch; 2 s, 1 d; *Heir* s, George William Owen Tapps-Gervis-Meyrick b 1970; *Style—* George Tapps-Gervis-Meyrick Esq; Waterditch House, Bransgore, Christchurch, Hants

TAPSCOTT, Paul Mais; s of Henry John Tapscott (d 1960), and Marjorie Phyllis, *née* Brooks; *b* 23 May 1919; *Educ* Uppingham, Trinity Coll Cambridge (BA); *m* 1946, Babette Alison, da of Joseph Blackham, of Birmingham (d 1941); 1 da; *Career* economist and memb Stock Exchange 1956-85; chm: Laurence Scott Ltd 1961-80, Lesney Products & Co Ltd 1960-80, Associated Fisheries Ltd 1969-78; dir Friends Provident Life Office 1964-, chm and dep chm Francis Industs Ltd 1964-84; *Recreations* swimming, gardening, DIY; *Clubs* RAC, Phyllis Court; *Style—* Paul Tapscott, Esq; Brampton, Green Dene, E Horsley, Leatherhead, Surrey KT24 5RF ☎ 048 65 2058); 256 Southbank House, Black Prince Rd, London SE1 7SJ (☎ 01 587 1571)

TAPSELL, Sir Peter Hannay Bailey; MP (Cons 1959, and East Lindsey 1983-); s of late Eustace Tapsell; *b* 1 Feb 1930; *Educ* Tonbridge, Merton Coll Oxford (MA); *m* 1, 1963 (m dis 1971), Hon Cecilia, 3 da of 9 Baron Hawke; m 2, 1974, Gabrielle Mahieu, of Normandy, France; *Career* 2 Lt Royal Sussex Regt ME 1948-50, hon life memb 6 Sqdn RAF 1971; hon postmaster Merton Coll 1953, librarian Oxford Union 1953, (rep in debating tour of US 1954), PA to PM (Sir Anthony Eden) 1955 election campaign, Cons Res Dept 1954-57; stockbroker James Capel & Co Stockbrokers 1957-, advsr to centl banks on mgmnt of int reserves; chm Coningsby Club 1957-58; contested (C) Wednesbury 1957; MP (C): Nottingham W 1959-64, Horncastle (Lincs) 1966-83; front bench spokesman on: Foreign and Cwlth Affairs 1976-77, Treasy and Econ Affairs 1977-78; chm Br Caribbean Assoc 1963-64, hon tres Anglo-Chinese Parly Gp 1974-77; memb: Cncl of Inst for Fiscal studies, Trilateral Cmmn, organising ctee Zaire River Expedition 1974-75, Ct of Nottingham and Hull Univs; hon memb Brunei Govt Investmt Advsy Bd 1976-85; Brunei Dato (Datuk) 1971; vice pres Tennyson Soc; Tstee Oxford Union Soc; vice chm Mitsubishi Oxford Fndn kt 1985; *Clubs* Carlton, Hurlingham; *Style—* Sir Peter Tapsell, MP; Albany, Piccadilly, London W1 (☎ 01 734 6641); Roughton Hall, Nr Woodhall Spa, Lincolnshire (☎ 065 82 2572); House of Commons, London SW1 (☎ 01 219 3000)

TARASSENKO, Lady Ann Mary Elizabeth; da (by 2 m) of late 6 Earl of Craven; *b* 9 April 1959; *m* 1978, Lionel Tarassenko; 1 s (Luke b 1988); *Style—* Lady Ann Tarassenko; 12 Squitchey Lane, Oxford

TARBAT, Viscount; John Ruaridh Blunt Grant MacKenzie; s and h of 4 Earl of Cromartie, *qv*; *b* 12 June 1948; *Educ* Rannoch Sch Perthshire, Strathclyde Univ; *m* 1, 1973, Helen, da of John Murray; 1 s (decd); m 2, 1985 Janet, da of Christopher Harley; 1 s (Colin Ruaridh b 7 Sept (1987); *Career* memb Inst Explosive Engrs 1982-, explosives conslt, editor Explosives Engineering; *Books* Rock and Ice Climbs in Skye (SMT); part author: Cold Climbs, Classic Rock, Wild Walks and many magazine articles both in the climbing press and in explosives; *Recreations* mountaineering, geology, art; *Clubs* Scottish Mountaineering, Army and Navy, Pratts; *Style—* Viscount Tarbat; Castle Leod, Strathpeffer, Ross-shire

TARDIF, Graham Mackenzie de Putron; s of Frederick Graham Charles Tardif (d 1972), and Mabel Marion, *née* Mackenzie (d 1987); *b* 27 June 1935; *Educ* Tonbridge; *m* 1, 9 April 1960 (m dis 1971), Judith Helen, da of Col Ferdinand Livock of Eastbourne; 1 s (Simon b 1963, d 1987), 1 da (Michele b 1962); m 2, 8 Jan 1972, Lucinda, da of John Hoskyns-Abrahall; 1 s (Ben b 1972), 2 da (Kate b 1975, Lucy b 1981); *Career* Nat Serv RAF 1953-55; dir: J H Minet UK 1968, Frank B Hall UK 1970, Wigham Poland UK 1973, Frizzell Gp 1976; pres and chief exec Canadian Internat Insur Mgmnt Ltd Bermuda USA 1981, chm Soberbiew Ltd and Graham Tardif Assoc Ltd 1988; Freeman City of London 1989; ABIBA; *Recreations* golf, rugby football, dog-walking, cooking; *Clubs* Royal St Georges GC, Richmond FC, London RC; *Style—* Graham Tardif, Esq; Kippen, Frinsted, Sittingbourne, Kent ME9 OSN (☎ 062 784 202); 133 Ebury St, London SW1 9PU (☎ 01 730 8291, fax 01 730 1677, telex 24681 HAROAK)

TARLING, Keith Ellis; s of Ellis John Tarling (d 1930), of Newhouse Farm, N Weald, Essex, and Margaret Madeline, *née* Cockerell (d 1954); *b* 22 July 1900; *Educ* Haileybury, Keble Coll Oxford; *m* 1, Aug 1934, Ethel Marjorie Joy, da of John Waugh Harris, of Stone, Staffs (d 1920); 1 s (Nikolas b 1941); m 2, March 1976, Margaret, da of D'Arcy Brabazon Ellis, of Stoke-on-Trent (d 1947); *Career* headmaster Yarlet Pre Sch 1934-70; memb Cncl of IAPS 1960-62; *Recreations* golf, tennis, bridge; *Clubs* Trentham Golf; *Style—* Keith Tarling, Esq; Yarlet, Stafford ST16 9SU (☎ Sandon 317)

TARLING, Nikolas Daniel; s of Keith Ellis Tarling, of Yarlet, Stafford, and Ethel Marjorie Joy, *née* Harris (d 1967); *b* 1 May 1941; *Educ* Repton, and Oxford Univ (MA); *m* 14 Feb 1969, Elizabeth Helen Margaret, da of Maj Alexander David Duncan Lawson, MBE, of Blinkbonny, Newburgh, Fife; 3 da (Rebecca, Camilla, Serena); *Career* slr 1966, ptnr Freshfields 1974-; *Recreations* fishing, skiing, music, old master drawings; *Clubs* City of London, Hurlingham; *Style—* Nikolas Tarling, Esq; 13 Markham Sq, London SW3; Fontaine St Donat, 06140 VENCE; 25 Newgate St, London EC1

TARN, Prof John Nelson; s of Percival Nelson Tarn (d 1976), and Mary Isabell, *née* Purvis (d 1972); *b* 23 Nov 1934; *Educ* Royal GS Newcastle Upon Tyne, Kings Coll Newcastle (BArch), Gonville and Caius Coll Cambridge (PhD); *Career* architectural asst W B Edwards and Ptnrs Newcastle 1960-63, sr lectr in architecture Univ of Sheffield 1970 (lectr 1963-70), prof of architecture and head of dept Univ of Nottingham 1970-73, Roscoe prof of architecture and head of Liverpool Sch of Architecture 1974-86, head of Liverpool Sch of Architecture and Building Engrg 1986-, pro-vice-chllr Liverpool Univ 1988; memb Peak Park Planning Bd 1973-86: chm planning control ctee 1979-, vice-chm of bd 1981-86, co-opted memb planning control ctee 1986-; RIBA: chm examinations sub ctee 1975-, memb professional literature ctee 1968-77, memb educn and professional devpt ctee 1978-; memb: technol ctee UGC 1974-84, architecture ctee CNAA 1981-86, Built Environment Ctee 1986-; ARCUK: chm bd of educn 1983-86, vice chm cncl 1985-86, chm 1987; FRIBA, FRHistS, FSA, FRSA; *Books* Working Class Housing in Nineteenth Century Britain (1971), Five Per Cent Philanthropy (1973), The Peak District, Its Architecture (1973), Working Class Housing in Nineteenth Century Britain (1971), Five Per Cent Philanthropy (1973), The Peak District Its Architecture (1973); *Clubs* Athenaeum; *Style—* Prof John Tarn; 2 Ashmore Close, Barton Hey Dr, Caldy, Wirral Merseyside L48 2JX; Piping Stones, Stanton in Peak, Matlock, Derbyshire DE4 2LR; Liverpool School of Arch and Building Engrg, Liverpool University, PO Box 147, Liverpool L69 3BX (☎ 051 794 2602, fax 051 708 6502, telex 627095 UNILPL G)

TARNOWSKI, Hon Mrs (Bridget Mary); *née* Astor; eldest da of 2 Baron Astor of Hever (d 1984), and Dowager Baroness Astor of Hever, *qv*; *b* 16 Feb 1948; *m* 31 Oct 1980, Count Arthur Tarnowski, s of Count Hieronym Tarnowski (a supposed Polish cr of Sigismund III has been claimed dated 1588; more tenable is that by Ferdinand III in his capacity as King of Hungary 1655 and subsequent recognition as an Austrian title by Emperor Joseph II 1785); 2 s (Sebastian b 1981, Lucian b 1984); *Career* photographer; freelance and with Harpers and Queen 1968-; author of childrens' book; *Books* Darling Dennis; *Style—* Hon Mrs Tarnowski

TARRANT, Lucius Frederick Charles; s of Hugh Sherrard Tarrant (d 1963), of Cork, Ireland and Doreen Kathleen Beatrice, *née* Harvey (d 1981); *b* 17 August 1928; *Educ* Cork GS, Portura Royal Sch, Dublin Univ (BA, BAI); *m* 16 march 1956, Yvonne Anne, da of George Stephen Sheffield (d 1956); 2 da (Sally-Ann b 1957, Julie b 1959); *Career* with Public Works Dept Nigeria 1950-52, md Costain Gp Plc 1952-; FICE; *Recreations* sailing, gardening; *Clubs* Bosham Sailing; *Style—* Lucius Tarrant, Esq; Costain International Limited, Costain House, West Street, Working, Surrey GU21 1EA (☎ 04862 27911, fax 04862 77331, telex 859375 COSWOK G)

TARRING, Trevor John; s of Leslie Herbert Tarring (d 1964), of Cobham Surrey, and Ethel Anne, (d 1976) *née* Rosser; *b* 5 July 1932; *Educ* Brentwood Sch, Brasenose Coll Oxford (MA); *m* 21 March 1959, Marjorie Jane, da of John Henry Colbert (d 1966), of Malvern, Worcs; 1 da (Emma Jane b 1964); *Career* dir Metal Bureau Ltd 1964, chief exec Metal Bulletin 1987- (jt ed 1968, md 1978); Freeman Stationers Co; MinstMet 1963; *Books* Trading in Metals (1953), Nonferrous Metal Works of the World (ed 1974); *Recreations* vintage car competitions; *Clubs* Vintage Sports Car; *Style—* Trevor Tarring, Esq; Metal Bulletin plc, P.O. Box 28E, Worcester Park, London KT4 7HY (☎ 01 330 4311, fax 01 337 8943, telex 21 383)

TARUA, H E Ilinome Frank; CBE (1988); s of Peni Frank Tarua, of Alotau, Papua New Guinea, and Anaiele, *née* Ketaloi; *b* 23 Sept 1941; *Educ* Church Mission Sch Kwato, Logea Sch Papua New Guinea, Sogeri Papua New Guinea, Sydney Univ Australia, Papua New Guinea Univ (BL); *m* 17 Feb 1969, Susan Christine, da of James Walter Reeves (d 1985), of Sydney Australia; 2 da (Anaiele Louise b 20 May 1976, Liasi Grace b 19 April 1980); *Career* legal offr dept of law 1971-72, constitutional law advsr 1972-75, dep perm head dept of PM 1976-77, dir Bougainville Copper Co 1974-77, sec to Cabinet Nat Exec Cncl 1977-79, high cmmr New Zealand 1980, Ambass UN 1980-81, perm head Dept of the Public Serv Cmmn 1982, perm head PM's Dept 1982-83; high Cmmr UK 1983-; ambass (non res): W Germany 1984-86, Italy 1984-, Greece 1984-, Israel 1984-; memb Australian House CC; Independence Medal 1975 of Papua New Guinea; *Recreations* cricket, golf; *Style—* HE Mr Ilinome F Tarua, CBE; Papua New Guinea High Commission, 14 Waterloo Place, London SW1Y 4AR (☎ 01 930 0922, fax 01 930 0828, telex 25827 KUNDU G)

TASKER, John Mellis (Jack); MBE (1954); s of Sir Theodore James Tasker, CIE,

OBE, ICS (d 1981), of Southover Swanage, Dorset, and Lady Jessie Helen Tasker (d 1974); *b* 18 Jan 1919; *Educ* Westminster, Trinity Coll Cambridge (BA); *m* 8 Oct 1949 (m dis 1988), (Cecile) Juliet, da of George Walter Frederick MCGwire (d 1959), of Hayes, Durlston, Swanage, Dorset; 3 s (Nigel b 1950, Richard b 1959, Patrick b 1961), 2 da (Madeline b 1952, Elizabeth b 1956); *Career* cmmnd 2 Lt RA 1939, Lt 1941, Capt 1942, demobbed 1946; HMOCS 1947-69: asst sec Gibraltar 1947-51, admin offr The Gambia 1951-56, under sec Kenya 1956-69; sec to the bd Milton Keynes Devpt Corpn 1969-81, ret 1981; *Style*— Jack Tasker, Esq, MBE; Brook Farm House, Milton Keynes Village, Milton Keynes (☎ 0908 665 360)

TATCH, Brian; s of David Tatch, of London and formerly of Glasgow (d 1958), and Gertrude Tatch (now Gertrude Alper); *b* 24 April 1943; *Educ* Central Fndn Grammar, Univ Coll London (BSc); *m* 1965, Denise Ann, da of William Eugene Puckett (d 1979), of London and formerly of Louisville, Kentucky; 2 s, 1 da; *Career* consulting actuary; ptnr Clay & Partners 1975-; fndr memb Assoc of Pensioneer Tstees (chm 1981-85); chm: Clay Clark Whitehill Ltd 1987- (jt chm 1985-87), The Bridford Gp Ltd 1987; FIA, FPMI; *Style*— Brian Tatch, Esq; c/o Clay & Partners, 61 Brook St, London W1Y 2HN (☎ 01 408 1600, telex 27167); 4 Eversley Crescent, London N21 1EJ (☎ 01 360 6243)

TATE, Alan George; s of George Tate (d 1967), of Beckenham, Kent, and Margaret Grace, *née* Holmes (d 1988); *b* 19 Nov 1927; *Educ* Colfe's GS Lewisham, London Univ (BSc); *m* 14 June 1952, Barbara Victoria, da of Donald Mason (d 1973), of Mottingham; 1 s (Neil), 2 da (Jill, Karen); *Career* dir G Tate and Son Ltd civil engrg contractors 1949-63, fndr ptnr A G Tate & Ptnrs conslt civil and structural engrs 1963-; memb ct Worshipful Co Paviors 1980 (ordinary memb 1957-80); FICE 1964, FIStructE 1961, MConsE 1967; *Recreations* photography, foreign travel; *Clubs* City Livery; *Style*— Alan Tate, Esq; 17 Orchard Rd, Bromley, Kent BR1 2PR (☎ 01 464 2830); 39-41 High St, Bromley, Kent BR1 1LE (☎ 01 464 7438)

TATE, David Alfred; s of Alfred James Tate (d 1982), of Hastings, Sussex, and Marie, *née* Coe (d 1985); *b* 23 Oct 1934; *Educ* Latymer Upper Sch Hammersmith; *m* 21 June 1958, Doreen Hilda, da of Wilfrid George Wilson (d 1985) of Wembley, Middx; 2 s (Nigel David b 1963, Peter Robert b 1966), 1 da (Jennifer Mary b 1968); *Career* CA; clerk to the Worshipful Co of Joiners and Ceilers 1978; FCA; *Style*— David Tate, Esq; Parkville House, Bridge St, Pinner, Middx, HA5 3JD, (☎ 01 429 0605, fax 01 866 8856, car tel 0836 261282)

TATE, David Read; s of Maurice Tate, of Penarth, S Glam, and Florence, *née* Read; *b* 10 Feb 1955; *Educ* Penarth GS, Jesus Coll Oxford (BA), UCL (MSc); *Career* Deloitte Haskins & Sells CAs 1977-80 (mgmnt consultancy div 1980-83) dir corporate fin div Barclays de Zoete Wedd Ltd; ACA 1980; *Recreations* golf, hillwalking, opera, theatre; *Clubs* Royal Porthcawl GC, Utd Oxford and Cambridge; *Style*— David Tate, Esq; Barclays de Zoete Wedd Ltd, Ebbgate House, 2 Swan La, London EC4R 3TS (☎ 01 623 2323, fax 01 929 3846)

TATE, Sir Henry; 4 Bt (UK 1898), TD, DL (Rutland 1964); s of Sir Ernest William Tate, 3 Bt, JP, DL (d 1939); *b* 29 June 1902; *Educ* Uppingham, RMC; *m* 1, 1927, Lilian Nairne (d 1984), da of late Col Saxon Gregson-Ellis, JP; 2 s; m 2, 6 Aug 1988, Edna, *née* Stokes; *Heir* s, (Henry) Saxon Tate; *Career* formerly Lt Grenadier Gds, Hon Lt-Col RWF; cncllr Rutland CC 1958-69, 1970-74; High Sheriff of Rutland 1949-50, jt master Cottesmore Foxhounds 1946-58, pres Cottesmore Hunt 1974-, dep pres Burghley Horse Trials 1960-82, chm Rutland Agric Soc 1946-66; *Recreations* hunting, fishing, gardening, shooting; *Clubs* Buck's; *Style*— Sir Henry Tate, Bt, TD, DL; Preston Lodge, Withcote, Oakham, Rutland, Leics LE15 8PP; The Cottage, Galltfaenan, Trefnant, Clwyd

TATE, John Frederick Peter; s of Alfred Herbert Tate (d 1930), and Elsie Louisa Vincent, *née* Jelf-Petit (d 1957); ggs of Sir Henry Tate, Bt; *b* 31 Jan 1923; *Educ* Stowe, Trinity Coll Cambridge; *m* 24 June 1949, Celia Judith, da of Adrian Gray Corbett (d 1936) of Sussex; 1 s (Christopher b 1953), 3 da (Teresa b 1951, Nicola b 1955, Sophia b 1958); *Career* Flt Lt RAF 1942-48; dir Tate & Lyle Ltd 1954-80 (joined 1948); chm: Caroni Trinidad 1970 (dir 1957), Belize Sugar 1969 (dir 1964), Illovo Sugar Durban 1975 (dir 1970), W Indies Sugar 1969 (dir 1959); ret O/seas sugar cos 1978 as interests transferred to local shareholders; dir Nigeria Sugar Vo 1978-80; pres RWHA 1970- (memb cncl from 1958), vice-pres W India Ctee 1977- (chm 1975-77, memb from 1958); chm fin ctee Indust Co-operative Programme FAO 1974-78, dir and tres Ind Cncl for Dvpt UNDP 1979-84; *Recreations* photography, music; *Clubs* RAF; *Style*— John F P Tate, Esq; The Old Rectory, Boscombe, Salisbury, Wiltshire SP4 0AB (☎ 0980 610240)

TATE, (William) Nicolas; yr s of Lt-Col Sir Henry Tate, 4 Bt, TD, DL, *qv*; *b* 19 Nov 1934; *Educ* Eton, Ch Ch Oxford (MA); *m* 7 Dec 1960, Sarah, er da of Lt-Col Angus John Campbell Rose (d 1980), of Dunira Garden House, Comrie, Perthshire; 2 s (Rupert Sebastian b 13 Nov 1962, Adrian b 27 July 1966, d 1966), 2 da (Melissa Nairne b 4 July 1964 d 1969, Georgina Nairne b 8 March 1969); *Career* cmmnd Grenadier Gds 1956, Lt 1958; dir CBI 1972-81; dir gen Salisbury Cathedral Spire Tst 1985-; *Style*— Nicolas Tate, Esq; Sauvey Castle Farm, Withcote, Oakham, Rutland LE15 8DT; Wren Hall, 56c The Close, Salisbury, Wilts SP1 2EC; 13A North Audley St, London W1Y 1WF (☎ 01 493 4623, fax 01 409 2027)

TATE, (Henry) Saxon; s and h of Lt-Col Sir Henry Tate, 4 Bt, TD, DL; *b* 28 Nov 1931; *Educ* Eton, Ch Ch Oxford; *m* 1, 3 Oct 1953 (m dis 1975), Sheila Ann, da of Duncan Robertson; 4 s (Edward Nicholas b 1966, Duncan Saxon b 1968, John William b 1969, Paul Henry (twin) b 1969); m 2, 31 Jan 1975, Virginia Joan Sturm; *Career* 2 Lt Life Guards 1949-51 (Lt Special Reserve 1951-); prodn trainee Tate & Lyle Liverpool 1952, various appts to refiner dir 1958-65, CBO Redpath Industs 1965-73, md and chm exec ctee Tate & Lyle plc 1973-80 (vice chm 1980-92), chief exec Industl Devpt Bd for NI 1982-85, chm and chief exec London Future and Options Exchange (trading as London Fox) 1985-; *Clubs* Buck's; *Style*— Saxon Tate, Esq; 26 Cleaver Square, London SE11 4BA (☎ 01 582 6507); 1 Commodity Quay, St Katherines Dock, London E1 9AX (☎ 01 481 2080, fax 01 702 9923, telex 884370)

TATHAM, Maj (Clifford Jackson) John; MBE (1946); s of Maj Clifford Tatham (d 1960), of Charnwood, Cotes Rd, Barrow-upon-Soar, nr Loughborough, Leics, and Gertrude Elizabeth, *née* White (d 1962); *b* 27 August 1916; *Educ* Rawlins Sch Quorn, Loughborough Sch; *m* 27 June 1942, (Mary) Noëlle, da of William Edward Carr Lazenby, CBE (d 1968), of 38 Cotes Rd, Barrow-upon-Soar, nr Loughborough, Leics; 2 da (Angela (Mrs Murphy) b 28 Sept 1949, Jemma (Mrs Peters) b 24 May 1954); *Career* WWII: TA 1939, 2 Lt 11 AA Div 1941, Capt 27 S/L Regt RASC Platoon 1942, A/Lt-Col 79 Armd Div 1945 (Maj 1944), demob, transferred to RASC Res of Offrs 1945; John Ellis & Sons Ltd: laboratory technician 1931, I/C Laboratory new Pipe Works Potters Marston 1934-36, departmental mangr 1946, commercial mangr 1950, gen mangr 1951; dir Redland Hldgs (take over co) 1960-70, chm Emalyx of Leicester Ltd 1970-76, Chief recruitment offr Bldg Employers Confedn 1976-; chm Barrow-upon-Soar RDC 1968-72, 1 Mayor Charnwood Borough Cncl; chm 1971-: Br Butterfly Conservation Soc, Leics Rail Servs Action Gp, Nat Paving and Kerb Assoc Midlands area; fell Royal Entomological Soc London; *Recreations* philately, motor racing, natural history, butterflies; *Clubs* RCT, Lighthouse, Loughborough Naturalists, BBCS; *Style*— Maj John Tatham, MBE; Tudor House, 102 Chaveney Rd, Quorn, nr Loughborough, Leics LE12 8AD (☎ 0509 412870); Bldg Employers Confedn, 82 New Cavendish St, London W1M 8AD (☎ 01 580 5588, fax 01 631 3872, telex 265763)

TATHAM, Nigel John; s of Col Eric Tillyer Tatham, and Hon Lettice Theresa (d 1967), eldest da of 10 Baron Digby; *b* 10 Oct 1927; *Educ* Pinewood, Rothesay Collegiate Sch; *m* 7 July 1951, Elizabeth Anne, da of Sir (William) Errington Keville, CBE; 4 da (Joanna b 1956, Caroline b 1958, Edwina b 1962, Charlotte b 1966); *Career* shipping co dir; dir Subsidiaries of Furness Withy & Co Ltd 1959-72; dir Furness Withy & Co Ltd 1970-72; vice-pres Sea Containers Ltd 1973-87; *Recreations* skiing, sailing, golf, tennis, gardening, music; *Style*— Nigel Tatham, Esq; 5 Avenue Ct, Draycott Ave, London SW3 (☎ 01 589 3379); Sea Containers House, 20 Upper Ground, London SE1 (☎ 01 928 6969), car (☎ 0836 242092)

TATHAM, Capt Richard Heathcote; s of Lt-Col William Heathcote Tatham, OBE, TD (d 1955), of Marylea, Heathside Rd, Woking, Surrey, and Mary, *née* Leigh-Wood (d 1975); *b* 19 August 1932; *Educ* Eton; *m* 6 Aug 1962, Ilona Eva, da of Janos Zelei (d 1988), of 61 Hungaria Krt, Budapest, Hungary; 1 s (William b 1964), 1 step da (Melinda (Mrs Lowe) b 1953); *Career* cmmnd Coldstream Gds 1951, Captain 1955, ADC to Govr of Tasmania 1957-58, ADC to Govr of S Aust 1958-60, ret 1962; dir Omnia Hldgs Gp 1962-68, chm Overland Gp 1968-76, corp rels dept George Wimpey plc 1976-; memb cncl People's Dispensary for Sick Animals; Freeman City of London, Liveryman Worshipful Co of Merchant Taylors 1970; *Recreations* collecting militaria, gardening; *Clubs* Cavalry and Guards, Household Div YC; *Style*— Capt Richard Tatham; 47 Strawberry Vale, Twickenham, Middx TW1 4RX (☎ 01 892 6775); George Wimpey plc, 26 Hammersmith Grove, London W6 7EN (☎ 01 748 2000, fax 01 748 0076, telex 25666)

TATTERSALL, David Nowell; s of David Lawrence Tattersall (d 1979), and Mary Ellen, *née* Gott (d 1979); *b* 12 April 1930; *Educ* The Leys School Cambridge; *m* 29 Aug 1959, Susan Elisabeth, da of John Heap (d 1961); 2 s (John b 1972, Michael b 1973); *Career* Nat Serv RAPC 1953-55; articled clerk Waterworth Rudd & Hove Blackburn 1947-53, dir James Tattersall & Sons Ltd Nelson 1955-57, accountant English sewing Cotton Co Ltd 1957-70, fin dir Overseas Div English Calico Ltd 1970-73, gp accountant Tootal Ltd 1973-79, dir Tootal Gp plc 1979-83, ptnr Dastat CAs 1983-; hon tres Family Welfare Assoc of Manchester Ltd; FCA 1956, FCT 1981; *Recreations* motoring, gardening, photography; *Style*— David Tattersall, Esq; Greycot, Castle Hill, Prestbury, Macclesfield, Cheshire, SK10 4AS (☎ 0625 829664)

TATTERSALL, John Hartley; s of Robert Herman Tattersall (d 1958), of Roewen, Conwy, Gwynedd, and Jean, *née* Stevens; *b* 5 April 1952; *Educ* Shrewsbury, Christ's Coll Cambridge (MA); *m* 8 Sept 1984, Madeleine Virginia, da of Robert Edward Hugh Coles, of Reading, Berks; 2 s (Robert b 1985, Luke 1987); *Career* ptnr Coopers & Lybrand 1985-; churchwarden St Jude's Church London 1984-, dir London City Ballet Tst Ltd 1987-; Freeman Worshipful Co of Horners 1980; ACA 1978; *Recreations* walking, opera, ballet; *Style*— John Tattersall, Esq; 3 St Ann's Villas, Holland Park, London, W11 4RU (☎ 01 603 1053); Coopers & Lybrand, Plumtree Ct, London, EC4A 4HT (☎ 01 583 5000, fax 01 822 4652, telex 887470 COLYLN G)

TATTERSALL-WALKER, George; s of George Tattersall-Walker (d 1947); *b* 2 Sept 1920; *Educ* The Leys Sch; *m* 1947, Edith; 2 s; *Career* CA 1949; exec brewery and hotels 1950-; planning dir John Smith's Tadcaster Brewery Ltd 1969-83, dir James Hole & Co Ltd 1975-; chm: Anchor Hotels & Taverns Ltd 1977-82, Cantrell & Cochrane Pension Tst 1977-, John Smith's Brewery SA Belgium 1970-82, Immo Smiths SA Brussels 1972-82, Vivoldi SA Brussels 1972-82, H&G Simmonds Pension Tst Ltd 1972-87, BIM Regnl Bd 1980, CAs Tstees Ltd 1986-; pres West Yorkshire Soc CAs 1980-81, memb York Soc CAs 1988; lectr accountancy 1950-; lay preacher 1944-; memb cncl Inst of CAs 1966-85; *Recreations* gardening, donkeys, public speaking; *Clubs* Anglo-Belgian, Overseas; *Style*— George Tattersall-Walker, Esq; Woodside, Oaks Lane, Boston Spa, W Yorks (☎ 0937 842250)

TATTON-BROWN, Lady Kenya Eleanor; *née* Kitchener; da of Viscount Broome (d 1928), by his w Adela Mary Evelyn; sis of 3 Earl Kitchener of Khartoum; *b* 12 July 1923; *Educ* Open Univ (BA); *m* 1947, as his 2 wife, John Stewart Tatton-Brown (d 1971), s of Eden Tatton-Brown, CB, of Westergate Wood, Chichester; 3 da; *Career* war serv 3 Offr WRNS; MCSP, state registered physiotherapist, chartered physiotherapist in private practice 1946-; govr Whitelands Coll, Putney; *Recreations* tennis; *Style*— Lady Kenya Tatton-Brown; Westergate Wood, Level Mare Lane, Chichester, W Sussex PO20 6SB (☎ 024 354 3061)

TATUM, Hon Mrs (Marguerite Betty); *née* Cadman; 1 da of 1 Baron Cadman, GCMG, FRS; *b* 1913; *m* 1940, Rev John Tatum (d 1966); 2 s, 1 da; *Style*— The Hon Mrs Tatum; Gorsedown, Birling Gap, Eastbourne, Sussex

TAUNTON, Bishop of; Rt Rev Nigel Simeon McCulloch; s of Pilot Offr Kenneth McCulloch, RAFVR (ka 1943), and Audrey Muriel, *née* Ball; *b* 17 Jan 1942; *Educ* Liverpool Coll, Selwyn Coll Cambridge (Kitchener scholar) (BA 1964, MA 1969) Cuddesdon Theol Coll Oxford; *m* 15 April 1974, Celia Hume, da of Rev Canon Horace Lyle Hume Townshend, of Norwich, Norfolk (*see* Burke's Irish Family Records, 1976); 2 da (Kathleen b 1975, Elizabeth b 1977); *Career* ordained 1966, curate of Ellesmere Port Merseyside 1966-70; chaplain Christs Coll Cambridge 1970-73, dir theol studies Christs Coll Cambridge 1970-75 (permission to officiate Dio of Liverpool 1970-73); diocesan missioner Norwich Diocese 1973-78, chaplain Young Friends of Norwich Cathedral 1974-78, rector St Thomas's and St Edmund's Salisbury 1978-86, archdeacon of Sarum 1979-86, hon canon Salisbury Cathedral and prebendary of Ogbourne 1979-86, prebendary of Wanstrow in Wells Cathedral 1986-; chm Cambridge War on Want 1971-73; memb: Br Cncl of Churches USA Exchange (Church Growth) 1972-75, Archbishops Cncl for Evangelism, res and trg Gp 1974-79; govr: Westwood St Thomas, St Edmund & St Mark's Salisbury 1979-86, Salisbury-Wells Theol Coll 1981-82, Royal Sch of Church Music 1984-, Marlborough Coll 1985-, Kings Bruton

1987-, Somerset Coll of Art and Technol 1987-, pres Somerset Rural Music Sch 1986-; memb Gen Synod Working Gp Organists & Choirmasters 1984-85; ldr Bath and Wells Zambia Link Programme 1987-; chm fin ctee ACCM 1987-; *Recreations* music, walking in the Lake District, broadcasting, gardening; *Clubs* Royal Cwlth Soc; *Style—* The Rt Rev the Bishop of Taunton; Sherford Farm House, Taunton TA1 3RF (☎ Taunton 288759)

TAUSIG, Peter; s of Dr Walter Charles Tausig (d 1969), and Judith, *née* Morris; *b* 15 August 1943; *Educ* Battersea GS, Univ Coll London (BSc); *m* 28 June 1987, Geraldine Alice Angharad, da of Leslie Stanley, of Chelsea, London; 1 da (Eva Lily Ibolya b April 1988); *Career* economist Aust Bureau of Census and Statistics 1965-69, SG Warburg/Warburg Securities 1976-87 (dir 1983), Confedn of Br Indust 1969, Bank of London and S America 1970-74, Int Marine Banking Co 1977-78; non-exec dir: Eur-Clear Clearance System Société Co-operative 1987; *Recreations* theatre, literature, cinema, walking, skiing, travel; *Clubs* Zanzibar, Groucho; *Style—* Peter Tausig, Esq; Elm Lodge, Elm Row, Hampstead, London NW3 1AA (☎ 01 435 7099); Warburg Securities, 1 Finsbury Ave, London EC2M 2PA (☎ 01 280 2762)

TAUSKY, Vilem; CBE (1981); s of Dr Emil Tausky (d 1945), of Czechoslovakia, and Josephine, *née* Ascher (d 1935); *b* 20 July 1910; *Educ* Janacek Conservatoire Brno Czechoslovakia, Meisterschule Prague Czechoslovakia; *m* 1 Jan 1948, Margaret Helen, *née* Powell (d 1982); *Career* Czechoslovak Army; served: France 1939-40, Eng 1940-45; conductor Brno Opera House 1929-39, musical dir Carl Rosa Opera 1945-49; guest conductor: Royal Opera House 1951-, Sadlers Wells 1953-; dir of opera Guildhall Sch of Music 1977-87; Freeman: City of London, Worshipful Co of Musicians; FGSM 1979; Czechoslovakia Military Cross 1944, Czechoslovkia Order of Merit 1945; *Books* Vilem Tausky Tells His Story (1979), Leos Janacek - Leaves from his Life (1982), Conserto (1957), Concertino for Harmonica and Orch (1963), Soho Scherro for Orch (1966), Divertimento for Strings (1966); *Style—* Vilem Tausky, Esq, CBE; 44 Haven Green Court, Ealing, London W5 2UY (☎ 01 997 6512)

TAVARE, John; CBE (1983); s of Leon Alfred Tavaré (d 1976), and Grace Tavaré (d 1976); *b* 12 July 1920; *Educ* Chatham House Ramsgate, King's Coll London Univ (BSc); *m* 1949, Margaret Daphne Wray; 3 s; *Career* PA mgmnt conslt 1948-58, Unilever plc 1958-70, chm and md Whitecroft plc; *Recreations* golf; *Clubs* Prestbury Golf; *Style—* John Tavaré Esq, CBE; Whitecroft plc, 51 Water Lane, Wilmslow, Cheshire (☎ 0625 524677, telex 666150); The Gables, Macclesfield Rd, Prestbury, Cheshire (☎ 0625 829778)

TAVENER, Prof John Kenneth; s of Charles Kenneth Tavener, and Muriel Evelyn, *née* Brown (d 1985); *b* 28 Jan 1944; *Educ* Highgate Sch, RAM; *m* 17 Nov 1974 (m dis 1980), Victoria, da of Dr Costas Marangopoulos, of Athens; *Career* composer; organist St Johns Church London 1960-75, prof of composition Trinity Coll of Music 1968-; compositions incl: Cain and Abel 1966 (first prize Prince Rainier of Monaco 1965), The Whale 1968 (London), Celtic Requiem, Ultimos Ritos 1974 (Holland Festival), Akhmatova Requiem, Antigone, Thérèse 1979 (Covent Garden), Palintropos, Sappho Fragments, Towards the Son, Mandelion, A Gentle Spirit, Ikon of Light 1984 (Tallis Scholars), Liturgy of St John Chrysosstom, Risen!, In Memory of Cats, Let Not the Prince be Silent, Requiem for Father Malachy, Two Hymns to the Mother of God, Kyklike Kinesis, Collegium Regale 1987 (Kings Coll Cambridge), Hymn to the Holy Spirit, Acclamation for his All Holiness the Ecumenical Patriarch Demetrios I 1988 (Canterbury Cathedral), Akathist of Thanksgiving (Westminster Abbey 1988), Ikon of St Seraphim (Truro Cathedral 1988); memb Russian Orthodox Church; hon: FRAM, FTCL; *Recreations* collecting Ikons; *Style—* Prof John Tavener

TAVENER, Philip Brandon; s of George Frederick Tavener (d 1985), of Kingsbridge, Devon, and Muriel Edith Kathleen *née* Jensen; *b* 17 May 1943; *Educ* Haberdashers Aske's Hampstead Sch, Hertfordshire Coll of Agric; *m* 1, 26 July 1969, Pamela Denise, da of Arthur Sutherland; 1 da (Sarah b 1974); m 2, 6 May 1978, Sally, da of John McNeil (d 1956); 1 s (Andrew b 1982); *Career* agrochemical conslt; chm and md Chiltern Farm Chemicals 1980-; *Recreations* gardening, conservation, bird watching, renovating old property; *Style—* Philip Tavener, Esq; Chiltern Farm Chemicals, 11 High St, Thornborough, Buckingham MU18 2DF (☎ 0280 817099, telex 826715 ACRO G, fax 044 282 7272)

TAVENER, Robin Frederick; s of Harold William Tavener (d 1969); *b* 20 Nov 1929; *Educ* Leighton Park Sch Reading; *m* 1955, Pamela Beatrice, *née* Austin; 2 s, 1 da; *Career* fin dir ITT 1965; Stone-Platt Industs: fin dir electrical div 1969-74 (chm), md and chief exec 1980-81; ldr of a mgmnt team organised by Candover Investmts to purchase the electrical div of Stone-Platt Indust, chief exec Stone Int plc 1982-87, chief exec Claudius Peters AG of Hamburg 1987-; FCCA; *Recreations* theatre, walking, travelling, sailing, skiing; *Clubs* RAC; *Style—* Robin Tavener Esq; The Mill House, Wonersh, nr Guildford, Surrey; Claudius Peters AG, Schanzenstrasse 40 D2150 Buxtehude, Federal Republic of Germany (☎ 010 49 4161 706212, fax 010 49 4161 706220)

TAVERNE, Dick; QC (1965); s of Dr Nicolaas Jacobus Marie Taverne (d 1966), and Louise Victoria, *née* Koch; *b* 18 Oct 1928; *Educ* Charterhouse, Balliol Coll Oxford; *m* 6 Aug 1955, Janice, da of Dr Robert Stuart Fleming Hennessey, of Beckenham, Kent; 2 da (Suzanna b 1960, Caroline b 1963); *Career* barr 1954; MP (Lab) Lincoln 1962-72, Parly sec Home Office 1966-68, min of state treasy 1968-69, fin sec 1969-70; resigned Labour Party 1972, re-elected Independent Social Democrat MP Lincoln 1973-74; first dir Inst for Fiscal Studies 1971 (chm 1979-83), chm Public Policy Centre 1984-87; Br memb Spierenburg Ctee to examine working of Euro Cmmn 1979; dir: Equity & Law 1972-, BOC Gp 1975-, PRIMA Europe 1987-; *Books* The Future of the Left (1974); *Recreations* sailing, marathon running; *Style—* Dick Taverne, Esq, QC; 60 Cambridge Street, London SW1V 4QQ (☎ 01 828 0166); office: PRIMA Europe Ltd, 10 Cork Street, London W1X 1PO (☎ 01 437 8633)

TAVISTOCK, Marquess of; Henry Robin Ian Russell; s and h of 13 Duke of Bedford; *b* 21 Jan 1940; *Educ* Le Rosey Switzerland, Harvard Univ; *m* 20 June 1961, Henrietta Joan, da of Henry Frederic Tiarks; 3 s; *Career* chm: TR Property Investmt Tst plc 1982-, Berkeley Devpt Capital Ltd 1985-, Kennedy Meml Fund 1985-; dir Trafalgar House plc 1977-, Touche Remnant Hldgs 1977-88, Utd Racecourses 1977-, Berkeley Govett plc 1985-; *Clubs* White's, The Brook (NY); *Style—* Marquess of Tavistock; Woburn Abbey, Woburn, Bedfordshire MK43 0TP (☎ 0525 290 666); office: Mermaid House, 2 Puddle Dock, London EC4V 3AT

TAYLOR, Alan Broughton; s of Valentine James Broughton Taylor, of 34 Norman Ave, Birmingham, and Gladys Maud, *née* Williams (d 1988); *b* 23 Jan 1939; *Educ* Malvern, Geneva Univ, Birmingham Univ (LLB), Brasenose Coll Oxford (MLitt); *m* 15 Aug 1964, Diana, da of Dr James Robson Hindmarsh, (d 1970), of Peach Cottage, Lytchett Matravers, Dorset; 2 s (Stephen James b 30 Nov 1965, Robert David b 21 Feb 1968); *Career* barr Gray's Inn 1961, in practice 1962-, rec 1979-; govr St Matthew's Sch Smethwick W Mids 1988-; *Books* A Practical Guide to the Care of the Injured by P S London (contrib 1964); philately, fell walking; *Style—* Alan Taylor, Esq; 94 Augustus Rd, Edgbaston, Birmingham B15 3LT (☎ 021 454 8600); 2 Fountain Court, Birmingham B4 6DR (☎ 021 236 3882, fax 021 233 3205)

TAYLOR, Alan John Percivale; s of Percy Lees Taylor, and Constance Sumner Taylor; *b* 25 Mar 1906; *Educ* Bootham Sch York, Oriel Coll Oxford; *m* Eva Taylor; 4 s, 2 da; *Career* lectr in modern history Univ of Manchester, lectr in int history Univ of Oxford 1953-63; Magdalen Coll Oxford: tutor 1938-63, fell 1938-76, hon fell 1976-; hon fell Oriel Coll Oxford 1980-; lectures: Ford's (English History) Oxford Univ 1955-56, Leslie Stephen Cambridge Univ 1960-61, Creighton London Univ 1973, Andrew Lang St Andrew's Univ 1974, Romanes Oxford 1981; Benjamin Mealer visiting prof of history Bristol Univ 1976-78; pres City Music Soc London; foreign hon memb American Acad of Arts and Scis 1985; hon memb: Yugoslav Acad of Scis 1985, Hungarian Acad of Scis 1986; Hon DCL New Brunswick 1961, Hon DUniv York 1970; Hon DLitt: Bristol 1978, Warwick 1981, Manchester 1982; FBA 1956-80; *Books* The Italian Problem in European Diplomacy 1847-49 (1934), Germany's First Bid for Colonies 1884-85 (1938), The Hapsburg Monarchy 1915-1918 (rewritten 1948), The Course of German History (1945), From Napoleon to Stalin (1950), Rumours of Wars (1952), The Struggle for Mastery in Europe 1848-1918 (1954), Bismarck (1955), Englishmen and Others (1956), The Trouble Makers: Dissent Over Foreign Policy 1792-1939 (1957), The Russian Revolution of 1917 (script of first TV lectures, 1958), The Origins of the Second World War (1961), The First World War: an illustrated History (1963), Politics in Wartime and Other Essays (1964), English History 1914-45 (1965), From Sarajevo to Potsdam (1966), Europe: Grandeur and Decline (1967), War by Timetable (1969), Lloyd George: twelve essays (ed 1971), Lloyd George, a Diary by Frances Stevenson (ed 1971), Beaverbrook (1972), Off the Record: political interviews 1933-43 by W P Crajier (ed 1973), The Second World War: an illustrated history (1975), My Darling Pussy: the letters of Lloyd George and Frances Stevenson (1975), Essays in English History (1976), The Last of Old Europe (1976), The War Lords (1977), The Russian War (1978), How Wars Begin (1979), Revolutions and Revolutionaries (1980), Politicians, Socialism and Historians (1980), A Personal History (autobiography, 1983), An Old Man's Diary (1984), How War's End (1985); *Style—* A J P Taylor, Esq; 32 Twisden Road, London NW5 1DN (☎ 01 485 1507)

TAYLOR, Lady; Alda Cecilia; *née* Ignesti; *m* 1944, Sir Robert Mackinlay Taylor, CBE (sometime sr dep chm Standard Chartered Bank; d 1985), s of Cdr R Taylor; *Style—* Lady Taylor; Flat 8, 24 Park Road, London NW1

TAYLOR, Andrew Robert; s of Benjamin Clive Taylor, of 13 Inkerman Terr, Tredegar, Gwent, and Enid, *née* Jones; *b* 14 Feb 1961; *Educ* Tredegar comp Sch, Univ Coll Cardiff (BSc), Inns of Court Sch of Law; *Career* called to the Bar Gray's Inn 1985; chm Abergavenny Lawn Tennis Club 1987-89, sec Tredegar RFC 1987-88; Parly candidate (Cons) Blanenau Gwent 1987, currently prospective candidate S Wales Euro Constituency; *Recreations* rugby, tennis, theatre; *Style—* Andrew Taylor, Esq; 13 Inkerman Terr, Tredegar, Gwent NP2 3NP (☎ 0495 253630); 49 Westgate Chambers, Commercial St, Newport NPT 1JP(☎ 0633 67403, 0633 55855, car ☎ 0836 724 938)

TAYLOR, (Winifred) Ann; MP (L) Dewsbury 1987-; *b* 2 July 1947; *Educ* Bolon Sch, Bradford Univ, Sheffield Univ; married; 1 s (b 1982), 1 da (b 1983); *Career* oppn front bench spokesman 1981- (educn 1979-81), asst govt whip 1977-79; pps to: Def Sec 1976-77, Sec State DES 1975-76; MP (L) Bolton W 1974-87; former teacher, pt/t tutor OU; *Books* Political Action (with Jim Flin 1978); *Style—* Mrs Ann Taylor, MP; Glyn Garth, Stoney Bank Rd, Thongsbridge, Huddersfield, Yorks

TAYLOR, Annita; da of Romola Piapan, (d 1967), of Switzerland, and Rosalia Smak Piapan (d 1984); *b* 21 Sept 1925; *Educ* Avviamento Proffessionale Tecnico di Monfalcone Italy; *m* 10 Nov 1946, Alfred Oakley Taylor, s of George Oakley Taylor; 1 da (Ligmoi Hannah b 18 Oct 1947); *Career* md ABBA DG Co Ltd 1983- (dir 1978-); dir: Liglets Co Ltd 1982-, Rosalia Mgmnt Servs Co Ltd 1989-, involved Riding for the Disabled, Red Cross; *Recreations* racing, polo, shooting; *Clubs* Guards Polo, Jockey, Racehorse Owners Assoc; *Style—* Mrs Annita Taylor; Wadley Manor, Faringdon, Oxon; 19 Millers Court, Chiswick Mall, London W4 (☎ 0367 20556, 01 748 2997); 6 Witan Park Estate, Witney, Oxon (☎ 0993 774547, fax 0993 705895)

TAYLOR, Dr Arnold Joseph; CBE (1971); s of Dr John George Taylor (d 1942), of Battersea, and Mary Matilda, *née* Riley (d 1965); *b* 24 July 1911; *Educ* Sir Walter St John's Sch Battersea, Merchant Taylors', St John's Coll Oxford (MA); *m* 19 April 1940, Patricia Katharine, da of Samuel Arthur Guilbride (d 1950), of Victoria, Br Columbia; 1 s (John Guilbride b 1947), 1 da (Katherine Mary b 1953); *Career* RAF Intelligence served in UK, N Africa, Italy 1942-46; asst master Chard Sch Somerset 1934-35, HM Off of Works inspectorate of ancient monuments 1935, chief inspr of ancient monuments and historic bldgs Miny of Public Bldgs 1961, ret 1972; pres Soc of Antiquaries 1975-78 (awarded gold medal 1988); memb: Ancient Monuments Bds for Eng, Wales & Scotland 1973-81, Cathedrals Advsy Ctee 1964-80, advsy bd for Redundant Churches 1973-81 (chm 1975-77), Westminster Abbey architectural advsy panel 1979-; cmmr Royal Cmmns on Historic Monuments Wales 1956-83, Eng 1963-78; Freeman: City of London, Worshipful Co of Merchant Taylors'; Hon D Litt (Wales) 1969, Docteur hc (Caen) 1980; FBA 1972, FSA; *Recreations* observing the built environment, music; *Clubs* Athenaeum; *Style—* Dr Arnold Taylor, CBE; Rose Cottage, Chiddingfold, Surrey (☎ 042 879 2069)

TAYLOR, Arthur Wood; CB (1953); s of Richard Wood Taylor (d 1917), of Newcastle-under-Lyme, and Ann, *née* Shelley (d 1938); *b* 23 June 1909; *Educ* Royal Sch Wolverhampton, Wolverhampton GS, Sidney Sussex Coll Cambridge (BA); *m* 1936, Mary Beatrice (d 1982), da of Frederick James Forster (d 1950), of Streatham; 1 da (Nicolette); *Career* civil servant, HM Customs and Excise 1931-57, under-sec treasy 1957-63, cmmnr of customs and excise 1964-65, dep chm bd of customs and excise 1965-70; chm Horserace Totalisator Bd 1970-72 (dep chm 1972-73); *Books* History of Beaconsfield (1976); *Clubs* Reform; *Style—* Arthur Taylor Esq, CB; Old Bakery, Thames St, Charlesbury, Oxford OX7

TAYLOR, Basil Horace; s of Horace Webb Taylor (d 1964), and Lilian Matilda, *née* Johnson (d 1960); *b* 11 July 1924; *Educ* Whitgift Sch Croydon, Sch of Building; *m* 16

July 1955, Cynthia Joan, da of William Marsh Gill (d 1986); 1 s (Julian Matthew Corfield b 1962); *Career* served RN 1943-46; CA; sr ptnr Paton Pitt Taylor & Assocs London 1978-; worked in Aust 1963, Oman, Malaysia 1975-86; currently in UK ARIBA; *Clubs* Directors; *Style*— Basil H Taylor, Esq; Paton Pitt Taylor & Assocs, 26 Wilfred Street, London SW1E 6PL (☎ 01 834 8707)

TAYLOR, Hon Bernard Alfred; o s of Baron Taylor of Mansfield (Life Peer); *b* 7 Feb 1922; *m* 1952; *Style*— The Hon Bernard Taylor; 126 Mansfield St, Sherwood, Nottingham

TAYLOR, Bernard David; s of Thomas Taylor, of Coventry, and Winifred, *née* Smith; *b* 17 Oct 1935; *Educ* John Gulson GS Coventry, Univ of Wales Bangor (BSc), London Business Sch; *m* 5 Sept 1959, Nadine Barbara, da of Ben Maile, of Devoran, Cornwall; 2 s (Johnathan b 5 Oct 1964, Michael b 5 Nov 1966), 2 da (Sian b 30 Sept 1960, Sarah b 10 Oct 1962); *Career* md Glaxo Aust 1972-83, md Glaxo Pharmaceuticals UK 1984-86, chief exec Glaxo Hldgs plc 1985-; cncllr Victorian Coll of Pharmacy 1976-82; memb: CBI Europe Ctee 1987-, Br Overseas Trade Bd 1987-; fell London Business Sch 1988; *Style*— Bernard Taylor, Esq; Glaxo Hldgs plc, 6-12 Clarges St, London W1Y 8DH (☎ 01 493 4060, fax 01 493 4809, telex 25456)

TAYLOR, Bernard John; s of John Taylor (d 1962), and Evelyn Frances Taylor; *b* 2 Nov 1956; *Educ* Cheltenham Coll, St John's Coll Oxford (MA); *m* 16 June 1984, Sarah Jane, da of John Paskin Taylor, of Paris; *Career* dir med div Smiths Industs plc 1983-85 (business planning and acquisitions 1979-82), exec dir Baring Bros & Co Ltd 1985 (mangr and asst dir corp fin dept); non exec dir New Focus Healthcare 1986; memb: Royal Photographic Soc 1971, Royal Soc Chemistry 1972; *Books* Photosensitive Film Formation on Copper (I) (1974), Photosensitive Film Formation on Copper (II) (1976), Oxidation of Alcohols to Carbonyl Compounds, Synthesis (1979); *Recreations* photography, gardening, wine; *Clubs* United Oxford and Cambridge Univ; *Style*— Bernard Taylor, Esq; 8 Bishopsgate, London EC2N 4AE (☎ 01 283 8833)

TAYLOR, Hon Mrs ((Lavender Lilias) Carole); *née* Alport; yr da of Baron Alport, TD, PC, DL (Life Peer), and Rachel Cecilia, *née* Bingham (d 1983); *b* 13 Dec 1950; *m* 1974, Ian Colin Taylor, MBE, MP, *qv*; 2 s (Arthur Lawrence Alport b 1977, Ralph George Alport b 1980); *Style*— The Hon Mrs Taylor; 7 The Cooperage, Regents Bridge Gardens, London SW8 1JR (☎ 01 735 9500)

TAYLOR, Cavan; s of Albert William Taylor; *b* 23 Feb 1935; *Educ* King's Coll Sch Wimbledon, Emmanuel Cambridge (MA, LLM); *m* 1962, Helen, da of late Everard Tinling; 1 s (Sean b 1965), 2 da (Karen b 1983, Camilla b 1970); *Career* slr; ptnr Lovell White Durrant, dir Tissunique Ltd; former: chm Cooper Estate Ltd, dir Hampton Gold Mining Areas plc; chm of governing body of King's Coll Sch Wimbledon 1973-; *Recreations* reading, sailing, gardening; *Style*— Cavan Taylor, Esq; Lovell White Durrant, 73 Cheapside, London EC2V 6ER (☎ 01 236 0066); Covenham House, Broad Highway, Cobham, Surrey KT11 2RP (☎ 64258)

TAYLOR, Hon Charles Richard Herbert; yr s of Baron Taylor (Life Peer); *b* 27 Jan 1950; *Educ* Highgate, King's Coll Cambridge, Queen's and St Antony's Colls Oxford, Wharton Sch Pennsylvania; *m* 1977, Mary-Ellen, da of John Feeney, of Pa USA; *Career* devpt economist World Bank to 1981, private economic conslt 1981-; *Clubs* Washington Squash and Racquets; *Style*— The Hon Charles Taylor; 45 Alfriston Rd, London SW11

TAYLOR, Charles Spencer; s of Leonard Taylor, and Phyllis Rose, *née* Emerson (d 1982); *b* 18 Jan 1952; *Educ* William Fletcher Sch Bognor Regis, Hull Univ (LLB); *m* 7 Sept 1973, Elizabeth Mary (Liz), da of Ernest Richard Stephens; 1 s (Leo John Julius Taylor b 5 June 1987); *Career* barr Middle Temple 1974, SE Circuit; memb Hon Soc of the Middle Temple 1969; *Recreations* gardening; *Style*— Charles Taylor, Esq; 3 East Pallant, Chichester, West Sussex PO19 1TR (☎ 0243 784538, fax 780861)

TAYLOR, David George Pendleton; s of George James Pendleton Taylor (d 1972), and Dorothy May Taylor, *née* Williams (d 1978); *b* 5 July 1933; *Educ* Clifton Coll, Clare Coll Cambridge (MA); *Career* Sub-Lt (Special) RNVR 1952-54; dist offr and subsequently sr local govt offr Tanganyika (now Tanzania) 1958-63; with Booker McConnell 1964-83 (sr mgmnt post and dir, chm and ch exec Booker (Malawi) 1976-77); chief exec Falkland Islands Govt 1983-87; dir Booker Agr Ind, memb: Royal Cwlth Soc, Royal African Soc; *Recreations* painting, reading; *Clubs* MCC, United Oxford and Cambridge; *Style*— David Taylor, Esq; 53 Lillian Road, London SW13 9JF

TAYLOR, David Mills; s of Donald Charles Taylor (d 1940), and Elsa Marjorie Taylor (d 1967); *b* 22 Dec 1935; *Educ* Royal Commercial Travellers Schs; *m* 1960, Gillian Irene, da of George Edward Washford; 4 da; *Career* gp fin dir: Trafalgar House plc 1979-87, The Guthrie Corpn Ltd 1971-79, Brooke Bond Oxo Ltd 1968-71; fin dir The Fitzroy Robinson Ptnr; FCA, FCT; *Recreations* golf, oriental cooking, music; *Style*— David Taylor, Esq; Fairwood House, Fairmile Park Rd, Cobham, Surrey KT11 2PG (☎ 0932 63520); 77 Portland Place, London W1N 4EP (telex 21807)

TAYLOR, Dennis James; s of Thomas Taylor, of 24 Mourne Cres, Coalisland, Co Tyrone, NI, and Annie, *née* Donnelly (d 1984); *b* 19 Jan 1949; *Educ* Prima Dixon Sch; *m* 30 March 1970, Patricia Ann, da of Robert Burrows; 2 s (Damian Thomas b 26 June 1973, Brendon Martin b 21 Oct 1976), 1 da (Denise Ann b 27 April 1971); *Career* snooker player; turned professional 1971, winner: Rothmans Grand Prix 1984, Embassy World Championship 1985, BCE Canadian Masters 1985, Kit Kat Break for World Champions 1985, Carlsberg Challenge 1986, Benson & Hedges Masters 1987, Carting Champions 1987, Labatts Canadian Masters 1987, Matchroom Championship 1987; Irish Professional Champion 1982, 1985, 1986 and 1987; involved with the Snooker Golf Soc; *Style*— Dennis Taylor, Esq; c/o Barry Hurn, Ground Floor, 1 Arcade Place, South Street, Romford, Essex (☎ 0708 730 480)

TAYLOR, Derek Edmund; s of Jack Evans Taylor, and Mary Jane, *née* Quigley; *b* 30 Nov 1925; *Educ* Farnworth GS, Royal Tech Coll (now Salford Univ) (ARICS), London Univ (BSc); *m* 28 Sept 1965, Pamela Margaret, da of John Seymour (d 1974), of Australia; 2 da (Margaret Jane b 1966, Kathleen Anne b 1968); *Career* physicist ICI 1951-56, sr scientist NCB 1956-58, sr conslt HB Maynard Inc Pittsburgh 1958-61, md Eng Velvets Ltd 1961-64, sr supervisory conslt Coopers & Lybrand Assoc Ltd 1965-73, md Scandinavian Inst for Admin Res Planning Ltd 1973-75; dir mgmnt and bus devpt Kingston Regnl Mgmnt Centre 1975-; non exec dir Roehampton Club Ltd Glaxo Ins (Bermuda) Ltd, Market Garages (Spitalfields) Ltd, Stategic Planning Soc; Freeman City of London, Worshipful Co of Bakers; C Phys (1985), M Inst P (1978), FIMC (1986), FBIM (1978), F InstD (1965); *Books* New Organisations From Old; *Recreations* golf, skiing, bridge, opera music; *Clubs* Roehampton, Royal Wimbledon GC, City Livery; *Style*— Derek Taylor, Esq; Kingston Regnl Management Centre, Kingston Polytechnic, Kingston Hill, Kingston-On-Thames (☎ 01 549 1141)

TAYLOR, Edward (Teddy) Macmillan; MP (Cons Southend E 1980-); s of Edward Taylor (d 1962), and Minnie Hamilton Taylor; *b* 18 April 1937; *Educ* Glasgow HS, Glasgow Univ (MA); *m* 1970, Sheila, da of Alex Duncan, of 80 Wimborne Rd, Southend-on-Sea; 2 s, 1 da; *Career* MP (C) Glasgow Cathcart 1964-79, parly under-sec Scottish Office 1970-71 and 1974, opposition spokesman Trade 1977 and Scottish Affrs 1977-79; journalist with Glasgow Herald 1958-59, industl rels offr with Clyde Shipbuilders' Assoc 1959-64; *Recreations* golf, chess; *Style*— Teddy Taylor, Esq, MP; 12 Lynton Rd, Thorpe Bay, Southend, Essex (☎ 0586 586282); House of Commons, London SW1 (☎ 01 219 3476)

TAYLOR, Eric; s of Sydney Taylor (d 1979), of Wigan, Lancs, and Sarah Helen, *née* Lea (d 1982); *b* 22 Jan 1931; *Educ* Wigan GS, Manchester Univ (LLB, LLM), Dauntesey Senior Legal Scholar; *m* 7 April 1958 (Margaret) Jessie, da of Thomas Brown Gowland (d 1951); *Career* admitted slr 1955, ptnr Temperley Taylor 1957-, p/t lectr law Manchester Univ 1958-80 (hon special lectr law 1981-), examiner Law Soc Final exam 1968-81 (chief examiner 1978-83); chm: Manchester Young Slrs Gp 1963, Manchester Nat Insur Appeal Tribunal 1967-73, pres Oldham Law Assoc 1970-72, cncl memb Law Soc 1972-; chm: Educn & Trg Ctee 1980-83, Criminal Law Ctee 1984-87; govr Coll of Law 1984-; rec Crown Ct 1978-; memb: CNAA Legal Studies Bd 1975-84, Lord Chancellor's Advsy Ctee on Trg of Magistrates 1974-79; memb Law Soc 1955; *Books* Modern Conveyancy Precedents (1964, 2 ed 1989), Modern Wills Precedents 1987); *Recreations* horse riding, dressage; *Clubs* Farmers; *Style*— Eric Taylor, Esq; 10 Mercers Rd, Heywood, Lancs L10 2NP (☎ 0706 66630); Suffield House, Middleton, Manchester M24 4EL (☎ 061 643 2411, fax 061 655 3015)

TAYLOR, Hon Mrs (Frances Rochelle); *née* Bellow; er da of Baron Bellwin (Life Peer); *b* 1951; *m* 1971, Stephen Taylor; 3 s (Daniel Mark b 1973, Benjamin Paul b 1974, Edward David b 1976); *Career* co dir; *Style*— The Hon Mrs Taylor

TAYLOR, Frank Henry; s of George Henry Taylor (d 1935), of Garden Ave, Mitcham, Surrey, and Emma Rebecca, *née* Hodder (d 1965); *b* 10 Oct 1907; *Educ* Rutlish Sch Merton London; *m* 1, 1936, Dora Mackay (d 1944); 1 da (Margaret b 10 July 1938); m 2, 1948, Mabel Hills (d 1974); 2 s (Martin Henry b 11 Feb 1951, Nicholas b 14 June 1953); m 3, 28 Jan 1978, Glenys Mary, MBE, da of Mr Edwards (d 1923), of N Wales; *Career* Lt-Col 1 Caernarvonshire Bn HG 1943; CA 1930, fin dir of tea coffee cocoa and yeast Miny of Food 1942, tport fin rep Miny of War Overseas 1944, visited over 40 countries on fin and political missions, princ Frank H Taylor & Co London CA; parly candidate (C): contested Newcastle under Lyme 1955, Chorley 1959; MP (C) Manchester Moss Side 1961-74; govr Rutlish Sch 1946-; rugby Surrey Co, golf capt RAC 1962, sculliing Thames Championship punting several Thames championships; Freeman Worshipful Co of Air Pilots, Liveryman and Past Master Worshipful Co of Bakers; FCIS 1929, FCA 1930; *Recreations* rugby sculling, punting, shooting, golf; *Clubs* RAC, City Livery, British Sportsmans; *Style*— Frank Taylor, Esq; 4 Barrie House, Lancaster Gate, London W2 (☎ 01 262 5684); 114 Hedgate St, London EC1A 7AE (☎ 01 606 9485)

TAYLOR, Frank William; s of Frank Taylor (d 1963), and Mary Gibson, *née* Steward; *b* 7 Oct 1937; *Educ* Birkenhead Inst; *m* 3 Aug 1963, Ann Taylor; 1 s (Michael b 13 Oct 1965), 1 da (Steffanie b 28 April 1968); *Career* ptnr Arthur Young CA's, pres Insolvency Practioners Assoc (1973); FCA; *Recreations* golf; *Clubs* Heswall, Artists; *Style*— Frank Taylor, Esq; Stableford, Brook Lane, Parkgate, Wirral, Cheshire; Arthur Young, Silkhouse Court, Tithebarn St, Liverpool L2 2LE

TAYLOR, Geoffrey Newton; s of William Henry Taylor, of Bovingdon Green, Bucks, and Elsie May Taylor; *b* 25 April 1938; *Educ* Royal GS High Wycombe, Oxford Univ (MA); *m* 1 1963, Julia Nora Barnes; 2 s (Scott Geoffrey b 1967, Jon Michael b 1970); m 2 1976, Janice Darlene Swett; *Career* dir: Investors In Indust plc 1985-, Tech Devpt Capital Ltd 1980-83, Rodime plc 1981-; *Recreations* music, tennis, pilot; *Clubs* IOD; *Style*— Geoffrey Taylor, Esq; The Hill, Penn Rd, Beaconsfield, Bucks HP9 2TS; Investors in Industry plc, 91 Waterloo Rd, London SE1 8XP (telex 917844, fax 01 928 0058)

TAYLOR, Geoffrey William; s of Joseph William (d 1980), of Heckmondwike, Yorks, and Doris, *née* Parr (d 1984); *b* 4 Feb 1927; *Educ* Heckmondwike GS, London Univ (BCom); *m* 21 July 1951, Joyce, da of George Clifford Walker, (d 1952), of Liversedge, Yorks; 3 s (Nigel b 1954, Christopher b 1957, Julian b 1959), 1 da (Ruth b 1966); *Career* RN 1945-47; Midland Bank 1943-86: md Midland Bank Fin Corpn 1967-72, gp tres 1972-73, asst chief gen mangr 1974-80, dep gp chief exec 1980-81, gp chief exec 1982-86; chm Daiwa Europe Bank plc 1987-, memb Banking Servs Law Review Ctee 1987-88, dir Y J Lovell Hldgs plc; memb fin devpt bd NSPCC; Freeman City of London 1984; FCIOB 1975, FBIM 1979; *Recreations* golf, reading, music; *Clubs* Bucks, Overseas Bankers; *Style*— Geoffrey Taylor, Esq; The Mount, Parkfields, Stokesheath Road, Oxshott, Surrey KT22 OPW (☎ 037 842991); Daiwa Europe Bank plc, Level 19, City Tower, 40 Basinghall St, London EC2V 5DE (☎ 01 315 3900, fax 01 782 0875, telex 9419121 DIAFIN G)

TAYLOR, Sir George; s of George William Taylor of Edinburgh; *b* 15 Feb 1904; *Educ* George Heriot's Sch Edinburgh, Edinburgh Univ (DSc); *m* 1, 1929 (m dis 1965), Alice Helen (d 1977), da of Thomas William Pendrich of Edinburgh; 2 s; m 2, 1965, Norah (d 1967), da of William Christopher English of Carrycoats Hall, Northumberland; m 3, 1969, Beryl, Lady Colwyn (d 1987); *Career* keeper of botany Br Museum 1950-56; botanical sec Linnean Soc 1950-56, vice pres 1956; dir Royal Botanic Gardens Kew 1956-71, visiting prof Reading Univ 1969-, dir Stanley Smith Hort Tst 1970-, vice pres and prof of Botany Royal Hort Soc 1974-, pres Botanical Soc of Br Is; FRS, FRSE, FLS; kt 1962; *Recreations* angling, gardening; *Clubs* Athenaeum, New (Edinburgh); *Style*— Sir George Taylor; Belhaven House, Dunbar, East Lothian (☎ 0368 62392/ 63546)

TAYLOR, Sir (Arthur) Godfrey; *b* 1925,Aug; *Career* former London cncllr and alderman and former chm London Borough Assoc, chm Assoc of Met Authy 1978-80, managing tstee Municipal Mutual Insur Ltd 1979-86, chm Southern Water Authy 1981-85, chm London Residuary Body 1985-; kt 1980; *Style*— Sir Godfrey Taylor; 23 Somerhill Lodge, Somerhill Rd, Hove, E Sussex

TAYLOR, Gordon William; s of William Herbert Taylor (d 1973), and Elizabeth Ann, *née* Tucker (d 1946); *b* 26 June 1928; *Educ* Army Technical Sch Arborfield, London Univ (BSc Eng, PhD); *m* 3 April 1954, Audrey Catherine, da of Arthur Bull (d 1976), of Blackheath, London; 3 s (Mark b 1961, Zachary b 1962, Matthew b 1965), 2 da (Gemma b 1964, Katie b 1966); *Career* Kellog Int Corpn 1954-59, WR Grace 1960-62;

gen mangr: Nalco Ltd 1962-66, BTR Industs 1966-68; md: Kestrel Chemicals 1968-69, Astral Mktg 1969-70; Robson Refractories 1971-87; consulting engr 1987-; GLC Alderman 1972-77, memb Croydon Central 1977-80; chm: Public Servs Ctee 1977-78, London Tport Ctee 1978-79; MICE, MIMechE, AMIEE; *Recreations* reading, theatre, opera, tennis; *Clubs* Holland Park Lawn Tennis; *Style*— Gordon Taylor, Esq; 33 Royal Avenue, Chelsea, London SW3 4QE (☎ 01 730 3045)

TAYLOR, Sir Henry Milton; *b* 1903,Nov; *Career* Ed Hansard, Bahamas House of Assembly 1979-; kt 1980; *Style*— Sir Henry Taylor; PO Box N10846, Nassau, Bahamas

TAYLOR, Iain Scott; TD; s of John Ross Taylor (d 1963), of Kerryston House, Kellas, by Dundee, Angus, and Annie, *née* Scott Paterson (d 1982); *b* 1 June 1931; *Educ* Dundee HS, Merchiston Castle Sch; *m* 8 Aug 1956, Nancy Christine, da of Dr William Allison (d 1979), of Elmbank, 154 City Rd, Dundee; 2 s (Alastair b 1958, Andrew b 1964), 2 da (Shirley b 1960, Sandra b 1962); *Career* Nat Serv RAF Regt 1950-52 (pilot offr 1951, sqdn adjutant 23LAA sqdn 1951-52, flt cdr 1952); TA 1953-75: FFYEO: Troop Ldr 1953-56, Troop Ldr (FRY Scottish Horse) 1956-66, Maj Sqdn Cdr 1966-71, 2 i/c 1971; Highland Yeo offr commanding at disbandment 1975; ACF 1976-: Lt-Col Cmdt Angus-Dundee Bn 1976-79, Col 1979-, cadet Force Medal 1988; WS Taylor & Co Ltd 1952-56, sole ptnr A Watson & Co 1956-63, jt ptnr Taylor Stewart Ltd 1961-66, fin dir John Cooper & Sons Ltd; non exec dir: Century Aluminium Co Ltd 1969-77, Kinnes Oilfield Servs Ltd 1974-80, schs liason offr Tayside Regn Dundee Chamber of Commerce 1983; Chm Lord Armistead Tst, memb exec cncl Scottish Veterans Residences, hon tres (formerly founding chm), Murroes & Wellbank Community Cncl, elder Murroes Parish Church; curling, memb RCCC Cncl 1981-84, memb Scottish Team in Switzerland 1980; *Recreations* shooting, curling, swimming, sailing, philately, militaria; *Style*— Iain Taylor, Esq, TD; Tigh-Na-Torr, Kellas, Dundee DD5 3PD (☎ 082 625 327)

TAYLOR, Ian Charles Boucher; s of Leslie Charles Taylor, of Kidderminster, Worcs, and Freda May, *née* Bell; *b* 24 Sept 1954; *Educ* Queen Elizabeth GS Hartlebury Worcs, Borough Road Coll, West London Inst of Higher Educn London Univ (B Ed, Cert Ed); *m* 25 Oct 1980, Julie Ann, da of James William Whitehead, of Whitestone, Nuneaton, Warwicks; 2 s (Simon Christopher b 16 Nov 1984, Oliver Sebastian b 9 Nov 1986); *Career* England hockey career: World Cup Buenos Aires 1978, Euro Cup Hanover 1979 (Bronze), World Cup Bombay 1982-83, Euro Cup Amsterdam 1983, World Cup London 1986 (Silver); Euro Cup Moscow 1987 (Silver); GB career Champion's Trophy: Lahore 1978, Karachi 1981, 1982, 1984 (Bronze), Perth 1985 (Silver), Lahore 1986, Amsterdam 1987, Lahore 1988; Los Angeles Olympics 1984 (Bronze), Seoul Olympics 1988 (Gold), voted best goalkeeper for 11 consecutive years, captained World XI 12 times; 'ministers' nominee on Regnl Sports Cncl, memb Hockey Assoc tech ctee; *Books* Taylor On Hockey (1988) Behind The Mask (1989); *Recreations* golf, antiques; *Style*— Ian Taylor, Esq; c/o British Olympic Assoc, 1 Wandsworth Plain, London SW18 1EH

TAYLOR, Ian Colin; MBE (1974), MP (Cons) Esher 1987; s of Horace Stanley Taylor (ret), and Beryl, *née* Harper; *b* 18 April 1945, Coventry; *Educ* Whitley Abbey Sch Coventry, Keele Univ (BA), LSE; *m* 17 June 1974, Hon Carole Alport, da of Baron Alport (Life Peer), *qv*, of The Cross House, Layer de la Haye, Colchester, Essex; 2 s (Arthur b 1977, Ralph b 1980); *Career* dir: Fentiman Conslts Ltd 1979-, Mathercourt Securities Ltd 1980-87, Health Care Servs plc 1981-84; conslt Commercial Union plc 1988-; memb Cons Nat Union Exec Ctee 1967-75, nat chm Fedn of Cons Students 1968-69, chm Euro Union of Christian Democratic and Cons Students 1969-70, hon sec Br Cons Assoc in France 1976-78; chm: Cons Gp for Europe 1985-88, Cwlth Youth Exchange Cncl 1980-84 (vice-pres 1984), Foreign Affrs Select Ctee 1987, cons Book Bench Euro Affr Ctee 1988-; assoc Soc of Investmt Analysts 1972; *Pamphlets* Under Some Delusion (1972), Fair Shares for all the Workers (1988); *Recreations* playing cricket, opera, shooting; *Clubs* Carlton; *Style*— Ian Taylor, MBE, MP; 7 The Cooperage, Bridge Gardens, Regents, London SW8 1JR (☎ 01 735 9500); House of Commons, London SW1A 0AA (☎ 01 582 5213)

TAYLOR, Ian Compton; s of Colin Vaughan Taylor, (d 1940), and Marjorie Lydia (d 1968); *b* 4 July 1937; *Educ* Wellington, The Sorbonne, Christ's Coll Cambridge (MA); *m* 27 Nov 1965, Marylou Anne Jane, da of Cdr A J Watson, OBE, RN; 2 s (Leo P C Compton b 20 Sept 1966, Ian D C Compton b 30 Aug 1967), 2 da (Samantha J C Compton b 10 March 1970, Jennifer J C Compton b 27 Aug 1971); *Career* Lt Intelligence Corps 1955-57, Army Emergency Reserve 1957-88; export dir British SIDAC Ltd 1961-72; md Corrupllast Ltd 1972-74, Charter Cars Ltd 1977-80; dep md Midland Montagu Ventures Ltd 1980-; *Recreations* tennis, foreign travel, family; *Clubs* Hurlingham; *Style*— Ian Taylor, Esq; 1 Weltje Road, London W6 (☎ 01 748 9646); c/o Midland Montagu Ventures Ltd, 10 Lower Thames St, London EC3R 6AE (☎ 01 260 9836, fax 01 270 7265, car 0860 378004, telex 887213)

TAYLOR, His Hon Judge Ivor Ralph; QC (1973); s of Abraham Taylor, and Ruth Taylor; *b* 26 Oct 1927; *Educ* Stand GS Whitefield, Manchester Univ; *m* 1, 1954 (m dis 1974), Ruth Cassel; 1 s, 1 da; m 2, 1974 (m dis 1978) Jane Elizabeth Gibson; m 3, 1984, (Audrey) Joyce Goldman, *née* Wayne; *Career* RAF 1945; barr Grays Inn 1951, standing counsel to Inland Revenue N Circuit 1969-73, rec 1972-76; *Recreations* golf, walking; *Style*— His Hon Judge Ivor Taylor, QC; 5 Eagle Lodge, 19 Harrop Rd, Hale, Altrincham, Cheshire WA15 9DA (☎ 061 941 5591)

TAYLOR, Sir James; MBE (1945); s of James Taylor, of Sunderland; *b* 16 August 1902; *Educ* Bede Coll Sunderland, Rutherford Coll Newcastle upon Tyne, Durham Univ, Sorbonne, Utrecht Univ, Cambridge Univ; *m* 1929, Margaret Lennox, da of Robert Stewart, of Newcastle upon Tyne; 2 s, 1 da; *Career* dir ICI 1952-64; chm: Imperial Aluminium Co Ltd 1959-64, Imperial Metals Ltd 1962-64 (chm Yorkshire 1958-64); dep chm: Royal Ordnance Factories Bd 1959-72, Pyrotenax Ltd 1965-67; dir: BDH Gp Ltd 1965-67, Oldham Int 1965-72, Fulmer Res Inst (chm 1976-78); chm Chloride Silent Power Ltd 1975-81; pres Inst of Physics and Physical Soc 1966-68; memb: steering ctee Nat Physical Laboratory 1966, advsy cncl on Calibration and Measurement 1966, ct Brunel Univ 1967-82; chm cncl RSA 1969-71 (vice-pres 1969-87, hon vice-pres 1987-); FRSC; kt 1966; *Style*— Sir James Taylor, MBE; Culvers, Seale, Nr Farnham, Surrey (☎ 025 182210)

TAYLOR, Dame Jean Elizabeth; DCVO (1978, CVO 1976, LVO 1971); da of late Capt William Taylor (ka 1917); *b* 7 Nov 1916; *Career* joined Office of the Private Sec to the Queen 1958, chief clerk 1961-78; *Recreations* music, walking, looking at old buildings; *Style*— Dame Jean Taylor, DCVO; Balcombe Farm, Frittenden, Cranbrook, Kent

TAYLOR, Hon Jeremy Stephen; s of Baron Taylor (Life Peer); *b* 1940; *Educ* Highgate; *m* 1964, Christina, da of late John Bruce Holmes; children; *Career* television executive; *Style*— The Hon Jeremy Taylor; 19 Ayresome Av, Leeds LS8 1BB

TAYLOR, (Margaret) Jessie; OBE (1989); da of Thomas Brown Gowland (d 1951), of Middleton, Manchester, and Ann Goldie, *née* Brighouse (d 1962); *b* 30 Nov 1924; *Educ* Queen Elizabeth GS Middleton, Univ of Manchester (BA, DipEd); *m* 7 April 1958, Eric, da of Sydney Taylor (d 1979), of Wigan; *Career* jr classics teacher Cheadle Hulme Sch 1946-49; N Manchester GS for Girls: sr classics teacher 1950, sr mistress 1963, acting headmistress 1967; dep headteacher Wright Robinson HS 1967-75, headmistress Whalley Range HS for Girls 1976-88, chm Manchester HS Heads 1982-88; memb cncl esam ctee Assoc Lancs Schs examing Bd 1976-89, conslt course tutor NW Educn Mgmnt Centre 1980-82; memb: ct of Salford Univ 1982-88, Nurse Educn Ctee S Manchester Area 1976-88, Williams Ctee (Home Off ctee on obscenity and censorship) 1977-79, UNICEF 1984, Northern Dressage Gp, Middleton Musical Soc NE, Cheshire Drag Hunt, Middleton Parish Church; dir Piccadilly Radio 1980-; FRSA 1979; *Recreations* music, riding; *Clubs* Leigh Riding, Rochdale Riding; *Style*— Mrs Jessie Taylor, OBE; 10 Mercers Rd, Hopwood, Heywood, Lancs OL10 2NP (☎ 0706 66630)

TAYLOR, Hon Mrs (Joan Evelyn); *née* Underhill; da of Baron Underhill, CBE (Life Peer); *b* 11 April 1944; *Educ* Warren Farm Secdy Sch Birmingham, Brooklyn Tech Coll Birmingham, Open Univ; *m* 1973, Ian Taylor; 3 s; *Career* memb: Nottinghamshire CC 1985-; chm Social Servs Ctee; memb: Assoc of CCs Exec Ctee (sec of Lab Gp), Selston PC, Central Notts Health Authy JCC; active memb and office holder APEX (TU); memb Regnl Exec Ctee Lab Pty; *Style*— The Hon Mrs Taylor; 22 Royal Oak Drive, Selston, Notts NG16 6QF (☎ 0773 812655); County Hall, West Bridgford, Nottingham NG2 7QD (☎ 0602 823823, telex 37485)

TAYLOR, Sir Jock (John) Lang; KCMG (1979, CMG 1974); s of Sir John William Taylor, KBE, CMG; *b* 3 August 1924; *Educ* Prague, Vienna, ISC Windsor; *m* 1952, Molly, only da of James Rushworth; 5 s; *Career* For Serv 1949-84; ambass: to Bonn 1981-84, The Hague 1979-81, Venezuela 1975-79; under-sec Dept Energy 1974-75, asst under-sec FCO 1973-74; has also served Saigon, Hanoi, Beirut, Prague, Montevideo, Bonn, Buenos Aires; *Style*— Sir Jock Taylor, KCMG; The Old Flint, Boxgrove, nr Chichester, West Sussex

TAYLOR, Dr Joe; JP (City of Manchester) 1961; s of Sam Taylor and Anne Taylor; *b* 6 Sept 1906; *Educ* Leeds HS, Leeds Univ and Leeds Med Sch (MBCRB); *m* 1935, Edith, da of Philip Dante (d 1929); 2 s (Philip, chael); *Career* med practitioner Manchester 1935-84, memb Crossley Hosp Bd 1955-, cncllr Manchester City 1954-870, (alderman 1970-73), cncllr Gtr Manchester CC 1973-86 (chm 1981-82), memb appeals advsy ctees BBC and ITA; chm: N Regional 1961-67, Northern 1967-76, Central 1961-79; memb: Salvation Army advsy cncl 1965-, Manchester Literary and Philosophical Soc, Gtr Manchester Police Authy 1973-86; memb Ct Univ of: Manchester 1981-, Salford 1981-85; Palace Theatre Tst 1981-85, Royal Exchange Theatre Tst 1981-85, NW Water, Authy 1977-86, Gtr Manchester Co Disaster Relief Tst 1980-85, Hallé Concert Soc 1973-86; pres: Gtr Manchester Cncl for Voluntary Servs 1981-82, Gtr Manchester Schs Football Assoc 1981-82, vice-pres Gtr Manchester Youth Assoc 1981-82; dep chm Br American Assoc for Gtr Manchester County 1985-88; *Recreations* fishing, gardening, reading; *Style*— Dr Joe Taylor, JP; 32 Old Hall Rd, Salford, MY0 J11

TAYLOR, John; MBE (1981); s of Percival Henry Taylor (d 1969), and Florence, *née* Jeffries (d 1981); *b* 4 Mar 1928; *Educ* Peter Symonds, Winchester; *m* 1, 1949, Joyce, da of Harold Hodson (d 1970); 3 s (Patrick b 1951, Ian b 1953, Andrew b 1965), 2 da (Janet b 1956, Jillian b 1960); m 2, 1980, Christiane, da of Capt Edouard Jean Talou (d 1947); *Career* cmmnd RE 1947; chartered architect and designer; fndr: Taylor & Crowther (princ) 1952, John Taylor Architects (sole princ) 1963, Marshman Warren Taylor (jt princ) 1968, MWT Architects (chm) 1972, MWT Planning 1975, MWT Landscapes 1982, MWT Design 1986; fndr and chm the Co of Designers plc 1986-; 7 times Gold Medallist DOE Housing Award, 4 times Civic Tst Award; *Recreations* sailing, travel; *Style*— John Taylor, MBE; 'Milbury Barton', Exminster, Exeter (☎ 0392 832151); The Company of Designers, Renslade House, Bonhay Rd, Exeter (☎ 0392 51366, fax 0392 216561)

TAYLOR, His Hon Judge John Barrington; MBE (Mil 1945), TD 1957; s of Robert Edward Taylor (d 1957), of Bath, and Anne Barrington, *née* Coggan (d 1956); *b* 3 August 1914; *Educ* King Edwards Sch Bath, London Univ (LLB); *m* 7 June 1941, Constance Aleen, da of John Barkly Macadam, of Edinburgh, 3 s (1 decd), 3 da; *Career* Somerset Lt Inf 1939, DAAG HQ 5 Corps 1943; AAG Allied Cmmn for Austria 1945; slr 1936, practised Bath, Registrar Bath Gp of Co Cts 1960-77, rec 1972, circuit judge 1977, JP Somerset 1962-77; *Recreations* gardening; *Style*— His Hon Judge Taylor, MBE, TD; c/o Crown Court, Chelmsford, Essex

TAYLOR, Rt Rev John Bernard; *see*: St Albans, Bishop of

TAYLOR, John Charles; QC (1984); s of Sidney Herbert Taylor (d 1977), of St Ives Cambridgeshire and Gertrude Florence, *née* Law; *b* 22 April 1931; *Educ* Palmers Sch Essex, Queens' Coll Cambridge (MA, LIB), Harvard Univ USA (LIM); *m* 1964, Jean Aimée, da of William Rankin Monteith (d 1976), late of Purston Manor, Brackley, Northants; 1 da (Victoria b 1967); *Career* memb Stevens Ctee on Minerals Planning Control 1972-74; chm EIP Panel for Leics and Rutland Structure Plan 1985; *Recreations* country pursuits, boardsailing, ski-ing, sailing; *Clubs* Athenaeum, Travellers'; *Style*— John Taylor, Esq, QC; Clifton Grange, Clifton, Shefford, Beds; 2 Mitre Court Buildings, Temple, London EC4

TAYLOR, Rt Hon John David; PC (N Ireland) 1970, MP (UU) Strangford 1983-, MEP N Ireland 1979-; s of George David Taylor, of Armagh (d 1979), and Georgina, *née* Baird (d 1986); *b* 24 Dec 1937; *Educ* Royal Sch Armagh, Queen's Univ Belfast (BSc); *m* 1970, Mary Frances, da of Ernest Leslie Todd (d 1985); 1 s (Jonathan), 4 da (Jane, Rachel, Rowena, Alex); *Career* MP (UU) S Tyrone, N Ireland Parl 1965-73; min of state Miny of Home Affrs 1970-72; memb (UU): Fermanagh and S Tyrone, N Ireland Assembly 1973-75, memb (UU) N Down, N Ireland Constitutional Convention 1975-76; memb (UU) N Down, N Ireland Assembly 1982-86; chartered engr; dir: West Ulster Estates Ltd 1968-, West Ulster Hotels Ltd 1976-, Bramley Apple Restaurant Ltd 1974-, Ulster Gazette (Armagh) Ltd 1983-, Gosford Housing Assoc (Armagh) Ltd 1978-, Cerdac Print (Belfast) Ltd, Tyrone Printing Ltd, Tyrone Courier Ltd; *Clubs* Armagh County, Armagh City, Farmers' (Whitehall London); *Style*— The

Rt Hon John D Taylor, MP, MEP; Mullinure, Portadown Road, Armagh, N Ireland (☎ 0861 522409)

TAYLOR, John Edward; s of Jesse Taylor (d 1977), of Hadleigh, Suffolk, and Clarice Bowron, *née* Watling; *b* 11 Nov 1931; *Educ* Cockburn Sch Leeds, Leeds Coll of Technol, RAF Tech Coll Henlow; *m* 25 Aug 1956, Marion Eveline, da of Francis Charles Jordon (d 1932); 3 da (Valerie b 1957, Patricia b 1959, Carol (twin) b 1959); *Career* RAF 1952-55: tech offr RAF Rutzweilerhof 1953-54, M & E offr Airfield Construction branch RAF Wildenrath 1954-55; contracts, engr AEI Ltd 1956-66, sales mangr Distribution Transformers 1965-66, commercial mangr Eastern Electricity Bd 1976-80, centl dir mktg Electricity Cncl 1980-, dir Br Electrical Approvals Bd 1984-; chm Aitfield Construction Offrs Assoc 1982; CEng 1966, MIEE 1963, MBIM 1971; *Recreations* motor cruising, photography; *Clubs* RAF; *Style*— Flt-Lt John Taylor; Hill House, 59 Henley Rd, Ipswich IP1 3SN (☎ 0473 52094); The Electricity Cncl, 30 Millbank, London SW1P 4RD (☎ 01 834 2333, fax 01 931 0356, telex LONDON 23385)

TAYLOR, Prof John Gerald; s of Dr William Taylor (d 1984), and Elsie, *née* Boyd (d 1986); *b* 18 August 1931; *Educ* Lancaster GS, Blackburn GS, Chelmsford GS, Mid-Essex Tech Coll (BSc), Christs Coll Cambridge (BSc, BA, MA, PhD); *m* 1, (m dis), Patricia Joan, *née* Kenney; m 2, Pamela Nancy, da of late Matthew Cutmore; 2 s (Geoffrey b 1956, Robin b 1964), 3 da (Frances b 1958, Susan b 1966, Elizabeth b 1971); *Career* cwlth fell Inst for Advanced Study Princeton NJ USA 1956-58, res fell Christs Coll Cambridge 1958-60, (asst lectr faculty of maths 1959-60); memb: Inst Hautes Études Scientifiques Paris 1960-61, Inst for Advanced Study Princeton 1961-63; sr res fell Churchill Coll Cambridge 1963-64, prof of physics Rutger Univ NJ USA 1964-66, lectr Maths Inst and fell Hertford Coll Oxford 1966-67, lectr and reader QMC London 1967-69, prof of physics Univ of Southampton 1969-71, prof of maths Kings Coll London 1971-; chm maths physics gp Inst of Physics 1981-86 (vice chm 1988-); fell Camb Phil Soc, FInstP, FRAS; *Books* Quantum Mechanics (1969), The Shape of Minds to Come (1971), The New Physics (1972), Black Holes: The End of the Universe? (1973), Superminds (1975), Special Relativity (1975), Science and the Supernatural (1980), The Horizons of Knowledge (1982), and over 200 scientific papers and numerous radio and TV programmes on popular science; *Recreations* travelling, listening to music, theatre, reading, swimming; *Style*— Prof John Taylor; 33 Meredyth Rd, Barnes, London SW13 0DS (☎ 01 876 3361); Dept of Mathematics, Kings Coll, Strand, London WC2R 2LS (☎ 01 836 5454, fax 01 836 1799)

TAYLOR, John Mark; MP (Cons Solihull 1983-); s of Wilfred Taylor and Eileen Taylor; *b* 19 August 1941; *Educ* Bromsgrove, Coll of Law; *m* 1979, Catherine Ann Hall; *Career* slr 1966-; memb: Solihull cncl 1971-74, W Mid CC 1973-86 (ldr 1977-79); contested (C) Dudley East, Feb and Oct 1974; govr Birmingham Univ 1977-81, dep chm Cons Gp Euro Parl 1981-82; Member House of Commons Environment Select Ctee 1983-87; pps to chllr of the Duchy of Lancaster 1987-88; asst govt whip 1988-, MEP (EDG) Mids East 1979-87; *Recreations* cricket, golf and reading; *Clubs* Carlton, MCC; *Style*— John Taylor, Esq, MP; 211 Bernards Rd, Solihull, W Mids (☎ 021 707 1076)

TAYLOR, John Richard Creighton; s of Richard Henry Chase Taylor (d 1987), and Rachel Loveday, *née* Creighton; *b* 17 Dec 1942; *Educ* Malvern Coll, Ecole des Hautes Etudes Commerciales Paris; *m* 7 Feb 1970, Sarah Barbour, da of Peter Thomas Simon Brown; 2 s (Oliver b 1973, Humphrey b 1981), 2 da (Eliza b 1972, Sophie b 1976); *Career* dir: Vine Products and Whiteways 1981-84, Grants of St James 1984-, London Wine Bars 1984-, Trouncer Wine and Spirit Merchants 1985-; chm and md Hatch, Mansfield and Co 1984-; memb Distillers Co 1980; memb Inst of Masters of Wine 1972; *Recreations* opera, theatre, walking, foreign interests, all sports; *Clubs* RAC; *Style*— John Taylor, Esq; European Cellars Ltd, Guildford Cellars, Moorfield Rd, Guildford, Surrey (☎ 0483 64861, fax 0483 506691, telex 859328)

TAYLOR, John Russell; s of Arthur Russell Taylor (d 1966), of Dover Kent, and Kathleen Mary, *née* Picker; *b* 19 June 1935; *Educ* Dover GS, Jesus Coll Cambridge (BA, MA), Courtauld Inst of Art London; *Career* The Times: sub-ed Educnl Supplement 1959-60, ed asst Lit Supplement 1960-62, film critic 1962-73, art critic 1978-; prof of cinema div Univ of Southern California 1972-78, ed Films and Filming 1983-; memb: Critics Circle 1962, Private Libraries Assoc 1967 (pres 1986-89), Assoc Art Historians 1985; AICA 1978; *Books Incl:* Anger and After (1962), Cinema Eye Cinema Ear (1964), The Art Nouveau in Britain (1966), The Rise and Fall of the Well-Made Play (1967), The Art Dealers (1969), The Hollywood Musical (1971), The Second Wave (1971), Graham Greene on Film (ed 1972), Directors and Directions (1975), Hitch (1978), Impressionism (1981), Strangers in Paradise (1983), Alec Guinness (1984), Edward Wolfe (1986), Orson Welles (1986); *Recreations* buying books, talking to strange dogs; *Style*— John Russell Taylor, Esq; The Times, Virginia St, London E1 9BD (☎ 01 782 5000, telex 262141)

TAYLOR, John Stephen; s of Maj Gerald Howard Taylor (d 1963), and Helen Mary Rivett, *née* Harrington; *b* 26 Dec 1928; *Educ* Stowe, Trinity Coll Cambridge (MA), Architectural Assoc London (Dip Arch); *m* 1, 1956 (m dis 1963), Tye Pagan, da of Tully Grigg, of Biot, France; 1 s (Fred b 1963), 1 da (Nona b 1960); m 2, 1965 Susan Marriott Sweet; *Career* joined Irish Gds 1947, serv GHQ FARELF Singapore RE, Capt Cheshire Yeo 1949-58; sr ptnr Chapman Taylor Ptnrs whose London bldgs incl: Caxton House, DOE, one Drummond Gate (Met Police), Lansdowne House, Berkeley Sq; planning cnslts and prime architects to Crown Cmmnrs Millbank Estate; govr Stowe Sch 1962- (chm 1975-81), chm Allied Schs Cncl 1982-88; Freeman Worshipful Co of Chartered Architects; *Recreations* gardens, boats; *Clubs* RTYC; *Style*— J S Taylor, Esq; 35 Kinnerton St, London SW1X 8ED; Castell Gyrn, Llanbedr, Ruthin, Clwyd, N Wales; Isle of Scalpay, Harris, Western Isles, Scotland PA84 3YB; Chapman Taylor Partners, 96 Kensington High St, London W8 4SG (☎ 01 938 3333, fax 01 937 1391)

TAYLOR, John William Ransom; s of Victor Charles Taylor (d 1976), of Ely, Cambs, and Florence Hilda, *née* Ransom (d 1969); *b* 8 June 1922; *Educ* Ely Cathedral Choir Sch, Soham GS Cambs; *m* 7 Sept 1946, Doris Alice, da of George Arthur Haddrick (d 1933), of London; 1 s (Michael John Haddrick b 1949), 1 da (Susan Hilda Haddrick b 1947); *Career* design offr Hawker Aircraft Ltd 1941-47, air correspondent Meccano Magazine 1943-71; ed: publicity off Fairey Aviation Gp 1947-55, Air BP Magazine Br Petroleum 1956-72; ed and ed-in-chief Jane's All the World's Aircraft 1959-, contrib ed Air Force Magazine (US) 1971-, jt ed Guinness Book of Air Facts and Feats 1974-83, author of 231 books; dist cmmr Surbiton Scout Assoc 1965-69, dep warden and warden Christ Church Surbiton Hill 1971-80, pres Chiltern Aviation Soc Ruislip; vice-pres: Horse Rangers Assoc, Guild Aviation Artists, Croydon Airport Soc, Surbiton Scout Assoc; memb Central Flying Sch Assoc; Freeman City of London 1987, Liveryman Guild Air Pilots and Air Navigators 1987 (Freeman 1983); FRAeS, FRHistS; *Books Incl:* Spitfire (1946), Aircraft Annual (1949-75), Civil Aircraft Markings (1950-78), Picture History of Flight (1955), CFS, Birthplace of Air Power (1958, revised 1987), Combat Aircraft of the World (1969), Westland 50 (1965), Encyclopaedia of World Aircraft (with M J H Taylor 1966), Pictorial History of the Royal Air Force (3 vols 1968-71, revised 1980), Aircraft Aircraft (1967), The Lore of Flight (1971), Spies in the Sky (with D Mondey 1972), History of Aviation (with K Munson 1973); *Recreations* historical studies, travel, philately; *Clubs* City Livery, RAF, Royal Aero; *Style*— John W R Taylor, Esq; 36 Alexandra Drive, Surbiton, Surrey KT5 9AF (☎ 01 399 5435)

TAYLOR, Jonathan Francis; s of Sir Reginald William Taylor (d 1971), of Great Haseley, Oxford, and Lady (Sarah) Ruth, *née* Tyson; *b* 12 August 1935; *Educ* Winchester, CCC Oxford (BA, MA); *m* 8 April 1965 (Anthea) Gail, da of Robert Vergette Proctor (d 1985), of Sheffield; 3 s (Luke b 1968, Matthew b 1970, James b 1972); *Career* 2 Lt KAR 1954-56; Booker plc: joined 1959, chm agric div 1976-80, dir 1980, pres IBEC Inc (USA) 1980-84, chief exec Booker plc 1984, dir Sifida Investmt Bank Geneva, dir Tate & Lyle plc 1988; memb advsy cncl UNIDO 1986, govr SOAS 1988; CBIM 1984; *Recreations* travel, skiing, collecting watercolours; *Clubs* Travellers London, Knickerbocker NY; *Style*— Jonathan Taylor, Esq; Booker plc, Portland House, Stag Place, London SW1E 5AY (☎ 01 828 9850, fax 01 630 8029, telex 888169)

TAYLOR, Jonathan Jeremy Kirwan; s of Sir Charles Stuart Taylor, TD, DL *qv*; *b* 12 Oct 1943; *Educ* Eton, St Edmund Hall Oxford (BA); *m* 1966, Victoria Mary Caroline, da of Hon John Francis McLaren (d 1953); 4 da (Arabella b 1969, Lucinda b 1972, Caroline b 1976, Katherine b 1979); *Career* barr Middle Temple 1968; dir Baring Int Investmt Mgmnt Ltd 1976- and other Baring Investmt Gp Cos, md Onyx Country Estates Ltd; *Recreations* skiing (Br Olympic Team 1964), tennis, boating; *Clubs* Turf, Hong Kong; *Style*— Jonathan Taylor, Esq; 42 Addison Rd, London W14 9JH (☎ 01 603 7853); 49 Rue du Port Sud, Port Grimaud, Var, France (☎ 94 434507); office: Baring International, 9 Bishopsgate, London EC2N 3AQ (☎ 01 588 6133, telex 894989, fax 01 588 2591)

TAYLOR, Dr (John) Leahy; s of John Alan Taylor (d 1953), of Malton, and May Pauline Taylor (d 1979); *b* 11 Feb 1921; *Educ* Worksop Coll, St Mary's Hosp (MB, BS, DMJ); *m* 15 Nov 1948, Muriel Florence, da of William Osborne (d 1926), of Paignton; 1 s (Lance b 1950), 1 da (Charlotte b 1952); *Career* Maj RAMC 1945-47; sec Med Protection Soc 1972-83, memb Gen Med Cncl 1984-, examiner Nat Univ of Ireland 1985-88; memb Medico Legal Soc (former pres); Freeman City of London 1965, Liveryman Worshipful Co of Apothecaries 1965, MRCS, LRCP; *Books* Doctor and the Law (1969 and 1982), Doctor & Negligence (ed Medical Malpractice, 1980); *Recreations* boating, bowls, walking; *Style*— Dr Leahy Taylor; 18 Thameside, Staines, Middx TW18 2HA (☎ 0784 452331)

TAYLOR, Hon Mrs (Marilyn Ruth); da of Baron Fisher of Camden (Life Peer, d 1979); *b* 1940; *Educ* BA; *m* 1960, Mervyn Taylor, slr; *Style*— The Hon Mrs Taylor; 4 Springfield Rd, Templeogue, Dublin

TAYLOR, Martin Gibbeson; s of Roy Gibbeson Taylor (d 1955), of Worthing, Sussex, and Vera Constance, *née* Farmer; *b* 30 Jan 1935; *Educ* Haileybury, St Catharine's Coll Cambridge; *m* 18 June 1960, Gunilla Chaterina, da of Nils Bryner (d 1962), of Stockholm, Sweden; 2 s (Thomas b 1963, Seth b 1967); *Career* 2 Lt RA 1953-55; with Mann Judd & Co (CA) 1958-62; co sec Dow Chemical UK 1963-69; Hanson plc 1969-: dir 1976-, vice-chm 1988-; non-exec dir: Vickers plc, Securities Assoc; memb panel on take-overs and mergers; govr The Mall Sch; FCA 1961; *Recreations* pictures, books, theatre, sport; *Clubs* MCC; *Style*— Martin Taylor, Esq; 1 Grosvenor Square, London SW1X 7JH (☎ 01 245-1245, fax 01 245 9795, telex 917698)

TAYLOR, Martyn Graeme; s of John William Havelock Taylor (d 1977), of Calne, Wilts, and Betty Evelyn *née* Clarke; *b* 8 June 1938; *Educ* Marlborough, Pembroke Coll Oxford (MA); *m* 23 May 1964, Jean, da of Thomas Topping (d 1983), of Churchill, Somerset; 2 s (Jeremy b 1966, Bruce b 1968), 1 da (Kirsty b 1972); *Career* CA, ptnr Deloitte Haskins & Sells 1972- (staff memb 1959-72); reader C of E, memb Winchester Diocesan Bd of Fin 1984-; FCA; *Books* Financial Times World Survey of Bank Annual Reports (jtly 1982), Banks: An Accounting and Auditing Guide (jtly 1983); *Recreations* fell walking, history and statistics of cricket; *Style*— Martyn Taylor, Esq; Deloitte Haskins & Sells, PO Box 207, 128 Queen Victoria St, London, EC4P 4JX (☎ 01 248 3913, fax 01 248 3623, telex 894941)

TAYLOR, Matthew Owen John; MP (Democrats) Truro 1987; s of Kenneth Heywood Taylor, and Gillian Dorothea, *née* Black; *b* 3 Jan 1963; *Educ* St Pauls Sch, Tremorvah Sch, Treliske Sch, Univ Coll Sch, LMH Oxford (BA); *Career* pres Oxford Univ Student Union 1985-86; econ res asst Parly Lib Pty 1986-87 (attached to late David Penhaligon MP); Parly spokesman for: Energy 1987-88, Local Govt, Housing and Tport 1988-; *Style*— Matthew Taylor, Esq, MP; 1 Charles St, Truro, Cornwall (☎ 0872 73478); House of Commons London, SW1 (☎ 01 219 3483)

TAYLOR, Hon Mrs (Melinda Charlotte); da of 2 Viscount Brookeborough, PC, DL; *b* 13 April 1958; *m* 1982, Nicholas Taylor, eldest s of Ronald Taylor, of Bighton Wood, Alresford, Hants; 1 da (Alice b 1988); *Style*— The Hon Mrs Taylor; Holly Lodge, 79 Larkhall Rise, London SW4 6H5

TAYLOR, Michael Paul Gordon; s of Gordon Taylor, and Stella, *née* Marsh; *b* 2 Mar 1949; *Educ* Altrincham GS, St Johns Coll Cambridge (LLB); *m* 11 June 1977, Angela Evelyn, *née* Llewellyn; 2 da (Catherine Elizabeth b 2 May 1981, Eleanor Frances b 7 Aug 1983); *Career* ptnr Norton Rose 1979; memb: Int Bar Assoc, City of London Slrs Co, Law Soc; *Recreations* sport, theatre, reading; *Clubs* RAC, Cumberland Lawn Tennis; *Style*— Michael Taylor, Esq; Kempson House, Camomile St, London EC3A 7AW (☎ 01 283 2434)

TAYLOR, Neville; CB (1989); s of late Frederick Herbert Taylor, and late Lottie, *née* London; *b* 17 Nov 1930; *Educ* Sir Joseph Williamson's Mathematical Sch Rochester, Coll of Commerce Gillingham Kent; *m* 4 Sept 1954, Margaret Ann, da of late Thomas Bainbridge Vickers; 2 s (Andrew b 1956, Martin b 1958); *Career* RCS 1948-50; journalist 1950-58, press offr Admty 1958-63, fleet info offr Far East Fleet Singapore Malaysia 1963-65, chief press offr MOD 1966-68, info advsr NEDO/NEDC London 1968-70, dep dir PR RN 1970, head of info MAFF 1971-72; dir info DOE 1974-79 (dep dir 1972), DHSS 1979-82, chief of PR MOD 1982-85, dir gen Central Off of Info and head of Govt Info Serv 1985-88, ret 1988; *Recreations* fishing, bird watching; *Clubs* Castle, Rochester; *Style*— Neville Taylor, Esq, CB; Crow Lane House, Crow La, Rochester, Kent (☎ 0634 42 990)

TAYLOR, Cdr RN Patrick Hugh Bisset; OBE (mil) 1963, DL Norfolk (1977); s of Rear Adm Alfred Hugh Taylor, CB, OBE (d 1972), of Manor House, Diss, and Maude Violet, *née* Bisset (d 1959); *b* 19 Feb 1916; *Educ* RNC Dartmouth; *Career* RN: Gunnery Offr 1940 (Dunkirk), Gunnery Offr HMS Roberts 1941-42, staff offr Gunnery and Plans to Flag Offr Western Italy 1943-44; serv: Corsica, Sardinia, French Riviera, Toulon, Marseilles, Nice; Gunnery Offr HMS Ceylon (present at Singapore for Japanese surrender) 1945; various gunnery appts mainly at HMS Excellent, Whale Island Portsmouth 1945-60, weapons dept Admty Bath 1960-64; ret from RN active list 1964; Norfolk CC 1967-85, Norfolk Health Authy 1974-82, Diss Town Cncl 1964-, hon tres S Norfolk Cons Assoc 1965-79, pres Royal Br Legion Diss 1971-, churchwarden 1969-78; *Clubs* Naval and Mil, Norfolk; *Style*— Cdr Patrick Taylor, OBE, DL, RN; Manor House, Diss, Norfolk IP22 3QQ (☎ 0379 642 096)

TAYLOR, Paul Duncan; JP (1969); s of Edward Duncan Taylor; *b* 25 April 1936; *Educ* Mill Hill Sch; *m* 1964, Lindsay Veronica Moncrieff, *née* Smith; 2 s; *Career* CA ptnr Spicer and Oppenheim, chm Wagon Indust Hldgs plc, dir: John Foster Son plc, Leeds and Holbeck Bldg Soc; *Clubs* The Leeds; *Style*— Paul Taylor, Esq, JP; Oakwood House, Upper Batley, Batley, W Yorks (☎ 0924 473552)

TAYLOR, Hon Paul Nurton; s of Baron Taylor of Blackburn (Life Peer); *b* 1953; *m* 1978, Diane Brindle; *Style*— The Hon Paul Taylor; 601 Preston Old Rd, Blackburn, Lancs

TAYLOR, Peter Cranbourne; s of Maurice Ewan Taylor, OBE, of St Andrews, and Mary Ann, *née* Gorst; *b* 11 August 1938; *Educ* Edinburgh Univ (MA); *m* 27 June 1970, Lois Mary, da of Anthony Godard Templeton, TD (d 1986), of St Andrews; 1 s (Christopher b 13 Nov 1975), 1 da (Kerrie b 18 Dec 1972); *Career* CA 1962; ptnr: Romanes & Munro Edinburgh 1964-74, Deloitte Haskins & Sells 1974-; convenor ICAS Membs Servs Ctee 1984-; sec and tres Scottish Nat Blood Transfusion Assoc 1981-; *Recreations* shooting, country pursuits; *Clubs* New (Edinburgh), Lansdowne; *Style*— Peter Taylor, Esq; 29 Abercromby Place, Edinburgh (☎ 031 557 2111, fax 031 556 2751)

TAYLOR, Peter Duncan; s of Capt Arthur Gilbert Taylor (d 1968), of Manchester, and Amy Margaret, *née* Duncan (d 1958); *b* 4 May 1925; *Educ* Oakham Sch, Univ of St Andrews; *m* 20 June 1956, Barbara, da of Daniel Greenaway (d 1968); 1 s (John); *Career* pilot RAF; Simon Engrg plc, dir Simon-Carves Ltd and Lodge-Cottell Ltd 1951-72, dir and sec Turriff Corpn plc 1972-; FCA 1951; *Recreations* golf, antiques, bridge; *Style*— Peter Taylor, Esq; Tanglewood, 6 Woodside Way, Solihull, W Mids B91 1HB; Turriff Corpn plc, Budbrooke Rd, Warwick CV34 5XJ (☎ 0926 410 400, fax 0926 497 315, car tel 0836 525 799)

TAYLOR, Rt Hon Lord Justice; Rt Hon Sir Peter Murray Taylor; PC (1988), QC (1967); s of Herman Louis Taylor (d 1966), of Newcastle upon Tyne; *b* 1 May 1930; *Educ* Newcastle Royal GS, Pembroke Coll Cambridge; *m* 1956, Irene Shirley, da of Lionel Harris, of Newcastle; 1 s, 3 da; *Career* barr Inner Temple 1954, QC 1967, rec of Huddersfield 1969, dep chm Northumberland QS 1970; recorder of: Teesside 1970-71, Crown Ct 1972-80; leader of North-Eastern Circuit 1975-80, bencher 1975, High Ct judge Queen's Bench Div 1980-87; presiding judge NE Circuit 1984- 87; Lord Justice of the Ct of Appeal 1987-; kt 1980; *Style*— The Rt Hon Lord Justice Taylor; Royal Courts of Justice, The Strand, London WC2

TAYLOR, Philippe Arthur; s of Arthur Peach Taylor, (d 1974), of St Andrews, Fife, and Simone, *née* Vacquin; *b* 9 Feb 1937; *Educ* Trinity Coll Glenalmond, St Andrews Univ; *m* 10 Feb 1973, Margaret Nancy, s of Arnold Frederick Wilkins, OBE (d 1985), of Framlingham, Suffolk; 2 s (Rupert Arthur James b 1975, Charles Philip b 1976); *Career* Proctor and Gamble 1961-66, Masius Int 1966-70, Br Tourist Authy 1970-75; chief exec: Scottish Tourist Bd 1975-81, Birmingham Convention Bureau 1982-; chm Br Assoc of Conference Towns 1988-, vice chm Ikon Gallery 1988-, Chevalier de L'Ordre des Couteaux de Champagne 1985; FTS 1975; *Books* Captain Crossjack and the Lost Penguin (1969); *Recreations* sailing, painting, tourism, making things; *Clubs* Royal Northumberland YC, Orford Sailing; *Style*— Philippe Taylor, Esq; Cadogan House, Beauchamp Ave, Leamington Spa, 2 Perth St, Edinburgh (☎ 0926 831 925); 9 The Wharf, Birmingham, W Mids (☎ 021 631 2401, fax 021 643 5001)

TAYLOR, Phyllis Mary Constance; da of Cecil Tedder (d 1974), and Constance *née* Price (d 1984); *b* 29 Sept 1926; *Educ* Sudbury HS, Girton Coll Cambridge (BA,MA); *m* 31 Dec 1949, Peter Royston, s of John William Edward Taylor (d 1972); 1 s (Julian Peter Gerald Royston b 10 Nov 1954); *Career* head of history Loughton HS 1951-58 (asst mistress 1948-51), mistress Lancaster Royal Elementary Sch for Boys 1959; head of history: Casterton Sch Kirby Lonsdale 1960, Lancaster Girls GS 1961 (mistress 1960-61); dep head Carlyle Sch Chelsea 1962-64; headmistress: Walthamstow HS 1964-68, Walthamstow Sr HS 1968-76, Wanstead HS 1976-82; candidate (Lib): Essex CC 1982, Dunmow DGI 1987; chm Dunmow Lib Pty 1986-88; memb UGC 1978-83; *Books* under pen name Julianne Royston The Pen hale Heiress (1988); *Recreations* horses, gardening, theatre, ecology; *Clubs* Utd Oxford and Cambridge; *Style*— White Horses, High Roding, Gt Dunmow, Essex CM6 1NS; White Horses, High Roding, Gt Dunmow, Essex CM6 1NS (☎ 0371 3161)

TAYLOR, Lt-Col Richard Ian Griffith; DSO, MC, DL; s of Lt-Col Thomas George Taylor, DSO (d 1946); *b* 5 June 1911; *Educ* Harrow, Oxford Univ; *m* 1934 (m dis 1951), Hon Sylvia Alice, da of late 2 Baron Joicey; 2 s (Simon, James), 1 da (Valerie); m 2, 1952, Hon Cecily Eveline (d 1975), widow of Patrick Magor Leatham, MC, and da of 1 and last Baron Buckland; 2 da; *Career* Lt-Col; serv Greece, Western desert, France, Germany; farmer, landowner; *Recreations* shooting, fishing, hunting; *Style*— Lt-Col Richard Taylor, DSO, MC, DL; Chipchase Castle, Wark on Tyne, Northumberland

TAYLOR, His Hon Judge Robert Carruthers; s of John Houston Taylor, CBE (d 1983), and Barbara Mary, *née* Carruthers; *b* 6 Jan 1939; *Educ* Wycliffe Coll, St John's Coll Oxford (MA); *m* 16 April 1968, Jacqueline Marjorie, da of Nigel Geoffrey Randall Chambers, of West Yorks; 1 s (John b 1972), 1 da (Susannah b 1969); *Career* barr Middle Temple 1961, practised NE Circuit 1962-84, rec 1976-84, chm Agric Land Tbnl (Lancs/Yorks/Humberside) 1979-; *Recreations* reading, music, gardening, exercising whippets; *Clubs* Yorks CCC; *Style*— His Hon Judge Robert Taylor; The Courthouse, 1 Oxford Row, Leeds LS1 3BE

TAYLOR, Robert Julian Faussitt; s of Col GF Taylor, MBE; *b* 21 June 1929; *Educ* Dragon Sch, Trinity Coll Cambridge; *m* 1967, Jacqueline, nee Castaing; 2 s; *Career* md Manchester Ship Canal Co 1980-, dir Ocean Tport & Trading 1964-79, Br Antartic Survey 1953-57, the Wildfowl Survey 1973-81, RSPB Cncl 1978-81; *Recreations* the countryside, birds, deer, gardening, climbing, reading; *Clubs* Travellers'; *Style*— Robert Taylor, Esq; Bridgewater House, Runcorn, Ches; Home Lodge, Cholderton, Wilts

TAYLOR, Sheriff-Principal Robert Richardson; s of James Stevens Taylor (d 1949), of Lanarkshire, and Agnes Richardson (d 1942); *b* 16 Sept 1919; *Educ* Glasgow HS, Glasgow Univ (MA, LLB, PhD); *m* 1949, Birgitta, da of Ivan Bjorkling (d 1954); 2 s (Richard, Hamish), 1 da (Kristina); *Career* barr: Scotland 1944, Middle Temple 1948; lectr in int private law Edinburgh Univ 1947-69, Sheriff-Princ: Stirling Dumbarton & Clackmannen 1971-75, Tayside Central & Fife 1975-; contested (U & NL): Dundee E 1955, Dundee W 1950 & 1963; chm Central and Southern Region Scottish Cons Assoc 1969-71; chm Sheriff Cts Rules Cncl, Northern Lighthouse Bd 1985-86; *Recreations* fishing, lapidary and mineral collecting; *Style*— Dr Robert Taylor, QC; 51 Northumberland St, Edinburgh, (☎ 031 556 1722)

TAYLOR, (Robert Hunter) Robin; s of Robert Louis Taylor (d 1970), of Milngavie, Dunbartonshire, Scotland, and Jean Allan (d 1954); *b* 5 Nov 1932; *Educ* Aberdeen GS, Kelvinside Acad; *m* 11 Sept 1964, Kathleen Mabel, da of Capt Harold Percival Gibbs (d 1950), Dundee, Scotland; 2 s (Philip b 1966, Colin b 1968); *Career* builders merchant; chm and jt md, Scott RAE Stevenson Ltd, nat pres The Builders Merchants Fedn 1988-89; Freeman: City of London, City of Glasgow; Liveryman Worshipful Co of Builders Merchants; FInstD, FIMB (fndr memb); *Recreations* golf, gardening, photography, walking, reading, philately; *Clubs* RNVR Scotland , Buchanan Castle GC, Rotary (Strathendrick), Br Airways Exec; *Style*— Robin Taylor, Esq; The Rowans, Killearn, Stirlingshire G63 9LG (☎ 0360 50388); Scott Rae Stevenson Ltd, 265 Pollokshaws Rd, Glasgow G41 1PT (☎ 041 423 5461)

TAYLOR, Roger Heath; s of Frederick George Taylor (d 1969), of Kingston-Upon-Thames, and Gladys Florence, *née* Heath; *b* 27 Nov 1944; *Educ* Surbiton GS, Brunel Univ (BSc); *m* 5 Oct 1968, Ann Joan, da of Leslie Ernest Leonard, of Bramford, Suffolk; 2 s (James Hrothgar Heath b 4 May 1976, Samuel St John Cedric Edmond Heath), 1 da (Donna Katrina Heath); *Career* res chemist Metal Box Co 1965-66, prodn supervisor Harrington Bros 1966-69, sales mangr Reeve Angel Scientific 1969-74, dir and jt owner Int Chemicals Trading Co Interchem UK Ltd 1974-; vice chm Parish Cncl; chm: Playing Field Charity Tst, Community Covers, Govrs Co Sch & Educnl Ctee; local politics; *Recreations* squash, Motorsport; *Style*— Roger Taylor, Esq; Tintern, The Street Copdock, Suffolk (☎ 0473 86 439); B 10/11 Farthing Rd, Indust Estate, Ipswich, Suffolk (☎ 0473 463 701, fax 0473 43 521, car tel 0860 366 567)

TAYLOR, Ronald George; CBE (1988); s of Ernest Noel Taylor (d 1978), of Bristol, and May Elizabeth, *née* Besant (d 1955); *b* 12 Dec 1935; *Educ* Cotham Grammar Sch Bristol, Jesus Coll Oxford (BA); *m* 14 June 1960, Patricia, da of Septon Stoker, of Hemingbrough; 1 s (David Robert b 1963), 2 da (Gillian Mary b 1961, Alison Catherine b 1965); *Career* Nat Serv 2 Lt Royal Signals 1957-59; dir Leeds C of C and Indus 1974 (joined 1959), dir-gen Assoc of Br C of C 1984; FSAE 1988, FRSA 1988; *Recreations* bridge, rugby union football; *Style*— Ronald Taylor, Esq, CBE; 2 Holly Bush Lane, Harpenden, Herts (☎ 058 27 2139); Assoc of British Chambers of Commerce, Sovereign Ho, 212 Shaftesbury Ave, London (☎ 01 240 5831, fax 01 379 6331, telex 265871)

TAYLOR, Hon Mrs (Sarah Lovell); *née* Rippon; 2 da of Baron Rippon of Hexham, PC, QC (Life Peer); *b* 10 Mar 1950; *m* 1978, Michael Taylor; 2 s (James Geoffrey Bethune b 1979, Alexander Edward Yorke b 1982); *Style*— Hon Mrs Sarah Taylor

TAYLOR, Selwyn Francis; s of Alfred Petre Taylor (d 1958), of Brook Cottage, Coombe, Marlborough, S Devon, and Emily, *née* Edwards (d 1965); *b* 16 Sept 1913; *Educ* Peter Symonds Winchester, Keble Coll Oxford (MA), Stockholm, Harvard (DM); *m* 14 Oct 1939, Ruth Margaret, da of Sir Alfred Bakewell Howitt, CVO, MP (d 1950), of Wolfhall Manor, Burbage Wilts; 1 s (Simon b 8 Sept 1945), 1 da (Jane b 18 Nov 1950); *Career* serv WWII 1940-45; Surgn Lt Cdr 1944; surgical specialist: Kintyre, E Africa, Mobile Surgical Unit ET, Sydney; univ lectr and conslt surgn: 1947-78 Postgrad Med Sch Hammersmith Hosp, 1951-65 Kings Coll Hosp; dean Royal Postgrad Med Sch 1965-75; Rockefellar travelling fell Harvard 1948-49; visiting prof: Duke Univ, UCLA, Cincinnati, Chapel Hill, USA, Hong Kong, S Africa, memb: Gen Med Cncl, senate London Univ, (founding) European Thyroid Assoc, Cncl RCS 1965 (vice- pres 1976-78); pres: Harveian Soc, Med Educn Sec, RSM, (first) Int Assoc Endocrine Surgns 1978-81, chm London Thyroid Club, corresponding fell American Thyroid Assoc; Gold Staff Offr Coronation 1953; Freeman City of London, Liveryman Worshipful Soc of Apothecaries; hon FRCS Edinburgh,hon FCM S Africa; MCh, FRCS; *Books* Recent Advances in Surgery (edns 5-10, 1959-80), Short Text Book of Surgery (edns 1-7,1960-80), Surgical Management 1984; *Recreations* sailing, tennis, gardening, wine; *Clubs* Garrick, Hurlingham, RN Sailing Assoc, tstee Bosham Sailing, Saintsbury; *Style*— Selwyn Taylor, Esq; Trippets, Bosham, Chichester PO18 8JE (☎ 0243 573387)

TAYLOR, Stanley Thomas; Charles Taylor (d 1948), and Eleanor Miriam, *née* North (d 1969); *b* 26 Sept 1923; *Educ* Archbishop Tenisons's GS; *m* 12 Feb 1955, Valerie Mary, da of Ernest Whitmarsh-Everiss (d 1972), of Bristol; 1 s (Stephen Charles b 1960), 1 da (Helen Frances b 1956); *Career* war serv cmmnd RAFVR; admin of Hertfordshire Health Authy until 1979, chief exec and sec Children's Film & Television Fndn 1980-; Freeman City of London, fndr memb Worshipful Co Chartered Secretaries and Administrators; FHSM 1968, FCIS 1970; *Recreations* golf, reading (biographies), walking; *Clubs* RAF; *Style*— Stanley T Taylor, Esq; 22 Stakers Ct, Milton Rd, Harpenden, Herts AL5 5PA (☎ 058 27 5287); Children's Film & Television Foundation Ltd, Goldcrest Elstree Studios, Borehamwood, Herts WD6 1JG (☎ 01 953 0844)

TAYLOR, Hon Mrs (Sylvia Alice); da of 2 Baron Joicey (d 1940); *b* 1908; *m* 1934 (m dis 1951), Lt-Col Richard Ian Griffith Taylor, DSO, MC (d 1984); 2 s, 1 da; *Style*— The Hon Mrs Sylvia Taylor

TAYLOR, Hon Mrs Sylvia Alice; 2 da of 2 Baron Joicey (d 1940) and Georgina Wharton (d 1952), da of Maj Augustus Edward Burdon; *b* 5 August 1908; *m* 28 April 1934 (m dis 1951), Lt-Col Richard Ian Griffith Taylor, DSO, MC, eld s of late Lt-Col Thomas George Taylor, DSO, of Chipchase Castle, Wark-on-Tyne; 2 s, 1 da

TAYLOR, Lady Ursula Daphne; *née* Brudenell-Bruce; da of 6 Marquess of Ailesbury,

DSO, TD (d 1961), and Caroline Sydney Anne, *née* Madden (d 1941); *b* 21 Oct 1905; *Educ* at home; *m* 1944, Alec Taylor; 2 s (and 1 s decd); *Career* chiropodist 1944-; *Recreations* motoring; *Style—* Lady Ursula Taylor; 18 Cresswell Rd, Newbury, Berks (☎ Newbury 35957)

TAYLOR, Wendy Ann (Mrs Bruce Robertson); CBE (1988); da of Edward Philip Taylor, and Lilian Maude, *née* Wright; *b* 29 Jan 1945; *Educ* St Martins Sch of Art (LDAD); *m* 1982, Bruce Robertson, s of Maurice Robertson; 1 s (Matthew Thomas b 1984); *Career* sculptor; one man exhibitions: Axiom Gallery London 1970, Angela Flowers Gallery London 1972, 24 King's Lynn Festival Norfolk and World Trade Centre London 1974, Annely Juda Fine Art London 1975, Oxford Gallery Oxford 1976, Oliver Dowling Gallery Dublin 1976 and 1979, Bldg Art - the process Bldg Centre Gallery 1986; shown in over 100 gp exhibitions 1964-82; represented in collections in: GB, USA, Rep of Ireland, NZ, Germany, Sweeden, Qatar, Switzerland, Seychelles; maj chmmns: The Travellers London 1969, Gazebo (edn of 4) London NY Oxford Suffolk 1970-72, Triad Oxford 1971, Timepiece London 1973, Calthac Leics 1977, Octo Milton Keynes 1979, Counterpoise Birmingham 1980, compass Bowl Basildon 1980, Sentinel Reigate 1982, Bronze Relief Canterbury 1981, Equatorial Sundial Bletchley 1982, Essence Milton Keynes 1982, Opus Morley Coll 1983, Gazebo Golder's Hill Park London 1983, Network London 1984, Geo I and Geo II Stratford upon Avon 1985, Landscape and Tree of the Wood Fenhurst Surrey 1986, Pharos Peel Park E Kilbride 1986, Ceres Fenhurst Surrey 1986, Nexus Corby Northants 1986, Globe Sundial Swansea Maritime Quarter 1987, Spirit of Enterprise Isle of Dogs London 1987, Silver Fountain Guildford Surrey 1988, The Whirlies E Kilbride 1988, Pilot Kites Norwich Airport 1988; awards: Walter Neurath 1964, Pratt 1965, Sainsbury 1966, Arts Cncl 1977, Duais Na Riochta (Kingdom Prize), Gold Medal Rep of Ireland 1977, winner silk screen Barcham Green Print Competition 1978; examiner Univ of London 1982-83, memb ct RCA 1982-, cncl memb Morley Coll 1985-, conslt New Town Cmmn Basildon (formerly Basildon Devpt Corpn) 1985-, specialist advsr Fine Art Bd cncl of Nat Academic Awards 1985- (memb 1980-85), memb ctee for art design Royal Fine Art Cmmn 1988 (memb 1981-); *Recreations* gardening; *Style—* Ms Wendy Taylor, CBE; 73 Bow Rd, Bow, London EC3 2AN (☎ 01 981 2037)

TAYLOR, Prof William; CBE (1982); s of Herbert Taylor (d 1969), and Maud Ethel, *née* Peyto (d 1972); *b* 31 May 1930; *Educ* Erith GS, LSE, Univ of London (BSc), Westminster Coll London (PGCE), Univ London Inst of Educn (DipEd, DPhil); *m* 30 Dec 1954, Rita, da of Ronald Hague (d 1980); 1 s (Richard William James b 1964), 2 da (Anne Catherine (Mrs Mitchell), Rosemary Caroline (Mrs Williams)); *Career* Nat Serv Royal West Kent Regt 1948-49, Intelligence Corps 1950-53, 135 Field Security Section TA; teacher in Kent 1953-59, dep head Slade Green Secdy Sch 1956-59), sr lectr St Luke's Coll Exeter 1959-61, princ lectr and head of educn dept Bede Coll Durham 1961-64, tutor and lectr in educn Univ of Oxford 1964-66, prof of educn Univ of Bristol 1966-73, dir Univ of London Inst of Educn 1973-83, princ Univ of London 1983-85, vice chllr Univ of Hull 1985-; chm: educnl advsy cncl of the IBA 1977-83, Univs Cncl for the Educn of Teachers 1976-79, ctee for educnl res Cncl of Europe 1968-71, Nat Fndn for Educnl Res 1984-88, Cncl for the Accreditation of Teacher Educn (CATE) 1984-, NFER/Nelson Publishing Co 1988-; pres Assoc of Colls of Further and Higher Educn 1985-88; Freeman City of London 1986, Liveryman Worshipful Soc of Apothecaries 1986; Hon DSc Aston Univ 1977, Hon LittD Leeds Univ 1979, Hon DCL Kent Univ 1981, Hon DUniv Open Univ 1983, Hon DLit Loughborough Univ 1984; FCP 1977, FCCEA 1979, FWAIEA 1979; *Books* The Secondary Modern School (1963), Society and the Education of Teachers (1969), Towards a Policy for the Education of Teachers (ed 1969); Heading for Change (1971), Policy and Planning in Post Secondary Education (1971), Research Perspectives in Education (ed 1974), Research and Reform in Teacher Education (1978), Metaphors of Education (ed 1984), Universities under Scrutiny (1987); *Recreations* books, music; *Style—* Prof William Taylor, CBE; Vice Chancellor's Lodge, University of Hull, Hull HU1 4QB (☎ 0482 465131, 0482 46311, fax 0482 465936)

TAYLOR, William Bernard; s of Francis Augustus Taylor (d 1956), of Swansea, and Mary Elizabeth, *née* George; *b* 13 Dec 1930; *Educ* Dynevor Sch Swansea, Univ of Kent (MA); *m* 26 April 1956, Rachel May, da of Daniel Brynmor Davies (d 1959), of Godre Rhiw, Morriston, Swansea; 1 s (Simon b 1965), 2 da (Kim b 1959, Deborah b 1961); *Career* Nat Serv 1949-51, cmmnd RNVR 1950, Sub Lt RNVR 1951-53; dist audit serv 1951-61, tres Llwchwr UDC 1967-68 (dep tres 1961-67), asst educn offr fin and mgmnt Manchester Corpn 1969-72, co tres Kent 1980-87 (asst co tres 1972-73, dep co tres 1973-80); specialist local authy advsr 1987-: Arthur Young Mgmnt Conslts, MIM Ltd, Lombard N Central plc, Sedgwick UK (Nat) Ltd; memb exec ctee Soc of Co Tres 1983-86; fin advsr to Social Servs Ctee of Assoc of CCs 1983-86, Lloyds Underwriter 1988-; memb: Maidstone Rotary Club, Union St Methodist Church; life memb W Kent speakers Club, hon tres SE Eng Tst Bd 1980-87, govr Kent Inst of Art and Design; FRSA, memb IPFA; *Books* Terotechnology & The Pursuit of Life Cycle Costs (1980), author of numerous articles for learned magazines; *Recreations* public speaking, tennis, cricket, watching rugby; *Style—* William Taylor, Esq; Selby Shaw, Heath Rd, Boughton Monchelsea, Maidstone, Kent ME17 4JE (☎ 0622 450 22)

TAYLOR, (Brian) William; s of Alan Stuart Taylor (d 1975), of Chatham, Kent, and Dora Frances Mary, *née* Betts (d 1968); *b* 29 April 1933; *Educ* Emanuel Sch Battersea; *m* 15 Aug 1959, Mary Evelyn, da of William Henry Buckley (d 1976), of Great Bookham, Surrey; 2 s (Jeffrey William b 16 Feb 1967, Michael John b 20 Jan 1972), 2 da (Helen Mary (Mrs Compston) b 28 Jan 1963, Gillian Elizabeth b 30 Oct 1964); *Career* Miny of Nat Insur: exec offr 1952, higher exec offr 1963, princ 1968, asst sec 1976, under sec 1982; Dept of Social Security; *Recreations* music, theatre, walking, sport; *Clubs* Royal Cwlth Soc; *Style—* Bill Taylor, Esq; 3 Box Ridge Ave, Purley, Surrey CR2 3AR (☎ 01 668 1184); Dept of Social Security, New Court, Carey St, London WC2 (☎ 01 831 6111, ext 2539)

TAYLOR, (Peter) William Edward; QC (1981); s of Peter Taylor (d 1963), of Winchester, and Julia Anne, *née* North; *b* 27 July 1917; *Educ* Peter Symonds' Sch Winchester, Christ's Coll Cambridge (MA); *m* 2 Jan 1948, Julia Mary, da of Air Cdre Sir Vernon Brown, CB (d 1986), of Chelsea, London SW3; 2 s (Malcolm b 1950, Nigel b 1952); *Career* cmmd TA 1937, served RA 1939-46; France and Belgium 1939-40, N Africa 1942-43, N W Europe 1944-45 (despatches), acting Lt-Col 1945; Hon Maj TARO 1946; barr Inner Temple 1946, Lincoln's Inn 1953, in practice 1947-, lectr in construction of documents, Cncl of Legal Educn 1952-70, Conveyancing Counsel of the Ct 1974-81, bencher Lincoln's Inn 1976-; memb: Gen Cncl of the Bar 1971-74, Senate of the Inns of Ct and the Bar 1974-75, Inter-professional Ctee on Retirement Provision 1974-, Land Registration Rule Ctee 1976-81, Standing Ctee on Conveyancing 1985-87, Inc Cncl of Law Reporting 1977-87 (vice chm 1988-); *Recreations* sailing, music; *Style—* William Taylor, Esq, QC; 46 Onslow Sq, London SW7 3NZ (☎ 01 589 1301); Carey Sconce, Yarmouth, Isle of Wight, PO41 OSB

TAYLOR, William Horace; GC (1941), MBE (1973); s of William Arthur Taylor (d 1945), and Hilda Jane, *née* Nicholson; *b* 23 Oct 1908; *Educ* Manchester GS; *m* 19 Sept 1946, Joan Isabel, da of John Skaife D'Ingerthorpe; 1 s (William Norman b 1949), 3 da (Susan Rosemary b 1948, Jane Elizabeth b 1951, Belinda Mary b 1954); *Career* Dept of Torpedoes and Mines Admty (despatches and comendation for brave conduct 1941), fndr memb Naval Clearance Divers, HMS Vernon 1944; travelling cmmr Sea Scouts UK 1946, field cmmr SW Eng Scout Assoc 1952-74, estate mangr 1975-84; *Recreations* scouting, boating, music; *Style—* William Horace Taylor, Esq, GC, MBE; The Bungalow, Carbeth, Blanefield, Glasgow G63 9AT (☎ 0360 70847)

TAYLOR, William McCaughey; s of William Taylor (d 1959), of Co Down, and Georgina Lindsay, *née* McCaughey (d 1983); *b* 10 May 1926; *Educ* Campbell Coll Belfast, Trinity Coll Oxford (MA); *m* 1955, June Louise, da of William Ewart Macartney (d 1971), of Co Antrim; 2 s (Dwayne b 1963, Heath b 1966), 2 da (Karin b 1956, Nicola b 1958); *Career* serv WWII 1944-47 Lt The Royal Inniskilling Fusiliers; chief exec N Ireland Police Authy (detached under sec N Ireland Office) 1979-86; chm N Ireland Coal Importers Assoc 1986-; *Recreations* golf, bridge, gardening, piano; *Clubs* Royal Belfast Golf, Ulster Reform; *Style—* William McCaughey Taylor, Esq; 1 Knocktern Gardens, Belfast BT4 3LZ (☎ 0232 653400); Northern Ireland Coal Importers Assoc, 10 Royal Avenue, Belfast GT1 1DB (☎ 0232 241153)

TAYLOR OF BLACKBURN, Baron (Life Peer UK 1978); Thomas Taylor; CBE (1974, OBE 1969); s of James Taylor; *b* 10 June 1929; *Educ* Blakey Moor HS; *m* 1950, Kathleen, da of John Edward Nurton; 1 s; *Career* memb Blackburn Town Cncl 1954-76 (ldr, and chm Policy and Resources Ctee 1972-76), dep pro-chllr Lancaster Univ 1974-, chm Govt Ctee of Enquiry into Mgmnt and Govt of Schs, and of Nat Fndn for Visual Aids, past chm of Juvenile Bench, pres Free Church Council 1962-68, memb Norweb Bd and conslt Shorrock Security Systems Ltd and other cos; JP Blackburn 1960; *Style—* The Rt Hon the Lord Taylor of Blackburn, CBE, JP; 34 Tower Rd, Feniscliffe, Blackburn, Lancs

TAYLOR OF GRYFE, Baron (Life Peer UK 1968); Thomas Johnston Taylor; DL (Renfrewshire 1970); s of John Sharp Taylor, of Glasgow; *b* 27 April 1912; *Educ* Bellahouston Acad Glasgow; *m* 1943, Isobel, da of William Wands; 2 da; *Career* sits as SDP Peer in House of Lords; chm Econ Forestry Gp 1976-82, Morgan Grenfell (Scotland) Ltd 1973-86, chm Scottish Railways Bd 1971-80; memb: BR Bd 1968-80, bd Scottish Television Ltd 1968-82; dir: Scottish Civic Tst, Whiteaway Laidlaw & Co Ltd (Bankers) 1971-, Friends' Provident Life Off 1972-82, Scottish Metropolitan Property Co Ltd 1972, BR property bd 1972-82; Hon LLD Strathclyde 1974; chm Isaac and Edith Wolfson Tst; FRSE; *Clubs* Caledonian, Royal and Ancient (St Andrews); *Style—* The Rt Hon the Lord Taylor of Gryfe; The Cottage, Auchenames, Kilbarchan, Renfrewshire PA10 2PM (☎ 050 57 2648)

TAYLOR OF HADFIELD, Baron (Life Peer UK 1982), of Hadfield in the Co of Derby; Frank (Francis) Taylor; s of Francis Taylor and Sarah Ann Earnshaw; *b* 7 Jan 1905; *m* 1, 1929 (m dis); 2 da; m 2, 1956, Christine Enid, da of Charles Hughes; 1 da; *Career* fndr, life pres and exec dir Taylor Woodrow Gp (md 1921-79, chm 1937-74); dir: Taylor Woodrow Hldgs of Canada Ltd, Monarch Investmts Ltd Canada; vice-pres Aims 1978-; former dir BOAC; FCIOB (hon fell 1979); Hon DSc Salford; hon: FICE, FFB; kt 1974; *Style—* The Rt Hon The Lord Taylor of Hadfield; 10 Park Street, London W1Y 4DD (☎ 01 499 8871)

TAYLOR OF MANSFIELD, Baron (Life Peer UK 1966); Harry Bernard Taylor; CBE (1966); s of late Henry Taylor; *b* 18 Sept 1895; *Educ* Oxclose Lane Sch, Mansfield Woodhouse; *m* 1921, Clara Annie (d 1983), da of John Ashley; 1 s; *Career* MP (L) Mansfield Div of Nottinghamshire 1941-66, pps to min of Nat Insur 1945, parly sec Miny of Nat Insur 1950-51; *Books* Uphill all the Way (autobiog 1973); *Style—* The Rt Hon the Lord Taylor of Mansfield, CBE; 47 Shakespeare Ave, Mansfield Woodhouse, Nottinghamshire (T Mansfield 2392)

TAYLOR THOMPSON, (John) Derek; CB (1985); s of John Taylor Thompson (d 1964), of Herts, and Marjorie Bligh, *née* Westcott; *b* 6 August 1927; *Educ* St Peter's Sch York, Balliol Coll Oxford (MA); *m* 2 Oct 1954, Helen Margaret, da of George Laurie Walker (d 1934), of Wimbledon; 2 da (Catherine b 1957, Bopha b 1960); *Career* govt serv: bd memb Inland Revenue 1973-87; chm Fiscal Affairs Ctee, Orgn for Econ Co-op & Devpt 1984-89; *Recreations* rural pursuits, reading, writing; *Clubs* Utd Oxford and Cambridge; *Style—* Derek Taylor Thompson, Esq, CB; Jessops, Nutley, E Sussex TN22 3PD

TAYLOR-DOWNES, Michael; s of Lt-Col Francis Algenon Taylor-Downes (d 1951), of Colwyn Bay, Bay, N Wales, and Lillias Elsie, *née* Banks (d 1966); *b* 30 Dec 1930; *Educ* The Downs Sch Colwall, Westminster; *m* 1, 2 Dec 1950, Pamela Jane Firkins (d 1972); 2 da (Hon Mrs Ian Wills (Elizabeth Jane) b 1952, Amanda Charlotte b 1955); m 2, 5 Oct 1963, Audrey Elizabeth Jackson (d 1984); m 3, 29 Nov 1983, Remony Charmian, da of late Sir Charles Gerald Stewkley Shuckburgh 12 Bt, TD, DL; *Career* The Life Gds 1949-52, Inns of Ct Regt (TA) 1952-59; underwriting memb of Lloyds 1956; vice chm Cotswold District Cncl 1975-80; master: The Garth Fox Hounds 1955-60, Cotswold Vale Fox Hounds 1962-63, Hawkstone Otter Hounds 1965-72, Wye Valley Otter Hounds 1969-72; *Recreations* hunting, shooting, fishing,; *Style—* Michael Taylor-Downes, Esq; The Cottage, Sherbourne, Warwick, CV35 8AA (☎ 0926 624 073)

TAYLOR-JONES, Dr Thomas Henry Edward; DL (Kent 1981); s of Henry Taylor-Jones (d 1939); *b* 6 Feb 1906; *Educ* Dulwich, London Univ; *m* 1931, Dorothy Amy, da of John Corbett (d 1922); 1 s decd, 1 da; *Career* late orthopaedic house surgn Belgrave Hosp for Children, MO W View Hosp Teneterden; MRCS, LRCP, DCH; *Recreations* gardening, general practice; *Clubs* Band of Brothers; *Style—* Dr Thomas Taylor-Jones, DL; The Garden, St Michaels, Tenterden, Kent (☎ 3193)

TAYLOR-SCHOFIELD, Annette Ainscough; da of Brian Wormald, MY Hedonist 'B' Cannes, S France, and Maureen Daphne, *née* Goodman; *b* 26 July 1953; *Educ* Mill Mount GS for Girls York; *m* 1, 2 Jan 1971, (m dis 1977), Nigel Griffiths Ainsclough, s of Thomas Griffiths Ainsclough, of Bracknell Berks; 1 s (Matthew Sean b 1971), 1 da (Kathryn b 1973); m2, 3 Aug 1978, (m dis 1983), Timothy (Julian) Taylor-Schofield; *Career* sales mangr Impact Insulation Ltd 1975-76 (mktg mangr 1974-75), sales dir

Solarwall Ltd 1976-78, property renovator 1978-80, proper Insulation Agency 1980-83; co-owner Ziggy's Nightclub & Staircase Restaurant York 1983-, (winner Disco Mirror awards 1986-88, runner up Disco & club Int award 1987, Yorks Disco of the Year 1988, runner up Club Mirror award), chm and md Taylor-Schofield Leisure Ltd 1987-, dir and co sec Bellerby's Ltd York 1989-; memb mgmnt ctee One Parent Families Assoc; took part 25 guest speaker in educn video, film Women Mean Business by York Film Workshop; Network (1987), The Int Alliance (1989); *Recreations* snow skiing, canoeing, mountain walking, fitness training, tennis, music; *Clubs* Viking Leisure Club; *Style*— Ms A A Taylor-Schofield; Taylor Schoffield Leisure Ltd, 31-33, North Moor Rd, Huntingdon, York YO3 9QN (☎ 0904 764 399 & 763 131/2); Ziggy's Nightclub, Micklegate, York - evenings (☎ 0904 620 602)

TAYLOR-YOUNG, (Harold) Strang; s of Hugh Corbett Taylor Young, and Annie Rankin Strang; *b* 3 Mar 1902; *Educ* Rugby, Trinity Coll Cambridge (BA), St Thomas' Hosp (BCh); *m* 4 Sept 1930, Nancy Adelaide, da of Charles Read Seymour, of Winchfield, Hants; 1 s (Christopher b 1934), 1 da (Patricia b 1931); *Career* conslt surgn Salisbury Gen Hosp 1931-58; OStJ 1944, KStJ 1961, div surgn, county surgn, surgn in chief; memb Nat Tst (fndr chm Salisbury branch); fndr memb Probus Club Salisbury; FRCS; LRCP; *Recreations* bridge, St John Ambulance Brigade; *Clubs* MCC, Utd Univ; *Style*— Strang Taylor-Young, Esq; National Provincial Bank, Salisbury, Wiltshire

TAYLORSON, John Brown; s of John Brown Taylorson (d 1955), and Edith Maria Taylorson (d 1981); *b* 5 Mar 1931; *Educ* Forest Sch Snares Brook Essex; *m* 1960 (m dis), Barbara June Hagg; 1 s (Jonathan) 1 da (Sally); m 2 1985, Helen Anne; *Career* Flying Offr RAF 1959-61; md: Int Div Gardner Merchant Food Servs 1974-77, Fedics Food Servs Pty 1977-80; chief exec Civil Serv Catering Org 1980-81, head of catering BA plc 1981-, pres Int Flight Catering Assoc 1983-6; *Recreations* golf, walking, theatre, crosswords; *Clubs* Escorts, Jesters, Burhill GC, Wanderers; *Style*— John Taylorson, Esq; 10 Ruxley Ridge, Claygate, Esher, Surrey; British Airways, Europa House, PO Box 10, London Heathrow Airport, Hounslow, Middx

TAYLOUR, Lord William Desmond; s of 4 Marquess of Headfort (d 1943); *b* 1904; *Educ* Harrow, Trinity Coll Cambridge (BA, MA, PhD); *Career* Capt 2 Derbyshire Yeo (TA); pres The Strafford Club; FSA; kt cmdr of St Gregory the Great (Papal); *Books* The Mycehaeans; *Style*— Lord William Taylour; St Aubyns, 2 Woodlands Rd, Great Shelford, Cambridge CB2 5LW (☎ 0223 842262)

TAYSIDE, Baroness; Hilda Gwendoline Urquhart; *née* Harris; da of John Thomson Harris, of Dundee; *Educ* Dundee HS, St Andrews Univ (BSc); *m* 1939, Baron Tayside (Life Peer; d 1975); 2 s, 1 da; *Style*— The Rt Hon the Lady Tayside; Kalliste, 30 Turfbeg Place, Forfar, Angus (☎ 0307 63338)

TE ATAIRANGIKAAHU, Te Arikinui Dame; DBE (1970); da of Koroki Te Rata Mahuta V; *b* 23 July 1931; *Educ* Rakaumanga Maori Primary Sch Huntly, Waikato Diocesan Secdy Sch for Girls Hamilton; *m* 1952, Whatumoana Paki; 2 s, 5 da; *Career* Hon Doctorate (Waikato); The Maori Queen 1966-; Te Atairangikaahu (the soaring bird of the dawn); *Style*— Te Arikinui Dame Te Atairangikaahu, DBE; -BE, Turangawaewae, Ngaruawahia, NZ

TE KANAWA, Dame Kiri Janette; DBE (1982, OBE 1973); da of Thomas Te Kanawa, of Auckland, NZ, and late Elanor Te Kanawa; *b* 6 Mar 1944,Gisborne, NZ,; *Educ* St Mary's Coll Auckland, London Opera Centre; *m* 1967, Desmond Stephen Park, s of Joseph Frank Park, of Brisbane, Aust; 1 s, 1 da; *Career* opera singer; studied singing under Dame Sister Mary Leo, *qv* 1959-65; has sung major roles at: Royal Opera House (Covent Garden), Metropolitan Opera (New York), Paris Opera, San Francisco Opera, Sydney Opera, Cologne Opera, La Scala (Milan); sang at Royal Wedding of HRH Prince of Wales to Lady Diana Spencer 1981; Hon LLD Dundee; Hon DMus Durham 1982, Oxford 1983; *Style*— Dame Kiri Te Kanawa, DBE; c/o Basil Horsfield, L'Estoril (B), Avenue Princess Grace 31, Monte Carlo, Monaco

TEAGUE, (Edward) Thomas Henry; s of Harry John Teague, of Kelsall, Ches, and Anne Elizabeth, *née* Hunt; *b* 21 May 1954; *Educ* St Francis Xavier's Coll Liverpool, Christ's Coll Cambridge (MA); *m* 8 Aug 1980, Helen Mary Bernadette, da of Daniel Matthew Howard (d 1974); 2 s (Michael b 1983, Dominic b 1985); *Career* called to the Bar Inner Temple 1977, in practice on Wales and Chester circuit 1978-; memb Soc of Dorset Men, co-fndr and memb Soc of St Edmund Campion; *Recreations* playing the cello, fly-fishing, stargazing; *Style*— Thomas Teague, Esq; 2 Hoole Park, Chester CH2 3AW (☎ 0244 349594); 40 King St, Chester CH1 2AH (☎ 0244 323 886/329 273, fax 47732)

TEALL OF TEALLACH, Dr Dennistoun Gordon; s of Bernard John Teall (d 1966), of Radford Semele, and Agnes Mary, *née* Cottrell (d 1977); *b* 8 August 1924; *Educ* Warwick Sch, Cooper's Hill Coll (Ed Cert), Univ of Leicester (MEd, PhD), Coll of Preceptors (LCP); *m* 4 Oct 1946, Eleanor Joan, da of John Thomas Ackland (d 1967), of Quadring; 2 s (David b 1947, Richard b 1962), 2 da (Maryon b 1950, Christine b 1956); *Career* SERV WWII despatch rider Civil Def 1940-43, radio offr Merchant Navy 1945-46 (cadet 1943-44); works chemist Colas Products Ltd 1946-47; headmaster: Yarwell Sch 1952-60, Priory Prep Sch 1960-62, princ Priory Coll 1962-84; chm: Midlands area Independent Schs Assoc 1982-85, NE England and Scotland Independent Schs Assoc 1982-85; hon exec pres Scottish Tartans Soc 1983- (patron 1978-, chm 1979-83); memb: Manorial Soc of GB, Noble Leet of Feudal Lords, Royal Scottish Country Dance Assoc; chm bd of tstees Scottish Tartans Museum N Caroline USA 1988-; memb Lloyd's of London; cncllr: Oundle and Thrapston RDC 1961-67, Barrack RDC 1965-68, Nassington 1958-66, St Martins Without Parish Cncl 1965-68; Parish Cncl hon memb Clan Grant, memb House of Gordon; Lord of the Manor of Croyland; Royal Humane Soc's Award for Gallantry in Saving Life; MIOD, FCS 1945, FSA Scot 1978, FSTS 1981; Hon Lt-Col Militia of the State of Georgia 1987; *Books* May Festivals (1963), The Tradesmen and Corporation of Stamford 1485-1750 (1975), The Manx Tartans (1981), The District Tartans of Scotland (jtly, 1988), A Brief History of The Scottish Tartans Society (1988); *Recreations* sailing in strong winds, windsurfing in light airs, horse riding, scottish dancing, mountain walking, swimming in warm waters; *Clubs* Univ Centre (Cambridge), Manx Sc; *Style*— Dr Gordon Teall of Teallach; Cornaa House, Maughold, Iom (☎ 0624 813580); Scottish Tartans Museum, Comrie, Perthshire PH6 2DW (☎ 0724 70779, car tel 0860 640 234)

TEAR, Robert; CBE (1984); s of Thomas Arthur Tear, of Barry, S Glam, and Edith Marion Tear; *b* 8 Mar 1939; *Educ* Barry GS, King's Coll Cambridge (MA); *m* 10 Jan 1961, Hilary, da of William Thomas, of Cwmbran, Gwent; 2 da (Rebecca b 22 Nov 1961, Elizabeth b 11 Feb 1966); *Career* opera/concert singer and conductor; regular appearances: throughout America, Covent Garden, Munich, Park, Salzburg, Brussels and Geneva; holder of Chair of Int Vocal Studies at RAM; hon fell King's Coll Cambridge 1988, RAM, RCM; *Recreations* anything interesting; *Clubs* Garrick, Beefsteak; *Style*— Robert Tear, Esq, CBE; Bessborough House, 11 Ravenscourt Sq, London W6; Harold Holt Ltd, 31 Sinclair Rd, London W14 0NS (☎ 603 4600)

TEARE, Nigel John Martin; s of Eric John Teare (d 1980), and Mary Rackham, *née* Faragher (d 1985); *b* 8 Jan 1952; *Educ* King William's Coll Castletown IOM, St Peter's Coll Oxford (BA, MA); *m* 16 Aug 1975, (Elizabeth) Jane, da of Alan James Pentecost, of Beaulieu, Derby Rd, Nottingham; 2 s (Roland b 1981, David b 1984), 1 da (Charlotte b 1982); *Career* barr Lincoln's Inn 1974; *Recreations* trying to play golf and tennis; *Clubs* RAC; *Style*— Nigel Teare, Esq; The Towers, Hawkshill Place, Portsmouth Rd, Esher, Surrey KT10 9HY (☎ 0372 64552); 2 Essex Ct, Temple, London (☎ 01 583 8381, fax 01 353 0998, telex 8812528 ADROIT)

TEASDALE, Anthony Laurence; s of John S Teasdale, of Beverley, N Humberside, and Pauline, *née* Tomlinson (d 1983); *b* 4 June 1957; *Educ* Slough GS, Balliol Coll Oxford (MA), Nuffield Coll Oxford (MPhil); *Career* res asst to Rt Hon Nigel Lawson MP 1978-79; lectr in politics Corpus Christi Coll Oxford 1980-81, Magdalen Coll Oxford 1982; policy advsr Euro Democratic Gp (of Cons MEPs) Brussels and London 1982-86, asst to dir gen for economic and fin affairs EC Cncl of Ministers Brussels 1986-88; political advsr to Rt Hon Sir Geoffrey Howe QC MP 1988-; *Books* Righting The Balance: A New Agenda for Euro-Japanese Trade (with James Moorhouse MEP, 1987); *Recreations* music, reading, travel; *Clubs* Carlton; *Style*— Anthony Teasdale, Esq; Foreign & Commonwealth Office, London SW1A 2AH (☎ 01 270 2112)

TEASDALE, Lieut Cdr (Raymond) Geoffrey; s of Canham Teasdale (d 1977), of Aldbrough, Yorks, and Alma Arabella, *née* Hobbs; *b* 5 Sept 1931; *Educ* Hymers Hull, RNC Dartmouth; *m* 22 Aug 1980, Michele Evadne, da of Capt Godfrey Charles Gale; *Career* RN 1949-81; chief Counter-Pollution Advsr MOD 1981; chm Nautical Inst (Avon) 1986; FInstPed; MNI; *Recreations* fishing, golf; *Clubs* RN, RN Sailing Assoc; *Style*— Lt Cdr Geoffrey Teasdale; 11 St Martins Park, Marshfield, Avon (☎ 0225 891764); MOD (Navy), Foxhill, Bath (☎ 0225 882687)

TEBB, Robert Maxwell; s of Capt Harry Raymond Tebb, RA (d 1978), of Scarborough, and Kathleen Cheveley (d 1979); *b* 9 Feb 1927; *Educ* Leeds GS; *Career* food distributor; md Leigh Lineham & Sharphouse Ltd 1967-; chm: Leigh Lineham 1983-, Cith of Leeds Coll of Music 1980; dir Eng Summer Sch of Light Opera, dep admin Harveys Leeds Inst Pianoforte Competition; *Recreations* theatre, music; *Style*— Robert Tebb, Esq; Grove Court, Holt Ave, Church Lane, Adel, Leeds 16, W Yorks (☎ 679666); Leigh Lineham Ltd, 1 Cottage Rd, Headingley, Leeds LS6 4DD, W Yorks (☎ 782319)

TEBBIT, Sir Donald Claude; GCMG (1980, KCMG 1975, CMG 1965); s of Richard Claude Tebbit (d 1967), of The Old Farm, Toft, Cambridge; *b* 4 May 1920; *Educ* Perse Sch Cambridge, Trinity Hall Cambridge (MA); *m* 1947, Barbara, da of Rev Norman Matheson (d 1952), of Beauly, Inverness-shire; 1 s, 3 da; *Career* serv WWII RNVR; entered FO 1946, min Br Embassy Washington 1970-72, chief clerk FCO 1972-76, high cmmr Aust 1976-80, ret; chm Dip Appeals Bd 1980-87; dir-gen Br Property Fedn 1980-85; dir Rio Tinto Zinc Corpn 1980-; pres: (UK) Australian-Br C of C 1980-, Old Persean Soc 1981-82; govr (Dep Chm) Nuffield Hosps 1980-; chm Marshall Aid Commemoration Cmmn 1985-; memb appeals bd Cncl of Europe 1981-; chm: ESU of the Cwlth 1983-87, Jt Cwlth Socs Cncl 1987-; *Clubs* Travellers', Gog Magog Golf; *Style*— Sir Donald Tebbit, GCMG; Priory Cottage, Toft, Cambridge CB3 7RH

TEBBIT, Rt Hon Norman Beresford; CH (1987), PC 1981, MP (C) Chingford 1983-; 2 s of Leonard Albert and Edith Tebbit, of Enfield; *b* 29 Mar 1931; *Educ* Edmonton Co GS; *m* 1956, Margaret Elizabeth, da of Stanley Daines, of Chatteris; 2 s, 1 da; *Career* memb Cons Pty 1946, journalist 1947-49, RAF 1949-51, RAuxAF 1952-55, publishing and advtg 1951-53, airline pilot 1953-70 (memb BALPA and former official), MP (C): Epping 1970-74, Waltham Forest, Chingford 1974-1983; former: memb select ctee Science and Technol, chm Cons Aviation Ctee, vice-chm and sec Cons Housing and Construction Ctee, sec New Town MPs; PPS to Min of State Employment 1972-73, parly under-sec state Trade 1979-81, min of state Indust 1981, sec of state Employment 1981-Oct 1983, sec of state Trade and Indust Oct 1983-85; cnllr of Duchy of Lancaster 1985-87; chm Cons Pty 1985-87; *Books* Upwardley Mobile, an autobiography (1988); *Style*— The Rt Hon Norman Tebbit, CH, MP; House of Commons, SW1

TEBBUTT, Michael Laurence; s of Laurence Tebbutt, and Joan, *née* Payne; *b* 23 July 1931; *Educ* Stamford Sch Lincs; *m* 23 May 1959, Hazel, da of Andrew Taylor; 4 da (Fiona b 1960, Nicola b 1962, Davina b 1963, Rowena b 1965); y; *Career* RN; serv HMS: Vanguard 1950, Finisterre 1951, Vanguard 1953; FOSM Staff 1954, 3 Submarine Sqdn 1955, HMS Dolphin 1957; with Outward Bound Tst 1957-61, trg offr Jt Iron Cmd 1961-63, gen mangr Bowes Lyon House 1963-67, gen sec NFYFC's 1967-69, comptroller Knebworth House 1969-72; admin: Weston Park 1972-82, Culzean (NTS) 1982-; vice pres Wrekin Decorative and Fine Arts Soc; chm: Ayrshire Decorative and Fine Arts Soc (exec memb), Ayrshire and Burns Country Tourist Bd, Culzean Arts Guild; MBIM 1983; *Recreations* mountaineering, sailing, music; *Clubs* Glasgow Art; *Style*— Michael Tebbutt, Esq; Culzean Castle, Ayrshire, (☎ 06556 274); Culzean Castle, Ayrshire KA19 8LE, (☎ 06556 274)

TEDDER, Hon Andrew Jonathan; s of 2 Baron Tedder; *b* 1958; *Style*— The Hon Andrew Tedder

TEDDER, Hon Anne Rosalinde; da of 2 Baron Tedder; *b* 1963; *Style*— The Hon Anne Tedder

TEDDER, 2 Baron (UK 1946); John Michael Tedder; s of Marshal of the RAF 1 Baron Tedder, GCB, AOC-in-C M East 1941-42 & Med 1943, Dep Supreme Cmdr Allied Expeditionary Force 1943-45, Chief Air Staff 1946-49 and Chllr Cambridge Univ 1950-67 (d 1967); *b* 4 July 1926; *Educ* Dauntsey's Sch, Magdalene Coll Cambridge (ScD), Birmingham Univ (PhD, DSc); *m* 1952, Peggy Eileen, da of Samuel George Growcott, of Birmingham; 2 s, 1 da; *Heir* s, Hon Robin John Tedder; *Career* Purdie prof of chemistry St Salvator's Coll St Andrews Univ 1969-; memb RSC 1980-; FRSE, FRSC; *Style*— The Rt Hon the Lord Tedder; Little Rathmore, Kennedy Gdns, St Andrews, Fife, Scotland (T St Andrews 3546)

TEDDER, Hon Mina Una Margaret; da of 1 Baron Tedder, GCB (d 1967); *b* 1920; *Career* formerly asst librarian British Embassy Washington USA; BBC TV 1954-57, Scottish TV Glasgow 1957-65, dist cmmr Nat Savings Alnwick Northumberland;

Style— The Hon Mina Tedder

TEDDER, Philip Anthony; s of Arthur Henry Tedder (d 1988), and Winifred May, *née* Marshall; *b* 3 Sept 1945; *Educ* Sutton Co GS, Univ Coll of Wales (BSc); *m* 6 July 1968, Pauline, da of William Richarson, of Manchester; 1 s (Richard b 1977); *Career* Deloitte Haskins and Sells: joined 1968, panel on take overs and mergers 1979-81, ptnr CA's 1981-; FCA; *Recreations* tennis, swimming, walking, photography; *Clubs* RAC; *Style*— Philip Tedder, Esq; Deloitte Haskins & Sells, P O Box 207, 128 Queen Victoria St, London EC4P 4JX (☎ 01 248 3913, fax 01 248 3623, telex 894941)

TEDDER, Hon Robin John; s and h of 2 Baron Tedder; *b* 6 April 1955; *m* 1, 1977, Jennifer Peggy (d 1978), da of John Mangan; m 2, 1980, (Rita) Aristea, da of John Frangidis, of Sydney, NSW, Australia; 2 s (Benjamin John, b 1985, Christopher Arthur b 1986), 1 da (Jacqueline Christina b 1988); *Career* stockbroker/merchant banker; dir: Australian Gilt Securities, Bondlending Co Ltd; dir Kleinwort Benson Australia; Dep md Hattersley Maxwell Mall Ltd; *Recreations* sailing, golf; *Clubs* Royal Sydney Yacht Squadron, Royal & Ancient Golf (St Andrews); *Style*— The Hon Robin Tedder

TEDDY, Peter Julian; s of Francis Gerald Teddy, of Rhyl, N Wales, and Beryl Dorothy Fogg; *b* 2 Nov 1944; *Educ* Rhyl GS, Univ of Wales (BSc), Univ of Oxford (MA, DPhil, BM, BCh 1972); *m* 1 June 1974, Fiona Margaret, da of Richard Edward Millard, CBE, JP; 2 s (Alexander Francis b 1982, William Peter b 1986); *Career* conslt neurological surgn: Radcliffe Infirmary Oxford, Nat Spinal Injuries Centre Stoke Mandeville Hosp 1981-; sr res fell St Peter's Coll Oxford 1971-, clinical lectr dep dir of clinical studies Univ of Oxford Med Sch; *Recreations* tennis, dinghy sailing, squash; *Style*— Peter Teddy, Esq; Dept of Neurological Suringdon, Oxon OX5 3DP (☎ 0869 50034); Dept of Neurological Surgery, The Radcliffe Infirmary, Oxford OX2 6HE (☎ 0865 249891)

TEE, (Brian) Nicholas; s of James Haselden Tee, of Churchdown, Glos, and May, *née* Kent; *b* 19 Oct 1950; *Educ* The Kings Sch Glos, Manchester Univ, Loughborough Univ; *m* 21 Nov 1978, Hilary Josephine, da of Richard Evans (d 1980); 1 s (Charles Nicholas b 1984); *Career* princ Nicholas Tee CAs; FICA; *Recreations* property maintenance, redevelopment, swimming; *Style*— Nicholas Tee, Esq; Little Orchard, Lansdown Parade, Cheltenham, Glos GL50 2LH; The Old School House, Leckhampton Road, Cheltenham, Glos GL53 0AX (☎ 0242 513232), car telephone 0836 608183)

TEELOCK, HE Dr Boodhun; s of Ramessur Teelock (d 1945), and Sadny Jugdharree (d 1926); *b* 20 July 1922; *Educ* Edinburgh Univ (MB, ChB 1950), Liverpool Univ (DTM & H 1951), DPH (England) 1959; *m* 9 Jan 1956, Riziya, da of Anand Mohan Sahay, of India; 3 da (Vijayalakshmi b 29 Oct 1956, Neena b 24 March 1959, Sajni b 31 Aug 1960); *Career* sch med offr Mauritius 1952-59; princ med offr Mauritius 1960- 68; regnl advsr Public Health WHO and regnl offr for Africa at Brazzaville 1968-71; rep WHO: Tanzania 1971-74, Kenya and Seychelles 1974-79; immunisation med offr Air Mauritius 1980-89; High Cmmr for Mauritius in UK 1989-; memb BMA and Mauritius Med Assoc; *Style*— HE Dr Boodhun Teelock; Mauritius High Commission, 32-33 Elvaston Place, London SW7 5NW (☎ 01 581 0294)

TEELOCK, Lady; Vinaya Kumari; *née* Prasad; *Educ* BA; *m* Sir Leckraz Teelock, CBE (d 1982), High Cmmr for Mauritius in UK 1968-82 and Doyen of Dip Corps at his death; 1 s, 1 da; *Career* barr Middle Temple; *Style*— Lady Teelock; Flat 1, Chelsea House, Lowndes St, SW1

TEGNER, Ian Nicol; s of Sven Stuart Tegner, OBE (d 1971); *b* 11 July 1933; *Educ* Rugby; *m* 1961, Meriel Helen, da of Maurice Stanley Lush, CB, CBE, MC; 1 s, 1 da; *Career* CA (Scotland) 1957; Clarkson Gordon & Co Toronto Canada 1958-59, Barton Mayhew & Co 1959-71 (ptnr 1965), fin dir Bowater Industs plc 1971-86; dir gp fin Midland Bank plc 1987, vice-pres Inst of Scotland 1986-87, chm The 100 Gp of Fin Dirs 1988; *Recreations* book collecting, walking, choral singing, family life, travel; *Style*— Ian Tegner, Esq; 44 Norland Sq, London W11 4PZ (☎ 01 229 8604); Keepers Cottage, Kilninver, Argyll

TEIGNMOUTH, Baroness; Pamela; s of Harry Edmonds-Heath; *m* 1, George Meyer; m 2, 1979, as his 2 w, 7 & last Baron Teignmouth, DSC & bar (d 1981); *Style*— The Rt Hon the Lady Teignmouth

TEJAN-SIE, Sir Banja; GCMG (1970, CMG 1967); s of Alpha Ahmed Tejan-Sie (d 1957), and Ayesatu Tejan Sie (d 1958); *b* 7 August 1917; *Educ* Bo Sch, Prince of Wales Sch Sierra Leone, LSE; *m* 1945, Admire Stapleton; 5 s (1 s decd), 3 da; *Career* barr Lincoln's Inn 1951, vice-pres Sierra Leone People's Pty 1953-56; speaker Sierra Leone House of Reps 1962-67, Chief Justice 1967-70; actg govr-gen and govr-gen Sierra Leone 1967-70; hon tres Int African Inst London; GCON (Nigeria) 1970, Grand Band Star of Africa (Liberia) 1969, Order of Cedar (Lebanon) 1966, Special Grand Cordon (Taiwan) 1967; *Clubs* Commonwealth; *Style*— Sir Banja Tejan-Sie, GCMG; 3 Tracy Ave, London NW2 4AT (☎ 01 452 2324)

TELFER, Frederick Charles Edmund; s of Edmund Telfer (d 1953); *b* 10 Nov 1931; *Educ* Millfield, Pembroke Coll Oxford; *m* 1965, Patricia Mary, da of John George Abraham, TD (d 1973); 3 s, 1 da; *Career* stockbroker 1957; ptnr Joseph Sebag & Co 1965-, ptnr Carr Sebag & Co 1979-, ptnr Laurie Millbank & Co 1983-; memb cncl Stock Exchange 1975-81, Chase Manhattan Securities 1986; *Recreations* sailing, shooting, skiing; *Clubs* City of London, Royal Thames Yacht, Royal London Yacht, Royal Southern Yacht; *Style*— Frederick Telfer, Esq; West End House, Frensham, Surrey (025125 3549)

TELFER, Hon Mrs (Laetitia Mary); *née* Bruce; JP (Newcastle upon Tyne); da of 7 Lord Balfour of Burleigh (d 1967), and Violet Dorothy Evelyn, MBE, yr da of late Richard Henry Done, JP, DL, of Salterswell, Tarporley, Cheshire; sis of 8 (de facto) Lord; *b* 29 Dec 1920; *Educ* St Andrews Univ (MB, ChB); *m* 8 July 1955, Dr Ian Metcalfe Telfer (d 1988), er s of John Telfer, FSAA, of Kingarth, Moorside, Fenham, Newcastle-upon-Tyne; 2 s (John Bruce b 15 June 1956, George Metcalfe b 9 Oct 1961), 1 da (Mary Daubeny b 30 March 1958); *Style*— The Hon Mrs Telfer, JP; Wallbottle Hall, Newcastle-upon-Tyne NE15 8JD

TELFER, Dr Robert Gilmour Jamieson (Rab); CBE (1985); s of James Telfer (d 1987), of Edinburgh, and Helen Lambie, *née* Jamieson (d 1977), of Edinburgh; *b* 22 April 1928; *Educ* Bathgate Acad, Univ of Edinburgh (BsC, PhD); *m* 8 July 1953, Joan Audrey, da of George William Gunning (d 1964), of Swansea; 3 s (James Gilmour b 26 June 1957, Robin Gunning b 26 Jan 1959, John Telfer b 26 July 1961); *Career* shift chemist Atomic Energy Authy 1953-54, joined ICI 1954, R and D dir Petrochemical Div (dep chm 1975-76, chm 1976-81); dir: Phillips Imperial Petroleum Ltd 1976-81, Manchester Business Sch 1984-88, Renold plc 1984-, Volex Gp plc 1985-; chm and md Mather and Platt Ltd 1981-84, chm European Industl Servs Ltd 1988-; chm Advsy Cncl on Energy Conservation 1982-84, personal advsr to SOS for Energy 1984-87; memb: Advsy Cncl on R and D for Fuel and Power 1981-87, Civil Serv Coll Advsy Cncl 1985-; sr visiting fellowship Manchester Business Sch Univ of Manchester, CBIM; *Recreations* poetry, gardening, walking, swimming, supporting Middlesborough FC; *Clubs* Caledonian; *Style*— Dr Rab Telfer, CBE; Downings, Upleatham, Redcar, Cleveland TS11 8AG; 75 Porchfield Sq, St John's Gdns, Manchester (☎ 0297 23254); European Industrial Services Ltd, Woden Rd West, Kings Hill, Wednesbury, W Midlands WS10 2TT (☎ 021 556 1997, fax 021 502 6198, telex 335105)

TELFER SMOLLETT OF BONHILL, Georgina Myra Albinia; da of Sir Gifford Wheaton Grey Fox, 2 Bt (d 1959), and his 1 w, Hon Myra Newton, da of 1 Baron Eltisley, KBE; *b* 1930; *m* 1951, Patrick Telfer Smollett of Bonhill, MC, DL, *qv*; 1 s (David), 1 da (Gabrielle); *Style*— Mrs Patrick Telfer Smollett of Bonhill; Cameron, Alexandria, Dunbartonshire (☎ 0389 56226); 9 Cleveland Row, London SW1 (☎ 01 930 6319)

TELFER SMOLLETT OF BONHILL, Patrick Tobias Telfer; MC (1940), DL (Dunbartonshire 1957); s of Maj-Gen Alexander Patrick Drummond Telfer Smollett of Bonhill, CB, CBE, DSO, MC (d 1954) and late Marian Lucy, da of George Herbert Strutt, of Bridgehill, and of Kingairloch, Argyll; descendant of John Smollett, of Dunbartonshire, shipowner, who was instrumental in the destruction of the Florida, one of the ships of the Armada, off the Island of Mull 1588; also descendant of Tobias Smollett, historian and novelist, and of Sir James Smollett, signatory to the Act of Union; *b* 26 Dec 1914; *m* 1951, Georgina Myra Albina, *qv*, da of Sir Gifford Fox, 2 and last Bt, MP; 1 s, 1 da; *Heir* s, David Telfer Smollett yr of Bonhill b 1953; *Career* 2 Lt HLI 1936, served India 1936, Palestine 1938; serv: Eritrea, Egypt and Italy WW II, Mil Mission to Egypt 1942, Allied Kommandatura Berlin 1948-51, Cyprus 1955-56, Egypt 1956, Maj 1945, ret 1959; memb Royal Co of Archers (Queen's Body guard for Scotland) 1956; vice-cdre Loch Lomond Rowing Club, vice-pres Loch Lomond Motor Cycle Club; KJStJ; *Recreations* skiing, animal husbandry, conservation of rare animals; *Style*— Patrick Telfer Smollett of Bonhill, Esq, MC, DL; Cameron, Alexandria, Dunbartonshire (☎ 0389 56226); 9 Cleveland Row, SW1 (☎ 01 930 6319)

TELFORD, Sir Robert; CBE (1967), DL (Essex 1982); s of Robert Telford; *b* 1 Oct 1915; *Educ* Queen Elizabeth's GS Tamworth, Tamworth Quarry HS Liverpool, Christ's Coll Cambridge; *m* 1, 1941 (m dis 1950); 1 s; m 2, 1958, Elizabeth Mary, da of F W Shelley; 3 da; *Career* chm The Marconi Co Ltd 1981-, chm Marconi Avionics Ltd 1981- (md Marconi Co 1965-81 and previously md and mangr various Marconi subsids), md GEC-Marconi Electronics Ltd 1968-; dir: General Electric Co plc 1973-, Ericsson Radio Systems (Sweden), Canadian Marconi Co (Canada); pres Marconi Italiana (Italy) 1983-; pres Instn of Production Engrs 1982/83; chm: Electronics Avionics requirements Bd of DOI 1981-, Alvey Steering Gp 1983-; memb: Electronics Econ Devpt Ctee 1980-, Cncl of Essex Univ 1980-; Hon FIMechE 1983; Hon DSc: Salford 1981, Cranfield Inst of Technol 1982; FEng, FIEE, FIProdE, CBIM, FRSA; kt 1978; *Style*— Sir Robert Telford, CBE, DL; Marconi House, Chelmsford, Essex CM1 1PL (☎ 0245 353221); Rettendon House, Rettendon, Chelmsford, Essex (☎ 037 44 3131)

TELLING, Arthur Edward; s of Arthur Henry Telling, OBE (d 1972), and Eleanor Mary, *née* Soles (d 1955); *b* 22 April 1920; *Educ* William Ellis Sch London, Jesus Coll Oxford (MA); *m* 21 March 1959, Diana, da of William John Almond (d 1967), of Hessle, E Yorks; *Career* res asst later asst sec Bldg Indust Nat Cncl 1941-48, barr Inner Temple 1949, asst sec and legal advsr Nat Fedn of Property Owners 1949-52, private practice 1953-, lectr Trent Poly 1964-82; memb: Utd Reformed Church, Rotary Club (Nottingham) (Rotary fndn offr dist 122 1974-76, chm N dist London Congregational Union 1958-60); *Books* Planning Applications Appeals and Inquiries (jtly 1963), Planning Law and Procedure (7 edns 1963-86), Water Authorities (1974), contrib Halsbury's Laws of England (3 and 4 edns); *Recreations* reading, watching TV; *Style*— Arthur Telling, Esq; 43 Harrow Rd, W Bridgford, Nottingham NG2 7DW (☎ 0602 231889); 24 The Ropewalk, Nottingham NG1 5EF (☎ 0602 472581, fax 0602 476532)

TELLING, David Malcolm; s of Alfred Caleb Victor Telling, CBE, of Barley Farm, Branches Cross, Wrington, Avon, and Dorothy Lillie, *née* Miller (d 1974); *b* 12 August 1938; *Educ* Cheltenham; *m* 26 Sept 1964, (Margaret Elizabeth) Jane, da of Maj-Gen Francis James Claude Piggott, CB, CBE, DSO, *qv*; 2 da ((Jane Emma) Louise b 12 Aug 1965, (Lucy Jane) Susy b 12 Aug 1969); *Career* serv RM May-Dec 1957, cmmnd 1 Bn KOSB Dec 1957, served in Malaya and Berlin until May 1959; dir HAT Gp plc 1969-86, jt md 1973-76, chief exec 1976-86, chm 1983-86; chm: S Western Industl Cncl 1983-87, Avon Branch Game Conservancy 1987; Freeman City of London 1959, Liveryman of Worshipful Co of Plaisterers; memb Soc of Merchant Adventurers Bristol 1966; FCIOB; *Recreations* stalking, shooting, skiing, water skiing; *Style*— David Telling, Esq; 9/25 Lowndes St, London SW1; Meeting House Farm, Long Lane, Wrington, Bristol, Avon BS18 7SP (☎ 0934 862414); The Estate Office, The Stable Block, Barley Wood, Wrington, Avon BS18 7SA (☎ 0934 862006/862030/862287; fax 0934 862239); car ☎ 0836 506424/587987

TELLWRIGHT, Hon Mrs (Caroline Fiona); *née* Fitzherbert; 2 da of 14 Baron Stafford (d 1986); *b* 13 Oct 1956; *Educ* Sacred Heart Convent, Woldingham; *m* 1981, Kirkland Tellwright, er s of William Tellwright (d 1986), of Market Drayton, Shropshire; 2 da (Turia Mary b 1984, Laura Caroline b 1987); *Career* Housewife; *Recreations* hunting, point-to-point, racing; *Clubs* Pony; *Style*— The Hon Mrs Tellwright; The Sydnall Farm, Woodseaves, Market Drayton, Shropshire

TELTSCHER, Bernard Louis; s of Felix Teltscher (d 1978), of Kingston Upon Thames, and Lillie, *née* Knoepfmacher (d 1961); *b* 18 Feb 1923; *Educ* Czech GS, Breclav UC London (BSc), Trinity Coll Cambridge (MA); *m* 1, 11 Sept 1963 (m dis), Irene Gladys Valerie, da of George Nathaniel Hotten, of Carshalton, Surrey; 1 da (Lisa decd); m 2, 10 Nov 1978 (m dis), Jill Patricia, da of Ivor Cooper, of Cornwall Gdns, London SW7; 1 s (Mark b 1980), 1 da (Natalie b 1981); *Career* wine importer; dir: Teltscher Bros Ltd 1958-, (Chairman 1978-), Ducal Vinery Ltd 1947-, Latymer Wine Shippers Ltd 1974-, Lutomer Bonded Warehouse Co Ltd 1981-, Lutomer Wine Co Ltd 1958-, St James's Bridge Club Ltd 1982-, Wine & Spirit Assoc of GB & NI 1985-86, Wine Devpt Bd 1983-86; Yugoslav Flag with Gold Star; *Recreations* bridge; *Clubs* St James's Bridge, Hurlingham; *Style*— Bernard Teltscher, Esq; 17 Carlyle Square, London SW3 6EX (☎ 01 351 5091); Lutomer House, West India Dock, Prestons Road, London E14 9SB (telex 887896 TELBROG, fax 5153957)

TEMKIN, Prof Jennifer (Mrs Graham Zellick); da of Michael Temkin, of London, and Minnie, *née* Levy; *b* 6 June 1948; *Educ* South Hampstead HS for Girls, LSE, Univ of London (LLB, LLM), Inns of Court Sch of Law; *m* 18 Sept 1975, Prof Graham John Zellick, s of Reginald H Zellick, of Windsor, Berks; 1 s (Adam b 1977), 1 da (Lara b 1980); *Career* barr Middle Temple 1971, lectr in law LSE 1971-89, visiting prof of law Univ of Toronto 1978-79, dean sch of law Univ of Buckingham 1989- (prof of law 1989-); memb: ed advsy gp Howard Journal of Criminal Justice 1984-, scrutiny ctee on draft criminal code Old Bailey 1985-86, ed bd Jl of Criminal Law 1986-, Home Sec's advsy gp on use of video recordings in criminal proceedings 1988-, ctee of heads Univ Law Schs 1989-; *Books* Rape and the Legal Process (1987); *Style*— Prof Jennifer Temkin; Sch of Law, Univ of Buckingham, Buckingham MK18 1EG (☎ 0280 814080)

TEMPEST, Henry Roger; DL (N Yorks 1981); Lord of the Manors of Broughton, Burnsall and Thorpe; yr but only surviving s of Brig-Gen Roger Tempest, CMG, DSO, JP, DL; inherited Broughton Hall Estate on death of elder bro in 1970; *b* 2 April 1924; *Educ* Oratory Sch, Christ Church Oxford; *m* 1957, Janet Evelyn Mary, da of Harold Longton, of Johannesburg; 2 s (Roger Henry b 1963, Piers b 1973), 3 da (Bridget b 1957, Anne b 1959, Mary b 1961); *Career* Scots Gds 1943-47, serv NW Europe (wounded 1945), apptd to Q Staff HQ Gds Div 1945, Staff Capt 1946; Britannia Rubber Co Ltd 1947-51; emigrated to Lusaka (then in Northern Rhodesia) 1952; ACIS 1958, Incorporated Cost Accountant (AACWA) S Africa 1959; returned to UK 1961; fin offr Oxford Univ Dept of Nuclear Physics 1962-72; memb: Skipton Rural Dist Cncl 1973-74, memb Br Computer Soc 1973, exec ctee CLA Yorks 1973-87, cncl Order of St John N Yorks 1977-, pres Skipton Branch 1974, Royal Br Legion, memb N Yorks Co Cncl 1973-85; govr: Craven Coll of Further Educn 1974-85, Skipton Girls' HS 1976-85; FCIS 1971; Kt of Malta; *Clubs* Lansdowne, Pratt's; *Style*— Henry Tempest Esq, DL; Broughton Hall, Skipton, N Yorks BD23 3AE (☎ 0756 2267)

TEMPEST-MOGG, Brenden Dayne; JP (New S Wales 1967); s of Alan Reginald Mogg, JP (NSW), Capt RAAF, and Ethyl Mavis Tempest-Hay; *b* 10 April 1945; *Educ* The Scots Coll Sydney, Univ of NSW (BA), Essex Univ (MA), Hertford Coll Oxford (MLitt), George Washington Univ Washington DC; *m* 27 May 1984 (m dis 1989), Galina, da of Ivan Mikhailovich Kobzev, of Frunze, USSR; 1 da (Gloria Dela Hay b 27 Feb 1987); *Career* pres Warnborough Coll (The American Coll in Oxford) 1973-; visiting lectr in Aust, India, USA 1976-; guest ed Sociological Perspectives 1982-; publisher of Status Quo (Education Gazette) 1987-; conslt on higher educn admin 1988-; *Recreations* sailing, polo, travel, tennis; *Clubs* The Victoria League for Cwlth Friendship, United Oxford and Cambridge, Cowdray Park Polo, Cirencester Park Polo; *Style*— Brenden Tempest-Mogg, Esq, JP; Warnborough College (The American College in Oxford), Boar's Hill, Oxford OX1 5ED (☎ 0865 730901, fax 0865 327796, telex 837574)

TEMPLE, Anthony Dominic Afamado; QC; s of Sir Rawden John Afamado Temple CBE, QC, *qv*, and Margaret, *née* Gunson (d 1980); *b* 21 Sept 1945; *Educ* Haileybury and ISC, Worcester Coll Oxford (MA); *m* 28 May 1983, Susan Elizabeth, s of Ernst Bodansky, of Millmead, Broadbridge Heath, Sussex; 2 da (Jessica Elizabeth b 11 Dec 1985, Alexandra Louise b 21 Aug 1988); *Career* barr; Crown Law Off WAust 1968-69; UK practice 1970; asst recorder 1982; *Recreations* modern pentathlon, travel; *Style*— Anthony Temple, Esq, QC; 4 Pump Court, London EC4 (☎ 01 353 2656, fax 01 583 2036, telex 8813250 REFLEX G)

TEMPLE, Derek Anthony; s of late Oscar Vincent Athelstan Temple; *b* 8 June 1923; *Educ* Salvatorian Coll Harrow Weald, Royal Sch of Mines London (ARSM, BSc Eng), Trinity Hall Cambridge (PhD); *m* 1949, Peggy Jean, da of S E Dunn; 2 da; *Career* metallurgical engr; dir and chief exec ISP Ltd (RTZ Group) 1970-82, dir-gen Zinc and Lead Devpt Assocs 1982-86; pres Inst of Mining & Metallurgy 1979-80; govr Camborne Sch of Mines, Cornwall; Liveryman Worshipful Co of Engnrs 1984; FEng; *Recreations* domestic; *Clubs* Utd Oxford and Cambridge; *Style*— Dr Derek Temple; 18 Heathfield, Royston, S Cambs SG8 5BW (☎ 0763 41782)

TEMPLE, His Hon Judge Ernest Sanderson; MBE (1946), QC (1969); s of Ernest Temple (d 1957); *b* 23 May 1921; *Educ* Kendal Sch, Queen's Coll Oxford; *m* 1946, June Debonnaire, *née* Saunders; 1 s, 2 da; *Career* served Army, India and Burma Temp Lt-Col (despatches); barr Gray's Inn 1943; dep chm Westmorland QS 1967-68, chm 1968-71; former asst rec Salford and Blackburn, rec Crown Court 1971-77, hon rec of Kendal 1972, circuit-judge and rec of Liverpool 1977-; hon rec Lancaster 1987; former memb Bar Cncl, dep chm Agric Land Tbnl; jt master Vale of Lune Harriers 1963-85; hon fell Clerks of Works Soc; *Recreations* farming and horses; *Clubs* Racquet Liverpool; *Style*— His Hon Judge Temple, MBE, QC; Yealand Hall, Yealand Redmayne, nr Carnforth LA5 9TD (☎ 0524 781200)

TEMPLE, Lt-Col Guy; MC (1953); s of Maj-Gen B Temple, CB, CMG, MC (d 1973), and Dulcibella, *née* Radcliffe (d 1982); *b* 16 Sept 1928; *Educ* Radley, RMA Sandhurst; *m* 7 Jan 1956, Caroline, da of Capt H F Bone, DSO, DSC, RN (d 1982); 1 s (Piers b 1963), 3 da (Deborah b 1956, Bridget (Mrs Ter Haar) b 1958, Miranda (Mrs Leenen) b 1961); *Career* cmmnd Gloucestershire Regt 1948, served Jamaica 1949 and Korea (Battle of Imjin) 1950-53, dist mil intelligence offr Kenya 1955-57, Cyprus 1958-60, HQ Libya 1963-66, HQ Army Strategic Cmd 1968-70, Glasgow Univ 1970-72, Dubai Def Force 1972-79, dir of logistics HQ Central Cmd Dubai 1979-; fndr Dubai Offshore SC; Dubai Medal 1976, UAE Medal 1980; *Recreations* sailing, tennis; *Style*— Lt-Col Guy Temple, MC; HQ Central Mil Command, PO Box 854, Dubai, United Arab Emirates, Arabian Gulf (☎ Dubai 440454, car tel 050 28638, telex 45915 CMC EM)

TEMPLE, Sir John Meredith; JP (Cheshire 1949), DL (1975); s of Tom Temple (d 1955); *b* 9 June 1910; *Educ* Charterhouse, Clare Coll Cambridge; *m* 1942, Nancy Violet, da of Brig-Gen Robert Hare, CMG, DSO, DL; 1 s, 1 da; *Career* farmer, landowner; memb Lloyd's 1938; MP (C) Chester 1956-74, special rep from House of Commons at UN XXVI Gen Assembly 1971; High Sheriff Cheshire 1980-81; kt 1982; *Recreations* travel; *Clubs* Carlton, Army and Navy, Racquet (Liverpool), City (Chester); *Style*— Sir John Temple, JP, DL; Picton Gorse, Chester (☎ 0244 300239)

TEMPLE, Kenneth James Noel; s of Richard James Temple; *b* 10 Dec 1919; *Educ* Godalming Surrey; *m* 1943, Kathleen Mary; 1 child; *Career* RAF 1940-45, Flt Engr; sales rep 1951-76, dir Drake & Son Ltd 1976-, md 1980- (Weymouth, Torquay, Exeter, Yeovil); *Books* Travel; *Style*— Kenneth Temple, Esq; 42 Brunel Rd, Elberry Cove, Paignton, Devon TQ4 6HW

TEMPLE, Marie, Lady; Marie Wanda; da of late F C Henderson, of Bombay, India; *m* 1939, as his 2 w, Sir Richard Durand Temple, 3 Bt, DSO (d 1962); *Style*— Marie, Lady Temple

TEMPLE, Ralph; s of Harry Temple (d in active service 1941), and Julia, *née* Glassman; *b* 15 Nov 1933; *Educ* Hackney Downs GS; *m* 22 May 1955, Patricia Yvonne, da of Samuel Gould (of 1975) of London; 2 s (Graham Robin b 23 April 1958, Howard Jeremy b 28 March 1960); *Career* managing clerk Wilson Wright and Co CA's 1955-61; Tesco plc: sr exec 1961-73, gp fin dir 1973-83, jt gp md 1983-85; md Temple Conslts (fin conslts) 1986-; Freeman City Of London, FCA 1956, FCT 1979; *Recreations* travel, bridge, keepfit; *Style*— Ralph Temple, Esq; 2 Culverlands Close, Stanmore, Middx, HA7 3AG

TEMPLE, Sir Rawden John Afamado; CBE (1964), QC (1951); *b* 1908; *Educ* King Edward's Sch Birmingham, Queen's Coll Oxford; *m* 1936, Margaret (d 1980), da of Sir James Gunson, CMG, CBE; 2 s; *Career* barr 1931, master of bench Inner Temple 1960, tres 1983; chief social security cmmr 1975-81, child benefit referee 1976-; vice-chm General Cncl of the Bar 1960-64, memb Industl Injuries Advsy Cncl; kt 1980; *Recreations* fishing; *Style*— Sir Rawden Temple, CBE, QC; 3 North King's Bench Walk, Temple, EC4 (☎ 01 353 6420)

TEMPLE, Reginald Robert; CMG (1979); s of Lt-Gen R C Temple CB, OBE, RM (d 1959); gs of Col William Temple VC (d 1919) and of Vere David Urquhart Hunt, JP, of Cummer More, Co Tipperary; *b* 12 Feb 1922; *Educ* Wellington, Peterhouse Cambridge; *m* 1, 1952 (m dis 1979), Julia Anthony; 1 s, 1 da; m 2, 1979, Susan McCorquodale, *née* Pick; 1 da, 1 step s, 1 step da; *Career* Maj, RE serv ME and Europe 1940-46; American Silver Star 1944; stockbroking 1947-51; HM Dip Serv 1951-79; Sultanate of Oman Govt Serv 1979-85; Order of Oman 3rd Class 1985; *Recreations* sailing; *Clubs* Royal Cruising, Royal Ocean Racing, Army and Navy; *Style*— Reginald Temple, Esq, CMG; Scarlett House, Scarlett, Nr Castletown, Isle of Man

TEMPLE, Richard; s and h of Sir Richard Antony Purbeck Temple, 4 Bt, MC; *b* 17 August 1937; *m* 1964, Emma Rose, da of late Maj-Gen Sir Robert Edward Laycock, KCMG, CB, DSO; 3 da; *Style*— Richard Temple, Esq; 79 Lansdowne Rd, London W11

TEMPLE, Sir Richard Anthony Purbeck; 4 Bt (UK 1876), MC (1941); s of Sir Richard Durand Temple, 3 Bt, DSO (d 1962); *b* 19 Jan 1913; *Educ* Stowe, Trinity Hall Cambridge; *m* 1, 1936 (m dis 1946), Lucy Geils, da of late Alain Joly de Lotbiniere, of Montreal; 2 s; m 2, 1950, Jean, da of late James T Finnie, and widow of Oliver P Croom-Johnson; 1 da; *Heir* s, Richard Temple; *Career* serv WWII (wounded), former Maj KRRC; *Clubs* Army and Navy; *Style*— Sir Richard Temple, Bt, MC; c/o The National Westminster Bank Ltd, 94 Kensington High St, London W8

TEMPLE OF STOWE, 8 Earl (UK 1822); (Walter) Grenville Algernon Temple-Gore-Langton; o s of Cdr Hon Evelyn Arthur Grenville Temple-Gore-Langton, DSO, RN (d 1972; yst s of 4 Earl), and Irene, *née* Gartside- Spaight (d 1967); s his cousin 7 Earl Temple of Stowe 1988; *b* 2 Oct 1924; *Educ* Nautical Coll Pangbourne; *m* 1, 24 July 1954, Zillah Ray (d 1966), da of James Boxall, of Fir Grove, Tillington, Petworth, Sussex; 2 s (James Grenville, Lord Langton b 1955, Hon Robert Chandos b 1957), 1 da (Lady Anna Clare b 1960); m 2, 1 June 1968, (Margaret) Elizabeth Graham, o da of Col Henry William Scarth of Breckness, of Skaill House, Orkney; *Heir* s, Lord Langton, *qv*; *Style*— The Rt Hon the Earl Temple of Stowe; Garth, Outertown, Stromness, Orkney; The Cottage, Easton, Winchester, Hants

TEMPLE-GORE-LANGTON, Lady Anna Clare; o da of 8 Earl Temple of Stowe, *qv*; *b* 19 May 1960; *Style*— Lady Anna Temple-Gore-Langton

TEMPLE-GORE-LANGTON, Hon Robert Chandos; yr s of 8 Earl Temple of Stowe, *qv*; *b* 22 Nov 1957; *Educ* Eton; *m* 1985, Susan Penelope, er da of David Cavender, of Avishays, Chard, Somerset; 52 Archbishops Place, London SW2

TEMPLE-MORRIS, Peter; MP (Cons Leominster Feb 1974-); s of His Honour Sir Owen Temple-Morris, (d 1985), and Vera, *née* Thompson; *b* 12 Feb 1938, in Cardiff; *Educ* Malvern, St Catharine's Coll Cambridge; *m* 1964, Taheré, e da of H E Senator Khozeimé Alam, of Teheran; 2 s, 2 da; *Career* barr Inner Temple 1962, memb exec ctee Soc of Cons Lawyers 1968-71, chm Hampstead Cons Political Centre 1971-73, second prosecuting counsel Inland Revenue on SE Circuit 1971-74, PPS to sec of state for transport 1979; sec Br Iranian Parly Gp; chm: Br Lebanese Parly Gp, Br Gp Inter-Parly Union 1982-85 (exec 1976-); vice-chm: Cons Parly For Affrs Ctee, vice chm UK-USSR Parly Gp, All Pty Southern Africa Gp, nat tres UN Assoc Cncl, GB-USSR Assoc; memb Commons Select Ctee on Foreign Affairs; *Recreations* shooting, wine, food, family; *Style*— Peter Temple-Morris, Esq, MP; House of Commons, London SW1; Huntington Court, Three Elms, Hereford HR4 7RA (☎ 0432 272684)

TEMPLE-RICHARDS, Susan Mary; da of Capt Neville Roland Joseph Bradshaw (d 1975), of Withypool, Lewes, Sussex, and Dorothy Mary Arnold, *née* Saunders; *b* 8 June 1932; *Educ* Cheltenham Ladies Coll, Badminton Sch Bristol, Westfield Coll London (BA); *m* 6 June 1964, Peter Henry John Temple-Richards (d 1975), s of Brig Harold Beecham Temple-Richards (d 1969), of Hindringham Hall, Fakenham, Norfolk; *Career* MOD 1956-58 and 1974-86, PA to Lord Hunt (formerly Sir John Hunt) 1960-62, self employed charitable organiser 1966-74; tst memb Arts Educn Schs 1976, chm Newbury Duke of Edinburgh's Award Ctee 1977-80, cncl memb Br Epilepsy Assoc 1982-89; tstees' Duke of Edinburgh's Award Ctee 1962-66; sec Br Soviet Pamirs Expedition 1962; Freeman City of London 1976; FRGS 1963; *Recreations* sailing, gardening, travelling, opera; *Clubs* Cripplegate Ward; *Style*— Mrs Susan Temple-Richards; 13 Culmstock Rd, London SW11 6LZ (☎ 01 228 9815)

TEMPLEMAN, Hon Michael Richard; s of Baron Templeman (Life Peer); *b* 1951; *m* 1974, Lesley Frances, da of Henry Davis; children; *Style*— The Hon Michael Templeman

TEMPLEMAN, The Rev the Hon Peter Morton; er s of Baron Templeman (Life Peer); *b* 1949; *m* 1973, Ann Joyce, da of Peter Williams; children; *Style*— The Rev the Hon Peter Templeman

TEMPLEMAN, Baron (Life Peer 1982); Sydney William Templeman; MBE (1946), PC (1978); s of Herbert Templeman; *b* 3 Mar 1920; *Educ* Southall GS, St John's Cambridge (Hon Fellow 1982); *m* 1946, Margaret Joan, *née* Rowles; 2 s; *Career* barr 1947, QC 1964, memb Middle Temple & Lincoln's Inn, former memb Bar Cncl, bencher Middle Temple; tres 1987; lord justice of Appeal 1978-82, ld of appeal in ordinary 1982-, High Ct judge (Chancery) 1972-78, attorney-gen Duchy Lancaster 1970-72, pres Bar Assoc for Commerce Fin & Indust 1982-; Hon DLitt Reading 1980, Hon LLD Birmingham 1986; Hon Memb: Canadian & American Bar Assocs; former pres Senate of Inns of Ct & Bar; kt 1972; *Style*— The Rt Hon Lord Templeman, MBE, PC; Manor Heath, Knowl Hill, Woking, Surrey (☎ 048 62 61930)

TEMPLER, Maj-Gen James Robert; OBE (1978), MBE (1973); s of Brig Cecil

Robert Templer, DSO (d 1986), and Angela Mary, *née* Henderson; *b* 8 Jan 1936; *Educ* Charterhouse, RMA Sandhurst; *m* 1, 1963 (m dis 1979); 2 s (William b 1964, Tristram b 1969), 1 da (Sophie b 1966); m 2, 18 July 1981, Sarah Ann (Sally), da of Capt W K Rogers, DSC, RM, of Nether Wallop; *Career* 2 Lt 41 and 4 Regt BAOR 1956-59, Lt Kings Troop RHA 1960-63, Capt 6 Regt Borneo 1964-66, Staff Coll 1967, Maj GSO2 3 Div UK 1968-69, BC 5 and 3 Regt NI 1970-72, GSO2 Sch of Artillery 1973, Lt-Col instr Staff Coll 1974-75, CO 42 Regt 1976, CO 5 Regt 1977, GSO1 MOD 1978, Col (later Brig) CRA 2 Armd Div 1979-81, Study Artillery in 90's 1982, RCDS 1983, ACOS Trg HQ UKLF 1984-86, Maj-Gen ACDS MOD 1986-; Br Nat Cross Country Ski Champion 1958; riding: Euro Individual Champion 3 day event 1962, RA Gold Cup Sandown 1962 and 1963, Burghley 1962, Munich 1963, Badminton 1964; memb Br Olympic 3 day event team Tokyo; FBIM 1988; *Recreations* riding, sailing, skiing, gardening, shooting, fishing; *Style—* Maj-Gen James Templer, OBE; c/o Lloyds Bank Ltd, Crediton, Devon

TEMPLETON, Prof (Alexander) Allan; s of Richard Templeton (d 1968), of Aberdeen, and Minnie, *née* Whitfield; *b* 28 June 1946; *Educ* Aberdeen GS, Aberdeen Univ (MB, ChB, MD); *m* 17 Dec 1980, Gillian Constance, da of Geoffrey William Penney, of Eastbourne; 3 s (Richard b 1981, Robbie b 1983, Peter b 1987), 1 da (Kate b 1985); *Career* regius prof of obstetrics and gynaecology Aberdeen Univ 1985-; various pubns on Human Infertility and Gynacological Endocrinology; MRCOG 1974, FRCOG 1987; *Recreations* mountaineering; *Clubs* Royal Northern and Univ; *Style—* Prof Allan Templeton; Aultmore, Maryculter, Aberdeenshire AB1 OBJ (☎ 0224 733947)

TEMPLETON, (William) Berry; s of Douglas Joseph Templeton (d 1948), and Elizabeth Jane, *née* Caton (d 1964); *b* 13 Sept 1925; *Educ* Birkenhead Sch, Liverpool Univ; *m* 1, 5 Oct 1946 (m dis 1961), Sheila Joan, da of the Arthur Leuty; m 2, 3 April 1962, Adele Monica, da of late Louis Arthur Westley ; *Career* chm W Berry Templeton Ltd 1963-, vice-chm Gateway Bldg Soc 1985-88; dir: Woolwich Equitable Bldg Soc 1988-, Woolwich Homes 1988-, (Woolwich Homes (1987) Ltd) 1988-; KS & J; Freeman City of London, memb Guild of Freeman; memb: AMInstBE, MCIOB; FFB; *Recreations* horse racing, polo, music, ballet; *Clubs* Oriental, Guards Polo; *Style—* Berry Templeton, Esq; 39 York Terrace East, Regent's Park, London NW1 4PT (☎ 01 486 2209)

TEMPLETON, Richard; s of Capt John Templeton (d 1953), of Maelsllech Farm, Radyr, Cardiff, and Janet *née* Morgan; *b* 11 April 1945; *Educ* Clifton, Reading Univ (BA), Bradford Univ (MSc); *m* Belinda Susan, da of Tim Timlin, of Harewood House, Scotland End, Hook Norton, Oxon; *Career* trainee analyst Philips & Drew stockbrokers 1969-71, dir Robert Fleming Ltd 1980 (1971-); Freeman Town of Llantrisant; ASIA 1972; *Recreations* beagling, reading; *Clubs* Turf, MCC; *Style—* Richard Templeton, Esq; 25 Copthall Ave, London, EC2R 7DR (☎ 01 638 5858, 01 638 9100)

TENBY, 3 Viscount (UK 1957) William Lloyd-George; JP (Hants); s of 1 Viscount Tenby, TD, PC (d 1967), s of 1 Earl Lloyd George; suc bro, 2 Viscount 1983; *b* 7 Nov 1927; *Educ* Eastbourne Coll, St Catharine's Coll Cambridge (BA); *m* 1955, Ursula, da of late Lt-Col Henry Edward Medlicott, DSO; 1 s (Timothy b 1962), 2 da (Hon Sara Gwenfron b 1957, Clare Mair b 1961); *Heir* s, Timothy Henry Gwilym *qv*; *Career* Capt RWF (TA); PR advsr to chm Kleinwort Benson Ltd; *Style—* The Rt Hon the Viscount Tenby, JP; Triggs, Crondall, nr Farnham, Surrey GU10 5RU (☎ 0252 850592)

TENCH, William Henry; CBE (1980); s of Henry George Tench (d 1970), and Emma Rose, *née* Orsborn (d 1980); *b* 2 August 1921; *Educ* Portsmouth GS; *m* 4 Nov 1944, Margaret, da of Harry Edwin Ireland (d 1966); 1 da (Anne Margaret (Mrs Kingston) b 1950); *Career* RN 1939-46, pilot 1940-, released Lt (A) RNVR 1946, airline pilot 1947-55; inspr of accidents Miny of Tport 1955-73, chief inspr of accidents Dept of Trade 1974-81, ret 1981, conslt on aircraft accidnet investigation MOD 1986, advsr on air Safety to Cmmr for Tport EEC; FRAeS; *Books* Safety is no Accident (1985); *Recreations* sailing, music; *Style—* William Tench, Esq, CBE; Seaways, Restronguet Point, Feock, Cornwall TR3 6RB (☎ 0872 865 434)

TENISON; *see*: King-Tenison

TENNANT, Anthony John; s of Maj John Tennant, TD (d 1967), and Hon Antonia Mary Roby Benson (later Viscountess Radcliffe, d 1982), da of 1 Baron Charnwood; *b* 5 Nov 1930; *Educ* Eton, Trinity Coll Cambridge (BA); *m* 1954, Rosemary Violet, da of Col Henry Charles Minshull, of Stockdale (d 1982); 2 s (Christopher, Patrick); *Career* cmmnd Scots Guards, served in Malaya; account exec Ogilvy & Mather 1953, dir: Mather & Crowther 1960-66, Tennant & Sturge 1966-70, Watney Mann & Truman 1970-76; dep md Int Distillers & Vintners 1976, md Int Distillers & Vintners Ltd 1977-83, Bd of Grand Metropolitan plc 1977-87; gp md Grand Metropolitan plc 1983-87, chm Int Distillers & Vintners Ltd 1983-87; dir: Close Brothers Gp plc, El Oro Mining & Exploration plc, Exploration Co plc; joined Guinness plc as gp chief exec March 1987; cncl memb Food from Britain; *Clubs* Boodles; *Style—* Anthony Tennant Esq; Guinness plc, 39 Portman Square, London W1H 9HB (☎ 01 486 0288, telex 23368)

TENNANT, Hon Charles Edward Pevensey; s and h of 3 Baron Glenconner; *b* 15 Feb 1957; *Style—* The Hon Charles Tennant; 50 Victoria Rd, London W8

TENNANT, Hon Christopher Cary; 3 s of 3 Baron Glenconner; *b* 1967; *Educ* Stanbridge Earls; *Style—* The Hon Christopher Tennant

TENNANT, Lady Emma; *née* Cavendish; da of 11 Duke of Devonshire, MC, PC; *b* 1943; *m* 1963, Hon Tobias William Tennant (s by 2 m of late 2 Baron Glenconner); 1 s, 2 da; *Style—* Lady Emma Tennant; Shaws, Newcastleton, Roxburghshire

TENNANT, Hon Mrs Emma Christina; *née* Tennant; da of late 2 Baron Glenconner by his 2 w; *b* 20 Oct 1937; *Educ* St Paul's Girls Sch; *m* 1, 1957 (m dis 1962), Sebastian, s of Henry Yorke and Hon Mrs (Adelaide) Yorke, *qv*, da of 2 Baron Biddulph; m 2, 1963 (m dis), Christopher Booker, journalist and author, *qv*; m 3, 1968 (m dis 1973), Alexander, s of Claud Cockburn, the journalist, *qv*, and Patricia, da of John Arbuthnot, MVO, ggs of Sir William Arbuthnot, 1 Bt; *Career* novelist (as Emma Tennant); author of 8 novels, incl The Bad Sister, Wild Nights; latest work: The House of Hospitalities (1983); founder ed literary newspaper Bananas; FRSL; *Recreations* exploring, walking in Dorset; *Style—* The Hon Mrs Emma Tennant; c/o A.D. Peters Ltd

TENNANT, Lady Harriot; *née* Pleydell-Bouverie; da of 7 Earl of Radnor, KG, KCVO, JP, DL (d 1968), by his 1 w; *b* 18 Dec 1935; *m* 11 Dec 1965, Mark Iain Tennant of Balfluig, *qv*; 1 s (Lysander Philip Roby b 1968), 1 da (Sophia Roby b 1967); *Style—* Lady Harriot Tennant; Balfluig Castle, Alford, Aberdeenshire AB3 8EJ

TENNANT, Hon Henry Lovell; 2 s of 3 Baron Glenconner; *b* 1960; *Educ* Eton; *m* 1983, Teresa Mary, yst da of John McRae Cormack, AFC; 1 s (Euan Lovell b 1983); *Style—* The Hon Henry Tennant; Hill Lodge, Hillsleigh Rd, London W8

TENNANT, Sir Iain Mark; KT (1986), JP (Morayshire 1961); s of Lt-Col John Edward Tennant, DSO, MC (d 1942; gs of Sir Charles Tennant, 1 Bt, and n of 1 Baron Glenconner), of Innes House, Elgin, and his 1 w, Georgina Helen, da of Sir George Kirkpatrick, KCB, KCSI; *b* 11 Mar 1919; *Educ* Eton, Magdalene Coll Cambridge; *m* 11 July 1946, Lady Margaret Helen Isla Marion, *née* Ogilvy (*see* Lady Margaret Tennant); 2 s (Mark b 1947, Christopher b 1950), 1 da (Emma (Mrs Cheape) b 1954); *Career* Capt Scots Gds 1941, served N Africa 1940-42; memb Royal Co of Archers (Queen's Body Guard for Scotland) and Ensign 1981, Lt 1988; HM Lord-Lt for Morayshire 1963- (DL 1954); chm: Bd of Govrs of Gordonstoun Sch 1957-72, Glenlivet Distillers 1964-84, Scottish Northern Investmt Tst 1964-84, Grampian TV 1967-, Seagram Distillers 1979-84; Crown Estate cmmr 1970-; dir: Clydesdale Bank 1968-, Abbey National Bldg Soc 1981- (chm Scottish Advsy Bd 1981-, memb 1968-); former dir Times Publishing Co Ltd, memb Newspaper Panel Monopolies and Mergers Cmmn; FRSA 1971, CBIM 1983; *Recreations* country pursuits; *Style—* Sir Iain Tennant, JP; Lochnabo House, Lhanbryde, Morayshire (☎ 0343 84 2228); Innes House, Elgin, Morayshire (☎ 0343 84 2410, fax 0343 84 3053)

TENNANT, Hon Mrs (Irene Adelaide); *née* Gage; da of 5 Viscount Gage and Leila, *née* Peel (great niece of Sir Robert Peel, the PM); *b* 9 Feb 1898; *m* 1, 1923 (m annulled 1928), Capt Murray Shuldham-Legh; m 2, 1928, Maj Frederick Bull (m dis 1950); 1 s, 1 da; m 3, 1950, Ernest Tennant, OBE (d 1962, kinsman of the Barons Glenconner); *Style—* The Hon Mrs Tennant; Grove House, Great Bardfield, Essex (☎ 0371 810398)

TENNANT, Hon James Grey Herbert; 2 s of late 2 Baron Glenconner by his 1 w; *b* 5 Mar 1929; *Educ* Eton, Trinity Coll Cambridge; *m* 1, 1955, Emily (m dis 1962), da of George Licos, of Khartoum and Cairo; 1 s; m 2, 1962, Mrs Elizabeth Romer, da of James Daløes, of W Vancouver; *Career* 2 Lt RHG, asst adj 1949; Gold Staff Offr at Coronation of HM The Queen 1953; chm Tennant Guaranty Ltd; has Coronation Medal 1953; FRGS; *Recreations* shooting, riding; *Clubs* White's, RAC; *Style—* The Hon James Tennant; 25 St Leonard's Terrace, Londson SW3 (☎ 01 730 6984)

TENNANT, Julian William Fiaschi; s of Ernest William Dalrymple Tennant (s of William Tennant, who was 4 cous of 1 Baron Glenconner, Margot Asquith, Baroness Elliot of Harwood, late Lady Ribblesdale and late Lady Crathorne); *b* 1 August 1924; *Educ* Eton; *m* 1954, Miranda, da of Capt Sidney Fairbairn, of Steventon Rectory (a previous occupant of which was Jane Austen), Steventon, nr Basingstoke; 1 s (Mungo), 2 da (Nell, Angela); *Career* served Capt Coldstream Gds (Gds Armd Div); chm: C Tennant & Sons 1973-80, Ingersoll Locks 1956-80, Daphne's Restaurant 1970-, Jermyn Street Travel 1981-; *Recreations* gardening, good food; *Clubs* Saints & Sinners, Whites; *Style—* Julian Tennant, Esq; 112 Draycott Ave, London SW3 (☎ 01 589 9898); Plush Manor, Plush, Dorchester, Dorset (☎ Piddletrenthide 030 04 516)

TENNANT, Lady Margaret Isla Marion; *née* Ogilvy; 2 da of 12 Earl of Airlie, KT, GCVO, MC (d 1968), and Lady Alexandra Coke (d 1984), da of 3 Earl of Leicester; *b* 23 July 1920; *m* 11 July 1946, Sir Iain Mark Tennant, KT JP, *qv*; 2 s, 1 da; *Career* formerly with WRNS; vice-chm Cancer Relief 1981-; *Style—* Lady Margaret Tennant; Lochnabo House, Elgin, Morayshire (☎ 034 384 2228)

TENNANT, Sir Mark Dalcour; KCMG (1964, CMG 1951), CB (1961); s of N R D Tennant; *b* 26 Dec 1911; *Educ* Marlborough, New Coll Oxford; *m* 1936, Clare, da of Sir Ross Barker, KCIE, CB; *Career* served WWII RA, entered Miny of Lab 1935, memb UK Delgn Int Lab Conferences 1949-53, IDC 1856, sec gen Monkton Cmmn on Review of Constitution of Rhodesia and Nyasaland 1960, dir Orgn and Estabs Miny Labour 1960, see Centl African Off 1962-64, third sec Treasy 1970-71 (Miny Public Bldg and Works and DOE 1965-70); *Clubs* Travellers'; *Style—* Sir Mark Tennant, KCMG, CB; c/o Barclays Bank, 1 Pall Mall East, London SW1

TENNANT, Sir Peter Frank Dalrymple; CMG (1958), OBE (1944); s of late G F D Tennant, of St Margarets, Herts; *b* 29 Nov 1910; *Educ* Marlborough, Trinity Coll Cambridge, (MA Cambridge and Oxford); *m* 1, 1934 (m dis 1952), da of Prof Fellenius, of Stockholm; 1 s, 2 da; m 2, 1953, Galina Bosley, da of K Grunberg, of Helsinki; 1 s (step); *Career* fell and univ lectr Queens' Coll Cambridge 1934-39, press attaché Br Legation Stockholm 1939-45; info cnsllr Br Embassy Paris 1945-50, dep cmdt Br Sector Berlin 1950-52, overseas dir FBI 1952-63, dep dir-gen FBI 1963-64, formerly memb Cncl of Industl Design, dir-gen Br Nat Export Cncl 1965-71; dir: Barclays Bank SA Paris, Prudential Assur Co 1973-81, Prudential Corpn 1979-86, C Tennant Sons & Co Ltd, Anglo-Rumanian Bank, Northern Engrg Industs (Int) Ltd, Int Energy Bank; industl advsr Barclays Bank Int 1972-81; chm: Gabbitas Thring Educn Tst, pres and chm London C of C, memb bd Centre for Int Briefing, actg chm Wilton Park Academic Cncl to 1983, chm UK ctee Euro Culture Fndn, tstee and former chm Heinz Koeppler Tst for Wilton Park; kt 1972; *Books* Ibsen's Dramatic Technique, The Scandinavian Book; *Recreations* painting, writing, talking; *Clubs* Travellers; *Style—* Sir Peter Tennant, CMG, OBE; Blue Anchor House, Linchmere Rd, Haslemere, Surrey GU27 3QF (☎ 0428 3124)

TENNANT, Hon Tobias William; s of late 2 Baron Glenconner by his 2 w; *b* 1 June 1941; *Educ* Eton, New Coll Oxford; *m* 1963, Lady Emma Cavendish, er da of 11 Duke of Devonshire, MC, DL; 1 s, 2 da; *Career* sometime pres OUBC; *Style—* The Hon Tobias Tennant; Shaws, Newcastleton, Roxburghshire (☎ Steele Road 241)

TENNANT OF BALFLUIG, Mark Iain; Baron of Balfluig; s of Maj John Tennant, TD (d 1967), of Budds Farm, Wittersham, Kent, and Hon Antonia Mary Roby Benson (later Viscountess Radcliffe; d 1982), da of 1 Baron Charnwood; *b* 4 Dec 1932; *Educ* Eton, New Coll Oxford (MA 1959); *m* 11 Dec 1965, Lady Harriot Pleydell-Bouverie, da of 7 Earl of Radnor, KG, KCVO, JP, DL (d 1968); 1 s (Lysander Philip Roby b 1968), 1 da (Sophia Roby b 1967); *Career* Lt The Rifle Bde (SRO); barr Inner Temple 1958, Master of the Bench 1984, rec Crown Ct 1987, master of the Supreme Ct, Queen's Bench Div 1988; chm Royal Orchestral Soc for Amateur Musicians 1989; *Clubs* Brooks's; *Style—* Mr Tennant; Balfluig Castle, Aberdeenshire AB3 8EJ; Royal Courts of Justice, Strand, London WC2A 2LL

TENNENT, John Michael; s of Capt John Harvey Tennent, MC (d 1978), and Mary Lilian, *née* Stevenson (d 1958); *b* 5 Feb 1929; *Educ* Charterhouse; *m* 8 Sept 1956, Rosalind Jane Mallord, da of Charles Wilfrid Mallord Turner (d 1979); 2 s (Richard

Michael b and d 1960, John Charles Roger b 1964), 1 da (Julie Rosalind Mary b 1962); *Career* cmmnd Lt 1947-49; qualified CA 1954; md Corporate Advsrs Ltd, chm various cos; ctee memb: NASDIM, FIMBRA; Liveryman Worshipful Co of Coach Makers 1956; memb ICEAW 1954 ; *Books* Practical Liquidity Management (1974), The Hesitant Heart (1988); *Recreations* yachting, tennis; *Clubs* Cumberland Tennis, IOD; *Style*— Michael Tennent, Esq; 4 Brendon Close, Esher, Surrey (☎ 0372 64283)

TENNYSON, 4 Baron (UK 1884); Harold Christopher Tennyson; s of 3 Baron Tennyson (d 1951; a notable cricketer who captained Hants and (in four Test Matches v Australia in 1921) England; he was in turn gs of the Victorian Poet Laureate and 1 Baron), and of the Hon Clarissa, *née* Tennant (d 1960), da of 1 Baron Glenconner; *b* 25 Mar 1919; *Educ* Eton, Trinity Coll Cambridge (BA); *Heir* bro, Hon Mark Aubrey Tennyson, DSC, RN (ret); *Career* employed WO 1939-46; co-fndr (with Sir Charles Tennyson, CMG) of Tennyson Res Centre, Lincoln; Hon Freeman City of Lincoln 1964; *Clubs* White's, Royal Automobile, Royal and Ancient, Beefsteak; *Style*— The Rt Hon the Lord Tennyson; 18 Rue Galilée, 75016 Paris, France

TENNYSON, Hon Mark Aubrey; DSC (1943); s of 3 Baron Tennyson (d 1951), and hp of bro, 4 Baron; *b* 28 Mar 1920; *Educ* RNC Dartmouth; *m* 1964, Deline Celeste Budler; *Career* 1939-45 War (despatches, DSC), Cdr RN 1954; *Clubs* White's, Royal Yacht Squadron; *Style*— The Hon Mark Tennyson, DSC; 13 Cumnor Av, Kenilworth, 7700 Cape Town, SA

TENNYSON-D'EYNCOURT, Sir Giles Gervais; 4 Bt (UK 1930), of Carter's Corner Farm, Parish of Herstmonceux, Co Sussex; s of Sir (Eustace) Gervais Tennyson-d'Eyncourt, 2 Bt (d 1971); s bro, Sir Jeremy Tennyson-d'Eyncourt, 3 Bt (d 1988); *b* 16 April 1935; *Educ* Eton, Millfield; *m* 1966, Juanita, da of late Fortunato Borromeo; 1 s; *Heir* s, Mark Gervais Tennyson-d'Eyncourt b 12 March 1967; *Career* late Capt Coldstream Gds; *Style*— Sir Giles Tennyson-d'Eyncourt, Bt; 20 Cranmer Court, Sloane Avenue, London SW3

TENNYSON-D'EYNCOURT, Norah, Lady; Norah; *née* Gill; da of late Thomas Gill, of Sheffield; *m* 1977, as his 3 w, Sir (John) Jeremy Eustace Tennyson-d'Eyncourt, 3 Bt (d 1988); *Style*— George Carter Esq; Bayons House, Hinton St George, Somerset

TENNYSON-D'EYNCOURT, Vinnie, Lady; Vinnie Lorraine; da of late Andrew Pearson, of Minneapolis, USA ; *m* 1, Robert J O'Donnell (decd); m 2, 1964, as his 2 w, Sir (Eustace) Gervais Tennyson-d'Eyncourt, 2 Bt (d 1971); *Style*— Vinnie, Lady Tennyson-d'Eyncourt; Catalino Pueblo, 2556 Avenida Maria, Tucson, Arizona 85718, USA

TEO, Sir (Fiatau) Penitala; GCMG (1979), ISO (1970), MBE (1956); *b* 1911,July; married with children; *Career* govr-gen Tuvalu 1978-; *Style*— Sir Penitala Teō, GCMG, ISO, MBE; Alapi, Funafuti, Tuvalu

TERENGHI, Mario; s of Emilio Giuseppe Terenghi, and Luigia, *née* Ripamonti; *b* 28 May 1927; *Educ* HS of Commerce Monza, Universita Cattolica Milan; *m* 8 Dec 1983, Airdrie Melba Joyce, da of Robert Lloyd George Armstrong (d 1959); *Career* exec dir Orion Banking Gp 1975-80; dir: Orion Multinat Servs Ltd 1975-80 (chm), Orion Pacific Ltd Hong Kong 1975-80, Orion Leasing Hldgs Ltd 1975-80, Libra Banks Ltd 1975-84; sr mangr Credito Italiano SpA 1981-84 (1946-75), md Credito Italiano Int Ltd 1984-; FInstD; Knight of the Italian Republic; *Style*— Mario Terenghi, Esq; Lombard Assoc, Foreign Banks Assoc, 21 Redcliffe Rd, London SW10 9NP Credito Italiano Int Ltd, 17A Moorgate, London EC2R 6HX (☎ 01 600 3616, fax 01 826 8927, telex 8814392)

TERLEZKI, Stefan; MP (C) Cardiff West 1983-; s of Oleksa Terlezki, of Ukraine, and Olena Terlezki; *b* 29 Oct 1927; *Educ* HS, Cardiff Coll of Food Technol and Commerce; *m* 1955; 2 da; *Career* hotel and catering consits; memb Hotel and Catering Inst 1965-80, memb Chamber of Trade, memb Welsh Tourist Cncl 1965-80; chm Cardiff City AFC 1975-77; contested (C): Cardiff S E Feb and Oct 1974, candidate Kingswood Bristol 1975, S Wales Euro elections 1979; memb: Cardiff City Cncl 1968-83 (former press offr Cons gp), S Glamorgan CC 1973-; chm Cardiff HS Bd of Govrs 1975-83, chm Keep Br in Europe Campaign 1973; memb: Educn Authy for Cardiff CC and S Glam Co Cncl 1969-, Planning, Finance and Policy Ctees 1975-83, UN Orgn Temple of Peace Cardiff, Official Nat Speaking Panels Cons Party, Cons Gp for Euro Movement 1973; Queen's Silver Jubilee Medal 1977; *Style*— Stefan Terlezki Esq, MP; House of Commons, London SW1; 16 Bryngwyn Road, Cyncoed, Cardiff

TERRAS, (Christopher) Richard; s of Frederick Richard Terras (d 1976), and Katherine Joan, *née* Anning; *b* 17 Oct 1937; *Educ* Uppingham, Univ Coll Oxford (MA); *m* 27 Oct 1962, Janet Esther May, da of Leslie Harold Sydney Baxter (d 1980); 1 s (Nicholas b 1965), 3 da (Clare b 1964, Penelope b 1968, Joanna b 1971); *Career* CA; ptnr: Swanwick Terras & Co 1963-65, Abbott & Son 1963-65, Arthur Andersen & Co 1971-; *Recreations* cricket (played for Cheshire); *Clubs* Free Foresters, Cheshire Gentlemen, Leicestershire Gentlemen, Vincents, Fifteen St James (Manchester); *Style*— Richard Terras, Esq; Frog Castle, Macclesfield Rd, Alderley Edge, Cheshire (☎ 0625 583118); Arthur Andersen & Co, Bank House, 9 Charlotte St, Manchester MI 4EU (☎ 0836 609 615)

TERRINGTON, Derek Humphrey; s of Douglas Jack, of Bury St Edmunds, and Jean Mary, *née* Humphrey; *b* 25 Jan 1949; *Educ* Sea Point Boys HS, Univ Cape Town (MA); *m* 15 July 1978, Jennifer Mary, da of Leslie Vernon Jones; 1 da (Sarah b 29 Sept 1984); *Career* assoc ptnr Grievson Grant 1984, dir Phillips & Drew 1988 (asst dir 1987); memb Int Stock Exchange; *Style*— Derek Terrington, Esq; 16 St Winifred's Road, Teddington, Middlesex TW11 9JR; Phillips & Drew Ltd, 120 Moorgate, London EC2M 6XP (☎ 01 628 4444)

TERRINGTON, 4 Baron (UK 1918); James Allen David Woodhouse; s of 3 Baron Terrington, KBE (d 1961); *b* 30 Dec 1915; *Educ* Winchester, RMC Sandhurst; *m* 1942, Suzanne, da of Col T S Irwin, JP, DL, late Royal Dragoons, of Justicetown, Carlisle, and Mill House, Holton, Suffolk; 3 da (Hon Mrs Bolton, Hon Georgina W, Countess Alexander of Tunis); *Heir* bro, Hon Christopher Montague Woodhouse, DSO, OBE; *Career* Staff Coll Haifa 1944, psc 1944, served WW II in India, N Africa and Middle East (wounded); sits as Independent Peer in House of Lords; Maj (ret) Royal Norfolk Regt and Queen's Westminster Rifles (King's Royal Rifle Corps), TA, an ADC to GOC Madras 1940; former memb Stock Exchange, partner in Sheppards and Chase 1952-80, dep chm of Ctees House of Lords 1961-63; vice chm Nat Listening Library (talking books for the disabled); vice pres Small Farmers Assoc memb: Ecclesiastical Ctee sincew 1979, Int Advsy Bd of the American Univ Washington DC USA; exec memb Wider Share Ownership Cncl (formerly dep chm); *Recreations* racing, gardening; *Clubs* Boodle's, Pratt's; *Style*— The Rt Hon the Lord Terrington; The Manor House, Barford St Martin, Salisbury, Wilts SP3 4AH (☎ Salisbury 0722 742252)

TERRY; *see*: Imbert-Terry

TERRY, Sir George Walter Roberts; CBE (1976), QPM (1967, DL (E Sussex 1983)); s of Walter George Tygh Terry; *b* 29 May 1921; *Educ* Peterborough; *m* 1942, Charlotte Elisabeth, da of Stanley Kresina; 1 s; *Career* served WWII Northants Regt Capt Italy; chief constable Sussex 1973-83 (dep chief constable 1968-69), Lincs 1970-73, E Sussex 1965-67, Pembrokeshire 1958-65; pres Assoc Chief Police Offrs 1980-81 (chm Traffic Ctee 1976-79), memb Cncl Inst Advanced Motorists 1974; CStJ 1982; kt 1981; *Style*— Sir George Terry, CBE, QPM, DL; c/o National Westminster Bank plc, 173 High St, Lewes, E Sussex BN7 1YF (☎ 0273 471211)

TERRY, (Robert) Jeffrey; s of Robert James Terry, of Stockport, and Emily, *née* Davison (d 1975); *b* 10 Sept 1952; *Educ* William Hulme's Sch Manchester, King's Coll London (LLB), City of London Poly (MA); *m* 15 July 1978, Susan Terry, da of Reginald Trevor Kingston Gregory, of Bath; 2 da (Sarah Louise b 7 Aug 1983, Anna May Emily b 7 May 1987); *Career* barr 1976, community lawyer Southend CAB 1976-78, in private practice London 1978- and Manchester; memb: Hon Soc Lincoln's Inn 1975; *Recreations* walking, photography, reading (especially literature, classics, history); *Style*— Jeffrey Terry, Esq; Cairnside, 43 Canonbie Rd, London SE23; Sycamore Cottage, Burrells, Near Appleby-in-Westmoreland, Cumbria; 601 The Royal Exchange, Cross St, Manchester; 8 King St, Manchester (☎ 061 834 9560, fax 061 834 2733); Lamb Buildings, Temple, London EC4 (☎ 01 353 6701, fax 01 353 4686)

TERRY, Sir John Elliott; s of late Ernest Fairchild Terry, OBE, FRICS, of Pulborough, Sussex; *b* 11 June 1913; *Educ* Mill Hill Sch, London Univ; *m* 1940, Joan Christine, da of late Frank Alfred Ernest Howard, fell of Stoke D'Abernon Surrey; 1 s, 1 da; *Career* business mangr Film Producers' Guild 1946-47, slr: Rank Organisation Legal Dept 1947-49, Nat Film Finance Corpn 1949-57 (sec 1956-57) and md 1958-78, conslt Denton Hall & Burgin; govr: Nat Film Sch to 1981, Royal Nat Coll for the Blind 1980-, London Int Film Sch 1982-; kt 1976; *Style*— Sir John Terry; Still Point, Branscombe, Devon

TERRY, John Victor; s of Norman Victor Terry (d 1981), and Mary Josephine Terry; *b* 6 Sept 1942; *Educ* Leys Sch Cambridge, Jesus Coll Cambridge (MA), Harvard Business Sch (MBA); *m* 3 April 1965, Jane Gillian, da of Donald Pearson, of Cambridge; 2 s (Nicholas b 11 Jan 1969, Simon b 6 May 1971); *Career* gen mangr Herbert Terry and Sons Ltd 1971-75; purchased and formed independant co of Anglepoise Lighting 1975: md 1975-88, chm 1988-; pres Harvard Business Sch Assoc of Midlands 1983-85, pres Lighting Indust Fedn 1988-89; Freeman Worshipful Co of Lightmongers 1985; *Recreations* windsurfing, cars, sailing, real tennis; *Clubs* Royal London YC, Barnt Green SC, Leamington TC, British Racing Drivers; *Style*— John Terry, Esq; Wasperton House, Warwick LV35 8EB (☎ 0926 624264); Anglepoise Lighting, Redditch B97 8DR (☎ 0527 63771, fax 0527 61232, telex 336918, car tel 0836 757523)

TERRY, Air Chief Marshal Sir Peter David George; GCB (1983, KCB 1978, CB 1975), AFC (1968); s of (James) George Terry (d 1968), and Laura Chilton, *née* Powell (d 1980); *b* 18 Oct 1926; *Educ* Chatham House Sch Ramsgate; *m* 1946, Betty Martha Louisa, da of Arthur Thompson; 2 s (Stephen, David decd), 1 da (Elizabeth); *Career* RAF 1945-, cmmnd 1946, dir Air Staff Briefing MOD 1970-71, dir Forward Policy RAF 1971-75, asst COS Policy and Plans 1975-77, vice-chief Air Staff 1977-79, C-in-C RAF Germany and Cdr 2 Allied Tactical AF 1979-81, dep C-in-C Allied Forces Central Europe 1981, Dep Supreme Allied Cdr Europe 1981-84, Govr and C-in-C Gibraltar; Queen's Commendation for Valuable Service in Air 1959 and 1962; *Recreations* golf; *Clubs* RAF; *Style*— Air Chief Marshal Sir Peter Terry, GCB, AFC; The Convent, Gibraltar (BFPO 52)

TERRY, (John) Quinlan; s of Philip John Terry, of Suffolk, and Phyllis May Whiteman; *b* 24 July 1937; *Educ* Bryanston, Arch Assoc; *m* 9 Sept 1961, Christina Marie-Therese, da of Joachin Tadeusz de Ruttié (d 1968); 1 s (Francis Nathannel b 1969) 4 da (Elizabeth b 1964, Anna b 1965, Martha b 1979, Sophia b 1982); *Career* architect in private practice, works incl Country House in the classical style, Richmond Riverside Devpt, New Howard Bldg Downing Coll Cambridge; *Recreations* sketching; *Style*— Quinlan Terry, Esq; Old Exchange, High St, Dedham, Colchester

TERRY, Walter; s of Frederick George Terry (d 1974), and Helen, *née* MacKenzie Bruce (d 1963); *b* 18 August 1924; *m* 24 March 1950, Mavis, da of Edward Landen (d 1988); 2 s (Gulliver b 28 March 1962, d May 1963, Barnaby b 13 Nov 1963), 1 da (Candida b 31 Oct 1958); *Career* journalist, political corr Daily Mail 1959-65, political ed Daily Mail 1965-73, political ed Daily Express 1973-75, political journalist The Sun 1976-78, political ed The Sun 1978-83; *Style*— Walter Terry, Esq; 11 Eliot Place, London SE3 04L (☎ 01 852 2526); 8 Fort Rise, Newhaven Harbour, Sussex BN9 9DW (☎ 0273 514347)

TESH, Robert Mathieson; CMG (1968); s of Ernest Tesh (d 1972), of Exted, and Elsie, *née* Steel (d 1983); *b* 15 Sept 1922; *Educ* Queen Elizabeth Sch Wakefield, Queen's Coll Oxford (MA); *m* 1950, Jean, da of Harold Bowker (d 1968), of Morecambe; 2 s (John, Simon), 1 da (Gillian); *Career* WWII Lt RB Serv Tunisia and N Europe 1942-45; HM Dipl Serv; dep high cmmr: Acra 1965-66, Lusaka 1966; cnsllr Cairo 1966-68; IDC 1969; head of Def Dept FCO 1970-72; HM Ambass: Bahrain 1972-75, Vietnam 1976-78, Ethopia and OAU 1979-82; *Recreations* singing, acting; *Clubs* Travellers, Richmond Golf; *Style*— Robert Tesh Esq; 10 Albany Close, Blackhills, Esher, Surrey KT10 9JR (☎ 0372 64192)

TESLER, Brian; s of David Tesler (d 1972), and Esther Tesler; *b* 19 Feb 1929; *Educ* Chiswick Co Sch for Boys, Exeter Coll Oxford (MA); *m* 1959, Audrey Mary; 1 s; *Career* former television producer/dir; dir of programmes Thames TV 1968; chm and md London Weekend Television 1984- (dep chief exec 1974, md 1976-, dep chm 1982-84); dir: Channel 4 1980-85, ITN, Oracle Teletext Ltd; govr Nat Film and Television Sch, chm Ind TV Cos Assoc Cable & Satellite Working Party and Superchannel Steering Gp, dir Services Sound and Vision Corpn; memb Br Screen Advsy Cncl (formerly IAC), chm ITCA Cncl 1980-82; *Recreations* books, theatre, cinema, music; *Style*— Brian Tesler Esq; LWT Ltd, South Bank Television Centre, Kent House, Upper Ground, London SE1 9LT (☎ 01 261 3434, telex 918123)

TETLEY, Brian; s of Herbert Tetley (d 1957), of Little Gomersal, and Gladys, *née* Holliday (d 1985); *b* 5 Sept 1937; *Educ* Heckmondwike GS; *m* 29 Aug 1959, Winifred Mary, da of William Sylvester O'Neill (d 1981), of Birkenshaw, Bradford; 2 s (Mark Richard b 1963, Neil Jon b 1966); *Career* CA; fin dir and co sec The Bradford Property Tst plc; dir: Margrave Estates Ltd, Faside Estates Ltd, Bradwa Ltd, Ashday Property

Co Ltd, Sydenham Estates Ltd, and dir of various other cos; FCA; *Recreations* Rotary, golf; *Clubs* The Bradford; *Style—* Brian Tetley, Esq; Reighton, 123 Huddersfield Rd, Liversedge, W Yorks WF15 7DA; 69 Market St, Bradford BD1 1NE (☎ 0274 723 181)

TETLEY, Lieut-Col David Rimington; TD (1947), DL (N Yorks 1958); s of Lt-Col Francis Eric Tetley, DSO, TD (d 1966), of The Grove, North Lane, Leeds, and Katherine Agnes, *née* Goodall; *b* 10 Dec 1912; *Educ* Harrow, Jesus Coll Cambridge (MA); *m* 15 Aug 1946, Sarah Dorothea, da of Capt Robert Athole Hay (d 1939), of Marlfield, Roxburghshire (er bro of Sir Bache Hay, 11 Bt, who d 1966); 1 s (Christopher b 1948), 1 da (Catherine b 1950); *Career* served Yorks Hussars and 13/18 Hussars, ME and NW Europe 1939-45, Lt-Col 1953; chartered surveyor, land agent, farmer; High Sheriff N Yorks 1975-76; *Clubs* Army and Navy, Farmers'; *Style—* Lt-Col David Tetley, TD, DL; Brawby Parks, N Malton, N Yorks (☎ 065386 236)

TETLEY, Glen; s of Glenford Andrew Tetley (d 1985), and Mary Eleanor Byrne; *b* 3 Feb 1926; *Educ* Franklin and Marshall Coll, NY Univ (BSc); *Career* choreographer ballets include: Pierrot Lunaire 1962, The Anatomy Lesson 1964, Mythical Hunters 1965, Ricercare 1966, Ziggurat 1967, Circles 1968, Embrace Tiger and Return to Mountain 1968, Arena 1968, Field Figures 1971, Laborintus 1972, Gemini 1973, Voluntaries 1973, Sacre du Printemps 1974, Greening 1975, Sphinx 1978, The Tempest 1979, Firebird 1981, Revelation and Fall 1984, Alice 1986; artistic associate National Ballet of Canada 1987-; Queen Elizabeth II Coronation Award 1981, Prix Italia 1982, Tennant Caledonian Award Edinburgh Fest 1983, Ohloana Career Medal 1986-; dir Glen Tetley Dance Co 1962-69, co dir Nederlands Dans Theater 1969-71; dir Stuttgart Ballet 1972-74; choreographer: Royal Ballet Covent Garden, Ballet Rambert, Festival Ballet, American Ballet Theatre, Nat Ballet of Canada, Royal Danish Ballet, Royal Swedish Ballet, Nat Ballet of Norway, Australian Ballet, Stuttgart Ballet, Paris Opera, La Scala, Ater Balletto; *Style—* Glen Tetley, Esq; Highbank, Green Lane, Old Bosham, Chichester, W Sussex PO18 8NT; Susan Bloch and Co, 25 Charles St, New York, NY 10014 USA (☎ 212 807 6480, telex 65204)

TETLEY, Sir Herbert; KBE (1965), CB (1958); s of Albert Tetley (d 1926), of Leeds, and Mary Tetley (d 1947); *b* 23 April 1908; *Educ* Leeds GS, Queen's Coll Oxford (MA); *m* 1941, (Nancy) Agnes MacLean MacFarlane, da of John Macphee of Glasgow; 1 s; *Career* jt actuary Nat Provident Inst 1946-53, dep govt actuary 1953-58 (govt actuary 1958-73); chm Civil Service Insur Soc and assoc socs 1961-73, chm Ctee on Econs Road Res Bd 1962-65, pres Inst of Actuaries 1964-66, memb Research Ctee on Road Traffic 1966-72; *Style—* Sir Herbert Tetley, KBE, CB; 37 Upper Brighton Rd, Surbiton, Surrey KT6 6QX (☎ 01 399 3001)

TETLEY, Lady Patricia Maud; *née* Bowes-Lyon; raised to the rank of an Earl's da 1974; da (twin) of late Hon Michael Claude Hamilton Bowes-Lyon, 5 s of 14 Earl of Strathmore and Kinghorne; sis of 17 Earl; *b* 1932; *m* 1964 (m dis 1970), Oliver Robin Tetley; 1 s (Alexander b 1965); *Style—* Lady Patricia Tetley; Abbey Lodge, Chruch St, Wymondham, Norfolk (☎ 0953 602355)

TETLEY, Richard James; s of Brig James Noel Tetley, DSO, TD, ADC, DL, LLD (d 1970), of Moor House, Moortown, Leeds, and Joyce Carine, *née* Grierson; *b* 15 April 1930; *Educ* Bradfield, Queen's Coll Oxford (MA); *m* 24 Aug 1963, Margaret Claire, da of Prof Allwyn Charles Keys (d 1985), of Auckland, NZ; 4 s (Douglas b 1964, Andrew b 1966, Stuart b 1968, Iain b 1970); *Career* dir Allied Breweries 1969-79, with ICL plc 1983-, memb Cncl Leeds Univ 1965-88; *Style—* Richard J Tetley, Esq; Beacon Croft, Shaw Lane, Lichfield, Staffs WS13 7AG (☎ 0543 263 304)

TETT, Sir Hugh Charles; s of James Charles Tett (d 1955); *b* 28 Oct 1906; *Educ* Hele's Sch Exeter, RCS, Univ Coll Exeter; *m* 1, 1931, Katie Sargent (d 1948); 1 da; m 2, 1949, Joyce Lilian, *née* Mansell (d 1979); 1 da; m 3, 1980, Barbara Mary, *née* Mackenzie; *Career* joined Esso Petroleum Co 1928, chm Esso Petroleum Co 1959-67; pro-chllr Univ of Southampton 1967-79; fell Imperial Coll of Sci and Technol 1964; Hon DSc: Southampton 1965, Exeter 1970; kt 1966; *Clubs* Athenaeum; *Style—* Sir Hugh Tett; Primrose Cottage, Bosham, Chichester, W Sussex PO18 8HZ (☎ 0243 572705)

TETT, Peter Alfred; s of Norman Noel Tett, CBE (d 1979), and Irene Constance, *née* Edwards; *b* 5 Nov 1939; *Educ* Oundle, Clare Coll Cambridge (MA), Carnegie Melloń Univ Pittsburgh USA (MSc); *m* 15 Aug 1964, Romaine Joy Carley, da of Dr John Carley Read, DSc (d 1969); 1 da (Gillian b 1967), 1 s (Richard b 1969); *Career* dir: Halma plc 1984, London & Euro Gp plc 1978-82; *Recreations* squash, skiing, theatre; *Clubs* Moor Park Golf, East Devon Golf; *Style—* Peter A Tett, Esq; 5 Bedford Rd, Moor Park, Northwood, Middx HA6 2BA (☎ 092 74 22622); Kingsbury Rd, London NW9 8UU (☎ 01 205 0038, fax 01 200 4512)

TEVERSON, Hon Mrs (Joanna Rosamond Georgina); da of Baron Gore-Booth GCMG, KCVO (Life Baron) (d 1984), and his w, Patricia Mary, da of late Montague Ellerton, of Yokohama, Japan; *b* 1954; *Educ* Sherborne Sch, New Hall Cambridge (BA); *m* 1978, Paul Richard Teverson; 1 s (Richard Hugh b 1984), 1 da (Cathryn b 1986); *Style—* The Hon Mrs Teverson; 25 Silverton Road, Hammersmith, London W6 9NY

TEVIOT, 2 Baron (UK 1940); Charles John Kerr; s of 1 Baron Teviot, DSO, MC (d 1968, himself ggs of 6 Marquess of Lothian), by his 2 w Angela (d 1979), da of Lt-Col Charles Villiers, CBE, DSO (ggn of 4 Earl of Clarendon) by his w Lady Kathleen Cole (2 da of 4 Earl of Enniskillen); *b* 16 Dec 1934; *Educ* Eton; *m* 1965, Patricia Mary, da of late Alexander Harris; 1 s, 1 da (Hon Catherine b 1976); *Heir* s, Hon Charles Robert Kerr b 19 Sept 1971; *Career* memb Advsy Cncl on Public Records 1974-82, dir Debrett's Peerage Ltd 1977-83; fell Soc of Genealogists 1975; *Recreations* genealogy, walking; *Style—* The Rt Hon the Lord Teviot; 12 Grand Ave, Hassocks, W Sussex (☎ 079 18 4471)

TEWKESBURY, Bishop of 1986-; Rt Rev (Geoffrey David) Jeremy Walsh; s of Howard Wilton Walsh, OBE (d 1969), and Helen Maud Walsh, *née* Lovell (d 1985); *b* 7 Dec 1929; *Educ* Felsted Sch, Pembroke Coll Cambridge (MA), Lincoln Theol Coll; *m* 1961, Cynthia Helen, da of Francis Philip Knight (d 1985); 2 s (David b 1962, Andrew b 1967), 1 da (Helen b 1964); *Career* vicar St Matthew's Bristol 1961-66; rector: Marlborough 1966-76, Elmsett with Aldham Suffolk 1976-80; archdeacon of Ipswich 1976-86; *Recreations* golf, gardening, bird-watching; *Style—* The Rt Rev the Bishop of Tewkesbury; Green Acre, 166 Hempsted Lane, Gloucester GL2 6LG (☎ 0452 21824)

TEYNHAM, 20 Baron (E 1616); John Christopher Ingham Roper-Curzon; s of 19 Baron Teynham, DSO, DSC (d 1972), by his 1 w Elspeth (m dis 1956, she d 1976, having m 2, 1958, 6 Marquess of Northampton, DSO); *b* 25 Dec 1928; *Educ* Eton; *m* 1964, Elizabeth, da of Lt-Col the Hon David Scrymgeour-Wedderburn, DSO (ka 1944) 2 s of 10 Earl of Dundee); 5 s of 6 Duke of Buccleuch); 5 s (Hon David, Hon Jonathan b (twin) 27 April 1973, Hon Peter b 20 Nov 1977, Hon William b 27 July 1980, Hon Benjamin b 15 Sept 1982), 5 da (Hon Emma b 19 Sept 1966, Hon Sophie b 30 Nov 1967, Hon Lucy b 23 July 1969, Hon Hermione b (twin) 27 April 1973, Hon Alice b 18 Dec 1983); *Heir* s, Hon David John Henry Ingham Roper-Curzon, b 5 Oct 1965; *Career* late Capt The Buffs (TA) and 2 Lt Coldstream Gds, active serv Palestine 1948, ADC to Govr of Bermuda 1953 and 1955, ADC to Gov of Leeward Islands 1955 (also private sec 1956), ADC to govr of Jamaica 1962; pres Inst of Commerce 1972-, vice-pres Inst of Export memb cncl Sail Training Assoc 1964; memb Cncl of l'Orchestra du Monde 1987-; land agent; OStJ; *Clubs* Turf, House of Lords Yacht, Ocean Cruising, Beaulieu River Sailing, Puffins (Edinburgh); *Style—* The Rt Hon the Lord Teynham; Seat Pylewell Park, Lymington, Hants

THACKER, Arthur Doe; s of Gilbert Doe Dwyer Way Thacker (d 1986), and Judith Mary St Leger, *née* Fagan (d 1980); *b* 19 June 1931; *Educ* Haileybury, ISC, Christ's Coll Cambridge (BA, MA); *m* 18 June 1960, Maude April Beatrice Evelyn, da of Frederick Croysdale Waud (d 1949); 2 s (Thomas b 1962, Geoffrey b 1970), 2 da (Bridget b 1963, Judith b 1966); *Career* RCS 1949-56, actg Capt and adjt; Wiggins Teape GP 1954-58, until ret in 1988; proprietor ADT Business Consultancy Serv, territorial dir Far East etc, dir Wiggins Teape Overseas Ltd 1977, Overseas Hldgs Ltd 1978 and Wiggings Teape Hong Kong 1978, Malaysia 1978, NZ 1978, Japan 1978, Singapore 1978, Far East Holdings 1980, Australia 1983; dir Computer Farms Toppan Moore Pte Ltd, Singapore 1985; memb Inst Admin Mgmnt 1974-, borough cncllr St Mary Bourne Ward of Basingstoke and Deane Borough Cncl 1979, 1983, and 1987, chm Housing Ctee 1988-; *Recreations* golf, contract bridge, tennis, gardening, philately; *Clubs* The Hong Kong, Royal Hong Kong Golf, Royal Hong Kong Yacht, Royal Selangor GC, The Lake (Kuala Lumpur), Tidworth Garrison GC; *Style—* Arthur D Thacker, Esq; Bourne House, St Mary Bourne, Andover, Hants SP11 6AP (☎ 0264 738 464)

THAIN, Leslie Alister; s of Alexander Simpson Thain (d 1966); *b* 22 August 1939; *Educ* Fettes, Edinburgh Univ (MA, LLB); *m* 1968, Katherine Mary, *née* Hudson; 1 s, 1 da; *Career* slr, co dir; WS; *Recreations* golf, tennis, freemasonry, gardening; *Style—* Leslie Thain, Esq, WS; The Dean, Longniddry, E Lothian (☎ 0875 53272, office 031 226 6703)

THATCHER, Anthony Neville; s of Edwin Neville Thatcher (d 1978), and Elsie May, *née* Webster; *b* 10 Sept 1939; *Educ* Sir John Lawes Sch Harpenden, Luton Tech Coll, Manchester Univ (MSc); *m* 20 Oct 1968, Sally Margaret, da of Henry Joseph Clark, of Norfolk; *Career* student apprentice Haywards Tyler & Co Luton 1956-64, project engr Smiths Indust London 1964-65, ops res asst Ultra Electronics 1967-69, vice pres sales Ultra Electronics Inc USA 1970-73, mktg dir Ultra Electronics Ltd Acton 1973-77; md: Ultra Electronic Controls Ltd 1977, Dowty Electronics Controls Ltd 1978-82; gp chief exec Dowty Gp plc 1986- (md electronics div 1982-86, bd member 1983); memb: cncl Electronics Engrg Assoc 1983- (pres 1986), RARDE mgmnt bd (industl) 1986-, mgmnt bd Engrg Employers & Avionics Requirement Bd of DTI 1981-85, innovation advsy bd DTI 1988-, engrg mkts advsy ctee DTI 1988-; memb cncl The Cheltenham Ladies Coll-; Liveryman Worshipful Co of Glass Sellers; CEng, MIMechE; *Recreations* art, jazz piano, opera, fishing, gardening, bird watching; *Style—* Anthony Thatcher, Esq; Dowty Group plc, Arle Ct, Cheltenham, Glos GL51 0TP (☎ 0242 533614, fax 0242 521054, telex 43176)

THATCHER, Rt Hon Margaret Hilda; PC (1970), MP (C) Finchley 1983-; da of late Alfred Roberts, grocer, of Grantham, Lincs; *b* 13 Oct 1925; *Educ* Huntingtower Primary Sch Grantham, Kesteven and Grantham Girls' Sch, Somerville Coll Oxford (MA, BSc; hon fellow 1970); *m* 1951, Denis Thatcher, company director; 1 s (Mark), 1 da (Carol (twin), radio journalist, presenter (freelance) with LBC) former research chemist; barr Lincoln's Inn 1953 (hon bencher 1975), contested (C) Dartford 1950 and 1951; MP (C): Finchley 1959-74, Barnet, Finchley 1974-1983; jt parly sec Miny of Pensions and National Insurance 1961-64, memb Shadow Cabinet 1967-70 (spokesman on: Tport, Power, Treasury matters, Housing and Pensions), chief oppn spokesman educn 1969-70, sec of state Educn and Science (and co-chm Women's National Cmmn) 1970-74, chief oppn spokesman environment 1974-75, leader of the Opposition Feb 1975-79, prime minister and first lord of Treasury (first woman to hold this office) from 4 May 1979 (re-elected June 1983, 1987); minister for the Civil Service Jan 1981-; freedom of Borough of Barnet 1980; hon freeman of Worshipful Co of Grocers 1980; freedom of Falkland Islands 1983; Donovan Award USA 1981; FRS; *Style—* The Rt Hon Margaret Thatcher, MP; 10 Downing St, London SW1

THELLUSSON, Hon Peter Robert; s of Lt-Col Hon Hugh Thellusson, DSO, by his w Gwynnydd, da of Brig-Gen Sir Robert Colleton, 9 and last Bt, CB; bro of 8 Baron Rendlesham and was raised to rank of a Baron's s 1945; *b* 25 Jan 1920; *Educ* Eton; *m* 1, 1947 (m dis 1950), Pamela (d 1968), da of Oliver Parker (2 s of Hon Francis Parker, 4 s of 6 Earl of Macclesfield by Lady Mary Grosvenor, da of 2 Marquess of Westminster, KG) and former w of Maj Timothy Tufnell, MC; m 2, 1952, Celia, da of James Walsh; 2 s; *Career* served WWII, Capt KRRC; *Style—* The Hon Peter Thellusson; 29 Bramham Gdns, SW5

THELLUSSON, Hon Sarah Ann; da of 8 Baron Rendlesham by his 2 w, Clare; *b* 25 Jan 1949; *Style—* The Hon Sarah Thellusson; 28 Walham Grove, SW6

THELWELL, Norman; s of Christopher Thelwell (d 1974), and Emily, *née* Vick (d 1964); *b* 3 May 1923; *Educ* Rock Ferry HS, Liverpool Coll of Art (ATD); *m* 1948, Rhona Evelyn, da of Harold Clyde Ladbury (d 1961); 1 s (David), 1 da (Penelope); *Career* artist & cartoonist; lectr Wolverhampton Coll of Art 1950-56; regular contributor to Punch 1952-77, cartoonist to News Chronicle, Sunday Express, Sunday Dispatch, many other publications; *Books* Angels on Horseback (1957), Thelwell Country (1959), Thelwell in Orbit (1961), A Place of Your Own, A Leg at Each Corner, Thelwells Riding Academy, Top Dog, Up the Garden Path, The Compleat Tangler (1967), Thelwell's Book of Leisure (1968), This Desirable Plot (1970), The Effluent Society (1971), Penelope (1972), Three Sheets in the Wind, Belt Up (1974), Thelwell Goes West (1975), Thelwell's Brat Race (1977), Thelwell's Gymkhana, A Plank Bridge by a Pool (1978), a Millstone Round My Neck (1981), Pony Cavalcade, Some Damn Fool's signed the Rubens Again (1982), Thelwell's Magnificat (1983), Thelwells Sporting Prints (1984), autobiography Wrestling with a Pencil (1986), Play It As It Lies (1987); *Recreations* trout fishing; *Style—* Norman Thelwell Esq; Herons Mead, Timsbury, Romsey, Hants SO51 0NE (☎ 0794 68238)

THEOBALD, (Robert) Courtenay; s of Rev Bernard Gage Theobald (d 1945), and

Hannah Bradshaw, *née* Boyle; *b* 4 Oct 1903; *Educ* Silcoates Sch, UCL (BA Arch); *m* 30 June 1928, Virginia, da of Ormerod Maxwell Ayrton (d 1960), of 9 Church Row, Hampstead; 2 s (Randle b 1940, Quentin b 1943, d 1978), 3 da (Tessa b 1932, Gay b 1936, Claire b 1938); *Career* WWII HS 1939-40, RAFVR liaison offr RAF War Room 1940-45, rank Fl Lt retained for life by grant of Air Cncl 1954; architect; designs incl: Somerville Coll Chapel Oxford (exhibition RA), Hanover Lodge Hall of Residence, Regent's Park and other bldgs for Bedford Coll, Presbyterian Church and Church House Regent Sq London, various bldgs for MRC country inns and houses; fifty bridges mainly on M4 and M40 and Eton and Windsor Rd incl: Queen Elizabeth II Bridge (over Thames) Windsor (exhitited RA), Loudwater Viaduct M40, new Thames bridges at Chertsey and Marlow, flyover Windsor-Maidenhead Rd; tstee Wells and Camden Charity Hampstead, memb ctee Old Hampstead Preservation Soc; ARIBA 1926, FRIBA 1938, FRSA 1970; *Recreations* gardening, snooker, watercolours (exhibited RA, Arts Club 1976, Bucks Co Museum Aylesbury 1983); *Clubs* The Arts; *Style*— Courtenay Theobald, Esq; 10 Coldharbour, Wendover, Bucks HP22 6NR (☎ 0296 622823)

THEOBALD, Col Frederick Kenneth; MBE (1957), TD (1952 and 2 bars, DL (Kent 1971)); s of Capt Frederick Theobald, MBE (d 1962); *b* 28 June 1909; *Educ* Whitgift GS; *m* 1934, Anne Amelia, *née* Booth; *Career* served TA 1927-45, Col, Kent County Army Cadet Force 1952-70, assoc Chartered Insur Inst, pension schemes & house purchase specialist Sun Life Assur Soc (ret 1970); *Recreations* walking on Dartmoor; *Style*— Col Frederick Theobald, MBE, TD, DL; Keystones, Moretonhampstead, Devon (☎ 0647 40384)

THEOBALD, (George) Peter; JP (1974); s of George Oswald Theobald (d 1952), of Surrey, and Helen, *née* Moore (d 1972); *b* 5 August 1931; *Educ* Betteshanger Sch, Harrow; *m* 1955, Josephine Mary, da of Wilfrid Andrew Carmichael Boodle (d 1961); 2 s (Carmichael, Christopher), 3 da (Caroline, Jane, Kate); *Career* cmmnd 5 Regt RHA 1950-52, Lt 290 City of London Regt RA (TA) 1953-59; gp chief exec Robert Warner plc 1953-74; dir: Moran Tea Hldgs plc 1977-, Moran Tea Co (India) plc 1981-; memb: Tport Users Consultative Ctee for London 1969-84 (dep chm 1978-79), London Regional Passengers Ctee 1984-; church cmmnr for England 1978-79 (alderman City of London 1974-79), licensed asst diocese of Guildford 1970-; govr: Bridewell Royal Hosp 1974-, Christs Hosp 1976-, King Edwards Sch Witley 1974- (tstee Education Tst 1977-), St Leonards Mayfield Sch 1982-88; Harrow Club 1978-, Nat Flood and Tempest Distress Fund 1977-; Asst Worshipful Co of Merchant Taylors 1983-; *Recreations* gardening, transport, walking; *Clubs* Oriental, MCC; *Style*— Peter Theobald, Esq, JP; Towerhill Manor, Gomshall, Guildford, Surrey GU5 9LP (☎ 048 641 2381)

THEODOROU, Skevos Gregory; s of Gregory Alfred Theodorou (d 1970), and Irene, *née* Alakouzos (both of shipping families); *b* 12 Oct 1939; *Educ* Le Rosey Switzerland, Neuch`atel Univk (dip Business Admin); *m* 1, 1968 (m dis), Gillian Geraldine Anne, da of Maj-Gen Sir (Harold) John (Crossley) Hildreth, KBE, and sis of Jan Hildreth (sometime dir gen of IOD); 1 s (Alexander John (Skevos) Hildreth b 11 May 1976), 1 da (Charlotte Amanda Joanna Hildreth b 26 Oct 1978); m 2, Antonia de Galard Brassac, eld da of Count Jean de Bearn; 1 s (Gregory b 23 Oct 1986); *Career* shipping, memb Baltic Exchange 1964-, md Transmarine SA Paris 1967-79, dir Clarkson & Co Ltd 1975-; *Recreations* shooting, sailing; *Clubs* Royal Thames Yacht, Royal Hellenic Yacht (Athens); *Style*— Skevos Theodorou, Esq; 58d Blomfield Rd, London W9 2PA

THESIGER, Hon Dawn Loraine; da of late 2 Viscount Chelmsford; *b* 1934; *Style*— The Hon Dawn Thesiger; Hazelridge, Chiddingfold, Surrey

THESIGER, Hon Frederic Corin Piers; s and h of 3 Viscount Chelmsford; *b* 6 Mar 1962; *Style*— The Hon Frederic Thesiger; 26 Ormonde Gate, London SW3 4EX

THESIGER, Hon Philippa Merryn; da of late 2 Viscount Chelmsford; *b* 1939; *Style*— The Hon Philippa Thesiger; Hazelridge Court, Chiddingfold, Surrey

THESIGER, Wilfred Patrick; CBE (1968), DSO (1941); s of Capt the Hon Wilfred Gilbert Thesiger, DSO (d 1920), and Kathleen Mary, *née* Vigors, CBE (d 1973); *b* 3 June 1910; *Educ* Eton, Magdalen Coll Oxford (MA); *Career* hon attaché Duke of Gloucester's Mission to Haile Sellasie's Convocation 1930, explored Danakil Country and Aussa Sultanate of Abyssinia 1933-34, Sudan Political Serv Darfur Upper Nile 1935-37 and 1938-40, Sudan Def Force Abyssinian Campaign 1940-41, Maj SOE Syria 1941-42, SAS Regt W Desert 1942-43, advsr to the Crown Prince in Ethiopia 1944; explored in Southern Arabia 1945-50 (twice crossed the Empty Quarter by camel), living with the Madan in the marshes of Southern Iraq 1950-58; awarded Back Guards RGS 1935, Founder's Medal RGS 1948, Lawrence of Arabia Medal RCAS 1955, Livingston Medal RSGS 1962, W H Heinemann Award RSL 1964, Burton Meml Medal Royal Asiatic Soc 1966; hon fell: Magdalen Coll Oxford 1982, Bristol Acad 1982; Hon DLit Leicester Univ; FRSL 1966; Star of Ethiopia third class 1930; *Books* Arabian Sands (1959), The Marsh Arabs (1964), Desert, Marsh and Mountain (1979), The Life of My Choice (1987), Visions of a Nomad (1987); *Recreations* travel in remote areas, photography; *Clubs* Travellers, Beefsteak; *Style*— Wilfred Thesiger, Esq, CBE, DSO; 15 Shelley Court, Tite St, London SW3 4JB (☎ 01 352 7213)

THETFORD, Bishop Suffragan of, 1981-; Rt Rev Timothy Dudley-Smith; s of Arthur and Phyllis Dudley Smith, of Buxton, Derbys; *b* 26 Dec 1926; *Educ* Tonbridge, Pembroke Coll Cambridge, Ridley Hall Cambridge; *m* 1959, (June) Arlette MacDonald; 1 s, 2 da; *Career* ordained 1950, archdeacon of Norwich 1973-81; *Publications* Christian Literature and the Church Bookstall (1963), What Makes a Man a Christian? (1966), A Man Named Jesus (1971), Someone who Beckons (1978), Lift Every Heart (1984), A Flame of Love (1987); contributor to various hymn books; *Recreations* reading, verse, woodwork, family and friends; *Clubs* Norfolk (Norwich); *Style*— The Rt Rev the Bishop of Thetford; Rectory Meadow, Bramerton, Norwich NR14 7DW (☎ Surlingham 251)

THIESS, Sir Leslie Charles; CBE (1968); s of H Thiess; *b* 8 April 1909; *Educ* Drayton Sch Toowoomba; *m* 1929, Christina, da of L Erbacher; 2 s, 3 da; *Career* fndr Thiess Brothers 1934; chm: Drayton Investments Pty Ltd, Thiess Watkins Gp of Co's, Breakwater Island Ltd, Queensland Metals Corp NL, Thiess Toyota Pty Ltd, Daihatsu Australia Pty Ltd; awarded Third Order of Sacred Treasure by Japanese Govt; FCIT; kt 1971; *Style*— Sir Leslie Thiess, CBE; 121 King Arthur Terrace, Tennyson, Qld 4105, Australia

THIMBLEBY, Peter; s of Arthur Wilfrid Thimbleby, and Gertrude Mary, *née* Fovargue; *b* 12 Sept 1927; *Educ* Rugby, Leicester Sch of Architecture; *m* 19 Sept 1950, Angela Marion, da of Walter Harold Hodson (d 1982); 1 s (Harold William b 1955), 1 da (Elizabeth Angela b 1953); *Career* Grenfell Bains Gp 1951-57, princ in private practice 1957-; FRIBA, FIAAS; *Recreations* caravanning; *Style*— Peter Thimbleby, Esq; Ryedale, 9 Overslade Lane, Rugby CV22 6DU (☎ 0788 815019); 62 Regent St, Rugby CV21 2PS (☎ 0788 544513)

THISELTON, Rev Dr Anthony Charles; s of Eric Charles Thiselton (d 1979), of Woking, Surrey, and Hilda Winifred, *née* Kevan (d 1969); *b* 13 July 1937; *Educ* City of London, Kings Coll Univ of London (BD, MTh), Univ of Sheffield (PhD); *m* 21 Sept 1963, Rosemary Stella, da of Ernest Walter Harman (d 1979), of Eastbourne, Sussex; 2 s (Stephen b 1964, Martin b 1969), 1 da (Linda b 1966); *Career* curate Holy Trinity Sydenham 1960-63, chaplain Tyndale Hall Bristol 1963-67, recognised teacher in theology Univ of Bristol 1965-70, sr tutor Tyndale Hall 1967-70, lectr in biblical studies Univ of Sheffield 1970-79, sr lectr 1979-85, visiting prof and fell Calvin Coll Grand Rapids 1982-83; princ: St John's Coll Nottingham 1985-88, St John's Coll Univ of Durham 1988-; memb: C of E Doctrine Cmmn 1976, C of E Faith and Order Advsy Gp 1971-81 and 1986-, Cncl for Nat Academic Awards, Ctee for Arts and Humanities 1983-87, Ctee for Humanities 1987-, Revised Catechism Working Pty 1988-89, Studiorum Novi Testamenti Societas, Soc for the Study of Theol, American Acad of Religion; examining Chaplian to: Bishop of Sheffield 1976-80, Bishop of Leicester 1979-86; *Books* Language, Liturgy and Meaning (1975), The Two Horizons: New Testament Hermeneutics and Philosophical Description (1980), The Responsibility of Hermeneutics (co-author 1985); contributor to: Believing in the Church, We believe in God, Their Lord and Ours; *Recreations* organ, choral music, the sea; *Clubs* National Liberal; *Style*— The Rev Dr Anthony Thiselton; 20a South Street, Durham DH1 4QP; St John's College, Durham DH1 3RJ (☎ 091 374 3579/3561, fax 091 374 3740)

THISTLETHWAITE, Prof Frank; CBE (1979); s of Lee Thistlethwaite (d 1973), of Bibury, Glos, and Florence Nightingale, memb Thornber (d 1982); *b* 24 July 1915; *Educ* Bootham Sch York, St John's Coll Cambridge (MA), Univ of Minnesota USA; *m* 11 Aug 1940, Jane, da of Harry Lindley Hosford (d 1946), of Lyme, Connecticut, USA; 2 s (Stephen Lee b 1944, d 1951, Miles b 1949), 3 da (Jill (Mrs Pellew) b 1942, Harriet b 1953, Sarah Lee (Mrs More) b 1956); *Career* Br Press Serv NY 1940-41; RAF 1941-45, seconded to Offs of War Cabinet 1942-45; fell St John's Coll Cambridge 1945-61, lectr faculty of econs and politics Cambridge Univ 1949-61, Inst for Advanced Study Princeston 1954, founding chm Br Assoc for American Studies 1955-59, founding vice-chllr UEA 1961-80, visiting fell Henry E Huntingdon Library California 1973, chm ctee of mgmnt Inst of US Studies Univ of London, Hill visiting prof Univ of Minnesota 1986; memb: Inter-Univ Cncl for Higher Educn Overseas 1962-81 (chm 1977-81), Marshall Aid Commoration Cmmn 1964-80, bd (formerly exec ctee) Br Cncl 1971-82; Hon LHD Univ of Colorado 1972, hon fell St John's Coll Cambridge 1974, Hon DCL UEA 1980, Hon Prof of History Univ of Mauritius 1918; hon fell RIBA 1985; FRHistS 1963; *Books* The Great Experiment; and Introduction to the History of the American People (1955), The Anglo-American Connection in the Early Nineteenth Century (1958); *Recreations* playing the piano, historical writing; *Clubs* The Athenaeum; *Style*— Prof Frank Thistlethwaite, CBE; 15 Park Parade, Cambridge CB5 8AL (☎ 0223 352680); Island Cottage, Winson, Glos

THISTLETHWAITE, John; s of Robert Thistlethwaite (former dir of R Thistlethwaite Ltd, and Merchant Navy Offr 1916-19), of Salterforth, and Edith Mary, *née* Pickles; *b* 5 Mar 1943; *Educ* Ashville Coll, Harrogate; *m* 18 June 1966 (m dis 1976); 1 s (Simon b 1968); *Career* CA; co sec: Dale Electric Int 1967-70, Suter Electrical Ltd 1970-, Pennine Motor Gp 1970-73, Evans of Leeds plc 1984-87; sr ptnr John Thistlethwaite and Co 1975-; dir: R Thistlethwaite Ltd 1959-60, Simon James Motors Ltd 1972-78, Skipton Finance Ltd 1973-87, F R Evans (Admin) Ltd 1985-87, Erskine Systems Ltd 1968-70, Dale Electrical installations Ltd 1968-70, Dale Plant Hire Ltd 1968-70, Skipton Sports Cars Ltd 1978-85; FCA 1966; FSCA 1968; MICMK 1975; *Recreations* cricket, music, snooker, motoring; *Clubs* Craven Gentlemens, Skipton; *Style*— John Thistlethwaite, Esq; Hunters Moon, Embsay, Skipton, N Yorkshire (☎ 0756 5052)

THISTLETHWAYTE, John Robin; JP; s of Lt-Cdr Thomas Thistlethwayte, RNVR (d 1956), of Bursledon Lodge, Old Bursledon, Hants, and Hon Eileen Gwladys (d 1955), *née* Berry; eld da of 1st and last Baron Buckland; *b* 8 Dec 1935; *Educ* Bradfield, RAC Cirencester; *m* 22 Jan 1964, Mary Katherine Grasett, da of Lt-Gen Sir (Arthur) Edward Grasett KBE, CB, DSO, MC, of Adderbury, Oxfordshire; 2 s (Mark b 1964, Hugo b 1967), 1 da (Sophy b 1973); *Career* chartered surveyor; ptnr Savills 1961-86, conslt to Savills Ltd 1986-; mayor of Chipping 1964 and 1965; chm Chipping Norton Petty Sessional Div 1984 and 1985; chm N Oxfordshire and Chipping Norton PSD 1989-; FRICS; *Recreations* shooting, travel; *Clubs* Boodles, St James; *Style*— John R Thistlethwayte, Esq, JP; Sorbrook Manor, Adderbury, Oxfordshire OX17 3EG; The Estate Office, Southwick, Fareham, Hants PO17 6EA; Savills Ltd, 21 Horse Fair, Banbury, Oxfordshire (☎ 0295 3535, telex 837291 SAVBAN, fax 0295 50784)

THISTLETHWAYTE, Maj (Thomas) Noel; s of Lt Cdr Thomas Arthur Donald Claude Thistlethwayte, RNVR (d 1956), and Ethel Mary, *née* Hickie (d 1934); *b* 18 Oct 1925; *Educ* Eton; *m* 10 Oct 1953, Ann Patience Wallop, da of Capt Newton William-Powlett, DSC, RN, of Cadhay, Ottery-St-Mary, Devon; 1 s (Rupert b 19 Jan 1955), 1 da (Jane b 2 June 1957); *Career* cmmnd 60 Rifles KRRC 1944, seconded Para Regt 1947-50; serv: Palestine, N Africa, Egypt, Borneo, BAOR; Lt Col dir staff Army Staff Coll 1961-64, ret 1965; dir: Rupert Chetwynd & Ptnrs Advertising 1968-77, Chetwynd Streets Fin Advertising and Chetwynd Streets (Hldgs) Ltd 1973-77; govr Royal West of Eng Residential Sch for the Deaf, local chm Devon Historic Churches Tst; MIPA 1968-77; *Recreations* sailing, shooting; *Clubs* Naval & Military; *Style*— Maj Noel Thistlethwayte; Summerhayes, Throwleigh, Okehampton, Devon (☎ 064 723 425)

THOBURN, Ralph Wood; VRD (1968); s of Capt Ralph Wood Thoburn (d 1967), of South Shields, and Florence, *née* Hayton (d 1986); *b* 1 Feb 1926; *Educ* South Shields HS; *m* 29 Aug 1953, Heather Rosslyn Rosemary, da of Capt William Leslie Cruikshank, DSC (d 1955); 3 s (Ralph b 1962, Grant b 1963, Hamish b 1965); *Career* RN 1944-47, RNR Tyne Div (HMS Calliope) 1952-70, ret cdr; CA; self employed Thoburn & Charlton 1955-; hon tres S Tyneside Help The Aged, chm Tyne and Wear ctee Missions to Seamen (memb gen ctee OS, memb cncl), memb S Tyneside Family Practitioner Ctee; formerly: pres S Shields and Westoe Club, master Westoe Lodge of Freemasons; FCA 1948; *Recreations* golf, bridge, swimming; *Style*— Ralph Thoburn, Esq; Rose Cottage, 37 Sunderland Rd, Cleadon, Sunderland, Tyne & Wear SR6 7UW (☎ 091 536 670); Thoburn and Charlton, Coronation Bldgs, 2 Charlotte Terr, South Shields, Tyne and Wear NE33 1QQ (☎ 091 456 8021, fax 091 427 0246)

THOM, Timothy Ritchie; JP (1982); s of David Ritchie Thom (d 1957), and Edna Beryl, *née* May (d 1986); *b* 20 May 1940; *Educ* Bedford Sch; *m* 8 Feb 1964, Diana Monica Mae, da of Edward James Morrow Tait (d 1973); 2 da (Fiona b 1965, Belinda b 1967); *Career* CA; ptnr Price Waterhouse Bristol; memb Cncl of the Univ of Bristol; FCA (1964); *Recreations* golf, fishing, gardening; *Clubs* Clifton, Burnham and Berrow Golf; *Style—* Timothy Thom, Esq, JP; The Forge, Lower Langford, Bristol BS18 7HU (☎ 0934 862356); c/o Clifton Heights, Triangle West, Bristol BS8 1EB (☎ 0272 293701)

THOMAS, (John) Alan; s of Idris Thomas, of Cambridge Gardens, Langland, Swansea, and Ellen Constance Thomas; *b* 4 Jan 1943; *Educ* Dynevor Sch Swansea, Nottingham Univ (Bsc); *m* 1966, Angela, da of Fersil Owain Taylor (d 1969); 2 s (Andrew James b 1971, Alexander Michael b 1974); *Career* md Data Logic Ltd 1973-85, pres and chief exec offr Raytheon Europe 1985-, vice pres Raytheon Co (US); dir: Cossor Electronics Ltd 1978, A C Cossor Ltd 1985, Sterling Greengate Cable Co Ltd 1985, Electrical Installations Ltd 1985, Lacroix Kress (W Germany) 1985, TAG Semiconductors (Switzerland) 1985; pres Computing Servs Assoc 1980-81; visiting prof Sch of Business Studies & Social Scis Poly of Centl London 1982-; CEng, MIProdE, FCMA (prizewinner); *Recreations* music, sport; *Clubs* Annabel's, Les Ambassadeurs; *Style—* Alan Thomas, Esq; Highwood Park, London NW7 (☎ 01 959 1665); Raytheon Europe, Queens House, College Rd, Harrow, Middx (☎ 01 861 2525, telex 91957)

THOMAS, Alan Ritchie; s of William David Thomas (d 1958), and Nellie Ritchie (d 1958); *b* 1 May 1927; *Educ* Regent Poly, (Dip TP); *m* 1, Jul 1952 (m dis 1982), Rita Alice, da of Frederick Styles (d 1970); 2 s (Peter Stuart b 1957, William Neil b 1960), 1 da (Gillian Margaret b 1962); m 2, Brenda Amy, da of Joshua Hudlass Taylor (d 1984); *Career* RE 1945-48, serv Land Forces: Egypt, Greece; chartered architect and town planner, offr in planning depts of various boroughs and LCC 1948-57, ptnr Ardin & Brookes 1957-79, fndr PDA Architectural Ptnrships 1979-; ARIBA, MRTPI; *Recreations* motor sports, photography; *Clubs* RAC; *Style—* Alan Thomas, Esq; 3 Beechwood Drive, Wincham, Northwich, Cheshire; PDA Architectural Partnership, 62 Bridge St, Manchester M3 3BW (☎ 061 832 2393)

THOMAS, Alston Havard Rees; s of Ebenezer Gwyn (d 1971), of Longworth, Oxford, and Mary Ann, *née* Morris (d 1974); *b* 8 July 1925; *Career* reporter: West Wales Guardian 1939-44, Wiltshire Times 1944-46; Bristol Evening Post: local govt specialist writer (also sport and ecclesiatical affrs) 1946-70, diary ed 1970-84, fin and property writer 1984-; pres Inst of Journalists 1985-86 (memb 1974, chm 1981-84); memb: Press Cncl 1979-, Cncl of Newspaper Press Fund 1987-; pres Bristol and West of England Press Fund; memb Wales and West of England Newspaper Trg Cncl, memb Avon Cncl of St John Ambulance; *Books* Muddling Through (jtly 1988); *Recreations* rugby, rugby football; *Clubs* Savages (Bristol); *Style—* Alston Thomas, Esq; Havene, Maysmead Lane, Langford, Bristol BS18 7HX (☎ 0934 862515); Bristol United Press, Temple Way, Bristol (☎ 0272 260080)

THOMAS, Ambler Reginald; CMG (1951); s of John Frederick Ivor Thomas OBE (d 1940), and Elizabeth Thomas; *b* 12 Feb 1913; *Educ* Gresham's Sch Holt, CCC Cambridge; *m* 1943, Diana Beresford, da of Arthur Gresham, MC; 2 s, 3 da; *Career* Civil Serv 1935, transferred Colonial Off 1936, chief sec Govt of Aden 1947-49, under-sec Miny of Overseas Devpt 1964-70, under-sec FCO 1970-73, chm Ctee of Inquiry into Devpt Authy of Gilbert Is 1976, memb exec ctee Br Cncl 1965-69; chm Corona Club; *Recreations* gardening, reading, walking; *Clubs* United Oxford and Cambridge; *Style—* Ambler Thomas, Esq, CMG; Champsland, North Chideock, Bridport, Dorset (☎ 0297 89314)

THOMAS, Capt (John Anthony) Bruce; RN; s of John Haydn Thomas (d 1987), of Crowborough, and Hove, and Barbara Ann, *née* Jones (d 1974); *b* 15 Nov 1929; *Educ* Warden House, RNC Dartmouth, RNC Greenwich; *m* 30 Nov 1957, Genevieve Margaret, da of Walter Frederick Whiting (d 1985), of Felixstowe; 1 da (Rachel b 1965); *Career* Sub Lt 1949, Lt 1952, Lt Cdr 1960, Cdr 1964, in cmd HMS Houghton and sr offr 6 M Sqdn 1964-66, JSSC 1966/67, MOD (N) 1967-68, Exec Offr HMS Albion 1968-71, Dir Ser Intelligence FE Cmd 1971-72, Capt 1972, i/c HMS Phoebe 1973-74, ACOS (ops) NAVSOUTH 1974-76, i/c HMS Hermione and Capt 5 Frigate Sqdn 1977-78, Cdre 1978, Cdre Naval Ship Acceptance and dir of Naval Equipment 1978-82; ADC to HM The Queen 1981-82; head Ship Weapon Systems Br Aerospace (Dynamics) 1988- (shipyard and warship advsr 1982-88); bd memb Br Marine Equipment Cncl 1987-; *Recreations* golf, shooting, sailing; *Clubs* Army & Navy, Lansdown GC, Bosham Sailing; *Style—* Capt Bruce Thomas, RN; Church End, Hawkesbury Upton, Badminton GL9 1AU (☎ 045423 707); British Aerospace Dynamics Ltd, FPC 622, PO Box 5, Filton, Bristol BS12 7QN (☎ 0272 366414)

THOMAS, Hon Catherine Clare Mitchell; yr da of Baron Thomas of Gwydir, PC, QC (Life Peer), *qv*; *Style—* The Hon Catherine Thomas; 57 Stanhope Gardens, London N4

THOMAS, Hon Charles Inigo Gladwyn; er s of Baron Thomas of Swynnerton; *b* 11 Oct 1962; *Style—* The Hon Charles Thomas

THOMAS, Dr Dafydd Elis; MP (Plaid Cymru, Meirionnydd Nant Conwy 1983-); *b* 18 Oct 1946; *Educ* Univ Coll of North Wales; *Career* former adult educn tutor, writer and broadcaster; TGWU, contested (PlC) Conway 1970, MP (PlC) Merioneth Feb 1974-; pty spokesman: Social, Educn and Social Policy 1975, Agric and Rural devpt 1974; PlC vice pres 1979-81; hon sec: All Pty Mental Health Gp, Mind, Inst for Workers Control and Shelter; memb select ctee Educn, Science and Arts; *Style—* Dr Dafydd Thomas, MP; Bryn Meurig, Y Lawnt, Dolgellau, Gwynedd LL40 1DS

THOMAS, David Arthur; s of David Martell Thomas (d 1960), of Hampton, Middx, and Sybil Elizabeth, *née* Perry; *b* 7 April 1938; *Educ* RCA (Des RCA); *m* 1, 8 Aug 1976 (m dis 1986), Georgina Anne Caroline, da of Dr Joseph Linhart of London; 1 s (Edward b 14 Feb 1977); m 2, 12 Sept 1987, Gillian Mary, da of Norman Duncan Mussett (d 1983); 1 da (Jessica b 5 Jan 1988); *Career* md David Thomas Design Ltd 1965-(designing and producing fine jewellery and silver); one man exhibitions: St Louis and NY USA, Sydney Aust, Tokyo Japan, Goldsmiths Hall London, Florence Italy; princ cmmns: Masters badge Grocers Co, ladies badge of Goldsmiths Co, Sheriffs badges for City of London, trophy for King George VI and Queen Elizabeth II stakes; jewellery in perm collections: Worshipful Co of Goldsmiths, De Beers Diamonds, V & A; chm Goldsmiths Craft Cncl 1986-88; Freeman City of London 1964, Liveryman Worshipful Co of Goldsmiths 1985; FRSA 1964; *Style—* David Thomas, Esq; 65 Pimlico Rd, London SW1 (☎ 01 730 2389); Steep Cottage, Marle Hill, Chalford, Glos (☎ 0453 88 4058);

THOMAS, David Churchill; CMG (1982); s of David Bernard Thomas (d 1981), and Violet, *née* Quicke (d 1979); *b* 21 Oct 1933; *Educ* Eton, New Coll Oxford (BA); *m* 12 April 1958, Susan Petronella, da of John Arrow (d 1958); 1 s (David b 1959), 2 da (Clare b 1962, Harriet b 1963); *Career* 2 Lt Rifle Bde 1952-54; HM Diplomatic Serv 1957-86, FO 1957-59, third sec Moscow 1959-61, second sec Lisbon 1961-64, FO 1964-68, first sec (commercial) Lima 1968-70, FCO 1970-73, asst sec Cabinet Off 1973-78, political cncllr Washington 1978-81, HM ambass Havana 1981-84, asst under sec state (Americas), FCO 1984-86, ret 1986; *Recreations* photography, listening to music, running; *Style—* David Churchill Thomas, Esq, CMG; 54 Tournay Rd, London SW6 7UF (☎ 01 385 0860)

THOMAS, David Glyndor Treharne; s of Dr John Glyndor Treharne Thomas, MC (Capt RAMC) (d 1955), of Fairways, Hills Rd, Cambridge, and Ellen, *née* Geldart (d 1970); *b* 14 May 1941; *Educ* Perse Sch Cambridge, Gonville and Caius Coll Cambridge (BA, MA, MB, BChir); *m* 29 Dec 1970, Hazel Agnes Christina, da of William John Cockburn (d 1977), of 15 Tylney Road, Paisley, Renfrewshire; 1 s (William b 1972); *Career* St Marys Hosp London: house surgn 1966, asst lectr in anatomy 1967-68, sr house offr in neurology 1969, casualty offr 1969; Royal Post Grad Med Sch Hammersmith Hosp London: sr house offr in surgery 1970, registrar in cardio-thoracic surgery 1970-71; Inst of Neurological Scis Southern Gen Hosp Glasgow: registrar, sr registrar and lectr neuro surgery 1972-76; sr lectr Inst of Neurology and conslt neurosurgn Nat Hosps for Nervous Diseases and Northwick Park Hosp Harrow 1976-; memb: Med Acad Staff ctee BMA 1981-82, Jt Hosp Med Servs Ctee 1981-82; chm EORTC Experimental Neuro-Oncology Gp 1986-88; Freeman City of London 1969, Liveryman Worshipful Co of Apothecaries 1971; MRCS Eng 1966, MRCP (UK) 1970, FRCS Ed 1972, FRCP Glas 1985; *Books* Braintumours: Scientific Basis, Clinical Investigation and Current Therapy (ed with DI Graham 1980), Biology of Braintumour (ed with MD Walker 1986), Neurooncology: Primary Brain Tumours (ed 1989); *Recreations* mil and naval history; *Clubs* Athenaeum, RSM; *Style—* David Thomas, Esq; 34 Oppidans Road, Primrose Hill, London NW3 3AG (☎ 01 586 2262); The National Hospital, Queen Square, London WC1 3BG (☎ 01 837 3611 ext 3154/01 829 8765, fax 01 278 8874)

THOMAS, David Graeme; s of Edgar Henry Edwin Thomas (d 1975); *b* 22 Oct 1925; *Educ* St Paul's; *m* 1961, Muriel, *née* Rogers; *Career* sec Philip Hill Higginson Erlangers 1956-63, dep chm (dir 1963-) Robert Fleming, chm Aberdare Hldgs 1970-73, dir Save & Prosper Gp 1981-; CA; *Recreations* fox hunting, golf; *Clubs* Pratt's; *Style—* David Thomas, Esq; 151 Old Church St, Chelsea, London SW3 (☎ 01 351 2082)

THOMAS, David John Godfrey; s and h of Sir Godfrey Michael David Thomas, 11 Bt; *b* 11 June 1961; *Educ* Harrow; *Career* mangr; *Recreations* squash, tennis; *Clubs* Hurlingham, MCC, Jesters, Escorts; *Style—* David Thomas, Esq; 30 Orbain Rd, London SW6 7JY

THOMAS, Hon David Nigel Mitchell; er s of Baron Thomas of Gwydir, PC, QC (Life Peer), *qv*; *Style—* The Hon David Thomas; 72 Jerningham Road, London SE14

THOMAS, Sir Derek Morison David; KCMG (1987), CMG (1977); s of Kenneth Peter David Thomas (1982), of Hill House Hempstead, Saffron Walden, Essex, and Mali McLeod, *née* Morison (d 1972); *b* 31 Oct 1929; *Educ* Radley, Trinity Hall Cambridge (MA); *m* 1956, Lineke, da of Thijs Van der Mast (d 1988), of Eindhoven, Netherlands; 1 s (Matthew b 1967), 1 da (Caroline b 1963); *Career* Sub-Lt RNVR 1955 (Midshipman 1953-55); articled apprentice Dolphin Indust Devpts Ltd 1947, entered Dip Serv 1953: second sec (previously third sec) Moscow 1956-59, second sec Manila 1959-61, UK delgn to Brussels Conf 1961-62, FO 1962-64, first sec Sofia 1964-67, first sec Ottawa 1967-69, seconded to Treasy 1969-70, fin cnsllr Paris 1971-75, head of N American dept 1975-76, asst under sec of state econ affrs FCO 1976-79, min commercial (later min) Washington 1979-84, dep under sec of state for Europe and political dir FCO 1984-87, Br ambass to Italy 1987-; *Style—* Sir Derek Thomas, KCMG, CMG; Foreign and Commonwealth Office, London SW1 2AH

THOMAS, Derek Walter; s of Walter John Thomas (d 1974); *b* 18 Oct 1936; *Educ* Portsmouth Southern GS; *m* 1960, Maureen Janet, nee Smith; 1 s, 1 da; *Career* md: D W Thomas (Pensions) Ltd, Pensioneer Investmt Mgmnt Services Ltd; ctee memb Assoc Pensioneer Tstees; FIA; *Recreations* squash, cricket, singing, music; *Style—* Derek Thomas, Esq; Allingtons, 43 Beech Rd, Reygate, Surrey

THOMAS, Douglas Ronald; s of Harry Leonard Thomas; *b* 15 Feb 1925; *m* Shirley Edith Frances, da of Archibald Dixon; 1 s (David), 2 da (Susan (Mrs Taylor), Sally (Mrs Demain)); *Career* served Sgt RAF; md Rank Advertising Films Ltd; pres Cinema Advertising Assoc; vice-pres Screen Advertising World Assoc; FCIS, FBIM; *Clubs* arts; *Style—* Douglas Thomas, Esq

THOMAS, Edward Hugh Gwynne; s of Edward Gwynne Thomas, OBE, VRD (d 1976), and Lisbeth Helen Mair, *née* Thomas (d 1950); *b* 12 Dec 1938; *Educ* Canford; *m* 1 Dec 1973, Annemary Perry, da of Lawrence Walter Dixon, of Poole, Dorset; 3 da (Juliet b 1974, Annabel b 1977, Louisa 1979); *Career* slr 1963, ptnr Keene Marsland 1966-; Freeman: City of London 1966, Worshipful Co of Slrs 1966; memb: Law Soc 1963, Central and S Middlesex Law Soc 1966; *Recreations* golf, sailing; *Clubs* Beaconsfield GC; *Style—* Hugh Thomas, Esq; Orchard Corner, Curzon Ave, Beaconsfield Bucks HP9 2NN (☎ 0494 671056); 11/15 High St, Ruislip, Middlesex HA4 7AX (☎ 0895 634027, fax 0895 637728)

THOMAS, Hon Frances Jane Mitchell; er da of Baron Thomas of Gwydir, PC, QC (Life Peer), *qv*; 33 Oxford Road, Putney, London SW15

THOMAS, (John) Frank Phillips; s of John Phillips Thomas (d 1948), and Catherine Myfanwy, *née* Williams (d 1979); *b* 11 April 1920; *Educ* Christ's Coll Finchley, London Univ (BSc); *m* 12 Dec 1942, Edith Victory, da of Alexander Caskie Milne (d 1958); 1 s (Paul Alexander b 1945), 1 da (Jane Margaret b 1947); *Career* Br Telecom; dir network planning 1972-78, dir o'seas liaison 1978-81; dir Frank Thomas Consultants 1981-; vice pres Rickmansworth LT Club; MIEE; *Recreations* fly fishing; *Style—* Frank Thomas, Esq; 24 Moneyhill Road, Richmansworth, Herts WD3 2EQ (☎ 0923 772992)

THOMAS, Sir Frederick William; AE and 2 Bars; s of late F J Thomas; *b* 27 June 1906; *Educ* Melbourne G S; *m* 1, 1944; 3 s; m 2, 1968, Dorothy Alexa, da of Carlos Gordon (decd); *Career* Gp Capt RAAF; md W C Thomas & Sons Ltd, cllr City of Melbourne 1953-65, (lord mayor 1957-59); Cdr Order of Orange Nassau with Swords (Holland) 1943; kt 1959; *Style—* Sir Frederick Thomas, AE; 35 Hitchcock Ave, Barwon Heads, Vic 3227, Australia

THOMAS, Air Vice-Marshal Geoffrey Percy Sansom; CB (1970), OBE (1945); s of Reginald Ernest Sansom Thomas (d 1949); *b* 24 April 1915; *Educ* King's Coll Sch Wimbledon; *m* 1940, Sally, *née* Biddle; 1 s, 1 da; *Career* cmmnd RAF 1939, served with Turkish Air Force 1950-52, served with RAAF 1960-62, Air Cdre 1965, dir of Movements 1965, Air Vice-Marshal 1969, SASO Maintanance Cmd 1969-71 (ret 1971); *Style—* Air Vice-Marshal Geoffrey Thomas; Elms Wood House, Elms Vale, Dover, Kent (☎ 0304 206375)

THOMAS, Gervase Alan; s of Alan Ernest Wentworth Thomas, DSO, MC (d 1969); *b* 19 April 1930; *Educ* Eton, Clare Coll Cambridge; *m* 1961 (m dis 1984), Jane Elizabeth, *née* Ross-Lowe; 2 s , 2 da; m 2, 1988, Carey Yulan Adria Coren, *née* Ross; *Career* 2 Lt Gren Gds; dir York Tst Gp plc; *Recreations* fox hunting, shooting, boating, golf; *Clubs* Boodle's, MCC; *Style—* Gervase Thomas, Esq; Charlcot, Ripon, N Yorks (☎ 0765 89335); York Trust Ltd, St Pauls House, Park Sq, Leeds (☎ 0532 460132)

THOMAS, Glyn Collen; s of Graham Lewis Thomas, of Budleigh Salterton, Devon, and Pegi Joan, *née* Bingham; *b* 30 July 1951; *Educ* BEC GS London, Cardiff HS Glamorgan, Univ of Wales Cardiff (BSc); *m* 9 Sept 1983, Heather Audrey, da of Thomas Alexander Kerslick, of Fulham, London; 1 s (Gregory Lewis b 30 March 1984), 1 da (Chloe Elizabeth b 3 June 1988); *Career* Peat Marwick Mitchell 1972-76, Rothmans Int London and Zug 1976-86, Woolworth Hldgs 1986-; memb Chalfonts and Gerrards Cross Gp SDP; memb: Assoc Corporate Treasy 1982, ICAEW, FCA 1975; *Recreations* skiing, squash; *Style—* Glyn Thomas, Esq; 6 Old Mead, Chalfont St Peter, Bucks SL9 0SE (☎ 02407 3691); Woolworth Hldgs plc, 119 Marylebone Rd, London NW1 5PX (☎ 01 724 7749, fax 01 724 1160)

THOMAS, Godfrey Slee; s of Harold Charles Thomas, of Walberton, Arundel, West Sussex, and Freda Elisabeth, *née* Slee; *b* 14 Feb 1946; *Educ* Brighton Coll, New Coll Oxford (BA, MA); *m* 5 Nov 1977, Caroline Anne, da of Leslie Gordon Glynn Warne (d 1962); 2 da (Charlotte b 21 Nov 1978, Verity b 9 March 1981); *Career* dir: Cap Scientific Ltd 1980-82 (md 1988-), Cap Indust Ltd 1982-88, Dowty-Cap Ltd 1988-, Aerosystems Int Ltd 1988-; *Recreations* squash, singing; *Style—* Godfrey Thomas, Esq; Cap Scientific Ltd, Scientific House, 40-44 Coombe Rd, New Malden KT3 4QF (☎ 01 942 9661, fax 01 949 8067, telex 28863)

THOMAS, Graham Stuart; OBE (1975); s of William Richard Thomas (d 1947), of 169 Hills Rd, Cambridge, and Lilian, *née* Hays (d 1951); *b* 3 April 1909; *Educ* Botanic Garden Univ of Cambridge; *Career* foreman later mangr T Hilling & Co 1931, assoc dir Sunningdale Nurseries Windlesham Surrey 1968-71 (mangr 1956), gardens conslt The Nat Tst 1974- (advsr 1954-74); vice pres: Garden History Soc, Br Hosta and Hemerocallis Soc, hon vice pres Royal Nat Rose Soc; RHS: Veitch Meml Medal 1966, Victoria Medal of Hon 1968; Dean Hole Medal Royal Nat Rose Soc 1976, hon memb Irish Garden Plant Soc 1983; *Books* The Old Shrub Roses (1955), Colour in the Winter Garden (1957), Shrub Roses of Today (1962), Climbing Roses Old and New (1965), Plants for Ground Cover (1970), Perennial Garden Plants (1976), Gardens of the National Trust (1979), Three Gardens (1983), Trees in the Landscape (1983), Recreating the Period Garden (ed 1984), A Garden of Roses (1987), The Complete Paintings and Drawings of Graham Stuart Thomas (1987); *Recreations* music, painting flowers, reading; *Style—* Graham Thomas, Esq, OBE; Briar Cottage, 21 Kettlewell Close, Horsell, Woking, Surrey (☎ 048 62 4042)

THOMAS, Gwyn Edward Ward; CBE (1973), DFC; s of William John Thomas (d 1941), and Constance, *née* Ogden; *b* 1 August 1923; *Educ* Bloxham, Rouen Lycée; *m* 1945, Patricia, da of Cecil Cornelius; 1 da; *Career* served WWII Fl Lt RAF Bomber and Tport Cmd Europe and India; md Grampian TV 1960-67; former chm: Yorkshire TV, Don Robinson Hldgs, Scarborough Zoo and Marineland; former dir Survival Anglia Ltd, chm and md Trident Television to 1984, chief exec Playboy (acquired by Trident Jan 1982) 1982-; chm: Castlewood Investmts, Watts & Corry Ltd and various Trident assoc cos: Trident Int, Trident Hldgs Pty, Independent Television Enterprise SA, Trident Films Ltd; dir: Tyne Tees Television Ltd, chm United Cable Programmes Ltd 1984-85; chm Br Cable Services 1985-; ptnr Worldwide Television Associates; *Style—* G E Ward Thomas, Esq, CBE, DFC

THOMAS, (John) Harvey Noake; s of Col John Humphrey Kenneth Thomas (d 1984), of Leamington Spa, and Olga Rosina, *née* Noake; *b* 10 April 1939; *Educ* Westminster, Univ of Minnesota, Univ of Hawaii, North Western Bible Coll Minnesota; *m* 22 Dec 1978, Marlies, da of Erich Kram, of Wolmersen, Federal Germany; 2 da (Leah Elisabeth b 1984, Lani Christine b 1986); *Career* Billy Graham Evangelistic Assoc 1960-75, int PR conslt 1976-, dir presentation and promotion Cons Party 1985-, field dir PM's Election Tour 1987, dir The London Cremation Co 1984-; memb: Oakwood Baptist Church N London, Salvation Army Advsy Bd London; memb: Inst PR, Assoc of Conf Exec; fell Inst of Journalists; *Books* In The Face Of Fear (1985); *Recreations* travel; *Clubs* IOD; *Style—* Harvey Thomas, Esq; 105A High Rd, Wood Green, London N22 6BB (☎ 01 889 6466)

THOMAS, Hon Henry Isambard Tobias; 2 s of Baron Thomas of Swynnerton; *b* 28 Jan 1964; *Educ* Latymer Upper Sch, London Coll of Printing, St Martins Sch of Art; *Career* artistic director; *Style—* The Hon Henry Thomas

THOMAS, Hilary Joan; *née* Thompson; da of John MacMillan Thompson, of Shaftesbury, Dorset, and Vivienne Josephine, *née* Thomson; *b* 27 May 1935; *Educ* St Cyprian's Sch Cape Town; *m* 15 June 1963, Rowland Humphrey Thomas, s of Leonard Tennant Thomas (d 1968); 1 s (David James Hamilton b 1970), 1 da (Caroline Josephine b 1966); *Career* journalist; historical researcher and genealogist 1970-, SRN St Thomas' Hosp 1958 *publications*: travel books, nursing articles, London; research on biographies, genealogies; *Recreations* travel, theatre, music, books, country walking; *Clubs* Soc of Genealogists; *Style—* Mrs Hilary Thomas; 27 Grasvenor Ave, Barnet, Herts EN5 2BY (☎ 01 440 5662)

THOMAS, Hugh Miles; s of Dr Gwilym Dorrien Thomas, of 17 Bryn Hyfred, Cwmisfael, nr Camarthen, and Dorothy Gertrude, *née* Jones; *b* 14 Oct 1944; *Educ* Clifton, Southampton Univ (BSc); *m* 10 Sept 1966, Alison Mary, da of Lt-Col Richard Ryder Davies (d 1968); 2 s (Simon b 1 July 1970, Ryder b 24 May 1973); *Career* CA 1969; Price Waterhouse: articled 1966, ptnr 1978-, ptnr in charge Wales 1983-; pres S Wales Inst of CAs 1987-88; memb: cncl UWIST 1983-88, cncl Univ of Wales Coll of Cardiff 1988, mgmnt ctee Cardiff Business Sch, Prince of Wales' Ctee (chm fin and gen purposes ctee); vice pres Cardiff Business Club; FCA 1979; *Recreations* sailing, farming; *Clubs* Cardiff Co; *Style—* Hugh Thomas, Esq; Penprysg, Llangenny, Crickhowell, Powys (☎ 0873 811387); Price Waterhouse, Haywood House North, Dumfries Place, Cardiff CF1 4BA (☎ 0222 376255, fax 0222 374124, telex 497949)

THOMAS, Hon Huw Maynard Mitchell; yr s of Baron Thomas of Gwydir, PC, QC (Life Peer), *qv*; *m* Jane, *née* Perman; 2 da; *Style—* The Hon Huw Thomas; 2 Porden Rd, London SW2

THOMAS, Baroness; Hylda Nora; da of late George Church, of Littlemore, Oxon; *m* 1924, Baron Thomas, DFC (Life Peer d 1980); *Style—* The Rt Hon the Lady Thomas; Remenham Court, Henley-on-Thames, Oxon

THOMAS, Ian Mitchell; s of John Bythell Thomas (d 1977), of Sutton Coldfield, and Gladys Ethel, *née* Miller; *b* 17 May 1933; *Educ* Liverpool Coll, Selwyn Coll Cambridge (MA); *m* 1, 20 Aug 1960 (m dis 1976), Jenifer Diana, da of Dr George Thomas Lance Fletcher Morris, of Coggeshall, Essex; 2 s (James b 1961, Mark b 1965), 2 da (Emma b 1963, Victoria b 1969); m 2, 24 Oct 1977, Diana Lesley Kathryn, wid of Nicholas Thorne (d 1976), and da of Donald William Leslie (d 1984), of Wimbledon; 1 step s (Alexander b 1972), 1 step da (Camilla b 1976); *Career* Nat Serv 4 KORR 1952-54 (2 Lt 1953), PA to COS Br Cwlth Forces Korea 1953, Capt The Liverpool Scottish Queen's Own Cameron Highlanders TA; asst md Hobson Bates and Ptnrs 1965 (dir 1963), jt md Cavenham Foods Ltd 1965-67, md Fabbri and Ptnrs Ltd 1968-70, chm Culpeper Ltd 1972- (md 1972-); cncllr (C) Islington Cncl 1968-70, vice pres Herb Soc 1986-87 (cncl memb 1978-87); *Books* Culpeper's Book of Birth (1985), How to Grow Herbs (1988); *Recreations* running, tennis, skiing, gardening; *Style—* Ian Thomas, Esq; Floriston Hall, Wixoe, Halstead, Essex CO9 4AR (☎ 044 085 229); Culpeper Ltd, Hadstock Rd, Linton, Cambridge CB1 6NJ (☎ 0223 891196, fax 0223 893104, car 0836 232545, telex 81698)

THOMAS, Irene; da of Edmund Roberts Ready (d 1956), and Ethel, *née* Crapnell (d 1970); *b* 28 June 1920; *Educ* The County Sch Ashford Middx; *m* 1, 1940 (m dis 1949), Wesley J C Baldry; m 2, 23 Jan 1950, Edward Kenfig Thomas, s of Walter Thomas of Porth, Rhondda; *Career* NFS 1940-45, Covent Garden Opera 1946-49, free-lance singer 1950-68; broadcaster progs inc: Brain of Britain 1961, Brain of Brains 1962, Round Britain Quiz 1967 and 1973-, Round Europe Quiz, Transatlantic Quiz; tv progs inc: The 60-70-80 show (with Roy Hudd) 1974-80, About Face 1986; regular contrib Woman & Home Magazine; *Books* The Bandsman's Doughter (1979), The Almost Impossible Quiz Book (1982); *Recreations* watching cats, thinking; *Style—* Mrs Irene Thomas; c/o BBC, Broadcasting House, London W1A 1AA

THOMAS, Hon Isabella Pandora; da of Baron Thomas of Swynnerton; *b* 17 Mar 1966; *Style—* The Hon Isabella Thomas

THOMAS, Hon Mrs (Jacqueline); yst da of Baron Cooper of Stockton Heath (Life Peer, d 1988); *b* 1946; *m* 1972, J Bradford Thomas; *Style—* The Hon Mrs Thomas; 54 Stanley Road, East Sheen, London SW14 7DZ

THOMAS, Jeffrey; QC (1974); s of John Thomas and Phyllis, *née* Hile; *b* 12 Nov 1933; *Educ* Abertillery GS, King's Coll London; *m* 1, 1960 (m dis 1981), Margaret Jenkins; m 2, 1987, Valerie Ellerington; *Career* barr (Gray's Inn) 1957, Crown Court recorder 1975-, served RCT from 1959 and as Maj Dep Assist Directorate Army Legal Servs BAOR HQ 1961; fought Barry (Lab) 1966; MP (Lab to Dec 1981, thereafter SDP) Abertillery 1970-83; pps to Sec State Wales 1977-79, Labour Party 1986, vice-chm Br Gp IPU, oppn spokesman Legal Affrs 1979-81; chm Br-Caribbean Assoc; 1979-83, now vice-pres, memb Court Univ of London until 1986; *Style—* Jeffrey Thomas Esq, QC; 3 Temple Gdns, Temple, London EC4 (☎ 01 583 0010); 26 Ellington St, London N7

THOMAS, Jeremy Jack; s of Maj Phillip Thomas, MC, and Joy Eveleyn, *née* Spanjer; *b* 26 July 1949; *Educ* Millfield; *m* 1, (m dis 1977), Claudia Frolich; m2, 1982, Vivien Patricia, da of Adolph Coughman; 2 s (Jack Felix, Joshua Kit), 1 da (Jessica Emily); *Career* film prodr; Mad Dog Morgan (1976), The Shout (1977), The Great Rock 'N' Roll Swindle (1978), Bad Timing (1979), Eureka (1982), Merry Christmas Mr Lawrence (1982), The Hit (1983), Insignificance (1984), The Last Emperor (1988), winning nine Academy Awards including 'Best Picture'; *Style—* Jeremy Thomas, Esq; The Recorded Picture Co, 8-12 Broadwick Street, London W1V 1FH (☎ 01 439 0607, fax 01 434 1192. telex 941 9035 RECORD G)

THOMAS, Lady; Jill; da of Edward Gordon Cuthbert Quilter; *m* 1946, Gen Sir (John) Noel Thomas, KCB, DSO, MC (d 1983, master-gen of the Ordnance 1971-74 and vice-chm Cwlth War Graves Cmmn 1974-81); 2 s; *Style—* Lady Thomas; Chandlers House, The Trippet, Old Bosham, Sussex

THOMAS, John Richard; s of David Edgar Thomas (d 1954), of Talog, Manor Way, Petts Wood, Kent, and Daisy Thomas (d 1949); *b* 11 Sept 1927; *Educ* Dulwich; *m* 4 July 1953, Pamela Mary, da of Owen Henry White (d 1959), of Three Chimneys, Fittleworth, West Sussex; 2 s (Mark David b 2 May 1955, Richard Jeremy b 19 Sept 1958); *Career* Royal W Kent Regt: Private 1946, cmmnd 2 Lt 1947, demobilised 1948; chm and sr ptnr Baxter Payne & Lepper Chartered Surveyors 1973-87 (ptnr 1959, conslt 1987-); dir: S of Eng Bldg Soc 1967-82, Nationwide Anglia Soc 1987-, Surveyors Hldgs (RICS) Ltd 1986-, dep chm Anglia Bldg Soc 1985-87 (vice chm 1982-85); chm: Nationwide Anglia Estate Agents 1987-, Peter Ling plc (bldg contractors); chm Gtr London (SE) Scout Cncl 1973-, hon sec Bromley Literary and Music Soc 1970-85; pres gen practise RICS 1977-78, memb gen cncl RICS 1974-88, magistrate SE Cmmn 1975-; fndr memb Worshipful Co of Chartered Surveyors 1977-; FRICS 1954, FRSA 1973; *Books* Valuations for Loan Purposes (1981), Estate Agents Act 1979 (1982); *Recreations* golf, music, gardening; *Clubs* St Stephens, Ham Manor GC, Sundridge Park GC; *Style—* John Thomas, Esq; 6 Glenbyrne Lodge, Albemarle Rd, Becken Ham, Kent (☎ 01 464 1181); Nationwide Anglia Bldg Soc, Chesterfield House, Bloomsbury Way, London (☎ 01 242 8822/01 379 0101)

THOMAS, Keith Henry Westcott; CB (1982), OBE (1962); s of Henry Westcott Thomas (d 1957), and Norah Dorothy, *née* Stone (d 1985); *b* 20 May 1923; *Educ* Southern Secdy Sch for Boys Portsmouth, Royal Dockyard Sch Portsmouth, RN Engrg Coll Manadon, RNC Greenwich; *m* 31 Aug 1946, Brenda Jeanette, da of William Royston Crofton (d 1964); 2 s (Michael b 1948, David b 1951); *Career* RCNC 1946-: asst constructor Admty Experiment Works Haslar 1946-49, professional sec to dir of naval construction Admiralty 1949-52, admiralty constructor (HM Yacht Britannia) 1952-53, constructor on staff of dir Tactical and Staff Requirements Div Admty 1953-56, constructor large carrier design Admty Bath 1956-60, constructor HM Dockyard Portsmouth 1960-63, chief constructor 1963-66, dep planning mangr HM Dockyard Devonport 1966-68 (project mangr 1968-70), dir gen Naval design Canberra Aust 1970-73, planning mangr HM Dockyard Rosyth 1973-75 (gen mangr 1975-77), gen mangr HM Dockyard Devonport 1977-79, chief exec Royal Dockyards (hd RCNC) 1979-83, ret 1983; pres Portsmouth Royal Dockyard Historical Soc, chm Hayling

Island Gp Civil Serv Retirement Fellowship; FEng 1981, FRINA 1970, FIIM 1981; *Recreations* painting, music, lapidary; *Style—* Keith Thomas, Esq, CB, OBE; 6 Wyborn Close, Hayling Island, Hants PO11 9HY (☎ 0705 463 435)

THOMAS, Leslie; s of David James Thomas, MN (ka 1943), and Dorothy Hilda Court (d 1943); *b* 22 Mar 1931; *Educ* Dr Barnardo's Kingston-on-Thames, Kingston Tech Sch; *m* 1, 1956 (m dis 1971), Maureen, da of Charles Crane; 2 s (Mark, Gareth), 1 da (Lois); m 2, Nov 1971, Diana Miles; 1 s (Matthew); *Career* Nat Serv Singapore, Malaya 1949-51; journalist 1951-63 (Exchange Telagraph 1955-57, London Evening News 1957-63); many radio and tv appearances; *Books* The Virgin Soldiers (1966), Tropic of Ruislip (1974), The Magic Army (1981), The Dearest and The Best (1984), The Adventures of Goodnight and Loving (1986), This Time Next Week (1964), In My Wildest Dreams (1983), Some Lovely Islands (1968), A World of Islands (1983), The Hidden Place of Britain (1981); *Recreations* cricket, music, antiques, stamp collecting; *Clubs* Lords Taverners, Wig and Pen; *Style—* Leslie Thomas, Esq; Greatbridge House, Greatbridge, Romsey, Hants

THOMAS, Sir (John) Maldwyn; s of Daniel Thomas (d 1930), and Gladys Thomas Davies (d 1954); *b* 17 June 1918; *Educ* Porth Glamorgan GS; *m* 1975, Maureen Elizabeth; *Career* barr Gray's Inn 1954, slr 1965; chm Rank Xerox Ltd 1972 (co sec 1964, md 1970), dir Xerox Corpn 1974-79, non exec dep chm John Brown plc 1984-, non exec dir Westland plc 1985-, memb cncl The Richmond Fell 1984-; Drake Fellowship 1986-; vice-pres London Welsh Rugby FC; kt 1984; *Clubs* Reform; *Style—* Sir Maldwyn Thomas; 9 Chester Terrace, Regent's Park, London NW1 4ND (☎ 01 486 4368)

THOMAS, Margaret; da of Francis Stewart Thomas (d 1971), of London, and Grace Darling, *née* Whetherly (d 1978); *b* 26 Sept 1916; *Educ* Slade, Royal Acad Schs; *Career* artist (painter); solo shows: Leicester Galleries London (1949 and 51), Aitken Dotts and Scottish Gallery Edinburgh (1952-), Howard Roberts Cardiff, Canaletto Gallery London, Minories Colchester, Mall Galleries London, Octagon Gallery Belfast Maltings Concert Hall Gallery Snape; work in numerous public collections incl: Chantrey Bequest, Miny of Educn, Exeter Coll Oxford, Bath Univ, Scottish Nat Orchestra, Edinburgh City Corpn, Mitsukshi Ltd Tokyo; reg exhibitor at Royal Acad and Royal Scottish Acad, winner Hunter Gp Award Oil Painting of the Year 1981; memb: Royal W of Eng Acad, RSBA, NEAC; *Recreations* gardens, dogs, vintage cars; *Style—* Miss Margaret Thomas; 8 North Bank St, Edinburgh (☎ 031 225 3343); Ellingham Mill, Bungay, Suffolk (☎ 050 845 656)

THOMAS, Meyric Leslie; OBE (1987); s of Lt-Col Charles Leslie Thomas (d 1979), of Horton, Gower, Glam, and Edith Annie (d 1983); *b* 17 Nov 1928; *Educ* Clifton Coll, Jesus Coll Oxford (MA); *m* 2 March 1956, Jillian Hamilton, da of Lt-Col Robert William Armstrong (d 1975), of Oxford; 2 s (Peter Leslie b 1956, Charles Leslie b 1958), 1 da (Clare Leslie b 1960); *Career* Nat Serv 2 Lt Glos Regt 1947-49; slr 1953, ptnr LC Thomas & Sons 1953-; Neath Harbour Cmmrs, Oak, Neath Div Income Tax Cmmrs; Oxford Rowing Blue 1952 & 1953, pres OUBC 1953, former pres and chm Neath RFC; pres: Neath Br Legion, Neath Cons Assoc; *Clubs* Vincents, Neath Constitutional; *Style—* Meyric Thomas, Esq, OBE; 13 Westernmoor Rd, Neath, W Glam (☎ 0639 3322); LC Thomas & Son, 19 London Rd, Neath, W Glam (☎ 0639 65061, fax 0639 66792)

THOMAS, Sir (Godfrey) Michael (David); 11 Bt (E 1694), of Wenvoe, Glamorganshire; s of Rt Hon Sir Godfrey John Vignoles, 10 Bt, PC, GCVO, KCB, CSI (d 1968); *b* 10 Oct 1925; *Educ* Harrow; *m* 1956, Margaret Greta, da of John Cleland, of Stormont Court, Godden Green, Sevenoaks; 1 s, 2 da (of whom 1 s and 1 da are twins); *Heir* s, David John Godfrey Thomas; *Career* Capt The Rifle Bde 1944-56; memb Stock Exchange 1959-; *Clubs* MCC, Hurlingham; *Style—* Sir Michael Thomas, Bt; 2 Napier Ave, London SW6 3PS (☎ 01 736 6896)

THOMAS, Michael David; CMG (1985), QC (1973); s of D Cardigan Thomas and Kathleen Thomas; *b* 8 Sept 1933; *Educ* Chigwell Sch Essex, LSE; *m* 1, 1958 (m dis 1978), Jane Lena Mary, eldest da of late Francis Neate; 2 s, 2 da; m 2, 1981 (m dis 1986), Mrs Gabrielle Blakemore; m 3, 1988, Lydia Dunn; *Career* barr Middle Temple 1955 (Bencher 1982), jr counsel to Treasury in Admiralty Matters 1966-73, wreck cmmr, salvage arbitrator Lloyd's 1974-83, attorney-gen Hong Kong 1983-88; memb of Exec and Legislative Cncls Hong Kong 1983-88; *Style—* Michael Thomas, Esq, CMG, QC; 2 Essex Court, Temple, London EC4Y 9AP; Temple Chambers, One Pacific Place, 88 Queensway, Hong Kong

THOMAS, Michael John Glyn; s of Glyn Pritchard Thomas (d 1985), and Mary, *née* Moseley (d 1987); *b* 14 Feb 1938; *Educ* Haileybury and ISC, Cambridge Univ (MA, MB, BChir), St Bart's Hosp; *m* 23 May 1969, (Sheelagh) Jane, da of Harold Thorpe (d 1979); 1 da (Fleur b 1970); *Career* RMO 2 Bn Para Regt 1964-67, trainee in pathology BMH Singapore 1967-71; specialist in pathology: Colchester MH 1971-74, Singapore 1974-76, sr specialist in pathology and 2 i/c Army Blood Supply Depot (ABSD) 1977-82, exchange fell Walter Reed Army Medical Centre Washington DC 1982-83, offr i/c Leishman Lab 1984-87, CO ABSD 1987-; BMA: memb cncl 1973-74 and 1977-82, Armed Forces Ctee 1971-82 and 1988-, jr membs forum 1971-78 (chm 1974), bd of Sci and Educn 1987-, Rep Body 1972-82 and 1987-, expert ctee on Aids 1986-; memb ctee on Transfusion Equipment Br Standard Inst, expert witness on Gene Mapping ESC; memb: Assoc of Clinical Pathologists 1971, Br Blood Transfusion Soc 1987, Inst of Medical Ethics 1987; LMSSA, DTM and H; *Books* Co-Author: Control of Infection (1989), Nuclear Attack, Ethics and Casulty Selection (1988), Handbook of Medical Ethics (1979), and subsequent editions; Contribution to Dictionary of Medical Ethics; *Recreations* DIY, photography, philately; *Clubs* Tanglin (Singapore); *Style—* Dr Michael Thomas; Army Blood Supply Depot, Ordnance Rd, Aldershot, Hants GU11 2AF (☎ 0252 24 431 ext 2140/2141, fax 0252 24 431 ext 2207/2358)

THOMAS, Sir (William) Michael Marsh; 3 Bt (UK 1918), of Garreglwyd, Anglesey; s of Major Sir William Eustace Rhyddlad Thomas, 2 Bt, MBE (d 1958), and Enid Helena Marsh (d 1982); *b* 4 Dec 1930; *Educ* Oundle; *m* 1957, Geraldine, da of Robert Drysdale, of Trearddur Bay, Anglesey; 3 da; *Heir* unc, Robert Freeman Thomas; *Career* formerly md Gors Nurseries Ltd; *Style—* Sir Michael Thomas, Bt; Belan, Fawr, Rhosneigr, Anglesey (☎ 0407 810541)

THOMAS, Michael Stuart (Mike); s of Arthur Edward Thomas, of 33 Longmeade Gardens, Wilmslow, Cheshire, and Mona, *née* Parker; *b* 24 May 1944; *Educ* Latymer Upper Sch, King's Sch Macclesfield, Liverpool Univ (BA 1965); *m* 31 July 1975, Maureen Theresa, da of Denis Kelly, of Derrynane, Stevenage Rd, Knebworth, Herts; 1 s by 1 m, (Paul b 1973); *Career* pres Liverpool Univ Guild of Undergrads 1965, memb Nat Exec NUS, head res dept Co-Op Party 1966-68, sr res assoc Policy Studies Inst 1968-73, dir The Volunteer Centre 1973-74; MP (Lab and Co-op 1974-81, SDP 1981-83) Newcastle-upon-Tyne East 1974- 1983; pps to Rt Hon Roy Hattersley, MP 1974-76, memb Commons Select Ctee Nationalised Industries 1975-79, chm PLP Trade Gp 1979-81, SDP spokesman health and social security 1981-83; SDP candidate Exeter 1987; memb: SDP Policy Ctee 1981-83 and 1984-, SDP Nat Ctee 1981-; chm SDP Orgn Ctee 1981-88; (Fin Ctee 1988-), Communications conslt 1978- dir Dewe Rogerson Ltd (1984-88), md Corporate Communications Strategy (1988-); dir BR Western Region 1985-, memb USDAW; fndr Parls weekly jnl The House Magazine (1976), ed The BBC Guide to Parliament (1979 and 1983), various articles, reviews and pamphlets; fndr parly journal The House Magazine (1976-), editor BBC Guide to Parliament (1979 and 1983), various articles, reviews and pamphlets; *Recreations* collecting election pottery and medals, walking, countryside ; *Clubs* Devon and Exeter Inst; *Style—* Mike Thomas, Esq; 45 St Mary's Grove, London W4 3LN (☎ 01 995 8803, mobile ☎ 0836 729603)

THOMAS, Hon (William) Michael Webster; s of Baron Thomas, DFC (Life Peer d 1980); *b* 1926; *m* 1952, Ann, da of late Col Philip Kirby-Green; *Style—* The Hon Michael Thomas

THOMAS, Neil Philip; s of Simon David Thomas, of 149 Stanmore Hill, Stanmore, Middx, and Jesse, *née* Blagborough; *b* 29 April 1950; *Educ* Stowe, and Lond Univ (BSc 1971); *m* 1, 25 Jan 1974, Mary Josephine Christian (d 21 June 1977), da of AVM Patrick Joseph O'Connor, CB, OBE, MD, FRCP; 1 da (Joanna b 19 June 1977); 2, 29 April 1979, Julia Vera, da of J J Ashken, MB, BS; 1 s (James b 17 March 1981), 1 da (Gemma b 15 Oct 1982); *Career* late sr registrar in orthopaedics Royal Nat Orthopaedic Hosp, Univ Coll Hosp and the Westminster Hosp; conslt orthopaedic surgn N Hants Health Authy; memb: Int Knee Soc, Euro Soc of Knee and Arthroscopic Surgery, Br Assocn of Surgery of the Knee, RCS Rep Engrg in Med Gp Ctee; Sir Herbert Seddon Prize and Medal 1986; FRCS 1978, FRSM, Fell Br Orthopaedic Assoc; *Recreations* golf, horticulture, wine, fishing; *Style—* Neil Thomas, Esq; Little Bullington House, Bullington, Sutton Scotney, Winchester, Hampshire SO21 3QQ (☎ 0962 760233); Acute Unit, Basingstoke Strict Hosptial, Aldermaston Rd, Basingstoke, Hampshire RG24 9NA (☎ 0256 473202)

THOMAS, (Robert) Neville; QC (1975); s of Robert Derfel Thomas (d 1983), of Clwyd, and Enid Anne, *née* Edwards; *b* 31 Mar 1936; *Educ* Ruthin Sch, Oxford Univ (MA, BCL); *m* 28 March 1970, Jennifer Anne, da of Philip Henry Akerman Brownrigg, CMG, DSO, OBE, TD, *qv*; 1 s (Gerran b 19 March 1973), 1 da (Meriel b 21 Aug 1975); *Career* Lt Intelligence Corps 1955-57; barr Inner Temple 1962, rec Crown Ct 1975-82, master of the Bench Inner Temple 1985; *Recreations* fishing, walking, gardening; *Clubs* Garrick; *Style—* Neville Thomas, Esq, QC; Galnsevern, Berriew, Welshpool, Powys; 38 Courtfield Gardens, London SW5; 3 Gray's Inn Place, London WC1R 5EA (☎ 01 831 8441, 01 831 8479, fax 01 831 8479, telex 295119 LEXCOL G)

THOMAS, Nicholas Andrew; s of Stanley Thomas (d 1971), of Plymouth, Devon, and Phyllis Doreen, *née* Larman; *b* 14 April 1953; *Educ* Kelly Coll Tavistock Devon, Exeter Coll Oxford (BA); *Career* slr 1977; Macfarlanes 1975-: articled clerk 1975-77, asst slr 1977-82, ptnr 1982-; memb: City of London Slrs Co, Law Soc; *Recreations* golf, walking, classical music, opera; *Style—* Nicholas Thomas, Esq; 8 Oxford Road North, Chiswick, London W4 4DN (☎ 01 995 6921); Macfarlanes, 10 Norwich St, London EC4A 1BD (☎ 01 831 9222, fax 01 831 9607, telex 296381 MACFAR G)

THOMAS, Pamela; OBE (1983); da of Rev Llewlyn Thomas (d 1959), of All Saints' Vicarage, Glasbury, Powys, and Betty *née* Williams (d 1971); *b* 15 May 1929; *Educ* Roedean, King's Coll London; *Career* barr, broadcaster, co dir, lectr; barr Lincoln's Inn 1955, head of chambers 1983, memb Performing Right Tbnl 1987, sec Soc of Cons Lawyers 1963-82, chm political devpt ctee SOCL 1982-85, fndr memb Bow Gp; Parly candidate: St Pancras N for LCC 1958, (C) Swansea East 1963, (C) Willesden West 1966; former govr: Chelsea Sch for Boys, Chelsea-Hurlingham Comprehensive Sch; former vice-chm PCC St Augustine's Queen's Gate, vice pres Old Roedeanians Assoc 1982-88, govr Roedean Sch 1983, visiting lectr in law Poly of Central London 1959-75; *Style—* Miss Pamela Thomas, OBE; 2 Clareville Court, Clareville Grove, London SW7 (☎ 01 373 6947); Broomfield, Glasbury-on-Wye, via Hereford (☎ 049 74 338); 3 New Square, Lincoln's Inn, London WC2 (☎ 01 242 3436)

THOMAS, Patricia, Lady; Patricia; *née* Larkins; *m* 1957, as his 3 w, Major Sir William Eustace Rhyddlad Thomas, 2 Bt, MBE (d 1958); *Style—* Patricia, Lady Thomas

THOMAS, Patricia Anne; *née* Lofts; da of Frederick Sidney Lofts (d 1978), of Mitcham, Surrey, and Ann Elizabeth, *née* Brown (d 1982); *b* 3 April 1940; *Educ* Mitcham Co GS for Girls, King's Coll London (LLB, LLM), Univ of Illinois; *m* 20 July 1968, (Joseph) Glyn Thomas, s of Joseph Ernest Thomas of Holmesfield, Derbyshire (d 1975); 1 s (Paul b 1972), 2 da (Jacqueline b 1969, Ruth b 1970); *Career* lectr Univ of Leeds 1962-63 and 1964-68, sr (later princ lectr) Preston Poly 1973-78, hd sch of Law Lancs Poly 1978-85, vice pres (later pres) Gtr Manchester and Lancs Rent Assessment Panel 1984-85 (memb 1975-85), cmmr Local Admin 1985-; chm Blackpool Supplementary Benefit Appeal Tbnl 1980-85; *Books* Law of Evidence (1972); *Recreations* walking, cooking, reading, travel; *Style—* Mrs Patricia Thomas; Greenbank Farm, Over Kellet, Carnforth, Lancashire LA6 1BS (☎ 0524 733296); Commission for Local Administration in England, 29 Castlegate, York YO1 1RN (☎ 0904 301 51)

THOMAS, Sir Patrick Muirhead; DSO (1945), TD (1945), DL (1980); s of Herbert James Thomas (d 1960); *b* 31 Jan 1914; *Educ* Clifton Coll, CCC Cambridge (MA); *m* 1939, Ethel Elizabeth Mary, *née* Lawrence (d 1986), of Sheffield; 1 s, 3 da; *Career* RA; served: France, N Africa, Italy, Greece, Mid E, Austria 1939-45, Lt-Col cmdg 71 Field Regt RA; Col Cmdt City of Glasgow Army Cadet Force 1956, Hon Col 1963-70 and 1977-84; fell Inst of Tport; md Wm Beardmore & Co Ltd 1954-67 (dir 1967-76); dir: Scottish Opera 1965-81 (chm 1976-81), Brightside Engng Hldgs Ltd 1967-71, Midland Caledonian Investmt Tst 1972-75; chm Scottish Tport Gp 1968-77, Lloyd's Register of Shipping 1967-78; pres FBI Scottish Cncl 1961-62, pres Scottish Engng Employers Assoc 1967-68, pt/t memb Scottish Gas Bd 1966-72; memb: Ct Strathclyde Univ 1967-88 (chm 1970-75), panel Industl Tbnls 1967-77, exec ctee Earl Haig Fund (Scotland) 1964-75 (chm 1982-84), Artillery Cncl for Scotland 1978-84; govr Clifton Coll 1979-; Hon LLD Strathclyde 1973 fell Univ of Strathclyde 1988; OStJ 1970; kt 1974; *Recreations* gardening; *Style—* Sir Patrick Thomas, DSO, TD, DL; Bemersyde, Kilmacolm, Renfrewshire (☎ 050 587 2710)

THOMAS, Pauline Ann; da of Rupert Augustus Thomas, of Georgia, USA, and Beryl Leone, *née* Thomas; *b* 6 Feb 1956; *Educ* Saker Baptist Coll and CCAST, W Cameroon, LSE (LLB); *m* 19 April 1986, Stephen Neil Mobbs, s of Noel Edward Henry Mobbs, of Norwich, Norfolk; *Career* practice devpt mangr Lovell White & King 1986-, mgmnt conslt Intermatrix Ltd 1984-86; *Recreations* travel, theatre, reading, classical music; *Style*— Ms Pauline Thomas; Lovell, White & King, 21 Holborn Viaduct, London EC1A 2DY (☎ 01 236 6011, telex 887122, fax 01 248 4212)

THOMAS, Dr Reginald; s of Dr Leopold Thomas (d 1956), and Irma Thomas, *née* von Smekal; *b* 28 Feb 1928; *Educ* Vienna Univ (DL); *m* 26 Nov 1960, Ingrid Renate, da of Dr Franz Helmut Leitner (d 1976), late ambass; 3 s (Alexander b 1963, George b 1966, Michael b 1970), 1 da (Elisabeth b 1962); *Career* entered Austrian foreign service 1951, Austrian Legation Berne 1952-56, Legal Advsr Miny Foreign Affairs Vienna 1956-59, Austrian Embassy Tokyo 1959-62, Head of Office of Sec-Gen for Foreign Affairs Vienna 1962-68, ambassador Pakistan and concurrently accredited to the Union of Burma 1968-71, ambass to Japan 1971-75, Miny of Foreign Affairs Vienna: head of Personnel Dept 1975-76, head of Dept of Admin 1976-82; Austrian Ambass to the Court of St Jame's 1982-; Grand Cross: Order of the Rising Sun, Japan; Order of Diplomatic Service, Korea; Independence Order, Jordan; Order of F de Miranda, Venezuela; Hilal-o-Quaid-i-Azam, Pakistan; *Clubs* Queen's, Hurlingham, Austrian Assoc for Foreign Policy and Internat Relations; *Style*— Dr Reginald Thomas; 18 Belgrave Square, London SW1; A-1010 Wien, Schwarzenbergstrasse 8; Austrian Embassy, 18 Belgrave Mews West, London SW1; Federal Ministry of Foreign Affairs, Ballhausplatz 2, A-1014 Wien, Austria

THOMAS, Richard; s of Anthony Hugh Thomas, JP, of The Old School, Stone-In-Oxney, Tenterden, Kent and Molly, *née* Bourne, MBE; *b* 18 Feb 1938; *Educ* Leighton Park, Merton Coll Oxford (MA); *m* 12 Feb 1966, Catherine Jane, da of Daniel Hayes, (d 1969), of Richmond, NSW; 1 s (Alexander James b 1969), 2 da (Phoebe Elizabeth b 1967, Corinna Jane b 1971); *Career* Nat Serv 2 Lt RASC 1959-61; HM Diplomatic Serv: asst princ CRO 1961, private sec to Parly Under Sec 1962-63; second sec: Accra 1963-65, Lome 1965-66; first sec: UK Delgn NATO Paris and Brussels 1966-69, FCO 1969-72, New Dehli 1972-75, FCO (asst head of Dept) 1976-78; FCO visiting res fell RIIA 1978-79, cnsllr Prague 1979-83, ambass Iceland 1983-86, overseas inspr 1986-89, ambass Bulgaria 1989-; *Books* India's Emergence as an Industrial Power: Middle Eastern Contracts (1982); *Recreations* foreign parts, gossip, skiing; *Style*— Richard Thomas, Esq; Foreign and Commonwealth Office, King Charles St, London SW1

THOMAS, Richard James; s of Daniel Lewis Thomas, JP, of Southend-on-Sea, Essex, and Norah Mary *née* James; *b* 18 June 1949; *Educ* Bishop's Stortford Coll, Univ of Southampton (LLB); *m* 18 May 1974, Julia Delicia Thomas, da of Dr Edward Granville Woodchurch Clarke, MC, of Shurlock Row, Berks; 2 s (Andrew b 1977, Christopher b 1983), 1 da (Gemma b 1979); *Career* articled clerk and asst slr Freshfields 1971-74, slr CAB Legal Serv 1974-79, legal offr and head of resources gp Nat Consumer Cncl 1979-86, dir Consumer Affrs Off Fair Trading 1986-; tstee W London Fair Housing Gp 1976-79; memb: mgmnt ctee Gtr London CAB Serv 1977-79, Lord Chllr's Advsy Ctee on Fair Justice 1985-88; memb Law Soc; *Books* Reports, articles and broadcasts on a range of legal and consumer issues; *Recreations* family, maintenance of home and garden, travel; *Style*— Richard Thomas, Esq; Office of Fair Trading, Field House, Breams Buildings, London EC1A 1PR *née* 01 242 2858)

THOMAS, Vice Adm Sir (William) Richard Scott; KCB (1987), OBE (1974); s of Cdr William Scott Thomas, DSC, RN (d 1983), and Mary Hilda Bertha, *née* Hemelryk; *b* 22 Mar 1932; *Educ* Downside; *m* 1959, Patricia Margaret, da of Dr John Henry Cullinan (d 1957), of Fressingfield, Suffolk; 4 s (Dominic b 1972, Gareth b 1967, George b 1973, Gavin decd), 4 da (Victoria b 1970, Emma b 1974, Harriet b 1968, Jemima b 1970); *Career* Naval Off; CO HM Ships Buttress 1958, Wolverton 1960-61, Greetham 1962, Torquay 1965, Tronbridge 1966-68, Fearless 1977-78; Naval Sec 1983-85; Flag Offr Second Flotilla 1985-87; Dep Supreme Allied Cdr Atlantic 1987-89; Adm 1989; UK Mil Rep of NATO 1989-; student of Naval Staff Coll, Jt Services Staff Coll and Royal Coll of Defence Studies; *Recreations* family and gardening; *Style*— Adm Sir Richard Thomas, KCB, OBE

THOMAS, Robert (Bob) Ernest; s of William Edward Thomas (d 1965), and Laura Jane, *née* Willoughby; *b* 15 Sept 1932; *Educ* Bedford Modern Sch, King's Coll London, Univ of Lancaster (MA); *m* 1 (m dis 1972), Barbara, *née* Levelle; 1 s (Adam Teirnan b 1963), 1 da (Sarah Jane b 1959); m 2, Aug 1972, Jacqueline Phyllis, da of Prof Guy Marrian, CBE (d 1981); *Career* Nat Serv 2 Lt Royal Signals 1950-52; hd of mktg Univ of Lancaster 1969-71, client and programme dir Ashridge Mgmnt Coll 1974-, chm t2 Solutions Ltd 1982-87, dir Deeko plc 1983-86; chm: BCCH Ltd 1984-, Rockliffe Leisure Ltd 1984-, Team One Ltd 1987-, dir Sherwood Computer Gp plc 1988-; founding govr communications Advertising and Mktg Educ Fndn, served on two Indust Trg Bds; MCAM 1980; *Recreations* photography, music; *Clubs* Inst of Directors; *Style*— Bob Thomas, Esq; Cadman Square, Shenley Lodge, Milton Keynes MK5 7DN (☎ 0908 678 465); Ashridge Management College, Berkhamsted, Herts HP4 1NS (☎ 044 284 3491, fax 044 284 2382, telex 826434 ASHCOL G)

THOMAS, Sir Robert Evan; JP (Manchester 1948), DL (County Palatine of Greater Manchester 1974); s of Jesse Thomas, of Leigh, Lancs; *b* 8 Oct 1901; *Educ* St Peter's Leigh, Manchester Univ (MA) 1974; *m* 1924, Edna, da of William Isherwood, of Leigh; 1 s, 1 da; *Career* former bus driver and trade union official; Lord Mayor of Manchester 1962-63, DL County Palatine of Lancaster 1967-73, dep chm Manchester Ship Canal to 1974, ldr Greater Manchester Met CC 1973-77, chm Assoc of Met Authorities 1974-77; kt 1967; *Books* Sir Bob; *Recreations* Golf; *Clubs* Heaton Moor Golf; *Style*— Sir Robert Thomas, JP, DL; 29 Milwain Road, Manchester M19 2PX

THOMAS, Robert Freeman; s of late Sir Robert John Thomas, 1 Bt, and hp of n, Sir Michael Thomas, 3 Bt; *b* 8 Jan 1911; *m* 1947, Marcia, da of Walter Lucas; *Style*— Robert Thomas, Esq; Garreglwyd, Holyhead, Anglesey

THOMAS, Robin Edwin; s of Arthur Edwin Thomas (ka 1942), and Joan Cicely, *née* Parsons; *b* 17 Oct 1940; *Educ* Stowe, Lincoln Coll Oxford (BA,MA), Harvard Business Sch (MBA); *m* 2 Sept 1972, Janine Penelope Russell, da of James Robert Maitland Boothby (d 1974); 1 da (Aurelia b 1975); *Career* md Thomas & Edge Ltd 1962-71, mangr Continental Illinois Ltd 1973-77, vice-pres Continental Illinois Nat Bank 1977-; *Recreations* opera, bridge, skiing, tennis; *Style*— Robin Thomas, Esq; Worsley House, 4 West Side, London SW19 4TN (☎ 01 946 7187), Continental Bank, 162 Queen Victoria St, London, EC4V 4BS (☎ 01 860 5444, fax 01 248 1244, telex 883620)

THOMAS, Dr Roger Gareth; MP (Lab) Carmarthen May 1979-; *b* 14 Nov 1925; *Educ* Amman Valley GS, London Hospital Medical Coll; *m* 1958, Indeg Thomas; 1 s, 1 da; *Career* GP; memb: Dyfed CC 1977-, select ctee on Welsh Affairs 1979-; oppn front bench spokesman on Wales; *Style*— Dr Roger Thomas, MP; Ffynnon W'en, Capel Hendre, Ammanford, Dyfed (☎ 0269 843093)

THOMAS, Roger Geraint; s of Geraint Phillips Thomas, and Doreen Augusta, *née* Cooke (d 1975); *b* 22 July 1945; *Educ* Penarth Co Sch, Leighton Park Sch Reading, Birmingham Univ (LLB); *m* 23 Oct 1971, Rhian Elisabeth Kenyon, da of Erith Kenyon Thomas, of Cardigan (d 1975); *Career* ptnr Phillips & Buck slrs 1969-; memb: ct Nat Museum of Wales 1983- (cncl memb 1985-), Welsh Cncl CBI 1987-, Action Ctee and Techniquest Cncl Cardiff; chm Cardiff branch BIM 1988; memb Law Soc 1969, FBIM 1984; *Recreations* sailboarding, hill walking; *Clubs* Cardiff and County, Penarth Yacht; *Style*— Roger G Thomas, Esq; Phillips & Buck, Fitzalan House, Fitzalan Rd, Cardiff CF2 1XZ; Pinners Hall, Austin Friars, London EC2N 2HE (☎ 0222 471147, fax 0222 464347, telex 497625)

THOMAS, Roger John Laugharne; QC (1984); s of Roger Edward Laugharne Thomas (d 1970), of Ystradgynlais, and Dinah Agnes, *née* Jones; *b* 22 Oct 1947; *Educ* Rugby, Trinity Hall Cambridge (BA), Univ of Chicago Law Sch (JD); *m* 6 Jan 1973, Elizabeth Ann, da of Stephen James Buchanan (d 1984), of Ohio; 1 s (David b 1978), 1 da (Alison b 1980); *Career* teaching asst Mayo Coll India 1965-66, barr Gray's Inn 1969, QC Eastern Caribean Supreme Ct 1986, rec 1987; *Recreations* gardens, travel, walking, opera; *Style*— John L Thomas, Esq, QC; 4 Essex Ct, Temple, London, EC4 (☎ 01 583 9191, fax 01 353 3421, telex 888465 COMCAS)

THOMAS, Roger Lloyd; s of Trevor John Thomas (d 1972), of Barry, S Glam, and Eleanor Maud, *née* Jones (d 1973); *b* 7 Feb 1919; *Educ* Barry County Sch, Madgalen Coll Oxford (MA); *m* 27 Oct 1945, Stella Mary, da of Reginald Ernest Willmett (d 1957), of Newport; 3 s (Julian b 1947, Andrew b 1948, Rupert b 1951), 1 da (Ursula b 1950); *Career* WWII enlisted RA 1939, cmmnd RA 1940, seconded to 2 Indian Field Regt 1940, served 1941-43: India, Iraq, Syria, Egypt, Libya; Capt 1942 staff offr intelligence: GHQ Paiforce, GHQ M East, AFHQ Algiers 1943-44, HQ Allied Armies in Italy 1944-45, (Maj 1944), SHAEF Frankfurt 1945-46; civil servant: Miny of Fuel and Power 1948-50, Home Office 1950-60 (Private Sec, Permanent Under Sec of State 1950-51, Parliamentary Under Sec of State 1951-53); sec: Interdepartmental Ctee on Powers of Subpoena 1960, Treasury 1960-62, Home Office 1962-64, Welsh Office 1964-67, Aberfan Inquiry Tribunal 1966-67, Miny of Housing 1967-70; chm: Working Party on Building by Direct Labour Organisations 1968-69; gen mangr: Housing Corpn 1970-73; Dept of Environment 1974-79; advsr Central Policy Review Staff Cabinet Office 1979, sr clerk Ctee Office House of Commons 1979-84, clerk to Select Ctee on Welsh Affairs 1982-84, ret 1984; *Style*— R Lloyd Thomas, Esq; 5 Pk Ave, Caterham, Surrey CR3 6AH (☎ 0883 42080)

THOMAS, Rosalind Mary; da of John Wyndham Pain (d 1963), of Howey Hall, Llandrindod Wells, Radnorshire, Powys, and Nina Owena, *née* Lankester (d 1980); *b* 28 May 1921; *Educ* RCM; *m* 1, 16 Dec 1941, Lt John Stewart Hallam, KRRC (ka 1943) 1 da (Nina b 7 March 1943); m 2, 21 March 1952, Edward Thomas (d 1963); s of Capt Edward Aubrey thomas (d 1952), of Cefndyrys, Builth Wells, Powys; 1 s (Evan David b 19 Jan 1953), 1 da (Celia b 22 April 1954); *Career* Powys CC: cncl 1973-74, chm 1987-88; co cncllr Radnor 1964-73; memb: Radnor LEA 1964-73, Powys LEA 1973-; chm govrs Llandrindod Wells HS 1980-; former pres Radnor Fedn of YFC's, former pres Radnor Fedn of YFC's, former chm Adoption Panel Powys Social Servs 1974-87, former pres Brecon & Radnor CLA (memb exec ctee and cncl 1987), memb Brecon & Radnor HMC 1956, vice-chm SEW Arts Cncl; High Sheriff of Powys 1987-88; *Style*— Mrs Edward Thomas; Pengraig, Ceendyrys, Builth Wells, Powys LD2 3TF (☎ 0982 552726)

THOMAS, Stephen Richard; s of Maj Norman Arthur Thomas (d 1974), of E Horsley, and Norah Margaret, *née* Cooke; *b* 9 June 1947; *Educ* Elizabeth Coll Guernsey; *m* 17 July 1971, Felicity Ruth, da of Harold Arthur George Quaintance (Flt Sgt RAF Bomber Cmd), of Rowlstone; 2 s (Daniel b 1973, Peter b 1979), 2 da (Hannah b 1975, Elizabeth b and d 1977); *Career* Deloitte Haskins & Sells 1965-: ptnr 1981-, chm Deloitte Building Socs Indust Gp, Japanese Liaison ptnr, Fin Servs Sector ptnr; sr accounting advsr seconded to HM Treasy 1981-83; memb Alton Evangelical Free Church and Odiham Soc; FCA 1969; *Recreations* nets cricketer, stable lad and football manager for children; *Style*— Stephen Thomas, Esq; Deloitte Haskins & Sells, 128 Queen Victoria St, London EC4P 4JX (☎ 01 248 3913, fax 01 248 3623, telex 894941)

THOMAS, Sir Swinton Barclay; QC (1975); s of Brig William Bain Thomas, CBE, DSO (d 1967), and Mary Georgina Thomas (d 1986); *b* 12 Jan 1931; *Educ* Ampleforth, Lincoln Coll Oxford (MA); *m* 1967, Angela Rose Elizabeth, wid of Sir Anthony Cope, 15 Bt, da of James Alfred Snarey Wright (d 1975); 1 s (Dominic), 1 da (Melissa); *Career* Lt Cameronians (Scottish Rifles); barr Inner Temple 1955, bencher Inner Temple 1983; judge of the High Ct 1985; kt 1985; *Recreations* reading, travel; *Clubs* Garrick; *Style*— The Hon Sir Swinton Thomas; Royal Cts of Justice, Strand, London WC2 (☎ 01 936 6884)

THOMAS, Hon Mrs (Ursula Nancy); *née* Eden; da of 7 Baron Henley (d 1977); *b* 1950; *m* 1978, William Thomas; *Style*— The Hon Mrs Thomas

THOMAS, William Ernest Ghinn; s of Kenneth Dawson Thomas, of Sheffield, and Monica Isobel, *née* Markham; *b* 13 Feb 1948; *Educ* Dulwich, King's Coll London Univ (BSc), St George's Hosp Med Sch (MB BS); *m* 30 June 1973, Grace Violet, da of Alfred Henry Samways (d 1979), of London; 2 s (Christopher b 1977, Benjamin b 1985), 3 da (Nicola b 1974, Jacqueline b 1979, Hannah b 1983); *Career* Hunterian prof RCS 1987 (Arris and Gale lectr 1982, Bernard Sunley fell 1977), Moynihan fell Assoc of Surgns 1982, conslt surgn Royal Hallamshire Hosp Sheffield 1986; exec ed Current Practice in Surgery 1988; memb: BMA 1974, BSG 1980; SRS 1981; nat pres Gideons Int 1987-89; Royal Humane Soc Award for Bravery 1974, Dr of the Year Award 1985 European Soc for Surgical Res Prize 1981; FRCS 1976, SRS 1981; *Books* Preparation and Revision for the FRCS (1986), Self-assessment Exercises in Surgery (1986), Nuclear Medicine: Applications to Surgery (1988); *Recreations* skiing, photography, oil painting; *Style*— William Thomas, Esq; Ash Lodge, 65 Whirlow Park Rd, Whirlow, Sheffield, S Yorks S11 9NN (☎ 0742 620 852); Royal Hallamshire Hosp, Glossop Rd, Sheffield, S Yorks S10 2JF (☎ 0742 766 222)

THOMAS, Sir William James Cooper; 2 Bt (UK 1919), of Ynyshir, Co Glamorgan, TD, JP (Monmouthshire 1958), DL (1973); s of Sir (William) James Thomas, 1 Bt (d 1945); *b* 7 May 1919; *Educ* Harrow, Downing Coll Cambridge; *m* 1947, Freida

Dunbar, da of late F A Whyte, of Montcoffer, Banff; 2 s, 1 da; *Heir* s, William Michael Thomas; *Career* served RA WW II, barr Inner Temple 1948, High Sheriff Co Monmouthshire 1973-74; *Clubs* Army and Navy; *Style—* Sir William Thomas, Bt, TD, JP, DL; Tump House, Llanrothal, Monmouth, Gwent (☎ 0600 2757)

THOMAS, Ven William Jordison; s of Henry William Thomas (d 1978), of Middlesbrough and Italy, and Dorothy Newton (d 1968); *b* 16 Dec 1927; *Educ* Homewood Prep Sch, Acklam Hall, Giggleswick Sch, King's Coll Cambridge (MA); *m* 23 Nov 1953, Kathleen Jeffrey, da of late William Robson, of Northumberland; *Career* Nat Serv RN 1946-48; ordained: deacon 1953, priest 1954; asst curate: St Anthony Newcastle 1953-56, Berwick-upon-Tweed 1956-59; vicar: Alwinton with Holystone and Alnham and Lordship of Kidland 1959-70, Alston with Garrigill, Nenthead and Kirkhaugh 1970-80; priest in charge Knaresdale 1973-80, team rector Glendale 1980-82, archdeacon of Northumberland and canon residentiary 1982-; *Recreations* making pictures and magic, sailing; *Clubs* Victory Ex-Services; *Style—* The Ven the Archdeacon of Northumberland; 80 Moorside North, Fenham, Newcastle-upon-Tyne NE4 9DU (☎ 091 273 8245); Wark Cottage, Whittingham, Alnwick (☎ 066 574 300)

THOMAS, Wyndham; CBE (1982); s of Robert John Thomas (d 1959), and Hannah Mary, *née* Davies (d 1936); *b* 1 Feb 1924; *Educ* Maesteg GS, Cardiff Training Coll, Carnegie Coll, LSE; *m* 17 May 1947, Elizabeth Terry (Betty), *née* Hopkin; 1 s (Gareth b 1962), 2 da (Sally b 1956, Jenny b 1958, Tessa b 1960); *Career* RA and RCS 1943-45, cmmnd RWF 1945, demob Lt 1947; chm Inner City Enterprises plc 1983-; dir Town and Country Planning Assoc 1965-67, chm of the Housebuilders Fedn's Independent Cmmn of Private Housebuilding and the Inner Cities; memb: Cmmn for the Towns 1964-68, DOE Property Advsy Gp 1974, London Docklands Devpt Corpn 1981-88, Urban Investment Review Gp DOE 1985-87, RIBA Inner Cities Working Pty 1987-88; gen mangr Peterborough Devpt Corpn 1968-83, conslt to Letchworth Garden City Corpn 1985-; Mayor and Bailiff Borough Hemel Hempstead 1959-60, pres Sharpewood GC 1975-; hon memb Royal Town Planning Inst 1980; Offr of the Order of Orange Nassau 1982; *Recreations* golf, running, restoring old furniture; *Clubs* Royal Overseas League; *Style—* Wyndham Thomas, Esq, CBE; 8 Westwood Park Rd, Peterborough, Cambridgeshire (☎ 0733 64399); Inner City Enterprises plc, 23 Maddox St, London W1R OBN (☎ 01 629 3087)

THOMAS, Wynne Simpson; OBE (1972), DL (Carmarthenshire 1968, Dyfed 1974); s of Edgar Wynne Thomas, MBE (d 1967), and May, *née* Williams (d 1956); *b* 16 Feb 1912; *Educ* Llanelli GS, Swansea Univ Law Sch; *m* 1942, Mary Etta, da of William Dunn Jenkins, JP (d 1946), of Burry Port; *Career* served WW II N Africa & Italy as Maj RAPC & RA (despatches); admitted slr 1936, slr: Llanelli Borough Cncl 1936-40, Carmarthenshire CC 1946-52 (clerk of the Peace, clerk to Lt, clerk and chief exec 1952-72), clerk of Carmarthenshire & Cards Police Authority 1952-68, dep clerk Dyfed-Powys Police Authority 1968-72, clerk Magistrates Courts Ctee 1952-72; *Recreations* music, walking; *Clubs* Cefn Sidan Rotary, Llanelli RFC (past pres and tstee), Llanelli Bowling; *Style—* Wynne Thomas, Esq, OBE, DL; St Illtyd Rise, Pembrey, Burry Port, Dyfed SA16 0YY (☎ 055 46 2542)

THOMAS OF GWYDIR, Baron (Life Peer UK 1987); Peter John Mitchell Thomas; PC (1964), QC (1965); o s of late David Thomas, of Llanrwst, Denbighshire, and Anne Gwendoline, *née* Mitchell; *b* 31 July 1920; *Educ* Epworth Coll Rhyl, Jesus Coll Oxford (MA); *m* 1947, Frances Elizabeth Tessa (d 1985), o da of late Basil Dean, CBE, the theatrical producer, by his 2 w, Lady Mercy Greville, 2 da of 5 Earl of Warwick ; 2 s (Hon David Nigel Mitchell, Hon Hugh Basil Maynard Mitchell), 2 da (Hon Frances Jane Mitchell, Hon Catherine Clare Mitchell); *Career* served WW II with RAF (prisoner); barr Middle Temple 1947; memb Wales and Chester Circuit, dep chm Cheshire Quarter Sessions 1966-70, Denbighshire Quarter Sessions 1968-70; Bencher Middle Temple 1971; Crown Court Recorder 1974-88; Arbitrator of ICC Court of Arbitration, Paris 1974-88; MP (C): Conway 1951-66, Hendon S 1970-87; pps to Solicitor Gen 1954-59, parl sec Min of Labour 1959-61, parl under-sec of state for Foreign Affairs 1961-63, min of state for Foreign Affairs 1963-64, opposition front bench spokesman on Foreign Affairs and Law 1964-66; chm Conservative Party Organisation 1970-72, sec of state for Wales 1970-74; pres Nat Union of Cons and Unionist Assocs 1974-76; *Clubs* Carlton; *Style—* The Rt Hon Lord Thomas of Gwydir, PC, QC; Millicent Cottage, Elstead, Surrey; 37 Chester Way, London SE11 (☎ 01 735 6047)

THOMAS OF SWYNNERTON, Baron (Life Peer UK 1981); Hugh Swynnerton Thomas; s of Hugh Whitelegge Thomas, CMG (d 1960), himself s of Rev T W Thomas and sometime of the Colonial Serv, sec for Native Affairs in the Gold Coast; chief commissioner Ashanti 1932 and UK rep to League of Nations *re* Togoland Mandate Report 1931 & 1934, and Margery Angelo Augusta, *née* Swynnerton; *b* 21 Oct 1931; *Educ* Sherborne, Queens' Coll Cambridge (MA); *m* 1962, Hon Vanessa Mary Jebb, *qv*, da of 1 Baron Gladwyn; 2 s, 1 da; *Career* sits as Conservative in House of Lords; historian; with Foreign Office 1954-57, lecturer Sandhurst 1957, prof history Reading Univ 1966-76; chm Centre for Policy Studies 1979-; memb Amnesty International; *Books Incl:* The Spanish Civil War (1961, revised 1977), Cuba (1971), An Unfinished History of the World (1979, revised 1982); *Clubs* Beefsteak, Garrick, Travellers' (Paris); *Style—* Rt Hon Lord Thomas of Swynnerton; 29 Ladbroke Grove, London W11 3BB (☎ 01 727 2288)

THOMAS OF SWYNNERTON, Baroness; Hon Vanessa Mary; *née* Jebb; er da of 1 Baron Gladwyn, GCMG, GCVO, CB, and Cynthia, da of Sir Saxton William Armstrong Noble, 3 Bt; *b* 1931; *m* 1962, Baron Thomas of Swynnerton (Life Peer), *qv*; 2 s, 1 da; *Style—* The Rt Hon the Lady Thomas of Swynnerton; 29 Ladbroke Grove, London W11 3BB

THOMAS-EMBERSON, Steve; s of Colin Thomas-Emberson, of Carisbrooke, Stoneygate, Leics, and Jean, *née* Vezey-Walker (d 1986); *b* 4 June 1956; *Educ* The Bosworth Sch; *Career* mergers and acquisitions conslt; dir: Carter Hargrave Ltd 1987-, Link Jet plc 1988-, Pioneer Hdlgs Ltd 1988-, Grey Cat Communications Ltd 1988-; fndr memb Boswell St James Dining Soc, tstee Young Dancers Fndn; *Recreations* living well, conversation with intelligent ladies; *Clubs* Great Windsor and Ascot Yacht (hon Cdre); *Style—* Steve Thomas-Emberson, Esq; Alconleigh Cottage, Weir Rd, Kidworth Beauchamp, Leics (☎ 0533 793679); 14 Devonshire Sq, London EC2 (☎ 01 377 2800)

THOMAS-EVERARD, Christopher Philip; s of Maj Charles Richard Thomas, MA (ka 1944), and Prunella Peel Lewin-Harris, *née* Bentley-Taylor (d 1979); *see* Burke's Landed Gentry, 18 edn, vol 1, 1965; *b* 19 Mar 1941; *Educ* Stowe, RAC; *m* 1966, Rohaise Harriet Julia, da of Maj Eudo Tonson-Rye; 1 s (Guy Richard), 2 da; *Career* farmer, landowner, chartered surveyor, owner of Miltons Estate and Broford Farm 1966-, chm: W Som NFU 1978-80, Som NFU Hill Farming Ctee 1981-82, Devon and Som Exmoor Hill Farming Ctee 1985-88; SW rep on MAFF Hill Farming Advsy Ctee 1979-; memb of MAFF SW Regnl Panel 1977-83; underwriting memb of Lloyd's 1973-; *Recreations* sailing, hunting; *Style—* Christopher Thomas-Everard, Esq; Broford Farm, Dulverton, Somerset (☎ 0398 23569)

THOMASON, Prof George Frederick; CBE (1982); s of George Frederick Thomason (d 1967), of Hawkshead, Lancs, and Eva Elizabeth, *née* Walker (d 1977); *b* 27 Nov 1927; *Educ* Kelsick GS Ambleside, Univ of Sheffield (BA), Univ of Toronto (MA), Univ of Wales (PhD); *m* 5 Sept 1953, Jean Elizabeth, da of Henry Horsley (d 1982), of Montreal, Canada; 1 s (Geraint b 25 Nov 1960), 1 da (Sian b 1 March 1957); *Career* RASC 1946-48; Univ Coll Cardiff: res asst 1953-54, asst lectr 1954-56, res assoc 1956-59, lectr 1959-60, sr lectr 1963-69, head of dept 1966-84, reader 1969, prof 1969-84, prof emeritus 1984-; asst to md Flex Fasteners Ltd 1960-62; dir: Community Initiatives Res Tst 1986-, Enterprise & Trg Devpt Ltd 1989-; dep chm Wales Cncl for Voluntary Action, memb Opportunities for Volunteering (Wales) Ctee, memb of Ct and cncl Univ of Wales Coll of Cardiff; memb: ACAS Panel of Industrial Relations Arbitrators, two pay review bodies Drs, Dentists, Nurses, Midwives & Health Visitor; CIPM 1975, FBIM 1975; *Books* Textbook of Personnel Management (1975), Textbook of Industrial Relations Management (1984), Professional Approach to Community Work (1969); *Recreations* gardening; *Clubs* Athenaeum, Cardiff and County; *Style—* Prof George Thomason, CBE; 149 Lake Rd, West, Cardiff CF2 5PJ (☎ 0222 754236)

THOMASON, (Kenneth) Roy; OBE (1986); s of Thomas Roger Thomason, of Eastfield Court, Eastfield Lane, Ringwood, Hants, and Constance Dora, *née* Wilcox; *b* 14 Dec 1944; *Educ* Cheney Sch Oxford, London Univ (LLB); *m* 6 Sept 1969, Christine Ann, da of William Richard Parsons (d 1985), of Queen's Park, Bournemouth; 2 s (Richard b 1972, Edward b 1974); 2 da (Julia b 1978, Emily b 1981); *Career* ptnr Horden & George Bournemouth (sr ptnr 1979); dir various cos; ldr Bournemouth Borough Cncl 1974-82 (memb 1970); Cons Pty: constituency chm Bournemouth West 1981-82, chm Wessex area local govt advsy ctee 1981-83, local govt advsy ctee 1981- (vice-chm 1989), memb nat union exec 1989-; Assoc of Dist Cncls: cncl memb 1979, Cons gp ldr 1981-87, chm housing and enviromental health ctee 1983-87, chm of the assoc 1987-; *Recreations* sailing, architectural, history; *Style—* Roy Thomason, Esq, OBE; Culness House, 18 Wellington Rd, Bournemouth (☎ 0202 292113); 9 Buckingham Gate, London SW1 (☎ 01 828 7931)

THOMLINSON, John Howard; s of Ernest Claud Thomlinson (d 1954), and Lilian Matilda Jackson (d 1957); *b* 13 Mar 1921; *Educ* Stowe, Trinity Coll Cambridge (MA); *m* 1 Nov 1947, Lorna Diana, da of Col John Thomson-Glover, of India; 2 s (Antony b 1950, Nicholas b 1953); *Career* WWII RA (Capt) served NW Europe and Far East (despatches); admitted slr 1949; sr ptnr Durrantpiesse 1975-84; dir Scandinavian Bank 1969-84; *Recreations* sailing, tennis; *Clubs* Hurlingham, Gresham, RAC; *Style—* John H Thomlinson, Esq; 73 Rivermead Court, London SW6 3RZ; West Wittering

THOMPSON, Prof Alan Eric; s of Eric Joseph Thompson (d 1956), and Florence, *née* Holmes (d 1974); *b* 16 Sept 1924; *Educ* Univ of Edinburgh (MA, PhD); *m* 3 Dec 1960, da of Frank Long (d 1963); 3 s (Matthew b 1962, Andrew b 1967, Hamish b 1971); *Career* WWII (served with Infantry and Br Forces Network in Centl Med Forces, Italy and Austria); lectr in economics Univ of Edinburgh 1953-59 and 1964-71, AJ Balfour Prof of Economics Heriot Watt Univ 1972-87, visiting prof Stanford Univ USA 1966 and 1968; Parl advsr: Scottish TV 1966-67, Pharmaceutical Gen Cncl Scotland 1985-; pres Edinburgh Amenity and port Assoc 1970-75, hon vice-pres Assoc of Nazi War Camp Survivors 1960-; chm: Northern Offshore (Maritime) Resources Study 1974-84, Newbattle Abbey Coll, Edinburgh Ctee Peace Through NATO 1984-; govr Leith Nautical Coll 1981-84; memb: Royal Fine Art Cmmn for Scotland 1975-80, Local Govt Boundaries Cmmn (Scotland) 1975-82, Jt Military Educn Ctee Edinburgh and Heriot-Watt Univs 1975-, Scottish Cncl for Adult Educn in HM Forces 1973-; MP (Lab) Dunfermline 1959-64, Lab Parl candidate Galloway 1950 and 1951; FRSA 1972; *Books* Development of Economic Doctrine (jtly, 1980); *Recreations* bridge, croquet, writing children's stories, plays; *Clubs* New (Edinburgh), Edinburgh University Staff, Loch Earn Sailing; *Style—* Prof Alan Thompson; 11 Upper Gray Street, Edinburgh EH9 1SN; Ardtrostan Cottage, St Fillan's, Perthshire (☎ 031 667 2140, 076 485 275); School of Business and Financial Studies, Heriot-Watt Univ, 31-35 Grassmarket, Edinburgh EH1 2HJ

THOMPSON, Alec Geoffrey; OBE (1984); s of Alexander William Thompson (d 1968), and Edna May Thompson (d 1980); *b* 25 April 1926; *Educ* Preston GS, Manchester GS, Manchester Univ (BSc); *m* 1949, Irene Lilian, da of James Eatock; 2 s (John, Peter); *Career* dir J Bibby & Sons Ltd 1977-87, Majorfinch Ltd 1985-; md J Bibby & Sons plc 1979-82; vice-chm: J Bibby & Sons plc 1982-87, Petranol plc 1984-86, Fothergill-Harvey plc 1985-86, chm Westmorland Smoked Foods Ltd 1985-, hon tres and memb of cncl Univ of Lancaster 1983-; chm Francis Scott Chartable Tst 1985-, Lancaster & Dist Hosp Authy 1985-, CBIM, FRSA; *Recreations* fishing, shooting, travel; *Clubs* Carlton; *Style—* Alec Thompson, Esq, OBE; Barcaldene, Leighton Drive, Beetham, Milnthorpe, Cumbria (☎ 044 82 2276)

THOMPSON, Anthony Arthur Richard; QC (1980); s of William Frank McGregor Thompson (d 1934), and Doris Louise, *née* Hill (d 1988); *b* 4 July 1932; *Educ* Latymer, Univ Coll Oxford (MA), Sorbonne; *m* 1958, Francoise Alix Marie, da of Joseph Justin Reynier (d 1981); 2 s (Richard, Mark), 1 s decd, 1 da (Melissa); *Career* called to the Bar Inner Temple 1957; chm Bar Euro Gp 1984-86, recorder of the Crown Ct 1985, bencher Inner Temple 1986; Avocat of the Paris Bar 1988; *Recreations* food & wine, theatre, cinema, lawn tennis; *Clubs* Roehampton; *Style—* Anthony Thompson Esq, QC; Coln Manor, Coln St Aldwyns, Gloucestershire GL7 5AD 1 Essex Court, Temple, London EC4Y 9AR (☎ 01 353 5362, telex 889109 ESSEX G, fax 01 583 1118)

THOMPSON, Anthony Peter; s of Thomas George Thompson (d 1974), of Liverpool, and Florence Mary, *née* Bucke (d 1972); *b* 16 May 1928; *Educ* Liverpool Inst, Lancaster Royal GS, Shrewsbury, Downing Coll Cambridge (MA); *m* 1 , 6 Sept 1953, Norma Rachel (d 1973), da of Frederick Sidney Banks; 1 s (Anthony b 1959), 2 da (Rosemary b 1954, Pippa b 1962); m 2, 18 June 1988, Jennifer Mischa (Jenny), da of Col James William Power Saunders; *Career* 2 Lt RASC 1946-48; CA; ptnr: head of res Sheppards & Co 1961-64, de Zoete & Gorton, de Zoete & Bevan 1964-86; dir Barclays de Zoete Wedd 1986-88 (conslt 1988-); FCA; *Recreations* skiing, sailing, music, theatre; *Style*— Peter Thompson, Esq; BZW Ebbgate House, Swan Lane, London EC4

THOMPSON, Charles Norman; CBE (1978); s of Robert Norman Thompson (d 1962), of 85 Temple Road, Prenton, Birkenhead, Cheshire, and Evelyn Tivendale, *née* Woo (d 1960); *b* 23 Oct 1922; *Educ* Birkenhead Inst, Liverpool Univ (BSc); *m* 8 June 1946, Pamela Margaret, da of Alfred Christopher Francis Wicks, MBE, (d 1971), of 94 Aigburth Hall Avenue Liverpool; 1 da (Fiona Jane b 1954); *Career* res chemist Shell UK Ltd 1943, personnel supt Shell Int Petroleum Ltd 1958-61, dir res admin Shell Research Ltd 1961-78, head of res and dupt Shell UK Ltd 1978-82; memb cncl RIC 1972-80 (pres 1976-78), chm professional affairs board RSC 1980-84; memb; CSTI (chm 1981-83, chm Health Care Sci Advsy Ctee 1986-), Inst of Petroleum 1961-78, Tech Educn Cncl 1974-81, Ct Univ of Surrey 1978-, Bd Thames Water Authy 1980-87; FRSC; *Recreations* golf, bowls; *Clubs* West Byfleet Golf, Wey Valley Indoor Bowling Guildford; *Style*— Charles Thompson, Esq, CBE; Delamere, Horsell Park, Woking, Surrey GU21 4LW (☎ 048 62 4939)

THOMPSON, Lt-Col Sir Christopher Peile; 6 Bt (UK 1890), of Park Gate, Guiseley, Yorks; s of Lt-Col Sir Peile Thompson, OBE, 5 Bt (d 1985), and his wife, Barbara Johnson, da of late Horace Johnson Rampling; *b* 21 Dec 1944; *Educ* Marlborough, RMA Sandhurst, Staff Coll; *m* 22 Nov 1969, Anna Elizabeth, da of late Maj Arthur George Callander, of Silbury House, Avebury, Wilts; 1 s (Peile Richard b 1975), 1 da (Alandra Lucy b 1973); *Heir* s, Peile Richard Thompson b 3 March 1975; *Career* Royal Hussars (PWO), asst G2 British Allied Staff Berlin 1975-76, DAAG M2 (A) 1979-81, Sqn Ldr Royal Hussars 1981-83, SO2 (OR) HQ DRAC 1983-85, CO Royal Hussars 1985-87, S01 Snr Officers Tactics Div 1987-; Equerry to HRH Prince Michael of Kent 1989-; *Recreations* fishing, shooting, sailing, windsurfing, skiing, reading, gardening, cresta; *Clubs* Cavalry and Guard's, St Moritz Toboganning; *Style*— Lt-Col Sir Christopher Thompson, Bt; Hill House, The Village, Appleshaw, Andover, Hants

THOMPSON, Christopher Ronald; s of Col S J Thompson, DSO, DL (d 1956); *b* 14 Dec 1927; *Educ* Shrewsbury, Trinity Coll Cambridge; *m* 1949, Rachael Mary, *née* Meynell; 2 s (1 s decd), 1 da; *Career* sr ptnr Aldenham Business Servs; chm: Wynn Electronics Ltd, Hoccum Devpts Ltd; dir: Isotron plc, Barclay's Bank Ltd, Plessey Co plc, Saraswate Syndicate India, G T Japan Investmt Tst plc; chm: Anglo Venezuelan Soc 1982-85, Sino-British Trade Cncl 1981-85, John Sutcliffe (Shipping) Ltd; High Sheriff Shropshire 1984-85; *Recreations* flyfishing, shooting, gardening; *Clubs* Boodle's; *Style*— Christopher Thompson, Esq; Aldenham Pk, Bridgnorth, Shrops (☎ 074 631 218); Estate Off Aldenham Pk (☎ 074 631 351)

THOMPSON, Clive Malcolm; *b* 4 April 1943; *Educ* Clifton Coll, Univ of Birmingham (BSc); *Career* gp chief exec Rentokil Gp plc; non exec dir: Caradon plc, Farepak Ltd; *Style*— Clive Thompson, Esq; Rentokil Group plc, Felcourt, East Grinstead, West Sussex

THOMPSON, David; s of Bernard Thompson, of Castleford, and Violet, *née* Laidler; *b* 28 Oct 1944; *Educ* King's Sch Pontefract; *m* 24 Oct 1970, Glenys, da of Harry Colley, of Badsworth, nr Pontefract; 2 s (Anthony David b 24 Aug 1972, Richard Martin b 17 Feb 1976); *Career* John Gordon Walton CAs until 1967, sr ptnr Buckle Barton 1981- (ptnr 1978-81); dir and sec: Safe Hands Creche Ltd 1985-, Securicloak Ltd 1986-; fin dir Bradford City AFC 1986-; chm: Omnis Assocs Ltd 1986-, DT Fin Conslts Ltd 1986-; dir and sec Wondercourt Ltd 1987-; songster ldr Castleford Corps Salvation Army; ACA 1969, FCA 1979; *Recreations* football, most sports; *Clubs* Regency (Leeds), Napoleon's (Bradford); *Style*— David Thompson, Esq; Stone Lea, Badsworth Ct, Badsworth, Pontefract, W Yorks WF9 1NW (☎ 0977 454 67); Sanderson Ho, Station Rd, Horsforth, Leeds LS18 5NT (☎ 0532 588 216/ 581 640, fax 0532 390 270, car tel 0836 265 365)

THOMPSON, David (Robin) Bibby; TD (1987); s of Noel Denis Thompson (d 1967), of Sansaw Hall, Clive, Shrewsbury, Shrops, and Cynthia Joan, *née* Bibby (d 1971); *b* 23 July 1946; *Educ* Uppingham; *m* 21 July 1971, Caroline Ann, da of Lt-Col O H J Foster, of Ardraccan House, Navan, Co Meath, Ireland; 1 s (James Peter Bibby b 1975), 1 da (Alexandra Jane b 1976); *Career* Mons OCS 1964-65, cmmnd Queen's Royal Irish Hussars 1965-71, ADC to HE Gvnr Victoria 1970-71, cmd Queen's Own Yeo TA 1984-87 (cmmnd 1974), Col TA 1987, ADC to HM The Queen 1988; farmer and landowner 1971-, dir Bibby Line Ltd 1974-87; memb Shrops CLA Ctee 1971-; chm NAC Housing Assoc 1983-86, memb Rural Devpt Cmmn 1986-; cncl memb RASE 1985; *Recreations* skiing, gardening, conservation, horses; *Clubs* Cavalry and Guard's; *Style*— Robin Thompson, Esq, TD; Sansaw Hall, Clive, Shrewsbury, Shrops SY4 3JR; Estate Office, Hadnall, Shrewsbury SY4 3DL, (☎ 09397 226)

THOMPSON, Donald; MP (C) Calder Valley 1983-; s of Geoffrey Thompson; *b* 13 Nov 1931; *Educ* Hipperholme GS; *m* 1957, Patricia Hopkins; 2 s; *Career* farmer, owner of contract butchering company, md Armadillo Plastics; memb: West Riding CC 1967-74, West Yorkshire CC 1974-75, Calderdale District Cncl 1975-79; chm Cons Candidates' Assoc 1972-74, contested (C): Batley and Morley 1970, Sowerby Feb and Oct 1974, MP (C) Sowerby 1979-1983, asst govt whip 1981-1983, Lord Cmmr of the Treasury/ govt whip 1983-1986; Parliamentary Sec Min, Fish and Food 1986-; *Style*— Donald Thompson, Esq, MP; Moravian House, Lightcliffe, nr Halifax, W Yorks (☎ 0422 202920)

THOMPSON, Dudley Stuart; s of Joel Percy Thompson (d 1964), and Joan Evelyn, *née* Anstey (d 1984); *b* 4 Nov 1942; *Educ* Whitgift Sch; *m* 27 June 1970, Anne Elizabeth, da of John Egerton Coope (d 1964); 1 s (Paul Dudley Fitzgerald b April 1975), 2 da (Karen Juliette b July 1973, Hazel Joan b Sept 1978); *Career* sr mangr Touche Ross & Co 1969-78, gp chief accountant Imperial Continental Gas Assoc 1978-87, gp fin dir Goode Durrant plc 1988-; chm Merstham Village Tst; FCA 1965, FCT 1982, MBIM 1985; *Recreations* golf, theatre, sailing, gardening; *Clubs* Walton Heath Golf, Hunstanton Golf; *Style*— Dudley Thompson, Esq; The Georgian House, Rockshaw Rd, Merstham, Surrey RH1 3DB; Goode Durrant plc, 22 Buckingham St, London WCRN 6PU (☎ 01 782 0010)

THOMPSON, Lt-Col Sir Edward Hugh Dudley; MBE (1945), TD, DL (Derby 1978); s of Neale Dudley Thompson; *b* 12 May 1907; *Educ* Uppingham, Lincoln Coll Oxford; *m* 1, 1931, Ruth Monica, *née* Wainwright; 2 s; m 2, 1947, Doreen Maud, *née* Tibbitt; 1 s, 1 da; *Career* Lt-Col 1939-45; slr 1931-36; asst md Ind Coope & Co Ltd 1937-39 (chm 1955-62), chm Allied Breweries Ltd 1961-68; chm Brewers Soc 1959-61; High Sheriff Derby 1964; Dr of Laws Univ of Nottingham 1984; kt 1967; *Recreations* farming; *Clubs* Boodle's; *Style*— Lt-Col Sir Edward Thompson, MBE, TD, DL; Culland Hall, Brailsford, Derby (☎ 0335 60247)

THOMPSON, Sir Edward Walter; JP (Salop 1953); s of A E Thompson of Gatacre Park, Bridgnorth and formerly of Wolverhampton; *b* 1902; *Educ* Oundle, Trinity Hall Cambridge; *m* 1930, Ann Elizabeth, da of late Rev G L'Estrange Amphlett, of Four Ashes Hall, nr Stourbridge, Worcs; 1 s, 3 da; *Career* chm Watertube Boilermakers' Assoc 1951-54, high sheriff Staffs 1955, chm Birmingham Regnl Hosp Bd 1957-61, dir Barclays Bank Ltd 1957-71 (local dir Birmingham 1950-71), chm Redditch New Town Devpt Corpn 1964-74, hon pres and former chm John Thompson Ltd Wolverhampton; kt 1957; *Style*— Sir Edward Thompson, JP; Gatacre Park, Bridgnorth, Salop

THOMPSON, Eric John; s of Herbert William Thompson, of Beverley, N Humberside, and Florence, *née* Brewer (d 1937); *b* 26 Sept 1934; *Educ* Beverley GS, London Sch of Economics (BSc); *Career* (pilot offr RAF) 1956-58; dir: of Statistics, Dept of Transport 1960-; statistician in Computer Ind 1958-60, Oil Indust 1960-65, gen Register Off 1965-68, GLC 1967-74 (asst dir Intelligence 1972-74); chief statistican, Central Statistical Office (ed 'Social Trends' 1975-80); *Recreations* reading, collecting books, British medieval history, English literature; *Clubs* E Yorks Local History Soc, Houseman Soc, Richard III Soc (exec Ctee 1984), Friends of National Libraries, Tstee, Richard III, Yorkist History Tst; *Style*— Eric Thompson, Esq; Dept of Transport, Romney House, London SW1P 3PY (☎ 01 212 8363)

THOMPSON, Ernest Gerald (Tommy); OBE (1973); s of Joseph Thompson (d 1943), of Goodmayes, Essex, and Rhoda Annie, *née* Messinger (d 1970); *b* 22 Nov 1925; *Educ* Brentwood Sch, Trinity Coll Cambridge; *m* 14 Sept 1968, Janet Muriel, da of Philip Andrew Smith (d 1977), of Blackmore House, Blackmore, Essex; 1 s (Richard Michael b 1971); *Career* Navigator/Bomb Aimer RAF 1943-47, Flt Lt; Int Secretariat of the Euro Movement Paris 1951-55, joined Baird & Tatlock Ltd 1955 (instrument sales mangr 1962-68), dir Dannatt SA Paris 1963-68, chm and md Chemlab Instruments Ltd 1968-86, chm Chemlab Mfrg Ltd chm and md Chemlab Scientific Products Ltd 1986-; memb Honorary Lecturing Faculty Inst of Marketing 1966-78, hon sec Britain in Europe 1958-68, vice chm Cons Gp for Europe 1967-75; memb: Gen Cncl of Cons Gp for Europe 1975-; nat exec of the Euro Movement 1969-83, nat cncl of Euro Movement 1983-, int Fed ctee of Union Européen des Fédéralistes 1974-, Honorary Senator of the Belgium Movement for the Utd States of Europe; LRSC (1968), IOD; *Recreations* music, swimming, travel, gardening; *Style*— Tommy Thompson, Esq; Yew Tree House, Morgan Crescent, Theydon Bois, Essex (☎ 037 881 2486); Los Ruisenores Son Pieras, Calviá, Mallorca, Spain; Chemlab Scientific Products Ltd, Construction House, Grenfell Ave, Hornchurch, Essex RM12 4EH (☎ 04024 76162, telex 9419785)

THOMPSON, Frank Robert; s of Corpl Arthur Robert Thompson (d 1964), of Newark, Notts, and Margaret Ellen, *née* Fordham; *b* 1 Jan 1938; *Educ* Magnus GS Newark, Notts, Hull Univ (BA, DipEd); *m* 21 Dec 1963, (Janet) Deirdre, da of Robert Fraser Skinner, of Melton Mowbray, Leicestershire; 1 s (Alastair b 1966), 1 da (Virginia b 1965); *Career* dep head Park Further Educn Centre Swindon 1969-70, head Westbourne Further Educn Centre Swindon 1971-72; Pontypool Coll: head gen studies 1975-82, sr lectr Dept Arts and Gen Studies 1982-; parly candidate (Lab) S Norfolk 1964, Wells 1970, Monmouth 1974, memb Bristol Univ Ct 1981-86; cnllr for Coleford on Glos CC 1981-, (gp ldr Glos CC 1985- (dep ldr 1982-85), rep on Assoc of CCs 1985-), memb Assoc of CCs Planning and Tportation Ctee 1985-); memb Staunton Parish Cncl 1979-87 (chm 1981-87), Staunton Parish Cncl rep on Forest of Dean Citizen's Advice Bureau mgmnt ctee 1979-87, chm of govrs: Roy Forest of Dean GS 1982-85, Lakers Sch 1985-; memb NATFHE 1973;; *Recreations* long-distance walking, swimming, chess, listening to music; *Style*— Frank Thompson, Esq; Steep Meadow, Staunton, Coleford, Gloucestershire GL16 8PD (☎ 0594 33873); Pontypool Coll, Blaendare Rd, Pontypool, Gwent (☎ 049 55 55141)

THOMPSON, Harry William; s of Gordon William Thompson, of Nant Ddu, Rhandirmwyn, Llandovery, Dyfed, and Brenda, *née* Houghton; *b* 6 Feb 1960; *Educ* Highgate, Brasenose Coll Oxford (MA); *Career* BBC TV: researcher (Chronicle, Not the 9 O'Clock News) 1981-82, dir (Film 83, Destination D Day, Nationwide) 1982-84; producer radio comedy (The News Quiz, Weekending, Lenin of the Rovers, Beachcomber by the Way, Nightcap, Quote… Unquote) 1985-88; wrote TV documentary The Man in the Iron Mask; contributor to: Spitting Image, Not the 9 O'Clock News, Private Eye, The Independant, The Listener; *Books* The Prejudice Library (1986), The Man in the Iron Mask (1987), The News Quiz Book (1987), The Spitting Image Book (contrib 1988); *Recreations* cricket, old bookshops; *Clubs* Captain Scott; *Style*— Harry Thompson, Esq; Alexandra House, St Mary's Terr, London W2 (☎ 01 402 2157); BBC, 16 Langham St, London W1 (☎ 01 927 4867)

THOMPSON, Dr Ian McKim; s of John William Thompson (d 1976), of Solihull, and Dr Elizabeth Maria, *née* Williams; *b* 19 August 1938; *Educ* Epsom Coll, Univ of Birmingham (MB, ChB); *m* 8 Sept 1962, Dr (Veronica) Jane, da of John Dent Richards (d 1987), of Fladbury; 2 s (David b 1966, Peter b 1969), 1 da (Suzanne b 1972); *Career* lectr in pathology Univ of Birmingham 1964-67, conslt forensic pathologist to HM Coroner City of Birmingham 1966-, dep sec BMA 1969-, lectr dept of adult educn Keele Univ 1985-; fndr memb AMEC; memb GMC 1979-; hon Collegiate Med Coll of Spain 1975; BMA 1961, FRSM 1988; *Books* The Hospital Gazeteer (ed 1972), BMA Handbook for Hospital Junior Doctors (ed 1984), BMA Handbook for Trainee Doctors in General Practice (ed 1985); *Recreations* inland waterways, rambling; *Style*— Dr McKim Thompson; 9 Old Rectory Green, Fladbury, Pershore, Worcs WR10 2QX (☎ 0386 860 668); BMA House, Tavistock Sq, London WC1H 9JP (☎ 01 383 6005)

THOMPSON, James Craig; s of Alfred Thompson, of Newcastle-upon-Tyne, and Eleanor, *née* Craig; *b* 27 Oct 1933; *Educ* Heaton GS, Rutherford Coll Newcastle; *m* 4 Sept 1957, Catherine, da of James Warburton, of Newcastle-upon-Tyne; 1 s (Roderic b 1959), 1 da (Fiona b 1963); *Career* pres: The Maidstone Minor League 1976-, The Eastern Professional Floodlight League 1976-; chm: The Southern Football League 1977-79, The Alliance Premier Football League 1979-; memb of Cncl of Football Assoc 1982-; pres The Kent League 1984-; chm and md: Maidstone United Football Club Ltd 1970-, Adverkit International Ltd 1987-; commercial exec Belfast Telegraph, Newcastle Chronicle and Journal, Scotsman Publications, Liverpool Post and Echo 1960-76; advertising and marketing mangr Kent Messenger Gp 1976-79, dir 1972-79; md South Eastern Newspapers 1975-79; chm and md Eadons Newspaper Services Ltd 1982-, chm Harvest Publications Ltd 1983-; dir: Weekley Newspaper Advertising Bureau 1977-, Adbuilder Ltd 1971-; life govr Kent County Agric Soc 1976-; hon life memb Kent County CC 1978; memb MCC; Catenian Assoc (pres Maidstone Circle

1974-75); *Recreations* walking, Northumbrian history; *Clubs* East India, Maidstone; *Style*— James Thompson, Esq; Prescott House, Otham, Kent (☎ 0622 686005); Adverkit Int Ltd, Bowerdene House, Number One Bower Terrace, Maidstone, Kent (☎ 0622 687654, fax 0622 57054)

THOMPSON, Jeremy Sinclair; s of Norman Sinclair Thompson, CBE, of Shadrach House, Burton Bradstock, Dorset, and Peggy, *née* Sivil; *b* 6 April 1954; *Educ* Durham Sch, Keble Coll Oxford (MA); *m* 12 June 1982, Lucy Jane Thompson, da of Peter Joseph Wagner (d 1983); 1 da (Victoria b 1986); *Career* Peat Marwick Mitchell 1976-80, dir accounting servs Air Florida Europe Ltd 1980-82, cnslt Coopers & Lybrand Assocs 1982-84; md: Sinclair Thompson Assocs 1985-86, Tranwood Earl & Co Ltd 1986-; dir Tranwood plc 1987-; ACA 1980; *Recreations* rowing, sailing; *Clubs* Leander; *Style*— Jeremy Thompson, Esq; Hill Barn Farm, Broomers Hill, Pulborough, W Sussex (☎ 07982 2778); Tranwood Earl & Co Ltd, 123 Sloane St, London SW1 (☎ 01 730 3412, fax 01 730 5770, telex 932016)

THOMPSON, John; MP (Lab) Wansbeck 1983-; s of Nicholas Thompson, of Ashington, Northumberland (d 1966), and Lilian Thompson; *b* 27 August 1928; *Educ* Bothal Sch; *m* 1952, Margaret, da of John Robert Clarke (d 1974), of Newbiggin-by-Sea, Northumberland; 1 s, 1 da; *Career* electrical engineer 1966-83; dist cllr 1970-79, co cllr 1974-85, ldr and vice-chm Northumberland Co Cncl 1974-83, bd memb Northumbrian Water Authority 1981-83; *Recreations* caravanning, listening; *Style*— John Thompson, Esq, MP; House of Commons, London SW1 (☎ 01 219 4048); 20 Falstone Crescent, Ashington, Northumberland (☎ 0670 817830)

THOMPSON, John; s of John Thompson, of Myrtle Bank, Kersal Rd, Prestwich, Lancs (d 1964), and Ellen Anne, *née* Evans (d 1954); *b* 10 May 1932; *m* 2 April 1955, Eileen Joan, da of Ernest Neate, of Amesbury, Wilts; *Career* md Wincanton Motor Gp, operations, dir Arlington Motor Hldgs, exec dir: United Service Garages Ltd, Turnbulls (Plymouth) Ltd; dir: Zenith Motors Ltd, Wincanton Garages Ltd, Vogal Motors Ltd, Hewitts Garages Ltd, Kays Ltd, Charnwood Trucks Ltd, Shepshed Engr Ltd, Wincanton Body Works (Westbury) Ltd; Freemasonry Rank 1987, past provincial snr Grand Deacon (Prov of East Lancashire); acting rank-prov Grand Steward 1985-86; FBIM, FIMI; *Recreations* motor racing, golf, horse riding, all aspects sports; *Clubs* Directors Lodge, RAC, Inst Directors, Mansion House (Poole), Bramshaw Golf, BARC; *Style*— John Thompson, Esq; Whisper Wood, The Warren, Chalfont Heights, Gerrards Cross (☎ 0753 885263); Arlington Motor Hldgs, Ardent House, Gatesway, Stevenage SG1 3NF (telex 825548, car ☎ 0860 522 908)

THOMPSON, Sir John; s of Donald Thompson; *b* 16 Dec 1907; *Educ* Bellahouston Acad, Glasgow Univ, Oriel Coll Oxford; *m* 1934, Agnes, da of John Drummond, of Glasgow; 2 s; *Career* barr Middle Temple 1933, QC 1954, vice-chm gen cncl bar 1960-61, commissioner assize Birmingham 1961, High Court judge (Queen's Bench) 1961-82; kt 1961; *Recreations* golf; *Clubs* R and A, Sundridge Park Golf, Woking Golf; *Style*— Sir John Thompson; 73 Sevenoaks Rd, Orpington, Kent (☎ 22339)

THOMPSON, Col John Keith Lumley; TD, (1961, Bar 1963 and 1971), MBE (mil 1965), CMG (1982); s of John Vere Valentine Thompson, (d 1968), of Wallsend, Tyne and Wear, and Gertrude, *née* Herrington (d 1977); *b* 31 Mar 1923; *Educ* Wallsend GS, King's Coll Durham Univ (BSc); *m* 21 Nov 1950, Audrey, da of George Henderson (d 1977), Grantham; 1 s (John Robert b 1951); *Career* WWII 2 Lt (later Lt then Acting Capt) REME NW Europe; TAVR 1948-78: Maj 44 Para Bde (v) BEME 1948-70, Lt Col dep inspector REME (v) Southern Cmd 1970-72, Col Dep Cdr 44 Para Bde (v) 1972-75, ADC to HM The Queen 1974-78; res scientist: Road Res Lab (DSIE) 1948-55, AWRE (Aldermaston) 1955-64; memb staff Lord Zuckerman Chief sci Advsr MOD 1964-65, head E Midlands Regnl Office Miny of Technol 1965-70, head Int Affairs Atomic Energy Div Dept of Energy 1972-74, regnl dir W Midlands and Northern Regnl Offices DTI 1974-78 (formerly 1970-72), cnsllr (sci & technol) Br Embassy Washington USA 1978-83, pre Lumley Assocs Conslt 1983-89; Br Legion: vice-pres Baston and Laingtoft Branch, pres Bourne and Dist, hon rep offrs assoc Bourne and Dist; FBIM 1975, memb American Soc Automotive Engrs 1983; *Recreations* outdoor sports, riding, skiing, windsurfing; *Style*— Col John Thompson, CMG, MBE, TD; Clover Cottage, 7 School Lane, Baston, Peterborough PE6 9PD (☎ 077 836 374)

THOMPSON, Air Cdre John Marlow; CBE (1952), DSO (1943), DFC (1940) and bar (1942), AFC (1952); s of John Thompson (d 1926), and Florence Thompson (d 1973); *b* 16 August 1914; *Educ* Bristol GS; *m* 1938, Margaret Sylvia Barlow Morris, *née* Rowlands; 1 s, 1 da (1 s decd); *Career* Air Cdre RAF 1934-66, cmd 111 Sqdn Battle of Britain 1940, Fighter Wings Siege of Malta 1942, dir Air Defence Air Ministry 1958-60, AOC Mil Air Traffic Operations 1962-65 (ret 1966); gen mangr Airwork Services Saudi Arabia 1966-68; Sec Moor Park Golf Club 1969-1973, Monte Carlo Golf Club 1973-83; Sec Moor Park Golf Club 1969-1973, Monte Carlo Golf Club 1973-1983; *Recreations* golf, travel, reading; *Clubs* RAF, Moor Park Golf (sec 1969-73), Monte Carlo Golf (sec 1973-83); *Style*— Air Cdre John Thompson, CBE, DSO, DFC, AFC; Flat 3, 35 Adelaide Crescent, Hove, E Sussex, BN3 2JJ

THOMPSON, John Michael Anthony; s of George Edward Thompson (d 1982), of Deganwy, Gwynedd, N Wales, and Joan, *née* Smith; *b* 3 Feb 1941; *Educ* William Hulme's GS Manchester, Univ of Manchester (BA, MA); *m* 24 July 1965, Alison Sara, da of Walter Bowers, of Cheadle Hulme, Greater Manchester; 2 da (Hannah Jane b 19 March 1973, Harriet Mary b 13 Feb 1976); *Career* res asst Whitworth Art Gallery 1964-66, keeper Rutherston Collection Manchester City Art Gallery 1966-68; dir: NW Museum and Gallery Serv 1968-70, Arts and Museums Bradford 1970-75, Tyne and Wear Co Museums and Galleries 1975-86, Tyne and Wear Jt Museums Serv 1986-; fndr memb and hon sec Gp of Dirs of Museums in Br Isles, cncllr Museum North (former pres), memb Tyne and Wear Building Preservation Tst, advsr Assoc of Met Authorities, jt sponsor Shipbuilding Exhibition Centre South Tyneside; AMA 1970, FMA 1977; *Books* Manual of Curatorship, A Guide to Museum Practice (ed, second edn 1986); *Recreations* running, travel, visiting exhibitions; *Clubs* Museum Assoc; *Style*— John Thompson, Esq; 21 Linden Rd, Gosforth, Newcastle-upon-Tyne; Blandford House, Blandford Sq, Newcastle-upon-Tyne

THOMPSON, John William McWean; CBE (1986); s of Charles Stanley Thompson, of Ramsgill, Yorks (d 1962), and Charlotte Dring, *née* Pickering (d 1972); *b* 12 June 1920; *Educ* Roundhay Sch, Leeds; *m* 12 July 1947, Sallie Cynthia Margaret, da of Alfred Pyne Ledsham, of Brentford, Middx (d 1972); 1 s (Matthew b 1954); 1 da (Sarah b 1958); *Career* journalist; dep-ed The Spectator 1964-70, ed The Sunday Telegraph 1976-86; *Clubs* Travellers'; *Style*— John Thompson, Esq, CBE; Corner Cottage, Burnham Norton, King's Lynn, Norfolk (☎ 0328 738396)

THOMPSON, Rear Adm John Yelverton; CB (1960); s of Sir John Perronet Thompson, KCSI, KCIE, ICS (d 1935), and Ada Lucia, *née* Tyrrell (d 1957); *b* 25 May 1909; *Educ* Mourne Grange, Kilkeel Co Down, RNC Dartmouth (psc 1946); *m* 15 Dec 1934, Barbara Helen Mary Aston, da of Dr Benjamin William Martin Aston Key, OBE (d 1961), of Southsea; 2 s (Richard b 1935, Martin b 1939); *Career* Lt Cdr HMS Anson N Atlantic 1941-43, Cdr Naval Ordnance Dept Admty 1943-45, US 5 Fleet 1946, Liverpool 1947, Newcastle 1948; Capt Ordnance Bd 1948-50, Unicorn (Korean War) 1951-52 (despatches), dir Gunnery Div, Naval Staff 1952-54, IDC 1955; Cdre RN Barracks Portsmouth 1956-57; ADC to HM 1957-58; Rear Adm Admty Interview Bd 1958, Adm Supt HM Dockyard Chatham 1958-61 (ret); naval advsr Elliott-Automation 1961-66; gov Aldenham Sch 1967-75; chm Herts Scout Cncl 1962-71; DL Hertfordshire 1966-73, and Cornwall 1973-; American Legion of Merit (1953); *Style*— Rear Adm J Y Thompson, CB, DL; Flushing Meadow, Manaccan, nr Helston, Cornwall (☎ 032 623 354)

THOMPSON, Joseph Lefroy Courtenay; s of Joseph Matthew Thompson, of Belfast (d 1976); *b* 4 April 1943; *Educ* Rugby, Trin Coll Dublin; *m* 1967, Joan Lesley, *née*, Love; 1 s, 1 da; *Career* md Charleville Hldgs Ltd, dir: William Ewart Investmt Ltd Hicks Bullick Ltd, Sydney Pentland Ltd, Industl Therapy Orgn (Ulster) Ltd, govr Princes Gardens Sch; *Clubs* Lansdowne; *Style*— J L Thompson Esq; Charleville, 39 Manse Rd, Castlereagh, Belfast (☎ 0232 792412)

THOMPSON, (Rupert) Julian de la Mare; s of Rupert Spens Thompson (d 1952), and Florence Elizabeth de la Mare; *b* 23 July 1941; *Educ* Eton, King's Coll Cambridge (MA); *m* 6 March 1965, Jacqueline Mary, da of John William Linnell Ivimy; 3 da (Rebecca b 1966, Sophia b 1968, Cecilia b 1971); *Career* dir Sothebys 1969-; chm: Sothebys (UK) 1982-86 (dep-chm 1987-), ; *Style*— Julian Thompson, Esq; 43 Clarendon Rd, London W11 4JD (☎ 01 727 6039); Crossington Farm, Upton Bishop, Ross-on-Wye, Hereford (☎ 098 895 363); Sotheby's 34-45 New Bond St, London W1A 2AA (☎ 01 493 8080)

THOMPSON, Maj-Gen Julian Howard Atherden; CB (1982), OBE (1978); s of Maj A J Thompson, DSO, MC (d 1966), of Cornwall, and Mary Stearns, *née* Krause (d 1978); *b* 7 Oct 1934; *Educ* Sherborne; *m* 1960, Janet Avery, da of Richard Robinson Rodd, of Devon; 1 s (David), 1 da (Henrietta); *Career* Cdr Offr 40 Commando RM 1975-78; Cdr 3 Commando Bgde 1981-83, including Falklands Campaign 1982, Maj-Gen cmd Training and Special Forces Royal Marines; sr research fell Kings Coll London; *Books* No Picnic (1985); *Clubs* Army and Navy; *Style*— Maj-Gen Julian Thompson, CB, OBE; Lloyds Bank plc, 8 Royal Parade, Plymouth

THOMPSON, Keith Bruce; s of Charles Bruce Thompson (d 1982), and Eva Elizabeth, *née* Vidler (d 1966); *b* 13 Sept 1932; *Educ* Bishopshalt Sch Hillingdon, New Coll Oxford (BA, PP, MA), Oxford Univ Dept of Education (Dip, Ed), Bristol Univ (MEd); *m* 17 Aug 1956, Kathleen Anne, da of Sydney Reeves, OBE (d 1982); 1 s (Bruce b 1959), 1 da (Fiona b 1961); *Career* RAOC 1950-52; schoolmaster City of Bath Boys' Sch 1956-62, lectr Newton Park Coll Bath 1962-67, head of dept Philippa Fawcett Coll Streatham 1967-72, princ Madeley Coll Staffs 1972-78, dep dir Staffs Poly, (formerly N Staffs Poly) 1978-86, dir 1986-; chm: Standing Conf on Studies in educn 1980-82, Undergarduate Initial Training Bd (Educn) CNAA 1981-85; memb Nat Advsy Body for Public Sector Higher Educn 1983-88 (chm teacher educn gp 1983-85); *Books* Education and Philosophy (1972), Curriculum Development (jt author 1974), Education for Teaching 1968-74 (ed-journal); *Recreations* sport, music; *Style*— Keith Thompson, Esq; Staffs Poly, Beaconside, Staffs ST18 OAD (☎ 0785 52331, fax 0785 520858)

THOMPSON, Dr (Malcolm) Keith; s of Ralph Whittier Thompson (d 1962), of London, and Ethel Eva, *née* Smith (d 1972); *b* 30 June 1921; *Educ* Trinity Sch of John Whitgift, Univ of St Andrews (MB, ChB), Univ of London (D Obst); *m* 24 Oct 1953, Jeanne Sophie Auguste, da of Jean Bernard Struys (d 1971), of Brussels; 1 da (Chantal (Mrs Blake-Milton) b 18 July 1957); *Career* Friend's Ambulance Unit 1943-45; house physician to Sir Ian Hill 1952-53, house surgn Obstetrics & Gynaecology Wanstead Hosp 1953, princ in GP Woodside Health Centre SE25 1955-86; examiner for MRCGP Examination 1976-86, RCP examiner for diploma in Geriatric Med 1984-; Nuffield Travelling Fell 1970, Med Gilliland Travelling fell 1984; fndr assoc memb Royal Coll of GPs 1953; med ed Med Opinion 1978-79 and Geriatric med 1984-86, med correspondent Yours newspaper 1974-, lectr Coll of GP Hong Kong 1987, advsr WHO Copenhagen 1979 and DHSS 1980; distintions: Butterworth Gold Medal 1967, Hunterian Socs Gold Medal 1968, memb: advsr Help the Aged, govng body Age Concern, med advsy panel Parkinsons Desease Soc of Gt Br (chm Croydon branch), BMA, Br Geriatrics Soc 1971; RCOG 1954, MRCGP 1965, FRCGP 1977; *Books* Geriatrics and the General Practitioner Team (1969), Geriatrie Voor Die Huisarts (1971), The Care of the Elderly in General Practice (1984), Caring for an Elderly Relative (1986), Commonsense Geriatrics (1989); *Recreations* swimming, golf, music, theatre, walking; *Style*— Dr Keith Thompson; 28 Steep Hill, Stanhope Rd, Croydon CR0 5QS (☎ 01 686 7489)

THOMPSON, Sir (Thomas) Lionel Tennyson; 5 Bt (UK 1806), of Hartsbourne Manor, Hertfordshire; s of Lt-Col Sir Thomas Raikes Lovett Thompson, 4 Bt, MC (d 1964), and of late Millicent Ellen Jean, da of late Edmund Charles Tennyson-d'Eyncourt, of Bayons Manor, Lincs; *b* 19 June 1921; *Educ* Eton; *m* 1955 (m dis 1962), Mrs Margaret van Beers, da of late Walter Herbert Browne; 1 s, 1 da; *Heir* s, Thomas d'Eyncourt John Thompson; *Career* 1939-45 War as Flying Officer RAFVR (invalided), and subsequently as Able Seaman Royal Fleet Auxiliary (1939-45, and Aircrew (Europe) stars, Defence and Victory Medals); barr Lincoln's Inn 1952; *Style*— Sir Lionel Thompson, Bt; 184/5 Temple Chambers, Temple Avenue, EC4Y 0BB (☎ 01 353 5580)

THOMPSON, Lucy Ellen; da of William Chidgey (d 1956), of 7 Clarendon St, London, and Elizabeth, *née* Lightfoot (d 1972); *b* 25 June 1924, ; *Educ* Buckingham Gate Secdy Sch; *m* 3 April 1954, Jack Evans Thompson, s of Ralph Dean Henry Thompson (d 1946); *Career* sec Lloyds Bank 1947-54; md: RHD Thompson & Co Ltd 1954-89, Thompson Hydribind Equipment Co Ltd 1963-, Marine and Tidal Power Ltd 1973-; *Recreations* Scottish country dancing; *Clubs* Royal Highland Yacht, British Motor Yacht; *Style*— Mrs Lucy Thompson; 7 Clarendon St, London SW1V 2EN (☎ 01 834 1886); Maelstroma, Kilmelford By Oban, Argyll; RHD Thompson & Co Ltd, Hersham Trading Estate, Walton on Thames, Surrey (☎ 0932 226 351)

THOMPSON, Michael; s of Eric Thompson, of Eldwick, and Mary, *née* Shuttleworth; *b* 18 June 1954; *Educ* Bradford GS, Trinity Coll Cambridge (MA); *Career* RAF

Reservist 1973-76; Freshfields: articled clerk 1977-79, asst slr 1979-85, ptnr Corporate Tax Dept 1985-; memb Law Soc's Revenue Law Sub-ctee on Petroleum Taxation; rep City Deanery Synod, memb PCC St Helen's Church Bishopsgate; Freeman of City of London Slrs Co 1987; memb The Law Soc; *Recreations* sailing, fell walking; *Style—* Michael Thompson, Esq; Grindall House, 25 Newgate St, London EC1A 7LH (☎ 01 606 6677, fax 248 3487/8/9, telex 889292)

THOMPSON, Prof (Francis) Michael (Longstreth); s of Francis Longstreth-Thompson, OBE (d 1973), of Little Waltham, Essex, and Mildred Grace, *née* Corder (d 1963); *b* 13 August 1925; *Educ* Bootham Sch York, Queen's Coll Oxford (MA, DPhil), Merton Coll Oxford; *m* 11 Aug 1951, Anne Longstreth, da of Maj John Lovibond Challoner, TA, of Northumberland (d 1970); 2 s ((Francis) Jonathan Longstreth b 1958, Matthew Longstreth b 1964), 1 da (Suzanna Jane Longstreth b 1959); *Career* WWII 1943-47, Lt 1944, 7 Indian Field Regt RIA India and Sumatra 1945-46, Staff Capt 26 Indian Div E Bengal 1946-47, Capt 1946-47; reader in economic history UCL 1963-68 (lectr in history 1951-63), prof of modern history Bedford Coll London 1968-77, dir Inst of Historical Res and prof of history London Unvi 1977-; pres; Economic History Soc 1984-87, Royal Historical Soc 1988-, Br Agric History Soc 1989-; sec Br Nat Ctee of Historians 1977-, Br Acad rep humanities ctee Euro Sci Fndn 1983-, hon tres Int Econ History Assoc 1986-; ed Econ History Assoc 1986-; ed Econ History Review 1968-80; FRHistS 1963, ARICS 1968, FBA 1979; *Books* English Landed Society in the Nineteenth Century (1963), Victorian England: The Horse Drawn Society (1970), Chartered Surveyors: The Growth of a Profession (1968), Hampstead: Building a Borough (1974), The Rise of Suburbia (ed, 1982), Horses in European Economic History (ed, 1983), The Rise of Respectable Society (1988), The Cambridge Social History of Britain 1750-1950 (3 vols, 1989); *Recreations* gardening, walking, carpentry; *Style—* Prof Michael Thompson; Inst of Historical Res, Univ of London, Senate House, London WC1E 7HU (☎ 01 636 0272)

THOMPSON, (John) Michael (Strutt); s of John Thompson (d 1951), of Dale Farm, Weald, Sevenoaks, Kent, and Donnie Agnes Beatrice, *née* Strutt (d 1979); *b* 14 Dec 1931; *Educ* Felsted; *m* 24 Oct 1959, Fiona Mary, da of Wing Cdr Malcolm Glassford Begg, MC (d 1969), of Armsworth Park Farm, Alresford, Hants; 1 s (Marcus Peter Strutt b 1961), 1 da (Julia Mariette (Mrs Gallagher) b 1963); *Career* Nat Serv 2 Lt cmmnd Rifle Bde 1956-58; res sub agent RH & RW Clutton Hursley Estate Hants 1958-65, agent and sec Ernest Cook Tst Fairford Glos 1965-73, chief agent Fitzwilliam Estates Milton Park Peterborough Cambs 1974-; pres local Cons branch 1981-, gen cmmr Income Tax Peterborough 1981, pres land agency and agric div RICS 1985-86; chm Landowners Gp 1987-, vice-chm Cambs CLA 1988-; FRICS 1956, FAAV 1986; *Recreations* fishing, shooting, sailing; *Clubs* Farmers; *Style—* Michael Thompson, Esq; Stibbington House, Wansford, Peterborough, Cambs PE8 6JS (☎ 0780 782043); Estate Office, Milton Pk, Peterborough, Cambs PE6 7AH (☎ 0733 267740, fax 0733 331200)

THOMPSON, Michael Harry Rex; William Henry Thompson, of Guildford, and Beatrice Hilda, *née* Heard (d 1987); *b* 14 Jan 1931; *Educ* St John's Sch Leatherhead Surrey; *m* 1958, Joyce; 1 s (Ian b 1963), 1 da (Anne b 1959); *Career* joined Lloyds Bank 1948, joint gen mangr 1977; dir: Lloyds Bank California 1978-81, The National Bank of New Zealand 1978-82, Lloyds & Scottish Ltd 1981-85; exec dir Lloyds Bank Int 1982, asst chief exec 1985; dep chief exec 1987; *Recreations* rugby football; *Clubs* Guildford & Godalming RFC; *Style—* Michael Thompson, Esq; 71 Lombard St, London EC3P 3BS (☎ 01 626 1500)

THOMPSON, Nanne, Lady; Nanne; *née* Broome; da of late Charles Broome, of Walton, Liverpool; *b* 24 July 1912; *m* 1936, Sir Kenneth Pugh Thompson, 1 Bt (d 1984, formerly MP (C) for Walton Liverpool and asst postmaster gen 1957-59); 1 s (Paul, 2 Bt, *qv*), 1 da; *Style—* Nanne, Lady Thompson, JP; Atherton Cottage, via Kirklake Rd, Formby, Merseyside L37 2DD (☎ 070 48 72486)

THOMPSON, Nicholas Annesley Marler; s and h of Sir Richard Hilton Marler Thompson, 1 Bt; *b* 19 Mar 1947; *m* 1982, Venetia Catherine, yr da of John Horace Broke Heathcote, of Conington House, nr Peterborough; 2 s (Simon b 1985, Charles b 1986); *Career* solicitor 1973; memb Westminster City Cncl 1978-86; dep Lord Mayor of Westminster 1983-84; conservative candidate for Newham South 1983 general election; *Recreations* foreign travel, skiing, riding, tennis, walking, theatre, reading; *Clubs* Carlton; *Style—* Nicholas Thompson, Esq; 15 Westminster Gdns, London SW1 (☎ 01 834 6757); Denning House, 90 Chancery Lane, London WC1 (☎ 01 242 1212)

THOMPSON, Nicolas de la Mare; s of Rupert Spens Thompson (d 1951), and Florence Elizabeth, *née* de la Mare; *b* 4 June 1928; *Educ* Eton, Christ Church Oxford (MA); *m* 13 Sept 1956, (Fenella Mary) Erica, da of Powlett Pennell (d 1970); 2 s (Rupert b 1962, Simon b 1964), 1 da (Sarah b 1960); *Career* RAF 1949-51; md George Weidenfeld & Nicolson Ltd 1956-70, publishing dir Pitman plc 1976-84, md Heinemann Gp of Publishers Ltd 1985-87, dir Octopus Publishing Gp plc 1985-; chm: Book Devlp Cncl 1984-86, Heinemann Educnl Books Ltd, Heinemann Professional Publishing Ltd, Guin & Co Ltd, George Philip Ltd, Mitchell Beazley Ltd; *Style—* Nicolas Thompson, Esq; Flat A, 8 Ennismore Gdns, London SW7 (☎ 01 584 9769); Octopus Publishing Gp, 59 Grosvenor St, London W1 (☎ 01 493 5841)

THOMPSON, Dr Noel Brentnall Watson; s of George Watson Thompson (d 1980), and Mary Henrietta, *née* Gibson (d 1944); *b* 11 Dec 1932; *Educ* Manchester GS, Cambridge Univ (MA), Imperial Coll London (MSc, PhD); *m* Jan 1957, Margaret Angela Elizabeth, da of Ernest William Baston (d 1967), of Bristol; 1 s (Gareth b 1972); *Career* sub Lt RN 1951-53; sec Nat Libraries Ctee 1967-69; Univ lectr Birmingham 1961-65; under sec Dept of Educn and Science 1980-; cabinet Off Secretariat 1977-79;; *Recreations* railways of all sizes, electronics, mechanics, music, photography, walking; *Style—* Dr Noel B W Thompson; Department of Education and Science, Elizabeth House, York Rd, London SE1 7PH (☎ 01 934 9869)

THOMPSON, (Hugh) Patrick; MP (C) Norwich North 1983-; s of Gerald Leopold Thompson, of 11 Gretton Court, Girton, Cambridge, and Kathleen Mary Landsdown Thompson; *b* 21 Oct 1935; *Educ* Felsted, Emmanuel Coll Cambridge (MA); *m* 1 Sept 1962, Kathleen, da of Thomas Falkingham Howson (d 1963); *Career* nat serv 2 Lt KOY LI 1957-59; TA 1959-65; jr engr English Electric Value Co Chelmsford 1959-60; physics master: The Manchester GS 1960-65, Gresham's Sch Holt 1965-83 (Gresham's CCF, Cadet Force Medal, Major); contested (C): Bradford North Feb and Oct 1974, Barrow-in-Furness 1979; PPS to Min of State for Transport 1987-88; pps to Min of State for Social Security and the Disabled 1988-, fndr memb All Pty Gp for Engrg Devpt 1985-; MInstP; *Recreations* travel, music, gardening; *Clubs* The Norfolk; *Style—* Patrick Thompson, Esq, MP; The Cottage, St Giles Rd, Swanton Novers, Norfolk NR24 2RB; House of Commons, London SW1A OAA (☎ 01 219 6398)

THOMPSON, Sir Paul Anthony; 2 Bt (UK 1963), of Walton-on-the-Hill, City of Liverpool; s of Sir Kenneth Pugh Thompson, 1 Bt (d 1984; MP (C) for Walton Liverpool 1950-64, asst PMG 1957-59), and Nanne, Lady Thompson, JP, *qv*; *b* 6 Oct 1939; *m* 1971, Pauline Dorothy, da of Robert Orrell Spencer, of Tippett House, Smithills, Bolton, Lancs; 2 s (Richard, David), 2 da (Karena, Nicola); *Heir* s, Richard Thompson; *Career* company director; *Style—* Sir Paul Thompson, Bt; 28 Dowhills Rd, Blundellsands, Liverpool L23 8SW

THOMPSON, Sir Peter Anthony; *b* 14 April 1928; *Educ* Bradford GS, Leeds Univ BA (Econ); *m* 1958, Patricia Anne Norcott (d 1983); 1 s, 2 da; *Career* formerly with: Unilever, GKN, Rank Orgn, British Steel Corpn, British Road Services; exec vice-chm National Freight Corpn (later Company) 1976-77, dep chm and ch exec 1977-82, chm and ch exec National Freight Consortium 1982-; chm Community Hospitals plc; former pres Inst of Freight Forwarders; exec chm National Freight Consortium plc 1984-, chm Inst of Logistics and Distribution Mgmnt; dir: Pilkington plc, Granville & Co Ltd, Smiths Industries plc; FCIT, CBIM; kt 1984; *Recreations* golf, walking, music; *Clubs* RAC; *Style—* Sir Peter Thompson; National Freight Consortium plc, Merton Centre, 45 St Peter's St, Bedford MK40 2UB (☎ 0234 272222, telex 826803)

THOMPSON, Peter Kenneth James; s of Rt Rev Kenneth George Thompson (d 1976), first Bishop of Sherwood, and Doreen May Latchford; *b* 30 July 1937; *Educ* Worksop Coll, Christ's Coll Cmabridge (MA, LLB); *m* 10 Aug 1970, Sandy Lynne, da of Wallace Harder (d 1970); 2 da (Helena b 1978, Gemma b 1981); *Career* Barr Lincoln's Inn 1961, practised at Common Law Bar 1961-73; lawyer in Government Serv 1972-; under-sec in The Slrs Off, DHSS; *Recreations* writing; *Style—* Peter K J Thompson, Esq; B912 Alexander Fleming House, Elephant Castle, London SE1 (☎ 01 407 5522 ext 7484)

THOMPSON, Prof Raymond; CBE (1988); s of William Edward Thompson (d 1946), and Hilda, *née* Rowley; *b* 4 April 1925; *Educ* Longton HS, Nottingham Univ (MSc, PhD), Imperial Coll (DIC); *Career* dir Borax Holdings Ltd 1969-87; md Borax Research Ltd 1980-86, dep chm 1986-; dir RTZ Chemicals (Borides) Ltd 1988-; conslt to Borax Holdings, RTZ Chemicals & CRA Ltd 1988-; special prof of Chemistry Nottingham Univ 1975-; hon prof of Chemistry Warwick Univ 1975-; govr Kingston-upon-Thames Poly 1978-88; Freeman of City of London, Liveryman of Worshipful Co of Glass Sellers (1983), Worshipful Co of Engineers 1987; FEng 1985, FRSC 1957, FIMM 1972, FRSA 1985; *Books* Mellor's Comprehensive Treatise, Boron Supplement (1979), The Modern Inorganic Chemicals Industry (1977), Speciality Inorganic Chemicals (1980), Energy and Chemistry (1981), Trace Metal Removal from Aqueous Solution (1986); *Recreations* gardening; *Clubs* City Livery; *Style—* Prof Raymond Thompson; The Garth, 7 Winchester Close, Esher Place, Esher, Surrey KT10 8QH (☎ 0372 64428); Borax Research Ltd, Cox Lane, Chessington, Surrey KT9 1SJ (☎ 01 397 5141, fax 01 391 5744, telex 929612)

THOMPSON, Richard; JP (1970); s of John William Thompson (d 1960), of Horsforth, Leeds, and Annie Elizabeth Newton (d 1950); *b* 22 April 1913; *Educ* Aireborough GS, Leeds Sch of Architecture; *m* 14 June 1950, Eleanor Rosemary, da of Alfred Gillgrass (d 1946), of Roundhay, Leeds; *Career* architect, arbitrator (pupil master for chartered inst arbitrators), pres W Yorks Soc of Architects 1963-65; memb Cncl; RIBA 1963-67, Nat Jt Consultative Cncl Bldg Indust 1965-76, RIBA, rep on DOE Bldg and Civil Engrg Regnl Joint Consultative Ctee for Yorkshire and Humberside 1965-78, RIBA, MRTPI, FCIArb; *Recreations* horticulture, cricket, charity works (local); *Style—* Richard Thompson, Esq, JP; The Lanes, 121 Hall Lane, Horsforth, Leeds LS18 5LZ (☎ 0532 582739); Clarendon Chambers, 55 Clarendon Rd, Leeds LS2 9NZ (☎ 0532 434861/2)

THOMPSON, Sir Richard Hilton Marler; 1 Bt (UK 1963), of Reculver, Co Kent; s of Richard Smith Thompson (d 1952), and Kathleen Hilda *née* Marler (d 1916), of London and Calcutta; *b* 5 Oct 1912; *Educ* Malvern; *m* 9 Aug 1939, Anne Christabel de Vere, da of late Philip de Vere Annesley (bro of 13 Viscount Valentia); 1 s; *Heir* s, Nicholas Annesley Marler Thompson, *qv*; *Career* RNVR 1940-46, cmmnd 1941 (despatches 1942), Lt Cdr 1944; business in India 1930-39; MP (C) Croydon West 1950-55, asst-govt whip 1952, Lord cmmr of the Treasy 1954, MP (C) Croydon South 1955-66 and 1970-74, vice chamberlain of HM Household 1956, parly sec Miny of Health 1957-59, under-sec of state CRO 1959-60, parly sec Miny of Works 1960-62; tstee Br Museum 1951-84, memb Council Nat Tst 1978-84; dir: Rediffusion TV Ltd and Rediffusion Hldgs Ltd 1966-83; fndr memb and first elected Br Museum Soc 1970-74, chm Capital Counties Property Co Ltd 1971-77; pres Br Property Fedn 1976-77; *Recreations* gardening, country pursuits, reading; *Clubs* Carlton, Army and Navy; *Style—* Sir Richard Thompson, Bt; Rhodes House, Sellindge, Kent

THOMPSON, Richard Kenneth Spencer; s and h of Sir Paul Thompson, 2 Bt, of Walton-on-the-Hill, City of Liverpool; *b* 27 Jan 1976; *Style—* Richard Thompson, Esq

THOMPSON, Dr Richard Paul Hepworth; s of Stanley Henry Thompson (d 1966), and Winifred Lilian Collier; *b* 14 April 1940; *Educ* Epsom Coll, St Thomas's Hosp Med Sch, Oxford Univ (MA, DM); *m* 1974, Eleanor Mary, da of Timothy Noel Joseph Hughes (d 1979); *Career* conslt physician St Thomas's Hosp 1972-; examiner in med Soc of Apothecaries 1976-80, memb Faculty of Dental Surgery RC of Surg 1980-, memb of mgmnt ctee Inst of Psychiatry 1981-, govr Guy's Hosp Med Sch 1980-82, physician to the Royal Household 1982-, King Edward VII Hosp for Offrs 1982; FRCP; *Recreations* gardening; *Style—* Dr Richard Thompson; 36 Dealtry Rd, London SW15 (☎ 01 789 3839); St Thomas's Hospital, London SE1 (☎ 01 928 9292, ext 2650)

THOMPSON, Sir Robert Grainger Ker; KBE (1965), CMG (1961), DSO (1945), MC (1943); s of Rev Canon William Grainger Thompson (d 1966); *b* 12 April 1916; *Educ* Marlborough, Sidney Sussex Coll Cambridge; *m* 1950, Merryn, da of Sir Alec Newboult, KBE, CMG, MC (d 1964); 1 s, 1 da; *Career* Wing Cdr RAF 1939-45; Malayan Civil Serv 1938-61, sec for Def 1959-61, head Br Advsy Mission Vietnam 1961-65; author and conslt; *Recreations* all country pursuits; *Style—* Sir Robert Thompson, KBE, CMG, DSO, MC; Pitcott House, Winsford, Somerset

THOMPSON, Stuart Gordon; s of George Douglas Thompson, of Studley Green, High Wycombe, Bucks, and Irene, *née* Taws; *b* 28 Nov 1953; *Educ* John Hampden GS High Wycombe Bucks; *m* 19 June 1976, Angela Elizabeth, da of Norman Albert Leslie Keeping, of Wymondham, nr Norwich, Norfolk; *Career* marine broker Golding Adam Ltd (insur brokers) 1972-73, underwriting asst HL Price (marine syndicate 920) 1973-80, asst underwriter (marine) London and Hull Maritime Insur Co 1980-82; RAF Macmillan & Co Ltd: dep marine underwriter (for syndicates 80, 83, 843, 180) 1982, dir and underwriter (of 843) 1986, underwriter (80 and 843) 1988-; *Recreations* clay pigeon shooting, tennis, badminton; *Style*— Stuart Thompson, Esq; Field End, 2 Manor Farm Cottages, Marsworth, nr Tring, Herts (☎ 0296 661698); RAF MacMillan and Co Ltd, The Estate Office, Lewis Rd, Ringmer, Lewis, Sussex (☎ 01 623 7100 ext 3461)

THOMPSON, Thomas D'Eyncourt John; s and h of Sir Lionel Tennyson Thompson, 5 Bt; *b* 22 Dec 1956; *Educ* Eton; *Style*— Thomas Thompson, Esq; c/o Sir Lionel Thompson, Bt, 16 Old Buildings, Lincolns Inn, London WC2

THOMPSON HANCOCK, Dr Percy Ellis; s of Dr Frank Ryder Thompson Hancock (d 1957), and Ethel Cullen, *née* Ellis (d 1972); *b* 4 Feb 1904; *Educ* Wellington, Gonville and Caius Coll Cambridge, St Bart's Hosp London (MB, BChir); *m* 1, 4 June 1932, Dorothy Doris (d 1953), da of William Henry Barnes (d 1931); 2 da (Judith b 1933, Caroline b 1939); m 2, 3 March 1955, Laurie Newton Sharp, da of William Henry Charles Newton (d 1936); *Career* hon conslt physician: Nat Temperence Hosp London 1936, Potters Bar & Dist Hosp 1937, Royal Marsden Hosp London 1937, Royal Free Hosp & Sch of Medicine 1988; dir dept of clinical res Royal Marsden Hosp and Inst of Cancer Res 1963-72, external examiner in medicine Univ of London 1963-72; memb grand cncl Cancer Res Campaign 1948, rep Royal Coll of Physicians on Imp Cancer Res Fund, memb exec ctee Action on Smoking and Health (ASH) 1973, Hon Fell Royal Soc of Medicine (pres section of Oncology 1974-75) 1945, hosp visitor King Edward's Hosp Fund for London; MRCS, LRCP, FRCP, MRCP; Hon memb: American Gastroscopic Soc 1958, Societa Italiana Cancerologia 1967, Sociedad Chileana di Cancerologia 1969, Sociedad Chileana di Haematlogia 1969, Sociedad Medica di Valparaiso; *Recreations* dining and wining; *Style*— Dr Percy Ellis Thompson Hancock; 23 Wigmore Place, London WIH 9DD (☎ 01 631 4697)

THOMSEN, Leif; s of Orla Thomsen and Kirsten Caver; *b* 15 Mar 1936; *Educ* Gentofte Statsskole Denmark, Denmark Tech; *m* 1962, Anne Elisabeth, *née* Naested; *Career* civil engr Denmark and Peru 1960-63, mgmnt and commercial engrg positions F L Smidth & Co (Denmark) 1963-79, md F L Smidth & Co Ltd (UK) 1979-84, F L Smidth & Co Egypt 1984-; *Recreations* archaeology; *Style*— Leif Thomsen, Esq; 19 St Bernards, Chichester Rd, Croydon, Surrey

THOMSON; *see*: Hyde-Thomson, White-Thomson

THOMSON, Sir Adam; CBE (1976); s of Frank Thomson and Jemima Roger; *b* 7 July 1926; *Educ* Rutherglen Academy, Coatbridge Coll, Royal Tech Coll (Strathclyde Univ) Glasgow; *m* 1948, Dawn Elizabeth Burt; 2 s (Scott, Anthony); *Career* chm Gold Stag Ltd, chm and chief exec Caledonian Aviation Gp 1970-; Br Caledonian Airways; dep chm Martin Currie Pacific Tst 1985; non exec dir: Royal Bank of Scotland Gp 1982, Metropolitan Estates Property Co 1982; dir: Br Caldeonian Hotel Mgmnt Ltd, Br Caldeonian Helicopters Ltd, Bachelors Abroad Ltd, The Royal Bank of Scotland Gp plc; dep chm Martin Currie Pacific Tst plc, sr dir Stanford Res Int, chm Assoc of Euro Airlines 1977-78, won Scottish Free Enterprise Award Aims for Freedom and Enterprise 1976, Businessman of the Yr 1971; Hon LLD: Glasgow Univ 1979, Univ of Sussex 1984, Univ of Strathclyde 1986; FRAeS, FCIT, CBIM; kt 1983; *Recreations* golf, sailing; *Clubs* Caledonian, Walton Heath Golf, Old Prestwick Golf, Royal and Ancient Golf of St Andrews; *Style*— Sir Adam Thomson, CBE; 154 Buckswood Drive, Crawley, W Sussex; Caledonian House, Crawley, West Sussex (☎ 0293 27890)

THOMSON, Alexander McEwan; s of James Aitchison Thomson (d 1956), and Agnes McEwan, *née* Walls (d 1975); *b* 13 Nov 1917; *Educ* Daniel Stewart's Coll, George Heriot's Sch, Edinburgh Univ; *m* 10 May 1942, Marjorie May, da of John William Wood, MBE (d 1974); 2 s (Keith Robert b 1947, Neil Gordon b 1952), 1 da (Maureen Barbara b 1950); *Career* RASC 1939, N Ireland 1940-42, Sch of Artillery India 1942, cmmnd 1942 Madras 1942-44;ptnr: Fairbairn & Thomson 1956-60, Drummond & Reid 1960-69, Drummond & Co WS 1969-83 (sr ptnr 1970-83); slr: Gen Teaching Cncl for Scotland 1966-83, Edinburgh Assessor 1969-83; pres SSC Soc 1979-82; *Recreations* reading, tv; *Style*— Alexander Thomson, Esq

THOMSON, Andrew Gordon; s of James Thomson (d 1981), of 12 Duke St, Cromarty, Scotland, and Anne, *née* Skinner (d 1981); *b* 20 July 1928; *Educ* Nigg Sch, Tain Royal Acad Scotland; *m* 27 March 1954, Jean Ann, da of Leonard Walter Collison, MBE, (d 1974), of 19 Elmgate Gardens, Edgware, Middx; 1 s (Stuart), 1 da (Susan); *Career* Nat Serv 1946-48; engr, Waterman Ptnrship Ltd (formerly HL Waterman and Ptnrs); sr engr 1959, assoc 1961, ptnr 1962, sr ptnr 1983, chm 1988; memb Worshipful Co of Fletchers, Freeman City of London 1982; MSocIS France (Memb of Societe des Ingenieurs et Scientifiques de France); *Recreations* golf; *Clubs* St Stephens, City Livery, St George's Hill GC; *Style*— Andrew Thomson, Esq; 46-47 Blackfriars Rd, London SE1 8PN (☎ 01 928 7888, fax 928 3033, telex 24157)

THOMSON, Charles Grant; s of William Eddie Spalding Thomson, of 23 Thorn Drive, Bearsden, Glasgow, and Helen Donaldson, *née* Campbell; *b* 23 Sept 1948; *Educ* Jordanhill Coll Sch, Glasgow Univ (BSc); *m* 11 July 1970, Pamela Anne, da of Frederick Simpson Mackay (d 1987), of 38 Ballater Drive, Bearsden, Glasgow; 1 s (Richard b 1979), 1 da (Susan b 1975); *Career* Scottish Mutual Assur Soc 1969-, various official and exec appts 1974-, asst gen mangr Scottish Mutual Gp 1984-; Faculty of Actuaries: memb of cncl 1983-86, chm faculty examinations bd 1989- (memb 1982-, sec 1985); FFA 1973; *Recreations* golf, swimming; *Clubs* The Western, Windyhill Golf; *Style*— Charles Thomson, Esq; St Fillans, Ralston Rd, Bearsden, Glasgow; 109 St Vincent St, Glasgow G2 5HN (☎ 041 248 6321, fax 041 221 1230, telex 777145)

THOMSON, Christopher James; s of Ronald Stuart Thomson (d 1948), and Heather Mary Shrimpton; *b* 30 Jan 1933; *Educ* Wellington, Merton Coll Oxford (MA); *m* 1976, Daphne Moyna, da of Edward Maguire; 2 step da; *Career* 2 Lt Coldstream Guards (Egypt); md Bowater UK Paper Co Newsprint Div; dir Lamco Paper Sales 1983-; *Clubs* White's; *Style*— Christopher Thomson, Esq; 65 Arlington Ave, Westmount, Quebec H3Y 2W5 (☎ 514 935 2255)

THOMSON, Clive Benjamin; JP (Gloucester 1986); s of Benjamin Alfred Thomson, of Brighton, and Ivy Grace, *née* Smith; *b* 29 May 1935; *Educ* Westminster City Sch; *m* 11 Jan 1959, Mary Lilian (Molly), da of Eric Clements (d 1985); 1 s (Michael Clive b and d 1963), 2 da (Deborah Jane b 1962, Victoria Louise b 1965); *Career* Nat Serv 2 Lt Royal Berks Regt 1953-55, Capt Royal Berks Regt (TA) 1955-65, Capt HAC 1980-89; gen mangr Ecclesiastical Insur Gp; former chm: Wesbury Cons Assoc, Twickenham Cons Assoc, London SW Euro Cons Assoc; former dep chm Gtr London Cons Assoc, former pres Surbiton Griffins FC; currently memb: nat exec Nat Assoc Voluntary Hostels, Cheltenham Health Authy; JP Richmond 1975-85; Freeman City of London 1980, Liveryman Worshipful Co of Insurers 1980; F Inst M (1988); *Recreations* walking, politics, racing; *Clubs* United, Cecil; *Style*— Clive Thomson, Esq, JP; Chota Koti, Oakley Rd, Cheltenham, Glos GL52 6PA (☎ 0242 582 936); Ecclesiastical Ins Group, Beaufort House, Brunswick Rd, Gloucester, Glos (☎ 0452 419 221)

THOMSON, David; s of George Thomson (d 1972), and Frances Mary, *née* Eade (d 1983); *b* 20 Sept 1932; *Educ* Royal HS Edinburgh; *m* 10 Sept 1957, Dorothy Patricia, da of Edward Waterhouse (d 1978); 2 s (Michael b 1964, Ian b 1969), 1 da (Anne b 1959); *Career* Nat serv RASC (2 Lt); CA; with NRDC 1976-81, md Systems Programmes Hldgs 1981-83; dir Syntech Inf Technol Fnd 1987-; *Recreations* walking, music, antiquarian, books; *Style*— David Thomson, Esq; Swanston, Burtons Way, Chalfont St Giles, Bucks; 65 New Cavendish St, London (☎ 01 487 3870, fax 01 436 5245, car tel 0836 526702)

THOMSON, Sir (Frederick Douglas) David; 3 Bt (UK 1929), of Glendarroch, Co Midlothian; s of Sir (James) Douglas Wishart, 2 Bt (d 1972), and Bettina, er da of late Lt Cdr David William Shafto Douglas, RN; *b* 14 Feb 1940; *Educ* Eton, Univ Coll Oxford (BA); *m* 1967, Caroline Anne, da of Maj Timothy Stuart Lewis, Royal Scots Greys; 2 s, 1 da; *Heir* s, Simon Douglas Charles Thomson b 16 June 1969; *Career* dep chm: Ben Line Group 1987-; dir Ben Line Steamers Ltd 1964-; chm: Jove Investment Trust plc 1983-, Britannia Steamship Insurance Assoc Ltd (dir 1965-), Through Transport Mutual Insurance Assoc Ltd (dir 1973-); dir: dir Life Assoc of Scotland Ltd 1970-, Martin Currie Pacific Tst plc 1985-, Dance Investment Tst plc 1979-; memb Royal Co of Archers (Queen's Body Guard for Scotland); *Style*— Sir David Thomson, Bt; Glenbrook House, Balerno, Midlothian (☎ 031 449 4116); Ben Line Group Ltd, 33 St Mary's St, Edinburgh EH1 1TN (☎ 031 557 2323, telex 72611)

THOMSON, David John; s of David Barron Thomson, of Monifieth, Dundee (d 1979), and Margaret Seath Baxter (d 1955); gf David Thomson, of Anstruther, Capt of last windjammer to sail under British flag Garthpool; *b* 21 Feb 1941; *Educ* Forest Sch London, Glasgow Univ (MA); *m* 1966, Marjorie Rose, da of William Clifford Utting; 2 s (Andrew b 1967, Mark b 1967), 1 da (Kathryn b 1970); *Career* marketing dir: European Div Rowntree plc Ltd 1980-, Grocery Div 1975-80; dep chm Rowntree Europe 1985; md Rowntree Snack Foods 1986-; *Recreations* golf, gardening, sea fishing, walking, reading, light opera; *Clubs* Yorkshire, York Golf; *Style*— David Thomson, Esq; Ashurst, Usher Park Rd, Haxby, York (☎ 0904 769537); Rowntree plc, York YO1 1XY (☎ 0904 53071); Rowntree Snackfoods, Cottage Beck Rd, Scunthorpe, S Humberside DN16 1TT (☎ 0724 281222)

THOMSON, Hon David Kenneth Roy; s and h of 2 Baron Thomson of Fleet; *b* 12 June 1957; *Style*— The Hon David Thomson

THOMSON, David Paget; s of late Sir George Thomson, FRS, Nobel Laureate; *b* 19 Mar 1931; *Educ* Rugby, Trinity Coll Cambridge; *m* 1959, Patience Mary, da of late Sir Lawrence Bragg, CH, MC, FRS, Nobel Laureate; 2 s, 2 da; *Career* Lt Cdr RNR, joined Lazard Bros & Co Ltd 1956, md 1966, seconded HM Foreign Service 1971-73, economic counsellor Bonn, Lazards 1973-; *Clubs* Athenaeum, City Livery; *Style*— David Thomson, Esq; Little Stoke House, North Stoke, Oxon (☎ 0491 37161)

THOMSON, Dr Duncan; s of Duncan Murdoch Thomson (d 1958), and Jane McFarlane, *née* Wilson (d 1982); *b* 2 Oct 1934; *Educ* Airdrie Acad, Univ of Edinburgh (MA, PhD), Edinburgh Coll of Art; *m* 15 July 1964, Julia Jane, da of Donald Campbell MacPhail (d 1962); 1 da (Rebecca b 1974); *Career* art teacher 1959-67, keeper Scottish Nat Portrait Gallery 1982- (asst keeper 1967-82); *Recreations* literature; *Style*— Dr Duncan Thomson; 3 Eglinton Cresent, Edinburgh EH12 5DH (☎ 031 225 6430); Scottish National Portrait Gallery, 1 Queen St, Edinburgh EH2 1JD

THOMSON, Edward Arthur; s of Arthur Percival Thomson (d 1976), of Bognor Regis, and Lilian Emily, *née* Lawther (d 1976); *b* 2 Mar 1915; *Educ* Stationers' Co Sch London; *m* 1, 29 April 1939, (Madge) Beryl (d 1983), da of late George William Manly, of Hornsey, N8; 2 s (Ian b 1947, Peter b 1950); m 2, 1983, Ramchuan, *née* Pungsomboon; *Career* Territorial 61 AA Bde 1937, cmmnd RA 1942; md: (later chm) EA Thomson (Gems) Ltd 1958, chm Morris Goldmam Gems Ltd 1971-, precious stone trade section London C & C 1982-83, pres precious stone cmmn Int Confed of Jewellers Precious Stone Dealers Retailers and Wholesalers; chm of govrs Southwark Coll of FE 1968-71, vice-chm Finchley Boxing Club 1987-89; Freeman: City of London 1975, Liveryman Worshipful Co of Wheelwrites 1975, Worshipful Co of Stationers and Newspaper Makers 1987; Hon FGA 1985; *Recreations* gardening, travel; *Clubs* Directors, City Livery; *Style*— Edward Thomson, Esq; EA Thomson (Gems) Ltd, Chapel House, Hatton Place, Hatton Gdn, London EC1N 8RX, (☎ 01 242 3181, fax 01 831 1776, telex 27726 THOMCO G)

THOMSON, Hon Mrs (Elizabeth Frances); *née* Williams; da of Baron Francis-Williams (d 1970); *m* 1963, George Alexander Thomson; children; *Style*— The Hon Mrs Thomson; 27 Haverfield Gdns, Kew, Richmond, Surrey

THOMSON, Sir Evan Rees Whitaker; s of Frederick Thorpe Thomson (d 1969), and Ann Margaret, *née* Evans (d 1979); *b* 14 July 1919; *Educ* Brisbane Boys' Coll, Qld Univ (MB, BS); *m* 1955, Mary, da of William Newton Kennedy (d 1930); *Career* hon consulting surgn Princess Alexandra Hosp 1972-, chm Qld State Ctee Roy Aust Coll of Surgns 1967-79, pres Qld Cncl of Professions 1970-72, chm Ctee to Inquire into Future Needs and Training for Med Practice in Qld 1979-81; Queen's Silver Jubilee Medal 1977; kt 1977; *see Debrett's Handbook of Australia and New Zealand for further details*; *Style*— Sir Evan Thomson; Alexandra, 201 Wickham Terrace, Brisbane, Qld 4000, Australia

THOMSON, Bettina, Lady; Evelyn Margaret Isobel; *née* Douglas; eld da of late Lt-Cdr David William Sholto Douglas, RN; *b* 1 Jan 1915; *Educ* private; *m* 25 Sept 1935, Sir (James) Douglas Wishart Thomson, 2 Bt (d 1972); 2 s, 3 da; *Style*— Bettina, Lady Thomson; Old Caberston, Walkerburn, Peeblesshire

THOMSON, Ewen Cameron; CMG (1964); s of Francis Murphy Thomson (d 1950); *b* 12 April 1915; *Educ* Forfar Acad, St Andrew's Univ; *m* 1948, Betty, da of Lt-Col James Henry Preston, MBE; 1 s, 3 da; *Career* consultant to World Bank on Nutrition Admin 1974-, Colonial Admin Serv 1938-64, perm sec and min for Native Affairs 1962-63, Provincial Cmmnr and Snr Provincial Cmmnr 1957-64, perm sec Min of Transport and Works Gov of Zambia; *Recreations* winemaking, cooking; *Clubs* Royal Cwlth Soc; *Style*— Ewen Thomson, Esq, CMG; Acorns, Roundhill, Woking, Surrey (☎ 048 62 73223)

THOMSON, George Malcolm; s of Charles Thomson (d 1924), of Scotland, and Mary Arthur, *née* Eason (d 1952); *b* 2 August 1899; *Educ* David Stewart's Coll Edinburgh,

Edinburgh Univ (MA, BCom); *m* 1, Else (d 1954), da of Harold Ellefsen, of Norway; 1 s (Peter George Malcolm b 1935), 1 da (Anne (Mrs Brian Ettlinger) b 1930); m 2, 1963, Diana, da of Maj Charles Read, of Canada; *Career* RA 2 Lt 1918-19; author and journalist; political writer and ldr writer Daily Express, pol sec to Lord Beaverbrook, WWII; princ private sec: Miny of Aircraft Prodn Supply Miny, Lord Privy Seal's Off; after war returned to be ldr writer Daily Express; *Books* The Twelve Days (1964), The Crime of Mary Stuart (1967), Sir Francis Drake (1972), The North West Passage (1975), The First Churchill (1979), The Prime Ministers (1980), The Ball at Glencarron (1982), Kronstadt 21 (1985); *Recreations* reading; *Clubs* Garrick; *Style*— George Malcolm Thomson, Esq; 5 The Mount Sq, London NW3 (☎ 01 435 8775)

THOMSON, Ian Gray; s of Norman Gray Thomson, JP (d 1965), and Doris Inez, *née* Perring; *b* 7 June 1927; *Educ* Sherborne; *m* 24 June 1966, Bridget Anne, da of Harold Keith, of Bournemouth; 1 s (Andrew James Gray b 1967), 1 da (Alexandra Bridget b 1969); *Career* RA (AA) 1945-48, cmnd 105 HAA Regt 1947; md John Perring Ltd 1964-88 (joined 1948, dir 1957-88); dir: Perring Furnishing Ltd 1967-88, Avenue Trading Ltd 1986-, Perring Fin Ltd 1986-; Liveryman: Worshipful Co Haberdashers 1948, Worshipful Co Furniture Makers 1961; FInstD; *Recreations* gardening, travel, game fishing; *Clubs* RAC, City Livery; *Style*— Ian Thomson, Esq, JP; 16 The Moast, Traps Laine, New Malden, Surrey KT3 4SB; Seafield Hse, Woodbason Lane, Hayling Is, Hants PO11 0RL; Woodcock Hse, 36 High St, Wimbledon Village SW19 (☎ 01 944 1777, fax 01 944 1717)

THOMSON, Sir Ian Sutherland; KBE (1985, MBE mil 1945), CMG (1968); s of William Sutherland Thomson (d 1966), of Glasgow, and Jessie McCaig, *née* Malloch (d 1982); *b* 8 Jan 1920; *Educ* Glasgow HS, Univ of Glasgow (MA); *m* 1 Sept 1945, Nancy Marguerite (d 1988), da of William Kearsley (d 1956), of Suva, Fiji; 7 s (Andrew b 1947, Peter b 1948, John b 1950, David b 1953, Richard b 1954, Mark b 1956, Douglas b 1960), 1 da (Sally b 1958); *Career* The Royal Highland Regt The Black Watch 1940, Fiji Mil Forces, ret Capt 1945; HM Colonial Admin Serv Fiji 1946-54, seconded to W Africa dept and Civil Aviation dept Colonial Off 1954-56, chm Native Lands and Fisheries Cmmn Fiji 1957-63 (cmmr for native reserves), cmmr Western Div Fiji 1963-66, actg chief sec and ldr of govt business Fiji Legislative Cncl 1966, admin Br Virgin Is 1966-70, independent chm Fiji Sugar Indust 1971-84; chm: Fiji Econ Devpt Bd 1981-86, Air Pacific Ltd 1984-87, Sedgewick (Fiji) Ltd 1984-87, Thomson Pacific Resources Ltd 1988-; Freeman City of Glasgow 1946; fell Inst Mgmnt 1984-87; kt 1985; *Recreations* golf, gardening; *Style*— Sir Ian Thomson, KBE, CMG; Sonas, Ardentallen, by Oban, Strathclyde PA34 4SF (☎ 0631 628 46)

THOMSON, Sir Ivo Wilfrid Home; 2 Bt (UK 1925), of Old Nunthorpe, co York; s of Sir Wilfrid Thomson, 1 Bt (d 1939), and Ethel Henrietta, 2 da of late Hon Reginald Parker (6 s of 6 Earl of Macclesfield); *b* 14 Oct 1902; *Educ* Eton; *m* 1, 1933 (m dis 1954), Sybil Marguerite, da of Claude W Thompson, of the Red House, Escrick, York; 1 s (and 1 da decd); m 2, 1954, Viola Mabel, da of Roland Dudley, of Linkenholt Manor, Andover, Hants, and formerly w of Keith Home Thomson; *Heir* s, Mark Wilfrid Home Thomson; *Career* Sqdn-Ldr RAuxAF 608 Sqdn 1930-35, Sqdn-Ldr 1940-45 No 4 Gp Bomber Command, Gp Flying Control Offr (despatches); newspaper dir; *Recreations* formerly shooting, flying, fishing; *Style*— Sir Ivo Thomson, Bt; Barfield, Chapel Row, Bucklebury, Reading, Berks

THOMSON, Lady Jacqueline Rosemary Margot; *née* Rufus Isaacs; da of 3 Marquess of Reading, MBE, MC (d 1980); *b* 10 Nov 1946; *Educ* Southover Manor Lewes, Int Sch Geneva, Madrid Univ; *m* 1976, Mark Thomson, *qv*, s and h of Sir Ivo Thomson, 2 Bt; 3 s, 1 da; *Style*— Lady Jacqueline Thomson; 42 Glebe Place, London SW3 5JE (☎ 01 352 5015)

THOMSON, James Currie; MBE (Mil 1945), TD (1946), JP (Hertfordshire 1956), DL; s of James Thomson (d 1961), of Leith, Edinburgh, and Nell Gertrude, *née* Hutt (d 1943); *b* 4 Feb 1911; *Educ* Marlborough, Pembroke Coll Cambridge (MA); *m* 12 May 1945, Letitia Blanche, wid of Capt M V Fleming (POW d of wounds 1940), and da of Hon Malcolm Algernon Borthwick (d 1941), of Woodcote House, Oxon; 1 s (James Borthwick b 9 Feb 1946), 1 da (Clare Nell (Hon Mrs R C Denison-Pender b 9 Feb 1946 (twin)), 3 step s (Valentine Patrick b 1 Aug 1935, Christopher Michael b 8 May 1937, David Algernon b 24 Nov 1938), 1 step da (Gillian (Mrs N C Newbury) b 28 Jan 1940); *Career* London Scottish Regt: joined 1936, cmmnd 2 Lt 1938, Adj 1 Bn 1940 serv UK and PAIFORCE 1939-42, on staff N Africa and Italy 1943-44 (despatches), 2 i/c then CO 2 Bn Queens Own Cameron Highlanders (wounded) serv Italy Greece Austria 1944-45, hon rank Lt-Col; Charles Mackinlay & Co Ltd: apprentice 1932, dir then chm 1970-76; cncllr Hertford RDC 1948-66, chm Stevenage Bench 1980; High Sheriff 1971-72; chm Herts Soc 1974-80; Master Worshipful Co of Founders 1964-65; *Clubs* Boodle's; *Style*— James Thomson, Esq, MBE, TD, JP, DL; Stable Court, Walkern, nr Stevenage, Herts SG2 7JA

THOMSON, Sir John; KBE (1972), TD (1944); s of late Guy Thomson, JP; *b* 3 April 1908; *Educ* Winchester, Magdalen Coll Oxford; *m* 1, 1935, Elizabeth, JP (d 1977), *née* Brotherhood; m 2, 1979, Eva Elizabeth Dreaper, *née* Russell; *Career* Bt-Col Cmd Oxfordshire Yeo Regt RA 1942-44 and 1947-50; dir Union Discount Co of London Ltd 1960-74, chm Barclays Bank Ltd 1962-73 (dir 1947-78), chm Morland and Co Ltd 1979-83; pres Br Bankers Assoc 1964-66; memb: Royal Cmmn on Trade Unions and Employees Assocs 1965-68, BR Nat Export Cncl 1968; dep Steward Oxford Univ, Curator Oxford Univ Chest 1949-74, chm Nuffield Med Tstees 1951-82; High Sheriff Oxon 1957, DL Oxon 1947-57, vice-Ld-Lt 1957-63, Ld-Lt Oxon 1963-79; Freeman of the City of Oxford; Hon DCL Oxford 1957, Hon Fell St Catherine's Coll Oxford; FIB; KStJ (1973); *Recreations* steeplechase horse owner and breeder; *Clubs* Cavalry and Guard's, Jockey, Overseas Bankers'; *Style*— Sir John Thomson, KBE, TD; Manor Farm House, Spelsbury, Oxford (☎ 0608 810266)

THOMSON, Sir John Adam; GCMG (1985, KCMG 1978, CMG 1972); s of Sir George Paget Thomson, FRS (d 1975), sometime Master CCC Cambridge, and Kathleen Buchanan, *née* Smith (d 1941); *b* 27 April 1927; *Educ* Phillip's Exeter Acad USA, Aberdeen Univ, Trinity Coll Cambridge; *m* 1953, Elizabeth Anne McClure (d 1988); 3 s, 1 da; *Career* joined FO 1950, head planning staff FO 1967, on secondment to Cabinet Off as chief assessments staff 1968-71, min and dep perm Rep N Atlantic Cncl 1972-73, head UK Delgn MBFR Exploratory Talks in Vienna 1973, asst under-sec FCO 1973-76, high cmmr India 1977-82, UK perm rep UNO NY and UK Rep Security Cncl (with personal rank of ambass) 1982-87; dir Grindlays Bank 1987-; princ 21 Century Trust London 1987-, memb Cncl Int Inst of Strategic Studies 1987-, memb govng bodies of Inst of Dvpt Studies, Overseas Devpt Inst; Assoc Memb Nuffield Coll Oxford; *Books* Crusader Castles (co-author with R Fedden 1956); *Recreations* hill walking; *Clubs* Athenaeum, Century (New York); *Style*— Sir John Thomson, GCMG; c/o Heads of Mission Section, Foreign and Commonwealth Office, King Charles St, London SW1

THOMSON, Hon (Lesley) Lynne; da of 2 Baron Thomson of Fleet; *b* 2 Feb 1959; *Style*— The Hon Lynne Thomson

THOMSON, Mark Wilfrid Home; s and h of Sir Ivo Wilfrid Home Thomson, 2 Bt; *b* 29 Dec 1939; *m* 1976, Lady Jacqueline Rufus Isaacs, *qv*; 3 s, 1 da; *Style*— Mark Thomson, Esq; 42 Glebe Place, London SW3 5JE (☎ 01 352 5015; office: 01 408 1592)

THOMSON, (George) Michael Mackinnon; s of Wing Cdr George Reid Thomson (d 1986), of Kinellar House, and Phyllis Sarah, *née* Mackinnon (d 1985); *b* 29 Mar 1940; *Educ* Rugby, Heriot-Watt Univ (Dip town planning); *m* 3 June 1967, Caroline Mary, da of Lt-Col George Harold Hay (d 1967), of Berwickshire; 1 s (Jolyon b 1970), 1 da (Mary b 1970); *Career* principal of Mackinnon Thomson Planning, MRTPI, FFAS, ARIBA, ARIAS; *Recreations* films, filming, skiing; *Clubs* Royal Northern; *Style*— Michael Thomson, Esq; Mackinnon Thomson Planning, Moray House, 145 Crown Street, Aberdeen

THOMSON, Sheriff Nigel Ernest Drummond; s of Rev James Kyd Thomson (d 1939), of Edinburgh, and Joan Drummond (d 1929); *b* 19 June 1926; *Educ* George Watson's Boys' Coll Edinburgh, St Andrews Univ (MA), Edinburgh Univ (LLB); *m* 1964, Snjolaug, da of Consul Gen Sigursteinn Magnusson (d 1982), of Edinburgh; 1 s (Diggi b 1969), 1 da (Ingalo b 1967); *Career* Lt Indian Grenadiers; Advocate; Sheriff at: Hamilton 1966-1976, Edinburgh 1976-; chm music ctee Scottish Arts Cncl 1979-1984; chm Edinburgh Youth Orchestra 1986- hon pres: Scottish Assoc for Counselling, Strathaven Arts Guild, Tenovus-Edinburgh; *Recreations* music, woodwork, golf; *Clubs* New (Edinburgh), Bruntsfield GC, Strathaven Arts; *Style*— Sheriff Nigel Thomson; 50 Grange Rd, Edinburgh (☎ 031 667 2166); Sheriff Court, Lawnmarket, Edinburgh (☎ 031 226 7181)

THOMSON, Oliver Campbell Watt; s of (James) Oliver Thomson OBE (d 1972), of Milngavie, and Linda Marie, *née* Kelly; *b* 28 Feb 1936; *Educ* King Edward VI Sch Birmingham, Trinity Coll Cambridge (MA); *m* 10 Sept 1960, Jean Patricia Dawson, da of James Sellar Christie, CBE (d 1986), of Glasgow; 2 s (Calum b 1961, Iain b 1964), 1 da (Margaret b 1967); *Career* RN 1954-56, Lt RNR 1964-70; dir McCallum Advertising 1972-75, md Charees Barker Scotland 1975-85, mktg dir Holmes McDougall 1985-87, md Levy McCallum Ltd 1987-; chm Four Acres Charitable Tst; dir Westbourne Sch; MCAM, FBIM, FIPA; *Books* The Romans in Scotland (1965), Persuasion in History (1970); *Recreations* sailing, hillwalking; *Clubs* RSAC; *Style*— Oliver Thomson, Esq; 3 Kirklee Terr, Glasgow G12 (☎ 041 339 7453); Levy McCallum Advertising Agency, 203 St Vincent St, Glasgow, Strathclyde G2 5QF (☎ 041 248 7977, fax 041 221 5803)

THOMSON, Peter Alexander Bremner; CVO (1986); s of Alexander Bremner Thomson (d 1976), and Dorothy Davison, *née* Scurr; *b* 16 Jan 1938; *Educ* Canford Sch, RNC Dartmouth, Sch of Oriental and African Studies (BA, MPhil); *m* 31 July 1965, Lucinda Coleman, da of Colin Sellar (d 1965), of Morayshire; 3 s (Philip b 1970, Nicholas b 1972, Christopher b 1978); *Career* RN 1954-75 sub Lt and Lt in HM Ships: Albion, Plover, Tiger, Ark Royal and Eagle; Lt Cdr ashore Hong Kong and Taiwan; diplomatic serv 1975-, first sec: London, Lagos, Hong Kong; cnsllr Peking; *Recreations* sailing, walking; *Clubs* Travellers, Hong Kong; *Style*— Peter Thomson, Esq, CVO; The Red House, Charlton, Horethorne, Sherborne, Dorset (☎ 096 322 301); c/o FCO, King Charles Street, SW1

THOMSON, Hon Peter John; s of 2 Baron Thomson of Fleet; *b* 25 April 1965; *Style*— The Hon Peter Thomson

THOMSON, Robert Walter; s of Robert Clow Thomson, of Kirkabister, Shore Rd, Whiting Bay, Arran, and Anne B C Watson; *b* 3 Feb 1936; *Educ* Rutherglen Acad, Glasgow Sch of Art, Glasgow Coll of Tech (B Arch, Dip TP); *m* 1 Sept 1960, Janet Wilson, da of Thomas Ross Menzies, JP (d 1976); 1 s (Eric Douglas b 1964), 1 da (Kay Anne b 1966); *Career* chartered architect and planning conslt in private practice 1964-, FRIAS, RIBA, MRTPI, ACIarb, FFB; *Recreations* hill climbing; *Style*— Robert Thomson, Esq; 11 Calderwood Rd, Newlands, Glasgow G43 2RP (☎ 041 637 5345, fax 041 637 2263)

THOMSON, Stanley; CBE (1989); s of William Ingram Thomson (d 1971), and Annie Blanche Thomson (d 1975); *b* 23 June 1926; *Educ* Robert Gordon's Coll Aberdeen; *m* 8 June 1956, Elizabeth Wright, da of Erick Knox Wilson, of Scotland; 1 s (David Bruce b 1960); *Career* certified accountant; exec dir Ford Motor Co Ltd 1980- (dir of fin 1967-); pres Chartered Assoc of CAs 1987-88 (fell 1952, memb of cncl 1974); chm: Inflation Accounting Sub Ctee, CBI Industrial Policy Ctee; memb Industrial Devpt Advsy Bd 1978-86; vice-chm Accounting Standards Ctee (memb 1982-85); FCCA, CBIM; *Recreations* gardening, reading; *Style*— Stanley Thomson, Esq, CBE; 6 Belvedere Rd, Brentwood, Essex (☎ 0277 226111); Ford Motor Co Ltd, Eagle Way, Brentwood, Essex (☎ 0277 253188, fax 0277 232374)

THOMSON, Sue; da of Basil Raymond Hamilton (d 1942); *b* 6 August 1938; *Educ* Christ's Hosp; *m* 1978, André Davis; 1 da (Susannah b 1978); *Career* exec dir Octopus Publishing Gp Ltd 1971-, md Octopus Books Ltd 1971-77; dir Mandarin Publishers Ltd Hong Kong 1971-; *Recreations* family life, early domestic architecture; *Clubs* University Women's; *Style*— Miss Sue Thomson; 59 Grosvenor St, London W1 (☎ 01 493 5841)

THOMSON, Thomas Davidson; CMG (1962), OBE (1959); s of James Allan Thomson (d 1961), and Barbara Margaret Davidson (d 1920); *b* 1 April 1911; *Educ* George Watson's, Edinburgh Univ, Magdalene Coll Cambridge; *m* 1, 1938 (m dis 1946), Jean, *née* Annan; m 2, 1947, Marjorie Constance, *née* Aldred (d 1980); 1 s; m 3, 1981, Kathleen Ramsay, *née* Craig, later Pestereff; *Career* serv WWII 1940-45 KAR, Maj E Africa and Eritrea; Colonial Admin Serv Nyasaland 1934, cmmr Social Devpt 1959, ret 1963; BBC 'Brain of Britain' 1969; *Books* A Practical Approach to Chi Nyanja (1946), Coldingham Priory (1972); *Recreations* philately, contemplative archaeology, reading; *Style*— Thomas Thomson, Esq, CMG, OBE; The Hill, Coldingham, Eyemouth, Berwicks (☎ 089 0771209)

THOMSON, Dr Thomas James; CBE (1983, OBE 1978); s of Thomas Thomson (d 1949), of Stoer Park, Airdrie, Scotland, and Annie Jane, *née* Grant (d 1968); *b* 8 April 1923; *Educ* Airdrie Acad, Univ of Glasgow (MB, ChB); *m* 10 Jan 1948, Jessie Smith, da of George Edward Shotbolt (d 1953), of Balmaha, Seafield Drive, Ardrossan,

Scotland; 2 s (Ian b 1954, Alan b 1960), 1 da (Shona b 1955); *Career* Fl-Lt RAF 1946-48; conslt physician and gastroenterologist Stobhill Gen Hosp Glasgow 1961-87; Dept of Materia Medica Glasgow Univ: lectr 1953-61, hon lectr 1961-87; postgrad advsr to Glasgow Northern Hosps 1961-80, hon sec Royal Coll of Physicians and Surgns Glasgow 1965-73, sec specialist advsy ctee for Gen Internal Med for UK 1970-74; chm: Medica - Pharmaceutical Forum 1978-80 (chm educn advsy bd 1979-84); Conf of Royal Colls and Faculties in Scotland 1982-84, Nat Med Consultative Ctee for Scotland 1982-87; pres Royal Coll of Physicians and Surgns of Glasgow 1982-84, active in postgrad med educn ctees locally nationally and in EEC; chm Gtr Glasgow Health Bd 1987- (memb 1985-); Hon Fell American Coll of Physicians 1983, Hon LLD Univ of Glasgow 1988; FRCP (Glasgow) 1964, FRCP (London) 1969, FRCP (Edin) 1982, FRCP (Ireland) 1983; *Books* Dilling's Pharmacology (jt ed 1969), Gastroenterology - an integrated course (1972, 3 edn 1983); *Recreations* swimming, golfing; *Clubs* RAF London, RSAC (Glasgow); *Style*— Dr Thomas Thomson, CBE; 1 Varna Rd, Glasgow G14 9NE (☎ 041 959 5930); Gtr Glasgow Health Bd, 112 Ingram St, Glasgow G1 1ET (☎ 041 552 6222)

THOMSON, William Chalmers; s of William Thomson (d 1968), of Glasgow, and Catherine, *née* Chalmers (d 1943); *b* 22 Feb 1929; *Educ* Royal Coll of Science and Technol Strathclyde (Dip Arch, Dip Town Planning); *m* 2 April 1955, Elizabeth Penman, da of John Sinclair (d 1972), of Glasgow; 1 s (Alan Sinclair b 1963), 1 da (Karen Jane b 1966); *Career* architect/planner East Kilbride Dvpt Corp 1954-56; Cumbernauld Dvpt Corp 1957-61; Basingstoke Dvpt Corpn (actg Chief Architect & Planning Offr) 1962-64; Colin Buchanan and Ptnrs (dir) 1964-; RIBA, Fellow Royal Town Planning Inst; *Recreations* riding, target shooting, cycling; *Style*— William C Thomson, Esq; 3 Vine House, 4 St Johns Road, Sevenoaks, Kent TN13 3LW (☎ 0732 46024); Colin Buchanan & Ptnrs, 59 Queen Gdns, London W2 3AF (☎ 01 258 3799, telex 263802 COBPARG, fax 01 258 0299)

THOMSON, Dr William Oliver; s of Capt William Crosbie Thomson (d 1955), of Glasgow, and Mary Jolie, *née* Johnstone (d 1953); *b* 23 Mar 1925; *Educ* Allan Glen's Sch Glasgow, Univ of Glasgow (MB, ChB, MD, DPH, DPA); *m* 5 April 1956, Isobel Lauder Glendinning, da of Capt John Glendinning Brady (d 1942), of Montreal and Glasgow; 2 s (John b 2 Sept 1957, David b 18 Jan 1960); *Career* Capt RAMC 1948-50; Gp 1947-60, appts in admin med 1960-73, chief admin med offr Lanarkshire Health Bd 1973-88; involved in: samaritans, recording for blind, cancer res; memb Worshipful Co of Apothecaries; hon Dip of Scottish Cncl for Health Educn Edinburgh 1979; FRCP, FFCM; *Recreations* keeping busy; *Style*— Dr William Thomson; 7 Silverwells Ct, Bothwell G71 8LT

THOMSON GLOVER, Lady Sarah Jane; *née* Craven; da of 6 Earl of Craven (d 1965), and his 1 w, Irene Meyrick (who m 2, 1961, late Sir Andrew MacTaggart); *b* 9 Jan 1940; *m* 1961, David John Traill Thomson Glover; 2 da; *Style*— Lady Sarah Thomson Glover; La Gratitude, 6 de Villiers Street, Somerset West, 7130, Cape Province, South Africa

THOMSON OF FLEET, 2 Baron (UK 1964), of Northbridge in the City of Edinburgh; Kenneth Roy Thomson; s of 1 Baron Thomson of Fleet, GBE (d 1976), fndr of the Thomson newspapers; *b* 1 Sept 1923; *Educ* Upper Canada Coll Toronto, Cambridge Univ (MA); *m* 1956, Nora Marilyn, da of Albert Vernard Lavis, of Toronto; 2 s, 1 da; *Heir* s, Hon David Kenneth Roy Thomson; *Career* serv WWII RCAF; began in editorial dept Timmins Daily Press 1947, newspaper proprietor, chm: Int Thomson Orgn Ltd 1978-, Thomson Orgn 1976-78, co-pres Times Newspapers Ltd 1971-81, chm and dir Thomson Newspapers Ltd (owners of 38 daily newspapers in Canada), chm Thomson Newspapers Inc (owners of 82 newspapers in the US), dir Toronto Dominion Bank, Scottish and York Ltd, Abitibi Price Inc, Hudson's Bay Co, Simpsons Ltd; vice pres and dir: Cablevue (Quinte) Ltd, Veribest Products Ltd; pres and dir of many other newspapers and communications companies; *Recreations* collecting paintings and works of art, walking; *Clubs* York (Toronto), National Hunt, Granite (Toronto), York Downs; *Style*— The Rt Hon the Lord Thomson of Fleet; 8 Kensington Palace Gdns, London W8; 8 Castle Frank Rd, Toronto, Ontario M4W 2Z4, Canada; offices: Thomson Newspapers Ltd, 65 Queen Street West, Toronto Ontario M5H 2M8, Canada; International Thomson Organisation plc, PO Box, 4 Stratford Place, London W1A 4YG

THOMSON OF MONIFIETH, Baron (Life Peer UK 1977); George Morgan Thomson; KT (1981), PC (1966); s of late James Thomson, of Monifieth, Angus; *b* 16 Jan 1921; *Educ* Grove Acad Dundee; *m* 1948, Grace, da of Cunningham Jenkins, of Glasgow; 2 da; *Career* on staff of Dandy rising to chief sub-ed 1930s; asst Editor/Editor Forward 1946-53; MP (L) Dundee East 1952-72, min of state FO 1964-66, chllr of the Duchy of Lancaster 1966-67 and 1969-70, joint min of state FO 1967, sec of state for Cwlth Affrs 1967-68, min without portfolio 1968-69, shadow def min 1970-72; EEC cmmnr 1973-77; chm: Euro Movement in Br 1977-80, Advertising Standards Authty 1977-80; dir: Royal Bank of Scotland Gp 1982- ICI plc 1977-, Woolwich Equitable Bldg Soc 1979-; First Crown Estate cmmnr 1978-80, chm IBA 1981-88, vice-pres Royal TV Soc 1982-, chllr Heriot Watt Univ 1977-; Hon Hon LLD Dundee 1967, Hon DLitt Heriot-Watt 1973, Hon DSc Aston 1976; Hon DLitt New Univ of Ulster 1984; tstee: Pilgrim Trust, Thomson Fndn, Leeds Castle Fndn; *Clubs* Brooks's; *Style*— The Rt Hon the Lord Thomson of Monifieth, KT, PC; 9 Cavendish Pl, London W1 (☎ 01 436 5767)

THORBEK, Erik; s of Kai Birch (d 1988), of Denmark, and Dr Agro Grete Thorbek; *b* 10 Jan 1941; *Educ* Billum Coll Denmark; *m* 6 April 1963, Susan Margaret, da of Sidney Gair (d 1977); 2 s (Alexander b 1964, Nikolas b 1973), 2 da (Francesca b 1966, Natasha b 1975); *Career* chm and chief exec of H & T Walker Gp of Cos, dir 1964 - (md 1972, chm 1977); *Recreations* golf, skiing, racing (horse), shooting, sailing, travelling; *Clubs* Turf, Helford River Sailing, Neville GC;; *Style*— Erik Thorbek, Esq; Maynards, Matfield, Kent (☎ 0892 72 3966); H & T Walker Ltd, Walker House, London Rd, Riverhead, Sevenoaks, Kent (☎ 0732 450712, telex 95679, fax 0732 459288) (car ☎ 0836 230396)

THORBURN, Andrew; s of James Beresford Thorburn (d 1972), and Marjorie Clara Thorburn (d 1987); *b* 20 Mar 1934; *Educ* Univ of Southampton (BSc); *m* 1957, Margaret Anne, da of Reginald Crack (d 1964); 1 s (Edward), 2 da (Jenny, Anna); *Career* county planning offr of E Sussex 1973-83, chief exec English Tourist Bd 1983-85, dir Sussex Heritage Tst, hd of Tourism and Leisure Grant Thornton 1986-; pres Royal Town Planning Inst 1982; *Books* Planning Villages (1971); *Recreations* sailing (Lily); *Style*— Andrew Thorburn, Esq; Hyde Manor, Kingston, Lewes, E Sussex BN7 3PB (☎ 0273 476019

THORBURN, Eric Walter Andrew; s of Walter Thorburn (d 1987), of Giffnock Glasgow, and Catherine Graham, *née* Wales (d 1988); *b* 7 Feb 1940; *Educ* Leeds GS, Allan Glens Sch Glasgow, Royal Coll of Sci and Technol Glasgow (DA); *m* 2 March 1966, Elizabeth Anne, da of Robert Paton Brown (d 1975), of Mansewood, Glasgow; 1 s (Alan Graham Robert b 1969), 1 da (Rhona Elizabeth b 1967); *Career* chartered architect; Eric Thorburn Assoc 1986-; sr ptnr Thorburn Twigg Brown & Ptnrs 1980-86; assoc Ian Burke Assoc 1979; princ bldgs: Mitchel House Glasgow, Extension to King's Theatre Glasgow, Shopping Centre Polmont; RIBA 1967; ARIAS, FFB; *Recreations* swimming, curling; *Style*— Eric Thorburn, Esq; 5 Wellesley Crescent, Hairmyres, E Kilbrido G75 8TS (☎ 03552 32833); 5 Claremont Terrace, Glasgow G3 7XR (☎ 041 333 9250)

THORLEY, Simon Joe; s of Sir Gerald Thorley, TD (d 1988), and Beryl Preston, *née* Rhodes; *b* 22 May 1950; *Educ* Rugby, Keble Coll Oxford (MA); *m* 7 May 1983, Jane Elizabeth, da of Frank Cockcroft, of Saltburn by Sea, Cleveland; 2 s (Matthew b 1984, Nicholas b 1985), 1 da (Francesca b 1985); *Career* barr Inner Temple 1972- (specialising in patent matters); church-warden St Margaret's Wicken, Bonhunt; *Books* Terrell on Patents (jt ed, thirteenth edn); *Recreations* family, shooting, walking, golf; *Clubs* Royal West Norfolk GC; *Style*— Simon Thorley, Esq; 6 Pump Ct, Temple, London EC4Y 7AR (☎ 01 353 8588, fax 01 583 1516)

THORN, John Leonard; s of Stanley Leonard Thorn (d 1951), and Winifred Thorn; *b* 28 April 1925; *Educ* St Paul's, CCC Cambridge; *m* 1955, Veronica Laura, da of Sir Robert Maconochie, OBE, QC (d 1962); 1 s, 1 da; *Career* schoolmaster; asst master Clifton Coll 1949-61, headmaster: Repton Sch 1961-68, Winchester Coll 1968-85; dir Royal Opera House Covent Garden 1972-78, tstee Br Museum 1980-85; dir Winchester Cathedral Tst 1986-88; memb: Bd of The Securities Assoc Ltd 1987-, Exec Ctee Cancer Research Campaign 1987-, Hampshire Buildings Preservation Tst 1987-; *Books* A History of England (jtly 1961), Road to Winchester (1989), and num articles; *Recreations* all the arts; *Clubs* Garrick; *Style*— John Thorn, Esq; 6 Chilbolton Avenue, Winchester SO22 5HD (☎ 0962 55990)

THORNBER, Iain; JP (1988), DL (Lochaber, Inverness, Badenoch, Strathspey); s of James Thornber (d 1982), of Morvern, Argyll, and Jeannie Easton Campbell, *née* Stenhouse; *b* 3 Feb 1948; *Educ* Glenhurich Public Sch; *Career* company factor Glensanda Estate Morvern (Foster Yeoman Ltd) 1980; first prize The Game Conservancy Photo Competition 1977; life memb W Highland Museum Fort William, memb Forestry Cmmn local advsy panel, memb Morvern Red Deer Mgmnt Gp, rep memb Royal Soc for Nature Conservation Rahoy Hills Nature Res; Lochaber dist cncllr for Ardgour Sunart and Morvern; FSA Scot 1973, FRSA 1987, memb Country Life Museums Tst; *Books* The Castles of Morvern Argyll (1975), The Sculptured Stones of Cill Choluimchille Morvern Argyll (1975), Rats (1989), Bronze Age Cairns in the Aline Valley Morvern Argyll (jt author, proceedings of the Soc of Antiquaries of Scot vol 106, 1974-75); *Recreations* deer stalking, salmon fishing, photography, local history research; *Style*— Iain Thornber, Esq, JP, DL; Knock House, Morvern, by Oban, Argyll PA34 5UU; Lower Polnish, Lochailort, Inverness-shire, Glensanda, Morvern, Argyll (☎ 096 784 651); Glensanda Estate, Morvern, Argyll (☎ 063 173 415, fax 0631 73 460, telex 777792)

THORNE, Lady Anne Patricia; *née* Pery; o da of 5 Earl of Limerick, GBE, CH, KCB, DSO, TD (d 1967), and Angela Olivia, Countess of Limerick, GBE, CH, LLD (d 1981), *née* Trotter; *b* 3 Oct 1928; *Educ* North Foreland Lodge, St Hugh's Coll Oxford (MA, DPhil); *m* 16 May 1959, Sir Peter Francis Thorne, KCVO, CBE, GRD *qv*; 1 s, 3 da; *Career* sr lecturer Imperial Coll of Science and Technology, various scientific ctees, memb bd European Gp for Atomic Spectroscopy 1979-85 (chm 1982-85); memb: governing bodies of various schs, past and present; *Books* Spectrophysics (second edn 1988), author of various papers published in scientific journals; *Style*— Lady Anne Thorne; Chiddinglye Farmhouse, West Hoathly, East Grinstead, Sussex RH19 4QS (☎ 0342 810338)

THORNE, Maj-Gen Sir David Calthrop; KBE (1983, CBE 1979, OBE 1975); s of Richard Everard Thorne (d 1957), and Audrey Ursula, *née* Bone; identical twin bro of Brig Michael Thorne, CBE, *qv*; *b* 13 Dec 1933; *Educ* St Edward's Sch Oxford, RMA Sandhurst; *m* 1962, Suzan Anne, da of Edward Eaton Goldsmith; 1 s, 2 da; *Career* cmmnd Royal Norfolk Regt 1952, cmd 1 Bn Royal Anglian Regt 1972-74, Bde Cdr 3 Infantry Bde NI 1977-79, Maj-Gen 1981, Vice QMG 1981-82, Cdr British Forces Falkland Islands 1982-83, cmd 1 Armd Div 1983-5; Dep Col Royal Anglian Regt 1981-87; dir of Infantry 1986-88, Col Cmdt Queen's Div 1986-88; dir gen Cwlth Tst 1989-; *Recreations* cricket, squash, butterfly collecting; *Clubs* Army and Navy, MCC, I-Zingari, Free Foresters, Jesters; *Style*— Maj-Gen Sir David Thorne, KBE; c/o Barclays Bank, 52 Abbeygate St, Bury St Edmunds, Suffolk IP33 1LL

THORNE, Maj George; MC (1945), DL (Oxfordshire 1961); 2 s of Gen Sir (Augustus Francis) Andrew Nicol Thorne, KCB, CMG, DSO, DL (d 1970), of Knowl Hill House, nr Reading (*see* Burke's Landed Gentry, 18 edn, vol II, 1969), and Hon Margaret Douglas-Pennant (d 1967), 10 da of 2 Baron Penrhyn; *b* 1 July 1912; *Educ* Eton, Trin Coll Oxford; *m* 18 April 1942, Juliet Agnes, o da of Hon (Arthur) George Villiers Peel, JP, DL (d 1956), 2 s of 1 Viscount Peel; 2 s (Robert George (Robin) b 7 Feb 1943, Ian David Peel b 14 Oct 1944), 1 da (Viola Georgina Juliet (Mrs Nicholas Halsey) b 20 Sept 1948*qv*); *Career* Maj late Gren Guards (SR), serv in WWII, ADC to GOC 1 Div (Maj-Gen Hon Harold Alexander) 1939-40, OC No 3 Co 1 Bn Gren Gds 1941-44, Capt The King's Co 1 Bn Gren Gds 1944-45 (despatches); memb sales staff McVitie & Price Ltd 1934-39 and 1946-67; farmer 1950-; memb: Royal Br Legion (Peppard), Dunkirk Veterans Assoc (Henley); *Recreations* shooting, sailing, cricket; *Clubs* Farmers'; *Style*— Major George Thorne, MC, DL; Blounts Farm, Sonning Common, Reading, Berks (☎ 0734 723191)

THORNE, Ian David Peel; s of Maj George Thorne, MC, DL, *qv*; *b* 14 Oct 1944; *Educ* Eton, RMA Sandhurst, Trinity Coll Oxford (MA); *Career* served in Grenadier Guards 1965-73 (ret as Capt); country landowner 1974-; dep pres Newark and Notts Agric Soc, vice-pres Notts Assoc of Boys' and Keystone Clubs, former chm of various ctees; High Sheriff of Notts 1986-87; *Recreations* shooting, travel; *Clubs* Boodle's, I Zingari; *Style*— Ian D P Thorne, Esq

THORNE, Matthew Wadman John; s of Robin Horton John Thorne, CMG, OBE, of the Old Vicarage, Old Heathfield, E Sussex, and Joan Helen, *née* Wadman; *b* 27 June 1952; *Educ* Dragon Sch, King's Sch Canterbury, Trinity Coll Oxford (MA); *m* 1978, Sheila Leigh, da of Col Hon Robert George Hugh Phillimore, OBE (d 1984), 3 s of 2

Baron Phillimore, MC, DL; 2 s (Robin b 15 Feb 1983, Andrew b 27 Feb 1986), 1 (Aelene b 17 June 1981); *Career* Price Waterhouse 1975-78, County Natwest 1787-83, Beazer plc 1983- 89; FCA 1978; *Style*— Matthew Thorne, Esq; The Mount, Bannerdown Rd, Batheaston, Bath, Avon

THORNE, Dr Napier Arnold; s of Arnold Thorne (d 1959), of Kenilworth, Cape Town, SA, and Wilhelmina Rosa, *née* Ayson (d 1970); *b* 26 Dec 1920; *Educ* Eastbourne Coll, London Univ, St Bartholomew's Hosp (MB BS, MD); *m* 16 May 1953, Pamela Joan, da of Robert Thomas Frederick Houchin, of Turves, Ruckinge, Kent; 1 s (Robert Napier b 1959), 3 da (Susan b 1954, Jane b 1957, Katherine b 1959); *Career* conslt dermatologist: Prince of Wales Hosp 1955-85, The London Hosp 1968-81; hon conslt dermatologist: The Italian Hosp London 1969-, Hosp of St John and St Elizabeth 1976-; senator Univ of London 1970-80, pres Inst of Trichologists 1972-; Freeman: Worshipful Co of Farriers 1965, Worshipful Soc of Apothecaries of London 1978; MRCS 1945, LRCP 1945, memb BMA 1945, fell Hunterian Soc 1947, MRCP 1949, FRSM 1949, fell Med Soc of London 1961, FRCP 1972, FRSA 1982; *Recreations* gardening, music, travelling; *Clubs* RSM; *Style*— Dr Napier Thorne; 106 Orchard Rd, Tewin, Herts AL6 0LZ (☎ 043 879 294); 96 Harley St, London W1N 1AF (☎ 01 935 4811, car tel 0860 335 729)

THORNE, Neil Gordon; OBE (1980), TD (1969), MP (C) Redbridge, Ilford South 1979-; s of Henry Frederick Thorne (d 1964); *b* 8 August 1932; *Educ* City of London Sch, London Univ; *Career* memb TA 1952-82, Lt-Col RA; chartered surveyor 1961-, snr ptnr Hull & Co 1962-76, Borough of Redbridge: cncllr 1965-68, alderman 1975-78 memb GLC and chm Central Area Bd 1967-73, Silver Jubilee Medal 1977; CO London Univ OTC 1976-80; chm Nat Cncl of Civil Def 1982-86: memb: Ct of Referees 1987-; chm St Edward's Housing Assoc; OStJ (1988); *Recreations* riding, walking, tennis; *Clubs* Carlton; *Style*— Neil Thorne, Esq, OBE, TD, MP; 60 Gyllyngdune Gardens, Seven Kings, Ilford, Essex IG3 9HY (☎ 01 590 3262)

THORNE, Sir Peter Francis; KCVO (1981), CBE (1966), ERD; s of Gen Sir (Augustus Francis) Andrew Nicol Thorne, KCB, CMG, DSO (d 1970); *b* 6 August 1914; *Educ* Eton, Trinity Coll Oxford; *m* 16 May 1959, Lady Anne Patricia Pery, *qv*, da of 5 Earl of Limerick, GBE, CH, KCB, DSO; 1 s, 3 da; *Career* Hon Lt-Col Grenadier Guards 1945 (serv WWII France and SE Asia); with ICI Ltd 1946-48; asst serjeant-at-arms House of Commons 1948-57, dep serjeant-at-arms 1957-76, serjeant at arms 1976-82; *Clubs* Cavalry and Guards', Royal Yacht Sqdn; *Style*— Sir Peter Thorne, KCVO, CBE, ERD; Chiddinglye Farmhouse, West Hoathly, East Grinstead, Sussex RH19 4QS (☎ 0342 810338)

THORNE, Robert George; s of Maj George Thorne, MC, DL; *b* 7 Feb 1943; *Educ* Eton, RAC Cirencester; *Career* local dir Barclays Bank Ltd Bristol 1973-76; Newcastle-upon-Tyne 1977-80; London Northern 1980-83; Pall Mall 1983-; *Recreations* country pursuits; *Clubs* Brooks's; *Style*— Robert Thorne, Esq; Blounts Farm, Sonning Common, Reading, Berks

THORNE, Stanley George; MP (Lab) Preston 1983-; s of Frederick George Thorne (d 1975), and Emily Louisa Thorne (d 1956); *b* 22 July 1918; *Educ* Ruskin Coll Oxford (BA), Liverpool Univ; *m* Catherine Mary Rand; 2 s, 3 da; *Career* sometime lecturer in industrial sociology; former coalminer, semi-skilled fitter, railway signalmen, clerk, commercial mangr; Liverpool cllr 1963-66 and 1971-74 (former dep chm educ ctee), contested (Lab) Liverpool, Wavertree 1964, MP (Lab) Preston South Feb 1974-1983, former vice-chm PLP Health and Educn Gps, former chm Parly Lab CND, memb PLP Housing and Aviation Gps; former chm Tribune Gp of Labour MPs, chm NW Group of Lab MPs; *Style*— Stanley Thorne, Esq, MP; 26 Station Road, Gateacre, Liverpool

THORNELY, (Gervase) Michael Cobham; s of Maj John Thornely, OBE, and Hon Muriel (granted rank of Baron's da 1917, although her f did not survive to enjoy the Barony of Cobham called out of abeyance in 1916), *née* Alexander, yr sis of 12 and 13 (or 15 and 16 but for attainder) Barons Cobham; in remainder to abeyant Barony through his mother (who became a coheiress after the death of the 13 (or 16) Baron in 1951); *b* 21 Oct 1918; *Educ* Rugby, Trinity Hall Cambridge (MA); *m* 1954, Jennifer, da of Sir (Charles) Hilary Scott (solicitor and former pres Law Soc), of Knowle House, Addington, Surrey; 2 s (Richard b 1957, Charles b 1958), 2 da (Elizabeth b 1960, Jacqueline b 1965); *Career* headmaster Sedbergh Sch 1954-75 (asst master 1940-54); FRSA; *Recreations* music, fishing; *Style*— Michael Thornely, Esq; High Stangerthwaite, Killington, Sedbergh, Cumbria (☎ 05396 20444)

THORNELY TAYLOR, Edward John; s of John Thornely Taylor, JP (d 1960); *b* 27 May 1924; *Educ* Uppingham; *Career* landowner; Lord of The Manors of Scaftworth (Notts), Hoylandswaine, Thurnscoe and Oxspring (Yorks), High Sheriff Yorks 1975-76; *Recreations* shooting, cricket; *Clubs* MCC, Farmers'; *Style*— Edward Thornely Taylor, Esq; Scaftworth Hall, nr Doncaster DN10 6BL (☎ 0302 710323)

THORNEYCROFT, Hon John Hamo; s of Baron Thorneycroft, CH, PC (Life Peer), and his 1 w Sheila Wells Page; *b* 24 Mar 1940; *Educ* Eton, Cambridge, Univ of Wales Inst of Science and Technology (DipArch); *m* 1971, Delia, da of Arthur William Lloyd (d 1977), of Penallt, Mon; 1 s (Richard b 1977), 1 da (Eleanor b 1974); *Career* architect; Dept of Ancient Monuments and Historic Buildings (English Heritage); memb Order of Orange-Nassau 1982; *Style*— The Hon John Thorneycroft; 21 St Peters St, Islington, London N1 8JD (☎ 01 226 0578)

THORNEYCROFT, John Patrick; s of Gerald Hamo Thorneycroft (d 1967), of Park House, Codsall Wood, Staffs, and Kathleen Mary, *née* Wilson (d 1985); *b* 9 Dec 1939; *Educ* Wellington Coll, Pembroke Coll Cambridge (MA); *m* 16 Oct 1965, Rev Philippa (Pippa) Hazel Jeanetta, da of Philip Fitzgerald Mander (d 1972), of The Folley Stableford, nr Bridgnorth, Salop; 2 s (Hugh b 1967, Martin b 1977), 2 da (Veryan b 1971, Naomi b 1975); *Career* slr in legal ptnrship, Lichfield diocesan registrar, legal sec to Bishop of Lichfield; *Recreations* sport; *Style*— John Thorneycroft, Esq; Kemberton Hall, nr Shifnal, Shropshire (☎ 0952 580 588); Manby & Steward, 1 St Leonard's Close, Bridgnorth, Shropshire (☎ 0746 761 436, fax 0746 766 764, car tel 0836 69563)

THORNEYCROFT, Dr Malcolm; s of Alec Charles Thorneycroft (d 1974); *b* 7 June 1936; *Educ* Wellingborough GS, Nottingham Univ; *m* 1960, Margaret Rose, *née* Fisher; 1 s, 2 da; *Career* chartered electrical engr, engrg dir TI Churchill Ltd 1976-85, TI Machine Tools Ltd 1985-87, Mastrix Churchill Ltd 1987-; *Recreations* swimming, walking; *Clubs* 41 Club, Coventry; *Style*— Dr Malcolm Thorneycroft; 1 Riverford Croft, Kenilworth Grange, Coventry

THORNEYCROFT, Baron (Life Peer 1967); (George Edward) Peter Thorneycroft; CH (1979), PC (1951); s of late George Thorneycroft, DSO, of Dunston Hall, Staffs; *b* 26 July 1909; *Educ* Eton, RMA Woolwich; *m* 1, 1938 (m dis 1949), Sheila Wells, da of E W Page, of Tettenhall; 1 s; m 2, 1949, Countess Carla Roberti, da of late Count Malagola Cappi, of Ravenna, Italy; 1 da; *Career* RA 1930, resigned cmmn 1933; barr Inner Temple 1935, MP (C) Stafford 1938-45, Monmouth 1945-66, parly sec Miny of War Tport 1945, pres BOT 1951-57, chllr of the Exchequer 1957-58, resigned, min of Aviation 1960-2, min Def 1962-64; chm Cons Pty 1975-81; chm: Pirelli General Cable Works Ltd, Pirelli Ltd 1970-87 (pres 1987-), Pirelli UK plc 1987-, Trusthouse Forte Ltd 1970-82 (pres 1982-), Br Insur Co Ltd 1980-87, Cinzano (UK) Ltd 1982-85; memb Royal Soc of Br Artists 1978; Order of the Sacred Treasure (1 Class, Japan) 1983; *Recreations* painting; *Clubs* Army and Navy; *Style*— The Rt Hon the Lord Thorneycroft, CH, PC; 42c Eaton Sq, London SW1; House of Lords, London SW1 (☎ 01 748 5843)

THORNHILL, Andrew Robert; QC (1985); s of Edward Percy Thornhill, of Bristol, and Amelia Joy Thornhill; *b* 4 August 1943; *Educ* Clifton Coll, CCC Oxford; *m* 5 Aug 1971, Helen Mary, da of George William Livingston, of Gainsborough; 2 s (George Percy b 1 Dec 1973, Henry Robert b 26 May 1977), 2 da (Emily Mary b 12 June 1972, Eleanor Clare b 19 June 1980); *Career* barr; joined chambers of H H Monroe 1969; *Recreations* sailing, walking, education; *Clubs* Oxford and Cambridge, Taverners, Chew Valley Lake Sailing; *Style*— Andrew Thornhill, Esq, QC; 37 Conynge Rd, Clifton, Bristol; St Agnes, Cranshaws, by Duns, E Lothian; 4 Pump Ct, Temple, London EC4 (☎ 01 583 9770, 01 353 6336)

THORNHILL, Lt-Col (Edmund) Basil; MC (1918), DL (Cambs and Isle of Ely 1957-); s of Edmund Henry Thornhill (d 1936), of Manor House, Boxworth, Cambs, and Violet Nina, *née* Campbell (d 1922); *b* 27 Feb 1898; *Educ* St Bee's Cumberland, RMA Woolwich; *m* 1934, Diana Pearl Day, *née* Beales (d 1983), da of Hubert Day Beales (d 1950), of St Margaret's Rd, Cambridge; 2 s, 1 da; *Career* WWII Lt-Col RA (France, Belgium) 1917-18; WWII 1939-45 (France, Western Desert, Italy); chm Cambridge and Isle of Ely Territorial Assoc 1957-62, Vice Lord Lieutenant Cambs and Isle of Ely 1965-75; *Clubs* Army and Navy; *Style*— Lt-Col Basil Thornhill, MC, DL; Manor House, Boxworth, Cambridge CB3 8NF (☎ 095 47 209)

THORNHILL, (George Edmund) Peter; s of Lt-Col Edmund Basil Thornhill, MC, of Manor House, Boxworth, Cambs, and Diana Pearl Day, *née* Beales (d 1983);descendant in unbroken male line of the family of Thornhill of Thornhill, Yorkshire, landowners; *b* 13 April 1935; *Educ* Eton, Trinity Coll Cambridge (MA); *m* 12 Sept 1959, Margaret Daughne, o da of Cdr William Geoffrey Barnard Hartley (d 1983), of Houghton Hill House, Huntingdon; 1 s (Edmund George William b 1969), 3 da (Vanessa (Mrs Fairhead) b 1960, Claire b 1962, Harriet b 1965); *Career* Nat Serv 1953-55, 2 Lt RA; landowner; formerly ptnr Smith-Woolley and Co chartered surveyors and chartered land agents, resigned 1975; dir Thornhill Yorkshire Estates Co; chm Huntingdon/Peterborough Branch CLA 1983-85; FRICS, formerly FLAS ; *Recreations* shooting, travelling abroad; *Clubs* Farmers, Cambridge County, Eton Vikings; *Style*— Peter Thornhill, Esq; The Grove, Winthorpe, Newark, Notts NG24 2NR (☎ 0636 703577); Estate Off, The Gardens, Diddington, Huntingdon, Cambs PE18 9XU (☎ 0480 810240)

THORNHILL, Richard John; s of Richard Norwood Thornhill, and Eleanor Louise, *née* Hoey; *b* 13 Nov 1954; *Educ* Malvern, St John's Coll Oxford (MA); *m* 30 Aug 1980, Nicola, da of Peter John Dyke, of Cumbria; *Career* articled clerk Slaughter & May 1977-79, admitted slr 1979, ptnr Slaughter & May 1986- (admitted Hong Kong Supreme Ct 1982 and practised Hong Kong off 1982-84); memb Law Soc; *Recreations* walking, water skiing, theatre, opera; *Style*— Richard Thornhill, Esq; 36 Chipstead Street, London SW6 (☎ 01 736 4091); 35 Basinghall Street, London EC2V 5DB (☎ 01 600 1200, fax 726 0028)

THORNLEY, Lady; (Muriel) Betty; da of late Dr H O Hobson; *m* 1940, Sir Colin Hardwick Thornley, KCMG, CVO (d 1983, govr and C-in-C British Honduras 1955-61); 1 s, 2 da; *Style*— Lady Thornley; Spinaway Cottage, Church Lane, Slindon, nr Arundel, W Sussex (☎ Slindon 308)

THORNTON, Adrian Heber; s of Nigel Heber Thornton, Croix de Guerre (d 1941), and Margaret Marion Gwendolen, *née* Gault; *b* 17 Sept 1937; *Educ* Eton, Pembroke Coll Camb (MA), INSEAD (MBA); *m* 8 Feb 1972, Margaret Barbara, da of Cyril Arthur Wales (d 1983); 1 s (Jasper b 1975), 2 da (Emily b 1973, Rebecca b 1979); *Career* 2 Lt Green Jackets Cyprus 1956-58; md: Gallic Management Ltd, Gallic Shipping Ltd; *Clubs* City of London; *Style*— Adrian Thornton, Esq; 31 Cheyne Row, London SW3 5HW (☎ 01 352 6290); Gallic Shipping Ltd, Bell Court House, 11 Blomefield St, London EC2M 7AY (☎ 01 628 4851, fax 01 374 0408, telex 913062 GALLIC G)

THORNTON, Lady; Agnes Margaret; *née* Masson; *m* 1927, Sir Ronald Thornton, late dir Bank of England (d 1981); 1 s, 1 da; *Style*— Lady Thornton; South Bank, Rectory Lane, Brasted, Westerham, Kent

THORNTON, Christopher Cholmondeley; s of Reginald Trelawny Thornton, MBE, MC, MBE (d 1968), of Chepstow, and Elsie Barbara Anson, *née* Tate; *b* 28 Sept 1933; *Educ* St Andrews Sch Pangbourne, Marlborough; *m* 17 June 1961, Jennifer da of Ernest Charles Goldsworthy (d 1986); 1 s Philip Charles b 1965), 1 da Julia Lucy b 1967); *Career* Nat Serv midshipman HMS Perseus and HMS Excellent RN 1952-54; slr's articled clerk Mackrell Maton & Co 1954-60, admitted slr 1960, Stephenson Harwood Linklaters & Paines 1963-65; mangr Hill Smauel & Co Ltd 1965-68; dir: Rediffusion plc 1984-88 (exec 1968-84), BET Security Servs Ltd 1988-; cncllr Sevenoaks Urban DC 1967-70, chm WI Trade Advsy Gp to BOTB 1983-85, vice-pres West India Ctee 1988- (chm 1985-87); Liveryman Worshipful Co of City of London Slrs1967; memb Law Soc 1960, Fell IOD 1987; *Recreations* fly fishing, tennis, choral singing, gardening; *Clubs* East India; *Style*— Christopher Thornton, Esq; Chartside, Cross Keys, Sevenoaks, Kent TN13 1TB

THORNTON, Clive Edward Ian; CBE (1983); s of Albert Thornton (d 1963), of Newcastle-upon-Tyne, and Margaret, *née* Coil; *b* 12 Dec 1929; *Educ* St Anthony's Newcastle upon Tyne, Coll of Commerce Newcastle upon Tyne, London Univ (LLB); *m* 17 March 1956, Maureen Carmine, da of Michael Crane (d 1975), of London; 1 s (Richard b 1963), 1 da (Elizabeth b 1957); *Career* slr 1962, slr to First Nat Fin Corpn 1964-67, chief slr Abbey nat Building Soc 1967-78, dep chief exec 1978, chief exec and dir 1979-83; ptnr Stoneham Langton and Passmore Solicitors 1985-87; dir: Housing Corpn 1980-86, Investmt Data Servs Ltd 1986-, Melton Mowbray Building Soc 1988-; Mirror Newspapers 1983-84, Financial Weekly 1983-87, Thamesmead Town Ltd 1986-, Universe Publications 1986-, Burgon Hall Ltd 1988-, Armstrong Capital Hldgs

Ltd 1988-; *Recreations* breeding Devon cattle; *Clubs* City Livery; *Style*— Clive Thornton, Esq; The Old Rectory, Creeton, Grantham, Lincs (☎ 078 081 401); Thamesmead Town Offices, Harrow Manor Way, Thamesmead (☎ 01 310 6433)

THORNTON, Hon Mrs (Diana Cara); da of 3 Baron Fairhaven, JP; *b* 1961; *m* 1983, Guy D Thornton, eld s of B M Thornton, of Stansted House, Stansted, Essex; *Style*— The Hon Mrs Thornton; 40/42 Harcourt Terrace, London SW10

THORNTON, Col Dudley Edwin; CBE (1967), ERD (1953); s of Edwin Thornton (d 1952); *b* 1 May 1919; *Educ* Bristol GS; *m* 1940, Elizabeth Joan, da of Maj John Humphrey England, TD (d 1976); 1 s, 2 da; *Career* Col Welch Regt 1937-74; co emergency planning offr Leics, ret 1984; chief staff offr OPS/Plans/TRG ANZUK Force 1972-74, dep chief of staff and cdr Br Contingent UN Force in Cyprus 1970-72, Col Gen Staff Plans and Policy Div IMS NATO HQ 1968-70; *Recreations* army historical research; *Clubs* Naval and Mil; *Style*— Col Dudley Thornton, CBE, ERD; Pepper's Farm, Burton Lazars, Melton Mowbray, Leics LE14 2UP (☎ 0664 62265)

THORNTON, Ian Charles; s of Charles William Thornton (d 1977), and Fay, *née* Eastwood; *b* 23 Mar 1934; *Educ* Manchester GS, Schs of Architecture/Civic Design Univ of Liverpool (BArch, MCD); *m* 1 Oct 1959, Mary Doreen, da of Robert Thomas Evans (d 1956); 2 da (Jacqueline b 1960, Jennifer b 1962); *Career* asst architect Morter & Dobie 1956-59, ptnr Bruxby & Evans 1959-61, assoc and ptnr Ronald Fielding Ptnrship 1961-70, ptnr and dir Alec French Ptnrship 1970-84; fndg dir Thornton Hartnell 1985-; nat pres: Faculty of Bldg 1982-84, Concrete Soc 1985-86; vice-pres RIBA (practice) 1986-87; cncl memb RIBA 1984-87; vice-pres Bristol FC (Rugby); Freeman: Worshipful Co of Constructors, Worshipful Co of Chartered Architects; FRIBA, FFB; *Recreations* rugby, cricket, golf, snooker, walking; *Clubs* MCC, Royal Western Yacht; *Style*— Ian Thornton, Esq; Old Manor Farm, Ingst, Olveston, Bristol BS12 3AP (☎ 04545 2353); Thornton Hartnell, 7 Park St, Bristol BS1 5NF (☎ 0272 272525, fax 0272 297847)

THORNTON, Jack Edward Clive; CB (1978), OBE (1964, MBE 1945); s of Stanley Henry Thornton (d 1970), and Elizabeth Daisy, *née* Baxter (d 1972); *b* 22 Nov 1915; *Educ* Solihull Sch, Ecole des Roches France, Christ's Coll Cambridge (MA); *m* 1, Margaret, JP, da of John David Copeland, of Crewe; m 2, Helen Ann Elizabeth, JP, da of Heinz Meixner, of Ravenshoe, Queensland, Aust; *Career* serv WWII RASC 1939-46 (despatches), Lt-Col 1944; teaching and educn admin 1946-54, dep dir of educn Cumberland 1954-62, sec Bureau for External Aid to Educn Nigeria 1962-64, educn conslt IBRD and ODM 1964-65, controller appts British Cncl 1965-68, chief educn advsr and under-sec Miny of Overseas Devpt 1970-77 (dep educn advsr 1968-70); lectr: Dept of Educn in Developing Countries, Inst of Educn London Univ 1978-79; *Recreations* books, gardens, mountains, music, travel, trains; *Style*— Jack Thornton, Esq, CB, OBE; 131 Dalling Rd, London W6 0ET

THORNTON, John Henry; OBE (1987), QPM (1980); s of Sidney Thornton (d 1968), and Ethel, *née* Grinnell (d 1972); *b* 24 Dec 1930; *Educ* Prince Henry's GS Evesham; *m* 1, 13 Dec 1952 (m dis 1972), Norma Lucille, da of Alfred James Scrivenor, of Eltham, London SE9; 2 s (Christopher b 1954, Jonathan b 1963); m 2, 7 Jan 1972, Hazel Ann, da of William Butler, of Blackheath, London SE3; 2 s (James b 1974 d 1976, Joseph b 1976), 1 da (Amy b 1973); *Career* RN 1949-50; Metropolitan Police 1950, supt 1965, vice-pres Br Section Int Police Assoc 1969-79, cdr 1976, head of Community Rels 1977-80, Royal Coll of Defence Studies 1981, dep asst cmmnr 1981, dir of Info 1982-83, head of Trg 1983-85, dep asst cmmnr Metropolitan Police North West Africa 1985-86; vice-pres British Section Int Police Assoc 1969-79; lay canon of St Albans Cathedral 1988-; chm: Breakaway Theatre Co St Albans 1987-, Int Organ Festival 1988; Liveryman Worshipful Co of Glaziers 1983; CStJ 1985; *Recreations* music, gardening, learning; *Style*— John Thornton Esq; Metropolitan Police, North West Area HQ, 2 Harrow Rd, London W2

THORNTON, (George) Malcolm; MP (C) Crosby 1983-; s of George Edmund Thornton by his w Ethel; *b* 3 April 1939; *Educ* Wallasey GS, Liverpool Nautical Coll; *m* 1, 1962; m 2, 1972, Sue Banton; 1 step s, 1 step da; *Career* former River Mersey pilot; memb: Wallasey County Boro Cncl 1965-75, Wirral Metropolitan Cncl 1973-79 (ldr 1974-77), chm Merseyside Dists Liaison Ctee 1975-77, vice-pres Assoc Metropolitan Auths, memb Burnham Ctee 1978-79, chm: AMA Educn Ctee 1978-79, Cncl Local Educn Auths 1978-79; MP (C) Liverpool Garston 1979-83; sec Cons Parly Shipping and Shipbuilding Ctee 1979, Cons Parly Educn Ctee, memb Select Ctee on Environment 1979-81, pps to: Rt Hon Patrick Jenkin and (as industry sec) 1981-1983; (as Environment Sec) 1983-84; memb Select Ctee on Educ, Sci and the Arts; vice chm (C) Parly Constitutional Affairs Ctee; *Style*— Malcolm Thornton Esq, MP; House of Commons, London SW1 (☎ 01 219 4489)

THORNTON, Michael Stanley; s of Joseph Stanley Thornton, of The Close Farm, Ashbourne, Derbyshire, and Jeanetta, *née* Jamieson (d 1982); *b* 1 August 1936; *Educ* Uppingham; *m* 1, 3 Sept 1960 (m dis 1977), Marie Margaret, *née* Pepper; 2 da (Jill Susan b 18 Aug 1961, Sally-Ann Margaret b 6 March 1964); m 2, 1977, Jane Susan Hinckley, *née* Bourne; 1 s (Matthew Michael b 11 Sept 1978); *Career* Nat Serv, cmmnd RASC 1955, Lt 1956; joined family business JW Thornton Ltd (Thorntons plc 1988): joined 1957, dir 1963, now dep chm, chief exec and co sec; md Mary Morrison Ltd (subsid of Thorntons plc) 1984-; former: cmmr of taxation, memb bd of tstees St Elphins Sch; tstee The Bishop of Derby's Urban Fund; vice-pres: The Arkwright Soc, NSPCC ctee (Derby Branch), The Br Show Pony Soc Area 4A; vice-chm Royal Jubilee and Prince's Tst Ctee (Derbyshire), pres Midland Cos Show, pres Matlock Rugby Club; FCIS 1977 (Assoc 1963); *Style*— Michael S Thornton, Esq; Shirley House, Shirley, Derby DE6 3AZ (☎ 0335 60810), Thorntons plc, Derwent St, Belper, Derbyshire DE5 1WP (☎ 0773 824181, fax 0773 824874, car tel 0836 380127, telex 377 835)

THORNTON, Peter Anthony; s of Robert Thornton, of 11 Hollen Croft, Owlett Rd, Shipley, W Yorkshire, and Freda, *née* Willey; *b* 8 May 1944; *Educ* Bradford GS, Manchster Univ (BSc); *m* 1969 (m dis 1987); 1 s (James William b 1976), 2 da (Victoria Jane b 1973, Charlotte Sarah b 1974); *Career* chartered surveyor and engineer; joint md Greycoat plc; FRICS, MICE, FCIOB; *Recreations* squash, tennis, skiing; *Clubs* RAC, Hurlingham; *Style*— Peter A Thornton, Esq; Van Buren Cottage, Queens Ride, Barnes Common, London SW13 0JF (☎ 01 7881969); 27 Old Jewry, London EC2R 8DQ (☎ 01 606 08 206 609)

THORNTON, Sir Peter Eustace; KCB (1974); s of D O Thornton; *b* 1917; *Educ* Charterhouse, Gonville and Caius Cambridge; *m* 1946, Rosamond Hobart Myers; 2 s, 1 da; *Career* BOT 1946, asst under-sec of State Dept of Economic Affrs 1964-67, under-sec Cabinet Office 1967-70, dep sec 1970-72, dep sec Dept of Trade and Industry 1972-74, second perm sec Dept of Trade 1974, perm sec 1974-77; dir: Laird Gp Courtaulds, Rolls Royce, Hill Samuel Gp 1977-84, pro-chllr Open Univ 1979-83; *Style*— Sir Peter Thornton, KCB; 22 East St, Alresford, Hants SO24 9EE

THORNTON, Peter Kai; s of Sir Gerard Thornton (d 1977), of Kingsthorpe Hall, Northampton, and Gerda Norregaard, of Copenhagen; *b* 8 April 1925; *Educ* Bryanston Sch, De Havilland Aeronautical Tech Sch, Trinity Hall Cambridge (BA); *m* 22 Aug 1950, Mary Ann Rosamund, da of Arthur Helps (d 1976), of Cregane, Rosscarbery, Co Cork; 3 da (Emma b 10 July 1952, Mimma b 5 March 1954, Dora b 5 Dec 1961); *Career* serv Intelligence Corps Austria 1945-48; asst keeper V & A: dept of textiles 1954-62, dept of furniture and woodwork 1962-84 (keeper 1966-84); keeper-in-charge Ham House Osterley Park curator Sir John Soames Museum 1984-; memb: cncl Nat Tst 1983-84, London advsy ctee Eng Heritage 1986-88; chm Furniture History Soc 1974-84, memb local residents assoc Chelsea; FSA 1976; *Books* Baroque and Rococo Silks, (1965), Seventeenth Century Decoration (1978), The Furnishing and Decoration of Ham House (with M Tomlin), Authentic Decor- The Domestic Interior 1620-1920 (1984), Musical Instruments as Works of Art (1968); *Style*— Peter Thornton, Esq; 15 Cheniston Gardens, London W8, (☎ 01 937 8868); Carrigillihy, Union Hall, Co Cork, Rep of Ireland; Sir John Soane's Museum, 13 Lincolns Inn Fields, London WC2 (☎ 01 405 2107)

THORNTON, Peter Leonard; s of Walter lawrence (d 1959), and Alice, *née* Latham (d 1955); *b* 9 August 1945; *Educ* Queen Mary's GS Basingstoke, Regent St Poly Sch of Modern Languages London; *m* 6 Sept 1975, Gabrielle Mary, da of Theodore Cortazzi, of Costa Rica; *Career* journalist: The Daily Sketch 1965-67, The Daily Telegraph 1967-73; ed Independant Radio News 1977-83, ed dir LBC Radio 1983-; *Style*— Peter Thornton, Esq; LBC Radio, Communications House, Gough Square, London EC4 P 4LP (☎ 01 353 1010)

THORNTON, Maj Peter Norman; s of William Norman Thornton (d 1984), and Muriel Thornton; *b* 5 May 1933; *Educ* Repton; *m* 4 April 1983, Jocelyn Bernice, da of William Henry Poole (d 1969); 1 s (Miles b 1968), 2 da (Sarah b 1962, Samantha b 1965); *Career* Lt Royal Signals Malaya 1951-55, Hallamshire Bn (Major) 1955-61; dir (ret as chm) J W Thornton Ltd 1962-87; dir Buxton Festival Soc 1983-, chm Midland Asthma & Allergy Res Assoc 1976-79, fdr and tstee Sheffield Asthma Soc 1977, fdr mbr SDP; FIIM (1976), FIOD (1981); *Recreations* offshire sailing, small boat racing, music; *Clubs* IOD, Ogston Sailing; *Style*— Maj Peter Thornton, GSM; Field Farm, Wensley, Matlock, Derbyshire DB4 2LL (☎ 0629 732598); Peter Thornton Assocs, Belleclair House, Archer Rd, Sheffield, Yorkshire S8 0JW (☎ 0742 552379, car tel 0836 212713)

THORNTON, Robert Luke Grant (Bob); er s of Rev Canon Cecil Grant Thornton, of Leicester, and Winifred Dorothy, *née* Fawkes; *b* 22 Dec 1923; *Educ* Bromsgrove; *m* 1953, Helen, da of Rev C B Hodson; 3 s (James, John, Peter), 1 da (Catherine); *Career* Capt RIASC 1942-45, India 1942-43, 36 Br Div in N Burma 1944, with 3 Commando Bde Hong Kong 1945; combined dental med course Guy's Hosp 1946; orthodontic house surgn Royal Dental Hosp 1952; gen dental practitioner Salisbury 1952; dental surgn WDHO Wills Bristol 1953-79; hon tres (and life memb) assoc of Industl Dental Surgns 1968-78; gen dental practitioner Almonsbury 1978-; fndr JOGLE Club raising £73,700 in aid of the Nat Star Centre for Disabled Youth Cheltenham having walked 3 times and cycled once between John O'Groats and Lands End since 1972; *Recreations* amateur potter, foreign travel, gardening, reading about Sir Winston Churchill, raising money for the Star Centre; *Style*— Bob Thornton, Esq; 3 Red House Lane, Almondsbury, Bristol BS12 4BB (☎ 0454 612300)

THORNTON, Dr Robert Ribblesdale; s of Thomas Thornton, (d 1970), of 102 Filey Road, Scarborough, and Florence, *née* Gatenby, (d 1959); *b* 2 April 1913; *Educ* Leeds GS, St John's Coll Cambridge (BA, LLB, LLM, MA); *m* 27 Jan 1940, Ruth Eleonore, da of William Tuckson, (d 1938), of Beaconsfield Road, New Southgate, London; 1 s (Peter b 1946), 1 da (Ann Mitchell b 1941); *Career* serv WWII 1940-46; Adj 86 Field Regt 1943-45, Bde Maj RA 3 Divn 1945, 53 (Welsh) Divn 1945-46; asst slr: Leeds 1938-40 and 1946-47, Bristol 1947-53; dep town clerk Southampton 1953-54; town clerk: Salford 1954-66, Leicester 1966-73; chief exec Leicester CC 1973-76; memb Local Govt Boundary Cmmn for England 1976-82 (dep chm 1982); hon sec St Mary's Ch Winterborne Whitechurch; pres Soc of Town Clerks 1971, DL (Leics) 1974-85, tres Leicester Univ 1980-85; hon LLD (Leicester) 1987; Solace (1974); *Recreations* sport (watching), music (listening); *Clubs* Nat Lib; *Style*— Dr R R Thornton, CBE, LLD, DL; 16 St Marys Close, Winterborne Whitechurch, Blandford Forum, Dorset DT11 0DJ (☎ 0258 880 980)

THORNYCROFT, Col Guy Mytton; DL (Shropshire 1967); s of Lt-Col Charles Mytton Thornycroft, CBE, DSO (d 1948); *b* 1 April 1917; *Educ* Shrewsbury, RMA Sandhurst; *m* 1947, Kathleen, *née* Evans; 2 s; *Career* Col King's Shropshire LI 1937-60, Bde-Col LI 1959-60; High Sheriff Shropshire 1975; *Recreations* shooting, cricket; *Clubs* MCC; *Style*— Col Guy Thornycroft, DL; Bank Cottage, Kenley, Shropshire

THORNYCROFT, John Ward (Jack); CBE (1956); s of John Edward Thornycroft, KBE (d 1960), of Steyne, Bembridge, Isle of Wight, and Louisa Isabel, *née* Ward (d 1969); *b* 14 Oct 1899; *Educ* RNC: Osbourne Dartmouth, Keyham, Trinity Coll Cambridge (naval offrs course); *m* 3 Feb 1928, Esther Katherine (d 1985), da of John Ernest Pritchard (d 1920), of Sutton Coldfield, Warwicks; 1 s (Timothy Edward Pritchard b 1932), 1 da (Jill Elizabeth (Lady Inveforth) b 1935); *Career* Midshipman HMS Canada 1916-17; Sub Lt: HMS Spencer 1917, HM Submarines G10 & G12 1917-18; ret Lt Cdr 1920; John I Thornycroft & Co Ltd: sales mangr and dir 1929-43, jt md 1943-55, md 1955-60, chm & md 1960-68; MRINA, MIMechE; *Recreations* shooting, sailing, farming; *Clubs* Utd Serv, Bembridge Sailing; *Style*— Jack Thornycroft, Esq, CBE; Steyne, Bembridge, Isle of Wight

THOROGOOD, Alfreda; da of Edward Thorogood, (d 1966), and Alfreda Langham; *b* 17 August 1942; *Educ* Lady Eden's Sch, Royal Ballet Sch (jr and upper sch); *m* 1 Aug 1967, David Richard Wall, CBE, s of Charles Wall; 1 s (Daniel b 12 Dec 1974), 1 da (Annaliese b 15 Oct 1971); *Career* princ dancer Sadler's Wells Royal Ballet Co touring section 1968 (joined 1960, soloist 1966), as principal transferred to resident co 1970, danced all princ roles in the maj classical ballets; created roles for: Sir Frederick Ashton, Sir Kenneth MacMillan, Anthony Tudor, Geoffrey Cavley; danced many roles choreographed by: Dame Ninette de Valois, Glen Tetley, Jerome Robins, Rudolf Nureyev, Leonide Massine, John Cranko, John Neumier, David Bintley, André Howard; left Royal Ballet 1980, dip for PDTC from the Royal Acad of Dancing 1982, dir Bush Davies Sch 1988 (sr teacher 1982-85, dep Ballet Princ 1985-88); *Style*— Miss

Alfreda Thorogood

THOROLD, Sir Anthony Henry; 15 Bt (E 1642), OBE (1942), DSC (1942, and bar 1945), JP (Lincs 1961), DL (1959); s of Sir James Ernest Thorold, 14 Bt (d 1965), and Katharine (d 1959), eldest da of Rev William Rolfe Tindal-Atkinson, formerly vicar of St Andrew's, Burgess Hill; *b* 7 Sept 1903; *Educ* RNC: Osborne, Dartmouth; *m* 1939, Jocelyn Elaine Laura, da of Sir Clifford Edward Heathcote-Smith, KBE, CMG (d 1963); 1 s, 2 da; *Heir* s, (Anthony) Oliver Thorold; *Career* RN 1917, serv WWII in Home and Med Fleets as SO, ops in Force H and Western Approaches, Capt 1946, Cdre in Charge Hong Kong 1953-55, ADC to The Queen 1955-56, ret 1956; CC Kesteven 1958-74, High Sheriff Lincolns 1968, ldr Lincs CC 1973-81; chm: Grantham Hosp Mgmnt Ctee 1963-74, Lincoln Diocesan Tst and Bd of Fin 1966-71; *Recreations* shooting; *Clubs* Army and Navy; *Style*— Capt Sir Anthony Thorold, Bt, OBE, DSC, JP, DL; Syston Old Hall, Grantham, Lincs NG32 2BX (☎ 0400 50270)

THOROLD, (Anthony) Oliver; s and h of Sir Anthony Thorold, 15 Bt, OBE, DSC; *b* 15 April 1945; *Educ* Winchester, Lincoln Coll Oxford; *m* 1977, Genevra, da of John L Richardson, of Broadshaw, W Calder, W Lothian; 1 s (Henry b 1981), 1 da (Lydia b 1985); *Career* barr Inner Temple 1971; *Style*— Oliver Thorold, Esq; 8 Richmond Cres, London N1 (☎ 01 609 0437); Dr Johnson's Bldgs, Temple, London EC4(☎ 01 353 9328)

THOROLD, Peter Guy Henry; s of Sir Guy Thorold KCMG (d 1970); *b* 20 April 1930; *Educ* Eton, New Coll Oxford; *m* 1964, Anne, da of Robert Fender, AFC; 4 children; *Career* dir Bain Dawes Ltd 1972; *Clubs* Buck's; *Style*— Peter Thorold, Esq; 25 Stanley Cres, London W11 2NA

THOROLD, Hon Mrs (Phyllis Margaret); *née* Russell; OBE (1946); da of 2 Baron Ampthill, GCSI, GCIE, and Margaret, *née* Lygon, GBE, GCVO; *b* 3 June 1909; *Educ* RCM (LRAM, ARCM); *m* 1940 (m annulled on her petition 1942), Capt William Thorold (d 1943, gggs of Sir John Thorold, 9 Bt, MP); *Career* serv WWII Dep Cmmr Jt War Orgn Order of St John and Br Cross Soc; serv: N Africa (despatches), Russia, Manila, Hong Kong; musician, embroideress; OStJ 1941; *Style*— The Hon Mrs Thorold; 55 Ebury Mews, London SW1W 9NY (☎ 01 730 9097)

THORP, James Noble; s of Arthur Thorp (d 1953), and Annie, *née* Rollinson (d 1975); *b* 27 Oct 1934; *Educ* Rothwell GS, Leeds Coll of Art Sch of Architecture; *m* 18 Jan 1958, Jean, da of Arthur Brown (d 1972); 2 s (Ian James b 1958, Julian Alexander b 1969), 2 da (Sally Ann b 1961, Jayne Stella b 1964); *Career* architect, estab private practice 1961; lectr in design 1964-87: Leeds Coll of Art, Leeds Poly, Sheffield Univ; Civic Tst assessor; awards: Leeds Gold Medal 1964, dept of Environment Award for Design 1976, Civic Tst Commendation 1987; ARIBA; *Recreations* skiing, amateur theatre, scenic design, music; *Style*— James Thorp, Esq; 73 Church Street, Woodlesford, Leeds 26 (☎ 0532 826303); Design Studio, James Thorp & Partners, 21 Park Street, Leeds 1 (☎ 0532 455451)

THORPE; *see*: Gardner-Thorpe

THORPE, Adele Loraine; da of Lionel Raphael Le Wis, and Bettie Louise, *née* Frome; *b* 29 Sept 1952; *Educ* Henrietta Barnett; *m* 16 April 1982, Simon Peter Thorpe, s of Stanley Thorpe; 1 da (Katy b 1987); *Career* Northern European accountant Amdahl (UK) Ltd 1978-81; fin dir: Tendem Computer Ltd 1981-87, Sybase Software Ltd 1987-; chm BIM Slough Branch 1985-87 (ctee memb 1987-), cncl memb Inst Chartered Secretaries & Administrators BBO Branch 1984-, memb IOD; Liveryman Worshipful Co of Chartered Secretaries and Administrators; FCIS, FBIM; *Style*— Mrs Adèle Thorpe; Harmond House, St Hubert's Close, Gerrards Cross, Bucks; Farley Hall, London Rd, Binfield, Bracknell

THORPE, Adrian Charles; s of Prof Lewis Guy Malville Thorpe, and Dr Eva Mary Bargara Imeson, da of Alfred Reynolds composer and mus dir Lyric Theatre, Hammersmith; *b* 29 July 1942; *Educ* The Leys Sch, Christ's Coll Cambridge (BA, MA); *m* 26 Oct 1968, Miyoko, da of Taketaro Kosugi (d 1950), of Japan; *Career* HM dir ser Tokyo 1965-70, FCO 1970-75, Beirut 1973-76 (head of Chancery 1975-76), FCO 1976, Tokyo 1976-81, FCO 1981-85 (cnsllr and head of inf dept 1982-85); Bonn (econ cnsllr) 1985-; FRSA; *Recreations* opera, travel, comfort; *Clubs* Tokyo (Japan); *Style*— Adrian Thorpe, Esq; c/o FCO, King Charles St, London SW1A 2AH (☎ 01 270 3000); Britische Botscheft, Friedrich Ebert Allee 77, 5300 Bonnl FRG (☎ 49 228 234061, telex 0886 887, fax 49 228 234070)

THORPE, Clifford Malcolm (Mick); s of Clifford Padgett Thorpe (d 1977), of Hull and Phyllis Ivy, *née* Atkins (d 1980); *b* 2 April 1931; *Educ* Marist Coll Hull, Univ of Manchester (LLB); *m* 4 April 1961, Sheila Muir, da of Arthur Thomsom Macfarlane; 5 s (Martin Peter b 1962, Christopher Paul b 1963, Richard Michael b 1963, Malcolm James b 1965, Gregory Neil b 1969), 1 da (Fiona Mary b 1966); *Career* admitted slr 1954; fndr Thorpe and Co slrs 1955-; pres Scarborough Law Soc 1965, clerk to Gen Tax Cmmrs 1974-, dir Hull City AFC plc 1984-; chm: Scarborough Round Table 1966, Area 15 Round Table 1969, pres; Nat Assoc of Round Tables 1971, Scarborough Catenian Assoc 1962, Yorks Coast Pastoral Cncl 1985-88; fnd pres Rotary Club of Scarborough cavalier 1978, vice chm St Catherines Hospice Tst 1986-; memb Law Soc 1954-; *Recreations* walking, music, skiing, travel; *Style*— Mick Thorpe, Esq; 46 Stone Quarry Rd, Burniston, Scarborough YO13 ODF (☎ 0723 871155); Thorpe and Co Slrs, 17 Valley Bridge Parade, Scarborough YO11 2JX (☎ 0723 364321, fax 0723 500459)

THORPE, Geoffrey Digby; s of Gordon Digby Thorpe, of Scotland, and Agnes Joyce, *née* Haines; *b* 24 Sept 1949; *Educ* Windsor GS for Boys, Architectural Assoc Sch of Architecture (AA Dip); *m* 29 Sept 1973, Jane Florence, da of James Hay McElwee, of Havant, Hampshire; 1 da (Holly b 1980); *Career* indust gp architect; Milton Keynes Devpt Corpn 1974-78, asst co architect East Sussex 1978-80, chm Geoffrey Thorpe Practicel Ltd 1980-; dir Arundel Festival Soc; memb: RIBA 1975, ARCUK 1975; *Recreations* fly and game fishing; *Clubs* Leconsfield Flyfishing, Petworth; *Style*— Geoffrey Thorpe, Esq; Lower Farm, Madehurst, Arundel, West Sussex BN18 0NU (☎ 0243 65 612); Avola House, Tarrant St, Arundel, West Sussex BN18 9AD (☎ 0903 883 500, fax 0903 882 188, car tel 0836 536 678)

THORPE, Rt Hon (John) Jeremy; PC (1967); s of Capt John Henry Thorpe, OBE, KC, JP, sometime MP (C) for Rusholme and dep chm Middx QS (d 1944; he eld s of Ven John Thorpe, Archdeacon of Macclesfield), of Limpsfield, by his w Ursula, JP (er da of Sir John Norton-Griffiths, 1 Bt, KCB, DSO, sometime MP for Wednesbury and Wandsworth Central); *b* 29 April 1929; *Educ* Eton, Trinity Coll Oxford (hon fell 1972); *m* 1, 1968, Caroline (d 1970), da of Warwick Allpass, of Kingswood, Surrey; 1 s; m 2, 1973, Marion, Countess of Harewood (*see* Harewood, Earl of), da of Erwin Stein (d 1958); *Career* conslt Stramit Ltd; ldr Lib Pty 1967-76 (hon tres 1965-67), MP (Lib) Devon N 1959-79 (fought N Devon 1955); barr Inner Temple 1954, memb Devon Sessions, vice-pres Anti-Apartheid Movement 1969-76; pres Oxford Union 1951; exec chm UN Association 1975- chm Jeremy Thorpe Assoc Ltd (Devpt Conslts); Hon LLD Exeter Univ; FRSA; *Clubs* Nat Lib; *Style*— The Rt Hon Jeremy Thorpe, PC; 2 Orme Sq, London W2 4RS

THORPE, John Grafton; s of Grafton Gould Thorpe (d 1963), of Willow View, West Hill, Epsom, Surrey, and Ivy Dorothy, *née* Locks; *b* 29 Oct 1932; *Educ* St John's Sch Leatherhead; *m* 30 March 1957, Pamela, da of Thomas Francis Faithfull, of Leatherhead, Surrey; 1 s (Martin John Richard b 9 Sept 1958), 1 da (Caroline Jane b 31 May 1960); *Career* underwriter: Lloyds 1963, St Quintin Syndicate 1979-85; dir Alexander Howdon Underwriting 1979-84, underwriter Coster Syndicate 1986; vice-pres Leatherhead CC; Freeman City of London 1955, Liveryman: Worshipful Co of Glass Sellers 1955 (apprentice 1950-55), Worshipful Co of Makers of Playing Cards 1979 (Steward 1984-86, elected to Ct 1986, Junior Warden 1988); *Books* The Playing Cards of the Worshipful Company of Makers of Playing Cards (1980); *Recreations* playing cards, watching cricket; *Clubs* MCC; *Style*— John Thorpe, Esq; Epsom Rd, Leatherhead, Surrey; Coster & Ors, Lloyds, London EC3 (☎ 01 623 7100)

THORPE, Hon Mr Justice; Sir Mathew Alexander; QC (1980); yr s of Michael Alexander Thorpe, of Rectory Gate House, Petworth, Sussex, and Dorothea Margaret, *née* Lambert; *b* 30 July 1938; *Educ* Stowe, Balliol Coll Oxford; *m* 30 Dec 1966, Lavinia Hermione, da of Maj Robert James Buxton (d 1968); 3 s (Gervase b 1967, Alexander b 1969, Marcus b 1971); *Career* barr Inner Temple 1961, memb Matrimonial Causes Rule Ctee 1978-83, QC 1980, rec 1982, bencher Inner Temple 1985, High Ct judge 1988; *Clubs* Turf; *Style*— The Hon Mr Justice Thorpe; Royal Courts of Justice, Strand, London WC2

THORPE, Richard Malin; s of Capt Bernard Thorpe (d 1987), and Hilda Mary Thorpe (d 1971); *b* 15 Oct 1926; *Educ* Cranleigh Sch, Trinity Coll Cambridge (MA); *m* 31 Dec 1948, Alice Daisy, da of Henry Samuel Adlam; 1 s (Malin b 1950); *Career* cmmnd Irish Gds 1944, demob 1947; joined family firm Bernard Thorpe & Ptnrs land agents and surveyers 1951, managing ptnr and chm Main Equity Partnership 1973, chm and sr ptnr Nat Partnership 1983, churchwarden Parish church of St Lawrence Bidborough, former co and dist cncllr Kent, vice-chm Citicare St Clememts; pres: Cons Assoc Constit (Tunbridge Wells), local cons Assoc (Southborough), West Kent Hunt Supporters Club (farmer master Kent Hunt); former memb Westminster coc Fin & Gen Purposes ctee; Freeman and memb ct of Worshipful Co of Gold and Silver Wyre Drawers (Master 1987), Freeman and Liveryman Worshipful Co of Farmers 1967; FRICS 1954; *Recreations* gardening; *Clubs* Oriental; *Style*— Richard Thorpe, Esq; Home Farm, London Rd, Southborough, Tunbridge Wells, Kent TN4 0UH (☎ 0732 354744)

THORPE-TRACEY, Stephen Frederick; s of Rev Julian Stephen Victor Thorpe-Tracey (d 1949), of the Rectory, Monkokehampton, Devon, and Faith Catherine Gwendoline, *née* Powell; *b* 27 Dec 1929; *Educ* Plymouth Coll; *m* 1 Jan 1955, Shirley, da of Lt-Col George Frederick Byles (d 1951), of The Old Forge, Stoodleigh, Tiverton, Devon; 1 s (Jeremy), 2 da (Catherine, Barbara); *Career* emergency cmmn 1948, short serv cmmn 1950, regular cmmn DLI 1952, Staff Coll Camberley 1960 (DSC), GSO2 Def Operational Res Estab 1961-63, Trg Maj 8 DLI TA 1964-65, Maj 1 DLI 1965-66, GSO2 MOD 1966-70; direct entry Civil Serv: under sec DHSS 1986- (princ 1970-77, asst sec 1977-86), Controller Newcastle Central Off DSS; hon sec Civil Serv Chess Assoc 1974-77, cdre Goring Thames SC 1981-82, chm Northern Gp Royal Inst of Public Admin 1988-89; *Recreations* chess, golf,sailing, fell walking; *Clubs* Naval and Military; *Style*— Stephen Thorpe-Tracey, Esq; DSS, Newcastle-upon-Tyne NE98 1YX (☎ 091 279 3060)

THOURON, Sir John Rupert Hunt; KBE (1976), CBE (1967); s of John Longstreth Thouron, and Amelia Thouron; *b* 10 May 1908; *Educ* Sherborne; *m* 1 (m dis); 1 s; m 2, 1953, Esther duPont, da of Lammot duPont; *Career* br army offr, serv WWII Major Black Watch; with Lady Thouron, fndr of Thouron Univ of Pennsylvania Fund for British-American Student Exchange 1960; *Recreations* gardening, horticulture, racing, hunting, fishing, golf; *Clubs* Vicmead, Seminole, Jupiter Island, The Brook, (all US), White's, Sunningdale, Royal St George's; *Style*— Sir John Thouron, KBE; Summer: DOE RUN, Unionville, Chester County, Pa 19375, USA (☎ 215 384 5542); Winter: 416 South Beach Rd, Hobe Sound, Florida 33455, USA (☎ 407 546 3577); office: 3801 Kennett Pike, Greenville, Delaware 19807, USA (☎ 302 652 6350)

THREADGOLD, Andrew Richard; s of Stanley Dennis Threadgold, of Brentwood, Essex, and the late Phyllis Ethel, *née* Marsh; *b* 8 Feb 1944; *Educ* Brentwood Sch, Nottingham Univ (BA), Melbourne Univ (PhD); *m* 21 May 1966 (sep), Rosalind Threadgold; 2 s (Richard b 1967, Matthew b 1971); *Career* mangr econ info Int Wool Secretariat 1971-74, advsr econ divn Bank of England 1974-84, on secondment chief economist Postel Investmt Mgmnt Ltd 1984-86, head fin supervision gen divn Bank of England 1986-87; chief exec and dir securities investmnt Postel Investmt Mngmnt 1987-; *Style*— Andrew Threadgold, Esq; 5 Barnsbury St, London N1 1PW (☎ 01 354 0583); Postel Investment Management Ltd, Standon House, 21 Mansell St, London E1 8AA (☎ 01 702 0888, fax 01 702 9452, telex 8956577, 888947)

THRELFALL, (Richard) Ian; QC (1965); s of William Bernhard Threlfall (d 1965), and Evelyn Alice, *née* Maconochie (d 1987); *b* 14 Jan 1920; *Educ* Oundle, Gonville and Caius Coll Cambridge (BA); *m* 9 Sept 1948, Annette, da of George Cowper Hugh Matthey (d 1972); 3 s (George, Aidan (decd), Hugh), 3 da (Emma (Mrs Antonatos), Alexandra (Mrs Holloway), Victoria (Mrs Bathurst)); *Career* serv WWII Indian Armd Corps Probyn's Horse, staff appts GS02 HQ 14 Army 945 (despatches twice); barr Lincoln's Inn 1947, bencher 1973; memb: E Surrey Health Authy 1982-, Surrey Family Practioner Ctee 1982-; Liveryman Worshipful Co of Goldsmiths 1964 (memb ct of assts 1969, Prime Warden, 1978-79); FSA 1949; *Style*— Ian Threlfall, Esq, QC; Pebble Hill House, Limpsfield, Oxted, Surrey (☎ 0883 712452)

THRING, Jeremy John; DL (Avon); o s of late Christopher William Thring, MBE, TD, of King Meadow, Upton Lovell, Warminster, Wilts, and Joan Evelyn, *née* Graham; *b* 11 May 1936; *Educ* Winchester; *m* 30 June 1962, Cynthia Kay, da of late Gilbert Kilpatrick Smith, of Bath; 2 da (Lucinda Katharine b 8 Aug 1963, Candida Sara b 11 May 1965); *Career* Nat Serv cmmnd 3 Kings Own Hussars 1955; slr 1962, Notary Public 1962, govr Bath HS; tstee: Bath Inst for Theumatic Diseases, Bath Inst for Res into Care of the Elderly, Nat Eye Res Centre, Avon and Bristol Red Cross Tst Fund; memb Bath Dist Health Authy; memb: Law Soc, Soc of Provinical Notaries;

Recreations stalking, shooting, fishing; *Clubs* Bath and Co; Belcombe House, Bradford-on-Avon, Wilts (☎ 02216 2295); Thrings & Long, 4-5 North Parade, Midland Bridge, Bath BA1 2HQ (☎ 0225 448494; fax, 0225 319735/319660; telex 444712)

THRING, John Gale Wake; s of Walter Leonard Howard Thring, of New Place Stables, Lingfield, Surrey, *see* Burke's Landed Gentry, 18 Edn vol 3), and Elizabeth Mary Ann, *née* Vandenbergh; *b* 2 May 1943; *Educ* Wellington Coll USA; *m* 1 Oct 1966, Dianne Elizabeth, da of William Henry Jones, of Wembury Park, Newchapel, Surrey; 3 da (Victoria Elizabeth Sarah b 1967, Arabella Caroline b 1969, Henrietta Charlotte Anne b 1971); *Career* property developer, govr Fonthill Sch 1983; *Style—* John Thring, Esq; Rosslyn House, Dormansland, Surrey RH7 6QR (☎ 0342 833 587)

THRING, Prof Meredith Wooldridge; s of Capt W H Thring, CBE, RN (d 1949), and Dorothy Wooldridge (d 1922); *b* 17 Dec 1915; *Educ* Malvern, Trinity Coll Cambridge (BA, ScD); *m* 14 Dec 1940, (Alice) Margaret (d 1986), da of Robert Hooley (d 1949) of London; 2 s (John b 1944, Robert b 1949), 1 da (Susan (Mrs Kalaugher) b 1942); *Career* HG 1941-45; scientific offr Br Coal Utilisation Res Assoc 1937-46, head physics dept Br Iron & Steel Res Assoc 1944-53 (asst dir 1953), prof fuel technol and chem engrg Sheffield Univ 1953-64, prof mechanical engr Queen Mary Coll London 1964-81; lectured in: Aust, Canada, USA, France, Holland, Italy, Russia, Argentina, Mexico, W Germany, Bulgaria, Hungary, Czechoslavakia and Poland; Hadfield Medal Iron and Steel Inst 1949; jt fndr Int Flame Res Fndn 1949; memb: Clean Air Cncl 1957-62, educn ctee RAF 1968-76, UNESCO Cmmn to Bangladesh 1979, Fire Res Bd 1961-64, Advsy Cncl R & D Miny of Power 1960-66; Hon D Open Univ 1982; FIMechE 1968, FIEE 1968, FIChemE 1972 FEng 1976, FInstP 1944, SFInstFuel 1951 (pres 1962-63); memb: Royal Norwegian Scientific Soc 1974, corr memb Nat Acad of Engrg Mexico 1977; *Books* The Science of Flames and Furnaces (1952, 2 edn 1962), Machines - Masters or Slaves of Man? (1973), Man, Machines and Tomorrow (1973), How to Invent (1975), The Engineer's Conscience (1980), Robots and Telechirs (1983); *Recreations* wood carving, arboriculture; *Clubs* Athenaeum; *Style—* Prof Meredith Thring; Bell Farm, Brundish, Suffolk IP13 8BL (☎ 037 984 296)

THRING, Peter Streatfeild; TD (1970); s of Jack Reddie Thring (d 1975), and Eirene Helen, *née* Streatfeild (d 1983); *b* 31 Dec 1933; *Educ* Winchester, Oxford Univ (MA); *m* Joanna Elizabeth, da of Charles Gordon Duff, MC (d 1968); 1 s (Christopher b 1964), 1 da (Katharine b 1966); *Career* Nat Serv 2 Lt 157 Div Locating Batty RA 1952-54, 254 City of London Field Regt RA TA 1954-71, Maj 1969; CA; hon tres: The Mothers Union 1972-86, The Oxford Soc 1977-; FCA 1970; *Recreations* bee-keeping, sailing, gardening; *Clubs* United Oxford and Cambridge; *Style—* Peter Thring, Esq, TD; Old School House, Cheverells Green, Markyate, St Albans, Herts AL3 8AB (☎ 0582 840501); 1 Lambeth Palace Rd, London SE1 7EU (☎ 01 928 2000, fax 01 928 1345, telex 885234)

THROCKMORTON, Anthony John Benedict; s of late Capt Herbert John Anthony Throckmorton, RN (3 s of 10 Bt), and hp of cous, Sir Robert Throckmorton, 11 Bt; *b* 9 Feb 1916; *Educ* Beaumont Coll (Old Windsor); *m* 1972, Violet Virginia, da of late Anders William Anderson; *Style—* Anthony Throckmorton, Esq; 2006 Oakes Everett, Washington 98201, USA; University of Washington, Seattle, Washington 98195 (☎ 206 543 8757)

THROCKMORTON, Lady Isabel Violet Kathleen; *née* Manners; da of 9 Duke of Rutland; *b* 5 Jan 1918; *m* 1, 1936 (m dis 1951), Gp Capt Loel Guinness, OBE (d 1988); 1 s (William Loel Seymour Guinness, *qv*), 1 da (Marchioness of Dufferin and Ava, *qv*); m 2, 1953, Sir Robert Throckmorton, 11 Bt, *qv*; *Style—* Lady Isabel Throckmorton; Molland, S Molton, N Devon; Coughton Court, Alcester, Warwicks

THROCKMORTON, Sir Robert George Maxwell; 11 Bt (E 1642); s of late Lt-Col Richard Courtenay Brabazon Throckmorton (s of 10 Bt) and Lilian, JP, only da of Col Henry Brooke Langford Brooke, of Mere Hall, Cheshire (ka 1916); suc gf Sir Richard Charles Acton Throckmorton, 10 Bt, 1927; *b* 15 Feb 1908; *Educ* Downside, RMC Sandhurst; *m* 1, 1942 (m dis 1948), Jean, formerly w of Arthur Turberville Smith-Bingham (she m 1959, 3 Baron Ashcombe, and d 1973), and da of Charles Tuller Garland, of Moreton Hall, Warwicks; m 2, 1953, Lady Isabel Violet Kathleen, formerly w of Gp Capt (Thomas) Loel Evelyn Bulkeley Guinness, OBE, and yr da of 9 Duke of Rutland; *Heir* cous, Anthony John Benedict Throckmorton; *Career* 2 Lt Grenadier Gds 1928-30, Lt (A) RNVR 1940-44; *Clubs* Army and Navy, White's; *Style—* Sir Robert Throckmorton, Bt; Coughton Court, Alcester, Warwickshire (☎ 0789 763 370); Molland Bottreaux, South Molton, N Devon

THROWER, David John; s of Edward Thrower (d 1972), and Gladys Naomi Maude, *née* Talbot; *b* 19 Nov 1932; *Educ* St Joseph's Coll, Cranfield Sch of Mgmnt; *m* 10 Aug 1955, Marie Jeanette, da of Frederick White (d 1975); 1 s (Graham David b 1969), 4 da (Amanda Jane b 1956, Chritine Alyson b 1959, Karen Denise b 1961, Michelle Susan b 1967); *Career* RAF aircrew, sr NCO, Gunnery Offr; dir H Bradley Ltd 1957-, (md 1967-74), fndr Nailpak Ltd 1972 (md 1974), fndr and exec chm Thrower Bros Gp (Hldgs) Ltd 1974-, dir Thrower Leasing Ltd 1983-86, ptnr Lebrad Properties Syndicate 1967-87; pres Upper Norwood Rotary Club 1977-78, life pres 2nd Croydon Scout Gp, chm CBI S London Regn; FCIS, FBIM; *Recreations* golf, reading, touring; *Clubs* Upper Norwood Rotary, IOD, Croydon Dining, Air Gunners Assoc Assoc; *Style—* David J Thrower, Esq; "Heatherdene", Harewood Rd, S Croydon, Surrey; 32 Church Rd, London SE19

THRUSH, Prof Brian Arthur; s of Arthur Albert Thrush (d 1963), of Hampstead, London, and Dorothy Charlotte, *née* Money (d 1982); *b* 23 July 1928; *Educ* Haberdashers' Aske's Hampstead Sch, Emmanuel Coll Cambridge (BA,MA, PhD, ScD); *m* 31 May 1958, Rosemary Catherine, da of George Henry Terry (d 1970), of Ottawa, Canada; 1 s (Basil Mark Brian b 1965), 1 da (Felicity Elizabeth b 1967); *Career* conslt to US Nat Bureau of Standards 1957-58; Univ of Cambridge: demonstrator in physical chemistry 1953-58, asst dir of res 1959-64, lectr 1964-69, reader 1969-78, prof of physical chemistry 1978-, head of chemistry dept 1988, vice-master Emmanuel Coll 1986- (fell 1960-); visiting prof Chinese Acad of Sci 1980-; memb: Lawes Agric Tst Ctee 1979-, Natural Environment Res Cncl 1985-; Tilden Lectr of Chemical Soc 1965, Michael Polanyi Medallist Royal Soc of Chemistry 1980; FRS 1976, FRS Chem 1977; *Recreations* wine, walking; *Clubs* Athenaeum; *Style—* Prof Brian Thrush; Brook Cottage, Pemberton Terrace, Cambridge CB2 1JA (☎ 0223 357 637); Univ of Cambridge, Dept of Chemistry, Lensfield Rd, Cambridge CB2 1EW (☎ 0223 336 458, fax 0223 336 362, telex 81240); Emmanuel Coll, Cambridge CB2 3AP (☎ 0223 336 537)

THUM, Maximilien John Alexandre; s of Maximilien Francois Thum (d 1972), of Geneva, Switzerland, and Kathleen Isabel, *née* Crouch (d 1972); *b* 15 Feb 1933; *Educ* Ecole Internationale de Genéve, Chigwell Sch Essex, Law Socs Coll of Law; *m* 1, 15 Feb 1958 (m dis 1981), Freda, *née* Wray; 2 s (Nicolas Charles Maximilien b 3 Feb 1959, Jonathan Richard Alexandre b 25 March 1962), 1 da (Annabel Maxine Elizabeth 26 Nov 1963); m 2, 25 Feb 1982, Valerie, *née* Kay; *Career* RAF 1955-57, cmmnd Pilot Offr 1956; admitted slr of Supreme Court 1955, asst slr Lewis and Lewis and Gisborne 1955, slr Rodyk and Davidson Singapore 1957-60, called to Singapore Bar 1958, Professional Purposes Dept Law Soc 1961, ptnr Sharpe Pritchard and Co London 1962-66, sr litigation ptnr Ashurst Morris Crisp London 1967-; memb: Int Bar Assoc, American Bar Assoc; *Recreations* photography, opera, swimming, tennis, cars; *Clubs* RAC; *Style—* Max Thum, Esq; Eastfield Cottage, Mickleham, Surrey; 24 Stanhope Gardens, London SW7; Ashurst Morris Crisp, Solicitors, Broadgate House, 7 Eldon St, London EC2M 7HD (☎ 01 247 7666, fax 01 377 5659, telex 887067 ASHLAW)

THURLOW, David George; OBE (1987); s of Frederick Charles Thurlow (d 1986), of Bury St Edmunds, and Audrey Isabel Mary, *née* Farrow; *b* 31 Mar 1939; *Educ* King Edward VI Sch Bury St Edmunds, Cambridge Coll of Art dept of architecture, Canterbury Coll of Art sch of architecture, Cambridge Univ (MA); *m* 19 Dec 1959, Pamela Ann, da of Percy Adolphous Rumbelow; 3 da (Suzanne Elizabeth, Jane Ann, Emma Louise); *Career* fndr ptnr: Cambridge Design Gp 1970, Cambridge Design Architects 1975, Design Gp Cambrige 1988; Faculty of Architecture Univ of Cambridge 1970-77, exhibitor Royal Acad Summer Exhibition 1983-87, awards incl: RIBA Award 1976, 1984 and 1986, Civic Tst Award 1978 and 1986,DOE Housing Award 1985; fndr memb: Granta Housing Soc, Cambridge Forum for the Construction Indust 1981 (chm 1985-86); assessor: RIBA Awards 1979, 1984 and 1986 Civic Tst Awards 1979-88; memb PSA Design Panel 1987-; ARIBA 1965; *Recreations* cricket, golf, food; *Style—* David Thurlow, Esq, OBE; 9 Sylvester Rd, Cambridge (☎ 0223 316 378); Design Group Cambridge, Merlin Place, Milton Rd, Cambridge CB4 4DP (☎ 0223 420 228, fax 0223 420 566)

THURLOW, 8 Baron (GB 1792); Francis Edward Hovell-Thurlow-Cumming-Bruce; KCMG (1961, CMG 1957); 2 s of Rev 6 Baron Thurlow (d 1952), and Grace Catherine, *née* Trotter (d 1959); suc bro, 7 Baron Thurlow, CB, CBE, DSO, 1971; *b* 9 Mar 1912; *Educ* Shrewsbury, Trinity Coll Cambridge (MA); *m* 13 Aug 1949, Yvonne Diana, da of late Aubyn Harold Raymond Wilson, of Westerlee, St Andrews, Fife, and formerly w of Mandell Creighton Dormehl; 2 s, 2 da; *Heir* s, Hon Roualeyn Robert Hovell-Thurlow-Cumming-Bruce; *Career* Dept of Agric for Scotland 1935-37, sec to British High Cmmn in NZ 1939-44, and Canada 1944-45; private sec to sec of state for Commonwealth Relations 1947-49, counsellor British High Cmmn in New Delhi 1949-52, adviser to govr of Gold Coast 1955; dep high cmmr in Ghana 1957, and in Canada 1958; high cmmr for UK in NZ 1959-63, and in Nigeria 1963-66; dep under-sec FCO 1964, govr and C-in-C of Bahamas 1968-72; chm Inst of Comparative Study of History, Philosophy and the Sciences 1975; chm Khiron Fndn 1988; KStJ; *Recreations* chess; *Clubs* Travellers'; *Style—* The Rt Hon the Lord Thurlow, KCMG; 102 Leith Mansions, Grantully Road, London W9 1LJ (☎ 01 289 9664)

THURNHAM, Peter Giles; MP (C) Bolton North-East; s of Giles Rymer Thurnham (d 1975), and Marjorie May, *née* Preston; *b* 21 August 1938; *Educ* Oundle Sch, Peterhouse Cambridge, Harvard Business Sch, Cranfield Inst of Tech; *m* 1963, Sarah Janet, da of Harold Keenlyside Stroude (d 1974); 1 s, 3 da, 1 s adopted; *Career* professional engr running own business 1972-; memb S Lakeland Dist Cncl 1982-84; *Recreations* Lake Dist, family life; *Style—* Peter Thurnham, Esq, MP; Hollin Hall, Crook, Kendal, Cumbria LA8 9HP (☎ 0539 821 382); House of Commons, London SW1

THURSBY, Brig Patrick Dehany Francis; OBE (1965); s of Maj Francis Dehany Victor Thursby (d 1973), and Marjorie Frances Ralph, *née* Barrow; *b* 29 Dec 1922; *Educ* Cheltenham, Univ of Manchester; *m* 1946, Gay, da of Dr C D Newman (d 1964), of Durban, S Africa; 2 s; *Career* joined (2 Lt) RE 1942, Suffolk Regt 1944; War serv: India, Burma 1942-45; Para Regt 1958, cmd 1 Para 1962-64, Regtl Col Para Regt 1965-68, cmd 44 Para Bde 1968-70, Brig Gen Staff MOD (ret 1973); Hon Col 10 Bn Para Regt TA 1978-84, dir Army Sport Control Bd 1973-88 (ret); Freeman City of London; *Recreations* gardening, bird watching; *Clubs* Army & Navy, MCC; *Style—* Brig Patrick Thursby, OBE; Tipplers, Tilford, Farnham, Surrey GU10 2DD (☎ 025 125 2272)

THURSBY-PELHAM, Brig (Mervyn) Christopher; OBE (1986); s of Nevill Cressett Thursby-Pelham (d 1950), of Llangadock, Carmarthenshire, *see* Burke's Landed Gentry, 18 Edn, vol 1, and Yseulte, *née* Peel (d 1982); *b* 23 Mar 1921; *Educ* Wellington, Merton Coll Oxford; *m* 16 Jan 1943, Rachel Mary Latimer, da of Sir Walter Stuart James Willson (d 1952), of Tonbridge, Kent; 1 s (David Thomas Cressett b 1948), 1 da (Philippa Rachel Mary b 1943); *Career* cmmnd Welsh Gds 1941; serv 3 Bn: N Africs, Italy, Austria 1943-45, 1 Bn serv Palestine and Egypt, graduate Staff Coll Camberley 1950, GSO2 (Ops) 6 Armd Div BAOR 1951-53, Regtl Adj Welsh Gds 1956-57, DSD Coll Camberley 1957-60, Cmdt Gds Depot Pirbright 1960-63, GSO1 (Ops) Allied Staff Berlin 1963-64, Regtl Lt-Col cmdg WG 1964-67, COS Br Forces Guls 1967-69, COS London Dist 1969-72, Dep Fortress Cdr Gibraltar 1972-74, Dep Cdr Midwest Dist UK 1974-76 (ret); ADC to The Queen 1972-76; dir gen Br Heart Fndn 1976-86 and 1988-89, co pres Royal Br Legion Berks 1985-; *Recreations* fishing, sailing, skiing, travel; *Clubs* Cavalry and Gds, Royal Yacht Sqdn; *Style—* Brig Christopher Thursby-Pelham, OBE; Ridgeland House, Finchampstead, Berks RG11 3TA; King's Quay, Whippingham, IOW PO32 6NU

THURSBY-PELHAM, Vaughan Brian George; s of Brian Thursby-Pelham (d 1958, seventh in descent from Henry Pelham, Clerk of the Pells (one of the great sinecures of state) *ante* 1721, whereby is kin to the Dukes of Newcastle); *b* 27 Dec 1932; *Educ* Beaumont; *m* 1969, Brigid Kathleen O'Doherty, da of Edward O'Doherty, of Co Donegal; 2 s, 3 da; *Career* Chartered accountant; FCA, FInstD; *Recreations* philately; *Clubs* Catenian Assoc; *Style—* Vaughan Thursby-Pelham, Esq; 2 Woodlands Av, New Malden, Surrey KT3 3UN

THURSFIELD, John Richard; s of Maj Rupert MacNaghten Cecil Thursfield (d 1979), and Elizabeth Margaret Mary, *née* Gunning; *b* 2 Oct 1937; *Educ* Rugby Sch; *m* 29 April 1961, Sarah, da of Charles Clinton Dawkins (d 1985); 2 s (Peter John b 1964, Robert Charles b 1967), 2 da (Mary Elizabeth b 1963, Rachel Sarah b 1969); *Career* dir Union Discount Co Ltd; *Recreations* skiing; *Style—* John Thursfield, Esq; Hodges Farm, Lower Froyle, Alton, Hants, GU34 4LL (☎ 0420 23294); 39 Cornhll, London,

EC3V 3NU (☎ 01 623 1020)

THURSO, 2 Viscount (UK 1952); Sir Robin Macdonald Sinclair; 5 Bt (GB 1786), JP (Caithness 1959); s of 1 Viscount Thurso, KT, CMG, PC (d 1970, leader, as Sir Archibald Sinclair, of Lib Pty 1935-45), and Marigold (da of Lt-Col James Forbes, gs of Sir Charles Forbes, 3 Bt, by the Col's 1 w Lady Angela St Clair-Erskine, da of 4 Earl of Rosslyn); *b* 24 Dec 1922; *Educ* Eton, New Coll Oxford, Edinburgh Univ; *m* 1952, Margaret Beaumont, da of late Col Josiah James Robertson, DSO, TD, JP, DL, of Norwood, Wick, Caithness, and widow of Lt Guy Warwick Brokensha, DSC, RN; 2 s, 1 da; *Heir* s, Hon John Archibald Sinclair, yr of Ulbster; *Career* sits as Lib peer in House of Lords; Flt-Lt RAF 1939-45; farmer; CC for Caithness 1949-61 and 1965-73, town cncllr Thurso 1957-61 and 1965-73, baillie 1960 and 1969, dean of Guild 1968, police judge 1971; chm: Sinclair Family Tst Ltd, Lochdhu Hotels Ltd, Thurso Fisheries Ltd; dir Stephens (Plastics) Ltd; fndr & 1 chm Caithness Glass Ltd; Lord-Lieut Caithness 1973- (DL 1952, Vice-Lt 1964-73); pres Highland Soc of London 1980-83; Boys Bde 1985-; North Country Cheviot Sheep Soc 1951-54; Assoc of Scottish Dist Fishery Bds 1975-; chm Caithness & Sutherland Youth Employment Ctee 1957-75, memb Red Deer Cmmn 1965-74; *Recreations* shooting, fishing, amateur drama; *Clubs* RAF, New (Edinburgh); *Style*— The Rt Hon the Viscount Thurso, JP; Thurso East Mains, Thurso, Caithness, Scotland (☎ 0847 62600); Dalnawillan, Altnabreac, Caithness

THWAITE, Anthony Simon; s of Hartley Thwaite, JP, (d 1978), of Yorks, and Alice Evelyn, *née* Mallinson; *b* 23 June 1930; *Educ* Kingswood Sch Bath, Christ Church Oxford (MA); *m* 4 Aug 1955, Ann Barbara, da of Angus John Harrop (d 1963), of NZ and London; 4 da (Emily b 1957, Caroline b 1959, Lucy b 1961, Alice b 1965); *Career* Nat Serv Sgt Instr Rifle Bde and RAEC 1949-51; lectr English lit Tokyo Univ 1955-57, prodr BBC radio 1957-62, literary ed The Listener 1962-65, asst prof English Univ of Libya Benghazi 1965-67, literary ed New Statesman 1968-72, co-ed Encounter 1973-85, dir Andre Deutsch Ltd 1986-; Richard Hillary Meml Prize 1968, Cholmondeley Award for Poetry 1983, chm of judges Booker Prize 1986; former memb: ctee of mgmnt Soc of Authors, cncl RSL, lit panel Arts Cncl of GB; current memb lit advsy ctee Br Cncl; FRSL 1978; *Books* Poems 1953-83 (1984), Six Centuries of Verse (1984), Poetry Today (1985), Letter From Tokyo (1987), Philip Larkin: Collected Poems (ed 1988); *Recreations* archaeology, travel; *Style*— Anthony Thwaite, Esq; The Mill House, Low Tharston, Norfolk (☎ 050 841 569); Flat 5, 128 Gloucester Terrace, London W2 (☎ 01 402 3695)

THWAITES, Prof Sir Bryan; s of Ernest James Thwaites (d 1978), and Dorothy Marguerite, *née* Dickeson; *b* 6 Dec 1923; *Educ* Dulwich, Winchester, Clare Coll Cambridge (MA, PhD); *m* 11 Sept 1948, Lady Katharine Mary, da of H R Harries (d 1946); 4 s (Barnaby Christopher b 1953, Quentin Mark b 1956, Dominic John b 1958, Jacoby Michael b 1963), 2 da (Eleanor Jane b 1951, Matilda Bridget b 1966); *Career* sci offr Nat Physical Lab 1944-47, lectr Imperial Coll London 1947-51, asst master Winchester Coll 1951-59, prof mathematics Univ of Southampton 1959-66, princ Westfield Coll of London 1966-83; fndr Sch Mathematics Project (SMP) 1961 (chm of tstees 1968-83, life pres 1984); JP 1963-66; chm: mgmnt ctee Northwick Park Hosp 1970-74, Brent cncl Harrow AHA 1973-82, Wessex RHA 1982-88; FIMA, pres 1966; kt 1986; *Books* Incompressible Aerodynamics (1960), On Teaching Mathematics (1961), The SMP: The First Ten Years (1973), Education 2000 (1983); *Recreations* sailing, music; *Clubs* IOD; *Style*— Prof Sir Bryan Thwaites; Milnthorpe, Winchester, Hampshire SO22 4NF (☎ 0962 52394)

THWAITES, Brig Peter Trevenen; s of Lt-Col Norman Graham Thwaites, CBE, MVO, MC (d 1956), of Barley End, Tring, Herts, and Eleanor Lucia, *née* Whitridge; *b* 30 July 1926; *Educ* Rugby; *m* 1, 7 Oct 1950 (m dis), Ellen Theresa (d 1976), da of William J King, US Army (d 1970); 2 s (Thomas b 1952, d 1960, Christian b 1958), 2 da (Allegra (Mrs Martin) b 1956, Grania b 1959); m 2, Jacqueline Ann Inchbald, *née* Bromley; *Career* cmmnd Grenadier Gds 1944; serv: Germany, Egypt, Br Cameroons, Br Guiana; memb Sir William Penney's scientific pty UK atomic trials S Aust 1956, Staff Coll 1958, Bde Maj 1 (later 2) Fed Inf Bde Malaya 1959-60, Jt Servs Staff Coll 1965, MOD 1965-67, Aden 1967, cmd Muscat Regt Sultan of Muscats Armed Forces Dhofar Campaign 1967-70, AQMG HQ London Dist 1970-71, Col cmdg Br Army Staff Singapore and govr Singapore Int Sch 1970-73, dep dir Def Operational Plans (Army) 1973-74, Brig 1975, head of MOD logistics survey team to Saudi Arabia 1976, ret 1977; chm Jt Staff Sultan of Oman's Armed Forces 1977-81; playwright: Love or Money 1958 (with Charles Ross), Master of None 1960, Roger's Last Stand 1976, Caught in the Act 1981 (with Charles Ross), Relative Strangers (1984); chm Individual Sch Direction Ltd 1981-; chm Hurlingham Polo Assoc 1982-; Sultan of Oman's Bravery Medal Sultan's Commendation, Sultan of Oman's Distinguished Service Medal for Gallantry; *Recreations* shooting; *Clubs* White's, Beefsteak, Cavalry and Guards'; *Style*— Brig Peter Thwaites; The Manor House, Ayot St Lawrence, Herts; 32 Eccleston Sq, London SW1; 7 Eaton Gate, London SW1W 9BA (☎ 01 730 5508)

THWAITES, Ronald; QC (1987); s of Stanley Thwaites, of Stockton-on-Tees, and Aviva, *née* Cohen; *b* 21 Jan 1946; *Educ* Richard Hind Secdy Tech Sch Stockton, Grangefield GS Stockton, Kingston Coll of Technol (LLB); *m* 7 Aug 1972, Judith Adelaide Foley, da of Barry Baron Myers, of Surbiton and Adelaide Foley *née* Comer; 3 s (George b 1973, David b 1976, Richard b 1981, 1 da (Stephanie b 1980); *Career* called to the Bar Gray's Inn (ad eundem Inner Temple) 1970; co fndr and chm Normansfield Hosp Thursday Club 1980-87; *Recreations* swimming, squash, lighting bonfires; *Style*— Ronald Thwaites, Esq, QC; 10 Kings Bench Walk, Temple, London EC4Y 7EB (☎ 01 353 2501, fax 01 353 0658)

THYKIER, Hans; s of Svend Thykier (d 1986) and Emilie Marie Johansen (d 1980); *b* 22 April 1931; *Educ* Ostre Borgerdyd Skole Copenhagen Denmark, Univ of Copenhagen; *m* 1971, Gertrud Ilona Birgitta, da of Baron Oscar Didrik Staël von Holstein (d 1969); 4 children; *Career* A H Riise Copenhagen Denmark 1957-66, Mobil Europe Inc in Denmark, Austria, Switzerland and the UK 1966-71, marketing dir in Europe for Occidental Int Oil Inc 1971-74, exec dir Int Planned Parenthood Fedn (IPPF) 1974-76, American Express Co 1976-85, vice-pres American Express Bank in Europe, ME and Africa 1983-85; dir Foreign & Colonial Mgmnt (Jersey) Ltd 1985-88; dir: John Govett & Co mgmnt (Jersey) Ltd, John Govett (Channel Islands) Ltd 1988-; *Recreations* tennis, yachting; *Clubs* Brooks's, Oriental, Royal Thames Yacht, Royal Danish Yacht, Danish; *Style*— Hans Thykier, Esq; 14 Beaumont St, London W1 (☎ 01 486 3041); Naylands, Slaugham, W Sussex, (☎ 0444 400270); Casa Ararat, Penedo, Sintra, Portugal; 20 Dalen, FANO, Vesterhavsbad, FANO, Denmark

THYNE, Malcolm Tod; s of Andrew Tod Thyne (d 1982), and Margaret Melrose, *née* Davidson (d 1984); *b* 6 Nov 1942; *Educ* Leys Sch Cambridge, Clare Coll Cambridge (MA); *m* 31 July 1969, Eleanor Christine, da of James Fleming Scott, of Edinburgh; 2 s (Douglas b 1973, Iain b 1976); *Career* asst master: Edinburgh Acad 1965-69, Oundle Sch 1969-80 (housemaster 1972-80); headmaster: St Bees Sch Cumbria 1980-88, Fettes Coll 1988-; HMC 1980; *Books* Periodicity, Atomic Structure and Bonding (1976), contributions to Nuffield Chemistry pubns; *Recreations* mountaineering; *Style*— Malcolm Thyne, Esq; The Lodge, Fettes College, Edinburgh EH4 1QX; Fettes College, Edinburgh EH4 1QX (☎ 031 332 2281)

THYNNE, Lord Christopher John; 2 s of 6 Marquess of Bath, ED, by his 1 w, Hon Daphne Vivian, da of 4 Baron Vivian; *b* 9 April 1934; *Educ* Eton; *m* 1968, Antonia, da of Maj Sir Anthony Palmer, 5 Bt; 1 da; *Career* late 2 Lt Life Guards; runs Longleat House; *Recreations* photography, drawing; *Style*— Lord Christopher Thynne; The Hermitage, Horningsham, Wilts; Longleat, Warminster, Wilts (☎ 09853 551)

THYNNE, Lady Valentine; Liese-Maria; da of late Kenneth William Dennis, of Bristol, and Mrs George Jackaman, of Malta; *b* 1 May 1939; *Educ* Abbeydale Sch Sheffield; *m* 1977, as his 3 w, Lord Valentine Thynne (d 1979), s of 6 Marquess of Bath, ED; 1 da (Natasche Charlotte-Lara Luist Wolsley b 1986) da of Thomas Gerrard Wolsley of New York; *Career* artist; *Recreations* reading, painting, gardening, cooking, listening to baroque music, medieaval architecture, keeping house; *Style*— Lady Valentine Thynne; Bridge House, St John Street, Wells, Somerset

THYNNE, Lady Silvy Cerne; da of 6 Marquess of Bath by his 2 w, Virginia; *b* 22 Dec 1958; *Style*— Lady Silvy Thynne; 25 Almeric Rd, London SW11

THYSSEN-BORNEMISZA, Baroness Francesca; da of Baron Heinrich von Thyssen, of the German steel family, and Fiona Campbell-Walter, the mannequin; *b* 1958; *Educ* Le Rosey Switzerland, St Martin's Art Sch, ICA; *Career* photographer, singer and mannequin; apprentice to family business; *Style*— Baroness Francesca Thyssen-Bornemisza; 18 Seymour Walk, SW10 (☎ 01 352 7913)

TIARKS, Anthony John Phipps; er s of Lt-Cdr John Desmond Tiarks, RN; *b* 28 July 1952; *Educ* Millfield, Somerset City Univ (BSc); *m* 1979, Lesley, da of Dr Ian Verner, of 67 Harley Street, London; 1 da (Venetia b 1985); *Career* jt dep md ACLI Int Commodity Servs (UK subsid of Donaldson Lufkin Jenrette, a Wall Street investment banking firm) 1982-; md Tide (UK) Ltd; landowner; *Recreations* shooting, sailing; *Style*— Anthony Tiarks, Esq; c/o ACLI International Commodity Services Ltd, 52 Mark Lane, EC3 (☎ 01 623 5811); The Old Manor, Chawton, nr Alton, Hants; 2 South Audley Street, London W1 (☎ 01 409 3500)

TIBBALDS, Francis Eric; s of William Eric Tibbalds, of Beckenham, Kent, and Elsie Agnes, *née* Wood; gf changed family name from Teague to Tibbalds; *b* 16 Oct 1941; *Educ* Farnham GS, Regent St Poly (Dip Arch), Univ of London (MPhil, town planning); *m* 6 Sept 1969, Janet Grace, da of Kenneth Malcolm McDonald, of Hayes, Bromley, Kent; 2 s (Adam Dominic b 1971, Benedict Malcolm b 1973); *Career* snr architect planner Llewelyn-Davies, Weeks, Forestier-Walker & Bor 1969-70; princ architect planner Westminster City Cncl 1970-72; dep chief planning offr Lambeth Borough 1972-74; jt project dir Gp Five (Nigeria) 1974-75; dir of planning Llewelyn-Davies Weeks 1975-78; fndr ptnr Tibbalds Ptnrship 1978; Tibbalds Colbourne Ptnrship Ltd architects and planners 1988-; pres London Univ Town Planning Soc 1968; fndr Urban Design Gp (chm 1979-86); assoc memb Soc of Architect Artists, RIBA, pres Royal Town Planning Inst 1988 Freeman City of London 1988, memb Worshipful Co of Chartered Architects; RIBA 1968, FRTPI 1970, FRSA 1980, FFB 1985; *Books* Urban Sketchbook (1988); *Recreations* sketching, choral singing, fitness training; *Style*— Francis E Tibbalds, Esq; 37 Kelsey Park Ave, Beckenham, Kent BR3 2NL (☎ 01 658 3479); Tibbalds Colbourne Ptnrship Ltd, 39 Charing Cross Rd, London WC2H 0AW (☎ 01 439 9272, fax 01 439 0323)

TIBBELLS, John Terence; s of William Shearer Tibbells (d 1949), of Liverpool, and Martha, *née* Fox (d 1973); *b* 5 May 1931; *Educ* Liverpool Coll; *m* 12 March 1964, Sheila Myfanwy, da of Robert Ivor Roberts (d 1958), of Dyserth Hall, Dyserth, Clwyd; 2 da (Sally b 1967, Nicola b 1970); *Career* Subaltern S Lancs Regt (PWV) 1955-57, 24 Bde Barnard Castle and Berlin Ind Bde; chartered accountant Glass and Edwards Liverpool 1949-58, and other professional firms 1962-67; sec of Liverpool cos in Seagram Gp 1958-61, accountant of wine cos John Holt Gp 1961-62, princ J T Tibbells and Co 1968-; FCA, ATII; *Recreations* country life, travel, rugby; *Clubs* Liverpool St Helens FC (RU), Old Liverpudlian Soc; *Style*— John Tibbells, Esq; Clarence House, Bryniau, Dyserth, Rhyl, Clwyd LL18 6BY; J T Tibbells & Co, Chartered Accountants, Clarence House, Bryniau, Dyserth, Rhyl, Clwyd LL18 6BY

TIBBER, Judge Anthony Harris; s of Maurice Tibber (d 1969), and Priscilla, *née* Deyong (d 1970); *b* 23 June 1926; *Educ* Univ Coll Sch Hampstead, Magdalen Coll Sch, Brackley; *m* 1954, Rhona Ann, da of Julius Salter; 3 s (Peter, Clifford, Andrew); *Career* rec Crown Ct 1976, circuit judge 1977; *Style*— His Honour Judge Tibber; c/o Edmonton County Ct, Fore St, London N18 2TN (☎ 01 807 1666)

TIBBITS, Capt Sir David Stanley; DSC (1943); s of Hubert Tibbits, MB, BCh, MRCS, LRCP (d 1933) of Warwick, and Edith Lucy, *née* Harman (d 1965); *b* 11 April 1911; *Educ* Wells House Sch Malvern Wells, RNC Dartmouth; *m* 1938, Mary Florence, da of Harry St George Butterfield, of Bermuda; 2 da; *Career* joined RN 1925, served WW II, Navigating Offr, started RN Radar Plotting Sch 1943, Cdr 1946, Capt 1953, Dir Radio Equipment Dept Admiralty 1953-56, i/c HMS Manxman, Dryad and Hermes 1956-61, ret 1961; elder bro of Trinity House 1961, dep master and chm of Bd 1972-76; fndr chm The Pilots' Nat Pension Fund 1967-76; tstee Nat Maritime Museum 1973-77; govr Pangbourne Coll 1973-78; lay vice-pres Missions to Seamen 1973-; hon sec King George's Fund for Sailors 1974-80; FNI 1979 (and fndr memb 1972); Liveryman Worshipful Co of Shipwrights 1973 (memb court 1976); memb Bermuda Port Authy & chm Pilotage Cttee; pres Bermuda Soc for the Blind; lay memb BDA Diocesan Synod and Cathedral Vestry 1982-88; kt 1976; *Recreations* sailing (yacht 'Beacon of Bermuda'), photography, music; *Clubs* Army and Navy, Royal Yacht Sqdn, Hurlingham, Royal Bermuda Yacht, Royal Hamilton Amateur Dinghy; *Style*— Capt Sir David Tibbits, DSC, FNI, RN; Harting Hill, PO Box HM 1419, Hamilton, Bermuda HM FX (☎ 80929 54394)

TIBBS, (Geoffrey) Michael Graydon; OBE (1987); s of Rev Geoffrey Wilberforce Tibbs (d 1957), vicar of Lynchmere, Sussex, and Margaret Florence, *née* Skinner (d 1952); *b* 21 Nov 1921; *Educ* Berkhamsted Sch, St Peter's Coll Oxford (BA, MA); *m* 6 Oct 1951, Anne Rosemary, da of Donald Jocelyn Wortley (d 1981), of Bunchfield, Lynchmere, Sussex; 2 s (Philip b 1955, Chirstopher b 1957); *Career* serv WWII;

ordinary seaman HMS Cottesmore 1940; RNVR: Midshipman 1941, Sub Lt HMS Sheffield 1941, Lt HMS/M Tantulus 1943, HMS/M Varne 1945-46, (despatches); Sudan Political Serv 1949-55 (dist cmmr), seconded Middle E Centre of Arab Studies 1950; personnel orgn and overseas depts Automobile Assoc 1955-68, sec: RCP 1968-86 (hon fell 1968), Faculty Community Med 1971-72, Faculty of Occuptional Med 1978-86 (hon fell 1987), Jt Ctee on Higher Med Trg 1970-86; memb Lynchmere PCC and parish cncl, local pantomime prodr; Freeman City of London 1986; FRGS 1948, MIPM 1960, FInstM 1971 (memb 1959); *Recreations* local affairs, producing pantomimes, making bonfires; *Clubs* Naval; *Style*— Michael Tibbs, Esq, OBE; Welkin, Lynchmere Ridge, Haslemere, Surrey GU27 3PP (☎ 0428 3120)

TICKELL, Sir Crispin Charles Cervantes; GCMG (1989), KCVO (1983, MVO 1958); s of Jerrard Tickell, and Renée Oriana, *née* Haynes; *b* 25 August 1930; *Educ* Westminster, Christ Church Oxford (MA); *m* 1, 1954 (m dis 1976), Chloë, da of Sir James Gunn, RA; 2 s, 1 da; m 2, 1977, Penelope, da of Dr Vernon Thorne Thorne; *Career* serv Coldstream Gds, Lt, 1952-54; joined Dip Serv 1954-; fell Center for Int Affrs Harvard Univ 1975-76, chef de cabinet to Roy Jenkins as pres of EEC Cmmn 1977-81, visiting fell All Souls Coll Oxford 1981, ambass Mexico 1981-83, dep under-sec FCO 1983-84; perm sec Overseas Devpt Admin 1984-87; perm rep and Ambass UN 1987-, Offr Order of Orange Nassau (Netherlands) 1958; *Books* Climatic Change and World Affairs (1977, 1986); *Recreations* climatology, paleohistory, art (esp precolumbiana), mountains; *Clubs* Brooks's; *Style*— Sir Crispin Tickell, GCMG, KCVO; c/o Foreign and Commonwealth Office, London SW1A 2AH

TICKELL, Maj-Gen Marston Eustace; CBE (1973, MBE 1955), MC (1945); s of Maj-Gen Sir Eustace Francis Tickell, KBE, CB, MC (d 1972), and Mary Violet, *née* Buszard; *b* 18 Nov 1923; *Educ* Wellington, Peterhouse Cambridge; *m* 1961, Pamela Vere, da of Vice Adm Arthur Duncan Read, CB (d 1976); *Career* RE 1944, Col-Cmdt RE, Engr-in-Chief (Army) 1972-75, Cmdt RMCS 1975-78, ret as Maj-Gen 1978; pres Inst RE 1979-82, Hon Col Engr and Tport Staff Corps 1983-88; *Recreations* sailing; *Clubs* Royal Ocean Racing, Army and Navy; *Style*— Maj-Gen Marston Tickell, CBE, MC; The Old Vicarage, Branscombe, Seaton, Devon

TICKLE, Brian Percival; CB (1985); s of William Tickle, and Lucy, *née* Percival; *b* 31 Oct 1921; *Educ* The Judd Sch Tonbridge; *m* 3 March 1945, Margaret Alice; 1 s (John b 1948), 1 da (Margaret (Mrs Schofield) b 1949); *Career* WWII RCS 1941-46; Civil Serv 1938-70; sr registrar family div High Ct of Justice 1982-88 (registrar 1970-), ret 1988; co-chm Independent Schools Tribunal 1988-; *Books* Edited Rees Divorce Handbook (ed 1963), Atkins Court Forms and Precedents Probate (Second edn 1984); *Recreations* golf; *Clubs* RAC, Nevill GC; *Style*— B P Tickle, Esq, CB; 1A Roal Chase, Tunbridge Wells, Kent

TIDBOROUGH, Hon Mrs (Christine Gray); *née* Addison; yr da of 2 Viscount Addison (d 1976), and Brigit Helen Christine, *née* Williams (d 1980); *b* 3 Sept 1946; *m* 28 Feb 1966, Terry Frederick Tidborough, s of Victor Tidborough, of Cullompton, Devon; *Style*— The Hon Mrs Tidborough; 2 Silver Street, Willand, Cullompton, Devon

TIDBURY, Charles Henderson; s of late Brig O H Tidbury, MC, and Beryl, *née* Pearce (decd); *b* 26 Jan 1926; *Educ* Eton; *m* 1950, Anne, da of late Brig Hugh Edward Russell, DSO, and Dorothy (d 1989) (who m 2, 1963, Gen Sir Richard Nugent O'Connor, KT, GCB, DSO, MC, d 1981); 2 s, 3 da; *Career* servd KRRC 1943-52, Palestine 1946-48 (despatches), Queen's Westminster TA 1952-60; chm Whitbread & Co 1978-84, dir: Whitbread & Co plc 1984-88, Nabisco Gp Ltd 1985-88; Brickwoods Brewery Ltd 1966-71, dir Whitbread Investmt Co plc, Barclays Bank plc 1985-, Barclays Bank UK Ltd 1973-, Mercantile Credit Co Ltd 1985-, Vaux Gp plc 1985-, ICL Europe 1985-, Pearl Assurance plc 1986-; pres Shire Horse Soc 1986-88, Inst of Brewing 1976-78, (vice-pres 1978), pres British Inst of Innkeeping 1985-; chm Brewers Soc 1982-84, (vice-pres 1985-); chm: Brewing Res Fndn 1985-, Master Brewers' Co 1988-89, Mary Rose Devpt Tst 1980-86, William & Mary Tercentenary Tst 1985-89; tstee Nat Maritime Museum 1984-; govr: The Nat Heart & Chest Hosps 1988-, Portsmouth Poly 1988-; *Recreations* family, sailing, shooting, countryside; *Clubs* Brooks's, Royal Yacht Sqdn, Island Sailing, Bembridge Sailing; *Style*— Charles Tidbury, Esq; 22 Ursula St SW11 3DW; Crocker Hill Farm, Forest Lane, Wickham, Hants PO17 5DW; 20 Queen Anne's Gate SW1H 9AA (☎ 01 222 7060)

TIERNEY, Sydney; s of James Tierney (d 1977), and Mrs Eleanor Mould (d 1979); *b* 16 Sept 1923; *Educ* Oxford (DIP), Bolton-on-Dearne Secondary Modern Sch; *m* 2 da (Susan, Patricia); *Career* MP (Lab) Birmingham 1974-79, Yardley 1974-79; PPS to Minster of State for Agric and Food 1976; pres of Union of Shop Distributive & Allied Workers; chm Lab Party 1986-87; JP; *Style*— Sydney Tierney, Esq; 14 Low Meadow, Whaley Bridge, via Stockport SK12 7AY (☎ 066 333 128); USDAW, 188 Wilmslow Rd, Fallowfield, Mancester M14 4LJ

TIGHE, Maj-Gen Patrick Anthony Macartan; CB (1977), MBE (1958); s of Macartan H Tighe (d 1928), and Dorothy Isabel Vine (d 1988); *b* 26 Feb 1923; *Educ* Christ's Hosp; *m* 1, 1950, Elizabeth Frazer Stewart (d 1971); 2 s; m 2, 1972, Princine Merendino Calitri; *Career* RAF 1940-41; Army 1941-77 serv: NW Europe, Palestine 1947, Malaya 1956, Borneo 1963; Inspector Intelligence Corps 1972-74, Signal Officer in Chief 1974-77, Col Cmdt Royal Signals 1977-84, Maj-Gen, ret; gp personnel mangr Hong Kong Land Co 1977-84; chm Ex-Services Mental Welfare Soc 1987; *Recreations* golf; *Clubs* Army and Navy, Hong Kong, Worthing Golf; *Style*— Maj-Gen Patrick Tighe, CB, MBE; c/o Lloyds Bank, 6 Pall Mall, London SW1

TIKARAM, Hon Justice Sir Moti; KBE (1980); s of Tikaram and Singari; *b* 18 Mar 1925; *Educ* Marist Bros HS Suva, Victoria Univ, Wellington NZ (LLB); *m* 1944, Satyawati (d 1981); 2 s, 1 da; *Career* started law practice 1954, stipendiary magistrate 1960, puinse judge 1968; acted as chief justice 1971, ombudsman Fiji 1972-; patron Fiji Lawn Tennis Assoc; *Books* articles in The Pacific Way and in Recent Law 131; *Recreations* tennis; *Clubs* Fiji, Fiji GC (Suva); *Style*— The Hon Justice Sir Moti Tikaram, KBE; PO Box 514, 45 Domain Road, Suva, Fiji; office: PO Box 982, Suva (☎ 211652)

TILBERIS, Elizabeth Jane; da of Thomas Stuart-Black Kelly, and Janet Storrie, *née* Caldwell; *b* 7 Sept 1947; *Educ* Malvern Girls' Coll, Leicester Coll of Art (BA); *m* 17 July 1971, Andrew Tilberis; 2 s (Robert b 1981, Christopher b 985); *Career* Vogue Magazine: fashion asst 1970, fashion ed 1974, exec fashion ed 1981, fashion dir 1987, ed 1987-; ctee memb Br Fashion Cncl; *Recreations* gardening, music; *Style*— Ms Elizabeth Tilberis; Vogue Magazine, Vogue House, Hanover Sq, London W1 (☎ 01 499 9080)

TILBURY, Alan George; CBE (1966, OBE 1962); s of George Tilbury (d 1945); *b* 9 Dec 1925; *Educ* Sutton County GS, Natal SA, London Univ; *m* 1949, Jean-Mary McInnes, *née* Pinkerton; 3 da; *Career* advocate; entered Colonial Legal Serv 1954; attorney-gen: Bechuanaland 1963, Botswana 1966-69; The Brewers Soc London: head legal dept 1970-72, dep sec 1972-82, sec 1982-; chm UK Botswana Soc; *Recreations* sailing (yacht 'Corinna'), music; *Clubs* Tollesbury Cruising; *Style*— Alan Tilbury, Esq, CBE; Oakwood, Tolleshunt Major, Essex (☎ 0621 860656)

TILEY, Timothy Francis Thornhill; s of Rev George Edward Tiley (d 1985), and Cecilia Frances Mystica Thornhill (d 1982); descended from ancient family of Thornhill of Thornhill in Yorkshire, which can trace continuous line of descent from saxon theign Eisulf de Thornhill (1080-1165), membs of the family of Jordan de Thornhill (s of Eisulf) are portrayed in a group of the most famous of the 13 century miracle windows in the trinity chapel of Cantabury Cath; *b* 6 June 1949; *Educ* Malvern, St Peter's Coll Oxford (MA); *Career* fndr and md of Tim Tiley Ltd, (publishers of philosophical and religious prints 1978-); co-fndr of Brass Rubbing Centres: Oxford 1973, Bristol 1974, Stratford on Avon 1974, London 1975, Edinburgh 1976, Bath 1976, Glastonbury 1977, Washington DC 1977; *Recreations* piano, reading, cycling, travelling, historical studies; *Clubs* Royal Cwlth Soc; *Style*— Timothy Tiley, Esq; Eblana Lodge, 157 Cheltenham Road, Bristol, BS6 5RR Avon, (☎ 0272 423397);

TILL, Brian Marson; TD (1946); s of Thomas Marson Till, OBE (d 1957), of The Old Rectory, Inkpen, Berks, and Gladys Rhonda Alice, *née* Stedman (d 1963); *b* 17 July 1913; *Educ* Marlborough, Trinity Hall Cambridge (MA); *m* 1, 16 Aug 1950, Amy Anne Elkington (d 1981), da of late Laurence Craigle Maclagan Wedderburn, of N Berwick; 2 s (Thomas Laurence b 29 Aug 1953, William Dominic b 29 Dec 1954); m 2, 27 Nov 1982, Lydia Margaret Gardner, da of late Charles Burnett Morgan, of King Samborne, Hants; *Career* joined TA 52 HAA Regt RA 1938, served WW11, Maj 1943, demob 1945; qualified CA 1939, sr ptnr Black Geoghegan & Till 1957 (ptnr 1939-), ret 1978; memb Worshipful Co of Fishmongers 1935 (Prime Warden 1979-80); *Recreations* fishing, shooting, stalking, skiing; *Clubs* Flyfishers; *Style*— Brian Till, Esq, TD; The Granary, Piddletrenthide, Dorset DT2 7QX

TILL, Ian Jeremy; s of Francis Oughtred Till, of Ilkley, Yorks, and Kathleen Emily, *née* Munt; *b* 6 Sept 1938; *Educ* Ghyll Royd Sch Ilkley, The Leys Sch (JDip MA); *m* 25 July 1964, Caroline Elizabeth Minden, da of Ronald Minden Wilson (d 1987), of Capetown, SA; 2 s (Rodger, Rupert); *Career* CA; formerly working with: Robson Rhodes, Deloittes Haskins & Sells, Crompton Parkinson, Courtaulds, Air Products; gp chief accountant Shepherd Building Gp Ltd 1975-; cncl memb ICEAW, memb Bldg Employers Confedn Jt Tax Ctee; hon auditor Barbarian FC, memb Old Leysian Lodge; FCA; *Recreations* chess, rambling, music, financial markets; *Style*— Ian Till, Esq; 21 Hamilton Way, Acomb, York, N Yorks; Shepherd Building Gp Ltd, Blue Bridge Lane, York, N Yorks

TILL, Ven Michael Stanley; s of Stanley Brierley Till (d 1985), of Sunderland, and Charlotte Mary, *née* Pearse; *b* 19 Nov 1935; *Educ* Brighton Hove and Sussex GS, Lincoln Coll Oxford (BA), Westcott House Cambridge; *m* 5 Oct 1965, Theresa Sybil Henriette (Tessa), da of Capt Stephen Wentworth Roskill, CBE, DSC, RN (d 1982), of Cambridge; 1 s (Tobias b 1969), 1 da (Sophie Elizabeth b 1971); *Career* Nat Serv 2 Lt RASC 1955-57; asst curate St Johns St Johns Wood 1964-67, chaplain Kings Coll Cambridge 1967-70, dean and fell Kings Coll Cambridge 1970-81, vicar All Saints Fulham 1981-86, rural dean Hammersmith and Fulham 1982-86, archdeacon of Canterbury 1986-; *Recreations* painting, walking, building; *Style*— The Ven the Archdeacon of Canterbury; Chillenden Chambers, 29 The Precincts, Canterbury, Kent CT1 2EP (☎ 0227 463036)

TILLARD, Maj Gen Philip Blencowe; CBE (1973, OBE 1967); s of Brig John Arthur Stuart Tillard, OBE, MC (d 1975), and Margaret Penelope, *née* Blencowe (d 1966); *b* 2 Jan 1923; *Educ* Winchester, Staff Coll Camberley 1966, Jt Servs Staff Coll 1962; *m* 21 March 1953, Patricia Susan (d 21 June 1988), da of Leslie William Rose Robertson (d 1957), of Snitterfield, Warwicks; 3 s (James b 1954, Andrew b 1956, Richard b 1961), 1 da (Melinda b 1963); *Career* WWII cmmnd KRRC 1942, serv 11 Bn (Syria, Italy, Greece) 1943-45, ADC to GOC 2 Div and Army Cdr Malaya 1946, transferred to 13/18 Royal Hussars 1947; served: Libya, Malaya, 1950 (despatches) and 1960, Adj Warwicks Yeo 1951-53, BAOR 1954-55 and 1961-62, 13/18 Hussars 1964-66, DAQMG (ops) 2 Div 1957-59, GSO2 Int WO 1963, cmd GSO1 Princ Admin Offrs' Secretariat MOD 1966-67, Brig cdr RAC 3 Div Tidworth 1967-69, dep dir Army Trg WO 1970-73, Maj-Gen COS HQ BAOR 1973-76; asst/actg dir resort servs Brighton Borough Cncl 1977-84 (asst to chief exec 1985-87); pres Chailey Sports Assoc 1975-, chm East Sussex Br Field Sports So 1988-; ADC to HM The Queen 1970-73; *Books* Tillard Report on RMA Sandhurst (1972), Suffield Report on setting up Army tank training area in Canada; *Recreations* family, shooting and country pursuits, estate; *Clubs* Farmers, Sussex; *Style*— Maj-Gen P B Tillard, CBE; Church House, North Chailey, nr Lewes, E Sussex BN8 4DA (☎ 082572 2759)

TILLER, Rev John; s of Harry Maurice Tiller, and Lucille Tiller; *b* 22 June 1938; *Educ* St Albans Sch, Christ Church Oxford (MA), Bristol Univ (MLitt); *m* 5 Aug 1961, Ruth Alison, da of Charles Authur Watson (d 1966); 2 s (Andrew b 1964, Jonathan b 1967), 1 da (Rachel b 1965); *Career* lectr Trinity Coll Bristol 1967-73, p-in-c Christ Church Bedford 1973-78, chief sec advsy cncl for the Church's Miny 1978-84, chllr and canon residentiary Hereford Cath 1984; *Books* A Strategy for the Church's Ministry (1983), The Gospel Community (1987); *Style*— The Rev Canon John Tiller; Canon's House, 3 St John St, Hereford HR1 2NB (☎ 0432 265 659)

TILLEY, Clifford James; CBE (1981); s of Henry James Tilley (d 1952), of Burnham on Sea, Somerset, and Zenobia Ruth Tilley (d 1959); *b* 23 Oct 1911; *Educ* Wycliffe Coll, St John's Coll Oxford (BA); *m* 1936, Ingeborg Hildegard Erna, da of Dr Heinrich Hoepker (d 1958), of Berlin; 2 s (Christopher, Stephen); *Career* WWII Maj RA AA Cmd 1939-44, Staff Coll Camberley 1944, HQ Allied Land Forces Norway 1945; chm Willett & Son (Corn Merchants) Ltd Bristol 1962-; pres: Grain & Feed Trade Assoc London 1976-77, Bourse de Commerce Européenne Strasbourg 1976-78, Comité du Commerce des Céréales et des Aliments du Bétail de la Communauté Européenne Brussels 1978-79 and 1981-83 (hon pres 1983); *Recreations* travel; *Style*— Clifford Tilley, Esq, CBE; 17 Dennyview Rd, Abbots Leigh, Bristol BS8 3RD (☎ 027 581 2307); office: 51 Queen Sq, Bristol BS1 4LJ (☎ 0272 262231; telex 44169)

TILLEY, John Vincent; MP (Lab) Lambeth Central April 1978-; *b* 1941,June; *Career* memb Lambeth Police Monitoring Gp 1981-82; oppn front bench spokesman Home Affrs 1981-82 (sacked for opposing official Lab policy on Falklands crisis); fought Kensington Oct and Nov 1974; former memb Wandsworth Borough Cncl; memb: NUJ,

Co-Op Pty, Fabian Soc; *Style*— John Tilley Esq, MP; House of Commons, SW1A 0AA

TILLING, (George) Henry Garfield; s of late T G Tilling; *b* 24 Jan 1924; *Educ* Hardye's Sch Dorchester, Univ Coll Oxford; *m* 1956, Margaret Meriel, da of Rear Adm Sir Alexander Davidson McGlashan, KBE, CB, DSO (d 1976); 2 s, 2 da; *Career* Capt Dorsetshire Regt NW Europe; Post Off: asst princ 1948, princ 1953, private sec to PMG 1964, dep dir of fin 1965, dir Eastern Postal Regn 1967, the sec 1973, dir postal ops 1975, chm Scottish Postal Bd 1977-84; CStJ 1986; *Recreations* orders and medals, heraldry, uniforms; *Style*— Henry Tilling, Esq; Standpretty, Gorebridge, Midlothian, EH23 4QG (☎ 0875 22409)

TILLOTSON, Maj-Gen Henry Michael; CB (1983), CBE (1976, OBE 1970, MBE 1956); s of Henry Tillotson (d 1967), of Keighley, W Yorks, and May Elizabeth (d 1977); *b* 12 May 1928; *Educ* Chesterfield Sch, RMA Sandhurst; *m* 1956, Angela Jane Wadsworth Shaw, da of Capt Bertram Wadsworth Shaw, TD (d 1978), of Swanland, E Yorks; 2 s, 1 da; *Career* cmmnd E Yorks Regt 1948; served: Austria 1948-50, Germany 1951-52, Indo-China 1953, Malaya 1953-56, Germany 1956-57 and 1961-63, Malaysia 1964-65, S Arabia 1965-67, Cyprus 1970-71, Hong Kong 1974-75, COS UN Force Cyprus 1976-78, Maj-Gen 1980, COS to C-in-C UK Land Forces 1980-83, Col Prince of Wales's Own Regt of Yorks 1979-86; regnl dir SE Asia Int Mil Servs Ltd 1983-86; res dir Army Quarterly & Def Journal 1987; *Recreations* travel, birds, listening to music; *Clubs* Army & Navy; *Style*— Maj-Gen H M Tillotson, CB, CBE; c/o Lloyds Bank, 16 St James's St, London SW1A 1EY

TILLY, John; s of Charles Selby Tilly, Park House, Greatham, Hartlepool, and Allison, *née* MacFarlane; *b* 22 April 1940; *Educ* Repton Sch, Coll of Law Guildford; *m* 27 Feb 1965, Veronica Evelyn, da of Harold Pallister (d 1965), of Cambridge Rd, Middlesbrough; 1 s (Nicholas Charles b 1966), 1 da (Kate Fiona b 1969); *Career* slr 1972, dir The Hartlepools Water Co 1975, Notary Public 1970; pres Hartlepool Law Soc 1982 (memb 1972), memb Soc of Prov Notaries 1970; *Recreations* farming; *Style*— John Tilly, Esq; York Chambers, York Rd, Hartlepool (☎ 0429 264 101, fax 0429 274 796, telex 58349)

TILLY, Brig (Alfred) John; CBE (1953), DL (Cornwall 1961); s of Alfred Tilly (d 1937), of Henleaze Gdns, Westbury, Bristol, and Elizabeth, *née* Trounson (d 1952); *b* 27 August 1909; *Educ* Clifton, Sandhurst; *m* 22 Aug 1936, Joy Viola (d 1986), da of William Arthur Jeboult (d 1947); 2 da (Vanessa, Rosemary); *Career* cmmnd 2 DCLI 1930, Staff Coll Camberley 1940, Bde Maj 136 Int Bde 1940, DAAG 1 Corps 1940, instr Staff Coll 1940, 2 i/c 5 DCLI 1942, GSO1 combined ops 1943, 2 i/c 8 Para 1944, Co 12 Air Ldg Bn Devons 1944, Co 6 Royal Welsh Para 1945 (despatches NW Europe 1945), Jt Servs Staff Coll 1947, AAG WO 1948, instr Jt Servs Staff Coll, GSO1 Br Troops Egypt 1950, Cdr Quetta Staff Coll (Pakistan) 1951, Cdr 31 lorried Inf Bde 1954 Brig AQ 1 Corps 1956; TA sec Cornwall 1958, dep sec Western WX TAVR Assoc 1965-74; *Recreations* music, painting, horology, swimming, tennis; *Style*— Brig John Tilly, CBE, DL; Moonsgreen, Elysian Fields, Sidmouth, Devon EX10 8UH

TILLYER, Graham Ernest; s of Ernest Horace Tillyer (d 1983), of Exeter, and Betty Alice, *née* Toms; *b* 23 Sept 1939; *Educ* Exeter Sch, Univ of Manchester (BSc); *m* 27 Feb 1965, Margaret Hazel, da of John Farbon Moultrie, CBE, JP, of Hornchurch, Essex; 3 da (Elizabeth Margaret b 1965, Anne Charlotte b 1967, Sarah Louise b 1971); *Career* M1 motorway work with Sir Owen Williams & Ptnrs, bridge design 1961-64, supervision of construction 1965-68, design of cement works, tunnels, railway, off devpts Oscar Faber Partnership 1969-70 and 1974-77, supervision of construction of int telephone exchange Mondial House City of London Property Servs Agency 1971-74, project engrg and design of works for aviation fuel distrib on behalf of MOD and BP; Liveryman Worshipful Co of Bakers 1972; MICE 1967, memb Inst of Highways and Transportation 1969; *Recreations* sailing, horticulture, foreign travel; *Clubs* Old Etonian; *Style*— Graham Tillyer, Esq; 5 Ben Austins, West Common, Redbourn, Herts AL3 7DR (☎ 058285 4639); Lord Alexander House, Hemel Hempstead, Herts HP1 1ES (☎ 0442 218862)

TILNEY, Dame Guinevere (Lady Tilney); DBE (1984); yst da of Sir Alfred Hamilton Grant, 12 Bt, KCSI, KCIE (d 1937); *b* 8 Sept 1916; *Educ* Westonbirt Girls Sch; *m* 1, 19 Feb 1944, Capt K Lionel Hunter, Royal Canadian Dragoons (d 1947); 1 s; m 2, 3 June 1954, Sir John Tilney, *qv*; *Career* former 2 Offr WRNS; former DL Lancs (later Merseyside); memb BBC Gen Advsy Cncl 1967-75, pres Nat Cncl of Women of GB 1968-70, chm Women's Nat Cmmn 1969-71, Br rep of UN Status of Women Cmmn 1970-73, co-chm Women Caring Tst 1972-75; served in private and political off of Rt Hon Margaret Thatcher 1975-83; *Recreations* embroidery, reading, theatre; *Style*— Dame Guinevere Tilney, DBE; 3 Victoria Sq, London SW1 (☎ 01 828 8674)

TILNEY, James Frederick; s of Maximilian James Eccles Tilney (d 1938), of Watford, Herts, and Elaine Amy Muriel, *née* Griffin (d 1967); *b* 30 June 1910; *Educ* Clifton, UCL; *m* 15 March 1941, Angela Margaret Mary, da of Rev Christopher Watson (d 1968), of Malvern; 1 s (Hugh b 1943); *Career* WWII Lt Cdr RNVR 1940-45 served Admty and Italy; asst mangr Edmundons Electricity Corpn, jr ptnr GH Buckle & Ptnrs 1947-65, fndr ptnr Tilney Simmons & Ptnrs, consltg mech and electrical engrs 1965-78; contrib papers on engrg servs to learned jnls; *Recreations* fly fishing, yachting; *Clubs* Fly Fishers; *Style*— James Tilney, Esq; Old School House, Easton, Winchester (☎ 096 278 487)

TILNEY, Sir John Dudley Robert Tarleton; TD, JP (Liverpool 1946); yr s of Col R H Tilney, DSO, of Tattenhall, Cheshire; *b* 1907; *Educ* Eton, Magdalen Coll Oxford; *m* 3 June 1954, Dame Guinevere, DBE, *qv*, wid of Lionel Hunter, and da of Sir Alfred Hamilton Grant, 12 Bt, KCSI, KCIE (d 1937); 1 step s; *Career* WWII served 59 (4 W Lancs) Medium Regt RA and 11 Medium Regt (despatches, Croix de Guerre with Gilt Star 1945), Lt-Col 1947, Col 1961, Cdr 359 (4 W Lancs) Medium Regt RA (TA) 1947-49, formerly Hon Col 470 (3 W Lancs) LAA Regt RA (TA); former memb Utd Stock Exchange; MP (C) Liverpool Wavertree 1950-74; PPS to: sec state for War 1951-55, PMG 1957-59, min Tport 1959; chm Inter-Parly Union 1959-62, parly under-sec State Cwlth Relations Off 1962-63 and for Cwlth Relations and Colonies 1963-64, memb exec ctee Nat Union of Cons and Unionist Assocs 1965-74, tres Cwlth Parly Assoc UK 1968-70, memb select ctee on Foreign Affrs and Def sub-ctees 1971-74; chm Airey Neave Meml Tst until 1983; memb Cncl Imperial Soc Kts Bachelor 1978-89, Legion of Honour 1960; pres Assoc of Lancastrians in London 1980-81; kt 1973; *Clubs* Pratt's, Liverpool Racquet; *Style*— Sir John Tilney, TD, JP; 3 Victoria Square, London SW1 (☎ 01 828 8674)

TILSON, Joseph Charles (Joe); s of Frederick Albert Edward Tilson (d 1973), and Ethel Stapley Louise, *née* Saunders (d 1982); *b* 24 August 1928; *Educ* St Martins Sch of Art, RCA, Br Sch at Rome; *m* 2 Aug 1955, Joslyn, da of Alistair Morton (d 1963); 1 s (Jake b 1958), 2 da (Anna b 1959, Sophy b 1965); *Career* RAF 1946-49; painter, sculptor, printmaker; worked in Italy and Spain 1955-59; visiting lectr 1962-63: Slade Sch of Art, Kings Coll London, Durham Univ; Teacher Sch of Visual Arts NY 1966, visiting lectr Staatliche Hochschule für Bildende Kunste Hamburg 1971-72; memb Arts Panel and Cncl 1966-71, exhibitions incl Venice Biennale 1964; work at: Marlborough Gallery 1966, Waddington Galleries; retrospective exhibitions: Boymans Van Beuningen Museum Rotterdam 1973, Vancouver Art Gallery 1979, Volterra 1983; Biennele prizes Krakow 1974 (Ljubljana 1985), subject of TV films 1963 (1968 and 1974); ARCA 1955, ARA 1985; *Recreations* planting trees; *Style*— Joe Tilson, Esq; c/o Waddington Galleries, 11 Cork St, London W1X PD (☎ 01 437 8611/ 01 439 6262, fax 01 734 4146, telex 266772)

TIMBURY, Dr Morag Crichton; da of William McCulloch (d 1975), of Glasgow, Scotland, and Dr Esther Sinclair, *née* Hood (d 1981); *b* 29 Sept 1930; *Educ* St Bride's Sch Helensburgh, Univ of Glasgow (MB, MD, PhD); *m* 5 Oct 1954, Dr Gerald Charles (d 1985), s of Montague Timbury (d 1980), of Glasgow; 1 da (Judith Susan (Mrs Sawyer) b 16 Nov 1959); *Career* sr lectr reader in virology Inst of Virology Glasgow, prof bacteriology Univ of Glasgow Royal Infirmary 1978-88, head regnl virus laboratory Ruchill Hosp Glasgow 1983-88, dir Central Public Health Laboratory Colindale London 1988-; FRSE, FRCPath, FRCP (Glasgow); memb: BMA, Soc for Gen Microbiology; *Books* Notes on Medical Virology (eighth edn 1986), Notes on Medical Bacteriology (second edn 1986); *Recreations* reading, fortified houses & castles, military history; *Clubs* Royal Soc of Med; *Style*— Dr Morag Timbury; 9-2 Antrim Grove, Belsize Park, London NW3 4XR (☎ 01 722 5588); St Rules, South St, Elie, Fife; Central Public Health Laboratory, 61 Colindale Ave, London NW9 5HT (☎ 01 200 4400, fax 01 200 7874, telex 8953942 DEFEND G)

TIMMINS, John Bradford; OBE (1973), TD (1968 and Bar 1974), JP 1987; s of Capt John James Timmins (d 1972); *b* 23 June 1932; *Educ* Dudley GS Worcs, Aston Univ Birmingham (MSc); *m* 1956, Jean, *née* Edwards; 5 s, 1 da; *Career* Col TA; ADC to HM The Queen 1975-80, Hon Col 75 Engr Regt 1980-; civil engr and chartered builder, chm Warburton Properties Ltd 1973-; chm Greater Manchester Co Ctee TAVRA 1980-88, vice-pres TA & VRA for NW England and IOM 1987-; KStJ 1988, co pres Order of St John 1988-, High Sheriff Co of Gtr Manchester 1986-87, former cdre Manchester Cruising Assoc; *Recreations* gardening, sailing (yacht 'Blue Octopus'); *Clubs* Army and Navy, Manchester Literary and Philosophical, RE; *Style*— Col John Timmins, OBE, TD, JP; The Old Rectory, Warburton, Lymm, Ches

TIMMS, The Ven George Boorne; s of George Timms (d 1936), and Annie Elizabeth, *née* Boorne (d 1939); *b* 4 Oct 1910; *Educ* Derby Sch, St Edmund Hall Oxford (MA), Coll of the Resurrection Mirfield; *Career* clerk in Holy Orders; deacon 1935, priest 1936; curacies St Mary Magdalen Coventry 1935-38, St Bartholomew Reading 1938-49, Oxford Diocesan Inspr of schs 1944-49, sacrist Southwark Cath 1949-52, vicar St Mary the Virgin Primrose Hill 1952-65, rural dean Hampstead 1959-65, prebendary St Paul's Cath 1964-71, proctor in convocation: 1955-59, 1965-70, 1974-80; dir ordination trg and examining chaplain to Bishop of London 1965-81, archdeacon Hackney 1971-81 (emeritus 1981-); pres Sion Coll 1980-81, chm Alcuin Club 1968-87; chm and dir The English Hymnal Co Ltd 1968-; *Books* Dixit Cranmer (1946), The Liturgical Seasons (1965), The Cloud of Witnesses (1982), ed The New English Hymnal (1986); *Style*— The Ven George B Timms; Cleve Lodge, Minster-in-Thanet, Ramsgate, Kent CT12 4BA (☎ 0843 821777)

TIMMS, Neil Richard Frederick Charles; s of Maj John Charles Timms, OBE, of The Old Rectory, Sutton Benger, Wilts, and Margaret Hazel, *née* Roberts; *b* 23 April 1949; *Educ* Forest GS Stockport, St Catharine's Coll Cambridge (MA); *m* 23 Dec 1983 (m dis 1987), Yolande Pelly Victoria, *née* Sziedlar; 2 da (Georgina b 1984, Victoria b 1986); *Career* barr Inner Temple 1974, practises SE circuit, memb MO circuit; *Style*— Neil Timms, Esq; 6 Kings Bench Walk, Temple, London EC4 (☎ 01 353 9507, fax 01 583 2033 Groups 2 & 3)

TIMPSON, John Harry Robert; OBE (1987); s of John Hubert Victor Timpson (d 1955), and Caroline Willson (d 1970); *b* 2 July 1928; *Educ* Merchant Taylors'; *m* 1951, Muriel Patricia, da of Albert Edward Whale (d 1962); 2 s (Jeremy, Nicholas); *Career* reporter Eastern Daily Press 1951-59, radio and TV reporter BBC News 1959-70, co-presenter Today programme Radio 4 1970-86, chm Any Questions? Radio 4 1984-87; *Books* Today and Yesterday (1976), The Lighter Side of Today (1983), The John Timpson Early Morning Book (1986), Timpson's England - A Look Beyond The Obvious (1987); Today and Yesterday (1976), The Lighter Side of Today (1983), The John Timpson Early Morning Book (1986), Timpson's England - A Look Beyond The Obvious (1987); *Recreations* enjoying Norfolk; *Clubs* Durrants (Old Merchant Taylors' Soc); *Style*— John Timpson, Esq, OBE; The Ark Cottage, Wellingham, King's Lynn, Norfolk

TIMPSON, Lady Selina Catherine; *née* Meade; da of 6 Earl of Clanwilliam; *b* 1950; *m* 1972, Nicholas George Lawrence Timpson, gs of Sir George Reginald Houstoun-Boswall, 4 Bt (d 1914); 1 s (Lawrence b 1974), 1 da (Catherine b 1979); *Style*— Lady Selina Timpson; Ardington Croft, Wantage, Oxon

TIMSON, Mrs Rodney; Penelope Anne Constance; *see*: Keith, P A C

TINDALE, Lawrence Victor Dolman; CBE (1971); s of John Stephen Tindale, and Alice Lilian Tindale; *b* 24 April 1921; *Educ* Latymer Upper Sch; *m* 1946, Beatrice Mabel; 1 s, 1 da; *Career* CA; chm: C & J Clark Ltd, Edbro plc; dep chm 3i Gp plc; dir: BTG, Polly Peck Int plc; *Recreations* opera lover; *Clubs* Reform, St James's (Manchester); *Style*— Lawrence Tindale, Esq, CBE; 3 Amyand Park Gardens, Twickenham, Middx TW1 3HS (☎ 01 892 9457); office: 91 Waterloo Road, London SE1 8XP (☎ 01 928 7822, telex 917844)

TINDALE, Patricia Randall; da of Thomas John Tindale (d 1986), and Princess May, *née* Uttin (d 1986); *b* 11 Mar 1926; *Educ* Blatchington Ct Sch, Architectural Assoc Sch of Architecture (AA Dip); *Career* architect; Miny of Educn: welsh dept 1949-50, devpt gp 1951-61; Miny of Housing and Local Govt R & D Gp 1961-72; DOE: head bldg regulations professional div 1972-74, head housing devpt directorate, dir central unit of the built environment 1980-81, chief architect 1982-86; architectural conslt 1986-, chair Housing Design Awards 1986-, assessor Times RIBA Community Enterprise Scheme; RIBA 1950; *Books* Housebuilding in the USA (1965); *Recreations* weaving, sailing; *Clubs* Reform; *Style*— Miss Patricia Tindale; 34 Crescent Grove, London SW4 7AH (☎ 01 622 1926)

TINDALL, Gillian Elizabeth; da of D H Tindall; *b* 4 May 1938; *Educ* Oxford univ (BA, MA); *m* 1963, Richard G Lansdowne; 1 s; *Career* novelist/biographer/historian; freelance journalist; occasional articles and reviews for: The Observer, Guardian, New Statesman, London Evening Standard, The Times, Encounter, New Society; also occasional broadcasts for the BBC; *Books* novels: No Name in the Street (1959), The Water and the Sound (1961), The Edge of the Paper (1963), The Youngest (1967), Someone Else (1969, second Edn 1975), Fly Away Home (1971, Somerset Maugham Award 1972), The Traveller and His child (1975), The Intruder (1979), Looking Forward (1983), To the City (1987); short stories: Dances of Death (1973), The China Egg and Other Stories (1981); biography: The Born Exile (George Gissing, 1974); other non-fiction: A Handbook on Witchcraft (1965), The Field Beneath (1977), City of Gold: the biography of Bombay (1981), Rosamond Lenmann: an Appreciation (contribution 1985), Architecture of the British Empire (1986); *Recreations* keeping house, for travel; *Style—* Ms Gillian Tindall; c/o Curtis Brown Ltd, 162-168 Regent Street, London, W1

TINDLE, David; s of Ernest Edwin Cook (d 1975), and Dorothy, *née* Smith (who m 2, 1946, William Tindle, and d 1974); assumed surname of Tindle 1946; *b* 29 April 1932; *Educ* Coventry Secdy Mod Sch, Coventry Sch of Art; *m* 3 Jan 1969, Janet Freda, da of Felix Trollope (d 1988); 1 s (Nathan b 1975), 2 da (Saskia b 1970, Charlotte b 1972); *Career* artist: visiting tutor many art schs 1956-, tutor RCA 1972-83; Ruskin Master of Drawing and Fine Art Oxford 1985-87 (MA 1985); many one man exhibitions incl: Piccadilly Gallery 1954-83, Coventry City Art Gallery 1957, Galerie du Tours San Francisco 1964, Northern Art Gallery 1972, Fischer Fine Art 1985 and 1989, (also important one man show at Gallery XX Hamburg: 1974, 1977, 1980 and 1985); represented in exhibitions: Royal Acad 1954, 1968, 1970-83 (Winne Johnson Wax Award 1983), Salon de a Jeune Peinture (Paris) 1967, Internationale Biennale of Realist Art (Bologna) 1967; work represented at: The Tate Gallery, The Arts Cncl, Chantrey Bequest DOE, London Museum, De Beers Collection, Royal Acad, Nat Portrait Gallery etc; designed stage set for Tchaikovsky's Iolanta Aldeburgh Festival 1988; hon fell St Edmund Hall Oxford 1988; ARA 1973, RA 1979, FRCA 1981, RE (1988), hon FRCA 1983; *Style—* David Tindle, Esq, RA, RE; 56A Leam Terrace, Leamington Spa CV31 1DE; Studio Flat 1, 61 Holly Walk, Leamington Spa, Warwickshire CV32 4JG; c/o Fischer Fine Art Ltd, 30 King St, St James's, London SW1 (☎ 01 839 3942)

TINDLE, Ray Stanley; CBE (1987, OBE 1974); s of John Robert Tindle (d 1975), and Maud Bilney (d 1952); *b* 8 Oct 1926; *Educ* Torquay GS, Strand Sch; *m* 8 Oct 1949, Beryl Julia, da of David Charles Ellis (d 1968); 1 s (Owen b 1956); *Career* Capt Devonshire Regt 1944-47, served Far East; chm: Tindle Newspapers Ltd, Surrey Advertiser Newspaper Hldgs Ltd; dir Guardian & Manchester Evening News Ltd and 36 other newspaper cos; fndr Tindle Enterprise Centres for the Unemployed 1984, tres Newspaper Soc (pres 1971-72); memb: Monopolies and Mergers Cmmn Newspaper Panel, cncl of Cwlth Press Union; vice-pres Newspaper Press Fund; Master Worshipful Coo of Stationers and Newspaper Makers 1985-86; *Recreations* veteran cars, georgian silver; *Style—* Ray Tindle, Esq, CBE; Devonshire House, 92 West St, Farnham, Surrey GU9 7EN; Tindle Newspapers Ltd, 114 West St, Farnham, Surrey (☎ 0252 725224, fax 0252 724951)

TINHAM, Alan Clement John; s of Victor Robert Sydney Tinham (d 1964), of Broadstairs, Kent, and Ethel Mabel, *née* Clements (d 1985); *b* 25 Jan 1948; *Educ* Chatham House GS Ramsgate; *m* 27 Sept 1969, Margaret Catherine, da of John Handford, of Broadstairs, Kent; 1 s (Richard b 1975), 3 da (Rebecca b 1973, Victoria b 1979, Ruth b 1987); *Career* managing ptnr Margate branch of Reeves & Neylan CAs; FCA, ATII; *Recreations* windsurfing, sea angling; *Style—* Alan Tinham, Esq; Spindrift, Marine Drive, Kingsgate, Broadstairs, Kent CT10 3LU (☎ 0843 63450); Reeves and Neylan, Cecil Sq House, Cecil Sq, Margate, Kent (☎ 0843 227937)

TINKER, Dr (Philip) Bernard Hague; s of Philip Tinker (d 1978), and Gertrude, *née* Hague (d 1977); *b* 1 Feb 1930; *Educ* Rochdale, Sheffield Univ (BSc, PhD), Oxford Univ (MA, DSc); *m* 27 Aug 1955, Maureen Tinker; 1 s (John Philip b 1956), 1 da (Amanda Jane b 1960); *Career* overseas res serv 1955-62, Rothamsted Experimental Station 1962-65, lectr in soil sci Oxford Univ 1965-71, prof of agric botany Leeds Univ 1971-77, (head of soils and dep dir 1977-85), experimental station dir of sci NERC 1985-; FIBiol 1976, FRSC 1985, memb Norwegian Acad of Sci 1987; *Books* Solute Movement in the Root Soil System (1977), Endomycorrhizas (1975), Advances in Plant Nutrition (vol I 1984, vol II 1986, vol III 1988); *Recreations* gardening, map collecting; *Style—* Dr Bernard Tinker; The Glebe House, Broadwell, nr Lechlade, Glos GL7 3QS (☎ 034 786 436); Natural Environment Research Council, Polaris House, Swindon, Wilts (☎ 0793 411500, fax 0793 411502)

TINLEY, Gervase Edmund Newport; s of Robert Gervase William Newport Tinley; *b* 16 June 1930; *Educ* HMS Worcester; *m* 1965, Jean Lengden, *née* Allen; 2 s, 2 da; *Career* served MN 1946-51 and 1956-58; schoolmaster 1959-60; dir: Stewart Wrightson Assur Conslts 1973-, Army Dependants Assur Tst 1973-, Naval Dependents Income & Assur Tst 1976-; chm Electoral Reform Soc 1979- (dep chm 1977); dep chm: Centurion Housing Assoc 1980-, Cromwell Assoc; master mariner; fell Pensions Mgmnt Inst, FBIM; *Clubs* Reform, Mensa; *Style—* Gervase Tinley Esq; Kingston Bridge House, Church Grove, Kingston Upon Thames, Surrey; office: Kingston Bridge House, Church Grove, Kingston-upon-Thames, Surrey KT1 4AG (☎ 01 977 8888)

TINN, James; s of James Tinn, of Consett; *b* 23 August 1922; *Educ* Consett Elementary Sch, Ruskin Coll Oxford, Jesus Coll Oxford; *Career* WWII ground crew RAF 1941-46, teacher and former steelworker Cleveland 1964-74, Teesside Redcar 1974-1983; PPS to: sec state Cwlth (formerly Cwlth Relations) 1965-66, min Overseas Devpt 1966-67; chm Trade Union Gp 1969-71, asst govt whip 1976-79, oppn whip 1979-82, MP (Lab) 1964-87; *Clubs* Utd Oxford and Cambridge; *Style—* James Tinn Esq; 1 Norfolk Rd, Moorside, Consett, Co Durham (☎ 0207 509313)

TINTON, Stephen Christopher Ben; s of Ben Howard Tinton, and Joan Wanda Tinton; *b* 19 July 1948; *Educ* Royal GS High Wycombe, St Catharines Coll Cambridge (BA); *m* 9 Dec 1972, Dr Marilyn Margaret, da of Reginald St George Stead, FRCS, of Highcliffe, Dorset; 1 s (Paul b 28 May 1980), 1 da (Sarah b 26 June 1978); *Career* teacher Dehra Dun India 1967; audit and business advsy ptnr Price Waterhouse 1982- (audit mangr 1976-82); *Recreations* sport, music, theatre; *Clubs* RAC; *Style—* Steve Tinton, Esq; Price Waterhouse, Southwark Towers, 32 London Bridge Street, London SE1 (☎ 01 407 8987, fax 01 378 0647)

TIPPET, Vice-Adm Sir Anthony Sanders; KCB (1984); s of W Tippet and H W Kitley, *née* Sanders; *b* 2 Oct 1928; *Educ* W Buckland Sch Devon; *m* 1950, Lola, *née* Bassett; 2 s, 1 da (1 s decd); *Career* RN 1946, Rear Adm 1979, asst chief of fleet support MOD 1979-81, chief naval supply and secretariat offr 1981-83, flag offr and port adm Portsmouth 1981-83, Vice Adm 1983, chief of fleet support 1983-87; barr Grays Inn 1958; gen mangr Hosps for Sick Children London 1987; memb: RN Sailing Assoc 1986, RN Lay Readers Soc; CBIM; *Style—* Vice Adm Sir Anthony Tippet, KCB; c/o Barclays Bank, 46 North St, Taunton TA1 1LZ

TIPPETT, Sir Michael Kemp; KBE (1966, CBE 1959), OM (1983), CH (1979); s of late Henry William Tippett; *b* 2 Jan 1905; *Educ* Stamford Sch, RCM; *Career* composer; RCM 1923-28, private lessons with KO Morris 1930, dir of music Morley Coll London 1940-51, artistic dir Bath Festival 1969-74, pres London Coll of Music 1983-; imprisoned for 3 months as conscientious objector Wormwood Scrubs 1943, pres Peace Union, hon pres Bath CND; works incl: String Quartets 1-4, Piano Sonatas 1-4, Symphonies 1-4; operas: The Midsummer Marriage 1947-52, King Priam 1958-61, The Knot Garden 1966-70, The Ice Break 1973-76, New Year 1985-88; chorals: A Child of Our Time 1939-41, The Vision of St Augustine 1965, The Mask of Time 1980-82; chamber works: The Blue Guitar 1982, Sonata for Four Horns 1955; brass: Festal Brass with Blues 1983; Hon DMus: Cambridge 1964, Trinity Coll Dublin 1964, Leeds 1965, Oxford 1967, Leicester 1968, Wales 1968, Bristol 1970, London 1975, Sheffield 1976, Birmingham 1976, Lancaster 1977, Liverpool 1981, RCM 1982, Melbourne 1984, Keele 1986, Aberdeen 1987; FRCM 1961; memb: Akademie der Künste Berlin 1976, American Acad of Arts and Letters 1976; Gold Medal Royal Philharmonic Soc 1976, Prix de Composition (Monaco) 1984; Cdr de l'Ordre des Arts et des Lettres (France) 1988; *Books* Moving into Aquarius (1974), Music of the Angels (1980); *Style—* Sir Michael Tippett, KBE, OM, CH; c/o Schott & Co, 48 Great Marlborough St, London W1

TIPPING, Hon Mrs (Catherine Joy); *née* Davies; da of 2 Baron Darwen, of White Lodge, Sandelswood End, Beaconsfield, Bucks, by his w Kathleen Dora; *b* 10 July 1948; *Educ* High Wycombe HS, Cardiff Univ (BA), PGCE; *m* 1, 1970 (m dis 1976), Robert Nienhuis; m 2, 1976, Richard George Tipping; 2 s; *Career* pt/t lectr in english literature and english language; *Recreations* ballet, writing poetry, theatre-going and yoga; *Clubs* Droitwich Poetry Group, Grenville Dance Academy; *Style—* The Hon Mrs Tipping; Coombe Cottage, 44 Worcester Rd, Droitwich, Worcs WR9 8AJ (☎ 0905 775051)

TIPPING, Robert Marsh; s of Harry Neville Derek Tipping, of the Chase, Chigwell Row, Essex, and Anne Marsh, *née* Fletcher; *b* 22 July 1944; *Educ* privately, Chard Sch Chard Somerset; *Career* stockbroker: memb London Stock Exchange 1971-79, ptnr Smith Keen Cutler 1973, membs and clerks panel 1977, advsr to govt and Central Bank Barbados 1979-81, asst lectr Jesus Coll Cambridge 1981, dir of various private cos; Freeman: City of London 1977, Worshipful Co of Pattenmakers 1978; FBISL 1981; *Recreations* fishing, sailing; *Clubs* City Livery, City YC; *Style—* Robert Tipping, Esq; Millers Farm, Grove Lane, Chigwell Row, Essex (☎ 01 500 6596)

TIPTAFT, David Howard Palmer; JP (1972-); s of Capt Paxman Tiptaft, MC, JP (d 1984), of Wentworth, S Yorks, and Irene, *née* Palmer (d 1968); *b* 6 Jan 1938; *Educ* Goldsborough Hall N Yorks, Shrewsbury; *m* 1 June 1963, Jennifer Cherry, da of Gerald Richard Millward (d 1967), of Khartoum; 2 s (Justyn b 30 Sept 1965, Quintin b 19 June 1970), 2 da (Elgiva b 10 March 1964, Genovefa b 20 Dec 1966); *Career* qualified CA 1962, Arthur Young 1961-64, ptnr Tiptaft Smith & King 1966-; chm Don Valley Cons Assoc 1964-75, tres Rother Valley Cons Assoc 1976-83, chm Wentworth Cons Assoc 1983-, Yorks area tres Cons Central Off 1988-; govr Denaby Main Jr Sch, memb redundant churches uses ctee Sheffield Diocese; FCA 1973; *Recreations* flying, tennis, opera (Wagner), horticulture; *Style—* David Tiptaft, Esq, JP; Ashcroft House, Wentworth, nr Rotherham, S Yorks (☎ 0226 742 972); Tiptaft Smith and King, Waveney House, Adwick Rd, Mexborough, S Yorks (☎ 0709 582991)

TIRARD, Lady Nesta; *née* FitzGerald; da of 8 Duke of Leinster; *b* 1942; *m* 1977, Philip Tirard; 2 da; *Style—* Lady Nesta Tirard; Coolnabrune, Borris, Co Carlow, Ireland

TITCHENER, John Lanham Bradbury; CMG (1955), OBE (1947); s of Alfred Titchener (d 1956); *b* 28 Nov 1912; *Educ* City of London Sch, RCM; *m* 1958, Britta Frederikke Marian, da of Carl Bendixsen (hon consul); 2 step s; *Career* BBC TV prodr 1938-39, talks prodr 1939-43; seconded to HM Armed Forces 1943-46; HM Diplomatic Serv 1947-57, cncllr 1954-57 (resigned); dir: Int Insur Service (Iran) 1974-79, Hamworthy Engrg (Iran) 1974-79, Hagen Int A/S; *Recreations* music, gardening, fishing; *Clubs* Travellers'; *Style—* Lanham Titchener, Esq, CMG, OBE; 3 Impasse Du Chateau, 06190 Roquebrune Village, CM France (☎ France 93 35 07 85); Weysesgade 13, 2100 Copenhagen (☎ 01 200 871)

TITCHENER-BARRETT, Lt-Col Sir Dennis Charles; TD (1953); s of Charles William George Barrett (d 1974), and Edith Lambert Titchener (d 1964); *m* 1940, Joan Florence, da of Albert Robert Wilson, of Coleherne Ct, Old Brompton Rd, London SW5; 1 s (Robert), 3 da (Georgina, Caroline, Jacqueline); *Career* WWII RA 1939-46, cmd 415 Coast Regt RA (TA) 1950-56, memb Kent T & A AFA 1950-56; ILEA sch govr 1956-73; memb: Gtr London Central Valuation Panel 1964-75, Cons Bd of Finance 1968-75, Cons Policy Gp for Gtr London 1975-78, Cons Central Cncl 1968-78, Gen Purposes and Nat Exec Ctees 1968-75; tres Gtr London Area Cons and Unionist Assoc 1968-75, chm Gtr London area Cons & Unionists Assoc 1975-78, vice pres Nat Soc Cons Agents Gtr London Area 1975-, chm South Kensington Cons Assoc 1955-58 (pres and tstee), memb Kensington Cons Assoc 1975-; RUSI 1947-; underwriting memb Lloyds 1977-; High Sheriff Gtr London 1977-78, vice pres Greater London Area 1978-, chm Woodstock (London) Ltd 1962-89; kt 1981; *Clubs* Carlton; *Style—* Lt-Col Sir Dennis Titchener-Barrett, TD; 8 Launceston Place, London W8 5RL (☎ 01 937 0613)

TITCOMB, (Simon) James; s of Geoffrey Cowley Baden Titcomb (d 1960), of Brighton, and Molly Gwendolyn Titcomb (d 1985); *b* 10 July 1931; *Educ* Brighton Coll; *m* 1957, Ann Constance, da of Gerald Bernard Vokins; 2 s, 1 da; *Career* Lt Nat Serv 1955-57; memb Stock Exchange 1962, ptnr de Zoete & Bevan (Stockbrokers) 1962-76 (sr ptnr 1976-86); dir of public and private companies; FCA, CBIM; *Recreations* golf, tennis, bridge, travel, wild life; *Clubs* Brooks's, City of London; *Style—* James Titcomb, Esq; Plummerden House, Lindfield, Sussex RH16 2QS (☎ 2117); Barclays de Zoete Wedd, Ebbgate House, 25 Swan Lane, London EC4R 3TS (☎ 01 623 2323)

TITMAN, John Edward Powis; CVO, JP (Surrey 1971); s of late Sir George Titman,

CBE, MVO; *b* 23 May 1926; *Educ* City of London Sch; *m* 1953, Annabel Clare, da of late C F Naylor; 2 s; *Career* sec The Lord Chamberlain's Office 1978-, Serjeant at Arms to HM The Queen 1982-; Freeman Worshipful Co of Wax Chandlers (Master 1984); *Clubs* RAC, MCC; *Style*— John Titman, Esq, CVO, JP; Friars Garth, The Parade, Epsom, Surrey (☎ 037 272 2302)

TITTERTON, Prof Sir Ernest William; CMG (1957); s of William Alfred Titterton (d 1962), and Elizabeth Titterton (d 1958); *b* 4 Mar 1916; *Educ* Queen Elizabeth GS Tamworth, Birmingham Univ (BSc, MSc, PhD, DipEd); *m* 1942, Peggy Eileen, da of Capt Alfred Johnson (d 1967); 1 s, 2 da; *Career* nuclear physicist; memb British Mission to USA on Atomic Bomb Devpt 1943-46, sr memb timing gp first atomic bomb test 1945, advsr on instrumentation Bikini Weapon Tests 1946, head electronics div Los Alamos Lab 1946-47, prof of nuclear physics Aust Nat Univ 1950-81, dir Res Sch of Physical Sciences ANU 1965-73; kt 1970; *see Debrett's Handbook of Australia and New Zealand for further details*; *Style*— Prof Sir Ernest Titterton, CMG; P.O. Box 331, Jamison, ACT 2614, Australia (☎ enquiries 515609)

TIVERTON, Viscount; *see*: Giffard, Adam Edward

TIZARD, Prof Barbara Patricia; *née* Parker; da of Herbert Parker, and Elsie, *née* Kirk, sis to His Honour Judge Michael Clynes Parker qv; *b* 16 April 1926; *Educ* St Paul's, Somerville Coll Oxford (BA), Inst of Psychiatry London (PhD); *m* 15 Dec 1947, Prof Jack Tizard (d 1979), s of John Marsh Tizard, of Stratford, NZ; 3 s (William b 3 Jan 1951, John b 10 Dec 1952, d 1983, Martin b 17 Nov 1966, d 1975), 2 da (Jenny b 17 Dec 1955, Lucy b 26 Jan 1968); *Career* co ed Br Jl of Psychology 1975-, memb ed bd Jl Child Psychology and Psychiatry, reader in educn Inst of Educn 1978-80, dir Thomas Coram Res Inst 1980-, prof of educn Univ of London 1982-; former chm Assoc Child Psychology and Psychiatry; Fell Br Psychological Soc; *Publications*: Early Childhood Education (1975), Adoption a Second Chance (1977), Involving Parents in Nursery and Infant Schools (1981), Young Children Learning (with M Hughes, 1984), Young Children at School in the Inner City (with P Blatchford, J Burke, C Farquhar, I Plewis 1988); *Style*— Prof Barbara Tizard; Thomas Coram Research Unit, 41 Brunswick Square, London WC1N 1AZ (☎ 01 278 2424, fax 01 436 2186)

TIZARD, Prof Sir (John) Peter Mills; s of Sir Henry Tizard, GCB, AFC, FRS (d 1959), sometime pres Magdalen Oxford and memb Cncl of Min of Aircraft Production during WWII, Lady (Kathleen Eleanor) Tizard, *née* Wilson (d 1968); *b* 1 April 1916; *Educ* Rugby, Oriel Coll Oxford and Middx Hosp (BM BCh, MRCP, DCH); *m* 1945, Elisabeth Joy, da of Clifford Taylor; 2 s, 1 da; *Career* serv WWII RAMC (Temp Maj); prof paediatrics and fell Jesus Oxford 1972-83, hon conslt children's physician Oxford AHA (teaching) 1972-83, prof of paediatrics Inst Child Health Royal Postgrad Medical Sch London Univ 1964-72, hon conslt children's physician Hammersmith Hosp 1954-72, chm Hammersmith Hosp Medical Ctee 1970-71; , pres Br Paediatric Assoc 1982-85, memb Neonatal Soc 1959- (pres 1975-78), pres HArveian Soc 1977 (memb 1974-), memb Br Paediatric Neurological Assoc; Worshipful Soc of Apothecaries: memb Ct of Assts 1971, Jr Warden 1981-82, Sr Warden 1982-83, Master 1983-84; FRCP, FRSocMed; kt 1982; *Style*— Prof Sir Peter Tizard; Jesus College, Oxford OX1 3DW; Ickenham Manor, Ickenham, Uxbridge, Middx UB10 8QT (☎ Ruislip 32262)

TNYFORD, Donald Henry; s of Henry John Tnyford, of Ferring and Crowborough, Sussex, (d 1982), and Lily Hilda, *née* Ridler (d 1977); *b* 4 Feb 1931; *Educ* Wimbley Co Sch; *Career* Nat Serv educn branch 1949-51; joined Export Credits Guarantee Dept 1949, sr principal (chief underwriter) 1968, asst sec 1972, establishment offr 1976, under sec 1979, chm EC policy co-ordination Gp 1981; *Recreations* gardening, growing daffodils, travel, music; *Style*— Donald Tnyford, Esq; Barbican, London; Ferring, W Sussex; ECGD, Export House, PO Box No 272, 50 Ludgate Hill, London EC4M 7AY (☎ (01) 382 7043)

TOALSTER, John Raymond; s of Chief Petty Offr John Edward Toglster RNVR (ka 1944), and Adeline Enid, *née* Smith; *b* 12 Mar 1941; *Educ* Kingston HS Hull N Humberside, LSE (BSc); *m* 21 Sept 1963, Christine Anne, da of Edward Percival Paget (d 1970); 1 s (Quentin Simon Edward b 1966), 2 da (Rachel Jane b 1969, Bethan Claire b 1981); *Career* lectr econs Univ of Sierra Leone 1964-67, corporate planner Mobil Oil 1967-69, sr analyst (oils) stockbroking 1970-77, corporate fin mangr Kuwait Int Investmt Co 1977-81, energy specialist stockbroking 1982-; dir: Hoare Govett, Security Pacific; FInstPet 1988; private circulation to clients; *Recreations* swimming, sailing, badminton; *Style*— John Taolster, Esq; Fig St Farm, Sevenoaks, Kent (☎ 0732 453357); Hoare Govett, 4 Broadgate, London EC2N 7LE (☎ 01 601 0101, fax 01 256 8500, telex 297 801)

TOBIN, Julian Jacob; s of John Tobin (d 1966), and Georgina Tobin (d 1972); *b* 13 August 1927; *Educ* Great Yarmouth GS, Cambridge and Co HS, Magdalene Coll, Cambridge (MA, LLM); *m* 6 Dec 1959, Jocelyne, da of Bernard Prevezer (d 1958), of 30 Green St, London W1; 1 s (Rupert b 1963), 2 da (Sasha b 1965, Annabel b 1968); *Career* admitted slr 1953; sr ptnr Pritchard Englefield & Tobin 1973-, admitted slr Hong Kong, ptnr Robert W H Wang & Co and Pritchard Englefield & Wang 1983-; elected to Hampstead Borough Cncl 1956-65; chm of various ctees Camden Borough Cncl 1964- (dep ldr of Cons gp: 1968-73, 1974-79, 1985-; ldr of Cons gp 1979-81), tstee Athlone Tst 1979-, govr Univ Coll Sch 1981-87, tres Lib Jewish Synagogue 1984-; special tstee: London Hosps 1981-88, Univ Coll Hosps 1986-; dir Andre Deutsch Ltd 1983-; former chm Hampstead Cons Assoc (now sr tstee), former memb Home Off Ctee on Juveniles and Ctee on Rent Rebates and Rent Allowances DOE; memb nat advsy property ctee Cons Party; *Recreations* reading, watching cricket, opera, music generally; *Clubs* Carlton, Garrick, Savile; *Style*— Julian Tobin, Esq; 18 Eton Villas, Hampstead, London NW3 (☎ (01) 722 8000); Orchard Cottage, Thicket Rd, Houghton, Huntingdon; 23 Great Castle St, London W1 (☎ 01 629 8883, fax 01 493 1891)

TODD, Rev Alastair; CMG (1971); s of Prof James Eadie Todd (d 1949), and Margaret Simpson Johnstone Maybin (d 1940); *b* 21 Dec 1920; *Educ* Fettes Coll Edinburgh, Royal Belfast Academical Inst, Oxford Univ (BA), London Univ (Dip Theol), Salisbury and Wells Theological Coll; *m* 1952, Nancy Hazel, da of Alick Frederick Buyers (d 1947); 2 s (Martin, James), 2 da (Clare, Diana); *Career* Army Service 1940-46, Capt RHA Europe and Far East; Colonial Admin Serv Hong Kong 1946-71, dir of Soc Welfare 1966-68, defence sec 1968-71; vicar St Augustine's Brighton 1977-86; *Recreations* embroidery, walking, travel; *Style*— The Rev Alastair Todd, CMG; 59 Park Avenue, Eastbourne

TODD, Hon Alexander Henry; o s of Baron Todd, OM (Life Peer); *b* 11 Nov 1939; *Educ* The Leys Sch Cambridge, Oriel Coll Oxford (DPhil); *m* 1, 12 May 1967 (m dis), Joan Margaret, da of Frederick Wilbur Koester, of Campbell, Calif, USA; m 2, 3 Oct 1981, Patricia Mary, da of late Brig A Harvey Jones, of Somerford Booths, Cheshire; *Style*— The Hon Alexander Todd; The Chestnuts, Crown Lane, Lower Peover, Knutsford, Cheshire WA16 9QB (☎ 056581 2297)

TODD, Baron (Life Peer UK 1962); Alexander Robertus Todd; OM (1977); el s of Alexander Todd, JP (d 1952), of Glasgow; *b* 2 Oct 1907; *Educ* Allan Glen's Sch Glasgow, Glasgow Univ (DSc), Frankfurt-on-Main Univ (PhD), Oxford Univ (DPhil); *m* 1937, Alison Sarah (d 1987), da of Sir Henry Hallett Dale, OM, GBE, (d 1968); 1 s, 2 da; *Career* prof of chem: Manchester Univ 1938-44, Cambridge Univ 1944-71; master of Christ's Coll Cambridge 1963-78, managing tstee Nuffield Fndn 1950-79 (chm 1973-79), chllr Strathclyde Univ 1964-, chm Croucher Fndn (Hong Kong) 1980-88; FRS 1942 (pres 1975-80); Hon LLD: Glasgow, Melbourne, Edinburgh, Manchester and California; Hon DSc Durham; Hon DLitt Sydney; Nobel Prize for Chemistry 1957; kt 1954; *Recreations* golf; *Style*— The Rt Hon the Lord Todd, OM; 9 Parker St, Cambridge CB1 1JL (☎ 0223 356688)

TODD, Anthony Clive; s of George William Todd (d 1967), and Clarissa, *née* Looker (d 1984); *b* 18 Oct 1928; *Educ* Palmers Grays Essex, UCL (Dip Arch, Dip TP); *m* 13 Aug 1966, Theresa, da of Hugh Kelly, of Co Sligo; 2 s (Andrew b 1967, Richard b 1970); *Career* mil serv: architectural instructor No 3 Army Coll Welbeck Abbey; chartered architect and town planning conslt; ptnr: Howes Jackman & Ptnrs Architects London, Challen Floyd Slaski & Todd Architects London; Freeman of the City of London, memb Worshipful Co of Constructors; RIBA; FRTPI; FFB; *Recreations* music, motor sports; *Style*— Anthony C Todd, Esq; 1 Macaulay Court, Caterham, Surrey CR3 5HS (☎ 0883 42781)

TODD, Daphne Jane (Mrs Driscoll); da of Frank Todd (d 1976), of Whitstable, and Annie Mary, *née* Lord; *b* 27 Mar 1947; *Educ* Simon Langton GS for Girls Canterbury, Slade Sch of Fine Art (DFA, Higher Dip in Fine Art); *m* 31 Aug 1984, Lt-Col (Patrick Robert) Terence Driscoll, s of Patrick Driscoll (d 1979); 1 da (Mary Jane b 12 Nov 1977); *Career* artist; dir of studies Heatherley Sch of Art 1980-86; work in the collections of: Regtl HQ Irish Guards, Cambridge Univ, London Univ, Oxford Univ, Royal Holloway Museum and Art Gallery, Bishop's Palace Hereford, Royal Acad, Nat Portrait Gallery; second prize John Player Portrait Award Nat Portrait Gallery 1983, first prize Oil Painting of the Year Hunting Gp Nat Art Prize Competition 1984; retrospective exhibition Morley Gallery 1989; memb NEAC 1984, RP 1985; *Clubs* Chelsea Arts; *Style*— Miss Daphne Todd; Salters Green Farm, Mayfield, East Sussex TN20 6NP (☎ 089 285 2472)

TODD, George Archibald; s of John Todd (d 1920), of Glasgow, and Margaret Todd (d 1936); *b* 26 August 1904; *Educ* North Kelvinside Sch Glasgow; *m* 6 July 1935, Alice Joan (d 1977), da of William Roberts (d 1950), of London; 1 s (Robert Douglas b 4 June 1936), 1 da Margaret Anne b 7 May 1940); *Career* CA (ret), former ptnr Wrigley Cregan Todd Co (ret 1967), former chm: Brent Manufacturing 1935-69, (dep) Hume Holdings Investmt Tst 1972-74, Industl Funding Tst, Hume Corpn Bankers, Pembertons advertising agents; former sec and chm Amersham and Dist Scottish Assoc; memb Grand Lodge of England; Master Worshipful Co of Turners 1988-89; FRSA, MICAS 1927; *Recreations* gardening; *Clubs* Caledonian; *Style*— George Todd, Esq; Cornercroft, Devonshire Ave, Amersham, Bucks (☎ 0494 727156)

TODD, Hon Hilary Alison; da of Baron Todd, OM (Life Peer); *b* 25 June 1946; *Educ* Perse Sch for Girls Cambridge, Westonbirt, London Acad of Music & Dramatic Art; *Style*— The Hon Hilary Todd

TODD, Sir Ian Pelham; KBE (1989); s of late Alan Herapath Todd, and late Constance Edwards; *b* 23 Mar 1921; *Educ* Sherborne, St Bart's Hosp Med Coll, Toronto Univ (MRCS, LRCP, FRCS, MD, MS, DCH); *m* 25 July 1946, Jean Audrey Ann, da of late James Morton Noble; 2 s (Neil b 1947, Stuart b 1957), 3 da (Jocelyn b 1948, Jane b 1952, Caroline b 1955); *Career* Maj RAMC; conslt surgn King Edward VII Hosp for Offrs, hon consltg surgn St Barts and St Marks Hosps; pres RCS, vice pres Imperial Cancer Res Fund; former pres Med Soc of London; hon memb: Assoc of Surgns of India, Hellenic Surgical Assoc, American Soc Coloproctology; sec Coloproctology RACS; hon: FCS, SA 1986, FACS 1988, FRACS 1988; Star of Jordan 1973; FRGS; *Recreations* music, travel, philately, skiing; *Clubs* RSM; *Style*— Sir Ian P Todd, KBE; 34 Chester Close North, London NW1 4JE (☎ 486 7776)

TODD, James; s of Robert Nicol Todd (d 1959), and Catherina Buchanan, *née* Semple; *b* 3 July 1894; *Educ* John Street Sr Secdy Sch Glagow, Harvard Business Sch; *m* 2 Oct 1953, Isabella Smith Jack, da of John Green (d 1985); 1 s (Jeffrey b 1958), 3 da (Gail b 1960, Julie b 1963, Lindsay b 1966); *Career* RCS 1950-52; dir Lazard Bros & Co Ltd 1977, exec vice pres Korea Merchant Banking Corpn Seoul 1982-86; dir: Lazard Bros & Co Ltd Jersey 1987 (Guernsey 1987), Marchome 1988; ACIB 1963; *Clubs* RAC; *Style*— James Todd, Esq; Old Letton Ct, Letton, nr Hereford; 10 Morgans Walk, Battersea Bridge Rd, London SW11 (☎ 098 17 604); Lazard Brothers & Co Ltd, 21 Moorfields, London EC2 (☎ 01 588 2721)

TODD, John Gordon; s of George Todd, and Janet Brown, *née* Glass; *b* 7 June 1958; *Educ* Stewarts Melville Coll Edinburgh; *Career* Habitat Designs Ltd 1978-79, Wine Importers (Edinburgh) Ltd 1979-80, Scottish Industl & Trade Exhibitions Ltd (currently chief exec and dir) 1980-, Industl & Trade Exhibitions (NI) Ltd 1987-, dir Art in Partnership (Scotland) Ltd 1986-; *Recreations* music, art, friends; *Style*— John Todd, Esq; 46A Blacket Place, Edinburgh, EH9 1RJ (☎ 031 667 2998); Scottish Industrial & Trade Exhibitions Ltd (SITE) 8A Charlotte Sq, Edinburgh EH2 4DR (☎ 031 225 5486, fax 031 226 3848, telex 728117 SELEH G)

TODD, (Thomas) Keith; s of Thomas William Todd, and Cecile Olive Francis, *née* Hefti; *b* 22 June 1953; *m* 19 May 1979, Anne Elizabeth, da of Hilson Adam Henfrie, of Edinburgh; 2 s ((Thomas) Christopher b 1984, Andrew Adam Paul b 1986), 2 da (Fiona Elizabeth b 1980, Nicola Anne b 1982); *Career* chief fin offr Cincinnati Electronics 1981-86; fin dir: The Marconi Co 1986-87, ICL 1987-; FCMA; *Recreations* golf, swimming; *Style*— Keith Todd, Esq; ICL, Bridge House, Putney Bridge, Fulham, London SW6 (☎ 01 788 7272)

TODD, Prof Malcolm; s of Wilfrid Todd (d 1980), of Durham, and Rose Evelyn, *née* Johnson; *b* 27 Nov 1929; *Educ* Henry Smith Sch, Univ of Wales (BA, DLitt), Brasenose Coll Oxford (Dip); *m* 2 Sept 1964, Molly, da of Alexander John Tanner (d 1987), of London; 1 s (Malcolm Richard b 1966), 1 da (Katharine Grace b 1965); *Career* res asst Rheinisches Landesmuseum Bonn 1963-65, reader Univ of Nottingham 1977-79 (lectr 1965-74, sr lectr 1974-77), prof of archaeology Univ of Exeter 1979-, visiting fell All Souls Coll Oxford 1984; vice pres Roman Soc 1984-; memb: Royal

Cmmn on Historical Monuments 1986-, cncl Nat Tst 1986-; FSA 1970, memb German Archaeological Inst 1977; *Books* The Northern Barbarians (1975, fifth edn 1987), Roman Britain (1981, second edn 1985), The South-West To AD 1000 (1987), Britannia (ed, 1984-); *Recreations* reading, writing; *Style*— Prof Malcolm Todd; The University, Exeter, Devon EX4 4QH (☎ 0392 264 351)

TODD, Richard Andrew Palethorpe; s of Maj Andrew William Palethorpe Todd, MC, RAMC, (d 1941), of Clevedon Lodge, Wimborne, Dorset, and Marvilla Rose, *née* Agar-Daly; *b* 11 June 1919; *Educ* Norwood Sch Exeter, Shrewsbury, Queen Elizabeths Wimborne, and privately; *m* 1, 13 Aug 1949 (m dis 1970), Catherine Stewart Crawford, da of William Grant-Bogle (d 1967), of Hyndland Rd, Glasgow; 1 s (Peter Grant Palethorpe b 1952), 1 da (Fiona Margaret Palethorpe b 1956); m 2, 1970, Virginia Anne Rollo, da of Colin Cotterill Rollo Mailer; 2 s (Andrew Richard Palethorpe b 1973, Seumas Alexander Palethorpe b 1977); *Career* WWII; RMC Sandhurst 1940, cmmnd KOYLI 1941, seconded Parachute Regt 1943 served Normandy, GSO3 (ops) 1944 served Battle of the Bulge and Holland, 2 i/c 3 Para Bde in Palestine 1945/46; actor, prodr dir 1937-; entered films 1948 making many Br and American films incl: The Hasty Heart (with Ronald Reagan), Disney's Robin Hood, Rob Roy, The Dam Busters, The Virgin Queen, A Man Called Peter, Yantze Incident, Chase a Crooked Shadow, D-Day the 6th of June, The Longest Day; awarded Br Nat Film Award, Oscar nomination and Hollywood Golden Globe for The Hasty Heart 1950; returned theatre 1965 in An Ideal Husband, fndr dir Truimph Theatre Prodns 1970, led RSC N American tour of The Hollow Crown 1975, many theatre appearances since incl The Business of Murder 1981-88; pres: Henley and Dist Agric Assoc 1963, Thames Valley branch Save The Children Fund 1958-64, Grantham branch Inst of Advanced Motorists; life pres Friends of Smith Hosp Henley; *Books* Caught In The Act (1986), In Camera (1989); *Recreations* shooting, fishing, working; *Clubs* Army & Navy; *Style*— Richard Todd, Esq; Chinham Farm, Faringdon, Oxon SW7 8EZ (☎ 03677 294)

TODD, Rev Dr (Andrew) Stewart; s of William Stewart Todd (d 1977), of Alloa, Clackmannanshire, and Robina Victoria, *née* Fraser (d 1988); *b* 26 May 1926; *Educ* HS of Stirling, Edinburgh Univ (MA, BD), Univ of Basel; *m* 17 Sept 1953, Janet Agnes Brown, da of John Smith, JP, DL, of Woodemailing, Symington, Lanarkshire; 2 s (David b 1956, Philip b 1960), 2 da (Diana b 1955, Jane b 1958); *Career* asst minister St Cuthbert's Edinburgh 1951-52; minister: Symington Lanarkshire 1952-60, N Leith 1960-67, St Machar's Cath Old Aberdeen 1967-; memb Church Hymnary Revision Ctee 1963-73, convenor Gen Assembly's Ctee on Public Worship and Aids to Devotion 1974-78, moderator Aberdeen Presbytery 1980-81, vice convenor Gen Assembly's Panel on Doctrine 1988-; Hon DD Aberdeen Univ 1982; hon pres Church Service Soc, memb Societas Liturgica; *Recreations* music, gardening; *Style*— Rev Dr Stewart Todd; 18 The Chanonry, Old Aberdeen (☎ 0224 483688); Culearn, Balquhidder, Perthshire (☎ 08774 662)

TODD, Col Walter John Cambridge; OBE (1953), TD (1945 and two bars), DL (Cheshire 1975)); s of Ralph Todd (d 1963), of Hartlepool, Co Durham; *b* 2 Oct 1910; *Educ* Durham Sch, St John's Coll Cambridge (MA); *m* 1950, Sheila Gertrude, da of the late Dr A Stewart Macbeth, of Pitlochry, Perthshire; 1 da; *Career* 2 Lt Durham Heavy Regt RA (TA) 1930, WWII served: UK, India, Persia, Iraq; Lt-Col 1945, cmd 349 LAA Regt RA (TA) 1947-52, Bt-Col 1952; cmdt Cheshire Army Cadet Force 1959-67, Hon Col 1968-79; slr 1935, formerly dep clerk of the Peace and dep County slr (Cheshire); TAA & TA & VRA 1947- (successively) of: Cheshire, Lancs and Cheshire, NW of Eng and IOM; chm mgmnt ctee Cheshire Victims of Crimes Support Scheme 1984-86; pres Royal Chester Rowing Club 1988-; *Recreations* rowing, gardening; *Clubs* Army & Navy, Leander; *Style*— Col Walter Todd, OBE, TD, DL; 21 Dee Fords Ave, Chester CH3 5UP (☎ 0244 351170)

TODHUNTER, Michael John Benjamin; s of Brig Edward Joseph Todhunter (d 1976), and Agnes Mary, *née* Swire (d 1975); *b* 25 Mar 1935; *Educ* Eton, Magdalen Coll Oxford (MA); *m* 1959, Caroline Francesca, da of Maj William Walter Dowding (d 1980); 1 s (Charles), 2 da (Nicola, Emily); *Career* 2 Lt 11 Hussars (PAO); banker; dir: PK English Trust Co Ltd; dep chm: Clyde Shipping Co Ltd; dir: James Finlay plc, S H Lock & Co (Hldgs) Ltd, Newbury Racecourse plc; special tstee Great Ormond Street Hosp; *Recreations* shooting; *Clubs* White's, Pratt's, Western Glasgow; *Style*— Michael Todhunter, Esq; The Old Rectory, Farnborough, Wantage, Oxon (☎ Chaddleworth (048 82) 298); The Studio, 4 Lowndes St, London SW1 (☎ 01 235 6421); office: 4 Fore St, London EC2 (☎ 01 920 9120)

TOFIELD, Terence William; s of Herbert Russell Tofield (d 1981), and Mary Josephine (d 1971); *b* 5 July 1936; *Educ* Latymer Upper; *Career* PR dir Rumasa and Augustus Barnett & Son Ltd (now Lawlers Ltd); tstee: City of London Univ, Wine and Spirit Educn Tst; Liveryman Worshipful Co of Distillers; *Recreations* tennis, shooting, skiing; *Clubs* Hurlingham, RAC, Mardens; *Style*— Terence Tofield, Esq; 77 Swan Court, Chelsea Manor St, London SW3 (☎ 01 352 3444); Lionsmead House, Shalbourne nr Malborough, Wilts SN8 8DD; office: 88/92 South St, Dorking, Surrey (☎ 0306 884412 and 0672 870440)

TOLEMAN, Norman Edward (Ted); s of Albert Edward Toleman (d 1966), of Cherry Acre, 2 Courtland Drive, Chigwell, Essex, and Kathleen Eardley, *née* Templeton; *b* 14 Mar 1938; *Educ* Clarke's Ilford Essex; *m* 8 July 1961, Dianne Joan da of George Walter Prior, of Willow Cottage, Hoe, Dereham, Norfolk; 2 s (Gary b 1961, Michael (twin) b 1961); *Career* powerboat racing: Br Nat Champion 1980-83, Euro Champion 1980; 1981 Australian Champion, fifth in American Championship, set new Class 1 World Speed Record of 97.65 mph; 1982: runner-up World Championship, winner London-Calais London race, set new Class 1 World Speed Record of 110.41 mph Lake Windermere; 1983: European Championships Sweden and Italy, raised World Speed Record to 120.95 mph Lake Windermere; conceived and skippered the initial Spirit of Britain Transatlantic Challenge (Virgin) 1985; motor sport: formed Toleman Gp Motorsport 1969, 1 and 2 place Tolemen Gp Motorsport Formula Two Championship 1980, entered Formula One motor racing 1981, 2 position Monaco Grand Prix 1984, entered Paris-Dakar rally to promote Br tech leadership; business acquisition of: A & C McLennan 1969, James Car Deliveries 1973, Samual Eden 1977, Cougar Marine (UK largest vehicle tportation Co) 1980; vice-pres Stowmarket FC; patron racing for BR; Freeman City of London 1984; memb Worshipful Co of Carmen; FBIM; *Recreations* rallying, motor and offshore power racing; *Clubs* Royal Southern YC, Br Racing Drivers; *Style*— Ted Toleman, Esq, JP; Abilene Lodge, Drinkstone Rd, Gedding, Bury St, Edmunds, Suffolk, IP30 0QD (☎ 044 937 831); Toleman House, St Thomas Rd, Brentwood, Essex CM14 4ES (☎ 0277 226 060, fax 0277 220 343, car telephone 0836 720 777, telex 995259)

TOLER, Maj-Gen David Arthur Hodges; OBE (1963), MC (1945), DL (1982); s of Maj Thomas Clayton Toler, JP, DL (d 1940), and Gertrude Marianna, *née* Wilkinson (d 1962); *b* 13 Sept 1920; *Educ* Stowe, Christ Church Oxford (MA); *m* 11 Sept 1951, Judith Mary, da of late Maj James William Garden, DSO, of Foucausie, Grandholm, Aberdeenshire; 1 s (Hugh b 1953), 1 da (Jane b 1955); *Career* WWII 2 Lt Coldstream Gds 1940; served in WW II in N Africa and Italy 1942-45; Regt Adjt Coldstream Guards 1952-54, Bde Maj 4 Guards Bde 1956-57, Adj RMA Sandhurst 1958-60, British liaison offr US Continental Army Cmd (Col) 1960-62, cmd 2 Bn Coldstream Guards 1962-64, cmd Coldstream Guards 1964-65, cmd 4 Guards Bde 1965-68, Brig 1966, dep cmdt Staff Coll Camberley 1968-69, dep cmd (Army) NI Ireland 1969-70, Maj-Gen 1969, GOC E Midland Dist 1970-73; Dep Hon Col Lincs Royal Anglian Regt 1979-84; county emergency planning offr Lincs 1974-77; chm Lincoln Diocesan Advsy Ctee 1981-86; hon clerk to the Lieutenancy (Co of Lincoln) 1983-; chm Lincs TA & VR Ctee 1984-86; *Recreations* shooting, fishing; *Clubs* Army and Navy; *Style*— Maj-Gen David Toler, OBE, MC, DL; Rutland Farm, Fulbeck, Grantham, Lincs NG32 3LG (☎ 0400 72310)

TOLER, Major (Thomas) Ian Jodrell; DFC (1944), TD (1956), JP (1950); s of Maj Thomas Clayton Toler, DL, JP (d 1940), of Swettenham Hall, Congleton, Cheshire, and Gertrude Marianna, *née* Wilkinson (d 1962); gf John Morton Toler chief engr responsible for construction of Milford Docks; *b* 14 Mar 1912; *Educ* Kings Sch Macclesfield, Christ Church Oxford (MA); *m* 15 March 1940, Joan, da of Philip Henry Adshead (d 1965), of Chipping Norton, Oxon; 4 da (Anne b 1943 d 1986, Susan b 1945, Pamla b 1948, Celia b 1950); *Career* 2 Lt 7 Bn The Cheshire Regt (TA) 1930, Maj and Adj 56 Anti Tank Regt RA, cdr air landing Anti-Tank by RA 1940, glider pilot Army Air Corps Cmd B Sqdn Arnhem Op and Rhine Crossing 1945, CO 10 Cheshire Bn Home Gd; engr; engr and mangr ICI 1937-60, dir and gen mangr Ward Blenkinsop 1960-77, tech dir Seashore Electronics 1977-81, i/c Min of Supply Factory Randle (destruction of war gases); *Recreations* philately; *Style*— Maj Ian Toler, DFC, TD, JP; Yarrangall Green, Simmonds Hill, Manley via Warrington, Cheshire WA6 9DP (☎ 09284 200)

TOLKIEN, Emma Katherine de Cusance; da of Anthony de Cusance Cussans, of The Manor House, Totnes, Devon, and Cecilia Anne, *née* Ratcliffe; *b* 20 July 1953; *Educ* St Mary's Convent Shaftesbury Dorset, Holland Park Comprehensive London, Univ of Manchester (BA); *m* 19 Oct 1985, Michael Geoffrey Stuart Tolkien, s of Stuart Frederick Gerald Tolkien (d 1978), of Staverton, Devon; *Career* Yachting Monthly Magazine: features ed 1981-85, organiser outside events triangle race 1986 and 1988, classic yacht rally 1989; ed: Tall Ships News 1983-, West Country Cruising 1988, East Coast Rivers 1989; memb: Topsham Museum Soc, Topsham Soc, Devon Local Valuation Panel; memb Yachting Journalists Assoc 1982; *Recreations* sailing, dog walking; *Clubs* Royal Torbay YC, Topsham SC; *Style*— Mrs Michael Tolkien; 2 Swains Ct, Topsham, Exeter, Devon EX3 OHH (☎ 039287 7979)

TOLLEMACHE, Hon Hugh John Hamilton; s of 4 Baron Tollemache (d 1975); *b* 1946; *Educ* Eton; *m* m 1986, Rosie, da of The Hon Anthony Cayzer; *Style*— The Hon Hugh Tollemache; 19 Clarendon St, SW1

TOLLEMACHE, Maj-Gen Sir Humphry Thomas; 6 Bt (GB 1793), CB (1952), CBE (1950), DL (1965); s of Sir Lyonel Tollemache, 4 Bt (d 1952), of Ham House, Richmond, Surrey, and Langham House, Ham Common, Richmond, Surrey, by his w Hersilia Henrietta Diana (d 1953), da of Henry Richard Oliphant; suc bro, Sir Lyonel, 5 Bt, 1969; *b* 10 August 1897; *Educ* Eastbourne Coll; *m* 6 Feb 1926, Nora Priscilla, da of John Taylor (d 1935), of Broomhill, Eastbourne; 2 s, 2 da; *Heir* s, Lyonel Humphry John; *Career* served 1914-18 War with Grand Fleet, WWII served in Admty, Middle East and Far East (Brig), Maj-Gen cmdg Portsmouth Gp RM 1949-52; Hon Col Cmdt Portsmouth Group RM 1958-60, Col Cmdt RM 1961-62 (ret 1961); ccncllr Hants 1957, alderman Hants 1969-74; *Clubs* Army and Navy; *Style*— Maj-Gen Sir Humphry Tollemache, Bt, CB, CBE, DL; Sheet House, Petersfield, Hampshire (☎ 0730 63813)

TOLLEMACHE, Lyonel Humphry John; JP (Leics), DL (Leics); s and h of Maj-Gen Sir Humphry Tollemache 6 Bt, CB, CBE, DL; *b* 10 July 1931; *Educ* Uppingham, RAC Cirencester; *m* 6 Feb 1960, Mary Joscelyne, da of Col William Henry Whitbread, TD; 2 s, 2 da; *Career* cmmnd Coldstream Gds, Maj; High Sheriff Leicestershire 1978-79, ccncllr Leicestershire 1985-; FRICS; *Style*— Lyonel Tollemache, Esq, JP, DL; Buckminster Park, Grantham NG33 5RU (☎ 0476 860 349; office: 0476 860 471)

TOLLEMACHE, Hon Michael David Douglas; s of 4 Baron Tollemache (d 1975); *b* 23 August 1944; *Educ* Eton, Trinity Coll Cambridge (MA); *m* 5 Feb 1969, Thérèsa, da of Peter Bowring; 2 s (twins), 1 da; *Career* dir: Michael Tollemache Ltd 1967-, David Carritt Ltd 1983-, Artemis Fine Arts Ltd 1983-; *Clubs* White's; *Style*— The Hon Michael Tollemache; Framsden Hall, Helmingham, Stowmarket, Suffolk (☎ work 01 930 8733)

TOLLEMACHE, Hon (John) Nicholas Lyonel; s of 4 Baron Tollemache (d 1975); *b* 13 June 1941; *Educ* Eton, Trinity Coll Cambridge (MA), Harvard (MBA); *m* 1971 (m dis 1974), Heide Eva Marie, da of Gunther Wiedeck, of Bonn; m 2, 1982, Dietlinde Hannelore, da of Hannelore Riegel of Munich, W Germany; *Style*— The Hon Nicholas Tollemache; 1114 San Ysidro Dr, Beverley Hills, Calif 90210, USA

TOLLEMACHE, 5 Baron (UK 1876); Timothy John Edward Tollemache; DL (Suffolk 1984); s of 4 Baron Tollemache (d 1975) ; *b* 13 Dec 1939; *Educ* Eton; *m* 1970, Alexandra Dorothy Jean, da of Col Hugo Meynell, MC, JP, DL (d 1960); 2 s (Hon Edward, Hon James b 1980), 1 da (Hon Selina b 1973); *Heir* s, Hon Edward John Hugo Tollemache b 12 May 1976; *Career* cmmnd Coldstream Gds 1959-62; chm NRG Hldgs UK Ltd; dir: Tollemache & Cobbold Breweries Ltd 1973, AMEV Hldgs (UK) Ltd 1980, Kanga Collection Ltd 1983; farmer; pres; Suffolk Assoc of Local Cncls 1978-, Friends of Ipswich Museums 1980-, Cheshire Cereal Soc 1983-, Suffolk Agric Assoc 1988; chm: HHA (E Anglia) 1979-83, Cncl St John (Suffolk) 1982-; vice-pres Cheshire BRCS 1980-, St Edmundsbury Cathedral Appeal 1986-; patron Suffolk Accident Rescue Services 1983-; CStJ 1988; *Recreations* shooting, fishing; *Clubs* White's, Pratt's, Special Forces; *Style*— The Rt Hon Lord Tollemache, DL; Helmingham Hall, Stowmarket, Suffolk (☎ 047 339 217)

TOLLER, Mark Geoffrey Charles; s of Capt Charles Bolton Toller, and Eleanor Ann, *née* Pease; *b* 23 Oct 1950; *Educ* Harrow; *m* 22 May 1981, Anna Caroline, s of James Alastair McGregor; 1 s (Edward b 4 June 1983), 1 da (Annabel b 14 Jan 1987); *Career* asst dir Guinness Mahon & Co Ltd 1983-87, dir Br and Cwlth Merchant Bank plc 1987-; memb ICA; *Recreations* horse racing, golf, shooting; *Style*— Mark Tolller, Esq;

British and Commonwealth Merchant Bank plc, 19 Motcomb St, London SW1 (☎ 01 245 6616, fax 01 235 2048)

TOLLEY, Rev Canon George; s of George Enoch Frederick Tolley (d 1971), of Old Hill, Staffs, and Elsie, *née* Billingham (d 1977); *b* 24 May 1925; *Educ* Halesowen GS Worcs, Birmingham Central Tech Coll, Princeton Univ, Lincoln Theol Coll, London Univ (BSc, MSc, PhD); *m* 21 June 1947, Joan Amelia, da of Isaac Grosvenor (d 1984), of Blackheath, Worcs; 2 s (Christopher b 1951, Martin b 1952), 1 da (Jane b 1955); *Career* chief chemist Metallisation Ltd 1947-51, chemistry dept Birmingham Coll of Advanced Technol 1951-58 (head of dept 1954-58), head of research Allied Ironfounders Ltd 1958-61, princ Worcester Tech Coll 1961-65, sr dir of studies RAF Coll Cranwell 1965-66, princ Sheffield Poly 1966-82; Manpower Services Cmmn: dir open tech, head quality branch, chief offr review of vocational qualifications 1987, conslt educn and training 1988-; ordained priest C of E 1968, hon canon Sheffield 1976; one of the twelve Capital Burgesses of the Commonality of Sheffield 1980-; dep chm S Yorks Fndn 1986-, memb Yorks and Humberside Economic Planning Cncl 1974-79, hon sec Assoc of Colls of Higher and Further Educn 1974-83; chm: Further Educn Unit 1977-83, cncl Selly Oaks Colls 1983-, Educn-Industry Forum Industry Matters 1984-; memb: CNAA 1973-82, Cncl RSA 1985-; Hon DSc: Univ of Sheffield 1983, Open Univ 1983, CNAA 1986; Hon fell: City and Guilds of London, Sheffield Poly, Coll of Preceptors, Columbia Pacific Univ; FRSC 1954, fell Plastics and Rubber Inst 1973, CBIM 1978; *Books* Meaning and Purpose in Higher Education (1976); *Recreations* music, hill walking, bird watching; *Clubs* Athenaeum; *Style*— The Rev Canon George Tolley; 74 Furniss Ave, Dore Sheffield S17 3QP (☎ 0742 360 538); Department of Employment, Training Agency, Moorfoot, Sheffield S1 4PQ (☎ 0742 703 319)

TOLLEY, Leslie John; CBE; *b* 11 Nov 1913; *Career* engrg mfr; chm Renold plc (makers of power transmission and mechanical handling equipment) to July 1982; dir Lloyds Bank Ltd (NW Regional bd), chm Excelsior Industl Hldgs Ltd; *Style*— Leslie Tolley Esq, CBE; Excelsion Industrial Holdings Ltd, Whitelands Rd, Ashton under Lyne, Greater Manchester (☎ 061 344 2711; home: (0625) 829073)

TOLLIT, Mark Frederick; MBE (1985); s of C Clifton Tollit (d 1965), of Middx, and Francis F, *née* Green (d 1977); *b* 7 Sept 1925; *Educ* Eastbourne Coll, London Sch of Printing; *m* 1, 24 April 1948, Mary Jamieson (d 1971), da of J J Reid, OBE (d 1964); 2 s (Mark Nigel b 1950, Ian Clifton b 1952), 1 da (Clare Margaret b 1958); m 2, 24 Aug 1974, Gillian Marigold, da of Bertram Savage (d 1975); *Career* Capt Queens Royal Regt UK and Egypt; chm Tollit & Harvey Ltd (Norfolk), dir W Norfolk Enterprise Tst Ltd (Kings Lynn); Master Worshipful Co of Stationers and Newspaper Makers; FID 1958; *Recreations* sailing, gardening, affinity with four legged creatures; *Clubs* Sloane; *Style*— Mark Tollit, MBE; Tollit & Harvey Ltd, Oldmedow Rd, Kings Lynn, Norfolk PE30 4LW (☎ 0553 760774, fax 0553 767235)

TOLMAN, Jeffery Alexander Spencer; s of Gerald James Spencer, of Cornwall, and Doris Rosaline, *née* Lane (d 1966); *b* 12 July 1950; *Educ* St Clement Danes GS, Univ of Wales Sch of Int Politics; *Career* product mangr Birds Eye Foods (Unilever) 1971-73, account exec Ogilvy & Mather 1973-74; McCann Erickson 1974-79: account supervisor, account dir, assoc dir, dir; fndr ptnr Grandfield Rork Collins 1979-85; Saatchi & Saatchi Advertising: gp account dir 1985-86, dep chm 1987-; MIPA; *Recreations* walking, eating, drinking, politics; *Clubs* Reform, RAC, Grouchos; *Style*— Jeffery Tolman, Esq; 12 Stonor Rd, London W14 8RZ (☎ 01 603 6697); Lushers, Whitsbury, Hampshire; Saatchi & Saatchi Advertising, 80 Charlotte St, London W1 (☎ 01 636 5060, fax 01 637 8489, telex 261580, car tel 0836 677 871)

TOLSTOY, (Count); Dimitry (full surname Tolstoy-Miloslavsky); QC (1959); s of Count (Michael) Tolstoy-Miloslavsky (d 1947); *b* 8 Nov 1912; *Educ* Wellington, Trinity Coll Cambridge; *m* da of late Howard Wicksteed; 1 s (Count Nikolai T-M, *qv*), 1 da (Natasha or Natalie m 1974 Patrick John Bucknell); m 2, 1943, Natalie, da of Captain Vladimir Deytrikh (d 1951); 1 s (Count Andrei T-M, *qv*), 1 da (Tania or Tatiana (Mrs Illingworth); *Career* barr 1937, lectr in divorce to Inns of Court 1952-68; author; *Publications* Tolstoy on Divorce (7 editions 1946-71); *Style*— Dimitry Tolstoy Esq, QC; c/o Barclays Bank, High St, Guernsey, Channel Islands

TOLSTOY-MILOSLAVSKY, Count Andrei; s of (Count) Dimitry Tolstoy-Miloslavsky, QC, and Natalie; half-bro of Count Nikolai Tolstoy-Miloslavsky, *qv*; *b* 12 May 1949; *Educ* French Lycée, Wellington Coll, Surrey Univ; *m* 1976, Carolinda Beatrice Catherine, da of Maj Ralph Pilcher, Welsh Gds, of Hay Place, Binsted, Hants; 2 s (Igor b 1985, Oleg b 1986), 1 da (Liubov b 1979); *Career* businessman; *Recreations* tennis, sailing, guitar; *Clubs* Beefsteak; *Style*— Count Andrei Tolstoy-Miloslavsky; 8 Orlando Rd, London SW4 (☎ 01 720 6687)

TOLSTOY-MILOSLAVSKY, Count Nikolai Dmitrievich; s of (Count) Dimitry Tolstoy, *qv*; *b* 23 June 1935; *Educ* Wellington, Trinity Coll Dublin (MA); *m* 1971, Georgina Katherine, da of Maj Peter Brown, of Longworth, Berkshire; 1 s (Dmitri b 1978), 3 da (Alexandra b 1973, Anastasia b 1975, Xenia b 1980); *Heir* (Count) Dmitri Nikolaevich Tolstoy-Miloslavsky; *Career* pres Assoc for a Free Russia; chm the Monarchist League; author, historian, biographer; *Books*: The Founding of Evil Hold School (1968), Night of The Long Knives (1972), Victims of Yalta (1978), The Half-Mad Lord (1978), Stalin's Secret War (1981), The Tolstoys (1983); The Quest for Merlin (1985), The Minister and the Massacres (1986), The Coming of the King (1988), also monographs on Celtic studies; FRSL; *Recreations* walking, archery, broadsword-and-buckler play; *Style*— Count Nikolai Tolstoy-Miloslavsky; Court Close, Southmoor, Abingdon, Berks (☎ 0865 820186)

TOM, Peter William Gregory; s of John Gregory Tom, of Bardon Hill, Leicester, and Barbara Tom, *née* Lambden; *b* 26 July 1940; *Educ* Hinckley GS; *m* 28 Jan 1985, Patrice Alison, da of Ronald S Chandler, of Markfield, Leics; 2 da (Saffron b 1972, Layla b 1975); *Career* chm and chief exec Bardon Group plc; *Recreations* tennis, theatre, golf; *Style*— Peter W G Tom, Esq; Thurcaston Grange, Thurcaston, Leicester LE3 7JQ; Bardon Gp plc, Bardon Hill, Leicester LE6 2TL (☎ 0530 510088)

TOMALIN, Air Cdre Charles Douglas; CBE (1966, OBE 1953), DFC (1943, AFC 1942); s of Frederick Tomalin (d 1933); *b* 20 August 1914; *Educ* William Ellis Sch, RAF Staff Coll, US Armed Forces Staff Coll, IDC; *m* 1941, Margaret, da of Rev J J Ellis (d 1962); 2 s; *Career* joined RAF 1936, dir intelligence (A) 1961-63, head br def liaison staff and air attaché S Africa 1963-66, ret Air Cdre; represented England in diving events in the Br Empire Games: 1930, 1934, 1938 (1 Gold, 3 Silver medals); represented GB in high diving event in the 1936 Olympic Games; *Clubs* RAF; *Style*— Air Cdre Charles Tomalin, CBE, DFC; Rauceby, Nascot Wood Rd, Watford, Herts WD1 3SD (☎ 0923 229539)

TOMALIN, Claire; da of Emile Delavenay, and Muriel Emily, *née* Herbert (d 1984); *b* 20 June 1933; *Educ* Lycée Francais de Londres Girls GS Hitchin, Dartington Hall Sch, Newnham Coll Cambridge (BA, MA); *m* 17 Sept 1955, Nicholas Osborne Tomalin (d 1973), s of Miles Ridley Tomalin (d 1983); 2 s (Daniel b and d 1960, Thomas Nicholas Ronald b 1970), 3 da (Josephine Sarah b 1956, Susanna Lucy b 1958 d 1980, Emily Claire Elizabeth b 1961); *Career* publishers ed, reader, journalist 1953-67; literary ed: New Statesman 1974-78 (dep literary ed 1968-70), Sunday Times 1980-86; FRCS 1974; *Books* Life and Death of Mary Wollstonecraft (1974), Shelley and His World (1980), Katherine Mansfield: A Secret Life (1987); *Style*— Mrs Claire Tomalin; 57 Gloucester Cres, London NW1 7EG

TOMBA, Hon Mrs (Henrietta Jane); *née* Piercy, da of 2 Baron Piercy; *b* 1951; *Educ* Badminton Sch, St Andrews Univ (MA); *m* 1985, Tullio Luigi Giuseppe Tomba, s of Gualfardo Tomba (d 1945), of Udine, Italy; 1 s (Tommaso Piercy 1987); *Style*— The Hon Mrs Tomba; Via Corona 40, Campoformido (Udine) Italy (☎ 0432 662260)

TOMBS, Sir Francis Leonard; s of Joseph Tombs; *b* 17 May 1924; *Educ* Elmore Green Sch Walsall, Birmingham Coll of Technol, Univ of London (BSc); *m* 1949, Marjorie Evans; 3 da; *Career* trained with: GEC Ltd Birmingham 1939-45, Birmingham Corpn electricity supply dept 1946-47, Br Electricity Authy 1948-57; gen mangr GEC Ltd Kent 1958-67, dir and gen mangr James Howden & Co Glasgow 1967-68; South of Scotland Electricity Bd: dir of engrg 1969-73, dep chm 1973-74, chm 1974-77; chm: Electricity Cncl for England and Wales 1977-80, Weir Gp plc 1981-83, Turner & Newall plc 1982-, Rolls-Royce plc 1985-, The Engineering Cncl 1985-, The Advsy Cncl on Science and Technology 1987-, Molecule Theatre Co 1985-; dir: N M Rothschild & Sons Ltd 1981-, Rolls-Royce Ltd 1982-, Turner & Newall Int Ltd 1982-, Turner & Newall Welfare Tst Ltd 1982-, Shell-UK Ltd 1983-; pro-chllr and chm cncl Cranfield Inst of Technology 1985-, vice-pres Engineers for Disaster Relief 1985-; Liveryman and Assistant Warden Goldsmith's Co, Freeman City of London; Hon LLD Strathclyde Univ (visiting prof); Hon DSc: Aston Univ, Lodz Univ (Poland), Cranfield Inst of Technol, The City Univ London, Univ of Bradford, Queen's Univ Belfast, Surrey Univ; Hon DTech Loughborough Univ; FEng (past vice-pres), FIEE (past pres), FIMechE; Hon FICE, Hon FIChemE, Hon FIProdE, Hon memb Br Nuclear Energy Soc; kt 1978; *Style*— Sir Francis Tombs; Honington Lodge, Honington, Shipston-upon-Stour, Warwickshire CV36 5AA; Rolls-Royce plc, 65 Buckingham Gate, London SW1E 6AT (☎ 01 222 9020, telex 918091)

TOMKINS, Sir Edward Emile; GCMG (1975, KCMG 1969, CMG 1960), CVO (1957); s of Lt-Col Ernest Leith Tomkins; *b* 16 Nov 1915; *Educ* Ampleforth, Trinity Coll Cambridge; *m* 15 Nov 1955, Gillian, da of Air Cdre Constantine Evelyn Benson, CBE, DSO (yr bro of late Sir Rex Benson), by his w Lady Morvyth, *née* Ward (2 da of 2 Earl of Dudley and sis of 1 Viscount Ward of Witley); 1 s (Julian b 1956), 2 da (Sarah b 1958, Rosemary b 1961); *Career* served WWII 1940-43 (liaised with French Free Forces); diplomat, joined Foreign Service 1939; served: Moscow 1944-46, FO 1946-51, Washington 1951-54, cnsllr (Information) Paris 1954-59, FO 1959-63, min Bonn 1963-67, min Washington 1967-69; ambass: Netherlands 1970-72, France 1972-75, ret; memb Bucks CC 1977-, chm Friends of Univ Coll of Buckingham 1977; Croix de Guerre, Grand Officer Légion d'Honneur 1984; *Clubs* Turf, Garrick; *Style*— Sir Edward Tomkins, GCMG, CVO; Winslow Hall, Winslow, Bucks (☎ (029 671) 2323)

TOMKINSON, John Stanley; CBE (1981); s of Harry Stanley Tomkinson (d 1980), and Katie Mills Tomkinson (d 1976); *b* 8 Mar 1916; *Educ* Rydal Sch, Birmingham Univ Sch of Med, St Thomas' Hosp (MB ChB); *m* 31 March 1954, Barbara Marie, da of Tom Pilkington (d 1965); 2 s (Barnaby b 1957 (d 1986), Matthew b 1958), 1 da (Claudia b 1955); *Career* conslt surgn (obstetrics and gynaecology) Queen Charlotte's Maternity Hosp and Chelsea Hosp for Women and Guy's Hosp London; sec-gen Int Fedn of Gynaecology and Obstetrics 1976-85, now hon sec-gen conslt advsr in Ostetrics and Gynaecology DHSS 1966-81; late memb: Cncl RCS England and RCOG, dep chm Central Midwives Bd; visiting prof Spanish Hosp, Mexico City 1972; late examiner: Oxford, Cambridge, London, Birmingham, Belfast, Tripoli, Addis Ababa, Singapore, E Africa Univs, RCOG Conjoint Bd and Central Midwives Bd; hon fell and memb Continental Gynaecological Club of America (also Canada, Colombia, Nigeria, S Africa, Brazil, Jordan, Korea, Italy, Spain, Poland, Romania); ed Queen Charlotte's Textbook of Obstetrics; Copernicus Medal Acad of Med Cracow Poland, medal of Polish Nation for Aid and Cooperation in Med; FRCS, FRCOG; *Recreations* fly fishing; *Clubs* Athenaeum, Flyfishers, MCC; *Style*— John S Tomkinson, Esq, CBE; Rose Cottage, Up Somborne, Hants SO20 6QY; 3 Downside, St John's Ave, London SW15 2AE; Keats House, Guy's Hospital, London SE1 9RT

TOMKYS, William Roger; CMG (1984); s of William Arthur Tomkys (d 1973), of Harden, Yorks, and Edith Tomkys (d 1984); *b* 15 Mar 1937; *Educ* Bradford GS, Balliol Coll Oxford (MA); *m* 1963, Margaret Jean, da of Norman Beilby Abbey (d 1964), of Barrow in Furness; 1 s, 1 da; *Career* foreign service 1960-; seconded to Cabinet Off 1975, head Near East and N Africa dept FCO 1977-80, head chancery and cnsllr Rome 1980-81, ambass and consul-gen to Bahrain 1981-84, ambass to Syria 1984-86, princ fin offr FCO 1986-; also served: Athens, Benghazi, Amman; studied MECAS; Commendatore Dell'Ordin Al Merito (Italy) 1980, Order of Bahrain (first class) 1984; *Clubs* Utd Oxford and Cambridge, Royal Blackheath GC; *Style*— William Tomkys Esq, CMG; c/o Foreign & Commonwealth Office, King Charles Street, London SW1

TOMLIN, Ivan; s of Fred Tomlin (d 1961), and Alice, *née* Weston (d 1967); *b* 7 August 1924; *Educ* Broom Leys Sch Coalville, Leicester Coll of Art and Technol; *m* 18 March 1950, Patricia Anne, da of Leo Peter McCarthy (d 1974); 1 s (Stephen b 1953), 1 da (Susan b 1954); *Career* Bevan Boy 1944-46; joined Howard Farrow Ltd (bldg and civil engrg contractors) 1948: md 1962, company acquired by ICI and reorganised 1966, md Farrow Gp Ltd 1970, dir Farrow Property Devpts Ltd; chm: F Rendell & Sons Ltd, Devizes Farrow Construction Ltd, Heery Farrow Ltd; bldg and devpt conslt (managing devpts in and around City of London); Inst of Bldg: chartered 1980, chm London region 1970-71, nat pres 1974-75, chm professional practice bd 1975-81, hon tres 1981-86; guest ed Architects Jl for a series on the cost of bldg 1975-77; chm Harrow Round Table 1965, fndr memb Golders Green Rotary Club 1967, dep chm bd of govrs Tottenham Tech Coll 1973-77; gen cmmr of income tax 1970, JP Gore Div Middx 1968; Freeman City of London 1968, Liveryman Worshipful Co of Farriers 1968; AIOB 1959, FAIB 1974; *Books* guest ed of the Architect's Journal for a Series on The Cost of Building (1975-77); *Recreations* trout and salmon fishing; *Style*— Ivan Tomlin, Esq; 3 Anselm Rd, Hatch End, Pinner, Middx HA5 4LN (☎ 01 428 4025); 6 Hobart

Place, London SW1W 0HU (☎ 01 235 0505, fax 01 235 8722)

TOMLINSON, Sir Bernard Evans; CBE (1981); s of James Arthur Tomlinson (d 1980), and Doris Mary, *née* Evans (d 1985); *b* 13 July 1920; *Educ* Brunts Sch Mansfield Notts, UCL (MB BS), UCH (MD); *m* 9 Aug 1944, Betty, da of Edgar Oxley (d 1941); 1 s (David Andrew b 1945), 1 da (Elizabeth Oxley (Mrs Peerless) b 1950); *Career* Maj RAMC specialist pathologist 1947-49; trainee pathologist (EMS) 1943-47, conslt neuropathologist Gen Hosp Newcastle upon Tyne 1972-85 (conslt pathologist 1949-55, sr conslt pathologist 1955-82), prof pathology Univ of Newcastle 1985-(hon prof pathology 1972-85), pres Br Neuropathalogical Soc; chm Northern Regnl Health Authy 1982-; memb and vice-chm Newcastle Health Authy 1975-80, pres Northern Alzheimer Disease Soc 1986-; author of numerous book chapters and articles on the pathology of the brain in old age and the pathology of dementia; FRCP, FRCPath; kt 1988; *Recreations* golf, gardening, walking, music; *Clubs* Army & Navy, Pall Mall; *Style*— Sir Bernard Tomlinson, CBE; Greyholme, Wynbury Rd, Low Fell, Gateshead, Tyne & Wear NE9 6TS (☎ 091 487 5227); Northern Regnl Health Authy, Benfield Rd, Newcastle upon Tyne NE6 4PY

TOMLINSON, Prof (Alfred) Charles; s of Alfred Tomlinson, DCM (d 1973), of Stoke-on-Trent, and May, *née* Lucas (d 1972); *b* 8 Jan 1927; *Educ* Longton HS, Queens' Coll Cambridge (BA, MA), London Univ (MA); *m* 23 Oct 1948, Brenda, da of Edwin Albert Raybould (d 1977), of Stoke-on-Trent; 2 da (Justine, Juliet); *Career* visiting prof Univ of New Mexico 1962-63, O'Connell prof Colgate Univ NY 1967-68, visiting fell of humanities Princeton Univ 1981, prof of eng lit Bristol Univ 1982- (lectr 1956-68, reader 1968-82), Lamont prof Union Coll NY 1987, numerous public lectures and poetry readings throughout the world 1967-, graphics exhibited at Grimpel Fils and Leicester Galleries, one man shows at OUP London 1972 and Clare Coll Cambridge 1975, Arts Cncl touring exhibition The Graphics and Poetry of Charles Tomlinson opened at the Hayward Gallery London then toured England, Canada and the USA 1978-; Hon fell Queens' Coll Cambridge 1976; Hon DLitt: Univ of Keele 1981, Colgate Univ NY 1981, Univ of New Mexico 1986; FRSL 1975; *Books* incl: Collected Poems (1987), Renga and Airborn (with Octavio Paz), Some Americans (1981), Poetry and Metamorphosis (1983), Selected W C Williams (ed 1976), Selected Octavio Paz (ed 1979), Oxford Book of Verse in English Translation (ed 1980); Graphics incl Eden (1985); *Recreations* music, gardening, walking, travel; *Style*— Prof Charles Tomlinson; English Dept, University of Bristol, 3-5 Woodland Rd, Bristol, Avon (☎ 0272 303030)

TOMLINSON, Claire Janet; da of Lascelles Arthur Lucas (d 1988), of Woolmers Park, nr Hertford, Herts, and Ethel Barbara, *née* Daer; *b* 14 Feb 1944; *Educ* Wycombe Abbey, Millfield, Somerville Coll Oxford (MA); *m* 16 March 1968, (George) Simon Tomlinson, s of George Antony Tomlinson (d 1954); 2 s (Luke b 27 Jan 1977, Mark b 25 March 1982), 1 da (Emma b 30 Oct 1974); *Career* polo player; Oxford half blue 1964-66, first woman to play against Cambridge, capt Oxford Univ team 1966, pioneered breakthrough for woman to be allowed in high-goal polo 1978, memb winnning team Queen's Cup 1979, achieved highest ever lady's handicap 1986; fencing: Oxford half blue 1963-66, capt Oxford ladies team 1965-66, memb England under-21 team 1962-63; squash: Oxford half blue 1964-66; *Style*— Mrs Claire Tomlinson; Down Farm, Westonbirt, nr Tetbury, Glos (☎ 066 688 214)

TOMLINSON, David Cecil MacAlister; s of Clarence Samuel Tomlinson (d 1978), of New Bond St, London, and Folkestone, and Florence Elizabeth Sinclair Thomson (d 1968); maternal uncle Albert Borlase Armitage (1864-43) was second in cmd on Scott's first Antarctic Expedition 1901-04; uncle Sir Cecil Hamilton Armitage (1867-1933) Govr of Gambia 1924-30; *b* 7 May 1917; *Educ* Tonbridge Sch; *m* 1953, Audrey, da of Walter Redvers Freeman, of S Yorks; 4 s (David, James, William, Henry); *Career* Grenadier Gds 1935-36, WWII Flt Lt RAF, demob 1946; actor; chief roles incl: Henry in The Little Hut (Lyric 1950-53), Clive in All Mary (Duke of Yorks 1954-55), David in Dear Delinguent (Westminster Westminster and Aldwych 1957-58), Tom in The Ring of Truth (Savoy), Robert in Boeing-Boeing (Apollo 1962); acted and directed: Mother's Boy (Globe 1964), A Friend Indeed (Cambridge 1966), On the Rocks 1969, A Friend Indeed and A Song at Twilight (SA) 1973-74, The Turning Point (Duke of Yorks 1974); first appeared in films 1939, since then appeared in leading roles in over 50 films; *Recreations* collecting antiques; *Clubs* Traveller's; *Style*— David Tomlinson Esq; Brook Cottage, Mursley, Bucks MK17 0RS (☎ 029 672 213); 610 Chelsea Cloisters, Sloane Ave, London SW3 (☎ 01 589 7303)

TOMLINSON, Elvira Mary (Molly); da of Domingo Riccardo Busi (d 1962), and Mary Wright, *née* Webster (d 1968); *b* 13 Sept 1922; *Educ* Westonbirt; *m* 31 May 1947, (John) Michael Tomlinson, s of late Henry Harrison Tomlinson; *Career* chm: Busi & Stephenson Ltd and associated cos in Germany and Ghana, R Singlehurst & Co Ltd Liverpool, J Miller & Co (Liverpool) Ltd, C H Jones Burton & Co Ltd; dir C Zard & Co Ltd Nigeria; vice-chm Cons W Africa Ctee; MInstD; *Clubs* Royal Ocean Racing, Liverpool Racquet, Irish Cruising; *Style*— Mrs Michael Tomlinson; Moel-y-Don, Llanedwen, Llanfairpwll, Anglesey, Gwynedd LL61 6EZ (☎ 0248 714 430); Busi Stephenson Ltd, Tower Building, Water St, Liverpool L3 1BW (☎ 051 236 7766, fax UK 4451 236 3860, telex 627075)

TOMLINSON, John; s of Frank Tomlinson, of Whitecliff, Longsdon, Stoke-on-Trent, Staffs, and Barbara, *née* Mayer (d 1986); *b* 30 Jan 1941; *Educ* Eversley House Prep Sch, Lawton Hall, Alsager; *m* 31 March 1962, Christine Ann, da of Thomas Evan Jones, of Clifton Drive, Stafford; 2 s (Nicholas John b 1963, David Nigel b 1964), 1 da (Lisa Ann b 1969); *Career* jt md London Scottish Fin Corpn plc; memb Br Inst of Mgmnt 1972, fell Inst Admin Account 1975; dir: London Scottish fin Corpn plc, and subsidaries; Refuge Lending Co (N) Ld, Reliance Guarantee Co Ltd, Robinson Way & Co Ltd, Dupant Bros Ltd, Glengall Est Ltd; *Recreations* shooting, fishing; *Style*— John Tomlinson, Esq; Ford Hall Farm, Ford, nr Leek, Sraffs (☎ 05388 342); Arndale House, Manchester

TOMLINSON, Prof John Race Godfrey; CBE (1983); s of John Angell Tomlinson (d 1968) and, Beatrice Elizabeth Race, *née* Godfrey; *b* 24 April 1932; *Educ* Stretford GS, Manchester Univ (BA, MA), London Univ; *m* 27 March 1954, Audrey Mavis, da of John Barrett (d 1935); 2 s (John b 1958, Graham b 1962), 2 da (Susan b 1959, Janet b 1960); *Career* Fl Lt RAF 1955-58; teacher 1958-60; educn offr: Shropshire LEA 1960-63, Lancs LEA 1963-67; dir of educn Ches LEA 1972-84 (dep dir 1967-71), dir Inst of Educn Univ of Warwick 1985-; pres Soc Educn Offrs 1982-83; chm Further Educn Curriculum Devpt Unit 1976- 78, Schs Cncl 1978-82, tstees Schs Curriculum Award 1982-, RSA Examinations Bd 1985-; fell Coll of Preceptors, memb Royal Northern Coll of Music, FBIM 1977, FRSA 1976; *Books* Additional Grenville Papers (ed 1962), The Changing Government of Education (ed with S Ranson, 1986); *Recreations* walking, music, gardening; *Clubs* Atheneum, Army and Navy, Royal Overseas League; *Style*— Prof John Tomlinson, CBE; Institute of Education, Univ of Warwick, Westwood, Coventry CV4 7AL (☎ 0203 523821, telex 317472 UN IREG)

TOMLINSON, Maj-Gen Michael John; CB 1981, OBE (1973, MBE 1964); s of Sidney Cyril Tomlinson (d 1983), and Emily Rose, *née* Hodges (d 1986); *b* 20 May 1929; *Educ* The Skinners' Sch Tunbridge Wells, RMA Sandhurst; *m* 24 June 1955, Lily Patricia, da of Lt-Col A Rowland, OBE, MC (d 1971); 1 s (Peter b 1958), 1 da (Jane (Mrs Wallis) b 1962); *Career* cmmnd RA 1949; served 1962-64: Tripoli, Canal Zone, Jordon, Germany, GS02 ops to dir of ops Brunei (despatches); dep asst mil sec 1966-68, instr Staff Coll Camberley 1968-70, CO 2 Field Regt RA 1970-72, Col GS Staff Coll Camberley 1972-73, CRA 3 Div 1973-75, dep mil sec 1976-78, dir of manning (Army) 1978-79, Vice Adj Gen 1979-81, DRA 1981-84, ret May 1984; Col Cmdt RA 1982-, Hon Col 104 Regt RA (V) 1985-87, Hon Regt Col 2 Field Regt RA; vice pres Nat Artillery Assoc 1984-, pres central branch RA Assoc 1988-; sec The Dulverton Tst 1984-; FBIM 1984, FRSA 1985; *Recreations* gardening, music; *Clubs* Army and Navy; *Style*— Maj-Gen Michael Tomlinson, CB, OBE; The Dulverton Trust, 5 St James's Place, London SW1A 1NP (☎ 01 629 9121, fax 01 495 6201)

TOMLINSON, Sir (Frank) Stanley; KCMG (1966), CMG (1954); s of John Tomlinson (d 1955); *b* 21 Mar 1912; *Educ* High Pavement Sch, Nottingham Univ; *m* 1959, Nancy, yr da of E Gleeson-White (decd), of Hampstead and Sydney Australia; *Career* former: cnsllr Br Embassy Washington, head of SE Asia Dept FO, dep to GOC (Br Sector) Berlin, min UK Delgn to NATO 1961-64, consul-gen NY 1964-66, high cmmnr Ceylon 1966-69, dep under-sec state FCO 1969-72; Hon LLD Nottingham 1970; *Style*— Sir Stanley Tomlinson, KCMG, CMG; 32 Long Street, Devizes, Wilts

TOMLINSON, Stephen Miles; QC (1988); s of Capt Enoch Tomlinson, of Dudley, W Mids, and Mary Marjorie Cecelia, *née* Miles; *b* 29 Mar 1952; *Educ* King's Sch Worcester, Worcester Coll Oxford (MA); *m* 15 March 1980, Joanna Kathleen, da of Ian Joseph Greig; 1 s, 1 da; *Career* barr Inner Temple 1974; *Recreations* cricket, gardening, walking, family; *Clubs* Travellers', MCC; *Style*— Stephen Tomlinson, Esq, QC; 7 King's Bench Walk, Temple, London EC4Y 7DS (☎ 01 583 0404, fax 01 583 0950, telex 887491)

TOMPSON, Hon Mrs (Margaret-Ann Michelle); *née* Donaldson; er da of Baron Donaldson of Lymington, PC (Life Peer), *qv*; *b* 1946, ; *Educ* St Paul's Girls' Sch, London Sch of Occupational Therapy (Dip OT), Univ of Saskatchewan (MCEd); *m* 1969, Conal Tompson; 1 s (Douglas Conal b 4 Jan 1974), 1 da (Caroline Margaret b 11 Dec 1975); *Style*— The Hon Mrs Tompson; 736 University Drive, Saskatoon, Saskatchewan S7N 0J4, Canada

TOMS, Carl; OBE; s of Bernard Toms (d 1947), of Mansfield, Notts, and Edith Toms; *b* 29 May 1927; *Educ* RCA, Sch of Art Mansfield, Old Vic Sch; *Career* conscript WWII; asst to Oliver Messel 1953-59; first design cmmn Suzanna's Secret Glyndebourne 1960, theatre design 1960-, design conslt for investiture of Prince of Wales at Caernarvon Castle, Tony Award for prodn of Sherlock Holmes for the RSC in 1975, hd of design Young Vic Theatre - until 1980 (dir), Olivier Award for the Provoked Wife for NT 1981, worked on 14 prodns for the NT, 10 prodns for the Burg Theatre and Statsoper, Vienna, and also for NY City Opera, Metropolitan Opera, San Francisco Opera, and many West End prodns; active in charitable work; FRSA; *Recreations* work, theatre, art, architecture, gardens; *Clubs* Groucho's; *Style*— Carl Toms, Esq, OBE; The White Ho, Beaumont, nr Wormley, Broxbourne, Herts EN10 9QJ (☎ 0992 463961)

TOMS, Edward Ernest; s of Alfred William Toms (d 1981), and Julia, *née* Harrington (d 1980); *b* 10 Dec 1920; *Educ* St Boniface's Coll; *m* 1946, Veronica Rose, da of Francis Rose (d 1951), and Bridget Rose (d 1972), of Dovercourt, Essex; 3 s (Duncan, David, James), 1 da (Rosemary); *Career* RTR 1940-43, Special Forces 1943-45, Regt Offr Seaforth Highlanders 1943-59, Bde Maj Berlin Inf Bde 1959-61, Col Gen Staff UK C-in-C Ctte 1966-69; asst sec Dept of Employment 1969-77, cnsllr Br Embass Bonn and Br Embass Vienna 1977-81, Int labour advsr FO 1981-83, dir Porcelain & Pictures Ltd 1983-; chm Nat Framers and Retailers Ctte, memb of Ct of Fine Art Trade Guild 1987; *Recreations* hill walking, picture framing; *Clubs* Army & Navy, Special Forces; *Style*— Edward Toms, Esq; c/o Clydesdale Bank, Chief Office, 5 Castle St, Aberdeen; The Studio, Gastein Rd, London W6

TOMSETT, Alan Jeffrey; OBE (1974); s of Maurice Jeffrey Tomsett (d 1987), and Edith Sarah Mackelworth (d 1953); *b* 3 May 1922; *Educ* Trinity Sch of John Whitgift Croydon, Univ of London (BCom); *m* 1948, Joyce May, da of Walter Albert Hill (d 1959); 1 s (Ian), 1 da (Ann); *Career* served WW II 1941-46 with RAF (Middle East 1942-45); Hodgson Harris & Co Chartered Accountants London 1938, Smallfield Rawlins & Co 1951: Northern Mercantile & Investmt Corpn 1955, William Baird & Co Ltd 1962-63; finance dir Br Tport Docks Bd 1974-83 (ch accountant and financial controller 1964-73), dir Assoc Br Ports Hldgs plc 1983- (finance dir 1983-87); FCA, FCMA, JDipMA, FCIT (hon treas 1982-88); *Recreations* gardening; *Style*— Alan Jeffrey Tomsett, Esq; 102 Ballards Way, Croydon, Surrey CR0 5RG (☎ 01 657 5069)

TONGE, Hon Mrs (Judith Felicity); *née* Allen; da of Baron Allen of Fallowfield, CBE (Life Peer; d 1985); *b* 1946; *m* 1973, Graham Tonge; 1 s (Daniel Allen b 1974), 1 da (Lucy Clare b 1977); *Style*— The Hon Mrs Tonge; Little Hillers, Innhams Wood, Crowborough, E Sussex IN6 1TE

TONGUE, Carole; MEP (Lab London East 1984); da of Walter Archer Tongue, of Lausanne, Switzerland, and Muriel Esther, *née* Boyes; *b* 14 Oct 1955; *Educ* Brentwood Co HS, Loughborough Univ of Technol (BA); *Career* asst ed Laboratory Practice 1977-78, courier 1978-79, Robert Schumann Scholarship for res in socl affrs Euro Parl 1979-80, admin asst 1 sec Socialist Gp Euro Parl 1980-84; memb: Inst for the Study of Drug Dependence (ISDD), CND, END, One World, Friends of the Earth, Greenpeace, Fabian Soc; vice chm; AMA, SERA; memb: Ctee Environment Pub Health and Consumer Protection, Ctee Rights of Women; subst memb Econ and Monetary Ctee; memb RIIA; *Recreations* tennis, squash, skiing, piano, film, all music; *Style*— Ms Carole Tongue, MEP; 84 Endsleigh Gdns, Ilford, Essex (☎ 01 514 0198); 97a Ilford Lane, Ilford, Essex (☎ 01 0198, fax 01 553 4764)

TONKIN, Derek; CMG (1982); s of Henry James Tonkin (d 1947) and Norah, *née* Wearing; *b* 30 Dec 1929; *Educ* High Paverent GS Nottingham, St Catherine's Coll Oxford (MA); *m* 1953, Doreen, da of Horace Samuel Rooke (d 1967); 2 s (Christopher (decd), Jeremy), 2 da (Caroline, Susan); *Career* HM Diplomatic Service 1952-; ambass to Vietnam 1980-82, min to S Africa 1983-85, ambass to Thailand and Laos 1986-;

Recreations tennis, music; *Clubs* Royal Bangkok Sports; *Style—* Derek Tonkin Esq; British Embassy, Bangkok, Thailand (☎ Bangkok 253 0191, telex Bangkok 82263)

TONKS, Dr Clive Malcolm; s of Clarence Tonks, of York, and Annie, *née* Holt; *b* 21 Mar 1932; *Educ* Normanton GS, Leeds Univ (MB, ChB); *m* 25 Oct 1958, Joyce Margaret, da of Clarence Handby (d 1983); 1 s (David b 1964), 2 da (Susan b 1960, Alison b 1962); *Career* conslt psychiatrist St Mary's Hosp & Med Sch 1969-; hon clinical sr lectr Imperial Coll of Sci Technol and Med previously sr lectr psychiatry Univ of Leeds; assoc prof Psychiatry Yale Univ; chm Med Staff Paddington & North Kensington Health Authy 1983-87; author of papers and chapters on psychiatric topics; memb various Standing Cttees of the Royal Coll of Psychiatry; FRCP, FRCPsych, DPM Univ of London; *Recreations* geology, opera, walking; *Clubs* Royal Society of Medicine; *Style—* Dr Clive M Tonks; 10 Anselm Rd, Pinner, Middlesex (☎ 01 428 3894); St Mary's Hosp, Praed St, London W2 (☎ 01 725 6666)

TONYPANDY, 1 Viscount (UK 1983), of Rhondda, Co Mid Glamorgan; Rt Hon Thomas George; PC (1968); *b* 1909,Port Talbot,; *Educ* Tonypandy GS, Univ Coll Southampton; *Career* former schoolmaster and vice-pres Methodist Conference 1959-60; MP (Lab) Cardiff Central 1945-50, Cardiff W 1950-83; pps min of Civil Aviation 1951, chm Welsh Labour Party 1950-51, parly under-sec Home Office 1964-66, first chm Welsh Parly Grand Ctee, min of state Welsh Office 1966-67, Cwlth Off 1967-68, sec of state for Wales 1968-70, speaker of House of Commons 1976-83 (dep speaker and chm Ways and Means Ctee 1974-76); hon master bencher of the bench Gray's Inn 1982-; Freeman: Rhondda, City of Cardiff, City of London; hon memb: Worshipful Co of Blacksmiths 1977, hon fell St Hugh's Coll Oxford 1983, hon memb Cambridge Students Union 1982, hon fell Hertford Coll Oxford 1983; pres Coll of Preceptors 1983-87; Hon LLD: Asbury Coll Kentucky, Univ of Southampton, Univ of Wales, Birmingham, Oklahoma USA, Liverpool, Leeds; Hon DCL Oxford, Hon DD Shreveport Louisiana; Hon LLD Univ Open Univ; Dato Setia Negara Brunei 1971, Grand Cross of Peruvian Congress 1980, Gold Award for Work of Democracy, State of Carinthia, Austria 1982, hon fell Univ Coll Cardiff 1982; Hon LLD Warwick 1984; Hon LLD Keele 1984; chm Nat Home for children, pres Br Heart Fndn; *Books* Christian Heritage in Politics (1960), Memoirs of a Speaker (1985), My Wales (1986); *Recreations* travel; *Clubs* Travellers, Reform, United Oxford and Cambridge, County Club (Cardiff); *Style—* The Rt Hon the Viscount Tonypandy, PC; House of Lords, London SW1

TOOGOOD, James Anthony Gordon; s of Maj Leonard Gordon Toogood (d 1988), of St Albans, Herts, and Muriel Frances Georgina, *née* Robinson (d 1987); *b* 12 July 1932; *Educ* Aldenham, St John's Coll Cambridge (MA); *m* 12 Oct 1963, (Anne) Margaret, da of Charles Wilfred Robbins (d 1977), of St Albans, Herts; 3 s (Michael b 1964, Paul b 1967, Oliver b 1970); *Career* Nat Serv with RA 1951-53, Capt Herts Yeo 1953-59; admitted a slr 1959; sr ptnr Forrester & Forrester 1977-; mayor of Malmesbury 1978; chm bd of govrs Malmesbury Sch 1970-75 and 1988-; memb Law Soc; *Recreations* music, country pursuits, chairing ctees; *Style—* James Toogood, Esq; Riversdale, Malmesbury, Wiltshire (☎ 0666 822120); 59 High Street, Malmesbury, Wiltshire (☎ 0666 822671)

TOOGOOD, John; QPM (1977); s of James Waller Giddings Toogood, (d 1964), of Chippenham, Wilts, and Katherine Mary, *née* Winter (d 1956); *b* 19 August 1924; *Educ* Chippenham GS, Kings Coll London Univ (LLB, LLM); *m* 1, 19 Oct 1946 (m dis 1949), June, da of Lelie Llewellyn Rowlands (d 1970), of Plymouth, Devon; m 2, 20 Dec 1951, Josephine, *née* Curran (d 1984); 1 da (Katherine b 3 Sept 1962), m 3, 23 July 1986 (remarried), June Martin (Rowlands); *Career* RM 1942-46; Met Police 1946-83 (ret as Cdr); barr Grays Inn 1957, practice at bar 1983-; memb Medico-Legal Soc 1955; admitted as Serving Brother to the Order of St John 1984; *Recreations* family; *Style—* John Toogood, Esq, QPM; 4 Kings Bench Walk, Temple, London EC4V 7DL (☎ 01 353 0478)

TOOGOOD, John; s of Raymond George Toogood, of 44 Steep Hill, Lincoln, and Joan Charlotte, *née* Wallis; *b* 17 Dec 1944; *Educ* Lincoln Sch, Bristol Old Vic Theatre Sch; *m* 26 Oct 1973, Maris Deborah, da of Maj Joseph Frank Sharp (d 1964), of 153 Warm Lane, London NW2; 1 s (Julian Frank b 13 April 1976), 2 da (Rachel Louise b 29 March 1978, Rebecca Sarah b 25 June 1982); *Career* Lincoln Theatre Royal 1958-63, Bristol Old Vic 1963-66, Liverpool Playhouse 1966-71, Greenwich Theatre 1971-72, co mangr No 1 Tours 1972-74, freelance co mangr West End (1974-78 and 1980-81), prodn mangr The King and I Palladium 1979-80, asst tech dir MMA 1981-86, gen mangr Prince Edward Theatre 1986-; chm Stage Mgmnt Assoc, memb cncl Assoc of Br Theatre Technicians; *Recreations* allotment, cycling; *Style—* John Toogood, Esq; 13 Arran Road, London SE6 2LT (☎ 01 698 5775); Prince Edward Theatre, Old Compton Street, London W1 (☎ 01 437 2024)

TOOGOOD, John Michael; s of Charles Dutton Toogood (d 1951), and Inez Mary (d 1957); *b* 4 Sept 1928; *Educ* Malvern; *m* 1960, Barbara Grace, da of Maj Walter Grant Fanning (d 1964); 1 s, 1 da; *Career* chief exec Hill Samuel Shipping Hldgs, md Lambert Brothers Shipping Ltd; dir: Amatco Trading Ltd, Wallem & Co Hong Kong, Tokyo Shipbrokers Ltd, Cleaves Shipbroking; *Recreations* squash, walking; *Clubs* MCC; *Style—* John Toogood, Esq; 4a Phillimore Court, Kensington High Street, London W8 7DS (☎ 01 937 5532); Lambert Brothers Shipping Ltd, Lambert House, 43 Worship St, London EC2A 2LB (☎ 01 283 2000, telex 884971)

TOOHEY, Joyce; *née* Zinkin; CB (1977); da of Louis Zinkin (d 1924) and Lena, *née* Daiches (d 1969); *b* 20 Sept 1917; *Educ* Brondesbury and Kilburn H S, Girton Coll Cambridge, LSE, Harvard Business Sch; *m* 1947, Monty Isaac Toohey, MD, MRCP, DCH; 2 da; *Career* CS 1941-76, under-sec DOE 1970-76, under-sec Miny of Public Bldg and Works 1964-70 (asst sec 1956-64, princ 1948-56, asst princ 1946-48), asst princ Miny Supply 1941-46, ret; *Recreations* reading,, walking; *Clubs* Hurlingham; *Style—* Mrs Joyce Toohey, CB; 11 Kensington Court Gardens, Kensington Court Place, London W8 (☎ 01 937 1559)

TOOK, Barry; s of Charles William Took (d 1961), of Worthing, and Kate Louise Rose, *née* Cox (d 1969); *b* 19 June 1928; *Educ* Stationers Cos' Sch; *m* 1, 10 Aug 1950 (m dis 1965), Dorothy Bird, da of Richard Bird (d 1965), of Lincoln; 2 s (Barry b 1951, David b 1961), 1 da (Susan b 1956); m 2, 29 Oct 1965, Lynden L, da of Mark Leonard (d 1967), of Scunthorpe; 1 da (Elinor b 1968); *Career* aaa Serv RAF 1946-49; broadcaster; Late Extra 1959-60, Bootsie and Snudge 1960-63, Round the Horne 1964-68, Marty 1968-69, Rowan and Martins Laugh In 1969-70, On the Move (adult literary project) 1975-79, Points of View 1979-86; conslt to comedy dept Thames TV 1968-69, advsr to BBC TV 1969-70, head of light entertainment LWT 1971-72; hon cncllr NSPCC, pres Herts branch NDCS; *Books* Laughter in the Air (1976), Tooks Eye View (1983), Comedy Greats (1989); *Recreations* golf, travel, mischief; *Clubs* Garrick, MCC; *Style—* Barry Took, Esq; 17 Hanover House, St Johns Wood, London NW8 7DX (☎ 01 722 8049, fax 01 483 2834)

TOOKE, Brian Cecil; CBE (1983), JP (Suffolk 1965); s of Cecil George Tooke (d 1982), and Violet Mabel, *née* Rolfe (d 1988); *b* 29 Dec 1933; *Educ* St Joseph's Coll Ipswich; *m* 4 July 1959 (m dis 1987), Patricia Ann; 2 s (Robert James b 1964, Julian Charles George b 1968), 2 da (Clarissa Jane b 1961, Melissa Mary b 1972); *Career* chm and md Sadler Hldgs Ltd, chm Local Bd of Commercial Union Assur plc; chm East of England Area Young Cons 1962-64; memb: Cons Party Nat Union Exec 1962-64 and 1975-84, Nat Union GP Ctee 1980-83, Cons Party Nat Advsy Ctee for Local Govt 1968-77; memb Ipswich County Borough Cncl 1959-74, pres East of England Area Cons Assoc 1987- (chm 1980-83), chm Ipswich and Suffolk Industl Advsy Cncl 1985-88 (fndr memb 1972-), pres, tstee, past chm and fndr Suffolk Cncl Nat Assoc of Boys Clubs 1962-, memb East Anglian TAVR Assoc Cncl 1985- (Suffolk Ctee TAVR 1980-); chm: Ipswich and dist appeal Ctee Suffolk Tst for Nature Conservations 1983-85, East Anglian Regmt C of C 1984-87; govr St Joseph's Gp Coll Ipswich 1963-88; *Recreations* theatre, architecture; *Clubs* Carlton; *Style—* Brian Tooke, Esq, CBE, JP; Chattishm Hall, Suffolk IP8 3PX; Sadler Holdings Ltd, PO Box 21, Richmond House, Sproughton Rd, Ipswich, Suffolk IP1 5AW

TOOLEY, Sir John; yr s of late H R Tooley; *b* 1 June 1924; *Educ* Repton, Magdalene Coll Cambridge; *m* 1, 1951 (m dis 1965), Judith Craig Morris; 3 da; m 2, 1968, Patricia Janet Norah, 2 da of late G W Bagshawe; 1 s; *Career* served Rifle Bde 1943-47; sec Guildhall Sch of Music and Drama 1952-55; Royal Opera House: asst to gen administrator 1955-60, asst gen admin 1960-70, gen admin 1970-80, chm Nat Music Cncl Exec 1970-72; govr The Royal Ballet and The Royal Ballet Sch; dir: Royal Opera House Trust, English Music Theatre Co Ltd, Nat Opera Studio, Covent Garden Video Productions Ltd, Nat Video Corpn Ltd; govr Repton Sch; gen dir 1980; Commendatore Italian Republic 1976; Hon FRAM, Hon GSM, Hon RNCM; *Recreations* walking, theatre; *Clubs* Garrick, Arts; *Style—* Sir John Tooley; Avon Farm House, Stratford-sub-Castle, Salisbury, Wilts; 2 Mart St, London WC2; Royal Opera House, Covent Gdn, London WC2E 7QA (☎ 01 240 1200)

TOOLEY, Dr Peter John Hocart; s of Dr Patrick Hocart Tooley, of Kapri, Houmet Lane, Vale, Guernsey, CI, and Brenda Margaret, *née* Williams (d 1939); *b* 28 Feb 1939; *Educ* Elizabeth Coll Guernsey, St Georges Sch Harpenden, Univ of London, London Hosp Med Coll London Univ (MB BS, DObst RCOG, DMJ); *m* 1, 22 Sept 1966 (m dis 1983), Elizabeth Monica, da of Percy Roche, of 164 London Rd, Twyford, Reading, Berks; 1 s (Patrick b 1969), 2 da (Lucy b 1967, Josephine b 1971); m 2, 1987, Diana Edith, *née* Sturdy; *Career* sr ptnr gen practise Twyford Berks 1974-(princ 1966, trainer 1977-81), MO Marks & Spencer plc Reading 1980-, asst dep coroner Borough of Reading 1984-, med conslt gen practice affrs Janssen Pharmaceutical Ltd 1986-; MO Oxfordshire RFU 1970-; memb: Berks Local Med Ctee 1978-86, Reading Pathological Soc; chm Reading Med Club 1980-83 and 1987-(fndr memb), vice-chm Polehampton Charities 1986- (tstee 1975); Freeman City of London, Liveryman Worshipful Co Apothecaries 1965; MRCS, LRCP 1963, MRCGP 1971; memb: BMA, Br Acad Forensic Scis, Assoc Police Surgns GB, Br Assoc Pharmaceutical Physicians, Pharmaceutical Marketing Soc, Coroner's Soc GB; *Recreations* sports, gardening, travel; *Style—* Dr Peter Tooley; Siplak House, Station Rd, Lower Shiplake, Henley on Thames, Oxon RG9 3NY (☎ 073 522 3545); The Surgery, Loddon Hall Rd, Twyford, Reading, Berks RG10 9JA (☎ 0734 340 112); Janssen Pharmaceutical Ltd, Grove, Wantage, Oxon OX12 0DO (☎ 0235 722 966, fax 0235 772 121, car tel 0860 204 413, telex 0235 837301 E-MAIL BT GOLD JPL0040)

TOOP, Alan James; s of James Cecil Toop (d 1973), of Clephane Rd, London, N1, and Elsie Ada, *née* Lavers; *b* 25 Feb 1934; *Educ* Highbury GS, Univ Coll London (BA); *m* 12 Sept 1964, Tessa Peggy Elaine, da of Richard Eric Widdis (d 1966), of Kenton, Middx; 1 s (Adam b 1965), 2 da (Annie b 1968, Rose b 1972); *Career* chm The Sales Machine Ltd 1970-, account dir J Walter Thompson 1967-70, mktg mangr Lever Bros 1961-65, brand mangr Wall's Ice Cream 1958-61; FInstM; *Books* Choosing The Right Sales Promotion (1966), Positioning Brands Profitably (co-author 1987); *Recreations* exercise; *Clubs* IOD; *Style—* Alan Toop, Esq; 21 St Peters Square, London W6 9NW; The Sales Machine Ltd, 75-79 York Rd, London SE1 7NP (☎ 01 928 3355, fax 01 928 2484, telex 27163)

TOOTH, Simon John Geoffrey; s of Cyril John Tooth (d 1936), and Irene, *née* O'Connor (d 1976); *b* 27 May 1934; *Educ* Downside Coll Bath; *m* 1959, Melissa Mary (d 1981), da of Col Colwell Carney (d 1978), of Palm Beach, Florida; 1 s (John), 3 da (Tata, Clare, Alexa); *Career* memb London Stock Exchange 1959-84, exec research conslt 1982-84; London mangr Trans City Hldgs, Aust Investmt Bank 1985-; *Recreations* golf, sailing, deep sea fishing; *Clubs* IOD, Hurlingham; *Style—* Simon Tooth Esq; 52 St Mary Abbots Court, Warwick Gardens, London W14 8RA; 32 Lombard Street, London EC3 (☎ 01 929 2141)

TOPHAM, Robert Charles; s of William George Topham, and Violet Frances, *née* Eayrs; *b* 14 Mar 1925; *Educ* County Sch Cambridge; *m* 14 May 1965, Penelope de Warrenne, da of Lt-Col Richard Arthur Allicocke Young (d 1984); 1 da (Venetia b 1970); *Career* farmer, served on numerous NFU and other agric ctees also Ivel & Beds Internal Drainage Board; former chm NFU Branch County Machinery ctee & Machinery club; *Recreations* shooting, fishing, rare cattle, conservation; *Clubs* CLA, NFU; *Style—* Robert Topham, Esq; Manor Farm, Bygrave, Baldock, Herts (☎ 0462 893165)

TOPLEY, Kenneth Wallis Joseph; CMG (1976); s of Maj William Frederick Topley (d 1956), of London, and Daisy Elizabeth, *née* Wellings (d 1981); *b* 22 Oct 1922; *Educ* Dulwich Coll, Aberdeen Univ, London Sch of Economics (BSc), Chinese Studies in Macau; *m* 1949, Marjorie Doreen, da of William Wills (d 1967), of London; 2 s (William, Julian), 2 da (Celia, Victoria); *Career* Fl-LT RAF 1941-46 served Italy and Yugoslavia; cmmr for Co-op Devpt and Fisheries 1962-63, sec Univ Grants Ctee 1965-67, cmmr for Census and Statistics Hong Kong 1970-73, dir: Social Welfare Hong Kong 1973-74, Educ Hong Kong 1974-80; chm Ctee to Review Post-Secondary and Technical Educ 1980-81, sec for Educ and Manpower Hong Kong 1981-83, ret, sec Univ of E Macau; *Recreations* jogging, television, conversation; *Clubs* Roy Cwlth, Roy Hong Kong Jockey, Ladies' Recreation; *Style—* Ken Topley, Esq; Parkdale, Powdermill Lane, Battle, E Sussex TN3 0SP (☎ 04246 2484); Moulin de Bret, Coussac Bonneval, Haute Vienne, France (☎ 55 752661); 4B, Vila da Colina Guia,

Travessa do Engenheiro Trigo, Macau (☎ 78697)

TOPP, Air Cdre Roger Leslie; AFC (1950, and 2 Bars 1955 and 1957); s of Horace William Topp (d 1972), and Kathleen, *née* Peters; *b* 14 May 1923; *Educ* North Mundham Sch, RAF Cranwell; *m* 21 April 1945, Audrey Jane, da of Arther Stanley Jeffery (d 1969); 1 s (Jeffery b 12 Aug 1950), 1 da (Marilyn b 24 March 1946); *Career* WWII: cmmnd RAF 1944, Glider Pilot Regt E Sqdn rhine Crossing Operation Varisity 1945; pilot Nos 107 and 98 Mosquito Sqdns BAFO Germany 1947-50, Empire Test Pilots Sch Farnborough 1950; lead test pilot: Armament and structures flights Farnborough, Comet Flight tests after disasters 1951-55; oc No 111 Fighter Sqdn, formed and led Black Arrows aerobatic team 1955-58; ops staff: HQ AAFCE Fontainbleau 1959, HQ Brockzetel Sector Control Germany 1960-61; JSSC Latimer 1961; oc: Fighter Test Sqdn Boscombe Down 1952-64, RAF Coltishall 1964-66; Canadian Nat Defence Coll Ontario 1966-67; staff Ops Requirements MOD (air) 1966-67, cmdt Aeroplane & Armament Experimental Estab Boscombe Down 1970-72, dep gen mangr NATO Mult-role Combat Aircraft Mgmnt Agency Munich 1972-78 (head mil factors 1969-70), ret RAF 1978; conslt: Ferranti Def Systems Edinburgh 1978-88, Br Indust for mil aviation, avionic and gen equipment 1988-; *Recreations* golf, yachting; *Clubs* RAF, Royal Fowey Yacht; *Style—* Air Cdre Roger Topp, AFC; Cedar Lodge, Meadow Drive, Hoveton St John, Norfolk (☎ 0603 783887); Fairview, The Espanade, Fowey, Cornwall

TOPPIN, Leo Christian; s of Aubrey John Toppin, CVO (d 1969, formerly Norroy and Ulster King of Arms), and Agnes Louise (d 1951); *b* 14 June 1916; *Educ* Harrow; *m* 1938, Heather Mary, da of Capt Eric Schooling (d 1914), of Royal Warwickshire Regt; 2 s; *Career* serv Army 1939-42, Mid East Cmd 1942-46, Major; former dir of: Kelani Valley Rubber Estates Ltd, Hunasgeria Tea Estates Ltd (chm), Tea Corpn Ltd, Devituri Tea and Rubber Estates Ltd (chm and md), Highfields Ceylon Ltd, Consolidated Commerce Ltd (chm), Liverpool Grain Storage & Transit Ltd, Liverpool & Manchester Investmnt Tst Ltd, London and Manchester Securities plc, and other cos; underwriting memb Lloyd's 1938-; chm Leo C Toppin (Investmnts) Ltd; chm (dir to 1982) Carlton Real Estates 1982-83; *Recreations* swimming; *Clubs* Naval and Military; *Style—* Leo Toppin, Esq; Westering, Maple Ave, Cooden, Bexhill, E Sussex (☎ 042 43 3207); office: Westering, Maple Ave, Cooden, Bexhill, E Sussex

TOPPING, Rev Francis (Frank); s of Francis Bede Topping (d 1982), of Birkenhead, and Dorothy Veronica, *née* Kelly (d 1985); *b* 30 Mar 1937; *Educ* St Anselm's Coll Birkenhead, The North West Sch of Speech and Drama Southport, Didsbury Coll Bristol ; *m* 15 April 1958, June, da of Alfred Sydney Berry, 2 s (Simon b 1961, Mark b 1963), 1 da (Anne b 1959); *Career* RAF Nat Serv Cyprus 1955-57, temporary officiating Chaplain RSME Regt 1983-84; stage mangr, electrician, asst carpenter and actor Leatherhead Repertory Co 1957-58, stage mangr and actor Wolverhampton Grand Theatre 1959-60, played Krishna in Dear Augustine Royal Court Theatre 1959, actor and stage mangr Touring Co 1960-; Granada TV: stage hand, TV floormangr 1960, first asst film dir 1962-64; Theological Coll 1964-67, probationer Methodist Minister Woodingdean Brighton and univ chaplin Sussex Univ 1967-70, freelance bdcaster BBC Radio Brighton 1967-70, ordained Methodist Minister 1970, prodr BBC Radio Bristol 1970-72 (also short story editor and presenter), asst religious progs organizer for all religious progs in North Manchester BBC Network Centre 1972-73, Nat editor London 1973-80, progs on BBC radio include Thought for the Day, Pause for Thought; presenter: Sunday Best (ITV), Topping on Sunday (ITV) 1982-84, The 5 Minute Show (TVS) 1989-; nat chaplain Toch 1984-86 (hon chaplain 1985-), chaplain Kent Coll 1988-; with Donald Swann wrote songs and sketches for Radio and TV, also Swann with Topping (Ambassadors Theatre); presented three one-man plays ; *Books* Lord of the Morning (1977), Lord of the Evening (1979), Lord of my Days (1980), Working at Prayer (1981), Pause for Thought - with Frank Topping (1981), Lord of Life (1982), The Words of Christ (1940), 40 Meditations (1983), God Bless You Spoonbill (1984), Lord of Time (1985), An Impossible God (1985), Wings of the Morning (1987), Act Your Age (1989); *Recreations* sailing, sketching, waterclours; *Clubs* Naval, Hurst Castle Sailing; *Style—* The Rev Frank Topping; Osborn House, Kent College, Pembury, T Wells, Kent (☎ 0892 282 2887); 3 Springfield Cottages, Brede, Rye, E Sussex

TOPPING, John; s of John Topping ISO (d 1970), of Edinburgh, and Margaret May, *née* Cunningham; *b* 22 July 1936; *Educ* George Heriots Edinburgh; *m* 27 March 1967, Anne Fyfe; 2 da (Julia b 1969, Amy b 1974); *Career* fin dir BETEC plc Aylesbury Bucks 1983-; CA, FCT; *Recreations* golf, squash; *Clubs* Ashridge Golf; *Style—* John Topping, Esq; 'Windleshaw', Whiteleaf, Princes Risborough, Bucks HP17 0LX (☎ 08444 4097); BETEC plc, PO Box 2, Mandeville Rd, Aylesbury, Bucks HP21 8AB (☎ 0296 395911)

TORA, Brian Roberto; adopted s of Ernest Carlo Tora, and Betty Lilian, *née* Squires (d 1971); *b* 21 Sept 1945; *Educ* Bancroft's Sch Woodford Green Essex; *m* 4 July 1975 (m dis 1988) Jennifer, da of (Julius) Dennis (Israel) Blanckensee (d 1951); 2 s (Matthew b 26 Dec 1977, Thomas b 5 June 1979); *Career* with Grieveson Grant 1963-74, investmt mangr Singer & Friedlander 1974-79; investmt dir: Van Cutsem & Assocs 1979-82, Touche Remnant Fin Mgmnt 1982-85; head of retail mktg James Capel & Co 1985-; dir: James Capel Unit Tst Mgmnt 1985-, James Capel Fin Servs 1986-; tstee The Mobility Tst, reg bdcaster on LBC, contributor of articles on personal finance to several journals; memb Stock Exchange; *Recreations* bridge, reading, food and wine; *Style—* Brian Tora, Esq; Enniskillen Lodge, Little Waldingfield, Suffolk C010 0SU (☎ 0787 247 783); James Capel & Co, James Capel House, 6 Bevis Marks, London EC3A 7JQ (☎ 01 621 0011, fax 01 621 0496)

TORBOCK, Cdr Richard Henley; JP (Westmorland 1954), DL (1954); s of Joseph Torbock (d 1925), Crossrigg Hall, Penrith, and Florence Hoste Henley (d 1944, da of Col H C Henley, of Leigh House, nr Chard, Somerset; *b* 27 Jan 1904; *Educ* Aysgarth Sch, RNCs Osborne, Dartmouth and Greenwich; *Career* Cdr RN, served 1939-45 in HMS Valiant and HMS Chaser; high sheriff Westmorland 1953; *Recreations* shooting, fishing; *Clubs* Lansdowne; *Style—* Cdr Richard Torbock, RN, JP, DL; Crossrigg Hall, Cliburn, Penrith, Cumbria CA10 3AN (☎ 093 14 287)

TORDOFF, Ernest (Harvey); s of Ernest Tordoff (d 1982), and Margaret, *née* Barraclough (d 1982); *b* 14 August 1946; *Educ* Bradford GS; *m* 25 Sept 1967, Susan Margaret, da of Leslie Vickers, of Filey, North Yorks; 1 s (Benjamin b 1971); *Career* CA; dip Mgmnt Studies; *Recreations* theatre, opera; *Style—* E Harvey Tordoff, Esq; Abbots Bay, Manesty, Keswick, Cumbria CA12 5UG

TORDOFF, Hon Frances Jane; da of Baron Tordoff (Life Peer); *b* 1956; *Style—* The Hon Frances Tordoff

TORDOFF, Baron (Life Peer UK 1981); Geoffrey Johnson Tordoff; s of Stanley Acomb Tordoff, of Marple, Cheshire; *b* 11 Oct 1928; *Educ* N Manchester GS, Manchester GS, Manchester Univ; *m* 1953, Mary Patricia, da of Thomas Swarbrick, of Leeds; 2 s, 3 da; *Career* contested (Lib) Northwich 1964, Knutsford 1966 and 1970; chm Lib Party 1976-79, pres 1983-84; chm Campaigns and Elections Ctee 1982; *Style—* The Rt Hon the Lord Tordoff; House of Lords, London SW1

TORDOFF, Hon Mark Edmund; s of Baron Tordoff (Life Peer); *b* 1962; *Style—* The Hon Mark Tordoff

TORDOFF, Hon Mary Catherine; da of Baron Tordoff (Life Peer); *b* 1954; *Style—* The Hon Mary Tordoff

TORDOFF, Hon Nicholas Gregory; s of Baron Tordoff (Life Peer); *b* 1958; *Style—* The Hon Nicholas Tordoff

TORDOFF, Hon Paula Mary; da of Baron Tordoff (Life Peer); *b* 1960; *Style—* The Hon Paula Tordoff

TORINO, Peter Antony; s of Nello Torino (d 1955), and Anna, *née* Victoria; *b* 15 Sept 1954; *Educ* Cotton Coll, Univ of Bristol (BSc); *m* 2 Jan 1977, Moira, da of Martin Augustine Ansbro, of Reading; *Career* CA; mangr Peat Marwick McLintock 1981-84, UK accountant Control Data 1984-85, fin dir Grayling Gp 1985-; memb ICEAW; *Recreations* travel, squash, reading; *Style—* Peter Antony Torino, Esq; 29 Hartley Rd, London E11 (☎ 989 2413); 4 Bedford Sq, London WC1 (☎ 255 1100, fax 6310602)

TORLESSE, Rear-Adm Arthur David; CB (1953), DSO (1946); s of Capt Arthur Ward Torlesse, RN (d 1939), and Harriet Mary Jeans (d 1952); *b* 24 Jan 1902; *Educ* Stanmore Park Middx, RNCs Osborne and Dartmouth; *m* 1933, Sheila Mary Susan, da of Lt-Col Duncan Darroch, of Gourock; 2 s, 1 da; *Career* joined RN 1915, Lt-Cdr 1931, Cdr 1935, served 1939-45 in HMS Suffolk and cmd HMS Hunter, on Air Staff Admty 1940-44, cmd HMS Triumph in Far East 1950 (Korea despatches), Rear-Adm 1951; flag offr: Special Squad cdr Monte Bello atomic trial expedition 1952, Ground Trg 1953-54, ret 1954; Civil Def dir North Midland Region 1955-67; Offr US Legion of Merit 1954; *Recreations* fishing, entomology; *Clubs* Naval & Military; *Style—* Rear-Adm Arthur Torlesse, CB, DSO; 1 Sway Lodge, Sway, Lymington, Hants (☎ 0590 682 550)

TORNBOHM, (Peter) Noel; s of Eric Anthony Tornbohm (d 1986), of 6 Mowden Hall Drive, Darlington, and May, *née* Barrow (d 1969); *b* 11 Jan 1943; *Educ* Queen Elizabeth GS Darlington, UCL (LLB); *m* 1, 29 May 1965 (m dis 1982), Yvonne Hamilton (Mrs Way), da of Wilfred Vincent Miller, of Darlington; 1 s (Paul b 28 March 1971), 1 da (Catherine b 16 June 1969); m2, 1983 Maureen Roberta (MO), da of Frank Griffin, of Mickleover, Derby; *Career* slr 1967, Smith Roddam & Co 1967 (ptnr 1968-71), Gadsby Coxon & Copestake 1971-72 (ptnr 1972-85); former memb City & Derby 126 Round Table; memb: Derby 41 Club, Derby Beaujolais Fellowship, Derby S and W Derbys Cons Assoc; memb Law Soc slrs Benevolent Assoc; *Recreations* playing & listening to music, walking, keeping dogs; *Style—* Noel Tornbohm, Esq; Hillbank House, 2 The Common, Quarndon, Derby DE6 4JY (☎ 0332 553376); Gadsby Coxon & Copestake, Sterne House, Lodge Lane, Derby (☎ 0332 372372, fax 0332 365715)

TORNEY, Thomas William; JP (Derby 1969); *b* 2 July 1915; *Educ* elementary sch; *Career* joined Lab Pty 1930; election agent Wembley North 1945, Derby West 1964, and Derby and dist area organiser USDAW (sponsored by same) 1946-1970, MP (Lab) Bradford South 1970-87 (ret); memb: Parly Select Ctee Race Relations and Immigration 1970-, Select Ctee on Agric 1979-, Wine and Spirit Liaison Ctee; chm PLP Agric, Fish and Food Gp 1981-; *Style—* Thomas Torney Esq, JP; 8 Wesley Court, 2 Beckwith Road, London SE24 (☎ 01 274 6822)

TOROBERT, Sir Henry Thomas; KBE (1981); *Career* mangr Reserve Bank 1972, govt advsr on currency, first govr Bank of Papua New Guinea 1973- (and instrumental in its foundation); *Style—* Sir Henry ToRobert, KBE; PO Box 898, Port Moresby, Papua New Guinea

TORODE, John Arthur; s of Alfred Charles Torode (d 1980), Gen Sec Sign and Display Trades Union, and Dorothy Amelia Torode (d 1966); *b* 4 Jan 1939; *Educ* Lincoln Coll Oxford (BA), Cornell Univ Ithaca NY; *m* 1975, Naseem Fatima Khan, da of Dr Abdul Wasi Khan (d 1977); 1 s from previous marriage (Jonathan b 1970), 1 s (George b 1976), 1 da (Amelia b 1975); *Career* Policy editor The Independent 1986-; political leader writer and columnist The Guardian 1977-86, (labour ed 1967-72, diary ed 1974-77), memb Younger Ctee on privacy 1969-72, editorial bd New Statesman 1969-72, jt presenter Weekend World 1972, conslt India for UN World Food Programme 1982, chm Labour and Industl Corrs Gp 1969-72; Parly candidate: (Lab) Kingston on Thames 1979, (SDP) Saffron Walden 1983; exec ctee memb Friends of Cyprus 1982-; hon citizen of Huntsville Alabama; *Recreations* swimming, amateur archaeology; *Clubs* Reform, Zoological Society of London; *Style—* John Torode, Esq; 25 Platt's Lane, Hampstead NW3 (☎ 01 435 6105); The Independent, 40 City Road, London EC1

TORPHICHEN, Master of; Douglas Robert Alexander Sandilands; s of late Hon Walter Alexander Sandilands (s of 12 Lord Torphichen, d 1966), and hp of cous, 15 Lord Torphichen; *b* 31 August 1926; *m* 1, 1949, Ethel Louise Burkitt; 1 s; m 2, Suzette Véva, *née* Pernet; 2 s; *Style—* The Master of Torphichen; 109 Royal George Road, Burgess Hill, W. Sussex

TORPHICHEN, 15 Lord (S 1564); James Andrew Douglas Sandilands; s of 14 Lord Torphichen (d 1975); *see also* Sir Francis Sandilands; *b* 27 August 1946; *Educ* King's Sch Canterbury, Birmingham Univ; *m* 1976, Margaret Elizabeth, da of William Alfred Beale (d 1967), of Boston, Mass; 3 da (Margaret b 1979, Mary b 1981, Anne b 1985); *Heir* Master of Torphichen (first cous once removed); *Career* electronics engr; *Style—* The Rt Hon the Lord Torphichen; Calder House, Mid-Calder, West Lothian EH53 0HN

TORPHICHEN, Pamela, Lady; Pamela Mary; da of late John Howard Snow, and widow of Thomas Hodson-Pressinger; *b* 11 Sept 1926; *Educ* Old Palace Mayfield Sussex; *m* 1973, as his 3 w, 14 Lord Torphichen (d 1975); *Career* LRAM; *Recreations* writes music, interested in Russian ikons; *Style—* The Rt Hon Pamela, Lady Torphichen; 16 Moore St, London SW3

TORRANCE, (David) Andrew; s of James Torrance, of Blundellsands, Liverpool, and Gladys, *née* Riley; *b* 18 May 1953; *Educ* Merchant Taylors' Sch Crosby, Emmanuel Coll Univ of Cambridge (MA), London Business Sch (M Sc); *m* 30 Dec 1983, Ann Lesley, da of George Tasker (d 1972), of Bebington, Wirral; 1 s (James b 1987), 1 da (Lucy b 1984); *Career* vice-pres and dir The Boston Consulting Gp Ltd (joined 1976, mangr 1981); *Recreations* cars, tennis, food, wine; *Style*— Andrew Torrance, Esq; 117 Lansdowne Rd, London W11 2LF (☎ 01 727 9019); The Boston Consulting Group Ltd, Devonshire House, Mayfair Place, London W1 (☎ 01 493 3222, fax 01 499 3660, telex 28975)

TORRANCE, (Henry) Bruce; s of Maj Thomas Stirling Torrance (d 1976), of Edinburgh, and Isobel Smith Torrance (d 1981); *b* 12 Mar 1927; *Educ* Edinburgh Acad, Univ of Edinburgh (MB ChB); *m* 10 Sept 1956, Isobel Marjorie, da of Maj Jack Parr (d 1963), of Edinburgh; 2 s (Anthony b 9 July 1959, Fergus b 10 May 1968), 2 da (Caroline b 26 Sept 1956, Juliet b 26 July 1961); *Career* Sqdn Ldr (surgical specialist) RAF 1950-52; conslt surgn (later sr surgn and hon lectr) Manchester Royal Infirmary 1959-; Pancreatic Soc, North of England Gastroenterology Soc; vice pres and hon sec Br Digestive Fndn; FRCS Edinburgh 1953, FRCS 1961; *Recreations* sailing, golf; *Clubs* Wilmslow GC, West Linton GC; *Style*— Bruce Torrance, Esq; Persilands, Biggar, Lanarkshire MS12 6LX (☎ 0899 20813); 15 Lorne St, Manchester M13 OEZ (☎ 061 273 1265)

TORRANCE, Very Rev Prof Thomas Forsyth; MBE (1944) ; s of Rev Thomas Torrance (d 1959), of Edinburgh, and Annie Elizabeth, *née* Sharp; *b* 30 August 1913; *Educ* Canadian Sch Chengdu, Bellshill Acad Scotland, Edinburgh Univ (MA, BD, DLitt), Basel Univ (Dr Theol), Oriel Coll Oxford; *m* 2 Oct 1946, Margaret Edith, da of George Frederick Spear (d 1946), of Combe, Dawn, Bath; 2 s (Thomas Spear b 3 July 1947, Iain Richard b 13 Jan 1949), 1 da (Alison Meta Elizabeth b 15 April 1951); *Career* Chaplain Church of Scotland MEF and CMF 1943-45, Combined Ops and 10 Indian Div, Emergency Serv Palestine Police Force May 1936; prof systematic theol Auburn NY 1938-39, minister Alyth Barony Parish Perthshire 1940-47, minister Beechgrove Parish Church Aberdeen 1947-50, prof church history New Coll Univ of Edinburgh 1950-52, prof christian dogmatics Univ of Edinburgh 1952-79, moderator of the Gen Assembly of the Church of Scotland 1976-77; fndr and co-editor Scottish Journal of Theology 1948-82; memb: Academic Int de Philosophie des Sciences 1976-, Kuratorium Das Deutsche Inst für Bildung und Wissen Paderborn and Berlin, Europaeische Akademie für Umweltfragen Tübingen, Cmmn of Faith and Order of the World Cncl of Churches 1952-62, bd Center of Theological Inquiry Princeton 1979-; pres Academie Int des Sciences Religieuses 1972-81; Hon DD Presbyterian Coll Montreal 1950, Hon DTheol Univ of Geneva 1959, DTheol Facultesace Libre Paris 1959, Hon DD St Andrews 1960, Hon DTheol Oslo 1961, Hon DSc Heriot-Watt Univ 1983, Hon DTheol Debrecen Reformed Coll Hungary 1988; FRSE Edinburgh 1977, FBA 1982; Cross of St Mark Patriarchate of Alexandria 1973, Proto Presbyter of the Greek Orthodox Church Patriarchate of Alexandria 1973, Cross of Thyateira 1977; *Books include* The Doctrine in the Apostolic Fathers (1946 and 1948), Kingdon and Church (1956), When Christ Comes and Comes Again (1957), The Mystery of the Lord's Supper (1958), The School of Faith (1959), Conflict and Agreement in the Church, Vol 1 Order and Disorder (1959), The Apocalypse Today (1959), Conflict and Agreement in the Church, Vol II The Ministry and the Sacraments of the Gospel (1960), Theology in Reconstruction (1965), Theological Science (1969), Space Time and Incarnation (1969), God and Rationality (1971), Theology in Reconciliation (1975), Space, Time and Resurrection (1976), The Ground and Grammar of Theology (1980), Christian Theology and Scientific Culture (1980). Divine and Contingent Order (1981), Reality and Evangelical Theology (1982), The Mediation of Christ (1983), Transformation and Convergence in the Frame of Knowledge (1984), The Christian Frame of Mind (1985), Reality and Scientific Theology (1985), The Trinitarian Faith (1988), The Hermenentics of John Calvin (1988); works edited: Karl Barth church Dogmatics (with G Bromiley, 1956-77), Calvin's Tracts and Treatises (1959), Calvin's New Testament Commentaries (with D W Torrance, 1959-73), Belief in Science and the Christian Life (1980), Christian Theology and Scientific Culture (1980-83), James Clerk Maxwell, A Dynamical Theory of the Electromagnetic Field (1982), Theology and Science are the Frontiers of Knowledge (1985); *Recreations* golf, fishing; *Clubs* Edinburgh Univ Staff, New (Edinburgh); *Style*— The Very Rev Emeritus Professor Thomas F Torrance; 37 Braid Farm Road, Edinburgh EH10 6LE (☎ 031 447 3225)

TORRE DIAZ, 7 Conde (Count; cr of 1846 by Queen Isabel II of Spain); Paul Gerald de Zulueta; only s of Maj Peter Paul John de Zulueta, (Welsh Gds (d 1982; whose mother, Dora, m as her 2 husband, 5 Marquess of Bristol) by his w Tessa, er da of late Lt-Gen Sir Frederick Browning, GCVO, KBE, CB, DSO, and Daphne du Maurrier, the novelist; *b* 12 April 1956; *Educ* Ampleforth, RMA Sandhurst; *m* 18 June 1988, Susan, o da of Dr G J Pritchard, of The Old Mill House, Stanwell Moor; *Career* Maj Welsh Gds 1979; Adj 1983-85; *Recreations* skiing, mountaineering, loafing; *Clubs* Royal Fowey Yacht, Pratts, Chelsea Arts; *Style*— Maj P G de Zulueta

TORRENS-SPENCE, Capt (Frederick) Michael Alexander; DSO, DSC (1941, AFC 1944, JP); s of Lt-Col Herbert Frederick Torrens-Spence (d 1937), of Rosstulla, Whiteabbey, Co Antrim, and Eileen Torrens (d 1983); *b* 10 Mar 1914; *Educ* RN Coll Dartmouth; *m* 1944, Rachel Nora, da of Edward Stanley Clarke, JP, DL (d 1960), of Ballyaughlis Lodge, Lisburn, Co Down; 3 s, 1 da; *Career* cmmnd Sub Lt RN 1934, served Med 1940-42, chief instr Empire Test Pilots Sch 1947-48, dep dir air warfare div Naval Staff 1952-54; cmd: HMS Delight 1955-56, RNAS Lossiemouth 1956-58, HMS Albion 1959-61; Col Cmdt Ulster Special Constabulary 1961-70, CO 2 Bn UDR 1970-71; ADC to HM The Queen 1961; High Sheriff Co Armagh 1979, Lord-Lieut Co Armagh 1981-89 (formerly DL); landowner (115) acres; DFC Greece 1943; *Clubs* MCC; *Style*— Capt Michael Torrens-Spence DSO, DSC, AFC, JP, RN; Drumeullen House, Ballydugan, Downpatrick, Do Down, N Ireland

TORRINGTON, 11 Viscount (GB 1721); Sir Timothy Howard St George Byng; 11 Bt (GB 1715); Baron Byng of Southill (GB 1721); s of Hon George Byng, RN (d on active service 1944, himself s of 10 Viscount, whom present Viscount suc 1961), and Anne Yvonne Carpenter, *née* Wood; *b* 13 July 1943; *Educ* Harrow, St Edmund Hall Oxford (BA); *m* 1973, Susan Honour, da of Michael George Thomas Webster, of The Vale, Windsor Forest, Berks; 3 da (Hon Henrietta Rose b 1977, Hon Georgina Isobel b 1980, Hon Malaika Anne b 13 April 1982); *Heir* kinsman, John Cranmer-Byng, MC; *Career* chm Moray Firth Exploration plc, Exploration & Producn Servs (Hldgs) Ltd (Expro); dir Flextech plc; memb House of Lords Select Ctee on Science and Technology; *Recreations* travel and field sports; *Clubs* White's, Pratts, Muthaiga (Nairobi); *Style*— The Rt Hon the Viscount Torrington; Great Hunts Place, Owslebury, Winchester, Hants (☎ 096 274 234); London office: (☎ 01 245 6522)

TORY, Sir Geofroy William; KCMG (1958), CMG (1956); s of William Frank Tory, of Sheffield, and Edith Wreghitt; *b* 31 July 1912; *Educ* King Edward VII Sch Sheffield, Queens' Coll Cambridge; *m* 1, 1938, Emilia Strickland; 2 s, 1 da; m 2, 1950, Florence Hazel (d 1985), da of Arthur William Thomas, of Halifax, Nova Scotia; *Career* IDC, WWII serv RA; entered Dominions Off 1935, princ private sec to Sec State Dominion Affrs 1945-46, sr sec Office of High Cmmr Canada 1946-49, cnsllr British Embassy Dublin 1950-51; dep high cmmr: Pakistan (Peshawar) 1953-54, Australia 1954-57; asst under-sec state Cwlth Rels Office 1957, high cmmr Fedn of Malaya 1957-63, ambass Eire 1963-66, high cmmr Malta 1967-70, ret 1970; PMN (Malaysia) 1963; *Style*— Sir Geofroy Tory, KCMG, CMG; 2 Burlington Gardens, London W4 4LT

TOSH, Malcolm Charles; s of Charles William Tosh (d 1976), of London, and Marjorie Ann, *née* Grant; *b* 14 May 1934; *Educ* Clifton Coll; *m* 3 Dec 1960, Elizabeth Jane Holmes, da of Raymond Hugh Scott Piercy, of Walton-on-Thames; 2 s (David b 1964, Philip b 1967), 2 da (Lucinda b 1963, Camilla b 1970); *Career* RA 1957-59, Lt 1958; trainee accountant Peat Marwick McLintock 1952-57 (CA 1957), joined Hodgson Impey 1959 (qualified asst 1959-63, ptnr 1963-); church warden; Liveryman Worshipful Co of Glaziers 1981 (hon tres 1988-); *Recreations* bridge, tennis, golf, fell walking; *Clubs* City of London, Naval and Military, MCC, London Scottish; *Style*— Malcolm Tosh, Esq; Little Clandon, West Clandon, Surrey GU4 7ST (☎ 0483 222561); 20 Cursitor St, London EC4A 1HY (☎ 01 405 2088, fax 01 831 2206)

TOSSWILL, (Timothy Maurice) Stephen; s of Timothy Diamonds Tosswill, of Cullompton, Devon, and Sigrid, *née* Bohn (d 1985); *b* 28 April 1949; *Educ* Rugby, St Paul's, London Univ (LLB, LLM); *Career* criminal lawyer, admitted slr 1976; ptnr Tosswill & Co 1976-, memb Crown Cts Liaison Ctee 1984-, articles in Criminal Law Review and New Law Journal; *Recreations* music, photography, skiing, scuba diving; *Style*— Stephen Tosswill, Esq; 260 Brixton Hill, London SW2 1HP (☎ 01 674 9494, fax 01 671 8987)

TOTNES, Archdeacon of; *seé: Hawkins, The Ven Richard Stephen*

TOTTENHAM, Rev Lady Ann Elizabeth; da of 8 Marquess of Ely; *b* 21 July 1940; *Educ* Trin Coll Toronto U (BA STB), Union Seminary New York (MTB); *Career* headmistress Bishop Strachan Sch, Toronto; *Style*— Rev Lady Ann Tottenham

TOTTENHAM, Lord Richard Ivor; s (by 1 m) of 8 Marquess of Ely; *b* 1954; *Educ* Univ of Western Ontario (BA); *m* 1978, Virginia Murney, da of William Murney Morris (decd), of Toronto, Ontario; 2 da (Elizabeth b 1983, Katherine b 1985); *Style*— Lord Richard Tottenham; 819 Grace St, Newmarket, Ontario, L3Y 2L6 Canada

TOTTENHAM, Lord Timothy Craig; 2 s of 8 Marquess of Ely; *b* 17 Jan 1948; *Educ* Ottawa Teachers' Coll; *m* 1973, Elizabeth Jane, da of Grant McAllister, of Ottawa, Ontario; 2 s (Scott b 1977, John b 1981); *Career* teaching, principle of St Michaels Univ Sch, Victoria, BC, Canada; *Recreations* sailing, windsurfing, gardening; *Style*— Lord Timothy Tottenham

TOTTERMAN, Christian William Bjornson; s of Capt Bjorn Balder Totterman, consul (d 1948), and Katharine Clare Wimpenny (d 1975); *b* 3 Sept 1923; *Educ* HS of Econ Studies Helsinki; *m* 29 April 1950, Diana Morrison, da of Neville Clayton (d 1984); 1 s (Robin Bjorn Christian b 1960), 2 da (Clare b 1951, Nicola Jane b 1953); *Career* md Nikolajeff Oy 1960-76; chm bd of dirs: Nikolajeff Oy 1976-78, Transporter Oy 1976-78; Nordick bd memb Int Orgn for Motor Trades and Repairs (IOMTR) 1973-78; memb: Nordik Cncl for Motor Trade 1970-78, Employers Assoc for Motor Trade 1965-78, Bd of Boat and Engine Assoc 1966-69; consul gen for Monaco in Finland 1969-78; KLO (Finnish), KLJ, KOG (Monaco), LMZ (Finnish), CM 1939-40, CM 1941-44; *Recreations* sailing; *Style*— Christian Totterman, Esq; 9 Sion Hill Place, Bath BA1 5SJ (☎ 0225 466655)

TOUCHE, Eric MacLellan; s and h of Sir Rodney Touche, 2 Bt; *b* 22 Feb 1960; *Style*— Eric Touche Esq

TOUCHE, Sir Rodney Gordon; 2 Bt (UK 1962), of Dorking, co Surrey; s of Rt Hon Sir Gordon Cosmo Touche, 1 Bt (d 1972); *b* 5 Dec 1928; *Educ* Marlborough, Univ Coll Oxford; *m* 30 April 1955, Ouida Ann, er da of late Frederick Gerald MacLellan, of Moncton, New Brunswick, Canada; 1 s, 3 da; *Heir* s, Eric MacLellan Touche; *Style*— Sir Rodney Touche, Bt; 1100 8th Ave (Apt 2403), Calgary, Alberta, Canada (☎ 403 233 8800)

TOUCHE, Ruby, Lady; Ruby Anne Hume-Purves; da of late Sir Duncan James Macpherson, CIE; *m* 1926, Rt Hon Sir Gordon Cosmo Touche, 1 Bt (d 1972); *Style*— Ruby, Lady Touche; Gable End, Mill Rd, Holmwood, Surrey

TOULMIN, John Kelvin; QC (1980); s of A H Toulmin, slr, and Mrs B Toulmin, *née* Fraser; *b* 14 Feb 1941; *Educ* Winchester, Trin Hall Cambridge (BA 1963, MA 1966), Univ of Michigan Law Sch (LLM 1965); *m* 13 May 1967, Carolyn Merton, da of Merton Gullick (d 1953); 1 s (Geoffrey b 1969), 2 da (Alison b 1972. Hilary b 1975); *Career* barr 1965, bencher Middle Temple 1986, memb Bar Cncl/Senate 1971-77, 1978-81 and 1986-, memb Supreme Court Rules Ctee 1976-80, recorder Crown Ct 1984; govr The Maudsley and Bethlem Royal Hosps 1979-87, memb ctee of Mgmnt Inst of Psychiatry 1982,- chm Young Barr Ctee 1973-75; bar rep UK delegation to Cncl of the Bars and Law Societies of Europe 1984-; ldr of the UK delegation 1987, chm of Bar int practice ctee 1987-; *Books* DHSS report into Unnecessary Dental Treatment in NHS (Co-author) 1986; articles on rights of establishment & recognition of diplomas in Europe; *Recreations* cricket, listening to music; *Clubs* MCC; *Style*— John Toulmin, Esq, QC; 4 Paper Bldgs, Temple, EC4 (☎ 01 353 3366, fax 01 353 5778)

TOULSON, Roger Grenfell; QC (1986); s of Stanley Kilsha Toulson, of Redhill, Surrey, and Lilian Mary Toulson (d 1985); *b* 23 Sept 1946; *Educ* Mill Hill Sch, Jesus Coll Cambridge (MA, LLB); *m* 28 April 1973, Elizabeth, da of Henry Bertram Chrimes, of Bracken Bank, Dawstone Rd, Heswall, Wirral, Merseyside; 2 s (Henry b 1979, Thomas 1984), 2 da (Susanna b 1975, Rachel b 1977); *Career* barr Inner Temple 1969, recorder 1987; *Recreations* skiing, tennis, gardening; *Style*— Roger Toulson, Esq, QC; Billhurst Farm, Wood St Village, nr Guildford, Surrey GU3 3DZ (☎ 0483 235 246); 2 Crown Office Row, Temple, London EC4Y 7HJ (☎ 01 583 8155, fax 01 583 1205)

TOUT, Herbert; CMG (1946); s of Prof Thomas Frederick Tout (d 1929), and Mary, *née* Johnstone (d 1960); *b* 20 April 1904; *Educ* Sherborne, Oxford; *Career* univ teacher economics, instr Univ of Minnesota 1929-36, lectr Univ of Bristol 1936-45, temp princ BOT 1940-41, asst sec 1941-45, reader in Political Economy UCL 1947-68 (ret); *Recreations* walking, gardening; *Style*— Herbert Tout Esq, CMG; Little Greeting, W Hoathly, E Grinstead, W Sussex (☎ 0342 810400)

TOVEY, Sir Brian John Maynard; KCMG (1980); s of Rev Collett John Tovey (d 1967), and Kathleen Edith Maud Maynard (d 1972); *b* 15 April 1926; *Educ* St Edwards

Sch Oxford, St Edmund Hall Oxford, Sch of Oriental and African Studies London (BA); *Career* dir Govt Communications HQ 1978-83; Plessey Electronics Systems Ltd: def systems cnsltnt 1983-85, defence and political advsr 1985-; *Recreations* music, walking, 16th Century Italian art; *Clubs* Naval & Military; *Style*— Sir Brian Tovey, KCMG; c/o Naval & Military Club, 94 Piccadilly, London W1; Plessey Electronic Systems Ltd, Station Road, Addlestone, Weybridge, Surrey KT15 2PW

TOVEY, (Raymond Francis) Frank; s of Francis Raymond Tovey (d 1966), and Tamara Sarah, *née* Krimont (d 1985); *b* 13 Feb 1920; *Educ* Mill Hill, Lincoln Coll Oxford (MA); *m* 1970, Pamela Jean McDowall, *née* Currie; *Career* RA 1940-46: UK 1940-43, India (14 Army) and Burma (15 Ind Corp) 1943-46, Capt; slr, sr ptnr Field Fisher & Martineau, ret; *Recreations* golf, theatre, philately; *Style*— Frank Tovey, Esq; Mill End Cottage, Chapel Lane, Salford, Oxon OX7 5YN (☎ 0608 41181)

TOVEY, Dr Geoffrey Harold; CBE (1974); s of Harold John Tovey (d 1976), of Midsomer Norton, and Gertrude, *née* Taylor (d 1936); *b* 29 May 1916; *Educ* Wycliffe Coll, Univ of Bristol (MB ChB, MD); *m* 6 Sept 1941, Margaret Beryl, da of Frederick Charles Davies (d 1941), of Abertysswg; 2 s (Charles b 1943, d 1973, Stuart b 1946); *Career* RAMC 1941-46, 8 Field Ambulance 1941-42, Army Blood Transfusion Serv 1942-46, OC No 3 base transfusion unit India Cmmd 1945-46; dir SW Regnl blood Transfusion Serv 1946-79, conslt advsr in Blood transfusion DHSS 1978-81, hon conslt in blood transfusion MOD 1978-82, fndr and dir UK Transplant Serv 1969-79, conslt physician Southmead Hosp Bristol 1946-79, clinical lectr in haematology Univ of Bristol 1947-79; pres: Int Soc of Blood Transfusion 1973-76, Br Soc for Haematology 1977-78; Hellenic Soc for Transplantation Award 1976, Oliver Memorial Award 1977, Alwyn Zoutendyk Memorial Award Medal SA Inst for Med Res 1979; memb select ctee of Experts on Histocompatability Cncl of Europe 1970-79, memb select ctee of Experts on Immunohaematology 1978-81; fndr Rehabilitation at Home Serv for Adult Brain Damaged Eastbourne 1989, memb Eastbourne Dist Med Soc; FRCPath 1963, FRCP 1968; *Books* Technique of Fluid Balance (1957); *Recreations* walking, foreign travel; *Style*— Geoffrey Tovey, Esq, CBE; Lynton, 1B St John's Rd, Eastbourne, E Sussex

TOWER, Maj-Gen Philip Thomas; CB (1968), DSO (1944, MBE 1942); s of Vice-Adm Sir Thomas Tower, KBE, CB (d 1964); *b* 1 Mar 1917; *Educ* Harrow, RMA Woolwich; *m* 1943, Elizabeth, da of Thomas Ralph Sneyd-Kynnersley, OBE, MC (d 1965); *Career* RA 1937, GOC MELF 1967, Cmdt RMA Sandhurst 1968-72, Col Çmdt RA 1970 -80; co cmmnr St John Norfolk 1975-78; *Recreations* shooting, gardening; *Clubs* Army and Navy; *Style*— Maj-Gen Philip Tower, CB, DSO, MBE; Hall Farm, East Raynham, Fakenham, Norfolk NR21 7EE (☎ 0328 4904); Studio A, 414 Fulham Rd, London SW6 1EB (☎ 01 385 8538)

TOWERS, Jonathan Henry Nicholson; s of John Richard Hugh Towers, of Lund House Green, Harrogate, North Yorkshire, and Gwynneth Helen Marshall, *née* Nicholson; *b* 5 April 1939; *Educ* Radley, Clare Coll Cambridge (MA); *m* 29 Sept 1979, Vanessa Catherine, da of John Francis Milward, of Barlow Woodseats, Nr Chesterfield, Derbyshire; 2 s (Edward b 1982, Harry b 1988); *Career* sr ptnr Grays slrs York 1987, under sheriff Yorkshire and Hallamshire 1988; memb Law Soc 1966; *Recreations* golf, shooting, walking, reading, skiing; *Clubs* Yorkshire York; *Style*— Jonathan Towers, Esq; Grays, Solicitors, Duncombe Place, York YO1 2DY (☎ 0904 634 771, fax 0904 610 711)

TOWERS, (William) Lennox; s of John Maxwell Towers, of Peebles, and Elizabeth Torrance Aithcison, *née* Moodie (d 1977); *b* 24 Sept 1946; *Educ* Hutchesons' Boys' GS Glasgow, Leeds GS, Exeter Univ (LLB); *m* 23 Sept 1972, Jan Elaine, da of Frank Morrill, of Menston, W Yorks; 2 s (Alexander b 1977, Edmund b 1985), 1 da (Francesca b 1980); *Career* ptnr Booth & Co Slrs Leeds 1974-, chm H Foster & Co (Stearines) Ltd Gp 1978-, dir M 5 Ltd 1988-; memb Law Soc 1971; *Recreations* family pursuits; *Style*— Lennox Towers, Esq

TOWLE, Peter Frederic Harold; DSC 1945; s of Frederic Statham Towle, of Sutton Courtenay, Berks (d 1963), and Gwendolen Lucy (Hippisley) (d 1965); *b* 8 July 1923; *Educ* Shrewsbury Sch, Brazenose Coll Oxford; *m* 31 March 1951, Kathleen Mary, da of William Vickers BSc, of Cranleigh, Surrey; 2 s (Simon b 1952, Nicholas b 1954), 1 da (Helen b 1956); *Career* Lt (A) RNVR, N Atlantic 1944, Indian Ocean and Pacific 1945; chm Buttons Ltd 1962-64, and Brough Nicholson and Hall Ltd 1962-64; md AFA Minerva EMI Ltd 1968-71, and Int Time Recording Co Ltd 1972-75; dir: Brocks Gp plc 1972-75, Securicor Ltd 1976-88, Securicor Gp plc 1978-, Security Services plc 1978-, Telecom Securicor Cellular Radio Ltd 1984-, Datatrak Ltd 1986-, Serco plc 1987-, chm Securicor Ltd 1985-88, gp chief exec Securicor Gp plc 1985-88, exec consultant 1988-; *Recreations* sailing, shooting; *Clubs* Royal London Yacht, Royal Solent Yacht; *Style*— Peter Towle, Esq; 80 Eccleston Square, London SW1; Sutton Park Hse, Sutton, Surrey (☎ 01 770 7000)

TOWLER, Peter Jeremy Hamilton; s of Stuart Hamilton-Towler, MBE, of E Skirdle, Waterrow, nr Taunton, Somerset, and Betty Irene, *née* Hardwidge; *b* 21 Mar 1952; *Educ* Peter Symonds Winchester, Clare Coll Cambridge (BA, MA); *m* 15 Sept 1979, Dr Martha Crellin, da of Norman Langdon-Down, of River Lodge, Dunally Park, Shepperton-on-Thames, Middx; 1 s, 1 da; *Career* barr Middle Temple 1974; with Western Circuit 1976; memb: Admin Law Bar Assoc 1987-, Local Govt and Planning Bar Assoc 1988-; fndr memb and chm Ampfield Cons Tst 1988, churchwarden 1988-; memb: Romsey Deanery Synod 1985-88; Liveryman Worshipful Co of Weavers 1982, Freeman City of London 1982; ACIARB 1984; *Recreations* cricket, tennis, skiing, conservation; *Clubs* MCC; *Style*— Peter Towler, Esq; 17 Carlton Crescent, Southampton SO9 5AL (☎ 0703 636036)

TOWNELEY, Simon Peter Edmund Cosmo William; JP (Lancs 1956); assumed surname of Worsthorne by deed poll in 1923, but reverted to Koch de Gooreynd in 1937; Simon (Towneley) discontinued by deed poll the name of Worsthorne, and assumed by Royal Licence of 1955 the arms of Towneley, by reason of descent from the eldest da and sr co-heiress of Col Charles Towneley of Towneley; ancestors of the Towneley family were Lay Deans of Whalley Abbey and were granted lands near Burnley by Roger de Lacy, Earl of Lincoln, c 1200; assumed surname of Worsthorne by deed poll in 1923, Simon (Towneley) discontinued by deed poll the name of Worsthorne, and assumed by Royal Licence of 1955 the arms of Towneley, by reason of descent from the eldest da and sr co-heiress of Col Charles Towneley of Towneley; ancestors of the Towneley family were Lay Deans of Whalley Abbey and were granted lands near Burnley by Roger de Lacy, Earl of Lincoln, c 1200; s of Alexander Koch de Gooreynd, OBE, late Irish Gds (s of Manuela, da of Alexandre de Laski, and Joaquima, Marquessa de Souza Lisboa, herself da of Jose' Marques Lisboa, sometime min Plenipotentiary of Emperor of Brazil to Court of St James) and Priscilla, now Baroness Norman, *qv*; er bro of Peregrine Worsthorne; *b* 14 Dec 1921; *Educ* Stowe, Worcester Coll Oxford (MA, DPhil); *m* 30 June 1955, Mary, 2 da of Cuthbert Fitzherbert (d 1987); 1 s (Peregrine b 1962), 6 da (Alice b 1956, Charlotte b 1957, Katharine b 1958, Victoria b 1964, Cosima b 1967, Frances b 1969); *Career* served KRRC Italy 1941-46; lectr in history of music Worcester Coll Oxford 1949-55; cncllr Lancs 1961-66, High Sheriff Lancs 1971-72, HM Lord-Lieut and Custos Rotulorum Lancs 1976-, Hon Col Duke of Lancaster's Own Yeomanry 1979-88; non-exec dir Granada TV 1981-; Live Provident Northern Ballet Theatre; memb ct and cncl of: Manchester Univ, Royal Northern Coll of Music; memb Cncl Duchy of Lancaster 1986-; tstee Br Museum 1988-; KStJ 1976, KCSG (Papal decoration); *Books* Venetian Opera in the Seventeenth Century; *Clubs* Beefsteak, Pratt's, Boodle's; *Style*— Simon Towneley Esq, JP; Dyneley, Burnley, Lancs (☎ 0282 23322)

TOWNELEY STRACHEY, Hon Richard; s of Hon (Thomas) Anthony Edward Towneley Strachey (d 1955), by his w (now Lady Mary Gore, *qv*); hp of bro 4 Baron O'Hagan; *b* 29 Dec 1950; *Educ* Eton; *m* 1983, Sally Anne, yr da of Frederick Cecil Cross, of Upcompton, Compton Bishop, Somerset; *Style*— Hon Richard Towneley Strachey; 23 Thomas St, Bath

TOWNEND, James Barrie Stanley; QC (1978); s of Frederick Stanley Townend (d 1967), of Deal, Kent, and Marjorie Elizabeth, *née* Arnold; *b* 21 Feb 1938; *Educ* Tonbridge, Lincoln Coll Oxford (MA); *m* 20 June 1970, Airelle Claire, da of Hermann Dail Nies, of Wimbledon; 1 step da (Pascale Jéhanne Lucie Sallée-Townend); *Career* Nat Serv in BAOR and UK 1955-57, Lt RA; barr Middle Temple 1962, rec Crown Court 1979-; memb: Kingston and Esher DHA 1983-86, Senate of the Inns of Court and Bar 1984-86, Gen Cncl of the Bar 1984-88; chm of the Family Law Bar Assoc 1986-88, bencher Middle Temple 1987; *Recreations* fishing, sailing, writing verse; *Clubs* Bar Yacht; *Style*— James Barrie Stanley Townend, QC; 1 King's Bench Walk, Temple, London EC4Y 7DB (☎ 01 583 6266)

TOWNEND, John Coupe; s of Harry Norman Townend (d 1988), of Sherborne, Dorset, and Joyce Dentith, *née* Coupe; *b* 24 August 1947; *Educ* Liverpool Inst, LSE (BSC, MSc); *m* 15 March 1969, Dorothy, da of David William Allister (d 1971); 3 s (Andrew, Jonathan, Christopher); *Career* Bank of Eng 1968- (head of wholesale mkts supervision div 1986-); contrib articles to various economic jls; *Recreations* running, fell walking, opera, birds; *Style*— John Townend, Esq; Bank of England, Threadneedle St, London EC2R 8AH

TOWNEND, John Ernest; MP (C) Bridlington 1979-; s of Charles Hope and Dorothy Townend; *b* 12 June 1934; *Educ* Hymers Coll, Hull; *m* 1963, Jennifer Ann; 2 s, 2 da; *Career* chartered accountant 1951-56, divnl chm Haltemprice and Beverley Young Cons 1952-54, RAF 1957-59, govr Hymers Coll, chm J Townend & Sons (Hull) Ltd 1977-(dir and sec 1959-67, md 1967-77) memb Hull CC 1966-74, chm Humber Bridge bd 1969-71, contested (C) Kingston upon Hull North 1970, ldr Humberside CC (memb and Cons ldr of oppn 1973-77) 1977-79, pps to Hugh Rossi (Min of State for the Disabled) 1981-1983; dir: Merchant Vintners Ltd, East Surrey Building Soc; vice-chm: Backbench Finance Ctee 1983-, Cons Small Business Ctee 1983-; memb Treasy and Civil Service Select Ctee; memb Lloyds; *Clubs* Carlton; *Style*— John Townend Esq, MP; Sigglesthorne Hall, Sigglesthorne, Hull, N Humberside

TOWNEND, Hon Mrs; (Katherine Patricia); *née* Smith; da of 3 Viscount Hambleden and Lady Patricia Herbert, da of 15 Earl of Pembroke; *b* 1933; *m* 1, 1961, Ivan Moffat; 2 s; m 2, 1973, Peter Robert Gascoigne Townend; *Style*— The Hon Mrs Townend; 122 Hurlingham Rd, London SW6 (☎ 01 736 1530)

TOWNING HILL, Richard; s of Rupert Albert Hill (d 1972), and Henrietta Towning (d 1974); *b* 5 Feb 1922; *Educ* Wells Cathedral Sch, Wells Blue Sch, Birmingham Univ, Arch Assoc London; *m* 1956 (m dis 1980), Claude Diane, da of Dr Pierre-Alfred Chappuis (d 1960), of Switzerland; 1 s (Alexander b 1960), 1 da (Josephine b 1957); *Career* Capt RE 14 Army England, India, Assam & Burma 1940-45; qualified architectural assoc London 1948; assoc RIBA 1949, fell RIBA 1957; work inc Towingin Hill Bristol early 1950s, redevpt Brunswick Square (in conjunction with English Heritage); works illustrated in Homes and Bungalows, Town Houses, Book of Small Houses; *Recreations* travel, writing, photography, swimming; *Clubs* MCC; *Style*— Richard Towning Hill, Esq; 7 Clifton Wood Court, Clifton Wood Road, Bristol BS8 4UL

TOWNLEY, Sir John Barton; s of Barton Townley of Bailrig, Lancaster (d 1982), and Margaret Gorst (d 1936); *b* 14 June 1914; *Educ* Rydal Sch, Downing Coll Cambridge (PhD, MA) (hon fell), Sorbonne; *m* 1939, Gwendoline Mary Ann, da of Arthur Simmonds (d 1943), of London; 1 s, 3 da; *Career* Award of Merit Preston Sea Cadet Corps 1954-72; md and vice-chm Northern Commercial Vehicles and assic Cos; pres Preston Charities Assoc 1949-; life vice-pres Preston, Chroley and Leyland Cons Club Cncl (pres 1949), Cons Clubs Cncl of GB Medal 1957; life memb MW Industl Assoc Advsy Bd; hon plenipotentiary on granting of freedom of numerous Carribean islands including Barbados, Antiqua and Trindad, hon plenipotentiary to Cyprus and Me 1970-74; chm: Preston YMCA Special Appeals Ctee, Bristol Police Athletics Assoc 1949-60; fndr memb and pres Police Hothersall Hall Youth Camnp (now Lancs Boys Club); fndr memb: Nat Playing Fields Assoc, (and former pres) OAP's Assoc; chm Spastics Appeal 1950-53; kt 1960; *Recreations* talking about rugby, cricket, golf, horse racing; *Clubs* Hawks, Union, Pitt (Cambridge); *Style*— Sir John Townley; 24 Agnew Street, Lytham, Lancs

TOWNS, Robin Peter; s of Harold George Towns, of Steyning, W Sussex, and Mildred, *née* Evans; *b* 3 Nov 1943; *Educ* Ilford County HS, Univ Coll London (LLB); *m* 10 Aug 1968, (Isabel) Susan, da of Albert Partington (d 1966), of Bolton, Lancs; 3 da (Emma b 1971, Sarah b 1973, Rebecca b 1976); *Career* Nat Serv joined Army 1949, Eaton Hall OCS 1950, cmmn serv with Jamaica Bn 1950-51, regular cmmn Depot Royal Norfolk Regt 1951-54, 1 Bn Royal Norfolk Regt 1954-60 serv in Cyprus BAOR Berlin, HQ Mid East Cmd Aden 1960-62, 4 Bn Royal Norfolk Regt 1963-65, on loan to Malaysian Government in Barawak 1965-66, 4 Royal Anglian Regt serv Malta and Eng 1967-69, MOD 1969-71, Depot The Queens Div 1971-73, HQ NI 1973-75, HQ Wales 1975-80, HQ Western Dist 1980-82, ret 1982; burser Outward Bound Tst Sch Aberdovey 1982-84, freelance journalist (nat and provincial pubns); memb: ctee of Shrewsbury Theatre Guild, Attingham Writers, Shrewsbury Sch Community Choir, Shrewsbury Arts and Drama Assoc; *Style*— Robin Towns, Esq; Llechwedd, 65 Lincoln Wood, Haywards Heath, W Sussex RH16 1LJ (☎ 0444 412 393); Capital Ho, 1/5 Perrymovnt Rd, Haywards Heath, W Sussex RH16 3SP

TOWNSEND, (John) Anthony Victor; s of John R C Townseand, of Danvers St, London, and Carla Hillerns, *née* Lehmann; *b* 24 Jan 1948; *Educ* Harrow Sch, Selwyn Coll, Cambridge (MA); *m* 16 April 1971, Carolyn Ann, da of Sir Walter Salomon, Castlemaine House, 2 1/2 St James Place, London SW1 (d 1987); 1 s (Christopher b 1974), 1 da (Alexandra b 1976); *Career* dir: Platignum plc, Rea Brothers Ltd, Blue Ridge REal Est Co (USA), John Townsend & Co (Hldgs) Ltd; *Clubs* Gresham, RAC; *Style*— Anthony Townsend, Esq; Anthony Townsend Associates Ltd, Southbank House, Black Prince Rd, London SE1 7ST (☎ 01 793 0700)

TOWNSEND, Charles Peter; s of Major Sam Fletcher Townsend, MC, of Lowick Bridge, Cumbria, and Katherine Mary, *née* Reynolds; *b* 19 Nov 1949; *Educ* Ampleforth, Manchester Univ (BSc); *m* 7 Oct 1972, Barbara Anne, da of Robert William Bowes (d 1983); 1 s (Hugo b 1979), 2 da (Sophy b 1976, Emma b 1982); *Career* BOC Ltd 1971-81, chm and md Townsend Croquet Ltd 1981; cncl memb The Croquet Assoc 1986; *Books* Five Simple Business Games (1977), Townsend's Croquet Almanack (with John Walters 1988); *Recreations* croquet, performing magic tricks; *Clubs* Croquet Assoc, Harwich Town SC; *Style*— Charles Townsend, Esq; 30 West St, Harwich, Essex CO12 3DD (☎ 0255 553 408); Townsend Croquet Ltd, Claire Rd, Kirby Cross, Frinton-on-Sea, Essex CO13 0LX (☎ 0255 674 404, telex 98163 TCROQ G)

TOWNSEND, Cyril David; MP (C) Bexleyheath 1974-; s of Lt-Col Cyril Moseley Townsend, and Lois, *née* Henderson; *b* 21 Dec 1937,Woking,; *Educ* Bradfield Coll, RMA Sandhurst; *m* 1976, Anita Sarah Weldon, da of late Lt-Col F G W Walshe MC; 2 s (Hugh, John); *Career* cmmnd Durham Light Infantry 1958; served: Berlin, UK, Cyprus, Borneo; Adj 1966-68, ADC to govr and C-in-C Hong Kong (Sir David Trench GCMG, MC) 1964-66, PA to Rt Hon Edward Heath 1968-1970, CRD 1970-74; memb Select Ctees on: Violence in the Family 1976-77, Foreign Affairs (and Sub-Ctee on Overseas Devpt); PPS to min of state DHSS 1979, sponsor of Protection of Children Act 1979, vice chm Cons Parly Def Ctee, vice-chm Friends of Cyprus, chm All Pty Freedom for Rudolf Hess Campaign, jt-chm Cncl for Advancement of Arab-Br Understanding; chm: British-Cyprus CPA Gp, Select Ctee on Armed Forces Bill 1981; co fndr and chm South Atlantic Cncl, the Bow Gp Standing Ctee on Foreign Affairs 1977-84; vice chm Political Ctee of the UN Assoc, memb SE London Industl consultative Gp 1975-83, vice chm of Cons ME Cncl; fell of Ind and Parly Tst, Br Parly Observer at presidential election in Lebanon 1982; *Style*— Cyril Townsend Esq, MP; House of Commons, London SW1

TOWNSEND, Jonathan Richard Arthur; s of David Charles Humphrey Townsend, and Honor Stobart, *née* Hancock (d 1967); *b* 30 Nov 1942; *Educ* Winchester, Corpus Christi Coll Oxford (BA); *m* Sarah Elizabeth, da of Gordon Chalmers Fortin (Cdr RN), of Lavenham, Suffolk; 2 da (Honor Sarah b 2 Sept 1968, Louise Rosamond b 12 March 1971); *Career* prodn mangr DRG plc 1961-62 and 1965-68, ptnr Laing and Cruickshank 1972-73 (joined 1969), ptnr de Zoete and Bevan 1973-86, md Barclays de Zoete Securities 1986; *Recreations* cricket, tennis, shooting, bridge; *Clubs* Brooks's, MCC, Vincents; *Style*— Jonathan Townsend, Esq; Mount Farm, Thorpe Morieux, Bury St Edmunds, Suffolk; 73 Gloucester St, London SW1 (☎ 01 834 8650); Ebbgate House, Swan Lane, Upper Thames St, London EC4 (☎ 01 623 2323, fax 01 626 1753, telex 888221, 883 7G)

TOWNSEND, Lady Juliet Margaret; *née* Smith; MVO (1981); da of 2 Earl of Birkenhead, TD (d 1975); *b* 9 Sept 1941; *Educ* Westonbirt, Somerville Coll Oxford; *m* 1970, John Richard Townsend, s of Lt-Col Clarence Henry Southgate Townsend, OBE, MC, TD, MRCVS (d 1953); 3 da; *Career* lady-in-waiting to HRH The Princess Margaret, Countess of Snowdon 1965-71, extra lady-in-waiting 1971-; *Style*— Lady Juliet Townsend, MVO; Newbottle Manor, Banbury, Oxon (☎ Banbury 811295)

TOWNSEND, Rear-Adm Sir Leslie William; KCVO (1981), CBE (1973); s of William Bligh Townsend and Ellen, *née* Alford; *b* 22 Feb 1924; *Educ* Regent's Park Sch Southampton; *m* 1947, Marjorie Bennett; 1 s, 3 da; *Career* joined RN 1942; sec to: Vice-Chief of Naval Staff 1967-70, First Sea Lord and Chief of Naval Staff 1970-71; mil asst to: Chief Def Staff 1971-73, chm NATO Military Ctee 1974; dir Naval and WRNS Appointments 1977, Rear-Adm 1979, Defence Services sec 1979-82, ret 1982; memb of Lord Chllr's Panel of Independent Inspectors 1982-; *Style*— Rear Adm Sir Leslie Townsend, KCVO, CBE; 21 Osborne View Rd, Hill Head, Fareham, Hants PO14 3JW (☎ 0329 663446)

TOWNSEND, Prof Peter Brereton; s of Flt Lt Philip Brereton Townsend, of Knaresborough, N Yorks, and Alice Mary, *née* Southcote; *b* 6 April 1928; *Educ* Univ Coll Sch, Univ of Cambridge (BA), Free Univ Berlin; *m* 1, 18 June 1949 (m dis 1976), Ruth, *née* Pearce; 4 s (Matthew, Adam, Christian, Ben); m 2, 1976 (m dis 1981), Joy, *née* Skegg; 1 da (Lucy); m 3, 1985, Jean, *née* Corston; *Career* RASC and RAEC 1946-48; res sec Political and Econ Planning 1952-54, res offr Inst of Community Studies Bethnal Green 1954-57, res fell (later lectr) LSE 1957-63, prof of sociology Univ of Essex 1963-81, prof of social policy Univ of Bristol 1982-; chm Child Poverty Action Gp 1969-, Disability Alliance 1974-; former pres Psychiatric Rehabilition Assoc 1967-85; (pt/t govr advsr and conslt); memb: exec ctee Fabian Soc 1958- (chm 1965-66), chief scientists ctee DHSS 1976-79, res Working Gp on Inequalities in Health 1977-80, Br Sociological Assoc 1961-89, Assoc 1978-89; *Books* incl: Cambridge Anthology (ed 1952), The Family Life of Old People (1957), The Last Refuge: A Survey of Residential Institutions and Homes for the Aged in England and Wales (1962), The Poor and Poorest (with Brian Abel-Smith 1965), Old People in Three Industrial Societies (with Ethel Shanas and others 1968), The Concept of Poverty (ed 1970), The Social Minority (1973), Disability Rights Handbook (jtly 1973), Disability Rights Handbook (jtly 1976-, now largely the responsibility of the Disability Alliance), Sociology and Social Policy (1975), Poverty in the United Kingdom (1979), Inequalities in Health (with Sir Douglas Black and others 1980), Health and Deprivation: Inequality and the North (with Peter Phillimcre and Alastair Beattie 1987), Poverty and Labour in London (1987); *Recreations* life-long interest in athletics; *Style*— Prof Peter Townsend; School of Applied Social Studies, Univ of Bristol, 40 Berkeley Sq, Bristol BS8 1HY (☎ 0272 297403)

TOWNSHEND, Lady Carolyn Elizabeth Ann; has resumed surname Townshend; da of 7 Marquess Townshend; *b* 27 Sept 1940; *Educ* Univ of Florence Italy; *m* 13 Oct 1962 (m dis 1971), Antonio Capellini; 1 s; *Career* Int Promotions & PR; md Orchestra of St John's Smith Square; *Recreations* skiing, classical music; *Style*— Lady Carolyn Townshend

TOWNSHEND, (Harold) Frank; s of Thomas David Townshend, and Zuradah Eisie, *née* Sutherland; *b* 30 Dec 1937; *Educ* Milton (Jr), Tech HS Bulawayo, Zimbabwe; *m* 21 March 1964, Elaine Marguerite; 2 s (Simon Neville Thomas b 1964, Philip Harold Tristram b 1968), 1 da (Guinevere Zuradah Heléné b 1967); *Career* engr and inventor; b in Johannesburg, lived Bulawayo, Rhodesia 21 yrs, Merchant navy, world travel six yrs, to patent inventions submitted; author of published articles; watercolour artist; *Recreations* sketching, painting, writing, model enging; *Style*— Harold Townshend, Esq; Snaith, Goole, N Humberside (☎ 0405 860413)

TOWNSHEND, 7 Marquess (GB 1787); Sir George John Patrick Dominic Townshend; 11 Bt (E 1617); also Baron Townshend of Lynn Regis (E 1661) and Viscount Townshend of Raynham (E 1682); s of 6 Marquess (d 1921) whose forebear, 1 Marquess and Field Marshal commanded the field of Quebec after the death of Gen Wolfe; *b* 13 May 1916; *Educ* Harrow; *m* 1, 1939 (m dis 1960; she m 1960, Brig Sir James Gault, KCMG, MVO, OBE), Elizabeth Pamela Audrey, da of Maj Thomas Luby, late judicial cmmr ICS; 1 s, 2 da; m 2, 1960, Ann Frances (d 1988), da of late Arthur Pellew Darlow; 1 s, 1 da; *Heir* s, Viscount Raynham; *Career* Norfolk Yeomanry 1936-40, Scots Gds 1940-45; chm: Anglia TV Ltd 1958-86, Anglia TV Gp plc 1976-86, Survival Anglia Ltd 1971-86, AP Bank Ltd 1975-, Raynham Farm Co Ltd 1957-, Norfolk Agric Station 1973-87; dir: Norwich Union Life Insur Soc Ltd 1950-86 (vice chm 1973-86), Norwich Union Fire Insur Soc Ltd 1950-86 (vice chm 1975-86); DL Norfolk 1951-61; *Clubs* White's, Pratt's, MCC, Norfolk; *Style*— The Most Hon the Marquess Townshend; Raynham Hall, Fakenham, Norfolk (☎ 0328 2133)

TOWNSHEND, Lord John Patrick; s of 7 Marquess Townshend; *b* 1962; *Educ* Eton, London Univ; *m* 12 Sept 1987, Rachel Lucy, da of Lt-Gen Sir John Chapple, KBE; *Career* advertising copywriter; *Recreations* advertising, drumming, Norfolk; *Style*— Lord John Townshend

TOWNSHEND, Lady Katherine Ann; da of 7 Marquess Townshend; *b* 1963; *Style*— Lady Katherine Townshend

TOWNSHEND, Timothy John Hume; s of Canon Horace Lyle Hume Townshend, of The Close, Norwich, Norfolk, and Lorna Ethel, *née* Lutton; *b* 20 May 1949; *Educ* Ipswich Sch, Pembroke Coll Cambridge (BA, MA); *Career* barr Lincolns 1972, practises SE circuit; ctee memb Broadland Housing Assoc; *Recreations* sailing, skiing, gardening; *Clubs* Norfolk, Norwich; *Style*— Timothy Townshend, Esq; 24 Newmarket Rd, Norwich, Norfolk NR2 2LA (☎ 0603 661519); Octagon House, 19 Colegate, Norwich, Norfolk (☎ 0603 623186, fax 0603 760519)

TOWNSIN, Michael Farndon; s of Reginald Townsin, and Mary, *née* Tebbs; *b* 7 April 1940; *Educ* Kings Sch Peterborough; *m* 1, 17 Jun 1967 (m dis 1977), Denise Margaret, da of George Ellicott (d 1972), of Peterborough; 1 s (Luke William), 3 da (Tara Sophie, Talitha Lucy, Georgina Sarah); m 2, 3 Jan 1981, Christine Noelle, da of Leonard Barker (d 1969), of Perth, W Aust; *Career* exec offr DHSS 1960-64; jt md and dep chm Young & Rubicam 1980-83 (media exec 1964-74, media dir and bd dir 1974-80), chm and chief exec offr Havas Conseil Marsteller 1983-86, advtg and mktg conslt 1986-; FIPA; *Recreations* swimming, reading, films; *Clubs* Annabel's, Mark's, Harry's Bar; *Style*— Michael Townsin, Esq; 90 East Sheen Ave, London SW14 (☎ 01 876 4924, car 0836 216282)

TOWNSING, Sir Kenneth Joseph; CMG (1971), ISO (1966); s of J Townsing (decd); *b* 25 July 1914; *Educ* Perth Boys' Sch, Univ of WA; *m* 1942, Frances, da of G Daniel; 2 s, 1 da; *Career* Maj 2 AIF ME 1940-46; public serv inspr 1946-49; sec Pub Serv Cmmrs Off 1949-52; dep under tres 1952-59; Pub Serv Cmmn 1958-59; under tres (permanent head WA State Tresy) 1959-75; chm Salaries & Allowances Tbnl 1975-84; memb Senate Univ of WA 1954-70, pro-chllr 1968-70), cmmr Rural & Industs Bank 1959-65, memb Tertiary Educn Cmmn 1971-74, dir Western Mining Corpn 1975-87; kt 1982; *Style*— Sir Kenneth Townsing, CMG, ISO; 22 Robin St, Mount Lawley, W Australia 6050 (☎ 09 272 1393)

TOWNSLEY, Barry Stephen; s of Dr William Townsley; *b* 14 Oct 1946; *Educ* Hasmonean GS; *m* 3 Nov 1975, Hon Laura Helen, da of Lord Wolfson of Marylebone (Life Peer); 1 s (Charles b 2 June 1984), 2 da (Alexandra b 3 May 1977, Georgina b 26 May 1979); *Career* W Greenwell & Co 1964-69, dir Astaire & Co 1969-76, fndr and sr ptnr Jacobson Townsley & Co 1976-; tstee Serpentine Gallery London; *Recreations* contemporary art; *Clubs* Carlton; *Style*— Barry Townsley, Esq; Jacobson Townsley & Co, 44 Worship St, London EC2A 2JT (☎ 01 377 6161, fax 01 375 1380)

TOWNSON, John Rothwell (Ronnie); s of Ernest Townson (d 1956), and Anne Brown (d 1957); *b* 17 August 1913; *Educ* Rivington GS; *m* 1947, June Beryl, da of David Temple Phillips (d 1957); 4 s, 2 da; *Career* chm J R Townson Investmts Ltd until 1987, dir Nationwide Bldg Soc until 1981, govr Millfield Sch; Freeman City of London, Liveryman Worshipful Co of Gardeners'; patron Christ's Church Harwood, ACIB, CBIM, FRSA; *Recreations* fishing, piano; *Clubs* E India, Royal Cork Yacht; *Style*— John R Townson, Esq; Withnell Grange, Bury Lane, Withnell, Lancs PR6 8BH (☎ 0254 830685)

TOY, Rev Canon John; s of Sidney Toy, FSA, FRIBA (d 1967), of London, and Violet Mary, *née* Doudney (d 1952); *b* 25 Nov 1930; *Educ* Epsom Co GS, Hatfield Coll Durham (BA, MA), Leeds Univ (PhD); *m* 1963, Mollie, da of Eric Tilbury (s 1987), of Ross-on-Wye; 1 s (Paul Bernard James b 1964), 1 da (Katherine Violet b 1966); *Career* priest C of E 1956, curacy in London 1955-58, travelling sec with Student Christian Movement 1958-60, chaplain and lectr Ely Theol Coll 1960-64, chaplain St Andrew's Gothenburg Sweden 1965-69, lectr, sr lectr and princ lectr in theol St John's Coll York 1969-83, canon residentiary and chllr York Min 1983-; *Publications* Cathedral Booklets; Jesus: Man for God (1988); *Recreations* music, architecture, travel; *Clubs* Yorkshire (York); *Style*— The Rev Canon John Toy; 10 Precentor's Court, York YO1 2EJ (☎ 0904 620877)

TOYE, Bryan Edward; s of Herbert Graham Donovan Toye (d 1969), and Marion Alberta, *née* Montignani; *b* 17 Mar 1938; *Educ* Stowe; *m* 8 Oct 1982, Fiona Ann, da of Gordon Henry James Hogg, of Wellington, New Zealand; 2 s (Charles Edward Graham b 16 Dec 1983, Frederick b 6 Jan 1988), 1 da (Elisabeth Fiona Ann b 27 July 1985); *Career* Toye & Co 1956- (dir Toye Kinning & Spencer 1962-, chm Toye & Co plc & 23 assoc subsid companies 1969); City of London: Alderman the Ward of Lime St 1983 (pres Lime St Ward Club), vice-pres City Livery Club, former Master Worshipful Co of Gold & Silver Wyre Drawers, memb Ct of Asssts of Worshipful Co of Broderers, memb Guild of Freemen of the City of London, Liveryman Worshipful Co of Goldsmiths; memb of cncl Royal Warrant Holders Assoc 1982; FBIM 1983; FID 1966; memb of Lloyds; steward Henley Royal Regatta 1980; OStJ 1980; *Recreations* swimming, tennis, gardening, music, entertaining; *Clubs* Leander, Wig and Pen, RAC;

Style— Bryan Toye, Esq; Toye & Co plc, 19-21 Great Queen St, London WC2B 5BE (☎ 01 242 0471, fax 01 831 8692, telex 261285)

TOYE, Col (Claude) Hugh; OBE (1962), MBE (1947); s of Rev Percy Sheffield Toye (d 1968), and Sarah, *née* Griffiths (d 1966); *b* 28 Mar 1917; *Educ* Kingswood Sch Bath, Queens' Coll Cambridge (BA, MA); *m* 28 April 1958, Betty, da of Lionel Hayne (d 1932), of Oulton Broad, Suffolk; *Career* enlisted Private RAMC (TA) 1938, FD Ambulance France 1940 (despatches), cmmnd RA 1941, Capt, instr Intelligence Sch Karachi 1943-44, Maj CSDIC (India) 1944-46, GSO 11 (Intelligence) HQ ALFSEA 1946-47, DAA and QMG HQ 56 Armd Div (TA) 1951-53, GSO II Political Off MEF Cyprus 1956-58, Cmd 36 Battery RA Cyprus 1958 (UK 1959), Lt-Col Mil Attaché Vientiane 1960-62, GSO I (SD) SHAPE Paris 1962-64, Gwilym Gibbon res fell Nuffield Coll Oxford (DPhil) 1964-66, Col UK mil advsr's rep HQ SEATO Bangkok 1966-68, def advsr UK Mission to UN NY 1969-70, Dep Cdr Br Army Staff Washington 1970-72, ret 1972; reviewer of book on Indo-China 1965-75 (later on SE Asia); *Books* The Springing Tiger, a study of Subhas Chandra Bose (1959), Laos Buffer State or Battleground (1968); *Recreations* gardening, writing, playing the piano; *Clubs* Army and Navy; *Style*— Col Hugh Toye, OBE, MBE; Old Farm Close, Wheatley, Oxford OX9 1UG

TOYE, Prof John Francis Joseph; s of John Redmond Toye, of Sketty, Swansea, S Wales, and Adele, *née* Francis (d 1972); *b* 7 Oct 1942; *Educ* Christ's Coll Finchley, Jesus Coll Cambridge (BA, MA), Harvard, SOAS (MSc, PhD); *m* 18 March 1967, Janet, da of Richard Henry Reason, of Harrow, London; 1 s (Richard b 1973), 1 da (Eleanor b 1970); *Career* asst princ HM Treasy 1965-68, res fell SOAS London 1970-72, fell (later tutor) Wolfson Coll Cambridge 1972-80 (asst dir of devpt studies 1977-80); dir: Commodities Res Unit Ltd 1980-82, Centre for Devpt Studies Univ Coll Swansea 1982-87, Inst of Devpt Studies Sussex Univ (professorial fell) 1987-; memb: Wandsworth Community Rels Cncl 1968-72, Cambridge Cncl of Community Rels 1972-80, W Glamorgan Equal Opportunities Gp 1983-87; *Books* Taxation and Economic Development (1978), Trade and Poor Countries (1979), Public Expenditure and Indian Development Policy (1981), Dilemmas of Development (1987); *Recreations* music, walking, theatre; *Style*— Prof John Toye; Institute of Development Studies, University of Sussex, Falmer, Brighton, Sussex BN1 9RE

TOYE, Wendy; da of Ernest Walter Toye and Jessie Crichton, *née* Ramsay; *b* 1 May 1917; *Educ* privately; *m* Edward Selwyn Sharp (m dis); *Career* dir and dancer; studied dancing as a child and first appeared at the Royal Albert Hall in 1921, produced a ballet at the Palladium when only ten years of age, made her first appearance on the stage at the Old Vic as Mustard Seed in A Midsummer Night's Dream 1929, Choreographer Mother Earth Savoy 1929, danced with Ninette de Valois' Vic-Wells Ballet Co 1930, numerous roles, princ dancer in 'The Golden Toy', toured with Anton Dolin 1934-35, princ dancer in Aladdin 1937, arranged the dances for all George Black's prodns 1937-44, arranged the ballets for Gay Rosalinda Palace 1945, directed prodn of Big Ben for Sir Charles Cochran Prince's 1946, played princ girl in the pantomime Simple Simon Adelphi 1947, sent her co Ballet-Hoode Wendy Toye to Paris for a season 1948, directed Lady at the Wheel 1958 and many more; recent prodns incl: This Thing Called Love Ambassadors 1984, Noel and Gertie Princess Grace Theatre Monte Carlo 1984, assoc prodr Barnum, Victoria Palace, tribute to Joyce Grenfell 1985; Shaw Festival Theatre Canada: Celemare, Mad Woman of Chaillot; assoc prodr Torvill & Dean Ice Show World Tour 1985, Singing In The Rain London Palladium, dir and choreographer Kiss Me Kate Copenhamgen and Unholy Trinity Stephenville Festival 1986, Laburnham Grove Watford Palace 1987, Miranda Chichester Festival Theatre for Children 1987, Songbook Watermill Theatre 1988, Ziegfeld London Palladium 1988, Mrs Dot Watford Palace 1988, Family and Friends Sadlers Wells 1988, When That I Was Manitoba Theatre Center 1988; ENO prodns incl: Bluebeards Castle, The Telephone. Russalka, La Vie Parisienne, Orpheus In The Underworld, Italian Girl In Algiers, Fledermaus; Seraglio, The Impresario For Yehudi Menuhins Bath (with Menuhin conducting); directed films: The Stranger Left No Card (first prize Cannes Film Festival), On The Twentieth Day, Raising A Riot, We Joined The Navy, Three Cases of Murder, All For Mary, True As A Turtle, The King's Breakfast; lectured in Australia 1977, memb cncl LAMDA, original memb Accreditation BD instigated by NCDT for Acting Courses 1981-84, served Equity Cncl as first dirs rep 1974 (dirs sub ctee 1971); Queen's Silver Jubilee Medal 1977; *Recreations* embroidery, gardening; *Style*— Wendy Toye; c/o Simpson Fox, 52 Shaftesbury Ave, London

TOYN, His Hon Judge (Richard) John; s of Richard Thomas Millington Toyn (d 1961), of Leamington Spa, Warwicks, and Ethel Toyn, *née* Crimp (d 1981); *b* 24 Jan 1927; *Educ* Salishull Sch; Bristol GS; Bristle Univ (LLB); *m* 20 Aug 1955, Joyce Evelyn, da of Harold Llewelyn Goodwin (d 1970), of Solihall, W Midlands; 2 s (Andrew b 1956, Richard b 1960), 2 da (Julia b 1958, Louise b 1964); *Career* Royal Army Serv Corps 1948-50; Barr 1950; chief justice 1972; memb Parole Bd for England and Wales 1978-80; Contributing ed, Buttermoriths County Court Precedents and Peending; *Style*— His Hon Judge Toyn; c/o Queen Elizabeth II Law Courts, Birmingham

TOYNBEE, Lawrence Leifchild; s of Arnold Joseph Toynbee (d 1975), of London, and Rosalind Mary, *née* Murray (d 1967); *b* 21 Dec 1922; *Educ* New Coll Oxford, Rustin Sch of Drawing and Fine Arts (Cert in Fine Art); *m* 20 April 1945, Jean Constance, da of Brig Gen The Hon Arthur Melland Asquith, DSO (d 1939), of Clovelly Ct, Bideford, Devon; 6 da (Rosalind (Mrs Pennybacker) b 1946, Celia (Mrs Caulton) b 1948, Clare (Mrs Huxley) b 1949, Rachel (Mrs Fletcher) b 1950, Sarah b 1953, Frances (Mrs Wilson) b 1957); *Career* Sandhurst, WWII Lt 4 Bn Coldstream Gds 1942-44; art master St Edwards Sch Oxford 1947-62, visiting tutor Ruskin Sch of Drawing Oxford 1947-62, lectr Oxford Sch of Art 1960-63, sr lectr in painting Bradford Sch of Art 1963-67, dir fine art Morley Coll London 1967-72; one man exhibitions: Leicester Galleries 1961, 1963, 1965, 1967 and 1972 (and at Mayor Gallery), Agnews 1980, Fine Art Soc 1985 and 1989; various charitable works incl meals on wheels and visiting the blind; *Clubs* MCC, 12 FF; *Style*— Lawrence Toynbee, Esq; Chapel Cottage, Ganthorpe, Terrington, York YO6 4QD (☎ 065 384 383)

TOYNBEE, Michael Robert; JP; s of Ralph Victor Toynbee (d 1970); *b* 26 Nov 1925; *Educ* Winchester; *m* 1953, Yvonne Norah, *née* Cleland; 1 s, 1 da; *Career* Capt Rifle Bde 1945-52, WO 1949-52, chm Jessel Toynbee & Gillett plc 1977-84 (dir 1953-77); chm Alexanders Discount 1984-88; chm sch council Ardingly Coll; High Sheriff East Sussex 1985; tres Univ of Sussex 1987-; *Recreations* shooting, fishing, tennis; *Style*— Michael Toynbee, Esq, JP; Westerleigh, Wadhurst, E Sussex (☎ 089 288 3238)

TOYNBEE, Polly (Mrs Peter Jenkins); da of Philip Toynbee (d 1981), and Anne Barbara Denise Powell; gf historian Arnold Toynbee; *b* 27 Dec 1946; *Educ* Badminton Sch, Holland Park Comprehensive, St Anne's Coll Oxford; *m* 1970, Peter George James Jenkins, s of Kenneth Jenkins; 1 s (Nathaniel b 1985), 2 da (Millicent b 1971, Flora b 1975); *Career* reporter The Observer 1968-71, ed The Washington Monthly USA 1971-72, feature writer The Observer 1972-77, columnist The Guardian 1977-88, social affrs ed BCC 1988-; SDP candidate Lewisham East 1983; *Books* Leftovers (1966), A Working Life (1970), Hospital (1977), The Way We Live Now (1982), Lost Children (1985); *Recreations* children; *Style*— Miss Polly Toynbee; 1 Crescent Grove, London SW4 7AF; BBC, Television Centre, Wood Lane, London W2

TOYNBEE, Simon Victor; s of Ralph Victor Toynbee (d 1970), and Olive Bridget, *née* Monins; *b* 30 Jan 1944; *Educ* Winchester; *m* 12 Aug 1967, Antoinette Mary, da of John Walter Devonshire, of Appt 402, 2800 Neilson Way, Santa Monica, 90405 Calif, USA; 3 da (Georgina, Elizabeth, Susannah); *Career* 2 Lt The Rifle Bde 1963-66; Jessel, Toynbee and Co Ltd 1966-72, dir Singer and Friedlander Ltd 1977-82 (joined 1973), dir Henderson Admin Ltd 1987- (joined 1982); hon investmt advsr: Royal Greenjackets Funds, Church Army; *Recreations* gardening, deerstalking; *Clubs* Royal Greenjackets, MCC; *Style*— Simon Toynbee, Esq; Old Tong Farm, Brenchley, Kent TN12 7HT (☎ 0892 723552); 3 Finsbury Ave, London EC2M 2PA (☎ 01 638 5757, fax 01 377 5742, telex 884616)

TOYNE, Prof Peter; s of Harold Toyne, and Lavinia Doris, *née* Smith (d 1968); *b* 3 Dec 1939; *Educ* Ripon GS, Univ of Bristol (BA); *m* 2 Aug 1969, Angela, da of Rev John Alroy Wedderburn; 1 s (Simon b 1970); *Career* Univ of Exeter: lectr in geography 1965-75, sr lectr 1975-80, sub dean of social studies 1976-79; dir Dept of Educn and Sci Educnl Credit Transfer Feasibility Study 1977-80, dep dir W Sussex Inst of HE 1980-83, dep rector N E London Poly 1983-86, rector The Liverpool Poly 1986-present; chm BBC Radio Merseyside, memb BBC NW Advsy Cncl, bd memb The Liverpool Playhouse, memb ctee of Business Opportunities on Merseyside (BOOM), memb Merseyside Enterprise Forum, memb devpt ctee and educnl activities ctee Royal Liverpool Philharmonic Orchestra; chm credit accumulation and tansfer ctee CNAA, memb ctee for internat cooperation in HE Br Cncl, tstee H E Fndn, theological coll inspr House of Bishops; *Books* World Problems (1969), Techniques in Human Geography (1971), Recreation and Environment (1974), Organisation, Location and Behaviour (1974), Toyne Report on Credit Transfer (1979), and 35 articles in various professional jnls; *Recreations* music (orchestral and churchmusic), railways, gardening, travel; *Clubs* Liverpool Athenaeum; *Style*— Prof Peter Toyne; The Liverpool Poly, Rodney House, 70 Mount Pleasant, Liverpool L3 5UX (☎ 051 709 3676, fax 051 709 0172)

TRACE, Capt David Morley; RM; s of Lawrence Archibald Trace (d 1978), and Edith, *née* Morley; *b* 17 May 1927; *Educ* Cranleigh; *m* 1, 12 Feb 1951, Nena, *née* Hadjisavvas (d 1952); m 2, 6 Sept 1958, Joanne Edith, da of Charles William Clark, of Newtown, Powys, Wales; 1 s (Charles b 6 June 1959), 1 da (Emma b 1 Feb 1961); *Career* 2 Lt RM 1945, Lt 1947, Subaltern RM detachment HMS Euryalus 1947-48, Troop Subaltern 42 Commando 1948-50, trg offr special boat section 1950-53, G3 Intelligence HQ 3 Commando Bde 1953-56, Capt 1954, HQ co cdr Jt Servs Amphibious Warfare Sch 1957-58, ret 1958; md Photome Studies Ltd 1958-63, dir Br Automatic Co 1963-70, md Wittenborg UK Ltd 1970-; cncllr The Surrey Co Agric Soc; MInstM 1975; Prince Henrik's Medal of Honour Denmark; *Recreations* hockey, swimming; *Clubs* Army and Navy; *Style*— Capt David Trace, RM; Domus, 141 Shear Cross, Crockerton, Nr Warminster, Wiltshire (☎ 0985 212 380); Wittenborg UK Ltd, Wittenborg House, Plough Rd, Smallfield, Horley, Surrey RH6 9JW (☎ 034 284 3939, fax 034 284 3779, car phone 0860 322 508, telex 957245)

TRACEY, Eric Frank; s of Allan Lewis Tracey, of Auckland, NZ, and Marcelle Frances, *née* Petrie; *b* 3 July 1948; *Educ* Mount Albert GS Auckland NZ, Univ of Auckland (BCom, MCom); *m* 16 May 1970, Patricia, da of G S (Bill) Gamble, of Hatch End, Middx; *Career* Inland Revenue NZ 1965, lectr Univ of Auckland 1970-72, Touche Ross & Co London 1973- (ptnr 1980-); ACA (NZ) 1970, FCA 1975, ACIS 1972; *Recreations* walking, rugby, cricket, cooking, certain roses; *Style*— Eric Tracey, Esq; 6 De Beauvoir Sq, De Beauvoir Town, London N1 4LG (☎ 01 254 6057); Touche Ross & Co, Hill House, 1 Little New St, London EC4A 3TR (☎ 01 936 3000, fax 01 583 8517)

TRACEY, Richard Patrick; JP (1977), MP (C) Surbiton 1983-; s of P H (Dick) Tracey (d 1959), of Stratford-upon-Avon, and Hilda, *née* Timms; *b* 8 Feb 1943; *Educ* King Edward VI Sch Stratford-upon-Avon, Birmingham Univ (LLB); *m* 1974, Katharine R, da of John Gardner (d 1969), of Ealing; 1 s (Simon b 1974), 3 da (Nicola b 1976, Emma b 1980, Polly b 1982); *Career* presenter of current affrs programmes BBC Radio and TV 1966-78, documentaries BBC 1974-76, leader writer Daily Express 1964-66, dep chm Gtr London Cons Pty 1981-83; Parly under-sec of state for Environment and min for Sport 1985-87; Freeman City of London 1984; *Books* The World of Motor Sport (with R Hudson-Evans); Hickstead - the first Twelve Years (with M Clayton); *Recreations* boating, riding, wildlife conservation; *Clubs* Wig and Pen; *Style*— Richard Tracey, Esq, JP, MP; House of Commons, London SW1A 0AA (☎ 01 219 5196)

TRACEY, Stanley William; OBE (1986); s of Stanley Clark Tracey (d 1957), and Florence Louise, *née* Guest (d 1984); *b* 30 Dec 1926; *m* 1, 1946 (m dis), Joan Lower; m 2, 1957 Jean Richards (m dis 1960); m 3, 24 Dec 1960, Florence Mary (Jackie), da of Douglas Richard Buckland (d 1970), of London; 1 s (Clark b 1961), 1 da (Sarah b 1962); *Career* served RAF 1946-48; composer of over 300 titles, incl: Under Milkwood Suite 1965, Genesis and some 40 albums; resident pianist Ronnie Scotts Club London 1960-66, ptnr (with wife) steamed Record Co 1975-, toured Middle East 1982, South America 1980 with own quartet, pianist/leader quartet, quintet, sextet (Hexad), octet and 15 piece orchestra; hon RAM; memb RSM & JB; *Style*— Stanley Tracey, Esq, OBE; 8 Hadleyvale Court, 114-116 Hadley Rd, New Barnet, Herts EN5 5QY (☎ 01 440 7955)

TRACY, Rear Adm Hugh Gordon Henry; CB (1965), DSC (1945); s of Cdr Andrew Francis Gordon Tracy, RN (Capt-Supt NC Pangbourne 1921-35, d 1979), and Uta Gladys, *née* Challis (d 1981); *b* 15 Nov 1912; *Educ* NC Pangbourne, RNEC; *m* 1938, Muriel, da of Maj-Gen Sir Ralph Bignell Ainsworth (d 1952); 2 s (Ralph b 1941, Charles b 1945), 1 da (Angela b 1934); *Career* naval offr Engrg Branch, War Serv, Admty 1939-41, sr engr HMS Illustrious 1942-44, HM Dockyard Chatham 1944-46; Cdr 1946, Capt 1956, asst dir Marine Engrg Admty 1956-58; Capt HMS Sultan 1959-60, IDC 1961, Capt of the Base HM Dockyard Portland 1962-63, Rear Adm 1963; dir of marine engrg MOD 1963-66; conslt UKAEA 1967-72; chm Wiltshire Gardens Tst 1985-89; *Recreations* gardening, plant ecology; *Clubs* Army and Navy; *Style—* Rear Adm Hugh Tracy, CB, DSC; Orchard House, Claverton, Bath (☎ 0225 65650)

TRAFFORD, Baron (Life Peer, UK 1987), of Falmer, Co E Sussex; Sir (Joseph) Anthony (Porteous) Trafford; s of Dr Harold Trafford, of Warlingham, Surrey, and Laura Dorothy, *née* Porteous (d 1965); *b* 20 July 1932; *Educ* St Edmund's Hindhead, Charterhouse, Lincoln's Inn, Univ of London, Guy's Hosp (MB BS); *m* 1960, Helen Elizabeth, da of Albert Ralph Chalk, of Cambs; 1 s (Hon Mark b 1966), 1 da (Hon Tanya b 1968); *Career* sr registrar Guy's Hosp 1963-66, conslt physician and dir of renal unit Brighton 1965-; MP (C) The Wrekin 1970-74; sr pro-chllr and chm of cncl Univ of Sussex 1985-; MRCP, FRCP; kt 1985; *Recreations* golf, bridge; *Style—* Lord Trafford of Falmer; 103 The Drive, Hove, E Sussex (☎ 0273 731567)

TRAFFORD, Ian Colton; s of Dr Harold Trafford, of Warlingham, Surrey, and Laura Dorothy, *née* Porteous (d 1965); *b* 8 July 1928; *Educ* Charterhouse, St John's Coll Oxford (BA); *m* 20 July 1949 (m dis 1964), Nella, da of Petros Georgara (d 1958), of Athens, Greece; m 2, 12 Dec 1972, Jacqueline Carole, *née* Trenque; *Career* Intelligence Corps 1946-48, cmmnd 1947, Actg Capt 1948, GSO3 Br Mil Mission to Greece 1948; feature writer (subsequently features ed and industl corres); The Financial Times 1951-58, UK corr Barrons Weekly NY 1954-60, md Industl and Trade Fairs Hldgs 1966-71 (dir 1958-); dir gen Br Trade Fairs: Peking 1964, Moscow 1966, Bucharest 1968, Sao Paolo 1969, Buenos Aires 1970; md The Economist Newspaper Ltd 1971-81, chm The Economist Intelligence Unit Ltd 1971-79, local dir W London branch Commercial Union Insur 1974-83; publisher 1981-88: The Times Educnl Supplement, The Times Higher Educnl Supplement, The Times Literary Supplement; ret 1988; *Recreations* gardening; *Style—* Ian Trafford, Esq, OBE; Grafton House, Westhall Road, Warlingham, Surrey CR3 9HF (☎ 08832 2048)

TRAHERNE, Sir Cennydd George; KG (1970), TD (1950); s of late Cdr Llewellyn Edmund Traherne, RN and Dorothy *née* Sinclair, gda of Sir John George Tollemache Sinclair 3 Bt of Ulbster; *b* 14 Dec 1910; *Educ* Wellington, Brasenose Coll Oxford; *m* 1934, Olivera Rowena, OBE, JP (d 1986), da of James Binney (d 1935) and The Lady Marjory, *née* Brudenell-Bruce, da of 5 Marquess of Ailesbury; *Career* serv WWII Capt RA & CMP Home & NW Europe (despatches); barr Inner Temple 1938, HM Lt of Glamorgan 1952-74 and of Mid, S and W Glamorgan 1974-85, dir Cardiff Bldg Soc 1953-, dir Wales Gas Bd 1958-71, chm Wales Gas Consultative Cncl 1958-71, pres Welsh Nat Sch & Univ of Wales Coll of Medicine 1970-87, dir Commercial Bank of Wales 1972-88, pres Cambrian Archaelogical Assoc 1983-84, Hon Col Glamorgan Army Cadet Force 1983-85, memb of Gorsedd of the Bards of Wales, hon master of Bench of Inner Temple 1983; kt 1964; *Recreations* fishing, walking; *Clubs* Athenaeum, Cardiff and County; *Style—* Sir Cennydd Traherne, KG, TD,; Coedarhydyglyn, nr Cardiff, CF5 6SF (☎ 0446 760321)

TRAILL, Sir Alan Towers; s of George Traill and Margaret Eleanor, *née* Matthews; *b* 7 May 1935; *Educ* St Andrew's Sch Eastbourne, Charterhouse, Jesus Coll Cambridge (MA); *m* 1964, Sarah Jane, *née* Hutt; 1 s; *Career* cncl memb Br Insur Brokers Assoc 1978-79, chm Reinsur Brokers Ctee of the Assoc 1978, memb London Ct of Int Arbitration 1981-, dir Lyon Jago Webb 1983-; chm: Lyon Hldgs 1983-, dir Lyon Traill Attenborough (Lloyds brokers) 1983-, Lyon Lohr (Life & Pensions) 1983-; memb Lloyd's 1963-, memb Ct of Common Cncl City of London 1970-75, alderman Langbourn Ward 1975-, Sheriff 1982-83, Lord Mayor of London 1984-85; Master Worshipful Co of Cutlers 1979-, dir City Arts Tst 1980-, almoner Christ's Hosp Fndn 1980-; govr: King Edward's Sch Witley 1980-, tstee RSC 1982-; chllr London Univ 1984- (Hon DMus 1984); GBE 1984; *Recreations* shooting, skiing, DIY, travel, opera, assisting educn; *Clubs* City Livery, Royal Automobile; *Style—* The Rt Hon the Lord Mayor of London; Lyon House, 160-166 Borough High St, London SE1 1JR (☎ 01 407 7144)

TRAIN, Christopher John; CB (1986); s of Keith Sydney Sayer Train (d 1985), and Edna Ashby, *née* Ellis; *b* 12 Mar 1932; *Educ* Nottingham HS, Christ Church Oxford (BA, MA); *m* 24 Aug 1957, Sheila Mary, da of Wilfred Watson (d 1950); 1 s (Nicholas b 1959), 1 da (Helen (Mrs McCartney) b 1961); *Career* Sub Lt RNVR 1955-57; asst master St Paul's Sch 1957-67; Home Off 1968-: sec Royal Cmmn on Criminal Procedure 1978-80, princ fin offr 1981-83, dir gen of the Prison Serv of England and Wales 1983-; *Recreations* jogging, cooking, cricket; *Clubs* Vincent's (Oxford), Reform; *Style—* Christopher Train, Esq, CB; Home Office, Queen Anne's Gate, London SW1 (☎ 01 273 3000)

TRANGMAR, Donald George; s of George Edward Trangmar (d 1975), of Barrow-in-Furness, and Mabel Winifred, *née* Rose; *b* 16 Nov 1939; *Educ* Barrow-in-Furness GS; *m* 1, 1968 (m dis 1986), Norma, *née* Denison; 1 da (Natalie Jane b 26 Dec 1981); m 2, 14 Oct 1988, Christabelle, *née* Mitchell; *Career* joined Marks and Spencer 1965 (dir 1983-); *Recreations* cricket; *Style—* Donald Trangmar, Esq; Marks and Spencer plc, Michael House, 57 Baker St, London W1A 1DN (☎ 01 935 4422)

TRANMIRE, Baron (Life Peer UK 1974); Robin (Robert) Hugh Turton; KBE (1971), MC (1942), PC (1955), JP (N Riding Yorks 1936), DL (1962); 2 s of late Maj Robert Bell Turton, JP, DL, of Kildale Hall, Yorks, Lord of the Manor and Patron of the Living of Kildale (himself 2 s of Edmund Turton, JP, DL, by his w Lady Cecilia Leeson, yr da of 4 Earl of Milltown, KP; Following the death without issue of Lady Cecilia's 3 er bros, 5, 6 and 7 Earls (latter d 1891) the dignity has been dormant); Maj Robert Turton m Marion Edith, da of Lt-Col Godfrey Beaumont by Anne Maria (da of Sir Edmund Blackett, 6 Bt); *b* 8 August 1903; *Educ* Eton, Balliol Coll Oxford; *m* 1928, Ruby Christian, da of late Robert Thomas Scott, of Beechmont, Sevenoaks, Kent; 3 s, 1 da; *Career* served WWII, Lt-Col Green Howards; barr Inner Temple 1926; MP (C) Thirsk and Malton 1929-74, Parly sec Miny of Nat Insur 1951-53, min of Pensions and Nat Insur 1953-54, jt parly under-sec state for Foreign Affrs 1954-55, min Health 1955-57; *Style—* The Rt Hon the Lord Tranmire, KBE, MC, PC, JP, DL; Upsall Castle, Thirsk, N Yorks YO7 2QJ (☎ Thirsk 537202); 15 Grey Coat Gdns, London SW1P 2QA (☎ 01 834 1535)

TRANT, Patrick Murray; s of Philip Trant (d 1984), and Jane, *née* Wackley; *b* 31 Jan 1953; *Educ* St Marys Coll Southampton, Prestentation Coll Reading; *Career* co chm Trant Gp of Cos; *Recreations* horse racing, tennis, golf, greyhound breeding; *Clubs* Turf; *Style—* Patrick Trant, Esq; Stoneham Park Hse, Stoneham, Eastleigh, Hants SO5 3HT (☎ 0703 768 955)

TRANT, Gen Sir Richard Brooking; KCB (1982, CB 1979); s of Richard Brooking Trant and Dora Rodney, *née* Lancaster; *b* 28 Mar 1928; *m* 1957, Diana, da of Rev Stephen Zachary Edwards; 1 s (Richard b 1967), 2 da (Diana b 1962, Sarah b 1965); *Career* cmmnd RA 1947, Def Servs Staff Coll India 1962-63, Brig Maj Aden Protectorate Levies FRA 1963-65, Cmd 3 RHA 1968-71, sr instr Army Staff Coll 1971-72; cmd 5 Air Portable Bde 1972-74, cmd Landforces NI 1977-79, Dir Army Staff Duties 1979-81, GOC SE dist 1982-83, Land Dep C-in-C Falklands 1982; QMG and Gen 1983-86, Col Cmdt RAEC 1979-86, RA 1982-87, RAOC 1984-88, HAC 1984-, cmmr Duke of Yorks Royal Mil Sch 1987-88; sr def advsr Short Bros Belfast, conslt Peat Marwick McKlintock, dep chm Wilson's Hogg Robinson 1988-, chm Hunting Engrg Ltd 1988-; cmmr Royal Hosp Chelsea 1988-, memb Armed Forces Pay Review Body 1988; vice pres Defence Manufacturers Assoc 1987; Freeman City of London 1984; memb soc Br Aerospace Cos 1988-; *Recreations* field sports, sailing, golf; *Clubs* Army and Navy, Royal Fowey Yacht; *Style—* Gen Sir Richard Trant, KCB; c/o Lloyds Bank, Newquay, Cornwall

TRANTER, Nigel Godwin; OBE (1983); s of Gilbert Tredgold Tranter (d 1929), of Edinburgh, and Eleanor Annie Cass (d 1933); *b* 23 Nov 1909; *Educ* George Heriot's Sch Edinburgh, Edinburgh Univ (MA); *m* 1933, May Jean Campbell (d 1979), da of Thomas Douglas Grieve (d 1925), of Edinburgh; 1 s (Philip, d 1966), 1 da (Frances-May); *Career* author & novelist; published over 100 books, fiction & non-fiction; hon pres Scottish Pen Club, former chm Soc of Authors Scotland and Nat Book League Scotland, chm: St Andrew Soc of E Lothian, Nat Forth Rd Bridge Ctee 1953-57, E Lothian Lib Assoc 1960-70; *Books* Robert the Bruce Trilogy (1965-69), The Fortified House in Scotland (1962-71, 5 Vols), Nigel Tranter's Scotland (1981), Columbia (1987), The Story of Scotland (1987), Flowers of Chivalry, Mail Royal; *Recreations* walking, historical res, knighthood; *Clubs* Pen; *Style—* Nigel Tranter, Esq; Quarry House, Aberlady, East Lothian, Scotland EH32 0QB (☎ 087 57 258)

TRAPNELL, Dr David Hallam; s of Hallam Trapnell (d 1982), of Clifton, Bristol, and Ruth Louisa, *née* Walker; *b* 21 June 1928; *Educ* Clifton, Gonville and Caius Cambridge (MA, MD), Middx Hosp; *m* 14 Nov 1959, Mary Elizabeth, da of John Gray (d 1976), of Whitby, Yorkshire; 2 s (Simon, Philip); *Career* Nat Serv Capt RAMC (formerly Lt) 1954-56; registrar and sr registrar St Barts Hosp 1957-61; conslt radiologist: Queen Mary's Hosp Roehampton, Westminster Hosp 1962-84, London Clinic 1978-84; pres Br Inst of Radiology 1980-81, Int Fleischner Soc 1983-84, George Simon lectr Royal Coll of Radiologists 1983, pres Br Postmark Soc 1970-75; churchwarden All Souls Church Langham Place London W1 1967-84, fndr chm Soc for Wildlife Art of the Nations 1982-, hon dir Nature in Art, The Int Centre for Wildlife Art Gloucester 1987-FRCP 1975, FRCR 1975; *Books* Principles of X-Ray Diagnosis (1967), Dental Manifestations of Systemic Disease (jtly 1973), Radiology in Clinical Diagnosis (ed series); *Recreations* postal history, natural history; *Style—* Dr David Trapnell; Nature in Art, The International Centre for Wildlife Art, Wallsworth Hall, Sandhurst, Gloucester GL2 9PA (☎ 0452 731 422)

TRAPNELL, Rev Stephen Hallam; s of Hallam Trapnell (d 1982), late of Clifton, Bristol, and Ruth, *née* Walker; *b* 10 June 1930; *Educ* Clifton, Gonville and Caius Coll Cambridge (MA), Ridley Hall Cambridge, Virginia Seminary Alexandria Va USA (MDiv); *m* 6 May 1961, Ann Mary Hensleigh, da of Lt-Col Eric H L H Walter, of Chaldon, Surrey; 2 s (Andrew b 1964, Mark b 1967), 2 da (Rachel b 1962, Lydia b 1965); *Career* 2 Lt RASC 1949; ordained priest 1957; curate: St Matthias Upper Tulse Hill London 1956-59, St Mary's Reigate 1969-61; vicar: Christ Church Richmond Surrey 1961-72, Holy Trinity, Sydenham, London 1972-80; rector of Worthing, Basingstoke Hants 1980-; surrogate for marriages; *Publications* Teaching The Familes (1973); *Recreations* the study of wild flowers, especially orchids; *Clubs* The Co of All Faithful People (life memb); *Style—* The Rev Stephen Trapnell; The Rectory, Glebe Lane, Basingstoke RG23 8QA (☎ 0256 22095)

TRAPP, Prof Joseph Burney; s of Henry Mansfield Burney Trapp (d 1957), and Frances Melanie, *née* Wolters (d 1950); *b* 16 July 1925; *Educ* Dannevirke HS, Victoria Univ NZ (MA); *m* 9 June 1953, Elayne Margaret, da of Sir Robert Alexander Falla, KCMG, of Days Bay, Wellington, NZ (d 1980); 2 s (Michael b 1957, James b 1959); *Career* asst librarian Alexander Turnbull Library Wellington 1946-50; asst lectr: Victoria Univ Coll 1950-51, Univ of Reading 1951-53; Warburg Inst Univ of London: asst librarian 1953-66, librarian 1966-76, dir 1976-; FSA 1978, FRSA 1978, FBA 1980; *Books* The Apology of Sir Thomas More (ed 1979); *Style—* Prof Joseph Trapp; The Warburg Institute, Woburn Square, London WC1H OAB (☎ 01 580 9663)

TRASENSTER, Maj Michael Augustus Tulk; CVO (1954); s of Major William Augustus Trasenster, MC (d 1950), of Meonstoke, and Brenda de Courcy, *née* Barrett (d 1987); *b* 26 Jan 1923; *Educ* Winchester; *m* 11 Jan 1950, Fay Norrie, da of Thomas Darley (d 1982), of Yorks; 2 da (Anna b 1953, Julia b 1955); *Career* serv 4/7 Royal Dragoon Gds 1942, Normandy and NW Europe 1944-45, Middle East 1946; ADC to Govr S Aust 1947-49, Sch of Tank Technol and Tech Staff 1951; military sec and comptroller to Govr Gen of NZ 1952-55; brewing 1955-60; contributed photographs to various pubns; ARPS 1960; Chev Order Leopold II with palm 1944, Croix de Guerre with palm; *Recreations* art, painting, reading; *Style—* Maj Michael Trasenster, CVO; c/o Royal Bank of Scotland, High St, Winchester, Hampshire

TRAVERS, David; s of George Bowes Travers (d 1966), and Gertrude Colbert, *née* Chrunside; *b* 19 Mar 1957; *Educ* Spennymoor Secdy Sch, Kings Coll London (LLB, AKC, LLM); *m* 13 Oct 1984, Sheila Mary, da of Martin Killoran, CBE, QFSM; 1 da (Rosamond b 11 Oct 1988); *Career* barr Middle Temple 1981, Harmsworth scholar Northern circuit, pt/t lectr Accountancy Tuition Centre Manchester and Liverpool until 1983, memb exec Northern circuit 1985-87, occassional lectr dept of mgmnt scis UMIST 1986-87, occassional libel reader Express newspapers 1987-88, exec ed King's Counsel 1979 (ed 1978), joined chambers Birmingham 1988; memb delegacy govrg body King's Coll London 1977-78, sabbatical pres King's Coll London Union of Students 1979-80, pres Middle Temple Students Assoc 1980-81; memb: Manchester Literary and Phiosophical Soc, Hon Soc of the middle Temple 1978-; hon life memb King's Coll London Union of Students 1980; *Recreations* food, wine, words; *Style—* David Travers, Esq; 3 Fountain Ct, Steelhouse Lane, Birmingham B4 6DR Document Exchange: DX 16079 (☎ 021 236 5854, 021 236 2286, fax 021 236 7008)

TRAVERS, Lady; Therese Sara (Copper); *née* Keeley; *m* 1956, Lt-Gen Sir Paul Anthony Travers, KCB (d 1983); 1 s, 2 da; *Style—* Lady Travers; 61 Valiant House, Vicarage Crescent, London SW11 3LX (☎ 01 223 4928)

TRAVERS, Sir Thomas à Beckett; s of Walter Travers (d 1907), and Isabelle Mary, *née* à Beckett; *b* 16 August 1902; *Educ* Melbourne GS, Melbourne Univ (MB BS, DSc); *m* 1949, Tone, da of late Herbert Smith, and widow of R S Burnard; *Career*

Wing Cdr RAAF WWII; asst ophthalmologist Alfred Hosp 1930-39, hon ophthalmologist Royal Melbourne Hosp 1946-62, consulting ophthalmologist 1962-; MRCP, DOMS, FRACS; kt 1972; *Recreations* gardening; *Clubs* Melbourne; *Style—* Sir Thomas Travers; 6 Barrup St, Carlton 3053, Australia; 55 Victoria Parade, Fitzroy, 3065, Australia (☎ 417 1722)

TRAVERS, William Inglis Lindon (Bill); MBE (1945); s of William Halton Lindon Travers (d 1966), of Newcastle-upon-Tyne, and Florence, *née* Wheatley; *b* 3 Jan 1922; *Educ* Governess GS Newcastle upon Tyne, Hannah and Gash Private Sch Sunderland; *m* 1, 1950 (m dis 1957), Patricia Raine; 1 da (Anna Louise Lindon b 28 Jan 1951); m 2, 19 Sept 1957, Virginia Anne, *qv*, da of Terence Morrell McKenna (d 1948); 3 s (William Morrell Lindon b 4 Nov 1958, Justin McKenna Lindon b 6 March 1963, Daniel Inglis Lindon b 27 Feb 1967), 1 da (Louise Annabella b 6 July 1960); *Career* enlisted Royal Northumberland Fus 1940, cmmnd 9 Gurkha Rifles 1941, Lt Razmak NW Frontier India Pathan tribal warfare 1942, Wingate's second Chindit campaign India 1943 (cdr recce gp, promoted Capt in field), SOE 1944 (Maj cmdg re-formed 2/9 Gurkha Bn Force 136, parachuted behind enemy lines into Perak Malaya to organise Malayan Peoples Anti-Japanese Army, remained in Malaya until Allied troops landed), Maj Hiroshima Japan 1946; actor of stage and screen; films incl: Geordie 1954, Bhowani Junction 1955, Born Free 1966, Ring of Bright Water (also wrote screenplay) 1968, The Belstone Fox 1973: tv incl: Lorna Doone BBC TV 1963, The Admirable Crichton (acad award nomination for best actor) 1967, Wild Dogs of Africa (documentary) 1973, Bloody Ivory (prodr and writer) 1980; stage appearances incl: A Cook for Mr General (Playhouse Theatre NYC) 1961, (RSC Stafford upon Avon) 1962, Abraham Cochrance (Broadway NYC) 1964, Peter Pan (London) 1970; pres Beauty Without Cruelty UK, patron Captive Animals Protection Soc, fndr Zoo Check Charitable Tst; Freeman City of Houston 1966; *Books* On Playing with Lions (with Virginia McKenna, 1966), Beyond the Bars (jtly 1987); *Recreations* travelling, photography, gardening; *Clubs* Special Forces; *Style—* Bill Travers, Esq, MBE

TRAVERSE-HEALY, Tim; s of John Healy, MBE, and Gladys, *née* Traverse; *b* 25 Mar 1923; *Educ* Stonyhurst, St Mary's Hosp London Univ (Dip CAM); *m* 8 March 1946, Joan, da of Sidney Thompson (d 1968), of London and Sussex; 2 s (Sean b 1947, Kevin b 1949), 3 da (Sharon (Mrs Butterfield) b 1951, Corinne (Mrs Russell) b 1953, Jeannine b 1954); *Career* WWII RA Territorial Res, RM Commandos and Special Forces 1941-46; sr ptnr Traverse-Healy Ltd Corporate Affrs Counsel 1947-, bd memb Centre for Public Affrs Studies 1969-; dir: Charles Barker Traverse Healy PR Consits 1987-, Charles Barker PR 1988-; chm Charles Barker Consltg Gp 1988-, visiting lectr Stirling Univ, visiting prof Baylor Univ Texas USA, vice-pres Euro PR Confedn 1965-69, memb Professional Practices Ctee (UK) PR Consits Assoc 1988-; Int PR Assoc: fndr sec 1950-61, cncl memb 1961-68, pres 1968-73, emeritus memb 1982, Presidential Gold Medal 1985, pres World PR congress Tel Aviv 1970 and Geneva 1973; PR congress fndr lectures: Boston 1976, Bombay 1982, Melbourne 1988; pres: Int Fndn for PR Res and Educn 1983-85, Int Fndn for PR Studies 1986-87 (tstee 1987-); memb (US) Public Affairs Cncl 1975-; PR News Award 1983, PR Week Award 1987, hon FIPR 1988 (Tallents Gold Medal 1985); RM Officers Assoc, Commandos Assoc, London Flotilla; MIPR 1948, FIPR 1956 (pres 1967-68), FIPA 1957, FRSA 1953; *Recreations* Irish Soc, French politics; *Clubs* Athenaeum, Norwegian, RAC; *Style—* Tim Traverse-Healy, Esq; 8 Rockwells Gdns, Dulwich Wood Pk, London SE19; Girffoul, Montaigu de Quercy, 82150, Tarn et Garonne, France

TRAVIS, Ernest Raymond Anthony; s of Ernest Raymond and Constance Mary Travis; *b* 18 May 1943; *Educ* Harrow; *m* 1, 1967 (m dis 1977), Hon Rosemary Gail, *qv* da of Baron Pritchard of Haddon; m 2, 1978, Jean Heather, da of John MacDonald (d 1983); m 3 Peta Jane, da of Sir Peter Foster; *Career* barr Inner Temple 1965; chm Travis Perkins plc; *Style—* Anthony Travis, Esq; 320 Fulham Rd, London SW10; Travis Perkins plc, 149 Harrow Rd, Paddington, London W2 (☎ 01 402 0081)

TRAVIS, Norman John; s of Frederick Pickles (d 1949), of Bristol, and Ada Alice, *née* Travis (d 1947); *b* 7 Mar 1913; *Educ* Clifton Coll, Trinity Coll Oxford (MA, BSc); *m* 25 Feb 1939, Mary Elizabeth, da of Alan Dale-Harris (d 1962), of Iver, Bucks; 4 s (Rupert b 1940, Julian b 1942, Michael b 1947, Mark b 1955); *Career* cmmnd 2 Lt RE 1940, navigator RAF 1942, demob Sqdn ldr 1945; md Borax (Hldgs) Ltd 1966-70, dir Rio-Tinto-Zinc Corpn Ltd 1968-79; chm: RTZ-Borax Ltd 1970-79, US Borax & Chem Corpn Los Angeles 1966-80; dir First inter State Bank of California 1967-80; memb: bd Directors American Mining Congress, cncl Chem Indust Assoc; chm Clifton Coll Cncl 1971-78; memb: Bibliographical Soc, Assoc Internationalle de Bibliophile; *Books* The Tincal Trail (jtly 1984); *Recreations* collecting antiquarian books, golf, real tennis; *Clubs* RAF, MCC, Los Angeles CC; *Style—* Norman Travis, Esq; Howe Green Hall, Hertford, Herts SG13 8LH (☎ 07072 61243)

TRAVIS, (Henry) Stuart; s of Sidney Travis (d 1956), of Accrington, Lancs, and Mary Travis; *b* 7 Dec 1945; *Educ* Peel Park Sch Accrington, Accrington GS; *m* March 1969, Margaret, da of Frederic Ryden (d 1960), of Oswald Twistle, Lancs; 3 da (Joanne b 1972, Sally b 1975, Susannah b 1977); *Career* William Deacons Bank Ltd 1963-69, sr mangr Liverpool City Off Williams & Glyns Bank Ltd 1983-85 (joined 1970, mangr Torquay 1978-83); Arbuthnot Latham Bank Ltd: asst dir 1985-86, dir UK Banking 1986-88, dir hd of Banking Dept 1988; chm Arbuthnot Asset Fin 1987-, chief exec Arbuthnot Leasing Int Ltd 1988; dir: Palace Financial Services Ltd, Dataformat Ltd, Crescent Credit Mgmnt Ltd, Arbuthnot Fleet Servs Ltd; vice pres Torbay Inst of Bankers 1983; memb: Round Table 1968-86, Rotary 1981-87; *Recreations* shooting, sailing, bowling; *Clubs* Royal Torbay Yacht; *Style—* Stuart Travis, Esq; The Brown Cottage, Crowhurst, East Sussex; Arbuthnot Latham Bank Ltd, 131 Finsbury Pavement, London EC2 (☎ 01 280 8566, fax 01 280 8520)

TREACHER, Adm Sir John Devereux; KCB (1975); s of late Frank Charles Treacher, of Bentley Grove, Suffolk; *b* 23 Sept 1924,Chile; *Educ* St Paul's; *m* 1, 1953 (m dis 1968), Patcie, da of Dr F McGrath, of Evanston, Illinois; 1 s, 1 da; m 2, 1969, Kirsteen Forbes, da of D F Landale, of Dumfries; 1 s, 1 da; *Career* serv RN 1941-77 (qualified pilot 1946, Capt 1962, Rear Adm 1970, Vice Adm 1972, Vice Chief Naval Staff 1973-75, Adm 1975, C-in-C Fleet & Allied C-in-C Channel & E Atlantic 1975-77); non-press memb Press Cncl 1978-81, chief exec Nat Car Parks 1977-81 (dir 1977-85), dir Westland Group plc 1978-, (vice chm 1984, dep chm 1986); FRAeS 1973; *Clubs* Boodle's; *Style—* Adm Sir John Treacher, KCB; 4 Carlton Gardens London SW1 (☎ 01 839 4061)

TREADGOLD, Rev Canon John David; *b* 30 Dec 1931; *Educ* Nottingham Univ (BA), Wells Theol Coll; *m* Hazel Rhona *née* Bailey, 2 s, 1 da; *Career* deacon 1959, priest 1960, vicar choral Southwell Minster 1959-64, CF (TA) 1962-67, rector of Wollaton Nottingham 1964-74, CF (TAVR) 1974-78, vicar of Darlington 1974-81, surrogate 1976-81, canon of Windsor and chaplain of The Royal Chapel, Windsor Great Park 1981-; chaplain to HM The Queen 1983-; *Style—* The Rev Canon John Treadgold; The Cloisters, Windsor Castle, Windsor, Berks; Chaplain's Lodge, Windsor Great Park, Windsor, Berks (☎ 0784 32434)

TREADWELL, Lt-Col Gerald William; OBE (1964); s of Claude Mallam Treadwell (d 1931), and Emily Dorothy, *née* Mixer (d 1911); *b* 26 Nov 1905; *Educ* Stamford, King's Coll London; *m* 25 Jan 1941 (in Jerusalem Cathedral), Margaret, da of Frederick Rogers (d 1972), of Llanusk, Usk, Mon; 1 s (John b 1950), 1 da (Ann b 1945); *Career* Lt-Col serv Middle E (1 Cav Div), Italy and Austria 1939-48, mil prosecutor, Jerusalem Mil Court 1943-44; slr; pres: City of Westminster Law Soc 1969-70, Blackheath CC 1971-76; chm Bromby Cons Assoc 1958-62; vice-pres: Blackheath Rugby Club; *Books* Military Courts Manual; *Style—* Lt-Col Gerald Treadwell, OBE; Ashlawn, Bickley Road, Bickley, Kent BR1 2ND; 1 Pall Mall East, London SW1Y 5AY

TREANOR, Frances Mary Elizabeth; da of George Francis Treanor (d 1978), of London, and Biddy *née* Maunsell (d 1964); *b* 16 April 1944; *Educ* Convent of the Sacred Heart HS For Girls Hammersmith, Goldsmiths Coll London (NDD), Hornsey Coll of Art (ATC) (Lond); *m* 1, 9 Oct 1965 (m dis 1969), Francis John Elliott s of Aubrey Elliott (d 1988), of Wales; 1 da (Lizzie Taylor b 1966); m 2, 30 Oct 1969 (m dis 1982), (Thomas) Anthony Taylor, s of Thomas Taylor (d 1984), of Cornwall; *Career* artist; govt purchase Art of Govt Scheme Derry's Gift 1987, govt print purchase Inland Revenue and Custom & Excise 1988, set design cmmn OUD's prodn of Shakespeare's As You Like It summer tour Japan USA England 1988; Awards: L'Artiste Assoifée 1975, George Rowney, Pastel 1982, Frank Herring Award for Merit 1984, Willi Hoffman-Guth Award 1988; ILEA teacher DES 1966, pt/t teacher of art ILEA 1967-87, sessional lectr in art and design at American Coll in London (ACL) 1979-87, cncl memb Pastel Soc FBA 1982 and 1986; vice-chm Blackheath Art Soc (BAS) 1974, steering gp memb Greenwich Lone Parent Project (GRIPP) 1984, area co-ordinator Neighbourhood Watch Scheme 1988-89; memb: (PS); *Books* Pastel Painting Technique (1987), The Medici Society (1987), Statics (1988), Women's Artist Diary (1988), Canns Down Press (1988, 1989); *Recreations* tv, conversation, antique markets ; *Style—* Miss Frances Treanor; 121 Royal Hill, Greenwich, London SE10 8SS (☎ 01 692 3239)

TREASURE, Fred; s of Fred Treasure (d 1959), of Preston, Lancs, and Ann Mary, *née* Sadler (d 1966); *b* 5 May 1919; *Educ* Preston GS; *m* 21 Oct 1940, Doris Dixon, da of Harry Howarth (local artist) (d 1964), of Preston, Lancs; 1 s (John Philip b 1947), 1 da (Judith Ann b 1943); *Career* RAF 1939-46, Sgt; qualified inc accountant 1950, ptnr Ashworth Treasure & Co 1957-70, private practice 1951-57 and 1970-; co sec and dir Sadlers (Lytham) Ltd, engrs; FCA; *Recreations* football and cricket for sch, RAF and local clubs post-war; *Clubs* Rotary of Lytham (pres 1987-), chm Lytham St Annes and Flyde YMCA (pres 1978-); *Style—* Fred Treasure, Esq; Sadlers (Lytham) Ltd, Dock Rd, Lytham (☎ 0253 739123, telex 67322)

TREASURE, Prof John Albert Penberthy; s of Harold Paul Treasure (d 1969), and Constance Frances, *née* Shapland (d 1987); *b* 20 June 1924; *Educ* Cardiff HS, Univ of Wales (BA), Cambridge Univ (PhD); *m* 30 March 1954, Valerie Ellen Bell; 2 s (Julian b 1958, Simon b 1960), 1 step s (Jonathan b 1948); *Career* chm J Walter Thompson London 1967; vice-chm J Walter Thompson Gp 1971; vice-chm Saatchi & Saatchi UK 1983-; dean City Univ Business Sch 1978; Freeman City London 1979, memb Guild of Marketors 1980; fell Marketing Research Soc, FBIM, FIPA, fell Marketing Soc; *Recreations* golf, tennis, eating; *Clubs* Royal Mid-Surrey, Queens; *Style—* Prof John Treasure; Saatchi & Saatchi Ltd, 80 Charlotte St, London W1A 1AQ (☎ 01 636 5060)

TRECHMAN, Gavin; s of Capt John Ronald Gordon Trechman, RN, and Phyllis Morva Trechman; ggs of Lord Charles Greenway; *b* 4 Mar 1942; *Educ* Charterhouse; *m* 3 Dec 1975, Angela de Carvalho, da of late Arnaldo Luiz; 1 s (Richard b 1977), 1 da (Sara b 1978); *Career* oil exec, dir Alexander Duckham & Co; *Recreations* golf, tennis; *Clubs* Royal Wimbledon GC, Hurlingham; *Style—* Gavin Trechman, Esq; 8 Paultons St, London SW3 5DP (☎ 01 352 9118); BP Oil Ltd, Hemel Hempstead, Herts HP2 4UL (☎ 0442 225 604)

TREDINNICK, David; MP (C) Bosworth 1987-; *b* 19 Jan 1950; *Educ* Eton, Mons Officer Cadet Sch, Graduate Business Sch, Cape Town Univ (MBA), St John's Coll Oxford (MLitt); *m* Rebecca; 1 da (Sophie); *Career* Grenadier Gds 1968-71; mangr Malden Mitcham Properties; *Recreations* skiing, tennis, riding, backgammon, rifle and shotgun shooting, windsurfing, sailing, travel; *Style—* David Tredinnick, Esq, MP; House of Commons, London SW1 (☎ 01 219 3000)

TREDINNICK, Noël Harwood; s of Harold James Tredinnick, of Beckenham, Kent, and Nola Frewin, *née* Harwood; *b* 9 Mar 1949; *Educ* St Olave's GS for Boys, Southwark Cathedral, Guildhall Sch of Music and Drama, Inst of Educn London Univ (Dip Ed); *m* 3 July 1976, Fiona Jean, da of James Malcolm Couper-Johnston, of Beckenham, Kent; 1 da (Isabel Jane b 1983); *Career* school master Langley Park Sch for Boys Beckenham 1971-75, prof and memb acad bd Guildhall Sch 1975-, organist and dir of music All Souls Church Langham Place London 1972-, artist dir Langham Arts 1987-; composer, orchestrator and conductor: Beckenham Chorale 1971-72, All Souls Orch 1972-, BBC Concert Orch 1985-, BBC Radio Orch 1988-; musical dir: BBC Radio (Religious Dept), Songs of Praise BBC TV; fndr and conductor Prom Praise; numerous recordings and performances with Cliff Richard, Mary O'Hara and Wendy Craig; memb: Archbishop's Cmmn on Church Music, Cncl Music in Worship Tst; *Recreations* theatre, architecture, country-walking; *Clubs* ACG; *Style—* Noël Tredinnick, Esq; 2, All Souls Place, London WIN 3DB (☎ 01 580 0898, fax 01 436 3019)

TREE, Lady Anne Evelyn Beatrice; *née* Cavendish; da of late 10 Duke of Devonshire, KBE, MBE, TD; *b* 1927; *m* 1949, Michael Lambert Tree, *qv* ; 2 adopted da (Isabella, Esther); *Style—* Lady Anne Tree; 75 Eaton Sq, London SW1 (☎ 01 235 1320); Shute House, Donhead St Mary, nr Salisbury, Wilts (☎ 034 788 253)

TREE, (Arthur) Jeremy; s of Arthur Ronald (d 1976), and bro of Michael, *qv*; *b* 21 Dec 1925; *Educ* Eton; *Career* 2 Lt 1 Household Cavalry 1945-47; owner and trainer of racehorses; *Clubs* Turf; *Style—* Jeremy Tree, Esq; Beckhampton House, Marlborough, Wilts (☎ Avebury 244 204)

TREE, Michael Lambert; s of (Arthur) Ronald Lambert Field Tree, (sometime tstee of Wallace Collection and MP for Harborough (d 1976)) of New York, by his 1 w, Nancy, da of Moncure Perkins, of Richmond Virginia; *b* 5 Dec 1921; *Educ* Eton; *m* 3

Nov 1949, Lady Anne Cavendish *qv*, da of 10 Duke of Devonshire; 2 adopted da (Isabella b 1964, Esther b 1966); *Career* serv WWII Capt Household Cavalry: Middle East, Italy, Germany; Chicago Sun 1947-48, Hambro's Bank 1951-53; Christie's 1966 (dir 1967-73), dir Mint Fabrications; painter, exhibited in Jacobson Hochman Galleries New York 1982 and The Fine Art Soc London 1984; *Recreations* shooting, golf; *Clubs* White's, Buck's, Pratt's; *Style*— Michael Tree, Esq; 75 Eaton Sq, London SW1 (☎ 01 235 1320); Shute House, Donhead St Mary, nr Shaftesbury, Wilts (☎ 074 788 253)

TREFFRY, David Charles; OBE (1966); yr s of Col Roger Carpenter Treffry, MC, TD, RA (ret) (d 1945), and Dorothy Emma, *née* Gundry Mills (d 1970); descended from an old Cornish family which acquired the manor of Fowey and the house of Place by marriage with an heiress *ca* 1300 (*see* Burke's Landed Gentry, 18 edn, vol I, 1965); *b* 7 Oct 1926; *Educ* Marlborough, Magdalen Coll Oxford (MA); *Career* Capt Frontier Force Regt IA 1945-47; joined HM Overseas Colonial Serv 1952, political offr S Arabia 1952, asst chief sec Aden 1959, perm sec Miny of Finance S Arabian Fedn 1963, cabinet sec S Arabian Fedn 1966, ret 1968; Int Monetary Fund 1968-87; fin advsr Indonesia 1971-73; memb: cncl Royal Inst of Cornwall 1988, regnl ctee Nat Tst Devon and Cornwall; *Clubs* Travellers'; Place, Fowey, Cornwall; 1684 32nd Street NW, Washington, DC 20007, USA

TREFGARNE, 2 Baron (UK 1947); David Garro Trefgarne; PC (1989); s of 1 Baron Trefgarne (d 1960); *b* 31 Mar 1941; *Educ* Haileybury, Princeton Univ USA; *m* 1968, Rosalie, da of Sir Peter Lane, of Holywell, Hook Heath, Woking; 2 s (George, Justin b 1973), 1 da (Rebecca b 1976); *Heir* s, Hon George Garro Trefgarne b 4 Jan 1970; *Career* awarded Royal Aero Club Bronze Medal (jtly) for flight UK to Aust and back in light aircraft 1963; oppn whip House of Lords 1977-79, a Lord in Waiting (Government Whip) 1979-8, under-sec state: Dept of Trade 1981, FCO 1981-82, DHSS 1982-83, Def (for Armed Forces) 1983-85, min of state Def (for Def Support) 1985-86, min of state (Def Procurement) 1986-; *Recreations* flying, photography; *Style*— The Rt Hon the Lord Trefgarne, PC; House of Lords, London SW1

TREFGARNE, Hon Gwion George Garro; s of 1 Baron Trefgarne (d 1960); *b* 2 April 1953; *Educ* Milton Abbey Sch, Merrist Wood Agric Coll, Usk Coll of Agric; *m* 6 Sept 1986, Jaqualine Rees; *Career* form served TAVR; tree surgn; memb Severn Area Rescue Assoc; *Style*— The Hon Gwion Trefgarne; Brok Cottage, Chepstow, Gwent NP6 7PF

TREFGARNE, Hon Mary Elizabeth; da of 1 Baron Trefgarne (d 1960); *b* 1946; *Style*— The Hon Mary Trefgarne; 8 Carthew Villas, London W6

TREFGARNE, Hon Trevor Garro; 2 s of 1 Baron Trefgarne (d 1960); *b* 18 Jan 1944; *Educ* Cheltenham; *m* 1, 1967 (m dis 1979), Diana Elizabeth, da of late Michael Gibb, of Forge House, Taynton, Oxon, by his w Ursula (whose f, Maj Guy Gibbs, TD, was 1 cous of 1st Baron Wraxall); 2 s (Rupert b 1972, Oliver b 1974), 1 da (Susannah Julia b 1976); m 2, 1979, Caroline France, da of Michael Gosschalk, of Monte Carlo; 1 s (Mark b 1982); *Career* Cranfield Sch of Management 1968-69, chm Nesco Investments plc; *Style*— The Hon Trevor Trefgarne; 17 Avenue de l'Annonciade, Monaco

TREFUSIS, Nicholas John; JP (Cornwall); s of Henry Trefusis (d 1975), of Trefusis, and Sheila Margaret, *née* Bryan; *b* 21 Oct 1943; *Educ* Sherborne, Lincoln Coll Oxford; *m* 23 Oct 1973, Servane Marie, da of M Louis Melenec, of Brest, France; 1 s (Jan b 27 April 1977), 1 da (Tamara b 19 Dec 1974); *Career* RN 1964-81; specialised as hydrographic surveyor, exchange serv Royal Danish Navy 1977-80, CO HMS Egeria and sr offr Inshore Survey Sqdn 1980-81; farmer and landowner 1982-; pres: Royal Cornwall Poly Soc, Friends of Glasney; *Recreations* music, sailing; *Style*— Lt Cdr Nicholas Trefusis, JP, RN; Trefusis, Flushing, Falmouth, Cornwall TR11 5TD (☎ 0326 75351)

TREGLOWN, Jeremy Dickinson; s of Rev Geoffrey Leonard Treglown, MBE, Hon CF, of 36 Christ Church Rd, Cheltenham, Glos, and Beryl Miriam; *b* 24 May 1946; *Educ* Bristol GS, St Peter's Coll Saltley Birmingham, St Peter's Coll Oxford (MA, BLitt); *m* 1970 (m dis 1982), Rona Mary Bower; 1 s, 2 da; m 2 1984, Holly Mary Belinda Eley, *née* Urquhart; *Career* lectr in english: Lincoln Coll Oxford 1973-76, UCL 1976-79 (PhD); asst ed Times Literary Supplement 1980-82 (ed 1982-); contributor to: Sunday Times, Observer and many other journals; visiting fell All Souls Coll Oxford, Mellon visiting assoc California Inst of Technol, fell Huntingdon Library California 1988; *Publications* (ed) The Letters of John Wilmot, Earl of Rochester (1980), Spirit of Wit (1982), The Lantern-Bearers: Essays by Robert Louis Stevenson (1988); general ed Plays in Performance series 1981-85; author of various articles on poetry; drama and literary history; *Style*— Jeremy Treglown, Esq; Priory House, St John's Lane, London EC1M 4BX (☎ 01 253 3000; telex 264971); 102 Savernake Rd, London NW3

TREGONING, Christopher William Courtenay; s of John Langford Tregoning, MBE (d 1976), of Windrush House, Inkpen, Newbury, and Sioned Georgina Courtenay, *née* Strick; *b* 15 June 1948; *Educ* Harrow, Fitzwilliam Coll Cambridge; *m* 15 Sept 1973, Antonia Isabella Mary, da of John Albert Miles Critchley-Salmonson, of The Manor House, Great Barton, Bury St Edmunds; 3 s (Harry John William b 23 Jan 1976, Daniel Christopher Leonard b 30 Dec 1977, Thomas Anthony Cecil b 26 Jan 1982); *Career* messrs Thomson McLintock and Co 1970-74, Barclays Bank Ltd 1974-79, dep md Den Norske Creditbank plc (formerly Nordic Bank plc) 1986 (1979-88); FCA; *Recreations* field sports, racing; *Style*— Christopher Tregoning, Esq; The Old Vicarage, Chrishall, Royston, Herts; Den Norse Creditbank plc, 20 St Dunstan's Hill, London EC3R 8HY

TREHANE, Sir (Walter) Richard; s of James Trehane (d 1949), of Hampreston Manor Farm, Wimborne, Dorset, and Muriel Yeoman Cowl; *b* 14 July 1913; *Educ* Monkton Combe Sch (govr 1957-), Univ of Reading; *m* 1948, Elizabeth Mitchell, da of Martin Shaw, MC; 2 s; *Career* mangr Hampreston Manor Farm 1936-; dir: Rivers Estate Co 1964-, Southern TV 1968-81, Rank Orgn 1971-84; former memb: Dorset War Ag Exec Ctee, Milk Mktg Bd 1947-77 (chm 1958-77), Dorset CC; former chm: English Country Cheese Cncl 1955-77, UK Dairy Assoc; pres Int Dairy Fedn 1968-72; pres Euro Assoc Animal Prodn 1961-67 (hon pres 1967-); chm Alfa-Laval Co 1982-85 (dir 1977-85); Hon DSc Univ of Reading; FRAgSs; Cmdr Order of Merit (France) 1964; kt 1967; *Style*— Sir Richard Trehane; Hampreston Manor Farm, Wimborne, Dorset

TREHARNE, Jennet Mary Lloyd (Mrs Stephen Warren); da of William Alan Treharne, of Penarth, S Glamorgan, and Janet Gwendoline, *née* Lloyd; *b* 6 Sept 1953; *Educ* Sir Frederick Osborn Sch Welwyn Garden City, Mid Essex Tech Coll, London Univ (external LLB); *m* 15 March 1980, Dr Stephen Willis Warren, s of Philip Warren; 1 s (Huw b 18 Aug 1982), 1 da (Siân b 19 Jan 1984); *Career* barr Middle Temple 1975, moved to Abergavenny 1981; Newport Chambers, and criminal practice S Wales 1987-; *Recreations* family, walking in W Wales; *Style*— Miss Jennet Treharne; Glaslyn, Avenue Rd, Abergavenng, Gwent (☎ 0873 5539); 73 Blue Anchor Way, Dale, Dyfed; 49 Westgate Chambers, Newport, Gwent (☎ 0633 67403)

TRELFORD, Donald; s of Thomas Staplin Trelford, of Coventry, and Doris, *née* Gilchrist; *b* 9 Nov 1937; *Educ* Bablake Sch Coventry, Selwyn Coll Cambridge (MA); *m* 1, Janice; 2 s, 1 da; m 2, 1978, Katherine Louise, da of John Mark, of Guernsey; 1 da; *Career* ed Times of Malawi 1963-66; corr in Africa: The Observer, The Times, BBC; ed and dir The Observer 1975- (dep ed 1969-75); regular bdcasts on radio and television; memb Br exec ctee Int Press Inst; Freeman City of London; Liveryman Worshipful Co of Stationers; *Publications* County Champions (contributor 1982), Sunday Best (ed, annual anthology 1981-83), Siege (jt author 1980), Snookered (1986), Child of Change (with Garry Kasparov) 1987; *Recreations* golf, tennis, snooker; *Clubs* Garrick, RAF, MCC; *Style*— Donald Trelford, Esq; The Observer, 8 St Andrew's Hill, London EC4V 5JA (☎ 01 236 0202, telex 888963)

TRENCH, Sir Nigel Clive Cosby; KCMG (1976, CMG 1966); s of Clive Newcome Trench (d 1964, s of Hon Cosby Godolphin Trench, 2 s of 2 Baron Ashtown) and Kathleen, da of Maj Ivar MacIvor, CIE hp of kinsman, 6 Baron Ashtown; *b* 27 Oct 1916; *Educ* Eton, Corpus Christi Coll Cambridge; *m* 1 Dec 1939, Marcelle Catherine, da of Johan Jacob Clotterbooke Patyn van Kloetinge, of Zeist, Holland; 1 s; *Career* serv KRRC WWII (UK and NW Europe, despatches); Foreign Serv 1946, Cabinet Off 1967, ambass to Korea 1969-71, memb Civil Serv Selection Bd 1971, ambass to Portugal 1974-76, memb Police Fire and Prison Serv Selection Bds 1977-86; Order of Dip Serv Merit (Rep of Korea) 1984; *Recreations* golf, photography, looking at other people's gardens; *Clubs* Naval and Military, MCC; *Style*— Sir Nigel Trench, KCMG; 4 Kensington Court Gdns, Kensington Court Place, London W8 5QE

TRENCH, Sir Peter Edward; CBE (1964, OBE 1945), TD (1949); s of James Trench; *b* 16 June 1918; *Educ* privately, LSE, St John's Coll Cambridge (BSc); *m* 1940, Mary St Clair Morford; 1 s, 1 da; *Career* serv WWII Queen's Royal Regt; FCIOB, FCIArb, FRSA, CBIM, Hon FRIBA; JP Inner London 1963-71; chm Y J Lovell Hldgs to 1983, former chm Construction & Housing Res Advsy Cncl, chm Nat House Bldg Cncl 1978-84; vice-pres Bldg Centre, hon memb Arch Assoc; memb: cncl CBI, cncl RSA, ct govrs LSE; visiting prof Construction Mgmnt Reading Univ 1981-; dir: Capital & Counties plc, LEP Gp plc, Nationwide Bldg Soc, Crendon Concrete, The Builder Ltd, Haden plc, Middle East Bldg Serv Ltd, RICS Journals Ltd, Trench & Ptnrs Ltd; former md Bovis Ltd; kt 1979; *Style*— Sir Peter Trench, CBE, TD; 4 Napier Close, Napier Rd, London W14 8LG (☎ 01 602 3936)

TRENCHARD, 3 Viscount (UK 1936); Sir Hugh; 3 Bt (UK 1919); also Baron Trenchard (UK 1930); s of 2 Viscount Trenchard, MC, and of Patricia, da of Adm Sir Sidney Bailey, KBE, CB, DSO; *b* 12 Mar 1951; *Educ* Eton, Trinity Coll Cambridge; *m* 1975, Fiona Elizabeth, da of Hon James Ian Morrison, TD, DC, *qv*, s of 1 Baron Margadale; 2 s (Hon Alexander b 1978, Hon William b 1986), 2 da (Hon Katherine Clare b 1980, Hon Laura Mary b 1987); *Heir* s, Hon Alexander Thomas b 1978; *Career* Capt 4 Royal Green Jackets, TA 1973-80; pres Kleinwort Benson Int Incorporated 1988-, (joined 1973, chief rep in Japan 1980-85), gen mangr Tokyo 1985-88, Dover Japan Incorporated 1985-87; memb: gen affairs ctee Japan Security Dealers Assoc 1987-88, Japan Assoc of Corp Execs 1987-; *Style*— The Rt Hon the Viscount Trenchard; 85 Thurleigh Rd, London SW12 8TY

TRENCHARD, Hon John; 2 s of 2 Viscount Trenchard, MC (d 1987); *b* 13 Mar 1953; *Educ* Eton; *m* 9 June 1983, Clare, yst da of E de Burgh Marsh, of The Old Rectory, Salcott, Essex; 1 s (Thomas Edward b 13 May 1988); *Style*— The Hon John Trenchard

TRENCHARD, Hon Thomas Henry; s of 2 Viscount Trenchard, MC; *b* 1966; *Style*— The Hon Thomas Trenchard

TREND, Hon Michael St John; er s of Baron Trend, GCB, CVO, PC (Life Peer, d 1987); *b* 1952; *m* 28 Feb 1987, Jill E, er da of L A Kershaw; 1 da (Faith Charlotte b 1988); *Style*— The Hon Michael Trend

TREND, Baroness; Patricia Charlotte; da of late Rev Gilbert Shaw; *m* 1949, Baron Trend, GCB, CVO, PC (Life Peer, d 1987); 2 s, 1 da; *Style*— Lady Trend; Flat 10, 102 Rochester Row, London SW1P 1SP

TREND, Hon Patrick St John; yr s of Baron Trend, GCB, CVO, PC (Life Peer, d 1988); *Style*— The Hon Patrick Trend; Michaelmas House, 28 Tangier Road, Guildford, Surrey GU1 2DF (☎ 0483 576187); Arthur Andersen & Co, 1 Surrey St, London WC2R 2PS (☎ 01 836 1200, fax 01 831 1133)

TRENEMAN, Col Richard Howard Wotton; s of Harry Ewart Treneman (d 1970), of Ley, Plymton, Plymouth, Devon, and Gladys Helena, *née* Treleaven; *b* 21 Oct 1925; *Educ* St Boniface's Coll Plymouth, Univ of Liverpool, Royal Coll of Surgeons Ireland LRCP; *m* 13 Oct 1956, Claire, da of Michael Joseph O'Neil Quirk (d 1967), of Cregg Cottage, Carrick-on-Suir, Tipperary, Eire; 3 s ((Richard) Christopher Michael b 8 Dec 1960, Oliver b 15 May 1964, Brian b 21 Nov 1966), 3 da (Nichola b 12 April 1958, Jill b 4 May 1959, Judy b 4 Aug 1965); *Career* house offr Shrewsbury and Copthorne Hosps 1955-56, casualty offr Salisbury Gen Infirmary 1956-58; registrar ENT surgery: Salisbury Hosp Gp 1958-60, Brighton and Lewes Hosps 1960-62; civilian med practitioner MOD (Army) Bulford and Tidworth Garrisons 1962-63, cmmnd Maj RAMC 1963, registrar accident and emergency dept Tidworth Mil Hosp 1963-66, postgrad sr med offs course Royal Army Med Coll London 1966-67, sr med offr Medical Reception Station Sennelager W Germany 1967-68, 2 i/c 30 Field Ambulance RAMC 1968-69, Lt-Col 1969, sr med offr Br Forces Sharjah 1970, Co 7 Field Ambulance RAMC and sr med offr 12 Mechanised Bde 1970-73, dep asst dir gen Army Med Dept MOD 1973-75; asst dir med servs: Rhine Area BAOR 1975-76, HQ UKLF 1976-78, SE Dist 1978; dep dir med servs FAREUF 1978-80, Col 1979, Co Br Mil Hosp Rinteln BAOR 1980-86, Col enviromental med and res Def Med Servs Directotate MOD 1986-87, med advsr (Army) Chemical Def Estab Porton Down 1987-; govr Christ the King Sch Amesburg; LRCP, LRCSI; memb: BHA 1956, MPS 1956, RCGP 1981, Salisbury Med Soc 1986; *Recreations* music, theatre, reading, gardening, travel; *Style*— Col Richard Treneman; The Grange, Idmiston, Nr Salisbury, Wilts SP4 0AP (☎ 0980 610374); Chemical Defence Establishment, Porton Down, Salisbury, Wilts SP4 0JQ (☎ 0980 610211, ext 413)

TRENERRY, Hon Mrs; Hon Jennifer; *née* Hill; da of Baron Hill of Luton, PC (Life Peer); *b* 1933; *Educ* Sch of St Mary and St Anne Abbots Bromley, and London Univ; *m* 1, 1960 (m dis), Robert Duncan Barnaby Leicester, MB; 2 s (Andrew b 1961,

Stephen b 1963), 2 da (Sarah b 1963, Gillian b 1968); m 2, 1974, Thomas Trenerry; *Career* medical practitioner in paediatrics and community health; hon paediatric registrar Westmead Hosp, Sydney; child medical offr Parrannatta Child Health Centre, Sydney; *Recreations* tennis, bush-walking, crafts; *Style—* The Hon Mrs Trenerry; 33 Day Rd, Cheltenham, New South Wales, Australia

TRENERRY, Michael John Boulden; s of Leslie Trenerry, and Margaret Trenerry; *b* 27 Mar 1953; *Educ* Truro Sch, Essex Inst of Higher Educn, Bristol Poly (LLB, Dip ES); *m* 19 July 1975, Elizabeth Mary, da of Benny Pearce; 2 da (Samantha b 1980, Rebecca b 1985); *Career* formerly slr in private practice; md Michael Trenerry Ltd; sr lectr in legal and mgmnt studies; *Recreations* numismatics, Victorian Art; *Style—* Michael Trenerry, Esq; Newhaven, 1 Northfield Drive, Truro, Cornwall TR1 2BS (☎ 0872 77977)

TRESCOWTHICK, Sir Donald Henry; KBE (1979); s of Thomas Patrick Trescowthick; *b* 4 Dec 1930; *m* 1952, Norma Margaret Callaghan; 2 s, 2 da; *Career* memb Lloyd's (London); chm: Charles Davis Ltd, McEwan Ltd, Investmt and Merchant Fin Corpn Ltd and Subsidiaries, Perpetual Insur and Securities Ltd; dir DOXA Youth Welfare Fndn; chm: Australian Ballet, Australian Sports Aid Foundation, Nat Olympic Fndn, The Minus Children's Fund; FASA; *see Debrett's Handbook of Australia and New Zealand for further details*; *Style—* Sir Donald Trescowthick, KBE; 38A Lansell Rd, Toorak, Vic 3142, Australia

TRESS, Dr Ronald Charles; CBE (1968); s of Stephen Charles Tress (d 1953), and Emma Jane, *née* Blewitt (d 1975); *b* 11 Jan 1915; *Educ* Gillingham Co Sch, Univ Coll Southampton (BSc), Univ of London, St Deiniol's Library Hawarden, Univ of Manchester; *m* 25 July 1942, Josephine Kelly, da of Hubert James Medland (d 1968); 1 s (Thomas b 1949), 2 da (Sarah b 1944, Janet b 1946); *Career* asst lectr econs Univ Coll of SW Exeter 1938-41, econ asst War Cabinet Offs 1941-45, econ advsr Cabinet Sec 1945-47, reader in public fin Univ of London 1947-51, prof political economy Univ of Bristol 1951-68, master Birkbeck Coll London 1968-77, dir The Lever Tst 1977-84, vice-pres Royal Econ Soc 1979- (sec gen 1975-79); tstee City Parochial Fndn 1974-77, 1979-89, govr Christ Church Coll Canterbury 1975-89, cncl memb Univ of Kent Canterbury 1977-89, memb mgmnt ctee Seaside Camps for London Boys and Girls Hawkshill Deal 1986-; chm South West Econ Planning Cncl 1965-68, devpt cmmr 1959-81, chm Lord Chancellor's Advsy Ctee on Legal Aid 1979-84; Hon: DSc Bristol 1968, LLD Furman S Carolina 1973, DUniv Open Univ 1974, LLD Exeter 1976, DSc Southampton 1978, DCL Kent at Canterbury 1984; *Clubs* Athenaeum; *Style—* Dr R C Tress, CBE; 22 The Beach, Walmer, Deal, Kent CT14 7HJ (☎ 0304 373254)

TRETHOWAN, (Henry) Brock; s of Michael Trethowan, OBE (d 1968), of Hampshire, Phyllis Franklin, *née* Miles (d 1981);; *b* 22 June 1937; *Educ* Sherborne; *m* 11 April 1970, Virginia, da of Lt-Col Geoffrey Charles Lee, of Farnham, Surrey; 2 da (Rebecca b 1966, Henrietta b 1977); *Career* slr: ptnr Trethowans of Salisbury; pres Wilts Valuation and community charge Tbnl 1989-; Enham Village Centre and memb Papworth Village Settlement 1969-; asst rec Co and Crown Ct 1986-; tstee Salisbury Hospice Care Tst 1981- (vice chm 1988-); *Recreations* shooting, enjoying good food and wine; *Style—* Brock Trethowan, Esq; Penruddocke Cottage, Dinton, Salisbury, Wilts (☎ 0722 76418; College Chambers, New St, Salisbury, Wilts (☎ 0722 412512, telex 477668, fax 0722 4311300)

TRETHOWAN, Sir (James) Ian Raley; s of late Maj J Trethowan, MBE; *b* 20 Oct 1922; *Educ* Christ's Hospital; *m* 1963, Carolyn Reynolds; 3 da; *Career* former journalist with: Yorks Post (political corr 1947-55), The Economist 1953-58 and 1965-67, News Chronicle (political correspondent 1955-57), The Times 1967-68; dep ed and political ed ITN 1958-63; joined BBC as political and current affairs commentator 1963, md BBC Radio 1969-75, md BBC TV 1976-77, dir-gen BBC 1977-82, ret; memb Br Cncl Bd 1980-87, independent nat dir Times Newspapers Hldgs 1982-; dir: Barclays Bank (UK) Ltd 1982-, Thorn EMI 1986-, Thames TV plc 1985-; chm: Horserace Betting Levy Bd 1982-, Thames TV plc 1987-; advsr Thorn-EMI 1982-; tstee Glyndebourne Arts Tst 1982-, chm Br Museum Soc 1982-, tstee Br Museum 1984-; pres Cinema and Television Gp of European Cmmn 1988-; Hon DCL E Anglia Univ 1979; kt 1980; *Style—* Sir Ian Trethowan; 17-23 Southampton Row, London WC1B 5HH (☎ 01 405 5346/242 3453)

TRETHOWAN, Prof Sir William Henry; CBE (1975); s of William Henry Trethowan (d 1933), of Hampstead, and Joan Durham, *née* Hickson (d 1949); *b* 3 June 1917; *Educ* Oundle, Clare Coll Cambridge (MA), Guy's Hosp (MB, BChir); *m* 1, 1940, Pamela (d 1985), da of Jack Waters (d 1946); 1 s, 2 da; m 2, 1988, Heather Dalton; *Career* serv RAMC 1944-47, BAOR, India, Maj; prof of psychiatry: Sydney Univ Australia 1956-62, Univ of Birmingham 1962-82 (emeritus 1982-); hon conslt psychiatrist: Central Birmingham Health Dist 1962-82, Hollymoor Hosp 1964-82, Midland Centre for Neurosurgery 1975-82; dean of med faculty Birmingham Univ 1968-74; hon fell Royal Australian and NZ Coll of Psychiatry; Hon DSc Chinese Univ of Hong Kong; FRCP, FRACP, Hon FRCPsych, kt 1980; *Books* Textbook of Psychiatry (with A C P Sims), Uncommon Psychiatric Syndromes (with M D Enoch); *Recreations* music; *Clubs* Birmingham Med Inst; *Style—* Prof Sir William Trethowan, CBE; 99 Bristol Rd, Edgbaston, Birmingham B5 7TX (☎ 021 440 7590)

TREUHAFT, Hon Mrs (Jessica); *see*: Mitford, Jessica

TREVELYAN, Hon Catherine Mary; OBE (1977); da of Baron Trevelyan (Life Peer; d 1985); *b* 1943; *Career* gen mangr The Burlington Magazine 1980-; *Style—* The Hon Catherine Trevelyan, OBE

TREVELYAN, Dennis John; CB (1981); s of John Henry Trevelyan (d 1982), and Eliza Trevelyan; *b* 21 July 1929; *Educ* Enfield GS, Univ Coll Oxford; *m* 1960, Carol, da of John Coombes (d 1944); 1 s, 1 da; *Career* entered Home Office 1950, princ private sec to Lord Pres and Ldr of House 1964-67, asst under-sec state NI Office 1972-76, asst under-sec state Home Office Broadcasting Dept 1976-77, dep under-sec of state Home Office and dir-gen Prison Serv 1978-83, first Civil Serv cmmr 1983- (responsible to the Queen and the Privy Cncl for keeping unqualified persons out of the Civil Service); memb: City of London Univ Business Sch Cncl 1986, Exec Ctee of Industl Participation Assoc 1987-; govr London Contemporary Dance Tst 1986-; *Recreations* music, sailing; *Clubs* Athenaeum, MCC; *Style—* Dennis Trevelyan, Esq, CB; Civil Service Commission, Cabinet Office (Off of the Mini for the Civil Service), Horse Guards Rd, London SW1P 3AL (☎ 01 270 3000)

TREVELYAN, Edward Norman; s and h of Sir Norman Trevelyan, 10 Bt; *b* 14 August 1955; *Style—* Edward Trevelyan, Esq

TREVELYAN, Geoffrey Washington; s of late Rt Hon Sir Charles P Trevelyan, 3 Bt; hp of bro, Sir George Trevelyan, 4 Bt; *b* 4 July 1920; *Educ* Oundle, Cambridge Univ (MSc); *m* 1947, Gillian Isabel, da of late Alexander Wood; 1 s, 1 da; *Career* de Havilland AC Co Ltd 1941-61; dir: Chatto & Windus Ltd, Hogarth Press Ltd 1962-78, Chatto, Bodley Head and Jonathan Cape Ltd 1970-78; chm Thames North Regn of Abbeyfield Soc, technical writer, hon tres Family Planning Assoc; dir: Family Planning Sales Ltd, The Lake Hunts Ltd; *Style—* Geoffrey Trevelyan, Esq; Silkstead, 3 Abbey Mill End, St Albans, Herts (☎ 0727 64866)

TREVELYAN, Sir George Lowthian; 4 Bt (UK 1874), of Wallington, Northumberland; s of Rt Hon Sir Charles Philips Trevelyan, 3 Bt, PC, JP (d 1958), and Mary Katharine, OBE, JP (d 1966), yst da of Sir Hugh Bell, 2 Bt; *b* 5 Nov 1906; *Educ* Sidcot Sch, Trinity Coll Cambridge (MA); *m* 1940, Editha Helen, da of Col John Lindsay-Smith, CBE; 1 da (adopted); *Heir* bro, Geoffrey Washington Trevelyan; *Career* WWII Capt RB, transferred to GHQ Travelling Wings for Home Guard Trg Adj Highland Home Guard; taught at No1 Army College Dalkeith 1945-47; craftsman-designer of furniture Peter Waals workshops 1929-31, trained and qualified to teach F M Alexander Techniques for re-education 1931-36, taught at Gordonstone and Abinger Hill Sch 1936-41, princ Attingham Park, the Shropshire Adult Coll 1947-71; founded Wrekin Tst, an educnl charity concerned with spiritual nature of man and the universe; with Malcolm Lazarus as co-dir ran weekend courses and conferences countrywide 1971-83; presented with the Right Livelihood Award in Stockholm; lectured widely in Britain and abroad; pres and tstee Wrekin Tst; *Books* Twelve Seats at the Round Table (with Edmund Matchett 1976), A Vision of the Aquarian Age (1977), The Active Eye in Architecture (1977), Magic Casements (1980), Operation Redemption (1981), Summons to a High Crusade (1986); *Style—* Sir George Trevelyan, Bt, MA; Badminton, Avon GL9 1BW (☎ (045 423) 359)

TREVELYAN, Sir Norman Irving; 10 Bt (E 1662), of Nettlecombe, Somerset; s of Edward Trevelyan (gggs of Sir John Trevelyan, 4 Bt); suc 3 cous, Sir Willoughby Trevelyan, 9 Bt, 1976; *b* 29 Jan 1915; *m* 1951, Jennifer Mary, da of Arthur E Riddett, of Long Orchards, Copt Hill Lane, Burgh Heath, Surrey; 2 s, 1 da; *Heir* s, Edward Norman Trevelyan; *Style—* Sir Norman Trevelyan, Bt; 1041 Adella Av, Coronada, Calif 92118, USA

TREVELYAN, (Walter) Raleigh; s of Col Walter Raleigh Fetherstonhaugh Trevelyan (d 1953), and Olive Beatrice *née* Frost (d 1976); *b* 6 July 1923; *Educ* Winchester Coll; *Career* Capt Rifle Bde WWII; publisher 1948-88 with Collins, Hutchinson, Michael Joseph (as ed dir), Hamish Hamilton, Jonathan Cape, Bloomsbury; translator from Italian (John Florio Prize 1967), reviewer; contrib: Apollo, Connosseur, John Rylands Bulletin; FRSL (memb cncl); *Books* The Fortress (1955), A Hermit Disclosed (1960), The Big Tomato (1966), Princes Under The Volcano (1972), The Shadow of Vesuvius (1976), A Pre-Raphaelite Circle (1978), Rome '44 (1982), Shades of the Alhambra (1984), The Golden Oriole (1987); *Recreations* travel, gardening; *Clubs* Groucho; *Style—* Raleigh Trevelyan, Esq; 18 Hertford St, London W1Y 7DB (☎ 01 629 5879); St Cadix, St Veep, Lostwithiel, Cornwall PL22 0PB (☎ 0208 872313)

TREVELYAN, Baroness; Violet Margaret; o da of late Gen Sir William Henry Bartholomew, GCB, CMG, DSO; *m* 10 Nov 1937, Baron Trevelyan, KG, GCMG, CIE, OBE (Life Peer, d 1985); 2 da; *Style—* The Rt Hon the Lady Trevelyan; 24 Duchess of Bedford House, London W8 7QN

TREVES, Vanni Emanuele; s of Giuliano Treves (ka 1944), and Marianna, *née* Baer; *b* 3 Nov 1940; *Educ* St Paul's, Univ of Oxford (MA), Univ of Illinois (LLM); *m* 7 Jan 1971, Angela Veronica, da of Lt-Gen Sir Richard Fyffe, DSO, OBE, MC (d 1971); 2 s (Alexander b 1973, William b 1975), 1 da (Louise b 1983); *Career* slr; ptnr Macfarlanes 1970 (sr ptnr 1987); dir Oceonics Gp plc (1984), dir Saatchi & Saatchi Co plc 1987, dep chm BBA Gp plc 1987; tstee: J Paul Getty Jr Charitable Tst, 29th May 1961 Charitable Tst; hon tres London Fedn of Boys' Clubs; *Recreations* walking, eating, watercolours; *Clubs* Boodle's, Buck's, City of London; *Style—* Vanni Treves, Esq; 10 Norwich St, London EC4A 1BD (☎ 01 831 9222, fax 01 831 9607, telex 296381)

TREVETHIN, Baron; *see*: Oaksey, Baron

TREVETT, Peter George; s of George Albert Trevett, of 56 Berrylands, Surbiton, Surrey, and Janet, *née* Ayling; *b* 25 Nov 1947; *Educ* Kingston GS, Queens' Coll Cambridge (MA, LLM); *m* 12 July 1972, Vera Lucia; 2 s (Thomas b 1973, Philip b 1978), 1 da (Jessica b 1982); *Career* barr Lincoln's Inn 1971, practising revenue barr 1973-; memb hon soc Lincoln's Inn; *Books* various articles in professional journals; *Recreations* golf, collecting cactaceae, gardening, book collecting, reading; *Clubs* Bucks, Woking GC; *Style—* Peter Trevett, Esq; 11 New Sq, Lincoln's Inn, London WC1A 3QB (☎ 01 242 4017, fax 01 831 2391, telex 894189 TAXLAW G)

TREVILIAN; *see*: Cely-Trevilian

TREVOR, 4 Baron (UK 1880); Charles Edwin Hill-Trevor; JP (Clwyd 1959); s of 3 Baron Trevor (d 1950, himself gs of 3 Marquess of Downshire); *b* 13 August 1928; *Educ* Shrewsbury; *m* 1967, Susan Janet Elizabeth, da of Ronald Ivor Bence, DSC, VRD, BEM, of Birmingham; 2 s (Hon Marke Charles b 1970, Hon Iain Robert b 1971); *Heir* s, Hon Marke Charles Hill-Trevor; *Career* chm Berwyn Petty Sessional Division; tstee: Royal Forestry Soc of England, Wales & N Ireland, Inst of Orthopaedics Robert Jones & Agnes Hunt Orthopaedic Hospital; memb: Awe District Salmon Fishery Bd, River Orchy Fishery Assoc, N Wales Police Authy; patron of 2 livings; CStJ; *Recreations* fishing, shooting; *Clubs* East India; *Style—* The Rt Hon the Lord Trevor, JP; Brynkinalt, Chirk, Wrexham, Clwyd (☎ Chirk 3425); Auch, Bridge of Orchy, Argyllshire (☎ Tyndrum 282)

TREVOR, John Clyfford; s of Clyfford Trevor (d 1970), and Louisa Ryder Trevor, *née* Airey; *b* 16 August 1932; *Educ* USA, Millfield; *m* 14 Sept 1957, Jane Carolyn, da of Capt Charles Houstoun-Boswall (d 1946), Royal Scots Greys (*see* Baronetage); 2 s (Mark b 1961, Richard b 1969), 2 da (Carolyn b 1959, Emma b 1963); *Career* Nat Serv 2 Lt First Battalion The East Surrey Regt 1952-53, serv Libya and Egypt; sr ptnr J Trevor and Sons 1972-; chm: Central London branch of the Royal Inst of Chartered Surveyors 1978-79, gen practice div of the Central London Branch RICS 1973-74, RICS Working Pty on Conveyancing 1986-, J Trevor Mortleman and Poland Ltd, Lloyds Brokers 1985-88; memb: Gen Practice Divisional Gen Cncl 1985-, Divisional Exec 1986-; FRICS, ACI, ARIS; *Recreations* furniture restoration, gardening; *Clubs* Naval and Military, MCC; *Style—* John Trevor, Esq; J Trevors & Sons, 58 Grosvenor St, London W1X 0DD

TREVOR, Phyllis, Baroness; Phyllis; da of J A Sims, of Ings House, Kirton-in-Lindsey, Lincs; *m* 1927, 3 Baron Trevor (d 1950); *Career* OStJ; *Style—* The Rt Hon Phyllis, Lady Trevor; The Holt, Chirk, Wrexham

TREVOR COX, Maj Horace Brimson; s of Charles Horace Cox (d 1941), and Florence Ann, da of H D Read; *b* 14 June 1908; *Educ* Eton (played football, wall games and boxed for coll), and in Germany and USA; *m* 1957, Gwenda Mary Gordon, da of Alfred George Ellis (d 1967); 1 da (Rosemary); *Career* trained in Germany with AEG Berlin 1929-30, studied in NY USA with Gen Electric Co 1931-32; MP Stalybridge 1937-45, PPS at BOT, min of Health, min of Economic Warfare, serv WWII, Capt Welsh Guards 1939-44, with BEF France, Bde Maj 1940; dir and chm various cos; European Star France 1940, Gen Serv Medal and Victory Medal 1939-45, Russian Gold Medal; farmer and landowner; Parly candidate: Stalybridge 1937 and 1945, Birkenhead 1950, Romford and Brentwood 1952-55, and Parly candidate Salisbury 1963; *Recreations* shooting, fishing; *Clubs* Brooks's; *Style—* Maj Horace Trevor Cox; Roche Old Ct, Winterslow, Wilts

TREVOR-ROPER, Patrick Dacre; s of Dr Bertie William Edward Trevor-Roper (d 1978), of Aluwick, Northumberland, and Kathleen Elizabeth Trevor-Roper (d 1965); *b* 9 June 1916; *Educ* Charterhouse, Clare Coll Cambridge (MA, MD), Westminster Med Sch; *Career* Capt NZ Med Corps served Italy 1943-46; conslt ophthalmic surgn: Westminster Hosp 1947-82, Moorfields Eye Hosp 1963-81; teacher Univ of London 1949-82; ed Transactions of the Ophthalmic Soc UK 1949-88; pres ophthalmic section RSM 1978-80, vice pres Ophthalmic Soc of UK, chm ophthalmic qualifications ctee BMA; Freeman City of London, Liveryman Worshipful Co of Spectacle Makers; FRCS 1947, FRGS, FRZS, FRSA; *Books* The World Through Blunted Sight (1970), The Eye and its Disorders (second edn 1984), Lecture notes in Ophthalmology (seventh edn 1986), Recent Advances in Ophthalmology (1975); *Recreations* music, travel; *Clubs* Athenaeum, Beefsteak; *Style—* Patrick Trevor-Roper, Esq; 3 Park Sq West, London NW1 4LS (☎ 01 935 5052)

TREW, Francis Sidney Edward; CMG (1984); s of Major Harry Francis Trew (d 1968), and Alice Mary, *née* Sewell (d 1972); *b* 22 Feb 1931; *Educ* Taunton's Sch Southampton; *m* 1958, Marlene Laurette, da of late George Peter Regnery, of Stratford, Conn, USA; 3 da; *Career* HM Diplomatic Serv; served in: Lebanon 1952, Amman 1953, Bahrain 1953-54, Jedda 1954-56; vice-consul Philadelphia 1956-58, second sec Kuwait 1959-62, consul Guatemala City 1965-70, first sec Mexico City 1971-74, consul Algeciras 1977-79, high cmmr Belmopan Belize 1981-84, HM ambass Manama 1984-88; Order of Aztec Eagle (Mexico) 1975; *Recreations* fishing, carpentry; *Style—* Francis Trew, Esq, CMG; c/o Lloyds Bank, 6 Pall Mall, London SW1

TREW, Peter John Edward; s of Antony Francis Trew, DSC, and Nora, *née* Houthakker; *b* 30 April 1932; *Educ* Diocesan Coll Cape, RNC Dartmouth; *m* 1, 1955 (m dis 1985), Angela Margaret, da of Kenneth Patrick Rush, CBE (d 1982); 2 s (Robin b 1957, Martin b 1959), 1 da (Sarah b 1961); m 2, 1985, Joan, da of Allan Howarth; *Career* RN 1950-54; MP (C) for Dartford 1970-74; dir Rush-Tompkins Gp plc 1973-; *Style—* Peter Trew, Esq; 1 Painshill House, Cobham, Surrey (☎ 0932 63315)

TREWBY, Vice Adm Sir (George Francis) Allan; KCB (1974); s of Vice Adm George Trewby, CMG, DSO (d 1953), of Richmond, Surrey; *b* 8 July 1917; *Educ* RNC Dartmouth, RNEC Keyham, RNC Greenwich; *m* 1942, Sandra Coleridge, da of late G C Stedham, of Kenya; 2 s; *Career* joined RN 1931, Cdr 1950, Capt 1959, Rear Adm 1968, Vice Adm 1971, asst controller (Polaris) MOD 1968-71, Chief of Fleet Support and Memb of Admty Bd 1971-74, ret 1974; mangr Messrs Foster Wheeler Ltd 1975-77, conslt 1977-87, ret 1987; *Style—* Vice Adm Sir Allan Trewby, KCB; 2 Radnor Close, Henley-on-Thames, Oxon

TREWIN, Ion Courtenay Gill; s of John Courtenay Trewin, OBE, of 15 Eldon Grove, Hampstead, London NW3, and Wendy Elizabeth, *née* Monk; *b* 13 July 1943; *Educ* Highgate; *m* 7 Aug 1965, Susan Harriet, da of Walter Harry Merry (d 1953), of 48 Cholmeley Cres, Highgate, London N6; 1 s (Simon b 1966), 1 da (Maria b 1971); *Career* reporter: The Independent & South Devon Times Plymouth 1960-63, The Sunday Telegraph 1963-67, The Times 1967-79 (ed The Times Diary 1969-72, literary ed 1972-79); ed Drama Magazine 1979-81, editorial dir Hodder & Stoughton 1985-(sr ed 1979-85); chm: library ctee Highgate Literary & Scientific Inst 1970-, Soc of Bookmen 1986-88; chm of judges Booker Prize for fiction 1974, memb arts and library ctee MCC 1988-; mgmnt ctee Booker Prize 1989; *Books* Journalism (1975), Norfolk Cottage (1977); *Recreations* restoring clocks, watching cricket, gossip; *Clubs* Garrick, MCC; *Style—* Ion Trewin, Esq; 48 Cholmeley Cres, Highgate, London N6 (☎ 01 348 2130); Bank Cottage, Surrey St, Wiggenhall St Germans, King's Lynn, Norfolk; Hodder & Stoughton Ltd, 47 Bedford Sq, London WC1 (☎ 01 636 9851, fax 01 631 5248, 0732 460 134, telex 885 887, 95122)

TRIBBLE, Norman Reginald; s of Frederick John Tribble (d 1972), of Exeter, and Alice Maud, *née* Hooper (d 1980); *b* 17 Feb 1927; *Educ* St Luke's Coll Sch Exeter, Univ of London (BSc); *m* 20 July 1946, Christine Mary, da of Stuart Allen Moore (d 1960), of Folkestone; 1 da (Hilary b 1953); *Career* Lt 1 Bn Devonshire Regt 1945-48, serv Singapore 1946 and HongKong 1947; accountant Inst Prodn Engrs 1948-53; mgmt accountant: Shell-Mex and B P Ltd 1953-60; dir and proprietor Manchester Exchange and Investmt Bank Ltd 1960-89; vice-pres Assoc Corporate Tres (fnd chm 1979), churchwarden; Liveryman Worshipful Co of Musicians; FCCA 1953; *Recreations* music, swimming; *Clubs* Naval and Military; *Style—* Norman Tribble, Esq; 237 Forest Rd, Tunbridge Wells, Kent TN2 5H7 (☎ 0892 20149); Manchester Exchange and Investment Bank, 40 City Rd, London EC1Y 2AX (☎ 01 251 9261, fax 01 251 6483, telex 261238)

TRICKETT, (Mabel) Rachel; da of James Trickett, and Margaret, *née* Hesketh; *b* 20 Dec 1923; *Educ* Lady Margaret Hall Oxford (BA, MA); *Career* asst to curator Manchester City Art Galleries 1945-46, lectr Univ of Hull 1946-49 and 1950-54, Cwlth Fund fell Yale Univ 1949-50, fell St Hugh's Coll Oxford 1954-73 (princ 1973-); *Books* The Return Home (1952), The Course of Love (1954), Point of Honour (1958), A Changing Place (1952), The Elders (1966), The Honest Muse (1967), A Visit to Timon (1970); *Style—* Miss Mabel Trickett; St Hugh's Coll, Oxford OX2 6LE (☎ 0865 274919)

TRIDGELL, (Francis) Peter; TD (1954); s of Arthur Ernest Tridgell (d 1980), of Tottenham, and Florence Tridgell (d 1974); *b* 12 Feb 1925; *Educ* Tottenham Co Sch; *m* 17 March 1950, Lois Audrey, da of (Leonard Hugh) Cooper (d 1970), of Tottenham; 1 s (Mark b 1954, d 1968), 3 da (Helen b 1952, Rhona b 1957, Kathryn b 1962); *Career* RAFVR 1943, Royal Signals 1944, i/c communications United Provinces India Signals 1946, Sqdn Cdr Royal Signals TA 1948-62; Nat Westminster Bank: area dir N London 1969-75, transmission mangr 1975-78, dep gen mangr Business Devpt and Planning 1978-85; memb Eurocheque Working Gp Brussels 1975-78, vice-pres Euro Fin Mktg Assoc 1983-85, govr and tres Middx Poly, commodore Aldenham Sailing Club, fndr memb Enfield Nat Tst Assoc; Freeman City of London 1976, Liveryman Worshipful Co of Painter Stainers 1976; FCIB 1981, FInstM 1986; *Recreations* dinghy racing, tennis, singing; *Clubs* Livery; *Style—* Peter Tridgell, Esq, TD; 100 Prince George Ave, London N14 4ST (☎ 01 360 7158)

TRIER, Peter Eugene; CBE (1980); s of Ernst Joseph Trier (d 1938), and Nellie Marie, *née* Bender (d 1979); *b* 12 Sept 1919; *Educ* Mill Hill Sch, Trinity Hall Cambridge (Mathematical Wrangler 1941); *m* 1946, Margaret Nora, da of Frederick James Holloway (d 1964), of Shoreham-by-Sea; 3 s; *Career* RN Scientific Serv 1941-50; dir: Mullard Research Labs 1953-69, Philips Electronics 1969-85; chm Defence Scientific Advsy Cncl 1981-85, pro-chllr Brunel Univ 1980-, pres Inst of Mathematics 1982; Hon DTech Brunel 1975; FEng; Glazebrook Medal and Prize Inst of Physics 1984; *Recreations* travel, sailing, railway history; *Clubs* Savile; *Style—* Peter Trier, Esq, CBE; Yew Tree House, Bredon, Tewkesbury, Glos GL20 7HF (☎ 0684 72200)

TRIGGER, Ian James Campbell; s of Lt Walter James Trigger (d 1961), and Mary Elizabeth, *née* Roberts (d 1984); *b* 16 Nov 1943; *Educ* Ruthin Sch Wales, Univ Coll of Wales Aberystwyth (LLB), Downing Coll Cambridge (MA); *m* 28 Aug 1971, Jennifer Ann, da of Harry Colin Downs (d 1986); 2 s (Ieuan Mungo Campbell b 12 Oct 1973, Simon Huw Campbell b 21 April 1977); *Career* law lectr UWIST 1967-70, barr Inner Temple 1970, Northern circuit 1970-, asst rec 1986-; pt/t chm Socl Security Appeal Tbnl 1983-; churchwarden St Saviour's Church Oxton 1986-88; *Recreations* preserving the countryside from the ravages of greed and the C of E from mediocrity; *Style—* Ian Trigger, Esq; Heather Ridge, 37 Ashburton Rd Oxton, Birkenhead, Merseyside (☎ 051 236 7191); Oriel Chambers, 5 Covent Garden, Liverpool L2 8UD (☎ 051 236 7191)

TRILLING, Capt Ossia; s of Sani Trilling (d 1951), and Rachel, *née* Kaplan (d 1968); *b* 22 Sept 1913; *Educ* St Paul's, St John's Coll Oxford (BA); *m* 11 July 1951, Marie-Louise, da of Harald Otto William Crichton-Fock (d 1978); *Career* WWII enlisted RA 1940, cmmnd 2 Lt 1942, demob Actg Capt 1946; co fndr and dir Chesham Repertory Theatre 1939-40; ed: Theatre Newsletter 1946-51, Theatre News Agency 1946; regular contrib Theatre Worl 1954-65, theatre and music corr The Times; obituary contrib: The Times, The Daily Telegraph, The Independent; regular contrib: The Stage, BBC arts programmes, BBC World Servs, various Euro radio stations (ret 1989); corr numerous papers andd pubns, translator of foreign language dramas; lectr Br Cncl; memb bd of dirs Theatre Royal Stratford East 1975-89; vice pres Int Assoc of Theatre Critics 1956-77; cncl memb: Critics' Circle (UK), Br Theatre Inst; Offr Royal Order of the North Star Sweden 1980, kt first class Order of the Finnish Lion Finland 1983; *Books* International Theatre (1946); *Recreations* swimming, walking, theatre going, piano playing; *Style—* Capt Ossia Trilling; 9A Portland Place, London W1N 3AA (☎ 01 580 6440)

TRIMLESTOWN, 19 Baron (I 1461); Charles Aloysius Barnewall; s of 18 Baron Trimlestown (d 1937); *b* 2 June 1899; *Educ* Ampleforth; *m* 1, 1926, Muriel (d 1937), da of Edward Oskar Schneider, of Mansfield Lodge, Whalley Range, Manchester; 2 s, 1 da; m 2, 1952, Freda Kathleen Watkins, da of late Alfred Watkins, of Ross-on-Wye; *Heir* s, Hon Anthony Edward Barnewall; *Career* formerly Lt Irish Gds; *Style—* The Rt Hon the Lord Trimlestown; Tigley, Dartington, Totnes, Devon

TRINDER, Frederick William; s of Charles Elliott Trinder (d 1970), and Grace Johanna, *née* Hoadly (d 1974); *b* 18 Nov 1930; *Educ* Ruskin Coll Oxford, LSE (BSc); *m* 17 Oct 1974, Christiane Friederike Brigitte, da of Joachim Hase (d 1952); 1 s (Stefan Charles b 1979); *Career* slr 1966, dep charity cmmr 1974-84, cmmr 1984-85; tstee Charities Official Investmt Fund, John Hunt Award Tst; memb: BBC Central Appeals Advsy Ctee, IBA apeals advsy ctee; *Recreations* travel, reading; *Clubs* Royal Overseas League; *Style—* Frederick Trinder, Esq; 37 The Common, W Wratting, Cambridge CB1 5LR (☎ 0220 29469)

TRINGHAM, David Lawrence; s of George William Tringham (d 1985), of Grasse, France, and Madeleine Joyce, *née* De Courcy (d 1987); *b* 13 Mar 1935; *Educ* Bedford Modern, Preston Manor GS; *m* 24 Oct 1962, Annette Alberte, da of Raymond Andre Schmitt (d 1987), of Paris; 2 da (Andréa Fréderique b 18 March 1966, Gaia Frances b 3 April 1970); *Career* Nat Serv Bombardier 39 Heavy Field Regt 1953-55; entered film indust under Sir Michael Balcon at Ealing Studies 1955, asst dir Lawrence of Arabia 1961-62; first asst dir working with: David Lean, Joseph Losey, Richard Lester, Sidney Lumet, Don Siegel, Peter Hyams amongst others; writer of numerous screenplays, adaptor and dir The Last Chapter; *Recreations* painting and drawing, cycling, reading and writing in the sun; *Style—* David Tringham, Esq; 40 Langthorne St, London SW6 6JY

TRINICK, (George Edward) Michael; OBE (1984), DL (Cornwall 1988-); s of Cdr G W Trinick, OBE, RD, RNR (d 1959), of Mylor, Falmouth, Cornwall, and Rosamond Frances, *née* Lloyd; *b* 10 July 1924; *Educ* Haileybury, Christ's Coll Cambridge, RAC; *m* 30 sept 1950, (Maud) Elizabethg Lyon, da of Arthur Bickersteth Hutchinson (d 1952), of Godalming, Surrey; 2 s (Marcus b 1952, William b 1965), 2 da (Mary b 1954, Cecily b 1956); *Career* RE 1942-47, Substantive Lt, attached Bombay Sappers and Miners 1946-47; land agent Nat Tst Cornwall 1953, sec Nat Tst Ctee for Devon and Cornwall 1958-84, ret; pres Royal Inst of Cornwall 1971-72; High Sheriff of Cornwall 1989-; fell Chartered Land Agents Soc 1947, FLAS 1969, FRICS 1970; *Recreations* shooting; *Clubs* Farmer's; *Style—* Michael Trinick, Esq, OBE, DL; Newton House, Lanhydrock, Bodmin, Cornwall PL30 4AH (☎ 0208 72543)

TRIPONEL, Hon Mrs; Hon Angela Caroline; da of Baron Harris of High Cross (Life Peer); *m* 1977, Roland Triponel, of Lyon, France; 4 da; *Style—* The Hon Mrs Triponel; Oakhurst, 21 Warwick Rd, Hale, Cheshire WA15 9NS (☎ 061 928 8409)

TRIPPIER, David Austin; RD, JP (Rochdale 1975), MP (Cons) Rossendale and Darwen 1983-; s of Austin Trippier MC; *b* 15 May 1946; *Educ* Bury GS; *m* 1975, Ruth Worthington; 3 s; *Career* sec: Cons Parly Def Ctee, All Pty Parly Footwear Ctee; ldr Cons Gp Rochdale Cncl 1974-76 (memb cncl 1969-78); memb Stock Exchange 1968-; cmmnd offr Royal Marine Reserve 1968, MP (C) Rossendale 1979-1983, nat vice-chm Assoc Cons Clubs 1980, PPS to Kenneth Clarke as Min State (Health) DHSS 1982-83; parly under-sec state: Trade and Indust 1983-85, Dept of Employment 1985-87, Dept of the Environment 1987-; *Style—* David Trippier, Esq, RD, JP, MP; House of Commons, London SW1 (☎ 01 219 4186)

TRISTRAM, Maj Uvedale Francis Barrington; Major; s of Uvedale Barrington Tristram (d 1926), and Edla Mary, *née* Guarracino (d 1960); *b* 20 Mar 1915; *Educ* St Georges Coll Surrey ; *m* 8 Sept 1939, Elizabeth Frances, da of Capt Harold-Eden-

Pearson (d 1945); 1 da (Carloyn Frances, b 23 Oct 1940); *Career* cmmnd RASC 1941, Capt 1942; mil observer Italian Campaign: 7 Armoured Div, 1 Inf, 46 Infantry, 6 Armoured Div; Maj GSO2 8 Br Armd Corps 1945, DADPR Eastern Cmd 1946, SO2 (PR) War Off 1947-48; BP: dep mangr PR Tehran 1948-49, mangr PR oilfields Iran 1949-50, staff London 1950-60; managing ed Hulton Publications 1960-61, ed mngr Longacre Press 1961-62, dir of info Govt of Basutoland (colonial serv) 1962-66, head info servs UK Freedom from Hunger Campaign 1967-73, fndr and ed World Hunger, press advsr Voluntary Ctee on Overseas Aid & Devt 1973-76, press advsr Catholic Fund for Overseas Devt 1976-77; Master of the Keys (Guild of Catholic Writers) 1988-, memb Inst of Journalists; *Books* Adventure in Oil (with Henry Longhurst, 1959), Saint John Fisher (Mazenod Press Basutoland, 1966); *Clubs* PRESS; *Style*— Maj Uvedale Tristram; 19 Mallards Reach, Weybridge, Surrey KT13 9HQ (☎ 0932 248411)

TRITTON, Maj Sir Anthony John Ernest; 4 Bt (UK 1905); s of Maj Sir Geoffrey Ernest Tritton, 3 Bt, CBE (d 1976); *b* 4 Mar 1927; *Educ* Eton; *m* 1957, Diana, da of Rear Adm St John Aldrich Micklethwait, CB, DSO; 1 s, 1 da (Clarissa); *Heir* s, Jeremy Ernest Tritton; *Career* Maj (ret) The Queen's Own Hussars; farmer; *Recreations* shooting, fishing; *Clubs* Cavalry and Guard's; *Style*— Maj Sir Anthony Tritton, Bt; River House, Heytesbury, Warminster, Wilts BA12 0EE

TRITTON, Hon Mrs; Hon Georgina Anne; *née* Ward; da of 1 Viscount Ward of Witley, PC by his 1 w Anne Capel; *b* 12 Mar 1941; *Educ* Lawnside, Sorbonne; *m* 1, 1963 (m dis 1971), Alastair Forbes, the writer and journalist, s of late James Forbes, of Boston; m 2, Patrick Tritton, *qv*; 2 s; *Career* actress; *Recreations* bullfighting, reading; *Style*— The Hon Mrs Tritton; Quintana 23, Gustavo Madero, La Villa, Mexico City, Mexico

TRITTON, Jeremy Ernest; s and h of Sir Anthony Tritton, 4 Bt; *b* 6 Oct 1961; *Style*— Jeremy Tritton, Esq; 2A Beechmore Rd, London SW11 4ET, (☎ 01 627 8056)

TRITTON, Patrick Claude Henry; 2 s of Patrick Arthur Tritton (gn of Sir Charles Tritton, 1 Bt) by his 1 w, Judith, *née* Hurt; *b* 18 May 1934; *Educ* Eton, Cambridge Univ; *m* 1, 1962 (m dis), as her 2 husb, Nancy, da of Sir Harry Oakes, 1 Bt (*see* Nancy Oakes); m 2, Hon Georgina Ward, *qv*, da of 1 Viscount Ward of Witley, PC, and former w of Alastair Forbes; *Career* broker; *Recreations* bullfighting, falconry, reading; *Clubs* White's, Pratt's, Boodle's; *Style*— Patrick Tritton, Esq

TRITTON, Peter Robert Jolliffe; s of Lt-Col J H Tritton, MBE (d 1988), of Powers Hall, Witham, Essex, and Pamela, *née* Skewes-Cox; *b* 22 May 1951; *Educ* Charterhouse; *m* 9 Sept 1975, The Hon Sally Louise, da of 2 Baron Nelson of Stafford; 1 s (Jonathan James Hedley b 1981), 1 da (Emma Pamela Louise b 1986); *Career* memb Lloyds 1981-; dir: Alexander Howden Insurance Brokers 1980-85, P/R Alexander Howden Gp 1985-, P/R Alexander & Alexander Europe plc 1988-; *Recreations* shooting, skiing, organ music, good food; *Style*— Peter Tritton, Esq; Weasel Cottage, Brent Pelham, Herts (☎ 0279 78584); 8 Devonshire Square, London EC2M 4PL (☎ 01 623 5500, fax 01 626 1178, telex 882171 HOWDEN G)

TRITTON, Hon Mrs; Hon Sally Louise; *née* Nelson; yr da of 2 Baron Nelson of Stafford; *b* 20 Oct 1955; *m* 1975, Peter Robert Jolliffe Tritton; 1 s (Jonathan b 1981); *Style*— The Hon Mrs Tritton

TRODDEN, Paul John; s of Lawrence Trodden (d 1962), of Birmingham, and Lilian Jane Trodden; *b* 17 April 1950; *Educ* St Philips GS Birmingham; *m* 22 Dec 1973, Patricia Mary, da of Daniel Francis Duffy (d 1983), of Birmingham; 1 s (Matthew Lawrence b 1979), 2 da (Laura Cathrine b 1981, Kate Elizabeth b 1985); *Career* chartered and certified accountant; dir Natural Solutions Ltd; ACA; *Style*— Paul J Trodden, Esq; 4 Eachway Lane, Rednal, Birmingham; 30 St Mary's Row, Birmingham B13 8JG (☎ 021 449 8121)

TROLLOPE, Sir Anthony Simon; 17 Bt (E 1642), of Casewick, Co Lincoln; o s of Sir Anthony Owen Clavering Trollope, 16 Bt (d 1987), and Joan Mary Alexis, *née* Gibbes; *b* 31 August 1945; *Educ* Sydney Univ (BA); *m* 1969, Denise, da of Trevern Thompson, of N Sydney, NSW, Australia; 2 da (Kellie Yvette b 1970, Analese Christina b 1972); *Heir* bro, Hugh Irwin Trollope, b 31 March 1947; *Style*— Sir Anthony Trollope, Bt; Churinga Lodge, 28 Midson Road, Oakville, NSW 2765, Australia

TROLLOPE, Hugh Irwin; yr s of Sir Anthony Owen Clavering Trollope, 16 Bt (d 1987); bro and hp of Sir Anthony Simon Trollope, 17 Bt, *qv*; *b* 31 Mar 1947; *m* 1971, Barbara Anne, da of William Ian Jamieson, of Lawley Crescent, Pymble, NSW, Australia: 1 s (Andrew Ian b 1978), 2 da (Edwina Anne b 1976, Jennifer Kate b 1980); *Style*— Hugh Trollope, Esq; 26 Bayswater Road, Lindfield, NSW 2070, Australia

TROLLOPE, Dowager Lady; Joan Mary Alexis; *née* Gibbs; da of Alexis Robert Gibbs, of Manly, NSW, Autralia; *m* 1942, Sir Anthony Owen Clavering Trollope, 16 Bt (d 1987); 2 s; *Style*— The Dowager Lady Trollope; Clavering, 77 Roseville Ave, Roseville, NSE, Australia

TROLLOPE, Joanna (Mrs Curtis); da of Arthur George Cecil Trollope, of Overton, Hampshire, and Rosemary, *née* Hodson; *b* 9 Dec 1943; *Educ* Reigate Co Sch For Girls, St Hugh's Coll Oxford (MA); *m* 1, 14 May 1966 (dis 1985), David Roger William Potter, s of William Edward Potter, of Durweston, Dorset; 2 da (Louise b 15 Jan 1969, Antonia b 23 Oct 1971); m 2, 12 A;pril 1985, Ian Bayley Curteis, s of John Richard Jones, of Lydd, Romney Marsh; *Career* writer; info res dept FO 1965-67, english teacher in various schs, feature writer Harpers and Queen, freelance work for maj newspapers; memb : soc of Authors, PEN, ctee Trollope Soc; *Books* Parson Harding's Daughter (historical novel of the year, 1980), The Taverners' Place (1986), Britannia's Daughters (1983), The Choir (1988), A Village Affair (1989); *Style*— Miss Joanna Trollope ; The Mill House, Coln St Aldwybs, Cirencester, Gloucestershire

TROMANS, Christopher John; s of Percy Tromans (d 1979), and Phyllis Eileen, *née* Berryman; *b* 25 Nov 1942; *Educ* Truro Sch, St Edmund Hall Oxford (MA); *m* 31 May 1969, Gillian, da of John Delbridge Roberts (d 1966); 1 s (Andrew b 1972), 1 da (Sarah b 1970); *Career* slr 1968; ptnr: Sitwell Money and Murdoch Truro 1971-79, Murdoch Tromans and Hoskin Truro and Redruth 1979-88, Murdoch Tromans Truro 1988-; Notary Public 1970; memb No 4 SW Legal Aid Gen Ctee and Appeals Panel; dep high ct and co ct registrar W Circuit 1987-; memb Lions Club of Truro, dep chm of govrs Truro Sch; memb The Law Soc, ACI ARB 1978; *Recreations* boating, practical theatre, travel, military history; *Clubs* Oxford Union, Cornwall Farmers (Truro); *Style*— Christopher Tromans, Esq; 17 Knights Meadow, Carnon Downs, Truro, Cornwall TR3 6HU (0872 863 695); Murdoch Tromans, 95 Pydar St, Truro, Cornwall TR1 2BD (☎ 0872 79474, fax 0872 79137)

TROTMAN-DICKENSON, Dr Aubrey Fiennes; s of Edward Newton Trotman-Dickenson, MC, (d 1977), of Airesford, and Violet Murray *née* Nicoll; *b* 12 Feb 1926; *Educ* Winchester, Balliol Coll Oxford (MA, BSc), Manchester Univ (PhD), Edinburgh Univ (DSc); *m* 11 Aug 1953, Danusia Irena, da of Maj Eugeniusz Karel Hewell (d 1955), of Warsaw; 2 s (Casimir b 1955, Dominic b 1961), 1 da (Beatrice b 1957); *Career* tech offr EI Pont de Nemours USA 1953-54, lectr Univ of Edinburgh 1954-60, prof of chemistry Univ Coll of Wales Aberystwyth 1960-68, princ UWIST 1968-88, princ Univ Coll Cardiff 1987-88, princ Univ of Wales Coll Cardiff 1988-; memb Wales Gas Bd 1966-72, chm Job Creation Scheme 1975-78, govr Christ Coll Brecon 1985-; *Style*— Dr Aubrey Trotman-Dickenson; Radyr Chain, Llandaff, Cardiff (☎ 0222 563263); PO Box 68 Cardiff CF1 3XA (☎ 0222 874835, fax 0222 874478, telex 498635)

TROTT, John Francis Henry; s of Francis Herbert Trott (d 1969), of 31 The Ridge, Coulsdon, Surrey, and Ellen Jane, *née* Tilbury; *b* 23 Jan 1938; *Educ* Whitgift Sch, Merton Coll Oxford (BA); *m* 24 April 1965, Averil Margaret, da of Harold Charles Milestone, of 13 Loxford Way, Caterham, Surrey; 2 s (Christopher John b 1966, Jeremy Charles b 1973), 1 da (Nicola Margaret b 1968); *Career* merchant banker; dir Kleinwort Benson Ltd 1972-86, chm and chief exec Kleinwort Benson Int Investmt Ltd 1986, dir Standard Life Assur Co 1974-, chm Kleinworth Overseas Investmt Tst, dir: Merchants Tst, Brunner Investment Tst; *Recreations* golf, tennis; *Clubs* Union, New York; *Style*— John Trott, Esq; 'Odstock', Castle Square, Bletchingley, Surrey RH1 4LB (☎ 0883 843 100); Kleinwort Benson Ltd, 10 Fenchurch St, London EC3

TROTTER, Alexander Richard; DL (Berwicks 1987); s of Maj H R Trotter (d 1962), of Charterhall, Duns, Berwicks, and Rona M, *née* Murray; *b* 20 Feb 1939; *Educ* Eton, City of London Tech Coll; *m* 1 June 1970, Julia Henrietta, da of Sir Peter McClintock Greenwell, 3 Bt (d 1979); 3 s (Henry b 1972, Edward b 1973, Rupert b 1977); *Career* served Royal Scots Greys 1958-68; mangr Charterhall Estate and Farm 1969, chm Mortonhall Park Ltd 1973-, dir Tumber Gravers' GB Ltd 1977-82, vice-chm Border Grain Ltd 1984-; memb Berwickshire CC 1969-75 (chm roads ctee 1974-75), cncl memb Scottish Landowners' Fedn 1975- (chm Land Use Ctee 1975-78, covener 1982-85), memb dept of Agric Working Party on the Agric Holding (Scotland) Legislation 1981-82, chm Scottish Ctee of Nature Conservancy Cncl 1985-, memb UK Ctee for Euro Year of the Environment 1986-88; memb Royal Co of Archers (Queen's Body Guard for Scotland); FRSA 1987; *Recreations* skiing, riding, shooting; *Clubs* New (Edinburgh), Pratt's; *Style*— Alexander Trotter, Esq; Charterhall, Duns, Berwickshire TD11 3RE (☎ 089 084 210, office ☎ 089 084 301)

TROTTER, Geoffrey Wensley; OBE (1988); s of Alfred Wensley Trotter (d 1936), of Calver, Derbys, and Gladys, Styring (d 1980); *b* 31 Dec 1924; *Educ* High Storrs GS Sheffield, HMS St Vincent Gosport Hants; *m* 26 June 1948, Mary Elizabeth, da of Capt Gerald Fountaine Sanger, CBE, JP (d 1981), of Willingham Cottage, Send, Surrey; 2 s (John Geoffrey b 1951, Andrew James b 1954), 1 da (Rosemary Clare (Mrs Heaton) b 1958); *Career* Seaman HMS St Vincent 1943, Sub Lt USN 1944-46, Lt Pilot Fleet Air Arm 1946-48; md: London Cab Co Ltd 1958-; London Serv Stations Ltd 1958-: dir Datacab Ltd 1986, badge examiner Boy Scouts Assoc, parish cncllr; chm: London Taxi Bd 1958-, London Motor Cab Proprietors Assoc 1958-; FIMI, TEng; *Recreations* golf, squash, tennis, gardening; *Clubs* RAC; *Style*— Geoffrey Trotter, Esq, OBE; 74 Manor Drive, Surbiton, Surrey (☎ 01 735 7777); 1-3 Brixton Rd, London SW9 (☎ 01 735 2000)

TROTTER, Neville Guthrie; JP (Newcastle upon Tyne 1973), MP (Cons) Tynemouth 1974-; s of Capt Alexander Trotter (d 1940), and Elizabeth, *née* Guthrie; *b* 27 Jan 1932; *Educ* Shrewsbury, Durham Univ (BCom); *m* 1983, Caroline, da of Capt John Darley Farrow, OBE, RN, and Oona, *née* Hall; 1 da (Sophie b 1985); *Career* RAF 1955-58; CA; ptnr (now conslt) Thornton Baker & Co 1962-74 (now Great Thornton), chm Cons Parly Shipping and Shipbuilding Ctee 1979-85 (vice-chm 1976-79), memb: Select Ctee on Tport, US Naval Inst, Cncl Br Maritime League, RVSI; conslt to Br Marine Equipment Cncl, Northern Gen Tport; dir William Baird plc and Darchem Ltd; memb Private bills passed on Consumer Safety, Licensing Law, Glue Sniffing; memb Newcastle City Cncl 1963-74 (alderman 1970-74); formerly: memb Tyne & Wear Met Cncl, memb CAA airline users ctee, vice-chm Northumberland Police authy, mil sec Cons Parly Aviation Ctee, memb: Northern Econ Planning Cncl, Tyne Improvement Cmmn, Tyneside Passenger Tport Authy; memb cncl RUSI, FCA; *Recreations* aviation, gardening, fell walking; *Clubs* RAF, Northern Counties, Newcastle upon Tyne, Whitley Bay, Tynemouth Cons; *Style*— Neville Trotter, Esq, JP, MP; office: Grant Thornton, Higham House, Higham Place, Newcastle upon Tyne NE1 6LB (☎ 091 261 2631)

TROTTER, Sir Ronald Ramsay; s of Clement George Trotter, CBE (d 1970), of NZ, and Annie Euphemia, *née* Young (d 1979); *b* 9 Oct 1927; *Educ* Collegiate Sch Wanganui, Victoria Univ of Wellington (BCom), Lincoln Coll Canterbury (Cert in Agric); *m* 2 July 1955, Margaret Patricia, da of James Rainey (d 1977), of NZ; 3 s (John b 1956, William b 1958, Douglas b 1963), 1 da (Elizabeth b 1970); *Career* Wright Stephenson & Co Ltd 1958-72: dir 1962-68, md 1968-70, chm and md 1970-72; chm and md Challenge Corpn Ltd 1972-81, chm Fletcher Challenge Ltd 1987- (chm and chief exec 1981-87); tstee and chm NZ Inst of Econ Res (Inc) 1973-86, memb and chm Overseas Invesmt Cmmn 1974-77, chm NZ Business Roundtable 1985-; Pacific Basin Economic Cncl 1985-: (dep int pres 1985-86, int pres 1986-88, immediate past pres 1988-; dir Reserve Bank of NZ 1986-88; Aust amd NZ Banking Gp Ltd 1986-: Inaugural memb of Int Bd of Advice 1986-88, Director 1988-; chm Telecom Corpn of NZ Ltd 1987-; Hon LLD (Well); Silver Jubilee Medal 1977; kt 1985; *Style*— Sir Ronald Trotter; 16 Wesley Road, Wellington 1, New Zealand (☎ 644 726 628); Fletcher Challenge Ltd, 87-91 The Terrace, Wellington 1, New Zealand (☎ 644 738 267, telex NZ3418, fax (644) 721 856)

TROTTER, Thomas Andrew; s of His Hon Richard Stanley Trotter (d 1974), of Meswall, Merseyside, and Ruth Elizabeth, *née* Pierce (d 1982); *b* 4 April 1957; *Educ* Malvern, RCM, Cambridge Univ (MA); *Career* organist; scholar RCM 1974; organ scholar: St George's Chapel Windsor 1975-76, King's Coll Cambridge 1976-79; organist: St Margaret's Church Westminster 1982-, to the City of Birmingham 1983-; deput Royal Festival Hall 1980, Prom Royal Albert Hall 1986, festival performances in UK and Europe; tours to: USA, Aust, and the Far E; first prize winner: Bach Prize, St Albans Int Organ Competition 1979, Prix de Virtuosite, Conservatoire Rueil-Malmaison Paris 1981; ARCM, FRCO; *Style*— Thomas Trotter, Esq; c/o The Town Hall, Birmingham B3 3DQ (☎ 021 235 3942)

TROTTER, Maj William Kemp; s of Lt-Col William Dale Chaytor Trotter, of Gorst Hall, Staindrop, Darlington, Durham, and Gladys Mona, *née* Brendon; *b* 4 Sept 1929; *Educ* Canford; *m* 6 Aug 1960, (Mary) Virginia, da of Maj Sir Reginald Culcheth Holcroft, 2 Bt (d 19780, Wrentnall House, Pulverbatch, Shrewsbury, Shropshire; 3 (James William b 1964, Henry Edward b 1966, Philip b 1969), 1 da (Victoria Mary b 1962); *Career* cmmnd 2 Hussars PAO 1948, Capt 1956, Maj 1963, serv Malaya, NI, Aden, BAOR; ret 1972; chm: Bishops Auckland Constituency Cons Assoc 1974-79, Northern Area Cons Assoc 1987-; High Sheriff Co Durham 1977 ; *Recreations* field sports; *Clubs* Army and Navy; *Style*— Maj William Trotter; The Deanery, Staindrop, Darlington, Co Durham (☎ 0833 60253)

TROUBRIDGE, Thomas; s of Vice Adm Sir Thomas Hope Troubridge, KCB, DSO, RN (d 1949); uncle of Sir Thomas Troubridge, 7 Bt; *b* 26 Dec 1939; *Educ* Eton; *m* 1, 1971 (m dis 1977), Baroness Marie Christine, da of Baron Günther von Reibnitz, and now Princess Michael of Kent (*see* Royal Family); m 2, 1981, Mrs Petronella Forgan; *Career* Kleinwort Benson Ltd; *Recreations* shooting; *Clubs* White's, The Brook (New York); *Style*— Thomas Troubridge, Esq; 1b Gertrude St, SW10 0JN (☎ 01 352 6049)

TROUBRIDGE, Sir Thomas Richard; 7 Bt (GB 1799); s of Sir Peter Troubridge, 6 Bt (d 1988), and The Hon Lady Troubridge, *née* Weeks, da of 1 Baron Weeks; *b* 23 Jan 1955; *Educ* Eton, Univ Coll Durham; *m* 1984, Hon Rosemary Douglas-Pennant, da of 6 Baron Penrhyn, DSO, MBE, *qv*; 1 da (Emily Rose b 1987); *Heir* uncle, Edward St Vincent Troubridge, *qv*; *Career* CA, ptnr Price Waterhouse; *Recreations* sailing ("Blithe Spirit"), skiing; *Clubs* White's, Itchenor Sailing; *Style*— Thomas Troubridge, Esq; 28 Lilyville Rd, London SW6 5DW (☎ 01 736 5739); Price Waterhouse, Southwark Towers, 32 London Bridge St, London SE1 9SY

TROUBRIDGE, Hon Lady; Hon Venetia Daphne; *née* Weeks; da of Lt-Gen 1 and last Baron Weeks, KCB, CBE, DSO, MC, TD (d 1960), and Baroness Weeks (d 1985); *b* 29 August 1933; *m* 10 April 1954, Sir Peter Troubridge, 6 Bt (d 1988); 1 s, 2 da; *Style*— The Hon Lady Troubridge; The Manor House, Elsted, Midhurst, West Sussex

TROUGHTON, Alistair Anthony James Lionel; s of Capt James Cecil Martin Troughton, of High Wych, Sawbridgeworth, Herts, and Georgina Mary, *née* Madell; *b* 8 Jan 1954; *Educ* Wellington; *m* 24 April 1976, (Helen) Mary Claire, da of George Xenophon Constantinidi, of Marsh Mills Hse, Wargrave Rd, Henley-on-Thames, Oxon; 2 s (James Anthony George Lionel b 16 May 1980, Albert Henry William (Bertie) b 19 Aug 1987), 2 da (Sarah Emily Jane b 22 May 1978, Lucy Mary b 16 July 1982); *Career* Bland Welch and Sedgwick Payne 1973-79, Seascope Insur Servs 1979-82 (dir 1981), Steel Burrill Jones GP plc 1983- (dir 1988); *Recreations* shooting, racing, fishing, cricket; *Clubs* Boodle's, MCC; *Style*— Alistair Troughton, Esq; The Old Rectory, Grafham, nr Huntingdon, Cambs PE18 0BB (☎ 0480 810 261); Steel Burrill Jones, Bankside House, 107-112 Leadenhall St, London EC3 (☎ 01 623 4411, fax 01 621 1848, car tel 0836 260 741, mobile phone 0836 722 545, telex 887830 SBJ G)

TROUGHTON, Sir Charles Hugh Willis; CBE (1966), MC (1940), TD (1959); s of Charles Vivian Troughton (d 1955), of Woolleys Hambleden, Henley on Thames, and Constance Lilla *née* Tate (d 1973); *b* 27 August 1916; *Educ* Haileybury, Trinity Coll Cambridge; *m* 1947, Constance Gillean, yr da of Col Philip Mitford (7 in descent from Humphrey Mitford, whose yr bro John became a merchant in London and was ancestor of the Barons Redesdale) by his w Constance, da of Sir John Fowler, 2 Bt; 3 s (Peter b 1948, James b 1950, Simon b 1953), 1 da (Katrina b 1956); *Career* joined TA 1938, serv WWII Oxon and Bucks LI (POW); barr 1945, chm Br Cncl 1977-84; dir: Electric & Gen Investmnt Co 1967-86 (chm 1977-80); dir: William Collins & Sons 1977-79, Whitbread & Co 1978-85, Whitbread Investmnt Co 1981-; independent nat dir Times Newspaper Hldgs 1983-88; former chm W H Smith & Son (Hldgs) 1972-77; govr LSE 1975-; kt 1977; *Clubs* Garrick, Boodle's, MCC; *Style*— Sir Charles Troughton, CBE, MC, TD; Little Leckmelm House, Lochbroom, By Garve, Ross-shire

TROUP, His Hon Judge Alistair Mewburn; s of William Annandale Troup, MC, and Margaret Lois, *née* Mewburn (d 1966); *b* 23 Nov 1927; *Educ* Merchant Taylors', New Coll Oxford; *m* 1969, Marjorie Cynthia, da of Francis Graham Hutchinson (d 1976); by prev marriages, 1 s (Alistair b 1964), 3 da (Victoria b 1953, Rosalind b 1955, Claudia b 1956); *Career* barr Lincoln's Inn 1952, crown cnsl Tanganyika 1955-62, sr cnsl 1962-64, dep circuit judge 1975-77, rec Crown Ct 1977-80, circuit judge 1980-; *Recreations* walking, gardening, golf; *Clubs* Sloane, Seaford Golf, Wildernesse (Sevenoaks); *Style*— His Hon Judge Alistair Troup; Lewes Crown Ct, High St, Lewes, E Sussex (☎ 0273 480400); The Rough, Firle Rd, E Blatchington, Seaford, E Sussex BN25 2FD (☎ 0323 896636)

TROUP, Vice Adm Sir (John) Anthony Rose; KCB (1975), DSC (1943) and bar (1945); s of Capt H R Troup, RN; *b* 18 July 1921; *Educ* RNC Dartmouth; *m* 1, 1943 (m dis 1952), Joy Gordon-Smith; 2 s, 1 da; m 2, 1953, Cordelia Mary, da of W K T Hope, of Newbury, Berks; 2 s, 1 da; *Career* joined RN HMS Worcester and RNC Britannia 1934-38, submarine specialist 1941, war period in Submarines Turbulent and Strongbow (despatches 1943), Capt 1959, Rear Adm 1969, Flag Offr Sea Trg 1969-71, Cdr Far E Fleet 1971-72, Flag Offr Submarines and NATO Cdr Submarines E Atlantic Area 1972-74, Flag Offr Scotland and N Ireland and NATO Cdr N Atlantic 1974-77; def advsr Scicon (UK) 1979-88; *Recreations* sailing, shooting, gardening; *Clubs* Army and Navy, Royal Yacht Sqdn; *Style*— Vice Adm Sir Anthony Troup, KCB, DSC; Bridge Gdns, Hungerford, Berks

TROUP, Donald Alexander Gordon; OBE (1988); s of Francis Gordon Troup (d 1984), of Haselmere, and Olive Mary Katharine, *née* Mosse (d 1959); *b* 20 Dec 1927; *Educ* Radley, Corpus Christi Coll Cambridge; *m* 1, 22 May 1954, Alison Joyce (d 1985), da of Dr Clement Neve (d 1939), of Croydon; 3 s (Robert James b 1955, Andrew Richard b 1957, Nigel Francis b 1960); m 2, 20 Dec 1986, Anne Hanson Barnes, wid of Brian Dearden Barnes (d 1982), da of Walter Hanson Freeman, MC, TD (d 1949); *Career* ptnr Porter & Cobb 1963-85, dir Cobbs 1985-86, exec conslt G A Property Servs 1986-; cncl memb RURAL 1984-, pres Royal Inst of Chartered Surveyors 1986-87; tstee Richard Watts and City of Rochester Almhouse Charities 1969-; Freeman Worshipful Co of Chartered Surveyors 1978; FRICS 1954, FAAV 1970; *Books* Agricultural Holdings Act 1984; *Style*— Donald Troup, Esq, OBE; Leeds Lodge, Yalding, Kent (☎ office: 0622 690 160, home 0622 814169)

TROUP, Prof Malcolm; s of William John Troup (d 1971), of Toronto, and Wendela Mary Seymour, *née* Conway (d 1960); *b* 22 Feb 1930; *Educ* Royal Conservatory of Music Toronto (ARCT), Saarlandisches Konservatorium, Univ of York (DPhil Mus), Guildhall Sch of Music and Drama (FGSM); *m* 24 Feb 1962, Carmen Lamarca-Bello Subercaseaux, da of Arturo Lamarca-Bello (d 1963), of Paris, Santiago, and San Francisco; 1 da (Wendela b 1963); *Career* concert pianist 1954-70; toured world wide, int festivals incl: Prague, Berlin, York, Belfast, Montreal Expo, CBC Toronto, Halifax, Cwlth Arts Festival London; played with leading orchestras incl: LSO, Hallé, Berliner-Sinfonie, Hamburg, Bucharest, Warsaw, Oslo Philharmonic, Bergen Harmonien, Toronto, Winnipeg, Sao Paulo, Lima, Santiago; first performances of important modern works, numerous recordings; dir music Guildhall Sch of Music and Drama 1970-75, prof music and head dept City Univ London 1975-; judge of: CBC Nat Talent Competition, Chopin Competition of Aust 1988, EckhardF-Grammaté Piano Competition, Young Musicians of the Year; govr Music Therapy Charity Tst, chm Euro Piano Teachers Assoc, ed Piano Journal 1987-; external examiner: King's Coll London, York Univ, Keele Univ; music advsr: Royal Netherlands Govt, Br Cncl, Canada Cncl; Freeman City of London 1971, Liveryman Worshipful Co of Musicians 1973; hon prof Univ of Chile 1966, Hon LLD Meml Univ of Newfoundland Canada 1985; FRSA 1986, RSM 1988; *Books* Serial Strawinsky in 20th Century Music; articles in: Composer, Music and Musicians, Music Teacher, Piano Journal, Revista Universitaria de Chile; *Style*— Prof Malcolm Troup; Dept of Music, The City Univ, Northampton Sq, London EC1V 0HB (☎ 01 253 4399, ext 3265/3284, fax 01 250 0837)

TROWBRIDGE, Hon Mrs; Hon (Dorothy) Frances Lucy St George; *née* Caulfeild; er da of 12 Viscount Charlemont (d 1979); *b* 28 Sept 1915; *Educ* Queens Gate London, Brillantmont Lausanne; *m* 1945, Robert Hender Trowbridge, late Flt Lt RAAF; 2 s (Mark Robert b 1947, Richard Keith Giles b 1950); *Clubs* Overseas; *Style*— The Hon Mrs Trowbridge; Drumcairn, Lane End, Elmstead Market, Essex CO7 7BB (☎ 0206 22 2726)

TROWBRIDGE, Martin Edward O'Keeffe; CBE (1987); s of Edward Stanley Trowbridge (d 1962), of London, and Ida, *née* O'Keeffe (d 1981); *b* 9 May 1925; *Educ* Royal Coll of Sci, City and Guilds Coll, Imperial Coll London (BSc, AGCI), American Mgmnt Assoc Coll NY (Dip Bus Studies); *m* 1946, Valerie Ann, da of Royden Glazebrook (d 1948), of Eastbourne, Sussex; 1 s (Sean); *Career* dir (later gp md) Pennwalt Int Corpn 1953-72, gp md Pegler Hattersley Ltd 1972-73, chm and md Martin Towbridge Ltd 1972, dir gen Chemical Industs Assoc 1973-87; dir: Nat Radiological Protection Bd 1987-, Investmt Mangrs Regulatory Orgn 1987-; memb: (later chm) Conceil d'Administration CEFIC Brussels 1973-87, advsy ctee Euro Business Inst 1985-; tstee Catalyst Nat Chemical Museum 1986-; Hinchley Medal of Inst of Chemical Engrs, Int Medal of Soc of Chemical Indust; CEng, FIChemE, MSCI; *Books* Poems (1953), Exhibiting for Profit (with H M Carter), The Purification of Maurice Octs; *Recreations* shooting, painting, relief printing, mineralogy and petrology, wooden and metal containers; *Clubs* Old Siberians, Frensham Gun, Boffles (NY); *Style*— Martin Trowbridge, Esq, CBE; 51A Moreton Terrace, London SW1V 2NS

TROWBRIDGE, Rear Adm Sir Richard John; KCVO (1975); s of Albert George Trowbridge (d 1970); *b* 21 Jan 1920; *Educ* Andover GS; *m* 1955, Anne Mildred, da of Francis W Perceval; 2 s; *Career* joined RN 1935, serv WWII (despatches), Cdr 1953 (destroyer Carysfort 1956-58); exec offr: HMS Bermuda 1958-59, HMS Excellent 1959-60; Capt 1960, cmd Fishery Protection Sqdn 1962-64, Rear Adm 1970, Flag Offr Royal Yachts 1970-75; extra equerry to HM the Queen 1970-; yr bro Trinity House 1972; govr Western Australia 1980-83; KStJ 1980; *Recreations* sailing, golf, fishing; *Clubs* Army and Navy; *Style*— Rear Adm Sir Richard Trowbridge, KCVO; Old Idsworth Garden, Finchdean, Portsmouth, Hants (☎ 070 541 2714)

TROWER, Anthony Gosselin; s of Sir William Gosselin Trower (d 1963), of Stanstead Bury, Ware Herts, and Hon Joan Olivia, *née* Tomlin (d 1968, er da of Baron Tomlin of Ash, Lord of Appeal in Ordinary); *b* 12 July 1921; *Educ* Eton; *m* 27 June 1957, Catherine Joan, da of Col John Philip Kellet, DSO, MC; 4 s (Jonathan b 1958, William b 1959, Christopher b 1964, Richard b 1966) 1 da (Charlotte b 1961); *Career* joined TA (Herts Yeomanry) 1939 and serv WWII (cmmnd RA) Middle E and India (Intelligence Corps), Western Europe (1 SAS Regt) 1939-45; admitted slr 1949; ptnr Trower Still & Keeling (now sr ptnr and third generation in firm) 1952-; *Recreations* field sports, mountain walking, birds, most things to do with preserving the Herts countryside, beautifying my house; *Clubs* Travellers', St James's (Manchester), The Alpine; *Style*— Anthony G Trower, Esq; Stanstead Bury, Ware, Hertfordshire (☎ 0763 3205); Trowers & Hamlins, 6 New Square, Lincoln's Inn, London WC2A (☎ 01 831 6292)

TRUBSHAW, Ernest Brian; CBE (1970, OBE 1964), MVO (1948); s of Maj Harold Ernest Trubshaw, JP, DL (d 1952), of Pembrey, Carmarthenshire, and Lumley Victoria, *née* Carter (d 1980); *b* 29 Jan 1924; *Educ* Winchester; *m* 21 April 1973, Yvonne Patricia, wid of R H Edmondson, and da of late John Arthur Clapham, of Harrogate, Yorks; *Career* RAF 1942-50, Bomber Cmd 1944, Tport Cmd 1945, The King's Flight 1946-48, Empire Flying Sch 1949, RAF Flying Coll 1949-50; Vickers-Armstrong: experimental test pilot 1950-53, dep chief test pilot 1953-60, chief test pilot 1960-66; dir flight test BAC 1966-80, dir and gen mangr Br Aerospace 1980-86, pt/t memb CAA Bd 1986, dir A J Walker (Aviation) Ltd 1986, aviation conslt 1986-; Freeman City of London; memb Guild of Air Pilots and Air Navigators, Worshipful Co of Coachmakers and Coach Harness Makers; Hon DTech Loughborough 1986; Fell: Royal Aeronautical Soc, Soc of Experimental Test Pilots; French Aeronautical Medal 1976; *Clubs* RAF, MCC; *Style*— Ernest Trubshaw, Esq, CBE, MVO; The Garden House, Dodington, nr Chipping Sodbury, Avon BS17 6SG (☎ 0454 323 951, car tel 0836 270 432)

TRUDEAU, Rt Hon Pierre Elliott; CH (1984), PC (Canada), QC (Canada); responsible for repatriation of British North American Act 1983; s of Charles-Emile Trudeau and Grace, *née* Elliott; *b* 18 Oct 1919; *Educ* Jean-de-Brébeuf Coll Montreal, Univ of Montreal, Harvard Univ, Ecole des Sciences Politiques Paris, LSE; *m* 1971, Margaret, da of James Sinclair, of Vancouver; 3 s (Justin, Emmanuel 'Sasha', Michel); *Career* barr Quebec 1943; prof of law Univ of Montreal 1961-65; MP (Lib) 1965-84, parly sec to PM of Canada (Rt Hon Lester Pearson) 1966-67, min Justice and attorney-gen 1967-68, ldr of Lib Pty of Canada 1968-84, PM of Canada 1968-79 and 1980-84; fndg memb Montreal Civil Liberties Union; Hon LLD Univ of Alberta; hon fell LSE 1969; Freeman City of London; FRSC; *Books* Deux Innocents en Chine Rouge (1961; Two Innocents in Red China 1969), Le Fédéralisme et la Société canadienne-française (1968; Federalism and the French Canadians 1968), Réponses (1968); *Recreations* swimming, skiing, canoeing, scuba diving; *Style*— The Rt Hon Pierre Trudeau, CH, QC; House of Commons, Ottawa, Ontario K1A 0A2

TRUESDALE, Geoffrey Ashworth; s of Reginald Truesdale (d 1934), and Ellen, *née* Ashworth (d 1974); *b* 16 Mar 1927; *Educ* King Edward's HS Birmingham, Bishop Vesey's Sch Sutton Coldfield, London Univ (BSc); *m* 5 May 1951, Beryl, da of Leslie Charles Hathaway (d 1988); 1 s (David Geoffrey b 1953), 1 da (Carolyn (Mrs Mitchell) b 1957); *Career* tech offr Water Pollution Res Laboratory (now Water Res Centre) 1947-68, chemical inspr DOE 1968-70, conslt Balfours Consulting Engrs 1988- (joined 1970, ptnr 1976-88); pres: Inst of Water Pollution Control Assoc 1984-87, Inst of Water and Environment Mgmnt (UK) 1988-89 (fell 1987); FIWEM 1987, predecessor bodies FIWPC 1959, FIPHE 1966, FIWES 1979-87; *Recreations* music, gardening; *Style—* Geoffrey Truesdale, Esq; Balfours Consulting Engrs, Yeoman House, 63 Croydon Rd, London SE20 7TW (☎ 01 659 2221, fax 01 659 5702, telex 946448 BALFOR G)

TRUMPINGTON, Baroness (Life Peer UK 1980); Jean Alys Barker; da of late Maj Arthur Edward Campbell-Harris, MC, and Doris Marie, *née* Robson; *b* 23 Oct 1922; *Educ* privately in England and France; *m* 1954, William Alan Barker (d 1988); 1 s (Adam) ; *Career* sits as Cons peer in House of Lords; cons cllr Cambridge City Cncl Trumpington Ward 1963-73, Mayor of Cambridge 1971-72, Dep Mayor 1972-73, Cons Cllr Camb Trumpington Ward 1973-75, hon cllr City of Cambridge 1975-; JP: Cambridge 1972-75, S Westminster 1976-82; UK delegate to UN Status of Women Cmmn 1979-81, hon fell Lucy Cavendish Coll Cambridge 1980, baroness-in-waiting to HM The Queen 1983-85, parly under-sec of state: DHSS 1985-87, MAFF 1987-; *Recreations* bridge, racing, golf, antique hunting; *Style—* The Rt Hon the Baroness Trumpington; House of Lords, London SW1

TRURO, 12 Bishop of 1981-; Rt Rev Peter Mumford; patron of 2 archdeaconries, 24 canonries, 64 livings, one alternately with the Crown, one other alternately and three jointly; The See of Cornwall existed independently 865-1050, whereafter merged with Diocese of Exeter until 1876, when the See refounded; It comprises the old archdeaconry of Cornwall within the Diocese of Exeter; s of Peter Walter Mumford (d 1970), and Kathleen Eva, *née* Walshe; granted arms, based on old family usage, by letters patent 1982; *b* 14 Oct 1922; *Educ* Sherborne, Univ Coll Oxford (MA), Cuddesdon Theol Coll; *m* 1950, Lilian Jane, da of Capt George Henry Glover, 20 Hussars; 2 s, 1 da; *Career* serv WWII, Capt RA; ordained priest 1952; vicar: Leagrave Luton 1957-63, St Andrew Bedford 1963-69; rector Crawley 1969-73, canon and prebendary Ferring (Chichester Cathedral) 1972-73, archdeacon of St Albans 1973-74, suffragan bishop of Hertford 1974-81; vice-chm Central Bd of Fin C of E; *Clubs* Utd Oxford and Cambridge; *Style—* The Rt Rev the Bishop of Truro; Lis Escop, Feock, Truro, Cornwall TR3 6QQ (☎ 0872 862657)

TRUSCOTT, Sir George James Irving; 3 Bt (UK 1909), of Oakleigh, East Grinstead, Sussex; s of Sir Eric Homewood Stanham Truscott, 2 Bt (d 1973); *b* 24 Oct 1929; *Educ* Sherborne; *m* 1, 1954 (m dis 1958), Irene Marion Craig Barr Brown; m 2, 1962, Yvonne Dora, da of late Frank Edward Nicholson; 1 s, 1 da; *Heir* s, Ralph Eric Nicholson Truscott b 21 Feb 1966; *Style—* Sir George Truscott, Bt; BM QUILL, London WC1N 3XX

TRUSCOTT, Ralph Eric Nicholson; s and h of Sir George James Irving Truscott, 3 Bt; *b* 21 Feb 1966; *Style—* Ralph Truscott, Esq

TRUSSLER, John; s of Thomas Herbert Trussler (d 1969), of Middx, and Lillian Frances, *née* Bailey (d 1986); *b* 11 July 1937; *Educ* Willesden Coll of Technol, Harvard Graduate Business Sch; *m* 2 June 1962, Anne Patricia, da of Henry Vincent Sheriff (d 1971), of Middx; 2 s (Andrew John b 1966, Jonathan David b 1971); *Career* gp md Kyle Stewart Ltd; dir Kyle Stewart: Mgmnt Ltd, Specialworks Ltd, Properties Ltd, Investmts Ltd, (golf) Investmts Ltd, Investmts (Hounslow) Ltd, Homes Ltd; dir: KSG Design Services Ltd, Arlingdrive Ltd, Wembly Labs Ltd, Robin Alexander Plant Hire Ltd, Andrew Murray Joinery Ltd; dir US Kyle Stewart: Hldgs Inc, West Coast Inc; dir: London Open Golf (and chm), Lakers Process Engineering Ltd, Mine Flight Ltd (and md), Lockton Devpt plc, Stewart Osborne Ltd; *Recreations* travel, gardening, photography, reading, music; *Clubs* IOD, Harvard Business Sch of London; *Style—* John Trussler, Esq; Cobblestones Wood End Road, Harpenden, Hertfordshire AL5 3ED; Kyle Stewart Ltd, Ardshiel House, Empire Way, Wembley, Middlesex HA9 0NA

TRUST, Peter; s of Ernest Jones Travis (d 1979), and Lillian Varley, *née* Perason; *b* 1 Mar 1936; *Educ* Salford GS, Salford Royal Tech Coll, Art apprenticeship Spain; *m* 7 April 1970, Doreen, MBE, da of Ernest Duckett Runcorn (d 1973); *Career* artist and illustrator; charity fndr and chm; 29 one man shows; Art into Industry; murals; public portraits and commissions; paintings in public and private collections; creator 'Art Constructions' (pre-cursor to concrete poetry); lectr on disfigurement and guidance; memb Soc of Authors; *Recreations* detective novels, walking dog; *Style—* Peter Trust, Esq; Hillview, Wester Kinsleith, Luthrie, Fife KY15 4NR (☎ (03377) 281); Disfigurement Guidance Centre, 52 Crossgate, Cupar KY15 5HS (☎ (0334) 55746)

TRUSTRAM EVE, Hon Amy Comfort; da of 2 Baron Silsoe

TRUSTRAM EVE, Col Hon Peter Nanton; OBE (Mil 1978); yr twin s of 1 Baron Silsoe, GBE, MC, TD, QC (d 1976), by his 1 w Marguerite (da of Sir Augustus Meredith Nanton); *b* 2 May 1930; *Educ* Winchester, Christ Church Oxford; *m* 1961, Petronilla Letiere Sheldon, da of Jannion Steele Elliott, of Dowles Manor, Bewdley, Worcs; 2 s (Richard b 1963, Nicholas b 1965); *Career* late RWF, RB and RGJ, CO Oxford Univ OTC 1973, def and mil attaché Brussels 1980, gen mangr Churchill Hosp Oxford 1985-88; *Recreations* skiing, collecting antiques (particularly sixteenth and seventeenth century maps); *Clubs* Ski of GB, Anglo-Belgian; *Style—* Col the Hon Peter Trustram Eve, OBE; Priory Ct, Duns Tew, Oxon OX5 4JL (☎ 0869 40262); 82 Shuttleworth Rd, London SW11 (☎ 01 585 1012)

TRYON, 3 Baron (UK 1940); Anthony George Merrik Tryon; s of 2 Baron Tryon, GCVO, KCB, DSO, PC (d 1976), and Ethelreda (da of Sir Merrik Burrell, 7 Bt, CBE); *b* 26 May 1940; *Educ* Eton; *m* 1973, Dale Elizabeth, da of Barry Harper, of Melbourne, Aust; 2 s (Charles, Edward (twin) b 1979), 2 da (Zöe b 1974, Victoria (twin) b 1979); *Heir* s, Hon Charles George Barrington Tryon, b 15 May 1976; *Career* page of honour to HM 1954-56; Capt Royal Wilts Yeo; dir Lazard Bros & Co Ltd 1976-83, chm English & Scottish Investors Ltd 1977-87; *Recreations* fishing, shooting; *Clubs* White's, Pratt's; *Style—* The Rt Hon the Lord Tryon; Ogbury House, Great Durnford, Salisbury (☎ 0722 73225); office: 19 Great Winchester St, London EC2N 2BH (☎ 01 382 9864)

TRYON, Hon Aylmer Douglas; s of 1 Baron Tryon (d 1940); *b* 16 July 1909; *Educ* Eton, Trin Cambridge (BA); *Career* formerly Capt Gren Gds; fndr Tryon Gallery; *Books* Kingfisher Mill, Wildfowlers Year; *Recreations* Fishing, Shooting, Natural History; *Clubs* Boodle's, Flyfisher's, Pratt's; *Style—* The Hon Aylmer Tryon; Kingfisher Mill, Great Durnford, Salisbury, Wilts

TRYON, Ethelreda, Baroness; Ethelreda Josephine; da of Sir Merrik Burrell, 7 Bt, CBE, JP, by his 2 w, Coralie (da of John Porter, DL, of Belle Isle, Co Fermanagh and Clonbalt, Co Longford); *b* 20 June 1909; *m* 1939, Brig 2 Baron Tryon, GCVO, KCB, DSO, PC (d 1976); 1 s, 1 da; *Style—* The Rt Hon Ethelreda, Lady Tryon; Church Farm, Great Durnford, Salisbury, Wilts (☎ 072 273 281)

TRYTHALL, Maj Gen Anthony John (Tony); CB (1983); s of Eric Stewart Trythall (d 1963), and Irene, *née* Hollingham; *b* 30 Mar 1927; *Educ* Lawrence Sheriff Sch Rugby, St Edmund Hall Oxford (BA, DipEd), Kings Coll London (MA); *m* 2 Aug 1952, Celia, da of Sidney Richard Haddon, of Rugby; 2 s (Timothy b 1960, Peter b 1961), 1 da (Susan b 1967); *Career* Royal Army Educnl Corps Offr 1948-49 and 1953-84, serv Egypt, Transjordan, Malaya, W Germany, UK, Chief Inspr and Col Research 1973-74, Chief Educn Offr UK Land Forces 1976-80, Dir Army Educn 1980-84; md Brassey's Defence Publishers 1984-87, exec dep chm 1988-; memb: cncl Royal Utd Services Inst 1978-84, bd of War Studies London Univ 1983-; publisher to Int Inst for Strategic Studies 1989-; chm Gallipoli Memorial Lecture Tst 1986-; cncl memb RUSI 1978-84; First Prize Trench Gascoigne Essay 1969; *Books* Boney Fuller: The Intellectual General 1878-1966 (1977), The Downfall of Leslie Hore-Belisha in the Second World War (1982), articles in military and historical journals; *Recreations* garden, family, good food and wine, military thoughts; *Clubs* Naval and Military; *Style—* Maj Gen Anthony Trythall, CB; c/o Royal Bank of Scotland, Holts Farnborough Branch, Lawrie House, Victoria Rd, Farnborough, Hampshire GU14 7PA; 24 Gray's Inn Road, London WC1X 8HR (☎ 01 242 2363, fax 01 405 3194, telex 265871 MONREF G)

TRYTHALL, Rear Admiral John Douglas; CB (1970), OBE (1953); s of Alfonzo Charle Trythall (d 1958), of Camborne, Cornwall, and Hilda Elizabeth, *née* Monson (d 1951); *b* 21 June 1914; *Educ* Stretford GS; *m* 17 June 1943, Elizabeth Loveday, da of Walter Alan Donald (d 1974), of Auckland, NZ; 2 s (William b 1947, James b 1952), 2 da (Jenifer b 1949, Julia (Mrs Drury) b 1956); *Career* cadet RN 1931-32, WI Stn 1932-33, Hume Fleet 1933-34, E Indies Stn 1934-37, Signal Sch 1937-39, lent RNZN (Battle of River Plate) 1939-40, Western Approaches 1940-42, Br Delegation Washington 1942-44, Staff of Flag Offr Cmdg 11 Aircraft Carrier Sqdn 1944-45, staff of Govr and C-in-C Hong Kong 1945-46, Sec to Vice Adm (Air) and 2 i/c Med Fleet 1947-48, Sec to 2 Sea Lord 1948-50, Sec to C-in-C The Nore 1950-52, JSSC 19536, Sec to C-in-C Plymouth 1955-58, Asst Dir of Naval Plans 1960-62, IDC 1963, Capt of Fleet Med 1964-65, Head of Personnel Panel Admiralty 1966-67, Rear Adm 1968, Asst Chief of Personnel and Logistics MOD 1969-72; ret 1972; Admty Bd's Govr RN Benevolent Tst 1972-79 (vice patron 1980-), chm Taunton Cons Assoc 1974-75, Cmmr & Cdr St John Ambulance (Somerset) 1976-82; FCIS (1956); *Recreations* genealogy, heraldy, watching ball games (too old to play); *Clubs* MCC; *Style—* Rear Adm John Trythall, CB, OBE; The Old Vicarage, Corfe, Taunton, Somerset TA3 7AQ (☎ 082 342 463)

TUBY, John; OBE; s of Joseph Tuby (d 1983), and Georgette, *née* Ismalun (d 1970); *b* 17 June 1923; *Educ* Private; *m* 29 May 1958, (Edith) Joan Redmayne, da of Col William Eric Walker, CBE, TD (d 1949); *Career* WWII Army 1941-47; mangr feeds sales div Quaker Oats Ltd 1953-63, exec dir of subsidiary of Thomas Tilling Gp 1953-63, dir gen Franco Br C of C and Indust 1988-89 (pres 1982-84), govr Br Sch of Paris 1985-, pres The Br Luncheon Club (1916) 1981; *Style—* John Tuby, Esq, OBE; Le Coudray Saint Germer, 60850 Saint Germer De Fly, France (☎ 44 81 62 18)

TUCK, Dr (John) Anthony; s of Prof John Philip Tuck, of Chillingham House, Gt Gransden, Sandy, Beds, and Jane Adelaide, *née* Wall; *b* 14 Nov 1940; *Educ* Royal GS Newcastle upon Tyne, Jesus Coll Cambridge (BA, MA, PhD); *m* 17 July 1976, Amanda Jane, da of Dr Lawrence John Cawley, of the Old Hall, Carlton Husthwaite, Thirsk, Yorks; 2 s (Robert James b 1979, Michael Richard b 1982); *Career* sr lectr in history Univ of Lancaster 1975- (lectr 1965), master Collingwood Coll Univ of Durham 1978; reader in medieval history Univ of Bristol 1987-; FRHist S 1987; *Books* Richard II and the English Nobility (1973), Crown and Nobility 1272-1461 (1985), Royal Grammar School, Newcastle Upon Tyne (with B Mains and Others 1986); *Style—* Dr Anthony Tuck; 66 A Hill View, Henleaze, Bristol BS9 4PU (☎ 0272 622 953); Department of History, University of Bristol, 13 Woodland Rd, Bristol BS8 1TB (☎ 0272 303 030)

TUCK, Sir Bruce Adolph Reginald; 3 Bt (UK 1910); s of Major Sir (William) Reginald Tuck, 2 Bt (d 1954, s of Sir Adolph Tuck, 1 Bt, who was gs of Raphael Tuck, fine art publisher and chm and md of Raphael Tuck and Sons); *b* 29 June 1926; *Educ* Canford; *m* 1, 1949 (m dis in Jamaica 1964), Luise, da of John C Renfro, of San Angelo, Texas, USA; 2 s; m 2, 1968, Pamela Dorothy, da of Alfred Michael Nicholson, of London; 1 da; *Heir* s, Richard Bruce Tuck; *Career* Lt Scots Gds 1945-47; with Miller-Carnegie; *Clubs* Lansdowne; *Style—* Sir Bruce Tuck, Bt; Montego Bay, PO Box 274, Jamaica

TUCK, Richard Bruce; s and h of Sir Bruce Tuck, 3 Bt; *b* 7 Oct 1952; *Educ* Millfield; *Career* Firearm Sales; *Recreations* shooting, fishing; *Clubs* Ducks Unlimited; *Style—* Richard Tuck, Esq; 9449 Briar Forest, Houston, Texas 77056, USA

TUCKER, Alistair John James; s of James Charles Henry Tucker (d 1982), and Mary Hannah, *née* Featherstonehaugh (d 1975); *b* 17 Feb 1936; *Educ* Southend HS, Keble Coll Oxford (BA, MA); *m* 2 Sept 1967, Deirdre Ann Forster, da of George Moore, of Amersham, Bucks; 1 s (Alistair b 1976), 1 da (Hannah b 1972); *Career* Subaltern The Green Howards 1958-60; exec dir within Tport Hldg Co 1967-70; md Alistair Tucker Halcrow and Assoc (conslts in the mgmnt, economics, regulation and strategic planning of the air tport indust) 1970-; visiting prof Univ of Surrey 1987-; MCIT 1972, MRAeS 1980; *Recreations* walking, travel, archeology; *Clubs* Athenaeum; *Style—* Alistair Tucker, Esq; 50 Primrose Gardens, London NW3 4TP (☎ 01 586 0027); Vineyard Hse, 44 Brook Green, London W6 7BY (☎ 01 602 7282, fax 01 603 0095, telex 916148)

TUCKER, Christopher Robby; s of Lt Leslie Freeman Tucker, JP, of Kemsing, Kent, and Leila Annie, *née* Ison; *b* 23 Mar 1941; *Educ* Eversley Sch Southwald Suffolk, Elizabeth Coll Guernsey CI, Guildhall Sch of Music and Drama London; *m* 29 July 1971 (m dis 1977), Marion Edith, da of Philip John Flint, of Willingborough; *Career* princ special make-up effects on: films: Star Wars 1976, Boys from Brazil 1978, Elephant Man 1979, Quest for Fire 1980, Company of Wolves 1983, High Spirits 1988; TV: I Claudius 1975, Holocaust 1976, Willie Langtry 1979, Prince Regent 1980, War and Remembrance 1986; theatre: Richard III and Cyrano de Bergerac 1984, Phantom of the Opera 1986; active involvement in local history, archaeology, natural history;

Freeman City of London 1962, Freeman Worshipful Co of Haberdashers 1962; BFI 1982, BAFTA 1982, AIP 1984; *Recreations* antiquarian books, opera, antiquities; *Style*— Christopher Tucker, Esq; Bere Ct, Pangbourne, Berks RH8 8HT (☎ 07357 2393); Agent-Eric L'Epine-Smith, 10 Wyndham Pl, London W1H 1AS (☎ 01 724 0739/0)

TUCKER, His Hon Judge; Henry John Martin; QC (1975); s of Percival Albert Tucker, LDS, RCS (d 1959); *b* 8 April 1930; *Educ* Downside, Christ Church Oxford; *m* 1957, Sheila Helen, *née* Wateridge; 1 s, 4 da; *Career* barrister 1954, dep chm Somerset QS 1971-, rec 1972-81, circuit judge (Western) 1981-; *Recreations* walking the dog; *Clubs* Hampshire (Winchester); *Style*— His Hon Judge Tucker, QC; Chingri Khal, Sleepers Hill, Winchester, Hants (☎ Winchester 53927)

TUCKER, Herbert Harold; OBE (1965); o s of late Francis Tucker and late Mary Ann Tucker; *b* 4 Dec 1925; *Educ* Queen Elizabeth's Lincs, Rossington Main Yorks; *m* 1948, Mary Stewart, *née* Dunlop; 3 s; *Career* Econ Info Unit Treasy 1948-49, FO 1951, cnsllr and dir Br Info Servs Canberra 1974-78, consul-gen Vancouver 1979-83, disarmament info co-ordinator FCO 1983-84, ret; dir Roberts Centre 1984-, conslt Centre for Security and Conflict Studies 1986-; *Style*— Herbert Tucker, Esq, OBE; Pullens Cottage, Leigh, Hill Rd, Surrey KT11 2HX

TUCKER, Louis Newton; s of Sidney Tucker (d 1968), of Aust, and Elsie Louise Marion, *née* Newton (d 1971); *b* 3 August 1925; *Educ* Christs Hosp Horsham; *m* 1, Nov 1949 (m dis 1963), Beryl, da of Reginald White, of Epsom; 1 s (Nicholas b 6 July 1951); m 2, 19 Oct 1966, Vera Catherine Watkins, da of George Frederick Goodwin; 1 s (Marcus Newton b 12 July 1967), 1 da (Sarah b 6 March 1969); *Career* Maj N Staffs Regt 1942-46, serv Middle E; slr 1953, sr ptnr Helder Roberts & Co; dir: New Estates Ltd 1950-, Estates Property Investmt Co plc 1961-88, Property Security Investmt Tst plc 1961-, govr Christs Hosp; Freeman Worshipful Co of Merchant Taylors 1950; memb Law Soc, MIOD; *Recreations* tennis, gardening; *Style*— Louis Newton Tucker, Esq; Helder Roberts & Co, Ormond House, 2 High St, Epsom, Surrey (☎ 037 27 26567)

TUCKER, Hon Mr Justice; Sir Richard Howard; s of His Hon Judge Howard Archibald Tucker (d 1963), and Margaret Minton, *née* Thacker (d 1976);; *b* 9 July 1930; *Educ* Shrewsbury, Queen's Coll Oxford (MA); *m* 1, 1958 (m dis 1974), Paula Mary Bennxett Frost; 1 s (Stephen), 2 da (Anneli, Gemma); m 2, 1975, Wendy Kate Standbrook; *Career* barr Lincoln's Inn 1954, bencher 1979, rec 1972-85, judge of the High Ct Queen's Bench Div 1985-, presiding judge Midland and Oxford Circuit 1986-; *Recreations* shooting, gardening, sailing (yacht Classmate of Beaulieu); *Clubs* Garrick; *Style*— Sir Richard Tucker; Royal Courts of Justice

TUCKER, Dr Sam Michael; MB, BCH (1952), FRCP (1971); s of Harry Tucker (d 1970), and Ray Tucker (d 1982); *b* 15 Oct 1926; *Educ* Benoni HS SA, Witwatersrand Univ (MBBcH); *m* 13 Dec 1953, Barbara Helen, da of M Kaplan; 2 s (Mark b 1957, Trevor b 1962), 1 da (Dana b 1956); *Career* conslt paediatrician Hillingdon Hosp Uxbridge and 152 Harley St London, clinical tutor and examiner RCP; memb Hillingdon Dist Health Authy, pres section of paediatrics RSM 1987-88, chm med advsy ctee Portland Hosp 1987-88; *Recreations* football, golf; *Clubs* RSM; *Style*— Dr Sam Tucker; 65 Uphill Rd, Mill Hill, London NW7 4PT; 152 Harley St, London W1

TUCKEY, Andrew Marmaduke Lane; s of Henry Lane Tuckey (d 1982), and Aileen Rosemary Tuckey, *née* Newsom-Davis; *b* 28 August 1943; *Educ* Plumtree Sch, Zimbabwe; *m* 24 June 1967, Margaret Louise, da of Dr Clive Barnes (d 1979), 1 s (Jonathan b 1970), 2 da (Clara b 1972, Anna b 1982); *Career* dir: Baring Brothers plc and subsidaries, Bishopscourt Investmts Ltd, Iterate Investmts Ltd, Commerce Int Merchant Bankers Berhad, Sanma Financial Servs Ltd, Sanma Bank (underwriters) Ltd; dir and tres Friends of Covent Garden; chm Fin ctee Young Nat Tst Theatre; tstee Esmee Fairbairn Charitable Tst; *Recreations* music, tennis, windsurfing; *Clubs* Roehampton, City of London; *Style*— Andrew Tuckey, Esq; 36 Lonsdale Rd, Barnes, London SW13 9QR (☎ 01 748 9893); Baring Brothers & Co Ltd, 8 Bishopsgate, London EC2N 4AE (☎ 01 283 8833, fax 01 283 2633)

TUCKEY, Simon Lane; QC (1981); s of Henry Lane Tuckey (d 1982), and Aileen Rosemary *née* Newsom-Davis; *b* 17 Oct 1941; *Educ* Plumtree Sch Zimbabwe; *m* 1964, Jennifer Rosemary, da of Sir Charles Edgar Matthews Hardie, of Henley-on-Thames; 1 s (William b 1966), 2 da (Camilla b 1965, Kate b 1970); *Career* barr Lincoln's Inn 1964, rec 1984; *Recreations* sailing ('Java'), tennis; *Style*— Simon Tuckey, Esq, QC; 6 Regents Park Terrace, London NW1 (☎ 01 485 8952); 4 Pump Court, Temple, London EC4 (☎ 01 353 2656)

TUCKMAN, Fred(erick) Augustus; MEP (EDG) Leicester 1979-; s of Otto Tuchmann (d 1930), and Amy Tina, *née* Adler (d 1966); *b* 9 June 1922; *Educ* LSE (BSc); *m* 1966, Patricia Caroline, da of Sidney Sym Myers; 2 s (Michael b 1968, Jeremy b 1971), 1 da (Jane b 1970); *Career* mgmnt conslt; Hay Gp 1965-85, ptnr Hay Assocs 1975-85; Con spokesman in Euro Parl on Social and Employment Ctee; led Cons in Latin American Delgn 1982-87; chm Inter gp Small Business 1985; *Recreations* reading, swimming, family; *Clubs* Carlton, Atheneum; *Style*— Fred Tuckman, Esq, MEP; 6 Cumberland Rd, Barnes, London SW13 (☎ 01 748 2392, work 01 948 8645)

TUCKWELL, Barry Emmanuel; OBE (1963); s of Charles Robert Tuckwell (d 1986), and Elizabeth Jane, *née* Hill; *b* 5 Mar 1931; *Educ* Sydney Conservatorium; *m* 1, 1958 (m dis 1970), Dr Sally Newton; 2 s (David Michael, Thomas James), 1 da (Jane Madeleine); m 2, 1970 (m dis 1988); *Career* princ horn LSO 1955-68, princ conductor Tasmanian Symphony Orch 1980-83, music dir and conductor Maryland Orch 1982-; Hon RAM, Hon GSM; FRSA; *Clubs* Athenaeum; *Style*— Barry Tuckwell, Esq, OBE; c/o Harold Holt Ltd, 31 Sinclair Rd, London W14 ONS (☎ 01 603 4600)

TUCKWELL, Dr Gareth David; s of Sir Edward Tuckwell, KCVO (d 1988), and Phyllis Courthope, *née* Regester (d 1970); *b* 3 Dec 1946; *Educ* Charterhouse, London Univ and St Bartholomews Hosp Med Coll (MB BS, DObst RCOG); *m* 4 Aug 1973, (Susan) Mary, da of Dr Hugh Wilfred Sansom, OBE, of 29 Holmewood Ridge, Langton Green, Kent; 2 s (Jonathan b 1977, Paul b 1984), 1 da (Deborah b 1976); *Career* princ in gen practice 1974-86, clinical tutor in gen practice St Bartholomews Hosp Med Coll 1976-86, dir Dorothy Kerin Tst 1986-, med dir of Burrswood Tunbridge Wells 1986-; vice-pres Phyllis Tuckwell Memorial Hosp Farnham, memb Working Pty on The Churches Miny of Healing in the Light of Hospice Experience, Freeman City of London, Liveryman Worshipful Soc of Apothecaries 1971; MRCS 1971, LRCP 1971, MRCGP; memb: Assoc of Palliative Medicine, BMA; *Recreations* photography, walking, gardening; *Style*— Dr Gareth Tuckwell; St Lukes, Burrswood, Groombridge, Tunbridge Wells, Kent TN3 9PY, (☎ 0892 864349); Burrswood, Groombridge, Tunbridge Wells, Kent TN3 9PY, (☎ 0892 863637)

TUDOR, Hon Mrs; Hon (Noreen Rosamond) Anne; *née* Tufton; da of 2 Baron Hothfield (d 1961), by 1 w, Lady Ierne Louisa Arundel Hastings (d 1935), da of 13 Earl of Huntingdon; *b* 1903; *m* 1928, Lt-Col Owen Frederick Morton Tudor, 3 King's Own Hussars; 2 da; *Style*— The Hon Mrs Tudor; Ash Court, Hothfield, Ashford, Kent

TUDOR, Rev Dr (Richard) John; s of Rev Charles Leonard Tudor (d 1986), and Ellen, *née* Clay (d 1981); *b* 8 Feb 1930; *Educ* Clee GS Grimsby, Queen Elizabeth's Barnet, Univ of Manchester (BA); *m* 21 July 1956, Cynthia Campbell, da of Richard Anderson (d 1951); 1 s (Peter b 1964), 1 da (Helen b 1967); *Career* RAF 1948-51; jr Methodist Minister East Ham London 1954-57, ordained Newark 1957, minister Thornton Cleveleys Blackpool 1957-60; supt minister: Derby Methodist Mission 1960-71, Coventry Methodist Mission 1971-75, Brighton Dome Mission 1975-81, Westminster Central Hall 1981-; free-church chaplain Westminster Hosp 1982-, chm Westminster Christian Cncl 1988-; Hon Texan 1965, Freeman Fort Worth Texas 1970, Freeman Arkansas 1987; Hon DD Texas Wesleyan Coll Fort Worth Texas 1981; *Recreations* motoring, cooking, photography, the delights of family life; *Style*— The Rev Dr R John Tudor; Westminster Central Hall, Storey's Gate, London SW1H 9NU (☎ 01 222 8010, fax 01 222 6883)

TUDOR, (Alwyn) Kenneth; s of Alwyn Iewun Tudor, CBE (d 1984), and Edith Eleanor, *née* Taylor (d 1981); *b* 9 April 1921; *Educ* Felsted; *m* 9 July 1949, Hazel Edith; 1 s (David b 1959), 1 da (Wendy b 1961); *Career* Serv WWII RCS 1941-46, cmmnd 1942, Temp Maj 1946; London Life Assoc Ltd (life assur co) 1939-81: actuary and mangr 1966, dir 1977, ret gen mangr 1981, ret dir 1985; Freeman City of London 1979, Liveryman Worshipful Co of Actuaries 1980 (hon clerk 1981); FIA 1951, IOD 1977; *Recreations* bowls, gardening, walking, travelling holidays; *Style*— Kenneth Tudor, Esq

TUDOR EVANS, John Mr Justice; Sir Haydn; QC (1962); s of John Edgar Evans by his w Ellen Stringer; *b* 20 June 1920; *Educ* W Monmouth Sch, Lincoln Coll Oxford; *m* 1947, Sheilagh Isabella *née* Pilkington; 1 s; *Career* serv WWII RNVR; barr 1947; bencher Lincoln's Inn 1970, rec Crown Ct 1972-74, High Ct judge Family Div 1974-78, Queen's Bench Div 1978-, judge Employment Appeal Tbnl 1982-; kt 1974; *Clubs* Garrick, MCC; *Style*— The Hon Mr Justice Tudor Evans; c/o Royal Courts of Justice, Strand, London WC2

TUDOR JOHN, William; s of Mr Tudor John, of Castle House, Llantrisant, Mid Glamorgan, and Gwen, *née* Griffiths (d 1969); *b* 26 April 1944; *Educ* Cowbridge Sch, Downing Coll Cambridge; *m* 25 Feb 1967, Jane, da of Peter Clark, of Cowbridge, Mid Glam; 3 da (Rebecca b 1971, Katherine b 1974, Elizabeth b 1980); *Career* Allen & Overy: articled clerk 1967-69, asst slr 1969-70, ptnr 1972-, banker Orion Bank Ltd 1970-72; non exec chm: Suttons Seeds Ltd 1978-, Horticultural and Botanical Hldgs Ltd 1985-; appeal steward Br Boxing Bd of Control 1980-, assoc fell Downing Coll Cambridge 1986-; memb: Freeman City of London, City of London Slrs Co 1972; memb: Law Soc 1969, Int Bar Assoc 1976; *Recreations* shooting, rugby football, reading, music; *Clubs* The Justinians; *Style*— William Tudor John, Esq; Willian Bury, Willian, Herts SG6 2AF (☎ 0462 683532); Allen & Overy, 9 Cheapside, London EC2V 6AD (☎ 01 248 9898, fax 01 236 2192, car tel 0836 730 128, telex 8812801)

TUDWAY QUILTER, David Cuthbert; *see*: Quilter, David Cuthbert

TUFF, Col Charles Reginald; DL (Kent 1976); s of Sir Charles Tuff (d 1961); *b* 18 Mar 1909; *Educ* Malvern, Sandhurst; *m* 1940, Ruth, da Maj A E Hardy; 2 s, 1 da; *Career* 2 Lt The Buffs 1929, Capt Instr Sandhurst 1936, serv WWII, Lt-Col 1943, Col 1945 (despatches); chm Kent County Scout Assoc 1967-77; *Recreations* shooting, fishing; *Clubs* Farmers', Royal Cwlth Soc, MCC; *Style*— Col Charles Tuff, DL; Hogs Green, Sandling, Hythe, Kent CT21 4HG (☎ 0303 67837)

TUFNELL, Hon Mrs; Hon Anne Rosemary; *née* Trench; da of late 5 Baron Ashtown, OBE (d 1979), by his 1 w, Ellen Nancy (d 1949), da of late William Garton; *b* 1936; *m* 1, 1958, Capt Timothy Patrick Arnold Gosselin, Scots Gds (d 1961); 1 da; m 2, 1962, Col Greville Tufnell, *qv*; 3 da; *Style*— The Hon Mrs Tufnell; The Old Rectory, North Cerney, Cirencester, Glos GL7 7BX (☎ 028 583 464)

TUFNELL, Hon Mrs; Hon Georgina Mary; *née* Cavendish; da of 5 Baron Chesham; *b* 8 Sept 1944; *m* 1967, (Michael) Wynne Tufnell, *qv*; 3 s; *Style*— The Hon Mrs Tufnell; High Dell Farmhouse, Bighton, Alresford, Hants SO24 9RB (☎ 0962 73 3970)

TUFNELL, Col Greville Wyndham; s of Maj K E M Tufnell, MC (d 1976); *b* 7 April 1932; *Educ* Eton, RMA Sandhurst; *m* 1962, Hon Anne, *qv*; 3 da; *Career* 2 Lt Grenadier Gds 1952, Adj 2 Bn 1959-61, GSO 3 WO (MO2) 1962-63, Staff Coll 1964, Maj 1965, DAQMG London Dist 1966-67, GSO 2 HQ Div 1969-71, Lt-Col 1971, cmdg 1 Bn Grenadier Gds 1971-73 (despatches 1972), Bde Maj Household Div 1974-76, Col 1976, cmdg Grenadier Gds 1976-78, Yeoman of the Guard Exon 1979, Ensign 1985, Clerk to the Cheque and Adjutant 1987; Liveryman Worshipful Co of Grocers', Freeman City of London; FBIM; *Clubs* Cavalry and Guards, MCC; *Style*— Col G W Tufnell; The Old Rectory, North Cerney, Cirencester, Glos GL7 7BX (☎ 028 583 464)

TUFNELL, Capt John Jolliffe; er s of Maj Nevill Arthur Charles de Hirzel Tufnell, JP, DL (d 1935), of Langleys, Chelmsford; *b* 26 April 1900; *Educ* Cheltenham, RMC; *Career* Lt Grenadier Gds 1920, retired 1922, re-employed 1941, Capt 1943; local dir Barclays Bank Chelmsford, ret; JP Essex 1941-58; Lord of the Manors of S House, Chatham Hall, Sparrowhawks, High Easter and Waltham Bury; *Style*— Capt John Tufnell; South House Manor, Great Waltham, Chelmsford, Essex

TUFNELL, Capt Michael Neville; CVO (1976), DSC (1940); er s of Col Neville Charsley Tufnell (d 1951), of Fairfield, Sunninghill, Ascot, and Sybil Carlos, *née* Clarke (d 1958); *b* 28 Jan 1914; *Educ* RNC Dartmouth, Greenwich; *m* 1941, Patricia Wynne, da of Edward Wynne Chapman (ka 1914), of NZ; 1 s, 2 da; *Career* RN 1927, serv WWII, Cdr 1946, Capt 1953, naval attaché Tokyo 1952-54, CO HMS Decoy 1954-56, naval advsr Australia 1958-60, CO HMS St Vincent Jrs Trg Estab 1960-62, ret; gentleman usher to HM The Queen 1965, extra gentleman usher to HM The Queen 1984-; Freeman City of London, Liveryman Worshipful Co of Grocers; *Recreations* cricket; *Clubs* Royal Yacht Sqdn, Naval and Military, MCC; *Style*— Capt M N Tufnell, CVO, DSC; Curdridge Grange, Curdridge, Southampton, Hants (☎ 048 92 782454)

TUFNELL, Maj Timothy; MC (1945), ERD; s of Col Neville Charsley Tufnell (d 1951), of Fairfield, Sunninghill, Ascot; *b* 1920; *Educ* Eton; *m* 1944 (m dis 1947), Pamela Dione, only da of Oliver Parker (d 1967); *Career* serv WWII 1939-46: Grenadier Gds, Capt 1941, Maj 1944; underwriting memb Lloyd's, conslt Knight Frank & Rutley; chm St John Cncl for Berks; Liveryman Worshipful of Grocers; C St J;

Recreations racing; *Clubs* Bucks, MCC; *Style—* Major Timothy Tufnell, MC, ERD; Hernes Keep, North St, Winkfield, Windsor, Berks SL4 4BY

TUFNELL, (Michael) Wynne; only s of Capt M N Tufnell, CVO, DSC, RN, *qv*; *b* 30 Sept 1942; *Educ* Radley, RAC Cirencester; *m* 1967, Hon Georgina Mary, *qv*; 3 s; *Clubs* MCC, Kandahar Ski; *Style—* Wynne Tufnell Esq; High Dell Farmhouse, Bighton, Alresford, Hants SO24 9RB (☎ 0962 73 3970)

TUFTON, Hon Anthony Charles Sackville; s and h of 5 Baron Hothfield, TD; *b* 1939; *Educ* Eton, Magdalene Coll Cambridge (MA); *m* 1975, Lucinda Margorie, da of Capt Timothy John Gurney; 1 s (William Sackville b 1977), 1 da (Emma b 1976); *Career* amateur tennis champion (singles 1964, doubles 1962, 1963 and 1964); CEng, MICE; *Style—* The Hon Anthony Tufton; Drybeck Hall, Appleby-in-Westmorland, Cumbria CA16 6TF

TUGENDHAT, Christopher Samuel; er s of Dr Georg Tugendhat (d 1973), of London; *b* 23 Feb 1937; *Educ* Ampleforth, Gonville and Caius Coll Cambridge; *m* 1967, Julia Lissant, da of Kenneth D Dobson, of Keston, Kent; 2 s; *Career* ldr and feature writer Financial Times 1960-70; MP (C): Cities of London and Westminster 1970-74, City of London and Westminster South 1974-76; dir Sunningdale Oils 1971-76, consit Phillips Petroleum Int Ltd 1972-1976, former consit to Wood Mackenzie & Co Stockbrokers; Br EEC cmmr (responsible for budget, financial control, personnel and admin) 1977-80, vice-pres Cmmn of European Communities (responsible for budget, fin control, fin insts and taxation) 1981-85; dir: The BOC Gp 1985-, Nat Westminster Bank 1985-, Commercial Union Assur Co plc 1988-; chm: Civil Aviation Authority 1986-, Royal Inst of Int Affairs (Chatham House) 1986-; *Books* Oil: The Biggest Business (1968), The Multinationals (1971), Making Sense of Europe (1986), Options for British Foreign Policy in the 1990's (with William Wallace 1988), *pamphlets* Britain, Europe and the Third World (1976), Conservatives in Europe (1979), Is Reform Possible? (1981); *Recreations* conversation, reading, being with my family; *Clubs* Carlton, Anglo-Belgian; *Style—* Christopher Tugendhat, Esq; 35 Westbourne Park Rd, London W2 5QD

TUGENDHAT, Michael George; QC (1986); s of Dr Georg Tugendhat (d 1973), and Maire, *née* £ Littledale; *b* 21 Oct 1944; *Educ* Ampleforth, Gonville & Caius Coll Cambridge (MA), Yale Univ; *m* 6 June 1970, Blandine Marie, da of Comte Pierre-Charles Menche de Loisne, of France, 4 s (Charles b 1972, Thomas b 1973, Gregory b 1977, Henry b 1986); *Career* barr Inner Temple 1969, MO circuit; *Clubs* Brooks's; *Style—* Michael Tugendhat, Esq, QC; 10 South Sq, Gray's Inn, London WC1R 5EZ (☎ 01 242 2902)

TUGHAN, Frederick Charles; CBE (1968); s of William Tughan (d 1912); *b* 24 Jan 1909; *Educ* Bangor GS, Queen's Univ Belfast; *m* 1935, Mildred, *née* Patterson; 2 s, 3 da (1 decd); *Career* slr 1930, Mayor of Bangor 1956-60, chm Seed Potato Bd N Ireland 1961-68, dir: Lamont Life Assoc Co, Ulster Scot Friendly Soc, Bangor Provident Tst; *Recreations* golf; *Clubs* Royal Belfast, Ulster Reform, Carlton; *Style—* Frederick Tughan, Esq, CBE; 40 Kylestone Rd, Bangor, Co Down (☎ Hangladu 883993); Ralborough Securities Ltd, 20 Victoria St, Belfast BT1 3PD

TUGWELL, John; s of John James Arthur Tugwell, of Hove Sussex and Vera Olive, *née* Mockford (d 1984); *b* 1 Oct 1940; *Educ* Hove Co GS; *m* 12 May 1962, Janice Elizabeth, da of Leslie Walter Santer (d 1979); 1 s (Matthew b 8 Dec 1969), 1 da (Jane b 11 Oct 1965); *Career* dir and chief exec int business NatWest Bank plc (gen mangr business devpt div 1987-88 regnl gen mangr exec off N America 1984-87); memb: W Sussex ctee Br Heart Fndn, CBI Europe Ctee, mgmnt The Jubilee of Princes's Tst, America Europe Community Assoc; int advsr American Univ Washington DC; ACIB; *Recreations* cricket, gardening, walking; *Style—* John Tugwell, Esq; Roundways, 13 Oak Bank, Lindfield, West Sussex RH16 1RR (☎ 0444 450 019); National Westminster Bank plc, 41 Lothbury, London EC2P 2BP (☎ 01 726 1970)

TUGWELL, Richard Stuart; s of Reginald Wilfred Tugwell, of Cirencester, Glos, and Sarah, *née* Burrow (d 1982); *b* 5 Nov 1947; *Educ* Cirencester GS, Bognor Regis Coll of Educn; *m* 30 May 1970, Elisabeth Mary, da of Maj Garth Douglas Curtis, OBE, of Winchester, Hants; 2 da (Lisa b 15 Nov 1970, Anna b 3 May 1974); *Career* journalist Wilts & Glos Standard 1969-84 (sports ed 1978-84), sports ed Oxford Times 1984, Br Sportswriters Assoc/Sports Cncl Award, Weekly Newspaper Sports Writer of the Year 1987; *Recreations* cricket, golf; *Clubs* Cirencester CC (Capt), Cirencester GC, Glos Gypsies CC, S Oxfordshire Amateurs CC; *Style—* Richard Tugwell, Esq; Oxford and County Newspapers Ltd, Osney Mead, Oxford OX2 0EJ (☎ 0865 244 988)

TUITE, Sir Christopher Hugh; 14 Bt (I 1622), of Sonnagh, Westmeath; s of Sir Dennis George Harmsworth Tuite, 13 Bt, MBE (d 1981, descended from the Sir Richard de Tuite or Tuitt, who was one of Strongbow's followers in his invasion of Ireland in 1172); *b* 3 Nov 1949; *Educ* Wellington Coll, Leeds Univ (BSc), Bristol Univ (PhD); *m* 1976, Deborah Ann, da of A E Martz, of Pittsburgh, USA; 2 s (Thomas Livingstone b 1977, Jonathan Christopher Hannington b 1981); *Heir* s, Thomas Livingstone Tuite; *Career* res offr The Wildfowl Tst 1978-81; pres Spirutec Inc (Arizona) 1982-; *Style—* Sir Christopher Tuite, Bt; 1521 East June, Mesa, Arizona 85203, USA

TUITE, Margaret, Lady; Margaret Essie; da of Col Walter Leslie Dundas, DSO, of Farnham; *m* 1947, Sir Dennis Tuite, 13 Bt, MBE (d 1981); 3 s; *Style—* Margaret, Lady Tuite; 7 Vicarage Gardens, Grayshott, Hindhead, Surrey GU26 6NH (☎ Hindhead 5026)

TUIVAGA, Hon Mr Justice; Hon Sir Timoci Uluiburotu; *b* 1931,Oct; *Career* acting chief justice of Fiji 1974-80, chief justice 1980-; kt 1981; *Style—* Hon Mr Justice Tuivaga; 228 Ratu Sukuna Rd, Suva, Fiji

TUKE, Sir Anthony Favill; s of Anthony Tuke; *b* 22 August 1920; *Educ* Winchester, Magdalene Coll Cambridge; *m* 1946, Emilia Mila Antic; 1 s, 1 da; *Career* chm: Savoy Hotel plc 1984- (dir 1982-), RTZ Corpn 1981-85 (dir 1980-); dir: Barclays Bank 1965- (chm 1973-81), Barclays Bank UK 1971-81, Barclays Bank Int 1965-87 (chm 1972-79), Urban Fndn 1980-86, Merchants Tst 1969-, Royal Insur 1978- (dep chm 1985-), Whitbread Investmt Co plc 1984-; memb Trilateral Cmmn 1973-; govr Motability 1978-84, former vice-pres Inst of Bankers and Br Bankers Assoc; kt 1979; *Clubs* MCC (pres 1982-83, memb ctee, chm fin ctee 1983-); *Style—* Sir Anthony Tuke; Freelands, Wherwell, Andover, Hants

TUKE, Peter Godfrey; s of Dr Reginald Godfrey Tuke (d 1973), of Bournemouth, and Dorothy Beatrice, *née* Underwood (d 1948); *b* 14 June 1944; *Educ* Radley, Keble Coll Oxford (MA), Poly of Central London (Dip Arch); *m* 21 June 1975, Susan, da of Edward Albert Hamilton Lawrence (d 1978), of Handcross, Sussex; 2 s (Edward b 1978, William b 1980); *Career* corporate planning BP 1967-71, architect and ptnr Prior Manton Tuke Ptnrship 1981-; Oxford Univ rowing blue; memb RIBA 1979; *Recreations* theatre, sailing, walking; *Clubs* Vincents, Leander; *Style—* Peter Tuke, Esq; 48 Brodrick Rd, London SW17 (☎ 01 672 8678); 8 Rathbone Place, London W1 (☎ 01 636 9031, fax 01 436 4922)

TUKER, Lady; Cynthia Helen; da of Ronald Gale (d 1939), of Sevenoaks; *b* 29 May 1902; *Educ* Cambridge Univ (MA); *m* 1, 1931, Lt-Col R B Fawcett, MC, Indian Army (d 1945); m 2, 1948, as his 2 w, Lt-Gen Sir Francis Ivan Simms Tuker, KCIE, CB, DSO, OBE (d 1967); *Career* pres Cornwall BRCS 1952-64; Kaisar-i-Hind Silver Medal; *Style—* Lady Tuker; Trenelow, Carwinion Rd, Mawnan, Falmouth, Cornwall (☎ 0326 250588)

TULLO, Carol Anne; da of Edward Alan Dodgson, of Woolton, Liverpool, and Patricia, *née* Masterson; *b* 9 Jan 1956; *Educ* Holly Lodge, Hull Univ (LLB); *m* 5 May 1979, Robin Brownrigg Tullo, s of James Francis Swanzy Tullo, of Highgate, London; 1 da (Alice b 1986); *Career* barr Inner Temple 1977; dir: Stevens 1985, Sweet & Maxwell Ltd 1988; *Recreations* motherhood; *Style—* Mrs Robin Tullo; 38 Friern Park, London N12 9DA (☎ 01 445 9689); South Quay Plaza, 183 marsh Wall, London E14 9FT (☎ 01 538 8686, fax 01 538 8625, telex 9290 89)

TULLOCH, Hon Mrs; Hon Marion Hamilton; *née* Wills; da (by 1 m) of 2 Baron Dulverton, CBE, TD; *b* 11 Sept 1940; *m* 15 June 1964, John Glen Alexander Tulloch; 2 s, 1 da; *Style—* The Hon Mrs Tulloch; Courance, Lockerbie, Dumfries-shire

TULLY, David John; s of William Scarth Carlisle Tully, CBE (d 1987), and Patience Treby, *née* Betts; *b* 13 Mar 1942; *Educ* Twyford, Sherborne; *m* 7 May 1965, Susan Patricia, da of (James) Geoffrey Arnott; 1 s (James Herbert b 1967), 2 da (Louise Patience b 1969, Clare Jane b 1972); *Career* slr, ptnr Addleshaw in Latham Manchester 1969-; formerly chm: Manchester Young Slrs, Nat Young Slrs, formerly pres Manchester Law Soc; dir Cobden gp of Cos 1975; govr Manchester GS; *Recreations* shooting, fishing, golf; *Clubs* St James's (Manchester); Racquets (Manchester); *Style—* David Tully, Esq; 2 Warwick Drive, Hale, Altrincham, Cheshire WA15 9TA (☎ 061 928 3029); Dennis House, Marsden St, Manchester M2 1JD (☎ 061 832 5994, fax 061 832 2250)

TUMIM, His Hon Judge Stephen; s of Joseph Tumim, CBE (d 1957), and Renée Tumim (d 1941); *b* 15 August 1930; *Educ* St Edwards Sch Oxford, Worcester Coll Oxford; *m* 1 Feb 1962, Winifred Letitia, da of Col Algenon Borthwick (d 1976), of Essex; 3 da (Matilda b 1963, Emma b 1964, Olivia b 1969); *Career* barr Middle Temple 1955, rec Crown Ct 1977-78 circuit judge 1978-; chm Friends of Tate Gallery 1983-; HM Chief Insp of Prisons for England and Wales 1987-; *Books* Great Legal Disasters (1983), Great Legal Fiascos (1985); *Clubs* Garrick, Beefsteak; *Style—* His Hon Judge Tumim; River House, Upper Mall, Hammersmith, London W6

TUNBRIDGE, Lady; Dorothy; da of Henry Gregg, of Knottingley; *Educ* Leeds Univ (MSc, MA, DipEd); *m* 1935, Sir Ronald Ernest Tunbridge, OBE, JP (d 1984, prof of med Leeds Univ 1946-71); 2 s; *Career* vice-pres Yorks Ladies Cncl of Educn (hon sec 1960-71), chm Univ of Leeds Convocation 1953-56, memb Leeds (GP B) Hosp Mgmnt Ctee (vice chm 1972-74), first pres Knottingley Civic Soc; *Style—* Lady Tunbridge; 9 Ancaster Rd, Leeds LS16 5HH

TUNE, Laurence Kenneth; s of Elijah Thomas and Catherine Tune; *b* 30 Sept 1939; *Educ* Holywell GS, Univ of Wales (BSc); *m* 1964, Ann Bridget, da of Thomas William Jackson (d 1953), of Northwich; 1 s (Christopher b 1971), 1 da (Helen b 1969); *Career* memb: Mktg Soc, Inst of Mktg 1973; dir: PA Mgmnt Conslts Ltd 1979-83, Coopers & Lybrand Associates Ltd 1983-; FIMC; *Recreations* literature, theatre, cinema; *Clubs* Portico Library, Manchester Literary & Philosophical Soc; *Style—* Laurence Tune, Esq; 8 Dane Bank Rd, Lymm, Ches (☎ 092 575 3154); Coopers & Lybrand Associates Ltd, St James's House, Charlotte St, Manchester (☎ 061 236 9841, telex 667257)

TUNNEY, Kieran Patrick; s of Patrick Adam Tunney, and Julia O'Callaghan, *née* Clancy; *b* 14 Oct 1922; *Educ* Rep of Ireland, England and France; *Career* Offr Cadet Grenadier Gds 1942; playwright author; plays: The Patriot Cork Ireland 1938, Day After Tomorrow Q theatre 1946, Fortune theatre 1946, The Marriage Playground Q Theatre 1946, A Priest in the Family Westminster Theatre 1951, The Wedding Ring Manchester Opera House 1952, Royal Exit Cambridge 1953, God and Kate Murphy Broadway 1959, A House of glass London 1963; screenplays: The Rasputin Yousoupoff Affair, The Red Prophet, Justice Deferred; awards: A Priest in the Family Play of the Season Observer, God and Kate Murphy Broadway's best record of the theatrical year; also reporter, theatre corr; critic: Daily Sketch Queen Magazine, News Chronicle, Tatler and Truth Ballet; memb Dramatisis Guild NY; *Books* Tallulah Darling of the Gods; *Recreations* walking, tennis, reading; *Style—* Kieran Tunney, Esq; 510 Beatty House, Dolphin Square, London SW1V 3PL (☎ 01 834 9864)

TUPPER, Capt Anthony Charles; DSC (1945); s of Lt-Col Geoffrey William Henry Tupper, TD (d 1936), of Putney and Alicia Mary, *née* Livingstone-Learmonth (d 1947); *b* 28 Mar 1915; *Educ* RNC Dartmouth and Greenwich; *m* 14 Nov 1942, Agnes Anne, da of Lt-Col Sir Edward Hoblyn Warren Bolitho, KBE, CB, DSO (d 1969); *Career* Naval Offr Med Fleet 1932-34, China 1934-35, 1926-38, Atlantic and Home Fleets 1939-45, Home Fleet 1945-49, Admty NOD 1950-52, Far E and America, WI Station 1954-55, Admty Gunnery Div Naval Staff 1955-57, CSO to Flag Offr Malta 1958-59, Reserve Fleet Plymouth 1959-61, dairy farming (Jersey cattle) 1961-; Cmmr of Irish Lights 1971 (chm 1988); *Recreations* shooting, fishing; *Clubs* Army and Navy, Kildare St and Univ (Dublin), Pratt's; *Style—* Capt Anthony Tupper, Esq, DSC; Lyrath, Kilkenny, Co Kilkenny, Republic of Ireland (☎ 353 56 21382)

TUPPER, Sir Charles Hibbert; 5 Bt (UK 1888), of Armdale, Halifax, Nova Scotia; s of Sir James Macdonald Tupper, 4 Bt (d 1967), and Mary Agnes Jean, *née* Collins; Sir Charles, 1 Bt (d 1915), was PM of Nova Scotia 1864-67 (encompassing date of Union), PM of Canada 1896, ldr of Oppn 1896-1900; *b* 4 July 1930; *m* 1959 (m dis 1975); 1 s; *Heir* s, Charles Hibbert Tupper b 10 July 1964; *Career* asst cmmr (ret); *Style—* Sir Charles Tupper, Bt; Suite 1101, 955 Marine Drive, W Vancouver, BC V7T 1A9, Canada

TUPPER, Simon Richard Farquhar; s of John Otway Richard Tupper, of Blandford Forum, Dorset, and Suzanne Denise Boswell, *née* Tonks; *b* 17 April 1952; *Educ* Canford; *m* 24 Feb 1979, Sally, da of Col Eustace Frank Alfred, OBE, RM (d 1976); 1 s (Tobias b 1984), 1 da (Joanna b 1980); *Career* photographer and journalist specialising in agric and livestock 1981-, official championship photographer for Royal Agric Soc of England 1987-88, accredited photographer for: Rare Breeds Survival Tst,

Dairy and Beef Breed Socs, Nat Pig Breeding Assoc; *Recreations* hunting, trout fishing, shooting, photography; *Style*— Simon R F Tupper, Esq; c/o Barclays Bank, High St, Burford, Oxon

TURBOTT, Sir Ian Graham; CMG (1962), CVO (1966), JP (1971); s of Thomas Turbott (d 1956), of Auckland, NZ; *b* 9 Mar 1922; *Educ* Takapuna GS, Auckland Univ, Jesus Coll Cambridge, LSE; *m* 1952, Nancy, da of Lyman Lantz (d 1935), of Sacramento California; 3 da; *Career* Capt 2 NZEF (W Pacific and Italy) WWII, 1939-45 Star, Pacific Star, Italy Star, War Medal, Def Medal, NZ Medal; FRSA; entered Colonial Serv 1947, admin offr Gilbert and Ellice Islands 1947-56, seconded Colonial Off 1956-58; admin and HM The Queen's rep: Antigua 1958-64, Grenada 1964-67; govr Assoc State of Grenada 1967-68; chm: Chloride Batteries Australia Ltd, TNT GP 4 Pty Ltd, The Triple M Broadcasting Co Pty Ltd, Hamrod Prodns Ltd, Penrith Lakes Dvpt Corp Oty Ltd, Essington Hi-Tech Ltd, Spencer Stuart & Assoc Pty Ltd, The Sydney Int Piano Competition, Duke of Edinburgh's Award Scheme (NSW); chm (advsy bd) American Int Underwriters (Australia) Pty Ltd; dep chm Stenco F/M Ltd (NZ); dir: The City Mutual Life Assoc Soc Ltd, Standard Chartered Fin Ltd, The Suncoast Gp; tstee: Cancer Res Fndn, World Wildlife Fund Australia; CStJ 1964, Queen's Silver Jubilee Medal 1977; kt 1968; *see Debrett's Handbook of Australia and New Zealand for further details*; *Recreations* farming, fishing, golf, tennis, cricket; *Clubs* Australia (Sydney), Royal Sydney Yacht Sqdn, Elanora Country; *Style*— Sir Ian Turbott, CMG, CVO, JP; 27 Amiens Road, Clontarf, NSW 2093, Australia (☎ 02 949 1566)

TURCAN, Henry Watson; s of Henry Hutchison Turcan, TD (d 1977), of Lindores House, Newburgh, Fife, and Lilias Cheyne (d 1975); *b* 22 August 1941; *Educ* Rugby, Trinity Coll Oxford (MA); *m* 18 April 1969, Jane, da of Arthur Woodman Blair, WS of Dunbar, E Lothian; 1 s (Henry b 1974), 1 da (Chloë b 1972); *Career* barr 1965; legal assessor Gen Optical Cncl 1982-; rec Crown Ct 1985-; *Recreations* hunting, shooting, fishing, golf; *Clubs* Royal and Ancient Golf (St Andrews), Hon Co of Edin Golfers Muirfield; *Style*— Henry Turcan, Esq; 4 Paper Buildings Temple, London EC4 (☎ 01 353 3420)

TURCAN, Patrick Watson; s of John Watson Turcan (d 1935), of Murrayfield House, Edinburgh, and Mary Oliphant, *née* Hutchison (d 1967); *b* 17 Mar 1913; *Educ* Rugby, Oxford Univ (MA), Edinburgh Univ (LLB); *m* 9 Dec 1939, Barbara Christian, da of Harry Cheyne, WS (d 1917); 1 da (Johanna b 1949); *Career* serv WWII Lothians and Border Yeomanry; serv France 1940, (POW 1940-45 despatches); WS 1938, snr ptnr Dundas & Wilson CS 1966-78; chm: The Scottish Life Assur Co 1972-77, Gen Scottish Tst Ltd (now Smaller Cos Tst) 1972-83, The Scottish American Investmt Co Ltd 1977-85; dir Christian Salvesen Ltd 1957-83; slr to the Lord Advocate the Rt Hon W R Milligan QC (later Lord Milligan) 1956-60 and to the Rt Hon William Grant QC (later Lord Grant) 1960-62; chm the Trefoil Sch for Handicapped Children 1954-68; *Recreations* golf, shooting, fishing, photography; *Clubs* New (Edinburgh), Caledonian London, Royal and Ancient (St Andrews), Hon Co of Edinburgh Golfers; *Style*— Patrick W Turcan, Esq; Inchrye, Lindores, Cupar, Fife KY14 6JD (☎ 0337 40135)

TURING, Sir John Dermot; 12 Bt (NS 1638), of Feveran, Aberdeenshire; s of John Ferrier Turing (d 1983), and Beryl Mary Ada, *née* Hann; suc kinsman Sir John Leslie, 11 Bt, MC; *b* 2 Feb 1961; *Educ* New Coll Oxford; *Style*— Sir John Turing, Bt; 35 Tavistock Ave, London E17 6HP

TURL, Philip Austin; s of Lt-Col Henry William Turl RAOC (d 1988), of North Finchley, London, and Clara, *née* Pinnell (d 1980); *b* 23 May 1932; *Educ* City of London Sch, Jesus Coll Cambridge (MA); *m* 5 April 1969, Wendy Rosemary, da of Rev Frank Jones, of Dereham Norfolk; 2 s (Graham b 1970, Andrew b 1977), 1 da (Catherine b 1973); *Career* Lt RAOC (res); called to the Bar Middle Temple 1959; Freeman: City of London 1952, Worshipful Co of Glass Sellers; memb Methodist Church, Christian Youth Worker; *Books* Praises in Sorrow and Praises in Faith, fifth book of Psalms (1962); *Clubs* Wig and Pen; *Style*— Philip Turl, Esq; 22 Wolstonbury, Woodside Park, London N12 7BA; 1 Harcourt Bldgs, Temple, London EC4Y 9DA (☎ 01 353 9371, fax 01 583 1656)

TURLE, Arish Richard; MC (1974); s of Rear Adm Charles Edward Turle, CBE, DSO (d 1966), and Janes Gillies, *née* Gray; *b* 4 April 1939; *Educ* Wellington; *m* 7 Sept 1969, Susan De Witt, da of Jack Leslie Keith Brown; 1 s (Edward b 1974), 1 da (Serena b 1973); *Career* RMA Sandhurst 1958-59, 2 Lt Rifle Bde 1960, Capt 22 SAS Regt 1964, Base Ecole Des Troupeś Aeroportes (BETAP) France 1970-71, Army Staff Coll Camberley 1971-72, Maj 22 SAS 1973, ret 1977; Control Risks Ltd: joined 1977, md 1979, resigned 1987; md (int) Kroll Assocs Ltd 1988; FBIM; *Recreations* golf; *Clubs* Boodle's, Special Forces; *Style*— Arish Turle, Esq, MC; Kroll Assocs Ltd, Leconfield House, Curzon St, London W1Y 7FB (☎ 01 408 0766, fax 01 493 7954)

TURMEAU, Dr William Arthur; s of Frank Richard Turmeau (d 1972), of Stromness, Orkney, and Catherine Lyon, *née* Linklater; *b* 19 Sept 1929; *Educ* Stromness Acad, Univ of Edinburgh (BSc), Moray House Coll of Educn, Heriot-Watt Univ (PhD); *m* 4 April 1957, Margaret Moar, da of Arthur John Burnett; 1 da (Rachel Margaret b 1967); *Career* Nat Serv RCS 1947-49; res engr Northern Electric Co Ltd Montreal 1952-54, mech engr USAF Goose Bay Labrador 1954-56, contracts mangr Godfrey Engrg Co Ltd Montreal 1956-61, leetr Bristo Tech Inst Edinburgh 1962-64; Napier Coll Edinburgh: lectr and sr lectr 1964-68, head of dept of mech engrg 1968-75, asst princ and dean of faculty of technol 1975-82, princ 1982-; ctee memb: Scottish Econ Cncl, Br Cncl Inter-Univ Poly Cncl, Br Cncl Ctee for Cooperation in Higer Educn, European Soc for Engrg Educn, Dirs of Polys, IMechE standing ctee for degree accreditation, Scottish Examing Bd, Scottish Action on Smoking and Health, manpower policy ctee Scottish Cncl Devpt and Indust; FIMechE, CEng; *Recreations* study of Leonardo da Vinci, modern jazz; *Clubs* Caledonian; *Style*— Dr William Turmeau; 71 Morningside Park, Edinburgh EH10 5EZ (☎ 031 447 4639); Napier Polytechnic of Ediburgh, 219 Colinton Rd, Edinburgh EH14 1DJ (☎ 031 444 2266, car tel 0836 724 341)

TURNBULL, Andrew; s of anthony John Turnbull (d 1984), and Mary Gwyneth, *née* Williams; *b* 21 Jan 1945; *Educ* Enfield GS, Christ's Coll Cambridge (BA); *m* 8 Sept 1967, Diane Elizabeth, da of Roland Gordon Deightley Clarke; 2 s (Adam b 1974, Benet b 1977); *Career* economist Govt of Zambia 1968-70; HM Treas: asst princ 1970-72, princ 1972-76, seconded to IMF Washington 1976-78, asst sec 1978-83, under sec 1985-88; princ private sec to the PM 1988- (Private Sec 1983-85); *Recreations* watching football, playing cricket, fell walking, running, opera; *Style*— Andrew Turnbull, Esq; 10 Downing St, London SW1

TURNBULL, (George) Anthony Twentyman; s of Stuart John Twentyman Turnbull, and Hilda Joyce, *née* Taylor (d 1983); *b* 26 June 1938; *Educ* Charterhouse, Christ Church Oxford; *m* 14 June 1962, Petronel Jonette Rene, da of Maj James Williams Thursby Dunn (d 1969), of St Leonards Lodge, Clewer, Windsor, Berks; 2 s (Robert Edward Twentyman b 1965, Timothy William John b 1970), 1 da (Victoria Jonette Turnbull b 1963); *Career* barr 1962, Debenham Tewson & Chinnocks: joined 1962, ptnr 1965, chief exec 1987; Freeman Worshipful Co fo Fruiterers; FRICS; *Recreations* theatre, conversation, playing games; *Clubs* Savile, Brook St, London W1; *Style*— Anthony Turnbull, Esq; Park Cottage, Downside Rd, Downside, Cobham, Surrey KT11 3LZ; 67A Aylesford St, London SW1; 75 Davies St, London W1A 1DZ (☎ 01 408 1161)

TURNBULL, George Henry; s of late Bartholomew Turnbull, of 34 Rochester Rd, Earlson, Coventry, and late Pauline Anne, *née* Konrath; *b* 17 Oct 1926; *Educ* King Henry VIII Sch Coventry, Birmingham Univ (BSc); *m* 14 March 1950, Marion, da of Henry George Wing (d 1969); 1 s (Robert), 2 da (Deborah, Penny); *Career* Standard Motors Ltd: PA to tech dir 1950-51, exec i/c experimental dept 1954-55, divnl mangr (cars) 1956-59, gen mangr 1959-62; work mangr Petters Ltd 1955-56, dir and gen mangr Standard-Triumph Int 1962-; BL Motor Corpn: dir 1967, dep md 1968-73, md 1973; md BL Austin Morris 1968-73, chm BL Truck and Bus Div 1972-73, vice-pres and dir Hyundai Motors Seoul S Korea 1974-77, dep md Iran Nat Motor Co Tehran 1978-79 (conslt advsr to chm 1977-78), chm Talbot UK 1979-84; Inchape plc: gp md 1984-86, gp chief exec 1985-86, chm and chief exec 1986-; Freeman City of Coventry 1948; memb SMMT, FIMechE, FI ProdE; *Books* Report on Future of the Korean Car Industry (1976); *Recreations* skiing, tennis, golf, fishing; *Clubs* Moreton Morrell Tennis Court, Conventry RFC, Finham Park Golf, Royal and Ancient Golf; *Style*— George Turnbull, Esq; Morrell Ho, Moreton Morrell, Warwick CB35 9AL (☎ 0926 651 278); Inchcape plc, St James's Ho, 23 King St, London SW1Y 6QY (☎ 01 321 0110, fax 01 321 0604, car tel 0860 386 176, telex 885395)

TURNBULL, Jeffrey Alan; s of Alan Edward Turnbull (d 1986), of Monkseaton and Carlisle, and Alice May, *née* Slee (d 1940); *b* 14 August 1934; *Educ* Newcastle upon Tyne Royal GS, Liverpool Coll of Technol (DipTE); *m* 7 Aug 1957, Beryl, da of Walter Griffith (d 1974), of Crewe; 2 s (Martin John b 1964, Andrew Malcolm b 1972), 1 da (Alison Denise b 1962); *Career* Nat Serv Corpl RE 1956-58; jr engr Cheshire CC 1951-55, engr Herefordshire CC 1955-59, res engr Berks CC 1959-66; Mott Hay & Anderson 1966-89: dep chief designer (roads) 1966-68, chief designer (roads) 1968-78, assoc 1973-78, dir (int Ltd) 1975-89, dir 1978-, dir (hldgs Ltd) 1983-89, chief exec (hldgs Ltd) 1987-89; chm and dir Mott MacDonald Gp Ltd 1989-; memb editorial bd New Civil Engrg 1979-82; CEng 1959, FIHT 1966, FICE 1973, MInstD; *Books* Civil Engineers Reference Book (contrib fourth edn 1988), numerous papers to PIARC and IRF conferences; *Recreations* cruising, visiting France, cricket; *Clubs* Institute of Directors; *Style*— Jeffrey Turnbull, Esq; 63 Higher Drive, Banstead, Surrey SM7 1PW (☎ 01 393 1054); Mott MacDonald Gp Ltd, St Anne House, 20/26 Wellesley Rd, Croydon, Surrey CR9 2UL (☎ 01 686 5041, fax 01 681 5706/01 688 1814, telex 917241 MOTTAY G)

TURNBULL, Lt-Col John Hugh Stephenson; MC (1943,45); s of Lt-Col Sir Hugh Turnbull, KCVO, KBE, of Reidhaven, Grantown-on -Spey, Morayshire, and Jean, *née* Grant,; *b* 10 Jan 1916; *Educ* Haileybury; *m* 7 Nov 1964, Sophie Penelope, da of Frederick Bryan Landale, of Coopers Ground, E Knoyle, Wilt; 1 da (Penelope); *Career* London Scottish 1936, 1 Commando 1941-46 (cmd Far E 1945-46), cmmnd Gordon Highlanders 1945, Staff Coll 1946, 2 Para Bn 1948-51, various staff & regtn appts until ret 1960; memb Royal Co of Archers; *Style*— Lt-Col John Turnbull, MC; Rossdhal, Comrie, Perthshire; 27 Nelson St, Edinburgh (☎ 0764 70301); 24 Onslow Sq, London SW7

TURNBULL, Hon Mrs; Hon Mary Elizabeth; *née* Parnell; eldest da of 6 Baron Congleton (d 1932); *b* 21 Feb 1919; *Educ* private and boarding sch; *m* 20 July 1956, Percy Purvis Turnbull (d 1976) pianist/composer; *Career* Govt salary, modern school teacher 1947-51; ARCM; *Recreations* music; *Clubs* English Speaking Union, Special Forces, New Cavendish, British Music Soc, Turnbull Memorial Trust; *Style*— The Hon Mrs Turnbull; West Wing, Dean House, West Dean, Salisbury, Wilts SP5 1JQ

TURNBULL, Sir Richard Gordon; GCMG (1962, KCMG 1958, CMG 1953); s of Richard Francis Turnbull (d 1963); *b* 1909; *Educ* Univ Coll Sch, UCL (Fell), Magdalene Coll Cambridge (hon fell); *m* 1939, Beatrice, da of late John Wilson; 2 s, 1 da; *Career* entered Colonial Admin Serv 1931, dist offr Kenya 1931, provincial cmmr 1948, provincial cmmr Northern Frontier Province 1948-53, min for Internal Security and Def 1954, chief sec Kenya and govr's dep 1955-58; govr and c-in-c: Tanganyika Territory 1958-61, Govr gen and c-in-c Tanganyika 1961-62; chm Central Land Bd Kenya 1963-64, high cmmr for Aden and Protectorates of South Arabia 1965-67; KStJ 1958; *Style*— Sir Richard Turnbull, GCMG; Friars Neuk, Jedburgh, Roxburghshire TD8 6BN

TURNBULL, Steven Michael; s of Philip Peveril Turnbull (d 1987), of Rock, Cornwall, and Dorothy June Turnbull; *b* 24 Oct 1952; *Educ* Monkton Coll Sch, Univ Coll Oxford (BA); *m* 22 Sept 1985, Mary Ann, da of David M Colyer, of Cheltenham, Glos; 1 s (Matthew b 11 July 1987), 1 da (Clare b 21 Aug 1988); *Career* Linklater & Paines: joined 1975, slr 1978, joined corporate dept, ptnr 1985; memb Law Soc, memb City of London slrs Co; *Recreations* golf, tennis, family; *Clubs* Oxford and Cambridge Golfing Soc, Royal Wimbledon Golf; *Style*— Steven Turnbull, Esq; Linklaters & Paines, Barrington House, 59-67 Gresham St, London EC2V 7JA (☎ 01 606 7080)

TURNER, Adrian Geoffrey Leslie; LVO (1986); er s of Leslie Bertram Turner, MBE (d 1979), and Lillian Augusta, *née* Broad; *b* 28 April 1927; *Educ* Highgate, Clayesmore; *Career* Dip Serv 1948-87: Lahore, Pakistan 1955-57 (also broadcaster western music Radio Pakistan, external examiner Univ of the Punjab), Colombo, Sri Lanka 1960-63 (also broadcaster Radio Ceylon), Asuncion, Paraguay 1969-71, Holy See 1971-73; memb Br delegation: Int Lab Confce Geneva 1959, UN Gen Assembly New York 1965, UN Conf on the Law of Treaties, Vienna 1969, head Hons Section FCO 1979-87; memb: cncl Heraldry Soc 1947-86 (hon fell 1954), hon cncl of mgmnt The Royal Philharmonic Soc 1981-86 (fell 1951-), cncl St John Historical Soc 1985-, conslt false orders ctee Orders of St John of Jerusalem 1987; Freeman City of London 1978, Liveryman Worshipful Co of Scriveners; Sovereign Mil Order of Malta 1972, Knight of Obedience 1981, OStJ 1988; FRSA 1987; *Recreations* music, heraldry, genealogy, reading, the study of the Orders of St John; *Clubs* Royal Overseas League;

Style— Adrian Turner, Esq, LVO; Shelsley, 135 Cranley Gdns, Muswell Hill, London N10 3AG

TURNER, Amédée Edward; QC (1976), MEP (EDG) Suffolk and SE Cambs 1984-; s of Frederick William Turner (d 1948), and Ruth Hayson (d 1970); mother's side Huguenot Swiss; *b* 26 Mar 1929; *Educ* Ch Ch Oxford; *m* 1960, Deborah Dudley, da of Dr Philip Owen: 1s, 1 da; *Career* barr Inner Temple 1954, practised patent bar 1954-57, assoc Kenyon & Kenyon patent attorneys NY 1957-60, London practice 1960-; contested (C) Norwich N gen elections 1964, 1966 and 1970, Euro Parl: vice-chm Legal Ctee 1979, memb: Econ and Monetary Ctee 1979-, Tport Ctee 1981-, Energy Ctee 1983-; ACP Jt Ctee, MEP (C) Suffolk and Harwich 1979-84; *Books* The Law of Trade Secrets (1962, supplement 1968), The Law of the New European Patent (1979), many Cons Pty study papers on defence, oil and Middle East; *Recreations* garden designs, painting; *Clubs* Carlton, Coningsby, United and Cecil; *Style*— Amédée Turner, Esq, QC, MEP; 3 Montrose Place, London SW1X 7DU; The Barn, Westleton, Saxmundham, Suffolk (☎ 072 873 235)

TURNER, Hon Mrs; Hon Anne Mary Cameron; *née* Corbett; da of 3 Baron Rowallan and Eleanor Mary, only da of late Capt George Frederic Boyle; *b* 3 Sept 1953; *m* 1972, Rodney John Turner; 2 s, 2 da; *Recreations* hunting; *Style*— The Hon Mrs Turner; Leigh Court, Angersleigh, Somerset (☎ 82342 700)

TURNER, Ven Antony Hubert Michael; s of Frederick George Turner (d 1960), and Winifred Frances Turner (d 1956); *b* 17 June 1930; *Educ* Royal Liberty Sch Romford, Univ of London (Dip Theol); *m* 5 July 1956, Margaret Kathleen, da of Reginald McKenzie Phillips, of 133 Balgores Lane, Gidea Park, Essex; 1 s (Michael b 1961), 2 da (Ruth b 1958, Susan b 1960); *Career* ordained deacon 1956, curate St Ann's Nottingham 1956-59, curate in charge St Cuthbert's Cheadle Diocese of Chester 1959-62, vicar Christ Church Macclesfield 1962-68, home sec Bible Churchmen's Missionary Soc 1968-74, vicar St Jude's Southsea 1974-86, rural dean Portsmouth 1979-84, archdeacon of the IOW 1986-; church cmmr 1983-; vice chm C of E Pensions Bd; ACA 1952, FCA 1962; *Recreations* photography, caravanning; *Style*— Ven the Archdeacon of the IOW; The Archdeaconry, 3 Beech Grove, Ryde, IOW PO33 3AN

TURNER, (Charles) Brian Godsell; s of Ernest Joseph Turner (d 1964), of Holmwood, Clarendon Rd, Harpenden, and Bertha, *née* Harris (d 1968); *b* 26 Oct 1913; *Educ* Tottenham GS; *m* 1941, Helen, da of Cecil Robert Slowe (d 1968), of Tabley, Wadhurst, Sussex; 2 s, 1 da; *Career* HAC (TA) 1930, cmmnd KOYLI 1939, Capt 1940, transferred to RA 1941, serv WWII: UK, France, Belgium, Holland, Germany; CA London 1950-74, ret; chm: Bournemouth & Dist Water Co 1977, Mid Kent Water Co 1980-87, Eastbourne Waterworks Co 1987; hon tres Nat Assoc of Parish Cncls 1958-73; FRSA; FCA; *Recreations* gardening, philately, travel; *Style*— Brian Turner, Esq; Dellside, Tongswood Drive, Hawkhurst, Kent TN18 5DS (☎ 058 075 3145)

TURNER, Brian William; s of William Edward Turner (d 1949), of Surbiton, Surrey, and Caroline Rose, *née* Camp (d 1958); *b* 21 Sept 1936; *Educ* Royal Masonic Sch; *Career* admitted slr 1959, sr ptnr Messrs Gill, Turner & Tucker, Slrs, Maidstone, Kent; hon slr Age Concern Kent; memb of The Law Soc; *Style*— Brian Turner, Esq; Byne Cottage, Chart Sutton, Maidstone, Kent; Colman House, King St, Maidstone, Kent ME14 1JE (☎ 0622 590 51, fax 0622 621 92, telex 965343)

TURNER, Air Vice-Marshal Cameron Archer; CB (1968), CBE (1960, OBE 1947); s of James Oswald Turner (d 1961), and Vida Catherine, *née* Cockburn (d 1970); *b* 29 August 1915; *Educ* New Plymouth Boys' Sch, Victoria Univ (NZ), Imperial Def Coll London, Massey Univ (NZ); *m* 1941, Josephine Mary, da of George Richardson (d 1942); 2 s (Roscoe, Simon); *Career* joined RAF 1936, transferred to RNZAF 1938-69, serv Europe 1939 and Pacific 1940-45, Chief of Air Staff 1966-69; dir NZ Inventions Devpt Authy 1969-76; CEng, FIEE, FRAeS; *Recreations* golf, fishing, Polynesian studies; *Clubs* Wellington, Taranaki, Utd Serv Offrs'; *Style*— Air Vice-Marshal Cameron Turner, CBE; 37A Parkvale Rd, Wellington 5, NZ (☎ 766 063); 3 Constance St, Fitzroy, New Plymouth, NZ (☎ 85811)

TURNER, Brig Charles Edward Francis; CBE (1943, OBE 1941), DSO (1943); s of Lt Arthur Edward Turner (d 1901 in India), and Edith Blanche (d 1942), da of Gen Sir Charles Scott, KCB; *b* 23 April 1899; *Educ* Twyford, Wellington, RMA Woolwich, Christ's Coll Cambridge; *m* 1930, Mary Victoria, da of Herbert Leed Swift (d 1930), formerly a solicitor in York; 1 s (Martin), 2 da (Frances, Celia); *Career* 2 Lt RE 1917-50 (ret); serv: France 1918, Archangel 1919, Waziristan (despatches) 1920-21, Palestine (despatches) 1936, Middle E (including Western Desert and Sicily; despatches) 1940-43; (Staff Coll Camberley 1931-32), Brig 1944, Malaya 1949-50; appeals organiser Nat Cncl Social Servs 1950-58, sec Iona Appeal Tst 1958-61, appeals Organiser Rainer Fndn and Inst Rural Life at Home and Overseas 1962-64; *Recreations* family history; *Style*— Brig Charles Turner, CBE, DSO; The Colleens, Lower Cousley Wood, Wadhurst, Sussex TN5 6HE (☎ 089 288 2387)

TURNER, Christopher; s of Harry Turner, JP, of Harrogate, and Margaret, *née* Archer; *b* 28 July 1940; *Educ* Repton, Univ of Leeds (BCom); *m* 23 May 1969, Caroline Sue Hodgeson, da of the late George Potts, of Pontefract; 2 da (Rachel Louise b 21 June 1975, Lucy Georgina b 30 June 1979); *Career* ptnr Robson Rhodes CA's Bradford 1972- (chm 1984-85); govr Leeds Girls HS, circuit steward Methodist Church Horsforth and Bramley, memb Aireborough Rotary Club; FCA; *Recreations* golf; *Clubs* Headingly GC, Bradford; *Style*— Christopher Turner, Esq; Windy Lea, 36 Lee Lane East, Horsforth, Leeds LS18 5RE (☎ 0532 582520); Robson Rhodes, Commerce House, Cheapside, Bradford BD1 4JY (☎ 0274 725594, fax 0274 724595)

TURNER, Christopher Gilbert; s of Theodore Francis Turner, QC (d 1986), and Hon Elizabeth Alice, *née* Schuster (d 1983), da of 1 and last Baron Schuster, GCB (d 1956), permanent sec of the Lord Chancellor and Clerk of the Crown in Chancery 1915-44; *b* 23 Dec 1929; *Educ* Winchester, New Coll Oxford; *m* 3 Aug 1961, Lucia, da of Prof Stephen Ranulph Kingdon Glanville (d 1958, Provost of King's Coll, Cambridge and Herbert Thompson Prof of Egyptology); 1 s (Matthew b 1964), 2 da (Rosalie b 1962, Catherine b 1967); *Career* head of classics: Radley to 1961, Charterhouse 1961-68; headmaster: Dean Close Sch 1968-79, Stowe 1979-89; *Books* History in Comparative Study in Greek and Latin Literature (1969); *Recreations* violin playing, music generally, walking, manual labour, repairing books, reading; *Style*— Christopher Turner, Esq; Kinloss, Stowe, Buckingham (☎ 0280 812346); Stowe Sch, Buckingham (☎ 0280 813164)

TURNER, Colin Francis; s of Francis Sidney Turner (d 1987), of Penge, and Charlotte Clara, *née* Hathaway (d 1968); *b* 11 April 1930; *Educ* Beckenham GS, Kings Coll Univ London (LLB); *m* 14 April 1951, Josephine Alma, da of Charles Henry Jones (d 1924); 2 s (Christopher b 1956, Paul b 1957), 1 da (Elizabeth b 1952); *Career* entered Princ Probate Registry 1949, dist probate registrar York 1965-68, sr registrar Family Div of High Ct 1988 (registrar 1971-); memb: Supreme Ct Procedure Ctee, Matrimonial Causes Rule Ctee; *Books* Rayden on Divorce (jt ed of edns 9, 11, 12, 13), Supreme Court Practice (ed), Precedents in Matrimonial Causes and Ancillary Matters; *Recreations* birding, fishing; *Style*— Colin Turner, Esq; Lakers, Church Rd, Redhill, Surrey RH1 6QA (☎ 0737 761807); Principal Registry Family Division Somerset House, Strand, London WC2 (☎ 01 936 6934)

TURNER, Colin William Carstairs; CBE (1984), DFC (1944); s of Colin Carstairs William Turner (d 1963), of Enfield, Middx, and Phebe Marianne Miller (d 1945); *b* 14 Jan 1922; *Educ* Highgate Sch; *m* 7 May 1949, Evelyn Mary, da of Claude Horatio Buckard (d 1966), of Enfield; 3 s (Anthony b 18 Feb 1954, Nigel b 7 Jan 1956, Christopher b 1 Aug 1964), 1 da (Susan b 23 Aug 1951); *Career* air observer RAFVR, volunteered 1940, ITW Torquay 1941, 47 Air Sch Queenstown SA 1941, 31 Air Sch E London SA 1941, 70 OTU Nakuru Kenya 1942, 223 Sqdn Baltimores Desert Air Force Egypt 1942 (cmmnd 1943) Tunisia 1943, Malta 1943, Sicily 1943, Italy 1943, returned UK 1944, 527 Sqdn Digby Lincs (crashed 1944), RAF Hosp Northallerton and Rehabilitation Centre Loughborough 1944-45, invalided-out Flying Offr 1946; Colin Turner Gp of Cos (family co): joined 1940, dir 1945, md 1964-84, chm 1985-87, life pres 1988-; Overseas Press and Media Assoc: fndr pres 1965-67, hon tres 1974-82, life pres 1983-; Cwlth Press Union: assoc memb 1963-, chm PR ctee 1970-87, memb fin ctee 1972-87, exec ctee 1988-; ed Overseas Media Guide 1968-74; memb Nat Exec Cons Pty: 1946-53, 1968-73, 1976-82; chm Cons Cwlth and Overseas Cncl 1976-82 (vice-pres 1984-), parly candidate (C) Enfield East 1950 and 1951, MP (C) West Woolwich 1959-64; pres Enfield branch RAFA 1947-58 and 1966- (memb 1945-), chm 223 Sqdn Assoc 1947-, pres Old Cholmeleian Assoc 1985-86 (Highgate Sch Old Boys), ed The Cholmeleian 1982-; *Recreations* DIY, gardening, sailing, fishing; *Clubs* IOD; *Style*— Colin Turner, Esq, CBE, DFC; 55 Rowantree Rd, Enfield, Middx EN2 8PN (☎ 01 363 2403)

TURNER, David George Patrick; s of George Patrick Turner (d 1988), of Londonderry, and Elsie Bamford, *née* McClure; *b* 11 July 1954; *Educ* Foyle Coll Londonderry, King's Coll London (LLB, AKC), Coll of Law London; *m* 4 March 1978, Jean Patricia, da of Gerald William Hewett, of Carlton, Rode, Norfolk; 2 s (Robert b 7 Oct 1980, Richard b 30 Oct 1982); *Career* barr Grays Inn 1976, S Eastern Circuit, dir and co sec Whimbrell Pubns Ltd; churchwarden and lay reader All Souls' Langham Place, memb Marylebone Deanery Synod; tstee: Langham Tst, St Paul's Tst (Portman Sq); cncl memb UCCF; memb: Family Law Bar Assoc, Criminal Bar Assoc, Ecclesiastical Soc Law; *Recreations* reading, swimming, family; *Style*— David Turner, Esq; 14 Chatterton Road, London N4 2DZ (☎ 01 226 7357); 14 Grays Inn Sq, Grays Inn, London WC1R 5JP (☎ 01 242 0858, fax 01 242 5434)

TURNER, David John; s of Frederick Turner, of 66 Osmaston Rd, Prenton, Birkenhead, Merseyside, and Sheila Margaret, *née* Collinson; *b* 7 Feb 1945; *Educ* Birkenhead Sch; 1 s (Jonathon Frederick b 23 March 1978), 2 da (Sarah Frances b 28 Feb 1970, Catherine Margaret b 19 Feb 1974); *Career* CA: Cook & Co Liverpool 1963-68, Touche Ross & Co London 1968-69; mgmnt auditor Mobil Oil Corpn 1969-71, chief accountant Mobil Servs Ltd 1971-73, special projects co-ordinator Mobil Europe Inc 1973-74, fin dir Booker plc (formerly Booker McConnell Ltd) 1975-; FCA; *Recreations* squash, tennis, skiing; *Clubs* Surbiton Lawn Tennis and Squash; *Style*— David Turner, Esq; Portland House, Stag Place, London SW1 5AY (☎ 01 828 9850, fax 01 630 8029, telex 888169)

TURNER, Prof David Warren; s of Robert Cecil Turner (d 1983), of Leigh-on-Sea, Essex, and Constance Margaret, *née* Bonner (d 1969); *b* 16 July 1927; *Educ* Westcliff HS, Univ of Exeter (BSc), Imperial Coll Univ of London (PhD, DIC); *m* 11 Sept 1954, Barbara Marion, da of Cyril Fisher (d 1982), of Oxford; 1 s (Paul b 1958), 1 da (Susan b 1963); *Career* reader in organic chemistry Imperial Coll Univ of London 1965 (lectr 1958); Univ of Oxford: fell and tutor Balliol Coll 1967, lectr in physical chemistry 1968, reader in physical chemistry 1978, prof of electron spectroscopy 1984; memb IUPAC cmmn on Molecular Spectroscopy; Hon DTech Royal Tech Inst Stockholm 1971, Hon DPhil Univ of Basel 1980; FRS 1973; *Books* Molecular Photoelectron Spectroscopy (1970); *Recreations* music, gardening, tinkering with gadgets; *Style*— Prof David Turner; Balliol College, Oxford

TURNER, Dennis; MP (Lab) Wolverhampton SE 1987; s of Thomas Herbert Turner (d 1981), and Mary Elizabeth, *née* Peasley (d 1974); *b* 26 August 1942; *Educ* Stonefield Secdy Sch Bilston W Mids, Bilston Coll of Further Educn; *m* 19 June 1976, Patricia Mary, da of Joseph Henry Narroway (d 1984), of Bilston; 1 s (Brendon Robert b 1977), 1 da (Jenny Mary b 1980); *Career* chm: Springvale Co-op Ltd Bilston, Springvale Trg Ltd Bilston; dir: W Mids Co-op Fin Ltd, Black Country Devpt Agency; dep ldr Wolverhampton MDC 1979-86; former chm: Socl Servs Ctee, Housing Ctee, Further Educn Ctee, Econ Devpt Ctee; memb W Mids CC 1975-; pres: Bilston Community Assoc, Bradley Community Assoc, Ettingshall Darts League, Bradley and Wultrun Corps of Drums; sec and tstee Bradley and Dist Sr Citizens Centre; *Recreations* compereing, beer tasting, all card games; *Clubs* New Springvale Sports & Social (Bilston); *Style*— Dennis Turner, Esq, MP; Ambleside, King St, Bradley, Bilston, W Mids (☎ 0902 41822); Springvale House, Millfields Rd, Bilston, W Mids (0902 42364)

TURNER, Dame Eva; DBE (1962); *b* 10 Mar 1892,Oldham, Lancs; *Educ* Royal Academy of Music (FRAM); *Career* opera singer; joined Royal Carl Rosa Opera Co 1915 and remained, as prima donna, until 1924, sang La Scala 1924, Covent Garden Int Season 1928 when she sang in Turandot, Aida and other operas until outbreak of WWII, appeared throughout Europe, USA and South America; visiting prof of voice Faculty of Music Oklahoma Univ (USA) 1949-59, prof of voice Royal Academy of Music (London) 1959-66; pres Wagner Soc 1971-, hon int memb Sigma Alpha Iota 1951-, hon int soroptomist 1955-; memb Nat Assoc of Teachers of Singing (USA); Hon GSM 1968, FRCM 1974, FRNCM 1978, Hon FTCL 1982, Hon Citizen State of Oklahoma USA 1982; first Freeman Metropolitan Borough of Oldham 1982; Hon DMus Manchester 1979, Hon DMus Oxford 1984, Hon Fell St Hilda's Coll Oxford 1984, Hon Licentiate Western Ontario Conservatory of Music, 1986; *Style*— Dame Eva Turner, DBE; 26 Palace Court, London W2 4HZ

TURNER, Brig Dame Evelyn Marguerite; DBE (1965, MBE 1946), RRC (1956); da of late Thomas Turner, and Molly, *née* Bryan; *b* 10 May 1910; *Educ* St Bartholomew's

Hosp London; *Career* joined QAIMNS (later QARANC) 1937, served WWII (POW Sumatra 1942-45), matron-in-chief and dir Army Nursing Service 1964-68, ret; Col Cmdt QARANC 1969-74; CStJ 1966; *Style*— Brig Dame Margot Turner, DBE, RRC; 2 Chantry Court, Frimley, Surrey (☎ Camberley 22030)

TURNER, Admiral Sir (Arthur) Francis; KCB (1970, CB 1966), DSC (1945); s of Rear Adm A W J Turner (d 1964), and Agnes Maria Lochrane (d 1958); *b* 23 June 1912; *Educ* Stonyhurst; *m* 1963, Elizabeth Clare, da of Capt Hubert E F and Hon Mrs de Trafford, of Villa Bologna, Malta; 2 s (Francis b 1966, Michael b 1969); *Career* joined RN 1931, serv WW11 Atlantic and Pacific, Capt 1956, Rear Adm 1964, Dir-Gen Aircraft (Naval) MOD 1966-67, Chief of Fleet Support MOD 1967-71, Vice-Adm 1968, Adm 1970; *Clubs* Army and Navy, Union (Malta); *Style*— Adm Sir Francis Turner, KCB, DSC; Plantation House, Ockham Rd South, East Horsley, Surrey

TURNER, Geoffrey Howard; s of Charles William Turner, of Willaston-in-Wirral, and Evelyn Doris, *née* Harris; *b* 23 July 1945; *Educ* The Kings's Sch Chester, St Edmund Hall Oxford (BA, MA); *m* 31 May 1975, Margaret Linda, da of John Aitken Donaldson, of Sedgley, West Midlands; 2 da (Katherine b 1978, Charlotte b 1981); *Career* The Stock Exchange: mangr Membership Dept 1975-78 (asst mangr 1973-75), sec Wilson Evidence Ctee 1978, sec Planning Ctee 1977-78, sec Restrictive Practices Case Ctee 1978-83, head of membership 1983-86; the int stock dir of membership The Int Stock Exchange 1986-, dir of authorisations The Securities Assoc Ltd 1986- (sec 1986-88); chm govrs Wood End Jr and Infant Schs Harpenden; Freeman City of London 1980; *Recreations* visiting country churches, collecting books and prints; *Clubs* Vincents (Oxford); *Style*— Geoffrey Turner, Esq; 44 Roundwood Lane, Harpenden, Herts (☎ 0582 769882); The Securities Assoc, The Int Stock Exchange, London EC2N 1HP (☎ 01 256 9000, 01 588 2355, fax 01 628 1052)

TURNER, Prof Grenville; s of Anrold Turner, of Todmorden, and Florence Turner; *b* 1 Nov 1936; *Educ* Todmorden GS, St Johns Coll Cambridge (BA, MA), Balliol Coll Oxford (DPhil); *m* 8 April 1961, Kathleen, da of William Morris (d 1986), of Rochdale; 1 s (Patrick b 1968), 1 da (Charlotte b 1966); *Career* asst prof Univ of California Berkeley 1962-69, lectr in physics Sheffield Univ 1964-74, res assoc California Inst of Technol 1970-71, sr lectr Sheffield Univ 1974-79, prof of isotope geochemistry Manchester Univ 1988-, reader 1979-80, prof of physics 1980-88; memb ctees of: The Sci and Engrg Res Cncl, Br Nat Space Centre, Royal Society; FRS 1980; *Recreations* photography, walking, theatre; *Style*— Prof Grenville Turner, FRS; The Royd, Todmorden, Lancs OL14 8DW (☎ 0706 818 621); Dept of Geology, The Univ of Manchester M13 9PL (☎ 061 275 3804, fax 061 275 5584, telex 666517 UNIMAN)

TURNER, Harry Edward; s of Harry Turner (d 1967), of London, and Bessie Marguerite Jay (d 1984); *b* 28 Feb 1935; *Educ* Sloane Sch Chelsea; *m* 2 June 1956, Carolyn Louie, da of Frank Bird (d 1958), of Guernsey, CI; 1 s (Gregory Alexander b 1957), 1 da (Jane Louie b 195 9); *Career* RA 1953-55, cmmnd 2 Lt 1 Bn Middx Regt 1934; Westward TV: sales exec 1962, gen sales mangr 1966, hd of sales 1970, dir of sales 1972; md TSW 1985 (joined 1981), dir ITN; vice chm The Advertising Assoc; FRSA 1986; *Books* The Man Who Could Hear Fishes Scream (1978), The Gentle Art of Salesmanship (1985), So You Want to be a Sales Manager (1986); *Recreations* skiing, riding, tennis, writing; *Clubs* English Speaking Union, The White Elephant, Tramp, Mannheim (NY); *Style*— Harry Turner, Esq; Four Acres, Lake Road, Deepcut, Surrey GU16 6RB; Villa Cortayne, Benalmadena, Spain (☎ 0252 835527); TSW, Derrys Cross, Plymouth, Devon (☎ 0752 663322)

TURNER, (Robert) Ian; s of Major Lewis John Turner, of Grove House, Singleton, nr Chichester, W Sussex, and Jean Cleghorn, *née* Dashwood; *b* 22 Oct 1940; *Educ* Eton; *m* 4 May 1974, Alexandra Susan, da of Brig Peter Chamber Hinde, DSO (d 1983); 1 s (Peter b 1975), 1 da (Katharine b 1977); *Career* dir Fuller, Smith & Turner plc 1967; *Recreations* shooting, skiing; *Style*— Ian Turner, Esq; Fuller, Smith & Turner plc, Griffin Brewery, Chiswick, London W4 2QB (☎ 01 994 2691, telex 912000)

TURNER, James Francis; s of Rev Percy Reginald Turner, of The Old Rectory, Wem, Salop; *b* 14 Mar 1915; *Educ* Marlborough, Pembroke Coll Cambridge; *m* 1968, Hon Joanna Elizabeth, *née* Piercy; *Career* served WWII pilot and navigator RN, Ark Royal, including sinking of Bismarck, also in Caribbean, Coastal Command; commanded 828 and 830 Sqdns Malta, on staff Flag Offr Naval Air Stations 1944; mangr Estate Duties Investmt Tst 1958 (dir 1973-80); dir: Henry Boot & Sons 1973-, Bermaline and Bermaline Foods 1972-, Bloxwich Lock & Stamping 1973-; md Cavendish Mercantile Co 1981-; Hon Tres Friends of the Elderly 1976-82, formed Gourley Charitable Tst 1970, memb cncl Arts Educnl Schools 1972-; *Recreations* work, charities; *Clubs* Boodle's; *Style*— James F Turner, Esq; The Old Coach House, Burford, Oxon OX8 4HZ (☎ 099 382 2368)

TURNER, Hon Mrs; Hon (Dorothy) Joan; *née* Yerburgh; er da (by 1 w) of 1 Baron Alvingham (d 1955); *b* 12 April 1913; *m* 12 March 1934, Lt-Col William Aspinall Turner, late The Queen's Bays; 1 s, 1 da; *Style*— The Hon Mrs Turner; Rectory Cottage, Cheselbourne, Dorchester, Dorset

TURNER, Hon Mrs; Hon Joanna Elizabeth; 2 da of 1 Baron Piercy, CBE (d 1966); *b* 10 Jan 1923; *Educ* St Paul's, Somerville Coll Oxford; *m* 1968, James Francis Turner, *qv*; *Career* classics teacher Ellesmere Coll Salop 1975-80, headmistress Badminton Sch Bristol 1966-69 (asst 1948-65, Gordonstoun 1947-48); JP Inner London Juvenile Courts Panel 1970-75; *Style*— The Hon Mrs Turner; The Old Coach House, Burford, Oxon (☎ 099382 2368)

TURNER, Prof John Derfel; s of Joseph Turner (d 1962), of Manchester and Southport, and Dorothy Winifred, *née* Derfel (d 1979); *b* 27 Feb 1928; *Educ* Manchester GS, The Univ of Manchester (BA, MA, Dip Ed); *m* 6 June 1951, Susan Broady, da of Robert Baldwin Hovey, MC, OBE (d 1974), of Wheelock, Cheshire; 2 s (Stephen b 1953, Leigh b 1959); *Career* Educn Offr RAF 1948-50; teacher Prince Henry's GS Evesham 1951-53, sr lectr in educn Nigerian Coll of Arts Sci and Technol 1956-61 (lectr in English 1953-56), lectr in educn inst of educn Univ of Exeter 1961-64, prof of educn and dir sch of educn Univ of Botswana Lesotho and Swaziland 1964-70 (pro-vice chllr 1966-70, emeritus prof 1970), prof of adult and higher educn Univ of Manchester 1976-85 (prof of educn and dir sch of educn 1970-76), rector Univ Coll of Botswana Univ of Botswana and Swaziland 1981-82 (vice chllr 1982-84); memb: UK nat cmmn UNESCO 1975-81, IUC working parties on E and Central Africa and on rural devpt 1975-81, educn sub-ctee UGC 1980-81, working pty on academic devpt of Univ of Juba 1977-78; chm: cncl social studies advsy ctee Selly Oak Colls 1975-81, ed bd Int Journal of Educn and Devpt 1978-81, Univ's Cncl for Educn of Teachers 1979-81 and 1988 (vice-chm 1976-79), bd govrs Abbotsholme Sch 1980-; methodist local preacher; Hon LLD Ohio Univ 1982; Hon FCP 1985, Hon Fell Bolton Inst of Technol 1988; *Recreations* reading, music, theatre, walking; *Clubs* Royal Cwlth Soc, Royal Overseas League; *Style*— Prof John Turner; 13 Firswood Mount, Gatley, Cheadle, Cheshire SK8 4JY (☎ 061 428 2734); Sch of Educn, Univ of Manchester, Oxford Rd, Manchester M13 9PL (☎ 061 275 3458, fax 061 275 3519)

TURNER, John Warren; CBE (1988); s of Thomas Henry Huxley Turner, CBE (d 1973), of Cardiff, and Phebe Elvira, *née* Evans; *b* 12 Oct 1935; *Educ* Shrewsbury, St John's Coll Cambridge; *m* 8 Oct 1966, Jillian Fiona Geraldine, da of Thomas Ouchterlony Turton Hart; 1 s (Gavin b 1972); *Career* 2 Lt RE Middle East 1957-59, TA 1959-66, Capt ret; chm and md E Turner and Sons Ltd (dir 1964, chm 1976, md 1984); chm Bldg Regulations Advsy Ctee BRAC 1985- (memb 1971); memb Cncl Br Bd of Agrement (BBA) 1980-; chm Cncl for Bldg and Civil Engrg Br Standards Instn BSI 1985-; dir Principality Bldg Soc 1985-; pres: Bldg Employers Confedn 1985-86, Concrete Soc 1976-77, Wales Div IOD 1981-86; JP 1979-85; *Recreations* golf; *Clubs* Cardiff and County, Leander, Royal Porthcawl Golf, Royal and Ancient Golf; *Style*— John Turner, Esq, CBE; 38 Victoria Rd, Penarth, S Glamorgan CF6 2HX (☎ 0222 707924); Havelock Buildings, Penarth Rd, Cardiff CF1 7YD (☎ 0222 210002, fax 0222 388206)

TURNER, Hon Kate Belinda; da of 2 Baron Netherthorpe; *b* 12 Oct 1967; *Educ* St Mary's Sch; *Style*— The Hon Kate Turner

TURNER, Kenneth Charles; CBE (1968); s of late Charles Albert Turner, of Jevington, Littleover, Derbys; *b* 1911; *Educ* St James Sch Derby; *m* 1, 1937, Catherine Mary (d 1965), da of Frederick Larmer; m 2, 1975, Josephine Heather, da of Charles Hewitt, of Falmouth, Cornwall; *Career* md/chm General Industrial Cleaners Ltd Derby 1939-80, md A Bell & Sons Ltd Paisley 1967-73, jt md Allied Industrial Services Ltd 1967-68; dir: Bloomsbury Investmts Ltd 1969-74, Initial Services plc 1968-80; chm: Bermaline Ltd Haddington 1978-, Bermaline Foods Ltd Haddington 1978-, Pure Malt Products Ltd 1986-, Teleacoustic Systems Ltd 1984-, Nat Road Transport Fedn London 1961-62, Hokatex N V Holland 1970-78, Hokatex GmbH Germany 1973-78; dir; Kex Industrial Servs Ltd 1977-78, Henry Boot & Sons plc Sheffield 1980; pres: Traders Rd Transport Assoc London 1961-66, Int Road Transport Union Geneva 1965-66; memb: ctee Derbyshire CCC (chm 1974-75) 1955-81, Metrication Bd for Transport & Communications 1965-71, Min of Transports' Ctee Cars for Cities 1964-66; chm: Rd Transport Industry Training Bd 1966-78, Derbys Youth Cricket Cncl 1960-74; dir Derby Co Football Club 1961-71; *Clubs* MCC; *Style*— Kenneth C Turner, Esq, CBE; Heatherdene, Nottingham Rd, Borrowash, Derbys (☎ 0332 676881)

TURNER, Kenneth Edward; s of Frank Turner (d 1967), of 8 Queens Rd, Portsmouth, Hants, and Dorothy Lilian May, *née* Poling (d 1967); *b* 8 Nov 1920; *Educ* Taunton Sch; *m* 6 July 1946, Norah (Mona), da of Patrick Hearns (d 1960), of Mill St, Ballina, Co Mayo, Ireland; 2 s (John b 1947, Michael b 1949), 2 da (Catherine (Mrs) b 1956, Margaret b 1958); *Career* Rifleman KRRC 1940, 2 Lt Somerset LI 1941, Capt RIASC 1942-46; admitted slr 1947, Turner Garett & Co 1950, currently sr ptnr Mackrell Turner Garett; Lib cncllr Woking 1963-66, former chm Botley Park Hosp Chertsey, chm Second Achilles Housing Assoc; memb Law Soc 1950; *Recreations* sailing, golf; *Clubs* Royal Commonwealth Soc, Woking GC; *Style*— Kenneth Turner, Esq; The Well House, Firbank Lane, St Johns, Woking, Surrey (☎ 04862 23 045); 66 High Street, Horsell, Woking, Surrey (☎ 04862 70 951, fax 0483 755 818, telex 858 070 MTG LAW G)

TURNER, Lawrence Frederick; OBE (1982); s of Frederick Thomas Turner (d 1967), of Warwicks, and Edith Elizabeth Turner (d 1975); *b* 28 Jan 1929; *Educ* Moseley GS, Univ of Aston in Birmingham (BSc, CEng); *m* 5 June 1954, Jeanette, da of Wilfred Edwin Clements (d 1967), of Warwicks; 2 s (Adrian Richard Lawrence b 1957, (Anthony) Christopher b 1959), 1 da (Susan Kathryn b 1965); *Career* chartered electrical engr; chm Static Systems Gp plc 1964; pres Inst Hosp Engrg 1979-81; Freeman: Worshipful Co of Fanmakers, Worshipful Co of Engineers; FIEE, FCIBSE; *Recreations* sailing, music, opera, rowing; *Style*— Lawrence Turner, Esq, OBE; Harborough Hall, Blakedown, Worcs (☎ 0562 700129); Static Systems Gp plc, Heath Mill Rd, Wombourn, Staffs (☎ 0902 895551)

TURNER, Dr Leslie Howard; MBE (Mil); s of Aubrey Howard Turner (d 1958), of Raynes Park, and Elsie Louise, *née* Anderson (d 1962); *b* 30 Nov 1916; *Educ* King's Sch Canterbury, Middx Hosp London Univ (MB, BS, MD); *m* 1 Aug 1940, Kathleen Elizabeth (Nancy), da of Maj Denis Connors (d 1956), of Southsea; 1 s (Michael); *Career* WWII Lt 3 Field Ambulance Federated Malay States Vol Force 1942-45 (POW Singapore and Siam Burma Railway F Force); Colonial Med Serv Malaya 1940-59: med offr i/c med and admin in hosps 1946-52, med offr for Med Res 1952-59; conslt (YAWS) WHO 1959;, ref expert leptospirosis Wellcome Labs of Tropical Med 1960-64, dir leptospirosis ref laboratory Public Health Lab Serv and memb gp WHO 1964-78, sec Taxonomic Sub Ctee on Leptospirosis 1960-78; memb: BMA 1946, RSM 1962; *Recreations* reading (gardening is a chore, not recreational); *Clubs* Royal Overseas League; *Style*— Dr Leslie Turner, MBE

TURNER, Lady; Louise B; *née* Taylor; *m* 1940, Sir Eric Turner, CBE (d 1983), sometime Prof of Papyrology at London Univ; 1 s, 1 da; *Style*— Lady Turner; Thornheath, Cathedral Square, Fortrose, Ross-shire

TURNER, Brig Dame Margot; *see*: Turner, Brig Dame Evelyn Marguerite

TURNER, Martin Neely; s of Robert Gabriel Barnard Turner (d 1969), of Bourton on the Water, and Dorothy Margaret, *née* Neely; *b* 12 Dec 1954; *Educ* Solihull Sch, Birmingham Poly Coll of Commerce (HND); *m* 18 Sept 1982, Stephanie Pamela, da of Albert William Edmonds; 2 da (Claire b 24 April 1985, Penny b 16 June 1988); *Career* CA; mangr Peat Marwick McLintock Birmingham until 1985, co sec and co accountant insurance pensions personal finance planning Fraser Tudor Ltd 1985-87, gp fin analyst Littlewoods Organisation plc, princ M N Turner CAs; memb Solihull Centre Nat Tst; ICAEW 1980; *Recreations* rambling, squash; *Clubs* The Old Silhillians (Solihull), The Fentham (Hampton-in-Arden); *Style*— Martin Turner, Esq; 54 Grenfell Pk, Parkgate, Neston, South Wirral L64 6TT (☎ 051 336 7079); The Littlewoods Organisation plc, J M Centre, Old Hall St, Liverpool X L70 1AB (☎ 051 235 2517, fax 051 235 2670, car tel 0836 518 770, telex 628501)

TURNER, Martin William; s of William Alexander Turner (d 1972), of 24 Marshall Rd, Rainham, Kent, and Enine Felicity, *née* McCabe; *b* 3 Oct 1940; *Educ* Gravesend Tech Sch, Medway Coll of Art (Nat Dip in Design); *Career* artist; mural painting cmmnd by: MOD 1971, GEC Ltd 1976, Rochester upon Medway Civic Centre 1987;

series of paintings and limited edition prints based on the Medway Towns and exhibited requlariy at Royal Acad 1960-; chm local youth club 1957-65; memb ROI 1975; *Recreations* photography, walking, model making; *Style*— Martin Turner, Esq; 24 Marshall Rd, Rainham, Kent (☎ 0634 319 94)

TURNER, Michael James; s of James Henry Turner (d 1966), and Doris May, *née* Daniels (d 1983); *b* 8 July 1939; *Educ* BEC GS London, Imperial Coll London (BSc, ARCS), London Business Sch, Harvard Business Sch; *m* 29 Dec 1962, Elizabeth Joyce, da of George Edward Hanselman (d 1969); 1 s (David b 1964), 1 da (Anne b 1966); *Career* gen mangr (life and pensions) Sun Life Assur Soc plc 1985 (joined 1960); dir: Sun Life Pensions Mgmnt Ltd, Suntrust, Co Pensions Mgmnt Centre; elder Redland Park Utd Reformed Church; *Recreations* squash, overseas travel; *Style*— Michael Turner, Esq; Grey Roofs, The Scop, Almondsbury, Bristol (☎0272 612 137); Sun Life Assur Soc plc, Sun Life Court, St James Barton, Bristol BS99 7SL (☎ 0272 426 911, fax 3895)

TURNER, Michael John; s of Gerald Mortimer Turner, of Wood Cottage, Ashtead Woods, Ashtead, Surrey, and Joyce Isobel Marguerite, *née* Healy; *b* 12 June 1951; *Educ* Eton; *m* 17 July 1982, Diana Mary St Clair, da of David Michael St Clair Weir; 2 s (Freddie b 1985, Max b 1987); *Career* dir: Fuller Smith and Turner plc 1985-, Ringwoods Ltd 1985-, Leonard Tong 1982- (chm 1986-87), Fuller Smith and Turner Estates Ltd 1985; FCA; *Recreations* skiing, shooting, golf, tennis, motor racing, travel; *Clubs* Aldeburgh Golf, Eton Vikings, Wine Trade Sports; *Style*— Michael Turner, Esq; 5 Bowerdean St, London SW6 3TN; Fuller Smith & Turner plc, Griffin Brewery, Chiswick, London W4 2QB

TURNER, The Hon Mr Justice Turner; Hon Sir Michael John; QC (1973); s of Theodore Francis Turner, QC (d 1986), and Elizabeth Alice Turner, *née* Schuster (d 1983); *b* 31 May 1931; *Educ* Winchester, Magdalene Coll Cambridge (BA); *m* 26 July 1956 (m dis 1965), Hon Susan Money-Coutts, da of 7 Baron Latymer (d 1987); 1 s (Mark b 1958), 1 da (Louise b 1959); m 2, 1965, Frances Deborah, da of The Rt Hon Sir David Powell Croom-Johnson; 2 s (David b 1966, James b 1967); *Career* called to the Bar Inner Temple 1955, recorder 1970, chm E Midlands Agric Laws Tribunal 1972, High Ct judge 1985-; memb Judicial Studies Bd 1988-, co-chm Civil & Family Ctee Judicial Studies Bd 1988; Kt 1985; *Recreations* listening to music, horses; *Clubs* Army & Navy; *Style*— The Hon Mr Justice Turner; c/o Royal Courts of Justice, Strand WC2A 2AA

TURNER, Michael Ralph; *b* 26 Jan 1929; *Educ* BA; *Career* gp md and chief exec Associated Book Publishers plc 1982-87, chm Methuen Inc New York 1981-87, sr vice-pres publishing/information gp Int Thomson Organisation Ltd 1987-; memb pres Publishers Assoc 1987-; *Books* The Bluffer's Guide to the Theatre (1967); with Antony Miall: Parlour Poetry (1967), The Parlour Song Book (1972), Just a Song at Twilight (1975), The Edwardian Song Book (1982), Gluttony, Pride and Lust and Other Sins for the World of Books (with Michael Geare, 1984), translation of Tintin books (with Leslie Lonsdale-Cooper, 1958-); *Recreations* theatre, writing, maritime art; *Clubs* Garrick; *Style*— Michael Turner, Esq; International Thomson Organisation Ltd, First Floor, The Quadrangle, 180 Wardour Street, London W1A 4YG (☎ 01 437 9787)

TURNER, Dr Michael Skinner; s of Sir Michael William Turner, CBE (d 1980), of Egerton Gdns, London, and Lady (Wendy), *née* Stranack; *b* 12 August 1947; *Educ* Dragon Sch, Marlborough, London Univ and St Thomas's Hosp (MB, BS, MRCS, LRCP), Washington (MD); *m* 8 July 1972, Amanda Baldwin, s of John Baldwin Raper, DFC, of 52 Elm Pk Rd, London; 4 da (Lucinda b 6 Dec 1974, Nara b 9 Oct 1976, Camilla b 3 July 1980, Alexia b 29 Jan 1984); *Career* chief med advsr: Texaco, Vickers Ltd, Citibank, Inchcape, BZW, Henlys Ltd, Robert Fleming, Lloyds Register of Shipping, Hoare Govett/Security Pacific; med advsr: Hong Kong and Shangai Bank, Sedgwick Gp, ANZ/Grindlays Bank; memb med advsy ctee; UKODA, Inst Petroleum; hon med advsr Br Ski Fedn 1974, Alpine team doctor Winter Olympics Calgary 1988; Freeman City of London 1971, Liveryman Worhsipful Co of Skinners; BASM 1975, BMA 1976, FZS 1981; memb; RSM, Soc Occupational Med, Assur Med Soc, Med Book Soc; *Recreations* skiing, shooting, fishing, tennis; *Clubs* Annabel's; *Style*— Dr Michael Turner; 4 Tite St, London SW3 4HY (☎ 01 352 2285); The City Medical Centre, 17 St Helens Place, London EC3A 6DE (☎ 01 588 5477, fax 01 256 5295)

TURNER, Hon (Edward) Neil; s of 1 Baron Netherthorpe (d 1980), and Margaret Lucy, *née* Mattock; *b* 27 Jan 1941; *Educ* Rugby, RAC Cirencester, London Univ; *m* 12 Oct 1963, Gillian Mary, da of Christopher John King (d 1963); 1 s (Charles), 1 da (Sara); *Career* chm Edward Turner and Son Ltd 1971-; memb: Yorks and Humberside Econ Planning Cncl 1975-79, Residuary Body for S Yorks 1985-, Cncl BIM 1976-81 and 1982-88; gen cmmnr of Taxes 1973-; High Sheriff S Yorks 1983-84, Freeman Worshipful Co of Cutlers in Hallamshire; FRICS, QALAS, Dip FBA (Lond), FBIM; *Recreations* shooting, golf; *Clubs* Lindrick Golf; *Style*— The Hon Neil Turner; The Limes, Crowgate, South Anston, nr Sheffield, S Yorks S31 7AL; 312 Petre St, Sheffield S4 8LT (☎ 0742 430291)

TURNER, Philip; CBE (1975); s of George Francis Turner (d 1957), of Alverstoke, Hants, and Daisy Louise, *née* Frayn; *b* 1 June 1913; *Educ* Peter Symonds Winchester, London Univ (LLB Hons); *m* 1938, Hazel Edith, da of Douglas Anton Benda (d 1923); 1 da (and 1 da decd); *Career* Lt Cdr RNVR WWII (Atlantic convoys, Scapa Flow, Far East); slr 1935, asst slr GPO Solicitor's Dept 1953-62, princ asst slr GPO 1962-72, slr to Post Office 1972-75; chm: Civil Service Legal Soc 1957-58, Int Bar Assoc Ctee on Public Utility Law 1972-77; in private practice Infields, Hampton Wick, Surrey; FRSA; *Recreations* piano, golf; *Clubs* Naval, Royal Automobile, Hants and Surrey CC, Law Soc; *Style*— Philip Turner, Esq, CBE; 8 Walters Mead, Ashtead, Surrey KT21 2BP (☎ 0372 273656)

TURNER, Surgn Rear Adm Philip Stanley; CB (1963); s of Frank Overy Turner, of Tunbridge Wells, and Ellen Mary, *née* Holder; *b* 31 Oct 1905; *Educ* Cranbrook, Guy's Hosp (LDS, RCS); *m* 1934, Marguerite, da of John Donnelly, of Glasgow; 1 s (Ian), 1 da (Sarah); *Career* entered RN as Surgn Lt 1928, Surgn Capt (D) 1955, Surgn Rear Adm (D) 1961, sr specialist in Dental Surgery 1946-60, dir of dental services RN Admiralty and MOD 1961-64, QHDS 1960-64; fndn fell Br Assoc of Oral Surgns 1962, ret 1964; *Style*— Surgn Rear Adm Philip Turner, CB

TURNER, Robert Lockley; s of Capt James Lockley-Turner, OBE (d 1954), of Purley, Berks, and Maud Beatrice, *née* Hillyard; *b* 2 Sept 1935; *Educ* Clifton, St Catharine's Coll Cambridge (MA); *m* 5 Oct 1963, Jennifer Mary, da of Alan Guy Fishwick Leather, TD, of Chester; 1 s (Guy Lockley b 1967), 1 da (Claire Henrietta b 1969); *Career* barr; cmmnd Gloucestershire Regt 1959, Army Legal Serv 1969-66 (Maj 1962); practised Midland and Oxford Circuit 1967-84, master of the Queen's Bench Div of the Supreme Ct 1984-; *Recreations* sailing, gardening; *Clubs* Royal Fowey Yacht; *Style*— Robert Turner, Esq; Royal Courts of Justice, Strand, London WC2A 2LJ

TURNER, Lt Col (Michael) Robin Rogers; OBE (1963, MBE 1945); s of Maj George Rogers Turner (d 1965), of Gumfreston Tenby, Pembrokeshire, and Edith Marguerite, *née* Smith (d 1956); *b* 5 July 1917; *Educ* Radley, RMC Sandhurst, Staff Coll Quetta; *Career* RMC Sandhurst 1936-37, 2 Lt 15 Regt of Foot (E Yorks) 1938, BEF 1939-40, Staff Coll Quetta 1942, BM 37 Gurkha Bde (Imphal Campaign) 1943-44, DS Staff Coll Quetta 1944-45, BN 89 Gurkha Bde Malaya 1945-46, GS WO 1947, BN 48 Gurkha Bde, Malaya 1949-52; 1 E Yorks: Malaya 1954-55, BAOR 1955-57; GS N Cmd York 1957-59, GSO1 HQ Singapore Dist 1959-62; army recruiting offr Se London 1962-69; dir Hatton Ct Residents Co Ltd 1963-; *Recreations* golf; *Clubs* Sundridge Pk Golf; *Style*— Lt-Col Robin Turner, OBE; Hatton Ct, Chislehurst, Kent (☎ 01 467 6936)

TURNER, Simon Neville; JP (Derbyshire); s of David Neville Turner, JP (d 1956), and Mary Gwendolyn, *née* Young (d 1953); *b* 4 Mar 1905; *Educ* Downside; *m* 1, 7 Sept 1948, Norah Alice (d 1956), yr da of A J F Platt, of Newark, Notts; m 2, 21 July 1969, Diana Mary, o da of Capt R H Walker (d 1964), of Sand Hutton and Bawtry, Yorks; *Career* Capt Royal Signals (TA), Maj Anti-Aircraft (Gunners) 1942-45; mining engr, vice-chm and md Staveley; dir assoc Mining, Engrg & Chemical Cos; MIMinE; *Recreations* hunting, shooting, fishing; *Clubs* Carlton; *Style*— Simon Turner, Esq; Mertoun Glebe, St Boswells (☎ 0835 22238); The Garden Cottage, Achnashellach, Ross-shire (☎ 052 06 274)

TURNER, Wilfred; CMG (1977), CVO (1979); s of Allen Turner (d 1966), and Eliza, *née* Leech (d 1955); *b* 10 Oct 1921; *Educ* Heywood GS, Univ of London (BSc); *m* 26 March 1947, June Gladys, da of Leonard Ham Tite, MBE (d 1983); 2 s (Nicholas Hugh b 1950, Matthew Julian b 1955), 1 da (Harriett Louise Macrae b 1960); *Career* REME: cmmnd 2 Lt 1942, Capt 1945, demobbed 1947; Miny of Lab 1938-60, asst lab advsr India 1955-59, Miny of Health 1960-66 (sec Ctee of Safety of Drugs 1963-66), HM Dip Serv 1966-81 (Br high cmmr Botswana 1977-81), dir Southern Africa Assoc 1983-85, non exec dir Transmark (BR) 1987-; memb: Royal Inst of Int Affrs, Royal African Soc, exec ctee Zambia Soc, Royal Cwlth Soc (memb central ctee); *Recreations* hill walking; *Clubs* Royal Cwlth Soc; *Style*— Wilfred Turner, Esq, CMG, CVO; 44 Tower Rd, Twickenham, Middlesex TW1 4PE (☎ 01 892 1593)

TURNER, Lt-Gen Sir William Francis Robert; KBE (1962), CB (1959), DSO (1945); s of Francis Robert Turner (d 1938), of Kelso; *b* 12 Dec 1907; *Educ* Winchester, RMC Sandhurst; *m* 1938, Nancy Maude, eld da of Lt-Col J B L Stilwell; 1 s (Maj William Sitwell Turner, MC); *Career* cmmnd KOSB 1928, served GB and India 1928-39, Capt 1938, served WWII NW Europe (despatches), OC 5 Bn KOSB 1942-45, OC 1 Bn KOSB 1945-46, GSO1 M East and GB 1946-50, Col Br Mil Mission to Greece 1950-52, Brig cmdg 128 Infantry Bde (TA) 1952-54, BGS Western Cmd 1954-56, Maj-Gen 1956, GOC 44 (Home Counties) Infantry Div (TA) and dep constable Dover Castle 1956-59, pres Regular Cmmns Bd 1959-61, Lt-Gen 1961, GOC-in-C Scottish Cmd and govr Edinburgh Castle 1961-64; Col KOSB 1961-70; Lord-Lt Dumfriesshire 1972-82 (JP 1973, DL 1970-72); Ensign Royal Co Archers (Queen's Body Guard for Scotland), ret 1985; cmmr Queen Victoria Sch Dunblane 1965-85; Cdr with Star Order of St Olav Class II (Norway), Order of the Two Niles Class II (Republic of Sudan); *Clubs* Naval and Military, New (Edinburgh); *Style*— Lt-Gen Sir William Turner, KBE, CB, DSO; Milnhead, Kirkton, Dumfries (☎ 0387 710319)

TURNER, Brig William George Rhyll (Bill); CBE (1984, MBE 1967); s of Lt-Col G F G Turner, OBE, DCM (d 1968), and Nancy Mary Turner (d 1947); *b* 14 Oct 1933; *Educ* Dulwich Coll, RMA Sandhurst, Staff Coll Camberley, Nat Def Coll; *m* 17 Aug 1957, Rosemary Anne, da of The Hon V H O Herbert (d 1983); 3 da (Valerie b 1958, Penelope b 1960, Susan b 1964); *Career* cmmnd Wilts Regt 1954, Duke of Edinburgh's Royal Regt (Berks & Wilts) 1959, ret 1987; Col Duke of Edinburgh's Royal Regt 1988-, Hon Col Wilts Army Cadet Force 1988-; memb Lloyd's 1988; govr Alleyn's Coll of God's Gift Dulwich; pres East Woodhay Silver Band; FBIM 1986; *Recreations* visual arts, viticulture, gardening, tennis; *Clubs* Army & Navy; *Style*— Brig Bill Turner, CBE; The Holt, Woolton Hill, Newbury, Berkshire RG15 9XL (☎ 0635 253 680); The Wardrobe, 58 The Close, Salisbury, Wiltshire SP1 2EX (☎ 0722 336 222, ext 2683)

TURNER CAIN, Maj-Gen (George) Robert; CB (1967), CBE (1963), DSO (1944); s of Wing Cdr George Turner Cain (d 1967), and Jesse Mary Smith (d 1927); *b* 16 Feb 1912; *Educ* Norwich Sch, Sandhurst; *m* 1938, Lamorna Maturin, da of Col G B Hingston (ka 1916); 1 s (Michael), 1 da (Rosemary); *Career* gazetted Norfolk Regt 1932, India 1933-38, NW Frontier Waziristan Camp 1937 (despatches), WWII 1 Royal Norfolk and 1 Hereford, BLA 1944-45, BAOR 1945-48, Berlin Airlift 1948, Hong Kong communist China 1953-54, cmd 1 Fed IB Malaya 1957-59, BGS HQ BAOR 1961-64, MGA HQ FARELF 1964-66 (Confrontation of Indonesia), ADC to HM The Queen 1960-64; chm and dir: F & G Smith Ltd Maltsters, Walpole & Wright Ltd, Crisp Maltings Ltd and EDME Ltd, Anglia Maltings Gp (Hldgs) Ltd 1947-82; pres Anglia Maltings (Hldgs) Ltd 1982-; Croix de Guerre avec Palme 1945, Star of Kedah 1959; *Style*— Maj-Gen Robert Turner Cain, CB, CBE, DSO; Holbreck, Hollowlane, Stiffkey, Wells-next-the-Sea, Norfolk NR23 1QG (☎ 032 875 280)

TURNER-OXENHAM, (John) Brent; s of John Eric Turner Oxenham, and Eileen Madge, *née* Maycock; *b* 13 June 1938; *Educ* Kent Coll, Caius Coll Shoreham, Steyning GS; *m* 17 Dec 1971, Sandra Elizabeth, da of Maj Harold Roden, of 5 Promenade Reine Astrid, Menton, France; 2 da (Victoria Elizabeth b 1974, Rebecca Jane b 1976); *Career* independent professional antiques valuer and restorer; *Recreations* travelling, theatre, gardening, Dartmoor, countryside exploration; *Clubs* RAC, CGA; *Style*— John Turner-Oxenham, Esq; Huxbear House, Chudleigh, S Devon TQ13 0NY (☎ 0626 852 948)

TURNER-SAMUELS, David Jessel; QC (1972); s of Moss Turner-Samuels, MP, of London, and Gladys Deborah, *née* Belcher; *b* 5 April 1918; *Educ* Westminster; *m* 5 Nov 1939 (m dis 1976), Norma, da of Philip Verstone, of Worthing (d 1971); 1 s (Michael b 17 Aug 1946), 1 da (Elizabeth b 28 March 1958); m 2, 10 April 1977, Norma Florence, da of Geoge David Shellabean (d 1973), of Devon; *Career* WWII RA 1939-46; barr Middle Temple 1939, bencher Middle Temple, attorney at law Trinidad and Tobago; *Style*— David Turner-Samuels, Esq, QC; Cherry Tree Cottage, Petworth Rd, Haslemere, Surrey GU27 3BG; New Court, Temple, London EL4Y 9BE;

Cloister, Temple, London EC4Y 7AA (☎ 01 583 0303, fax 01 583 2254)

TURNER-WARWICK, Prof Margaret Elizabeth Harvey; da of William Harvey Moore, QC, and Maud Kirkdale, *née* Baden-Powell; *b* 19 Nov 1924; *Educ* St Pauls Sch for Girls, Lady Margaret Hall Oxford (MA, DM), Univ Coll Hosp (PhD); *m* 21 Jan 1950, Richard Trevor, s of William Turner-Warwick; 2 da (Gillian (Mrs Bathe), Lynne (Dr Turner Stokes)); *Career* conslt physician Elizabeth Garrett Anderson Hosp 1960-67, conslt physician London Chest Hosp and Brompton Hosp 1967, dean of Cardiothoracic Inst 1984-87 (sr lectr 1963-72, prof 1972-87); pres Br Thoracic Soc 1982-83, second vice pres RCP 1988; chm: Asthma Res Cncl 1988, Med Advsy Ctee CORDA 1985; memb: Imperial Cancer Res Fund Cncl 1988, NW Thames Regnl Health Authy 1988, senate London Univ 1983-87, systems bd MRC 1982-85, mgmnt ctee Cardiothoracic Inst, bd of govrs Nat Heart and Chest Hosps 1971-88; Hon DSc NY; FRCP 1969, FRCP (Edin) 1988, FRCAP 1983; memb: Alpha Omega Alpha (USA) 1988, Assoc of Physicians; *Recreations* family and their hobbies, classical music, watercolour painting; *Style—* Prof Margaret Turner-Warwick; 55 Fitzroy Park, Highgate, London N6; 61 Harley House, Marylebone Road, NW1 (☎ 01 935 2550)

TURPIN, (James) Alexander; CMG (1966); s of Samuel Alexander Turpin (d 1944), of Dublin, and Marie Louise, *née* Mitchell (d 1921); *b* 7 Jan 1917; *Educ* The King's Hospital Dublin, Trinity Coll Dublin (MA); *m* 1942, Kathleen Iris, da of Thomas Tait Eadie (d 1968), of Co Kerry; 1 da (Alexa); *Career* Royal Irish Fus 1942-46, Capt; HM Foreign (later Dip) Serv 1947; serv: Paris, Warsaw, Tokyo, The Hague, New Delhi, Manila; ambass Manila 1972-76; chm Br Phillippine Soc 1986-88; chm British Phillippine Soc 1986-88; *Publications* New Society's Challenge in the Philippines (1980), The Philippines: Problems of the Ageing New Society (1984); *Recreations* music, cookery, wine, tennis, swimming; *Style—* Alexander Turpin, Esq, CMG; 12 Grimwood Rd, Twickenham, Middlesex

TURPIN, Maj-Gen Patrick George; CB (1962), OBE (1943); s of Rev Julian James Turpin, MA, BD (d 1936), Vicar of Misterton Somerset, and Emily Hannah Bryant (d 1960); *b* 27 April 1911; *Educ* Haileybury, Exeter Coll Oxford (BA, MA); *m* 1947, Cherry Leslie Joy, da of Maj Kenneth Sydney Grove (d 1949), of Bleadon, Somerset; 1 s (Richard), 1 da (Annabel); *Career* cmmnd RASC 1933; served WWII in: Egypt, Western Desert, Sicily, Italy and Germany; AQMG 30 Corps 1943, AA & QMG 5 Div 1943-44, DA & QMG (Brig) 1 Corps BLA 1945, DAG HQ BAOR 1956-59, Brig 17 Gurkha Div Malaya 1959-60, dir of supplies and tport WO 1960-63, dir of movements MOD 1963-66, psc 1941, jssc 1949, idc 1955, Col Cmdt RCT 1965-71, Col Gurkha Army Service Corps 1960-65, Col Gurkha Tport Regt 1965-73; sec gen ABTA 1966-69; pres Army Lawn Tennis Assoc 1968-73; govr Royal Sch for Daughters of Officers of the Army Bath 1963-83; FCIT, FRHS; *Recreations* lawn tennis (rep Somerset and Army, Somerset Co Champion 1948), squash rackets (rep Bucks and Army), golf; *Clubs* Oxford Union Soc, All England Lawn Tennis, Int Lawn Tennis, Escorts Squash Rackets; *Style—* Maj-Gen Patrick Turpin, CB, OBE; c/o National Westminster Bank plc, 121 High St, Oxford OX1 4DD

TURRILL, Hon Mrs; Hon Jean Phyllis; *née* Wise; da of 1 Baron Wise, DL; *b* 11 July 1914; *m* 1939, Lt-Col John Turrill, OBE, TD; 1 s, 2 da; *Style—* The Hon Mrs Turrill; 94 Albert Rd, Caversham, Reading

TURTON, Eugenie Christine (Genie); da of Arthur Turton (d 1973), and Georgina, *née* Fairhurst; *b* 19 Feb 1946; *Educ* Nottingham Girls HS (GPDST), Girton Coll Cambridge (MA); *m* 1, 20 July 1968 (m dis 1972), Richard Lindsay Gordon; m 2, 14 June 1974 (m dis 1978), Gerrard Flanagan; *Career* princ private sec to Sec of State for Tport 1978-80, memb Channel Link Financing Gp Midland Bank 1981-82, hd of machinery govt div Cabinet Off 1982-85, dir heritage and royal estate DOE 1987 (under sec housing gp 1986-87); non-exec dir Woolwich Equitable Building Soc 1987-; FRSA 1986; *Recreations* music, books; *Style—* Miss Genie Turton; DOE, 2 Marsham St, London SW1 (☎ 01 276 3836)

TURTON, Hon Gerald Christopher; s of Baron Tranmire (Life Peer), and Ruby Christian, *née* Scott; *b* 12 May 1937; *Educ* Eton, RAC Cirencester; *m* 1967, Alexandra Susan, da of Lt-Col S Oliver, of Richmond, Yorks; 1 s, 2 da; *Career* farmer; *Style—* The Hon Gerald Turton; Park House, Upsall, Thirsk, N Yorks (☎ 0845 537383)

TURTON, Hon Michael Andrew; s of Baron Tranmire (Life Peer); *b* 1929; *Style—* The Hon Michael Turton

TURTON, Richard Charles; s of Charles Ernest Turton (d 1978), of Epperstone, Notts, and Aline Audrey Turton (d 1983); *b* 17 Dec 1936; *Educ* Uppingham; *m* 1, 15 Aug 1961 (m dis 1969), Rosemary Margaret, da of Arthur J C Moore, of Uppingham, Rutland; 2 s (Andrew b 20 June 1962, Philip b 6 Feb 1965); m 2, Susan Katharine, da of Capt Edward Norman Allan (d 1944); 1 s (Paul b 29 May 1970); *Career* qualified CA 1961; ptnr: Turton Ross & Co 1961-63, Chamberlain Turton & Dunn 1963-75, Spicer & Oppenheim (formerly Spicer & Pegler) 1975-; chm Insolvency Practitioners Assoc 1975-76, pres Insol Int 1985-; sec Nottingham Glyndebourne Assoc 1967, memb fin ctee Glyndebourne 1980-; pres Nottingham Hockey Club 1975-80, memb cncl ICEAW 1986; Freeman City of London, Memb Worshipful Co of CAs; FCA 1966, FIPA, MICM; *Books* Meet the Receiver (1985); *Recreations* singing, violin, classical music listening, gardening, hockey, tennis; *Style—* Richard Turton, Esq; Spicer & Oppenheim, Clumber Ave, Sherwood Rise, Nottingham NG5 1AH (☎ 0602 607131, fax 0602 607987, car 0836 610 130, telex 377 013 Esano G)

TURTON, Hon Timothy Robert Scott; s of Baron Tranmire (Life Peer); *b* 1934; *Style—* The Hon Timothy Turton

TURTON-HART, Sir Francis Edmund; KBE (1963, MBE Mil 1942); s of David Edwin Hart (d 1947), of New Hextalls, Bletchingley, Surrey, and Zoe Evelyn Turton (d 1964); *b* 29 May 1908; *Educ* Uppingham; *m* 1947, Margaret Frances Edith, da of Richard Hathorn Greaves (d 1955), of Cairo; 1 da; *Career* served WWII with RE, Hon Maj (E Africa 1924-38), Mid E, Western Desert and Italy, Nigeria 1947-65; dir Amalgamated Engrg Co Ltd Nigeria 1949-59; memb Nigerian Federal House of Representatives 1956-60; dir Dorman Long (Nigeria) Ltd 1959-65; pres Lagos C of C 1960-63; *Recreations* shooting, golf; *Clubs* Thurlestone Golf (pres); *Style—* Sir Francis Turton-Hart, KBE; 39 Hunters Moon, Dartington, Totnes, South Devon TQ9 6JT (☎ 0803 863126)

TURVEY, Peter James; s of Douglas Ronald Turvey, of Croydon, and Kathleen Mildred, *née* Smith; *b* 9 May 1943; *Educ* Whitgift Sch, Brasenose Coll Oxford (MA); *m* 23 Oct 1965, (Norah) Louise, da of Dr Peter O'Flynn, of Croydon; 1 s (Andrew b 1968), 3 da (Marie-Louise b 1967, Caroline b 1972, Fiona b 1975); *Career* asst gen mangr Swiss RE (UK) 1972-87, princ Mercer Fraser 1987-; vice pres Inst of Actuaries 1988- (hon sec 1984-86), chm Staple Inn Actuarial Soc 1988-; chm Croydon HS Scholarship Tst; memb Co of Actuaries 1980 (jr warden 1988-); FIA 1968; *Recreations* jogging, windsurfing, bridge; *Style—* Peter Turvey, Esq; William M Mercer Fraser Ltd, Telford House, 14 Tothill St, London SW1H 9NB (☎ 01 222 9121, fax 01 799 2449, telex 8813544)

TURVILL, Peter Barry; s of William Herbert Turvill (d 1988), of Worthing, W Sussex, and Evelyn Margaret, *née* Kennard (d 1970); *b* 16 August 1945; *Educ* Kingsway Coll London; *m* 8 April 1972, Jane Alexandra, da of Alexander John Langley, of Yapton, Sussex; 2 da (Joanne b 1976, Caroline b 1979); *Career* accountant; fin dir R A Marshall Ltd 1972-; *Recreations* charitable activities, reading, music; *Style—* Peter B Turvill, Esq; 127 Clarence Avenue, Clapham Park, London SW4 8LX (☎ 01 674 1756); Century House, 33 Station Road, London SE25 5AH (☎ 01 771 5119)

TURVILLE CONSTABLE-MAXWELL, Robert John; s of David Turville Constable-Maxwell (d 1985), and Mary Alethea Elizabeth Evelyn; *b* 4 Oct 1933; *Educ* Ampleforth; *m* 23 April 1960, Susan Mary, da of Stephen Francis Gaisford St Lawrence (d 1957), 2 s (Anthony Nicholas b 1961, Stephen Bernard b 1963), 1 da (Alice Marion b 1969); *Career* Lt Grenadier Gds 1952-54; Allied Lyons 1956-84, underwriting memb Lloyds; vice-chm Harborough Cons Assoc, pres Husbands Bosworth Sheepdog Trial Assoc, ctee memb local CLA; Freeman City of London 1975, memb Brewers Court; *Recreations* golf, shooting, tennis; *Clubs* Cavalry & Guards, Pratts; *Style—* Robert Turville Constable-Maxwell, Esq; Boswoth Hall, Husbands Bosworth, Nr Lutterworth, Leics LE15 7LZ (☎ 0858 880 730); PO Box 31, Oakham, Rutland (☎ 0572 2610)

TUSA, John; s of John Tusa, OBE, of Dorset, and Lydia, *née* Sklenarova; *b* 2 Mar 1936; *Educ* Gresham's Sch Holt, Trinity Coll Cambridge (BA); *m* 1960, Ann Hilary, da of Stanley Dowson, of Lancs; 2 s (John, James); *Career* presenter: Newsnight BBC 2 1980-86, Timewatch BBC 2 1982-84; md BBC World Service 1986-; Royal Television Soc Journalist of the Year 1984, BAFTA Richard Dimbleby Award 1984; memb: Cncl RIPA, RIIA; tstee Nat Portrait Gallery; *Books* The Nuremberg Trial (co-author with Ann Tusa, 1984), The Berlin Blockade (co-author with wife, 1988); *Recreations* squash, tennis, opera, music; *Clubs* United Oxford and Cambridge Univ; *Style—* John Tusa, Esq; 21 Christchurch Hill, London NW3 1JY (☎ 01 435 9495)

TUSHINGHAM, Rita; da of John Tushingham, of Liverpool, and Enid Ellen *née* Lott; *b* 14 Mar 1942; *Educ* La Sagesse Convent Liverpool; *m* 1, 1 Dec 1962 (m dis 1976), Terence William Bicknell; 2 da (Dodonna b 1 May 1964, Aisha b 16 June 1971); m 2, 27 Aug 1981, Dusama Rawi, s of Najib El-Rawi, of Geneva, Switzerland; *Career* actress; began career Liverpool Rep Theatre 1958, first film A Taste of Honey 1961 (Best Actress Cannes Film Festival), New York Film Critics Award, Golden Globe Award); other films incl: Gin with Green Eyes 1965 (Best Actress Variety Club of GB), The Knack 1965 (Best Actress Mexican Film Festival), Doctor Zhivago 1966, The Trap 1967, the Guru 1968, Bedsitting Room 1969, A Judgement in Stone 1986, Resurrected 1988; tv incl Bread 1988; *Recreations* cooking, painting, gardening; *Style—* Miss Rita Tushingham; c/o Michael Anderson, ICM 388 Oxford St, London WIN 9HE (☎ 01 885 974)

TUSTIN, Rt Rev David; *see*: Grimsby, Bishop of

TUTIN, Dorothy; CBE (1967); da of John Tutin, and Ada Evelyn Friars; *b* 8 April 1930; *Educ* St Catherine's Bramley, RADA (Dip); *m* 1964, Derek Barton-Chapple (stage name Derek Waring), s of Wing Cdr Harry John Barton-Chapple; 1 s (Nicholas b 1966), 1 da (Amanda b 1965); *Career* stage and film actress; began stage career 1959; stage rôles incl: many Shakespearian parts, Sally Bowles in I am a Camera; film rôles incl: Polly Peachum in The Beggar's Opera, Cecily in The Importance of Being Earnest, Lucie Manette in A Tale of Two Cities, Sophie Breslea in Savage Messiah, The Shooting Party; Variety Club of Gt Britain Film Actress Award 1972; *Style—* Miss Dorothy Tutin, CBE; c/o Barry Burnett, Suite 42-43, Graften House, 2-3 Golden Sq, London W1

TUTT, Dr Leslie William Godfrey; s of Charles Leslie Tutt, of London, and Emily Ditcham, *née* Wiseman; *b* 13 Oct 1921; *Educ* RMC of Sci (pac), Univ of London (MSc, PhD); *Career* RA 1940-46, Maj SO 1944; actuary and mathematical statistician in private practice; lectr, writer; memb: cncl Faculty Actuaries 1975-78 (bd examiners 1980-), exec ctee Pensions Res Accountants Gp 1976-85, cncl Nat Assoc Pension Funds 1979-83; examinations assessor CII 1980-, chm Inst Statisticians 1984-87, (memb cncl 1968-74 and 1975-81, vice-chm 1981-84); contrib numerous res papers and tech articles to actuarial, statistical and fin jls 1950-; Liveryman: Worshipful Co of Loriners 1975, Worshipful Co of Actuaries 1979; FFA 1949, FSS 1951, FIS 1951, assoc Soc Actuaries USA 1968, FPMI 1976; *Books* Private Pension Scheme Finance (1970), Pension Schemes, Investment, Communications and Overseas Aspects (1977), Pension Law and Taxation (1985), Financial Aspects of Pension Business (1986), Financial Aspects of Life Business (1987), Financial Services Marketing and Investor Protection (1988), Life Assurance (1988), Pensions (1988); *Recreations* running, riding the cresta run, bobsleighing, golf; *Clubs* Athenaeum, City Livery, New (Edinburgh); *Style—* Dr Leslie Tutt; 21 Sandilands, Croydon, Surrey CR0 5DF (☎ 01 654 2995)

TUTT, Penny; da of Frank Robert Pennell (d 1945), and Edith May, *née* Bingham; *b* 23 Mar 1925; *Educ* King Edward VI HS for Girls Birmingham; *m* 24 Aug 1956 (m dis 1986), Norman Leslie Tutt, s of George Tutt (d 1964), of Ealing, London; 1 s (Simon b 19 Feb 1960), 1 da (Sarah b 30 Sept 1962); *Career* Midland Bank 1943-46, Nat Cncl of Soc Servs 1946-49, Sigmund Pumps 1949-50, won Britain's Perfect Air Girl Award 1950 (travelled Australia, featured on radio and tv), passenger relations offr BOAC 1953-59 (air hostess 1950-53); FI Gp 1953-; PA to fndr, co sec, mangr, exec dir to subsidiaries, current dir community relations; chm: tstees Women into Technol, London Employers Advsy Cncl Apex; memb: exec ctee Industl Soc, Commerce/Indust liason ctee Royal Jubilee Tst, Business in the Community Women into Econ Devpt Initiative 1969-; MBIM 1981, AMJI 1983; *Recreations* family, talking with people; *Style—* Mrs Penny Tutt; F I Group plc, The Bury, Church St, Chesham, Bucks HP5 1HW (☎ 0494 791234, fax 0494 791381, telex 838872 FINGRP)

TUTT, Sylvia Irene Maud; da of Charles Leslie Tutt, of London, and Emily Ditcham, *née* Wiseman; *Career* chartered sec and admin in private practice, author; Inst of Chartered Secs and Admins: cncl memb 1975-76 and 1980-82, memb benevolent fund mgmnt ctee 1975-, rep memb Crossways Tst 1977- (memb educn ctee 1980-82, memb pubns and PR ctee 1980-82), pres Women's Soc 1975-76 (memb ctee 1968-71 and 1976-87, hon sec 1971-74, vice pres 1973-75, chm London branch 1984-85 (memb ctee 1974-82 and 1985-87, vice-chm 1982-84)); sr examiner CII 1975-, pres

Soroptimist Int of Central London 1976-78 (vice-pres 1974-76); Liveryman Worshipful Co of Scriveners 1978, Freeman Guild of Freeman City of London 1976; Worshipful Co of Chartered Secs and Admins: Liveryman 1977, memb Ct of Assts 1977-, Jr Warden 1981-82, Sr Warden 1982-83, Master 1983-84, managing tstee Charitable Tst 1978-; ACIS 1956, FRSA 1983; author of numerous technical articles in professional and financial journals 1956-; *Books* Private Pension Scheme Finance (jtly 1970), Pensions and Employee Benefits (contrib 1973), Pension Law and Taxation (jtly 1985), Financial Aspects of Pension Business (jtly 1986), Financial Aspects of Life Business (jtly 1987), A Mastership of a Livery Company (1988); *Recreations* horse-riding, golf, winter sports; *Clubs* City Livery, Royal Over-Seas League; *Style—* Miss Sylvia I M Tutt; 21 Sandilands, Croydon, Surrey CRO 5DF(☎ 01 654 2995)

TUTTON, Brig John Theodore Stevenson; CBE (1960); s of Dr Alfred Edwin Howard Tutton (d 1938), and Margaret Ethel MacLannahan Tutton (d 1941); *b* 15 Feb 1907; *Educ* Winchester, Trinity Coll Cambridge (MA); *m* 1940, Diana Cicely, yst da of Henry Bryan Godfrey-Faussett-Osborne (d 1945), of Queendown Warren, Hartlip, Kent; 2 da (Caroline, Matilda); *Career* 2 Lt RE 1926, Lt-Col WWII, Brig 1957, AA and QMG N Malaya 1948-51, CRE Kent 1951-53, Col E War Office 1953-56, chief engr Malaya 1956-59, dir Engr Equipment WO 1959-62 (ret); *Recreations* gardening, bell ringing; *Style—* Brig John Tutton, CBE; Woodend Cottage, Awre, Newnham, Glos GL14 1EP (☎ 0594 510371)

TUZO, Gen Sir Harry Craufurd; GCB (1973, KCB 1971), OBE (1961), MC (1945), DL (Norfolk 1983); s of John Tuzo and Annie, *née* Craufurd; *b* 26 August 1917; *Educ* Wellington, Oriel Coll Oxford (MA, hon fell); *m* 1943, Monica Salter; 1 da; *Career* WWII RA, on staff Far East 1946-49, RHA, Staff Sch Inf, GSO1 WO, Cdr 51 Gurkha Bde, Imperial Def Coll, chief of staff BAOR 1967-69, dir RA 1969-71, GOC and dir ops NI 1971-73, Gen 1973, cdr N Army Gp and C-in-C BAOR 1973-76, Dep Supreme Allied Cdr Europe 1976-78, ADC Gen to HM The Queen 1974-77; Col Cmdt RA 1971-83, and RHA 1976-83; chm Royal Utd Servs Inst 1980-83; chm Marconi Space and Def Systems 1979-83; master gunner St James's Park 1977-83; cncl memb Inst Study of Conflict; govr Wellington Coll 1977-87; chm King's Lynn Festival and Fermoy Centre 1982-87, Pensthorpe Wildfowl Tst 1986-; pres Norfolk Soc 1987-; *Clubs* Army and Navy; *Style—* Gen Sir Harry Tuzo, GCB, OBE, MC, DL; Heath Farmhouse, Fakenham, Norfolk NR21 8LZ (☎ 0328 3290)

TWEDDLE, Lady; Sheila; da of Dr C S Vartan, of Nottingham; *m* 1941, Sir William Tweddle, CBE, TD (d 1982), sometime chm Yorkshire RHA; 1 s (John), 1 da (Judy); *Style—* Lady Tweddle; Red Roof Mews, 41 Wetherby Rd, Leeds LS8 2JU (☎ 651506)

TWEED, David John; s of William Tweed, of 1 Hockenhall Crescent, Tarvin, Chester, and Margaret, *née* Gittus (d 1984); *b* 14 Dec 1946; *Educ* The King's Sch Chester, Manchester Univ (BA, BArch); *m* 26 April 1980, Helen Elspeth Hamilton, da of Frank Hamilton-Leckie, MD, TD, of Monklands, Uddington, Glasgow; 1 da (Hilary b 1986); *Career* founded John Assocs Architects Chester; pres Cheshire Soc of Architects 1985-86; memb: RIBA NW Regnl 1983-87, RIBA NW Educn Ctee 1987-, cncl The Architects Benevolent Soc 1986-; chm Mgmnt Ctee of Claverton Ct Chester 1985-; memb: cncl Chester Civic Tst 1986-, Chester Historic Buildings Preservation Tst 1987-, Chester Sprots and Leisure Assoc 1984-; chm Info and Interpretation Gp and memb of Steering Ctee Presenting Chester; RIBA 1974, ACIArb 1983; *Recreations* rowing, sailing, squash, boatbuilding; *Style—* David Tweed, Esq; 14 Victoria Pathway, Queens Park, Chester (☎ 0244 683179); Duncraig House, Salen, Argyll; John Tweed Associates, Chapel House, City Road, Chester CG1 3AE (☎ 0244 310388, fax 0244 325643)

TWEED, Jill (Mrs Hicks); da of late Maj Jack Robert Lowrie Tweed, and Kathleen Janie, *née* Freeth; *b* 7 Dec 1935; *Educ* Slade Sch of Art (BA); *m* Philip Lionel Sholto Hicks, s of Brig P Hicks; 1 s (David b 1971), 1 da (Nicola b 1960); *Career* sculptor; solo and gp exhibitions incl: New Grafton Gallery 1975, Royal Acad 1979, Embankment Gallery 1979, Festival Hall 1980, Barbican Centre 1981, Poole-Willis Gallery NYC 1984; cmmns incl: HM The Queen Elizabeth the Queen Mother 1980, HRH Prince Charles and Lady Diana Spencer 1981, HE The Governor of Guernsey; ARBS; *Recreations* horse riding; *Style—* Ms Jill Tweed; 15 Cleveland Rd, Barnes, London SW13 0AA (☎ 01 876 7889)

TWEEDIE, Hon Mrs (Prudence Mary); *née* Addington; eld da of 6 Viscount Sidmouth; *b* 11 June 1916; *m* 1 July 1939, Lt Cdr Hugo Edward Forbes Tweedie, DSC, RN, s of late Adm Sir Hugh Tweedie, KCB; 4 s, 3 da; *Style—* The Hon Mrs Tweedie; 8 Stafford Street, Boston, Lincs PE21 96N

TWEEDIE-SMITH, John Ian; s of Leslie Tweedie-Smith; *b* 17 Feb 1929; *Educ* Stowe; *m* 1954, Gillian Mary; 4 children; *Career* co dir; memb London CC 1961-65; md Rawlplug Co Ltd 1968-73, chm E H Mundy & Co Ltd 1977- (gp md 1973-75); *Recreations* swimming, golf; *Style—* John Tweedie-Smith, Esq; c/o EH Mundy & Co Ltd; The Albany Boathouse, Lower Ham Rd, Kingston Upon Thames, Surrey KT2 5BB

TWEEDSMUIR, 2 Baron (UK 1935); John Norman Stuart Buchan; CBE (1964, OBE 1945), CD (1964); s of 1 Baron Tweedsmuir, GCMG, GCVO, CH, sometime Govr-Gen Canada (the writer John Buchan, d 1940) and Susan Charlotte (d 1977), da of Hon Norman Grosvenor (s of 1 Baron Ebury); *b* 25 Nov 1911; *Educ* Eton, BNC Oxford; *m* 1, 1948, Priscilla Jean Fortescue (later Baroness Tweedsmuir of Belhelvie, PC; d 1978); 1 da; m 2 1980, Jean Margharita, da of late Capt Humphrey Douglas Tollemache, RN (gs of 1 Baron Tollemache), and widow of Capt Sir Francis Cullen Grant, 12 Bt; *Heir* bro, Hon William De L'Aigle Buchan; *Career* late Lt-Col Canadian Infantry Corps; HM Colonial Serv Uganda 1934-36; rector of Aberdeen Univ 1948-51; chm Jt East and Central African Bd 1950-52, UK delegate UN Assembly 1951-52, Council of Europe 1952, pres Cwealth and British Empire Chambers of Commerce 1955-57; govr: Cwealth Inst 1958-77 (tstee 1977-), Ditchley Fndn; pres: Inst of Rural Life at Home and Overseas 1951-84, London branch Oxford Soc, Inst of Export 1964-67, British Schs Exploring Soc 1964-85; chm: Advertising Standards Authy 1971-74, Cncl on Tbnls 1973-80, British Rheumatism and Arthritis Assoc 1971-78 (pres 1978-), chm West End bd Sun Alliance Insurance plc; Hon LLD Aberdeen, Queen's (Canada); FRSA, FRSE; *Recreations* fishing, forestry; *Clubs* Carlton, Travellers', Pratt's, Flyfishers'; *Style—* The Rt Hon the Lord Tweedsmuir, CBE, CD; Kingston House, Kingston Bagpuize, Oxon (☎ 0865 820259);

TWEEDY, Colin David; s of Clifford Harry Tweedy, of Abbotsbury, Dorset, and Kitty Audrey, *née* Matthews; *b* 26 Oct 1953; *Educ* City of Bath Boys Sch, St Catherine's Coll Oxford (MA); *Career* mangr Thorndike Theatre Leatherhead 1976-78, corp fin offr Guinness Mahon 1978-80, asst dir Streets Financial PR 1980-83, dir and chief exec Assoc for Business Sponsorship of the Arts 1983-; memb UK nat ctee Euro Cinema and TV Year 1988-89, memb exec ctee Japan Festival 1991; dir Oxford Stage Co, tstee Crusaid; Freeman City of London 1978; *Books* A Celebration of Ten Year's Business Sponsorship of the Arts (1987); *Clubs* Utd Oxford and Cambridge; *Style—* Colin Tweedy, Esq; 2 Chester St, London SW1X 7BB (☎ 01 235 9781)

TWEEDY, Brig (Oliver) Robert; s of Cdr G J D Tweedy, OBE, RN (d 1969), and V E Maurice (d 1984); *b* 4 Feb 1930; *Educ* Sedbergh, RMA Sandhurst; *m* 11 Aug 1956, April Dawn, da of E T Berrangé; 2 s (Christopher b 1962, Andrew b 1964), 1 da (Sareth b 1959); *Career* cmmnd The Black Watch 1949; CO 1 BW Scotland, N Ireland and Hong Kong 1971-73; cdr British Advsy Team Nigeria 1980-82; cdr 51 Highland Brigade 1982-84; ADC to HM The Queen 1983-85, ret 1985; *Recreations* golf, country pursuits; *Style—* Brig Robert Tweedy; Inverbraan, Little Dunkeld, Perthshire PH8 0AD; Commandant, Queen Victoria Sch, Dunblane, Perthshire FK15 0JY

TWELVETREES, Hon Mrs; Hon Catherine Simonne; *née* du Parcq; da of late Baron du Parcq (Life Peer); *m* 1939, Leslie Twelvetrees; children; *Style—* The Hon Mrs Twelvetrees; 14 Overdale Rd, Leicester

TWIGG, David Joseph; s of John Twigg (d 1960), of Tothby Manor, Lincs, and Edith Mary, *née* Waterfield (d 1982); *b* 7 Mar 1934; *Educ* Queen Elizabeth's Lincs; *m* 1, 9 May 1970 (m dis 1987), Hilary Ann, da of Maj Ronald Hedley Vickers (d 1977), of Gloucester; m 2, 15 July 1988, Nina, da of Ivan Prokopenko, of Moscow; *Career* Nat Serv RE 1958-60, serving Mil Engrg Experimental Estab Christchurch and No 1 Bomb Disposal Unit; civil engr Lincs and Bucks CC 1953-62, sr civil engr Huntingdonshire CC 1962-65, sr appts with consulting engrs 1965-70; ptnr: Donovan H Lee and Ptnrs Consulting Engrs 1970-79, The Henderson Busby Ptnrship Consulting Engrs (dir) 1979-82; fndr and sr ptnr: David Twigg Assocs 1983-, DTA Transportation Consulting Engrs and Planners 1987-; chm Merton Community Rels Cncl 1983; various offs Kingston Lib Assoc 1976-88; Parly candididate Wimbledon: (Lib) 1979, (Alliance) 1983; contested London SW Euro Seat 1984; CEng 1963, FICE 1973, FIHT 1968, MCONSE 1986; *Recreations* tennis, cricket, history; *Clubs* Nat Lib; *Style—* David Twigg, Esq; 87 Blenheim Gardens, Kingston Upon Thames, Surrey KT2 7BJ (☎ 01 549 3690); 91 East Hill, Wandsworth, London SW18 2QD (☎ 01 874 0834/3291, fax 01 877 1390)

TWIGG, Dr Graham Ira; s of John Twigg (d 1938), of Moscar, Derbyshire, and Lois, *née* Dearden (d 1975); *b* 15 Nov 1927; *Educ* Lady Manners Sch Bakewell, Sheffield Univ (BSc, PhD); *m* 29 Sept 1956, Mary Elizabeth, da of John William Hancock (d 1956), of Burrs Mount, Great Hucklow; 1 s (Dr John David Twigg); *Career* RAF 1945-48; colonial rodent liaison offr Colonial Office 1958-59, lectr Univ of London 1959-; former sec and Capt Royal Ascot Cricket Club; FZS 1960; *Books* The Brown Rat (1975), The Black Death: A biological reappraisal (1984); *Style—* Dr Graham Twigg; 6 Wentworth Way, Ascot, Berks SL5 8HU (☎ 0344 884442); Dept of Biology, Royal Holloway & Bedford New College, Egham, Surrey (☎ 0784 335553)

TWINCH, Richard William; s of Richard Herbert Twinch, of Burleydam House, Burleydam, Whitchurch, Salop, and Roma Bayliss, *née* Silver; *b* 29 Oct 1950; *Educ* Wellington, Clare Coll Cambridge (MA, Architectural Assoc AADip); *m* Hazel Cecilia, da of James Herbert Merrison (d 1987); 1 s (Oliver b 1975), 2 da (Jemila b 1977, Anna b 1981); *Career* architect and special technol conslt; author of tech software for architects incl: Condensation Control 1981-87, Heat Loss Performance 1983-87; dir: Richard Twinch Design, Chisholme Inst Beshara Sch of Esoteric Educn; commentator to Beshara Magazine, lectr and conslt in CAD; computer columnist to Building Design & Atrium magazines, numerous articles on CAD in architectural press; papers incl: Thermal Insulation and Condensation and Building Materials (1988); RIBA; *Recreations* listening to music, walking, tennis; *Style—* Richard Twinch, Esq; 9 Redan St, Ipswich, Suffolk IP1 3PQ (☎ 0473 54605/210001)

TWINE, George Edward; s of late L H M Twine; *b* 29 Oct 1909; *Educ* Hurstpierpoint Coll, St Catharine's Coll Cambridge (MA, LLM); *m* 1939, Barbara Opal Onslow, *née* Perkins; 2 s; *Career* Maj RA, North Sea and India; slr of the Supreme Ct; memb Cncl of Nat Rifle Assoc; twice winner Queen's Prize at Bisley; pres English Twenty Club; *Recreations* target rifle and match rifle shooting, game shooting; *Style—* George Twine, Esq; Kolkinnon House, Up Nately, Basingstoke, Hants (☎ 025 672 2273)

TWINING, Hon John Peter; s of Baron Twining (Life Peer d 1967); *b* 8 June 1929; *Educ* Charterhouse, BNC Oxford; *m* 1954, Mary Avice, da of Brig Joseph Hector Dealy Bennett, CBE (d 1979); 2 s; *Career* Colonial Serv 1953-63; admin offr City & Guilds of London Inst 1963-78, chm Guildford Educnl Servs; ed: EDUCA, Open Learning for Technicians (1982); *Style—* The Hon John Twining; 3 The Ridgeway, Guildford, Surrey

TWINING, Prof William Lawrence; s of Baron Twining (Life Peer d 1967); *b* 1934; *Educ* Charterhouse, BNC Oxford, Chicago Univ (JD, LLD, MA); *m* 1957, Penelope Elizabeth, da of Richard Wall Morris; 1 s, 1 da; *Career* prof of jurisprudence Queen's Univ Belfast 1965-72, prof of law Warwick Univ 1972-82, Quain prof of jurisprudence UCL 1983-; pres Soc of Public Teachers of Law 1978-79; chm Cwlth Legal Educn Assoc 1983-; *Books* Karl Llewellyn and the Realist Movement (1973), How to do Things with Rules (2 edn, with David Miers, 1982), Theories of Evidence: Bentham & Wigmore (1985); *Style—* Prof William Twining; 10 Mill Lane, Iffley, Oxford OX4 4EJ

TWINN, Dr Ian David; MP (C) Edmonton 1983-; s of David Twinn and Gwynneth Irene, *née* Ellis; *b* 26 April 1950; *Educ* Netherhall Secdy Modern Sch, Cambridge GS for Boys, Univ Coll of Wales Aberystwyth, Reading Univ (BA, PhD); *m* 1973, Frances Elizabeth, da of Godfrey Nall Holtby, of Poltesco Cornwall; 2 s (David b 1983, John b 1986); *Career* sr lectr in Town Planning Southbank Poly; PPS to Rt Hon Peter Morrison, MP, hon sec all-party Parly Greek ctee; *Recreations* antique furniture restoration, collecting second-hand books; *Style—* Dr Ian Twinn, MP; House of Commons, London SW1A 0AA (☎ 01 219 3512)

TWISLETON-WYKEHAM-FIENNES *see also*: Fiennes

TWISLETON-WYKEHAM-FIENNES, Audrey, Lady; Audrey Joan; da of Sir Percy Wilson Newson, 1 and last Bt; sis of Dowager Lady Napier and Ettrick; *b* 21 July 1912; *Educ* Heathfield; *m* 1931, Lt-Col Sir Ranulph Twisleton-Wykeham-Fiennes, 2 Bt, DSO (d of wounds received in action 1943), s of Col Hon Sir Eustace T-W-F 1 Bt (2 s of 17 Baron Saye and Sele); 1 s (present Bt), 3 da (Susan, m 1957 Lt-Col John Scott, Blues and Royals, Celia, m 1963 Dr Robert Brown, Gillian m 1960 Timothy Hoult); *Style—* Audrey, Lady Twisleton-Wykeham-Fiennes; Robins, Lodsworth, W Sussex GU28 9DE

TWISLETON-WYKEHAM-FIENNES, Sir John Saye Wingfield; KCB (1970, CB 1953), QC (1972); 3 s of Gerard Twisleton-Wykeham-Fiennes, CBE (d 1926, s of Rev Hon Wingfield Twisleton-Wykeham-Fiennes, 4 s of 16 Baron Saye and Sele); *b* 14 April 1911; *Educ* Winchester, Balliol Coll Oxford; *m* 1 Sep 1937, Sylvia (d 1979), da of Rev Charles McDowall (d 1956); 2 s, 1 da; *Career* barr; served Parly Counsel Off 1939-76, first Parly counsel 1968-72 ; *Style*— Sir John Twisleton-Wykeham-Fiennes, KCB, QC; Mill House, Preston St Mary, Sudbury, Suffolk (☎ 0787 247125)

TWISLETON-WYKEHAM-FIENNES, Sir Maurice Alberic; s of Alberic Twisleton-Wykeham-Fiennes (d 1919, himself gs of 16 Baron Saye and Sele) and Gertrude Colley, paternal ggda of 4 Viscount Harberton, and ggda through her mother of 4 Viscount Powerscourt; *b* 1 Mar 1907; *Educ* Repton, Armstrong Coll Newcastle; *m* 1, 1932 (m dis 1963), Sylvia, da of Maj David Finlay; 2 s, 3 da; m 2, 1967, Erika, da of Dr Herbert Hueller von Huellenried, of Vienna; *Career* Lt Suffolk Yeo; engrg apprentice with Ransomes and Rapier; engr: Armstrong Whitworth, Utd Steel Cos, Brush Electrical Engrg; md and later chm Davy-Ashmore Gp; govr Yehudi Menuhin Sch 1969-84; CEng, FIMechE; kt 1965; *Recreations* music; *Clubs* Carlton, Naval and Military; *Style*— Sir Maurice Twisleton-Wykeham-Fiennes; 11 Heath Rise, Kersfield Rd, Putney Hill, London SW15 3HF (☎ 01 785 7489)

TWISLETON-WYKEHAM-FIENNES, Very Rev the Hon Oliver William; s of 20 Baron Saye and Sele, OBE, MC (d 1968), and Hersey Cecilia Hester (d 1968), da of Capt Sir Thomas Dacres Butler, KCVO; *b* 17 May 1926; *Educ* Eton, New Coll Oxford (MA); *m* 26 June 1956, Juliet, yr da of Dr Trevor Braby Heaton, OBE; 2 s, 2 da; *Career* late Lt Rifle Bde; ordained 1954, rector of Lambeth 1963-68, dean of Lincoln 1968-89, dean emeritus 1989; CStJ; *Style*— The Very Rev the Hon Oliver Twisleton-Wykeham-Fiennes; Home Farm House, Colsterworth, nr Grantham, Lincs NG33 5NE (☎ 0476 860811)

TWISLETON-WYKEHAM-FIENNES, Sir Ranulph; 3 Bt (UK 1916); s of Lt-Col Sir Ranulph Twisleton-Wykeham-Fiennes, 2 Bt, DSO (d 1943, gs of 17 Baron Saye and Sele), and Audrey, Lady Twisleton-Wykeham-Fiennes, *qv*; *b* 7 Mar 1944, (posthumously); *Educ* Eton, Mons; *m* 1970, Virginia, da of Thomas Pepper; *Career* Capt Royal Scots Greys, Capt 22 SAS Regt 1966; ret; author and explorer, leader of the first polar circumnavigation of earth, the Transglobe Expedition that arrived back in UK in Sept 1982 after 3 years non-stop travel; Man of the Year Award 1982; awarded: French Parachute Wings 1968, Gold Medal of New York Explorers Club 1984, Livingstone Gold Medal by Royal Scottish Geographical Soc 1983, Fndr's Medal of RGS 1984; Dhofar Campaign Medal 1968, Sultan's Bravery Medal 1970; awarded the Polar Medal by HM The Queen 1987 (wife is only woman to have received Polar Medal); *Books* Talent for Trouble (1968), Icefall in Norway (1971), The Headless Valley (1972), Where Soldiers Fear to Tread (1975), Hell on Ice (1978), To the Ends of the Earth: Transglobe Expedition 1979-82 (1983), Bothie The Polar Dog (1984, co written with wife), Living Dangerously (1987); *Recreations* travel, photography; *Style*— Sir Ranulph Twisleton-Wykeham-Fiennes, Bt; Greenlands, Exford, nr Minehead, W Somerset TA24 7NU (☎ 064 383 350)

TWISS, Charles Edward Hartley; s of Edward Whalley Twiss (d 1983), of Grappenhall, Cheshire, and Margaret Gertrude, *née* Hartley; *b* 10 April 1943; *Educ* Boteler GS Warrington Cheshire, Hertford Coll Oxford (MA); *m* 6 Oct 1967, Sylvia, da of Frank Ellis (d 1968), of Elland, W Yorks; 1 s (Simon Charles Ellis b 1971), 1 da (Rebecca Catherine b 1973); *Career* slr 1967; ptnr Streat Daunt & Farmiloe Southampton 1969-76, asst controller (legal) London Borough of Harrow 1976-80, slr to the bd Eastern Electricity 1980-85; HQ dir of legal servs, Br Gas plc 1985-; *Recreations* tennis, sailing, music; *Clubs* Royal Harwich Yacht; *Style*— Charles Twiss, Esq; Mallards, Martins Lane, Polstead, nr Colchester (☎ 0206 262093); British Gas plc, Rivermill House, 152 Grosvenor Rd, London (☎ 01 821 1444, telex 938529)

TWISS, Adm Sir Frank Roddam; KCB (1965, CB 1962), KCVO (1978), DSC (1945); s of Col E K Twiss, DSO, and Margaret Edmondson Twiss, *née* Tate (d 1950); *b* 7 July 1910; *Educ* RNC Dartmouth; *m* 1, 1936, Prudence (d 1974), da of Rear Adm John de Mestre Hutchison, CMG (d 1932); 2 s, 1 da; m 2, 1978, Rosemary Maitland, *née* Howe, wid of Capt Denis Chilton, RN; *Career* joined RN 1924, Rear Adm 1960, Naval Sec to First Lord of Admiralty 1960-62, Flag Offr Flotillas Home Fleet 1962-64, Cdr Far E Fleet 1965-67, Adm 1967, Second Sea Lord and Chief of Naval Personnel 1967-70; gentleman usher of the Black Rod House of Lords 1970-78 (serjeant-at-arms House of Lords and sec to Lord Great Chamberlain 1971-78), memb Cwlth War Graves Cmmn 1970-79; younger bro of Trinity House 1956-; *Clubs* Army and Navy; *Style*— Admiral Sir Frank Twiss, KCB, KCVO, DSC; East Marsh Farm, Bratton, nr Westbury, Wilts

TWISS, (Lionel) Peter; OBE (1956), DSC (1942, and bar 1943); s of Col Dudley Cyril Twiss, South Staffordshire Regt (d 1964), of Lindfield Sussex, and Laura Georgina Smith, *née* Chapman (d 1980); *b* 23 July 1921; *Educ* Sherborne; *m* 1, Oct 1944; m 2, 1949; 2 da (Joanna d 1954, Sarah b 1954); m 3, 1960; 1 da (Miranda b 1961); m 4, 4 Nov 1964, Heather Linda, da of Strachan Goldingham (d 1981), of Palmerston North, NI, New Zealand; *Career* fleet air arm 804 sqdn 1939-46, Med Convoys 807 Sqdn, Nightfighters 1 Seafire Sqndn N Africa Op Torch, NFIU, Br Air Cmmn Patuxent River USA, A & AEE Boscombe Down Empire Test Pilots Sch, Naval Test Sqdn A & AEE Lt RNVR; Fairey Aviation test pilot 1946-60, chief test pilot 1957; Worlds absolute speed record 1956; Fairey Marine sales mangr; dir: Fairey Marine, Fairey Yacht Harbours; gen mangr and dir Hamble Point Marina; *Recreations* ornithology, yachting, gardening; *Clubs* Royal London Yacht, Royal Southern Yacht, Island Sailing; *Style*— Peter Twiss, Esq, OBE, DSC; Nettleworth, 33 South St, Titchfield, Hampshire PO14 4DL; Hamble Point Marina Ltd, School Lane, Hamble Southampton SO3 5NB (☎ 0703 452464, telex 47235, fax 0703 456440)

TWIST, Stephen John; s of James Twist, of Darlington, Co Durham, and Kathleen Marion, *née* Gamble; *b* 26 Sept 1950; *Educ* Queen Elizabeth GS Darlington, Liverpool Univ (LLB); *Career* former policy offr Met Police; called to the Bar Middle Temple 1979; memb: Hon Soc of Middle Temple, Hon Soc Gray's Inn; *Style*— Stephen Twist, Esq; 2 Harcourt Bldgs, Temple, London EC4Y 9DB

TWISTON-DAVIES, Audley William; s of William Anthony Twiston-Davies, DL (d 1989), of The Mynde, Much Dewchurch, Herefordshire, and Rosemary, *née* Archdale; *b* 13 Nov 1950; *Educ* Radley; *m* 9 Feb 1985, Hon Caroline Harbord-Hamond, da of Lord Suffield, of Wood Norton, Dereham, Norfolk; 1 da (Antonia Rose b 22 Oct 1987); *Career* dir: For & Colonial Mgmnt Ltd, Brazilian Securties Ltd, Brazilain Investmt Co; Liveryman Haberdashers Co; *Clubs* City; *Style*— Audley Twiston-Davies, Esq; 67 Oakley Gardens, London SW3 (☎ 01 351 4796); 1 Laurence Pountney Hill, London EC4 (☎ 01 929 2701, fax 01 621 9589)

TWISTON-DAVIES, Hon Mrs (Caroline Mary Elaine); *née* Harbord-Hamond; da of 11 Baron Suffield, MC; *b* 15 Dec 1960; *m* 1985 (m dis 1987), Audley William Twiston-Davies, er s of William Anthony Twiston-Davies (d 1989), of The Mynde, Much Dewchurch, Hereford, and his w Rosemary, *née* Archdale (gda of Rt Hon Sir Edward Mervyn Archdale, 1 Bt); *Style*— The Hon Mrs Twiston-Davies; 67 Oakley Gardens, London SW3

TWITE, Robin; s of Reginald John Twite (d 1973), of Rugby, Warwicks, and May Elizabeth Twite (d 1963); *b* 2 May 1932; *Educ* Lawrence Sheriff Sch Rugby, Balliol Coll Oxford (MA); *m* 1, July 1955 (m dis 1979), Sally Patricia, *née* Randall; 1 s (Daniel b 7 Feb 1963); m 2, 25 March 1980, Sonia, *née* Yaari; 3 step da (Naomi b 1952, Zohara b 1954, Lital b 1963); *Career* RCS 1950-52; Br Cncl 1955-87: sec overseas students fees awards SCITECH 1966-68, rep Israel 1968-73, rep Calcutta 1980-84, controller books libraries and info 1984-87, resigned 1987; sec Open Univ of Israel 1973-76, advsr to chm Hebrew Univ Res and Devpt Authy; *Recreations* travel, meditation, free-lance journalism; *Style*— Robin Twite, Esq, OBE; 45 Christchurch Ave, London NW6; 36 Gimel, Ein Kerem, Jerusalem, Israel; c/o Chairman, Hebrew Univ, Research and Dev Authority, Hebrew Univ, Jerusalem

TWIVY, Paul Christopher Barstow; s of Dr Samuel Barstow Twivy, of Dunstable, and Sheila, *née* Webster; *b* 19 Oct 1958; *Educ* Haberdashers' Aske's Sch, Magdalen Coll Oxford (BA); *m* 31 July 1982, Martha Mary Sladden; 2 s (Samuel b 1985, Joshua b 1988); *Career* bd dir Hedger Mitchell Stark 1982-83, md Still Price Court Twivy D'Souza 1984-; memb: steering ctee Comic Relief, exec ctee The Healthcare Fndn; spokesman for: advtg indust, RCN, Healthcare Fndn; memb Mktg Soc, MIPA; *Recreations* freelance comedy writer, playwright, poetry, reading, swimming, music: guitar and piano; *Clubs* Oxford Union, Groucho's; *Style*— Paul Twivy, Esq; 55D, Cavendish Rd, London NW6 (☎ 01 459 7953); Still Price Court Twivy D'Souza, 30 New Oxford St, London WC1A 1AP (☎ 01 636 3377, fax 01 631 4322)

TWYFORD, Donald Harry; s of Henry John Twyford (d 1982), of Crowborough, and Ferring Sussex, and Lily Hilda, *née* Ridler (d 1977); *b* 4 Feb 1931; *Educ* Wembley County Sch; *Career* Nat Serv Educn Branch 1949-51; joined ECGD 1949: sr princ (chief underwriter) 1968, asst sec 1972, estab offr 1976, under sec 1979, chm EC policy co-ordination Gp 1981, dir, chm Project Gp Bd 1986; *Style*— Donald H Twyford, Esq; Barbican, London; Ferring, W Sussex; ECGD, Export House, PO Box No.272, 50 Ludgate Hill, London EC4M 7AY (☎ 01 382 7043); Javea, Spain

TWYFORD, Sidney Hamilton; s of Robert James Twyford (d 1924), and Sarah Hamilton, *née* Taylor (d 1937); *b* 6 Oct 1906; *m* 16 Feb 1943, Williamina, da of Donald Campbell MacDonald (d 1936); 3 s (Robert b 28 March 1945, John b 20 June 1946, d 1946, Kenneth b 2 Oct 1947); *Career* WWII 1939-45: hon artillery boy 1939, cmmnd 2 Lt RA 1940, Acting Maj, War Substantive Capt 1945; md Campbell Hamilton & Co Ltd 1950-86, memb Lloyds 1977; Freeman City of London 1977, Liveryman Worshipful Co of Upholders 1977; MIOD 1958; *Recreations* rugby, hockey, cricket; *Clubs* RAC, Caledonian, The City Livery; *Style*— Sidney Twyford, Esq; Flat 2, Braidley, Cliffe Drive, Canford Cliffs, Dorset; Longwood Hse, Heather Close, Kingswood (☎ 0737 832 947)

TWYMAN, Paul Hadleigh; s of late Lawrence Alfred Twyman, and Gladys Mary, *née* Williams; *b* 24 July 1943; *Educ* Chatham House Sch Ramsgate, Univ of Sheffield (BA), LSE (MSc); *Career* schoolmaster 1963-64; Civil Serv: asst princ Bd of Trade 1967-71, memb Secretariat Cmmn on the Third London Airport 1969-71, private sec to Sec of State for Trade and Indust 1971-83, princ anti-dumping unit DTI 1976-78, asst sec and head of overseas projects gp DTI 1978-81, civil aviation div 1981-83, Dept of Tport 1983, Cabinet Off 1984, under sec and dir enterprise and deregulation unit Dept of Employment 1985-87; econ advsr to chm of Cons Pty and head of econ section Cons Res Dept 1987, chm and chief exec Political Strategy Ltd 1988; dir: Anglia Bldg Soc 1983, Nationwide Anglia Bldg Soc 1987-; Irospective Euro Parly candidate Greater Manchester 1989-; FBIM; *Recreations* hill walking, gardening, observing gorillas; *Style*— Paul Twyman, Esq; 2 St James's Sq, London SW1Y 4JN (☎ 01 839 3422)

TYACKE, Maj-Gen David Noel Hugh; CB (1970), OBE (1957); s of Capt Charles Noel Walker Tyacke (ka 1918), and Phoebe Coulthard (d 1969); *b* 18 Nov 1915; *Educ* Malvern, RMA Sandhurst; *m* 1940, Diana, da of Aubrey Hare Duke (d 1972); 1 s (Nicholas); *Career* cmmnd DCLI 1935 RA, cmd 1 Bn DCLI 1957-59, cmd 130 Inf Bde (TA) 1961-63, GOC Singapore District 1966-70; *Recreations* walking, motoring, bird watching; *Style*— Maj-Gen David Tyacke, CB, OBE; c/o Lloyds Bank, 6 Pall Mall, London SW1Y 5NH

TYACKE, Maj Humphry John; s of Col Ashley John Tyacke (d 1985), of Grayswood, Fareham, Hampshire, and L M A Tyacke (d 1984); direct descendant of Sir Joseph Paxton, creator of the Crystal Palace; *b* 4 Dec 1930; *Educ* Wellington, RMA Sandhurst; *m* 17 Sept 1980, Barbara Mary, da of W E Hunter (surgeon) (d 1980), of Cefn Mawr Hall, nr Mold, Flintshire; 2 step s (Anthony b 1951, Michael b 1954); *Career* Maj 13/18 Royal Hussars (Queen Mary's Own): Malaya, Aden, Malaysia, Falkland Islands; *Recreations* sailing; *Style*— Maj Humphry Tyacke; Crossways, Hoe, Dereham, Norfolk (☎ 860550); Mijas (Spain)

TYE, Alan; *b* 18 Sept 1933; *Educ* Regent St Poly Sch of Architecture (Dip Arch, RIBA); *m* 1966, Anita Brigitta, Goethe-Tye; 2 s (Nicolas b 1969, Kevin b 1973), 1 da (Madeleine b 1967); *Career* formed Alan Tye Design 1962-; civic tst award assessor 1968, 1969, visiting tutor RCA 1978-83 (external assessor 1987-), specialist advsr on Ind Design CNAA 1980, London regnl assessor RIBA 1981, RSA bursary judge 1983-87; recipient Int Design Prize Rome 1962, Cncl of Ind Design Award 1965 (1966, 1981), Br Aluminium Design Award 1966, 1 prize GAI award 1969, Observer (London) Design award 1969, Ringling Mus of Art (Fla) award 1969, Gold Medal Graphic Design 1970, 1 Prize GAI award Int Bldg Exhibn 1971, British Aluminium Eros Trophy 1973, 4 Awards for Design Excellence Aust 1973, Commendation for Arch 1977, IBD Int Award (NY) 1982, Internat Bldg Exhibits Top Design Award 1983 (1985), memb selection ctee cncl of Industl Design 1967, Royal Designer for Indust 1986; *Recreations* tai chi, aikido, badminton, fly dressing; *Style*— Alan Tye, Esq; Great West Plantation, Tring, Herts HP23 6DA (☎ 044282 5353, telex 826715 Aero G, fax 044282 7723)

TYLDESLEY, Reginald George; s of Bertrand Joseph Jennings Tyldesley (d 1966), of Woking, and Isabel, *née* Hughes (d 1972); *b* 4 Sept 1923; *Educ* Lancing; *Career* RAC; Sandhurst 1943-44, cmmnd 1944, attached Royal Mil Police 1944-47, served in India, Malaya, French Indochina, Java, appt Capt and Dep Asst Provost Marshall 1945, dep asst cmmr of Police Batavia Djakarta 1946; CA 1949, Deloitte Haskins & Sells 1947-84, ret as sr mangr; dir Friends of St Paul's Enterprises Ltd 1987-; cncl memb Friends of St Paul's Cathedral; memb: Royal Hort Soc, Horsellcommon Preservation Soc, Surrey & Hampshire Canal Soc, Genealogical Soc; Freeman City of London 1959, Liveryman Worshipful Co of Goldsmiths 1959; FCA; *Recreations* genealogy, gardening, fine arts, conservation; *Clubs* Royal Overseas League; *Style*— Reginald Tyldesley, Esq; Craigmore, Horsell Park, Woking, Surrey GU21 4LW (☎ 048 62 724 96)

TYLDESLEY, Robert John Ross; s of John Tyldesley; *b* 3 Feb 1935; *Educ* Headlands GS, London Sch of Economics, London Univ; *m* Cynthia Ann; 1 s, 1 da; *Career* former md F Hewitt & Son Ltd, dir and gen mangr Wester Morning News Co Ltd Plymouth, md Western Mail & Echo, Cardiff, Thomson Regnl Newspapers Ltd, Watford; cncl memb: Newspaper Soc, Cwlth Press Union; *Recreations* skiing, shooting; *Clubs* Royal Western Yacht, Cardiff and County; *Style*— Robert Tyldesley, Esq; Glan Avon Lodge, Peterston Super Ely, South Glamorgan

TYLER, Arthur Catchmay (Hugh); CBE (1960), MC (1945), DL (Surrey 1968); s of Hugh Griffin Tyler, JP (d 1953), of Cleddon House, nr Monmouth, and Muriel Barnes (d 1976); *b* 20 August 1913; *Educ* Allhallows Sch, RMC Sandhurst; *m* 1938, Sheila Maysie, da of James Kinloch, of Meigle, Perthshire; 3 s, 1 da; *Career* WWII serv Africa, Burma (despatches), Bt-Lt-Col 1953, Col 1957, Brig 1960, sec British Jt Servs Mission Washington 1952-54, WO 1957-60, sr UK liaison offr and mil advsr to High Cmmr Canada 1960-63, asst COS Allied Forces Centl Europe 1963-65, sec Cncl of TA and VR Assocs 1965-72, Hon Col 7 (V) Bn The Queens Regt 1971-75; govr Allhallows Sch 1967 (chm 1976-79); Mil Knight of Windsor 1978-; *Style*— Brig A C Tyler, CBE, MC, DL; 19 Lower Ward, Windsor Castle, Berks SL4 1NJ (☎ 0753 851471)

TYLER, Maj-Gen Christopher; CB (1989); s of Maj-Gen Sir Leslie Tyler, KBE, CB, *qv*, of Liphook, Hants, and Louie Teresa, *née* Franklin (d 1950); *b* 9 July 1934; *Educ* Beaumont Coll Old Windsor, RMA Sandhurst, Trinity Coll Cambridge (MA); *m* 12 July 1958, Suzanne, da of (Hubert John) Patrick Whitcomb (d 1962); 1 s (William 1959), 3 da (Catherine b 1961, Louisa b 1965, Sophie b 1967); *Career* cmmnd REME 1954, Army Staff Coll 1966-67, Lt-Col CO 1 Parachute Logistic Regt 1974-76, asst mil sec (MS6) 1976-77, Col Asst Adj Gen (AG21) 1977-80, chief aircraft engr Army Air Corps 1980-82, Brig Dir EME Mgmnt Servs 1982-83, cdr maintenance 1 (BR) Corps 1983-85, Dep Cmdt Royal Mil Coll of Sci 1985-87, Maj-Gen dep chief of staff (support) HQ AFNORTH 1987-89; hon sec RFU Referee Advsy Panel 1979-83; memb Worshipful Co of Turners 1979; CEng 1964, FRAES 1981, FIMechE 1982, FBIM 1982; *Recreations* most sports but especially Rugby Union Football; *Clubs* Lansdowne; *Style*— Maj-Gen Christopher Tyler, CB; c/o Lloyds Bank plc, 19 Obelisk Way, Camberley, Surrey GU15 3SE; HQ AFNORTH, BFPO 50, Oslo (☎ 02 47 21 18)

TYLER, Maj-Gen Sir Leslie Norman; KBE (1961), OBE (1942, CB 1955); s of Maj Norman Tyler, RA (TA) (d 1931), and Aurora Tyler (d 1930); *b* 26 April 1904; *Educ* Diocesan Coll S Africa, RNC Osborne and Dartmouth, King's Coll London (BSc Eng); *m* 1, 1930, Louie Teresa (d 1950), da of Lt-Col R J Franklin (d 1944); 1 s, 1 da; m 2, 1953, Sheila, wid of Maj-Gen L H Cox, CB, CBE, MC (d 1949); 2 s, 2 step da; *Career* Lt RAOC 1927, transfd REME 1942, Brig WWII, served Malta, NW Europe; DEME War Off 1957-60 (ret); regnl dir Miny of Public Bldg and Works Central Mediterranean 1963-69, chm and vice chm Royal Hosp and Home for Incurables Putney 1970-81; Master Turners' Co 1982-83 (Upper Warden 1981-85); FIMechE, FKC; upper warden 1981-85; *Recreations* music, watching rugby football, cricket, lawn tennis; *Clubs* Army and Navy; *Style*— Maj-Gen Sir Leslie Tyler, KBE, CB; 51 Chiltley Way, Liphook, Hants GU30 7HE (☎ 0428 722335)

TYLER, Mary Caroline; da of Bernard Southcombe (d 1934), of Milborne Port, Somerset, and Caroline Edith, *née* Raves (d 1964); *b* 5 Sept 1921; *Educ* Sherborne Sch for Girls, Bedford Coll London (BA); *m* 4 Sept 1947, Frederick Lockwood Tyler, s of Frederick Richard Tyler (d 1956), of Whiteladies, Poole, Dorset; 1 s (Bernard b 1951), 3 da (Rosalind b 1949, Caroline b 1956, Elizabeth b 1959); *Career* campaigner for a Family Responsibility Benefit for mothers of young children; schizophrenia researcher; *Recreations* golf, archaeology; *Style*— Mrs Mary Tyler; 2 Corringway, London NW11 7ED (☎ 01 455 3123)

TYLER, Richard Michael Townsend; s of James Tyler-Stewart-Mackenzie (d 1956), of Brahan, Cononbridge, Ross-shire, and Kathleen Audrey, *née* Townsend (d 1941); *b* 9 Nov 1916; *Educ* Charterhouse, RWA Sch of Arch; *m* 15 July 1944, Anne Henrietta, er da of Cdr Sir Geoffrey Cecil Congreve, 1 Bt, DSO (ka 1942), of Congreve Manor, Staffs; 2 s (Christian b 1945, Felix b 1954), 2 da (Camilla b 1946, Amelia b 1950); *Career* served RE WWII, Capt wounded 1941 W Desert; architect; ptnr Bird and Tyler Assocs 1954-83, principally engaged on country houses and buildings for the disabled; Civic Tst Awards; ARIBA; *Clubs* Boodles; *Style*— Richard Tyler, Esq; Brachamfield House, Burstock, Beaminster, Dorset

TYLOR, John Edward; s of Maj Vyvian Alfred Tylor, MC (d 1968), and M S Tylor; *b* 1 July 1942; *Educ* Eton, Trinity Coll Dublin (MA); *m* 18 Oct 1975, Heather Catherine, da of Richard Alan Budgett, of Kirtlington, Oxon; 2 s (Sam Vyvian b 1980, Hugo Alexander b 1985); *Career* slr Herbert Smith & Co 1967-73, Samuel Montagu & Co 1973-, exec dir corp fin dept 1981-; *Recreations* field sports, polo; *Style*— John Tylor, Esq; Stud Farm, Chesterton, Bicester; 10 Lower Thames St, London EC2 (☎ 01 260 9000)

TYNAN, Prof Oliver; s of John Tynan (d 1949), and Ethelwyn Tynan, MBE (d 1980); *b* 3 April 1928; *Educ* Dragon Sch, Marlborough, Oxford Univ (BA), London Univ; *m* 1 Sept 1959, Carol, da of Arthur James Penrose Booth, of Craven Arms, Shropshire; 1 s (Christopher b 1957), 1 da (Clare b 1959); *Career* advsr on the human aspects of industry; visiting prof Brunel, The Univ of W London; dir: Work Res Univ ACAS 1979-86, Technet Ltd 1987-; *Recreations* wine making, gardening, goose breeding; *Clubs* Devonshire House Management; *Style*— Prof Oliver Tynan; Tudor Cottage, Brockley, Bury St Edmunds, Suffolk IP29 4AG (☎ 0284 830321)

TYREE, Daniel C; *b* 4 June 1948; *Educ* St Louis Univ (BA), Rutgers Grad Sch of Business (MBA), Rutgers Law Sch (JD) Degrees; *m* 1975, Teri L, da of Dwight Pattee, of 2079 Lincoln Lane, Salt Lake City, Utah, USA; 1 s (Ian Stuart b 19 Dec 1982), 1 da (Heather Alise b 7 Jan 1980); *Career* practised law on Wall St 1974-75; Salomon Brothers Inc 1975-: head equipment of lease fin gp, head of transportation lease fin and equipment gps, head of project fin gp, md head of int investmt banking 1984-; memb: NY and New Jersey Bar Assoc, Int Advsy Ctee NY Stock Exchange; *Clubs* Mark's, Annabel's, The Down Town Assoc of NY; *Style*— Daniel C Tyree, Esq; 45 Eaton Place, London SW1X 8DE; Salomon Brothers Int Ltd, Victoria Plaza, 111 Buckingham Palace Rd, London SW1W OSB (☎ 01 721 3777, fax 01 222 7062, telex 886441)

TYREE, Sir (Alfred) William; OBE (1971); s of J V Tyree; *b* 4 Nov 1921; *Educ* Auckland GS, Sydney Tech Coll; *m* 1946, Joyce, da of F Lyndon; 2 s, 1 da; *Career* fndr Tyree Industries Ltd; chm and fndr: Medicheck, Reinhausen (Aust) Pty Ltd, A W Tyree Fndn, Tycan Aust Pty Ltd, CPR Constructions Pty Ltd; pres Nat Assoc for Training the Disabled in Office and Computer Work; kt 1975; *Style*— Sir William Tyree, KCVO; 3 Lindsay Ave, Darling Point, NSW 2027, Australia

TYRELL-KENYON, Hon Lloyd; s and h of 5 Baron Kenyon, CBE; *b* 13 July 1947; *Educ* Eton, Magdalene Coll Cambridge; *m* 1971, Sally Carolyn, da of J F P Matthews, of The Firs, Thurston, Bury St Edmunds; 2 s; *Style*— The Hon Lloyd Tyrell-Kenyon; Gredington, Whitchurch, Shropshire SY13 3DH (☎ 094874 550)

TYRELL-KENYON, Hon Thomas; s of 5 Baron Kenyon, CBE; *b* 1954; *Style*— The Hon Thomas Tyrell-Kenyon

TYRER, Christopher John Meese; s of Jack Meese Tyrer, of 57 Thornhill Rd, Rhiwbina, Cardiff, South Glamorgan, Wales, and Margaret Joan, *née* Wyatt; *b* 22 May 1944; *Educ* Wellington, Bristol Univ (LLB); *m* 9 Feb 1974, (Monica) Jane, JP, da of Peter Beckett, of Daisy Nook, Carleton, Pontefract, Yorkshire; 1 s (David b 1981), 1 da (Rebecca b 1979); *Career* barr Inner Temple 1968; dep judiciary 1979 (dep judge 1979-82), asst rec 1982-83, rec 1983-; *Recreations* music, reading, photography, growing things; *Style*— Christopher Tyrer, Esq; Randalls Cottage, Loosley Row, Princes Risborough, Aylesbury, Bucks HP17 0NU (☎ 084 44 4650); Devereux Chambers, Devereux Ct, London WC2R 3JJ (☎ 01 353 7534)

TYRONE, Earl of; Henry Nicholas de la Poer Beresford; s and h of 8 Marquess of Waterford by his w Lady Caroline Wyndham-Quin, da of 6 Earl of Dunraven and Mount-Earl; *b* 23 Mar 1958; *Educ* Harrow; *m* 1986, Amanda, da of Norman Thompson, of The Castle, Boris in Ossory, Co Laois; 1 s; *Heir* s, Richard John (Baron la Poer) b 19 Aug 1987; *Style*— Earl of Tyrone; Garden House, Curraghmore, Portlaw, Co Waterford, Eire (T 051 87 186)

TYRRELL; *see*: Smyth-Tyrrell

TYRRELL, Alan Rupert; QC (1976), MEP (EDG) London East 1979-84; *b* 1933,June; *Career* barr Gray's Inn 1956, bencher 1986, rec Crown Ct 1972-; MEP (EDG) London East 1979-84, chm Bar European Gp 1986-88; chm Int Practice Ctee Bar Cncl 1988; *Style*— Alan Tyrrell, Esq, QC; 15 Willifield Way, Hampstead Garden Suburb, London NW11; 42 Rue du Taciturne, 1040 Bruxelles, Belgium; Francis Taylor Bldg, Temple, London EC4

TYRRELL, Lady Caroline Susan Elizabeth; da of late Lt-Col Lord Edward Douglas John Hay (3 s of 10 Marquess of Tweeddale) and sis of 12 Marquess; raised to the rank of a Marquess's da 1970; *b* 1930; *m* 1, 1953 (m dis 1970), Richard Noel Marshall Armitage; 2 s; m 2, 1970, Reginald Charles Tyrrell; *Style*— Lady Caroline Tyrrell; Capplegill, Moffat, Dumfriesshire

TYRRELL, Dr David Arthur John; CBE (1980); s of late Lt Col Sidney Charles Tyrrell, of Stalham, Norfolk, and Agnes, *née* Blewett; *b* 19 June 1925; *Educ* Ashford Co Sch Middx, King Edward VII Sch Sheffield, Sheffield Univ (MB ChB, MD); *m* 13 April 1950, Betty Moyra, da of Dr John Wylie, MC, of Woodlands, Doncaster, Yorks; 1 s (Stephen b 1955, d 1979), 2 da (Frances b 1951, Susan b 1953); *Career* res registrar Sheffield Utd Hosps 1950-51, asst physician and res asst Rockefeller Inst Hosp NY 1951-54, memb MRC scientific staff Virus Res Laboratory Univ of Sheffield 1954, Common Cold Unit Salisbury 1957 (head 1962), dir of WHO Virus Res Laboratory 1962, head div of communicable diseases Clinical Res Centre Harrow 1967-84 (dep dir 1970-84); hon conslt physician: West Hendon Hosp 1967-70, Northwick Park Hosp Harrow 1970-85, Wessex RHA 1985-; dir MRC Common Cold Unit Salisbury 1982-; chm ACDP; memb: governing body Animal Virus Disease Res Inst Pirbright, biological prods sub-ctee of Ctee on Safety of Med, steering ctee AIDS Directed Prog; The Rock Carling Lecture 1982, The Leewenhock Lecture; author of numerous scientific pubns; Hon DSc Univ of Sheffield 1979; FRCP 1965, FRS 1970, FRCPath 1971, memb Assoc of Physicians; hon memb: Infectious Disease Soc of America, Australian Soc of Infectious Diseases, American Assoc of Physicians; *Books* Common Colds and Related diseases (1965); *Recreations* music, gardening, walking; *Style*— Dr David Tyrrell, CBE; Ash Lodge, Dean Lane, Whiteparish, Salisbury SP5 2RN (☎ 0749 884 352); MRC Common Cold Unit, Harvard Hosp, Coombe Road, Salisbury SP2 8BW (☎ 0722 22485)

TYRRELL, George Edward; s of William George Tyrrell (d 1937); *b* 21 Sept 1920; *Educ* Whitgift Middle Sch Croydon; *m* 1950, Mildred Hilda; 1 s, 1 da; *Career* consulting engr; former dir of John Miles & Ptnrs (London) Ltd; chartered engineer; Freeman City of London; FIEE; *Recreations* shooting; *Clubs* IOD; *Style*— George Tyrrell, Esq; 1 Leigham Court, Dawlish, Devon (☎ 0626 867054)

TYRRELL, Prof Henry John Valentine; s of John Rice Tyrell (d 1954), of Prittlewell, Essex, and Josephine Magdalene, *née* MacGuinness (d 1960); *b* 14 Feb 1920; *Educ* Newport HS, Jesus Coll Oxford, (MA, BSc, DSc); *m* 1, 15 July 1947, Sheila Mabel, da of Philip Henry Straw (d 1985), of London; 3 s (Michael b 1948, Patrick b 1950, Sebastian b 1961), 3 da (Jennifer b 1951, Philippa b 1956, Fiona b 1965); m 2, Sept 1986 Bethan, da of Ben Davies; *Career* WWII RA 1939 (transfd to res) discharged 1942; scientific offr; ICI Gen Chemicals 1943-45, Br Non-Ferrous Metals Res Assoc 1945-47; memb academic staff Sheffield Univ 1947-65, prof physical chemistry Chelsea Coll Univ of London 1965-84 (princ 1984-85), vice-princ Kings Coll KQC Univ of London 1985-87; Royal Inst of GB: hon sec 1978-84, memb cncl 1985-, chm 1986-; chm cncl Greenacre Sch Banstead Surrey 1989; fell Royal Soc of Chemistry 1968; *Books* Diffusion and Heat Flow in Liquids (1961), Thermometric Titimetry (1968), Diffusion in Liquids (1984); *Recreations* music, walking, gardening; *Clubs* Athenaeum (memb gen ctee); *Style*— Prof Valentine Tyrrell; Fair Oaks, Coombe Hill Rd, Kingston-upon-Thames, KT2 7DU (☎ 01 949 6623)

TYRRELL, Jean Margaret; OBE (1982), DL (W Yorks 1983); da of Fredrick Harrap (d 1960), of Woodthorpe House, Wakefield, and Bertha Harrap (d 1977); *b* 1 July 1918; *Educ* St Leonards Sch St Andrews Fife, Geneva Univ; *m* 15 July 1944, James Hall Tyrrell, s of Robert Tyrrell (d 1942); 3 da (Susan Gaye (Mrs Ainslie), Anne Maureen (Mrs Upsdell), Carolyn Jane); *Career* served WWII with Mechanised Tport Corps; joined Harrap Bros (Sirdar Wools) Ltd 1939, dir Sirdar plc 1953 (jt md 1959, chm and md 1960); former memb: Local Manpower Services Cmmn, advsy ctee on Womens Employment (Dept of Employment); gen cmmr of taxes; Taxes; The Times Veuve Cliquot Business Woman of the Year 1980; hon vice-chm British Hand Knitting

Assoc; memb IOD; Hon LLD Leeds 1988; *Recreations* golf, sailing, bridge; *Clubs* Wakefield Golf; *Style—* Mrs Jean Tyrrell, OBE, DL; Sirdar Group, Bective Mills, Alverthorpe, Wakefield, W Yorks (☎ 0924 371501, fax 0924 290506, telex 557426); Invermor, 23 Woodthorpe Lane, Wakefield, W Yorks WF2 6JC (☎ 0924 255468); Reewaydin, Golf Rd, Abersoch, Gwynedd, N Wales

TYRRELL, Sir Murray Louis; KCVO (1968, CVO 1954), CBE (1959), JP; s of late Thomas Michael Tyrell and Florence Evelyn Tyrrell; *b* 1 Dec 1913; *Educ* Orbost HS, Melbourne HS; *m* 1939, Ellen St Clair, da of late E W St Clair Greig; 1 s, 2 da; *Career* private sec to mins of the Crown 1939-47, official sec to govr-gen of Australia 1947-74, comptroller 1947-53; attached Royal Household Buckingham Palace 1962; CStJ; *Style—* Sir Murray Tyrrell, KCVO, CBE, JP

TYRWHITT, John Edward Charles; s of Adm Sir St John Reginald Joseph Tyrwhitt, 2 Bt, KCB, DSO, DSC, and bro of Sir Reginald Tyrwhitt, 3 Bt; *b* 27 July 1953; *Educ* Worth Sch, Magdalene Coll Cambridge (MA); *m* 1978, Melinda Ngaire, da of Capt Anthony Philip Towell, MC, of Ridge Rd, Long Island, NY, USA; 3 s (St John b 5 Jan 1980, Oliver b 9 May 1982, Alexander b 15 Feb 1984); *Career* ACA; *Style—* John Tyrwhitt, Esq

TYRWHITT, Dame Mary Joan Caroline; DBE (1949, OBE 1946), TD; er da of Adm of the Fleet Sir Reginald Tyrwhitt, 1 Bt, GCB, DSO; *b* 27 Dec 1903; *Career* sr controller ATS (dir 1946-49), Brig WRAC 1949-50; Hon ADC to George VI 1949-50, asst admin WRVS Southern Region 1953-72; *Style—* Brig Dame Mary Tyrwhitt, DBE, TD

TYRWHITT, Sir Reginald Thomas Newman; 3 Bt (UK 1919), of Terschelling, and of Oxford; s of Adm Sir St John Reginald Joseph Tyrwhitt, 2 Bt, KCB, DSO, DSC (d 1961), and Nancy Veronica, da of Charles Newman Gilbey (gn of Sir Walter Gilbey, 1 Bt); Sir St John's gf's gf, Richard, was 3 s of Capt John Tyrwhitt, RN (d 1812), of Netherclay House, Somerset, by his w Katherine (paternal gda of Lady Susan Clinton, da of 6 Earl of Lincoln (a dignity now subsumed in the Duchy of Newcastle); Richard's er bro was (Sir) Thomas, *née* Tyrwhitt, who assumed (1790) the name of Jones (although subsequent holders of the Btcy appear to have been known as Tyrwhitt) & was cr a Bt 1808; Sir Thomas's ggs, Sir Raymond Tyrwhitt, 4 Bt, inherited his mother's Barony of Berners, *qv*, the Btcy becoming extinct 1950; John Tyrwhitt of Netherclay was seventh in descent from Marmaduke Tyrwhitt, yr s of Sir William Tyrwhitt, of Kettilby; *b* 21 Feb 1947; *Educ* Downside; *m* 1972 (m dis 1980 and annulled 1984), Sheila Gail, da of William Alistair Crawford Nicoll, of Liphook, Hants; m 2, 1984, Charlotte, o da of Capt Angus Jeremy Christopher Hildyard, DL, RA; 1 s (b 1987); *Heir* s, Robert St John Hildyard b 1987; *Career* 2 Lt RA 1966, Lt 1969, RARO 1969; *Style—* Sir Reginald Tyrwhitt, Bt; c/o Lloyds Bank, 21 High St, Ascot, Berks SL5 7JE

TYSER, Hon Mrs; Hon Susan Frances; *née* Remnant; da of 2 Baron Remnant, MBE (d 1967); *b* 9 May 1938; *m* 29 Mar 1967, Alan Tyser, s of Granville Tyser, of Park Lane, London W1; 1 s; *Style—* The Hon Mrs Tyser; West Hanney House, Wantage, Oxon

TYSON, Dr Alan Walker; CBE (1989); s of Lt Henry Alan Maurice Tyson (d 1975), of Edinburgh, and Dorothy Allan, *née* Walker (d 1959); *b* 27 Oct 1926; *Educ* Rugby, Magdalen Coll Oxford (BA, MA), Univ Coll London and Univ Coll Hosp Med Sch (MB BS); *Career* sr res fell All Souls Coll Oxford 1971- (fell 1952-), on editorial staff standard edn of Freud's works 1952-74, visiting lectr in psychiatry Montefiore Hosp NY 1967-68, lectr in psychopathology and developmental psychology Oxford Univ 1968-70, visiting prof of music Columbia Univ NY 1969, James PR Lyell reader in bibliography Oxford Univ 1973-74, Ernest Bloch prof of music Univ of California Berkeley 1977-78, memb Inst for Advanced Studies Princeton 1983-84, visiting prof of music Graduate Center City Univ of NY 1985; assoc memb Br Psychoanalytical Soc 1957-, MRCPsych 1972, FBA 1978; *Books* The Authentic English Editions of Beethoven (1963), English Music Publishers' Plate Numbers (with O W Neighbour, 1965), Selected Letters of Beethoven (ed 1967), Thematic Catalogue of the Works of Muzio Clementi (1967), Beethoven Studies (ed Vol 1 1973, Vol 2 1977, Vol 3 1982), The Beethoven Sketchbooks (with D Johnson and R Winter, 1985), Mozart: Studies of the Autograph Scores (1987); *Style—* Dr Alan Tyson, CBE; 7 Southcote Road, London N19 5BJ (☎ 01 609 2981); All Souls College, Oxford OX1 4AL (☎ 0865 279363)

TYSON, John Vernon; s of Gilbert John Gilbanks Tyson (d 1942), and Caroline, *née* Smith (d 1985); *b* 16 Feb 1937; *Educ* Keswick Sch, Fitzwilliam Coll Cambridge (MA); *m* 30 July 1966, Nigella Jane, da of Frederick John Sewry (d 1978); 1 s (Robin b 1971), 2 da (Rachel b 1969, Helen b 1976); *Career* asst master Abingdon Sch 1960-66, head of mathematics and headmaster's admin asst Bradfield Coll 1966-78; headmaster St Edmund's Sch Canterbury 1978-; chm: Canterbury Cathedral Old Choristers' Assoc, Canterbury Squash Racquets, Ellis Ctee Mathematics Panel 1980-84; *Books* School Mathematic Project (books 1-5 co-author), Individualised Mathematics (co-author); *Recreations* music, chess, crossword, printing, DIY; *Style—* John V Tyson, Esq; Headmaster's House, St Edmund's Sch, Canterbury, Kent CT2 8HT (☎ 0227 464496)

TYSON, William Leslie; OBE (1966); s of William Ernest Tyson, OBE (d 1971), and Ada Alice, *née* Smith (d 1953); *b* 17 July 1907; *Educ* Merchant Taylors' Crosby; *m* 29 Aug 1946, Kathleen Emily, da of Capt Burnham William Adamson (d 1956), marine supt Bibby Shipping Line (in charge of Bibby Line Shipping Fleet during evacuation from Dunkirk 1940); *Career* RAF Air Crew Gunner, served India 1942-45; surveyor USA 1928-29; pres Regnl Fed Building Trades Employers 1938-39 and 1966; memb: IOD 1956-, Royal Agric Society, The Br Friesian Cattle Soc; Hon memb RIBA 1979-87; govr Liverpool Coll of Building 1967-83; personally responsible for building of Queen Elizabeth II Crown Courts Liverpool opened by the Queen 1984; chm and md Tysons (contractors) plc Liverpool; *Recreations* rugby, tennis, swimming; *Clubs* Secretary Liverpool Round Table; *Style—* Leslie Tyson, Esq, OBE; Hilstone Grange, Stanley Road, Hoylake, Wirral, Cheshire L47 1HN (☎ 051 632 3676; Dryden Street, Liverpool L69 5AA

TYZACK, Margaret; OBE (1970); da of Thomas Edward Tyzack, and Doris, *née* Moseley; *Educ* St Angela's Ursuline Convent, RADA; *m* 26 March 1958, Alan Stephenson, s of Thomas Stephenson; 1 s (Matthew b 10 Aug 1964); *Career* actress; Royal Court Theatre: Progress to the Park, the Ginger Man, Tom and Viv (also Public Theatre New York, nominated for US Drama Desk Award); RSC: Coriolanus, Julius Caesar, Titus Andronicus, Summerfolk (also New York, Stratford, Ontario), Ghosts, Richard III, All's Well that End's Well, Lower Depths (at Art's theatre); other theatre work incl: The Cherry Orchard and Sisters Exeter and UK tour, A Man for All Seasons and Macbeth Nottingham and European tour, Find your Way Home, Open Space, Vivat Vivat Regina Piccadilly Theatre, People are Living There Royal Exchange Manchester, Veronica's Room Palace Watford, Mornings at Seven Westminster Theatre, An Inspector Calls and Night Must Fall Greenwich Theatre; SWET Best Actress Award for Martha in Who's Afraid of Virginia Woolf? National Theatre, Tony Nomination for the countess in All's Well that Ends Well RSC New York, Variety Club Best Actress Award for Lettice and Lovage Globe Theatre; films incl: Prick Up Your Ears, 2001, A Clockwork Orange, A Touch of Love, The Whisperers, Ring of Spies, The Wars, Mr Love; tv incl: The Forsyte Sage, The First Churchills (BAFTA Best Actress Award), Cousin Bette (US Emmy Nomination), A Winter's Tale, I Claudius, The Reason of things, Another Man's Life, Waters of the Moon, The Silver Box, Dear Octopus, Amelia Edwards, The Flowering Cherry, An Inspector Calls; *Style—* Ms Margaret Tyzack, OBE; c/o Joyce Edwards, 275 Kennington Road, London SE11 (☎ 01 735 5736)

U

UATIOA, Dame Mere; DBE (1978); da of Aberam Takenibeia and Bereti Bamatang; *b* 19 Jan 1924; *Educ* Hiram Bingham HS Beru Island; *m* 1950, Reuben Uatioa, MBE (d 1977); 3 s, 1 da; *Career* awarded DBE in recognition of her support for her husband throughout his public career as a Gilbertese nationalist; *Style*— Dame Mere Uatioa, DBE; Erik House, Antebuka, Tarawa, Gilbert Islands

UDALL, David Victor; s of George Edward Udall, of Woldingham, Surrey; *b* 8 Nov 1937; *Educ* Hampton GS; *m* 1974, Ann, da of John Daniel Ellwood; 2 s, 1 da; *Career* CA (own practice); md: Casetrend Ltd, Casetrend Property Investmt Co Ltd; fin dir: Ellmall Properties Ltd, Ellmall Hldgs Ltd, Dereham Produce Co Ltd; *Recreations* tennis, landscape gardening, travelling; *Style*— David Udall, Esq; Dukes Edge, Lunghurst Rd, Woldingham, Surrey (☎ 088 385 2340);

UDOMA, Hon Sir (Egbert) Udo; CFR (1978); s of Chief Udoma Inam of Ibekwe Ntanaran Akama Ikot Abasi, of Akwa Ibom State, Nigeria and Adiaha Edem; *b* 21 June 1917; *Educ* Methodist Coll Uzuakoli, Trinity Coll Dublin, St Catherine's Oxford (LLB, MA, PhD); *m* 1950, Grace Bassey; 5 s (and 1 s decd), 1 da; *Career* barr Gray's Inn 1945, practised as barr and slr Supreme Ct Nigeria 1946-61, MHR Nigeria 1952-59, High Ct judge Lagos 1961-63, govr gen 1963, chief justice of Uganda 1963-69, justice Supreme Ct of Nigeria 1969-82, ret; nat pres Ibibio State Union 1947-61, memb Nigeria Mktg Co 1952-54, mangr ctee W Africa Inst for Oil Palm Research 1953-63, chm bd of tstees King George V Memorial Fund 1964-69, patron Nigeria Soc of Int Law 1968, chllr Ahmadu Bello Univ 1972-75, chm Constituent Assembly Nigerian Constitution 1977-78, dir and presiding justice Seminar for Judges Nigeria 1980 and 1981, memb Nigerian Inst of Int Affrs 1979-; awarded title of Obong Ikpa Isong Ibibio 1961; Hon LLD: Univ of Ibadan 1967, Ahamadu Bello Univ 1972, Trinity Dublin 1973; kt 1964; *Publications* The Lion and the Oil Palm and other essays (1943), The Human Right to Individual Freedom - a Symposium on World Habeas Corpus (jty 1970), The Story of the Ibibio Union (1987); *Clubs* Metropolitan, Island (both Lagos); *Style*— Hon Sir Udo Udoma, CFR; Mfut Itiat Enin, 8 Dr Udoma St, Ikot Abasi, Akaw Ibom State, Nigeria

UFLAND, Richard Mark; s of Bertram Ufland, and Shirley, *née* Gross; *b* 4 May 1957; *Educ* St Paul's Sch, Downing Coll Cambridge (BA, MA); *m* 20 Oct 1985, Jane Camilla, da of Louis Rapaport, 1 s (James b 1987); *Career* ptnr Stephenson Harwood 1986- (articled 1979-81, asst slr 1981-86); Freeman: City of London, Worshipful Co of Solicitors of the City of London; memb Law Soc; *Recreations* music, bridge, skiing; *Style*— Richard Ufland, Esq; 10 Folly Close, Radlett, Herts WD7 8DR (☎ 0923 854378); One St Paul's Churchyard, London EC4M 8SH (☎ 01 329 4422, fax 01 606 8822, telex 886789 SHSPC G)

UHLMAN, Hon Mrs (Nancy Diana Joyce); da of 1 Baron Croft, CMG, TD, PC (d 1947), and Hon Nancy, da of 1 Baron Borwick; *b* 1912; *m* 1936, Dr Manfred Uhlman (d 1985); 1 s (Francis Raymond Croft b 1943), 1 da (Caroline Ann b 1940); *Style*— The Hon Mrs Uhlman; Croft Castle, nr Leominster, Herefordshire HR6 9PW

UJIELL-HAMILTON, Adrianne Pualine; da of late Dr Marcus Grantham, and Ella Grantham; *b* 14 May 1932; *Educ* Maria Gray's Acad for Girls; *m* 1952, Maria Reginald Ujiell-Hamilton; 1 s, 1 da; *Career* called to the Bar Middle Temple 1965 (ad eundem Inner Temple 1976-), head of chambers 1976-, rec Crown Ct 1985-; memb: Legal Aid Panel 1969-, Gen Cncl of the Bar 1970-74 (exec ctee 1973-74); govr Poly of N London 1986-; author of various articles on marriage contracts; FRSA; *Recreations* collecting theatre and ballet costume design, cooking, conversation; *Clubs* Lloyds; *Style*— Mrs Adrianne Ujiell-Hamilton; 3 Dr Johnson's Bldgs, Temple, London EC4 (☎ 01 353 8778)

ULLMAN, Hon Mrs (Julian Mary); *née* Russell; da of Baron Russell of Killowen, PC; *b* 1935; *m* 1, 1955 (m dis 1974), Anthony Allfrey, s of Lady Holman, *qv*, by her 1 husb Capt Basil Allfrey; 1 s, 2 da; m 2, Mr Ullman, of Norfolk, Virginia, USA; *Style*— The Hon Mrs Ullman

ULLSTEIM, Augustus Rupert Patrick Anthony; s of Frederick Charles Leopold Ullsteim (d 1988), of Chiswick, and Patricia, *née* Guinness; *b* 21 Mar 1947; *Educ* Bradfield, LSE (LLB); *m* 12 Sept 1970, Pamela Margaret, da of Claude Wells (d 1974), of Woodford, Essex; 2 s (William b 3 July 1980, George b 29 April 1983), 2 da (Elizabeth b 1 June 1977, Caroline b 28 Oct 1978); *Career* called to the Bar Inner Temple 1970, dep registrar Family Div 1987; dir Saxon Radio 1980-87; Freeman City of London 1982, Liveryman Worshipful Co of Bowyer 1982; *Books* The Law of Restrictive Trade Practices and Monopolies (second supplement to second edn, 1973), Matrimonial and Domestic Injunctions (1982); *Recreations* after dinner speaking, television, my children; *Clubs* Farmers; *Style*— Augustus Ullsteim, Esq; 74 Duke's Ave, Chiswick, London W4; 5 Paper Buildings, Temple, London EC4 (☎ 01 353 8494, fax 01 583 1926, car 0836 250 954)

ULLSWATER, 2 Viscount (UK 1921); Nicholas James Christopher Lowther; s of Lt John Arthur Lowther, MVO, RNVR (d 1942); suc ggf, 1 Viscount Ullswater, GCB (s of late Hon William Lowther, bro of late 3 Earl of Lonsdale), 1949; *b* 9 Jan 1942; *Educ* Eton, Trinity Cambridge; *m* 1967, Susan, da of James Howard Weatherby, of Salisbury, Wilts, by his w Mary (4 da of Sir Hereward Wake, 13 Bt, CB, CMG, DSO, JP, DL); 2 s (Hon Benjamin b 1975, Hon Edward b 8 Oct 1981), 2 da (Hon Emma b 1968, Hon Clare b 1970); *Heir* s, Hon Benjamin James Lowther b 26 Nov 1975; *Career* Capt Royal Wessex Yeo TAVR 1973-78; farmer; *Style*— The Rt Hon the Viscount Ullswater; Barrow Street House, nr Mere, Warminster, Wilts BA12 6AB (☎ 0747 860621)

ULRICK, Alan Henry; s of Henry Alexander Ulrick, of Hayes, Middlesex, and the late Ivy Beatrice, *née* Wright; *b* 25 June 1928; *Educ* Principal Sch, Chiswick Poly; *m* 10 Sept 1961, (Lily) Bronwen Gwen, da of the late Robert Lee; 2 da (Caroline Louise b 1963, d 1971, Susannah Elizabeth b 1965); *Career* Nat Serv RAF 1946-49; Chase Manhattan Bank NA London: joined 1944, asst gen mangr 1977, sr vice-pres capital mkts and foreign exchange sector 1987-; *Recreations* bridge, sailing, horseriding, gardening; *Clubs* Overseas Bankers, Int Forex Assoc; *Style*— Alan Ulrick, Esq; Twintops, 38 Oatlands Chase, Weybridge, Surrey (☎ 0932 223 316); The Chase Manhattan Bank NA, Woolgate House, Coleman St, London EC2 (☎ 01 726 5611)

ULSTER, Earl of; Alexander Patrick Gregers Richard Windsor; only s of HRH The Duke of Gloucester, GCVO; *b* 24 Oct 1974; *Style*— Earl of Ulster

ULYATE, Hon Mrs (Frances Margaret); *née* Douglas; da of Baron Douglas of Barloch, KCMG (d 1980), by 1 w, Minnie, *née* Smith (d 1969); *b* 22 May 1920; *Educ* St Pauls Girls Sch, London Sch of Medicine for Women; *m* 1943, Kenneth Ulyate, PhD, MSc; 2 s, 1 da; *Career* conslt anaesthetist (ret); memb RSM; *Books* contributed to Active Learnings in Hospitals (R W Revans); *Recreations* music, gardening, enmbroidery; *Style*— The Hon Mrs Ulyate; 8 Cambridge Road, London SW11 4RS (☎ 01 228 2247); 8 Market Place, Tetbury Glos GL8 8DA (☎ 0666 54009)

ULYATE, Hon Mrs (Katharine Hilda); *née* Borwick; da of 3 Baron Borwick (d 1961), by 1 w, Irene Phyllis (d 1969), da of Thomas Main Patterson; *b* 1914; *m* 1938, Ashton Jack Ulyate; 2 s (Stanley, Raymond b 1955), 1 da (Mrs Berry); *Style*— The Hon Mrs Ulyate; 5 Elgarth, 19 St Patrick Road, Scottsville, Pietermaritzburg 3201, Natal, S Africa

UNDERHILL, Nicholas Peter; s of Kenneth Underhill, and Evelyn Ellen, *née* Barnard; *b* 15 Jan 1955; *Educ* William Ellis Sch; *m* 28 July 1973, Julie Ann Evelyn, da of William Augustus Michael Chard, of London; 3 s (Matthew, James, Julian), 1 da (Lyndsey); *Career* property advertising mangr Evening Standard 1974-75, ptnr Druce & Co 1978-81, equity ptnr Hampton & Sons 1986-87, md Hamptons (estate agents) 1988; memb Hampstead and Highgate Cons Assoc; MLandInst; *Recreations* shooting, rugby, skiing, opera, power boating; *Clubs* Saracens RFC, Lords Taverners; *Style*— Nicholas Underhill, Esq; Wellfield Ave, London N10 (☎ 01 444 2248); Ile Des Quatre Vents, Port Grimaud, S France; Hamptons, 6 Arlington St, St James, London SW1 (☎ 01 493 8222, car tel 0860 205 497)

UNDERHILL, Baron (Life Peer UK 1979); (Henry) Reginall Underhill (Reg); CBE (1976); s of Henry James Underhill (d 1943), and Alice Maud Underhill (d 1957), of Walthamstow; *b* 8 May 1914; *Educ* Tom Hood Central Sch Leyton; *m* 1937, Flora Janet, da of Leonard Philbrick; 2 s (Hon Terry Leonard m 1959 Dorothy Askew, Hon Robert m 1970 Christine Vinson), 1 da (Hon Mrs (Joan Evelyn) Ian Taylor); *Career* takes Labour whip in House of Lords; memb APEX 1931-; propaganda offr Lab Pty 1947, regional organiser W Midlands 1948, asst nat agent 1960, nat agent of the Lab Pty 1972-79, advsr Home Sec 1980-84, memb Parly delgn to Zimbabwe 1980, memb IPU delgn to USSR 1986, dep ldr Lab Oppn 1983-, oppn spokesman (Lords) Electoral Affairs and Transport 1980-; pres Assoc of Metropolitan Authorities; memb: Houghton Ctee on Financial Aid to Political Parties 1975-76, Kilbrandon Ctee on New Ireland Forum 1984; *Recreations* golf, life-long supporter Leyton Orient FC; *Style*— The Rt Hon the Lord Underhill, CBE; 94 Loughton Way, Buckhurst Hill, Essex IG9 6AH (☎ 01 504 1910)

UNDERHILL, Hon Robert; s of Baron Underhill, CBE (Life Peer); *b* 26 Feb 1948; *Educ* Handsworth GS, Chingford County HS, Queen Mary Coll London (BSc); *m* 1970, Christine Ann, da of Ernest Edward Lawrence Vinsen; 1 s (Bruce), 1 da (Helen); *Career* sr mangr Touche Ross & Co; fin dir: Ritz Design Gp plc 1986-87, Campbell & Armstrong plc; FCA; *Recreations* gardening, sport and other outdoor pursuits; *Style*— The Hon Robert Underhill; Campbell & Armstrong plc, Broom House, Highfield Road, Levenshulme, Manchester M19 3WD

UNDERHILL, Hon Terry Leonard; s of Baron Underhill, CBE (Life Peer); *b* 1938; *m* 1960, Dorothy, da of late Edwin Askew; 3 s (Philip b 1964, Richard b 1967, Duncan b 1969); *Style*— The Hon Terry Underhill; Fairlight, Mill Cross, Rattery, S Brent, Devon TQ10 9LB (☎ 036 47 2314)

UNDERWOOD, Derek Leslie; MBE (1981); s of Leslie Frank Underwood (d 1978), of Kent, and Evelyn Ann Underwood, *née* Wells; *b* 8 June 1945; *Educ* Dulwich Coll Prep Sch Beckenham and Penge GS; *m* 1973, Dawn, da of Gerald Daniel Sullivan, of Surrey; 2 da (Heather Fiona b 1977); *Career* cricketer; joined Kent 1962, County Cap 1964, England debut 1966, left-arm spin bowler, 86 Test matches - 297 test wickets; yst player ever to take 100 wickets in debut season, ret from first class cricket 1987; md Kent Indoor Cricket plc 1988-; *Style*— Derek Underwood, MBE; Kent CCC, St Lawrence Ground, Canterbury, Kent (☎ 0227 456886)

UNDERWOOD, Flt Lt Rory; s of James Ashley Underwood (d 1982), and Anne, *née* Tan; *b* 19 June 1963; *Educ* Barnard Castle Sch; *m* 19 Sept 1987, Wendy, da of Laurence Sydney Blanshard, of East Halton, Grimsby, S Humberside; *Career* RAFC Cranwell 1983-84, Pilot Offr 1984, advanced flying trg RAF Valley 1985, Flying Offr 1985, tactical weapons unit RAF Chivenor 1985-86, Tornado trg estab RAF Cottesmore 1986, Canberra OCU (later 360 sqdn) RAF Wyton 1986, Flt Lt 1988; rugby player representing: Leicester, Yorks, Northern Div, England (29 Caps), Barbarians Br Lions; *Recreations* rugby; *Style*— Flt Lt Rory Underwood; 360 Squadron, RAF Wyton, Huntingdon, Cambs (☎ 0480 52 451, ext 335)

UNGER, Michael Ronald; s of Ronald Unger, CBE, of Carvoeiro, Algarve, Portugal, and Joan Maureen Unger; *b* 8 Dec 1943; *Educ* Wirral GS; *m* 20 Aug 1966, Eunice; 1 s (Paul b 1973), 1 da (Sarah decd); *Career* ed: Daily Post Liverpool 1977-82, Liverpool

Echo 1982-83, Manchester Evening News 1983-; dir: the Guardian & Manchester Evening News plc 1983-; tstee the Scott Tst 1986-; *Books* The Memoirs of Bridget Hitler; *Recreations* reading, walking; *Clubs* Press (Manchester); *Style*— Michael Unger, Esq; The Moorings, Lees Lane, Little Neston, S Wirral, Cheshire (☎ 051 336 5186); 164 Deansgate, Manchester (☎ 061 832 7200)

UNIACKE, Hon Mrs (Susan Geraldine); *née* Verney; da of 20 Baron Willoughby de Broke, MC, AFC, AE, JP; *b* 2 Dec 1942; *m* 1, 1964 (m dis 1969), Jeremy Wagg, gs of Sir James Horlick, 4 Bt, OBE; m 2, 1972, Robie Uniacke; 1 s, 1 da (decd); *Style*— The Hon Mrs Uniacke; Challens Yarde, Easebourne, Midhurst, Sussex; 41A Prince of Wales Mansions, Prince of Wales Drive, London SW11

UNMACK, Timothy Stuart Brooke; s of Randall Carter Unmack (d 1978), and Anne Roberta, *née* Stuart (d 1972); *b* 5 August 1937; *Educ* Radley, Christ Church Oxford (MA); *m* 21 May 1966, Eleanor Gillian, da of George Aidan Drury Tait (d 1970); 2 s (Guy Douglas b 13 March 1975, Neil Alexander b 29 July 1977); *Career* Nat Serv RN; admitted slr 1965, sr ptnr Beaumont & Son 1987 (ptnr 1968-); memb ctee on legal aspects of air traffic control of Int Law Soc; former chm Royal Philanthropic Soc Redhill; memb Worshipful Co of Barbers; memb: Law Soc 1965, Royal Aeronautical Soc 1987, Royal Soc for Asian Affairs 1987; *Recreations* squash, sailing, languages; *Clubs* Utd Oxford & Cambridge; *Style*— Timothy Unmack, Esq; Lloyds Chambers, 1 Portsoken St, London E1 8AW (☎ 01 481 3100, fax 01 481 3353, telex 889018 BOSUN G)

UNSWORTH, Sir Edgar Ignatius Godfrey; CMG (1954), QC (N Rhodesia, now Zambia, 1951); s of John Unsworth; *b* 18 April 1906; *Educ* Stonyhurst, Manchester Univ; *m* 1964, Eileen, widow of Raymond Ritzema; *Career* barr Gray's Inn 1930, fought Farnworth (C) 1935 Gen Election; Crown counsel: Nigeria 1937, N Rhodesia 1942 (slr-gen 1946, then slr-gen Malaya Fedn), attorney-gen N Rhodesia 1951-56, attorney-gen Nigeria 1956-60, federal justice Supreme Court of Nigeria 1960-62; CJ: Nyasaland 1962-64, Gibraltar 1965-76; justice appeal Gibraltar 1976-81; kt 1963; *Style*— Sir Edgar Unsworth, CMG, QC; Pedro el Grande 9, Sotogrande, (Cadiz), Spain

UNSWORTH, Michael Anthony; s of Lt Cdr John Geoffrey Unsworth, MBE, of Hayling Island, Hants, and Joan Rhyllis, *née* Clemes; *b* 29 Oct 1949; *Educ* St John's Coll Southsea Hants, Enfield Coll of Tech (BA); *m* 1 Dec 1973, Masa, da of Prof Zitomir Lozica, of Orebic, Yugoslavia; 2 da (Tania Elizabeth b 1978, Tessa Joanna b 1981); *Career* res analyst Grieveson Grant & Co 1972-79, ptnr Scott Goff Hancock & Co 1981-86 (sr oil analyst 1979-81, Scott Goff Hancock merged with Smith Bros to form Smith New Ct), dir i/c of res Smith New Ct 1989- (dir i/c of energy res 1986-); memb Stock Exchange; assoc: Soc of Investmt Analysts, Inst of Petroleum; memb: London Oil Analysts Gp (former chm), Nat Assoc of Petroleum Investmt Analysts (USA), Edinburgh and Leith Petroleum Club; *Recreations* sailing, opera, theatre, skiing; *Clubs* Little Ship, Cruising Assoc; *Style*— Michael Unsworth, Esq; Smith New Court plc, Chetwynd House, 30 St Swithins' Lane, London EC4N 8AE (☎ 01 626 1544, fax 01 623 3213, telex 941 391)

UNWIN, (James) Brian; s of Reginald Unwin (d 1975), and Winifred Annie, *née* Walthall; *b* 21 Sept 1935; *Educ* Chesterfield Sch, New Coll Oxford (MA), Yale Univ (MA); *m* 5 May 1964, Diana Susan, da of Sir David Aubrey Scott, GCMG, *qv*; 3 s (Michael Alexander, Christopher James, Nicholas Edward); *Career* HM Civil Serv: asst princ CRO 1960, second later first sec Br High Cmmn Salisbury Southern Rhodesia 1961-64, first sec Br High Cmmn Accra 1964-65, FCO 1965-68, HM Treasy 1968-81 (asst sec 1972, under sec 1975), dep sec Cabinet Off 1985-87 (under sec 1981-83), dep sec HM Treasy 1983-85, chm of the bd HM Customs & Excise 1987-; UK dir Euro Investmt Bank 1983-85, hon sec bd of dirs ENO 1987-; CBIM 1988 ; *Recreations* bird watching, cricket, Wellington, Trollope; *Clubs* Reform, Vincents, Kingswood Village (Surrey); *Style*— Brian Unwin, Esq, CB; H M Customs & Excise, New King's Beam House, 22 Upper Ground, London SE1 9PJ (☎ 01 382 5001)

UNWIN, David Storr; s of Sir Stanley Unwin, KCMG (d 1968), and Alice Mary Storr (d 1971); *b* 3 Dec 1918; *Educ* Abbotsholme Sch Derbys; *m* 31 July 1945, Bridget Mary Periwinkle, da of Capt (E) Sydney Jasper Herbert, RN (d 1941); 1 da (Phyllida b 1950), 1 s (Corydon b 1950); *Career* author; *Books Incl:* The Governor's Wife (1954), A View of the Heath (1956); biography: Fifty Years with Father (1982); books for children: Rickafire! (1942), Dream Gold (1948), Drumbeats (1953), The Future Took Us (1957), Foxy-Boy (1959), The Girl in the Grove (1974), The Wishing Bone (1977); *Recreations* travel; *Clubs* Pen; *Style*— David S Unwin, Esq; Garden Flat, 31 Belsize Park, London NW3 4DX (☎ 01 435 5198)

UNWIN, Sir Keith; KBE (1964, OBE 1937), CMG (1954); s of Edwin Ernest Unwin, and Jessie M Black; *b* 3 August 1909; *Educ* Merchant Taylors', Lycée Condorcet Paris, St John's Coll Oxford (MA); *m* 1935, Linda Giersé; 1 s, 2 da; *Career* joined commercial Dip Serv, served Madrid, Istanbul, San Sebastian, Mexico City, Paris, Prague, Buenos Aires, Rome; foreign service inspr 1959-62, UK rep Econ and Social Cncl UN 1962-66, ambass Uruguay 1966-69, UK memb UN Commission Human Rights 1970-78; *Style*— Sir Keith Unwin, KBE, CMG; Great Kingley, Dodington Lane, Chipping Sodbury, Bristol BS17 6SB (☎ 0454 310913)

UNWIN, Ven Kenneth; s of Percy Unwin (d 1971), and Elsie, *née* Holmes (d 1979); *b* 16 Sept 1926; *Educ* Chesterfield Sch, St Edmund Hall Oxford (MA); *m* 1958, Beryl, da of Arthur Riley, of Leeds; 1 s (Michael b 1973), 4 da (Katharine b 1959, Helen b 1961, Sarah b 1963, Ruth b 1965); *Career* vicar: St John Baptist Dodworth 1959-69, St John Baptist Royston Barnsley 1969-73, St John Baptist Wakefield 1973-82; archdeacon of Pontefract 1981-; *Style*— Ven The Archdeacon of Pontefract; Pontefract House, 19a Tithe Barn Street, Horbury, Wakefield WF4 6LJ (☎ Wakefield 263777)

UNWIN, Peter William; CMG (1981); s of Arnold and Norah Unwin; *b* 20 May 1932; *Educ* Ampleforth, Ch Ch Oxford (MA); *m* 1955, Monica Steven; 2 s, 2 da; *Career* army 1954-56; entered Foreign Off 1956, cnsllr (econ) Bonn 1973-75, head Personnel Policy Dept FCO 1976-78, min (econ) Bonn 1980-82, ambass to Hungary 1983-86, ambass to Denmark 1986; *Style*— HE Mr Peter Unwin, CMG; British Embassy, Kastelsvet 40, Copenhagen, Denmark; Foreign and Commonwealth Office, King Charles St, London SW1

UNWIN, Rayner Stephens; CBE; s of Sir Stanley Unwin (d 1968), and Alice Mary Storr (d 1971); *b* 23 Dec 1925; *Educ* Abbotsholme Sch, Trinity Coll Oxford (MA), Harvard USA (MA); *m* 1952, Carol Margaret, *née* Curwen; 1 s (Merlin b 1954), 3 da (Camilla b 1955, Tamara b 1958, Sharon b 1958); *Career* publisher; *Recreations* skiing downhill, walking up-hill, birds, gardens; *Clubs* Garrick; *Style*— Rayner Unwin, Esq, CBE; Limes Cottage, Little Missenden, Nr Amersham, Bucks; 15-17 Broadwick St, London W1V 1FP

UPHAM, Charles Hazlitt; VC (1943) and Bar (1943), JP; s of John Hazlitt Upham (barr, d 1951), and Agatha Upham (d 1975); *b* 21 Sept 1908; *Educ* Christ's Coll NZ, Lincoln Agric Coll (Post Grad Land Valuation); *m* 1945, Mary, da of James McTamney (d 1916); 3 da; *Career* Capt WWII (POW Colditz, amongst others camps); sheep farmer 1700 acres, now semi-retired; *Recreations* riding, fishing, reading; *Clubs* Christchurch, Canterbury and Officers (all NZ); hon memb Sydney RSL; *Style*— Charles Upham, Esq, VC; Landsdowne, Parnassus Rd, N Canterbury, New Zealand

UPJOHN, Baroness; Marjorie Dorothy Bertha; da of late Maj Ernest Murray Lucas; *Educ* privately; *m* 1947, Baron Upjohn (Life Peer d 1971); *Style*— The Rt Hon the Lady Upjohn; 91 High St, Earls Colne, Colchester

UPTON, John; s of Ernest Upton (d 1940); *b* 3 Dec 1905; *m* 1951, Kathleen Ruth; 2 s, 2 da; *Career* md The Liverpool Warehousing Co Ltd, chm The Br Public Warehousekeepers Ctee 1979-80; dir: Lukwa Storage Ltd, North West Storage Co, Cheshire Storage; *Recreations* golf; *Clubs* Royal Birkdale Golf; *Style*— John Upton Esq; 5 Westbourne Rd, Birkdale, Southport

UPTON, Peter Thomas; s of Frank Harry Upton (d 1985), of Wilts, and Rachel Amelia, *née* Cain; n of Charles W Cain the artist known as the 'Etcher of the East'; *b* 1 Jan 1937; *Educ* Headlands GS Wilts, Newlands Park Coll (Art Teachers Cert), Reading Univ (Post Grad Res in Psychology); *m* 14 Aug 1963, Janet Harnell, da of Maj Thomas Joyce Parry (d 1958); 1 s (Simon Dominic b 1966), 1 da (Fiona Sorolla b 1964); *Career* artist; equestrian painter and sculptor; exhibition and 1 man shows held in London, America, France, Sweden, Dubai; works in private and Royal collections; hd of art and housemaster Pierrepont Sch 1961-89; pres Arab Horse Soc of GB 1986-87, int judge and expert on the Arab Horse, breeder and judge of Dartmoor ponies; *Books* Desert Heritage (1980), The Classic Arab Horse (1987), The First Arab Horses Imported From the Desert (1989), author of numerous articles on the Arab horse for nat and int magazines; *Recreations* travelling in the deserts of Arabia, falconry, riding, hunting, an avid bibliophile; *Style*— Peter T Upton, Esq; The Old Vicarage, Clun, Shropshire

UPTON, Robin James; JP (1969); s of Col Philip Valentine Upton, MBE, TD, JP, DL (d 1985), of Park Lodge, and Coptfold, Margaretting, Essex, and Veronica Rosemary, da of Lt-Col Leslie Heber Thornton, CMG, DSO, of Lewes, Sussex; *b* 18 Mar 1931; *Educ* Trinity Coll Glenalmond, Trinity Coll Cambridge (MA); *m* 1961, Priscilla Mary, yr da of Dr William Sydney Charles Copeman, CBE, TD, (d 1970), of 12 Hyde Pk Pl, London W2; 2 s (Hugo, Simon), 1 da (Victoria); *Career* farmer; magistrate; dir: R J Upton Farms Ltd 1969-, Reed & Upton 1971-, Mereacre Farms Ltd 1983-, Assoc Farmers plc 1983-; county chm Suffolk Country Landowners Assoc 1981-84, High Sheriff of Suffolk 1988-89; *Recreations* conservation, shooting, fishing; *Style*— R J Upton, Esq; Park Farm, Herringswell, Bury St Edmunds, Suffolk (☎ 0638 750317)

UPTON, Roger Charles; s of Frank Harry Upton (d 1985), of Wilts, and Rachel Amelia, *née* Cain; *b* 1 Jan 1937; *m* 9 Aug 1961, Jean, da of Andrew Robert Turnell (d 1982), of Ogbourne, Marlborough, Wilts; 2 s (Mark Lundy, Guy); *Career* Royal Horse Gds; artist and sculptor; works in: USA, UK, Arabia, Europe; contrib of articles on: falconry, coursing, the Middle East, poetry; memb advsy ctee to HO and DOE on Protection of Birds 1967-80; *Books* A Bird In The Hand, O For A Falconers Voice; *Recreations* falconry, coursing, hunting, punting, driving horses; *Clubs* British Falconers'; *Style*— Roger Upton, Esq; (☎ 067 286 656)

URE, Alan Willis; CBE (1984), RD (1969); s of Colin McGregor Ure (d 1963), Edith Hannah Eileen Willis Swinburne (d 1945); *b* 30 Mar 1926; *Educ* Kelvinside Acad, Merchiston Castle Sch, Pembroke Coll Cambridge; *m* 1953, Mary Christine, *née* Henry; 1 s, 2 da; *Career* memb Construction Indust Trg Bd 1982-85, pres Nat Fedn of Bldg Trades Employers 1981-82, memb Royal Cmmn on Civil Liability and Compensation for Personal Injury 1974-78; dep md Trollope and Colls Hldgs, formerly md Trollope and Colls Ltd and Trollope and Colls Mgmnt Ltd; vice-pres Fed Internationale Européenne de Construction 1982-85; *Recreations* vintage motoring, bell ringing, walking, reading, sailing; *Clubs* Naval; *Style*— Alan Ure, Esq, CBE, RD; 28 Hambleside Court, Hamble SO3 5QE; 20 Eastbourne Terrace, London W2 6LE

URE, Sir John Burns; KCMG (1987), LVO (1968); s of Tam Ure, MBE (d 1963), Mrs Mary Jeanie, *née* Bosworth (d 1963); *b* 5 July 1931; *Educ* Uppingham Sch, Magdalene Coll Cambridge (MA), Harvard Business Sch (AMP); *m* 1972, Caroline, da of Charles Allan, of Roxburghshire; 1 s (Alasdair b 1978), 1 da (Arabella b 1981); *Career* 2 Lt Cameronians (Scottish Rifles) 1949-51, active service during Emergency in Malaya; Lt London Scottish (Gordon Highlanders) 1951-55 (TA), served at Br Embassies in Moscow, Leopoldville, Santiago and in the Foreign and Cwlth Off in London 1956-71; cncllr and chargé d'affaires at Lisbon 1972-77; head of S America Dept Foreign and Cwlth Off 1977-79, ambass to Cuba 1979-81, asst under-sec of State Foreign and Cwlth Off 1981-84, ambass to Brazil 1984-87, ambass to Sweden 1987-; Cdr of Military Order of Christ (Portugal) 1973; *Books* Cucumber Sandwiches in the Andes (1973), The Trail of Tamerlane (1980), The Quest for Captain Morgan (1983), Trespassers on the Amazon (1986), Prince Henry The Navigator (1977), book reviews for TLS; *Recreations* travelling uncomfortably in remote places and writing about it comfortably afterwards; *Clubs* Whites, Beefsteak, Royal Geographical Soc; *Style*— Sir John Ure, KCMG, LVO; FCO (Stockholm), King Charles St, London SW1A 2AH; British Embassy, Stockholm, Sweden

URQUHART, Alastair Hugh; CBE (1967); s of late Geoffrey Urquhart, of Collaroy, NSW, Australia; *b* 3 Nov 1919; *Educ* Sydney C of E GS; *m* 1947, Joyce Muriel, *née* Oswald; 2 da; *Career* serv WWII, T/Capt N Africa (Tobruk, El Alamein); UK POW rehabilitation work 1944-45; stockbroker; conslt BBL Mullens Ltd, memb Sydney Stock Exchange Ltd 1949- (vice-chm 1956 and 1958-59, chm 1959-66), pres Aust Assoc Stock Exchanges 1959 and 1964-66 (vice-pres 1960-63), memb exec cmmn ctee Aust Red Cross Soc (NSW div) 1950-85 (vice-chm 1964-65, vice pres 1985-); tstee Sydney Opera House 1969-81, memb Devpt Corpn of NSW 1967-75; chm: Chubbs Australia Ltd, NSW Building Soc Ltd (now Advance Bank Australia Ltd); dir P & O Australia Ltd 1976-87; *Recreations* swimming, golf, yachting; *Clubs* Union, Royal Sydney Golf, Royal Sydney Yacht Sqdn, Rotary (Australia); *Style*— Alastair Urquhart, Esq, CBE; 4 Wentworth Place, Point Pier, NSW, Australia 2027 (☎ Home 3274424, off: 2336277)

URQUHART, Barry; s of Kenneth Hector Urquhart, of Horsham, Sussex, and Lillian Rosina, *née* Batten (d 1983); *b* 19 Oct 1943; *Educ* St Paul's Sch, Poly of N London (Dip Arch); *m* 23 Nov 1977, Susan Corrie, da of Henry William Albert Griffiths, (d

1985), of Spindrift Cottages, Roedean Way, Brighton; 1 s (David Alexander b 29 Nov 1985), 1 da (Rebecca Elizabeth b 8 March 1983); *Career* formed own architecture practice 1977, opened additional office 1988; dir: Living Water Ltd, BU Design Ltd; nat and int lectr on designing for the mentally ill and mentally handicapped; contrib to learned jls; elder Living Water Fellowship; memb: Weybridge Soc, IOD; RIBA, FASI, FIAA; *Clubs* Old Pauline; *Style*— Barry Urquhart, Esq; 80 Onslow Rd, Burwood Park, Walton on Thames, Surrey KT12 5AY (☎ 0932 229 463); BUA Barry Urquhart Assocs, 23 Monument Green, Weybridge, Surrey KT13 8QW (☎ 0932 856 551, fax 0932 859 735)

URQUHART, Sir Brian Edward; KCMG (1986), MBE (1945); s of Murray Urquhart (d 1977), and Bertha Rendall Urquhart (d 1984); *b* 28 Feb 1919; *Educ* Westminster, Christ Church Oxford; *m* 1, 1944 (m dis 1963), Alfreda, da of Constant Huntington (d 1964), of London; 2 s (Thomas b 1944, Robert b 1948), 1 da (Katherine b 1946); m 2, 1963, Sidney, da of Sidney Howard (d 1939), of USA; 1 s (Charles b 1967), 1 da (Rachel b 1963); *Career* Maj Dorset Regt and Airborne Forces Africa and Europe 1939-45; UN Secretariat 1945-86 (under sec-gen special political affrs 1972-86), scholar-in-residence The Ford Fndn 1986-; Hon DCL Oxford; *Books* Hammarskjold (1972), A Life in Peace and War (1987); *Recreations* reading, writing; *Clubs* Century (New York); *Style*— Sir Brian Urquhart, KCMG, MBE; 131 East 66th St, New York, New York 10021; Howard Farm, Tyringham, Massachusetts 01264; The Ford Foundation, 320 East 43rd St, New York, New York 10017 (☎ 212 573 4952)

URQUHART, Dennis Alexander; *b* 5 Mar 1929; *Educ* King Edward VI Sch Southampton, The Queen's Coll Oxford (BA 1952); *m* 24 Aug 1957, Chrystal Walton; 2 s, 2 da; *Career* dir: Bass plc and subsidiary; chm: Hedges & Butler Ltd, Charrington & Co Ltd, Bass Wales & West Ltd, Alexis Lichine & Co; *Recreations* music, opera, English cricket, Welsh rugby; *Style*— Dennis Urquhart, Esq; Little Acre, Byes Lane, Silchester, Nr Reading, Berks RG7 2QB; Bass plc, 20 Portland Place, London W1N 3DF

URQUHART, Donald John; CBE (1970); s of late Roderick Urquhart; *b* 27 Nov 1909; *Educ* Barnard Castle Sch, Sheffield Univ (BSc, PhD); *m* 1939, Beatrice Winifride, *née* Sheffield; 2 s; *Career* dir National Lending Library for Science and Technology 1961-73, dir gen British Library Lending Division 1973-74, Hon DSc: Sheffield Univ 1974, Salford Univ 1974, Heriot Watt Univ 1974; *Clubs* Athenaeum; *Style*— Donald Urquhart, Esq, CBE; Wood Garth, 15 First Ave, Bardsey, Leeds (☎ 0937 73228)

URQUHART, James Graham; CVO (1983); s of James Urquhart (d 1982), of Edinburgh, and Mary, *née* Clark (d 1984); *b* 23 April 1925; *Educ* Berwickshire HS; *m* 1 Oct 1949, Margaret, da of Earnest Hutchinson (d 1982), of Rock Ferry; 2 da (Janet b 10 May 1952, Alison b 18 May 1955); *Career* BR 1949-86; mgmnt trainee 1949-52, dist traffic supt Perth 1960-62, divnl mangr Glasgow 1964-67, asst gen mangr York 1967-69, chief operating offr BR HQ 1969-72, personnel dir 1972-74, gen mangr London Midlands Region 1975-77; chm: Br Tport Police 1977-86, BR Engrg 1982-86, Transmark 1983-86, Freightliner 1983-86; memb BR Bd 1977-86: ops and productivity 1977-85, exports 1985-86; dir: Park Air Electronics Ltd 1986-, Waterslides plc 1987-, Sonic Tape plc 1988-; MIT 1978, MIMH 1979, CBIM 1982, FIPersonnel 1983; *Recreations* golf, reading; *Style*— James Urquhart, Esq, CVO; 10 Wychcotes, Caversham, Reading (☎ 0734 479 071); 22A High St, Hungerford (☎ 0448 84141)

URQUHART, Lawrence McAllister; s of Robert Urquhart, of 36 West Way, Cirencester, Gloucestershire, and Josephine McEwan, *née* Bissell (d 1988); *b* 24 Sept 1935; *Educ* Strathallan Sch Perthshire, Kings Coll London (LLB); *m* 26 Aug 1961, Elizabeth Catherine, da of William Burns (d 1952); 3 s (Douglas b 1964, Ross b 1965, Guy b 1971), 1 da (Caroline b 1972); *Career* CA; appts: Price Waterhouse 1957-62, Shell Int Petroleum 1962-64, PA Mgmnt Conslts 1964-68; sr gp exec Charterhouse Gp Ltd 1968-74; gp fin dir: Tozer Kemsley and Millbourn Hldgs 1974-77, Burmah Oil Co Ltd 1977-82; chief exec Castrol Ltd 1982-85, gp md Burmah Oil plc 1985-88 (gp chief exec 1988-); Liveryman Worshipful Co of Coachmakers and Coach Harness Makers 1984; CBIM, FInstPet; *Recreations* golf, music; *Clubs* Lilley Brook GC, Frilford Heath GC, Goutherness GC; *Style*— Lawrence Urquhart, Esq; The Burmah Oil plc, Burmah House, Pipers Way, Swindon, Wiltshire, SN3 1RE (☎ 0793 511 521, car tel 0836 615 453, telex 449221)

URQUHART, Peter William; s of Maj-Gen Ronald Walton Urquhart, CB, DSO, DL (d 1968), of Meredith, Tibberton, Gloucestershire, and Jean Margaret, *née* Moir; *b* 10 July 1944; *Educ* Bedford Sch, Pembroke Coll Cambridge (BA, MA); *m* 1 May 1976, The Hon Anne Serena, da of Lord Griffiths, of Kensington, London; 1 s (James b 1980), 3 da (Katherine b 1978, Flora b 1981, Serena b 1984); *Career* RMA Sandhurst 1963-64, Lt RE 1964-69; stockbroker: James Capel 1969- 75, Gilbert Elliot 1975-76, Sheppards & Chase 1976-79, Mercury Asset Mgmnt (formerly Warburg Investmt Mgmnt) 1981- (dir 1984-); *Recreations* field sports, racing, golf, gardening; *Style*— Peter Urquhart, Esq; 33 King William Street, London EC4 (☎ 01 280 2187)

URQUHART, Hon Ronald Douglas Lauchlan; yr s of Baron Tayside, OBE (Life Peer d 1975), and Hilda Gwendoline, *née* Harris; name of Lauchlan derives from ancestor in 1745 rebellion nicknamed 'the Big Sword' or 'Lauchlan'; *b* 20 Feb 1948; *Educ* Fettes Coll, Edinburgh Univ (LLB); *m* 1975, Dorothy May Jackson; *Career* chartered accountant; gp chief financial off Jardine Insurance Brokers, dir of various gp cos 1984-; *Recreations* golf; *Clubs* Caledonian, Hong Kong, Gresham; *Style*— The Hon Ronald Urquhart; Ash Park, East Prawle, nr Kingsbridge, Devon TQ7 2BX; 19 Eastcheap, London EC3

URQUHART, Hon William James Lauchlan; s of Baron Tayside (Life Peer, d 1975); *b* 18 Oct 1944; *Educ* Fettes Coll, Univ of Glasgow (BSc); *m* 1967, Wendy Helen Cook; 3 da (Carolyn, Suzanne, Jacqueline); *Career* CA, company dir; ATTI; *Style*— The Hon William Urquhart; Magicwell House, Balmullo, St Andrews, Fife

URRY, (John) Brian (Marshall); s of John Marshall Urry (d 1972); *b* 11 Mar 1938; *Educ* Solihull Sch, Aston Univ (BSc); *m* 1968, Carol Elizabeth, *née* Blakely; 2 s; *Career* chm and md: Powell-Piggott Ltd, Hudson Edmunds & Co Ltd; Peerless Stampings Ltd, Econa Bilston Ltd, Outward Tools Ltd; hon sec Warwicks Union of Golf Clubs, jt hon sec Public Schs Old Boys Golf Assoc; *Recreations* golf; *Clubs* St Pauls (Birmingham), Olton Golf, St Enodoc Golf; *Style*— Brian Urry, Esq; Dormers, Dickens Heath Rd, Shirley, Solihull, W Midlands (☎ 056 482 3114); Newman Tonks Metals Division, Priory Road, Aston, Birmingham B6 7LF (☎ 021 328 5665, telex 339987)

URSELL, Bruce Anthony; s of Stuart Ursell, of Edgware, London, and Nancy, *née* Fallowes; *b* 28 August 1942; *Educ* William Ellis Sch Highgate; *m* 19 Feb 1966, Anne Carole, da of John Pitt (1970); 1 s (Piers John b 1971), 2 da (Philippa Anne b 1972, Virginia Anne b 1974); *Career* mangr Standard Chartered Bank 1961-68, gen mangr Western American Bank 1968-74, md Guiness Mahon & Co Ltd 1984-87 (dir 1974-84), chief exec Br & Cwlth Merchant Bank plc 1987-, dir Br & Cwlth Hldgs plc 1987-; *Recreations* tennis, theatre, cinema, reading; *Style*— Bruce Ursell, Esq; Roundwood Park, Harpenden, Hertfordshire (☎ 05827 2784); 66 Cannons St, London EC4N 6AE (☎ 01 248 0900, fax 01 248 0917, telex 884 040)

URSELL, Rev Philip Elliott; s of Clifford Edwin Ursell, of Porthcawl, S Wales, and Hilda Jane, *née* Tucker; *b* 3 Dec 1942; *Educ* Cathays HS Cardiff, Univ Coll Cardiff (BA), St Stephen's House Oxford (MA); *Career* ordained Llandaff Cathedral: deacon 1968, priest 1969; asst curate Newton Nottage 1968-71, asst chaplain Univ Coll Cardiff 1971-77, chaplain The Poly of Wales 1974-77, fell Wales 1974-77, fell chaplain and dir of studies in music Emmanuel Coll Cambridge 1977-82, princ Pusey House Oxford 1982-, fell St Cross Coll Oxford 1982-, warden Soc of the Holy and Undivided Trinity Ascot Priory 1986-, examining chaplain to the Bishop of London 1986-; *Style*— The Rev Philip Ursell; Pusey House, Oxford OX1 3LZ (☎ 0865 278415, fax 0865 270708); Ascot Priory, Berks SL5 8RT (☎ 0344 885157)

URWICK, Sir Alan Bedford; KCVO (1984), CMG (1978); s of Col L F Urwick; *b* 2 May 1930; *Educ* The Dragon Sch, Rugby, New Coll Oxford (BA); *m* 1960, Marta Yolanda, da of Adhemar Montagne (formerly Peruvian ambass in London 1969-78); 3 s (Christopher, Richard, Michael); *Career* FO 1952-; served: Brussels, Moscow, Baghdad, Amman, Washington, Cairo; memb Central Policy Review Staff Cabinet 1973-75, head Near East and N Africa dept FCO 1975-76, minister Madrid 1977-79; ambassador: Jordan 1979-84, Egypt 1984-87; High Commissioner Canada 1987-; KStJ 1983; Jordanian Order of Independence 1 Class 1984; *Clubs* Garrick; *Style*— Sir Alan Urwick, KCVO, CMG; c/o Foreign and Commonwealth Office, King Charles St, London SW1

URWICK, Lt-Col Anthony Christopher Moore; DL (1971); s of Col Frank Davidson Urwick, DSO, TD, JP (d 1936); *b* 31 May 1913; *Educ* Malvern, RMC; *m* 1947, Jacqueline Denise, da of Judge John Doyle, ICS (d 1934); 2 da; *Career* Lt-Col Sudan Def Force 1939-48, E African Campaign and N Africa, cmd 9 Bn 1944-45, Western Arab Corps 1945-48, regtl offr Som LI 1933-53, regtl sec (ret offr) 1955-79; *Style*— Lt-Col Anthony Urwick, DL; Flat 3, No 13 Mount St, Taunton, Somerset TA1 3QB (☎ 0823 337399)

URWIN, Peter Michael; s of Denis John Urwin (ka 1943), of Longthorpe Peterborough, and Vera May, *née* Frost; *b* 22 April 1941; *Educ* Stamford Sch, Kings Peterborough; *m* 27 April 1968, Jean Maureen, da of J J George W Jepson, of Christchurch, Hants; 2 s (Simon Christopher James b 1977, James Alexander Edward b 1980); *Career* Royal Insurance 1959-65, Shaw & Sons Insurance Brokers 1965-66, United Africa Co (Unilever) Freetown Sierra Leone 1966-71, dir own cos incl Peter Urwin Holdings Ltd 1971-; md Birchgrey Ltd (promoters of European Open Golf Championship) 1981-; Sierra Leone Open Golf Champion 1970, Capt Freetown GC 1970; ACII 1962; *Recreations* golf, bridge, philately; *Clubs* Roehampton, Kingswood Golf; *Style*— Peter Urwin, Esq; Alverstone, Beeches Wood, Kingswood, Surrey; Broadway House, The The Broadway, Wimbledon, London SW19 1RL (☎ 01 542 9048, fax 01 543 0314, telex 9413321)

USHER, Andrew Michael; s of Francis George Usher; *b* 15 Oct 1938; *Educ* Cheltenham Coll; *m* 1964, Anne, *née* Whittington; 3 s, 1 da; *Career* slr 1964; sec Br Investmnt Tst plc 1979-86, dir The Fleming Fledgeling Investmt Tst plc 1978-, ptnr Baillie Gifford & Co 1986-; *Recreations* genealogy, music, golf; *Clubs* New (Edinburgh), memb Hon Co of Edinburgh Golfers Muirfield; *Style*— Andrew Usher Esq; 12 Blackford Rd, Edinburgh EH9 2DS

USHER, Peter Joseph; OBE (1980); s of Philip Usher, of Homestead, St Marys Rd, Dymchurch, Kent (d 1960), and Gertrude Usher *née* Capon (d 1964); *b* 28 July 1926; *Educ* Maidstone Tech Sch, Royal Naval Coll, Greenwich; *m* 31 March 1951, Pamela; 2 s (Martin b 1952, David b 1954); *Career* constructor cdr RN Staff of Flag Offr (submarines) 1960-64, Naval constructor overseer 1964-66; tech gen mangr Vosper Thornycroft (UK) Ltd 1966-68 (tech dir 1968-74, dep md 1974-81, md 1981-); FEng, FRINA, RCNC; *Recreations* golf, music; *Clubs* Naval and Military; *Style*— Peter Usher, OBE; Vosper Thornycroft (UK) Ltd, Victoria Rd, Woolston, Southampton SO9 5GR (fax 0703 421539, telex 47682 VT WOOL (G))

USHER, Sir Peter Lionel; 5 Bt (UK 1899), of Norton, Midlothian, and of Wells, Co Roxburgh; s of Sir (Robert) Stuart Usher, 4 Bt (d 1962); *b* 1 Oct 1931; *Educ* privately; *Heir* bro, Robert Edward Usher; *Style*— Sir Peter Usher, Bt; Hallrule, Hawick, Roxburghshire

USHER, (Thomas) Raymond; s of Thomas Edward Usher (d 1987), of Easington, Co Durham, and Catherine, *née* McGourley; *b* 10 April 1932; *Educ* Ryhope Robert Richardson GS Co Durham, Univ of Sheffield (BA); *m* 11 Feb 1956, Clare, da of Antony Wear Elliott, of Durham (d 1976); 1 s (Antony Edward b 1965); *Career* dir: Nat Employers Gen Insur Co Ltd (S Africa) 1972-86, Nat Employers Life Assoc Co Ltd (UK) 1976-84, Nat Underwriters (Reinsurance) Ltd (Bermuda) 1979-85, Nat Employers' Mutual Gen Insur Assoc (UK) Ltd 1976-, The Chancellor Group Ltd (Canada) 1986-, American Fam Ltd 1985-, American Family Health & Sec Co Ltd 1985-, American Fam Life Assoc Co Ltd 1985-, East West Insur Co Ltd 1987-; chm Chancellor Insur Co Ltd (UK) 1985-; *Recreations* golf, sailing, horse racing; *Clubs* Royal Thames Yacht, City Livery; *Style*— Raymond Usher, Esq; Parsonage Farmhouse, Church Rd, Wanborough, Wiltshire SN4 0BZ (☎ (0793) 790 818); Flat 1, 10 Craven St, London WC2 (☎ 01 930 5627); Chancellor Insurance Co Ltd, 40 Lime St, London EC3 (☎ 01 481 0827)

USHER, Robert Edward; s of Sir Robert Stuart Usher, 4 Bt (d 1962), and hp of bro, Sir Peter Usher, 5 Bt; *b* 18 April 1934; *Style*— Robert Usher, Esq

USHERWOOD, Stephen Dean; s of John Frederick Usherwood (d 1964), and Grace Ellen, *née* Crush (d 1966); *b* 14 Sept 1907; *Educ* St Dunstan's Coll London, Oriel Coll Oxford (MA); *m* 1, 27 July 1935, Hazel Doreen, *née* Weston (d 1968); 1 s (Nicholas John b 1943), 1 da (Susan Clare b 1939); m 2, 24 Oct 1970, Elizabeth Ada, *née* Beauington; *Career* Flt Lt RAF attached FO 1941-46; educn and current affrs depts BBC 1946-68; author, coll lectr and broadcaster 1968-; *Books* Reign by Reign (1960), The Bible, Book by Book (1962), Shakespeare, Play by Play (1967), History from Familiar Things (1970), Britain, Century by Century (1972), Europe, Century by Century (1972), Food, Drink and History (1972), The Great Enterprise, The Story of the Spanish Armada (1982); with Elizabeth Usherwood: Visit Some London Catholic

Churches (1982), The Counter Armada 1596: The Journal of the Mary Rose (1983), We Die For The Old Religion (1987); *Recreations* travel, theatre, music; *Clubs* Soc of Authors; *Style*— Stephen Usherwood, Esq; 24 St Mary's Grove, Canonbury, London N1 2NT (☎ 01 226 9813)

USTINOV, Peter; CBE (1975); s of late (Peter) Iona Ustinov, journalist, and of late Nadia Benois, painter (niece of Alexandre Benois, the stage designer); *b* 16 April 1921; *Educ* Westminster, London Theatre Sch; *m* 1, 8 Aug 1940 (m dis 1950), Isolde Denham, actress, da of Reginald Denham, actor (and half-sister of Angela Lansbury, *qv*); 1 da (Tamara b 1945); m 2, 15 Feb 1954 (m dis 1971), Suzanne Cloutier; 1 s (Igor b 1956), 2 da (Pavla, Andrea b 1959); m 3, 21 June 1972, Hélène du Lau d'Allemans; *Career* actor, prodr, dir, author and playwright; WWII 1942-46 Royal Sussex Regt, Army Kinematograph Service, Directorate of Army Psychiatry; plays incl: Blow Your Own Trumpet (1943), Man in the Raincoat (1949), The Moment of Truth (1951), High Balcony (1952), Romanoff and Juliet (1956), Paris Not So Gay (1956), Photo Finish (1962), Half Way Up the Tree (1967), The Unknown Soldier and His Wife (1967), Overhead (1981), Beethoven's Tenth (1983); films written incl: The Way Ahead (1942), School for Secrets (1946), Private Angelo (1949), Billy Budd (1962), The Lady L (1964), Hot Millions (1968), Memed My Hawk (1982); books incl: Add A Dash of Pit (1960), The Loser (1961), Krumnagel (1971), Dear Me (1977), My Russia (1983), Ustinov in Russia (1987); TV includes: History of Europe (BBC), Einstein's Universe (1979), The Well Tempered Bach (1985; nominated for an Emmy), 13 At Dinner (1985), Deadman's Folly (1986), Appointment With Death (1987), Peter Ustinov's Russia (1987); films incl: Private Angelo (1949), Odette (1950), Quo Vadis (1951), Beau Brummel (1954), We're No Angels (1955), The Spies (1955), The Sundowners (1960), Spartacus (1960), Ramanoff and Juliet (1961), Billy Budd (1962), Topkapi (1963), Blackbeard's Ghost (1967), The Comedians (1967), Hot Millions (1968), Hammersmith Is Out (1971), One of Our Dinosaurs Is Missing (1974), Purple Taxi (1977), Death on the Nile (1977), The Thief of Baghdad (1978), Ashanti (1979), Charlie Chan and the Curse of the Dragon Queen (1980), Evil Under the Sun (1981), Memed My Hawk (1982); phonographic recordings incl: Mock Mozard, Peter and the Wolf, Hary Janos, The Old Man of Lochnager; also dir several operas incl: The Magic Flute (Hamburg 1968), Les Brigands (Berlin 1978), The Marriage (Piccola Scala 1981), Mavra (1982), Katja Kabanowa (Hamburg 1985); Benjamin Franklin Medal RSA 1957, Hon DMus Cleveland Inst of Music 1967, Hon LLD Dundee Univ 1969 (rector 1968 and 1971-73), Hon LLD La Salle Coll of Philadelphia 1971, Hon DLitt Lancaster Univ 1972, Hon doctorate Toronto Univ 1984, UNICEF Award for Distinguished Service 1978, Prix de la Butte (French Award for 'Dear Me' 1978), Variety Club Award of GB for Best Actor 1979, Commandeur des Arts et des Lettres 1985; *Recreations* sailing, music, motor cars; *Clubs* Garrick, Arts Theatre, Queens, RAC; *Style*— Peter Ustinov, Esq; 11 Rue de Silly, 921000 Boulogne, France (☎ 010 3314 603 8753)

UTIGER, Ronald Ernest; CBE; *b* 1926; *Educ* Shrewsbury, Worcester Coll Oxford (MA); *m* 1953, Barbara von Mohl; 1 s, 1 da; *Career* economist Courtaulds Ltd 1950-61; Br Aluminium Ltd: fin controller 1961-64, comm dir 1965-68, md 1968-79, chm 1979-82; dir: Br Alcan Aluminium plc 1982-, Ultramar plc 1983-; chm TI Gp 1984- (md 1982-86, dep chm & md 1982-84); pres NIESR 1986-; memb Br Library Bd 1987-; FRSA, CBIM; *Style*— Ronald Utiger, Esq, CBE; 9 Ailsa Rd, St Margaret's, Twickenham, Middx

UTTLEY, Hon Mrs (Katherine Barbara); da (by 1 m) of late 18 Baron St John of Bletso; *b* 1907; *m* 1945, George William Uttley (d 1986), late Flt Lt RAF; 1 da; *Career* S/O WAAF; *Style*— The Hon Mrs Uttley; 44 Heath Crescent, Free School Lane, Halifax HX1 2PW

UTTLEY, Roger Miles; s of James Stuart Uttley, and Peggy, *née* Howarth; *b* 11 Sept 1949; *Educ* Montgomery Secondary Modern, Blackpool GS, Northumberland Coll of Educ (MA); *m* 1971, Kristine, da of Arthur Samuel Gibbs; 2 s (Simon b 1976, Benjamin b 1978); *Career* dir of physical education Harrow Sch; England RFU player 1973-80, 23 Caps, Capt season 1976-77, British Lions 1974 to S Africa, played all four test matches; *Books* Pride in England (autobiography), Captaincy in Rugby Football; *Style*— Roger Uttley, Esq; 1 Deyne Court, Harrow Park, Harrow on Hill, Middlesex (☎ 01 422 2556); Harrow Sch Sports Centre, Football Lane, Harrow on Hill (☎ 01 422 2196, telex 304)

UVAROV, Dame Olga; DBE (1983, CBE 1978); da of Nikolas Uvarov and Elena Uvarov; *Educ* Royal Veterinary Coll; *Career* private veterinary practice 1934-53, clinical res pharmaceutical indust 1953-70, head of veterinary advsy dept Glaxo Laboratories 1967-70, Br Veterinary Assoc Tech Info Serv 1970-76, worked on MAFF cttes (under Medicines Act 1968) 1972-77, advsr on tech info BVA 1976-78, memb Medicines Cmmn 1978-82; vice pres: Res Def Soc 1982 (hon sec 1978-82), Inst of Animal Technicians 1983; pres: Soc of Women Veterinary Surgeons 1947-49, Central Veterinary Soc 1952-53, Assoc of Veterinary Teachers and Res Workers 1967-68, Comparative Medicine Section RSM 1967-68 (sec Int Affairs 1983-), Royal Coll of Veterinary Surgeons 1976-77 (memb cncl 1968-), Laboratory Animal Science Assoc 1984- (vice pres 1983-85); memb cncl Univ Fedn of Animal Welfare 1983 (vice pres 1986-); fell RVC 1979, FRCVS 1973 (memb 1934, memb cncl 1968-88), FIBiol 1983, hon fell RSM 1982; Hon DSc Guelph Canada 1976, Victory Gold Medal Central Veterinary Soc 1965; *Books* The Veterinary Annual, Int Encyclopaedia of Veterinary Medicine, many publications in the Veterinary Record and other journals; *Style*— Dame Olga Uvarov, DBE; 76 Elm Park Ct, Elm Park Rd, Pinner, Middx HA5 3LL

UXBRIDGE, Earl of; Charles Alexander Vaughan Paget; s and h of 7 Marquess of Anglesey, DL; *b* 13 Nov 1950; *Educ* Eton, Exeter Coll Oxford; *m* 1986, Georganne Elizabeth Elliott, da of Col John Alfred Downes, MBE, MC, of Tudor Cottage, Whittlesford, Cambs; 1 s (Lord Paget de Beaudesert b 11 April 1986); *Heir* s, (b 1986); *Style*— Earl of Uxbridge; Pl^as Newydd, Llanfairpwll, Gwynedd

UZIELL-HAMILTON, Mario Reginald; s of Don Nino Uziell (d 1951), and Dona Louisa Sevilla de Uziell (d 1976); *b* 4 May 1922; *Educ* Brentwood, Sorbonne, St Catharine's Coll Cambridge; *m* 1952, Adrianne Pauline, da of Prof Marcus Grantham (d 1975); 1 s (Fabian b 1955), 1 da (Amanda b 1956); *Career* Intelligence Corps 1942-46; barr Middle Temple 1951, slr 1959-, sr ptnr Hooper Holt & Co (slrs London, Redhill, Marbella Spain); chm: Fabian Properties Ltd, Commercial & Continental Ltd; dir Mercantile Asset Corpn Ltd; chm: Anglo Ivory Coast Soc 1973-, Anglo Afrique Gp 1983-86; Trustee National Benevolent Fund for the Aged 1984-; Cruz Vermeila Portugal 1945, Ordre National Cote d'Ivoire 1983; War medals;; *Recreations* watching football (particularly Queens Park Rangers); *Style*— Mario Uziell-Hamilton, Esq; 12 Jeymer Ave, London NW2 4PL (☎ 01 450 6462); office: One Beaumont Court, 38/40 Beaumont Street, London WIN 1FA (☎ 01 486 1366); Chandos St, Cavendish Sq, London W1M 0HP (☎ 01 580 6562)

UZIELLI, (William) John; s of Herbert Rex Uzielli, CIE, JP, ICS (d 1961); *b* 2 Mar 1937; *Educ* Marlborough, Trinity Coll Oxford (MA); *m* 1968, Angela Mary, *née* Carrick; 1 s, 1 da; *Career* insurance broker and memb of Lloyd's; chm Hogg Robinson & Gardner Mountain Marine Div; *Recreations* golf, gardening; *Clubs* Royal and Ancient Golf, Berkshire Golf, Trevose Golf, City of London; *Style*— John Uzielli, Esq; Buckhurst Park Cottage, Cheapside, Ascot, Berks (☎ 0990 22932, office 01 480 4000)

V

VACHER, Peter John; s of Edwin John Vacher, of Westcott, Surrey, and Deira Beatrice, *née* Paxman; *b* 28 June 1942; *Educ* Marlborough, London Sch of Printing (Dip Mgmnt); *m* 11 June 1966, Mary Anne (Polly), da of Gerald King, of Britannia RNC, Dartmouth; 3 s (Julian, Clive, Brian); *Career* md Burgess & Son (Abindon) Ltd 1972- (joined 1963); held various posts in BPIF and PIRA 1970-; chm Oxford Section Rolls Royce Enthusiasts 1987; *Recreations* restoration of vintage motor cars; *Style—* Peter Vacher, Esq; Gilbournes Farm, Drayton, Abindon, Oxon OX14 4HA (☎ 0235 31540); Burgess & Son (Abingdon) Ltd, Thames View, Abingdon, Oxon OX14 3LE (☎ 0235 555555, fax 0235 555544, car tel 0836 593931, telex 837316)

VAES, Baron Robert R L; Hon KCMG 1968; *Educ* Brussels Univ (LLD); *m* 22 July 1947, Anne Albers; 1 da (Corinne (Lady John Wellesley)); *Career* joined Belgian Dip Serv 1946; served: Washington, Paris, Hong Kong, London, Rome Madrid; personal priv sec to Min of Foreign Trade 1958-60, dir-gen of political affairs 1964-66, perm under-sec Min of Foreign Affairs (foreign trade and Devpt Cooperation 1966-72), ambass: Spain 1972-76, UK 1976- 84; dir Sotheby's 1984-; cr Baron (Kingdom of Belgium) 1985; Grand Offr Order of Leopold Belgium, Grand Offr Legion of Honour France, Grand Cross Order of Isabel the Catholic Spain; *Recreations* bridge; *Clubs* White's, Beefsteak, Pratt's, Anglo-Belgian; *Style—* Baron Robert Vaes; The Orangery Cottage, Langley Park, Bucks; Sotheby's, 34/35 New Bond Street, London W1A 2AA (☎ 01 493 8080)

VAIL, John Richard; s of Lionel Stuart Vail, JP, and Catherine Grace, *née* Ridler; *b* 7 May 1937; *Educ* Clifton Coll; *m* 21 Oct 1961, Anne, da of Cdr Peter Ward, RN, of 2 Herne Court, Petersfield, Hampshire; 2 s (Paul Dominic b 29 Sept 1962, Thomas Edward b 19 Jan 1967), 1 da (Joanna b 5 Nov 1964); *Career* chartered surveyor; ptnr LS Vail & Son Farnham 1961-88 (sr ptnr 1966 -88), sr ptnr Vail Williams Conslt Surveyors and Commercial Property Agents 1988-; farmer; dir: Portsmouth Building Soc, Ajax Insurance Holdings; memb Wessex Ctee (former chm) RICS, fndr ctee memb Hampshire Devpt Corpn, govr Farleigh Sch, memb cncl St Dismas Soc; former player Rugby Union for Hampshire; FRICS 1961; *Recreations* fox hunting, tennis, shooting; *Clubs* Carlton; *Style—* John Vail, Esq; The Old Rectory, Upham, Hants, SO3 1JH; 20 Brunswick Place, Southampton SO1 2AQ (☎ 0703 631973, fax 0703 223884, car tel 0836 221 485)

VAILE, (Philip) Bryn; MBE (1989); s of Philip Edward Burdock Vaile, of Lymington, Hants, and Florence, *née* Hughes (d 1983); *b* 16 August 1956; *Educ* Beltairs HS, Singapore Int Sch, Thames Poly, Portsmouth Poly; *Career* Mobil Oil Co Ltd: retail mktg 1978-, credit controller 1982-, liquid petroleum gas mktg admin 1986-; sec Int Star Class Solent Fleet 1984-, memb ctee Contessa 32 Class Assoc; *Recreations* yacht racing, golf, photography, music, walking; *Clubs* Royal Lymington Yacht; *Style—* Bryn Vaile, Esq, MBE; 22 Terrington Hill, Marlow, Bucks SL7 2RF (☎ 06284 76082); The Clockhouse, Frogmoor, High Wycombe, Bucks HP13 5DB (☎ 0494 459222, fax 0494 453000, telex 837611 MOBHNY G)

VAISEY, David George; s of William Thomas Vaisey, and Minnie, *née* Payne (d 1987); *b* 15 Mar 1935; *Educ* Rendcomb Coll Glos, Exeter Coll Oxford (BA, MA); *m* 7 Aug 1965, Maureen Anne, da of August Alfred Mansell (d 1939); 2 da (Katharine b 1968, Elizabeth, b 1969); *Career* Nat Serv 1954-56, 2 Lt Glos Regt, seconded KAR 1955-56 serv Kenya; archivist Staffs CC 1960-63, asst (later sr asst) librarian Bodleian Library Oxford 1963-75, dep keeper Oxford Univ Archives 1966-75, keeper of western manuscripts Bodleian Library Oxford 1975-86 (librarian 1986-); professorial fell Exeter Coll Oxford 1975-, visiting prof library studies UCLA 1985, memb Royal Cmmn on Historical Manuscripts 1986-, hon res fell Sch of Library Archive and Info Studies UCL 1987-; FRCHistS 1973, FSA 1974; *Books* Staffordshire and the Great Rebellion (jtly 1964), Probate Inventories of Lichfield and District 1568-1680 (1969), Victorian and Edwardian Oxford from Old Photographs (jtly 1971), Oxford Shops and Shopping (1972), Art for Commerce (jtly 1973), Oxfordshire, A Handbook for Local Historians (jtly 1973, 2 edn 1974), The Diary of Thomas Turner 1754-65 (1984); *Style—* David Vaisey, Esq; 12 Hernes Rd, Oxford, OX2 7PU (☎ 0865 59258); Bodleian Library, Oxford OX1 3BG (☎ 0865 277 166, fax 0865 277 182, telex 83656)

VAIZEY, Hon Edward; s of Baron Vaizey (Life Peer); *b* 1968; *Educ* St Paul's; *Style—* The Hon Edward Vaizey

VAIZEY, Baroness; Marina Alandra; da of Lyman Stansky, of New York, USA; *b* 16 Jan 1938; *Educ* Brearley Sch New York, Putney Sch Putney Vermont, Radcliffe Coll, Harvard Univ (BA), Girton Coll Cambridge (MA); *m* 1961, Baron Vaizey; 2 s, 1 da; *Career* art critic: Financial Times 1970-74, Sunday Times 1974-; dance critic Now! 1979-81; author, broadcaster, occasional exhibition organiser, lecturer, ctee memb; *Books* 100 Masterpieces of Art (1979), Artist as Photographer (1982), Peter Blake (1985); *Recreations* arts, travel; *Style—* The Rt Hon the Lady Vaizey; 24 Heathfield Terrace, London W4 4JE (☎ 01 994 7994)

VAIZEY, Hon Polly; da of Baron Vaizey (Life Peer); *b* 3 Dec 1962; *Educ* St Paul's Girls' Sch, LMH Oxford; *Career* stockbroker; *Style—* The Hon Polly Vaizey

VAIZEY, Hon Thomas Peter John; s of Baron Vaizey (Life Peer); *b* 1964; *Educ* St Paul's, Worcester Coll Oxford (BA), City Univ (Dip Law); *Career* called to the Bar Inner Temple 1988; *Recreations* travel; *Style—* The Hon Thomas Vaizey

VALDINGER, Jan Robin; s of Maj Stefan Valdinger-Vajda, MC, of Chertsey, Surrey, and Peggy, *née* Chadwick; *b* 28 Sept 1945; *Educ* Univ of Newcastle upon Tyne (LLB); *m* 28 Sept 1974, Rosemary Jane, da of Brendan O'Conor Donelan, of Esher, Surrey; 1 s (Stefan b 1975), 2 da (Anna b 1977, Juliet b 1980); *Career* articled clerk Pinsent & Co 1968-70, slr Clifford Turner & Co 1970-74, corporate fin exec Morgan Grenfell & Co 1974-79; Standard Chartered Merchant Bank Ltd: chief exec merchant banking div India 1979-83, md Hong Kong 1983-87, dir advsy servs London 1987-; memb Law Soc; *Clubs* Hong Kong, Royal Hong Kong Jockey; *Style—* Jan Valdinger, Esq; Michael Court, More Lane, Esher, Surrey KT10 8AJ (☎ 0372 68362); Standard Chartered Merchant Bank, 33-36 Gracechurch St, London EC3V 0AX (☎ 01 623 8711, fax 01 626 1610, telex 884689)

VALE, Brian; OBE (1977); s of Leslie Vale, of Headcorn, Kent (d 1986), and May, *née* Knowles (d 1983); *b* 26 May 1938; *Educ* Sir Joseph Williamson's Mathematical Sch Rochester, Keele Univ (BA, Dip Ed), Kings Coll London (MPhil); *m* 12 Dec 1966, Margaret Mary, da of Thomas Ernest Cookson, of Cockerham, Lancs (d 1983); 2 s (Nicholas b 1970, Jonathan b 1977); *Career* Overseas Civil Serv: Northern Rhodesia 1960-63, asst cmmr N Rhodesia London 1964, educn attaché Zambia High Cmmn London 1964-65; Br Cncl: Rio de Janiero Brazil 1965-68, appts div London 1968-71, educn and sci div 1972-75; rep Riyadh Saudi Arabia 1975-78, dep controller educn and sci div London 1978-83, dir gen TETOC 1980-81, controller sci technol and educn div, rep and cultural cnsllr Cairo Embassy 1983-87, asst dir gen Br Cncl London 1987-; *Recreations* reading, talking, naval history; *Clubs* Travellers; *Style—* Brian Vale, Esq, OBE; 40 Gloucester Circus, Greenwich, London SE10; 10 Spring Gardens, London SW1A 2BN (☎ 01 930 8466)

VALENTIA, Gladys, Viscountess; Gladys May Kathleen; da of Uriah Fowler (d 1941), and Emily (d 1938); *b* 19 Feb 1903; *Educ* Ridley Hall Cambridge; *m* 1938, 13 Viscount Valentia (d 1951); *Style—* The Rt Hon Gladys, Viscountess Valentia; 34 Uphills, Bruton, Somerset (☎ Bruton (074 981) 1524)

VALENTIA, 15 Viscount (I 1642, with precedence of 1622); Sir Richard John Dighton Annesley; Bt (I 1620, Premier Baronet of Ireland); also Baron Mountnorris (I 1628); s of 14 Viscount Valentia (d 1983), and Joan, Viscountess Valentia (d 1986); *b* 15 August 1929; *Educ* Marlborough, RMA; *m* 10 Aug 1957, Anita Phyllis, o da of William Arthur Joy, of Bristol; 3 s, 1 da; *Heir* s, Hon Francis Annesley, *qv*; *Career* Capt RA (ret); *Style—* The Rt Hon the Viscount Valentia

VALENTIN, Friedrich Heinrich Hermann; s of Kurt Heinrich Valentin (d 1940), and Margarete Hedwig Eva, *née* Beermann (d 1957); *b* 10 Jan 1918; *Educ* Grunewald Gymnasium Berlin, Univ of Edinburgh, Univ of Witwatersrand (BSc,MSc, PhD); *m* 31 Jan 1953, Nancy, da of George Henry Hitchin (d 1962), of Bury, Lancs; 2 s (Peter Henry b 1959, Leo Kurt b 1964), 1 da (Claire Marguerite b 1955); *Career* offr S African MOD 1942-45, lectr Univ of Natal 1946-49, chem engr Petrocarbon Ltd 1949-51, sr chem engr British Oxygen Co Ltd 1951-55, sr lectr Univ of Cape Town 1955-56, prof of chem engrg Univ of Natal 1957-62, dep dir (res) Warren Spring Labs 1970-82 (head chem engrg 1962-69); consulting chem engr 1982-; Eur Ing, C Eng, FIChemE, FIWEM, MConsE, memb Br Acad Experts; *Books* Absorption in Gas Liquid Dispersions (1965), Odour Control - A Concise Guide (1980), Silos - Draft Design Code for Silos, Bins, Bunkers and Hoppers (1987); *Recreations* gardening, family, writing computer programmes; *Style—* Dr Friedrich Valentin; Elm Tree House, Letchworth Lane, Letchworth, Herts SG6 3ND (☎ 0462 684940, fax 0462 671436, telex 825644)

VALENTINE, David Aitken; s of David Aitken Valentine (d 1979), of Balgrummo, Perth, and Isabella, *née* Dow (d 1983); *b* 31 Jan 1939; *Educ* Perth Acad, CPU California (BA, MBA); *m* 15 Nov 1963, Sheena Mairi, da of John McLean (d 1984), of Perth; 1 da (Janine Lynne b 12 July 1966); *Career* corporate planning mangr and lectr in Australia 1972, Airfix Prods Ltd 1973-76, BSG Int (special and subsids) 1976-80, chief exec Bullers plc and subsids 1983-88, search dir Kay Exec Search 1988-; FRSA; *Books* Insolvency Prevention (1985); *Recreations* shooting, water colour painting; *Clubs* Carlton, RAC, Phyllis Ct; *Style—* David Valentine, Esq; Sussex House, Berkeley Gardens, Claygate, Esher, Surrey (☎ 0372 68430); Res Gordon Bennett, Boulevard Gordon Bennett, Beaulieu-sur- Mer, Cote d'Azur, France (☎ 010 33 93 01 10 87); office, 1 New Bond St, London W1Y 9PE (☎ 01 493 7232, fax 01 499 6015, car tel 0860 372 435)

VALENTINE, Dr Donald Graham; s of Rev Cyril Henry Valentine (d 1957), and Ada Grace, *née* Herington (d 1982); *b* 5 Nov 1929; *Educ* East Grinstead Co GS, Trinity Coll Cambridge (BA, MA, LLB), Utrecht Univ Netherlands (Dr Jur); *m* 25 March 1961, Vera Ruth, da of Robert Klinger (d 1954); 2 da (Tessa, Jill); *Career* asst lectr LSE 1954, barr Lincolns Inn 1956, lectr LSE 1957, prof of law Univ of Nigeria 1966-67, reader in law LSE 1967-81; Freeman: Worshipful Co of Arbitrators 1985, City of London 1988; FCI Arb; *Books* The Court of Justice of the European Coal and Steel Community (1956), The Court of Justice of the European Communities (2 vols, 1966); *Recreations* greenhouse gardening; *Clubs* Garrick; *Style—* Dr D G Valentine; 3 Park Lane, Appleton, Oxfordshire (☎ 0865 864658); 1 Atkin Building, Gray's Inn, London WC1 (☎ 01 404 0102, fax 01 405 7456, telex 298623 HUDSON)

VALENTINE, Hon Mrs (Janet Sibella); *née* Weir; da of 2 Viscount Weir, CBE; *b* 13 April 1947; *m* 1978, Francis Anthony Valentine, 2 s of Dr Francis Valentine and Lady Freda, *née* Butler, half-sis of 9 Earl of Lanesborough, TD, JP, DL; 1 s (b 1983), 1 da (b 1981); *Style—* The Hon Mrs Valentine; The Gate House, Astrop, Banbury, Oxon

VALENTINE, Michael Robert; s of Alfred Buyers Valentine (d 1971), and Violet Elise; *b* 16 Jan 1928; *Educ* Shrewsbury, Corpus Christi Coll Cambridge (MA); *m* 1957, Shirley Josephine, *née* Hall; 1 s (James b 1964), 2 da (Josephine b 1958, Helen b 1960); *Career* Lt RCS; dir: S G Warburg & Co Ltd 1966-88 (vice-chm 1986-88), dir: Mercury Securities Ltd 1974-86, S G Warburg Gp plc 1986- (non exec 1988-); non exec vice-chm Croda Int plc 1982-, non exec dir Reckitt & Colman plc 1986-; FCA;

Recreations opera, vintage cars, social life, travel; *Clubs* London Rowing, VSCC, Lagonda; *Style*— Michael Valentine, Esq; 2 Finsbury Ave, London EC2M 2PA (☎ 01 860 1090)

VALENTINI, Baroness - Princess Giovanna Ethel; da of late Prince Giambattista Pia Sigismondo Francesco Rospigliosi (s of Lady Elena Maria Concetta Isabella Gioacchina Giuseppa Giustiniani-Bandini *Princess Camillo Rospigliosi*, 3 da of late 8 Earl of Newburgh) and sis of 11 Earl of Newburgh; *b* 1911; *m* 1937, Baron Umberto Duranti Valentini; *Style*— Princess Giovanna Valentini; Piazza Adriana, 10 Rome, Italy

VALÈRE, Hon Mrs; Hon Gloria Theresa; da of Baron Constantine (Life Peer; d 1971); *b* 2 April 1928; *Educ* St Andrew's Univ (MA), Inst of Educn London Univ (DipEd); *m* 1954, André Joseph Valère; 1 s; *Career* public service Medal of Merit of Order of the Trinity 1982 (MOM); *Style*— The Hon Mrs Valère; 202A Terrace Vale, Goodwood Park, Point Cumana, Trinidad and Tobago (☎ 637 4840)

VALIN, Reginald Pierre (Reg); s of Pierre Louis Valin (d 1962), of Nice, France, and Molly Doreen, *née* Butler; *b* 8 Mar 1938; *Educ* Emanuel Sch; *m* 16 July 1960, Brigitte Karin; 1 da (Claire Suzanne b 1962); *Career* Nat Serv RAF; dir Charles Barker City 1970-73, (chief exec 1976-79, md 1973-76), chm and chief exec: Valin Pollen 1979-84, Valin Pollen Int plc 1984-87, The VPI Plc 1987-88; dir Business in the Community, memb Oxfam Fundraising Ctee; *Style*— Reg Valin, Esq; The VPI Group Plc, 32 Grosvenor Gdns, London, SW1, (☎ 01 730 3456, fax 01 730 6663, telex 296846)

VALLANCE, Anthony (Tony) Thomas Frederick; s of Reece Henry Vallance (d 1942), and Elizabeth Beatrice Vallance, *née* Gibson (d 1944); *b* 3 April 1921; *Educ* King Edward's Sch Birmingham, Univ of Birmingham (LLB); *m* 18 March 1944, Geraldine Lilian Mary, da of William George Burrough, of Somerset (d 1939); 2 s (Richard b 1947, John b 1958), 2 da (Clare b 1950, d 1957, Paula b 1952); *Career* serv WWII RN, Sub Lt RNVR (wounded 1944, invalided from serv); slr: formerly sr ptnr now conslt Messrs Cole & Cole Slrs of Oxford; pres Berks Bucks & Oxfordshire Law Soc 1968-69; Under Sheriff Oxfordshire 1972-85; *Clubs* The Frewen (Oxford); *Style*— A T F Vallance, Esq; 15 Godstow Rd, Upper Wolvercote, Oxford OX2 8AJ (☎ Oxford 58396); St Georges Mansions, George St, Oxford OX1 2AR (☎ Oxford 791122)

VALLANCE, Dr Elizabeth Mary; da of William Henderson McGonnigill, and Jane Brown, *née* Kirkwood; *b* 8 April 1945; *Educ* Univ of St Andrew's (MA), LSE (MSc), Univ of London (PhD); *m* 5 Aug 1967, Iain David Thomas Vallance, s of Edmund Thomas Vallance, CBE, ERD; 1 s (Edmund William Thomas b 1975), 1 da (Rachel Emma b 1972); *Career* univ lectr; reader in politics Univ of London; head dept of political studies, QMC London 1985-88; author, books: The State, Society and Self-Destruction (1975), Women in the House (1979), Women of Europe (1985), Member of Parliament (jt 1987); *Style*— Dr Elizabeth Vallance; Dept of Political Studies, Queen Mary Coll, Univ of London, Mile End Rd, London E1 4NS (☎ 01 980 4811)

VALLANCE, Col James Newton; OBE (1955), TD (1948) and bar, DL (Notts 1966); s of C J Vallance (d 1939); *b* 23 Jan 1906; *Educ* Malvern; *m* 1, 1931, Edith Mary, *née* Hart (d 1974); 2 da; m 2, 1976, Muriel Hattie, *née* Prentice; *Career* slr of the Supreme Ct; *Recreations* shooting; *Clubs* Army and Navy; *Style*— Col James Vallance OBE, TD, DL; The Hermitage, Hermitage Lane, Mansfield, Notts

VALLANCE, Michael Wilson; s of Vivian Victor Wilson Vallance (d 1967), of Wandsworth and Helston, Cornwall, and Kate, *née* Edwards (d 1986); *b* 9 Sept 1933; *Educ* Brighton Coll, St John's Coll Cambridge (MA); *m* 1 April 1970, Mary Winifred Ann, da of John Steele Garnett (d 1969) of Runcorn, Cheshire; 3 da (Vivian b 1974, Rachel b 1971, Emma b b 1972); *Career* staff memb Utd Steel Cos Ltd 1952-53, asst master: Abingdon Sch 1957-61, Harrow Sch 1961-72, headmaster: Durham Sch 1972-82, Bloxham Sch 1982-; chm: Ctee of Northern ISIS 1976-77, NE Div of Headmasters Conf 1981-82; memb: steering ctee Bloxham Project 1986-, Headmasters Conf 1972; *Recreations* books, cricket, the sea; *Clubs* MCC, Jesters; *Style*— Michael Vallance, Esq; Bloxham Sch, nr Banbury, Oxfordshire OX15 4PE (☎ 0295 720 206)

VALLAT, Prof Sir Francis Aimé; GBE (1981), KCMG (1962, CMG 1955), QC (1961); s of Col Frederick Vallat, OBE (d 1922); *b* 25 May 1912; *Educ* Univ Coll Toronto, Gonville and Caius Coll Cambridge; *m* 1, 1939 (m dis 1973), Mary Alison, da of F H Cockell, of Barnham, Sussex; 1 s, 1 da; m 2, 1988, Patricia Maria, da of Capt Hamish Morten Anderson, MB, ChB, RAMC; *Career* serv WWII as Flt Lt RAFVR; barr Gray's Inn 1935; joined FO 1945, legal advsr Perm UK Delegation to UN 1950-54, dep legal advsr FO 1954-60, legal advsr 1960-68, visiting prof McGill Univ 1965-66; dir Int Law Studies King's Coll London 1968-76, reader Int Law London Univ 1969-70, prof 1970-76, prof emeritus Int Law London Univ 1976-; bencher Gray's Inn 1971-; memb: Int Law Cmmn 1973-81 (chm 1977-78), Permanent Ct of Arbitration 1981-, Curatorium Hague Acad of Int Law 1982-; Dr en dr hc Lausanne Univ 1979; *Clubs* Hurlingham; *Style*— Prof Sir Francis Vallat, GBE,; 3 Essex Court, Temple, London EC4 (☎ 01 583 9294); 17 Ranelagh Grove, London SW1W 8PA (☎ 01 730 6656)

VALLINGS, Vice Adm Sir George Montague Francis; KCB (1986); s of Robert Archibald Vallings, DSC (d 1970), of Perth, Scotland, and Alice Mary Joan, *née* Bramsden (d 1964); *b* 31 May 1932; *Educ* Belhahen Hill Dunbar, RNC Dartmouth; *m* 12 Sept 1964, Tessa Julia, da of Bernard Delacourt Cousins (d 1968), of Haslemere; 3 s (Sam b 10 Jan 1966, Tom b 1 Oct 1968, Andrew b 28 June 1970); *Career* Cdr 1965, CO HMS Defender 1967-68, exec offr HMS Bristol 1970-73, Capt 1974, NA Canberra Aust 1974-76, Capt 2 Frigate Sqdn 1977-78, dir Naval Op and Trade 1978-80, Cdre Clyde 1980-82, Rear Adm 1983, Flag Offr Gibraltar 1983-85, Vice Adm 1985, Flag Offr Scotland and NI 1985-87; sec Chartered Inst Mgmnt Accountants 1987-, chm race ctee Sail Trg Assoc; cncl memb: Royal Nat Mission to Deep Sea Fisherman, Bede House Assoc (Bermondsey); MNI 1976; *Recreations* various sports; *Clubs* Royal Ocean Racing; *Style*— Vice Adm Sir George Vallings, KCB; Meadowcroft, 25 St Marys Rd, Long Ditton, Surrey KT6 5EU (☎ 01 398 6932); 63 Portland Place, London W1 4AB (☎ 01 637 2311)

VALLIS, Rear-Adm Michael Anthony; CB (1986); s of Ronald William Harvey Vallis (d 1980), of Frome, Somerset, and Sarah Josephine (d 1964); *b* 30 June 1929; *Educ* RNC Dartmouth, RNEC Manadon, RNC Greenwich; *m* 1959, Pauline Dorothy, da of George Abbott (d 1967), of Wymondham, Leics; 3 s, 1 da; *Career* dir Naval Recruiting 1979-82, dir-gen Surface Ships MOD 1983-84, dir-gen Marine Engrg MOD 1984-86 and sr naval rep Bath 1983-86, dir Darchem Ltd 1987, dep pres Inst of Marine Engrs 1987-; FEng; *Recreations* fishing, walking, music, theatre; *Clubs* Royal Cwlth Soc; *Style*— Rear Adm Michael Vallis, CB; 54 Bloomfield Park, Bath BA2 2BX (☎ 0225 314286)

VALLS, Rafael Francisco Jose; LVO (1986); s of Aurelio Valls, (d 1968), and Maria de los Angeles, *née* Carreras (d 1970); *b* 10 Jan 1912; *Educ* Chamatin De La Rosa Madrid, Stonyhurst, Madrid Univ; *m* 1 March 1947, Diana Seymour, da of John Chadwick Greaves (d 1950); 2 s (Rafael Rhidian b 1948, Jilan Allrelio b 1949); *Career* called to the Bar Middle Temple 1933, barr Spanish Bar Madrid 1934, practising barr Spanish and English Law 1934-75, legal advsr to Spanish Embassy London 1939, legal attache to Spanish Embassy London 1975-; Blackstone Prizeman 1931, 1932; memb: various Spanish Govt Delegations for negotiating Legal Conventions, Bar Cncl Foreign Relations Ctee 1965-70; rep Spanish Bar Cncl 1950-73; memb: British Maritime Law Assoc, Spanish Maritime Law Assoc; Kt Grand Cross Order of Civil Merit Spain 1986, Kt Car Order of Isabel the Catholic Spain 1970, Car Order Civil Merit 1954 Spain; *Books* many articles on Spanish law, author of 21 summaries of relevant Spanish laws currently available; *Recreations* music, sailing, motoring; *Clubs* Pegasus, Bar YC, Royal Southern YC; *Style*— HE Don Rafael Valls, LVO; 26 Hans Crescent, SW1 (☎ 01 235 5555); Casa Bermudas, Altea, Spain; Spanish Embassy, 24 Belgrave Square, London SW1X 89A

VAN ALLAN, Richard; s of Joseph Arthur Jones, of Private Sherwood Foresters Mansfield, Notts, and Irene Hannah, *née* Taylor; *b* 28 May 1935; *Educ* Brunts GS Mansfield, Worcester Coll of Educ (Dip Ed), Brimingham Sch of Mus; *m* 1, 1963 (m dis 1974), Elizabeth Mary, da of Bib Peabody, (d 1983), of Leamington SPA; 1 s (Guy Richard b 1967); m 2 31 Dec 1976 (m dis 1987), Elisabeth Rosemary, da of Richard Pickering, DM, of Cape Town SA; 1 s (Robert Tristan b 1979), 1 da (Emma Mary b 1983); *Career* Sgt Special Investigation Branch, RMP 1953-56; sch teacher, opera singer, debut 1964, principal bass at; Glyndebourne, WNO, ENO, Scottish Opera, Royal Opera House Covent Garden, Nice, Bordeaux, Paris, Marseille, Bruxelles, San Diego, Miami, Boston, Seattie, Metropolitan NY, Buenos Aires; dir Nat Opera Studio; Hon RAM; *Recordings* Cosi Fan Tutte, Don Alfonso (Grammy award), Don Giovanni, Leporello (Grammy nomination); *Recreations* cricket, golf, shooting; *Style*— Richard Van Allen, Esq; 18 Octavia St, London SW11 3DN (☎ 01 228 8462)

VAN CUTSEM, Geoffrey Neil; yr s of Bernard van Cutsem (d 1975), and Mary, da of Capt Edward Compton, JP, DL (s of Lord Alwyne Compton, 2 s of 4 Marquess of Northampton, KG), of Newby Hall, Ripon; yr bro of Hugh van Cutsem, *qv*; *b* 23 Nov 1944; *Educ* Ampleforth; *m* 30 Oct 1969, Sarah, only da of Alastair McCorquodale, *qv*; 2 da (Sophie b 5 Aug 1975, Zara b 11 Dec 1978); *Career* served Royal Horse Gds (Blues and Royals) 1963-68, Capt 1967; joined Savills 1969, exec dir 1987-; memb nat appeals ctee Cancer Res campaign; FRICS 1973; *Clubs* White's, Pratt's; *Style*— Geoffrey van Cutsem, Esq; 9a Elm Park Rd, London SW3 6BP (☎ 01 352 8281); The Old Rectory, Old Somerby, Grantham, Lincs NG33 4AG (☎ 0476 63167); Savills, 20 Grosvenor Hill, London W1X 0HQ (☎ 01 499 8644)

VAN CUTSEM, Hugh Bernard Edward; s of Bernard van Cutsem (d 1975), and Mary, da of Capt Edward Compton, JP, DL (himself s of Lord Alwyne Compton, 2 s of 4 Marquess of Northampton, KG), of Newby Hall, Ripon; er bro of Geoffrey van Cutsem, *qv*; *b* 21 July 1941; *Educ* Ampleforth; *m* 1971, Jonkvrouwe Emilie Elise Christine, da of Jonkheer Pieter Quarles van Ufford (Netherlands cr of Willem I 1814), of Ackworth House, E Bergholt, Suffolk; 4 s; *Career* Lt Life Gds; bloodstock breeder, farmer, co chm; *Clubs* White's, Jockey; *Style*— Hugh van Cutsem, Esq; Northmore, Exning, Newmarket, Suffolk CB8 7JR (☎ 063 877 332)

VAN CUYLENBURG, Peter; s of Flt Lt Brian Van Cuylenburg, of Auckland, NZ, and Margaret, *née* Budd; *b* 5 Mar 1948; *Educ* Sir William Berlase Marlow Bucks, St John's Singapore, Bristol Poly; *m* 5 Aug 1972, Mary-Rose, da of Harry Sabberton, of Cambridge (d 1984); 1 s (Jamie b 1981), 1 da (Nicola b 1984); *Career* md Texas Instruments Ltd 1984-87; vice-pres Data Systems Gp, Texas Instruments 1987; CBIM; *Recreations* sailing; *Style*— Peter van Cuylenburg, Esq; Texas Instruments Ltd, Manton Lane, Bedford (☎ 0234 223201)

VAN DER NOOT, Hon Mrs; (Barbara Mary); *née* Cokayne; da of late 1 Baron Cullen of Ashbourne and Grace, da of the late Rev the Hon John Marsham (s of 3 Earl of Romney); *b* 1905; *m* 1929, Maj Gilbert Edgar Francis Van der Noot (d 1981); 1 da; *Style*— The Hon Mrs Van der Noot; Oak Cottage, Hartley Wintney, Hants

VAN DER WERFF, His Hon Judge Jonathan Ervine; s of James van der Werff (d 1960), of London, and Clare Poupart, *née* Ervine; *b* 23 June 1935; *Educ* Harrow, RMA Sandhurst; *m* 17 Sept 1968, Katharine Bridget, da of Maj James Colvin, of Newland Hse, Withypool, Somerset; 2 da (Olivia b 1971, Claudia b 1976); *Career* joined Coldstream Gds 1953, RMA Sandhurst 1954-55, cmmnd 1955, Adj 1 Bn 1962-64, Maj 1967, ret 1968; barr Inner Temple 1969, rec 1986, circuit judge 1986; *Clubs* Pratt's, Hurlingham, Bembridge Sailing, Something; *Style*— His Hon Judge van der Werff; Knightsbridge Crown Ct, Hans Crescent, London SW3

VAN DER WOUDE, Lady (Anne) Penelope Marian; *née* Herbert; da (by 1 m) of 6 Earl of Carnarvon; *b* 1925; *m* 1945, Gerrit van der Woude, Grenadier Gds; 2 s (and 1 da decd); *Style*— Lady Penelope van der Woude; Heronden, Eastry, Sandwich, Kent

VAN DER WYCK, Jonkheer Herman Constantyn; s of Jonkheer Hendrik Lodewyk van der Wyck, OBE (d 1986), Col Royal Netherlands Artillery, and Berendina Johanna van Welderen, Baroness Rengers (d 1963); *b* 17 Mar 1934; *Educ* Inst for Int Studies Univ of Geneva (MA), Rotterdam/Ann Arbour Business Sch (MA); *m* 1, 1959 (m dis 1969), Danielle Mourgue d'Algue; 1 s (Patrick Henri Louis b 5 Dec 1962), 1 da (Edina Nathalie b 8 Aug 1960); m 2, 1977 (m dis 1988), Viviana Olga Paulina van Reigersberg Versluys; 2 s (Edzard Lorillard b 10 Oct 1980, Alexander Lodewyk b 5 Aug 1985); *Career* ret Capt Royal Dutch Cavalry; chm S G Warburg & Co Ltd; vice-chm S G Warburg Gp plc; dir: Automobiles Peugeot, Peugeot Talbot UK Ltd, Energy Int NV; *Recreations* skiing, water skiing, swimming, tennis, reading, music; *Style*— Herman C Van Der Wyck, Esq; 27 South Terrace, London SW7 (☎ 01 584 9931); S G Warburg Group plc, 1 Finsbury Avenue, London EC2 (☎ 01 382 4086)

VAN GEEST, Leonard Waling; s of Leonard van Geest; *b* 1 April 1950; *Educ* Spalding GS; *m* 1978, Gillian Denise, *née* Fox; 1 s; *Career* chief exec Geest plc; non-exec dir The Littlewoods Orgn; *Recreations* tennis; *Style*— Leonard van Geest Esq; Wool Hall, Cross Gate, Wykeham, Spalding (☎ 0775 66256)

VAN HEE, David William; s of Victor George Van Hee, of Coventry, Warwickshire, and Vera, *née* Gibson; *b* 26 Feb 1949; *Educ* King Henry VIII Sch Coventry, Downing Coll Cambridge (MA, LLB); *Career* called to the Bar Middle Temple 1972, barr South Eastern Circuit; *Recreations* gliding; *Clubs* Utd Oxford and Cambridge; *Style*— David Van Hee, Esq; 3 Dr Johnson's Buildings, Temple EC4 (☎ 01 353 4854, fax 01 583 8784)

VAN KLAVEREN, Dr George (John); s of Wilhelm Gottfried Van Klaveren (d 1963), and Gladys Joan Van Klaveren, *née* Bickmore (d 1962); *b* 9 April 1925; *Educ* Marlborough, Cambridge Univ, St Mary's Hosp (MRCS, LRCP); *m* 10 Aug 1949, Doreen Maud, da of William Benjamin Riceveal Berriman (d 1964); 1 s (Geoffrey b 1960), 1 da (Juliana b 1952); *Career* Flt Lt RAF 1950-52, physician and surgn in gen practice 1952-70; sr med offr to Br Rail Bd 1986-, chm Br Coll of Acupuncture 1986-; *Recreations* badminton, philately, gardening; *Clubs* AA; *Style—* Dr George Van Klaveren; Hunting Delight, 3 Rotherfield Rd, Henley-on-Thames, Oxon RG9 1NR (☎ 0491 575736); Medical Centre, West Colonnade, Euston Station, London (☎ 01 928 5151, ext 40997)

VAN KOETSVELD, Hon Mrs (Margaret Ross); *née* Geddes; o da of 2 Baron Geddes, KBE (d 1975), and Enid, Baroness Geddes, *qv*; *b* 5 May 1934; *Educ* Benenden; *m* 6 May 1961, Ralph Emilius Quintus van Koetsveld, s of Johan Emilius van Koetsveld, of Rotterdam; 3 s (Michael, Guy, Dirk); *Career* memb Assoc of Occupational Therapists; chm Hydon Hill Cheshire Home, Godalming 1984-88; tstee Leonard Cheshire Fndn; *Recreations* needlework, canalling, singing; *Style—* The Hon Mrs van Koetsveld; Northacre, Grenville Rd, Shackleford, Godalming, Surrey GU8 6AX

VAN LENNEP, Edward David Ogilvy; s of Cyril Charles Ogilvy van Lennep (d 1959), and Ella Theresa, *née* Gruning (d 1927); Dutch subject, naturalised British on coming of age, yst s of Charles David van Lennep, landowner in Turkey and Swedish Consul in Smyrna; *b* 17 August 1921; *Educ* RNC Dartmouth; *m* 1 July 1950, June Denise, da of James Reginald Bromley, of Billericay, Essex; 2 da (Jane b 1952, Felicity (Mrs Gillott) b 1953); *Career* serv WWII RN, Midshipman Home Fleet 1939-41, (HMS Birmingham, HMS Renown, and HMS Reaper), 1 Lt i/c HMS Farndale 1948, NID Germany 1948 (ret at own request); farmer, established Rawreth Riding Sch 1956, memb Arab Horse Soc, fndr Heron Stream Stud (ret); MN 1973-80; 1 Offr: Crescent Shipping, Turnbull Scott, Weston Shipping (FG Masters Cert); co-organiser first police underwater search and recovery gp in UK; *Recreations* photography, volunteer driver for Riding for Disabled Assoc; *Style—* David van Lennep, Esq; Burrells Farm, Church Rd, Rawreth, Wickford, Essex SS11 8SH (☎ 0268 762001)

VAN MARLE, (Johan) Tyo; s of Tyo Henrik van Marle and Catharina Alida van Marle of St Jeaume, Chatenauneuf, AM France; *b* 20 Oct 1940; *Educ* Baarns Lyceum, Amsterdam Univ, Harvard Bus Sch USA; *m* 1972, Isabella Christina, da of Rudolph Maximilliam Crommelin; 2 s (John b 1977, Francis b 1980); *Career* mangr Pierson, Heldring and Pierson (bankers) Amsterdam 1966-72; dir J Henry Schroder Wagg and Co Ltd (merchant bankers) 1972-82; md Schroder & Chartered (merchant bankers) Hong Kong 1982-84; exec dir Credit Suisse First Boston (Investmt Bankers) 1984-, chief exec offr Credit Suisse First Boston Nederland NV Amsterdam 1987-; *Recreations* opera, golf, skiing; *Clubs* Sunningdale Golf, Annabelle's, Hong Kong, Sheh-OGC; *Style—* Tyo van Marle, Esq; Jagtlust Eemnesserweg 38B, 1261 HJ Blassicum, The Netherlands, (☎ 02153 11706); Herengracht 478, 1017 CB Amsterdam (☎ 020 556 7222, telex 14517 CSFB NL)

VAN PRAAGH, Dame (Margaret) Peggy; DBE (1970, OBE 1966); da of Harold John Van Praagh; *b* 1 Sept 1910; *Educ* King Alfred Sch Hampstead London; *Career* memb Sadler's Wells Ballet (now Royal Ballet Organisation) 1940-56, dir Norsk Ballet 1957-58, Edinburgh Int Festival Ballet 1958, artistic dir Borovansky Ballet Co 1960-61, founding artistic dir The Australian Ballet 1962-74 and memb cncl and guest teacher 1975-, dance conslt to Vic Miny for the Arts (and memb cncl 1975-); Queen Elizabeth II Coronation Award Royal Academy of Dancing 1965, Distinguished Artist Award Aust Cncl 1974; Hon DLitt Univ of New England NSW; *Style—* Dame Peggy Van Praagh, DBE; Flat 5, 248 The Avenue, Parkville, Vic 3052, Australia

VAN RAALTE, Hon Mrs (Mary Anne); *née* Berry; eldest da of 2 Viscount Kemsley; *b* 30 April 1934; *m* 26 July 1960, Charles Henry van Raalte, s of late Noel van Raalte; 1 s, 2 da; *Style—* The Hon Mrs van Raalte; c/o Rt Hon Viscount Kemsley, Thorpe Lubenhall Hall, Market Harborough, Leics

VAN STRAUBENZEE, Lt-Col Henry Hamilton; DSO (1945), OBE (1949); s of Henry Turner van Straubenzee (d 1914), of Spennithorne House, Leyburn, Yorks, and Elfreda Mowbray (d 1963), da of William Houston Rogers, of Johannesburg; family descends from Philip William Casimir van Staubenzee, Capt Dutch Gds (naturalised by Act of Parliament 1759) (*see* Burke's Landed Gentry, 18th Edn, vol 1); *b* 7 Mar 1914; *Educ* Winchester, RMC Sandhurst; *m* 2 April 1943, Angela de Laune, da of Capt Charles Harry Fenwick, 60th Rifles (d 1938); 3 s (Charles b 1945, Alexander b 1951, William b 1952), 1 da (Philippa (Mrs Whitaker), b 1944); *Career* regular army offr; cmmnd Oxford and Bucks LI 1934; serv WWII: Bde Maj 11 Armoured Bde 1941-42, GSOI (Lt-Col) 10 Armd Div MEF 1943 (despatches), Italy 1944, cmd 145 (Duke of Wellington's Regt RAC and 12 Bn RTR Palestine 1945-46, GSOI 1 Inf Div, cmd 2 Bn Oxford and Bucks LI, GSOI 6 Airborn Div, Instr Staff Coll Camberley 1948-50, GSOI 11 Armd Divn Germany 1950-53, mil assist to CIGS WO 1953-56, cmd 4/7 Royal Drag Gds 1956-57, invalided out of Army 1957; joined W H Smith & Son Ltd 1957, dir 1960, md 1968 (ret 1974); *Recreations* dry fly trout fishing, gardening; *Clubs* Army and Navy; *Style—* Lt-Col van Straubenzee, DSO, OBE; Kingscote, Binfield Rd, Wokingham, Berks (☎ Bracknell 54491)

VAN STRAUBENZEE, Col Philip Turner; DSO (1944); elder s of Henry Turner van Straubenzee, of Spennithorne House, Leyburn, NJ Yorks (d 1914), and Elfred Mowbray, *née* Rogers (d 1963); paternal family of Dutch Extraction, Philip William Casimir van Straubenzee was naturalised by Act of Parliament 1759 (*see* Burke's Landed Gentry, 18th Edn, vol i); *b* 2 Mar 1912; *Educ* Sherborne, RMA Sandhurst; *m* 29 May 1954, Rosemary Imogen Atterbury (d 1980), 2nd da of Maj-Gen Walter Edmond Clutterbuck, DSO, MC, of Hornby Castle, Bedale, N Yorks (d 1986); 2 da (Henrietta Jane b 1956, Joanna Rosemary b 1958); *Career* cmmnd Oxford and Bucks LI 1952, serv WWII with Royal W African Frontier Force in E Africa Campaign, Somaliland and Abyssinia (despatches), cmd 1 Bn Sierra Regt RWAFF in Burma Campaign 1942-43 (DSO), cmd 4 Bn Green Howards (TA) 1955-59; appted Dep Bde Cmd 151 Inf Bde (TA); CC Leyburn Dist N Yorks 1959-64, chm Yorks Dales Nat Park Ctee 1970-83, chm of Govrs Wenlseydale Sch 1970-72; JP 1955-75, DL N Yorks 1959-87; *Recreations* cricket, golf, shooting, fishing; *Clubs* Army and Navy, I Zingari, Free Foresters Cricket; *Style—* Col Philip Van Straubenzee, DSO, DL; Spennithorne House, Leyburn, N Yorks (☎ 0969 23200)

VAN STRAUBENZEE, Sir William Radcliffe; MBE (1954); s of late Brig A B van Straubenzee, DSO, MC, and Margaret Joan, da of A N Radcliffe, of Bag Park, Widecombe-in-the-Moor, Newton Abbot, S Devon; *b* 27 Jan 1924; *Educ* Westminster; *Career* serv WWII Maj RA; slr 1952; memb Gen Synod C of E, chm Dioceses Cmmn 1978-86, church cmmr 1968-87; MP (C) Wokingham 1959-87; PPS to Min Educn 1960-62, jt parly under-sec of State Dept of Educn and Sci 1970-72, Min State NI 1972-74, second church estates cmmr 1979-87, chm YCs Nat Advsy Ctee 1951-53; chm: Cons Parly Educn Ctee 1979-83, Select Ctee Assistance to Private Membs 1975-77, (memb Exec 1922 Ctee 1979-87); former chm Nat Cncl for Drama Trg; kt 1981; *Clubs* Carlton, Garrick; *Style—* Sir William van Straubenzee, MBE; York House, 199 Westminster Bridge Rd, London SE1 (☎ 01 928 6855)

VAN VEEN, Marcella; da of Marcel Fresco, of Holland, and Barbara, *née* Zoeteman; *b* 28 Mar 1943; *Educ* Holland; *m* 4 Aug 1963, Peter Vincent, s of Johan van Veen; 1 s (Robert b 1964), 1 da (Julie b 1968); *Career* md: DAC (Dial a Char) Ltd, Frobishers Limousine Servs Ltd, DAC Prods Ltd; *Recreations* theatre, opera, travel; *Clubs* IOD; *Style—* Mrs Marcella Van Veen; 46 Goffs Park Rd, Crawley, Sussex (☎ 0293 21834); DAC Ltd, 77 London Rd, East Grinstead, Sussex (☎ 0342 315556, car ☎: 0836 514017)

VAN ZUYDAM, Paul Johannes; *b* 13 Mar 1938; *m* 4 children; *Career* chm chief exec Prestige Gp plc 1983-; dir Gallaher Ltd 1986-; *Clubs* Hurlingham; *Style—* Paul van Zuydam, Esq; The Prestige Gp plc, Prestige House, 14-18 Holborn, London EC1N 2LQ (☎ 01 405 6711, telex PRESLOW G 24162)

VANCE, Charles Ivan; s of E Goldblatt; *b* 1929; *Educ* Royal Sch Dungannon, Queen's Univ Belfast; *m* 1966, Hon Imogen Moynihan, *qv*; 1 da (Jacqueline); *Career* actor and theatrical dir/prodr/publisher and ed; dep chm Festival of Br Theatre 1974- (vice chm 1975), chm standing advsy ctee on Local Authy and the Theatre 1983-; chm Charles Vance Ltd and Beck Theatre Prodns Ltd, pres Theatrical Mgmnt Assoc 1971-76; vice-chm: Theatres Advy Cncl 1974; dir: Empire Theatre York 1987-, Top Hat Catering 1986-; chm Platform Pubns Ltd; FRSA, FInstD; *Books* Amateur Stage (ed), Br Theatre Directory (1971-75), Br Theatre Review (1973), Stage Adaption: Jane Eyre and Wuthering Heights; *Recreations* travel, cooking, sailing (in 1956 single handed crossing Atlantic), dog breeding; *Clubs* RAC, Kennel, Hurlingham, Tenterden GC, Wig and Pen; *Style—* Charles Vance, Esq; Quince Cottage, Bilsington, nr Ashford, Kent

VANCE, Hon Mrs; Hon Imogen Anne Ierne; *née* Moynihan; da of 2 Baron Moynihan, OBE, TD (d 1965); *b* 1932; *m* 1, 1953 (m dis 1965), Michael Edward Peter Williams; m 2, 1965, Charles Ivan Vance, *qv*; 1 da; *Style—* The Hon Mrs Vance; Oak Lodge, Perry Hill, Farway, nr Colyton, E Devon EX13 6DH

VANDELEUR, Major (William) David (Boyle); s of Lt-Col Thomas Boyle Vandeleur, DSO (d 1968), of Co Down, N Ireland, and Marcella, *née* Barker (d 1981); *b* 10 June 1928; *Educ* Sedbergh, RMA Sandhurst; *m* 12 July 1954, Iona, da of Maj G J R Tomkin (d 1980); 2 s ((David) Simon b 1956, Alexander b 1963), 1 da (Christina Mary b 1958); *Career* ret Army 1968; DL Co Antrim 1977; High Sherrif Co Antrim 1980; *Recreations* sailing, gardening; *Clubs* Royal Dublin Soc; *Style—* Maj David Vandeleur; Long Acre, Briningham, Melton Constable, Norfolk

VANDEN-BEMPDE-JOHNSTONE; *see*: Johnstone

VANDER SPIEGEL, Joseph Anthony; s of Joseph Vander Spiegel (d 1977), of Grimsby, and Helen, *née* Kelly (d 1948); *b* 2 July 1923; *Educ* Wintringham GS Grimsby; *m* 15 Oct 1949, Margaret Mary, da of Clarence Thwaites (d 1971), of London; 1 s (Mark b 1954), 2 da (Catherine b 1951, Josephine b 1957); *Career* Corpl RASC 1942-47; Charringtons Solid Fuel: dir 1974, md 1976-86; pres Coal Merchants Fedn GB 1985-86; chm Chamber of Coal Traders 1985-; Freeman: City of London 1984, Worshipful Co of Fuellers 1985; *Recreations* tennis, allotment gardening; *Clubs* Nat Lib, Cricketers; *Style—* Joseph Vander Spiegel, Esq; 44 Drapers Rd, Enfield, Middx EN2 8LY (☎ 01 367 6248); Victoria House, Southampton Row, London WC1B 4DH (☎ 01 405 8218)

VANDER-MOLEN, Jack; s of Leon Vandermolen (d 1941), of Berwick St, London W1, and Rosetta, *née* Defries (d 1952); *b* 9 August 1923; *Educ* Archibishop Tenisons GS; *m* 23 March 1950, Muriel, da of Louis Walters (d 1981), of Edgware, Middx; 3 s (Jonathan Mark b 1954, Paul Nicholas b 1956, d 1985, Leon Richard b 1960), 1 da (Lesley Rebecca b 1952); *Career* WWII, RM 1942-46 (Middle E combined ops 1943-45); orthotic conslt V-M Orthopaedics Ltd 1948- (chm and md 1963-), pt/t conslt Camp Ltd; chm of tstees Paul Vander-Molen Fndn 1986-, expedition ldr Breakthrough Disability 1986 (expedition to Iceland involving disabled explorers) collaborated with Channel 4 in making film A Different Frontier; pres Br Surgical Trade Assoc 1987- (chm 1984-87; pres IV Hendon Scouts and Guides, hon vice-pres Hendon and Edgware Dist Scouts and Guides, awarded Chief Scouts Medal of Merit for outstanding servs to Scouting 1984; Freeman City of London 1973, memb: Worshipful Co of Basketmakers 1973, Guild of World Traders in London 1986, United Wards 1973; FRGS 1986, Fell Br Inst Surgical Technologists 1958; *Books* Iceland Breakthrough (jt author 1985); *Recreations* outdoor adventure activities, music: organ playing, writing, boating; *Style—* Jack Vander-Molen, Esq; The Model Farm House, Church End, London NW4 4JS; 10 Garrick Alt, Hampton on Thames, Middx (☎ 01 203 1214, 01 203 2344)

VANDERFELT, Sir Robin Victor; KBE (1973), OBE (1954); s of Sydney Vanderfelt, OBE; *b* 24 July 1921; *Educ* Haileybury, Peterhouse Cambridge; *m* 1962, Jean Becker, da of John Steward; 2 s; *Career* serv WWII Burma and India; asst sec Cwlth Parly Assoc UK branch 1949-59, sec 1960-61, sec-gen 1961-86; *Recreations* gardening; *Clubs* Royal Cwlth Soc; *Style—* Sir Robin Vanderfelt, KBE, OBE; No 6 Saddler's Mead, Wilton, Salisbury, Wilts SP2 0DE

VANDERSTEEN, Martin Hugh; s of William Martin Vandersteen (d 1983), and Dorothy Margaret, *née* Leith; *b* 9 August 1935; *Educ* Harrow Co GS; *m* 3 April 1967, Catherine Susan Mary, da of John Cansdale Webb; 2 s (Anthony b 1970, William b 1973); *Career* md European Mgmnt consultancy practices Arthur Andersen & Co 1987- (mgmnt ptnr 1973-86, ptnr since 1968, joined 1957); chm UK Mgmnt Consulting Assoc 1981, FCA; *Recreations* sailing, fishing, golf, swimming; *Clubs* Royal Ocean Racing, Royal Southern Yacht, Otter Swimming; *Style—* Martin H Vandersteen, Esq; 2 Bristol Gardens, Putney Heath, London SW15 3TG (☎ 01 788 9026); 1 Surrey Street, London WC2R 2PS (☎ 01 438 3106)

VANE, Hon Carolyn Mary; da of 11 Baron Barnard, TD, JP, and Lady Davina, *née* Cecil, da of 6 Marquess of Exeter; *b* 5 May 1954; *Style—* The Hon Carolyn Vane

VANE, Hon Christopher John Fletcher-; yr s of 1 Baron Inglewood, TD, *qv*; *b* 27 Mar 1953; *Educ* Eton, Trinity Coll Cambridge; *Career* barr Inner Temple 1976; *Clubs*

Travellers', Northern Counties (Newcastle-upon-Tyne); *Style*— The Hon Christopher Vane; Hutton-in-the-Forest, Penrith, Cumbria CA11 9TH (☎ 085 34 400); 3c Lambton Rd, Newcastle-upon-Tyne NE2 4RX (☎ 091 2810930)

VANE, Eric Digby Tempest; s of Harry Tempest Vane, CBE (d 1942), and Florence Emmara Maud *née* Burley (d 1936); *b* 27 Dec 1912; *Educ* Mill Hill, LSE (BSc); *m* 1936, Kathleen Doreen, da of Henry Edward Libby (d 1947); 2 s, (Christopher, Charles) 2 da (Fiona, Susan); *Career* engrg and mgmnt conslt; mangr Messrs Young & Widsmith Ltd 1937-39, dir Noma Electric Co Ltd 1939-47 (md 1946-50, changed its name to EDTV Ltd 1950, md EDTV Ltd 1950-81), md and chm Shalibane Ltd 1948-80, md and chm Eilean Shona Res & Advsy Servs Ltd 1973-85, chm Shalibane Hldgs Ltd 1980-85; landowner King's Stag (40 acres), Liveryman Worshipful Co of Scientific Instrument Makers (fndr memb); *Recreations* viticulture; *Clubs* RAC; *Style*— Digby Vane, Esq; Lyddon House, King's Stag, Sturminster Newton, Dorset DT10 2AU (☎ 02586 303)

VANE, Hon Gerald Raby; yr s of 10 Baron Barnard, CMG, OBE, MC, TD (d 1964); *b* 2 Dec 1926; *Educ* Eton, Trinity Coll Cambridge (BA); *Career* Durham LI; chm Watermill Theatre Bangor Newbury 1975-83; memb: Southern Arts Assoc Exec; chm: Western Area Planning Newbury DC 1979-82, Devpt Servs Ctee Newbury DC 1983-86; *Recreations* politics, local govt, architecture, gardens; *Style*— The Hon Gerald Vane; 1 Hartforth, Gilling West, Richmond, N Yorks DL10 5JR (☎ 0748 2716)

VANE, Hon Henry Francis Cecil; s and h of 11 Baron Barnard, TD, JP, and Lady Davina, *née* Cecil, da of 6 Marquess of Exeter; *b* 11 Mar 1959; *Educ* Edinburgh Univ (BSc); *Style*— The Hon Henry Vane

VANE, Sir John Robert; s of Maurice Vane, and Frances Florence, *née* Fisher; *b* 1927; *Educ* King Edward's HS Birmingham, Birmingham Univ (BSc), St Catherine's Coll Oxford (BSc, DPhil, DSc); *m* 1948, Elizabeth Daphne Page; 2 da; *Career* RCS: sr lectr in pharmacology Inst of Basic Med Scis 1955-61, reader in pharmacology 1961-65, prof of experimental pharmacology 1966-73; gp res and devpt dir The Wellcome Fndn 1973-85; dir The William Harvey Res Inst 1986-; tstee Migraine Tst 1988- (and memb scientific advsry ctee); recipient of numerous int prizes and awards including Nobel Prize for Physiology or Med (jt) 1982; FRS; kt 1984; *Recreations* underwater photography; *Clubs* Athenaeum, Garrick; *Style*— Sir John Vane; St Bartholemew's Hosp Medical Coll, Charterhouse Sq, London EC1M 6BQ (☎ 01 251 1683, fax 01 251 1685)

VANE, Hon Louise Cicely; da of 11 Baron Barnard, TD, JP, by his w, Lady Davina, *née* Cecil, da of 6 Marquess of Exeter; *b* 30 May 1968; *Style*— The Hon Louise Vane

VANE, Hon (William) Richard Fletcher; s and h of 1 Baron Inglewood, TD, DL, *qv*; *b* 31 July 1951; *Educ* Eton, Trinity Coll Cambridge (MA), Cumbria Coll of Agric and Forestry; *m* 29 Aug 1986, Cressida R, yst da of late (Alan) Desmond Frederick Pemberton-Pigott, CMG, of Fawe Park, Keswick; 1 da (Miranda Mary b 19 May 1987); *Career* barr Lincoln's Inn 1975; contested (C) Houghton and Washington Gen Election 1983; Durham Euro-Election 1983; memb: Lake Dist Special Planning Bd 1984, regnl land drainage ctee NWWA 1985, ct Univ of Lancaster 1985, NWWA 1987; ARICS; *Clubs* Travellers', Pratt's; *Style*— The Hon Richard Vane; Hutton-in-the-Forest, Penrith, Cumbria CA11 9TH (☎ 085 34 500); Flat 4, 111 Alderney St, London SW1 (☎ 01 821 8127)

VANE PERCY, Hon Mrs (Linda Denise); *née* Grosvenor; da of late 5 Baron Ebury, DSO by 2 w, Hon Denise Yarde-Buller (da of 3 Baron Churston); *b* 1948; *m* 1973, Christopher D Vane Percy; 1 s (Maximillian b 1979), 1 da (Grace Dorothy b 1981); *Style*— The Hon Mrs Vane Percy

VANE-TEMPEST-STEWART, Lord Reginald Alexander; s of 9 Marquess of Londonderry

VANGEKE, Most Rev Sir Louis; MSC, KBE (1980, OBE 1974); *b* 1904June; *Career* aux to Archbishop V P Copas (RC) 1974-76, bishop of Bereina Papua New Guinea 1976-80; *Style*— Most Rev Sir Louis Vangeke, MSC, KBE; Catholic Parish, Kubana CP, PO Box 177, Port Moresby, Papua New Guinea

VANNECK, Hon Joshua Charles; s and h of 6 Baron Huntingfield; *b* 10 August 1954; *Educ* Eton, Magdalene Coll Cambridge (MA); *m* 1982, Arabella Mary, da of Maj Alastair Hugh Joseph Fraser, MC, of Moniack Castle, Kirkhill, Inverness; 1 s (Gerard b 1985), 1 da (Vanessa b 1983); *Career* businessman; *Clubs* Pratt's; *Style*— The Hon Joshua Vanneck; Flat 1, Clanricarde Mansions, Clanricarde Gdns, London W2

VANNER, Michael John; s of Walter Geoffrey Vanner (d 1933), of Winkfield, Berks, and Doris Ellen, *née* Hall (d 1977); *b* 6 Dec 1932; *Educ* Blundells, Sidney Sussex Coll Cambridge (BA, MA); *m* 1 July 1961, Myra, da of William John Sharpe (d 1982), of Fetcham, Surrey; 2 s (Luke b 1967, Guy b 1970); *Career* res engr Electrical Res Assoc 1955-64, chief devpt engr BICC Construction Co Ltd 1964-75, engrg conslt Balfour Beatty Power Construction Ltd 1981-86 (engrg mangr 1973-81), princ Construction and Material Servs (int consulting) 1986-; chm IEE PG Power Cables and Overhead Lines 1988- (memb 1985-); CEng, MIEE 1984, CPhys, MInstP 1962, MBGS 1961; *Books* The Structure of Soil and A Critical Review of The Mechanisms of Soil Moisture Retention And Migration (1961); *Recreations* walking in the country, sailing; *Style*— Michael Vanner, Esq; 17 Wolsey Way, Loughborough, Leics LE11 1PR (☎ 0509 236 877); Construction And Material Services, 1 Blanford Rd, Reigate, Surrey RH2 7DP (☎ 0737 222 173)

VANSTONE, Hon Mrs (Mary Rose); *née* Brock; da of Baron Brock (Life Peer, d 1980) and Baroness Brock, *qv*; *b* 1933; *m* 1959, Keith Vanstone; children; *Style*— The Hon Mrs Vanstone; Blakes Farm, Ashurst, Steyning, W Sussex

VARAH, Prebendary Dr (Edward) Chad; OBE (1969); s of Canon William Edward Varah (d 1945), of Barton on Humber, and Mary, *née* Atkinson (d 1965); *b* 12 Nov 1911; *Educ* Worksop Coll Notts, Keble Coll Oxford, Lincoln Theological Coll; *m* 1940, Doris Susan, OBE, da of Harry Whanslaw (d 1961), of Putney; 4 s (Michael, Andrew, David, Charles), 1 da (Felicity); *Career* staff scriptwriter Eagle 1950-62; C of E clerk in holy orders, rector Lord Mayor's Parish Church of St Stephen Walbrook 1953-; fndr: The Samaritans 1953, Befrienders Int 1974; pres ctee publishing Russian Church Music 1960-80; chm: The Samaritans Inc 1963-66, Befrienders Int 1974-83 (pres 1983-86); patron Terrence Higgins Tst; preb St Paul's 1975-; Albert Schweitzer Gold Medal 1972, Louis Dublin Award American Assoc Suicidology 1974, Prix de l'Inst de la Vie 1977, Roumanian Patriarchal Cross 1968; *Recreations* reading, writing autobiography, watching TV nature programmes; *Clubs* Oxford Union, Sion Coll (City); *Style*— Preb Dr Chad Varah; St Stephen Walbrook, London EC4N 8BN (☎ 01 283 4444, 626 8242)

VARCOE, (Christopher) Stephen; s of Philip William Varcoe, OBE (d 1980), of Lanescot, Par, Cornwall, and Mary Northwood, *née* Mercier; *b* 19 May 1949; *Educ* King's Sch Canterbury, King's Coll Cambridge, (BA, MA), Guildhall Sch of Music; *m* 22 April 1972, Melinda, da of William Arthur Davies, of 11 Sackville Road, Cheam, Surrey; 3 s (Josiah b 6 March 1979, Amyas b 16 Nov 1982, Leander 26 March 1986, d 1986), 2 da (Flora b 22 Nov 1975, Oriana b 9 April 1988); *Career* baritone, freelance concert opera singer 1970-; Calouste Gulbenkian Fndn Fellowship 1977; *Recreations* building, painting, gardening; *Style*— Stephen Varcoe, Esq; Ron Gonsalves, 10 Dagnan Rd, London SW12 9LQ (☎ 01 673 6507, fax 01 675 7276, telex 265871 MONREF G REF MUS033)

VARDE, John; s of Shamrao Varde (d 1949), and Helen, *née* Leontzini; *b* 2 Jan 1935; *Educ* Malvern; *m* 1964, Elizabeth Lilian, da of James Hudson Foskett (d 1985); 1 s (Andrew b 1965), 1 da (Nicola b 1967); *Career* mechanical and manufacturing engr, md Plessey Aerospace Ltd 1982-; *Recreations* music; *Clubs* RAC; *Style*— John Varde Esq; 32 Richmond Road, Sherborne, Dorset; Plessey Aerospace Ltd, Abbey Works, Titchfield, Hants PO14 4QA (☎ 0329 43031; telex 86214)

VARDY, Peter Christian; s of Mark Vardy; *b* 29 July 1945; *Educ* Charterhouse, Southampton Univ, King's Coll London; *m* 1974, Anne Maree, da of Patrick Moore; 2 s, 3 da; *Career* management consultant; chm H Young Holdings Gp 1979-; dir of various cos; FCA; *Recreations* philosophy of religion, forestry, walking, travel; *Clubs* East India, Sports & Public Schools; *Style*— Peter Vardy Esq; 14 Croft Gdns, Alton, Hants

VARLEY, Hon Mrs (Elizabeth Susan); *née* Douglas-Scott-Montagu; da of 2 Baron Montagu of Beaulieu, KCIE, CSI (d 1929); *b* 1909; *m* 1962, Col Arthur Noel Claude Varley, CBE (d 1985); *Style*— The Hon Mrs Varley; The Mill Race, Beaulieu, Hants

VARLEY, Rt Hon Eric Graham; PC (1974); s of Frank Varley by his w Eva; *b* 11 August 1932; *Educ* Ruskin Coll Oxford; *m* 1955, Marjorie Turner; 1 s; *Career* worked in engineering and mining industry; branch sec NUM 1955-64 (memb Derbys Area Exec Ctee 1956-64); MP (Lab) Chesterfield 1964-84, asst govt whip 1967-68, PPS to Harold Wilson as PM 1968-69, min of state Technology 1969-70; energy sec 1974-75, industry sec 1975-79; chief oppn spokesman Employment 1979-83, tres Labour Pty 1981-83, oppn front bench spokesman Employment 1981-83; chm and chief exec Coalite Gp 1984- (dep exec chm 1983-84); steward and bailiff of the Manor of Northstead 1984-; *Style*— The Rt Hon Eric Varley

VARLEY, Ian Mansergh; s of William Mansergh Varley (d 1956), of Brighton, and Hephzibah, *née* Walker (d 1957); *b* 25 June 1926; *Educ* Brighton Coll, Brighton Tech Coll, London Univ (BSc); *m* 1 Sept 1951, Jean Margaret, da of Jack Spencer Searle (d 1956), of Brighton; 1 s (Christopher Mansergh b 1960), 1 da (Alison Elizabeth b 1954); *Career* chartered engr; ptnr: Chester & Varley Singapore 1953-60, Steen Sehested & Ptnrs Singapore 1960-65, TF Burns & Ptnrs London & Hove 1965- (conslt 1986-); dist govr Rotary Int Dist 125, cncl memb Brighton Poly 1985; CEng, FICE 1963, MConsE 1963, FIE (Malaysia); *Recreations* sailing, golf, gardening, rotary; *Clubs* Dyke Golf (Brighton); *Style*— Ian Varley, Esq; Newtimber, The Common, Henfield, W Sussex BN5 9RL (☎ 0273 492 538); TF Burns & Partners, 41 Portland Road, Hove, E Sussex BN3 5DQ (☎ 0273 720 626, fax 0273 735 292)

VARLEY, Dame Joan Fleetwood; DBE (1985, CBE 1974); da of Fleetwood Ireton Varley (d 1941), of London, and Harriet Elizabeth, *née* Heenan; *b* 22 Feb 1920; *Educ* Cheltenham Ladies, LSE (BSc); *Career* WAAF Corpl Fighter Cmd radio operator, section offr Fighter Cmd Meteorological Offr; cons; dep agent Warwick & Leamington Constituency 1949-52, agent Shrewsbury constituency 1952-56, cpc offr W Midlands Area Cons Central Off 1956-57, dep central off agent NW Area 1957-64, dep chief orgn offr Cons Central Off 1965-66, dep dir of orgn Cons Central Off 1966-74, chief asst to dir gen and chief woman exec 1974-75, dir of central admin Cons Central Off 1975-76, dir of local govt orgn 1976-84; churchwarden St Clements & St James Norlands Jt Parish, chm Friends of St James Norlands Assoc, memb Brighter Kensington & Chelsea Scheme Ctee; govr Thames Poly 1980 (vice-chm ct of govrs 1986-), pt/t memb VAT Appeals Tbnl 1986-; *Recreations* gardening, walking; *Clubs* St Stephens, Utd and Cecil; *Style*— Dame Joan Varley, DBE; 9 Quennsdale Walk, Holland Park, London WN4QQ (☎ 01 727 1292)

VARLEY, (John) Philip; TD; s of John Varley (d 1952), of Leamington Spa, and Frances, *née* Gould (d 1976); *b* 14 May 1920; *Educ* Downside, Birmingham Univ (LLB); *m* 12 July 1952, Jacqueline Mary, da of Lt Col George Taylor, DSO, TD, DL (d 1983), of Kirkheaton, nr Huddersfield; 1 s (John Silvester b 1956), 1 da (Mrs Philippa Jane O'Gorman b 1954); *Career* Maj Royal Warwicks Regt, Europe, POW 1940-45; slr; sr ptnr Varley Hibbs and Co; pres Warwicks Law Soc 1984-85; OStJ; *Recreations* shooting; *Clubs* Army and Navy; *Style*— Philip Varley, Esq; Garden House, Barford Hill, Barford, nr Warwick; 16 Hamilton Terrace, Leamington Spa, Warwickshire (☎ 0926 311223)

VARNEY, Lady Mary (Bethune); *née* Lindesay-Bethune; da of 14 Earl of Lindsay; *b* 1935; *m* 1956, Capt Owen Buckingham Varney; 2 s, 1 da; *Style*— Lady Mary Varney; Hill House, Dedham, Nr Colchester, Essex CO7 6EA

VARNEY, Michael Arthur; s of Sydney Albert Varney (d 1986), and Vera Margaret, *née* Fisher (d 1962); *b* 19 Nov 1933; *Educ* Ealing County GS; *m* 4 Sept 1965 (m dis 1988), Carol Elizabeth, da of John Little; 1 s (Andrew Michael), 1 da (Joanne Claire); *Career* Nat Serv SAC 1952-54; asst sec Globe Building Soc 1965-70, exec accountant London Investmt Building Soc 1970-76, asst accountant East Surrey Building Soc 1976-80, gen mangr and sec Bexhill-on-Sea Building Soc 1980-; ctee memb Bexhill Horticultural Soc; FCBSI 1971, FCIS 1975; *Recreations* computers, badminton, photography, bridge; *Style*— Michael Varney, Esq; Badgers, 5 Woodland Way, Crowhurst, Battle, East Sussex TN33 9AP (☎ 0424 83 286); 2 Devonshire Square, Bexhill-on-Sea, East Sussex TN40 1AE (☎ 0424 210 542)

VARTAN, John Brian Robertson; s of Dr Ronald Hepworth Vartan; *b* 13 Sept 1937; *Educ* Uppingham, Gonville and Caius Coll Cambridge; *m* 1963, Frances Margaret, *née* Bowser; 2 children; *Career* stockbroker; memb Cncl The Stock Exchange 1976-83, chm Provincial Unit of Stock Exchange 1980-83; memb Central Exec Ctee NSPCC 1972-81; *Recreations* shooting, fishing, golf, tennis; *Clubs* IOD; *Style*— John B R Vartan Esq; Castor Heights, Castor, Peterborough (☎ 073 121 315)

VASARY, Tamas; s of Josef Vasary (d 1975), and Elisabeth, *née* Baltazar (d 1977); *b* 11 August 1933; *Educ* Franz Liszt Music Acad Budapest; *m* 30 March 1967, Ildiko, da of Lajos Kovács, of Sao Paulo, Brazil; *Career* pianist and conductor, first concert at age of 8, asst prof Budapest Music Acad at 21; prizes at int competitions: Paris 1955,

Warsaw 1955, Brussels 1956, Rio de Janeiro 1957; debut in London 1960 (New York 1961); recording incl: Chopin, Liszt, Brahms, Mozart, Rachmaninoff; conducting debut 1969; conducted many major orchestras including: Berlin Philharmonic, London Symphony, Royal Philharmonic; music dir Northern Sinfonietta 1979-82; awarded Bach and Poaderewski medals 1961; *Recreations* yoga, writing; *Style*— Tamas Vasary, Esq; 9 Village Road, London N3 1TL (☎ 01 346 2381); Harold Holt Ltd, 31 Sinclair Road, London W14 0NS (☎ 01 603 4600)

VASQUEZ, Sir Alfred Joseph; CBE (1974), QC (1986); s of Alfred J Vasquez (d 1971), of Gibraltar, and Maria Josefa, *née* Rugeroni (d 1942); *b* 2 Mar 1923; *Educ* Mount St Mary's Sch, Millfield, Fitzwilliam Coll Cambridge (MA); *m* 10 April 1950, Carmen, da of Lt-Col Robert Michael Sheppard-Capurro, OBE, JP, of Cloister Ramp, Gibraltar; 3 s (Alfred b 1951, Robert b 1952, Peter b 1953), 1 da (Mrs Maurice Sewe b 1958); *Career* served Gibraltar Def Force 1943-45, Gibraltar Regt 1957-64, Capt; barr Inner Temple 1950, sr ptnr Vasquez Benady and Co, barristers and solicitors; speaker Gibraltar House of Assembly 1970-, Mayor of Gibraltar 1970-76; chm: Gibraltar Regt Assoc, Gibraltar Bursary and Scholarship Bd, Cwlth Parly Assoc Gibraltar Branch; memb: Gibraltar Public Serv Cmmn, Ctee Gibraltar Lawyers Assoc, Ctee Gibraltar Soc for Cancer Relief; kt 1987; *Recreations* golf, shooting, bridge; *Clubs* Sotogrande Golf (Cadiz), Mediterranean Racing (Gibraltar), Calpe Rowing; *Style*— The Hon Sir Alfred Vasquez, CBE, QC; 2 St Bernards Road, Gibraltar (☎ 010 350 73710); 26A St Georges Drive, London SW1 (☎ 01 821 0987); Cloister House, Fountain Ramp, Gibraltar (☎ 010 350 76108)

VASSAR-SMITH, John Rathborne; s and h of Sir Richard Vassar-Smith, 3 Bt, TD; *b* 23 July 1936; *Educ* Eton; *m* 1971, Roberta Elaine, da of Wing Cdr Norman Williamson; 2 s (Richard b 1975, David b 1978); *Career* runs St Ronans Prep Sch with father; *Style*— John Vassar-Smith, Esq; St Ronans, Hawkhurst, Kent

VASSAR-SMITH, Sir Richard Rathborne; 3 Bt (UK 1917), of Charlton Park, Charlton Kings, TD (1950); s of late Maj Charles Martin Vassar-Smith (2 s of 1 Bt); suc unc, Sir John George Lawley Vassar-Smith (d 1942); *b* 24 Nov 1909; *Educ* Sancing, Pembroke Coll Cambridge; *m* 1932, Dawn Mary, da of Sir Raymond Wybrow Woods, CBE (d 1943); 1 s, 1 da (and 1 child decd); *Heir* s, John Rathborne Vassar-Smith; *Career* Maj RA 1939-45, headmaster St Ronans Prep Sch 1957- (ptnr 1946-57, ptnr with son John Vassar-Smith, *qv* 1957-); *Recreations* golf; *Clubs* Hawks (Cambridge), Rye Golf; *Style*— Sir Richard Vassar-Smith, Bt, TD; Orchard House, St Ronans, Hawkhurst, Kent (☎ 058 05 2300)

VASSILTCHIKOV, Prince George; s of Prince Illarion Vassiltchikov (d 1969), and Princess Lydia Viazemsky (d 1948); descended from one Indris, who is said to have arrived in Russia in the 14th c; Boyars of the Great Prince of Muscovy since the late 15th c; Anna Vassiltchikova was the 5th wife of Tsar Ivan IV 'the Terrible'; in senior court, state, and military positions in Russia from the 16th c until 1917; *b* 22 Nov 1919; *Educ* secondary education in France (Lycée Condorcet) & Lithuania (Russian gymnasium), Univ Education in Italy (Rome), Germany (Berlin), France (Paris Ecole Libre des Sciences Politiques et Sociales); *m* 1964, Barbarina, da of Ambass Guy de Keller, of Rougemont, Switzerland; 1 s (Alexander b 1966), 1 da (Nathalia b 1965); *Career* Agence France-Presse (Paris) 1944-45; Int Military Tribunal (Nüremberg) 1945-46, UN Secretariat 1948-60 and 1966-77, in business 1977-; *Books* author (pseud 'Geoffrey Bailey' The Conspirators (1960/61); Ed. The Berlin Diaries 1940-45, of Marie ('Missie') Vassiltchikov (1985); *Recreations* reading, writing, music, travel; *Clubs* Beefsteak; *Style*— Prince George Vassiltchikov; 73 Durrels House, Warwick Gardens, London W14; 7 Grande Avenue, Rolle Vaud, Switzerland

VAUGHAN, Lady Auriel Rosemary Malet; da of 7 Earl of Lisburne (d 1965); *b* 1923; *Career* writer as Oriel Malet; *Style*— Lady Auriel Vaughan

VAUGHAN, Dr Caroline Lesley; da of Frederick Alan Vaughan (d 1970), and Helen Mary, *née* Brackett (d 1983); *b* 5 Feb 1941; *Educ* Croydon HS, Manchester Univ (BSc), Chelsea Coll London (PhD); *Career* post doctoral fell: MD Anderson Hosp Houston USA 1965-68, King's Coll London 1968-69; fin analyst and mktg mangr WR Grace Euro Consumer Products Div Paris 1969-74, commerical planner Tube Investmts (domestic appliances div and head off) 1974-78, divnl exec Nat Enterprise Bd 1978-80; dir: business devpt Celltech Ltd 1980-84, Newmarket Venture Capital plc 1984-; *Recreations* theatre, opera, travel; *Style*— Dr Caroline Vaughan; 14-20 Chiswell St, London EC1Y 4TY (☎ 01 638 2521, fax 01 638 8409, telex 934084 NEWVCG)

VAUGHAN, David Bertram; s of Leonard Lionel Vaughan (d 1980), and Elizabeth Vaughan, *née* Gibbins; *b* 21 July 1936; *Educ* Wilson GS; *m* 3 Sept 1960, Pamela Druscilla, da of Charles James Brewood; 2 da (Catherine b 1968, Margaret b 1970); *Career* chartered accountant; gen ptnr Peat Marwick McLintock 1980- (ptnr 1972-); dep chm The Welton Foundation; govr: Nat Heart and Chest SHA, The Cardiothoracic Inst; FCA; *Recreations* golf, music, reading; *Clubs* Athenaeum, MCC, West Hill Golf; *Style*— David Vaughan, Esq; Mount Lodge, Malthouse Lane, Worplesdon, Surrey (☎ Worplesdon 232 048); 1 Puddle Dock, Blackfriars, London EC4V 3PO (☎ 01 236 8000, fax 01 248 6552, telex 8811541 PMM Lon G)

VAUGHAN, Viscount; David John Francis Malet Vaughan; s and h of 8 Earl of Lisburne; *b* 15 June 1945; *Educ* Ampleforth; *m* 1973, Jennifer Jane (an artist), da of late James Desiré John William Fraser Campbell, of Glengarry, Inverness-shire; 1 s (Hon Digby b 3 Jan 1973 but since b before f's marriage legitimated for all purposes except succession to f's and gf's titles), 1 da (Hon Lucy b 2 Aug 1971); *Heir* bro, Hon Michael Vaughan; *Career* artist; *Style*— Viscount Vaughan

VAUGHAN, Sir (George) Edgar; KBE (1963, CBE 1956, OBE 1937); s of William John Vaughan (d 1919), of Cardiff, and Emma Kate Caudle (d 1966); *b* 24 Feb 1907; *Educ* Cheltenham GS, Jesus Coll Oxford; *m* 1, 1933, (Elsie) Winifred (d 1982), da of late Louis Deubert; 1 s (John), 2 da (Doreen, Pauline); m 2, 12 Nov 1987, Mrs Caroleen Mary Sayers, da of late Frank Selley; *Career* former memb Dip Serv; joined Consular Serv 1930, serving at Hamburg, La Paz, Barcelona, Buenos Aires; chargé d'affaires Monrovia 1945-46, consul Seattle 1946-49; consul-gen: Lourenço Marques 1949-53, Amsterdam 1953-56, Buenos Aires 1956-60 (where also minister); ambass and consul-gen Panama 1960-63, ambass Colombia 1964-66; FRHistS; Dean Arts and Science Saskatchewan Univ 1969-73 (prof history 1967-74, lectr 1966-67); *Books* author of articles in learned journals mostly concerning British relations with Latin America; *Clubs* Travellers'; *Style*— Sir Edgar Vaughan, KBE; 9 The Glade, Sandy Lane, Cheam, Surrey SM2 7NZ

VAUGHAN, Sir Gerard Folliott; MP (C) Reading E 1983-; s of Leonard A Vaughan, DSO, DFC, by his w Joan, *née* Folliott; *b* 11 June 1923; *Educ* privately, London Univ, Guy's Hospital (MB BS), London (DPM); *m* 1955, Joyce Thurle, *née* Laver; 1 s, 1 da; *Career* medical specialist Guy's Hosp; lectr and author; Party candidate (C) Poplar 1955; alderman GLC 1966-72 (LCC 1955-64); MP (C) Reading 1970-74, Reading S 1974-83; PPS to NI sec 1974, oppn whip 1974, oppn spokesman on Health 1975-79, min for Health (rank of min of state) DHSS 1979-82, min of state for Trade with responsibility for Consumer Affrs 1982-1983; Hon FFAS; Liveryman Worshipful Co of Barbers; MRCP FRCP, FRCPsych; kt 1984; *Clubs* Carlton; *Style*— Sir Gerard Vaughan, MP; House of Commons, London SW1

VAUGHAN, Hugh Garraway; s of Lt-Col P H Vaughan, of 6 Stort Lodge, Bishops Stortford, Herts, and Dora Mary, *née* Garraway; *b* 23 June 1943; *Educ* Highgate Sch London; *m* 23 March 1968, Diana, da of Frank William Matthews, of Oaklands, Woburn Sands, Bucks; 1 s (Nicholas James b 3 Jan 1972), 1 da (Claire Louise b 31 Jan 1974); *Career* dir M & J Engineers Ltd (assoc co Abbey plc) 1969-; FBIM; *Recreations* swimming, archaeology, boats; *Style*— Hugh Vaughan, Esq; Meadow Ct, Tyrells End, Eversholt, Beds (☎ 0525 28 513); Cashel House, Cadwell Lane, Hitchin, Herts (☎ 0462 52 861)

VAUGHAN, Dame Janet Maria; DBE (1957, OBE 1944); da of William Wyamar Vaughan, MVO (sometime headmaster of Rugby and Wellington) and his 1 w, Margaret, *née* Symonds; *b* 18 Oct 1899; *Educ* North Foreland Lodge, Somerville Oxford, UCH; *m* 1930, David Gourlay (d 1963); 2 da; *Career* formerly asst clinical pathologist UCH and Br Post-Grad Med Sch, MO i/c NW London Blood Supply Depot for MRC; princ Somerville Oxford 1945-67 (hon fell), chm Oxford Regnl Hosp Bd 1950-51; hon fell Watson Coll Oxford; Hon DCL: Oxford, London, Bristol; Hon DSc: Wales, Leeds; Hon FRSM, DM, FRCP, FRS; *Books* numerous books and papers on scientific literature; *Style*— Dame Janet Vaughan, DBE; 5 Fairlawn Flats, First Turn, Wolvercote, Oxford (☎ 0865 514 069)

VAUGHAN, Hon John Edward Malet; s of 8 Earl of Lisburne, and Shelagh Mary Countess of Lisburne; *b* 3 Oct 1952; *Educ* Ampleforth, RAC Cirencester; *m* 1977 (m dis 1983), Catherine Euphan, da of J P Waterer, of Norton Canon, Hereford; *Career* land agent, agricultural marketing, publishing; dir Property Data Services Ltd 1985; journalist; *Books* Sir Herbert (1985); *Clubs* Boodle's; *Style*— The Hon John Vaughan; 13 Dancer Rd, London SW6 4DU; Fullbrook, Tregaron, Dyfed; Property Data Services ltd, 114 Brompton Road, London SW3 (☎ 01 581 5351)

VAUGHAN, Hon Mrs (Mary Patricia); *née* Monck; raised to rank of Viscount's da 1928; da of Capt the Hon Charles Henry Stanley Monck (ka 1918), and Mary Florence, *née* Portal (d 1919); sis of 6 Viscount Monck, OBE (d 1982); *b* 20 June 1911; *Educ* Belstead Southover; *m* 28 Nov 1935, Brig (Charles) Hilary Pritchard, DSO, JP, DL (d 1976, who assumed by deed poll of 1956 the surname Vaughan in lieu of his patronymic), s of Col Charles Hamerton Pritchard (d 1912), late Indian Political Service; 4 da (Susan (Mrs Muirhead) b 1936, Molly (Mrs Davies) b 1941, Patricia (Mrs Engel) b (twin) 1941, Jane (Mrs Allen) b 1945); *Recreations* gardening; *Style*— The Hon Mrs Vaughan; The Old Rectory, Pen Selwood, Wincanton, Somerset (☎ 0747 840 836)

VAUGHAN, Hon Michael John Wilmot Malet; 2 s of 8 Earl of Lisburne; hp to er bro's courtesy title of Viscount Vaughan; *b* 1948; *Educ* Ampleforth, New Coll Oxford; *m* 1978, Lucinda Mary Louisa, da of the Hon Sir John Francis Harcourt Baring (himself er s & h of 6 Baron Ashburton); *Style*— The Hon Michael Vaughan; 44 Pembroke Sq, London W8

VAUGHAN, Col Peter David Wyamar; MBE (1971), TD (1964); s of David Wyamar Vaughan, CBE, JP (d 1984), of The Old Rectory, Wherwell, Andover, Hampshire, and Norah Agnes, *née* Burn (d 1963); *b* 27 May 1931; *Educ* Rugby; *m* 1, Sept 1956 (m dis 1976), Elizabeth Dobree, *née* Burn; 1 s (David John Wyamar b Nov 1957), 1 da (Laura Katherine b 1960);m 2, 23 May 1978, (Signe) Monica Karin, da of Thor Janzon, of Helsinki, Finland; 1 s (Henry Arthur Peter b 1981); *Career* Nat Serv 1949-51: Welsh Bde Trg Centre 1949-50, Eaton Hall OTS 1950, 2 Lt 1 Bn Royal Welch Fusiliers 1950-51; TA: Maj (formerly: 2 Lt, Lt, Capt) 4/5 Bn Royal Northumberland Fusiliers 1951-66, 4/5 16 Bn Royal Northumberland Fusiliers 1967-70 (Co Lt-Col 1970), OC 103 Field Sqdn (1 Newcastle) RE (V) 1971-74, Col Dep Cdr NE Dist 1974-76; Hon Col 72 Engr Regt RE (V) 1986-; Burn Fireclay Co Ltd 1952-: works mangr 1955, dir 1958, md 1978, chm and md 1980-; memb Nat Assoc Boys' Clubs; memb Inst Refractory Engrs; *Recreations* walking, bird-watching, gardening, shooting; *Style*— Col Peter Vaughan, MBE, TD; Heatherlea, Tranwell Woods, Morpeth, Northumberland (☎ 0670 512225); The Burn Fireclay Co Ltd, Stobswood, Morpeth, Northumberland (☎ 0670 790234, telex 53526 BURN G)

VAUGHAN, Ven Peter St George; s of Dr Victor St George Vaughan, of 50 Sedlescombe Road South, St Leonards-on-Sea, East Sussex, and Dorothy Marguerite, *née* Longworth-Dames; 27 Nov 1930; *b* 27 Nov 1930; *Educ* Dean Close Jr Sch, Charterhouse, Selwyn Coll Cambridge (MA), Ridley Hall Cambridge, (MA); *m* 2 Sep 1961, Elisabeth Fielding, da of late Dr Fielding Parker, of Selwyn Village, Auckland, NZ; 1 s (Richard b 1969), 2 da (Sarah b 1963, Merle b 1966); *Career* Army NS RHA and RAPC (Lt) 1949; asst curate Birmingham Parish Church 1957-62; chaplain: Oxford Pastorate, Brasenose Coll Oxford 1963-67; vicar Christ Church Galle Face Colombo Sri Lanka 1967-72, precentor Auckland Cathedral NZ 1972-75, princ Crowther Hall Selly Oak Coll 1975-83, archdeacon of Westmorland and Furness 1983-89; appointed Bishop Suffragan of Ramsbury (diocese of Salisbury) 1989; *Recreations* swimming, walking, gardening, reading; *Style*— The Archdeacon of Westmorland and Furness; Helsfell House, 235 Windermere Road, Kendal, Cumbria LA9 5EY (☎ 0539 23553)

VAUGHAN, Lady Rose Mary Sydney; *née* Yorke; da of 9 Earl of Hardwicke; *b* 1951; *Educ* St Mary's Convent Ascot; *m* 1 (m dis), Kenneth Delbray; resumed maiden name of Yorke; m 2, 1981, (m dis 1985), (Herbert) Richard Vaughan (publisher, d 1987); *Style*— Lady Rose Vaughan; Bryn Tami Fawr, Llannor, Pwllheli, Gwyned, North Wales (☎ 0758 614515)

VAUGHAN DAVIES, Geoffrey; s of Hubert Vaughan Davies (d 1963), of Colwyn Bay, N Wales, and Elsie Fielding, *née* Turner (d 1931); *b* 21 July 1928; *Educ* Bishop Vesey's GS, Carlisle GS, Cambridge (MA); *m* 11 Aug 1956, Esther Lockie Menzies, da of Rev Andrew Henderson Anderson (d 1955); 1 s (Andrew b 1966), 2 da (Angela b 1960, Elizabeth b 1962); *Career* RN 1947-49, HMS Wizard 1948-49; barr Inner Temple 1953, practice Northern circuit 1953-70, dep asst registrar Criminal Appeal Off 1970-74, asst dir Legal Div Off of Fair Trading 1974- legal advsr comsumer affrs div DTI 1988-; er St Pauls' Utd Reform Church S Croydon 1970-, chm Unified Appeal Ctee Utd Reformed Church 1972-79; Party candidate Withington div of Manchester

1955, 1959, 1964 and 1966; *Recreations* chess, croquet, walking; *Style*— Geoffrey Vaughan Davies, Esq; Ardmore, 13 Norfolk Ave, Sanderstead, South Croydon, Surrey CR2 8BT (☎ 01 657 1449)

VAUX, John Cuthbert; s of Col Cuthbert Vaux MC (d 1960), of Moulton Manor, Richmond, N Yorks, and Brenda Mary, *née* Palmer (d 1955); *b* 21 Sept 1933; *Educ* Sandroyd Sch Salisbury, Eton, RMA Sandhurst; *m* 25 June 1964, Sara Penelope, da of Gerald Richard Powlett Wilson, JP (d 1986), of Cliffe Hall, Piercebridge, Co Durham; 2 s (Andrew b 1955, Hugo b 1956), 1 da (Camilla b 1972); *Career* 12 Royal Lancers 1954-60, ADC to the Govt Cyprus 1959-60, Northumberland Hussars Yeo 1962-67; T Pease wine merchants 1961-80, bursor Aysgarth Sch 1980-; Master of Beagles: Eton 1951-52, Sandhurst 1953-54; jt Master of Bedale hunt 1961-66 and 1969-72; *Recreations* country sports; *Style*— Capt John Vaux; Moulton Manor, Richmond, N Yorks; Aysgarth School, Bedale, N Yorks (☎ 0677 50240)

VAUX, Maj-Gen Nicholas Frances; DSO (1982); s of Harry Vaux, and Penelope Vaux; *b* 15 April 1936; *Educ* Stonyhurst; *m* 1966, Zoya, da of Gen Sir Peter Hellings, KCN, DSC, MC; 1 s (Piers b 1973), 2 da (Zoya b 1967, Tara b 1969); *Career* cmmnd RM 1954, Suez 1956, Far East 1958-61, frigate W Indies 1962-64, Staff Coll Camberley 1969, MOD (Army) 1975-77, 2 i/c 42 Commando 1977-79, Lt Col Special advsr US Marine Corps Educn Centre Quantico Virginia 1979-81, CO 42 Commando (Operation Corporate) 1981-83, Col 1983, COS to Maj Gen Trg Reserve and Special Forces 1983-85, Royal Coll of Def Studies 1985, COS Maj- Gen RM Commando Forces 1986, Maj Gen RM Commando Forces 1987-; *Books* March to the South Atlantic (1986); *Recreations* skiing, field sports; *Clubs* Farmers; *Style*— Maj-Gen Nicholas Vaux, DSO; c/o Nat West Bank, Old Town St, Plymouth; Headquarters Commando Forces Royal Marines, Hamoaze House, Mount Wise, Plymouth (☎ 0752 563 777 ext 4000)

VAUX OF HARROWDEN, 10 Baron (E 1523); John Hugh Philip Gilbey; s of William Gordon Gilbey (d 1965), and Grace Mary Eleanor, Baroness Vaux of Harrowden (d 1958); suc bro, 9 Baron, 1977; *b* 4 August 1915; *Educ* Ampleforth, Ch Ch Oxford; *m* 5 July 1939, his 1 cous Maureen Pamela, eld da of late Hugh Gilbey, of Shellwood Bend, Leigh, Reigate, Surrey; 3 s, 1 da; *Heir* s, Hon Anthony William Gilbey; *Career* Maj, Duke of Wellington's Regt, served War of 1939-45; sits as Conservative in House of Lords; *Style*— The Rt Hon the Lord Vaux of Harrowden; Cholmondeley Cottage, 2 Cholmondeley Walk, Richmond, Surrey

VAVASOUR, Sir Geoffrey William; 5 Bt (UK 1828), DSC (1943); s of Capt Sir Leonard Pius Vavasour, 4 Bt (d 1961, himself ggs of Hon Sir Edward Vavasour, 1 Bt, *née* Stourton and 2 surviving s of 17 Baron Stourton, but who changed his name to Vavasour on inheriting the estates of his mother's 1 cous, Sir Thomas Vavasour, 7 & last Bt of the 1628 cr; the 1 Bt of this previous cr was Knight Marshal of the King's Household and ggs through his mother of the 1 Earl of Rutland, while his w Ursula was one of the Giffards of Chillington); *b* 5 Sept 1914; *Educ* RNC Dartmouth; *m* 1, 1940 (m dis 1947), Joan Millicent Kirkland, da of Arthur John Robb; 2 da; m 2, 1971, (m dis 1980), (Marcia) Christine, da of Marshall Shaw Lodge, of Batley, Yorks; *Heir* kinsman, Hugh Bernard Moore Vavasour; *Career* RN (ret) dir W M Still & Sons; *Clubs* All England Lawn Tennis; *Style*— Sir Geoffrey Vavasour, Bt, DSC; 8 Bede House, Manor Fields, Putney, SW15 (☎ 01 788 0707)

VAVASOUR, Hugh Bernard Moore; s of Oswald Joseph Stanislaus Vavasour (d 1973, himself n of Sir William Vavasour, 3 Bt), and hp of 2 cous, Sir Geoffrey Vavasour, 5 Bt, DSC; *b* 4 July 1918; *Educ* Stonyhurst; *m* 1952, Monique Pauline Marie Madeleine (d 1982), da of Maurice Erick Beck, of St Aubin sur Scie, Seine Maritime, France; 1 s, 1 da; *Career* 1939-45 War as Capt RA served UK and S and SE Asia; former: dep md Blythe Colours Ltd, pres Blythe-Karel Italy; former dir: Colores Blythe SA Spain, Blythe Vidrados de Portugal; ret 1983; *Recreations* golf; *Style*— Hugh Vavasour, Esq; Blakeley House, Draycott, Stoke-on-Trent ST11 9AQ (☎ 078 18 3348)

VAZ, (Nigel) Keith Anthony Standish; MP (Lab) Leicester East 1987; s of Tony Vaz, and Merlyn Verona Rosemary, *née* Pereira; *b* 26 Nov 1956; *Educ* Latymer Upper Sch, Gonville & Caius Coll Cambridge; *Career* slr; *Style*— Keith Vaz, Esq, MP; 144 Uppingham Rd, Leicester (☎ 0533 768834) (car ☎ 0860 646 479 ask for 2532888); House of Commons, London SW1A 0AA

VEALE, Sir Alan John Ralph; s of Leslie Henry Veale (d 1971); *b* 2 Feb 1920; *Educ* Exeter Sch, Manchester Coll of Technology; *m* 1946, Muriel, da of John William Edwards; 2 children; *Career* chartered engr; dir and gen mangr AEI Motor & Control Gp 1966-68; md: GEC Diesels Ltd 1968-70, GEC Power Engrg Ltd 1970-85; dir GEC 1973-85, chm Rossmore Warwick Ltd 1986-, pres Instn of Prodn Engrs 1985-; kt 1984; *Recreations* sailing, walking; *Style*— Sir Alan Veale; 41 Northumberland Rd, Leamington Spa, Warwickshire CV32 6HF (☎ 0926 24349)

VEALE, Dr Michael Henry Dumergue; s of Rawdon Augustus Veale (d 1954), and Frances Adeline Lowe, *née* Drury (d 1956); *b* 7 Jan 1920; *Educ* Shrewsbury, Peterhouse Camb (BA, MB BChir); *m* 5 Oct 1957, Angela Barbara Mary, da of Maj Charles Robert Thropp Thorp, MC, KOYLI (d 1935), by his w Joan (d 1983), 3 da of Sir James de Hoghton, 11 Bt, CBE, of Hoghton Tower, Preston, Lancs; 2 s (Jonathan b 2 Dec 1962, Richard b 26 Sept 1965), 2 da (Claire b 4 Aug 1958, Annabel (Mrs Nigel Costantine), b 19 March 1960); *Career* Surgn Lt RNVR 1944-47 in North Sea and Far East; GP (ret); Pres RNA Fairford and Dist Branch, Pres Fairford Cricket Club 1954-79; MRCS, LRCP; *Recreations* sailing, shooting, gardening, cricket; *Clubs* Royal Cruising, Naval; *Style*— Dr Michael Veale; Hantone House, Mersey Hampton, Cirencester, Glos (☎ 0285 85 301)

VEARNCOMBE, Roderick Andrew George; s of Maj Colin Alexander Vearncombe, of 3 Coxwell Court, Coxwell St, Cirencester, Glos, and Theresa Mary, *née* Bendixson; *b* 9 April 1959; *Educ* Monkton Combe Sch, UCL (BSc, Dip Arch); *Career* architect and designer; sole ptnr Roderick A G Vearncombe, chm Hogarth Trading Co; Memb RIBA; *Recreations* tennis, hockey, theatre, film, opera; *Style*— Roderick Vearncombe, Esq; 18a Walberswick St, London SW8 (☎ 01 582 8524)

VELATE, Anthony Spencer; s of Louis Anthony Velate (d 1942), of Altrincham, Cheshire, and Doris Emily, of London (d 1983); *b* 18 Dec 1925; *Educ* Bradbury Central Sch, Birkbeck Coll London (BSc); *m* 29 March 1952, (Gwendoline) Mary, da of Philip David Scott (d 1967), of E Finchley; 1 s (Simon J A b 27 Feb 1956), 2 da (Sara J b 9 May 1960, Rebecca H b 10 Oct 1961); *Career* leading Aircraft Radar Fitter (A) RAFVR 1944-48 (serv in SEAC India 1945-48); experimental staff IMA Ltd 1942-44, devpt engr electro med Electronic and X Ray Applications Ltd 1948-57, chief technician electro-physiology Nat Hosp London 1957-63, res fell MRC St Mary's Hosp Med Sch 1964-67, system conslt patient monitoring TEM Instruments Ltd 1967-71, sales and mktg mangr TEM Engrg Ltd 1971-81, owner Mktg Technol Consultancy 1982-83, membership and qualification mangr Inst of Electronic and Radio Engrs 1983-88, sr trg admin IEE 1988-; chm UK liaison ctee for Sci Allied to Med & Biology 1972-74; fndr memb SDP (vice chm Horsham Area 1982-84) Horsham Soc: exec ctee 1973-79, chm 1975-77; Thakeham PC 1983-88, chm Emergency Planning Ctee 1984-88; CEng 1964, FIEE 1987, CPhys 1986, MIERE 1964, MInst P 1964, MBES 1960; *Recreations* photography, travel, genealogy; *Style*— Anthony Velate, Esq; Goffsland House, Coolham Rd, West Chiltington, Pulborough, West Sussex RH20 2LT (☎ 07983 3120); Inst of Electrical Engrs, Savoy Place, London WC2R 0BL (☎ 01 240 1871, fax 01 240 7735, telex 261 176 IEELDN G)

VELISSAROPOULOS, Hon Mrs (Penelope Jane); *née* Allsopp; da of 4 Baron Hindlip (d 1966); *b* 1940; *m* 1965, Theodore D Velissaropoulos; *Style*— The Hon Mrs Velissaropoulos; c/o First National City Bank, Athens 118, Greece

VELLACOTT, David Norman Strain; s of James Millner Vellacott (d 1983), and Alice Irene, *née* Strain; *b* 23 Oct 1930; *Educ* Rugby, St John Coll Cambridge (MA); *m* 17 Sept 1955, Patricia Le Souef, da of Dr Robert Baxendale Coleman (d 1963), of Bromley, Kent; 2 s (Iain b 1960, Nicholas b 1968), 1 da (Jacqueline b 1956); *Career* land agent to Sir Francis and Lady Whitmore Orsett Estate Essex 1954-61, estates bursar Winchester Coll 1961-82, bursar Winchester Coll 1982-; chm elect Ind Schs Bursars Assoc; govr Pilgrims Sch Winchester; FRICS; *Recreations* family, photography, golf; *Style*— David Vellacott, Esq; 52 Kingsgate St, Winchester, Hampshire SO23 9PF (☎ 0962 653 31); Winchester Coll, Winchester, Hampshire SO23 9NA (☎ 0962 642 42)

VENABLES, Harold David Spenser; s of Maj Cedric Venables TD, of Oatlands, Warborough, Oxford (d 1976), and Gladys, *née* Hall (d 1973); *b* 14 Oct 1932; *Educ* Denstone Coll; *m* 18 July 1964, Teresa Grace, da of James Cornelius Watts, Hove, Sussex (d 1960); 1 da (Louise b 1965), 1 s (Julian b 1967); *Career* pilot off RAF 1957-58 central reconnaissance estab; admitted slr 1956; entered official Slr Off 1960; memb Lord Chllrs Ctee on Age of Majority 1965-67, asst Official Slr 1977-80; Official Slr 1980-; *Books* A guide to the Law Affecting Mental Patients (1975), Contributor Halsbury's Laws of England (4 ed), The Racing Fifteen-Hundreds: A History of Voiturette Racing 1931-40 (1984); *Recreations* vintage motor cars, military and motoring history; *Style*— David Venables, Esq; Penderel House, 287 High Holborn, London WC1V 7HP (☎ 01 936 7116, tax 01 936 7105)

VENABLES, Robert; s of Walter Edwin Venables, MM, of 30 Boswell Rd, Wath upon Dearne, Rotherham, and Mildred Daisy Robson, *née* Taylor; *b* 1 Oct 1947; *Educ* Wath upon Dearne Co GS, Merton Coll Oxford (MA), LSE (LLM); *Career* lectr: Merton Coll Oxford 1972-75, UCL 1973-75; Oxford Univ 1975-80: official fell and tutor in jurisprudence St Edmund Hall, CUF lectr; barr Middle Temple 1973, in practice 1976-; FTII 1983; *Books* Trusts and Estate Planning (1987), Inheritance Tax Planning (1988), Non-Resident Trusts (1988), Preserving the Family Farm (1989), Tax Planning and Fundraising for Charities (1989); *Recreations* music making; *Clubs* Travellers; *Style*— Robert Venables, Esq; 62 Harrington Gardens, London SW7; Rue de L'Ormeau, Claviers, Var, France; Chambers, 24 Old Buildings, Lincoln's Inn, London WC2A 3UJ (☎ 01 242 2744, fax 01 831 8095)

VENABLES-LLEWELYN, Sir John Michael Dillwyn-; 4 Bt (UK 1890) of Penllergaer, Llangyfelach and Ynis-y-gerwn, Cadoxton juxta Neath, of Glamorganshire; s of Brig Sir (Charles) Michael Dillwyn-Venables-Llewelyn, 3 Bt, MVO (d 1976); *b* 12 August 1938; *Educ* Eton, Magdalene Coll Cambridge; *m* 1, 1963 (m dis 1972), Nina, da of late J S Hallan; 2 da; m 2, 1975, Nina Gay Richardson Oliver; *Career* farmer; *Style*— Sir John Venables-Llewelyn, Bt; Talwen Uchaf Farm, Garthbrengy, Brecon, Powys LD3 9TE; Llysdinam, Newbridge-on-Wye, Llandrindod Wells, Powys (☎ Newbridge-on-Wye 351)

VENABLES-VERNON, Hon Georgina Frances; da of 10 Baron Vernon; *b* 1963; *Style*— The Hon Georgina Venables-Vernon

VENABLES-VERNON, Hon Joanna Elizabeth; da of 10 Baron Vernon; *b* 1965; *Style*— The Hon Joanna Venables-Vernon

VENESS, George Thomas Lionel; s of Robert Veness (d 1962), and Florence Frances, *née* Randall (d 1984); *b* 23 August 1936; *Educ* Cuckoo Schs Hanwell; *m* 4 July 1959 (sep), Kathleen, da of late Alfred Powell; 2 da (Jacqueline Susan b 4 Nov 1960, Sharon Nicole b 28 Sept 1962); *Career* Nat Serv RAF 1954-56; md Wilven Finishing Ltd 1972-; *Recreations* art; *Style*— George Veness, Esq; Wilven Finishing Ltd, Burlington House, Reynolds Rd, Chiswick, London W4 5AR (☎ 01 994 6551 23)

VENNING, Martin John Wentworth; s of Major Peter Wentworth Venning, of Surrey, and Vera Venning, *née* Heley (d 1956); *b* 30 June 1942; *Educ* Cranleigh Sch Surrey; *m* 1, 5 May 1973, Barbara Lesley; 2 da (Zoe b 1974, Nicola b 1976); m 2, 4 Dec 1982, Marian Kay, da of Ronald Rupert Arthur, of Surrey; *Career* CA; managing ptnr Sheffield office Finnie & Co; hon tres: High Peak Cons Assoc, Sheffield & District Soc of CAs 1984-87, W Yorks Soc of CAs 1981-83; chm Hope Valley Tourist Assoc; Insolvency Practitioners Licence; *Recreations* hockey (Yorkshire Co 1972-73), squash, tennis; *Clubs* Purley Hockey, Farsley Hockey, Bamford Tennis; *Style*— Martin J W Venning, Esq; The Old Vicarage, Church Bank, Hathersage, Sheffield S30 1AB (☎ 04 33 51099); Business: Nimrod House, 42 Kingfield Road, Sheffield S11 9AT (☎ 0742 556591)

VENNING, Philip Duncombe Riley; s of Roger Riley Venning, MBE (d 1953), and Rosemary Stella Cenzi, *née* Mann; *b* 24 Mar 1947; *Educ* Sherborne, Principia Coll Illinois USA, Trinity Hall Cambridge (MA); *m* 4 April 1987, Elizabeth Frances Ann, da of Michael Anthony Robelou Powers, of Grove Terr Mews Highgate London; *Career* journalist Times Educational Supplement 1970-81 (asst ed 1978), freelance writer 1981-84, sec Soc for the Protection of Ancient Buildings 1984-; sec William Morris Craft Fellowship Ctee 1986-, memb Cncl for Occupation Standards and Qualifications in Environmental Conservation 1988-; *Recreations* archaeology, book collecting; *Style*— Philip Venning, Esq; 17 Highgate High St, London N6 5JT (☎ 01 341 0925); 37 Spital Sq, London E1 6DY (☎ 01 377 1644)

VENNING, Virginia Margaret; s of John Venning, MC (d 1964), of Kendals Hall, nr Radlett, Herts, and Marjorie Beatrice Venning, *née* Close-Brooks (d 1947); *b* 25 Jan 1913; *Educ* private, Regent St Poly (Sculpture Sch), RA Schs; *m* 11 July 1939, Capt E A T Churcher, CBE, RN; *Career* 2 Offr WRNS; sculptor and painter; exhibited: RA, RWA, annually at own studio and locally; cmmnd work on and in churches, gardens in London, Somerset, Dorset, and N Africa; memb SWA; *Recreations* travelling, bridge;

Clubs (assoc) Army and Navy; *Style*— Miss Virginia Venning; 22 Bimport, Shaftesbury, Dorset SP7 8AZ

VENTHAM, Michael John; s of Percy Ventham, of Rettendon Common, nr Chelmsford, Essex, and Grace Winifred, *née* Rogers; *b* 13 June 1951; *Educ* Wimbledon County Sch for Boys; *m* 14 Sept 1974, Janis, da of Cleaveland Philip Johnson, of Hockley, Essex; 2 s (Mark b 18 June 1975, Graham b 6 June 1977), 1 da (Victoria b 28 Feb 1984); *Career* CA; sr ptnr M J Ventham 1974-; dir: Focusmeer Ltd 1975-, Cotti's House Ltd 1975-, M J Ventham & Co Ltd 1986, Ventham Employment Ltd 1986-, M J Ventham & Co (Computer Services) Ltd 1986-, M J Ventham & Co (Tstees) 1986-, Balance control plc 1987-, Somerly Publications 1987-, M J Ventham & Co (Management Conslts) Ltd 1986-; govr Greensward Sch Hockley Essex; FCA 1978 (ACA 1973), FBIM 1986, FIOD 1987; *Recreations* watching and playing football, cricket, reading, travel ; *Style*— Michael J Ventham, Esq; Warren House, 10-20 Main Rd, Hockley, Essex SS5 4RY (☎ 0702 206333, fax 0702 207488, car ☎ 0836 252760, telex 946240)

VENTRY, 8 Baron (I 1800) Sir Andrew Wesley Daubeny de Moleyns; 8 Bt (1797); assumed by deed poll 1966 the surname of Daubeny de Moleyns; s (by 2nd w) of Hon Francis Alexander Innys Eveleigh-Ross-de-Moleyns (d 1964), s of 6 Baron Ventry, and his 2 w Joan (now Mrs Nigel Springett), eldest da of Harold Wesley, of Surrey; suc uncle, 7 Baron, 1987; *b* 28 May 1943; *Educ* Aldenham; *m* 1, 20 Feb 1963 (m dis 1979), Nelly Edouard Renée, da of Abel Chaumillon, of Loma de los Riseos, Villa Angel, Torremolinos, Malaga, Spain; 1 s, 2 da (Hon Elizabeth-Ann b 1964, Hon Brigitte b 1967); m 2, 1983, Jill Rosemary, da of Cecil Walter Oram; 1 da (Hon Lisa b 1985); *Heir* s, Hon Francis Wesley Daubeny de Moleyns b 1 May 1965, ed Gordonstoun; *Style*— The Rt Hon the Lord Ventry; Hill of Errol House, Errol, Perthshire

VENUS, Rev John Charles; s of Ernest De Lacey Venus, of St Annes, Binstead, Isle of Wight (d 1971), and Mary Jessie Venus (d 1938); *b* 27 July 1929; *Educ* Newport County GS, Kings Coll London (AKC); *Career* curate Havant Hants 1954-59, chaplain/housemaster St George's GS Cape Town 1960-65; chaplain: RN 1966-70 and 1979-83, Glenalmond Coll 1970-78; rector of Abinger with Coldharbour 1983-; *Recreations* walking, theatre, painting; *Style*— The Rev John Venus; The Rectory, Abinger Common, Dorking, Surrey RH5 6HZ (☎ 0306 730746)

VERCO, Sir Walter John George; KCVO (1981, CVO 1970, MVO 1952); s of John Walter Verco; *b* 18 Jan 1907; *m* 1929, Ada Rose (d 1989), da of Bertram Leonard Bennett, of Lymington, Hants; 1 s, 1 da; *Career* served WWII RAFVR; sec to Garter King of Arms 1949-60, sec Order of Garter 1974-88, sec to Earl Marshal 1961-; Rouge Croix Pursuivant 1954-60, Chester Herald 1960-71, Norroy and Ulster King of Arms 1971-80, Surrey Herald of Arms Extraordinary 1980-; hon genealogist to: Order Br Empire 1959-, Royal Victorian Order 1968-88; inspr: RAF Badges 1970-, RAAF Badges 1971-; advsr on Naval Heraldry 1970-; tstee Coll of Arms Tst; OStJ; *Recreations* travel; *Style*— Sir Walter Verco, KCVO, Surrey Herald of Arms Extraordinary; College of Arms, Queen Victoria St, London EC4 (☎ 01 248 6185); 8 Park Court, Linkfield Lane, Redhill, Surrey (☎ 0737 71794)

VERDIN, Anthony; s of Jack Arthur Verdin, and Doris Hilda; *b* 16 Nov 1922; *Educ* Christ's Hosp, Merton Coll Oxford (MA, MSc); *m* 1, 1958, Greta; 1 s (John b 1965), 2 da (Julia b 1962, Annemarie b 1963); m 2, 1986, Araminta, da of Michael Henry Carlile Morris; 1 s (Arthur b 1987), 1 da (Aurelia b 1986); *Career* managing ptnr Cherwell Boathouse 1968-; dir: Chelart Ltd 1978-, Chelsea Arts Club Ltd 1987-, Morris & Verdin Ltd 1981-; md Analysis Automation Ltd 1971-; chm first Sch on Process Analytical Instrumentation Warwick Univ 1972; toured USA and W Indies with Golden Oldies and Miami Rugby Club 1977; CEng; *Publications* books incl: Gas Analysis Instrumentation (1973), and numerous articles and lectures on instrumentation techniques and air pollution; *Recreations* family, rugby football, tennis (lawn and real), cricket, music, reading, wine tasting; *Clubs* Chelsea Arts, Henley RFC; *Style*— Anthony Verdin, Esq; Analysis Automation Ltd, Southfield House, Eynsham, Oxon OX8 1JD (☎ 0865 881888, telex 837509)

VERDIN, Peter Anthony; s of Norman Verdin of Northwich, Cheshire (d 1985), and Mary Winifred, *née* McCormack; *b* 4 Mar 1934; *Educ* Ushaw Coll Durham, Durham Univ (LLB); *m* 16 Jan 1965, Patricia Marie, da of Joseph Patrick Burke, of Paington, Devon; 2 s (Christopher b 1966, Michael b 1971), 2 da (Catherine b 1968, Caroline b 1972); *Career* admitted slr 1957; ptnr Healds, Wigan; memb Law Soc (memb cncl 1974); *Recreations* golf, opera, watching Liverpool FC; *Clubs* RAC, Lymm Golf; *Style*— Peter A Verdin, Esq; 15 Mill Bank, Lymm, Cheshire, WA13 9DG (☎ Lymm 3433); Moot Hall Chambers, 8 Wallgate, Wigan, WN1 1JE (☎ 0942 41511, fax 0942 826 639)

VERDIN, Maj Philip George; MC (1943), DL (1979); s of Lt-Col R N H Verdin, DL, of Garnstone Castle, Weobley, Hereford, (d 1956) and Alison Macfie, *née* Barbour; *b* 27 May 1917; *Educ* Harrow, RMC Sandhurst; *m* 4 Jul 1961, Juliet, da of John Fitzadam Ormiston of Misesden, Glos; 2 s (Richard b 1962, Michael b 1965); *Career* cmmnd 4/7 Royal Dragon Guards 1937, wounded at Dunkirk, instr RMC 1941-42, wounded in accident 1942, returned to regt 1943, took part in D Day, (despatches 1945), invalided from army 1950; farmer and landowner; High Sheriff of Herefordshire 1966, chm Hereford Race Course, tax cmmr, pres of Royal Br Legion; *Recreations* shooting, fishing; *Clubs* Cavalry, Guards; *Style*— Maj Philip G Verdin, MC, DL; The Buttas, Canon Pyon, Herefordshire (☎ 0432 71231)

VERDON-SMITH, Sir (William) Reginald; DL (Avon 1974); s of Sir William George Verdon-Smith, CBE (d 1957), and Florence Diana, *née* Anders (d 1928); *b* 5 Nov 1912; *Educ* Repton, BNC Oxford (MA, BCL); *m* 1946, Jane Margaret, da of Victor William Hobbs (ka 1918); 1 s, 1 da, 2 step da; *Career* barr; dir Br Aeroplane Co Ltd 1942-66, pres SBAC 1946-48; dir: Br Aircraft Corpn 1960-72 (chm 1955-66), Bristol Siddeley Ltd 1960-66; dep chm Rolls Royce Ltd 1966-68, chm Br Aircraft Hldgs 1969-72, dir Babcock & Wilcox Ltd 1950-70 (dep chm 1960-70), dep chm Lloyds Bank Ltd 1952-83; chm: Lloyds Bank Int Ltd 1973-79, Lloyds Bristol Regnl Bd 1977-83; ptnr George White Evans Tribe & Co Stockbrokers 1952-80; Master: Worshipful Co of Coachmakers 1960-61, Soc of Merchant Venturers of Bristol 1968-69; pro-chllr Univ of Bristol 1970-86 (chm of cncl 1949-56), vice lord-lt for Avon 1980-; hon fell Brasenose Coll Oxford, hon LLD, and Hon Fell Bristol, Hon DSc Cranfield; kt 1953; *Recreations* sailing, golf; *Clubs* Royal Yacht Squadron, Royal Cruising, Royal Lymington Yacht, Oxford and Cambridge; *Style*— Sir Reginald Verdon-Smith, DL; 3 Spring Leigh, Church Road, Leigh Woods, Bristol BS8 3PG

VERE HODGE, Rev Prebendary Francis; MC (1943); s of Rev Roger Cuthbert Vere Hodge (d 1975), of Somerset, and Juliette Bornèque, *née* Peter (d 1975); *b* 31 Oct 1919; *Educ* Sherborne, Worcester Coll Oxford (MA); *m* 10 Oct 1942, Eleanor Mary, da of Arthur Bentley Connor (d 1960), of Somerset; 2 s (Anthony b 1943, David b 1945), 1 da (Felicity b 1949); *Career* joined Oxford Univ OTC (RA) 1938, 458 Ind Lt Bty RA, 1 Airborne Div 1941-43, No 1 COBU 1943-45, T/Capt 1943, Sicily (attached 2 Para Bn), Italy (attached 1 Para Bde), France (attached 7 Para Bn); Cuddesdon Theol Coll 1946-48; ordained: deacon 1948, priest 1949; curate of Battle 1948-54, rector of Iping and Linch 1954-58; vicar: Kingswood 1958-65, Moorlinch 1965-79; rector: Greinton 1968-79, Lydeard St Lawrence 1979-84; prebendary St Decuman's Wells Cathedral 1979-, chm Glastonbury Abbey Tstees 1986-; *Books* A Handbook for the Newly Ordained and Other Clergy (1986); *Recreations* birdwatching; *Style*— The Rev Prebendary Francis Vere Hodge, MC; Rose Cottage, Ham St, Baltonsborough, Glastonbury, Somerset BA6 8PN (☎ 0458 50032)

VERE NICOLL, Charles Fiennes; s of Maj Raymond Guy Vere Nicoll, MC (d 1981), of Mont Plaisant House, Catel, Guernsey, CI, and Shirley Eugenie Mary, *née* Allen; *b* 2 April 1955; *Educ* Eton; *m* 17 Jan 1985 (m dis 1983), Amanda Mary Howell Crichton-Stuart, da of Michael Pollock Howell Williams, of Orchards, Fordingbridge, Hants; 1 step s (Frederick James b 1981), 1 step da (Katherine Rose b 1979); *Career* admitted slr 1979; co dir Tellydisc Ltd 1980-83; chief exec offr: Telegroup Hldgs 1981-83, Ventech Ltd 1983-, Ventech Healthcare Corpn Inc 1986-; *Recreations* shooting; *Clubs* Turf; *Style*— Charles Vere Nicoll, Esq; Drifthouse, Ashampstead, Berkshire; 11 Old Queen St, London SW1

VERE-LAURIE, Lt-Col George Edward; o s of Lt-Col George Halliburton Foster Peel Vere-Laurie, JP, DL (d 1981), of Carlton Hall, Notts, and (Caroline) Judith, *née* Francklin (d 1987); Carlton Hall was purchased in 1832 by John Vere (d 1881), descended in an illegitimate line from the de Vere Earls of Oxford, and passed on his death to his niece Clementina Isabella Margaret, Mrs Craig, whose eldest da (by her 1 m to Hon Sydney William Foster-Skeffington (3 s of 10 Viscount Massereene and 3 Viscount Ferrard) Florence Clementina Vere m 1, Lt- Col George Brenton Laurie (ka 1915) and assumed the additional surname of Vere for herself and issue (*see* Burke's Landed Gentry, 18 edn, Vol III, 1972); *b* 3 Sept 1935; *Educ* Eton, RMA Sandhurst, London Univ (BSc); *Career* cmmnd 9 Lancers 1955, cmd 9/12 Royal Lancers (PWO) 1974-77; md Trackpower Transmissions Ltd 1979-; Lord of the Manors of Carlton-on-Trent and Willoughby-in-Norwell Notts; Freeman City of London, Key Warden and Master Elect Worshipful Co of Saddlers; FBIM 1981; *Recreations* horses, fox hunting, country life; *Style*— Lt-Col George Vere-Laurie; Carlton Hall, Carlton-on-Trent, Newark, Notts (☎ 0636 821421)

VEREKER, Hon Elizabeth Jane; da of 8 Viscount Gort; *b* 1948; *Educ* Hillcourt Dublin; *m* ; 1 s (Jason b 1974), 1 da (Sara Jayne b 1976); *Career* rep for Phillips Fine Arts, auctioneers with IOW and Rep of Ireland Offices; *Style*— The Hon Elizabeth Vereker

VEREKER, Hon Foley Robert Standish Prendergast; s and h of 8 Viscount Gort; *b* 24 Oct 1951; *Educ* Harrow; *m* 1979 (m dis 1987), Julie Denise, only da of D W Jones; *Career* Photographer; *Style*— The Hon Foley Vereker

VEREKER, John Michael Medlicott; s of Cdr Charles William Medlicott Vereker, and Marjorie Hughes, *née* Whatley (d 1984); *b* 9 August 1944; *Educ* Marlborough, Univ of Keele (BA); *m* 7 Nov 1971, Judith, da of Hobart Rowen, of Washington, DC; 1 s (Andrew b 1975), 1 da (Jennifer b 1973); *Career* asst princ: ODM 1967-69, World Bank Washington 1970-72; princ ODM 1972, private sec to successive Mins at ODM; asst sec 1978, PMs Off 1980-83; under sec 1983- and princ fin offr FCO ODA 1986-88, dep sec (teachers) DES 1988, dep sec (further and higher educn sci) DES 1988-; *Style*— John Vereker, Esq; c/o Dept of Education and Science, Elizabeth House, York Rd, London SE7 7PH (☎ 01 934 9000)

VEREKER, Hon Nicholas Leopold Prendergast; s of 8 Viscount Gort; *b* 1954; *Educ* Harrow; *m* 1985, Nicola F, yst da of Michael W Pitt, of Lias Cottage, Compton Dundon, Somerton, Som; *Style*— The Hon Nicholas Vereker

VEREKER, Peter William Medlicott; s of Cdr C W M Vereker, of Wylye, Wilts, and Marjorie Hughes, *née* Whatley (d 1984); *b* 13 Oct 1939; *Educ* Marlborough, Trinity Coll Cambridge (MA), Harvard Univ; *m* 7 April 1967, Susan Elisabeth, da of Maj-Gen A J Dyball, CBE, MC, TD (d 1985); 3 s (Connel b 1971, Toby b 1973, Rory b 1981); *Career* Dip Serv; head Chancery Athens 1975-78, RCDS 1982, csllr and consul-gen HM Embassy Bangkok 1983-86 (chargé d'affaires 1984 and 1986), dep perm rep UK Mission Geneva 1987-; *Recreations* tennis, sailing, skiing, poetry; *Clubs* Royal Bangkok Sports, New Sporting (Geneva); *Style*— Peter W M Vereker, Esq; c/o FCO, King Charles St, London SW1A 2AH; UK Mission at Geneva (☎ 34 38 00)

VEREKER, Hon Mrs Charles; Yvonne Frances; da of late Maj Geoffrey Arthur Barnett, MBE; *m* 1938, Hon Charles Standish Vereker (d 1941), s of Field Marshal 6 Viscount Gort, VC, GCB, CBE, DSO, MVO, MC (d 1946); *Style*— The Hon Mrs Charles Vereker; Serge Hill, Abbots Langley, Herts

VEREY, Michael John; TD (1945); s of Henry Edward Verey, DSO (d 1968), of Bridge House, Twyford, Berks, and Lucy Alice, *née* Longstaffe (d 1968); *b* 12 Oct 1912; *Educ* Eton, Trinity Coll Cambridge (MA); *m* 26 March 1947, Sylvia Mary, da of Lt-Col Denis Wilson, MC (k 1916); 2 s (Geoffrey b 1949, David b 1950), 1 da (Angela b 1948); *Career* joined Warwicks Yeo 1936, serv: Middle East, Iraq, Syria and Persia Campaigns 1941, El Alamein 1942, Italy 1943; Lt-Col 1945; dir: Helbert Wagg & Co Ltd 1948-77 (joined 1934), Aust Mercantile Land & Fin Co 1950-70; dep chm Commercial Union Assur Co 1951-82, vice chm The Boots Co 1962-83, Br Petroleum Co 1974-82; Invest Int SA 1968-; chm: Broadstone Investmt Tst 1962-83, Brixton Estate Co 1971-83, Schroders Ltd 1973-77; chm: Charities Official Investmt Fund Accepting Houses Ctee 1974-77; vice pres Br Bankers Fedn 1974-77, memb Covent Garden Mkt Authy 1961-66; High Sheriff Berks 1968; *Recreations* gardening, travel; *Clubs* Boodles; *Style*— Michael Verey, Esq, TD; Little Bowden, Pangbourne, Berkshire (☎ 073 57 2210); 120 Cheapside, London EC2 (☎ 01 382 6000)

VERMES, Dr Geza; s of Ernö Vermes (d 1944), and Terezia, *née* Riesz (d 1944); *b* 22 June 1924; *Educ* Gymnasium of Gyula Hungary, Budapest Univ, Louvain Univ, Coll St Albert of Louvain; *m* 12 May 1958, (Noreen) Pamela, da of Dr Edward Ernest Hobson (Capt RAMC); *Career* lectr (later lectr biblical studies) Univ of Newcastle 1957-65, reader in Jewish studies and professorial fell Wolfson Coll Oxford 1965-; govr Oxford Centre for Hebrew Studies 1972-, chm Oxford Cncl of Christians and Jews 1980-86; FBA 1985; *Books* Discovery in the Judean Desert (1956), Scripture and Tradition in

Judaism (1961), Jesus the Jew (1973), Post Biblical Jewish Studies (1975), Jesus and the World of Judaism (1983), History of the Jewish People in the Age of Jesus by E Schürer (jt reviser, 1973-87), The Dead Sea Scrolls in English (1987); *Recreations* Watching Wildlife; *Style*— Dr Geza Vermes; West Wood Cottage, Foxcombe Lane, Boars Hill, Oxford OX1 5DH (☎ 0865 735 384); Oriental Institute, Pusey Lane, Oxford OX1 2LE (☎ 0865 278 200/278 208)

VERMONT, David Neville; s of Leon Vermont (d 1949), and Anne MacDonald, *née* Hardy (d 1972); *b* 13 Feb 1931; *Educ* Mercers Sch, Christ's Coll Univ of Cambridge (BA, MA); *m* 16 March 1957, Ann Marion, da of late Lloyd Wilson; 2 s (Christopher b 1959, Charles b 1961), 1 da (Rachel b 1964); *Career* Cadet Bn HAC 1947-50, Nat Serv 2 Regt RHA 1950-52 (served Germany BAOR, cmmnd 1951), 1 Regt HAC RHA 1952-62 (cmmnd 1956); Sedgwick Gp plc 1955-88: dep chm gp reinsur subsid E W Payne Cos Ltd 1975-87, dir Sumitomo Marine & Fire Insur Co (Europe) Ltd and City Fire Insur Co Ltd, London Rep Compagnie de Réassurance d'Ile de France (Corifrance), gen rep UK of New India Assur Co Ltd; memb Lloyds 1969-; chm: Reinsur Brokers Assoc 1976-77, Brokers Reinsur Ctee 1977-78; chm: Argentine Diocesan Assoc (vice pres 1988-), cncl Gresham Coll, Anglo-Norse (London) Fund for Disabled;vice pres Argentine Diocesan Assoc (chm 1973-88); dir London Handel Orchestra Ltd, govr St Paul's Schls (chm 1981-82); memb: cncl City Univ, city and insur advsy panels of City Univ Business Sch; tstee Whitechapel Art Gallery Fndn; Freeman City of London 1952, Master Worshipful Co Mercers 1981-82; FCII; *Recreations* walking, opera, chamber music; *Clubs* Garrick, MCC, United Oxford & Cambridge, City Livery, Nikaen; *Style*— David Vermont, Esq; Frodsham, Sawbridgeworth, Herts CM21 9EP (☎ 0279 723 415); AGF House, 41 Botolph Lane, London EC3R 8DL (☎ 01 929 2414, fax 01 626 2099)

VERNER-JEFFREYS, Robert Gerard; s of Lt Robert David Verner-Jeffreys, RN (ka 1942), and Audrey Marion, *née* Bray; *b* 30 Sept 1937; *Educ* Marlborough, RNC Dartmouth; *m* 12 Sept 1964, Anne, da of Col Samuel Alexander Holwell Kirkby, MC (ka 1943); 1 s (Robert b 1969), 1 da (Annabel b 1966); *Career* insur broker; dir John Broadwood & Sons Ltd 1983-86, Pendlehill Ltd 1986-, C T Bowring Reinsurance Ltd 1987-, Bowring Insur Bankers Ltd 1988-; tstee: Broadwood Tst, Fullers Almshouses, Neale's Charity; ACII, ABIBA; *Recreations* genealogy, music; *Style*— Robert G Verner-Jeffreys, Esq; Little Barn, Elstead, Surrey (☎ 0252 702179); Ct Bowring & Co Ltd (☎ 01 283 3100); Bowring Building, London EC3 & at Lloyds

VERNEY, Lt-Cdr David; DL (Cornwall 1982); 2 s of Sir Ralph Verney, 1 Bt, and bro of Sir John Verney, 2 Bt, MC; *b* 31 May 1918; *Educ* Eton; *m* 1948, Hon Mary Kathleen Boscawen, JP, da of 8 Viscount Falmouth; 1 s, 2 da (including Mrs Peter Bickford-Smith); *Career* WWII served RN (ret); High Sheriff Cornwall 1964; *Recreations* fishing; *Clubs* Naval and Military; *Style*— Lt-Cdr David Verney, DL, RN; Trevella, St Erme, Truro, Cornwall

VERNEY, Hon Mrs (Dorothy Cecily); *née* Tollemache; da of 3 Baron Tollemache (d 1955); *b* 1907; *m* 1942, Air Cdre Reynell Henry Verney, CBE, RAF (d 1974); *Style*— The Hon Mrs Verney; Stone House, Bishop's Hill, Lighthorne, Warwick

VERNEY, Edmund Ralph; s and h of Sir Ralph Verney, 5 Bt; *b* 28 June 1950; *Educ* Harrow, York Univ; *m* 1982, Daphne Fausset-Farquhar, of Lovelocks House, Shefford Woodlands, Hungerford; 1 s (b 1983); *Career* ARICS; *Clubs* Brooks's; *Style*— Edmund Verney, Esq; Rectory Close, Middle Claydon, Buckingham

VERNEY, Sir John; 2 Bt (UK 1946), of Eaton Square, City of Westminster, MC (1944), TD (1970); s of Lt-Col Sir Ralph Verney, 1 Bt, CB, CIE, CVO (d 1959); Sir Ralph's f, Frederick, was 4 s of Sir Harry Verney, 2 Bt, of Claydon (*see* Sir Ralph Bruce Verney, 5 Bt); *b* 30 Sept 1913; *Educ* Eton, Christ Church Oxford; *m* 1939, Jeanie Lucinda, da of late Maj Herbert Musgrave, DSO, RE; 1 s, 5 da (and 1 s decd); *Heir* s, John Sebastian Verney; *Career* served 1939-45 War as Maj RAC; painter, illustrator and author; Légion d'Honneur 1945; *Style*— Sir John Verney, Bt, MC, TD; The White House, Clare, Suffolk (☎ 0787 277 494)

VERNEY, His Hon Judge Lawrence John; TD (1955), DL (Bucks 1967); 5 s of Sir Harry Verney, 4 Bt (d 1974), by his w Lady Rachel Bruce (d 1964), da of 9 Earl of Elgin and Kincardine, KG; *b* 19 July 1924; *Educ* Harrow, Oriel Coll Oxford; *m* 1972, Zoë Auriel, da of Lt-Col P G Goodeve-Docker; *Career* Capt Grenadier Gds 1943-46, Lt-Col Royal Bucks Yeo TA 1947-68, Hon Col Bucks Army Cadet Force 1975-80; barr Inner Temple 1952; dep chm QS: Bucks 1962-71, Middx 1971; circuit judge 1972-; govr Harrow Sch 1972-87; *Style*— His Hon Judge Verney, TD, DL; Windmill House, Church Lane, Oving, Aylesbury, Bucks HP22 4HL

VERNEY, Hon Mrs (Mary Kathleen); *née* Boscawen; JP (Cornwall 1960); da of 8 Viscount Falmouth; *b* 11 June 1926; *Educ* Heathfield Ascot; *m* 1948, David (*qv*), yr s of Sir Ralph Verney, 1 Bt; 1 s, 2 da; *Style*— The Hon Mrs Verney, JP; Trevella, St Erme, Truro, Cornwall

VERNEY, Sir Ralph Bruce; 5 Bt (UK 1818), of Claydon House, Buckinghamshire, KBE (1974), JP (Bucks 1954), DL (Bucks); s of Sir Harry Calvert Williams Verney, 4 Bt, DSO (d 1974); *b* 18 Jan 1915; *Educ* Canford, Balliol Coll Oxford (BA); *m* 7 July 1948, Mary, da of late Percy Charles Vestey (3 s of Sir Edmund Vestey, 1 Bt) and 2 cous of the present Lord Vestey; 1 s, 3 da; *Heir* s, Edmund Ralph Verney; *Career* Maj RA Java 1945; Vice Lord-Lieut for Bucks 1965-85, High Sheriff 1957, ccncllr 1952-73, co alderman 1961-73, chm Nat Ctee for England of Forestry Cmmn 1968-80 (produced plan for Chiltern Hills 1971), pres CLA 1961-63, memb Royal Cmmn on Environmental Pollution 1973-79; trtee: Radcliffe, Ernest Cook and Chequers Tsts-, chm Nature Conservancy Cncl 1980-83; hon FRIBA 1977, hon fell Green Coll Oxford; *Clubs* Cavalry and Guards'; *Style*— Sir Ralph Verney, Bt, KBE, JP, DL; Claydon House, Middle Claydon, Buckingham MK18 2EX (☎ 029 673 297); Plas Rhoscolyn, Holyhead LL65 2NZ (☎ 0407 860288)

VERNEY, Rt Rev Stephen Edmund; MBE (1945); 2 s of Sir Harry Verney, 4 Bt, DSO, by Lady Rachel Bruce, da of 9 Earl of Elgin and Kincardine; *b* 17 April 1919; *Educ* Harrow, Balliol Coll Oxford; *m* 1, 1947, Priscilla (d 1974), da of George Schwerdt, of Alresford; 1 s, 3 da; m 2, 1981, as her 2 husband, Sandra Bailey, of Llandeilo; 1 s (Harry, decd); *Career* late Lt and Temp Capt Intelligence Corps; canon St George's Chapel Windsor 1970-77, suffragan bishop Repton 1977-85; *Books* Fire in Coventry (1964), People & Cities (1969), Into the New Age (1976), Water into Wine (1985), The Dance of Love (1989); *Recreations* conversation and aloneness, music, gardening, walking; *Clubs* English Speaking Union; *Style*— The Rt Rev Stephen Verney, MBE; Charity School House, Church Rd, Blewbury, Didcot, Oxon OX11 9PY (☎ 0235 850004)

VERNON, Anthony John; s of John Bloor Vernon; *b* 21 May 1937; *Educ* Abbotsholme Sch Rocester Derbys; *m* 1962, Beatrice Jane, *née* Murray; 2 s; *Career* chm and md Murray Vernon Ltd; chm: Sandfield Securities Ltd, Leyfos Plastics Ltd, Fastnet Fish Ltd, Sheppard (International Traders) Ltd, UK Provision Trade Fedn; govr Ellesmere Coll Salop, pres Haslington Cons Assoc, fell of the Woodard Schools (Midland Div), vice-chm Congleton Constituency Cons Assoc; *Recreations* shooting, sailing; *Clubs* Royal Ocean Racing; *Style*— Anthony Vernon, Esq; Haslington Hall, Haslington, Crewe, Cheshire (☎ 0270 582662)

VERNON, Denis Stewart; s of Eric Stewart Vernon (d 1964), and Bessie Ferguson, *née* Alder; *b* 11 Feb 1931; *Educ* Rossall, King's Coll Newcastle, London Business Sch; *m* ; 2 s, 2 da; *Career* Nat Serv 2 Lt RASC 1954-56; slr; sr ptnr in Newcastle firm 1956-78; chm and chief exec Ferguson Industl Hldgs plc 1968-; chm: Utd Merchants Ltd 1978-87, Rare Breeds Survival Tst Ltd 1988-; *Recreations* sailing, skiing, ornithology, art, conservation; *Clubs* Farmers; *Style*— Denis Vernon, Esq; Ferguson Industrial Holdings plc, Appleby Castle, Appleby, Cumbria (☎ 07683 51402, telex 64100)

VERNON, (John) Fane; s of Capt John Edward Vernon (d 1951), of Co Cavan, Ireland, and Dolores Arnold (d 1931); *b* 16 Jan 1924; *Educ* Winchester; *m* 1948, Pamela Elizabeth, da of Archibald Evander McIver (d 1962), of Dublin; 1 s (John), 1 da (Katharine); *Career* mil serv 1942-46, 820 Naval Air Sqdn, HMS Formidable, HMS Indefatigable, Home Fleet, Med and Pacific, demob Lt (A) RNVR; joined Ash & Lacy plc 1951 (chm 1970-89); chm: Br Dredging plc 1980-, Brooke Tool Engrg (Hldgs) plc 1984-; dir: Shipton Communications Ltd 1982-86, Hargreaves Gp plc 1984-87, Davenports Brewery (Hldgs) plc 1985-86; *Recreations* golf, bridge; *Style*— Fane Vernon, Esq; 60 Richmond Hill Rd, Edgbaston, Birmingham B15 3RZ (☎ 021 454 2047)

VERNON, Hon Grant; s of 6 Baron Lyveden; *b* 1952; *Style*— The Hon Grant Vernon

VERNON, Hon Jack Leslie; s and h of 6 Baron Lyveden; *b* 10 Nov 1938; *m* 1961, Lynette June, da of William Herbert Lilley; 1 s, 2 da; *Style*— The Hon Jack Vernon; 17 Carlton St, Te Aroha, New Zealand

VERNON, Sir James; AC (1980), CBE (1962, OBE 1960); s of Donald Vernon, of Tamworth, NSW; *b* 1910; *Educ* Sydney Univ (BSc), UCL (PhD); *m* 1935, Mavis (d 1980), da of C Lonsdale Smith; 2 da; *Career* Colonial Sugar Refining Co Ltd: chief chemist 1938-51, sr exec offr 1951-55, asst gen mangr 1956-57, gen mangr 1958-72, dir 1958-82, chm 1978-80; dir Westham Dredging Co Pty Ltd; chm Volvo Aust Pty Ltd; Hon DSc: Sydney, Newcastle; FRACI; FTS; FAIM; Order of the Sacred Treasure (1 class) Japan 1983; kt 1965; *Clubs* Australian, Union, Royal Sydney Golf; *Style*— Sir James Vernon, AC, CBE; 27 Manning Rd, Double Bay, NSW 2028, Australia

VERNON, James Loudon; s of Capt Reginald Thornycroft Vernon, RFC (d 1977); *b* 27 Oct 1940; *Educ* Eton, Trinity Coll Dublin; *m* 1971, Elspeth Mary Stewart, da of Rev Cyril Raby Thomson; 2 s, 2 da; *Career* dir Constantine Hldgs Ltd 1977, underwriting memb Lloyd's 1980, Liveryman Worshipful Co of Skinners 1979; *Recreations* sailing (yachts 'Archon' and 'Minx'), shooting, skiing, music (particulary opera); *Clubs* Royal Yacht Sqdn, RAC, Royal St George; *Style*— James Vernon, Esq; 45 Egerton Crescent, London SW3 2ED (☎ 01 589 0858)

VERNON, James William; s and h of Sir Nigel Vernon, 4 Bt; *b* 2 April 1949; *Educ* Shrewsbury; *m* 1981, Davinia, da of Christopher David Howard, of Ryton Corner, Ryton, Shrewsbury; 1 da (Harriet Lucy Howard b 1985), 1 s (George William Howard b 1987); *Career* chartered accountant; *Style*— James Vernon, Esq; The Hall, Lygan-y-Wern, Pentre Halkyn, Holywell, Clwyd

VERNON, John Humphrey; s of Major Humphrey Bagnall Vernon, MC (d 1979), and Sibyl Mason Vernon, of Beechdale House, Stonecross, Exford, Somerset; *b* 7 Dec 1940; *Educ* Charterhouse, Magdalen Coll Oxford; *m* 1973, Alison Margaret, da of William Warnock Watt (d 1986), of Knowlegate, Sheriffhales, Shifnal, Shropshire; 1 s (Andrew b 1981), 1 da (Nicola b 1978); *Career* div chief exec Newship Gp Ltd 1987-, exec with Babcock Int plc 1974-87; md: Dynamo & Electrical Services Ltd 1977-80, Secundalax Emergency Lighting Ltd 1977-80, Piranha Ignition Ltd 1977-80; dep chm Piranha Ignition Ltd 1980-82; dir Pexit Precision Ltd 1981-82; chief exec: Babcock Gardner Ltd 1982-84, Babcock Gears Ltd 1982-85, Babcock Wire Equipment Ltd 1982-85; *Recreations* fishing, photography; *Style*— John Vernon, Esq; Maybank, 36 G;em Brook Rd, Priorslee, Telford, Shropshire (☎ Telford 0952 615381); Newship Gp Ltd, Clive House, Queens Rd, Weybridge (☎ 0932 858044)

VERNON, 10 Baron (GB 1762); John Lawrance Venables-Vernon; s of 9 Baron Vernon (d 1963); *b* 1 Feb 1923; *Educ* Eton, Magdalen Coll Oxford; *m* 1, 1955 (m dis 1982), Sheila Jean, da of W Marshall Clark, OBE, of Johannesburg, S Africa; 2 da; m 2, 1982, Sally June, da of Robin Stratford, QC, and formerly w of (1) Colin Fyfe-Jamieson and (2) Sir (John) Jeremy Eustace Tennyson d'Eyncourt, 3 Bt; *Heir* kinsman, Robert Vernon-Harcourt; *Career* WWII Capt Scots Gds, took Conservative Whip in Lords to 1981, since when has sat as SDP Peer; barr Lincoln's Inn 1949; served: Cabinet Office 1953-57, Colonial Office Kenya 1957-58, Foreign Office 1958-60; JP Derbys 1965-77; *Style*— The Rt Hon The Lord Vernon; Sudbury House, Sudbury, Derbyshire DE6 5HT (☎ (028 378) 208); 10 Ringmer Ave, Fulham, London SW6 (☎ 01 736 5900)

VERNON, Sir Nigel John Douglas; 4 Bt (UK 1914), of Shotwick Park, Co Chester; s of Sir (William) Norman Vernon, 3 Bt (d 1967); *b* 2 May 1924; *Educ* Charterhouse; *m* 29 Nov 1947, Margaret Ellen, da of late Robert Lyle Dobell, of The Mount, Waverton, Chester; 2 s (1 s decd), 1 da; *Heir* s, James William Vernon; *Career* Lt RNVR 1942-45; dir Travel Fin Ltd 1971-87, conslt Hogg Robinson Ltd 1984-; *Recreations* gardening, shooting, golf; *Clubs* Naval; *Style*— Sir Nigel Vernon, Bt; Top-y-Fron Hall, Kelsterton, nr Flint, Clywd CH6 5TF

VERNON, Richard Wallace; s of Herbert Wallace Vernon (d 1974), of Aldeburgh, Suffolk, and Gertrude Mary, *née* Jackson (d 1959); *b* 18 Oct 1927; *Educ* Loretto, Cambridge Univ (MA); *m* 8 Jan 1955, Pamela Violet, da of Lt-Col Alexander George William Grierson, RM (d 1951), of Walmer, Kent; 2 s (David Grierson b 1956, Simon Richard b 1958), 2 da (Sally Pamela Clare Daniell b 1960, Joanna Caroline Bennett b 1963); *Career* Lt RA 1945-48; dir: R K Harrison J I Jacobs (Insur) Ltd 1967-82, R K Harrison & Co 1975-82, Harrison Horncastle (Insur) Ltd 1982-84; md Towry Law (Int) Ltd 1984-88 (conslt 1988-); Freeman City of London, memb Worshipful Co of Fanmakers; *Recreations* sailing; *Clubs* Aldeburgh YC, Lloyds YC, Little Ship; *Style*— Richard Vernon, Esq; Scotch Corner, Wildernesse Avenue, Sevenoaks, Kent TN15

0EA (☎ 0732 61 567)

VERNON, Hon Robert Howard; s of 6 Baron Lyveden; *b* 1942; *m* 1968, Louise Smith; 1 s

VERNON, Hon Mrs; Hon Victoria; *née* Arthur; da of 3 Baron Glenarthur, OBE, DL, by his 2 w; *b* 20 June 1946; *m* 1976, Hugh (Richard) Vernon, 2 s of Mervyn Vernon, MVO (2 s of Rupert Vernon, DSO, JP, 5 s of Hon Greville Vernon, JP, DL, sometime MP Ayrshire and 4 s of 1 Baron Lyveden), by his w, Lady Violet Baring, yr da of 2 Earl of Cromer; 1 s (Andrew Robert Richard b 21 Aug 1979), 2 da (Catherine Victoria b 13 Oct 1977, Emma Mary b 12 Oct 1983); *Style*— The Hon Mrs Vernon; Pierhill, Annbank, Ayrshire

VERNON, William Michael; s of Sir Wilfred Douglas Vernon (d 1973), of Anningsley Park, Ottershaw, Surrey, and Nancy Elizabeth, *née* Jackson; *b* 17 April 1926; *Educ* Marlborough, Trinity Coll Cambridge (MA); *m* 1, 25 April 1952 (m dis 1977), Rosheen Elizabeth Mary, da of George O'Meara (d 1932), of Johannesburg, S Africa; 1 s (Mark Thornycroft Vernon b 7 March 1958); m 2, 7 Sept 1977, Jane Olivia Colston, da of Denys Kilham-Roberts (d 1975); *Career* Lt RM 1944-46; chm and chief exec Spillers Ltd 1968-80 (joined 1948, dir 1960, jt md 1962), dir EMI Ltd 1973-80, chm Famous Names Ltd 1981-85; pres: Nat Assoc of Br and Irish Millers 1965, Br Food Export Cncl 1977-80; vice-chm Millers' Mutual Assoc 1968-80, vice- pres and dep chm RNLI; dir Strong & Fisher (Hldgs) plc 1980-, chm Granville Meat Co Ltd 1981-; CBIM; *Recreations* sailing (ASSEGAI VI), skiing, shooting; *Clubs* Roy Yacht Sqdn, Roy Ocean Racing, Hurlingham; *Style*— Michael Vernon, Esq; Fyfield Manor, Andover, Hants

VERULAM, 7 Earl of (UK 1815); Sir John Duncan Grimston; 14 Bt (E 1629); also Lord Forrester (S 1633), Baron Dunboyne and Viscount Grimston (I 1719), Baron Verulam (GB 1790), Viscount Grimston (UK 1815); s of 6 Earl of Verulam (d 1973); *b* 21 April 1951; *Educ* Eton, Christ Church Oxford; *m* 1976, Dione Angela, da of Jeremy F E Smith, *qv*, of Balcombe House, Balcombe, Sussex; 3 s (Viscount Grimston b 1978, Hon Hugo Guy Sylvester b 1979, Hon Sam George b 1983), 1 da (Lady Flora Hermione b 1981); *Heir* s, Viscount Grimston; *Career* dir Baring Brothers Co Ltd; *Recreations* country pursuits; *Clubs* Beefsteak, White's, Turf; *Style*— The Rt Hon the Earl of Verulam; Gorhambury, St Albans, Herts AL3 6AH (☎ St Albans 55000)

VERULAM, Dowager Countess of; Marjorie Ray; da of late Walter Atholl Duncan; *m* 1938, Hon John Grimston, 6 Earl of Verulam (d 1973); 1 s, 4 da; *Style*— The Rt Hon the Dowager Countess of Verulam; Pré Mill House, Redbourn Rd, St Albans, Herts

VESEY, Sir (Nathaniel) Henry Peniston; CBE (1953); s of Hon Nathaniel Vesey, of Devonshire, Bermuda; *b* 1 June 1901; *Educ* Saltus GS; *m* 1920, Louise, da of Capt J Stubbs; 2 s; *Career* chm: H A & E Smith 1939-, Bank of N T Butterfield & Son 1970-; memb House of Assembly Bermuda 1938-72; kt 1965; *Style*— Sir Henry Vesey, CBE; Windward, Shelly Bay, Bermuda (☎ 3 0186)

VESSEY, Prof Martin Paterson; s of Sydney James Vessey, of Mill Hill, London, and Catherine, *née* Thompson; *b* 22 July 1936; *Educ* Univ Coll Sch Hampstead, UCL, Univ Coll Hosp Med Sch (MD, MA Oxon); *m* 21 May 1959, Anne, da of Prof Benjamin Stanley Platt, CMG. (d 1969); 2 s (Rupert b 1964, Ben b 1967), 1 da (Alice b 1970); *Career* prof of social and community medicine Univ of Oxford 1974-, fell St Cross Coll Oxford 1974-; memb: Oxford Preservation Tst, Nat Tst, Cncl for the Preservation of Rural England, Ctee on Safety of Medicines and Royal Cmmn on Environmental Pollution, BMA, Soc for Social Medicine; author of 3 books and 300 scientific papers; *Recreations* walking, motoring, singing, conservation; *Style*— Prof Martin Vessey; 8 Wamborough Road, Oxford OX2 6HZ (☎ 0865 52698); Dept of Community Medicine and General Practice, Radcliffe (☎ 0865 511293)

VESTEY, Sir (John) Derek; 2 Bt (UK 1921); s of late John Joseph Vestey (eldest s of Sir Edmund Vestey, 1 Bt, the latter being bro of 1 Baron Vestey); suc gf 1953; *b* 4 June 1914; *Educ* The Leys Sch; *m* 21 June 1938, Phyllis Irene, o da of Harry Brewer, of Banstead; 1 s, 1 da; *Heir* s, Paul Edmund Vestey; *Career* WWII Flt Lt RAFVR 1940-45; *Clubs* MCC, RAC; *Style*— Sir Derek Vestey, Bt; 5 Carlton Gdns, London SW1 (☎ 01 930 1610)

VESTEY, Edmund Hoyle; DL (Essex 1978); only s of Ronald Vestey, DL; *b* 1932; *Educ* Eton; *m* 1960, Anne Moubray, yr da of Gen Sir Geoffry Scoones, KCB, KBE, CSI, DSO, MC; 4 s (Timothy b 1961, James b 1962, George b 1964, Robin b 1968); *Career* served as 2 Lt Queen's Bays 1951; chm: Union Int Blue Star Line, Lamport & Holt Line, Albion Insurance; pres Gen Cncl Br Shipping 1981-82; jt master Puckeridge & Thurlow Foxhounds, pres Essex County Scouts Council 1979-87; High Sheriff Essex 1977-78; Lt City of London Yeomanry; *Clubs* Cavalry, Carlton; *Style*— Edmund Vestey, Esq, DL; Glencanisp Lodge, Lochinver, Sutherland; Sunnyside Farmhouse, Hawick, Roxburghshire; Little Thurlow Hall, nr Haverhill, Suffolk CB9 7LQ

VESTEY, Hon Mark William; s of Capt the Hon William Howarth Vestey (ka 1944), and bro of 3 Baron Vestey; raised to the rank of a Baron's younger son 1955; *b* 16 April 1943; *Educ* Eton; *m* 1975, Rose Amelia, da of Lt-Col Peter Thomas Clifton, DSO; 1 s, 2 da; *Career* 2 Lt Scots Gds; *Style*— The Hon Mark Vestey; 20 Eaton Mews South, SW1 (☎ 01 235 8932); Stowell Park, Northleach, nr Cheltenham, Glos

VESTEY, Paul Edmund; s and h of Sir (John) Derek Vestey, 2 Bt; *b* 15 Feb 1944; *Educ* Radley; *m* 1971, Victoria Anne Scudamore, da of John Salter, of Old Ford House, Tiverton, Devon; 3 da; *Clubs* British Racing Drivers', Farmers', Royal Automobile; *Style*— Paul Vestey Esq; 53 Cheval Place, London SW7 (☎ 01 589 0562); Manor House Farm, Bishops Sutton, Hants

VESTEY, 3 Baron (UK 1922); Sir Samuel George Armstrong Vestey; 3 Bt (UK 1913), DL (Glos 1982); s of l Capt the Hon William Howarth Vestey, Scots Gds (ka Italy 1944, only s of 2 Baron Vestey), and Pamela, da of George Nesbitt Armstrong, s of Charles Nesbitt Frederick Armstrong and Dame Nellie Melba, the opera singer; suc gf 1954; *b* 19 Mar 1941; *Educ* Eton; *m* 1, 1970 (m dis), Kathryn Mary, da of John Eccles, of Moor Park, Herts; 2 da (Hon Saffron b 1971, Hon Flora b 1978); m 2, 1981, Celia Elizabeth, yr da of Maj (Hubert) Guy Knight, MC, of Lockinge Manor, Wantage, and Hester, sis of Countess (w of 6 Earl) of Clanwilliam; 2 s; *Heir* s, Hon William Guy Vestey b 27 Aug 1983; *Career* Lt Scots Gds; dir Union International Co Ltd, Albion Insurance, Blue Star Line, Booth Steamship Co, Frederick Leyland & Co, Lamport & Holt Line, R F Kershaw Ltd, Robert Barrow Ltd, W Angliss & Co Pty (Australia), Western United Investment Co; pres London Meat Trade and Drovers Benevolent Assoc 1973, Inst of Meat 1978-83, Glos Assoc of Boys' Clubs; Liveryman Worshipful Co of Butchers'; patron of one living; GCStJ, Bailiff of Egle; *Clubs* White's, Jockey (Newmarket), Melbourne (Melbourne); *Style*— The Rt Hon the Lord Vestey, DL; Stowell Park, Northleach, Glos

VEVERS, David Michael; s of Maj John Bewlay Vevers, MBE (d 1979), of 6 Armit Road, Greenfield, Oldham, Lancs, and Kathleen Mary, *née* Wright; *b* 12 June 1942; *Educ* Felsted; *Career* head of PR Charterhouse Gp plc 1975-83, dep chm IPR City and Fin Gp (IPR cncl memb 1989), dir communications J Rothschild Hldgs plc 1983-85, gp public affrs mangr Prudential Corpn plc 1985-; MinstPR 1975, MInstM 1970; *Recreations* bridge, collecting contemporary art; *Clubs* Cavalry and Guards; *Style*— David Vevers, Esq; 91 Lexham Gdns, London W8 6JN (☎ 01 373 0141); Prudential Corporation plc, 142 Holborn Bars, London EC1N 2NH (☎ 01 405 9222, fax 01 831 1740, telex 266431)

VEY, Hon Mrs (Catharine Gina Amita); *née* Noble; da of Baron Glenkinglas, PC (Life Peer, d 1984), and Baroness Glenkinglas, *qv*; *b* 1943; *m* 1964, Peter Conrad Hamilton Vey; 1 s; *Style*— The Hon Mrs Vey; Godsfield Manor, Alresford, Hants

VIAL, Sir Kenneth Harold; CBE (1968); s of G O Vial, of Melbourne; *b* 11 August 1912; *Educ* Scotch Coll Melbourne; *m* 1937, Adele, da of R G R Ball; 1 s, 2 da; *Career* WWII Flt Lt RAAF 1941-46; chartered accountant; partner Arthur Andersen & Co 1946-67; chm: Yarra Falls Ltd 1967-74, Aust Nat Airlines Cmmn 1975-79, Rocke Tompsitt & Co Ltd 1976-79, Michaelis Bayley Ltd; dir Mono Pumps (Australia) Ltd, F H Faulding & Co Ltd; dep chllr La Trobe Univ 1970-72, memb Melbourne Rail Loop Authority 1971-; kt 1978; *Style*— Sir Kenneth Vial, CBE; 6-393 Barkers Rd, Kew, Vic 3101, Australia

VIBRAYE; *see*: de Vibraye

VICARS-HARRIS, Noel Hedley; CMG (1953); s of Charles Frederic Harris (d 1953), of the Gate House, Rugby, and Evelyn Clara Vicars (d 1942); *b* 22 Nov 1901; *Educ* Charterhouse, St John's Coll Cambridge (BA); *m* 1, 1926 (m dis 1939), Maria Guimaraes; 2 s; m 2, 1940, Joan Marguerite, da of Col C A Francis (d 1924); 1 s; *Career* served WWII RA 1939-43, Capt; HM Colonial Admin Service 1927-55: asst dir Tsetse Research 1930-36, sec Lands and Mines 1937-45, asst chief sec 1945-46, dir of establishments 1946-50, memb for Lands and Mines Tanganyika 1950-55; *Recreations* gardening; *Style*— Noël Vicars-Harris, Esq, CMG; Bampfylde Cottage, Sparkford, Yeovil, Somerset BA22 7LL (☎ 0963 40454)

VICARY, Rev Canon Douglas Reginald; s of Reginald William Vicary (d 1982), of Walthamstow, and Nellie Mary, *née* Fairman (d 1969); *b* 24 Sept 1916; *Educ* Sir George Monoux GS Walthamstow, Trinity Coll Oxford, Wycliffe Hall Oxford (MA, BSc, Dip Th); *m* 1947, Ruth, da of Frederick John Long Hickinbotham (d 1951); 2 s (Joseph, Simon), 2 da (Teresa, Margaret); *Career* dir of educn Diocese of Rochester 1948-57, canon of Rochester Cathedral 1952-75, headmaster King's Sch Rochester 1957-75, canon of Wells Cathedral and precentor 1975-88; chaplain to HM The Queen 1976-86; *Recreations* hill walking, music, reading; *Style*— The Rev Canon Douglas Vicary; 8 Tar St, Wells, Somerset (☎ 0749 79137)

VICE, (Henry) Anthony; s of S J Vice (d 1981), and L I Vice; *b* 24 Dec 1930; *Educ* Hymers Coll Hull, Queen's Coll Oxford (MA); *m* 4 Sept 1954, Elizabeth Joan Spencer, da of Prof J N Wright (d 1982); 1 s (John b 6 Aug 1962), 2 da (Susan b 6 Feb 1961, Philippa b 24 Aug 1965); *Career* Somerset LI 1948-50; dir: N M Rothschild 1972-, Bowthorpe Hldgs 1978-, Drummond Gp 1986-, Cavaghan & Gray 1988-; chm I J Dewhirst 1988-; *Style*— Anthony Vice, Esq; New Court, St Swithin's Lane, London EC4 (☎ 01 280 5000)

VICK, Sir (Francis) Arthur; OBE (1945); s of Wallace Devenport Vick (d 1952), of Birmingham, and Clara, *née* Taylor (d 1932); *b* 5 June 1911; *Educ* Waverley GS Birmingham, Birmingham Univ (BSc, PhD); *m* 1943, Elizabeth Dorothy, da of Ernest Story; 1 da; *Career* physicist; lectr UCL 1936-44, asst dir scientific res Miny of Supply 1939-44, sr lectr Manchester Univ 1947-50 (lectr 1944-47), physics prof Univ Coll North Staffs (now Keele Univ) 1950-59 (vice princ 1950-54), dir AERE Harwell 1960-64, memb for res UKAEA 1964-66, pres and vice-chllr Queen's Univ Belfast 1966-76, pro-chllr and chm of cncl Warwick Univ 1977-; Hon DSc: Keele, Nat Univ of Ireland, Birmingham; Hon LLD: Dublin, Belfast; Hon DCL Kent; memb UGC 1959-66; kt 1973, FIEE, FInstP, MRIA; *Recreations* music, gardening, DIY; *Clubs* Athenaeum, Savile; *Style*— Sir Arthur Vick, OBE; Fieldhead Cottage, Fieldhead Lane, Myton Rd, Warwick CV34 6QF (☎ 0926 491822)

VICK, Dr John Alexander Stewart; s of John Oliver Curtis Vick, of 8 Churchfields House, Guessens Rd, Welwyn Garden City, Herts; and Mary Macfarlane, *née* Stewart (d 1988); *b* 4 April 1937; *Educ* Taunton Sch, The London Hosp Med Coll and London Univ (MB BS); *m* 14 Sept 1963, Patricia Anne Marie, da of William Vincent Cassidy (d 1963), of 7 Grafton St, Londonderry, NI; 1 s (Peter John William b 1965), 1 da (Emma Mary Louise b 1969); *Career* receiving room offr London Hosp 1960, house surgn and house physician Brighton Gen Hosp 1961, sr house offr surgery Lister Hosp Hitchin 1962 (medical and paediatric registrar 1962-64), med registrar Queen Elizabeth II Hosp Welwyn Garden City 1964-66, ptnr Drs Vick, Dines, Tidy, Christie, Ingram and Cooper, paediatric hosp practitioner Lister Hosp Stevenage, med offr William Ransom & Son Hitchin, dep coroner Hitchin Dist Herts 1979-; former: divnl surgn Hitchin St John Ambulance Bde, memb Herts Local Med Ctee, memb Herts Family Practitioner Ctee, chm E Herts BMA Div; LRCP, MRCS, memb BMA, MRCGP; *Recreations* bridge, croquet, philately, photography; *Style*— Dr John Vick; The Pines, 7 Wymondley Close, Hitchin, Herts SG4 9PW (☎ 0462 32904); The Portmill Surgery, 114 Queen St, Hitchin, Herts SG4 9TH (☎ 0462 34246)

VICK, His Hon Judge Russell; (Arnold Oughtred) Russell Vick; QC (1980); yr s of His Honour Judge Sir Godfrey Russell Vick, QC, of Seal, Kent (d 1958), and Marjorie Hester, Lady Russell Vick, JP (d 1985); *b* 14 Sept 1933; *Educ* The Leys School, Jesus Coll Cambridge (MA); *m* 1959, Zinnia Mary, da of T B Yates (d 1968), of Godalming; 2 s, 1 da; *Career* barr Inner Temple 1958, prosecuting counsel to Post Office 1964-69, recorder Crown Court 1972-82, circuit judge (SE) 1982-; Master Worshipful Co of Curriers' 1976-77; *Recreations* golf, cricket, bridge; *Clubs* MCC, Hawks (Cambridge), Wildernesse Golf; *Style*— His Honour Judge Russell Vick, QC; The Law Courts, Barker Road, Maidstone (☎ 0622 54966)

VICKERMAN, Prof Keith; s of Jack Vickerman, and Mabel, *née* Dyson; *b* 21 Mar 1933; *Educ* King James Gs Almondbury, UCL (BSc, PhD, DSc), Exeter Univ; *m* 16 Sept 1961, Moira, da of Wilfrid Dutton, MC; 1 da (Louise Charlotte b 1973); *Career* Royal Soc tropical res fell UCL 1963-68 (Wellcome lectr 1958-63), regius prof of zoology Univ of Glasgow 1984- (head of dept 1979-85, prof 1974-84, reader 1968-74); served on various ctees of WHO, ODA and SERC; fell UCL 1985; FRSE (1970), FRS (1984); *Books* The Protozoa (with FEG Cox, 1967); author numerous articles and res papers in learned jls; *Recreations* sketching, gardening; *Style*— Prof Keith Vickerman; 16 Mirrlees Drive, Glasgow G12 0SH (☎ 041 334 2794); Dept of Zoology, Univ of Glasgow, Glasgow G12 8QQ (☎ 041 339 8855)

VICKERS, Angus Douglas; TD; s of Douglas Vickers (d 1937); *b* 15 Feb 1904; *Educ* Eton, Magdalen Coll Oxford; *m* 1937, Phyllis Maud, da of Norton Francis, CMG (d 1939); *Career* serv RA (TA) 2 Lt 1939, Bt-Col 1953 (despatches); underwriter Lloyd's; memb Royal Co of Archers (Queen's Body Guard for Scotland); JP 1946-68, DL 1950-68 Ross and Cromarty; hon Sheriff Substitute Inverness, Moray, Nairn, Ross and Cromarty 1949-; Feudal Baron of Tulloch;; *Recreations* photography; *Clubs* New (Edinburgh); *Style*— Angus Vickers, Esq, TD; Casa Sta Catarina, Parque Da Praia, Luz 8600 Lagos, Algarve, Portugal (☎ 082 69660)

VICKERS, Hugo Ralph; s of Ralph Cecil Vickers, MC, *qv*; *b* 12 Nov 1951; *Educ* Eton, Strasbourg Univ; *Career* author, reviewer, and broadcaster; worked with London Celebrations Committee for Queen's Silver Jubilee 1977, administrator Great Children's Party 1979; literary executor to the late Sir Charles Johnston and the late Sir Cecil Beaton; *Books* We Want The Queen (1977), Gladys, Duchess of Marlborough (1979, reissue 1987), Debrett's Book of the Royal Wedding (1981), Cocktails and Laughter (ed,1983), Cecil Beaton - the Authorized Biography (1985, reissue 1986), Vivien Leigh (1988); *Recreations* photography, reading, music, travel; *Style*— Hugo Vickers, Esq; 62 Lexham Gardens, London W8 5JA

VICKERS, Jeffrey; s of Edward Vickers (d 1984), and Rose, *née* Soloman; *b* 3 June 1937; *Educ* Harold Co Sch Stratford; *m* 1 (m dis 1982), Angela Vickers; 1 s (Andrew b 11 Feb 1967), 1 da (Joanne b 1 May 1965); m 2, 22 July 1982, Barbara, da of James Ebury Clair May, DSM, RN (d 1986); *Career* chm: DPM Gp of Cos 1959-, Chromacopy 1979- (fndr and ptnr Chromacopy of America 1979-), Magog Industs 1984-, Vecone Devpt Corpn 1984-, Blasteeh Gp of Cos 1985-; finalist Prince of Wales Award for Industl Innovation and Production; memb Fulham Cons Assoc; FIOD 1983; *Recreations* skiing, sailing, swimming, class music/opera; *Clubs* Hurlingham; *Style*— Jeffrey Vickers, Esq; DPM Design Consultants Ltd, 63 Poland St, London W1V 3DF (☎ 01 439 7786, fax 01 434 1528, telex 296328)

VICKERS, Baroness (Life Peer UK 1974); Joan Helen Vickers; DBE (1964, MBE 1946); da of late Horace Cecil Vickers; *b* 1907; *Educ* St Monica's Coll Burgh Heath Surrey; *Career* served BRCS in SE Asia; memb LCC 1937-45, with Colonial Office 1946-50, chm Anglo-Indonesian Soc 1958-, pres Int Bureau for Suppression of Traffic in Persons, Inst for Qualified Private Secretaries 1969-, Int Friendship League 1972-, Status of Women Ctee, Europe China Ctee, London Centre for Homeless Young Persons 1977-; MP (C) Devonport 1955-74; Freedom City of Plymouth 1982; Netherlands Red Cross Medal 1946, Polish Medal 1972; *Style*— The Rt Hon The Lady Vickers, DBE; The Manor House, East Chisenbury, Pewsey, Wilts

VICKERS, The Rt Rev Michael Edwin; s of Mr William Edwin Vickers (d 1967), and Florence Alice, *née* Parsons (d 1975); *b* 13 Jan 1929; *Educ* St Lawrence Coll, Worcester Coll Oxford (MA), Cranmer Hall, Durham (Dip in Theology); *m* 3 Sept 1960, Janet Cynthia, da of Arthur Herbert Croasdale (d 1944), of Rostead, Cark-in-Cartmel, N Lancashire; 3 da (Lorna b 1963, Fiona b 1965, Nicola b 1966); *Career* Military Serv 1947-49, Warrant Offr II RAEC serving with Br Troops in Austria; co sec Hoares (Ceylon) Ltd Colombo 1952-56, refugee admin Br Cncl for Aid to Refugees 1956-57; asst curate Christ Church Bexleyheath 1959-62, sr chaplain Lee Abbey 1962-67, vicar Newland Hull 1967-81, area dean Central Hull 1972-81, chm York Diocesan House of Clergy 1975-85, canon and prependary York 1981-88, archdeacon of the East Riding. 1981-88, bishop of Colchester 1988-; int rugby union caps for Ceylon 1954-55; *Recreations* fell-walking, photography, gardening; *Style*— The Rt Rev Michael E Vickers; 1 Fitzwalter Rd, Lexden, Colchester, Essex CO3 3SS (☎ 0206 576 648)

VICKERS, Ralph Cecil; MC (1944); s of Horace Cecil Vickers (d 1944), and Lilian, *née* Grose (d 1922); brother of Baroness Vickers, DBE; *b* 14 Nov 1913; *Educ* Uppingham, Trinity Coll Cambridge; *m* 1, 1950 (m dis 1986), Dulcie, da of John Metcalf; 1 s (Hugo, *qv*, 1 da (Imogen); m 2 1987, Khurshid da of Prince Abdual Hossain Farman Farmbian; *Career* served 2 Lt 1 RHA 1939-40, Capt Royal Devon Yeo Artillery 1942-44, Actg Maj; chm: Acorn Investmt Tst, Bridge Mgmnt Hong Kong; hon fell commoner St Catharine's Coll Cambridge; *Recreations* fishing, shooting; *Clubs* BRDC; *Style*— Ralph Vickers, Esq, MC; 33 Egerton Terr, London SW3 2BU (☎ 01 589 5975); Vickers da Costa Ltd, Regis House, King William St, London EC4R 9AR (☎ 01 623 2494, telex 886004)

VICKERS, Rex Adrian; s of Henry Allen Hamilton Vickers (d 1972), and Gladys May, *née* Hardy (d 1976); *b* 27 July 1934; *Educ* Chingford GS, SW Essex Tech Coll; *m* 23 July 1960, Gillian Elizabeth, da of Leonard Frank Edmonds, of Oxted, Surrey; 4 s (Mark b 1961 d 1975, Andrew b 1963, James b 1965, Nicholas b 1972), 1 da (Lucy b 1976); *Career* Nat Serv RE 1955-57; dir: Mott Hay of Anderson Conslt Engrs 1979- (assoc 1978-79, dir overseas ptnrships 1979-), chm SE Gp Assoc Conslt Engrs 1988, memb bd examiners ICE; pres Chinghoppers Cricket Club; CEng 1962, FICE 1973, FFB 1980, M Cons E 1980; *Recreations* cricket, rugby, football, golf, gardening; *Clubs* MCC; *Style*— Rex Vickers, Esq; Neb Corner, Neb Lane, Old Oxted, Surrey RH8 9JN; Mott Hay & Anderson, 22/26 Wellesley Rd, Croydon CR9 2UL (☎ 01 686 5041, fax 01 6814 5706, telex 917 241 MOTTAY G)

VICKERS, Lt-Gen Sir Richard Maurice Hilton; KCB (1982), LVO (1959), OBE (1970, MBE 1964); s of Lt-Gen Wilmot Gordon Hilton Vickers, CB, OBE, DL (d 1987); *b* 21 August 1928; *Educ* Haileybury and, Imperial Serv Coll, RMA Sandhurst; *m* 1957, Gaie Bradley, da of Maj-Gen George Philip Bradley Roberts, CB, DSO, MC; 3 da; *Career* Capt Tank Regt 1954, Equerry to HM The Queen 1956-59, Maj 1961, Lt-Col 1967, CO The Blues and Royals 1968-70, Brig 1972, dep dir Army Trg 1975-77, GOC 4 Armd Div 1977-79, Cmdt RMA Sandhurst 1979-82; dir-gen: Army Trg 1982-83, Winston Churchill Meml Tst 1983-; Gentleman Usher to The Queen; *Clubs* Cavalry and Guards'; *Style*— Lt-Gen Sir Richard Vickers, KCB, LVO, OBE; Little Minterne, Dorchester, Dorset

VICKERS, Thomas Douglas; CMG (1956); *b* 25 Sept 1916; *Educ* Eton, King's Coll Cambridge; *m* 1951, Margaret Awdry; 1 s, 1 da; *Career* served WW II Coldstream Gds; HM Overseas Civil Service 1938-40 and 1945-68, colonial sec British Honduras 1953-60, chief sec Mauritius 1960-67, dep govr Mauritius 1968, head of personnel services Imperial Cancer Research Fund 1969-81; *Clubs* Army and Navy; *Style*— Thomas Vickers, Esq, CMG; Wood End, Worplesdon, Surrey GU3 3RJ (☎ 0483 233468)

VICKERY, Hon Mrs (Melanie Frances Isobel Connell); *née* Murton; da of Baron Murton of Lindisfarne. (Life Peer), OBE, TD, PC; *b* 1946; *m* 1971, Ian Lee Vickery; 1 s, 1 da; *Style*— The Hon Mrs Vickery; Lawnswood, 3 Clifton Rd, Chesham Bois, Amersham, Bucks HP6 5PU

VICTOR, Ed; s of Jack Victor (d 1987), of Los Angeles, and Lydia Victor; *b* 9 Sept 1939; *Educ* Dartmouth Coll USA (BA), Pembroke Coll Cambridge (MLitt); *m* 1, 1963, Michelene Dinah, da of Avram Samuels (d 1985); 3 s (Adam b 1964, Ivan b 1966, Ryan b 1984); m 2, 1980, Carol Ryan, da of Clifton Boggs, of Diego, California; *Career* ed dir: Weidenfeld & Nicolson 1965-67, Jonathan Cape Ltd 1967-70; sr ed Alfred A Knopf Inc NY USA 1971-72, dir John Farquharson Ltd 1973-77; chm and md Ed Victor Ltd 1977-; *Recreations* opera, tennis travel; *Clubs* Groucho; *Style*— Ed Victor, Esq; 10 Cambridge Gate, Regents Park, London NW1 (☎ 01 224 3030); Ed Victor Ltd, 162 Wardour St, London W1 (☎ 01 734 4795, fax 494 3400, car ☎ 0836 225173)

VIELER, Geoffrey Herbert; s of Herbert Charles Stuart Vieler (d 1950), of Bexhill on Sea, and Emily Mary Vale (d 1964); *b* 21 August 1910; *Educ* Fairway Sch Bexhill on Sea; *m* 25 Aug 1934, Phyllis Violet, da of George Thomas Kedge (d 1943), of Reading; 1 da (Margaret b 1945); *Career* WWII RAOC 1941-46, Maj India 1944-46; CA, chm taxation ctee of the Assoc of Br Chambers of Commerce; memb taxation events working pty and the technical (taxation) sub-ctee London Soc of CAS, md and bd memb Posts and Nat Giro 1969-71, chm London Soc of CA 1976-77 (main ctee memb 1969-82), memb tech advsy ctee ICAEW 1967-74; FCA; *Recreations* gardening, philately; *Style*— Geoffrey H Vieler, FCA; Robins Wood, Monks Drive, South Ascot, Berks SL5 9BB (☎ 0344 20 564)

VIGGERS, Peter John; MP (C) Gosport Feb 1974-); s of John Sidney Viggers (d 1969), of Gosport; *b* 13 Mar 1938; *Educ* Alverstoke Sch, Portsmouth GS, Trinity Hall Cambridge (MA); *m* 1968, Jennifer Mary, da of Dr R B McMillan (d 1975); 2 s, 1 da; *Career* RAF pilot 1956-58, TA 1963-70; co slr Chrysler (UK) Ltd 1968-70; dir: Premier Consolidated Oilfields Ltd 1973-86, Sweetheart Int Ltd; vice chm Cons Energy Ctee 1977-79 (sec 1975-76), PPS to Slr Gen 1979-83, delegate to N Atlantic Assembly 1980-86, PPS to Chief Sec to Treasy 1983-85; memb Nat Ctee RNLI 1980-; Parly under sec of state for NI 1986-; *Style*— Peter Viggers, Esq, MP; House of Commons, London SW1

VIGIER; *see*: de Vigier

VIGORS, Lt-Col Richard de Cliffe; DSO (1945); s of Thomas Mercer de Cliffe Vigors (d 1951), of Coln St Denys Manor Fossebridge, Glos, and Marjorie Caroline Mary, *née* Walwyn (d 1965); *b* 24 Nov 1914; *Educ* Marlborough Coll, RMC Sandhurst; *m* 29 Nov 1939, (Evelyn) Rosa, da of Edward Mansfield Weatherby (d 1957), of Brill House, Brill, Bucks; 2 s (Richard (Robin) b 1941, Martin b 1944); *Career* 2 Lt 5 Royal Inniskilling Dragoon Gds 1934, ADC to Cdr Mobile Div (later 1 Armd Div) 1938, BEF France 1940, 1 Lothians & Border Yeomanry: Sqdn Ldr UK 1941, BELF France 1944; 2 i/c then CO 1 Fife & Forfar Yeomanry BELF 1945, Armd Corps Instr, Sch of Combined Ops 1946-48; 5 Royal Inniskilling Dragoon Gds: 2 i/c BAOR 1950, CO Korea 1951, (despatches) 1952, CO serv Korea Canal Zone of Egypt and UK; Cmdt RAC Tactical Sch Lulworth 1955, ret 1958; gen mangr CSE Aviation Ltd Oxford Airport 1963-67; pres Brill & Dist Royal Br Legion, vice pres CPRE Aylesbury Vale branch; *Recreations* shooting; *Style*— Lt-Col Richard Vigors, DSO; The Stable House, Brill, Buckinghamshire (☎ 0844 237 567)

VILLA, (Charles) Peter Wolferstan; s of Sqdn Ldr John Villa, DFC (d 1983), and Sheila Margaret, *née* Reed; *b* 14 Mar 1940; *Educ* Berkhamsted Sch Herts; *m* 26 March1966, Jennifer Edith, da of Leonard Alfred Croker; 1 s (Paul Wolferstan Villa b 11 Feb 1967), 2 da (Sarah Villa b 29 April 1968, Anne Villa b 5 June 1970); *Career* chief internal auditor Mobil African Servs Ltd 1965-68, co sec Cyclax Ltd 1968-70; md Br Island Airways Ltd 1976-80, (fin controller 1970-76, chm 1982-), Air UK Ltd 1980-82; FCA 1964; *Recreations* sailing, flying; *Style*— Peter Villa, Esq; Apollo House, Church Road, Lowfield Heath, Crawley, Sussex RH11 0PQ (☎ 0293 546301, fax 0293 545270, car tel 0836 212324, telex 87218 BIA L6W)

VILLAR, Anthony Sidney Rex; s of Arthur Andrew Sidney Villar (d 1966), and Betty Helen, Fyfe-Jamieson, *née* Cohen MBE; *b* 4 Sept 1934; *Educ* Stowe; *m* 21 Oct 1961, Clare, da of Henry William Pearson-Rogers, CBE; 4 da (Sally b 1962, Francesca b 1954, Caroline b 1968, Alexandra b 1975); *Career* RNVR ret 1955; past pres: Racehorse Owners Assoc, St Moritz Curling Club; farmer; *Recreations* shooting, curling, racing; *Clubs* Turf, Naval, St Moritz Curling; *Style*— Anthony Villar, Esq; Tostock Old Rectory, Bury St Edmunds, Suffolk IP30 9NU; Little Haugh Farm, Norton, Bury St Edmunds, Suffolk (tel: 0359 30468)

VILLIERS, Sir Charles English Hyde; MC (1945); s of Algernon Hyde Villiers (ka 1917, 3 s of Rt Hon Sir Francis Hyde Villiers, GCMG, GCVO, CB, sometime ambass to Belgium and 4 s of 4 Earl of Clarendon), and Beatrix Elinor, *née* Paul (d 1978, m 1919, 4 Baron Aldenham and (2) Hunsdon, by whom she was mother of the present (5 and 3) Lord Aldenham and Hunsdon; *b* 14 August 1912; *Educ* Eton, New Coll Oxford; *m* 1, 9 June 1938, Pamela Constance (d 1943), da of Maj John Flower; 1 s (Nicholas b 1939) & 1 s decd; m 2, 26 Oct 1946, Marie José de la Barre, da of Comte Henri de la Barre d'Erquelinnes (d 1961, original Austrian Netherlands cr of 1722 by Letters Patent by Emperor Charles VI; title recognised by William I of The Netherlands (subsequently Belgium) 1829, while a Countship in the Kingdom of Belgium was also conferred on the 5 Count by King Leopold I of the Belgians in 1844; the original guarantee of the eighteenth century dignity, François Léonard de la Barre, was Seigneur de Maurage et d'Erquelinnes and was descended from the noble Hugues de la Barre, on whom the post of trésorier-général de guerre was conferred by Letters Patent in 1536), of Jurbise, Belgium; 2 da (Diana, Anne); *Career* SRO Grenadier Gds 1936-46, Dunkirk 1940, wounded 1942, SOE Yugoslavia, Italy and Austria (parachuted to Tito Partisans 1944) Lt Col cmd 6 SFSS (1945), MC (1945); md: Glyn Mills and Co Bankers 1931-46, Helbert Wagg (Schroder Wagg) 1947-67, Indust Reorganisation Corpn 1967-71; memb Inst Int Etudes Bancaires 1959-76 (pres 1964); chm: Guinness Mahon and Co 1971-76, Br Steel Corpn 1976-80, BSC (Industry) Ltd 1976-; exec dep chm Guinness Peat Gp 1973-76; dir: Bass Charrington, Courtaulds, Sun Life Assurance, Banque Belge, Financor SA, Darling and Co Pty Ltd; advsr Deloitte Haskins & Sells (accountants) 1982-; chm: Theatre Royal Windsor, Small Business Research Tst; former Tstee Royal Opera Tst, former memb NEDC; 1973 Review of NI Ind; chm: NI Finance Corpn till 1975, thirteenth Int Small Business Congress 1986; Order of People of Yugoslavia, Grande Officier de l'Ordre de Leopold II of Belgium (1974); kt 1975; *Recreations* gardening; *Clubs* Special Forces; *Style*— Sir Charles

Villiers, MC; 65 Eaton Sq, London SW1 (☎ 01 235 7634); Blacknest House, Sunninghill, Berks (☎ 0990 22137)

VILLIERS, Charles Nigel; s of Capt Robert Alexander Villiers, CBE, RN, of Robinsgreen, Warnham, Sussex, and Elizabeth Mary, *née* Friend (d 1985); *b* 25 Jan 1941; *Educ* Winchester, New Coll Oxford (MA); *m* 7 Aug 1970, Sally Priscilla, da of Capt David Henry Magnay, RN (d 1968); 1 s (Christopher b 1976), 1 da (Caroline b 1974); *Career* Arthur Andersen & Co 1963-67, Industl & Commercial Fin Corpn 1967-72; County Bank (subsid of NatWest Bank): dir 1974, dep chief exec 1977, chm and chief exec 1984-86; dir NatWest Bank 1985-88, chm County NatWest 1986-88, md corporate devpt Abbey Nat Building Soc 1988-; ACA 1966, FCA 1976; *Recreations* opera, skiing, squash, tennis; *Clubs* Hurlingham; *Style—* Charles Villiers, Esq; 8 Sutherland St, London SW1V 4LB; Abbey House, Baker St, London NW1 6XL

VILLIERS, George Edward; TD; s of Algernon Edward Villiers, of 15 Salterns Lande, Hayline Island, Hants, and Annie Augusta Merewether, *née* Massy (d 1979); *b* 23 August 1931; *Educ* Wellington Coll, Brasenose Coll Oxford (MA); *m* 25 Aug 1962, (Anne) Virginia, da of Cuthbert Raymond Forster Threlfass, MC (d 1965), formerly of Warstone House, Bewdley, Worcs; 2 s (Edward b 1963, Henry b 1965), 1 da (Theresa b 1968); *Career* Nat Serv 2 Lt RHA 1949-51, TA 1951-65 (Maj Berks and Westminster Dragoon); stockjobber Moir & Shaw 1956-64, memb Stock Exchange 1960; stockbroker: assoc Sorrell Lamb & Co 1964-65, ptnr H Evans Gordon & Co 1966-70, ptnr Beardsley Bishop & Co 1970-83; assoc Cawood Smithie 1983-; pres Oxford Univ Athletic Club 1953-54; Freeman City of London (1977), Liveryman Worshipful Co of Fanmakers (1977); AMSIA; *Recreations* golf, bridge; *Clubs* Boodles, Wentworth; *Style—* George Villiers, Esq, TD; 73 Carlton Hill, London NW8 0EN (☎ 01 624 2778); Cawood Smithie & Co, 22 East Parade, Harrogate, N Yorks HG1 5LT (☎ 0423 530 035, fax 0423 507 312)

VILLIERS, Viscount; George Henry Child Villiers; s and h of 9 Earl of Jersey; *b* 29 August 1948; *Educ* Eton, Millfield; *m* 1, 1969 (m dis 1973), Verna, da of K A Stott, of St Mary, Jersey; 1 da (Hon Sophia Georgiana b 25 June 1971); m 2, 1974, Sacha Jane Hooper, da of Peter Hooper Valpy, step da of Harold Briginshaw, and former w of K F Lauder; 1 s, 2 da (Hon Helen Katherine Luisa b 21 Oct 1978, Hon Luciana Dorothea Sacha b 23 July 1981); *Heir* s, Hon George Francis William Child Villiers b 5 Feb 1976; *Career* late 2 Lt 11 Hussars and the Royal Hussars; md Rouse Woodstock (Jersey) Ltd; *Style—* Viscount Villiers; Bel Respiro, Mont-au-Pretre, St Helier, Jersey, CI (☎ 0534 20371); Rouse Woodstock (Jersey) Ltd, 4 Broad St, St Helier, Jersey (☎ 0534 75989; telex 4192418)

VILLIERS, Vice-Adm Sir (John) Michael; KCB (1962, CB 1960), OBE (1943); s of Rear-Adm E C Villiers CMG (d 1939); *b* 22 June 1907; *Educ* Oundle; *m* 1936, Rosemary, da of Lt-Col B S Grissell, DSO (ka 1917); 2 da; *Career* joined RN 1925, served WWII Atlantic and Med (despatches); commanded: HMS Ursa 1945, HMS Snipe 1946-47, HMS Bulwark 1954-57; Capt 1948, Queen's Harbour Master Malta 1952-54, Rear-Adm 1958, chief of Naval Staff RNZN 1958-60, Vice-Adm 1960, Fourth Sea Lord 1960-63, ret 1963; Lt-Govr and C-in-C Jersey 1964-69; KStJ; *Clubs* Army and Navy; *Style—* Vice-Adm Sir Michael Villiers, KCB, OBE; Decoy House, Melton, Woodbridge, Suffolk

VILLIERS, Hon (William) Nicholas Somers Laurence Hyde; JP (Hants); s of late 6 Earl of Clarendon; *b* 1916; *Educ* Eton, New Coll Oxford; *m* 1939, Mary Cecilia Georgina, da of Maj the Hon Edric Weld-Forester, CVO (6 s of 5 Baron Forester); 3 da; *Career* Maj Grenadier Gds (Supplementary Res), served ME N Africa and Italy 1943-47; OStJ (pres N Wilts branch), memb Lloyd's, div & sec Anderson Finch Villiers (Agencies) Ltd (ret); *Recreations* all field sports, cricket, golf; *Clubs* White's; *Style—* Maj The Hon Nicholas Villiers, ERD, JP; Firs Farm, Milbourne, Malmesbury, Wilts SN16 9JA

VILLIERS, Lady Sarah Katherine Jane; da of 7 Earl of Clarendon; *b* 20 Oct 1977; *Style—* Lady Sarah Villiers; 5 Astell St, London SW3 3RT (☎ 01 352 9131)

VILLIERS, Lt-Col Tim (Timothy Charles); s of Brig Richard Villiers, DSO (d 1973), and Nancy Villiers, *née* Godwin; *b* 16 Mar 1943; *Educ* Eton, RMA Sandhurst; *m* 30 Jan 1971, Maureen Gwendolen, da of The Ven Reginald George Henry McCahearty (d 1966); 2 s (Nicholas b 1976, Richard b 1980), 1 da (Louise b 1973); *Career* offr 15/19 The Kings Royal Hussars 1963-87, cmdg offr, Royal Hong Kong Regt (the Volunteers) 1983-86; *Recreations* field sports, horses, family life; *Style—* Lt-Col Tim Villiers; Kyrle Rd, London SW11 6BB (☎ 01 350 2531)

VINCENT, Helen, Lady; Helen Millicent; da of Field Marshal Sir William Robertson, 1 Bt, GCB, GCMG, GCVO, DSO; sis of 1 Baron Robertson of Oakridge, GCB, GBE, KCMG, KCVO, DSO, MC; *b* 17 Dec 1905; *m* 18 Oct 1938, Sir Lacey Eric Vincent, 2 Bt (d 1963); 1 s (Sir William Vincent, 3 Bt), 1 da; *Style—* Helen, Lady Vincent; 44 Eresby House, Rutland Gate, London SW7 (☎ 01 589 4217)

VINCENT, John Anthony; s of Frederick John Vincent (d 1956); *b* 28 Sept 1936; *Educ* Wandsworth Technical Grammar, Hammersmith Coll of Building; *m* 1956, Frances Ruth; 3 da; *Career* princ J A Vincent & Associates, Business Conslts 1984-; sales and marketing dir HY-Ten Reinforcement Co Ltd 1974-83; sales mangr Pioneer Concrete Ltd 1967-74; chief buyer Pitchers Ltd (Contractors), 1962-67; assoc memb Inst of Civil Engineers; *Recreations* swimming, riding; *Clubs* The Lighthouse; *Style—* John Vincent, Esq; 'Silverdell', Golf Drive, Camberley, Surrey

VINCENT, Paul Howard; s of Stanley Howard Vincent (d 1975); *b* 9 April 1924; *Educ* Bishops Stortford Coll, St Johns Coll Cambridge; *m* 1957, Jean, *née* Ford; 1 s, 2 da; *Career* RAF 1942-47; dir: Vincent Fin Co (Yeovil) Ltd, Binding and Payne Ltd, H and C Services Ltd, CB Morgan (Shaftesbury) Ltd, S M V Commercials (Wells) Ltd, Sugg-Vincent Ltd, Vincents Self-Drive Hire Ltd; *Style—* Paul Vincent, Esq; Watermeadows, Turners Barn Lane, Yeovil, Somerset (☎ 0935 23201)

VINCENT, Paul Stephen; s of Ralph Henry Morley Vincent (d 1984) of New Malden, Surrey, and Gladys, *née* Jones; *b* 8 April 1945; *Educ* Stonleigh West Co Tech Sch; *m* 19 Sept 1970, Lynne Patricia, da of Stanley Lawrence Connors, of New Malden, Surrey; 1 s (Edward b 1986), 3 da (Rebecca b 1977, Victoria b 1979, Helena b 1984 d 1985); *Career* audit mangr Cape & Dagleish, fin dir Metal Bulletin plc (formerly Metal Bulletin Ltd) 1980- (accountant 1972, co sec 1973); *Recreations* DIY; *Style—* Paul Vincent, Esq; Metal Bulletin Plc, Park House, Park Terrace, Worcester Park, Surrey KT4 7HY (☎ 01 330 4311, fax 01 337 8943, telex 21383 METBUL G)

VINCENT, Gen Sir Richard Frederick; KCB (1984), DSO (1972); s of Frederick Vincent and Frances Elizabeth, *née* Coleshill; *b* 23 August 1931; *Educ* Aldenham, Royal Mil Coll of Science Shrivenham; *m* 1955, Jean Paterson, da of Kenneth Stewart and Jane, *née* Banks; 1 s, 1 da (and 1 s decd); *Career* Cmdt Royal Mil Coll of Sci 1980-83, Master Gen of the Ordnance MOD 1983-87; Col Cmdt: REME 1983-87, RA 1983; Hon Col: 100 (Yeo) Field Regt RA (Volunteers) TA, 12 Air Def Regt; Vice Chief of the Def Staff 1987-; pres: Combined Servs Winter Sports Assoc 1983-, Army Skiing Assoc 1983-87; memb ct Cranfield Inst of Technol 1981-83; govr Alderham Sch 1987; Kermit Roosevelt lectr USA 1988; DSc Cranfield 1985; *Recreations* travel, reading, film making, theatre; *Clubs* Army and Navy; *Style—* Gen Sir Richard Vincent, KCB, DSO; Vice Chief of the Defence Staff, MOD Main Building (Room 6177), Whitehall, London SW1A 2HB (☎ 01 218 9000)

VINCENT, Sir William Percy Maxwell; 3 Bt (UK 1936), of Watton, Co Norfolk; s of Sir Lacey Vincent, 2 Bt (d 1963), and Helen, Lady Vincent, *qv*; *b* 1 Feb 1945; *Educ* Eton, New York Inst of Finance; *m* 1976, Christine Margaret, da of Rev Edward Gibson Walton, of Petersfield; 3 s; *Heir* s, Edward Mark William Vincent b 6 March 1978; *Career* late 2 Lt Irish Gds, served Malaya; dir Save & Prosper Investment Tst 1980-85, Touche Remnant & Co 1985, md and invest dir Touche Remnant Holdings Co 1987; *Recreations* sailing (yacht Jouet 1080), skiing; *Clubs* Household Div Yacht, Chichester Cruiser Racing, City Yacht, Hayling Island Sailing; *Style—* Sir William Vincent, Bt; Whistlers, Buriton, Petersfield, Hants (☎ 0730 63532)

VINCENZI, Penny; da of Stanley George Hannaford (d 1985), of New Milton, Hants, and Mary Blanche, *née* Hawkey (d 1987); *b* 10 April 1939; *Educ* Notting Hill and Ealing HS; *m* 27 May 1960, Paul Robert, s of Julius Vincenzi, of Essex; 4 da (Polly b 1963, Sophie b 1965, Emily b 1975, Claudia b 1979); *Career* freelance journalist and author; contrib to : Cosmopolitan, Nova, Honey, Options, Over 21, You Magazine, Daily Mail, The Times, Sunday Mirror, Sunday Times, Mail on Sunday; *Books* The Complete Liar (1979), There's One Born Every Minute (1985); *Recreations* family life, surfing, riding; *Style—* Mrs Penny Vincenzi

VINCZE, Ernest; *b* 1942; *Career* dir photography; started in the field of documentaries winning several awards incl: Flaherty Award, Prix Italia, Golden Gate San Francisco, trento, BAFTA; Pt/t tutor and tech Cinematography RCA and Nat Film Sch, nominated Br Acad Award for Best Cinematography 1984; features, serials and made-for-TV movies incl: Business As Usual, Escape From Sobibor, Shangai Surprise, Biggles, Behind Enemy Lines, Hitler's SS, A Woman of Substance, Kennedy, Scrubbers, Cream In My Coffee, Roseland, Winstanley, Tell Me No Lies, The Secret Policeman's Ball, A Very British Coup (Emmy Award 1988); memb Br Soc Cinematographers 1978, ACTT; *Style—* Ernest Vincze, Esq; 25 Marville Rd, London SW6 7BB (☎ 01 385 3413); Freddie Vale, CCa Personal Management, 4 Court Lodge, 48 Sloane Square, London SW1 8AT (☎ 01 730 8857)

VINE, Brian John; s of Frank Alexander Vine, of St Leonard's-on-sea, Sussex, and Edith Ellen, *née* Sharp; *b* 11 July 1932; *Educ* Winton House, St Dunstans Coll London; *m* 18 Sept 1972, Beverley Jacqueline, da of Dr Alan Wardle, of Dunedin, NZ; 1 s (Alexander Charles b 1979); *Career* Nat Serv RAF (2 yrs) Zimbabwe; home reporter News Chronicle 1956-60; Daily Express 1960-84: William Hickey Column 1960-69, chief of bureau, New York (This is America Columnist) 1969-73, foreign ed 1973-74, asst ed 1974-84; Daily Mail: foreign ed 1985-86, asst ed 1986-87, managing ed 1987-; memb Press Cncl, judge Br Press Award; *Books* Zola; *Recreations* racehorse ownership, game shooting, tennis; *Clubs* Turf, Scribes, University NY; *Style—* Brian Vine, Esq; 14 Lisgar Terrace, London W14; Lower Farm Cottage, Haywards Bottom, nr Hungerford, Berkshire (☎ 01 602 3298); Northcliffe House, Kensington High St, London W8

VINE, Col (Roland) Stephen; s of Joseph Soutter Vine (d 1944), and Margaret Mary Josephine, *née* Moylan (d 1976); *b* 26 Dec 1910; *Educ* Southend-on-Sea Boys' HS, London Univ and Guys Hosp Med Sch (BSc, MRCS, LRCP); *m* 14 Dec 1935, Flora Betty, da of Charles Strutton Brookes, MBE (d 1960), of Dovercourt, Essex; 3 da (Jill (Mrs De Bretton-Gordon) b 8 Jan 1937, Sallie (Mrs Maclay) b 10 May 1939, Joanna (Mrs Marley) b 19 Aug 1950); *Career* short serv cmmn Lt RAMC 1934, Capt 1935, regular cmmn 1939; served in OC mil hosps in India 1936-39, war serv N Africa 1939-44, OC HDS Dover 1944, ADMS Northern France 1944, CO 174 (Highland) Field Ambulance Europe 1944-45 (wounded and invalided to UK), CO 4 Field Ambulance Salonika 1946-47, RAM Coll Millbank 1947-48, qualified as specialist in pathology 1949; asst dir pathology: Northern Cmd UK 1949-51, Canal Zone Egypt 1951-52, Scottish Cmd 1954; OC David Bruce mil hosp Malta 1952-54, Temp Col OC mil hosp Catterick Camp 1955-60, ret 1960 awarded rank of Hon Col; Inspr under the Cruelty to Animals Act at the HO 1960 (chief inspr 1962-75), ret 1975; fndr Fell Coll of Pathologists 1962, memb of Cncl Res & Def Soc 1976-79, memb res team and cnslt Biorex Res Laboratories 1976-81; church warden High Hurstwood Trinity Church E Sussex 1970-80; FZS; *Style—* Col Stephen Vine; Shola, Fielden Road, Crowborough, East Sussex TN6 1TR (☎ 0892 661 381)

VINELOTT, Hon Mr Justice; Hon Sir John Evelyn Vinelott; QC (1968); s of Frederick George Vine-Lott (d 1984), and Vera Lilian Mockford (d 1957); *b* 15 Oct 1923; *Educ* Queen Elizabeth's GS Faversham, Queens' Coll Cambridge (MA); *m* 1956, Sally Elizabeth, da of His Hon Sir Walker Kelly Carter (decd), *qv*; 2 s, 1 da; *Career* served WW II Sub-Lt RNVR; barr Gray's Inn 1953, High Court judge (Chancery Div) 1978-; chm Insolvency Rules Advsy Ctee 1984-; kt 1978; *Clubs* Garrick; *Style—* The Hon Mr Justice Vinelott; 22 Portland Rd, London W11 (☎ 01 727 4778); Dolphin House, Market Hill, Orford, Suffolk (☎ 039 45 357)

VINER, Gordon; s of Joseph Viner (d 1982), of Liverpool, and Muriel, *née* Sharp; *b* 14 Nov 1940; *Educ* Kings Sch Chester; *m* 9 Oct 1966, Helen Frances, da of Philip Waters, of London; 3 s (Andrew b 1970, Paul b 1970, Richard b 1974), 1 da (Michelle b 1972); *Career* CA; trainee CA Chester 1957-63, H & J Supplies Ltd Chester 1963, ptnr Lerman Quaile & Co Birkenhead 1966-; former chm: Chester and N Wales CAs Students Assoc, Merseyside Branch of Inst of Taxation 1984-87; chm Chester Jewish Community; memb MENSA; FCA 1963, ATII 1965; *Recreations* golf, tennis, bridge, ball games; *Clubs* Upton by Chester GC, Chester Tennis; *Style—* Gordon Viner, Esq; 5 Nield Court, Upton-By-Chester, Cheshire CH2 1DN (☎ 0244 383 745); Lerman Quaile & Co, 17 Brandon St, Birkenhead, Merseyside L41 5HN (☎ 051 647 7171, fax 051 666 2585)

VINER, Ruben; OBE; s of Adolf Viner (d 1953); *b* 21 August 1907; *Educ* King Edward VII Sheffield; *m* 1932, Elaine Rhoda, *née* Aubrey; 2 children; *Career* pres Viners Ltd; pres and tres Sheffield C of C 1965, pres Sheffield Cutlery Manufacturers' Assoc 1958-61; chm: Talbot Tsts, Kelham Is Industl Museum Tst; Freeman Cutlers' Co, Liveryman Worshipful Co Clockmakers, Guardian of the Assay; underwriting memb of

Lloyd's; *Recreations* gardening, walking; *Style*— Ruben Viner Esq, OBE; 4 Ivy Park Ct, Ivy Park Rd, Sheffield S10 3LA (☎ 0742 306036; work: 684503)

VINES, Eric Victor; CMG (1984), OBE (1981); s of late Henry E Vines; *b* 28 May 1929; *Educ* St Dunstan's Coll London, St Catharine's Coll Cambridge (MA); *m* 1953, Ellen-Grethe Ella Küppers; 1 s; *Career* served in Army 1947-49; Cwlth Rels Off 1952: Colombo 1954-55, 1 sec Singapore 1958-61, Canberra 1961-65; Diplomatic Service Admin Office 1965-68, 1 sec Information Mexico City 1968-70, cnsllr Exec Sec-Gen SEATO Conference London 1971, head Cultural Exchange Dept FCO 1971-74; cnsllr (commercial) Tel Aviv 1974-77, Stockholm 1977-80; consul-gen Barcelona 1980-83, ambass: Maputo 1984-85, Montevideo 1986-; *Style*— HE Mr Eric Vines, CMG, OBE; British Embassy, Montevideo, Uruguay; c/o Foreign & Commonwealth Office, King Charles St, London SW1A 2AH

VINES, Sir William Joshua; AC (1987), CMG (1969); s of P Vines, of Canterbury, Victoria, Aust; *b* 27 May 1916; *Educ* Haileybury Coll, Victoria; *m* 1939, Thelma Jean, *née* Ogden (d 1988); 1 s (Geoffrey), 2 da (Judith, Susan); *Career* chm: ANZ Banking Gp 1982-89 (dep chm to 1981), Assoc Pulp & Paper Mills, Dalgety Aust Ltd; formerly dep chm: Tubemakers of Aust Ltd; dir: Conzinc Rio Tinto of Aust, Port Phillip Mills Pty; md Int Wool Secretariat, directorships with Lewis Berger & Sons; grazier; chm cncl Hawkesbury Agric Coll 1975-, memb Aust NZ Fndn 1979-, chm Sir Robert Menzies Meml Tst; ACIS, FASA; kt 1977; *see Debrett's Handbook of Australia and New Zealand for further details*; *Style*— Sir William Vines, AC, CMG; 38 Bridge St, Sydney, NSW 2000, Australia

VINEY, Hon Mrs (Anne Margaret); *née* Morton; JP; da of Baron Morton of Henryton, PC, MC (Life Peer, d 1973); *b* 14 June 1926; *Educ* Priorsfield; *m* 1947, Peter Andrew Hopwood Viney, DFC; 1 s, 2 da; *Career* barr Lincoln's Inn 1979; former cllr Kensington & Chelsea Borough Cncl 1960-62; publicity worker with Int Wool Secretariat 1945-47; chm Consumer Protection Advsy Ctee 1973-, jt co-chm Hackney Juvenile Court, chm Inner London Juvenile Court panel 1970 (appointed to panel 1961) (ret 1987); co-fndr (sec 1962-69) London Adventure Playground Assoc 1962; *Style*— The Hon Mrs Viney, JP; Worth House, Worth Matravers, Dorset (☎ Worth Matravers 248)

VINEY, Elliott Merriam; DSO (1945), MBE (1946), TD, DL (Bucks 1952); s of Col Oscar Viney (d 1976), of Green End House, Aylesbury; *b* 21 August 1913; *Educ* Oundle, Univ Coll Oxford (MA); *m* 1950, Rosamund Ann, da of E P L Pelly (d 1978); 2 da; *Career* dir: Hazell Watson & Viney, printers 1947-78, British Printing Corpn 1964-75; pres British Fedn of Master Printers 1972-73; Master Grocers' Co 1970-71, High Sheriff Bucks 1964; FSA; *Clubs* Alpine, County Hall (Aylesbury); *Style*— Elliott Viney, Esq, DSO, MBE, TD, DL; Cross Farmhouse, Quainton, Aylesbury, Bucks HP22 4AR (☎ 029 675 537)

VINK; *see*: de Vink

VINNICOMBE, John; s of Francis William Vinnicombe (d 1964), of St Saviour, Jersey, CI, and Marjorie Florence, nee Shuff (d 1972); *b* 17 Jan 1930; *Educ* Godalming GS, St Johns Coll Cambridge (MA), St Thomas's Hosp Med Sch (MB MChir); *m* 12 July 1958, Diana Mary, da of Maj-Gen Dennis Charles Tarrant Swan, CB, CBE of Lordington, Chichester; 3 da (Sarah b 1959, Amanda b 1961, Jane b 1964); *Career* Nat Serv Capt RAEC 1948-49; conslt urological surgn: Portsmouth Dist Hosp 1966, King Edward VII Hosp Midhurst 1970; Br Assoc of Urological Surgns: memb cncl 1976-79 and 1985-88, hon sec 1981-84, hon tres 1985-86; former pres Portsmouth div BMA 1981-82; Freeman City of London, Liveryman Worshipful Co of Apothecaries 1972; FRCS, FRSM (pres Urol section 1982-88); *Recreations* travel, sailing, skiing; *Style*— John Vinnicombe, Esq; Hindon House, Emsworth, Hants, (☎ 0243 37 2528); Department of Urology, Saint Mary's Hospital, Portsmouth, Hants, PO3 6AD (☎ 0705 822 331 Extn 2302)

VINSON, Baron (Life Peer UK 1985) Nigel; LVO (1979); s of late Ronald Vinson, of Wateringbury, Kent, by his first wife, Bettina Myra Olivia, da of Dr Gerald Southwell-Sanders; *b* 27 Jan 1931; *Educ* RNC Pangbourne; *m* 1972, Yvonne Ann, da of Dr Olaf Collin, of Forest Row; 3 da (Bettina b 1974, Rowena b 1977, Antonia b 1979); *Career* Lt Queen's Royal Regt 1949-51; donor Martin Mere Wildfowl Tst; fndr Plastic Coatings Ltd (chm 1952-72); dir: Sugar Bd 1968-75, British Airports Authority 1973-80, Centre for Policy Studies 1974-80, Electra Investmt Tst 1975-, Barclay's Bank UK 1982-; memb Cncl King George V Jubilee Tst 1974-78; hon dir Queen's Silver Jubilee Tst 1974-78: dep chm CBI Smaller Firms Council 1979-, chm: Council for Small Industries in Rural Areas 1980-82, Newcastle Technol Centre 1985-, Industry Year Steering Ctee 1985-, Dvpt Cmmn 1980-; pres Industrial Participation Assoc 1979- (chm 1971-78): FRSA; *Clubs* Boodles; *Style*— The Rt Hon Lord Nigel Vinson, Bt; 34 Kynance Mews, London SW7

VINTON, Anna-Maria; da of Charles Dugan-Chapman, and Mary Elizabeth Chapman; *b* 17 Nov 1947; *Educ* Chatelard Sch Les Avants Switzerland, Guildhall Sch of Music and Drama; *m* 1, 1970 (m dis 1982), Anthony Greatrex Hawser; m 2, Alfred Merton Vinton; 1 s (George Oliver b 21 Oct 1987), 1 da (Isabel Anusha b 3 Dec 1985); *Career* theatre agent: Cochrane Theatrical Agency 1967-68, Norma Skemp Agency 1969-70; ran private property co 1970-72; fndr and mangr: The Reject Linenshop Beauchamp Place London SW1 1972, The Reject Shops plc 1973 (currently jt md); memb Northamptonshire Ctee Wishing Well Appeal 1987-88; *Recreations* skiing, riding, gardening, theatre, reading; *Style*— Mrs Anna-Maria Vinton; Stoke Albany House, Near Market Harborough, Leics; 25 Pont St, London SW1; The Reject Shop plc, RMC House Townmead Rd, London SW6 (☎ 01 736 7474)

VIOT, Jacques Edmond; s of Edmond Viot (d 1974), and Irma, *née* Pelletant; *b* 25 August 1921; *Educ* Bordeaux and Paris Lycées, École Normale Superieure, École Nationale d'Administration; *m* 1950, Jeanne, da of Comte Xavier de Martimprey de Romecourt (d 1972); *Career* FO (Euro) 1951-53, second sec London 1953-57, first sec Rabat 1957-61, tech advsr Foreign Min 1961-62; head Tech Coop 1962-68, dir Personnel & Gen Admin 1968-72, ambass Canada 1972-77, gen inspr for Foreign Affairs 1977-78, dir de cabinet to Foreign Minister 1978-81, gen inspr Foreign Affrs 1981-84, ambass: Court of St James 1984-86, de France 1986-; chm: Review Ctee on Foreign Affairs Paris 1986, Entrance Exam Bd Ecole Nationale d'Administration 1987-, Assoc France Grande-Bretagne 1987-; Officier de la Légion d'Honneur 1973; commandeur de l'Ordre National du Mérite 1979; *Style*— M Jacques Viot, Esq; 19 rue de Civry, 75016 Paris (☎ 46517379)

VISSER, John Bancroft; s of Gilbert Frederick Visser (d 1964), and Ethel Frances Elizabeth, *née* Smith; *b* 29 Jan 1928; *Educ* Mill Hill Sch London, New Coll Oxford Univ (BA, MA); *m* 3 Sept 1955, (Astrid) Margareta, da of Sven Ragnar Olson (d 1976), of London; 2 s (Andrew b 1961, Michael b 1964), 1 da (Helen b 1962); *Career* Nat Serv 1946-48, 2 Lt RA; Civil Serv: entered 1951, princ Miny of Supply 1956 (asst princ 1951), Miny of Aviation 1959, Admin Staff Coll Henley 1965, asst sec 1965, Miny of Technol 1967, RCDS 1970, Civil Serv Dept 1971, procurement exec MOD 1971, sec of Nat Def Industs Cncl 1971-74, under sec 1974, dir admin SERC (formerly SRC) 1974-88, ret 1988; chm mgmnt ctee Cirencester CAB, ctee memb Churn Valley Decorative and Fine Arts Soc, ordinary memb Cirencester Civic Soc; *Recreations* music, antique furniture and longcase clocks, gardening; *Clubs* Old Millhillians; *Style*— John Visser, Esq; Rosslyn, 3 Berkeley Road, Cirencester, Glos GL7 1TY (☎ 0285 652626)

VIVIAN, Hon Amanda Ursula Georgina; *née* Vivian; da of 4 Baron Swansea; *b* 22 Nov 1958; *m* Hugh Lowther; *Style*— The Hon Amanda Vivian Lowther; Nortoft Grange, Guilsborough, Northants

VIVIAN, 5 Baron (UK 1841); Sir Anthony Crespigny Claud Vivian; 5 Bt (UK 1828); s of 4 Baron Vivian, DSO (d 1940); *b* 4 Mar 1906; *Educ* Eton; *m* 1930, Victoria (d 1985), da of late Capt Henry Gerard Laurence Oliphant, DSO, MVO, RN; 2 s, 1 da; *Heir* s, Hon Nicholas Crespigny Laurence Vivian; *Career* WWII 1939-40: RA, Special Constabulary, War correspondent; *Style*— The Rt Hon the Lord Vivian; 154 Coleherne Court, London SW5 (☎ 01 373 1050); Boskenna Ros, St Buryan, nr Penzance, Cornwall

VIVIAN, Rev (Thomas) Keith; s of William Vivian (d 1945), of Cornwall, and Glady Irene, *née* Thomas (d 1979); *b* 19 Feb 1927; *Educ* Truro Sch, St John's Coll Cambridge (MA); *m* 2 Aug 1952, Audrey Campbell, da of Norman Cowan, of Newcastle-on-Tyne; 1 s (Jonathan Mark b 1954), 1 da (Jenefer Clare b 1956); *Career* schoolmaster: Christ's Hosp Horsham 1949-54, Rugby Sch 1954-62; headmaster Lucton Sch Leominster 1962-84; ordained deacon 1980, priest 1981; priest i/c Chew Stoke, Norton Malreward and Nempnett Thrubwell 1985, Rector 1988-; noted Univ and Co Rugby Football players 1945-57; *Recreations* fishing, golf watching sport, walking; *Clubs* Hawkes (Cambridge), Rotary, Burnham & Berrow Golf; *Style*— The Rev Keith Vivian; The Rectory, Chew Stoke, Bristol BS18 8TV (☎ 0272 332554)

VIVIAN, Hon Louisa Caroline Sarah; da of 4 Baron Swansea; *b* 13 Feb 1963; *Style*— The Hon Louisa Vivian

VIVIAN, Hon Mrs Douglas; Mary Alice; da of late Francis John Gordon Borthwick; *m* 1943, Lt-Cdr the Hon Douglas David Edward Vivian, DSC, RN (d 1973, yr s of 4 Baron Vivian); 5 da; *Style*— The Hon Mrs Douglas Vivian; Monastery Garden, Edington, Westbury, Wilts

VIVIAN, Col Hon Nicholas Crespigny Laurence; s and h of 5 Baron Vivian; *b* 11 Dec 1935; *Educ* Eton, Madrid Univ; *m* 1, 1960 (m dis 1972), Catherine Joyce, da of James Kenneth Hope, CBE, DL; 1 s, 1 da; m 2, 1972, Carol, da of F Alan Martineau, MBE, JP, of Valley End House, Chobham, Surrey; 2 da; *Career* Col (1982) 16/5 The Queen's Royal Lancers; *Clubs* White's, Cavalry and Guards'; *Style*— Colonel The Hon Nicholas Vivian

VIVIAN, Hon Richard Anthony Hussey; s and h of 4 Baron Swansea; *b* 24 Jan 1957; *Educ* Eton, Durham Univ (BA); *Career* Journalist; *Clubs* North London Rifle; *Style*— The Hon Richard Vivian; Flat 3, 37 Dafforne Rd, London SW17 8TY (☎ 01 682 0603)

VIVIAN, Hon Victor Anthony Ralph Brabazon; yr s of 5 Baron Vivian and Victoria Ruth Mary Rosamund, *née* Oliphant (d 1985); *b* 26 Mar 1940; *Educ* Ludgrove, Nautical Coll Pangbourne, Southampton Univ; *m* 1966, Inger Johanne, da of Advokat Per Gulliksen (d 1981), of Sandejord, Norway; 1 s (Thomas b 1971), 1 da (Arabella b 1973); *Career* Br Merchant Navy 1957-61; overseas managerial contracts 1977-; *Recreations* sports, shooting; *Clubs* Royal Overseas League; *Style*— The Hon V R B Vivian; Prades, St Martin de Boubaux, 48160 Le Collet de Deze, France (☎ 66455613)

VOGT, (Susan) Harriet; da of Richard Vogt, of Washington DC, and Joan *née* Davis; *b* 31 July 1952; *Educ* Sidwell Friends Sch Washington DC, Westonbirt Sch, Sussex Univ (BA) ; common law husband, Philip Gallagher, s of Patrick Gallagher, DFC; *Career* dir of planning Ayer Barker (advertising agency, subsid Charles Barker plc) 1985-, (dir 1984-); *Recreations* consuming books, films, Italian food, culture, swimming; *Clubs* YMCA; *Style*— Mrs Philip Vogt; 2 Dunollie Place, London NW5 (☎ 0 486 7635); Ayer Barker, Metropolis House, 22 Percy St, London WIP 9FF (☎ 01 528 8888, fax 01 636 1119, telex 883588)

VOGT, John Julian Charles; s of Charles Vogt, and Evelyn Maude, *née* Smythe; *b* 2 April 1942; *Educ* St Paul's Sch London, The Coll of Law London; *m* 18 April 1970, Patricia, da of Jack McConnel, of 159 Woodstock Rd, Oxford; 1 s (Simon), 1 da (Caroline); *Career* slr Parker Chamberlain (private country practice) Wantage, Oxon; memb Law Soc, memb Br Legal Assoc; *Recreations* skiing, bridge; *Style*— John Vogt, Esq; 159 Woodstock Rd, Oxford (☎ 0865 515197); Parker Chamberlain, 9 Victoria Gallery, Wantage, Oxon (☎ 96 65651, fax 023577921)

VOKINS, Trevor William Derek; s of William Howard Gilburd Vokins (d 1984), and Gladys Florence Vokins; *b* 14 May 1935; *Educ* Eastbourne Coll; *m* 2 June 1962, Gillian Christine, da of Hugh A Kinney; 3 da (Susan b 1964, Amanda b 1966, Kathryn b 1968); *Career* dir: Anston Hldgs plc 1972-78, Vokins Ltd 1972-, Citizens Regency Building Soc 1973-85, Regency Building Soc 1987; memb Inst Chartered Accountants in England and Wales; FCA; *Recreations* travel, gardening; *Clubs* Brighton and Hove Soiree Rotary; *Style*— Trevor Vokins, Esq; 323 Dyke Road, Hove, E Sussex BN3 6PE (☎ 0273 556317); Vokins Ltd, North Street, Brighton BN1 1FD

VOLES, Dr Roger; s of Bertram Richard Edward (d 1978), and Winifred Mabel, *née* Barnes (d 1988); *b* 20 July 1930; *Educ* Ranelagh Sch, Univ of London (BSc), Brunel Univ (MTech, CNAA (DTech); *m* 24 Sept 1966, Vida Margaret Murray, da of Alec Riley (d 1973); *Career* chief scientist THORN EMI Electronics 1974-, papers to jls of IEE and IEEE, organised 6 int confs, 80 patents, past chm AGARD Avionics Panel, chm EEA res advsy ctee; Freeman Worshipful Co of Engrs 1984; FIEE 1971, FInstP 1971, FEng 1983; *Recreations* mountain walking, genealogy, travel; *Style*— Dr Roger Voles; THORN EMI Electronics, 120 Blyth Rd, Hayes, Middx UB3 1DL

VOLLAM, Dr (Frederick) Harman; s of Frederick William Vollam (d 1940), and Katie Leonora, *née* Harman (d 1973); *b* 6 Jan 1914; *Educ* King Edward's Sch Birmingham, Birmingham (MB, CLB, MRCS, LRCP); *m* 14 Sept 1939, Eleanor (d 1987), da of Jon Heath Davis (d 1920); 1 da (Katherine Elizabeth Anne b 1939); *Career* ret medical practitioner; *Recreations* music; *Clubs* Royal Western Yacht Plymouth; *Style*— Dr Harman Vollam; Flat 2, Moondara, The Crescent, Hannafore, W Looe, Cornwall PL13

2EL (☎ 05036 2620)

VON BERGEN, Hon Mrs; Hon Sheila; da of Baron Thomas, DFC (Life Peer d 1980); *b* 1925; *m* 1948, Julian von Bergen; *Style—* The Hon Mrs von Bergen; Ellicombe, Minehead, Somerset

VON BRENTANO (DI TREMEZZO), (Georg) Michael Robert; s of Bernard von Brentano (d 1964), of Wiesbaden, and Margot, *née* Gerlach; *b* 6 August 1933; *m* 26 Feb 1966, Elke, da of Walter Hassel (d 1978), of Frankfurt; 1 da (Meline b 15 Aug 1969); *Career* sr vice pres: Berliner Handels - Gesellschaft Frankfurt until 1964, Deutsche Bank AG Frankfurt 1974-85; md Deutsche Bank Capital Mkts Ltd London 1985-; *Recreations* collecting first editions, golf; *Clubs* IOD, Royal Mid-Surrey GC, Frankfurter Gesellschaft fuer Handel Industrie und Wissenschaft; *Style—* Michael von Brentano, Esq; Deutsche Bank Capital Mkts Ltd, 150 Leadenhall Street, London EC3V 4RJ (☎ 01 826 5104)

VON DER HEYDE, Helmut Heinrich Sigismund; s of Wolf Heinrich Sigismund Paul Von der Heyde (d 1953), and Anna Milicent Caroline Rose Wall, *née* Woltmer; *b* 25 July 1927; *Educ* Landschulheim Neubern Bavaria, Bootham Sch York, Oxford Univ (BA, MA); *m* 19 July 1952, Bronwen, da of Vincent Burr (d 1975); 3 s (Paul Heinrich Sigismund b 1953, Stephen Peter b 1959, Alexander Peter b 1966), 1 da (Jane Margaret b 1955); *Career* chm and md: Von Der Heyde Ltd 1963, Bielomatik London Ltd 1957, Evd Engrg Ltd 1963; dir Hills Electrical Engrs Ltd; *Recreations* golf, gardening; *Clubs* RAC; *Style—* Helmut Von Der Heyde, Esq; Luth House, Wisborough Green, Billingshurst, W Sussex RH14 0BJ (☎ 0403 700 440); Bielomatik London Ltd, Cotswold Street, London SE27 0DP (☎ 01 761 1211, telex 24995, fax 01 761 2847)

VON HAYEK, Prof Friedrich August; CH (1984); came to Britain 1931, naturalised 1938; *b* Vienna; *Career* Tooke prof of econs London Univ 1931-50, prof of econ sci and statistics Univ of Chicago 1950-62, prof of econs Univ of Freiburg 1962-69, Hon DLitt Univ of Dallas 1975, Hon Doctorate in social scis, Marroquin Univ Guatemala 1977, Santa Maria Univ Valparaiso 1977, Univ of Buenos Aires 1977, Univ of Gessen 1982; Nobel Prize in Econ Science (jtly) 1974; Austrian Distinction for Sci and Art 1975; memb Orders pour le Mérite fur Wissenschaften und Künste Fed Rep of Germany 1977; hon fell: LSE, Austrian Acad of Sci, American Econ Assoc; *Publications* Prices and Production (1931), Monetary Theory and the Trade Cycle (1933, German ed 1929), Monetary Nationalism and International Stability (1937), Profits, Interest and Investment (1939), The Pure Theory of Capital (1941), The Road to Serfdom (1944), Individualism and Economic Order (1948), John Stuart Mill and Harriet Taylor (1950), The Counter-revolution of Science (1952), The Sensory Order (1952), The Political ideal of the Rule of Law (1955), The Constitution of Liberty (1960), Studies in Philosophy, Politics and Economics and the History of Ideas (1978), Beitrage zur Geldtheorie (ed 1933), Collectivist Econ Planning (1935), Capitalism and the Historians (1954); the works of: HH Gossen (1927), F Wieser (1929), C Menger (1933-36), H Thornton (1939); articles in Economic Journal, Economica, and other English and foreign jls; *Clubs* Reform; *Style—* Prof Friedrich von Hayek, CH; c/o Central Chancery of the Order of Knighthood, St James's Palace, London SW1

VON HOYNINGEN-HUENE, Baroness Nancy; *née* Oakes; da of Sir Harry Oakes, 1 Bt; *b* 17 May 1925; *m* 1, 1942 (m annulled 1949), Marie-Alfred Fouquerreaux de Marigny, of Mauritius; m 2, 1952 (m dis 1961), Baron Ernst von Hoyningen-Huene, 2 s of Baron Hermann von Hoyningen-Huene, of Munich; 1 s (Baron Alexander George Lyssardt, b 17 Feb 1955); m 3, 1962 (m dis), Patrick Tritton, *qv*; resumed surname of 2 husb; *Style—* Baroness Nancy von Hoyningen-Huene; PO Box N1002, 28 Queen St, Nassau, Bahamas; Marsella 44, Mexico 6, DF Mexico

VON MALLINCKRODT, Georg Wilhelm Gustav; s of Arnold Wilhelm von Mallinckrodt (d 1982), of 8110 Riegsee, nr Murnau, Germany, and Valentine *née* von Joest; *b* 19 August 1930; *Educ* Schule Schloss Salem, Sch of Econ Hamburg; *m* 1958, Charmaine Brenda, da of Helmut Schroder, of Dunlossit, Isle of Islay (d 1967); 2 s (Philip, Edward), 2 da (Claire, Sophie); *Career* merchant banker; joined J Henry Schroder Banking Corpn NY 1954, exec chm Schroders plc London 1984-, chm and chief exec Schroders Inc NY 1983-, chm J Henry Schroder Bank AG Zurich 1984, chm and pres Schroder Int Ltd 1984-; dir: Schroder Australia (Holdings) Ltd Sydney 1984-, Wertheim Schroder & Co Inc NY 1986-, J Henry Schroder Wagg & Co Ltd London 1967-; dir NM UK Ltd 1986-; memb European Advsy Ctee McGraw-Hill Inc NY 1986-, vice pres German Chamber of Industry and Commerce in UK, pres German YMCA London 1971-; Cross of Order of Merit German Federal Republic 1986; *Recreations* shooting, ski-ing, gardening, classical music; *Clubs* River, New York; *Style—* Georg von Mallinckrodt, Esq; Schroders plc, 120 Cheapside, London EC2 (☎ 01 382 6000, telex 885029)

VON PREUSSEN, Princess Nicholas; Hon Victoria; *née* Mancroft; da of 2 Baron Mancroft, KBE, TD; *b* 1952; *m* 1980, HRH Prince (Frederick) Nicholas von Preussen; 2 da (Beatrice b 1981, Florence b 1983); *Style—* Princess Nicholas von Preussen; Maperton House, Wincanton, Somerset

VON SAXE DILLEY, Tatiana Alexandra; da of Enrique Sigismundo Von Saxe Tourowitz (d 1979), and Consuelo Trinidad, *née* Yépez; *b* 27 April 1944; *Educ* Lima Peru (Business Admin); *m* 1, 8 June 1968, late Eric A Dilley; *Career* sr ptnr Von Saxe Assocs 1970, chm Mainline Corpn 1980, md Mainline Restaurants Ltd 1980; Order of Merit for Distinguished Servs Peru 1980; *Recreations* tennis; *Clubs* St James's, IOD; *Style—* Ms Tatiana Von Saxe Dilley; 4 Delancey Passage, London NW1 7NN (☎ 01 387 3544, fax 01 385 314, telex 23291 DILLEY G)

VON SCHRAMEK, Sir Eric Emil; s of Emil von Schramek (d 1947), and Annie von Schramek (d 1981); *b* 4 April 1921; *Educ* Stefans Gymnasium Prague, Tech Univ Prague (Dip Ing Arch); *m* 1948, Edith, da of Dipl Ing W Popper; 1 s (Charles), 2 da (Annette, Therese); *Career* town planner Bavaria 1946-48; sr supervising architect Dept of Works and Housing, Darwin, NT 1948-51; Evans, Bruer & Ptnrs (now von Schramek and Dawes) 1951-, work includes Nat Mutual Centre, State Govt Insur Building, Wales Ho, TAA Building; numerous churches throughout Australia and New Guinea; nat pres Building Sci Forum of Australia 1970-72; pres RAIA 1974-76; former nat dep chm Austcare; former cncllr Cncl of Professions; former chm Lutheran Church of Australia; life fellow RAIA; FRIBA, FIArbA, Affiliate RAPI; kt 1982; *Publications* contributions and articles in architectural pubns; *Style—* Sir Eric von Schramek; 4 Burlington St, Walkerville, S Australia 5081

VON SIMSON, HSH Princess Marie-Anne of Salm-Reiffersheidt, Krautheim und Dyck; Mrs Marie-Anne Helena Emmanuela; da of HSH 6 Prince (Franz Joseph), zu Salm-Reiffersheidt, Krautheim und Dyck; *m* 1, 1964, as his 2 w, Col Hon Alexander Campbell Geddes, OBE, MC, TD, (d 1972, s of 1 Baron Geddes); 1 s (Stephen George b 1969), 1 da (Camilla Johanna Isabel b 1966); m 2, 1978, Prof Dr Otto Georg von Simson, of Berlin; *Style—* HSH Princess Marie-Anne zu Salm-Reif; Petersham Lodge, Richmond, Surrey

VON WESTENHOLZ, Lady Mary (Marianella Anne); *née* Kerr; da of 12 Marquess of Lothian, by his w Antonella Newland; *b* 20 Mar 1944; *Educ* Open Univ (BA); *m* 1970, Charles von Westenholz; 3 s; *Recreations* skiing, tennis, guitar playing, knitting; *Style—* Lady Mary von Westenholz; Little Blakesware, Widford, Ware, Herts

VON WESTENHOLZ, Piers Patrick Frederick; Baron; s of Baron Henry Frederick Everard von Westenholz (d 1984), of Crackney, Widford, Herts; *b* 10 Dec 1943; *Educ* Downside; *m* 1, 1964 (m dis 1969), Sarah, da of Raimund von Hofmannstahl (s of the poet Hugo von Hofmannstahl) by his 2 w, Lady Elizabeth Paget (da of 6 Marquess of Anglesey, GCVO); m 2, 1979, Jane, da of Arthur Leveson, of Hall Place, Ropley, Hants; 1 s, 2 da; *Career* antique dealer and decorator; *Recreations* shooting, fishing, skiing; *Clubs* Turf; *Style—* Baron Piers von Westenholz; Letterellan, by Aberfeldy, Perthshire (☎ Kenmore 221); Barrow Farm, Widford, Herts (☎ 027 984 2146)

VOS, Geoffrey Charles; s of Bernard Vos (d 1974), of London, and Pamela Celeste Rose, *née* Heilbuth; *b* 22 April 1955; *Educ* UCS, Gonville and Caius Coll Cambridge (MA); *m* 31 Mar 1984, Vivien Mary, da of Albert Edward Dowdeswell (d 1982), of Birmingham; 1 da (Charlotte b 1985), 1 step s (Carl b 1973), 2 step da (Maria b 1965, Louise b 1965); *Career* called to the Bar 1977 Inner Temple 1977, in practice Chambers of DR Stanford 1979-; memb Chancery Bar Assoc; subscriber Senate of the Inns of Ct; memb: Inner Temple, Lincoln's Inn; *Recreations* sheep farming, wine, photography; *Clubs* United Oxford and Cambridge, Worcs GC; *Style—* Geoffrey Vos, Esq; 46 Fordington Rd, Highgate, London N6 4TJ (☎ 01 444 9547); Woodlands, Crumpton Hill, Storridge, Nr Malvern, Worcs (☎ 0886 32556); 3 Stone Buildings, Lincoln's Inn, London WC2A 3XL (☎ 01 242 4937, fax 01 405 3896, telex 892300 ADVICE G REF: TW)

VOWLES, Paul Foster; s of Ernest Foster Vowles (d 1929), of Bristol, and Georgina May, *née* Lawrence (d 1983), of Bristol; *b* 12 June 1919; *Educ* Bristol GS, Corpus Christi Coll Oxford (MA); *m* 8 Jan 1948, Valerie Eleanor, da of Ralph Theodore Hickman (d 1967); 1 s (John b 1949), 2 da (Penelope b 1952, Deborah b 1955); *Career* army 1939-46; cmmnd 1940, Gloucs Regt, KAR 1942 (despatches) Maj; asst sec: Univ of Birmingham Appts Bd 1947, Inter-Univ Cncl for HE Overseas 1948-51, registrar Makerere Univ Coll East Africa 1951-63; Univ of London: sr asst to princ 1964-68, external registrar 1968-73, academic registrar 1973-82; vice-chm Cncl of Westfield Coll Univ of London; *Clubs* Athenaeum; *Style—* Paul Vowles, Esq; 13 Dale Close, Oxford OX1 1TU (☎ 0845 244042)

VULLIAMY, Patrick David; s of Maj Gen Lolwyn Henry Hughes Vulliamy, CB, DSO (d 1972), of Fleet, Hants, and Veronica Mary, *née* Ellis, (d 1978) ; *b* 25 May 1927; *Educ* Bedford Sch, Peterhouse Cambridge (BA, MA); *m* July 1954, Pamela Elsie, da of Frederick Cottier (d 1974), of Lausanne, Switzerland; 1 s (Christopher Patrick Colwyn b 19 Oct 1956), 1 da (Dominique Fiona b 1 Oct 1958); *Career* Lt Royal Signals 1947 (served 1945-49); mgmnt trainee Purchase Dept Ford Motor Co 1952-54, ptnr Scott Wilson Kirkpatrick Ptnrs Consulting Engrs 1968- (joined 1956); FICE, FASCE; *Recreations* golf, skiing, bridge; *Clubs* NZ GC, Oxford and Cambridge; *Style—* Patrick Vulliamy, Esq; The Stables, Coldharbour, Kingsley, nr Bordon, Hants GU35 9LB (☎ 04203 3008); Scott House, Basing View, Basingstoke, Hants (☎ 0256 461161)

VYVYAN, (Ralph) Ferrers Alexander; s and h of Sir John Vyvyan, 12 Bt; *b* 21 August 1960; *Educ* Charterhouse, Sandhurst; *Career* short term cmmn Light Infantry; estate mgmnt in conjunction with Sir John Vyvyan Bt; *Recreations* dinghy sailing; *Style—* Ralph Vyvyan, Esq; Trelowarreb, Mawgan, Helston, Cornwall TR12 6AF (☎ 0326 22 224)

VYVYAN, Sir John Stanley; 12 Bt (E 1645); s of late Maj-Gen Ralph Ernest Vyvyan, CBE, MC (himself only s of late Capt Herbert Reginald Vyvyan, OBE, who was in turn 2 s of Rev Herbert Francis Vyvyan, while the Rev Herbert was 3 s of Rev Vyell Francis Vyvyan, the latter being 2 s of Sir Vell Vyvyan, 7 Bt); suc cous Sir Richard Philip Vyvyan, 11 Bt, 1978; *b* 20 Jan 1916; *Educ* Charterhouse, London Sch of Oriental Studies; *m* 1, 1940 (m dis 1946), Joyce Lilia, da of late Frederick Marsh, of Kailan Mining Admin, Peking; 1 da (decd); m 2 1948 (m dis 1958), Marie, da of late Dr O'Shea, of Hamilton, Ont; m 3, 1958, Jonet Noel, da of Lt-Col Alexander Hubert Barclay, DSO, MC; 1 s, 1 da; *Heir* s, Ralph Ferrers Alexander Vyvyan; *Career* 1939-45 War as Maj Royal Signals, in India and Arakan; owner and manager of Trelowarren Estate 1950-; *Clubs* Army and Navy, Royal Cornwall Yacht (Falmouth); *Style—* Sir John Vyvyan, Bt; Trelowarren Mill, Mawgan, Helston, Cornwall (☎ 0326 22 505)

WADDELL, Sir Alexander Nicol Anton; KCMG (1959), CMG (1955, DSC 1944); s of Rev Alexander Waddell; *b* 8 Nov 1913; *Educ* Fettes, Edinburgh Univ, Gonville & Caius Cambridge; *m* 1949, Jean Margot Lesbia, da of W Masters; *Career* district offr Br Solomon Islands 1938, DC 1945, princ asst sec N Borneo 1947-52, colonial sec: Gambia 1952-56, Sierra Leone 1956-58 (dep govr 1958-60), govr & c-in-c Sarawak 1960-63; UK Cmmr Br Phosphate Commis 1965-78, memb Panel Ind Inspectors Dept Environment 1979-85; *Recreations* golf, hill walking; *Clubs* East India & Sports; *Style*— Sir Alexander Waddell, KCMG, CMS, DSC; Pilgrim Cottage, Ashton Keynes, Wilts

WADDELL, Sir James Henderson; CB (1960); s of Donald M Waddell and J C Fleming; *b* 5 Oct 1914; *Educ* George Heriot's Sch, Edinburgh Univ (MA); *m* 1940, Dorothy Abbie, da of Horace Wright; 1 s, 1 da; *Career* Civil Serv 1936-75: under sec Cabinet Off 1961-63, dep sec Miny Housing and Local Govt 1963-66, dep under-sec H O 1966-75; dep chm Police Complaints Bd 1977-81; kt 1974; *Style*— Sir James Waddell, CB; Longmeadows, East Lavant, Chichester, W Sussex (☎ 0243 527 129)

WADDELL, Michael Richard; s of Arthur Smith Waddell, and Mabel Louise *née* Skilton; *b* 12 Oct 1937; *Educ* Ashborton Sch Croydon, Wellington Coll (New Zealand); *m* 1958, Margaret Ann, da of Arthur Charles Petchey; 2 da (Beverley b 1963, Suzanne b 1965); *Career* serv RA 1958-60; div mktg dir Reed Bldg Products Ltd 1978-81, div md Rentokil Gp (timber presevation) and dir numerous cos inc Rentokil Ltd, Celcore (m) Sdn Bhd, Treztim Ltd, Fuller Energy Ltd; FInstM; Freeman City of London, memb Worshipful Co of Feltmakers; *Recreations* travel, walking, gardening; *Style*— M R Waddell, Esq; Ashlands, Oast Ct, Yalding, Kent (☎ 0622 813570); Rentokil Gp plc, Felcourt, East Grinstead, W Sussex (☎ 0342 833022, telex 95456, fax 0342 26229)

WADDELL, Robert Steele (Robin); s of Herbert Waddell, CBE (Col HLI, d 1988), of 14A Ledcameroch Road, Bearsden, Glasgow, and Jean Cameron, *née* Wallace; *b* 3 August 1931; *Educ* Glasgow Acad, St Mary's Melrose, Fettes, Cambridge Univ; *m* 8 July 1960, (Margaret) Eileen Monro, da of Dr John Sturrock; 4 da (Mrs Elizabeth-Anne Wilson b 1961, Dr Nicola Markland b 1963, Alexandra b 1966, Victoria b 1967); *Career* Nat Serv 41 Field Regt RA, Egypt; with Thomson McLintock Glasgow 1955-59, sr dir Speirs and Jeffrey Ltd; memb: R and A Finance Ctee, sec Scottish Wayfarers Over 50's 1982-; *Recreations* golf; *Clubs* Elie Golf, Prestwick Golf, Glasgow Golf, Muirfield, R and A; *Style*— Robin Waddell, Esq; Fairmount, 17 Ledcameroch Road, Bearsden, Glasgow B61 4AB (☎ 041 942 0455); Speirs and Jeffrey Ltd, 36 Renfield Street, Glasgow G2 1NA (☎ 041 248 4311, fax 041 221 4764, telex 777902)

WADDELL, Rear-Adm William Angus; CB (1981), OBE (1966); s of James Whitefield Waddell (decd), and Christina Maclean (decd); *b* 5 Nov 1924; *Educ* Glasgow Univ (BSc); *m* 1950, Thelma Evelyn Tomlins; 1 s, 1 da; *Career* Sub Lt RNVR (Special Branch) 1945, Offr i/c RN Polaris Sch 1966-68, Instr Capt Staff of SACLANT (Dir Information Systems Gp) 1969-72, Dean RN Coll Greenwich 1973-75, Dir Naval Offr Appointments (Instructor) 1975-78, Rear-Adm 1979, Chief Naval Instr Offr 1978-81, Flag Offr Admiralty Interview Bd 1979-81; sec and chief Exec Royal Inst of Public Health and Hygiene 1982-; FIEE ; ADC to HM The Queen 1976-79; *Style*— Rear-Adm William Waddell, CB, OBE; c/o National Westminster Bank Ltd, 1 Lee Rd, Blackheath, London SE3

WADDICOR, (James) Richard; s of William Waddicor (d 1960), of Bolton, and Marian, *née* Cookson; *b* 2 May 1937; *Educ* Uppingham Sch; *m* 1 March 1962, (Margaret) Gillian, da of Rev Richard Greville Norburn (d 1978 Canon and Rural Dean of Botlon and of Edgbaston); 1 s (James b 1965), 1 da (Frances b 1963); *Career* fin dir Hawker Siddeley Dynamics Engrg Ltd 1972-79, md Water Engrg Ltd 1979- (formerly Hawker Siddeley Water Engrg Ltd); MIWE, FCA 1970; *Recreations* fly fishing, squash; *Style*— Richard Waddicor, Esq; Oaken Hedges, Enborne Rd, Newbury, Berks (☎ 0635 344 65); Water Engineering Ltd, Aynho Rd, Adderbury, Banbury, Oxon OX17 3NL (☎ 0295 810 581, fax 0295 811 997, telex 83655)

WADDILOVE, Lewis Edgar; CBE (1978), OBE (1965, JP York 1968); s of Alfred Waddilove (d 1946), of Leigh on Sea Essex, and Edith Emily Waddilove, *née* Javens (d 1966); *b* 5 Sept 1914; *Educ* Westcliff HS, London Univ (DPA); *m* 1969, Maureen, da of Alfred Piper, resident in Spain; from previous marriage: 1 s (Trevor), 1 da (Pamela); *Career* dir Joseph Rowntree Meml Tst 1946-79, dep chm Housing Corpn 1978-83 (memb 1968-); chm: Friends Serv Cncl 1961-67, Nat Fedn of Housing Assocs 1965-73 and 1977-79 (now vice-pres), Central Appeals Advsy Ctee (BBC and IBA) 1978-84, York City Charities 1957-65 and 1972-, York Univ Cncl 1977-87, Personal Social Servs Cncl 1977-80, Coal Mining Subsidence Compensation Review Ctee 1983-84, Bootham and Mount Schs 1974-81; memb: Ctee on Housing in Gtr London 1963-65, Nat Ctee on Cwlth Immigrants 1966-68, Soc Sci Res Cncl 1967-71, Pub Schs Cmmn 1968-70, Central Housing Advsy Ctee 1960-75, Legal Aid Advsy Ctee 1972-78; presiding clerk Fourth World Conf of Soc of Friends in N Carolina 1967; govr Merchant Adventurers of City of York 1978-79; DUniv Brunel 1978; DUniv York 1987; *Books* One Man's Vision (1954), Housing Associations (1962), Private Philanthropy and Public Welfare (1983); *Recreations* inland waterways, gardening; *Style*— Lewis E Waddilove, Esq, CBE, OBE, JP; Red Oaks, 27 Hawthorn Terrace, New Earswick, York YO3 8AJ (☎ 0904 768696)

WADDINGTON, David Charles; PC (1987), QC (1971), MP (Cons Ribble Valley 1983-); s of Charles Waddington, JP, of The Old Vicarage, Read, Lancs; *b* 2 August 1929; *Educ* Sedbergh, Hertford Coll Oxford; *m* 1958, Gillian Rosemary, da of Alan Green of Sabden, Lancs; 3 s, 2 da; *Career* 2 Lt 12 Royal Lancers 1951-53; barr Gray's Inn 1951, rec Crown Ct 1972; former dir: J J Broadley Ltd, J and J Roberts Ltd, Wolstenholme Rink Ltd; cons candidate: Farmworth 1955, Nelson and Colne 1964, Heywood and Royton 1966; MP (Cons): Nelson and Colne 1968-Oct 1974, Clitheroe March 1979-1983; lord cmmmr treasy 1979-81, parly under sec Employment 1981-83, min of state Home Off 1983-87; govt chief whip 1987-; *Style*— The Rt Hon David Waddington, Esq, QC, MP; Whins House, Sabden, Nr Blackburn, Lancs (☎ 0282 71070); 9 Denny St, London SE11 (☎ 01 735 5886)

WADDINGTON, Prof David James; s of Eric James Waddington (d 1958), of 43 Caroline House, London, and Marjorie Edith, *née* Harding; *b* 27 May 1932; *Educ* Marlborough, Imperial Coll (BSc, ARCS, DIC, PhD); *m* 17 Aug 1957, Isobel, da of Ernest Hesketh, of Eastbourne; 2 s (Matthew b 1963, Rupert b 1964), 1 da (Jessica b 1970); *Career* head sci dept Wellington Coll 1961-64 (teacher 1956-64); York Univ 1965-: prof of chemical educn 1978-, head dept 1983-, pro vice chllr 1985-; pres educn div Royal Soc Chem 1981-83, chm ctee teaching chemistry, Int Union Pure and Applied Chem 1981-85, sec ctee teaching sci Int Cncl Sci Unions 1985-, Nyholm Medal Royal Soc Chem 1985; *Books* Modern Organic Chemistry (1985), Kinetics and Mechanism: Case Studies (1977), Chemistry, The Salters' Approach (1989), Teaching Sch Chemistry (ed 1984), Chemistry in Action (ed 1987), Education Industry and Technology (ed 1987); *Recreations* golf; *Style*— Prof David Waddington; Murton Hall, York YO1 3UQ (☎ 0904 489 393); Dept of Chem, Univ of York, Heslington, York YO1 5DD (☎ 0904 432 500/1, fax 0904 433 433, telex 57933 YORKUL)

WADDINGTON, Robert; s of George Waddington (d 1967), of Lytham, Lancs, and Mary Gwendoline, *née* Briggs; *b* 20 Jan 1942; *Educ* Uppingham; *m* 24 Jan 1976, Jennifer Ann, da of Sir Anthony Banks Jenkinson 13 Bt, of Georgetown, Grand Cayman; 2 s (Thomas Anthony b 10 May 1977, Guy George b 6 Sept 1979); *Career* Hambros Bank Ltd 1971- (dir 1984); FCA; *Recreations* shooting, golf, gardening; *Style*— Robert Waddington, Esq; 51 Ranelagh Grove, London, SW1W 8PB; 41 Tower Hill, London EC3 (☎ 01 480 5000, fax 01 702 9725)

WADDINGTON, Very Rev Robert Murray; s of Percy Nevill Waddington, MBE (d 1971), and Dorothy, *née* Murray (d 1983); *b* 24 Oct 1927; *Educ* Dulwich Coll, Selwyn Coll Cambridge (MA); *Career* asst curate St John's Bethnal Green 1953-55, chaplain Slade Sch Warwick Qld Aust 1955-59, curate St Luke's Cambridge 1959-61, headmaster St Barnados Sch Ravenshoe N Qld Aust 1961-70, Oxford Univ Dept of Education 1971-72, residentiary canon Carlisle Cathedral 1972-77; gen sec C of E Bd of Educn and Nat Soc for Promoting Religious Edn 1977-84; dean of Manchester 1984-; *Recreations* cinema, cooking, sociology, travel; *Clubs* St James (Manchester); *Style*— The Very Rev The Dean of Manchester; 44 Shrewsbury Rd, Prestwich, Manchester M25 8GQ (☎ 061 773 2959); The Cathedral, Manchester M3 1SX (☎ 061 834 0019)

WADDY, Col John Llewellyn; OBE (1963); s of Lt-Col Richard Henry Waddy (d 1952), of Westhay, Kingston St Mary, Taunton, Somerset, and Olive Meriel, *née* Llewellyn (d 1961); *b* 7 June 1920; *Educ* St Neot's Eversley, Wellington Coll, RMC Sandhurst; *m* 14 July 1945, Megan Ann, da of Alwcyn Penry Davies (d 1960), of West Bridgford Nottingham; *Career* cmmnd Somerset Light Infantry 1939, India 1939-41, Parachute Bn Dehli India 1941, Parachute Regt Middle East, N Africa, Italy and UK; wounded POW, Maj 156 Para Bu Battle of Arnhem 1944; Palestine 1945-48; Libya, Egypt, Malaya (despatches), Canada; Parachute Regt, Jordan, Cyprus and UK; Col SAS (1959-67), BAS Washington DC; Def Advisor Saigon S Vietnam (1970-72) , ret Col 1974; military advsr Westland Helicopters Ltd 1974-87, mil advsr on film A Bridge Too Far 1976; *Recreations* walking my dogs in the wild woods, gardening; *Clubs* Army and Navy; *Style*— Col John Waddy, OBE; Jack O'Knights, Spaxton, Bridgwater, Somerset TA5 1AJ

WADDY, Lady Olivia Sheelin Davina Anne; *née* Taylour; da of 6 Marquess of Headfort, by his 1 w, *see* Hon Mrs Knight; *b* 4 Oct 1963; *m* 19 April 1986, David Charles Henry Waddy, er s of Ian Waddy, of Mirza Downs, Ward Marlborough, New Zealand; *Style*— Lady Olivia Waddy; c/o The Hon Mrs Knight, Northfield, Kirk Andreas, Isle of Man

WADE, Derwent Malcolm Mercer; s of Roland Henry Wade, CBE, JP, and Margaret Elizabeth Wade; n of Baron Wade (Life Peer); *b* 26 June 1939; *Educ* Marlborough, Selwyn Coll Cambridge (MA); *m* 1967, Rosemary, da of Eric Cyprian Perry Whiteley, TD (d 1970); 1 s, 1 da; *Career* solicitor 1965, ptnr Booth & Co 1968-; dir: Wade Gp of Cos 1972-80, BNL Hldgs 1979-82, FTL Hldgs 1974-, Kaye & Co (Huddersfield) 1983-; *Recreations* hunting, gardening; *Clubs* Leeds; *Style*— Derwent Wade, Esq; The Barn House, Bulmer, York YO6 7BL (☎ 065 381 212); PO Box 8, Soverign House, South Parade, Leeds LS1 1HQ (☎ 0532 469655)

WADE, Hon Donald William Mercer; er s of Baron Wade, DL (Life Peer, d 1988); *b* 1 June 1941; *Educ* Silcoates Sch, Trin Hall Cambridge (BA 1963, MA 1967); *Style*— The Hon Donald Wade; 18 Pinewood Grove, London W5

WADE, Maj-Gen Douglas (Ashton) Lofft; CB (1945), OBE (1940), MC (1918); s of late C S D Wade, of Saffron Walden; *b* 13 Mar 1898; *Educ* St Lawrence Coll, RMA Woolwich, Clare Coll Cambridge (BA); *m* 1, 1926, Heather, *née* Bulmer (d 1968); 1 da; m 2, 1972, Cynthia, *née* Allen; *Career* cmmnd RA 1916, served: France and Italy WW I, S Russia 1919, France and India WW II, Malaya 1948; Br memb Indian Armed Forces Nationalisation Ctee 1947, special appointments War Office 1948-50, ret 1950; telecommuncations attaché Br Embassy Washington DC 1951-54, sr engr ITA 1954-60 (regnl offr 1960-64), chm Royal Signals Inst 1957-63, chm SE Forum for Closed Circuit TV in Higher Educn 1967-73, HQ WRVS 1970-75; vice-pres Dunkirk Veterans Assoc 1962- (vice-chm 1962-67, chm 1967-74); CEng, MIEE; *Books* A Life on the Line (autobiography 1988); *Recreations* gardening, writing; *Style*— Maj-Gen Ashton

Wade, CB, OBE, MC; Phoenix Cottage, 6 Church St, Old Catton, Norwich (☎ 0603 45755)

WADE, Baroness; Ellenora Beatrice; da of late Frank Bentham Holdsworth, of Ilkley; *m* 18 June 1932, Baron Wade, DL (Life Peer UK 1964; d 1988); 2 s (Hon Donald William Mercer, Hon Robert Alexander Mercer), 2 da (Hon Mrs Wickham, Hon Mrs Morrish); *Style*— The Rt Hon Lady Wade; Meadowbank, Wath Road, Pateley Bridge, N Yorkshire (☎ 0423 711431)

WADE, Sir Henry William Rawson; QC (1968); s of Col Henry Oswald Wade, DSO, TD (d 1962), and Mrs Eileen Lucy Wade, *née* Rawson-Ackroyd (d 1973); *b* 16 Jan 1918; *Educ* Shrewsbury Sch, Gonville and Caius Coll Cambrige (BA, MA, LLD), Harvard USA; *m* 1943, Marie (d 1980), da of G E Osland-Hill (d 1958), of Bucks; 2 s (Michael, Edward); m 2, 1982, Marjorie Grace Hope, wid of B C Browne, da of Surgn-Capt H Hope Gill RN (d 1956), of Devon; *Career* barr Lincoln's Inn, honorary bencher 1964; prof of law: Oxford 1961-76, Cambridge 1978-83; master Gonville and Caius Coll Cambridge 1976-88; kt 1985; Fell Br Acad 1969 (vice pres 1981-83); *Books* numerous Books and articles on administrative, constitutional and real property law; *Recreations* climbing, gardening, music; *Clubs* United Oxford & Cambridge U, Alpine; *Style*— Sir William Wade, QC; Gonville and Caius Coll, Cambridge CB2 1TA (☎ 0223 332400); 1A Ludlow Lane, Fulbourn, Cambridge (☎ 0223 881745)

WADE, Michael John; s of Peter Wade, and Lorna A M Harris; *b* 22 May 1954; *Educ* Royal Russell, N Staffs Coll; *Career* fndr Holman Wade Ltd 1980, memb of Lloyd's 1980, chm Holman Wade Ltd, dir Horace Clarkson plc, Horace Holman Gp, cncl and ctee Lloyd's 1987-92, memb Baltic Exchange 1987; *Recreations* music, shooting, flying; *Clubs* Turf; *Style*— Michael J Wade, Esq; 6 Vincent Sq, London SW1; 12 Camomile St, London EC3 (☎ 01 283 7522)

WADE, Sir (William) Oulton; *m* ; 1 s, 1 da; *Career* md of family farming co, chm Mollington Gp of Cos involved in food and farming; former Cheshire cllr, jt hon tres Cons Pty 1982-; JP Cheshire 1967, Liveryman Worshipful Co Farmers; kt 1982; *Style*— Sir Oulton Wade; Chorlton Lodge Farm, Chorlton by Backford, Chester

WADE, Prof Owen Lyndon; CBE (1983); s of James Owen David Wade, OBE (d 1962), of 25 Park Place, Cardiff, and Kate, *née* Jones (d 1974); *b* 17 May 1921; *Educ* Repton, Emmanuel Coll Cambridge, UCH (MA, MB BCh, MD); *m* 6 March 1948, Margaret, da of Reginald John Burton (d 1972), of Ilfracoombe and New Milton; 3 da (Robin Elizabeth b 1949, Josephine b 1951, Sian Mary b 1953); *Career* RMO UCH 1946, clinical asst pneumkoniosis res unit MRC 1948-51, lectr dept of med Birmingham Univ 1951-56, sr lectr and conslt physician Utd Birmingham Hosps 1956-57, Whitla prof of therapeutics Queen's Univ Belfast and conslt physician NI Hosps Authy 1957-71, dep dean faculty of med Queen's Univ Belfast 1968-71, prof of therapeutics and clinical pharmacology Birmingham Univ and conslt physician Queen Elizabeth Hosp Birmingham 1971-85, vice princ and pro vice-chllr Birmingham Univ 1984-85 (dean faculty of med and dentistry 1978-84); memb: NI Gen Health Servs Bd 1957-71, standing med advsy ctee Min of Health and Social Security NI 1968-71 (chm sub ctees on community med and psychogeriatric care 1969), jt formulary ctee for the Br Nat Formulary 1963-85 (chm 1978-85), Dunlop ctee on Safety of Drugs Miny of Health London 1963-70 (chm sub of Adverse Reactions to Drugs 1967-70), Medicines Cmmn DHSS London 1969-77, chm Ctee of Review of Medicines 1977-83, clinical res bd MRC 1970-74; conslt advsr WHO: med educn 1960, 1963 and 1965, drug monitoring 1964, intensive hosp drug monitoring 1968, drug monitoring 1968, drug consumption in Europe 1969, drug utilisation res gp 1968-86; chm of tstees Arthur Thomson Charitable Tst 1984- (tstee 1978-), Hon MD Queen's Univ of Belfast 1989; memb: Physiological Soc, Br Pharmacological Soc, Assoc of Physicians of GB and Ireland, Med Res Soc; FRCP 1962, MRCP 1948, FRSA; *Books* Adverse Reactions to Drugs (second edn 1976), Cardiac Output and Regional Blood Flow (with JM Bishop 1962); contrib: J Physiology, Clinical Science, J Clinical Investigation; *Recreations* sailing, reading, grandchildren; *Clubs* Athenaeum; *Style*— Prof Owen Wade, CBE; The Medical School, Univ of Birmingham, Birmingham B15 2TJ (☎ 021 414 4049)

WADE, Hon Robert Alexander Mercer; yr s of Baron Wade, DL (Life Peer, d 1988); *b* 22 May 1943; *Educ* Mill Hill, Trin Coll Camb (BA 1965, LLB 1966, MA 1969) ; *m* 1, 29 July 1967, Jennifer Jane, da of Leslie Elliott, of Grantley Grange, High Grantley, nr Ripon; 1 s (Michael Richard b 1968), 1 da (Juliet Helen b 1970); m 2, 1978, Elizabeth, da of James Lobban, of Dundee; *Career* admitted a solicitor 1968; *Style*— The Hon Robert Wade; The Old Rectory, Barwick-in-Elmet, Leeds, W Yorks

WADE, Air Chief Marshal Sir Ruthven Lowry; KCB (1974), CB (1970, DFC 1944); *b* 1920; *Educ* Cheltenham, RAF Cranwell; *Career* RAF 1939-78: Staff Offr Air HQ Malta, Cdr RAF Gaydon 1962-65, Air Exec to Dep for Nuclear Afgfrs SHAPE 1967-68, AOC 1 Gp Strike Command 1968-71, Dep Cdr RAF Germany 1971-72, vice-chief Air Staff 1973-76, Air Marshal 1974, Air Chief Marshal 1976, Chief Personell & Logistics MOD 1976-78; *Style*— Air Chief Marshal Sir Ruthven Wade, KCB, CB, DFC; White Gables, Westlington, Dinton, Aylesbury, Bucks HP17 8UR (☎ 0296 748884)

WADE-GERY, Sir Robert Lucian; KCMG (1982), CMG (1979, KCVO 1983); o s of late Prof Henry Theodore Wade-Gery, MC, FBA, and Vivian, *née* Whitfield; *b* 22 April 1929; *Educ* Winchester, New Coll Oxford; *m* 16 June 1962, Sarah, da of Adam Denzil Marris, of Hampen House, Andoversford, Glos; 1 s (William Richard b 1967), 1 da (Laura Katharine b 1965); *Career* entered For Serv 1951; served: London, Bonn, Tel Aviv and Saigon; under sec Central Policy Review Staff 1971-73; min: Madrid 1973-77, Moscow 1977-79; dep sec of the Cabinet 1979-82, high cmmr New Delhi 1982-87; exec dir Barclays de Zoete Wedd Ltd 1987-; fell All Souls Oxford 1951-73 and 1987-; *Recreations* walking, sailing, travel; *Clubs* Athenaeum; *Style*— Sir Robert Wade-Gery, KCMG, CMG, KCVO; 7 Rothwell St, London NW1A 8YH (☎ 01 722 4754); c/o BZW, Ebbgate House, 2 Swan Lane, London EC4R 3TS (☎ 01 623 2323); Church Cottage, Cold Aston, Cheltenham GL54 3BN (☎ 0451 21115)

WADE-GERY, William Alexander (Sandy); o s of William Robertson Wade-Gery, JP (d 1967), of Bushmead Priory, and Margaret Frances, *née* Dymond; descended from Rev Hugh Wade (d 1832), who assumed the additional name and arms of Gery by Royal Licence on his marriage (1792) to Hester, 3 da and co-heiress of William Gery, of Bushmead Priory (*see* Burke's Landed Gentry, 18 edn, vol II, 1969); *b* 28 Feb 1950; *Educ* Bloxham; *Career* farmer and landowner; *Style*— Mr Wade-Gery; Bushmead Priory, Bushmead, nr Colmworth, Beds; Bushmead Farm Office, nr Colmworth, Beds MK44 2LH (☎ 0230 62376, car tel 0860 627290)

WADSWORTH, Arthur John; s of John Edwin Wadsworth, of Epsom, Surrey, and Vera May, *née* Merrett; *b* 13 June 1939; *Educ* Kings Coll Sch Wimbledon; *m* 2 July 1966, Sheila, da of Charles William Blythe, of Tunbridge Wells, Kent; 1 s (Daniel b 9 Nov 1972), 2 da (Faye b 7 Aug 1970, Zoe b 5 April 1975); *Career* asst gen mangr Midland Bank Plc 1982-86 (joined 1958, with various depts/ branches in London 1958-67, appts in Leicester Nottingham London 1967-82), co sec Midland Montagu (Hldgs) Ltd 1987-, co sec and exec dir Samuel Montagu & Co Ltd 1987-, dir of London Int Fin Futures Exchange Ltd 1982-85; dir Epsom Sports Club Ltd; Freeman City of London 1979; ACIB 1964, MBIM 1974; *Recreations* playing hockey, gardening; *Clubs* Epsom Hockey; *Style*— Arthur Wadsworth, Esq; Samuel Montagu & Co Ltd, 10 Lower Thames St, London, EC3R 6AE (☎ (☎ 01 260 9777)

WADSWORTH, David Jeffrey; s of Arthur Jeffrey Wadsworth, and Gweneth Phyllis, *née* Horsman; *b* 11 Dec 1949; *Educ* Reading Sch, New Coll Oxford (MA); *m* 29 July 1972, Susan Mary, da of Eric Thomas Hardiman; *Career* CA; Peat Marwick Mitchell & Co 1971-79, ptnr Kidsons 1981- (sr mangr 1979-81); non exec dir: Columbia House Nominees Ltd 1985, Kidsons Corporate Fin Ltd 1988, Penington Ltd 1988; dir: Green and Grey Ltd 1988, Morworth Ltd 1988, Bramley Heritage Ltd 1988; tres Tring Festival Co Ltd until 1985, memb Investors in Indust Non-Exec Directors Resource; FCA, IOD; *Recreations* collecting first edition Penguin books, walking, music, gardening; *Style*— David Wadsworth, Esq; Bramley Cottage, Hastoe, Tring, Herts (☎ 044282 6208); Kidsons, Russel Sq House, 10-12 Russel Sq, London WC1B 5AE (☎ 01 436 3636, fax 01 436 6603, car 0836 766069, telex 263901)

WADSWORTH, Roger Leonard; s of Leonard Wadsworth (d 1985), and Irene Nellie, *née* Hughes; *b* 2 May 1950; *Educ* Hurstpierpoint, Kingston Poly (BA); *Career* chm and md Roger Wadsworth & Co (Hldgs) Ltd; chm: Wadsworth Electronics Ltd, Leonard Wadsworth Gp Ltd; dir: Sachs (Holdings) Ltd; *Recreations* stalking, big game hunting, shooting ; *Clubs* RAC; *Style*— Roger Wadsworth, Esq; Wadsworth Electronics Ltd, Central Avenue, East Molesey, Surrey KT8 0QB; Camusrory Estate, Mallaig, Inverness-shire

WADSWORTH, Thomas Gordon; s of Samuel Bertram Wadsworth (d 1955), and Elizabeth Jane, *née* Brown (d 1987); *b* 13 Jan 1930; *Educ* Liverpool Coll, Univs of Liverpool and Wales (MChOrth); *Career* conslt orthopaedic surgn, St Bartholomew's Hosp and Homerton Hosp London; examiner: in pathology and section chm Primary FRCS England, in pathology, surgical pathology and clinical surgery FRCS Edinburgh; corresponding memb: American Acad of Orthopaedic Surgns, American Soc for Surgery of the Hand; memb American Shoulder and Elbow Surgns, hon lectr, Med Coll of St Bartholomew's Hosp; memb cncl Br Soc for Surgery of the Hand; Freeman City of London; FB OrthA; FRCS; FRCSE; FACS; FICS; *Recreations* walking in country, classical music, travel; *Clubs* Reform; *Style*— Thomas Wadsworth, Esq; 35 Shepherd St, Mayfair, London W1Y 7LH (☎ 01 723 5785); Department of Orthopaedic Surgery, St Bartholomew's Hospital, West Smithfield, London EC1A 7BE (☎ 01 601 8888)

WADWELL, David Martin; s of George Wadwell, of 10 Virginia Beeches, Callow Hill, Virginia Water, Surrey, and Marie, *née* Pickering; *b* 12 Mar 1946; *Educ* Ipswich Sch, Southampton Univ (BSc), LSE (MSc); *m* 5 June 1971 (m dis 1978), Valerie, da of Peter Arthur Wilks; *Career* CA Ernst & Whinney 1968-72, ptnr de Zoete & Bevan Stockbrokers 1972- 86, dir Barclays de Zoete Wedd 1986-; FCA; *Recreations* sailing, travel; *Style*— David Wadwell, Esq; 7 Hippodrome Mews, Clarendom Cross, Kensington, London W11 4NN (☎ 01 229 0493); Barclays De Zoete Wedd Securities Ltd, Ebbgate House, 2 Swan Lane London EC4R 3TS (☎ 01 623 2323, fax 01 626 1879, telex 888 221)

WAEBER, Hon Mrs (Jill); *née* Taylor; da of Baron Taylor of Gryfe (Life Peer), and Isobel, *née* Wands; *b* 15 Sept 1945; *Educ* Hutcheson's Girls' GS, Glasgow Sch of Art, Jordanhill Coll of Educn; *m* 1, 1969, Dr Thomas Egli; m 2, 1976, Hans René Waeber; 1 s (Alexander b 1979), 2 da (Kirstie b 1977, Jennifer b 1980); *Career* teacher; *Style*— The Hon Mrs Waeber; Marchbachstrasse 24, 4108 Witterswil, Switzerland

WAGEMAKERS, Monique Huberdina Yvonne Maria; da of Corneluis Johannes Maria Wagemaker (d 1972), and Francisca Geertruida Maria, *née* Verbeeten; *b* 29 Sept 1951; *Educ* Brabants Conservatorium; *m* 23 Aug 1985, Aart Bouwmeester, s of Max Eric Bouwmeester, of Stuifzand, Nederland; 1 s (Sebastiaan b 8 Dec 1985), 1 da (Laura b 16 May 1988); *Career* asst dir De Nederlandse Opera Amsterdam 1976-; asst to: Götz Friedrich, Harry Kupfer, John Cox, Gian Carlo Menotti, Lotfi Mansouri, David Poutney, Dario Fo, Tito Capobianco, Michael Geliot; revival dir: The Fantasticks, Don Giovanni, La Vie Parisienne, La Fanciulla del west, Fidelio; debut as dir: Madama Butterfly 1983, Don Giovanni 1986; 1987 Rigoletto Choreographies for: La Traviata, son Giovanni, I due Foscari, Intemezzo, rodelinda la vie Parisienne, Arabella; Glyndebourne Festival Opera: asst dir and choreographer Intermezzo 1983, assoc dir and choreographer Arabella 1984 and 1985, revival dir Arabella 1989; *Recreations* photography, video; *Style*— Miss Monique Wagemakers; Amsterda, Gaaspstraat 58, 1079 VG Amsterdam (☎ 020 449 465); De Nederlandse Opera, Waterlooplein 22, 1011PG Amsterdam, Nederland (☎ 020 551 8922)

WAGGETT, Ralph Whitell; s of John Waggett, and Mary, *née* Whitell; *b* 30 Nov 1924; *Educ* Richmond Sch Yorkshire; *Career* RAF 1943-47; slr (ret); tstee: The Yorkshire Museum of Horse Drawn Carriages, The Richmondshire Museum; re-fndr first warden and present clerk of Co of Fellmongers of Richmond Yorks; Liveryman Worshipful Co of Glovers; *Books* Transcript of the Archives (1580-1980) of the Company of Mercers Grocers and Haberdashers of Richmond Yorkshire (1988); *Recreations* walking, painting, the study of local history, antiquarian book collecting; *Style*— Ralph Waggett, Esq; Hill Hse Cottage, Frenchgate, Richmond, N Yorks (☎ 0748 3000)

WAGNER, Sir Anthony Richard; KCB (1978), KCVO (1961, CVO 1953); s of Orlando Wagner (gggs of one George Wagner, godson of George I and hatter to George III. George's f Melchior was hatter to George I and George II and was 2 s of Hans Heinrich Wagner, hatter to the court of Coburg. The Wagners are of Silesian origin). Sir Anthony's sis is m to Rt Hon Sir Melford Stevenson *qv*; *b* 6 Sept 1908; *Educ* Eton, Balliol Coll Oxford (MA); *m* 26 Feb 1953, Gillian Mary Millicent, *qv*, eldest da of Maj Henry Graham (d 1970), of Micheldever, Hants; 2 s, 1 da; *Career* serv WWII War Off and Miny Town and Country Planning; Portcullis Pursuivant 1931-43, Richmond Herald 1943-61, Garter 1961-78, Clarenceux King of Arms 1978-; ed Soc of Antiquaries' Dictionary of Br Arms 1940-, sec Order of the Garter 1952-61, registrar Coll of Arms 1953-60, jt register Ct of Chivalry 1954-, genealogist Order of the Bath 1961-72 and Order of St John 1961-75, kt princ Imperial Soc of Kts Bachelor 1962-83, dir Heralds' Museum Tower of London 1978-83, pres Aldeburgh Soc 1970-83; former: memb Cncl Nat Trust, trustee Nat Portrait Gallery; hon fellow: Balliol Coll Oxford 1979, Heraldry Soc of Canada; KStJ; *Publications include* Heralds and Heraldry in the Middle Ages (1939), Heraldry in England (1946), The Records and Collections of the College of Arms (1952), English Genealogy (1960), Pedigree and Progress (1975); *Style*— Sir Anthony Wagner, KCB, KCVO, Clarenceux King of Arms; 68A Chelsea Sq, London SW3 (☎ 01 352 0934); Wyndham Cottage, Aldeburgh, Suffolk (☎ (072 885) 2596); College of Arms, Queen Victoria St, London EC4 (☎ 01 248 4300)

WAGNER, Lady; Gillian Mary Millicent; *née* Graham; eldest da of Maj Henry Archibald Roger Graham (d 1970), of Old Mill House, Micheldever, Hants, and Hon Margaret Beatrice Lopes (d 1983), 3 da of 1 Baron Roborough; *b* 25 Oct 1927; *Educ* Cheltenham Ladies' Coll, Geneva Univ (Licencée ès Sciences Morales), LSE (Dip Social Admin, PhD); *m* 26 Feb 1953, Sir Anthony Richard Wagner, KCB, KCVO, *qv*; 2 s (Roger Henry Melchior b 28 Feb 1957, Mark Anthony b 18 Dec 1958), 1 da (Lucy Elizabeth Millicent (Mrs Page) b 22 Oct 1954) ; *Career* chm: Review into Residential Care 1985-88, Barnardo 1978-84 (memb cncl 1984-), Volunteer Centre 1984-; pres IAPS 1984-; chm Felixstowe Coll 1978- 86; pres SKILL Nat Bureau for Students with Disabilities; tstee: Carnegie UK Tst, Leche Tst; Freeman of City of London; *Books* Barnardo (1977), Children of the Empire (1982), The Chocolate Conscience (1987); *Recreations* sailing, gardening, travelling; *Clubs* Aldeburgh Yacht; *Style*— Lady Wagner; 68A Chelsea Sq, London SW3 6LD (☎ 01 352 0934); Wyndham Cottage, Crespigny Rd, Aldeburgh, Suffolk

WAGNER, Maj Michael Stanley; MBE (1944); s of Capt Alfred Fenner Wagner (d 1967), and Violet Ethel, *née* Henderson; *b* 2 Nov 1917; *Educ* UCS, Rhenania Coll Neuhausen Switzerland; *m* 30 Sept 1946, Nan Elizabeth Russell, da of Robert Wilson (d 1950); 1 s (Robert Michael b 24 Sept 1947), 2 da (Margaret Anne b 7 June 1949, Patricia Jane b 4 Jan 1957); *Career* TA 1936-39, cmmnd Welch Regt 1940, WWII (Maj), served N Ireland, W Desert, POW Cyrenaica 1941, escaped 1943 and joined partisans in Italy until joined HQ 21 Army Gp 1944-45; cmd 636 Regt RA; demobilised with rank of Maj; joined Colonial Administrative Service 1946, served N Rhodesia as dist offr, dist commnr, rising to under sec and acting perm sec Zambia, ret 1968; *Recreations* golf, skiing; *Clubs* Ski of GB; *Style*— Maj Michael Wagner, MBE; Rose Cottage, Holton, Wincanton, Somerset (☎ 0963 32220)

WAGNER, Dr Nicholas Alan Giles; s of Thomas Donald Wagner, of Croydon, Surrey (d 1980), and Valerie Jacqueline Cameron Peers, *née* Kemp; *b* 17 Jan 1945; *Educ* Whitgift Sch, The Med Coll of St Bartholomew's Hosp, Univ of London (MB, BS); *m* 1, 14 Aug 1971, Patsy (m dis 1982), da of Fred Doherty-Bullock, of Worcester (d 1982); m 2, 16 April 1987, Linda, da of James Halstead, of Brentford, Middx; 1 s (Alexander b 1984); *Career* conslt: psychiatrist W Middx Univ Hosp 1978-88, mental health in elderly Herts Health Authy 1988-; *Recreations* gardening, gastronomy; *Style*— Nicholas Wagner, Esq; Dept of Mental Health of the Elderly, Cantilupe Wing, General Hosp, Hereford HR1 2PA (☎ 0432 272561)

WAGSTAFF, Ven Christopher John Harold; s of Harold Maurice Wagstaff (d 1982), of London, and Kathleen Mary, *née* Bean (d 1979); *b* 25 June 1936; *Educ* Bishops Stortford Coll, Essex Inst of Agriculture, St Davids Coll Lampeter (BA); *m* 1964, Margaret Louise, da of John Park Alan Macdonald, of Scotland; 2 s (Alasdair b 1966, Robert b 1968), 1 da (Marianne b 1972); *Career* curate All Saints Queensbury London 1963-68; vicar: St Michael Wembley 1968-72, Coleford with Staunton Gloucester 1972-82; rural dean South Forest 1975-82; archdeacon of Gloucester 1982-; Freeman City of London, Liveryman Worshipful Co of Armourers and Brasiers; *Recreations* gardening, travel; *Style*— The Ven the Archdeacon of Gloucester; Christchurch Vicarage, Montpellier, Gloucester GL1 1LB (☎ 0452 28500)

WAGSTAFF, David St John Rivers; s of John Edward Pretty Wagstaff (d 1973), and Dorothy Margaret Wagstaff, *née* McRobie (d 1980); *b* 22 June 1930; *Educ* Winchester, Trinity Coll Cambridge (MA, LLB); *m* 31 March 1970, Dorothy Elizabeth, da of Robert Carter Starkie (d 1982), of Pool-in-Wharfedale, nr Leeds; 2 da (Susan b 1971, Patricia b 1973); *Career* barr Lincoln's Inn 1954, NE circuit, rec of the Crown Court 1974; *Recreations* mountaineering; *Clubs* Alpine, Fell and Rock Climbing (Leeds); *Style*— David Wagstaff, Esq; 8 Breary Lane East, Bramhope, Leeds LS16 9BJ; 22 East Parade, Leeds 1 (☎ 0532 452702)

WAGSTAFF, Edward Malise Wynter; s of Col Henry Wynter Wagstaff, and Jean Everil, *née* Mathieson (d 1965); *b* 27 June 1930; *Educ* Wellington Coll, RMA Sandhurst, Pembroke Coll Cambridge (MA), Staff Coll Camberley; *m* 14 Dec 1957, Eva Margot, da of Fred Erik Oscar Hedelius, Kammarratsrad (Justice), Judge of the Swedish Appeal Court; 1 s (James b 1973), 2 da (Kersti b 1959, Anna b 1962); *Career* cmmnd RE 1949; served UK, Germany, Gibraltar 1950-62; seconded to Fed Regular Army, Fedn of South Arabia 1963-65; asst Mil Attaché Amman 1967-69 (Major 1962); joined FCO 1969: first sec Embassy Saigon 1973, FCO 1975, Oslo 1976, Copenhagen 1978, FCO 1981, cnsllr 1983; Gen Serv Medal; South Arabia Radfan Bar 1965; Knight, first degree, order of Dannebrog 1979 (Danish decoration); *Recreations* church work, psychotherapy, house repair; *Clubs* Travellers'; *Style*— Edward Wagstaff, Esq; c/o Lloyds Bank plc, 32 Commercial Way, Woking, Surrey GU21 1ER

WAGSTAFF, Col Henry Wynter; CSI, MC; s of Edward Wynter Wagstaff (d 1939); *b* 19 July 1890; *Educ* Woodbridge Sch, RMA Woolwich; *m* 1, 1918, Jean Everil, *née* Mathieson; 2 s; m 2, 1967, Margaret Annie, *née* Marshall; *Career* RE 1910, Col, WW I Mesopotamia, WW II India; memb Railway Bd Govt of India 1939-46; FCIT; *Recreations* reading, writing; *Style*— Col Henry Wagstaff, CSI, MC; 8 Meadow Close, Milford, Godalming, Surrey GU8 5HN (☎ 048 68 5941)

WAGSTAFFE, Michael Christopher; s of Keith Desmond Wagstaffe, of Kent, and Louisette Nita Atkinson; *b* 26 Sept 1945; *Educ* Rossall Sch, Exeter Univ (BA); *m* 5 Aug 1972, Helen Pattullo, da of Henry Stanley May, of Sussex; 1 s (Richard b 1976), 2 da (Anna b 1979, Caroline b 1980); *Career* tea planter 1965-68; schoolmaster: Clifton Coll 1972-75, Dulwich Coll 1975-80 master, cricket, Byanston Sch 1980- housemaster; cricket: Oxford v Cambridge 1972, Devon 1972-80, Dorset 1980-84 (Capt); *Recreations* cricket, rugby, tennis, squash; *Clubs* Arabs, Oxford Univ, Devon CCC, Dorset CCC (Capt); *Style*— Michael C Wagstaffe, Esq; The Old Parsonage, Winterborne, Kingston, nr Blandford, Dorset DT11 9BQ; Bryanston Sch, Blandford, Dorset (☎ 0929 471220)

WAIN, John Barrington; CBE (1984); s of Arnold A Wain, and Anne, *née* Turner (d 1963); *b* 14 Mar 1925; *Educ* The High Sch Newcastle-under-Lyme, St John's Coll Oxford (BA,MA); *m* 1, 1947 (m dis 1956), Marianne da, of Julius Urmston; m 2, 1960, Eirian (d 1988), da of TE James; 3 s (William Brunswick b 1960, Ianto Samuel b 1962, Tobias Hamnet b 1966); m 3, Patricia Anne, da of R Dunn; *Career* Fereday fell St John's Coll Oxford 1946-49, lectr eng lit reading Univ 1949-55, prof of poetry Oxford Univ 1973-78, lectr at various univs in Eng, USA, Fr, Greece, India, Scandinavia; Hon D Litt: Loughborough Univ 1984, Keele 1984; *Books* publications incl: fiction- Hurry on Down (1953), The Smaller Sky (1967), A Winter in the Hills (1970), Young Shoulders (Whitbread Award 1982), Where the Rivers Meet (1988), poetry- Poems 1947-79 (1963), Memoirs - Dear Shadows (1986), biography - Samuel Johnson (James Tait Black Prize, William Heinemann Award 1974), Memoirs Dear Shadows (1987); *Recreations* walking, travelling by train especially in France; *Style*— John Wain, Esq, CBE

WAIN, Roger Henry Ashley; s of Ernest Wain (decd), and Muriel Maimie Wain (decd), of Caton, Lancashire; *b* 28 May 1938; *Educ* Lancaster Royal GS, St Peter's Coll Oxford (MA); *m* 1965, Rosalind, da of John Laycock of Moorgarth, Lancaster (decd); 1 s, 2 da (twins); *Career* 2 Lt The Lancashire Regt; dir and chief exec for GB The Imperial Life Assurance Co of Canada 1981-; dir: Abercorn Gen Investmts Ltd, Castlemere Properties Ltd (chm), Chesterfield Properties PLC, Centaur Communications Ltd, Impco Properties (GB) Ltd, Imperial Life (UK) Ltd (md), Invicta Investmt Co Ltd, Laurentian Financial Services Ltd (chm), Property Investmt & Finance Ltd; pres Canada/UK Chamber of Commerce; chm: Life Insurance Mgmnt and Research Assoc UK Advsy Ctee, Laurentian Investmt Mgmnt Ltd, Laurentian Unit Tst Mgmnt Ltd, British Empire Securities and Gen Tst Ltd Ch; dep chm Trident Life Ltd; hon fell Life Insurance Assoc 1983 & National Playbus Assoc; dir Foundation for Canadian Studies; *Recreations* hunting, tennis, travel, shooting, skiing; *Clubs* Buck's; *Style*— Roger Wain, Esq; 15 Lansdowne Walk, London W11 3AH (☎ 01 727 4485)

WAINE, Peter Edward; s of Dr Theodore Edward Waine, of Bilton, Rugby, Warwickshire, and Mary Florence, *née* Goodson; *b* 27 June 1949; *Educ* Bilton Grange, Worksop Coll, Bradford Univ (BSc); *m* 21 June 1973, Stefanie Dale (niece of C P Snow, novelist), da of Philip Albert Snow, OBE, of Gables, Station Rd, Angmering, Sussex; 1 da (Philippa Wigmore b 21 May 1981); *Career* personnel mangr: GEC 1970-74, Cape Industs 1974-79, Coopers & Lybrand 1979-83; dir: CBI 1983-88, Blue Arrow 1988-, W R Royle & Sons (non-exec) 1988-; chm Welwyn Garden City Soc; memb: cncl Euro Business Sch, English Speaking Union current affairs ctee, ctee Br Atlantic; parly candidate (Cons) Nottingham North 1979, Nat vice chm The Bow Gp 1972 (chm Birmingham Gp 1971), dist cncllr Rugby 1973-77; Freeman: City of London 1978, Worshipful Co of Carmen; FBIM (former memb cncl); *Publications* Spring Cleaning Britain (1974), Withering Heights (1976), Weekly Columnist under pseudonym for London Newspaper (1984-87); *Recreations* gardening, walking, tennis; *Clubs* MCC, ESU; *Style*— Peter Waine, Esq; West House, Digswell Place, Welwyn Garden City, Herts (☎ 0707 330 714); Blue Arrow plc, 31 Worship St, London E1 (☎ 01 638 7788, fax 01 374 8412)

WAINWRIGHT, (Harold) Anthony; s of Herbert Wainwright (d 1945), of Prenton, Ches, and Louise, *née* Stewart; *b* 30 Dec 1919; *Educ* Birkenhead Sch; *m* 29 March 1947, (Frances) Jean, da of Edgar Warren (d 1950), of Heswall, Wirral; 2 s (Nicholas b 1948, Michael b 1957), 2 da (Sarah b 1950, Louise b 1960); *Career* RA 1940-45, Lt 1941, Capt 1943, Maj 1945, served 28 LAA Regt (RA) with 14 Army in Burma and Assam 1942-45; chm Boodle and Dunthorne Ltd 1984- (md 1945-84), Hon Consul of Thailand 1965, chm Nat Jewellers Assoc (JIC) 1971-75, Br rep De Beers Euro Diamond Cncl 1972-75; govr Blue Coat Sch 1974-, sec Birkenhead Boys Club, assoc on ctees of other Boys Clubs; Freeman: Worshipful Co of Goldsmiths 1966, City of London 1966; *Recreations* golf, game shooting, gardening; *Clubs* Royal Liverpool GC (Hoylake), Athenaeum (Liverpool); *Style*— Anthony Wainwright, Esq; Boodle & Dunthorne Ltd, Boodles House, Lord St, Liverpool L2 9SQ (☎ 051 227 2525, fax 051 255 1070)

WAINWRIGHT, Edgar Worthington; s of John Andrew Worthington Wainwright, of Twyford, Winchester, Hants, and Kathleen, *née* Gillibiand; *b* 17 Mar 1943; *Educ* Westminster; *m* 14 June 1969, Jill Rosamond, da of Capt Anthony Wilmott Adams, MC; 1 s (Timothy John Alexander Worthington b 26 Sept 1978), 2 da (Amanda Jane b 9 Sept 1970, Lucianne Clare b 2 Sept 1972); *Career* chartered shipbroker and freight forwarder; dir Wainwright Bros & Co Ltd and assoc cos 1969-; FICS 1972, FIFF 1975; *Recreations* sailing; *Clubs* Baltic Exchange, Royal Southampton YC, Bosham SC; *Style*— Edgar Wainwright, Esq; Crofton, Cheriton Rd, Winchester, Hants; Wainwright Bros & Co Ltd, Bowling Green House, Orchard Place, Southampton Hants (☎ 0703 223671, fax 0703 330880, telex 47 620)

WAINWRIGHT, John Andrew Worthington; s of Edgar Worthington Wainwright (d 1941), and Alice Maude, *née* La Mude (d 1979); *b* 11 Jan 1918; *Educ* Heath Mount Sch Hampstead, Westminster Sch; *m* 1, 1939 (m dis 1945), Dathleen, *née* Gillibrand; 1 s (Edgar Worthington, 1 da (Angela); m 2, 1948, Betty Margaret, *née* Schluter; 1 s (Robert Edward Worthington); *Career* dir: Br Transit Ltd, H Chaplin & Co Ltd, General Transit Services Ltd, Maccabe-Bower Shipping Ltd, Oscar Harris Son & Co Ltd, Packing and Warehousing Ltd, Bussey Freight Service Ltd, Wainwright Bros & Co Ltd; FICS, FInstFF; Liveryman Worshipful Company of Shipwrights; *Recreations* gardening, reading, travelling, motoring; *Clubs* Royal Southampton Yacht; *Style*— John Wainwright, Esq; Knighton, Twyford, nr Winchester, Hants SO21 1QU; Bowling Green House, 1 Orchard Place, Southampton, Hants SO1 1BR

WAINWRIGHT, Richard Scurrah; s of H S Wainwright, OBE (d 1968), of Leeds; *b* 11 April 1918; *Educ* Shrewsbury, Clare Coll Cambridge (open scholar); *m* 1948, Joyce Mary da of Arthur Hollis of Leeds; *Career* Friends Ambulance Unit (NW Europe) 1939-46; sometime: ptnr Peat, Marwick Mitchell & Co, Chartered Accountants, pres Leeds-Bradford Soc of Chartered Accountants 1966; contested (Lib) Colne Valley: 1959, 1963 by-election, 1964, gained and held same 1966-70 and MP Colne Valley 1974-87; chm Lib Pty Research Dept 1968-70, chm Lib Pty 1970-72; former Lib spokesman on: the economy 1979-85, employment 1985-87, trade and industry; memb select ctee on Treasy 1985-87; *Style*— Richard Wainwright Esq, MP; The Heath, Adel, Leeds LS16 8EG (☎ 0532 673938)

WAINWRIGHT, Robert Everard (Robin); CMG (1959); s of Dr George Bertram Wainwright, OBE, MB (d 1950), and Florence Maud, *née* Everard; *b* 24 June 1913; *Educ* Marlborough Coll, Trinity Coll Cambridge (BA); *m* 1939, Bridget Doris, da of Lt Cdr K B Wiliams, RN (d 1926); 2 s (Ian, Christopher); *Career* HMOCS Kenya 1935-63, prov cmmr 1953-59, IDC 1959, chief cmmr 1960-63, admin Turks & Caicos Islands WI 1966-71; *Recreations* sailing, cabinet making; *Clubs* Mombasa; *Style*—

Robin Wainwright, Esq, CMG; Wagoner's Cottage, Cann Common, Shaftesbury, Dorset SP7 0DL (☎ 0747 2877)

WAINWRIGHT, Rear-Adm Rupert Charles Purchas; CB (1966), DSC (1943); s of Lt-Cdr Oswald Johnson Wainwright, RN (ka 1918), and Sybil, *née* Purchas (d 1975); *b* 16 Oct 1913; *Educ* RNC Dartmouth; *m* 1937, Patricia Mary Helen, da of Col Frederick Herbert Blackwood, DSO (d 1926) and Nora, *née* Widdup (d 1941); 2 s (Michael, Richard), 2 da (Rosemary Pockley, Sara Raynes); *Career* joined RN 1927, served WW II (HMS Cardiff, Scylla, Jamaica), cmd HM ships and estabs (Actaeon, Tintagel Castle, Zephyr, Cambridge) 1952-57, Capt 1955, COS S Atlantic & S America Station 1958-60, dir Naval Recruiting 1960-62, Cdre Naval Drafting 1962-64, ADC to HM The Queen 1964, Rear Adm 1965, Vice Naval Dep to SACEUR 1965-67, ret 1967; memb: Redditch Devpt Corpn 1968-77, Stratford-upon-Avon Dist Cncl 1973-86 (vice-chm 1983-84, chm 1984-85), Assoc of Dist Cncls 1976-83; vice-pres Keep Britain Tidy Gp and Beautiful Britain Campaign; *Recreations* hockey (vice-pres Eng Hockey Assoc), swimming (RN), tennis; *Clubs* Royal Navy; *Style*— Rear Adm Rupert Wainwright, CB, DSC, RN; Regency Cottage, 30 Maidenhead Rd, Stratford-upon-Avon, Warwicks (☎ 0789 293 574)

WAINWRIGHT, Sam; CBE (1982); *Educ* LSE; *Career* dep City ed Glasgow Herald 1952, md Rea Bros (merchant bankers) until 1977, md Nat Girobank 1977-87, dep chm Post Office Bd 1981-85, dir BICC plc 1985-, chm Manders (Hldgs) plc 1986-87; memb of Monopolies and Mergers Cmmn 1985-; *Style*— Sam Wainwright, Esq, CBE; 6 Heath Close, London NW11 7DX (☎ 01 455 4448)

WAITE, Hon Mr Justice; Hon Sir John Douglas Waite; QC (1975); s of Archibald Waite; *b* 3 July 1932; *Educ* Sherborne, CCC Cambridge; *m* 1966, Julia Mary, da of Joseph Tangye; 3 s and 2 step s; *Career* 2 Lt RA 1951-52; barr Gray's Inn 1956, memb Gen Cncl Bar 1968-69, bencher 1981, High Ct Judge 1982-, pres Employment Appeal Tribunal 1983-85; kt 1982; *Style*— The Hon Sir John Waite; Royal Courts of Justice, Strand, London WC2A 2LL (☎ 01 405 7641)

WAITE, Jonathan Gilbert Stokes; s of Capt Henry David Stokes Waite, of 8 Priory Close, Aldwick Bay, West Sussex, and Joan Winifred, *née* Paull; *b* 15 Feb 1956; *Educ* Scaitcliffe Sch Surrey, Sherborne, Trinity Coll Cambridge (MA); *Career* called to the bar Inner Temple 1978, practised in common Law SE Circuit 1978-; hon sec Bar Golfing Soc; *Recreations* golf, skiing, the turf; *Clubs* Woking GC; *Style*— Jonathan Waite, Esq; 1 Paper Buildings, Temple, London EC4Y 7EP (☎ 01 583 7355, fax 01 353 2144)

WAKE, Lady Doune Mabell; *née* Ogilvy; da of 13 Earl of Airlie, DL; *b* 13 August 1953; *m* 1977, Hereward Charles, s and h of Sir Hereward Wake, 14 Bt; 1 s; *Style*— Lady Doune Wake; The Stables, Courteenhall, Northants

WAKE, Sir Hereward; 14 Bt (E 1621), of Clevedon, Somerset, MC (1942), DL (Northants 1955); s of Maj-Gen Sir Hereward Wake, 13 Bt, CB, CMG, DSO, JP, DL (d 1963, himself tenth in descent from the 1 Bt; the latter was in turn fifteenth in descent from Hugh Wac or Wake, feudal Baron by tenure of Bourne and Deeping *temp* King Stephen; this family's descent from Hereward the Wake, albeit in the female line, seems probable although not proven); *b* 7 Oct 1916; *Educ* Eton, RMC; *m* 1952, Julia Rosemary, JP, da of Capt Geoffrey W M Lees, of Falcutt House, nr Brackley, Northants; 1 s, 3 da; *Heir* s, Hereward Charles, b 22 Nov 1952; *Career* served 1937-46 with 1, 2, 7 and 9 Bns 60 Rifles (Burma Egypt, N Africa, NW Europe and Greece), Maj, ret 1947; High Sheriff Northants 1955; *Style*— Sir Hereward Wake, Bt, MC, DL; Courteenhall, Northampton (☎ 0604 204)

WAKE-WALKER, Lady Anne; *née* Spencer; only da of 7 Earl Spencer, TD (d 1975), and Lady Cynthia, *née* Hamilton, DCVO, OBE, da of 3 Duke of Abercorn; aunt of HRH The Princess of Wales; *b* 4 August 1920; *m* 1944, Capt Christopher Wake-Walker, DL, RN, *qv*; 3 s, 2 da; *Career* served WW II, Third Offr WRNS; *Style*— Lady Anne Wake-Walker; East Bergholt Lodge, Suffolk (via Colchester) CO7 6QU (☎ 0206 298278)

WAKE-WALKER, Capt Christopher Baldwin Hughes; DL (Suffolk 1983); assumed additional surname of Hughes; s of Adm Sir (William) Frederic Wake Walker, KCB, CBE (d 1945), Third Sea Lord and Controller of the Navy 1943-45, and Muriel Elsie (d 1963), only da of Sir Collingwood Hughes, 10 Bt; *b* 16 May 1920; *Educ* RNC Dartmouth; *m* 1944, Lady Anne, *qv*, da of The Earl Spencer (d 1975); 3 s, 2 da; *Career* served RN, WW II, Cdr RNC Greenwich 1959-61, Naval Attaché Paris 1962-64, Capt Dartmouth Training Sqdn 1964-66, Dir Naval Signals 1966-68, ret 1968; High Sheriff Suffolk 1985; *Recreations* gardening; *Clubs* Army & Navy; *Style*— Capt Christopher Wake-Walker, DL, RN; East Bergholt Lodge, Suffolk (via Colchester) CO7 6QU (☎ 0206 298278)

WAKE-WALKER, David Christopher; s of Capt Christopher Baldwin Hughes Wake-Walker, RN, and Lady Anne, da of 7 Earl Spencer; 1 cous to HRH The Princess of Wales; *b* 11 Mar 1947; *Educ* Winchester, St Andrews Univ; *m* 1979, Jennifer Rosemary, only da of Capt Patrick Vaulkhard, of 4 The Terrace, Snape, Suffolk; 2 s (Frederic b 1981, Nicholas b 1985); *Career* dir Kleinwort Benson Ltd 1980, md Kleinwort Benson (Hong Kong) Ltd 1983-86; *Clubs* Wanderers, Aldeburgh Yacht, Hong Kong, Shek O Country, Hurlingham; *Style*— David Wake-Walker Esq; 82 Royal Hill, London SE10 8RT, (☎ 01 691 4666); 20 Fenchurch St, London EC3P 3DB, (☎ 01 623 8000)

WAKEFIELD, 10 Bishop of 1985-; Rt Rev David Michael Hope; patron of 74 livings and the archdeaconries and canonries in his cathedral; s of Jack Hope, by his w Florence; *b* 14 April 1940; *Educ* Queen Elizabeth GS, Wakefield, Nottingham Univ (BA), Linacre House Oxford (D PHIL), St Stephens House Oxford; *Career* princ St Stephens Hse Oxford 1974-82; Vicar of All Saints Margaret St London 1982-85; *Recreations* theatre, walking, travel; *Style*— The Rt Rev the Lord Bishop of Wakefield; Bishop's Lodge, Woodthorpe Lane, Wakefield, W Yorks (☎ 0924 255349)

WAKEFIELD, Derek John; CB (1982); s of Archibald John Thomas Wakefield (d 1971), and Evelyn Bessie, *née* Goddard (d 1971); *b* 21 Jan 1922; *Educ* The Commonweal Sch; *m* 1951, Audrey Ellen, da of Johnathan Smith (d 1961); 1 da (Isobel); *Career* Lt Royal Pioneer Corps 1942-47, served in N Africa, Italy and ME; Air Miny 1939-42 and 1947-52; GCHQ 1952-82 (under sec 1978-82); govr Barnwood Ho Tst Gloucester 1973-; memb Airship Assoc; *Recreations* airships; *Clubs* Naval and Military; *Style*— Derek Wakefield, Esq, CB; Dunhurst, Bay Lane, Gillingham, Dorset SP8 4ER (☎ 07476 2932)

WAKEFIELD, Gerald Hugo Cropper (Hady); yr s of Sir Edward Birkbeck Wakefield, 1 Bt, CIE (d 1969), and (Constance) Lalage, *née* Thompson; *b* 15 Sept 1938; *Educ* Eton, Trinity Coll Cambridge (MA); *m* 4 Dec 1971, Victoria Rose, da of Maj Cecil Henry Feilden; 1 s (Edward Cecil b 7 March 1973); *Career* Nat Serv Lt 12 Royal Lancers 1957; memb of Lloyd's; joined Joseph W Hobbs & Co 1961, Anderson Finch Villiers (Insur) Ltd 1963, C T Bowring & Co 1968 (dir 1983-); dir CTB (Insur) Ltd 1972; chm CTB Reinsurance Ltd 1988-; *Recreations* skiing, shooting, fishing; *Clubs* White's; Bramdean House, Alresford, Hants; C T Bowring Reinsurance Ltd, Bowring Building, Tower Place, London EC3 (☎ 01 283 3100; fax, 01 929 2705; telex 882 191)

WAKEFIELD, Sir (Edward) Humphry (Tyrrell); 2 Bt (UK 1962), of Kendal, Co Westmorland; s of Sir Edward Birkbeck Wakefield, 1 Bt, CIE (d 1969, himself yr bro of 1 Baron Wakefield of Kendal); *b* 11 July 1936; *Educ* Gordonstoun and Trinity Coll Cambridge (MA); *m* 1, 1960, Priscilla (m dis 1964), da of (Oliver) Robin Bagot; m 2, 1966, Hon Elizabeth Sophia Sidney (m dis 1971), da of 1 Viscount de L'Isle, KG, VC, GCMG, GCVO, PC (d 1973); 1 s; m 3, 1974, Hon Katherine Mary Alice Baring, da of 1 Baron Howick of Glendale, GCMG, KCVO (d 1973); 1 s (and 1 s decd), 1 da; *Heir* s, Maximilian Edward Vereker Wakefield b 1977; *Career* Capt 10 Royal Hussars; fndr Stately Homes Collection, exec vice-pres Mallett America Ltd 1970-75 and former dir Mallett & Son (Antiques) Ltd; chm: Tyrrell & Moore Ltd, Sir Humphry Wakefield & Ptnrs Ltd; dir: Spoleto Festival, Tree of Life Fndn (a UK charity); memb Standing Cncl Baronetage; awarded Freedom of City of Kansas, hon citizen of City of: Houston and New Orleans (and also Hon Col in Louisiana); *Articles* on antique furniture and architecture; *Clubs* Harlequins, Cavalry and Guards, Turf; *Style*— Sir Humphry Wakefield, Bt; Chillingham Castle, Alnwick, Northumberland; c/o Barclays Bank, St James' St, Derby

WAKEFIELD, Hon Lady; Hon Katherine Mary; *née* Baring; da of 1 Baron Howick of Glendale, KG, GCMG, KCVO (d 1973); *b* 1936; *m* 1974, as his 3 wife, Sir (Edward) Humphry Tyrrell Wakefield, 2 Bt; *Style*— The Hon Lady Wakefield

WAKEFIELD, Dowager Lady; (Constance) Lalage; da of Sir John Perronet Thompson, KCSI, KCIE; *b* 2 Oct 1906; *m* 1929, Sir Edward Wakefield, 1 Bt, CIE (d 1969); *Style*— Dowager Lady Wakefield; 13 St Mary Abbots Terrace, W 14 8NX (☎ 01 602 3042)

WAKEFIELD, Sir Peter George Arthur; KBE (1977), CMG (1973); s of John Bunting Wakefield; *b* 13 May 1922; *Educ* Cranleigh Sch, Corpus Christi Coll Oxford; *m* 1951, Felicity Maurice-Jones; 4 s, 1 da; *Career* RA 1942-47, Mil Govt Eritrea 1946-47; Hulton Press 1947-49; joined Dip Serv 1949, ME Staff Coll for Arab Studies, 2 sec Amman, 1 sec: Nicosia, Cairo; Admin Staff Coll Henley; 1 sec, commercial: Vienna, Tokyo; consul-gen and cnsllr Benghazi 1966-69; Tokyo: econ and commercial cnsllr 1970-72, min 1973; seconded BOTB as Japanese mkt special advsr 1973-75; ambass: Lebanon 1975-78, Belgium 1979-82, ret; dir Nat Art Collections Fund 1982-; *Clubs* Travellers'; *Style*— Sir Peter Wakefield, KBE, CMG; Lincoln House, Montpelier Row, Twickenham, Middx TW1 2NQ (☎ 01 892 6390); La Molineta, Frigiliana, nr Malaga, Spain; National Art Collections Fund, 20 John Islip St, London SW1P 2LL (☎ 01 821 0404)

WAKEFORD, Air Marshal Sir Richard Gordon; KCB (1976), LVO (1961), OBE (1958), AFC (1952); s of Charles Edward Augustus Wakeford; *b* 20 April 1922; *Educ* Kelly Coll; *m* 1948, Anne Butler; 2 s, 1 da (and 1 da decd); *Career* served RAF 1941-78, Cdr The Queen's Flight 1958-61, Air Offr Scotland and NI 1970-72, dir Service Intelligence MOD 1972-73, ANZUK Force cdr Singapore 1974-75, dep chief Def Staff MOD (Intelligence) 1975-78; dir RAF Benevolent Fund Scotland 1978-, vice-chm (air) Lowland TA & VRA; tstee McRoberts Tsts, (chm 1982-); dir: Thistle Fndn, Cromar Nominees; cmmr Queen Victoria Sch Dunblane; OStJ 1981; C St J 1986; *Style*— Air Marshal Sir Richard Wakeford, KCB LVO, OBE, AFC; Earlston House, Forgandenny, Perth (☎ 073 881 2392)

WAKEHAM, Bryan Redvers James; s of Stanley Redvers Wakeham (d 1971), and Alice Rose, *née* Taylor (d 1979); *b* 9 April 1929; *Educ* Essex Co Sch Leyton; *m* 11 Sept 1954, Patricia Claire, da of Arthur St Clair-Marston (d 1959); 1 da (Hilary Clair (Mrs Rhodri Huw Williams) b 14 Dec 1960); *Career* Nat Serv LG 1947-49; Thomas Stephens & Sons (Lloyds broker) 1943-: dir 1961 (co merged into Baindawes 1969), md 1971, resigned 1979; dir Leslie & Godwin Marine, Richard Wood Int Ltd Tampa Florida, Wake Forest Univ Winston Salem N Carolina; Freeman City of London 1981, Liveryman Worshipful Co of Poulters 1981; *Recreations* swimming, gardening, cricket; *Clubs* City of London, MCC; *Style*— Bryan Wakeham, Esq; Windrush, High Trees Rd, Reigate, Surrey, RH2 7EJ (☎ 07372 44696); Leslie & Godwin Ltd, 6 Braham St, London E1 8ED (☎ 01 480 7200, fax 01 480 7450, telex 8950221)

WAKEHAM, Rt Hon John; PC (1983), JP (Inner London 1972), MP (Cons Colchester South and Maldon 1983-); s of Maj Walter John Wakeham (d 1965), of Godalming; *b* 22 June 1932; *Educ* Charterhouse; *m* 1, 1965, Anne Roberta Bailey (d 1984, in IRA bomb blast at Brighton), 2 s; m 2, 1985, Alison Bridget, MBE, da of Venerable Edwin J G Ward, of Dorset, 1 s; *Career* CA: memb of Lloyd's, contested (C): Coventry East 1966, Putney Wandsworth 1970; former sec Cons Small Businesses Ctee, govt whip 1979, Ld Cmmr of the Treasy 1981, under sec of state Indust 1981-82, min state Treasy 1982-1983, parly sec to the Treasy and Chief Whip 1983-87, Lord Privy Seal and Ldr of House of Commons 1987-88, Lord Pres of the Cncl and Ldr of House of Commons 1988-; *Recreations* sailing (ketch 'Tias Dancer'), farming, reading; *Clubs* Royal Yacht Squadron, Banks, Carlton, St Stephen's; *Style*— The Rt Hon John Wakeham JP, MP; House of Commons, London SW1A 0AA

WAKEHURST, 3 Baron (UK 1934); (John) Christopher Loder; s of 2 Baron Wakehurst, KG, KCMG (d 1970). and Margaret, Lady Wakehurst, DBE, *qv* ; *b* 23 Sept 1925; *Educ* Eton, King's Sch Sydney, Trinity Coll Cambridge (MA, LLB); *m* 1, 27 Oct 1956, Ingeborg (d 1977), da of Walter Krumbholz-Hess; 1 s, 1 da; m 2, 10 Sept 1983, (Francine) Brigid, da of William Noble, of Cirencester, Glos; *Heir* s, Hon Timothy Loder; *Career* serv WWII RANVR and RNVR; barr 1950; chm: Anglo & Overseas Tst plc, The Overseas Investmt Tst plc, Philadelphia Nat Ltd; dep chm London and Manchester Gp plc; CStJ; *Clubs* City of London, Chelsea Arts; *Style*— The Rt Hon the Lord Wakehurst; 26 Wakehurst Road, London SW11 6BY (☎ 01 223 9410); c/o London and Manchester Gp plc, Eldon House, Eldon Street, London EC2M 7LB (☎ 01 247 2000; fax, 01 247 2859)

WAKEHURST, Margaret, Baroness; Dame Margaret; DBE (1965); 6 da of Sir Charles Tennant, 1 Bt, MP, JP, DL, by his 2 w Marguerite; half sis of Margot Asquith and 1 Baron Glenconner; *b* 4 Nov 1899; *m* 1920, 2 Baron Wakehurst, KG, KCMG (d 1970); 3 s, 1 da; *Career* GStJ; Hon LLD Belfast; *Style*— Rt Hon Margaret, Lady

Wakehurst DBE; 31 Lennox Gdns, SW1 (☎ 01 589 0956)

WAKELEY, Sir John Cecil Nicholson; 2 Bt (UK 1952), of Liss, Co Southampton; s of Sir Cecil Pembrey Grey Wakeley, 1 Bt, KBE, CB, FRCS (d 1979), and Elizabeth Muriel, *née* Nicholson-Smith; *b* 27 August 1926; *Educ* Canford, London Univ (MB BS), FRCS Eng FACS; *m* 10 April 1954, June, o da of Donald Frank Leney; 2 s, 1 da; *Heir* s, Nicholas Jeremy Wakeley b 17 Oct 1957; *Career* former chief inspr City of London Special Constabulary; sr consulting surgn W Cheshire Gp of Hosps; memb: Liverpool Regional Hosp Bd, Mersey Regnl Health Authy, cncl Royal Coll of Surgns of Eng; conslt advsr (civilian) to RAF; CStJ 1957; *Recreations* photography, music; *Style—* Sir John Wakeley, Bt; Mickle Lodge, Mickle Trafford, Chester CH2 4EB (☎ 0244 300316)

WAKELEY, Dr Richard Michael; s of Sir Cecil Wakeley (d 1979), and Dr Elizabeth Muriel, *née* Nicholson-Smith (d 1985); *b* 21 Jan 1933; *Educ* Winchester, King's Coll London (MB, BS); *Career* house surgn King's Coll Hosp 1958, actor 1960-66, lit agent 1968-; Freeman City of London 1956; memb City Co of Barber Surgns, Worshipful Soc of Apothecaries; *Recreations* music, tennis; *Style—* Dr Richard Wakeley; 1 Wordsworth Mansions, Queens Club Gdns, W14 9TE (☎ 01 385 0908); Coves Cottage, St Peters, Broadstairs, Kent CT10 2TH; Peters Fraser & Dunlop, 5th floor, The Chambers, Chelsea Harbour, Lots Rd, London SW10 0XF (☎ 01 376 7676, fax 01 352 7356)

WAKELING, Rt Rev (John) Denis; MC (1945); s of Rev John Lucas Wakeling (d 1939), and Mary Louisa, *née* Glover (d 1923); *b* 12 Dec 1918; *Educ* Dean Close Sch Cheltenham, St Catharine's Coll Cambridge (MA), Ridley Hall Cambridge; *m* 4 April 1941, Josephine Margaret, da of Benjamin Charles Broomhall, FRCS (d 1961); 3 s (Antony James b 1943, (John) Gerald b 1949, (John) Jeremy b 1954); *Career* Actg Maj Royal Marines 1939-45; clerk in Holy Orders; ordained: deacon 1947, priest 1948; asst curate Barwell Leics 1947-50; chaplain Clare Coll Cambridge and Cambridge Pastorate 1950-52; vicar Emmanuel Plymouth 1952-59; prebendary Exeter Cathedral 1957 and prebendary emeritus 1959; vicar Barking Essex 1959-65; archdeacon of West Ham 1965-70; Bishop of Southwell 1970-85, entered House of Lords 1974; Hon DD Nottingham Univ 1985; *Recreations* walking, camping, gardening, hockey, cricket, classical music; *Clubs* Hawks (Cambridge); *Style—* The Rt Rev Denis Wakeling, MC; The Maples, The Avenue, Porton, Salisbury, Wilts SP4 0NT

WAKEMAN, Sir (Offley) David; 5 Bt (UK 1828), of Perdiswell Hall, Worcestershire; s of Sir Offley Wakeman, 4 Bt, CBE (d 1975); *b* 6 Mar 1922; *Educ* Canford; *m* 16 Nov 1946, Pamela Rose Arabella, o da of late Lt-Col Cecil Hunter Little, DSO, MBE; *Heir* half-bro Edward Offley Bertram Wakeman, b 31 July 1934; *Career* formerly employed by Herefordshire War Agricultural Exec Ctee; *Clubs* Lansdowne, Shropshire; *Style—* Sir David Wakeman, Bt; Peverey House, Bomere Heath, Shrewsbury, Salop (☎ 0743 850561)

WAKERLEY, (John) Charles; OBE (1974); s of Charles William Wakerley (d 1978), of Welton, nr Lincoln, and Gladys McLennan, *née* Skelton (d 1986); *b* 18 Jan 1936; *Educ* Lincoln Sch, Nottingham Univ (LLB); *m* 1, 1958 (m dis 1987) Peggy, da of late George Hayward of Lincoln; m2, 1987. Diana Louise Seton Adams, da of Fenmore Roger Seton of N Haven, Conn, USA (pres Rehabilitation Int); 2 step s (Christopher Adams b 1969, James Adams b 1971); *Career* with Army Legal serv 1960-74 (asst dir Army Legal Serv HQ NI 1972-74, ret as Lt-Col 1974); called to The Bar Gray's Inn 1960; currently legal dir and sec Int Divn Beecham Pharmaceuticals (joined 1974); admitted NY Bar 1982; *Recreations* gardening, american civil war; *Clubs* IOD; *Style—* Charles Wakerley, Esq, OBE; Beecham Pharmaceuticals, Beecham House, Great West Road, Brentford, Middlesex, TW8 9BD (☎ 01 560 5151)

WAKERLEY, Richard MacLennon; QC (1982); s of Charles William Wakerley (d 1978), and Gladys MacLennon Wakerley, *née* Skelton (d 1986), of Lincoln; *b* 7 June 1942; *Educ* De Aston Sch Market Rasen, Emmanuel Coll Cambridge (MA); *m* 1966, Marian Heather, da of Stanley William Dawson, of Lincoln; 2 s (Paul b 1968, Simon b 1971), 2 da (Helen b 1966, Emma b 1973); *Career* barr Gray's Inn 1965; rec Crown Ct 1982-; dep ldr Midland and and Oxford Circuit 1989-; *Recreations* bridge, gardening, theatre; *Style—* Richard Wakerley, Esq, QC; Croft House, Grendon, Atherstone, Warwickshire (☎ 0827 712 329); 4 Fountain Ct, Steelhouse Lane, Birmingham (☎ 021 236 3476); 2 Dr Johnson's Buildings, Temple, London (☎ 01 353 4197)

WAKLEY, His Hon Judge Bertram Joseph; MBE (1945); s of Maj Bertram Joseph Wakley (d 1917), and Hon Dorothy Henrietta, *née* Hamilton (d 1951); *b* 7 July 1917; *Educ* Wellington, Christ Church Oxford (MA); *m* 30 July 1953, Alice Margaret, da of Archibald McErvel Lorimer (d 1939), of Linden, 39 Osborne Park, Belfast, NI; *Career* Maj S Lancashire Reg; serv: N Africa, Italy Greece 1939-46 (despatches); barr Gray's Inn 1948; Circuit judge 1973-; Diocesan l reader Southwark 1977; *Books* History of the Wimbledon Cricket Club (1954), Bradman the Great (1959), Classic Centuries (1964); *Recreations* golf, cricket; *Clubs* Carlton, Roehampton, MCC; *Style—* His Hon Judge Bertram Wakley, MBE; Hamilton House, Kingston Hill, Surrey KT2 7LX (☎ 01 546 9961)

WALDEGRAVE, 12 Earl (GB 1729); Sir Geoffrey Noel Waldegrave; 16 Bt (E 1643), of Hever Castle, Co Kent; KG (1971), GCVO (1976), TD, DL (Somerset 1951); also Baron Waldegrave (E 1686) and Viscount Chewton (GB 1729); s of 11 Earl Waldegrave (d 1936; descended from Sir Richard Walgrave, Speaker of the House of Commons *temp* Richard II), and Anne, da of Rev William Pollexfen Bastard, of Buckland Court, Ashburton, and Kitley, Yealmpton, Devon ; *b* 21 Nov 1905; *Educ* Winchester, Trinity Coll Cambridge (BA); *m* 1930, Mary, da of Lt-Col Arthur Grenfell, DSO; 2 s, 5 da ; *Heir* s, Viscount Chewton; *Career* memb Prince's Cncl Duchy of Cornwall 1951-58 and 1965-76; Lord Warden of the Stannaries 1965-76; Vice-Lt Somerset 1955-60; jt parly sec Miny Ag and Fish 1958-62; chm Forestry Cmmn 1963-65; Offr Legion of Merit (US); *Clubs* Travellers', Farmers'; *Style—* Rt Hon Earl Waldegrave, KG, GCVO, TD, DL; Chewton House, Chewton Mendip, Bath

WALDEGRAVE, Hon William Arthur; MP (C) Bristol W 1979-; 2 s of 12 Earl Waldegrave (whose ancestor, 1 Baron Waldegrave, m Henrietta FitzJames, child of Arabella Churchill by James II); through the 4 Earl Waldegrave's marriage with his cous Lady Elizabeth Waldegrave, William is direct descendent of Great Britain's First PM, Sir Robert Walpole; William's ancestor the 2 Earl Waldegrave (f of Lady Elizabeth) was also briefly PM (in 'the two days ministry' of 1746), and Mary Hermione Grenfell; *b* 15 August 1946; *Educ* Eton, Corpus Christi Coll Oxford, Harvard Univ; *m* 1977, Caroline (MA), da of Maj Richard Burrows, of The Malt House, Kemsing, Kent ; 1 s (James b 1984), 3 da (Katharine b 1980, Elizabeth b 1983, Harriet b 1988); *Career* fell All Souls Oxford 1971-78, 1979-; CPRS 1971-73, political staff 10 Downing St 1973-74, head of Rt Hon Edward Heath's (oppn ldr) Political Office 1974-75; GEC Ltd 1975-81, memb IBA Advsy Cncl 1980-; jt vice-chm Fin Ctee to Sept 1981, under-sec state DES (for higher educn) 1981-1983, chm ctee for Local Authy Higher Educn 1982-83, under-sec state DOE 1983-85; min of state DOE 1985; *Books* The Binding of Leviathan - Conservatism and the Future (1977); *pamphlet*: Changing Gear: What the Government Should Do Next (co-author, 1981); *Clubs* Beefsteak, Pratts; *Style—* The Hon William Waldegrave, MP; c/o House of Commons, Westminster, London SW1A 0AA

WALDEN, George Gordon Harvey; CMG 1981, MP (Cons Buckingham 1983-); s of G G Walden; *b* 15 Sept 1939; *Educ* Latymer Upper Sch, Jesus Coll Cambridge, Moscow Univ, Hong Kong Univ (reading Chinese); *m* 1970, Sarah Nicolette Hunt; 2 s, 1 da; *Career* FO 1962-65, second sec Peking 1967-70, first sec Soviet desk FCO 1970-73, Ecole Nationale d'Administration Paris 1973-74, first sec Paris 1974-78, princ private sec to: Rt Hon David Owen (-1979), Rt Hon Lord Carrington 1978-81, fell Harvard Univ 1981-82, head of planning staff FCO 1982-83, ret 1983; PPS to Sec of State for Educn and Sci 1984-85, parly under-sec of state, DES 1985-; *Style—* George Walden, Esq, CMG, MP; House of Commons, London SW1A 0AA (☎ 01 219 6346)

WALDEN, Herbert Richard Charles; CBE (1986); s of Reginald George Walden (d 1954), and late Matilda Ethel, *née* Baker; *b* 6 Oct 1926; *Educ* Westgate Sch Warwick; *m* 1950, Margaret, da of Percy Harold Walker (d 1957); 2 da (Ann, Judith); *Career* serv WWII 1944-47, Royal Warwicks Regt, Royal Leicestershire, serv UK and Gold Coast; dir and gen mangr: Warwicks Bldg Soc 1962-67, Rugby and Warwick Building Soc 1967-74; Heart of Eng Bldg Soc 1974-86; chm S Warwickshire HMC 1964-72, memb cncl The Building Societies Assoc 1974-86 (chm 1983-85), memb bd Housing Corpn 1985-88, Chm Warwicks Schs Fndn, vice-pres Warwicks Scout Cncl (former co tres), fndr pres Warwick Rotary Club 1965, cmmnr of taxes, tstee various Warwick charities; pt/t cmmr Bldg Socs Cmmn 1986-; *Recreations* watching cricket and soccer; *Clubs* Naval and Military; *Style—* Herbert Walden, Esq, CBE; Fieldgate House, 24 Hill Wootton Road, Leek Wootton, Warwick CV35 7QL (☎ 0926 54291)

WALDER WESIERSKA, Ruth Christabel; *née* Walder; OBE (1956); da of Ernest Walder (d 1951), former rector of Bincombe with Broadwey, and Jane, *née* Bull (d 1920); *b* 15 Jan 1906; *Educ* Cheltenham Ladies Coll; *m* 6 Jan 1955, late Maj Gen Jerzy Wasierski, s of Vincent Wasierski; *Career* serv WWII Admty 1940-41, air raid warden Chelsea 1941-45; gen organizer Nat Fedn of Womens Insts 1934-40, FO 1942-44, UN Relief and Rehabilitation Admin 1944-47, sec UN Appeal for Children (UK) 1948, nat gen sec YWCA (UK) 1949-67; memb RIIA, IAMS, vice pres Dorset Co Decorative and Fine Arts Soc; memb: Prayer Book Soc, Nat Tst, RSPB; Polish Gold Cross of Merit 1969; *Recreations* reading, writing, lecturing, gardening; *Clubs* Naval and Military, Royal Dorset Yacht; *Style—* Mrs Ruth Walder Wesierska; Westhope, Langton Herring, nr Weymouth, Dorset DT3 4HZ (☎ 0305 871 233)

WALDRON, Lady Olivia Elsie June; *née* Taylour; da of 5 Marquess of Headfort, TD (d 1960), by his w Elsie Faith (formerly w of Sir Rupert Clarke, Bt); *b* 20 June 1929; *Educ* St Catherine's Melbourne Australia, St Mary's Convent Ascot; *m* 1955, Victor Echevarri Waldron, s of Ernest Victor Echevarri; 2 da; *Career* co dir; *Style—* Lady Olivia Waldron; Hunters Close, Downton, Salisbury, Wilts (☎ 01 370 3273)

WALDRON, Robert Sydney (Robin); s of Robert Waldron (d 1950), of The Cedars, Marlow, Bucks, and Alice *née* Hull (d 1976); *b* 30 Nov 1922; *Educ* Sir William Borlase's Sch (FCA, FACCA, CA, CPA (New York), FCIArb, FBIM, FRSA); *m* 12 June 1954, Marjorie Elizabeth, da of Thomas Victor Scott (d 1987) of 135 Palace View, Bromley, Kent; 2 s (Nigel, Laurence), 1 da (Sally); *Career* Home Guard 1940-42 and 1951-53, RAPC 1942-44, TA Reserve of Officers 1946-52; ptnr Hill Vellacott (CA) 1951-74, fin dir Employment Conditions Bd 1972-88; chm GMS Syndicate 1972-; dir: W Pearce and Brothers Inc (USA), Overseas Productrs BV, The Wellclose Tst Ltd; dep chm United Merchants 1974-80; lay reader C of E St Marks Church Bromley, churchwarden St Margarets Church Lothbury London EC2, memb Lord Chief Justice Cross Ctee to enquire into unsatisfactory work by accountants; *Recreations* drama, family history, cinema, writing; *Clubs* Royal Cwlth, IoD; *Style—* Robin Waldron, Esq; 8 Broadoaks Way, Bromley, Kent BR2 0UB (☎ 01 460 8595)

WALDRON, Victor Echevarri; s of Ernest Echevarri; adopted additional surname of Waldron 1947; *m* 1, 1947, Gladys Leila (d 1958), o da of Col Sir William Waldron; 1 s, 1 da; 2, 1955, Lady Olivia Elsie June, o da of 5 Marquess of Headfort (d 1960); 2 da; *Career* serv RN 1940-45, Lt RNVR; memb Cons Central Off 1946-53, Parly candidate 1951, fin advsr to Constituencies 1954, exec memb Nat Fedn of Property Owners, hon tres Property Cncl; chm: Waldron Gp of Cos, Roundwood Devpt Ltd; memb: Dip & Cwlth Writers Assoc, For Press Assoc, Journalists Devpt Gp of CWDE; *Clubs* Naval and Military; *Style—* Victor Waldron, Esq; Roundwood Devpts Ltd, 81 Cromwell Rd, London SW7 5BS; Idleigh Cottage; Meopham, Kent; 362 President St, New York (☎ NY 112 321)

WALDUCK, (Hugh) Richard; JP (Middx 1974); s of Hugh Stanley Walduck (d 1975), of Long Meadow, Hatfield, Herts, and Enid Rosalind (Wendy) Walduck; *b* 21 Nov 1941; *Educ* Harrow, Univ of Cambridge (MA); *m* 1, 1969 (m dis 1979), Meintje Marianne, *née* Stubbe; 2 s (Alexander b 1971, Nicholas b 1972), 2 step s (Richard b 1966, Simon b 1968), 1 step da (Nicola b 1971); m 2, 27 Aug 1980, Susan Marion, da of Frank Sherwood; *Career* dir and sec Imperial London Hotels Ltd 1964-; Liveryman Worshipful Co of Basketmakers 1968; *Recreations* history, skiing, beekeeping; *Style—* Richard Walduck, Esq, JP; Lower Woodside, Hatfield, Herts AL9 6DJ; c/o Directors Off, Imperial Hotel, Russell Sq, London WC1B 5BB (☎ 01 837 3655, fax 01 837 4653, telex 263951 RUSIMP LDN)

WALERAN, Baroness; Valentine; da of Eric Oswald Anderson, CBE; *m* 1954, as his 3 w, 2 and last Baron Waleran (d 1966); *Style—* Rt Hon Lady Waleran; 42a Cathcart Rd, London SW10 9NN

WALES, Hon Mrs; Hon (Susan) Clare; *née* Richardson; da of Baron Richardson, MVO; *b* 25 Mar 1940; *m* 1970, Robert Wales; 1 s; *Style—* The Hon Mrs Wales; 2 Thorne St, London SW13

WALES, Archbishop of 1987-; Most Rev George Noakes; s of David John Noakes (d 1948), of Bwlchllan, Lampeter, Dyfed, and Elizabeth Mary Noakes (d 1987); *b* 13 Sept 1924; *Educ* Tregaron Co Sch, Univ Coll of Wales Abeystwyth (BA), Wycliffe Hall Oxford; *m* 23 April 1957, Jean Margaretta, da of Samuel Richard Davies (d 1933); *Career* ordained: deacon 1950, priest 1952; curate of Lampeter 195-56; vicar: Eglwyswrw with Meline 1956-59, Tregaron 1959-67, Eglwys Dewi Sant Cardiff 1967-

76; rector Aberystwyth 1976-80, canon St Davids Cath 1977-79, archdeacon of Cardigan 1979-82, vicar Llanychearn with Llanddeiniol 1980-82, bishop of St Davids 1982-; *Recreations* angling; *Style*— The Most Rev the Lord Archbishop of Wales; Llys Esgob, Abergwili, Carmarthen, Dyfed SA31 2JG (☎ 0267 236 597)

WALES, Gregory John; s of A J Wales, of Guildford, Surrey, and B F Wales, *née* Read; *b* 17 May 1949; *Educ* Guildford RGS; *m* 29 Jul 1972, Jennifer Hilary, da of E Brown, of St Albans; 2 s (Nicholas b 1978, Andrew b 1981); *Career* qualified accoutant 1974, sr lectr City 1976-79, mgmnt conslt 1976-80, mangr Arthur Andersen & Co 1980-82, ptnr Coombes Wales & Co 1982-; Freeman City of London; FCA; *Recreations* cricket, squash, real tennis; *Clubs* MCC; *Style*— Gregory Wales, Esq; 31 Selwyn Ave, Richmond, Surrey TW9 2HB (☎ 01 910 4398); Coombes, Wales & Co, 100 Baker St, London W1M 1LA (☎ 01 486 9788)

WALES, Roland John; s of William Frederick Wales (d 1979), of West End, nr Eastleigh, Hants, and Margaret Loise, *née* Landeryou (d 1982); *b* 15 April 1932; *Educ* Brockley Cross, SE London Tech Coll, Borough Poly (NC); *m* 1, 22 March 1958 (m dis 1981), Audrey Mary, da of Sqt Walter Mepsted, of Carshalton, Surrey; m 2, 7 April 1984, Gillian Yvonne, da of Terence Addy, of Upper Tysoe, Warwicks; 2 da (Jeanette Deborah (Mrs Scola), Joanne Dorothy); *Career* Nat Serv RAF (air radar fitter and jr technician) 1953-55; electro-optic systems devpt Hilger & Watts 1955-57, missile testing Av Roe Ltd 1957-59; Beckman Instruments: tech serv 1959-61, UK sales mangr 1962-64, UK mktg mangr 1965-67, int mktg mangr 1968-72; biochemical product gp mangr Rank Hilger 1972-74, euro Devpts 1982-84, md Ferranti Astron Ltd 1984-88; memb nanotechnology strategy ctee DTI; MInstM; *Recreations* skiing, sailing; *Style*— Roland Wales, Esq; 5 Burham Rd, Hughenden Valley, Bucks (☎ 024 024 2633); Ferranti Astron Ltd, Unit 1, Aerodrome Way, Cranford Lane, Hounslow TW5 9QB (☎ 01 897 3123, fax 01 759 0029)

WALEY, His Hon Judge (Andrew) Felix; QC (1973), VRD (1962, clasp 1972); s of Guy Felix Waley (d 1959), and Anne Elizabeth, *née* Dickson (d 1959); *b* 14 April 1926; *Educ* Charterhouse, Worcester Coll Oxford (MA); *m* 3 Sept 1955, Petica Mary, da of Sir Philip Rose, 3 Bt (d 1980); 1 s (Simon b 9 Sept 1964), 4 da (Sarah b 17 Feb 1958, Jane b 27 Feb 1959, Juliet b 10 Feb 1960, Victoria b 21 Jan 1961, d 1963); *Career* barr Middle Temple 1953; Cdr RN Reserve 1965; Parly candidate Dagenham (C) 1957-60; bencher Middle Temple 1980, circuit judge 1982, resident judge County of Kent 1985; Judge Advocate of the Fleet 1986; *Recreations* gardens, boats, birds; *Clubs* Garrick, RNSA; *Style*— His Hon Judge Felix Waley, VRD, QC; The Law Cts, Barker Rd, Maidstone, Kent ME16 8EQ (☎ 0622 54966)

WALEY-COHEN, Sir Bernard Nathaniel; 1 Bt (UK 1961), of Honeymead, Co Somerset; s of late Sir Robert Waley Cohen, KBE (d 1952, first md of Shell Co and WWI petroleum advsr to WO; chm of Palestine Corpn; 1 cous of Sir Herbert Cohen, 2 and last Bt, OBE); assumed by deed poll 1950 his f's final forename as an additional surname; 2 cous of late Baron Cohen (Life Peer d 1973); *b* 29 May 1914; *Educ* HMS Britannia (RNC Dartmouth), Clifton, Magdalene Coll Cambridge; *m* Hon Joyce Nathan (*see* Hon Lady Waley-Cohen); 2 s (Stephen b 1946 m Pamela Doniger, Robert b 1948, m 1975 Hon Felicity Samuel, da of 3 Visc Bearsted), 2 da (Rosalind b 1945, m 1966 Philip Burdon of NZ; Eleanor b 1952, m 1977 Keith Gallant of Connecticut, USA); *Heir* s, Stephen Harry Waley-Cohen; *Career* serv WWII: River Emergency Serv, Home Gd, princ Miny Fuel and Power 1940-47; underwriting memb Lloyd's 1939, chm Palestine Corpn 1952-54 (vice-chm 1947-52), Exmoor farmer 1952-, chm Simo Properties Ltd 1955-70, dep chm Burston Gp 1971-75(dir: Messrs N Burston & Co Ltd 1962-68, Burston & Texas Commerce Bank Ltd 1968-75); dir: O & M Kleeman Ltd 1957-65, Kleeman Industl Hldgs Ltd 1965-84, Mathews Wrightson Pulbrook Ltd 1971-84; one of HM Lts for City of London 1949-, Sheriff 1955-56, Lord Mayor of London 1960-61; govr Nat Corpn for Care of Old People 1965-72; pres Jewish Museum 1964-84; vice-pres: Trades Advsy Cncl 1963- (pres 1981), Anglo-Jewish Assoc 1962-, Jewish Ctee for HM Forces 1980- (memb 1947-), Fndn Ctee Cambridge Soc 1980- (memb 1975-); chm: Investmts Ctee London U 1966-78, Public Works Loan Bd 1972-79, governing body UCL 1971-80 (memb 1953-80); hon tres Jewish Bd of Guardians 1948-53 tstee College of Arms 1970-; memb: exec ctee Jewish Memorial Cncl 1947-, Senate London Univ 1962-78 and of Ct 1966-78, Girton Coll investmts ctee 1971-78; Liveryamn Worshipful Co of Clothworkers'1936- (Master 1975), hon Liveryman Worshipful Co of Farmers' 1961-, hon fell UCL 1963, Hon LLD London Univ 1961, associate KStJ 1961; kt 1957; - tstee College of Arms 1970-; memb: Exec Ctee Jewish Memorial Cncl 1947-, Senate London Univ 1962-78 and of Court 1966-78, Girton Coll Investments Ctee 1971-78; liveryman of Clothworkers' Co 1936- (master 1975), hon liveryman Farmers' Co 1961-, hon fellow UCL 1963, Hon LLD London Univ 1961, associate KStJ 1961; kt 1957; *Recreations* hunting, racing, shooting, rugger; *Clubs* Boodle's, Pratt's, City Livery, MCC, Pitt, Harlequins RFC; *Style*— Sir Bernard Waley-Cohen, Bt; Honeymead, Simonsbath, Minehead, Somerset TA24 7JX (☎ 064 383 242)

WALEY-COHEN, Hon Mrs (Felicity Ann); *née* Samuel; da of 3 Viscount Bearsted, TD, DL, and his 1 w, (Elizabeth) Heather, da of G Firmston-Williams, now Mrs R H Grierson; *b* 3 April 1948; *m* 1975, Robert, 2 s of Sir Bernard Waley-Cohen, 1 Bt, *qv*Waley-Cohen; 3 s (Marcus b 1977, Sam b 1982, Thomas b 1984), 1 da (Jessica 1979); *Career* Felicity Samuel Gallery 1972-81; chm Patrons of New Art, Tate Gallery 1982-87; tstee Tate Fndn 1986; *Style*— The Hon Mrs Waley-Cohen; Honeymead, Simonsbath, Minehead, Somerset TA24 7JX

WALEY-COHEN, Hon Lady; Joyce Constance Ina; *née* Nathan; JP (Somerset 1959) supplemental list 1987; only da of 1 Baron Nathan, TD, PC (d 1963); *b* 20 Jan 1920; *Educ* St Felix Sch, Girton Coll Cambridge (MA); *m* 1943, Sir Bernard Nathaniel Waley-Cohen, 1 Bt, *qv*; 2 s, 2 da; *Career* JP Middx 1949-59; memb bd of govrs Westminster Hosp Gp 1952-68; chm: Westminster Children's Hosp 1952-68, Gordon Hosp 1961-68, governing body St Felix Sch 1970-83 (memb 1945-83), Governing Bodies of Girls Schs Assoc 1974-79 (memb 1963-), Independent Schs Jt Ctee 1977-80; govr: Taunton Sch 1978-, Wellington Coll 1979-; pres Independent Schs Info Serv Cncl 1981-86 (memb 1972-86) and memb Mgmnt Ctee; *Style*— The Hon Lady Waley-Cohen, JP; Honeymead, Simonsbath, Minehead, Somerset TA24 7JX (☎ 064 383 242)

WALEY-COHEN, Robert Bernard; 2 s of Sir Bernard Waley-Cohen, 1 Bt, and Hon Joyce Nathan, da of 1 Baron Nathan; *b* 10 Nov 1948; *Educ* Eton; *m* 1975, Hon Felicity Anne, da of 3 Viscount Bearsted, TD; 3 s (Marcus Richard b 1977, Sam Bernard b 1982, Thomas Andrew b 1984), 1 da (Jessica Suzanna b 1979); *Career* exec Christie's 1969-81, (gen mangr USA 1970-73); dir Samuel Properties 1977-86; chm and chief exec offr Alliance Imaging Inc 1987-88; *Recreations* the arts, hunting, racing (racehorses include: Sun Lion, Rustle, The Dragon Master); *Clubs* Boodle's, Queen's, Jockey; *Style*— Robert Waley-Cohen, Esq; 18 Gilston Rd, London SW10

WALEY-COHEN, Stephen Harry; s and h of Sir Bernard Waley-Cohen, 1 Bt, and Hon Lady Waley-Cohen, *qqv*; *b* 22 June 1946; *Educ* Eton, Magdalene Coll Cambridge; *m* 1, 1972 (m dis 1986), Pamela Elizabeth, da of J E Doniger, of Knutsford, Cheshire; 2 s (Lionel Robert b 7 Aug 1974, Jack David b 7 Sept 1979), 1 da (Harriet Ann b 20 June 1976); m 2, 1986, Josephine, da of Duncan Spencer, of New York; 2 da (Tamsin Alice b 4 April 1986, Freya Charlotte b 20 Feb 1989); *Career* financial journalist Daily Mail 1968-73, ed Money Mail Handbook 1972-74, dir and publisher Euromoney Publications Ltd 1969-83, chief exec Maybox Gp plc (theatre and cinema owners and managers 1984-); dir Publishing Hldgs plc 1986-, Stewart Wrightson Member Agency Ltd 1987-; govr Wellesley House Sch; memb fin ctee Univ Coll London 1984, cncl memb Jewish Colonisation Assoc 1984-; *Style*— Stephen Waley-Cohen, Esq; 1 Wallingford Ave, London W10

WALFORD, Hon Mrs (Angela Mary); *née* Bellew; only da of 7 Baron Bellew; *b* 11 April 1944; *m* 1964, Capt Simon Hugh Walford, 17/21 Lancers, s of Lt-Col Hugh Walford (of a family which has been traced to one Sir Hugo de Walford, who held, as a knight's fee, the lordship of Walford, Herefordshire, 1109); 2 da (Jeanie Anne b 1966, Caroline Sarah b 1968); *Style*— The Hon Mrs Walford; Summerstown House, Trim, Co Meath, Eire (☎ 046 31245)

WALFORD, Hon Mrs; (Claire Elizabeth); *née* Pennock; da of Baron Pennock (Life Peer); *b* 1958; *m* 1985, Peter Vivian Walford, s of Edward Walford, of 108 High Street, Norton, Cleveland; *Style*— The Hon Mrs Walford

WALFORD, John Howard; s of Henry Howard Walford (d 1928), and Marjorie Josephine, *née* Solomon (d 1983); *b* 16 May 1927; *Educ* Cheltenham, Gonville and Caius Coll Cambridge (MA); *m* 6 Aug 1953, Peggy Ann, da of Cdr Richard Frederick Jessel, DSO, OBE, DSC, RN (ret) (d 1988); 2 s (Charles b 1955, Richard b 1960), 2 da (Veronica b 1957, Rosemary b 1964); *Career* conslt to Bischoff & Co; slr 1950; memb Cncl Law Soc 1961-69; govr: Coll of Law 1967-88, St John's Hosp for Diseases of the Skin 1967-82; sr ptnr Bischoff & Co 1979-88, pres Slrs Disciplinary Tribunal 1979- 88; chm: Skin Disease Res Fund Appeal Ctee, chm: bd of mgmnt Petworth Cottage Nursing and Convalescent Home 1988-; Master City of London Solicitors Co 1981; Cdr Order of Bernardo O'Higgins (Chile) 1972; *Recreations* being in the country, fly-fishing, travelling abroad; *Clubs* Garrick, City Law; *Style*— John Walford Esq; Pheasant Ct, Northchapel, Petworth, West Sussex (☎ 042 878 550); office: Epworth House, 25 City Rd, London EC1 (☎ 01 628 4222, fax 01 638 3345, telex 885062)

WALKDEN, Hon Margaret; da of 1 Baron Walkden; *b* 1914; *Style*— The Hon Margaret Walkden; 7 Priory Av, Hastings, Sussex

WALKER; *see*: Forestier-Walker

WALKER, Sir Allan Grierson; QC (Scot); s of Joseph Walker; *b* 1 May 1907; *Educ* Whitgift Sch, Edinburgh Univ; *m* 1935, Audrey, da of Dr T Glover; 1 s; *Career* Scottish bar 1931-39, sheriff-substitute at: Selkirk and Peebles 1942-45, Dumbarton 1945-50, Glasgow 1950-63; sheriff princ Lanarks 1963-74; chm Sheriff Ct Rules Cncl 1972-74, memb Law Reform Ctee for Scotland 1964-70; hon LLD Glasgow 1967; kt 1968; *Style*— Sir Allan Walker, QC; 24 Moffat Rd, Dumfries (☎ 0387 53583)

WALKER, Andrew David; s of Alexander MacPherson Walker, of Norfolk, and Viola Maisie, *née* Pearce; *b* 18 April 1948; *Educ* Norwich Sch, Univ of Bristol (LLB), Univ of Warwick (LLM); *m* 4 Sept 1976, Christine Joan, da of Clifford Horace Hall, of Bedford; 1 s (Alexander Henry b 1982), 1 da (Helen Victoria b 1985); *Career* lectr Univ of Aston 1974-81; slr 1974, private practise Curtler & Hallmark 1981-; memb Malvern Hills Dist Cncl, chm Social Security Appeal Tbnl; memb Law Soc 1981; *Books* Law of Industrial Pollution Control (1979); *Recreations* antique collecting, book collecting, cookery; *Style*— Andrew Walker, Esq; 31 Hornyold Rd, Malvern, Hereford & Worcester (☎ 0684 566 991); 4 & 5 Sansome Place, Worcester WR1 1UQ (☎ 0905 726 600, fax 0905 611 093)

WALKER, Hon Mrs (Anna Elizabeth Blackstock); *née* Butterworth; er da of Baron Butterworth, CBE (Life Peer), *qv*; *b* 1951; *Educ* Benenden, Lady Margaret Hall Oxford; *m* 1983, Timothy John Hanson Walker; *Style*— The Hon Mrs Walker; 24 Old Park Ave, London SW12 8RH

WALKER, Lt-Gen Sir Antony Kenneth Frederick; KCB (1987); s of Kenneth Frederick Andrews Walker (d 1966), and Iris Mary Walker (d 1983); *b* 16 May 1934; *Educ* Merchant Taylors', RMA Sandhurst; *m* 1, 1961 (m dis 1983), Diana Merran Steward; 1 s, 1 da; m 2, 1985, Susan Carol, da of Derrick Stuart Holmes, of Bournemouth; *Career* cmmnd RTR 1954; serv: BAOR, Libya, Ghana, NI (despatches), Hong Kong, UN Force in Cyprus; CO 1 RTR 1974-76, Dep Cdr 4 Armd Div 1978-80, Maj-Gen 1982, GOC 3 Armd Div 1982-84, Col Cmdt RTR 1983-; COS HQ UKLF 1985-87, Dep CDS (Commitments) 1987-; *Recreations* bird-watching, music, theatre, country sports, practical study of wine; *Style*— Lt-Gen Sir Antony Walker, KCB; c/o National Westminster Bank, 151 The Parade, Watford, Herts

WALKER, Archibald George Orr; s of George Edward Orr Walker, MBE, TD, QC (d 1973), of Newark Castle, Alloway, Ayr, and Margaret Sybil, *née* Orr; *b* 14 Feb 1937; *Educ* Eton; *m* 11 Feb 1967, Fiona Mary Elizabeth, da of Alison Lyle Barr MC d 1970), of Brannochlie, Bridge of Weir; 1 s (James b 1968), 1 da (Rosamund b 1970); *Career* Nat Serv 2 Lt Coldstream Gds 1955-57; apprentice CA McClelland Moores Glasgow 1957-62, qualified AC 1962, dir John Beresford and Co (Devpts) Ltd 1965-67 (joined 1962), dep chm Singer and Friedlander Ltd 1983 (joined 1968, dir 1973), non exec dir Clyde Petroleum plc 1973-88, non exec dir Scottish Nat Tst plc 1984, exec dir Singer and Friedlander Gp plc 1987-, chm Pionshead Gp plc 1987-, chm Irvine Devpt Corpn 1987; memb Queens Bodyguard for Scot, memb Royal Co of Archers 1968; FICA (Scot); *Recreations* golf, tennis, stalking, skiing; *Clubs* Wester (Glasgow), Prestwick Golf, The Honourable, Company of Edinburgh Golfers, Machrihanish Golf; *Style*— Archibald Walker, Esq; Newark Castle, Alloway, Ayr (☎ 0292 41587); 19 St Vincents Place Glasgow, G1 2DT (☎ 041 221 9996, fax 041 221 1088, telex 886977)

WALKER, Sir Baldwin Patrick; 4 Bt (UK 1856), of Oakley House, Suffolk; also hereditary Pasha of the Ottoman Empire; s of late Cdr Baldwin Charles Walker, himself s of Sir Francis Walker, 3 Bt (d 1928, in his turn 2 surviving s of Adm Sir Baldwin Wake Walker, 1 Bt, KCB, who was Comptroller of the (Royal) Navy and sometime Adm in the Turkish service, whereby he was cr a Pasha); *b* 10 Sept 1924; *Educ* Gordonstoun; *m* 1, 1948 (m dis 1954), Joy Yvonne, da of Sir Arrol Moir, 2 Bt (d 1957); m 2, 1954, Sandra Stewart; m 3, 1966, Rosemary Ann, da of late Henry

Hollingdrake; 1 s, 1 da; *Heir* s, Christopher-Robert Baldwin, b 25 Oct 1969; *Career* formerly London regional man Planned Music Ltd, Planned Equipment Ltd, Planned Communications Ltd; *Style*— Sir Baldwin Walker, Bt; 8 Waltham Way, Meadowridge, Cape Town 7800, SA

WALKER, Barry Matthew; s of George Edward Walker, OBE, JP (d 1977), of Cobham Surrey, and Muriel Edith, *née* Brown (d 1981); *b* 30 August 1939; *Educ* Cranleigh; *m* 18 feb 1961, Hazel Mary Philippa, da of Wilfred John Oakley Jenkins, of Oxshott, Surrey; 2 s (Simon b 1 Oct 1964, Dominic b 3 March 1973) 2 da (Nicola b 15 June 1962, Philippa b 11 May 1966); *Career* slr; articled clerk Gouldens 1957-63, ptnr Paisner & Co 1967-74 (asst slr 1963-67), ptnr Ashurst Morris Crisp 1974-; non-exec dir: Sterling Guarantee Tst 1969-80, Town & City Properties plc 1969-80, Dipolma plc 1982-; memb: Law Soc 1961, City of London Law Soc 1985 ; *Recreations* golf, gardening, squash, tennis, bridge; *Style*— Barry Walker, Esq; 7 Eldon St, London EC2 (☎ 01 247 7666, fax 01 377 5659)

WALKER, Brian Wilson; s of Arthur Harrison Walker (d 1960), and Eleanor Charlotte Mary, *née* Wilson; *b* 31 Oct 1930; *Educ* Heversham Sch Westmorland 1940-50, Leicester Coll of Technol, Manchester Univ, Oxford Univ (MA); *m* 5 April 1954, Nancy Margaret, da of Samuel Henry Gawith (d 1967); 1 s (Peter b 1955), 5 da (Clare b 1957, Dorcas b 1958, Grainne b 1964, Siobhan b 1967, Sarah b 1968); *Career* pres Int Inst for Environment and Devpt 1985-, dir Independent Cmmn on Int Humanitarian Issues 1983-85; dir gen Oxfam 1974-83; gen mangr Bridge Port Brass Ltd 1961-74; fndr chm New Ulster Movement 1969; chm: Band Aid, Live Aid 1985-; *Recreations* gardening, walking, reading; *Style*— Brian Walker, Esq; 14 Upland Park Rd, Oxford OX2 7RU (☎ 0865 515473); IIED, 3 Endsleigh St, London WC1H 0DD (☎ 01 388 2117)

WALKER, (Alfred) Cecil; JP (1966), MP (UU) Belfast N 1983-; s of Alfred George and Margaret Lucinda Walker (d 1983); *b* 17 Dec 1924; *Educ* Methodist Coll Belfast; *m* 1953, Ann May Joan; 2 s; *Career* contested (UU): NI Assembly 1973, Belfast N 1979; sales mngr; *Recreations* sailing (yacht 'Nekita'); *Clubs* Down Cruising; *Style*— A Cecil Walker, Esq, JP, MP; 1 Wynnland Rd, Newtownabbey, Belfast BT36 6RZ, NI (☎ (023 13) 3463)

WALKER, Prof David Alan; s of Cyril Walker, of 33 Hayman Way, Falmouth, and Dorothy *née* Dobson; *b* 18 August 1928; *Educ* South Shields HS, Univ of Durham (BSc, PhD, DSc); *m* 7 July 1956, Shirley Wynne, da of William Chambers Mason (d 1980); 1 s (Rick b 1960), 1 da (Marney b 1957); *Career* RNAS 1946-48; ICI post-doctoral res fell 1956-58, reader in botany QMC London 1963-65 (lectr 1958-63, Charles F Kettering Res Fellowship 1962), reader in enymology Imperial Coll London 1965-70; Univ of Sheffield: prof of biology 1970-84, dir res inst for photosynthesis 1984-88, prof of photosynthesis Robert Hill inst 1988-; corr memb American Soc of Plant Physiologists; exec cncl Save British Science, FIBiol 1971, FRS 1979; *Books* Energy, Plants and Man (1979), C3 C4 mechanisms and Cellular and Enviromental regulation of photosynthesis (1983), The use of the oxygen electrode and fluorescence probes in simple measurements of photsynthesis (1987); *Recreations* singing the Sheffield carols, walking, eating and drinking in good company; *Style*— Prof David Walker; Research Institute for Photosynthesis, The University, Sheffield S10 2TN (☎ 0742 768555 ext 6401, fax 0742 682521)

WALKER, Prof David Maxwell; CBE (1986), QC (Scot 1958); s of James Mitchell Walker (d 1934), of Woodbank, Bishopbriggs, Glasgow, and Mary Paton Colquhoun, *née* Irvine (d 1971); *b* 9 April 1920; *Educ* Glasgow HS, Univ of Glasgow (MA, LLB, LLD), Univ of Edinburgh (PhD, LLD), Univ of London (LLB, LLD); *m* 1 Sept 1954, Margaret, da of Robert Knox (d 1970), of Haystone, Brookfield, Renfrewshire; *Career* WWII: NCO Cameronians (Scottish Rifles) 1939, 2 Lt HLI 1940, transferred to RIASC 1941, served with 8 Indian Div India 1941-42, N Africa 1942-43, Italy 1943-46 (Bde Supply and Tport Offr HQ 21 Indian Inf Brig); advocate Scottish Bar 1948, practising Scottish Bar 1948-53, barr Middle Temple 1957; regius prof of law Univ of Glasgow 1958- (prof of jurisprudence 1954-58), dean Faculty of Law 1956-59, dir Scottish Univs' Law Inst 1974-80, convenor Sch of Law 1984-88; chm: HS of Glasgow Educn Tst, Ed Ctee Juridical Review; govr HS of Glasgow, hon pres Friends of Glasgow Univ Library; hon LLD Univ of Edinburgh 1974; memb Faculty of Advocates 1948, Middle Temple 1957, FBA 1976, FRSE 1980; *Books* Law of Damages in Scotland (1955), The Scottish Legal System (1959, fifth edn 1981), Law of Delict in Scotland (1966, second edn 1981), Principles of Scottish Private Law (2 vols 1970, fourth edn 4 vols 1988-89), Law of Prescription and Limitation in Scotland (1973, thilrd edn 1981, supplement 1984), Law of Civil Remedies in Scotland (1974), Law of Contracts and Related Obligations in Scotland (1979, second edn 1985), The Oxford Companion to Law (1980), Stair's Institutions of the Law of Scotland (ed 1981), Stair Tercentenary Studies (ed 1981), The Scottish Jurists (1985), A Legal History of Scotland (vol 1, 1988); numerous papers in legal journals; *Recreations* book-collecting, Scottish history; *Clubs* Royal Scottish Automobile; *Style*— Prof David M Walker, CBE, QC; 1 Beaumont Gate, Glasgow G12 9EE (☎ 041 339 2802); Dept of Private Law, Univ of Glasgow, Glasgow, Scotland G12 8QQ (☎ 041 339 8855 ext 4556, telex 777070 UNIGLA)

WALKER, (Thomas) Dickson; MBE (1945); s of Tom Brunton Walker (d 1964), and Letitia Flora McDonald, *née* Dickson (d 1964); *b* 23 Sept 1912; *Educ* Mill Hill; *m* 24 June 1939, Joan Mary, da of Herbert Joseph Hawes (d 1966); 1 s (Humphrey 1943), 2 da (Elizabeth b 1941, Janet b 1949); *Career* WW11 RASC 1939-46, enlisted as cadet 1939, cmmnd 1940, 2 Lt Tport UK 1940-42, Capt 1942, Tport N Africa 1942-43 (despatches), Tport Italy 1943-46 (despatches), Maj 1945, released 1946; temporarily recalled Z Reserve Trg; CA; ptnr Josolyne Layton-Bennett & Co (formerly Layton Bennett Billingham & Co) 1949-78 (sr ptnr 1971-78); non exec dir of various public cos latest appts inc: Scapa Gp plc 1962-88, chm Sheldon Jones plc 1975-88, William Nash plc 1977-; sec/chm Alford House Youth Club Lambeth 1934-; govr and tres Mill Hill Sch 1953-88, pres Old Millhilltons Club 1969-70, ctee memb The Buttle Tst for Children, elder Utd Reformed Church; FCA 1954, FRSA 1977; *Recreations* gardening, natural history (particularly wildflowers), studying art; *Clubs* East India; *Style*— Dickson Walker, Esq, MBE

WALKER, Esme; *née* Burnett; CBE (1985); da of David Burnett (d 1968), and Jane, *née* Thornton (d 1967); *b* 7 Jan 1932; *Educ* St George's Sch for Girls Edinburgh, Univ of Edinburgh (MA, LLB); *m* 17 March 1956, Ian Macfarlane Walker (d 1988), s of James Walker (d 1950); 1 s (Angus David b 9 Aug 1960); *Career* lectr Queen Margaret Coll Edinburgh 1977-83; chm: Scottish Consumer Cncl 1981-85, Scottish Assoc of CAB 1986-88; vice chm Nat Consumer Cncl 1984-87, cmmnr Equal Opportunities Cmmn 1986-; tstee John Watson's Tst, memb: Scottish Consumer Cncl 1980-81, Scottish Ctee of the Cncl on Tbnls 1986-, cncl St George's Sch for Girls; FRSA 1987, memb Law Soc of Scotland 1974; *Recreations* crosswords; *Clubs* New (Edinburgh); *Style*— Mrs Esme Walker, CBE; 13 Clinton Rd, Edinburgh (☎ 031 447 5191); Barrelfield, Waterfoot, by Carradale, Kintyre

WALKER, Geoffrey Hurst; s of Raymond Bennet Walker, of Perth, Scotland, and Joan Edith Agnes, *née* Michie; *b* 7 Feb 1956; *Educ* Bell Baxter HS Cupar Fife, Edinburgh Univ (BCom); *Career* audit mangr Athur Young 1978-87, fin dir Serif Cowells plc 1987-; ACA 1981; *Recreations* sailing, badminton, philately; *Style*— Geoffrey Walker, Esq; 2 Ransome Close, Sproughton, Ipswich, Suffolk IP8 3DG (☎ 0473 419 76); Serif Hse, Hadleigh Rd, Ipswich, Suffolk IP2 0EE (☎ 0473 225 941, fax 0473 221 979/ 987532)

WALKER, George Alfred; s of William James Walker and Ellen, *née* Page; *b* 14 April 1929; *m* 1957, Jean Maureen, *née* Hatton; 1 s (Jason), 2 da (Sarah (Marchioness of Milford Haven), Romla); *Career* chm (and md) The Brent Walker Group plc (leisure gp) 1981-; *Recreations* skiing, climbing, sailing; *Clubs* RAC; *Style*— George Walker, Esq; c/o Brent Walker Group plc, Knightsbridge House, 197 Knightsbridge, London SW7 1RB (☎ 01 225 1941)

WALKER, Sir Gervas George; JP (Bristol 1969), DL (Avon 1982); s of Harry Walker; *b* 12 Sept 1920; *Educ* Monmouth Sch; *m* 1944, Eileen, *née* Maxwell; 2 s; *Career* formerly: chm Bristol Avon River Authy, memb SW Regnl Planning Cncl, ldr and oppn ldr Bristol City Cncl, chm and ldr Avon CC 1973-81, chm Bristol Cons Assoc 1975-79 and Assoc of CCs 1979-81 (vice-chm 1978-79); kt 1979; *Style*— Sir Gervas Walker, JP, DL; Bulverton Well Farm, Sidmouth, Devon EX10 9DW (☎ 0395 516902); The Lodge, Cobblestone Mews, Clifton Park, Bristol BS8 3DQ (☎ 0272 737063)

WALKER, (Victor) Gordon; DL (Co of IOW 1987); s of Edgar Frederick Walker (d 1959), of Mitcham, Melbourne, Victoria, Australia, and Myra Gaskell, *née* Jones (d 1973); *b* 27 Jan 1919; *Educ* Wesley Coll Melbourne, Queen's Coll Univ of Melbourne (MB, BS); *m* 1 Sept 1948, Judith Mary, da of Arnold Augustus Phillips (d 1961), of Melbourne, Australia; 2 s (Nicholas b 1949, Jeremy b 1955), 2 da (Philippa b 1951, Belinda b 1956); *Career* Flt Lt RAAF; serv: Australia, France, and UK 1942-47; conslt surg: IOW Gp of Hosps 1954-86, Home Office 1959-86; memb ct of examiners RCS (Eng) 1970-76; High Sheriff Co of IOW 1985-86; FRCS (Eng); *Recreations* sailing, shooting; *Clubs* Royal Yacht Sqdn, Melbourne Cricket, Army and Navy; *Style*— Gordon Walker, Esq, DL; Stonelands, Binstead, IOW PO33 3NJ (☎ 0983 63980)

WALKER, Rt Hon Harold; PC (1979), MP (Doncaster Central 1983 and 1987); s of Harold Walker, and Phyllis Walker; *b* 12 July 1927; *Educ* Manchester Coll of Technol; *m* 1, 1956, late Barbara, da of Cecil Hague; 1 da; m 2, 1984, Mary Griffin; *Career* Fleet Air Arm 1946-48; MP (Lab) Doncaster 1964-1983, asst govt whip 1967, parly under-sec state employment and productivity 1968-70, oppn front bench spokesman industl rels 1970-74, parly under-sec state employment 1974-76, min state 1976-79, oppn spokesman 1979-1983; chm Ways and Means Ctee (dep speaker 1983-); *Style*— The Rt Hon Harold Walker, MP; House of Commons, London SW1A 0AA

WALKER, Maj Sir Hugh Ronald Walker; 4 Bt (UK 1906), of Pembroke House, City of Dublin; s of Maj Sir Cecil Edward Walker, 3 Bt, DSO, MC (d 1964), and Violet, *née* McMaster; *b* 13 Dec 1925; *Educ* Wellington; *m* 1971, Norna, da of Lt-Cdr R D Baird; 2 s (Robert Cecil, Roy Edward b 10 Aug 1977); *Heir* s, Robert Cecil Walker, b 26 Sept 1974; *Career* Maj RA, ret; memb Assoc of Supervisory and Exec Engrs; *Style*— Maj Sir Hugh Walker, Bt; Ballinamona Stud Hospital, Killmallock, Co Limerick, Eire; c/o Lloyds Bank Ltd, Somerton, Somerset

WALKER, Sir Hugh Selby; *see*: Norman-Walker

WALKER, Ian Hugh; s of John Walker, and Joan, *née* Crowther; *b* 3 Jan 1950; *Educ* Huntley's Tunbridge Wells; *m* 15 July 1975, Lorraine, da of George Armstrong; 2 s (Matthew James Hugh b 1979, Robert George b 1982); *Career* estate agent; ptnr Page & Wells Maidstone, dir Page & Wells Fin Servs Ltd; chm Bearsted Round Table 1989-; FNAEA; *Recreations* golf, squash, running, skiing; *Clubs* Tudor Park, Mote Squash, Bearsted; *Style*— Ian Walker, Esq; 132 Ashford Road, Bearsted, Maidstone, Kent (☎ 0622 39574)

WALKER, Sqdn Ldr James; CBE (1974); s of James Walker (d 1952); *b* 8 Mar 1916; *Educ* HS Stirling, Univ of Glasgow Univ (BSc, MD); *m* 1940, Catherine Clark, da of George Raphael Agnew Johnston; 1 s, 2 da;; *Career* served RAF Actg Wing Cdr RAF Med Service SE Asia; reader London Univ 1954-56; prof obstetrics gynaecology: St Andrews 1956-67, Univ of Dundee 1967-81, Malaysia 1982-83; visiting prof: Florida Univ, New York State, McGill, Riyadh, Pennsylvania, Stellen Bosch; former chm Nat Med Consultative Ctee (Scotland); former chm 1976-88: Standing Ctee Definitions, Int Fedn Obstet Gyn 1976-; FRCP Glasgow, FRCOG; *Books* ed combined textbook Obstetrics Gynaecology; *Clubs* RAF; *Style*— Prof James Walker, CBE; 31 Ravenscraig Gardens, Broughty Ferry, Dundee DD5 1LT (☎ 0382 79238)

WALKER, Rev Dr James Bernard; s of Rev Dr Robert Bernard William Walker, MB, CLB, of Edinburgh, and Grace Brownlee, *née* Torrance; *b* 7 May 1946; *Educ* Hamilton Acad Lanarkshire, Edinburgh Univ (MA, BD), Merton Coll Oxford (D Phil); *m* 18 Aug 1972, Sheila Mary, da of Alexander Ballantyne Easton (d 1948), of Ilford, London; 3 s (Colin Alexander b 1975, Alastair Robert b 1975, Peter Donald b 1978); *Career* ordained Church of Scotland 1975, assoc minister Mid Craigre Parish Church (with Wallacetown) Dundee 1975-78, minister Old St Paul's Parish Church Galashiels 1978-87, princ Queen's Theol Coll Birmingham 1987-; *Books* Israel - Covenant and Land (1986); *Recreations* hill walking, squash, swimming; *Style*— The Rt Rev Dr James Wakker; The Queen's College, Somerset Road, Edgbaston, Birmingham B15 2QH (☎ 021 454 1527)

WALKER, Sir James Graham; MBE (1963); s of Albert Edward Walker (decd), and Adelaide Walker (decd); *b* 7 May 1913; *Educ* New England GS NSW; *m* 1939, (Mary) Vivienne (Maude), da of W R Poole (d 1935); 2 s, 3 da; *Career* cllr Longreach Shire Cncl 1953- (chm 1957-87), dep chm Longreach Pastoral Coll 1966-78 (chm 1979-87), exec memb Central Western Qld Local Authorities Assoc 1964-79, chm Central Western Electricity Bd 1966-76, chm Capricorn Electricity Bd 1979-86, dir Longreach Printing Co; Hon LLD Queensland Univ 1985; kt 1972; *see Debrett's Handbook of Australia and New Zealand for further details*; *Style*— Sir James Walker, MBE; Lambeth, Longreach, Qld 4730, Australia

WALKER, Jason; s of George Alfred Walker, and Jean Maureen, (*née* Hatton); *b* 31

May 1960; *Educ* Millfield; *Career* dir Brent Walker Casino's Ltd; *Recreations* flying (H), shooting, skiing; *Clubs* St James', RAC; *Style*— Jason Walker, Esq; Brent Walker Casino's Ltd, 41 Upper Brook St, London W1Y 1PF (☎ 01 499 7602, telex 297902, fax 01 629 6935)

WALKER, His Hon Judge John David; DL (Humberside); s of late Lawrence Cecil Walker, and late Jessie Walker; *b* 13 Mar 1924; *Educ* Oundle, Cambridge Univ (MA); *m* 1954, Elizabeth Mary Emma, da of late Victor William Owbridge, of Yorks; 1 s (Nicholas b 1958), 2 da (Belinda b 1955, Emma b 1962); *Career* serv WWII Capt Frontier Force Rifles IA 1942-47; barr Middle Temple 1951, rec 1972; circuit judge 1972-; pres Mental Health Revue Tbnls; *Recreations* shooting, fishing; *Clubs* Lansdowne; *Style*— His Hon Judge John Walker; Arden House, North Bar Without, Beverley, North Humberside

WALKER, Prof John Hilton; s of Lt Col Arthur Walker (d 1966), of Allendale, Northumberland, and Effie Lilian, *née* Cheetham (d 1979); *b* 28 April 1928; *Educ* Samuel Kings Sch Alston Cumberland, Kings Coll Univ of Durham (MB, BS, MD), Univ of Newcastle Upon Tyne (DPH, MFCM, MRCGP); *m* 9 March 1957, (Margaret) June, da of Capt William Reay Simpson (d 1980), of Allendale, Northumberland; 3 da (Gillian Amanda b 1958, Shona Ruth b 1960, Penelope Kate b 1964); *Career* RNR 1947-49; Luccock res fell Univ Durham 1957-59, lectr in gen practice Univ of Edinburgh 1959-63; Univ of Newcastle: lectr in public health 1964-68, sr lectr and head of dept family and community med 1968-76, prof and head of dept 1976-88; chm Assoc of Univ Teachers of Gen Practice, chief examiner and chm membership div RCGP 1972-83; FRCGP, FFCM 1977; *Recreations* gardening,skiing, motoring, building; *Style*— Prof John Walker; Low Luddick House, Woolsington, Newcastle NE13 8DE, (☎ 2860551)

WALKER, John James; s of Patrick Walker, of Flat 1, Glebe Cottage, Grove Lane, Weston-S-Mare, Avon, and Claudine, *née* Brown; *b* 26 July 1949; *Educ* Sidcot Sch Winscombe Somerset, Bournemouth Coll of Art (Dip in Design); *Career* freelance film ed 1970-80, dir Bumper Films Ltd 1980-88, prodn of Stop Frame Puppet; Animation Films: Rocky Hollow, Fireman Sam; *Recreations* skiing, squash, wine, travel; *Style*— John Walker, Esq; Bumper Films Ltd, 115 High St, Weston-S-Mare, Avon (☎ 0934 418 961, fax 0934 623 608)

WALKER, Jonathan Gervas; s of Sir Gervas Walker, JP, DL, of Bulverton Well Farm, Sidmouth, Devon, and Lady Jessie Eileen, *née* Maxwell; *b* 26 June 1953; *Educ* Clifton; *m* 25 Feb 1984, Gillian, da of Dr Colin Dodds Drew, of Weston-Super-Mare, Avon; 1 s (Edward b 20 May 1986); *Career* accountant Grant Thornton 1973-80, dir Terrett Taylor Ltd 1987-; *Recreations* tennis, shooting; *Clubs* Clifton (Bristol); *Style*— Jonathan Walker, Esq; Old Manor Cottage, Bulverton, Sidmouth, Devon (☎ 0395 514114); Ottery Moor, Honiton, Devon (☎ 0404 41117)

WALKER, Julian Fortay; CMG (1982), MBE (1960); s of Kenneth MacFarlane Walker (d 1963), of Woodcutters, Little London, Ambersham Common, nr Midhurst, W Sussex, and Eileen Marjorie Walker, later Mrs Dahlberg (d 1983); *b* 7 May 1929; *Educ* Harvey Sch NY, Stow Bryanston, Cambridge (MA); *m* Aug 1983, Virginia Anne (Mrs Austin), da of Michael Stevens, of Lechdale, Glos; 3 step da (Rachel b 17 Feb 1969, Katheryn b 6 Oct 1970, Elizabeth b 21 Oct 1972); *Career* Nat Serv RN 1947-49; Cambridge 1949-52, London Univ Sch of African and Oriental Studies 1952; For Serv: MECAS 1953, asst political agent Trucial States 1953-55, 3 then 2 sec Bahrain 1955-57, FCO and frontier settlement Oman 1957-60, 2 then 1 sec Oslo 1960-63, news dept spokesman FCO 1963-67, 1 sec Baghdad 1967, 1 sec Rabat Morocco 1967-69, FCO 1969-71, political agent Dubai Trucial States 1971, consul gen and cnsllr HM Embassy Dubai United Arab Emirates 1971-72, sabbatical leave Cambridge Univ 1972-73, political advsr and head of chancery Br Mil Govt Berlin 1973-76, NI off Stormont Castle 1976-77, dir MECAS 1977-78, ambass to Arab Rep Yemen and Rep of Jibuti 1979-84, ambass to Qatar 1984-87; HM Dip Serv: special advsr (Syria) res dept FCO 1987-; order of Isthqaq 1st Class (Qatar, 1985); *Recreations* sailing and sailboarding, music, gardening, tennis; *Clubs* RAC; *Style*— Julian Walker, Esq, CMG, MBE; 23 Woodlands Grove, Isleworth, Middx TW7 6NS (☎ 560 8795); Research Dept, Foreign and Commonwealth Office, Whitehall, London SW1A 2AH (☎ 01 210 6214)

WALKER, Kenneth Lane; s of Herbert Arthur Walker (d 1961), and Verona Sophie, *née* Thomas; *b* 26 Feb 1936; *Educ* Moseley GS, Univ Coll Oxford; *m* 1964, Isabella Mary, da of John Moffat (d 1966); *Career* CA, dir of Mono Containers Ltd 1967-77, vice-chm Mono Containers Int Ltd 1975-77 (dir 1971-77), md Mono Containers: GmbH FDR and (Hldgs) AG Switzerland 1975-77; vice-chm: Pontneau Mono & Cie SA France 1970-77, Monoplast SA Spain 1972-77, Thurbaform Ltd 1975-77; dir: Kode Int Ltd, Kode Investmts Ltd and Kode Europe SA Belgium 1977-85; mgmnt conslt 1985-; chm Wilts Centre IOD 1983-; *Recreations* gliding, reading, philately; *Clubs* City Livery; *Style*— Kenneth Walker, Esq; Whitley Grange, Whitley, nr Melksham, Wilts (☎ 0225 702242)

WALKER, Prof Kenneth Richard; s of Arthur Bedford Walker (d 1972), of Yorks, and Olive, *née* Thornton (d 1988); *b* 17 Oct 1931; *Educ* Prince Henry's GS Otley Yorks, Univ of Leeds (BA), Lincoln Coll Oxford (DPhil); *m* 28 July 1959, Dr June Abercrombie, da of George Morrison Collie, of Aberdeen; 1 s (Neil George Arthur b 1965), 1 da (Ruth Abercrombie b 1967); *Career* asst in political economy Univ of Aberdeen 1956-59; memb academic staff SOAS Univ of London 1959-: res fell 1959-61, lectr 1961-65, reader 1965-72, prof of econs 1972-, head of dept econ and political studies 1969-86, writer of various articles on the Chinese Economy in learned jls; memb exec ed board of the China Quarterly; *Books* Planning in Chinese Agriculture (1965), Food Grain Procurement and Consumption in China (1984); *Recreations* choral singing, hill walking, bird watching, golf; *Style*— Prof Kenneth Walker; 4 Harpenden Rd, St Albans, Herts; South Lodge, Eden, Banff, Scotland; Dept of Economic & Political Studies, School of Oriental & African Studies, Univ of London WC1 (☎ 01 637 2388)

WALKER, (David) Lindsay; s of Rev David Sloan Walker, of Perthshire, and Mary Allan, *née* Ogilvie (d 1987); *b* 11 Sept 1940; *Educ* Stranraer HS, Alloa Acad; *m* 1963, Margaret Anne, da of Capt James Simpson Binnie, of Argyll; 1 s (David b 1969), 1 da (Valerie b 1966); *Career* corporate devpt dir Clydesdale Bank plc; dir: Banff & Buchan Nurseries Ltd 1982, Rhu Marina Ltd 1983, Freeport Scotland Ltd 1984, Clydesdale Bank Equity Ltd 1985, Clydesdale Bank Industl Investmts Ltd 1985, The Buy-Out Syndicate Ltd 1986; memb: Trade Devpt Ctee, Scottish Cncl Devpt and Indust, Rhu and Shandon Community Cncl; Churchill fell 1970; ACIB, FIBScot; *Recreations* sailing; *Style*— Lindsay Walker, Esq; Alt-na-Coille, Shandon, Helensburgh, Dunbartonshire G84 8NP (☎ 0436 820 264); Clydesdale Bank plc, 30 St Vincent Place, Glasgow G1 2HL (☎ 041 248 7070 ext 2581, fax 0436 820 264, telex 77135)

WALKER, Michael; s of Wilfred Arthur Walker, of Sudbury, Suffolk, and Molly, *née* Castle; *b* 1 Nov 1948; *Educ* Thomas Lethaby Sch London; *m* 6 June 1970, Jacqueline Margaret, da of John Alexander Bowen, of Witham, Essex; 1 s (Christopher Andrew James b 1984), 2 da (Sarah Jane b 1973, Lucy Anne b 1975); *Career* banker; dir: Clive Discount Co Ltd 1985, Clive Discount Hldgs Ltd 1988, Clivwell Securities Ltd 1988; *Recreations* various sports, photography; *Style*— Michael Walker, Esq; 9 Augustus Way, Lodge Park, Witham, Essex CM8 1HH (☎ 0376 513 911); Clive Discount Co Ltd, 9 Devonshire Square, London EC2M 4HP (☎ 01 548 4294, fax 01 548 5306, telex 8958901)

WALKER, Sir (Charles) Michael; GCMG (1976, KCMG 1963, CMG 1960); s of Col Charles William Garne Walker, CMG, DSO (d 1974), and Dorothy Frances (d 1965), da of F Hughes-Gibb, JP, of Manor House, Tarrant Gunville, Dorset; *b* 22 Nov 1916; *Educ* Charterhouse, New Coll Oxford; *m* 1945, Enid Dorothy, da of William Alexander McAdam, CMG (d 1961); 1 s, 1 da; *Career* clerk House of Lords 1939, serv WWII RA (attained rank of Lt-Col), serv Dominions Off 1947, 1 sec UK Embassy Washington DC 1949-51, High Cmmn New Delhi & Calcutta 1952-55, CRO 1955-58, IDC 1958, asst under-sec CRO 1959-62, high cmmr Ceylon 1962-65 & concurrently ambass Maldives 1965, high cmmr Malaysia 1966-71, perm sec Overseas Dvpt Admin 1971-73, high cmmr India 1974-76; chm: Cwlth Scholarship Cmmn UK 1977-87, Festival of India Tst 1980-83; *Style*— Sir Michael Walker, GCMG; Herongate House, West Chiltington Common, Pulborough, W Sussex (☎ 079 83 3473)

WALKER, Dr Paul Crawford; JP (Essex Cmmn for the Peace 1980-85); s of Dr Joseph Viccars Walker (d 1986), of Northants, and Mary Tilley *née* Crawford (d 1984); *b* 9 Dec 1940; *Educ* Queen Elizabeth GS Darlington, Downing Coll Cambridge (BA, MB BChir); *m* 1962, Barbara Georgina, da of Albert Edward Bliss, of Cambridgeshire; 3 da (Kate, Victoria, Caroline); *Career* Capt RAMC(V) 1975-78; area medical offr Wakefield Area Health Authority 1976-77, regional medical offr NE Thames Regional Health Authority 1977-85, gen mangr Frenchay Health Authority 1985-, chm CAER Consortium 1985, memb: NHS Computer Policy Ctee 1984-85, Advsy Ctee on Misuse of Drugs, exec ctee Gtr London Alcohol Advsy Service 1978-85, Mgmnt Ctee Kings Fund Centre 1980-84; hon sr lectr London Sch of Hygiene and Tropical Medicine 1983-, visiting prof Queen Mary Coll London 1985-, Avon Cmmn for the Peace 1985-; vice-chm Professional advisory gp NHSTA, 1987-; *Recreations* railway history, anthropology; *Style*— Dr Paul Walker, JP; Chagford, 8 Church Avenue, Stoke Bishop, Bristol BS9 1LD (☎ (0272) 687378); Frenchay District Headquarters, Beckspool Road, Frenchay Common, Bristol BS16 1ND (☎ (0272) 574505)

WALKER, Rt Hon Peter Edward; MBE (1960), PC (1970), MP (C) Worcester 1961-; s of Sydney Walker by his w Rose; *b* 25 Mar 1932; *Educ* Latymer Upper Sch; *m* 1969, Tessa, da of G Pout; 3 s, 2 da; *Career* contested (C) Dartford 1955 and 1959, memb Cons NEC 1956, nat chm Young Cons 1958-60, PPS to ldr House of Commons 1963-64, oppn spokesman: Fin and Econ 1964-66, Transport 1966-68, Local Govt, Housing and Land 1968-70; min Housing and Local Govt DOE June-Oct 1970, sec state: Environment 1970-72, Trade and Indust 1972-74; oppn spokesman: Trade and Indust and Consumer Affrs Feb-June 1974, Defence 1974-75; min Ag, Fish and Food 1979-83, sec state Energy June 1983-87, sec for Wales 1988-; *Style*— The Rt Hon Peter Walker, MBE, MP; Abbots Morton Manor, Gooms Hill, Abbots Morton, Worcestershire

WALKER, Peter Frank; s of Wilfrid Herbert Hornsey Walker (d 1965), and Mildred Sheila, *née* Caddell (d 1984); *b* 27 June 1937; *Educ* Oundle, Kings Coll London (BSc); *m* 27 March 1965, Susan Margaret, da of Geoffrey Hugh Sharp, of Leciester; 1 s (Richard b 1972), 2 da (Fiona b 1967, Julia b 1969); *Career* Nat Serv 2 Lt RE 1955-57; chm and md Usher Walker plc 1985- (md 1974-); pres Soc of Br Printing Ink Mfrs 1985-86 (cncl memb: 1973-76, 1979-82, 1983-87); CChem, MRIC, MIOP; *Recreations* racing, antiques, bridge; *Clubs* RAC; *Style*— Peter Walker, Esq; Usher-Walker plc, Chancery House, Chancery Lane, London WC2A 1SA (☎ 01 405 3642, fax 01 831 9921, telex 261293)

WALKER, Vice Adm Sir (Charles) Peter Graham; KBE (1967), CB (1964, DSC 1944); s of Charles Walker; *b* 23 Feb 1911; *Educ* Worksop Coll; *m* 1938, Pamela, da of George Hawley; 1 s, 1 da; *Career* serv WWII, HMS: Cornwall, Georgetown, Duke of York, Berwick (also at Admty); Rear Adm 1962, dir gen Dockyards and Maintenance MOD (RN) 1962-67 and ch naval engr offr 1963-67, Vice-Admiral 1965, ret 1967; non-exec dir Cammell Laird (Shipbuilder & Engrs) Ltd Birkenhead 1969-71, chm Civil Serv Cmmn Interview Bds 1971-82; *Style*— Vice Adm Sir Peter Walker, KBE, CB, DSC; Brookfield Coach House, Weston Lane, Bath BA1 4AG (☎ 0225 23863)

WALKER, Rt Rev Peter Knight; *see*: Ely, Bishop of

WALKER, Peter Michael; s of Oliver Walker (d 1965), of S Africa, and Freda Miller; *b* 17 Feb 1936; *Educ* Highlands North HS, Johannesburg S Africa; *m* 2, 1979, Susan, da of Harold Davies (d 1969); 1 s (Daniel), (1s Justin, 1 da Sarah by previous marriage); *Career* former Glamorgan and England cricketer (3 caps v S Africa 1960), former chm Cricketers Assoc, sports columnist for variety of papers and periodicals including The Times, Sunday Telegraph and Mail on Sunday, BBC 2, Refuge Assurance Sunday League, presenter, numerous radio programmes on news, current affairs, sport; md Merlin Film & Video Co Ltd; *Books* Winning Cricket, Cricket Conversations, The All Rounder; *Recreations* golf, music; *Style*— Peter Walker, Esq; 14 Chargot Rd, Llandaff, Cardiff (☎ 0222 563959); Merlin Film & Video Co Ltd, "Merlin House", 1 Pontcanna Place, Pontcanna, Cardiff CF5 1JY (☎ 0222 223456)

WALKER, Richard; s of Edwin Roland Walker (d 1980), of Epsom, and Barbara Joan, *née* Swann (d 1985); *b* 9 Mar 1942; *Educ* Epsom Coll, Worcester Coll Oxford (MA); *m* 29 March 1969, Angela Joan, da of John Robert Hodgkinson, of Minehead; 2 da (Rosemary b 1972, Sarah b 1974); *Career* barr Inner Temple 1966; asst cmmr: Parly Boundary Cmmn 1978-, Local Govt Boundary Cmmn 1982-; chm Pathfinders (Anglican Youth Movement) 1978-84, vice-chm Church Pastoral-Aid Soc 1978-85; *Books* Carter-Ruck on Libel and Slander (jt ed, 3 edn 1985); *Style*— Richard Walker, Esq; 1 Brick Court, Temple, London, EC4Y 9BY, (LDE Box No 468) (☎ 01 353 8845, fax 01 583 9144)

WALKER, (Edward) Rognvald Lindsay; s of James Alexander Walker, CBE (d 1967), of Edinburgh, and Edith Marion, *née* Liddle; *b* 30 Jan 1931; *Educ* Edinburgh Acad; *m* 18 April 1956, Lillias McGregor, da of Gregor Eadie, of Edinburgh; 2 s

(Douglas b 1958, David b 1964), 1 da (Fiona (Mrs Drew) b 1960); *Career* Nat Serv cmmnd Pilot Offr 1954-56; ptnr: Howden & Molleson CA 1957-64, Scott-Moncrieft Thomson & Shiells 1964-; auditor: St Andrews Tst plc 1964-, Scottish Equitable Life Assur Soc 1967-, Inst of CAs of Scotland 1980-85; dir: Melville Securities Ltd 1971-, Scott-Moncrieft Life & Pensions Ltd 1988-; chm: Pentland Cons Assoc 1969-72, Local Govt Auditors (Scotland) Assoc 1977-79; MICAS; *Recreations* golf, music, photography, reading; *Clubs* New (Edinburgh), The Hon Co of Edinburgh Golfers, Bruntsfield Links Golfing Soc; *Style*— Rognvald Lindsay, Esq; 9 Woodhall Rd, Edinburgh EH13 0DQ (☎ 031 441 3283); Scott-Moncrieff Thomson & Shiells, 17 Melville St, Edinburgh EH3 7PH (☎ 031 226 6281, fax 031 225 9829, tele 727 186)

WALKER, Dame Susan Armour; DBE (1972, CBE 1963); *Educ* Dunbar GS; *Career* chief agent Cons Central Office Yorkshire 1950-56, dep chief orgn offr Cons Central Office 1956-64, dep chm Cons Pty Orgn 1964-68, ret 1968; vice-chm WRVS 1969-75; *Style*— Dame Susan Walker, DBE; The Glebe House, Hownam, Kelso, Roxburghshire (☎ 057 34 277)

WALKER, Victor Stewart Heron; s and h of Sir James Walker, 5 Bt, by his 1 w Angela; *b* 8 Oct 1942; *Educ* Eton; *m* 1, 1969 (m dis 1982), Caroline Louisa, yst da of late Lt-Col Frederick Edwin Barton Wignall; 2 s, 1 da; m 2, 1982, Svea Borg, only da of late Capt Ernest Hugo Gothard Knutson Borg and Mary Hilary Borg; *Career* late 2 Lt Gren Gds & Lt Roy Wilts Yeo & Royal Yeo; *Clubs* Royal Yacht Sqdn; *Style*— Victor Walker Esq; Villa Josephine, Madliena, Malta

WALKER, Walter Basil Scarlett (Bobby); s of Col James Scarlett Walker, TA (d 1952), of Southport, and Hilda, *née* Sykes (d 1973); *b* 19 Dec 1915; *Educ* Rugby, Clare Coll Cambridge; *m* 10 April 1946, Teresa Mary Louise (Terry), *née* John; 1 s (Peter b 1947, d 1964), 1 da (Sara b 1953); *Career* serv RN 1940-46: Sub Lt (S) RNVR HMS Clavermouse Edinburgh 1940, HMS Kenya 1940-42 (Home Fleet), Operation "TORCH" (Algiers Landing) Staff of Adm 1942, asst sec to Adm Gibraltar 1943-45 (Lt Cdr 1945), Staff of Adm Cdr Expeditionary Force Paris and Minden (later C-in-C Germany); CA; ptnr Peat Marwick Mitchell & Co 1956-82 (joined 1937-39 and returned 1946); pt/t dir UK Atomic Energy Authy 1972-81, govr Royal Ballet Covent Gdn 1980-; chm local Gdn Soc; FCA 1940; *Recreations* gardening, golf; *Style*— Walter Walker, Esq; 11 Sloane Ave, London SW3 3JD (☎ 01 589 4133); Coles Privett, Nr Alton, Hants GU34 3PH (☎ 073 088 223)

WALKER, Gen Sir Walter Colyear; KCB (1968, CB 1964), CBE (1959, OBE 1949), DSO (1946) and Bars (1953, 1965); s of Arthur Colyear Walker; *b* 11 Nov 1912; *Educ* Blundell's, RMC Sandhurst; *m* 1938, Beryl Catherine, da of E N W Johnston; 2 s, 1 da; *Career* served Bde of Gurkhas: Waziristan 1939-41 (despatches twice), Burma 1942 and 1944-46 (despatches), Malaya 1949-59 (Brevet Lt-Col, despatches twice), Atomic Trials Maralinga S Australia 1956, Maj-Gen 1961, dir of ops Borneo 1962-65, Col 7 Duke of Edinburgh's Own Gurkha Rifles 1964-75, dep ch staff Allied Forces Central Europe 1965-67, Lt-Gen 1967, GOC-in-C Northern Cmd 1967-69, Gen 1969, C-in-C Allied Forces Northern Europe 1969-72; Paduka Stia Negara, Brunei 1 class 1964, hon Panglima Mangku Negara, Malaysia 1965; *Books* The Bear at the Back Door (1978), The Next Domino (1980); *Recreations* normal; *Clubs* Army & Navy; *Style*— General Sir Walter Walker, KCB, CBE, DSO; Haydon Farmhouse, Sherborne, Dorset DT9 5JB

WALKER, William Connoll; MP (C) Tayside North 1983-; s of Charles and Willamina Walker; *b* 20 Feb 1929; *Educ* Dundee: Logie and Blackness Schs, Trades Coll, Coll of Arts; Coll of Distributive Trades London; *m* 1956, Mavis Lambert, 3 da; *Career* Sqdn-Ldr RAFVR; contested (C) Dundee East Oct 1974, gained Perth and E Perthshire from SNP 1979-1983, memb: select ctee on Scottish Affairs 1979-, select ctee on Parly Commission for Administration 1979-; jt sec Aviation Ctee, jt vice-chm Cons Backbench European Affairs ctee 1982-; chm: Cons for European Reform, Walker Associates; *Clubs* RAF; *Style*— Bill Walker Esq, MP; Candletrees, Golf Course Road, Rosemount, Blairgowrie, Perthshire (☎ (0250) 2660)

WALKER, Hon Mrs (Yvonne Marie); *née* Wall; da of Baron Wall, OBE (Life Peer d 1980); *b* 1942; *m* 1970, Hugh Walker; *Style*— The Hon Mrs Walker; Fieldfare, Seven Hills Close, Walton-on-Thames, Surrey

WALKER-ARNOTT, Edward Ian; s of Charles Douglas Walker-Arnott (d 1980), of Woodford, Essex, and Kathleen Margaret, *née* Brittain; *b* 18 Sept 1939; *Educ* Haileybury Coll, London Univ (LLB), UCL (LLM); *m* 11 Sept 1971, (Phyllis) Jane, da of Lt-Col JM Ricketts, MC (d 1987), of Weston, Honiton, Devon; 1 s (William b 9 Nov 1981), 2 da (Emily b 7 April 1974, Hannah b 9 July 1979); *Career* slr 1963, ptnr Herbert Smith 1968; memb: Cork Ctee on Review of Insolvency Law 1977-82, Insolvency Practitioners Tbnl; cncl memb: Lloyds 1983-88 (hon memb 1988), Haileybury Coll (tres 1977-88), Benenden Sch; Freeman Worshipful Co of Slrs, Asst of Ct Worshipful Co of Loriners; memb Law Soc; *Recreations* cricket, tennis, gardening; *Clubs* City of London; *Style*— Edward Walker-Arnott, Esq; Manuden Hall, Manuden, nr Bishops Stortford, Herts CM23 1 DY; Herbert Smith, Watling House, 35 Cannon St, London EC4 (☎ 01 489 8000)

WALKER-MUNRO, Hon Mrs; Hon Marjorie Amy; *née* Biddulph; da of 3 Baron Biddulph (d 1972), and Amy Louise (d 1983), da of 4 Earl of Normanton; *b* 1927; *m* 1947, Thomas Ian Michael Walker-Munro; 1 s, 1 da; *Style*— Hon Mrs Walker-Munro; Balgersho, Coupar Angus, Perthshire PH13 9JE

WALKER-OKEOVER, Elizabeth, Lady; (Dorothy) Elizabeth; yr da of Josceline Reginald Heber-Percy, DL (gs of Algernon Heber- Percy, n of 5 Duke of Northumberland), and his w, Katharine, da of Lord Algernon Percy, s of 6 Duke of Northumberland; *b* 23 June 1913; *m* 1938, Lt-Col Sir Ian Walker-Okeover, 3 Bt, DSO & bar, TD, JP (d 1982), sometime Ld-Lt Derbyshire; 1 s (Sir Peter W-O, 4 Bt, *qv*), 2 da (Mrs Timothy Clowes, Jane W-O); *Style*— Elizabeth, Lady Walker-Okeover; Park Cottage, Osmaston, Ashbourne, Derbys

WALKER-OKEOVER, Sir Peter Ralph Leopold; 4 Bt (UK 1886), of Gateacre Grange, Co Lancaster, and Osmaston Manor, Co Derby; s of Sir Ian Peter Andrew Monro Walker-Okeover, 3 Bt, DSO, TD (d 1982); *b* 22 July 1947, (King Leopold III of the Belgians stood sponsor); *Educ* Eton, RMA Sandhurst; *m* 1972, Catherine Mary Maule, da of Col George Patrick Maule Ramsay (s of Archibald Ramsay by his w Hon Ismay Preston, formerly w of Lord Ninian Crichton-Stuart (2 s of 3 Marquess of Bute) and da of 14 Viscount Gormanston; Archibald was great nephew of 12 Earl of Dalhousie); 2 s (Andrew b 1978, Ralph b 1982), 1 da (Georgina b 1976); *Heir* s, Andrew Peter Monro Walker-Okeover, b 1978; *Career* Capt Blues and Royals; *Style*— Captain Sir Peter Walker-Okeover, Bt; Okeover Hall, Ashbourne, Derbyshire; House of Glenmuick, Ballater, Aberdeenshire, Scotland

WALKER-SMITH, John Angus; Prof; s of Dr Angus Buchanan Walker-Smith (d 1975), of Sydney, Australia, and Alexandra Buckingham, *née* Trindall (d 1970); *b* 1 Dec 1936; *Educ* Sydney C of E GS, Univ of Sydney (MB, BS, MD); *m* 29 Aug 1969, Elizabeth Cantley, da of George Blaikie, of Edinburgh; 1 s (James b 15 July 1978), 2 da (Louise b 13 Aug 1970, Laura b 17 March 1975); *Career* house physician: Hammersmith Hosp 1963, Brompton Hosp 1963; res fell: Gastroenterology Royal Prince Alfred Hosp Sydney 1964-66 (res med offr 1960-61), Kinderklinik Zurich Switzerland 1968; student supervisor and hon assoc physician Royal Alexandra Hosp for Children 1969-72 (professorial registrar 1967, res med offr 1962) conslt paediatrician St Bartholomew's Hosp 1973 - (prof paediatric gastroenterology 1985); memb: All Saints Parish Church Woodford Green, Wanstead and Woodford Cons Assoc; Freeman City of London, Liveryman Worshipful Soc Apothecaries; FRACP, FRCP (London and Edinburgh); memb: BMA, Br Paediatric Assoc, Br Soc Gastroenterology; *Books* Diseases of small intestine in childhood (3 edns 1975, 1979, 1988), Practical Paediatric Gastroenterology (with JR Hamilton and WA Walker 1983); *Recreations* swimming, photography, philately; *Style*— Prof John Walker-Smith; 16 Monkham's Drive, Woodford Green, Essex IG8 0LQ (☎ 01 505 7756); Acad Dept of Paediatric Gastroenterology, St Bartholomew's Hosp, London EC1A (☎ 01 601 8888)

WALKER-SMITH, Hon John Jonah; s (and h to btcy), of Baron Broxbourne (Life Peer); *b* 6 Sept 1939; *Educ* Westminster, Ch Ch Oxford; *m* 1974, Aileen Marie, only da of late Joseph Smith; 1 da (Lucinda b 1977); *Career* barrister; *Style*— The Hon John Walker-Smith; 1 Garden Court, London EC4 (☎ 01 353 5524)

WALKEY, Maj Gen (John) Christopher; CB (1953), CBE (1943); s of late Samuel Walkey, of Dawlish Devon, and Kathleen, *née* White; *b* 18 Oct 1903; *Educ* Newton Coll Devon, RMA Woolwich; *m* 24 Feb 1947, Beatrice Record, da of late Maj Frank McCabe Brown, of Yew Close, Wells, Somerset; 1 da (Barbara d 1949; *Career* cmmnd RE 1923, chief engr 13 Corps 1943-47, Asst Cmdt RMA Sandhurst 1949-51, chief engr MELF 1951-54, engr-in-chief WO 1954-57, ret 1957, Col Cmdt RE 1958-68, Hon Col RE Resourses Unit 1959-64; Offr Legion of Merit USA 1945; *Style*— Maj-Gen Christopher Walkey, CB, CBE; Holcombe House, Moreton Hampstead, Devon (☎ 0647 40576)

WALKINSHAW, Nicholas John Coode; s of David Walkinshaw (d 1966), of Isle of Wight, and Barbara Betty Coode Walkinshaw, *née* Coode-Adams; *b* 30 July 1940; *Educ* Marlborough, St John's Coll Cambridge (MA); *m* 1, 14 Sept 1963 (m dis), Sibyl Mary, da of William S Hutton, of Cambs; 2 s (Christopher b 1965, Anthony b 1967); m 2, 28 May 1977, Barbara Hazel, da of Bertie Ward, of Doncaster; *Career* md Vandenbergh Walkinshaw Ltd Windsor 1972-76, chm Walkinshaw Hldgs Ltd Kingsclere Newbury 1976-87, md Walkinshaw Handling Ltd 1987; Freeman: City of London, Worshipful Co of Merchant Taylors; *Recreations* riding/horse trials, sailing; *Clubs* Leander, Henley Royal Regatta; *Style*— Nicholas J C Walkinshaw, Esq; Keepers, Sydmonton, Newbury, Berks; c/o Lloyds Bank, Thames Street, Windsor; King John House, Kingsclere Park, Kingsclere, Newbury, Berks (☎ 0635 298171, telex 848648, fax 0632 297936)

WALL, (Dame) (Alice) Anne; DCVO (1981, CVO 1972, MVO 1964); da of Adm Sir Geoffrey Alan Brooke Hawkins, KBE, CB, MVO, DSC (d 1980), by his w Lady Margaret Ida, *née* Montagu-Douglas-Scott (d 1976), eldest da of 7 Duke of Buccleuch; *b* 31 Mar 1928; *Educ* Miss Faunce's PNEU Sch, Portsmouth Tech Coll; *m* 1975, Cdr Michael Edward St Quintin Wall, RN, s of Capt Bernard St Quintin Wall, Grenadier Gds (d 1976); *Career* asst press sec to HM The Queen 1958-81, extra woman of bedchamber to HM The Queen 1981-; *Style*— Mrs Michael Wall, DCVO; Ivy House, Lambourn, Berks RG16 7PB (☎ 0488 72348); 6 Chester Way, Kennington, London SE11 4UT (☎ 01 582 0692)

WALL, Brian Owen; s of Maurice Stanley Wall (d 1983), of Newport, Gwent, and Ruby Wall, *née* Holmes; *b* 17 June 1933; *Educ* Newport HS Monmouthshire, Imp Coll of Sci and Technol (BSc, ACGI), RNC Greenwich; *m* 4 Aug 1960, Patricia Thora, da of Percival Spencer Hughes (d 1965), of Langstone, Mon; 1 s (Andrew b 1969); *Career* with MOD in Bath: ship vulnerability 1958-61, submarine design 1961-66; head of propeller design Admty Experiment Works Haslar 1966-71, Staff of C in C Fleet Portsmouth 1971-73, submarine support and modernisation gp 1973-77, RCDS 1977; MOD Bath: Ship Prodn Div 1978-79, project dir New SSBN Design 1979-84, dir cost estimating and analysis 1985, chief naval architect 1985-; memb RCNC, CEng 1969, FRINA 1986; *Recreations* photography, golf, music, walking; *Style*— Brian Wall, Esq; Wychwood, 39 High Bannerdown, Batheaston, Bath, Avon BA1 7JZ (☎ 0225 858 694); Ministry of Defence, Foxhill, Bath (☎ 0225 88 2793)

WALL, David Richard; CBE (1985); s of Charles Wall, and Dorothy Irene, *née* Barden; *b* 15 Mar 1946; *Educ* Haliford House Shepperton, Royal Ballet Sch White Lodge Richmond, Royal Ballet Sch Upper Sch; *m* 1 Aug 1967, Alfreda, da of Edward Thorogood (d 1966); 1 s (Daniel b 12 Dec 1974), 1 da (Annaliese b 15 Oct 1971); *Career* Royal Ballet 1963-: soloist 1964, princ dancer 1966-84, danced all maj classical roles incl Rakes Progress 1965, Swan Lake (with Margot Fonteyn) 1966, Giselle (Peter Wright prodn) 1968, Walk to the Paradise Garden 1972, Manon 1974, Dancers at a Gathering 1974, Romeo and Juliet 1975, La Bayadere 1975, Rituals 1975, Mayerling 1977; *Style*— David Wall, Esq, CBE; 34 Croham Manor Rd, South Croydon, Surrey; c/o Royal Academy of Dancing, 48 Vicarage Crescent, London SW11 3LT (☎ 01 223 0091, fax 01 924 3129, telex 8952105 RADANC G)

WALL, Edward Alfred (Ted); ERD (1967); s of Alfred Ernest Wall (d 1944), of Rotherham Yorks, and Katherine Hannah Walker (d 1952); *b* 11 July 1925; *Educ* Spurley Hey Sch Rotherham, Harvard Bus Sch Vevey Switzerland (sr mgmnt programme); *m* 21 Dec 1946, Phyllis Doreen Jean, da of Reginald Harry Pearce (d 1957), of Monmouth; 1 s (Adrian b 1955), 1 da (Vanessa b 1951); *Career* served S Staffs Regt 1943-45, Worcs Regt 1945-47, cmmnd RASC 1947, invalid out 1949; Capt AER 1954-67; articled R A Williams & Co 1949-54, chief accountant Wincanton Tport 1954-68, fin accountant Kuwait Nat Petroleum Co Kuwait 1968; Unigate Ltd: cnslt 1969, md Wincanton Tport and dep chm Tport Eng Div 1970-78; NFC: joined 1978, chm NFC Int Hldgs Ltd 1987- (md 1984-87), appointed Main Bd 1985-; past chm Road Haulage Assoc: Milk Carriers Gp, Dairy Trade Fedn Carriers Gp; *Recreations* fishing, swimming, music, reading, travel; *Clubs* Naval and Military; *Style*— Ted Wall, Esq, ERD; Cherry Trees, The Hocket, Northfield End, Henley-on-Thames, Oxon RG9 2JJ (☎ 0491 573 673); NFC plc, The Merton Centre, St Peters St, Bedford MK40 2UB (☎ 0234 272222, fax 0234 270 900, car tel 0860 530 732, telex 826803)

WALL, Baroness; Gladys Evelyn; da of William Wright and Martha Naomi Cox; *m*

1939, Baron Wall, OBE (Life Peer, d 1980); 2 s, 1 da; *Style—* The Rt Hon the Lady Wall; Wychwood, Coombe End, Coombe Hill, Kingston, Surrey

WALL, Hon Martin John; er twin s of Baron Wall, OBE (Life Peer d 1980); *b* 1948; *m* 1976, Margaret, da of L J Scott, of Alton, Hants; *Style—* The Hon Martin Wall

WALL, Prof Patrick David; s of Capt Thomas Wall, MC (d 1976), and Ruth, *née* Cresswell (d 1978); *b* 5 April 1925; *Educ* St Pauls, Christ Church Oxford (BM, BCH, DM); *Career* instr physiology Yale 1948-50, asst prof anatomy Chicago Univ 1950-53, instr physiology Harvard 1953-55, assoc prof and prof biology MIT 1955-67, prof anatomy UCL 1967- ; visiting prof Hebrew Univ Jerusalem 1972-; hon MD Siena 1987; FRCP 1984; *Books* Challenge of Pain (with R Melzack, 2 ed 1988), Textbook of Pain (2 ed 1989); *Style—* Prof Patrick Wall; 141 Grays Inn Rd, London WC1X 8UB (☎ 01 833 0451)

WALL, Maj Sir Patrick Henry Bligh; MC (1945), VRD (1957); s of Henry Benedict Wall; *b* 14 Oct 1916; *Educ* Downside; *m* 1953, Sheila Elizabeth Putnam (d 1983); 1 da; *Career* servs 1935-50 with RM, Maj 1944; RN Staff Coll 1946, jt services Staff Coll 1947; memb Westminster City Cncl 1953-63; MP (C): Haltemprice 1954-55, E Yorkshire 1955-83, Beverley 1983-87; pps to: min AFF 1955-57, chllr exchequer 1958-59; delegate to UN Gen Assembly 1962, vice-chm Cons Pty Def Ctee 1965-77, Select Ctee Def 1979-84; chm: Br SA Parly Gp 1970-87, Monday Club 1977-79, Br Taiwan Parly Gp 1979-87, Br Portugese Parly Gp 1979-87; pres North Atlantic Assembly 1983-85 (chm Mil Ctee 1977-79, vice-pres 1980-82); US Legion of Merit 1944, Kt SMO Malta; kt 1981, Brilliant Star of Taiwan 1987;; *Books* Soviet Maritime Thrust, Indian Ocean and the Threat to the West, Southern Ocean and the Security of the Free World; *Recreations* model ships & aircraft; *Clubs* Royal Yacht Squadron; *Style—* Maj Sir Patrick Wall, MC, VRD, RM (ret); Brantinghamthorp, Brantingham, nr Brough, North Humberside HU15 1QG (☎ 0482 667248); 8 Westminster Gdns, Marsham St, London SW1P 4JA (☎ 01 828 1803)

WALL, Maj-Gen Robert Percival Walter; CB (1978); s of Frank Ernest Wall, of Goodmayes Essex (d 1986), and Ethel Elizabeth, *née* Collins (d 1980); *b* 23 August 1927; *Educ* Army & Jt Servs Staff Coll and Royal Coll of Defence Studies; *m* 1, 1953 (m dis 1985), Patricia Kathleen O'Brien; 2 s (Malcolm b 1956, Patrick b 1958), 1 da (Clare b 1961); m 2, 7 Feb 1986, Jennifer Hilary Anning; *Career* RM 1945; served Middle East, Far East; various MOD appointments; dir Staff JSS Coll 1969-71; maj-gen RM chief of Staff 1976-79; dir (Land) Decade Educn Cncl 1980-; mgmnt conslt 1983-; chm Essex Family Practitioner Ctee 1985; Freeman City of London 1978, Craft Owning Freeman Co of Watermen and Lightermen 1979; fell BR Inst of Mgmnt 1980; FRSA, JP City of London 1982; *Recreations* reading, walking, cricket, rugby; *Clubs* Army and Navy, MCC; *Style—* Maj-Gen Robert Wall; c/o Barclays Bank, 116 Goodmayes Road, Goodmayes, Ilford, Essex

WALL, Sir Robert William; OBE (1980); s of William George Wall, of Sellack (d 1980), and Gladys Perina, *née* Powell (d 1958); *b* 27 Sept 1929; *Educ* Monmouth Sch, Bristol Coll of Technol; *m* 24 Feb 1968, Jean, da of Harry Clifford Ashworth; 1 s (Matthew b 1970, d 1986), 1 da (Gabrielle b 1971); *Career* cmmnd RAF 1955-58, OC Mountain Rescue Team RAF Valley 1956-58; engr 1958-88: Bristol Aeroplane Co, Br Aerospace plc; cncl memb: Univ of Bristol (chm Bldgs ctee), ss Great Britain Project; govr Bristol Vic Theatre Tst, pres Bristol Soc of Model & Experimental Engrs, memb The Audit Cmmn; ldr: Cons Gp, Bristol City Cncl; chm: Tport Users Consultative ctee for W Eng, Western Provincial Area Nat Union of Cons & Unionist Assocs; Freeman City of London 1986, Freeman Co of Watermen and Lightermen; Hon MA Univ of Bristol 1982; MBIM 1980, AMRAeS 1985; kt 1987; *Books* Bristol Channel Paddle Steamers (1973), Ocean Liners (1979), Airliners (1981), Bristol-Maritime City (1981), The Story of HMS Bristol (1986); *Recreations* hill walking, collecting postcards; *Clubs* Royal Overseas League, Clifton, Bristol Savages; *Style—* Sir Robert Wall, OBE; 1 Ormerod Rd, Stoke Bishop, Bristol BS9 1BA; Lower Deems, Branscombe, Devon (☎ 0272 682 910); The Council House, College Green, Bristol BS1 5TR (☎ 0272 266 031, fax 0272 294 512, telex 449819 CITBRI)

WALL, Hon Robin John; yr twin s of Baron Wall, OBE (Life Peer d 1980); *b* 1948; *Style—* The Hon Robin Wall

WALL, Prof (Charles) Terence Clegg; s of Charles Wall (d 1976), of Woodfield, Dursley, Glos, and Ruth, *née* Clegg; *b* 14 Dec 1936; *Educ* Marlborough Coll, Trinity Coll Cambridge (BA, PhD); *m* 22 Aug 1959, Alexandra Joy, da of Prof Leslie Spencer Hearnshaw, of W Kirby; 2 s (Nicholas b 1962, Alexander b 1967), 2 da (Catherine b 1963, Lucy b 1965); *Career* fell Trinity Coll Cambridge 1959-64, Harkness fell 1960-61, lectr Cambridge Univ 1961-64, Univ reader and fell St Catherine's Coll Oxford 1964-65, prof of pure mathematics Liverpool Univ 1965-; Royal Soc Leverhulme visiting prof Mexico 1967, SERC sr fell 1983-88; tres: Wirral Area SDP 1985-88, W Wirral SLD 1988-; fell: Cambridge Phil Soc 1958-, American Math Soc 1961-, London Math Soc 1961 (memb Cncl 1973-80, pres 1978-80); FRS 1969 (memb Cncl 1974-76); winner of Junior Berwick Prize 1965, Whitehead Prize 1976, Polya Prize 1988, Sylvester Medal 1988; *Books* Surgery on Compact Manifolds (1970), A Geometric Introduction to Topology (1971); *Recreations* gardening, home winemaking; *Style—* Prof Terence C Wall; 5 Kirby Park, West Kirby, Wirral, Merseyside, L48 2HA (☎ 051 625 5063); Dept of Pure Maths, Liverpool Univ, Liverpool, L69 3BX (☎ 051 794 4062, fax 051 708 6502)

WALL MORRIS, George Malcolm; s of Richard Wall Morris, of Fuengirola, Spain, and Doris Wall Morris; *b* 16 Sept 1937; *Educ* Radley; *m* 6 Dec 1969, Katherine Mary Lucy, da of Gen Sir Malcolm Cartwright-Taylor, KCB (d 1969); 2 s (Malcolm b 1971, Andrew b 1974); *Career* short service cmmn, 10 Royal Hussars Lt; direct mktg conslt, sales dir Merit Direct Ltd; *Recreations* gourmet, gardening, sailing; *Clubs* Royal Irish Yacht; *Style—* George Wall Morris, Esq; Harlyn House, Manor Rd, Stratford upon Avon, Warks CV37 7EA; Merit Direct Ltd, Conrad Hse, Brimingham Rd, Stratford upon Avon, Warks CV37 0AZ (☎ 0789 299622, telex 312607 MERIT G, fax 0789 292341, car ☎ 0860 541316)

WALLACE, Gp Capt Albert Frederick; CBE (1963, OBE 1955), DFC (1943); s of Maj Frederick Wallace, late RA (d 1952), and Ada, *née* Betts (d 1981); *b* 22 August 1921; *Educ* Roan Sch Blackheath; *m* 26 Nov 1940, Evelyn, da of Charles White (d 1950), of Streatham, London; 1 s (Robert b 1943), 1 da (Hazel b 1951); *Career* joined RAF 1939, trained as Air Observer (Navigator), cmmnd 1940; served WWII with 108 Sqdn 1939-40, 40 Sqdn 1940, 93 Sqdn 1941, 214 Sqdn 1943, 620 Sqdn 1943-44; one of the first navigators to be promoted Sqdn Ldr and the yst (at 23) to be promoted Wing Cdr 1945; permanent cmmn 1946; post-war service included: Jt Admin Planning Staff (MOD) 1949-53, Air Staff Plans Middle East 1953-55, head of organisation branch MEAF (Cyprus) 1960-62, Station Cdr RAF Shawbury 1963-66; Dep Dir RAF (Personnel) Establishments MOD 1966-69; graduate of RAF staff coll 1945, Nat Defence Coll 1960, and RN War Coll Greenwich 1963; ret 1969; joined Local Authorities' Mgmnt Services and Computer Ctee as Regnl Offr W Midlands and Manpower Specialist 1969; head of Mgmnt Services Warwickshire CC 1971-73; County Personnel Offr W Midlands (Metropolitan) CC 1973-78; dir W Midlands Passenger Transport Exec 1977-78; controller of manpower GLC 1978-82; MBIM 1969, MIPM 1971, MILGA (later AICS) 1974; *Recreations* bridge, golf; *Clubs* RAF; *Style—* Gp Capt A F Wallace, CBE, DFC; 24 Kepplestone, Staveley Road, Eastbourne BN20 7JZ (☎ 0323 30668)

WALLACE, Alistair James Wishart Falconer; s of Alexander Lewis Paget Falconer Wallace, TD (d 1975), of Strathdon, Aberdeenshire, and Lois, *née* Wishart-Thomson (d 1940); *b* 17 August 1935; *Educ* Eton, Gordonstoun; *m* 1, (m dis 1965), Eileen Mary, *née* Macnaughton; 1 s (James Alexander Falconer b 22 June 1960), 2 da (Caroline Jane b 9 Sept 1958, Emma Mary b 26 Aug 1962); m 2, 10 Feb 1966, Alice Julia, da of Charles John Addison Doughty QC (d 1973), of London; 1 s (Adam William Doughty Falconer b 29 Aug 1969), 1 da (Arabella Lois b 11 June 1971); *Career* Nat Serv The Lifeguards 1954-56, TA Inns of Ct and City Yeomanry 1957-67, ret Lt TARO; dir Maynard Reeve and Wallace Ltd (Lloyds Brokers) 1964, dir Edinburgh Gen Insur Servs 1972-83, chm Maynard Wallace and Coffrey (Lloyds underwriting agents) 1975, chm Andrew Booth Gp 1975-83, dir Laurence Philips Agencies 1986, chm Aragon Agencies 1988 (dir 1983-), chm Alpwood Hldgs 1988 (dir 1984-); former jt chm Dockland Settlements (res 1981); Liveryman Worshipful Co of Gunmakers; *Recreations* shooting, fishing, golf; *Clubs* Whites, Turf, Pratts, City of London; *Style—* Alistair Wallace, Esq; Manor Farm House, Damerham, Fordingbridge, Hants SP6 3HN (☎ 0725 3229); 11 Aylesford St, London SW1V 3RY (☎ 01 821 8393); Aragon Agencies Ltd, 100 Fenchurch St, London EC3M 5JB (☎ 01 265 1711, fax 01 702 4760)

WALLACE, Constance Armine Louise; da of Maj Graeme Roper Wallace, of North Tregeare Farmhouse, Tresmeer, Launceston, Cornwall, and Katherine Jane Armine, *née* Wodehouse; *b* 27 Sept 1960; *Educ* West Wing Sch Kyneton House Thornbury, Monmouth Sch for girls, Cambridge Univ; *Career* slr Bond Pearce Plymouth 1984-88, Simpson Curtis Leeds 1989-; memb Jr C of C; memb Law Soc 1986; *Recreations* haute cuisine, art; *Style—* Miss Constance Wallace; North Tregeare Farmhouse, Tresmeer, Launceston, Cornwall (☎ 0566 81319); Simpson Curtis, 41 Park Sq, Leeds (☎ 0532 433433, fax 0532 445598, telex 55376)

WALLACE, Hon Mrs (Elizabeth Anne Hoyer); *née* Millar; da of 1 Baron Inchyra, GCMG, CVO; *b* 1933; *m* 1965, William Euan Wallace (d 1977); *Style—* The Hon Mrs Wallace; Egbury House, St Mary Bourne, Andover, Hants

WALLACE, (James) Fleming; QC (1985); s of James Fleming Baird Wallace (d 1957), and Margaret Braidwood, *née* Gray; *b* 19 Mar 1931; *Educ* The Edinburgh Acad, Edinburgh Univ (MA, LLB); *m* 15 Sept 1964, Valerie Mary (d 1986), da of Leslie Lawrence (d 1957), of Wilts; 2 da (Jennifer b 1966, Gillian b 1969); *Career* Nat Serv RA 2 Lt 1954-56, TA RA Lt 1956-60; advocate Scots Bar 1957-60, Scottish parly draftsman and legal sec to the Lord Advocate London 1960-79, counsel Scottish Law Cmmn Edinburgh 1979-; memb Faculty of Advocates 1957; *Books* contributor to Stair Memorial Encyclopaedia of the Laws of Scotland (1988); *Recreations* choral singing, hill walking, golf, badminton; *Clubs* Royal Mid Surrey GC; *Style—* Fleming Wallace, Esq, QC; The Scottish Law Cmmn, 140 Causewayside, Edinburgh (☎ 031 668 2131)

WALLACE, Ian Bryce; OBE (1983); s of Sir John Wallace (d 1949), of London, and Mary McAdam Bryce Temple; *b* 10 July 1919; *Educ* Charterhouse, Trinity Hall Cambridge (MA); *m* 1948, Patricia Gordon, da of Michael Gordon Black, OBE (d 1946), of Scotland; 1 s (John), 1 da (Rosemary); *Career* singer, actor, writer & broadcaster; *Books* Promise Me You'll Sing Mud (1975), Nothing Quite Like It (1982); *Recreations* walking, reading, photography & watching sport; *Clubs* Garrick, MCC; *Style—* Ian Wallace, Esq, OBE; c/o Fraser & Dunlop Ltd, 91 Regent St, W1R 8RU (☎ 01 734 7311)

WALLACE, Sir Ian James; CBE (1971, OBE 1942); s of John Madder Wallace, CBE; *b* 25 Feb 1916; *Educ* Uppingham, Jesus Coll Cambridge; *m* 1942, Catherine Frost Mitchell; 1 s, 1 da; *Career* Cdr (A) RNVR Fleet Air Arm WWII; chm SNR (Bearings) UK Ltd 1978-85; dir: Massey Ferguson Hldgs 1952-72, Coventry Motor and Sundries Ltd 1986-; commercial conslt TRW Valves; Lloyd's underwriter; vice pres W Midlands Cons Cncl (chm 1967-70, pres 1972-74); Coventry C of C 1972-74; chm: CBI Midland Regnl Cncl 1967-69, Fedn of Coventry Cons Assoc 1968-; (chm 1968-87, pres 1987-); former memb: W Midlands Econ Planning Cncl and Severn-Trent Water Authy; pres Worcestershire Rifle Assoc; kt 1982; *Recreations* rifle shooting, antiquarian horology; *Clubs* Carlton, Naval and Mil, North London RC, Drapers Coventry; *Style—* Sir Ian Wallace, CBE; Little House, 156 High St, Broadway, Worcs WR12 7AJ (☎ 0386 852414)

WALLACE, Ian Norman Duncan; QC (1973); s of Duncan Gardner Wallace (d 1939, HBM Crown Advocate in Egypt), of Alexandria, Egypt, and Eileen Agnes Wilkin, of Smyrna, Turkey; *b* 21 April 1922; *Educ* Loretto Sch, Midlothian and Oriel Coll Oxford (MA) ; *m* 25 March 1961 (m dis 1965), Valerie Mary, da of Rudolf Karl Walter Hollmann of Beckenham, Kent; *Career* Ordinary Seaman RN 1940-41, Lieut RNVR 1941-46; barr Middle Temple 1948, visiting scholar Univ of California at Berkeley 1977, visiting prof Kings Coll London 1987, practicing barr and arbitrator specialising in Construction Law; author Hudson on Building and Civil Engineering Contracts (1959, 65, 70 and 79 edns), Building and Civil Engineering Standard Forms (1969), Further Building Standard Forms (1973), ICE Conditions (1978), The International Civil Engineering Contract (1980), Construction Contracts Principals and Policies (1986), contributor: Law Quarterly Review, Construction Law Journal, International Construction Law Review, memb editorial bd Construction Law Journal; *Recreations* tennis, shooting; *Clubs* Lansdowne, Hurlingham; *Style—* Ian N D Wallace, Esq, QC; 53 Holland Park, London, W11 3RS (☎ 01 727 7640); 1 Atkin Building, Gray's Inn, London, WC1R 5BQ, (☎ 01 404 0102), fax 01 405 7456, telex 298 623 HUDSON G

WALLACE, James Robert; MP (Lib) Orkney and Shetland 1983-(Soc & Lib Dem 1988-); s of John Fergus Thomson Wallace, of Annan Dumfriesshire, and Grace Hannah, *née* Maxwell; *b* 25 August 1954; *Educ* Annan Acad Dumfriesshire, Downing Coll (BA, MA), Edinburgh Univ (LLB); *m* 1983, Rosemary Janet, da of William Grant Paton Fraser, OBE, TD, of Barloch, Mugdock Rd, Milngavie, Glasgow; 2 da (Helen b 1985, Clare b 1987); *Career* memb Scottish Lib Pty Nat Exec 1976-85 (vice-chm

1982-85); contested (Lib): Dumfries 1979, S Scotland Euro elections June 1979; admitted to Faculty of Advocates 1979, Lib parly spokesman on defence and dep whip 1985-87; Alliance election spokesman on tport 1987; dep whip 1985-87, elected chief whip and reappointed defence spokesman Oct 1987, elected chief whip Social & Lib Democrats, appointed employed spokesman 1988; *Recreations* golf, music, travel, croquet; *Clubs* Scottish Liberal; *Style*— James Wallace, Esq, MP; Northwood House, Tankerness, Orkney (☎ 0856 86383); House of Commons, London SW1

WALLACE, Hon Jim Anthony Hill; s of Baroness Dudley and late Guy Wallace and h to Barony; *b* 9 Nov 1930; *Educ* Lancing; *m* 1962, Nicola Jane, nee Dunsterville; 2 s; *Style*— The Hon Jim Wallace; Little Grange, Napleton, Kempsey, Worcs

WALLACE, John Malcolm Agnew; JP (Wigtownshire), DL (1971); s of Maj John Alexander Agnew Wallace, MC (d 1956); *b* 30 Jan 1928; *Educ* Brooks Sch Andover Mass USA, Harrow; *m* 1955, Louise Arden, *née* Haworth-Booth; 1 s, 2 da; *Career* farmer; *Style*— Malcolm Wallace, Esq, JP, DL; Lochryan, Stranraer, Wigtownshire

WALLACE, John Williamson; s of Christopher Kidd Wallace, of Glenrothes, Fife, and Ann Drummond, *née* Allan; *b* 14 April 1949; *Educ* Buckhaven HS, King's Coll Cambridge (MA); *m* 3 July 1971, Elizabeth Jane, da of Prof Ronald Max Hartwell, of Oxford; 2 s (Cosmo b 1979, Esme b 1982); *Career* asst principal trumpet LSO 1974-76, principal trumpet Philharmonia 1976-, performed obligato trumpet at Royal Wedding 1981, performed first performance of Sir Peter Maxwell Davies trumpet concerto Hiroshima 1988; hon memb RCM 1982, ARAM, memb Royal Soc of Musicians; *Books* First Book of Trumpet Solos (1985), Second Book of Trumpet Solos (1985); *Recreations* playing the trumpet; *Style*— John Wallace, Esq; 16 Woodstock Rd, Croydon, Surrey CR0 1JR (☎ 01 688 1170); Seven Muses, 5 Milton Ave, Highgate N6 (☎ 01 348 7256, telex 918774)

WALLACE, Hon Mrs (Karis Valerie Violet); *née* Mond; o da of 2 Baron Melchett (d 1949), and Gwen, *née* Wilson; *b* 26 July 1927; *m* 1, 15 Dec 1949 (m dis 1956), John Hackman Sumner, yt s of late Thomas Hackman Sumner, of Redruth, Cornwall; 1 s (Justin b 1953); m 2, 1956, Brian Albert Wallace (d 1986), o s of Peter Daniel Wallace, of Melbourne, Australia; 2 da (Jessica b 1957, Arabella b 1959); *Career* theatre director; *Style*— The Hon Mrs Wallace; Greenways, Lambourn, Berks

WALLACE, Lt Col Malcolm Robert; s of Col Robert Francis Hurter Wallace, CMG (d 1970), and Euphemia, *née* Hoskyns (d 1972); chief of House of Wallace and represents in direct male line families of Wallace, of Riccarton, of Craigie, of Elderslie; *b* 14 Dec 1921; *Educ* Stowe; *Career* serv Black Watch WWII (despatches), serv in Korean War with Argyll and Sutherland Highlanders and Black Watch, Aust Staff Coll 1955, serv Malaya, Cyprus, War Off, Singapore and Borneo, cmd Argyll and Sutherland Highlanders 1964-67, Regimental Sec The Black Watch 1967-77; memb Queen's Body Gd for Scotland The Royal Co of Archers; *Recreations* shooting, fishing; *Clubs* Army and Navy, Royal Perth Golfing Soc; *Style*— Lt Col M R Wallace; Hilton of Gask, Auchterarder, Perthshire (☎ 073 873 278)

WALLACE, Hon Michael George; s of Baron Wallace of Coslany; *b* 1944; *m* 1974, Susan, da of Henry Price; has issue; *Recreations* gardening, amateur radio; *Style*— The Hon Michael Wallace; 17 Leaminton Ave, Orpington, Kent

WALLACE, Nicholas Patrick (Nicky); s of James Wallace, of 54 South Main Street, Wexford, Ireland, and Brigid Ita, *née* Lambert; *b* 12 Sept 1952; *Educ* De La Salle Coll Waterford, Jacob Kramer Coll Leeds (Dip Fashion and Design); *m* 2 Sept 1978 (m dis 1988), Carmel Marie Therese, da of Desmond Corish; 1 s (Karl Nicholas b 28 Feb 1981), 1 da (Lauren Catherine b 19 Jan 1985); *Career* int fashion designer (supplies top mkts worldwide), designer wardrobes for TVs Miami Vice, produced own name designer collections for 5 yrs; *Recreations* diving, windsurfing, reading, art; *Style*— Nicky Wallace, Esq; 6 Islington Terrace, Sandy Cove, Co Dublin, Ireland; Nicky Wallace International Trading Ltd, 2c Rockview Terrace, Montenotte, Cork, Ireland (☎ 021 506 930)

WALLACE, Richard Lindsay; CBE (1946), AFC (1941); s of William James Lindsay Wallace (d 1937); *b* 28 Feb 1909; *Educ* Sedbergh, RAF Coll Cranwell; *m* 1, 1940, Lorna Elspeth, *née* Comrie (d 1960); 1 s, 1 da; m 2, 1962, Mary Helen, *née* Marsden; *Career* Gp Capt RAF Co 36 (TB) Singapore 1938-39, Flying Instr 1939-42, RAF Station Leuchars (Coastal Cmd) 1943-44, OC 298 Wing (gen reconnaissance) W Africa 1944-45; asst administrator: London Hosp 1953-57, Nuffield Orthopaedic Centre and Utd Oxford Hosps 1957-1975; *Recreations* painting; *Style*— Richard Wallace Esq, CBE, AFC; 6 Abberbury Rd, Iffley, Oxford OX4 4ES (☎ 0865 777056)

WALLACE, Robert; TD (1956); s of late Joseph Duncan Wallace; *b* 4 July 1915; *Educ* Glasgow Academy; *m* 1949, Jeanne Houlden, da of Thomas Beswick; 2 children; *Career* dir Brookhurst Switchgear Ltd 1954-58; chm: The Automatic Sprinkler Co Ltd 1958-79, The Atlas and Automatic Sprinkler Co Ltd 1977-79; memb Inst of CA of Scotland 1946-; *Recreations* golf, gardening; *Style*— Robert Wallace, Esq, TD; Spey House, Legh Rd, Knutsford, Cheshire WA16 8NT (☎ 0565 3254)

WALLACE, Hon Robin Guy Hill; s of Baroness Dudley and late Guy Wallace; *b* 1936; *Educ* Malvern; *m* 1959, Jill Alexandra, *née* Williams; 2 s; *Style*— The Hon Robin Wallace; Pond House, Ham Hill, Powick, Worcs WR2 4RD (☎ 0905 830445)

WALLACE, (Wellesley) Theodore Octavius; s of Dr Caleb Paul Wallace, O St J (d 1981), and Dr Lucy Elizabeth Rainsford, *née* Pigott (d 1968); *b* 10 April 1938; *Educ* Charterhouse, Christ Church Oxford (MA); *m* 23 Jan 1988, Maria Amelia, da of Sir Ian George Abercromby, Bt; *Career* 2 Lt RA 1958, Lt Surrey Yeomanry 1959; called to the Bar Inner Temple 1963, memb Lloyds; Inner London Sch govr 1966-86, chm Chelsea Cons Assoc 1981-84; pt/t chm Value Added Tax Tribunals 1989; Cons candidate: Pontypool Feb 1974, South Battersea Oct 1974 and May 1979; *Publications*: The Case Against Wealth Tax (1968), A History of Hans Town Chelsea (1986); *Recreations* tennis, skiing; *Clubs* Carlton; *Style*— Theodore Wallace, Esq; Whitecroft, West Clandon, Surrey (☎ 0483 222574); 17 Old Buildings, Lincoln's Inn, London WC2A 3UP (☎ 01 405 9653, fax 01 405 5032)

WALLACE, Vivien Rosemary Lumsdaine; da of late Capt James Edward Lumsdaine Wallace, and late Gwynne Wallace, *née* Jones; *b* 11 Feb 1944; *Educ* St Martin's Sch Solihull, Emma Willard Troy New York (on English speaking Union Scholarship), Arts Cncl of GB bursary to study theatre admin; *m* 1, 2 Sept 1964, Anthony Thomas Etridge; m 2, Terence Fracis Frank Coleman; 1 s (Jack b 1984), 1 da (Eliza b 1983); *Career* press offr London Festival Ballet 1969-71, first ever press offr Royal Ballet, Covent Garden 1972-74, chief press offr National Theatre 1975-77; Granada TV Int 1979-: head of sales 1981, dir of sales 1983, chief exec 1987; *Style*— Miss Vivien R L Wallace; Granada Television International, 36 Golden Square, London W1R 4AH (☎ 01 734 8080, fax 01 734 8080 ext 2152, telex 27937)

WALLACE, Hon William John Sutton; s of Baroness Dudley, and late Guy Wallace; *b* 1938; *Educ* Malvern; *m* 1962, Jean Carol Ann, *née* Shipton; 2 s (Guy Edward John Sutton b 18 Dec 1963, Piers William Somery b 25 April 1965); *Style*— The Hon William Wallace; Beechmount House, Hallow, Worcs (☎ 0905 640413)

WALLACE OF CAMPSIE, Baron (Life Peer UK 1974); George Wallace; JP (1968), DL (Glasgow 1971); s of John Wallace; *b* 13 Feb 1915; *Educ* Glasgow Univ; *m* 1977, Irene Phipps; *Career* pres Wallace Cameron Hldgs 1977-; slr Supreme Cts 1950-, Hon Sheriff Hamilton 1971-; memb: Law Soc Scotland, Royal Faculty of Procurators, Int Bar Assoc, Bd of Smith and Nephew plc 1972-77, South of Scotland Electricity Bd 1966-69; chm East Kilbride Devpt Corpn 1969-75, fndr memb Scottish Devpt Agency 1976-78, vice pres Scottish Assoc of Youth Clubs, pres East Kilbride Business Centre; chm: Community Indust Support Gp Scotland, Advsy Bd Salvation Army Strathcylde; active with many other gps and assocs; FRSA, FInstM, MBIM; KStJ; *Style*— The Lord Wallace of Campsie, JP, DL; 14 Fernleigh Rd, Newlands, Glasgow (☎ 041 637 3337)

WALLACE OF COSLANY, Baron (Life Peer UK 1974); George Douglas Wallace; s of George Wallace; arms granted 1985; *b* 18 April 1906; *Educ* Central Sch Cheltenham; *m* 1932, Vera, da of William Randall; 1 s (Michael), 1 da (Anne); *Career* sits as Lab Peer in House of Lords; MP (Lab): Chislehurst 1945-50, Norwich N 1964-74; govt whip 1947-50, lord in waiting 1977-79, oppn whip 1979-84, oppn spokesman (Lords) Health 1983-84; pres: Radio Soc GB 1977, SE London SSAFA, London Soc of Recreational Gardeners; pres League of Friends Queen Marys Hosp Sidcup; *Recreations* gardening, amateur radio; *Style*— The Rt Hon the Lord Wallace of Coslany; 44 Shuttle Close, Sidcup, Kent (☎ 01 300 3634)

WALLACE-TURNER, Isobel; da of Dr William Turner (d 1918), of Saltcoats, Ayrshire, and Isabella Wallace-Barr; *b* 4 Dec 1906; *Educ* The Acad Ardrossan Ayrshire, London Univ (extra mural); *Career* OC Women's Naval Vol Res Hong Kong 1945-56, i/c physiotherapy Miny of Health Colonial Off Hong Kong 1945-56, i/c physical med Hacathepe Univ Ankara Turkey, head Med Trg Centre Nairobi Univ Kenya 1966-74, warden in charge Hong Kong House Lancaster Gate London; sec and chm Hong Kong Cncl of Women, del to Manilla representing Hong Kong to Pan-Pacific Conf of 21 Nations; currently free-lance journalist; cncllr Cove and Kilcreggan Community Cncl (Strathclyde Reg), life memb Nat Tst of Scotland; FRCS, MCSP; *Recreations* manifold, non-competitive; *Clubs* Naval; *Style*— Miss Isobel Wallace-Turner; Craigrownie Castle, Cove, Dunbartonshire, Scotland G84 0LT (☎ 042 684 2529)

WALLACE-TURNER, Robert John Aufrère Carr; s of Alfred Wallace Wallace-Turner (d 1968); *b* 22 July 1931; *Educ* Eton, Trinity Coll Oxford (MA); *m* 1966, Sabine, *née* de Falguerolles; 3 da; *Career* Lt Gren Gds; currently with Springfield Capital Mgmnt Ltd; FCA; *Recreations* France, carpentry; *Clubs* City of London, First Guards; *Style*— Robert Wallace-Turner, Esq; 39 Marryat Rd, London SW19 5BE (☎ 01 946 6418); Cayenne Par St Germain-des-Prés, Tarn, France; Springfield Capital Mgmnt Ltd, 37 Lombard Street, London EC3V 9BS (☎ 01 626 3074)

WALLDEN, Richard James; s of Frederick Edward Wallden, of Frinton on Sea, Essex, and Olive Maud, *née* Jones; *b* 7 Oct 1946; *Educ* Bancroft's Sch Woodford Green Essex; *m* 9 Oct 1971, Sally Barbara, da of Herbert James Ford, of Woodford Green, Essex; 4 s (James b 1975, Toby b 1977, Luke b 1980, Benjamin b 1981); *Career* Barclays Bank plc: mangr 1977-85, dir London NW Regn 1985-; memb Fyfield PCC 1974-; ACIB; *Recreations* rugby football; *Clubs* Bancroft RFC; *Style*— Richard Wallden, Esq; North West House, 119-127 Marylebone Rd, London NW1 5BX (☎ 01 723 9211, fax 01 402 6831)

WALLER, (Trevor) Alfred Morfey; s of Canon Trevor Waller, of Waldringfield, nr Woodbridge, Suffolk, and Nora Mary, *née* Morfey (d 1973); *b* 23 Sept 1937; *Educ* Ipswich Sch, Selwyn Coll Cambridge (MA); *m* 20 May 1966, (Katherine) Jane, da of Sir Steward Crawford, GCMG, of Henley-On-Thames, Oxon; 2 s (Charles, Edward); *Career* Lt attachment Br Gurkhas (Nepal), 1 Bn Suffolk Regt Cyprus 1957-59; md Evans-Methuen SA 1967-70, books offr Br Cncl 1970-72, publisher Prentice-Hall Int 1972-75, ed dir Pitman Publishing Ltd 1976-85, md Mary Glasgow Gp 1985-88; former bd memb Univ Coll Ad Professional Cncl Publishers Assoc, chm Further Educn Ctee Publishers Assoc; *Recreations* tennis, sailing, ornithology, entomology; *Clubs* Holland Park Lawn Tennis; *Style*— Alfred Waller, Esq; Orchards, Fawley, Nr Henley-On-Thames, Oxon (☎ 049 163 694)

WALLER, Hon Lady Elizabeth Margery; JP (Petersfield); da of 1 Baron Hacking, OBE, PC (d 1950); aunt of 3 Baron *qv*; *b* 1916; *m* 1936, Rt Hon Sir George Waller, *qv*; 2 s, 1 da; *Style*— The Hon Lady Waller, JP; Hatchway, Hatch Lane, Kingsley Green, Haslemere, Surrey GU27 3LJ (☎ 0428 4629)

WALLER, Gary Peter Anthony; MP (C) Keighley 1983-; s of John Waller (d 1965), and Elizabeth Waller; *b* 24 June 1945; *Educ* Rugby, Lancaster Univ; *Career* contested (C) Rother Valley Feb and Oct 1974, MP (C) Brighouse and Spenborough 1979-83; memb House of Commons Select Ctee on Transport 1979-82, pps to David Howell as sec state Transport 1982-83; chm All Party Wool Textile Gp 1984-; *Style*— Gary Waller, Esq, MP; House of Commons, London SW1A OAA (☎ 01 219 4010)

WALLER, Rt Hon Sir George Stanley Waller; OBE (1945), QC (1954), PC (1976); s of James Stanley Waller; *b* 3 August 1911; *Educ* Oundle, Queens' Coll Cambridge; *m* 1936, Hon Elizabeth Margery, *qv*, da of 1 Baron Hacking; 2 s, 1 da; *Career* RAFO 1931-36; served WWII: RAFVR, 502 Sqdn 1940-41, Wing Cdr 1943 (despatches); barr Gray's Inn 1934, rec: Doncaster 1953-54, Sunderland 1954-55, Bradford 1955-57, Sheffield 1957-61, Leeds 1961-65; slr-gen Durham 1957-61, attorney-gen Co Palatine Durham 1961-65; judge High Ct Queen's Bench 1965-76, presiding judge NE circuit 1973-76, Lord Justice of Appeal 1976-84, ret; former memb: Gen Cncl Bar, Parole Bd, Criminal Law Revision Ctee 1977-85; chm Policy Advsy Ctee Sexual Offences 1977-85; kt 1965; *Style*— The Rt Hon Sir George Waller, OBE; Hatchway, Hatch Lane, Kingsley Green, Haslemere, Surrey GU27 3LJ (☎ 0428 4629)

WALLER, Sir John Stainier Waller; 7 Bt (UK 1815), of Braywick Lodge, Berkshire; s of late Capt Stanier Edmund William Waller, gs of the late Rev Ernest Adolphus Waller, 2 s of 1 Bt; *b* 1917; *Educ* Weymouth Coll, Worcester Coll Oxford; *Career* serv 1940-46 RASC Middle E, Capt 1942; features ed and Min of State Cairo 1943-45, cheif press offr Br Embassy Baghdad 1945, editorial offr MIME Cairo 1945-46; information offr London Press Serv, Central Off of Information 1954-59; author, poet, journalist, co dir; *Style*— Sir John Waller, Bt; 21 Lyndhurst Road, Hove, East

Sussex BN3 6FA

WALLER, Sir (John) Keith; CBE (1961, OBE 1957); s of late A J Waller; *b* 19 Feb 1914; *Educ* Scotch Coll Melbourne, Melbourne Univ; *m* 1943, Alison Irwin, da of late J I Dent; 2 da; *Career* entered Dept of External Affairs 1936, consul-gen Manila 1948, asst sec Dept of External Affairs Canberra 1953-57 and 1962-64; Aust ambass to: Thailand 1957-60, USSR 1960-62, USA 1964-70; sec Dept of Foreign Affairs 1970-74; kt 1968; *see Debrett's Handbook of Australia and New Zealand for further details*; *Style—* Sir Keith Waller, CBE; 17 Canterbury Cres, Deakin, ACT 2600, Australia

WALLER, Hon Mrs (Margery Edith); *née* Sugden; da of late Hon Henry Frank Sugden, bro of 2 Baron St Leonards, ggda of 1 Baron St Leonards; raised to the rank of a Baron's da 1912; *b* 1885; *m* 1918, Maj Robert Jocelyn Rowan Waller, DSO (d 1968); 2 da; *Style—* The Hon Mrs Waller; Ickford House, Little Ickford, nr Aylesbury, Bucks

WALLER, (George) Mark; QC (1979); s of The Rt Hon Sir George Stanley Waller, OBE (ret Lord Justice of Appeal 1985), of Haslemere, Surrey, and Elizabeth Margery Waller; *b* 13 Oct 1940; *Educ* Oundle, Durham Univ (LLB); *m* 1967, Rachel Elizabeth, da of His Hon Judge Beaumont, MBE, of Boroughbridge, N Yorks; 3 s (Charles b 1968, Richard b 1969, Philip b 1973); *Career* barr Gray's Inn 1964, rec 1986; *Recreations* tennis; *Clubs* Garrick, MCC; *Style—* G M Waller, Esq, QC; Mead House, Bradfield, Reading, Berkshire RG7 6HU (☎ 0734 744218); 1 Hare Ct, The Temple EC4 (☎ 01 353 3171)

WALLER, Maj Patrick John Ronald; MBE (1959), JP (Herefordshire 1972), DL (Gwent 1983); s of Brig Robert Peel Waller, DSO, MC (d 1978), formerly of Wyastone Leys, Monmouth, and Olave Harriet (d 1966), da of Henry Edward William Fock, 5 Baron de Robeck; *b* 24 Nov 1923; *Educ* St Aubyn's Rottingdean, Wellington; *m* 14 May 1952, Mary Joyce, da of Lt-Col Laton Frewen, DSO (d 1977), of Round Oak Cottage, Bridstow, Herefordshire; 1 s (Richard Patrick b 7 March 1958), 1 da (Olivia Louise (Mrs Stirling) b 14 Nov 1954); *Career* enlisted TA engagement 1941; cmmnd 12 Royal Lancers 1943, serv N Africa, Italy, Palestine, Staff Coll 1952, special military intelligence staff (Malaya) 1957-59, ret 1968; dir A R Mountain & Son (Lloyd's agents) 1983; past pres Gwent branch CLA, (chm Welsh Ctee 1985-); memb Herefordshire CC 1970-74, parish cncllr 1970-83, govr Haberdashers' Monmouth Schs 1971- (chm boys' sch 1979-), chm mangrs Whitchurch VA Sch; memb Agric Land Tbnl (Wales) 1977-; High Sheriff of Gwent 1978; Freeman of City of London 1982, Liveryman Worshipful Co of Haberdashers 1982; *Recreations* country sports; *Clubs* Cavalry and Guards'; Hadnock Court, Monmouth, Gwent NP5 3NJ (☎ 0600 2768)

WALLER, Sir Robert William; 9 Bt (I 1780), of Newport, Tipperary; s of 8 Bt (d 1958); *b* 16 June 1934; *Educ* Newark Coll of Engineering, Farleigh Dickinson Univ; *m* 1960 (m dis 1975), Carol Anne, da of John Edward Hines, of Hampton, New Hampshire, and Lynn, Mass, USA; 3 s (1 decd), 2 da; *Heir* s, John Michael Waller b 14 May 1962; *Career* engineer General Electric Co; *Style—* Sir Robert Waller, Bt; 5 Lookout Ter, Lynnfield, Mass 01940, USA

WALLEY, Joan Lorraine; MP (Lab) Stoke-on-Trust North 1987-; da of Arthur Simeon Walley (d 1968), and Mary Emma, *née* Pass; *b* 23 Jan 1949; *Educ* Biddulph GS, Univ of Hull (BA), Univ Coll of Swansea (Dip); *m* 2 Aug 1980, Jan Ostrowski, s of Adam Ostrowski; 2 s (Daniel b 1981, Tom b 1983); *Career* Lambeth cncllr 1982-86; *Style—* Joan Walley, MP; House of Commons, London SW1A 0AA

WALLEY, Sir John; KBE (1965), CB (1950); s of R M Walley; *b* 3 April 1906; *Educ* Hereford HS, Hereford Cathedral Sch, Merton Coll Oxford; *m* 1934, Elisabeth Pinhorn; 2 s, 2 da; *Career* postmaster Merton Coll Oxford 1924-28; asst princ Miny of Labour 1929, sec Cabinet Ctee on Unemployment 1932, princ 1934, asst sec Miny of Nat Serv 1941, promoted under-sec to take charge of legislation and other preparations for Beveridge Nat Insur Scheme in New Miny of Nat Insur 1945, dep sec 1958-66; chm Dental Benefit Cncl 1945-48; chm Hampstead Centre Nat Tst 1969-79, (pres 1980-); *Books* Social Security - Another British Failure? (1972); *Style—* Sir John Walley, KBE, CB; 46 Rotherwick Rd, London NW11 (☎ 01 455 6528)

WALLIKER, Christopher John; RD (1971); s of Richard Harold Walliker, of Wimbledon, and Phyllis Muriel Frances Vincent, *née* Williams (d 1981); *b* 26 April 1936; *Educ* Oundle; *m* 26 Sept 1962, Susan May, da of Eric Windsor Berry (d 1963); 1 s (Michael John Delane b 5 Sept 1964), 1 da (Emma May Delane b 1 May 1967); *Career* Nat Serv RN 1955-56, Sub Lt RNVR, Lt Cdr RNR 1957-72; chief accountant Euckyl Gp Ltd 1965-69, divnl fin dir Delta Gp 1969-76 (manpower dir 1976-83, main bd dir 1977-), chm Benjamin Priest Gp plc 1984- (vice-chm 1983); chm cncl CBI W Mids 1980-82 (memb 1976-83), vice pres mgmnt bd Engrg Employers W Mids Assoc 1988- (memb 1976-, hon tres 1981-87), chm Central Birmingham Dist Health Authy 1983-; Freeman City of London, memb Worshipful Co of Chartered Accountants; *Recreations* golf, bridge; *Clubs* Naval; *Style—* Christopher Walliker, Esq; 73 Willes Rd, Leamington Spa, Warwicks; P O Box 38, Cradley Heath, Warley, W Mids, B64 6JW (☎ 0384 66501, fax 0384 64598)

WALLINGER, John David Arnold; s of Sir Geoffrey Arnold Wallinger, GBE, KCMG (d 1979), and Diana Peel, *née* Nelson (d 1986); *b* 1 May 1940; *Educ* Winchester, Clare Coll Cambridge (BA); *m* 16 Feb 1966, Rosamund Elizabeth, da of Jack Philip Albert Gavin Clifford-Wolff, MBE; 2 da (Rosamund b 1944, Antoinette b 1946); *Career* ptnr: Panmure Gordon & Co 1972-75, Rowe & Pitman 1975-86; dir S G Warburg Securities 1986-; SIA; *Recreations* tennis, skiing, fishing, shooting, racing; *Style—* John Wallinger, Esq; S G Warburg Securities, 1 Finsbury Ave, London, EC2M 2PA (☎ 01 606 1066, fax 01 382 4800, car tel 0836 232 530, telex 937011)

WALLIS, Capt Arthur Hammond; CBE (1952); s of late Harold Tom Wallis; *b* 16 Sept 1903; *Educ* RNC Osborne, Dartmouth; *m* 1940, Lucy Joyce, *née* Becher; 1 s, 1 da; *Career* RN 1917, torpedo offr HMS Nelson 1938-41, i/c Torpedo Experimental Dept HMS Vernon 1941-43, HMS Illustrious 1943-45, Capt 1947, cmd Underwater Detection Estab Portland 1948-50, Cdre HMS Mauritius (Persian Gulf) 1951, RN del to NATO Mil Agency for Standardisation 1952-53, dir Underwater Weapons Admty 1953-56, Naval ADC to HM The Queen 1956, chief of Naval Info Admty 1957-1964; *Recreations* now an onlooker; *Clubs* Naval & Military; *Style—* Capt Arthur Wallis, CBE, RN; Compton's Barn, Woodstreet, Guildford, Surrey

WALLIS, David Anthony; s of George Arthur Wallis (d 1950), and Marjorie Jane, *née* Faulkner (d 1940); *b* 24 Nov 1932; *Educ* Victoria Sch Watford, Goldsmiths Coll New Cross (City & Guilds); *m* 11 Aug 1956, Edna, da of Thomas Harold Harrison (d 1977), of Croydon; *Career* Nat Serv RAF 1950-52, instrument specialist, jr technician; apprentice instrument maker Charles Baker & Sons Ltd Holborn, salesman in wholesale optical products with CS Pyser Ltd of Holborn 1952-56; ptnrship with Pyser family formed Survey & Gen Instrument Co Ltd (md 1956-86, chm of bd 1986); cncl memb Drawing Off Material Mfrs and Dealers Assoc, past pres Photogrammetric Soc, memb UK nat ctee Photogrammetry and Remote Sensing; Freeman: City of London 1977, Worshipful Co of Scientific Instrument Makers 1977 (memb of Ct); ARICS 1986, FCIM 1988, FRGS 1981; *Recreations* golf, sea fishing, sailing, carriage driving; *Clubs* Shortlands GC, City Livery, Utd Wards; *Style—* David A Wallis, Esq; Pyser (Hldgs) plc, Fircroft Way, Edenbridge, Kent TN8 6HA (☎ 0732 864 111, fax 0732 865 544, car tel 0860 391 113, telex 95527 OPTSLS G)

WALLIS, Jeffrey Joseph; s of Nathaniel Wallis (d 1948), and Rebecca Wallis (d 1967); *b* 25 Nov 1923; *Educ* Owens Coll of Aeronautical Engrg; *m* 27 Jan 1948, Barbara Rosalind, da of Leonard Brickman, of 22 Devonshire Place, London; 1 da (Sandi Norman b 1952), 1 s (Nicholas Wallis b 1955); *Career* co dir, Monopolies Cmmn 1981-85; md Wallis Shops 1948-80; formerly memb CNAA Textile (NEDC); various governorships; *Recreations* offshore boating, art, industrial design, motor racing; *Style—* Jeffrey J Wallis, Esq; 37 Avenue Close, London NW8 (☎ 01 722 8665); 21 Grafton St, W1 (☎ 01 491 4683, fax 409 0243)

WALLIS, Hon Mrs (Juliet); er da of 2 Baron Sinclair of Cleeve, OBE (d 1985); *b* 16 Oct 1951; *m* 1983, Philip Wallis, only s of A P Wallis, of Beaumont, Clacton, Essex; *Style—* The Hon Mrs Wallis

WALLIS, (William) Roger; s of Charles Edward Wallis (d 1974), of Nettleham, Lincoln, and Marjorie, *née* Scupham; *b* 8 Oct 1945; *Educ* De Aston Sch Market Rasen; *m* 27 Dec 1975, Clare, da of Maurice Mills, of Louth, Lincolnshire; 2 s (Edward b 1981, James b 1985), 1 da (Katherine b 1979); *Career* admitted slr 1969; asst slr Nottingham 1969 and Louth 1970-73; barr Inner Temple 1973, practised Midland and Oxford Circuit 1974-76; readmitted slr 1976, sole princ Sills & Betteridge Lincoln 1976-79 (sr ptnr 1979-); hon sec Lincolnshire Law Soc 1983-86 (vice-pres 1987-); dep county ct registrar and dep district registrar High Ct 1983-; memb No 10 Legal Aid Area Ctee 1984-; *Recreations* gardening, literature; *Style—* William Wallis, Esq; c/o Sills & Betteridge, St Peter's Churchyard, Silver St, Lincoln LN2 1EG (☎ (0522) 42211, fax (0522) 510463)

WALLIS, Col Rupert Lionel; s of Frank Wallis (d 1958), of Henwick, nr Newbury, Berks, and Edith Gwendoline, *née* Brooks (d 1971); *b* 31 Jan 1927; *Educ* St Edward's, Univ Oxford; *m* 9 June 1956, Pamela Ann Paine, da of Col Frederick George Arnold, OBE (d 1980); 1 s (Martin b 1959), 1 da (Caroline b 1963); *Career* cmmnd Royal Berks Regt 1946, transferred RASC with regular cmmn 1948, ADC to GOC Aldershot Dist 1951-52, serv Korea in 1 Cwlth Div 1952-53, Malaya 1953-55, student Staff Coll Camberley 1960, DAQMG (Movements) HQ Northern Cmd 1961-64, cmd 55 Air Despatch Co RASC (later RCT) Malayasia during Indonesian confrontation 1964-66, GS02 Def Intelligence Staff MOD 1967-68, Lt-Col cmd Army Air Transport Trg and Devpt Centre 1968-70, GSO1 Logistics at Joint Warfare Estab 1970-72, HQ UK LF as SO1 Tport 1972, Col 1974, cmd 27 Regt RCT and LSG 1974, Col Movements HQ UKLF 1977, ret 1982; Hon Col 160 Regt RCT (TA) 1980; memb Lloyds 1974-; *Recreations* history, genealogy, gardening; *Clubs* Naval and Military; *Style—* Col Rupert Wallis; Northacre, Broughton, nr Stockbridge, Hants (☎ 0794 301307)

WALLIS, Victor Harry; s of Harry Stewart Wallis, MBE (d 1966), and Ada Elizabeth, *née* Jarratt (d 1978); *b* 21 Dec 1922; *Educ* Wilson's GS, SOAS; *m* 1 March 1948, (Margaret) Teresa, da of Samuel Meadowcroft (d 1964); 1 s (Stewart Scott b 1949), 3 da (Nicola b 1950, Amanda b 1954, Debra Jane b 1957); *Career* enlisted Royal Scots 1941, Maj (attached Indian Army) 1942-47, Maj RARO 1947-49, TA (Intelligence Corps) 1949-54, TARO (Intelligence Corps) 1954-77; Home Office: Immigration Serv 1947-52, regnl offr 1952-58, Policy and Trg Divs 1958-67, chief trg offr 1967-68, princ estabs 1968-72, asst sec estabs 1972-80, under sec of state Fire and Police Dept 1980-82; assoc BIET 1939; *Books* many HMSO publications on home defence matters (1958-56); *Recreations* philately, military history, painting; *Clubs* Civil Service, St Stephen's Constitutional, British Legion, Old Wilsonians; *Style—* Victor Wallis, Esq; 26 Lumley Rd, Horley, Surrey RH6 7JL (☎ 0293 771925)

WALLIS-JONES, His Hon Ewan Perrins Wallis-Jones; s of William James Wallis-Jones, MBE (d 1944); *b* 22 June 1913; *Educ* Mill Hill Sch, Univ Coll of Wales Aberystwyth, Balliol Coll Oxford; *m* 1940, Veronica Mary, *née* Fowler; 1 s, 2 da; *Career* barr, county ct judge 1964-72, dep chm Carmarthonshire QS 1965-66 (chm 1966-71), circuit judge 1972-84; *Recreations* music, photography; *Style—* His Hon Ewan Wallis-Jones; 25 Cotham Grove, Bristol, BS6 6AN (☎ 0272 48908)

WALLIS-KING, Maj-Gen Colin Sainthill; CBE (1975, OBE 1971); s of Lt-Col Frank King, DSO, OBE (d 1934), of Hill Hse, Northrepps, nr Cromer, Norfolk, and Colline Ammabel, *née* St Hill (d 1985); *b* 13 Sept 1926; *Educ* Stowe; *m* 10 Nov 1962, Lisabeth, da of Swan P Swanstrom (d 1970), of Oslo, Norway; 2 da (Kathrine, Marianne); *Career* HG 1942-44, enlisted Coldstream Gds 1944 (cmmnd 1945), liason offr Fleet Air Arm 1954-60, Army Staff Coll 1960-61, Regtl Adj Coldstream Gds 1961-63, seconded to Parachute Regt 1963, ACOS G4 Comland Norway 1965-68, 2 i/c 1BN Coldstream Gds 1968-69, Cdr 2 Bn Coldstream Gds 1969-72, Dep Cdr 8 inf Bde 1972, Col GS Combat Devpt MOD 1972-73, Cdr 3 Inf Bde 1973-75, Brig Intelligence MOD 1975-77, dir Serv Intelligence 1977-80, ret 1980; dir Kongsberg Ltd 1982-87, UK rep Norsk Forsvarsteknologi 1987-; churchwarden Stubbings Parish Church; *Recreations* equitation, fishing, sailing, music, cross-country skiing; *Clubs* Cavalry & Guards; *Style—* Maj-Gen C S Wallis-King, CBE; c/o Royal Bank of Scotland, 21 Gosvenor Gardens, London SW1W 0BW; Weir House, 62 King St, Maidenhead, Berks SL6 1EQ (☎ 0628 73 212, fax 0628 25 791, telex 846 366)

WALLOP, Lady Jane Alianora Borlace; da of 9 Earl of Portsmouth (d 1984); *b* 1939; *Style—* Lady Jane Wallop

WALLOP, Hon Nicholas Valoynes Bermingham; s of 9 Earl of Portsmouth (d 1984); *b* 1946; *Educ* Stowe; *m* 1969, Lavinia, da of David Karmel, CBE, QC; 1 s, 1 da; *Career* art dealer; *Clubs* Boodles; *Style—* The Hon Nicholas Wallop; 15 Tregunter Rd, London SW10; 90 Jermyn Street, London SW1Y 6JD (☎ 01 930 4221)

WALLROCK, John; s of Samuel Wallrock (d 1955), and Marie Kate Wallrock (d 1943); *b* 14 Nov 1922; *Educ* Bradfield; *m* 1967, Audrey Louise, *née* Ariow; 1 s (Giles), 2 da (Marina, Camilla); *Career* Lt RNR 1943, master mariner 1948; chm: J H Minet & Co Ltd 1972-79 (dir 1955-72), Minet Hldgs Ltd 1972-82, Conocean Int Conslts Gp Hong Kong 1984-; dir Tugu Insurance Co Hong Kong 1976-84; memb: Lloyd's Underwriting 1950-84, cncl of mgmnt White Ensign Assoc 1974-83; memb: Hon Co Master Mariners, Nautical Inst (MNI) 1970-; Freeman City of London 1965; *Recreations* yachting, painting; *Clubs* Royal London YC, Royal South YC, East India; *Style*— John Wallrock, Esq; Conocean Int Conslts Gp, Suite 804A Admiralty Centre (Tower I), 18 Harcourt Rd, Hong Kong

WALLROCK, Raphael John; s of William Wallrock (d 1960), of Westcliff-on-Sea, Essex, and Julia, *née* Joseph (d 1981); ggf Austrian Count Von Tempel Wollrock; *b* 28 August 1948; *Educ* Westcliff HS Essex; *m* 28 Jan 1948, Renée, da of Paul Green (d 1961); 1 da (Louise b 1949), 1 s (David b 1954); *Career* RAF 1939-45; chm Magnolia Gp (Mouldings) plc 1966-; Grantee of the Royal Warrant; FBIM 1973; *Style*— Raphael Wallrock, Esq; Magnolia Group (Mouldings) plc, Sutton Rd, Rochford, Essex SS4 1NA (☎ (0702) 547121, telex 99320, fax (0702) 540348)

WALLS, (William) Alan; s of Harold Walls, of Sedgefield, Cleveland, and Marjorie, *née* Orton; *b* 18 Sept 1956; *Educ* Ferryhill GS, Trinity Hall Cambridge (MA); *m* 29 July 1978, Julie, da of John Brown, of Windlestone, Co Durham; 1 s (Thomas b 1985), 1 da (Rachel b 1987); *Career* admitted slr 1981, ptnr Linklater & Paines 1987 (articled 1979-88); Freeman City of London Slrs Co 1987; memb: Law Soc, Int Bar Assoc; assoc member Assoc Europeenne des Practiciens des Procedures Collectives; *Recreations* walking, sailing; *Style*— Alan Walls, Esq; Barrington House, 59/67 Gresham St, London EC2V 7JA (☎ 01 606 7080, fax 01 606 5113, telex 884349/ 888167)

WALLS, Geoffrey Nowell; s of Andrew Nowell Walls, of Canberra, Aust, and Hilda Margaret, *née* Thompson; *b* 17 Feb 1945; *Educ* Trinity GS Melbourne Aust, Univ of Melbourne Aust (BComm); *m* 8 Aug 1975, Vanessa, da of Capt Alan John Bodger, DFC, of Boston, USA; 1 s (Robert Walls b 20 Jan 1968), 3 da (Tanya b 12 Nov 1969, Jennie b 18 Jan 1977, Sacha b 21 March 1978); *Career* 2 Lt RAAOC 1966-69, active serv S Vietman 1968; Aust Dip Serv: asst trade cmmr (Bahrain, Cairo, Singapore, Jakarta, Mecas) 1970-75, trade cmmr Manila 1975-76, asst dir M East section Dept of Trade and Resources Canberra 1976-78, trade cmmr Baghdad 1978-79, regnl dir Cwlth Depts of Trade and Indust and Commerce 1980-83; gen mangr central region ATCO Industs Aust 1983-86, agent gen State of S Aust London 1986-; *Recreations* gardening, golf, reading, tennis; *Clubs* RAC, East India; *Style*— Geoffrey Walls, Esq; 31 Belvedere Grove, Wimbledon, London SW19 7RQ (☎ 01 946 9491); South Australia House, 50 Strand, London WC2N 5LW (☎ 01 930 7471, fax 01 930 1660, car 0836 588056, telex 918749)

WALMSLEY, Air Marshal Sir Hugh Sydney Porter; KCB (1952, CB 1944), KCIE (1947), CBE (1943, OBE 1937), MC (1918), DFC (1922); s of James Walmsley; *b* 6 June 1898; *Educ* Dover Coll; *m* 1928, Audrey, da of Dr Pim; 3 s; *Career* AOC-in-C Flying Training Cmmd RAF 1950-52, princ Coll Air Trg Hamble 1960; *Style*— Air Marshal Sir Hugh Walmsley, KCB, KCIE, CBE, MC, DFC; Upwood, Tiptoe, Lymington, Hants

WALMSLEY, Kevin; s of James Walmsley, and Evelyn Grace, *née* Bunnett; *b* 20 August 1959; *Educ* Runshaw Coll Lanc, Liverpool Univ (BA); *Career* cncllr Dartford Borough Cncl 1983-: ctee memb Fin and Personnel (later chm), ctee memb Policy, Planning, Contracts, Resources and Housing; *Recreations* travel, walking, current affairs, reading; *Style*— Kevin Walmsley, Esq; Fairhaven, 28 Miskin Rd, Dartford, Kent DA1 2LS (☎ 0322 27398); King & Co Chartered Accountants, 12 Fife Rd, Kingston-upon-Thames, Surrey KT1 1S2 (☎ 546 7562, fax 01 541 1387)

WALMSLEY, Peter James; MBE (1975); s of George Stanley Walmsley (d 1985), of Cringle, Whyteleafe, Surrey, and Elizabeth Martin, *née* Martin (d 1977); *b* 29 April 1929; *Educ* Caterham Sch, Royal Sch of Mines, Imperial Coll London Univ (BSc, ARSM); *m* 1, 1958 (m dis 1967), Jane Mary, *née* Budgen; 1 s 1 da; m 2, Edna, *née* Gallagher; 2 step s; *Career* geologist: IRAQ Petroleum Co 1951-59, BP Trinidad 1959-65, BP London 1965-72; exploration mangr BP Aberdeen 1972-78, dep chief geologist BP London 1978-79, regnl exploration mangr BP London 1979-81; dir petroleum engrg div Dept of Energy 1981-87 (dir-gen 1987); chm Petroleum Exploration Soc of GB 1971-72; *Style*— Peter Walmsley, Esq; Petroleum Engineering Div, Dept of Energy, Thames House South, Millbank, London SW1P 4QJ (☎ (01) 211 6141)

WALPOLE, Dowager Baroness; Nancy Louisa; *née* Jones; OBE, JP (Norfolk 1941); yst da of late Frank Harding Jones, of 21 Abingdon Court, London W8; *m* 14 July 1937, 9 Baron Walpole (d 1989); 1 s (10 Baron), 1 da (Hon Mrs Phillida Hurn) and 1 s and 1 da decd; *Career* pres Norfolk Red Cross for 25 yrs, now patron; *Style*— The Rt Hon Nancy, Lady Walpole, OBE, JP; Wolterton Hall, Norwich, Norfolk NR11 7LY (☎ 0263 761210, 0263 77274)

WALPOLE, Hon Pamela Frances; OBE (1960, MBE 1954); da of Lt Horatio Walpole and sis of 9 Baron Walpole, TD; *b* 22 Feb 1908; *Career* raised to rank of Baron's da 1939; former JP Norfolk; *Recreations* bridge, travelling; *Style*— The Hon Pamela Walpole, OBE; Green Tops, 5 Orpen Lane, Kenilworth, SA

WALPOLE, 10 Baron (GB 1723); Robert Horatio Walpole; JP (Norfolk); also 8 Baron Walpole of Wolterton (GB 1756); patron of 6 livings; s of 9 Baron Walpole, TD (d 1989); *b* 8 Dec 1938; *Educ* Eton, King's Coll Cambridge (BA, MA, Dip Agric); *m* 1, 30 June 1962 (m dis 1979), (Sybil) Judith, yr da of Theodore Thomas Schofield, of Stockingwood House, Harpenden, Herts; 2 s (Hon Jonathan Robert Hugh, Hon Benedict Thomas Orford b 1 June 1969), 2 da (Hon Alice Louise b 1 Sept 1963, Hon Emma Judith b 10 Oct 1964); m 2, 1980, Laurel Celia, o da of S T Ball, of Swindon; 2 s (Hon Roger Horatio Calibut b 1980, Hon Henry William b 1982), 1 da; *Heir* s, Hon Jonathan Robert Hugh Walpole b 16 Nov 1967; *Style*— The Rt Hon Lord Walpole, JP; Mannington Hall, Norwich, Norfolk NR11 7BD

WALSER, Ven David; s of Rev William Walser (d 1952, formerly vicar of Imber, Wilts), and Eleanor Marguerite Davida, *née* Corelli (d 1923); *b* 12 Mar 1923; *Educ* Clayesmore Sch, St Edmund Hall Oxford (MA, Dip Theol), St Stephen's House Oxford; *m* 15 Nov 1975, Elizabeth Enid, da of James Francis Shillito, of Old Forge, Staple Cross, Robertsbridge, Sussex; *Career* RA, Capt Royal Indian Artillery serv UK, India, Burma, French, Indo-China, Malaya 1942-46; ordained: deacon 1950, priest 1951; curate St Gregory's Horfield, vice-princ St Stephen's House 1954-60, chaplain the King's Sch Ely and minor canon Ely Cathedral 1961-71, vicar Linton Cambs 1971-81, rector Bartlow Cambs 1973-81, rural dean Linton 1976-81, rector St Botolph's Cambridge 1981-, archdeacon of Ely 1981-; hon canon Ely Cathedral 1981-, priest in charge St Clements Cambridge 1985-; *Recreations* hill walking, caravanning, music, hymn-writing; *Style*— The Ven the Archdeacon of Ely; St Botolph's Rectory, Summerfield, Cambridge CB3 9HE (☎ 0223 350684)

WALSH, Sir Alan; s of late Thomas Haworth Walsh, and late Betsy Alice Walsh; *b* 19 Dec 1916; *Educ* Darwen GS, Univ of Manchester (BSc, MSc, DSc); *m* 1949, Audrey Dale, da of G A Hutchinson; 2 s; *Career* Br Non-Ferrous Metals Res Assoc 1939-42 and 1944-46, DSIRO 1946-77 (asst chief of div 1961-77); winner of numerous scientific awards; hon fell Royal Soc Chemistry; Hon DSc Monash; FRS; kt 1977; *Style*— Sir Alan Walsh; 11 Norwood Ave, Brighton, Vic 3186, Australia (☎ 592 4897)

WALSH, Andrew Geoffrey; s of Dr Geoffrey Parkin Walsh, of Blackburn, Lancs, and Dorothy, *née* Baldwin; *b* 26 July 1954; *Educ* Westholme Sch Blackburn, Queen Elizabeth GS Blackburn, Magdalen Coll Oxford (MA), Trinity Hall Cambridge (LLB); *m* (m dis); *Career* articled clerk Payne Hicks Beach 1977-79, asst slr Norton Rose Botterell and Roche 1979-83, ptnr McKenna and Co Slrs 1986- (asst slr 1983-86); memb City of London Slrs Co; *Books* Global Mergers and Acquisitions (chapter, 1988); *Recreations* soccer, squash, cycling, visiting historic churches and buildings, theatre; *Clubs* Cannons; *Style*— Andrew Walsh, Esq; 71 Queen Victoria Street, London EC4V 4EB (☎ 01 236 4340, fax 01 236 4485, telex 264824)

WALSH, (Bernard) David James; TD (1956); s of Maj Bernard John Merlin Walsh (d 1928), of Stourbank, Nayland, Suffolk, and Violet Jennie, *née* Pearson (d 1973); *b* 12 July 1923; *Educ* Eton, Trinity Hall Cambridge; *m* 28 Aug 1954, (Gladys) Angela Margot, da of Maj Henry Berry Lees, MC (d 1967), of Stour House, Nayland, Suffolk; 3 da (Sarah (Mrs Blake) b 1955, Jenny (Mrs Pickford) b 1957, Charlotte (Mrs Johnston) b 1960); *Career* WWII RA 1943, cmmnd 1944, served Field and Medium Regts in UK 1944-45, instr Army Signal Sch India 1945 (cmd Artillery & Engrg Wing 1946-47), 304 Essex Yeo RHA Field Regt RA (UK) 1948-57, ret Maj 1957; barr Inner Temple 1952, private practice and SE Circuit 1954-62 and 1974-81, Govt Legal Serv (MPNI) 1962-63, asst registrar Criminal Appeals 1969-74 (dep asst registrar 1963-69), standing counsel for DHSS 1979-81, chm Social Security Appeal Tribunals 1983; vice-pres Stour Valley Railway Preservation Soc 1971-, pres Gt Eastern Railway Soc 1973-, chm Consltative Panel for the Preservation of Br Transport Relics 1977-82 (hon sec and tres 1958-61), pres Railway Club 1982-(hon sec 1951-68, vice pres 1968-82); hon sec Essex Yeo Assoc 1981-; *Books* The Stour Valley Railway (1971), various articles Railway Magazine and other periodicals; *Recreations* study of railway operating and history, photography; *Clubs* Carlton, Railway; *Style*— B D J Walsh, Esq, TD; The Old Rectory, Burgate, DISS, Norfolk IP22 1QD

WALSH, Dennis Maxton; OBE, JP; s of Walter Walsh (d 1947), of Bradford, W Yorkshire, and Edith, *née* Gorrod (d 1955); *b* 28 Dec 1925; *Educ* Hanson HS; *m* (m dis); 1 da (Moira Kay); *Career* travel agent; chm: Briggs and Hill (Insurance Consultants) Ltd, Naita Systems Ltd, BFD Image Ltd; princ Briggs and Hill World Travel Serv; past pres: Bradford C of C, Nat Assoc of Independent Travel Agents; former pres and chm ABTA,chm Bradford Magistrates 1985; FTS; *Recreations* foreign travel, walking; *Style*— Dennis Walsh, Esq, OBE, JP; Wellfield Cottage, Lane Side, West Scholes, Queensbury, W Yorks BD13 1NE; Briggs and Hill, 20 Rawson Place, Bradford, W Yorks BD1 3QN (☎ 0274 724167)

WALSH, Hon Jane Emily Mary; da of 5 Baron Ormathwaite, MVO (d 1944); *b* 1910; *Career* lady-in-waiting to HRH Princess Alice Duchess of Gloucester 1969-75; *Style*— The Hon Jane Walsh; 13 Mount St, London W1

WALSH, Jonathan George Michael; s of Charles Arthur Walsh (d 1978), of Surrey, and Joan Violet Braidwood, *née* Allen (d 1969); *b* 21 April 1944; *Educ* Eton, Sorbonne Univ; *m* 24 Feb 1968, Angela Mary, da of Rear-Adm Sir Anthony Cecil Capel Miers, VC, KBE, CB, DSO (d 1985), of 8 Highdonn Rd; 4 s (David b 1969, William b 1971, James b 1974, Harry b 1981); *Career* admitted slr 1969, ptnr Joynson-Hicks London; Freeman of City of London 1982, Liveryman Worshipful Co of Tin Plate Workers 1982; memb Law Soc 1969; *Recreations* real tennis, lawn tennis, shooting; *Clubs* Boodles, Queens, Hurlingham, MCC; *Style*— Jonathan Walsh, Esq; 12 Briar Walk, London SW15 (☎ 01 788 9907); Joynson-Hicks, 10 Maltravers St, London WC2 (☎ 01 836 8456, fax 01 379 7196, telex 268014 JHICKS G)

WALSH, (William) Neville; s of Cyril Mervyn Walsh (d 1957), of 236 Neath Rd, Briton Ferry, Neath, W Glamorgan, and Hannah, *née* Williams (d 1957); *b* 31 Jan 1928; *Educ* Llandovery Coll, Cambridge Univ (MA); *m* 1, 5 Sept 1953 (m dis), Margaret, da of William Watson (d 1956); 2 da (Catherine b 1954, Julia b 1960); m 2, Hilary Mary, da of Norman Phillip Elliott (d 1987); *Career* Sgt Royal Fusiliers RAEC W Germany; slr, dep coroner for Western Dist of Glam, pt/t chm Medical Appeals Tbnl 1988-, sr ptnr Howe Walsh & Ambrose; hon slr and hon team mangr Aberavon RFC, hon life vice-pres Crawshay's Welsh RFC; pres Bridgend RFC Former Players Assoc, patron Llanelli RFC and Pontarddulais RFC; life memb Ruthin RFC, life vice-pres Aberavon Green Stars RFC, country memb London Welsh RFC; *Style*— Neville Walsh, Esq; 129 Mayals Rd, Mayals, Swansea, W Glam SA3 5DH (☎ 0792 402143); c/o Howe, Walsh & Ambrose, 42 Station Rd, Port Talbot, W Glam (☎ 0639 882256, fax 0639 891028)

WALSH, Dr Nigel Dennis; s of Arthur Edward Walsh, MBE (d 1974), and Lilian Freda, *née* Schmidt; *b* 17 Oct 1928; *Educ* Epsom, St Georges Hosp Med Sch London; *m* 29 Sept 1956, Walburga Ann, da of George Rugby Haywood (d 1941); 1 s (Philip b 1965), 3 da (Victoria b 1957, Rosamund b 1961, Elizabeth b 1962); *Career* Maj RAMC 1952-54, serv E Africa; conslt in pharmaceutical med; med dir: Park Davis and Co UK 1971-79, Europe Warner Lambert Int 1981-87; hon med offr Dorrigo Hosp NSW Aust 1966-69; RSM; *Style*— Dr Nigel D Walsh; Bodenham Steppes, Bodenham, Mill House, Bodenham Moor, Hereford HR1 3HS (☎ 056884 404)

WALSH, Lt-Col Noel Perrings; s of John Walsh (d 1937), of Emsworth, Hants, and Nancy, *née* Perrings (d 1953); *b* 25 Dec 1919; *Educ* Purbrook Park GS, Open Univ (BA), currently at Birmingham Univ; *m* 1, 9 July 1945, Olive Mary (d 1987), da of Thomas Walsh (d 1921), of Waterford, Eire; 3 s (John b 1947, Richard b 1950, Colin b 1960), 1 da (Mary b 1954); m 2, 27 June 1988, Mary Ruth, da of Rev Reginald David Morgan Hughes (d 1956); *Career* WWII 2 Lt RA Aug 1940-42, Capt RA 1942 (India, Arakan, Burma); Capt 33 Airborne Regt RA BAOR 1949, Staff Coll 1950, Maj DAQMG 52 (Ll Div 1951-53, 53 LAA Regt AA BAOR 1953-55, GSO 2 RA HQ BAOR 1955-57, 58 Medium Regt RA 1951-61, GSO2 PR WO 1961-64, Lt Col GSO1 PR MOD 1964-66; Civil Serv: princ MPBW 1966-69, sr princ dir Far East 1969-71, regnl dir Midlands 1971-76, under sec dir of home regnl serv DOE 1976-80; vice chm Midland Study Centre for Building Team 1982-, chm West Midland Regn CIOB 1988-; govr Henry Thornton Sch Clapham 1977-80, chm Westminster Dioscese Handicapped Childrens Soc 1964-69; FCIOB 1973, FBIM 1980, FRSA 1986; *Recreations* econmomic history, gardening, squash, railway modelling; *Clubs* Naval and Miltary, Edgbaston Priory (Birmingham); *Style*— Lt-Col Noel Walsh; 25 Oakfield Rd, Selly Park, Birmingham B29 7HH (☎ 021 472 2031)

WALSH, Peter Anthony Joseph; s of Michael Walsh, of Yorkshire, and Eileen, *née* Duffy; *b* 24 May 1956; *Educ* Ushaw Coll Durham, London Univ (LLB); *Career* barr 1978; memb: MENCAP, Action Aid; *Recreations* tennis, swimming, cycling; *Clubs* Little Ship, Naval; *Style*— Peter Walsh, Esq; Queen Elizabeth Building, Temple, London, EC4, (☎ (01) 353 7181

WALSH, Peter Banbury; s of Raymond Nevile Walsh (d 1950), and Kathleen Mary, *née* Banbury (d 1973); *b* 18 June 1936; *Educ* Cranleigh, New Coll Oxford (BA); *Career* ptnr Coopers 7 Lybrand Cas 1970-; FCA; *Style*— Peter Walsh, Esq; 28 Shawfield St, London SW3 4BD (☎ 01 351 4290); Coopers & Lybrand, Plumtree Ct, London EC4A 4HT (☎ 01 822 4602, fax 01 822 4652)

WALSH, Hon Mrs (Sarah Louise); *née* Wedderburn; da of Baron Wedderburn of Charlton by his 1 w, Nina, da of Dr Myer Salaman; *b* 1954; *m* 1975, Michael Walsh; *Style*— The Hon Mrs Walsh; 76 Cromwell Avenue, London N6

WALSHAM, Rear Adm Sir John Scarlett Warren; 4 Bt (UK 1831), of Knill Court, Herefordshire, CB (1963), OBE (1944); s of Sir John Walsham, 3 Bt (d 1940), by his w Bessie (gda of Sir John Warren, 4 Bt); *b* 29 Nov 1910; *Educ* Rugby; *m* 1936, Sheila Christina, da of late Cdr Bertrand Bannerman, DSO, RN, and herself 2 cous of Sir Donald Bannerman, 13 Bt; 1 s, 2 da; *Heir* s, Timothy John Walsham b 26 April 1939; *Career* Lt RN 1933, Cdr 1944, Capt 1953, chief engr Singapore Dockyard 1956, CO RNEC Plymouth, Adm Supt HM Dockyard Portsmouth, Rear Adm 1961, ret 1965; *Style*— Rear Adm Sir John Walsham, Bt, CB, OBE; Priory Cottage, Middle Coombe, Shaftesbury, Dorset

WALSINGHAM, 9 Baron (GB 1780); John de Grey; MC (1951); patron of 3 livings; s of 8 Baron Walsingham, DSO, OBE, JP, DL (d 1965, half-n of 6 Baron, considered by some the best game shot of his generation, also a noted cricketer (Cambridge blue) and lepidopterist); *b* 21 Feb 1925; *Educ* Wellington, Aberdeen Univ, Magdalen Coll Oxford (MA), Royal Mil Coll of Sci; *m* 30 July 1963, Wendy, er da of Edward Sidney Hoare; 1 s, 2 da (Hon Sarah b 1964, Hon Elizabeth b 1966); *Heir* s, Hon Robert de Grey, b 21 June 1969; *Career* Lt-Col RA; co dir; landowner and farmer; FInstD; *Recreations* etymology; *Clubs* Army and Navy, Special Forces, Farmers, Norfolk; *Style*— The Rt Hon the Lord Walsingham, MC; Merton Hall, nr Watton, Thetford, Norfolk IP25 6QJ (☎ 0953 881226, office 883370, telex 97228)

WALSTON, Baron (Life Peer UK 1961), of Newton; Henry David Leonard George Walston; CVO (1976), JP (Cambridge 1944); s of Sir Charles Walston, *née* Waldstein, archaeologist, and Florence, da of David Einstein, of NY; *b* 16 June 1912; *Educ* Eton, King's Coll Cambridge (MA); *m* 1, Catherine Macdonald (d 1978); 3 s, 2 da (and 1 s decd); m 2, 1979, Elizabeth, da of late John Bissett-Robinson and formerly w of Nicholas Scott, MP; *Career* sits as SDP Peer House of Lords (formerly Lab 1961-1981); chief whip SDP Peers 1988-89; contested: (Lib) Hunts 1945, (Lab) Cambs 1951, 1955, Gainsborough 1957, 1959; farmer, agriculturist; res fell Bacteriology Harvard USA 1934-35; dir of Agric Br Zone of Germany 1946-47, agric advsr on Germany to FO 1947-48; cnsllr Duchy of Lancaster 1948-54; parly under-sec: FO 1964-67, BOT 1967; sometime special ambass, cmmr Crown Estates 1968-75, chm Inst of Race Relations 1968-71, memb UK delgn to Cncl of Europe and WEU 1970-75, nominated memb Euro Parl 1975-77, dep chm Cwlth Devpt Corpn 1980-83 (memb 1975-83); dir Bayer UK Ltd; chm: East Anglia Econ Planning Cncl 1969-79, GB/East Europe Centre 1972-86; vice-pres Royal Cwlth Soc 1970-; Hon DCL East Anglia; *Publications include* : From Forces to Farming (1944), Land Nationalisation, for and against, (1958), The Farm Gate to Europe (1970), Dealing With Hunger (1976); *Recreations* shooting, sailing; *Clubs* Brooks's, MCC, House of Lords Yacht; *Style*— The Rt Hon the Lord Walston, CVO, JP; Selwood Manor, Frome, Somerset

WALSTON, Hon James Patrick Francis; 3 surviving s of Baron Walston, CVO, JP; *b* 18 July 1949; *Educ* Ampleforth, Eton, Jesus Coll Cambridge, Univ of Rome, Cambridge (PhD); *Books* The Mafia and Clientelism (1988); *Style*— The Hon James Walston; Via Stelletta 14, Rome, Italy

WALSTON, Hon Oliver; s of Baron Walston, CVO, JP; *b* 1941; *Educ* Eton, King's Cambridge; *m* 1, 1966, Leslie, da of Milton Gordon, of New York (m dis); m 2, 1969, Anne Dunbar, of Washington DC; issue includes 1 s (David Charles b 30 May 1982); *Style*— The Hon Oliver Walston; Thriplow Farm, Thriplow, Royston, Herts

WALSTON, Hon Susan; da of Baron Walston, CVO, JP; *b* 18 Nov 1942, (twin with bro William); *Style*— The Hon Susan Walston; 27 Ennis St, Balmain, Sydney, NSW, Australia

WALSTON, Hon William; 2 surviving s of Baron Walston, CVO, JP; *b* 18 Nov 1942, (twin with sis Susan); *Educ* Eton, Downside, King's Coll Cambridge; *m* 1963, Hilary, da of William Galbraith, of Malaga; children; *Style*— The Hon William Walston; Cochrane's Farm, Thriplow, Royston, Herts

WALTER, Hon Sir Harold Edward; s of Rev Edward Walter; *b* 17 April 1920; *Educ* Royal Coll Mauritius; *m* 1942, Yvette Nidza, MBE, da of James Toolsy; *Career* MLA Mauritius 1959-, min External Affrs, Tourism and Emigration 1976-; kt 1972; *Style*— Hon Sir Harold Walter; La Rocca, Eau Coulée, Mauritius

WALTER, Harriet Mary; da of Roderick Walter, of Flat 5, 41 Lexham Gdns, London W8, and Xandra Carandini, *née* Lee; *b* 24 Sept 1950; *Educ* Cranbourne Chase Sch, LAMDA; *Career* actress; began career Duke's Playhouse Lancaster 1974; nat tours 1975-78 with: 7:84, Joint Stock, Paines Plough; Royal Court Theatre 1980-81 incl: Cloud Nine, The Seagull, Ophelia in Hamlet (with Jonathan Pryce dir Richard Eyre); RSC 1981-83 incl: Nicholas Nickleby, Helena in A Midsummers Night's Dream, Helena in All's Well That Ends Well (with Dame Peggy Ashcroft dir Trevor Num, toured Broadway 1983): Maria in The Possessed (dir Yuri Luibimov) Almeida Thaetre 1985 (toured Paris, Milan, Bologna), Skinner in The Castle by Howard Barker RSC 1985 (nominated Best Actress Olivier Awards), Portia in The Merchant of Venice Royal Exchange Manchester 1987, RSC Stratford Imogen in Cymbeline, Viola in Twelfth Night, Dacha in A Question of Geography, Masha in The Three Sisters (winner of Best Actress Laurence Olivier Awards); TV incl: The Invitation Game (by Ian McEwan), Harriet Vane in Dorothy L Sayers Mysteries, Frances in The Price (with Peter Barkworth Channel 4); films incl: Turtle Diary (with Ben Kingsley and Glenda Jackson), Otilie in Reflections, Emmy in The Good Father (with Atnhony Hopkins); winner Sony Radio Best Actress 1988; assoc artist RSC 1987; memb: Amnesty Int, CND, AAA for Labour; *Books* contrib: Women and Theatre (1984), Clamorous Voices Shakespeare's Women Today (1988), Players of Shakespeare Vol 3; *Recreations* music, travel, cinema, theatre, riding, flying, photography; *Style*— Miss Harriet Walter; Meg Poole - Richard Stone Partnership, 25 Whitehall, London SW1A 2BS (☎ 01 839 6421)

WALTER, Jeremy Canning; s of Maj Richard Walter, OBE, and Beryl, *née* Pugh; *b* 22 August 1948; *Educ* King's Sch Canterbury, Sidney Sussex Coll Cambridge (MA, LLB); *m* 24 Aug 1973, (m dis 1985), Judith Jane, da of Dr Denton Rowlands, of Tamworth, Staffs (d 1987); 2 da (Emma b 1976, Alison b 1979); *Career* Ellis Piers & Young Jackson 1971-73, slr 1973, ptnr Simmons & Simmons 1976- (slr 1973-); memb Law Soc; *Recreations* theatre, cricket, reading, squash; *Clubs* MCC; *Style*— Jeremy Walter, Esq; 14 Dominion St, London EC2 (☎ 01 628 2020, fax 01 588 4129)

WALTER, Michael; s of Leonard Walter, of 4 Griffin Close, Saxon Park, Blacon, Chester, and Anne, *née* Rue; *b* 6 May 1956; *Educ* The King's Sch, Christ's Coll Cambridge (BA, MA); *m* 27 Nov 1982, Joan Margaret, da of Arthur Colin Hubbard (d 1978), of Paeroa, Nr Auckland, NZ; 1 s (Matthew b 1987), 1 da (Helen b 1984); *Career* admitted slr 1981 (Hong Kong 1981); Stephenson Harwood: articled clerk 1979-81, asst slr 1981-86, ptnr 1986-; Freeman: City of London 1987, Worshipful Co of Slrs 1987; memb: Law Soc, Law Soc of Hong Kong; *Books* Moores & Rowlands Orange Tax Guide 1987/88 and 1988/89; *Recreations* sailing, scuba diving, running, reading, music; *Clubs* Royal Hong Kong Yacht, Hong Kong FC, London Road Runners; *Style*— Michael Walter, Esq; 4 Melbourne Terr, Moore Park Rd, London SW6 2JU (☎ 01 736 7367); Le Grenier, Chemin Du Rocher Nay, Le Tour, Chamonix 74400, France (☎ 50 54 13 92); Flat B-20, Po Shan Mansions, 10 Po Shan Rd, Hong Kong (852 5 8581124); One St Paul's Churchyard, London EC4M 8SH (☎ 01 329 4422, fax 01 606 0822, telex 886789 SHSPC G); 1802 Edinburgh Tower, The Landmark, 15 Queen's Rd Central, Hong Kong (☎ 852 5 8680789, fax 852 5 8681504, telex 66278 SHL HX)

WALTER, Robert John; s of Richard John Walter, of Warminster, Wilts, and Irene Gladys, *née* Clements; *b* 30 May 1948; *Educ* Warminster, Univ of Aston (BSc); *m* 28 Aug 1970, Sally, da of Donald Middleton, (d 1976); 2 s (Charles b 1976, Alexander b 1977), 1 da (Elizabeth b 1974); *Career* investmt banker and farmer; dir: FW Holst (Europe) Ltd 1984-86, and vice pres Aubrey G Lanston & Co Inc 1986-, TV-UK Ltd 1988-, Willow Films Ltd 1989; visiting lectr Central London Poly, farmer in W Country; memb Stock Exchange; Parly candidate (C) Bedwellty 1979, chm Foreign Affrs Forum 1985-87 vice-chm Cons Gp for Europe 1984-86; chm Euro Democrat forum 1979-84, Aston Univ cons Assoc 1967-69, W Wilts Young Cons 1972-75; chm govrs Tachbrook Sch 1980-; Freeman City of London 1983, Liveryman Worshipful Co of Needlemakers 1983; AMSIA; *Recreations* sailing, shooting; *Clubs* Carlton; *Style*— Robert Walter, Esq; 110 Grosvenor Rd, London SW1, (☎ 0364 73433); Staddon, South Brent, Devon, TQ10 9E4; Aubrey G Lanston & Co Inc, 3 Queen Victoria St, London EC4N 8HR (☎ 01 248 3955, fax 01 236 2781, telex 945771)

WALTER, Lady Sarah (Marion); *née* Coke; yst da of 5 Earl of Leicester (d 1976); *b* 23 July 1944; *m* 1970, Maj David Finlayson Wylie Hill Walter; 2 s; *Style*— Lady Sarah Walter; 14 Hyde Park St, W2; Westwood, Balthayock, by Perth

WALTERS, Prof Sir Alan Arthur; s of James Arthur Walters, and Claribel, *née* Heywood; *b* 17 June 1926; *Educ* Alderman Newtons Sch Leicester, Univ Coll Leicester (BSc London), Nuffield Coll Oxford (MA); *m* 1975, Margaret Patricia, da of Leonard Wilson, of Leeds, Yorks; 1 da by previous m (Louise); *Career* Cassel prof of econs LSE 1968-76, prof of political economy Johns Hopkins Univ Maryland USA 1976-, personal econ advsr to PM 1981-84; Hon DLitt Leicester 1981, Hon DSocSc Birmingham 1984; kt 1983; *Clubs* Athenaeum, Political Economy; *Style*— Prof Sir Alan Walters; 2820 P Street NW, Washington, DC 20007, USA; American Enterprise Institute, 1150 17th Street NW, Washington DC 20036, USA (☎ 202 862 6407)

WALTERS, Beverley Hugh (Bev); s of Hugh Edward Walters (d 1986), and Florence Mary (d 1987); *b* 1 April 1942; *Educ* St John's Coll Johannesburg, Univ of Witwatersrand (BSc), Univ of South Africa (B COMM, MBA); *m* 16 Jan 1965, Helen Paris, da of Patrick Llyod Gooderham, of Johannesburg; 1 s (Mark Hugh b 1965), 2 da (Caren b 1967, Cathy b 1972); *Career* regnl mining geologist Gen Mining & Fin Ltd Johannesburg 1964-69, gen mangr Citicorp Johannesburg 1969-78, vice pres Bank of Montreal (Toronto, London, Australia) 1978-86, md ANZ Merchant Bank (Australia and London) 1986-; SAGS 1965, SATS 1965, IBSA 1970, AAIS 1968; *Recreations* golf; *Clubs* Hindheard GC, Metropolitian GC (Melbourne), Australian GC (Sydney); *Style*— Bev Walters, Esq; 34 Onslow Gdns, South Kensington, London SW7; ANZ Merchant Bank, 65 Holborn Viaduct, London EC1A 2EU (☎ 01 489 0021, fax 01 3248 1103, telex 888981)

WALTERS, David Grenville; s of Claude Grenville Walter (d 1971), of Notts, and Agnes, *née* Dunkerley; *b* 19 August 1942; *Educ* Nottingham HS; *m* 4 Sept 1965, Frances Mary, da of Robert James Cumming (d 1979), of Banff; 1 s (Nigel b 1967), 1 da (Lynne b 1970); *Career* cmmnd TA 1973, Regt Offr 101 (FD) Regt RA (V) 1974, 2 i/c 203 (FD) Battery RA (V) 1983, SO (TA) HQ RA 2 Inf Div 1986-, Maj; landowner, sr exec Thomson Regnl Newspapers 1968-72, chm Grentex Mfrg Ltd 1972-, Lloyds underwriter 1973-, pres Grenville SA France 1974-78, chm Grenville Marine 1988-; vice-chm Ponteland Cons Assoc, hon tres Hexham Constituency Cons Assoc; memb: bd visitors HM Prisons, parole bd Local Review Ctee, Northumberland Assoc Boys' Clubs; MInstM 1970; *Recreations* flying, sailing, rugby, hill walking, wine; *Style*— David Walters, Esq, TD; Mill Close, Runnymede Rd, Ponteland, Northumberland NE20 9HL (☎ 0661 24624); 54 West St, Oundle, Northants

WALTERS, Sir Dennis Murray; MBE (1960), MP (C) Westbury 1964-; s of Douglas L Walters (d 1964), and Clara, *née* Pomello; *b* 28 Nov 1928; *Educ* Downside, St Catharine's Coll Cambridge (MA); *m* 1, 1955 (m dis 1969), Vanora, da of Sir Archibald McIndoe, CBE, MB, ChB (d 1960); 1 s (Nicholas McIndoe b 1957), 1 da (Lorian b 1960); m 2, 1970 (m dis 1979), Hon Celia Mary, da of Baron Duncan Sandys, CH (d 1987), 1 s (Dominic b 1971); m 3, 22 Jan 1981, Bridgett Louise, da of J F Shearer, CBE, of Wimbledon; 1 s (Oliver Charles b 1985), 1 da (Camilla Clare b 1982); *Career* interned in Italy during early part of WWII, joined Resistance Movement for 11 months; dir Cluff Oil Inc; tstee ANAF Foundation; memb Kuwait Investment Advsy Ctee; conslt to Balfour Beatty Construction Ltd; writer and broadcaster; contested (C) Blyth 1959 and 1960 by-election; fndr memb Bow Group; chm Fedn of Univ Cons and Unionist Assocs 1949-50; PA to to Rt Hon Quintin Hogg, QC (Lord Hailsham of Saint Marylebone) as chm of Cons Pty 1957-69; jt sec Cons Parly Foreign Affairs Ctee 1965-71, jt vice-chm 1974-78; chm Asthma Research Cncl 1968-88;, jt-chm Cncl of Advancement of Arab-Br Understanding 1970-82; chm Cons Middle E Cncl 1980-; Order of the Cedar of Lebanon 1969; kt 1988; *Recreations* reading, tennis; *Clubs* Boodle's; *Style*— Sir Dennis Walters, MBE, MP; Orchardleigh, Corton, Warminster, Wiltshire (☎ 098 55 369); 43 Royal Avenue, London SW3 4QE (☎ 01 730 9431, fax

01 823 5938); car ☎ 0836 233617

WALTERS, Very Rev (Rhys) Derrick Chamberlain; s of Ivor Chamberlain Walters, and Rosamund Grace, *née* Jackson; *b* 10 Mar 1932; *Educ* Gowerton Boys' GS, LSE, Ripon Hall Oxford (BSc); *m* 28 Dec 1959, Joan, da of William George Fisher, 2 s (David b 1962, Michael b 1964); *Career* curate Manselton Swansea 1957-58, anglican chaplain Univ Coll Swansea and curate St Mary's 1958-62; vicar: All Saints Totley 1962-67, St Mary's Boulton by Derby 1967-74; diocesan missioner Diocese of Salisbury 1974-82, vicar Burcombe 1974-79, non-residentiary canon Salisbury Cath 1978 (canon and tres 1979-82), dean Liverpool 1983-; hon fell Liverpool Poly 1988; *Recreations* escapist, literature, croquet, classical music; *Style—* The Very Rev the Dean of Liverpool; Liverpool Cathedral, St James Mount, Liverpool L1 7AZ (☎ 051 709 6271, fax 051 709 1112)

WALTERS, Sir (Frederick) Donald; s of Percival Donald Walters, and Irene Walters; *b* 5 Oct 1925; *Educ* Howardian HS Cardiff, LSE (LLB); *m* 1950, Adelaide Jean, *née* McQuistin; 1 s; *Career* barr Inner Temple 1946; practised Wales and Chester circuit 1948-59; memb: bd Welsh Devpt Agency 1980- (dep chm 1984-), Devpt Bd for Rural Wales 1984-; dir Chartered Tst plc 1959-85; cncl chm Univ of Wales Coll of Cardiff 1988-; High Sheriff S Glamorgan 1987-88; *Style—* Sir Donald Walters; 120 Cyncoed Rd, Cardiff CF2 6BL

WALTERS, Geraint Gwynn; CBE (1958); s of Rev David D Walters (d 1968), of Gaiman, Argentian, and Brynsiencyn, Anglesey, and Rachel Gwynn, *née* Williams (d 1955); *b* 6 June 1910; *Educ* Univ Coll Bangor (BA); *m* 1, July 1942, Doreena (d 1959), da of John Owen (d 1955), of Bethesda, N Wales; m 2, 2 July 1968, (Sarah Ann) Ruth, da of Henry Roberts Price (d 1963), of Mathry, Dyfed; *Career* regnl organiser under Rt Hon David Lloyd George 1935-40, dep regnl dir Miny of Info 1940-45, dir Miny of Public Bldgs and Works 1945-72: Wales 1948-53 and 1966-72, Far E 1963-66; Parly housing cmmr Borough of Merthyr Tydfil 1972-73; memb Gorsedd of Bards 1961, memb Cole Cmmn on Broadcasting in Wales 1962-63, ldr Overseas Welsh at Royal Nat eisteddfad 1965, pres Singapore Welsh Soc 1965-66, former pres S Wales Soc of Public Admin, cncl memb UWIST 1968-76 (vice hcm 1970-73), memb of ct Univ of Wales 1980-86, life memb of ct Univ of Wales Coll Cardiff; *Recreations* reading (talking books for the blind); *Clubs* Cardiff and County, Civil Service (London); *Style—* Geraint Walters, Esq, CBE; 1 The Mount, Cardiff Rd, Llandaff, Cardiff CF5 2AR (☎ 0222 568739)

WALTERS, Lt Col John Henry; s of the late Henry Blanchard Walters, OBE, and the late Grace Walters; *b* 17 May 1909; *Educ* Clifton Coll, Corpus Christi Coll Cambridge (MD, BCh); *m* 7 Aug 1937, Janet Isobel Norah, da of Ernest McIntyre (d 1964); 1 s (Humphrey b 1942), 1 da (Julia (Mrs Duprée b 1940); *Career* IMS 1937-46 (specialist physician 1942-), MO i/c MRC Nutritional Res Stn The Gambia 1948-51, Specialist Physician and dep SMO Kuwait State Med Serv 1951-54, MO i/c and sec W African Cncl for Med Res Lagos 1952-54; conslt physician: Hosp for Tropical Diseases London, Tropical Diseases Unit Queens Mary's Hosp Roehampton 1955-63; FRCP 1958 (London), 1960 (Edin); *Publications incl:* contribs to Manson's Tropcial Diseases (17 edn, 1972), Recent Advances in Tropical Medicine (3 edn, 1961), Fundamentals of Current Medical Treatment (1965), and papers in many learned jnls; *Recreations* observing natural history, fishing, gardening; *Clubs* MCC; *Style—* Lt Col John Walters; Higher Lawn, Chudleigh, S Devon (☎ 0626 853 160)

WALTERS, Rear Adm John William Townshend; CB (1984); s of William Bernard Walters and Lilian Martha, *née* Hartridge; *b* 23 April 1926; *Educ* John Fisher Sch Purley; *m* 1949, Margaret Sarah Patricia Jeffkins; 2 s, 1 da; *Career* joined RN 1944, barr Middle Temple 1956, Supply Offr HMS Albion 1967-69, Sec to Chief of Fleet Support 1969-72, Chief Naval Judge Advocate 1972-75, Capt Naval Drafting 1975-78, Dir Naval Admin Planning 1978-80, asst chief of Def Staff (Personnel and Logistics) 1981-84, ret RN 1984; chm Industl Tbnls 1984, dep chm Data Protection Tbnl 1985; *Recreations* sailing (yacht 'Lady Macbeth'); *Clubs* Army and Navy, Royal Naval Sailing Assoc; *Style—* Rear Adm John Walters, CB; Good Holding, 5 Hollycombe Close, Liphook, Hants GU30 7HR

WALTERS, Joyce Dora; da of Wilfred John Davies (d 1961), and Florence May, *née* Fisher; *b* 10 Dec 1932; *Educ* St Anne's Coll Oxford (MA); *m* 29 July 1979, Lt Col Howard Corey Walters IV (d 1983), s of Col Howard Corey Walters III (d 1982), of California; by prev m, 1 s (Nicholas John Warwick Bailey b 18 Sep 1962); *Career* headmistress: St Mary's Calne 1972-85 Clifton HS 1985-; *Recreations* reading, cooking, travel; *Clubs* Utd Oxford and Cambridge; *Style—* Mrs Joyce Walters; 4 Longwood House, Failand, Bristol (☎ 0272 392092); Clifton High Sch, College Rd, Bristol (☎ 0272 730201)

WALTERS, (Thomas) Mervyn Llewellyn; MBE (1966); s of Hon Canon Thomas William Walters (d 1951), of Whitwick Vicarage, Leics, and Emmeline Florence, *née* Cocks (d 1958); *b* 8 April 1910; *Educ* Loughborough GS; *m* 1, 22 Sept 1942, Jean Margaret (d 1972), da of late Roy Wallace Murray, of Lincoln; 2 s ((Thomas) Rhodri Murray b 1944, Malcolm Hywel b 1948), 1 da (Gwyneth Margaret (Mrs Page) b 1945); m 2, 26 March 1976, Eileen Mary, da of late Sholto Douglas, of Keniworth; *Career* slr 1931, Cruikshank Bird & Witford 1931-, Notary Public 1938; pres Loughborough Rotary Club 1974-75; memb: Cncl Leics 1970-88, gen synod C of E 1975-85; lay canon Leicester Cathedral 1977-; govr: Warner C of E Sch 1944-, Gardendon HS 1955-87; chm review ctee Loughborough Charities (under charities act 1960); scout cmmr: dist 1937, asst county 1954, dep conty 1963, hon 1977-, Silverwolf 1957; memb: nat cncl Scout Assoc 1967-77, Co Youth Ctee 1954-77, first chm Leics Standing Conf of Youth Orgns 1965; memb Law Soc; *Books* Loughborough 1888-1988 The Birth Of A Borough jtly; *Recreations* travel, caravanning, history, photography, philately; *Style—* Mervyn Walters, Esq, MBE; 32 Sandalwood Rd, Loughborough, Leics (☎ 0509 212 349); 20 Church Gate, Loughborough, Leics (☎ 0509 232 611, fax 0509 239 081, telex 341995428)

WALTERS, Michael Quentin; s of Leslie and Helen Marie Walters; *b* 14 Oct 1927; *Educ* Merchant Taylors', Worcester Coll Oxford (MA); *m* 1954, Lysbeth Ann Falconer; *Career* admitted slr 1954; chm EIS Gp plc 1977-; dir Delta Gp plc 1980-; sr ptnr Theodore Godd and, Solicitors 1983-; *Style—* Michael Walters, Esq; c/o EIS Group plc, 6 Sloane Sq, London SW1W 8EE (☎ 01 730 9187)

WALTERS, Sir Peter Ingram; s of Stephen Walters (d 1945), and Edna, *née* Redgate; *b* 11 Mar 1931; *Educ* King Edward's Sch Birmingham, Birmingham Univ; *m* 1960, Patricia Anne, *née* Tulloch; 2 s, 1 da; *Career* Lt RASC; md BP Co Ltd 1973, dep chm 1980-81, chm 1981-; chm BP America Inc 1987-, vice-pres BP North America 1965-67; chm: BP Chemicals 1976-81, BP Chemicals Int 1981; dir Nat Westminster Bank 1981-; memb Indust Soc Cncl 1975-; Post Off Bd 1978-79; Gen Ctee Lloyds Register of Shipping 1976; pres: Soc of Chem Indust 1978-80, Gen Cncl of Br Shipping 1977-78, memb Inst of Manpower Studies 1980- (vice-pres 1977-80, pres 1980-86, Inst of Manpower Studies 1980- (vice-pres 1977-80); Govr chm of Govg Body London Business Sch 1987- (dep-chm 1986, Gov 1981-), London Business Sch 1981-; Int Mgmnt Inst Memb Fdn Bd 1982- (chm 1984-86); memb Fndn Bd 1982-83, chm 1984-, Int Mgmnt Inst, pres ctee CBI 1982-; Tstee: Nat Maritime Museum 1983-, E Malling Res Station 1983-; memb Police Fndn 1985-, memb Inst of Econ Affairs 1986, pres IOD 1986-, hon D Stirling Univ 1987, hon DSc Birmingham 1986; Cdr Order of Leopold (Belgium); kt 1984; *Recreations* golf, gardening, sailing; *Style—* Sir Peter Walters; British Petroleum Co Ltd, Britannic House, Moor Lane, London EC2Y 9BU (☎ 01 920 8000, telex 888811)

WALTERS, Sir Roger Talbot; KBE (1971, CBE 1965); s of Alfred Walters, of Sudbury, Suffolk; *b* 31 Mar 1917; *Educ* Oundle, Architectural Assoc Sch of Architecture, Liverpool Univ; *m* 1976, Claire Chappell; *Career* serv RE WWII; chief architect (devpt) Directorate of works WO 1959-62, dep dir-gen res and devpt Miny Public Bldgs and Works 1962-67 (dir-gen prodn 1967-69), architect and controller construction servs GLC 1971-78; hon FAIA; FRIBA, FIStructE; *Clubs* Reform; *Style—* Sir Roger Walters, KBE; 46 Princess Rd, London NW1 (☎ 01 722 3740)

WALTERS, William Charles; s of William Dyke Walters (d 1977), of Walsall, and Georgina May, *née* Bayford, JP (d 1975); *b* 5 Dec 1921; *Educ* Edward Shelley HS Walsall, Coll of Accountancy; *m* 6 Feb 1944, Margaret Joan, da of George Gavan (d 1977); 1 s (Michael b 1948); *Career* secretarial branch RN 1942-46; serv: Africa, India, Ceylon, Aust, Philipines, Hong Kong; NCO in Cmd Admin Gp Ldr Ship: frigates on Ceylon and Burma Patrols, aircraft carriers Br Pacific Fleet; rescue work (food and medicines); CA, joined Kimberley Morrison Moore & Co 1951 (ptnr 1965, sr ptnr 1976); church choirman (formerly choirboy) Walsall Parish Church 1930-; memb: Royal Sch of Church Music (chm Lichfield branch 1972-), Br Legion 1948-, Church Neighbourhood Care 1968-; FICA 1949, ATII 1950; *Recreations* classical music, photography, travel; *Style—* William Walters, Esq; 7 Seckham Rd, Beacon Place, Lichfield, Staffs WS13 7AN (☎ 0543 251068; Kimberley Morrison Moore and Co, St Philips House, St Philips Place, Birmingham B3 2PP; (☎ 021 200 3077, fax 021 200 2454)

WALTHALL, Capt (Leigh) Edward (Delves); CBE (1961), DSC (1941); s of Henry Douglas Delves Walthall, OBE (d 1931), and Hilda Maude, *née* Hancock (d 1979); *b* 21 August 1914; *Educ* RNC Dartmouth; *m* 7 April 1951, Dorothy Margaret, da of Hugh Robert Leonard (d 1969); 3 da (Fiona b 1953, Louisa b 1956, Serena b 1959); *Career* Capt RN Pilot Fleet Air Arm, serv WWII mostly N Atlantic, responsible in USA for adaptation to Br requirements of US Navy Aircraft supplied under Lend-Lease, cmd HMS Delight 1956-58; dir Air Equipment Admty 1958-61; farmer 1961-; *Recreations* tennis, skiing; *Clubs* Army and Navy; *Style—* Capt L E D Walthall, CBE, DSC; Hillhouse Farm, Sapperton, Cirencester, Glos GL7 6LP (☎ 028 576 256)

WALTHER, Robert Philippe; s of Prof David Philippe Walther (d 1973), and Barbara *née* Brook; *b* 31 July 1943; *Educ* Charterhouse, Christ Church Oxford (MA); *m* 21 June 1969, Anne, da of Lionel Wigglesworth, of Hill Brow, Woldingham, Surrey; 1 s (Luke b 1978), 1 da (Julie Clare b 1973); *Career* Clerical Med Investmt Gp: joined 1965, dep investmt mangr 1972, investmt mangr 1976, asst gen mangr (investments) 1980, dir 1985-; dep chm investmt ctee Assoc of Br Insurers; FIA 1970, ASIA 1969; *Recreations* hockey, golf, bridge, squash, sailing; *Clubs* Utd Oxford and Cambridge; *Style—* Robert Walther, Esq; Ashwell's Barn, Chesham Lane, Chalfont St, Giles, Bucks HP8 4AS (☎ 024 07 5575); Clerical Medical Investment Group 15 St James's Square, London SW1Y 4LQ (☎ 01 930 5474, fax 01 321 1846, telex 27432 CMG LDN)

WALTON, Anthony Michael; QC (1970); s of Henry Herbert Walton (d 1975), of Dulwich, and Clara Martha *née* Dobrantz (d 1974); *b* 4 May 1925; *Educ* Dulwich, Hertford Coll Oxford (MA, BCL); *m* 1955, Jean Frederica, da of William Montague Hey (d 1936), of London; 1 s (Martin b 1969); *Career* bencher Middle Temple 1978; Liveryman Worshipful Co of Gunmakers; *Publications* Patent Law of Europe and the UK (1978), Russell on Arbitration (1982); *Style—* Anthony Walton, Esq, QC; 62 Kingsmead Rd, Tulse Hill, London SW2 3JG (☎ 01 674 9159); Francis Taylor Building, The Temple EC4Y 7BY (☎ 01 353 5657);

WALTON, Col Dennis; CBE (1967, OBE 1962), MC, TD; s of Harry Walton (d 1966), and Eva Kathleen Walton (d 1969), of Bury, Lancs; *b* 7 Feb 1920; *Educ* Bury GS, Emmanuel Coll Cambridge (MA); *m* 1949, Barbara Shirley, da of Leonard Bertram Jones, JP (d 1948), a former Mayor of Bury; 2 da; *Career* serv WWII N Africa and Europe; Col RA (TA), dep cdr 42 Div 1962-67; md Dalkeith Knitwear Ltd 1963-78, bd memb Coats Patons Knitwear Div 1976-78; pres Nottingham and Dist Hosiery Mfrs Assoc 1967-69; chm: E Midland Further Educn Cncl Textiles Panel 1973-77, Technician Educn Cncl Ctee 1975-80; sr advsr Small Firms Serv (DE) 1978-; memb cncl Nat Artillery Assoc 1962-; chm E Midland Further Educ Cncl 1985-; pres: RA Offrs' Assoc of the North-West 1985-; Bolton Volunteer Artillery Assoc 1985-; Cambridge Soccer blue 1940; FBIM, FInstD; *Clubs* Royal Overseas League; *Style—* Col Dennis Walton, CBE, MC, TD; Riber Manor, Matlock, Derbyshire DE4 5JU (☎ 0629 583864)

WALTON, The Ven Geoffrey Elmer; s of Maj Harold Walton (d 1978), and Edith Margaret Dawson (d 1983); *b* 19 Feb 1934; *Educ* West Bridgford GS, Univ of Durham (BA), Queens Coll Birmingham (Diploma in Theology); *m* 9 Sept 1961, Edith Mollie, da of John Patrick O'Connor (d 1970); 1 s (Jeremy Mark b 1968); *Career* vicar of Norwell, Notts and Diocesan Youth chaplain 1965-69, recruitment and selection sec, Advsy Cncl for the Church's Ministry London 1969-75; hon Canon of Salisbury Cathedral 1981; Rural Dean of Weymouth 1980-82; Archdeacon of 1982-, Dorset 1982-, incumbent of Witchampton with Long Crichel and Moor Crichel 1982-, Dorset Co Scout Chaplain, chm Diocesan Bd for Social Responsibility; *Recreations* religious drama, conjuring, walking; *Style—* The Ven the Archdeacon of Dorset; The Vicarage, Witchampton, Wimborne, Dorset BH21 5AP (☎ 0258 840422)

WALTON, Lt-Col John Cusack; DL (1987); s of Col Granville Walton, CMG, OBE, DL, JP (d 1974), and Joan, *née* McCraken (d 1975); *b* 16 April 1928; *Educ* Marlborough; *m* 31 Jan 1971, Elsabe, da of Brig James Whetstone, OBE (d 1956); 1 s (David b 29 Feb 1972), 1 da (Joanna b 7 Nov 1973); *Career* cmmnd Royal Scots Greys 1947: Capt 1949-58, Adj 1955-58, Maj 1960-71, Lt-Col 1971-77, ret 1977; chm and tstee Regtl Assoc 1984-; chm: Old Berks Hunt 1984-; Oxon Scout Cncl 1984, Thames Valley Police Authy 1985-; memb E Wessex TAVR Assoc 1981-, ccncllr Oxon 1981-; *Recreations* hunting; *Clubs* Cavalry and Guards'; *Style*— Lt-Col John Walton, DL; Longworth Manor, Abingdon, Oxfordshire (☎ 0865 820223)

WALTON, Sir John Nicholas; TD (1962); s of Herbert Walton; *b* 16 Sept 1922; *Educ* Alderman Wraith GS, King's Coll Med Sch Durham Univ (MD); *m* 1946, Mary Harrison; 1 s, 2 da; *Career* Col (late RAMC) CO I(N) Gen Hosp (TA) 1963-66, Hon Col 201 (N) Gen Hosp (T and AVR) 1968-73; conslt neurologist Newcastle Univ Hosps 1958-83, Prof Neurology Newcastle Univ 1968-83, chm Muscular Dystrophy Gp GB 1970-, memb Gen Med Cncl 1971- (chm Educn Ctee 1975-82, pres 1982-89), pres BMA 1980-82, ASME 1982-, ABN 1987-8; first vice-pres World Fedn Neurologists 1981-; warden Green Coll Oxford 1983-89; pres RSM 1984-86; FRCP; DSc Newcastle; kt 1979; *Clubs* Athenaeum, United Oxford and Cambridge; *Style*— Sir John Walton, TD; 1a Observatory St, Oxford OH2 6EW (☎ 0865 59846); Green College, Radcliffe Observatory, Oxford OX2 6HG (☎ 0865 274774)

WALTON, Sir John Robert; s of late John Thomas Walton, and Dorothy Amelia Walton; *b* 7 Feb 1904; *Educ* Scots Coll Sydney; *m* 1938, Peggy Everley, da of late W S H Gamble; 1 s, 1 da; *Career* Nat Cash Register Co Pty Ltd: NSW mangr 1934, md in Australia 1946-51; dir Waltons Ltd Group (md 1951-72, chm 1966-73), chm FNCB-Waltons Corpn Ltd 1966-73; kt 1971; *Style*— Sir John Walton; 9a Longwood, 5 Thornton St, Darling Point, NSW 2027, Australia

WALTON, John Victor; s of Eric Roscoe Walton (d 1961), of 18 Beech Ave, Radlett, Herts, and Ethel Marjorie, *née* Addinsell (d 1983); *b* 5 Dec 1925; *Educ* Aldenham, Ruskin Sch of Drawing Oxford, Slade Sch of Fine Art London, Univ of London (dip fine art); *m* 1950 (m dis 1970), Annette Rolande Francoise D'Exea; 2 s (James Andre b 1950, Roland Dominic b 1966), 1 da (Victoria Ann b 1953); *Career* portrait painter; princ Heatherley Sch of Fine Art 1974-; Exhibitions Incl: RA, Royal Soc of Portrait Painters, Paris Salon (hon mention), Institut de France, Academic des Beaux Arts; paintings in national instns and private collections in GB & abroad; co sec Thomas Heatherley Educnl Tst 1976-, govr FBA 1982- (chm constitutional advsy ctee 1983-86), memb cncl RSPP 1983- (previously 1979-81); *Recreations* painting, cycling, history; *Clubs* Chelsea Arts; *Style*— John Walton, Esq; 30 Park Road, Radlett, Herts; The Heatherley School of Fine Art, Upcerne Road, Chelsea SW10 0SH (☎ 01 351 4190)

WALTON, Leonard Joseph; *b* 30 May 1911; *Educ* Wallasey GS; *m* 10 Jul 1937, Vera Freda; 1 da (Deryn); *Career* Gunner RA (TA) 1938, WWII commnd RA 1940 (Capt 1941, Maj 1942), served BAOR (despatches) 1939-45; TEM; dep chief gen mangr Martins Bank Ltd 1965-69, gen mangr Barclays Bank plc (on merger) 1969-71, dep chm & chief exec Barclays Merchant Bank and dir various Barclays subsidiaries 1971-76, dep chm Riggs AP Bank Ltd 1976; chm: Riggs AP Leasing Ltd 1988-, Riggs AP Servs Ltd 1988-, Regalian Properties Plc 1983-; chm inst of Laryngology (Univ of London) 1971-76, govr Royal Throat Nose & Ear Hosp 1971-76, hon tres & dep chm Victoria League for Cwlth Friendship 1972-88; FCIB (hon tres 1966-80); *Recreations* fishing, golf; *Clubs* Roy Liverpool Golf, Hoylare Ches - Wynesdale Anglers; *Style*— L J Walton, Esq; 16 Clifton Place, Hyde Park, London W2 2SN (☎ 01 723 0382); Riggs AP Bank Ltd, 21 Great Winchester St, London EC2N 2HH (☎ 01 588 7575, car tel 0836 286 938); Regalian Properties Plc, 44 Grosvenor Hill, London W1X 9JE (☎ 01 493 9613)

WALTON, Malcolm Cranston; s of Cranston Graham Walton, of Amwell, Wheathampstead, nr St Albans, Herts, and Pamela Beatrice, *née* Sharpe; *b* 29 Jan 1950; *Educ* Stowe; *m* 6 Nov 1971, Henrietta Elizabeth, da of Lt-Col Henry Leonard Boultbee; 2 s (Richard b 1974, Henry b 1984), 2 da (Lucy b 1977, Anna b 1979); *Career* admitted slr 1974, ptnr Waltons 1975-77; md and fndr Cambridge Tst plc (property investmt and devpt) 1982-; memb Law Soc; *Recreations* fishing, shooting, gardening, tennis; *Clubs* Lansdowne; *Style*— Malcolm Walton, Esq; Crave Hall, Cow Lane, Gt Chesterford, Saffron Walden, Essex CB10 5JH (☎ 0799 30803); Cambridge Tst plc, Pound Hill House, Pound Hill, Cambridge CB3 OAE (☎ 0223 312457, fax 0223 460401, car 0860 224654)

WALTON, Hon Mrs Mary Synolda; *née* Butler; eldest da of 28 Baron Dunboyne, *qv*; *b* 29 April 1954; *Educ* Benenden, Girton Coll Cambridge (BA, MA); *m* 1984, Alastair Henry Walton, o s of late Sir Raymond Henry Walton; 3 da (Alexandra Mary b 1985, Christina Frances b 1986, Stephanie Katharine b 1988); *Career* admitted slr 1980; *Recreations* Tennis (Cambridge 1/2 Blue 1974 and 1975); *Style*— The Hon Mrs Walton; 26 Paradise Walk, London SW3 4LJ

WALTON, Miles Henry; s of Rae Walton, MC, AFC, TD, of Tynemouth, and Anne Elizabeth, *née* Flisher; *b* 15 July 1955; *Educ* Ratcliffe Coll, Brasenose Coll Oxford (MA); *m* 11 May 1985, Lorraine, da of Jack Nunn (d 1965); 1 s (Jack b 14 Nov 1986); *Career* slr 1980; currently ptnr Wilde Sapte; memb Law Soc, ATII; *Recreations* wine, sailing, saxophone, scuba diving, skiing; *Style*— Miles Walton, Esq; Wilde Sapte, Queensbridge House, Upper Thames St, London EC2 (☎ 01 236 3050, fax 01 236 9624)

WALTON, Hon Mrs (Sarah Lucy); *née* Pym; yr da of Baron Pym (Life Peer), *qv*; *b* 18 Dec 1958; *m* 1985, Peter Walton, s of W C Walton; 1 s (James Peter b 1986), 1 da (Victoria Lucy b 1988); *Style*— The Hon Mrs Walton; c/o The Rt Hon Lord Pym, PC, MC, DL, Everton Park, Sandy, Beds SG19 2DE

WALTON, Lady; Susana; da of Enrique Gil, of Buenos Aires; *m* 1948, Sir William Walton, OM, the composer (d 1983); *Style*— Lady Walton; La Mortella, Forio d'Ischia, Italy

WALTON, William Robert; s of Wiliam Redman Walton (d 1970) and Edith Alice, *née* Levit (d 1980); *b* 4 July 1925; *Educ* Loughborough Coll; *m* 1949, Joyce, da of Ernest Edward Baldwin (d 1960); 1 da (Jacqueline); *Career* mechanical engr; dir Hathorn Davey & Co 1971-, jt md Sulzer Bros (UK) Ltd 1978- (dir 1971-), chm Sulzer (UK) Pumps Ltd 1987-; past pres Yorkshire & Humberside Employers Assoc; FIMechE, CEng; *Recreations* golf, photography, gardening; *Style*— William Walton, Esq; Willow Court, Tripp Garth, Linton, Wetherby, W Yorks; Sulzer (UK) Pumps Ltd, Manor Mill Lane, Leeds LS11 8BR (☎ 0532 701244, telex 55471)

WALTON JONES, Howard; s of Alfred Hayter Walton Jones, of Majorca, and Carmen Mary, *née* Rowlands; ggf A Jones founded A Jones & Sons 1857 London; Co now has 120 shops in England with int reputation for high quality; *b* 18 Feb 1945; *Educ* Monkton Combe Sch nr Bath; *m* 20 July 1968, Susan Dorothy Ann, da of John Brian Edwards Penn (d 1980); 2 da (Emma b 1972, Katy b 1975); *Career* md A Jones & Sons plc (shoe retailers) 1976-; dir: Church & Co plc (shoe manufacturers) 1976-, Babers of Oxford St (show retailers) 1976-; *Recreations* tennis; *Clubs* East India; *Style*— Howard Walton Jones, Esq; 18 Maple Road, Eastbourne, E Sussex BN23 6NZ (☎ 0323 30532, telex JONESA 878252)

WALWYN, Peter Tyndall; s of Lt-Col C T Walwyn, DSO, OBE, MC (d 1959), and Alexandra Adelaide Walwyn (d 1959); *b* 1 July 1933; *Educ* Charterhouse; *m* 5 Jan 1960, Virginia Clementina, da of Auriol S Gaselee (d 1987); 1 s (Edward b 1969), 1 da (Kate b 1972); *Career* racehorse trainer; leading trainer on the Flat 1974-75, leading trainer Ireland 1974-75; major races won incl: The Thousand Guineas 1970, Oaks Stakes 1974, Irish Derby 1971, King George and Queen Elizabeth Stakes, Epsom Derby, Irish Derby, Irish 2000 Guineas; *Recreations* foxhunting, shooting; *Clubs* Turf, Jockey; *Style*— Peter Walwyn, Esq; Seven Barrows, Lambourn, Berks

WANAMAKER, Samuel (Sam); s of Maurice Wanamaker (d 1983), of Los Angeles, and Molly, *née* Bobele (d 1978); *b* 14 June 1919; *Educ* Tuley HS Chicago, Drake Univ Des Moines Iowa, Godman Theatre Chicago Art Inst (BDA); *m* 26 May 1940, Charlotte, da of Arnold Holland (d 1936), of Chicago; 3 da (Abby b 14 July 1942, Zoe Mora b 13 May 1948, Jessica Lee b 24 January 1954); *Career* WWII serv: NCO Special Servs Div US Army 1944-46 (serv Pacific with invasion forces in capture of Iwo Jima); Globe players Co (Great Lakes Fair) 1936, dir JPI Theatres Chicago 1939-40; acted in and directed Broadway shows incl: Café Crown 1941, Counterattack 1942, "This Too Shall Pass" (1946), Joan of Lorraine 1947, Goodbye My Fancy 1949, Caesar and Cleopatra 1950, A Far Country 1961, Children from their Games, Case of Libel, Murder Among US 1962-63; acted in and directed over 50 films incl: My Girl Tisa 1947, Christ in Concrete 1949, Tara Bulba 1962, Those Magnificent Men in Their Flying Machines 1964, The Spy Who Came in From The Cold 1965, Death on the Nile 1978, Private Benjamin 1980, Superman IV 1986, Baby Boom 1987; acted in and directed over 20 TV shows in UK and US incl: Holocaust 1977, The Berrengers 1984, Baby Boom 1988-89; Dir ABC TV Movie "Colombo" 1989, prodr opera incl: King Priam, Forza del Destino, Ice Break (all at Covent Garden), War and Peace (Sydney), Aida (San Francisco), Tosca (San Diego); narrator Oedipus Rex BBC, artistic dir New Shakespeare Theatre Liverpool 1957-59, played Othello RSC 1959-60, played title role and directed Macbeth Chicago 1964, prodr seasons Globe Playhouse Tst 1972-74; fndr: The Globe Playhouse Tst, World Centre for Shakespeare Studies 1970-71, Shakespeare Globe Tst, Int Shakespeare Globe Centre, Bear Gardens Museum and Arts Centre 1982; Hon LLD Univ of New Brunswick 1988; memb BAFTA; *Recreations* jogging, tennis, swimming; *Clubs* Athenaeum; *Style*— Sam Wanamaker, Esq; International Shakespeare Globe Centre, Bear Gardens, Bankside, Liberty of the Clink, London SE1 9EB (☎ 01 620 0202/, US 213 383 383 7040, fax 01 928 7968)

WANDRAG, Graham David; s of late Fl Lt Sarel Johannes Wandrag, MBE, of Pretoria, SA, and Florence Belle Adath, *née* Chedzey; *b* 23 Sept 1949; *Educ* Stationers Co Sch; *m* 1, (m dis 1983), Christine Ann, *née* Johnson; 1 da (Olivia Maria b 14 Feb 1981); m 2, 6 Oct 1986, Jenefer Catherine; *Career* ptnr City Deposit Brokers 1974-87, md Tradition UK Ltd 1987-88; dir Tradition UK Ltd 1989-, md Tradition Bensford LP New York 1989-; TSA fell RSPB, SRA, fell RZS; *Recreations* squash, wildlife conservation, golf; *Clubs* Roehampton; *Style*— Graham Wandrag, Esq; 14 Wadham Rd, Putney, London SW15 2LR (☎ 01 870 8340); Apt 19h River Terrace 515E 72nd St, Manhattan NY NY 10021 (☎ 1 212 628 6316); Staple Hall, Stone House Ct, 87-90 Houndsditch, London EC3A 7AX (☎ 01 283 7971, 01 623 0088, fax 01 621 1213, car tel 0836 211 722, telex 894711); 61 Broadway, New York NY 100006 (☎ 1 212 797 7200, fax 1 212 7427)

WANE, Peter Ingle; s of Richard Soloman Wane, and Hazel, *née* Whitalker; *b* 15 Mar 1949; *Educ* Harrogate Sch of Art, Stoke-on-Trent Coll of Art and Design, RCA; *Career* graphic designer BBC 1975-; programmes worked on incl: Bread, Arena, Omnibus, An Ocean Apart, Life without George, You Must be the Husband, Playschool, Fast Forward, Sword and Spirit, The Two Ronnies Antiques Road Show; also various documentary features, music and art childrens programmes; Illustrator Annual, Illustrated: The Pilgrims Progress by John Bunyan; illustrator various George McDonald Books incl: The Lost Princess, The Princess and the Goblin; illustrator various magazine articles; *Clubs* BBc Squash; *Style*— Peter Wane, Esq; 45 Woodheyes Rd, London NW9 9DE (☎01 451 4706); BBC Television Centre, Woodlane, Shepherds Bush, London W7 (☎ 01 576 1339, fax 01 743 0377)

WARBURTON, Col Alfred Arthur; CBE (1960), DSO (1946, JP Notts 1968, DL 1966); s of Alfred Victor Warburton, and Margaret Elizabeth, *née* Wall; *b* 12 April 1913; *Educ* Sedbergh; *Career* served with RA Essex Yeomanry 1939-45, Lt-Col cmd S Notts Hussars Yeomanry 1953-58 (Hon Col 1966-76), Col Dep Cdr RA 49 Inf Div TA 1958-60; ADC to HM The Queen 1961-66; High Sheriff Notts 1968; chm Notts County TA Assoc 1973-78; pres Royal Br Legion: E Midlands Area 1976-77, 1981-82 and 1986-87, Notts County 1979-; *Recreations* shooting, fishing, gardening; *Clubs* Cavalry and Guards'; *Style*— Col Alfred Warburton, CBE, DSO, JP, DL; Wigthorpe House, Wigthorpe, Worksop, Notts S81 8BT (☎ 0909 730357)

WARBURTON, Dame Anne (Marion); DCVO (1979, CVO 1965, CMG 1977); da of Capt Eliot Warburton, MC; *b* 8 June 1927; *Educ* Barnard Coll, Columbia Univ, Somerville Coll Oxford; *Career* NATO Paris 1952-54, Lazard Bros 1955-57; joined FO 1957, served FO/FCO and: UN New York 1959-62, Bonn 1962-65; head Guidance and Info Policy Dept FCO 1975-76, ambass Denmark 1976-83; ambass and perm UK rep to UN and other int orgns, Geneva 1983- (formerly cnsllr UK Mission to UN Geneva 1970-75), pres Lucy Cavendish Coll Cambridge 1985-; cmmr Equal Opportunities Cmmn 1986-; FRSA 1986; *Style*— Dame Anne Warburton, DCVO, CVO, CMG; Lucy Cavendish Coll, Lady Margaret Road, Cambridge

WARBURTON, Hon Mrs; Hon Belinda Anne; *née* Hewitt; da of 8 Viscount Lifford; *b* 1939; *m* 1963, Rev Piers Eliot de Dutton Warburton; 1 s, 1 da; *Style*— The Hon Mrs Warburton; St Andrew's Rectory, Guernsey, Channel Isles

WARBURTON, David; s of Harold Warburton, (d 1988), of Shipley Yorks, and Ada, *née* Sinfield (d 1960); *b* 10 Jan 1942; *Educ* St Walburgas Sch Shipley, Cottingley Manor Sch Bingley, Coleg Harlech N Wales; *m* 15 Oct 1966, Carole Ann Susan, da of Frank Tomney (d 1984), of Rickmansworth, and former MP for Hammersmith; 2 da (Sara Anne b 25 Sept 1968, Caroline Susan b 28 July 1970); *Career* GMWU educn offr 1965-67 (regnl offr 1967-73), Nat industl offr GMBATU 1973-; vice pres Int Fedn Chemical and Energy Workers 1986-, sec UK Chemical Unions Cncl 1978-85, chm TUC gen purpose ctee 1984-; memb: NEDC 1973-86, Cwlth Devpt Corpn 1979-87, MOD Industl Cncl 1988-; vice pres Friends of Palestine 1983-; memb: Yorkshire Soc

1983-, Upper Wharfedale Museum Soc 1978-; *Books* Pharmaceuticals for the People (1973), Drug Industry (1975), UK Chemicals: The Way Forward (1977), Economic Detente (1980), The Case for Voters Tax Credits (1983), Forward Labour (1985), Facts Figures and Damned Statistics (1987); contrib num articles to leading jnls; *Recreations* hill climbing, music, 1930-40 film memorabilia; *Clubs* Victoria (Westminster); *Style—* David Warburton, Esq; 47 Hill Rise, Chorleywood, Rickmansworth, Herts WD3 2NY (☎ 0923 778726); GMB Thorne House, Ruxley Ridge Claygate, Esher, Surrey (☎ 0372 62081, fax 0372 67164)

WARBURTON, John Kenneth; CBE (1983); s of Frederick Hammond Warburton, of Wolstanton, Newcastle-under- Lyme, and Winifred Eva, *née* Abbotts; *b* 7 May 1932; *Educ* Newcastle-under-Lyme HS, Keble Coll Oxford (MA); *m* 25 June 1960, Patricia Naomi Margaret, da of Stewart Frank Glennie Gordon, ISM (d 1962), of Shrewsbury; 1 da (Moira b 1961); *Career* RAOC 1950-52; barr Gray's Inn 1977; with London C of C 1956-59, dir and chief exec Birmingham Chamber of Industry and Commerce 1978 (joined 1959-); memb: Steering Ctee Int Bureau of C of C 1976-, Nat Cncl Assoc of Br C of C 1978-, Euro Trade Ctee & Business Link Gp BOTB 1979-87, review body on Doctors & Dentists Remuneration 1982-, E Euro Trade Cncl BOTB 1984-, MSC Task Gp on Employment Trg 1987-88; regnl sec W Midlands Regnl Gp of C of C 1978-; dir: Business in the Community 1981-, Nat Garden Festival 1986 Ltd 1983-87, Birmingham Convention & Visitor Bureau 1986-, Black Business in Birmingham 1986-; alternate dir Birmingham Heartlands Ltd 1988-; chm: advsy cncl W Midlands Industl Devpt Assoc 1983-86, Birmingham Chamber Trg Ltd 1987-; pres Br C of C Execs 1979-81, govr Univ of Birmingham 1982-; *Style—* John Warburton, Esq, CBE; 35 Hampshire Drive, Edgbaston, Birmingham B15 3NY (☎ 021 454 6764); Birmingham Chamber of Industry & Commerce, PO Box 360, 75 Harborne Rd, Birmingham B15 3DH (☎ 021 454 6171, fax 021 455 8670, telex 338024)

WARBURTON, Laurence; s of John Urquhart Warburton, of Esher, Surrey, and Edith Mary, *née* Rhodes; *b* 8 April 1943; *Educ* Kingston GS, Surbiton GS; *m* 2, 14 Feb 1986, Geraldine; children by previous m, 1 s (Julian b 1974), 1 da (Sarah b 1972),; *Career* md Regency Fin Gp plc 1985, nat sales mangr Life Assoc of Scotland 1983-85, marketing dir Trident Life 1974-83; *Recreations* skiing, travel, opera; *Style—* Laurence Warburton, Esq; Little Oak, Fee Farm Rd, Claygate, Surrey KT10 0JX (☎ 0372 68 453); Regency Financial Group plc, 55-57 High Holborn, WC1 (☎ 831 7481); Regency House, Lanark Square, Crossharbour, London E14 9XS (☎ 01 538 8800)

WARBURTON, Richard Maurice; OBE (1987); s of Richard Warburton (d 1954), of 63 Chorley Rd, Standish, nr Wigan, and Phyllis Abbott (d 1972); *b* 14 June 1928; *Educ* Wigan GS, Birmingham Univ (BA); *m* 13 Feb 1952, Lois May, da of Sydney Green, of 16 Romney Way, Wigan; 2 s (Jan Richard b 1952, Nicholas b 1953); *Career* HM inspectorate of Factories 1953-79: HM superintending inspector, dir accident prevention advsy unit 1972-79, chm jt standing ctee safety in paper mills 1976-78; dir gen Royal Soc for the Prevention of Accidents 1979-; advsr Worshipful Co of Carmen 1980-; *Recreations* golf, hill walking, gardening, reading; *Style—* Richard Warburton, Esq, OBE; Cornaa, Wyfordby Ave, Blackburn BB2 7AR (☎ 0254 56824); ROSPA, Cannon House, The Priory, Queensway, Birmingham (☎ 021 200 2461. telex 336546, fax 021 200 1254)

WARD, Dr Adam Anthony; s of Dennis Harold Ward, of Avening, Mark Cross, Crowborough, East Sussex, and Margaret Maud, *née* Record; *b* 15 June 1947; *Educ* Tonbridge Sch, Springhill Sch, Kings Coll, Westminster Med Sch, London Univ (MB, BS), London Sch of Hygiene and Tropical Med (MSc), Hotel Dieu Univ of Paris (Dip Orth Med); *Career* ed Broadway Magazine 1970, lectr and hon sr registrar (Epidemiology) Westminster Med Sch 1978-79; physician: Dept of Orthopaedic Med Hotel Dieu Paris 1982-83, Royal London Homoeopathic Hosp 1983-; memb: Cncl The Faculty of Homoeopathy London, Medical Homoeopathic Res Gp London; specialist in complementary med, clinician, lectr, Broadcaster; *Style—* Dr Adam A Ward; 41 Frankfield Rise, Tunbridge Wells, Kent TN2 5LF (☎ 0892 25799)

WARD, Sir Alan Hylton; s of Stanley Victor Ward (d 1974), and Mary, *née* Whittingham; *b* 15 Feb 1938; *Educ* Christian Bros Coll Pretoria, Univ of Pretoria (BA, LLB), Cambridge Univ (MA, LLB); *m* 1, 22 June 1963 (m dis 1982); 1 s (Mark b 1968), 2 da (Wendy b 1965, Emma b 1966); m 2, Helen Madeleine, da of Keith Gilbert, of Berkswell, Warwicks; 2 da (Amelia b 1984, Katharine (twin) b 1984); *Career* attorney Supreme Ct SA 1959-61, called to the Bar Gray's Inn 1964, QC (1984), Justice of the High Ct assigned to the Family Div 1988; kt 1988; *Recreations* knocking balls about; *Clubs* MCC; *Style—* The Hon Sir Alan Ward; Royal Cts of Justice, Strand, London WC2A 2LL (☎ 01 936 6000)

WARD, Hon Mrs; Hon Alathea Gwendolen Alys Mary; *née* Fitzalan-Howard; da of late 2 Viscount Fitzalan of Derwent and Joyce Elizabeth, now Countess Fitzwilliam, *qv*; *b* 24 Nov 1923; *m* 1953, Hon Edward Frederick Ward (d 1987), s of 2 Earl of Dudley; *Style—* The Hon Mrs Ward; 21b Ave du Temple, Lausanne, Switzerland (☎ 021 32 69 86)

WARD, Lady Amelia Maureen Erica; da (by 2 m) of 4 Earl of Dudley; *b* 1967; *Style—* Lady Amelia Ward

WARD, Anthony John Hedderley; s of Dudley John Hedderley Ward (d 1980), of Matchine Green, Harlow, Essex, and Winifred Marjorie, *née* Bidwell (d 1979); *b* 21 May 1926; *Educ* Bowden House Sch Seaford Sussex, Eton; *Career* joined Goldstream Gds 1944, cmmnd 1945, ret with rank of capt 1948; chm and md N J Randell Ltd (family firm), Hitchin, Herts (joined 1948), chm and md Hydrophane Ltd Hitchin, Herts, former dir Ward and Ward (Australia) Ltd and Bliss Chemicals and Pharmaceuticals (India) Ltd; pres N Herts Cons Assoc 1980-85 (former chm 1975-78); pres The Queens Club 1984-89 (chm 1977-80); Liveryman Worshipful Co of Mercers 1967; *Recreations* real tennis, lawn tennis, golf; *Clubs* All England Lawn Tennis, The Queen's, Royal Worlington GC; *Style—* Anthony Ward, Esq; Bunyans Cottage, Preston, Hitchin, Herts SG4 7RS (☎ 0462 452 147); Ickleford Manor, Hitchin, Herts SG5 3XE (☎ 0462 432 596, fax 0462 420 423, car tel 0860 720 528, telex 82311)

WARD, Antony John (Tony); s of Edgar Frank Ward (d 1979), of Northampton, and Kathleen Muriel Ward MBE, *née* Hobbs; *b* 23 June 1947; *Educ* Northampton Trinity HS, Lanchester Poly Coventry (LLB); *Career* legal govt legal serv 1969-78, slr of Supreme Ct 1971, ptnr Coward Chance 1985-87 (joined 1978), ptnr Clifford Chance 1987-, memb Law Soc Planning Law Ctee 1985-; chm: Bar Cncl, RICS, Law Soc Jt Planning Law Conference Ctee 1987-88; numerous lectures and articles for professional orgns and pubns; Freedom City of London 1980, Liveryman Worshipful Co of Slrs 1983; memb Law Soc 1980, Internat Bar Assoc 1981; *Recreations* tennis, squash; *Style—* Tony Ward, Esq; 111 Willoughby House, Barbican, London EC2Y 8BL (☎ 01 628 8200); Clifford Chance, Blackfriars House, 19 New Bridge St, London EC4V6BY (☎ 01 353 0211, fax 01 489 0046, telex 887 847 LEGIS G)

WARD, Hon Bethany Rowena; da (by 2 m) of 4 Earl of Dudley

WARD, Brian; s of Stanhope Llewellyn Ward (d 1958), of Huddersfield, and Lily, *née* Wilkinson (d 1982); *b* 12 Dec 1924; *Educ* King James GS, Almondbury Huddersfield; *m* 24 March 1951, Joan Ward, da of Arthur George Enoch (d 1963), of Huddersfield; 2 da (Valerie Ann b 1954, Helen Virginia Wells b 1957); *Career* RNVR 1943-46, Sub Lieut; qualified chartered accountant 1949, sr ptnr Revell Ward W Yorks; business interests: machine tools, builders' merchants, graphic art materials, venture capital; memb: Bd of Govrs for Poly of Huddersfield, Colne Valley Conservative Assoc; FICA 1949; *Recreations* golf, private flying, travel; *Clubs* Woodsome Hall GC Ltd, Yorkshire Aeroplane; *Style—* Brian Ward, Esq; 8 Occupation Rd, Lindley, Huddersfield, W Yorks HD3 3AZ (☎ 0484 21005); Revell Ward, Chartered Accountants, Norwich Union House, High St, Huddersfield, W Yorks HD1 2LN(☎ 0484 538 351, fax 0484 513522, telex 265871 MONREF G CJJOII)

WARD, Christopher John Ferguson; s of Maj Harry Leeming Ferguson Ward, and Barbara Dorothy, *née* Gurney; *b* 26 Dec 1942; *Educ* Magdalen Coll Oxford; *m* Janet Theresa, da of Ronald Kelly; 3 s (Julian b 1963, Alexander b 1969, Rupert b 1986), 2 da (Samantha b 1967, Sarah b 1984); *Career* admitted slr 1965; MP for Swindon 1969-70, former memb Berks CC (ldr 1979-81); chm Chiltern Nursery Trg Coll; *Clubs* Carlton, United and Cecil (hon sec 1982-87); *Style—* Christopher Ward, Esq; Ramblings, Maidenhead Thicket, Berks SL6 3QE; Gt Western House, Station Rd, Reading RG1 1SX (☎ 0734 585 321)

WARD, Clive Richard; s of William Herbert Ward (d 1982), and Muriel, *née* Wright; *b* 30 July 1945; *Educ* Sevenoaks Sch, Cambridge Univ (MA); *m* 9 Sept 1972, Catherine Angela, da of Lt Cdr Godfrey Joseph Hines, of Droxford, Hants; 3 da (Joanna b 1975, Diana b 1977, Emily b 1979); *Career* CA 1971, asst sec take over panel 1975-77, ptnr Ernst and Whinney 1979, head corp fin London 1987; Freeman Worshipful Co of Barbers 1985, Worshipful Co of Tobacco Pipe Makers and Tobacco Blenders 1975; FCA 1971; *Recreations* fishing, music, gardening; *Style—* Clive Ward, Esq; Market Heath House, Brenchley, Tonbridge, Kent TN12 7PA (☎ 089272 2172); Ernst and Whinney, Becket House, 1 Lambeth Palace Rd, London SE1 7EU (☎ 01 928 2000, fax 01 928 1345)

WARD, Lady (Emma Sophia) Cressida; da (by 2 m) of 4 Earl of Dudley; *b* 1970; *Style—* Lady Cressida Ward

WARD, Denis John; s of George Ward (d 1978), and Enid Joyce, *née* Randall (d 1982); *b* 3 Dec 1923; *Educ* Kings Sch Rochester; *m* 1959, Mary Rosina; 1 s (Timothy), 1 da (Claire); *Career* Army 1943-46, Sgt Bomb Disposal SE England, W Africa Frontier Force (WAE), served Nigeria and Burma; chm and md: Ward Hldgs plc, Ward's Construction (Medway), Wards Construction (London) Ltd, AB Panels Manufacturers Ltd, Ward Bros (Gillingham) Ltd, Wards Construction (Industrial) Ltd; dir: Troy Dvpts, White Seal Stairways; chm Homecare Window Systems Ltd; memb IOD; landowner (25 acres); *Recreations* tennis, squash; *Style—* Denis Ward, Esq; Ward Holdings plc, 2 Ashtree Lane, Chatham, Kent ME5 7BZ (☎ 0634 50177)

WARD, Donald Albert; s of Albert Goerge Ward, and Rosie, *née* Smith; *b* 30 Mar 1920; *Educ* Southend HS, Queen's Coll Univ of Oxford (MA); *m* 1 Sept 1948, Mary Theresa, da of Michael Molloy; 5 s (Michael b 1949, Anthony John b 1951, Adrian b 1953, Julian Patrick b 1956, Gregory Peter b 1958); *Career* IA 1940-45: RIASC served Middle East and Italy, (despatches), final appt OC 10 Indian Inf Bde Tport Co; Miny of Food 1946-53, under sec Export Credits Guarantee Dept 1971-74 (joined 1953), sec gen Int Union Credit and Investmt Insurers (Berne Union) 1974-86; *Clubs* Oxford and Cambridge; *Style—* Donald Ward, Esq; Lindisfarne, St Nicholas Hill, Leatherhead, Surrey

WARD, Gen Sir Dudley; GCB (1959), KCB (1957, CB 1945, KBE 1953, CBE 1945, DSO 1944, DL (Suffolk 1968-85)); s of Lionel Howell Ward of Wimborne Dorset; *Educ* Queen Elizabeth's GS Wimborne, RMC Sandhurst; *m* 1, 1933, Beatrice Constance (d 1962), da of late Rev T F Griffith (d 1950); 1 da; m 2, 1963, Joan Elspeth de Pechell, da of late Col D C Scott, CBE; *Career* O Lt Dorset Regt 1929, transferred King's Regt, Capt 1937; served WW II: Central Med Theatre (Italy (despatches), Greece), Cdr 4 Div 1944-45; (acting: Lt-Col 1941, Brig 1942, Maj-Gen 1944) COS 1945, 1945, Maj-Gen 1946, cmdt Staff Coll Camberley 1948-51, cdr 1 Corps BAOR 1951, dep CIGS 1953-56, Gen 1957, cdr Northag and C-in-C BAOR 1957-59, C-in-C Near East 1960-62, govr and C-in-C Gibraltar 1962-65, ret 1965; Col King's Regt 1947-57, Col Cmdt REME 1958-63, ADC Gen to HM The Queen 1958-61, memb Security Cmmn to 1982; KStJ, Order of Suvorov 3 class (USSR) 1944, Cdr Legion Merit (USA) 1946; *Recreations* golf; *Clubs* Army and Navy; *Style—* Gen Sir Dudley Ward, GCB, KCB, CB, KBE, CBE, DSO, DL; Wynney's Farmhouse, Dennington, Woodbridge, Suffolk (☎ 072 875 663)

WARD, Dudley Arthur Jonathan; s of Charles Thomas Ward (d 1924), of Colchester, and Eva Louisa Ward (d 1944); *b* 12 Sept 1915; *Educ* Felsted Sch; *m* 17 Nov 1939, Laila, da of Brox Bergum (d 1942), of Norway; 2 s (Christopher b 1943, Tim b 1945), 1 da (Rita b 1941); *Career* war serv: Capt RASC France, Belgium, Holland, Germany, N Ireland 1939-45; CA, Ward & Co Frinton Walton & Colchester 1946-83, ptnr Bland Fielden Colchester 1983-85, dir Burkill & Co Ltd; ACA; *Recreations* golf, yoga; *Clubs* Frinton Golf; *Style—* Dudley A J Ward, Esq; 34 Upper Third Ave, Frinton, Essex CO13 9PS (☎ 0255 674599); 12521 Coldstream D V 508 Fort Myers, Florida, USA (☎ 813 7689510)

WARD, Hon Edward Nicholas; s (by 4 w) of 7 Viscount Bangor, *qv*; *b* 16 Jan 1953; *m* 1985, Rachel Mary, 2 da of Hon Hugh Waldorf Astor, *qv*; 1 da (Anna Roxelana b 1987); *Style—* The Hon Edward Ward; 9 Kildare Terrace, London W2

WARD, Ven Edwin James Greenfield; LVO (1963); s of Canon Frederick Greenfield Ward, MC (d 1963); *b* 26 Oct 1919; *Educ* St John's Leatherhead, Christ's Coll Cambridge; *m* 1946, Grizell Evelyn (d 1985), da of Capt Harry Gurney Buxton (d 1936); 1 s, 2 da; *Career* Lt King's Dragoon Guards 1940-46; ordained 1948, vicar of North Elmham 1950-55; chaplain to: HM The Queen 1955-, Windsor Great Park 1955-67, archdeacon of Sherborne and rector of W Stafford 1967-84, archdeacon emeritus 1985-; *Recreations* fishing; *Style—* The Ven Edwin Ward, LVO; Manor Cottage, Poxwell, Dorchester, Dorset

WARD, Geoffrey Wesley; OBE (1982), VRD (1960); s of Rev Clarence Oliver Ward (d 1981), and Beatrice Ellen Ward, (d 1940); *b* 6 Oct 1923; *Educ* Kingswood Sch

Bath; *m* 1950, Patricia, da of Leonard Bowman Beevers (d 1980); 2 s, 1 da; *Career* joined RNVR 1942, Lt Cdr 1958; dir James Neill (Sheffield) Ltd 1966, md 1972-, dir James Neill Hldgs Ltd 1976-, dep chm and marketing dir Neill Tools Gp Ltd 1982-, chm Stubs Welding Ltd 1979-, dir Edward Pryor and Son Ltd 1981-; *Recreations* golf, gardening, caravanning; *Clubs* RNVR; *Style—* Geoffrey Ward, Esq, OBE, VRD; Robin Hill, Water Lane, Eyam, Sheffield S30 1RG; Neill Tool Ltd, Handsworth Rd, Sheffield S13 9BR (☎ 0742 449 911)

WARD, Gerald John; s of Col Edward John Sutton Ward LVO, MC; *b* 31 May 1938; *Educ* Eton, Sandhurst, RAC Cirencester; *m* 1967 (m dis 1983), Rosalind Elizabeth, da of Hon Richard Lygon (d 1972), 2 da; m 2, 1984, Amanda, da of Sir Lacey Vincent, 2 Bt (d 1963); *Career* Capt RHG; industrialist and farmer; chm: UK Solenoid Ltd, Chilton Farms Ltd, Nat Cncl of YMCAs; Extra Equerry to HRH The Prince of Wales 1987; *Clubs* White's, Portland; *Style—* Gerald Ward, Esq; Chilton Park Farm, Hungerford, Berks (☎ 0488 82329); 179 Cranmer Court, Whiteheads Grove, London SW3 (☎ 01 589 6955)

WARD, Hon Helen Elizabeth; da of 6 Viscount Ward, OBE, PC (d 1950), of Castle Ward, Downpatrick, NI, and Agnes Elizabeth Hamilton (d 1972), da of Dacre Hamilton; *b* 9 May 1912; *Style—* The Hon Helen Ward; 7 Sydney St, London SW3

WARD, Ivor William (Bill); OBE (1969); s of Stanley James (d 1943), of Plymouth, and Emily, *née* Smith (d 1944); *b* 19 Jan 1989; *Educ* Hoe GS; *m* 1, 1939, Patricia Aston, *née* Gold (m dis 1967); m 2, 1970, Betty, *née* Wager (m dis 1981); m 3, 22 Dec 1987, Sandra Calkins Hastie, da of Cdr William Calkins, USN, of Pacific Grove, California, USA; 2 s (David Terence, Martin Sean), 1 da (Mary Kathleen); *Career* gunner RA TA 1939, WO1 REME TA 1942-46 seconded to SAS 1946; BBC: engr's asst 1932, tech asst Alexandra Palace 1936, maintenance engr 1937, returned to Alexandra Place as studio mangr 1946, light entertainment to prodr 1947 (responsible for "How do you View", "This is Show Business", and others), sr light entertainment producer 1951; ITV: head of light entertainment ATV 1935, prodn controller ATV 1956, exec controller TV 1963, bd memb ATV (Network) Ltd 1955, dir of progs and exec dir ATV Ltd 1968, memb ITV Network prog ctee 1970, chm network sports ctee 1971, memb EBU sports working party 1973, chm EBU football ctee 1974, dep md ATV Ltd 1974, head EBU ops gp for all euro broadcasters for coverage of FIFA World Football Cup in Argentina 1978 (summer olympic games in Moscow 1980), assisted Thomson Fndn in improving Thailand's TV prodn techniques 1981, memb UNESCO team assisting Ethiopian Govt in media devpt plan 1982, exec prodr Highway 1983; responsible for shows such as Sunday Night at The Palladium and the Royal Variety Shows working with performers such as: Bob Hope, Nat King Cole, Bing Crosby, Sir Harry Secombe, Shirley Bassey, and many others; Guild of TV Producers-Light Entertainment Producer 1959, BAFTA Desmond Davies Award 1976; Liveryman Fletchers' Co; FRSA 1974 year 1959; memb London Guild of Fletchers; FRSA 1974; *Recreations* golf; *Clubs* Lord Taverners; *Style—* Bill Ward, Esq, OBE; 28A Talbot Rd, Lyme Regis, Dorset DT7 3BB; Richmond Film and TV, 87 Charlotte St, London WC1 (☎ 01 631 5424, 01 831 0337)

WARD, Joan, Lady; Joan Mary Haden; da of Maj Thames Patrick Laffey, of Auckland NZ; *m* 1944, Sir Joseph Ward, 3 Bt, LLM (d 1970); 3 s (including 4 Bt), 3 da; *Style—* Joan, Lady Ward

WARD, (Christoher) John (William); s of Gp Capt Thomas Maxfield Ward, CBE, DFC (d 1969), and Peggy, *née* Field; *b* 21 June 1942; *Educ* CCC Oxford, Univ of E Anglia (Dip Econ); *m* 1971 (m dis 1988), Diane, *née* Lelliott; *Career* Bank of Eng 1965-74; gen sec: Bank of Eng Staff Orgn 1974-80, Assoc First Div Civil Servants 1980-88; head of Devpt Opera North 1988-; chm Swindon Supporters in London 1987-88; *Style—* John Ward, Esq; Opera North, Grand Theatre, 46 New Briggate, Leeds LS1 6NU (☎ 0532 439 999)

WARD, John Anthony; s of Alfred Bernard Ward, of Lythm St Annes Lancs, and Mildred, *née* Wall; *b* 26 Feb 1948; *Educ* Stand GS Lancs, Univ of Liverpool (BA); *m* 8 March 1975, Arlene Joan, da of Dr John Fraser-Butchart, of Weston-Super-Mark, Avon; 2 da (Anne-Marie b 28 Feb 1981, Joanna Louise b 18 Dec 1982); *Career* with J Walter Thompson 1970-7, dir planning Collett Dickenson Pearce 1974-81, vice chm Aspect Advertising 1982-85, dep md BSB Dorland 1988-; chm Telford Park Residents Assoc 1986; *Books* Account Planning (1987); *Recreations* reading, surfing, skiing, France, social history; *Style—* John Ward, Esq; BSB Dorland, 121-141 Westbourne Tce, London W26JR (☎ 262 5077, fax 258 3757, telex 27778)

WARD, John Devereux; CBE (1973), MP (C) Poole 1979-; s of Thomas Edward Ward (d 1981), and Evelyn Victoria Ward (d 1986); *b* 8 Mar 1925; *Educ* Romford County Tech Sch, St Andrews Univ (BSc Eng); *m* 1955, Jean Miller, da of Andrew Aitken (d 1974); 1 s, 1 da; *Career* RAF 1943-47, chartered civil and structural engr; joined Taylor Woodrow Ltd 1958, md Taylor Woodrow Arcon 1976-78; contested (C) Portsmouth North Oct 1974; fndr memb Cons Cwlth Cncl; memb: nat union exec Cons Pty 1965-78, Cons Pty central bd of finance 1969-78, Cons Political Centre Nat Advsy Ctee, European Movement, Cons Gp for Europe; jt sec Cons backbench Industry Ctee 1982-83, vice-chm Trade and Industry Ctee (C) 1983-84, parly private sec to Financial Sec to Treasy 1984-86, parly private sec to Sec of State for Social Security 1987-; *Style—* John Ward, Esq, CBE, MP; 54 Parkstone Road, Poole, Dorset (☎ 0202 674771); House of Commons, London SW1A 0AA

WARD, Sir John Guthrie; GCMG (1967), KCMG (1956, CMG 1947); s of Herbert John Ward; *b* 3 Mar 1909; *Educ* Wellington, Pembroke Coll Cambridge; *m* 1, 1933, Bettine (d 1941), da of Col Sydney Hankey; 1 s, 1 da; m 2, 1942, Daphne Norah, late Sr Cdr ATS, only child of Capt Hon Andrew Mulholland (ka 1914, eldest s of 2 Baron Dunleath, JP, DL) and Lady Hester Joan Byng, DBE, da of 10 Earl of Cavan; 2 da (Jane b 1943, m 1968 Fabrice Gauguier; Joanna b 1950); *Career* served FO 1931-67: Baghdad, Cairo, Moscow Conferences 1943, 1944, 1945, Potsdam Conference 1945, head UN Dept FO 1946, cnsllr Rome 1946-49, IDC 1950, dep UK high commissioner Germany 1951-54, dep under-sec FO 1954-56, ambass Argentina 1957-61, Italy 1962-66; chm Br-Italian Soc 1967-74, former memb cncl RSPCA; pres ISPA; hon fell Pembroke Coll Cambridge; *Style—* Sir John Ward, GCMG; Lenox, St Margarets Bay, Dover; Flat 5, 15 Herbert Crescent, SW1

WARD, John William; s of George Ward, and Margaret, *née* Ellaway; *b* 25 Dec 1940; *Educ* Elliot Secondary Sch Putney; *Career* PR conslt Medway Shoes Ltd 1977-82, PR conslt Mary West PR 1982-87, owner and mangr John Ward PR and Promos; active participant in sports fund raising events for charities incl: Cystic Fibrosis, Save the Children, Haemophiliac Soc; *Recreations* marathon running, reading; *Clubs* Gardens Running and Tennis Wimbledon; *Style—* John Ward, Esq; 31 Trentham St, Southfields, London SW18 3DU; John Ward Public Relations and Promotions, 11 Bolt Ct, Fleet St, London EC4A 3DQ (☎ 01 353 7887/01 936 2127, fax 01 583 2800)

WARD, Sir Joseph James Laffey; 4 Bt (UK 1911), of Wellington, New Zealand; s of 3 Bt (d 1970); *b* 11 Nov 1946; *m* 1968, Robyn Allison, da of William Maitland Martin, of Rotorua, NZ; *Heir* bro, Roderic Anthony Ward b 23 April 1948; *Style—* Sir Joseph Ward, Bt

WARD, Keith John; s of Thomas B Ward; *b* 10 Sept 1933; *Educ* St Christopher's Sch Herts; *m* 1960, Susan Jean Robson; 2 s; *Career* builder's merchant, timber merchant, timber importer; dir The Graham Gp 1974 (devpt dir 1981); md: Graham-Reeves Ltd 1974-81, Ward Assocs Commerical Consits 1982-; pres Soc of Builders Merchants 1982-84; princ and md Brock's Fireplaces Ltd 1984-; *Recreations* sailing, fishing, shooting, hortilculture; *Clubs* Reform; *Style—* Keith Ward, Esq; Brock's Fireplaces Limited, Centurion Works, Union Road, Kingsbridge, Devon TQ7 1EF

WARD, Hon Lalla - (Sarah); *née* Ward; da of 7 Viscount Bangor, *qv*, and his 4 w, Marjorie Alice, *née* Banks; *b* 28 June 1951; *m* 1980 (m dis 1984), Tom Baker, the actor; *Career* actress and illustrator; *Style—* The Hon Lalla Ward; 13 Durham Terrace, London W2

WARD, Hon Leander Grenville Dudley; s (by 2 m) of 4 Earl of Dudley; *b* 1971; *Style—* The Hon Leander Ward

WARD, Hon Mrs ((Elizabeth) Louise); *née* Astor; 2 da of 2 Baron Astor of Hever (d 1984), and Dowager Baroness Astor of Hever, *qv*; *b* 1951; *Educ* St Agnes and St Michael Convent, Madrid Univ, Westminster Hosp London; *m* 1, 1979 (m dis 1981), David John Shelton Herring; m 2, 1985, David Joseph Ward, s of Joseph Ward, of Canterbury, Kent; 1 s (Oliver Gavin Joseph b 1985), 1 da (Victoria Mary Ward b 1987); *Career* registered nurse; *Recreations* riding (master of foxhounds), painting; *Style—* The Hon Mrs Ward; Chelworth House, Chelwood Gate, Haywards Heath, West Sussex RH17 7JZ (☎ 082 574 615)

WARD, His Hon Judge Malcolm Beverley; s of Edgar Ward (d 1966), and Dora Mary, *née* Dutton (d 1974); *b* 3 Mar 1931; *Educ* Wolverhampton GS, St John's Coll Cambridge (MA, LLM); *m* 12 July 1958, Muriel Winifred, da of Dr Edwin Daniel Mackay Wallace (d 1973); 2 s (Simon b 1963, Nicholas b 1967), 2 da (Louise b 1965, Amanda b 1970); *Career* called to the Bar 1956, rec 1974, circuit judge 1979-; chm Wolverhampton GS 1981-(govr 1972-); *Recreations* golf, music, (in theory) horticulture; *Style—* His Hon Judge Malcolm Ward; 1 Fountain Court, Birmingham B4 6DR

WARD, Malcolm Stanley; s of Hugh Ward (d 1979), and Rebecca, *née* Rogerson; *b* 24 Sept 1951; *Educ* Gilberd Sch Colchester; *Career* dep ed Gulf News (Dubais) 1978-79, ed Woodham and Wickford Chronicle (Essex) 1979-81, dep ed Gulf Times (Qatar) 1981-84, dir Daily News 1986- (ed 1986-); memb Guild Br Newspaper Eds; *Recreations* writing, soccer, tennis, travel; *Style—* Malcolm Ward, Esq; Drayton House, 28 Comberton Road, Kidderminster, Worcs DY10 3DL (☎ 0562 67447); Daily News, 78 Franics Road, Edgbaston, Birmingham B16 8SP (☎ 021 454 8800, fax 021 455 9458)

WARD, Lady; Margaret Mary; da of Anthony Davis, of New York; *m* 1, Capt Ralph Risley, USN (decd); m 2, 1965, as his 3 w, Cdr Sir Melvill Ward, 3 and last Bt, DSC, RN (d 1973); *Style—* Lady Ward; Box 276, Southport, Conn, USA

WARD, Hon Mr Justice; Martyn Eric Ward; s of Arthur George Ward, DSM (d 1969), and Dorothy, *née* Perkins (d 1982); *b* 10 Oct 1927; *m* 1, 1957, Rosaleen Iona Soloman; 1 da (Belinda); m 2, 25 March 1966, Rosanna Maria; 2 s (Rufus b 1969, Henry b 1971); *Career* RN 1945-48 (Palestine); barr Lincoln's Inn 1955-72; HM CJ 1972-87; Judge Supreme Ct Bermuda 1987-; *Recreations* skiing, swimming, tennis, reading; *Style—* The Hon Mr Justice Ward; c/o The Supreme Court, 21 Parliament St, Hamilton HL12, Bermuda

WARD, Maxwell Colin Bernard; s of Maj Bernard Maxwell Ward, LVD, of Rockalls Hall, Polstead, Colchester, Essex, and Margaret Sunniva, *née* Neven-Spence (d 1962); *b* 22 August 1949; *Educ* Harrow, St Catherines Coll Cambridge (MA); *m* 17 April 1982, Sarah, da of Lt Col Peter William Marsham, MBE (1970); 1 s (Charles Bernard Maxwell b 27 Feb 1986), 1 da (Laura Sunniva b 2 April 1984); *Career* investment trainee Ballie Gifford and Co 1971-74 (ptnr 1975-), dir Scottish Equitable Life Assur Soc; main bd memb Scottish Cncl for Spastics 1981-; *Recreations* tennis, squash, bridge, country pursuits; *Clubs* New (Edinburgh); *Style—* Maxwell Ward, Esq; The Old Manse, Crichton, Pathhead, Mid Lothian (☎ 0875 320702); Baillie Gifford and Co, 3 Glenfinlas St, Edinburgh EH3 6YY (☎ 031 225 2587, fax 031 225 2358, telex 72310)

WARD, Lady Melissa Patricia Eileen; da (by 2 m) of 4 Earl of Dudley; *b* 1964; *Style—* Lady Melissa Ward

WARD, Michael Jackson; CBE (1980); s of Harry Ward, CBE (d 1988), and Dorothy Julia, *née* Clutterbuck (d 1974); *b* 16 Sept 1931; *Educ* Drayton Manor GS, Univ Coll London (BA), Univ of Freiburg Germany, CCC Oxford; *m* 1 Oct 1955, Eileen Patricia, da of John Foster (d 1985); 1 s (Michael b 1959), 1 da (Victoria b 1962); *Career* Nat Serv 2 Lt Royal Signals 1953-55; dist cmmr and asst sec to govt Gilbert and Ellice Islands HMCOS 1956-61; Br Cncl Schs Recruitment Dept 1961-64, regnl rep Sarawak 1964-68, dep rep Pakistan 1968-70, dir Appts Servs Dept 1970-72, dir Personnel Dept 1972-75, controller Personnel and Appts Div 1975-77, rep Italy 1977-81, controller Home Div 1981-85 (asst dir gen 1985-); *Recreations* music, golf; *Clubs* Nat Lib, Gog Magog GC; *Style—* Michael Ward, Esq, CBE; Flat 39, Westminster Palace Gardens, Artillery Row, London SW1P 1RR (☎ 01 222 2921); The British Council, 10 Spring Gardens, London SW1A 2BN (☎ 01 389 4889)

WARD, Michael John; s of Stanley William Ward (d 1985), of Romford, and Margaret Annie, *née* Gill (d 1986); *b* 7 April 1931; *Educ* Royal Liberty GS Gidea Park Essex, Univ of Manchester (BA); *m* 1953, Lilian, da of Frederick Lomas, of Hadleigh, Essex; 2 da (Alison, Susan); *Career* Fl Lt RAF 1952-57; MP (Lab) Peterborough 1974-79, ldr London Borough & Mavering Cncl 1971-74 (memb 1958-74), sponsored Unfair Contract Terms Act 1977, pps to Sec of State Educn and Science, min for Overseas Dvpt, min of state Foreign and Cwlth Off 1976-79, joined SDP 1982, dir of info Inner London Educn Authy 1984-86, Public Affrs Offr, Gas Consumers Cncl 1986-88; exec offr to Rt Hon Paddy Ashdown MP, Leaden, Social and Liberal Democrats 1988-, parly candidate National Liberal (SDP/Lib All) Tonbridge & Malling 1987; MIPR; *Recreations* music, gardens; *Clubs* Reform; *Style—* Michael Ward, Esq; Leaders Office, Social and Liberal Democrats, House of Commons, London SW1A 0AA (☎ 01 219 6690)

WARD, Hon Peter Alistair; 3 s of 3 Earl of Dudley, MC, TD (d 1969), and his 1 w, Rosemary Millicent Ednam, *née* Leveson-Gower, RRC (who d 1930 prior to 2 Earl's death in 1932), da of 4 Duke of Sutherland, KG; *b* 8 Feb 1926; *Educ* Eton, Univ of British Columbia, Ch Ch Oxford; *m* 1, 1956 (m dis 1974), Claire Leonora, only da of A E G Baring; 1 s (Alexander b 1961), 2 da (Rachel b 1957, Tracy b 1958); m 2, 1974, Elizabeth Rose, da of Richard V C Westmacott, of Ascona, Switzerland; 2 s (Jeremy b 1975, Benjamin b 1978); *Career* Royal Canadian Air Force 1943-45 and Fleet Air Arm; chm Baggeridge Brick plc; dir Kleen-e-ze Hldgs plc; *Clubs* White's, Pratt's, Royal Yacht Squadron; *Style—* The Hon Peter Ward; Cornwell Manor, Kingham, Oxon (☎ (060 871) 555); 6 Thackeray Court, Elystan Place, London SW3 (☎ 01 581 4301)

WARD, Peter Michaeljohn; s of Lt-Col Francis Ward, OBE, MC (d 1950), of 69 Cheyne Ct, Chelsea, London, and Dorothy Aline Augusta, *née* Peile (d 1950); *b* 24 July 1924; *Educ* St Ronan's Sch, Stowe, Clare Coll Cambridge; *m* 16 Sept 1950, Janet Mary, da of Brig IRCGM Bruce, DSO, MBE (d 1956), of The Old Manor House, Letcombe Regis, nr Wantage, Berks; 4 s (Jonathan Francis Bruce b 6 Oct 1954, Robert Richard Craufurd b 29 July 1959, Edmund Giles William b 15 May 1962, Damian Peter Michael b 29 Jan 1966), 4 da (Clare Dorothy b 27 Aug 1951, Catharine Joan b 5 Dec 1952, Magdalen Mary b 6 Dec 1955, Hester Janet Teresa b 30 March 1964); *Career* WWII serv: Lt 3 (Tank) Bn Scots Guards 1944, Sports Gds Div 1946, Staff Capt A (PS2) Branch HQ 1 Br Corps 1947, demob 1947; Gulf Oil 1947-85: chm Gulf UK pension scheme ctee 1973-85, gen mangr Human Resources 1976-85, dir Eastern Gulf Oil Co Ltd 1976-85; dir Kuwait Oil Co Tstees Ltd 1975-85; chm: David Brown Staff Pension Tstee Ltd 1987-, David Brown Works Pension Tstee Ltd 1987-; p/t ambulance driver Arthritis Care 1986-; *Recreations* sport, theatre, films, music; *Clubs* Oriental; *Style—* Peter Ward, Esq; Waterdell House, Little Green Lane, Croxley Green, Rickmansworth, Herts WD3 3JH (☎ 0923 772 775)

WARD, Maj-Gen Sir Philip John Newling; KCVO (1976), CBE (1971, OBE 1967), DL (W Sussex 1981); s of George William Newling Ward (d 1953), of The Old Rectory, Clapham, nr Worthing, and Mary Florence Ward; *b* 10 July 1924; *Educ* Monkton Combe Sch; *m* 1948, Pamela Ann, da of William Horace Edmund Glennie; 2 s, 2 da; *Career* cmd 1 Bn Welsh Gds 1965-67, Cdr LF Gulf 1969-71, GOC London Dist and Maj-Gen Cmd Household Div 1973-76, cmdt RMA Sandhurst 1976-79 (Adj 1960-62); dir: Corporate Affrs (IDV), Int Distillers & Vintners (UK) 1980-, Gilbey Vintners 1980-, Morgan Furze, Justerini & Brooks; chm: Peter Hamilton Security Consits, Securipol; memb southern regnl bd Lloyds Bank 1983-; communar of Chichester Cathedral 1980-83; chm: Royal Soldiers' Daughters' Sch until 1983, Queen Alexandra's Hosp Home; govr cmdt Church Lads and Church Girls Bde until 1986; High Sheriff of W Sussex 1985-86; Freeman City of London; *Recreations* gardening; *Clubs* Cavalry and Guards (chm 1987), Buck's; *Style—* Maj-Gen Sir Philip Ward, KCVO, CBE, DL; The Old Rectory, Patching, nr Worthing, W Sussex (☎ 090 674 369); Morgan Furze & Co Ltd, 12 Brick St, London W1 (☎ 01 493 9861)

WARD, Richard; s of Louis Ward, and Rose, *née* Shafer; *b* 14 Jan 1945; *Educ* John Kelly Sch for Boys; *m* 14 Jan 1968, Simone Maureen, da of Samuel Lestor; 1 s (Ellis Andrew b 20 Oct 1972), 1 da (Jannie Laura b 15 Nov 1968); *Career* md G F Dietary Supplies Ltd 1977-85, chm G F Dietary Gp of Cos Ltd 1985-; advsr to: Euro Dietary Cmmn, Health Food Mfrs Assoc, Br Health Food Trade Assoc; memb Harrow Cons Business Club, advsr to Young Enterprise; FInstD 1984, FBIM 1985; memb Ceoliac Soc, Nat Sov of Phenylketonuria; *Recreations* tennis, swimming, opera, sailing; *Clubs* Dyrham Park (Barnett); *Style—* Richard Ward, Esq; G F Dietary Gp of Cos Ltd, 494-496 Honeyport Lane, Stanmore, Middx HA7 1JH (☎ 01 951 5155, fax 01 951 5623, car 0860 413401, 0836 207012, telex 21875 GFS)

WARD, Gen Sir Richard Erskine; GBE (1975), KCB (1971, CB 1969), DSO (and bar 1943), MC (1942); s of John Petty Ward (d 1956, 2 s of Sir William Ward, KCSI (n of 3 Viscount Bangor)), and Rose Gladys May (d 1937), *née* Marsh-Dunn; *b* 15 Oct 1917; *Educ* Marlborough, RMC Sandhurst; *m* 1947, Stella Elizabeth, 2 da of Brig Philip Neville Ellis (d 1947); 2 s (Anthony b 1960, Jeremy b 1961), 2 da (Léonie b 1949, Stephanie b 1952); *Career* cmmnd Royal Tank Corps 1937, CO Westminster Dragoons 1945, Co 3 Royal Tank Regt 1957-59, Cdr 20 Armoured Bde 1963-66; GOC 1 Div 1966-68; Cdr Br Forces Hong Kong 1970-73, Gen 1974, chief Personnel and Logistics MOD 1974-76; *Clubs* Army and Navy; *Style—* Gen Sir Richard Ward, GBE, KCB DSO, MC; Bellsburn, 18 Lower Street, Rode, Somerset BA3 6PU

WARD, Maj-Gen Robert William; CB (1989), MBE (1972); s of Lt Col William Denby Ward (d 1973), of Fleet, Hants, and Monica Thérese, *née* Collett-White, (d 1985); *b* 17 Oct 1935; *Educ* Rugby, RMA Sandhurst; *m* 16 April 1966, Lavinia Dorothy, da of Col (Alexander James) Henry Cramsie OBE, DL, JP (d 1982), of O'Harabrook, Ballymoney, Co Antrim, N Ireland; 2 s (Thomas b 1968, James b 1973), 1 da (Gemma b 1970); *Career* cmmnd The Queen's Bays (later Queen's Dragoon Gds) 1955; served: Jordan, Libya, Germany, NI, Borneo, 1955-64; student RN Staff Coll 1967, GSO2 Intelligence Bahrain 1968-69, cdr A Squadron, QDG Berlin 1970-72, Nat Def Coll 1972-73, MA to C in C BAOR 1973-75, CO 1 Queen's Dragoon Gds 1975-77, Col GS Army Staff Coll 1977-78, cmd 22 Armoured Bde 1979-82, student Nat Def Coll Canada 1982-83, asst COS Northern Army Gp 1983-86, GOC Western District 1986; *Recreations* gardening, outdoor sports, country pursuits, food, wine, travel; *Clubs* Cavalry and Guards, MCC, I Zingari; *Style—* Maj-Gen Robert Ward, CB, MBE; Springways Cottage, Sutton Veny, Warminster, Wiltshire (☎ 0985 40001); Headquarters, Western District, Shrewsbury, Shropshire (☎ 0743 52234)

WARD, Simon Charles Vivian; s of Maj Vivian Horrocks Ward, of Long Meadow House, Little Cornard, Sudbury, Suffolk, and Leila Penelope, *née* Every; *b* 23 Mar 1942; *Educ* Shrewsbury, Trinity Coll Cambridge (MA); *m* 18 Sept 1965, Jillian Eileen, da of Thomas Roycroft East (d 1980), of Dublin; 3 da (Victoria Penelope Jane b 1969, Antonia Lisa b 1971, Lucinda Fiona (twin) b 1971); *Career* trainee stockbroker Govett Sons & Co 1963-65; ptnrs asst: Hedderwick Hunt Cox and Co 1965-67, Hedderwick Borthwick and Co 1967-70; ptnr Montagu Loebl Stanley and Co 1972-, dir Fleming Montagu Stanley Ltd 1986-; memb Int Stock Exchange 1968; *Recreations* skiing, tennis, gardening, opera, ballet; *Style—* Simon Ward, Esq; The Dower House, Bulmer, Sudbury, Suffolk CO10 7EH (☎ 0787 73257); 107 Andrews House, The Barbican, London EC2 (☎ 01 588 3290); Fleming Montagu Stanley Ltd, 31 Sun St, London EC2M 2QP (☎ 01 377 9242, fax 01 247 3594, telex 885941)

WARD, Simon Roderick; s of Edward John Ward (d 1976), of Grey Barn, Pagham Harbour, W Sussex, and Vera, *née* Braun (d 1985); *b* 4 August 1928; *Educ* Clifton, Lincoln Coll Oxford (BA), Cornell Univ NY (MA); *m* 11 Dec 1965, Diana Strafford, da of Col Rowland Marshall Davies (d 1980), of India; 2 da (Clare Lara b 1969, Charlotte Kate b 1972); *Career* 2 Lt 1 Bn Malay Regt 1948-49; Malayan Starr 1949; barr Lincolns Inn 1953-56, slr Slaughter & May 1956-; memb cncl Charing Cross and Westminster Med Sch; *Style—* Simon R Ward, Esq; 26 Ladbroke Grove, London, W11 3BQ; 35 Basinghall St, London EC2V 5DB (☎ 01 600 1200)

WARD, Lady Susanna Louise; da (by 2 m) of 4 Earl of Dudley; *b* 1963; *Style—* Lady Susanna Ward

WARD, Sir Terence George; CBE (1961, MBE mil 1945); *b* 16 Jan 1906; *Educ* Edinburgh (DDS, DO); *m* 1931, Elizabeth Wilson (d 1981); 1 s, 1 da; m 2, 1982, Sheila Elizabeth Lawry; *Career* oral surgeon; dean faculty of dental surgery RCS 1965-68; former consulting dental surgeon to: DHSS, RAF, Army, Navy; now conslt emeritus to Navy and Army and hon conslt to RAF and Queen Victoria Hosp East Grinstead; FRCS, FDSRCS, FFDRCSI, FDS Aust, FACD; *Recreations* golf; *Style—* Sir Terence Ward, CBE; 22 Marina Court Ave, Bexhill-on-Sea, E Sussex (☎ 0424 214760)

WARD, Lady Victoria Cecilia Larissa; da (by 2 m) of of 4 Earl of Dudley; *b* 1966; *Style—* Lady Victoria Ward

WARD, Walter; s of Alfred Ward, of Edgware, Middx, and Mary, *née* Beck; *b* 22 May 1930; *Educ* Grocers' Co Sch; *m* 1, 21 June 1955, Joan Frances, da of Alfred Cash, of Wembley; 1 da (Lorraine b 1960); m 2, 7 July 1968, Alma, da of Samuel Baars (d 1986); 1 da (Lisa Melanie b 1969); *Career* Corporal RAF 1952-54, Fighter Cmd N Weald Essex, Malta 1953; *Recreations* video filming, painting oils, travel, skiing; *Style—* Walter Ward, Esq; 29 Welbeck Street, London W1M 8DA

WARD, Hon William Maxwell David; s (by 3 m) and h of 7 Viscount Bangor, *qv*; *b* 9 August 1948; *Educ* St Edward's Sch Oxford; *m* 1976, Mrs Sarah Bradford, da of Brig Hilary Anthony Hayes, DSO, OBE; *Style—* The Hon William Bangor; 31 Britannia Road, London SW6

WARD HUNT, Wing Cdr Peter; DFC (1941, bar 1943); s of Capt Wilfrid Ward Hunt, DSO, RN (d 1970), of Hereford, and Sophy Alice (d 1973), da of Adm Sir George Morant; ggf Rt Hon George Ward Hunt, Chllr of the Exchequer 1868, first Lord of the Admiralty 1874; *b* 6 Dec 1916; *Educ* Imp Service Coll; *m* 30 March 1940, Erica Dorothy, da of Cdr Eric B Turtle, RN (d 1973), of Kent; 2 s (David b 1941, John b 1945), 1 da (Angela b 1947); *Career* RAF 1937-46, pilot 5 Gp Bomber Cmd 1939-43, Wing Cdr operations 1 Gp Bomber Cmd 1944-45, CAA 1946-70 (despatches 1946), Royal Aircraft Estab 1970-76; tstee Wadenhoe Tst; *Recreations* gardening, wood turning; *Clubs* RAF; *Style—* Wing Cdr Peter Ward Hunt, DFC; The Old Cottage, Sharnbrook, Bedford MK44 1PE (☎ 0234 781 142)

WARD-BOOTH, Maj-Gen John Antony; OBE (1969); s of Rev John Vernon Ward Ward-Booth (d 1973); *b* 18 July 1927; *Educ* Worksop Coll; *m* 1952, Margaret Joan, da of Rev Aubrey Hooper, MC; 2 s, 2 da; *Career* joined Army 1945, CO 3 Bn Parachute Regt 1967-69, Cdr 16 Parachute Bde 1970-73, Nat Defence Coll Canada 1973-74, DAG HQ BAOR 1974-75, Maj-Gen 1976, Dir Army Air Corps 1976-79, GOC Western Div 1979-82, ret; sec Eastern Wessex TA and 1 VRA 1982-; chm Southampton Div SSAFA 1982-, Dep Col R Anglian Regt 1982-86; memb Paracute Regt Cncl 1982; govr: Clayesmore Sch 1985, Enham Village Centre 1982; *Recreations* sports; *Clubs* Army and Navy, MCC; *Style—* Maj-Gen John Ward-Booth, OBE; 22 Winchester Gardens, Andover, Hants SP10 2EH (☎ 0264 54317); work: 30 Carlton Place, Southampton (☎ 0703 28661)

WARD-HOWLETT, Ronald Peter Henry; s of Ronald Desmond Ward-Howlett (d 1972), of Gerrards Cross, Bucks, and Hilda May (d 1970), *née* Stopforth-Rimmer; *b* 5 May 1932; *Educ* Ealing Coll; *Career* served RAF 1950-52; fin investmt controller Arthur Young 1984-, md and chief exec Silkhouse Fin Services Ltd 1987-, dir Berklay Devere (Hldgs) Ltd; life memb Br Herpetological Soc, fndr memb Jersey Wildlife Preservation Soc; FBIM, FInstAA, FZS, fell Linnean Soc; *Recreations* herpetology, numismatics; *Clubs* Royal Overseas, The Victory Services; *Style—* Ronald Ward-Howlett, Esq; 13 Brandon Park Court, Argyle Road, Southport, Lancashire PR9 9LG (☎ 45366); Arthur Young, Silkhouse Court, Tithebarn Street, Liverpool L2 2LE (☎ 051 2368214, telex 629179 AYLI, fax 051 2360258)

WARD-JACKSON, (Audrey) Muriel; *née* Jenkins; da of William James Jenkins (d 1974), of Roehampton, and Alice, *née* Glyde (d 1967); *b* 30 Oct 1914; *Educ* Queenswood Hatfield Herts, Lady Margaret Hall Oxford (BA, MA); *m* 14 March 1946, George Ralph Norman Ward-Jackson (d 1982), s of late Ralph Stapleton Ward-Jackson; *Career* Civil Serv: asst princ 1937, princ 1942, asst sec 1946-55 (served in Miny of Works, Town and Country Planning, HM Treasy, Housing and Local Govt); John Lewis Partnership 1955-74: gen inspr and fin dir, dir 1957-74, dir John Lewis Properties Ltd 1969-74, chm Pensions Tst 1964-74; serv Civil Serv Arbitration Tbnl 1959-64, memb Nat Savings Review Ctee 1971-73, chm Consumer Ctees (Agric Mktg) 1971-75, memb Royal Cmmn on Standards of Conduct in Public Life 1974-76; a govr Br Film Inst 1962-65, memb Cncl of Bedford Coll London Univ 1967-72; fund-raiser for St Luke's Church Chelsea 1984-(hon tres and memb ctee Restoration Fund); *Recreations* swimming; *Clubs* Lansdowme, Naval & Military; *Style—* Mrs Muriel Ward-Jackson; 195 Cranmer Court, Whiteheads Grove, Chelsea, London SW3 3HG (☎ 01 581 1926)

WARD-JONES, Norman Arthur; VRD (1959), JP (N Westminster 1966); s of Alfred Thomas Ward-Jones, and Claire Mayall, *née* Lees; *b* 19 Sept 1922; *Educ* Oundle, Brasenose Coll Oxford; *m* Pamela Catherine Ainslie, *née* Glessing; *Career* Capt RM 1941-46; RM Reserve 1948-64, Lt-Col RMR (City of London) 1961-64, (Hon Col 1968-74); admitted slr 1950, conslt Lawrence Messer Co (sr ptnr 1981-85), hon slr Magistrates' Assoc 1960-85; chm: East Anglian Real Property Co Ltd 1970-80 (non exec dir 1980), Gaming Bd GB (memb 1984-); *Recreations* wine drinking; *Clubs* East India; *Style—* Norman Ward-Jones, Esq; Gaming Board For Great Britain, Berkshire House, 168-173 High Holborn, London WC1V 7AA (☎ 01 240 0821)

WARDALE, Sir Geoffrey Charles; KCB (1979, CB 1974); *b* 29 Nov 1919; *Educ* Altrincham GS, Queens' Coll Cambridge; *m* 1944, Rosemary Octavia Dyer; 1 s, 1 da; *Career* entered Civil Service; Miny Tport 1942-70: asst sec 1957-66, under-sec 1966-70; DOE 1970-80: dep sec 1972-78, second perm sec 1978-80; *Style—* Sir Geoffrey Wardale, KCB; 89 Paddock Lane, Lewes, E Sussex (☎ 0273 47368)

WARDE, His Hon Judge John Robins; *b* 25 April 1920; *Educ* Radley, Corpus Christi Coll Oxford (MA); *m* 16 Aug 1941, Edna Holliday (Holly), *née* Gipson; 3 s (Robin b 1944, Simon b 1946, Nicholas b 1952); *Career* WWII served 1940-45 Lt RA, liaison offr with HQRA 53 (W) Div, awarded C-in-C's certificate for oustanding good service in the campaign in NW Europe; admitted slr 1950, ptnr in Waugh & Co Haywards Heath and East Grinstead Sussex 1960-70, registrar of Clerkenwell County Ct 1970-77, rec of the Crown Ct 1972-77, circuit judge SE circuit 1977-; memb: Devon CC 1946-49, Devon Agric Exec Ctee 1948-53, W regnl advsy cncl of BBC 1950-53; *Recreations* mountaineering, watching cricket, listening to music; *Clubs* MCC, Forty, Law Soc, Assoc of Br Members of the Swiss Alpine, Br Schools Exploring Soc; *Style—* His Honour Judge John Warde; 20 Clifton Terrace, Brighton, Sussex BN1 3HA

WARDE, John St Andrew; o s of Major John Roberts O'Brien Warde, TD, DL (d 1975), of Squerryes Court, Westerham, Kent, and Millicent Anne, CBE (d 1982), o da of Ralph Montagu Cook, of Roydon Hall, Paddock Wood, Kent; descended from Sir John Warde, Lord Mayor of London 1719, whose son John acquired Squerryes Court (house built 1681), where the family has resided ever since (*see* Burke's Landed Gentry, 18 edn, Vol III, 1972); *b* 8 Mar 1940; *Educ* Eton, Trinity Coll Cambridge (BA, MA); *m* 16 April 1973, Anthea, da of Anthony Holland, MC; 2 s (Charles b 1974, Henry b 1976), 1 da (Charlotte b 1982); *Career* served with Kent and Co of London Yeo (Sharpshooters) TA 1960-68; farmer and landowner; dir private cos; past chm: Kent Branch CLA, South East Region Historic Houses Assoc, Home Counties Region Timber Growers UK; memb Sevenoaks Dist Cncl 1976-87 (chm 1980); *Recreations* field sports; *Clubs* Cavalry and Guards'; *Style—* John Warde, Esq; Squerryes Court, Westerham, Kent TN16 1SJ (☎ 0959 63118)

WARDE-ALDAM, Maj William; JP (S Yorks 1972), DL (S Yorks 1979); s of Lt-Col John Ralph Patientius Warde-Aldam, TD (d 1973); *b* 14 June 1925; *Educ* Eton; *m* 1960, Gillian Margaret, da of Malcolm Scott, of Lyons Hall, Great Leighs, Essex; 2 s, 1 da; *Career* served with Coldstream Guards: Germany, Italy, Norway, Malaya, Kenya 1943-64; High Sheriff Hallamshire 1971; *Clubs* Cavalry and Guards', MCC, Pratt's; *Style—* Maj William Warde-Aldam, JP, DL; Frickley Hall, Doncaster DN5 7BU (☎ 0977 42854); Ederline, Ford, Lochgilphead, Argyll PA31 8RJ (☎ 054 681 284)

WARDE-NORBURY, (William George) Antony; s of Harold George Warde-Norbury, of Hooton Pagnell Hall, nr Doncaster, Yorks, and Mary Betty Warde-Aldam; *b* 2 Mar 1904; *Educ* Aysgarth Sch, Eton, Sandhurst; *m* 15 April 1961, Philippa Marjorie, da of Col Philip Ralph Davies-Cooke, CBE, of Gwysaney Hall, Mold, N Wales; 2 s (Mark b 1962, Alistair b 1966); *Career* Capt Coldstream Gds 1957-64; joined Allied Lyons 1964, bd memb Allied Breweries Bd 1979 (jt md 1986-88); dir : Allied Lyons, Euro Cellars and Britvic Corona 1986-88, Skol Int (also chm), Ind Coope African Investmts, Providents Fin Gp, Selection Res Ltd; *Recreations* shooting, agriculture, golf, music; *Clubs* Cavalry and Guards, RAC; *Style—* Antony Warde-Norbury, Esq; Hooton Pagnell Hall, Doncaster DN5 7BW (☎ 0977 42850, car tel 0860 31193)

WARDELL, Gareth Lodwig; MP (Lab) Gower 1982-; s of John Thomas and Jenny Ceridwen Wardell; *b* 29 Nov 1944; *Educ* Gwendraeth GS, LSE (BSc, MSc); *m* 1967, Jennifer Dawn Evans; 1 s (Alistair); *Career* college lecturer in Carmarthen; *Recreations* swimming, cross-country running; *Style—* Gareth Wardell, Esq, MP; 67 Elder Grove, Carmarthen, Dyfed SA31 2H

WARDINGTON, 2 Baron (UK 1936); Christopher Henry Beaumont Pease; s of 1 Baron Wardington (d 1950), and Dorothy Charlotte, *née* Forster (d 1983); *b* 22 Jan 1924; *Educ* Eton; *m* 9 Sept 1964, Margaret Audrey, da of John White (d 1962), and former w of Jack Dunfee; 1 adopted s (Christopher William Beaumont b 18 April 1970), 2 adopted da (Lucy Anne b 23 Sept 1966, Helen Elizabeth b 24 Dec 1967); *Heir* bro, Hon William Simon Pease; *Career* served Scots Gds Italy, Capt 1942-47; ptnr Hoare Govett Ltd 1950-86; cmmr Public Works Loan Bd 1964-69; memb: cncl of Stock Exchange 1963-81, Corpn for Bond Holders 1967-; Alderman Broad St Ward London 1960-63, tstee Royal Jubilee Tsts, chm Friends of British Library; *Recreations* books, gardening, golf; *Clubs* RAC, Garrick, Roxburgh, All England, Wimbledon Lawn Tennis; *Style—* The Lord Wardington; 29 Moore St, London SW3 (☎ 01 584 5245); Manor House, Wardington, Banbury, Oxon (☎ 0295 750202)

WARDLAW, Sir Henry; 20 Bt (NS 1631), of Pitreavie, Fifeshire; s of Sir Henry Wardlaw, 19 Bt (d 1954, himself ninth in descent from Sir Henry Wardlaw, 1 Bt, who was Chamberlain to James I's Queen, Anne of Denmark); *b* 30 August 1894; *m* 1929, Ellen, da of late John Francis Brady, of Hawthorn, Victoria, Australia; 4 s, 1 da; *Heir* gs, Henry Justin Wardlaw b 10 Aug 1963; *Style—* Sir Henry Wardlaw, Bt; 10120 Florence Rd, Surrey Hills, Victoria, Australia 3127

WARDLE, Charles Frederick; MP (C) Bexhill and Battle 1983-; s of Frederick Maclean Wardle (d 1975), and Constance, *née* Roach; *b* 23 August 1959; *Educ* Tonbridge, Lincoln Coll Oxford, Harvard Business Sch; *m* 1964, Lesley Ann, da of Sidney Wells (d 1967); 1 da (Sarah b 1969); *Career* chm: Benjamin Priest Gp 1977-84, Warne Wright & Rowland; MP Bexhill and Battle 1983; PPS to sec of state for Social Services 1984; memb CBI Cncl 1980-84; *Style—* Charles Wardle, Esq, MP; The Dodo House, Caldbec Hill, Battle, E Sussex; House of Commons Westminster; c/o Benjamin Priest & Sons (Holdings) Ltd, P O Box 38, Priest St, Cradley Heath, Warley, W Midlands (☎ 0384 69662)

WARDLE, John Malcolm; s of Hubert Stanley Wardle, of Minehead, Somerset, and Annie, *née* Lambert (d 1964); *b* 30 Dec 1928; *Educ* St Edwards Sch Oxford, Birmingham Univ (LLB); *m* 1958, (Nora) Patricia Hilda JP, da of John Gilbert Saville (d 1982); 1 s (Guy), 1 da (Jocelyn), 1 step da (Geraldine); *Career* Flying Offr RAF 1951-53; slr and co dir; chm: Metalrax Gp, Hampson Industs, OF Bevan Hldgs, Rex Williams Leisure; dep chm Joseph Webb; dir: Caparo Industs plc, Galliford plc, Peerless, The Deritend Stamping plc; *Recreations* golf, theatre writing (for amusement only); *Style—* John Wardle, Esq; Norton Grange, Norton Green Lane, Knowle, Solihull, West Midlands (☎ 05645 2548); Rutland House, 148 Edmund St, Birmingham B3 2JR (☎ 021 236 7022, telex 336370)

WARDLE, Sir Thomas Edward Jewell; s of Walter Wardle (d 1961), and Lily, *née* Jewell; *b* 18 August 1912; *Educ* Perth Boys' HS; *m* 1940, Hulda May, da of John Olson; 1 s, 1 da; *Career* Lord Mayor of Perth 1967-72, chm Trustees WA Museum 1973-82, chm Aboriginal Loans Cmmn 1974-; Hon LLD WA; kt 1970; *Style—* Sir Thomas Wardle; 3 Kent St, Bicton, W Australia 6157

WARDMAN, Arthur Stewart; s of Gp Capt Rex Wardman, OBE, AFC (d 1985), and Edith, *née* Harper; *b* 13 Sept 1941; *Educ* Brighton Coll; *m* 1965 (m dis 1971); 1 s (Iain b 1968), 1 da (Joanne b 1970); *Career* chm and gp md Kigass Ltd 1985-; md: Kigass Engrg Ltd 1975-85, Kigass Aero Components Ltd 1975-85, Abex Plastic Products Ltd 1976-, Apco Int Ltd 1984-; dir Premier Springs and Pressings Ltd 1985-; *Recreations* sailing, shooting, skiing, sub-aqua diving; *Clubs* Royal Ocean Racing, Royal Lymington Yacht, British Sub Aqua No 217; *Style—* Arthur Wardman, Esq; Kigass Ltd, Kigass House, Chapel St, Leamington Spa, Warwicks CV31 1EL (☎ 0926 422241, telex 311071, fax 0926 421454)

WARDROPER, Lt-Col Michael John Ferrerc; s of Kingsley Ronald Wardroper (d 1970), and Ruth Elizabeth Bunbury (d 1948); *b* 24 July 1935; *Educ* Bedford Sch, Canford; *m* 30 Aug 1969, Angela Yvonne, da of John Kenneth Stanley, of Eastbourne; 2 s (James b 1970, David b 1972); *Career* Lt-Col cmmnd from RMA Sandhurst into 10 Princess Mary's Own Gurkha Rifles 1956, Army Staff Coll 1967-68, Nat Defence Coll 1974-75, cmd 6 Queen Elizabeth's Own Gurkha Rifles 1975-78; (served principally in Far East); gp co-ordinator LEP Gp plc 1985; *Recreations* shooting, gardening, riding; *Style—* Lt-Col Michael Wardroper; LEP Gp plc, 87 East St, Epsom, Surrey KT17 1DT (telex 268716 LEPGRP G, fax 03727 44307)

WARE, Cyril George; CB (1980); s of Frederick George Ware (d 1969), of Essex, and Elizabeth Mary, *née* Root (d 1983); *b* 25 May 1922; *Educ* County HS Leyton; *m* 1946, Gwennie, da of William Sydney Wooding (d 1963), of Stafford; 2 s (Richard, Peter), 1 da (Judith); *Career* sr princ inspr of taxes 1969-74, under sec Bd of Inland Revenue 1974-82, ret; *Recreations* reading, music, swimming, carpentry, photography; *Style—* Cyril Ware, Esq, CB; 86 Tycehurst Hill, Loughton, Essex IG10 1DA (☎ 01 508 3588)

WARE, Sir Henry Gabriel; KCB (1972, CB 1971); s of Charles Martin Ware, and Dorothy, da of Howel Gwyn Jeffreys, JP; *b* 23 July 1912; *Educ* Marlborough, St John's Coll Oxford; *m* 1939, Gloria Platt (d 1986); 3 s (and 1 s decd); *Career* served WWII RA; admitted slr 1933, procurator-gen and Treasy slr 1971-75 (dep 1969-71); *Recreations* fly fishing; *Style—* Sir Henry Ware, KCB; The Little House, Tilford, Farnham, Surrey (☎ 025125 2151)

WARE, Jeremy John; s of Col Robert Remington Ware (d 1952), of Collingham, Newark, Notts, and Barbara, *née* Lewellyn; *b* 29 Oct 1932; *Educ* Winchester, Lincoln Coll Oxford (MA); *m* 23 April 1960, Patricia Jane, da of Maj Horace Maylin Vipan Wright; 3 s (Julian b 1963, Henry b 1965, Maylin b 1968); *Career* slr ; ptnr Tallents Godfrey & Co; pres: Notts Law Soc 1986-87, Grantham Div Cons Assoc 1986- (chm 1978-86); chm Lincs & E Notts Euro Parly Constituency 1988-; memb Law Soc; *Recreations* shooting, fishing, gardening; *Style—* J J Ware, Esq; Lister Place, Brant Broughton, Lincoln; 3 Middlegate, Newark, Notts (☎ 0636 7188)

WARE, John Desmond; s of Ralph Ernest Ware, MBE (d 1957), of Exeter, and Hilda Marguerite, *née* Croom-Johnson (d 1955); *b* 12 Jan 1920; *Educ* Sherborne; *m* 19 Nov 1966, Constance Wiltshire, da of Sir John Hampden Inskip, KBE (d 1960); 1 s (Nicholas John b 29 Nov 1967); *Career* WWII serv Royal Gloucestershire Hussars (TA) 1937-40, Lt Devonshire Regt 1940-43, Capt Chindits 54 Column 1943-44, Maj Para Regt 1944; WD & HO Wills: mangr Swindon 1949-53, gen factor mangr 1953-59; gen mangr Wills/Clarke Dublin 1959-63; dir: Irish Carton Printers 1959-63, Imperial Tobacco Co 1963-69, WD & HO Wills 1963-69; chm: Imperial Athletic Club, Wills Branches Royal Br Legion; memb cncl St Monica Home, hon tres Bristol Benevolent Inst, govr Milton Abbey Sch, pres elect Colston Soc; former pres: Anchor Soc, Colston Res Soc; *Recreations* golf, gardening; *Clubs* Bristol & Clifton; *Style—* John D Ware, Esq; Coach House, 4 Cooks Folly Rd, Bristol BS9 1PL (☎ 0272 681 550)

WARE, Dr Lancelot Lionel; OBE (1987); s of Frederick Richard Ware (d 1940), of Astolat, The Chase, Wallington, Surrey, and Eleanor Gwynne, *née* Emslie (d 1952); *b* 5 June 1915; *Educ* Steyning GS, Royal Coll of Science (BSc, PhD, ARCS, DIC), Lincoln Coll Oxford (MA); *m* 14 June 1980, Joan Francesca Rae Ware; *Career* res worker Nat Inst Med Res 1938-39, lectr in biochemistry St Thomas' Hosp Med Sch 1941-46; barr Lincoln's Inn 1949, practised 1949-87; Surrey Cncllr 1949-55, Alderman London CC 1955-61, memb Cncl of Euro Municipalities 1958-70; vice pres Eurotalent 1988-, chm Tstees of Shakespearean Authorship Tst, vice pres Royal Asiastic Soc, vice pres Inst of Patentees and Inventors (formerly chm), former pres Int Assoc of Inventors Assocs; former chm: Assoc of Voluntary Aided Secdy Schs, Cons Graduate Assoc; formerly govr: Wye Agric Coll, Coll of St Mark and St John, Imperial Coll, LSE, LSHTM, SOAS St, Olave's and St Saviour's Fndn (warden), St Olave's GS, St Saviour's GS, Weybridge Tech Coll, St Thomas' Hosp; FRIC, FRACS, FCIArb; *Recreations* field sports, real tennis, rackets, chess (former univ and co player); *Clubs* Athenaeum, Carlton; *Style—* Dr Lancelot Ware, OBE; Homewood, Quarry Rd, Hurtmore, Godalming, Surrey GU7 2RW (☎ 048 68 22711); 11 Old Sq, Lincoln's Inn, London WC2A 3TS (☎ 01 242 6995)

WARE, Michael John; CB (1985); s of Kenneth George Ware (d 1967), and Phyllis Matilda, *née* Joynes (d 1984); *b* 7 May 1932; *Educ* Cheltenham GS, Trinity Hall Cambridge (BA, LLB); *m* 4 June 1966, Susan Ann, da of Gp Capt C E Maitland, DFC, AFC, of Home Green, Haslemere, Surrey; 3 da (Victoria b 1967, Johanna b 1970, Katherine b 1974); *Career* barr Middle Temple 1955; Legal Dept Bd of Trade, (later Dept of Trade and Industry) 1957-73, legal advsr Offr of Fair Trading 1973-77; under-sec (legal) Dept of Trade and Industry (Co Inspections and Prosecutions) 1977-80; slr Dept of Environment 1980-; *Style—* Michael J Ware, CB; Department of the Environment, 2 Marsham St, London SW1P 3EB (☎ (012) 212 4731)

WARE, Peter Morrell; s of late Arthur Coates Ware; *b* 14 Sept 1922; *Educ* Malvern; *m* 1955, Elizabeth Ann, *née* Farrell; 1 s, 2 da; *Career* Warrant Officer 11 UK; md CPC (UK) Ltd 1975-, gen mangr CPC Benelux and Scandinavia 1966-70, chm British Maize Refiners Assoc 1976-77, pres Assoc des Amidonneries de Maîs de la CEE 1978-79; *Recreations* cricket, tennis; *Clubs* MCC; *Style—* Peter Ware, Esq; 1 Fairacres, Roehampton Lane, London SW15 (☎ 01 878 1979)

WAREING, Robert Nelson; MP (Lab) Liverpool, West Derby 1983-; s of Robert Wareing (d 1960), and Florence Patricia, *née* Mallon (d 1964); *b* 20 August 1930; *Educ* Ranworth Square Sch, Alsop HS Liverpool, Bolton Coll of Educn, London Univ (BSc, external degree); *m* 1962, Betty, da of Thomas Coward (d 1964); *Career* local govt offr 1946-48, LAC RAF 1948-50, local govt offr 1950-56, college lecturer 1957-83; contested (Lab): Berwick-upon-Tweed 1970, Liverpool Edge Hill March 1979 (by-election), May 1979; Merseyside Cllr, chief whip Lab gp 1981-83, chm Merseyside Economic Devpt Co Ltd 1981-; vice-chm British-Yugoslav Parly Gp; *Recreations* concert-going, soccer, travel; *Clubs* Pirrie Labour, Dovecot Labour (Liverpool); *Style—* Robert Wareing, Esq, MP; House of Commons, London SW1A 0AA (☎ 01 219 3482)

WARHURST, Alan; s of William Warhurst (d 1965), and Margaret, *née* Holden (d 1953); *b* 6 Feb 1927; *Educ* Canon Slade GS Bolton, Manchester Univ (BA); *m* 5 Sept 1953, Sheila Lilian, da of John Bradbury (d 1957), of Atherton; 1 s (Nicholas b 1964), 2

da (Alyson b 1958, Frances b 1960); *Career* Nat Serv cmmnd Lancs Fus 1946-48; dir: City Museum Bristol 1960-70, Ulster Museum Belfast 1970-77, Manchester Museum 1977-; pres South Western Fedn Museums and Galleries 1966-68, chm Irish Nat Ctee ICOM 1973-75; pres: The Museums Assoc 1975-76, North Western Fedn Museums and Galleries 1979-80; hon sec The Univ Museum Gp 1987, dep chm: North West Museum and Art Gallery Serv 1987-, Gt Manchester Archaeological Fedn; tstee Canon Slade GS, chm Hulme Hall Ctee Manchester Univ, memb Bolton Educn Ctee; MA Queens Univ Belfast 1983; FSA 1953, FMA 1958; *Recreations* English ceramics, hillwalking; *Style*— Alan Warhurst, Esq; Calabar Cottage, Woodville Road, Altrincham, Cheshire WA14 2AL (☎ 061 928 0730); The Manchester Museum, The University, Oxford Rd, Manchester M13 9PL (☎ 061 275 2650)

WARING, Sir Alfred Holburt; 3 Bt (UK 1935); s of Sir Alfred Waring, 2 Bt (d 1981), and Winifred, Lady Waring; *b* 2 August 1933; *Educ* Rossall; *m* 1958, Ana, da of Valentine Medinilla; 1 s, 2 da; *Heir* s, Michael Holburt Waring, b 3 Jan 1964; *Career* dir: SRM Plastics, Waring Investments, Property Realisation Co Ltd; *Recreations* tennis, golf, squash, swimming; *Clubs* Moor Park Golf, Northwood Squash; *Style*— Sir Alfred Waring, Bt; 30 Russell Rd, Moor Park, Northwood, Middx

WARING, John; s of Samuel Hugh Waring (d 1940), of Leek, and Mary, *née* Whittington (d 1972); *b* 13 Dec 1927; *Educ* Leek HS, Sacred Heart Coll Droitwich; *m* 1951, Jean Margaret, da of John Norman Hill (d 1968), of Worcs; 1 s (Richard), 2 da (Susan, Claire); *Career* chm John Waring Gp of Cos 1969- (involved in grain shipping, seed and animal feed prodn, intensive pig and cattle farming); *Recreations* shooting, swimming, painting; *Style*— John Waring, Esq; Wellingore Hall, Wellingore, Lincoln LN5 0HX (☎ Lincoln 810810)

WARING, Maj John Charles Thomas Tremayne; s of Capt Rupert Thomas Tremayne Waring, RFC, and Jeannette Kathleen Begbie, *née* Morrison; *b* 14 May 1923; *Educ* Sherborne; *m* 1, 13 Aug 1955 (m dis), Susan Bendicke, *née* Moller; m 2, 25 Oct 1958, June, *née* Tilden (d 1969); m 3, 26 July 1983, Judith Ann, *née* Rogerson; *Career* cmmnd KRRC 1942, serv with GHQ Liaison Regt (Phantom) NW Europe 1944-45, Maj GS02 30 Corps Rhine Army 1946, Capt Queens Westminsters 1948-50;co sec and dir FE Charman Ltd 1948-83; contrib to various mil jls 1960-; patron NW London Br Legion 1959-64, memb Surrey CC 1965-68, parly candidate (Cons) Hackney Central 1959, JP Surrey 1966-69; tstee Royal Toxophilite Soc; Freeman City of London 1974, Liveryman Worshipful Co of Bowyers 1974; *Recreations* history, swimming, walking; *Clubs* Carlton; *Style*— John Waring, Esq; Merton House, Westcott, Surrey (☎ 0306 881 636)

WARING, Winifred, Lady; Winifred; da of Albert Boston, of Stockton-on-Tees; *m* 1930, Sir Harold Waring, 2 Bt (d 1981); 1 s (Sir Alfred W, 3 Bt), 2 da (Mrs Michael Mark, Mrs John Holderness); *Style*— Winifred, Lady Waring; Pen Moel, Tidenham, Glos

WARMAN, Oliver Byrne; *b* 10 June 1932; *Educ* Stowe, Exeter Univ, Balliol Coll Oxford; *Career* cmmnd Welsh Guards 1953, GSO III Cabinet Office, instr Staff Coll RMCS, ret 1970; artist: first exhibited RA 1980; exhibited: RBA, RWA, FSMA, ROI, NEAC; work in public collections incl: US Embassy, Natwest Bank, Co-op Bank Crown Cmmn; dir: Ship & Boat Builders Fedn 1972, Falmarine 1973, Ashlyns' - Wine Shippers 1978, Tulsemead Wine Shippers 1983; chief exec Fedn of Br Artists 1984-; memb cncl: CBI, Army Ski Assoc; RBA 1984; *Books* Arnhem 1944 (1970), Royal Society of Portrait Painters (1986); contrib to anthologies on wine, painting, military history; *Recreations* painting, France, food, military history, sailing, wine; *Clubs* Cavalry & Guards, Chelsea Arts, Royal Cornwall YC; *Style*— Oliver Warman, Esq; 17 Carlton Hse Terr, London SW1Y 5BD (☎ 01 930 6844)

WARMINGTON, Sir Marshall George Clitheroe; 3 Bt (UK 1908); s of Sir Marshall Denham Warmington, 2 Bt, JP (d 1935), and his 1 w Alice Daisy, *née* Ing; *b* 26 May 1910; *Educ* Charterhouse; *m* 1, 1933 (m dis 1941), Mollie, da of late Capt Malcolm Alfred Kennard RN; 1 s, 1 da; m 2, 1942, Eileen Mary (d 1969), da of late P J Howes; 2 s; m 3, 1972 (m dis 1977), Sheila (d 1988), da of Stanley Brotherhood, JP, of Thornhaugh Hall, Peterborough, and widow of Adm the Hon Sir Cyril Eustace Douglas-Pennant, KCB, CBE, DSO, DSC (d 1961, s of 5 Baron Penrhyn); *Heir* s, Marshall Denham Malcolm Warmington b 1934; *Career* Lt Cdr RN 1928-54, co sec Securicor 1963-69; *Recreations* fishing, golf; *Clubs* MCC; *Style*— Sir Marshall Warmington, Bt; Swallowfield Park, Reading, Berks (☎ 0734 882210)

WARNE, (Ernest) John David; CB (1982); s of John Warne (d 1954), and Amelia, *née* Hawking (d 1928); *b* 4 Dec 1926; *Educ* Univ of London (BA); *m* 1953, Rena, da of Col Vladimir Vasilievich Alexandrov (d 1937), of Leningrad, USSR; 3 s (Anthony, Steven, Richard); *Career* univ lectr 1951-53; CS: princ 1953-64, asst sec 1964-72, under sec 1972-79, dep sec 1979-82; sec ICAEW 1982-; *Recreations* reading, collecting prints, theatre, walking; *Clubs* Reform; *Style*— John Warne, Esq, CB; 3 Woodville Rd, Ealing, London W5 (☎ 01 998 0215); Inst of CA in England and Wales, Moorgate Place, London EC2 (☎ 01 628 7060, telex 827502)

WARNER, Alan Tristram Nicholas; s of Sir Edward Warner, KCMG, OBE, of Blockley, Glouc, and Grizel Margaret, *née* Clerk-Rattray; *b* 18 Oct 1949; *Educ* Rugby, St Andrews Univ (MA); *m* 7 Jan 1984, Susan Voase, da of Richard Boyle Adderley, MBE, of Pickering, N Yorks; 1 s (Nicholas b 15 April 1985), 1 da (Harriet b 9 Feb 1988); *Career* accountant Touche Ross & Co 1974-78; Douglas Deakin Young Ltd: joined 1978, dir 1981, md 1988; Citycall Unit Tst Review 1987-; Liveryman Worshipful Co of Grocers 1980; ACA; *Recreations* family, shooting, skiing; *Clubs* RAC; *Style*— Alan Warner, Esq; 43 Thornhill Rd, London N1 1JS (☎ 01 607 6577); Douglas Deakin Young Ltd, Byron House, 7/9 St James's St, London SW1A 1EE (☎ 01 839 6734 fax 01 930 3950)

WARNER, Sir Edward Redston; KCMG (1965, CMG 1955), OBE (1948); s of Sir George Redston Warner, KCVO, CMG (d 1978), and Margery Catherine, *née* Nichol (d 1963); *b* 23 Mar 1911; *Educ* Oundle, King's Coll Cambridge; *m* 1943, Grizel Margaret, da of Col Paul Robert Clerk Rattray, CBE, JP, DL, RE (d 1937); 3 s (Paul now Ramsay of Bamff, Nigel, Alan), 1 da (Elizabeth); *Career* FO 1935-70: served Athens, dep UK delegate OEEC Paris 1956-59, min Tokyo 1959-62, ambass Cameroon 1963-66, UK rep econ and social cncl UN 1966-67, ambass Tunisia 1968-70, memb staff appeals bd OECD Paris 1971-83; pt/t ed Historical Manuscripts Cmmn 1971-74; *Clubs* Utd Oxford and Cambridge, Royal Cwlth Soc; *Style*— Sir Edward Warner, KCMG, OBE; Old Royal Oak, Blockley, Glos GL56 9EX

WARNER, Francis Robert Le Plastrier; s of Rev Hugh Compton Warner, (d 1955), of Epsom, Surrey, and Nancy Le Plastrier, *née* Owen; *b* 21 Oct 1937; *Educ* Christ's Hosp, London Coll of Music, St Catharine's Coll Cambridge (BA, MA), Oxford Univ (MA); *m* 1, 1958 (m dis 1972), Mary, *née* Hall; 2 da (Georgina b 1962, Lucy b 1967); m2, 2 July 1983, Penelope Anne, da of John Hugh Davis, of Blagdon, Nr Bristol; 1 s (Benedict b 1988), 1 da (Miranda b 1985); *Career* poet and dramatist; Cambridge Univ: supervisor St Catherine's Coll 1959-63, staff tutor in Eng, memb bd of extramural studies 1963-65; Oxford Univ Sir Gordon White fell in Eng lit and sr Eng tutor St Peter's Coll 1965-, fell librarian 1966-76, dean of degrees 1984-, vice-master 1987-, pro-proctor 1988-; univ lectr Cambridge Univ Fund 1965-, Messing Int Award for Distinguished Contribs to Lit 1972; memb southern arts drama panel Arts Cncl of GB 1976-78 (chm 1978-79 and 1979-80); *poetry:* Petennia (1962), Early Poems (1964), Experimental Sonnets (1965), Madrigals (1967), The Poetry of Francis Warner (USA, 1970), Lucca Quartet (1975), Morning Vespers (1980), Spring Harvest (1981), Epithalamium (1983), collected Poems 1960-84 (1985); *plays:* Maquettes, a trilogy of one-act plays (1972); Reguiem: Pt1 Lying Figures (1972), Pt 2 Killing Time (1976), Pt 3 Meeting Ends (1974); A Conception of Love (1978), Light Shadows (1980), Moving Reflections (1983), Living Creation (1985), Healing Nature: The Athens of Pericles (1987); *ed:* Eleken Peoms by Edmund Blunden (1965), Garland (1968), Studies in the Arts (1968); *Recreations* children, cathedral music, travel; *Clubs* Athenaeum; *Style*— Francis Warner, Esq; St Peter's College, Oxford OX1 2DL (☎0865 278 900)

WARNER, Frank Ernest; MBE (1945), TEM (1950); s of Stanley Theodore Warner (d 1953), of Henley-on-Thames, and Ursula Marguerite, *née* Harrison; *b* 7 Jan 1920; *Educ* Reading Sch; *m* 28 Nov 1942, Joan Vera, da of Joseph Cotton (d 1938), of Reading; 1 s (David b 1948), 2 da (Ann b 1944, Jill b 1948); *Career* serv WWII, Maj (1944) RCS UK and Europe, TA 1938-39 and 1947-50; Turquand Youngs & Co 1946-48, co sec and accountant Thresher & Co 1948-50, sr ptnr Urwick Orr & Ptnrs (chm UK and o/seas cos) 1950-75; conslt and CA in pte practice 1975-88; hon nat tres The Abbeyfield Soc 1977-83; FCA (1948), FIOD (1964); *Clubs* Army & Navy; *Style*— Frank Warner, Esq, MBE, TEM; 7 Lewes Crescent, Brighton BN2 1FH (☎ 0273 691 093)

WARNER, Sir Fred Archibald; GCVO (1975), KCMG (1972, CMG 1963), MEP (EDG) Somerset 1979-; s of Cdr Frederick Archibald Warner, DSO, RN (ka 1917); *b* 2 May 1918; *Educ* Wixenford Berks, RNC Dartmouth, Magdalen Coll Oxford; *m* 1971, Simone Georgina, formerly w of Basil de Ferranti, MEP (by whom she had 1 da: Alexa Georgina Ziani), and da of Lt-Col Hubert Jocelyn Nangle, DSO (d 1968, tenth in descent from Walter Nangle, 8 s of Sir Thomas Nangle (*floruit temp* Henry VIII), 17 ('Palatine') Baron of Navan, by Sir Thomas's w Elizabeth, eldest da of 3 Viscount Gormanston; This 'Palatine' Barony of Navan was first granted to Jocelyn De Angulo by Hugh de Lacy after Jocelyn accompanied Strongbow to Ireland from Pembrokeshire (in which county the place name Angle, whence De Angulo, is to be found) 1169); 2 s (Valentine b 1972, Orlando b 1974); *Career* Lt Cdr RNVR; served FO (later FCO) 1946-75: ambass (Laos 1965-67, UN 1969-71, Japan 1972-75); dir: Guinness Peat Gp, Loral Int, Job Creation Ltd; chm Nat Tst Wessex Region 1976-78; farmer 1958-82; chm overseas ctee CBI; *Clubs* Puffin's, Beefsteak, Turf; *Style*— Sir Fred Warner, GCVO, KCMG, MEP; 4 The Porticos, Kings Road SW3 (☎ 01 351 3645); Inkpen House, Newbury, Berks

WARNER, Prof Sir Frederick Edward; s of Frederick Warner; *b* 31 Mar 1910; *Educ* Bancrofts Sch, UCL; *m* 1, Margaret Anderson McCrea; 2 s, 2 da; m 2, Barbara Reynolds; *Career* Chemical engr; joined Cremer & Warner 1956, sr ptnr 1963-80, now emeritus ptnr; visiting prof: Bartlett Sch Architecture UCL 1970-73, Imperial Coll London 1970-78, Essex Univ 1983-; chm London Univ Sch of Pharmacy 1971-78, pro-chllr Open Univ 1974-79, pres Br Standards Inst 1980-83 (formerly chm exec bd and dep-pres), memb ct: Cranfield Inst Technol, Essex Univ; fell UCL 1967; DUniv Open U, Hon DSc: Aston, Cranfield, Heriot-Watt, Newcastle; Hon DTech Bradford; FRS; kt 1968; *Style*— Prof Sir Frederick Warner, FEng, FRS; Univ of Essex, Wivenhoe Park, Colchester CO4 3SQ (☎ 0206 873370); Cellar House, Brightlingsea, Essex CO7 0JR

WARNER, Gerald Chierici; CMG (1984); s of Howard Warner and Elizabeth, *née* Chierici-Kendall; *b* 27 Sept 1931; *Educ* Oxford Univ (BA); *m* 1956, Mary Wynne Davies; 1 s, 2 da; *Career* 3 sec Peking 1956-58, 2 sec Rangoon 1960-61, 1 sec Warsaw 1964-66 and Geneva 1966-68, cnsllr Kuala Lumpur 1974-76, cnsllr FCO 1976-; *Style*— Gerald Warner Esq, CMG; c/o Foreign & Commonwealth Office, London SW1A 2AH

WARNER, Sir (Edward Courtenay) Henry; 3 Bt (UK 1910), of Brettenham, Suffolk; s of Col Sir Edward Warner, 2 Bt, DSO, MC (d 1955); *b* 3 August 1922; *Educ* Eton, Christ Church Oxford; *m* 1949, Jocelyn Mary, da of Cdr Sir Thomas Lubbock Beevor, 6 Bt, RN (ka 1943); 3 s; *Heir* s, Philip Warner; *Career* served WWII 1939-45 with Scots Gds; chm Law Land Co Ltd 1975-81; *Style*— Sir Henry Warner, Bt; The Grove, Great Baddow, Essex

WARNER, Hon Mr Justice; Hon Sir Jean-Pierre Frank Eugene; s of Frank Cloudesley ffolliott Warner, and Louise Marie Blanche, *née* Gouet; *b* 24 Sept 1924; *Educ* Sainte Croix de Neuilly, Ecole des Roches, Harrow, Trinity Coll Cambridge; *m* 1950, Sylvia Frances, da of Sir Ernest Goodale, CBE, MC; 2 da; *Career* serv WWII Rifle Bde; barr Lincoln's Inn 1950, jr counsel: Restrictive Trading Agreements Registrar 1961-64, Treasury (Chancery) 1964-72; QC 1972, advocate-gen European Communities Ct of Justice 1973-81, vice-pres UK Assoc European Law 1975-83 (pres 1983-), High Ct judge (Chancery) 1981-, judge of Restictive Practices Ct 1982-; master of the walks Lincoln's Inn 1982, keeper of the Black Book 1983, dean of the chapel 1984; tres 1985; former cllr Kensington and Chelsea; former dir Warner & Sons; Hon LLD Exeter 1983; Leicester 1984, Edinburgh 1987; kt 1981; *Style*— The Hon Mr Justice Warner; 32 Abingdon Villas, London W8 6BX (☎ 01 937 7023); Royal Courts of Justice, Strand, London WC2 2LL (☎ 01 936 6769)

WARNER, Capt John Rudyerd; s of Lt-Col Harold Rudyerd Warner, 1/131 UP Regt and Imp Indian Police (d 1964), and Ethel Norah, *née* Elliott (d 1966); *see* Burkes Landed Gentry, 18 edn, vol I, 1965, *sub* Warner formerly of Framlingham; *b* 22 Mar 1923; *Educ* Pangbourne, London Univ (BSc 1966); *m* 1, 11 Oct 1958 (m dis 1963), Sheila Lesley, da of Edward Andrew, of Guernsey, CI; m 2, 30 Nov 1974 (m dis 1987), Lesley Ann Collier; 4 da (Madeleine b 26 Sept 1975, Lucy b 27 Nov 1979, Louise b 17 March 1982, Marie b 24 April 1984); *Career* served in IA, Capt RE, co cdr 10 Pathan Engr Bn, India, Burma, France and Germany 1941-46; chm Republic Lands Ltd 1973-; LRSC; *Recreations* tennis, swimming, photography; *Clubs* Naval; *Style*— Capt J R Warner; 131 Wellington Close, Walton-on-Thames, Surrey (☎ 0932 245028); Los Altos, Marbella, Spain

WARNER, Kenneth; CBE (1978); s of John Warner (d 1961), of Penzance, and Mabel, *née* Rogers (d 1973); *b* 22 July 1922; *Educ* Hayle GS; *m* 24 Jan 1948, (Edith Zenobia) Zoe, da of Archibald Kitchen (d 1972), of St Ives Cornwall; 1 da (Karen b 1956); *Career* serv WWII RAF UK and India; banker; gen mangr Western India Grindlays Bank Ltd 1975-76, regn mangr 1971-73, dep gen mangr 1973-75, regnl dir South Asia Grindlays Bank Ltd 1976/78; dir: Grindlays Bank Ltd UK 1978-79, Grindlays Bank (Overseas Mgmnt) Ltd 1976-79, Hatton Nat Bank Ltd Sri Lanka 1976-79, Grindlays Dao Heng Bank Ltd Hong Kong 1978-79; pres Bombay C of C & Indust 1976-77, dep pres Assoc Chambers of Commerce & Industry 1975-76, dep chm Indian Banks' Assoc 1977-78, cncl memb Indian Inst of Bankers 1975-78; memb: Nat Inst of Bank Mgmnt 1975-78, adv cncl Bankers' Trg Coll 1975-78, Indian Cncl of Arbitration 1975-78, advsy ctee Export Credit Guarantee Corpn Ltd 1975-78, Banking & Trade Facilitation Cmmn 1976-78, Indian Nat Ctee Int C of C 1976-78, Assocham Fin & Banking Expert Panel 1976-78, Employers' Fedn of India 1976-78, negotiating ctee State Apex Body on Lab 1976-78, Nat Apex Body on Lab 1976-78; *Recreations* fishing, wood-turning, photography; *Clubs* The Himalayan (life memb); *Style*— Kenneth Warner, Esq, CBE; Trenkesten, Tregenna Parc, Trelyon, St Ives, Cornwall TR26 2AT (☎ 0736 795450)

WARNER, Marina Sarah (Mrs John Mathews); da of Col Esmond Pelham Warner, TD (d 1982), of Cambridge, ant Emilia, *née* Terzulli; *b* 9 Nov 1946; *Educ* Lady Margaret Hall Oxford (MA); *m* 1, 31 Jan 1972 (m dis 1980), Hon William Hartley Hume Shawcross, s of Baron Shawcross, *qv*; 1 s (Conrad Hartley Pelham b 1977); m 2, 16 Dec 1981, John Piers Dewe Mathews, s of Denys Cosmo Mathews (d 1986), of London; *Career* writer; Getty Scholar Getty Center for the History of Art and the Humanities 1987-88; memb: Public Art Devpt Tst, Advsy Bd Royal Mint; chm Advsy Bd Inst of Contemporary Arts; FRSL 1985; *Books* The Dragon Empress (1972), Alone of All Her Sex: the myth and the cult of the Virgin Mary (1976), Queen Victoria's Sketchbook (1980), Joan of Arc: the image of female heroism (1981), Monuments and Maidens: the allegory of the female form (1985); fiction: In A Dark Wood (1977), The Skating Party (1983), The Lost Father (1988); children's books: The Impossible Day (1981), The Impossible Night (1981), The Impossible Bath (1982), The Impossible Rocket (1982), The Wobbly Tooth (1984); juvenile: The Crack in the Teacup (1979); contrib: Times Literary Supplement, Independent; *Recreations* travel, gardening, photography, looking at pictures; *Style*— Miss Marina Warner; c/o Peters, Fraser, Dunlop, Fifth Floor, The Chambers, Lots Rd, London SW10 (☎ 01 376 7676)

WARNER, Michael John Pelham; s of John Jellico Pelham Francis Warner (s of Sir Pelham (Plum) Warner, England Cricket Capt and Pres MCC), and Jean Mary, *née* McWatters; *b* 8 Dec 1943; *Educ* Eton; *m* 27 Feb 1982, Jennifer Jane, da of Nicholas John Inman, of Wendover, Bucks; 3 s (Richard Pelham b 1973, Giles Peter b 1975, James William b 1987); 1 da (Victoria Jean b 1984); *Career* CA; snr ptnr in Warner Marsh; pres Southern Soc of CAs 1983-84; *Recreations* golf, theatre, opera; *Clubs* Stoneham Golf; *Style*— Michael J P Warner, Esq; Quarry Cottage, Quarry Rd, Winchester, Hants (☎ 0962 55799); 11 College Place, Southampton (☎ 0703 38237)

WARNER, Philip Arthur William; s of W T Warner (d 1964), of Whitacre, Warks, and M Whitacre, *née* Rowley (d 1933); *b* 19 May 1914; *Educ* St Catherine's Coll Cambridge (MA); *m* 11 Sept 1946, Patricia Kathleen (d 1971), da of R G Rollinson; 2 s (Richard, John), 1 da (Diana); *Career* Army 1939-46; asst princ HM Treasy 1946, lectr (Spain) Br Cncl 1947, snr lectr RMA Sandhurst 1948-80 fndr Dept of Communication; *Recreations* fly fishing, tennis, travel, archeology; *Clubs* Athenaeum, Wig and Pen, Harlequin RFC, Jesters Squash; *Style*— Philip Warner, Esq; The White Cottage, 21 Heatherdale Rd, Camberley, Surrey GU15 2LT (☎ 0276 63623)

WARNER, Philip Courtenay Thomas; s and h of Sir (Edward Courtenay) Henry Warner, 3 Bt, and Jocelyn Mary Beevor; *b* 3 April 1951; *Educ* Eton; *m* 1982, Penelope Anne, yr da of John Lack Elmer (d 1973) 2 da; *Career* dir: Lewin & Warner Ltd, Warner Estate Hldgs plc; *Recreations* power-boating, sailing, skiing; *Style*— Philip Warner, Esq; work: 151-155 New North Rd, London N1 6TA

WARNFORD-DAVIS, (Karelyn) Mandy; da of John David Warnford-Davis, and Ruth Grace, *née* Clift; *b* 19 June 1954; *Educ* Heathfield Sch Ascot Berks, St Hugh's Coll Oxford (MA); *Career* slr 1979, slr Titmuss Sainer and Webb 1979-82, ptnr Rowe and Maw 1985- (joined 1982); memb Law Soc; *Recreations* opera, theatre, music, travel; *Style*— Miss Mandy Warnford-Davis; Rowe & Maw, 20 Black Friars Lane, London EC4V 6HD (☎ 01 248 4282, fax 01 248 2009, telex 262787 MAWLAW G)

WARNOCK, Hon Felix Geoffrey; er s of Sir Geoffrey James Warnock and Baroness Warnock (Life Peer), *qqv*; *b* 18 Jan 1952; *Educ* Winchester, Royal Coll of Music (ARCM); *m* 27 Aug 1975, Juliet, da of Arthur Robert Lehwalder, of Seattle, Wasington, USA; 1 s (Daniel Arthur Richard b 1985), 2 da (Eleanor Denise b 1982, Polly Patricia b 1986); *Career* bassoonist Acad of St Martin-in-the-Fields 1975-89; principal bassoon London Classical Players 1978-88; memb Albion Ensemble 1980-; principal bassoon Acad of Ancient Music 1981-89; prof of bassoon Trin Coll of Music 1985-; memb musical advsry panel to Arts Cncl of Great Britain 1987-89; gen mangr Orchestra of the Age of Enlightenment 1989-; memb Musicians' Union; *Recreations* cricket, golf; *Style*— The Hon Felix Warnock; 5 Kingsbridge Road, London W10 6PU (☎ 01 969 5738); Age of Enlightenment, 259 New Kings Road, London SW6 4RB (☎ 01 384 2622)

WARNOCK, Sir Geoffrey; s of James Warnock, OBE, MD (d 1953), of Leeds, Yorks, and Kathleen, *née* Hall (d 1976); *b* 16 August 1923; *Educ* Winchester, New Coll Oxford (MA); *m* 1949, Helen Mary, Baroness Warnock, *qv*, da of Archibald Wilson, of Winchester (d 1924); 2 s (Felix, James), 3 da (Kathleen, Stephana, Grizel); *Career* fell and tutor Brasenose Coll Oxford, fell and tutor in philosophy Magdalen Coll Oxford 1952-71 (now hon fell), hon fell New Coll Oxford, princ Hertford Coll Oxford 1971-88 (now hon fell), vice-chllr Oxford Univ 1981-85; kt 1986; *Books* Berkeley (1953), English Philosophy since 1900 (1958), Contemporary Moral Philosophy (1967), The Object of Morality (1971), Morality and Language (1983); *Style*— Sir Geoffrey Warnock; Brick House, Axford, Marlborough, Wilts SN8 2EX

WARNOCK, Hon Grizel Maria; da of Sir Geoffrey Warnock and Baroness Warnock, DBE (Life Peer), *qqv*; *b* 17 July 1961; *Educ* Oxford High Sch, W Surrey Coll of Art & Design, Liverpool Poly; *Career* dir and memb exec cncl Breakout Children's Holidays; *Recreations* music; *Style*— The Hon Grizel Warnock; 24e Falkner Square, Liverpool L8 7NY

WARNOCK, James; yr s of Baroness Warnock (Life Peer) and Sir Geoffrey Warnock; *m* 31 March 1986, Fiona Margaret, da of Matthew Stewart Hair, of Stratford-upon-Avon; 1 da; 12 Gambier Terrace, Liverpool 1

WARNOCK, Baroness (Life Peer UK 1985), of Weeke in the City of Winchester; (Helen) Mary Warnock; DBE (1984); da of Archibald Edward Wilson, of Winchester (d 1924), and Ethel Mary, *née* Schuster (d 1952); *b* 14 April 1924; *Educ* St Swithun's Winchester, Lady Margaret Hall Oxford (MA, BPhil); *m* 1949, Sir Geoffrey Warnock, *qv*; 2 s (Felix, James), 3 da (Kitty, Stephana, Grizel); *Career* fell and tutor in philosophy St Hugh's Coll Oxford 1949-66; former headmistress Oxford HS; memb SSRC; chm ctee of enquiry into Human Fertilisation; former memb IBA; chm: advsy ctee on Animal Experiments, ctee of enquiry into Education of Handicapped; memb Royal Cmmn on Environmental Pollution 1979-; Talbot Research Fell LMH to 1976; FCP; mistress Girton Coll Cambridge 1985-; hon degrees: Open Univ, Essex, Melbourne, Bath, Exeter, Manchester, Glasgow, York; author of numerous books, journalist (womens magazines and educ journals); *Books* Ethics Since 1900, Existentialism, Imagination, Schools of Thought, What Must We Teach? (with T Devlin), Education: A Way Forward, Memory: A Common Policy for Education; *Recreations* gardening, music; *Style*— The Rt Hon Lady Warnock, DBE; Girton College, Cambridge; Brick House, Axford, nr Marlborough, Wiltshire SN8 2EX

WARREN, Very Rev Alan Christopher; s of Arthur Henry Warren (d 1987), of Durdham Court, Bristol, and Gwendoline Catherine, *née* Hallett; *b* 27 June 1932; *Educ* Dulwich Coll, Corpus Christi Coll Cambridge (MA), Ridley Hall Theol Coll; *m* 24 Aug 1957, Sylvia Mary, da of Charles Edwin Matthews (d 1988), of West Wickham, Kent; 3 da (Susan Rachel b 1958, Catherine Linda b 1960, Helen Judith b 1963); *Career* curate: St Paul's Margate 1957-59, St Andrew's Plymouth 1959-62; chaplain Kelly Coll Tavistock 1962-64, vicar Holy Apostles Leicester 1964-72, Coventry diocesan missioner 1972-78, hon canon Coventry Cathedral 1972-78, proctor in convocation 1977-78 and 1980-85, provost Leicester Cathedral 1978-; memb Cathedral's Statutes Cmmns 1981-, chm Leicester Cncl of Christians and Jews; pres: Leicester Civic Soc, Leicester Cncl of Churches; vice-pres Leicester Bach Choir; formerly MCC and minor counties cricketer; *Books* Putting it Across (1975); *organ prelude* Et incarnatus Est (1979); *Recreations* music, golf, steam trains; *Clubs* Free Foresters, The Leicestershire, Hunstanton Golf, Leicestershire Golf; *Style*— The Very Rev the Provost of Leicester; Provost's House, St Martin's East, Leicester LE1 5FX (☎ 0533 25295); 9 Queen's Drive, Hunstanton, Norfolk; Cathedral Office, St Martin's East, Leicester (☎ 0533 25294)

WARREN, Dr Alan George; s of George James Warren (d 1964), of Beckenham, Kent, and Edith Elizabeth, *née* Court (d 1982); *b* 15 August 1923; *Educ* Co Sch For Boys Beckenham and Penge, Univ of Reading, Royal Vet Coll Univ of London (BSc), Univ of Zurich (Dr medvet), RCS (anaesthesia course 1960); *m* 4 Sept 1948, Elsa, da of Friedrich Franz Uhrig (d 1976), of Bassersdorf, Zurich, Switzerland; 2 s (Louis George b 1960, Jeremy James Alan b 1965), 1 da (Angela Elizabeth b 1951); *Career* Offr Cadet Corps Reading Univ 1941-43, Home Gd 7 BRX 1943-45; asst lectr in animal husbandry Royal Vet Coll 1947-48, lectr in vet surgery and clinical med Gordon Memorial Coll Khartoum (later Univ Coll of Khartoum) 1948-53, vet offr Colonial Vet Serv Nyasaland (later Malawis) 1953-64, inspr under Cruelty to Animals Act 1876 in the Home Off 1965-86, inspr Animals (Sientific Procedures) in Home Office 1987-88; biologist and biomedical advsr 1988-; memb: BVA, BSAVA, Assoc of Anaesthetists 1960, Assoc of Vet Anaesthetists 1964, Laboratory Animal Sci Assoc 1965, Assoc of Faculty of Homoeopathy 1982, Br Assoc of Homoeopathy Vet Surgeons 1982, Int Assoc for Vet Homoeopathy 1984; Sco of London; MRCVS, FIBiol; *Books* Cyclopropane Ancesthesia in Animals (1961); *Recreations* travel, walking, photogrphy, cookery, dowsing, countryman; *Style*— Dr Alan Warren

WARREN, Alastair Kennedy; TD (1952); s of Maj John Russell Warren, MC (d 1941); *b* 17 July 1922; *Educ* Glasgow Acad, Loretto, Glasgow Univ; *m* 1952, Ann Lindsay, *née* Maclean; 2 c; *Career* Maj served with Highland LI 1939-45; journalist, ed Glasgow Herald 1965-74, Dumfries and Galloway Standard 1976-86; provost Royal Borough of New Galloway and Kells Community Cncl 1978-81; *Recreations* writing poetry, hill walking, swimming, marathon running; *Clubs* Glasgow Academicals; *Style*— Alastair Warren, Esq, TD; Rathan, New Galloway, Kirkcudbrightshire (☎ 064 42 257)

WARREN, Sir Alfred; *see*: Warren, Sir Freddie

WARREN, Andrew David; s of Walter Warren, of 18 Yarnells Hill, Oxford, and Monica Joyce Warren; *b* 9 May 1944; *Educ* Royal GS High Wycombe, Wadham Coll Oxford (MA); *m* 27 Oct 1973, Joan Mary, da of Arthur Webb; 2 s (Paul b 1978, Ian b 1980), 1 da (Clare b 1976); *Career* Centrefile 1966-69; Deloitte Haskins & Sells 1969-: ptnr mgmnt consultancy 1975- 79, ptnr i/c computer servs div 1979-85, ptnr i/c mgmnt consultancy div 1985-; MBCS 1968, FIMC 1987; *Recreations* sailing, theatre, photography; *Clubs* Le Micro; *Style*— Andrew Warren, Esq; 10 Tring Avenue, Ealing, London W5 3QA (☎ 01 992 0673; Deloitte Haskins & Sells, PO Box 198, Hillgate House, 26 Old Bailey, London EC4M 7PL (☎ 01 248 3913, fax 01 248 1368, telex 8955899)

WARREN, Sir (Harold) Brian (Seymour); s of late Harold Warren and late Marian, *née* Emlyn, of St Ives, Huntingdonshire; *b* 19 Dec 1914; *Educ* Bishop's Stortford Coll, UCL, Univ Coll Hosp; *m* 1, 1942 (m dis 1964), Dame Josephine Barnes; 1 s, 2 da; m 2, 1964, (Elizabeth) Anne (d 1983), da of Walter Marsh; 2 s; *Career* served WWII (Regtl MO 1 Bn Grenadier Gds and DADMS Gds Div, despatches; house physician and surgn UCH 1942-, pres Chelsea Clinical Soc 1955-56, personal physician to PM 1970-74, memb: cncl King Edward VII Hosp for offrs, governing body Westminster Hosp 1970-74; former memb: LCC, Westminster City Cncl 1955-64 and 1968-78; fought (C) Brixton Gen Election 1959; Freeman City of London; MRCS, LRCP; kt 1974; *Recreations* travel, shooting, gardening, listening to music; *Clubs* Boodle's, Pratt's; *Style*— Sir Brian Warren; 94 Oakley St, London SW3 5NR (☎ 01 351 6462)

WARREN, Lady Carolyn Penelope; *née* Herbert; da of 7 Earl of Carnarvon; *b* 27 Jan 1962; *m* 1985, John F R Warren, s of John Warren, of Harlow, Essex; 1 da (Susanna b 1988); *Career* video dept of Pacemaker; *Style*— Lady Carolyn Warren

WARREN, Sir (Brian) Charles Pennefather; 9 Bt (I 1784), of Warren's Court, Co Cork; s of Sir Thomas Warren, 8 Bt, CBE, DL (d 1961); *b* 23 June 1923; *Educ* Wellington; *m* 1976, Nicola, da of Capt Edward Cazenove, of Great Dalby, Leics, and his w Grania (ggda of Sir John Kennedy, 1 Bt); *Heir* kinsman, Michael Blackley Warren b 1918; *Career* serv with 2 (Armoured) Bn Irish Gds 1941-45; *Style*— Sir Charles Warren, Bt; The Wilderness, Castle Oliver, Kilmallock, Co Limerick, Ireland

WARREN, Charles Wyatt; JP (1968), DL (1969); s of Charles Wyatt Warren (d 1931); *b* 15 August 1908; *Educ* Caernarvon GS, London Univ (DPA); *m* 1938, Margaret Mary, *née* Lewis; 2 da; *Career* landscape painter; *Recreations* hill walking, reading, music, foreign travel; *Style—* Charles Warren, Esq, JP, DL; High Meadows, Caernarvon, Gwynedd (☎ 0286 67 3108)

WARREN, Sir Freddie - Alfred Henry; CBE (1970, MBE 1957); s of William Warren (d 1917), and Clara Wooff; *b* 19 Dec 1915; *Educ* Sir Walter St John's GS Battersea; *m* 1940, Margaret Anne, da of John Murphy; 1 s, 1 da; *Career* Capt RAPC; Cabinet Office 1947, asst private sec to Sec of Cabinet 1951-58, sec to Govt Chief Whip 1958-79; kt 1976; *Recreations* the press; *Clubs* Inst of Directors; *Style—* Sir Freddie Warren, CBE; 93 South Eden Park Rd, Beckenham, Kent BR3 3BA (☎ 01 658 6951)

WARREN, Prof Graham Barry; s of Charles Graham Thomas Warren, and Joyce Thelma, *née* Roberts; *b* 25 Feb 1948; *Educ* Willesden Co GS, Pembroke Coll Cambridge (BA, MA, PhD); *m* 18 June 1966, Philippa Mary Adeline, da of Alexander Edward Temple-Cole (d 1981), of Shoreham, Kent; 4 da (Joanna b 5 Nov 1966, Eleanor b 20 Aug 1969, Katya b 13 Nov 1979, Alexandra b 7 Dec 1980); *Career* MRC jr res fell Nat Inst for Med Res London 1972-74, res fell Gonville and Caius Coll Cambridge and Stothert res fell of the Royal Soc biochemistry dept Cambridge Univ 1975-77, sr scientist Euro Molecular Biology Lab Heidelberg W Germany (formerly gp ldr) 1977-85, prof and head of dept of biochemistry Univ of Dundee 1985-88, princ scientist Imperial Cancer Res Fund 1988-; memb European Molecular Biology Orgn; *Style—* Prof Graham Warren; 17 Grosvenor Rd, London N10 2DR (☎ 01 444 5808); Imperial Cancer Research Fund, P O Box 123, Lincoln's Inn Fields, London WC2A 3PX (☎ 01 242 0200)

WARREN, John Cecil Turnbull; s of Cecil George Warren (d 1971), and Jessie Eileen, *née* Parker; *b* 25 April 1931; *Educ* Collyers Sch Horsham, Univ of Durham (BArch), Univ of Newcastle (MLitt); *m* 11 Sept 1957, Judith Boulton, da of Ernest Kershaw (d 1985); 1 s (Philip Heath b 1963), 1 da (Rebecca Jane b 1966); *Career* Pilot Offr RAF 1957; architect and town planner, fndr and sr ptnr architectural and planning partnership; author, exhibitor RA Summer Exhibitions; fnding tstee: Weald and Downland Open Air Museum Singleton Chichester, Chalkpits Museum Amberley; ARIBA 1959, FRTPI 1961, FRAS 1970 FSA 1981; *Books* Greek Mathematics and the Architects to Justinian I (1980), Traditional Houses in Baghdad (1982), Conservation in Baghdad (1983) contributor to History of Architecture by Sir Bannister Fletcher (18 and 19 edns), The World's Great Architecture, ed Nuttgens, Architecture of the Islamic World, ed Michell, Edwardian Architecture, ed Service, Conservation and Rehabilitation of Buildings, ed Markus; Cambridge Illustrated Encyclopedia Modern Architecture, contributor to Architectural Review, Art and Archaeology Research Papers, Architectural Design, Industrial Archaeology; *Recreations* painting, writing, travelling; *Clubs* Oriental; *Style—* John Warren, Esq; Parsons Farm, Coltstaple Lane, Horsham, W Sussex RH13 7BB (☎ 0403 730022); The Architectural and Planning Partnership, APP House, 100 Station Rd, Horsham, W Sussex RH13 5EU (☎ 0403 210 612, fax 0403 210617, telex 877058 APP HG)

WARREN, Kenneth Robin; MP (cons Hastings and Rye 1983-); s of Edward Charles Warren (d 1987), of St Leonards on Sea, East Sussex; *b* 15 August 1926; *Educ* Midsomer Norton, Aldenham, De Havilland Aeronautical Tech Sch, London Univ; *m* 1962, Elizabeth Anne, da of Russell Chamberlain; *Career* aero and electronics engr; De Havilland Aircraft 1947-51, BOAC 1951-57, Smith Industs Ltd 1957-60, Elliott Automation Ltd 1960-69; memb Paddington Borough Cncl 1953-65, chm Warren Woodfield Assocs; dir: Datapoint (UK) Ltd, Gulf Guaranty Bank Ltd, Loral Int; contested (C) St Pancras North 1964, MP (C) Hastings 1970-1983; chm: Parly Ctee on Offshore Technol 1974-75, Cons Parly Aviation Ctee 1974-76, Western European Univ Sci, Technol and Aerospace Ctee 1977-80; memb Select Ctee on Sci and Technol, pps to Rt Hon Sir Keith Joseph, Bt, MP Sec of State industry 1979-81 (educn and sci 1981-83); chm: Select Ctee on Trade & Indust 1983-; Br-Soviet Party Gp 1986; Freeman City of London; Liveryman: Worshipful Co Coachmaker's and Harness Maker's Co, Worshipful Co Air Pilots and Navigaters; CEng, FRAeS, FCIT FRSA; *Clubs* Special Forces; *Style—* Kenneth Warren, Esq, MP; Woodfield House, Goudhurst, Kent (☎ 0580 211 590)

WARREN, Margaret Patricia; da of Basil Louis Watkins (d 1983), of Kirby Muxloe, Leics, and Muriel, *née* Wheeldon; *b* 1 August 1945; *Educ* Ravenhurst Rd Primary Sch, Nativity Convent Leics, Anstey Martin HS, Loughborough Coll; *m* 31 Aug 1968, Michael Peter Warren, s of Montague Warren (d 1980), of Kirby Muxloe, Leics; 1 s (Matthew Charles b 7 March 1973), 1 da (Rebecca Louise b 25 March 1971); *Career* sec family business 1965-68; dir: S W Wilkinson & Co Ltd 1980-, Warren Beale Ltd 1980-; past memb WRVS and tres local branch Red Cross; *Recreations* swimming, cooking; *Style—* Mrs M P Warren; 78 Oakcroft Ave, Kirby Muxloe, Leics (☎ 0533 392655); S W Wilkinson & Co Ltd, 374 Western Rd, Leics (☎ 0533 546525)

WARREN, Maurice Eric; s of Frederick Leonard Warren, and Winifred Warren (d 1936); *b* 21 June 1933; *Educ* St Brendans Coll Bristol; *m* 21 Aug 1954, Molly, da of Herbert Slater, of Bristol; 1 s (Stephen), 1 da (Sally (Mrs Wilkinson)); *Career* RAF 1951-53; md Dalgety: Agric Ltd 1976-81, UK Ltd 1981-87, plc 1987-; FCCA; *Recreations* golf; *Clubs* RAC, Lansdowne; *Style—* Maurice Warren, Esq; Dalgety plc, 19 Hanover Sq, London W1R 9DA (☎ 01 499 7712, fax 01 493 0892, telex 23874)

WARREN, Prof Michael Donald; s of Charles Warren (d 1966), of Brook Vale, Rattlesden, Bury St Edmunds, Suffolk, and Dorothy Gladys Thornton, *née* Reeks (d 1979); *b* 19 Dec 1923; *Educ* Bedford Sch, Guy's Hosp Med Sch (MB BS), London Sch of Hygiene and Tropical Med (MD, DPH, DIH); *m* 8 March 1946, Joan Lavina, da of Robert Horace Peacock (d 1955), of Green Acre, New Farm Dr, Abridge, Romford, Essex; 1 s (David b 1947), 2 da (Dorothy b 1948, Penelope b 1958); *Career* RAF Med Branch 1947-51, Sqdn Ldr 1948-51; dep med offr of health Hampstead 1952-54, asst princ med offr London CC 1954-58, sr lectr in social and preventive med Royal Free Sch of Med and London Sch of Hygiene and Tropical Med 1958-64, hon conslt in social and rehabilitation med Royal Free Hosp 1958-64, reader in public health London Univ 1964-71, prof of social med and dir of the health servs res unit Univ of Kent Canterbury 1971-83 (emeritus prof of social med 1984); chm Soc for Social Med 1982-83, academic registrar faculty of community med RCP 1971-77; memb: Cncl for Postgrad Med Educn 1972-76, regnl res ctee SE Thames Regnl Health Authy 1974-83, exec cncl Kent Postgrad Med Centre Canterbury 1974-88; FFCM 1972, FRCP 1975; *Books* Public Health and Social Services (3 edn 1965), Physically Disabeled People Living at Home (1978), Recalling the Medical Officer of Health (1987); *Recreations* reading, genealogy, light gardening; *Clubs* RSM, Kent CCC; *Style—* Prof Michael Warren; 2 Bridge Down, Bridge, Canterbury, Kent CT4 5AZ (☎ 0227 830 233)

WARREN, Prof Peter Michael; s of Arthur George Warren (d 1946), and Alison Joan, *née* White (d 1942); *b* 23 June 1938; *Educ* Sandbach Sch, Llandovery Coll, Univ Coll of N Wales Bangor (BA), Corpus Christi Coll Cambridge (BA, MA, PhD); *m* 18 June 1966, Elizabeth Margaret, da of Percy Halliday, of Beaconsfield, Bucks; 1 s (Damian b 1984), 1 Da (Diktynna b 1979); *Career* reader in Aegean Archaeology Birmingham Univ 1976 (lectr 1972-74, sr lectr 1974-76), dean Faculty of Arts Bristol Univ 1988- (prof of Ancient History and Classical Archaeology 1977-), visiting prof Univ of Minnesota 1981, Geddes-Harrower prof of greek art and archaeology Univ of Aberdeen 1986-87, Félix Neubergh Lectr 1986 Univ of Güteborg 1986; chm Bristol and Glos Archaeological Soc Cncl 1981-83 (vice-chm 1980-81); pres: Wotton-under-Edge Historical Soc 1986-89, Bristol Anglo-Hellenic Cultural Soc 1987-; chm managing ctee Br Sch at Athens 1979-83 (memb 1973-77, 1978-79, 1986-), memb cncl Soc for the Promotion of Hellenic Studies 1978-81; FSA 1973, Hon Fell Archaeological Soc of Athens (1987); *Books* Minoan Stone Vases (1969), Myrtos An Early Bronze Age Settlement in Crete (1972), The Aegean Civilizations (1975), Minoan Religion as Ritual Action (1988); *Recreations* contemporary Br politics, med travel, history of med botany; *Style—* Prof Peter Warren; Claremont House, Merlin Haven, Wotton-under-Edge, Glos GL12 7BA (☎ 0453 842 290); Dept of Classics and Archaeology, University of Bristol, 11 Woodland Rd, Bristol BS8 1TB (☎ 0272 303 030 ext 3476)

WARREN, Dr Peter Tolman; s of Hugh Alan Warren, OBE, of 35 West Hill, Sanderstead, Surrey, and Florence Christine, *née* Tolman; *b* 20 Dec 1937; *Educ* Whitgift Sch S Croydon, Queens' Coll Cambridge (BA, MA); *m* 9 Sept 1961, Angela Mary, da of Thomas Henry Curtis, of 8 Teresa's Walk, Sanderstead, Surrey; 2 s (Simon b 1965, Timothy b 1970), 1 da (Katherine b 1967); *Career* princ sci offr Br Geological Survey (prev Inst Geological Sci, formerly Geological Survey & Museum) 1962-72 (sci offr), chief sci advsr dept Cabinet Off Whitehall 1972-76, safety advsr NERC 1976-77, exec sec The Royal Soc of London 1985- (dep exec sec 1977-1985); govr Croydon HS for Girls; FGS FInst Geol;; *Books* Geology of the Country around Rhyl and Denbigh (jtly 1984); *Recreations* gardening, geology; *Clubs* Athenaeum; *Style—* Dr Peter Warren; Flat 1, 6 Carlton Hse Terrace, London, SW1Y 5AG (☎ 01 839 5260); The Royal Society, 6 Carlton Hse Terrace, London, SW1Y 5AG (☎ 01 839 5561, fax 01 930 2170, telex 917876)

WARREN, Col (Ernest) Ralph; s of Ernest Ralph Warren (d 1972), of Tonypandy, Wales, and Gwen, *née* Beynon (d 1975); *b* 18 Jan 1913; *Educ* Tonypandy GS, St Luke Coll Univ of Exeter, Royal Mil Coll of Sci; *m* 26 Jan 1943, Lilian Mabel (Mabs), da of Capt Harry Shearwood (d 1952), of Stockton-on-Tees; 1 da (Carol Anne Beynon b 11 Feb 1944); *Career* imspr of guns CIA 1941-44, OC carriages branch Royal Mil Coll of Sci 1944-47, GSO2 SD (tech) BAOR 1947-50, design offr Royal Armaments R & Dl Estab 1950-53, OC trials wing Royal Sch of Artillery 1953-55, mil attaché Berne 1955-58, asst mil attaché (tech) Belgrade 1955-58, GSO1 Dept Res Washington DC 1958-61; dep conslt 1961-75 for various firms incl: Sterling Armament Co, Ferranti, Hasler, Westley Richards & Co Ltd; UK dir: Sidem Int, Firearms Co Ltd, Manser Atkins Ltd, Erwood Int Ltd, Paxpress Ltd; formed Ralph Warren & Ptnrs 1975 (resigning from all directorships and consultancies); Freeman City of London 1979, Liveryman Worshipful Co of Gunmakers 1979; assoc IMechE 1969, MIQA 1972, FBIM 1979; *Clubs* Wellington; *Style—* Col Ralph Warren; Spring Wood, Foxhill Village, Haywards Heath, W Sussex RH16 4QZ (☎ 0444 413 894)

WARREN, Stanley Anthony Treleaven (Tony); CB (1984); s of Stanley Howard Warren, and Mable Harriet, *née* Ham; *b* 26 Sept 1925; *Educ* King's Coll London; *m* 1950, Sheila Gloria May, *née* Rowe; 2 s, 1 da; *Career* Sub Lt RN 1945-47, Constructor Lt RCNC 1947-51, design Royal Yacht Brittania 1951-54, frigate modernisations 1954-57, constructor HM Dockyard Malta 1957-60, Admty constructor overseer John Brown and Yarrow 1960-64, Polaris submarine design 1964-67, dep dir of Submarines (Polaris) MOD (PE) 1976-79, dir gen Submarines MOD (PE) 1979-85; CEng, FRINA, FIMechE, RCNC; *Style—* Tony Warren, Esq, CB

WARRENDER, Hon Anthony Michael; s (by 2 m) of 1 Baron Bruntisfield, MC; *b* 17 July 1950; *Educ* Eton, Christ Church Oxford; *m* 1, 1976, Christine, da of Serge Semenenko, of Boston, Mass; m 2, 1983, Mrs Patricia Connors Kelly, da of Philip Connors, of Middleburg, VA; 1 s (Patrick Victor Anthony b 1984); *Career* ACA; pres Warrender Associates Inc 1983-; *Clubs* Turf, White's; *Style—* The Hon Anthony Warrender; Little Cotland Farm, PO Box 1431, Middleburg, Virginia 22117, USA

WARRENDER, Col Hon John Robert; OBE (1963), MC (1943), TD (1967), DL (Somerset 1965); s (by 1 m), and h of 1 Baron Bruntisfield, MC; *b* 7 Feb 1921; *Educ* Eton, RMC Sandhurst; *m* 1, 1948, Ann Moireen (d 1976), 2 da of Lt-Col Sir Walter Fendall Campbell, KCIE; 2 s, 2 da; m 2, 1977, Shirley (d 1981), formerly w of Jonathan J Crawley, and da of Sqdn Ldr Edward Ross, RAF ret; m 3, 1985, Joanna (Jan), formerly w of Colin Hugh Campbell, and da of late David Chancellor, of Pencaitland, E Lothian; 2 step s, 1 step da; *Career* Col RARO, memb Queen's Body Guard for Scotland (Royal Co of Archers), late Capt 2 Dragoons, Royal Scots Greys, ADC to Gov of Madras 1946-48 and cmdg N Som Yeo 44, Royal Tank Regt 1957-62,; *Clubs* Pratt's, New (Edinburgh); *Style—* Col the Hon John Warrender, OBE, MC, TD, DL; 18 Warriston Crescent, Edinburgh, EH3 5LB

WARRENDER, Hon Robin Hugh; 3 s of 1 Baron Bruntisfield, MC; *b* 24 Dec 1927; *Educ* Eton, Trinity Coll Oxford; *m* 1951, Gillian Elizabeth, da of Leonard Lewis Rossiter and his w Elsie Rose, da of late Sir Bernard Oppenheimer, 1 Bt; 1 s, 2 da; *Career* chm London Wall Hldgs plc 1986-; underwriting memb of Lloyd's 1953; Tudor & Co (Insurance) Ltd, 1958-62; md Fenchurch Insurance Holdings Ltd, 1963-69; dep chm A W Bain & Sons Ltd, 1970; chm Bain Dawes plc and other group companies, 1973-86; dir: Comindus SA (France), 1980-, Worms & Co, 1981-; varity Corporation (Canada), 1982; Varity Holdings Ltd, 1982-; Heritable Group Holdings Ltd, 1983-; Societe Centrale Preservatrice Fonciere Assurances, 1986-; mem cncl and ctee of Lloyd's 1983-86, mem cncl of Bath Univ 1979-; hon tres Governing Ctee; Royal Choral Soc 1979-; *Clubs* City of London, Portland, White's; *Style—* The Hon Robin Warrender; Widcombe Manor, Church St, Bath (☎ 0225 317116)

WARRENDER, Hon Simon George; DSC; s of 1 Baron Bruntisfield, MC, and Dorothy Etta Rawson (d 1982); *b* 11 August 1922; *Educ* Eton; *m* 1950, Pamela, da of Sir Norman Myer (d 1956), of Toorak, Vic, Australia; 2 s, 2 da; *Career* Lt RNVR, serv WWII (DSC); co dir; conslt Aviation and Travel, ptnr and dir Australia World Air; Score of Years Biography (1973); *Recreations* fencing, fishing, flying; *Clubs* Turf, Melbourne; *Style—* The Hon Simon Warrender; 35 Barkly Avenue, Armadale, Vic 3143, Australia; PO Box 145, Toorak, Vic 3142, Australia

WARRINGTON, Anthony; s of Stanley Warrington, CBE (d 1951), and Gladys, *née* Sutcliffe (d 1969); *b* 15 August 1929; *Educ* Welwyn Garden City GS, LSE (BSc); *m* 30 March 1955, Lavinia Rose, da of G Lord, MBE, (d 1985); 3 s (Richard b 1957, Stuart b 1959, Robert b 1961); *Career* Nat Serv 1947-49, Beds and Herts Regt, Essex Regt; asst statistician: Admty 1953, Br Electricity Authy 1954-56, economist Br Tport Cmmn 1956-58; statistician Miny of Power 1958-66, asst sec Miny of Power and Miny of Indust and Trade 1966-73, under sec air div Miny of Indust 1973-78, co sec and dir policy coordination Rolls-Royce plc 1978-; chm of govrs Welwyn Garden City GS then Stanborough Sch 1957-77; cncl memb Soc of Br Aerospace Co's (chm jt review bd advsy ctee for govt contracts); *Recreations* golf, hockey, theatre; *Clubs* Mid Herts GC; *Style*— Anthony Warrington, Esq; 9 Fern Grove, Welwyn Garden City, Herts AL8 7ND (☎ 0707 326110); 65 Buckingham Gate, London SW1E 6AT (☎ 01 222 9020, fax 01 222 9020 ext 607)

WARSOP, Rear Adm John Charles; CB (1984); s of John Charles Warsop, of Leicester, and Elsie Mary Warsop; *b* 9 May 1927; *Educ* Eaton Hall RNC, RN Engrg Coll; *m* 1958, Josephine; 2 da; *Career* joined RN 1943, RNC Keyham and Greenwich, sr engr HMS Ark Royal 1959-61, staff engr offr Def Staff Washington 1965-68, MOD 1968-70, marine engr offr HMS Blake 1970-72, Capt 1972, MOD 1972-75, CO HMS Fisgard 1975-78, Dep Dir Systems Design and Ch Marine Engr Offr Ship Dept 1979-81, Rear Adm 1981, Port Adm Rosyth 1981-83, Flag Offr and Naval Base Cdr Portsmouth 1983- ret 1986; hon consulting engr HMS Warrior; FIMechE; *Recreations* sailing (yacht 'Filjo'), golf, rugby, tennis, water polo; *Style*— Rear Adm John Warsop, CB; 1 Garden Terr, Southsea, Hants

WARWICK, Alban Maurice; JP (1973); s of Frederick Maurice Warwick (d 1964), and Constance Mabel, *née* Brightman; *b* 13 Nov 1933; *Educ* St Albans Sch; *m* 1, 1958 (m dis 1980), Janet Rose; 2 s (Neil b 1963, Bruce b 1964); m 2, 1981, Susan Marilyn, da of Walter Arthur Wells (d 1951); 2 step s (William b 1975, Charles b 1976), 1 step da (Zoe b 1973); *Career* dir: Warwicks Ltd 1957-, Rodney Maurice (St Albans) Ltd 1982; chm St Albans Round Table 1973-74; pres St Albans & Dist C of C 1984-85; govr Heathlands Sch; *Recreations* golf, shooting, gardening, cricket; *Clubs* St Albans Rotary, St Albans and Professional; *Style*— Alban M Warwick, JP; Hill End Farm, Gorhambury, St Albans AL3 6AR (☎ 0727 50351)

WARWICK, Diana; *b* 16 July 1945; *Educ* London Univ (BA); *m* 1969, Sean Terence Bowes Young; *Career* gen sec Assoc of Univ Teachers 1983-, asst sec civil and Public Services Assoc 1972-83, tech asst National Union of Teachers 1979-83, memb Bd of the British Council 1984-; *Style*— Ms Diana Warwick; Flat A, 51 Elm Park Gardens, London SW10 9PA; Assoc of Univ Teachers, United House, 1 Pembridge Road, London W11 3HJ (☎ 01 221 4370)

WARWICK, Edwin Stanley Ransom; s of Sir Norman Richard Combe Warwick, KCVO (d 1962), and Joyce Huskinson; *b* 22 Mar 1928; *Educ* Marlborough; *m* 26 Jan 1963, Marjorie, da of Eden White (d 1982); 1 s (Hugh b 1966), 1 da (Tessa b 1969); *Career* shipowner; dir: Thos and Jas Harrison Ltd 1980-, Liverpool & London P and I Club, Liverpool & London War Risks Club (vice-chm 1985-86), Thos Tweddle & Co Ltd 1980-86; *Recreations* music, swimming; *Clubs* Liverpool Racquet; *Style*— Edwin Warwick, Esq; Fieldings, 167 Lache Lane, Chester CH4 7LU (☎ 0244 676983)

WARWICK, Frederick Richard; MC (1942), TD (1946), JP (Notts 1960); s of Col Philip H Warwick DSO, TD (d 1954); *b* 22 May 1919; *Educ* Eton, Trinity Coll Oxford; *m* 1955, Kathleen, *née* Walker; 1 s, 1 da; *Career* Maj, served with Sherwood Rangers Yeomanry 1939-45; chm: John Smith's Tadcaster Brewery Ltd 1975-80 (dir 1962, md 1966-75), dir Courage Ltd 1971-80; *Style*— Maj Frederick Warwick, MC, TD, JP; Cherry Tree House, Skelton-on-Ure, nr Ripon, N Yorks HG4 5AJ (☎ 0423 322786)

WARWICK, John William; s of John Alfred Warwick, of Plumstead, London, and Lillian Rose, *née* Stothard; *b* 10 Feb 1932; *Educ* Stratford GS, Univ of Birmingham (BSc); *m* 28 March 1963, Thea Susan, da of Bernard Leeming, of Perth, Western Australia; 1 s (David b 1964), 1 da (Jennifer b 1969); *Career* RA 1953-55; 44 Regt, 5 Army Gp, Br Army of The Rhine; Exploration Geophysicist: Pakistan 1957-60, Australia 1961-64, Saudi Arabia 1965-66, USA 1966-67, Singapore 1969-73, UK 1973-76; geophysical conslt Texas Instruments Inc (Petroleum Exploration Div) 1976-85, geophysical advsr Sirte Oil Co 1986-; memb: Soc of Exploration Geophysicists 1975, American Assoc of Petroleum Geologists 1975, IOD; *Style*— John Warwick, Esq; 32 Bramley Ave, Coulsdon, Surrey CR32DP (☎ 01 660 1232); 13/15 High St, Weybridge, Surrey (☎ 0932 852 021)

WARWICK, Lady; Joyce Huskinson; da of Herbert Charles Ransom, of Winscombe, Somerset; *m* 1921, Sir Norman Richard Combe Warwick, KCVO, OBE (d 1962); 2 s (*see* Warwick, Edwin Stanley Ransom); *Style*— Lady Warwick; High Down, Holmewood Ridge, Langton Green, Tunbridge Wells

WARWICK-SMITH, Myles Humphrey (Mike); s of Cdr Reginald Warwick-Smith, RN (d 1944), and Eileen, *née* Maclean (d 1984); *b* 26 Dec 1929; *Educ* Nautical Coll Worcester; *m* 1952, Diana Mary Stella, da of Capt R Calum Freeman (d 1982); 2 s (Robert, Peter), 2 da (Penelope, Fenella); *Career* Capt (Leicesters) TA, served Korea; md: LRC Industrial Holdings Ltd, LRC Overseas Ltd; chm United Photographic Laboratories until 1981; chm and md Elsan Ltd and Horton Hygiene Co 1981-; *Recreations* riding, tennis, travel; *Clubs* IOD; *Style*— Mike Warwick-Smith, Esq; Elsan Group Ltd, Buxted, Sussex TN22 4LW (☎ 0825 813 291, telex 957236)

WASE-ROGERS, Nicholas John; s of Lt-Col John Alistair Wase-Rogers (d 1984), and Margery Lillian, *née* Hall; *b* 19 June 1945; *Educ* Shrewsbury Sch; *m* 28 July 1973, Christine Linda, da of Ernest Williams, of Droitwich, Worcs; 1 s (James b 1974), 1 da (Melissa b 1975); *Career* solicitor, sr ptnr Rigbey Loose & Mills; *Recreations* golf, tennis, skiing, shooting; *Clubs* Blackwell Golf, Priory Tennis; *Style*— Nicholas Wase-Rogers, Esq; Oakfield Farmhouse, Cakebole, Chaddesley Corbett, Worcs (☎ 056 283 737); 18 Bennetts Hill, Birmingham (☎ 021 643 1831)

WASHINGTON, Lt-Col Timothy John Clulow; s of Peter Washington (d 1984), and Catherine Marguerite Beauchamp Waddell (d 1972); *b* 26 June 1923; *Educ* Shrewsbury Sch, Trinity Coll Cambridge; *m* 10 July 1956, Margaret Helen, da of Maj Edward William Hasell (d 1972), 2 da; *Career* served in Army 1941-78, 27 Lancers 1942-45, 12 Lancers 1945-60, 9/12 Lancers 1960-78; *Recreations* horses, farming; *Clubs* Cavalry and Guards'; *Style*— Lt-Col Timothy J C Washington; Dacre Lodge, Penrith CA11 0HH (☎ 08536 221)

WASILEWSKI, Mark Alexander; s of Stanislaw Wasilewski (d 1979), and Vera, *née* Hudson; *b* 22 June 1960; *Educ* Culcheth HS, Brasenose Coll Oxford; *Career* investmt analyst NCB Pension Fund, dir Marketable Securities, portfolio mangr UK Equities; *Recreations* most sports, football, cricket, golf, music, cinema/theatre; *Clubs* ICPG FC; *Style*— Mark Wasilewski, Esq; 14 Forsyth House, Tachbrook St, London, SW1V 2LE, Cin Management Ltd, PO Box 10, Hobart House, Grosvenor Place, London, SW1X 7AD (☎ 245 6911)

WASON, (Robert) Graham; s of Cathcart Roland Wason, and Margaret Ogilvie, *née* Lamb, gs of Rear Adm Cathcart Romer Wason, CMG, CIE (d 1941), ggs of Rt Hon Eugene Wason, MP (Liberal MP and Chm Scottish Liberal Party), gggs of P R Wason, MP for Ipswich, Promoter of Reform Bill 1832 and co-founder of Reform Club; *b* 6 Jan 1951; *Educ* Alleyne's GS, Stevenage; Univ of Surrey Hons Degree (BSc) in Hotel and Catering Administration; *Career* dir Greene Belfield-Smith & Co Ltd 1986-; *Recreations* tennis, badminton, squash; *Style*— Graham Wason, Esq; Greene Belfield-Smith, Victoria House, Vernon Place, London WL1B 4DB (☎ 01 242 3959, telex 24292 GBS, fax 01 831 8626)

WASS, Sir Douglas William Gretton; GCB (1980, KCB 1975, CB 1971); s of Arthur William Wass (d 1978), of Hampton, Middx, and Winifred Elsie, *née* Gretton (d 1955); *b* 15 April 1923; *Educ* Nottingham HS, St John's Coll Cambridge (BA 1944, MA 1947); *m* 14 July 1954, Dr Milica, da of Tomislav Pavicic (d 1932), of Belgrade, Yugoslavia; 1 s (Andrew b 1960), 1 da (Alexandra b 1958); *Career* entered HM Treasy 1946, private sec to: Chllr of Exchequer 1959-61, Chief Sec Treasy 1961-62; asst sec Treasy 1962, alternate exec dir IMF and fin cnsllr Br Embassy Washington 1965-67, Treasy: under-sec 1968, dep-sec 1970-73, second perm sec 1973-74, perm sec 1974-83; jt head Home Civil Serv 1981-83; dir Barclays Bank 1984-87, De La Rue Company plc 1984-, Compagnie du Midi SA 1987-; chm: Equity & Law plc 1986-, Nomura Int Ltd 1986-; Reith lectr 1983, Shell Int lectr St Andrews 1985, Harry Street memorial lectr Manchester Univ 1987; dep chm Centre for Policy Studies Inst 1980-84; chm: Br Selection Ctee of Harkness Fellowships 1981-84, UN Advsy Gp on Fin Flows to Africa 1987-88; govr Centre for Econ Policy Res, pres Mkt Res Soc; memb of cncl Univ of Bath, govr Ditchley Fndn; Hon Fell St John's Coll Cambridge, Hon DLitt Univ of Bath 1985; *Books* Government and the Governed (1984); *Recreations* swimming, golf; *Clubs* Reform; *Style*— Sir Douglas Wass, GCB; 6 Dora Rd, London SW19 7HH (☎ 01 946 5556); Nomura International Ltd, 24 Monument St, London EC3R 8AJ (☎ 01 283 8811, fax 01 621 1286, telex 883119)

WASS, Francis Harry; s of Frank Wass, of Burton Coggles, Grantham, Lincs (d 1955); *b* 6 August 1927; *Educ* King's Sch Grantham, Newark Tech Coll; *m* 1951, Phyllis May; 1 s, 1 da; *Career* chartered engr: asst chief engr Aveling Barford Ltd 1966-75, dir Goodwin Barsby Ltd 1977-82, tech conslt (design and drawing serv); MIMechE; *Recreations* author tech papers on Compaction, Hydrostatic Transmissions; *Style*— Francis H Wass, Esq; 57 Priory Close, Beeston Regis, Sheringham, Norfolk (☎ 0263 825707)

WASS, Lawrence Farbon; CBE (1963), JP (1957); s of William Henry Wass (d 1963); *b* 19 Feb 1912; *Educ* Southend HS, McGill Univ, Queen's Univ Canada; *m* 1938, Margaret Kate, *née* Wilson; 1 s, 1 da; *Career* served RE 1940-45: Maj Normandy 1944 (despatches), asst dir Survey First Canadian Army 1945; memb Enfield Boro Cncl 1946-60, chm Enfield Cons Assoc 1964-68; dep chm Edmonton PSD 1974-82; chm Wass Pritchard Ltd 1964-78; *Recreations* music, garden; *Style*— Lawrence Wass, Esq, CBE, JP; 141 Green Dragon Lane, Southgate, London N21 1EU (☎ 01 360 3870)

WASSERMAN, Ian; s of John J Wasserman, QC (d 1985), and Rachel Chait-Wasserman (d 1963); *b* 4 Sept 1939; *Educ* City of London Sch; *m* 23 Sep 1981, Nicola Viveca, da of Major John Bromley MVO (d 1979); 3 s (Nicholas, Alexander, Joshua), 2 da (Caron, Tanya); *Career* chm: GM Firth plc, Slug & Lettuce Ltd; *Recreations* fishing, travel, bridge, investment; *Clubs* East India; *Style*— Ian Wasserman, Esq; Cotswold Park, Cirencester, Glos (☎ 0285 83414); 40 Catherine Place, London SW1 (☎ 01 828 7425)

WASTELL, Prof Christopher; s of Edgar Barker Wastell (d 1963), and Doris Emmeline, *née* Pett (d 1965); *b* 13 Oct 1932; *Educ* Drax GS; Guy's Hosp Med Sch (MB, BS), London Univ Med Sch (MS); *m* 2 April 1958, Margaret Anne, da of Joseph Fletcher (d 1976); 1 s (Giles Richard b 1965), 2 da (Jackie b 1961, Vivien b 1963); *Career* house physician Joyce Green, house surgn Franborough Kent, sr house offr Bristol Royal Infirmary, house surgn Great Ormond St, registrar Westminster Hosp, lectr Westminster Med Sch 1964-67, C and H J Gaisman Res Fell Mount Sinai Hosp NY USA 1965-66, sr lectr and hon conslt surgn Westminster Med Sch and Hosp 1968-73 (rdr 1973-82), prof and hon conslt surgn Charing Cross and Westminster Med Sch London Univ at Westminster Hosp 1983-, conslt to accident and emergency Westminster Hosp 1971-; FRCS; *Books* Chronic Duodenal Ulcer (1972), Westminster Hospital Sumposium on Chronic Duodenal Ulcer (1974), Surgery for Nurses (with Ellis 1976), Surgery of the Stomach and Duodenum (with Nyhus, 1977 and 1986), Cimetidine, The Westminster Hospital Symposium (1978); *Recreations* sailing, gardening, walking; *Clubs* Wilsonian Sailing, RSM; *Style*— Prof Christopher Wastell; 7 Manor Way, Beckenham, Kent BR3 3LH; 3 North Rd, Kingsdown, Deal, Kent CT14 8AG (☎ 01 650 5882); Surgical Unit, Westminster Hosp, Page St Wing, London SW1P 2AP (☎ 01 828 9811 ext 2548/2544, fax 01 834 4240, telex 919263 RHIVA G)

WASTELL, William; s of Capt Charles Henry Wastell, MN (d 1939), and Elsie Alice Perham; *b* 13 Dec 1939; *Educ* Brentwood Sch, Regent St Poly Sch of Architecture, ARIBA; *m* 26 Nov 1966, Rosamund, da of Harold Geoffrey Haden; 3 da (Kerry b 1969, Miranda b 1970, Cindy b 1972); *Career* md William Wastell Architects Ltd; *Recreations* archery, bridge, travel; *Style*— William Wastell, Esq; Oak House, Mardley Heights, Welwyn, Herts (☎ 043 871 6808); Troopers Yard, 23 Bancroft, Hitchin Herts (☎ 0462 422440, fax 0462 420403)

WATANABE, Nobuyuki; s of Akio Watanabe, of Fujisawa-City Japan, and Keiko Gorin (d 1970); *b* 13 Dec 1939; *Educ* Keio Univ (BA Economics); *m* 25 Oct 1970, Mariko, da of Haruichi Eguchi (d 1986); 1 s (Clayton b 1973), 1 da (Meme b 1971); *Career* md Sony (UK) Ltd 1984-; md: Sony Broadcasting Ltd 1978-86, Sony of Canada Ltd 1974-78; *Recreations* golf, tennis; *Style*— Nobuyuki Watanabe, Esq; Hakoyanagi, Queens Hill Rise, Ascot, Berkshire (☎ 0990 26930); Sony (UK) Ltd, South St, Staines, Middlesex TW18 4PF (☎ 0784 467202, car tel 0836 237584)

WATCH, Cecil; s of Samuel Watch (d 1977), of Manchester, and Emma Watch (d 1988); *b* 5 Dec 1934; *Educ* Manchester GS; *m* 9 Sept 1973, (Valerie) Angela, da of Paul Field (d 1983), of Cheshire; 1 s (Jonathan Franklin b 1977), 2 da (Helen Victoria b 1974, Lisa Ruth b 1976); *Career* ptnr Woolfson Watch & Co Manchester; FCA, ATII; *Recreations* sport; *Style*— Cecil Watch, Esq; Reedham House, 31-33 King St, Manchester M3 2PF (☎ 061 834 2432)

WATERFIELD, John Percival; elder s of Sir Percival Waterfield, KBE, CB (d 1965), and Doris Mary, *née* Siepmann (d 1988); *b* 5 Oct 1921; *Educ* Dragon Sch Oxford, Charterhouse, Ch Ch Oxford; *m* 5 Feb 1950 (Margaret) Lee, da of late Prof H R Thomas, of Univ of Illinois, USA; 2 s (John, James), 1 da (Polly); *Career* WWII 1940-45, 1 Bn KRRC (Adj) served W Desert, Tunisia, Italy and Austria (despatches); Foreign (later Dip) Service: entered 1946, third sec Moscow 1947, second sec Tokyo 1950, FO 1952, first sec Santiago 1954, consul (commercial) NY 1957, FO 1960, ambass to Mali Rep 1964-65 (concurrently to Guinea 1965), duties connected with NATO 1966, cnsllr and head of chancery New Delhi 1966-68, head Western Orgns FCO 1969, md BEAMA, princ estabs and fin offr NI Off 1973-79 (on secondment to Int Mil Services Ltd 1979-80); chm and dir various cos 1981-84; *Recreations* fishing, water colour painting, gardening; *Clubs* Boodle's; *Style—* John Waterfield, Esq; 5 North St, Somerton, Somerset TA11 7NY

WATERFORD, Marchioness of; Lady Caroline Olein Geraldine; *née* Wyndham-Quin; da of late 6 Earl of Dunraven and Mount-Earl, CB, CBE, MC; *b* 1936; *m* 1957, 8 Marquess of Waterford; *Style—* The Most Hon the Marchioness of Waterford

WATERFORD, 8 Marquess of (I 1789); Sir John Hubert de la Poer Beresford; 12 Bt (I 1665); also Baron of Le Power and Coroghmore (I 1535; the 8 Baron's da Katherine claimed 1763 an alleged Barony of La Poer, said to have been cr by writ of summons 1375, but leading authorities dismiss any such right, though George III (1767) confirmed the I House of Lords's ruling that her claim was valid), Viscount Tyrone, Baron Beresford (both I 1720), Earl of Tyrone (I 1746), and Baron Tyrone (GB 1786, in which title he sits in House of Lords); s of 7 Marquess of Waterford (d 1934); *b* 14 July 1933; *Educ* Eton; *m* 1957, Lady Caroline Wyndham-Quin, da of 6 Earl of Dunraven and Mount-Earl; 3 s, 1 da (Lady Alice Rose de la Poer b 31 July 1970); *Heir* s, Earl of Tyrone; *Career* Lt RHG Supp Reserve; *Clubs* Whites; *Style—* The Most Hon the Marquess of Waterford; Curraghmore, Portlaw, Co Waterford (☎ 87102)

WATERHOUSE, Lady Caroline; *née* Spencer-Churchill; da of 10 Duke of Marlborough (d 1972); *b* 1923; *m* 1946, Maj (Charles) Hugo Waterhouse *qv*; 2 s, 1 da; *Career* an extra Lady-in-Waiting to HRH Princess Alexandra, The Hon Lady Ogilvy 1970-; *Style—* Lady Caroline Waterhouse; Middleton Hall, Bakewell, Derbys (☎ 062 986 224)

WATERHOUSE, Douglas Frew; AO (1980), CMG (1970); s of Prof Eben Gowrie Waterhouse, CMG, OBE (d 1977), and Janet Frew, *née* Kellie (d 1974); paternal ggf arrived in Australia 1839 to establish the first Methodist church in Tasmania (Hobart); *b* 3 June 1916; *Educ* Sydney Church of England GS, Sydney Univ (BSc, MSc, DSc), Australian Nat Univ (DSc), Canberra Coll of Advanced Educn (Hon Fell); *m* 1944, Allison Dawn, da of John Henry Calthorpe (d 1950); 3 s (Douglas, Jonathan, Gowrie), 1 da (Jill); *Career* res scientist CSIR 1938; chief Div of Entomology CSIRO 1960-81, hon research fell CSIRO 1981-; chm of cncl Canberra Coll of Advanced Educn 1968-84, pres National Tst of Australia (ACT) 1984-, conslt Australian Centre for Int Agric Res 1984-; capt Australian Papua New Guinea; Queens Jubilee Medal 1977; *Books* over 125 scientific publications, a number of collaborative scientific books; *Recreations* gardening, fishing, gyotaku (ancient Japanese art of fish printing); *Clubs* Commonwealth (Canberra); *Style—* Dr D F Waterhouse, AO, CMG; 60 National Circuit, Canberra, ACT 260, Australia (☎ 062 731 772); 133 Annetts Parade, Mossy Point, NSW (☎ 044 717 554); Division of Entomology, CS 1RO, Box 1700, City Canberra 2601, ACT Australia (☎ 062 465 833)

WATERHOUSE, Maj (Charles) Hugo; DL (Derbyshire); s of Capt Rt Hon Charles Waterhouse, MC, JP, DL, and Beryl, *née* Ford; *b* 11 June 1918; *Educ* Eton, Trinity Coll Cambridge; 5 Dec 1946, Lady Caroline Spencer-Churchill, *qv*; 2 s, 1 da; *Career* cmmnd Life Guards, served Europe (despatches, Croix de Guerre) WW II, Maj, ret; High Sheriff of Derbys 1981; *Recreations* shooting; *Clubs* White's; *Style—* Maj Hugo Waterhouse, DL; 57 St George's Drive, London SW1 (☎ 01 834 3950); Middleton Hall, Bakewell, Derbys DE4 1RS (☎ 0629 636224)

WATERHOUSE, Keith Spencer; s of Ernest Waterhouse, and Elsie Edith Waterhouse; *b* 6 Feb 1929; *Educ* Osmondthorpe Cncl Sch Leeds, Leeds Coll of Commerce; *m* 1 (m dis); 1 s, 2 da; m 2, 1984, Stella Bingham; *Career* serv RAF 1947-49; freelance writer and journalist 1950-; Columnist: Daily Mirror 1970-86, Daily Mail 1986-; contrib Punch 1966-, memb Punch Table 1979; plays (with Willis Hall) incl: Billy Liar 1960, Celebration 1961, England Our England (revue, music by Dudley Moore), Squat Betty & the Sponge Room, All Things Bright and Beautiful 1963, Say Who You Are 1965, Childrens Day 1969, Who's Who 1972, Saturday, Sunday, Monday; Filuemena (adaption from Edwards de Filippo) 1973, The Card (musical adaption from novel by Arnold Bennet, music and lyrics Tony Hatch and Jackie Trent) 1973, Worzel Gummidge (music Dennis King), Budgie (musical, lyrics Don Black, music Mort Schuman); Mr & Mrs Nobody (play) 1986; Screenplays (with Willis Hall) incl: Whistle Down the Wind, Billy Liar, A Kind of Loving, Man in the Middle, Pretty Polly, Lock up your Daughters; TV Films incl: There is a Happy Land, The Warmonger, Charlie Muffin (from Brian Freemantle's novel) 1983, This Office Life (from own novel) 1985, Slip Up (from the book by Anthony Delano) 1986; TV Series incl: The Upchat Line, The Upchat Connection, West End Tales, The Happy Apple, Charters and Caldicott, Andy Capp; Play with Willis Hall: Queenie's Castle, Budgie, The Upper Crusts, Billy Liar, Worzel Gummidge (character created by Barbara Euphan Todd); Awards: Granada Columnist of the Year 1970, IPC Descriptive Writer of the Year 1970, IPC Columnist of the Year 1973, Br Press Columnist of the Year 1978, Granada Special Quarter Century Award 1982; *Books* Novels incl: There is a Happy Land (1957), Billy Liar (1959), Jubb (1963), The Bucket Shop (1968), Billy Liar on the Moon (1975), Office Life (1978), Maggie Muggins (1981), In the Mood (1983), Thinks (1984), Our Song; general: The Passing of the Third Floor Buck (anthology of Punch pieces, 1974), Mondays, Thursdays (Daily Mirror columns 1976), Rhubarb, Rhubarb (1979), Daily Mirror Style (1980), Fanny Peculiar (1983), Mrs Pooter's Diary (1983), Waterhouse at Large (1985), The Collected Letters of a Nobody (1986), The Theory and Practise of Lunch (1986), The Theory and Practise of Travel; *Clubs* Garrick, Pen, Chelsea Arts, Savile; *Style—* Keith Waterhouse, Esq; 29 Kenway Rd, London SW5 0RP; Agent: London Mgmnt, 235/241 Regent St, London W1; Literary Agent: David Higham Assocs, 5-8 Lower John St, London W1

WATERHOUSE, Rachel Elizabeth; *née* Franklin; CBE (1980); da of Percival John Franklin (d 1955), and Ruby Susanna, *née* Knight; *b* 2 Jan 1923; *Educ* King Edward's HS for Girls Birmingham, St Hugh's Coll Oxford (MA), Univ of Birmingham (PhD); *m* 16 Aug 1947, John Alfred Humphrey Waterhouse, s of (Thomas Alfred) Foster Waterhouse, of 60 Hagley Road, Edgbaston, Birmingham; 2 s (Matthew b 21 Sept 1950, Edmund b 4 Feb 1952), 2 da (Deborah (Mrs De Haes) b 11 March 1956, Rebecca (Mrs Morgan) b 20 Oct 1958); *Career* WEA/extra-mural tutor 1944-47; res fell Univ of Birmingham 1948-52; memb: Potato Mktg Bd 1969-81, Price Cmmn 1977-79, Nat Consumer Cncl 1975-86, Duke of Edinburgh's Enquiry into Br Housing 1984-85; chm Consumers' Assoc 1982- (cncl memb 1966-); memb: Nat Economic Devpt Cncl 1981-, Securities & Investmts Bd 1983-, Cncl of Banking Ombudsman 1986-advsy bd Inst of Food Res 1988; chm Cncl for Licensed Conveyancers 1986-89; Hon D Litt Loughborough; Hon CGIA 1988; CBIM 1988; *Books* History of the Birmingham and Midland Institute 1854-1954 (1954), A Hundred Years of Engineering Craftsmanship (1957), Children in Hospital, 100 Years Child Care in Birmingham (1962); *Clubs* Royal Cwlth Soc; *Style—* Mrs Rachel Waterhouse; 252 Bristol Rd, Birmingham B5 7SL (☎ 021 472 0427); Consumers' Association, 2 Marylebone Rd, London NW1 4DX (☎ 01 486 5544, fax 01 935 1606, telex 918197); car ☎ 0836 734673

WATERHOUSE, Hon Mr Justice; Hon Sir Ronald Gough Waterhouse; QC (1969); s of Thomas Waterhouse, CBE (d 1961), and Doris Helena Gough, of Holywell, Clwyd; *b* 8 May 1926; *Educ* Holywell GS, St John's Coll Cambridge (MA, LLM); *m* 1960, Sarah Selina, da of Capt Ernest Augustus Ingram (d 1954), of Bletchley Park Stud; 1 s, 2 da; *Career* RAFVR 1944-48; barr Middle Temple 1952; dep chm: Cheshire QS 1964-71, Flintshire QS 1966-71; Crown Ct rec 1972-77, High Ct judge (Family Div) 1978-88, (Queen's Bench Div) 1988-, judge of Employment Appeal Tbnl 1979-88, presiding judge Wales and Chester Circuit 1980-84; chm Local Govt Boundary Cmmn for Wales 1974-78, vice-pres Zoological Soc of London 1981-84 (cncl memb 1972-74); Hon LLD Univ of Wales 1986; kt 1978; *Recreations* golf, cricket, music; *Clubs* Garrick, MCC, Cardiff and County; *Style—* The Hon Mr Justice Waterhouse; Royal Courts of Justice, Strand, London WC2A 2LL

WATERLOW, Sir Christopher Rupert; 5 Bt (UK 1873), of London; s of (Peter) Rupert Waterlow (d 1969), of Knightsbridge, London, and Jill Elizabeth, *née* Gourlay (d 1961); gs of Sir Philip Alexander Waterlow, 4 Bt (d 1973), and 3 cous twice removed of Sir Thomas Waterlow, 3 Bt, CBE, of Harrow Weald; *b* 12 August 1959; *Educ* Stonyhurst; *m* 6 Sept 1986, Sally-Ann, o da of Maurice Bitten, of Abbey Wood, London; *Career* Met Police civil staff; memb: Stonyhurst Assoc, Civil Service Sports Cncl; *Recreations* music, American football, NFL supporter (UK), shooting; *Style—* Sir Christopher Waterlow, Bt; 58D St John's Park, Blackheath, London SE3 (☎ 01 853 4900); New Scotland Yard, Broadway, London SW1 (☎ 01 230 1212)

WATERLOW, Lady; Diana Suzanne; *née* Skyrme; da of Sir Thomas Skyrme, KCVO, of Elm Barns, Blockley, Gloucs, and Hon Barbara Suzanne Lyle, da of 1 Baron Lyle of Westbourne; *b* 21 Mar 1943; *m* 10 July 1965, Sir (James) Gerard Waterlow, 4 Bt, *qv*; 1 s, 1 da; *Career* actress 1963-68; appointed JP S Westminster 1972, transferred to W Berkshire 1982; memb: of Bd of Holloway Prison, Securities Assoc Appeal Tbnl; memb of many ctees including: Gaming and Betting, Parole Review, Crime and Juvenile Delinquency; dir Securities Assoc, ptnrship in interior design business W Squared Interiors 1986; *Recreations* tennis, bridge; *Style—* Lady Waterlow; Windhills House, Hurstbourne Tarrant, nr Andover, Hants SP11 0DQ (☎ 026476 547)

WATERLOW, Sir (James) Gerard; 4 Bt (UK 1930), of Harrow Weald, Middlesex; s of Sir Thomas Waterlow, 3 Bt, CBE (d 1982); *b* 3 Sept 1939; *Educ* Marlborough, Trinity Coll Cambridge; *m* 1965, Diana Suzanne, *qv*, yr da of Sir Thomas Skyrme, KCVO, CB, CBE, TD, JP, *qv*; 1 s, 1 da (Amanda b 1968); *Heir* s, Thomas James Waterlow b 20 March 1970; *Style—* Sir Gerard Waterlow, Bt; Windhills House, Hurstbourne Tarrant, nr Andover, Hants SP11 0DQ (☎ 026476 547)

WATERLOW, Prof John Conrad; CMG (1969); Sir Sydney Philip Perigal Waterlow, KCMG, CBE, Chev Legion of Honour (d 1944), and Helen Margery, *née* Eckhard (d 1978); *b* 13 June 1916; *Educ* Eton, Trinity Coll Cambridge (BA, MB, Bch, MA, MD, ScD); *m* 1939, Angela Pauline Cecil, da of George Wynter Gray (d 1945), of Galhampton Manor, Yeovil, Somerset; 2 s (Oliver, Richard), 1 da (Sarah); *Career* dir Medical Res Cncl Tropical Metabolism Res Unit Univ of the West Indies Jamaica 1954-70, prof of Human Nutrition Univ of London 1970-82; FRS; *Clubs* Savile; *Style—* Prof John Waterlow, CMG, FRS; Parsonage House, Oare, Marlborough, Wilts

WATERLOW, John William; s of Sir Thomas Gordon Waterlow, 3 Bt, CBE, LLD (d 1982), of Edinburg and Helen Elizabeth, *née* Robinson (d 1970); *b* 14 Nov 1945; *Educ* Marlborough; *m* 15 July 1972, Camilla Dudley, da of Wing-Cdr Dudley Farmer, AFC, DFC, of Frieth, Oxon; 2 s (Rufus b 1976, Alec b 1980); *Career* Burrup Mathieson Sales 1969-81 (assoc dir 1984-85, sales dir 1985); sales dir Jarroid & Sons 1981-83: Liveryman Worshipful Co of Stationers E Newspapermakers; *Recreations* tennis, golf, fishing, skiing; *Clubs* MCC, Lansdowne, Den Norske; *Style—* John Waterlow, Esq; 81 Streathbourne Rd, London SW17 8RA (☎ 01 767 1398); Crane House, Lavington St, London SE1 0NX (☎ 01 928 8911)

WATERMAN, Clive Adrian; s of Harvey Waterman (d 1967), of Hendon, London, and Hannah, *née* Spector; *b* 13 August 1949; *Educ* Haberdashers' Aske's Sch Elstree, London Hosp Med Coll (BDS), Royal Dental Hosp of London (MSc); *Career* clinical asst London Hosp 1973-75 (house surgn 1973), registrar Eastman Dental Hosp 1976-77, pt/t clinical asst Guy's Hosp 1977-84, gen and specialist practice 1977-, pt/t lectr King's Coll 1985-; chm elect GP Section Br Soc of Periodontology; memb: Kingston and Richmond local Dental Ctee, Rotary Club Barnes; memb BSP 1973, LDC 1988; *Recreations* cricket, skiing, squash, wine, dinning; *Clubs* Riverside, Reform; *Style—* Clive Waterman, Esq; 4 Elm Grove Rd, Barnes, London SW13 0BT (☎ 01 392 2288, office 01 878 8986)

WATERMAN, Fanny; OBE (1971); da of Myer Waterman (d 1984), of Leeds, and Mary, *née* Behrmann (d 1978); *b* 22 Mar 1920; *Educ* Chapel Allerton HS Leeds, RCM; *m* Dr Geoffrey de Keyser; *Career* concert pianist and teacher of int repute; chm Haney Leeds Int Pianoforte Competition, jury memb of prestigious piano competitions incl the Tchaikovsky and Rubinstein (vice-pres), regular broadcaster tv and radio, author of over twenty books on piano-playing and teaching: FRCM; *Recreations* travel, reading, voluntary work, cooking; *Style—* Miss Fanny Waterman, OBE; Woodgarth, Oakwood Grove, Leeds, W Yorks LS8 2PA (☎ 0532 655 771)

WATERMAN, Howard John; *b* 23 May 1953; *Educ* Southampton Univ (LLB), Coll of Law; *m* 1 Nov 1981, Sharon; 1 da (Lauren b 1 Sept 1988); *Career* slr 1977, ptnr Cameron Markby 1984- (departmental mangr Banking Dept 1987-); City of London Slrs Co; memb Law Soc 1977; *Recreations* chess, bridge, sports; *Style—* Howard

Waterman, Esq; 20 Beaumont Place, Hadley Highstone, Herts (☎ 01 440 7839); Sceptre Court, 40 Tower Hill, London EC3N 4BB (☎ 01 702 2345)

WATERS, Alexander James Garland; s of Rev Alexander Waters, MA, BD (d 1924), and Isabella Jane, *née* Garland (d 1956); *b* 24 Mar 1912; *Educ* Sorbonne, Heidelberg, McGill Univ (BSc Eng); *m* 6 March 1940, Eileen Mary, da of Rev Arthur Edwin Thomas Mcnamara, MA, BD (d 1949), of Westbury-on-Severn, Glos; 1 da (Ann Garland b 1943); *Career* engr; research engr Rolls Royce and Rotal Ltd 1938-43, gen sales mangr Landley Alloys Ltd 1943-45; chm: A J G Waters Ltd 1956-, Realm Engineering Ltd 1960, Realm Control, Systems Ltd 1983, Proclin Int 1972; *Recreations* cricket, golf, rugby, squash; *Clubs* MCC, Berkshire Golf, Royal Aero, London Scottish and Wasps Rugby; *Style—* Alexander J G Waters, Esq; Rolls Farm, Tismans Common, Rudawick, Horsham, W Sussex; 8/28 Milton Ave, Croydon, Surrey C24 2JP (☎ 01 639 5521, telex 945411, fax 01 689 1715)

WATERS, Brian Richard Anthony; s of Montague Waters, QC, of London, and Jessica Freedman; *b* 27 Mar 1944; *Educ* City of London Sch, St John's Coll Cambridge (MA, Arch & Fine Arts), Dip in Arch, PCL Dip in Town Planning; *m* 1 Nov 1974, Myriam Leiva, da of Jose Ramon Leiva Alvarez, of Bogota, Colombia; *Career* chartered architect & town planner; memb RIBA, RTPI; pres Cities of London and Westminster Soc of Architects 1980-82; vice pres RIBA 1988 (cncl memb 1987); princ The Boisot Waters Cohen Partnership; ptnr: Sant Design, Studio Crown Reach; dir Gray Lucas Mgmnt Ltd; Architectural Journalist of the Year commendation 1979, 1982, 1984, 1986; *Books* articles and reviews for various architectural pubns; *Recreations* tennis, dressage, pots, Siberian huskies; *Clubs* RAC, Hurlingham; *Style—* Brian R A Waters, Esq; Studio Crown Reach, 149a Grosvenor Road, London SW1V 3JY (☎ 01 828 6555, fax 01 834 9470)

WATERS, Brian Wallace; s of Stanley Wallace Waters, of Harpenden, Herts, and Kathleen, *née* Thake; *b* 24 Nov 1936; *Educ* City of London Sch, Harvard Business Sch; *m* 1 April 1961, Gillian, da of Herbert William Harris (d 1976); 4 s (Andrew b 1963, James b 1965, Richard b 1967, Mark b 1975); *Career* Arthur Young: ptnr 1968, exec vice-chm (Europe) 1979-82, chm (Europe) 1982-85, managing ptnr Arthur Young Cambridge 1984-, dir of Euro affrs UK 1986-, memb mgmnt ctee 1986-; chm London Soc of Chartered Accountants, and memb ICAEW 1983-87, memb exec ctee Union Européennes des Expert Compatables 1983-87; memb of the Horserace Betting Levy Appeal Tbnl 1986-; Liveryman: Worshipful Co of Chartered Accountants, Drapers; FCA 1960, FCMA 1962; *Recreations* cricket, field sports, horseracing, real tennis; *Clubs* MCC, Institute of Directors, City Livery, Wig and Pen; *Style—* Brian Waters, Esq; Arthur Young, Compass House, 80 Newmarket Rd, Cambridge CB5 8DZ (☎ 0223 461200)

WATERS, Mrs Frank; Denise Jeanne Marie Lebreton; *see*: Brown, D J M L

WATERS, Donald Henry; s of Henry Lethbridge Waters (d 1978), of Edinburgh, and Jean Manson, *née* Baxter (d 1987); *b* 17 Dec 1937; *Educ* George Watson's Coll Edinburgh, Inverness Royal Acad; *m* 5 May 1962, June Leslie, da of Andrew Hutchison (d 1984), of Forres, Moray; 1 s (Andrew Henry Lethbridge b 1969), 2 da (Jennifer Dawn b 1963, Gillian Claire b 1966); *Career* dir: John M Henderson Ltd 1972-75, Glenburnie Properties Ltd 1976-, Blenheim Travel Ltd 1981-, Moray Firth Radio Ltd 1982-, Ind TV Pubns Ltd 1987-, Cablevision Scot plc 1987-; chief exec Grampian TV plc 1987-(dir 1979-); former chm Royal Northern and Univ Club Aberdeen; MICAS; *Recreations* gardening, travel, hillwalking; *Clubs* Royal Northern and Univ Aberdeen; *Style—* Donald Waters, Esq; Balquhidder, 141 North Deeside Rd, Milltimber, Aberdeen AB1 0JS (☎ 0224 867 131); Grampian TV plc, Queens Cross, Aberdeen AB9 2XJ (☎ 0224 646 464)

WATERS, Lt-Gen Sir (Charles) John; KCB (1988), CBE (1981, OBE 1977); s of Patrick George Waters (d 1952), and Margaret Ronaldson, *née* Clark; *b* 2 Sept 1935; *Educ* Oundle, RMA Sandhurst; *m* 1962, Hilary Doyle, da of Harry Sylvester Nettleton (d 1983); 3 s; *Career* CO 1 Bn Gloucs Regt 1975-77, Col Gen Staff 1 Armd Div 1977-79, Cdr 3 Inf Bde 1979-81, RCDS 1982, Dep Cdr Land Forces Falklands 1982, Cdr 4 Armd Div 1983-85, Col Gloucs Regt 1985-, Cmdt Staff Coll Camberley 1986-88, GOC and dir of ops NI 1988-, Col Cmdt Prince of Wales Div, Lt-Gen 1988; *Recreations* sailing (yacht 'Momentilla'), skiing, painting, reading, walking; *Clubs* Army and Navy, Ski of GB, Eagle Ski; *Style—* Lt-Gen Sir C J Waters, KCB, CBE; c/o National Westminster Bank, 4-6 Broad St, Reading, Berks

WATERTON, John Brian; s of Laurence Maude Waterton (d 1976); *b* 10 Mar 1934; *Educ* Giggleswick Sch Yorks; *m* 1959, Jane Pollack, da of Harry Anthony Pitt Wilkinson (d 1966); 2 s, 2 da; *Career* co dir, gp mktg dir Dawson Int plc; *Recreations* golf; *Clubs* Caledonian; *Style—* John Waterton, Esq; Dawson International plc, 9 Charlotte Square, Edinburgh EH2 4DR

WATHEN, Julian Philip Gerard; s of Gerard Anstruther Wathen, CIE (d 1958), and Melicent Louis, *née* Buxton (d 1984); *b* 21 May 1923; *Educ* Harrow; *m* 1948, Priscilla Florence, da of Maj-Gen Bevil Thomson Wilson (d 1975); 1 s (Simon), 2 da (Lucy m 1987 Andrew Floyer-Acland, Henrietta m 1986 Edward Goodall); *Career* joined Barclays Bank DCO 1948, served Kenya, Tanganyika, Cyprus, New York, Sudan, Ghana; vice-chm Barclays Bank 1979-84 (gen mangr 1966); dir Mercantile & Gen Reinsurance; chm Hall Sch Tst; pres Royal African Soc, vice-chm London House for Overseas Graduates; govr: St Paul's Schs, Dauntseys, Abingdon, SOAS; Master Mercers' Co 1984-85; *Clubs* Travellers'; *Style—* Julian Wathen, Esq; Woodcock House, Owlpen, Dursley GL11 5BY (☎ 0453 860214); 1 Montagu Place, Marylebone, London W1H 1RG (☎ 01 935 8569)

WATHEN, Rev Mark William Gerard; TD (1946); s of Gerard Anstruther Wathen, CIE (d 1958), and Melicent Louis, *née* Buxton (d 1984); *b* 18 Sept 1912; *Educ* Gresham's Sch Holt; *m* 1940, Rosemary, da of Charles Hartridge, of Findon Place, W Sussex, and his w Kathleen, er da of Sir Fortescue Flannery, 1 Bt; 2 s (Roderick b 1940, Jonathan b 1951), 2 da (Primula b 1946, Erica b 1949); *Career* dir Barclays Bank (City, Ipswich, Norwich) 1948-72; high sheriff Norfolk 1968; memb Gen Synod C of E 1970-80, church cmmr 1973-78, ordained deacon and priest 1982, priest i/c St Columba's Church Isle of Skye 1982-; master Mercers' Co 1963; FRSA; *Recreations* shooting, fishing, writing; *Clubs* Brooks's, MCC; *Style—* The Rev Mark Wathen, TD; Talisker House, Carbost, Isle of Skye IV47 8SF (☎ 047 842 245); Bolwick Hall Farm, Marsham, Norwich (☎ 026 373 3130)

WATHERSTON, (John) Michael; s of John Robert Watherston (d 1983); *b* 30 June 1932; *Educ* Sedbergh; *m* 1960, Lorna Kathryn, da of George Warren (d 1956), of Enniskillen; 1 s, 1 da; *Career* exec dir Murray Johnstone Ltd; dir: Murray Johnstone Unit Trust Mgmnt Ltd, MJ Finance Ltd, Murraystone Investment Ltd, and other cos; high constable Holyrood; MICAS; Holyrood High Constable; *Recreations* golf, shooting, skiing; *Clubs* Honourable Co of Edinburgh Golfers, Western (Glasgow); *Style—* Michael Watherston, Esq; 22 Murrayfield Drive, Edinburgh EH12 6EB (☎ 031 337 2948); Murray Johnstone Ltd, 7 West Nile Street, Glasgow G2 (☎ 041 226 3131)

WATKIN, Mr (Francis) David; s of John Wilfrid Watkin and Beatrice Lynda Dadswell; *b* 23 Mar 1925; *Career* British Army 1944-47; dir of photography; documentary films incl The England of Elizabeth; feature films incl: The Knack, Help, Marat Sade, The Charge of the Light Brigade, Catch 22, The Devils, The Boyfriend, Jesus of Nazareth, Chariots of Fire, White Nights, Out of Africa, Moonstruck; American Academy Award 1985, British Academy Award 1986; *Recreations* music, reading; *Style—* David Watkin, Esq; 6 Sussex Mews, Brighton BN2 1GZ

WATKIN WILLIAMS, Sir Peter; s of Robert Thesiger Watkin Williams; *b* 8 July 1911; *Educ* Sherborne, Pembroke Coll Cambridge; *m* 1938, Jane Dickinson, *née* Wilkin; 2 da; *Career* served WWII; ptnr Hansons (lawyers) Shanghai 1937-40, resident magistrate Uganda 1946-55, puisne judge: Trinidad & Tobago 1955-58, Sierra Leone 1958-61; plebiscite judge Cameroons 1961; CJ: Basutoland, Bechuanaland and Swaziland (also pres Ct Appeal) 1961-65, high court judge Malawi 1967-69, CJ Malawi 1969-70, ret; kt 1963; *Style—* Sir Peter Watkin Williams; Lower East Horner, Stockland, Honiton, Devon (☎ 040 488 374)

WATKINS, Brian; s of James Edward Watkins (d 1981), of Newport, Gwent, and Gladys Ann, *née* Fletcher (d 1942); *b* 26 July 1933; *Educ* Newport HS, LSE (BSc), Worcester Coll of Oxford; *m* 1, 26 Oct 1957 (m dis 1979), Thelma, da of Thomas Horace Waite (d 1963), of Newport, Gwent; 1 s (Mark b 1958), m 2, 31 Dec 1982, Elizabeth, da of Arfon Jones, of Littleton Hall, Littleton, Chester; 1 da (Caroline b 1985); *Career* RAF 1954-58, HMOCS Sierra Leone 1959-63, local govt 1963-66, admin Tristan da Cunha 1966-69, slr 1970, lectr Univ of Manchester 1969-71; HM Dip Serv: FCO 1971-73, NY 1973-76, NI Off 1976-78, FCO 1978-81, cnsllr and dep govr Bermuda 1981-83, cnsllr (econ) Islamabad 1983-86, consul gen Vancouver 1986; memb Law Soc; *Recreations* reading, dancing, theatre; *Clubs* Royal Bermuda Yacht, Vancouver; *Style—* Brian Watkins, Esq; British Consulate General, 800-111 Melville St, Vancouver, BC, Canada V6E 3V6 (☎ 604 683 4421, fax 604 681 0693)

WATKINS, Rev Gordon Derek; s of Clifford Henry Watkins (d 1967), of Bristol, and Margaret Caroline, *née* Grimley (d 1974); *b* 16 July 1929; *Educ* St Brendan's Coll Clifton; *m* 3 Jan 1957, Beryl Evelyn Watkins, da of Thomas Henry Whitaker (d 1959), of Sydney, NSW; *Career* Nat Serv RAOC 1947-49; minor canon Grafton Cathedral NSW 1953-56, vicar Texas Queensland 1956-61, curate St Wilfrid's Harrogate 1961-63, vicar Upton Park 1963-67; rector: Great and Little Bentley 1967-73, Great Canfield 1973-78; asst sec Chelmsford Diocesan Synod 1973-78, sec Chelmsford Redundant Churches Uses Ctee 1973-78, pastoral sec Diocese of London 1978-84, vicar St Martin-within-Ludgate City of London 1984-89, sec London Diocesan Advsy Ctee 1984-, priest vicar of Westminster Abbey 1984; Priest-in-Ordinary HM The Queen 1984-; chaplain: Ward of Farringdon within City of London 1984-89, Knights of the Round Table 1984-89; Freeman City of London 1984; Chaplain: Co of Makers of Playing Cards 1987-88, Co of Pipe Makers and Tobacco Blenders 1985-; *Recreations* reading, television, the country; *Clubs* Athenaeum, Oriental; *Style—* The Rev Gordon Watkins; 30 Causton St, London SW1P 4AU

WATKINS, Maj-Gen Guy Hansard; CB (1986), OBE (1974); s of Col Alfred Norman Mitchell Watkins (d 1970), of Milford-on-Sea, Hants, and Sylvia Christine, *née* Downing (d 1988); *b* 30 Nov 1933; *Educ* The King's Sch Canterbury; *m* 15 Feb 1958, Sylvia Margaret, da of William Lawrence Grant, of Walton-on-the-Hill, Surrey; 2 s (Michael b 1959, Peter b 1971), 2 da (Anne-Marie b 1961, Carol b 1965); *Career* cmmnd RA 1953, Battery Cdr (BAOR) 1969, Instr Staff Coll 1971, Co 39 Regt RA (BAOR) 1973, Dep Cmd 1 Armoured Div (BAOR) 1977, Dir Public Relations (Army) 1980, Cmd Artillery Div (BAOR) 1982, Dir Gen Army Manning and Recruiting 1985, ret 1986; chm exec The Royal Hong Kong Jockey Club 1986; *Recreations* riding, golf, fishing; *Clubs* Royal Hong Kong Jockey, Shek-O Country, Army and Navy, Littlehampton Golf; *Style—* Maj-Gen Guy Watkins; c/o Nat Westminster Bank, 60 High St, Bognor Regis, West Sussex; The Royal Hong Kong Jockey Club, Sports Road, Happy Valley, Hong Kong (☎ Hong Kong 0-4856925, telex 65581 RHKJC HX, fax 052 5 8902946)

WATKINS, Nowell St John; s of Josceline Charles Shaw Watkins (d 1974) and Anne Agnes St John Beddow *née* Hickman; *b* 20 August 1930; *Educ* Haileybury; *m* 27 April 1957, Penelope Mary, da of James Herbert Harris, MC (d 1981), of Mayfield; 1 s (Timothy James b 16 May 1961), 1 da (Amanda Mary St John b 14 Jun 1959); *Career* slr, NP and ptnr in firm variously known as Steward Vulliamy & Watkins & Stewards 1960 -86; sr ptnr Watkins Stewart & Ross 1986-; HM Coroner for Ipswich Dist of Suffolk, chm Ipswich SSAFA; *Recreations* cricket, racing and getting our into the garden; *Clubs* MCC; *Style—* Nowell Watkins, Esq; 8 Lower Brook St, Ipswich Suffolk, IP4 1AP (☎ 0473 226 266, fax 0473 230 052)

WATKINS, Robert; *see*: Roach, Jill

WATKINS, Rt Hon Lord Justice; Rt Hon Sir Tasker Watkins; VC (1944), DL (Glamorgan 1956), PC (1980); s of Bertram Watkins; *b* 18 Nov 1918; *Educ* Pontypridd GS; *m* 1941, Eirwen Evans; 1 s, 1 da; *Career* WWII Maj Welch Regt; batt Middle Temple 1948, QC 1965, Carmarthenshire QS 1966-71, dep chm Radnor QS 1962-71, rec: Merthyr Tydfil 1968-70, Swansea 1970-71; high ct judge: Family Div 1971-74, Queen's Bench 1974-80; presiding judge Wales and Chester Circuit 1975-80 (ldr 1970-71), ld justice of Appeal 1980-, sr presiding judge England and Wales 1983-, dep chief justice 1988; chm Judicial Studies Bd 1979-; Hon LLD Wales 1979; Kt 1971; *Style—* The Rt Hon Lord Justice Watkins, VC, DL; 5 Pump Court, Middle Temple, London EC4 (☎ 01 353 1993); Fairwater Lodge, Fairwater Rd, Llandaff, Glamorgan

WATKINS, Baron (Life Peer UK 1972); Tudor Elwyn Watkins; s of Howell Watkins, JP; *b* 9 May 1903; *Educ* Harlech Coll; *m* 1936, Bronwen Richards, da of Thomas Stather, of Talgarth; *Career* MP (L) Brecon and Radnor 1945-70, pps Sec State Wales 1964-68; formerly miner and political agent; chm Brecon Beacons Nat Park Ctee 1974-78; *Style—* The Rt Hon Lord Watkins; Bronafon, Penyfan Rd, Brecon, Powys (☎ 0874 2961)

WATKINS-PITCHFORD, Denys James; s of Rev Walter Watkins-Pitchford, and Edith Elizabeth, *née* Wilson; *b* 25 July 1905; *Educ* privately, Paris; *m* Aug 1939, Cecily Mary (decd), da of late Frank Adnitt, of Northampton; 1 s (Robin John (decd)), 1 da (Angela Jane b 1943); *Career* Capt Home Gd 1939; artist, illustrator, author under pen name 'BB'; bdcaster and contributor to various journals; books include: Little Grey

Men, Brendon Chase, Manka, Fishermans Bedside Book, Shooting Man's Bedside Book; Hon MA; FRSA, ARCA; *Recreations* shooting, fishing, natural history, butterfly rearing and conservation; *Style*— Denys Watkins-Pitchford, Esq; Round House, Sudboro', Kettering, Northants (☎ 08012 3215)

WATKINS-PITCHFORD, Dr John; CB (1968); s of Wilfred Watkins-Pitchford (d 1952), and Olive Mary, *née* Beynon Nicholl (d 1960); *b* 20 April 1912; *Educ* Shrewsbury Sch, St Thomas's Hosp (MB BS, MD, DPH, DIH); *m* 14 Aug 1945, (Elizabeth) Patricia, da of Hubert Wright (d 1959), of Guernsey; 1 s (Michael); *Career* WW11 sqdn Ldr RAF 1939-46; chief med offr Miny Soc Security, chief med advsr in Soc Security Miny of Health; memb: Industl Injuries Advsy Cncl 1975-84, cncl Chest, Heart & Stroke Assoc; Queens Hon Physician 1971; MRCS (1937), LTCP (1937); *Recreations* gardening; *Style*— Dr John Watkins-Pitchford, CB; Hill House, Farley Lane, Westerham, Kent TN16 1UD (☎ 0959 64448)

WATKINSON, 1 Viscount (UK 1964); Harold Arthur Watkinson; CH (1962), PC (1955); s of Arthur Watkinson; *b* 25 Jan 1910; *Educ* Queen's Coll Taunton, King's Coll London; *m* 1939, Vera, da of John Langmead; 2 da; *Heir* none; *Career* sits as Conservative in House of Lords; MP (C) Woking 1950-64, min Transport and Civil Aviation 1955-59, min Defence 1959-62; chm Cadbury Schweppes 1969-74, pres CBI 1976-77; *Books* Blueprint for Industrial Survival, Turning Points, The Mountain; *Recreations* sailing, walking; *Style*— The Rt Hon the Viscount Watkinson, PC, CH; Tyma House, Shore Rd, Bosham, nr Chichester, Sussex

WATKINSON, John Taylor; s of William Forshaw Watkinson (d 1963), of Bristol, and Muriel Beatrice, *née* Taylor (d 1979); *b* 25 Jan 1941; *Educ* Bristol GS, Worcester Coll Oxford (MA, PPE); *m* 29 Aug 1969, Jane Elizabeth, da of Ian Gerald Miller; 2 s (Benjamin Harry, Harry John), 2 da (Anna Rose, Polly Rachel); *Career* schoolmaster: Repton 1964-66, Rugby 1966-71; barr 1971-86; MP (Lab) W Gloucs 1974-79, PPS Home Off 1976-79, memb Public Accounts Ctee 1976-79, memb cncl Europe and Western European Union 1976-79, rapporteur Legal Affairs Ctee 1978-79; reporter Money Pragramme BBC 1979-83, dir 1984-, slr 1986; *Books* UK Telecommunications Approvals Manual (jtly 1987); *Recreations* golf, curst, squash; *Clubs* Jesters; *Style*— John Watkinson, Esq; Canna Lodge, Alvington, Lydney, Gloucs (☎ 0594 42475)

WATKINSON, Leonard James; s of Leonard Watkinson (d 1966); *b* 27 June 1928; *Educ* W Leeds HS, Leeds Univ (MSc, PhD); *m* 1957, Norma, *née* Schofield; 1 s, 2 da; *Career* tech dir Universal Ink Co Ltd 1960-64, dir of Research W H Howson Ltd 1964-70, tech dir Howson-Algraphy Gp of Vickers plc 1970-85, dir Wychem Ltd 1980-85; graphic arts conslt 1985-; CChem, FRSC; *Recreations* fell-walking, photography, botany, choral music; *Style*— Leonard Watkinson, Esq; 95 Cookridge Lane, Leeds, LS16 7NE (☎ 0532 673853)

WATKISS, Barbara Anne; *née* Needham; da of Ernest Needham (d 1984), and Gertrude Agnes, *née* Glover; *b* 19 Feb 1934; *Educ* St Albans Girls' GS, Bath Domestic Sci Coll Bristol Univ (Dip Teaching); *m* 31 March 1956, Christopher Robin Watkiss, s of Arthur Edwin Watkiss (d 1975), of Middlesborough; 1 s (Michael Christopher b 1957), 2 da (Susan Barbara (Mrs Attew) b 1960, Julia Anne b 1963); *Career* teacher Herts CC 1955-59, dir and co sec: Watkiss Studio's Ltd 1959-, Watkiss Gp Aviation Ltd 1971-, Multiplex Techniques Ltd 1972-, Multiplex Medway Ltd 1979-; md and co sec Watkiss Automation Ltd 1972-, ptnr Holme Grove Farm 1983-, md Franshams Ltd 1988-; chm: Competition Stallions Int Ltd 1988-, NEBC Ltd 1988-; memb BFPMS; *Recreations* supporting equestrian competition, tennis, skiing; *Style*— Mrs Barbara Watkiss; Holme Grove Hse, Biggleswade, Beds SG18 9SS (☎ 0767 315 182); Holme Ct, Biggleswade, Beds SG18 9ST (☎ 0767 313 853, fax 0767 317 945, telex 826053)

WATKISS, Ronald Frederick; CBE (1981); s of Bertie Miles Watkiss (d 1943), of 71 Pentre St, Cardiff, and Isabella, *née* Blake (d 1966); *b* 21 May 1920; *Educ* Howard Gardens HS Cardiff; *m* 30 April 1941, Marion, da of Harry Preston (d 1976), of Fishguard Close, Cardiff; 1 s (Derek b 21 Jan 1943, d 1964), 1 da (Carolyn b 12 Oct 1955); *Career* TA, RCS 1938, served 1939-43, Combined Ops 1943-46, Sgt: md Lloyd and Watkiss Ltd 1950-86; pres: Cardiff Credit Traders Assoc 1953-54 and 1963-64, Heath Community Assoc (Cardiff) 1982-(chm 1970-72); vice-chm Cardiff 94 Cwlth Games Ctee 1985-88, memb People and Work Unit 1988; Cardiff City Cncl: cncllr 1960, alderman 1967-74, re-elected cncllr 1973, cncl leader 1976-79 and 1983-87, ldr Cons Party 1974-; Hon Fell Univ Coll of Cardiff 1986; Queen's Silver Jubilee Medal 1977; *Recreations* all forms of sport (spectator only now); *Clubs* Victory Services, Crockford's; *Style*— Ronald Watkiss, Esq, CBE; 69 King George V Drive, Heath, Cardiff CF4 4EF (☎ 0222 752 716, fax 0222 747 184)

WATLING, His Honour Judge; (David) Brian Watling; QC (1979); s of Vernon Watling and Edith, nee Ridley; *b* 18 June 1935; *Educ* Charterhouse, King's Coll London; *m* 1964, Noelle Bugden, WRNS; *Career* barr 1957, Crown Ct recorder 1979-81, Circuit judge (SE) 1981-, visiting prof law Univ Coll Buckingham 1980; *Style*— His Hon Judge Watling, QC; Queen Elizabeth Building, Temple, EC4 (☎ 01 353 6453)

WATMORE, Leslie John; s of Arthur Watmore (d 1962), of London, and Edith Alice, *née* Giles (d 1986), of London; *b* 8 May 1929; *Educ* St Olaves GS, Keble Coll Oxford (MA); *m* 19 Dec 1953, Iris Daphne, da of Charles William Enever (d 1981), of London; 2 s (Stephen Charles b 26 Nov 1954, David Anthony b 22 Oct 1960); *Career* admitted slr 1957, ptnr L Bingham and Co 1959-76, sr ptnr L Watmore and Co 1976-, chm Legal Aid Area 1981-84; former Capt and chm West Kent GC; Freeman City of London, Liveryman Worshipful Co of Slrs 1966; memb Law Soc; *Recreations* golf, hill walking; *Clubs* RAC, City Livery, Cordwainer Ward, West Kent Golf; *Style*— Leslie Watmore, Esq; Tudor Cottage, 10 Downs Hill, Beckenham, Kent (☎ 01 650 4807); L Watmore & Co, Chancery House, 53/66 Chancery Lane, London WC2A 1QU (☎ 01 430 1512, fax 01 405 7382)

WATNEY, Lady Katherine Felicity; *née* Courtenay; da of 17 Earl of Devon; *b* 1940; *m* 1966, Antony Stephen Pope Watney (d 1986); 1 s; *Style*— Lady Katherine Watney; 1 Playhatch Cottages, nr Reading, Berks RG4 9QX

WATSON *see also*: Inglefield-Watson, Milne-Watson

WATSON, Alan John; CBE (1985); s of Rev John William Watson (d 1980), of Bognor Regis, and Edna Mary, *née* Peters (d 1985); *b* 3 Feb 1941; *Educ* Kingswood Sch Bath, Jesus Coll Cambridge (MA); *m* 1965, Karen, da of Hartwig Lederer (d 1966), of Frankfurt-on-Main; 2 s (Stephen b 1966, Martin b 1968); *Career* history scholar and res asst to Regius Prof of Modern History Cambridge 1962-64; broadcaster: presenter of The Money Programme BBC 2 and Panorama BBC 1 1964-76; head of radio & TV EEC Cmmn 1976-80; chief exec Charles Barker City Ltd 1980-83, pres Liberal Party 1984-85, dep chm Sterling PR Ltd 1985-86, chm City & Corporate Cncl Ltd 1987-; gov Kingswood Sch 1984-; memb: UNICEF Exec Bd 1985- chm of governors Westminster Coll Oxford 1988-, Jesus Coll Cambridge Soc Ctee 1987-;; Gov Kingswood Sch 1984-; memb: UNICEF Exec Bd 1985-, NCH Nat Appeals Cttee 1985-, Jesus Coll Cambridge Soc Ctee 1987-; *Books* Europe at Risk (1974); *Recreations* travel, wines, theatre; *Clubs* Brooks's, RAC, Oxford and Cambridge, Kennel; *Style*— Alan Watson, Esq, CBE; Cholmondeley House, 3 Cholmondeley Walk, Richmond, Surrey; 18 Bolton St London W1 (☎ 01 491 1253)

WATSON, Alexander Stuart; s of William Alexander Stuart Watson of Shanghai (d 1960), and Frances Dorothy, *née* Hawes (d 1963); *b* 16 July 1920; *Educ* Worksop Coll, Notts Coll of Aeronautical Engrg Chelsea; *m* 1949, Jean Patricia, da of Capt Charles Geoffrey Kerswell; 1 s (Roderick), 2 da (Katie, Fiona); *Career* Lt (A) RNVR 1942-46, sales dir: Hawker Siddeley Aviation Ltd 1972-77, Dowty-Rotol Ltd 1962-72, dir Dowty Exports Ltd, Bolton Paul Aircraft Ltd; pres and chm Hawker Siddeley Aviation Inc; mktg dir (Aircraft) Br Aerospace plc 1977-82, conslt aeronautical engr 1982-; *Recreations* sailing (yacht 'Kit V'); *Clubs* Royal Motor Yacht (Poole); *Style*— Alexander Watson, Esq; Saxon Hill, South Cadbury, Somerset (☎ 0963 40516)

WATSON, Sir (James) Andrew; 5 Bt (UK 1866), of Henrietta Street, Cavendish Sq, St Marylebone, Co Middx; s of Sir Thomas Watson, 4 Bt (d 1941), and Ella, Lady Watson, *qv*; *b* 30 Dec 1937; *Educ* Eton; *m* 1965, Christabel Mary, da of Kenneth Ralph Malcolm Carlisle; 2 s, 1 da; *Heir* s, Roland Victor Watson; *Career* Lt Life Gds; barr; *Style*— Sir Andrew Watson, Bt; Talton House, Newbold-on-Stour, Stratford-on-Avon, Warwicks

WATSON, Maj-Gen Andrew Linton; CB (1981); s of Col W L Watson, OBE (d 1961), and Dorothy Ellen, *née* Lea (d 1950); *b* 9 April 1927; *Educ* Wellington; *m* 23 Feb 1952, Mary Elizabeth (Ginty), da of Albert S Rigby (d 1968), of Edina, Warren Point, Co Down; 2 s (Alastair Alexander Linton b 15 Feb 1953, Patrick Adrian Richard John b 4 April 1955), 1 da (Shane Elizabeth Annabel b 2 Aug 1960); *Career* cmmnd Black Watch 1946; 1 and 2 Bns served: UK, Germany, Cyprus, Br Guiana, UN Force Cyprus; Staff Coll 1958, Jt Servs Staff Coll 1964, GSO1 HQ 17 Div Malaya Dist 1966-68; cmd 1 Bn Black Watch 1969-71: Malaya, UK, Gibraltar, NI; Royal Coll Def Studies 1974, cdr Br Army Staff and mil attaché Washington DC 1975-77, GOC Eastern Dist 1977-80, chief of staff Allied Forces Northern Europe 1980-82; Col The Black Watch 1981-; lt-govr Royal Hosp Chelsea 1984-, chm Inner London branch Army Benevolent Fund 1983-; *Recreations* shooting, tennis, classical music, walking; *Clubs* Army and Navy; *Style*— Major-Gen Andrew Watson, CB; c/o Royal Bank of Scotland, 18 South Methven St, Perth; Lieutenant-Governor's House, Royal Hospital, Chelsea, London SW1

WATSON, Anthony; s of Lt-Cdr Andrew Patrick Watson, RNR, and Harriet, *née* Hewardine (d 1981); *b* 1 April 1945; *Educ* Campbell Coll Belfast, Queen's Univ Belfast (BSc); *m* 29 July 1972, Heather Jane, da of Lt Cdr Wilfred Norman Dye, RNR (d 1988); 2 s (Edward b 1975, Tom b 1976), 1 da (Tilly b 1980); *Career* barr Lincoln's Inn; dir: Touche Remnant & Co 1978-85, Touche Remnant Hldgs 1978-85; chief investmt offr Citibank NA 1985; chm: Citifunds Ltd 1985-, Citicare ltd 1985-; played for London Irish RFC first XV 1967-68; AMSIA 1971; *Clubs* RAC; *Style*— Anthony Watson, Esq

WATSON, Antony Edward Douglas; QC (1986); s of William Edward Watson, of Honchurch, Staffs, and Margaret Douglas; *b* 6 Mar 1945; *Educ* Sedbergh Sch, Sidney Sussex Coll Cambridge (MA); *m* 15 Sept 1972, Gillian Mary, da of Alfred John Beran-Arthur, of Brainshall, Staffs; 2 da (Edwina b 1978, Willa b 1981); *Career* 2LT Staffs Yeomanry (TA) 1964-67; called to the barr Inner Temple 1968, specialising in Intellectual Property Law; *Recreations* country pursuits, wine, opera; *Style*— Antony Watson, Esq, QC; The Old Rectory, Milden, Suffolk IP7 7HF (☎ 0449 740227); 6 Pump Court, Temple, London EC4 (☎ 01 353 8588, cartel 0860 304709)

WATSON, Lady; Beryl; da of Alfred Norris; *m* 1, Sqdn Ldr Basil Davis, RAF (decd); m 2 (m dis 1973), Sir Frances Cyril Rose, 4 Bt (d 1979); m 3, 1974, Sir Norman James Watson, 2 Bt (d 1983, when title became extinct); *Style*— Lady Watson; Flat 132, 55 Park Lane, London W1

WATSON, Brig Bruce Edmeston; s of Prof Herbert Edmeston Watson (d 1980), and Margaret Kathleen, *née* Rowson (d 1952); *b* 5 April 1918; *Educ* Marlborough, UCL; *m* 1941, Joan Elizabeth, da of Maj William Moore (d 1950); 1 s (Andrew), 2 da (Susan, Gillian); *Career* served RA 1939-73: dep dir Inspectorate of Armaments 1967-70, dir Heavy Weapons Projects 1970-73, ret; MBIM 1969, FBIM 1980, dir FN (Eng) Ltd 1973-85; *Recreations* photography, gardening; *Style*— Brig Bruce Watson; Chestnut Cottage, 12 Longdon Wood, Keston Park, Kent BR2 6EW (☎ 0689 52619)

WATSON, Hon Mrs (Catriona Mary Antonia); da of Baron Swann (Life Peer); *b* 15 Mar 1953; *Educ* St George's Sch for Girls Edinburgh, N of Scotland Coll of Agric; *m* Robert Noble Watson, s of Robert John Watson; 1 s, 1 da; *Career* farmer; *Recreations* riding, sailing, skiing, gardening; *Style*— The Hon Mrs Watson; Ballingall Farm, Leslie, Fife (☎ 0592 742963)

WATSON, Duncan Amos; CBE (1986); s of Duncan Watson (d 1980), of Sheffield, and Sybil Watson (d 1984); *b* 10 May 1926; *Educ* Worcester Coll for the Blind, St Edmund Hall Oxford (BA); *m* 2 June 1954, Mercia Margaret, da of Gilbert S Casey (d 1963), of Auckland, NZ; *Career* Treasy slrs dept 1957-86, ret as princ Treasy slr; chm exec cncl Royal Nat Inst for the Blind 1975-, pres World Blind Union 1988-; *Recreations* reading, listening to music; *Clubs* Reform, MCC; *Style*— Duncan Watson, Esq, CBE; 19 Great Russell Mansions, 60 Great Russell St, London, WC1B 3BE (☎ 01 242 7284)

WATSON, Sir (Noel) Duncan; KCMG (1967, CMG 1960); s of Harry Watson; *b* 16 Dec 1915; *Educ* Bradford GS, New Coll Oxford; *m* 1951, Aileen (d 1980), da of Charles Bell, of Dublin; *Career* Colonial Admin Serv: admin offr Cyprus 1938-43, asst colonial sec Trinidad 1943-45; seconded to Colonial Off 1946, princ private sec to Sec State Colonies 1947-50, asst sec Colonial Off 1950-62 under-sec Central Africa Office, 1963, asst under-sec Colonial Office & CRO 1964-67; transfered to HM Diplomatic Serv 1965-; political advsr to C-in-C Far East 1967-70, high Cmmr Malta 1970-72, dep under-sec FCO 1972-75; ret HM diplomatic service 1975; dep chm Central Cncl of Royal Cwlth Soc 1983-87 (vice pres for life 1987); *Style*— Sir Duncan Watson, KCMG; Sconce, Steels Lane, Oxshott, Surrey

WATSON, Edward Howsley; CB (1968); s of Ernest Watson (d 1945); *b* 16 June 1910; *Educ* Harrogate GS, Univ of Leeds (LLB); *m* 1951, Alice Mary, *née* Atkinson; 1 s; *Career* served RA, WW II, Maj; joined Civil Serv, Miny of Health 1946; slr and legal advsr: Miny of Health 1965-68, Miny of Housing and Local Govt 1965-70; *Style*—

Edward Watson Esq, CB; 10 The Terrace, Hales Place, Canterbury, Kent CT2 7AJ (☎ 0227 450 978)

WATSON, Ella, Lady; Ella Marguerite; da of Sir George Farrar, DSO, 1 and last Bt (d 1915); sis of Viscountess Lowther m of 7 Earl of Lonsdale; *m* 1935, Sir Thomas Watson, 4 Bt (ka 1941); 1 s (5 Bt); *Style*— Ella, Lady Watson; Talton Lodge, Newbold-on-Stour, Stratford-on-Avon, Warwicks

WATSON, Sir Francis John Bagott; KCVO (1973, CVO 1965, MVO 1959); s of Hugh Watson, and Helen Marian, *née* Bagott; *b* 24 August 1907; *Educ* Shrewsbury, St John's Coll Cambridge (BA); *m* 1941, Mary Rosalie Gray (d 1969), da of George Strong; 1 adopted s; *Career* dir Wallace Collection 1963-74 (asst keeper and dep dir 1938-63), surveyor Queen's Works of Art 1963-72 (Dep 1947-63), advsr Works of Art 1972-, tstee White Chapel Art Gallery, Slade Prof of Fine Art, Oxford 1969-70, Wrightsman Prof NY Univ 1970-71, Kress Prof Nat Gallery Washington DC 1975-76, visiting lectr Univ of California 1970; FBA, FSA; *Books* numerous learned journals including: Canaletto (1947), Wallace Collection Catalogue of Furniture (1956), Louis XVI Furniture (1959), Gt Family Collections (1965), The Guardi Family of Painters (1966), Tiepolo (1966), The Wrightsman Collection Catalogue (5 Vols 1966-70), Fragonard (1967), Systematic Catalogue of 17th and 18th Century French Furniture Nat Gallery of Washington DC 1989; *Style*— Sir Francis Watson, KCVO; West Farm House, Corton, Wilts BA12 0SY

WATSON, Rear Adm (John) Garth; CB (1965); el s of Alexander Henry St Croix Watson (d 1963), and Gladys Margaret, *née* Payne; *b* 20 Feb 1914; *Educ* UCL, Northampton Engrg Coll London Univ; *m* 1943, Barbara Elizabeth, da of Cecil Hugh Falloon (d 1959), of Moor Park, Middx; 2 s (John, Peter), 1 da (Jane); *Career* served WWII, Br Jt Servs Mission Washington 1945-48, Admty 1948-50, 5 Destroyer Sqdn 1950-53, fleet electrical offr Staff of C in C Home Fleet 1955-57, HM Dockyard Gibraltar 1957-60, asst dir electrical engrg Admty 1960-63, Adm Supt HM Dockyard Rosyth 1963-66, ADC to HM The Queen 1962; md Thomas Telford Ltd 1971-79, chm Inst of Civil Engrs Queens Jubilee Scholarship Tst 1980-85, vice chm Civil Engrs Club 1980-86; Hon DSc City Univ 1984; Freeman City of London 1986, Liveryman Worshipful Co of Engrs 1986; *Books* The Civils (1987), The Smeatonians (1989), contrib to Encyclopedia Britannica 15 Edn (1974); *Recreations* sailing, gardening; *Clubs* Athenaeum, Royal Thames Yacht, Royal Naval & Royal Albert Yacht; *Style*— Rear Adm Garth Watson, CB; Little Hall Court, Shedfield, nr Southampton, Hants (☎ 0329 833216)

WATSON, (Angus) Gavin; s of Herbert Edward Watson, of Carlisle, and Marjorie, *née* Reid; *b* 14 April 1944; *Educ* Carlisle GS, Merton Coll Oxford, Peterhouse Cambridge; *m* 29 April 1967, Susan Naomi, da of Eric Beal, of Manchester; 2 s (Matthew b 1974, Nicholas b 1980); *Career* DOE 1971-: princ 1974, sec of state's private off 1975-78, asst sec 1979, under sec 1986-; chm environment and tport branch Assoc of First Div Civil Servants 1983-85; hon fell Inst of Bldg Control 1987; *Recreations* industrial history, architecture, fell walking; *Style*— Gavin Watson, Esq; Dept of the Environment, 2 Marsham St, London SW1 (☎ 01 276 3467)

WATSON, George Menzies; s of William George Watson; *b* 15 July 1941; *Educ* Barnard Castle Sch; *m* 1969, Irene, da of Albert Johnson; l s, l da; *Career* fin dir and co sec: Wailes Dove Bitumastic plc, proprietor C and G Model Railways; FCA; *Recreations* golf, photography, railways; *Style*— George Watson, Esq; Avenue House, High Shincliffe, Co Durham DH1 2PY (☎ 091 384 2143)

WATSON, Gerald Walter; s of Reginald Harold Watson (d 1970), and Gertrude Hilda, *née* Ruffell (d 1979); *b* 13 Dec 1934; *Educ* King Edward VI Norwich Sch, CCC Cambridge (MA); *m* 30 Dec 1961, Janet Rosemary, da of Benjamin Henry Hovey (d 1954); 1 s (Rupert b 1968), 2 da (Candida b 1966, Meriel b 1971); *Career* Pilot Offr RAF 1953-55; W O 1958-64, MOD 1964-69; Civ Serv Dept 1969-73 (and 1975-81), NI off 1973-75, HM Treasy 1981-86; dir: Central Computer and Telecommunications Agency 1978-82, Bank of England 1983, dep chm Bldg Socs Cmmn 1986-88; ptnr Arthur Young mgmnt conslts 1989-; FBCS 1980; *Recreations* opera, theatre, equestrian sports; *Style*— Gerald Watson, Esq; c/o Holts Branch, Royal Bank of Scotland, Kirkland House, Whitehall, London SW1

WATSON, J Jordan; CMG (1972); s of John Henry Watson (d 1928); *b* 15 Dec 1912; *Educ* Gosforth GS; *m* 1940, Marjorie, *née* Lumb; 1 s, 1 da; *Career* Dept Employment 1930, seconded to For Serv 1945-53, cnsllr (Lab) Br Embassy Washington DC 1966-72; *Recreations* angling, golf; *Style*— J Jordan Watson, Esq, CMG; West Cottage, 19 Riverside Rd, Alnmouth, Alnwick, Northumberland (☎ 0665 830573)

WATSON, James Kenneth; s of James Edward Watson, of Phillips Rd, Birchington, Kent, and Helen Grace, *née* Kilby (d 1959); *b* 16 Jan 1935; *Educ* Watford GS, Stanford Univ California; *m* 23 Aug 1959, Eileen Fay, da of Sydney Purtiss, of Amberway, Nancy Downs, Oxhey, Herts; 2 s (Jamie Nicholas b 6 April 1970, Mark Robin b (twin 6 April 1970), 1 da (Sara Ann b 11 Dec 1968); *Career* CA; dir fin Br Rd Servs 1968-75, dep chm Nat Freight Consortium 1982 - (dir fin 1976-82); Freeman City of London, Liveryman Worshipful Co Carmen; FCA; *Recreations* cricket, tennis, theatre, history; *Clubs* MCC, Tring Tennis; *Style*— James Watson, Esq; Ingnawds, Lower Ickwieldway, Buckland, Nr Aylesbury, Bucks (☎ 0296 630829); Merton Centre, 45 St Peters St, Bedford (☎ 0234 272222)

WATSON, Prof James Patrick; s of Hubert Timothy Watson (d 1964), of London, and Grace Emily, *née* Mizen (d 1957); *b* 14 May 1936; *Educ* Roan Sch Greenwich, Trinity Coll Cambridge (BA, MB, MD); *m* 4 April 1962, Christine Mary, da of Rev Norman Tasker Colley (d 1987), of Midsomer Norton; 4 s (Peter b 1963, Andrew b 1964, John b 1970, Robert b 1972); *Career* jr hosp appts 1960-64, trainee psychiatrist Inst of Psychiatry 1964-70, sr lectr and hon conslt psychiatrist St George's Hosp and Med Sch 1970-74, prof of psychiatry Guy's Hosp Med Sch 1974- (The United Med and Dental Schs of Guy's and St Thomas's Hosp 1984-); FRCPsych 1977, FRCP 1978; *Recreations* music (especially Mozart), sport in gen; *Clubs* Nat Lib; *Style*— Prof James Watson; Guy's Hosp, London SE1 9RT (☎ 01 407 7600)

WATSON, Jennifer; da of Edward Gordon, of Bower's Hill House, Bower's Lane, Burpham, Surrey, and June Elizabeth, *née* Cobb; *b* 31 August 1952; *Educ* St Mary's Convent Shaftesbury, Branson's Coll Playford Suffolk, St Mathias Coll of Educ Bristol (Cert Ed), King Alfred's Coll Winchester (B Ed); *m* 23 July 1977, Thomas Alexandera Watson, *qv*, so of Donald Fletcher Watson, of Australia; 2 s (James Donald b 18 Feb 1981, Alexander Edward 4 Jan 1987), 1 da (Laura Helen 15 Jan 1983); *Career* dir and co sec Hallmark Mktg Servs Ltd 1986-, co sec Hallmark NCL Communications Ltd 1987-; tres and sec Macleod Soc 1983-, chm of govrs Southdown Sch Campton, Winchester 1985-87 (govr 1981-87); *Recreations* tennis; *Clubs* Littleton Tennis; *Style*— Mrs Jennifer Watson; 12 Stoke Rd, Winchester, Hants; 21 Northgate Place, Staple Gardens, Winchester SO23 85R (☎ 0962 63850, fax 0962 841 820, telex 477104)

WATSON, Hon Mrs Alastair; Joan; da of late Capt Philip Wyndham Cobbold; *m* 1925, Hon Alastair Joseph Watson (d 1955), s of 1 Baron Manton; 2 s (Michael b 1926, Andrew b 1930); *Style*— The Hon Mrs Alastair Watson; c/o Chillesford Lodge, Sudbourne, Woodbridge, Suffolk

WATSON, John Gillard; s of Albert Watson (d 1962), of Cheapside, Wakefield, Yorkshire, and Margaret Elizabeth, *née* Gillard (d 1981); *b* 30 April 1919; *Educ* Driffield Sch, Ruskin Coll, St Peter's Coll, Univ of Oxford (BA, MA); *m* 26 July 1954, Kathleen Mary, da of William Harold Raymond (d 1987), of Essex; 1 s (John Stephen b 1959), 1 da (Margaret Mary b 1957); *Career* RASC (England, France, India, Burma) 1939-46 (Sgt); librarian Oxford Univ Inst of Econ & Statistics 1961-86, nat exec ctee memb Assoc of Univ Teachers 1985-; *Recreations* watching cricket, mountain walking; *Clubs* United Oxford and Cambridge University, Oxford Union; *Style*— John Gilliard Watson, Esq; 11 Beaumont Buildings, Oxford OX1 2LL (☎ 0865 54583)

WATSON, John Grenville Bernard; MP (C) Skipton and Ripon 1983-; s of Norman V and Ruby E Watson; *b* 21 Feb 1943; *Educ* Bootham Sch York, Guildford Coll of Law; *m* 1965, Deanna Wood; 1 s, 2 da; *Career* slr 1967, fought (C) York Feb and Oct 1974, PA to Edward Heath 1970, chm Nat Young Cons 1971, former chm Cons Candidates Assoc; MP (C) Skipton 1979-83, memb Parly Select Energy Ctee, pres Br Youth Cncl 1980-83; pps NI Office 1982-83, pps to Alick Buchanan-Smith (Min State Energy) 1983-; dir John Waddington 1979- (joined 1968, md Waddington Games 1977, chief exec security printing div 1983); Master Co of Makers of Playing Cards; *Books* Home from Home (1976), Changing Gear (1981), View from the Terrace (1986); *Recreations* walking, climbing, dining, running; *Style*— John Watson, Esq, MP; 21 Ashley Ct, Westminster, SW1

WATSON, John Henry; s of Henry William Watson (d 1963), and Rose Hannah, *née* Abley (d 1982); *b* 25 Jan 1944; *Educ* Wolverhampton GS; *m* 1966, Marigold Anne, da of Rev William Young Milne, Rector of Malvern Wells; 1 s (decd), 3 da; *Career* articled with Worcester Country Practice 1960-66, mgmnt conslt Touche Ross & Co 1968-71, fin dir Pillsbury UK Ltd 1975-85, sr vice-pres Pillsbury Cunnda Ltd 1985; vice-pres Finance Int The Pillsbury Co USA; FCA; *Recreations* music; *Style*— John Watson, Esq; 1678 The Pillsbury Center, Minneapolis, Minnesota 55402, USA

WATSON, Kenneth Tomalin; CBE (1965); s of John William Watson (d 1959); *b* 14 August 1922; *Educ* Henry Mellish Sch Nottingham, Nottingham Univ Coll; *m* 1948, Gwendoline, da of Henry Park; *Career* chartered civil engr; engr asst and later asst civil engr Air Min Works Directorate 1943-47, engr asst Merton and Morden UDC 1947-48, exec engr HMOCS Nigeria 1949-58, prov engr 1958-59, sr exec Engr 1959-60, progress engr 1960-63; chief engr Miny of Works N Nigeria 1963-67, ret 1967; civil engr BAA 1967-73, sr civil engr 1973-85; ret 1985; FICE; *Clubs* Walton-on-Thames, Conservative; *Style*— Kenneth Watson, Esq, CBE; 1 Mandeville Rd, Shepperton, Middlesex (☎ 0932 224898)

WATSON, Lt-Col Leslie Kenyon; MBE (1944), TD (1944); s of Maj William Ernest Watson, TD (1950), of Gray's Inn Place, and Edith Mary, *née* Kenyon (d 1958); *b* 8 Sept 1906; *Educ* Bradfield Coll, Pembroke Coll Cambridge (MA); *m* 15 June 1929, Josephine Ida (d 1983), da of Edward Gosset-Tanner (d 1922); 2 s (Niall b 1934, Robin b 1941), 1 da (Diana b 1931); *Career* Lt-Col serv RA W Desert, Italy (P.O.W., 4 escapes); architect; town planner; worked under Louis de Soissons, Cyril Farey, Sir Guy Dawber, Sir Giles Scott, Sir Edward Maufe; site architect of Bomber Cmd HQ building 1938; own practice 1950, later in ptnrship with H J Coates; Power Stations at Ferrybridge, Thorpe Marsh, Richborough, Rugeley A and B, offices LEB, offices Tyne Tunnel, New Scotswood Bridge; memb RTPI, FCIArb, jt fndr High Wycombe Arts Assoc 1947, The Assoc of Private Architects 1959, The Doric Club 1973, first chm West Wycombe Parish Cncl 1987; RIBA; *Recreations* hunting, fishing, gardening; *Clubs* The Arts; *Style*— Lt-Col Leslie K Watson, MBE, TD; Silver Birches, W. Wycombe, Bucks HP14 3AH (☎ 0494 27905)

WATSON, Marilyn Jane; da of Edwin John Watson, DFC, of Norfolk, and Mary Irene Love, *née* Willmott; *b* 17 Sept 1952; *Educ* St Mary's Convent Bishop's Stortford, Cambridge Coll of Arts and Technol; *m* 1 s (Luke b 1988); *Career* dir MPR Leedex Gp Ltd (formerly known as MPR Communications Ltd) 1986-; MIPR; *Recreations* sailing, riding, swimming; *Style*— Ms Marilyn Watson; West End House, Hills Place, London W1R 1AG (☎ 01 734 9681, fax 01 734 4913)

WATSON, Martin Yorke; CBE (1948); s of Ven Arthur Herbert Watson (d 1952), formerly Canon of Ripon and Archdeacon of Richmond Yorks, and Louisa Caroline, *née* Yorke (d 1957); *b* 10 Nov 1905; *Educ* Lancing, Ch Ch Oxford (MA); *m* 1936, Ursula Catherine, da of Maj Harold Hunter Grotrian (d 1951), of North Stainley Hall, Ripon; 3 s, 1 da; *Career* entered HM Consular Serv 1928; vice-consul: San Francisco 1928-31, Valparaiso 1931-34; princ 1939-42 and asst sec 1942-45 Miny Economic Warfare, dep dir Jt Intelligence Bureau 1945-58, dir Economic Intelligence MOD 1958-65; *Recreations* gardening, woodworking; *Style*— Martin Watson Esq, CBE; 3 Saxon Way, Saffron Walden, Essex CB11 4EQ (☎ 0799 23069)

WATSON, Col Michael Colvin; OBE (1966), MC (1944), TD, DL (Wilts 1979-86, Gloucs 1986-); s of Lt-Col Forrester Colvin Watson, OBE, MC (d 1951), and Cecilia, *née* Grimston (descended from 1 Earl of Verulam, d 1960); *b* 30 Sept 1918; *Educ* Stowe, Sandhurst; *m* 18 April 1942, Hon (Joan) Sybil, *née* Berry, da of 1 Baron Buckland (d 1928); 1 s (Rupert b 1949), 2 da (Mrs Langsdon b 1946, Virginia b 1951); *Career* cmmnd 17/21 Lancers 1938, ret 1947; cmd Royal Wilts Yeo 1961-65 (joined 1954), Col TAVR 1967-73, ADC (TAVR) to HM The Queen 1969-73, Col 17/21 Lancers 1975-83; High Sheriff Gloucestershire 1981, Vice-Lord Lieut Gloucestershire 1987-;; *Recreations* field sports; *Clubs* Cavalry and Guard's; *Style*— Col M C Watson, OBE, MC, TD, DL; The Dower Hse, Barnsley, Cirencester, Gloucestershire GL7 5EF (☎ 028 574 508)

WATSON, Hon Miles Ronald Marcus; s and h of 3 Baron Manton; (triplet with Hon Thomas and Hon Victoria); *b* 7 May 1958; *Educ* Eton; *Career* Lt Life Guards; *Recreations* shooting, skiing, hunting; *Style*— Lt the Hon Miles Watson

WATSON, Vice Adm Sir Philip Alexander; KBE (1976), LVO (1960); s of Alexander Henry St Croix Watson (d 1963); *b* 7 Oct 1919; *Educ* St Albans Sch; *m* 1948, Jennifer Beatrice, *née* Tanner; 1 s, 2 da; *Career* joined RNVR 1940, transferred to RN 1945, Dir-Gen Weapons (Navy) MOD 1970-77, Vice Adm 1974, Chief Naval Engr Offr 1974-76, ret 1976; Adm Pres Midland Naval Offrs Assoc 1979-85; dir

Marconi Int Marine Co Ltd, naval conslt GEC Marconi Electronics Ltd 1977-85, chm Marconi Radar Systems Ltd 1981-85, conslt to Marconi Gp of Companies 1985-87; *Clubs* Army and Navy; *Style*— Vice Adm Sir Philip Watson, KBE, LVO; The Hermitage, Bodicote, Banbury, Oxon OX15 4BZ

WATSON, Rt Rev Richard Charles Challinor; s of Col Francis William Watson, CB, MC, DL (d 1966), of the Glebe House, Dinton, Aylesbury, Bucks, and Alice Madelein, *née* Collings Wells (d 1952); *b* 16 Feb 1923; *Educ* Rugby, New Coll Oxford, Westcott House Cambridge; *m* 1955, Anna, da of Rt Rev Christopher Maude Chavasse, OBE, MC, MA, DD (d 1962), Bishop of Rochester; 1 s (David b 1956), 1 da (Rachel b 1959); *Career* served WW II Indian Artillery, Capt RA SE Asia 1942-45; curate Stratford E London 1952-53, tutor and chaplain Wycliffe Hall Oxford 1954-57, chaplain Wadham Coll and Oxford Pastorate 1957-61, vicar of Hornchurch 1962-70; examining chaplain to: Bishop of Rochester 1956-61, Bishop of Chelmsford 1962-70; asst rural dean of Havering 1967-70, rector of Burnley 1970-77, bishop suffragan of Burnley 1970-87; *Recreations* reading, gardening; *Clubs* Lansdowne; *Style*— The Rt Rev Richard Watson; 6 Church Rd, Thame, Oxon OX9 3AJ (☎ 0844 213853)

WATSON, Richard James Lea; s of Col William Linton Watson, OBE, IMS (d 1961), and Dorothy Ellen Lea (d 1950); *b* 11 Dec 1928; *Educ* Charterhouse, Cambridge (BA); *m* 1961, Daphne Christian, da of Capt H S Bowlby, RN (d 1977); 1 s (Malcolm b 1966), 1 da (Fiona b 1969); *Career* Lt Malaya; chief exec Construction Div of Norcros Industry (EEC) Ltd; dir Darlington and Simpson Rolling Mills; chm: Crittal Warmlife Ltd, Archtectural Installation Services Ltd, Anglian Building Products Ltd, Crittall Windows Ltd, Crittall Tectonic Ltd, Dow-Mac Concrete Ltd, Security Computing Services Ltd, UBM Glass Ltd; dir Metal Window Federation Ltd; *Recreations* fishing, shooting, local affairs; *Clubs* Oxford and Cambridge; *Style*— Richard Watson, Esq; Stocks, Castle Hedingham, Halstead, Essex; Manor Works, Braintree, Essex CM7 6DF (☎ 0376 24106, telex 98244)

WATSON, Robert John; s of Donald George James Watson, and Nabiha, *née* Bulis; *b* 29 June 1955; *Educ* Sir Walter St John Sch, Oxford Sch of Architecture (BA Dip Arch); *m* 11 Aug 1984, Au, da of Dr Hing Tsung Lam; *Career* ptnr Lam and Watson and Woods Partnership, dir and ptnr First Design Gp, dir Mitrech Ltd; hon consulting architect to London Chinatown Assoc and specialist in traditional Chinese architecture and oriental design; fdr memb Progress Architectural Gp; RIBA; *Recreations* private aviation, vintage transport, speed, futurism; *Style*— Robert Watson, Esq; 23 Rydal Rd, London SW16 (☎ 01 769 5853); Lam, Watson & Woods Architects, Astra House, 19 Clapham High St, London SW4

WATSON, (Lawrence) Roger; s of Lawrence Watson (d 1983), of Alford Lincs, and Alberta Gertrude, *née* Baker; *b* 25 Jan 1941; *Educ* Maidenhead GS; Univ of London (BA); *m* 19 Oct 1963, Sheila, da of Victor Orlando Dandridge (d 1976), of Bourne End Bucks; 1 da (Rachel Helen b 1967), 1 s (Neil Lawrence b 1969); *Career* Insur Co dir; dir: Paramount Insur Co Ltd 1972 (md 1986), Robert A Rushton (life pensions) Ltd; *Recreations* sport, reading, walking; *Style*— Roger Watson, Esq; 202 Beech Rd, St Albans, Herts AL3 5AX (☎ 0727 63367); 188-196 St Albans Rd, Watford, Herts (☎ 0923 37111, car ☎ 359485)

WATSON, Ronald Norman Stewart; s of Kenneth Watson, of Yeovil, Somerset, and Dorothy Fraser, *née* Peat; *b* 12 Feb 1942; *Educ* Tauntons' GS Southampton; *m* 2 Dec 1972, Sally Virginia, da of Arthur John Wilson; 2 s (Ben b 1974, Ross b 1979); *Career* mangr data servs Conoco Europe 1969-74, mgmnt conslt Booz, Allen & Hamilton 1974-76, fin mangr BNOC 1977-83, fin mangr Britoil 1983-86, gp fin dir Hornden Group plc 1987-; FCA 1964; *Recreations* sailing, golf; *Clubs* RNCYC, Cardross GC; *Style*— Ronald Watson, Esq; Howden Group plc, 195 Scotland St, Glasgow G5 8PJ (☎ 041 429 4747, fax 041 429 4244)

WATSON, Prof Stephen Roger; s of John Cole Watson, MBE (d 1987), of Steyning, Sussex, and Marguerite Freda Rose, *née* Seagrief; *b* 29 August 1943; *Educ* Univ Coll Sch Hampstead, Emmanuel Coll Cambridge (BA, MA, PhD); *m* 26 July 1969, Rosemary Victoria, da of Rt Rev Cyril James Tucker, CBE, of Cambridge; 1 s (Oliver b 5 Feb 1972), 1 da (Emily b 18 Feb 1975); *Career* planning asst Shell Int Petroleum Co 1970-71, fell Emmanuel Coll Cambridge 1971- (res fell 1968-70); Cambridge Univ: lectr engrg dept 1971-86, Peat Marwick prof mgmnt studies 1986-; dir Cambridge Descision Analysts 1984-; chm ctee Cambridge Christian Aid; FSS, AFIMA; *Books* Decision Synthesis (with D M Buede, 1988); *Recreations* overseas development, music, singing, politics; *Style*— Prof Stephen Watson; 120 Huntingdon Rd, Cambridge CB3 0HL (☎ 0223 625 36); Management Studies Gp, Cambridge Univ Engineering Dept, Mill Lane, Cambridge CB2 1RX (☎ 0223 388 170, fax 0223 338 076, telex 81239)

WATSON, Steuart Charles; s of Edwin Charles Watson, of 10 Ancrum Gdns, Dundee, and Betty, *née* Cuthbert; *b* 29 June 1952; *Educ* Harris Acad Dundee, Canterbury Sch of Architecture (dip arch); *m* 10 June 1980, Claire-Marie, da of Dr Desmond M Burns (d 1985), of Dundee; *Career* architect, qualified 1977; principal in private practice 1979-80 and 1983-85, conslt architect E African Breweries Ltd 1980-83, ptnr Campbell Watson and Waker Architects and Surveyors 1985-; Br Inst's Prize in Arch awarded by the RA 1975; RIBA; *Recreations* golf; *Style*— Steuart C Watson, Esq; c/o Natwest Bank, 98 High Street, Wimbledon, London SW19 5EJ; Campbell Watson & Walker, 2 Wimpole Street, London W1M 7AA (☎ 01 637 4266, fax 409 0165)

WATSON, Maj-Gen (Henry) Stuart (Ramsay); CBE (1973, MBE 1954); s of Maj Henry Angus Watson, CBE, MVO (d 1952), and Dorothy Bannerman Watson, OBE, *née* Ramsay (d 1968); *b* 9 July 1922; *Educ* Winchester Coll; *m* 1965, Susan, o da of Col William Hall Jackson, CBE, DL, of Barford, nr Warwick; 2 s (Angus b 1967, William b 1969), 1 da (Edwina b 1971); *Career* cmmnd 2 Lt 13/18 Royal Hussars 1942, Lt 1943, Capt 1945, Adjt 13/18 H 1945-46 and 1948-50; psc 1951, GS02 HQ 1 Corps, 1952-53, Instr RMA Sandhurst 1955-57, Instr Staff Coll Camberley 1960-62, CO 13/18 Royal Hussars 1962-64, Col GS, SHAPE 1965-68, Col Def Policy Staff MOD 1968, idc 1969, BGS HQ BAOR 1970-73, Dir Defence Policy MOD 1973-74, Sr Army Directing Staff RCDS 1974-76, Col 13/18 Royal Hussars 1979-; dep dir gen IOD 1985-88 (exec dir 1977-85); *Recreations* golf, gardening, shooting; *Clubs* Cavalry and Guard's; *Style*— Maj-Gen Stuart Watson, CBE; The Glebe House, Little Kimble, Aylesbury, Bucks HP17 0UE (☎ 029661 2200)

WATSON, Lady Susan Diana; *née* Wood; yr da of 2 Earl of Halifax (d 1980); *b* 22 Sept 1938; *m* 10 Oct 1959, Brig Ian Darsie Watson, CBE, TD, s of late Darsie Watson, of Blackeshours, Upper Hartfield, Sussex; 2 s (David Charles Darsie b 1960, Richard Ian b 1962); *Style*— Lady Susan Watson

WATSON, Thomas Alexander (Tom); s of Donald Fletcher Watson, of Bowral, NSW, Aust, and Helen Mary Spedding, *née* Irvine; *b* 17 Sept 1950; *Educ* Grafton HS NSW, Hunters Hill HS NSW, Univ NSW, Sydney, Aust (BA); *m* 23 July 1977, Jennifer, *qv* da of Edward Gordon Eliott; 2 s (James Donald b 1981, Alexander Edward b 1987), 1 da (Laura Helen 1983); *Career* md: Hallmark Mktg Servs Ltd 1984-, Hallmark NCL Communications Ltd 1987-; vice-chm: Wessex Area Inst of PR, Macleod Soc; dir Prince's Youth Business Tst Southern Counties, cncllr Hampshire CC 1981-85, govr Westgate Sch Winchester 1981-85, memb consultancy mgmnt ctee PR Cnslts Assoc 1985; MIPR 1983; *Recreations* yacht racing and cruising, reading, politics; *Clubs* Warsash Sailing; *Style*— Tom Watson, Esq; 21 Northgate Place, Staple Gardens, Winchester SO23 8SR (☎ 0962 63850, fax 0962 841 820, telex 477104)

WATSON, Hon Thomas Philip; 2 s of 3 Baron Manton; (triplet with Hon Miles and Hon Victoria); *b* 7 May 1958; *Educ* Eton, RAC; *Career* Lt QOH TAVR 1981, ret 1981, Lt Yorks Yeo; *Style*— The Hon Thomas Watson

WATSON, Victor Hugo; CBE (1987); s of Norman and Ruby Ernestine Watson; *b* 26 Sept 1928; *Educ* Clare Coll Cambridge (MA); *m* 1952, Sheila *née* Bryan; 2 da; *Career* served Royal Engr, 2 Lt 1946-48; joined Waddingtons 1951, chm John Waddington plc 1977-, chm John Foster and Son plc 1985; dir: Leeds and Holbeck Building Soc 1985, Yorkshire TV 1987; pres Inst of Packaging 1984; *Recreations* sailing, golf, music; *Style*— Victor H Watson, Esq, CBE; John Waddington plc, Wakefield Rd, Leeds LS10 3TP

WATSON, Hon Victoria Monica; da of 3 Baron Manton; *b* 7 May 1958, (triplet, with Hon Miles and Hon Thomas); *Educ* Convent Woldingham; *Career* landscape gardener; *Style*— The Hon Victoria Watson

WATSON-SMYTH, Edward Michael; DFC (1943); s of George Robert Watson-Smyth (d 1968: Capt 13th Hussars, ret) and Madeleine Mary Pedder (d 1971); perfumiers in Bond St W1 1697-1939 Trading as Smyth & Son; James Smyth was a friend of Handel and his home at Wadhurst Castle remained in the family until 1930; *b* 25 Mar 1923; *Educ* Sunningdale Sch Berks, Fettes Coll Edinburgh, Univ of Miami USA; *m* 7 Aug 1954, Monica Amy Merrick, da of Thomas Alderson Scott (d 1951); 1 s (Miles b 1966), 5 da (Melanie b 1955, Madeleine b 1956, Miranda b 1957, Marianne b 1959, Millicent b 1963); *Career* flight Lt RAEVR; navigator: 150 squadron N Africa 1943, (DFC), 161 Sqad Tempsford's 1944-45; chm: Window-Boxes Ltd, Yard Arm Club Ltd, Continuous Laminates Ltd; dir Country House Hotels Ltd, Veritair Ltd; memb of Lloyds; *Recreations* cricket, music, Times Crossword; *Clubs* MCC, Turf; *Style*— Edward Watson-Smyth, DFC; Middle Hill Park, Broadway, Worcs (☎ 0386 858888); 5 Melina Place, London NW8 9SA

WATT; *see*: Harvie-Watt

WATT, Col Alexander James; MBE (1942), TD (1948, JP 1972, DL (1988); s of Maj James Watt, MC, DL (d 1975), of Dest Linton, Peebleshire, and Emily, *née* Burns (d 1972); *b* 3 May 1915; *Educ* Royal HS Edinburgh, Leys Sch Cambridge; *m* 15 March 1946, Margaret Laura Evelyn, da of Lt Col John Gibson Anderson (d 1955), of Edinburgh; 2 s (James b 1947, Ian b 1953), 1 da (Pamela b 1950); *Career* WWII joined London Scottish 1939, cmmnd Black Watch 1940, 51 Highland Div, Served: N Africa, Sicily, Normandy, Holland, Germany; demob 1946; Maj 6/7 Bn Black Watch TA (Lt-Col cmdg 1956-60, Hon Col 1/51 Bn Highland Volunteers 1976-80; chm and md McEwens Perth 1982; involved locally with the Order of St John, hospitaller for Scotland KStJ 1981; FSA (Scotland) 1974; *Recreations* fishing; *Clubs* Royal Golf (Perth), Army and Navy; *Style*— Col Alexander Watt, MBE, TD, JP, DL; Ballanquhal House, Glenfarg, Perthshire PH2 9QD (☎ 057 73 261)

WATT, Arthur Alexander; *b* 22 May 1940; *Educ* George Heriot's Sch Edinburgh, Falkirk H S; *m* 1, 1965 (dis 1977), Judith Mary, nee Mangles; 2 s, 1 da; *m* 2, 1979; *Career* chartered accountant, gp md Aurora Holdings Ltd 1974-, gp fin dir Cooper & Turner Ltd 1971-74, consultant PA Management Consultants Ltd 1968-71; *Recreations* running, climbing, squash; *Clubs* Oriental; *Style*— Arthur Watt Esq; Priory Farmhouse, S Leverton, Notts (☎ 0427 880250)

WATT, Hew Matthew Brown; OBE (1973), JP (Essex 1951); s of William Orr Watt (d 1949), of Heath Place, Orsett, Grays, Essex and Jeanie, *née* Dunlop (d 1951); *b* 16 Sept 1915; *Educ* Palmers GS Grays Essex, Essex Inst of Agric; *m* 9 Oct 1937, Molly Annie, da of William John Payne (d 1972), of Gaypenant, Lodge Lane, Grays, Essex; 1 da (Dr Trudy Watt b Jan 1953); *Career* Lt Army Cadet Corp 1941-45; agric broadcaster and writer 1951-, chm Thurrock Licensing Ctee 1961-85, memb Agric Advsy Ctee BBC 1964-76, agric visits to 22 countries incl China and Soviet Union 1967-86, dep chm Thurrock Bench 1970-85, memb Guild Agric Journalists 1970-, chm Apple & Pear Devpt Cncl 1972-77, memb Nature Conservancy Cncl 1972-82; memb and pres Thurrock Rotary Club 1947-, organiser Orsett Agric Show 1950-71, tres and deacon Orsett Congregational Church 1964-, memb and pres Farmers Club London 1964-, fndr chm: Thurrock Christian Social Cncl 1965-75, chm Thurrock Marriage Guidance Cncl 1968-75, vice-pres Royal Agric Benevolent Inst; Freeman City of London, Liveryman Worshipful Co Fruiterers 1977; fell Royal Agric Socs 1985; *Recreations* talking, live theatre; *Style*— Hew Watt, Esq, OBE, JP; Wingfield Cottage, Prince Charles Ave, Orsett, Grays, Essex RM16 3HS

WATT, Iain Alasdair; s of Andrew Watt, FRCSE, of Edinburgh, and Margaret Fawns, *née* Brown (d 1967); *b* 30 Mar 1945; *Educ* Edinburgh Acad, Hull Univ (BSc); *m* 30 Jun 1971, Lynne Neilson, da of Harold Livingston (d 1984), of Kirkcaldy; 3 s (Nicholas b 1973, Christopher Nial b 1975, Oliver Noel b 1980), 1 da (Gemma Stephanie Margaret b 1985); *Career* with Bank of Scotland 1964-86; dir British Liwen Bank 1986-; other directoring inc: Crescent Japan Invest Tst, New Tokyo Invest Tst, Euro Assets Tst NV, Continental Assets Tst, EFM Dragon Tst, Edinburgh Fund Managers; memb Cncl Queens Nursing Inst in Scotland; AIB; *Recreations* tennis, golf; *Clubs* N Berwick Golf, Aberdour Tennis, Dean Tennis; *Style*— I A Watt, Esq; Sycamore Bank, North Queensferry, Fife (☎ 0383 413645); 4 Melville Crescent, Edinburgh (☎ 031 226 4931, fax 031 226 2359, telex 72453)

WATT, Ian Glendinning; s of Edward Glendinning Watt (d 1974), of Eastbourne, and Violet Isabel, *née* Eeley; *b* 6 Dec 1932; *Educ* Eastbourne Coll; *m* 27 Sept 1958, Pauline Ann, da of Bertram Roy Shaw (d 1972), of Fareham; 1 s (Jonathan b 1962), 1 da (Louise b 1963); *Career* CA 1957-; ptnr: KMG Thomson McLintock 1963-1987 (chm 1987), Peat Marwick McLintock 1987-,jt liquidator Rolls Royce Ltd 1977; DTI inspr: Alexander Howden Gp plc 1982, Guinness plc 1986; FCA; *Recreations* fishing, cricket, golf; *Clubs* MCC, Caledonian, Royal Ashdown Forest GC; *Style*— Ian Watt,

Esq; Rough Acre, Furners Green, Uckfield, Sussex TN22 3RP (☎ 082 574 392); Peat Marwick McLintock, 1 Puddle Dock, Blackfriars, London EC4V 3PD (☎ 01 236 8000, telex 8811541 PMM LONG)

WATT, Surgn Vice Adm Sir James; KBE (1975); s of Thomas Watt (d 1944), and Sarah Alice, *née* Clarkson; *b* 19 August 1914; *Educ* King Edward VI Sch Morpeth, Durham Univ (MB BS, MS), Univ of Newcastle (MD); *Career* joined RN as Surgn Lt RNVR 1941; served: HMS Emerald Far East, HMS Roxborough N Atlantic 1943, HMS Asbury USA 1944, HMS Arbiter Pacific 1945, Surgn Lt Cdr, demobbed 1946; rejoined RN as surgical registrar RN Hosp Haslar 1948; surgical specialist: NI 1949, HM Hosp Ship Maine (Korean War) 1951, RN Hosp Hong Kong 1954; conslt in surgery: RN Hosp Plymouth 1956 (Surgn Cdr), RN Hosp Haslar 1959, RN Hosp Malta 1961, RN Hosp Haslar 1963, Surgn Capt and first jt prof of naval surgery RCS and RN Hosp Haslar 1965, Surgn Rear Adm first dean of naval medicine and med offr i/c New Inst of Naval Medicine 1969, Surgn Vice Adm and med dir gen of the Navy 1972, ret 1977; visiting fell Univ House Aust Nat Univ Canberra 1986; author of numerous papers on: surgery, burns injury, hyperbaric oxygen therapy, christian ethics, med aspects of the history of sea warfare, voyages of discovery, the slave trade and the founding of Aust; pres: Med Soc of London 1980-81 (tstee 1983-), Royal Soc of Medicine 1982-84; vice pres: Soc for Nautical Res, Churches Cncl for Health and Healing 1988-; pres Inst of Religion and Medicine 1989-; chm bd of tstees Naval Christian Fellowship 1968-75, tstee Royal Sailors Rests 1972-81, pres RN Lay Readers Soc 1974-83; Erroll Eldridge Prize 1968, Gilbert Blane Gold Medal 1971; Hon Freeman Worshipful Co of Barbers 1978, hon memb Smeatonian Soc of Civil Engrs 1978; Hon FRCS Edinburgh 1976, Hon DCh Newcastle 1978; FRCS, FRCP, FRSM, FICS, FRGS, fell Assoc of Surgns of GB & Ireland; *Books* Starving Sailors (ed 1981), Talking Health: Conventional and Complementary Approaches (ed 1988); *Recreations* mountain walking; *Clubs* English Speaking Union; *Style*— Surgeon Vice Adm Sir James Watt, KBE

WATT, James Muir; OBE (1968); s of James Watt (d 1944), of Ayr, Scotland and Hove, Sussex, and Mary Hewitt, *née* Muir (d 1971); *b* 13 July 1909; *Educ* Glasgow HS, Glasgow Univ (MA), Balliol Coll Oxford (MA); *m* 28 June 1940, Merlyn Keigwin Duncombe, da of Capt Frederick Duncombe Mann, of Kent and Somerset; 4 da (Betty b 1943, Barbara b 1946, Horatia b 1957, Julia b 1961); *Career* gunner 97 HAA Regt 1940, non cmmnd ranks to SSM 1940-43, staff appts: Lt, Capt, Maj 1943-45; Maj i/c Statistical Branch Northern Cmd; barr Inner Temple 1935, asst (later dep sec) Chartered Auctioneers and Estate Agents Inst 1946-70, sec Livestock Autioneers Market Ctee for England and Wales 1970-73, legal advsr and vice-pres London Rent Assessment Panel 1973-82; chm St Margarets Sch for Girls Hampstead 1952-80; ARICS 1973, hon memb CAAV 1973; *Books* Agricultural Holidays (Latest Edn 1987), jt ed 11 edn Megarry's Rent Accts (1988); *Recreations* reading, walking; *Clubs* Naval and Military; *Style*— James Watt Esq, OBE; 47 Fort Street, Ayr, Scotland, KA7 1DH (☎ 0292 283 102)

WATT, Capt Kenneth Rupert; s of Gerald Allingham Watt, of Thornhill, Co Londonderry, NI, and Gladys Kathleen, *née* Macky; *b* 12 Sept 1914; *Educ* Malvern, Sandhurst, Trinity Coll Cambridge, (MA); *m* 1946, Elizabeth, da of Capt Edward Hodgson, of Barnfield, Cowfold, Sussex; *Career* regular soldier 15/19 The King's Royal Hussars, active Serv France, invalided 1945; in Tattersalls sr ptnr 1951-85 (currently and chief Shareholder); landowner, salmon fishery owner, shoot and bird reserve owner; Lord of the Manor of Boulge (Suffolk); *Recreations* hunting, polo, shooting, fishing, music, opera, wildlife, sanctuary (private); *Clubs* White's, Cavalry; *Style*— Capt Kenneth Watt; Dingle Estate, Dunwich, Suffolk, Barclays, Cambridge; Tattersalls, Terrace House, New Market, Suffolk

WATT, Hon Mrs (Mary); *née* Mackintosh; da of 1 Viscount Mackintosh of Halifax (d 1964); *b* 1927; *m* 1949, (Charles) Michael Watt; 2 s (Charles b 1950, Henry b 1962), 1 da (Susan b 1953); *Career* JP Norfolk, chm Norwich Juvenile Ct 1978-82; dir: Thick Thorn Farm Ltd, dir The Constance Spry and Cordon Bleu Gp Ltd; *Recreations* horse racing; *Clubs* Jockey Club Rooms; *Style*— The Hon Mrs Watt; Wychwood House, Hethersett, nr Norwich, Norfolk NR9 3AT

WATT, Dr Robert Mackay; s of Robert Mackay Watt, of Southfield Cottage, Summerfield Rd, Dunbar, Scotland, and Helen Good, *née* Pollock (d 1975); *b* 5 Feb 1941; *Educ* Aberdeen Gs, Manchester GS, Univ of Edinburgh (BSc, MB, ChB, PhD, Dip Comm Med); *m* 28 June 1969, Christine Wendy, da of James Clifford Gregory, of Innisfree, 10 Outgaits Close, Hunmanby, Filey, Yorks; 2 s (Andrew b 1970, Mark b 1972); *Career* lectr in physiology Edinburgh Univ Med Sch 1970-75 (fell in community med 1975-77), superintending inspr Cruelty to Animals Act 1876 1984-87 (inspr 1977-84), chief inspr Animals (Scientific Procedures) Act 1987-; CBiol, FIBiol 1989; *Recreations* painting, model making, wood carving, DIY, aviation; *Style*— Dr Robert Watt; Home Office, Animals (Scientific Procedures) Inspectorate, 50 Queen Anne's Gate, London SW1H 9AT (☎ 01 273 2347)

WATT, Prof William Smith; s of John Watt, and Agnes, *née* Smith; *b* 20 June 1913; *Educ* Univ of Glasgow (MA), Balliol Coll Oxford; *m* 7 July 1944, Dorothea, da of Robert James Codington Smith; 1 s (Robert b 1951); *Career* lectr in greek Univ of Glasgow 1937-38; Balliol Coll Oxford: fell and tutor in classics 1938-52, lectr latin lit 1947-52; civilian offr admty Naval Intelligence Div 1941-45; Univ of Aberdeen: regius prof of humanity 1952-79, curator of library 1954-59, dean of faculty of arts 1963-66; Univ Ct 1966-77, vice-princ 1969-72; chm governing body Aberdeen Coll of Educn 1971-75 (vice-chm 1964-67, govr 1959-75); memb: Scottish Cncl for Trg of Teachers 1955-67, Gen Teaching Cncl 1967-71, 1975-78, Scottish Univs Cncl on Entrance 1968-77 (convener 1973-77); pres Scottish Classical Assoc 1983-88,; *Books* Ciceronis Epistulae (vol 3 1958, vol 21 1965, vol 1 1982), George Buchanan's Miscellaneorum Liber (jtly 1982), Vellei Paterculi Historiae (1988); *Clubs* Aberdeen Business and Professional; *Style*— Prof William Watt; 38 Woodburn Grdns, Aberdeen AB1 8JA (☎ 0224 314 369)

WATTERS, James Andrew Donaldson; s of Andrew James Watters, of Dumfriesshire, and Elsa Donaldson, *née* Broatch; *b* 16 Mar 1948; *Educ* Kings Coll Sch Wimbledon, Pembroke Coll Oxford (BA); *m* 27 July 1973, Lesley Jane Aves, da of Cyril Joseph Churchman (d 1963); 2 s (Alexander b 4 March 1978, Rupert b 11 June 1980), 1 da (Flora b 16 May 1985); *Career* articled clerk and slr Stephenson Harwood 1970-75, slr Norton Rose Botterell & Roche 1976-79, sr legal advsr Investors in Industry plc 1980-82, ptnr Goodwille & Co 1982-85, ptnr Stephenson Harwood 1985-; Freeman: City of London, Worhipful Co Slrs, memb Law Soc 1972; *Style*— James Watters, Esq; 59 De Beauvoir Rd, London N1 5AU (☎ 01 254 9221); Stephenson Harwood, 1 St Pauls Churchyard, London EC4M 8SH (☎ 01 329 4422, fax 01 606 0822, telex 886789)

WATTS, Anthony Venning; s of William Andrews Watts (d 1954), and Dorothy, *née* Moody; *b* 30 Dec 1933; *Educ* Hymers Coll Hull, Sch of Architecture Hull Coll of Art (Dip Arch); *m* 28 March 1959, Patricia, da of Wilfred Edgar Blake; 3 s (Jonathan b 14 Nov 1961, Andrew b 2 Feb 1963, Matthew b 16 Jan 1966) ; *Career* architect; ptnr Fisher Hollingsworth Ptnrship Hull; vice chm Hull Missions to Seamen; memb RIBA 1959; *Books* The Humber (1980); *Recreations* sailing, golf, watercolour painting; *Clubs* Humber Yawl, Hull Golf; *Style*— Anthony Watts, Esq; Greenways, Seven Corners Lane, Beverley, Humberside (☎ 0482 882 269); Fisher Hollingsworth Partnership, Haworth House, Clough Road, Hull (☎ 0428 41 455, fax 0428 45 768)

WATTS, Sir Arthur Desmond; KCMG (1989, CMG 1977), QC (1988); s of Col Arthur Edward Watts (d 1958), and Eileen May, *née* Challons (d 1981); *b* 14 Nov 1931; *Educ* Haileybury, RMA Sandhurst, Downing Coll Cambridge (MA, LLB, Whewell Scholar in Int Law); *m* 1957, Iris Ann; 1 s (Christopher), 1 da (Catherine); *Career* called to the Bar Gray's Inn 1957, legal asst FO 1957-59, legal advsr Br Property Cmmn (later Br Embassy) Cairo 1959-62, asst legal advsr FO 1962-67, legal advsr Br Embassy Bonn 1967-69, asst slr Law/Offrs Dept 1969-70, legal cnsllr FCO 1970-73, cnsllr (legal advsr) Office of UK permanent rep to EEC 1973-77, legal cnsllr FCO 1977-82, dep legal advsr FCO 1982-87 and legal advsr 1987-; *Books* Legal Effects of War (4th edn with Lord McNair, 1966), Encyclopaedic Dictionary of Int Law (jt ed 1986); contributions to: Br Year Book Int Law, Int and Comparative Law Quarterly, Egyptian Review of Int Law; *Style*— Sir Arthur Watts, KCMG; Foreign and Cwlth Office, Whitehall, London SW1

WATTS, Christopher Charles Philip; s of Rev Bertram Philip Knight Watts (d 1978), and Ethel Mary, *née* Palmer; unc Sir Henry Lumby of Ormskirk, Lord Lieut of Lancs; *b* 21 Jan 1943; *Educ* St John's Leatherhead, Northern Poly London (Dip Arch); *m* 5 Sept 1964, Anne Elizabeth, da of George Richard Harding; 1 da (Melanie-Ann b 1969); *Career* architect of TV Station (Superchannel), TV Technical Facilities Sound Recording Studios (Virgin Olympic); designer patentee of Frolic fun boat; *Recreations* mountains, art; *Style*— Christopher C P Watts, Esq; Tressan House, Chapmans Lane, Deddington, Oxon OX5 4SU (☎ 0869 38883), car telephone 0860 343641

WATTS, Christopher Nigel Stuart; s of Maj Ronald Watts (d 1982), of Carlisle, and Eva Maria-Louise Gliese; *b* 6 Mar 1954; *Educ* Univ of Aberdeen (MA); *m* 24 Dec 1986, Nicola Clare, da of Wilfred Albert Mason; *Career* slr 1980, ptnr Rutherfords of Tamworth, Birmingham, and dir Mason-Watts Fine Art; legal memb Mental Health Cmmn; *Recreations* theatre, opera; *Clubs* Lansdowne; *Style*— Christopher Watts, Esq; 16 Lansdowne Circus, Leamington Spa, Warwicks; Drystones, Stainton, Cumbria (☎ 0926 316192); 112 High St, Coleshill, Birmingham, W Mids B46 3BL (☎ 0675 63855, car 0860 305 271)

WATTS, Maj David Glynn Tracey; s of William John Vicary Watts, JP (d 1972), of The Firs, Newton Abbot, Devon, and Ella Winifred, *née* Bonsall (d 1962); *b* 28 July 1924; *Educ* Clifton; *Career* 2 Lt France 1944 (wounded), regular cmmn 3 The King's Own Hussars 1945, served: Palestine, Middle East, Germany, UK; Adj 1947-49, Staff Capt WO 1950-52, GSO3 London Div 1954-56, Maj 1956, 2 i/c The Queen's Own Hussars 1962, ret 1964; former memb Devon CC (representing Dartmouth and serving on various ctees); dir and hon sec Devon and Exeter Race course, cncl memb and vice pres Devon Co Agric Assoc 1979-, govr Royal West of England Sch for the Deaf, memb mgmnt ctee Exeter Hosp Aid Soc; *Recreations* racing, shooting, gardening, travel, antiques; *Clubs* Cavalry; *Style*— Maj David Watts; Charlecombe, Combe-In-Teignhead, Nr Newton Abbot, Devon TQ12 4RE (☎ 0626 872 359)

WATTS, Geoffrey Alan Howard; s of Arthur Josiah Watts (d 1977), and Mary Louise *née* Baber; *b* 26 August 1921; *Educ* Wycliffe Coll, Glasgow Univ (BSc Eng); *m* 28 May 1955, Phyllis Mary, da of James Joseph Harris (d 1977); 2 s (John b 1956, Arthur b 1965), 2 da (Louise b 1958, Rebecca b 1961); *Career* WWII RNVR HMS Hunter (air eng offr) serv India and Malaya 1942-46; chief engr Red & White Services 1947, dir: Utd Tport Co Ltd 1948-82, Uganda Tport Co Ltd 1953-63, Kenya Bus Serv Ltd 1953-63, African Tport Co ltd 1954-63, Rhodesia Omnibus Co 1953-63, Bulwark Tport Co ltd 1963-82, BET 1976-82, Electrical Press Ltd 1982-87, num current dirships inc: Lloyds Bank Ltd S Wales 1977-, BET plant Servs 1982-, Edison Plant Ltd 1982-, Watts of Lydney Gp 1949-; vice pres Wycliffe Coll Inc 1965-; dir St John's-on-the -Hill Sch tst ltd 1965-, BSc Eng, FCIT, FInst Nuc Eng, MIME; *Recreations* tennis, squash, golf, sailing, skiing, swimming, flying; *Clubs* Lansdowne, St Pierre, Cardiff Business; *Style*— Geoffrey Watts, Esq; Stroat House, Stroat, Glos NP6 7LR (☎ 0594 52330); Watts of Lydney Gp Ltd, High St, Lydney, Glos

WATTS, Gerald Edward; s of Reginald Edward Watts, of West Huntspill, Somerset, and late Gladys May, *née* Hussey; *b* 21 Oct 1934; *Educ* Blundell's, Selwyn Coll Cambridge (MA); *m* 1, 16 Aug 1958 (m dis 1981), Anne, da of Thomas Henry Clarke (d 1965), of Battlefields, Bath; 2 da (Philippa Anne, Susannah Jane); m 2, 21 Dec 1981, Barbara Ann, da of Oliver Rawson (d 1952) of Swindon; *Career* headmaster: Malsis Sch Cross Hills Keighley Yorks 1965-75, Hawtreys Savernake Forest Marlborough 1975-; athletics for Cambridge Univ and Western Cos; cricket for MCC, I Zingari and Free Foresters, rugby for Blackheath, Bath, Bedford and Headingley; cncl memb St Christopher's Sch Burnham-on-Sea; *Recreations* collecting prints, sporting, ephemera, golf; *Clubs* Hawks, MCC; *Style*— Gerald Watts, Esq; Hawtreys, Savernake Forest, Marlborough, Wilts; (☎ 0672 870331)

WATTS, John Arthur; MP (C) Slough 1983-; *b* 19 April 1947; *Educ* Bishopshalt GS, Hillingdon, Gonville Caius Coll Cambridge (MA); *m* 1974, Susan Jennifer, *née* Swan; 1 s, 3 da; *Career* CA, under sec Parly and Law Affairs Inst of CA in Eng and Wales, former chm Cambridge Univ Cons Assoc, chm Uxbridge Cons Assoc 1973-76, memb: Hillingdon Boro Cncl 1973-86 (former dep ldr and leader of oppn) ldr 1978-84, Treasy and CS Select Ctee 1986, Cncl of Brunel Univ, Uxbridge and Hillingdon Health Authy; PPS to Min Housing and Construction 1984-85, Min of State Treasy 1985; FCA; *Style*— John Watts, Esq, MP; House of Commons, London SW1

WATTS, (William) John Bonsall; s of William John Vickery Watts, JP (d 1972), of The Firs, Neton Abbot, Devon, and Ella Winifred, *née* Bonsall; *Educ* Leighton Park Sch Reading; *m* 1940, Myrae Gertrude; 1 s (William John Christpher b 8 Jan 1949); *Career* serv WWII RNVR; dir (later pres) Watts Blake Beame & Co plc; chm Teignmouth Harbour Cmmn, memb Newton Abbot UDC, capt and pres Teignmouth GC, memb Trinity House Pilot Cmmn; Br Legion Gold Medal awarded for servs rendered; memb CBI; *Recreations* golf, shooting, conservation, gardening; *Style—* John Watts, Esq; Coombe Hatch, Bishopsteignton, Teighmouth, Devon (☎ 0626 775 228); Watts Blake Bearne & Co plc, Park House, Newton Abbot, Devon (☎ 0626 52 345)

WATTS, Col John Cadman; OBE (1959), MC (1945); 21 Feb 1938, Joan Lilian, da of Maj Charles Inwood, OBE, MC (d 1944); 3 s John Inwood Michael b 1941, Jeremy Christopher b 1945, Richard Charles b 1947); 1 da (Stephanie Carol b 1938); *b* 13 April 1913; *Career* cmmnd Lt RAMC 1937, Surgical Specialist: 2/s CCS Palestine 1938, Western Desert 1939-41, 8 Gen Hosp Alexandria 1941, 9 Gen Hosp Cairo 1942, 2 CCS Syria 1942, 3 CCS WDF 1943; Offr cdr 31 FSU Italy 1943-44, Surgical Specialist 1944, DADMS 6 Airburne Div 1944 (despatches 1944), CO 225 Para FD AMB Malaya, Java 1945-46 (despatches 1946), CO 195 Para FD AMR Palestine 1946-47, Surgical Specialist BCOF Hosp Japan 1950-57, Adust in Surgery Br Troops Austria 1953-55, Surgical Specialist Cyprus 1955-59, prof of mil surgery Royal Coll & Surgns England 1960-64; conslt surgn Bedford Cen Hosp 1965-76, cncl memb BMA 1969-76, cmmr St John Ambulance Bedford 1966-68, chm Armed Forces Ctee BMA 1977-80, OStJ 1968; pres E Suffolk BMA 1982-84; LRCP 1936, FRCS Eng 1949; *Books* Surgeon at War (1955); *Recreations* sailing, gardening; *Clubs* Deben Yacht Utd Hosp Sailing; *Style—* Colonel Watts; Lowood Lodge, Hasketon, Woodbridge, Suffolk (☎ 047 335 326)

WATTS, John Clifford; s of Clifford Watts, master builder, of Hull, and Edith, *née* Fenby (d 1972); *b* 13 June 1933; *Educ* Hull GS, Hull Coll of Technol; *m* 1954, Marion Edith, da of John Holroyd (d 1983), of Hull; 2 s (Christopher, Nicholas); *Career* chm and md Lovell Construction Ltd and subsidiaries, dir Y J Lovell (Hldgs) plc; gp chief exec John E Witshier Gp plc; *Recreations* flying (holder of private pilot's licence); *Clubs* IOD; *Style—* John Watts, Esq; 11 West Drive, Sonning, nr Reading, Berks (☎ 0734 695789); Manor Court, Harmondsworth, Middx (☎ 01 759 331; fax 01 564 7545)

WATTS, Lesley Mary; *née* Samuel; da of Prof Eric Samuel, CBE, of S Africa, and Uera Eileen; *b* 19 Sept 1953; *Educ* Cheltenham Ladies Coll, Cambridge Univ (MA); *m* 1983, Ian Roscoe, s of William Watts, of Lancs; *Career* dir Kleinwort Benson Ltd; *Recreations* fly fishing, piano, collector of comtemporary art; *Style—* Mrs Lesley Watts; Kleinwort Benson Ltd, 20 Fenchurch Street, London EC3 (☎ 01-623-8000)

WATTS, Rev Michael; s of Henry Moseley Watts (d 1959), of Gloucester, and Kathleen Evelyn, *née* Powell (d 1981); *b* 18 Jan 1932; *Educ* Sir Thomas Rich's Sch Gloucester, St David's Univ Coll Lampeter (BA), St Catherine's Coll Oxford (BA, MA), St Stephen's House Oxford; *Career* asst curate St Michael Summertown Oxford 1958-60, chaplain and precentor Christ Church Oxford 1960-80, admin asst to Dean of Christ Church 1969-80, gen sec Soc for the Maintenance of the Faith 1983-, rector Sulhamstead Abbots Berks 1980-, warden Burnham Abbey Bucks 1988-, priest vicar Westminster Abbey 1982-87; chaplain to the County High Sheriff Berks 1984; *Books* Christ Church Oxford (1971), The Life of Christ (1975), Oxford City and University (1974), Pope John Paul II - His Life and Travels (1979); *Recreations* music, church architecture; *Style—* The Rev Michael Watts; The Rectory, Ufton Nervet, Reading RG7 4DH (☎ 073 529 2328)

WATTS, Reginald John; s of Wilfred John Lionel Watts (d 1963), and Julia Doris Watts; *b* 28 Jan 1931; *Educ* Bishops Stortford Coll; Susan Roscoe Watts; 2 children; *Career* chm Burson Marsteller 1968-85, fndr chm Reginald Watts Assoc 1985-; cncllr Southend Borough Cncl 1954-63, cncllr Westminster City Cncl 1974-82, Dep Lord Mayor City of Westminster 1981-82; hon sr visiting fell City Univ Business Sch, memb CBI London Regnl Cncl, chm BIM Public Affairs Ctee, govnr London Festival Ballet, pres Inst PR 1989; FIPR; *Books* Public Relations for Top Management Reaching the Consumer, The Businessman's Guide to Marketing, The Corporate Revolution; *Recreations* art, ballet, polo, squash; *Clubs* Carlton; *Style—* Reginald Watts, Esq; Reginald Watts Assoc Ltd, 1-11 Hay Hill, London W1X 7LF (☎ 01 491 2121, fax 01 409 1424)

WATTS, Roy; CBE (1978); *b* 17 August 1925; *Educ* Doncaster GS, Edinburgh Univ (MA); *m* 1951, Jean Rosaline; 1 s, 2 da; *Career* Army 1943-47, cmmnd Sandhurst; joined BEA 1955, chm European Airlines 1982; former dep chm and chief exec BEA 1972-74, BEA 1974-77; chm: Thames Water Authy 1983-, Cabeltime Installations Ltd 1984, Armstrong Equipment plc; Water Aid 1984; dep chm: Brymen Airways; jt dep chm BA Bd 1980-83; (memb 1974-83); FCIPEA, FRAeS, FCIT, Hon DBA 1987; *Recreations* cricket, squash; *Clubs* Reform; *Style—* Roy Watts, Esq, CBE; Thames Water Authority, Thorny House, 34 Smith Square, London, SW1P 3HF

WATTS, Thomas (Tom) Rowland; CBE (1978); s of Thomas William Watts (d 1947), of Colchester, and Daisy Maud Watts, *née* Bultitude (d 1949); *b* 1 Jan 1917; *Educ* Gresham's Sch Holt Norfolk; *m* 1955, (Hester) Zoë, da of William Kenrick Armitstead (d 1961), of Colchester; 1 s (Nigel), 2 da (Felicity, Claudia); *Career* TA 1939-41, RM 1941-46, Capt; CA; ptnr Price Waterhouse until retirement 1982 (joined as an articled clerk 1934); dir Jarrold and Sons Ltd Norwich 1982-87; chm: Accounting Standards Ctee (UK and I) 1978-82, EEC Ctees of Accountancy Profession 1974-79; advsr Dept of Trade on EEC Co Law 1974-82; pres D'honneur Gp d'etudes des Experts Comptables de la Cee 1979-87 (vice-pres 1975-79), chm: EEC Liason Ctee of UK Accountancy Bodies 1985-, Dental Rates Study Gp 1982-85; gen cmmr for Income Tax 1986-; hon visiting prof City of London Poly 1983-87, Laureate Founding Socs Centenary Award 1982; author and editor various professional books and papers; *Recreations* travel, music, opera costume designs; *Style—* Tom Watts Esq, CBE; 13 Fitzwalter Road, Colchester, Essex CO3 3SY (☎ Colchester 573520); 29 Capstan Square, Isle of Dogs, London E14

WATTS, His Hon Judge Victor Brian; s of Percy William King Watts Esq, of 77 Harland Rd, Lee SE12 (d 1981), and Doris Milicent *née* Peat (d 1971); *b* 7 Jan 1927; *Educ* Coffe's GS, Univ Coll Oxford (MA, BCL); *m* 21 July 1965, Patricia Eileen, da of Richard Cuthbert Steer Ferndown, Dorset (d 1982); 1 s (Martin b 1969), 1 da (Julia b 1967); *Career* Flying Offr RAF educn branch 1950-52; barr Middle Temple 1950; memb Western circuit; rec Crown Ct 1972- 80; circuit judge 1980; *Recreations* the arts, tennis, walking; *Clubs* Hurlingham; *Style—* His Honour Judge Victor Watts; 28 Abinger Rd, Bedford Park, London W4 1EL (☎ 01 994 4435)

WATTS-FARMER, Air Cdre James Nigel; DFC (1940); s of James Watts-Farmer (d 1947), of Howle Manor, Newport, Salop, and Caroline Betrice, *née* Clayton (d 1978); *b* 11 Mar 1915; *Educ* Shrewsbury; *m* 3 May 1941, Joé Barbara Gabrielle, da of Capt Archibald Goodman Frazer-Nash, RFC (d 1965), of Ardua, Kingston Hill, Surrey; 2 s (Peter b 1947, Michael b 1950); *Career* regular offr RAF 1935-60, Air Cdre Battle of Br Clasp & Burma Star (despatches thrice) and other campaign medals, inc Defence Cdr Calcutta, India; farmer 1960-84 (ret); RAF show jumping, home and abroad, winner HM Queen's Cup Windsor & Inter-Serv; *Recreations* hunting, show jumping, racing, sailing; *Clubs* RAF Piccadilly; *Style—* Air Cdre James Watts-Farmer, DFC; Field House, Morston Rd, Blakeney, Norfolk

WATTS-RUSSELL, David O'Reilly; s of Cdr Neville David Watts-Russell (d 1961), and Jean, *née* McNair (d 1974); *see* Burkes Landed Gentry 18 edn vol II; *b* 21 Jan 1944; *Educ* Gordonstoun; *m* 5 April 1974, Susan; 1 s (Edward David b 1976), 3 da (Miranda Jane b 1980, Emily Susan b 1983, Tabitha Rose b 1986); *Career* dir Greig, Middleton & Co Ltd 1986-, bd memb Ayshire and Arran Health Bd 1987-; *Recreations* music, reading, shooting, fishing, travel; *Clubs* Western (Glasgow), Glasgow Arts; *Style—* David Watts-Russell, Esq; Glenlogan, Sorn, Mauchline, Ayshire KA5 6JP; 70 Wellington St G2 6SB, Glasgow

WAUGH, Auberon Alexander; s of Evelyn Waugh, the novelist, by his 2 w Laura da of Hon Aubrey Herbert, 2 s of 4 Earl of Carnarvon; *b* 17 Nov 1939; *Educ* Downside, Christ Church Oxford; *m* 1961, Lady Teresa Onslow, da of 6 Earl of Onslow, KBE, MC; 2 s (Alexander b 1963, Nathaniel b 1968), 2 da (Sophia b 1962, Daisy b 1967); *Career* served Royal Horse Guards 1957-58; journalist and novelist; formerly with: Catholic Herald, Mirror Group, Times; former chief fiction reviewer Evening Standard 1973-80; columnist: Private Eye 1970-86, The Spectator 1976- (chief fiction reviewer 1970-73), The Sunday Telegraph 1981; chief book reviewer Daily Mail 1981-; former contributor Books and Bookmen; stood for N Devon 1979 Gen Election as Dog Lovers Party Candidate; Ed of Literary Review 1986 Nat Press Critic of the Year Commendations 1976, 1978; Granada TV What the Papers Say 1979; *Books* Foxglove Saga (1960), Who are the Violets Now? (1966), A Bed of Flowers (1971), Four Crowded Years (Diaries of f 1976), The Diaries of Waugh 1976-85 (1985), Waugh on Wine (1986); *Recreations* gossip, wine; *Style—* Auberon Waugh Esq; Combe Florey House, Combe Florey, Taunton, Somerset (☎ 0823 432297)

WAUGH, Rev Eric Alexander; s of Hugh Waugh, of 73 Philip Ave, Linlithgow, Scotland, and Marion, *née* McLay (d 1972); *b* 9 May 1933; *Educ* Glasgow Univ, Edinburgh Univ (LTh); *m* 26 Aug 1955, Agnes-Jean (Sheena), da of James Renton Saunders (d 1985); 2 s (Euan b 1959, Eric James b 1961); *Career* local govt offr 1948-64, asst minster High Church Bathgate 1969-70, missionary Kenya Highlands 1970-73, minister Mowbray Presbyterian Church Cape Town 1973-78, minister Presbyterian Church of Southern Africa 1978-85, minster The City Temple URC London 1986-; *Recreations* hill walking, gardening; *Style—* The Rev Eric Waugh; 124 Rotherfield St, Islington, London N1 3DA (☎ 01 359 7961); The City Temple, Holborn Viaduct, London EC1A 2DE (☎ 01 583 5532)

WAUGH, Dr Michael Anthony; s of Anthony Lawrence Waugh, of Richmond, Surrey, and Nancy Genevieve, *née* Vernon; *b* 19 Sept 1943; *Educ* St George's Coll Weybridge Surrey, Charing Cross Hos Med Sch Univ of London (MB, BS); *Career* conslt physician genito urinaty medicine Gen Infirmary Leeds 1975-, hon sec Med Soc Study of Veneral Diseases 1981-, sec gen Int Union Against Veneral Diseases and Treponematoses 1984-, observer venereology dermatovenereology specialists ctee Union Euro Med Specialists 1984-, hon sr lectr Univ of Leeds 1985- (Soc Apotliecaries lectr in history of medicine 1984-); DHMSA 1970, Dip Vennereology 1974; Liveryman Worshipful Co Apothecaries 1970; *Books* venereology section of Oxford Companion to Medicine (1986); *Recreations* gardening, browsing in second hand bookshops, travelling; *Style—* Dr Michael Waugh; Wellfield House, 151 Roker Lane, Pudsey, Leeds LS28 9ND (☎ 0532 565 255); Dept of Genito Virinary Medicine, Gen Infirmary Leeds, LS1 3EX (☎ 0532 432 799)

WAUGH, Lady Teresa (Lorraine); *née* Onslow; da of 6 Earl of Onslow, KBE, MC, TD (d 1971); sister of 7 Earl of Onslow; *b* 1940; *m* 1961, Auberon Waugh, *qv*; 2 s, 2 da; *Style—* Lady Teresa Waugh; Combe Florey House, Combe Florey, Taunton, Somerset (☎ 0823 432297)

WAVERLEY, 2 Viscount (UK 1952); David Alastair Pearson Anderson; s of 1 Viscount Waverley, GCB, OM, GCSI, GCIE, PC, FRS, Chllr of Exchequer 1943-45 (d 1958), by his 1 w, Christina Anderson; *b* 18 Feb 1911; *Educ* Malvern, Pembroke Coll Cambridge (MA), Frankfurt Univ; *m* 1948, Lorna Myrtle Ann, da of Lt-Col Frederick Ledgerwood; 1 s, 1 da (and 1 da decd); *Heir* s, Hon John Desmond Forbes Anderson; *Career* formerly at St Thomas' Hosp, resident asst physician and registrar Dept Clinical Pathology 1946-50, consultant Reading Gp of Hosps 1951-75; FRCP; *Recreations* golf, fishing; *Clubs* Travellers', Hawks (Cambridge); *Style—* The Rt Hon Viscount Waverley; Chanders, Aldworth, Berks (☎ 063 522 377)

WAY, Col Anthony Gerald; MC (1945); s of Maj Roger Hill Way, of Badminton House, Gerrards Cross, Bucks (d 1957), and Brenda, *née* Lathbury (d 1976); *see* Ways of Denham Place, Burke's Landed Gentry 18 edn Vol II; Descent from Sir Roger Hill (kt 1688) who completed Denham Place in 1701 and passed the estate to his sole male heir Benjamin Way; *b* 5 Nov 1920; *Educ* Stowe, RMC Sandhurst; *m* 28 Aug 1946, Elizabeth Leslie (d 1986), da of Maj George Mitchell Richmond (d 1957) of Kincairney, Dunkeld, Perths and Mogila, Goodooga, NSW, Aust; 1 s (Gerald b 1952), 1 da (Elizabeth Anne b 1948); *Career* serv WWII Grenadier Gds, 3 Bn Grenadier Gds N Africa Italy CO 3 BN Grenadier Gds 1960-61, Lt-Col cmdg Grenadier Gds 1961-64, memb HM Body Guard of the Hon Corps of Gentlemen of Arms 1972; *Recreations* shooting, gardening; *Clubs* Pratt's; *Style—* Col Anthony Way, MC; Kincairney, Dunkeld, Perthshire, PH8 0RE (☎ 073871 304)

WAY, Dr Geoffrey Leslie; s of Lt-Col Leslie Ferguson Kennedy, DSO (d 1958), and Gladys Elizabeth May, *née* Pixel (d 1918); *b* 6 Mar 1914; *Educ* ISC, London Univ St Bart's Hosp (DA); *m* 4 April 1941, Edith Mairi Reid, da of Frederick Reid Corson (d 1941); 1 s (Ian Frederick Leslie b 1942); *Career* WWII Lt-Col SMO GHQ Troops 21 Army Gp 1934-46; chief anaesthetist Geneva Univ 1949-50; conslt anaesthetist: Dreadnought Hosp 1951-56, Royal London Homeopathic Hosp 1954-60, Royal Surrey Country Hosp 1959-74, King Edward VII Hosp 1973-83; dir St John Ambulance (IOW County) 1974-78; OStJ; MRCP, LRCP, FFARCS; *Recreations* golf and sailing; *Clubs* Royal Solent Yacht; *Style—* Dr Geoffrey Way; 8 Grove Place, Lymington, Hampshire SO41 9SS

WAY, John Stanley; s of Stanley George Godwin Way (d 1985), of Weybridge, Surrey, and Margaret Jean, *née* Edwards; *b* 18 Dec 1946; *Educ* St John's Sch Leatherhead; *m* 1 Feb 1975, (Diana) Jayne, da of maj Thomas Herbert Sills, Esq, MBE, TD, DL (d 1988), of Sandy, Beds; 2 s (Robert b 1979, Duncan b 1986); *Career* Coopers & Lybrand 1969-73; Continental Illinois Nat Bank & Tst Chicago: far east regnl auditor 1974-79, euro/latin america regnl auditor London 1979-83, int auditor

1983-87; int auditor worldwide Prudential Insur Co of America 1987-; FCA 1969, FHKSA 1977, MBIM 1978, MENSA, IIA 1978; *Recreations* golf, tennis; *Style—* John Way, Esq; Fairfield, Pyrford Woods, Pyrford, Woking, Surrey GU22 8UT; 9 Devonshire Square, London EC2M 4HP (☎ 01 548 5045)

WAY, Sir Richard George Kitchener; KCB (1961, CB 1957), CBE (1952); s of Frederick Way; *b* 15 Sept 1914; *Educ* Poly Secdy Sch London; *m* 1947, Ursula Starr; 1 s, 2 da; *Career* dep sec Miny Supply 1958-59, perm under-sec WO 1960-63, perm sec Miny Aviation 1963-66; chm: Lansing Bagnall 1967-69, London Transport 1970-74, Royal Cmmn for Exhibition of 1851 1978-87; princ King's Coll London 1975-80; dir Dobson Pk Industs Ltd 1975-85; tres cncl London Zoological Soc 1983-84 (memb 1977, vice-pres 1979-82 and 1984-87); hon DSC Loughborough Univ; CStJ; *Clubs* MCC, Brooks's; *Style—* Sir Richard Way, KCB, CBE; Manor Farm, Shalden, Alton, Hants (☎ 0420 82383)

WAYE, Ranulph; MBE (1949), TD (1950); s of late James Thomas Waye, of The Hawthorns, Belle Vue, Shrewsbury, Salop, and Lucy, *née* Edgecombe; *b* 27 Oct 1908; *Educ* Shrewsbury, St Edmund Hall Oxford; *m* 19 April 1938, Rachel Hope, da of late Dr David Alfred Alexander of 112 Pembroke Rd, Clifton, Bristol; 3 s (Christopher b 1939, Robert b 1940, dec'd, Alexander b 1943), 1 da (Julia b 1955); *Career* serv WWII: instr 162 OCTU HAC 1939, capt, laster Lt-Col TA general list; schoolmaster: Birkenhead Sch 1931-83, Radley 1933-69; *Recreations* reading, gardening, walking; *Clubs* OU Authentics CC, OU Centaurs AFC, Nat Tst; *Style—* Ranulph Waye Esq, MBE, TD; Curly Cottge, West Hendred, Wantage, Oxon OX12 8RR (☎ 0235 833284)

WAYMOUTH, Peter Gordon; s of Capt Gilbert Ridley Waymouth, RN, CBE (d 1974), and Gwyneth Lilian, *née* Rice (d 1987); *b* 11 Nov 1932; *Educ* Radley, Pembroke Coll Cambridge; *m* 2 June 1956, Jean Myddleton, da of Neil Sutherland Eaton (d 1964); 1 s (Harry b 1962), 2 da (Claire b 1958, Sophie b 1960); *Career* Lt RTR serv Germany 1952-53; chief exec Containerbase Federation Ltd and dir assoc cos 1968-70, mangr Blue Star Line 1970-73, mangr Union Int Ltd and dir subsidiary cos 1973-78, chm Continental N Atlantic Westbound Freight Conf 1978-79, dir and md T S Engineering Ltd 1979-86, dir Turnbull Scott Holdings plc 1981-86; dir: Acoustat Ltd, Hurry & Ptnrs 1984-86, Perth Corp Hldgs Ltd 1988-; md Ailsa Perth Shipbuilders Ltd 1987-; govr Radley Coll 1981-86; *Recreations* golf, painting, walking, fishing, shooting; *Clubs* Woking, Prestwick Golf; *Style—* Peter G Waymouth, Esq; c/o Ailsa-Perth Shipbuilders, Harbour Rd, Troon, Ayrshire KA10 6DN (☎ 0292 311311, fax 0292 317613, telex 778027 AILSA G)

WAYMOUTH, Lady Victoria Mary Verenia Braganza; *née* Yorke; da of 9 Earl of Hardwicke (d 1974); *b* 22 Feb 1947; *Educ* St Mary's Convent Ascot; *m* 1976, Nigel Norman de Glanville, artist, s of Wing Cdr T G Waymouth, of Bideford; 2 s; *Career* interior designer; *Style—* Lady Victoria Waymouth; 36 Elms Rd, SW4 (☎ 01 622 2985)

WAYNE, Sir Edward Johnson; s of William Wayne, of Leeds, and Ellen Rawding; *b* 3 June 1902; *Educ* Leeds Univ & Medical Sch, Manchester Univ; *m* 1932, Honora Halloran; 1 s, 1 da; *Career* Regius prof practice of med Glasgow Univ 1954-67, physician to Western Infirmary Glasgow; Hon Physician to HM The Queen in Scotland 1954-67, chm: Br Pharmacepoeia Cmmn 1958-63, Advsy Ctee Drug Dependence 1967-69; Hon DSc Sheffield 1967; MD 1938, MSc, PhD, FRCP; kt 1964; *Style—* Sir Edward Wayne; Lingwood Lodge, Lingwood, Norfolk, NR13 4ES (☎ Gt Yarmouth 751370)

WAYNE, Francis Tudor; s of Rev Canon St John Wayne (d 1951), of Conington, Hunts, and Dorothy, *née* Williams (d 1950); see Wayne of Eisg Brachaidh and Stansted, Burke's Landed Gentry 18 Edn Vol III; *b* 30 April 1909; *Educ* Winchester, Magdalene Coll Cambridge (MA); *m* 9 Sept 1939, Joan Margaret, da of J Arthur Findlay, JP (d 1964), of Stansted Hall, Essex; 3 s (Peter b 1941, Anthony b 1946, Richard b 1951), 1 da (Margaret (Signora Starace Janfolla) b 1944); *Career* with Price Waterhouse & Co 1930-36, FCA (CA) PE Consulting Grp (mgmt conslts) 1936-64; dir of various industl and investmt cos 1960-74; landowner, Eisg Brachaidh 5000 acres; FCA 1939 (ACA 1934), MIMC 1963; *Books* Energy for Future Transport (1980); *Recreations* fishing, sailing, trees and shrubs, doggerel; *Clubs* Flyfishers' (pres 1964); *Style—* Francis Wayne, Esq; Eisg-Brachaidh, Lochinver, Sutherland IV27 4LR (☎ 05714 277)

WAYNE, Peter Howard; s of Kurt Wolff (d 1944), of Berlin, and Lilli, *née* Wallerstein; *b* 8 May 1920; *Educ* Friends' Sch Great Ayton, Germany, Switzerland; *m* 19 Oct 1968, Waltraud Charlotte, da of Carl Kirsch (d 1985), of Frankfurt, Germany; 1 s (Alexander Simon Howard b 1970), 1 da (Nicola Martina Suzanne b 1973); *Career* mil serv 1941-46 UK, France, Belgium, Germany; mil govt head interpreter at Minden War Crimes Ct Interpreter & Investigator of German Financial Institutions; CA, ptnr Thomas Theobald & Son 1952-67; finance dir: Engway Properties Ltd 1958, Lynjohn Investmts Ltd 1959, Waldron Flats Ltd 1973, Brompton Flats Ltd 1973, Roundwood Devpts Ltd 1973; *Recreations* skiing, music, historic research; *Clubs* Army Ski Assoc; *Style—* Peter H Wayne, Esq; 11 Kensington Park Gdns, London W11 3HD (☎ 01 727 3476); 81 Cromwell Rd, London SW7 (☎ 01 370 3273)

WAYT, John Lancaster; s of Arthur George Wayt, MBE, of Netherstones, Oxshott Way, Cobham, Surrey, and Leonora Lancaster, *née* Shaw; *b* 8 Mar 1937; *Educ* Cranleigh, Keble Coll Oxford (MA); *m* 30 Sept 1965, Margaret, da of Henry Morris, of Woodcote Ave, Nuneaton, Warks; 3 s (Anthony b 1967, James b 1970, David b 1970); *Career* admitted slr 1961; exec deputy chm and chief exec Nat Countries Bldg Soc 1982-89; dir: Nat Countries 1967-89, St Martins-le-Grand plc 1967-89 (chm 1982-89), Lancaster Scott and Co Ltd; sr ptnr Lancaster Scott and Co Ltd 1963-89, dir and chm Lancaster Shaw Insurance Conslts plc 1972-89; chm: Lancasters Business Mgmnt Ltd, Nat Countries Fin Servs; md Nat Counties Estate Agents Ltd, London dir Guardian Royal Exchange Assurance, tstee Nat Counties (1978) Pension Scheme; memb Law Soc; FCIFA, FAAI, FBIM, ACIArb; *Recreations* art appreciation, gardening, reading; *Clubs* RAC; *Style—* John Wayt, Esq; Lancaster House, 35 Blackhills, Esher, Surrey KT10 9JW; Waterloo House, 147-153 High St, Epsom, Surrey KT19 8EL (☎ 037 27 24931)

WEALE, Graham Alexander; s of Prof Robert Alexander Weale, of London, and Margaret Elizabeth, *née* Drury; *b* 26 August 1953; *Educ* Highgate Sch, Lincoln Coll Oxford (MA), City Univ (MSc), Cranfield Sch of Mgmnt (MBA); *m* 15 March 1978, Anthea, da of Thomas Crompton (d 1986), of Christchurch; 2 s (Thomas b 1979, James b 1983); *Career* supply co-ordinator Esso Petroleum Co 1977-81, mgmnt conslt Touche Ross & Co 1982-84, sr energy conslt DRI: Europe (McGraw Hill) 1984-86, mangr euro energy servs Wharton Econometric Forecasting Assocs 1987-: conslt to various Euro gas, oil and power cos; memb: Hayes Town Chapel, Reformed Evangelical Church; Freeman City of London 1983, memb Worshipful Co of Tin Plate and Wire Workers; MInst Pet; *Books* European Gas Markets After Troll, European Coal Markets - Prospects and Risks; *Recreations* chamber music, travel; *Style—* Graham Weale, Esq; 28 Winscombe Crescent, Ealing, London W5 1AZ (☎ 01 997 9859); Wharton Econometric Forecasting Associates, Ebury Gate, 23 Lower Belgrave St, London SW1W ONW (☎ 01 823 4201, fax 01 730 1400)

WEALE, Timothy Donald; s of Donald Jones Weale (d 1971), of Basingstoke, Hants, and Freda Jessy, *née* Gardiner; *b* 10 April 1951; *Educ* Magdalen Coll Oxford, Coll of Estate Mgmnt Reading; *m* 12 Oct 1974, Pamela Anne, da of Gerard Gordon Moore (d 1972), of Tadley, Hants; 1 s (Edward b 15 April 1981), 1 da (Alice b 21 April 1983); *Career* Wessex Regt (Rifle Vols) (TA) 1979-86, Capt Inns of Ct and City Yeo 1986; ptnr Pearsens (auctioneers, estate agents surveyors) 1984-86, dir Prudential Property Servs 1986-; FSVA 1978, ARVA 1979; *Recreations* field sports, sailing, skiing, vintage cars, gardening; *Clubs* VSCC, Island Sailing; *Style—* Timothy Weale, Esq; Thackham Ct, Hartley Wintney, nr Basingstoke, Hants RG27 8JG (☎ 025 126 3900); Dolphin Hse, St Peter St, Winchester, Hants (☎ 0962 843 300, fax 0962 840 602, car tel 0836 243 083)

WEARING, Hon Mrs (Caroline Ruth); *née* Addison; da of 3 Viscount Addison; *b* 30 July 1942; *m* 1965, John Wearing; 1 s (Patrick b 1969), 1 da (Jacalyn b 1966); *Style—* The Hon Mrs Wearing; 12 Hill St North, Richmond, Nelson, N Z

WEATHERALL, Prof Sir David John; s of Harry Weatherall (d 1973), and Gwendoline Charlotte Miriam, *née* Tharme (d 1985); *b* 9 Mar 1933; *Educ* Calday Grange GS, Univ of Liverpool; *m* 20 June 1962, Stella Mayorga Isobel, da of Rev Campo Mayorga, of Bogota, Colombia; 1 s (Mark b 1968); *Career* Nuffield prof of Clinical Medicine, Univ of Oxford 1974-; Hon dir MRC Molecular Haematology Unit 1980; hon dir Inst of Molecular Medicine Oxford Univ; Hon MD Leeds Univ, Hon DSc Manchester Univ; *Books* The Thalassaemia Syndromes (with J B Clegg, third edn 1982), Blood and Its Disorders (with R M Hardisty second edn 1982), The Oxford Textbook of Medicine (with J G G Ledingham and D A Warrell second edn 1987), The New Genetics and Clinical Practice (second edn 1986); MB ChB, MD, FRCP, FRCPath, FRCPE, FRS; *Recreations* music, oriental food; *Style—* Prof Sir David Weatherall; 8 Cumnor Rise Rd, Cumnor Hill, Oxford OX2 9HD (☎ 0865 862467); Nuffield Dept of Clinical Medicine, John Radcliffe Hosp, Oxford (☎ 0865 60201, telex 83147 viaor GJRH2, fax 0865 750506)

WEATHERALL, Rear Adm James Lame (Jim); s of Lt Cdr Alwyne Thomas Hirst Weatherall, RNR (d 1939), and Olive Catherine Joan, *née* Cuthbert (d 1977); *b* 28 Feb 1936; *Educ* Gordonstun; *m* 12 May 1962, Jean Stewart, *née* Macpherson, da of 1 Baron Drumalbyn, KBE, PC; 2 s (Niall b 1967, Ian b 1976), 3 da (Sarah b 1968, Annie b 1974, Elizabeth b 1976); *Career* cadet BRNC Dartmouth, HMS Truimph 1954, midshipman HMS Albion 1955-56; Sub Lt: HMS Scotsman 1956, HMY Britannia 1958; Lt: HMS Lagos 1959-60, HMS Wizard 1960-61, HMS Houghton 1962-64, HMS Tartar 1964, HMS Eastbourne 1965-66; Lt Cdr Advanced Navigation Course 1966, HMS Soberton 1966-67, HMS London 1968-70; Lt Cdr/Cdr HMS Ulster 1970-72 (i/c); Cdr: MOD 1972-74, HMS Tarter 1975-76 (i/c), Sea Trng 1976-77, HMS Ark Royal 1978; Capt: Nato Defence Coll 1979, MOD-Naval Plans 1979-81, HMS Andromeda (i/c), and 8 Frigate Sqdn 1982-84 (inc Falklands), RN Presentation Team 1984-85, HMS Ark Royal (i/c) 1985-87; ADC HM The Queen 1986-87; Rear Adm Staff of Supreme Allied Cdr Europe 1987-89; pres: Bishop's Waltham Branch Royal Br Legion 1983-, London Area Sea Cadet Corps 1973-, Leicestershire Fleet Air Arm Assoc 1984-; Liveryman Worshipful Co of Shipwrights 1985, Freeman City of London 1985, Younger Brother Trinity House 1986; *Recreations* fishing, stamp collecting, hockey; *Clubs* RN of 1765 and 1785; *Style—* Rear Adm Jim Weatherall

WEATHERALL, Hon Mrs (Jean Stewart); *née* Macpherson; da of 1 Baron Niall Malcolm Stewart Drumalbyn, KBE, PC, of Claytons, Bishops Waltham, Hants, and Margaret Phyllis Runge (d 1979); *b* 1938; *m* 1962, Rear Admiral James Lamb, s of Alwyn Thomas Lamb Weatherall, RN (d 1939); 2 s (Niall b 1967, Ian b 1976), 3 da (Sarah b 1968, Annie b 1974, Elizabeth b 1976); *Style—* The Hon Mrs Weatherall; Craig House, Bishop's Waltham, Hants

WEATHERBY, Charles (Edward); s of Edward William Weatherby (d 1967); and Ida Rosemary Weatherby, *née* Stratton (d 1984); *b* 28 Dec 1932; *Educ* Winchester; *m* 2 April 1960, Susan (Alison), da of Sir Francis Ley, Bt, MBE, TD; 2 da (Camilla b 1963, Fiona b 1965); *Career* Nat Serv 1 Bn Coldstream Gds (Lt) 1951-53 (Cyprus and Middle E); dep sec and dir of Field Servs of the Jockey Club; dir of Weatherbys 1956; *Recreations* fishing, gardening, travelling; *Clubs* Boodle's; *Style—* Charles Weatherby, Esq; Mixbury Lodge Farm, Brackley, Northants, NN13 5RW; Jockey Club Office, 42 Portman Sq, London WIH 0EN

WEATHERHEAD, Alexander Stewart (Sandy); OBE (1985), TD (1964 and Clasp 1973); s of Kenneth Kilpatrick Weatherhead (d 1979), and Katharine, *née* Stewart, of Glasgow; *b* 3 August 1931; *Educ* George Watsons Edinburgh, Larchfield Sch Helensburgh, Glasgow Acad, Glasgow Univ (MA, LLB); *m* 22 Dec 1972, (Harriett) Foye, da of Rev Arthur Organ, of Toronto, Canada; 2 da (Foye b 1974, Alison b 1975); *Career* Nat Serv 2 Lt 1950-52 RA 1950; TA 1952-76; Lt Col cmdg: 277 A & SH Field Regt RA 1965-67, Lowland Regt RA 1967, Glasgow and Strathclyde Univs OTC 1971-73; Col TAVR (Lowlands West) 1974-76, ADC to HM The Queen 1977-81, Hon Col Glasgow and Strathclyde Univs OTC 1982-; slr 1958, ptnr Tindal Oatts 1960-, hon vice pres Law Soc of Scotland 1983-84 (cncl memb 1971-84); Temp Sheriff 1985-; memb: Royal Cmmn on Legal Servs in Scotland 1976-80, Law Soc of Scotland 1958-; *Recreations* reading, sailing, music, tennis; *Clubs* New (Edinburgh), Royal Western Yacht, Royal Highland Yacht; *Style—* A S Weatherhead, Esq, OBE, TD; 52 Partickhill Rd, Glasgow G11 5AB (☎ 041 334 6277); 48 St Vincent St, Glasgow G2 5HS (☎ fax 041 221 8012, 041 221 7803, telex 778309)

WEATHERILL, Rt Hon (Bruce) Bernard; PC (1980), MP (C) Croydon NE 1964-; s of Bernard Weatherill, of Guildford, by his w Annie Gertrude, *née* Creak; *b* 25 Nov 1920; *Educ* Malvern; *m* 1949, Lyn, da of H Eatwell; 2 s, 1 da (Virginia); *Career* serv WWII 4/7th Royal Dragoon Gds & Indian Army; former md Bernard Weatherill Ltd; former chm Guildford Cons Assoc and memb Nat Union Cons Party; oppn whip 1967, lord cmmr Tresy 1970-71, vice-chamberlain HM Household 1971-72, comptroller 1972-73, tres HM Household and dep chief govt whip 1973-74, oppn dep ch whip 1974-79, chm Ways and Means Ctee 1979-83; elected speaker House of Commons

1983-; *Style—* The Rt Hon Bernard Weatherill, PC, MP; Speaker's House, Westminster, London SW1

WEATHERILL, John Arthur Morrell; DFC (1945); s of Arthur Ernest (d 1950), of Ascot, Berks, and Susan Edith, *née* Story (d 1961); *b* 10 Sept 1915; *Educ* St Michael's, Sunninghill, Ascot Tailor & Cutter Acad (hons dip); *m* 1, 10 June 1937, Hilda Constance (d 1965), da of George Kenneth Kirkin (d 1960), 1 s (Bruce b 1943), 1 da (Susan b 1946); m 2, 7 Dec 1968, Nancy Jane, da of Franklin Davenport Haynes Price of Philadelphia USA; 1 s (Jonathan b 1970); *Career* RAF 1941-46, Fl-Lt Euro theatre; tailor (family businrss) 1932-37, tailoring mangr Trimingham Bros Ltd Bermuda 1937-40, buyer AS Cooper & Sons Ltd Bermuda 1946-56; author, photographer, dir photography Bermuda Dept of Tourism 1956-76; *Books* contrib Br Jl of Photography, Faces of Bermuda (1985), Queen of the East (1988); *Recreations* music, reading, walking; *Clubs* RAF, Piccadilly; *Style—* John Weatherill, Esq, DFC; Wylye Head, Kilmington, Wilts BA12 6RD (☎ 09853 348)

WEATHERLEY, Dr Michael (Mike); s of Joseph Weatherley (d 1970), of Colchester, Essex, and Louisa Frances, *née* Fowler; *b* 10 July 1935; *Educ* Dean Close Sch Cheltenham, Haberdashers' Aske's, The City Univ (BSc), Univ of Bristol (PhD); *m* 11 Sept 1959 (m dis 1981), Jean Dawn Howard, da of John Pexton, of Colchester, Essex; 1 s (Julian b 1965), 1 da (Helen b 1961); *Career* Nat Serv RAF 1954-56, writer DJ and announcer Aden Forces Bdcadting Assoc; res and devpt engr GEC Ltd 1957-66, res assoc Univ of Bristol 1966-69, prodr/dir BBC TV 1969-, programmes incl: Open Univ tech courses, Bellamy on Botany (1972), Bellamy's Britain (1974), Bellamy's Europe (1976), Up a Gum Tree (1979), Bellamy's Backyard Safari (1981), Bellamy's New World (1983), Favourite Walks (1985), The Trouble with Sex (1987), Business Matters (1989); *Recreations* walking, travel, opera, theatre; *Style—* Dr Mike Weatherley; 73 Archel Rd, London W14 9QL (☎ 01 381 2427); BBC Television, Villiers Ho, Haven Green, London W5 (☎ 01 743 8000)

WEATHERSBEE, Robin Charles Henry; s of Oliver Charles Weathersbee (d 1973), of Farnham Royal, Berks, and Eileen Daisy, *née* Anstee; *b* 13 April 1938; *Educ* Aldenham Sch Elstree, Northampton Coll of Advanced Technol; *m* 29 July 1961, Jennifer Margaret, da of Richard Frank Sibley (d 1983), of Yeovil, Somerset; 1 s (Michael), 1 da (Sally); *Style—* Robin Weathersbee, Esq; Parkfield, Farthing, Green Lane, Stoke Pages, Bucks SL2 1HA (☎ 02814 3459)

WEAVER, Edward John Martin; s of Edward Algernon Weaver (d 1964), of Berwyn, Mill Lane, Codsall, nr Wolverhampton, and May Evelyn Edwards (d 1974); *b* 7 Nov 1921; *Educ* Clifton, Gonville and Caius Coll, Cambridge: St Thomas's Hosp, (MA, MB, BChir); *m* 2 Sept 1953, Mary Elaine, da of Charles Spitteler (d 1961), of Shevaroy Hill, S India; 3 s (Peter b 1954, James b 1955, Timothy b 1958); *Career* hon conslt cardis thoracic surgeon to The London Hosp, (former head of dept of cardis thoracic surgery at Lond Hosp) conslt thoracic surgeon Royal Masonic Hosp, former conslt thoracic surgeon Whipps Cross Hosp and Princess Alexander Hosp Harlow; FRCS, LRCP, MRCS; *Recreations* gardening, do-it-yourself; *Style—* John Weaver, Esq; The Lone Pine, Matching Green, nr Harlow, Essex CM17 0QB (☎ 0279 731295); London Independent Hospital, Stepney Green E1 (☎ 01 791 3422)

WEAVER, (Christopher) Giles Herron; s of Lt Col J F H Weaver, of Greywalls, Gullane, Lothian, and Ursula Priscilla Marie Gabrielle, *née* Horlick; *b* 4 April 1946; *Educ* Eton, London Business Sch (MSc); *m* 30 July 1974, Rosamund Betty, da of Lionel Mayhew, of Whittlesfield, Higher Burwardsley, Tattenhall; 2 s (Freddy b 1977, Jack b 1986), 2 da (Flora b 1975, Johanna b 1983); *Career* CA, Arthur Young 1966-71, asst to chm: Jessel Securities 1973-75, Berry Wiggins 1975-76; dir in charge of pension funds Ivory and Sime plc 1976-86, md pensions mgmnt Prudential Portfolia Mangrs 1986-; prop Greywalls Hotel Gullane Lothian 1976-; mangr New Club (Edinburgh); ACA 1970, FCA 1977; *Recreations* skiing, golf, tennis, stalking, bridge; *Clubs* New (Edinburgh), HCEG (Muirfield), Hurlingham, Denham; *Style—* Giles Weaver, Esq; Greywalls, Gullane, Lothian; 48 Thurloe Sq, London SW7 (☎ 0620 843205); PPM, 142 Holborn Bars, London EC1 (☎ 01 405 9222, fax 01 936 8424, car 0860 527076, telex 265082)

WEAVER, Leonard John; s of Alfred Wallace Weaver and Anne, *née* Geleyns; *b* 10 June 1936; *Educ* St Mary's Sch, Surrey Univ; *m* 1963, Penelope Ann, *née* Sturge-Young; 5 s, 1 da; *Career* served Kenya Regt 1955-57; AEI Ltd 1962-64, works mangr PYE-TMC 1964-66; P E Consulting Gp: joined 1966, dir 1975, md 1979-82; chm: Polymark Int plc 1982-, Jones & Shipman 1988-, Manifold Industs Ltd 1982-; memb: BIM Cncl 1978-83, IProdE Cncl 1980- (vice-pres 1986-); pres Inst Mngmt Conslts 1983-84; Freeman City of London, Liveryman Worshipful Co of Engrs; CEng, FIEE, FIProdE, CBIM, FIMC, FRSA; *Recreations* cricket, book-collecting, shooting; *Clubs* Reform, MCC; *Style—* Leonard Weaver, Esq; Crab Apple Court, Oxshott Rd, Leatherhead, Surrey (☎ 0374 843647); Polymark International plc, Polymark House, Abbeydale Road, Wembley, Middlesex HA0 1LQ (☎ 01 991 0011)

WEAVER, Simon John; s of Kenneth John Weaver (d 1973), and Hilda Nora *née* Rooke;; *b* 4 Mar 1946; *Educ* King's Sch Canterbury; *m* 28 Oct 1980, Rosemary Jane, da of Leslie John Fuhr (d 1966), of Beckenham; 2 s (Matthew b 1974, Thomas b 1982 twin), 2 da (Lara, Samantha b 1987 (twin));; *Career* account exec W Nally Sports Promotions Gp 1970-75, dir Barwell Sports Mngmnt 1976-83, fndr and ptnr Simon Weaver Sports 1983- assoc memb Inst of Leisure and Amenity Mgmnt; *Recreations* cricket, squash, gardening, walking, conservation; *Clubs* Band of Brothers, Buccaneers, St Lawrence and Highland Ct CC; *Style—* Simon J Weaver, Esq; Castle House, Clifford, Hay-on-Wye, Hereford HR3 5EP (☎ 04973 484 ext 491)

WEAVER, Sir Tobias Rushton (Toby); CB (1962); s of Sir Lawrence Weaver, KBE (d 1930), of London, and Kathleen Purcell (d 1927); *b* 19 July 1911; *Educ* Clifton, Corpus Christi Coll Cambridge (MA); *m* 1941, Marjorie, da of Rt Hon Sir Charles Trevelyan, 3 Bt, of Wallington Hall, Northumberland; 1 s (Lawrence b 1948), 3 da (Kathleen m Nicholas Abbott, Caroline m Michael Baker, Rachel m Charles Munn); *Career* former master Eton and Barking, Admty 1941, civil servant DES 1946-73; dep sec 1962-73; prof of educn: Southampton Univ 1973, London Univ Inst of Educnl 1974, Open Univ 1976-78; fell Imp Coll 1986; *Recreations* playing piano; *Style—* Sir Toby Weaver, CB; 14 Marston Close, London NW6 4EU

WEAVERS, Frank Paton; s of Frank Paton Weavers (d 1969), and Ellen, *née* Billing (d 1969); *b* 30 Jan 1927; *Educ* Holly Lodge GS Smethwick; *m* 22 Sept 1951, Meryl June, da of Victor Robert Dixon (d 1984), of Moseley, Birmingham; 2 s (Malcolm Dixon b 1959, Stewart Paton (twin) b 1959); *Career* Nat Serv RAF, mainly in Malaya 1946-48; with Carter & Co, chartered accountants 1943-61, investmt banking exec and co sec Birmingham Indust Tst Ltd 1962-68, dir and investmt mangr Britannic Assur plc 1980- (investmt mangr 1972-79, joined 1969); FCA; *Recreations* walking, reading, opera; *Style—* FP Weavers, Esq; 8 Beechnut Lane, Solihull B91 2NN (☎ 021 704 1543); Britannic Assurance plc, Moor Green, Moseley, Birmingham B13 (☎ 021 449 4444, fax 021 449 0456)

WEBB, Anthony Allan; s of Robert McGraw Webb (d 1967), of Washington DC, and Ruth, *née* Webb (d 1986); *b* 24 May 1943; *Educ* Univ of Colorado (BA, B Int mgmnt); *m* 10 July 1971, Micheline, da of Alphonse Touchette (d 1983), of Montreal, Canada; 1 s (Christian b 1981), 1 da (Annie b 1978); *Career* Lt US Navy 1965-69; Royal Bank of Canada 1970-, The Royal Bank of Canada (Suisse) 1984-88; chm The Royal Bank of Canada: AG Frankfurt, Brussels, Belgium, Paris France; *Recreations* skiing; *Clubs* Club Baur au Lac (Zurich), Annabel's, Overseas Bankers; *Style—* Anthony Webb, Esq; 56 Sheldon Ave, Highgate, London N6 4NS (☎ 01 340 7399); The Royal Bank of Canada, 71 Queen Victoria St, London EC4V 4DE (☎ 01 489 1188, fax 01 329 6144, telex 8811837)

WEBB, Anthony Michael Francis; CMG (1963), JP (1966), QC (1961); s of Sir Ambrose Henry Webb, QC (d 1964), and Agnes Ellen, *née* Gunn (d 1969); *b* 27 Dec 1914; *Educ* Ampleforth, Magdalen Oxford (MA); *m* 1948, Diana Mary, da of Capt Graham Farley IA (d 1942) and Hilda Uvedale, *née* Pyper (d 1974); 1 s (Simon), 1 da (Amanda); *Career* 2 Lt Queen's Bays 1940; SOE Middle East and Europe 1941-46, Maj; barr Gray's Inn 1939, Colonial Legal Serv: Malaya 1947-55, Kenya 1955-64 (Attorney-Gen & Min for Legal Affairs); Lord Chllrs Off 1964-78 (dep sec of Commissions and head of Ct Business); chm Indust Tribunals 1978-87; *Clubs* Special Forces; *Style—* Anthony Webb Esq, CMG, JP, QC; Yew Tree Cottage, Speldhurst Rd, Langton Green, Tunbridge Wells, Kent TN3 0JH

WEBB, Anthony Ronald; s of Ronald Alfred Webb, of East Sutton, Kent, and Muriel Dorothy, *née* Empleton; *b* 17 July 1947; *Educ* Chislehurst and Sidcup GS, Univ of Bristol (LLB); *m* 29 Sept 1979, Sarah Lynette, da of Denzil Edward Kieft, of Lagos, Portugal; 1 da (Camilla); *Career* called to Bar Inner Temple 1970; *Recreations* equestrian, travel, gardening; *Clubs* Kent CCC; *Style—* Anthony Webb, Esq; Capel Cross, Grovehurst Lane, Horsmonden, Tonbridge, Kent TN12 8BB (☎ 0892 72 3973); Farrar's Building, Temple, London EC4Y 7BD (☎ 01 583 9241, fax 01 583 0090)

WEBB, Douglas Geoffrey Larwood; s of Geoffrey Royce Webb (d 1968), of Gt Shelford, Cambs, and Gwendoline Doris, *née* Larwood; *b* 25 Sept 1932; *Educ* Aldenham, Cambridge Univ (MA, LLM); *m* 29 March 1972, Janet Elizabeth, da of Claud James Walsingham, of Diss, Norfolk; 1 s (Cameron Patrick Walsingham b 1975); *Career* admitted slr 1959, sr ptnr Smart & Webb (Cambridge); *Recreations* sailing, fishing; *Style—* Douglas G L Webb, Esq; 11 Cavendish Ave, Cambridge CB1 4UP; 1 St Mary's Passage, Cambridge CB2 3PH (☎ 0223 358227)

WEBB, George Hannam; CMG (1984), OBE (1974); s of late George Ernest Webb and Mary Hannam, *née* Stephens; *b* 24 Dec 1929; *Educ* Malvern Coll, King's Coll Cambridge (MA); *m* 1956, Josephine Chatterton, JP; 2 s, 2 da; *Career* serv 14/20 King's Hussars 1948-49, Parachute Regt (TA) 1950-53; Colonial Serv Kenya 1953-63 (Dist Offr Centl and North Nyanza, Dist Cmmr Moyale, Secretariat Nairobi); Diplomatic Serv 1963-85 (First Sec Bangkok and Accra; Cnsllr Tehran and Washington); dir Mgmnt Devpt, City Univ, London 1985-; memb Cncl of Royal Soc for Asian Affairs 1984-; tstee Hakluyt Soc 1986-, memb cncl of Gresham Coll 1988-, dep chm cncl of Friends of Nat Army Museum 1988-; FRSA; *publications* Kipling Journal (ed 1980-), The Bigger Bang: Growth of a Financial Revolution (1987), Kipling's Japan (1988, ed with Sir Hugh Cortazzi); *Clubs* Travellers', Beefsteak, Royal Cwlth Soc; *Style—* G H Webb, Esq, CMG, OBE; Weavers, Danes Hill, Woking, Surrey GU22 7HQ

WEBB, Hon Mrs (Janet Diana); *née* Allanson-Winn; da of 7 Baron Headley; *b* 1932; *m* 1, 1955 (m dis 1969), Antony John Vlassopulos; 2 s; m 2, 1975, David Walter Webb; *Style—* The Hon Mrs Webb; Springs, Rookery Drive, Westcott, Surrey

WEBB, Jeremy Richard; s of C R Webb, OBE, MC (d 1976); *b* 25 Mar 1931; *Educ* Radley, Hertford Coll Oxford; *m* 1956, Clover Margaret, da of Maj J Suckling (d 1981); 3 s; *Career* 2 Lt Royal Sussex Regt; advertising (creative dir): Foote Cone & Beldins 1956-61, Lintas Ltd 1961-65, Wasey Campbell Ewald 1966-71, Ferrero & Co Spa Turin 1971-74, Wasey Campbell Ewald 1974-75, Everetts Ltd 1975-85; dir and creative dept mangr Allen Brady and Marsh 1985-87; dir The Word Process 1987-; *Recreations* bridge, swimming, painting, writing; *Style—* Jeremy Webb, Esq; 79 Cowleigh Rd, Malvern, Worcs WR14 1QL (☎ 0684 574748)

WEBB, John Harold; s of Donald Percy Webb (d 1945), and Helen, *née* Jackson (d 1968); *b* 25 Feb 1929; *Educ* Kings Sch Macclesfield; *m* 1, 25 April 1956 (m dis 1966), Muriel Joan, *née* Gittins; 2 s (Duncan, Simon), 3 da (Jacqueline, Elizabeth, Sophie); m 2, 23 Oct 1968, Sandra Benita, da of late Benjamin Keeling; *Career* md: Kay Metzeler 1960-67, Tangent Ltd 1960-67, Draka Foam Ltd 1970- 86; chm and chief exec Hyman plc; Freeman Worshipful Co of Furniture Manufacturers 1988, Freeman City of London 1989; BRMA; *Recreations* gardening, shooting; *Style—* John Webb, Esq; Henbury Farm, Henbury, Macclesfield, Cheshire SK11 9PY (☎ 0625 34442; Hyman Plc, Spinners Lane, Poynton, Cheshire SK12 IFF (☎ 0625 879944, fax 0625 879943, telex 668307)

WEBB, Prof Joseph Ernest; s of Joseph Webb (d 1975), of Worcester Pk, Surrey, and Constance, *née* Inman (d 1967); *b* 22 Mar 1915; *Educ* Rutlish Sch Merton, Birkbeck Coll Univ of London (BSc, PhD, DSc); *m* 10 Aug 1940, Gwenlilian Clara, da of Herbert Samuel Coldwell (d 1949), of Stoneleigh, Surrey; 3 s (David John b 1943, Ian b 1945, Peter Joseph b 1954); *Career* res entomo and parasitologist Cooper Tech Bureau 1940-46, lectr zoology Univ of Aberdeen 1946-48, sr lectr zoology Univ Coll Ibadan Nigeria 1948-50 (prof 1950-60), prof zoology Westfield Coll Univ of London 1960-80 (vice princ 1976-80, hon fell 1986); emeritus prof zoology Univ of London 1980-; FZS 1943, FLS 1972, MIBiol 1952, MIBiol 1963; *Books* with J A Wallwork and J H Elgood: Guide to Invertebrate Animals (second edn 1978), Guide to Living Mammals (second edn 1979), Guide to Living Reptiles (1978), Guide to Living Birds (1979), Guide to Living Fishes (1981), Guide to Living Amphibians (1981), various pubns on insect physiology, insecticides, systematics, populations, tropical ecology, marine biology and sedimentology; *Recreations* art, music, photography, gardening; *Clubs* Athenaeum; *Style—* Prof J E Webb; 43 Hill Top, London NW11 6EA (☎ 01 458 2571)

WEBB, Kaye; MBE (1974); da of Arthur Webb, and Ann, *née* Stevens; *b* 26 Jan 1944;

Educ Hornsey HS, Ashburton GS; *m* 1, Christopher Brierley; m 2, Gp Capt Keith Hunter, OBE; m 3, Ronald Searle *qv*, 1 s (John b 17 July 1947), 1 da (Kate (twin) b 17 July 1947); *Career* journalist: ed: Picturegoer 1931, Picture Post 1938; Lilliput 1939-47, theatre corr The Leader 1947-49, feature writer News Chronicle 1949-55, ed Elizabethan (children's magazine) 1955-58, theatre critic Nat Review 1957-58, children's ed Puffin Books and publishing dir Penguin Books Ltd 1961-79; currently: conslt Goldcrest Films and Curtis Brown Literary Agency, ed in chief Puffin Books, dir Penguin Books; Eleanor Farjeon Award for Servs to Children's Literature; *Books* ed; with C Fry: Experience of Critics, Penguin Patrick Campbell, The Friday Miracle, The St Trinian's Story, I Like This Poem (1979), All the Day Round (1981), dil Lilliput Goes to War (1985), I Like This Story (1986); with Ronald Searle: Looking at London, Paris Sketchbook, Refugees 1960; *Recreations* theatre, antiques, reading and working with children; *Style—* Ms Kaye Webb, MBE; 8 Lampard Ho, 8 Maida Ave, London W2 1SS (☎ 01 262 4695)

WEBB, Lawrence Desmond; s of Maj George Lawrence Webb, and Evelyn Annie Alice, *née* Wardale; *b* 18 April 1939; *Educ* Harrow and Neuchatel Switzerland; *Career* slr; dir The Investmt Co plc 1965-, fin conslt Tico A G Zürich 1981-; *Recreations* squash, sailing/sailboarding, golf; *Clubs* Carlton, Lansdowne; *Style—* Lawrence Webb, Esq; Barclays Bank plc, 6 Clarence St, Kingston-upon-Thames, Surrey KT1 1NY; Credit Suisse, Paradeplatz 8001, Zürich

WEBB, Hon Mrs (Marigold Elizabeth Cassandra); *née* Neave; da of Airey Neave, DSO, OBE, MC, TD, MP (assas 1979), and The Baroness Airey of Abingdon, *née* Diana Barbara Josceline Giffard; *b* 5 May 1944; *Educ* St Mary's Sch Wantage Oxon, Pershore Coll of Horticulture, Architectural Assoc (Dip Garden Conservation); *m* 1968, (William) Richard Broughton, s of late Lt-Cdr William Frank Broughton Webb, DSC, RN, of Caulin Court, Droitwich; 1 s (Edward Alexander Broughton b 1974), 1 da (Katharine Angela Mary b 1970); *Career* garden designer; *Recreations* hunting, gardening; *Style—* The Hon Mrs Webb; Barbers, Martley, Worcs (☎ 08866 362)

WEBB, Patrick John Ryall; s of Kenneth Edmund Ryall Webb, of Tadworth, Surrey, and Marjorie Eveline Ryall, *née* Nuthall; *b* 31 Mar 1944; *Educ* St Edward's Sch Oxford, Trinity Hall Cambridge; *m* 22 March 1969, Dr Joanna Webb, da of Thomas Gilbert Burton (d 1976), of Hull; 1 s (Edward b 1970), 2 da (Georgina b 1971, Elly b 1975); *Career* articled clerk Ernst and Whinney 1965-69, mangr Peat Marwick McLintock 1969-81; co sec: Touche Remnant and Co 1981-85, James Capel and Co 1986-; govr Bramley Sch, tres Betchworth Cons Assoc; FCA 1970; *Recreations* golf, music, tennis; *Style—* Patrick Webb, Esq; Ravenleigh, Betchworth, Surrey RH3 7DF (☎ 073 784 3327); James Capel and Co, 6 Bevis Marks, London EC3A 7JQ (☎ 01 626 0566, fax 01 626 2192, telex 886720)

WEBB, Pauline Mary; da of Rev Leonard Frederick Webb (d 1973), and Daisy Winifred, *née* Barnes (d 1972); *b* 28 June 1927; *Educ* King's Coll London Univ (BA), Union Theol Seminary New York (STM), Univ of Brussels (DTheol), Univ of Victoria Toronto (DLitt), Univ of Mt St Vincent Halifax (DLitt); *Career* ed Methodist Missionary Soc 1955-66; dir: Lay Tning Methodist Church 1966-72, First Conf Estate 1978-; exec offr Methodist Overseas Div 1972-79; organiser Religious Broadcasting Overseas BBC External Services 1979-87; dir Hinksey Centre Westminster Coll Oxford 1987-; *Books* Women of Our Company, Women of Our Time, Salvation Today, Faith and Faithfulness, Celebrating Friendship; film scripts: Bright Diadem, New Life in Nigeria, Beauty for Ashes, The Road to Dabou; *Recreations* theatre, travel; *Clubs* Univ Women's, BBC; *Style—* Dr Pauline Webb; 14 Paddocks Green, Salmon St, London NW9 8NH (☎ 01 904 9088)

WEBB, Philip Alun; s of Frederick Albert George Webb, of Glamorgan, Wales, and Dilys Maud, *née* Williams (d 1968); *b* 23 Nov 1955; *Educ* Ferndale Glamorgan, Univ Coll of Wales Aberystwyth; *Career* dir public affairs Barry Hook Assoc Ltd (advertising and public relations) 1987; sr exec The Public Affairs Dept of Sea Containers/ SEACO Inc London 1985-87; conservative central off Community Affairs Dept 1979-82; memb Monarchist League, regional rep Monarchist League in the Principality of Wales 1975-77; memb The Heraldry Soc; memb Middle Temple Inn of Court; *Recreations* tennis, riding, reading; *Style—* Philip A Webb, Esq; Apartment 11, Parsonage Court, Palatine Rd, Withington, Manchester M20 (☎ 061 434 5903); 94 Churchgate, Stockport, Cheshire (☎ 061 477 0854)

WEBB, Richard; s of Lt-Col Richard Webb (d 1988); *b* 26 July 1943; *Educ* Marlborough; *Career* dir: Michael Joseph Ltd London (publishers) 1970-74, co-fndr and md Webb & Bower (publishers) 1975-; *Style—* Richard Webb, Esq; Wixels, Ferry Rd, Topsham, Exeter, Devon; Webb & Bower (publishers) Ltd, 9 Colleton Crescent, Exeter, Devon (☎ 0392 435362, telex WEBBOW 42544, fax 03072 211652)

WEBB, Sir Thomas Langley; s of Robert Langley Webb and Alice Mary Webb; *b* 25 April 1908; *Educ* Melbourne C of E GS; *m* 1942, Jeanette Alison, da of Dr A Lang; 1 s, 1 da; *Career* AIF 1940-45; joined Huddart & Parker Ltd 1926 (dir 1951-, md 1955-61); dir: Bulkships Pty Ltd, McIlwraith McEacharn Ltd (vice-chm); chm CBA Ltd 1970-78, ret; kt 1975; *Style—* Sir Thomas Webb; 6 Yarradale Rd, Toorak, Vic 3142, Australia

WEBB, Tom Peel (Tim); MBE (1946); s of Thomas Webb (d 1918), and May Safford (d 1962); *b* 11 Feb 1919; *Educ* Glossop GS, Manchester Coll of Technol; *m* 18 May 1945, Nancy Eileen, da of Frederick Denny Farrow, OBE; 3 da (Susan b 1946, Anne b 1948, Charlotte b 1958); *Career* Manchester Regt (TA) 1938, serv NW Europe 1939-40, cmmnd RA 1941, Capt/Adj 20 LAA Regt 1944-45, serv NW Europe, Maj DAA & QMG 106 AA Bde 1945-46; md Northide Ltd 1946-53, dir Fergusson Wild & Co Ltd 1953-60, exec dir Rank Relay Servs Ltd 1960-61; sec GB Project 1972-81, dir G B Trading Ltd 1969-83; govr G B Project 1983-; ctee memb Nat Union of Mfrs Manchester 1949-53, parish cncllr W Peckham Kent 1963-69; *Recreations* travel, sketching; *Style—* Tim Webb, Esq, MBE; 16 Riverbank Way, Shirebrook Park, Glossop, Derbyshire SK13 8SN (☎ 04574 69579)

WEBB CARTER, Brig David Brian Wynn; OBE (1983), MC (1967); s of Brig Brian Wolseley Webb Carter, DSO, OBE (d 1982), and Evelyn Rosemary, *née* Hood (d 1978); *b* 5 Nov 1940; *Educ* Eton, RMA Sandhurst; *m* 1973, Felicity, da of W L R de B Young, DL, of Co Antrim; 1 s (Oliver b 1975), 2 da (Margot b 1977, Camilla b 1983); *Career* served BAOR, Aden, Cyprus, Hong Kong and Belize, Co 1 Bn Irish Guards 1979-81, Cdr Br Forces Belize 1984-87; *Clubs* Whites, MCC; *Style—* Brig David Webb Carter, OBE, MC; c/o Guards & Cavalry Section, Lloyds Bank, 6 Pall Mall, London SW1

WEBB-CARTER, Hon Mrs (Anne Celia); *née* Wigram; da of 2 Baron Wigram, MC, JP, DL; *b* 23 April 1945; *m* 1973, Maj Evelyn Webb-Carter, Gren Gds, s of Brig Brian Webb-Carter, DSO, OBE (s of Maj-Gen Sir John Carter, KCMG, of Ixworth Court, Bedford), by Evelyn Hood, gt niece of 4 Viscount Hood; 1 s, 2 da; *Style—* The Hon Mrs Webb-Carter; Ashton Cottage, Bishop's Waltham, Hants

WEBER, David Henry; s of Humphrey N Weber of London, and Queenie Weber; *b* 11 August 1953; *Educ* Haberdashers Askes Sch Herts, Clare Coll Cambridge (MA), Coll of Law London; *m* 14 Aug 1977, Dorothy Broughton *née* Fairhust; 2 da (Clare Louise b 10 July 1981, Helen Victoria b 29 Aug 1984); *Career* articled clerk Linklaters & Paines London 1976, slr 1978, seconded Fulbright & Jaworski (attorneys) Houston Texas 1980-81, ptnr Linklaters & Paines 1984- (advsr to arranging banks on financing of Channel Tunnel project 1985-88); memb: Law Soc, Int Bar Assoc; memb Worshipful Co of Slrs; *Style—* David Weber, Esq; Barrington House, 59-67 Gresham Street, London EC2V 7JA (☎ 01 606 7080, fax 01 606 5113, telex 884349/888167)

WEBSTER, Rev Dr Alan Brunskill; KCVO (1988); *b* 1 July 1918; *Educ* Oxford (MA, BD), City Univ (DD Hons); *m* 1961, Margaret; 2 s, 2 da; *Career* curate in Sheffield 1942-46, warden of Lincoln 1959-70, dean of Norwich 1970-78, dean of St Pauls 1978-87; *Books* Joshua Watson, Broken Bones May Joy; Contrib: Historic Episcopate, Strategist of the Spirit, The Reality of God; *Recreations* writing, gardening, travel; *Style—* The Rev Dr Alan Webster, KCVO; 20 Beech Bank, Unthank Road, Norwich NR22AL (☎ 0603 55833)

WEBSTER, Maj-Gen Bryan Courtney; CB (1986), CBE (1981); s of Capt Herbert John Webster (ka 1940), and Mabel, *née* Harrison (d 1970); *b* 2 Feb 1931; *Educ* Haileybury, RMA Sandhurst; *m* 1957, Elizabeth Rowland Waldron, da of Prof Sir David Waldron Smithers; 2 s (Julian, Justin), 1 da (Lucinda); *Career* cmmnd Royal Fusiliers 1951, Airborne Forces 1953-56; served: Ger, Korea, Egypt, Gibraltar, Hong Kong, Malta; directing staff Staff Coll 1969-71, cmd: 1 RRF 1971-73, 8 Inf Bde 1975-77; MID 1977, Chief of Staff SE Dist 1977-78, Planning (Army) 1980-82, Army Quartering 1982-86; Dep Col (City of London) RRF 1976-79; FBIM City of London 1984; *Recreations* field sports, ornithology; *Style—* Maj-Gen Bryan Webster, CB, CBE; Ewshot Lodge, Ewshot, Surrey

WEBSTER, David Gordon Comyn; s of Alfred Edward Comyn Webster, of St John's Town of Dalry, Castle Douglas, Scotland, and Meryl Mary, *née* Clutterbuck (d 1970); *b* 11 Feb 1945; *Educ* Glasgow Acad, Glasgow Univ (LLB); *m* 12 Feb 1972, (Pamela) Gail, da of Dr Dennis Frank Runnicles, of Sevenoaks, Kent; 3 s (Michael Gordon Comyn b 2 Sept 1974, Nicholas Gordon Comyn b 9 Jan 1978, Jonathan Hugo Comyn b 9 Feb 1983); *Career* Lt RNR ret 1970; slr 1968; corporate fin Samuel Montagu & Co 1968-72; fin dir: Oriel Foods Ltd 1973-76, Argyll Gp plc 1977-; govr Lockers Park Sch Tst Ltd; *Recreations* military history, gardening, skiing, shooting; *Style—* David Webster, Esq; Rodinghead, Ashridge Park, Berkhamsted, Hertfordshire; 7 Chelsea Cres, Chelsea Harbour, London SW10; Argyll Group plc, 8 Chesterfield Hill, London W1X 7RG (☎ 01 493 0808)

WEBSTER, David John; s of Maj Edgar Webster, and Gladys; *b* 14 Jan 1947; *Educ* All Saints, Emerson Coll Michigan USA; *m* 12 Aug 1973, Julie; 1 s (Piers b 1978); *Career* lectr; artist; works: largest historical mural in UK, historical restorations, signed David John sold worldwide; NSPCC suporter; donated works sold 1987 raised £2,500; *Recreations* photography, shooting, hunting; *Clubs* Historic Wine of GB Sloane Square, Dorset; *Style—* David Webster, Esq; 26b Abbey St, Crewkerne, Somerset (☎ 0460 74665)

WEBSTER, Derek Adrian; CBE (1979); s of James Tulloch and Isobel Webster; *b* 24 Mar 1927; *Educ* St Peter's Bournemouth; *m* 1966, Dorothy Frances Johnson; 2 s, 1 da; *Career* RN 1944-48; reporter West Morning News 1943, staff journalist Daily Mail 1949-51, joined Mirror Gp 1952, Northern ed Daily Mirror 1964-67, ed Daily Record 1967-72, dep-chm Scottish Daily Record and Sunday Mail Ltd 1972-74, (chm and editorial dir 1974-87), dir Mirror Gp Newspapers 1974-87; memb Press Cncl 1981- (jt vice chm 1982-83), vice chm Age Concern Scotland 1977-83, hon vice pres Newspaper Press Fund; *Recreations* boating, gardening; *Style—* Derek Webster Esq, CBE; Kessog Bank, 60 Glasgow Rd, Blanefield, Glasgow G63 9BP (☎ 0360 70252); Scottish Daily Record and Sunday Mail Ltd, Anderston Quay, Glasgow G3 8DA (☎ 041 242 3350; telex 778277)

WEBSTER, His Honour Judge; Ian Stevenson; s of Harvey Webster by his w Annabella, *née* MacBain; *b* 20 Mar 1925,; *Educ* Rochdale GS, Manchester Univ; *m* 1951, Margaret, *née* Sharples; 2 s; *Career* serv Sub-Lt RNVR in WWII; barr 1948; rec Crown Ct 1972-76 (asst rec Oldham 1970, Salford 1971); chm Manchester Industl Tribunals 1976-; Circuit Judge (Northern) 1981-; *Style—* His Honour Judge Webster

WEBSTER, John Dudley; *b* 13 Nov 1939; *Educ* Merchant Taylors Sch, London (BSc); *m* 1967, Barbara Joan; 1 da (Katherine b 1969); *Career* dir and gen mangr (investmt) Sun Life Assur Soc plc; dir Sapphire Petroleum plc 1981-88, chm Br Insur Assoc Investmt Protection Ctee 1982-84; dir: Gp Investors plc 1984-86; Save and Prosper Return of Assets Investmt Tst plc 1984-; lay memb Cncl of Stock Exchange 1985-86 and 1988-; ind dir Securities Assoc 1986-; FIA; *Style—* John Webster Esq; c/o Sun Life Assurance Society plc, 107 Cheapside London, EC2V 6DU (☎ 01 606 7788); 10 Merrydown Way, Chislehurst, Kent

WEBSTER, John Lawrence Harvey; CMG (1963); s of Sydney Webster (d 1970), of Grayshott, Surrey, and Elsie Gwendoline, *née* Harvey (d 1970); *b* 10 Mar 1913; *Educ* Rugby, Balliol Coll Oxford (MA, DipEd); *m* 1, 9 Jan 1940 (m dis 1959), Elizabeth Angela, da of Dr H Gilbertson (d 1972), of Hitchin, Herts; 2 da (Diana b 17 July 1942, Hilary b 10 May 1949); m 2 Jan 1960, Jessica Lilian, *née* Royston-Smith; *Career* Colonial Admin Serv Kenya: dist offr 1935-46, dist cmmr 1947-48, asst sec 1949-50, sec for devpt 1950-54, admin sec 1954-56, sec to cabinet 1956-58, perm sec for Forest Game and Fisheries 1958-62, perm sec for Info and Broadcasting 1963-; ret HMOCS at Kenya Self Govt; served with Br Cncl 1964-80 in: Thailand, Sri Lanka, Hong Kong, Istanbul, London; *Recreations* swimming, badminton; *Clubs* Nairobi, Royal Commonwealth Society, Leander; *Style—* John Webster, Esq, CMG; Timbercroft, 11 Pevensey Rd, Worthing, Sussex (☎ 0903 48617)

WEBSTER, Vice Adm Sir John Morrison; KCB (1986); s of Frank Martin Webster (d 1986), of Lea House, Lymington, and Kathleen Mary, *née* Morrison (d 1986); *b* 3 Nov 1932; *Educ* Pangbourne Coll; *m* 15 Dec 1962, Valerie Anne, da of Vice Adm Sir Michael Villiers KCB, OBE, of Decoy House, Melton, Woodbridge; 1 s (Thomas b 1970), 2 da (Lucilla b 1964, Rozelle b 1966); *Career* joined RN 1951, specialised in navigation 1959, served UK, Far East and Australia, staff appts at Dartmouth and MoD; cmd: HMS Argonaut 1970-71, HMS Cleopatra 1977-79; Naval Advsr and RNLO

Ottawa 1974-76; dir Naval Warfare (MoD) 1980-81; Rear Adm 1982; Flag Offr Sea 1982-84; chief of Staff to CinC Fleet 1984-86; Vice Adm 1985; Flag Offr Plymouth and Naval Base Cmdr Devonport 1987-; landscape and marine painter, exhibitions in Canada and London (King St Gallery 1981, 1984, Oliver Swann Gallery 1986); govr of Canford Sch; yr bro of Trinity House 1970; *Recreations* painting, sailing; *Clubs* Royal Cruising, Royal Naval Sailing Assoc, Armed Forces Art Soc; *Style*— Vice Adm Sir John Webster, KCB; c/o Royal Bank of Scotland, 62/62 Threadneedle St EC2R 8LA

WEBSTER, John Walter; s of Norman Alan Webster (d 1982), and Francis Kate, *née* Simons; *b* 21 Jan 1936; *Educ* De Aston Sch Market Rasen Lincs, LSE (BSc); *m* 12 Aug 1961, Constance Anne, da of Arthur Cartwright (d 1944, of Sch House, Admaston, Rugeley, Staffs; 1 da (Elizabeth b 1966), 1 s (Graham b 1968); *Career* mangr Price Waterhouse & Co 1961-71; finance dir The Penguin Gp; dir: The Penguin Publishing Co Ltd 1980, Penguin Books Ltd 1976, Penguin Books Australia Ltd 1982, Penguin Books Canada Ltd 1982, Penguin Books (NZ) Ltd 1982, NAL Penguin Inc 1986, NAL Canada Ltd 1987, Viking Penguin Inc 1980, Penguin India (Private) Ltd 1984, Frederick Warne & Co Ltd 1983; FCA; *Recreations* skiing, travel, reading; *Style*— John Webster, Esq; Woodmans Cottage, Bramley Rd, Silchester, Hants (☎ 0734 700670); School House, Admaston, nr Rugeley, Staffs (☎ 088921 285); Penguin Books Ltd, Bath Rd, Harmondsworth, Middx 1JK (☎ 01 759 2184, fax 01 897 6774), car ☎ 0836 246689)

WEBSTER, Patrick; s of Francis Glyn Webster, and Ann Webster, *née* Harrington (d 1980); *b* 6 Jan 1928; *Educ* Swansea GS; Rockwell Coll, Eire, St Edmund's Coll Ware Downing Coll Cambridge (BA); *m* 6 Aug 1955, Elizabeth, da of Trevor David Knight (d 1976); 2 s (David b 1956, Patrick 1962), 4 da (Anne b 1957, Elizabeth b 1959, Mary b 1961, Catherine b 1965); *Career* called to Bar Gray's Inn 1950, practised at Bar in Swansea, ISCOED Chambers -1975, Crown Ct Rec 1972, chm of Tribunals Cardiff Region 1976 (pt/t chm 1965-75); pt/t chm Med Appeals Tribunal 1971-75; *Recreations* music, rowing, sailing (watching); *Clubs* Penarth Yacht (Penarth), Beechwood; *Style*— Patrick Webster, Esq; 103 Plymouth Road, Penarth, S Glamorgan CF6 2DE; Caradog House, St Andrews Place, Cardiff

WEBSTER, Hon Mr Justice; Hon Sir Peter Edlin Webster; QC (1967); s of Herbert Edlin Webster, of Cookham, by his w Florence Helen; *b* 16 Feb 1924; *Educ* Haileybury, Merton Coll Oxford; *m* 1, 1955 (m dis), Susan Elizabeth, da of the late Benjamin William Richards, 1 s, 2 da; m 2, 1968, Avril Carolyn Simpson, da of the late Dr John Ernest McCrae Harrisson; *Career* served RNVR 1943-46 and 1950; law lectr Lincoln Coll Oxford 1950-52, barr Middle Temple 1952, standing jr counsel to Labour Miny 1964-67, chm: London Common Law Bar Assoc 1975-79, Senate of the Inns of Court and the Bar 1976-77; dir Boster Cauldwell 1978-79; high ct judge (Queen's Bench) 1980, chm Judicial Studies Bd 1981-83; kt 1980; *Style*— The Hon Mr Justice Webster, QC; Royal Courts of Justice, Strand, London WC2

WEBSTER, Richard Joseph; s of Peter Joseph Webster, of Dulwich,London; *b* 7 July 1953; *Educ* William Penn Dulwich; *m* 1980, Patricia Catherine, da of Gerald Stanley Edwards (former Chief Supt Sussex Police), of East Grinstead; 1 s (James Joseph b April 1985), 1 da (Victoria Catherine b Sept 1983); *Career* Lloyd's insur broker; dir: Howden Cross Ltd 1977-82, Alexander Howden insur Brokers Ltd 1978-82, Hogg Robinson & Gardner Mountain (reinsurance and non marine) Ltd 1982-87, Hogg Robinson (London) Ltd 1983-87, Hogg Robinson Ltd 1986-87, Hispano American Reinsurance Brokers Ltd 1984-87, J Besso & Co Ltd 1987-; chm: R J Webster Insur Brokers Ltd, R J Webster Insur Serv Ltd 1987-; *Recreations* riding, squash, swimming, badminton; *Clubs* Lloyd's of London; *Style*— Richard Webster, Esq; 23a The Glen, Farnborough Park, Locksbotton, Kent BR6 8LP; Plantation House, 31-35 Fenchurch St, London EC3M 3DX (☎ 01 283 8944, telex 938046 BESSOG)

WEBSTER, Richard Stanley; s of Maurice Stanley Webster, JP (d 1971), of Liverpool, and Dorothea Marie, *née* Thompson; *b* 25 Mar 1938; *Educ* Sedbergh Sch; *m* 6 June 1964, Sheila Elizabeth, da of Richard Stephenson (d 1975), of North Berwick; 2 da (Karen b 1966, Fiona b 1968); *Career* CA; chm James Webster & Bro Ltd and subsidiaries; dir: Diversion Insurance (Timber) Assoc Ltd, Age Concern Liverpool, Union Pour Le Commerce Des Bois Tropicaux Dans Le CEE; FCA; *Recreations* gardening, gastronomy; *Style*— Richard Webster, Esq; The White Cottage, 11 Derby Road, Formby, Merseyside L37 7BN (☎ 07048 73730); James Webster & Bro Ltd, 165 Derby Road, Bootle, Merseyside L20 8LE

WEBSTER, Prof (John) Roger; OBE (1988); s of Samuel Webster (d 1974), and Jessie, *née* Farbrother (d 1951); *b* 24 June 1926; *Educ* Llangefni Co Sch, Univ Coll of Wales Aberystwyth (MA, PhD); *m* 17 April 1963, Ivy Mary, da of Frederick Garlick (d 1956); 1 s (Matthew b 1964), 1 da (Catrin b 1966); *Career* lectr Trinity Coll Carmarthen 1948, lectr in educn Univ Coll Swansea 1951, dir for Wales Art Cncl of GB 1961; prof of educn: Univ Coll of N Wales Bangor 1966, Univ Coll of Wales Aberystwyth 1978; James ctee on Teacher Trg 1971; chm: Standing Conf on Studies in Educn 1972-76, Wales Telecommunications Advsrs Ctee 1984-88; memb: Lloyd Ctee on Nat Film Sch 1965-66, Welsh Jt Educn Ctee 1967-, cncl Open Univ 1969-78, Venables Ctee on Continuing Educn 1974-76, Standing Conf on Studies in Educn 1972-76, CNAA 1976-79, Post Office Users Nat Cncl (chm Wales) 1981-88, educn sub ctee UGC 1988-; govr Cwlth Inst; *Style*— Prof Roger Webster, OBE; Bron Y Glyn, Rhyd Y Felin, Aberystwyth, Dyfed SY23 4QD; Dept of Educn, Univ Coll of Wales, Old College, King St, Aberystwyth

WEDDERBURN, Hon David Roland; s of Baron Wedderburn of Charlton and his 1 w, Nina, da of Dr Myer Salaman; *b* 1956; *Career* BSc, ACA; *Style*— The Hon David Wedderburn; c/o 29 Woodside Av, Highgate, London N6

WEDDERBURN, Prof Dorothy; s of Frederick C Barnard (d 1953), and Ethel L, *née* Lawrence (d 1969); *b* 18 Sept 1925; *Educ* Walthamstow HS For Girls, Girton Coll Cambridge (MA); *Career* res offr Dept of Applied Economics Cambridge Univ 1950-65; Imperial Coll of Sci and Technol: lectr in industl sociology 1965-70, reader 1970-77, prof 1977-81, dir Industl sociology unit 1973-81, head dept of social and economic studies 1978-81; princ: Bedford Coll 1981-85, Royal Holloway and Bedford New Coll 1985-; hon pres Fawcett Soc 1986-, pt/t memb Royal Cmmn on the Distribution of Income and Wealth 1974- 78; memb: cncl Advsy Conciliation and Arbitration Serv 1976-82, Social Science Res Cncl 1976-82; Hon DLitt Warwick Univ 1984, Hon fell Imperial Coll London Univ 1986, fell Ealing Coll of Higher Educn 1985; *Books* White Collar Redundancy (1964), Redundancy and the Railwaymen (1964), The Aged in the Welfare State (with P Townsend 1965), Workers' Attitudes and Technology (1972); *Recreations* politics, walking, cooking; *Style*— Prof Dorothy Wedderburn; Royal Holloway and Bedford New College, Egham Hill, Egham, Surrey TW20 OEX (☎ 0784 34455)

WEDDERBURN, Hon Jonathan Michael; s of Baron Wedderburn of Charlton by his 3 w, Frances, da of Basil Knight; *b* 1972; *Style*— The Hon Jonathan Wedderburn; 29 Woodside Avenue, London N6 4SP

WEDDERBURN, Hon Lucy Rachel; da of Baron Wedderburn of Charlton by his 1 w, Nina, da of Dr Myer Salaman; *b* 1960; *Style*— The Hon Lucy Wedderburn

WEDDERBURN OF CHARLTON, Prof Baron (Life Peer UK 1977); Kenneth William Wedderburn; s of Herbert Wedderburn; *b* 13 April 1927; *Educ* Aske's Hatcham Sch, Whitgift Sch, Queens' Coll Cambridge (MA, LLB); *m* 1, 1951 (m dis 1962), Nina, da of Dr Myer Salaman; 1 s, 2 da; m 2, 1962 (m dis 1969), Dorothy, da of Frederick Barnard and formerly w of William Cole; m 3, 1969, Frances, da of Basil Knight; 1 s; *Career* served RAF 1949-51; sits as Lab peer in House of Lords; barr Middle Temple 1953, former lectr at Clare Coll and Faculty of Law Cambridge Univ, Cassel Prof Commercial Law LSE 1964-; visiting prof: Univ of California Los Angeles Law Sch 1967, Harvard Law Sch 1969-70; chm: London and Provincial Theatre Cncls 1973-, Ind Review Ctee 1976-, ed Modern Law Review 1970-88; fell Br Acad 1981; Hon Dott Givr (Univ of Pavia) 1987; *Publications include* The Worker and the Law (1986), Cases and Materials on Labour Law (1967), Employment Grievances and Disputes Procedures (with P L Davies, 1969), Labour Law and Industl Relations (with R Lewis and J Clark, 1982), Diritto del Lavoro in Europa (with B Veneziani and S Ghimpu, 1987); *Recreations* Charlton Athletic FC; *Style*— Prof the Rt Hon the Lord Wedderburn of Charlton; 29 Woodside Avenue, Highgate, London N6 4SP (☎ 01 444 8472); LSE, Aldwych, London WC2A 2AE (☎ 01 405 7686, telex 24655 BLPES G)

WEDDERBURN-OGILVY, Caryl Eustace; s (by 1 m) of late Donald Wedderburn-Ogilvy; hp of cous, Sir Andrew Ogilvy-Wedderburn, 7 Bt; *b* 10 Dec 1925; *m* 1953, Katharine Mary, da of William Steele, of Dundee; 1 s, 2 da; *Career* ARIBA; *Style*— Caryl Wedderburn-Ogilvy Esq; Pucklepeggies, 21 Sth Glassford St, Milngavie, Strathclyde G62 6AT

WEDELL, Prof (Eberhard Arthur Otto) George; s of Rev Dr H Wedell (d 1964), of Haslemere and Dusseldorf, and Gertrude, *née* Bonhoeffer (d 1982); *b* 4 April 1927; *Educ* Cranbrook Sch, LSE (BSc); *m* 5 April 1948, Rosemarie, da of Rev Dr Paul Winckler; 3 s (Martin b 1950, Crispin b 1954, Philip b 1956) 1 da (Rebecca b 1957) ; *Career* princ Miny of Educn 1955-60 (asst princ 1950-55), fndr sec-gen bd for social responsibility Gen Assembly of the C of E 1958-60 (secondment from Civil Serv), sec ITA 1961-64 (dep sec 1960-61) prof of adult educn and dir extramural studies Univ of Manchester 1964-75, head of community employment div Cmmn of the Euro Communities 1973-82, visiting prof of employment policy Manchester Business Sch 1975-83, prof of communications policy Univ of Manchester and dir of the Euro Inst for the Media 1983-; chm: Wyndham Place Tst, Beatrice Hankey Fndn; dir: Royal Exchange Theatre 1968-88, Manchester Arts Centre 1983-; vice pres Greater Manchester Lib Pty; candidate (Lib) Greater Manchester West Euro elections 1979, Greater Manchester Central (Alliance) in Euro elections 1984; pres Friends of the Manchester Coll of Adult Educn; Lord of the Manor of Clotton Hoofield; Hon MEd Manchester 1968; memb Int Inst of communications 1969, FRTS 1982, FRSA 1972; *Books* The Use of Television in Education (1963), Broadcasting and Public Policy (1968), Teaching at a Distance (with HD Perraton, 1968), Structures of Broadcasting (ed 1970), Study by Correspondence (with R Glatter, 1971), Correspondence Education in Europe (1971), Teachers and Educational Development in Cyprus (1971), Education and the Development of Malawi (ed 1973), Broadcasting in the Third World (with E Katz, 1977) Mass Communications in Western Europe (with G M Luyken and R Leonard, 1985), Making Broadcasting Useful (ed 1986), Media in Competition (with G M Luyken, 1986); *Recreations* gardening, music, theatre; *Clubs* Athenaeum Fonclation Univ (Brussels); *Style*— Prof George Wedell; 18 Cranmer Rd, Manchester M20 OAW (☎ 061 445 5106); 94 Eton Place, London NW3 (☎ 01 722 0299); Vigneau, Lachapelle 47350 Seyches, France (☎ 58 83 88 71); The European Institute for the Media, The University of Mânchester M13 9PL (☎ 061 273 2754, fax 273 8788)

WEDGWOOD, Chester Dwight; s of Paul Wedgwood, and Phyllis May (now Mrs King); *b* 25 July 1943; *Educ* Catford Tech Coll; *m* 1, (m dis 1978), Linda Hunt; m 2, 6 Oct 1978, Elizabeth Blanche, da of Edmund Hutchinson (d 1983), of 64 Marlow Rd, High Wycombe, Bucks; 1 s (Simon John b 6 Aug 1980); *Career* The Rank Orgn 1960-64: mgmnt trainee 1960-62, mangr The Pye Record Co 1962-64; mangr The Tan-Sqd Chair Co Ltd 1964-70, sales mangr Godfrey Syrett Ltd 1970-72, md and fndr memb Gordon Russell plc (formerly Giroflex Ltd) 1972-; fndr DIA Gordon Russell Awards; memb Design Cncl with New Designers; memb Worshipful Co of Furniture Makers 1988; FCSD 1988; *Recreations* motor racing, collecting cars, reading, resting; *Style*— Chester Wedgwood, Esq; Gordon Russell plc, 44 Eagle St, London WC1 (☎ 01 831 0031, fax 01 831 9172)

WEDGWOOD, Hon Mrs (Elfrida Sandra); *née* MacLehose; er da of Baron MacLehose of Beoch; *b* 1949; *m* 1971, Martin Amery Wedgwood; 1 s (Richard Martin b 1975), 1 da (Lois Elfrida b 1977); *Style*— The Hon Mrs Wedgwood; Beoch, Maybole, Ayrshire

WEDGWOOD, Hon Elizabeth Julia; da of 1 Baron Wedgwood (d 1943), by 1 w, Hon Ethel Kate, da of 1 Baron Bowen; *b* 1907; *Style*— The Hon Elizabeth Wedgwood; 55 Gretton Court, High St, Groton, Cambs

WEDGWOOD, Baroness; Jane Weymouth; da of William Poulton, of Kenya; *m* 1949, as his 2 w, 3 Baron Wedgwood (d 1970); 1 s (4 Baron), 2 da (Hon Susan Wedgwood and Hon Mrs Wedgwood Bitove); *Style*— The Rt Hon Lady Wedgwood; Harewood Cottage, Chicksgrove, Tisbury, Wilts

WEDGWOOD, Jill; da of George William Thomas Garrood, AFC (d 1968), of The Sheraton, Kenilworth, Capetown, SA, and Winifed Irene, *née* Jeffery (d 1968); *b* 20 Mar 1931; *Educ* Malvern Girls Coll; *m* 1, 9 March 1959, James Stirrat (d 1966), s of James Stirrat (d 1914), of 16 Westbourne Gdns, Glasgow; 1 s (Hamish b 1959); m 2, 29 Sept 1972, (Arthur) Anthony Wedgwood, s of Robert Amery Wedgwood, TD, DL (D 1988), of The Mill House, Helensburgh; *Career* chm Scottish Trading Co Ltd 1964-67, dir Goosewing Products 1984-86; dist pres Stirlingshire Red Cross 1967-68, memb Tenovus (Scotland) Strathclyde Ladies Ctee 1986-89; *Recreations* art, swimming, tennis, journalism; *Clubs* The Royal Overseas League; *Style*— Mrs Anthony Wedgwood; Artarman Cottage, Rhu, Dunbartonshire G84 8LQ (☎ 0436 820 866)

WEDGWOOD, Dr John; CBE (1987); s of Hon Josiah Wedgwood (d 1968, yr s of 1 Baron Wedgwood and sometime chm of Josiah Wedgwood and Sons and dir of Bank of England 1942-46), of Damson Hill, Stone, Staffs, and Dorothy Mary, OBE, *née* Winser; hp to 1 cous once removed, 4 Baron Wedgwood; *b* 28 Sept 1919; *Educ* Abbotsholme, Trin Coll Cambridge (MA, MD); *m* 1, 17 July 1943 (m dis 1971), Margaret, da of Alfred Sidell Mason, of Bury St Edmunds; 3 s (Anthony John b 31 Jan 1944 (m 1969 Angela Page), Simon James Josiah b 3 Oct 1949, Nicholas Ralph b 30 June 1951), 2 da (Judith Margaret b 24 Aug 1946 (m 1967 Christopher Tracy), Katherine Sarah b 24 Nov 1955); m 2, 1972, Jo Alice, da of Harold Swann Ripsher (d 1958); *Career* Surgn-Lt RNVR, Europe and Far East 1943-46; conslt Middx Hosp 1968-80; med dir Royal Hosp for Incurables 1980-86, conslt emeritus Middx Hosp 1980-; chm Royal Surgical Aid Soc 1987-; dir Wedgwood Ltd plc 1967-; FRCP; *Recreations* ceramics, history, sailing; *Clubs* Savile, Athenaeum, Liveryman Soc of Apothecaries; *Style*— Dr John Wedgwood, CBE; 227 Ashley Gdns, Emery Hill St, London SW1P 1PA (☎ 01 828 8319)

WEDGWOOD, Sir John Hamilton; 2 Bt (UK 1942), of Etruria, Co Stafford, TD (1948); s of Brig-Gen Sir Ralph Wedgwood, 1 Bt, CB, CMG, TD (d 1956, himself yr bro of 1 Baron Wedgwood), and Iris Veronica Pawson (d 1982); bro of (Dame) C(icely) V(eronica) Wedgwood, OM, DBE, the historian; direct 6 generation descendant of Josiah Wedgwood whose other descendants include Charles Darwin, the evolutionist, and Ralph Vaughan Williams, the composer; *b* 16 Nov 1907; *Educ* Winchester, Trin Coll Cambridge; *m* 1, 1933, Diana Mildred (d 1976), da of Col Oliver Hawkshaw, TD (d 1949); 4 s (1 decd), 1 da; m 2, 1982, Dr Pamela Tudor-Craig, PhD, FSA, art historian, wid of James Tudor-Craig, FSA (d 1969); *Heir* s, (Hugo) Martin Wedgwood, b 27 Dec 1933; *Career* Maj CSO 11 1939-45; pottery mfr Josiah Wedgwood & Sons 1931-66 (dir 1935, dep chm 1955-66); memb Br Nat Export Cncl 1964-66; JP (Staffs) 1952-59; pres: Utd Commercial Travellers' Assoc 1959, Samuel Johnson Soc 1959; chm Anglo-American Community Rels Ctee Lakenheath Airbase 1972-76; hon citizen: Lubock Texas 1963, Winnipeg Manitoba 1961, St Petersburg Florida 1964; alcade of San Antonio Texas 1963; Hon LLD Birmingham, Hon DLitt Wm Jewell Coll Kansas; *Recreations* mountaineering, foreign travel; *Clubs* Alpine, Wessex Cave, Travellers Century (Los Angeles - for those who have visited 100 countries), Eng Speaking Union, Arts, Br Pottery Manufacturer's Assoc; *Style*— Sir John Wedgwood, Bt, TD; Home Farm, Leighton Bromswold, nr Huntingdon PE18 0FL (☎ 0480 890 340)

WEDGWOOD, 4 Baron (UK 1942); Piers Anthony Weymouth Wedgwood; s of 3 Baron Wedgwood (d 1970, 5 in descent from Josiah Wedgwood, first MP for the newly enfranchised Stoke-on-Trent 1832-34 and s of Josiah Wedgwood, FRS, who founded the pottery), by his 2 w, Jane Weymouth, *née* Poulton; *b* 20 Sept 1954; *Educ* Marlborough, RMA Sandhurst; *m* 30 May 1985, Mary Regina Margaret Kavanagh, da of late Edward Quinn, of Philadelphia, USA; 1 da (Alexandra Mary Kavanagh b 3 Oct 1987); *Heir* first cous once removed, Dr John Wedgwood, CBE; *Career* late Lt Royal Scots (The Royal Regt); *Style*— The Rt Hon the Lord Wedgwood; Harewood Cottage, Chicksgrove, Tisbury, Wilts (☎ Fovant 325)

WEDGWOOD, Hon Susan Margaret; da of 3 Baron Wedgwood (d 1970), by his 2 w Jane, Baroness Wedgwood, *qv*; *b* 22 July 1950; *Style*— The Hon Susan Wedgwood

WEDGWOOD, Dame (Cicely) Veronica; OM (1969), DBE (1968, CBE 1956); da of Sir Ralph Wedgwood, 1 Bt, sis of Sir John Wedgwood, 2 Bt, and 1 cous twice removed of 4 Baron Wedgwood; *b* 20 July 1910; *Educ* privately, Lady Margaret Hall Oxford; *Career* historian, particularly of sixteenth and seventeenth centuries; former memb: bd Nat Gallery, Arts Cncl, advsy cncl V & A, Inst for Advanced Studies Princeton; hon bencher Middle Temple; hon memb: Am Soc Arts & Scis, Am Philosophical Soc, Am Hist Assoc; *Books Incl:* The Thirty Years' War (1938), The King's Peace (1955), The King's War (1958), The Trial of Charles I (1964), The Political Career of Rubens (1975), The Spoils of Time (1984); *Style*— Dame Veronica Wedgwood, OM, DBE; c/o Messrs Collins, 8 Grafton St, London W1 (☎ 01 493 7070)

WEEDON, Dr Basil Charles Leicester; CBE (1974); s of Charles William Weedon (d 1954), and Florence May Weedon (d 1963); *b* 18 July 1923; *Educ* Wardsworth Sch, Imp Coll of Science and Technology (PhD, DSc); *m* 21 March 1959, Barbara Mary, da of Leonard Sydney Dawe (d 1963); 1 s (Matthew b 1967), 1 da (Sarah b 1962); *Career* vice-chllr Univ of Nottingham 1976-88; prof Organic Chemistry, Queen Mary Coll, Univ of London 1960-76; FRS 1971; hon D Tech Brunel Univ 1975; fell Queen Mary Coll 1984; scientific ed, Pure and Applied Chemistry 1960-75; chum Food Additives and Contaminants Ctee 1968-83; chm cncl Nat Stone Centre 1985-; *Recreations* reading, music, walking; *Style*— Dr Basil Weedon, CBE; Sheepwash Grange, Heighington Rd, Canwick, Lincoln LN4 2RJ; University of Nottingham, University Park, Nottingham NG7 2RD (☎ 0602 506101)

WEEDON, Dudley William; s of Reginald Percy Weedon (d 1965), and Ada Kate Weedon (d 1964); *b* 25 June 1920; *Educ* Northampton Polytech, Univ of London (BSc); *m* 28 July 1951, Monica Rose, da of Emerson Edward Smith, of Colchester (d 1975); 2 s (Michael b 1959, John b 1962), 1 da (Sarah b 1957); *Career* dir Cable & Wireless Ltd 1979-81; chm Energy Communications Ltd 1980-82; dir Hogg-Robinson Space & Telecommunications Ltd; FIEE; *Recreations* sailing

WEEKES, Rt Rev Ambrose Walter Marcus; s of Lt Cdr William Charles Tinnoth Weekes (d 1958); *b* 25 April 1919; *Educ* Rochester Cathedral Choir Sch, Sir Joseph Williamson's Rochester, King's Coll London, AKC 1941, FKC 1970, Scholoe Cancellarii Lincoln; *Career* deacon 1942, priest 1943, Chaplain RN 1944-72, Chaplain of the Fleet 1969-72; QHC 1969, Dean of Gibraltar 1973-78; asst bp of Gibraltar 1978; suffragan bishop of Gibraltar in Europe 1980-86; Dean, Pro-Cathedral of the Holy Trinity, Brussels 1980-86; Hon Asst Bp of Rochester 1986-88; *Recreations* music, yachting; *Clubs* RAC; *Style*— The Rt Rev Ambrose Weekes; Deanery Lodge, Kings Orchard, The Precinct, Rochester, Kent (☎ 0634 44165); St John's House, Avenue de Chillon 92, CH-1820 Territet (Montreux), Switzerland

WEEKS, Alan Frederick; s of Frederick Charles Weeks, Master Mariner (d 1961), and Ada Frances Taylor (d 1959); *b* 8 Sept 1923; *Educ* Brighton, Hove and Sussex GS; *m* 6 Sept 1947, Barbara Jane, da of Harold Burleigh Huckle (d 1936); 2 s (Nigel b 1953 (d 1981), Roderick b 1958), 1 da (Beverly b 1948); *Career* Lt RNR served: HMS Renown, HMS Rother, HMS Helmsdale 1941-46; PRO - Brighton Sports Stadium 1946-65, commentator BBC (sports) 1951-, dir Sports Aid Fdn 1976-83, govr Sports Aid Fndn 1983-, life vice-pres Brighton and Hove Entertainment Mangrs Assoc, life memb Nat Skating Assoc GB; memb cncl Ice Hockey Assoc; *Recreations* swimming, ice sports; *Style*— Alan Weeks, Esq; 102 Wick Hall, Furze Hill, Hove, E Sussex BN3 1NH (☎ 0273 779769)

WEEKS, John; CBE (1986); s of Victor John Weeks (d 1983), and Beatrice Anne Beasley (d 1975); *b* 5 Mar 1921; *Educ* Dulwich Coll, Architectural Assoc Sch (Dip); *m* 7 Sept 1955, Barbara Lilian, da of Thomas Harry Nunn, RIBA (d 1937); 1 s (Timothy b 1959), 1 da (Julia b 1957); *Career* dep dir Nuffield Foundation Division of Arch Studies 1956-60, architect in partnership with Richard Llewelyn-Davies (cr. Baron 1963, d 1981) 1960-81, chm Llewelyn-Davies Weeks 1981-86, Conslt Llewelyn-Davies Weeks 1986-, sr lectr Univ Coll London 1961-72; cncl memb Architectural Assoc London 1975-83 (vice-pres 1976-78), Br Health-Care Export Cncl (chm 1982-84, exec cncl memb 1967-); works include: Student Housing Imperial Coll of Agric Trinidad (1960), Northwick Park Hospital Harrow (1961), Univ Childrens Hosps Leuven Belgium (1970), Flinders Medical Centre Adelaide S Aust (1972), redevelopment of St Mary's Hosp Paddington London (1978); exhibitions: This is Tomorrow (London 1956), Cybernetic Serendipidity (London 1968); *Books* Indeterminate Architecture (1964), Multi-Strategy Buildings (1969), Design for Research-Principles of Laboratory Architecture (1986); *Clubs* Architectural Assoc; *Style*— John Weeks, Esq, CBE; Llewelyn-Davies Weeks, Brook House, Torrington Place, London WC1E 7HN (☎ 01 637 0181)

WEETCH, Kenneth Thomas; MP (Lab) Ipswich Oct 1974-; s of Kenneth George Weetch of Cwmcarn; *b* 17 Sept 1933,Abercarn,; *Educ* Newbridge GS, LSE, London Inst of Educn; *m* 1961, Audrey Jill Wilson; 2 da; *Career* lectr in econ history, head of history dept Hockerill Coll of Educn Bishop's Stortford 1966-75; contested (Lab): Saffron Walden 1970, Ipswich Feb 1974; pres Nat Houseowners Soc 1975-78, parly private sec Dept of Tport 1976-77; memb: Home Affairs Select Ctee 1981-83, Select Ctee for Parly Cmmr for Admin; *Recreations* assoc football, playing pianos in pubs, eating junk food; *Clubs* Labour (Ipswich); *Style*— Kenneth Weetch Esq, MP; House of Commons, London SW1

WEIDEMANN, Hon Mrs (Hilary Mary); *née* Carron; da of Baron Carron (Life Peer, d 1969); *b* 1933; *m* 1959, John Simon, s of late Sidney Weidemann, of Sussex; 1 s, 1 da; *Style*— The Hon Mrs Weidemann; The Gables, 27 Bromley Rd, SE6 (☎ 01 697 3188)

WEIDENFELD, Baron (Life Peer UK 1976); (Arthur) George Weidenfeld; s of Max and Rosa Weidenfeld; *b* 13 Sept 1919; *Educ* Piaristen Gymnasium Vienna, Vienna U, Konsular Akademie; *m* 1, 1952, Jane, da of J Edward Sieff; 1 da; m 2, 1956 (m dis 1961), Mrs Barbara Connolly, da of Maj George Skelton and former wife of Cyril Connolly; m 3 (m dis 1973), Sandra, da of Charles Payson; *Career* takes SDP whip in House of Lords; kt 1969; chm Weidenfeld & Nicolson 1948- & assoc cos, served during WW II in BBC monitoring serv, 1939-42; news commentator with BBC 1942-45 & News Chronicle Columnist 1945-46; fndr Contact Magazine and Books 1945; spent 1 year as political advsr and chief of cabinet to Pres Weizmann of Israel; memb Royal Opera House Tst; vice chm Bd of Govrs Ben Gurion Univ of Negev Beer-Sheva; govr: Univ of Tel Aviv, Weizmann Inst of Sci, Bezalel Acad of Arts Jerusalem; tstee Emeritus Aspen Inst Colorado, Wolfson History Prize, chm Mitchell Prize for History of Art; memb of South Bank Bd 1986, bd memb of English nat Opera 1988, tstee Nat Portrait Gallery 1988; *Recreations* opera, travel; *Clubs* Garrick; *Style*— The Rt Hon Lord Weidenfeld; 9 Chelsea Embankment, SW3 (☎ 01 351 0042)

WEIGH, Brian; CBE (1982), QPM (1976); s of Edwin Walter Weigh (d 1958), and Ellen, *née* Wignall (d 1969); *b* 22 Sept 1926; *Educ* St Joseph's Coll Blackpool, Queens Univ Belfast; *m* 1952, Audrey, da of Arthur Leonard Barker (d 1968); 1 da (Amanda); *Career* Metropolitan Police 1948-67, dep chief constable Somerset and Bath Constabulary 1969-74 (asst chief constable 1967-69), dep chief constable Avon and Somerset Constabulary 1974-75; chief constable: Gloucestershire Constabulary 1975-79, Avon and Somerset 1979-83; HM inspr of constabulary for SW England and pt of E Anglia 1983-88; memb Royal Life Saving Soc (dep pres UK Branch, Cwlth Vices Pres); *Recreations* golf, fell walking, gardening; *Style*— Brian Weigh, Esq, CBE, QPM; c/o Home Office, HM Ch Insp of Constabulary, Queen Anne's Gate London SW1H 9AT

WEIGHTMAN, John; s of James Weightman, of Newcastle upon Tyne, and Grace Doreen, *née* Fenton; *b* 6 Sept 1949; *Educ* George Stephenson GS, Univ of London (BSc, external); *m* 1 July 1971, Helena Ruby (d 1986), s of Lt Cdr George Daisley, of Horsham, Sussex; 1 da (Kyle b 17 April 1984); *Career* H M Inspr of Taxes Bd of Inland Revenue 1970-75, tax mangr Deloitte and Co 1975-77, co dir Concord Pater Sales 1977-84, tax conslt 1984-, fin conslt New Life Assocs; tax conslt to CAB Bureau and NFU, choirmaster Berwick Baptist Church; ATII 1974, LIA 1987; *Recreations* angling, sailing; *Clubs* Co Gentlemans, Berwick Sailing; *Style*— John Weightman, Esq; Twizel Smithy, Cornhill-on-Tweed, Northumberland TD12 4DY (☎ 0289 82573); New Life Associates Ltd, 38 High St, Hungtingdon, Cambs PE18 6AQ (☎ 0480 412479, car 0836 211339)

WEIL, Peter Leo John; s of Robert Weil of Berlin, Germany, and Renate Schener; *b* 7 Sept 1951; *Educ* Methodist Coll Belfast, Queen's Coll Cambridge (BA); *Career* researcher Granada TV 1973-77 (Granada Reports, World in Action), prodr BBC TV Current Affairs 1977-84, (Nationwide, Newsnight, Panorama), hd of Youth Progs BBC NI 1984-86 (actg hd of progs 1986), ed Open Air BBC NW 1986-88, series prodr Wogan 1988; *Recreations* cinema, eating, day dreaming, gossip; *Style*— Peter Weil, Esq; 307 Willoughby House, Barbican, London EC2 (☎ 01 628 6602); BBC TV, TV Centre, Wood Lane, London W12 (☎ 01 743 8000)

WEINBERG, Prof Felix Jiri; s of Victor Weinberg (d 1988), and late Nelly, *née* Altschul; *Educ* London Univ (BSc, DIC, PhD, DSc); *m* 26 July 1954, Jill Nesta, da of Jack Alfred Piggott (d 1970); 3 s (John Felix b 27 April 1958, Peter David (twin) b 27 April 1958, Michael Jonathan b 8 Jan 1969); *Career* dept of chemical engrg and chemical technol Imperial Coll London: res asst 1951-54, asst lectr 1954-56, lectr 1956-60, sr lectr in combustion 1960-64, reader in combustion 1964-67, prof combustion physics 1967-; visiting prof at various univs and insts across the world, fndr and first chm combustion physics gp Inst of Physics 1974-, chm Br section Combustion Inst 1975-80, cncl memb Inst of Energy (formerly Inst of Fuel) 1976-79; conslt to numerous bodies incl: BHP, Tioxide UK, Frazer Nash, BP, US Army, Univ of California; Silver Combustion Medal The Combustion Inst Pittsburgh 1972, Bernard Lewis Gold Medal Univ of Waterloo Canada 1980, Rumford Medal of the Royal Soc 1988; prolific contrib to scientific literature and memb editorial bds of various specialist jls; fell: Inst of Physics 1960, Inst of Energy 1960, CEng 1960, fell Royal Soc 1983;

Style— Prof Felix Weinberg; Dept of Chemical Engineering and Chemical Technology, Imperial Coll, Prince Consort Rd, London SW7 2BY (☎ 01 589 5111, ext 4360 and 4498, fax 01 584 7596, telex 92984)

WEINBERG, Sir Mark Aubrey; s of Philip Weinberg (d 1933); *b* 9 August 1931; *Educ* King Edwards, Johannesburg, Witwatersrand Univ, LSE; *m* 1980, Anouska, da of Albert Geissler (d 1980); *Career* md Abbey Life Assurance 1961-70, dep chm (formerly md) Hambro Life Assurance (1971-), now renamed Allied Dunbar Assurance; dir BAT Industs 1985-; dep chm of Securities and Investments Bd 1986-; kt 1987; *Recreations* riding, tennis, skiing; *Style*— Sir Mark Weinberg; Allied Dunbar Assurance plc, 9-15 Sackville Street, London W1X 1DE (☎ 01 434 3211)

WEINSTOCK, Baron (Life Peer UK 1980); Arnold Weinstock; s of Simon and Golda Weinstock; *b* 29 July 1924; *Educ* Albion Road Central Sch N London, LSE; *m* 1949, Netta, da of Sir Michael Sobell; 1 s, 1 da; *Career* sits as independent in House of Lords; md GEC 1963-, dir Rolls-Royce Ltd 1971-73, hon master of the bench Gray's Inn 1982-; tstee: Br Museum 1985-, Royal Philharmonic Soc Fndn Fund; hon FRCS; hon DSc: Salford 1975, Aston 1976, Bath 1978, Reading 1978, Ulster 1987; hon LLD: Leeds 1978, Wales 1985; hon DTech Loughborough 1981; hon fell LSE, hon fell Peterhouse Cambridge; kt 1970; *Recreations* racing, music; *Clubs* Jockey; *Style*— The Rt Hon Lord Weinstock; 7 Grosvenor Sq, London W1 (☎ 01 493 7676)

WEINSTOCK, Hon Simon Andrew; s of Baron Weinstock (Life Peer) (*qv*); *b* 1952; *Educ* Winchester, Magdalen Coll Oxford; *m* 1976, Laura Helen, only da of Maj Hon Francis Michael Legh, KCVO (d 1984); 2 da; *Style*— Hon Simon Weinstock

WEIPERS, Sir William Lee; s of Rev John Weipers and Evelyn Bovelle, *née* Lee; *b* 21 Jan 1904; *Educ* Whitehill Higher Grade Sch Glasgow, Glasgow Veterinary Coll (DVSM); *m* 1939, Mary (d 1984), da of late Joseph MacLean, of Barra; 1 da; *Career* dir Veterinary Educn 1949-68, dean Faculty Veterinary Medicine 1968-74, dean of faculties Glasgow Univ; BSc Glasgow 1951; Hon DUniv Stirling 1978, Hon DVMS Glasgow Univ 1981; kt 1966; FRSE, FRCVS; *Style*— Sir William Weipers; Snab Cottage, Duntocher, Clydebank G81 5QS (☎ 0389 73216)

WEIR, Rear-Adm Alexander Fortune Rose; CB (1981), JP (Bodmin 1985-); s of Cdr Patrick Wylie Rose Weir RN, (d 1971), and Minna Ranken Forrester, *née* Fortune (d 1983); *b* 17 June 1928; *Educ* RNC Dartmouth, RNC Greenwich; *m* 5 Sept 1953, Ann Ross Hamilton, da of Col John Atchison Crawford, RAMC (d 1982); 4 da (Phillipa b 1954, Joanna b 1956, Margaret b 1958, Nicola b 1959); *Career* Cadet 1945-46, Midshipman 1946-47, Actg Sub-Lt HMS Zephyr, Portland 1947, Sub-Lt professional courses 1947-48, Sub-Lt and Lieut, HMS Loch Arkaig 1949-51, ADC to Govr of Victoria Aust 1951-53; HMS Mariner 1953-54, Navigating Offr 1954, HMS St Austell Bay WI, Navigating Offr 1955-56, HMS Wave, Fishery Protection Sqdn Home Arctic and Iceland 1956-58, Lt-Cdr Advanced Navigation Course, 1958; Staff ND Offr, Flag Offr Sea Trng at Portland Dorset 1958-61, HMS Plymouth, Staff Offr Ops, 4 Frigate Sqdn, Far East Station 1961-62, Cdr 1962, Trng Cdr, BRNC Dartmouth 1962-64, CO HMS Rothesay WI Station 1965-66, Staff of C-in-C Portsmouth, Staff Offr Ops 1966-68, 2 in Cmd and Exec Offr HMS Eagle 1968-69, Capt 1969; jssc 1969-70; pres Far East Cmd Midshipman's Bd 1970, Asst Dir Naval Operational Requirments, MoD(N) 1970-72, Capt (F) 6 Frigate Sqdn (8 ships) and HMS Andromeda FEast Mediterranean & Home Waters 1972-74, NATO Def Coll Rome 1974-75, ACOS Strategic Policy Requirements and Long Range Objectives, SACLANT 1975-77, Capt HMS Bristol 1977-78; Rear-Adm 1978; Dep Asst Chief of Staff (Ops) to SACEUR 1978-81; ret RN 1981; joined Capt Colin McMullen and Associates, Marine Consultants 1981 and took over 1983-; FBIM, Assoc Victoria Coll of Music, memb: Nautical Inst, Royal Inst of Navigation; licensed RN lay reader, licensed reader St Kew Parish Diocese of Truro 1984-; JP: Chichester 1982-84, Bodmin 1985-; *Recreations* sailing, shooting, golf; *Clubs* Inst of Dir; RYS, RYA, RNSA; *Style*— Rear-Adm Alexander Weir, CB, JP; Tipton, St Kew, Bodmin, Cornwall PL30 3ET (☎ 020 884 289); Captain Colin McMullen and Associates, Yeoman House, Croydon Rd, Penge SE20 7TP (☎ 01 778 6060, telex 946171)

WEIR, The Hon Lord; David Bruce; QC (1971); s of James Douglas Weir (d 1981), of Argyll, and Kathleen Maxwell, *née* Auld (d 1975); *b* 19 Dec 1931; *Educ* The Leys Sch Cambridge, Glasgow Univ (MA, LLB); *m* 1964, Katharine Lindsay, da of The Hon Lord Cameron; 3 s (Donald b 1965, Robert b 1967, John b 1971); *Career* senator of the Coll of Justice in Scotland, pres Pension Appeals Tribunal (Scotland) 1984, memb Criminal Injuries Compensation Bd 1974-79 and 1984-85; *Recreations* sailing (Tryad), music; *Clubs* New (Edinburgh), Royal Highland Yacht; *Style*— The Hon Lord Weir; Parliament House, High St, Edinburgh (☎ 031 225 2595)

WEIR, Dorothy, Viscountess; Dorothy; da of William Yerrington Dear; *m* 1, Edward Hutton (decd); m 2, 1973, as his 2 w, 2nd Viscount Weir, CBE (d 1975); *Style*— The Rt Hon Dorothy, Viscountess Weir; Little Pennbrook, Lake Road, Far Hills, N.J. USA 07931

WEIR, Hon Douglas Nigel; s of 2 Viscount Weir, CBE; *b* 6 Oct 1935; *Educ* Eton, Trinity Cambridge; *m* 1964, Penelope, da of Gp Capt John Whitehead; 3 da; *Style*— The Hon Douglas Weir; Creagdubh Lodge, Newtonmore, Inverness-shire

WEIR, Hon George Anthony; s of 2 Viscount Weir, CBE (d 1975), and Dorothy Isobel Lucy, *née* Crowdy (d 1972) ; *b* 27 April 1940; *Educ* Winchester, Trinity Cambridge, MIT (BA, SM, PhD); *m* 1962, Hon Jane Caroline, da of The Rt Hon Sir William John St Clair Anstruther-Gray, OC, MC, Baron Kilmany, of Kilmany, Cupar, Fife; 2 s (William b 1971, Edward b 1972), 1 da (Belinda b 1974); *Career* eng, presently md Webtec Indust Technol Ltd 1984; dir The Weir Gp plc since 1972; memb Scottish Devpt Agency 1975-82; *Books* The Attraction of Mobile Investments, Scottish and Irish Experience, Centre for Business Strategy (1986); *Recreations* shooting, fishing, racing, bridge; *Clubs* Jockey, Turf; *Style*— The Hon George Weir; 17 Ainslie Place, Edinburgh EH3 6AU (☎ 031 220 4466)

WEIR, Hon Mrs; Hon (Grania Rachel); *née* O'Brien; da of 16 Baron Inchiquin (d 1968), and Anne Molyneux, *née* Thesiger (d 1973); *b* 31 May 1928; *m* 1973, Hugh William Lindsay Weir, *qv*, s of Maj Terence John Collison Weir (d 1958); *Career* sec to Rt Hon Sir Arthur Salter, MP 1947-52; social sec to Br ambass to: Spain 1952, Japan 1954-57, Peru 1958-60; pres (Ennis branch) RNLI, dir Craggaunowen Project and Hunt Museum Co Clare; *Recreations* writing, gardening, sewing, reading; *Style*— The Hon Mrs Weir; Ballinakella Lodge, Whitegate, Co Clare, Republic of Ireland (☎ 0619 27030)

WEIR, Hugh William Lindsay; s of Maj Terence John Collison Weir (d 1958), and Rosamund Suzanne, *née* Gibson; *b* 29 August 1934; *Educ* Portora Royal Sch; *m* 1973, Hon Grania Rachel O'Brien, da of 16 Baron Inchiquin (d 1968); *Career* md Weir Machinery Ltd; memb Church of Ireland Representative Body 1980-; Irish Heritage historian 1980-; pres: Young Environmentalist Fedn, Clare Youth Impact; teacher, journalist, author and publisher; FRGS; *Books* Houses of Clare, O'Brien - People and Places, Ireland - A Thousand Kings (1988); *Recreations* writing, drawing, angling, travel, youth work; *Style*— Hugh Weir, Esq; Ballinakella Lodge, Whitegate, Co Clare, Ireland (☎ 0619 27 030)

WEIR, Hon James Richard Canning; 4 s of 2 Viscount Weir, CBE; *b* 1 May 1949; *Educ* Winchester, Strathclyde Univ; *m* 1977, Haude Chantal Gabrielle, da of Marc Charpentier, of Paris; 2 da; *Career* venture capital; *Recreations* shooting, fishing, golf; *Clubs* Prestwick Golf, Gatineau Fish and Game; *Style*— The Hon James Weir; 25 Chester Street, London SW1 (☎01 245 6182)

WEIR, Hon James William Hartland; s and h of 3 Viscount Weir; *b* 6 June 1965; *Career* accountant; *Style*— The Hon James Weir; 27 Albany St, Edinburgh EH1 3QN

WEIR, Hon Mrs (Jane Caroline); *née* Anstruther-Gray; da of Baron Kilmany, MC, PC (Life Peer; d 1985); *b* 1943; *m* 1962, Hon George Anthony Weir, s of 2 Viscount Weir (d 1975); 2 s, 1 da; *Career* farmer; *Style*— The Hon Mrs Weir; Kilmany, Cupar, Fife KY15 4QW (☎ 082 624 753)

WEIR, Kenneth George; s of Thomas Weir, 30 Hospital Road, Annan, Dumfriesshire; *b* 30 Oct 1921; *Educ* Alloa Academy; *m* 1950, Mary Whittingham; 2 c; *Career* past pres: Society of Pension Consultants 1972-74, Pensions Management Institute 1979-80; dep chm Hogg Robinson Europe Ltd and Hogg Robinson (Benefit Consultants) Ltd; fell of the Faculty of Actuaries; *Recreations* bridge, tennis, swimming; *Style*— Kenneth Weir Esq; Castle Point, 11 Harebell Hill, Cobham, Surrey (☎ Cobham 4604)

WEIR, Malcolm Donald; s of Malcolm Weir (d 1944), of Craigend, Craigmore, Isle of Bute, and Helen Begg, *née* Saunders (d 1960); *b* 8 Sept 1921; *Educ* Rothesay Acad, Merchiston Castle Sch Edinburgh; *m* 30 June 1950, Angela Christine, da of Alexander Murray (d 1958), of Brora, Sutherland; 2 da (Pauline Helen b 1951, Angela Rosemary b 1955); *Career* WWII OCTU Bangalore India cmmnd Maj Indian Army 1941 served: India, Burma, Malaya RIASC; Maj; mentioned in despatches, demob 1946; Maj TA 1947-50; John Bruce & Co Shipowners Glasgow 1939-65: ptnr 1950-57, dir 1957-65; Westcott & Laurence Line Ltd London 1965-72: dir 1965-69, md 1969-72; md Ellerman City Liners London 1972-; memb Glasgow Jr Chamber of Commerce 1955-65, chm stewardship ctee Busbridge Church Godalming 1970-84; Freeman City of London 1980, Liveryman Worshipful Co of Shipwrights 1980; FICS 1947; *Recreations* golf; *Clubs* Caledonian; *Style*— Donald Weir, Esq; The Gables, Munstead, Godalming, Surrey GU8 4AR (☎ 0483 892 554)

WEIR, Sir Michael Scott; KCMG (1980), CMG (1974); s of Archibald Weir; *b* 28 Jan 1925; *Educ* Dunfermline HS, Balliol Coll Oxford; *m* 1, 1953, Alison Walker; 2 s, 2 da; m 2, 1976, Hilary Reid; 2 s; *Career* WWII RAF; joined FO 1950, served: Trucial States, San Francisco, Washington, Cairo; chllr and head Arabian Dept FO 1966-68, dep political resident Bahrain 1968-71, head of chancery, UK Mission to UN (NYC) 1971-73, asst under-sec FCO 1974-79, ambassador Cairo 1979-85, ret 1985; pres Egypt Exploration Soc 1988-, memb West Lambeth Health Authy 1987-; *Style*— Sir Michael Weir, KCMG, CMG; 37 Lansdowne Gardens, London SW8

WEIR, Richard Stanton; s of Brig Richard Ambrose Weir, OBE (d 1972), and Dr Margaret Lucretia, *née* Cowan; *b* 5 Jan 1933; *Educ* Repton, Christ Church Oxford (MA); *m* 1961, Helen Eugenie, da of Andrew Guthrie (d 1978); 1 da (Nicola b 1964); *Career* cmmnd 3 Carabiniers (Prince of Wales' Dragoon Guards) 1952; barr 1957; head of legal dept Soc of Motor Mfrs and Traders Ltd 1958-61, exec Br Motor Corpn Ltd 1961-64; dep co sec Rank Orgn Ltd 1964-67, head of admin Rank Leisure Services 1967-69, sec CWS Ltd 1969-74; dir: The Retail Consortium 1975-81, Br Retailer Assoc 1986-; sec gen £chief exec) Bldg Socs Assoc 1981-86; memb Consumer Protection Advsy Ctee 1973-76, dir gen The Retail Consortium; *Recreations* walking, shooting; *Clubs* Utd Oxford and Cambridge, The Royal Overseas League; *Style*— Richard Weir, Esq; 2 Lamont Rd, London SW10 0HL (☎ 01 352 4809); The Retail Consortium, Commonwealth House, 1-19 New Oxford St, London WC1A 1PA (☎ 01 404 4622)

WEIR, Hon (John) Vincent; 2 and yr s of Andrew Alexander Morton Weir, 2 Baron Inverforth of Southgate (d 1975), and Iris, Baroness Inverforth, *qv*; *b* 8 Feb 1935; *Educ* Malvern Coll; *Career* chm: Andrew Weir Insur Brokers Ltd 1964-, Andrew Weir & Co Ltd 1982-, Andrew Weir Finance Co Ltd 1982-, Andrew Weir Insur Co Ltd 1982-, Andrew Weir Investmt Co Ltd 1982-, Andrew Weir Mgmnt Services Ltd 1982-, Andrew Weir Leasing Co Ltd 1983-, The Bank Line Ltd 1982-, Initial Metals Engrg Ltd 1982-, MacAndrews & Co Ltd 1982-, Spink & Son Ltd 1979-, Utd Baltic Corpn 1982-, Andrew Weir Commodities Ltd 1982; *Recreations* natural history, wildlife conservation; *Style*— The Hon Vincent Weir; 85 Whitehall Court, London SW1A 2EL (☎ 01 930 3160); Andrew Weir & Co Ltd, 21 Bury St, London EC3A 5AU (☎ 01 283 1266, telex 887392)

WEIR, William; s of David Weir (d 1949), of Enfield, Middx, and Agnes Craig, *née* Morton (d 1969); *b* 8 Nov 1909; *Educ* Mill Hill Sch, Clare Coll Cambridge (MA); *m* 1, 26 Oct 1937, Jenny (d 1980), da of Dr James Allan Wilson (d 1944), of Glasgow; 1 s (Allan b 1942), 1 da (Joan b 1944); m 2, 26 May 1982, Christine Margaret; *Career* res asst GEC 1931-34, dir Bryce Weir Ltd 1934-72, princ tech offr on radar Royal Aircraft Estab Farnborough 1942-45; former: chm Watford Mfrg Assoc, dir Watford Sheltered Workshop, vol worker CAB; Liveryman Worshipful Co Needlemakers 1974; CPhys, FInstP, FBIM; *Recreations* bridge, golf; *Clubs* Cambridge Soc; *Style*— William Weir, Esq; 3 Caroon Drive, Sarratt, Herts WD3 6DD (☎ 092 776 7036)

WEIR, 3 Viscount (UK 1938); William Kenneth James Weir; also Baron Weir (UK 1918); s of 2 Viscount Weir, CBE (d 1975), of Montgreenan, Kilwinning, Ayrshire, and his 1 w, Lucette Isabel, *née* Crowdy (d 1972); *b* 9 Nov 1933; *Educ* Eton, Trinity Coll Cambridge (BA); *m* 1, 1964 (m dis 1972), Diana Lucy, da of late Peter Lewis MacDougall of Ottawa, Canada; 1 s (Hon James William Hartland), 1 da (Hon Lorna Elizabeth b 17 May 1967); m 2, 6 Nov 1976, Mrs Jacqueline Mary Marr, da of late Baron Louis de Chollet, of Fribourg, Switzerland; *Heir* s, Hon James William Hartland Weir b 6 June 1965; *Career* Nat Serv with RN 1955-57; chm: Great Northern Investmnt Tst Ltd 1975-82, Weir Gp plc 1983- (vice-chm 1981-83, chm and chief exec 1972-81); co-chm RIT and Northern plc 1982-83, vice-chm J Rothschild Hldgs; dir: British Steel Corpn 1972-76, Br Bank of the Middle East 1977-79 (memb London Advsy Ctee of Hongkong and Shanghai Banking Corpn 1980-), BICC plc 1977-, L F Rothschild Unterberg Towbin 1983-85; memb: Ct of Bank of England 1972-84,

Scottish Econ Cncl 1972-84, Engrg Industries Cncl 1975-80; FIBF 1984, MIES 1985, FRSA 1987; *Recreations* golf, shooting; *Clubs* White's; *Style—* The Rt Hon the Viscount Weir; Rodinghead, Mauchline, Ayrshire KA5 5TR (☎ 056 384 233); The Weir Group plc, Cathcart, Glasgow G44 4EX (☎ 041 637 7111, fax 041 637 2221, telex 77161 WPLCRT G)

WEISKRANTZ, Prof Lawrence; s of Benjamin Weiskrantz (d 1935), of Russia and the USA, and Rose, *née* Rifkin; *b* 28 Mar 1926; *Educ* Swarthmore Coll (BA), Oxford Univ (MSc), Harvard (PhD); *m* 11 Feb 1954, Barbara Edna, da of William Collins (d 1979); 1 s (Conrad b 1963), 1 da (Julia b 1966); *Career* cryptographer USAF 1944-46, served Europe Africa, Middle East assoc Inst of Living 1952-55, teaching asst Harvard Univ 1952-53, pt/t lectr Tufts Univ 1952, sr post-doctoral fell US Nat Acad of Sci Oxford Univ (prof of psychology 1967-); Cambridge Univ: res assoc 1956-61, asst dir of res 1961-66, reader in physiological psychology 1966-67; FRS 1980, memb US Nat Acad of Sci 1987; *Recreations* music, walking; *Style—* Prof Lawrence Weiskrantz; c/o Magdalen Coll, Oxford; Dept of Experimental Psychology, South Parks Rd, Oxford OX1 3UD (☎ 0865 271 356)

WEISMAN, Lorenzo David; s of Eduardo Weisman (d 1988), of Guatemala, and Suzanne, *née* Loeb; *b* 22 April 1945; *Educ* Moses Brown Sch Providence Rhode Island USA, Harvard Coll Cambridge Mass USA (BA), Univ of Columbia NY USA (MBA); *m* 21 June 1971, Danielle Yvonne Camille Maysonnave; 1 s (Thomas b 3 Oct 1980), 2 da (Melissa b 26 July 1973, Alexia b 27 Oct 1976); *Career* Dillon Read and Co Inc NY: joined 1973, vice pres 1977, md 1981, pres (London) 1984; Memb Societé Francaise des Auteurs; *Clubs* Spee (Harvard), Travellers (Paris), RAC, Hurlingham; *Style—* Lorenzo Weisman, Esq; 24 The Little Boltons, London SW10 (☎ 01 373 8092); Dillon Rd Limited, Devonshire House, Mayfair Place, London W1 (☎ 01 493 1239, telex 8811055)

WEISMAN, Malcolm; s of David Weisman (d 1969), and Jeanie Pearl Weisman (d 1980); *Educ* Parmiter's Sch, Harrogate GS, London Sch of Econs, St Catherine's Coll Oxford (MA); *m* 1958, Rosalie, da of Dr A A Spiro (d 1963), of St John's Wood; 2 s (Brian b 1959, Daniel b 1963); *Career* barr Middle Temple 1961, rec Crown Ct 1980; asst cmmr Parly Boundaries 1976; Jewish chaplain RAF 1956, sr chaplain HM Forces 1972, sec gen Allied Air Forces Chiefs of Chaplains Ctee 1980, chaplain Oxford Univ 1971; memb of Cts of Univs of East Anglia, Lancaster and Warwick; ed Menorah magazine; memb: Advsy Ctee on Mil Chaplaincy, Cabinet of Chief Rabbi of Cwlth, Man of Year Award 1980; religious advsr to small Jewish communities and Hillel cnsllr to New Univs; *Recreations* reading, walking, doing nothing; *Style—* Malcolm Weisman, Esq; 1 Grays Inn Square, London WC1R 5AA (☎ 01 405 8946)

WEISS, Charles; CBE (1974); s of Frank Weiss (d 1944); *b* 29 Jan 1914; *Educ* Bolyai GS Budapest, Florence Univ; *m* 1, 1935, Isabel Katherine; m 2, 1964, Lesley Anne, *née* Ryan; 4 da; *Career* Maj RE (India, Assam, Burma), consulting engr; *Recreations* cinephotography, history, music; *Clubs* White Elephant; *Style—* Charles Weiss Esq, CBE; 30 Westcoombe Ave, London SW20 0RQ (☎ 01 946 4429)

WEISS, Sir Eric; s of (Siegfried) Solomon Weiss (decd); *b* 30 Dec 1908; *Educ* Augustinius Gymnasium Weiden (Germany), Neues Gymnasium Nürnberg; *m* 1934, Maria Margarete Gertrud (Greta), da of Jean Kobaltzky (d 1953); 2 s, 2 da; *Career* fnder Foundry Services Ltd (original co of Foseco Minsep Gp) 1932; chm Minerals Separation Ltd 1964; chm Foseco Minsep Ltd 1969, pres 1979; Lloyds underwriter 1976-79; dep presiding memb UK Cmmn of United World Colls 1973-76, memb Int Cncl 1969-76, memb bd of dirs 1970-76, memb Inst Br Foundrymen; kt 1980; *Recreations* golf, travel; *Clubs* Garrick; *Style—* Sir Eric Weiss; Flat 6, 3 West Eaton Place, London SW1X 8LU; 3rd Floor, 1-6 Ely Place, London EC1N 6RY (☎ 01 405 5092); The Manor House, Little Marlow, Bucks (☎ (062 84) 2824)

WELANDER, Rev Canon David Charles St Vincent; s of Charles Ernest Sven Welander, of Uppsala, Sweden, and Lousia Georgina, Downes, *née* Panter; *b* 22 Jan 1925; *Educ* Unthank Coll Norwich, London Univ (BD), Univ of Toronto; *m* 12 July 1952, Nancy O'Rourke, da of Dr George Weldale Stanley, MC (d 1960); 2 s (Richard David Edward b 1955, Christopher Peter Graham b 1959), 3 da (Rosemary Eileen Nancy b 1953, Sarah Jane Mary b 1957, Claire Elizabeth Georgina b 1960); *Career* chaplain and lectr in New Testament studies London Coll of Divinity Univ of London 1950-56; vicar: Iver Bucks 1956-61, Christ Church Cheltenham 1962-74; rural dean Cheltenham 1972-75, memb Gen Synod of C of E 1970-85, sr inspr Theol Coll 1975-82, canon residentiary Gloucester Cath 1975-; cncl memb: Friends of Gloucester Cath, Sch for Miny Diocese of Gloucester, Malvern Girls Coll, King's Sch Gloucester; FSA 1979; *Books* Gloucester Cathedral (with David Verey, 1979), The Stained Glass of Gloucester Cathedral (1985), Gloucester Cathedral: Its History, Art and Architecture (1989); *Recreations* walking, golf, music, European travel; *Clubs* Royal Cwlth Soc; *Style—* The Rev Canon David Welander; 6 College Green, Gloucester GL1 2LX (☎ 0452 21954)

WELBY, Sir (Richard) Bruno Gregory Welby; 7 Bt (UK 1801), of Denton Manor, Lincolnshire; s of Sir Oliver Welby, 6 Bt, TD (d 1977, s of Lady Maria Hervey, sis of 4 Marquess of Bristol), by his w, Barbara Angela, da of John Gregory, CB, CMG, and gda of Sir Philip Gregory; n of Dowager Lady Saltoun and Viscountess Portal of Hungerford, *qqv*; *b* 11 Mar 1928; *Educ* Eton, Ch Ch Oxford; *m* 1952, Jane Biddulph, da of the late Ralph Hodder-Williams, MC; 3 s, 1 da; *Heir* s, Charles William Hodder Welby; *Style—* Sir Bruno Welby, Bt; 23 Hanover Gdns, London SE11

WELBY, Charles William Hodder; s and h of Sir (Richard) Bruno Welby, 7 Bt, of Denton by Jane Biddulph; *b* 6 May 1953; *Educ* Eton, RAC; *m* 1978, Suzanna, da of Maj Ian Stuart-Routledge (d 1981), of Harston Hall, Grantham; 2 da (Venetia b 1981, Zinnia b 1985); *Career* 2 Lt 1974 Worcestershire and Sherwood Foresters TAVR; chartered surveyor, conslt Humber's, dep dir Cons Bd of Finance 1987; contested (C) Caerphilly 1983; ARICS; *Style—* Charles Welby, Esq; Stroxton House, Grantham, Lincs (☎ 047 683 232)

WELBY-EVERARD, Maj-Gen Sir Christopher Earle; KBE (1965), OBE (1945, CB 1961), DL (Lincs 1966); s of Edward Everard Earle Welby-Everard (d 1951); *b* 9 August 1909; *Educ* Charterhouse, Corpus Christi Coll Oxford; *m* 1938, Sybil Juliet Wake, *née* Shorrock; 2 s; *Career* 2 Lt Lincoln Regt 1930, served WWII UK and Normandy, Lt-Col 1944, Brig 1957, Maj-Gen 1959, COS to C-in-C Allied Forces Northern Europe 1959-61, GOC Nigerian Army, ret; High Sheriff Lincs 1974-75; *Style—* Maj-Gen Sir Christopher Welby-Everard, KBE, CB, OBE, DL; The Manor House, Sapperton, Sleaford, Lincs NG34 0TB (☎ 047 685 273)

WELCH, David Reginald Stuart; s of Reginald Welch, and Margaret Cynthia, *née* Hughes; *b* 14 April 1954; *Educ* Moseley Hall GS, Manchester Poly; *m* 25 Sept 1976, Anne, da of Leslie James Vaux (d 1984); 1 s (Mark b 1986), 2 da (Sarah b 1979, Rachael b 1980); *Career* CA; FCA; *Recreations* Sunday sch teacher, reading, poetry; *Style—* David R S Welch, Esq; 3 Alvington Grove, Hazel Grove, Stockport, Cheshire SK7 5LS (☎ 061 456 9140); 220 Wellington Rd South, Stockport, Cheshire SK2 6RT (☎ 061 480 2480)

WELCH, Ivan Edwin; s of William Edwin Welch, Police Inspector, and Edith May Welch; *b* 14 Nov 1926; *Educ* Lansdowne, Leicester Sch of Arch; *m* 10 May 1951, Eileen, da of Leonard Towers, 1 da (Elaine b 1960); *Career* chartered architect; ptnr Welch, Dood, Wright Ptnrship 1966; ARIBA 1966, FFAS 1984; *Recreations* golf, art; *Style—* Ivan Welch, Esq; Launde House, Harborough Rd, Oadby, Leicester (☎ 0533 714141)

WELCH, Sir John Reader; 2 Bt (UK 1957), of Chard, Co Somerset; s of Sir Cullum Welch, 1 Bt, OBE, MC (d 1980); *b* 26 July 1933; *Educ* Marlborough, Hertford Coll Oxford; *m* 25 Sept 1962, Margaret Kerry, o da of Kenneth Victor Douglass; 1 s, 2 da; *Heir* s, James Douglass Cullum, b 10 Nov 1973; *Career* slr; ptnr: Bell Brodrick & Gray 1961-71, Wedlake Bell 1972-; chm: John Fairfax (UK) Ltd, London Homes for the Elderly; registrar Archdeaconry of London, memb Court of Common Cncl (City of London) 1975-86 and chm Planning and Communications Ctee 1981-1982; Liveryman and memb of Ct of Assts Haberdashers' Co, Freeman and past master Parish Clerks' Co; pres (1986-87) and hon slr City Livery Club; chm Walbrook Ward Club 1978-79; CStJ 1981; *Clubs* MCC, Surrey County Cricket; *Style—* Sir John Welch, Bt; 28 Rivermead Court, Ranelagh Gardens, London SW6 3RU; office: 16 Bedford St, Covent Gdn, London WC2E 9HF (☎ 01 379 7266)

WELCH, Peter John; s of Cyril Vincent Welch (d 1961), of Sutton Colfield, and Elsie Lilian Ramsden; *b* 4 Jan 1940; *Educ* St Philip's Sch Edgbaston; *m* 12 June 1962, Margaret Mary, da of John Lavelle Bates, of Birmingham; 4 s (Peter b 1963, Andrew b 1964, Julian b 1966, Ian b 1975), 1 da (Elspeth b 1968); *Career* dir: Unicorn Inds plc 1972-78 and 1980-87 (chm 1980-84), Foseco MINSEP plc 1978-87, Thermal Scientific plc & Jeyes Hldgs Ltd 1987-; chm Unitary Tax Campaign (Ltd) 1978-; FCA 1961; *Recreations* bridge, music, reading, private flying; *Style—* Peter Welch, Esq; Frankfield, Spinfield Lane, Marlow, Buckinghamshire SL7 2LB (☎ 06284 5975, car tel 0836 508766)

WELD, Col Sir Joseph William; OBE (1946), TD & 2 bars (1947), JP (Dorset 1938); yr s of Wilfrid Weld (whose paternal grandmother was Hon Elizabeth Stourton, da of 17 Baron Stourton). Sir Joseph is fourth in descent from Thomas Weld, of Lulworth Castle, who founded Stonyhurst Coll and whose er bro's 2 wife subsequently married Thomas Fitzherbert and, after being widowed as Mrs Fitzherbert, The Prince of Wales, later George IV; *b* 22 Sept 1909; *Educ* Stonyhurst, Balliol Oxford; *m* 1933, Elizabeth Agnes Mary, da of Edmund Joseph Bellord, of Kensington; 1 s (Wilfrid b 1934), 5 da (Magdalen b 1937, Elizabeth b 1939, Clare b 1945, Katherine b 1948, Georgina b 1952) & 1 da decd; *Career* served WW II: Staff Coll Camberley 1941 and 1942-43, GSO 2 GHQ Home Forces, GSO 1 HQ SEAC; cmd 4 Bn Dorset Regt 1947-51 (Hon Col TA, served 1932-41), Col 1951; ld-lt Dorset 1964- (DL 1952, High Sheriff 1951, ccllr 1961), lord of the manors of Lulworth, Combe Keynes, Winfrith Newburgh, Sutton Pointz; Privy Chamberlain of Sword and Cape to Pope Pius XII; chm Dorset CLA 1949-60, S Dorset Cons Assoc 1952-55 (pres 1955-59); kStJ 1967; kt 1937; *Clubs* Royal Dorset Yacht; *Style—* Colonel Sir Joseph Weld, OBE, TD, JP; Lulworth Manor, East Lulworth, Dorset (☎ 092 941 2352)

WELD-FORESTER, Hon Kythé Priscilla; da of late 7 Baron Forester; *b* 1941; *Career* farmer; *Style—* The Hon Kythé Weld-Forester

WELDON, Anthony Henry David; s of Max Weldon (d 1979), and Regina Charlotte, *née* Gideon; *b* 23 Dec 1945; *Educ* Uppingham; *m* 1970 (m dis 1984), Claire Ellen, *née* Gessler; 2 s (Julian b 1972, Oliver b 1975), 1 da (Alexandra b 1974); m 2, 1984, Manina Anne, *née* Mitchell; *Career* chm Durrington Corpn Ltd 1984, mangr Cocoa Merchants Gp Ltd; dir Storeylake Ltd 1981, Impexlord Ltd 1985, Maylight Ltd 1985, Print Permanising Ltd 1985, Emos Information Systems Ltd 1985, SGL Communications plc 1985, Royal Acad Tst Ltd; tstee Royal Opera House, chm advsy bd Royal Acad of Arts, memb RCM, chm appeal ctee The Exploratory; memb Worshipful Co of Masons; *Recreations* sport, opera; *Clubs* MCC, RAC, Royal Tennis, Annabel's, Mark's, Brooks', Hurlingham, Riverside, Cumberland Lawn Tennis, Highgate GC; *Style—* Anthony Weldon, Esq; Flat 2, 83-85 Onslow Gardens, London SW7 3BU (☎ 01 373 6263); Durrington Corporation Ltd, 4/5 Grosvenor Place, London SW1X 7HJ (☎ 01 235 6146)

WELDON, Sir Anthony William; 9 Bt (I 1723), of Dunmore, Co Carlow; s of Sir Thomas Weldon, 8 Bt (d 1979), by his w Marie, Lady Weldon, now Countess Cathcart *qv*; *b* 11 May 1947; *Educ* Sherborne; *m* 1980, Amanda, formerly w of Anthony Wigan and da of Maj Geoffrey North, MC, by his w, Hon Margaret de Grey (2 da of 8 Baron Walsingham, DSO, OBE, JP, DL); 2 da (Alice Louise b 13 Nov 1981, Oonagh Leone b 6 Oct 1983); *Heir* 2 cous, Kevin Weldon; *Career* late Lt Irish Gds, awarded S Arabian GSM; *Recreations* stalking, champagne, cricket; *Clubs* White's, The Stranded Whales; *Style—* Sir Anthony Weldon, Bt

WELDON, Duncan Clark; s of Clarence Weldon, of Southport, and Margaret Mary Weldon; *b* 19 Mar 1941; *Educ* King George V GS Southport; *m* 1, Helen Shapiro (m dis 1971); m 2, July 1973, Janet, da of Walter Mahoney (d 1982); 1 da (Lucy Jane b Oct 1977); *Career* theatrical prodr presented over 135 prodns in London notably: When We Are Married 1970, The Chalk Garden 1971, Waters of the Moon 1978, Man and Superman 1982, School for Scandal 1983, Heartbreak House 1983, A Patriot for Me 1983, The Aspern Papers 1984, Aren't We All 1984, The Way of the World 1984, Sweet Bird of Youth 1985, Waste 1985, Mr and Mrs Nobody 1986, Antony and Cleopatra 1986, The Taming of the Shrew 1986, Long Day's Journey into Night 1986, Breaking the Code 1986, Melon 1987, Kiss Me Kate 1987, A Touch of the Poet 1988, The Admirable Crichton 1988, Richard II 1988, A Walk in the Woods 1988, Orpheus Descending 1988; first Broadway prodn Brief Lives 1974; *Recreations* photography; *Style—* Duncan Weldon, Esq; Brackenhill, Munstead Park, Godalming, Surrey (☎ 04868 5508); Triumph Theatre Productions Ltd, Wardolf Chambers, 11 Aldwych, London, WC2 (☎ 01 836 0186)

WELDON, Fay; da of Dr Frank Birkinshaw (d 1947), of N Zealand, and Margaret, *née* Jepson; *b* 22 Sept 1931; *Educ* Christ Church Girls HS (NZ); South Hampstead HS; St Andrews Univ (MA) Economics and Psychology (1952); *m* June 1961, Weldon Ron; 4 s (Nicholas b 1954, Daniel b 1963, Thomas b 1970, Samuel b 1977); *Career* screenwriter, novelist, critic, essayist; chm of judges Booker McConnell Prize 1983; The Fat Woman's Joke 1967, Down Among the Women 1971, Female Friends 1975, Remember Me 1976, Little Sisters 1978, Praxis 1978 (Booker Prize Nomin), Puffball 1980, Watching Me Watching You 1981, The President's Child 1982, Life and Loves' of a She Devil 1984 (televised 1986), Letters to Alice-on First Reading Jane Austen 1984, Polaris and other Stories 1985, Rebecca West 1985, The Shrapnel Academy 1986, Heart of the Country 1987 (televised 1987), The Hearts and Lives of Men 1987, The Rules of Life 1987; *Books* Down Among the Women (1968), Female Friends (1970), Puffball (1978), The Shapnee Academy (1983), Life and Loves of a She Devil (1984), Hearts and Lives of Men (1987); *Style—* Mrs Fay Weldon; c/o Giles Gordon, Anthony Shiels Associates, 43 Doughty St, WC1N 2LF; c/o Phil Kelvin, Goodwin Associates, 12 Rabbit Row, Kinsington Church St, W8 4DX

WELENSKY, Rt Hon Sir Roy - Rowland; KCMG (1959), CMG (1946, PC 1960); s of Michael Welensky; *b* 20 Jan 1907,Salisbury, S Rhodesia; *Educ* Salisbury, Rhodesia; *m* 1, 1928, Elizabeth Henderson (d 1969); 1 s, 1 da; m 2, 1972, Valerie Scott; 2 da; *Career* former engine driver; Fedn Rhodesia and Nyasaland: MLC N Rhodesia (now Zambia) 1938, memb Exec Cncl 1940-53, dir Manpower N Rhodesia 1941-46, Min Tport Communications and Posts 1953-56, Ldr House and Dep Pm 1955-56, Pm and Min External Affrs 1956-63; kt 1953; *Style—* The Rt Hon Sir Roy Welensky, KCMG, CMG, PC; Shaftesbury House, Milldown Rd, Blandford Forum, Dorset DT11 7DE

WELFARE, Mary Katharine; *née* Gordon; er adopted da of 4 Marquess of Aberdeen and Temair (d 1974); *b* 30 May 1946; *m* 1968, Simon Piers Welfare, 2 son of late Kenneth William Welfare, of The Old Doctor's House, Stradbrooke, Suffolk; *Style—* Mrs Simon Welfare; 7 St Edward's Terr, Clifford, Boston Spa, Lincs

WELFORD, George Henry (Harry) Ettrick; AE (1945); s of George Henry Welford, OBE (d 1966), and Flora Welford (d 1950); *b* 4 Dec 1916; *Educ* HMS Worcester, Kings Coll, Durham Univ (BSc Mech Eng); *m* 2 Nov 1940, Betty Elise, da of Svere an Hjersing (d 1956), of Norway;4 s (Stuart Ettrick Welford b 1942, Michael Sverre b 1945, Jonathan b 1953, Robert Anthony Hylton b 1957); *Career* RAF 1938-46: fighter pilot 607 Sqdn Battle of Britain, Tactical Air Force 222 Sqdn 135 Wing; conslt engr Prod Engrg 1948-52; export mangr John HEATHCOTE 1952-70, dir Mid Devon Engr Gp Tning 1970-80; *Recreations* painting, yacht cruising (RYA yachtmaster offshore 1983); *Clubs* Royal Overseas League, RAF Assoc, RYA, Battle of Britain Figher Assoc; *Style—* Harry Welford, AE

WELLBELOVED, James; MP (L but resigned Whip and joined SDP July 1981) Bexley, Erith and Crayford 1974-; s of Wilfred Wellbeloved; *b* 29 July 1926; *Educ* SE London Tech; *m* 1948, Mavis Ratcliff; 2 s, 1 da; *Career* MP (L) Erith and Crayford 1965-74, pps MOD 1967-69, sec of State Foreign and Cwlth Affrs 1969-70, oppn whip 1972-74, parly under-sec Def (RAF) 1976-79; dep chm London MPs Parly Gp 1970-; commercial conslt; writer and bdcaster on foreign and def matters; *Style—* James Wellbeloved Esq, MP; House of Commons, SW1 (☎ 01 219 4563/4077)

WELLESLEY, Lady Alexia Anne Elizabeth; da of 6 Earl Cowley (d 1975), and Maria, da of Enrique Buenãno of Buenos Aires; *b* 1973; *Style—* Lady Alexia Wellesley

WELLESLEY, Hon Brian Timothy; s (by 2 m) of 4 Earl Cowley; *b* 1938; *Educ* Arizona State Coll, Denver Univ, Colorado and Nevada U (BS); *m* 1, 1961 (m dis 1964), Patricia Tribbey; m 2, 1966, Karen Elizabeth Bradbury, of Reno, Nevada, USA; *Career* ch of intelligence div US Treasury Dept Alaska; *Style—* The Hon Brian Wellesley; PO Box 974, Anchorage, Alaska, 99510 USA

WELLESLEY, Lady Caroline; da of 6 Earl Cowley (d 1975), and Maria, da of Enrique Buenãno of Buenos Aires

WELLESLEY, Lord (James) Christopher Douglas; 4 s of 8 Duke of Wellington; *b* 16 Dec 1964; *Style—* Lord Christopher Wellesley; Stratfield Saye House, Reading, Berks

WELLESLEY, Lady George; Jean; da of John Mcgillivray, of The Braes of Glenlivet, Banffshire; *b* 18 August 1905; *m* 1955, as his 2 w, Lt-Col Lord George Wellesley (d 1967), 4 s of 4 Duke of Wellington and bro of 5 and 7 Dukes; *Style—* Lady George Wellesley; 14 Melbury Rd, London W14 8LS (☎ 01 602 3031)

WELLESLEY, Lord John Henry; 3 s of 8 Duke of Wellington; *b* 20 April 1954; *Educ* Eton; *m* 1977, Corinne, da of HE Robert Vaes, Belgian ambass; 1 s (b 6 June 1981), 1 da (b 23 July 1983); *Style—* Lord John Wellesley; 58, Elm Park Road, London SW3 6AU

WELLESLEY, Julian Valerian; s of Gerald Wellesley, MC, of Highfield Park, Sussex (gn of 1 Earl Cowley, KG, GCB, PC, and ggs of 1 Baron Cowley, bro of 1 Duke of Wellington), by Elizabeth, da of Otho Ball, of Chicago, and formerly w of Quintin Gilbey, the racing correspondent; *b* 9 August 1933; *Educ* RNCs Dartmouth & Greenwich; *m* 1965, Elizabeth, da of Cyril Stocken and formerly w of David Hall; 1 s (William Valerian b 1966), 1 da (Kate Elizabeth b 1970), 3 step da; *Career* late Lt RN; jt md Ayer Barker 1971-78, chm Charles Barker Gp 1978-83; dir: Horizon Travel plc 1984-87,; Chatsworth Food Ltd 1986-; memb Eastbourne Health Authy 1986-; ctee memb Assoc of Lloyds Members 1985-; *Recreations* reading, music, family, tennis, watching cricket; *Clubs* Brooks's, Sussex; *Style—* Julian Wellesley, Esq; Tidebrook Manor, Wadhurst, Sussex

WELLESLEY, Lord Richard Gerald; 2 s of 8 Duke of Wellington; *b* 20 June 1949; *Educ* Eton, RAC Cirencester; *m* 1973, Joanna, da of John Sumner; 2 da; *Style—* Lord Richard Wellesley; Knockdolian, Colmonell, Girvan, Ayrshire

WELLESLEY, Robin Alfred; s of Quintin Gilbey (d 1979), of London; step s of Gerald Wellesley (d 1961), of Withyham, Sussex; *b* 23 July 1928; *Educ* Eton; *m* 1953, Marianne, da of John McDonald, of Chicago; 1 s (Gerald), 2 da (Diana, Laura); *Career* dir: Prestige Gp 1965-82, Aust Br C of C 1984-, NZ UK C of C and Indust 1984-; *Recreations* gardening, cricket, travel; *Clubs* Buck's; *Style—* Robin Wellesley, Esq; Shingle Barn, Dwelly Lane, Edenbridge, Kent (☎ 0732 862251); 36 Edge St, London W8 (☎ 01 727 4503); Suite 615, 162-168 Regent Street, London W1R 5TB

WELLESLEY, Lady Tara Lennon; da (by 1 m) of 7 Earl Cowley; *b* 1962; *Style—* Lady Tara Wellesley

WELLESLEY, Hon Mrs Henry; Valerie Rose; *née* Pitman; da of late Christian Ernest Pitman, CBE, of Doynton House, Doynton, nr Bath, and Eileen Winifred, *née* Clarke; *m* 1969, as her 4 w, Hon Henry Gerald Valerian Francis Wellesley (d 1981), yr s of 3 Earl Cowley (d 1919); 2 s; *Style—* The Hon Mrs Henry Wellesley; Priestown House, Mulhuddart, Co Dublin, Eire

WELLESLEY, Hon Mrs (Youla Edithe); *née* Littleton; 4 da of 4 Baron Hatherton (d 1944); *b* 13 Mar 1904; *m* 5 Oct 1927 (m dis 1938), John Elvine Harris (d 1965), eldest, s of John Waugh Harris, of Stone, Staffs; 3 s; *Career* assumed by deed poll 1939, the surname of Wellesley in lieu of that of Harris; *Style—* The Hon Mrs Wellesley

WELLING, Mark Ronald; s of Kenneth Ronald Welling, of Derby, and Margaret Dorothy, *née* Hunter; *b* 22 Mar 1956; *Educ* Derby Sch, Emmanuel Coll Cambridge (MA); *m* 28 March 1987, Vanessa Jane, da of W Richard Barker, of Farnley Tyas, W Yorks; *Career* slr 1981, ptnr Allen and Overy 1987-; cncllr Royal Borough of Kingston upon Thames 1986; memb City of London Slrs Co 1987; memb Law Soc 1981-; *Recreations* bassoon, clarinet, and piano playing; *Style—* Mark Welling, Esq; 52 Grove Cres, Kingston upon Thames, Surrey KT1 2DG (☎ 01 541 3405); Allen and Overy, 9 Cheapside, London EC2V 6AD (☎ 01 248 9898, fax 01 236 2192, telex 8812801)

WELLINGHAM, Air Cdre (John) Bernard; s of Claude Bernard Wellingham (d 1963), and Annetta, *née* Jagoe (d 1980); *b* 21 June 1925; *Educ* Trinity Sch Croydon, Christs Coll Cambridge (MA), Royal Coll of Military Sci Shrivenham, RAF Staff Coll Bracknell, Jt Servs Staff Coll Latimer; *m* 24 July 1948, Patricia Margaret, da of Wing Cdr Patrick John Murphy (d 1965); 2 s (John b 1949, Charles b 1953); *Career* RAF 1945, cmmnd 1946, communications devpt Royal Aircraft Establishment Farnborough 1946-50, serv RAF Shaluffa and Abu Sueir 1951-53, HQ RAF Fighter Cmd 1953-54, sr tech offr RAF Patrington 1954-56, Guided Wpns Devpt Royal Radar Establishment Malvern 1957-60, Operational Requirements Staff Air Miny 1961-63, Cmd Telecomms Offr NEAF 1964-67, chief instr RAF Coll Cranwell 1967-68, memb Air Force Bd Ctee on RAF Career Structure 1968-69, asst dir signals MOD 1969-72, controller Def Communications Network 1972-74, Air Offr Wales and Station Cdr RAF St Athan 1974-76, Air Cdre Signals RAF Support Cmd 1976-78; Mid Suffolk DC 1983-: chm environmental health ctee 1986-88 (vice-chm 1984-86), currently vice-chm policy and resources ctee; chm Wingfield Parish Cncl, vice-chm Govrs Stradbroke HS, and Churchwarden; CEng, FRAes 1976, FBIM 1976; *Recreations* tennis, shooting, horticulture; *Clubs* RAF; *Style—* Air Cdre Bernard Wellingham; The White House, Wingfield, Diss, Norfolk IP21 5QT

WELLINGS, Sir Jack Alfred; CBE (1970); s of late Edward Josiah Wellings, of Surrey; *b* 16 August 1917; *Educ* Selhurst GS, London Poly; *m* 1946, Greta, da of late George Tidey, of Sunderland; 1 s, 2 da; *Career* vice-pres Hawker Siddeley (Canada) Ltd 1952-62, chm and md George Cohen 600 Gp Ltd 1968-, memb Nat Enterprise Bd 1977-79, pt-t memb: NCB 1971-, Br Aerospace 1980-; kt 1975; *Style—* Sir Jack Wellings, CBE; Boundary Meadow, Collum Green Rd, Stoke Poges, Bucks (☎ 395 2978); George Cohen 600 Group Ltd, Wood Lane, London W12 (☎ 01 743 2070)

WELLINGS, Victor Gordon; QC (1973); s of late Gordon Arthur Wellings, and Alice Adelaide Wellings (who later m Charles Arthur Poole, decd); *b* 19 July 1919; *Educ* Reading Sch, Exeter Coll Oxford (MA); *m* 1948, Helen Margaret Jill, da of late Henry Lovell; 3 s; *Career* barr 1949-73, pres Lands Tribunal 1989- (memb 1973-88); dep High Court judge 1975-; *Recreations* golf, fishing; *Clubs* Oxford and Cambridge; *Style—* Victor Wellings, Esq, QC; Cherry Tree Cottage, Whitchurch Hill, Pangbourne, Berks; 48-49 Chancery Lane, London WC2 (☎ 01 936 7169)

WELLINGTON, 8 Duke of (UK 1814); Arthur Valerian Wellesley; MVO (1952), OBE (1957), MC (1941), DL (Hants 1975); also Baron of Mornington (I 1746), Earl of Mornington, Viscount Wellesley (both I 1760), Viscount Wellington of Talavera and of Wellington, Baron Douro (both UK 1809), Conde do Vimeiro (Portugal 1811), Earl of Wellington (UK 1812), Marquess of Wellington (UK 1812), Duque de Ciudad Rodrigo and a Grandee of the 1 Class (Spain 1812), Duque da Vittoria, Marques de Torres Vedras (both Portugal 1812), Marquess of Douro (UK 1814), and Prince of Waterloo (Netherlands 1815); s of 7 Duke of Wellington, KG (d 1972, but ceded Sp Dukedom and Grandeeship to present Duke 1966); *b* 2 July 1915; *Educ* Eton, New Coll Oxford; *m* 1944, Diana, da of Maj-Gen Douglas McConnel, CB, CBE, DSO, of Ayrshire; 4 s, 1 da; *Heir* s, Marquess of Douro; *Career* patron of 4 livings, Brig (ret) RHG; Silver Stick in Waiting & Lt-Col cmdg Household Cav 1959-60 & OC 22 Armd Bde 1960-61; defence attaché Madrid 1964-67; Col-in-Chief The Duke of Wellington's Regt 1974-; Hon Col 2 Bn Wessex Regt TA & VRA, pres SE Roy Br Legion; dir Massey Ferguson Holdings 1967 and Massey Ferguson Ltd 1973, vice pres and cncl memb Zoological Soc of London, dep-pres the Game Conservancy 1982-; pres: Rare Breeds Survival Trust 1982-, Cncl for Environmental Conservation 1983-, Atlantic Salmon Trust 1983-; Queen's trustee bd of Tower Armouries 1983-; chm Pitt Club, govr Wellington Coll; trustee: St Cross Winchester, Wilderness Fndn; Cncl memb: RASE, OStJ Hants; *Clubs* Turf, Buck's; *Style—* His Grace the Duke of Wellington; Stratfield Saye House, Reading, Berks; Apsley House, Piccadilly, London W1

WELLMAN, Derek Morris; s of Moris Francis Ernest Wellman, of 33 Partis Way, Bath, and Doris Laurena Rose, *née* Chappell; *b* 12 April 1944; *Educ* Crypt GS Gloucester, Selwyn Coll Cambridge (MA); *m* 8 Jan 1972, (Evelyn) Barbara Hall, da of Thomas Richard Lennox (d 1985); 1 s (Edwrd b 1972), 1 da (Katherine b 1975); *Career* slr Supreme Ct 1969, registrar Diocese of Lincoln 1978; Notary Public 1978; tstee Lincs Old Church Tst, chm Lincoln area RSCM, amateur musician; memb: Law Soc 1969, Ecclesiastical Law Assoc 1978, Ecclesiastical Law Assoc 1978, Ecclesiastical Law Soc 1987; *Recreations* music, sport; *Style—* Derek Wellman, Esq; 52 Nettleman Road, Lincoln (☎ 0522 32619); 28 West Parade, Lincoln (☎ 0522 536161)

WELLS, (William Arthur) Andrew; TD (1984); s of Sir John Wells, *qv* ; *b* 14 June 1949; *Educ* Eton, North London Poly; *m* 19 Oct 1974, Tessa Margaret, da of Lt-Col Jocelyn Eustace Gurney, DSO, MC, DL (d 1973), of Tacolneston Hall, and Sprowston, Norfolk, and niece of John Gurney, *qv*; 2 s (William b 1980, Frederick b 1982), 1 da (Augusta b 1984); *Career* TA: cmmnd 1971, extra lectr JDSC 1978-79, Maj Royal Green Jackets (V) 1981-; publisher and book ed 1969-81; chief exec and corporate sec Minories Hldgs Ltd 1981-; landowner Mereworth, Kent; memb exec ctee Friends of Kent Churches; div chm: N Battersea Cons Assoc 1977-80 (pres 1981-83), Tooting Cons Assoc 1983-86; Liveryman Stationers' Co 1977, Clerk Watermen's Co 1986-; *Recreations* country interests, gardening, architectural history; *Style—* Andrew Wells, Esq, TD; Mere House, Mereworth, Maidstone, Kent ME18 5NB; 47 Streathbourne Rd, London SW17 8QZ; Minories Hldgs Ltd, 16 St Mary-at-Hill, London EC3R 8SE

WELLS, Benjamin Weston; TD (1954); s of Sir William Henry Wells (d 1933), of Wimbledon, and Dorothy Kate, *née* Horne, JP (d 1946); *b* 17 Feb 1918; *Educ* Bromsgrove, London Univ, St Thomas's Hosp (MB, MS); *m* 7 May 1945, Jean Lowson, da of Millar Mudie, of Madeley, Shropshire; 1 s (Graham b 1947, d 1959), 2 da (Fiona b 1949, Jane b 1960); *Career* cmmnd RAMC 1942, serv MEF Hosps, Arab Legion 1943-44, surgn CMF 1944-45, Maj RAMC TA 1945-66; conslt surgn 1952-83:

St Helier Hosp Carshalton, Nelson Hosp Wimbledon, Wilson Hosp Mitcham; ret from NHS 1983, conslt surgn Parkside Hosp Wimbledon and New Victoria Hosp Kingston 1983-; Freeman City of London 1959-, Liveryman Worshipful Soc of Apothecaries 1953; FRSM 1946, MRCS, LRCP, FRCS, EDIIV, FRCS (Eng); *Publications* numerous papers on bowel cancer in Br Jl of Surgery, The Lancet, Br Jl of Oncology; *Recreations* shooting, golf; *Clubs* Roehampton; *Style—* Benjamin Wells, Esq, TD; Oakleigh, 20 Sunnyside, Wimbledon SW19 4SH (☎ 01 946 3191)

WELLS, (Petrie) Bowen; MP (C) Hertford & Stortford 1983-; s of Reginald Laird Wells by his w Agnes, *née* Hunter; *b* 4 August 1935; *Educ* St Paul's, Exeter Univ, Regent St Poly Mgmnt Sch; *m* 1975, Rennie Heyde; 2 s; *Career* RN; schoolmaster, sales trainee Br Aluminium, with Cwlth Devpts Corpn, co sec & industl rels mangr Guyana Timbers and owner mangr Substation Gp Servs, MP (C) Hertford and Stevenage 1979-1983, PPS to Michael Alison as Min State Employment 1982-83; memb Foreign Affrs Select Ctee; memb Euro Legislation Select Ctee; chm: Utd Nat Parly Gp, Br Caribbean Gp; govr Inst of Devpt Studies Sussex Univ, tstee Industry and Parly Tst, bd memb Outward Bound Wales; govr Centre for Caribbean Studies, Warwick Univ; chm Soc for Int Dev UK Chapter; memb cncl of World Devpt Movement; memb cncl Centre for World Devpt Educn; *Books* Managing Third World Debt; *Style—* Bowen Wells, Esq, MP; House of Commons, London, SW1A 0AA

WELLS, Boyan Stewart; s of Gordon Tebbutt Wells, of 6 Edmund Close, Downend, Bristol BS16 5EJ, and Vera, *née* Stanisic; *b* 3 June 1956; *Educ* Colston's Sch Bristol, Wadham Coll Oxford (MA); *m* 11 Aug 1984, Alison Jayne, da of Michael Albert Good, of 45 Henbury Rd, Westbury-on-Tryma, Bristol; 2 da (Holly Catharine b 8 May 1987, Elena Rose b 2 Dec 1988); *Career* ptnr Allen & Overy 1987- (joined 1979); Oxford blue hockey; Freeman: City of London, Worshipful Co of Slrs 1987; memb: Friends of Dulwich Soc, Law Soc; *Recreations* hockey, squash, cinema; *Clubs* Richmond Hockey; *Style—* Boyan Wells, Esq; Allen & Overy, 9 Cheapside, London EC2V 6AD (☎ 01 248 9898, fax 01 236 2192)

WELLS, Sir Charles Maltby; 2 Bt (UK 1944), of Felmersham, Co Bedford, TD; s of Sir (Sydney) Richard Wells, 1 Bt, DL (d 1956), and Mary Dorothy (d 1956), da of Christopher Maltby; *b* 24 July 1908; *Educ* Bedford Sch, Pembroke Coll Cambridge; *m* 1935, Katharine Boulton, da of Frank Boteler Kenrick, of Toronto, Canada; 2 s (Christopher *qv*, Anthony Richard b 2 July 1947); *Heir* s, Christopher Wells; *Career* joined RE (TA) 1933, Capt 1939, served 54 Div 1939-41 and 76 Div 1941-43, Lt-Col 1941, Br Army Staff Washington 1943-45, Acting Col 1945; *Style—* Sir Charles Wells, Bt, TD; Apt 507, 350 Lonsdale Road, Toronto, Canada

WELLS, Christopher Charles; s and h of Sir Charles Wells, 2 Bt, TD; *b* 12 August 1936; *Educ* McGill Univ, Toronto Univ; *m* 1960, (m dis 1984), Elizabeth, da of I Griffiths, of Outrement, Quebec; 2 s (Michael b 1966, Geoffrey b 1970), 2 da (Felicity b 1964, Megan b 1969); m 2, 1985, Lynda Anne Cormack, of Toronto, Ontario; 1 s (Andrew b 1983); *Career* md in family practice; *Style—* Christopher Wells, Esq; St Michael's Family Practice, 30 Bond St, Toronto, Ontario M5B 1W8, Canada

WELLS, Prof David Arthur; s of Arthur William Wells, and Rosina Elizabeth, *née* Jones (d 1986); *b* 26 April 1941; *Educ* Christs Hosp Horsham, Gonville and Caius Coll Cambridge (MA, PhD); *Career* lectr in german: Univ of Southampton 1966-69, Bedford Coll Univ of London 1969-74; prof german: The Queens Univ of Belfast 1974-87, Birkbeck Coll Univ of London 1987-; hon sec Modern Humanities Res Assoc 1969-, sec-gen Int Fedn for Modern Languages and Literatures 1981-; FRSA 1985; *Books* The Vorau Moses and Balaam (1970), The Wild Man from the Epic of Gilgamesh to Hartmann von Ave's Iwein (1975), A Complete Concordance to the Vorauer Bücher Moses (1976), The Years Work in Modern Language Studies (jt ed 1976-); *Recreations* travel, theatre, music; *Style—* Prof David Wells; 128 Belgrave Rd, London SW1V 2BL (☎ 01 834 6558); Dept of German, Birkbeck College, 43 Gordon Square, London WC1H 0PD (☎ 01 631 6103)

WELLS, David George; s of George Henry Wells, of Welford, Northants, and Marian, *née* Trolley (d 1988); *b* 6 August 1941; *Educ* Market Harborough GS, Univ of Reading (BA); *m* 27 Oct 1967, Patricia Ann, da of George Fenwick (d 1983), of Southampton; 2 s (Jonathan b 1968, Colin b 1971); *Career* Hancock Gilbert & Morris 1962-67, Esso Chemical Ltd 1967-69, Gas Cncl 1969-72; Br Gas: chief investmt accountant (HQ) 1976 (chief accountant admin 1973-76), dir fin (SE Region) 1976-83, dep chm (W Midlands regn) 1983-88, SE regnl chm (plc) 1988-; FCA 1966, FBIM 1983, Companion IGasE 1988; *Recreations* walking, reading, photography, gardening; *Style—* David Wells, Esq; British Gas plc South Eastern, Katharine St, Croydon, Surrey CR9 1JU (☎ 01 688 4466)

WELLS, David John; s of Ralph Weston Wells, (d 1973) of Purley, Berks, and Mary Angela, *née* Crawford g da of 17 Baron Saye & Sele (d 1973); *b* 6 Oct 1935; *Educ* Cheltenham, Royal Agric Coll Cirencester (Dip Estate Mgmnt),; *m* 9 July 1960, Patricia Meriel, da of Percy Tyson (d 1962), of Lowick, Cumbria; 2 s (Andrew William b 1963, Alan David b 1966) ; *Career* Nat Serv Midshipman RNVR 1952-54; Lt (SCC) RNVR 1955-63; estate mgmnt in N Wales; branch chm (N Wales); CAAV 1977-78, RICS 1984-85; assoc ptnr Strutt & Parker, external tutor Coll of Estate Mgmnt (founded by gt the late Sir William Wells); licensed lay reader Diocese of St Asaph; memb: governing body Church in Wales 1966-, representative body Church in Wales 1972-, Electors Coll for Appt of Bishops (Church in Wales) 1973-; Community Cncllr; FRICS, FAAV, MRAC (DIST); *Recreations* Wrexham FC, philumeny; *Style—* D J Wells, Esq; 46 High Park, Gwernaffield, Mold, Clwyd CH7 5EE; Strutt & Parker, Victoria House, Grosvenor St, Mold, Clywd CH7 1AY (☎ 0352 2301)

WELLS, Prof George Albert; s of George J Wells (d 1960), and Lilian Maud, *née* Bird (d 1986); *b* 22 May 1926; *Educ* Stationers' Company's Sch, UCL (BA, MA, PhD, BSc); *m* 29 May 1969, Elisabeth, da of Franz Delhey, of Aachen; *Career* war service in Coal Mines 1944-45; lectr in germany, UCL 1949-64 (reader 1964-68), prof of germany Birkbeck Coll London 1968-; chm Rationalist Press Assoc; *Books* Erder and After (1959), The Plays of Grillparzer (1969), The Jesus of the Early Christians (1971), Goethe and the Development of Science (1978), The Historical Evidence for Jesus (1982), Did Jesus Exist ? (1986), The Origin of Language (1987), Religious Postures (1988); Who Was Jesus?, A Critique of the New Testament Record (1989); editor of J M Robertson, Liberal, Rationalist and Scholar (1987); co-ed F R H Englefield's Language, Its Origin and Relation to Thought (1977) and the same author's The Mind at Work and Play (1985); *Recreations* walking; *Style—* Prof George Wells; German Department, Birkbeck College, 43 Gordon Square, London WC1H 0PD (☎ 01 636 6105)

WELLS, Hon Mrs (Gillian Hermione Christian); *née* Turton; da of Baron Tranmire (Life Peer); *b* 1930; *Educ* Slade School of Art, London; *m* 1960, David Poulett Wells; 2 s (Quinton Robert b 1 Feb 1962, Nicholas Michael b 1966, d 1966), 2 da (Fiona Mary b 8 May 1963, Olivia Rosalind b 21 Jan 1969); *Career* artist; *Recreations* dancing, tennis; *Style—* The Hon Mrs Wells; Hilperton House, Hilperton, Trowbridge, Wilts (☎ 0225 75 3845)

WELLS, Lt-Col Herbert James; CBE (1958), MC (1918), JP (Surrey 1952), DL (1962); s of late James J Wells, of NSW, Aust; *b* 27 Mar 1897; *Educ* Newcastle NSW; *m* 1926, Rose Hamilton (d 1983), da of late H D Brown, of Bournemouth; *Career* AIF and Aust Flying Corps WWI, 55 Surrey Bn Home Gd WWII, Lt-Col 1954; former memb Surrey T & AFA; chm Queen Mary's Hosp Carshalton 1958-60; vice chm Surrey CC 1959-62, chm 1962-65; High Sheriff Surrey 1965; chm Wallington Bench 1961-70, a gen cmmr for income tax, Baker Tilley CAs; Freeman City of London; vice chm Carshalton UDC, (chm 1950-52 and 1955-56); Hon DUniv Surrey 1975; FCA; *Clubs* RAC; *Style—* Lt-Col Herbert Wells, CBE, MC, JP, DL; 17 Oakhurst Rise, Carshalton Beeches, Surrey SM5 4AG (☎ 01 643 4125); Baker Tilley Chartered Accountants, Clement House, 99 Aldwych, London WC2B 4JY (☎ 01 242 0211; telex 268002)

WELLS, John Campbell; s of Rev Eric George Wells (d 1984), and Dorothy Mary, *née* Thompson (d 1960); *b* 17 Nov 1936; *Educ* Eastbourne Coll, St Edmund Hall Oxford (MA); *m* Teresa, da of Sir Christopher Chancellor, of The Old Priory, Ditcheat, Somerset; *Career* 2 Lt Royal Sussex Regt 1955; author: Mrs Wilson's Diary (with Richard Ingrams), The Dear Bill Letters (with Richard Ingrams), Anyone for Denis? (in which he played the lead Whitehall Theatre 1982); various translations include: Danton's Death, The Marriage of Figaro (Nat Theatre), La Vie Parisienne (Scottish Opera), The Magic Flute (City of Birmingham Touring Opera); dir: La Vie Parisienne, Mikado (D'Oyly Carte); memb The Literary Soc; *Recreations* walking, talking; *Style—* John Wells, Esq; 1A Scarsdale Villas, London W8 6PT (☎ 01 937 0534)

WELLS, Capt John Gerard; CBE (1964), DSC (1940); s of Vice Adm Sir Gerard Aylmer Wells, KBE (d 1943); *b* 22 Sept 1915; *Educ* Britannia RNC Darmouth; *m* 1947, Diana, da of Lt-Gen Sir Edmond Schreiber, KCB, DSO; 2 s; *Career* WWII served RN 1929-64; served Atlantic, Med and Pacific, cmd: HMS Dainty 1959, HMS Excellent 1961, HMS Kent 1963-: ret Capt; gen mangr Aviemore Centre 1965-70, dir Clarkson Holiday 1970-74, conslt Wakeman Trower & Ptnrs 1975-76, gen mangr Gulfspan 1977-78, Mgmnt Business Servs (London) 1980-, res historian HMS Warrior (1860) 1981-87, chm Warrier Assoc 1985; *Books* Whaley - The Story of HMS Excellent 1830-1980, The Immortal Warrior, Britain's first and last battleship; *Recreations* sailing, skiing, shooting, stalking, naval historical research; *Clubs* Army and Navy, Royal Cruising; *Style—* Capt John Wells, CBE, DSC, RN; High Firs House, Hatch Lane, Liss, Hants (☎ 0730 893343)

WELLS, Sir John Julius; o s of Rev (Arthur) Reginald Kemble Wells (d 1964), and Margaret Evelyn, *née* Hodgson; ggg nephew of John Wells, JP, DL, MP for Maidstone 1820-30; *b* 30 Mar 1925; *Educ* Eton, CCC Oxford (MA); *m* 31 July 1948, Lucinda Mary Helen Francis, eldest da of Francis Ralph Meath Baker, JP, of Hasfield Court, Glos; 2 s ((William Arthur) Andrew *qv*, Oliver Reginald b 5 Nov 1955), 2 da (Julia Jane b 1 Feb 1951, Henrietta Frances b 27 Feb 1952); *Career* served WWII in HM Submarines; contested (C) Smethwick 1955 MP (C) Maidstone 1959-87; chm: Cons Pty Horticultural Ctee 1965-71 and 1973-87, Horticulture sub-ctee of Agric Select Ctee 1968, Parly Waterways Gp 1974-80; vice-chm Cons Agric Ctee 1970; memb Mr Speaker's Panel of Chairmen 1974-87; pres Nat Inst of Fresh Produce 1984-; Master Worshipful Co of Fruiterers 1977, Hon Freeman of Maidstone 1979; Kt Cdr Order of Civil Merit (Spain) 1972, Cdr Order of Lion (Finland) 1984; kt 1984; *Clubs* Army and Navy; *Style—* Sir John Wells; Mere House, Mereworth, Kent

WELLS, John Lawrence; s of Sidney Lawrence Wells (d 1957), and Margaret Robin, *née* Milligan (d 1977); *b* 27 Feb 1921; *Educ* Kings Coll Sch Wimbledon; *m* 10 April 1947, Betty-May Moya, da of Mark Tweddell, of Toronto, Canada; 1 s (William b 5 Sept 1957), 2 da (Elisabeth b 26 Oct 1948, Jane b 5 Nov 1952); *Career* RNVR 1939; WWII: Midshipman, Sub Lt and Lt HM Minesweepers 1939-40, served Dunkirk, Armd Merchant Cruiser Signals Offr Atlantic Convoys (sunk 1941, POW Germany until 1945); served M19 Far East and Italy 1945-46; chm (master tailor and dir) Wells of Mayfair (and other small cos), pres Trade Guild 1956, memb Trade Wages Cncl (sometime ldr), pres Masters Tailors Benevolent Assoc 1982-87; Westminster City Cncl: memb 1956-78, chm housing ctee, Lord Mayor 1971-72, dep ldr 1974-78; additional memb GLC; cncl memb Br Lung Fndn (nat), fndr chm Westminster Arts Cncl 1965, chm London Regnl Arts Assoc 1967-73; Freeman City of London, Liveryman Worshipful Co Needelmakers; FRSA 1953; memb Order of Sacred Treasure of Japan 1971, Cdr Order of Orange Nassau 1972, KSG (Vatican) 1987; *Recreations* reading, cricket, philately; *Clubs* Arts, MCC; *Style—* John Wells, Esq; 145B Ashley Gdns, Thirleby Rd, Westminster, London SW1P 1HN (☎ 01 828 0659)

WELLS, Kasan Heybourn; JP (1961-); s of Arthur George Wells, JP (d 1971), and Violet Caroline Annie Heybourn (d 1929); *b* 6 June 1917; *Educ* Brighton Coll, Merton Coll Oxford (MA); *m* 9 Dec 1944, Delicia Mary, da of Edwin Lawrence Mitchell, CB, CBE (d 1960); 2 s (Graham b 1948, Robert b 1953 (decd)), 2 da (Tina b 1945, Fiona b 1956); *Career* served BEF Jan-June 1940, Staff Sgt 8 Army Middle East, N Africa 1940-44, 21 Army Gp France, Belgium, Germany 1945-46; sr ptnr Brandiston Farms 1950-86, farmer, landowner; memb Norfolk Local Valuation Panel 1979-88, govr Taverham Hall Prep Sch 1967-88; *Recreations* golf, music, contract bridge; *Clubs* Royal W Norfolk Golf (Brancaster), Sheringham Golf, Magistrates Golf (vice-pres), Norfolk and Norwich Bridge; *Style—* Kasan Wells, Esq, JP; Church Farm, Brandiston, Norwich, Norfolk NR10 4PJ (☎ 0603 871264)

WELLS, Malcolm Henry Weston; s of Lt Cdr Geoffrey Weston Wells (d 1988), and Inez Brenda, *née* Williams (d 1967); *b* 27 July 1927; *Educ* Eton; *m* 20 Dec 1952, (Helen) Elizabeth Agnes, da of Rt Rev Bishop Maurice Henry Harland (d 1986); 1 s (Nicholas Weston b 1954), 1 da (Caroline Felicity b 1956); *Career* RN 1945-48; Peat Marwick Mitchell 1948-58 (articled clerk, latterly asst mangr), SIEBE plc 1958-63 (sec, latterly md); dir: Charterhouse Japhet plc 1963-73 (chm 1973-80), Charterhouse Gp 1964-80 (joined 1963), CAA 1974-77; chm: Charterhouse Petroleum plc 1977-82, BWD Securities plc 1987-; dep chm: Carclo Engrg Gp plc 1982-, German Securities Investmt Tst plc 1985-89; dir Nat Home Loans Corpn 1989-; Bank Liechtenstein plc 1981- (London rep, currently md); memb Solicitors Disciplinary Tbnl 1975-81;

Recreations sailing; *Clubs* City of London, Overseas Bankers; *Style*— M H W Wells, Esq; Bank Liechtenstein plc, 1 Devonshire Square, Bishopsgate, London EC2M 4UJ (☎ 01 377 0404, fax 01 247 1171, telex 8811714)

WELLS, Wing Cdr Oliver John; DL (Beds 1964); s of Sir Richard Wells, 1 Bt, of Felmersham Grange, nr Bedford (d 1956); *b* 10 Mar 1922; *Educ* Uppingham, RAF Staff Coll; *m* 1949, Felicity Anne, da of Brig M E Mascall, DSO, OBE (d 1958); 2 s, 1 da; *Career* served RAF 1941-56, High Sheriff of Bedfordshire 1970, chm of brewery co and malting co; *Recreations* flying, sailing; *Clubs* RAF; *Style*— Wing Cdr Oliver Wells DL; Ickwell Grange, nr Biggleswade, Beds (☎ 076 727 274)

WELLS, Ronald Alfred; OBE (1965); s of Alfred John Wells (d 1973), and Winifred Jessica Lambert (d 1972); *b* 11 Feb 1920; *Educ* Wallington County Sch for Boys, London Univ (BSc); *m* 1953, Anne Brebner, da of Dr Harold Frederick Lanshe, of Penna, USA; 2 s (Andrew, Michael); *Career* RN Science Serv 1940-47; joined NCL 1947, head Radio Chem Gp 1956-63, memb UK Science Mission Washington 1957, head Div Inorganic Chem 1963, dep dir NCL 1963, dir Nat Chem Lab 1964, res dir TBA T & N 1965-69; jt md TBA T & N 1969-77, dir Rochdale Private Surgical Unit 1977-81, md AMFU T & N 1977-81; dir: MRL T & N 1981-83, Salford Univ Ind Centre 1981-83; gp scientist Turner & Newall 1981-84, industl conslt 1984-87, ret 1987; non-exec dir Eversave Ltd (UK) 1984-85; FRCS, FIMM; *Recreations* golf, gardening, mineralogy; *Style*— Ronald Wells, Esq, OBE; Westbury, 19 First Ave, Charmandean, Worthing, Sussex BN14 9NJ (☎ 0903 33844)

WELLS, Prof Stanley William; s of Stanley William Wells, MBE (d 1952), of Hull, and Doris, *née* Atkinson (d 1986); *b* 21 May 1930; *Educ* Kingston HS Hull, UCL (BA), The Shakespeare Inst Univ of Birmingham (PhD); *m* 23 April 1975, Susan Elizabeth, *née* Hill; 3 da (Jessica b 1977, Imogen b and d 1984, Clemency b 1985); *Career* Nat Serv RAF 1951 (invalided out); Shakespeare Inst: fell 1962-77, lectr 1962, sr lectr 1971, reader 1973-77, hon fell 1979-88, conslt in Eng Wroxton Coll 1964-80, head of Shakespeare dept OUP 1978-88, gen ed Oxford Shakespeare 1978-, sr res fell Balliol Coll Oxford 1980-88, prof of Shakespeare studies and dir Shakespeare Inst Univ of Birmingham 1988-, dir Royal Shakespeare Theatre Summer Sch 1971-, pres Shakespeare Club of Stratford upon Avon 1972-73; memb: exec cncl Royal Shakespeare Theatre 1976- (govr 1974-), exec ctee Shakespeare's Birthplace 1976-78 (tstee 1975-81 and 1984-); guest lectr at Br and overseas univs, Br Acad Annual Shakespeare lectr 1987; govr King Edward VI GS for Boys 1973-77; assoc ed New Penguin Shakespeare 1967-77, ed Shakespeare Survey 1980-; Hon DLitt Furman Univ 1976; memb: Soc for Theatre Res 1963-, cncl Malone Soc 1967-; *Books* Thomas Nashe, Selected Writings (ed 1964), A Midsummer Night's Dream (ed 1967), Richard II (ed 1969), Shakespeare, A Reading Guide (1969 and 1970), Literature and Drama (1970), The Comedy of Errors (ed 1972), Shakespeare (ed 1973), English Drama Excluding Shakespeare (ed 1975), Royal Shakespeare (1977 and 1978), Nineteenth Century Burlesques (compiled in 5 vols, 1977), Shakespeare: An Illustrated Dictionary (1978 and 1985), Shakespeare: The Writer and his Work (1978), Thomas Diekker, The Shoemaker's Holiday (ed with RL Smallwood 1979), Modernising Shakespeare's Spelling with three studies in the text of Henry V (with Gary Taylor 1979), re-editing Shakespeare for the Modern Reader (1984), Shakespeare's Sonnets (ed 1985), The Complete Oxford Shakespeare (ed with Gary Taylor *et al*, 1986), The Cambridge Companion to Shakespeare Studies (ed 1986), William Shakespeare: a textual companion (with Gary Taylor *et al*, 1987), An Oxford Anthology of Shakespeare (1987); contrib: Shakespeare Survey, Shakespeare Quarterly, Shakespeare Jahrbuch, Theatre Notebook, Stratford upon Avon Studies, TLS, and others; *Recreations* music, travel; *Style*— Prof Stanley Wells; Midsummer Cottage, Church Lane, Beckley, Oxford (☎ 086735 252); 38 College St, Stratford upon Avon, Warwicks (☎ 0789296 047); The Shakespeare Inst, Stratford upon Avon, Warwicks (☎ 0789 293138)

WELLS, Thomas Leonard; s of Leonard Wells, and Lillian May, *née* Butler; *b* 2 May 1930; *Educ* Univ of Toronto; *m* 24 April 1954, Audrey Alice, da of Arthur C Richardson; 1 s (Andrew Thomas), 2 da (Brenda Elizabeth, Beverley Gail); *Career* advertising mangr: Canadian Hosp Jl 1951-61, Canadian Med Assoc Jl 1961-67; chm: Scarborough Ontario Bd Educn 1961 and 1962, MLA (Progressive C) Scarborough N Ontario 1963-85; min: without portfolio responsible for youth affrs 1966-69, of health 1969-71, of social and family servs 1971-72, of educn 1972-78, of intergovernmental affrs 1978-85; govt house ldr Ontario 1980-85, agent gen for Ontario in UK 1985-; *Recreations* photography, walking, theatre, cinema; *Clubs* RAC, Royal Over seas League, Royal Cwlth Soc, Albany and Empire (Toronto), United Wards; *Style*— Thomas Wells, Esq; 6-12 Reeves Mews, London WIY 3PB (☎ 01 245 1222); Ontario House 21 Knightsbridge, London SWIX 7LY

WELLS, William Henry Weston; s of Sir Henry Wells, CBE (d 1970), and Rosemary Halliday, *née* Whitchurch (d 1977); *b* 3 May 1940; *Educ* Radley, Magdalene Coll Cambridge (BA); *m* 1 Jan 1966, Penelope Jean, da of Col R B Broadbent (d 1979); 3 s (Rupert d 1969, George b 1971, Henry b 1972); *Career* chm: Land and House Property Gp 1977, Frincon Hldgs Ltd 1977-87, Chesteron 1983-; dir London Life Assoc 1984; memb board of governors: Royal Free Hosp (1968-74), Camden and Islington AHA 1972-82; chm Spl Tstee of the Roy Free Hosps 1979-; memb Cncl Royal Free Hosp Sch of Medicine 1977-; chm Hampstead Health Auth 1982-; FRICS; *Recreations* family, philately, gardening; *Clubs* Boodle's; *Style*— William Wells, Esq; 54 Brook St, London W1A 2BU (☎ 01 499 0404)

WELLS, William Thomas; QC (1955); s of William Colins Wells (d 1945), of Bexhill-on-Sea, Sussex, and Gertrude Mary Wells, *née* Fortnam (d 1964); *b* 10 August 1908; *Educ* Lancing, Balliol Coll Oxford (BA, MA); *m* 4 April 1936, Angela Mary, da of Robert Emilius Noble, KSG (d 1936), of Chester Square, London SW1; 2 s (Martin b 1937, John b and d 19500, 2 da (Gillian (Mrs Wilson-Smith) b 1939, Catherine (Mrs Macdonald b 1944); *Career* Army 1940-45, GSO2 dir of mil trg War Office 1942-45; called to the Bar Middle Temple 1932, bencher 1963, QC Hong Kong 1968, dep chm Herts Quarter Sessions 1961-71, rec Kings Lynn 1965-71, rec Crown Ct 1972-80, chm Industl Tribunals 1976-80; MP Walsall 1945-55, Walsall North 1955-74; Freedom of Walsall 1974; memb Cncl of Legal Educ 1972-86; *Books* How English Law Works (1946); frequent contributor since 1934 to: Political Quarterly, Times Literary Supplement, The Fortnightly, The Spectator, The Tablet; *Clubs* Athenaeum; *Style*— William Wells, Esq; 2 Mays House, 44 Sydenham Hill, London SW26 6ND (☎ 01 693 2758); 1 Grays Inn Square, Grays Inn, London WC1R 5AA (☎ 01 405 8946)

WELLS-PESTELL, Hon Philip Anthony; s of Baron Wells-Pestell; *b* 31 July 1941; *Educ* City of London Sch, London Univ; *m* 1965, Holly, da of Lorne Hopkins, of Conn, USA; has issue; *Style*— The Hon Philip Wells-Pestell; 7 Woodberry Av, Winchmore Hill, N21

WELLS-PESTELL, Baron (Life Peer UK 1965), of Combs, Co Suffolk; Reginald Alfred Wells-Pestell; CBE (1988)); assumed additional surname of Wells by deed poll; s of Robert Thomas Pestell of Highgate (d 1957) and Mary Ann *née* Manning (d 1952); *b* 27 Jan 1910; *Educ* Lyulph Stanley GS, London Univ, Geneva Theological Coll North Carolina USA (MA, Hon LLD); *m* 1935, Irene Mabel, da of Arthur Wells; 2 s; *Career* Capt KRRC; sits as Lab Peer in House of Lords; sociologist; memb Inner London Probation Ctee, fndr memb Nat Marriage Guidance Cncl; lord in waiting (govt whip) 1974-79, parly under-sec DHSS 1979, dep chief oppn whip 1979-81, dep speaker House of Lords and dep chm of Ctees 1981-; *Recreations* music, opera; *Style*— The Rt Hon the Lord Wells-Pestell; 22 Vicarage Close, Oxford OX4 4PL (☎ 0865 771142)

WELLWOOD, James McKinney; s of James Wellwood (d 1967: general medical practitioner), of Belfast, and Violet Armstrong McKinney (d 1978); *b* 18 Dec 1940; *Educ* Fettes, Cambridge Univ and St Thomas' Hosp Medical Sch London; *m* 1, 8 March 1975, Frances Alexandria Ruth, da of Stephen Howard, of Hertfordshire, England; m 2, 24 July 1982, Anne Margaret, da of Sydney Jones Samuel, of Llanelli, Wales; 1 s (James b 1984); *Career* conslt surgn Whipps Cross Hosp Leytonstone London 1979; lectr to Medical Coll of St Bartholomew Smithfield London 1979, clinical tutor Waltham Forest District 1983; hon sec The Br Assoc Surgical Oncology 1982-86; hon overseas sec The Br Assoc Surgical Oncology 1986-; Br Del The European Soc of Surgical Oncology 1986-; memb of educn advsy ctee, Assoc of Surgns of GB and Ireland 1987; memb of Waltham Forest DHA 1983-; Queen's Commendation for Brave Conduct (1971); *Recreations* skiing, shooting, travel; *Clubs* Athenanaeum, Royal Soc of Medicine; *Style*— James Wellwood, Esq; 24 Willoughby Rd, Hampstead, London NW3 1SA (☎ 01 794 5708); Whipps Cross Hospital, Leytonstone, London E17 (☎ 01 539 5522); 134 Harley St, London W1N 1AH (☎ 01 487 4212)

WELMAN, Douglas Pole (Pat); CBE (1966); s of late Col Arthur Pole Welman, and late Lady Scott; *b* 22 June 1902; *Educ* Tonbridge, Faraday House Engrg Coll; *m* 1, 1929, Denise, da of Charles Steers Peel; 1 da; m 2, 1946, Betty Majorie, da of late Henry Huth; *Career* electrical and mechanical engr; Indies 1928-32, consulting practice 1932-38, md Forster Yates & Thom Ltd (heavy precision engrs) 1938-50; involved in various wartime ctees in Lancs incl: ESO and armaments prodn 1942, seconded to Miny of Aircraft Prodn as dir of engr prodn 1942, dep dir-gen 1943, control of directorate-gen (incl propellor and accessory prodn) 1944; chm NW Gas Bd 1950-64 (pt/t memb 1949), memb Gas Cncl 1950-67, chm Southern Gas Bd 1964-67; chm and md Allspeeds Hldgs Ltd 1967-72; memb ct of govrs Univ of Manchester Inst of Sci and Technol 1956-64 and 1968-72 (cncl memb 1960-64 and 1968-72); CStJ 1968 (OStJ 1964); author of articles and papers on company mgmnt; FRSA; *Recreations* Royal Thames Yacht; *Style*— Pat Welman, Esq, CBE; 11 St Michael's Gardens, St Cross, Winchester SO23 9JD (☎ 0962 68091)

WELSBY, John Kay; *b* 26 May 1938; *Educ* Exeter Univ (BA), London Univ (MSc); *Career* Br: dir prov services 1981-83, dir Mfrg and Maintenance policy 1984-86, md procurement and special projects 1986-87; bd memb Br Bd 1987; md Procurement & Special Projects; *Style*— John Welsby, Esq; British Railways Board, Euston House, 24 Eversholt St, London NW1 1DZ (☎ 01 922 6928)

WELSBY, Dr Paul Antony; *b* 18 August 1920; *Educ* Alcester GS, Univ of Durham (MA), Lincoln Theol Coll, Univ of Sheffield (PhD); *m* 1948, Cynthia Mary Hosmer; 1 da (Rosamund); *Career* curate: Boxley Kent 1944-47, St Mary Le Tower Ipswich 1947-52; rector Copdock with Washbrook Suffolk 1952-66, rural dean Samford 1964-66, canon residentiary of Rochester Cathedral 1966-88, dir post-ordination training for diocese of Rochester 1966-88, examining chaplain to Bishop of Rochester 1966-88, canon emeritus Rochester Cathedral 1988-, personal chaplain to Bishop of Rochester 1988-; memb: Church Assembly 1964-70, Gen Synod 1970-80; chm House of Clergy of Gen Synod, prolocutor of Convocation of Canterbury 1974-80; chaplain to HM The Queen 1980-; former chm City of Rochester Soc; *Books* A Modern Catechism (1956), Lancelot Andrewes (1958), The Unwanted Archbishop: Life of George Abbot (1962), The Bond of Church and State (1962), Sermons and Society (1970), A History of the Church of England 1945-80 (1984), How the Church of England Works (1985); *Recreations* reading detective fiction, genealogy; *Style*— The Rev Dr Paul Welsby; 20 Knights Ridge, Pembury, Tunbridge Wells, Kent TN2 4HP (☎ 089 282 3053)

WELSH, Andrew Paton; s of William (d 1979), and Agnes Paton Reid (d 1977); *b* 19 April 1944; *Educ* Univ of Glasgow (MA, Dip Ed); *m* 1971, Sheena Margaret, da of Douglas Henry Cannon (d 1972); 1 da (Jane b 1980); *Career* MP (SNP) Angus Sth (spokesman on Housing, Agric, self employed) 1974-79 (chief whip 1978-79), sr lectr (business studies & pub admin) Dundee Coll of Commerce 1979-87; MP (SNP) Angus E Chief Whip and spokesman local govt, self-employed, small businesses and employment 1987-; provert Angus DC 1984-87; SNP exec vice chm: Admin 1979-82, Local Govt 1983-86; SNP vice pres 1987-; *Recreations* music, horseriding, languages; *Style*— Andrew Welsh; 22 Monymusk Road, Arbroath DD11 2DB; House of Commons, London SW1A 0AA

WELSH, Frank Reeson; s of Francis Cox Welsh (d 1974), of Westmorland, and Doris (Reeson) Ibbet; *b* 16 August 1931; *Educ* Blaydon GS, Magdalene Coll Cambridge (MA); *m* 1954, Agnes, da of John Embleton Cowley, OBE, of Co Durham; 2 s (Benjamin, John), 2 da (Jane, Sophie); *Career* dir: William Branots Sons 1965-72, Grindlays Bank 1972-85, The Trireme Tst 1983-; chm: Cox & Kings 1972-77, Jensen Motors, Hadfields, Robey of Lincoln 1967-78, The London Industl Assoc 1984-; memb: Royal Cmmn on the Nat Health Service, Br Waterways Bd, Gen Advsy Cncl of the IBA, Health Educn Cncl; *Books* The Profit of the State (1982), The Afflicted State (1983), First Blood (1985), Bend'or (with George Ridley, 1985); *Recreations* sailing (Remercie), building triremes; *Clubs* Savile, Utd Oxford & Cambridge; *Style*— Frank Welsh Esq; Bridge House, Bungay, Suffolk NR35 1HD (☎ 0986 5300)

WELSH, Michael Collins; MP (Lab) Doncaster N 1983-; s of Danny Welsh, and Winnie Welsh; *b* 23 Nov 1926; *Educ* Univ of Sheffield, Ruskin Coll; *m* 1950, Brenda Nicholson, 2 s; *Career* miner, memb Doncaster Cncl 1962-, MP (Lab) Don Valley 1979-83 and 1987-, sponsored by NUM; *Style*— Michael Welsh, Esq, MP; House of Commons, London SW1A 0AA

WELSH, Michael John; MEP (EDG) Lancs Central 1979-; s of Cdr David Welsh, RN; *b* 22 May 1942; *Educ* Dover Coll, Lincoln Coll Oxford; *m* 1963, Jennifer Pollitt; 1 s, 1 da; *Career* formerly with Levi Strauss & Co Europe (dir mkt devpt 1976), non-exec dir Initial 1982-; *Publications* Textiles in the Eighties (1980), Trade Equals Jobs (1981); *Clubs* Carlton; *Style—* Michael Welsh, Esq, MEP; Watercrook, 181 Town Lane, Whittle le Woods, Chorley, Lancs (☎ 025 72 76992)

WELSH, Maj-Gen Peter Miles; OBE (1973), MC (1966); s of Brig William Miles Moss O'Donnell Welsh, DSO, MC (d 1965), of Lismore, Sonning, Berks, and Mary Margaret Edith Gertrude Louise, *née* Hearn; *b* 23 Dec 1930; *Educ* Winchester, RMA Sandhurst; *m* 1974, June Patricia, da of Francis MacAdam, of Buenos Aires, Argentine, widow of M E McCausland; 2 step s, 1 step da; *Career* Army Offr; directing staff Staff Coll 1968-71, CO 2 Royal Green Jackets 1971-74, cmd 5 Inf Bde 1974-76, RCDS 1977, BGS HQ BAOR 1978-80, Brig Lt Div 1980-83, pres Regular Cmmns Bd 1983-; *Recreations* golf, shooting; *Clubs* MCC, I-Zingari, Free Foresters, Berks Golf; *Style—* Maj-Gen Peter Welsh, OBE, MC; c/o Lloyds Bank, Maidenhead, Berks;

WELTON, Hon Mrs (Kirstin Elizabeth); *née* Lowther; da of late Lt John Arthur Lowther, MVO, RNVR, gs of 1 Viscount Ullswater; sister of 2 Viscount Ullswater; raised to the rank of a Viscount's da 1951; *b* 1939; *m* 1, 1966, Capt Caledon Alexander, late 7 Queen's Own Hussars; 1 s, 1 da; m 2, 1976, Antony Edward Ord Welton; *Style—* The Hon Mrs Welton; Willowbrook House, Lower Dean, North Leach, Glos

WEMYSS, Rear Adm Martin La Touche; CB (1981); s of Cdr David Edward Gillespie Wemyss, DSO, DSC, RN, of Luthrie Fife, and Edith Mary (d 1930); *b* 5 Dec 1927; *Educ* Shrewsbury; *m* 1 (m dis), Ann Hall; 1 s, 1 da; m 2, 1973, Elizabeth Loveday, da of Col Robert Harper Alexander, RAMC, of Kingston Gorse, Sussex (d 1969); 1 s, 1 da; *Career* Cmdg Offr: HMS Sentinel, HMS Alliance, Submarine COs Qualifying Course, HMS Norfolk, 3 Submarine Sqdn; Dir Naval Warfare 1974-76, Flag Offr Second Flotilla 1977-78, Rear Adm 1977, asst chief of Naval Staff (Ops) 1979-81; clerk Worshipful Co of Brewers 1981; *Recreations* sailing, shooting, gardening; *Clubs* White's, Army & Navy; *Style—* Rear-Adm Martin Wemyss, CB; The Old Post House, Emberton, nr Olney, Bucks MK46 5BX (☎ 0234 713838); Brewers' Hall, Aldermanbury Sq, London EC2 (☎ 01 606 1301)

WEMYSS, Lady Victoria Alexandrina Violet; *née* Cavendish-Bentinck; CVO (1953); da of 6 Duke of Portland, KG, GCVO, TD, PC (d 1943); *b* 1890; *m* 1918, Capt Michael John Wemyss, late Household Cavalry; *Career* appointed an extra woman of the bedchamber to HM Queen Elizabeth, the Queen Mother 1937; *Style—* The Lady Victoria Wemyss, CVO; Wemyss Castle, East Wemyss, Fife

WEMYSS AND MARCH, 12 (and 8) Earl of (S 1633 & 1697); Francis David Charteris; KT (1966), JP (E Lothian); also Lord Wemyss of Elcho (S 1628), Lord Elcho and Methil (S 1633), Viscount of Peebles, Lord Douglas of Neidpath, Lyne, and Munard (both S 1697), and Baron Wemyss of Wemyss (UK 1821); s of Lord Elcho (ka 1916, s and h of 11 Earl, but predeceased him) and Lady Violet Manners (d 1971), 2 da of 8 Duke of Rutland; suc gf 1937; *b* 19 Jan 1912; *Educ* Eton, Balliol Coll Oxford, Trinity Coll Cambridge; *m* 24 Feb 1940, Mavis Lynete Gordon (d 1988), er da of Edwin Edward Murray, of Cape Province, SA; 1 s, 1 da (and 1 s, 1 da decd); *Heir* s, Lord Neidpath; *Career* Basutoland Admin Serv 1937-44 (war serv with Basuto troops ME 1941-44); landowner; former dir: Standard Life Assur, STV; conslt Wemyss and March Estate Mgmnt Co Ltd; chm Royal Cmmn on Ancient and Hist Monuments and Constructions of Scotland 1949-84, Lord High Cmmr to Gen Assembly of Church of Scotland 1959 (1960 and 1977), pres Nat Bible Soc of Scotland 1962-83, Lord Lt E Lothian 1976-87, pres Nat Tst for Scotland, Lord Clerk Register of Scotland and Keeper of the Signet 1974-, Ensign Royal Co of Archers (Queen's Bodyguard for Scotland), hon pres The Thistle Fndn; Hon LLD St Andrews 1953, Hon DUniv Edinburgh 1983; *Clubs* New (Edinburgh); *Style—* The Rt Hon the Earl of Wemyss and March, KT, LLD, JP; Gosford House, Longniddry, East Lothian (☎ (087 57) 200/389)

WEMYSS OF WEMYSS, Lady Jean Christian; *née* Bruce; da of late 10 Earl of Elgin and (14 of) Kincardine, KT, CMG, TD, CD and Hon Dame Katherine Cochrane, DBE, da of late 1 Baron Cochrane of Cults and Lady Gertrude Boyle, OBE, da of 6 Earl of Glasgow; *b* 1923; *m* 1945, Capt David Wemyss of Wemyss, late Royal Corps of Signals; 2 s; *Career* formerly in WAAF; *Style—* Lady Jean Wemyss; Invermay, Forteviot, Perthshire (☎ 0764 84276)

WENNIKE, Helge; *b* 10 Nov 1944; *Educ* Commercial Coll Copenhagen; *m* 17 Feb 1973, Grete Else-Marie; 1 s (Nicolai b 1973), 1 da (Anne-Marie b 1976); *Career* mangr Privatbanken unitl 1978; md: RB-Banken 1978-80, Finansbank 1980-81, Jyske Bank 1981-84; dep md Scandinavian Bank GP plc 1984-; *Recreations* golf, tennis; *Clubs* RAC; *Style—* Helge Wennike, Esq; 10a Pelhams Walk, Esher, Surrey (☎ 0372 674 53); 2/6 Cannon St, London EC4M 6XX (☎ 01 236 6090, fax 01 243 6612)

WENT, David; s of Arthur Edward James Went (d 1980), of Dublin, and Phyllis, *née* Howell (d 1980); *b* 25 Mar 1947; *Educ* High Sch Dublin, Trinity Coll Dublin (BA, LLB); *m* 4 Nov 1972, Mary, da of Jack Milligan (d 1972), of Belfast; 1 s (James b 1976), 1 da (Kate b 1978); *Career* barr King's Inn Dublin; gen mangr Citibank Dublin 1974 (Jeddah 1975), banking dir Ulster Investmt Bank Dublin 1976 (chief exec 1982), chief exec Ulster Bank 1988-; FIBI 1978; *Recreations* tennis, squash, reading; *Clubs* Univ; *Style—* David Went, Esq; c/o Ulster Bank, Belfast, NI

WENTWORTH, Stephen; s of Ronald Wentworth, OBE (d 1983), of London, and Elizabeth Mary, *née* Collins (d 1967); *b* 23 August 1943; *Educ* King's Coll Sch Wimbledon, Merton Coll Oxford (MA, MSc); *m* 9 May 1970, Katharine Laura, da of Rev Arthur John Hopkinson, CIE (d 1953), of, Aislaby, N Yorks; 3 da; *Career* Civil Serv: princ MAFF 1970-74 (asst princ 1967-70), on loan to civil serv selection bd 1974-75, personnel div MAFF 1975-76, on loan to HM Dip Serv as first sec (agric), Office of the UK Perm Rep to the Euro Communities Brussels 1976-78, asst sec head of beef div MAFF 1978-80, seconded Cabinet Off 1980-82, head of milk div MAFF 1982-85, head of Euro Communities div 1985-86, promoted grade 3 head of meat gp 1986; *Style—* Stephen Wentworth, Esq; Ministry of Agriculture Fisheries and Food, Whitehall Place, London SW1A 2HH

WENTWORTH PING, (William) Hugh; s of Capt Andrew Wentworth Ping (d 1973), of York, and Anne Margaret, *née* Varley (d 1977); *b* 7 June 1924; *Educ* St Peters Sch York, Leeds Coll of Commerce, Sheffield Univ Business Sch, Henley Staff Coll; *m* 7 July 1956, (Joan) Carol, da of Carl Eric Holmstrom (d 1968), of Sheffield; 2 s (Jonathan b 25 Sept 1957, Richard b 3 July 1959); *Career* WWI RNVR 1942-47 served on: HMS Thruster, HMS Lizard, HMS Saunders; ranks: Ordinary Seaman, Able Seaman, Midshipman, Sub-Lt, Lt Staff Offr to C-in-C Mediterranean 1946-47; Lt RNR Humber Div 1947-59; Firth-Vickers Stainless Steels Ltd Sheffield 1948-70: sales rep, asst publicity mangr, sales devpt mangr, special dir (sales); commercial dir PI Castings Ltd 1970-72, commercial mangr Br Steel Corpn forges foundries and engrg 1973-82, commercial mangr Tech Commercial Intertrade Ltd 1983-89, chm Quasco Wear Systems Ltd Barnsley 1989-; memb Sheffield C of C 1956-70, dist cmmr Scouts 1961-66; chm: Sheffield Croft House Boxing Club, Sheffield Sea Cadets 1979-85, Conservation Sheffield Antiquities; rep GB World Bobsleigh Championships 1955; High Sheriff South Yorks 1988-89; Freeman Co of Cutlers in Hallamshire (1961); *Recreations* golf, riding, advanced motor cycling, vintage cars, stamps, winter sports; *Clubs* Sickleholme, St Moritz Tobogganing, Shrievalty; *Style—* Hugh Wentworth Ping, Esq; Nicholas Hall, Thornhill, Bamford, Sheffield S30 2BR (☎ 0433 51403); Business Innovation Centre, Innovation Way, Barnsley S78 1JL (☎ 0226 249590, fax 0226 249629, telex 84687 BBIC)

WENTWORTH-STANLEY, Charles Wroughton; s of Charles Sidney Bowen Wentworth-Stanley, CBE (d 1960), of High Wych Grange, and Edith Katherine (Nancy) Brockle Bank JP (d 1948); *b* 22 Nov 1919; *Educ* Eton and Magdalene Coll, Cambridge MA; *m* 4 Dec 1946, Sonia Patricia Molesworth, da of Lt-Col Temple Percy Molesworth Bevan, MC, Grenadier Gds (d 1981), of Longstowe Hall, Cambridgeshire (d 1981); 2 s (Charles Richard b 15 Nov 1947, Jeremy Wroughton b 25 July 1950), 1 da (Henrietta Sara b 30 July 1954); *Career* served 1940-46 with RAFVR (UK and SE Asia, despatches) Sqdn-Ldr 1945; export mangr English Electric Co Ltd 1963-69; dir: Gray Dawes & Co Ltd 1969-71, Inchcape Export Ltd 1969-72; memb: Ctee Middle East Trade 1964-65, Br Nat Export Cncl and Ctee Australia and N Zealand 1968-71, Br Cncl The Australian Br Trade Assoc 1968-74 (chm 1972-74); md laxberry Ltd 1973, ret 1984; High Sheriff Hertfordshire 1973-74; pres Bishop's Stortford & District Angling Soc 1963-; CEng, MIEE, MIMECHE; *Recreations* fishing, shooting, gardening; *Clubs* Bucks, Naval and Military, MCC; *Style—* Charles Wentworth-Stanley, Esq; High Wych Granbe, Sawbridgeworth, Herts CM21 0JB

WENTWORTH-STANLEY, (Geoffrey) David; s of Charles Sidney Bowen Wentworth-Stanley, CBE (d 1960), and Edith Katherine, *née* Brockleback (d 1948); *b* 28 May 1924; *Educ* Eton, RMA Sandhurst; *m* 1951, Bridget, da of late Maj Philip Ivan Pease; 4 s; *Career* served 9 Queen's Royal Lancers, Italy 1944-47; memb Stock Exchange 1948, ptnr Cazenove & Co 1958-88, High Sheriff Herts 1972; *Clubs* White's, Cavalry; *Style—* David Wentworth-Stanley Esq; Great Munden House, nr Ware, Herts SG11 1HU (☎ 092 084 244)

WENTWORTH-STANLEY, Maj Oliver Montagu; MC (1944), TEM (HAC) 1945; 2 s of Charles Sidney Bowen Wentworth-Stanley, CBE (d 1960), of High Wych Grange, Sawbridgeworth, Hertfordshire, and Edith Katherine, *née* Brocklebank, JP (d 1948); *b* 7 Nov 1921; *Educ* Eton; Sandhurst; *m* 1959 (m dis 1975), Priscilla Margaret, yst da of Norman Selwyn Pryor, DL, JP (d 1982), of Manuden House, Manuden, nr Bishops Stortford, Herts, 1 s, 2 da; *Career* served HAC (TA), 1939, WWII; 11 (HAC) Regt RHA, 1939, 11 Hussars (PAO), 1941, M East (W Desert, Paiforce, BNAF), Central Med (Italy, CMF) NW Europe (France, Germany, BLA, BAOR) Malaya 1953, RAC Southern Command 1959; *Clubs* Cavalry and Guards, MCC, HAC, Armoury House; *Style—* Maj Oliver Wentworth-Stanley, MC, TEM; Stonards Farm High Wych, Sawbridgeworth, Hertfordshire

WENTZELL, Pamela; *née* Moran; da of Herbert Thomas Moran, of London, and Teresa McDaid, *née* Conway; *b* 3 Feb 1950; *Educ* Pitman's Sch Ealing, Marlborough Coll London; *m* 18 Oct 1969, Christopher John, s of Charles John Wentzell, of Gurnard, IOW; *Career* md JP Communicators Ltd PR Consultancy 1980-; former chm Southampton Publicity Assoc 1985-86; MIPR 1980; *Recreations* theatre going, classical music, gardening; *Style—* Mrs Pamela Wentzell; Roke Hollow, Woodington Lane, East Wellow, Hampshire (☎ 0794 517583); Bedford House, 81 Bedford Place, Southampton SO1 2DF (☎ 0703 632738, fax 0703 332283)

WERNICK, Joseph; s of Samuel Wernick (d 1967), and Bertha Wernick (d 1955); *b* 28 August 1920; *Educ* Wolverhampton Municipal GS, Wolverhampton & Staffs Tech Coll, Licentiate Inst of Technol; *m* 22 Aug 1942, Eileen, da of Harold Berry (d 1976); 3 s (Andrew b 1945, Julian b 1950, Simon b 1952); *Career* Capt RE BAOR 1945-47; chm and jt md Wernick Gp of Companies; pres Birmingham Progressive Synagogue 1982-85; magistrate Wolverhampton; chm Wolverhampton S Lib Assoc 1970-73 and 1987-; Parly candidate: (Lib) Wolverhampton SW Feb 1974, Oct 1974, 1979, and as (Alliance) Wolverhampton SE 1983; *Recreations* bridge, foreign travel, music, tennis (ex); *Clubs* Tettenhall Bridge, Wolverhampton Lawn Tennis, Squash; *Style—* Joseph Wernick, Esq; 39 Newbridge Cres, Wolverhampton, W Midlands WV6 0LH; S Wernick & Sons Ltd, Lindon Rd, Brownhills, Walsall, W Midlands (☎ 0543 3742)

WERNICK, Lionel Rufus; s of Samuel Wernick (d 1967); *b* 6 Nov 1928; *Educ* Wolverhampton Municipal GS, London Univ; *m* 1955, Sheila Faye, *née* Lambert; 4 children; *Career* former Lt Royal Signal Corps; chm & md The Wernick Group, Lloyds underwriter; memb cncl Nat Prefabricated Building Assoc Ltd, chm Essex ctee The Royal Jubilee and Prince's Tst, chm Essex bd Prince's Youth Business Tst, pres Essex Community Relations Cncl; Liveryman Worshipful Co of Wheelwrights, Freeman City of London; *Recreations* bridge, travel, spectator sports; *Style—* Lionel Wernick, Esq; The Lyches, Greenway, Hutton, Brentwood, Essex (☎ 0277 220535)

WESKER, Arnold; s of Joseph Wesker (d 1959), and Leah, *née* Perlmutter (d 1976); *b* 24 May 1932; *Educ* Upton House Central Sch Hackney; *m* 1958, Doreen Cecile, da of Edwin Bicker, of Norfolk; 2 s (Daniel, Lindsay Joe), 1 da (Tanya Jo); *Career* playwright and dir; chm Br Centre of Int Theatre Inst 1978-83, pres Int Playwrights' Ctee 1981-83; 28 stage plays include The Kitchen (1957), Chicken Soup with Barley (1958), Roots (1959), Chips with Everything (1962), The Four Seasons (1965), The Old Ones (1970), The Journalists (1972), The Wedding Feast (1974), One More Ride on the Merry-Go-Round (1978), Caritas (1980), Anne Wobbler (1982), Yarsdale (1983), When God wanted a Son (1986), The Mistress (1988); radio, film and tv plays incl: Menace (1971), The Wesker Trilogy (19740, Breakfast (1981), Bluey (1984), Thieves in the Night (4 part adaptation of Arthur Koestler's novel, 1984-85), Caritas (lidretto for opera, 1988); stories, essays and other writings incl: Six Sundays in January (1971), Love Letters on Blue Paper (1974), Fatlips (1978), Distinctions (1985), A Mini-biography (1988); plays directed incl: The Four Seasons (Havana, 1968), The Old Ones (Munich, 1973), The Entertainer (1983), Yarsdale (1985 and 1987); FRSL; *Clubs* Groucho; *Style—* Arnold Wesker, Esq; 37 Ashley Road, London N19 3AG (☎ 01 272 0034); Nat Westminster Bank plc, 298 Seven Sisters Rd, London N4 2AF

WEST; *see*: Granville-West

WEST; *see*: Alston-Roberts-West

WEST, Christopher John Rodney; s of Norman (Peter) Hartley West (d 1963), of Rio de Janerio Brazil, Epsom, and Lucy Catherine West *née* Skey (d 1962); *b* 6 April 1932; *Educ* St Ginger Coll Benon Ainen Australia, Haileybury, Univ Coll London (BSc); *m* 31 March 1956, Patricia Anne, da of Kenneth Arthur Alexander Neilson (d 1972); 1 da (Helen b 1958), 2 s (Martin b 1960, Ian b 1964); *Career* Nat Serv Sub Lt RNVR; indust career plant mangr in ICI Plastics div and Br Visqueen Ltd 1955-68; BOC Laser Div in gen mgmnt 1968-71; Courtnay Mgmnt Selection Consultant; chm Assoc for Marriage Enrichment (a registered charity); *Recreations* sailing, walking; *Clubs* Naval; *Style*— Christopher West, Esq; Courteney, 3 Hanover Sq, London W1R 9OAT (☎ 01 491 4014, fax 01 408 1667)

WEST, Denison Hayton; s of George Stephen West (d 1918), of Birmingham Univ, and Minnie Bullock, *née* Pratt (d 1972); *b* 12 June 1914; *Educ* St Peters York, St Johns Coll Oxford (MA); *m* 11 Nov 1944, Sheila, da of Wilfrid Allport (d 1950); 3 da (Jane b 1947, Phillipa b 1949, Jill b 1951); *Career* WWII Maj 7 Ghurka Rifles IA, NW Frontier and Burma; dir Forestry Grosvenor Estates 1966; FICFor; *Recreations* fishing, golf; *Clubs* Farmers; *Style*— Denison West, Esq; The Kennels, Belgrave, Chester CH4 9DF (☎ 0244 671555)

WEST, Prof John Clifford; CBE (1977); s of John Herbert West (d 1958), of Hindley, Lancs, and Ada, *née* Ascroft (d 1984); *b* 4 June 1922; *Educ* Hindley and Abram GS, Manchester Univ (BSc, PhD, DSc); *m* 7 Jan 1946, Winefride Mary, da of Herbert Francis Turner, of Blackpool, Lancs (d 1973); 3 da (Angela b 1946, Julia b 1951, Clare b 1960); *Career* electrical Lt anti-submarine warfare branch RNVR 1943-46; lectr Univ of Manchester 1946-57, prof electrical engrg Queens Univ Belfast 1958-65, dean of applied sciences Univ of Sussex 1965-78, vice-chancellor Univ of Bradford 1979-; pres IEE 1984-85; chm: Cncl for Educnl Technol 1980-85, Civil Serv Cmmn Special Merit Promotions Panel 1966-72, Crawford Cmmn on Broadcasting Coverage 1973-74, Asian Inst of Business Bradford 1987-; memb UGC 1973-78; Hon DSc Sussex Univ 1988; FIEE 1962, FEng 1983, FInstMC 1984, FRPSL 1970, FRGS 1988; *Books* Servomechanisms (1953), Analytical Techniques for Non-Linear Control Systems (1960); *Recreations* philately; *Clubs* Athenaeum, Royal Cwlth Soc; *Style*— Prof John West, CBE; 6 Park Crescent, Guiseley, Leeds LS20 8EL (☎ 0943 72605); 11 Windlesham Hall, Windlesham Ave, Brighton BN1 3AH (☎ 0273 726915); University of Bradford, Richmond Rd, Bradford BD7 1DP (☎ 0274 728390, 733466, fax 0274 726365, telex 51309 UNIBFD G)

WEST, (Sidney) John; s of Robert Osborn West (d 1964), of Willowhurst, Earith, Huntingdonshire, and Rose Emma, *née* French (d 1964); *b* 4 Oct 1918; *Educ* Kingswood Sch Bath; *m* 27 April 1946, Lorna Marion, da of Harry Cecil Cooper (d 1971), of The Mill House, Unstone, nr Sheffield; 2 s (Stephen John b 1956, Peter James b 1959), 3 da (Jane b 1947, Mary b 1949, Sarah b 1952); *Career* War Serv 1939-46 104 (Essex Yeo) Regt TA RHA, Br Military Mission Pretoria; RA HAA TA Service 1948-55 482 (M) HAA Regt RA (Maj 1954); TA Reserve of Offrs 1957-; joined Barclays Bank Ltd 1935; mangr Colchester 1964-68 (Framlingham 1961-64), local dir Exeter Dist 1968-80; chm Dartington & Co Ltd 1984- (dir 1980-); pres Inst of Bankers: local centre Ipswich 1956, local centre Exeter 1972; Exeter City AFC Ltd 1978-83, chm Exeter and Dist C of C 1972, FCIB 1962; *Recreations* gardening (memb Nat Gardens Scheme); *Style*— John West, Esq; The Glebe Ho, Whitestone, nr Exeter, Devon EX4 2LF (☎ 0392 81 200); Dartington & Co Ltd, Linacre Ho, Southernhay Gardens, Exeter EX1 1UG (☎ 0392 410 599, fax 0392 411 135)

WEST, Kenneth; s of Albert West of Barlby, Selby (d 1978); *b* 1 Sept 1930; *Educ* Archbishop Holgate's GS, Univ Coll Oxford; *m* 1, 1957 (m dis 1982), Doreen Isabel; 3 da; m 2, 1982, Elizabeth Ann Borland; 1 s; *Career* Corpl REME; chemist; dir: South African Nylon Spinners 1976-83, Fiber Industries Inc USA 1977-83, Seahorse Int 1985-, ICI Fibres 1978-83; md Thomas Water 1983-85; chm: Harrogate WEA 1960-67, Granby HS PTA 1973-81; govr Granby HS 1980-83, FRIC, FRSA; *Recreations* flying (pilot), sailing (yacht 'Indemood Again'), theatre (producing), violin playing; *Clubs* Yorks Aeroplane, Royal Lymington Yacht; *Style*— Kenneth West, Esq; Sonning Mead, Thames St, Sonning, Reading, Berks, HG4 0UR; Seahorse International Ltd, Crescent House, The Crescent, Eastleigh, Hants S05 4BS (☎ 0703 620 448)

WEST, Martin Graham; s of Edward Graham West, of Bury, and Dorothy West (d 1987); *b* 7 Nov 1938; *Educ* Bury GS; *m* 1962, Jacqueline, da of Alfred Eric Allen (d 1959); 1 s (Jeremy b 1970), 2 da (Angela b 1965, Janine b 1967); *Career* CA; dir: British Mail Order Corpn Ltd 1973-76, London Scottish Bank plc 1976- (chief exec 1988-); FCA; *Recreations* classic car restoration, bridge; *Clubs* St James's (Manchester), Mere Golf and Country; *Style*— Martin Graham West, Esq; The Chaplain's House, West Lane, High Legh, Knutsford, Cheshire WA16 6LR (☎ 092 575 4448); Arndale House, Arndale Centre, Manchester M4 3AQ (☎ 061 834 2861, telex 669004, fax 061 834 2536)

WEST, Peter; s of Harold William West (d 1975), and Dorcas Ann West (d 1972); *b* 12 August 1920; *Educ* Cranbrook Sch; *m* 1946, Pauline Mary, da of Lt Cdr Evan Cuthbert Pike, RNVR (d 1929); 2 s (Simon, Stephen), 1 da (Jacqueline); *Career* radio and television sports commentator/presenter 1947-; sports journalist, rugby corr The Times 1971-82; *Books* Fight for the Ashes (1953), Fight for the Ashes (1956), Flannelled Fool and Muddied Oaf (autobiography 1986), Clean Sweep (1987); *Recreations* gardening; *Style*— Peter West, Esq; The Paddock, Duntisbourne Abbotts, Cirencester, Glos (☎ 028 582 380)

WEST, Prof Richard Gilbert; s of Arthur Gilbert Dixon West (d 1949), and Daisy Elizabeth Lovesay, MBE; *b* 31 May 1926; *Educ* Kings Sch Canterbury, Clare Coll Cambridge (MA, PhD, ScD); *m* 30 June 1973, Hazel Violet; *Career* Univ of Cambridge: dir sub-dept quaternary res 1966-87, prof botany 1977-; FRS 1968, FGS, FSA, Hon MRIA; *Books* Pleistocene Geology and Biology (second edn 1977), Preglacial Pleistocene of the Norfolk and Suffolk Coasts (1986); *Style*— Prof Richard West; 3A Woollards Lane, Gt Shelford, Cambridge CB2 5LZ; Department of Botany, Univ of Cambridge

WEST, Dr Richard John; s of Cecil John West (d 1987), and Alice B, *née* Court; *b* 8 May 1939; *Educ* Tiffin Boys Sch, Middx Hosp Med Sch (MB BS, MD); *m* 15 Dec 1962, Dr Jenny Winn, da of Leslie Gaius Hawkins (d 1976); 1 s (Simon b 1964), 2 da (Sarah b 1967, Sophie b 1982); *Career* lectr Inst of Child Health 1974-75, sr lectr and conslt paediatrician St George's Hosp and Med Sch 1975- (dean 1982-87); chm dist med ctee Wandsworth & E Merton 1978-80; memb: cncl Br Paediatric Assoc 1974-76, Wandsworth Health Authy 1981-82, S W Thames RHA 1982-88, cncl Inst of Med Ethics 1986-; gp scout master 2 Stoneleigh 1978-80; sch govr Tiffin Boys Sch 1983-86, Wimbledon HS 1987-; MRCP 1967, FRCP 1979; *Books* The Family Guide to Children's Ailments (1983); *Recreations* reading, travel, collecting pap boats; *Style*— Dr Richard West; 6 Dorset Rd, Merton Park, London SW19 (☎ 01 542 5119); Dept of Child Health, St George's Hosp Med Sch, London SW17 ORE (☎ 01 672 9944)

WEST, Timothy Lancaster; CBE (1984); s of (Harry) Lockwood West (d 1989), actor, and Olive Carleton-Crowe; *b* 20 Oct 1934; *Educ* John Lyon Sch Harrow, Regent St Poly; *m* 1, 1956 (m dis), Jacqueline Boyer; 1 da; m 2, 1963, Prunella Scales; 2 s; *Career* actor; memb RSC 1964-66, Prospect Theatre Co 1966-72, artistic dir Old Vic Co 1980-81; *Style*— Timothy West Esq, CBE; James Sharkey Associates, 15 Golden Square, London W1

WEST, William Todd; s of Alfred William West (d 1963), of Humberside, and Annie Beatrice, *née* Todd (d 1969); *b* 7 August 1924; *Educ* Sedbergh, Univ of London (LLB); *m* 7 July 1956, Beryl Josephine, da of William Fletcher Taylor (d 1966), of Scarborough, N Yorks; 1 s (Nicholas William b 1958); *Career* slr; elected legal memb of Royal Town Planning Inst 1975; *Books* Drugs Law (1982), The County Court (1983), A Shop Hours Casebook (1984), The Trial of Lord de Clifford (1985); *Recreations* watching county cricket, exercising a rabbiting terrier, bowls; *Style*— William West, Esq; Lindis, Roundhay Road, Bridlington, North Humberside YO15 3JZ (☎ 0262 673116); 10 Wellington Road, Bridlington, N Humberside YO15 2BL (☎ 0262 672747/672677)

WEST CUMBERLAND, Archdeacon of; *see*: Hodgson, Ven Thomas Richard Burnham

WEST INDIES, Archbishop of; Most Rev George Cuthbert Manning Woodroffe; KBE (1980, CBE 1973); *b* 1918,May; *Educ* Grenada Boys' Secondary Sch, Codrington Coll, Univ of Durham (MA); *m* 1947, Alice Aileen, da of Sybleboyle Cowley Connel, MBE (d 1970); 1 s (Andrew), 1 da (Paula); *Career* priest 1945, bishop of the Windward Islands 1969-80; civil servant Grenada 1936-42; archbishop of the West Indies 1980-; *Recreations* music, cooking; *Clubs* Royal Cwlth Soc; *Style*— The Most Rev the Lord Archbishop of the West Indies, KBE; Bishop's House, PO Box 128, St Vincent, West Indies (☎ 809 45 61895)

WEST-RUSSELL, His Honour Judge Sir David Sturrock; s of Sir Alexander West-Russell, KB (d 1962), and Agnes, *née* Sturrock (d 1930); *b* 17 July 1921; *Educ* Rugby, Pembroke Coll Cambridge (MA); *m* 30 April 1949, Christine, *née* Tyler; 1 s (Christopher), 2 da (Fiona, Sarah); *Career* War Serv 1940-46: cmmnd Queens Own Cameron Highlanders 1941, Parachute Regt 1942, N Africa, Italy, France, Greece, Norway, Palestine (despatches) Maj; mgmnt trainee Guest Keen & Nettlefold 1948-50; barr Middle Temple 1953, bencher 1986, practising SE circuit; dep chm Inner London QS 1966-72, circuit judge 1972, sr circuit judge Inner London Crown Ct 1979-82 and Southwark Crown Ct 1983-84, pres Industl Tbnls for England and Wales 1984, memb Departmental Ctee on Legal Aid in Criminal Proceedings 1964-65, cmmr NI Emergency Provisions Act 1974-; chm: Lord Chancellors advsy ctee on Appointments of Magistrates for Inner London 1976-87, Home Sec's advsy bd on Restricted Patients 1985; pres Inner London Magistrates Assoc 1979-83; memb: Inner London Probation Ctee 1979 (chm 1988), Lord Chancellor's Advsy Ctee on Training of Magistrates 1980-85, Judicial Studies Bd 1980-84 and 1987-, Parole Bd 1980-82, Parole Review 1987-88; *Recreations* gardening, photography, walking; *Clubs* Garrick; *Style*— His Hon Judge Sir David West-Russell; 24 Hamilton Terrace, St Johns Wood, London NW8 (☎ 01 286 3718)

WESTBROOK, Brig Geoffrey Tom Edney; OBE (1960), DL (Durham 1982); s of Maj Tom Westbrook (d 1922), and Edith Elizabeth Westbrook (d 1969); *b* 12 August 1920; *Educ* St Lawrence Coll; *m* 1943, Elizabeth Norah Scott; 1 s, 1 da (and 1 s decd); *Career* RE, Dep Engr-in-Chief, ret 1973; sec North of England TAVR Assoc 1973-83, ret; *Recreations* ornithology, conservation; *Style*— Brig Geoffrey Westbrook, OBE, DL; Hinkhams Cottage, Whitchurch Canonicorum, Bridport, Dorset

WESTBROOK, Hon Mrs (Mary Joan); *née* Fraser; da of late 1 Baron Strathalmond, CBE; *b* 1922; *m* 1945, Neil Gowanloch Westbrook; 1 s, 1 da; *Style*— The Hon Lady Westbrook; White Gables, Prestbury, Cheshire

WESTBROOK, Sir Neil Gowanloch; CBE (1981); s of Frank Westbrook, and Dorothy; *b* 21 Jan 1917; *Educ* Oundle, Clare Coll Cambridge (MA); *m* 1945, Hon Mary Joan Fraser, da of 1 Baron Strathalmond, CBE; 1 s, 1 da; *Career* WWII Actg Lt Col RE and Gen Staff Offr (despatches); chm and mangr: Trafford Park Est plc, Port of Manchester Warehouses Ltd; farmer; memb CBI NW regnl cncl 1982-88, chm CBI NW inner cities study gp 1985-88, memb IOD Manchester and area branch ctee 1967-86, dep chm Trafford ctee Manchester C of C and Indust 1983-86; memb: Trafford Indust Cncl 1975-86, Assoc of Br C of C Ctee on Rates and Local Govt Fin 1975-77, Cons Party memb Cons Bd of Fin 1984-87, chm NW Indust Cncl 1982-87; memb: Nat Union Industl and Trade Forum 1982-87, Nat Union Exec Ctee 1975-81, NW Area Fin and Gen Purposes Ctee 1974-87; chm of Manchester Cons Assoc 1974-83 (vice chm 1973-74, hon tres 1964-73), chm Greater Manchester Co-ordinating Ctee 1978-86, memb Manchester City Cncl 1949-72 (dep ldr 1968-69), Lord Mayor C of Manchester 1969-70, chm Greater Manchester South Euro Div 1978-84; Kt 1988; *Recreations* shooting, fishing; *Clubs* Carlton London, Manchester Tennis and Racquets; *Style*— Sir Neil Westbrook, CBE; Estate Office, Trafford Park, Manchester M17 1AU (☎ 061 872 5426)

WESTBROOK, Roger; s of Edward George Westbrook, of Sandy Mount, Bearsted, Kent, and Beatrice Minnie, *née* Marshall; *b* 26 May 1941; *Educ* Dulwich, Hertford Coll Oxford (MA); *Career* HM Dip Serv: FO 1964, asst private sec to the Chllr of Lancaster and Min of State FCO 1965, Yaoundé 1967, Rio de Janeiro 1971, Brasilia 1972, private sec to min of State FCO 1975, head of chancery Lisbon 1977, dep head news dept FCO 1980, dep head Falkland Islands dept FCO 1982, overseas inspectorate FCO 1984, high cmmr Negara Brunei Darussalam 1986; *Clubs* Travellers', Royal Brunei Polo; *Style*— Roger Westbrook, Esq; British High Commission, Bandar Seri Begawan, Negara Brunei Darussalam

WESTBURY, 5 Baron (UK 1861); David Alan Bethell; MC (1942), DL (N Yorks 1973); s of Capt Hon Richard Bethell (d 1929, s of 3 Baron, whom he predecesased), and Lady Agatha Tollemache, sis of 9 Earl of Dysart; suc bro, 4 Baron, 1961; *b* 16 July 1922; *Educ* Harrow, RMC; *m* 21 Oct 1947, Ursula Mary Rose, er da of Hon Robert James (3 s of 2 Baron Northbourne), and his 2 w, Lady Serena Lumley, da of 10 Earl of Scarbrough; 2 s, 1 da; *Heir* s, Maj Hon Richard Bethell, MBE; *Career* served WWII with Scots Guards in N Africa & Italy (despatches); sits as Conservative peer in House of Lords; equerry to HRH Duke of Gloucester 1947-49; pres British Paraplegic Sports Soc; chm Cncl and Care for the Elderly; pres Northern Police Convalescent Home; tstee Berkeley Square Ball; memb exec ctee of Int Fedn of Multiple Sclerosis Socs; patron Action Around Bethlehem Children with Disability; KStJ 1977, Bailiff of Egle GCStJ 1987; Registrar OstJ, chm CCE; pres: BPSS, YABC, Northern Convalescent Home; tstee Berkeley Square Ball; Registrar OStJ, pres BPSS, chm CCE, pres YABC, pres Northern Clonvalescent Home; Tstee Berkeley Square Ball;; *Clubs* Jockey, Pratt's; *Style—* The Rt Hon the Lord Westbury, MC, DL; Barton Cottage, Malton, N Yorks (☎ 0653 692293); 8 Ropers Orchard, Danvers St, London SW3 (☎ 01 352 7911)

WESTCOTT, Richard Henry; s of Charles Westcott (d 1984), of S Molton, Devon, and Ruby Alice, *née* Addicott (d 1979); *b* 5 Nov 1947; *Educ* Barnstaple Boys' GS; *m* 26 Nov 1983, Susan, da of George Frederick Read, of Middlesbrough, Cleveland; 1 s (Charles George Frederick b 20 April 1987), 1 da (Emily Margaret Alice b 29 Aug 1985); *Career* barr Lincoln's Inn 1978; articled/sr clerk Moore Bedworth & Co CAs Barnstaple 1964-73, tax mangr Arthur Andersen CAs London 1973-75, exec mangr Morgan Grenfell & Co Ltd London 1975-83 (dir 1983-); dir Warburg, Akroyd, Rowe & Pitman, Mullens Securites Ltd; FCA 1970, FTII 1974, ACIB 1979; *Recreations* walking, reading, carpentry, music, golf; *Style—* Richard Westcott, Esq; 1 Finsbury Ave, London, EC2M 2PA (☎ 01 606 1066, fax 01 247 4984 telex 8952485)

WESTENRA, Hon Mrs Brigid Mary; da of 6 Baron Rossmore; *b* 23 Sept 1928; *m* 1956 (m dis 1969), Hon Jonathan Howard, s of 3 Baron Strathcona and Mountroyal; 2 da; *Career* reverted to maiden name; *Style—* The Hon Mrs Brigid Westenra; Pratolino, Radda-in-Chianti, Siena, Italy

WESTERMAN, Sir (Wilfred) Alan; CBE (1962, OBE 1957); s of John Walter Westerman (d 1941), and Ena Westerman (d 1957); *b* 25 Mar 1913; *Educ* Knox GS, Univ of Tas (MA), Melbourne Univ (BEd), Columbia Univ NY (EdD); *m* 1970, Margaret; 2 s (from previous marriage); *Career* dir of Trade Promotion and Int Relations in Dept of Commerce and Agric 1949-58, chm Tariff Bd 1958-60, sec Devpt of Trade and Indust 1960-71, exec chm Aust Indust Dvpt Corpn 1971-77; kt 1963; *see Debrett's Handbook of Australia and New Zealand for further details*; *Style—* Sir Alan Westerman, CBE; PO Box 1483, Canberra City, ACT 2601, Australia

WESTHEAD, John Michael; s of Percy Westhead (d 1961); *b* 13 Nov 1928; *Educ* St John's Coll and St Antony's Coll Oxford; *m* 1958, Portia Joan Peters, da of Capt John Wentworth Rooke, OBE; 2 s; *Career* gp md Bowthorpe Holdings Ltd; *Recreations* squash, music, reading; *Clubs* Oxford & Cambridge, RSA; *Style—* John Westhead, Esq; Hapstead Green Cottage, 63 High St, Ardingly, W Sussex (☎ 0444 892 362); 6 Wetherby Mews, Bolton Gdns, London SW5 (☎ 01 370 3685)

WESTLAKE, Gp Capt George Herbert; DSO (1945), DFC (1943); s of Herbert Westlake (d 1953), and Edith Florence Forder (d 1966); *b* 21 April 1918; *Educ* Shoreham-by-Sea GS, De Havilland Aeronautical Tech Sch, Hatfield, Herts; *m* 1, 14 Oct 1946, Margaret Lesley, da of John Iddon (d 1956), of Lancs; 1 s (Richard b 1953), 1 da (Jennifer b 1955); m 2, 23 June 1976, Susan Frances Chilton, da of John Kennedy, of Northants; 1 step s (Myles Chilton b 1965), 1 step da (Mimi Lucy Chilton b 1968); *Career* aeronautical student 1936-39, RAF service 1939-69; war serv Battle of Britain, Syria, KI Desert, Cyprus, Central Med, Sicily, Italy; post war serv UK, Germany, USA, NATO (Fontainebleau), Singapore, Hong Kong, Cyprus; aviation and gen mangr in Kuwait 1975-; Air Efficiency Award 1944, despatches 1943; *Recreations* game fishing, reading, TV; *Clubs* RAF, Flyfishers'; *Style—* Gp Capt George H Westlake, DSO, DFC; 17 Main Street, Seaton, nr Uppingham, Leics (☎ 057 287 451); Kuwait Overseas Agencies, PO Box 301, 13004 Safat, Kuwait (☎ 2424477/88)

WESTLAKE, Rev Peter Alan Grant; CMG (1972), MC (1943); s of Alan Robert Cecil Westlake, CSI, CIE (d 1978), and Dorothy Louise (d 1966), *née* Turner; *b* 2 Feb 1919; *Educ* Sherborne, CCC Oxford (MA), Univ of Wales (MSc, BD); *m* 1943, Katherine Gertrude, da of Rev Harold Charles Spackman; 2 s; *Career* FRAS; RA in Libya and Tobruk (adj 1 RHA) and Italy (despatches), Capt, 1939-46; entered Foreign Service 1946, head of Chancery Tel Aviv 1955-57; cnsllr: Washington 1965, Canberra 1967-71; min Br Embassy Toyko 1971-76, UK cmmr gen Int Ocean Expo Okinawa 1975; deacon 1981, priest Church in Wales 1982-; Order of Rising Sun (Japan) 1975; *Recreations* sailing, oceanography; *Clubs* RAYC; *Style—* Rev Peter Westlake, CMG, MC; 53 Church St, Beaumaris, Gwynedd LL58 8AB (☎ 0248 810114)

WESTLEY, Alan; s of Frederick Westley (d 1956), of Wellingborough Rd, Northampton, and Alice Westley (d 1944); *b* 30 April 1912; *Educ* John Clare Sch Northampton; *m* 21 Sept 1939, (Alice) Betsy, da of Arthur Cotton (d 1965), of Heath End, Nuneaton; 2 s (Clive Alan b 1 Feb 1945, Mark Julian b 30 Dec 1949), 1 da (Sally Ann b 12 Aug 1953); *Career* entered motor industry 1926; worked with: Arthur Mulliner coach builder Northampton, Pytchley Autocar Co coach builder Northampton, Salmon & Sons Newport Pagnell coachbuilders, motor panels for Coventry Body Pressings, metalwork for Motor Industry, Sir W G Armstrong Whitworth Aircraft aircraft manufacturers Coventry; jt fndr and jt md Airflow Streamlines Ltd 1941-68, chm and chief exec Airflow Streamlines plc 1968-88; *Recreations* golf, boating, gardening, travel; *Clubs* Valletta YC (Malta), Northamptonshire Co GC, Northampton GC, Northampton Co; *Style—* Alan Westley, Esq; The Knowle, 502 Wellingborough Rd, Abington Park, Northampton NN3 3HX (☎ 0604 406 098); Airflow Streamlines plc, Main Rd, Far Cotton, Northampton NN3 3HX (☎ 0604 762 261, fax 0604 701 405, telex 316319)

WESTMACOTT, Richard Kelso; s of Cdr John Rowe Westmacott, RN (d 1983), and Ruth Pharazyn (d 1971); *b* 20 Feb 1934; *Educ* Eton, Royal Navy; *m* 1965, Karen; 1 s (John b 1969), 1 da (Camilla b 1967); *Career* RN 1952-54; stockbroker, joined Hoare & Co 1955; memb Stock Exchange 1960, chm: Hoare Govett Ltd 1975, Security Pacific Hoare Govett (Hldgs) Ltd 1985, Hoare Govett Corporate Fin Ltd; *Recreations* sailing, shooting; *Clubs* Whites, City of London, Royal Yacht Squadron; *Style—* Richard Westmacott Esq; 9 Alexander Sq, London SW3 2AY (☎ 584 9073); Security Pacific House, 4 Broadgate, London EC2M 7LE (☎ 01 601 0101, telex 887887)

WESTMEATH, 13 Earl of (I 1621); William Anthony Nugent; also Baron Delvin (I before 1489, evolved from a feudal Barony, of which the date of origin is uncertain); s of 12 Earl of Westmeath (d 1971); *b* 21 Nov 1928; *Educ* Marlborough, RMA Sandhurst; *m* 31 July 1963, Susanna Margaret, o da of His Hon Judge James Charles Beresford Whyte Leonard, of Sutton Courtenay, Berks; 2 s; *Heir* s, Lord Delvin; *Career* RA 1947-61, ret as Capt; sr master St Andrew's Sch Pangbourne, ret 1988; *Style—* The Rt Hon the Earl of Westmeath; Farthings, Tutts Clump, Reading, Berks (☎ 0734 744426)

WESTMINSTER, Anne, Duchess of; Anne Winifred; da of Brig-Gen Edward Sullivan, CB, CMG, of Glanmire House, Co Cork; *m* 1947, as his 4 w, 2 Duke of Westminster, GCVO, DSO (d 1953); *Style—* Her Grace Anne, Duchess of Westminster; Lochmore, Lairg, Sutherland; Eaton Lodge, Eccleston, Chester

WESTMINSTER, Archbishop (RC) of, 1976-; His Eminence (George) Basil Hume; s of late Sir William Errington Hume, CMG, and late Marie Elizabeth, *née* Tisseyre; *b* 2 Mar 1923; *Educ* Ampleforth, St Benet's Hall Oxford, Fribourg Univ Switzerland; *Career* ordained priest 1950; Ampleforth: sr modern language master 1952-63, housemaster 1955-63, prof of Dogmatic Theology 1955-63, magister scholarum of the English Benedictine Congregation 1957-63, abbot 1963-76; Cardinal 1976; pres: Euro Ctee of Bishops' Conferences 1979-87, Bishops' Conference England and Wales 1979-; memb Cncl for Secretariat of Int Synod of Bishops 1978-87; Hon Bencher Inner Temple; Hon DD: Cambridge 1979, Newcastle 1979, London 1980, Oxford 1981, York 1982, Kent 1983, Durham 1987, Collegio S Anselmo Rome 1987; Hon DHL: Manhattan Coll NY USA 1980, Catholic Univ of America 1980; *Books* Searching for God (1977), In Praise of Benedict (1981), To Be a Pilgrim (1984); *Style—* His Eminence the Cardinal Archbishop of Westminster; Archbishop's House, Westminster, London SW1 (☎ 01 834 4717)

WESTMINSTER, 6 Duke of (UK 1874); Sir Gerald Cavendish Grosvenor; 15 Bt (E 1622), DL (Cheshire 1982); also Baron Grosvenor (GB 1761), Earl Grosvenor, Viscount Belgrave (both GB 1784), and Marquess of Westminster (UK 1831); s of 5 Duke of Westminster, TD (d 1979), and Hon Viola Lyttelton (*see* Viola, Dowager Duchess of Westminster (d 1987)), da of 9 Viscount Cobham; bro of Countess of Lichfield and Duchess of Roxburghe; *b* 22 Dec 1951; *Educ* Harrow; *m* 1978, Natalia Ayesha, yst da of Lt-Col Harold Pedro Joseph Phillips, and Georgina (da of Sir Harold Wernher, 3 Bt, GCVO, TD, and Lady Zia, CBE, *née* Countess Anastasia Mikhailovna, da of HIH Grand Duke Michael of Russia); sis of Duchess of Abercorn; 2 da (Lady Tamara Katherine b 20 Dec 1979, Lady Edwina Louise b 4 Nov 1981); *Heir* to Dukedom none, to Marquessate and all inferior honours: *see* 7 Earl of Wilton; *Career* sits as Cons Peer in House of Lords; landowner; cmmnd Cheshire Sqdn QOY 1984-87; tstee Grosvenor Estate 1971-; pres: Chester City Cons Assoc 1975-, NW Industl Cncl 1979-, freemen of England 1979-, Coal Trade Benevolent Assoc 1980-82, London Tourist Bd 1980-, Spastics Soc 1982-, St John's Ambulance London (Prince of Wales) Dist 1983-; chm Hennel, Frazer & Haws Ltd 1979-87; dir: Sun Alliance Insurance London, Stuart-Devlin Ltd 1979-86, Marcher Sound Ltd, Harland & Wolff Ltd 1983-87; govr: King's Sch 1976-87, Int Students Tst 1978-, Chester Teaching Training Coll 1978-; patron: Br Kidney Patients Assoc 1980-86, Br Holestein Soc 1981-, pro chancellor Keele Univ 1986-; pres: RNIB 1986-, National Kidney Research Fund 1986-, London Federation Boys Clubs 1985-, Arthritis Care 1986-, Game Conservancy 1986-, Royal Assoc British, Dairy Farmers 1987-, Industrial Cncl N Wales; patron: British Holstein Soc 1985-, Worcester CCC 1986; The Continuing Professional Devpt Fndn 1983-; tstee Civic Tst 1983-; memb Cons NW Area Exec 1979-; Freeman City: Chester 1975, London 1981; OStJ 1982; CStJ 1987; FRSA 1987; FID 1985; *Recreations* shooting, fishing, scuba diving; *Clubs* Royal Yacht Sqdn, Brooks's, Cavalry & Guards, MCC; *Style—* His Grace the Duke of Westminster, DL; Eaton Hall, Chester, Cheshire; Eaton Estate Office, Eccleston Chester (☎ 0244 680333)

WESTMINSTER, Sally, Duchess of; Sally; twin da of late George Perry, and late Mrs Alfred Scott-Hewitt; *m* 11 April 1945, 4 Duke of Westminster, DSO, PC, DL (d 1967); *Style—* Her Grace Sally, Duchess of Westminster; Hill House, Wickwar, Glos (☎ 045 424 304)

WESTMORE, Geoffrey David; s of Alan Herbert Westmore, of Guildford, Surrey, and Mary Elspeth, *née* Brooking; *b* 28 Sept 1950; *Educ* Royal GS Guildford; *m* 21 July 1979, Paula, *née* Clemett; 1 s (Jonathan Henry Clemett b 1987), 1 da (Kathryn May Clemett b 1983); *Career* Deloitte Haskins & Sells: mangr 1975-83, ptnr 1983-; FCA 1972; *Recreations* sport, music, theatre, films; *Style—* Geoffrey Westmore, Esq; 26 Old Bailey, London EC4 M 7PL (☎ 01 248 3913, fax 01 236 2367)

WESTMORLAND, 15 Earl of (E 1624); David Anthony Thomas Fane; KCVO (1970); also Baron Burghersh (E 1624); s of 14 Earl of Westmorland (d 1948), and Diana, Countess of Westmorland (d 1983); Lord Westmorland is fourth in descent from 11 Earl, soldier, diplomat, ambass Berlin 1841-51, fndr and pres Royal Academy of Music; *b* 31 Mar 1924; *Educ* Eton; *m* 1950, Barbara, da of Lt-Col Sir Roland Lewis Findlay, 3 Bt; 2 s, 1 da; *Heir* s, Lord Burghersh; *Career* served RHG, wounded WWII, Capt, ret 1950; lord in waiting to HM The Queen 1955-78, master of the horse 1978-; chm Sotheby's 1980-82 (dir 1982-); dir: Westmoreland Coal Co (Philadelphia), I U Int, Crown Life of Canada; OStJ 1981; *Clubs* White's, Buck's; *Style—* The Rt Hon the Earl of Westmorland, KCVO; Kingsmead, Didmarton, Glos (☎ 045 423 634); 23 Chester Row, London SW1 (☎ 01 730 3389)

WESTOLL, James; DL (Cumbria 1963); s of James Westoll (d 1969); *b* 26 July 1918; *Educ* Eton, Trinity Coll Cambridge (MA); *m* 1946, Sylvia Jane, MBE, da of Lord Justice Luxmoore (d 1944); 2 s, 2 da; *Career* served 1939-46 NW Europe (despatches), Maj Border Regt; farmer; called to the Bar 1952, memb NW Electricity Bd 1959-66; chm: Cumberland CC 1958-74, Cumbria CC 1973-76; dep chm Cumberland QS 1960-71, High Sheriff 1964; Master Worshipful Co of Clothworkers 1983-84; Hon LLD Leeds Univ 1984; CStJ 1977, KStJ 1984; *Recreations* gardening, shooting; *Clubs* Boodle's, Farmers'; *Style—* James Westoll, Esq, DL; Dykeside, Longtown, Cumbria (☎ 0228 791235)

WESTON, Adrian Robert; s of Harold Gibbons Weston MA, LLB (d 1987), of Leicester, and Alwyne Gabrielle Weston, *née* Applebee; *b* 7 June 1935; *Educ* Ratcliffe Coll, Queens Coll Oxford (MA); *m* 28 Sept 1963, Bridget Ann, da of William Henry Smith (d 1964), of Leicester; 1 s (Thomas b 1968), 1 da (Alexandra b 1967); *Career* admitted slr 1961; dir: Everards Brewery Ltd 1984-, Burgess Gp plc 1982-88, Pal Int Ltd 1985-, Akinson Design Assoc Ltd 1982-; sr ptnr Harvey Ingram Stone and Simpson Slrs; dir Portland Hse Sch Tst Ltd 1982-84; govr Ratcliffe Coll Leicester 1988-; capt Leics Co Hockey Assoc 1965-66; vice pres: The Hockey Assoc 1979- (chm 1972-78), Leics Co CC ; *Recreations* golf, reading, music; *Clubs* Leicestershire Golf, Br Sportsmens, Leicestershire County Cricket; *Style—* Adrian R Weston, Esq; Home Farm, Smeeton Westerby, Leicester LE8 0JQ (☎ 0533 792514); Harvey Ingram Stone & Simpson Solicitors, 20 New Walk, Leicester LE1 6TX (☎ 0533 545454)

WESTON, Anthony Paul Cartade (Tony); s of Robert Jean Marcel Cartade Weston, of Bristol, and Edna Lavinia Jago-Burton (d 1949); *b* 14 May 1936; *Educ* King Edwards Southampton, Farfield Bristol, The West of England Coll of Art (NDD, ATD, MAH); *m* 28 Dec 1961, Jennifer Anne Blaise, da of Arthur Frederick Gore Bird (d 1971); 1 s (Nicholas b 1964), 1 da (Rebecca b 1965); *Career* painter, sculptor, antiquarian, paintings in many private collections, author; exhibiter at The Royal West of Englan Acad; *Books* The Late Drawings of Mantegna, Paduan Sculpture, West of England Horology et al; *Recreations* riding to hounds, literary research; *Clubs* The Clifton Yacht; *Style—* Tony Weston, Esq; Eaton House, Clifton Down, Clifton, Bristol BS8 3HT

WESTON, Benjamin Charles; s of Robert H Weston, and Alice E Weston; *b* 19 August 1954; *Educ* Miami Univ Ohio (BA), The Johns Hopkins Sch of Advanced Int Studies Washington DC (MA); *m* 29 July 1978, Sara, da of Jack W Sigler; 1 da (Emily b 1985); *Career* asst tres Morgan Guaranty Tst Co 1978-82, mangr Morgan Guaranty Ltd 1982-83, exec dir Bankers Tst Int Ltd 1988- (vice-pres 1983-), md Bankers Tst Co 1986-; *Recreations* golf, classic cars, house renovation; *Style—* Benjamin Weston, Esq; Bankers Trust Int Ltd, Dashwood House, 69 Old Broad St, London EC2P 2EE (☎ 01 382 2566, fax 01 382 2274, telex 888707)

WESTON, Hon Mrs (Berenice Mary); *née* Walker-Smith; da of Baron Broxbourne (Life Peer); *b* 1946; *m* 1967, William Andrew Weston; *Style—* The Hon Mrs Weston; 7 Royal Arcade, Albemarle Street, London W1X 3HD

WESTON, Brian Henry; s of Horace Henry Weston, of Stisted, Essex, and Ethel May, *née* Steel; *b* 29 Nov 1933; *Educ* Cornwall Sch, City of London Coll; *m* 21 July 1956, Sheila Elizabeth, da of Edwin George Howard (d 1971); 2 s (Simon Neil b 1964, David Andrew b 1968), 1 da (Amanda Jane b 1963); *Career* Nat Serv RAF 1952-54; with Bank of Nova Scotia 1955-73, gen mangr First Interstate Bank 1973-83; chm and chief exec HFC Bank plc 1983-; memb exec cncl Young Enterprise (chm E Berks Bd); FCIB, FAAI, FIOD; *Recreations* gardening, art, reading; *Clubs* Les Ambassadeurs, Wig and Pen, Wellington; *Style—* Brian Weston, Esq; Rallywood, Munstead, Godalming, Surrey GU8 4AA (☎ 04868 23232); HFC Bank Plc, North St, Winkfield, Windsor, Berks (☎ 0344 890000, fax 0344 489604)

WESTON, Bryan Henry; s of Henry James Weston (d 1973), and Rose Kate Weston (d 1989); *b* 9 April 1930; *Educ* St George GS Bristol, Bristol Rutherford and Oxford Technical Colls; *m* 21 July 1956, Heather Grace, da of Henry Gordon West, of Redhill, Avon; 2 s (Richard b 21 Jan 1958, Robert b 21 Dec 1960), 2 da (Rebecca b 13 Sept 1962, Rachel b 21 Sept 1967); *Career* 2 Lt RE 1954-56; apprentice engr SW Electricity Bd 1949, various engrg and commercial posts with SW Electricity Bd 1956-73 (latterly commerical mangr 1973); dep chm Yorks Electricity Bd 1977, chm MANWEB (Merseyside and N Wales Electricity Bd) 1985; dir : Br Electrotech Approvals Bd, Chloride Silent Power Ltd, Deeside Enterprise Tst; CEng, MIEE, CBIM; *Recreations* gardening, walking, caravanning, DIY; *Style—* Bryan Weston, Esq; Fountainhead Cottage, Brassey Green, nr Tarporley, Cheshire CW6 9UG; MANWEB (Merseyside & North Wales Electricity Board), Head Office, Sealand Rd, Chester CH1 4LR (☎ 0244 377 111, fax 0244 390 725)

WESTON, Hon Mrs (Caroline Cecily); *née* Douglas-Scott-Montagu; da of 2 Baron, KCIE, CSI (d 1929); *b* 1925; *m* 1950 (George) Grainger Weston; 3 s, 1 da; *Style—* The Hon Mrs Weston; Santa Clara Ranch, Marion, Texas, USA; 301 Wiltshire, San Antonio, Texas, USA

WESTON, Rear Adm Charles Arthur Winfield; CB (1978); s of Charles Winfield Weston (d 1958), of Barton-on-Sea, Hants; *b* 12 July 1922; *Educ* Merchant Taylors'; *m* 1946, Jeanie Findlay, da of William Dick Brown Miller; 1 s, 1 da; *Career* joined RN as cadet 1940, serv WWII: in home waters, Med, Indian Ocean, Atlantic; sec to 2 Sea Lord 1965-67, Capt 1967, cso to C-in-C Naval Home Cmd 1969-71, dir Naval Physical Trg and Sport 1972, dir: Def Admin Planning Staff 1973-75, Quartering (RN) 1975-76; ADC to HM The Queen 1976, adm pres RNC Greenwich 1976-78, appeals sec King Edward VII's Hosp for Offrs 1979-87; *Recreations* cricket, golf, gardening; *Clubs* MCC, Army and Navy; *Style—* Rear Adm Charles Weston, CB; Westacre, Liphook, Hants (☎ 0428 723337)

WESTON, Christopher John; s of Eric Tudor Weston, of Plaxton, Kent, and Evelyn, *née* Snell; *b* 3 Mar 1937; *Educ* Lancing Coll; *m* 7 July 1969, Josephine; 1 da (Annabel); *Career* RAF 1955-57; chm and chief exec Phillips Son & Neale and assoc cos; dir: F & C Pacific Investmt plc 1984-, Headline Publishing 1986-, F & C Enterprise Tst plc 1987-, F & C Ventures Advsrs Ltd 1988-, Nationwide Anglia Estate Agents 1988-, Nationwide Anglia Estate Agents (Scotland) Ltd 1988-, Ventris Securities Ltd 1988-; chm Bradford Peters (Hldgs) Ltd 1987-; cncl memb: Royal Soc for Encouragement of Arts, Manufactures and Commerce, Royal Soc of Arts; Liveryman Worshipful Co of Painter Stainers, Freeman City of London; FIA (Scot), FRSA; *Recreations* theatre, music; *Clubs* Oriental; *Style—* Christopher Weston, Esq; Blenstock House, 7 Blenheim St, New Bond St, London W1Y 0AS (☎ 01 629 6602, fax 01 629 8876, telex 298855 Blen G)

WESTON, Rev David Wilfrid Valentine; s of The Rev William Valentine Weston (d 1937), and Gertrude Hamilton, *née* Erby (d 1979); *b* 8 Dec 1937; *Educ* St Edmund's Sch Canterbury; *m* 9 June 1984, Helen Strachan, da of James R Macdonald; 1 s (Luke b 1986); *Career* monk of Nashdom Abbey 1960; ordained: deacon 1967, priest 1968; novice master 1969-74, prior of Nashdom 1971-74, (abbot 1974-84), vicar of Pilling 1985; Freedom of the City of London 1959, memb Slaters' co 1959; *Recreations* local history; *Style—* The Rev David Weston; The Vicarage, Pilling, Preston PR3 6AA (☎ 0253 790 231)

WESTON, Ven Frank Valentine; s of Rev William Valentine Weston (d 1937), and Gertrude Hamilton Erby (d 1979); *b* 16 Sept 1935; *Educ* Christ's Hosp, Queen's Coll Oxford (MA); *m* 1963, Penelope Brighid, da of Marmaduke Carver Middleton Athorpe (d 1973); 1 s, 2 da; *Career* curate St John Baptist Atherton 1961-65, chaplain Coll of the Ascension Selly Oak 1965-69, princ 1969-76; princ and Pantonian prof of theology Edinburgh Theological Coll 1976-82; archdeacon of Oxford and canon of Christ Church Oxford 1982-; *Recreations* music, books, stamps, exploring the countryside; *Style—* The Ven the Archdeacon of Oxford; Archdeacon's Lodging, Christ Church, Oxford OX1 1DP (☎ 0865 276185)

WESTON, (Willard Gordon) Galen; s of W Garfield Weston (d 1978, sometime Cons MP), of Toronto, Canada, and London, by his 1 w, Reta Lila Howard (d 1967); yr bro of Garry *see* Garfield Howard Weston; *for further details see: Debrett's Illustrated Guide to The Canadian Establishment*; *b* 29 Oct 1940; *m* 1966, Hilary Frayne; 2 children; *Career* chm and pres: George Weston Ltd, Wittington Investmts Ltd; chm: Brown Thomas Gp Ltd (Ireland), Holt Renfrew & Co Ltd, Loblaw Companies Ltd, Weston Foods Ltd, Weston Resources Ltd; vice chm Fortnum & Mason plc (UK); dir: Associated British Foods plc (UK), Canadian Imperial Bank of Commerce, George Weston Hldgs Ltd (UK), Ritz - Carlton Hotel Inc (Montreal); chm The Lester B Pearson Coll of the Pacific; dir: Operation Raleigh - Canada, Utd World Colls (UK); pres: The W Garfield Weston Fndn, The Weston Canada Fndn; life memb: Art Gallery of Ontario, Royal Ontario Museum; Hon LLD Univ of Western Ontario; *Recreations* polo, tennis; *Clubs* Badminton & Racquet (Toronto), Guards Polo (UK), Lyford Cay (Bahamas), Toronto Club, York (Toronto); *Style—* Galen Weston, Esq; George Weston Ltd, 22 St Clair Avenue East, Toronto, Canada (416 922 2500, telex 06 22781 WESTLOB)

WESTON, Garfield Howard (Garry); s of W Garfield Weston (d 1978, sometime Cons MP), of Toronto Canada and London, by his 1 w, Reta Lila Howard (d 1967); er bro of Galen Weston, *qv*; *for further details see: Debrett's Illustrated Guide to The Canadian Establishment*; *b* 28 April 1927; *Educ* New College Oxford, Harvard Univ; *m* 1959, Mary Ruth, da of Maj-Gen Sir Howard Kippenberger; 3 s, 3 da; *Career* chm: Assoc Br Foods plc, Fortnum & Mason plc, George Weston Hldgs Ltd, Twining Crosfield & Co Ltd; dir: Allied Bakeries, Allied Mills, Burton's Gold Medal Biscuits, Fine Fare (Hldgs), Allied Foods (Hldgs) Ltd, Ryvita Co, George Weston Foods Ltd Australia; *Style—* Garry Weston Esq; Associated British Foods plc, Weston Centre, 68 Knightsbridge, London SW1X 7LR (☎ 01 589 6363)

WESTON, John Henry Mortimer; s of Dr Henry James Weston (d 1954), of Woodlands, Sedlescombe, Sussex, and Ruth Woltera, *née* Nihill; *b* 20 May 1910; *Educ* Charterhouse, Gonville and Caius Coll Cambridge (MA) ; *m* 17 June 1939, Helen Mary Meta Mathilde, da of Prof Frederic Spencer Chevalier Légion d'Honneur, of Worthing, Sussex; 1 s (Timothy b 1940), 2 da (Verity b 1942, Nicola b 1944); *Career* Lt KSLI 1942; slr (Richmond, Surrey); pres Mid-Surrey Law Soc 1959-60; cnllr Richmond BC 1961-65; JP Borough of Windsor 1962-70; founder sec Richmond Fellowship (mental rehabilitation); Liveryman Worshipful Co of the Fishmongers 1931-; memb Law Soc; *Recreations* walking, gardening, foreign travel; *Clubs* Law Society; *Style—* John Weston, Esq; Medlars, Ufford, Nr Stamford, Lincs (☎ 0780 740533)

WESTON, (Philip) John; CMG (1985); s of Philip George Weston, of London (d 1969), and Edith Alice Bray, *née* Ansell (d 1976); *b* 13 April 1938; *Educ* Sherborne, Worcester Coll Oxford; *m* 28 Jan 1967, Margaret Sally, da of Robert Hermann Ehlers, of Bridgwater; 2 s (Ben b 1969, Rufus b 1973), 1 da (Gabriel b 1970); *Career* served as 2 Lt with 42 Commando RM 1956-58; entered Dip Serv 1962: FO 1962-63; Treasy Centre for Admin Studies 1964; Chinese languages student Hong Kong 1964-66, Peking 1967-68, FO 1969-71, Off of Perm Rep to EEC 1972-74; asst private sec to Sec of State for Foreign and Cwlth Affrs (Rt Hon James Callaghan, Rt Hon Anthony Crosland) 1974-76, head of EEC Presidency Secretariat FCO 1976-77; visiting fell All Souls Coll Oxford 1977-78, cncllr Washington 1978-81; head Def Dept FCO 1981-84; asst under-sec of State FCO 1984-85; min Paris 1985-88; dep sec to the Cabinet 1988-89; dep under sec of state FCO 1989-; *Recreations* fly-fishing, running, chess, poetry; *Clubs* Utd Oxford and Cambridge, Fly Fishers; *Style—* John Weston, Esq, CMG; c/o Foreign and Commonwealth Office, London SW1

WESTON, John Pix; s of Lt John Pix Weston (d 1968), of "Stickley", Margaret Road, Harborne, Birmingham, and Margaret Elizabeth, *née* Cox (d 1946); *b* 3 Jan 1920; *Educ* King Edward's Birmingham, Univ of Aston Birmingham (BSc), LSE (BSc), Univ of Geogia USA (Dip); *m* 5 Aug 1948, Ivy, da of Walter Glover, of 21 East Road, Northallerton, Yorks; 3 s (John b 1951, David b 1958, Christopher b 1963); *Career* Sgt RAMC 1939, 203 Mil Liaison Mission SA 1940-44, Allied Mil Liaison HQ Albania and GHQ (Southern) Cairo 1944-45, HQ NI Dist 1945-46; City of Birmingham Police Dept 1936-39, City of Birmingham Electricity Supply Dept 1939-48 (released for war service), third dist engr Mids Electricity Bd 1948-50, Switchgear Eng EF Co Ltd 1950-51, second asst area engr (technical) N Western Electricity Bd Kendal 1951-58, sr asst commercial engr Eastern Electricity Bd 1958-60, seconded dep op mangr Jamaica Public Serv Co 1960-61, princ tech engr and princ commercial engr Mids Electricity Bd 1961-64, asst chief commerce offr S of Scotland Electricity Bd 1964-66, advsr to Min of Transport 1966-69, sr economist and engr Int Bank for Reconstruction and Devpt Washington 1968-70, sr mangr Michelin Tyre Co 1970-72, dir post experience courses Open Univ 1972-75, dir gen Royal Soc for the Prevention of Accidents 1974-78, industl devpt offr Argyll and Bute DC 1977-79, health and safety advsr Newcastle Poly and Northants Ct 1979, chief admin offr W Bromich Coll of Commerce and Technol 1979-85, conslt engr and economist 1985-; Birmingham Photographic Soc 1979-85: prog sec, competition sec, outings sec, cncl memb; memb cncl Midland Counties Photographic Fedn 1982-85, chm Upper Malbrook Residents Assoc 1982-87; lect: Allen Tech Inst Kendal 1951-58, Ipswich Civic Coll 1958-60, Halesowen Coll of Further Educn 1961-64, Broomsgrove Coll of Further Educn 1964-64, Univ of Aston in Birmingham 1961-64, SBStJ 1965, author of numerous papers on edn, eng, tport and safety, CEng 1953, AMIEE 1958, MAPLE 1958, FSS 1957, FREconS 1957, MIEE 1964, FIEE 1966, FBIM 1973; *Recreations* fell walking, swimming, gardening, cine and still photography; *Clubs* Farmers, St John House; *Style—* John Weston, Esq; Brook Mill and Woodside, Brook, Pendine, Dyfed SA33 4NX (☎ 099421 477)

WESTON, Dame Margaret (Kate); DBE (1979); da of Charles Edward and Margaret Weston; *b* 7 Mar 1926; *Educ* Stroud HS, Coll of Technology Birmingham (now Univ of Aston); *Career* engrg apprenticeship and past Gen Electric Co Ltd; asst keeper Dept of Electrical Engrg and Communications, Science Museum 1955 (dep keeper 1962, keeper of Dept of Museum Servs 1967); dir Sci Museum 1973-86; govr: Imp Coll of Sci & Technol, Ditchley Fndn 1985 (and memb of cncl of mgmnt); pres Assoc of Rway Preservation Socs; vice-pres Tport Tst; tstee: Brooklands Museum Tst Queen's Gate Tst, Hunterian Collection; memb: Museum and Galleries Cmmn 1851 Cmmn Ct of Royal Coll of Art, SE Electricty Bd 1981-, cncl RSA; hon doctorate: Sci Univ of Aston 1974, Sci Univ of Salford 1984, Engrg Univ of Bradford 1984, Sci Univ of Leeds 1987, D Univ of Open Univ 1987, Loughborough; fell: Imperial Coll London 1975, Newham Coll Cambridge 1986; sr fell RCA 1986-, FMA, FINucE, FRSA, Companies BIM; Medal of Inst of Engrs and Shipbuilders in Scotland 1988;; *Recreations* music, travel gardening, getting involved in a few things; *Style—* Dame Margaret Weston, DBE; 7 Shawley Way, Epsom, Surrey KT18 5NZ (☎ 0737 355885)

WESTON, Richard Miles; s of Maj Eric Cecil Knowles Weston (d 1944), and Joan, *née* Price (d 1975); *b* 31 July 1944; *Educ* Sherborne Sch; *m* 5 May 1975, Ella Patricia, da of Eric Drewett, of Somerset; *Career* slr; *Recreations* hockey, tennis, cricket, horse racing, life; *Style*— Richard M Weston, Esq; Tatt House, Kingston St Mary, Taunton, Somerset TA2 8HY (☎ 0823 45489); The Post House, Church Square, Taunton, Somerset TA1 1SD (☎ 0823 257999)

WESTON, Ronald; CB, (1987); s of Arthur Weston (d 1968), of Derbyshire, and Edna Olive, *née* Jackson; *b* 17 Feb 1929; *Educ* Swanwick Hall GS Derbyshire; *m* 1953, Brenda Vera, da of Horace Edward Townshend, of Derbyshire; 2 s (Andrew b 1954, Ian b 1957), 1 da (Sally b 1961); *Career* offr Customs & Excise 1952-, princ Customs and Excise 1972, Collector Birmingham Customs & Excise 1977, cmmr bd memb Customs & Excise 1982-88; *Recreations* choral music, golf, walking; *Clubs* Moor Park Golf; *Style*— Ronald Weston, Esq; Alphin Heights, 133 Manchester Rd, Garenfield, Oldham, Lancs OL3 7HJ (☎ 04577 2176)

WESTON SMITH, Ian; s of Albert Alexander Smith (d 1921), of Glasgow, and Jessie Lailey Weston (d 1964); *b* 21 Feb 1918; *Educ* Fettes Coll; *m* 1956, Angela Janet, da of Hugh Lloyd Thomas (d 1938); 2 s (Richard, Dominic); *Career* Capt Scots Gds 1940-47, served Western Desert and Italy; (POW Germany 1943, escaped 1945); md The Morgan Crucible Co plc (chm 1975-82), non exec dir Avon Rubber Co, chm Biomechanics Int 1983-87, memb cncl Prince of Wales Business Tst; *Recreations* shooting, breeding steeplechasers; *Clubs* Guards, Pratt's; *Style*— Ian Weston Smith, Esq; The Old Rectory, Hinton Waldrist, Faringdon, Oxon SN7 8SA

WESTON SMITH, John Harry; s of Cdr Weston Smith, OBE, RN (1986); *b* 3 Feb 1932; *Educ* Fettes, St John's Coll Cambridge (MA); *m* 1955, Margaret Fraser, da of Prof E A Milne (d 1954); 1 s (Hugh b 1961), 2 da (Miranda b 1956, Lucinda b 1964); *Career* jt gen mangr Abbey National 1968-69 (sec 1961-68), dir British Land Co plc 1973-, and dir of other cos; chm Govrs of St Christopher's Sch Hampstead; *Style*— John Weston Smith, Esq; 10 Eldon Grove, London NW3 (☎ 01 435 5069); Sydenhams Farm Hse, Bisley, Glos (☎ 0453 770047)

WESTPHAL, William Henry (Bob); OBE (1972), DFC (1944); s of William Mathias Westphal (d 1950), of Sydney Aust, and Madeline May, *née* Pepper (d 1962); *b* 5 Nov 1921; *Educ* North Sydney Heights Sch, Sydney Univ (LLB); *m* 23 July 1945, Daphne Meta Astrid; 3 s (John b 1947, Michael b 1949, David b 1954), 1 da (Pamela b 1951); *Career* WWII RAAF Sqdn Ldr 83 Pathfinder Sqdn Europe; dir Rentokil Gp plc 1956-87 (chm 1981-87); FRSA; *Recreations* golf, travel; *Clubs* Pathfinder; *Style*—, WH Westphal, Esq, OBE, DFC; The Grove, Penshurst, Kent (☎ 0892 870 504); Penshurst Vineyards, Penshurst, Kent (☎ 0892 870255)

WESTROPP, Anthony Henry; s of Col L H M Westropp of Berry House, Chilham, Kent, and Muriel Jorgensen; *b* 22 Dec 1944; *Educ* Sherborne, King's Coll London Univ; *m* 1977, Zoe Rosaleen, da of Charles Douglas Walker; *Career* dir Trafalgar House Investment Mgmnt Ltd, 1972-75, md Bardsey plc and subsidiaries 1975-, chm: Rabone Chesterman Ltd, R C F Tools plc; dir Regency Building Soc; *Recreations* hunting, fishing, tennis; *Clubs* Boodle's, City of London; *Style*— Anthony Westropp, Esq; Ludwell Farm, Glympton, Oxon; office: Regent House, 89 Kingsway, London WC2 (☎ 01 405 9082)

WESTROPP, Eric Mountefort; CBE (1982); s of Col Lionel Henry Mountefort Westropp, and Muriel Constance Lilian, *née* Jorgensen; *see* Burkes Irish Family Records; *b* 30 Mar 1939; *Educ* Wellington, Camberley Staff Coll; *m* 18 Oct 1963, Jill Mary, da of Rear Adm I G Aylen, of Tracy Mill Barn, Honiton, Devon; 2 s (Richard b 1965, Patrick b 1966), 1 da (Victoria b 1969); *Career* cmmnd 11 Hussars (PAO) 1958, serv Armd Car Troop Ldr NI, Aden, Aden, Sharjah, Kuwait; Regt Offr BAOR, Bde Maj 51 Inf Bde Honk Kong 1972-74, exec Offr to Dep SACEUR at SHAPE in Belgium 1976-78, cmd Royal Hussars (PWO) 1978-80, Brig 33 Armd Bde BAOR 1983-85, ret; joined Control Risks Ltd 1985 (dir 1986), md Control Risks Response Servs Ltd 1987-; *Recreations* riding, skiing, photography, reading; *Clubs* Cavalry and Guard's; *Style*— Eric Westropp, Esq, CBE; The White House, Bloxworth, Wareham, Dorset (☎ 092945 356); 83 Victoria St, London SW1 (☎ 01 222 1552)

WESTROPP, George Victor; s of Edward L Westropp (d 1962), of Epsom, Surrey, and Mary Breward, *née* Hughes (d 1973); *b* 2 Nov 1943; *Educ* Bedford Sch; *m* 12 Jan 1972, (m dis 1973), Alexander Jeanne, da of Joseph Steinberg; m 2, 9 May 1977, (m dis 1988), Christine June, da of Alan Ashley, of London; 2 s (Edward b 1980, Kit b 1982); *Career* reporter City Press 1961-63, city reporter Sunday Express 1963, fin journalist Evening Standard 1963-68, (asst city ed 1968-69); dir Shareholder Relations Ltd 1969-73, fin PR exec PPR Int Ltd 1974-76, md Hemingway Public Relations Ltd 1977-79, dir public affrs UK and Europe Touche Ross & Co 1979- (ptnr 1985-); MIPR; *Books* The Lake Vyrnwy Fishing Book (1979); *Recreations* salmon and trout fishing; *Clubs* London Press, Room 74; *Style*— George Westropp, Esq; 36 Holley Rd, London W3 7TS (☎ 01 743 1752); Touche Ross & Co, Hill House, 1 Little New St, London EC4 3TR (☎ 01 936 3000, fax 01 583 8517, car tel 0860 299 350, telex 884739 TRLNDN G)

WESTWELL, Alan Reynolds; s of Stanley Westwell, (d 1980), of Liverpool, and Margaret, *née* Reynolds (d 1962); *b* 11 April 1940; *Educ* Old Swan Coll, Liverpool Poly (ACT), Univ of Salford (MSc); *m* 30 Oct 1967, (Elizabeth) Aileen, da of John Birrell, (d 1975), of Fife, Scotland; 2 s (Stephen b 1972, Colin (twin) b 1972), 1 da (Julie b 1970); *Career* asst works mangr (previously engrg apprentice and tech asst) Liverpool City Tport Dept 1956-67; chief engr: Southport Corpn Tport Dept 1967-69, Coventry Corpn Tport Dept 1969-72, Glasgow Corpn Tport Dept 1972-74 (dir of public tport 1974-79); dir gen Strathclyde Passenger Tport Exec 1979-86, chm and md Strathclyde Buses Ltd; deacon Congregational Church; FCIT, MIMechE, MIProdE; *Recreations* golf, swimming, tennis, music, reading; *Clubs* Helensburgh Golf; *Style*— Alan Westwell, Esq; 12 Glen Dr, Helensburgh, Dunbartonshire G84 9BJ (☎ 0436 71709); Strathclyde Buses Ltd, 197 Victoria Rd, Glasgow (☎ 041 423 6600, fax 041 636 3223, telex 779748)

WESTWOOD, David John Morris; s of Sydney Westwood, of W Midlands, and Florence, *née* Thornycroft (d 1973); *b* 21 June 1931; *Educ* Denstone Coll; *m* 1, 20 June 1956 Valerie Ann Dallison, da of Valentine White (d 1956); 1 s (Mark Westwood b 1959), 1 da (Johanna Cole b 1957); m 2, 29 May 1982, Patricia, da of Frederick Higgs (d 1973); *Career* md Utd Spring & Steel Gp plc; magistrate 1974-80; FCA; *Recreations* foxhunting, coursing, golf; *Style*— David J M Westwood, Esq; Wales End Farm, Barton-under-Needwood, Burton-on-Trent, Staffordshire DE13 8JN (☎ 028371 3769); Blews St, Birmingham B6 4EP (☎ 021 333 3494)

WESTWOOD, Hon (William) Gavin; s and h of 2 Baron Westwood, JP; *b* 30 Jan 1944; *Educ* Fettes; *m* l1969, Penelope, da of Charles Shafto, VRD, MB; 2 s; *Career* Co dir; FRSA; *Style*— The Hon Gavin Westwood; 'Ferndale', Clayton Road, Newcastle-upon-Tyne, NE2 1TL

WESTWOOD, Hon James Young Shaw; 3 s of 1 Baron Westwood, OBE; *b* 1915; *m* 1941 (m dis 1969), Joan, da of Raymond Potts; 1 s; *Style*— The Hon James Westwood

WESTWOOD, Hon Mrs Douglas (Mary Katherine); da of John Carter; *m* 1939, Hon Douglas Westwood (d 1968); 1 da; *Style*— The Hon Mrs Douglas Westwood; Landover Place, Burlington Place, Eastbourne, E Sussex

WESTWOOD, Hon Nigel Alistair; 2 s of 2 Baron Westwood, JP; *b* 1950; *Educ* Fettes; *m* 1977, Joan Ibison; 2 s; *Career* chartered surveyor; hon Norwegian Consul; FRICS, FRSA; *Clubs* The Northern Counties; *Style*— The Hon Nigel Westwood; 7 Fernville Rd, Gosforth, Newcastle-upon-Tyne NE3 4HT

WESTWOOD, 2 Baron (UK 1944); William Westwood; JP (Newcastle 1949); s of 1 Baron Westwood (d 1953) by his 1 w, Margaret; *b* 25 Dec 1907; *Educ* Glasgow; *m* 1937, Marjorie, da of Arthur Bonwick; 2 s; *Heir* s, Hon (William) Gavin Westwood; *Career* former pres Football League, now life memb; hon vice-pres FA; FRSA, FCIS; *Style*— The Rt Hon the Lord Westwood, JP; 55 Moor Court, Westfield, Gosforth, Newcastle-upon-Tyne NE3 4YD

WETHERED, Simon Richard; s of Dr Rodney Richard Wethered, Nupend House, Stonehouse, Glos, and Sarah Meriel, *née* Long-Price; *b* 1 Mar 1945; *Educ* Clifton, Worcester Coll Oxford (BA); *m* 9 Sept 1978, Victoria, da of Adm of the Fleet Sir Michael Le Fanu, GCB, DSC (d 1970); 2 s (Edward b 1983, Charles b 1988), 1 da (Anna b 1981); *Career* admited slr 1970; ptnr: Simmons & Simmons 1974-78, Alsop Wilkinson (formerly Wilkinson Kimbers) 1978-; licenced insolvency practitioner 1987-; memb Holy Innocents Community Centre and PCC, dir Academy Concerts Soc 1984-; FIMBRA 1987-, memb Law Soc 1970-; visitor HMP Wormwood Scrubs 1984-; *Recreations* wine, music, walking; *Style*— Simon Wethered, Esq; 14 Ashchurch Park Villas, London W12 9SP (☎ 01 743 5440); 6 Dowgate Hill, London EC4R 2SS (☎ 01 623 5141, car phone 0860 828 664, fax 6238286, telex 885543)

WETHERELL, John Michael Hugh Paxton; s of Paxton Wetherell, MBE (d 1978), of Whitstable, Kent, and Catherine Wilson, *née* Collins; *b* 24 Oct 1942; *Educ* Ampleforth; *m* 2 May 1964, Elizabeth Ann, da of Harold Thompson (d 1988), of Broadstairs, Kent; 1 s (Joseph b 1979), 5 da (Laura b 1966, Kate b 1968, Beatrice b 1972, Gabrielle b 1974, Jessica b 1978); *Career* Lloyd's underwriter Janson Green/ Bolton Ingham Non-marine syndicate 1983; dir: Bolton Ingham Agency Ltd 1983-88, Janson Green Mgmnt Ltd 1986; memb Lloyd's 1973; *Recreations* reading, music, racing; *Clubs* City University; *Style*— John Wetherell, Esq ; Claremont House, Claremont Rd, Tunbridge Wells, Kent (☎ 0892 36481); Lloyds Lime Street, London EC3 (☎ 01 623 5190)

WETZEL, Dave; s of Fred Wetzel (d 1982), and Ivy, *née* Donaldson (d 1981); *b* 9 Oct 1942; *Educ* Spring Grove GS Isleworth, Southall Tech Coll (ONC), Ealing Coll, Henry George Sch of Soc Sci; *m* 14 Feb 1973, Heather Jacqueline, da of Edmond John Allman (d 1976), of Staines; 2 da (Emma b 1968, Chantel b 1974); *Career* apprentice Wilkinson Sword 1959-62, inspector LRT (conductor, driver) 1962-69, branch mangr Initial Serv 1969-70, pilot roster offr BA 1970-74, political organiser London Co-op 1974-81; Sch Govr, Ed of Civil Aviation News 1978-81, convenor Trade Union & Co-op Esperanto Gp, chm Labour Land Campaign; ldr London Borough of Hounslow 1987-(cllr 1964-68 and 1986-), transport chair GLC 1981-86; TGWU; *Recreations* politics, swimming, windsurfing, reading; *Clubs* Feltham Lab; *Style*— Dave Wetzel, Esq; Civic Centre, Lampton Rd, Hounslow, London, TW3 4DN (☎ 01 572 0615)

WEYER, Deryk Vander; s of Clement Vander Weyer of Bridlington, North Humberside (d 1963), and Harriet Annie, *née* Raper (d 1948); *b* 21 Jan 1925; *Educ* Bridlington Sch Yorks; *m* 1950, Marguerite, da of Laurence Henry Warden (d 1953), of Bridlington, North Humberside; 1 s (Martin), 1 da (Linda); *Career* dep chm British Telecom 1983- (former chm Barclays Bank UK); *Recreations* music; *Style*— Deryk Vander Weyer Esq; British Telecom Centre, 81 Newgate Street, London EC1A 7AJ (☎ 01 356 5000)

WEYMES, John Barnard; OBE (1975); s of William Stanley Weymes (d 1965), of Fawdon, Newcastle-on-Tyne, and Irene Innes, *née* Horn (d 1976); *b* 18 Oct 1927; *Educ* King's Coll Durham Univ; *m* 1, 13 Oct 1951 (m dis 1978), Hazel Madaline, *née* Bellairs; 1 s (James b 1959), 2 da (Barbara (Mrs Doré) b 1952, Jan (Mrs Watson) b 1955); m 2, 15 April 1978, Beverley Pauline, *née* Gliddon; *Career* RAC 1945-48, 8 Royal Tank Regt; HM Dip Serv 1949-81: third sec Panama 1952-56, second sec Bogota 1956-60, vice consul Berlin 1960-63, dep consul Tamsui 1963-65, first sec FCO 1965-68, PM's Off 1968-70, consul Guatemala City 1970-74, FCO 1974-77, consul gen Vancouver 1977-78, ambass Tegucigalpa 1978-81; dir Cayman Islands News Bureau 1981-83, ret 1983; *Recreations* cricket, tennis, chess, reading; *Clubs* MCC; *Style*— John Weymes, Esq, OBE; Nuthatches, Balcombe Green, Sedlescombe, Battle, E Sussex TN33 0QL (☎ 042 487 455)

WEYMOUTH, Viscount; Alexander George Thynn (*sic*, reverted to this spelling); s and h of 6 Marquess of Bath, ED; *b* 6 May 1932; *Educ* Eton, Christ Church Oxford (MA); *m* 1969, Anna, da of Laszlo Gyarmathy, of Los Angeles (Anna Gael, the actress, journalist and novelist); 1 s, 1 da (Hon Lenka Abigail b 1969); *Heir* s, Hon Ceawlin Henry Laszlo Thynn b 6 June 1974; *Career* late Lt Life Gds & Royal Wilts Yeo; contested: Westbury (Feb 1974) & Wells (1979) in Wessex Regionalist Pty's interest, Wessex (Euro elections 1979) Wessex Regionalist and European Fed Pty; painter; opened perm exhibition of murals in private apartments of Longleat 1973; dir Longleat Enterprises incl Cheddar Caves; *Books* as Alexander Thynne before 1976, Thynn thereafter); The Carry Cot (1972), Lord Weymouth's Murals (1974), A Regionalist Manifesto (1975), The King is Dead (1976), Pillars of The Establishment (1980); *Record* I Play the Host (1974, singing own compositions); *Style*— Viscount Weymouth; Longleat, Warminster, Wilts (☎ 098 53 300)

WHADDON, Baron (Life Peer UK 1978); (John) Derek Page; s of John Page and Clare, *née* Maher; *b* 14 August 1927; *Educ* St Bede's Coll Manchester, London Univ (BSc); *m* 1, 1948, Catherine Audrey (d 1979), da of John William Halls; 1 s, 1 da; m 2, 1981, Angela Rixson, da of Luigi della Bella, of Treviso; *Career* dir Cambridge Chemicals 1962-; MP (Lab) King's Lynn 1964-70, joined SDP 1981; memb cncl management CoSIRA to 1976-83; chm: Microautomatics Ltd 1981-87, Daltrade 1983-, Skorimpex-Rind 1985-; dir Rindalbourne 1983-; *Recreations* flying; *Clubs* Reform; *Style*— The Rt Hon Lord Whaddon; Letterbock, Liscarney, Westport, Co Mayo, Republic of Ireland; The Old Vicarage, Whaddon, Royston, Herts (☎ 0223 207209)

WHALEN, Geoffrey Henry; s of Henry Charles Whalen (d 1981), and Mabel Elizabeth

Whalen (d 1965); *b* 8 Jan 1936; *Educ* East Ham GS, Magdalen Coll Oxford (MA); *m* 1961, Elizabeth Charlotte, da of Dr Eric Ward, of Helperby, Yorks; 2 s (Thomas b 1967, Henry b 1977), 3 da (Catherine, Anna b 1965, Georgina b.1975); *Career* personnel dir Leyland Cars, British Leyland 1975-78, asst md Peugeot Talbot Motor Co Ltd 1981-84, (md 1984-), dir: Robins and Day Ltd, Talbot Ireland Ltd, Proptal UK Ltd, Motaquip Ltd, Sunbeam-Talbot Ltd; pres Soc of Motor Manufacturers & Traders 1988-89, FIPM, Companion BIM, FIMI; *Recreations* cricket, tennis; *Clubs* Utd Oxford and Cambridge; *Style—* Geoffrey Whalen, Esq; 8 Park Crescent, Abingdon, Oxfordshire; Peugeot Talbot Motor Co Ltd, International House, PO Box 712, Bickenhill Lane, Birmingham B37 7HZ (☎ 021 779 6565, telex 334698)

WHALLEY, Anthony; s of Frederic Edward Whalley, of Hurstbourne, Southwell Park Rd, Camberley, Surrey, and, Kathleen, *née* Rowan (d 1956); *b* 5 July 1941; *Educ* Salesian Coll Farnborough, St Joseph's Coll Mark Cross; *m* 8 Oct 1966, Eileen Angela, da of Gp Capt Harold Robert Withers, OBE (d 1986); 2 s (Frederick b 1968, James b 1972), 1 da (Caroline b 1967); *Career* chm Neotech Gp Ltd (formerly Aeronautical Radio Serv Ltd) 1978-; non-exec dir: Medusa Communications Ltd, PSL Freight Ltd, Consort Equipment Prods Ltd, Kemutec Gp Ltd, WLS Holdings Ltd; memb: CBI, SE Regnl Cncl 1980-86, Co Ctee 1984-88; ACA 1966, FCA 1976; *Recreations* music, literature; *Clubs* Nat Lib; *Style—* Anthony Whalley, Esq; 27 Clarence Rd, Windsor, Berks; 311 Willoughby House, Barbican, London EC2 (☎ 01 628 0026); Neotech Gp Ltd, Doman Rd, Camberley, Surrey (☎ 0276 685005, fax 0276 61524, telex 858779)

WHALLEY, Guy Ainsworth; s of Philip Guy Rothay Whalley, CBE (d 1950), and Norah Helen, *née* Mawdsley (d 1981), direct descendant of Col Edward Whalley, cousin of Oliver Cromwell and Signatory of The Death Warrant of King Charles I; *b* 26 May 1933; *Educ* Rugby, Gonville and Caius Coll, Cambridge (BA, MA); *m* 22 Aug 1959, Sarah, da of Walter William Knight (d 1966); 1 s (Philip Mark b 1961), 1 da (Katherine Jane b 1962); *Career* Nat Serv 2 Lt Royal Fus 1951-53, active serv Korean War 1952-53; slr Supreme Ct 1959, ptnr Freshfields Slrs 1964-, non exec dir Higgs and Hill plc 1972-, dir and memb ctee of mgmnt RAM 1982-, govr Beechwood Park Sch 1974-88 (chm 1975-84), co-opted memb Oxford Univ Appts Ctee 1982-; tstee: Rugby Sch War Meml Fund 1980-, Rugby Sch Gen Charitable Tst 1986-; *Recreations* gardening, music, cricket, golf, painting; *Clubs* MCC; *Style—* Guy Whalley, Esq; Woodmans Farm, Chipperfield, Hertfordshire (☎ 09277 63795); Grindall House, 25 Newgate St, London EC1A 7LH (☎ 01 606 6677, telex 889292, fax 01 248 3487/8/9)

WHARNCLIFFE, Dowager Countess of Aline Margaret Montagu-Stuart-Wortley-Mackenzie; *née* Bruce; o da of Robert Fernie Dunlop Bruce (d 1952), of Dyson Holmes House, Wharncliffe Side, nr Sheffield; *m* 1957, 4 Earl of Wharncliffe (d 1987); 2 da (Lady Joanna Margaret b 1959, d 1981, Lady Rowena Hunt, *qv*); *Style—* The Rt Hon the Dowager Countess of Wharncliffe; Wharncliffe House, Wortley, Sheffield

WHARNCLIFFE, 5 Earl of (UK 1876) Richard Alan Montagu Stuart Wortley; also Baron Wharncliffe (UK 1826) and Viscount Carlton (UK 1876); er s of Alan Ralph Montagu Stuart Wortley (d 1986), and Virginia Ann, *née* Claybaugh; suc his kinsman 4 Earl of Wharncliffe (d 1987); *b* 26 May 1953; *Educ* Wesleyan Univ; *m* 1979, Mary Elizabeth, da of Rev William Reed, of Keene, NH, USA; 2 s (Viscount Carlton, Hon Christopher James b 1983); *Heir* s, Reed Montagu Stuart Wortley, Viscount Carlton, b 5 Feb 1980; *Career* construction foreman; *Style—* The Rt Hon the Earl of Wharncliffe; 270 Main Street, Cumberland Center, Maine, USA

WHARTON, Dr Christopher Lloyd; s of Maj John Robert Wharton (d 1950), of Ledbury, Herefordshire, and Marjorie, *née* Haynes (d 1981); *b* 20 June 1915; *Educ* Eton, Trinity Coll Cambridge (BA); *m* 4 Feb 1944, Eleanor Mary, da of Kenneth Henry Wilson, OBE (d 1969), of Kidderminster, Worcs; 1 s (Richard b 1953), 3 da (Marion b 1945, Elizabeth b 1947, Julia b 1950); *Career* doctor of medicine; MRCS; LRCP; *Recreations* music, shooting game; *Clubs* BMA; *Style—* Dr Christopher L Wharton; Monks Bridge, Butlers Marston, Warwickshire (☎ 0926 640218)

WHARTON, (John) Steven; s of Jack Illingworth Wharton (d 1969), and Gladys May Wharton, *née* Cundall; *b* 5 Oct 1943; *Educ* Burton-Stather Primary, Oundle; *m* 26 Oct 1978, Fiona Lisbeth, da of Thomas Windle; 1 s (Joseph William b 1981), 1 da (Angela Claire b 1979); *Career* chm J Wharton (shipping) Ltd 1986- (md from 1969); chm and md of many assoc coys inc: Trent Lighterage Ltd, JS Wharton (Hldgs) Ltd, J Wharton (Farms) Ltd; *Recreations* hockey (over 150 cups for Lincs), hunting, tennis, squash; *Clubs* Farmers; *Style—* J Wharton, Esq; JI Wharton (Shipping) Ltd, Grove Wharf, Gunness, Scunthorpe, South Humberside (☎ 0724 782371, telex 52213, fax 782610)

WHATMORE, Andrew; s of Charles Sydney Whatmore, of Palmer's Lodge, Tunbridge Wells, Kent TN3 9AD, and Monica Mabel, *née* Tucker; *b* 18 June 1946; *Educ* The Skinners' Sch Tunbridge Wells, Woolwich Poly, London Univ; *m* 17 Dec 1983, Elizabeth, da of James Stewart Morrison Sim, of 32 McNabb St, Dollar, Clacks; 1 s (Charles Stewart b 1984), 1 da (Kathryn Elizabeth b 1985); *Career* resident engr: (EAEC) Kenya 1980, Roughton and Ptnrs Al Ain UAE 1981; chief engr Taylor Woodrow Int Ghana 1983, agent Christiani & Nielsen S Wales 1987; CEng, MICE; *Style—* Mr Andrew Whatmore, Esq; Garth Hall, Abertridwr, Caerphilly, Mid-Glamorgan CF8 2DS (☎ 0222 830261); Geoffrey Osborne Ltd, Stockbridge Rd, Chichester PO19 2LL (☎ 0243 787811)

WHEADON, Richard Anthony; s of Ivor Cecil Newman Wheadon (d 1981), and Margarita Augusta; *b* 31 August 1933; *Educ* Cranleigh Sch, Balliol Coll Oxford (MA); *m* 1961, Ann Mary, da of Gp Capt Frederick Charles Richardson, CBE; 3 s; *Career* Sword of Honour RAF 1955, Air Radar Offr 1955-57; asst master Eton 1957-66, Eton CCF 1958-66, dep headmaster and head of science dept Dauntsey's Sch 1966-71, contingent cdr, Dauntsey's Sch CCF 1969-70; memb Wilts Educn Ctee's Science Advsy Panel; princ Elizabeth Coll Guernsey 1972-88; rowing: pres Balliol Coll Boat Club 1954 and 1955, Bow Oxford Univ 100 Boat Race, Capt and coach RAF eight 1956-57, in Br VIII Euro Championships and Olympic Games 1956, coach Oxford Boat Race 1957, nat coach and Olympic selector 1965-66; *Books* The Principles of Light and Optics (1968); *Recreations* french horn, photography, sailing, singing, swimming; *Style—* Richard Wheadon, Esq; L'Enclos Gallienne, Rue du Court Laurent, Torteval, Guernsey, CI (☎ 0481 64988)

WHEARE, Thomas David; s of Sir Kenneth Clinton Wheare, CMG (d 1979), of Oxford, and Joan, *née* Randell, MA; *b* 11 Oct 1944; *Educ* Dragon Sch, Magdalen Coll Sch Oxford, King's Coll Cambridge (MA), Christ Church Oxford (DipEd); *m* 29 Oct 1977, Rosalind Clare, da of J E Spice, of Winchester; 2 da (Clare b 1980, Frances b 1981); *Career* asst master Eton 1967-76, housemaster Shrewsbury 1976-83, headmaster Bryanston 1983-; *Recreations* music; *Style—* Thomas Wheare, Esq; The Headmaster's Ho, Bryanston Sch, Blandford, Dorset (☎ 0258 527 28); Bryanston Sch, Blandford, Dorset (☎ 0258 527 28)

WHEAT, Kenneth James (Ken); s of Arthur James Wheat, of Kenilworth, Warwickshire, and Freda, *née* Glasson; *b* 16 April 1948; *Educ* Castle HS, Kenilworth, Royal Agricultural Coll Cirencester (MRAC); *m* 2 Oct 1981, Trudi Elizabeth, da of Percival McDonald, of Stratford upon Avon, Warwick; *Career* sr writer: KMP Manchester 1975-77, Cogent Elliot 1977-82, Ayer Barker 1982-83, Crawford Halls 1984-86; creative dir Brookes and Vernons 1986-; memb South Warwicks Flying Sch; *Recreations* athletics, flying, skiing, gardening, rare breeds; *Clubs* Leamington Cycling and Athletics; *Style—* Ken Wheat, Esq; Brookes & Vernons, 109 Hagley Rd, Edgbaston, Birmingham B16 8LA (☎ 021 455 9481)

WHEATLEY, Baroness; Agnes Mary; *née* Nichol; da of Samuel Nichol; *m* 1935,Baron Wheatley, PC, QC (Life Peer, d 1988); 4 s, 1 da; *Style—* The Rt Hon Lady Wheatley; 3 Greenhill Gardens, Edinburgh EH10 4BN

WHEATLEY, Alan Edward; s of Edward Wheatley, Ret Investment Analyst, of 135 Upney Lane, Barking, Essex, and Margaret Rosina Turner; *b* 23 May 1938; *Educ* Ilford GS; *m* 30 June 1962, Marion Frances, da of John Douglas Wilson (d 1968); 1 da (Susan b 1966), 2 s (Michael b 1968, Jonathan b 1974); *Career* Price Waterhouse 1960-, sr ptnr London Off 1985-; Br Steel Corp, non-exec bd memb 1984-; bd-memb Industrial Development Advisory Bd 1985-; non-exec dir EBS Investments Ltd (Bank of England subsidiary) 1977-; govt dir Cable & Wireless plc 1981-84, non-exec dept chm 1984-85; govr Solefield Sch; FCA; *Recreations* golf, tennis, badminton, music, bridge; *Clubs* Wildernesse Golf; *Style—* Alan E Wheatley, Esq; Price Waterhouse, Southwark Towers, 32 London Bridge St, London SE1 (☎ 01 407 8989, fax 01 378 0647, telex 884 657/8)

WHEATLEY, Sir (George) Andrew; CBE (1960); s of Robert Wheatley; *b* 1908; *Educ* Rugby, Exeter Coll Oxford; *m* 1937, Mary Vera Hunt; 3 s, 2 da; *Career* BCL, DL Hants 1967-70, clerk of the Peace & clerk Hants CC 1946-67; memb English Local Govt Boundary Commission 1971-; kt 1967; *Style—* Sir Andrew Wheatley, CBE

WHEATLEY, Rear Adm Anthony; CB (1988); s of Edgar Christian Wheatley, and Audrey Grace Barton Hall, *née* Phillips; *b* 3 Oct 1933; *Educ* Berkhamsted Sch, RNC Dartmouth, RN Engng Coll Manadon; *m* 17 Nov 1962, Iona Sheila, da of Major Oliver Peter Haig (d 1987); 1 da (Charlotte b 1 Oct 1963); *Career* RN Joined 1950, HMS Ceylon 1958-60, HMS Ganges 1960-61, HMS Cambrian 1962-64, Staff of RNEC, Manadon 1964-67, Staff of Cdr Br Navy Staff, Washington 1967-69, HMS Diomede 1970-72, Staff of C-in-C Fleet 1972-74, Exec Offr RNEC, Manadon 1975-76, MOD Procurement Exec 1977-79, Br naval attaché Brasilia 1979-81, RCDS 1982, HMS Collingwood (in cmnd) 1982-85; Flag Offr Portsmouth, Naval Base Cdr and Head of Estab of Fleet Maintenance and Repair Orgn, Portsmouth 1985-87; placed on ref list 1988; gen mangr Nat Hosps for Nervous Diseases 1988- 77; *Recreations* cricket, (pres, royal navy cricket club), golf, music; *Clubs* Army and Navy, Free Foresters; *Style—* Rear Adm Anthony Wheatley, CB; 2 Claridge Court, Munster Rd, Fulham, London SW6 4EY

WHEATLEY, Rev Canon Arthur; s of George Wilson Wheatley (d 1971), of Edinburgh, and Elizabeth, *née* Mackenzie (d 1987); *b* 4 Mar 1931; *Educ* Alloa Acad, The Episcopal Theol Coll Edinburgh; *m* 1 Aug 1959, (Sheena) Morag, *née* Wilde; 2 s (Christopher b 2 Oct 1961, Kenneth b 3 Nov 1969), 2 da (Paula b 1 Sept 1960, Virginia b 14 June 1964); *Career* ordained: deacon 1970, priest 1970; curate St Salvador Dundee Brechin and St Ninian Dundee 1970-71, priest i/c St Nimian Dundee 1971-76, rector Holy Trinity Elgin with St Margarets Church Lossiemonth Diocese of Moray Ross and Caithness 1976-80, canon St Andrew's Cath 1978-80 (provost 1980-83, canon 1983-); priest i/c: Grantown-on-Spey 1983, Rothiemurchus 1983-; *Recreations* shooting, fishing, bee-keeping; *Style—* Rev Canon Arthur Wheatley; The Rectory, Grant Rd, Grantown-on-Spey PH26 3ER (☎ 0479 2866)

WHEATLEY, Derek Peter Francis; QC (1981); s of Edward Pearse Wheatley (d 1967), of Exeter, and Gladys Eugenie, *née* Williams; *b* 18 Dec 1925; *Educ* The Leys Sch Cambridge, Univ Coll Oxford (MA); *m* 1955, Elisabeth Pamela, da of John Morgan Reynolds Fairlawn (d 1983), of Penarth; 2 s (Simon, Jonathan), 1 da (Claire); *Career* 8 King's Royal Hussars, WS Lt 1946-48; served BAOR in Germany; barr 1951, practised until 1974, memb Hon Soc of the Middle Temple, recorder Crown Ct 1971-74, memb Bar Cncl 1975-78, 1980-83, 1986-; chm Legal Ctee, Ctee of London and Scottish Bankers 1984-86, chief legal advsr Lloyds Bank plc, vice-pres Bar Assoc for Commerce Finance and Industry, memb Commercial Ct Ctee 1976-; *Recreations* yachting; *Clubs* Bar Yacht; *Style—* Derek Wheatley, Esq, QC; 3 The Wardrobe, Old Palace Yard, Richmond, Surrey (☎ 01 940 6242); 71 Lombard St, EC 3 (☎ 01 626 1500 ext 2026, telex 893855)

WHEATLEY, John Edward Clive; MC, JP; s of Edward Pearse Wheatley (d 1968, former alderman and sheriff of Exeter), by his w Gladwys Eugenie, *née* Williams; *b* 7 Mar 1921; *Educ* The Leys Sch Cambridge, Exeter Univ; *m* 1945, Rosemarie Joy Malet, da of Victor Samuel Rowbotham of Johannesburg, SA; 3 s (Robin, Adam, Benedict), 1 da (Candida); *Career* Staff Capt N Africa, Italy; Staff Capt RMC Sandhurst; metal merchant; former chm: E Pearse & Co Ltd, Pearse Complex Alloys Ltd, C Philipp & Son Ltd; former chm: South Western Industrial Gases Ltd (SWIG), Exeter Housing Soc Ltd, chm Parks (Exeter) Ltd, pres British Scrap Fedn 1978-79; former chm: E Pearse and Co Ltd, C Phillips & Son (Bristol) Ltd, Bay City Radio; former dir West One Prodns Ltd; memb Police Authority for Devon and Cornwall; *Recreations* travel, photography, collecting old books; *Clubs* Army and Navy; *Style—* John Wheatley, Esq, MC, JP; Bellenden, Wreford's Lane, Exeter (☎ 0392 56087); Parks (Exeter) Ltd, 11/12 West St, Exeter (☎ 0392 32145)

WHEATLEY, Hon John Francis; s of Baron Wheatley (Life Peer, d 1988), and Agnes Mary, da of Samuel Nichol; *b* 9 May 1941; *Educ* Mount St Mary's College Derbyshire, Edinburgh Univ (BL); *m* 1970, Bronwen Catherine, da of Alastair Fraser of Dollar; 2 s; *Career* Scottish bar 1966, advocate depute 1974-78, Sheriff of Perthshire and Kinross-shire 1980-; *Recreations* gardening, music; *Style—* The Hon John Wheatley; Braefoot Farmhouse, Fossoway, Kinross-shire (☎ 057 74 212); Sheriff Court House, Tay St, Perth (☎ 0738 20546)

WHEATLEY, Hon Michael; yst s of Baron Wheatley, PC (Life Peer, d 1988); *b* 1949; *Educ* Mount St Mary's Coll Derbyshire; *m* 1971, Anne, da of Thomas Barry; *Clubs* MCC; *Style—* The Hon Michael Wheatley; Millburn, Old Philpstoun, W Lothian EH49 7RY

WHEATLEY, Hon Patrick; 2 s of Baron Wheatley, PC (Life Peer, d 1988); *b* 1943; *m* 1968, Sheena, da of Douglas Lawrie; *Style*— The Hon Patrick Wheatley; c/o The Rt Hon Lady Wheatley, 3 Greenhill Gardens, Edinburgh EH10 4BN

WHEATLEY, Robert Larke Andrew; s of Sir (George) Andrew Wheatley, CBE, of Broad Lane, Lymington, and the late Vera, *née* Hunt; *b* 14 August 1938; *Educ* Rugby, McGill Univ Montreal; *m* 22 Aug 1964, Elizabeth Marian, da of Leonard Amos Oakden, of Winchelsea, Sussex; 1 s (Andrew b 1966), 1 da (Nicola b 1968); *Career* 2 Lt Rifle Bde, Malaya 1957; co sec R & G Cuthbert Ltd 1970-71, product mangr IBM (UK) Ltd 1986-; CA, ACMA; *Recreations* gardening, singing, school governor; *Style*— Robert Wheatley, Esq; The Pines, Edward Rd, St Cross, Winchester, Hants SO23 9RB

WHEATLEY, Simon Derek John Pearse; s of Derek Peter Francis Wheatley, QC, of 3 The Wardrobe, Old Palace Yard, Richmond, Surrey, and Elizabeth Pamela, *née* Reynolds; *b* 8 August 1956; *Educ* Marlborough, Univ of Brunel (LLB); *Career* barr Middle Temple 1979; *Recreations* broadcasting; *Style*— Simon Wheatley, Esq; 22 Cedar Terrace, Richmond, Surrey (☎ 01 948 7815); 1 Harcourt Bldgs, Temple, London (☎ 01 353 0375, fax 583 5816)

WHEATLEY-HUBBARD, (Evelyn) Raymond; s of Eric Wyndham Hubbard (d 1946); assumed additional name of Wheatley by Deed Poll 1949; *b* 22 Feb 1921; *Educ* Eton; *m* 1949, Ann Christobel, OBE, da of late Col Charles Joshua Hirst Wheatley, TD, DL, JP; 1 s, 1 da; *Career* Coldstream Gds 1940-46; chartered surveyor and land agent; *Clubs* Cavalry and Guard's; *Style*— Raymond Wheatley-Hubbard, Esq; Broadleaze, Boyton, Warminster, Wilts (☎ 0985 50214)

WHEATLY, Richard John Norwood; s of Patrick Wheatly (d 1986), of Watford, and Doris Mary; *b* 9 Feb 1946; *Educ* Watford Boys GS, St John's Coll Cambridge (MA); *m* 1, 8 July 1968, (m dis 1974), Jane Margaret Phillips, da of Frank Thomas, of Rickmansworth, Herts; 1 da (Sophie b 26 June 1970); m 2, 9 Feb 1980, Susan Angela, da of Stuart Masson, of Watford, Herts; *Career* mktg mangr Unilever 1968-72; gp exec Garland Compton Advertising 1972-73, McCann Erickson Advertising 1973-74; divnl mangr Johnson & Johnson 1974-78; chm Leo Burnett Advertising 1978-; memb: cncl IPA 1986, Mktg Gp of GB 1987; *Recreations* riding, shooting; *Style*— Richard Wheatly, Esq; Matley House, Beaulieu Rd, Lyndhurst, Hants (☎ 042 128 3900); Leo Burnett Ltd, 48 St Martin's La, London WC2N 4EJ (☎ 01 836 2424, fax 01 829 7026/7, car tel 0036 223647, telex 24243)

WHEATON, Rev Canon David Harry; s of Harry Wheaton, MBE (d 1982), and Kathleen Mary, *née* Hyde-Frost (d 1957); *b* 2 June 1930; *Educ* Abingdon, St John's Coll Oxford (MA), London Bible Coll (BD); *m* 23 March 1956, (Helen Joy), da of Leonard Forrer (d 1953); 1 s (Mark b 1965), 2 da (Mary b 1964, Joanna b 1967); *Career* tutor Oak Hill Coll 1954-62; rector Ludgershall Bucks 1962-66, vicar St Paul's Onslow Sq London 1966-71, chaplain Brompton Hosp 1969-71; princ Oak Hill Coll 1971-86, rural dean Hereford 1988-; vicar Christ Church, Ware 1986-; Hon Canon of St Albans 1976; rural dean of Hertford 1988-; dir: Church Soc Tst (chm, 1981-88), Church Pastoral-Aid Society Tst; *Books* New Bible Dictionary (contributor 1962), New Bible Commentary (revised 1970), Evangelical Dictionary of Theology (1984), Here We Stand (1986); *Recreations* walking, DIY; *Style*— The Rev Canon David Wheaton; Christchurch Vicarage, 15 Hanbury Close, Ware, Herts SG12 7BZ (☎ 0920 3165); Dalegarth, Hare Lane, Buckland St Mary, Chard, Somerset (☎ 046 034 377)

WHEELDON, Rt Rev Philip William; OBE (1946); s of Alfred Leonard Wheeldon (d 1936); *b* 20 May 1913; *Educ* Clifton, Downing Coll Cambridge; *m* 1966, Margaret, *née* Redfearn; *Career* ordained: deacon 1937, priest 1938; Farnham Parish Church 1937-39, chaplain to the Forces 1939-46, chaplain 1 Bn Coldstream Gds 1939-42, hon chaplain Forces 1946-, domestic chaplain to Archbishop of York 1946-49, hon chaplain 1949-54, gen sec CACTM 1949-54, prebendary of Wedmore II in Wells Cathedral 1952-54, suffragan bishop of Whitby 1954-61, bishop of Kimberly and Kuruman 1961-65 and 1968-76, asst bishop Diocese of Worcester 1965-68, hon asst bishop Diocese of Wakefield 1977-83; ret 1985; *Recreations* music, gardens; *Style*— The Rt Rev Philip Wheeldon, OBE; Westgate Close, Clifton, Brighouse, W Yorks

WHEELER, Alice, Lady; Alice Webster; *née* Stones; yst da of George Heath Stones, of Rutherglen, Lanarkshire; *m* 7 Jan 1938, Sir Arthur Frederick Pullman Wheeler, 2 Bt (d 16 Dec 1964); *Style*— Alice, Lady Wheeler; E12, Marine Gate, Marine Parade, Brighton 7, Sussex

WHEELER, Sir (Harry) Anthony; OBE (1973); s of Herbert George Wheeler (d 1976), and Laura Emma, *née* Groom (d 1966); *b* 7 Nov 1919; *Educ* Stranraer HS, Royal Tech Coll Glasgoe, Glasgow Sch of Art, Univ of Strathclyde (B Arch); *m* 10 June 1944, Dorothy Jean, da of David Campbell; 1 da (Pamela Jane b 1954); *Career* RA 1939-46 121 OCTU Alton Towers, RA RHA HAC, cmmnd 170 Field Regt, 77 Medium Regt RA Duke of Lancaster Yeo, serv: France, Belgium, Holland, Germany; Capt RA, demob 1946; asst to city architect Oxford 1948, asst to Sir Herbert Baker and Scott London 1949, sr architect Glenrothes New Town 1950-51, sr lectr Dundee Sch of Architecture 1952-58, private practice Fife 1952; sr ptnr Wheeler and Sproson Kircaldy and Edinburgh 1952-86; princ works incl: Woodside Shopping Centre Glenrothes, St Columba's church Glenrothers, reconstruction of Giles Pittenweem, redevpt Dysart and Old Buckhaven, Grangemouth Towncentre, SU Bldg Univ St Andrews, Hunter Bldg Edinburgh Coll of Art, St Peters Episcopal Church Kirkcaldy; memb Royal Fine Art Cmmn for Scot 1967-86, memb Scot Housing Advsy Ctee 1971-75, tstee Scot Civic Tst 1970-83, pres Royal Incorp of Architects in Scotland 1973-75, vice pres RIBA 1973-75, pres Royal Scot Acad 1983-; Hon RA 1983, Hon RGI 1986, FRIBA, FRIAS, MRTPI; *Recreations* water colour painting, fishing, gardens; *Clubs* New, (Edinburgh), Scottish Arts; *Style*— Sir Anthony Wheeler, OBE; Hawthornbank House, Dean Village; Edinburgh EH4 3BH (☎ 031 225 2334); 118 Hanover St, Edinburgh (☎ 031 226 3338)

WHEELER, Arthur William Edge; CBE (1979, OBE 1967); eldest s of Arthur William Wheeler, (d 1969), of Dublin, and Rowena, *née* Edge; *b* 1 August 1930; *Educ* Mountjoy Sch, Trinity Coll Dublin; *m* 1956, Gay, *née* Brady; 2 s, 1 da; *Career* barr, crown cncl Nigeria 1955, acting legal sec Southern Cameroons and memb Exec Cncl and House of Assembly 1958, princ crown cncl Fedn of Nigeria 1961, dir Public Prosecutions N Nigeria 1966, high ct judge N Nigeria 1967, Circuit Judge Kaduna State of Nigeria 1975, cmmr for Revision of the Laws of Northern States of Nigeria 1980; chm Foreign Compensation Cmmn 1983-; *Recreations* tennis, golf, music; *Clubs* Royal Cwlth Soc, Kildare Street and University (Dublin); *Style*— Arthur Wheeler, Esq, CBE; c/o Barclays Bank plc, Bowater House, 68 Knightsbridge, London SW1X 7LW; Foreign Compensation Commission, Alexandra House, Kingsway, London WC2B 6TT

WHEELER, (Selwyn) Charles; s of Wing Cdr Charles C Wheeler (d 1971), of Dormansland, and Winifred Agnes, *née* Rees (d 1972); *b* 26 Mar 1923; *Educ* Cranbrook; *m* 29 March 1962, Dip, da of Dr Harbans Singh, of Delhi; 1 da (Shirin b 1963, Marina b 1964); *Career* joined RM 1941, cmmnd 1942, 3 Bn RM, served Force S Normandy 1944, RN Forward Intelligence Unit, 30 Assault Unit RN/RM (despatches 1945), demobbed as Capt RM; joined Daily Sketch 1940; BBC 1947-78: prodr, reporter, foreign corr (Berlin 1949-53, S Asia 1958-62, Berlin 1962-65, USA 1965-73), freelance bdcaster with Panorama and Newsnight 1973-; documentaries incl The Road to War; *Recreations* gardening, travel; *Style*— Charles Wheeler, Esq; 10A Portland Rd, London W11 (☎ 01 221 4300); c/o BBC Television Wood Lane, London W14 (☎ 01 743 8000, telex 934 323)

WHEELER, Sir Frederick Henry; AC (1979), CBE (1962); s of A H Wheeler; *b* 9 Jan 1914; *Educ* Scotch Coll Melbourne, Melbourne Univ (BCom); *m* 1939, Peggy (d 1975), da of Basil Bell; 1 s, 2 da; *Career* State Savings Bank of Victoria 1929-39; tres: Research Officer 1939-52; Economist 1944; tres Int Labour Orgn Geneva 1952-60, chm Cwlth Pub Service Bd 1960-71, sec to Treasury Australia 1971-79, ret; dir Amatil Ltd 1979-84, & Alliance Hldgs Ltd 1979-86, Commonwealth govt Defence Ctee 1981-82; kt 1967; *see Debrett's Handbook of Australia and New Zealand for further details*; *Style*— Sir Frederick Wheeler, AC, CBE; 9 Charlotte St, Red Hill, Canberra, ACT 2603, Australia

WHEELER, Brig Guy Philip Mowbray Cato; s of Philip John Wheeler (d 1927), and Constance Rosa Tasman, *née* Cato (d 1953); *b* 23 Feb 1921; *Educ* Brighton Coll, Christ's Coll Cambridge (Cert Competent Knowledge in Russian); *m* 28 May 1955, Stephanie Ruth, da of Brig Harold Sealy Woodhouse (d 1941), of W Lodge, Blandford, Dorset; 5 s (Rupert b 1956, Jonathan b 1958, Felix b 1961, Dominic b 1969, Marcus (twin) b 1969); *Career* cmmnd 4 Queen's Own Hussars 1941, serv: Egypt, Libya and Cyrenaica 1941-43, Italy 1944-45, Malaya 1951-52, asst Mil Att HBM Embassy Prague 1948-51; Scots Greys 1958 (CO 1964-66); Col GS Armour HBM Embassy Washington 1966-69; Comd Brig RAC UK Land Forces 1971-73; vice-pres Army Regular Cmmns Bd 1973-76, AdC HM The Queen 1972-76; contribute The Times, Country Life, Field 1958-71; *Books* The Year Round in USA 1968 (1971), Cato's War (1980); *Recreations* music, mil and social history, languages, hunting, fishing; *Clubs* Cavalry and Guards; *Style*— Brig Guy Wheeler, Esq; Wambrook House, Wambrook, Chard, Somerset (☎ 046 06 3225)

WHEELER, John Daniel; JP (Inner London 1978), MP (C) Westminster North 1983-; *b* 1940; *Educ* Staff Coll Wakefield; *m* 1967, Laura; 1 s, 1 da; *Career* former asst prison governor, MP (C) Paddington 1979-1983; *Style*— John Wheeler, Esq, JP, MP; House of Commons, London SW1 (☎ 01 219 4615)

WHEELER, John Frederick; s and h of Sir John Wheeler, 3 Bt, and Gwendolen Alice, da of late Alfred Ernest Oram; *b* 3 May 1933; *Educ* Bedales, London Sch of Printing; *m* 1963, Barbara Mary, da of Raymond Flint, of Stoneygate, Leicester; 2 s (John Radford b 1965, Andrew Charles b 1969), 1 da (Jane Louise b 1964); *Career* company dir and farmer; *Recreations* sailing, field sports; *Style*— John F Wheeler, Esq; Frostenden Hall, Beccles, East Suffolk NR34 7HS (☎ 050 275 232)

WHEELER, Sir John Hieron; 3 Bt (UK 1920), of Woodhouse Eaves, Co Leicester; s of Sir Arthur Wheeler, 1 Bt, DL, JP, (d 1943), and Mary, *née* Pullman (d 1938); bro of 2 Bt (d 1964); *b* 22 July 1905; *Educ* Charterhouse; *m* 24 July 1929, Gwendolen Alice, da of late Alfred Ernest Oram, of Walberton, Kirby Muxloe, nr Leicester; 2 s (John Frederick, Benjamin b 1935); *Heir* s, John Frederick Wheeler b 3 May 1933; *Style*— Sir John Wheeler, Bt; 39 Morland Ave, Stoneygate, Leicester

WHEELER, John Michael; s of Sir Charles Wheeler, KBE (d 1976), and Frieda, *née* Close (d 1972); *b* 8 Nov 1931; *Educ* Shrewsbury, Queens' Coll Cambridge (BA), Harvard Bus Sch (PMD); *m* 22 Sept 1956, (Jean Ruth) Kirsty,da of John McMyn Gilmour, MC (d 1950); 1 s (Richard b 1960), 2 da (Fiona b 1962, Tanya b 1963); *Career* Nat Serv cmmnd 2 Lt Gren Guards 1950-52; dir: H Clarkson & Co Ltd 1967-72, Elder Austral Chartering Pty Ltd 1973-84, Baltic Freight Futures Exchange 1985-88, Baltic Futures Exchange 1988-; dir H Clarkson & Co Ltd 1967-, Elder Austral Chartering Pty Ltd 1973-, Baltic Futures Exchange 1988-, Baltic Freight Futures Exchange 1985-88; Master Old Berkeley Beagles, memb Cncl Int Social Serv of GB; Freeman City of London, Liveryman Worshipful Co of Broderers; *Recreations* beagling, wine tasting, golf; *Clubs* MCC, City Univ (chm), The Tasting, Leander; *Style*— John Wheeler, Esq; Great Missenden, Bucks; H Clarkson & Co Ltd, 12 Camomile St, London EC3A 7BP (☎ 01 283 8977, fax 01 626 4189)

WHEELER, John Vashon Tyrwhitt; s of Wing-Cdr Vashon James Wheeler, MC, DFC (ka 1944), of Bitterley Court, Ludlow, Shropshire, and Josephine Hermione, *née* Spencer-Phillips (d 1974); *b* 24 Oct 1931; *Educ* Eton, Trinity Coll Cambridge (BA, MA); *m* 1, 7 Sept 1957, Geraldine (d 1970), da of William Noel Jones (d 1982), of Little Gables, Glasllwch Lane, Newport; 3 s (James Vashon b 1960, Nicholas Charles Tyrwhitt b 1965, Justin Alexander Noel b 1970), 1 da (Susan Verity (Mrs Cummings) b 1958); m 2, 1978, Mrs Caroline Susan Chance, da of Patrick Edward Michael Holmes, MBE; 2 step s (Timothy William Holmes b 1966, Henry Charles Hugh b 1968), 1 step da (Lucy Emma b 1971); *Career* Nat Serv Flying Offr; dir Wolseley-Hughes plc 1970-82, chief exec agric div; chm and md: Benson Heating Ltd 1982-84, Benson Gp plc 1984-; chief exec agric machinery div Wolseley plc 1960-82; memb Bitterley Parish Cncl; MIMechE 1965, FIAgrE 1978; *Recreations* land management; *Clubs* RAF; *Style*— John Wheeler, Esq; Bitterley Court, Ludlow, Shropshire (☎ 0584 890 265); Benson Works, Ludlow Rd, Knighton, Powys LD7 1LP (☎ 0547 528534, fax 0547 520399, telex 35323, car ☎ 0860 626905)

WHEELER, Hon Mrs (Katharine Jane); er da of Baron Briggs (Life Peer); *b* 1956; *m* July 1980, David Robert Wheeler, er s of C R Wheeler, of Wimbledon SW19; 1 s (Timothy b 1985), 2 da (Caroline b 1982, Charlotte Rose 1987); *Style*— The Hon Mrs Wheeler; 30 Alexandra Rd, Epsom, Surrey

WHEELER, Hon Sir Kenneth Henry; s of William Henry Wheeler (d 1958), and Alma Nellie Wheeler; *b* 9 Sept 1912; *Educ* Mernda State Sch Vic; *m* 1934, Hazel Jean, da of Leonard Collins; 1 s, 1 da; *Career* mayor City of Coburg Vic 1955-56, MLA (Lib) Essendon Vic 1958-79, speaker of Legislative Assembly Vic 1973-79; kt 1976; *Style*— The Hon Sir Kenneth Wheeler; 27 Downes St, Strathmore, 3041, Australia

WHEELER, Air Vice-Marshal Leslie William Frederick; s of George Douglas Wheeler (d 1982), and Susan Wheeler; *b* 4 July 1930; *Educ* Creighton Sch Carlisle; *m* 1960, Joan Elizabeth, da of Harry Newton Carpenter (d 1969); 2 da; *Career* RAF;

cmmnd 1952, OC 360 Sqdn 1970-72, Station Cdr RAF Finningley 1977-79, Dir-Gen RAF Personal Services 1983-84; independent inspr Public Inquiries 1984-, chm appt bd for Civil Serv Cmmn and MOD; *Recreations* walking, philately; *Clubs* RAF; *Style*— Air Vice-Marshal Leslie Wheeler; c/o Midland Bank plc, Brampton, Cumbria

WHEELER, Lady; Marcelle; *née* Ades; 2 da of (Abdul) Edward Ades, of Alexandria, Egypt, and Alice, *née* Yabes; *b* 7 Feb 1914,Alexandria; *m* 1, 31 Aug 1950 (m dis 1973), as his 2 w, HH Prince Ibrahim Fazil of Egypt (d 1978), s of HH Prince Ali Fazil Pasha (d 1925), and ggs of Ibrahim Pasha, Vali of Egypt; m 2, 9 Nov 1973, Sir Charles Reginald (Mike) Wheeler, KBE (d 1975); *Style*— Lady Wheeler

WHEELER, Michael Mortimer; QC (1961), TD (1971); s of Sir (Robert Eric) Mortimer Wheeler MC, TD (d 1975), and 1st wife Tessa Verney Wheeler (d 1936); *b* 8 Jan 1915; *Educ* Dragon Sch, Rugby, Christ Church Oxford (MA); *m* 30 Oct 1939, Sheila, er da of Stephen Mayou (d 1936); 2 da (Susan Patricia (Mrs Donnellan) b 1940, Caroline Jane (Mrs Pettman) b 1943); *Career* serv WWII 1938-46: RA (TA) UK and Italy, Lt-Col 1945; called to Bar Gray's Inn 1938, joined Lincoln's Inn 1946 (tres 1986), dep High Ct Judge 1973-, ret from Bar 1988; *Recreations* golf, watching cricket; *Clubs* Garrick, MCC, Berks Golf; *Style*— Michael Wheeler, Esq, QC, TD; 114 Hallam St, London W1N 5LW (☎ 01 580 7284); Clare Cottage, Maidens Green, nr Windsor, Berks

WHEELER, Air Chief Marshal Sir (Henry) Neil George; GCB (1975, KCB 1969, CB 1967), CBE (1957, OBE 1949), DSO (1943), DFC and bar (1941, 1943), AFC (1954); s of Thomas Henry Wheeler (d 1933), of Pretoria, S Africa; *b* 8 July 1917; *Educ* St Helen's Coll Southsea; *m* 1942, Alice Elizabeth, da of William Henry Weightman, CMG (d 1970); 2 s, 1 da; *Career* joined RAF 1935, serv in Bomber Fighter and Coastal Cmds WW II, Gp Capt 1954, ADC to HM The Queen 1957-61, Air Cdre 1961, Air memb Research Policy Staff MOD 1962-63, Air Vice-Marshal 1963, SASO RAF Ger 1963-66, Asst Chief of Defence Staff (Operational Requirements) MOD 1966-67 and Dep Chief 1967, Air Marshal 1967, Cdr Far East Air Force 1969-70, Air memb Supply and Organisation MOD 1970, Air Chief Marshal 1972, controller of Aircraft MOD Procurement Exec 1973-75, ret 1976; dir: Rolls Royce Ltd 1977-82, Flight Refuelling Ltd 1977-85; memb Cncl of the Air League; Liveryman Guild of Air Pilots and Air Navigators (Master 1986-87); chm Anglo-Ecuadorian Soc 1986-; CBIM, FRAeS; *Recreations* flyfishing, painting, gardening; *Clubs* Flyfishers', RAF; *Style*— Air Chief Marshal Sir Neil Wheeler, GCB, CBE, DSO, DFC, AFC; Boundary Hall, Cooksbridge, Lewes, Sussex (☎ 0273 400201)

WHEELER, Maj-Gen (Thomas) Norman Samuel; CB (1967), CBE (1964, OBE 1958); s of Thomas Henry Wheeler (d 1933), and Wilhelmina, *née* Abernethy (d 1982); *b* 16 June 1915; *Educ* Waterkloof House SA, St Helens Coll Southsea Hants, RMC Sandhurst, Staff Coll Camberley, Armed Forces Staff Coll Norfolk Virginia USA; *m* 1 Sept 1939, Helen Clifford, da of Frederick Herbert Edwin Webber (Capt RE TA, d 1927); 1 s (Roger b 16 Dec 1941), 1 da (Alison b 3 March 1945); *Career* cmmnd Royal Ulster Rifles 1935, (despatches 1938, 1943, 1945, 1958), Palestine Rebellion 1937-39, Bde Maj 38 (Irish) Bde 1941-42, MEF Sudan and Eritrea 1942-43, Br Mil Mission to Albania (SOE) 1943-44, 2 Bn Royal Ulster Rifles BLA 1944-45, AAQMG 6 Airborne Div Palestine 1945-46, HQ Airborne Estabs Aldershot 1946-47, MA to Adj Gen 1949-50, UK Liaison Staff Melbourne Aust 1951-52, 1 Bn Royal Ulster Rifles Hong Kong 1953, GSO 1 and Col GS HQ BAOR 1954-57, Cdr 1 Bn RUR Cyprus 1957-59, Cdr 39 Inf Bde Gp NI 1959-62, COS 1 (Br) Corps BAOR 1962-63, GOC 2 Inf Div 1964-66, COS Contingency Planning SHAPE 1966-68, COS HQ BAOR 1968-71; dir and sec Independent Stores Assoc 1971-76, Associated Independent Stores dep md 1976-80; chm: J E Beale plc 1980-83, John Elmes Beale Tst Co Ltd 1983-88; pres Royal Ulster Rifles Assoc 1975-, chm Army Benevolent Fund Suffolk; independent memb Cinematograph Film Cncl 1980-83; cncl memb: Royal Patriotic Fund Corpn 1971-, Lord Kitchener Meml Fund 1982-; *Recreations* travel; *Clubs* Army & Navy, Airborne, Special Forces; *Style*— Maj-Gen Norman Wheeler, CB, CBE; Glebe House, Liston, Sudbury, Suffolk CO10 7HS (☎ 0787 756 40)

WHEELER, Paul; s of Dennis Wheeler, and Joan Margaret, *née* Crawte; *b* 8 Nov 1952; *Educ* Wallingford GS, Coll of Law Guildford; *m* 17 Dec 1977, Sally Anne, da of Arthur (Bob) Robert; 2 s (Lewis b 1983, Nicholas b 1986); *Career* slr 1977; lectr Coll of Law 1977-78, prosecuting slr Thames Valley Police 1978-82, ptnr Hedges & Son Wallingford and Widcot 1985; memb: Law Soc 1985 (Berks, Bucks and Oxon), Oxford Dist Slrs Assoc 1987; *Recreations* hockey; *Clubs* Wallingford Sports and Social, Wallingford Dist Lions; *Style*— Paul Wheeler, Esq; 10 Brookmead Drive, Wallingford, Oxon (☎ 0491 35 252); 144a Broadway, Didcot, Oxon (☎ 0235 812 842, fax 0235 815 696)

WHEELER, Raymond Leslie; s of Edmund Francis Wheeler (d 1969), and Ivy Geraldine, *née* Fryer (d 1979); *b* 25 Oct 1927; *Educ* Mewport Co Secdy GS, Univ Coll Southampton (BSc), Imperial Coll London (MSc); *m* 22 March 1950, Jean, da of Colin McInnes (d 1942); 1 s (Douglas b 1956), 2 da (Lesley (Mrs Rathmann) b 1952, Jennifer (Mrs Harrison) b 1954); *Career* chief structural designer Saunders-Roe Div Westland Aircraft Ltd 1965-66 (chief struc engr 1962-65), tech dir Br Hovercraft Corpn Ltd 1972-85 (chief designer 1966-85), business devpt dir Westland Aerospace Ltd 1985-; pres IOW area bd Young Enterprise, chm of govrs Whippingham Co Primary Sch, govr IOW Coll of Arts and Technol; FRAeS, FRINA, FRSA; *Books* From Sea to Air - The Heritage of Sam Saunders (with A E Tagg 1989); *Recreations* hockey, photography, archaeology; *Style*— Raymond Wheeler, Esq; Brovacum, Old Rd, East Cowes, IOW PO32 6AX (☎ 0983 292 994); Westland Aerospace Ltd, East Cowes, IOW PO32 6RH (☎ 0983 294 101, fax 0983 291 006, telex 86761)

WHEELER, Lt Cdr Sir (Ernest) Richard; KCVO (1981, CVO 1969, MVO 1965), MBE (1943); s of Rev Harold W Wheeler, and Margaret Laura Wheeler; *b* 21 July 1917; *Educ* Marlborough, HMS Frobisher; *m* 1, 1939, Yvonne Burns (d 1973); 1 da; m 2, 1974, Auriel Clifford; *Career* served RN 1935-49, ret (invalid); asst bursar Epsom Coll 1949-52; Duchy of Lancaster: chief clerk 1952-70, clerk of cncl and keeper of records 1970-81; *Style*— Lt Cdr Sir Richard Wheeler, KCVO, MBE, RN; 40 The Street, Marden, Devizes, Wilts

WHEELER, (John) Richard; s of John Wheeler, MBE (d 1982), of 10 Alton Drive, Colchester, and Christine Mary, *née* Everett; *b* 16 May 1932; *Educ* Framlingham Coll Suffolk; *m* 16 June 1956, (Christine) Mary, da of Octavius Blyth (d 1947), of Sunnyside, Yorick Rd, West Mersea, Essex; 1 s (Johnny b 1967), 3 da (Bridget b 1958, Susie b 1959, Sacha b 1962); *Career* Nat Serv cmmnd 2 Lt RASC 1950; md Lay & Wheeler Ltd 1958-(chm 1982-); memb Colchester Borough Cncl 1960-88; hon alderman 1988; Freeman Worshipful Co of Distillers 1976; Chevalier du Merite Agricole France 1988; *Recreations* salmon fising, walking; *Clubs* Colchester Garrison Offrs, West Mersea Yacht; *Style*— Richard Wheeler, Esq; West Mersea Hall, West Mersea, Colchester, Essex CO5 8QD (☎ 0206 382 391); Lay & Wheeler Ltd, 6 Culver Street West, Colchester, Essex CO1 1JA (☎ 0206 764 446, fax 0206 562 792, telex 987070 LAY WLR)

WHEELER-BENNETT, Richard Clement; s of Dr Clement Wheeler Wheeler-Bennett (d 1957), and Enid Lucy, *née* Boosey (d 1975); *b* 14 June 1927; *Educ* Radley, Christ Church Oxford (MA), Harvard Business Sch; *m* 8 May 1954, Joan Ellen, da of the late Prof Eric Alfred Havelock, of Connecticut, USA; 1 s (Clement b 1965 d 1986), 2 da (Joanna b 1957, Emily b 1960); *Career* RM Lt Commando 1944-48; banker; mangr First Nat City Bank of N York 1960-66, gen mangr (Europe) Aust and NZ Banking Gp 1978-80 (exec dir 1967-78), chm Thomas Borthwick & Sons Ltd 1980-85; dir Fleming Technol Tst 1983-; exec chm Roehampton Club Ltd 1988-; *Recreations* fishing, golf, shooting, viticulture; *Clubs* Brooks's, Pratts, MCC; *Style*— Richard Wheeler-Bennett, Esq; The Mill House, Calstone Wellington, nr Calne, Wilts SN11 8QF (☎ 0249 813241); 94 Rosebank, London SW6 6LJ (☎ 01 385 4970); Roehampton Club Ltd, Roehampton Lane, London SW15 (☎ 01 876 5505)

WHEELER-BOOTH, Michael Addison John; s of Addison James Wheeler, and Mary Angela, *née* Blakeney-Booth; *b* 25 Feb 1934; *Educ* Leighton Park Sch, Magdalen Coll Oxford (MA); *m* 1982, Emily Frances Smith; 2 da (Kate Charlotte); *Career* reading clerk House of Lords 1983-88, clerk asst of the Parl 1988-; *Style*— M A J Wheeler-Booth, Esq; House of Lords, London SW1

WHEELHOUSE, Alan; s of George William Wheelhouse, of Nottingham, and Dorothy Marion, *née* Hickling (d 1974); *b* 4 Mar 1934; *Educ* Nottingham HS, Emmanuel Coll Cambridge (MA, LLB); *m* 1963, Jennifer Mary, da of Donald Stewart Robinson (d 1974), of Nottingham; 3 da (Heather Jane b 1964, Julie Ann b 1966, Emma Louise b 1969); *Career* slr, sr ptnr Freeth Cartwright & Sketchley, pres Nottinghamshire Law Soc 1985-86; Cambridge Cricket Blue 1959, Nottinghamshire Co Cricket 1961, ctee 1987-; Capt Notts 50+ Cricket XI 1985-88, XL Club Dist Chm 1985-; chm Gunn & Moore Club Cricket Alliance 1983-85, pres Old Nottinghamians Soc 1982, pres Old Nottinghamians Cricket Club 1988; govr Nottingham HS 1988-; *Recreations* cricket, watching sport, concert and theatre going, eating-out; *Clubs* Old Nottinghamians CC (former captain), XL Club, Notts CCC, Nottinghamshire Football (vice-pres); *Style*— Alan Wheelhouse, Esq; The White House, 64 Breckhill Road, Woodthorpe, Nottingham NG5 4GQ (☎ Nottm 262754); Willoughby House, 20 Low Pavement, Nottingham (☎ Nottm 506861, fax Nottm 585079)

WHEEN, Rear Adm Charles Kerr Thorneycroft; CB (1966); s of Francis Thorneycroft Wheen (d 1974), of Holmbury, Chislehurst, Kent; *b* 28 Sept 1912; *Educ* RNC Dartmouth; *m* 1940, Veryan Rosamond, da of late William Acworth, of Chobham, Surrey; 3 s, 1 da; *Career* naval attaché Beirut, Amman, Addis Ababa 1958-60; Admty 1960-63, Rear Adm 1964, Flag Offr Admty Interview Bd 1964-66, ret 1966; dir Cement Makers Fedn 1967-79; chm of govrs Gordon Boys Sch 1971-85; *Recreations* golf, fishing, painting; *Clubs* Worplesdon Golf, MCC; *Style*— Rear Adm Charles Wheen, CB; Willow House, Philpot Lane, Chobham, Surrey (☎ 099 05 8118)

WHEEN, Richard Francis; s of Rear Adm Charles Kerr Thorneycroft Wheen, CB, of Surrey, and Veryan Rosamond, *née* Acworth; *b* 27 May 1941; *Educ* Harrow, Peterhouse Cambridge (MA); *m* 14 Jan 1983, Anne, da of Patrick Joseph Keegan, of Ireland (d 1980); 5 s (Timothy b 1983, Patrick (twins) b 1983, Jonathan b 1985 (d 1987), Christopher b 1986, Peter b 1988); *Career* slr; ptnr Linklaters & Paines; Lt/ Cdr RNR, ret 1979; author 'Bridge Player' series of programs for home computers 1983-; *Recreations* bridge, shooting, computer programming, golf; *Clubs* Army and Navy, Worplesdon Golf; *Style*— Richard F Wheen, Esq; The Grange, Rectory Lane, Buckland, Betchworth, Surrey RH3 7BH (☎ 073784 2193); Linklaters & Paines, Barrington House, 59-67 Gresham St, London EC2 (☎ 01 606 7080)

WHELAN, Michael Joseph; s of Michael Whelan (d 1972), and Mary T, *née* Hynes; *b* 1 May 1932; *Educ* Castleknock Coll Dublin, Univ Coll Dublin (BA), Columbia Univ NY (MSc); *m* 3 June 1955, Maureen Therese, da of John Ryan (d 1972); 3 s (Gerard b 1959, Brian b 1962, Roger b 1966), 1 da (Ann-Maeve b 1956); *Career* called to the Bar King's Inn Dublin 1953; corporate lawyer Shell Oil; Toronto 1955-59, NY 1959-60; devpt and commercial mangr Aer Lingus NY and Dublin 1960-63, mktg dir Irish Tourist Bd Dublin 1963-71, fndr and chief exec Aran Energy plc Dublin and London 1972-; FInstPet, FInstD; *Recreations* sailing; *Clubs* Royal Irish Yacht, Fitzwilliam, St Stephens Green, Milltown Golf, Royal Irish Automobile (All Dublin); *Style*— Michael J Whelan, Esq; 51 Mount St, Mayfair, London W1; The Cove, Baltimore, Co Cork; Ardoyne House, Ballsbridge, Dublin 4; 37 Maddox St, London W1 (☎ 01 629 2080); Clanwilliam Court, Dublin 2 (☎ 0001 760 696)

WHELER, Sir Edward Woodford; 14 Bt (E 1660, of City of Westminster, Co London); s and h of Sir Trevor Wood Wheler, 13 Bt (d 1986), and Margaret Idris, *née* Birch (d 1987); *b* 13 June 1920; *Educ* Radley; *m* 2 July 1945, Molly Ashworth, da of late Thomas Lever; 1 s (Trevor), 1 da (Dinah); *Heir* s, Trevor Woodford b 11 April 1946; *Career* Royal Sussex Regt and 15 Punjab Regt Indian Army 1941-47, Capt; Colonial Audit Dept 1948-58; *Style*— Sir Edward Wheler, Bt; 25 Cavendish Rd, Chesham, Bucks (☎ 0494 784766); 19 St James's St, London SW1 (☎ 01 930 3787)

WHELER, Margaret, Lady; Margaret Idris; *née* Birch; da of late Sir Ernest Woodford Birch, KCMG; *m* 1915, Sir Trevor Wood Wheler, 13 Bt (d 1986); 1 s (Sir Edward Wheler, 13 Bt), 2 da (Audrey Idris, Diana Edmee); *Style*— Lady Margaret Wheler; 5A Motcombe Court, Bedford Avenue, Bexhill-on-Sea, Sussex

WHELON, (Charles) Patrick Clavell; s of Charles Eric Whelon (d 1975), and Margaret Ethel Salter (d 1960); *b* 18 Jan 1930; *Educ* Wellington Coll, Pembroke Coll Cambridge (BA); *m* 6 Jan 1968, Prudence Mary, da of Samuel Lesley Potter (d 1966); 1 s (Charles b 1969), 1 da (Emily b 1971); *Career* barr, rec Crown Ct 1978-; *Recreations* gardening, travel, drawing; *Clubs* Liveryman of Vintners Company; *Style*— Patrick Whelon, Esq; Russetts, Pyott's Hill, Old Basing, Hants; 2 Harcourt Buildings, Temple, London EC4 (☎ 01 353 2112)

WHELPTON, Robert Anthony (Tony); s of Francis Clair William Whelpton (d 1983), and Alice Beatrice, *née* Cresswell (d 1976); *b* 27 Jan 1933; *Educ* High Pavement Sch Nottingham, Goldsmiths' Coll London (BA, PGCE), Birkbeck Coll London (BA), Univ of Lille (Lè SL); *m* 1, 4 Feb 1956, Kathryn, da of Joseph Evans (d 1984), of Nottingham; 2 da (Fiona b 1957, Rachel b 1959); m 2, 5 Sept 1981, Joan Valerie, *née* Williams; *Career* Nat Serv RAF, Sr Aircraftman 1951-53; schoolmaster 1957-65, sr lectr in french Nottingham Coll of Educn 1965-74, princ lectr in french Trent Poly 1974-82; chief examiner: GCE (N Ireland) 1969-72, GCE (Associated Examining Bd 1973-87, Malawi Cert of Educn 1979, GCSE French Southern Examining Gp; freelance writer, author numerous newspaper, magazine articles and school text-books; *Recreations* squash, choral singing, genealogy; *Style—* Tony Whelpton, Esq; 25 Hartlebury Way, Charlton Kings, Cheltenham, Glos GL52 6YB (☎ 0242 36692)

WHETHERLY, Hon Mrs; Hon Rosemary Gertrude Alexandra; *née* Lever; yr da of 2 Viscount Leverhulme (d 1949), and his 1 w Marion Beatrice, *née* Smith; *b* 23 April 1919; *m* 19 Oct 1938, Lt-Col William Erskine Stobart Whetherly, er s of late Lt-Col William Stobart Whetherly, DSO; 2 s, 1 da; *Style—* The Hon Mrs Whetherly; Hallam, Ogbourne St George, Marlborough, Wilts SN8 1SG (☎ 067 284 212)

WHETHERLY, Lt-Col William Erskine Stobart (Toby); s of Lt-Col W S Whetherly, DSO (d 1956), and Marjorie, *née* Holmes (d 1966); *b* 1 July 1909; *Educ* Harrow, Sandhurst; *m* 19 Oct 1938, Rosemary Gertrude Alexandra, da of 2 Viscount Leverhulme (d 1949), of Thornton Manor, Wirral, Cheshire; 2 s (Dennis b 27 Jan 1940, Robin b 19 Oct 1947), 1 da (Dawn b 12 Feb 1946); *Career* 2 Lt Dragoon Gds 1929, Maj cmdg sqdn Western Desert 1940, Lt-Col cmdg Mil Mission Yugoslavia 1944, Gen Staff Italy, Lt-Col GSO1 WO 1945, ret 1947; High Sheriff of Wiltshire 1973-74; *Clubs* Boodle's; *Style—* Lt-Col Toby Whetherly; Hallam, Ogbourne St George, Marlborough, Wilts (☎ 067 284 212); Flat 12A, 17 Grosvenor Sq, London W1 (☎ 01 493 9111)

WHETSTONE, Lt Cdr (Norman) Keith; VRD (1964), OBE (1983); s of Albert Whetstone (d 1949), of Coventry, and Hannah Elizabeth, *née* Hubbard (d 1963); *b* 17 June 1930; *Educ* King Henry VIII Sch Coventry; *m* 6 Dec 1952, Monica Joan, da of Allan Clayton, of Leamington Spa; 3 s (William b 1954, Neil b 1956, Alastair b 1959); *Career* RNVR 1949-50 and 1952-53 Korea; journalist Coventry Evening Telegraph 1950-52, rugby football corr Western Morning News Plymouth 1953-55, sub-ed The Birmingham Post 1955-58, theatre corr Coventry Evening Telegraph 1958-63; ed: Cambridge Evening News 1963-70, Coventry Evening Telegraph 1970-80; ed dir The Birmingham Post and Mail Ltd 1980-86, ed The Birmingham Evening Mail 1980-85, ed in chief The Birmingham Post and Birmingham Evening Mail Series 1984-86; ret 1986, ed conslt freelance writer; memb: Guild of Br Newspaper Editors 1964 (Nat Pres 1976-77), Press Cncl 1980-86; *Recreations* rugby football (former Warwickshire sch player), golf, squash, theatre, DIY; *Clubs* Coventry and North Warwickshire CC, Coventry FC (rugby); *Style—* Lt Cdr Keith Whetsone, VRD, OBE; Tudor House, Benton Green Lane, Berkswell, Coventry CV7 7AY (☎ 0676 32323)

WHEWELL, Roger William; s of Alfred Thomas Whewell (d 1969), and Dorothy Annie Whewell (d 1988); *b* 24 Jan 1940; *Educ* Harrison Coll Barbados, Clifton Coll Bristol; *m* 9 May 1964, (Edith) Elaine, da of George Turcan Chiene, DSO, TD, MC, of Edinburgh; 2 s (Andrew b 1966, Rupert b 1969), 1 da (Lisa b 1968); *Career* CA; articled clerk Jackson Taylor Aberhethy & Co 1958-64; Peat Marwick McLintock: joined 1964, ptnr 1974, gen ptnr 1985, chm insur indust ctee 1989; chm indust ctee and memb parly and law ctee ICEAW, co-chm interprofessional working party accountants/actuaries; inspr under Lloyd's Act 1982 (Re-extended Warranty Insur); Liveryman Worshipful Co of Chartered Accountants; FCA 1964; *Recreations* hunting, stalking, fishing, shooting; *Style—* Roger Whewell, Esq; Innerwick, Glenlyon, By Aberfeldy, Perthshire; 10 Lexham House, 45 Lexham Gdns, London W8; Peat Marwick Mclintak, 1 Puddle Dock, Blackfriars, London EL4V 3PD (☎ 01 236 8000, fax 01 248 6552 (GROUP 3), telex 811541 PMMLOW G)

WHICKER, Alan Donald; s of late Charles Henry Whicker, and Anne Jane, *née* Cross; *b* 2 August 1925; *Educ* Haberdashers' Aske's; *Career* Devonshire Regt, Capt, dir Army Film and Photo Section with 8 Army and US 5 Army, war corr in Korea; foreign corr, novelist, writer, television and radio broadcaster; joined BBC TV 1957, Tonight programme; TV series: Whicker's World 1959-60, Whicker Down Under 1961, Whicker on Top of the World! 1962, Whicker in Sweden, Whicker in the Heart of Texas, Whicker down Mexico Way 1963; The Alan Whicker Report series including The Solitary Billionaire (J Paul Getty); wrote and appeared in own series of monthly documentaries on BBC-2 (subsequently repeated on BBC-1 under series title Whicker's World) 1965-76; BBC radio programmes and articles for various publications; Sunday newspaper columns; left BBC 1968; various cinema films including: The Angry Silence 1967; completed 16 documentaries for Yorkshire TV during its first year of operation including Whicker's New World series, and specials on Gen Stroessner of Paraguay, Count von Rosen and Pres Duvalier of Haiti, Whicker in Europe, Whicker's Walkabout, Broken Hill-Walled City, Gairy's Grenada; documentary series: World of Whicker, Whicker's Orient, Whicker Within a Woman's World 1972, Whicker's South Seas, Whicker Way Out West 1973, Whicker's World series on Cities 1974, Whicker's World - Down Under 1976; Whicker's World: US 1977, India 1978, Indonesia 1979, California 1980, Peter Sellers meml programme 1980, Whicker's World aboard the Orient Express 1982, Around Whickers World in 25 years 1982; returned to BBC TV 1982-83, Whicker's World - the First Million Miles 1982; BBC Radio: chaired Start the Week, Whicker's Wireless World 1983; BBC 1 Whicker's World - a Fast Boat to China 1984; BBC-2: Talk Show Whicker! 1984, Whicker's World - Living with Uncle Sam 1985, Whicker's World - Living with Waltzing Matilda 1988; various awards including Screenwriters' Guild best Documentary Script 1963, Guild of Television Producers and Directors Personality of the Year 1964, Silver Medal Royal Television Soc 1968, Dumont Award Univ of California 1970, Best Interview Programme Award 1978; FRSA; *Books* Some Rise By Sin (1949), Away - with Alan Whicker (1963), Within Whicker's World (1982), Whicker's New World (1985), Whicker's World Down Under (1988); *Style—* Alan Whicker, Esq; Le Gallais Chambers, St Helier, Jersey

WHICKER, (Mary) Eileen; da of Patrick Alexander Creighton, of 2 Ivanhoe Place, Stirling, Scotland, and Agnes, *née* Gavin (d 1980); *b* 29 Oct 1937; *Educ* St Modans HS; *m* 2 June 1962, Paul Jonathan Owen Whicker, s of James Whicker (d 1982); 1 da (Karen Suzanne); *Career* psychotherapist, mgmnt consit, trainer; fndr Assoc for Neuro Linguistic Programming 1984 (chm 1985-86); *Recreations* reading, theatre, sculpture, travelling; *Clubs* Network; *Style—* Mrs Eileen Whicker; 14 Weston Park, Thames Ditton, Surrey KT7 0HQ

WHIDBORNE, Hon Mrs (Elaine Barbara Julia); o da of Lt-Col Hon Rowland Tudor St John, DLI (d 1948, s of 16 Baron St John of Bletso), and Katherine Madge, *née* Lockwood (d 1954); sis of late 20 Baron; raised to the rank of a Baron's da 1977; *b* 19 June 1921; *m* 25 Aug 1939, Lt-Col John Francis Whidborne, RA, o s of John Herbert Whidborne, of Stockleigh English, Devon; 1 s (and 1 s decd), 1 da; *Style—* The Hon Mrs Whidborne; Holly Mount, Pethybridge, Lustleigh, Devon TQ13 9TG (☎ 064 77 267)

WHILEY, Reginald Raymond; JP (1979); s of Harry Hewitt Whiley (d 1957); *b* 7 July 1924; *Educ* Kilburn GS; *Career* memb of Lloyds 1969-; dir CT Bowring (UK) 1974-79, chm Shipton Insurance Services 1976-81; hon tres Snowdon Award Scheme 1979-88, Nat Fund for Research into Crippling Diseases 1979-88; govr: Southlands Coll 1979-, Luton Indust Coll 1981-; *Recreations* walking, watching sport, opera; *Clubs* RAC, MCC; *Style—* Reginald Whiley, Esq, JP; 21 Francis Rd, Pinner, Middx, HA5 2ST (☎ 01 866 6147)

WHINNEY, Rt Rev Michael Humphrey Dickins; *see*: Southwell, Bishop of

WHINNEY, Capt Reginald Fife; DSC (1943 and 2 bars 1944); s of Lt-Col Harold Fife Whinney, DSO, OBE (d 1956), and Sarah Mary Meredith Parsons (d 1962); *b* 8 Feb 1909; *Educ* RNC Dartmouth, RNC Greenwich; *m* 1, 27 Dec 1939 (m dis), Nora Reade, da of B Reade (d 1959), of Vanchurch, Dorchester; m 2, 29 July 1957, Bridget, da of Arthur Coote; 1 s (Christopher), 2 da (Rosalind, Alison); *Career* Capt RN, served Abyssinian and Spanish Civil Wars 1935-36, HMS Cossack N Sea (sinking of Bismarck) 1940-41, Fleet A/S Offr S Atlantic 1941-42, CO HMS Wanderer, Atlantic and Arctic 1943-44, sr offr 104 Escort Gp 1944; exec cdr: HMS Dolphin (submarine base) 1945-47, HMS Euraylus (Mountbatten's cruiser sqdn Med) 1947; i/c Seaward Defence Sch Plymouth 1950-52, promoted Capt and dep dir Underwater Weapons Admiralty 1952-54, CSO intelligence Med and Middle East 1954-57, sr offr Reserve Fleet E Coast 1957-59, NA Belgrade 1959-61; ret; research and devpt Int Computers progress and external relations dept 1962-65; worked on Cancer Research Campaign Appeals Wessex and CI 1965-77; chm NABC Stevenage 1961-65; pres Mere (Wilts) and Dist Royal Br Legion 1967-77; life memb RN Equestrian Soc; *Books* The U-boat Peril (1986); *Recreations* fishing, grass cutting, writing, politics (penal reform); *Clubs* RN, Royal Albert Yacht, Royal Lymington Yacht; *Style—* Capt Regindald Whinney, DSC; Lentune Ford, Walhampton, Lymington, Hampshire SO41 5RB

WHIPHAM, Thomas Henry Martin; s of Harry Rowland Whipham (d 1942), and Anne Hilda Muriel Martin (d 1975); *b* 18 May 1923; *Educ* Malvern Coll; *m* 6 May 1972, Bridget Elizabeth, da of Hugh Roger Greville Montgomery (d 1952); 1 da (Sandra Claire b 24 June 1975); *Career* WWII Army 1941-46, cmmnd Lt RAC Duke of Wellington's Regt 1943 served: N Africa, Italy, Middle East; called to the Bar Lincolns Inn 1949 (ad eundem Middle Temple); pres London Rent Assessment Panel 1986- (a vice pres 1978-86), chm Central London Valuation Panel 1987-, hon steward Westminster Abbey 1985-; Parly candidate (Cons) Shoreditch and Finsbury by-election 1958 (also gen election 1959); memb: London Electricity Consultative cncl 1961-70, Friern Hosp mgmnt ctee 1960-73, Marlylebone Borough Cncl 1962-65, Westminster City Cncl 1968-86 (chm ctees on: Road Safety, Highways and Works, Town Planning), Lord Mayor of Westminster 1982-83; Freeman City of London, Worshipful Co of Goldsmiths; Cdr of Order of Orange Nassau 1982; *Recreations* swimming, walking, opera, theatre, reading, travel, enjoying life; *Clubs* MCC, Carlton, Hurlingham; *Style—* Thomas Whipham, Esq; 73 Clifton Hill, St John's Wood, London NW8 0JN (☎ 01 624 9837); 37-40 Berners St, London W1 (☎ 01 580 2000)

WHISHAW, Sir Charles Percival Law; 2 s of Montague Law Whishaw (d 1946), of London, and Erna Louise, *née* Spies; *b* 29 Oct 1909; *Educ* Charterhouse, Worcester Coll Oxford; *m* 1936, (Margaret) Joan, da of Col Thomas Henry Hawkins, CMG (d 1944), of Formby, Lancs; 1 s, 2 da; *Career* barr 1932, became slr 1938, ptnr Freshfields 1943-74; tstee Calouste Gulbenkian Fndn 1956-81; Comendador of Order of Infante D Henrique Portugal 1982; kt 1969; *Style—* Sir Charles Whishaw; Clare Park, Nr Farnham, Surrey GU10 5DT (☎ 0252 851333, 0252 850681)

WHISKARD, John Mason; s of Sir Geoffrey Granville Whiskard, KCB, KCMG (d 1957), of Suffolk, and Cynthia Salome Caroline, *née* Reeves (d 1940); *b* 28 Feb 1924; *Educ* Westminster Sch, Corpus Christi Coll Oxford; *m* 26 June 1952, Elizabeth Dorothy, da of Lt-Col Edward Darby Jackson, DSO, OBE, DL (d 1962), of Roxburghshire; 2 s (Richard b 1959, Timothy b 1965); *Career* Sub Lt RNVR 1944, Lt 1946, served combined ops; OUP: asst mangr Calcutta branch 1947-50, personal asst to publisher to the univ 1950-52, prodn mangr overseas educn dept 1952-56, Gilmour & Dean Ltd (Printers) Glasgow 1956-65 (dir 1961-65), chm and md Three Birds Press 1965-69; sr sales appts with: Life & Equity Assur Ltd, Barclays Unicorn, Sun Life Unit Services Ltd; govr Glasgow Sch of Ar 1960-65; hon steward Westminster Abbey 1951-84 (dep chief hon steward 1984-); *Recreations* small-press printing; *Clubs* Naval; *Style—* John M Whiskard, Esq; Bellingham Farmhouse, Sevenhampton, Swindon, Wilts SN6 7QA (☎ 0793 762425)

WHISTLER, Laurence; CBE (1973), OBE (1955); s of Henry Whistler (d 1940), of 69 The Close, Salisbury Cathedral, and Helen, *née* Ward; *b* 21 Jan 1912; *Educ* Stowe, Balliol Coll Oxford (MA); *m* 1, 12 Sep 1939, Jill (d 1944), da of Sir Ralph Fure, KCMG (d 1963); 1 s (Simon b 1940), 1 da (Caroline b 1944); m 2, 15 Aug 1950 (m dis 1986), Theresa, yr sis Jill Fure; 1 s (Daniel b 1954), 1 da (Frances b 1957); m 3, 24 March 1987, Carol, da of John Groves, CB; *Career* WWII RCS 1940-41, 2 Lt RB 1941, Capt RB 1942-45; glass engraver and author; work on glass incl: engraved church windows and panels Sherborne Abbey Dorset, Guards Chapel London, Salisbury Cathedral, Curry Rivel Somerset; exhibitions: Agnews Bond St 1969, Marble Hill Twickenham 1972, Corning Museum USA 1974, Ashmolean 1976 and 1985; hon fell Balliol Coll Oxford 1974, first pres Guild Glass Engravers 1975-80; FRSL 1955; *Books* on glass incl: The Engraved Glass of Laurence Whistler (1952), Engraved Glass 1952-58 (1959), Pictures on Glass (1972), The Image on The Glass (1975), Scenes And Signs On Glass (1985); Poetry incl: The World's Room Collected Poems (1949), To Celebrate Her Living (1967), Enter (1987); prose incl: The English Festivals (1947), The Initials In The Heart, The Story of a Marriage (1975); on his brother: Rex Whistler, His Life and Drawings (1948), The Work of Rex Whistler (with Ronald Fuller 1969), The Laughter And The Urn (biography 1985); on architecture incl: Sir John Vanbrugh (biography 1938), The Imagination of Vanbrugh (1954); *Style—* Laurence Whistler, Esq, CBE; c/o Lloyds Bank, F Section, 6 Pall Mall, London SW1Y 5NH

WHISTLER, Maj-Gen (Alwyne) Michael Webster; CB (1963), CBE (1960); s of Rev W W Whistle, MA (d 1969), of Battle Abbey, Sussex, and Lilian, *née* Meade (d 1969); *b* 30 Dec 1909; *Educ* Gresham's Sch Holt, RMA Woolwich; *m* 1 Jan 1936, Margaret Louise Michelette (d 1986), da of Brig-Gen M H E Welch, CB, CMG, JP, of Sussex; 1 s (Hugh b 1931), 2 da (Bridget b 1938, Clare b 1942); *Recreations* field sports, gardening; *Style—* Maj-Gen Michael Whistler; 8 Shirley Road, Wareham,

Dorset BH20 4QE (☎ 092385 2605)

WHITAKER, Alan Arthur; s of Sir (Frederick) Arthur Whitaker, KCB (d 1968, formerly civil engr-in-chief Admiralty 1940-53) of Northwood, Middx, and Florence, *née* Overend (d 1978); *b* 21 Mar 1925; *Educ* Aldenham, Christ Church Oxford (MA); *m* 1957, Beulah, da of Ernest C Hatcher (d 1978), of Northwood, Middx; *Career* dir: Pearson plc 1969-, Yorkshire Television Holdings plc 1985-, Osprey Communications plc, Madame Tussaud's Ltd, Société Civile du Vignoble de Chateau Latour 1981-; FCA; *Recreations* gardening; *Style*— Alan Whitaker, Esq; Hartfield, Martinsend Lane, Gt Missenden, Bucks (☎ (024 06) 5124); Pearson plc, Millbank Tower, Millbank, London SW1P 4QZ (☎ 01 828 9020, telex 8953869)

WHITAKER, Barry Carnaby; s of Maj Kenneth Henry Whitaker (d 1987), of Tilford House, Tilford, Surrey, and Millicent, *née* Carnaby (d 1984); *b* 5 Nov 1940; *Educ* Marlborough; *m* 21 Nov 1968, Jacqueline, da of Sqdn Ldr Harold Rothwell; 2 s (Jason b 7 Feb 1970, Max b 11 Dec 1975); *Career* CA; Peat Marwick Mitchell & Co 1959-64, ptnr Joseph Sebag & Co 1970-79 (joined 1965); ptnr: Carr Sebag & Co 1979-84, Grieveson Grant & Co 1984-86, Kleinwort Griveson & Co 1986-88, C L Alexanders Laing & Cruickshank Gilts Ltd 1987-; dep chm Tilford Parish Cncl 1987- (memb 1977-), pres Tilford Cons Assoc 1988- (chm 1983-88); ACA 1964, FCA 1974, memb Stock Exchange 1961; *Recreations* country sports, bridge, reading; *Clubs* Boodle's; *Style*— Barry Whitaker, Esq; Tilford House, Tilford, Farnham, Surrey GU10 2BX (☎ 025 125 2962); 65 Cornhill, London EC3V 3PP (☎ 01 283 3030, fax 01 623 1116, car phone 0836 266763)

WHITAKER, Benjamin Charles George (Ben); 3 s of Maj-Gen Sir John Albert Charles Whitaker, 2 Bt, CB, OBE (d 1957), and Pamela Lucy Mary, *née* Snowden (d 1945); bro of Sir James Whitaker, 3 Bt, *qv*; *b* 15 Sept 1934; *Educ* Eton, New Coll Oxford (BA); *m* 18 Dec 1964, Janet Alison, da of Alan Harrison Stewart, of The Small House, Station Rd, Beeston, Notts; 2 s (Daniel b 1966, Rasaq b 1972), 1 da (Quincy b 1968); *Career* Lt Coldstream Guards; barr Inner Temple 1959; MP (LAB) Hampstead 1966-70, Parly sec for Overseas Devpt 1969-70, exec dir The Minority Rights Gp 1971-, UK memb The UN Human Rights Sub Cmmn 1975-; *Books* Parks for People (ed, 1971), The Police in Society (1979), A Bridge of People (1983); The Global Connection (1987); *Recreations* writing; *Style*— Benjamin Whitaker, Esq; 13 Elsworthy Rd, London NW3

WHITAKER, Hugh; MBE (1966), JP (1966); s of Hugh Whitaker, of Ivydene, The Hollow, Littleover, Derbys, and Mary Cowper, *née* Stanton; *b* 5 April 1912; *Educ* Derby Sch, Nottingham Univ; *m* 31 Dec 1949, Kathleen Mary, da of Archibald Rudkin, of Woodbank, Blaby, Leicester; 2 s (Hugh Rudkin, Anthony Kim); *Career* schoolmaster: asst master Merchant Taylor's Sch Crosby, warden/headmaster Holt Hall Norfolk, (on retirement) pt-t asst master Gresham's Sch Holt; chm: govrs Beeston Hall Prep Sch 1974-84, Whitaker Tst Beeston Hall Sch, Fakenham Bench 1982-83; Co cmmr Norfolk Scout Assoc 1970-75; ldr Scout Expeditions to: Iceland, Norway, Morocco, Greece 1963-69; *Recreations* cricket, association football, rugby football, ornithology, hill walking; *Style*— Hugh Whitaker, Esq, MBE, JP; Cornerways, 15 Peasons Close, Holt, Norfolk NR25 6EH (☎ 0263 711 284)

WHITAKER, James Edward Anthony; s of George Edward Dudley Whitaker, OBE (d 1983), and Mary Evelyn Austin, *née* Haslett; *b* 4 Oct 1940; *Educ* Cheltenham Coll; *m* 1965, Iwona, da of late Andrzej Karol Milde, of Poland; 2 s (Edward b 1965, Thomas b 1966), 1 da (Victoria b 1973); *Career* journalist: Daily Mail, Daily Express, Sun, Daily Star; *Books* Prince Charles, Prince of Wales; *Recreations* racing, shooting, skiing; *Clubs* City Golf; *Style*— James Whitaker, Esq; c/o Mirror Gp Newspapers, Holborn Circus EC1 (☎ 01 353 0246)

WHITAKER, Sir James Herbert Ingham Whitaker; 3 Bt (UK 1936), of Babworth, Nottinghamshire; s of Maj-Gen Sir John Albert Charles Whitaker, 2 Bt, CB, CBE (d 1957), and Pamela Lucy Mary, *née* Snowden (d 1945); bro of Benjamin Charles George Whitaker, *qv*; *b* 27 July 1925; *Educ* Eton; *m* 26 July 1948, Mary Elisabeth Lander, JP (who m 1940, Capt David Urling Clark, MC, d 1942), da of Ernest Johnston (d 1965), of Cockshut, Reigate, Surrey, and sis of Sir Charles Hepburn Johnston, GCMG (d 1986); 1 s, 1 da (Shervie m David W J Price, *qv*); *Heir* s, John James Ingham Whitaker b 23 Oct 1952, *qv*; *Career* 2 Lt Coldstream Gds 1944, served in N W Europe, Egypt and Palestine 1945, ret 1947; dep chm Halifax Bldg Soc 1973- (chm of London Bd); chm bd of govrs Atlantic Coll; High Sheriff Notts 1969; *Recreations* shooting; *Clubs* Boodle's; *Style*— Sir James Whitaker, Bt; Auchnafree, Dunkeld, Perthshire (☎ 035 05 233); Babworth Hall, Retford, Notts (☎ 0777 703454)

WHITAKER, Maj Jeremy Ingham; s of Maj Leith Ingham Tomkins Whitaker, DL (d 1971), and Myrtle Clare, *née* Van de Weyer; *b* 10 Nov 1934; *Educ* Eton, Sandhurst; *m* 18 April 1974, Philippa, da of Lt-Col HH van Straubenzee, DSO, OBE, of Kingscote, Binfield, Berkshire; 1 s (Benjamin Ingham b 17 April 1979), 2 da (Alexandra Marilyn b 27 June 1975, Camilla Isabelle b 31 May 1980); *Career* cmmnd Coldstream Gds 1954, Capt 1960, ADC to Govr Gen Nigeria 1960-61, UNO forces Congo West Africa Frontier Force GSO3 Nigerian Bde 1961, ADC to High Cmmn Malaysia 1963-65, Maj 1 Bn Coldstream Gds Aden 1965-66; prof architecture photographer 1967-; MCSD 1976; *Recreations* ski-ing, gardening, carpentry; *Clubs* Pratts; *Style*— Maj Jeremy Whitaker; Land of Nod, Headley, Bordon, Hampshire GU35 8SJ (☎ 0428 713609, 0428 712292)

WHITAKER, John James Ingham (Jack); s and h of Sir James Herbert Ingham Whitaker, 3 Bt; *b* 23 Oct 1952; *Educ* Eton, (BSc); *m* 31 Jan 1981, Elizabeth Jane Ravenscroft, da of L J R Starke, of NZ; 1 s (Harry James Ingham b 1984), 2 da (Lucy Harriet Ravenscroft b 1982, Alix Catherine Hepburn b 1987); *Career* FCA, AMIEE; *Style*— Jack Whitaker, Esq; The Cottage, Babworth, Retford, Notts DN22 8EW

WHITAKER, Martin; s of Maj Robert Edmund Whitaker, TD, of Shropshire, and Priscilla Kynaston, *née* Mainwaring; *b* 24 Sept 1938; *Educ* Sherborne, RAC Cirencester; *m* 16 July 1966, Susan Mary Sheila, da of Francis Spenceleigh Walker, of Standlake, Oxon; 1 s (Alexander b 1972), 1 da (Anabel b 1969); *Career* chartered surveyor; dir: Cleghorn & Harris Ltd 1979-, Lane Fox and Ptnrs Ltd 1987-; FRICS; *Recreations* shooting, hunting; *Style*— Martin Whitaker, Esq; Dovecote House, Driffield, Cirencester, Glos GL7 5PY (☎ 028 585 465); The Mead House, Thomas St, Cirencester, Glos

WHITAKER, Steven Dixon; s of George Dixon Whitaker, of Exeter, and Elsie Whitaker; *b* 28 Jan 1950; *Educ* Burnley GS, Churchill Coll Cambridge (MA); *m* 4 Sept 1976, Jacqueline, da of William Ernest Branter (d 1985), 1 da (Emma Louise); *Career* called to the Bar Middle Temple 1973; chm bd govrs Rosemead Prep Sch London; *Recreations* choral singing, music, the arts, for travel; *Style*— Steven Whitaker, Esq; Beulah Cottage, Queen Mary Rd, Upper Norwood, London SE19 3NN (☎ 01 670 0861); Il Poggiolo, Via Marconi, Brucciano, Lucca, Italy; 3 Paper Bldgs, Temple, London EC4Y 7EU (☎ 01 583 8055, fax 01 353 6271)

WHITAKER, Wolstan John; (formerly Churchwood, name changed by deed poll 1954); s of Capt Paul Rycaut de Shordiche Churchward (d 1981), and Clair Isabel, *née* Whitaker who m 2 Richard Rusby Kaye (d 1981); *b* 8 Sept 1935; *Educ* Northaw Sch, Tabley House Sch; *m* 1961 June, Rosemary, da of Capt Stanley William Culverhouse (d 1973); 2 s (Charles James Stanbury b 1963, Piers Francis John b 1955); *Recreations* hunting, shooting; *Style*— Wolstan Whitaker, Esq; Winsley Hall, Westbury, Shrewsbury, Shropshire SY5 9HB

WHITBREAD, Fatima; MBE (1987); *b* 3 Mar 1961; *Career* javelin thrower; Cwlth Games: Bronze Medallist 1982, Silver Medallist 1986; Euro Champs Gold Medallist 1986; World Champs: Silver Medallist 1983, Gold Medallist 1987; Olympic Games: Bronze Medallist 1984, Silver Medallist 1988; World record holder 1986-; womens rep Br Olympic Assoc; memb Mazda Track Club; *Books* Fatima (autobiography, 1988); *Recreations* theatre; *Style*— Miss Fatima Whitbread, MBE; c/o AAA, Francis House, Francis St, London SW1P 1DL (☎ 01 821 1487, fax 01 630 6328, telex 942601 BAAB)

WHITBREAD, Hugh William; s of Col William Henry Whitbread, TD, and Betty Parr, *née* Russell; *b* 11 Feb 1942; *Educ* Eton, Cambridge Univ, Harvard Univ; *m* 1972, Katherine Elizabeth, *née* Hall; 3 c; *Career* brewing industry exec, specialist dir Whitbread & Co, md Thomas Wethereds of Marlow 1976-81; HM Diplomatic Serv 1966-71, second sec Vientiane 1968-70 (third sec 1966-68); *Recreations* fishing, shooting, private flying; *Clubs* Brook's, RAC; *Style*— Hugh Whitbread Esq; The Old Rectory, Dennington, Woodbridge, Suffolk; Kinlochewe Lodge, Achnasheen, Ross-shire

WHITBREAD, Michael William; 2 s of Col William William Whitbread; *b* 25 June 1930; *Educ* Stowe; *m* 1965, Helen Mary, *née* Aikenhead; 1 s, 1 da; *Career* brewery dir, pres Licenced Victualler's Nat Homes 1981-82; ret; *Recreations* shooting, fishing, rugby; *Style*— Michael Whitbread, Esq; The Grey House, Turkdean, Northleach, Glos (☎ 0457 60389)

WHITBREAD, Samuel Charles; DL (1974); s of Maj Simon Whitbread (d 1985), of Bedford, and Helen Beatrice Margaret, *née* Trefusis; family settled in Bedfordshire at time of Conquest, founded Brewery 1742, 1 Tory and 5 Whig/Liberal MPs; *b* 22 Feb 1937; *Educ* Eton, Trinity Coll Cambridge; *m* 1961, Jane Mary, da of Charles William John Hugh Hayter (d 1985), of Oxfordshire; 3 s (Charles, Henry, William), 1 da (Victoria); *Career* dir: Whitbread & Co plc 1972 (chm 1984), Whitbread Investmt Co plc 1977, Brewers' Soc Cncl 1984, Whitbread Share Ownership Tstees Ltd 1984, Whitbread Pension Tstees Ltd 1984, SC Whitbread Farms 1985; landowner (10800 acres); *Recreations* shooting, photography, music, travel; *Clubs* Brooks's; *Style*— Samuel Whitbread, Esq, DL; Southill Park, Biggleswade, Bedfordshire (☎ 0462 813272); Brewery, Chiswell St, London EC1Y 4SD (☎ 01 606 4455, telex 888640)

WHITBREAD, Col William Henry; TD 2 Bars; s of Henry William Whitbread (d 1947), of Norton Bavant, Westbury, Wilts and Mary *née* Ryamond (d 1925); Landed Gentry Family, Robert Wytbred of Gravenhurst mentioned in the subsidy Rolls 1309 Samuel Whitbread (d 1796) the eminent brewer was MP Bedford 1768-90 and had his seat at Southilll rebuilt by Holland, his s Samuel (d 1815) MP Bedford 1790-1815, m Lady Elizabeth Grey eld da 1 Earl Grey, subsequent Whitbread's have been MPs and m into the Peerage.; *b* 22 Nov 1900; *Educ* Eton, Corpus Christi Coll Cambridge (MA); *m* 1, 27 April 1927, Anne Joscelyne (d 1936), da of Samuel Howard Whitbread, CB (d 1944), of Southill Park, Beds; 2 s (Henry Charles b 1928, Michael William b 1930), 1 da (Mary Joscelyne, Mrs Humphry T Tollemache, (*see* Baronetage) b 1933); m 2, 26 April 1941, Betty Parr, da of Samuel Russell (d 1940), of 18 Grange Road, Eastbourne; 1 s (Hugh William b 1942), 2 da (Isabella Margaret Ruth b 1946, Sarah Maud b 1950); *Career* chm Whitbread Investment Co and Whitbread Int 1944-70 (dir: 1927); dir: Barclays Bank, Eagle Star Insurance Co; vice pres Brewers Soc (chm 1952-53), Inst of Brewing (chm research ctee); memb: Hurlingham Polo Ctee 1932-45, Field Sports Ctee 1950; Master Trinity Foot Beagles 1921-23; *Recreations* hunting, stalking, shooting, fishing, sailing; *Clubs* Brook's, Pratts, Thames Yacht, Royal Yacht Squadron, Jockey; *Style*— Col William Whitbread, TD; Haslehurst, Haslemere, Surrey; Farleaze, nr Malmesbury, Wilts; The Heights of Kinlochewe, Ross-shire

WHITBY, Charles Harley; QC (1970); s of Arthur William Whitby (d 1983), of Acton, Middx, and Florence, *née* Edwards (d 1982); *b* 2 April 1926; *Educ* St Johns Leatherhead, Peterhouse Cambridge (MA); *m* 11 Sept 1981, Eileen May, da of Albert George Scott (d 1978), of Palmers Green, London N13; *Career* RAFVR 1944-48; barr Middle Temple 1952, bencher 1977, memb Bar Cncl 1969-71 and 1972-78, rec Crown Court 1972-; Criminal Injuries Compensation Bd 1975-; contrib: Halsbury Laws of Eng, Atkins Encyclopedia of Court Forms; *Recreations* reading, golf, watching soccer, fishing, swimming; *Clubs* Utd Oxford and Cambridge Univ, RAC (steward 1985-), Garrick, Woking Golf; *Style*— Charles H Whitby, Esq, QC; 12 Kings Bench Walk, Temple, EC4 (☎ 01 583 0811)

WHITBY, Prof (Lionel) Gordon; s of Sir Lionel Ernest Howard Whitby, CVO, MC, MD (d 1956), of The Masters Lodge, Downing Coll, Cambridge, and Ethel, *née* Murgatroyd; *b* 18 July 1926; *Educ* Eton, King's Coll Cambridge (BA, MA, PhD, MB BChir, MD), Middx Hosp Med Sch London; *m* 29 July 1949, Joan Hunter, da of William Sanderson (d 1969), of 14 Blackford Rd, Edinburgh; 1 s ((Lionel) Michael b 1952), 2 da (Anne Rosemary (Mrs Priestley) b 1950, Pamela Jean (Mrs Molyneaux) b 1954); *Career* fell King's Coll Cambridge 1951-55, jr med appts in London 1956-59, Rockefeller travelling scholarship in med Nat Inst of Health USA 1959-60, univ biochemist Addenbrooke's Hosp Cambridge 1960-63, fell Peterhouse Cambridge 1961-62, prof of clinical chemistry Edinburgh Univ 1963- (dean faculty of med 1969-72 and 1983-86, vice princ 1979-83); tstee Nat Library of Scotland 1982-, vice pres Royal Soc of Edinburgh 1983-86, memb Br Library Advsy cncl 1986-; memb: Dept of Health, Scottish Home and Health dept, professional advsy ctees 1965-81, Med Laboratory Technicians Bd, Cncl for Professions supplementary to MED 1978-; memb Worshipful Co of Glovers of London; MRCS, LRCP 1956, FRCPE 1968, FRCP 1972, FRCPath 1972, FIBiol 1988; *Books* Lecture Notes on Clinical Chemistry (with A F Smith and G J Beckett, fourth edn 1988), Principles & Practice of Medical Computing 1971); *Recreations* gardening, photography; *Clubs* RSM; *Style*— Prof Gordon Whitby; 51 Dick Place, Edinburgh EH9 2JA (☎ 031 667 4358); Dept of Clinical Chemistry, The Royal

Infirmary of Edinburgh, Edinburgh EH3 9YW (☎ 031 667 1011 ext 2533)

WHITCOMBE, Maj John Douglas Hawkes; s of Eric Aubrey Hawkes Whitcombe, (of Christchurch, NZ, later of Sevenoaks Kent and Wallingford Oxon (d 1967, 4 s of George Hawkes Whitcombe, fndr of publishing firm of Whitcombe and Tombs NZ), and Anna Templeton (d 1977), da of D Young, JP, DL, of Glasgow, and sis of Sir Arthur Stewart Leslie Young, 1 Bt, MP, Min of State SO 1950; *b* 3 Nov 1917; *Educ* Winchester, RMC Sandhurst; *m* 4 Nov 1943, Heather Madeline, da of Capt Geoffrey William Sherston, MC (d 1944), of Olliver, Richmond, Yorks; 4 s (Jonathan b 1950, James b 1951, Mark b 1954, Nicholas b 1959), 1 da (Rosemary b 1947, d 1968); *Career* cmmnd Highland LI 1937, Temp Capt France and Belgium 1939-40, Temp Maj Italy and Greece 1944-47, Maj Hong Kong and Malaya 1949-52, Egypt 1952-54, Fort George Inverness-shire 1954-55, Cyprus 1956, BAOR 1957-58, UK HQ Scottish Cmd and Inf Records 1959-69, Royal Highland Fusiliers, ret 1969 (despatches 1940, 1957); churchwarden Goldsborough Parish Church; *Recreations* most games, shooting; *Style—* Maj J D M Whitcombe; Allerton House, Knaresborough, Yorks (☎ 0423 330488)

WHITCOMBE, Hon Mrs; Hon Rosemary Anne Heather; *née* Colville; da of late 1 Baron Clydesmuir, GCIE, TD, PC; *b* 1927; *m* 1954, Philip Arthur Whitcombe; 1 s, 1 da; *Style—* The Hon Mrs Whitcombe; Green Cross Farm, Churt, Farnham, Surrey

WHITE, Hon Caroline Davina; da of 5 Baron Annaly by his 2 w, Jennifer; *b* 8 Feb 1963; *Style—* The Hon Caroline White

WHITE, (James George) Charles; s of James Samuel Michie White (d 1954), and Sophia, *née* Mortimer (d 1956); *b* 14 Dec 1921; *Educ* Robert Gordon's Coll Aberdeen, Univ of Aberdeen (MA), St John's Coll Cambridge (BA); *m* 12 Aug 1947, Katharine Isobel Mary, da of William Peterkin Masson, of Nethy Bridge, Inverness-shire; 4 s (David b 1948, Peter b 1953, John b 1955, Christopher b 1962), 2 da (Ann b 1951, Patricia b 1960); *Career* Royal Fus 1942 (SOAS London), Corpl transferred to Intelligence Corps Interrogation centre Delhi 1943, cmmnd Lt 1944, served Burma 1944-45, Capt 1945, Maj 2 i/c of intelligence unit and head of interrogation wing SE Asia Singapore 1946, demob 1947; Baillie Gifford & Co Investmt Mangrs: investmt mgmnt trainee 1949-55, ptnr 1955-75, sr ptnr 1975-84; non-exec dir: Scottish Mortgage and Tst 1978-, New Ct Tst 1979-87, Equity Consort Investmt Tst 1979-, The Baillie Gifford Japan Tst 1981-; memb Scottish Equitable Life Assoc Soc 1971-, tstee memb exec ctee and chm investmt ctee Carnegie Tst for the Univ's of Scotland, ct memb and fin ctee convenor Heriot-Watt Univ 1977-83; Hon DLitt Heriot-Watt Univ 1986; *Recreations* reading, photography, steam locomotives; *Clubs* New (Edinburgh); *Style—* Charles White, Esq; 51 Braid Ave, Edinburgh EH10 6EB (☎ 031 447 2395); Glebe Cottage, Longformacus, Dune, Berwickshire TD11 3PE (☎ 03617 256)

WHITE, Christoher John Waring; s of Arthur John Stanley White, CMG, OBE, of The Red House, Mere, Wilts, and Joan, *née* Elston-Davies; *b* 21 Nov 1933; *Educ* Marlborough, Clare Coll Cambridge (BA); *m* 11 April 1959, Shirley Diana, da of Sir Kenneth Oswald Peppiatt, KBE, MC (d 1983); 1 da (Annabel b 1961); *Career* Lt Royal Hampshire Regt 1952-54; Joseph Travers & Sons Ltd 1957-60, George Harker & Co Ltd 1960-70; chm F & E Clarke Ltd 1983- (joined 1970), dir The Corn Exchange Co Ltd; memb Chiltern Dist Cncl 1979-83, chm Penn Parish Cncl 1983- (memb 1976-); Freeman Worshipful Co of Makers of Playing Cards 1969-; *Style—* Christopher White, Esq; Ray's Yard, Penn, Bucks (☎ 049 481 3238); 52 Mark Lane, London EC3 (☎ 01 481 8707, fax 01 702 3716, telex 886881)

WHITE, Sir Christopher Robert Meadows White; 3 Bt (UK 1937), of Boulge Hall, Co Suffolk; s of Sir (Eric) Richard Meadows White, 2 Bt (d 1972); *b* 26 August 1940; *Educ* Bradfield; *m* 1962, Anne Marie Ghislaine (m dis 1968), da of late Maj Tom Brown, OBE, MC; m 2, 1968, Dinah Mary Sutton (m dis 1972); m 3, 1976, Ingrid Carolyn, da of Eric Jowett, of Gt Baddow, Essex; *Heir* none; *Career* formerly schoolmaster; housemaster St Michael's Sch Ingoldisthorpe Norfolk 1963-69; *Style—* Sir Christopher White, Bt; 101 Thunder Lane, Norwich, Norfolk

WHITE, David Julian; s of Arthur John Stanley White, CMG, OBE; *b* 17 July 1942; *Educ* Marlborough; *m* 1967, Claire Rosemary, *née* Emett; 3 da; *Career* dep chm Cater Allen Holdings plc;; *Style—* David White Esq; Flint House, Penn Street, nr Amersham, Bucks (☎ 0494 713262); Cater Allen Ltd, 1 King William St, London EC4N 7AU (☎ 01 623 2070, telex 888553/4)

WHITE, Diane, Lady; Diane Eleanor Abdy; da of late Bernard Abdy Collins, CIE, of Deccan House, Aldeburgh; *m* 1939, Sir George Stanley Midelton White, 3 Bt (d 1983); 1 s (Sir George White, 4 Bt, *qv*), 1 da; *Style—* Diana, Lady White; Acton House, Park Street, Iron Acton, nr Bristol

WHITE, Sir Dick Goldsmith; KCMG (1960), KBE (CBE 1950, OBE 1942); s of Percy Hall White; *b* 20 Dec 1906; *Educ* Bishop's Stortford Coll, Ch Ch Oxford, Michigan Univ, California Univ; *m* 1945, Kathleen Somers Bellamy; 2 s; *Career* previously with FCO until 1972; *Style—* Sir Dick White, KCMG, KBE; The Leat, Burpham, Arundel, W Sussex

WHITE, Hon Doone Patricia; da of 5 Baron Annaly by his 2 w, Jennifer; *b* 16 June 1961; *Style—* The Hon Doone White

WHITE, Baroness (Life Peeress UK 1970); Eirene Lloyd White; da of Thomas Jones, CH, of Aberystwyth; *b* 7 Nov 1909; *Educ* St Paul's Girls' Sch, Somerville Oxford; *m* 1948, John White (d 1968); *Career* former journalist and civil servant; MP (Lab) Flint E 1950-70; min state: Foreign Affrs 1966-67, Welsh Off 1967-70; chm Labour NEC 1968-69, takes l whip in Lords; chm select ctee EEC and princ dep chm Ctees House of Lords 1979-82, a dep Speaker House of Lords 1979; memb Royal Commission on Environmental Pollution 1974-80, pres Montgomeryshire Soc 1981-82; chm cncl UNWIST Cardiff 1984-; hon fell Somerville Coll Oxford; Hon LLD: Wales 1979, Queen's Univ Belfast 1982, Bath 1983; *Style—* The Rt Hon The Lady White; 64 Vandon Court, Petty France, SW1H 9HF (☎ 01 222 5107); House of Lords SW1A 0PW (☎ 01 219 5435)

WHITE, Lady; Elizabeth Victoria Mary; da of Wilfrid Wrightson, JP (3 s of Sir Thomas Wrightson, 1 Bt, JP, DL, sometime MP Stockton and St Pancras E); *m* 1943, Sir Headley White, 3 Bt (d 1971); 1 s (Sir John Woolmer White, 4 Bt, *qv*), 2 da (Morna b 1944, Isabelle b 1948); *Style—* Lady White; Salle Park, Reepham, Norfolk

WHITE, Hon Mrs; Hon Frances Alice; da (by 1 m) of 3 Baron Fisher; *b* 1951; *m* 1981, Angus J White; 1 s (Thomas, b 1983), 1 da (Sally b 1985); *Style—* The Hon Mrs White; Cooks Farm, Nuthurst, nr Horsham, Sussex

WHITE, His Hon Judge Frank John; s of Frank Byron White (d 1984), of Reading, and Renée Marie Therése, *née* Cachou (d 1972); *b* 12 April 1927; *Educ* Reading Sch, King's Coll London (LLB, LLM); *m* 11 April 1953, Anne Rowlandson, da of Sir Harold Gibson Howitt, GBE, DSO, MC; 2 s (Stephen b 29 Sept 1955, Simon b 27 Aug 1963), 2 da (Teresa b 31 Aug 1958, Louise b 8 Sept 1961); *Career* Sub Lt RNVR 1945-47; barr Grays Inn 1951, memb Gen Cncl of The Bar 1969-73, dep chm Berks QS 1970-72, rec Crown Ct 1972-74, circuit judge 1974-; memb: Lord Chllrs Legal Aid Advsy Ctee 1977-83, Judicial Studies Bd 1985-; *Books* Bench Notes for Assistant Recorders (1988); *Recreations* walking, gardening; *Clubs* Athenaeum, Roehampton; *Style—* His Hon Judge Frank White; 8 Queens Ride, London SW13 0JB

WHITE, Sir Frederick William George; KBE (1962, CBE 1954); s of late William Henry White; *b* 26 May 1905; *Educ* Wellington Coll, Vic Univ Wellington, NZ Univ (MSc), Cambridge Univ (PhD); *m* 1932, Elizabeth Cooper; 1 s, 1 da; *Career* chm: CSIRO 1959-70, Aust and NZ Assoc for the Advancement of Science 1970-; FAA, FRS, FInstP, FAIRE; *see Debrett's Handbook of Australia and New Zealand for further details*; *Style—* Sir Frederick White, KBE; 57 Investigator St, Red Hill, Canberra, ACT 2603, Australia (☎ 957 424)

WHITE, Geoffrey Ian; s of Alderman George White (d 1970); *b* 16 Nov 1928; *Educ* Dulwich Coll, Corpus Christi Coll Oxford; *m* 1956, (m dis 1985), Hazel, *née* Allenby; 2 s, 1 da; *Career* memb Beckenham Borough Cncl 1955-65; conslt Fleming Montagu Stanley): 1987- (formerly Montagu Leobl Stanley, dir 1986, dep sr ptnr 1978-, fin ptnr 1984-83, ptnr 1959); FRSA; *Recreations* theatre, opera, gardening, watching rugby, cricket, wine; *Clubs* City of London; *Style—* Geoffrey White, Esq; Pilgrim Cottage, Godstone, Surrey RH9 8BL (☎ 0883 842232); Montagu, Loebl, Stanley, 31 Sun St, London EC2M 2QP (☎ 01 377 9242, telex 885941)

WHITE, Air Vice-Marshal George Alan; CB (1984), AFC (1973); s of James Magee White, and Evangeline, *née* Henderson; *b* 11 Mar 1932; *Educ* Univ of London (LLB); *m* 1955, Mary Esmé, *née* Magowan; 2 da; *Career* pilot 1956, RAF Staff Coll 1964, HQ Middle East Command 1966-67, 11 Sqdn 1968-70, 5 Sqdn 1970-72, Nat Defence Coll 1972-73, dir of ops (air defence and overseas) 1977-78, Air Cdre Plans HQ Strike Cmd 1981-82, dep cdr RAF Germany 1982-; *Style—* Air Vice-Marshal George White, CB, AFC; c/o Williams & Glyn's Bank Ltd, Kirkland House, Whitehall, London SW1A 2EB

WHITE, Sir George Stanley James; 4 Bt (UK 1904), of Cotham House, Bristol; s of Sir George Stanley Midelton White, 3 Bt (d 1983, md Bristol Aeroplane Co, and gs of Sir George White, 1 Bt, pioneer of Electric Street Traction, fndr first Eng aeroplane factory and responsible for introduction of Bristol Biplanes and Monoplanes), and Diane, Lady White, *qv*; *b* 4 Nov 1948; *Educ* Harrow; *m* 1974 (m dis 1979), Susan, da of John Ford; 1 da; m 2, Elizabeth, da of Sir William Reginald Verdon-Smith, and formerly w of Robert Clinton; 1 da; *Career* horologist; Keeper of the Collection of the Worshipful Co of Clockmakers; *Books* English Lantern Clocks (1988); *Style—* Sir George White, Bt

WHITE, Maj-Gen Gilbert Anthony; MBE (1944) ; s of Cecil James Lawrence White (ka 1918), and Muriel, *née* Collins (d 1985); *b* 10 June 1916; *Educ* Christ's Hosp; *m* 22 Sept 1939, Margaret Isabel Duncan (Joy), da of Arthur Wallet (d 1952); 2 da (Susan (Mrs Neil Weir), Caroline); *Career* joined Artists Rifles TA 1936, cmmnd E Surrey Regt 1938, Adj 1/6 Surreys BEF France 1940, Tunisian Campaign 1943, Staff Coll Camberley 1944, Bde Maj 10 Inf Bde Italy 1944, directing staff Staff Coll Haifa 1945, memb UK delgn to mil staff ctee UN NYC 1946-48, regtl duty Egypt and UK 1948-54, mil asst CIGS 1954, regtl duty and instr Latimer 1954-59, cmd 1 Bn E Surrey Regt 1959-61, personal staff to Lord Mountbatten MCD 1961-62, Brig cmd 56 (London) TA Bde 1962-64, Imperial Def Coll 1965, BGS HQ BAOR 1966-69, Maj-Gen JSLO 1969-71; clerk with Lloyd's Brokers 1933-39, memb Lloyd's 1938-; memb cncl Guide Dogs for the Blind 1972-; *Recreations* indifferent golfer and even worse shot; *Clubs* Army and Navy; *Style—* Maj-Gen Gilbert White, MBE; Speedkell, Tekels Avenue, Camberley, Surrey (☎ 0276 23812)

WHITE, Sir (Vincent) Gordon Lindsay; KBE (1979); s of Charles White; *b* 11 May 1923; *Educ* De Aston Sch Lincs; *m* 1; 2 da; m 2, 1974 (m dis), Virginia Anne; 1 s; *Career* WWII served SOE; chm Welbecson Ltd 1947-65, dep chm Hanson Tst 1965-73, chm Hanson Industs 1983-; memb and chm Int Ctee USA Congressional Award Fndn 1984-; hon fell St Peter's Coll Oxford 1984-; Nat Voluntary Leadership Award Congressional Award 1984; memb: cncl for the Police Rehabilitation Appeal 1985-, bd of dirs Shakespeare Theatre Folger Library Washington 1985-, cncl City Technol Colls Tst 1987-, chm Zoological Soc of London Devpt Tst 1988; Aims of Industry Free Enterprise Award 1985-; *Clubs* Special Forces, The Brook (NY); *Style—* Sir Gordon White, KBE; 410 Park Ave, New York, NY 10022, USA (☎ 212 759 8477; telex 96 17 75)

WHITE, Hugh Collins; s of William Mitchell White, of Maybole, Ayrshire, and Mary Ann Luke, *née* Collins; *b* 21 Oct 1944; *Educ* Kilmarnock Acad, MacIntosh Sch of Arch (Cert in Arch); *m* 23 Aug 1968, Betsy, da of Bernard Lizar Zive (d 1977), of Ayr; 2 da (Kirstine b 1971, Sheona b 1974); *Career* chartered architect in private practice; corp memb RIBA; *Recreations* equestrian driving, photography, restoring horse drawn vehicles; *Style—* Hugh White, Esq; 17 Cargill Rd, Maybole, Strathclyde KA19 8AF (☎ (0655) 82188)

WHITE, Rear Admiral Hugo Moresby; CBE; s of Hugh Fortescue Moresby White, CMG (d 1979), and Betty Sophia Pennington, *née* Brandt; *b* 22 Oct 1939; *Educ* Dragon Sch, BRNC Pangbourne, RNC Dartmouth; *m* 16 April 1966, Josephine Mary Lorimer, da of Dr John Meavious Pedler, of Adelaide, S Aust; 2 s (Jonathan b 26 Feb 1968, Thomas b 8 Jan 1971); *Career* RN; Lt HMS Blackpool 1960-61 Kuwait; on diesel submarines: HMS Tabard 1962-64, HMS Tiptoe 1964, HMS Odin 1964-65; navigation course HMS Dryad 1966, navigator HMS Warspite 1966-68, Lt Cdr HMS Osiris 1968-69, CO HMS Oracle 1970-71, staff BRNC Dartmouth 1971-73 Cdr submarine sea trg HMS Neptune 1973-75, CO HMS Salisbury 1975-77 (Cod War), with naval secs dept MOD 1977-78, Capt naval plans MOD 1978-80, CO HMS Avenger and Capt 4 Frigate Sqdn (Falklands) 1980-82, Cdre PSO to CDS MOD 1982-85, CO HMS Bristol and Flag Capt to FOF2 1985-87, Rear Adm Flag Offr Flotilla 3 and cdr ASW Strike Force 1987-88, asst chief of naval staff MOD 1988- ; *Recreations* sailing, travelling, gardening; *Clubs* Army and Navy; *Style—* Rear Adm Hugo White, CBE; c/o Naval Secretary, Old Admiralty Building, Whitehall, London SW1A 2BE

WHITE, Ian Jeremy; s of Walter Douglas White, of Melcombe, Lewes Rd, Haywards Heath, Sussex, and Eileen Gordon, *née* Ford; *b* 19 Feb 1943; *Educ* Brighton Coll, Coll of Estate Mgmnt, Univ of London; *m* 14 Sept 1968, Julia Louise, da of Charles Leonard Walker (d 1945), and Helen Maud Walker; 1 s (Jeremy Mark b 27 Feb 1975), 2 da (Samantha Louise b 14 Oct 1970, Justine Ruth b 28 June 1972); *Career* dir Richard Ellis SA 1986 (ptnr UK 1982, joined 1962); Brighton Coll: memb gen cncl, memb fin and gen purposes ctee, memb property ctee, former tstee scholarships funds; ctee memb city branch Guide Dogs for Blind Assoc; Freeman City of London, Liveryman Worshipful Co Innholders and Worshipful Co of Surveyors; FRICS 1968; *Recreations* cricket, tennis; *Clubs* MCC, Free Forester, Roehampton; *Style—* Ian White, Esq; Hyannis, Brook Lane, Haywards Heath, Sussex RH16 1SG (☎ 0444 414836); Richard Ellis, Berkeley Sq House, London W1X 6AN (☎ 01 629 6290, car tel 0836 225285)

WHITE, Ian Shaw; s of Frank White, of May Hill, Glos, and Joan, *née* Shaw; *b* 30 July 1952; *Educ* Bromsgrove Sch Worcs, Churchill Coll Cambridge (MA); *m* 18 Oct 1980, Susan Elizabeth, da of Capt Alan Francis Bacon, of Purley, Surrey; 2 s (Duncan b 1985, Gordon b 1988); *Career* ptnr W Greenwell and Co 1984-86; dir: Greenwell Montagu 1986-88 (head of research 1987-88), Kleinwort Benson Securities 1988-; memb AMSIA; *Recreations* travel, philosophy, family; *Style—* Ian White, Esq; 12 Dove Park, Chorleywood, Herts (☎ 092 78 3051); Kleinwort Benson Securities, 20 Fenchurch St, London EC3P 3DB (☎ 01 623 8000, fax 01 623 5606, telex 922241)

WHITE, James; s of John White (d 1985), of Cleland, Lanarkshire, and Helen, *née* Beattie; *b* 22 Oct 1937; *m* 1961, Mary, da of Alex Jardine (d 1940); 2 da (Jane b 1975, Helen b 1976); *Career* chartered accountant (Scotland); former dir: sales and marketing SKF (UK), Lex Service Gp; chm Bunzl plc 1988- (md 1981-88); dir: Lucas Industries plc 1985-, Redland plc, Beecham plc; chm Ashley Gp plc; *Recreations* golf, gardening, athletics; *Clubs* St Stephen's Constitutional; *Style—* James White, Esq; The Moat House, Annables Lane, Kinsbourne Green, Harpenden, Herts (☎ 0582 64387); Bunzl plc, Stoke House, Stoke Green, Stoke Poges, Slough SL2 4JN (☎ 0753 693, fax 0753 694 694, telex 847503)

WHITE, James; s of James White of Whiteinch, Glasgow; *b* 1922; *Educ* Knightswood Secdy Sch; *m* 1948, Mary Elizabeth, da of Peter Dempsey, of Glasgow; 1 s, 2 da; *Career* joined Lab Pty 1946, sponsored by TGWU, md Glasgow Car Collection Ltd 1959-; memb Cwlth Parly Assoc Delgn: Bangladesh 1973, Nepal 1981; MP (Lab) Glasgow Pollok 1970-87; *Style—* James White Esq, MP; 23 Alder Road, Glasgow

WHITE, Hon Mrs; Hon Jessica Jane Vronwy; *née* Scott-Ellis; da of 9 Baron Howard de Walden and 5 Baron Seaford; co-heiress of Barony of Howard de Walden; *b* 6 August 1941; *m* 1966, Adrian Tancred White; 4 s; *Style—* The Hon Mrs White; Farnborough Downs Farm, Wantage, Oxon

WHITE, John; s of John Wesley White (d 1972), and Emily, *née* Brown (d 1981); *b* 21 Dec 1934; *Educ* Brentwood Sch Essex; *m* 28 Aug 1960, Annette Kitty, da of Godfrey William Allnutt (d 1985); 2 s (Jeremy b 1965, Timothy b 1968), 1 da (Philippa b 1963); *Career* CA, sr ptnr Peat Marwick and McLintock 1986- (ptnr Middle East 1972-85); memb: PCC, Essex Naturalists Tst; FCA 1958, AMCA 1961; *Recreations* walking, gardening, cricket; *Clubs* Reform; *Style—* John White, Esq; Crownfields, Kelvedon Hatch, Brentwood, Essex; 1 Puddle Dock, Blackfriars, London EC4

WHITE, Rev Canon John Austin; s of Charles White (d 1976), and Alice Emily, *née* Precious (d 1967); *b* 27 June 1942; *Educ* Batley GS Yorks, Univ of Hull (BA), Coll of the Resurrection Mirfield; *Career* asst curate St Aidan's Church Leeds 1966-69, asst chaplain Leeds Univ 1969-73, Chaplain Northern Ordination Course 1973-82, canon St George's Chapel Windsor Castle 1982- (canon precentor 1984-); memb directing staff St George's House Windsor Castle 1982-, convenor Nat Conf on the Care of the Dying, vice-chm govrs Princess Margaret Royal Free Sch Windsor; *Recreations* medieval iconography, cooking, poetry; *Style—* The Rev Canon John White; 8 The Cloisters, Windsor Castle, Windsor SL4 1NJ (☎ 0753 860 409); 2 Queen's Staithe Mews, York

WHITE, John Dudley George; s of John Leslie White (d 1962), of Strathdale, Streatham, London and Winifred Emily, *née* Bachelor (d 1962); *b* 6 August 1937; *Educ* Emanuel Sch London; *m* 20 March 1965, Lorraine Judith Anne, da of Raymond Stanley Ives (d 1981), of Dial House, Chipstead, Surrey; 2 s (Harvey b 1966, Gregory b 1969); *Career* chm and md Electrowares Gp of Cos 1979-86; chm: WC Pickering Ltd 1972-87, E & M Construction Ltd 1969-88, Electrical Wholesalers Fedn; cnclr Electrical and Electronic Industs Benevolent Assoc; Freeman City of London 1971, Master Worshipful Co Lightmongers 1981, Liveryman Worshipful Co of Tallow Chandlers 1975; FBIM 1973; *Recreations* yachting (The City of London); *Clubs* RAC, Royal Southern YC, City Livery; *Style—* John White, Esq; High Woods, The Glade, Kingswood, Surrey KTZO 6LH; Forge Cottage, West Lulworth, Dorset (☎ 0737 832052)

WHITE, Prof John Edward Clement Twarowski; CBE 1983; s of Brig A E White, and Suzanne, *née* Twarowska; *b* 4 Oct 1924; *Educ* Ampleforth, Trinity Coll Oxford, Courtauld Inst of Art (BA), Warburg Institute (PhD); *m* 19 Oct 1950, Xenia, *née* Joannides; *Career* WWII Pilot RAF 1943-47, demob as Flt Lt; reader in history of art Courtauld Inst 1958-59 (lectr 1952-58), Alexander White visiting prof Univ of Chicago 1958, Pilkington prof of history of art Manchester Univ and dir of Whitworth Art Gallery 1959-66, Ferens visiting prof of fine art University of Hull 1961-62, chm art advsy panel NW Museum and Art Gallery Servs 1962-66, prof of history of art and chm of dept of history of art John Hopkins Univ Baltimore 1966-71, Durning-Lawrence prof of history of art UCL 1971- (vice-provost 1984-88); vice pres Comite Int d'Histoire de l'Art 1986-, chm Assoc of Art Historians 1976-80; memb: bd of dirs Coll Art Assoc 1970, advsy cncl V & A 1973-76, exec ctee Assoc of Art Historians 1974-81, art panel of Arts Cncl 1974-78, reviewing ctee on Export of Works of Art 1975-82, visiting ctee RÇA 1976-86, Armed Forces Pay Review Body 1986-; tstee Whitechapel Art Gallery; FSA; *Books* Perspective in Ancient Drawing and Painting (1956), The Birth and Rebirth of Pictorial Space (third edn, 1987), Arts and Architecture in Italy 1250-1400 (second edn, 1987), Duccio: Tuscan Art and the Medieval Workshop (1979), Studies in Renaissance Art (1983); articles in: Art History, Arts Bulletin, Burlington Magazine, Jl of Warburg and Courtauld Insts; *Recreations* Athenaeum; *Style—* Prof John White, CBE; 25 Cadogan Place, London SW1; Department of History of Art, University coll, 39-41 Gordon Sq, London WC1H OPD (☎ 01 387 7050, fax 01 387 0857)

WHITE, Prof John William; CMG (1981); s of George Alexander John White (d 1977), of New Lambton HTS, Newcastle, and Jean, *née* Mackay; *b* 25 April 1937; *Educ* Newcastle Boys HS (NSW), Aust, Sydney Univ (BSc, MSc), Oxford Univ (MA, DPhil); *m* 24 July 1966, Ailsa Barbara, da of Arthur Ambrose Vise, of Southport, Queensland; 1 s (David George Blithe b 1973), 3 da (Sarah Kirsten Jean b 1968, Catherine Naomi b 1970, Rachel Mary b 1974); *Career* ICI fell Lincoln Coll Oxford 1961-63, official fell St Johns Coll Oxford 1963-85, Marlowe Medal Faraday Soc 1968, Tilden lectr Royal Soc of Chem 1976, neutron beam co-ordinator AERE Harwell 1973-75, dir Institut von Laue Langevin Grenoble 1977-80 (dep dir 1975-77), assessor Oxford Univ 1981-82, prof of physical and theoretical chem Aust Nat Univ Canberra 1985-; Argonne fell Univ of Chicago and Argonne Nat Laboratory USA 1985-; prof of physical and theoretical chem Hulme Project for Schs Oxford 1983-85; churchwarden Rhowe Alps Parish 1976-80, memb cncl: Epsom Coll 1980-85, Wycliffe Hall Oxford 1981-85; pres: Royal Aust Chem Inst (Canberra 1987), Aust Soc of Crystallographers 1987; FRS Chem 1981, FRAust Chem Inst 1985, FAust Inst Phys 1986; *Recreations* skiing, squash, family; *Style—* Prof John White, CMG; 2 Spencer St, Turner Act 2601, Australia (☎ 062 486836); Research Sch of Chemistry, Australian Univ, PO Box 4, Acton 2601, Act, Australia (☎ 062 493578, fax 062 487817)

WHITE, Sir John Woolmer; 4 Bt (UK 1922), of Salle Park, Norfolk; s of Sir Headley Dymoke White, 3 Bt (d 1971); *b* 4 Feb 1947; *Educ* Cheltenham, Royal Agric Coll Cirencester; *m* Joan, da of late T D Borland, of Flemington, W Linton, Peeblesshire; 1 s; *Heir* s, Kyle Kymoke Wilfrid White b 16 March 1988; *Style—* Sir John White, Bt; Salle Park, Reepham, Norfolk

WHITE, Hon Luke Richard; s and h of 5 Baron Annaly by his 1 w, Lady Marye Pepys, da of 7 Earl of Cottenham; *b* 29 June 1954; *Educ* Eton, RAC Cirencester; *m* 1983, Caroline Nina, yr da of Col Robert Garnett, MBE, of Hope Bowdler House, Church Stretton, Shropshire, 1 da (b 1987); *Career* late Lt Royal Hussars; *Style—* The Hon Luke White

WHITE, Sir Lynton Stuart; MBE (1943), TD, DL (Hants); s of Sir Dymoke White, 2 Bt, JP, DL (d 1968), *qv*, and Isabelle Stuart, *née* MacGowan (d 1982) ; *b* 11 August 1916; *Educ* Harrow, Trinity Coll Cambridge (MA); *m* 1945, Phyllis, da of Sir Newnham Worley, KBE (d 1976); 4 s (Anthony, Richard, Robert, Philip), 1 da; *Career* TA; 2 Lt RA 1939, served WWII UK 1939-40, Far East 1940-45 (despatches), Hon Lt-Col RA (TA) 1946, TARO 1948-71; memb Hampshire CC 1970 (vice-chm 1976, chm 1977-85); kt 1985; *Recreations* country pursuits; *Clubs* United Oxford and Cambridge Univ, East India; *Style—* Sir Lynton White, MBE, TD, DL; Oxenbourne House, East Meon, Petersfield, Hants

WHITE, (Edward) Martin Everatt; s of Frank White (d 1983), of Shrewsbury, and Norah Kathleen, *née* Everatt (d 1959); *b* 22 Feb 1938; *Educ* Priory Boys GS Shrewsbury, King's Coll Cambridge (MA); *m* 10 May 1969, Jean Catherine, da of James Orr Armour (d 1987), of Manchester; 1 s (Robert b 1978), 1 da (Susannah b 1975); *Career* admitted slr 1962; chief exec: Winchester City Cncl 1974-80, Bucks CC 1980-88, Nat Assoc of Citizens Advice Bureaux 1988-; govr Ashfold Sch; CBIM 1987; *Books* The Role of the Chief Executive in Information Technology (1987); *Recreations* gardening, walking, other outdoor pursuits; *Style—* Martin White, Esq; The Spinney, Sevenacres, Long Crendon, Aylesbury, Bucks HP18 9DU (☎ 0844 208914); National Association of Citizens Advice Bureaux, 115-123 Pentonville Road, London N1 9LZ (☎ 01 833 2181)

WHITE, Michael John; s of Albert Ernest White (d 1979), and Doris Mary White, *née* Harvey; *b* 4 April 1955; *Educ* Langdon Sch, Oxford Univ (MA); *Career* barr Middle Temple, music critic and librettist; *Books* The Adjudicator (opera libretto); *Recreations* travel, composition, The Church of England (occasionally); *Style—* Michael John White, Esq; c/o The Independent, 40 City Road, London EC1

WHITE, Michael Simon; s of Victor R White and Doris G White; *b* 16 Jan 1936; *Educ* Lyceum Alpinum Zuoz Switzerland, Pisa Univ, Sorbonne Paris; *m* 1, 1965, (m dis 1973), Sarah Hillsdon; 2 s, 1 da; m 2, 1985, Louise, da of Nigel Moores (d 1977); 1 s (b 1985); *Career* theatre and film producer; asst to Sir Peter Daubeny 1956-61; *stage prodns* (London) incl: Rocky Horror Show, Sleuth, America Hurrah, Oh, Calcutta!, The Connection, Joseph and the Amazing Technicolour Dreamcoat, Loot, The Blood Knot, A Chorus Line, Deathtrap, Annie, Pirates of Penzance, On Your Toes, Metropolis; films incl: Monty Python and the Holy Grail, Rocky Horror Picture Show, My dinner with André, Ploughman's Lunch, Moonlighting, Stranger's Kiss, The Comic Strip presents Supergrass, High Season, Eat The Rich, White Mischief; *Books* Empty Seats (1984); *Recreations* art, ski-ing, racing; *Clubs* Turf, RAC, Rocks (LA); *Style—* Michael White, Esq; 13 Duke St, St James's, SW1 (☎ 01 839 3971)

WHITE, Dr Norman Arthur; s of Charles Brewster White (d 1969), of Co Durham, and Lilian Sarah, *née* Finch (d 1975), of Great Malvern; *b* 11 April 1922; *Educ* London Univ, Manchester Inst of Science and Technol (BSc, AMCT), Harvard Business Sch, Univ of Philippines, LSE (PhD, MSc, DMS, AMP); *m* 1, 1944, Joyce Marjorie (d 1982), *née* Rogers; 1 s (Howard Russell b 1945), 1 da (Lorraine Avril b 1949); m 2, 1983, Marjorie Iris, da of William Colenso Rushton (d 1947), of London; *Career* Royal Dutch Shell Gp 1945-72; petroleum res engr Thornton Research Centre 1945-51, tech mangr Shell Co Philippines 1951-55; Shell Int Petroleum: dep mangr product devpt div 1955-61, gen mangr lubricants bitumen and LPG Divs 1963-66, dir mktg devpt and dep to gp mktg co-ordinator 1966-68; chm and dir Shell Oil and mining cos in UK and Europe 1963-72, chief exec new enterprises div 1968-72, plural assignments 1972-; dir and princ exec Norman White Assocs 1972-; dir: Environmental Resources Ltd 1973-87, Henley Centre for Forecasting 1974- (dep chm 1974-87); dir chm Exec Ctee Tanks Oil & Gas Ltd 1974-85, dep chm Strategy Int Ltd 1976-82; chm: KBC Advanced Technologies Ltd 1979-, American Oil Field Systems plc 1980-85; dep chm Br Canadian Resources Ltd 1980-83; chm: Ocean Thermal Energy Conversion Systems Ltd 1982-, Tesel plc 1983-85 (dir 1980-85), Process Automation & Computer Systems Ltd 1984-, Kelt Energy plc 1986-87 (dir 1985-88), Andaman Resources plc 1986-; memb int energy/petroleum delgns to: USSR, China, Rumania, East Germany, Japan, Korea, India, Mexico, Argentine, Brazil 1979-; memb Parly and scientific ctee House of Commons 1977-83 and 1987-; chm Br nat ctee World Petroleum Congresses (WPC) 1987- (vice chm 1977-87); memb: cncl IMechE 1980-85 and 1987-, cncl InstPet (vice pres) 1975-81, Royal Soc Mission to People's Republic of China 1985, UK CAA Ctee of Enquiry on Flight Time Limitations (Bader Ctee) 1972-73; visiting prof Univ of Manchester 1981-; memb of senate London Univ 1974-87; govr: King Edward VI Royal GS Guildford 1976-, Reigate GS 1976-; Freeman City of London 1983, Liveryman: Worshipful Co of Engineers 1984, Worshipful Co of Spectacle Makers 1986; memb Royal Inst of Int Affrs and Royal Inst; CEng; FInstD, FBIM, FRSA, FIMechE; *Books* Financing the International Petroleum Industry (1979); *Recreations* family, country and coastal walking, wild life, browsing, international affairs, comparative religions, domestic odd-jobbing; *Clubs* Athenaeum, City Livery, Harvard (London), IOD; *Style—* Dr Norman A White; Green Ridges, Downside Road, Guildford, Surrey GU4 8PH (☎ 0483 67523); 9 Park House; 123/125 Harley Street,

London W1N 1HE (☎ 01 935 7387, telex 21792, fax 01 935 5573)

WHITE, Adm Sir Peter; GBE (1977), KBE (1976, CBE 1960, MBE 1944); s of William White (d 1936), and Gertrude Frances, *née* Turner (d 1972), of Amersham, Bucks; *b* 25 Jan 1919; *Educ* Dover Coll; *m* 1947, Audrey Eileen, da of Ernest Wallin, of Kingsthorpe, Northampton; 2 s; *Career* served RN 1937-1977, Adm (princ staff offr to CDS 1967-69, dir-gen Fleet Services 1969-71, Port Adm Rosyth 1972-74, chief of fleet support 1974-77); conslt Wilkinson Match Ltd 1978-79; assoc dir Educn for Industl Soc 1979-88, chm cncl Offrs Pension Soc 1982-, memb Fndn Ctee Gordon Boys' Sch 1980-; *Recreations* riding, gardening; *Clubs* Army and Navy; *Style—* Adm Sir Peter White, GBE, KBE; c/o Westminster Bank, 26 The Haymarket, London SW1Y 4ER

WHITE, Capt Richard Taylor; DSO (1940, and bars 1941 and 1942); s of Sir Archibald Woolaston White, 4 Bt (d 1954), and hp of bro, 5 Bt; *b* 29 Jan 1908; *Educ* RNC Dartmouth; *m* 1936, Gabrielle Ursula, yr da of Capt Robert Style, JP (n of Sir William Style, 9 Bt); 3 s, 2 da; *Career* WWII RN served: Atlantic, Med, Far East; Capt RN Coll Dartmouth 1951-53; *Style—* Captain Richard White, DSO, RN; Tilts House, Boughton Monchelsea, Maidstone, Kent ME17 4JE (☎ 0622 43465)

WHITE, Roger; s of Geoffrey White, of Home Cottage, Didmarton, Badminton, Avon, and Zoe, *née* Bowler; *b* 1 Sept 1950; *Educ* Ifield GS, Christs Coll Cambridge (BA), Wadham Coll Oxford; *Career* hist building div GLC 1979-83, sec the Georgian Gp 1984-; pres Oxford Univ Architectural Soc 1975-76, memb ctee Painswick Rococo Garden 1985-; FSA 1986; *Books* John Vardy (in The Architectural Outsiders, 1985), Georgian Arcadia: Architecture for the Park and Garden (exhibition catalogue, 1987); *Recreations* looking at old buildings; *Style—* Roger White, Esq; The Georgian Gp, 37 Spital Sq, London E1 6DY (☎ 01 377 1722)

WHITE, Roger John Graham; s of Alfred James White (d 1976), of Kingston Hill, Kingston, and Doris Elizabeth, *née* Robinson (d 1973); *b* 30 April 1940; *Educ* Tiffen Sch; *m* 18 Jun 1966, Elizabeth, da of Tom Lionel Greenwood, of Knap Hill, Woking, Surrey; 2 s (Graham b 1968, Andrew b 1970), 1 da (Katherine b 1977); *Career* chartered accountant; ptnr Peat Marwick McLintock 1974- (sr tax ptnr 1981); FCA 1962, FTII 1970; *Books* The Trading Company (1978), Purchase of Own Shares (1983); *Recreations* bridge, gardening, books; *Style—* Roger White, Esq ; 1 Puddle Dock, Blackfriars, London EC4V 3PD (☎ 01 236 8000, fax 01 248 6552 (Group 3), telex 8811541 PMM LON G

WHITE, (Wilfred) St John; s of Richard St John White (d 1932), of Wellington Lodge, Bristol, and (Gladys) Lucy, *née* Jones; *b* 28 Nov 1922; *Educ* Merchant Venturers Coll Univ of Bristol; *m* 22 Aug 1974, Kyoko (d 1978), da of Dr Ray Igarashi (d 1938), of Tokyo, Japan; *Career* res engr Telecommunications Res Estab 1942-46 (devpt of RADAR for RAF); Decca Ltd (later Racal Decca Ltd) 1946-: devpt engr 1946-, dir of up to forty cos within the gp Electronic Position Fixing System (won Queen's Award for Technological Innovation 1969), dir responsible for mktg of Decca Navigational System (internatoinal standard), dir Decca Avionics Mktg, involved in devpt North Sea Resources 1963-, currently dir Racal Oil and Gas; dir SENA Ltd and DSKK Ltd of Japan 1965-; memb sales and export ctee, Soc Br Aerospace Cos 1982; MIEE 1947, FInstD 1954, MRIN 1955, cncl memb Electronic Engr Assoc 1975-88; memb: Air League 1982, Royal Aeronautical Soc 1986; *Books* Christmas Island Cracker (1987); *Recreations* swimming and squash; *Clubs* The Naval & Military; *Style—* St John White, Esq; Dolphin Sq, London SW1 (☎ 01 828 3600); Mukoyama, Nerimaku, Tokyo (☎ 03 990 2546); Racal-Decca Ltd, New Malden, Surrey (☎ 01 942 2460, fax 01 949 1273, telex 22852)

WHITE, Stephen Frank; s of Judge Frank John White, of Queens Ride, London, and Anne Rowlandson, *née* Howitt, MBE; *b* 29 Sept 1955; *Educ* Eton, Bristol Univ (BA); *Career* accountant Price Waterhouse and Co 1977-81, Phillips and Drew 1981-83, Hill Samuel Investmt Mgmnt Ltd 1983-85, Foreign and Colonial Mgmnt, F & C Euro Fund SA, F & C Nordic Fund SICAV; Freeman Worshipful Co of Merchant Taylors; ACAG; *Recreations* opera, gardening, swimming; *Style—* Stephen F White, Esq; 86 Archel Road, London, W14 9QP (☎ 01 385 5815); c/o Foreign and Colonial Management Ltd, 1 Laurence Pountney Hill, London, EC4R 0BA (☎ 01 623 4680)

WHITE, Stephen John; s of George Edward White, and Doreen Ivy White; *b* 23 July 1948; *Educ* St Olaves GS; *m* 24 April 1971; 2 da (Claire Louise b 1975, Victoria Emily b 1978); *Career* dir WCRS Gp plc, dep chm WCRS-Mathews Marcantonio; MAA, MIPA, MCAM; *Recreations* tennis, swimming, boating, vintage cars; *Clubs* RAC, Vanderbilt; *Style—* Stephen White, Esq; c/o Lloyds Bank, 9 High Street, Bromley, Kent; W.C.R.S Group plc, 41/44 Gt Queen St, London WC2B 5AR

WHITE, Terence de Vere; s of Frederick S de Vere White, and Ethel, *née* Perry; *b* 29 April 1912; *Educ* St Stephen's Green Sch Dublin, Trinity Coll Dublin (BA, LLB); *m* 1, 1941 (m dis 1982), Mary O'Farrell; 2 s, 1 da; m 2, 1982, Hon Victoria Glendinning, *qv*; *Career* admitted slr 1933, memb cncl Incorporated Law Soc, ret 1961; author; literary editor Irish Times 1961-77, vice-chm bd of govrs National Gallery of Ireland; trustee: National Library 1946-79, Chester Beatty Library 1959-80; dir Gate Theatre 1969-81, memb Irish Academy of Letters 1968; Hon RHA 1968, hon prof of literature RHA 1973, FRSL; *Books* The Road of Excess, Kevin O'Higgins, The Story of the Royal Dublin Society, A Fretful Midge, A Leaf from the Yellow Book, An Affair with the Moon, Prenez Garde, The Remainder Man, Lucifer Falling, The Parents of Oscar Wilde, Tara, Leinster, Ireland, The Lambert Mile, The March Hare (1970), Mr Stephen (1971), The Anglo-Irish (1972), The Distance and the Dark (1973), The Radish Memoirs (1974), Big Fleas and Little Fleas (1976), Chimes at Midnight (1977), Tom Moore (1977), My Name is Norval (1978), Birds of Prey (1980), Johnnie Cross (1983), Chat Show (1987); *Clubs* Garrick, Kildare St and University (Dublin); *Style—* Terence White, Esq; c/o Allied Irish Banks, 100 Grafton St, Dublin 2, Eire

WHITE, Sir Thomas Astley Wollaston; 5 Bt (UK 1802), of Wallingwells, Nottinghamshire; JP (Wigtownshire 1952); s of Lt-Col Sir Archibald White, 4 Bt, TD (d 1945); *b* 13 May 1904; *Educ* Wellington; *m* 1935, Daphne Margaret, da of Lt-Col Francis Remi Imbert Athill, CMG, OBE, DL (d 1958), of Harbottle Castle, Morpeth, Northumberland; *Heir* bro, Capt Richard Taylor White, DSO, RN, *qv*; *Career* FRICS, Hon Sheriff Substitute Wigtownshire; *Style—* Sir Thomas White, Bt, JP; HA Hill, Torhousemuir, Wigtown, Newton Stewart DG8 9DJ (☎ 09884 2238)

WHITE, Victor Oscar; s of Arthur Albert White (d 1976), and Gisela Lydia, *née* Wilde; *b* 30 August 1936; *Educ* Michael Hall Sch Forest Row, London Univ (LLB); *m* 28 March 1967, Susan Raynor, da of Raynor Leslie Jones, of Praia, Daluz, Portugal; 2 s (Christopher b 1968, Jonathan b 1974), 1 da (Katherine b 1971); *Career* slr; joined ICI Legal Dept 1965, appointed gp slr ICI 1980; memb Law Soc; *Style—* Victor White, Esq; Ballards, Tompsets Bank, Forest Row, Susex; ICI Gp Legal Dept, 9 Millbank, London SW1P 2JF (☎ 01 834 4444, fax 01 834 2042, telex 21324)

WHITE-THOMSON, Christopher Trefusis; yr s of Maj Walter Norman White-Thomson (3 s of Rt Rev Leonard W-T, sometime Bishop of Ely, by his w Hon Margaret Trefusis, 3 da of 20 Baron Clinton); *b* 22 Feb 1940; *Educ* Harrow, RMA Sandhurst; *m* 1967, Juanita Maria, da of Frederick Arthur Rowlands, of Catania, Sicily; 1 s (Charles b 1969), 1 da (Kate b 1971); *Career* formerly Capt Royal Fusiliers; joined Cater Ryder & Co 1969, chief exec Oppenheimer Fund Management 1982-87, dir Mercantile House Hldgs 1980-87, Parrish plc 1988-; *Clubs* Army and Navy; *Style—* Christopher White-Thomson, Esq; Parrish plc, 4 London Wall Bldgs, London EC2M 5NX (☎ 01 638 1282)

WHITE-THOMSON, Very Rev Ian Hugh; s of Rt Rev Leonard Jauncey White-Thomson, Bishop of Ely (d 1933), and Margaret Adela Hepburn Stuart Forbes Trefusis (d 1939); *b* 18 Dec 1904; *Educ* Harrow, Oxford Univ; *m* 1954, Wendy Ernesta, da of Gp Capt Frank Hawker Woolliams (d 1980); 2 s, 2 da; *Career* ordained 1929, rector St Martin with St Paul Canterbury 1934-39, chaplain to Archbishops of Canterbury (Lang, Temple, and Fisher) 1939-47, vicar of Folkestone 1947-55; chaplain to: HM King George VI 1947-52, HM The Queen 1952-63; archdeacon of Northumberland 1955-63, dean of Canterbury 1963-76; *Recreations* painting; *Style—* The Very Rev Ian White-Thomson; Camphill, Wye, Kent (☎ 0233 812210)

WHITECROSS, Richard Peter; s of John Francis Whitecross (d 1977), and Edna Margaret, *née* Robbins (d 1979); *b* 28 July 1945; *Educ* Univ Coll of Wales Aberystwyth (BA); *m* 14 July 1972, Cristina Elvira, da of German Lange Rosario, of Argentina; 2 s (Mathew b 1977, Thomas b 1980); *Career* regnl dir OUP Consortium Latin America 1970-76, dir Blackwell's Mainstream Book Club 1978-79, mktg conslt Phillips Fine Art Auctioneers 1984-; *Recreations* book collecting; *Style—* Richard P Whitecross, Esq; 35 Linkside Ave, Oxford OX2 8JE; Phillips Auctioneers, 39 Park End Street, Oxford OX1 1JD (☎ 0865 723524)

WHITEFIELD, Robert Henry; s of Henry Whitefield (d 1987), and Lily Josephine, *née* Rolt; *b* 9 Jan 1937; *Educ* Charterhouse; *m* 4 Dec 1965, Diana, da of Lt-Col R C Barrow (d 1968), of Farmington, Glos; 1 s (George b 1983), 3 da (Melanie b 1968, Anna b 1970, Serena b 1984); *Career* Nat Serv 1956-58, 2 Lt RE; dir Jamesons Chocolates plc 1960 (md 1972, chm 1987); *Recreations* sailing, skiing, water colour painting, gardening, photography; *Clubs* Royal Cruising, Royal Ocean Racing, Old Carthusian; *Style—* Robert H Whitefield, Esq; The Old Rectory, Stocking Pelham, Buntingford, Herts SG9 0HU (☎ 027 978 303); Jamesons Chocolates plc, Willoughby Lane, London N17 0RX (☎ 01 807 4417)

WHITEHEAD, Hon Mrs; Hon Annabel Alice Hoyer; *née* Millar; LVO (1986); da of 1 Baron Inchyra, GCMG, CVO; *b* 25 Jan 1943; *m* 1973, Christopher James Bovill Whitehead; 1 s, 1 da; *Career* lady-in-waiting to HRH The Princess Margaret, Countess of Snowdon 1971-75, extra lady-in-waiting 1975-; *Style—* The Hon Mrs Whitehead, LVO; 5 Vicarage Gdns, London W8

WHITEHEAD, Christopher James Bovill; s of Thomas Bovill Whitehead, of Wiltshire, and Christine Margaret, *née* Dixon; *b* 9 Feb 1939; *Educ* Eton Coll; *m* 1973, Annabel Alice, da of Lord Inchyra, of Perthshire; 1 s (Robert William Bovill b 1977), 1 da (Christina Daisy Elizabeth b 1975); *Career* memb The Stock Exchange London 1962-; chm TC Coombs & Co 1979-; *Clubs* White's, City of London, MCC; *Style—* Christopher Whitehead, Esq; 4-5 Bonhill Street, London EC2A 4BX (☎ 01-588 6209, telex 881 3804, fax 01-628 5174)

WHITEHEAD, Capt David; s of Herbert John Whitehead (d 1984), of Sparsholt, Winchester, Hants, and Doreen Mary, *née* Knight; *b* 10 Mar 1934; *Educ* Bickley Hall Kent, Wrekin Sch; *m* 24 Oct 1959, Annarosa, da of Lt-Col Leonard Henry Dismore, OBE, TD (d 1956), of Canterbury, Kent; 2 s (Nicholas b 9 Oct 1960, James b 23 Oct 1962), 2 da (Tanya b 9 June 1964, Deborah b 10 Jan 1969); *Career* cadet Britannia RN Coll 1950, cmmnd Sub Lt 1954, OC HMS Droxford 1958-60, Long Communications Course 1961, Lt Cdr Flag Lt to Flag Offr Flotillas (Home) 1962, CO HMS Wakeful 1968, CO HMS Grenville 1969, staff communications offr to Cdr Hong Kong and CO Hong Kong Naval Wireless Station 1970, Cdr sr offr Hong Kong Sqdn and CO HMS Yarnton 1971, OC user requirements and trials section Directorate of Naval Signals 1972, Naval Staff 1974-77, exchange serv with US Naval Staff with responsibility for int interoperability in cmd control and communications (cited for Legion of Merit) 1978-80, Capt asst dir cmd control and communications policy Def Staff 1980, dir def fixed telecommunications system Def Staff 1982, Dep Chief Naval Signal Offr 1984, ret 1985; dir tech liaison Racal Gp Servs Ltd 1985-, dir (UK) Nuits St James Ltd 1988; FBIM 1978, MNI 1979, memb Lloyds; *Recreations* maritime affairs, photography, travel; *Clubs* Special Forces; *Style—* Capt David Whitehead, RN; 33 Harewood Ave, London NW1 6LE (☎ 01 723 0551); Swanmore Pk, Hants SO3 2QS; Chez Spaud, 24410 St Aulaye, France; Racal Group Services Ltd, Western Rd, Bracknell, Berks RG12 1RG (☎ 0344 483 244 ext 2120, fax 0344 54119, telex 848239)

WHITEHEAD, Dr Denis Sword; s of Henry Whitehead (d 1979), and Alice, *née* Nicholson (d 1942); *b* 8 May 1927; *Educ* Uppingham Sch, Cambridge Univ (MA, PhD); *m* 21 June 1951, Frances Cabot Paine (Frankie), da of Frank Cabot Paine (d 1952), yacht designer and builder of Wayland, Mass; 3 s (Henry, Frank, Ian), 1 da (Anne (Mrs Prebensen)); *Career* with Rolls-Royce 1948-54, lectr and reader Cambridge Univ 1957-85; engrg conslt 1985-; fell Jesus Coll Cambridge 1962-; contrib chapter on Aerolasticity in Turbomachines to AGARD Manual; MIMechE, MRAeS, CEng; *Recreations* sailing, golf, fishing; *Clubs* RAC; *Style—* Dr Denis Whitehead; Inwoods, Earleigh Wick, Bradford-on-Avon, Wilts BA15 2PU (☎ 02216 3207)

WHITEHEAD, His Hon Judge (Garnet) George Archie; DFC (1944); s of Archibald Payne Whitehead (d 1943), and Margaret Elizabeth Whitehead (d 1919); *b* 22 July 1916; *m* 1946, Monica, da of Bertie Watson (d 1974), of York; 2 da (Margaret Elizabeth b 1949, Monica Jane b 1955); *Career* joined RAF 1939, Flt Lt (pilot) Bomber Cmd and Tport Cmd; slr admitted 1949, circuit judge appointed 1977; *Recreations* walking, photography; *Style—* His Hon Judge Whitehead, DFC; 15 Burton Close, Boston, Lincs PE21 9QW (☎ 0205 64977)

WHITEHEAD, John Michael Stannage; JP (1968), DL (1988); s of (Arthur) Stannage Whitehead, JP (d 1946), of Stechford, Elms Rd, Leicester, and Isaline, *née* Baker, JP (d 1974); *b* 19 Dec 1927; *Educ* Uppingham, Leicester Tech Coll (now Leicester Poly); *m* 28 April 1962, Alanda Joy, da of Geoffrey Taylor Bentley (d 1987), of Acorns, Esher Park Ave, Esher, Surrey; 1 s (Michael John Stannage b 1968), 2 da

(Penelope Josephine b 1963, Belinda Louise (Mrs Kearns) b 1964); *Career* 2 Lt Army Cadet Corps 1945-48, Special Constabulary 1950-68; dir: G Stibble & Co Ltd 1948-74, J & H Hadden Ltd 1954-63; md Stibbe-Hadden Ltd 1963-74 (chm 1963-72), chm John Whitehead Textiles Ltd 1974-, name Lloyds of London 1979-, chm H Harrison & Co Finishers Ltd 1987-; tax cmmr 1966; chm govrs: Leicester Poly 1974-(vice-chm 1971-74), Leicester Poly Higher Educn Corpn 1988-; memb various charities; Freeman: City of London, City of Leicester; Liveryman Worshipful Co Merchant Taylors 1951, Master Worshipful Co Framework Knitters 1978 (Liveryman 1952); FRSA 1978; *Recreations* watching rugby football, sailing, gardening, reading; *Clubs* Leicestershire; *Style—* John Whitehead, Esq, JP, DL; The Poplars, Main St, Houghton on the Hill, Leicester LE7 9GD (☎ 0533 412 244); John Whitehead Textiles Ltd, 23 Lancaster St, Leicester LE5 4GD (☎ 0533 762 861, fax 0533 460 215, telex 34376 WP LSTR)

WHITEHEAD, Sir John Stainton; KCMG (1986), CVO (1978); s of John William Whitehead (d 1946), and Kathleen Mary Whitehead (d 1981); *b* 20 Sept 1932; *Educ* Christ's Hosp Horsham, Hertford Coll Oxford (MA); *m* 1 Feb 1964, (Mary) Carolyn, da of Henry Whitworth Hilton (d 1985); 2 s (Simon b 1966, James b 1973), 2 da (Sarah b 1968, Jessica b 1971); *Career* chief clerk FCO 1984-86; HM ambass to Japan 1986-; *Recreations* music, travel, golf, tree-felling, chess; *Clubs* Beefsteak United Oxford and Cambridge Univ, Liphook Golf; *Style—* Sir John Whitehead, KCMG, CVO; Bracken Edge, High Pitfold, Hindhead, Surrey GU26 6BN; British Embassy, Tokyo, Japan

WHITEHEAD, Hon Mrs (Lucia Edith); *née* Lawson; da of Maj-Gen 4 Baron Burnham, CB, DSO, MC, TD (d 1963); *b* 29 August 1922; *m* 1, 1946 (m dis 1953), Hon Roger David Marquis (later 2 Earl of Woolton; d 1969); m 2, 1966, John Whitehead (d 1982); *Career* served WW II 1941-46 as CSM ATS (despatches); *Style—* The Hon Mrs Whitehead; Hallin, 18 Burnham Avenue, Beaconsfield, Bucks

WHITEHEAD, Dr (John Ernest) Michael; s of Dr Charles Ernest Whitehead (d 1939), of London, and Bertha Ivy, *née* Harding (d 1945); *b* 7 August 1920; *Educ* Merchant Taylors' Sch, Gonville and Caius Coll Cambridge (MA, MB BChir), St Thomas's Hosp Med Sch (Dip Bact); *m* 3 Aug 1946, Elizabeth Bacchus, da of Col George Walker Cochran, DSO (d 1970); 1 s (Stephen Michael b 1947), 1 da (Anne Elizabeth b 1951); *Career* co cdr 7 Bn Cambridgeshire HG 1940-42; first lectr in bacteriology St Thomas' Hosp Med Sch London 1949-51, dep dir Public Health Laboratory Sheffield 1953-58, hon lectr in bacteriology Univ of Sheffield 1954-58, dir Public Health Laboratory Coventry 1958-75, hon lectr in bacteriology Univ of Birmingham 1962-75, dir Public Health Laboratory Serv 1981-85 (dep dir 1975-81), conslt advsr in med microbiology DHSS 1981-85, temp advsr WHO 1976-81; specialist advsr to House of Commons select ctee on Agric 1988-; FRCPath (1974, vice pres 1983-86), chm Assoc of Med Microbiologists 1983-85; *Recreations* skiing, modern languages, house and garden maintenance; *Clubs* Athenaeum; *Style—* Dr Michael Whitehead; Martins, Lee Common, Great Missenden, Bucks HP16 9JP (☎ 0240 20492)

WHITEHEAD, Philip Henry Rathbone; s and h of Sir Rowland Whitehead, 5 Bt; *b* 13 Oct 1957; *Educ* Eton, Bristol Univ; *m* 1987, Emma Charlotte, da of Capt Alexander Michael Darley Milne Home, RN, of Sydney, Australia; *Career* late Lt Welsh Gds; GSM; *Clubs* Special Forces, Cavalry and Gds, Royal Geographical Soc; *Style—* Philip Whitehead, Esq; 8 Herbert Crescent, London SW1X 0EZ

WHITEHEAD, Phillip; s of Harold Whitehead (d 1961), and Frances May *née* Kingman (d 1966); *b* 30 May 1937; *Educ* Lady Manners Sch Bakewell, Exeter Coll Oxford (MA); *m* 1967, Christine Hilary, da of Thomas George Usborne, of Surrey; 2 s (Joshua b 1969, Robert b 1971), 1 da (Lucy b 1974); *Career* cmmnd Sherwood Foresters 1956 Lt Oxford 1958-61; writer and TV prodr, BBC producer 1961-67; ed The Week Thames TV 1967-70; MP (Lab) Derby N 1970-83, front bench spokesman Higher Educn 1981-83; chm Fabian Soc 1978-79; presenter Credo LWT 1983-85; columnist The Times 1983-85; dir: Goldcrest Film & TV Hldgs 1984-, Consumers Assoc 1982-; chm: New Society Ltd 1984-, Statesman Nation Publications 1984- (chm 1985-); FRSA; *Style—* Phillip Whitehead, Esq; Mill House, Rowsley, Matlock, Derbys DE4 2EB (☎ (0629) 732 659); Brook Productions, 103 Wardour St, London W1V 1LM (☎ 01 439 9871)

WHITEHEAD, Sir Rowland John Rathbone; 5 Bt (UK 1889), of Highfield House, Catford Bridge, Kent; ggs of 1 Bt, sometime Lord Mayor of London; s of Maj Sir Philip Henry Rathbone Whitehead, 4 Bt (d 1953); *b* 24 June 1930; *Educ* Radley, Trinity Hall Cambridge (BA); *m* 3 April 1954, Marie-Louise, da of Arnold Christian Gausel, of Stavanger, Norway; 1 s, 1 da; *Heir* s, Philip Henry Rathbone Whitehead, *qv*; *Career* chm: Rowland Hill Benevolent Fund (PO) 1983-, govrs of Appleby Sch Cumbria, chm and fndr The Baronets' Trust; chm exec ctee of Standing Cncl of the Baronetage 1984-86; Liveryman Fruiterers Co, Freeman City of London; *Books* Cybernetics: Communication of Control (Handbook of Management Technology); *Recreations* poetry, rural indolence; *Clubs* Arts; *Style—* Sir Rowland Whitehead, Bt; Sutton House, Chiswick Mall, London W4 (☎ 01 994 2710)

WHITEHEAD, Prof Thomas Patterson; CBE (1985); *b* 7 May 1923; *Educ* Salford Royal Tech Coll, Birmingham Univ (Ph D); *m* 20 Sept 1947, Doreen Grace, *née* Whitton; 2 s (Paul b 1948, David b 1952), 1 da (Jill b 1955); *Career* biochemist S Warwicks Hosp Gp 1950-60, conslt biochemist Queen Elizabeth Hosp Birmingham 1968-86, dir Wolfson Res Laboratories 1972-84, Dean of Faculty of Medicine Birmingham Univ 1984-87, scientific advsr BUPA Health Care; MRCP (Hon), FRCPath, FRSC; *Books* Quality Control in Clinical Chemistry (1976); *Recreations* growing and exhibiting sweet peas; *Clubs* Athenaeum; *Style—* Prof Tom Whitehead, CBE; 70 Northumberland Rd, Leamington Spa, Warwickshire CV32 6HB (☎ 0926 21974); BUPA Medical Research BUPA Medical Centre, 300 Grays Inn Rd, London WC1X 8DU (☎ 01 837 6484, fax 01 837 6646)

WHITEHORN, John Roland Malcolm; CMG (1974); s of Alan Drummond Whitehorn (d 1980), and Edith Marcia Whitehorn (d 1981); *b* 19 May 1924; *Educ* Rugby, Trinity Coll Cambridge (BA); *m* 1, 1951 (m dis 1973) Josephine, *née* Plummer; m 2, 1973, Marion, *née* Gutmann; *Career* Flying Offr RAFVR 1943-46, Far East; overseas dir: FBI 1963 (joined 1947), CBI 1965-68; dep dir-gen CBI 1966-78, dir Mitchell Cotts plc 1978-86, conslt dir Lilly Industs Ltd 1978-; memb: BOTB 1975-78, Gen Advsy Ctee BBC 1976-82, bd Br Cncl 1968-82; *Clubs* Reform; *Style—* John Whitehorn, Esq, CMG; Casters Brook, Cocking, Midhurst, W Sussex GU29 0HJ

WHITEHORN, Katharine Elizabeth; da of Alan Drummond Whitehorn (d 1980), of Marlborough and London, and Edith Marcia, *née* Gray (d 1982); *Educ* Blunt House, Roedean, Glasgow HS for Girls, Newnham Coll Cambridge (MA); *m* 4 Jan 1958, Gavin Tudor Lyall, s of Joseph Tudor Lyall; 2 s (Bernard b 1964, Jake b 1967); *Career* publisher's reader 1950-53, secdy teacher Finland 1953-54, graduate asst Cornell Univ USA 1954-55, Picture Post 1956-57, Woman's Own 1958, Spectator 1959-61; columnist The Observer 1960- (assoc ed 1980-88); dir: Nationwide Anglia (formerly Nationwide) Bldg Soc 1983-, Nationwide Anglia Estate Agents 1987-; memb: Latey ctee on Age of Majority 1965-67, BBC advsy gp on Social Effects of Television 1971-72, bd Br Airports Authy 1972-77, cncl RSM 1982-85; rector St Andrew's Univ 1982-85; Hon LLD St Andrews 1985; memb NUJ; *Books* Cooking in a Bedsitter (1960), Roundabout (1961), Only on Sundays (1966), Whitehorn's Social Survival (1968), Observations (1970), How to Survive in Hospital (1972), How to Survive Children (1975), Sunday Best (1976), How to Survive in the Kitchen (1979), View from a Column (1981), How to Survive your Money Problems (1983); *Recreations* a small river boat; *Clubs* Royal Soc of Med; *Style—* Ms Katharine Whitehorn; c/o The Observer, Chelsea Bridge House, Queenstown Road, London SW8 4NN (☎ 01 627 0700)

WHITEHOUSE, Brian Paul; s of Rev Sydney Paul Whitehouse (d 1978); *b* 24 May 1933; *Educ* Manchester GS, CCC Oxford; *m* 1958, Jane Margaret da of Lt Cmdr John Roberts-West (d 1942); 4 c; *Career* 2 Lt Northamptonshire Regt; dir Hambros Bank 1970-; *Recreations* croquet, bridge, racing; *Style—* Brian Whitehouse, Esq; Hambros Bank, 41 Bishopsgate, EC2

WHITEHOUSE, David Rae Beckwith; s of (David) Barry Beckwith Whitehouse, MA, FRCS, FRCOG, MD, and Mary, *née* Boffey; *b* 5 Sept 1945; *Educ* Ellesmere, The Choate Sch Wallingford Connecticut USA, Trinity Coll Cambridge (MA); *m* 1 Jan 1971, Linda Jane, o da of Eric Vickers, CB, of Oakham, Rutland, Leics; 1 s (Benedict Harry Beckwith b 1978); *Career* barr Gray's Inn 1969; asst Recorder 1983; Recorder 1987; *Style—* David Whitehouse, Esq; 3 Raymond Buildings, Gray's Inn, London WC2

WHITEHOUSE, Gerard Victor; s of Cyril Whitehouse (d 1961), and Rita Jamieson, *née* Rose; *b* 4 Sept 1955; *Educ* Bishop Vesey's GS Sutton Coldfield, Sheffield Univ (LLB); *m* 9 Sept 1978, Margaret, da of Ronald Winter, of Bainbridge, Sunderland; 2 da (Louise b 1984, Emma b 1986); *Career* slr, enrolled 1980; ptnr Blakemores Slrs 1981-; *Style—* Gerard Whitehouse, Esq; Watling House, Orton on the Hill, Leicestershire (☎ 0827 880292); 8 Davenport Rd, Coventry, West Midlands (☎ 0203 716161, fax 0203 711611)

WHITEHOUSE, Mary; CBE (1980); da of James Hutcheson, and Beatrice Ethel, *née* Searanckle; *b* 13 June 1910; *Educ* Chester City GS For Girls, Cheshire Co Training Coll Grewe; *m* 23 March 1940, Ernest Raymond Whitehouse; 3 s (Paul b 4 Jan 1941, Richard 8 June 1944, Christopher 30 Dec 1945); *Career* Art Specialist at Wednesfield Sch Wolverhampton 1932-40, Bremwood GS 1943, sr mistress and sr art mistress Madeley Sch Shrops 1960-64; co-fndr Clean up TV campaign 1964, hon gen sec Nat Viewer's and Listener's Assoc 1965-80 (pres 1980-), freelance journalist/broadcaster; *Books* Cleaning Up TV (1966), Who Does She Think She is? (1971), Whatever Happened to Sex? (1977), A most Dangerous Woman (1982), Mightier than the Sword (1985); *Recreations* reading, walking, gardening; *Style—* Mrs Mary Whitehouse, CBE; Ardleigh, Colchester, Essex C07 7RH (☎ 0206 230 123)

WHITEHOUSE, Prof (Julian) Michael Arthur; s of Arthur Arnold Keer Whitehouse, of Olney, Bucks, and Kathleen Ida Elizabeth, *née* Elliston; *b* 2 June 1940; *Educ* Queens' Coll Univ of Cambridge (MA, MB, BChir), St Bartholomews Hosp of London (MD); *m* 10 April 1965, Diane France, da of Dr Raymond Maximillien Theodore de Saussure (d 1972), of Geneva, Switzerland; 1 s (Michael Alexander de Saussure b 1968) 2 da (Fiona Geraldine b 1968, Vanessa Caroline b 1972); *Career* St Barts Hosp 1976: sr lectr and acting dir dept med oncology, hon conslt physician; visiting prof: Univ of Boston 1981, Christchurch Clinical Sch of Med NZ 1986; former: vice-pres Euro Soc Med Oncology first chm UICC Cancer Chemotherapy Ctee; currently: prof med oncology and hon conslt physician Southampton Hosps, dir CRC and Wessex Regnl Med Oncology Unit Southampton; ed Hematological Oncology; govr Canford Sch Dorset; Freeman City of London, Liveryman Worshipful Co Apothecaries; FRCP, FRSM; *Books* CNS Complications of Malignant Disease (1979), A Pocket Consultant in Medical Oncology (1983), Investigation and Management (with Christopher J Williams 1984-85), Recent Advances in Clinical Oncology (1982 and 1986); *Recreations* skiing, sailing, travelling; *Clubs* Athenaeum; *Style—* Prof Michael Whitehouse; CRC Wessex Regnl Med Oncology Unit, CF99 Southampton Gen Hosp, Tremona Rd, Southampton SO9 4XY (☎ 0703 777222, ext 4296/7, fax 0703 783839)

WHITEHOUSE, Patrick Bruce; OBE (1967), JP (1971); s of Cecil Norman Whitehouse (d 1952), and Phylis Mabel, *née* Bucknall (d 1976); *b* 25 Feb 1922; *Educ* Ellesmere Coll, Warwick Sch; *m* 16 Oct 1948, Thelma, da of Capt G H Crosbie (d 1967), of Birmingham; 1 s (Christopher Michael b 1952), 1 da (Margaret Anne b 1956); *Career* WWII RAF Flt Navigator/WT Middle East, Greece, N Africa 1941-46; articled pupil OA Wainwright Chartered Quantity Surveyor 1939-41, presenter BBC Railway Roundabout 1959-63, gp bd dir Holland Hannen & Cubitts Ltd (Int Contractors) 1968-71; chm: B Whitehouse & Sons Ltd, Millbrook House Ltd (Publishers) 1976-; memb Birmingham & District Industl Safety Gp 1963-70, vice-chm licensing ctee Birmingham Magistrates 1985-, HM Cmmr Income Tax 1971-87; tstee Birmingham Railway Museum Tst, fndr memb Talyllyn Railway Soc 1950-, assoc Royal Photographic Soc 1954, memb Ho Ctee Birmingham Assoc Youth Clubs, memb Birmingham Assoc Boys Club 1972-; author over of 35 books on railway subjects; FCIB; *Recreations* photography, travel, railway history; *Clubs* Birmingham Chamber of Commerce & Industry; *Style—* Patrick B Whitehouse, Esq, OBE, JP; 32 Augustus Road, Edgbaston, Birmingham B15 3PQ; Millbrook House Ltd, 90 Hagley Road, Edgbaston, Birmingham B16 5YH (☎ 021 454 1308)

WHITELAW, Billie Honor; s of Percival Whitelaw, (d 1942), of Bradford, Yorks, and Frances Mary, *née* Williams (d 1980); *b* 6 June 1932; *Educ* Thornton GS; *m* 1, 1952 (m dis 1965), Peter Vaughan; m 2, Robert Muller; 1 s (Matthew Norreys b 1967); *Career* actress; first appearance aged 11 BBC Northern Region 1943, first West End appearance Hotel Paradiso 1954; later theatre (Joan Littlewood) 1959-60; National Theatre at Old Vic 1964- incl: Desdemona to Olivier's Othello, work with Samuel Beckett on Play, performance at Chichester, Moscow and Berlin; RSC incl: After Haggerty 1971, The Greeks; close work with Samuel Beckett 1973- incl Not I, Happy Days, Footfalls, (written especially for her) 1976, opened Samuel Beckett Theatre New York with one woman plays (also performed in Los Angeles); films incl: Charlie Bubbles 1967 (American Film Critics Award and Br Film Acad Best Supporting Actress), The Chain, Shadey, Old Girlfriends, Maurice, The Dressmaker; over 100

TV appearances incl: No Trains to Lime St, Wessex Tales, Jamaica Inn, Private Schultz, The Picnic, Imaginary Friends; awards incl: TV Actress of the Year 1960, Best TV Actress 1972, Evening Standard Best Actress 1977, Variety Club Best Actress 1977, Best Radio Actress 1987, Br Film Award Evening Standard Best Actress; active memb Amnesty International; Hon D Litt Bradford Univ 1981; *Style*— Ms Billie Whitelaw; Rose Cottage, Plum St, Glemsford, nr Sudbury, Suffolk (☎ 01 485 3252); Duncan Heath Associates (agent), Paramount House, Wardour St, London W1 (☎ 01 439 1471)

WHITELAW, Prof James Hunter (Jim); s of James Whitelaw, and Jean Ross, *née* Scott; *b* 28 Jan 1936; *Educ* Glasgow HS, Glasgow Univ (BSc, PhD), London Univ (DSc); *m* 10 July 1959, Elizabeth, da of David Dewar Williamson Shields; 3 s (Alan Scott b 1962, David Stuart b 1964, James Douglas b 1968); *Career* res assoc Brown Univ 1961-63, prof Imperial Coll 1974-(lectr 1963-69, reader 1969-74), ed Experiments in Fluids 1982-; Hon DSc Univ of Lisbon 1980; FIMechE; *Books* Principles and Practice of Laser-Doppler Anemometry (with F Durst and A Melling, 1981), Calculation Methods for Engineering Flows (with P Bradshaw and T Cebeci, 1981), Series ed Combustion Treatise also over 300 technical papers; *Recreations* music, garden, travel; *Style*— Prof Jim Whitelaw; 149A Coombe La West, Kingston Upon Thames, Surrey KT2 7DH (☎ 01 942 1836); Dept of Mechanical Engineering, Imperial Coll, London SW7 2BX (☎ 01 589 5111 ext 6207/8)

WHITELAW, 1 Viscount (UK 1983), of Penrith, Co Cumbria; William Stephen Ian Whitelaw; CH (1974), MC (1944), PC (1967), DL (Cumbria 1974, Cumberland 1967); s of William Alexander Whitelaw (s of William Whitelaw, MP Perth and chm LNER, whose unc, Alexander *m* Dorothy, da of Ralph Disraeli and niece of Benjamin, 1 and last Earl of Beaconsfield) and Helen (da of Maj-Gen Francis Russell, CMG, JP, DL, of a family long domiciled in Scotland, one of whom served under Edward III at the siege of Berwick and saw action at Hallydon Hill in 1333; her mother was Philippa, maternal gda of 6 Viscount Strangford, diplomat and author; 7 Viscount Strangford was George Smythe, supposed model for Disraeli's Coningsby); *b* 28 June 1918; *Educ* Winchester, Trinity Coll Cambridge; *m* 1943, Cecilia Doriel, yr da of Maj Mark Sprot, Royal Scots Greys, of Roxburghshire, and Meliora, herself er da of Sir John Hay, 9 Bt; 4 da; *Career* served Scots Gds WW II; landowner; DL Dunbartonshire 1952-66; MP (C) Penrith and Cumberland Borders 1955-83; pps to pres BOT 1956 and to chllr of Exchequer 1957-58, asst govt whip 1959-61, lord cmmr of Treasury 1961-62, parly sec Miny of Labour 1962-64, chief oppn whip 1964-70, lord pres of Cncl and leader of House of Commons 1970-72, sec state Northern Ireland 1972-73, for Employment 1973-74, chm Cons Party 1974-75, dep leader of Oppn and Home Affairs spokesman 1975-79, home secretary 1979-83, lord pres of Cncl and leader of House of Lords 1983-88, ret; *Clubs* White's, Carlton, County (Carlisle), Royal and Ancient Golf Club of St Andrew's; *Style*— The Rt Hon the Viscount Whitelaw, CH MC, PC, DL; Ennim, Penrith, Cumbria

WHITELEY; *see*: Huntington-Whiteley

WHITELEY, Lady Angela Mary; *née* North; yr da of Francis George, Lord North (d 1940), er s of 8 Earl of Guilford; sister of 9 Earl; raised to the rank of an Earl's da 1950; *b* 28 May 1931; *m* 18 July 1955, Peter John Henry Whiteley, eldest s of late Brig John Percival Whiteley, OBE, TD, MP, of The Grange, Bletchley, Bucks; 2 s, 1 da; *Style*— Lady Angela Whiteley; Harsfold Farmhouse, Wisborough Green, Billingshurst, Sussex

WHITELEY, Lady Anne Patricia; *née* Nevill; da of 5 Marquess of Abergavenny, KG, OBE, JP; *b* 25 Oct 1938; *m* 1971, Martin Whiteley (d 1984); 3 da (Camilla Mary b 1972, Davina Marian Beatrice b 1973, Lucinda Jane b 1978); *Style*— Lady Anne Whiteley; Dalmar House, Culworth, Banbury, Oxon OX17 2BD

WHITELEY, Gen Sir Peter John Frederick; GCB (1979, KCB 1976), OBE (1960), DL (Devon 1987); s of John George Whiteley (d 1958), by his w Irene *née* Course (d 1964); *b* 13 Dec 1920; *Educ* Bishop's Stortford Coll, Bembridge Sch, Ecole des Roches; *m* 1948, Nancy Vivian, da of William Carter Clayden (d 1943); 2 s, 2 da; *Career* joined RM 1940, Fleet Air Arm 1946-51, Staff Offr Staff Coll Camberley 1960-63, CO 42 Commando Malaysia 1965-66 (despatches), NATO Def Coll 1968, Cdr 3 Commando Bde 1968-70, Maj-Gen Commando Forces 1970-72, COS Allied Forces Northern Europe 1972-75, Cmdt Gen RM 1975-77, C-in-C Allied Forces Northern Europe 1977-79, Lt-Govr and C-in-C Jersey 1979-85; pres Devon St John's Ambulance Bde; trustee Jersey Wildlife Preservation Trust; KStJ 1980; *Recreations* sailing, skiing, music, dogs; *Clubs* Royal Western Yacht, Royal Commonwealth Society; *Style*— Gen Sir Peter Whiteley, GCB, OBE, DL; Stoneycross, Yealmpton, Devon PL8 2JZ (☎ 0752 880 462)

WHITELOCKE, Rodger Alexander Frederick; s of Leslie W S Whitelocke (d 1955), of Bulstrode, Jamaica, and Ruth M *née* Hopwood; descendent of Sir James Whitelocke b 1570 (and Family Tree in Plantagenet Roll Exeter Vol) and Bulstrode Whitelocke, Keeper of the Great Seal b 1605 (s Sir James); *b* 28 Feb 1943; *Educ* Taunton Sch, London Univ, Bart's London (MB, BS); *m* 28 July 1973, Eleonora Valerie, da of Professor W F Maunder, of Tiverton Devon; 2 s (Nicholas b 1979, James b 1984), 1 da (Katherine b 1978); *Career* house surgn St Bartholomews Hosp 1969-70, research on Prostaglandins in Ocular Inflammation Inst of Ophthalmology 1971-73, sr resident surgical offr Moorfields Eye Hosp 1976, sr registrar St Bartholomews Hosp 1977-80; conslt opthalmic surgn: St Bartholomews Hosp London, Royal Marsden Hosp London; hon conslt St Lukes Hosp for Clergy, visiting prof of visual scis City Univ London; FRCS; *Recreations* music, antiques, travel, gardening; *Clubs* The Fountain; *Style*— Rodger Whitelocke, Esq; Westwood, Heather Drive, Sunningdale, Berks; 152 Harley Street, London W1N 1HH (☎ 01 935 3834)

WHITEMAN, Prof John Robert; s of Robert Whiteman, and Rita, *née* Neale; *b* 7 Dec 1938; *Educ* Bromsgrove Sch, Univ of St Andrew's (BSc), Worcester Coll Oxford (Dip Ed), Univ of London (PhD); *m* 8 Aug 1964, Caroline Mary, da of Oswald B Leigh (d 1941); 2 s (Angus b 1967, Hamish b 1969); *Career* sr lectr RMCS Shrivenham 1963-67; asst prof: Univ of Wisconsin USA 1967-68, Univ of Texas at Austin USA 1968-70; Brunel Univ 1970-: reader numerical analysis 1970-76, (on leave Richard Merton Gäst professor Univ of Münster FRG 1975-76) prof numerical analysis and dir Brunel Inst of Computational Mathematics 1976-, (head dept mathematics and statistics 1982-); visiting prof: Univ of Kuwait 1986, Texas A and M Univ USA 1986-; memb: SERC Mathematics Ctee 1981-86, Amersham Deanery Synod C of E; Freeman City of London 1979, Liveryman Worshipful Co of Glass Sellers 1979; FIMA 1970; *Books* numerous pubns on numerical solution of differential equations (particularly finite element methods) incl: The Mathematics of Finite Elements and Applications vols 1-6 (ed 1973-88), Numerical Methods for Partial Differential Equations (ed journal); *Recreations* walking, swimming, golf, tennis, squash; *Style*— Prof John Whiteman; Institute of Computational Mathematics, Brunel Univ, Uxbridge, Middlesex UB8 3PH (☎ 0895 74 000)

WHITEMAN, Michael Norman; s of Norman Vincent Whiteman (RAFR, d 1943), and Alma Meads Whiteman; *b* 28 May 1937; *Educ* Whitgift Sch; *m* 21 Nov 1959, Josephine, da of George Henry Hobbs, of Garden Cottage, Great Durnford, Salisbury, Wilts; 1 s (James Michael b 1 April 1966), 1 da (Sarah Jane b 15 April 1963); *Career* RAF 1955-75, gen duties navigator, Sqdn Ldr; Ferranti Computer Systems Ltd 1975-82, mktg dir Mel Philips 1982-83, md Plessey Avionics Ltd 1983-; dir: Soc Br Aerospace Cos Ltd 1984-, Identification Projects Ltd 1986-; chm: Candlestar Plessey BV1 1988-, Skytrading Hldgs Ltd BV1 1988-, Skytrading BV 1989-; *Recreations* golf, gardening, reading; *Clubs* Liphook GC; *Style*— Michael Whiteman, Esq; Plessey Avionics Ltd, Martin Rd, Havant, Hants PO9 5DH (☎ 0705 493218, fax 0705 493140, car tel 0836 212 306, telex 86227)

WHITEMAN, Prof Peter George; QC (1977); s of David Whiteman (d 1988), and Betsy Bessie, *née* Coster; *b* 8 August 1942; *Educ* Warwick Secdy Mod Sch, Leyton HS, LSE (LLB, LLM); *m* 24 Oct 1971, Katherine Ruth, da of Gershon Ellenbogen; 2 da (Victoria Elizabeth b 1975, Caroline Venetia b 1977); *Career* lectr London Univ 1966-70, barr Lincoln's Inn 1967, QC 1977; vis prof: Univ of Virginia 1978, Univ of California at Berkeley 1980; memb Faculty of Laws Univ of Florida 1977-, prof of Law Univ of Virginia 1980-; attorney and cnsllr NY State 1982, bencher Lincoln's Inn 1985, recorder Crown Ct 1986-; memb ctee Unitary Tax Campaign (UK) 1982-, pres Dulwich Village Preservation Soc 1987-, memb advsy ctee Dulwich Estates Govrs Scheme of Mgmnt-; memb Bar Council; *Books* Whiteman on Income Tax (1988), Whiteman on Capital Gains Tax (1988), British Tax Encyclopedia (1965), and author num articles in learned jnls; *Recreations* tennis, jogging, hill-walking, croquet; *Style*— Prof Peter Whiteman, QC; Queen Elizabeth Building, The Temple, London EC4Y 9BS (☎ 01 353 0551, fax 01 353 1937, telex 8951414)

WHITEMORE, Hugh John; s of Samuel George Whitemore (d 1987), and Kathleen, *née* Fletcher; *b* 16 June 1936; *Educ* Judd Sch Tonbridge, King Edward VI Sch Southampton, RADA; *m* 1, July 1961 (dis 1976) Jill, *née* Brooke; m 2, May 1976, Sheila, *née* Lemon; 1 s (Tom b 1976); *Career* playwright; stage plays: Stevie 1977, Pack of Lies 1983, Breaking the Code 1986, The Best of Friends 1988, films incl 84 Charing Cross Rd (Royal Film Performance 1987); also many TV plays, dramatisations, and contribs to: The Wednesday Play, Armchair Theatre, Play for Today, etc; *Recreations* music, movies, reading; *Style*— Hugh Whitemore, Esq; c/o Judy Daish Assocs, 83 Eastbourne Mews, London W2

WHITEOAK, John Edward Harrison; s of Frank Whiteoak, and Marion Whiteoak (d 1955); *b* 5 July 1947; *Educ* Keighley Secdy Tech, Sheffield Univ (MA); *m* 1, Margaret Elisabeth, *née* Blakey (d 1980); 1 s (Roger b 1969), 2 da (Juliet b 1971, Olivia b 1973); m 2, 23 Sept 1983, Dr Karen Lynne Wallace, *née* Stevenson; *Career* positions 1966-76 with: Skipton UDC, Skipton RDC, Solihull CBC; asst co tres Cleveland CC 1976-79; gp dir fin and mgmnt servs Cheshire CC 1988- (dep co tres 1979-81, co tres 1981-88); fin advsr ACC 1984-; memb: Soc of Co Tres 1981-, Accounting Standards Ctee 1984-87, tech ctee CIPFA 1984-87, exec ctee SCT 1987; Lord of the Manor of Huntington and Cheaveley; CIPFA; *Recreations* golf, tennis; *Clubs* Eaton GC; *Style*— John Whiteoak, Esq; Huntington Hall, Huntington, Chester CH3 6EA (☎ 0244 312 901); County Hall, Chester, Cheshire (☎ 0244 602 000)

WHITER, Lt Col David Stuart; MBE (1968); s of Frank Shirley Stuart Whiter (d 1979), and Ethel Marjorie, *née* Shorland (d 1980); *b* 30 July 1930; *Educ* Radley, RMA Sandhurst; *m* 8 Feb 1958, Marcia, da of Norman Ingrey (d 1977); 1 s (Christopher b 1959), 1 da (Carey b 1965); *Career* personal staff Chief of Def MOD 1970-71 (Germany, Aden, Netherlands) Co 20 Medium Regt RA 1972-73, chief plans and exercises Intelligence HQ Allied Forces Central Europe 1973-75, Cabinet Off 1975-78, service attaché liaison offr FCO 1978-83, admin dir Br Field Sports Soc 1983 ; *Recreations* gardening, birdwatching; *Style*— Lt Col David Whiter, MBE; Shorlands, Birch Grove, Pyrford, Woking, Surrey (☎ 09323 43 771) 59 Kennington Road, London (☎ 01 928 4742)

WHITER, John Lindsay Pearce; s of Nugent Whiter (d 1966), and Jean Dorothy, *née* Pearce; *b* 10 May 1950; *Educ* Eastbourne GS; *m* 5 July 1975, Janet Dulcie Sarah, da of Dr Kenneth Oswald Albert Vickery, of Eastbourne; 1 s (Timothy b 1976), 1 da (Nancy b 1979); *Career* articled clerk and audit sr Honey Barrett & Co Eastbourne 1968-72, mangr Brebner Allen & Trapp 1973-74; managing ptnr Neville Russell 1988- (ptnr 1977-88); hon tres The Nat Club; FCA 1973; *Recreations* golf, tennis, the arts; *Clubs* The Nat; *Style*— John Whiter, Esq; 9 Papillons Walk, Blackheath Park, London SE3 9SF (☎ 01 852 3879); Neville Russell, 246 Bishopsgate, London EC2M 4PB (☎ 01 377 1000, fax 01 377 8931, telex 883410)

WHITFELD, Hon Mrs; Hon Deborah Mary; *née* Vaughan-Morgan; da of Baron Reigate, PC, *qv*; *b* 1 Sept 1944; *Educ* West Heath Sevenoaks; *m* 3 May 1966, Michael Whitfield, s of Lt-Col Ernest Hamilton Whitfeld (d 1973, whose m, Mary, *née* Curzon, was gda of 1 Earl Howe), and Iris E, *née* Scully; 2 s (Nicholas b 1968, Mark b 1971), 1 da (Melanie b 1976); *Style*— The Hon Mrs Whitfeld; Querns, Goring Heath, Oxon RG8 7RH (☎ 0491 680400)

WHITFIELD, Adrian; QC (1983); s of Peter Henry Whitfield (d 1967), and Margaret Mary Whitfield; *b* 10 July 1937; *Educ* Ampleforth Coll, Magdalen Coll Oxford (MA); *m* 1, 1962 (m dis), Lucy Caroline, *née* Beckett; 2 da (Teresa, Emily); m 2, 1971, Niamh, da of Prof Cormac O'Ceallaigh, of Dublin; 1 s (Adam), 1 da (Katharine Anna); *Career* barr Middle Temple 1964, practising on Western circuit, asst parly boundary cmmr, recorder 1981-; *Style*— Adrian Whitfield, Esq, QC; 47 Faroe Rd, London W14 0EL (☎ 01 603 8982); 3 Serjeants' Inn, EC4Y 1BQ (☎ 01 353 5537)

WHITFIELD, Hon Anna Louise; da of 2 Baron Kenswood; *b* 6 June 1964; *Style*— The Hon Anna Whitfield

WHITFIELD, Lady Fiona Catherine; *née* Sinclair; da (by 1st marr) of late 19 Earl of Caithness; *b* 27 Oct 1941; *m* 10 Jan 1969, Maj Michael Stephen Whitfield; 1 s, 1 da; *Style*— Lady Fiona Whitfield; Plyntree Farm, PO Box 721, Marondera, Zimbabwe

WHITFIELD, Rev George Joshua Newbold; s of Joshua Newbold Whitfield; *b* 2 June 1909; *Educ* Bede GS Sunderland, King's Coll London, Bishops' Coll Cheshunt; *m* 1937, Audrey Priscilla, *née* Dence; 2 s, 2 da; *Career* headmaster: Tavistock GS 1943-46, Stockport Sch 1946-50, Hampton Sch 1950-68; ordained priest 1963; pres

Headmasters' Assoc 1967, gen sec Bd of Educn of Gen Synod of C of E 1968-74, memb of Corpn of Church House Westminster 1974-, chm Exeter Diocesan Educn Ctee 1981-88; *Books Incl:* God and Man in the Old Testament (1949), Philosophy and Religion (1955); *Recreations* gardening, photography; *Clubs* Athenaeum; *Style—* The Rev George Whitfield; Bede Lodge, 31A Rolle Rd, Exmouth, Devon EX8 2AW (☎ 0395 274 162)

WHITFIELD, John; MP (C) Dewsbury 1983-; s of Sydney Richard Whitfield and Mary Rishworth Whitfield; *b* 31 Oct 1941; *Educ* Sedbergh Sch, Leeds Univ (LLB); *m* 1967, Mary Ann *née* Moy; 3 s;; *Career* slr and memb family firm Whitfield Son and Hallam of Batley, Dewsbury and Mirfield 1965-; MP (C) Dewsbury 1983-87, contested (C) Dewsbury 1987; dir: Caldaire Ind Hosp plc, Cullingworth Textiles Ltd; *Clubs* Headingley Football, Mirfield Constitutional, Tanfield Angling; *Style—* John Whitfield Esq, MP; The Old Rectory, Badsworth, Pontefract, W Yorks

WHITFIELD, John Flett; JP (1971), DL (1982); s of John Herbert Whitfield of London (d 1955), and Bertha Georgina, *née* Flett (d 1982); *b* 1 June 1922; *Educ* Epsom Coll Surrey; *m* 10 Aug 1946, Rosemary Elisabeth Joan, da of Col Raymond Theobald Hartman of London (d 1961); 2 da (Christine b 1947, Veronica b 1949); *Career* WWII Capt KRRC 1939-46; HM Foreign Service served M East, Roumania and Finland 1946-57; export dir Materials Handling Equipment (GB) Ltd 1957-61, London dir Hunslet (Hldgs) Ltd 1961-64, dir Sunningdale Golf Club 1973-77; memb Surrey CC 1961-(chm 1981-84); chm: Police ctee Assoc of Co Cncls 1985-88, Surrey Police Authy 1985-, Windsor Co Bench 1978-80, cncl Univ of Surrey 1986-; High Sheriff Surrey 1985-86; parly candidate (Con) Pontefract 1964; *Recreations* golf, foreign languages, bookbinding; *Clubs* R & A, Sunningdale Rye GC; *Style—* John F Whitfield, Esq, JP, DL; 4 Holiday House, Priory Road, Sunningdale, Berks, SL5 9RW (☎ 0990 20997)

WHITFIELD, Prof John Humphreys; s of late John Allen Whitfield; *b* 2 Oct 1906; *Educ* Handsworth GS, Magdalen Coll Oxford; *m* 1936, Joan Herrin, ARCA; 2 s; *Career* asst master King Edward VII Sch Sheffield 1930-36, lectr Italian Oxford Univ 1936-46, serena prof: Italian language and literature Birmingham Univ 1946-74, emeritus 1974-; chm Soc for Italian Studies 1962-74, sr ed Italian Studies 1967-74; Commendatore Ordine al Merito della Repubblica Italiana 1972; fell of the Inst for Advanced Research in the Humanities Univ of Birmingham 1984; Serena Medal for Italian Studies (British Acadamy) 1984; *Books Incl:* Petrarch and the Renascence (1943), Machiavelli (1947), Giacomo Leopardi (1954), A Short History of Italian Literature (1960), Discourses on Machiavelli (1969); *Style—* Prof John Whitfield; 2 Woodbourne Rd, Edgbaston, Birmingham 15 (☎ 021 454 1035)

WHITFIELD, John Robert; s of Wesley Simpson Whitfield (d 1976); *b* 6 May 1930; *Educ* Consett GS, Coll of Technol Leeds; *m* 1960, May, da of Robert Hindhaugh (d 1974); 2 s (Ian Robert, Andrew Wesley); *Career* dir Brims & Co Ltd 1976-; pres Newcastle, Tyne & Northumberland Building Employers Confederation 1981-82; *Recreations* sailing, golf, caravanning; *Style—* John Whitfield, Esq; 3l Earnshaw Way, Beaumont Park, Whitley Bay, Tyne and Wear (☎ 091 2534591); Brims & Co Ltd, Clayton House, Regent Centre, Gosforth, Newcastle-upon-Tyne (☎ 091 2856606)

WHITFIELD, Hon Michael Christopher; s and h of 2 Baron Kenswood; *b* 3 July 1955; *Style—* The Hon Michael Whitfield

WHITFIELD, Paul Martin; s of Christopher Gilbert Whitfield, FSA (d 1968), of Chipping Campden, Glos, and Frances Audrey, *née* Chandler; *b* 9 Dec 1942; *Educ* Stowe, The Middle Temple; *m* 1, 3 July 1965, Rowan. da of late Norman Fleming, of Broadway, Worcs; 1 s (Benjamin b 1971), 1 da (Lucy b 1968); m 2, 22 Sept 1982, Alison, da of Dr I A B Cathie, of Barton House, Warwick; 1 s (Orlando b 1987); *Career* deputy chm W & FC Bonham Ltd (auctioneers) 1987-; dir Christie's Internat and Gp Companies (resigned 1987); govr Stowe Sch 1980; chm Stowe Garden Bldgs Tst 1986; *Recreations* music, literature; *Clubs* Brooks's; *Style—* Paul Whitfield, Esq; Bonhams, Montpelier Street, London SW1 (☎ 01 584 9161, fax 01 589 4072, telex 916477 BONHAMG, car ☎ 0836 245 030)

WHITFIELD, Prof Roderick; s of Prof John Humphreys Whitfield, and Joan, *née* Herrin; *b* 20 July 1937; *Educ* King Edward's Sch Birmingham, Sch of Oriental and African Studies, St Johns Coll Cambridge (BA, MA), Princeton Univ (MFA, PhD); *m* 1, 11 July 1963 (m dis 1983), Frances Elizabeth, PhD, da of Prof Richard Charles Oldfield; 1 s (Aldus b 1970), 2 da (Martha-Ming b 1965, Tanya b 1967); m 2, 25 Aug 1983, Youngsook Pak, PhD; *Career* Offr Cadet Jt Serv Sch for Linguists, RAF 1955-57, PO RAFVR 1957, Flying Offr RAFVR; res assoc and lectr Princeton Univ 1964-66, res fell St John's Coll Cambridge 1966-68, asst keeper 1st class dept of oriental antiquities The Br Museum 1968-84, prof of chinese and east asian art Univ of London and head of Percival David Fndn of Chinese Art 1984-; memb cncl Oriental Ceramic Soc, tstee Inst of Buddhist Studies; *Books* In Pursuit of Antiquity (1969), The Art of Central Asia, The Stein Collection at the British Museum (3 vols, 1982-85), Treasures From Korea (ed 1984), Korean Art Treasures (ed 1986); *Style—* Prof Roderick Whitfield; Percival David Fndn of Chinese Art, 53 Gordon Sq, London WC1H OPD (☎ 01 387 3909)

WHITFORD, Hon Mr Justice; Hon Sir John Norman Keates Whitford; s of Harry Whitford; *b* 24 June 1913; *Educ* Univ Coll Sch, Munich Univ, Peterhouse Cambridge; *m* 1946, Rosemary, da of John Barcham Green by his w Emily Paillard; 4 da; *Career* served WW II RAFVR; QC 1965; High Court judge (Chancery) 1970-, barr: Inner Temple 1935, Middle Temple 1946; chm Departmental Ctee Copyright & Design Law 1974-76; kt 1970; *Style—* The Hon Mr Justice Whitford; Royal Courts of Justice, WC2

WHITING, Derek Alan; s of William Thomas Whiting (d 1981), of Beckenham, Kent, and Gladys Dudfield Whiting (d 1970); *b* 2 August 1931; *Educ* Tonbridge Sch; *m* 1, 5 June 1962, Lady Frances Esmee, *née* Curzon, da of 5 Earl Howe, PC (d 1964); 2 s (Frances b 1965, Alexander b 1967); m 2, 14 Dec 1972, Angela Clare Forbes, da of Sir Archibald Forbes GBE, of Orchard Ct, Portman Square, London SW1;; *Career* Commodity Trading & Broking 1952-; chm: Int Petroleum exch 1985, London Sugar Futures Mkt 1984, AFBD 1984-87, Comfin Hldgs Ltd 1980, Sucden (UK) Ltd 1980-; played rugby football for Harlequins & Kent; Liveryman Worshipful Co of Skinners; *Recreations* shooting, squash, golf, reading; *Clubs* Swinley Forest, Hurlingham, Harlequins; *Style—* Derek Whiting, Esq; 4 Gertrude St, London SW10 0JN (☎ 352 6220); 5 London Bridge St London SE1 9SG (☎ 01 378 6322, fax 01 378 6556, car telephone 0836 237518, telex 883780/89)

WHITING, Rev Peter Graham; CBE (1984); s of Rev Arthur Whiting, of Wimborne, Dorset, and Olive, *née* Stebbings (d 1986); *b* 7 Nov 1930; *Educ* Yeovil GS, Irish Baptist Coll, Dublin (Dip Theol); *m* 9 Jan 1960, Lorena, da of Albert Inns (d 1982), of Northampton; 2 s (Julian b 1962, Toby b 1964), 3 da (Clare b 1960, Sophie b 1967, Anna b 1973); *Career* cmmnd RAChD 1962, Regtl Chaplain 1962-69, Chaplain 1 Bn Parachute Regt 1964-66, Sr Chaplain 20 Armd Bde BAOR and Lippe Garrison BAOR 1969-72, Staff Chaplain HQ BAOR 1972-74, Sr Chaplain 20 Airportable Bde 1974-75, Dep Asst Chaplain Gen W Midland Dist Shrewsbury 1975-78, Sr Chaplain Young Entry Units 1976-78, Asst Chaplain Gen 1 Br Corps BAOR 1978-81, Dep Chaplain Gen to the Forces (Army) 1981-84; ordained Baptist Minister 1956; minister: Kings Heath Northampton 1956-62, Beechen Grove Baptist Church Watford 1985-; Queen's Hon Chaplain 1981-84; memb Cncl of Churches; *Style—* The Rev P G Whiting, CBE; The Manse, 264 Hempstead Rd, Watford, Herts WD1 3LY (☎ 0923 53 197); Beechen Grove Baptist Church, Clarendon Rd, Watford WD1 1JJ (☎ 0923 241 858)

WHITLEY, Air Marshal Sir John Rene; KBE (1956, CBE 1945), CB (1946), DSO (1943), AFC and bar (1937, 1956); s of Arthur Noel Joseph Whitley (d 1940); *b* 7 Sept 1905; *Educ* Haileybury; *m* 1, 1932, Barbara Alice Patricia (d 1965), da of F R Liscombe; 3 s (Christopher, David, Piers) and 1 s (Guy d 1978); m 2, 1967, Alison (d 1986), widow of John Howard Russell, and da of Sir Nigel Campbell (d 1948, s of Adela Harriet, 2 da of Lord Charles Pelham Clinton, 2 s of 4 Duke of Newcastle), sometime jt MFH Old Berkeley; *Career* served RAF 1926-62: India 1932-37, Bomber Cmd 1937-45, Singapore 1946, India 1947, Dir Organisation (Estabs) Air Miny 1948-49, IDC 1950, AO Admin 2 TAF Germany 1951-52, AOC 1 Gp Bomber Cmd 1953-56, air memb Personnel 1957-59, Inspr-Gen RAF 1959-62, ret; controller RAF Benevolent Fund 1962-68; *Recreations* sailing (yacht 'Condette'), fishing, skiing; *Clubs* RAF, Royal Lymington Yacht; *Style—* Air Marshal Sir John Whitley, KBE, CB, DSO, AFC*; 2 Woodside Close, Woodside Ave, Lymington, Hants SO41 8FH (☎ (0590) 76920)

WHITLEY, Lady Mary Ilona Margaret; *née* Cambridge; da of 2 and last Marquess of Cambridge, GCVO (d 1981; HSH Prince George of Teck until 1917; himself s of 1 Marquess of Cambridge, 2 and last Duke of Teck, which latter title was resigned 1917, by the 1 Marquess's w Lady Margaret Evelyn Grosvenor, da of 1 Duke of Westminster. The 1 Marquess was eldest s of HH The 1 Prince and Duke of Teck, GCB, GCVO, and bro of late Queen Mary, The 1 Marquess's mother was HRH Princess Mary Adelaide, da of HRH 1 Duke of Cambridge, KG, GCB, GCMG, GCH, 7 s of George III) and Dorothy Isabel Westenra, *née* Hastings (d 1988); *b* 24 Sept 1924; *m* 1950, Peter Whitley, s of Sir Norman Henry Pownall Whitley, MC, and Florence May, *née* Erskine; 1 s (Charles Francis Peter b 1961), 1 da (Sarah Elizabeth b 1954, m 1982, Timothy J F Felton; 2 da); *Career* bridesmaid to HM The Queen; *Recreations* bird watching, beagling, gardening, sailing; *Clubs* Ladies' side Boodle's; *Style—* Lady Mary Whitley; Leighland House, Road Water, Watchet, Somerset TA23 ORP (☎ 0984 40996)

WHITLEY, Oliver John; s of Rt Hon J H Whitley, MP (d 1981), Speaker House of Commons, chm BBC and, Marguerite Marchetti; *b* 12 Feb 1912; *Educ* Clifton, New Coll Oxford; *m* 1939, Elspeth Catherine, *née* Forrester-Paton; 4 s, 1 da; *Career* RNVR 1942-46; Coastal Forces, Combined Ops; barr 1935; BBC 1935-41, and 1946-72, head overseas serv 1950-57 (asst controller 1955-57), appointments offr 1957-60, controller staff trg 1960-64, chief asst to dir gen 1964-68, md external servs; Valiant for Truth Award 1974; *Recreations* gardening, reading; *Style—* Oliver J Whitley, Esq; Greenacre, Ganavan Rd, Oban, Argyll PA34 5TU (☎ 0631 62555)

WHITLEY, (Samuel) Peter; s of Alfred William Whitley, JP (d 1945), of Old Brantwood, Halifax, and Elizabeth Lucas Sutcliffe (d 1962), (nephew of Rt Hon J H Whitley MP (d 1981), Speaker House of Commons and chm BBC); *b* 27 June 1916; *Educ* Loretto Sch; Jesus Coll Oxford (MA); *Career* Civil Servant; RA 1940-46, parachutist, attached as FOD to 6 Airborne Div, Normandy 1944 POW, Staff Capt Mil Gov Germany 1946; asst prcpl NI 1939-40, control cmmn Germany 1947-50, pncpl Min of Pensions 1950-54, treasy 1954-56, Col Off 1957-66, first sec and head of Chancery, UK Cmmn Singapore 1959-62, asst sec 1963, Central African Off and CRO Dept Educn and Science 1966-73, dir S Whitley & Co, Cotton Spinners Halifax 1950-57 (chm and md 1956-57); voluntary work for community service volunteers (CSV) 1975-85; actively developed "Study Service' in higher and further educn, initiating a Maj nat pilot project in Coventry, now hon consultant; *Recreations* philosophy, the arts, walking; *Clubs* United Oxford and Cambridge Univ; *Style—* Peter Whitley, Esq; Flat 2, 5 Palmeira Ave, Hove, E Sussex (☎ Brighton 737201)

WHITLEY, Hon Tara Olivia; *née* Chichester-Clark; da of Baron Moyola (Life Peer); *b* 8 July 1962; *Educ* Sherborne Sch for Girls Dorset; *m* 1984, Edward Thomas Whitley, s of John Whitley, of Hamsey Lodge, nr Lewes, E Sussex; *Career* conference and public relations dir; *Clubs* The Hong Kong; *Style—* The Hon Mrs Whitley; 402 May Tower, 7 May Road, Hong Kong

WHITLOCK, Ralph; s of Edwin Whitlock (d 1964), of Pitton, Wilts, and Alice *née* White (d 1958); *b* 7 Feb 1914; *Educ* Bishop Wordsworth's Sch Salisbury; *m* 1 Nov 1939, Hilda, da of Alexander Pearce (d 1963), of Pitton, Wilts; 1 s (Edward Ralph b 1948), 2 da (Wendy Anne (Mrs Beauchamp) b 1940, Rosalie Margaret (Mrs Price) b 1945); *Career* WWII serv Home Gd; writer; farming in Wilts-1968, agric conslt Methodist Missionary Soc 1968-73; journalist/broadcaster; Western Gazette 1932, farming corr/farming ed The Field 1946-73, script writer & lead part Cowlease Farm (BBC Children's Hour) 1946-62, resident panellist Slightly Quizzical (BBC TV programme) 1971-74, written many plays for BBC incl The Odstock Curse, numerous articles for many magazines and nat newspapers incl The Times and Daily Telegraph, weekly column The Guardian Weekly 1981-; former co chm Wilts Fedn of Young Farmers' Club 1947, vice-pres Salisbury Nat History Soc, memb Guild of Agric Journalists; organiser & ldr pioneer ornithological safari to The Gambia 1971-72; *Books* numerous books published incl: nat history: The Great Cattle Plague (1959), Bulls through the Ages (1977), Rare Breeds (1980), Bird Watch in an English Village (1982); folklore: In Search of Lost Gods (1979), Here be Dragons (1984); history: The Everyday Life of the Maya (1976), The Warrior Kings of Saxon England (1977); children's books: Cowlease Farm, Royal Farmer (a major work prepared with special encouragement from HM The Queen), Gentle Giant, The English Farm, The Lost Village; *Recreations* natural history, writing; *Style—* Ralph Whitlock, Esq; The Penchet, Winterslow, Salisbury, Wilts SP5 1PY (☎ 0980 862 949)

WHITMORE, Sir Clive Anthony; GCB (1988, KCB 1983), CVO 1983; s of Charles Arthur Whitmore, by his w Louisa; *b* 18 Jan 1935; *Educ* Sutton GS, Christ's Coll Cambridge; *m* 1961, Jennifer Mary Thorpe; 1 s, 2 da; *Career* private sec to perm under-sec state War Off 1961, asst private sec to sec of state for War 1962 (princ 1964), private sec to perm under-sec state MOD 1969, asst sec 1971, asst under-sec of state (Def Staff) MOD 1975, under-sec Cabinet Off 1977, princ private sec to PM 1979-82, perm under-sec state MOD 1983-88; perm under-sec state Home Off 1988-; *Recreations* music, gardening; *Style—* Sir Clive Whitmore, GCB, KCB, CVO; Home Office, 50 Queen Anne's Gate, London SW1H 9AT

WHITMORE, Dowager Lady; Ellis Christense; *née* Johnsen; da of Herr Direktor Knud Christian Johnsen (d 1945), of Bergen, Norway, and Thora Heltberg, *née* Lampe (d 1978); *b* 29 August 1904; *Educ* U Phils Coll Bergen Norway; *m* 1 Oct 1931, as his 2 w, Sir Francis Henry Douglas Charlton Whitmore, 1 Bt, KCB, CMG, DSO, TD (d 1962); 1 s (Sir John Henry Douglas, 2 Bt, *qv*), 1 da (Anne Catherine (Mrs D J E O'Connell) b 1933); *Career* D St J; *Recreations* gardening, canvas embroidery; *Style—* Dowager Lady Whitmore; c/o Barclays Bank, 155 Beehive Lane, Chelmsford, Essex CM29 9SG

WHITMORE, Sir John Henry Douglas; 2 Bt (UK 1954), of Orsett, Co Essex; s of Col Sir Francis Henry Douglas Charlton Whitmore, 1 Bt, KCB, CMG, DSO, TD (d 1962, maternal gs of Sir William Cradock-Hartopp, 3 Bt, while his paternal grandmother was Lady Louisa Douglas, eldest da of 5 Marquess of Queensberry); *b* 16 Oct 1937; *Educ* Eton; *m* 1, 1962, Ella Gunilla, (m dis 1969), da of Sven A Hansson, of Danderyd, Sweden; 1 da; m 2, 1977, Diana Elaine, da of Fred A Becchetti, of California USA; 1 s; *Heir* s, Jason Whitmore b 26 Jan 1983; *Career* sports psychologist, also concerned with psychology of int relations; dep dir Centre for Int Peacebuilding, author of books on the mental aspects of sport, life and work; *Recreations* squash, skiing, motor racing; *Clubs* British Racing Drivers; *Style—* Sir John Whitmore, Bt; Southfield, Leigh, Nr Tonbridge, Kent TN11 8PJ, (☎ 0732 454490)

WHITNEY, John Norton Braithwaite; s of Dr Willis Bevan Whitney, and Dorothy Anne, *née* Robertson; *b* 20 Dec 1930; *Educ* Leighton Park Friends' Sch; *m* 9 June 1956, Roma Elizabeth Duncan (former dancer with London Festival Ballet), da of George Hodgson; 1 s (Alexander b 31 Jan 1961), 1 da (Fiona b 17 Nov 1958); *Career* formed Ross Radio Producns 1951, Ross TV Producns, Ross Scripts & Sagitta Producns for devising and writing series and plays for ITV (inc Upstairs, Downstairs, Danger UXB and The Flame Trees of Thika, etc); chm autocue 1950-70; co-fndr and chm Local Radio Assoc 1964, chm Assoc of Independent Radio Contractors 1973-75 and 1980, md Capital Radio 1973-82, dir Consolidated Productions (UK) 1980-82, dir-gen IBA 1982-; vice-pres Royal Nat Inst for the Deaf 1988-; bd memb Nat Theatre 1982-; chm: Artsline 1983-, Soundaround 1981-; memb cncl Royal London Aid Soc 1966; Hon Fell RCM, memb British Cncl's Films, TV and Video Advsy Ctee; FRSA, RNID (vice pres 1988-); *Recreations* chess, photography, sculpture; *Clubs* Garrick, Whitefriars, Pilgrims; *Style—* John N B Whitney, Esq; 10 Wadham Gardens, London NW3 3DP; IBA, 70 Brompton Rd, London SW3 1EY (☎ 01 584 7011, telex 24345)

WHITNEY, Raymond William; OBE (1968), MP (C) Wycombe (by-election) April 1978-; o s of late George Whitney, of Northampton; *b* 28 Nov 1930; *Educ* Wellingborough Sch, RMA Sandhurst, London Univ (BA), Hong Kong and Australia Nat Univs; *m* 1956, Sheila Margot Beswick Prince; 2 s; *Career* RA Northants Regt 1951-64, seconded to Australian Army HQ 1960-63, served Trieste, Korea, Hong Kong, Germany; FO 1964-78: served Peking, head Chancery Buenos Aires 1969-72, dep high cmmr Dacca 1973-76, head Overseas Info Dept FCO 1977-78; parly private sec to Treasy Mins 1979-80, vice-chm Cons Backbench Employment Ctee 1980-83, chm Cons For Affrs Ctee 1981-83, parly under-sec state FCO 1983-84; parly under-sec of state for: Social Security 1984-85, Health 1985-86; *Style—* Ray Whitney, Esq, OBE, MP; The Dial House, Sunninghill, Berks SL5 0AG (☎ 0990 23164); House of Commons, London SW1A 0AA (☎ 01 219 5099)

WHITNEY-LONG, Simon Anthony; *b* 25 April 1943; *Career* exec dir Union Discount Co plc 1982-, exec dir The Discount Company of London plc; *Style—* Simon Whitney-Long, Esq; 39 Cornhill, London EC3V 3NU (☎ 01 623 1020, fax 01 929 2110, telex 886434)

WHITSEY, Fred; *b* 18 July 1919; *m* 1947, Patricia Searle; *Career* ed Popular Gardening 1967-82 (asst ed 1948-64, assoc ed 1964-67); gardening corr Sunday Telegraph 1961-71 and Daily Telegraph 1971-; contrib Country Life and The Guardian; Gold Veitch Mem Medal 1979, Victoria Medal of Honour 1986; *Books* Sunday Telegraph Gardening Book (1966), Fred Whitsey's Garden Calendar (1985); *Recreations* music, gardening; *Style—* Fred Whitsey Esq; Avens Mead, 20 Oast Rd, Oxted, Surrey RH8 9DU

WHITSON, Harold Alexander; CBE (1968); s of Ralph A Whitson, MICE, of Carlton, Symington, Lanarks (d 1949), and Annie Laura Morton Greig (d 1970); *b* 20 Sept 1916; *Educ* Rugby, Cambridge Univ (BA); *m* 1942, Rowena, da of George Stanhope Pitt, of Broadlands, Warlingham, Surrey; 1 s (and 1 s decd), 2 da (and 1 da decd); *Career* former pres Glasgow C of C; former chm: M D W (Hldgs) Ltd, Publ Construction Co, Irvine New Town Dvpt Corpn; dir Ailsa Investmnt Tst Ltd; *Recreations* gardening, shooting; *Clubs* East India, New (Edinburgh), RSAC; *Style—* Harold Whitson, Esq, CBE; Edmonston House, Biggar, Lanarks (☎ 0899 20063)

WHITSON, Keith Roderick; s of William Cleghorn Whitson, and Ellen, *née* Wade; *b* 25 Mar 1943; *Educ* Alleyn's Sch Dulwich; *m* 26 July 1968, Sabine Marita, da of Ulrich Wiechert; 1 s (Mark James b 26 July 1980), 2 da (Claudia Sharon b 31 Aug 1971, Julia Caroline b 2 May 1973); *Career* The Hong Kong and Shanghai Banking Corpn 1961-: mangr Frankfurt 1978-80, mangr Indonesia 1981-84, asst gen mangr fin Hong Kong 1985-87, chief exec offr UK 1987-; dir: Gibbs Insur Hldgs Ltd 1987, James Capel & Co 1987, Wardley Investmt Servs Int Ltd 1987, Euro-Clear Clearance Systems 1987, HBL Property Fin 1988; chm Br Overseas and Cwlth Banks Assoc 1988, exec ctee memb Br Banks Assoc 1988; *Style—* Keith Whitson, Esq; Hong Kong Bank Group, 99 Bishopsgate, London EC2P 2LA (☎ 01 638 2300)

WHITSON, Cmdt Thomas Jackson; OBE; s of Thomas Whitson, QPM (d 1974), of Springlea, Aberlady, E Lothian, and Susan, *née* Steele; *b* 5 Sept 1930; *Educ* North Berwick HS, Knox Acad; *m* 5 Sept 1953, Patricia Marion, da of Robert Bugden (d 1968), of Soutra Fair Oak Hamps; 2 s (Kenneth b 17 June 1956, Kevan b 19 Dec 1958); *Career* RN 1949-51; chief supt Lothian and Borders Police 1976-80, dep chief constable Central Scotland Police 1980-87, cmdt Scottish Police Coll; memb Rotary Club of Polmont; *Recreations* golf, curling, reading; *Style—* Cmdt Thomas Whitson, OBE; 10 Glasclune Court, North Berwick; Tulliallan Castle, Kincardine, Alloa FK10 4BE (☎ 0259 303333)

WHITTAKER, (Thomas) Geoffrey; s of Maj William Whittaker (d 1983), and Nellie May, *née* Crabtree; *b* 2 Mar 1937; *Educ* Ermysted's Sch Skipton, Lincoln Coll Oxford (MA), London Coll of Violinists; *m* 8 Nov 1960, Florence McKay, da of John Glasgow (d 1943); 2 s (William Robert b 1961, Edward Norman b 1963), 1 da (Katherine Margaret (Mrs Saner) b 1966); *Career* Nat Serv radar tech Cyprus 1955-57; dir and gen mangr Harlander Coats AG Austria 1969, md Laidlaw & Fairgrieve Scotland 1983, dir Invergordon Distillers plc Scotland 1983-; playing memb Edinburgh Symphony Orchestra; memb: Galashiels Mfrs Corpn 1975, Soc of Coopers of Glasgow 1984, Keepers of the Quaich 1988, Br Wool Textiles Export Cncl; former deacon Galashiels Mfrs Assoc, former chm Scottish Wool Spinners Fedn; Liveryman Worshipful Co of Grocers of Paisley 1962, Liveryman Glasgow Co of Coopers 1984, Freeman Citizen of Glasgow at Far Hand 1984; *Recreations* music, bridge; *Clubs* Caledonian (Edinburgh); *Style—* Geoffrey Whittaker, Esq; Beechlaw Langside Dr, Peebles, Tweeddale EH45 8RF (☎ 0721 214 52); Invergordon Distillers Ltd, 21 Salamander Place, Leith, Edinburgh (☎ 031 554 4404)

WHITTAKER, George Anthony; s of George Whittaker (d 1980), by his w Muriel (d 1975); *b* 10 May 1930; *Educ* McGill Univ Montreal (BEng), Inst of Technol Charlottesville Virginia USA (MS); *m* 1964, Elizabeth Anne, da of R E Smyth; 1 s, 2 da; *Career* 2 Lt REME; dir: Smith and Nephew Overseas Ltd 1956-63, Deering Milliken 1963-68 (and int vice-pres), Guinness Peat Gp Ltd 1968-82, Robin Marlar Ltd 1983-84; non exec dir: Spillers Ltd 1979-80, Albert Fisher Gp plc 1982-, Norman Reeves plc 1983-86, Edeco Hldgs Ltd 1985-, UK Paper plc 1988-; md Grosvenor Place Amalgamations Ltd 1982-; chm: Bright Walton Homes plc 1986-, Corroless Int Ltd 1987- (dir 1984-87); *Recreations* cricket, walking, fishing; *Clubs* IOD; *Style—* G Anthony Whittaker, Esq; Craigie Lea, Church Lane, Stoke Poges, Bucks SL2 4NZ Grosvenor Place Amalgamations Ltd, 14 Grosvenor Place, London SW1X 7HH (☎ 01 235 0111, telex 261260 ASM G, fax 01 235 0961)

WHITTAKER, Roger Henry Brough; s of Edward Whittaker, and Valda Viola *née* Showan; *b* 22 Mar 1936; *Educ* Prince of Wales Sch, Nairobi Kenya, Univ of Cape Town SA, Nairobi Kenya, Univ of Wales Bangor (BSc); *m* 15 Aug 1964, Natalie Deidre, da of Edward (Toby) O'Brien (d 1979); 2 s (Edward Guy b 1974, Alexander Michael b 1978), 3 da (Emily, Claire b 1968, Lauren Marie b 1970, Jessica Jane b 1973); *Career* Nat Serv Kenya Regt in Kenya, TA; singer/songwriter; first recorded hit Steelmen (1962), first continental hit If I were a Richman, Mexican Whistler (1967), first UK hit Durham Town (1969), I Don't Believe In If Anymore (1970), New World in the Morning (1970), What Love is (1971), Why (1971), Mammy Blue (1971); first USA hit The Last Farewell 1976, over 11 million copies sold worldwide, earning major acclaim throughout Europe, Canada, Australia, N Zealand and the third world; Skye Boat Song (with Des O' Connor) 1986; TV series incl: Whittaker's World of Music (LWT 1971), Hallelujah It's Christmas (Thames 1975), Roger Whittaker Show (Westward 1977) Sing Out (Ulster 1987); tv specials in Denmark, Germany, Canada, USA, Australia; Films inc Roger Whittaker in Kenya (a musical safari) SOS (Stars Orgn for Spastics), Birthright (fund raising aim of Royal Soc of Gynaecologists), Rescue the Rhino, Lords Taverners, Br Acad of Songwriters and Composers; L'Invite d'Honneur (Juan Les Pins, Antibes) 1971, key to the City of Atlanta 1975; hon citizen: Baltimore 1978, Winnipeg 1978, Houston 1983, Lowell Mass 1985; B'Nai B'Rith Humanitarian Award 1980, Ambassador of Goodwill (Chatanooga) 1983, Seal of the Cwlth of Mass 1985; MCPS (pres); *Books* So Far So Good; *Recreations* squash, golf, fishing, photography, backgammon, gardening; *Style—* Roger Whittaker, Esq; Irene Collis, 50 Regents Park Road, Primrose Hill, London, NW1 7SX (☎ 01 586 5591)

WHITTALL, (Harold) Astley; CBE (1978); s of Harold and Margaret Whittall; *b* 8 Sept 1925; *Educ* Handsworth GS, Tech Coll Birmingham; *m* 1952, Diana Margharita Berner; *Career* former chm Amalgmated Power Engg; former pres Engineering Employers' Fedn; chm Ransomes Sims & Jefferies, BSG Int; chm Turriff Corporation plc, Engineering Industry; training bd dir Adv-Baker plc, chm BRISCC (British Iron & Steel Consumers Council); CE, FIMechE, FI ProdE, FIMarE, CBIM; *Recreations* shooting; *Clubs* RAC, Institute of Directors; *Style—* Astley Whittall, Esq

WHITTAM, Prof Ronald; s of Edward Whittam (d 1966); *b* 21 Mar 1925; *Educ* cncl and tech schs Oldham and Manchester, Sheffield Univ, Cambridge Univ; *m* 1957, Christina Patricia Margaret, *née* Lamb; 1 s, 1 da; *Career* prof of physiology 1966-83, formerly lectr in biochem Oxford Univ 1960-66, dean of the Faculty of Sci Leicester Univ 1979-82, emeritus prof 1983-; FRS; *Recreations* walking, gardening; *Style—* Professor Ronald Whittam; 9 Guilford Rd, Stoneygate, Leicester (☎ 0533 707132)

WHITTELL, James Michael Scott; OBE (1984); s of Edward Arther Whittel (d 1972), and Helen Elizabeth Whittell (d 1971); *b* 17 Feb 1939; *Educ* Greshams Sch Holt, Magdalen Coll Oxford, (MA, BSc), Mancherster Univ; *m* 30 July 1962, Eleanor Jane, da of Allen Frederick Reynolds Carling, CBE, of Henfield, Sussex; 3 s (Matthew b 11 Oct 1964, Giles b 19 March 1966, Crispin b 19 Dec 1969); *Career* schoolmaster Sherborne Sch 1962-65 and 1966-69, researcher Oxford Univ 1965-66, Nairobi Sch Kenya and Swedish Int Devpt Agency 1969-72; Br Cncl: Nigeria 1973-78, dir gen's dept London 1978-81, rep Algeria 1981-85, hd dir gen's dept and sec to cncl 1985; *Recreations* walking, mountaineering, reading, music; *Clubs* Alpine, Traveller's; *Style—* The Brittish Council, 10 Spring Gardens, London SW1 (☎ 01 930 8466)

WHITTEMORE, Hon Mrs (Ivy Lorna); *née* Jervis; da of late 6 Viscount St Vincent and Marion, *née* Brown; *b* 1895; *m* 1920, W Laurence Whittemore, MC; 1 s, 1 da; *Style—* The Hon Mrs Whittemore; Box 512, St James 11780, New York, USA

WHITTERIDGE, Sir Gordon Coligny; KCMG (1964, CMG 1956), OBE (1946); s of Walter Whitteridge; *b* 6 Nov 1908; *Educ* Whitgift Sch Croydon, Cambridge Univ; *m* 1, 1938, Margaret Lungley (d 1942); 1 s, 1 da (decd); m 2, 1951, Jane (d 1979), da of Frederick Driscoll, of Mass, USA; 1 s; m 3, 1983, Mrs Jill Stanley, da of Bertram Belcham; *Career* joined Consular Serv 1932, 1 sec Moscow 1948-49, consul-gen Stuttgart 1949-51, cnsllr Bangkok 1951-56, consul-gen: Seattle 1956-60, Istanbul 1960-62; ambass: Burma 1962-65, Afghanistan 1965-68; hon tres Soc Afghan Studies 1972-; *Clubs* Travellers'; *Style—* Sir Gordon Whitteridge, KCMG, OBE

WHITTICK, Richard James; s of Ernest George Whittick (d 1947); *b* 21 August 1912; *Educ* George Heriot's Sch, Edinburgh Univ; *m* 1938, Violet Enid Elizabeth, *née* Mason; 2 s; *Career* asst keeper Br Museum (Natural History) 1936; HO 1940, princ private sec to Home Sec 1952-53, Asst Sec 1953, Asst Under-Sec State 1967-72; *Recreations* gardening, photography FRPS 1988; *Style—* Richard Whittick, Esq; Coombe Cottage, Coombe, Sherborne, Dorset DT9 4BX (☎ 0935 814 488)

WHITTINGTON, (Thomas) Alan; CB (1977), TD (1986); s of George Whittington, JP (d 1932), of Northcote, Old Park Rd, Leeds, and Mary Elizabeth, *née* Miller (d 1955); *b* 15 May 1916; *Educ* Uppingham, Leeds Univ (LLB); *m* 1939, Audrey Elizabeth, da of Craven Gilpin (d 1951), of The Mansion, Roundhay, Leeds; 4 s (Richard, Christopher, Jeremy, Peter); *Career* cmmnd W Yorks Regt (Leeds Rifles) TA 1937, serv WWII UK and Maj 14 Army India; admitted slr 1945; clerk of the peace for City of Leeds 1952-70, sr ptnr Marklands Leeds 1967-70; under sec Lord Chllr's dept 1970; admin: Northern circuit 1970-74, NE circuit 1974-81; *Recreations* gardening, fishing; *Style*— Alan Whittington, Esq, CB, TD; The Cottage, School Lane, Collingham, Wetherby LS22 5BQ (☎ 0937 73881); Marklands Stansfield Chambers, 6 Great George St, Leeds LS1 3BW (☎ 0532 455 310)

WHITTINGTON, Dr Richard Michael; s of Dr Theodore Henry Whittington (d 1982), and Cecily Grace, *née* Woodman (d 1973); *b* 9 Sept 1929; *Educ* St Edwards Sch Oxford, Oriel Coll Oxford (MA); *m* 1954, Dorothy Margaret, da of William Fraser Darroch Gardner (d 1977); 1 s (Richard), 1 da (Alison); *Career* HM Coroner Birmingham and Solihull 1976; tstee Parly Advsy Ctee on Tport Safety 1980; univ physician Aston Univ Midlands 1985; contrib many papers related to sudden death in medical journals; memb Br Acad of Forensic Sci, FRSM; *Recreations* contact bridge, mirror dinghy (Allegretto); *Style*— Dr Richard Whittington; Clanrickarde House, 11 Fouroaks Rd, Sutton Coldfield, W Midlands B74 2XP; Coroners Court, Newton St, Birmingham B4 6NE (☎ 021 236 5000)

WHITTLE, Air Cdre Sir Frank; OM (1986), KBE (1948, CBE 1944), CB (1947); *b* 1 June 1907; *Educ* Leamington Coll, RAF Coll Cranwell, Peterhouse Cambridge (MA); *m* 1, 1930 (m dis 1976), Dorothy Lee; 2 s; m 2, 1976, Hazel Hall; *Career* served RAF 1928-48, former test pilot and involved in dvpt of jet engine; former hon tech advsr BOAC, Shell Gp; former conslt Bristol Siddeley & Rolls Royce; memb faculty US Naval Acad Annapolis Md 1977-; FRS, FEng, Hon FRAeS, Hon FAeSI, Hon FIMechE, Hon FAIAA, hon fellow Peterhouse Cambridge, Hon DSc: Oxford, Manchester, Leicester, Bath, Warwick, Exetere; Hon LLD: Edinburgh; Hon ScD Cantab, Hon DTech Trondheim; US Legion of Merit (Cdr) 1946; *Style*— Air Cdre Sir Frank Whittle, OM, KBE, CB; - CB, 10327 Wilde Lake Terrace, Columbia, MD 21044, USA

WHITTON, Cuthbert Henry; s of Henry McManus Whitton (d 1951), of Clonsheagh Castle, Co Dublin, and Eleanor Constance, *née* Beatty (d 1956); *b* 18 Feb 1905; *Educ* St Andrew's Coll Dublin, Dublin Univ (BA); *m* 30 July 1938, Iris Elva, da of James Hawke Moody, of Port Talbot, Wales; 1 s (Brian b 1941 d 1942), 1 da (Jennifer b 1948); *Career* cadet Malayan Civil Serv 1929; transferred to Colonial Legal Serv 1939; barr Gray's Inn 1939; Puisne Judge Singapore and Malaya 1951, served in Malaya 1951-53 and in Singapore 1953-57; ret 1957; in legal dept Foreign Compensation Cmmn London 1957-71; ret; *Recreations* gardening; *Clubs* Royal Commonwealth Soc, Kildare St and Univ (Dublin); *Style*— Cuthbert Whitton Esq; Far End, Hill Waye, Gerrards Cross, Bucks (☎ 0753 885608)

WHITTY, (John) Lawrence; s of Frederick James Whitty (d 1981), and Kathleen May Whitty (d 1967); *b* 15 June 1943; *m* 11 Jan 1969 (m dis 1986), Tanya Margaret, da of Tom Gibson; 2 s (Michael Sean b 1970, David James b 1972); *Career* aviator Hawker Siddeley 19-62; Civil Serv 1965-70, Miny of Aviation, UKAEA, Miny of Technol; economics dept TUC 1970-73, nat res and political offr GMBATU (formerly Gen and Municipal Workers Union), gen sec Lab Pty 1985-; memb: Lab Pty (Islington, Greenwich, Dulwich, Peckham), Fabian Soc; *Recreations* swimming, walking, theatre; *Style*— Lawrence Whitty, Esq; 64 Coleman Rd, London SE5 7TG; Labour Party, 150 Walworth Rd, London, SE17 (☎ 01 703 0833)

WHITWORTH, Anthony Elliott; s of Geoffrey Maden Whitworth; *b* 12 Feb 1935; *Educ* Bromsgrove; *m* Elizabeth; 2 s, 2 da; *Career* chm Frijole Ltd; dir: Benjamin Priest Gp plc and subsidiaries; Mallett Machinery Ltd; Triland Metals Ltd; Ryleys Sch Ltd; FCA; *Recreations* sailing, business; *Clubs* Army and Navy; *Style*— Anthony E Whitworth, Esq; Clover Cottage, Snelson Lane, Snelson, Macclesfield, Cheshire SK11 9BL (☎ 0565 861236)

WHITWORTH, Gp Capt Frank; QC (1965); s of Daniel Arthur Whitworth (d 1958), of Didsbury, Manchester, and Gertrude, *née* Hodge (d 1969); *b* 13 May 1910; *Educ* Shrewsbury, Trinity Hall Cambridge (MA); *m* 1, 30 Sept 1939, (Mary) Lucy (d 1979), da of Sir John Holdsworth Robinson (d 1927), of Bradford; m 2, 24 May 1980, Irene Violet, da of late William Davidson, of S Africa, and wid of David Lannon; *Career* WWII Pilot Offr RAF 1940, Gp Capt special duties 1944, invalided out 1945; barr Gray's Inn 1934; contested (C) St Helens Gen Election 1945; rec Crown Ct 1972-82; judge of Cts of Appeal of Jersey and Guernsey 1971-80; memb Dorking & Horley RDC 1940-60; tstee Whiteley Homes 1963-; Sr Past Master Worshipful Co of Clockmakers; *Recreations* reading, writing; *Clubs* Utd Oxford and Cambridge; *Style*— Gp Capt Frank Whitworth, QC; Little Manor House, Westcott, Dorking, Surrey (☎ 0306 889966)

WHITWORTH, John Leslie; DFC (1945); s of Frank Sunderland Whitworth (d 1959), and Edith, *née* Chinn (d 1963); *b* 9 Jan 1921; *Educ* Bishop Vesey GS Sutton Coldfield; *m* 1950, Audrey Beatrice, da of Cyril Stanley Frank Girling (d 1980); 2 s; *Career* Actg Sqdn Ldr Pilot Bomber Cmd RAF 1942-43, Bomber Cmd Pathfinder Force Europe 1944-45, RAF Transport Cmd Burma 1945-46; engr and dir Heaton Ward Ltd 1951-1971, (md 1971-84, chm 1978-84), ret 1984; *Recreations* DIY, golf (Warwicks Co champion 1959, Eng sr champion 1982, Midlands sr champion 1985); *Clubs* Pathfinder, Walmley Golf; *Style*— John Whitworth, Esq, DFC; Brelade, 4 Upper Clifton Rd, Sutton Coldfield, W Midlands B73 6BP (☎ 021 354 6379)

WHITWORTH, Maj-Gen Reginald Henry; CB (1969), CBE (1963); s of Aymer William Whitworth (d 1976), and Alice Lucy Patience (d 1973), *née* Hervey, gda of Lord Arthur Hervey (d 1894), Bishop of Bath and Wells and s of 1 Marquis of Bristol; *b* 27 August 1916; *Educ* Eton, Balliol Coll and Queen's Coll Oxford; *m* 1946, June Rachel, da of Col Sir Bartle Mordaunt Edwards, CVO, MC, JP, DL, (d 1977), of Hardingham Hall, Norfolk; 2 s (and 1 decd), 1 da; *Career* Grenadier Gds 1940, GSO3 1944, Bde Maj 24 Gds Bde 1945-46, instr Staff Coll Camberley 1953-55, Cdr: 1 Gren Gds 1956-57, Berlin Inf Bde Gp 1961-63, GOC Yorks and Northumberland Dists 1966-68, COS Southern Cmd 1968-70; fell and bursar Exeter Coll Oxford 1970-81, chm: St Mary's Sch Wantage, Army Museums Ogilby Tst; tstee Historic Churches Preservation Tst USA Bronze Star 1946; *Books* Field Marshal Earl Ligonier, Famous Regiments: The Grenadier Guards; Le Gunner at Large (1988); *Recreations* riding, fishing, military history; *Clubs* Army and Navy; *Style*— Maj-Gen Reginald Whitworth, CB, CBE; Abbey Farm, Goosey, Oxon (☎ 03677 252)

WHYBROW, Christopher John; s of Herbert William Whybrow, OBE (d 1973), of Colchester, Essex, and Ruby Kathleen, *née* Watson; *b* 7 August 1942; *Educ* Colchester Royal GS, King's Coll London (LLB); *m* 1, 11 Sep 1969 (m dis 1976), Marian, da of John Macaulay, Ramsey of Essex; m 2, 4 April 1979, Susan, da of Edward Christie Younge, of Loddiswell, Devon; *Career* called to the Bar Inner Temple 1965; church warden St Matthews Leavenheath, vice-chm Leavenheath CC; *Recreations* cricket, tennis, country life; *Clubs* Lansdowne, Offrs (Colchester); *Style*— Christopher Whybrow, Esq; Spring Farm, Leavenheath, Suffolk; 2 Mitre Court Buildings, Temple, London EC4Y 7BX

WHYTE, Donald; JP (City of Edinburgh); s of late John Whyte, of Almondhill, Kirkliston, and late Catherine Dunachie; descended from Archibald Whyte in Tignafaolin, LochECKside, Argyll who flourished c1740; *b* 26 Mar 1926; *Educ* Crookston Sch Musselburgh, Inst of Heraldic and Genealogical Studies Canterbury; *m* 1950, Mary, da of George Laird Burton; 3 da; *Career* conslt genealogist, author, lectr; memb pres Assoc Scottish Genealogists and Record Agents; vice-pres: Scottish Genealogy Soc, family history socs Glasgow, Aberdeen and Dundee; granted armorial bearings Lyon Office 1986; Citation of Recognition, Ontario Geneaological Soc 1987; *Books* Kirkliston: a Short Parish History (third edn 1975), Dictionary of Scottish Emigrants to the USA pre-1855 (1972, repr 1981, vol 2 1986), Introducing Genealogical Research (fifth edn 1985), Dictionary of Scottish Emigrants to Canada Before Confederation (1986), Walter MacFarlane: Clan Chief and Antiquary (1988), contrib to numerous academic jnls; FHGT, FSG; *Recreations* motoring, black and white photography; *Clubs* Edinburgh Airport Social; *Style*— Donald Whyte, Esq, JP; 4 Carmel Rd, Kirkliston, West Lothian EH29 9DD (☎ 031 333 3245)

WHYTE, Sir (William Erskine) Hamilton; CMG (1979); s of Prof William Hamilton Whyte (d 1972), of Univ of Bristol, and Janet, *née* Williamson; *b* 28 May 1927; *Educ* King's Sch Bruton, Queen's Coll Oxford (BA); *m* 1953, Sheila Annie, da of William James Townsend Duck (d 1964); 3 da (Lucy d 1984, Polly, Kate); *Career* RN 1945-48, Able Seaman; Caribbean and BWI Station; civil asst War Off 1952-55; FO 1955-, HM Embassy: Vienna 1956-59, Bangkok 1959-62; UK Mission to the UN New York 1963-66, FO 1966-70, HM Embassy Kinshasa 1970-72; dir-gen British Info Servs New York 1972-76; FCO, head of News Dept 1976-79; min, subsequently ambassador and dep permanent rep UK Mission to the UN NY 1979-83, high cmmr Nigeria, ambass Benin 1983-84, high commr Singapore 1985-87; *Recreations* gardening, photography; *Clubs* The Century Assoc (New York); *Style*— Sir Hamilton Whyte, CMG; Eden Hall, 28 Nassim Rd, Singapore 1024 (☎ 2357252); The Lodge, Ford Lane, Ford, W Sussex (☎ Yapton 551477); British High Cmmn, Tanglin Rd, Singapore 1024 (☎ 4739333)

WHYTE, John Stuart; CBE (1976); s of William Walter Whyte (d 1951), and Ethel Kate, *née* Budd (d 1983); *b* 20 July 1923; *Educ* The John Lyon Sch Harrow, Northampton Engrg Coll London Univ (BSc (Eng), MSc); *m* 10 March 1953, (Edna) Joan Mary, da of Frank Stark Budd (d 1942); 1 s (Peter b 1954), 1 da (Anne (Mrs McCulloch) b 1959); *Career* HM Treasy 1965-68; Post Off Telecommunications 1968-79; dep md Br Telecom 1979-81; md and engr-in-chief Br Telecom 1981-83; chm Plessey Telecoms Int 1983-88; pres Stromberg Carlson Corpn (USA) 1984-85; chm: Astronet Corpn 1984-86, GEC/Plessey Telecoms Int 1988-; pres Assoc of Br Membs of Swiss Alpine Club 1988-; vice-pres: Royal Inst 1972-74, Inst of Electrical Engrs 1981-84; dep chm Nat Electronics Cncl 1976-; pres Inst of Telecommunications Engrs 1977-83; govr Int Cncl for Computer Communications 1982-; Freeman City London 1979, Liveryman Worshipful Co of Scientific Instrument Makers 1979; FEng 1982, FIEE 1966, CEng 1951, CBIM 1982; *Recreations* mountaineering, opera; *Clubs* Alpine; *Style*— John Whyte, Esq, CBE; Wild Hatch, Coleshill Lane, Amersham, Bucks HP7 0NT (☎ 0494 722663); GPT (Int), Vanwall Business Park, Vanwall Rd, Maidenhead, Berks SL6 4UN (☎ 0628 23351)

WIBBERLEY, Prof Gerald Percy; CBE (1972); s of Percy Wibberley (d 1915), of Abergavenny, Gwent, and Ellen Mary, *née* Jackson (d 1962); *b* 15 April 1915; *Educ* King Henry V111 GS Abergavenny, Univ Coll of Wales Aberystwyth (BSc,PhD), Univ of Oxford, Univ of Illinois USA (MSc); *m* 1, 18 Sept 1943, Helen Cecilia (d 1964), da of John Youmans (d 1967), of Newport, Indiana, USA; 1 da (Jane b 1945); m 2, Sept 1972, Peggy, *née* Samways; *Career* E Sussex Agric Exex Ctee 1941, chief res offr land use Miny of Agric 1948 (asst 1945), head econs dept Wye Coll Univ of London 1954: (Wye Coll and UCL); personal chair in rural economy 1963, personal chair in countryside planning; conslt to Kent CC on rural planning; memb Kent Educn Ctee 1982-89; cncl memb: Ctee for Small Industs in Rural Areas 1960-86, Nature Conservancy 1972-80; hon memb Royal Town Planning Inst 1949; Hon DSc Univ of Bradford 1984; memb: Br Agric Econ Soc 1939- (Pres 1975), Int Assoc of Agric Econs; Order of Merit Univ of Padua Italy 1982; *Books* Agriculture and Urban Growth (1959), Planning and The Rural Environment (with J Davidson, 1977); *Recreations* choral music; *Clubs* Farmers; *Style*— Prof Gerald Wibberley, CBE; Vicarage Cottage, 7 Upper Bridge St, Wye Nr Ashford, Kent TN25 5AN (☎ 0233 812 377)

WICK, Patricia Joyce; da of Dr Douglas George Pollard, of Bristol, and Dorothea Mary, *née* Hunter; *b* 31 August 1953; *Educ* Rose Green HS Bristol, Birmingham Univ (BA); *m* 28 Sept 1984, Graham David, s of Norman Wick, of Tadworth, Surrey; 1 da (Holly b 19 July 1986); *Career* dir FT Int Ltd Farnborough 1986-; *Recreations* art; *Style*— Mrs Patricia Wick; 41 Queens Rd, Farnborough, Hants (☎ 0252 549 775, fax 0252 548 800, telex 859804)

WICKENS, Dr Alan Herbert; OBE (1980); s of Leslie Herbert Wickens (d 1986), of Birmingham, and Sylvia Amelia, *née* Hazelgrove (d 1968); *b* 29 Mar 1929; *Educ* Ashville Coll Harrogate, Loughborough Univ (DLC, DSc), London Univ (BSc); *m* 1, 12 Dec 1953, Eleanor Joyce Waggot (d 1984); 1 da (Valerie Joanne b 1958); m 2, 2 July 1987, Patricia Anne McNeil, da of Willoughby Jervaise Cooper, of Dawlish; *Career* res engr Armstrong Whitworth Aircraft Ltd 1951-55, Canadair Ltd Montreal 1955-59, Airvoe & Co Ltd 1959-62; British Rail: res dept 1962-68, dir advanced projects 1968-71, dir res 1971-84, dir engrg r & d 1984; industl prof Loughborough Univ of Technol 1972-76, chm off res and experiment Union Internationale de Chemin de Fer Utrecht 1988-, writer of various pubns on dynamics of railway vehicles, high speed trains and railway technol; pres Int Assoc of Vehicle System Dynamics 1981-86, jt winner Macrobert Award 1975; Hon DTech CNAA 1978, Hon Doctorate Open Univ 1980, Hon Fell Derbyshire Coll of Higher Educn 1984; MAIAA 1958, MRAeS 1963, FIMechE 1971, FEng 1980; *Recreations* gardening, travel, music; *Style*— Dr Alan Wickens, OBE; Railway Technical Centre, London Rd, Derby DE2 8UP (☎ 0332 43301)

WICKERSON, Sir John Michael; s of Walter Wickerson, of London, and Ruth Ivy

Constance Field; *b* 22 Sept 1937; *Educ* Christ's Hosp, London Univ (LLB); *m* 1963, Shirley Maud, da of Andrew Best (d 1980); 1 s (Andrew b 1968); *Career* qualified slr 1960; pres: London Criminal Cts Slrs Assoc 1981-83, Law Soc England and Wales 1986-87; dir R Mansell Ltd; hon memb: American Bar Assoc, Canadian Bar Assoc, NZ Law Assoc; *Books* Motorist and the Law; kt 1987; *Recreations* sport, music; *Style—* Sir John Wickerson; 10 High St, Croydon, Surrey (☎ 01 686 3841)

WICKHAM, Rt Rev Dr Edward Ralph; s of Edward Wickham, and Minnie, *née* Wanty; *b* 3 Nov 1911; *Educ* Univ of London (BD), St Stephen's House Oxford; *m* June 1944, (Dorothy) Helen, da of Prof K N Moss; 1 s, 2 da; *Career* ordained 1938, curate Christ Church Newcastle upon Tyne 1938-41, chaplain Royal Ordnance Factory No 5 1941-44, fndr and dir Sheffield Industl Mission 1944-59, bishop of Middleton in the Diocese of Manchester 1960-84, asst bishop Diocese of Manchester 1984-; Hon DLitt Univ of Salford 1973; FRSA; *Books* Church and People in an Industrial City (1959), Encounter with Modern Society (1964); *Recreations* rock-climbing, mountaineering; *Style—* The Rt Rev Dr E R Wickham; 12 Westminster Rd, Eccles, Salford, Manchester M30 9HF (☎ 061 789 3144)

WICKHAM, Hon Mrs (Helen Mary); *née* Wade; er da of Baron Wade, DL (Life Peer, d 1988); *b* 14 April 1933; *m* 28 Sept 1963, Rev Dr Lionel Ralph Wickham, s of Harry Temple Wickham, formerly of Bromley, Kent; children; *Style—* The Hon Mrs Wickham; c/o Divinity Faculty, Divinity School, Trinity St, Cambridge

WICKHAM, Henry Lewis; s of Henry Albert Wickham (d 1974), and Alice Emily (d 1967); *b* 30 July 1927; *Educ* St Dunstans Coll Catford, Pinner County Sch, Hammersmith Sch of Architecture (Dip Arch); *m* 5 Oct 1957, Patricia Rose, da of Thomas Pearce (d 1978), of Boreham, Herts; 1 da (Susan b 1959); *Career* architect: London Tport 1955-58, Sir Robert McAlpine and Sons 1958-64, BR 1964-65, Arndale Property Tst 1965-67, London Borough of Ealing 1967-72; ptnr G M Assocs 1972-79, in own private practice 1979-; memb: Guild of Freemen of the City of London, Planning and Tport Ctee Exeter C of C and Trade; project coordinator RIBA Community Gp E Devon; assoc Faculty of Architects and Surveyors, ARIBA; *Recreations* walking, cycling, photography; *Style—* Henry L Wickham, Esq; 2 Clinton Ave, Exeter, Devon EX4 7BA (☎ 0392 51993)

WICKHAM, (William) Jeffry Alexander; RD (1974); s of Lt Col Edward Thomas, Ruscombe Wickham, MVO (d 1957), and Rachel Marguerite, *née* Alexander (d 1955); *b* 5 August 1933; *Educ* Eton, Balliol Coll Oxford (BA, MA), LAMDA; *m* April 1962, Clare Marion, da of A R M Stewart (d 1958), of Fearnan; 2 s (Caspar (Fred) b 1962, Rupert b 1964), 1 da (Saskia b 1967); *Career* Nat Serv RN 1962-64, Russian interpreter 1964; actor; West End appearances incl: Othello Old Vic 1963, Catch My Soul (The Rock Othello) Prince of Wales 1970, The Unknown Soldier and his Wife New London 1973, The Marrying of Ann Leete Aldwych 1975, Donkey's Years Globe 1976, The Family Reunion Vaudeville 1979, Anyone for Denis? Whitehall 1981, Amadeus Her Majesty's 1982, Interpreters Queen's 1985, Beyond Reasonable Doubt Queen's 1987; Nat Theatre 1983-85 and 1986-87: Saint Joan, The Spanish Tragedy, A Little Hotel on the Side, The Magistrate; cncllr Br Actors Equity Assoc (vice pres 1986-89), memb cncl Actors' Benevolent Fund; Liveryman Worshipful Co of Skinners 1956; *Recreations* walking, languages; *Style—* Jeffry Wickham, Esq, RD; c/o Plant & Froggati Ltd, 4 Windmill St, London W1 (☎ 01 636 4412)

WICKHAM, John Ewart Alfred; s of Alfred James Wickham (d 1931), of Chichester, Sussex, and Hilda May, *née* Cummins (d 1977); *b* 10 Dec 1927; *Educ* Chichester GS, London Univ St Bartholomew's Med Coll (BSc, MB, BS, MS); *m* 28 July 1961, (Gwendoline) Ann, da of James Henry Honey (d 1975); 3 da (Susan Jane b 31 May 1962, Caroline Elizabeth b 28 July 1963, (Ann) Clare b 4 July 1966); *Career* Nat Serv RAF 1947-49; sr conslt urological surgn St Bart's Hosp London 1966-, surgn St Peters Hosp London 1967-, sr lectr Inst of Urology London 1967-, surgn King Edward VIII Hosp for Offrs London 1973, surgn urologist RAF 1973-, dir academic unit Inst of Urology Univ of London 1979-, dir London Clinic Lithotriptor Unit 1987-, dir N E Thames Regnl Lithotriptor Unit 1987-, pres RSM Urological Section 1984; dir: Rencal Ltd, London Lithotriptor Co Ltd, Aquaplastics Ltd, BPI Couferences Ltd; Freeman City of London 1971, Liveryman Worshipful Co of Barber Surgns 1971; Hunterian Prof and Medal RCS 1970, James Berry Prize and Medal for contribs to renal surgery 1982, Cutlers Prize Assoc Surgns GB for surgical instrument design 1985, St Peters Medal Br Assoc of Urological Surgns 1985; FRCS 1959, FRSM; Fulbright Scholars of USA 1964; *Books* Urinary Calculous Disease (1979), Percutaneous Royal Surgery (1983), Intra-Reval Surgery (1984), Lithotripsy II (1987), Urinary Stone Metabolic Basis and Clinical Practice (1989); *Recreations* mechanical engineering, tennis; *Clubs* Athenaeum; *Style—* John Wickham, Esq; Stowe Maries, Balchinslawe, Westcott, Surrey RH4 3LR (☎ 0306 885557); 29 Devonshire Pl, London W1N 1PE (☎ 01 935 2232)

WICKHAM, Julyan Michael; s of Michael Whalley Wickham (painter, designer), and Tatiana, *née* van Langandoc (d 1976); *b* 14 August 1942; *Educ* Pinewood Sch Herts/ Devon, Holloway Comprehensive, Tulse Hill Comprehensive, Architectural Assoc (AADipl, RIBA); *m* 1969, Tess, da of Prof Aldo Ernest van Eyck, of Loenen a/d Vecht, Holland; 1 s (Rufus b 1971), 1 da (Pola Alexandra b 1969); *Career* architect ARCUK, memb RIBA, princ ptnr Wickham & Assocs (established 1971); *Clubs* Zanzibar, Groucho, FREDS; *Style—* Julyan M Wickham, Esq; 46 St Mary's Mansions, St Mary's Terrace, London W2; 4-5 Crawford Passage, London EC1R 3DP (☎ 01 833 2631, fax 01 833 4993, car ☎ 0836 612 998)

WICKHAM, His Hon Judge; William Rayley; s of Rayley Esmond Wickham (d 1970), and Mary Joyce, *née* Thom (d 1965); *b* 22 Sept 1926; *Educ* Sedbergh, Brasenose Coll Oxford (MA, BCL); *m* 11 May 1957, Elizabeth Mary, da of John Harrison Thompson (d 1957); 1 s (Christopher b 1961), 2 da (Katharine b 1958, Sarah b 1959); *Career* Army 1944-47 Lt; called to Bar Inner Temple 1951; magistrate Aden 1953 (chief magistrate 1957), crown cnsl Tanganyika 1959, asst to law offrs Tanganyika 1961-63, rec 1972, circuit judge 1975; *Style—* His Honour Judge Wickham; 115 Vyner Rd South, Bidston, Birkenhead, Merseyside (☎ 652 2095); Queen Elizabeth II Law Courts, Liverpool

WICKHAM-BOYNTON, Marcus William; DL North Humberside; s of Capt Thomas Lamplugh Wickham-Boynton, JP, DL, of Driffield, and Cycley Mabel (d 1947), da and heiress of Sir Henry Somerville Boynton, 11 Bt; proprietor of Burton Agnes Estate by descent for 900 years from gift after Norman Conquest to Robert de Bruis, and hence through the Sentevilles, Merlays and Somervilles to the Griffiths 1365; the last of whom Sir Henry Griffith Bt built in 1600 the magnificient Elizabethan house which was later acquired in marriage by the 1st Bt Boynton (cr 1618) whose family's home it has thus been for the last 380 years; *b* 6 April 1904; *Educ* Eton, France; *Career* Capt Welsh Gds, serv WWII GHQ 1942-44; chm York Race Ctee; owner Burton Agnes Stud; *Clubs* Jockey Club Rooms, Boodles; *Style—* Marcus Wickham-Boyton, Esq, DL; Burton Agnes Hall, Driffield, N Humberside Y025 0ND (☎ 026 289 388)

WICKINS, David Allen; s of James Samuel Wickins (d 1940), and Edith Hannah (d 1973); ggs of Adm Sir Robert Henry Wickins; *b* 15 Feb 1920; *Educ* St George's Coll Weybridge; *m* 1960, Dorothy Covington; 1 s, 5 da; *Career* serv South Afican Naval Forces, seconded to RN Coastal Forces (Lt) WWII; chm: British Car Auction Gp plc, Attwoods plc, Gp of Lotus Car Cos plc; memb IOD; *Recreations* golf, sailing (yacht 'Stavros II'), racing (race-horses: Return to Power and Indianapolis, winner Schweppes Gold Cup); *Clubs* Royal Thames Yacht, Sunningdale Golf; *Style—* David Wickins Esq; 16 Rutland Mews South, London SW7 (☎ 01 589 6047); The British Car Auction Gp plc, Expedier House, Portsmouth Rd, Hindhead, Surrey (☎ (042 873) 7440, telex 858192)

WICKLOW, Countess of; Eleanor; da of Prof Rudolph Butler, of Dublin; *m* 1959, 8 and last Earl of Wicklow (d 1978); *Career* memb Irish Senate 1948-51; *Style—* The Rt Hon Countess of Wicklow; Sea Grange, Sandycove Ave East, Dun Laoghaire, Co Dublin, Eire

WICKRAMASINGHE, Prof (Nalin) Chandra; s of Percival Herbert Wickramasinghe, of Sri Lanka, and Theresa Elizabeth, *née* Soysa; *b* 20 Jan 1939; *Educ* Royal Coll Colombo, Univ of Ceylon, (BSc), Univ of Cambridge (MA, Phd, ScD); *m* 5 April 1966, (Nelum) Priyadarshini, da of Cecil Eustace Pereira; 1 s (Anil Nissanka b 1970), 2 da (Kamala Chandrika b 1972, Janaki Tara b 1981); *Career* fell Jesus Coll Cambridge 1963-73, prof and head Dept of Applied Mathematics & Astronomy Univ Coll Cardiff 1973-88; professor Applied Maths & Astronomy Univ of Wales 1988-; dir Inst of Fundamental Studies and advsr Pres of Sri Lanka 1982-84; co-author with Prof Sir Fred Hoyle of a series of books of cosmic theory of life 1978-88; Powell Prize for English Verse Trinity Coll Cambridge 1962, Int Dag Hammarskjöld Gold Medal for Science 1986, Scholarly Achievement Award Inst of Oriental Philosophy Japan 1988; *Books* Interstellar Grains (1967), Light Scattering Functions (1973); with F Hoyle: Lifecloud (1978), Diseases from Space (1979), Evolution from Space (1981), Space Travellers (1981), Living Comets (1985), From Grains to Bacteria (1984), Archaeopteryx (1986), Cosmic Life Force (1988); *Recreations* photography, poetry, history of sci; *Clubs* Icosahedron Dining Club (Cardiff); *Style—* Prof Chandra Wickramasinghe; 24 Llwynypia Rd, Lisvane, Cardiff CF4 5SY (☎ 0222 752 146); School of Mathematics, University of Wales College of Cardiff, Senghennydd Rd, Cardiff CF2 4AG (☎ 0222 874 811, fax 0222 371 921, telex 498635)

WICKS, Brian Cairns; TD; s of Henry Gillies Wicks (d 1970), of Eastbourne, and Ethel (d 1968); *b* 26 Mar 1934; *Educ* Sedbergh, Cambridge Univ (BA); *m* 31 March 1959, Judith Anne, da of Kennedy Harrison (d 1961); 1 s (Robert b 1965), 1 da (Pippa b 1962); *Career* Maj 4/5 Btn Green Howards (TA), A/G AVT 1 W African Field Battery Nigeria 1952-54; dir sec ICI plc Paints Div 1975-86, dep dir gen Nat Farmers Union 1986, pres S Bucks and E Berks C of C and Ind 1981-83, chm Berks Business Gp 1983-87; Freeman City of London, Liveryman Worshipful Co of Glovers 1988; *Recreations* fishing, shooting, squash, gardening; *Style—* Brian C Wicks, Esq; Gracefield Main Road, Lacey Green, Aylesbury, Bucks HP17 0QU; Knightsbridge, London SW1 (☎ 01 235 5077)

WICKS, Sir James; s of James Wicks (d 1964), and Lilian Mary, *née* Purser (d 1966); *b* 20 June 1909; *Educ* Royal GS Guildford, King's Coll London (LLB), Ch Ch Oxford (MA, BLitt); *m* 1960, Doris Mary, da of G Sutton; *Career* serv RAF WWII; chartered surveyor 1931; barr Gray's Inn 1939, former crown counsel Palestine and judiciary Hong Kong; Kenya: puisne judge 1958-69, sr puisne judge 1969-71, chief justice 1971-82 and Court of Appeal 1977-82, ret; kt 1972; *Style—* Sir James Wicks; Cote de Vauxlaurens, Cambridge Park, St Peter Port, Guernsey, CI (☎ 0481 20249)

WICKSTEED, Capt Denis George; s of George Frederick Wicksteed (d 1949), of Stourton Mill, Warwicks and Christina Nesta Wicksteed (d 1981); *b* 30 Jan 1919; *Educ* King Edward VI Sch Stratford Upon Avon; *m* 14 March 1942, Beryl Sutton da of Albert Gellion (d 1983) of Port St Mary, Isle of Man; 2 s (Antony Sutton b 1943, Michael John b 1946, d 1978); *Career* Midshipman-Chief Offr Elder Dempster Lines 1935-46, (camp ldr NW Africa POW Camp 1942-43), King's Commendation for Brave conduct 1943, Third Offr (later Chief Offr) Cunard Line 1946-58, Lt RNR 1949; Lt: HMS Contest 1950-51, HMS Crossbow 1953-54; Lt Cdr RNR 1957, ADC to Lord High Com Holyrood Palace 1957, Insp and later Dep Chief Insp RNLI 1958-70; cdr RNR 1960 RD 1965; Adm Cmdg: Reserves Advsy Cncl 1967-70, Flag and COs Ctee 1971-73; Capt RNR 1966; cmdg in Paicfic Int Line 1977-83; Freeman City of London 1973, Liveryman Honourable Co of Master Mariners; *Recreations* fishing; *Style—* Capt Denis Wicksteed, RD, RNR; 13 The Shimmings, Guildford, Surrey GU1 2NG (☎ 0483 63827);

WIDDECOMBE, Ann Noreen; da of James Murray Widdecombe, CB, OBE, and Rita Noreen Widdecombe; *b* 4 Oct 1947; *Educ* La Sainte Union Convent, Bath; Univs of Birmingham and Oxford (LMH), MA (Oxon); *Career* Sr Admin London U 1975-87; Runymede dist cncllr 1976-78, Fndr and vice-chm Women & Families for Def 1983-85, contested gen elections (C) (Burnley 1979, Plymouth Devonport 1983); MP (C) Maidstone 1987-; *Books* Laymans Guide to Defence (1984); *Recreations* riding, reading; *Style—* Miss Ann Widdecombe; 9 Tamar House, Kennington Lane, London SE11 4AX (☎ 01 735 5192); House of Commons (☎ 01 219 5091)

WIDDECOMBE, (James) Murray; CB (1968), OBE (1959); s of Charles Frederick Widdecombe (d 1944), of Saltash Cornwall, and Alice Beatrice Lillian (d 1972); *b* 7 Jan 1910; *Educ* Devonport HS; *m* 1936, Rita Noreen, da of James Plummer (d 1929), of St Budeaux, Devonport; 1 s (Malcolm Murray m 1965 Ann Meryl Jones), 1 da (Ann Noreen); *Career* Admty: entered Exec Offr Admty 1929, sr Armament Supply Offr, Capt RNVR, staff of C-in-C Med 1944-46; dep-dir Armament Supply Admty 1959-61, dir Victualling Admty 1961-66; head RN Supply and Tport Serv MOD 1966-68, dir-gen: Supplies and Tport (Naval) MOD 1968-70, Special Duties Mgmnt Servs MOD 1970-73, gen-sec Civil Serv Retirement Fellowship 1973-79; pres Navy Dept Golfing Soc; FBIM, FIPS; *Recreations* golf, gardening, amateur dramatics; *Clubs* Hindhead Golf; *Style—* Murray Widdecombe, Esq, CB, OBE; Keng Hua, 1 Manor Close, Haslemere, Surrey GU27 1PP (☎ 0428 2899)

WIDDIS, William Thomas (Bill); s of Capt George Thomas Widdis (d 1979), of Bitterne Park, Southampton, and Maud, *née* Jamieson (d 1979); *b* 19 Dec 1940; *Educ*

Duke of York's Royal Mil School Dover; *m* 8 Oct 1966, Anne, da of Leslie Robert Biddlesden, of Reading; 1 s (Robert Thomas b 1 June 1969), 1 da (Patricia Anne b 23 Feb 1971); *Career* offr Customs & Excise 1960-70, official assignee The Stock Exchange 1984-86 (systems mangr 1975-85), systems devpt dir The Int Stock Exchange 1986; *Recreations* golf, squash, bridge; *Clubs* Sonning Golf; *Style—* Bill Widdis, Esq; Woodley cottage, Loddon Bridge, Woodley, Reading, Berks (☎ 0734 695379); The Int Stock Exchange, London EC2N 1HP (☎ 01 588 2355, fax 01 588 7653, telex 886557)

WIDDOWS, Hon Mrs; Angela Hermione; *née* Marshall; da of Baron Marshall of Leeds; *b* 9 Feb 1944; *Educ* Queen Margaret's Sch Escrick York, Les Ambassadrices Paris, The Cygnets House London, Yorkshire Ladies Cncl of Educn; *m* 1, 1966 (m dis 1979), Myles Spencer Harrison Hartley; 1 s (Robert b 1974), 2 da (Annabelle b 1967, Alexandra b 1972) 1986 Major Geoffrey Widdows 15/19 Hussars, yr s of Air Cdre Charles Widdows *qv*, of Guernsey CI; *Recreations* field sports, music and church music; *Style—* The Hon Mrs Widdows; The Home Farm, Sand Hutton, York

WIDDOWS, Air Cdre (Stanley) Charles; CB (1959), DFC (1941); s of Percy Lionel Widdows and Beatrice Olive, *née* Warner; *b* 4 Oct 1909; *Educ* St Bartholemew's Sch Newbury, No 1 School of Tech Trg RAF Halton, RAF Coll Cranwell; *m* 1939, Irene Ethel, da of Sidney Rawlings; 2 s; *Career* cmmnd RAF 1931, Fighting Area (RAF) 1931-32, serv Middle E, Egypt, Sudan, Palestine 1933-37, Aeroplane and Armament Experimental Estab 1937-40, OC: 29 (Fighter) Sqdn 1940-41, RAF West Malling 1941-42; Gp Capt Night Ops HQ 11 and 12 Gp 1942, SASO No 85 (Base Def) Gp 1943-44 (Op Overlord), Gp Capt Organisation HQ AEAF 1944, OC RAF Wahn (Ger) 1944-46, RAF Dir Sr Offrs War Course RNC Greenwich 1946-48; Fighter Cmnd 1948-54: SASO HQ No 12 Gp, Chief Instr (Air Def Wing) Sch of Land/Air Warfare, Eastern Sector Cdr; IDC 1955, Dir Ops (Air Def) Air Miny 1956-58, twice mentioned in despatches; People's Dep States of Guernsey 1973-79; Bailiwick rep RAF Benevolent Fund,; *Style—* Air Cdre Charles Widdows, CB, DFC; Les Granges de Beauvoir, Rohais, St Peter Port, Guernsey, CI (☎ 0481 20219)

WIDDOWSON, Prof Henry George; s of George Percival Widdowson (d 1986), of East Runton, Norfolk, and Edna May, *née* Garrison (d 1980); *b* 28 May 1935; *Educ* Alderman Newton's Sch Leicester, King's Coll Cambridge (MA), Univ of Edinburgh (PhD); *m* 15 July 1966, Dominique Nicole Helene, da of Jean Dixmier, of Paris; 2 s (Marc Alain b 24 May 1968, Arnold b 18 Oct 1972); *Career* Nat Serv RN 1956; english language offr Br Cncl Sri Lanka and Bangladesh 1962-68, lectr dep of linguistics Univ of Edinburgh 1968-77, prof of educn Inst of Educn London Univ, chm advsy ctee Br Cncl English Teaching, vice chm Bell Educn Tst, fndr ed Applied Linguistics; memb Kingman ctee on the Teaching of English Language; *Books* Stylistics and the Teaching of Literature (1975), Teaching Language as Communication (1978), Explorations in Applied Linguistics (vol I 1979, vol II 1984), Learning Purpose and Language use (1983), Language Teaching: A Scheme for Teacher Education (ed), English in the World (with Randolph Quirk, 1985); *Recreations* reading, walking, travel, poetry; *Style—* Prof Henry Widdowson; 151 Sheen Rd, Richmond upon Thames, Surrey (☎ 01 948 0854); Institute of Education, 20 Bedford Way, London (☎ 01 636 1500)

WIDDRINGTON, Francis Nathaniel Heron; yr s of Brig-Gen Bertram FitzHerbert Widdrington, CMG, DSO, DL, JP (d 1942), of Newton Hall, Newton on the Moor, Morpeth, Northumberland, and Clothilde Enid (d 1952); da of Edward Onslow-Ford, RA, the sculptor; *b* 5 Jan 1920; *Educ* Stowe, RMC Sandhurst; *m* 21 April 1949, Gabrielle, da of Loris Emerson Mather, CBE (d 1976), and formerly wife of John Marcus Garforth-Bles; *Career* Capt Welsh Gds 1939-49, serv: Gibraltar, NW Europe 1939-45, Palestine 1945-48, (wounded twice); JP Northumberland 1957, High Sheriff 1966-67; *Recreations* field sports; *Style—* Francis Widdrington, Esq; Newton Hall, Newton on the Moor, Morpeth, Northumberland (☎ 666 575 273)

WIDGERY, Baroness; Ann; da of William Kermode, of Peel, IOM; *m* 1948, Baron Widgery, OBE, TD, PC, DL (Life Peer cr 1971, d 1981); *Style—* The Rt Hon Lady Widgery; 56 Jubilee Place, Chelsea SW3 3QT

WIELAND, Barry Raymond; s of Otto Charles Wieland, and Hilda Victoria, *née* Ayling (d 1985); *b* 13 Oct 1922; *Educ* St Josephs Coll Beulah Hill London; *m* 4 May 1957, Mary Evelyn (Meryl) (d 1986), da of late Murdo Macrae; 1 da (Alexandra Mary b 23 Jan 1965); *Career* enlisted 1942, RMA, cmmnd Buffs, serv E Africa, Cmd 3 Bn KAR, 2 Bn N Rhodesia Regt Somali Scouts, appt ADC to Mil Govr of Br Somaliland; joined Schlesinger Orgn S Africa 1952; dir: Odeon Cinema Hldgs Ltd, African Consolidated Investmt Corpn Ltd, African Caterers Ltd, African Theatres Ltd, African Amalgamated Advtg Ltd; res dir Schlesinger Orgn London, dir Int Variety & Theatrical Agency, ptnr Collingwood of Conduit St Ltd 1959, joined Chaumet Jewellers 1980; grand council Monarchist League; Freeman City of London; holder Malaysian Illustrious Order of Kinabalu (Datuk) 1975; *Clubs* Oriental, Hurlingham, Anabells, Marks; *Style—* Barry Wieland, Esq; 83 Hamlet Gdns, London W6 0SX; Chaumet (UK) Ltd, 178 New Bond St, London W1Y 9PD (☎ 01 493 5403/629 0136)

WIELD, (William) Adrian Cunningham; s of Captain Ronald Cunningham Wield, CBE, RN (d 1981), of Coburg, Chudleigh, S Devon, and Mary, *née* MacDonald; *b* 19 Feb 1937; *Educ* Downside; *m* 8 June 1979, Benedicte, da of Poul Preben Schoning (d 1984), of Copenhagen; 1 s (Alexander b 1983), 1 da (Isobel b 1980); *Career* 2 Lt Duke of Cornwall LI 1955-57; stockbroker; ptnr W Mortimer 1967-68, dir EB Savory Milln (later SBC1 Savory Milln) 1985-88 (ptr 1968-85), dir Albert Sharp & Co 1988-; memb London Stock Exchange 1959-1988; *Books* 1973 The Special Steel Indust (pub ptely, 1973); *Recreations* golf, shooting, sailing; *Clubs* Reform; *Style—* Adrian Wield, Esq; Tysoe Manor, Tysoe, Warwicks; Scott House Sekforde St, London EC1 (☎ 029 588 709); c/o Albert Sharp & Co, Davies House, 1 Sun St, London EC2 (☎ 01 638 7275, fax 01 638 7270, telex 336550)

WIELER, Anthony Eric; s of Brig Leslie Frederic Ethelbert Wieler, CB, CBE, JP (d 1965), of Feathercombe, Hambledon, Surrey, and Elisabeth Anne, *née* Parker (d 1984); *b* 12 June 1937; *Educ* Shrewsbury, Trinity Coll Oxford (MA); *Career* Nat Serv 1958-60, 2 Lt 7 Duke of Edinburgh's Own Gurkha Rifles (in 1967 organised the appeal which raised £1.5m for Gurkha Welfare Tsts); joined L Messel & Co, memb London Stock Exchange until 1967, sr investmt mangr Ionian Bank Ltd until 1972; fndr chm: Anthony Wieler & Co Ltd 1972, Anthony Wieler Unit Tst Mgmnt 1982; dir Lorne House Tst IOM 1987 dir Arbuthnot Fund Mangrs Ltd 1988; fndr Oxford Univ Modern Pentathlon Assoc 1957 (organised first match against Cambridge), chm Hambledon PCC 1965-76, initial subscriber Centre for Policy Studies 1972 (Wider Ownership sub ctee), hon sec AIIM, 1974-88; *Recreations* tennis; *Clubs* Boodle's; *Style—* Anthony Wieler, Esq; Feathercombe, Hambledon, nr Godalming, Surrey, GU8 4DP (☎ 048632 200); Anthony Wieler & Co Ltd, 19 Widegate St, off Bishopsgate, London, E1 7HP (☎ 01 377 1010, fax 01 247 5000, telex 886307)

WIGAN, Sir Alan Lewis; 5 Bt (UK 1898), of Clare Lawn, Mortlake, Surrey, and Purland Chase, Ross, Herefordshire; s of Sir Roderick Grey Wigan, 3 Bt (d 1954), and bro of Sir Frederick Adair Wigan, 4 Bt (d 1979); *b* 19 Nov 1913; *Educ* Eton, Magdalen Coll Oxford; *m* 1950, Robina, sis of Countess of Arran (w of 8 Earl), aunt of Duchess of Argyll (w of 12 Duke), and da of Lt-Col Sir Iain Colquhoun of Luss, 7 Bt, KT, DSO; 1 s, 1 da (Rebecca, b 1953, m 1, 1976 (m dis 1977), John Spearman; m 2, 1978 (m dis 1986), James Compton, s of Robin Compton, *qv*; 2 s, 1 da); *Heir* s, Michael Iain, b 3 Oct 1951; m 1984, Frances, da of late Flt Lt Angus Barr Fawcett; *Career* serv WWII KRRC (wounded and POW 1940); former dep chm Charrington & Co (Brewers), Master Brewers Co 1959-60; *Style—* Sir Alan Wigan, Bt; Badingham House, Badingham, Woodbridge, Suffolk (☎ 072 875 664); Moorburn, The Lake, Kircudbright

WIGAN, Hon Mrs Caroline; *née* Kinnaird; da of 13 Lord Kinnaird; *m* 1970, Christopher Wigan, s of Algernon Wigan; 1 s, 1 da; *Style—* The Hon Mrs Wigan; 14 Zetland House, Marloes Rd, W8

WIGAN, Christopher; 3 s of Maj Algernon Desmond Wigan, MC, TD, Mary, da of Capt Eric Butler-Henderson, 6 s of 1st Baron Faringdon, and Hon Sophia Massey (da of 5th Baron Clarina); *b* 2 Jan 1947; *Educ* Eton; *m* 1970, Hon Caroline Kinnaird (b 1949), eldest da of 13th Lord Kinnaird; 1 s (George b 1977), 1 da (Leila b 1974); *Career* dir Samuel Montagu & Co Ltd Merchant Bankers; FCA; *Recreations* tennis, cinema, theatre; *Clubs* Brooks's; *Style—* Christopher Wigan, Esq; 14 Zetland House, Marloes Rd, W8 (☎ 01 937 4401)

WIGAN, Michael Christian; s of Maj John Derek Wigan (d 1985), and Anne Geraldine Wigan; *b* 3 Nov 1945; *Educ* Heatherdown, Eton; *m* 14 Oct 1971, Eugenie Mary Felicity, da of Peter Egbert Cadbury, of Armsworth Hill, Old Alresford, Hants; 3 s (Charlie Christian b 1976, James Patrick Cameron b 1978, Rollo Richard b 1980); *Career* chm and dir Wigan Richardson Int Ltd, Hop Devpts Ltd, Fanfire Ltd, Wild Neame Gasgain Ltd, Interhop Ltd, Hopair Ltd, sr ptnr Wigan Richardson and Co; memb Lloyd's; *Clubs* White's; *Style—* Michael Wigan, Esq; Brighton House, nr Alresford, Hants; c/o Wigan Richardson & Co, Church Rd, Paddock Wood, Tonbridge, Kent TN12 6EP (☎ 089283 2235, fax 089283 6008, telex 957022)

WIGGIN, Maj Charles Rupert John; s and h of Sir John Wiggin, 4 Bt, MC, and his 1 w, Lady Cecilia, *née* Anson, da of 4 Earl of Lichfield; *b* 2 July 1949; *Educ* Eton; *m* 1979, Mrs Mary Burnett-Hitchcock; 1 s (Richard b 1980), 1 da (Cecilia b 1984); *Career* Maj Grenadier Gds; *Style—* Maj Charles Wiggin; 10 Ovington St, London SW3

WIGGIN, Fergus Tredennick Francis; s of Clarence Ethelred Wiggin, MBE (1975); *b* 2 Nov 1930; *Educ* Queen's Coll Taunton, Faraday House Electrical Engrg Coll London; *m* 1952, Jennifer Phillis Louise, *née* Burbidge; 3 c; *Career* chartered engr in field of power utilities; sr engr CEGB 1964-68, mangr GLC 1968-75, dir and generation mangr Slough Industl Estates Ltd 1975-82, dir and gen mangr utilies servs div Slough Trading Estate Ltd 1982-; *Recreations* sailing, fishing; *Style—* Fergus Wiggin, Esq; 24 Clarefield Drive, Pinkneys Green, Maidenhead, Berks SL6 5DP; Slough Estates plc, 234 Bath Rd, Slough, Berks SL1 4EE (☎ 0753 37171, telex 847604)

WIGGIN, Jerry - Alfred William; TD (1970), MP (C) Weston Super Mare 1969-; s of Col Sir William Wiggin, KCB, DSO and Bar, TD, DL, JP, sometime chm Worcs TA & AF Assoc (gs of Sir Henry Wiggin, 1 Bt, being s of Alfred Wiggin, Sir Henry's 4 s, and Margaret, da of Edward John Nettlefold, whose f was founder of the firm of Nettlefold & Chamberlain and J S Nettlefold & Sons, the latter eventually becoming part of the Guest Keen & Nettlefold conglomerate); *b* 24 Feb 1937; *Educ* Eton, Trinity Coll Cambridge; *m* 1964 (m dis 1981), Rosemary Janet, da of David Orr; 2 s, 1 da; *Career* 2 Lt Queen's Own Warwicks & Worcs Yeo (TA) 1959, Maj Royal Yeo 1975-78; contested Montgomeryshire (C) 1964 & 1966; pps to Lord Balniel (MOD then FCO) 1970-74, to Sir Ian Gilmour (MOD) 1971-72, parly sec Miny of Ag, Fish and Food 1979-81, parly under-sec of state MOD 1981-83, chm select ctee on Agri 1987-; *Clubs* Beefsteak, Pratt's, Royal Yacht Squadron; *Style—* Jerry Wiggin Esq, TD, MP; The Court, Axbridge, Somerset BS26 2BN (☎ 0934 732527); House of Commons, SW1A 0AA (☎ 01 219 4522)

WIGGIN, Sir John Henry; 4 Bt (UK 1892), of Metchley Grange, Harborne, Staffs, MC (1946); s of Col Sir Charles Richard Henry Wiggin, 3 Bt, TD, JP, DL (d 1972), and Mabel, da of Sir William Jaffray, 2 Bt; *b* 3 Mar 1921; *Educ* Eton, Trinity Coll Cambridge; *m* 1, 1947 (m dis 1961), Lady Cecilia Evelyn Anson (d 1963), da of 4 Earl of Lichfield; 2 s; m 2, 1963, Sarah, da of Brig Stewart A Forster; 2 s; *Heir* s, Maj Charles Wiggin, Grenadier Gds; *Career* serv WWII Europe and Middle E (POW); Maj Grenadier Gds Reserve; JP Berks 1966-72, High Sheriff Warwicks 1976-77; DL Warwicks 1985; *Clubs* Boodle's; *Style—* Sir John Wiggin, Bt, MC; Honington Hall, Shipston-on-Stour, Warwicks (☎ 0608 61434)

WIGGINS, Brian Seymour; s of Edwin Seymour Wiggins, sr civil servant (d 1976), and Lillian May, *née* Clarke; *b* 30 April 1926; *Educ* Purley and Rhyl GS, Liverpool Univ (BSc); *m* 11 Jan 1958, Margaret, da of Edward Byron (d 1978); 4 da (Janet Elizabeth b 1959, Pamela Margaret b 1960, Moira Frances b 1963, Sandra Joan b 1966); *Career* chm in Temple 1978-87 (ret 1987); chm Marlborough Biopolymers Ltd 1983-87; md: Seal Sands Chemical Co Ltd 1978-80, N W Oil Co Ltd 1971-73, Tekchem Ltd 1973-76, Magnachem Ltd 1974-78, vice-pres Magna Corp (USA) 1977-78, founder of numerous chemical and other cos in the North of England principally: MTM plc, Seal Sands Chemcal Co Ltd, Fine Organics Ltd, Tekchem Ltd, Marchem Ltd, Marlborough Special Products Ltd, Marlborough Biopolymers Ltd, Marlborough Chemicals Inc (USA), Marlborough Chemicals (Far E) Ltd (Hong Kong); *Recreations* vintage motor cars, sailing; *Clubs* Bentley Drivers, Rolls Royce Enthusiast, Institute of Directors; *Style—* Brian S Wiggins, Esq; The Old Hall, Coxwold, York YO6 4AD (☎ (03476) 676, fax (03476) 677); Flat 11, Roseberry, Charles St, London W1

WIGGINS, (Anthony) John; s of Rev Sydney Arthur Wiggins, of Wilts, and Mavis Ellen, *née* Brown; *b* 8 July 1938; *Educ* Highgate, The Hotchkiss Sch USA, Oriel Coll Oxford (MA), Harvard Univ (MPA); *m* 1962, Jennifer Anne, da of John Wilson Walkden, of Northampton; 1 s (Nicholas b 1963), 1 da (Victoria b 1967); *Career* asst princ HM Treasy 1961, prince Dept of Econ Affrs 1966, asst sec HM Treasy 1972, princ private sec Chllr of the Exchequer 1980-81, bd memb BNOC 1980-84, under sec head of oil dev Dept of Energy 1981-84, under sec Cabinet Office 1985-86, under sec Dept of Educn and Sci 1987-88, dep sec 1988-; *Recreations* mountaineering, skiing, opera; *Clubs* Alpine; *Style*— John Wiggins, Esq; Dept of Education & Science, Elizabeth House, York Road, London SE1

WIGGINS, Linda Margaret; da of Frederick John Coe, of 58 Park Lane, Snettisham, King's Lynn, Norfolk, and Edna May, *née* Winner; *b* 21 Dec 1949; *Educ* West Norfolk King's Lynn HS for Girls, Univ of Essex (BA); *m* 12 Feb 1972, Derek Ernest, s of Frank Wiggins, of 33 Fourth Cross Road, Twickenham (d 1976); *Career* CA 1975-; started own practice Wiggins & Co 1984; ptnr in local firm 1978-84; *Recreations* riding, embroidery; *Style*— Mrs Linda Wiggins; 5 Granada House, Gabriel's Hill, Maidstone, Kent (☎ 0622 688 189)

WIGGINTON, Michael (John); s of Lt-Col Sydney Isaac Wigginton, OBE (d 1945), and Eunice Olive, *née* Piper; *b* 26 Mar 1941; *Educ* Nottingham HS, Gonville and Caius Coll Cambridge (MA, Dip Arch); *m* (m dis), Julia; 1 s (Alexander b 1974), 1 da (Julia b 1972); m 2, 1988, Jennifer Bennett; *Career* architect and author; with YRM architects and planners 1982-85 (responsible for the design of a series of bldgs inc: an innovatory off bldg in the Netherlands, a maj energy sensitive hosp in Singapore and co-designer The Sultan Qaboos Univ in Oman), organiser Glass in the Environment Conference Crafts Cncl 1986; ptnr Richard Horden Assoc 1987-; architect memb UK/USA Govt sponsored res on energy responsive bldg envelopes; winner (with Richard Horden) The Stag plc Competition (London 1987); FRSA; *Publications* Window Design (1969), Office Buildings (1973), Practice in the Netherlands (1976), Design of Health Building in Hot Climates (1976), Glass To-day (1987), Glass in Architecture (1989); *Recreations* music, reading, tennis; *Style*— Michael Wigginton, Esq; 55 Winchester St, London SW1V 4NY (☎ 01 828 4432); Richard Horden Associates, 4 Golden Square, London W1 (☎ 01 439 0241)

WIGGLESWORTH, David Cade; s of Air Cdre Cecil George Wigglesworth, CB, AFC, (d 1961), and Margaret *née* Cade Bemrose (d 1963); *b* 25 Mar 1930; *Educ* Tonbridge, London Coll of Printing; *m* 11 Feb 1956, Anne, da of John Cairns Hubbard, of Esher, Surrey; 2 s (George b 1957, Lloyd b 1959), 2 da (Sally b 1962, Joanna b 1963); *Career* Nat Serv PO, FO RAFVR 1948-50; Bemrose Corpn Plc: Salesman in London 1952-55, London Sales mangr 1955, London Sales dir 1956-65, gen mangr Bemrose Flexible Packaging Spandon Derbyshire 1965-69, md Bemrose Derby Ops 1969-71, gp chief exec 1971-, started acquisitions in USA; capt Derbyshire Co Golf team 1974-75, memb bd of govrs Trent Coll Long Eaton Notts, chm CBI Economic Situation Ctee; Freeman City of London, Liveryman Woshipful Co of Stationers; memb Faculty Assoc of Mgmnt Centre Europe (of American Mgmnt Assoc); *Recreations* golf, gardening, skiing, tennis, photography; *Clubs* Carlton, Chevin Golf Derby, Pine Valley Golf (USA); *Style*— David Wigglesworth, Esq; Manor Quarry, Duffield, Derbyshire, DE6 4BG (☎ 0332 840330); Bemrose Corporation Plc, Wayzoose Drive, Derby DE2 6XP (☎ 0332 294242, fax 0332 290367, car tel 0836 513677, telex 37482 BEMPNT G)

WIGGLESWORTH, Sir Vincent Brian; CBE (1951); s of Sidney Wigglesworth, MRCS (d 1944), and Margaret Emmeline, *née* Pierce (d 1953); *b* 17 April 1899; *Educ* Repton, Gonville and Caius Coll Cambridge (MA, MD, BCh), St Thomas's Hosp; *m* 1928, Mabel Katherine, da of Col Sir David Semple, IMS (d 1936); 3 s, 1 da; *Career* 2 Lt RFA (France) 1917-18; lectr med entomology London Sch of Hygience and Tropical Med 1926, reader entomology: London Univ 1936-44, Cambridge Univ 1945-52; dir ARC Unit of Insect Physiology 1943-67, Quick Prof biology Cambridge 1952-66; FRS, FRES, fell Gonville and Caius Coll Cambridge 1945; awarded hon doctorates and membership of various UK and foreign Socs, Acads and Insts; medals gained incl Royal Medal (Royal Soc) 1955, Gregor Mendel Gold Medal (Czechoslovak Acad of Science) 1967; kt 1964; *Publications include* Insect Hormones (1970), The Principles of Insect Physiology (fourth edn 1972), Insect and the Life of Man (1976), Insect Physiology (fourth edn 1984); *Style*— Sir Vincent Wigglesworth, CBE; 14 Shilling St, Lavenham, Suffolk (☎ 0787 247 293); Gonville and Caius Coll, Cambridge

WIGGLESWORTH, William Robert Brian; s of Sir Vincent Brian Wigglesworth, of Suffolk, and Mabel Katherine Semple (d 1986); *b* 8 August 1937; *Educ* Marlborough, Magdalen Coll Oxford (BA); *m* 1969, Susan Mary, da of Arthur Baker, JP (d 1980), of Suffolk; 1 da (Elizabeth b 1979), 1 s (Benjamin b 1982); *Career* Nat Serv 2 Lt Royal Signals 1956-58; dep dir gen of Telecommunications 1984-; Ranks Hovis McDougall Ltd 1961-70, gen mgmnt and PA to chief exec Bd of Trade 1970; dept of Prices and Consumer Protection exec 1975; asst sec dept of Indust 1978; *Recreations* fishing, gardening, history; *Style*— William Wigglesworth, Esq; Office of Telecommunications, Atlantic House, Holborn Viaduct, London EC1 2HQ (☎ 01 822 1604, telex 883584, fax 01 822 1643)

WIGHT, Robin Alexander Fairbairn; s of William Fairbairn Wight (d 1972), of Alwoodley, Leeds, and Olivia Peterina, *née* Clouston (d 1988); *b* 5 June 1938; *Educ* Dollar Acad, Magdalene Coll Cambridge (MA); *m* 27 July 1963, Sheila Mary Lindsay, da of James Forber (d 1963), of Edinburgh; 3 s (James William Fairbairn b 1966, Alasdair Robin Forbes b 1968, Douglas Clouston Fullerton b 1973), 1 da (Catriona Mary Susan b 1965); *Career* ptnr Coopers & Lybrand CAs 1971-, regl ptnr Coopers & Lybrand Scotland 1977-; FCA 1976; *Recreations* golf, skiing, hill walking, bridge; *Clubs* Caledonian, RAC; *Style*— Robin Wight, Esq; 22 Regent Terrace, Edinburgh EH7 5BS (☎ 031 556 2100); George House, 126 George St, Edinburgh EH2 4JZ (☎ 031 226 2595, fax 031 226 2692, car tel 0860 620202, telex 727803)

WIGHTMAN, Gerald; s of Harold Wightman (d 1978), and Evelyn, *née* Reader (d 1963); *b* 18 Sept 1937; *Educ* Hillhouse; *m* 17 Jan 1959, Mavis, da of William Wilson, (d 1988); 1 da (Andrea Yvonne (Mrs Peel) b 1965), 1 s (Ian Stewart b 1967); *Career* fin dir Allied Textile Cos plc and subsid cos, Allintex Co Ltd Hong Kong; *Recreations* sport, music; *Clubs* Huddersfield, Brough, FCA; *Style*— Gerald Wightman, Esq; Belmont, 110 Knowle Rd, Mirfield, W Yorks WF14 9RJ (☎ 0924 494231); Allied Textile Companies plc, Highburton, Huddersfield, W Yorks (☎ 0484 604301, fax 0484 605740)

WIGHTMAN, John Martin; s of John William Wightman, of Leatherhead, Surrey, and Nora *née* Martin; *b* 27 Jan 1944; *Educ* The Oratory; *m* 17 Oct 1970, Anne Leigh, da of William Laurence Paynter, MBE, of Leatherhead, Surrey; 2 s (Dominic Martin b 20 Dec 1972, Patrick John b 22 March 1983), 5 da (Antonia Leigh b 7 Dec 1971, Georgina Mary b 13 July 1975, Francesca Katherine b 13 May 1978, Gemma Theresa b 25 June 19801, Christiana Bernadette b 11 March 1986); *Career* joined David A Bevan Simpson & Co (now Barclays de Zoete Wedd) 1968: ptnr 1978-, dir de Zoete & Bevan Ltd 1986-; dir Barclays de Zoete Wedd Securities Ltd 1986-; memb: Knights of St Columba Guildford, Cons Assoc Shamley Green; AMSIA; *Recreations* sports; *Clubs* Gresham, Guildford and Godalming RFC; *Style*— John Wightman, Esq; The Manor House, Shamley Green, Surrey GU5 0UD (☎ 0483 893269); de Zoete & Bevan Ltd, Ebbgate House, 2 Swan Lane, London EC4R 3TS (☎ 01 623 2323)

WIGHTMAN, Nigel David; s of Gerald Wightman (d 1983), of Church Brampton, Northants, and Margaret Audrey, *née* Shorrock; *b* 19 July 1953; *Educ* Bolton Sch, Kent Coll, Dundee HS, Brasenose Coll Oxford (MA), Nuffield Coll Oxford (MPhil); *m* 21 Feb 1987, Christine Dorothy, da of Hubert Alexander Nesbitt, of Bangor, Co Down, NI; 1 s (Patrick Gerald Wisdom b 1987); *Career* Samuel Montagu and Co 1976-80, Chemical Bank 1980-84, NM Rothschild and Sons 1984-, md NM Rothschild Int Asset Mgmnt Ltd; *Recreations* seasonal; *Clubs* RAC; *Style*— Nigel Wightman, Esq; Five Arrows House, St Swithins Lane, London EC4N 8NR

WIGHTMAN, Richard Edward John; s of Charles Prest Wightman, of Fairfax Hall, Menston, Ilkley, West Yorks; *b* 21 August 1944; *Educ* Uppingham, Edinburgh Univ (BCom); *m* 15 Oct 1966, Elizabeth Constance, da of James Birnie (d 1960), of Dufftown, Banff, Scotland; 2 s (Charles, Alasdair); *Career* chm: Beecrofts Gp Ltd, Beecrofts Transport Ltd; dir: Beecrofts Boards Ltd, B & W (Scaffold Bds) Ltd, Davenport Engineering Co Ltd, Davenport Hldgs Ltd, Normanton Wood Servs Ltd, RG Fowler Ltd, Tait of Hull Ltd, Wightwood Joinery Ltd; dep ledr Bradford Met DC 1988- (memb 1983); *Style*— Richard Wightman, Esq; Fairfax Hall, Menston, Ilkley, West Yorks LS29 6EY; 70 Harris St, Bradford, West Yorks BD1 5JB (☎ 0274 729744, fax 0274 307380, telex 517153)

WIGLEY, Dafydd; MP (Welsh Nationalist Party) Plaid Cymrua Caernarfon Feb 1974-; s of Elfyn Edward Wigley; *b* 1 April 1943; *Educ* Caernarfon GS, Rydal Sch Colwyn Bay, Univ of Manchester; *m* Elinor, da of Emrys Bennett Owen, of Dolgellau; 3 s (2 s dêcd), 1 da; *Career* industl economist; formerly with: Ford Motor Co, Mars Ltd, Hoover Ltd; chm Alpha Dyffryn Ltd (Medical equipment manufacturers), Electoral Reform Nat Ctee; Plaid Cymru: industry and econ affrs spokesman and parly whip, pty pres 1981-84; vice-pres Fedn of Industl Devpt Authys, pres Spastics Soc Wales; *Style*— Dafydd Wigley, Esq MP; 21 Penllyn, Caernarfon; House of Commons, London SW1 (☎ 01 219 5021; constituency office ☎ 0286 2076)

WIGLEY, John Robert; s of Jack Wigley, and Eileen Ellen, *née* Murphy; *b* 22 Dec 1945; *Educ* Latymer Upper Sch, Jesus Coll Cambridge (MA); *m* 12 May 1973, Susan Anne (Sam), da of David Thomas Major (d 1974); 2 s (Robert b 1978, Peter b 1982); *Career* ptnr R Watson & Sons 1972 (joined 1969), dir Combined Actuarial Performance Servs Ltd 1984; FIA 1970; *Recreations* music, sport; *Style*— John Wigley, Esq; Bellapais, 9 Beeches Wood, Kingswood, Surrey (☎ 0737 833664); R Watson & Sons, Watson House, London Rd, Reigate, Surrey RH2 9PQ (☎ 0737 241144, fax 0737 241496, telex 946070)

WIGLEY, (Francis) Spencer; s of Francis Spencer Wigley (d 1970), dep cmmr of Police of Fiji, and Lorna Yvonne *née* Wattley; gf Sir Wilfrid Wigley, chief justice of Leeward Islands, WI; *b* 28 Oct 1952; *Educ* Dean Close Sch, Nottingham Univ, (BA); *m* 15 March 1969, Caroline, da of George Jarratt, consultant radiotherapist, of Nottingham General Hosp, of Garden Cottage, Colston Bassett, Notts; 2 s (Francis b 1972, Edward b 1973); 1 da (Elizabeth b 1979); *Career* slr 1967; memb Law Society; sec and slr The RTZ Corp plc 1983-; chm Amesbury Sch 1987-; *Recreations* sailing, tennis, golf, photography; *Clubs* RAC, Pall Mall; *Style*— Spencer Wigley, Esq; 6 St James's Square London SW1V 4LD (☎ 01 930 23999, telex 24639, fax 01 930 3249)

WIGODER, Baron (Life Peer UK 1974); Basil Thomas Wigoder; QC (1966); s of Phillip Wigoder, LRCPI, LRCSI, of Manchester; *b* 12 Feb 1921; *Educ* Manchester GS, Oriel Coll Oxford (MA); *m* 1948, Yoland, da of Ben Levinson; 3 s, 1 da; *Career* serv WWII Lt RA N Africa, Italy, Greece; sits as Lib in House of Lords; contested (Lib): Bournemouth 1945, Westbury 1959 and 1964; pres Oxford Union 1946, barr 1946, vice-pres Lib Pty 1966-, memb Crown Ct Rules Ctee 1971-80, master of bench Gray's Inn 1972 (tres 1989), rec Crown Ct 1972-87; Lib dep whip House of Lords 1976-77, chief whip 1977-86; chm Health Servs Bd 1977-80, memb Cncl on Tbnls 1980-86, chm BUPA and dir BUPA Hosps 1981-; *Recreations* cricket, music; *Clubs* Nat Lib, MCC; *Style*— The Rt Hon the Lord Wigoder, QC; BUPA, Provident House, Essex St, London WC2R 3AX; House of Lords, London SW1 (☎ 01 219 3114)

WIGODER, Hon Carolyn; da (twin with bro Giles) of Baron Wigoder, QC; *b* 17 August 1963; *Style*— The Hon Carolyn Wigoder

WIGODER, Hon Giles; s (twin with sis Carolyn) of Baron Wigoder, QC; *b* 17 August 1963; *Style*— The Hon Giles Wigoder

WIGODER, Hon Justin; s of Baron Wigoder, QC; *b* 11 May 1951; *m* 1981, Heather, da of late J H Bugler and Mrs William Storey, and step da of William Storey, of Newark-upon-Trent; *Style*— The Hon Justin Wigoder

WIGRAM, Hon Andrew Francis Clive; MVO (1986); s and h of 2 Baron Wigram, MC, JP, DL; *b* 18 Mar 1949; *Educ* Winchester, RMA Sandhurst; *m* 1974, Gabrielle, yst da of R Moore, of NZ; 3 s (Harry Richard Clive b 1977, Robert Christopher Clive b 1980, William Michael Clive b 1984); *Career* Maj Gren Guards 1969-86; Extra Equerry to HRH The Duke of Edinburgh 1982-86; *Clubs* Leander; *Style*— Maj the Hon Andrew Wigram, MVO; Garden House, Poulton, Cirencester, Glos (☎ 028 585 388)

WIGRAM, Rev Canon Sir Clifford Woolmore; 7 Bt (UK 1805), of Walthamstow, Essex; s of Robert Ainger Wigram (d 1915), and Evelyn Dorothy *née* Henslowe (d 1960); suc unc, Sir Edgar Thomas Ainger Wigram, 6 Bt (d 1935); *b* 24 Jan 1911; *Educ* Winchester, Trinity Coll Cambridge (MA); *m* 24 Aug 1948, Christobel Joan (d 1983; who m 1, Eric Llewellyn Marriott, CIE d 1945), da of late William Winter Goode, of Curry Rivel, Somerset; 1 step s, 1 step da; *Heir* bro Edward Robert Woolmore Wigram, b 19 July 1913; *Career* ordained 1934, vicar of Marston St Lawrence with Warkworth and Thenford, non-residentiary canon of Peterborough Cathedral 1973, ret 1983, canon-emeritus of Peterborough Cathedral; *Style*— The Rev Canon Sir Clifford Wigram, Bt; Little Lyon Mead, 40 High St, Chard, Somerset TA20 1QL (T (0460) 61634)

WIGRAM, Edward Robert Woolmore; s of Robert Ainger Wigram (d 1915), and Evelyn Dorothy, *née* Henslowe (d 1960); hp of bro, Rev Canon Sir Clifford Wigram, 7 Bt; *b* 19 July 1913; *Educ* Winchester, Trinity Coll Cambridge; *m* 12 Aug 1944, Viva, da of Douglas Bailey, of Laughton Lodge, nr Lewes; 1 da (Mrs Fredrik Procopé); *Career* Maj IA; former master Westminster Sch; *Style*— Robert Wigram, Esq; Hilliers Lodge, St Mary Bourne, Andover, Hants

WIGRAM, 2 Baron (UK 1935); (George) Neville Clive Wigram; MC (1945), JP (Glos 1959), DL (1969); s of 1 Baron Wigram, GCB, GCVO, CSI, PC, Equerry to

George V both as Prince of Wales and King (d 1960, himself ggs of Sir Robert Wigram, 1 Bt), and his w Nora, da of Sir Neville Chamberlain; *b* 2 August 1915; *Educ* Winchester, Magdalen Coll Oxford; *m* 19 July 1941, Margaret Helen (d 1986), da of Gen Sir Andrew Thorne, KCB, CMG, DSO, and Hon Margaret Douglas-Pennant, 10 da of 2 Baron Penrhyn, JP, DL; 1 s, 2 da; *Heir* s, Hon Andrew Wigram; *Career* late Lt-Col Gren Gds; page of honour to HM 1925-32; mil sec and comptroller to Govr-Gen NZ 1946-49; *Clubs* Cavalry and Guards', MCC; *Style*— The Rt Hon Lord Wigram, MC, JP, DL; Poulton Fields, Cirencester, Glos (☎ Poulton 250)

WIGRAM, Hon Mrs; Hon Sally Ann; *née* Bethell; da of Hon William Gladstone Bethell (3 s of 1 Baron) and sis of 4 Baron Bethell, MEP;; *b* 1943; *m* 1965, Anthony Francis Wigram; 1 s, 2 da (twin); *Style*— The Hon Mrs Wigram; 7 Gloucester Sq, London W2 (☎ 01 262 8419)

WILBERFORCE, (William) John Antony; CMG (1981); s of Lt-Col William B Wilberforce, DSO (ka 1943), of Markington Hall, Yorks, and Cecilia, *née* Dormer (d 1974); sr descendant of William Wilberforce, The Emancipator; *b* 3 Jan 1930; *Educ* Ampleforth, Christ Church Oxford (MA); *m* 20 Aug 1953, Laura Lyon, da of Howard Sykes (d 1966), of Englewood, NJ, USA; 1 s (William b 1958), 2 da (Anne b 1954, Mary b 1955); *Career* Nat Serv (2nd Lt KOYLI, Malaya 1948-49); Dip Serv 1953-88; asst under-sec RCDS 1979, ldr UK Del to Madrid CSCE Review Meeting 1980-82, high cmmr Cyprus 1982-88; *Recreations* the turf, travel, gardening; *Clubs* Athenaeum; *Style*— John Wilberforce, Esq, CMG; Markington Hall, via Harrogate, N Yorks (☎ 0765 87356);

WILBERFORCE, Baron (Life Peer UK 1964); Richard Orme Wilberforce; (CMG 1965, OBE 1944, PC 1964); s of Samuel Wilberforce, of Lavington House, Petworth, Sussex (d 1954, 4 s of Reginald Wilberforce, JP, DL, by Anna Maria, da of Hon Richard Denman, 3 s of 1 Baron Denman; Reginald was 2 s of the Bp of Oxford who founded Cuddesdon Theological Coll and was himself 3 s of William Wilberforce, the philanthropist) and Katherine, *née* Sheepshanks (d 1963); the family name derives from a Yorkshire village, Wilberfoss (Wild-Boar-Foss); *b* 11 Mar 1907; *Educ* Winchester, New Coll Oxford (MA); *m* 10 July 1947, Yvette Marie, da of Roger Lenoan, Judge of the Cour de Cassation, Paris; 1 s, 1 da; *Career* served WWII Norway, France and Germany as Brig; barr 1932, QC 1954, high ct judge (Chancery) 1961-64, lord of appeal in ordinary 1964-82, chm Exec Cncl Int Law Assoc, memb Perm Ct of Arbitration, pres Fédération Internationale du Droit Européen 1978; fell All Souls Oxford 1932-, hon fell New Coll Oxford 1965, high steward Oxford Univ 1967-, chllr Hull Univ 1978-; hon FRCM, Hon CRAeS, hon memb Scottish Faculty of Advocates and Canadian Bar, hon DCL Oxford 1967, hon LLD London 1972, Hull 1973 and Bristol 1983; Diplôme d'Honneur Corp des Vignerons de Champagne, Bronze Star (US 1944); kt 1961; *Clubs* Athenaeum; *Style*— The Rt Hon The Lord Wilberforce, CMG, OBE, PC; c/o House of Lords, SW1

WILBERFORCE, Hon Samuel Herbert (Sam); s of Baron Wilberforce, CMG, OBE, PC; *b* 15 Dec 1951; *Educ* Eton, New Coll Oxford (MA, PGCE, Dip Ed); *m* 1978, Sarah, da of late Arthur Allen, of Northampton; *Style*— Sam Wilberforce, Esq

WILBRAHAM; *see*: Baker Wilbraham

WILBRAHAM, David Charles; s of Anthony Basil Wilbraham, and Sheila Eleanor, *née* Neville; *b* 16 August 1957; *Educ* Radley; *m* 2 Oct 1982, Debra Ann, da of Bryan Windass; 2 da (Annabel b 1984, Jennifer b 1984); *Career* dir: North Br Maritime Gp Ltd, North Br Fin Gp Ltd; *Recreations* golf, shooting; *Style*— David C Wilbraham, Esq; Rosemount, 9 Sands Lane, Elloughton Brough, N Humberside HU15 1JH (☎ 0482 666942); Boston House, St Andrew's Dock, Hull, N Humberside HU3 4PR (☎ 0482 224 181, fax 0482 24669)

WILBRAHAM, Hugh Dudley; s of Ralph Venables Wilbraham (d 1983), of Cheshire, and Katharine Mary, *née* Kershaw (d 1984); *b* 18 Feb 1929; *Educ* Wellington; *m* 27 April 1957, Laura Jane, da of George McCorquodale (d 1979), of Bucks; 3 s (Ian b 1958, Philip b 1960, James b 1964), 1 da (Fiona b 1967); *Career* Nat Serv 1947-49, 2 Lt W Yorks Regt; gen mangr Hyde Park Hotel London 1966-71, dir Russell & McIver (wine merchants); *Recreations* tennis, real tennis; *Clubs* Boodle's, RAC; *Style*— Hugh D Wilbraham, Esq; The Gage, Little Berkhamsted, Hertfords SG13 8LR (☎ 099286 233); Russell & McIver Ltd, The Rectory, St Mary-at-Hill, London E3R 8EE (☎ 01 283 3575)

WILBRAHAM, Philip Neville; s of Anthony Basil Wilbraham, of N Humberside, and Sheila Eleanor, *née* Neville; *b* 25 Nov 1958; *Educ* Woodleigh Sch, Radley, Univ of Aston Birmingham (BSc); *m* 1981, Stephanie Jane, da of Ian William McClaren Witty; 2 s (Samuel b 1984, Dominic b 1987), 2 da (Rachel b 1982, Rosemary b 1986); *Career* jt dep chief exec North British Maritime Gp Ltd, North British Shipping Ltd, North British Mgmnt Service Ltd, Cochrane Shipbuilders Ltd (chm), Maritime Brokers Ltd, Maritime Ship Mgmnt Ltd, Humber Tugs Ltd (chm), United Towing Ltd (chm), Walfred Motors Ltd, Norbrit Inter Ltd, Joseph Bentley Ltd, Joseph Bentley Distributors Ltd, Boston Deep Sea Fisheries Ltd (chm), Carry on Fishing Ltd, Fleetwood Near Water Trawlers Ltd, Grimsby Near Water Trawlers Ltd, North Cape Fishing Ltd, W H Kerr (Ships Chandlers) Ltd, Fleetwood Tankers Ltd, Boston Putford Offshore Safety Ltd; Cyclade Overseas Ltd, North British Finance Gp Ltd, Spey Salmon fisheries Ltd, North British Securities Ltd, Standby Ship Operators Association Ltd; *Recreations* shooting, politics; *Clubs* Carlton; *Style*— Philip Wilbraham, Esq; 58 Southfield, Hessle, N Humberside HU13 0EU; Boston House, St Andrews Dock, Hull HU13 4PR (☎ 0482 224181, telex 597682 NBMG, fax 0482 24669)

WILBY, David Christopher; s of Alan Wilby, of Baildon, Yorks, and June, *née* Uppard; *b* 14 June 1952; *Educ* Roundhay Sch Leeds, Downing Coll Cambridge (MA, CANTAB); *m* 23 July 1976, Susan Christine, da of Eric Arding (d 1977), of Bardsey, nr Wetherby, Yorks; 1 s (Edward b 1985), 3 da (Victoria b 1981, Christina b 1983, Charlotte b 1987); *Career* called to the bar 1974; memb: NE Circuit Hon Soc of Inner Temple; *Recreations* golf, watching assocation and rugby football, being in Tenerife; *Clubs* Pannal Golf, Golf Del Sur (Tenerife), 100 (Leeds) United AFC, memb Harrogate Round Table 1978-; *Style*— David Wilby, Esq; Stray Holt, Slingsby Walk, Harrogate, North Yorks (☎ 0423 888 019); San Andres, San Miguel, Tenerife, CI; 5th Floor, St Paul's House, 23 Park Square, Leeds LS1 2NI (☎ 0532 455 866, car tel 0860 204 121), 2 Harcourt Buildings, Temple, London

WILCOX, Albert Frederick; s of Albert Clements Wilcox (d 1925), and Ada, *née* Elliott (d 1946); *b* 18 April 1909; *Educ* Fairfield GS Bristol, Hendon Police Coll; *m* 22 Dec 1939, Ethel Edith, da of Ernest Wilmott (d 1963), of Manor House, Whitchurch, nr Bristol; 1 s (Stephen b 1948), 2 da (Susan b 1941, Bridget b 1943); *Career* served WWII Italy 1943 (Maj), Lt-Col Austria 1945; policeman Bristol City 1928, Met Police 1934, asst chief constable Bucks 1946, chief constable Herts 1947; pres Assoc of Chief Police Offrs 1966-67, memb Parole Bd of England and Wales 1969, memb ed bd of Criminal Land Rev 1970; author of Decision To Prosecute (1972); *Style*— Albert Wilcox, Esq; 34 Roundwood Park, Harpenden, Herts (☎ 058 27 2098)

WILCOX, The Rt Rev David Peter; see: Dorking, Bishop of

WILCOX, Desmond John; s of John Wallace Wilcox, and Alice May, *née* Whittle; *b* 21 May 1931; *Educ* Cheltenham GS, Christ's Coll London, Outward Bound Sea Sch (sail trg apprentice); *m* 1, 6 Jan 1954, Patsy, da of late Harry Price; 1 s (Adam b 1961), 2 da (Cassandra b 1959, Claire (twin) b 1961); m 2, 2 Dec 1977, Esther, da of Harry Rantzen; 1 s (Joshua b 1981), 2 da (Emily b 1978, Rebecca b 1980); *Career* Nat Serv Army 1949-51; deckhand Merchant Marine 1948; reporter weekly papers 1949, news agency reporter 1951-52, reporter and foreign corr, Daily Mirror (incl New York bureau and UN) 1952-60, reporter This Week ITV 1960-65; joined BBC 1965, co-ed and presenter Man Alive 1965, formed Man Alive Unit 1968, head of gen features BBC TV 1972-80, writer and presenter Americans (TV documentaries) 1979, presenter and chm Where it Matters (ITV discussion series), 1981; prodr and presenter BBC TV series: The Visit 1982 (1984-86), The Marriage (series) 1986; presenter 60 Minutes BBC TV 1983-84; SFTA Award for best factual programme series 1967; Richard Dimbleby Award SFTA for Most Important Personal Contrib in Factual TV 1971; tstee Walk Fund (Walk Again Limb Kinetics); memb Conservation Fndn; dir Wilcox Bulmer prodns: corporate videos, and independent prodn; *Publications* (jtly) Explorers (1975), Americans (1978), with Esther Rantzen: Kill the Chocolate Biscuit: or Behind the Screen (1981), Baby Love (1985); *Recreations* riding; *Clubs* Arts, BBC; *Style*— Desmond Wilcox, Esq; East Heath Lodge, 1, East Heath Rd, Hampstead, London NW3 1BN (☎ 01 435 1950)

WILCOX, Lady; Judith Ann; *née* Freeman; *b* 31 Dec 1939; *Educ* St Mary's Convent Wantage; *m* 1986, as his 2 w, Sir Malcolm George Wilcox, CBE (d 1986); *Career* pres dir gen Pecheries de la Morinie, France; dir Channel Foods Ltd; FRSA; *Recreations* fishing, sailing, bird preservation; *Style*— Lady Wilcox; Flat 15, 50 Queen's Gate, London SW7 (☎ 01 584 7256)

WILD, (James) Anthony; s of James Wild, of Bolton, and Margaret, *née* Warburton; *b* 11 May 1941; *Educ* Bedstone Sch Shropshire; *m* 1964, Jean Margaret, da of Ashton Dootson, of Bolton; 1 s (Daniel b 1976), 2 da (Sarah b 1968, Suzanne b 1970); *Career* CA, ptnr J Wild & Co 1964-87, conslt 1987-; dir: Associated Credits Ltd 1986-, Dean Property Gp Ltd 1984-, Forshaw Watson Hldgs Ltd 1986-; *Recreations* farming, working; *Style*— Anthony Wild, Esq; Orrell Cote Farm, Edgworth, Bolton, Lancs BL7 0JZ (☎ 0204 852771); Lancaster House, Blackburn St, Radcliffe, Manchester M26 9TS (☎ 061 723 3211, fax 061 723 3911)

WILD, (Charles) Barrie; s of Charles wild (d 1960), of Skellow, Doncaster, and Dorothy Mary Wild (d 1982); *b* 6 August 1934; *Educ* Sir Percy Jackson GS; *m* 22 Aug 1959, Beryl Margaret, da of Reginald Joseph Lowe, of 9 Reginald Grove, Bishopthorpe Rd, York; 2 da (Karen Beverley b 1962, Katrina Lorraine b 1964); *Career* ptnr Wild & Co (accountants and auditors); auditor: Milk Mktg Bd 1979-, Thomson McLintock (now Peat Marwick McLintock) 1969-79; FCA; *Recreations* cricket, rugby league, horse racing; *Style*— Barrie Wild, Esq; 34 Dringthorpe Rd, Dringhouses, York YO2 2LG (☎ 0904 707227)

WILD, Dr David; s of Frederick Wild (d 1981), of 213 Manchester Road, Heywood, Lancs, and Lena, *née* Thomson (d 1981); *b* 27 Jan 1930; *Educ* Manchester GS, Manchester Univ (MA, ChB), Liverpool Univ (DPM); *m* 19 June 1954, Sheila, da of Thomas Wightman (d 1981), of 76 Yew Tree Lane, Manchester 23; 1 s (Tom b 1962), 1 da (Christina b 1960); *Career* Nat Serv Capt RAMC 1954-56; dep co Med Offr W Sussex CC 1963-74 (area med offr 1974-81), regnl med offr SW Thames Regnl Health Authy 1982-86 (dir professional servs 1986-); FRSM 1978, FFCM 1980; *Recreations* conversation, reading; *Clubs* Royal Soc of Medicine; *Style*— Dr David Wild; 16 Brandy Hold Lane, Chichester, W Sussex PO19 4RY (☎ 024 352 7125); 13 Surrendale Place, London W9 3QW (☎ 01 289 7257); 40 Eastbourne Terrace, London W2 3QR (☎ 01 262 6505, 262 8011 ext 4112)

WILD, (John) David; s of Herbert Winston Wild (d 1982), and Beatrice Mary, *née* Barraclough (d 1982); *b* 15 August 1937; *Educ* Bishop Vesey's GS, Sutton Coldfield; *m* 10 Aug 1962, Janet Rosemary, da of Edwin Clover Askew, of 94 Bonsall Rd, Erdington, W Midlands; 2 s (Jonathan b 1966, Zoe b 1974); *Career* memb Institute of CA in England and Wales; *Recreations* watching rugby union football, opera; *Style*— David Wild, Esq; 210 Birmingham Rd, Wylde Green, Sutton Coldfield, W Midlands BT2 1DD; 7 Vine Terrace, 318 High St, Harborne, Birmingham B17 9PU (☎ 021 427 5333)

WILD, John Vernon; CMG (1960), OBE (1955); s of James Wild (d 1964), and Ada Gertrude, *née* Clark (d 1947); *b* 26 April 1915; *Educ* Taunton Sch, Kings Coll Cambridge (MA); *m* 1, 17 Oct 1942, Margaret Patricia, *née* Rendell (d 1975); 1 s (Paul b 1949, d 1986), 1 da (Judith b 1944); m 2, 30 Dec 1976, Marjorie Mary Lovatt Robertson, da of Francis William Lovatt Smith (d 1975); *Career* Colonial Admin Serv Uganda: asst dist offr 1938, asst chief sec 1950, estab sec 1951, admin sec 1955-60, chm constitutional ctee 1959; teacher mathematics Hele's Sch Exeter 1960-71, lectr in maths Exeter Sixth Form and Tech Coll 1971-76; *Books* The Story of the Uganda Agreement (1957), The Uganda Mutiny (1953), Early Travellers in Acholi (1950); *Recreations* cricket (Cambridge Blue 1938), golf, music; *Clubs* Rye GC; *Style*— J V Wild, Esq, CMG, OBE; Maplestone Farm, Brede, Nr Rye, E Sussex TN31 6EP (☎ 0424 882261)

WILD, Jonathan; s of John William Howard Wild, CO (RAF), of Poole, Dorset, and Madeleine Clifford, *née* Hole; *b* 4 August 1951; *Educ* Woking GS for Boys, Univ Coll London (BSc); *m* 27 April 1979, Jacqueline Ann, da of Roland Oliver Cise, of Walton-on-Thames, Surrey; 1 s (Nicholas James b 1980), 1 da (Anna Loise Julie b 1969); *Career* chartered architect, sole princ Wild Assocs, Wild Alliance and Penwild; RIBA; *Recreations* motor sport, windsurfing; *Style*— Jonathan Wild, Esq; Wild Associates, Rosemount Studios, Pyrford Rd, West Byfleet, Surrey KT14 6LD (☎ 09323 49926 or 0932 336270)

WILD, Kenneth (Ken); s of Ernest Wild, and Ethel Harriet, *née* Singleton; *b* 25 July 1949; *Educ* Chadderton GS, Univ of York (BA); *m* 6 April 1974, Johanna Regina Elizabeth, da of Karl Heinrich Christian Wolf, of Cheltenham; 1 s (Philip b 1981), 1 da (Victoria b 1978); *Career* CA; Peat, Marwick Mitchell & Co 1974-78, under ICEAW 1978-80, tech ptnr Touche Ross & Co 1984- (mangr and sr mangr 1980-84); FCA

1978; *Books* An Accountants Digest guide to Accounting Standards - Accounting for Associated Companies (1982), Company Accounting Requirements, A Practical Guide (jtly 1985); *Recreations* reading, gardening; *Style*— Ken Wild, Esq; Touche Ross & Co, Hill House, 1 Little New St, London EC4A 3TR (☎ 01 936 3000, fax 01 583 8517, telex 884739 TRLNDN G)

WILD, Prof Ray(mond); s of Frank Wild, of Chinley, Derbyshire, and Alice, *née* Large; *b* 24 Dec 1940; *Educ* Glossop GS, Stockport Tech Coll, Salford Coll of Tech, John Dalton Coll, Univ of Bradford (MSc (Mgt), PhD, MSc (Eng), DSc), Brunel Univ; *m* 25 Sept 1965, Carol Ann, da of William Mellor, of Birchvale, Derbys; 1 s (Duncan Francis b 19 March 1970), 1 da (Virginia Kate b 10 June 1972); *Career* Indust: apprentice and draughtsman 1957-62, design engr 1962-64, res engr 1964-66, prodn controller 1966-67; Bradford Univ: res fell 1967-69, lectr 1969-73; Henley Admin Staff Coll: prof fell 1975-77, prof 1973-; Brunel Univ: head of dept 1977-, pro-vice-chllr 1988-; coll govnr; Whitworth fell; FIMechE, FIProdE, FBIM, FRSA, CEng; *Books* Work Organization (1975), Concepts For Operations Management (1977), Mass Production Management (1972), Techniques of Production Management (1971), Management And Production (1972), Production and Operations Management (1978), How To Manage (1982), and 7 others; *Recreations* writing, travel, theatre, skiing, tennis, DIY; *Style*— Prof Ray Wild; Broomfield, New Rd, Shiplake, Henley-on-Thames, Oxfordshire RG9 3LA (☎ 073522 4102); Brunel Univ, Uxbridge, Middx UB8 3PH (☎ 0895 74000, fax 0895 32806, telex 261173G)

WILD, (John) Robin; JP (Ettrick and Lauderdale 1982-); s of John Edward Brooke Wild (ka 1943), of Whin Brow, Cloughton, Scarborough, Yorks, and Teresa, *née* Ballance; *b* 12 Sept 1941; *Educ* Sedbergh, Edinburgh Univ (BDS), Dundee Univ (DPD); *m* 31 July 1965, (Eleanor) Daphne, da of Walter Gifford Kerr (d 1975), of Edinburgh; 1 s (Richard b 1978), 2 da (Alison b 1967, Rosemary b 1977); *Career* princ in gen dental practice Scarborough Yorks 1965-71, dental offr E Lothian CC 1971-74, chief admin dental offr Borders Health Bd 1974-87, regnl dental postgrad advsr SE Regnl Ctee for Postgrad Med Educn 1982-87, dir of studies (dental) Edinburgh Postgrad Bd for Med 1986-87, dep chief dental offr Scottish Home and Health Dept 1987-; vice chm Tweeddale Ettrick & Lauderdale Cons & Unionist Assoc 1982-87, chm Scottish Cncl of British Dental Assoc 1985-87; Hon Fell Univ of Edinburgh 1984; *Recreations* restoration and driving of vintage cars, music, gardening, photography; *Clubs* Royal Cwlth Soc; *Style*— Robin Wild, Esq, JP; Braehead House, St Boswells, Roxburghshire TD6 0AZ (☎ 0835 23203); Nether Craigwell, Calton Rd, Edinburgh EH8 8DR (☎ 031 557 6057); Scottish Home & Health Dept, St Andrew's House, Edinburgh EH1 3DR (☎ 031 244 2305)

WILDASH, Richard James; s of Arthur Ernest Wildash, of London, and Sheila Howard, *née* Smith; *b* 24 Dec 1955; *Educ* St Paul's, Corpus Christi Coll Camb (MA); *m* 29 Aug 1981, (Elizabeth) Jane, da of Peter Edward Walmsley, of Dundee; 1 da (Joanna b 1987); *Career* Dip Serv: FCO 1977, E Berlin 1979, Abidjan 1981, FCO 1984, first sec Br High Cmmn Harave 1988-; *Recreations* music, literature, the country; *Style*— Richard Wildash, Esq; British High Commission, P O Box 4490, Harare, Zimbabwe (☎ 793781); Foreign and Cwlth Office, King Charles St, London SW1A 2AH (☎ 01 270 3000)

WILDBLOOD, (Christopher) Michael Garside; s of Richard Garside Wildblood, of Villars, Switzerland, and Rita Muriel, *née* Jellings; *b* 9 Oct 1945; *Educ* Rugby, Corpus Christi Coll Cambridge (MA, Dip Arch); *m* 30 July 1971, Anne Somerville, da of Alun Roberts, of Radyr, Glamorgan; 1 s (Thomas Garside b 1976), 2 da (Shân Catherine Somerville b 1978, Jane Somerville b 1987); *Career* chartered architect; ptnr and principal Wildblood Macdonald Partnership 1975-; chm: RIBA Leeds Soc of Architects 1985-87, RIBA Yorkshire Region 1985-86; ARIBA; *Recreations* golf, choral singing, water-colour painting; *Clubs* Alwoodley GC, Old Rugbeian Golfing Soc (Northern Sec); *Style*— Michael Wildblood, Esq; 24 Gledhow Lane, Leeds LS8 1SA; Wildblood Macdonald Partnership, Aubdy Studio, Audby Lane, Wetherby LS22 4FD (☎ 0937 65225)

WILDE, Malcolm James; s of Malcolm John Wilde, and Irene Doris, *née* Rickwood; *b* 9 Oct 1950; *Educ* Bishopshalt Sch; *m* 1 Sept 1973, (Helen) Elaine, da of John Bartley; 1 s (Alastair James Rory b 27 Feb 1987), 2 da (Joanne Caroline b 6 July 1976, Julia Felicity b 10 Feb 1981); *Career* mangr Western American Bank (Europe) Ltd 1970-75, vice pres Crocker Nat Bank 1975-77; dir: Guinness Mahon Hldgs Ltd, Guinness Mahon & Co Ltd 1977-87, Stock Beech & Co; md: Br & Commonwealth Merchant Bank plc 1987-, BCMB Gp Ltd; chm: Stock Beech Securities Ltd, Spry Finance Ltd; *Recreations* golf, tennis, music, antique furniture; *Style*— Malcolm Wilde, Esq; Copyhold House, Copyhold Lane, Cuckfield, Sussex; British & Commonwealth Merchant Bank plc, 66 Cannon St, London EC4N 6AE (☎ 01 248 0900, fax 01 248 0906, telex 884040)

WILDING, Richard William Longworth; CB (1979); s of Longworth Allen Wilding (d 1963), of Oxford, and Elizabeth Olga Fenwick, *née* Stokes (d 1968); *b* 22 April 1929; *Educ* Winchester, New Coll Oxford; *m* 1954, Mary Rosamund, da of Sir Nicolas de Villiers (d 1958), of London; 1 s (James), 2 da (Lucy, Clare); *Career* civil servant; head of the Off of Arts and Libraries 1984-; previously dep sec: HM Tresy, Civil Service Dept; *Style*— Richard Wilding Esq, CB; Office of Arts and Libraries, Gt George St, London SW1

WILDING, Thomas Henry (Tom); s of Jack Wilding (d 1985), and Ivy, *née* Spicer (d 1963); *b* 29 Mar 1930; *m* 27 Feb 1954, Ruby Edna, da of Charles William Wix (d 1954); 3 s (Andrew b 1958, Gavin b 1960, Mark b 1961), 1 da (Julia b 1967); *Career* chief chemist St Andrews Paper Mill 1950-57; Mill mangr: Bowater Scott Walthamstow 1960-62 (dep 1957), Bowaters 1965 (Mill dir 1968); dir: Kemsley Mill 1968-71, Southern Mills 1971, Independent Sea Terminals Ltd, Bowaters UK Paper Co Ltd 1971, Thames Mill 1973, Paper and Bd Div 1973 (and gen mangr); md: Paper and Bd Div 1977, Bowaters UK Paper Co Ltd 1978 (chm and md 1981); exec dir Bowaters Industries plc 1984, chief exec UK Paper plc 1988; memb bd of Wilding Office Equipment Ltd; pres: CEPAC, Euro Paper Indust Fndn; memb bd of Clares Equipment Hldgs Ltd; appeals pres Nat Playing Fields Assoc; *Recreations* golf, skiing; *Clubs* Tudor Park GC and Country; *Style*— Tom Wilding, Esq; Garden Lodge, Boxley, Maidstone, Kent ME14 3CX; UK Paper plc, UK Paper House, Kemsley, Sittingbourne, Kent ME10 2SG (☎ 0795 24488, telex 96102, fax 0795 78038)

WILDMAN, Hon Mrs; Hon Corinna; da of 2 Baron Cunliffe (d 1963); *b* 18 April 1929; *m* 18 May 1957 (m dis 1965), Frederick Starr Wildman; 1 s; *Books* Hand of Fortune (1985), Play of Hearts (1986), The Unsuitable Chaperone (1988); *Style*— The Hon Mrs Wildman; The Applehouse, RR1 Box 979, Dorset, Vermont 05251, USA

WILDMAN, David Aubrey; s of Ronald Aubrey Wildman, of Luton, Beds, and Bridget Teresa, *née* Cotter; *b* 4 July 1955; *Educ* Denbigh HS, Luton Coll; *m* 11 Oct 1975, Gillian, da of Edward Ambrose Close, of Richmond, N Yorks; 1 s (Philip b 1986); *Career* Chase Manhattan Bank 1973-75, Mobil Oil Co 1975-80, Herald Fin Servs 1980-88, owner of Gen and Med Fin 1988-; *Recreations* theatre, antiques, collecting paintings; *Clubs* Oundle and Thrapston Round Table; *Style*— David A Wildman, Esq; Forest Thatch, Pilton, Oundle, Peterborough PI8 5SN (☎ 080 15 692)

WILDSMITH, Brian Lawrence; s of Paul Wildsmith, of Yorks, and Annie Elizabeth Oxley (d 1984); *b* 22 Jan 1930; *Educ* De La Salle Coll, Slade Sch of Fine Art UCL (DFA); *m* 1955, Aurélie Janet Craigie, da of Bernard I Thurbide (d 1957); 1 s (Simon), 3 da (Clare, Rebecca, Anna); *Career* freelance artist 1957-, prodn design, illustrations, titles and graphics for first USA-USSR Leningrad film co-prodn of the Blue Bird, artist and maker of picture books for young children; Kate Greenaway Medal 1962; *Books* ABC (1962), The Lion and the Rat (1963), The North Wind and the Sun (1964), Mother Goose (1964), 123 (1965), The Rich Man and the Shoemaker (1965), The Hare and the Tortoise (1966), Birds (1967), Animals (1967), Fish (1968), The Miller, the Boy, and the Donkey (1969), The Circus (1970), Puzzles (1970), The Owl and the Woodpecker (1971), The Twelve Days of Christmas (1972), The Little Wood Duck (1972), Squirrels (1974), Pythons Party (1974), Blue Bird (1976), The True Cross (1977), What The Moon Saw (1978), Hunter and his Dog (1979), Animal Shapes (1980), Animal Homes (1980), Animal Games (1980), Animal Tricks (1980), Seasons (1980), Professor Noah's Spaceship (1980), Bears Adventure (1981), Cat on the Mat (1982), The Trunk (1982), Pelican (1982), Apple Bird (1983), The Island (1983), All Fall Down (1983), The Nest (1983), Who's Shoes (1984), Toot Toot (1984), Daisy (1984), Give a Dog a Bone (1985), What A Tale (1986), My Dream (1986), Goats Trail (1986), Giddy Up (1987), If I Were You (1987), Carousel (1988); *Recreations* piano, tennis; *Clubs* Reform; *Style*— Brian L Wildsmith, Esq; 11 Castellaras, 06370 Mouans-Sartoux, Alpes-Maritimes, France (☎ 93752411)

WILDY, Michael Charles William; s of Cyril William Wildy (d 1980), of Woldingham, Surrey, and Isabel Stewart, *née* Ensell (d 1984); *b* 26 Sept 1926; *Educ* Charterhouse; *m* 3 Dec 1954 (m dis 1987), Rosemary Susan, da of late Christopher Browne; 2 s (Guy b 1955, Hugh b 1957), 1 da (Joanna b 1961); *Career* Nat Serv RN Sub Lt RNVR Northern Europe 1945-48; CA 1951; articles with Deloitte Haskins Sells 1958-51, professional experience London and Australia 1951-54, Booker plc 1954-57; 1959-84: fin dir 1964-84, vice chm 1980-84; chm: authors div 1971-77, Engrg 1973-76, food distribution div 1981-82; tstee and invest ctee memb Booker Pension Fund 1985-; non exec dir J W Spear and Sons plc 1985-; memb advsy ctee Causeway Develop Capital Funds 1985-, cncl memb C of E Childrens Soc 1982- (finance ctee memb 1978-, chm 1988-) FCA; *Recreations* golf (past club Capt), tennis, bridge, ornithology; *Clubs* Reform, Roehampton; *Style*— Michael Wildy, Esq; 7 The Layne, Middleton on Sea, nr Bognor Regis, W Sussex PO22 6JJ (☎ 024369 5900)

WILEMAN, John Malcolm Hayes; s of Harry Wileman (d 1967), of Mill House, Bishop Burton, Yorkshire, and Doris Hayes (d 1971); *b* 16 April 1938; *Educ* Rydal Sch North Wales, Westminster Hotel Sch; *m* 1 March 1974, Sandra Beatrice, da of Dennis George Russell Northern, of Brambles, Morecombelake, Dorset; 1 s (James b 1978); *Career* Nat Serv Army Catering Corps 1958-60; hotel gen mangr 1966-; memb Worshipful Co of Innholders 1980; hon memb The Society of Master Chefs; chm and fndr memb The Jersey Etching Gp; hon sec Asthma Soc (Jersey Branch) and Friends of the Asthma Research Cncl; FHCIMA; MCFA; *Recreations* etching, painting, concert-going, writing cookery articles; *Style*— John Wileman, Esq; Le Petit Chêne, La Rue de La Botellerie, St Ouen, Jersey, Channel Islands (☎ 0534 82410); Hotel L'Horizon, Jersey, Channel Islands (☎ 0534 43101)

WILEY, Lady (Jane Lily) Serena; *née* Lumley; da of 11 Earl of Scarbrough, KG, GCSI, GCIE, GCVO, TD, PC (d 1969), and Katharine, *née* McEwen, DCVO; *b* 1935; *m* 1963, Hugh Wiley; 3 s; *Style*— Lady Serena Wiley; Oak Hill, Palmyra, Virginia, USA (☎ 804 589 3475)

WILEY, (William) Struan Ferguson; s of John Nixon Wiley (d 1968), of Hartlepool, and Muriel Isobel, *née* Ferguson (d 1969); *b* 13 Feb 1938; *Educ* Fettes, Univ of New Hampshire USA; *m* 1, 25 Jan 1964 (m dis 1977), Margaret Louise, da of Ian Graham Forsyth, of Crinan, Scotland; 1 s (Fergus b 1966), 2 da (Sarah b 1964, Anna b 1969); m 2, 21 Dec 1977, Rosemary Anne, da of Sir John Cameron, OBE, of Cowesby, Yorks; *Career* Nat Serv 2 Lt 10 Royal Hussars 1956-58, TA 1958-68, Lt Queens Own Yorks Yeo 1958-68; dir: Chunky Chicks (Nichols) Ltd 1962, Sterling Poultry Prods Ltd 1965, Ross Poultry Ltd 1970, Allied Farm Foods Ltd 1970, Imperial Foods Ltd 1975, Golden Lay Eggs UK Ltd (non-exec); chm and md Ross Poultry and Ross Buxted Nitrovit Ltd 1977; chm: J B Eastwood Ltd 1978, J Lyons Catering Ltd 1981, Normand Ltd 1981, Embassy Hotels Ltd 1983; asst md J Lyons & Co Ltd 1981, dir Allied-Lyons plc 1986, non-exec dir Wembley Stadium Ltd; chm Br Poultry Breeders and Hatcheries Assoc 1976; memb: governing body Houghton Poultry Res Station 1974-82, grand cncl Hotel Catering Benevolent Assoc 1983, leisure industs ctee NEDC 1987; winner Poultry Indust Mktg Award 1977; Freeman: City of London 1980, Worshipful Co of Poulters 1981; *Recreations* golf, shooting, fishing; *Clubs* Cavalry and Guards, Woodhall Spa GC; *Style*— Struan Wiley, Esq; Old Rectory, Withcall, Louth, Lincs LN11 9RL (☎ 050 784 218); J Lyons & Co Ltd, Cadby Hall, London W14 0PA (☎ 01 603 2040)

WILFORD, Sir (Kenneth) Michael; GCMG (1980), KCMG (1976, CMG 1967); s of George McLean Wilford (d 1965), and Dorothy Veronica, *née* Wilson, MBE (d 1945); gs of Sir Thomas Wilford, KCMG, KC, formerly NZ high cmmr in London 1929-33; *b* 31 Jan 1922,Wellington, NZ; *Educ* Wrekin Coll Shropshire, Pembroke Coll Cambridge (MA); *m* 1944, Joan Mary, da of Capt E F B Law, RN (d 1977); 3 da; *Career* RE WW II (despatches); entered Foreign Service 1947, Berlin 1947-49, asst private sec to Sec State Foreign Affrs 1949-52 and 1959-60, Paris 1952-55, Singapore 1955-59, private sec to Lord Privy Seal 1960-62, Rabat 1962-64, consul-gen Peking 1964-66, cnsllr Washington 1967-69, asst under-sec FCO 1969-73, dep under-sec 1973-75, ambass Japan 1975-80; dir Lloyds Bank Inter 1982-87; advsr Baring Int Investment Mgmnt 1982-; visiting fell All Souls 1966-67, memb IOD; hon pres Japan Assoc 1981-, chm Royal Soc for Asian Affairs 1984-; *Recreations* golf, gardening; *Style*— Sir Michael Wilford, GCMG, KCMG, CMG; Brook Cottage, Abbotts Ann, Andover, Hants SP11 7DS (☎ 0264 710509)

WILKES, Prof Maurice Vincent; s of Vincent J Wilkes, OBE (d 1971), of Hagley,

Worcestershire, and Helen, *née* Malone (d 1968); *b* 26 June 1913; *Educ* King Edward's Sch Stourbridge, St John's Coll, Cambridge (BA, MA, PhD); *m* 1947, Bertie Mary (Nina), da of Bertie Twyman (d 1914), of Shanghai, China; 1 s (Anthony b 1950), 2 da (Helen b 1951, Margaret b 1953); *Career* WWII serv: sci offr ADRDE Army Ops Res Gp TRE 1939-42 (sr sci offr 1942-45); computer engr; Cambridge Univ: univ demonstrator 1937-45, head computer laboratory (formerly mathematical laboratory) 1945-80, prof computer technol (now emeritus prof) 1965-80, fell St John's Coll 1950-; computer engr Digital Equipment Corp Maynard MA USA 1980-86, memb for res strategy Olivetti Res Bd 1986-; hon DSc: Newcastle, Hull, Kent, City, Amsterdam, Munich, Bath; hon DTech Linköpung Sweden; FRS, FEng, FBCS, FIEE; foreign assoc: US Nat Acad of Sci, US Nat Acad of Engrg; foreign hon memb American, Acad of Arts & Sciences; *Books* Memoirs of a Computer Pioneer (1985), technical books, papers in sci jls; *Clubs* Athenaeum; *Style*— Prof Maurice V Wilkes; 130 Huntingdon Rd, Cambridge CB3 0HL; Olivetti Research Ltd, 24A Trumpington St, Cambridge CB2 1QA (☎ 0223 343 300, fax 0223 313 542, telex 818226)

WILKES, Richard Geoffrey; OBE (1969), TD (1958, DL (Leics 1967)); s of Geoffrey William Wilkes (d 1963), of Leicestershire, and Kathleen Mary, *née* Quinn (d 1932); *b* 12 June 1928; *Educ* Repton; *m* 1953, Wendy Elaine, da of Rev Clarence Oliver Ward (d 1982) of Hampshire; 1 s (Timothy), 3 da (Judi, Jane, Louise); *Career* cmmr RHA 1947, serv in TA in Leics 1948-72, cdr Royal Leicestershire Regt (TA) 1965-69, TA Col E Midlands Dist 1969-72, ADC (TAVR) to HM The Queen 1972-77, dep hon Col (TA) Royal Anglian Regt (Leics) 1981-88; chm Leicester Co TAVRA 1981-89, vice chm E Midland TAVRA 1981-89; chartered accountant, ptnr Price Waterhouse London 1969-; pres ICAEW 1980-81, pres Int Fed of Accountants 1987-, advsr to Lloyds of London on self-regulation 1983-85, cmdt Leics Special Constabulary 1972-79, govr Care for Mentally Handicapped 1972-; FCA 1952; *Recreations* shooting, sailing; *Clubs* Army and Navy; *Style*— Richard Wilkes, Esq, OBE, TD, DL; The Hermitage, Foxton, Leicestershire (☎ 085 884213); Price Waterhouse, Southwark Towers, 32 London Bridge St, London SE1 9SY (☎ 01 407 8989)

WILKIE, Alex Ian; s of Frederick James Wilkie (d 1976), and Florence Gladys Bell; direct descendant of Sir David Wilkie, RA (1785-1841); *b* 1 Sept 1935; *Educ* Lancing, Poole Coll of Tech, Brighton Tech Coll (HNC Metallurgy); *m* 4 May 1963, Pamela May, da of William Frank Ross, of Hove, Sussex; 1 s (Andrew), 2 da (Jill, Philippa); *Career* Military Service: The Gordon Highlanders; dir The Assoc of Br Pewter Craftsmen Ltd, md Br Pewter Designs Ltd, dir Anzon Ltd subsid to Cookson Gp plc 1980-84, hd of corporate relations, worldwide Cookson Gp plc; capt London Metal Exchange; memb Country Landowners Assoc; regular contributor of articles on: marketing and advertising, visiting London, the industrial society; *Recreations* shooting, golf, gardening, property restoration; *Clubs* East India, Wig and Pen; *Style*— Alex I Wilkie, Esq; The Old Post Office, Hall Weston, Cambs; 416 Horsey Road, London W19; 29 Mona Road, Sheffield; 14 Gresham Street, London EC2V 7AT (☎ 01 606 4400, car telephone 0836 235869)

WILKIE, Liam; s of William Douglas Wilkie, of Kirkintilloch, and Kathleen, *née* Gormley (d 1984); *b* 15 Dec 1956; *Educ* St Ninian's HS, Kirkintilloch, Strathclyde Univ (LLB); *m* 25 May 1984, Anne, da of Alexander Barrie, of Blantyre; *Career* slr and notary public, for 8 years; *Recreations* swimming, walking, mountaineering, the arts, theatre; *Clubs* Glasgow Bar Assoc; *Style*— Liam Wilkie, Esq; Kennedy Court, 2 Braidholm Crescent, Giffnock, Glasgow (☎ (041) 638 2874); Wilkie & Co, Solicitors, 686 Dumbarton Rd, Glasgow (☎ (041) 339 0843/7715)

WILKINS, Christopher Scott; s of R S Wilkins (Ronald "Ronny" Scott), and Nora, *née* Mills; *b* 27 Mar 1945; *Educ* Emanuel Sch, King Coll Cambridge (MA English); *m* 2 Aug 1966 (m dis 1979); 2 s (Ben b 1969, Toby b 1972); *Career* advertiser; copywriter Saatchi & Saatchi 1975-77, creative dir Young & Rubicam 1977-85, fndr Davis Wilkins Advertising Ltd 1985-; TV plays: The Late Wife (Thames 1975), The Day of the Janitor (LWT 1979); *Publications* Finger (P Davies 1971, Pan 1973); *Recreations* cooking, skiing, music; *Clubs* Annabel's, Mark's, Groucho; *Style*— Christopher Wilkins, Esq; 44-50 New Oxford St, WC1 (☎ 01 631 3300)

WILKINS, Sir Graham John (Bob); s of George Wilkins; *b* 22 Jan 1924; *Educ* Yeovil Sch, Univ Coll Exeter; *m* 1945, Daphne Haynes; *Career* chm and chief exec: Thorn EMI 1985-88 (dir 1978, chm 1988-89), Beecham Gp 1975-84 (exec vice-chm 1974); dir: Beecham Inc 1967-86, Beecham AG 1973-74, Courtaulds 1975-85, Hill Samuel 1977-88, Rowntree Mackintosh 1984-88; memb Doctors and Dentists Rem Rev Body 1980-87 (chm 1987-); pres Advertising Assoc 1983-; chm ICC UK 1985-; pres: Assoc of Br Pharm Ind 1969-71, European Fed Pharm Inds Assoc 1978-82; memb BOTB 1977-80; Cncl Sch of Pharmacy London Univ 1984-88 (chm 1988-); Hon FRCP 1985; *Style*— Sir Graham Wilkins; Alceda, Walton Lane, Shepperton-on-Thames, Middx TW17 8LQ (☎ 0932 27714)

WILKINS, Prof Malcolm Barrett; s of Barrett Charles Wilkins (d 1962), of 28 Heath Park Av, Cardiff, and Eleanor Mary, *née* Jenkins; *b* 27 Feb 1933; *Educ* Monkton House Sch Cardiff, King's Coll London Univ (BSc, PhD, DSc); *m* 10 July 1959, (Mary) Patricia, da of Lt-Cdr James Edward Maltby, RNR, RD; 1 s (Nigel Edward Barrett b 7 Aug 1961), 1 da (Fiona Louise Emma Barrett b 14 Jan 1965, d 1980); *Career* lectr in botany Kings Coll London 1959-64 (assr lectr 1958-59), prof biol Univ of E Anglia 1965-67 (lectr 1964-65), prof plant physiology Univ of Nottingham 1967-70, regius prof botany Glasgow Univ 1970-; chm: life sciences advsy ctee Euro Space Agency 1987-89, Laurel Bank Sch Co Ltd Glasgow 1980-87; memb Incorpn of Gardeners City of Glasgow; hon memb American Soc for Plant Physiology; FRSE, FRSA; *Books* Plantwatching (1988), Advanced Plant Physiology (ed 1984), The Physiology of Plant Growth and Development (ed 1969); *Recreations* fishing, sailing; *Clubs* Caledonian; *Style*— Prof Malcolm Wilkins; 5 Hughenden Drive, Glasgow G12 9XS (☎ 041 334 8079); Botany Dept, Glasgow Univ, Glasgow G12 8QQ (☎ 041 330 4450/041 339 8855, ext 4450, fax 041 330 4808, telex 777070 UNIGLA)

WILKINSON, Rev Canon Alan Bassindale; s of Rev John Thomas Wilkinson (d 1980), Knighton, Powys, and Marian, *née* Elliott (d 1980); *b* 26 Jan 1931; *Educ* William Hulme's GS Manchester, St Catharine's Coll Cambridge (BA, MA, PhD), Coll of the Resurrection Mirfield; *m* 1, 27 July 1961 (m dis 1975), Eva Leonore, da of Curt Michelson (d 1981), of Lausanne; 2 s (John b 1964, Conrad b 1968), 1 da (Sarah b 1962); m 2, 29 Dec 1975, Fenella Ruth, da of Col Rupert Thurstan Holland, CBE, DSO, MC (d 1959), of Salisbury; *Career* ordained: deacon 1959, priest 1960; asst curate St Augustine's Kilburn 1959-61, chaplain St Catharine's Coll Cambridge 1961-67, vicar Barrow Gurney 1967-70, chaplain and lectr St Matthias' Coll Bristol 1967-70, princ Chichester Theol Coll 1970-74, warden Verulam House St Alban's 1974-75, sr lectr Crewe and Alsager Coll 1975-78, dir of training Ripon Diocese 1978-84, p-in-c Darley Thornthwaite and Thruscross 1984-88, hon priest Portsmouth Cathedral 1988-; Open Univ tutor 1988-; select preacher: Cambridge 1967, Oxford 1982; memb: Gen Synod Bd of Educn 1982-86, Governing Body Coll of Ripon and York St John 1984-88, Governing Body SPCK 1982-; Hon Canon: Chichester 1970, Ripon 1984; *Books* The Church of England and the First World War (1978), Would You Believe It? (1983), Christian Choices (1983), More Ready to Hear (1983), Dissent or Conform? War, Peace and the English Churches 1900-1945 (1986); *Style*— The Rev Canon Alan Wilkinson; 5 Chadderton Gardens, Pembroke Park, Old Portsmouth PO1 2TE (☎ 0705 825 788)

WILKINSON, Alan Richard; s of Rev Richard Brindle Wilkinson, OBE (d 1966), and Mary, *née* Bretherton (d 1970); *b* 19 July 1923; *Educ* Culford Sch Bury St Edmunds; *m* 9 May 1953, Margaret Ruth, da of Dr Cuthwin Eagleston Donaldson (d 1988); 2 s (Andrew b 1956, Richard b 1962), 1 da (Jane b 1959); *Career* RE: sapper 1942, Offr/Cadet 1943, 2 Lt trg unit 1944, Lt 1 Para Sqdn Rye 1944-45, Lt first Airborne Div Burma, engrs Field Co 1946, Capt and Adj Depot Burma Engrs 1946-47; design engr Lewis & Duvivier and later Coode & Ptnrs (consltg engrs) 1947-54; Coode & Ptnrs: asst resident engr (Baghdad Iraq) 1954-57, resident engr (Mombasa Port Kenya) 1957-60, engr (London) 1960-62, resident engr (Mailsi Siphon Pakistan) 1962-65, resident chief engr (Indus Basin Barrages Pakistan) 1965-68, ptnr 1969, sr ptnr and md 1985-89, (Coode & Ptnrs later became Coode Blizard); MICE 1956, FICE 1964, MConsE 1969; *Recreations* wood carving, sculpture, swimming, gardening; *Style*— Alan Wilkinson, Esq; Coode Blizard, Royal Oak House, Brighton Rd, Purley, Surrey CR2 2BG, (☎ 01 668 0711, telex 947020 COODES)

WILKINSON, Sheriff Alexander Birrell; s of Capt Alexander Wilkinson, MBE (d 1938), of Perth, Scotland, and Isabella Bell, *née* Birrell (d 1977); *b* 2 Feb 1932; *Educ* Perth Acad, Univ of St Andrews (MA), Univ of Edinburgh (LLB); *m* 10 Sept 1965, Wendy Imogen, da of Capt Ernest Albert Barrett, RE (d 1949), of Belfast; 1 s (Alan b 1974), 1 da (Jennifer b 1970); *Career* Nat Serv RAEC 1954-56; faculty of advocates 1959, practice Scottish Bar 1959-69, lectr in Scots Law Univ of Edinburgh 1965-69, Sheriff of Stirling Dunbaton and Clackmannon at Stirling and Alloa 1969-72, chm Industl Tbnls (Scotland) 1972-86, dean of faculty of law Univ of Dundee 1974-76 and 1986 (prof of private law 1972-86), Sheriff of Tayside Central and Fife at Falkirk 1986-; chm: Scottish Marriage Guidance Cncl 1974-77, Legal Servs Gp Scottish Assoc of CAB 1979-83; memb ed bd Scottish Acad Press, chllr Dioceses of Brechin and of Argyll and The Isles; *Books* Gloag and Henderson's Introduction To The Law of Scotland (jt ed 1980 and 1987), The Scottish Law of Evidence (1986); *Recreations* collecting books and pictures, reading, travel; *Clubs* New (Edinburgh); *Style*— Sheriff Alexander Wilkinson; 267 Perth Rd, Dundee DD2 1JP (☎ 0382 689 39); Sheriffs Chambers, Sheriff's Ct House, Falkirk (☎ 0324 20 822)

WILKINSON, Prof Andrew Wood; CBE; s of late Andrew Wood Wilkinson, of 134 Greenway Rd, Taunton, Somerset, and Caroline, *née* Robinson (d 1921); *b* 19 April 1914; *Educ* Huish Taunton, Weymouth Coll Dorset, Univ of Edinburgh (MB, ChB); *m* 18 Sept 1941, Joan Elizabeth Longair, da of Cdr Guy Descarriéres Sharp, RN, of Edinburgh; 2 s (Peter, Angus), 2 da (Caroline, Jane); *Career* surgical specialist RAMC; Lt, Capt, Maj, Lt-Col; clinical tutor and asst surgn Royal Infirmary Edinburgh, asst surgn Hosp for Sick Children, sr lectr surgery Univ of Aberdeen, asst surgn Royal Infirmary Aberdeen, surgn Hosp for Sick Children Aberdeen (ret); Freeman Worshipful Co of Apothecaries; FRCS (Edin); *Style*— Prof Andrew Wilkinson, CBE; Auchenbrae, Rockcliffe, Dalbeattie, Kircudbrightshire

WILKINSON, Hon Mrs; Hon Anthea Mary; *née* Hall; yr da of Baron Roberthall, KCMG, CB (Life Peer), and his 1 w (Laura) Margaret, *née* Linfoot, now Lady MacDougall; *b* 3 June 1939; *Educ* Oxford HS for Girls, LMH Oxford; *m* 19 March 1966, (David) Max Wilkinson, s of Roger Wilkinson, of York; 1 s, 1 da; *Career* journalist with The Sunday Telegraph; *Recreations* music, being a housewife; *Style*— The Hon Mrs Wilkinson; 112 Hemingford Rd, London N1 1DE; The Sunday Telegraph, 1 Peterborough Court, At South Quay, 181 Marsh Wall, London E14 9SR (☎ 01 538 7356)

WILKINSON, Charles Edmund; s of Dr Oliver Charles Wilkinson (d 1987), of Riverholme, Thames St, Wallingford, Oxon, and Sheila Muriel, *née* McMullan; *b* 6 June 1943; *Educ* Haileybury and ISC, Clare Coll Cambridge; *m* 3 June 1967, Gillian Margaret, da of Thomas Patrick Madden Alexander, of Forest Row, East Grinstead, Sussex; 2 da (Claire b 10 March 1972, Juliet b 13 June 1973); *Career* slr, sr ptnr Blyth Dutton 1980- (ptnr 1974-); memb of Law Soc; memb Worshipful Co of Coachmakers and Coack Harness Makers, Freeman City of London; *Clubs* Hurlingham, Roehampton; *Style*— Charles Wilkinson, Esq; 8/9 Lincolns Inn Fields, London WC2A 3DW (☎ 01 242 3399, fax 01 404 4788)

WILKINSON, Brig Charles Edward; CBE (1982), OBE (1977, TD 1964 and Clasp 1976, DL (Derbyshire 1985-)); s of Charles Dean Wilkinson, of Woking, Surrey, and Florence, *née* Wakefield; *b* 5 May 1932; *Educ* Repton, Manchester Business Sch; *m* 15 Sep 1956, Joy Maureen, da of Arthur Locke, of Colchester, Essex (d 1946); 1 s (Timothy), 1 da (Sarah); *Career* Nat Serv cmmnd Sherwood Foresters 1951, Mercian volunteers Worcester-Foresters staff 1952-85 (Brig TA 1982); dir numerous cos including Leigh Interests plc 1978-; Liveryman Co of Fuellers, Freeman City of London; Hon Col 3 Worcester Foresters 1983-; *Recreations* territorial army, flying, photography, spectator sports; *Clubs* Army and Navy, City Livery; *Style*— Brigadier Edward Wilkinson, CBE, TD, DL; Thornbury, Ashford in the Water, Bakewell, Derbyshire DE4 1QH (☎ 062981 2535); Leigh Interests plc, Lindon Rd, Brownhills, Walsall, W Midlands WS8 7BB (☎ 0543 452121, car ☎ 0836 500917)

WILKINSON, Christopher John; s of Maj Edward Anthony Wilkinson, of Welwyn Garden City, Herts, and Norma Doreen, *née* Trevelyan-Beer; *b* 1 July 1945; *Educ* St Albans Sch, Regent Street Poly Sch of Architecture (Dip Arch, RIBA); *m* 3 April 1976, Diana Mary, da of Alan Oakley Edmunds, of Limpsfield Chart, Surrey; 1 s (Dominic b 1980), 1 da (Zoe b 1978); *Career* princ ptnr Chris Wilkinson Architects 1983-; formerly with Richard Rogers and Ptnrs, Michael Hopkins Architects and Foster Assocs; visiting lectr Liverpool Univ; assessor on BSC Colorcoat Award 1986 and 1987; works exhibited at Royal Acad Summer Exhibition 1986, 1987 and 1988; *Recreations* golf, sketching, travel; *Style*— Christopher J Wilkinson, Esq; 52 Park Hill Rd, West Dulwich, London SE1 (☎ 01 761 7021); 1 Horseshoe Yard, Brook St, London W1Y 1AB (☎ 01 409 2887, fax 01 499 0451)

WILKINSON, (Thomas) David; s of Thomas Lancelot Wilkinson, of Standdlestones, Stitching Lane, Hilcott, Pewsey, and Ruth Margaret, *née* Hedley; *b* 1 May 1940; *Educ* St John's Sch Leatherhead Surrey; *m* 25 July 1964, Angela Mary, da of Peter Martineau, of 54 St Ann St, Salisbury SP1 2DX; 1 s (Edward Rupert b 23 June 1969); 1 da (Camilla b 10 May 1974); *Career* 5 Royal Inniskilling Dragoon Guards 1959-63, cmmnd 2 Lt 1960, Lt 1961; mktg dir: Del Monte Int 1972, Bacardi Int 1974-79, gen mangr Fourcroy UK 1982, md Finnish Nat Distiller (Alko) Ltd 1983, memb Mattingley Parish Cncl 1974-82, Freeman: City of London 1969, Worshipful Co of Grocers 1969 (Liveryman 1977); *Recreations* sailing, skiing; *Clubs* Anglo-Belgian; *Style—* David Wilkinson, Esq; Heath House, Hazeley Lea, Hartley Wintney, Basingstoke, Hants RG27 8ND (☎ 0734 326 298); Finnish National Distillers (Alko) Ltd, 40/41 Pall Mall, London SW1 (☎ 01 930 1916, fax 01 930 0199, telex 8950542 FNDLK)

WILKINSON, Sir Denys Haigh; s of Charles Wilkinson, and Hilda Wilkinson; *b* 5 Sept 1922; *Educ* Loughborough GS, Jesus Coll Cambridge; *m* 1, 1947 (m dis 1967), Christiane, *née* Clavier; 3 da; m 2, 1967, Helen, *née*Sellschop; 2 step da; *Career* dir Int Sch Nuclear Physics Erice Sicily 1974-83, vice-chllr Sussex Univ 1976-87; chm: Br Cncl Scientific Advsy Panel and Ctee 1977-86, Radioactive Waste Mgmnt Advsy Ctee 1978-83; pres Inst of Physics 1980-82; memb: Wilton Park Acad Cncl 1979-83, Cncl Assoc Cwlth Univs 1980-87; for memb Royal Swedish Acad of Sciences 1980-, Hon FilDr Uppsala; Hon DSc: Saskatchewan, Utah State, Guelph, Queen's (Kingston); Hon LLD Univ of Sussex; FRS 1956; kt 1974; *Style—* Sir Denys Wilkinson; Gayles Orchard, Friston, Eastbourne, E Sussex BN20 0BA (☎ 032 15 3333)

WILKINSON, Hon Mrs; Hon Elizabeth Jane Molyneux; *née* Fletcher; da of Baron Fletcher, PC (Life Peer); *b* 1938; *m* 1962, David Blair Wilkinson; 3 s, 1 da; *Style—* The Hon Mrs Wilkinson; Charnwood Lodge, Burton Rd, Repton, Derby DE6 6FN (☎ 0283 702339)

WILKINSON, Prof Sir Geoffrey; s of Henry Wilkinson (d 1978), of Todmorden, Yorks, and Ruth Crowther (d 1971); *b* 14 July 1921; *Educ* Imperial Coll London, in the USA; *m* 1951, Lise Søolver, da of Rektor Prof Svend Aa Schou, of Copenhagen; 2 da; *Career* Sir Edward Frankland prof of inorganic chemistry London Univ 1956-; foreign memb: Nat Acad of Sciences (US), Royal Danish Acad of Sciences; hon fell Spanish Science Research Cncl, centennial foreign fell American Chemical Soc; Hon DSc: Edinburgh, Granada, Columbia, Bath; awarded: Lavoisier Medal (Fr Chemical Soc), jt Nobel Prize for Chemistry 1973, Galileo Medal Univ of Pisa; FRS; kt 1976; *Books* Advanced Inorganic Chemistry (jt author, 4th edn 1980); *Style—* Prof Sir Geoffrey Wilkinson; Imperial College, London SW7 2AY (☎ 01 589 5111 ext 4501)

WILKINSON, Geoffrey Crichton; CBE (1986), AFC (1957); s of Col William Edward Duncan Wilkinson (d 1980), of 15 High St, Rode, Bath, Avon, and Evelyn Katherine Wilkinson; *b* 7 Nov 1926; *Educ* Bedford Sch, Royal Indian Mil Coll; *m* 6 dec 1958, Virginia Mary, da of Russell Broom (d 1963), of Rodinghead, Mauchline, Ayrshire; 2 da (Susannah (Mrs Wright) b 1961, Samantha b 1963); *Career* aeronautical engrg trg RN 1948-49 (flying trg 1944-47); pilot RAF 1949-59, seconded UASF Korea 1952-53, Empire Test Pilot Sch 1956, engrg test pilot 1957-59, ret 1959; Turner and Newall 1959-61, dir Mercury Airlines 1961-65, dep chief inspr air accidents Dept of Trade 1981 (inspr 1965, ret as chief inspr accidents 1986); Air Medal USA 1953; FRSAeS 1970; *Recreations* sailing; *Clubs* RAF, RAF YC; *Style—* Geoffrey Wilkinson, Esq, CBE, AFC; Buckingham House, 50 Hyde St, Winchester, Hants SO23 7DY (☎ 01 0962 65823)

WILKINSON, Sir (David) Graham Brook; 3 Bt (UK 1941), of Brook, Witley, Co Surrey; s of Sir David Wilkinson, 2 Bt, DSC (d 1972); *b* 18 May 1947; *Educ* Millfield, Ch Ch Oxford; *m* 1977, Sandra Caroline, da of Dr Richard Rossdale; 1 da (Louise Caroline Sylvia b 1980); *Heir* none; *Career* exec dir Orion Royal Bank Ltd; OStJ; *Style—* Sir Graham Wilkinson, Bt; 28 Sheffield Terrace, London W8

WILKINSON, James Arthur; s of James Arthur Wilkinson (d 1972), and Mary Allaby (d 1970); *b* 16 July 1928; *Educ* Westham GS, Chelmsford Poly (HNC); *m* 22 July 1961, Margaret, da of John Welsh (d 1958); *Career* engr Crompton Parkinson 1952-68; fndr dir Indust Control Services plc 1968-; developed wind turbine powered catamaran; FLOD, memb Instrument Soc of America; *Publications* author of numerous articles in learned jls on risks in chem, oil and nuclear installations; *Recreations* sailing, golf; *Clubs* Maldon Little Ship, Burnham Golf; *Style—* James Wilkinson, Esq; Beacon Hill House, St Lawrence, Southminster, Essex CM0 7LP (☎ 0621 87721); Industrial Control Services plc, Hall Road, Madon, Essex

WILKINSON, Jeffrey Vernon; s of Arthur Wilkinson (d 1965), and Winifred May; *b* 21 August 1930; *Educ* Midlandsmberstone Sch, King's Coll Cambridge; *m* 1955, Jean Vera, da of George Farrow Nurse (d 1959); 2 da (Julie Katherine b 1962, Elizabeth Jane b 1964); *Career* dir and gen mangr Lucas Electrical 1974, dir Lucas Exec Bd 1974 (divnl md 1978); memb Lucas Industs bd; joint gp md Lucas Industs 1979-84; dir Alan Patric & Assocs, chm and chief exec offr: Rel Ltd 1985-, Rotaprint Industs Lld 1988; chm Nedo Plastic Processing Economic Devpt Ctee 1985-88; *Recreations* tennis, swimming, water skiing, reading, theatre; *Style—* Jeffrey Wilkinson, Esq; Hillcroft, 15 Mearse Lane, Barnt Green, Birmingham B45 8HG (☎ 021 445 1747)

WILKINSON, Jeremy Squire; s of Philip Squire Wilkinson (d 1979) of Butley Rise, Prestbury, Cheshire, and Mary, *née* Betteridge; *b* 4 June 1936; *Educ* Rugby, Cambridge (MA, LLM); *m* 29 Sept 1962, Alison Margaret, da of Walter Thomas Isaac, OBE, of Pierce Close, Prestbury, Cheshire; 1 s (Timothy), 1 da (Emma); *Career* Nat Serv 2 Lt RCS 1954; admitted slr 1962, ptnr Addleshaw Sons and Latham; chm: bd of mangrs Cheadle Royal Hosp, Talyllyn Railway Preservation Soc; govr Cheadle Hulme Sch, tstee Narrow Gauge Railway Museum; *Recreations* history of mines, quarries and railways; *Style—* Jeremy Wilkinson, Esq; 3 Old Orchard, Wilmslow, Cheshire SK9 5DH (☎ 0625 524535); Dennis House, Marsden Street, Manchester M2 1JD (☎ 061 832 5994, fax 061 832 2250, telex 668886)

WILKINSON, John Arbuthnot Ducane; MP (C) Ruislip-Northwood 1979-; s of Denys Wilkinson; *b* 23 Sept 1940; *Educ* Eton, RAF Coll Cranwell, Churchill Cambridge; *m* 1969, Paula, da of Josepf Adey; 1 da; *Career* RAF Flying Instructor; MP (C): Bradford W 1970-74 (fought Bradford W Sept and Oct 1974); pps to: min of State Industry 1979-80, to John Nott as min of Defence 1981-82; chm Bow Gp Standing Ctee Defence, Anglo-Asian Conservative Soc 1979-, vice-chm Anglo-Somali Partly Gp 1981-, sec Anglo-Bangladesh Parly Gp 1979-, chm Anglo-Malawi Parly Gp 1981-; pa to chm BAC, sales mangr Klingair Ltd, tutor OU, head Universities Dept UCO and and ex regular RAF, also SAS (TA); delegate to Cncl of Europe and WEU 1979-; chm: EMC and EMC (Conns) Ltd 1984-, chm Cons Aviation Ctee 1983-; vice-chm Cons Defence and Space Ctees 1983-; *Books* The Uncertain Ally- British Defence Policy 1960-90 (co-author with Michael Chichester); *Recreations* flying; *Clubs* RAF, Inst of Dir; *Style—* John Wilkinson Esq, MP; House of Commons, London SW1

WILKINSON, Rev Keith Howard; s of Kenneth John Wilkinson, of Leicester, and Grace Winifred, *née* Bowler; *b* 25 June 1948; *Educ* Beaumont Leys Coll Leicester, The Gateway GS Leicester, Univ of Hull (BA), Emmanuel Coll Cambridge (MA), Westcott House Cambridge; *m* 27 Aug 1972, Carolyn, da of Lewis John Gilbert (d 1985), of Wokingham; 2 da (Rachel b 1979, Claire b 1979); *Career* head of religous studies Bricknell HS 1970-72, head of faculties (humanities) Kelvin Hall Comprehensive Sch Kingston upon Hull 1972-74; ordained: deacon 1976, priest 1977; asst priest St Jude Westwood Peterborough 1976-79, educn offr to the church Peterborough 1977-79, asst master and chaplain Eton Coll 1979-84, sr chaplain and head of religions studies Malvern Coll 1984-89 (sr tutor 1988-89), headmaster Berkhamsted Sch 1989-; chaplain Oxford Conf on Educn 1987-, memb steering ctee The Bloxham Project 1988-; *Recreations* films, music, drama, ecology, walking, buildings, building; *Clubs* United Ushers; *Style—* The Rev Keith Wilkinson; Wilson House, The School, Castle St, Berkhamsted, Herts HP4 2BE (☎ 0442 864827)

WILKINSON, Kenneth Grahame; CBE (1979); s of Bertie Wilkinson; *b* 14 July 1917; *Educ* Shooter's Hill, Imperial Coll London (DIC, BSc); *m* 1941, Mary Victory; 1 s, 1 da; *Career* aviation conslt; dir: British Rail Eng Ltd 1981-88, Airways Aero Assoc Ltd 1984-; chm New Media Prods Ltd; memb cncl Cranfield Inst of Technol 1971- (dep chm and visiting prof), former md and vice-chm Rolls Royce, chm and chief exec BEA 1972, bd memb BOAC 1972; bd memb British Airways 1971-72 and 1976-81 (engrg dir 1976-79, dep chm 1979-80), bd memb Airworthiness Requirements Bd CAA 1976-85, chm Air Transport and Travel Indust Training Bd 1981-82; Hon DSc; FEng, CBIM, FCIT, FSLAET, FRSA, FCGI, Hon FRaeS (pres 1972); *Recreations* gardening, flying, boating, travel; *Style—* Kenneth Wilkinson, Esq, CBE; Pheasants, Mill End, Hambleden, Henley-on-Thames, Oxon RG9 3BL (☎ 070 132 368)

WILKINSON, Sir (Robert Francis) Martin; s of Sir Robert Pelham Wilkinson; *b* 4 June 1911; *Educ* Repton; *m* 1936, Dora Esmé, da of William John Arendt; 3 da; *Career* ptnr de Zoete & Gorton 1936 and sr ptnr de Zoete & Bevan 1970-1976; chm: Stock Exchange 1965-73 (memb 1933, memb cncl 1959, dep chm 1963-65), Fedn Stock Exchange in GB and Ireland 1965-73; one of HM's Lts City London 1973-; kt 1969; *Clubs* City of London; *Style—* Sir Martin Wilkinson; Hurst-An-Clays, Ship St, East Grinstead, W Sussex RH19 4EE

WILKINSON, Prof Paul; s of Walter Ross Wilkinson (d 1985), of Bristol, and Joan Rosemary, *née* Paul; *b* 9 May 1937; *Educ* Lower Sch of John Lyon Harrow, Univ Coll Swansea (MA); *m* 19 March 1960, Susan Sherwyn, da of Charles William John Flook (d 1968), of Newport, Mon; 2 s (John Paul b 1964, Charles Ross b 1969), 1 da (Rachel Margaret b 1962); *Career* served RAF 1959-65, ret as Flt Lt; asst lectr in politics Univ Coll Cardiff 1966-68, lectr 1968-75, visiting prof Simon Fraser Univ Canada 1973, sr lectr in politics Univ Coll Cardiff 1975-78; reader in politics Univ of Wales 1978-79; prof int relations 1979- and head dept politics and int relations 1985- Univ of Aberdeen; chm Res Fndn Study of Terrorism 1986-89, dir Res Inst for Study of Conflict and Terrorism 1989-; conslt ITN London and CBS News NY 1986-, jt ed Terrorism And Political Violence (scholarly journal) 1988-; hon fell Univ Coll Swansea; memb: RIIA, Br Int Studies Assoc, Political Studies Assoc; *Books* Social Movement (1971), Political Terrorism (1974), Terrorism versus Liberal Democracy (1976), Terrorism and the Liberal State (1977, revised edn 1986), Terrorism: Theory versus Practice (jtly, 1978), British Perspectives on Terrorism (1981), The New Fascists (revised edn, 1983), Contemporary Research on Terrorism (1987); *Recreations* walking, modern painting, poetry; *Clubs* Savile, Aberdeen Business and Professional; *Style—* Prof Paul Wilkinson; Dept Politics and Int Relations, University of Aberdeen, Aberdeen AB9 2TY (☎ 0224 272713/4/7, fax 0224 487048, telex 73458 UNIABN G)

WILKINSON, Lt-Col Sir Peter Allix; KCMG (1970), CMG (1960, DSO 1944, OBE 1944); child of Capt Osborn Cecil Wilkinson (ka 1915), by his w Esmé Barbara, da of Sir Alexander Wilson; *b* 15 April 1914; *Educ* Rugby, CCC Cambridge; *m* 1945, Mary Theresa (d 1984), da of Algernon Hyde Villiers (ka 1917, 3 s of Rt Hon Sir Francis Hyde Villiers, GCMG, GCVO, CB, sometime ambass Brussels, 4 s of 4 Earl of Clarendon) by his w Beatrix (who subsequently m (1919) 4 Baron Aldenham & (2 Baron) Hunsdon, by whom she was mother of 5 Baron Aldenham); 2 da (Virginia b 1947, m 1971, Daniel Worsley; 1 s, 1 da; Alexandra b 1953; 1 s, 2 da); *Career* cmmnd 2 Bn Royal Fusiliers 1935, served WW II (Poland, Fr, Balkans, Italy) Lt-Col, ret 1947; joined Dip Serv 1947, 1 sec: Vienna 1947, Washington 1952; cnsllr Bonn 1955-60, under-sec Cabinet Office 1963-64, sr civilian instr IDC 1964-66, ambass Vietnam 1966-67, asst under-sec FO 1967-68, dep under sec and chief admin Dip Serv 1968-70, ambass Vienna 1970-71, ret 1972; re-employed as dep under sec Cabinet Office 1972-73; Polish Cross of Valour 1940, Czech Order of White Lion 1945; Order of Yugoslav Banner (hon) 1984; *Recreations* reading, trout-fishing; *Clubs* White's, Army and Navy; *Style—* Lt-Col Sir Peter Wilkinson, KCMG, CMG, DSO, OBE; Mill House, Charing, Kent (☎ 023 371 2306)

WILKINSON, Sir Philip William; *b* 8 May 1927; *Educ* Leyton County HS; *m* 1951, Eileen Patricia, *née* Malkin; 1 s, 2 da; *Career* dep chm Nat Westminster Bank plc 1987- (gp ch exec 1983-87, dir 1979-, dep gp ch exec 1980); dir: Int Westminster Bank 1982, Handelsbank NW Zürich (dep chm), British Aerospace plc; memb cncl: Confedn of British Industry 1983, Industrial Soc 1982-; FCIB; kt 1988; *Recreations* golf, watching sport; *Clubs* RAC; *Style—* Sir Philip Wilkinson; National Westminster Bank plc, 41 Lothbury, London EC2P 2BP (☎ 01 726 1266)

WILKINSON, Rev Canon Raymond Stewart; s of Sidney Ewart Wilkinson, and Florence Miriam, *née* Lawrence; *b* 5 June 1919; *Educ* Luton GS, King's Coll London (AKC), Bishop's Coll Cheshunt; *m* 8 Sept 1945, Dorothy Elinor, da of Robert Jacob Church (d 1984); 4 s (Francis John b 1946, Andrew Peter b 1948, Mark Lawrence b 1950, Paul Richard b 1953); *Career* curate of Croxley Green, Herts 1943; vicar: St Oswald's, Croxley Green 1945- 50, Abbots Langley 1950-61; rector of Woodchurch 1961-71, proctor in convocation and memb Church Assembly 1964-71, rector of Solihull 1971- 87; Hon Canon of Birmingham 1976; Chaplain to HM The Queen 1982; FRSA; *Books* The More Edifying (1952), Church and Parish of Abbots Langley (1955), My Confirmation Search Book (10 edn 1984), An Adult Confirmation Handbook (6 edn 1985), Gospel Sermons for Alternative Service Book (1983), Pocket Guide for Servers (1986); *Recreations* producing, acting in and conducting Gilbert and Sullivan operas, church architecture, gardening; *Clubs* Royal Cwlth, Royal Soc of Arts; *Style—* The

Rev Canon Raymond Wilkinson; 42 Coten End, Warwick CV34 4NP (☎ 0926 493 510)

WILKINSON, Richard Denys; s of Denys Cooper Wilkinson (d 1961), of Pill House, Llanmadoc, and Gillian Avice, *née* Nairn (d 1973); *b* 11 May 1946; *Educ* Eton, Trinity Coll Cambridge (MA, MLitt), Ecole Nationale des Langues Orientales Vivantes, Paris, Ecole des Langues Orientales Anciennes Institut Catholique de Paris; *m* 8 Dec 1972, (Maria) Angela, da of Frederick Edward Morris, of London; 2 s (Wilfred b 17 Dec 1983, Samuel b 4 Feb 1986); *Career* Hayter post-doctor in Soviet Studies Sch Slavonic and East Europ Studies London Univ 1971-72, dip serv 1972, Madrid 1973-77, FCO 1977-79, visiting prof faculty of history Univ of Michigan Ann Arbor 1980, FCO 1980-83, Ankara 1983-85, cnsllr and head of chancery Mexico City 1985-88, info cnsllr Paris 1988-; *Recreations* sightseeing, oriental studies; *Clubs* United Oxford and Cambridge; *Style*— Richard Wilkinson, Esq; c/o FCO, London SW1A 2AH

WILKINSON, Samuel William; s of Samuel William Wilkinson (d 1981), of Tabbey House, Cirencester and Louisa, *née* Eggitt (d 1978); *b* 31 Dec 1935; *Educ* Dudley GS, Tetenhall Coll Wolverhampton, Swansea GS, UCL (LLB); *m* 2 Sept 1961, Jane Margaret, da of Henry de Witt West (d 1974), of Porteynon, nr Swansea; 1 s (william b 1962), 2 da (Anna b 1965, Mary b 1968); *Career* admitted slr 1961; with Collins Woods and Vaughan Jones Swansea 1958-62, sr ptnr Davey Son and Jones (Cirencester) 1981- (joined 1962, ptnr 1965); soc and tres N Corney C C, past chm Cirencester Round Table, team memb Cirencester Squash Club; memb: Law Soc; *Recreations* cricket, squash, tennis, walking, motor racing; *Style*— Samuel Wilkinson, Esq; Pennings, North Cerney, Cirencester GL7 7BZ (☎ 028 583 342); 10/12 Dollar Street, Cirencester, Glos GL7 2AL (☎ 0285 4875)

WILKINSON, Sir William Henry Nairn; s of Denys Cooper Wilkinson (d 1961), and Gillian Avice Wilkinson, *née* Nairn (d 1973); *b* 22 July 1932; *Educ* Eton, Trinity Coll Cambridge; *m* 25 July 1964, Katharine Louise Frederica, da of William Francis Hope Loudon (d 1986); 1 s (Matthew b 1969), 2 da (Sophia b 1971, Alice b 1974); *Career* dir: Kleinwort Benson Ltd 1973-85, TSL Gp plc 1976-88 (chm 1984-88), John Mowlem & Co plc 1977-87; memb: RSPB 1970-76 (hon tres 1971-76 and 1977-83, chm info ctee 1980-81), Game Conservancy Cncl 1976-83 (vice-chm 1981-83); chm Nature Conservancy Cncl 1983-, memb cncl Winston Churchill Meml Tst 1985-, memb CEGB 1986-; FRSA; kt 1989; *Recreations* ornithology, opera, music, shooting, archaeology; *Clubs* Brooks; *Style*— Sir William Wilkinson; 119 Castelnau, Barnes, London SW13 9EL (☎ 01 748 9964); Northminster House, Peterborough PE1 1UA

WILKINSON, Dr William Lionel; CBE (1986); s of Lionel Wilkinson (d 1978), and Dorothy, *née* Steels; *b* 16 Feb 1931; *Educ* Holgate GS Barnsley, Christ's Coll Cambridge (MA, PhD, ScD); *m* 3 Sept 1955, (Josephine) Anne, da of Charles Dennis Pilgrim (d 1954), of Bedford; 5 s (David William b 6 March 1957, Andrew Charles b 15 Nov 1958, Iain Francis b 5 March 1962, Richard John b 24 March 1965, Stephen James b 6 Feb 1970); *Career* lectr Univ Coll Swansea 1956-59, UKAEA 1959-67, prof of chemical engrg Bradford Univ 1967-79, BNF 1979- (dep chief exec and dir of engrg 1986-); memb London Salters Co 1985; FIChemE 1957, FEng 1980; *Books* Non-Newtonian Fluids (1960); *Recreations* fell walking; *Clubs* Atheneum; *Style*— Dr William Wilkinson, CBE; Tree Tops, Legh Rd, Knutsford WA16 8LP (☎ 0565 533 44); BNF plc, Risley, Warrington (☎ 0925 832 000)

WILKS, Capt Antony Hugh Francis; s of Walter Hugh Wilks (d 1964), of Bushey, Herts, and Frances Mary Bradford, *née* Pratt; *b* 29 Dec 1936; *Educ* Oundle; *m* 4 Sept 1971, Susan Chaloner, *née* Reed; 1 s (Rupert b 1973), 1 da (Lalage b 1976); *Career* serv HM Submarines 1958-67, i/c HMS Belton 1967-69, Staff Coll India 1970, HMS Jupiter 1971-72, BRNC Dartmouth 1973-75, ADC to HE Govr Hong Kong 1976, Naval Staff 1977-78; i/c: Royal Brunei Navy 1979-80, HMS Aurora 1981-82, RNC Greenwich 1983-85; Dep Cdr Naval Base Rosyth Scotland and Queen's Harbourmaster Rosyth and Cromarty 1986-; chm Forth Maritime Planning Ctee, memb Forth Pilotage Ctee; Yr Brother Trinity House London 1976; Liveryman Worshipful Co of Wheelwrights 1965 (Ct Asst); Perwira Agong Negara Brunei (first class) 1979, Derja Seri Laila Jasa (Brunei Knighthood) 1980; *Recreations* music, squash; *Clubs* St Moritz Tobogganing, Jesters; *Style*— Capt Antony Wilks, MBE, RN; Orchardhead House, Rosyth, Fife (☎ 0383 417086); Easter Fossoway, Carnbo, Kinrosshire; HM Naval Base, Rosyth, Fife (☎ 0383 412121 ext 3496)

WILKS, Capt Carey Lovell; s of Richard Lovell Wilks, of Bailing Hill Farm, Warnham, Horsham, W Sussex, and Shelia Gillian Jean, *née* Bowack; *b* 10 May 1960; *Educ* Malvern Coll, Lincoln Coll Oxford Univ (MA); *m* 7 May 1983, Alyson Jane Prior, da of Capt Peter Arnold Prior-Willeard; 1 s (Michael b 17 Sept 1987); *Career* cmmnd RE 1978, Troop Cdr Germany 1982-84, Support Troop Cdr UK 1984-86, professional engr trg (elec and mech) 1986-88 (incl attachment to John Holland Engrg Australia); Adj Germany 1989-; target rifle shooting: Capt Oxford Univ Rifle Club tour of Kenya 1982, shot for England 1983, Combined Services; MIEAust (1988), AMIEE (1987); *Recreations* target rifle shooting, country sports; *Clubs* Vincents; *Style*— Capt Carey Wilks; c/o Bailing Hill Farm, Warnham, Horsham, Sussex

WILKS, Stanley David (Jim); CB (1979); *b* 1 August 1920; *Educ* Polytechnic Sch London; *m* 1947, Dorothy Irene, *née* Adamthwaite; 1 s, 1 da; *Career* Royal Armoured Corps 1939-46, serv with 48 Bn Royal Tank Regt; 3 Carabiniers Imphal 1944; Home Off 1946-50, Bd of Trade, later Dept of Trade and Indust 1950-80, 1 sec Br Embassy Washington 1950-53; GATT non-ferrous metals, ECGD, airports policy, chief exec BOTB 1980-85; dep-chm: Technol Transfer Gp 1986-, (formerly dir-gen 1981-86); dir: Matthew Hall Business Devpt Ltd 1981-87, Hadson Petroleum Int plc 1981-, Hadson Corpn (USA) 1985-, Associated Gas Supplies Ltd 1987-; chm Export Network Ltd 1985-, consultant dir Strategy Internat Ltd 1981-87 (dep-chm 1987-), regional dir James Hallam Ltd 1984-; MIEx; *Recreations* dinghy racing, water skiing; *Clubs* Royal Overseas League, World Traders, Civil Service, Lloyds Yacht, Medway Yacht (Rochester), Tamesis (Kingston); *Style*— Stanley Wilks, Esq, CB; 6 Foxgrove Ave, Beckenham, Kent

WILLACY, Michael James Ormerod; s of James Willacy (d 1977), of Plymouth, Devon, and Majorie Winifred, *née* Sanders; *b* 7 June 1933; *Educ* Taunton Sch Somerset; *m* 1, 25 Nov 1961, Merle Louise, da of Johannes Schrier, of Denia, Spain; 2 s (Richard b 1962, Peter b 1969), 1 da (Jennifer b 1963); m 2, Victoria Stuart, da of Cecil Stuart John, of Mobberley, Ches; 2 s (James b 1985, Michael b 1986), 1 da (Elizabeth b 1988); *Career* dir HM Govt Central Unit on Purchasing 1985-, gen mangr Shell UK Materials Services 1983-85; chm Macclesfield C of C 1981-83; fndr chm: Macclesfield Business Ventures 1982-83, gen sec Old Tauntonian Assoc 1978- (pres 1988-89); FInstPS; *Recreations* golf, travel, gardening; *Clubs* Royal Cwlth Soc; *Style*— Michael Willacy, Esq; 144 Hadlow Rd, Tonbridge, Kent TN9 1PB (☎ 0732 353081)

WILLAMS, John Robert; s of Edward S Williams (d 1986) of London, and Frances Madge, *née* Porter; *b* 7 April 1931; *Educ* Enfield GS, Queen's Coll Cambridge (MA Hons); *m* 12 Sept 1959, Teresa, da of Joseph Wareing (d 1956) of Preston, Lancs; 3 da (Catherine b 1960, Joanna b 1962, Helen b 1967); *Career* Ogilvy & Mather: res exec, mktg mangr, res dir, account dir, client servs dir, int mgmnt supervisor 1956-68, appointed to bd 1968, vice-chm 1981; chm Wimbledon CC 1974-89, chm The Wimbledon Club (cricket, lawn tennis, hockey clubs, Lakeside squash club); FIPA 1968; *Recreations* cricket, tennis, squash, theatre; *Clubs* MCC, RAC

WILLAN, Edward Gervase; CMG (1964); s of Capt Francis George Loveless Willan, RNR (d 1957), and Gladys Gordon Bushe (d 1981); *b* 17 May 1917; *Educ* Radley, Pembroke Coll Cambridge (MA); *m* 1944, Mary Bickley, da of Lt-Col Henry Alexander Joy (d 1964); *Career* Indian Civil Serv 1940-47; HM Foreign (later HM Diplomatic) Serv 1948-77, 2 later 1 sec New Delhi 1947-49, Foreign Off 1949-51, 1 sec: The Hague 1952-55, Bucharest 1956-58; head Communications Dept FO 1958-62, political advsr Hong Kong 1962-65, head Scientific Relations Dept FO 1966-68, min Lagos 1968-70; ambass: Rangoon 1970-74, Prague 1974-77; ret 1977; *Recreations* walking, gardening; *Clubs* Utd Oxford and Cambridge Univ; *Style*— Edward Willan Esq, CMG; Cherry Tree Cottage, Shappen Hill, Burley, Nr Ringwood, Hants BH24 4AH

WILLAN, Richard Martin; s of Gp Capt Frank Andrew Willan, CBE, DFC, MA, DL (d 1982), of Salisbury, Wilts, and Joan Frances Strathern, *née* Wickham Legg; *b* 22 Nov 1946; *Educ* Eton; *m* 17 April 1971, Susan St John, da of Maurice St John Howe, of Dorchester, Dorset; 1 da (Clare b 1976); *Career* short service cmmn Royal Green Jackets 1966-76; dir Christie Tyler plc 1982-; *Recreations* shooting, walking, swimming; *Clubs* Army and Navy, RAC; *Style*— Richard Willan, Esq; Tyn yr Heol, Heol y Cyw, Bridgend, Mid Glamorgan CF35 6NL (☎ 0656 860236); Christie Tyler plc, Brynmenyn, Bridgend, Glamorgan (☎ 0656 721367)

WILLATT, Sir Hugh; s of Robert John Willatt, OBE, JP, of Nottingham; *b* 25 April 1909; *Educ* Repton, Pembroke Coll Oxford; *m* 1945, Evelyn May, ARE, ARCA, da of Horace Edward Gibbs; *Career* serv RAF WWII; practising slr; sec gen Arts Cncl of GB 1968-75 (and sometime chm of Drama Panel), chm Nat Opera Studio, pres Riverside Studios; formerly memb bd: Nat Theatre, English Stage Co (Royal Ct Theatre), Mercury Trust (Ballet Rambert), Nottingham Theatre Trust; Hon MA Nottingham Univ; FRSA; kt 1972; *Style*— Sir Hugh Willatt; 4 St Peter's Wharf, Hammersmith Terrace, London W6 (☎ 01 741 2707)

WILLCOCK, David Charles; s of Clarence Harry Willcock (d 1952), of Horsforth, Leeds, and Lena Gladys, *née* Crabtree (d 1960); *b* 5 Oct 1924; *Educ* Woodhouse Grove Sch Yorks, Leeds Univ; *m* 8 Oct 1953, Kathleen Mary, da of Capt Alfred Pilley (d 1965), of Calverley, Yorks; 1 s (Charles b 1961), 2 da (Louise b 1963, Frances b 1965); *Career* serv Koyli 1943-47, Middle E, Italy and E Africa; slr; pres Bradford Law Soc 1974-75, chm Legal Aid Area Ctee 1986-; *Books* St Peters Church Rawdon (1984); *Recreations* walking, theatre, geneology, local history; *Style*— David Willcock, Esq; Calvi, Carr Close, Rawdon, Leeds (☎ 0532 502297); 43 Cheapside, Bradford (☎ 0274 721104)

WILLCOCKS, Sir David Valentine; CBE (1971), MC (1944); s of late Theophilus Herbert Willcocks and Dorothy, *née* Harding; *b* 30 Dec 1919; *Educ* Clifton, King's Coll Cambridge (MA, MusB); *m* 1947, Rachel Gordon Blyth, da of late Rev Arthur Cecil Blyth, fellow of Selwyn Coll Cambridge; 2 s, 2 da; *Career* serv WWII DCLI, Capt NW Europe; organist Salisbury Cathedral 1947-50, master choristers and organist Worcester Cathedral 1950-57, music lectr Cambridge 1957-74, fell and organist King's Coll Cambridge 1957-73 (hon fell 1979), Univ organist 1958-74, musical dir Bach Choir 1960-, gen ed OUP Church Music 1961-; past pres: RCO, ISM, Birmingham and Midland Inst; former chm assoc bd Royal Schs of Music; former conductor: Cambridge Philharmonic, Salisbury Music Soc, Worcester Festival Choral Soc, City of Birmingham Choir, Cambridge Univ Music Soc; dir Royal Coll of Music 1974-84, pres Nat Fedn of Music Socs 1980-; dir of orchestras at wedding of HRH The Prince of Wales to Lady Diana Spencer 1981; Hon RAM, Hon GSM, Hon FTCL, Hon MA Bradford; Hon DMus: Exeter, Leicester, Bristol, Westminster Choir Coll, Princeton; Hon DLit Sussex; Hon Dr Sacred Letters Trinity Coll Toronto; FRCM, FRCO, FRNCM, FRSAMD, FRSCM; hon fellow Royal Canadian College of Organists; kt 1977; *Clubs* Athenaeum, Arts; *Style*— Sir David Willcocks, CBE, MC; 13 Grange Road, Cambridge CB3 9AS (☎ 0223 359559)

WILLCOX, John Horace; s of Sir William Henry Willcox, KCIE, CB, CMG, FRCP (d 1941), of 40 Wilbeck St, London W1, and Mildred, *née* Griffin; *b* 1 Feb 1909; *Educ* Oundle, Christ's Coll Cambridge (BA); *m* 19 Jan 1946, Diana Tilden, da of John Sydney Walker, JP (d 1939), of Fellcourt, Coulsdon, Surrey; 3 da (Elisabeth b 1946, Jane b 1950, Joanna b 1953); *Career* WWII serv 1942-46: cmmnd Lt RAOC (serv Persia/Iraq Force, Egypt, Italy, Austria), Capt OC Light Aid Detachment REME 104 Regt RHA (Essex Yeo) 1943-45; J & E Hall Ltd Dartford Kent 1930-35; Anglo Ecuadorian Oilfields Ltd 1936-57: asst chief engr 1938-41, chief engr, asst field mangr, local dir; exec engr Regent Oil Co and Esso Petroleum Co 1958-68; CEng, MIMechE 1941; *Recreations* riding, gardening; *Style*— John Willcox, Esq; Blegberry, Shootersway, Berkhamsted, Herts HP4 3NN (☎ 0442 865083)

WILLCOX, Toyah Ann; da of Beric Arnold Willcox, of Birmingham, and Barbara Joy, *née* Rollinson; *b* 18 May 1958; *Educ* Edgbaston Cofe Coll, Birmingham Old Rep Theatre Sch; *m* 16 May 1986, Robert Fripp, s of Aurthur Fripp (d 1985), of Wimbourne; *Career* actress and singer songwriter; films incl: Jubilee 1978, The Corn is Green 1978, Quadrophenia 1978, The Tempest 1979, URG The Music War 1979, Battle Ship Redwing 1985, Murder 1985, Midnight Breaks 1987; theatre incl: Tales from the Vienna Woods (National Theatre 1977), American Days (ICA 1978), Sugar and Spice (Royal Court 1979), Trafford Tanzi (Mermaid Theatre 1983), Cabaret (Strand Theatre 1987), Three Men on a Horse (National Theatre 1987), A Midsummer Nights Dream (Birmingham Rep 1988); tv incl: Little Girls Don't 1980, Ebony Tower 1983; albums: Sheep Farming in Barnet 1978, Blue Meaning 1979, Toyah Toyah, 1980, Anthem 1981, Changeling 1982, Warrior Rock 1982, Love is the Law 1983, Minx 1985, Lady or the Tiger 1985, Desire 1987 Pro 1988; Singles incl: It's a Mystery, I Wanna be Free, Thunder in the Mountains, Good Morning Universe, Brave New World, World in Action, Echo Beach; vice-pres Nat Assoc of Youth Clubs; patron: Birmingham Rape Crisis Centre, Bournemouth Hosp, Salisbury Festival, Sch for the Performing Arts; *Style*— Ms Toyah Willcox; 63A King's Rd, Chelsea, London SW3 (☎ 01 730 2162)

WILLETT, Peter Stirling; s of Maj Kingsley Willett, MC (d 1946), of South Cadbury House, Yeovil, Somerset, and Agnes Mary, *née* Stirling (d 1972); *b* 19 July 1919; *Educ* Wellington Coll, Cambridge Univ (MA History); *m* 1, 1954 Anne Marjorie, *née* Watkins (d 1965); 2 s (David Henry Stirling b 1955, Stephen Murray b 1958); m 2, 1971, Chloë Lister Beamish; *Career* The Queen's Bays 1941-46 (Middle East, Italy); author, journalist, thoroughbred breeding consultant; pres Thoroughbred Breeders Assoc 1980-85; dir: Goodwood Racecourse 1977, Nat Stud 1985-; chm tstee Br Euro Breeders Fund 1983; author: An Introduction to the Thoroughbred (1960), The Thoroughbred (1970), The Classic Racehorse (1981), Makers of the Modern Thoroughbred (1986), Tattersalls (1987); FRSA; *Recreations* tennis, following cricket, reading, history; *Clubs* Army and Navy, Jockey; *Style—* Peter Willett, Esq; Paddock House, Rotherwick, Basingstoke, Hants RG27 9BG (☎ 0256 672 2488)

WILLETTS, Roger William; s of Leonard Willetts (d 1984), and Doreen May Joyce, *née* Hutchinson; *b* 21 August 1946; *Educ* Cavendish Sch Eastbourne Sussex; *m* 23 Oct 1970, Linda, da of Robert Mullins; 1 s (Timothy b 7 Aug 1974), 1 da (Karen b 9 Feb 1977); *Career* Abbey Life Assur: sales agent 1969, unit mangr 1971, branch mangr 1974, exec dir 1984; Head of Sales City of Westminster Assurance (1989-); charter pres Woodley and Earley Lions Club FLIA, FInstSM; *Recreations* squash, golf, tennis (Sussex Co player); *Style—* Roger Willetts, Esq; 16 Alyth Rd, Talbot Woods, Bournemouth, Dorset (☎ 0202 769079); City of Westminster Assurance Co Ltd, 500 Avebury Boulevard, Central Milton Keynes MK9 2NU (☎ 0908 690 888)

WILLEY, Spencer Frank; CBE (1978); s of Frank Richardson Willey (d 1977), of Herne, Kent, and Sarah, *née* Foreman (d 1986); *b* 6 August 1926; *Educ* King's Coll Sch Wimbledon; *m* 6 Oct 1951, Glenys, da of John Andrew Dingwall, DCM (d 1958); 1 s (Mark b 1956), 1 da (Laura b (twin) 1956); *Career* Intelligence Corps (Sgt); md Johnson and Johnson Malaya 1962-68, chm and md Malayan Cement 1968-79; vice-pres Fedn of Malaysian Mfrs 1972-74, vice-chm Malaysian Employers' Fedn 1972-79, pres Malaysian Int C of C and Indust 1977-79, vice-pres Malaysian Inst of Mgmnt 1976-79; *Recreations* singing; *Clubs* Selangor, Lake, Royal Selangor Golf (all Malaysia), Singapore Cricket; *Style—* Spencer Willey, Esq, CBE; Hill House, Abbotsham, Bideford, Devon EX39 5AU (☎ 023 72 72025)

WILLIAM-POWLETT, Hon Mrs (Katherine Elizabeth); *née* Keyes; 2 da of Adm of the Fleet 1 Baron Keyes, GCB, KCVO, CMG, DSO (d 1945); *b* 24 Oct 1911; *m* 30 July 1935, Major Peter de Barton Vernon Wallop William-Powlett, MC, yst son of late Maj Barton Newton Wallop William-Powlett, of Cadhay, Ottery St Mary, Devon; 1 s, 1 da; *Career* artist; *Clubs* Hurlingham; *Style—* The Hon Mrs William-Powlett; 22 St Leonard's Terrace, London SW3

WILLIAMS; *see*: Ffowcs Williams

WILLIAMS, Rt Hon Alan John; PC (1977), MP (Lab) Swansea W 1964-; s of Emlyn Williams (d 1951); *b* 14 Oct 1930; *Educ* Cardiff HS, Cardiff Coll Technol, Univ Coll Oxford; *m* 1957, (Mary) Patricia Rees; 2 s, 1 da; *Career* serv RAF 1956-58; former econ lectr and journalist; memb: Lab Pty 1950-, Fabian Soc and Co-op Pty; contested (Lab) Poole 1959; chm Welsh PLP and PPS to PMG 1966-67, Parly under-sec Dept Econ Affrs 1967-69, Parly sec Miny Technol 1969-70, oppn spokesman: Consumer Protection, Small Businesses and Minerals 1970-74; min state: prices and consumer protection 1974-76, indust 1976-79; oppn spokesman: Wales 1979-81, civil service 1981-83, indust 1983-; dep shadow leader of the House 1983-, shadow sec of State for Wales 1987-; *Style—* The Rt Hon Alan Williams, MP; Hill View, Plunch Lane, Limeslade, Swansea (☎ 0792 60475); House of Commons, London SW1

WILLIAMS, Dr Alan Wynne; MP (Lab) Carmarthen 1987; s of Tom Williams (d 1980), and Mary Hannah Williams, *née* Thomas; *b* 21 Dec 1945; *Educ* Carmarthen GS, Jesus Coll Oxford , BA (Chemistry), DPhil; *m* 1973, Marian, da of Tom Williams, of Gwynedd; *Career* lectr Environmental Science Trinity Coll 1970-87; *Recreations* reading, watching sport; *Style—* Dr Alan Williams, MP; Cwmaber, Alltycnar Road, Carmarthen, Dyfed (☎ 0267 235 825); House of Commons, London (☎ 01 219 4533)

WILLIAMS, Sir Alwyn; s of D D Williams; *b* 8 June 1921; *Educ* Aberdare Boys' GS, Univ Coll of Wales, Aberystwyth, US Nat Museum; *m* 1949, Joan Bevan; 1 s, 1 da; *Career* prof of geology Queen's Univ Belfast 1954-74, pro-vice chllr 1965-74; Lapworth prof of geology and head of dept Birmingham Univ 1974-76, princ and vice-chllr Glasgow Univ 1976-; FRS, FRSE, MRIA; kt 1983; University of Wales Fellow 1947-48; Harkness Fellow 1948-50; chm of Board of Trustees BM (NH) 1974-79; pres RSE 1985-; *Books* Treatises and Monographs in Geology and Palaeontology; *Recreations* music, art; *Style—* Sir Alwyn Williams; The Principal's Lodging, 12 The University, Glasgow G12 8QG

WILLIAMS, Dr (Hugh) Amphlett; s of Edwin George Williams (d 1917), of Latimers, Knotty Green, Beaconsfield, Bucks, and Florence Mary, *née* Amphlett (d 1948); *b* 5 June 1906; *Educ* City of London Sch, London Univ (PhD); *m* 9 Sept 1933, Mary Eileen, da of Arthur Ernest Blackwell (d 1951); *Career* public analyst: City of Port and London, Greenwich, Kensington, Chelsea, Hackney, Woolwich, Bermondsey 1933-71; gas identification offr 1939-45; contrib var scientific journals on food analysis for harmful substances; Freeman City of London 1927, Liveryman Worshipful Co of Goldsmiths 1944 (Freeman 1927); Fell City and Guilds Inst 1968; FRSC, MChemA, FIFST, FRSH, memb Soc of Public Analysts, Chem Ind; *Recreations* tennis, countryside; *Clubs* Nat Lib, English Speaking Union; *Style—* Dr Amphlett Williams; Wood End, 11 Leazes Ave, Chaldon, nr Caterham, Surrey CR3 5AG (☎ 0883 45 766)

WILLIAMS, Sir Anthony James; KCMG (1983, CMG 1971); s of late Bernard Warren Williams, MB, ChB, FRCS, and late Hon Muriel Burton, Buckley, da of 1 Baron Wrenbury, PC; *b* 28 May 1923; *Educ* Oundle, Trinity Coll Oxford (MA); *m* 12 April 1955, (Maria) Hedwig Gabrielle Nathalie Benedicta Lioba Laurentia, 2 da of late Count Erwin von Neipperg (d 1957), of Schwaigern, Württemberg; 2 s (1 decd), 2 da (1 decd); *Career* diplomatic serv 1945-, serv: Prague, Montevideo, Cairo, UK Mission to UN, Buenos Aires, Geneva (Disarmament Negotiations), cnsllr Moscow 1965-67, Washington 1968-70, ambass Khmer Republic 1970-73, min Rome 1973-76; ambass: Libyan Arab Jamahariya 1977-79, Argentine Republic 1980-82; ldr UK Delgn to Conf on Security and Co-operation 1982-83 and to CSCE Experts Meetings in Ottawa and Berne, 1984-85; UK rep UN Human Rights Cmmn 1984-87; dep UK memb exec bd UNESCO 1984-86; *Recreations* arts, history; *Clubs* Beefsteak, Canning; *Style—* Sir Anthony Williams, KCMG; Jollys Farmhouse, Salehurst, E Sussex

WILLIAMS, Anthony Touzeau; s of Frank Chauncy Williams (d 1971), of Keymer, of Sussex, and Yvonne Romaine,*née* Touzeau (d 1967); *b* 14 Mar 1927; *Educ* Crainleigh Sch, A A Sch of Architecture (Dip Arch) ; *m* 16 May 1953, Eleanor Brigitte, da of Dr Ernst Jellinek (d 1977), of Harpenden; 3 s (Simon b 1956, Michael b 1959, Peter b 1962); *Career* asst architect Herts CC 1949-56, Br Standards Inst 1956-58, head tech dept RIBA 1958-63; ptnr: Alex Gordon & Ptnrs 1963-66, Anthony Williams & Burles 1966-76; (series ed Building Dossiers 1973-), Anthony Williams & Ptnrs 1976-; chm Yarsley Quality Assured Firms 1985-; cncl memb Bldg Standards Gp of Br Standards Soc, memb BSI Ctee, past chm Modular Soc; FRIBA, FCSD, FRSA; *Books* Signs (1984), Energy Design Guide (1985); *Recreations* historic gardens; *Style—* Anthony Williams, Esq; 43A West Common, Harpenden, Herts AL5 2JW (☎ 0582 460 994)

WILLIAMS, Arthur Laurence (Laurie); s of Percival Arthur Williams (d 1956), and Beatrice Georgina Powell (d 1956); *b* 21 July 1924; *Educ* Bassaleg Elimentary Sch, Cathays (Cardiff) Boys; *m* 4 April 1953, Marion, da of Edward Sydney Griffiths (d 1982); 1 s (Nicholas Symers b 4 Dec 1957), 1 da (Louise Georgina b 2 June 1960); *Career* WWII served NW Eur and Far East 1944-46; DipArch 1949, elected to RIBA; *Recreations* jazz violinist, painting, ham radio GW3NKZ; *Clubs* Victory Services, Gibbs; *Style—* Arthur Williams, Esq; Wren House, 3 Portland Place, Lisuane, Cardiff CF4 6EQ

WILLIAMS, Betty, Lady; Betty Kathleen; da of John Taylor, of Hitchin; *m* 1950, Sir William Williams, 8 Bt, of Tregullow (d 1960); *Style—* Betty, Lady Williams; The Flat, St Brannocks House, Braunton, N Devon

WILLIAMS, Professor Sir Bruce Rodda; KBE (1980); s of Rev W J Williams; *b* 10 Jan 1919; *Educ* Wesley Coll, Queen's Coll Univ of Melbourne; *m* 1942, Roma Olive Hotten; 5 da; *Career* formerly econ lectr Adelaide Univ, Queen's Univ Belfast; Prof of Econ: Univ of Keele 1949-59, Manchester 1959-67; memb Nat Bds for Prices and Incomes, econ advsr Miny Tech 1966-67; chm NSW State cancer cncl 1967-81, dep chm Paramatta Hosps Bd 1979-81; vice-chllr and princ Sydney Univ 1967-81, memb Aust Reserve Bank Bd 1969-81; dir Technical Change Centre London 1981-86; chm Australian Review of Engineering 1986-88; *Clubs* Athenaeum, Royal Cmwlth Soc; *Style—* Prof Sir Bruce Williams, KBE; 106 Grange Rd, London N5 3PJ; 68 Stuart Street, Canberra, Australia, 2604

WILLIAMS, Bryn Owen; s of Hugh James Owen Williams (d 1983), and Ivy, *née* Heffer; *b* 20 August 1933; *Educ* Southgate County GS, Pitman's Coll, Italia Conti Stage Sch; *m* 6 July 1957, Ann Elizabeth Rheidol, da of David Rheidol Powell (d 1932), adopted da of Stephen Llewellyn Jones (d 1963), of Dulwich; 1 s (Timothy Dorian b 7 April 1959), 1 da (Tracy-Jane b 11 June 1961); *Career* professional toastmaster 1950; co fndr (with father) Nat Assoc of Toastmasters 1956 (pres 1962 and 1989-90, life vice-pres 1984), officiated at over twelve thousand events in over twenty countries; memb Grand Order Water Rats 1965; Freeman City of London 1980, Liveryman Worshipful Co of Butchers 1985; *Recreations* golf, classical music; *Clubs* Wig & Pen, Muswell Hill GS, Concert Artists Assoc, City Livery, Variety Club of GB Golf Soc (life memb), Jaguar Drivers (life memb); *Style—* Bryn Williams, Esq; Tanglewood, 50 The Ridgway, Enfield, Middx EN2 8QS (☎ 01 366 0012); Bryn Williams Enterprise, 6 Gladstone Hse, High Rd, Wood Green N22 6JS (☎ 01 888 2398)

WILLIAMS, Catrin Mary; da of Richard Williams, JP (d 1966), of Y Ddol, Pwllheli, Gwynedd, and Margaret, *née* Jones (d 1986); *b* 19 May 1922; *Educ* Pwllheli GS, Welsh Nat Sch of Med; *Career* conslt ear nose and throat surgn Clwyd Health Authy (North) 1956-86; pres Med Women's Fedn 1973-74, elected co-chm Women's Nat Cmmn 1981-83, vice-chm Memiere's Soc, chm Wales Cncl for the Deaf 1986-88, memb cncl exec ctee Royal Nat Inst for Deaf, exec memb Wales Cncl for the Disabled; memb: BMA, Med Women's Int Assoc; *Recreations* reading, embroidery; *Style—* Miss Catrin Williams; Gwrych House, Abergele, Clwyd LL22 8EU (☎ 0745 832256)

WILLIAMS, Clifford Sydney; s of George Frederick Williams (d 1932), and Florence Maud Gapper Williams Maycock; *b* 30 Dec 1926; *Educ* Highbury County GS London; *m* 1962, Josiane Eugenie, da of Auguste Camille Joseph Peset (d 1972), of Paris; 2 da (Anouk, Tara); *Career* Lt RAOC 1946-48; founded and directed Mime Theatre Co 1950-53, dir of productions Marlow Theatre, Canterbury 1956, and Queen's Theatre Hornchurch 1957, assoc dir Royal Shakespeare Co 1963-, has directed for Nat Theatres of UK, Finland, Yugoslavia, Bulgaria, Mexico and Spain, and in France, Denmark, Sweden, W Germany, Japan, Canada and USA; productions in London and New York incl premieres of plays by: Friedrich Dürrenmatt, Eugene Ionesco, David Rudkin, Anthony Shaffer, Alan Bennett, Peter Ustinov, Rolf Hochhuth, Alexander Solzhenitsyn and Hugh Whitemore; Man and Superman (film 1988); author of plays incl: The Sleeping Princess, The Goose Girl, The Secret Kingdom (with Donald Jonson) Stephen Hero (adaptation of James Joyce with Donald Jonson); fell Trin Coll of Music 1956, govr Welsh Coll of Music and Drama 1980-; chm: British Theatre Assoc 1978-, UK Centre of Int Amateur Theatre Assoc 1980-; *Recreations* motor sport; *Style—* Clifford Williams, Esq; 62 Maltings Place, London SW6 2BY (☎ 01 736 4673)

WILLIAMS, David; s of Trevor Kenneth Stuart Williams (d 1961), and Peri Rene Mavis, *née* Morgan (d 1987); *b* 8 June 1926; *Educ* Cathedral Sch Hereford, St John's Coll Oxford (MA); *m* 18 Aug 1951, Brenda Yvonne, da of Dan Campbell Holmes, OBE (d 1964); 1 s (Jonathan b 1955), 1 da (Linda b 1957); *Career* Sub Lt RNVR 1944-47; dir Gordon and Gotch Advertising 1950-58, chm David Williams and Ketchum 1958-78, dir Ketchum Communications Inc USA 1968-86; govr Pusey House Oxford 1963-; vice-chm Royal Cwlth Soc for the Blind 1969-85; cncl memb: Advertising Assoc 1963-78, Advertising Standards Authy 1976-80, Impact Fndn 1985-, Chest Heart and Stroke Assoc 1987-; Freedom City of London 1959, Liveryman Worshipful Co of Stationers and Newspaper Makers 1960; MCAM 1959, FIPA 1962; *Novels*: Unholy Writ (1976), Treasure by Degrees (1977), Treasure up in Smoke (1978), Murder for Treasure (1980), Copper, Gold & Treasure (1982), Treasure Preserved (1983), Advertise for Treasure (1984), Wedding Treasure (1985), Murder in Advent (1985), Treasure in Roubles (1986), Divided Treasure (1987), Treasure in Oxford (1988), Holy Treasure (1989), and numerous short stories; *Recreations* golf, music, looking at churches; *Clubs* Carlton, Wentworth GC; *Style—* David Williams, Esq; Blandings, Pinewood Rd, Wentworth, Virginia Water, Surrey GU25 4PA (☎ 09904 2055)

WILLIAMS, Adm Sir David; GCB (1977, KCB 1975), DL (Devon 1981); s of A Williams; *b* 22 Oct 1921; *Educ* Yardley Ct Sch Tonbridge, RNC Dartmouth; *m* 1947, Philippa Stevens; 2 s; *Career* joined RN as Cadet 1935, Flag Offr and 2 i/c Far East Fleet 1970-72, dir-gen Naval Manpower and Trg 1972-74, Vice-Adm 1973, Adm 1974, Chief Naval Personnel and Second Sea Lord 1974-77, C-in-C Naval Home Cmd and ADC to HM The Queen 1977-79, Gentleman Usher to HM The Queen 1979-82, Extra Gentleman Usher 1982-, govr and C-in-C Gibraltar 1982-85; memb Cwlth War Graves Cmmn 1980-89 (vice-chm 1986-89); KStJ 1983; *Clubs* Royal Yacht Sqdn, Army and

Navy; *Style*— Admiral Sir David Williams, GCB, DL; Brockholt, Strete, Dartmouth, Devon TQ6 0RR

WILLIAMS, Rear Adm David Apthorp; CB (1965), DSC (1942); s of Thomas Pettit Williams (d 1962), of 37 Auckland Rd East, Southsea, Hants, and Vera Frederica Dudley, *née* Apthorp (d 1955); *b* 27 Jan 1911; *Educ* Cheltenham; *m* 27 April 1951, Susan Eastlake (d 1987), da of Wharram Henry Lamplough (d 1945), of Bredon, Foster Rd, Alverstoke, Hants; 1 s (Nigel Lamplough Williams), 2 step da (Sarah Ley (Mrs Bradey) b 1939, Shirley Anne (Mrs Palmes) b 1942); *Career* Naval Cadet HMS Erebus (trg ship) 1929-30, Midshipman (E) (later Sub Lt (E)) RN Engrg Coll Keyham 1930-34, Sub Lt (E) (later Lt (E)) HMS Nelson 1934-35, Lt (E) sr engine room watchkeeper HMS Barham 1935-37, Lt (E) Mechanical Trg Estab Chatham (HMS Pembroke) 1937-39; Lt (E) (later Lt Cdr (E)) engrg offr HMS Hasty 1939-42: 2 Destroyer Flotilla, Med Fleet, S Atlantic Station, Home Fleet, E Med Fleet (sunk Malta convoy 1942, despatches four times); Lt Cdr (E) sr engr HMS Implacable 1942-45 Home Fleet and 1 Aircraft Carrier Sqdn Br Pacific Fleet (C-in-C's Commendation) Cdr (E) 1945, Cdr (E) HMS Argonaut Br Pacific Fleet and Portsmouth 1945-47, RN Engrg Coll Plymouth (HMS Thunderer) 1947, air engrg course 1947, prodn mangr RN Aircraft Repair Yard Gosport 1947-49, Air Equipment and naval photography dept Admty 1949-52, trg cdr and air engrg offr RN Air Station Yeovilton 1952-53, trg cdr and air engrg offr RN Air Station St Merryn 1953-55, Capt 1955, First Admty Interview Bd Dartmouth and HMS Sultan 1955-57, cmd tech offr staff of Flag Offr Air (Home) HMS Daedalus 1957-59, Co RN Air Station Abbotsinch 1959-61, cmd engr offr staff of Flag Offr Air (Home) 1961, chief staff offr (tech) staff of C-in-C Plymouth 1961-62, Rear Adm dir gen (aircraft) Admty (later dir gen aircraft (naval) MOD) 1962-65; ret 1965; memb panel of interviewers for Professional and Tech Grades and Retired Offrs (Civil Serv Cmmn) 1965-82; chm: Gosport local ctee Cancer Res Campaign 1967-, Portsmouth annual area meeting Offrs' Pension Soc 1986-; CENG, MIMechE 1947; *Clubs* Army and Navy; *Style*— Rear Adm David Williams, CB, DSC; 3 Ellachie Gdns, Alverstoke, Gosport, Hants PO12 2DS (☎ 0705 583 375)

WILLIAMS, His Honour Judge David Barry; QC (1975), TD (1964); s of William Barry Williams (d 1967), of Sully Glam and Gwyneth Williams, *née* John; *b* 20 Feb 1931; *Educ* Cardiff HS for Boys, Wellington Sch Somerset, Exeter Coll Oxford (MA); *m* 1961, Angela Joy, da of David Thomas Davies of 52 Cyncoed Road, Cardiff; 3 s (Rhodri, Cristyn, Rhidian), 1 da (Catrin); *Career* Nat Serv S Wales Borderers 1949-51, 2 Bn The Monmouthshire Regt (TA) 1951-67 (ret as Maj); barr Gray's Inn 1955, Wales and Chester Circuit 1957-79, rec of Crown Ct 1972-79; asst cmmr Local Govt Boundary Cmmn for Wales 1976-79, cmmr for trial of Local Govt Election Petitions 1978-79; circuit judge 1979-; chm: Glamorgan RFC 1974-78, Ctee Cardiff and Country Club 1979-80, Legal Affairs Ctee Welsh Centre for Int Affairs 1979-; memb Ct: Govrs Univ Coll Glamorgan 1981-, Ct of Govrs Univ Wales Inst Sci and Tech (and of cncl of same 1982-); vice-chm Cncl UWIST 1983- (vice-pres UWIST 1984-); dep sr Judge (non-resident) Sovereign Base Areas Cyprus 1983-, liason judge W Glamorgan 1983-; pres Mental Health Review Tribunals 1983-; *Recreations* rugby football (administration), mountain walking; *Clubs* Army & Navy, Cardiff and County, Glam Wanderers RFC; *Style*— His Honour David Williams; 52 Cyncoed Road, Cardiff (☎ 0222 498 189); The Law Courts, Guildhall, Swansea, W Glamorgan

WILLIAMS, Sir David Innes; s of Gwynne Evan Owen Williams (d 1957), and Cecily Mary, *née* Innes; *b* 12 June 1919; *Educ* Sherborne, Trinity Hall Cambridge, Univ Coll Hosp Med Sch (MB, BCh, MA, MD, MCh); *m* 19 Sept 1944, Margaret Eileen, da of Victor Harding (d 1956); 2 s (Martin Gwynne b 13 March 1948, Michael Innes b 14 Nov 1949); *Career* Maj RAMC 1945-48 (surgical specialist); surgn St Peters Hosp London 1950-78, urological surgn The Hosp for Sick Children Gt Ormond St 1952-78; urologist: King Edward VII Hosp for Offrs 1961-72, Royal Masonic Hosp 1962-72, civil conslt urologist to RN 1971-78, dir Br Post Grad Med Fedn Univ of London 1978-86, pro vice-chllr Univ of London 1985-87, pres Br Assoc of Urological Surgns 1976-78; vice pres: Int Soc of Urology 1973-74, RCS 1983-85; chm: Cncl for Post Grad Med Educn Eng and Wales 1985-88, cncl Imperial Cancer Res Fund 1982-; pres BMA 1988-89; Hon Fell UCL 1986; FRCS Eng 1944, hon FACS 1983, hon FRCSI 1984, hon FDSRCS Eng 1986; kt 1985; *Books* Urology of Childhood (1952), Urology of Childhood (1958), Paediatric Urology (1968, 1982); *Recreations* gardening; *Clubs* RSM; *Style*— Sir David Williams; 66 Murray Road, Wimbledon Common, London SW19 4PE (☎ 01 879 1042); The Old Rectory, East Knoyle, Salisbury, Wilts; Imperial dr Cancer Research Fund, 44 Lincolns Inn Fields, London WC2A 3PX (☎ 01 242 0200)

WILLIAMS, David Lincoln; s of Lewis Bernard Williams (d 1976), of Cardiff, and Eileen Elizabeth, *née* Cadogan; *b* 10 Feb 1937; *Educ* Cheltenham Coll; *m* 1959, Gillian Elisabeth, da of Dr William Phillips (d 1977); 1 s (Jonathan), 1 da (Sophie); *Career* chm: Allied Profiles Ltd 1981-, John Williams of Cardiff plc 1983-88 (dir 1969-88), Cox (Penarth) Ltd 1987-, Costa Rica Coffee Co 1988-; chm: Vale of Glamorgan Festival 1978-, Cardiff Broadcasting plc 1979-84, Friends of Welsh Nat Opera 1980-; *Recreations* opera, sailing; *Clubs* Cardiff & County; *Style*— David Williams, Esq; Rose Revived, Llantrithyd, Cowbridge, S Glam (☎ 04468 357)

WILLIAMS, Lt-Col David William Bulkeley; s of Capt RA Williams, MC (d 1932), of Porth Yr Aur, Caernarvon, and Winifred, *née* Baker Brown (d 1979); *b* 22 Jan 1922; *Educ* Dover Coll, Birmingham Univ (special war course), Jesus Coll Cambridge (Mechanical Sci Tripos), Army Staff Coll Camberley; *m* 11 Jan 1947, Frances Felicity, da of Lt-Col GH Latham (d 1969), of Robin Post, Hailsham, Sussex; 1 s (Kenneth David Bulkeley b 4 Feb 1950), 2 da (Marion Dilys Bulkeley b 17 March 1948, Christine Frances Bulkeley b 27 July 1951); *Career* WWII cmmnd Maj RE serv 1941-46: Guards Armoured Div UK and NW Europe, M East, Greece, Egypt, Palestine; staff appointment; sr planning engr Thames Conservancy 1972-82; former memb: IEE, InstP; memb: 1WEM, Geologists Assoc; *Recreations* gardening, wood working, geology; *Style*— Lt-Col David Williams; Maen Melin, Peasemore, nr Newbury, Berks RG16 0JF (☎ 0635 248 415)

WILLIAMS, Dr Denis John; CBE (1954); s of Rev Daniel Jenkin Williams, and Elsie Leonora, *née* Edwards; *b* 4 Dec 1908; *Educ* Manchester GS, Manchester Univ (MB, MD, DSc), Harvard (hon res fell, Rockefeller fell); *m* 2 Sept 1937, Joyce Beverley, MBE, JP, da of Frank Jewson, of Norwich; 2 s (1 decd), 2 da; *Career* RAF 1936-45, Wing Cdr, civil conslt RAF 1945-72, mil hosp for head injuries St Hugh's Coll Oxford (electro-encephalography and res into psychological problems in air crews); seconded RN: prof Tom Johnes res fell in surgery Univ of Manchester: 1934, 1935 and 1960; visiting prof Univ of Cincinnatti Ohio 1963 and 1969, hon physician Univ of Sydney 1965; conslt physician (neurology): St George's Hosp London, King Edward VII Hosp for Offrs, Nat Hosp Queen Sq London; ed: Brain Jl of neurology 1954-75, Modern Trends in Neurology; chm sec of state's hon med panel on Safety in Driving 1967-83, advsr on neurology DHSS; chm academic bd Inst of Neurology 1965-74, pres neurology section Royal Soc of Med 1967 (hon memb), vice pres Royal Coll of Physicians 1972-74, pres Assoc Br Neurologists 1972-74, fndr and vice pres Br Epilepsy Assoc (hon memb); Freeman City of London, Liveryman Worshipful Soc of Apothecaries; FRCP 1943; auth of scientific articles on brain functions, electro encephalography and disorders, especially epilepsy; author of numerous scientific articles on brain functions and disorders, especially epilepsy; *Recreations* dairy and sheep farming in W Wales, gardening, nostalgia, Welsh Affairs; *Clubs* Savile, Wayfarers; *Style*— Dr Denis Williams, CBE; 11 Frognal Way, London NW3 6XE (☎ 01 435 4030); Woodlands Farm, Dyfed SA9 5UT

WILLIAMS, Derek Gordon; *b* 22 July 1931; *m* Stephanie Anne, *née* Briggs; 2 c; *Career* CA; chm Charterhall plc 1969-87; FCA; *Clubs* East India; *Style*— Derek Williams, Esq; 9 Paultons Sq, London SW3 5AP, (☎ 01 352 0519)

WILLIAMS, Sir Donald Mark; 10 Bt (UK 1866), of Tregullow, Cornwall; s of Sir Robert Ernest Williams, 9 Bt (d 1976); *b* 7 Nov 1954; *Educ* W Buckland Sch; *Heir* bro, Barton Matthew, b 21 Nov 1956; *Style*— Sir Donald Williams, Bt; Kamsack, Saskatchewan, Canada; Upcott House, Barnstaple, N Devon

WILLIAMS, Douglas; CB (1977), CVO (1966); s of James Eli Williams (d 1977), and Elizabeth Williams (d 1943); *b* 14 May 1917; *Educ* Wolverhampton Sch, Exeter Coll Oxford (MA); *m* 4 Dec 1948, Marie, da of Charles Leon Jacquot (d 1960); *Career* WWII Maj RA (despatches 1945); princ Colonial Off 1947, colonial attaché Br Embassy Washington 1956-60, memb and Br Co- chm Caribbean Cmmn 1960, asst sec Colonial Office (Head of West Indian Div) 1960-67, Miny of Overseas Devpt 1967, undersec in charge of multilateral aid 1968, govr Asian Devpt Bank & African Devpt Bank 1968-73 (dep sec 1973-77), retired 1977; memb: Bd of Crown Agents 1978-84, Econ and Social Ctee Euro Community 1978-82, Overseas Devpt Inst Govng Cncl 1979-85; tstee Help the Aged 1984, chm various ctees, memb Exec Ctee David Davies Memorial Inst of Int Relations 1984-; *Books* The Specialised Agencies and the United Nations (1987), Human Rights Economics Development and Aid to the Third World (1978); *Clubs* United Oxford & Cambridge; *Style*— Douglas Williams, Esq, CB, CVO; 14 Gomshall Rd, Cheam, Sutton, Surrey SM2 7JZ (☎01 393 7306)

WILLIAMS, Dr Dudley Howard; s of Lawrence Williams, and Evelyn Williams (d 1982); *b* 25 May 1937; *Educ* Pudsey GS Yorks, Univ of Leeds (BSc, PhD), Univ of Cambridge (MA, ScD); *m* 9 March 1963, Lorna Patricia Phyllis, da of Phillip Anthony Herbert Bedford; 2 s (Mark Howard b 1966, Simon Bedford b 1968); *Career* post doctoral fell and res assoc Stanford Univ USA 1961-64; Cambridge Univ: fell Churchill Coll 1964-, asst dir of res 1966-74, reader in organic chem 1974-; author of numerous sci pubns and books; FRS 1983; *Books* Spectroscopic Methods in Organic Chemistry (with I Fleming, fourth edn); *Recreations* squash, skiing, piano playing; *Style*— Dr Dudley Williams; 7 Balsham Rd, Fulbourn, Cambridge CB1 5BZ (☎ 0223 880 592); University Chemical Laboratory, Lensfield Rd, Cambridge CB2 1EW (☎ 0223 336 368)

WILLIAMS, Sir Edgar Trevor; CB (1946), CBE (1944, DSO 1943, DL Oxon 1964-); s of Rev Joseph Edgar Williams, of Greenbank, Chester; *b* 20 Nov 1912; *Educ* Tettenhall Coll, King Edward's Sch Sheffield, Merton Oxford; *m* 1, 1938, Monica, da of Prof P Robertson; 1 da; m 2, 1946, Gillian, yr da of Maj-Gen Michael Denman Gambier-Parry, MC (gs of Thomas Gambier-Parry, JP, DL, whose mother was niece of Adm 1 and last Baron Gambier, GCB, the man who failed to destroy the French fleet at the Basque Roads in 1809 but was acquitted at the subsequent court martial owing to political considerations. The general's maternal gf was Hon George Denman, 4 s of 1 Baron Denman) by his w Barbara (paternal gda of Eleanor, herself yst da of Rt Rev George Murray, sometime Bp of Rochester, by the Bp's w Lady Sarah Hay, 2 da of 10 Earl of Kinnoull. The Bishop's f was 2 s of 3 Duke of Atholl); 1 s, 1 da; *Career* serv WWII 1 King's Dragoon Gds; GSO: N Africa, Italy, Normandy Rhine Army; with UN Secretariat 1946-47; asst lectr Liverpool Univ 1936, govr St Edward's Sch Oxford 1964-, emeritus fell Balliol Oxford 1980- (fell 1945-80), pro-vice-chllr Oxford Univ 1968-80; chm Nuffield Provincial Hosps Tst 1966-88, Radcliffe tstee 1960-; Freeman Chester; hon fell Wolfson Coll Oxford, Merton Coll Oxford; UK Observer Rhodesian Elections 1980, sec Rhodesian Tst 1951-80, memb Devlin Nyasaland Cmmn 1959; ed DNB 1949-80; FRHistS; kt 1973; *Clubs* Athenaeum, Savile, Vinvent's; *Style*— Sir Edgar Williams, CB, CBE, DSO, DL; 94 Lonsdale Rd, Oxford OX2 7ER (☎ 0865 515199)

WILLIAMS, Air Cdre Edward Stanley; CBE (1975, OBE 1968); s of William Stanley Williams (d 1957), of Wallasey, Cheshire, and Ethel, *née* Jones (d 1953); *b* 27 Sept 1924; *Educ* Wallasey Central Sch, Sch of Slavonic and Eastern European Studies London Univ, Univ Coll London, St John's Coll Cambridge (M Phil); *m* 12 July 1947, Maureem, da of William Joseph Donovan (d 1974), of Oxton, Merseyside; 2 da ((Susan) Jane b 3 Feb 1950, Sally (Ann) b 23 June 1955); *Career* joined RAF 1942, WWII training in Canada, serv in flying boats 1944, seconded BOAC 1944-48, 18 Sqdn RAF Waterbeach 1949, instr Central Navigation Sch RAF Shawbury 1950-52, Russian language study 1952-54; flying appts 1954-61: MEAF, A & AEE Boscombe Down, 216 Sqdn Tpt Cmd; OC RAF Element Army Intelligence Centre 1961-64, asst air attaché Moscow 1964-67, first RAF def fell 1967-68, Sch of Serv Intelligence 1968-71, chief Target Plans HQ Second ATAF 1971-73, chief intelligence offr Br Forces Near East 1973-75, cmd Jt Air Reconnaissance Intelligence Centre (UK) 1976-77, def and air attaché Moscow 1978-81, ret RAF 1981; conslt Soviet mil affrs MOD 1982-85, Soviet res assoc RUSI 1985-; vice-chm (air) TAVR and RAFVR Assoc (NW Area); *Books* The Soviet Military (1987); *Recreations* walking; *Clubs* RAF; *Style*— Air Cdre E S Williams, CBE; c/o Midland Bank, 2 Liscard Way, Wallasey, Merseyside L44 5TR

WILLIAMS, Hon Sir Edward Stratten; KCMG (1983), KBE (1981); s of Edward Stratten Williams (d 1929), and Zilla Claudia Williams (d 1930); *b* 29 Dec 1921; *Educ* Yungaburra State Sch, Mt Carmel Coll, London Univ (LLB) Hons; *m* 1949, Dorothy, da of Reginald Murray; 3 s (Edward, Sydney, Anthony), (Michael decd), 4 da (Zilla, Judith, Therese, Elizabeth); *Career* RAAF (Pilot) UK 1943-46; Qld barr 1946, judge of Supreme Ct of Qld 1971-84, chm Qld Parole Bd 1976-83; chm XII Cwlth Games Fndn 1976-82, Royal cmmnr Aust Royal Cmmn of Inquiry into Drugs 1977-80, memb int Narcotics Control Bd Vienna 1982-87, comm-gen of Expo 88 1984-89; chm Queensland Turf Club; dir Elders IXL Ltd, Aust Hydrocarbons NL; chm Queensland Carlton Board of Advice; patron Nat Basketball Federation and League; Trustee Queensland Overseas Foundation since 1976; Received Australian of The Year Award 1982 and Queenslander of the Year Award 1983; *Recreations* horse racing, golf, gardening; *Clubs* Brisbane, United Services, Tattersalls, Qld Turf, Bris Amateur Turf, Albion Park Trotting, Far North Qld Amateur Turf; *Style—* The Hon Sir Edward Williams, KCMG, KBE; 150 Adelaide St, East Clayfield, Qld 4011, Australia (☎ 262 4802)

WILLIAMS, Edward Thomas; s of Capt Thomas Williams, (d 1960), and Mabel Elvira, *née* Thomas (d 1985); *b* 21 Feb 1927; *Educ* Porth Co Sch, Kingswood Sch Bath, Trinity Hall Cambridge (MA, LLM); *m* 22 March 1955, (Marjorie) Jane Stanley, da of Capt Richard Stanley Evans (d 1949), of Bron-wydd Pontypridd; 1 s (Rhodri Clive b 30 Nov 1957), 2 da (Anne Judith b 10 July 1956, Susan Jane b 18 May 1961); *Career* Nat Serv RN 1945-48; slr 1954; pt/t chm: Nat Insur Local Tbnl 1966, Med Appeals Tbnls for Wales 1985; sec advsy ctee on Gen Cmmrs of Income Tax Mid Glamorgan 1986; pres: Pontypridd and Rhondda Dist Law Soc 1968-69, Assoc Law Socs of Wales 1976-77, Bridgend and Dist Law Soc 1977-78, clerk to Gen Cmmrs of Income Tax for Pontypridd 1973-; chm S Wales Autistic Soc, pres Rotary Club of Porthcawl 1987-88, former dir Pontypridd Mkts Fairs and Town Hall Co Ltd (resigned 1988); memb Law Soc 1954; *Recreations* golf; *Clubs* Royal Porthcawl; *Style—* Edward Williams, Esq; 2 Mallard Way, Porthcawl, Mid Glamorgan, CF36 3TS (☎ 065 671 4031);65 Mary Street, Porthcawl, Mid Glamorgan (☎ 065 671 4151, fax 5532)

WILLIAMS, Eirian John; s of Rev Prof Cyril G Williams, of St. Davids Coll, Univ of Wales, Lampeter, and Irene Williams; *b* 15 May 1952; *Educ* Carleton Univ Ottawa Canada (BA), Univ Coll of Wales Aberystwyth (LLB); *m* 10 Sept 1978, Glesni, da of Glyn Evans, of Tregaron County Sch, Dyfed; 2 s (Iwan Marc b 1982, Dylan Sion b 1985); *Career* admitted Canadian (Alberta) Bar 1978, admitted Br Slrs Roll 1983, ptnr Amphlett Lewis & Evans in assoc with Ungoed Thames & King; *Style—* Eirian Williams, Esq; 4/5 Bridge St, LLandysul, Dyfed (☎ 055932 3244, fax 055932 3733)

WILLIAMS, Elizabeth, Lady; Elizabeth Mary Garneys; JP (Dorset 1959), DL (Dorset 1983); da of William Ralph Garneys Bond, JP (d 1952, whose mother was da of Sir Harry Meysey-Thompson, 1 Bt, also sis of 1 and last Baron Knaresborough and the late Countess of Iddesleigh, w of 2 Earl) of Tyneham, Dorset and Evelyn Isobel, OBE, *née* Blake (d 1954); *b* 1 May 1921; *Educ* Downe House; *m* 1948, as his 2 w, Sir David Williams, 3 Bt (d 1970), s of Sir Philip Williams, 2 Bt (d 1958), of Bridehead, Littlebredy, Dorset; 2 s (Philip 4 Bt *qv*, Michael b 1955), 1 da (Ruth b 1951, m Michael Widén 1975); *Career* ATS (FANY) 1939-46, cmmnd 1942; High Sheriff Dorset 1979; Territorial Medal; *Recreations* country pursuits; *Style—* Elizabeth, Lady Williams, JP, DL; Stable House, Moigne Combe, Nr Dorchester, Dorset DT2 8JA (☎ 0305 852418)

WILLIAMS, Eric Charles; s of Herbert Reginald (d 1969), of Upper House, Clunbury, Shrops, and May Williams (d 1975); *b* 14 Nov 1921; *Educ* Wellingborough GS; *m* 18 Aug 1947, Margaret Goldsworthy, da of Thomas Peregrine (d 1956), of London; 2 s (Simon Eric b 1969, Philip Charles Peregrine b 1966), 3 da (Susan b 1951, Anne (twin) b 1951, Caroline b 1963); *Career* WWII Capt's sec HMS Agamemnon RNR 1943-44, RNVR 1943-46, paymaster branch HMS Rajah 1944, Capts Sec HMS Highway 1944, official naval reporter CNI Admty 1944-46; journalist provincial newspapers Northampton 1938-41, Reuters 1946, Sunday Dispatch 1946-47; dir Gainsborough Studios 1948-49, PR Foote Cone & Belding Ltd 1949- 56 (Greece 1951-52), PR Mangr Notley Advtg Ltd 1957-60, PR dir McCann-Erickson Ltd 1960-62, md PR Plan Ltd 1962-67, fndr and md Eric Williams & Ptnrs Ltd 1967-83, sold co to Daniel J Edelman Ltd and joined their board until ret 1987; chm Esher and Dist Christian Aid Ctee; Freeman City of London 1975, Liveryman Worshipful Co of Fruiterers 1975 (Hon Asst 1986-88); FInst PR 1970, FIOD, memb Int PR Assoc; *Recreations* dry fly fishing, boating, travel, gardening, conversation; *Clubs* Solus; *Style—* Eric Williams, Esq; Fair Acre, 20 Meadway, Esher, Surrey KT10 9HF (☎ 0372 64489)

WILLIAMS, Lady; Florence Alice; da of John Exley; *m* 1925, Sir Charles Henry Trelease Williams, CBE (d 1982); *Style—* Lady Williams; Overdales, 4 Brunswick Rd, Rotherham, Yorks S60 2RH (☎ 0709 67192)

WILLIAMS, Sir Francis John Watkin; 8 Bt (GB 1798), of Bodelwyddan, Flintshire, QC (1952); s of Col Lawrence Williams, OBE, JP, DL (d 1958, himself gs of Sir John Williams, 1 Bt, whose gggf was Speaker of the House of Commons); suc bro, Sir Reginald Williams, 7 Bt, MBE, TD (d 1971); *b* 24 Jan 1905; *Educ* Malvern, Trinity Hall Cambridge; *m* 1932, Brenda, JP, da of Sir (Joseph) John Jarvis, 1 Bt (d 1950); 4 da; *Heir* half-bro Lawrence Hugh Williams, b 25 Aug 1929; *Career* serv WWII, Wing Cdr RAFVR; barr Middle Temple 1928; rec of: Birkenhead 1950-58, Chester 1958-71; chm: Anglesey QS 1960-71 (dep chm 1949-60), Flint QS 1961-71 (dep chm 1953-61); dep chm Cheshire QS 1952-71, rec of the Crown Ct 1972-75; chm Med Appeal Tbnl N Wales Area 1954-57; JP Denbighshire 1951-74; high sheriff: Denbighshire 1957, Anglesey 1963; chllr Diocese of St Asaph 1966-83; Freeman City of Chester 1960; hon memb Wales and Chester Circuit 1987; *Recreations* gardening, golf; *Clubs* United Oxford and Cambridge; *Style—* Sir Francis Williams, Bt, QC; Llys, Middle Lane, Denbigh

WILLIAMS, Frank - Francis Owen; CBE (1987); s of Owen Garbett Williams, Liverpool; *b* 16 April 1942; *Educ* St Joseph's Coll Dumfries; *m* 1974, Virginia Jane, da of Raymond Berry, of Marlow, Bucks; 3 c; *Career* md Williams Grand Prix Engrg; *Recreations* running; *Clubs* BRDC; *Style—* Frank Williams, Esq, CBE; Boxford House, Boxford, Nr Newbury, Berks; Williams Grand Prix Engineering Ltd, Station Road Industrial Estate, Didcot, Oxon OX11 7NA (☎ (0235) 818161, telex 837632)

WILLIAMS, Col (John) Gage; OBE (1987); s of Col George Torquil Gage Williams, DL, of Menkee, St Mabyn, Cornwall, and Yvonne Marguerite, *née* Ogilvy; *b* 12 Mar 1946; *Educ* Eton, RMA Sandhurst, Magdalene Coll Cambridge (MA); *m* 4 Jul 1970, Elizabeth Anne Kyffin, da of Stephen Marriott Fox (d 1971), of Burlorne, Weybridge, Surrey; 1 s (James b 1973), 2 da (Rebecca b 1971, Meg b 1978); *Career* cmmnd Somerset and Cornwall Light Inf 1966 (The Light Inf 1967); Platoon Cdr: Ethiopia, Aden, Canada, Norway, Kenya, Germany; GSO 3 ops 19 Airportable Bde England and Cyprus 1974-75, instr tactics Sch of Inf Fort Benning USA 1975-77, Royal Mil Coll Sci 1977, Royal Staff Course Greenwich 1978; Co Cdr: Ireland, Canada, Cyprus (UN) 1978-80; GSO2 Jt Warfare MO1 1980-82, Special Ops Liaison Offr Washington DC 1982-83, Mil Asst GOC NI 1983-84; cmmd 1 Bn Light Inf: Lancs, Falklands, Canada, NI 1985-87; liaison Col to Sch of Advanced Mil Studies Fort Leavenworth Kansas 1987-88, Col Higher Comd and Staff Course Camberley 1988-89; RUSI; *Recreations* shooting, fishing, stalking, golf, skiing, squash, tennis; *Clubs* Light Infantry, Hawks, Cornish, Beefsteak, Stenodoc GC; *Style—* Col Gage Williams, OBE; Staff College, Camberley, Surrey, GU15 4NP (☎ 0276 63344 Ext 2654)

WILLIAMS, Prof Gareth Howel; JP (Brent Petty Sessions Area); s of Morgan John Williams (d 1970), of Harrow, Middx, and Miriam, *née* Jones (d 1979); *b* 17 June 1925; *Educ* Pentre GS, UCL (BSc, PhD, DSc); *m* 2 April 1955, Marie Jessie Thomson, da of William Mitchell (d 1951), of Llanrwst, Gwynedd; 1 s (John b 1956), 1 da (Barbara b 1959); *Career* lectr in chemistry King's Coll London 1950-60 (asst lectr 1947-50), reader in organic chemistry Birkbeck Coll London 1960-67, visiting lectr Univ of Life Nigeria 1965, prof of chemistry 1967-84 and head chemistry dept 1967-84 Bedford Coll London, Rose Morgan visiting prof Univ of Kansas 1969-70, visiting prof Univ of Auckland NZ 1977, emeritus prof Univ of London 1984-, pt/t prof of chemistry Royal Holloway and Bedford New Coll London 1984-87; memb ctee Magistrates Cts and dep chm Juvenile Panel Brent Petty Sessions area; chm: London Welsh Assoc 1987-, Harrow Philharmonic Choir 1987-; Freeman City of London 1984, Liveryman Worshipful Co of Fletchers 1984-, memb Hon Soc Cymmrodorion; FRSC 1945-; *Books* Homolytic Aromatic Substitution (1960), Advances in Free Radical Chemistry (ed vol 1-6 1965-80), Organic Chemistry: A Conceptual Approach (1977); *Recreations* music; *Clubs* Athenaeum; *Style—* Prof Gareth Williams, JP; Hillside, 22 Watford Rd, Northwood, Middx HA6 3NT (☎ 09274 25297)

WILLIAMS, Gareth James; s of Rev Daniel James Williams, (d 1967), of Cardiff, and Elizabeth Beatrice May, *née* Walters (d 1974); *b* 22 Dec 1944; *Educ* Cardiff HS, Univ of Exeter; *m* 2 Aug 1970, Ruth Elizabeth, s of Sub-Lt Albert Gordon Laugharne (d 1944); 1 s (Geraint b 1975), 2 da (Rhian b 1971, Catherine b 1974); *Career* Marks and Spencer plc: joined 1967, exec responsibilities for buying and distribution systems 1974-86, sr exec 1986-87, business devpt gp NY USA 1987-88, divnl dir for Physical Distribution, Retail Systems and Info Tech; memb Cons Pty, memb Chalfont St Giles Parish Church, Friend of Covent Garden, hon vice pres Cardiff HSOB RFC; sport: Cardiff and Cardiff HSOB Rugby Clubs 1964-67, capt Univ of Exeter RFC 1967, played for Br Univs Athletic Union 1967, advsr Br Acad 1985-87, memb UK cncl of Inst of Logistics and Distribution Mgmnt 1989; *Recreations* sport esp rugby, music esp opera, education; *Clubs* Rugby (London), Cardiff HSOBRFC; *Style—* Gareth Williams, Esq; Larksfield, Amersham Rd, Little Chalfont, Bucks HP6 6SW (☎ 0240 743012); Michael House, Baker St, London W1A 1DN (☎ 01 935 4422)

WILLIAMS, Gareth Wyn; QC (1978); s of Albert Thomas Williams (d 1964), and Selina Williams (d 1985); *b* 5 Feb 1941; *Educ* Rhyl GS; Queens' Coll, Cambridge (MA, LLM); *m* Aug 1962, Pauline, da of Ernest Clarke (d 1962); 1 s (Daniel b 1969), 2 da (Martha b 1963, Emma b 1966); *Career* barr, recorder Crown Court 1978; ldr Wales and Chester circuit 1987; *Style—* Gareth Williams, Esq; Southlake House, Shurlock Row, Berks RG10 0PS; Farrars Building Temple, London EC4Y 7BD (☎ 01 583 9241, fax 01 583 0090)

WILLIAMS, Geoffrey Copeland Meirioty; s of William Meirion Williams (d 1939), of Hastings, and Winifred Marjorie, *née* Brice (d 1987); *b* 31 August 1937; *Educ* Eastbourne Coll; *m* 29 May 1965, (Carin) Marianne, da of Col Arne Persson (d 1971), of Stockholm; 1 s (Anthony b 1977), 2 da (Ingela b 1968, Kathrine b 1968); *Career* md Ansvar Insur Co Ltd 1977- (gen mangr 1969-77); other directorships inl: Eastbourne Mutual Bldg Soc, UK Temperance Alliance Ltd; chm Friends of the Towner Gallery Eastbourne, vice-chm Eastbourne Health Authy; FCII 1970; *Recreations* reading, jazz; *Style—* Geoffrey Williams, Esq; Ansvar House, St Leonards Rd, Eastbourne, E Sussex BN21 3UR (☎ 0323 37541, fax 0323 39355)

WILLIAMS, Geoffrey Guy; s of Capt Alfred Guy Williams, OBE (d 1956), and Margaret, *née* Thomas; *b* 12 July 1930; *Educ* Blundell's, Christ's Coll Cambridge (MA, LLM); *Career* slr; ptnr Slaughter & May 1961-66 (joined 1952); J Henry Shroder Wagg & Co Ltd: dir 1966-, vice chm 1974, dep chm 1977-; chm Nat Film Fin Corpn 1976-85 (dir 1970); dir: Bass plc 1971-, Shroders plc 1976-, John Brown plc 1977-85; chm Issuing Houses Assoc 1979-81; Freeman City of London; *Clubs* Brooks's; *Style—* Geoffrey Williams, Esq; 18G Eaton Square, London SW1W 9DD (☎ 01 235 5212); 120 Cheapside, London EC2V 6DS (☎ 01 382 6000, fax 01 382 6878, telex 885029)

WILLIAMS, George; CBE (1983, OBE 1968); s of Charles Henry Williams (d 1971), of Saliabury, Wilts, and Thirza Ann, *née* Chamings (d 1980); *b* 6 August 1917; *Educ* Truro Sch, St John's Coll Cambridge (MA); *m* 5 April 1941, (Margaret) Jean, da of John William Hoyle (d 1941), of Clyderhow, Garston Drive, Garston, Herts; 1 da (Susan Thirza Brett b 24 July 1954); *Career* joined RAF 1939, Pilot Offr No 53 Sqdn 1941, Flying Offr/Flt Lt/Sqdn Ldr No 608 Sqdn 1942, Sqdn Leader/Wing Cdr HQ MACAF 1943, HQ 242 Gp 1944, CO No 36 Sqdn 1944-45, CO No 6 PCC 1945-46; joined Shell Gp 1946; chief exec Shell Cos Br Borneo 1963-64; md: Shell UK Exploration & Prodn 1964-73, Trafalgar House Offshore Ltd 1973-74; dir gen UK Offshore Operators Assoc 1975-84; pres Assoc Br Offshore Industries 1984-89; Hon DSc Heriot-Watt Univ 1979; FGS, FInstPet, FSUT; cdr Most Hon Order of Crown of Brunei 1965; *Recreations* golf; *Clubs* Berkshire Golf, Royal and Ancient Golf, RAF; *Style—* George Williams, Esq, CBE; Sarum House, Hancocks Mount, Sunningdale, Berks SL5 9PQ (☎ 0990 23549)

WILLIAMS, George Mervyn; CBE (1977), MC (1944), DL (Glamorgan 1967); yr s of Owain Lloyd Joseph Williams (d 1930), and Maude Elizabeth, *née* Morgan (d 1941); *b* 30 Oct 1918; *Educ* Radley; *m* 1, 8 March 1941 (m dis 1946), Penelope, da of late Sir Frank Herbert Mitchell, KCVO, CBE; m 2, 19 Aug 1950, Grizel Margaretta Cochrane, DStJ, da of Maj Walter Peter Stewart, DSO, late Highland LI, of Davo House, Kincardineshire; 1 s (Owain Anthony Mervyn b 8 Jan 1955); *Career* Maj Royal Fusiliers N Africa, Italy, Greece; chm: Christie-Tyler plc 1950-86, S Wales Regnl Bd Lloyds Bank Ltd 1975-87, Williams & Morgan Ltd 1986-; High Sheriff Glamorgan 1966, Vice Lord Lt Mid Glamorgan 1986-, JP 1965-70, DL 1967-86; *Clubs* Brooks's, RAC, Cardiff and County; *Style—* George Williams Esq, CBE, MC; Llanharan House, Llanharan, Mid Glamorgan CF7 9NR; Craig y Bwla, Crickhowell, Powys NP8 1SU; Williams & Morgan Ltd, 10 St James Crescent, Swansea SA1 6DZ (☎ 0792 473782, fax 0792 51165)

WILLIAMS, Colonel George Torquil Gage; s of Capt John Gage Williams, 19 Hussars (ka 1943), and Nevil Thorne George; *b* 17 May 1920; *Educ* Cheltenham Coll, RMC Sandhurst; *m* 6 Jan 1945, Yvonne Marguerite, da of Louis William Ogilvy (d 1922), of Calcuta & St Jean de Luz, France; 2 s (Gage, Peter), 2 da (Louella (Mrs Hanbury-Tenison *qv*), Rosemary (Mrs Anderson)); *Career* cmmnd Duke of Cornwall's LI 1939, served India, Iraq, M East until 1942, POW in Italy, escaped, served

Palestine 1945-47, 1947-49, 10 Gurkha Rifles 1949-51 Duke of Cornwall's LI BAOR, W Indies, Cmd Regtl Depot 1958-62, Cmd TA Bn 1962-65, Cmdt Hong-Kong Mil Serv Corps 1965-68, ret 1968; DL (1968) clerk to Lieutenancy of Cornwall 1968; Hon Col 6 Bn Light Infantry (TA) 1978-88; *Recreations* shooting, fishing; *Style*— Col G T G Williams; Menkee, St Mabyn, Bodmin, Cornwall

WILLIAMS, Gerald Wellington; JP (Tunbridge Wells 1957); s of Wellington Archbold Williams, JP (d 1926); *b* 9 August 1903; *Educ* Eton, Ch Ch Oxford (MA); *m* 1930, Mary Katharine Victoria, da of Josceline Heber-Percy, DL (gs of Algernon Heber-Percy, JP, DL, n of 5 Duke of Northumberland), by his w Katharine, da of Lord Algernon Percy (s of 6 Duke of Northumberland) and her husband's 3 cous; 1 s (John b 1937), 2 da (Brioni (Mrs Maurice Armytage), Annette (Mrs Andrew Watson); *Career* Lt-Cdr RNVR Europe 1939-45; MP (Cons) Tonbridge 1945-56; High Sheriff Kent 1968-69; *Clubs* Carlton, MCC; *Style*— Gerald Williams, Esq, JP; 13 Woodsford Square, London W14 8DP (☎ 01 602 0084)

WILLIAMS, Prof Glanmor; CBE (1981); s of Daniel Williams (d 1957), of Dowlais, Glamorganshire, and Ceinwen, *née* Evans (d 1970); *b* 5 May 1920; *Educ* Cyfarthfa Sch Merthyr Tydfil, Univ Coll of Wales Aberystwyth (BA, MA, DLitt); *m* 6 April 1946, (Margaret) Fay, da of late William Harold Davies, of Cardiff; 1 s (Huw b 1 Dec 1953), 1 da (Margaret b 31 March 1952); *Career* Univ Coll of Swansea: asst lectr 1945, sr lectr 1952-57, prof of history 1957-82, vice princ 1975-78; vice pres Univ of Coll of Wales 1986-; chm Royal Cmmn on Ancient Monuments (Wales) 1986- (memb 1962-), memb: Historic Bldg Cncl (Wales) 1962-, bd of Celtic studies Univ of Wales 1969-, Ancient Monuments Bd (Wales) 1983-, ctee Welsh Nat Folk Museum 1986-; chm: Nat Broadcasting Cncl of Wales 1965-71, Br Library Bd 1973-80, Br Library Advsy Cncl 1980-85; govr BBC 1965-71, pres Assoc of Teachers of History of Wales 1983-; FR Hist Soc 1954, FSA 1979, FBA 1986; *Books* The Welsh Church From Conquest to Reformation (1962), Welsh Reformation Essays (1967), Religion Language and Literature in Wales (1979), Wales 1415-1642 (1987), Glamorgan County History Vols I-VI (ed 1971-88); *Recreations* gramophone, walking, cine-photography; *Style*— Prof Glanmor Williams, CBE; 11 Grosvenor Rd, Sketty, Swansea SA2 0SP (☎ 792 204 113)

WILLIAMS, Air Vice-Marshal Graham Charles; AFC (1971, and bar 1975); s of Charles Francis Williams (d 1968), and Molly, *née* Chapman (d 1988); *b* 4 June 1937; *Educ* Marlborough, RAF Coll Cranwell; *m* 3 March 1962, Judy Teresa Ann, da of Reginald Walker (d 1972); 1 s (Mark b 1963), 1 da (Kim b 1966); *Career* Pilot 54 Sqdn Odiham 1958-60, instr 229 OCU Chivenor 1961-63, Flt-Cdr 8 Sqdn Khormaskar 1964-65, Empire Test Pilot's Sch 1966, 'A' Sqdn (fighter test) A and AEE Boscombe Down 1967-70, RAF Staff Coll Bracknell 1971, OC 3 (F) Sqdn Wildenrath 1972-74, jr directing staff RCDS 1975-77, Stn Cdr RAF Bruggen 1978-79, Gp Capt Ops HQ RAF Germany 1980-82, CO Experimental Flying RAF Farnborough 1983, Cmdt A and AEE Boscombe Down 1984-85, DOR (Air) MOD 1986, asst chief of def staff Operational Requirements (Air) 1987-; FRAeS 1984; Harmon Trophy USA 1970; *Recreations* squash, golf; *Clubs* RAF; *Style*— Air Vice-Marshal Graham Williams; 3 The Ramparts, Knightrider St, Sandwich, Kent CT13 9ER (☎ 0304 613030); 31 Chester Way, London SE11; MOD, Whitehall, London SW1A 2HB (☎ 01 218 7221)

WILLIAMS, Sir Gwilym Tecwyn; CBE (1966); s of late David Williams; *b* 9 August 1913; *Educ* Llanfyllin CSS, Harper Adams Agricultural Coll; *m* 1936, Kathleen Isabel Rishworth, *née* Edwards (d 1989); 2 s (Rev John Roger,David Edward), 1 da (Bridget Anne Kemp); *Career* farmer (ret), vice-pres and dep pres NFU 1952-55 and 1960-66, chm Potato Marketing Bd 1955-59, pres NFU 1966-70, dir Dalgety (UK) Ltd 1976-, chm of governors Harper Adams Coll; kt 1970; *Recreations* golf, shooting, trout fishing; *Clubs* Farmers'; *Style*— Sir Gwilym Williams, CBE; Red Gables, Longford, Newport, Shropshire (☎ (0952) 810439)

WILLIAMS, Prof (John) Gwynn; s of Rev John Ellis Williams (d 1969), of 26 Stanley Ave, Rhyl, Clwyd, and Annie Maude, *née* Rowlands; *b* 19 June 1924; *Educ* Holywell GS Clwyd, Univ Coll of N Wales Bangor (BA, DipEd, MA); *m* 24 July 1954, Beryl, da of Rev Stafford Henry Morgan Thomas (d 1968); 3 s (William Gwynn b 1965, Gruffudd Rowland b 1969, Thomas Ellis b 1972); *Career* RN 1943-46; staff tutor dept of extra mural studies Univ of Liverpool 1951-54; Univ of N Wales: asst lectr 1955, prof of welsh history 1963-83, dean faculty of arts 1972-74, vice princ 1974-79; chm press bd Univ of Wales 1979- (memb cncl 1973-85), dir Gregynog Press 1979-; pres: Nat Library of Wales 1986- (vice pres 1984-86), Cambrian Archaeological Assoc 1987-88; vice pres Hon Soc of Cymmrodorion 1988-, hon memb Gorsedd of Bards (White Robe), memb Royal Cmmn on Ancient and Historical Monuments in Wales 1987 (1967 and 1977); *Publications* The University College of North Wales: Foundations (1985), contrib on seventeenth Century Wales to learned jnls; *Recreations* travelling, walking; *Style*— Prof J Gwynn Williams; Llywenan, Siliwen, Bangor, Gwynedd LL57 2BS (☎ 0248 353065)

WILLIAMS, Sir Henry Morton Leech; MBE (1945); s of late Owen Richard Williams, of Kitemore House, Faringdon, Oxon, and late Helen Dykes, *née* Morton; *b* 19 Mar 1913; *Educ* Harrow, CCC Cambridge (BA); *m* 1945, Bridget Mary, da of late Charles Gordon Dowding; 2 s, 2 da; *Career* served WWII REME, Maj, Middle East and Italy (despatches); pres: Bengal C of C and Industry, Assoc Cs of C India 1960; md GKW Ltd India 1952-62, ccllr Berks 1967; now farming; kt 1961; *Clubs* Oriental; *Style*— Sir Henry Williams, MBE; Grounds Farm, Uffington, Faringdon, Oxon SN7 7RD (☎ 0367 82614)

WILLIAMS, Hon Horace; s of Baron Williams of Barnburgh (Life Peer, d 1967); *b* 1914; *m* 1, 1941 (m dis 1948), Hon Mary Morrison, da of Baron Morrison of Lambeth; m 2, Margaret Chisholm, da of William Green; *Style*— The Hon Horace Williams

WILLIAMS, Hubert Glyn; AE (1944); s of John Christmas Williams (d 1944), of Denbigh, and Florence Jane, *née* Jones (d 1958); *b* 18 Dec 1912; *Educ* Ruthin; *m* 1952, Audrey Elizabeth, da of George Alfred Righton (d 1970), of Gosport; 1 s, 1 da; *Career* served WW II UK, Egypt, E Africa, Palestine: AAF 1939-41, RAFVR 1941-45, Sqdn Ldr; slr 1934; sr ptnr Blake Lapthorn Rea & Williams of Portsmouth 1973-83, rec Crown Ct 1974-77; pres Hants Inc Law Soc 1977-78; *Recreations* cricket; *Clubs* MCC; *Style*— Hubert Williams, Esq, AE; 29 The Ave, Alverstoke, Gosport, Hants PO12 2JS (☎ 0705 583058)

WILLIAMS, James Sinclair; OBE (1957); s of James Annand Williams, CBE (d 1963), and Jessie Catherine, *née* McPherson (d 1968); *b* 27 April 1910; *Educ* King's Coll Sch Wimbledon, George Watson's Coll Edinburgh, Edinburgh Univ (B Com); *m* 1 Sept 1945, Audrey Irvine Wiliams, da of Douglas Irvine Watson, BSc, AIC; *Career* dir Coal Utilisation Cncl 1946-60 (sec 1937-45), jt sec Govt Fuel Efficiency Ctee 1940-44, dep dir gen of mktg NCB 1960-64, dir gen Advertising Assoc 1964-75; UK delegate to Int C & S Paris, pres Nat Fedn of Publicity Assocs 1974-75, chm Euro Assoc of Advertising Assoc 1967-75; chm History of Advertising Tst 1978-85; memb W Sussex CC 1977-85, chm Arundel constituency Cons Assoc, pres Adwick W Cons branch; hon memb: Int Advertising Assoc, Communication Advertising and Marketing Fndn; *Recreations* gardening, reading, parties, relaxing; *Clubs* Caledonian, London, Bognor (chm); *Style*— James Williams, Esq, OBE; Sea Cottage, 126 Manor Way, Aldwick Bay, West Sussex PO21 4HN (☎ 0243 262 871)

WILLIAMS, John Charles Wallis; s of Peter Alfred Williams, of Menston, West Yorks, and Mary, *née* Bower; *b* 12 Dec 1953; *Educ* St Peter's York, Queen's Coll Oxford (MA); *m* 28 June 1980, Wendy Irene, da of Harold Doe, of Whitton, Middx; 2 da (Sarah b 1984, Clare b 1988); *Career* advertising exec J Walter Thompson Co 1975-86, Walin Pollen Ltd 1988-(head res and planning 1988-); *Recreations* cinema, music, good food and wine; *Clubs* RAC; *Style*— John Williams, Esq; 128 Rusthall Ave, London W4 1BS (☎ 01 995 8747); Valin Pollen Ltd, 18 Grosvenor Gdns, London SW1W 0DH (☎ 01 730 3456, fax 01 730 7445, telex 296846 BIZCOM G)

WILLIAMS, Dr John Garret Pascoe; s of Surgn Cdr Edward Rex Pascoe Williams, OBE, RN (d 1950), and Marion May Gibson, *née* Jarvie; *b* 15 Sept 1932; *Educ* Beaumont Coll, Gonville and Caius Coll Cambridge (MB, BChir, MD), St Mary's Hosp Sch London W2 (DPhysMed, MSc, MRCS, LRCP); *m* 20 Sept 1958, Sally Jennifer, da of Ranald Montague Handfield-Jones, MC (d 1972); 2 s (Stephen b 1960, David b 1965), 1 da (Philippa b 1962); *Career* conslt physical med and dir dept physical med and rehabilition 1965-76, Mount Vernon Hosp, Harefield Hosp; med dir Farnham Park rehabilition centre Farnham Royal 1965-88, conslt rehabilitation med and dir dept rehabilition med Wexham Park Hosp Slough 1965-, fell (former sec gen) Int Fedn Sports Med 1970-80 (Gold Medal 1980), civil conslt rehabilition med RN 1981-, chm ctee PSM 31 Br Standards Inst, med advsr Squash Rackets Assoc; pres Bourne End Jr Sports Club; Philip Noel Baker Res Prize UNESCO ICSPE 1974, Winston Churchill Travelling Fellowship; Liveryman Worshipful Soc of Apothecaries; FRCS 1963, FRCP 1986; *Books* Sports Medicine (contrib and ed 1962 2 edn 1976), Medical Aspects of Sport and Physical Fitness (1965), Rowing - A Scientific Approach (contrib and ed with A C Scott 1967), Atlas on Injury in Sport (1980), Diagnostic Picture Tests in Injury in Sport (1988); *Recreations* naval history, music, model making, real tennis; *Clubs* Queens, Leander Henley on Thames; *Style*— Dr John Williams; Little Paddocks, Brantridge Lane, Bourne End, Bucks SL8 5BZ (☎ 06285 20834); Wexham Pk Hosp, Rehabilitation Departmt, Slough, Berks SL2 4HL (☎ 02814 2271, 0753 34567, 0836 640384)

WILLIAMS, John Godfrey; s of Godfrey Williams (d 1927), of Chapel Farm, and Clara Ellen, *née* Hughes (d 1974); *b* 15 May 1922; *Educ* King Henry the Eigth GS Abergavenny; *m* 10 Nov 1960, Margaret Jean, da of Richard Morgan David (d 1959); 1 s (Richard John b 1961); *Career* served RN 1941-46; slr 1950, clerk to the Justices of the Hay-on-Wye and Talgarth Divs 1957-66, supt registrar Hay-on-Wye Div 1957-74; pres Herefordshire Breconshire & Radnorshire Incorporated Law Soc 1977; life memb Cambria Archaeological Assoc 1955-; memb: British Dowsers Soc 1963-, Research into Lost Knowledge Organisation 1960-; *Recreations* investigating prehistoric standing stones; *Clubs* Abergavenny Conservative, Hay-on-Wye, Hereford Conservative; *Style*— John Williams, Esq; Aurora, 129 Chapel Road, Abergavenny, Gwent (☎ 0873 3141); Williams Beales & Co, Solicitors, 2 Baker Street, Abergavenny (☎ 0873 2293); 9 Broad Street, Hay-on-Wye, Hereford (☎ 0497 820302)

WILLIAMS, John Griffith; QC (1985); s of Maj Griffith John Williams, TD, of Heddyr-Ynys, Common Lane, Beer, Seaton, Devon, and Alison Rundle, *née* Bennett; *b* 20 Dec 1944; *Educ* Kings Sch Bruton, Somerset, The Queen's Coll Oxford (MA); *m* 3 April 1971, Mair, o da of Major The Right Hon Sir Tasker Watkins VC, PC, DL; 2 da (Joanna b 1972, Sarah b 1976); *Career* Lt 4 Bn Royal Welsh Fus (TA) Welsh Volunteers (TAVR); barr Grays Inn 1968, practice Wales and Chester circuit, recorder Crown Ct 1984-; *Recreations* golf; *Clubs* Army and Navy, Cardiff and County, Cardiff, Royal Porthcawl Golf; *Style*— J G Williams, QC; 144 Pencisely Rd, Llandaff, Cardiff CF5 1DR (☎ 0222 562981); Goldsmith Building, Temple, EC4Y 7BL (☎ 01353 788, fax 01 353 5319)

WILLIAMS, Rev John Herbert; s of Thomas Williams (d 1932), of Gwent, and Mary Williams, *née* Davies (d 1956); *b* 15 August 1919; *Educ* Lewis Sch Pengam, St David's Coll Lampeter (BA), Salisbury Theological Coll; *m* 1948, Joan Elizabeth, da of Archibald Morgan, of Gwent; 1 s (Michael); *Career* clerk in holy orders; chaplain (Prison Dept): Manchester 1951, Holloway 1952, Birmingham 1955, Wormwood Scrubs 1964; regional chaplain SE 1971, dep chaplain gen (Home Off) 1974-83, priest-in-ordinary to HM The Queen 1979-83; chaplain of the Queen's Chapel of the Savoy; chaplain of the Royal Victorian Order 1983; chaplain to HM The Queen 1988; *Recreations* music (classical, opera, church), rugby, stamp collecting; *Clubs* City Livery; *Style*— The Rev John Williams; 18 Coombe Lane West, Kingston-upon-Thames, Surrey KT2 7BX (☎ 01 942 1196); The Queen's Chapel of the Savoy, Savoy Hill, Strand, London WC2R 0DA (☎ 01 836 7221)

WILLIAMS, Rev Canon John James; TD (1961, clasp 1967); s of John Ifor Williams (d 1956), of Bromfield, Shaun Drive, Rhyl, Flints, and Marie Williams (d 1969); *b* 4 May 1920; *Educ* Grove Park Sch Wrexham, Lincoln Coll Oxford (MA); *m* 18 March 1953, Kaye, da of Bertram Law (d 1949), of Westroyd, Penrhyn Bay, Llandudno: 2 s (John b 1956, David b 1959), 1 da (Karen b 1961); *Career* ordained: deacon 1944, priest 1945; chaplain Flint and Denbigh Yeo 1949, 4 Bn KSLI (TA) 1955, sr chaplain HQ 48 W Midlands Div (TA) 1962, chaplain 202 (M) Gen Hosp RAMC (TAVR) 1967, ret 1968; Rhosymedre 1944, Flint 1947, Eglwys Rhos 1950; vicar: Whixhall Salop 1953, Prees Salop 1957, Powyke Worcs 1964, ret 1985; chaplain Powick Psychiatric Hosp 1967-, hon canon Worcester Cath 1977; *Style*— The Rev Canon John Williams; 9 St Nicholas Rd, Peopleton, Pershore, Worcs WR10 2EN (☎ 0905 840032)

WILLIAMS, John Leighton; QC (1986); s of Reginald John Williams, of Skewen, Neath, Glamorgan, and Beatrice Beynon; *b* 15 August 1941; *Educ* Neath Boys GS; Kings Coll London, (LLB); Trinity Hall Cambridge (MA); *m* 9 Oct 1969, Sally Elizabeth, of Howard Jones Williams, of Abergavenny, Gwent; 2 s (Nicholas b 1970, Thomas b 1972); *Career* barr Grays Inn 1964; Rec 1985; QC 1986; *Recreations* sales bargains; *Style*— J L Williams, QC; Farrar's Building, Temple, London EC4 (☎ 583 92141)

WILLIAMS, Hon John Melville; QC (1977); s of Baron Francis-Williams (Life Peer, d

1970); *b* 20 June 1931; *Educ* St Christopher Sch Letchworth, St John's Coll Cambridge (BA); *m* 1955, Jean Margaret, da of Harold Lucas, of Huddersfield; 3 s, 1 da; *Career* barrister Inner Temple 1955; recorder 1986; *Style*— The Hon John Melville Williams, QC; 15 Old Square, Lincoln's Inn, London WC2A 3UH (☎ 01 831 0801); Deers Hill, Abinger Hammer, Dorking, Surrey

WILLIAMS, John Michael; JP; s of William Robert John Williams (d 1976), of West Wickham, Kent, and Alice Gladys, *née* Holbrow; *b* 13 Nov 1935; *Educ* Beckenham & Penge GS, Downing Coll Cambridge (MA, LLB); *m* 18 Aug 1962, Patricia May, da of James Francis Logan (d 1960), of Beckenham, Kent; 3 s (Duncan b 1965, Daniel b 1967, Benjamin b 1980), 1 da (Kate b 1963); *Career* slr Supreme Ct of Judicature 1962, NP 1966; hon sec Magistrates Assoc SE London Branch, dir Churchill Theatre Tst Bromley; cncl memb Magistrates Assoc, cncl memb cwlth Magistrates and Judges Assoc; memb Law Soc, memb Prov Notaries Soc; *Recreations* hockey, cricket, theatre, singing; *Clubs* Langley Park Rotary, Kentish Opera Group; *Style*— John Williams, Esq, JP; Normanhurst, Bishops Walk, Croydon CRO 5BA (☎ 01 656 2445); Norwich Union House, 96 George Street, Croydon CR9 1ZT (☎ 01 688 7128, fax 01 680 8127)

WILLIAMS, Sir John Protheroe; CMG (1960), OBE (1950); s of late John James Williams, and late Ruth Williams; *b* 5 Mar 1896; *Educ* Queen Elizabeth GS, Camarthen Wales; *m* 1, 1922, Gladys (d 1962); 1 s, 3 da; m 2, 1974, Althea Florence, da of Frederick Michael Partridge (d 1930); *Career* master mariner; offr i/c Bank of England bullion salvage operation of RMS Niagra; chm: Aust National Line 1956-71, United Salvage Pty Ltd, underwriting memb Lloyd's of London; kt 1967; *see Debrett's Handbook of Australia and New Zealand for further details*; *Style*— Sir John Williams, CMG, OBE; 77 St George's St, Toorak, Vic 3142, Australia (☎ 241 2440)

WILLIAMS, John Robert; s of Edward S Williams (d 1986), of London, and Frances Madge, *née* Porter; *b* 7 April 1931; *Educ* Enfield GS, Queens' Coll Cambridge (MA); *m* 12 Sept 1959, Teresa, da of Joseph Wareing (d 1956), of Preston, Lancs; 3 da (Catherine b 1960, Joanna b 1962, Helen b 1967); *Career* Ogilvy & Mather: res exec, mktg mangr, res dir, account dir, client servs dir, int mgmnt supervisor 1956-68, appointed to bd 1968, vice-chm 1981; chm: Wimbledon CC 1974-89, The Wimbledon Club (cricket, lawn tennis, hockey clubs, Lakeside squash club); FIPA 1968; *Recreations* cricket, tennis, squash, theatre; *Clubs* MCC, RAC; *Style*— John Williams, Esq; 61 Murray Rd, London SW19 4PF (☎ 01 946 9363)

WILLIAMS, Sir John Robert; KCMG (1982, CMG 1973); s of Sydney James Williams, of Salisbury; *b* 15 Sept 1922; *Educ* Sheen Co Sch, Fitzwilliam Coll Cambridge; *m* 1958, Helga Elizabeth, da of Frederick Konow Lund, of Bergen; 2 s, 2 da; *Career* CRO New Delhi and N Malaya; high cmmr Suva 1970-74, min Lagos and non-resident ambass Benin 1974-79, asst under-sec FCO 1979, high cmmr Nairobi and perm Br rep UN Environment Programme and HABITAT (UN Centre for Human Settlements) 1979-82, ret; chm Cwlth Inst London 1984-87; hon fell Fitzwilliam Coll Cambridge 1983; *Style*— Sir John Williams, KCMG; Eton House, Hanging Langford, Salisbury

WILLIAMS, Juliet Susan Durrant; da of Robert Noel Williams (d 1972), of Gower, W Glamorgan, and Frances Alice, *née* Durrant; *b* 17 April 1943; *Educ* Leeds Girls HS, Cheltenham Ladies' Coll, Bedford Coll London (BSc), Hughes Hall Cambridge (PGCE); *Career* ed MacMillan & Co (publishers) 1966-68, asst ed The Geographical Magazine 1968-73, md Readers Union gp of books and clubs 1978-79, chief exec Marshall Cavendish Mail Order 1979-82, md Christian Brann Ltd 1982-88, dir The BIS Gp Ltd 1985-, chief exec BIS Brann Gp 1988-; non exec dir Oxfam Trading; cncl memb: Br Direct Mktg Assoc, Advertising Assoc; full blue lacrosse Univ of London and Cambridge; FRGS 1970, MInstM 1975; *Recreations* labrador retrievers, the countryside, motor sport; *Style*— Ms Juliet Williams; Treeton Cottage, Abbotskerswell, Newton Abbot, Devon TQ12 5PW; 5 Coach House Mews, The Avenue, Circencester, Glos GL7 1EJ (☎ 0626 61655); BIS-Brann Ltd, Phoenix Way, Circencester, Glos GL7 1RY (☎ 0285 644 744, fax 0285 654 952, car tel 0860 535 637, telex 43473)

WILLIAMS, Hon Mrs (Katharine Lucy); *née* Roskill; da of Baron Roskill, PC, QC, JP, DL (Life Baron); *b* 1953; *Educ* St Mary's School Calne Wilts; *m* 1977, Nicholas Richard Melville Williams; 1 s (George Nicholas Melville b 1981), 1 da (Olivia Katharine Elisabeth b 1978); *Clubs* Hurlingham; *Style*— The Hon Mrs Williams; 37 Perrymead Street, London SW6

WILLIAMS, Lawrence Hugh; s of Col Lawrence Williams, OBE, JP, DL, by his 2 w and 1 cous once removed, Elinor, da of Sir William Williams, 4 Bt, JP, DL; hp of half-bro Sir Francis Williams, 8 Bt, QC, JP; *b* 25 August 1929; *Educ* RNC Dartmouth; *m* 1952, Sara, da of Prof Sir Harry Platt, 1 Bt, MD, MS, FRCS; 2 da (Emma b 1961, Antonia b 1963); *Career* Capt RM, ret; High Sheriff Anglesey 1970; *Clubs* Army and Navy; *Style*— Lawrence Williams, Esq; Parciau, Marianglas, Anglesey

WILLIAMS, Sir Leonard; KBE (1981), CB (1975); *b* 19 Sept 1919; *Educ* St Olave's GS, King's Coll London; *m* Anne Taylor Witherley; 3 da; *Career* dir-gen Energy Commission of the European Communities 1976-81, served formerly Inland Revenue, MOD, NATO, Miny Supply, Miny Technology, IDC, Energy Dept; *Style*— Sir Leonard Williams, KBE, CB; 200 rue de la Loi, 1049 Brussels, Belgium

WILLIAMS, Leonard Edmund Henry; CBE (1981), DFC (1944); s of William Edmund Williams (d 1965), and Elizabeth, *née* Restall (d 1969); *b* 6 Dec 1919; *Educ* Acton Co Sch; *m* 23 March 1946, Marie Eirina, da of John Harries-Jones (d 1939); 4 s (Graham b 1949, Martin b 1957, Simon b 1961, Andrew b 1965), 1 da (Jennifer b 1947); *Career* served RAF WWII; chm Nationwide Bldg Soc 1982-87 (gen offr 1954-61, dep gen mangr 1961-67, chief exec 1967-81, dir 1975), dir Y J Lovell (Hldgs) plc 1982-, chm Nationwide Anglia Bldg Soc 1987-88, dep chm Br Utd Provident Assoc Ltd 1988- (govr 1982-); FCA, CBIM, FRSA; *Books* Building Society Accounts (1966); *Recreations* golf, reading; *Clubs* RAF; *Style*— Leonard Williams Esq, CBE, DFC; 11 Albury Rd, Burwood Park, Walton-on-Thames, Surrey KT12 5DY (☎ 0932 242758)

WILLIAMS, Hon Mrs (Margaret de Hauteville); *née* Udny-Hamilton; da of 11 Lord Belhaven and Stenton, CIE (d 1950, assumed additional surname of Udny 1934); *b* 1939; *m* 1, 1964 (m dis), Keith Schellenberg; 1 s, 2 da, m 2 1983, James Frank Williams; *Style*— The Hon Mrs Williams; Udny Castle, Udny, Aberdeenshire (☎ 0224 2428)

WILLIAMS, Martin John; CVO (1983), OBE (1979); s of John Henry Stroud Williams, of Cricklade, Wilts, and Barbara, *née* Benington; *b* 3 Nov 1941; *Educ* Manchester GS, Corpus Christ Coll Oxford (BA); *m* 6 April 1964, Susan, da of Albert Mervin (Peter Dent, (d 1984); 2 s (Nicholas b 1966, Peter b 1967); *Career* CRO 1963, Dip Serv: joined 1968, Manila 1966-69, Milan 1970-72, Tehran 1977-80, New Delhi 1982-86, Rome 1986-; *Style*— Martin Williams, Esq; British Embassy, Rome Italy (☎ 396 475 5441)

WILLIAMS, Lady Mary Rose; *née* FitzRoy; da of late William Henry Alfred, Viscount Ipswich; sister of 9 Duke of Grafton; co-heiress to Barony of Arlington and Earldom of Arlington; *b* 1918,posthumous; *m* 1945 (m dis), Francis Trelawny Williams, late Lt KRRC; 1 da (Linda Jane Auriol b 1947) da; *Career* show jumping (memb of Br S J Team for 6 years); *Recreations* teaching showjumping, building courses, judging horses and ponies; *Style*— Lady Mary Rose Williams; The Green, Oddington, Moreton-in-Marsh, Glos (☎ 0451 31008)

WILLIAMS, Sir (William) Maxwell Harries; s of Llwyd and Hilary Williams; *b* 18 Feb 1926; *Educ* Nautical Coll Pangbourne; *m* 1951, Jenifer, da of Rt Hon Edward Leslie Burgin, LLD (d 1945); 2 da; *Career* served 178 Assault Fd Regt RA, Far East (Capt) 1943-47; slr 1950, memb Cncl Law Soc 1962-85 (pres 1982-83), Royal Cmmn on Legal Servs 1976-79, memb ctee of Mgmnt of Inst of Advanced Legal Studies 1980-86, Crown Agents for Overseas Govts and Admin 1982-86; lay memb Stock Exchange Cncl 1984-, sr ptnr Clifford turner 1984-87 (jt sr ptnr Clifford Chance 1987) dir: Royal Insur plc 1985-, 3i plc 1988-; chm Review Bd for Govt contracts 1986-; hon memb: Canadian Bar Assoc, American Bar Assoc; memb cncl Wildfowl Trust (hon tres 1974-80); pres City of London Law Soc 1986-87; Master Solicitors' Co 1986-87; Hon LLD Birmingham 1983; kt 1983; *Recreations* fishing, ornithology; *Clubs* Garrick, Flyfishers; *Style*— Sir Maxwell Williams; Clifford Chance, Blackfriars House, 19 New Bridge St, London EC4V 6BY (☎ 01 353 0211, telex 887847)

WILLIAMS, Michael; s of Michael Leonard Williams (d 1987), of Stratford upon Avon, and Elizabeth, *née* Mulligan (d 1982); *b* 9 July 1935; *Educ* St Edward's Coll Liverpool, RADA; *m* 5 Feb 1971, (Judi) Olivia Dench, DBE, BE, da of Dr Reginald Arthur Dench (d 1964), of York; 1 da (Finty b 24 Sept 1972); *Career* Nat Serv RAF 1953-55; Coronation Scholarship winner RADA 1959, Nottingham Playhouse 1959-61, West End debut 1961, memb RSC 1963-77 roles include: Pick (Midsummer Night's Dream), the herald (Marat/Sade) London & N York, Arthur (Tango), Petruchio (Taming of the Shrew), Troilus (Troilus & Cressida), Orlando (As You Like It), the Fool (King Lear), Charles courtly (London Assurance), title role (Henry V) Private Meek (Too True to be Good), Autolycus (Winter's Tale); TV: Elizabeth R, A Raging Calm, My Son, My Son, Love in A Cold Climate, A Fine Romance, Bukovsky, Blunt, Double First, Angel Voices; films: Dead Cert, Enigma, Educating Rita, Henry V; chm Catholic Stage Guild 1977-88; patron: The Surrey Soc of Cncl for the Protection of Rural England, Cumbria Theatre Tst, Chicken Shed, Imperial Cancer Fund; *Recreations* cricket, gardening; *Clubs* Garrick; *Style*— Michael Williams, Esq; c/o Michael Whitehall Ltd, 125 Gloucester Rd, London SW7 4TE (☎ 01 244 8466)

WILLIAMS, (John) Michael; s of George Keith Williams (d 1980), and Joan Doreen, *née* Selby (d 1969); *b* 15 Oct 1942; *Educ* Cheltenham Coll, Worcester Coll Oxford (MA); *Career* admitted slr 1967, ptnr Cooper Sons Hartley & Williams; conductor Buxton Musical Soc 1968-, sec Buxton & High Peak Law Soc 1984-, organist St Johns Buxton 1985-, vice-chm Buxton Opera House 1978-; *Recreations* music, cricket; *Style*— Michael Williams, Esq; 143 Lightwood Rd, Buxton (☎ 0298 4185); Cooper Sons Hartley & Williams, 25 Market St, Chapel-en-le-Frith, via Stockport (☎ 0298 81 2138)

WILLIAMS, (Garnet) Montague Eveleigh; s of Garnett Montague Williams (d 1939), of Coulsdon, Surrey, and Ellen, *née* Eveleigh (d 1968); *b* 19 Dec 1917; *Educ* Reigate GS, London Poly (BSc); *m* 8 May 1948, Phyllis Olive, da of Capt Thomas Mann (d 1950), of Margate, Kent; 1 s (Oliver b 19 March 1961 d 26 Dec 1973), 1 da (Sara b 5 Nov 1957); *Career* sr sci offr Armament Res & Devpt Estab Miny of Supply 1941-55, sr engr tech div PE Consltg Gp 1955-59, head of dept City Univ London and Northampton CA 1959-67, tech dir Ferraris Med Ltd & Assocs 1967-86, pt/t conslt chartered engr; life memb Old Reigatian Assoc (chm 1960-61), memb: Barbican Assoc London, Parly and Sci Ctee 1971-74; chm UK Automation Cncl 1971-74, common cncllr Aldersgate Ward of London 1985-; Freeman: City of London 1966, Worshipful Co of Instrument Makers 1966, Worshipful Co of Engrs 1988; MIEE 1954, FIProdE 1962, FInst MC 1976, FRSA 1969; *Recreations* reading, theatre, cinema, photography, good living, France; *Clubs* City Livery, Guildhall; *Style*— Montague Williams, Esq; 154 Thomas More House, Barbican, London EC2Y 8BU; Milton House, 24 Richmond Rd, Horsham, Sussex, (☎ 01 638 5339)

WILLIAMS, Hon Mrs (Ursula) Moyra; *née* Lubbock; da of late Capt the Hon Harold Fox Pitt Lubbock (4 s of 1 Baron Avebury ka 1918); sister of late 3 Baron; raised to the rank of a Baron's da 1931; *b* 1917; *Educ* private, Oxford Univ; *m* 1938 (m dis 1949), Dorian Joseph George Williams, OBE (d 1985), BBC TV equestrian commentator; *Career* clinical psychologist; *Books* Brain Damage of the Mind (Wiley), Horse Psychology (J A Allen); *Recreations* anything with horses; *Style*— The Hon Mrs Williams; Leyland Farm, Gawcott, Buckingham

WILLIAMS, Nicholas Michael Heathcote; s of Sir Edgar Trevor Williams, CB, CBE, DSO, DL, of 94 Lonsdale Rd, Oxford, and Gillian, *née* Gambier-Parry; *b* 5 Nov 1954; *Educ* Marlborough, St Catharine's Coll Cambridge (BA, MA); *m* 19 Dec 1987, Corinna Mary, da of David Mitchell, of Oxford; 1 s (Benjamin b 1988); *Career* RMA Sandhurst 1977, 2 Lt Royal Green Jackets 1977, Lt 1977; barr Inner Temple 1976; *Recreations* reading, looking at pictures, walking, cricket; *Clubs* Royal Green Jackets, Friends of Tate Gallery, Theberton; *Style*— NM Heathcote Williams, Esq; 12 King's Bench Walk, Inner Temple, London EC4 (☎ 01 583 0811, fax 01 583 7228)

WILLIAMS, Nigel Christopher Ransome; CMG (1985); s of Cecil Gwynne Ransome Williams, and Corinne Belden, *née* Rudd; *b* 29 April 1937; *Educ* Merchant Taylors, St John's Coll Oxford; *Career* entered Foreign Serv 1961: Tokyo 1961-66, FO 1966-70, first sec UK mission to the UN 1970-73, FO 1973-76, econ cnsllr Tokyo 1976-80, head of UN dept FCO 1980-85, min Bonn 1985-88, hon ambass Copenhagen 1989-; *Style*— NCR Williams, Esq; c/o Foreign and Commonwealth Office, 1 King Charles St, London SW1

WILLIAMS, Noel Laurence; s of Walter Parry Williams (d 1959), of School House, Branston, Nr Lincoln, and Marion, *née* Ward (d 1971); *b* 4 Mar 1926; *Educ* City GS Lincoln, Loughborough Univ (Miny of Educn Teacher Cert), Harvard Univ Graduate Sch of Business, Birmingham Univ; *m* 7 March 1953, Margaret, da of Horace Gray (d 1988), of Penryn, Lincoln Rd, Metheringham, Nr Lincoln; 3 da (Alison b 7 Oct 1956, Anne b 9 April 1959, Jacqueline b 3 May 1961); *Career* cmmnd 1 Lt Royal Lincs Regt

1946, Capt transferred to Army Educn Corps 1947; Stanley Tools Ltd: brand and selling mgmnt 1953-62, mktg mangr 1962-70, mktg dir 1970-84; md The Stanley Works Ltd 1984-; memb Yorks & Humberside Regnl Cncl of the CBI, past pres Fedn of Br Hand Tool Mfrs; Freeman Worshipful Co of Cutlers Hallamshire York; FInstD, memb Inst of Mktg; *Recreations* tennis, Walking, Golf; *Style—* Noel Williams, Esq; 9 Birchitt Close, Bradway, Sheffield S17 4QJ (☎ 0742 364 755); Stanley Tools, Woodside, Sheffield S3 9PD (☎ 0742 768 888, fax 0742 739 038, telex 54150)

WILLIAMS, Sir (Michael) Osmond; 2 Bt (UK 1909), of Castell Deudraeth, and Borthwen, Co Merioneth; MC (1944), JP (Gwynedd 1960); s of Capt Osmond Trahairn Deudraeth Williams, DSO (d 1915), by his w Lady Gladys Finch-Hatton (da of 13 Earl of Winchilsea); suc gf, Sir Arthur Osmond Williams, 1 Bt, JP, sometime Lord-Lt and MP Merionethshire, 1927; *b* 22 April 1914; *Educ* Eton, Freiburg Univ; *m* 1947, Benita Mary, da of G Henry Booker (d 1953); 2 da; *Heir* none; *Career* 2 Lt Royal Scots Greys 1933-37 and 1939; Mid East, Italy and NW Europe WW II 1939-45, Capt 1940, Maj 1945; memb Merioneth Pk Planning Ctee 1971-74, govr Rainer Fndn Outdoor Pursuits Centre 1963-75, chm Quarry Tours Ltd 1973-77; Chev Order of Leopold II with Palm, Croix de Guerre with Palm (Belgium) 1940; *Recreations* music, travelling; *Clubs* Travellers'; *Style—* Sir Osmond Williams, Bt, MC; Borthwen, Penrhyndeudraeth, Gwynedd LL48 6EN (☎ 0766 770215)

WILLIAMS, Owen Tudor; CBE (1969); s of Sir Evan Owen Williams, KBE (d 1969), of Gladys Clarissa, *née* Tustian (d 1947); *b* 4 Oct 1916; *Educ* Shrewsbury, St Catharines Coll Cambridge (MA); *m* 15 Sept 1943, Rosemary Louisa, da of James Curzon Mander (d 1962); 4 s (Richard Owen b 1945, Robert Tudor Owen b 1948, Hugh Curzon b 1951, Shon Gwyn Owen b 1962); *Career* asst engr chief engrs dept Admty 1942-46; Sir Owen Williams and Ptnrs (consulting civil and structural engrs): asst engrs 1937-42, ptnr 1946-62, managing and sr ptnr 1962-87, conslt 1987-; engrg work incl: Luton to Doncaster M1 Motorway, Birmingham link of M1, M5 and M6 Motorways, second peripheral highway of Istanbul Turkey; FEng, FICE, FIHT, MIAT, M Cons E; *Clubs* Naval and Military; *Style—* Owen Williams, Esq; 18 Little Gaddesden, Herts HP4 1PA

WILLIAMS, Paul Glyn; s of Samuel O Williams (d 1967), of Alnmouth, Northumberland, and Esmée Ingledew, *née* Cail (d 1974); *b* 14 Nov 1922; *Educ* Marlborough, Trinity Hall Cambridge (MA); *m* 1, Sept 1947 (m dis 1964), Barbara Joan, da of late Alan Hardy; 2 da ((Heather) Jane b 1949, Jennifer Ann b 1952); m 2, 13 Aug 1964, Gillian Dawtrey, step da of late James Foote, MBE; 1 da (Henrietta Caroline b 1966); *Career* serv RAF Canada and Europe 1942-46; MP (Cons) Sunderland S 1953-57, ind candidate 1957-58 (after resignation of Pty whip in protest against UK withdrawal from Suez); candidate (Cons) 1958-64; former chm and md of Mount Charlotte Investmts Ltd, dir Backer Electric Co Ltd; conslt PE Consulting Servs; chm Monday Club 1964-69; FInstD, FBIM; *Recreations* music, literature, watching Rugby; *Clubs* Boodle's, IOD; *Style—* Paul Williams, Esq; 65 Perrymead St, London SW6 3SN (☎ 01 731 0045); 34 Grosvenor Gdns, London SW1W ODH (☎ 01 730 4599, fax 01 730 7096, telex 933783 PECG G)

WILLIAMS, Paul Raymond; s of Raymond Williams (d 1979), and Majorie Joyce, *née* Ashby; *b* 11 Feb 1947; *Educ* King Edward GS Sturbridge W Mid; *m* 12 Oct 1970 (m dis 1985); 1 s (Robert Paul 16 May 1974), 1 da (Joanne 28 Oct 1971); *Career* chief accountant - BSG Int Fin Co 1970-73, business mgmnt accountant - BSG Int plc 1973-82, gen mangr Bristol Street Morrs, Long Acre 1982-85 (md Cheltenham Ltd 1985); memb: Cheltenham C of C, bd of govrs Arle Sch Cheltenham; FCCA 1974, FBIM 1983, FInstD 1988; *Recreations* squash, reading, sports writing; *Style—* Paul Williams, Esq; 24, Bafford Approach, Charlton Kings, Cheltenham, Gloucs, GL53 9HT (☎ 0242 51140); Bristol Street Motors (Cheltenham) Ltd, 71/93, Winchcombe St, Cheltenham, Gloucs (☎ 0242 527 061, fax 0242 221 809, car telephone 0836 511 631, telex 43131)

WILLIAMS, Dr Penry Herbert; s of Douglas Herbert Williams (d 1939), of Cheshunt, Herts, and Dorothea Adelaide Blanche, *née* Murray (d 1982); *b* 25 Feb 1925; *Educ* Marlborough, New Coll Oxford, St Antony's Coll Oxford (MA, DPhil); *m* 10 Sept 1952, June Carey, da of George Carey Hobson (d 1945), of Cape Town; 1 s (Jonathan b 1960), 1 da (Sarah b 1957); *Career* RA 1943-45 (cmmnd 1945), Royal Indian Artillary 1945-47 (Lt 1946); Univ of Manchester: asst lectr 1951-54, lectr 1954-63, sr lectr 1963-64, fell lectr and tutor New Coll Oxford 1964; ed Eng Historical Review 1982-; FRS; *Books* The Council in the Marches of Wales (1958), Life in Tudor England (1964), The Tudor Regime (1979); *Recreations* hill walking, opera; *Style—* Dr Penry Williams; 53 Park Town, Oxford OX2 6SL (☎ 0865 57613); Brook House Llanigon, via Hereford (☎ 0497 820964) New College, Oxford OX1 3BN (☎ 0865 248451)

WILLIAMS, Peter; CBE (1984); s of late Humphrey Richard Williams; *b* 4 Oct 1916; *Educ* St Paul's; *m* 1940, Nona, da of late William Cook-Davies; 1 da (Lowri); *Career* dep chm Wedgwood plc 1975-84, chm: Staffs Devpt Assoc 1984-; FCA; *Recreations* golf, reading, music; *Style—* Peter Williams, Esq, CBE; Una, Barlaston, Stoke-on-Trent (☎ 078 139 2566)

WILLIAMS, Peter John Frederick; s of Clifford Thomas Williams, of Westwinds, Nash, Newport, Gwent, and Ethel, *née* Holmes; *b* 20 August 1935; *Educ* Bassaleg GS, Newport Tech Coll, Newport Coll of Art, Welsh Sch of Architecture Cardiff (dip Arch); *m* 20 Dec 1958, Gladys Bronwen, da of Albert Colbourne (d 1966), of Chestnut Tree Cottage, Goldcliff, Newport, Gwent; 2 s (Simon Nicholas Alexander b 5 April 1960, Andrew John b 11 Oct 1961); *Career* princ: Stowfield Ltd Newport, OLP/Y & H London, OLP/Peter Williams Ltd London, Shoredene Ltd Newport; dir Detention Corp Ltd London; cllr Magor & Mellons RDC 1966-67; memb: Westminster C of C, Br Consits Bureau, CLAWSA, Inst of Welsh Affairs; Freeman: City of London 1984, Worshipful Co of Chartered Architects memb ARIBA 1960, FRIBA 1970, fell Faculty of Building 1983; *Recreations* sailing, golf, shooting, fishing; *Clubs* St Pierre Golf & Country Club, Chepstow, City Livery; *Style—* Peter Williams, Esq; Bali Hai, Whitson, Newport, Gwent; 310 Nelson House, Dolphin Square, London SW1 (☎ 0633 274040); OLP/Peter Williams Ltd, 96 St George Sq, London SW1V 3RA; OLP/Peter Williams Ltd, 15 Goldtops, Newport, Gwent (☎ 01 821 1488/0633 246325, FAX 01 821 7477/0633 244671, car 0836 713761, telex 21792/ref 693)

WILLIAMS, Peter Keegan; s of William Edward Williams and Lilian *née* Spright; *b* 3 April 1938; *Educ* FCalday Grange GS, Univ de Lille, Pembroke Coll Oxford (MA); *m* 1969, Rosamund Mary de Worms; 2 da; *Career* joined Dip Serv 1962, first sec FCO 1973, first sec, head of Chancery and Consul Rabat 1976 (chargé d'Affaires 1978 and 1979), cnsllr GATT UK Mission Geneva 1979-83, ambass S Yemen 1983-85; head UN Dept FCO 1986-; *Recreations* wine, walking; *Clubs* Travellers', United Oxford and Cambridge Univ; *Style—* HE Mr Peter Williams; British Embassy, 28 Shara Ho Chi Minh, Khormaksar, Aden, South Yemen; c/o Foreign and Commonwealth Office, King Charles St, London SW1

WILLIAMS, Brig Peter Richard Godber; s of Maj William Washington Williams, TD, FRGS, of Am Bogha, Appin, Argyll, and Katherine Beatrice, *née* Godber; *b* 2 Jan 1936; *Educ* The Leys Sch Cambridge, RMA Sandhurst; *m* 30 Oct 1964, Margaret Ellen Nina, da of Maj-Gen John MacKenzie, Matheson, OBE, TD, of 2 Orchard Brae, Edinburgh; 1 s (Richard b 12 March 1968, 1 da (Charlotte b 18 Dec 1965); *Career* Nat Serv 1954, cmmnd Welsh Gds 1957, 1 Bn Welsh Gds UK/BAOR 1957-61, Gds Parachute Co 1962-63, Staff Captain Cyprus 1964, Co-Cdr Welsh Gds 1964-66, Staff Coll 1967, Bde-Maj 16 Para Bde 1967-70, 2 Ic 1 Bn Welsh Gds BAOR N Ireland 1970-72, Lt-Col 1972, Staff Cdr 1 Bn Welsh Gds UK Cyprus Berlin 1975-77, Col MOD and HQ UKLF 1977- 85, Brig cdr 54 Inf Bde E Midlands Area 1985-88, ret 1989; bursar St Mary's Sch Cambridge 1989; rugby Army XV 1958; *Books* various articles in mil pubns; *Recreations* tennis, shooting, fishing, music; *Clubs* Army and Navy; *Style—* Brig Peter Williams; Croxton Old Rectory, Eltisley, Huntingdon, Cambs PE19 4SU (☎ 048 087 344)

WILLIAMS, Sir (Robert) Philip Nathaniel; 4 Bt (UK 1915), of Bridehead, Co Dorset; s of Sir David Philip Williams, 3 Bt, DL (d 1970), by his 2 w, Elizabeth, Lady Williams, *qv*; *b* 3 May 1950; *Educ* Marlborough, St Andrews Univ (MA); *m* 1979, Catherine Margaret Godwin, da of Canon Cosmo Gabriel Rivers Pouncey, of Gannicox, Birlingham, Pershore, Worcs; 1 s (David b 1980), 3 da (Sarah b 1982, Margaret b 1984, Clare b 1987); *Heir* s David Robert Mark Williams b 31 Oct 1980; *Career* landowner (2500 acres); *Clubs* MCC; *Style—* Sir Philip Williams, Bt; Bridehead, Littlebredy, Dorchester, Dorset DT2 9JA (☎ 030 83232)

WILLIAMS, Richard Grenville; s of Gordon Williams of Chester, and Rhianwen Lloyd Williams; *b* 10 August 1957; *Educ* Ellesmore Port GS; *m* 1981, Helen Laura, da of Ronald Gerald Williams, of Yardley Gobion, Northampton; *Career* professional cricketer, carpenter; *Recreations* trout fishing, golf, shooting; *Style—* Richard Williams, Esq

WILLIAMS, Col Richard Thomas Meurig; CBE (1985, OBE 1957), MC, TD, DL (S Glam 1981); s of Rev D Williams and Mrs A Bartley Williams; *b* 16 Oct 1919; *Educ* N Wales; *m* da of J A Anderson (d 1954), aviation pioneer; 4 s; *Career* WWII, evacuated Dunkirk, serv Normandy (despatches 1944), Germany; Cdr 384 Light Regt RA (RWF) TA 1952-55, (dr 372 medium Regt RA (TA) forming flint and Denbigh Yeomanry, dep Cdr RA 53 (W) Div 1958-65; ADC (Hun) to HM the Queen 1960-66 and 1974-80; memb Cncl Univ Coll Cardiff, chm Wales Appeal Army Benevolent Fund 1980, chm Wales TAVRA 1980-85; *Recreations* travel; *Clubs* Army and Navy, Cardiff and Co, Br American Club (Palma); *Style—* Col Richard Williams, CBE, MC, TD, DL; Ty-Newydd, Castleton, Cardiff (☎ Castleton 680342)

WILLIAMS, Robert Charles; s of (Charles) Bertram Williams, of Sutton Coldfield, and Marjorie Iris, *née* Jones; *b* 29 Sept 1949; *Educ* Bromsgrove Sch, Worcester Coll Oxford (MA); *m* 4 Aug 1976, Caroline Ursula Eanswythe, da of Rev David Allan Pope; 3 s (Henry b 1979, George b 1981, Alfred b 1982); *Career* barr Inner Temple 1973, asst ed The Weekly Law Reports 1983-; hon sec PCC All Saints Blackheath London; *Style—* Robert Williams, Esq; 65, Micheldever Rd, London SE12 8LU (☎ 01 318 0410); 1 Crown Office Row, Temple, London EC4Y 7HH

WILLIAMS, Prof Robert Charles Gooding; OBE (1969); s of Robert Williams (d 1941), of Westminster, London, and Alice Grace, *née* Gooding (d 1935); *b* 28 Dec 1907; *Educ* Westminster City, Imperial Coll of Sci and Technol (BSc, DIC, PhD); *m* 16 Dec 1937, Edith Emma (Molly) (d 1974), da of Albert James Morrow (d 1948), of Highgate, London; 1 da (Fiona Molly (Mrs Hunt) b 1940); *Career* chief engr Murphy Radio Ltd 1935-45, exec engr N American Philips Inc NY 1946-47, chief engr Philips Electronics and Assoc Industs 1948-69, dir Guildford and Counties Broadcasting Co Ltd 1970-, chm Professional and Scientific Servs Ltd 1974-, vice-pres and tech conslt County Sound plc 1982-; chm Int Confs on: ferrites 1958, transistors 1959, med electronics 1960, tv 1962, educn 1974; memb cncl IEE 1962-65 (chm: former radio and telecommunications section 1956-57, electronics div 1963-64); dir IEEE USA 1967-68 (fndr chm UK and Repub Ireland section 1961-66), memb Br Electrotechnical Approvals Bd 1967-86, visiting prof of electronics Univ of Surrey 1969-74, pres IEEIE 1969-75 (chm cncl 1966-69); memb ctee: Cncl Royal TV Soc 1958-60 and 1963-65, Res Degrees of CNAA 1964-68, Nat Cncl Educnl Technol 1967-72; chm ctee: Int Electrotechnical Cmmn on Safety of Household Appliances 1967-74 (Data Processing Equipment 1974-84); memb: bd govrs Guildford Coll Technol, bd tstees Yvonne Arnaud Theatre Guildford; Freeman City of London, Liveryman Worshipful Co of Clothworkers 1946; FCGI, hon FIEIE, FIEEE (USA), FInstP, CEng, FIMechE, FIEE; *Books* numerous professional papers incl: Tuning Devices for Broadcast Radio Receivers in Journal of the Institution of Electrical Engineers (1946), Industrial Television in Telecommunications Journal (1953), The Technical Opportunities for Community Television in The Royal Television Society Journal (1965), Electronics in the Classroom in Journal of the Royal Society of Arts (1970); feature articles incl: Engineers Look Ahead - What we many expect in The Times Radio and Television Supplement (1956), Colour - A Progress Report in Contrast Autumn (1961), By Wire: An Electronic Grid in The Guardian (1962); *Clubs* Athenaeum, Pilgrims of GB; *Style—* Prof Robert C G Williams, OBE; Field Plot, The Flower Walk, Guildford, Surrey GU2 5EP (☎ 0483 577 777); Professional and Scientific Servs Ltd, PO Box 7, Guildford, Surrey GU2 5HH

WILLIAMS, Sir Robert Evan Owen; s of Gwynne Williams; *b* 30 June 1916; *Educ* Sherborne, UCL, Univ Coll Hosp (MD); *m* 1944, Margaret Lumsden; 1 s, 2 da; *Career* former memb MRC and pres RCPath; prof bacteriology London Univ 1960-73, dean St Mary's Hosp Medical Sch 1967-73, dir Public Health Laboratory Service 1973-81, chm Genetic Manipulation Advsy Gp and Ctee on Genetic Manipulation (HSE) 1981-86; fellow UCL 1968; Hon FRCPA, Hon MD Uppsala, Hon DSc Bath; FRCP, FRCPath, FFCM; kt 1976; *Recreations* horticulture; *Clubs* Athenaeum; *Style—* Sir Robert Williams; Little Platt, Plush, Dorchester, Dorset (☎ 030 04 320)

WILLIAMS, Robert James; s of Capt Thomas Edwin Williams, MBE, of Malta, and Joan Winifred, *née* Nelson; *b* 20 Sept 1948; *Educ* King Edward VII Sch Sheffield, Univ Coll Oxford (BA); *m* 29 July 1972, Margaret, da of Charles Neville Hillier, of Guernsey; 2 da (Katherine b 6 Aug 1979, Caroline b 24 Aug 1983); *Career* Linklanters & Paines: articled clerk 1971-73, asst slr 1973-81, Hong Kong Off 1978-80, ptnr 1981-; Friend of Dulwich Coll; memb City of London Slrs Co 1980; memb Law Soc

1973; *Recreations* swimming, walking, eating, sleeping; *Style—* RJ Williams, Esq; 84 Alleyn Rd, London SE21 8AH (☎ 01 761 1536); Barrington Ho, 59/67 Gresham St, London EC2V 7JA (☎ 01 606 7080, fax 01 606 5113, telex 884349)

WILLIAMS, Sir Robin Philip; 2 Bt (UK 1953), of Cilgeraint, Co Caernarvon; s of Sir Herbert Geraint Williams, 1 Bt, sometime MP (Reading and also Croydon S) and parly sec BOT 1928-29 (d 1954), and Dorothy Frances, *née* Jones (d 1957); *b* 27 May 1928; *Educ* Eton, St John's Coll Cambridge; *m* 19 Feb 1955, Wendy Adele Marguerite, da of late Felix Joseph Alexander (decd) of Hong Kong; 2 s; *Heir* s, Anthony Geraint Williams, b 22 Dec 1958; *Career* Lt RA 1947; barr Middle Temple 1954; insurance broker 1952- and memb Lloyds 1961-; chm: Bow Gp 1954, Anti-Common Mkt League 1969; borough cllr Haringay 1968-74; *Style—* Sir Robin Williams, Bt; 1 Broadlands Close, Broadlands Rd, Highgate, London N6 4AF

WILLIAMS, Rev (John) Roger; s of Sir Gwilym Tecwyn Williams, CBE, *qv*, and Kathleen Isabel Rishworth, *née* Edwards; *b* 6 Oct 1937; *Educ* Denstone Coll, Lichfield Theol Coll; *Career* ordained Lichfield Cath; deacon 1963, priest 1964; asst curate: Wem Shropshire 1963-66, St Peter's Colegiate Church Wolverhampton 1966-69; rector Pudleston-cum-Whyle with Hatfield and priest i/c Stoke Prior Humber and Docklow Hereford 1969-74, vicar Christ Church Fenton Stoke-on-Trent 1974-81, rector Shipston-on-Stour with Honington and Idlicote 1981-, rural dean Shipston 1983-; chaplain to High Sheriff of Warwicks 1987-88; *Recreations* art, architecture, walking, travel; *Style—* The Rev Roger Williams; The Rectory, 8 Glen Close, Shipston-on-Stour, Warwickshire CV36 4ED (☎ 0608 62661)

WILLIAMS, Dr Roger Stanley; s of Stanley George Williams, and Doris, *née* Dagmar; *b* 28 August 1931; *Educ* St Mary's Coll Southampton, London Hosp Med Coll (MB, MD); *m* 1, 8 Aug 1954 (m dis 1977), Lindsay Mary, *née* Elliott; 2 s (Robert b 8 March 1956, Andrew b 3 Jan 1964), 3 da (Anne b 5 March 1958, Fiona b 24 April 1959, Deborah b 12 July 1961); m 2, 15 Sept 1978, Stephanie Gay, da of Gp Capt Patrick De Laszlo (d 1980); 1 s (Aiden b 16 May 1981), 2 da (Clemency b 28 June 1979, Octavia b 4 Sept 1983); *Career* Capt RAMC 1956-58; jr med specialist Queen Alexandra Hosp Millbank 1956-58, med registrar and tutor Royal Postgraduate Med Sch 1958-59, lectr med Royal Free Hosp 1959-65, conslt physician Royal S Hants and Southampton Gen Hosp 1965-66, dir Liver Res Unit and conslt physician King's Coll Hosp and Med Sch 1966-, memb scientific gp on viral hepatitis WHO Geneva 1972, conslt Liver Res Unit Tst 1974-, memb advsy gp on hepatitis DHSS 1980- (memb transplant advsy panel 1974-83), attended Melrose Meml Lecture Glasgow 1970, Goulstonian Lecture RCP 1970, Searle Lecture American Assoc for Study of Liver Disease 1972, fleming lecture Glasgow Coll of Physicians and Surgns 1975, Sir Arthur Hurst Meml Lecture Br Soc of Gastroenterology 1975, Skinner Lecture Royal Coll of Radiologists 1978; Sir Ernest Finch visiting prof Sheffield 1974, hon conslt in medicine to Army 1988-; memb: RSM (sec of section 1962-71), Euro Assoc for Study of the Liver (sec and tres 1968-71, pres 1984); pres elect Br Soc of Gastroenterology 1989, UK rep select Ctee of Experts Organ Transplantation 1989-; Freeman City of London, Liveryman Worshipful Co of Apolliecaries; MRCS, LRCP, MRCP, FRCP, FRCS; *Books* ed: Fifth Symposium on Advanced Medicine (1969), Immunology of the Liver (1971), Artificial Liver Support (1975), Immune Reactions in Liver Diseases (1978), Drug Reactions and the Liver (1981), Variceal Bleeding (1982); author of over 500 scientific papers, review articles and book chapters; *Recreations* tennis, sailing, opera; *Clubs* Saints and Sinners, Royal Yacht Sqdn, Royal Ocean Racing; *Style—* Dr Roger Williams; 8 Eldon Rd, London W8 (☎ 01 937 5301); Reed Hse, Satchell Lane, Hamble, Hants; Liver Unit, King's Coll Hosp, Denmark Hill, London SE5 9RS (☎ 01 326 3169, fax 01 326 4789)

WILLIAMS, Roy; CB (1989); s of Eric and Ellen Williams; *b* 31 Dec 1934; *Educ* Univ of Liverpool (BA), Univs of Chicago and Berkeley USA; *m* 1959, Shirley, da of Capt O Warwick; 1 s (Justin b 1966), 1 da (Adela b 1961); *Career* asst principal Min of Power 1956 (principal 1961), principal priv sec Min of Power 1969, Paymaster Gen 1969, asst sec DTI 1971, principal private Sec of State for Indust 1974, (under sec 1976), dep permanent sec DTI 1984-; *Style—* Roy Williams, Esq, CB; Department of Trade and Industry, 123 Victoria St, London SW1

WILLIAMS, Lady; Ruth Margaret; da of Charles Butcher, of Hudson Bay; *m* 1948, Sir Robert Williams, 9 Bt, of Tregullow (d 1976); 3 s (1 decd, 10 Bt, Barton), 1 da (Phyllis); *Style—* Lady Williams; Kamsack, Saskatchewan, Canada; Upcott House, Barnstaple, N Devon

WILLIAMS, Hon Mrs (Sarah Sophia Rhiannon); *née* Rhys; 2 da of 9 Baron Dynevor, *qv*; *b* 1963; *m* 1987, Dyfrug Williams, eldest s of Daniel Thomas Williams, of Carmarthen; 1 s (Stefan Orlando b 1988); *Style—* The Hon Mrs Williams; c/o The Rt Hon Lord Dynevor, The Walk, Carmarthen Road, Llandeilo, Dyfed

WILLIAMS, Rt Hon Shirley Vivien Teresa Brittain (Mrs Richard Neustadt); PC (1974); da of Prof Sir George Catlin and the writer, Vera Brittain (Mrs Catlin); *b* 27 July 1930; *Educ* Somerville Coll Oxford, Columbia Univ New York; *m* 1, 1955 (m dis 1974), Prof Bernard Williams; 1 da; m 2, 19 Dec 1987, Prof Richard E Neustadt; *Career* contested (Lab): Harwich 1954 and 1955, Southampton Test 1959; MP (Lab) Hitchin 1964-74, Hertford and Stevenage 1974-79; MP SDP Crosby (by-election, converted Cons majority of 19,272 to SDP one of 5,289) 1981-83; PPS to Min Health 1964-66, Parly sec: Miny Lab 1966-67, Min State Educn and Sci 1967-69, Home Off 1969-70; oppn spokesman: Social Serv 1970-71, Home Affrs 1971-73, Prices and Consumer Protection 1973-74 (sec state 1974-76); sec state Educn and Sci and paymaster gen 1976-79, chm Fabian Soc 1980 (gen sec 1960-64), memb Lab NEC 1970-81, co-fndr SDP 1981, pres 1982-88; fell Inst of Politics Harvard Univ 1979-80, OECD examiner 1979-, prof fell Policy Studies Inst 1979-85, memb Sr Advsy Ctee Inst of Politics, Harvard; tstee, Twinhick Century Fund (New York), Learning by Experience Tst; dir Turing Inst, Univ of Strathcylde, prof elective politics Kennedy Sch of Govt Harvard Univ 1988-, acting dir Inst of Politics (1988-); *Style—* The Rt Hon Shirley Williams; SDP, 4 Cowley St, London SW1P 3NB (☎ 01 222 7999)

WILLIAMS, Susan Eva; MBE (1958); da of Robert Henry Williams (d 1963), of Bonvilston House, S Glam, by his w, Dorothy Marie (d 1976); *b* 17 August 1915; *Educ* St James's Sch W Malvern; *m* 1950, Charles Crofts Llewellyn Williams (d 1952), s of Charles Williams, of The Heath, Cardiff (d 1912); *Career* Wing Offr WAAF WWII; JP Glam 1961, High Sheriff 1968; DL Glam 1973, HM Lt for S Glam 1981-; Lord Lt S Glam 1985; *Recreations* nat hunt racing; *Clubs* RAF; *Style—* Mrs Susan Williams, MBE; Caercady, Welsh St Donat's, Cowbridge, S Glamorgan CF7 7ST (☎ 044 63 2346)

WILLIAMS, Prof Thomas Eifion Hopkins; CBE (1980); s of David Garfield Williams (d 1974), of Cwmtwrch, Breconshire, and Annie Mary, *née* Hopkins (d 1949); *b* 14 June 1923; *Educ* Ystradgynlais GS, Univ of Wales (BSc, MSc), Univ of Durham (PhD), Univ of California Berkeley (Post-Doctoral); *m* 28 June 1947, (Elizabeth) Lois, da of Evan Rees Davies (d 1979), of Cwmtwrch, Breconshire; 1 s (Huw b 2 Feb 1960), 2 da (Maelor b 5 April 1948, Amanda b 19 May 1955); *Career* res Stressman Sir WG Armstrong Whitworth Aircraft 1945, asst engr Glamorgan CC trunk rds div 1946, asst lectr Univ Coll of Swansea 1947, lectr-reader King's Coll Univ of Durham 1948-63, resident conslt engr RT James & Ptnrs 1952, visiting prof Northwestern Univ Illinois 1957, reader-prof Univ of Newcastle upon Tyne 1963-67; Univ of Southampton dept of civil engrg and transportation: prof 1967-83, res prof 1983-; memb and chm NEDO EDC Civil Engrg 1969-78, chm Dept of Tport Trunk Rd Assessment Standing Advsy Ctee 1980-87; pres Inst of Highway Engrs 1979-80, memb public policy ctee RAC 1981-, cncl memb Church Schs Co 1982-, visitor traffic engr div Tport & Rd Res Laboratory 1982-88, specialist advsr H of C Tport Select Ctee 1989; CEng, FICE, FIHT, FCIT, FRSA; *Books* ed: Urban Survival & Traffic (1961), Inter-City VTOL: Traffic & Sites (1969), Transportation & Environment (1973), Urban Road Appraisal Report (chm 1986); *Recreations* music; *Clubs* RAC; *Style—* Prof Thomas Williams, CBE; Willowdale, Woodlea Way, Ampfield, Romsey, Hants SO51 9DA (☎ 0703 253 352); Transportation Res Gp, Dept of Civil Engrg, Univ of Southampton S0G 5NH (☎ 0703 595 000, telex 47661)

WILLIAMS, Dr Trevor Illtyd; s of Illtyd Williams (d 1947), of Bristol, and Alma Mathilde, *née* Sohlberg (d 1956); *b* 16 July 1921; *Educ* Clifton Coll, The Queen's Coll Oxford (MA, Bsc, DPhil); *m* 13 Sept 1952, Sylvia Iréne, da of Archibald Armstead (d 1942), of Bromley; 4 s (Darryl, Lloyd, Adam, Benjamin), 1 da (Clare); *Career* ed Endeavour 1954-, Outlook on Agriculture 1982-, academic relations advsr ICI 1962-74; chm: World List of Scientific Periodicals 1966-88, Soc for the History of Alchemy & Chemistry 1967-84, Ctee for Selection of Low-Priced Books for Overseas 1982-84; FRCS 1947, FRHistS 1977; *Books* The Chemical Industry (1953), A History of Technology (jt ed 8 vols 1954-84), A Biographical Dictionary of Scientists (ed 1968), Industrial Research in the United Kingdom (ed 1980), History of the British Gas Industry (1981), Florey, Penicillin and After (1984), The Triumph of Invention (1987); *Recreations* gardening, hill walking; *Clubs* Athenaeum; *Style—* Dr Trevor Williams; 20 Blenheim Drive, Oxford OX2 8DG (☎ 0865 58591); Pen-Y-Cwm, Corris Uchaf, Machynlleth, Powys SY20 7HN

WILLIAMS, Walter Gordon Mason; CB (1983); s of Rees John Williams DSO (d 1960), of Cardiff, and Gladys Maud Williams, *née* Hull (d 1967); *b* 10 June 1923; *Educ* Cardiff HS, Coll of Estate Mgmnt; *m* 1950, Gwyneth Joyce, da of Thomas Swyn Lawrence (d 1941), of Caerphilly; 2 da (Lois, Ann); *Career* chartered surveyor, district valuer: Tower Hamlet 1967-68, Westminster 1968-69, superintending valuer North Midlands 1969-73, asst chief valuer 1973-79, dep chief valuer (under sec) 1979-83, vice-pres London Rent Assessment Panel 1984-; *Recreations* reading, music, theatre, rugby union football; *Style—* Walter Williams Esq, CB; 33A Sydenham Hill, London, SE26 6SH (☎ 01 670 8580); Newlands House, 37-40, Berners St, London W1P 4BP (☎ 01 580 2000)

WILLIAMS, William Trevor (Bill); s of Percy Trevor Williams (d 1987), of Liverpool, and Edith, *née* Hible; *b* 3 June 1935; *Educ* Liverpool Coll Sch; *m* 1, 23 June 1956, Jane Williams; 2 s (Bruce b 1957, Shaun b 1959); 1 da (Heidi b 1961); m 2, 25 March 1967, Pamela Hilda, da of Albert Victor Saunders (d 1988), of Westminster; 1 da (Justine b 1970); *Career* Nat Serv RAF 1953-55; dir gen mangr RMC Ltd: Wales 1963-73, E Midlands 1973-76, London 1976-78; div dir north of England RMC (UK) Ltd 1978-84, md Hall & Co Ltd 1984-; Freeman City of London, Liveryman Worshipful Co of Builders Merchants; *Recreations* fly fishing, gardening; *Style—* Bill Williams, Esq; Quarry House, Springbottom Lane, White Hill, Bletchingley, Surrey RH1 4QZ (☎ 07374 3876); Hall & Co Ltd, RMC House, Victoria Wharf, Brighton Rd, Redhill, Surrey RH1 6QZ (☎ 0737 772415, fax 0737 760567)

WILLIAMS OF ELVEL, Baron (Life Peer UK 1985) Charles Cuthbert Powell; CBE (1980); s of Dr Norman Powell Williams, DD (d 1943), and Muriel de Lerisson (d 1979), da of Arthur Philip Cazenove; *b* 9 Feb 1933; *Educ* Westminster, Christ Church Oxford (MA), LSE; *m* 1 March 1975, Jane Gillian, da of Maj Gervase Edward Portal (d 1960) and formerly w of Gavin Welby; *Career* British Petroleum Co Ltd 1958-64, Bank of London and Montreal 1964-66, Eurofinance SA, Paris 1966-70, Baring Brothers & Co Ltd 1970-77 (md 1971-77), chm Price Cmmn 1977-79, md Henry Ansbacher & Co Ltd 1980-82, chief Exec Henry Ansbacher Holdings plc, chm Henry Ansbacher & Co Ltd 1982-85; *Clubs* Reform, MCC; *Style—* The Rt Hon Lord Williams of Elvel; 48 Thurloe Sq, London SW7 2SX

WILLIAMS-BULKELEY, Michael; s of Lt-Col Sir R H D Williams-Bulkeley, Bart, of Plas Meigan, Beaumaris, Anglesey, Gwynedd, and Renée Arundell, *née* Neave; see Debrett's Peerage and Baronetage 1985 Edn; *b* 2 April 1943; *Educ* Eton; *m* 4 May 1968, Ellen-Marie, da of L Falkum-Hansen (d 1972); 2 s (James b 1970, David b 1973); *Career* Lt Welsh Gds, served Aden 1965-66; dir CT Bowring Reinsurance Ltd 1981-89, Bowring Int Insur Brokers Ltd 1988-; md Marsh & McLennan Worldwide 1988-; insur broker; *Recreations* golf, gardening, shooting; *Style—* Michael Williams-Bulkeley, Esq; Pigeon Hill, Lilley Bottom, nr Luton LU2 8NH (☎ 0582 31971; Bowring Int Insur Brokers Ltd, PO Box 145, The Bowring Bldg, Tower Place, London EC3 (☎ 01 283 3100)

WILLIAMS-BULKELEY, Sir Richard Harry David; 13 Bt (E 1661), TD, JP (1934); s of late Maj Richard Gerard Wellesley Williams-Bulkeley, MC, only s of 12 Bt; suc gf, Sir Richard Henry Williams-Bulkeley, 12 Bt, KCB, 1942; *b* 5 Oct 1911; *Educ* Eton; *m* 1938, Renée Arundell, da of Sir Thomas Lewis Hughes Neave, 5 Bt; 2 s; *Heir* s, Capt Richard Thomas Williams-Bulkeley; *Career* serv WWII Maj Royal Welsh Fus; former Lt-Col Cmdt of Caernarvonshire and Anglesey Army Cadet Force; Maj of Beaumars 1949-51-; Lord-Lt of: Anglesey 1947-74, Gwynedd 1974-83; memb Anglesey CC 1946-74 (chm 1956-58); CStJ; *Clubs* Army and Navy, Royal Anglesey, Yacht; *Style—* Sir Richard Williams-Bulkeley, Bt, TD, JP; Plas Meigan, Beaumaris, Gwynedd

WILLIAMS-BULKELEY, Richard Thomas; s and h of Sir Richard Willliams-Bulkeley, 13 Bt; *b* 25 May 1939; *Educ* Eton; *m* 1964, Susan Sarah, da of late Rt Hon Lord Justice (Sir Henry Josceline) Phillimore, OBE; 2 s (twin), 1 da; *Career* Capt Welsh Gds 1963; ARICS; *Recreations* astronomy; *Clubs* Army and Navy; *Style—* Richard Williams-Bulkeley, Esq; Red Hill, Beaumaris, Anglesey, Gwynedd

WILLIAMS-ELLIS, Elizabeth Ann; JP (Carnarvonshire 1966, Inner London 1977); da of Gp Capt Evan Christopher Lewis, RAF (d 1960), of Berwick Ct, E Sussex, and Madge Constance, *née* Pilkington; *b* 10 Nov 1935; *Educ* Rosemead Littlehampton; *m* 31 May 1958 (m dis 1975), Roger Clough Williams-Ellis, DL, s of Rupert Greaves William-Ellis, JP, DL, of Glasfryn, Caerrarvonshire; 3 s (Jonathan b 1959, Christoper b 1960, Mark b 1961); *Career* Christies 1972-74, Winchester Bowring 1977-80, memb Lloyd's 1978-; memb: arts purchasing ctee Nat Gallery and Museum of Wales 1966-74, Home Off Bail Project 1975-77; ctee memb N Wales Family Planning Assoc 1963-72, vice-pres Caernarvonshire Red Cross 1964-72, chm Pencoenewydd WI 1963-66, life memb Cambrian Archaelogical Soc 1959, memb Nat Health exec ctee Caernarvonshire 1970-73; vice-chm: Warwick Square Residents' Assoc 1981-83, Belgravia NADFAS 1989; memb: ctee Westminster Soc 1987-, selection panel for most outstanding new building in City of Westminster 1989, Hon Soc of Cymroddrian; *Recreations* history, sailing; *Clubs* Berkley; *Style—* Mrs Elizabeth Williams-Ellis, JP; 18 Wilton St, London SW1X 7AX

WILLIAMS-ELLIS, Roger Clough; DL (Caernarfonshire/Gwynedd); s of Rupert Greaves Williams-Ellis, JP (d 1951), of Glasfryn, Pencaenewydd, Pwllheli, and Cecily Edith (MBE), *née* Hambro ; *b* 12 April 1923; *Educ* Eton; *m* 1 1958 (m dis 1974), Elizabeth Ann, da of Gp Capt E Christopher Lewis (d 1965), of Berwick Court Farm, Polegate, nr Eastbourne; 3 s (Jonathan b 1959, Christopher b 1960, Mark b 1961); m 2 1 Aug 1975, Jane Susan, da of Wing-Cdr Ralph Seymour Pearce; *Career* cmmd RE 1944, served India, Capt SORE III 14 Army 1945 (despatches), Maj SORE II ALFSEA 1946, Singapore 1946, demobilised 1947; mgmnt and devpt Glasfryn Estate, primarily forestry; EAHY Prince of Wales Award; High Sheriff Caernarfonshire 1965; *Style—* Roger Williams-Ellis, Esq, DL; Glasfryn, Pencaenewydd, Pwllheli, Gwynedd LL53 6RE (☎ 0766 810 203)

WILLIAMS-FREEMAN, Lady Jean Elisabeth; da of Brig 19 Earl of Caithness (d 1965), by his 1 w, Grizel Margaret (d 1943); *b* 11 Feb 1936; *Educ* Seymour Lodge Sch Crieff, Atholl Crescent Domestic Science Coll; *m* 1961, David Peere Williams-Freeman, s of Cdr Frederick Arthur Peere Williams-Freeman, DSO and bar, RN (d 1939), of Constantia Cape; 1 s, 3 da; *Style—* Lady Jean Williams-Freeman; Glendean Farm, Nottingham Rd, Natal, S Africa

WILLIAMS-THOMAS, Lt-Col Reginald Silvers; DSO (1940), TD (1946), JP (Worcs and Staffs), DL (Worcs 1953-); s of Hubert Silvers Williams-Thomas, (d 1973), of The Old Rectory, Broome, Stourbridge, Worcs, and Eleanor, *née* Walker (d 1975); *b* 11 Feb 1914; *Educ* Shrewsbury, Univ of Birmingham; *m* 1, 23 April 1938 (m dis 1961), Esmée Florence, da of Maj William Herbert Taylor, JP, DL, of The Moors, Birlingham, nr Pershore, Worcs; 2 s (David b 1939, Simon b 1946), 1 da (Angela (Mrs Williams) b 1942); m 2, 24 Oct 1963, Sonia Margot, da of Maj Maurice Frederick Stewart Jewell, CBE, JP, DL, of The Hill, Upton-on-Severn, Worcs; *Career* joined TA 1932, Queen's Own Worcestershire Hussars 1937, Capt and Adjt 1939, serv WWII in France, Maj 1940, psc 1942, GSO II 43 Wessex Divn 1942, Lt-Col and GSOI SHAEF Mission to Belgium 1945; md, later chm and pres Royal Brierley Ltd (crystal table glass mfrs) 1946-85; memb Kidderminster RDC; Freeman of City London, former Master Worshipful Co of Glass Sellers; Cdr Order of the Crown of Belgium 1945, Croix de Guerre (France) 1944; OStJ 1946; *Books* The Crystal Years (1983); *Recreations* shooting, fishing, archery, gardening, philately, embroidery, cooking, antique glass collecting; *Clubs* Royal Toxopholite Soc, Midland, Flyfishers'; *Style—* Lt Col Reginald S Williams-Thomas, DSO, TD, DL; The Tythe House, Broome, Clent, nr Stourbridge, W Mids DY9 OET (☎ 0562 700632); Royal Brierley Crystal (☎ 0384 700)

WILLIAMS-WYNN, Maj Sir (David) Watkin; 11 Bt (E 1688), of Gray's Inn, Co Middx; DL (Clwyd 1969); s of Sir Watkin Williams-Wynn, 10 Bt, CBE, JP (d 1988), and his 1 w, Margaret Jean, *née* McBean; *b* 18 Feb 1940; *Educ* Eton; *m* 1, 1968 (m dis 1981), Harriet, da of Gen Sir Norman Tailyour, KCB, DSO; 2 s (Charles b 1970, Robert b 1977), twin da (Alexandra, Lucinda b 1972); m 2, 1983, Victoria Jane Dillon, da of Lt-Col Ian Dudley De Ath, DSO, MBE (d 1960); twin s (Nicholas Watkin, Harry Watkin b 1988); *Heir* s, Charles Williams-Wynn b 1970; *Career* Lt Royal Dragoons 1959, Maj Queen's Own Yeo 1970; memb Agricultural Lands Tbnl (Wales) 1978; *Style—* Maj Sir Watkin Williams-Wynn, Bt, DL; Plas-yn-Cefn, St Asaph, Clwyd LL17 0EY (☎ 0745 582200)

WILLIAMS-WYNNE, Col John Francis; CBE (1972), DSO (1945), JP (Gwynedd 1974); s of Maj Frederick Williams-Wynn, CB (s of Lady Annora Williams-Wynne, yr da of 2 Earl Manvers (Earldom extinct 1955), and ggs of Sir Watkin Williams-Wynn, 4 Bt, by his 2 w Charlotte, *née* Grenville, aunt of Richard Grenville, 1 Duke of Buckingham); Col Williams-Wynne took the name Williams-Wynne instead of Williams-Wynn in 1940; *b* 9 June 1908; *Educ* Oundle, Magdalene Coll Cambridge; *m* 1938, Margaret Gwendolen Hayward, da of Rev George Eliot Roper; 1 s (*see* Williams-Wynne, Hon Mrs), 2 da (Merion b 1941, m 1, 1964 Maj Peter Abbot-Davies, 2 s, m 2, HH Sayyid Faher bin Taimour Al-Said; Hon Mrs David Douglas-Home, *qv*); *Career* RA 2 Lt 1929, serv WWII India and Burma, Col 1954, Hon Col 7 Cadet Bn Roy Welsh Fus 1964-74; contested (C) Merioneth 1950; pres: Wales and Monmouth Cons and Unionist Assoc 1948-49, Royal Welsh Agric Soc 1967-68 (chm Cncl 1972-76), Timber Growers' Orgn 1974-76; former chm BBC Wales Agric Advsy Ctee, chm and md Cross Foxes Ltd; chm: Advsy Ctee Miny of Agric Experimental Farm Trawscoed 1955-76, Flying-Farmers Assoc 1974-82 (pres 1982-); memb: Gwynedd River Bd 1957-63, Nat Parks Cmmn 1961-66, Forestry Cmmn 1963-65, Forestry Ctee of GB 1967-76, Prince of Wales's Ctee 1971-76, Airline Users' Ctee CAA 1973-80; part-time memb Merseyside and N Wales Electricity Bd 1953-65; JP Merioneth 1950; constable of Harlech Castle 1964-; Vice Lord-Lt Gwynedd 1980- (lt 1974-80; Merioneth: DL 1953, Vice-lt 1954, lt 1957-74); CStJ, FRAgS; *Clubs* Pratt's, Army & Navy; *Style—* Col John Williams-Wynne, CBE, DSO, JP; Peniarth, Tywyn, Merioneth, Gwynedd LL36 9UD (☎ (0654) 710328)

WILLIAMS-WYNNE, Hon Mrs (Veronica Frances); *née* Buxton; 3 da of Baron Buxton of Alsa by his w Pamela Mary; *b* 24 Mar 1953; *Educ* St Mary's Convent Ascot; *m* 1975, William Robert Charles, s of Col John Williams-Wynne, CBE, DSO, JP, *qv*; 3 da (Chloë b 1978, Leonora b 1980, Rose b 1983); *Career* farmer; *Style—* The Hon Mrs Williams-Wynne; Talybont, Tywyn, Gwynedd (☎ 0654 710101)

WILLIAMSON, Anthony Evelyn (Tony); s of Arthur Evelyn Williamson (d 1944), and Lucy; *b* 2 Jan 1932; *Educ* East Lane Secondary Modern Willesden Techn Coll; *m* 17 Sept 1953, Sylvia Elizabeth, da of James Alowler (d 1969); 2 da (Sandra b 1960, Joanne b 1960); *Career* md Hoover plc UK 1986-; vice-chm Queens Park Ranger FC res 1987; Freeman City of London; Liveryman Worshipful Co of the Makers of Playing Cards; memb AMDEA BD; *Recreations* sport, golf; *Style—* Anthony Williamson, Esq; 7 Crofta, Lisvane, Cardiff CF4 5EW; Hoover plc, Dragonparc, Abercanaid, Merthyr Tydfil, Mid Glamorgan CF48 1PQ

WILLIAMSON, Rev Anthony William (Tony); s of Rev Joseph Williamson (d 1988), of St Paul's, Dock St, London, and Audrey Hollist, *née* Barnes (d 1974); *b* 2 Sept 1933; *Educ* Marlborough, Trinity Coll Oxford, Cuddesdon Theological Coll Oxford; *m* 10 Oct 1959, Barbara Jane, da of Louis Freeman (d 1970), of South Gullet Lane, Kirby Muxlue, Leicester; 3 s (Paul Joseph b 19 March 1962, Hugh Anthony b 3 May 1964, Ian Thomas b 17 Jan 1967), 1 da (Ruth Elizabeth (Mrs Lever) b 16 Sept 1960); *Career* Nat Serv 1951-53; fork-lift driver Pressed Steel Co Cowley Oxford (now Austin Rover Cowley Body Plant) 1958-87; ordained: deacon 1960, priest 1961; chm: BBC Radio Oxford local radio cncl 1970-73, TGWU Cowley body plant 1971-87; memb Oxfordshire Co Cncl 1973-88 (jt ldr 1985-87, jt chm of educn 1987-88), memb Oxford City Cncl 1961-67 and 1970-88 (former chm of housing, ldr 1980-83, Lord Mayor 1982-83); *Recreations* squash, tennis, hill walking; *Style—* The Rev Tony Williamson, OBE; 9 The Goggs, Watlington, Oxford OX9 5JX (☎ 049 161 2143); Education Dept (Schools), Diocesen Church House, Oxford OX2 0NB (☎ 0865 244 566)

WILLIAMSON, (Robert) Brian; OBE; *b* 16 Feb 1945; *Educ* Trinity Coll Dublin (MA); *m* June 1986, Diane Marie Christine de Jacquier de Rosee; *Career* cmmnd HAC 1975-; PA to Rt Hon Maurice Macmillan MP (later Viscount Macmillan) 1967-71, ed Int Currency Review 1971, contested (C) Sheffield Hillsborough 1974, prospective Parly candidate Truro 1976-77, md Gerrard Nat 1978-; chm: London Int Fin Futures Exchange 1985-88 (dir 1980-) GNI Ltd 1985; cncl memb Br Invisible Exports Cncl 1985-88; dir: Bank of Ireland Br Hldgs 1986-, Securities and Investmts Bd 1986-; memb: Br Invisible Export Cncl Euro Ctee 1988-, Globe Theatre Project Fund Raising Ctee 1987; *Clubs* Kildare Univ (Dublin); *Style—* Brian Williamson, Esq, CBE; Gerrard National Hldgs Plc, 33 Lombard St, London EC3 (☎ 01 623 9981)

WILLIAMSON, David Francis; CB (1984); s of Samuel Charles Wathen Williamson, of Bath, and late Marie Eileen; *b* 8 May 1934; *Educ* Tonbridge, Exeter Coll Oxford (MA); *m* 1961, Patricia Margaret, da of Eric Cade Smith of Broadclyst, Exeter; 2 s; *Career* civil servant: MAFF 1958-65 and 1967-77; seconded to HM Dip Serv for Kennedy Round Trade Negotiations 1965-67; dep-dir gen agric European Cmmn Brussels 1977-83, dep sec Cabinet Off 1983-87; sec gen Euro Cmmn Brussels 1987-; *Style—* David Williamson, Esq, CB; European Commission, 200 Rue de la Loi, 1049 Brussels, Belgium

WILLIAMSON, David Stewart Whittaker; s of John Watt Williamson (d 1951), and Annie Simpson Williamson, *née* Stewart; *b* 18 Jan 1943; *Educ* Hamilton Acad, Glasgow; *m* 1 March 1969, Joy Delia Francis, da of Walter Elliot Francis Wilson (d 1959); 2 s (Robin b 1970, John b 1979), 2 da (Jill b 1972, Nicola b 1975); *Career* CA in pte practice, ptnr McMurodo & Williamson 1967-; pt/t lectr in accountancy Glasgow Univ 1966-76; memb Local Authy Accounts in Scotland 1986-; cncllr (Con): Burgh of Hamilton 1966-75, Hamilton Dist 1975-84; JP 1972-, magistrate 1973-75; *Recreations* tennis, hillwalking, swimming, politics; *Style—* David Williamson, Esq; 3 Alder Ave, Hamilton, Lanarkshire ML3 7LL (☎ 0698 422882); McMurdo and Williamson, Chartered Accountants, 47 Cadzow St, Hamilton ML3 6ED (☎ 0698 284888)

WILLIAMSON, Ian Gordon; s of Edgar Williamson (d 1939), of Hove, Sussex, and Silvia Beatrice, *née* Pilkington (d 1987); *b* 28 Nov 1931; *Educ* Stowe, London Univ (LLB); *m* 31 Aug 1974, Hylda Josephine, da of Austin Hugh Percival Carbery (d 1969), of Dartry, Dublin 6; 2 da (Sarah Louise b 1976, Charlotte Lucy b 1977); *Career* admitted slr 1957; ptnr J Elliott Brooks Southall & Co; clerk to Worshipful Co of: Poulters 1968-87, Farmers 1979-86, Framework Knitter 1978-80 (creating a record of 3 clerkships of livery cos held simultaneously); *Recreations* tennis, squash, walking, fishing, genealogy, music; *Clubs* Naval and Military, Lansdowne, Ski; *Style—* Ian G Williamson, Esq; 47 Newstead Way, Wimbledon, London SW19 5HR (☎01 947 4496); J Elliott Brooks Southall & Co, 84 Brook St, Grosvenor Square, London W1Y 1YG

WILLIAMSON, John Peter; s of John William Stephen Williamson (d 1979), of Camberwell, and Ellen Gladys, *née* Noells; *b* 19 Jan 1943; *Educ* Addey and Stanhope GS, Hackney Tech Coll, Thames Poly (FCA, FInstSMM, MInstM, FInstD, MBIM, MIIM, MInstAM); *m* 17 Oct 1964, Dorothy Shirley Esther, da of Leonard Frederick, Farmer of Blackheath; 2 s (Earl John Grant b 1975, Craig Stephen b 1980); *Career* engr mangr Production Dept Rolex Watch Co 1960-63; jt md financial controller Dynamic Reading Inst 1968-69; memb Found Exec BIM Younger Mangr Assoc 1969-70; gp financial controller, co sec and asst md Hunter-Print Gp plc 1971-74; Co Comptrollers Sen Analyst ITT, STC 1975; UK chm Investigations and Operational Reviews (mangr 1976-80), ITT Bd (USA), consult CE Health 1985-86; princ J P Williamson Co 1981, fndr memb I Fin Planning 1987, co fndr Assoc of London Hobby Computer Clubs; *Books* author ITT/STC EDP Audit Manual; *Recreations* shooting, martial arts; *Style—* John Williamson, Esq; c/o Nat West Bank plc, 17 Camberwell Green, London SE15 (☎ 01 851 4195)

WILLIAMSON, John Robin; s of Samuel Charles Wathen Williamson, of Waterhouse, Monkton Combe, Bath, Avon, and Marie Eileen, *née* Denney (d 1962); *b* 11 May 1931; *Educ* Tonbridge, St John's Coll Cambridge (MA); *m* 28 June 1958, Rosemarie Dorothea, da of Rev Carl Hugo Stelzner (d 1967), of St Jacobus, Pesterwitz, Germany; 2 da (Catherine Anne b 1959, (Susan) Jane b 1962); *Career* Iraq Petroleum Co 1956-68, Qatar and Abu Dhabi Petroleum Cos 1968-77, BP plc 1977-82 (mangr Forties Oilfield, gen mangr exploration and prodn, dir BP Pet Devpt Ltd), Trafalgar House plc 1982 (dir and md oil and gas subsidiary cos 1984-); FIMechE, FInstPet; *Recreations* gardening, travel; *Style—* John Williamson, Esq; 28 Hornton St, London W8

WILLIAMSON, Marshal of the RAF Sir Keith Alec; GCB (1982, KCB 1979), AFC (1968); s of Percy and Gertrude Williamson; *b* 25 Feb 1928; *Educ* Bancroft's Sch, Market Harborough GS, RAF Coll Cranwell; *m* 1953, Patricia Anne, da of Wing Cdr F M N Watts; 2 s, 2 da; *Career* cmmnd 1950, served with RAAF in Korea, cmd RAF Gütersloh W Germany 1968-70, Royal Coll of Def Studies 1971, Dir of Air Staff Plans 1972-75, Cmdt RAF Staff Coll 1975-77, ACOS SHAPE Plans and Policy 1977-78, AOC-in-C: RAF Support Cmd 1978-80, RAF Strike Cmd and C-in-C UK Air Forces 1980-82, Chief of Air Staff 1982-85, Air ADC to HM The Queen 1982-85, Marshal of the RAF 1985; *Style—* Marshal of the RAF Sir Keith Williamson, GCB, AFC; c/o Midland Bank Ltd, 25 Notting Hill Gate, London W11

WILLIAMSON, Malcolm Benjamin Graham Christopher; CBE (1976); s of Rev

George Williamson, of Sydney; *b* 1931; *Educ* Barker Coll Hornsby NSW, Sydney Conservatorium; *m* 1960, Dolores Daniel; 1 s, 2 da; *Career* composer; Master of The Queen's Music 1975-, pres Royal Philharmonic Orchestra (London) 1977-82; Hon Degree Open Univ 1983; *Style—* Malcolm Williamson, Esq, CBE; c/o Josef Weinberger Ltd, 10-16 Rathbone St, London W1P 2BJ

WILLIAMSON, Dame (Elsie) Marjorie; DBE (1973); da of Leonard Williamson; *b* 30 July 1913; *Educ* Royal Holloway Coll; *Career* dep vice-chllr London Univ 1970-71 and 1971-72; princ: St Mary's Coll Durham Univ 1955-62, Royal Holloway Coll 1962-73; lectr physics Bedford 1945-55; memb Cwlth Scholarship Cmmn 1975-84 fell Bedford Coll London; *Style—* Dame Marjorie Williamson, DBE; Priory Barn, Lower Raydon, Ipswich, Suffolk (☎ 0473 824033)

WILLIAMSON, Prof Mark Herbert; s of Herbert Stansfield Williamson (d 1955), and Winifred Lilian, *née* Kenyon; *b* 8 June 1928; *Educ* Groton Sch Mass USA, Rugby Christ Church Oxford (DPhil); *m* 5 April 1958, Charlotte Clara Dallas, da of Hugh Macdonald (d 1958); 1 s (Hugh b 1961), 2 da (Emma b 1963, Sophia b 1965); *Career* Nat Serv 2 Lt Oxfordshire and Buckinghamshire LI 1950-52, Capt 100 APIU TA 1952-57; demonstrator in zoology Oxford Univ 1952-58, i/c herring section Scottish Marine Biological Assoc oceanographic lab Edinburgh 1958-62, lectr in zoology Univ of Edinburgh 1962-65, prof (fndr and head of dept) dept of biology Univ of York 1965-; memb 1965-: SERC, NERC, UGC, HSE, Royal soc; chm Br Nat Ctee on Problems of the Environment 1988-, conslt OECD 1988-; memb: cncl Yorks Wildlife Tst, York Archaeological Tst; FIBiol 1966; *Books* Analysis of Biological Populations (19720, Ecological Stability (1974), Island Populations (1981), Biological Invasions (1986); *Recreations* natural history, walking, photography; *Style—* Prof Mark Williamson; Dalby Old Rectory, Terrington, York YO6 4PF (☎ 03475 244); Department of Biology, University of York, York YO1 5DD (☎ 0904 432806, fax 0904 415185, telex 57933 YORKUL)

WILLIAMSON, Sir Nicholas (Frederick Hedworth); 11 Bt (E 1642), of East Markham, Notts; s of Maj William Hedworth Williamson (ka 1942), and Diana (who m 2, 1 and last Baron Hailes, and d 1980), o da of Brig-Gen Hon Charles Lambton, DSO, 4 s of 2 Earl of Durham; suc unc, Sir Charles Williamson, 10 Bt (d 1946) ; *b* 26 Oct 1937; *Educ* Eton; *Heir* none; *Career* cmmnd 4/7 Royal Dragoon Gds 1957 (Nat Serv); farmer; *Style—* Sir Nicholas Williamson, Bt; Abbey Croft, Mortimer, Reading, Berks (☎ 0734 332324)

WILLIAMSON, Nigel; s of Neville Albert Williamson, of Arizona, and Ann Maureen Kitson; *b* 4 July 1954; *Educ* Chislehurst and Sidcup Grammar, UCL; *m* 1976, Magali Patricia; 2 s (Adam b 1977, Piers b 1978); *Career* editor Tribune 1984-87, Labour Party News 1987-, New Socialist 1987-; *Books* The SDP (1982), The New Right (1984); *Recreations* cricket, opera, gardening, boating; *Clubs* Skyliners Cricket; *Style—* Nigel Williamson, Esq; Flat 2, 15 Shortlands Grove, Bromley, Kent BR2 0LS (☎ 01 466 5633); Labour Party News/New Socialist, c/o The Labour Party, 150 Walworth Road, London SE17 (☎ 01 703 0833)

WILLIAMSON, Philip (Nigel); s of Leonard James Williamson, and Doris, *née* Chapell; *b* 23 Sept 1948; *Educ* Mill Hill, Newcastle Univ (CBA, BArch); *m* 27 May 1983, Victoria Lois, da of Joseph Samuel Brown, of Clwyd, N Wales; 1 s (Nicholas James b 1984); *Career* architect; princ PNW Design & Co 1979-; chm and md: PNW Assocs Ltd (architects and interior designers) 1985-, PNW Properties Ltd 1985-; RIBA; *Recreations* sailing, tennis, winter sports; *Clubs* The Queens, London Riverside Racquet Centre; *Style—* Philip Williamson, Esq; 8 Netherton Rd, St Margarets, Twickenham, Middlesex (☎ 01 892 3076); 6 North Rd, Richmond, Surrey (☎ 01 878 8427)

WILLIAMSON, Rt Rev Robert (Roy) Kerr; *see* Bradford, Bishop of

WILLIAMSON, Robert Algie; s of Thomas Algie Williamson (d 1955), of Glasgow, and Laura Evelyn, *née* Littler; *b* 11 August 1931; *Educ* Merchiston Castle Edinburgh, Harvard Business Sch (Advanced Mgmnt Prog); *m* 25 Aug 1956, (Sheila) Patricia Langdon (d 1985), da of Air-Cdre Richard Grice, OBE, DFC (d 1952);2 s (Eric Duncan b 26 June 1958, d 1958, Roy Eric b 26 Oct 1963), 2 da (Susan Kay b 18 Feb 1960, Lois Ann b 31 Aug 1961); *Career* RAF Pilot Offr Flying Trg 1954-56; sec and fin dir John Brown & Co (Clydebank) Ltd 1958-67; fin dir: Upper Clyde Shipbuilders Ltd Glasgow 1967-68, Surface Electronics Ltd Poole, Dorset 1984-; gp fin dir Samuel Osborn & Co Ltd Sheffield 1968-78; dir: Seatic Marine Ltd Dorset 1984-, Forelle Ltd 1987-, Bourne Steel Ltd 1988-; Freeman Worshipful Co of Cutlers of Hallamshire 1972; FBIM; *Recreations* fishing, sailing; *Clubs* RAF; *Style—* Robert Williamson, Esq; Chamberlaynes Farm House, Bere Regis, nr Wareham, Dorset BH20 7LS (☎ 0929 471 357); office: (☎ 0202 674 333, fax 0202 678 028, telex, 41184 SURFEL S)

WILLIAMSON MACDOUGALL, Major James; MC (1946); s of George Taylor Williamson (d 1967), of Argyll, and Helen Dorothy, *née* Patten MacDougall (d 1977); *b* 22 May 1919; *Educ* Fettes; *m* 10 Feb 1953, Marie-Claire Thérese Huberte Marie Ghislaine, da of Charles Louis Ghislain van Wambeke (d 1933), of Belgium; 1 s (Charles b 1965), 4 da (Elspeth b 1954, Isabel b 1955, Cecile b 1957, Anne b 1958); *Career* serv RSF 1939-59 (Major) Madagascar, India, Middle E, Sicily, Italy, NW Europe, Malaya; farmer and landowner; *Recreations* sport & country life; *Clubs* Sport and Country Life; *Style—* Major James Williamson MacDougass, MC; Gallanach, by Oban, Argyll PA34 4QL (☎ 0631 62176)

WILLINGDON, Marchioness of; Daphne; da of Seymour Caldwell; *m* 1943, as his 3 w, 2 and last Marquess of Willingdon (d 1979); *Style—* The Most Hon The Marchioness of Willingdon; Kilbees Farm, Winkfield, Windsor Forest

WILLINGHAM, Derrick; *b* 29 Dec 1932; *Educ* Brunts GS, Mansfield Notts, Nottingham Univ (BA); *m* 1956, Nancy Patricia, *née* Webb; 1 s, 1 da; *Career* chm Hayward Tyler Pump Gp 1977-86; pres chartered Inst of Mgmnt Accountants 1982-83 (memb cncl 1975-86, vice-pres 1980-82); sr vice-pres Vulcan Indust Serv 1985-87; pres Sterling Pump Co's 1984-85; chm Br Pump Mfrs Assoc 1984-85 (memb cncl 1977-85); FCMA; *Recreations* golf, tennis, travelj; *Clubs* RAC, Woburn Golf and Country, Dunstable Downs Golf; *Style—* Derrick Willingham, Esq; TWIL Limited, PO Box 119, Shepchote Lane, Sheffield S9 1TY (☎ 0742 443388); Lindrick Lodge, Lindrick Road, Woodsetts, Nr Worksop, Notts S818 A7 (☎ 0909 568276)

WILLINK, Alma Marion; JP (City of Manchester 1949), DL (Gter Manchester 1981); da of Rev Hendrick Chignell, sometime Rector of Northenden, Cheshire; *Educ* Manchester Univ (MA); *m* 1930, Lt-Col Francis Arthur Willink (sometime dep chm Lancashire United Transport Ltd), and 2 s of Henry Willink, JP (1 cousin of Wiliam Willink, f of Sir Henry Urmston Willink, 1 Bt, MC, PC, QC); *Career* chm City of Manchester Bench 1978 and 1979; pres Manchester Luncheon Club 1984-85; *Style—* Mrs Francis Willink, JP, DL; 141 The Green, Worsley, M28 4PA

WILLINK, Sir Charles William; 2 Bt (UK 1957), of Dingle Bank, City of Liverpool; s of The Rt Hon Sir Henry Urmston Willink, 1 Bt, MC, QC (d 1973, ggs of Daniel Willink, sometime Dutch Consul in Liverpool), and his 1 w, Cynthia Frances (d 1959), da of Herbert Morley Fletcher, MD, FRCP, of Harley Street; *b* 10 Sept 1929; *Educ* Eton, Trinity Coll Cambridge (MA, PhD); *m* 7 Aug 1954, Elizabeth, er da of Humfrey Andrewes, of North Grove, Highgate; 1 s, 1 da; *Heir* s, Edward Daniel Willink b 17 Feb 1957; *Career* housemaster Eton 1964-77; *Books* Euripides Orestes (ed with commentary, 1986); *Style—* Sir Charles Willink, Bt; 20 North Grove, Highgate N6 4SL (☎ 01 340 3996)

WILLINK, William Alfred; s of Derek Edward Willink (d 1985), of Mirefoot, Burneside, Cumbria, and Joan Leslie, *née* Smallwood; *b* 11 July 1931; *Educ* Marlborough, St John's Coll Oxford (BA, MA); *m* 7 April 1956, Hester Anne Dymond, da of Wilfred Edmund Mounsey, of Helsington Lodge, Brigsteer, Cumbria; 1 s (Daniel b 1961), 2 da (Jessica b 1963, Priscilla b 1965); *Career* Barclays Bank: local dir Reading 1962-66, local dir Maidstone 1966-70, sr local dir Maidstone 1970-81, sr local dir Preston 1981-87; chm: Kent Nat Savings Ctee 1973-77, Maidstone Cancer Res Campaign 1978-81; fndr govr Satro Cumbria 1982-87, tstee Francis C Scott Charitable Tst 1983-; *Recreations* fly fishing, travel, fell walking; *Style—* William Willink, Esq; Dalton House, Burton-in-Kendal, Cumbria (☎ 0524 781203)

WILLIS, Antony Martin Derek; s of Thomas Martin Willis, of Marton, NZ, and Dawn Marie, *née* Christensen; *b* 29 Nov 1941; *Educ* Wanganui Collegiate Sch Wanganui NZ, Victoria Univ Wellington NZ (LLB 1966); *m* 1, 10 Feb 1962 (m dis), Diane Elizabeth, da of late Frederick Willis Gorton (d 1987), of Feilding, NZ; 3 da (Kirsty Elizabeth b 13 April 1963, Sara Jane b 7 June 1966, Nicola Mary b 6 Nov 1968); m 2, 12 April 1975, Diana Alice, da of Robert Dermot McMahon Williams, of Lenham, Kent; 1 s (Matthew William Dermot b 22 Aug 1988), 2 da (Charlotte Emily Christensen b 5 Jan 1978, Joanna Catherine Dalrymple b 7 Dec 1981); *Career* slr; ptnr: Perry Wylie Pope & Page NZ 1967-70, Coward Chance London 1970-87 (managing ptnr 1987); jt managing ptnr Clifford Chance (merged firm of Coward Chance with Clifford Turner) 1987-88, sr litigation qand arbitration ptnr 1989-; memb: Law Soc, City of London Slrs Co, American Arbitration Assoc, Int Bar Assoc, Wellington Dist Law Soc (NZ); Freeman City of London 1975, Liveryman of Worshipful Co of Slrs; ACIArb; *Recreations* music, gardening; *Clubs* Reform, Hurlingham; *Style—* Antony Willis, Esq; 28 Chipstead St, London SW6 (☎ 01 731 4735); Clifford Chance, Royex House, Aldermanbury Sq, London EC2V 7LO (☎ 01 600 0808, fax 01 726 8561, telex 8959991 COWARD G)

WILLIS, David; s of William Willis (d 1986), of Consett, Co Durham, and Rachael Elizabeth, *née* Cant; *b* 13 Jan 1949; *Educ* Consett GS, Edinburgh Univ (BArch (Summa cum Laude)); *m* 12 July 1970, Patricia Ann, da of Charles Cedric Endley, DSO, of Cape Town, S Africa; 2 s (Robert b 1984, Steven b 1988), 1 da (Jennifer b 1988); *Career* architect, ptnr Lang, Willis & Galloway; architect Thirlestane Castle Tst 1987-; dir: The Caledonian Racing Club, Cobbscot New Lanark restoration 1974-, (awards include RICS. The Times Conservation, Europn Nostra Medal of Honours 1988), Old Coll Univ of Edinburgh 1974-87; RIBA, RIAS; *Recreations* racehorse owner; *Clubs* Br Thoroughbred and Racing Breeding; *Style—* David Willis, Esq; 3 Maryfield Place, Bonnyrigg, Midlothian (☎ 031 663 5487); 3 Walker St, Edinburgh EH3 7JY (☎ 031 226 7031)

WILLIS, Baron (Life Peer UK 1963); Edward Henry Willis (Ted); s of Alfred Willis, of Tottenham; *b* 13 Jan 1918; *Educ* Downhills Central Sch Tottenham; *m* 1944, Audrey, da of Alfred Hale; 1 s, 1 da; *Career* served WWII Royal Fus; sits as Lab Peer in House of Lords; playwright and writer; dir: World Wide Pictures 1967-, Vitalcall Ltd 1983-; pres Authors' Lending and Copyright Soc; FRTS, FRSA; *Books Incl:* Whatever Happened to Tom Mix? (auto-biography 1970), The Churchill Commando (1977), The Naked Sun (1980), Spring at the Winged Horse (1983), The Green Leaves of Summer (1988), A Problem for Mother Christmas (1988); *Plays include* Hot Summer Night, New (1957), A Slow Roll of Drums (1964), Mr Polly (1977), Stardust (1983), Battle at Lavender Lodge (1985), The Green Leaves of Summer (1987), It Takes Two to Make a Murder (1989), Doctor on the Boil (1989); *Films include* Woman in a Dressing Gown (1958, later also a play), A Long Way to Shiloh (1969), Mrs Harris Goes to Monte Carlo (1986), Spy on Ice (1987), The Valley of the Dream (1987), Mrs Harris Goes to Moscow (1988); *TV scripts include* Dixon of Dock Green, Crime of Passion, Black Beauty, Valley of Kings, Sergeant Cork, A Home for Animals; *Clubs* Garrick, Wig and Pen; *Style—* The Rt Hon the Lord Willis; 5 Shepherds Green, Chislehurst, Kent

WILLIS, Hon Sir Eric Archibald; KBE (1975), CMG (1974); s of Archibald Clarence Willis and Vida Mabel, *née* Buttenshaw; *b* 15 Jan 1922; *Educ* Murwillumbah HS, Sydney U (BA); *m* 1951, Norma Dorothy Knight; 2 s, 1 da; *Career* MLA (Lib) for Earlwood NSW 1950-78, dep ldr of the opposition 1959-65, min for Labour and Indust NSW 1965-71, chief sec Govt of NSW 1965-72, min for Educn NSW 1972-76, ldr NSW Parly Lib Party 1976-78, ret; exec sec Royal Australian Coll of Ophthalmologists 1978-; *Style—* The Hon Sir Eric Willis, KBE, CMG; 1/51 Upper Pitt St, Kirribilli, NSW 2061, Australia (☎ 929 9251)

WILLIS, Dr Hector Ford; CB (1960); s of William Frank (d 1941), and Jemima Gillies Willis (d 1949); *b* 3 Mar 1909; *Educ* Univ Coll Cardiff (MSc), Cambridge Univ (PhD); *m* 1936, Maria Iddon, da of Joseph Renwick (d 1975); *Career* scientist; Br Cotton Indust Res Assoc 1935-38, Admiralty 1938-62, chief of Royal Naval Scientific Serv 1954-62, scientific advsr MOD 1962-70, ret 1970; US Medal of Freedom with Silver Palm 1947; *Recreations* chess; *Style—* Dr Hector Willis, CB; Fulwood, Eaton Park, Cobham, Surrey (☎ 093 26 3395)

WILLIS, Vice Adm Sir (Guido) James; KBE (1981), AO (1976); s of Dr Jack R L Willis (d 1969), and Thea Willis (d 1939); *b* 18 Oct 1923; *Educ* Wesley Coll Melbourne, RAN Coll; *m* 1, 1949; 1 s, 2 da; m 2, 1976, Marjorie Joyce; *Career* RAN, Asst Chief of Def Force Staff 1976-78, Flag Offr cmdg HMA Fleet 1978-79, Chief of Naval Staff 1979-82, ret; *see Debrett's Handbook of Australia and New Zealand for further details*; *Style—* Vice Adm Sir James Willis, KBE, AO; Toragy, Kyla Park, Tuross Head, NSW 2537, Australia

WILLIS, Maj Gen John Brooker; CB (1981); William Noel Willis (d 1976), and Elaine (d 1978); *b* 28 July 1926; *Educ* Redhill Tech Coll; *m* 1959, Yda Belinda Jane, da of Lt-Col G C Firbank, MC (d 1947); 2 s (Christopher b 1960, Hugo b 1968), 2 da

(Richenda b 1961, Abigail b 1967); *Career* cmmnd 10 Hussars 1947, cmd 1964-67, Brig 1974, Maj-Gen 1977, dir gen Fighting Vehicles and Engr Equip 1977-81, army advsr IMS Ltd; *Recreations* golf, aviation, amateur dramatics; *Clubs* Army and Navy; *Style*— Maj-Gen John Willis, CB; c/o Lloyds Bank plc, 26 Hammersmith Broadway, London W6 7AH

WILLIS, John Frederic Earle d'Anyers; OBE (1945); s of Rev Canon F E d'A Willis (d 1940), and Agnes Hilda, *née* Postlethwaite (d 1954); (paternal ancestry, *see* Burke's Landed Gentry 18th Edn, vol ii); *b* 14 Mar 1908; *Educ* Marlborough Coll; *m* 1, 6 Aug 1938 (m dis 1946), Constance Flora Margaret, da of late Frederick Edward Hooper, of Madras, India; 1 s (John b 1940); m 2, 20 July 1946, Joan Mary Granvaile, da of late Lt-Col Charles Loughlin Meyler O'Malley, RFA; 1 s (Peter b 1949), 1 da (Anne b 1952); *Career* serv WWII Lt-Col 1940-45 Paiforce, Iraq, Persia, Egypt, Lebanon; chm Gillanders Arbuthnot & Co Ltd India, dir: Anglo Thai Corpn Ltd, AD Int Ltd (dep chm), Charrington Gardner & Locket Ltd, Home County Newspapers, and chm J Gerrard & Sons Ltd; *Recreations* shooting, bridge; *Clubs* Bourne Farnham Surrey; *Style*— John Willis, OBE; South Court, Crondall, Farnham, Surrey GU10 5QF (☎ 0252 850711)

WILLIS, Rear Adm Kenneth Henry George; CB (1981); s of Henry (d 1926), and Elsie Nellie Willis; *Educ* St Olaves GS, Jesus Coll Cambridge (BA); *m* m, Sheila Catherine; 3 da (Lois, Laura, Sharon); *Career* Chief of Staff to CIC Naval Home Cmmnd to Sept 1981; dir-gen Home Farm Trust Ltd Bristol 1982-; memb Inst of directors; FRSA; *Recreations* rowing, life-saving, amateur theatricals; *Style*— Rear Adm Kenneth H G Willis, CB; c/o Barclays Bank, 1 Manvers St, Bath, Avon

WILLIS, Robert George Dylan; MBE (1982); s of Edward Woodcock Willis (d 1982), and Anne Margaret, *née* Huntington; *b* 30 May 1949; *Educ* King Edward VI Royal GS Guildford; *m* 1980, Juliet, da of William and Barbara Smail, of Wilts; 1 da (Katie-Anne b 1984); *Career* professional cricketer and broadcaster; capt: Warwickshire 1980-84, England 1982-84; 90 tests for England, record number of wickets for England on retirement (325); chm In Style Promotions Ltd; *Books* co-author of eight cricket books; *Recreations* classical music, golf, tennis, real ale; *Clubs* MCC, Corinthian Casuals Football, International Luncheon Club at the Cafe Royal, Warwickshire CCC; *Style*— Robert Willis, Esq, MBE; 22 Fitzwilliam Rd, Lodnon SW4 0DN; Café Royal, 68 Regent St, London W1R 6EL (☎ 01 437 0144)

WILLIS, (Joseph) Robert McKenzie; CB (1952), CMG (1946); s of Charles Frederick Willis (d 1949), and Lucy Alice, *née* McKenzie (d 1952); *b* 18 Mar 1909; *Educ* Eton, Christ Church Oxford (MA); *m* 1945, Elizabeth Browning, da of James Ewing (d 1975); 1 s (Robert James), 1 da (Ann-Margaret); *Career* dep chm Bd of Inland Revenue 1957-71, res prof Univ of Bath 1972-79; *Style*— Robert Willis, Esq, CB, CMG; Bunbury, Lower Shiplake, Henley-on-Thames, Oxon RG9 3PD (☎ 073 522 2726)

WILLIS, His Hon Judge Stephen Murrell; s of John Henry Willis (d 1936), of Hadleigh, Suffolk, and Eileen Marian, *née* Heard (d 1984); *b* 21 June 1929; *Educ* Chorister Christ Church Cathedral Choir Sch Oxford, Bloxham Sch; *m* 1, 1953 (m dis 1974), Jean Irene, *née* Eve; 1 s (Geoffrey Willis), 3 da (Susanna (Mrs Ravestein-Willis), Barbara, Jill (Mrs Warner)); m 2, 1975, Doris Florence Davies, *née* Redding; 2 step da (Mrs Jill Lockhart, Mrs Janette Davies); *Career* Nat Serv RS 16 Ind Para Bde Gp 1948-50; articles Gotetee and Goldsmith 1950-55, admitted slr 1955; ptnr: Chamberlin Talbot and Bracey 1955-63, Pearless de Rougemont Co 1964-85; dep circuit judge 1975-80, rec 1980-85, circuit judge 1986-; fndr The Suffolk Singers 1962, fndr and dir The Prodigal Singers 1964-; *Recreations* performing early music, sailing, walking, travel; *Clubs* The Noblemen and Gentlemen's Catch; *Style*— His Hon Judge Willis; Croydon Combined Court Centre, Altyre Rd, Croydon CR9 5AB (☎ 01 681 2533)

WILLIS-FLEMING, Hon Mrs (Elizabeth Sarah); *née* James; da of 4 Baron Northbourne; *b* 1933; *m* 1960, Michael Edward Willis-Fleming; 1 s, 1 da; *Style*— The Hon Mrs Willis-Fleming; Updown Farm, Betteshanger Deal, Kent

WILLISON, Lt-Gen Sir David John; KCB (1973), OBE (1958), MC (1945); s of Brig Arthur Cecil Willison, DSO, MC, of Trentishoe Manor, Parracombe, N Devon, and Hyacinth D'Arcy, er da of Maj Philip Urban Walter Vigors, DSO, of Basingstoke; *b* 25 Dec 1919; *Educ* Wellington, RMA Woolwich; *m* 1941, Betty Vernon, da of Air Vice-Marshal Sir Leslie Bates, KBE; 1 s, 2 da; *Career* 2 Lt RE 1939; serv NW Europe, Malaya, Egypt, Middle E, Berlin, Aden; CO 38 Engr Regt 1960-63, BGS: Intelligence MOD 1967-70, HQ Northag 1970-71; dir of Service Intelligence MOD 1971-72, dep chief of Def Staff Intelligence MOD 1972-75, dir-gen Intelligence 1975-78, Col Cmdt RE 1973-82, Chief RE 1977-82; conslt: int affrs Nat Westminster Bank Gp 1980-84, affrs NatWest Investmnts 1984-; pres SJA Western Area Hants 1987-, chm RE Widows' Soc 1987-, Freeman City of London; *Clubs* Naval and Military, Royal Lymington Yacht; *Style*— Lt-Gen Sir David Willison, KCB, OBE, MC; Long Barton, Lower Pennington Lane, Lymington, Hants (☎ 0590 77194)

WILLISON, Sir John Alexander; OBE (1964), QPM (1970), DL (Worcs 1968); s of John Willison Gow Willison (d 1942), and Mabel (d 1964); *b* 3 Jan 1914; *Educ* Sedbergh; *m* 1947, Jess Morris, da of late John Bruce; *Career* chief constable: Berwick Roxburgh and Selkirk Police 1952-58, Worcs Constabulary 1958-67, W Mercia Constabulary 1967-74; KStJ 1970; kt 1970; *Recreations* country pursuits; *Style*— Sir John Willison, OBE, QPM, DL; Ravenhills Green, Lulsley, Worcs (☎ 0886 21688)

WILLMAN, John Romain; s of John Sydney Willman, and Millicent Charlotte, *née* Thornton; *b* 27 May 1949; *Educ* Bolton Sch Lancs, Jesus Coll Cambridge (MA), Westminster Coll (Oxford (Cert Educn); *m* 1 April 1978, Margaret, da of Dr John Shanahan (d 1981), of Maida Vale; 1 s (Michael b 1982), 2 da (Kate b 1984, Claire b 1987); *Career* asst teacher Brentford Sch for Girls Middx 1972-76, fin researcher Consumer's Assoc 1976-79, ed of Taxes and Assessment (jls of Inland Revenue Staff Fedn) 1979-83, pubns mangr Peat Marwick Mitchell & Co 1983-85, gen sec Fabian Soc 1985-; *Books* Lloyds Bank Tax Guide (2 edn 1988); *Recreations* skiing, making the Lab Pty think; *Clubs* Wessex Cave, Inst of Contemporary Art; *Style*— John Willman, Esq; 33 Reservoir Road, London SE4 2NU (☎ 01 639 3845); 11 Dartmouth St, London SW1H 9BN (☎ 01 222 8877)

WILLMER, John Franklin; QC (1967); s of Rt Hon Sir Henry Gordon Willmer (d 1983), of London, and Mary Barbara, *née* Hurd; according to the privately printed History of the Wilmer Family (1888), the name in various spellings is found in public records from the 12th century and existed prior to the Norman Conquest; *b* 30 May 1930; *Educ* Winchester, Corpus Christi Coll Oxford (MA); *m* 1, 1958 (m dis 1979), Nicola Ann Dickinson; 1 s (Stephen), 3 da (Susan, Jennifer, Katherine); m 2, 1979, Margaret Lilian, da of Chester B Berryman, of Marlborough, Wilts; *Career* Nat Serv 1949-50, 2 Lt TA 1950-57, Capt; called to the Bar Inner Temple 1955, bencher 1975, memb panel of Lloyd's arbitrators in Salvage Cases 1967; panel from which Wreck cmmrs apptd 1967-79; gen cmmr Income Tax for Inner Temple 1982, re-appointed a Wreck cmmr 1987; *Recreations* walking; *Clubs* Utd Oxford and Cambridge; *Style*— J F Willmer, Esq, QC; Flat 4, 23 Lymington Road, London NW6 1HZ (☎ 01 435 9245); 7 King's Bench Walk, Temple, London EC4Y 7DS (☎ 01 583 0404, telex 887491 KBLAW)

WILLMER, John Honour; OBE (1989); s of Richard Newman Willmer (d 1963), of Friars Ct, Clanfield, Oxford, and Mary Elizabeth Willmer (d 1974); *b* 11 Nov 1920; *Educ* Kingswood Sch Bath, Bradford Tech Coll; *m* 8 Feb 1964, Frances Irene, da of Alan Amory Jackson (d 1959); 1 s (Charles b 1970), 2 da (Carol b 1966, d 1985, Mary b 1967, d 1975); *Career* environmentally sensitive farming open to public; West Oxon Tech Coll 1959-(currently actg chm), county chm Oxfordshire NFU 1965-, Westminster Teacher Trg Coll 1965-, Luton Industl Coll 1975-, Cliff Coll 1975-; memb Thames Water Western CCC NFU (memb land drainage ctee 1974-86), chm Oxfordshire YFC 1959 (memb mgmnt and travel ctee), memb Clanfield Parish Cncl 1970- (Former chm), jt divnl tres Methodist Home Mission Div Westminster 1975-; ARAgS; *Recreations* conservation; *Style*— John Willmer, Esq, OBE; Friars Ct, Clanfield, Oxford OX8 2SU

WILLMOTT, Dennis James; CBE (1988), QFSM (1981); s of James Arthur Willmott (d 1970), and Esther Winifred Maude Styles; *b* 10 July 1932; *Educ* St Albans County GS; *m* 1958, Mary Patricia, da of Walter Ball-Currey (d 1975), of Liverpool; 2 s (Christopher, Andrew); *Career* served Korea 1951-52, Royal Norfolk Regt 1950-57, Sgt; joined Fire Serv 1957, dep chief fire offr: Isle of Wight Fire Bde 1972-74, Wilstshire 1976, London Fire Bde 1976-81, London 1981-83; chief fire offr Merseyside Fire Bde 1983-88; gp contingency mangr Avon Rubber plc 1988; *Recreations* walking; *Clubs* Royal Br Legion; *Style*— Dennis Willmott, Esq, CBE, QFSM; 27 Highlands, Potterne, Devizes (☎ 0380 5672)

WILLMOTT, Maj-Gen Edward George; OBE (1980); s of Thomas Edward Willmott (d 1983), of 33 Witheybed La, Alvechurch, Worcs, and Eileen Ruth, *née* Murphy; *b* 18 Feb 1936; *Educ* Redditch Co HS, Gonville and Caius Coll Cambridge (MA); *m* 18 June 1960, Sally Penelope, da of George Philip Banyard (d 1946), of Long Rd, Cambridge; 2 s (Philip b 1961, Christopher b 1964), 1 da (Georgina b 1962); *Career* RMCS Shrivenham and Camberley 1967-68, DAA & QMG 8 Inf Bde 1969-70, OC 8 Field Sqdn RE 1971-73, directing staff RMCS Shrivenham 1973-75; CO: 23 Engr Regt 1976, 2 Armd Div Engr Regt 1976-78, Col MGO Secretariat MOD (PE) 1979-80, Cdr 30 Engr Bde, RCDS 1983, dep Cmdt RMCS Shrivenham 1984-85, pres (army) ordnance bd MOD 1986-88 (vice- pres 1985-86), dir gen weapons (army) MOD 1988-; *Recreations* sailing, skiing, walking, gardening; *Clubs* IOD; *Style*— Maj-Gen Edward Willmott, OBE; St Christopher House, Southwark St, London SE1 (☎ 01 928 7999 ext 1786, car tel 01 921 1786)

WILLMOTT, John Charles; CBE (1983); s of Arthur George Willmott (d 1960), of Goodmayes, Essex, and Annie Elizabeth, *née* Darby (d 1964); *b* 1 April 1922; *Educ* Bancroft's Sch Woodford, Imperial Coll London (ARCS, BSc, PhD); *m* 10 May 1952, Sheila Madeleine, da of Stanley Dumbell, OBE (d 1966), of Birkenhead; 2 s (Nigel b 24 Sept 1956, Philip b 13 March 1963), 1 da (Stella b 19 Apr 1954); *Career* serv WWII Lt REME 1942-46; Univ of Liverpool: asst lectr 1948-49, lectr 1949-58, sr lectr 1958-63, reader 1963-64; Univ of Manchester: prof nuclear physics 1964-67, dir physical labs 1967- (pro vice-chllr 1982-85); memb: physics bd SERC 1968-73 and 1976-82 (cncl 1978-82), physical sciences sub-ctee UGC 1970-80, NATO Science for Stability Steering Gp 1981-; FInst P 1968; *Books* Tables of Coefficients for the Analysis of Triple Angular Correlations of Gamma-Rays from Aligned Nuclei (1968), Atomic Physics (1975); *Recreations* walking; *Style*— Prof John Willmott, CBE; 37 Hall Moss Lane, Bramhall, Cheshire SK7 1RB (☎ 061 439 4169); Department of Physics, Schuster Laboratory, University of Manchester Manchester M13 9PL (☎ 061 275 4200)

WILLMOTT, Peter; s of Benjamin Merriman Willmott (d 1959), and Dorothy Nellie, *née* Waymouth (d 1926); *b* 18 Sept 1923; *Educ* London Univ (BSc); *m* 31 July 1948, Phyllis Mary, da of Alec George Noble (d 1966); 2 s (Lewis b 1949, Michael b 1952); *Career* co-dir Inst of Community Studies 1964-78 (res offr 1954-64), dir Centre for Enviromental Studies 1978-81, head central policy unit GLC 1981-83, sr fell Policy Studies Inst 1983-; *Books incl*: Family and Kinship in East London (with Michael Young, 1957), Adolescent Boys of East London (1966), The Symmetrical Family (with Michael Young, 1973), Friendship Networks and Social Support (1987); *Style*— Peter Willmott, Esq; Policy Studies Institute, 100 Park Village East, London NW1 3SR (☎ 01 387 2171, fax 01 388 0914)

WILLNER, Stuart; s of Dr Hugo Willner (d 1946), and Elsa, *née* Gruenbaum (d 1981); *b* 31 August 1925; *Educ* Taunton's GS Southampton, Univ Coll Southampton (BSc); *m* 1 Sept 1954, Lesley Anita, da of Alexander Kari (d 1957); 1 s (Andrew b 1960), 1 da (Alexandra b 1958); *Career* buyer United Africa Co (Unilever) 1954-59, sales mangr Viners of Sheffield 1959-62, int mktg mangr Wilkinson Sword 1962-65, md sheaffer Pen Co 1965-70, owner Senger Promotional Gifts 1970-; gen cmmr of tax Barnet Div 1985-; Freeman City of London 1981, Liveryman Worshipful Co of Tobacco Pipe Makers and Tobacco Blenders 1981; memb IOD 1967; *Recreations* theatre, music, sport; *Style*— Stuart Willner, Esq; 17 Church Crescent, Whetstone, London N20 OJR (☎ 01 368 2989); Pilgrim Cottage, Coleman Green, Wheathampstead, Herts AL4 8ES (☎ 058283 4238, fax 058283 3918)

WILLOUGHBY, Brig the Hon (Henry Ernest) Christopher; 2 s of 11 Baron Middleton, KG, MC, TD (d 1970) ; *b* 12 June 1932; *Educ* Eton, RMA Sandhurst; *m* 7 May 1955, Jean Adini, er da of Lt-Col John David Hills, MC (d 1976), of House by the Dyke, Chirk, Clwyd, and Lady Rosemary Ethel Hills, *née* Baring, da of 2 Earl of Cromer, GCB, GCIE, GCVO, PC; 1 s (Guy Nesbit John b 2 June 1960), 2 da (Angela Jane b 5 Feb 1956, Caroline Rosemary b 22 May 1957); *Career* cmmnd Coldstream Gds 1952; passed Staff Coll 1962; serv BAOR Cyprus, Kenya, S Arabia, Mauritius, Washington DC, N Ireland and Gibraltar; cmd 2 Bn Coldstream Gds 1974-76; finally def and mil attaché in Turkey 1980-83 Brig, presently dept cmdt Corps of Commissionaires; *Recreations* field sports; *Clubs* Army and Navy; *Style*— Brig the Hon Christopher Willoughby; National Westminster Bank Plc, 4 High St, Pangbourne, Berkshire; 3 Crane Court, Fleet St EC4A 2EJ (☎ 01 353 1125)

WILLOUGHBY, Ven David Albert; s of John Robert Willoughby (d 1982), and Jane May, *née* Lilley; *b* 8 Feb 1931; *Educ* Bradford GS, St John's Coll Univ of Durham (BA, Dip Theol); *m* 1959, Brenda Mary, da of Dennis Watson (d 1953); 2 s (Simon, Andrew); *Career* asst curate: St Peter's Shipley 1957-60, Barnoldswick with Bracewell 1960-62; rector St Chad's New Moston Manchester 1962-72; vicar: Marown IOM 1972-80, St Georges with all Saints Douglas IOM 1980-; rural dean of Douglas 1980-82, archdeacon of IOM 1982-; memb Gen Synod 1982-; *Recreations* motor cycling, involvement in light entertainment; *Clubs* Victory Services (London); *Style—* The Ven the Archdeacon of the Isle of Man; St George's with All Saints Vicarage,16 Devonshire Rd, Douglas, Isle of Man (☎ 0624 75430)

WILLOUGHBY, Geoffrey David Mortimer; s of John Lucas Willoughby, OBE (d 1985), and Hilary Winifred Tweedale, *née* Tait; *b* 22 Nov 1936; *Educ* Westminster, Pembroke Coll Cambridge (MA); *m* 28 Oct 1967, Alexandra Hay (Sandy), da of Edward Charlton Mitchell; 2 da (Martha b 16 Jan 1969, Jennifer b 4 March 1972); *Career* Sub Lt RNR 1955-57; Herbert Smith 1964-68 (ptnr 1968); tstee The Petroleum and Mineral Law Educn Tst; *Books* United Kingdom Oil and Gas Law (2 edn ed with Prof Daintith, 1984); *Recreations* sailing, music; *Clubs* Garrick, New York Yacht, American Yacht; *Style—* Geoffrey Willoughby, Esq; 17 Holly Lodge Gdns, London N6 6AA (☎ 01 348 7218); Herbert Smith, Watling House, 35 Cannon St, London EC4M 5SD (☎ 01 489 8000, fax 01 236 5733)

WILLOUGHBY, Hon (John) Hugh Francis; s of 12 Baron Middleton, MC, of Birdsall House, Malton, Yorks, and Janet Marshall-Cornwall, Lady Middleton; *b* 13 July 1951; *Educ* Eton; *Career* Capt Coldstream Gds, served Dhofar War 1974-76, with Sultan of Omans Armed Forces, Actg Maj; conslt IPS Gp; Distinguished Service Medal (Oman) 1976; *Recreations* country pursuits, skiing; *Style—* The Hon John Willoughby; c/o Birdsall House, Malton, N Yorks; 4 Westmoreland Terrace, London SW1

WILLOUGHBY, Maj-Gen Sir John Edward Francis; KBE (1967, CBE 1963, OBE 1953), CB (1966); s of late Maj Noel Edward Grey Willoughby of Manor House, East Horsley and Heytesbury; *b* 18 June 1913; *m* 1938, Muriel, da of Maj Roger Douglas Scott; 3 da; *Career* cmmnd Middx Regt 1933, WW II (BEF, Pacific and NW Europe), in Korea 1950-51, cmd 1 bn in Cyprus 1955, Col AAG WO 1956, Col Middx Regt 1959-65, cmd Inf Bde (TA) 1959-61, COS Hong Kong 1961-62, GOC 48 Div (TA) W Midland Dist 1963-64, Maj-Gen 1963; GOC MELF, Inspr-Gen S Arabian Regular Fed Army, Security Cdr Aden State 1965-67, ret 1967; recalled to active list as Def Advsr to United Arab Emirates 1968, ret 1972; *Clubs* Naval and Military; *Style—* Maj-Gen Sir John Willoughby, KBE, CB; c/o Naval & Military Club, 94 Piccadilly, London W1V 0BP

WILLOUGHBY, Hon Mrs (Lucy Corinna Agneta); *née* Sidney; da of 1 Viscount De L'Isle, VC, KG, GCMG, GCVO, PC, of Penshurst Place, by his 1 w, Jacqueline, *née* Vereker (d 1962), da of Field Marshal 6 Visvount Gort, VC, GCB, CBE, DSO, MVO, MC; *b* 21 Feb 1953; *m* 1974, Hon Michael Charles James Willoughby, s and h of 12 Baron Middleton; 2 s, 3 da; *Style—* The Hon Mrs Michael Willoughby; North Grimston House, Malton, N Yorks

WILLOUGHBY, Hon Michael Charles James; s and h of 12 Baron Middleton, MC; *b* 14 July 1948; *Educ* Eton; *m* 1974, Hon Lucy Corinna Agneta Sidney, da of 1 Viscount De L'Isle, VC, KG, GCMG, GCVO, PC; 2 s (James William Michael b 1976, Charles Edward Henry b 1986), 3 da (Charlotte Jacqueline Louise b 1978, Emma Coralie Sarah b 1981, Rose Arabella Julia b 1984); *Career* Lt Coldstream Gds and Queen's Own Yeomanry; farmer; *Style—* The Hon Michael Willoughby; North Grimston House, Malton, N Yorks YO17 8AX (☎ 094 46 204)

WILLOUGHBY, Rt Rev Noel Vincent; *see*: Cashel and Ossory, Bishop of

WILLOUGHBY, Prof Peter Geoffrey; JP (Hong Kong 1984); s of George James Willoughby (d 1976), and Enid Alberta, *née* Nye; *b* 17 Feb 1937; *Educ* Merchant Taylors', LSE (LLB, LLM); *m* 20 Jan 1962, Ruth Marlyn, da of Frederick William Brunwin (d 1981); 1 s (Richard Stephen William b 1967), 1 da (Sara Jane Bandele b 1964); *Career* RNVR 1954-59; admitted slr 1962, lectr Gibson & Weldon Law Tutor 1962, barr and slr Nigeria 1962, sr lectr The Nigerian Law Sch 1962-66, princ lectr (formerly lectr and sr lectr) The Coll of Law 1966-73, slr Hong Kong 1973, dir of professional legal educn Univ of Hong Kong 1973 (prof of law 1975-86), ptnr Turner Kenneth Brown (London and Hong Kong) 1986-; Hong Kong: memb Advsy Ctee on Legal Educn, chm ctee of inquiry into Public Works Dept 1977, chm ctee on snsur law reform Hong Kong Law Soc; chm revenue law ctee 1973-, memb disciplinary panel 1983-, memb free legal advice panel; memb VAT sub ctee 1973-; memb: Hong Kong Inland Revenue Bd of Review 1977-, Hong Kong Law Reform Cmmn 1980-87, Hong Kong Standing Ctee on Company Law Reform 1983-, Hong Kong Securities Cmmn 1984-, Air Traffic Licensing Authy (Hong Kong 1987), chm Jt Liaison Ctee on Hong Kong Taxation 1986-, memb city of London Slrs Co 1987-; memb Soc 1962; *Books publications*: Hong Kong Revenue Law (Encyclopaedia in 3 looseleaf vols with sixth monthly updates); *Recreations* sailing, sport generally, music, gardening, Siamese cats; *Clubs* RORC, Royal Hong Kong YC, Royal Fowry YC, Lagos YC; *Style—* Prof Peter Willoughby, JP; Littleholme Cottage, 8 Upper Guildown Rd, Guildford, Surrey (☎ 0483 571585); Turner Kenneth Brown, 100 Fetter Lane, London EC4A 1DD (☎ 01 242 6006); 1901 Des Vaeux Rd, Hong Kong (☎ 5 8105081)

WILLOUGHBY, Philip John; s of George James Willoughby (d 1976), of Cawsand, Cornwall, and Enid Alberta, *née* Nye; *b* 6 Oct 1939; *Educ* Merchant Taylors'; *m* 16 May 1964, Susan Elizabeth, da of John Humphriss (d 1971), of Northwood, Middlesex; 1 s (Andrew James b 17 Sept 1965), 1 da (Caroline Louise b 3 March 1969); *Career* RNVR Seaman's Branch 1957-60; articled to predecessor of Clark Whitehill 1957, ptnr 1968; hon tres (formerly chm) Pottery and Glass Trades Benevolent Inst, govr Northwood Coll Sch; Freeman of London 1971, Liveryman of Glass Sellers Co 1971 (Master 1986-87, Hon clerk 1976-); FCA 1968; *Recreations* sailing, cricket, rugby, football, music, the family, golf; *Clubs* MCC, City Livery, OMT Soc, Moor Park GC, Castletown GE (IOM); *Style—* Philip Willoughby, Esq; Penlee, 28 Valley Road, Rickmansworth, Herts WD3 4DS (☎ 0923 775409); Clark Whitehill, 25 New Street Sq, London EC4A 3LN (☎ 01 353 1577, fax 01 583 1720)

WILLOUGHBY, Hon (Thomas Henry) Richard; 3 s of 12 Baron Middleton, MC; *b* 20 Nov 1955; *Educ* Harrow, Univ of Manchester (BSc); *Career* electronics engineer; *Style—* The Hon Richard Willoughby; The Croft, Batts Lane, Steeple, Essex

WILLOUGHBY, Trevor Willoughby; s of Frederick Thomas Willoughby (d 1964), of Red Stacks, Beverly Rd Kirkella, Nr Hull, Yorkshire, and Vera, *née* Ohlson (d 1982); *b* 9 Dec 1926; *Educ* Hymers Coll Hull, Hull Reg Coll of Art; *m* 1, Nov 1957 (m dis), Katherine Anne McLaren, da of Mr Fulton (d 1987), of Johannesburg SA; 2 s (Mark b 1958, Simon b 1959, d 1987); m 2, 12 Aug 1969, Nicola Jane, da of Steven Macoun of Godalming Surrey; 2 s (John b 1973, George Henry b 1981); *Career* WWII Merchant Navy Cadet 1943-47; freelance illustrator (magazines and leading advertisers), painter exhibitions incl: Eight one Man exhibitions, RA, RP mixed; portraits incl: Lord Birkett, James Fisher, Mrs Basil Ferranti, late princ and vice chllr Edinburgh Univ Sir Hugh Robson; memb Royal Soc Portrait Painters 1967; *Recreations* reading, carpentry; *Clubs* Chelsea Arts; *Style—* Trevor Willoughby, Esq; 4 Offerton Rd, Grafton Square, Clapham Old Town, London SW4 0DH (☎ 01 720 5415)

WILLOUGHBY DE BROKE, 21 Baron (E 1491); (Leopold) David Verney; s of 20 Baron Willoughby de Broke (d 1986, descendend from the 1 Baron, who was so cr after after being on the winning side at Bosworth, and was 4 in descent from 4 Baron Willoughby de Eresby); *b* 14 Sept 1938; *Educ* Le Rosey, New Coll Oxford; *m* 1965, his kinswoman Petra, 2 da of Col Sir John Aird, 3 Bt, MVO, MC, and Lady Priscilla Heathcote-Drummond-Willoughby (yr da of 2 Earl of Ancaster); 3 s (Rupert Greville b 1966, John Mark b 1967, Edmund Peyto b 1973); *Heir* s, Rupert Greville b 1966; *Clubs* Whites; *Style—* The Rt Hon Lord Willoughby de Broke; Ditchford Farm, Moreton-in-Marsh, Glos

WILLOUGHBY DE ERESBY, Baroness (E 1313) (Nancy) Jane Marie Heathcote-Drummond-Willoughby; da of 3 Earl of Ancaster (d 1983, when Earldom of Ancaster and Barony of Aveland became extinct, and the Baronetcy of Heathcote passed to his kinsman) and Hon (Nancy) Phyllis Louise Astor (d 1975), da of 2 Viscount Astor; succeeded father in Barony of Willoughby de Eresby; *b* 1 Dec 1934; *Career* a train bearer to HM The Queen at the Coronation 1953; *Style—* The Rt Hon the Lady Willoughby de Eresby; Grimsthorpe Castle, Lincs

WILLS, Dr Arthur William; s of Archibald Wills (d 1950), of Market St, Warwick, and Violet Elizabeth, *née* Davies (d 1971); *b* 19 Sept 1926; *Educ* St John's Sch Coventry, St Nicholas Coll Canterbury, Durham Univ (BMus, DMus); *m* 14 Nov 1953, Mary Elizabeth, da of John Titterton (d 1955), of Downham Rd, Ely; 1 s (Colin b 1956), 1 da (Rachel b 1958); *Career* dir of music King's Sch Ely 1953-65, composer organist Ely Cathedral 1958-, prof and academic tutor RAM 1964-, examiner Royal Schools of Music 1964-; recitals in: Europe, USA, Australia, Hong Kong; Hon RAM, Hon FLCM, ARSCM; FRCO 1948 (cncl memb 1966); *Books* Organ (Menuhin Music Guide Series 1984); compositions: Symphonic Suite The Fenlands (for brass band and organ), Symphony in A Minor, Piano Sonata "1984", Opera "1984", Sonata (for guitar), Concerto (for guitar and organ), A Music of Fire (overture for brass band and organ), Concerto Lirice (for guitar quartet); song cycles: Love's Torment (for counter tenor and guitar or piano/harpsochord), The Dark Lady (for baritone and piano), When the Spirit Comes (for mezzo and piano), A Woman in Love (for Mezzo and guitar), Three Poems of EE Cummings (for terror, oboe and piano); sacrae symphonrae: Veni Creator Spirits (for double wind quartet), Benedicite Miss Eliensis, Resurrection (for organ); *Recreations* travel, antiques, reading; *Clubs* RAM; *Style—* Dr Arthur Wills; The Old Sacristy, The College, Ely, Cambs CB7 4JU (☎ 0353 662 084)

WILLS, Colin Spencer; s of Sir John Spencer Wills, of E Sussex & London, and Elizabeth D A C, *née* Garcke; *b* 25 June 1937; *Educ* Eton, Queens' Coll Cambridge (MA); *Career* dir: Thames Television plc 1970-, Euston Films Co 1971-, English Nat Opera 1975-87, BAFTA 1980-, Wembley Stadium 1975-84, English Nat Ballet 1988-; *Recreations* music, theatre, walking; *Clubs* Whites; *Style—* Colin S Wills, Esq; 12 Campden Hill Square, London W8 7LB; Old Brick Farm, Burwash, E Sussex (☎ 0435 882 234)

WILLS, Sir (Hugh) David Hamilton; CBE (1971), MBE (1946) TD 1964, DL 1967); yr s of Frederick Noel Hamilton Wills (d 1927, himself yr bro of 1 Baron Dulverton) by his w Margery Hamilton, da of Hon Sir Hugh Fraser, sometime High Court Judge. Mrs Wills m, 1942, as her 2 husb, Wing Cdr Huntly Sinclair, Roy Canadian Air Force; *b* 19 June 1917; *Educ* Eton, Magdalen Coll Oxford; *m* 1949, Eva Helen, JP, yst da of Maj Arthur Thomas McMorrough Kavanagh, MC (decd); 1 s, 1 da; *Career* serv WWII Queen's Own Cameron Highlanders (TA); chm of tstees Rendcomb Coll 1955-84, memb governing body Atlantic Coll 1963-73 and 1980-; High Sheriff Oxfordshire 1961; dir Batsford Estates, Farmington Tst pres Ditchley Fndn; kt 1980; *Recreations* fishing and sailing; *Clubs* Boodles, Grillions; *Style—* Sir David Wills, CBE, MBE, TD, DL; Sandford Park, Sandford St Martin, Middle Barton, Oxford (☎ 060 883 238)

WILLS, David James Vernon; s and h of Sir John Vernon Wills, 4 Bt, *qv*; *b* 2 Jan 1955; memb cncl Royal Bath & West and Southern Countries Soc; *Recreations* shooting; *Style—* David Wills Esq

WILLS, Hon Mrs; Hon Elizabeth Anne; *née* Cecil; da of 2 Baron Rockley and Anne Margaret, er da of late Adm Hon Sir Herbert Meade-Featherstonhaugh, GCVO, CB, DSO; *b* 6 July 1939; *m* 1961, Andrew Wills, late Life Gds, s of Maj John Wills (himself gs of Sir Edward Wills, 1 Bt, KCB), of Allanbay Park, Binfield, Berks by Hon Jean, 2 da of 16 Lord Elphinstone, KT, by Lady Mary Bowes-Lyon, DCVO (da of 14 Earl of Strathmore and sis of HM Queen Elizabeth The Queen Mother); 2 s (Richard b 1962, Alexander b 1967), 1 da (Tessa b 1963); *Style—* The Hon Mrs Wills; Middleton House, Longparish, Andover, Hants (☎ 026 472 206)

WILLS, Frederick Hugh Philip Hamilton; s of Capt Michael Desmond Hamilton Wills, MC (ka 1943), and Mary Margaret Gibbs, *née* Mitford; *b* 31 May 1940; *Educ* Eton; *m* 2 Dec 1969, Priscilla Annabelle, da of Capt Alec David Charles Francis, of Malmesbury, Wilts; 2 s (Michael b 1972, Edward b (twin) 1974), 1 da (Clare b (twin) 1974); *Career* Capt II Hussars (PAO): served: N Ireland, Aden, Persian Gulf, Muscat & Oman, BAOR Germany 1959-66; TA Royal Wilts Yeomanry 1967-75; landowner, farmer, forester; hon tres Cirencester and Tewkesbury Cons Assoc 1976-86; *Recreations* fishing, stalking; *Style—* Frederick Wills, Esq; The Old House, Rendcomb, Cirencester, Glos GL7 7EY (☎ 028583 671); Coulin Lodge, Kinlochewe by Achnasheen, Ross-shire, Scotland IV22 2ES (☎ 044584 210)

WILLS, Hon (Robert) Ian Hamilton; yr s of 2 Baron Dulverton, CBE, TD by his 1 w, Judith Betty Dulverton, *née* Leslie Melville (d 1983); *b* 28 June 1948; *Educ* Harrow, Warwick Univ (BA), Royal Agric Coll Cirencester; *m* 1979, Elizabeth Jane, da of Michael Taylor Downes; 1 s (James b 1984), 1 da (Emma b 1982); *Career* farmer; *Recreations* all field sports; *Style—* The Hon Ian Wills; Soundborough Farm, Andoversford, Cheltenham (☎ 0242 820576)

WILLS, Hon Mrs (Jean Constance); *née* Elphinstone; LVO (1983); da of 16 Lord Elphinstone, KT, (d 1955), and Lady Mary Bowes-Lyon, DCVO (d 1961), 2 da of 14 Earl of Strathmore and sis of HM Queen Elizabeth The Queen Mother; *m* 1936, Maj

John Lycett Wills, Life Gds (ret), s of Capt Arnold Wills and gs of Sir Edward Wills, 1 Bt, KCB; 1 s (Andrew *see* Hon Mrs Elizabeth Wills), 1 da (Susan, 2 da decd); *Career* extra Lady-in-Waiting to HRH The Princess Margaret 1970-; *Style*— The Hon Mrs Wills, LVO; Allanbay Park, Binfield, Berks; 11 Rutland Mews, East London SW7

WILLS, Sir John Spencer; s of Cedric Spencer Wills by his w Cécile; *b* 10 August 1904; *Educ* Merchant Taylors' Sch; *m* 1936, Elizabeth Drusilla Garcke; 2 s; *Career* chm British Electric Traction 1966-82 (remains full time exec, md 1946-73, dep chm 1951-66); chm: Birmingham & Dist Investmnt Tst, Electrical & Industl Investmnt Co Wembley Stadium Ltd; former chm Rediffusion TV, Birmingham & Midland Motor Omnibus Co; vice-patron Theatre Royal Windsor Tst, memb UK Cncl European Movement 1966-; FCIT; kt 1969; *Style*— Sir John Spencer Wills; Beech Farm, Battle, E Sussex (☎ 042 46 2950); 1 Campden House Terrace, Kensington Church St, London W8 4BQ (☎ 01 727 5981)

WILLS, Sir John Vernon; 4 Bt (UK 1923), of Blagdon, Co Somerset, TD, JP ((Somerset 1962), DL (1968)); s of Sir George Vernon Proctor Wills, 2 Bt, (d 1931) and bro of 3 Bt (ka 1945); Sir George, 1 Bt, was pres of Imperial Tobacco Co of GB and Ireland of which 2 Bt was a dir; *b* 3 July 1928; *Educ* Eton; *m* 1953, Diana Veronica Cecil (Jane), da of Douglas Ryan Midelton Baker of Winsford, Minehead, Somerset; 4 s (David, Anthony, Rupert, Julian); *Heir* s, David James Vernon, *qv*; *Career* Lt-Col (TA) 1965-67, Bt-Col 1967; Somerset Co alderman 1970, High Sheriff 1968, DL 1968, Ld-Lt and Custos Rotulorum of Avon 1974-; chm Wessex Water Authority to 1982; dep chm: (dir 1973-) Bristol Evening Post 1978-, Bristol Waterworks Co 1983- (chm 1986); chm Bristol & West Building Soc; memb: Nat Water Cncl 1973-82, Bristol local bd Barclays Bank to 1987; pro-chllr Univ of Bath 1979-; KStJ 1978; hon LLD Bristol Univ 1986; hon Capt RNR 1988, FRICS; *Clubs* Cavalry and Guards; *Style*— Sir John Wills, Bt, TD, JP, DL; Langford Court, Langford, Bristol (☎ 0934 862338)

WILLS, Juliet, Lady; Juliet Eve; *née* Graham-Clarke; yr da of late Capt John Eagles Henry Graham-Clarke, JP, of Frocester Manor, Glos; *b* 30 Nov 1920; *m* 29 June 1949, as his 2 w, Sir (Ernest) Edward de Winton Wills, 4 Bt (d 1983; suc by n Sir Seton Wills, Bt, *qv*); *Style*— Juliet, Lady Wills; Mount Prosperous, Hungerford, Berks RG17 0RP; Lochs Lodge, Glen Lyon, Perthshire, PH15 2PU

WILLS, (Thomas) Justin; s of Philip Aubrey Wills, CBE (1978), and Katharine, *née* Fisher; *b* 20 August 1946; *Educ* Bryanston Sch, Pembroke Coll Oxford (MA); *m* 1980, Gillian, da of Maj Samuel Francis Maxwell Howe; *Career* dir of Wills Gp plc 1973-; dep chief exec Wills Tp plc 1984- (dir 1983-); current holder of 10 UK Gliding Recorder Inc Distance Record, Br Team memb World Gliding Championships 1985 and 1987; memb HAC; *Recreations* gliding, fishing, kayaking, skiing; *Style*— Justin Wills, Esq; 55 Holland Park Mews, London W11 (☎ 01 727 0375); Wills Gp plc, 25/35 City Rd, London EC1 (☎ 01 606 6331, fax 01 628 4379, telex 883323)

WILLS, Lady Katharine Anne; da of 6 Earl of Clanwilliam (d 1989); *b* 10 August 1959; *m* 7 Feb 1987, Christopher Aubrey Hamilton Wills, s of Hon (Victor) Patrick Hamilton Wills, *qv*, and Hon Mrs Henry Douglas-Home; *Style*— Lady Katharine Wills; Litchfield Down, Whitchurch, Hants

WILLS, Hon (Gilbert) Michael Hamilton; s (by 1 m) and h of 2 Baron Dulverton, CBE, TD, DL; *b* 2 May 1944; *Educ* Gordonstoun; *m* 1980, Rosalind J M, da of J van der Velde; 1 s (b 20 Oct 1983), 1 da; *Style*— The Hon Michael Wills

WILLS, Nicholas Kenneth Spencer; s of Sir John Spencer Wills of Beech Farm, Battle, Sussex, and Elizabeth Drusilla Alice Clare Fanoke; *b* 18 May 1941; *Educ* Rugby, Queens' Coll Cambridge (MA); *m* 1973 (m dis 1983), Hilary Ann Flood; 2 s, 2 da; m 2, 1985, Philippa Trench Casson; 1 da; *Career* chm: Argus Press Hldgs plc 1974-83, Electrical Press plc 1974-83, Initial plc 1979-87; md: Birmingham & District Investmnt Tst plc 1970-, Electrical & Industl Investmnt plc 1970-, Nat Electric Construction plc 1971-, BET plc 1982- (dir 1975-); dir: American Chamber of Commerce (UK) 1985-, St George Assurance Co Ltd 1974-81, Nat Mutual Life Assurance Soc 1974-85, Colonial Securities Tst Co Ltd 1976-82, Cable Tst Ltd 1976-77, Globe Investment Tst plc 1977-, Drayton Consolidated Tst plc 1982-, Nat Westminster Bank plc (City & West End Advsy Bds) 1982-, United World Colleges (International) Ltd 1987-; tres and churchwarden Church of St Bride Fleet St 1978-, asst Worshipful Co of Haberdashers' 1981-; Boulton and Paul plc 1979-84; chm: BET Building Services Ltd 1984-87, Bradbury Agnew and Co Ltd 1974-83; memb of Cncl CBI 1987-; FCA; CBIM, FCT, FRSA; *Recreations* shooting, sailing, trying to farm in the Highlands; *Clubs* White's, RAC, Clyde Cruising; *Style*— Nicholas Wills Esq; BET plc, Stratton House, Stratton St, Piccadilly, London W1X 6AS (☎ 01 629 8886; telex 299573 Betcl G)

WILLS, Hon (Victor) Patrick Hamilton; DL (Hants); s of late 1 Baron Dulverton, OBE; *b* 1926; *Educ* Eton, Coll of Estate Mgmnt; *m* 1, 1948 (m dis 1962), Felicity Betty, da of late Maj Aubrey Jonsson, Royal Irish Rifles; 2 s, 1 da; m 2, 1963, Jean Felicity Strutt, da of late Hon Francis Erskine (s of 12 Earl of Mar and Kellie); m 3, 2 Jan 1988, Mrs Elizabeth Gilmor Shaw; *Career* Grenadier Gds and Para Regt (ret); CC Hants 1965-73, chm Hants Playing Fields Assoc 1969-79; tstee Dulverton Tst 1949-81; govr Int Students Tst 1965 (dep chm 1971, chm 1984); vice-chm Trident Tst 1972 (chm 1978-80); chm Atlantic Salmon Conservation Tst (Scotland); fell Chartered Land Agents Soc 1957; *Style*— The Hon Patrick Wills, DL; Litchfield Manor, Whitchurch, Hants

WILLS, Peter Gordon Bethune; TD (1967); s of Lionel Wills (d 1967), of Trieste, Italy, and Sita, *née* Stapleton (d 1982); *b* 25 Oct 1931; *Educ* Malvern, CCC Cambridge; *m* 1, 1957, Miss Linda Hutton; 2 s, 1 da; m 2, 1982, Faith Hines; *Career* serv Royal Inniskilling Fusiliers in N Ireland and Korea 1950-52, London Irish Rifles (TA) 1952-67; memb Stock Exchange 1960, ptnr Sheppards and Chase (stockbrokers) 1960-85 (joined 1955), chm Sheppards Moneybrokers Ltd 1985-, memb Cncl of Stock Exchange 1973- (dep chm 1979-82); dir: The Securities Assoc 1986-, London Clear Ltd 1987-, BAII Hldg Ltd 1986-; *Style*— Peter Wills, Esq, TD; 54 Frant Rd, Tunbridge Wells, Kent (☎ 0892 26705)

WILLS, Hon (Edward) Robert Hamilton; s of late 1 Baron Dulverton, OBE; *b* 1918; *Educ* Eton; *Career* Maj late Grenadier Gds (wounded) 1939-45; *Style*— The Hon Robert Wills; Farmington Lodge, Northleach, Glos

WILLS, Hon Sarah May Hamilton; da (by 1 m) of 2 Baron Dulverton, CBE, TD, DL; *b* 1942; *Style*— The Hon Sarah Wills; 8 Montrose Court, Prince's Gate, London SW7

WILLS, Sir (David) Seton; 5 Bt (UK 1904), of Hazelwood, Stoke Bishop, Westbury-on-Trym, Glos, and Clapton-in-Gordano, Somerset; s of Maj George Wills by his first w, Lilah, da of Capt Percy Hare, gs of 2 Earl of Listowel; suc unc, Sir Edward Wills, 4 Bt, (d 1983, *see also* his widow, Juliet, Lady Wills); *b* 29 Dec 1939; *Educ* Eton; *m* 1968, Gillian, twin da of Albert Eastoe; 1 s, 3 da; *Heir* s, James Seton Wills, b 1970; *Career* FRICS; *Style*— Sir Seton Wills, Bt; Eastridge House, Ramsbury, Marlborough, Wilts SN8 2HJ (☎ 0672 20015); Estate office (☎ 0672 20042)

WILLS, Maj (Michael) Thomas Noel Hamilton; s of Capt Michael Desmond Hamilton Wills, MC (d 1943), and Mary Margaret, *née* Mitford; *b* 31 May 1940; *Educ* Eton, Royal Agric Coll Cirencester; *m* 23 Oct 1982, Penelope Ann, da of Ben Howard-Baker, of Glascoed Hall, Llansilin, Oswestry, Shropshire; 1 s (Nicholas James Noel Hamilton b 9 Sept 1983), 1 da (Camilla Jane Hamilton b 27 June 1985); *Career* Coldstream Gds 1959-73; memb: country Landowners Assoc, Timber Growers UK, Royal Forestry Soc, chm League of Friends Stroud Hosp; chm Gloucs Scout Assoc, chm of tstees Rendcomb Coll, jt master Cotswold Hunt; High Sheriff Gloucs 1985; *Recreations* country pursuits; *Clubs* Boodles; *Style*— Major Thomas Wills; Misarden Park, Stroud, Gloucs (☎ 028 582 309); Coulags, Achnashellach, Ross-shire

WILLSON, Hon Mrs Anne Mildred; *née* Curzon; da of 2 Viscount Scarsdale (decd); *b* 1923; *m* 1942 (m dis 1960), Maj Walter James Latimer Willson, DSO, Gren Gds, s of Sir Walter Willson; 1 s, 1 da; *Career* ATS 1942-44; *Style*— The Hon Mrs Anne Willson; Hill Farm, Garsdale, Sedbergh, Cumbria

WILLSON, Prof (Francis Michael) Glenn; s of Christopher Glenn Willson (d 1940), and Elsie Katrine, *née* Mattick (1924); *b* 29 Sept 1924; *Educ* Carlisle GS, Univ of Manchester (BA), Balliol and Nuffield Coll Oxford (MA, DPhil); *m* 23 June 1945, Jean, da of Malcolm Nicol Carlyle (d 1957); 2 da (Judith b 1946, Rosanne b 1953); *Career* MN 1941-42, RAF 1943-47, PO 1944, Flying Offr 1945, Fl-Lt 1946; res offr Royal Inst Pub Admin 1953-60; Univ of Oxford: res fell Nuffield Coll 1955-60, lectr in politics St Edmund Hall 1958-60; Univ Coll of Rhodesia & Nyansaland: prof of govt 1960-64, dean faculty social studies 1962-64; Univ of California Santa Cruz, prof of govt/politics 1965-74, provost Adlai Stevenson Coll 1967-74, vice chllr coll and student affairs 1973-74, visiting prof 1985-; princ Univ of London 1975-78 (warden Goldsmith's Coll 1974-75); Murdoch Univ W Aust: vice chllr 1978-84, emeritus prof 1985; memb: Royal Inst Pub Admin, Political Studies Assoc of UK; *Books* The Organization of British Central Govenment (with D N Chester, 2 ed 1964), Administrators in Action (1961); *Recreations* reading, listening to music; *Style*— Prof Glenn Willson; 32 Digby Mansions, Hammersmith Bridge Rd, London W6 9DF (☎ 01 741 1247)

WILLSON, John Michael; CMG (1988); s of Richard Willson (d 1972), of New Malden, Surrey, and Kathleen, *née* Aldridge (d 1983); *b* 15 July 1931; *Educ* Wimbledon Coll, University Coll Oxford (MA), Trinity Hall Cambridge; *m* 25 Sept 1954, (Phyllis Marian) Dawn, da of William John Richards (d 1970), of Barcombe, Sussex; 2 s (Simon b 8 July 1955, Richard b 17 May 1957), 2 da (Melanie b 2 April 1960, Amanda b 5 March 1962); *Career* Nat Serv Army 1949-51; HM Overseas Civil Serv Nothern Rhodesia 1955-64, Min Overseas Devpt London 1965-70, FCO 1970-: HM ambassador 1983-87 (Ivory Coast, Niger, Burkina), Br high cmmn Zambia 1988-; *Recreations* photography, music, gardening; *Clubs* Royal Cwlth Soc; *Style*— John Willson, Esq, CMG; British High Commission, Po Box 50050, Lusaka, Zambia (☎ 010 260 1 216770, telex 41150)

WILLSON, Stanley William; s of late Stephen Willson; *b* 17 May 1927; *Educ* George Dixon GS; *m* 1957, Rachel, *née* Nickerson; 3 c; *Career* dir: Guardian Royal Exchange Gp (Birmingham) 1960-, Birmingham Citizens Building Soc 1968-77; chm: Co Devpts Ltd 1965-, Cheylesmore Garages Ltd 1968-, Kean & Scott Ltd 1971-79, Aston Martin Lagonda Ltd 1972-75, chm Birmingham Building Soc 1980-82 (dir 1977-80), chm Birmingham & Bridgewater Building Soc 1984-86 (dir 1982-84), Marston Green Garage Ltd 1985-, Birmingham Midshires Building Soc 1986-88; dir St Peters Urban Village Tst; memb cncl soc of Motor Manufacturers and Traders 1973-75; *Recreations* preservation of wild life and countryside, photography; *Style*— Stanley William Willson, Esq; Lapworth House, Wharf Lane, Lapworth, Warwicks R94 5QH (☎ 056 43 3224/ 2994)

WILMOT, Sir Henry Robert; 9 Bt (GB 1759), of Chaddesden, Derbyshire; s of Capt Sir Robert Arthur Wilmot, 8 Bt (d 1974, sometime equerry to HRH The Duke of Gloucester) of Pitcarlie Farm, Auchtermuchty, Fife, and Mrs Juliet Elvira Wilmot, *née* Tufnell; *b* 10 April 1967; *Educ* Eton; *Heir* bro, Charles Sacheverel Wilmot, b 13 Feb 1969; *Recreations* origami, marathon running; *Style*— Sir Henry Wilmot, Bt; 12 Saxe-Coburg Place, Edinburgh EH3 5BR (☎ 031 332 3295)

WILMOT, Michael John Assheton Eardley; s and h of Sir John Eardley-Wilmot, 5 Bt, MVO, DSC; *b* 13 Jan 1941; *Educ* Clifton; *m* 1, 1971, Wendy, da of A J Wolstenholme; 2 s, 1 da; m 2, 1987, Diana, da of R Wallis; 1 da; *Career* md Famous Names Hldgs 1974-86, md Beaufort Hotel; *Style*— Michael Wilmot, Esq; Beaufort Hotel, 33 Beaufort Gardens, London SW3 (☎ 01 584 5252, telex 929200)

WILMOT-SITWELL, Peter Sacheverell; s of Capt Robert Bradshaw Wilmot-Sitwell, RN (d 1946), and Barbara Elizabeth Fisher; *b* 28 Mar 1935; *Educ* Eton, Oxford Univ (BA); *m* 1960, Clare Veronica, da of Ralph H Cobbold; 2 s, 1 da; *Career* memb Stock Exchange 1960, 1982-86 sr ptnr Rowe & Pitman (stockbrokers), until merger with Mercury International Group, jt chm Warburg Securities, chm Rowe & Pitman Ltd 1986; *Recreations* shooting, golf; *Clubs* White's, Swinley Forest Golf, Pratt's; *Style*— Peter Wilmot-Sitwell, Esq; Portman House, Dummer, nr Basingstoke, Hants; Warburg Securities, 1 Finsbury Avenue, London EC2M 2PA (☎ 01606 1066; telex 937011 8952485)

WILMSHURST, John; s of Alfred William Wilmshurst, and Frances May, *née* Handy; *b* 30 Jan 1926; *Educ* Maidstone GS, Univ Coll Oxford (MA); *m* 31 March 1951, Patricia Edith, da of R John W Hollis, MBE; 1 s (Jonathon 1968), 3 da (Letitia 1953, Felicity 1955, Priscilla 1960); *Career* Lt RASC 1945-58; patents offr Glaxo Laboratories Ltd 1950-52, gp advertising mangr Reed Int Ltd 1952-59, dir Roles & Parker Ltd 1959-67, md Stuart Advertising Ltd 1967-71, chm and chief exec John Wilmshurst Mktg Consultants Ltd 1971-; memb: gen cncl Church Missionary Soc 1970-78, church warden Farleigh Parish Church 1979-82, Kent Playing Fields Assoc, Chartered Inst of Mktg (chm Kent branch 1972), SE Publicity Club, ctee Oxford Soc; Freeman City of London, Liveryman Worshipful Co of Carmen; FCIM 1986, FCAM 1982; *Books* The Fundamentals and Practice of Marketing (1978), The Fundamentals of Advertising (1985); *Recreations* birdwatching, horse-racing, theatre, music, collecting first editions; *Clubs* City Livery; *Style*— John Wilmshurst, Esq; The Stable Cottage, East Farleigh, Kent (☎ 0622 28241)

WILSHERE, Jonathan Edward Owen; s of H Owen Wilshere MBE (d 1963), of Kirby Muxloe, Leicestershire, and Margaret Elsie, *née* Hughes, LRAM (d 1981); *b* 24 June 1936; *Educ* Rugby Sch; *m* 27 July 1974, Daphne Vivien Maureen, da of Reuben Racey (d 1977), of Leicester; 2 s (Nicholas Edward Antony b 1978, Andrew Thomas Hugh b 1984); *Career* proprietor: Chamberlain Music & Books 1970-, Leicester Research Services 1968-; memb Leics CC 1970-; fndr and chm Leics Family History Soc (vice-pres and life memb 1987); ACIS 1965, FCII 1961, FRMetS 1984, memb AGRA 1976; *Recreations* historical research, photography, music, cricket statistics, meteorology; *Clubs* Leicestershire County CC (life memb), Leicestershire Tst for Nature Conservation (life memb); *Style*— Jonathan Wilshere, Esq; 134 London Rd, Leicester (☎ 0533 543405)

WILSHIRE, David; MP (Cons Spelthorne 1987-); *b* 16 Sept 1943; *Educ* Kingswood Sch Bath, Fitzwilliam Coll Cambridge; *m* 1967, Margaret; 1 s (Simon b 1971), 1 da (Sarah b 1969, d 1981); *Career* sr ptnr Western Political Res Servs, co-dir political mgmnt programme Brunel Univ; former ldr Wansdyke DC (Avon); *Style*— David Wilshire, Esq, MP; 55 Cherry Orchard, Staines, Middx (☎ 0784 50822); House of Commons, London SW1A 0AA (☎ 01 219 4017)

WILSKI, Andrew; s of Ingénieur Boguslaw Jaloszynski, of Piotrowek, Warsaw, and Janina Zofia Zalewska; *b* 2 April 1947; *Educ* Reytan GS, Med Acad Warsaw (DM), Univ of London (DPM, MRC Psych); *m* 2 April 1982, Phillippa, da of Patrick Green, of Freshfields, Harpenden, Herts; 3 s (Alexis b 1983, Nicholas b 1984, Piers b 1986); *Career* conslt psychiatrist Royal Tunbridge Wells Health Authy; former conslt psychotherapist Univ of Essex; lectr Herts Coll of Art; community psychiatrist Mental Health Centre London; sr registrar Westminster Hosp; memb Assoc of Christian Psychiatrists; *Books* Cultural Resources and Psychiatric Rehabilitation (1985); *Recreations* travel, reading, arts, photography; *Style*— Andrew Wilski, Esq; 4 Berkeley Rd, Mount Sion, Royal Tunbridge Wells, Kent (☎ 0892 27304)

WILSON, Prof Alan Geoffrey; s of Harry Wilson (d 1987), of Darlington, County Durham, and Gladys, *née* Naylor; *b* 8 Jan 1939; *Educ* Queen Elizabeth GS Darlington, Corpus Christi Coll Cambridge (BA, MA); *m* 17 April 1987, Sarah Caroline Fildes; *Career* scientific offr Rutherford Laboratory 1961-64, res offr Inst of Econs and Statistics Univ of Oxford 1964-66, mathematical advsr Miny of Transport 1966-68, asst dir Centre for Environmental Studies 1968-70; Univ of Leeds: prof of urban and regnl geography 1970-, chm bd of arts econs and social studies and law 1984-86, pro-vice-chancellor 1989-; memb Oxford City Cncl 1964-67, memb and vice-chm Kirklees AHA 1979-81, vice-chm Dewsbury Dist Health Authy 1982-86; *Books* Entropy in urban and regional modelling (1970), Catastrophe theory and bifuration (1981), Geography and the environment (1981); *Recreations* fell running; *Style*— Prof Alan Wilson; Colton House, Burnsall, N Yorks BD23 6BN (☎ 075 672 682); School of Geography, Univ of Leeds, Leeds LS2 9JT (☎ 0532 333320, fax 0532 333308)

WILSON, Alan Herbert; s of Herbert Wilson (d 1968), and Muriel Rahab Penelope, *née* Morley (d 1966); *b* 6 Sept 1918; *Educ* Doncaster GS, Leeds Sch of Architecture (DipArch); *m* 6 Oct 1952, Gwendoline, da of William Watt (d 1960); 2 da (Janet Ruth (Mrs Warburton) b 2 Oct 1954, Judith Helen b 13 Oct 1960); *Career* RE 1939-46; chief draughtsman to Chief Engr Aerodromes 1942-44 (despatches 1944), superintending draughtsman to Chief Engr MEF 1944-45 (certificate for outstanding serv 1945), chief instr (building) Army Formation Coll Scotland 1945-46; sr ptnr T H Johnson & Son 1968-77 (asst 1948-49, jr ptnr 1949-61, full ptnr 1962-77); sr hon architect Sue Ryder Fndn 1977-, hon architect Burghley House Preservation Tst 1982-; second prize London Airport Competition 1945, Civic Tst Award, Design Award for Stone 1981; chm: Doncaster Round Table 1952, Doncaster Devpt Ctee 1970-74, Potteric Carr Drainage Bd 1968-82, Doncaster Civic Tst 1969-77, Sue Ryder Fndn; sec Collyweston Slaters Tst; Doncaster Borough CC: cncllr 1966-68, Alderman 1968-74, ldr of cncl 1968-70, cncllr S Yorks Co Cncl; ARIBA 1949, FRIBA 1957; *Recreations* gardening, bridge; *Style*— Alan Wilson, Esq; Ostlers House, 1 Stamford Rd, South Luffenham, Rutland LE15 8NT (☎ 0780 721 224); 11 Rue de Noisitiers, Llauro, Thuir, France 66 300 (☎ 010 3368 394 036)

WILSON, Sir Alan Herries; s of H Wilson; *b* 2 July 1906; *Educ* Wallasey GS, Emmanuel Coll Cambridge; *m* 1934, Margaret Monks (d 1961); 2 s; *Career* fellow Emmanuel Coll Cambridge 1929-33; fellow and lectr Trinity Coll and lectr mathematics Cambridge Univ 1933-45; former chm: Glaxo Gp, Ctee Coal Derivatives, Ctee on Noise, Nuclear Safety Advsy Ctee, Central Advsy Water Ctee; chm: governing body Nat Inst Agric Engrg 1971-76, govrs Bethlehem Royal and Maudsley Hosps 1973-80; dep chm Courtaulds 1957-62 (joined 1945, md 1954); part-time memb and dep chm Electricity Cncl 1959; prime warden Goldsmiths' Co 1969-70; hon fell Emmanuel Coll 1929-33; FRS, Hon FIChemE, Hon FInstP, Hon FIMA; Hon DSc: Oxon, Edinburgh Univ; *Style*— Sir Alan Wilson; 65 Oakleigh Park South, Whetstone, London N20 9JL (☎ 01 445 3030)

WILSON, Lady Alexandra Patricia Gwendoline; da of 2 Earl Jellicoe, DSO, MC, PC; *b* 1944; *m* 1970, (Edward) Philip Wilson *qv*, s of Peter Wilson, CBE, *qv*; *Style*— Lady Alexandra Wilson; 28 Highbury Place, London N5

WILSON, (Francis) Amcotts; s of Cdr Alec Thomas Lee Wilson, RN (d 1956), of Garth Hse, Llangammard Wells, Powys, and Margaret Mina Philipina, *née* Hirsch (d 1966); *b* 3 Jan 1922; *Educ* Shrewsbury, (Nat Cert Mechanical Engrg); *m* 1 March 1968, Katherine Mary, da of Robert Charles Bruce, MC (d 1952), of 79 Cadogan Sq, London SW1; 1 s (Robert Mathew b 21 March 1970), 1 da (Jane Mary b 22 Jan 1972); *Career* HO rating RN 1941, Sub Lt RNVR served Atlantic, home waters and Med 1942-45; farmer 1950, memb Lloyds 1962; memb: Builth RDC 1960-67, Breconshire CC 1967-74; chm St John Cncl Brecknock 1980-, Community Cncl 1986-; High Sheriff Powys 1974-75; *Recreations* shooting, fishing; *Clubs* Army & Navy; *Style*— Amcotts Wilson, Esq; Garth Hse, Llangammarch Wells, Powys LN4 4AL

WILSON, Andrew Norman; s of Lt-Col Norman Wilson (d 1985), and Jean Dorothy, *née* Crowder; *b* 27 Oct 1950; *Educ* Rugby, New Coll Oxford (MA); *m* 1971, Katherine Dorothea, da of late Prof Austin Ernest Duncan-Jones; 2 da; *Career* author; Chancellor's Essay Prize 1971, Ellerton Theological Prize 1975, John Llewellyn Rhys Memorial Prize 1978, Somerset Maugham Prize, Arts Cncl Nat Book Award, Southern Arts Prizes 1981, W H Smith Prize 1983; FRSL 1981; *Books* The Sweets of Pimlico (1977), Unguarded Hours (1978), Kindly Light (1979), The Laird of Abbotsford (1980), The Healing Art (1980), Who Was Oswald Fish? (1981), Wise Virgin (1982), The Life of John Milton (1983), Scandal (1983), Hilaire Belloc (1984), How Can We Know? (1985), Gentlemen in England (1985), Love Unknown (1986), Stray (1987), Penfriends from Porlock (1988), Tolstoy (1988), Incline Or Hearts (1988), The Tabitha Stories (1988); *Clubs* Travellers', Scottish Arts (Edinburgh); *Style*— Andrew Wilson, Esq; c/o A D Peters Ltd, 10 Buckingham St, London WC2 (☎ 01 839 2556)

WILSON, Sir Angus Frank Johnstone; CBE (1968); s of William Johnstone-Wilson; *b* 11 August 1913; *Educ* Westminster, Merton Coll Oxford; *Career* novelist and playwright; prof Eng literature Univ of E Anglia 1966-78 (emeritus 1978); memb: Royal Literary Fund 1966, Arts Cncl 1967; pres: Powys Soc 1970-80, Dickens Fellowship 1974-75, Kipling Soc 1981-88, Royal Society of Literature 1982-88; chm Nat Book League 1971-74; FRSL, CLitt; Hon LittD Liverpool; Hon DLit: Leicester, E Anglia, Sussex, Sorbonne; Chev de l'Ordre des Arts et des Lettres 1972; kt 1980; *Books incl*: The Wrong Set (1949), Such Darling Dodos (1950), Hemlock and After (1952), The Middle Age of Mrs Eliot (1958, winner of James Black Memorial Prize and Prix du Meilleur Roman Etranger), The Old Men at the Zoo (1961), Late Call (1964), As If By Magic (1973); *biographies* Emile Zola (1952), The World of Charles Dickens (1970), The Strange Ride of Rudyard Kipling (1976), Setting the World on Fire (1980); *Style*— Sir Angus Wilson, CBE; BP 95, 13533 St Remy Cedex, France (☎ 909 23 436)

WILSON, Sir Anthony; s of Charles Ernest Wilson (d 1930), of Kirkstall, Leeds, and Martha Clarice, *née* Mee (d 1943); *b* 17 Feb 1928; *Educ* Giggleswick Sch; *m* 18 June 1955, (Margaret) Josephine, da of Maj Joseph Henry Hudson, CBE, MC, DL (d 1977), of Hill Top House, Wetherby, Yorkshire; 2 s (Duncan Henry b 1957, Oliver Charles b 1964), 1 da (Victoria Margaret (Mrs Mathews) b 1960); *Career* CA, head Government Accountancy Serv and accountancy advsr to HM Treasury 1984-; ptnr Price Waterhouse 1961-84; memb Mgmnt Bd of South West Arts 1983-; cncl memb of Inst of Chartered Accountants in England and Wales 1985-; memb: Accounting Standards Ctee 1984-, Auditing Practices Ctee 1987-; pres Chandos Chamber Choir 1986-88, chm Dorset Opera 1988-; Freeman of City of London, memb Court of Worshipful Co of Needlemakers 1988, Liveryman of Worshipful Co of Chartered Accountants; FCA, AIIA; kt 1988; *Recreations* fishing, golf, gardening, opera, music; *Clubs* Reform; *Style*— Sir Anthony Wilson; The Barn House, 89 Newland, Sherborne, Dorset DT9 3AG (☎ 0935 815674); HM Treasury, Parliament Street, London SW1P 3AG (☎ 01 270 5177)

WILSON, Brian John; s of Andrew Wilson (d 1983), and Alice Margaret,*née* Dickel; *b* 17 May 1944; *Educ* Enfield GS; *m* 26 March 1966, Pamela Florence, da of Joseph Thomas Wansell; 2 da (Jane b 1967, Susan b 1971); *Career* articled clerk Charles Comins & Co 1960-66, CA 1966; Ernst & Whinney 1966- : joined 1966, ptnr 1973-, i/c public sector services 1983-88, ptnr i/c specialist industries 1988-; FCA; *Recreations* sailing; *Clubs* Stone SC; *Style*— B J Wilson, Esq; Ernst & Whinney, Becket House, 1 Lambeth Palace Rd, London SE1 7EU (☎ 01 928 2000, fax 01 928 1345)

WILSON, Brian Vincent; s of Reginald Wilson (d 1976), of Dublin, and Josephine, *née* Murphy (d 1980); *b* 10 July 1945; *Educ* Clongowes Wood Coll Co Kildare Ireland, Univ Coll Dublin (BA), Trinity Coll Dublin (MBA); *m* 16 Oct 1968, Frances Mary Carroll, da of Thomas Carroll (d 1978), of Dublin; 1 s (Stephen b 11 Dec 1973), 2 da (Samantha b 24 July 1969, Eugenie b 25 May 1971); *Career* private indust 1968-71, sr exec Industl Credit Co 1971-73, mangr banking (later dir and gen mangr GB) Allied Investment Bank 1974-83, gp gen mangr GB Allied Irish Banks 1983-; *Recreations* cricket, golf, rugby, opera; *Clubs* Reform, Wentworth GC, MCC; *Style*— Brian Wilson, Esq; Allied Irish Bank Plc, Belmont Rd, Uxbridge, Middx UB8 1SA (☎ 0895 72222, fax 0895 39774)

WILSON, Charles Martin; s of Adam Wilson (d 1964), and Ruth Ann Wilson (d 1974); *b* 18 August 1935; *Educ* Eastbank Acad Glasgow; *m* 1, 18 Jan 1968 (m dis 1973), Anne Josephine, da of Bernard Robinson; 1 da (Emma Alexandra b 1970); m 2, 2 Oct 1980, Sally Angela O'Sullivan, da of L J Connell; 1 s (Luke Adam b 1981), 1 da (Lily Joan b 1985); *Career* dep night news ed Daily Mail 1963, followed by exec jobs at The Daily Mail including sports ed and dep Northern ed, asst ed London Evening News; ed: Glasgow Evening Times 1976, Glasgow Herald 1981, The Sunday Standard from its launch 1982; exec ed Times 1982, ed Chicago Sunday Times 1984, jt dep ed The Times 1984, ed The Times Nov 1985-; *Recreations* writing, reading, watching steeplechasing; *Clubs* Reform; *Style*— Charles M Wilson, Esq; The Times, 1 Pennington St, London E1 (☎ 01 782 5145, fax 01 782 5142)

WILSON, Hon Charles Thomas; s of 3 Baron Nunburnholme (d 1974) by his 1 w, late Lady Mary Alexander Thynne, youngest da of 5 Marquess of Bath; hp of bro, 4 Baron; *b* 27 May 1935; *Educ* Ludgrove, Eton; *m* 1969 (m dis), Linda Kay, only da of Cyril James Stephens of Woodlands, Challock Lees, Ashford, Kent; 1 s (Stephen), 1 da (Nathalia); *Career* page of honour to HM King George VI 1950-52; memb Stock Exchange 1956-66; co dir; *Clubs* White's; *Style*— The Hon Charles Wilson; c/o Banco Fonseca Y Burnay, Portimao, Portugal

WILSON, Colin Christopher; s of late Ninian Jameson Reid-Wilson, of Bournemouth, England, and Margaret Elizabeth, *née* Briscoe (d 1958); *b* 6 Sept 1941; *Educ* St Peter's Sch Bournemouth, Coll of Law; *m* 11 Sept 1965, Priscilla Joan, da of Bruce Osborne (d 1960), of Calcutta, India; 2 s (Simon Christopher b 1971, Daniel James b 1977); *Career* slr 1966, sr ptnr Turners Bournemouth 1985-; hon slr: Wimborne and Dist Community Assoc, St Thomas Garnet Sch; memb Law Soc; *Recreations* sailing, tennis, skiing; *Style*— Colin Wilson, Esq; Chalbury Grange, Chalbury, Wimborne, Dorset (☎ 0258 840465); 1 Poole Rd, Bournemouth, Dorset (☎ 0202 291291, fax 0202 23606, telex 41158 JUMBOS G)

WILSON, Colin Henry; s of Arthur Wilson, and Annetta Wilson; *b* 26 June 1931; *Educ* Leicester Gateway Sch; *m* 2, 1973, Pamela Joy, da of John Arthur Stewart (d 1972); 1 s (Roderick, from 1 m); 2 s (Damon, Rowan), 1 da (Sally); *Career* writer in residence Hollins (VA) Coll 1966-67; visiting prof: Univ of Washington Seattle 1967, Rutgers Univ New Brunswick NJ 1974; author; *books incl*: The Outsider (1956), Ritual in the Dark (1960), The Mind Parasites (1966), The Black Room (1970), The Occult (1971), Criminal History of Mankind (1983), The Essential Colin Wilson (1984), The Personality Surgeon (1986), Spiderworld 1987; *Recreations* walking, swimming; *Clubs* Savage; *Style*— Colin Wilson, Esq; Gorran Haven, Cornwall PL26 6NT

WILSON, Sir David; 3 Bt (UK 1920), of Carbeth, Killearn, Co Stirling; s of Sir John Mitchell Harvey Wilson, 2 Bt, KCVO (d 1975), by his w, Mary Elizabeth (d 1979); *b* 30 Oct 1928; *Educ* Deerfield Acad Mass USA, Harrow, Oriel Coll Oxford; *m* 1955, Eva Margareta, da of Tore Lindell, of Malmö, Sweden; 2 s, 1 da; *Heir* s, Thomas David Wilson; *Career* barr Lincoln's Inn 1953, solicitor 1962, ptnr Simmons & Simmons 1963-; *Recreations* sailing; *Clubs* Arts, Royal Southern Yacht; *Style*— Sir

David Wilson, Bt; Tandem House, Queen's Drive, Oxshott, Surrey KT22 0PH (☎ 037 284 2061); Simmons & Simmons, 14 Dominion St, London EC2M 2RJ (☎ 01 628 2020, telex 888562)

WILSON, (Christopher) David; CBE (1968), MC (1945); s of James Anthony Wilson (d 1921); *b* 17 Dec 1916; *Educ* St George's Sch Windsor, Aldenham; *m* 1947, Jean Barbara, nee Smith; *Career* Capt RA; business mangr Assoc Newpapers Ltd 1955-57, dir Assoc Rediffusion Ltd 1956-57; chm: Southern TV Ltd (dir and gen mangr 1957-59, md 1956-76) 1976-81, ITN Ltd 1970-72 (dir 1967-72); FCA; *Recreations* music, sailing; *Clubs* MCC, Royal Southern Yacht; *Style—* David Wilson, Esq, CBE, MC; Little Croft, Upham, Southampton, Hants (☎ 048 96 204); Avenida De La Marina, Espanola 14-4, Javea, Alecante, Spain

WILSON, Sir David Mackenzie; s of Rev Joseph Wilson (d 1988), of Castletown, Isle of Man; *b* 30 Oct 1931; *Educ* Kingswood Sch, St John's Coll Cambridge (MA, LittD), Lund Univ Sweden; *m* 1955, Eva, da of late Dr G Sjögren, of Stockholm; 1 s, 1 da; *Career* asst keeper British Museum 1954-66 (dir 1977-); reader archaeology of Anglo-Saxon period Univ of London 1966-71 (prof medieval archaeology 1971-76); jt head Dept Scandinavian Studies UCL 1973-76 (dean of Faculty of Arts 1973-76); govr Museum of London 1976-81, tstee Nat Museums of Scotland 1985-87; memb Ancient Monuments Bd for England 1976-84, former pres British Archaeological Assoc; hon fell: St John's Cambridge, Univ Coll London; FSA, FBA; Order of Polar Star (Sweden, first class) 1977; kt 1984; *books incl*: The Anglo Saxons, Viking Art, Catalogue of Anglo-Saxon Metalwork 700-1100 in the British Museum; and publications on the Vikings and St Ninian's Isle Treasure and the Bayeux Tapestry; *Clubs* Athenaeum; *Style—* Sir David Wilson; British Museum, London WC1B 3DG

WILSON, Des; s of Albert Wilson, of Oamuru NZ, and Ellen, *née* Hoskins; *b* 5 Mar 1941; *Educ* Waitiki Boys HS NZ; *m* 1, (m dis 1984); 1 s (Timothy), 1 da (Jacqueline); m 2, 24 May 1985, Jane, da of Maurice Dunmore, of Brighton; *Career* journalist; columnist: The Guardian 1968-71, The Observer 1971-75, ed Social Work Today 1976-79, dep ed The Illustrated London News 1979-81; dir Shelter 1967-71, memb nat exec Nat Cncl for Civil Liberties 1971-73, head public affairs RSC 1974-76; chm: CLEAR 1982-, Friends of the Earth 1983-86, Citizens Action 1984-, Campaign for Freedom of Info 1984-; Lib pty: memb cncl 1973-74 and 1984-85, memb Fed Exec 1988-89; *Books* I know it was the Place's Fault (1970), Des Wilson's Minority Report - a diary of protest (1973), So you want to be a Prime Minister; a personal view of British politics (1979), The Head Scandal (1982), Pressure, the A to Z of Campaigning in Britain (1984), The Environmental Crisis (ed 1984), The Secrets File (ed 1984), The Citizen Action Handbook (1986), Battle for Power - Inside the Alliance General Election Campaign (1987); *Clubs* National Liberal, Groucho's; *Style—* Des Wilson, Esq; 46 Arundel St, Brighton, Sussex; 3 Endsleigh St, London WC1 (☎ 01 278 9686)

WILSON, Sir (Robert) Donald; DL (Cheshire 1987-); s of John Wilson, and Kate Wilson; *b* 6 June 1922; *Educ* Grove Park Sch Wrexham Clwyd; *m* 1946, Elizabeth; *Career* RAF; landowners; Tyre industry 1946-60, dir of various farming and property cos 1954-; chm: Electricity Consultative Cncl (NW) 1981-85, Mersey Regnl Health Authy 1982-, Cheshire CLA 1979-81; bd memb NW Electricity Bd (NORWEB) 1981-85, memb Lloyds 1970-; pres Ayreshire Cattle Soc 1966-67; High Sheriff Cheshire 1985-86; kt 1987; *Recreations* fishing, countryside generally; *Clubs* Chester City, Farmers; *Style—* Sir Donald Wilson; The Oldfields, Pulford, Chester

WILSON, Douglas George; CB (1984); s of William John Wilson (d 1932), of Ipswich Qld, and Mary Catherine Mitchell (d 1966); *b* 21 Jan 1924; *Educ* St Joseph's Coll Nudgee Qld (MB BS); *m* 1951, Heloise, da of John Joseph McCormack (d 1972), of Ipswich Qld; 1 s (Drewe); *Career* served Royal Aust Artillery AIF 1942-44, Pacific Area, RAAMC 1953-64 (RL) Capt; RMO Brisbane Hosp 1952-33, Gen Practice Coloundra Qld 1954-65, dep MOH NSW Dept of Pub Health 1965-67, chief govt medical offr Qld 1968-84 (ret 1984); memb: Br Acad of Forensic Sciences, Forensic Science Soc, Int Assoc for Accident of Traffic Medicine, Australian & Pacific Area Police Medical Offrs Assoc, Qld Traffic Advsy Ctee 1975-, dep chm Medical Div and memb Int Medical Cmmn XII Cwlth Games Brisbane 1982; Nat Health & Medical Research Cncl Travelling Fellowship in Forensic Medicine 1975, Fulbright sr scholar in Traffic Medicine, Central Missouri State Univ 1978, IAATM Gold Medal for Achievement in Traffic Medicine 1985; DPH, DMJ, SA; *Publications* Rationale of the Determination of Blood Alcohol Concentration by Breath Analysis (Trg Manual, 1968), numerous papers on alcohol, drugs and traffic safety, and forensic subjects in learned journals; *Recreations* swimming, boating, golf, tropical fruit farming; *Clubs* Univ of Qld Caloundre Services, Power Boat, Golf; *Style—* Dr Douglas George Wilson; 3 Alfred St, Caloundra, Qld 4551, Australia (☎ 071 911610)

WILSON, Lady; Elizabeth Anne Martin; da of Charles James Nicol Fleming (d 1947), and Katherine, *née* Cunningham; *b* 7 Sept 1911; *Educ* St Leonard's Scotland, Lady Margaret Hall Oxford (MA); *m* 1937, Sir (Archibald) Duncan Wilson, GCMG (d 1983, ambass to Yugoslavia and USSR, and master of Corpus Christi Coll Cambridge), s of Archibald Edward Wilson (d 1924); 1 s decd, 2 da; *Publications* The Modern Russian Dictionary for English Speakers (1981); *Style—* Lady Wilson; Cala Na Ruadh, Port Charlotte, Islay, Argyll PA48 7TS (☎ 049 685 289)

WILSON, Hon Geoffrey Hazlitt; yr s of 1 Baron Moran, MC (d 1977), and Dorothy, *née* Dufton, MBE (d 1983); *b* 28 Dec 1929; *Educ* Eton, King's Coll Cambridge (BA); *m* 19 May 1955, (Barbara) Jane, o da of William Edward Hilary Hebblethwaite, of Itchen Stoke, Alresford, Hants; 2 s (Nicholas b 1957, Hugo b 1963), 2 da (Laura b 1966, Jessica b 1967); *Career* 2 Lt RHG 1948-49; joined English Electric 1956, dep comptroller 1965, fin controller (overseas) GEC 1968; Delta plc: fin dir cables divn 1969, elected to main bd as gp fin dir 1972, jt md 1977, dep ch exec 1980, ch exec 1981-88, chm 1982-; dir: Blue Circle Industries plc, English & Int Tst plc, Nat Westminster Bank plc (W Midlands and Wales region); dep pres Engrg Employers Fedn 1986-, pres British Electro- technical and Allied Manufacturers' Assocs 1987-88; hon memb Hundred Gp 1985 (chm 1979-81); memb: cncl Inst of Company and Management Accountants 1972-78, Accounting Standards Ctee 1978-79, admin cncl The Royal Jubilee Tsts 1979-88 (hon tres 1980-89), cncl Winchester Cathedral Tst, cncl St Mary's Hosp Med Sch 1985-88, mgmnt bd Prince's Royal Jubilee Tsts 1988-89; memb Ct of Assistants, Worshipful Co of CAs (jr warden 1986-87, sr warden 1987-88, master 1988-89); FCA 1955, FCMA 1959; *Recreations* family, reading, vintage cars; *Clubs* Boodle's, RAC; *Style—* The Hon Geoffrey Wilson; Delta plc, 1 Kingsway, London WC2B 6XF (☎ 01 836 3535, telex 27762)

WILSON, Sir Geoffrey Masterman; KCB (1969, CB 1968), CMG (1962); s of Alexander Wilson; *b* 7 April 1910; *Educ* Manchester GS, Oriel Oxford; *m* 1946, Julie Stafford Trowbridge; 2 s, 2 da; *Career* chm Oxfam 1977-, chm Race Rels Bd 1971-77, dep sec-gen Cwlth Secretariat 1971, perm sec Miny Overseas Devpt 1968-70 (dep sec 1966-68), vice-pres Int Bank Washington DC 1961; hon fellow Wolfson Coll Cambridge 1971; *Style—* Sir Geoffrey Wilson, KCB, CMG; 4 Polstead Rd, Oxford

WILSON, (William) George; OBE (1960); s of William James Wilson (d 1965), and Susannah, *née* Barnfather (d 1967); *b* 19 Feb 1921; *Educ* Blaydon GS; *m* 29 March 1948, Freda, da of David Richard Huddleston (d 1927); 3 s (David b 1951, Richard b 1962, Edward b 1966); *Career* Royal Signals 1940-46; Min of Health 1939-40, Colonial Off 1947-57, fin sec Mauritius 1957-60, Dept of Tech Co-op 1960-62; Min of Health: hosp planning and design 1962-1968, DHSS 1970-81, under sec NHS Mgmnt and controller Social Security Mgmnt, ret 1981; admin UK- Kuwait Health Services Co-op 1981-83, dir and chief exec Paul James & George Wilson Ltd Health Serv Devpt Advsrs 1983-; memb N Tyneside Community Health Cncl 1976-80, librarian Soc of Antiquaries Newcastle Upon Tyne 1977-81; *Recreations* gardening; *Clubs* Royal Cwlth, Royal Overseas; *Style—* George Wilson, Esq, OBE; Clarghyll Hall, Alston, Cumbria CA9 3NF; Paul James & George Wilson Ltd, 207 Victoria St, London SW1E 5NE (☎ 01 630 9693, fax 01 630 9840)

WILSON, Gerald Robertson; s of Charles Robertson Wilson, of Edinburgh, and Margaret, *née* Early; *b* 7 Sept 1939; *Educ* Edinburgh Univ (MA); *m* 11 May 1963, Margaret Anne, da of John Wight, of Edinburgh (d 1970); 1 s (Christopher b 1968), 1 da (Catherine b 1964); *Career* civil serv Private Sec (Lord Privy Seal) 1972-74, cllr UK Representation Brussels 1977-82, asst sec Scottish Off 1974-77 (1982-84), under sec Indust Dept for Scotland 1984-88, sec Scottish Educn Dept 1988-; *Recreations* music; *Clubs* Royal Cwlth Soc, New (Edinburgh); *Style—* Gerald Wilson, Esq; Scottish Educn Dept, Scottish Office, New St Andrews House, Edinburgh

WILSON, (Robert) Gordon; s of Robert George Wilson, of Glasgow; *b* 16 April 1938; *Educ* Douglas HS, Edinburgh Univ (BL), Dundee Univ (LLD); *m* 1965, Edith Margaret Hassall; 2 da; *Career* MP (SNP) Dundee East Feb 1974-87; SNP: nat sec 1964-71, vice-chm 1972-73, sr vice-chm 1973-74, dep ldr Parly Gp 1974-79, chm 1979-; rector Dundee Univ 1983-86; solicitor; *Style—* Gordon Wilson, Esq; 48 Monifieth Rd, Broughty Ferry, Dundee DD5 2RX (☎ 0382 79009)

WILSON, Graeme McDonald; CMG (1975); s of Robert Linton McDonald Wilson (d 1929), and Sophie Hamilton, *née* Milner (d 1953); *b* 9 May 1919; *Educ* Rendcomb Coll, Schloss Schule Salem, Lincoln Coll Oxford (war degree); *m* 6 Nov 1968, Masae (Mayumi), da of Tokichi Yabu, of Fukui, Japan; 3 s (Mark, Jiro, Christopher); *Career* Lt Cdr Fleet Air Arm RNVR 1950-53 (Lt 1939-46), Lt Cdr RCNR 1953-56; private sec to parly sec Miny of Civil Aviation 1946-49, planning 1 Miny of Civil Aviation 1945-53, dep UK rep Cncl of Int Civil Aviation Orgn 1953-56, int rels 1 Miny of Tport and Civil Aviation 1956-61; asst sec Miny of Aviation 1961-64: interdependence, exports, electronics; cllr Br civil aviation rep in Far East FCO 1964-81, UN expert on air servs agreements ICAO 1984-; fell Ford Fndn Nat Translation Centre Austin Texas 1968; *Books* Face at the Bottom of the World: Poems by Hagiwara Sakutaro (1969), Three Contemporary Japanese Poets (1972), Natsume Soseki's I Am a Cat (vol 1 1972, vol 2 1979, vol 3 1986), Natsume Soseki's Ten Nights of Dream (1974); *Clubs* Naval, Pen Club of Japan (Tokyo); *Style—* Graeme Wilson, Esq, CMG; 42 Cranford Ave, Exmouth, Devon (☎ 0395 264786)

WILSON, Guy Edward Nairne Sandilands; s of John Sandilands Wilson (d 1963), of 36 Egerton Crescent, London, and Penelope Ann, *née* Fisher-Rowe; *b* 10 April 1948; *Educ* Heatherdown Sch, Eton, Univ of Aix-en-Provence; *m* 20 Oct 1979, (Marianne) Susan, da of James Drummond D'Arcy Clark, of Oxwold Ho, Barnsley, Glos; 2 s (John b 5 Feb 1984, Hugh b 27 Aug 1986); *Career* CA, ptnr Ernst & Whinney 1979- (joined 1967); FCA; *Recreations* cricket, golf, tennis, squash, football, gardening; *Clubs* Brooks's, MCC, IZ, Arabs, Royal St George's Golf, Berkshire Golf; *Style—* Guy Wilson, Esq; Ernst & Whinney, Becket House, 1 Lambeth Palace Rd, London SE1 7EU (☎ 01 928 2000, fax 01 928 0467)

WILSON, Ven (John) Hewitt; CB (1978); s of John Joseph Wilson (d 1959), of Ireland, and Marion Wilson, *née* Green (d 1980); *b* 14 Feb 1924; *Educ* Kilkenny Coll, Mountjoy Sch Dublin, Trinity Coll Dublin (BA, MA); *m* 1951, Gertrude Elsie Joan, da of Rev Robert Edward Weir (d 1957), of Dublin; 3 s (John, Peter, Timothy), 2 da (Kathryn, Sarah); *Career* clergyman; ordained 1947 for St Georges Church Dublin; joined RAF 1950, Staff Chaplain Air Miny 1961-63, Asst Chaplain in Chief Far E Air Force 1966-69, Strike Cmd 1969-73, Chaplain in Chief RAF 1973-80; hon chaplain to HM The Queen 1972-80; *Recreations* tennis, gardening, motoring; *Clubs* RAF; *Style—* Ven Hewitt Wilson, CB; Glencree, Philcote St, Deddington, Oxford OX5 4TB (☎ 0869 38903)

WILSON, Ian; s of John Wilson, of S Sheilds, Tyne & Wear, and Gladys Irene, *née* Lascelles; *b* 2 Mar 1944; *Educ* Argyle House Private GS for Boys Sunderland, Marine Sch S Sheilds; *m* 28 Dec 1968, Elizabeth Rebecca, da of George Wilson Brownless, of Westoe S Shields; 1 s (Nicholas Ian b 9 Feb 1971), 1 d (Rebecca Jane b 11 Sept 1973); *Career* night ed Newcastle Journal 1979-82 (chief sub-ed 1975-79), features ed Evening Chronicle Newcastle 1981-; memb: Bd of Govrs Sunderland Church HS for Girls, Newspaper Press Fund; *Style—* Ian Wilson, Esq; 10 Luffness Drive, Cleadon, S Shields, NE34 8AJ (☎ 091 4561092) Evening Chronicle, Thomson House, Newcastle (☎ 232 7500, fax 091 2322256)

WILSON, Ian Matthew; CB (1985); s of Matthew Thomson Wilson, OBE, 114 Morningside Drive, Edinburgh, EH10 5NS, and Mary Lily *née* Barnett (d 1968); *b* 12 Dec 1926; *Educ* George Watson's Coll, Edinburgh Univ (MA); *m* 4 July 1953, Anne, da of Thomas Allan Chalmers (d 1962); 3 s (Alan b 1957, David b 1959, Alastair b 1962); *Career* Nat Serv 1948-50; Capt RAEC 1949-50; asst under sec of state Scottish Off 1974-77, under sec Scottish Educn Dept 1977-86, sec of comms for Scotland 1986-; *Style—* Ian Wilson, Esq, CB; 1 Bonaly Drive, Edinburgh, EH13 OEJ (☎ 031 441 2541)

WILSON, Lt-Gen Sir (Alexander) James; KBE (1974), CBE (1966, MBE 1948, MC (1945); s of late Maj-Gen Bevil Thomson Wilson, CB, DSO, of Chelsea, and Florence Erica, da of Sir John Starkey, 1 Bt, JP, DL; *b* 13 April 1921; *Educ* Winchester, New Coll Oxford (BA); *m* 30 Oct 1958, Hon Jean Margaret, *qv*, da of 2 Baron Rankeillour (d 1958); 2 s, 1 step s, 2 step da; *Career* served Rifle Bde, WWII: N Africa and Italy (despatches); Adj Indian Mil Acad Dehra Dun 1945-47, priv sec to C-in-C Pakistan 1947-49, psc 1950, Co Cdr 1 Bn Rifle Bde BAOR 1951-52, Bde Maj 11 Armd Div BAOR 1952-54, Kenya (despatches) 1954-55, Lt-Col 1955, Instr Staff Coll Camberley

1955-58, 2 cmd 3 Green Jackets BAOR, GSO1 Sandhurst 1960-62, CO 1 Bn XX Lancs Fus 1962-64, COS UN Force Cyprus 1964-66, Actg Force Cdr 1965-66), Cdr 147 Inf Bde (TA) 1966-67, dir Army Recruiting MOD 1967-70, GOC NW Dist 1970-72, Vice Adj-Gen 1972-74, GOC SE Dist 1974-77; Dep Col (Lancs) R&F 1973-77; Col Royal Regt Fus 1977-82; Col Cmdt: Queen's Div 1974-77, RAEC 1975-79, Royal Green Jackets 1977-81; Hon Col Oxford Univ OTC 1978-82; Sunday Times football corr 1957-, chm Tobacco Advsy Cncl 1977-83 (chief exec 1983-85); memb: Sports Cncl 1973-82, Cncl CBI 1977-85; hon vice-pres FA 1976-82, vice-chm NABC 1977-, chm Russ 1973-76; *Recreations* cricket, association football; *Clubs* Travellers, MCC, Nottinghamshire County Cricket; *Style—* Lt-Gen Sir James Wilson, KBE, CBE, MBE, MC; 151 Rivermead Court, London SW6 3SF (☎ 01 736 7228)

WILSON, Hon James McMoran; er s of 2 Baron Moran; *b* 6 August 1952; *Educ* Eton, Trinity Coll Cambridge; *m* 7 June 1980, Hon (Mary) Jane Hepburne-Scott, yst da of 10 Lord Polwarth; *Career* dir Boston Ventures Management; *Clubs* Somerset, Flyfishers; *Style—* Hon James Wilson; 65 Upland Rd, Brookline, Mass 02146, USA

WILSON, James Noël Chalmers Barclay; s of Alexander Wilson (d 1957), and Isobel Barbara, *née* Fairweather (d 1961); *b* 25 Dec 1919; *Educ* King Henry VIII Sch Coventry, Univ of Birmingham (MB ChB, ChM); *m* 3 Sept 1945, Patricia Norah, da of Harold Norman McCullough (d 1927); 2 s (Michael b 3 Dec 1956, Richard b 24 March 1960), 2 da (Sheila (Mrs Edwards) b 20 Aug 1947, Jane (Mrs Wentworth b 30 April 1950); *Career* regtl MO RAMC 1943-46, discharged W/S Capt, qualified as parachutist and served 1 Airborne Div; resident surgical posts: Birmingham Gen Hosp 1943 and 1947, Coventry and Warwicks Hosp 1948, Robert Jones and Agnes Hunt Orthopaedic Hosp 1949-52; conslt orthopaedic surgn: Cardiff Utd Hosps and Welsh Regnl Bd 1952-55, Royal Nat Orthopaedic Hosp London and Stanmore 1955-84 Cardiff Utd Hosps and Welsh Regnl Bd 1952-55, Nat Hosp Queen Square 1962-84; surgn i/c accident serv Stanmore 1955-84, hon conslt orthopaedic surgn Garston Med Rehabilitation Centre Watford 1955-84, teacher in orthopaedics Univ of London 1955-84, BOA travelling fell USA 1954; emeritus orthopaedic surgn and conslt: Royal Nat Orthopaedic Hosp, Nat Hosp for Nervous Diseases Queen Square; UK chm World Orthopaedic Concern (pres 1979-84), vice chm IMPACT (Initiative Against Avoidable Disablement); MRCS 1943, LRCP 1943, FRCS 1948, Fell Br Orthopaedic Assoc (editorial sec 1972-76); memb: Egyptian Orthopaedic Assoc, Bangladesh Orthopaedic Soc; *Books* Fractures and Joint Injuries (ed sixth edn); *Recreations* golf, gardening, photography, old cars; *Clubs* RSM; *Style—* J N Wilson, Esq; The Chequers, Waterdell, nr Watford, Herts WD2 7LP (☎ 0923 672364)

WILSON, Air Vice-Marshal James Stewart; CBE (1959); s of James Wilson (d 1937), of Wentworth, Westferry, Dundee, and Helen Fyfe (d 1914); *b* 4 Sept 1909; *Educ* Dundee HS, St Andrew's Univ (MB, ChB), London Univ (DPH), Royal Coll of Physicians; *m* 1937, Elizabeth Letitia, da of Benjamin Elias (d 1944), of Goodwick, Pembrokeshire; 2 s (Malcolm, Peter d 1952); *Career* medical branch RAF 1935-65, N Africa 1941-45, DGMS RAAF 1961-63, QHP 1961-65, special advsr to RAF in applied entomology and epidemiology 1973-84; hon civil conslt (Preventive Medicine) to RAF 1984; FFCM 1984; memb 1953-59: Miny of Supply biology ctee and clinical defence ctee, Med Res Ctee on Influenza and Allied Viruses, aeromedical panel of advsy gp for auronautical res and devpt NATO; UK chm Anglo- Netherlands Working Gp on Personnel Res MOD 1957-59; hon Civil Consultant (Preventive Medicine) RAF, 1984; *Recreations* fishing, shooting, golf (rugby-formerly rugby int player 1931and 1932); *Clubs* RAF, Ashridge Golf; *Style—* Air Vice-Marshal James Wilson; Eucumbene, Buckland, Aylesbury, Bucks HP22 5HY (☎ 0296 630062)

WILSON, Sir James William Douglas; 5 Bt (UK 1906), of Airdrie, New Monkland, Co Lanark; s of Sir Thomas Douglas Wilson, 5 Bt, MC (d 1984), and Pamela Aileen, da of Sir Griffin Wyndham Edward Hanmer, 7 Bt; *b* 8 Oct 1960; *Educ* Marlborough, London Univ; *m* 1985, Julia Margaret Louise, da of Joseph Charles Francis Mutty, of Mulberry Hall, Melbourn, nr Royston, Herts; *Career* farmer; *Style—* Sir James Wilson, Bt; Lillingstone Lovell Manor, Buckingham MK18 5BQ (☎ 028 06 237)

WILSON, Hon Lady (Jean Margaret); *née* Hope; JP (inner London); 2 da of 2 Baron Rankeillour, GCIE, MC (d 1958, sometime govr of Madras), by his w Grizel (d 1975), da of Brig-Gen Sir Robert Gordon Gilmour, 1 Bt, CB, CVO, DSO; *b* 7 Jan 1923; *m* 1, 1942 (m dis 1955), Capt Anthony Paul, adopted s of F Paul; 1 s (Anthony), 2 da (Sarah (Mrs Oliphant), Susan d 1986); m 2, 1958, Lt-Gen Sir James Wilson, KBE, MC, *qv*; 2 (William, Rupert); *Style—* The Hon Lady Wilson, JP; Goldhill Farm House, Edingley, Newark, Notts (☎ 0636 813308); 151 Rivermead Court, Ranelagh Gdns, London SW6 3SF

WILSON, Jeffery Graham; s of Herbert Charles Wilson (d 1983), and Dora Gladys Wilson; *b* 28 Sept 1939; *Educ* Monkton Combe Sch; *m* 8 June 1962, Lise-Francoise, da of Marcel Fritz Robert (d 1977); 3 s Anthony Charles b 1964, Martin James b 1965, Richard Graham b 1967), 1 da (Sarah Rachel Jane b 1970); *Career* ptnr Wilson & Watford 1964 (joined 1958), memb Stock Exchange 1961, dir Baring Wilson & Watford 1986-; *Recreations* golf; *Style—* Jeffery Wilson, Esq; 1 Grove Rd, Northwood, Middx HA6 2AP (☎ 09274 25495); Baring Bros, 8 Bishopsgate, London EC2N 4AE (☎ 01 283 8833)

WILSON, Lady; Jessie; da of John Winston Foley Winnington (3 s of Sir Francis Winnington, 5 Bt, JP, DL, by his w, Jane, eldest da of Lord Alfred Spencer Churchill, himself 2 s of 6 Duke of Marlborough), by his w Gladys Cooke; *b* 16 Mar 1912; *m* 1933, Sir Michael Thomond Wilson, MBE (d 1983), former vice-chm Lloyds Bank and chm Export Guarantees Advsy Cncl, eldest s of Sir Roy Wilson (decd), of Wood End, Pryford, Woking; 2 s (Michael, b 1934, m 1968 Katharine Fanshawe; Simon b 1937), 1 da (Patricia, twin with Simon, m 1966 Maj Charles Halkett); *Style—* Lady Wilson; Clytha, S Ascot, Berks (☎ 0990 20833)

WILSON, John; s of George Wilson (d 1988), and Mable Wilson; *b* 20 Dec 1932; *Educ* Audley Cncl Sch Blackburn Lancs; *m* 6 Sept 1958, Margaret, da of Stanley Holmes (d 1965); 3 da (Edwina Jane b 1961, Clare Margaret b 1963, Joanne Sarah b 1966); *Career* Nat Serv RAF 1951-53; various posts incl chief accountant Jackson Steeple Gp 1946-62, conslt Cotton Bd Productivity Centre 1962-65, chief mgmnt accountant (later fin dir) Viyella Internat Ltd (later Carrington Viyella plc) 1965-80, dep chief exec KCA Internat plc 1981-83, exec chm H Young Hldgs plc 1984-; FCMA 1959, FCT 1978; *Recreations* ballet, cricket; *Style—* John Wilson, Esq; Worleys Hills, Wargrave, Berks RG10 8PA (☎ 0491 572 226); H Young Howings plc, Old Dominion Hse, 5 Gravel Hill, Henley-on-Thames, Oxon (☎ 0491 578 988, fax 0491 572 360)

WILSON, Sir John Foster; CBE (1965, OBE 1955); s of Rev George Henry Wilson (d 1959); *b* 20 Jan 1919; *Educ* Worcester Coll for the Blind, St Catherine's Oxford; *m* 1944, Chloe Jean, *née* McDermid, OBE; 2 da; *Career* international health administrator; dir Royal Commonwealth Soc for the Blind 1950-83, pres Int Agency for the Prevention of Blindness 1975-83 (now hon life pres); sr conslt UN Devpt Programme (IMPACT) 1983-; kt 1975; *Books* various publications on disability and travel; *Clubs* Royal Commonwealth Society; *Style—* Sir John Wilson, CBE; 22 The Cliff, Roedean, Brighton, E Sussex (☎ 0273 607667)

WILSON, Sir John Gardiner; CBE (1972); s of J S Wilson; *b* 13 July 1913; *Educ* Melbourne GS, Clare Coll Cambridge; *m* 1944, Margaret Louise, da of S M De Ravin; 3 da; *Career* Aust Paper Manufacturers Ltd: joined 1947, dep md 1953-59, md 1959-78, chm 1978-; kt 1982; *see Debrett's Handbook of Australia and New Zealand for further details*; *Style—* Sir John Wilson, CBE; 20 Martin Place, Sydney, NSW 2000, Australia

WILSON, John Gilmour (Gil); s of John Gilmour Wilson (d 1964), of Torr Hall, Bridge of Weir, Renfrewshire, and Helen Muirhead, *née* Clark; *b* 22 May 1943; *Educ* Loretto Sch, Paisley Coll (HNC); *m* 28 April 1971, Sally Edgar, da of Dr Edgar Rentoul, MBE, JP, of West Manse, Houston, Scotland; 2 s (Edgar b 8 June 1975, Gregory b 18 Aug 1979), 1 da (Nicola b 4 Aug 1981); *Career* chm and md Carlton Die Castings Ltd 1964-, chm and md Tool Manufacturing & Servs (Glasgow) Ltd 1973-, md Vacuseal Ltd 1977-, chm and md Millstream Devpts Ltd 1981-87, dir Ronnoco Engrg 1985-88; dir Paisley TSB 1975-80; *Recreations* fishing, shooting, photography, gardening; *Style—* Gil Wilson, Esq; Rowallan Mill, Kilmaurs, Kilmarnock, Ayrshire KA3 2LJ (☎ 0563 384 92); Carlton Die Casting Ltd, 88 Greenhill Rd, Paisley PA3 1RG (☎ 041 887 8355, fax 041 848 1157)

WILSON, Sir John Martindale; KCB (1974, CB 1960); s of John Wilson of Edinburgh (d 1920), and Kate Benson Martindale (d 1963); *b* 3 Sept 1915; *Educ* Bradfield, Gonville and Caius Coll Cambridge (MA); *m* 1941, Penelope Beatrice, da of Francis Alfred Bolton, JP, of Moor Court, Oakamoor, Staffs; 1 s, 1 da; *Career* RA India and Burma (despatches) 1940-46, Maj; civil servant 1938-75: under-sec Miny Supply 1954-55 (private sec 1947-50), Cabinet Off 1955-58, dep sec Miny Aviation 1960-65, dep under-sec state MOD 1965-72, second perm under-sec state MOD 1972-75; chm: Crown Housing Assoc 1975-78, Civil Service Appeal Bd 1978-81; Civil Service Retirement Fellowship 1978-82; vice-pres Civil Service Retirement Fellowship 1982-; *Recreations* gardening; *Clubs* Army & Navy; *Style—* Sir John Wilson, KCB; Bourne Close, Bourne Lane, Twyford, Winchester, Hants SO21 1NX (☎ 0962 713488)

WILSON, His Hon Judge John Warley; s of John Pearson Wilson, of Kenilworth, and Nancy Wade, *née* Harston; *b* 13 April 1936; *Educ* Warwick Sch, St Catharines Coll Cambridge (MA); *m* 2 June 1962, Rosalind Mary, da of Raymond Harry Pulford; *Career* barr Lincolns Inn 1960, practised Midland and Oxford circuit until 1982, recorder 1979-82, circuit judge 1982; *Recreations* gardening, nat hunt racing; *Style—* His Hon Judge John Wilson; Victoria House, Farm St, Harbury, Leamington Spa CU33 9LR (☎ 0926 612572)

WILSON, Hon Mrs (Joyce Margaret); *née* Davison; da of 1 Baron Broughshane (d 1953), by first wife; *b* 1900; *Educ* North Foreland School; *m* 1922, Humphrey Bowstead Wilson, OBE, MB; 1 s, 1 da; *Career* worked for 10 years or so in Bodleian, Oxford Library, on catalogue of Dept Western medieval literature & MSS; *Style—* The Hon Mrs Wilson; Fyfield Close, Fyfield, Abingdon, Oxon

WILSON, Kenneth; s of Leslie Wilson (d 1936), of NY, and Theresa Mary, *née* Holmes (d 1973); *b* 3 Jan 1927; *Educ* Bideford GS, Univ of London (LLB); *m* 6 Sept 1958, Jean Margaret, da of Herbert Fletcher, of Maidstone, Kent; 2 s (Peter b 1960, Grenville b 1966), 2 da (Heidi b 1962, Serena b 1969); *Career* War Serv RE 1945-48; ctee clerk Kent CC 1952-58, clerk of the cncl Hailsham Dist Cncl 1963-73 (dep clerk 1958-63), chief exec Wealden Dist Cncl 1974-85, ret 1985; chm Sussex branch Inst Chartered Secretaries and Administrators 1972-74, pres Rotary Club of Hailsham 1975, tstee Thomas Scanlon Tst, hon sec S Wealden Foster Care Assoc, govr Hailsham Grovelands CP Sch; memb: Hon Soc Middle Temple, Bar Cncl, ICSA (FCCS); *Recreations* ornithology, phyiology; *Style—* Kenneth Wilson, Esq; 42 Hawthylands Rd, Hailsham, East Sussex BN27 1EY (☎ 0323 840 966)

WILSON, (William) Lawrence; CB (1967), OBE (1954); s of Joseph Osmond Wilson (d 1976), and Hannah, *née* Ransome (d 1914); *b* 11 Sept 1912; *Educ* Constantine Coll; *m* 2, 1964, Constance Violet, da of Samuel Richards (d 1970), of Kent; 2 s (Graham, Andrew); *Career* chief engr Miny of Pub Buildings and Works 1962-69, dep sec Dept of Environment 1969-72, conslt; papers presented home and abroad on energy production and waste disposal; Coronation Medal; *Recreations* fly fishing, travel; *Style—* Lawrence Wilson, Esq, CB, OBE; Oakwood, 34 Chestnut Ave, Chorleywood, Herts WD3 4HB (☎ 0923 774 419)

WILSON, Hon Lorraine Mary Charmiane Nicole; da of 4 Baron Nunburnholme; *b* 1959; *Style—* The Hon Lorraine Wilson

WILSON, Hon Mrs; (Margaret Eleanor); *née* Maybray-King; JP (Havant); da of Baron Maybray-King, PC (Life Peer); *b* 1926; *m* 1945, Roy Wilson; *Style—* The Hon Mrs Wilson, JP; 26 Blenheim Road, Westbury Park, Bristol

WILSON, (Alan) Martin; QC (1982); s of Joseph Norris Wilson (1986), of London, and Kate, *née* Clusky (d 1982); *b* 12 Feb 1940; *Educ* Kilburn GS, Univ of Nottingham (LLB); *m* 1966 (m dis 1975), Pauline Frances Kibart; 2 da (Rebecca b 1968, Anna b 1971); m 2, Julia Mary, da of Patrick Maurice George Carter, OBE, of Worcestershire; 1 da (Alexandra b 1980); *Career* recorder of the Crown Ct 1979; *Recreations* sailing, shooting, literature; *Clubs* Bar Yacht, Sloane; *Style—* Martin Wilson, Esq, QC; Langland House, Peopleton, Nr Pershore, Worcestershire; 8 Arielle, Domaine Des Mas De St Pierre, 83120, Plan De La Tour, France; 6 King's Bench Walk, Temple, London EC4

WILSON, Sir (Mathew) Martin; 5 Bt (UK 1874), of Eshton Hall, Co York; s of Sir Mathew Richard Henry Wilson, 4 Bt, CSI, DSO (d 1958), by his w Hon Barbara Lister (da of 4 & last Baron Ribblesdale); bro of Peter, *qv*; *b* 2 July 1906; *Educ* Eton; *Heir* n, Mathew Wilson, MBE, MC, *qv*; *Career* patron of four livings; *Style—* Sir Martin Wilson, Bt; 1 Sandgate Esplanade, Folkestone, Kent

WILSON, Hon Mrs (Mary Jane); *née* Hepburne-Scott; da of 10 Lord Polwarth, TD; *b* 16 Feb 1955; *m* 7 June 1980, Hon James McMoran Wilson, s of 2 Baron Moran, CMG; *Style—* The Hon Mrs Wilson; 65 Upland Road, Brookline, Mass 02146, USA

WILSON, Hon Mrs; (Mary Stewart); *née* Macpherson; da of 1 Baron Drumalbyn, KBE, PC; *b* 1942; *m* 1967, Philip D Wilson; *Style—* The Hon Mrs Wilson; 5 Clancarty Rd, London SW6

WILSON, Brig Mathew John Anthony; OBE (Mil 1979), MBE (Mil 1971), MC (1972); s of Anthony Thomas Wilson (d 1982), by his 1 w Margaret, formerly w of Vernon Motion and da of Alfred Holden (decd); hp to unc, Sir Martin Wilson, 5 Bt; *b* 2 Oct 1935; *Educ* Trin Coll Sch Port Hope Ontario; *m* 1962, Janet Mary, er da of Edward Worsfold Mowll, JP (decd), of Walmer; 1 s (Mathew Edward Amcotts b 1966), 1 da (Victoria Mary b 1968); *Career* Brig King's Own Yorks LI, ret 1983; exec dir Wilderness Fndn (UK) 1983-85; *Clubs* Explorers; *Style*— Brig Mathew Wilson, OBE, MC

WILSON, Hon Maud Maitland; da of 1 Baron Wilson; *b* 19 Nov 1917; *Style*— The Hon Maud Wilson; c/o Barclays Bank plc, PO 544, 54 Lombard Street, London EC3V 9EX

WILSON, Michael John Francis Thomond; s of Sir Michael Thomond Wilson KB, MBE, of Clytha, South Ascot, Berks (d 1983), and Lady Jessie Babette *née* Winnington (d 1984); *b* 9 Sept 1934; *Educ* Rugby, Oriel Coll Oxford (MA); *m* 4 May 1968, (Katharine) Mary Rose, da of Lt Col Robert Macauley Fanshawe (d 1974), of Church Cottage, Longborough, Moreton-in-Marsh, Glos; 3 s (James b 1970, Andrew b 1972, Richard b 1976); *Career* Nat Serv, Lt RA 1953-55; admitted slr 1961; head of litigation dept Stephenson Harwood 1969- (formerly Stephenson Harwood and Tatham, ptnr 1966-); memb City of London Slrs Co; memb Law Soc; *Recreations* horse racing, tennis; *Style*— Michael Wilson, Esq; Andridge House, Radnage, High Wycombe, Bucks, HP14 4DZ (☎ 024 026 2215); Stephenson Harwood, 1 St Paul's Churchyard, London, EC4M 8SH (☎ 01 329 4422, fax 01 606 0822, telex 886789 SHSPC G)

WILSON, Michael Stuart; s of Claude Stuart Wilson, of 39 Bury Fields, Guildford, Surrey, and Vivienne Sinclair Dalrymple Morton, *née* Bell; *b* 22 June 1939; *Educ* Marlborough; *m* 26 Dec 1964, Alyson, da of Sidney Arthur Starkey (d 1982), of 4 Warwick New Road, Leamington Spa; 2 s (Piers b 1967, Neil b 1969); *Career* ptnr Deloitte Haskins & Sells 1969-; memb Crafts Cncl 1988; FCA 1969; *Recreations* gardening, vintage cars; *Clubs* City of London; *Style*— Michael Wilson, Esq; 22 Crescent Grove, London SW4 7AH (☎ 01 622 6360); Faiths Cottage, Church Lane, Sidlesham, Chichester, W Sussex; Deloitte Haskins & Sells, 12b Queen Victoria St, London EC4P 4JX (☎ 01 248 3913, fax 01 248 3623, telex 894941)

WILSON, Michael Sumner; s of Cdr Peter Sumner Wilson, AFC, Lower Middlewood, Dorstone, Hereford, and Margaret Kathleen, *née* Letchworth; *b* 5 Dec 1943; *Educ* St Edwards Sch Oxford; *m* 5 June 1975, Mary Dorothy Wordsworth, da of John Alexander Drysdale (d 1986); 1 da (Amanda Wordsworth b 12 March 1976); *Career* Equity & Law 1963-68, Abbey Life 1968-71: Hambro Life/Allied Dunbar 1971-: broker mangr 1971-73, exec dir 1973-76, main bd dir 1976-82, jt dep md 1982-84, jt md 1984-88, gp chief exec 1988-dir BAT Industs 1989-, memb Lloyds; Tstee Mental Health Fndn; *Recreations* tennis, racing; *Style*— Michael Wilson, Esq; Warrens Gorse, nr Cirencester, Glos GL7 7JD; Allied Dunbar, Allied Dunbar Centre, Swindon SN1 1EL (☎ 0793 514 514, fax 0793 512 371, telex 449129 Allied G)

WILSON, Michael Thomas; s of Thomas Wilson (d 1967), and Blanche, *née* Dunne; *b* 27 April 1938; *Educ* Rothwell GS, Manchester Univ (BA); *m* 1 Sept 1962, Diana Frances, da of Harold Frank Pettit (d 1968); 1 s (Simon b 1964), 2 da (Victoria b 1966, Emmeline b 1977); *Career* supervisor truck mktg Ford Motor Co 1959-62, dir residential studies Inst of Mktg 1962-64, md Marketing Improvements Ltd 1964-88, chm Mktg Improvements Gp plc 1988-, visiting prof Cranfield Sch of Mgmnt 1989; FInstM (1985), FInstD (1966); *Books* Managing a Sales Force (1970), The Management of Marketing (1980); *Recreations* sport, theatre, cinema, reading; *Style*— Michael Wilson, Esq; Ulster House, 17 Ulster Terrace, Regents Park Outer Circle, London NW1 (☎ 01 487 5811, fax 01 935 4839, telex 299723 MARIMP G)

WILSON, Miles Robert; s of Maurice James Wilson (d 1969), of Greensleeves, Welshwood Park, and Kathleen Isobel Wilson; *b* 28 Sept 1946; *Educ* Chinthurst Sch Tadworth Surrey, Carshalton Coll Surrey; *m* 15 Nov 1985, Sarah, da of Cyril Deakin (d 1976), of Sheffield; *Career* professional broadcaster and radio presenter 1964-78, involved in the tourist indust, set up PR-advtg agency 1983, chm and md Wasp Gp Worthing Sussex 1986-; chm Sussex Coast Business Club 1985-; vice chm Worthing Post Off Advsy Cncl 1988-; exec memb: Worthing Coll Tourism Liaison Ctee 1987-; memb Tourism Soc 1983, MInstPR 1985, MBIM 1989; *Recreations* sailing, country pursuits, equestrian; *Style*— Miles Wilson, Esq; The Old Dairy, 65A Kingsland Rd, Worthing, W Sussex (☎ 0903 209327, fax 0903 38242, car 0860 716359, mobile 0860 622526)

WILSON, Nicholas Allan Roy; QC (1987); s of (Roderick) Peter Garratt Wilson, of Three Chimneys, Fittleworth, Pulborough, W Sussex, and (Dorothy) Anne, *née* Chenevix-Trench; *b* 9 May 1945; *Educ* Bryanston Sch, Worcester Coll Oxford (BA); *m* 14 Dec 1974, Margaret, da of Reginald Frank Higgins (d 1986); 1 s (Matthew b 1977), 1 da (Camilla b 1981); *Career* barr Inner Temple 1967, W circuit, 1987 recorder Crown Ct; *Style*— Nicholas Wilson, Esq, QC; Queen Elizabeth Building, Temple, London EC4Y 9BS (☎ 01 583 7837, fax 01 353 5422)

WILSON, Nicholas Samuel; s of Dr John Alexander George Wilson, of Sheffield (d 1985), and Grace, *née* Twiselton (d 1974); *b* 27 Sept 1935; *Educ* Repton, Univ of Sheffield (LLB), Harvard Univ (LLM), Univ of California at Berkeley (post grad res); *m* 1, 1961 (m dis 1980), Rosemary Ann Wilson; 2 s (Simon John b 1964, Justin Nicholas b 1966), 1 da (Sophie Rachael b 1973); m 2, 11 Oct 1982, Penelope Mary Elizabeth Moore; *Career* Nat Serv 2 Lt RA 1954-56, capt TA 1956-61; articled with Keeble Hawson Steele Carr & Co Sheffield 1956-61, asst slr Slaughter and May 1961-67 (ptnr 1968-); memb: DTI Advsy Ctee on Company Law 1970-74, Ctee of Inquiry on Indust Democracy 1975-76, City Capital Markets Ctee 1980-; Freeman Worshipful Co of Slrs; memb Law Soc; *Recreations* music, gardening; *Style*— Nicholas Wilson, Esq; Whitnorth, The Street, Shalford, Guildford, Surrey GU4 8BU (☎ 0483 572 644); Slaughter and May, 35 Basinghall St, London EC2V 5DB (☎ 01 600 1200, fax 01 726 0038/600 0289, telex 883486/888926)

WILSON, Nigel Guy; s of Noel Wilson, and Joan Louise, *née* Lovibond; *b* 23 July 1935; *Educ* Univ Coll Sch, CCC Oxford (BA, MA); *Career* lectr Merton Coll Oxford 1957-62, fell and tutor in classics Lincoln Coll 1962-; visiting prof: Univ of Padua 1985, Ecole Normale Supérieure Paris 1986; FBA 1980; *Books* Scribes and Scholars (with L D Reynolds, second edn 1974), Scholars of Byzantium (1983); *Recreations* tennis (not lawn), squash, bridge; *Style*— Nigel Wilson, Esq; Lincoln College, Oxford, Oxfordshire

WILSON, Nigel Richard; s of Lt Col Richard Wilson, of Stamford, Lincolnshire, and Jean Dorothy, *née* Jamieson; *b* 18 Feb 1946; *Educ* Radley; *m* 8 July 1971, Eliza Ann, da of John Rowlands, of Canada; 1 s (William Pennington b 1974), 1 da (Rebecca Pennington b 1977); *Career* ptnr McAnally Mongomery 1980-83 (memb mgmnt ctee 1982-83), ptnr F Laing of Cruickshank 1983, dir Alexanders Laing & Cruickshank 1987-88, md Laing & Cruickshank Investmt Mgmnt Servs Ltd 1987-88, dir CS Investmt Ltd 1988-; chm Ski Club of GB 1979-82, dir Nat Ski Fedn 1979-82, hon steward All England Lawn Tennis of Croquet Club 1969-, memb Multiple Sclerosis fin ctee 1983-; Freeman City of London 1972, Liveryman of the Worshipful Co of Skinners 1982; *Books* Silk Cut Ski Guide (1974); *Recreations* skiing, golf, tennis, cricket, shooting; *Clubs* Ski Club of GB; *Style*— Nigel Wilson, Esq; Old Manor Farm, Cublinton, Leighton Buzzard, Bedfordshire LU7 0LE (☎ 0296 681279); CS Investments Ltd, 125 High Holborn, London WC1V 6PY (☎ 01 242 1142, fax 01 430 0742)

WILSON, 2 Baron (UK 1946); Patrick Maitland Wilson; s of 1 Baron Wilson, GCB, GBE, DSO, Supreme Allied Mil Cdr Mediterranean 1944 (d 1964); *b* 14 Sept 1915; *Educ* Eton, King's Coll Cambridge; *m* 1945, Storeen Violet, da of Maj Archibald James Douglas Campbell, OBE (d 1936), of Blythswood, and Hon Anna, *née* Massey (4 da of 5 Baron Clarina, by his 2 w Sophia, and half sis of 6 Baron who d 1952, from which date the title has been extinct); *Heir* none; *Style*— The Rt Hon the Lord Wilson; c/o Barclays Bank, Cambridge

WILSON, Peter George Kirke; s of Col H W Wilson, OBE, TD (d 1965), of Enton, Surrey, and Lilian Rosemary, *née* Kirke; *b* 22 Oct 1942; *Educ* Winchester; *m* 18 Sept 1965 Susan Mary, da of Capt David Baynes, MC, DSO (d 1958); 2 s (Nigel b 1968, David b 1971), 1 da (Fiona b 1967); *Career* formerly with Deloittes Hoskins & Sells, currently md Mgmnt Appts Ltd; FCA 1966; *Recreations* golf, tennis, study of WWII, old Morris's; *Style*— Peter Wilson, Esq; Dormers, Kiln Way, Graysheat, Hindhead, Surrey; 84 Ashbury Rd, London SW11; Finland House, Management Appointments Ltd, 56 Haymarket, London SW1

WILSON, Peter Michael; s of Michael de Lancey Wilson, of Bolney, Blandford Forum, Dorset, and Mary Elizabeth, *née* Craufurd (d 1972); *b* 9 June 1941; *Educ* Downside, Oriel Coll Oxford (MA); *m* 5 Sept 1964, Lissa, da of Olaf Trab, of Copenhagen; 1 s (Mark b 1974), 1 da (Juliet b 1972); *Career* dep chm Gallaher Ltd 1987; chm Gallaher Tobacco Ltd 1987; *Style*— Peter Wilson, Esq; 191 Sycamore Rd, Farnborough, Hants (☎ 0252 512512); Gallaher Ltd, Members' Hill, Brooklands Rd, Weybridge, Surrey (☎ 0932 859777)

WILSON, Prof Peter Northcote; CBE (1987); s of L William Charles Montgomery Wilson (d 1980), and Fanny Louise, *née* White (d 1975); *b* 4 April 1928; *Educ* Whitgift Sch, Wye Coll London (BSc, MSc), Univ of Edinburgh, London Univ (PhD); *m* 9 Sept 1950, (Maud Ethel) Bunny, da of William Ernest Bunn (d 1962); 2 s (David Richard b 1953, John Peter b 1959), 1 da (Rosemary Margaret b 1951); *Career* lectr in agric Makerere Coll Uganda 1951-57, sr lectr in animal prodn Imp Coll of Tropical Agric 1957-61, prof agric Univ of W Indies, dir Trinidad & Tobago Agric Credit Bank 1962-64, sr scientist and head of biometrics Unilever Res 1968-71, chief agric scientist BOCM Silcock 1971-83, prof of agric and rural economy Univ of Edinburgh 1984-, princ E of Scotland Coll of Agric 1984-, head Edinburgh Sch of Agric 1984-; visiting prof Univ of Reading 1975-83; govr Eastern Caribbean Farm Inst 1961-64, chm Frank Parkinson Agric Tst 1972-, pres Br Soc of Animal Prodn 1977-78, memb Medicines Cmmn 1976-79, vice pres Inst of Biology 1977-79, sec-gen Scottish Agric Colls 1986-87, memb Univ Grants Ctee (agric sub ctee) 1987-; CBiol 1963, FIBiol 1963, FRSE 1987; *Books* Agriculture in The Tropics, Improved Feeding of Cattle and Sheep; *Recreations* photography, philately, ornithology, hill walking; *Clubs* Farmers; *Style*— Prof Peter Wilson, CBE; 8 St Thomas Rd, Edinburgh EH9 2LQ (☎ 031 667 3182); Sch of Agric, W Mains Rd, Edinburgh EH9 3JG (☎ 031 667 1041)

WILSON, (Edward) Philip; s of Peter Wilson, *qv*, and Grace Helen; *b* 2 Nov 1940; *Educ* Bryanston, Conservatoire de Musique Paris; *m* 1970, Lady Alexandra Jellicoe, *qv*, er da of 2 Earl Jellicoe, PC, DSO, MC; *Career* md Sotheby Publications; *Style*— Philip Wilson Esq; 24 Highbury Place London N5; Sotheby Publications, Russell Chambers, Covent Gdn, London WC2E 8AA (☎ 01 379 7886, telex 22158)

WILSON, Philip John Maurice; s of Col Maurice James Hartley Wilson, OBE (d 1978), by his w, Muriel Rose (d 1983); *b* 5 Nov 1927; *Educ* Trinity Coll Glenalmond; *m* 1956, June Valerie Fairburn, da of Arthur Bibby (d 1954), Ziwa of Kenya; 1 s, 1 da; *Career* asst md Caltex in Europe 1965-67, md Chevron Int Oil Co Ltd 1967-75, md and chief exec Chevron Oil (UK) Ltd 1975-, pres Chevron Serv Co Ltd 1975-84; chm Exeter Oil and Gas 1986; *Recreations* shooting, fishing, golf; *Clubs* Naval & Military, Muthaiga Country; *Style*— Philip Wilson, Esq; Merstham Lodge, Harps Oak Lane, Merstham, Surrey RH1 3AN (☎ 07374 2160)

WILSON, Sir Reginald Holmes; s of Alexander Wilson; *b* 1905; *Educ* St Lawrence Ramsgate, London Univ (BCom); *m* 1, 1930, Rose Marie von Arnim; 1 s, 1 da; m 2, 1938, Sonia Havell; *Career* CA (Scot) 1927, ptnr Whinney, Murray & Co 1937-72, princ asst sec Miny Shipping 1941, dir fin Miny War Tport 1941, under-sec Miny Tport 1945, memb Royal Cmmn on the Press 1946, vice-chm Hemel Hempstead Devpt Corpn 1946-56, comptroller Br Tport Cmmn (BTC) 1947, govr LSE 1954-58; chm BTC: Eastern Area Bd 1955-60, London Midland Area Bd 1960-62; memb Ctee of Enquiry into Civil Air Transport 1967-69; chm: Thomas Cook & Son Ltd 1966- 75, Transport Hldg Co 1967-70 (dep chm 1962-67), Nat Freight Corpn 1969-70, Transport Dvpt Gp Ltd 1971-75, bd for Simplication of Int Trade Procedures 1976-79; chm Brompton Hosp Cardiographic Inst 1960-80; chm bd govrs: Hosp for Diseases of the Chest 1960-71, Nat Heart Hosp 1969-71, Nat Heart and Chest Hosps 1971-80; hon tres Int Hosp Fedn; FCIT, FBIM; kt 1951; *Style*— Sir Reginald Wilson; 49 Gloucester Sq, London W2

WILSON, Robert Harold; s of Harold Wilson (d 1969), of London, and Emily May Wilson (d 1972); *b* 11 August 1930; *Educ* Latymer GS; *m* 1, 4 Dec 1954, Hilda May (1986), da of Henry Charles Christopher Stoneman (d 1972); 1 s (Guy Nicholas Robert b 1963), 1 da (Jane Frances b 1955); m 2, 29 April 1988, Jean, da of William Clayton Riley (d 1976); 2 step da (Juliet Contance Robertson b 1972, Jane Margaret Robertson b 1975); *Career* sales dir Speedwork Labels Ltd 1971-73; sales and mktg dir: Harlands of Hull Ltd 1972-76, Harland Gp of Cos 1976- (vice chm 1988); vice pres Fedn Internationale D'Adhesifs et Theomocollants 1987- (bd memb 1982-), bd memb Article Number Assoc (UK) Ltd London 1974-79; Freeman City of London 1980, Liveryman Worshipful Co of Marketors 1980 (Middle Warden 1989); FInstM 1980; *Recreations* riding, antiques restoration; *Clubs* Carlton, Farmers'; *Style*— Robert Wilson, Esq; No 6 Newbegin, Beverley HU17 8EG (☎ 0482 881 487); The Harland Gp, Hull HU10 6RN (☎ 0482 561 166, fax 0482 532 40, car tel 0836 615 141, telex 597138)

WILSON, Robert Peter; s of Alfred Wilson (d 1951), and Dorothy Eileen, *née* Matthews, MBE; *b* 2 Sept 1943; *Educ* Epsom Coll, Sussex Univ (BA); *m* 7 Feb 1975, Shirley Elisabeth, da of George Robson, of Hunmanby, Yorks; 1 s (Andrew), 1 da (Nicola); *Career* asst economist Dunlop Ltd 1966-67, economist Mobil Oil Co Ltd 1968-70; Rio Tinto Zinc Gp 1970-: md Am and s Europe Ltd 1979-82, head of planning and devpt RTZ plc 1982-87, dir RTZ Corp plc 1987-; *Recreations* theatre, literature, squash, tennis; *Style—* Robert Wilson, Esq; The RTZ Corporation plc, 6 St James's Square, London SW17 4LD (☎ 01 930 2399, 01 895 9077, fax 01 930 3249, telex 24639)

WILSON, Robert William; s of Alfred Wilson (d 1968), of Retford, Notts, and Winifred, *née* Scarborough (d 1964); *b* 18 Sept 1926; *Educ* Retford GS; *m* 24 March 1951, Pamela Marjorie, da of Horace Utley Dixon (d 1962), of Retford; 2 da (Jillian b 1954, Carol b 1956); *Career* served in Intelligence Corps 1945-48 (latterly in India); solicitor 1951, cmmr for oaths 1957, HM Coroner for E Berks 1970-, sr ptnr Colemans Solicitors Maidenhead 1980; chm Waltham St Lawrence Parish Cncl 1986; memb: Law Soc 1960, Coroners' Soc for England and Wales 1970; *Recreations* yachting (yacht 'Josephine'); *Clubs* Arun Yacht; *Style—* Robert Wilson, Esq; Oak Trees, West End, Waltham St Lawrence, Reading, Berks RG10 0NN (☎ 0734 343406, fax 0734 320599); office: 10 Bridge Avenue, Maidenhead, Berks SL6 1RR (☎ 0628 31051, fax 0628 773916, telex 847660)

WILSON, Hon Robin James; Dr The Hon; elder s of Baron Wilson of Rievaulx (Life Peer); *b* 5 Dec 1943; *Educ* University Coll Sch Hampstead, Balliol Coll Oxford, Univ of Pennsylvania, MIT; *m* 1968, Margaret Elizabeth Joy, da of Brian and Sallie Crispin, of Dawlish; 2 da (Jennifer b 1975, Catherine (twin) b 1975); *Career* lectr in mathematics: Jesus Coll Oxford 1969-72, Open Univ 1972-79 (sr lectr 1979-), Keble Coll Oxford (pt/t) 1980-; several times visiting prof of mathematics Colorado Coll USA; *Books* Instruction to Graph Theory (1972), twelve other mathematics books, Gilbert and Sullivan: The D'Oyly Carte Years (jtly), three other music books; *Recreations* music (performing and listening), travel, philately; *Style—* Dr The Hon Robin Wilson; 15 Chalfont Rd, Oxford OX2 6TL

WILSON, Rt Rev Roger Plumpton; KCVO (1974); s of Canon Clifford Plumpton Wilson; *b* 3 August 1905; *Educ* Winchester, Keble Coll Oxford; *m* 1935, Mabel Avery; 2 s, 1 da; *Career* former classical master Shrewsbury and St Andrew's Grahamstown; archdeacon of Nottingham 1945-49, bishop of Wakefield 1949-58, bishop of Chichester 1958-74; clerk of the closet to HM The Queen 1963-75; DD Lambeth; *Style—* The Rt Rev Roger Wilson, KCVO; Kingsett, Wrington, Bristol, Avon

WILSON, Sir Roland; KBE (1965, CBE 1941); s of Thomas Wilson (d 1956), and Mabel, *née* Inglis (d 1937); *b* 7 April 1904; *Educ* Devonport HS Tas, Univ of Tas (BCom), Oriel Coll Oxford (DPhil), Univ of Chicago (PhD); *m* 1, 1930, Valeska (d 1971), da of William Thompson; m 2, 1975, Joyce Clarice, da of Clarence Henry Chivers (d 1977); *Career* Cwlth statistician and econ advsr to the Treasy 1936-40 and 1946-51; perm hd Dept of Labour and Nat Service 1940-46; sec to Treasy 1951-66; dir: Cwlth Bank of Australia 1951-59, Reserve Bank of Australia 1960-66; chm: Cwlth Banking Corpn 1966-75, Qantas Airways Ltd 1966-73, Wentworth Hotel Ltd 1966-73; kt 1955 *see Debrett's Handbook of Australia and New Zealand for further details*; *Books* Capital Imports and The Terms of Trade (1931); *Clubs* Commonwealth (Canberra); *Style—* Sir Roland Wilson, KBE; 64 Empire Circuit, Forrest, ACT 2603, Australia (☎ 062 95 2560)

WILSON, Air Vice- Marshal Ronald Andrew Fellowes (Sandy); AFC (1978); s of Mr Ronald Denis Wilson (d 1983), of Great Bookham, Surrey, and Gladys Vera; *b* 27 Feb 1941; *Educ* Tonbridge, RAF Coll Cranwell; *m* 1, 4 Aug 1962 (m dis 1979), Patricia Lesley, da of Mr BD Cauthery (d 1986), of Effingham, Surrey; 1 da (Hayley Ann Fellowes b 7 Oct 1972); m 2, 21 May 1979, Mary Christine, da of Stanley Anderson (d 1978), of Darfield, Yorks; *Career* Flying Instr RAF Leeming 1963-65, Pilot 2 Sqdn RAF Gutersloh 1966-67, ADC to C-in-C RAF Germany 1967-68, Fl Cdr 2 Sqdn RAF Gutersloh 1968-70, Sqdn Ldr 1970, Flt Cdr 2 Sqdn RAf Laarbruch 1970-72, RAF Staff Coll Bracknell 1973, SO HQ Strike Cmd 1974-75, Wing Cdr 1975 OC 2 Sqdn 1975-77, SO Air Plans MOD 1977-79 Gp Capt 1980, OC RAF Lossiemouth 1980-82, Air Cdr Falkland Is and OC RAF Stanley 1982, SO Cent Commitments Staff MOD 1983-85 Air Cdre 1985, dir of ops (Strike) MOD 1985, dir air offensive MOD 1986-87 Air Vice-Marshal 1987, SASO Strike Cmd and DCSO HQUKAR 1987-88 AOC 1 Gp 1989-; awarded: Queens Commendation for Valuable Servs in the Air 1973, Arthur Barratt Meml Prize 1973; govr Tonbridge 1984-87, memb Cncl of Br Ski Fedn 1986; Freeman City of London 1966, Liveryman of Worshipful Co of Skinners 1970 (Extra Memb of Ct 1984-87); FBIM; *Recreations* skiing, golf, painting, furniture restoration, photography; *Clubs* Royal Air Force; *Style—* Air Vice-Marshal RAF Wilson, AFC; c/o Royal Bank of Scotland, Holts Branch, Whitehall, London SW1

WILSON, Hon Mr Justice; Sir Ronald Darling; KBE (1979), CMG (1978), QC (1963); s of Harold Wilson, and Jean Ferguson, *née* Darling; *b* 23 August 1922; *Educ* Geraldton State Sch, WA U (LLB), Pennsylvania Univ (LLM), Hon LLD West Aust Univ; *m* 1950, Leila Amy Gibson, da of W G Smith; 3 s, 2 da; *Career* asst Crown prosecutor WA 1954-59, chief Crown prosecutor WA 1959-61, Crown counsel 1961-69, solicitor-gen WA 1969-79, justice of the High Ct of Australia 1979-89; *see Debrett's Handbook of Australia and New Zealand for further details*; *Style—* Sir Ronald Wilson, KBE, CMG, QC; 38 Webster St, Nedlands WA 6009 Australia

WILSON, (Gerald) Roy; s of Fred Wilson (d 1934), of Oldham, Lancs, and Elsie, *née* Morrison (d 1968); *b* 11 Jan 1930; *Educ* Oldham HS; *m* 18 Sept 1965, Doreen, da of Albert Edward Chadderton (d 1970), of Failsworth, Manchester; 1 s (Jonathan b 1973), 1 da (Susan b 1969); *Career* Min of Works, HMSO, sr systems designer PO HQ 1965-66, branch mangr Girobank 1966-69 (sr systems designer 1966); Nat Savings: asst controller IT systems Durham 1972-78 (mangr 1969-72), controller Savings Certificate Off Durham 1978-86, dep dir of Savings London (under sec rank) 1986-; memb: Rotary Club of Durham, mgmnt res Gp BIM; FBIM 1984; *Recreations* swimming, reading, drawing, photography, watching sport; *Clubs* Civil Service, Dunelm (Durham), Durham City Swimming; *Style—* Roy Wilson, Esq; c/o Department for National Savings, Charles House, 375 Kensington High St, London W14 8SD

WILSON, Hon Mrs; Hon Sally Anne Marie Gabrielle; da of 5 Baron Vivian; *b* 1930; *m* 1, 1954 (m dis 1962), Robin Lowe; m 2, 1963, Charles William Munro Wilson; 1 s; *Style—* The Hon Mrs Wilson; 150 Cranmer Ct, Whitehead's Grove, London SW3 (☎ 01 589 8864)

WILSON, Hon Mrs (Shirley Cynthia); da of late 2 Baron Cunliffe; *b* 1926; *m* 1959, Alan Desmond Wilson; 1 s (Matthew Crispin b 1961), 1 da (Richenda Catherine b 1963); *Style—* The Hon Mrs Wilson; Ashbrook, Aston Tirrold, Didcot, Oxon OX11 9DL

WILSON, Snoo; s of Leslie Wilson, and Pamela Mary Wilson; *b* 2 August 1948; *Educ* Bradfield, East Anglia Univ (BA); *m* 1976, Ann, *née* McFerran; 2 s, 1 da; *Career* writer 1969-, assoc dir Portable Theatre 1970-75, Dramaturge RSC 1975-76, script ed Play for Today 1976, Henfield Fell Univ of E Anglia 1978, US Bicentennial Fell in Playwriting 1981-82, adapted Gounod's La Colombe Buxton Fextival 1983, assoc prof of theatre Univ of California San Diego 1987; filmscrip: Shadey 1986; Plays: Layby (jtly 1972), Pignight (1972), The Pleasure Principle (1973), Blowjob (1974), Soul of the White Ant (1976), England England (1978), Vampire (1978), The Glad Hand (1978), A Greenish Man (1978), The Number of the Beast (1982), Flaming Bodies (1982), Grass Widow (1983), Loving Reno (1983), Hamlyn (1984), More Light (1987), 80 days (book, musical 1988) etc; novels: Spaceache (1984), Inside Babel (1985); operas: Orpheus in the Underworld (new version 1984); *Recreations* beekeeping, space travel; *Style—* Snoo Wilson, Esq; 41 The Chase, London SW4 0NP

WILSON, Stanley John; CBE (1981); *b* 23 Oct 1921; *m* 1952, Molly Ann; 2 step s; *Career* md Burmah Oil 1975-82, chief exec 1980-82; chm Burmah SA Ltd 1983-; *Clubs* City of London, City, Rand; *Style—* Stanley Wilson, Esq, CBE; The Jetty, PO Box 751, Plettenberg Bay, Cape Province 6600, Republic of South Africa (☎ Plettenberg Bay 9624)

WILSON, Stephen Shipley; CB (1950); s of Alexander Cowan Wilson (d 1955), of London, and Edith Jane Brayshaw (d 1953); *b* 4 August 1904; *Educ* Leighton Park, Queen's Coll Oxford; *m* 1933, Martha Mott, da of Albert Bartram Kelley (d 1932), of Philadelphia; 2 s (Alexander, Guy), 1 da (Sarah); *Career* civil servant; keeper of Public Records 1960-66; historical section Cabinet Off 1966-77; *Clubs* Reform; *Style—* Stephen Wilson, Esq, CB; 3 Willow Rd, London NW3 1 TH (☎ 01 435 0148)

WILSON, (Catherine) Thelma; da of John Matters (d 1964), of Ashington, Northumberland, and Eleanor Irene, *née* Hudson (d 1979); *b* 9 June 1929; *Educ* St Margaret's HS Gosforth, Central Newcastle HS, King's College Durham Univ (BA); *m* 26 Sept 1953, Noel, s of the late Andrew Wilson, Ashington, Northumberland; 2 s ((Peter) Lawrence b 16 Jan 1956, Michael David b 5 Aug 1959); *Career* geriatric social worker Wimbledon Guild of Social Welfare 1952-56, lectr several Colls in London 1958-65, princ lectr in social policy NE London Poly 1965-, conslt on preparation for retirement Tate & Lyle Refineries London 1968-, cncl memb for the educn and trg of health visitors 1973-83, short term expert Social Devpt Fund UN 1973, expert assignment Regnl Off for Euro World Health Orgn 1981, UK rep on the int ctee Euro Regnl Clearing House for Community Work 1971-78; advsr Nursing and Social Work Serv Soldiers' Sailors & Airmen's Families Assoc 1983-, hon sec social admin & social work ctees of the J Univ Cncl for Social & Public Admin 1972-79, memb exam ctee local Govt Trg Bd and several related activities 1979-; Freeman City of London 1984, Liveryman Worshipful Co of Chartered Secs and Admins 1984; ACIS 1964, MISW 1964, FCIS 1974; *Books* over 40 pubns including Penal Services for Offenders; comparative studies of England and Poland 1984-85 (1987); *Recreations* reading, travel; *Clubs* Royal Overseas League; *Style—* Mrs Thelma Wilson; Polytechnic of East London, Dept of Medical Sciences and Health Studies, Romford Rd, London E15 4LZ (☎ 01 590 7722 ext 4225/4241, fax 01 519 3740)

WILSON, Prof Thomas; OBE (1946); s of John B Wilson (d 1945), and Margaret, *née* Ellison (d 1977); *b* 23 June 1916; *Educ* Methodist Coll Belfast, Queen's Univ Belfast (BA), London Univ (PhD), Oxford (MA); *m* 6 July 1943, Dorothy Joan, da of Arthur Parry; 1 s (John), 2 da (Moya, Margaret); *Career* WWII Miny Econ Warfare 1940-41, Miny Aircraft Prodn 1941-42, War Cabinet Offs 1942-45, Econ Section Cabinet 1945-46, fell Univ Coll Oxford 1946-58, Adam Smith Prof political econ Univ of Glasgow 1958-82, numerous govt consultancies; hon fell LSE, Hon DUniv of Stirling 1981; FBA, FRSE; *Books* Fluctuations in Income and Employment (1942), Oxford Studies in the Price Mechanism (1951), Inflation (1961), Planning and Growth (1964) Essays on Adam Smith (jt ed with A S Skinner 1975), The Market and the State (jt ed, with A S Skinner 1976), Welfare State (with D J Wilson 1982), Inflation Unemployment and the Market (1984), Ulster - Conflict and Consent (1989); *Recreations* hill walking, photography; *Clubs* Athenaeum; *Style—* Prof Thomas Wilson, OBE; 1 Chatford House, The Promenade, Clifton Down, Bristol BJ8 3NC (☎ 0272 730741)

WILSON, Thomas Charles; s of Jeremy Charles Wilson, DFC, of Fulmer, Bucks, and June Patricia, *née* Bucknill; *b* 2 June 1946; *Educ* Eton, Aix-en-Provence Univ; *m* 5 Dec 1980, (Elizabeth) Jane, da of Lt-Gen Sir Napier Crookenden KCB, DSO, OBE; 1 s (James b 1984), 1 da (Tobina b 1981), 1 step s (Geoffrey b 1977); *Career* hd corporate fin Price Waterhouse 1987- (articled clerk 1965-77, ptnr 1977-); FCA 1974; *Recreations* golf, tennis, fishing, bridge; *Clubs* Hurlingham Denham Golf; *Style—* Thomas Wilson, Esq; Price Waterhouse, Southwark Towers, 32 London Bridge St, London SE1 9SY (☎ 01 407 8989, fax 01 378 0647)

WILSON, Thomas David; s and h of Sir David Wilson, 3 Bt, *qv*; *b* 6 Jan 1959; *m* 21 July 1984, Valerie, er da of V D D Stopdale, of Shotover, Oxon; *Style—* Thomas Wilson, Esq

WILSON, Thomas Dunlop; s of William Wilson (d 1977), of Annwill, Grahamston Rd, Barrhead, Glasgow, and Annie, *née* Stewart (d 1986); *b* 5 Feb 1919; *Educ* Allan Gilens Sch Glasgow, Univ of Glasgow (BSc); *m* 29 Nov 1946, (Marie) Paule Juliette, da of Mathieu Durand (d 1974), of Souar, Tunisia; 1 s (William Mark Dunlop b 23 Jan 1949), 2 da (Anne-Marie Paule (Mrs Grove) b 3 April 1953, Gillian Francoise b 31 March 1959); *Career* WWII enlisted RE 1941 served UK, cmmnd 1942, 1 Army N Africa 1942-43, Italy and Austria 1943-46 (Maj dep asst dir tport railways GHQ CHF 1945-46); civil engr asst: Paisley 1946-49, Lanarkshire 1949-54; res engr Miny of Devpt Iraq 1954-58, sr civil engr (bridges) Lanarkshire 1958-60, chief project engr M5 Motorway (Worcs) 1960-62, dep co surveyor bridgemaster and engr Cumberland 1962-68, dir NW road construction unit Dept of Tport 1969-72, dep chief engr Dept of Tport 1972-74, ptnr Mott Hay & Anderson (consulting engrs) 1974-79, private consulting practice in civil engrg (arbitrator) 1979-; memb Rotary Club Glasgow, elder Neilston Church of Scotland; memb int ctees on roads and tunnels; CEng, FICE, FIStructE, FAMunE, FCIArb, FIHT, MAConsE; memb French Soc Civil Engrs; *Books* Civil Engineers Reference Book (highways chapter, 1975); *Recreations* hill-walking, fishing, shooting; *Clubs* Naval and Military; *Style—* Thomas Wilson, Esq; Kilmartin, Neilston, Glasgow G78 3EA (☎ 041 881 1346); 114 Main St, Neilston, Glasgow G78 3EA (☎ 041 881 1346, fax 041 248 4032)

WILSON, Col Timothy John Michael; s of Lt-Col AC Wilson (d 1975), of Kent and Devon, and Margaret Beverley, *née* Iliffe; *b* 23 Mar 1932; *Educ* Cranbrook Sch Kent, Canadian Army Staff Coll, Nat Defence Coll, Indian Nat Defence Coll; *m* 23 Sept 1961, Kitty Maxine, da of Maj Seymour Norton-Taylor, of Poole, Dorset; 2 da (Vanessa b 1963, Jennifer b 1965); *Career* 2 Lt and Lt 1950-53, Lt 2 i/c RM Detachment HMS Gambia 1953-55 (memb earthquake relief team Zante Ionian Islands 1953), Troop Subaltern 40 Commando RM 1955-57 served Cyprus, Near East (severely wounded at Port Said landings 1956, despatches), housemaster RM Sch of Music 1957-59, motor tport course 1959-60, local Capt ADC to C-in-C Near East HQ Near East Cyprus 1960-61, Capt Motor Tport Offr RM Poole 1961-63, staff course Canadian Army Staff Coll 1963-65, Adj 40 Commando RM (subsequently Maj) 1965-68 (served Malaysia 1965-67), Maj GSO 2 (instr) Jr Div Army Staff Coll Warminster 1968-70, Bde Maj UK Commandos GSO 2 Ops and Planning HQ Commando Forces RM 1970-72, staff course Nat Def Coll 1972-73, Lt-Col Royal Marines Rep USMC Devpt and Educn Cmd 1973-75, CO 42 Commando RM 1975-78 (served N Ireland 1976), Col Dir drafting and records RM HMS Centurion 1978-79, staff course Indian Nat Def Coll New Delhi 1979-80, Asst Adj Gen to Cmdt Gen RM MOD London 1980-83; Ptnrship sec Radcliffes & Co Slrs Westminster; memb HM Bodyguard of the Hon Corps of Gentlemen of Arms 1984; hon MSc (def studies) Allahabad 1980; FBIM 1980, FInstAM 1982; *Recreations* beagling, golf, tennis, travel; *Clubs* Army and Navy; *Style—* Col Timothy Wilson

WILSON, Hon William Edward Alexander; yr s of 2 Baron Moran, KCMG; *b* 16 Dec 1956; *Educ* Eton, Inns of Court Sch of Law; *Career* barr Dept of the Dir of Public Prosecutions; *Style—* The Hon William Wilson

WILSON, Hon Ysabelle; da of 4 Baron Nunburnholme; *b* 1962; *Style—* The Hon Ysabelle Wilson

WILSON, Hon Mrs (Yvette Latham); o da of 1 Baron Baillieu, KBE, CMG (d 1967), and Ruby Florence Evelyn, *née* Clark (d 1962); *b* 30 Sept 1922; *m* 20 July 1946, Robert Ruttan Wilson, s of late Arthur Alling Wilson (ggs of Rev George Wilson, bro of 9 and 10 Barons Berners), of San Francisco, California, USA; 4 da; *Style—* The Hon Mrs Wilson; Durford Knoll, Upper Durford Wood, Petersfield, Hants

WILSON OF HIGH WRAY, Baroness; Valerie Frances Elizabeth; da of William Baron Fletcher, of Cape Town; *m* 1935, Baron Wilson of High Wray, OBE, DSC (d 1980); *Style—* The Rt Hon Lady Wilson of High Wray; Gillingate House, Kendal, Cumbria

WILSON OF LANGSIDE, Baron (Life Peer UK 1967); Henry Stephen Wilson; PC (1967), QC (Scot 1965); s of James Wilson, slr of Glasgow; *b* 21 Mar 1916; *Educ* Glasgow HS, Glasgow Univ; *m* 1942, Jessie, da of William Waters, of Paisley; *Career* serv WWII HLI & RAC; barr 1946, slr-gen Scotland 1965-67, ld-advocate 1967-70, Sheriff Princ Glasgow and Strathkelvin 1975-77; contested (Lab): Dumfriesshire 1950 and 1955, Edinburgh W 1951; joined SDP 1981, sits as SDP peer in House of Lords; *Style—* The Rt Hon the Lord Wilson of Langside, PC, QC; Dunallan, Kippen, Stirlingshire (☎ 078 687 210)

WILSON OF RADCLIFFE, Baroness Freda; *née* Mather; *b* 23 Jan 1930; *m* 1976, as his 2 w, Baron Wilson of Radcliffe (d 1983, former Lab Peer and chief exec offr Co-operative Wholesale Soc); 1 step da; *Style—* The Rt Hon the Lady Wilson of Radcliffe; The Bungalow, 4 Hey House Mews, off Lumb Carr Road, Holcombe, Nr Bury BL8 4NS

WILSON OF RIEVAULX, Baron (Life Peer UK 1983), of Kirklees, Co W Yorks; Rt Hon Sir (James) Harold Wilson; KG (1976), OBE (1945), PC (1947); s of James Herbert Wilson (d 1971, sometime Lib dep election agent to Sir Winston Churchill), of Rievaulx, Biscovey, Par, Cornwall, formerly of Huddersfield and of Manchester, and Ethel Wilson; *b* 11 Mar 1916; *Educ* Milnsbridge Cncl Sch, Royds Hall Sch Huddersfield, Wirral GS Bebington, Jesus Coll Oxford; *m* 1940, (Gladys) Mary, da of late Rev Daniel Baldwin, of The Manse, Duxford, Cambridge; 2 s; *Career* lectr in economics New Coll Oxford 1937, fellow Univ Coll Oxford 1938, praelector in Economics and domestic bursar 1945; MP (Lab): Ormskirk 1945-50, Huyton 1950-83; dir economics and statistics Miny of Fuel and Power 1943-44, parly sec Miny of Works 1945-47, sec Overseas Trade 1947, pres BOT 1947-51, chm Labour Party exec ctee 1961-62 (vice-chm 1960-61) leader Oppn 1963-64 and 1970-74, prime minister and first lord of the Treasury 1964-70 and 1974-76; chllr Bradford Univ 1966-85, pres Royal Statistical Soc 1972-73, chm Ctee to Review Financing of Financial Instns 1976-80; hon pres GB-USSR Assoc 1976-87; pres Royal Shakespeare Co 1976-86; hon fellow Jesus and Univ Colls Oxford 1963; elder bro Trinity House, hon freeman City of London; Hon DCL Oxford 1965; Hon LLD: Lancaster, Liverpool, Nottingham, Sussex; HonDTech Bradford; DUniv: Essex and Open Univ (which he founded); FRS; *Clubs* Athenaeum; *Style—* The Rt Hon the Lord Wilson of Rievaulx, KG, OBE, PC; House of Lords, London SW1A 0AA

WILSON SMITH, Lt-Col John Logan; OBE (1976); s of William Arthur Wilson Smith, (d 1948), and Dorothy Grace, *née* Lawes (d 1974); *b* 4 July 1927; *Educ* Wellington Coll; *m* 14 April 1961, Ann Winifred Lyon, da of Kenneth Charles Corsar (d 1967), of Cairniehill; 3 da (Susan b 1962, Caroline b 1964, Jane b 1969); *Career* Regular Army offr cmmnd The Royal Scots 1946, served Palestine, Korea, Aden, Cyprus, NI, The Staff Coll (psc) 1961 jssc 1965, ret Lt Col 1977, regt sec The Royal Scots; chm The Royal Scots Assoc; dir The Royal Scots Regt Shop Ltd; pres SSAFA/FHS Edinburgh and Midlothian; *Recreations* shooting, forestry, horticulture; *Clubs* The Royal Scots; *Style—* Lt-Col John L Wilson Smith, OBE; Cumledge, Duns, Berwickshire TD11 3TB; The Castle, Edinburgh EH1 2YT (☎ 031 336 1761 ext 4265)

WILSON-FISH, Peter; s of Wilfred Fish, of Longton, Preston, Lancs, and Muriel, *née* Wilson; *b* 20 Oct 1933; *Educ* Giggleswick Sch, London Univ; *m* 1, 20 July 1961 (m dis) Shirley Gertrude, da of Leopold Augustus Henry Rohlehr (d 1961), of New Amsterdam Guiana; 1 da (Jacqueline b 1963); m 2, 8 Oct 1975, Stella Dawn, da of Sidney Charman (d 1982); 2 s (James b 1977, Oliver b 1979); *Career* RE 1956-; in Pharmaceutical Indust 1979; *Recreations* beagling, sailing, thrashing the water, gardening; *Style—* Peter Wilson-Fish, Esq; Hilltop, Colby, Appleby in Westmorland, Cumbria CA16 6BD

WILSON-JOHNSON, David Robert; s of Harry Kenneth Johnson, of Irthlingborough, Northants, and Sylvia Constance, *née* Wilson; *b* 16 Nov 1950; *Educ* Wellingborough Sch, Br Inst of Florence, St Catharine's Coll Cambridge (BA), RAM; *Career* baritone, Royal Opera House, performances incl: We Come to the River (debut) 1976, Billy Budd 1982, L'Enfant et les Sortilèges 1983 and 1987, Boris Godunov 1984, Die Zauberflöte 1985, 86 and 87, Turandot 1987, Madame Butterfly 1988, Paris Opera debut Die Meistersinger 1988; Eight Songs for a Mad King Paris 1979, Last Night of the Proms 1981 and 1986; festival appearances at: Glyndebourne, Edinburgh, Bath, Bergen, Berlin, Geneva, Graz, Holland, Hong Kong, Jerusalem, Orange, Paris, Vienna; recordings incl: Schubert, Winterreise, Schoenberg's Ode to Napoleon, La Traviata, Lucrezia Borgia, Mozart Masses from King's College, Nelson Mass Haydn; films incl: The Midsummer Marriage (Tippett), The Lighthouse (Maxwell Davies); ARAM 1984, FRAM 1988; *Recreations* swimming, slimming, gardening, growing walnuts at house in Dordogne; *Style—* David Wilson-Johnson, Esq; 28 Englefield Rd, London N1 4ET (☎ 01 254 0941); Lies Askonas Ltd, 186 Drury Lane, London WC23B 5RY (☎ 01 405 1808, fax 01 242 1831, telex 265914 ASKONA G)

WILTON, Francis George (Frank); s of William Charles Wilton (d 1985), of Swindon, and Clara May, *née* Boyce (d 1987); *b* 20 Feb 1934; *Educ* Swindon GS; *m* 16 June 1962, Betty Eileen, da of William Francis Radford (d 1958); 2 s (Mark b 1968, Darren b 1970), 2 da (Carole b 1964, Shula b 1966); *Career* sub offr Wilts Fire Bde 1961 (fireman 1954, leading fireman 1960), station offr Worcester City and Co Fire Bde 1963, station offr Wolverhampton Fire and Ambulance Serv 1964, instr Fire Serv Tech Coll 1969, dep chief fire offr Gloucester City Fire Bde 1971, dep chief fire offr Gloucestershire Fire Serv 1976, firemaster Central Region Scotland Fire Bde 1983, chief fire offr Co of Avon Fire Bde 1984; chm: Avon Fire Liaison Panel; pres: Co of Avon Fire Bde Sports Assoc, Co of Avon Fire Bde Offrs Club, Avon branch Fire Servs Nat Benevolent Fund; vice pres Eastern area St John in Avon; cncl memb St John in Avon, memb Bristol Rotary Club; MIFireE 1962, FBIM 1981, MICD 1986; *Recreations* golf, campanology, philately, calligraphy; *Style—* Frank Wilton, Esq, QFSM; 16 Charles Close, Thornbury, Bristol, Avon BS12 1LN (☎ 0454 416 870); Fire Brigade HQ, Temple Black, Bristol BS1 6EU (☎ 0272 262 061, fax 0272 250 980, car tel 0836 745 036, telex 9312110719 (AFG))

WILTON, Sir (Arthur) John; KCMG (1979, CMG 1967), KCVO (1979), MC (1945); s of Walter Wilton (d 1944); *b* 21 Oct 1921; *Educ* Wanstead HS, St John's Coll Oxford; *m* 1950, Maureen Elizabeth Alison, *née* Meaker; 4 s, 1 da; *Career* Royal Ulster Rifles 1942 (despatches), Maj; HM Dip Serv 1947-79: dir MECAS Shemlan 1960-65, dep high cmmr Aden 1966-67, ambass Kuwait 1970-74, under-sec FCO 1974-75, ambass Jedda 1976-79; dir London House for Overseas Graduates 1979-86; chm Arab-Br Centre 1981-86, FRSA 1982; *Recreations* reading and current affairs, gardening; *Style—* Sir John Wilton, KCMG, KCVO, MC

WILTON, (John) Michael; s of Herbert George Wilton (d 1959), of East Carleton Lodge, Norfolk and Ethel Jane, *née* Brumwell (d 1967); *b* 7 July 1917; *Educ* Gresham's Sch Holt; *m* 16 Dec 1944, Joan Adelene, da of Donald Edward Brown (d 1943), of Ifield Place, Shorne Ifield, Kent; 1 s (Simon Edward b 1950), 1 da (Jane Katharine b 1948); *Career* Capt RA, serv GB and Ceylon 1940-46; slr 1947; Norwich Union Life Insur Soc: asst slr 1948, slr 1957, sr chief slr 1965; ret and ceased to practice as slr 1977; memb Tunstead Parish Cncl Norfolk 1970-83 (chm 1970-82); memb Law Soc; OStJ 1965; *Recreations* carpentry, photography, gardening; *Style—* Michael Wilton, Esq; Barnside, Skelton, Penrith, Cumbria CA11 9TE (☎ 085 34 386)

WILTON, Rosalyn Susan; *née* Trup; da of Samuel Trup, and Celia, *née* Aronson; *b* 25 Jan 1952; *Educ* Copthall Co GS, L'Alliance Francaise Paris, London Univ (BSc); *m* 11 April 1978, Gerald Parselle Wilton, s of Orville Wilton; 2 da (Georgina b 1979, Emily b 1981); *Career* sterling money broker Butler Till Ltd 1973-79, dir GNI Ltd 1982-84, md Drexel Burnham Lambert Ltd (institutional financial futures and options) 1984-; dir The London Int Financial Futures Exchange 1985-; *Style—* Mrs Rosalyn Wilton; Drexel Burnham Lambert Ltd, Winchester House, 100 Old Broad St, London EC2N 1BE (☎ 01 920 9797, fax 01 920 9799, telex 884 845)

WILTON, 7 Earl of (UK 1801); Seymour William Arthur John Egerton; also Viscount Grey de Wilton (UK 1801); s of 6 Earl of Wilton (d 1927, gs of 2 Earl, himself yr bro of 2 Marquess of Westminster and er bro of 1 Baron Ebury; hence Lord Wilton is hp to Marquessate of W, and all lesser attendant honours, at present held by 6 Duke of Westminster (tho' not the Dukedom itself), while his kinsman, Lord Ebury, is in turn hp to Lord Wilton) and Brenda, da of Sir William Petersen, KBE; *b* 29 May 1921; *Educ* Eton; *m* 1962, Diana, da of Royal Galway and formerly w of David Naylor-Leyland, MVO, 3 s of Sir Edward Naylor-Leyland, 2 Bt; *Heir* 4 cous, 6 Baron Ebury; *Clubs* White's; *Style—* The Rt Hon The Earl of Wilton; Warrens Boyes 2 Archer, 20 Hartford Road, Huntingdon

WILTSHIRE, Earl of; Christopher John Hilton Paulet; s and h of 18 Marquess of Winchester; *b* 30 July 1969; *Style—* Earl of Wiltshire

WILTSHIRE, Sir Frederick Munro; CBE (1970, OBE 1967); *b* 5 June 1911; *m* 1938, Jennie L, da of F M Frencham; 1 da; *Career* md Wiltshire File Co Ltd 1938-77, indust memb Sci and Indust Forum Acad of Sci 1967-80, memb of exec CSIRO 1974-78, memb Aust Indust Devpt Assoc 1954-80 (pres 1966-69); kt 1976; *see Debrett's Handbook of Australia and New Zealand for further details*; *Style—* Sir Frederick Wiltshire, CBE; 38 Rockley Rd, S Yarra, Vic 3141, Australia

WILTSHIRE, James Gordon; s of Arthur Thomas Wiltshire (d 1984), of Oxshott, and Barbara Gordon, *née* Donald; *b* 17 Jan 1928; *Educ* Dean Close Sch Cheltenham, Queens' Coll Cambridge (BA); *m* 19 May 1961, Philippa Katharine, da of Philip Milholland (d 1976), of Wimbledon; 1 s (Philip Gordon b 1965), 2 da (Nicola Viva b 1962, Penelope Ara 1967); *Career* Lt RE Gold Coast (Ghana) 1947-48; asst engr Kennedy & Donkin, Consulting Engrs 1951-57, ptnr 1958-, jt sr ptnr 1975-86, chief exec 1984-86; ptnr Kennedy & Donkin Int Hong Kong 1960-86, Africa, Malawi 1960-, Africa Uganda 1960-74, Africa Botswana 1960-; gp conslt Kennedy & Donkin Gp Ltd 1987-; dir Kennedy & Donkin Africa Pty Ltd 1987-; memb Smeatonian Soc of Civil Engrs 1977- (hon tres 1981-); serv on cncls of Assoc of Consulting Engrs and of Br Conslts Bureau; FEng, FICE, FIEE, FRSA; *Recreations* tennis, golf, sailing, DIY; *Clubs* Royal Wimbledon Golf; *Style—* James Wiltshire, Esq; Willow Bend, Moles Hill, Oxshott, Surrey KT22 0QB (☎ 0372 842316); Kennedy & Donkin Group Ltd, Westbrook Mills, Godalming, Surrey GU7 2AZ (☎ 04868 25900, telex 859373 KDHO G, fax 04868 25136)

WILTSHIRE, Timothy John; s of Raymond Wiltshire (d 1983), of Farmborough, Bath, Avon, and Kathleen Grace Wiltshire; *b* 18 April 1953; *Educ* S Bristol Poly (Dip Engrg), Lackham Coll of Agric; *m* 14 June 1975, Bridget Eileen, da of Rodney Holbrook Acheson-Crow, of Bristol, Avon; 3 s (Benjamin b 1978, Robert b 1980, Jonathon b 1986) 1 da (Eleanor b 1983); *Career* branch mangr Lloyds Abbey Life plc

1973-82, mgmnt fin serv Property Growth Assur Ltd 1982-83, formed financial servs brokerage 1983, chm and md County Mgmnt Conslts Ltd (business and property investmt servs) 1987; memb C of C, govr Royal Bath & West Soc, community advsr Civil Def Wilts CC; FLIA 1979, MInst M 1984;; *Recreations* shooting, water sports, historic building conservation; *Style—* Timothy Wiltshire, Esq; Driffield Manor, Driffield, Cirencester, Gloucester (☎ 0285 85359); County Management Consultants, Cirencester, Glos GL7 5PY (☎ 0285 853559, fax 0666 52701, cellnet 0860 369392)

WIMBERLEY, Maj Neil Campbell; MBE (1956); s of Maj-Gen Douglas Wimberley, CB, DSO, MC, DL, LLD (d 1983), of Foxhall, Coupar Angus, Perthshire, and Myrtle Livington Campbell; Wimberley - see Burkes Landed Gentry 1 Ed Vol I; *b* 23 Nov 1927; *Educ* Geelong GS Victoria Aust, Army Staff Coll (psc); *m* 10 Aug 1953, Ann, da of Lt-Col Walter Lloyd Stewart-Meiklejohn (d 1963, late Indian Army); 1 s (Michael Campbell b 1954), 1 da (Sarah b 1958); *Career* serv Queen's Own Cameron Highlanders, Malaya, Suez, Korea, Aden, Brunei, Borneo 1945-67; co dir Appleyard Scottish Div Ltd 1975-79, estates mangr Wm Low & Co Plc 1980-; cncl memb Econ League (Scotland) 1972-, memb Queen's Bodyguard for Scotland, Royal Co of Archers; *Recreations* shooting, fishing, gardening; *Clubs* Army and Navy, Highland Society of London; *Style—* Major Neil Wimberley; The Old Manse, Lundie by Dundee, Angus (☎ 0382 581230); Wm Low & Co Plc, Baird Avenue, Dundee (☎ 0382 814022)

WIMBORNE, 3 Viscount (UK 1918); Sir Ivor Fox-Strangways Guest; 5 Bt (UK 1838); also Baron Wimborne (UK 1880) and Baron Ashby St Ledgers (UK 1910); s of 2 Viscount Wimborne, OBE (d 1967), and Lady Mabel Fox-Strangways, da of 6 Earl of Ilchester; *b* 2 Dec 1939; *Educ* Eton; *m* 1, 1966 (m dis), Victoria (who m subsequently, 1982, Vincent Poklewski-Koziell), da of Col Mervyn Vigors, DSO, MC, by his 2 w Margaret (da of Maj-Gen Sir George Aston, KCB); 1 s; m 2, 1983, Venetia Margaret, er da of Richard Bridges St John Quarry, and former w of Capt Frederick G Barker; 1 da; *Heir* s, Hon Ivor Mervyn Vigors Guest b 19 Sept 1968; *Career* chm Harris & Dixon 1972-76, jt master Pytchley 1968-76, chm Harris & Dixon Holdings Ltd 1977-; *Clubs* Travellers', Cercle Interalliée, Polo; *Style—* The Rt Hon the Viscount Wimborne; c/o Travellers' Club, 25 Champs Elysées, 75008 Paris, France

WIMBORNE, Dowager Viscountess; Lady Mabel Edith; *née* Fox-Strangways; da of 6 Earl of Ilchester, GBE, and Lady Helen Mary Theresa Vane-Tempest-Stewart , da of 6 Marquess of Londonderry; *b* 17 Feb 1918; *m* 1938, 2 Viscount Wimborne; 3 s (3 Viscount, Hon Julian and Hon Charles Guest), 1 da (Hon Mrs Johnson), *qv*; *Style—* The Rt Hon the Dowager Viscountess Wimborne; Magnolia House, Candie, St Peter Port, Guernsey

WIMBUSH, Rt Rev Richard Knyvet; s of Rev Canon James Sedgewick Wimbush (d 1941), and Judith Isabel, *née* Fox (d 1957); *b* 18 Mar 1909; *Educ* Haileybury Coll, Oriel Coll Oxford (BA, MA), Cuddesdon Theol Coll; *m* 25 Sept 1937, Mary (Mollie) Margaret, da of Rev Ezekiel Harry Smith (d 1934), Vicar of Ripponden, Halifax, and Illingworth, Halifax; 3 s (Martin b 1943, Stephen b 1944, John b 1950), 1 da (Judith b 1940); *Career* ordained: deacon 1934, priest 1935; chaplain Cuddesdon Coll 1934-37; asst curate: Pocklington E Yorks 1937-39, St Wilfred's Harrogate 1939-42; rector Melsonby N Yorks 1942-48, princ Edinburgh Theol Coll (Scottish Episcopal Church), 1948-62, bishop of Argyll and The Isles 1963-77, primus Scottish Episcopal Church 1974-77, incumbent of Etton with Dalton Holme N Humberside 1977-83, asst bishop diocese of York 1977-; *Clubs* New (Edinburgh); *Style—* The Rt Rev Richard Wimbush; 5 Tower Place, York YO1 1RZ (☎ 0904 641971)

WINBERG, Max Henry; s of Abraham Winberg (d 1973), and Betty *née* Singer; *b* 11 Oct 1937; *Educ* Northwold and Mount Pleasant Secdy Modern Sch; *m* 20 Aug 1981, Jean, da of Robert Ruthen (d 1976); 2 da (Lucy b 1981, Emma b 1985); *Career* chm and md: Tacbrook Ltd, Shedmoor Ltd, Cycloacre Ltd; *Recreations* chess, windsurfing, amateur poker player; *Style—* Max Winberg, Esq; Costa Blanca Villas, 13/17 Newbury St, Wantage, Oxon OX12 8BU (☎ 02357 65305, telex 837071 CBVROK, fax 02357 60256)

WINCH, Hon Mrs; Hon Jean Rosemary Vera; *née* Cary; da of 14 Viscount Falkland, by his 1 w Joan Sylvia, only da of Capt Charles Bonham Southey; *b* 30 Oct 1928; *Educ* Lady Walsingham's Sch; *m* 1950, Henry Herman Montagu Winch, s of Henry Louis Winch (d 1903), and Vera, Lady Newborough (1 w of 5 Baron); *Recreations* country pursuits, flat racing (racehorses: My Solitaire, Sparkling Halo); *Clubs* Turf; *Style—* The Hon Mrs Winch; Castle Barn, Penrhyndeudraeth, Gwynedd (☎ 0766 770313)

WINCH, Richard Anthony Brooke; s of Maj Stanley Brooke Winch, OBE (d 1959), of Swanington Manor, Norwich, and Eleanor Boville, *née* Morris (d 1951); *b* 6 Sept 1921; *Educ* Charterhouse, Trin Coll Camb (MA); *m* 29 Aug 1959, Frances Evelyn Barbara, da of Robert Ives, of Erpingham House, Erpingham, Norfolk; 1 da (Eleanor Charlotte (Mrs Buxton) b 21 March 1963); *Career* High Sheriff of Norfolk 1972; memb Worshipful Co of Farmers; *Recreations* gardens, shooting; *Style—* Richard Anthony Winch, Esq; Swanington Manor, Norwich, Norfolk (☎ 0603 860700)

WINCH, Thomas Beverley Charles; s of Eric William Winch (d 1964), of St Peter Port, Guernsey, CI, and Jessie Kathleen Jeanette, *née* Garrould; *b* 8 April 1930; *Educ* Rugby, St John's Cambridge (MA); *m* 19 Oct 1963, Jane, da of Col Nathaniel Montague Barnardiston (d 1986), of Cirencester, Glos; 1 s (William Montague b 1970), 1 da (Katherine Jane Amicia b 1972); *Career* fine arts valuer; borough cncllr Mayor 1977-78; *Recreations* historical research and analysis; *Style—* Thomas B C Winch, Esq; Westport Granary, Malmesbury, Wilts (☎ Malmesbury 822119)

WINCHESTER, Archdeacon of; *see*: Clarkson, Ven Alan Geoffrey

WINCHESTER, Bapsy, Marchioness of; Bapsy; *née* Pavry; da of Most Rev Khurshedji Pavry, High Priest of the Parsees in India; *Educ* Columbia Univ New York (MA); *m* 1952, as 3 wife, 16 Marquess of Winchester (d 1962); *Career* memb cncl World Alliance for Int Peace through Religion; Order of Merit of Iran; *Books* Heroines of Ancient Iran (1930); *Style—* The Most Hon Bapsy, Marchioness of Winchester

WINCHESTER, 95 Bishop of (AD 636) 1985-; Rt Rev Colin Clement Walter James; patron of 78 livings, and 29 alternately with other patrons, the Canonries in his Cathedral, and the Archdeaconries of Winchester and Basingstoke; s of late Canon Charles Clement Hancock James, and Gwenyth Mary James; *b* 20 Sept 1926; *Educ* Aldenham, King's Coll Cambridge (MA), Cuddesdon Theological Coll; *m* 1962, Margaret Joan Henshaw; 1 s, 2 da; *Career* asst curate Stepney Parish Church 1952-55, chaplain Stowe Sch 1955-59, BBC Religious Broadcasting Dept 1959-67, vicar St Peter's Bournemouth 1967-73, bishop suffragan of Basingstoke 1973-77, chm Church Information Ctee 1976-79, bishop of Wakefield 1977-85, chm Central Religious Advsy Ctees to BBC and IBA 1979-84; *Recreations* theatre, travelling, radio and television; *Style—* The Rt Rev the Bishop of Winchester; Wolvesey, Winchester, Hants SO23 9ND

WINCHESTER, Colin Robert John; s of Stanley Robert John Winchester (d 1968), of Herts, and Daisy Florence Griffiths; *b* 5 Dec 1933; *Educ* Queen Elizabeth's Barnet; *m* 25 March 1961, Jane Hillier, da of Rodney Guy Margetts (d 1961), of Grange Farm, Stratford upon Avon; 2 s (Dominic b 1969, Luke b 1975); *Career* Nat Serv; RA 1952-54; dir Ogilvy & Mather Ltd 1975-; *Recreations* golf, squash, skiing; *Clubs* Army and Navy; *Style—* Colin Winchester, Esq; Cranard Broomrigg Rd, Fleet, Hants (☎ 0252 614808); Ogilvy & Mather Ltd, Brettenham House, Lancaster Place, London WC2

WINCHESTER, Ian Sinclair; CMG (1982); s of Dr Alexander Hugh Winchester FRCS Ed, of Redroofs, 16 Melville Ave, S Croydon, Surrey, and Mary Stewart Duguid (d 1954); *b* 14 Mar 1931; *Educ* Lewes County GS, Oxford Univ (BA); *m* 9 Nov 1957, Shirley Louise, da of Frederic Milner CMG (d 1957); 3 s (Charles b 1959, Andrew b 1962, Robert b 1967); *Career* HM Dip Serv; dir Communications and Tech Servs 1985-; min Br Embassy Saudi Arabia 1982-83; commercial cnsllr Br Embassy Brussels 1973-76; *Style—* Ian S Winchester, Esq, CMG

WINCHESTER, 18 Marquess of (Premier Marquess of England, cr 1551); Nigel George Paulet; also Baron St John of Basing (E 1539) and Earl of Wiltshire (E 1550); s of George Paulet (1 cous of 17 Marquess, who d 1968; also eighth in descent from 5 Marquess); *b* 23 Dec 1941; *m* 1967, Rosemary, da of Maj Aubrey Hilton, of Harare, Zimbabwe; 2 s (Earl of Wiltshire, Lord Richard b 1971), 1 da (Lady Susan b 1976); *Heir* s, Earl of Wiltshire; *Career* dir Rhodesia Mineral Ventures Ltd, Sani-Dan Servs Ltd, Rhodesia Prospectors Ltd; *Style—* The Most Hon the Marquess of Winchester; Lydford Cottage, 35 Whyteladies Lane, Borrowdale, Salisbury, Zimbabwe

WINCHILSEA AND NOTTINGHAM, 16 and 11 Earl of (E 1628 and 1681); Sir Christopher Denys Stormont Finch Hatton; 17 and 11 Bt (E 1611 and 1660), of Eastwell and Raunston respectively; also Baron Finch (E 1675), Viscount Maidstone (E 1623) and Hereditary Lord of Royal Manor of Wye; s of 15 and 10 Earl of Winchilsea and Nottingham (d 1950), by his 1 w, Countess Gladys Széchényi, 3 da of Count Lászlo Széchényi (sometime Hungarian min in London); *b* 17 Nov 1936; *Educ* Eton, Gordonstoun; *m* 1962, Shirley, da of late Bernard Hatfield, of Wylde Green, Sutton Coldfield; 1 s (Viscount Maidstone), 1 da (Lady Alice b 2 May 1970); *Heir* s, Viscount Maidstone; *Style—* The Rt Hon the Earl of Winchilsea and Nottingham; South Cadbury House, nr Yeovil, Somerset

WINCKWORTH, Archibald Norman; s of William Norman Winckworth (d 1941), of Dunchideock House, Exeter, and Mary Russell Watson (d 1954), f int footballer (assoc) against Scotland and Wales 1892-93; *b* 14 Oct 1917; *Educ* Westminster, Reading Univ; *Career* Capt RA 1943, Adj 1943-46, serv M East 1941-45; social worker 1946-51, schmaster 1952-65; antique dealer 1965-; *Books* My Twenty One Short Stories; *Recreations* gardening, bridge, antique bottle collecting; *Style—* Archibald Winckworth, Esq; Dunchideock House, nr Exeter EX2 9TS (☎ 0392 832429)

WINDELER, John Robert; s of Alfred Stewart, and Ethela Marie, *née* Boremuth; *b* 21 Mar 1943; *Educ* Ohio State Univ USA (BA, MBA); *m* 15 June 1965, Judith Lynn, da of Robert Francis Taylor; 2 s (Stewart, James); *Career* Irving Tst Co NY: vice pres liability mgmnt 1973-75, sr vice pres money market div 1975-80, mangr loan syndication devpt 1981, gen mangr London 1981-83, exec vice pres investmt banking gp 1984; md Irving Tst Int Ltd London 1984-, pres Irving Securities Inc NY 1987-; dir: Trans City Hldgs Sydney Aust, Irving Tst Int Singapore, Little Red Sch House Inc; former dir Int Commercial Bank London; memb: Securities Assoc, Assoc Int Bond Dealers; *Recreations* skiing, tennis, running, history; *Clubs* Hurlingham; *Style—* John Windeler, Esq; 18 Margaretta Terrace, London SW3 (☎ 01 352 5183); 10 Mayfair Place, London W1X 5FJ (☎ 01 322 6100, fax 01 322 6074, telex 888479)

WINDER, (Alexander) John Henry; s of Lt Col Alexander Stuart Monck Winder (d 1969), of Finches, Castlewalk, Wadhurst, Sussex, and Helen Mary, *née* Swayne (d 1985); *b* 23 Oct 1921; *Educ* Shrewsbury, New Coll Oxford (BA, MA); *m* 2 May 1959, Shirlie (Cherry), da of Norman James Lewis (d 1969), of Tunbridge Wells; 2 s (Mark Henry Stuart b 1960, Paul Alexander Lewis b 1962), 2 da (Rachel Emily b 1965, Jane Helen Esther b 1966); *Career* cmmnd RCS 1941, Signal Off 90 Field Regt RA 1942-45, Capt 1 Corps HQ Germany 1945-46; served: Sicily Landings with 231 Brigade 50 Div 1943, D Day Landings 50 Div 1944; Colonial Engrg Serv N Rhodesia 1949-52; Binnie & Ptnrs Consulting Engrs 1952-56: sr asst resident engr Hong Kong 1953-56, chief resident engr Grafham Water 1957-66; resident engr Hong Kong 1953-56; Binnie & Ptnrs conslt engr 1966-70, chief resident engr for Rutland Water,T & C Hawksley Consulting Engrs 1978-85; author of various papers for Inst of Civil Engrs and Inst of Water and Enviromental Mgmnt; memb Br Section of the Int on Large Dams, 1969 appointed memb of Panel AR under the Reservoir's Act; chm of various research project steering ctees for CIRIA; FICE 1986, FIWEM 1960, MASCE 1980, FBIS; *Recreations* music, walking, tennis, woodworking; *Style—* John Winder, Esq; 10 Mary Vale, Godalming, Surrey, GU7 1SW; c/o Watson Hawksley, Terriers Hse, Amersham Rd, High Wycombe, Bucks, HP13 5AJ (☎ 0494 26240)

WINDER, John Lindsay; s of Harold Vickers Winder (d 1969), of Barrow-in-Furness, and Mary Dick, *née* Card; *b* 8 Nov 1935; *Educ* Barrow GS; *Career* chartered accountant 1959; vice-chm (dir 1973-) Furness Building Soc 1988-; pres Barrow Scout Mgmt Ctee, chm Barrow Rambling Club; JP (dep chm Barrow-on-Furness with Bootle Bench 1988); FCA; *Recreations* fell walking, gardening, golf; *Style—* John L Winder, Esq, JP; 32 Dane Avenue, Barrow-in-Furness LA14 4JS (☎ 0229 217 26); 125 Ramsden Square, Barrow-in-Furness, Cumbria LA14 1XA (☎ 0229 203 90)

WINDEYER, Sir Brian Wellingham; s of Richard Windeyer, KC, of Sydney, NSW; *b* 7 Feb 1904; *Educ* Sydney C of E GS, St Andrew's Coll Sydney Univ (Hon MD); *m* 1, 1928, Joyce, da of Harry Russell; 1 s, 1 da; m 2, 1948, Elspeth, da of H Bowry; 1 s, 2 da; *Career* prof radiology Middx Hosp Med Sch 1942-69 (dean 1954-67), vice-chllr London Univ 1969-72; Hon FRACS, Hon FCRA, Hon FACR; Hon DSc: Br Columbia, Wales, Cantab; Hon LLD Glasgow; FRCP, FRCS, FRCSE, FRSM, FRCR, DMRE; kt 1961; *Style—* Sir Brian Windeyer; 9 Dale Close, St Ebbe's, Oxford OX1 1TU (☎ (0865) 242816);

WINDHAM, John Jeremy; er s of Sir Ralph Windham (d 1980), formerly of Waghen Hall, Yorks and later of Tetbury, and Kathleen Mary, *née* FitzHerbert, *qv*; descended from the ancient family of Wyndham of Felbrigg and Crownthorpe (NW of Wymondham) Norfolk; kinsman and hp of Sir Thomas Bowyer-Smyth, 15 Bt; *b* 22 Nov

1948; *Educ* Wellington Coll; *m* 1976, (Rachel) Mary, da of Lt-Col (Walter) George Finney, TD (d 1973); 1 s ((Thomas) Ralph b 1985), 2 da (Katharine b 1981, Emma b 1983); *Career* Capt Irish Gds and SAS, ret; Br Trans-Americas Expdn (Darien Gap) 1972; Kleinwort, Benson Ltd 1978-84, dir Def Systems Ltd 1980-85; joined Enterprise Oil plc 1984; *Recreations* tennis, shooting, sailing; *Style*— John Windham, Esq; 81 Broxash Rd, London SW11 6AD (☎ 01 223 7461); The Hyde, Woolhope, Herefordshire; Enterprise Oil plc, 5 Strand, London WC2N 5HU (☎ 01 930 1212, telex 8950611)

WINDHAM, Lady Kathleen Mary; da of Capt Cecil Henry FitzHerbert, DSC (d 1952), of Latimerstown, Co Wexford, and Ellen Katherine Lowndes (d 1975); *b* 19 Feb 1918; *Educ* Langford Grove Essex; *m* 1946, Sir Ralph Windham (d 1980), s of Maj Ashe Windham, of Waghen Hall, Hull; 2 s (John, *qv*, Andrew), 2 da (Penelope, Belinda); *Career* served WW II WRNS; *Style*— Lady Windham; Hook's Cottage, Kingscote, nr Tetbury, Glos (☎ 0453 860461)

WINDLESHAM, 3 Baron (UK 1937); Sir David James George Hennessy; 3 Bt (UK 1927), CVO, PC (1973); s of 2 Baron Windlesham (d 1962), by his 1 w Angela (d 1956), da of Julian Duggan; *b* 28 Jan 1932; *Educ* Ampleforth, Trinity Coll Oxford; *m* 22 May 1965, Prudence Loveday (d 1986), yr da of Lt-Col Rupert Trevor Wallace Glynn, MC; 1 s (Hon James b 1968), 1 da (Hon Victoria b 1966); *Heir* s, Hon James Rupert Hennessy b 9 Nov 1968; *Career* served Grenadier Gds, Lt; sits as Cons peer in House of Lords; min state: Home Off 1970-72, NI 1972-73; ld privy seal and ldr House of Lords 1973-74; chm: ATV Network 1981 (md 1975-81), Parole Bd 1982-88; dir: The Observer 1981-, W H Smith Gp 1986-; chm: Oxford Preservation Tst 1979-, Oxford Soc 1985-88; tstee; Br Museum 1981- (chm 1986-), Community Service Volunteers 1981-; memb Museums and Galleries Cmmn 1984-86; hon fell Trinity Coll Oxford 1982; visiting fell All Souls' Coll 1986; *Books* Communication and Political Power (1966), Politics in Practice (1975), Broadcasting in a Free Society (1980), Responses to Crime (1987); *Style*— The Rt Hon the Lord Windlesham, CVO, PC; House of Lords, London SW1

WINDOWS, Anthony Robin (Tony); s of Frederick Ernest Windows (Lt, RNVR, d 1986), of 9 Ridgewood, Knoll Hill, Sneyd Park, Bristol and Freda Marjorie *née* Bateman; *b* 25 Sept 1942; *Educ* Clifton, Jesus Coll Cambridge (MA); *m* 28 June 1969, Carolyn Mary, da of Eric Spencer, of 3 Norfolk Rd, Portishead, Avon; 2 s (Matthew b 5 Aug 1973, Tom b 12 Jan 1975); *Career* Cambridge cricket blue 1962-64, Glos CCC 1960-69 (capped 1967), MCC under 25 tour Pakistan 1967/68, best bowling 8-78 W Indies v Glos 1966; Cambridge Rugby Fives Blue 1961-63 (capt 1963); slr 1969, Glos CCC, Bristol Savages; memb Law Soc; *Clubs* MCC, T & RA, Clifton Club Bristol; *Style*— Tony Windows, Esq; Harley Cottage, Clifton Pk, Clifton, Bristol

WINDSOR *see also*: Royal Family

WINDSOR, Viscount; Ivor Edward Other Windsor-Clive; s and h of 3 Earl of Plymouth, DL, and Caroline, *née* Rice; *b* 19 Nov 1951; *Educ* Harrow, RAC Cirencester; *m* 1979, Caroline, da of Frederick Nettlefold and Hon Mrs Juliana Roberts (da of 2 Viscount Scarsdale) ; 2 s (Hon Robert, Hon Frederick b 1983); *Heir* s, Hon Robert Other Ivor Windsor-Clive b 25 March 1981; *Career* co-fndr and dir Centre for Study of Modern Art 1973; *Recreations* cricket, football; *Style*— Viscount Windsor; The Stables, Oakly Park, Ludlow, Shropshire (☎ Bromfield 393); 6 Oakley Street, London, SW3

WINDSOR, Rodney Francis Maurice; CBE (1972), DL (Co Antrim); s of Maurice Windsor, MBE (d 1945), and Elsie, *née* Meredith (d 1959); *b* 22 Feb 1925; *Educ* Tonbridge; *m* 26 April 1951, Deirdre Willa, da of Col Arthur O'Neill Cubitt Chichester, OBE, MC, DL (d 1972), of Co Antrim; 2 s (Anthony b 1955, Nicholas b 1961), 1 da (Patricia b 1953); *Career* The Queens Bays 1944-52, Capt 1949, ADC to High Cmmr and C-in-C Austria 1949-50; N Irish Horse TA 1959-67 (Lt-Col cmdg 1964-67), Col TA N Ireland 1967-71, ADC TA to HM The Queen 1970-75; *Recreations* shooting, fishing; *Style*— Rodney F M Windsor, Esq, CBE; Byth House, Newbyth, Turriff, Aberdeenshire (☎ 08883 230)

WINDSOR CLIVE, Hon Simon Percy; s of 3 Earl of Plymouth; *b* 1956; *Educ* Harrow; *Style*— The Hon Simon Windsor Clive; c/o Oakly Park, Ludlow

WINDSOR-CLIVE, Hon Mrs; Hon (Mary) Alice; *née* Jolliffe; da of 4 Baron Hylton (d 1967); *b* 1937; *m* 1, 1959 (m dis 1968), John Paget Chancellor; 1 s, 3 da; m 2, 1968, Hon Richard Windsor-Clive, *qv*; *Style*— The Hon Mrs Windsor-Clive; Combe, Nettlecombe, Taunton, Somerset (☎ 098 44 0212)

WINDSOR-CLIVE, Hon David Justin; 3 s of 3 Earl of Plymouth; *b* 4 Sept 1960; *Educ* Harrow, RAC Cirencester; *m* 18 Sept 1986, Camilla Jane, *née* Squire; *Career* banker; *Recreations* football, tennis, shooting, racing; *Style*— The Hon David Windsor-Clive; 29 Cheyne Court, Flood Street, London SW3; King and Shaxson Ltd, 52 Cornhill, London EC3 (☎ 01 623 5433)

WINDSOR-CLIVE, Hon Richard Archer Alan; s of 2 Earl of Plymouth, PC (d 1943); *b* 1928; *Educ* Eton, Trinity Coll Cambridge; *m* 1, 1955 (m dis 1968), Joanna Mary, da of Edward Corbet Woodall, OBE; 1 s, 1 da; m 2, 1968, Hon (Mary) Alice Chancellor; 1 da; *Career* chm Bayfine Ltd 1973-85; *Style*— The Hon Richard Windsor-Clive; Combe, Nettlecombe, Taunton, Somerset (☎ 098 44 0212)

WINDUST, Jeremy Paul; s of Norman Albert Windust (d 1963), of Glos, and Pamela Rosie, *née* Frampton (d 1969); *b* 6 Jan 1952; *Educ* Marling Sch Stroud, Middx Poly (BA), Brunel Univ; *m* 8 Jan 1972, Elaine Rosemary, da of Lionel Hubert Jordan; 2 s (Alexander b 1973, Benjamin b 1976), 1 da (Kathryn b 1978); *Career* exec offr GCHQ Cheltenham 1975-87; memb ctee to re-establish trade union rights at GCHQ, co-applicant against Govt's union ban at GCHQ in High Ct, Ct of Appeal and House of Lords 1984 and before European Ct of Human Rights Strasbourg 1987; ed Warning Signal 1985-87; proprietor Willow Press (letterpress printing shop); exec sec (chief negotiator) RBA 1988; *Recreations* playing guitar; *Style*— Jeremy Windust, Esq; 189 Prestbury Rd, Cheltenham, Glos

WINFIELD, (Elaine Margaret) Maggie; da of Maj Richard Vivian Taylor (d 1980), and Enid Josephine, *née* Fair; *b* 14 Dec 1957; *Educ* Dudley Girls HS, City of Birmingham Poly (BA); *m* 23 July 1977, Stephen Winfield, s of John William Winfield; 1 da (Anna b 1983); *Career* ptnr Myles Communication Gp 1985-; fndr memb Soc of E Midlands Businesswomen 1987; *Recreations* running, gardening; *Style*— Mrs Maggie Winfield; Hatfield View, Forest Rd, Oxton, nr Southwell, Notts NG25 OHF (☎ 0602 654479); Myles Communication Group, 2 First Ave, Sherwood Rise, Nottingham NG7 6JL (☎ 0602 691692, fax 0602 691221)

WINFIELD, Peter Stevens; s of Harold Stevens Winfield (d 1945), of Chelsea, and Susan, *née* Cooper (d 1973); *b* 24 Mar 1927; *Educ* Sloane Sch Chelsea, West London Coll of Commerce; *m* 29 June 1955, Mary Gabrielle, da of Patrick John Kenrick (d 1955), of Chelsea; 4 s (John b 28 May 1961, Michael b 18 Jan 1965, Peter Anthony b 18 May 1966, Edward b 4 April 1968), 2 da (Susan (Mrs Wood) b 10 March 1958, Katherine (Mrs Cardona) b 18 Nov 1959); *Career* RA 1944-48, BQMS, India, Egypt and Palestine; joined Healey & Baker 1951 (sr ptnr 1975), dir London Auction Mart Ltd 1970 (chm 1980-); memb: Lloyds of London 1978-, property investmt ctee Save and Prosper Gp Ltd 1980-, Horserace Totalisator Bd 1981-; property conslt Manders Hldgs plc 1985-, chm Letinvest plc 1987-; govr Guys Hosp 1973-74 (special tstee 1974-); Liveryman: Worshipful Co of Farriers 1967-, Worshipful C of Feltmakers 1972-87; (third warden 1987-88; asst to court 1979-86); FRICS 1953; *Recreations* horseracing, cricket, swimming, reading; *Clubs* Buck's, United and Cecil, MCC, Turf, RAC; *Style*— Peter Winfield, Esq; 29 St George St, Hanover Square, London W1A 3BG (☎ 01 629 9292, telex 21800 HEABAK G, fax 01 355 4299)

WING, Prof John Kenneth; *b* 22 Oct 1923; *Educ* Strand Sch, UCL (MB BS, MD, PhD); *Career* RNVR 1942-46, Lt (A); medical and specialist trg 1947-56; scientific staff Med Research Cncl 1957-64; dir Med Research Cncl Social Psychiatry Research Unit 1965-; prof of social psychiatry Inst of Psychiatry and London Sch of Hygiene 1970-, conslt psychiatrist Bethlem Royal Hosp and Maudslay Hosp 1960-; memb bd of govrs Nat Inst for Social Work 1981-87, tstee Mental Health Fndn 1983-; memb: Med Research Cncl 1985-, departmental research ctee Dept of Health 1987-; Hon MD Univ of Heidelberg 1976; FRCPsych ; *Books* Institutionalism and Schizophrenia (1970), Measurement and Classification of Psychiatric Symptoms (1974), Reasoning about Madness (1978); *Style*— Professor J K Wing; MRC Social Psychiatry Unit, Institute of Psychiatry, London SE5 8AF (☎ 01 708 3235, 01 703 5411, ext 3509, fax 01 703 0458)

WINGATE, Michael Gerald; s of Dr Henry Paul Wingate (later Henry Paul Hamblin; d 1984), and Barbara Mervyn (later Hamblin), *née* Wyatt; *b* 29 August 1945; *Educ* Epsom Coll, Univ Coll London, Arch Assoc Sch; *m* 10 July 1971, Frances Nichola, da of David John Petty, MBE; 1 s (Samuel b 1983), 2 da (Jennifer b 1975, Tessa b 1978); *Career* chartered architect; sole princ Michael Wingate Architect 1985- (formerly of Purcell Miller Tritton and Ptnrs 1981-85); new buildings incl: Chapel of Reconciliation RC Nat Shrine of Our Lady at Walsingham 1981, Church of the Holy Family (RC) Kings Lynn 1985; major appts in the care of historic bldgs: cmmnd arch for the State and for Churches Scheme 1980-, Anglesey Abbey for The Nat Tst 1976-84; arch: to the RC Cath of St John the Baptist Norwich 1985-, The Carmelite Monastery Quidenham 1986-; memb The Bldg Materials Panel, Intermediate Technol Dept Gp 1986-, Norwich Cons Area Advsy Ctee 1980-85; *Books* Small-Scale Lime-Burning (1985); *Recreations* cycling; *Clubs* Society for the Protection of Ancient Buildings; *Style*— Michael G Wingate, Esq; Michael Wingate Architect, 82 The Street, Hindolveston, Dereham, Norfolk NR20 5DF (☎ 0263 860257)

WINGATE, Capt Sir Miles Buckley; KCVO (1981); s of Terrence Wingate; *b* 17 May 1923; *Educ* Taunton GS, Prior Park Coll; *m* 1947, Alicia Forbes Philip; 3 da; *Career* with Royal Mail Lines 1939; master mariner; memb bd Trinity House 1968-, (dep master 1976-); *Style*— Captain Sir Miles Wingate, KCVO; Trinity House, Tower Hill, London EC3N 4DH (☎ 01 480 6601)

WINGATE, His Honour Judge; William Granville; QC (1963); s of Col George Wingate, CIE (d 1936); *b* 28 May 1911; *Educ* Brighton Coll, Lincoln Coll Oxford; *m* 1960, Judith Rosemary, da of late Lt-Col J H B Evatt; 1 s, 1 da (twins); *Career* barr Inner Temple 1933, memb Bar Council 1961-65 and 1966-67, dep chm Essex QS 1965-71, a circuit judge (E Sussex) 1967-, memb: County Court Rule Ctee and Lord Chancellor's Legal Aid Advisory Ctee 1971-77, Ld Chllr's Law Reform Ctee 1974-87; chm of govrs of Brighton Coll 1978-87; *Clubs* Bar Yacht, Royal Corinthian Yacht; *Style*— His Honour Granville Wingate, QC; Cox's Mill, Dallington, Heathfield, Sussex (☎ Rushlake Green (0435) 830 217); 2 Garden Court, Temple, London EC4 (☎ 01 236 4741)

WINGATE-ROUTLEDGE, Robin Charles Mark; s of Lt-Col Stanley Wingate-Routledge (d 1972), and Ilse Anne-Marie, da of Marquard BöDecker; *b* 26 April 1944; *Educ* Int Diplomatic HS, Nikolaus Cosanus Gymnasium Bonn W Germany; *Career* farmer; breeds pedigree sheep (Suffolk); *Recreations* music, theatre, art, wild life and conservation, walking, horses; *Clubs* Guards' Polo, Henley Royal Regatta; *Style*— Robin Wingate-Routledge, Esq; New Barn Farm, Sibford Gower, nr Banbury, Oxon OX15 5RY (☎ 029 578 330)

WINGATE-SAUL, Michael Anthony; s of Anthony Slyvester Wingate-Saul, and Brenda Maxwell, *née* Stoddart (d 1987); *b* 8 Feb 1938; *Educ* Rugby, King's Coll Cambridge MA (Hons); *m* 23 Sept 1967, Eleanor Jane, da of Alan Lawrence Brodie (d 1972); 2 da (Polly b 1969, Rebecca b 1971); *Career* Nat Serv 1956-58, 2 Lt 4 Regt RHA Germany; slr, ptnr Letcher & Son, Notary Public; govr Bryanston Sch 1982-; *Recreations* music, theatre, amateur dramatics, shooting, tennis skiing; *Style*— Michael A Wingate-Saul, Esq; Sandle Lodge, Sandleheath, Hampshire SP6 1PF (☎ 0425 52261); 24 Market Place, Ringwood, Hampshire BH24 1BS (☎ 0425 471424, telex 41124, fax 0425 470917)

WINGFIELD, Hon (Mervyn) Anthony; s and h of 10 Viscount Powerscourt; *b* 21 August 1963; *Style*— The Hon Mervyn Wingfield

WINGFIELD, Charles John; s of Lt-Col Charles Ralph Borlase Wingfield (d 1923), of Onslow, Shrewbury, and Mary Nesta Harriet, *née* Williams (d 1947); *b* 9 May 1917; *Educ* Eton; *m* 14 June 1956, (Cecily) Maxine d'Eyncourt, da of Percy George Meighar-Lovett, OBE (d 1970), of 71 Cadogan Square, London SW1; 1 s (John b 1957), 2 da (Elisabeth b 1959, Helen b 1963); *Career* KSLI Supplementary Res 1938, France and Belgium 1939-40, Somaliland Scouts, KAR E Africa 1941-45; patron of one living Bicton; chm Midland Gliding Club 1947-50, jt master S Shrops Hunt 1954-57; JP Salop 1949, High Sheriff 1953; *Recreations* gliding, fishing, shooting; *Style*— Charles Wingfield, Esq; Onslow, Bicton Heath, Shrewsbury

WINGFIELD, Hon Mrs; Hon Cynthia Meriel; *née* Hill; da of 6 Baron Sandys; *b* 1929; *m* 1954, Charles Talbot Rhys Wingfield; 1 s, 3 da; *Style*— The Hon Mrs Wingfield; Barrington Park, Burford, Oxon (☎ Windrush 045 14 302)

WINGFIELD, Hon Guy Claude Patrick; s of 9 Viscount Powerscourt (d 1973), and Sheila, Viscountess Powerscourt, *qv*; bro of 10 Viscount and Hon Lady Langrishe; *b* 5 Oct 1940; *Educ* Millfield; *Style*— The Hon Guy Wingfield

WINGFIELD, Hon Julia Margaret; da of 10 Viscount Powerscourt; *b* 5 August 1965; *Style*— The Hon Julia Wingfield

WINGFIELD, Lady Norah Beryl Cayzer; *née* Jellicoe; da of Adm of the Fleet 1 Earl Jellicoe, GCB, OM, GCVO (d 1935); *b* 1910; *m* 1935, Maj Edward William Rhys Wingfield (d 1984), late King's Royal Rifle Corps; 2 s, 2 da; *Style*— Lady Norah Wingfield; Salterbridge, Cappoquin, Co Waterford

WINGFIELD DIGBY, Very Rev Richard Shuttleworth; s of George Everard Wingfield Digby (d 1915), and his 2 w Dorothy Loughnan (d 1921); *b* 19 August 1911; *Educ* Nautical Coll Pangbourne, Christ's Coll Cambridge (MA); *m* 1936, Rosamond Frances, da of Lt-Col William Trench Digby (d 1952); 2 s, 1 da; *Career* RN 1928-30, ordained deacon in C of E 1936; WWII: defence of Calais, army chaplain (4 class emergency) and POW 1940-45; vicar of All Saints Newmarket 1946-53, rector of Bury Lancs 1953-66, dean of Peterborough Cathedral 1966-80 (dean emeritus 1980-); *Recreations* golf, walking; *Clubs* Army and Navy; *Style*— The Very Rev Richard Wingfield Digby; Byways, Higher Holton, Wincanton, Somerset (☎ 0963 32137)

WINGFIELD DIGBY, (Kenelm) Simon Digby; TD (1946), DL (1953); s of Col Frederick James Bosworth Wingfield Digby, DSO (d 1952), and Gwendolen *née* Hamilton Fletcher (d 1975); Sir Simon Digby and his brothers fought beside Henry Tudor at Bosworth Field, granted Manor of Coleshill which is still in the family; *b* 13 Feb 1910; *Educ* Harrow, Trinity Coll Cambridge (MA); *m* 1936, Kathleen Elizabeth, da of Hon Mr Justice Courtney Kingstone, of Canada; 1 s (John), 1 da (Venetia); *Career* barr; MP (C) West Dorset 1941-74, Cons whip 1948-51, Civil Lord of Admiralty 1951-57, ldr Br Delgn Cncl Europe Assembly 1972-74; Order of Leopold, Order of the White Lion; landowner (estates at Sherborne, Dorset and Coleshill, Warwickshire); *Recreations* shooting, fishing; *Clubs* Carlton; *Style*— Simon Wingfield Digby, Esq, TD, DL; Sherborne Castle, Sherborne, Dorset (☎ 07476 2650); Coleshill House, Warwickshire; Digby Estate Office, Sherborne, Dorset (☎ 0935 813182)

WINGFIELD DIGBY, Stephen Hatton; s of Archdeacon Basil Wingfield Digby, of Salisbury, and Barbara Hatton Budge (d 1987); *b* 17 Nov 1944; *Educ* Sherborne, Bristol Univ (BSc, Queen's Univ Belfast (MBA); *m* 1968, Sarah Jane, da of Osborne Lovell, of Dorset; 2 s (William b 1974, Alexander b 1983), 1 da (Claire b 1972); *Career* dir: Bass Sales Ltd 1978-81, Bass Wales & West Ltd 1981-83, The Harp Lager Co 1983-; vice-chm London Brewers' Cncl 1987; *Recreations* fishing, shooting; *Clubs* MCC; *Style*— Stephen Wingfield Digby, Esq; The Coach House, Gregories Farm Lane, Beaconsfield; The Harp Lager Co, Southway House, Park Royal, London NW1

WINGROVE, David Terence; s of Alfred Wingrove, of Holmer Green, Bucks, and Kathleen Rose Wingrove; *b* 22 Dec 1947; *Educ* John Hampden Sch High Wycombe, Poly of Central London; *m* 29 April 1973; *Career* chartered surveyor; dir: Howden Mgmnt Servs Ltd 1984-, Alexander Howden Gp Mgmnt Servs Ltd 1986-; FRICS; *Recreations* travel, horticulture, walking, photography, reading, seeking-out good food and drink; *Style*— David Wingrove, Esq; Stable Cottage, Wilderwick, Dormansland, E Grinstead, W Sussex (☎ 034287 367); 8 Devonshire Sq, London EC2M 4PL (☎ 01 623 5500, telex 882171, fax 01 621 1511)

WINKLE, Anthony Webbe; s of Harry Downing Winkle (d 1974), of Edinburgh, and Gladys, *née* Hughes (d 1977); *b* 28 Dec 1931; *Educ* Newcastle HS, George Watsons Coll, Heriot-Watt Univ; *m* 1959, Patricia Emily Mary, da of George Alfred Parker (d 1984), of Edinburgh; 2 s (Philip b 1964, Paul b 1966); *Career* Nat Serv RAF pilot, Flying Offr 1956-58; chartered surveyor; ptnr Gibson & Simpson Edinburgh; farmer; *Clubs* New (Edinburgh); *Style*— Anthony W Winkle, Esq; Whitmuir Lamancha, West Linton, Peeblesshire EH46 7BB (☎ (0968) 60431); Gibson & Simpson, Chartered Surveyors, 3 Melville Cres, Edinburgh EA3 6HP (☎ (031 225) 3397, fax (031 225) 8990)

WINKLER, Audrey; JP (1977); da of Ronald Bowers (d 1979), of Netherton, nr Wakefield, and Glarice Hirst; *b* 8 Mar 1935; *Educ* Ossett GS; *m* 30 March 1955, Andrew Winkler, s of Sandor Winkler (d 1956), of Deak Ferenc Utca, Budapest, Hungary; 2 s (Alex b 10 March 1958, Michael (twin) b 10 March 1958), 1 da (Kay b 12 June 1963); *Career* co sec Profifex Ltd 1987, manufacturer and retailer, dir Derby Arts Festival 1985-; memb: Wirksworth and Dist Chamber of Trade and Commerce (pres 1984-86); *Style*— Mrs Audrey Winkler, JP; Winkler, The Dale, Wirksworth, Derby DE4 4EJ (☎ 062 982 4949)

WINKS, David John Ffoulkes; s of Capt Geoffrey Ffoulkes Winks, TD (d 1976), and Marjorie Mary, *née* Hoggarth; *b* 16 Oct 1938; *Educ* Wycliffe Coll Glos; *m* Diane Pamela; 1 s (Peter John b 1966), 1 da (Sian Mary b 1969); *Career* ptnr Peat Marwick McLintock 1968-, chm Milton Keynes Business Venture 1983-; pres Beds Bucks & Herts Soc of CAs 1987-88; FCA, ATII; *Recreations* golf; *Clubs* Royal Porthcawl Golf, Woburn Golf and Country, Br Sportsmans; *Style*— David Winks, Esq; Manor Lodge, Milton Bryan, Milton Keynes MK17 9HS (☎ 0525 210015); Norfolk House, 499 Silbury Boulevard, Milton Keynes MK9 2HA (☎ 0908 661881)

WINKWORTH, Peter Leslie; s of Francis William Henry Winkworth (d 1975), and Ruth Margaret Llewllin, *née* Notley; *b* 9 August 1948; *Educ* Tonbridge; *m* 16 June 1973, Tessa Anne, da of Sir Alexander Warren Page; 1 s (Piers b 1976), 2 da (Victoria b 1975, Jessica b 1978); *Career* merchant banker and CA, dir: Close Bros Gp plc 1984-, Close Bros Ltd 1977, Safeguard Investmts Ltd 1984-, Arkstar Ltd (1984-88), Clifford Bown Opticians Ltd 1987-; *Recreations* tennis, horse riding, national horse racing; *Clubs* St George's Hill Lawn Tennis; *Style*— Peter Winkworth, Esq; Saxes Plat, Tismans Common, West Sussex; Close Bros Ltd, 36 Great St Helens, London EC3A 6AP (☎ 01 283 2241, telex 88142744, fax 01 6239699)

WINN, Hon Charles Rowland Andrew; s and h of 5 Baron St Oswald, *qv*; *b* 22 July 1959; *m* 1985 Louise Alexandra Scott; 1 s (Rowland Charles Sebastian b 1986); *Career* landowner; *Style*— The Hon Charles Winn

WINN, Geoffrey Frank; s of Capt Frank Winn (d 1987), of Scarborough, and Hettie *née* Croft (d 1983); *b* 13 Dec 1938; *Educ* Scarborough HS, Univ of Leeds (BComm); *m* 9 July 1966, Jennifer Lynne, JP, da of Jack Winter, DFC, of Scarborough; 2 da (Deborah b 1967, Susie b 1970); *Career* CA; Winn & Co (Scarborough and branch offs) 1962-; dir: Belvedere Hosps Ltd 1979-88, Scarborough Bldg Soc 1984-; Lloyds External name 1985-; memb: Rotary Club of Scarborough Caveliers 1978- (pres 1985-86), Scarborough Round Table 1964-79 (chm 1971-72), Scarborough Flower Fund Homes 1970- (chm 1986); tstee Scarborough CC; FCA 1962, FCCA 1980; *Recreations* golf, swimming, badminton; *Clubs* Royal Overseas League, CLA; *Style*— Geoffrey Winn, Esq; Barmoor House, Scalby, Scarborough, N Yorks YO13 OPG, (☎ 0723 362 414); 62/63 Westborough, Scarborough, N Yorks YO11 1TS, (☎ 0723 364341, car tel 0836 768902)

WINN, Hon Reginald Henry; s of late 2 Baron St Oswald and Mabel, da of Sir Charles Forbes, 4 Bt; *b* 1899; *Educ* Eton, Christ Church Oxford; *m* 1924, Alice, da of late Moncure Perkins, of Virginia, USA; 2 da (*see* Hon Mark Wyndham, MC; *Career* formerly Maj Gren Gds; *Clubs* White's, Buck's; *Style*— The Hon Reginald Winn

WINNER, Michael Robert; s of George Joseph Winner (d 1972), and Helen, *née* Zlota (d 1984); *b* 30 Oct 1935; *Educ* St Christopher Sch Letchworth Herts, Downing Coll Cambridge (MA); *Career* chm: Scimitar Films Ltd, Michael Winner Ltd, Motion Picture & Theatrical Investmts Ltd 1957-; memb cncl and chief censorship off Directors Guild of GB 1983-, fndr and chm Police Meml Tst 1984-; dir: Play It Cool 1962, West Eleven 1963, The Mechanic 1972; dir and writer The Cool Mikado 1962; producer and dir: The System 1963, I'll Never Forget What's 'is name 1967, The Games 1969, Lawman 1970, The Night Comers 1971, Chato's Land 1971, Scorpio 1972, The Stone Killer 1973, Death Wish 1974, Won Ton Ton The Dog That Saved Hollywood 1975, Firepower 1978, Scream for Help 1984, Death Wish Three 1985; prodr dir and writer: You Must be Joking 1965, The Jokers 1966, Hannibal Brooks 1968, The Sentinel 1976, The Big Sleep 1977, Death Wish Two 1981, The Wicked Lady 1982, Appointment with Death 1987, A Chorus of Disapproval 1988; theatre prodns: The Tempest 1974, A Day in Hollywood A Night in the Ukraine 1978; *Recreations* walking around art galleries, museums and antique shops; *Style*— Michael Winner, Esq; 6-8 Sackville St, London W1X 1DD (☎ 01 734 8385)

WINNICK, David Julian; MP (Lab) Walsall North 1979-; *b* 26 June 1933; *Educ* LSE; *Career* memb: Willesden Cncl 1959-64, Brent Cncl 1964-66; contested (Lab) Harwich 1964, MP (Lab) Croydon South 1966-70, contested Croydon Central Oct 1974 and Walsall Nov 1976 (regained Walsall North for Lab 1979), memb Select Ctees on: Race Relations and Immigration 1969-70, Environment 1980-; vice-pres APEX; *Style*— David Winnick Esq, MP; House of Commons, London SW1

WINNIFRITH, Sir (Alfred) John Digby; KCB (1959, CB 1950); s of Rev Bertram Thomas Winnifrith, Rector of Ightham, Kent; *b* 16 Oct 1908; *Educ* Westminster, Christ Church Oxford; *m* 1935, Lesbia Margaret (d 1981), eldest da of Sir Arthur Cochrane, KCVO, sometime Clarenceux King of Arms; 2 s, 1 da; *Career* civil servant 1932-67: BOT to 1934, transferred to Treasy 1934, asst sec War Cabinet and civil sec Combined Ops HQ 1942-44, 3 sec Treasy 1951-59, perm sec MAFF 1959-67; tstee Nat History section Br Museum 1967-72, dir-gen Nat Tst 1968-70, memb Cwlth War Graves Cmmn 1969-83; *Style*— Sir John Winnifrith, KCB; Hallhouse Farm, Appledore, Ashford, Kent (☎ 023 383 264)

WINNING, Most Rev Thomas Joseph; *see*: Glasgow, Archbishop of

WINNINGTON, Anthony Edward; s of Col Thomas Foley Churchill Winnington, MBE, of 182 Rivermeade Ct, Hurlingham, London, and Lady Betty, *née* Anson, da of 4 Earl of Lichfield; *b* 13 May 1948; *Educ* Eton, Grenoble Univ; *m* 5 Dec 1978, Karyn Kathryn Kettles, da of William Alan Dayton, of Palm Beach, Florida, USA; 1 s (Edward b 1987), 2 da (Victoria b 1981, Sophia b 1985); *Career* dir (equity sales) Hoare Govett Securities Ltd 1984- (joined 1969); memb Stock Exchange 1984; *Recreations* travel, opera, music, reading; *Clubs* Boodles; *Style*— Anthony Winnington, Esq; 20 Baskerville Rd, London SW18 3RW (☎ 01 870 8466); Hoare Govett, 4 Broadgate, London EC2M 7CE (☎ 01 374 1116)

WINNINGTON, Lady Betty (Marjorie); *née* Anson; da of 4 Earl of Lichfield (d 1960); *b* 12 Mar 1917; *m* 20 May 1944, Col Thomas Foley Churchill Winnington, MBE, yr bro of Sir Francis Winnington, 6 Bt; 2 s, 2 da; *Style*— Lady Betty Winnington; 182 Rivermead Court, Ranelagh Gardens, London SW6 3SG

WINNINGTON, Sir Francis Salwey William; 6 Bt (GB 1755), of Stanford Court, Worcestershire; s of Francis Salwey Winnington (d 1913), and gs of Sir Francis Winnington, 5 Bt, JP, DL (d 1931); *b* 24 June 1907; *Educ* Eton; *m* 1944, Anne Beryl Jane, da of late Capt Lawrence Drury-Lowe, Scots Gds; 1 da; *Heir* bro, Col Thomas Foley Churchill Winnington, MBE b 16 Aug 1910; *Career* Lt Welsh Gds 1928-32; re-employed 1939 (despatches); patron of three livings; landed proprietor (4,700 acres); *Clubs* Cavalry and Guards'; *Style*— Sir Francis Winnington, Bt; Brockhill Court, Shelsley Beauchamp, Worcs

WINNINGTON, Col Thomas Foley Churchill; MBE (1948); s of Francis Winnington (d 1913), and Blanche Emma, *née* Casberd-Boteler, (d 1968); hp to bro, Sir Francis Winnington, 6 Bt; *b* 16 August 1910; *Educ* Eton, Balliol Coll Oxford (BA); *m* 20 May 1944, Lady Betty Anson, da of 4 Earl of Lichfield (d 1960); 2 s (Anthony b 1948, m 1978 Karyn Kettles, 1 s (Henry b 1961), 2 da (Viscountess Campden, da-in-law of 5 Earl of Gainsborough; Emma b 1956, m 1981 Christopher Milne); *Career* joined Gren Gds 1933: served WWIIA Dunkirk and NW Europe (despatches), cmd 3 Bn Malaya (despatches) 1948, Col cmdg 1952-55; pres WO Selection Bd 1955, ret 1957; Reed Int 1958-75; appeals advsr Help The Aged 1976-; *Clubs* Pratt's; *Style*— Col Thomas Winnington, MBE; 182 Rivermead Ct, Ranelagh Gdns, London SW6 3SG (☎ 01 731 0697); Help The Aged, St James Walk, London EC1R 0BE (☎ 01 253 0253)

WINNINGTON-INGRAM, (Edward) John; s of Rev Preb Edward F Winnington-Ingram (d 1963), and Gladys, *née* Armstrong; gn of Rt Rev Arthur Foley Winnington-Ingram, PC, KCVO, Bishop of London 1901-39; *b* 20 April 1926; *Educ* Shrewsbury, Keble Coll Oxford (BA); *m* 1, 1953 (m dis 1966), Shirley Yvoire, da of Gerald Lamotte; 2 s (Edward b 1957, Gerald b 1960); m 2, Elizabeth Linda, da of Geoffrey Milling (d 1983); *Career* serv WWII RN 1944-74 (Sub-Lt RNVR); joined Assoc Newspapers 1949, circ mangr Daily Mail 1960; gen mangr Mancester 1965-70; dir assoc Newspapers 1971; md The Mail on Sunday 1982; md Mail Newspapers plc 1986-; dir Assoc Newspapers Hldgs 1986-; *Recreations* tennis, shooting, music, beagling, gardening; *Clubs* Buck's; *Style*— John Winnington-Ingram, Esq; Old Manor Farm, Cottisford, Brackley, Northants NN13 5SW (☎ Finmere 367); Mail Newspapers plc, New Carmelite House, Carmelite St, London EC4Y 0JA (☎ 01 353 6000)

WINROW, Frank Reginald; s of Reginald Winrow, of Southport, and Phylis, *née* Greenhalgh; *b* 8 Mar 1937; *Educ* King George V GS Southport; *m* 1958, Dorothy Rosalie Moffat, da of Stuart Moffat Walker (d 1983), of Southport; 2 s (Andrew, Michael); *Career* SAC RAF 1955-57, HM inspr of taxes, pres Inland Revenue Staff Fedn; memb: arts, entertainment and sports advsy ctee of TUC, gen cncl of NW Regional TUC, Cncl of Civil Serv Unions, exec ctee Lancs Assoc of Boys Clubs, Lab Pty; former referee Assoc Football; *Recreations* trade union and labour movement, assoc football, gardening, reading, photography; *Style*— Frank Winrow, Esq; 8 Everard Rd, Southport, Merseyside PR8 6NA (☎ 0704 32930); Inland Revenue Staff Federation, 231 Vauxhall Bridge Rd, London SW1V 1EH

WINSHIP, James Gunn; s of James Gunn Winship (d 1965), of Shearwater, Bishopstone, nr Salisbury, Wilts, and Gladys Winefred, *née* Pine-Coffin; *b* 29 Jan 1950;

Educ Redrice Public Sch Andover; *m* 6 April 1974, Sarah Jane, da of James Henry Manners, of Hill View, Sevenhampton, Highworth, Wilts; 1 s (Christian b 21 Oct 1981), 1 da (Charlotte); *Career* reporter Southern Evening Echo Southampton 1970-73, industl corres United Newspapers London 1973-75, sub ed Aldershot News Series 1975-76, account exec Infoplan PR 1976-78, account mangr Bolton Dickinson Assocs 1978-80; fndr/chm: Shearwater PR 1980-, Stephen Gray Assocs 1986-, Kestrel Publishing 1986-; memb Southern Region Cncl of CBI; *Style*— James Winship, Esq; Manor Farmhouse, Manor Lane, West Hendred, Oxfordshire (☎ 0235 833 396); Shearwater Public Relations Ltd, 29 Market Place, Wantage, Oxfordshire OX12 8BG (☎ 02357 66339, fax 02357 69044)

WINSKELL, Cyril; MBE (1982); s of Robert Winskell (d 1963), of South Shields, and Margaret Wiley (d 1970); *b* 29 August 1932; *Educ* South Shields HS, Rutherford GS, King's Coll Newcastle-upon-Tyne, Durham Univ (certificate in architecture); *m* 24 Sept 1960, Patricia, da of Leonard George Dolby (d 1967), of North Shields; 4 s (Cy b 1961, Scott b 1962, Dane b 1968, Mark b 1968), 1 da (Patricia b 1965); *Career* Nat Serv, Sapper Christmas Island 1956-57; ARIBA 1956, visiting critic and occasional lectr at various schs of architecture 1972-, one man show Gallery Colbert Durham City 1977, chm Northern Region RIBA 1980-82; chm Northumbria Branch RIBA 1984-86, convenor "Newcastle Cityscape" 1984-; external examiner sch of architecture, Queen's Univ Belfast 1987-88, architect for the restoration of: St Thomas's Neighbourhood, Newcastle-upon-Tyne 1978-81, Canning Area, Liverpool 1984-87; founded Winstell Chartered Architects Urban Conslts 1982, memb Historic Areas Advs Ctee English Heritage 1987-88 FRSA 1981; FRIBA 1971; *Recreations* painting, travel; *Style*— Cyril Winskell, Esq, MBE; 7 Collingwood St, Newcastle-upon-Tyne NE1 1JE (☎ 091 261 4436)

WINSKILL, Air Cdre Sir Archie (Archibald) Little; KCVO (1980, CVO 1973), CBE (1960), DFC and bar, AE; s of James Winskill, of Penrith; *b* 24 Jan 1917; *Educ* Carlisle GS; *m* 1947, Christiane Amélie Pauline, da of M Bailleux, of Calais; 1 s, 1 da; *Career* serv WWII: Fighter Pilot Battle of Britain, memb of Fr Resistance N Africa; Air Cdre 1963, air attaché Paris 1964-67, dir PR (Air) MOD 1967-68, Capt of HM The Queen's Flight 1968-82, extra equerry to HM The Queen 1968-; ret RAF 1982; *Clubs* RAF; *Style*— Air Cdre Sir Archie Winskill, KCVO, CBE, DFE, AE, MRAeS; Anchors, Coastal Rd, West Kingston, East Preston, W Sussex BN16 1SN (☎ 0903 775439)

WINSOR, Thomas Philip; WS; s of Dr Thomas Valentine Marrs Winsor, of 1 Bayfield Rd, Broughty Ferry, Dundee DD5 1AW, and Phyllis Margaret, *née* Bonsor; *b* 7 Dec 1957; *Educ* Grove Acad Broughty Ferry Dundee, Univ of Edinburgh (LLB), Univ of Dundee (Dip Petroleum Law); *Career* slr: Thornton Oliver WS Dundee 1981-82, Dundas & Wilson CS Edinburgh 1983-84, Norton Rose London 1984-; Notary Public (Scotland) 1981; memb UK Oil Lawyers Gp 1985, pres The Soc of Scottish Lawyers in London 1987-89, pres of Univ Dundee Petroleum and Mineral Law Soc 1987-89; memb: Law Soc of Scot 1981, Int Bar Assoc 1983, Soc of Writers to HM Signet 1984, American Soc of Int Law 1984, The Law Soc 1986; *Recreations* Scottish legal history, antique books, reading, golf, politics, travel; *Clubs* Caledonian; *Style*— Thomas P Winsor, Esq, WS; 179 Lavender Hill, Battersea, London SW11 5TE (☎ 01 585 2662); Kempson House, Camomile St, London EC3A 7AN (☎ 01 283 2434, fax 01 588 1181, telex 883652 NOROSE G)

WINSTANLEY, Hon Diana Christine; da of Baron Winstanley and his 2 w, Joyce, *née* Woodhouse; *b* 1960; *Style*— The Hon Diana Winstanley

WINSTANLEY, John; MC (1944), TD (1951); s of Capt Bernard Joseph Winstanley (d 1919), and Grace Frances, *née* Taunton (d 1970); *b* 11 May 1919; *Educ* Wellington, Univ of London (MB BS), St Thomas' Hosp Med Sch; *m* 10 Jan 1959, Jane Mary, da of Geoffrey Ryan Frost; 1 s (Richard b 28 May 1964), 2 da (Emma b 1 April 1960, Sophie b 27 April 1962); *Career* cmmnd 4 Bn Queens Own Royal W Kent Regt (TA) 1937, serv BEF (despatches) 1940, 8 Army MB Middle E Forces 1942, India and Burma 1943-45, ret hon Maj 1945; hon civilian conslt opthalmic surgn Army 1963-84, hon conslt opthalmologist Royal Hosp Chelsea 1963-86, hon conslt ophthalmic surgn St Thomas' Hosp 1984- (conslt ophthalmic surgn 1960-84); memb cncl Med Protection Soc 1979-; exec ctee memb Ex-Servs Mental Welfare Soc 1980, vice-pres Iris Fund 1984; Liveryman Worshipful Co of Apothecaries; FRCS, FCOphth; *Recreations* field sports, history; *Clubs* Fly-Fishers, Army and Navy; *Style*— John Winstanley, Esq, MC, TD; 10 Pembroke Villas, The Green, Richmond, Surrey TW9 1QF (☎ 01 904 6247)

WINSTANLEY, Baron (Life Peer UK 1975); Michael Platt Winstanley; s of Dr Sydney Winstanley; *b* 27 August 1918; *Educ* Manchester GS, Manchester Univ; *m* 1, 1945 (m dis 1952), Nancey Penney; 1 s; m 2, 1955, Joyce, da of Arthur Woodhouse; 1 s, 1 da; *Career* sits as Lib in House of Lords; MP (Lib) Cheadle 1966-70, Hazel Grove Feb-Oct 1974; chm Lib Pty Health Cttee 1965-66, Lib Spokesman Health, PO and Broadcasting; memb Water Space Amenity Commission 1980-; GP Urmston Manchester 1948-66; broadcaster; MRCS, LRCP; *Style*— The Rt Hon Lord Winstanley; 30 Broad Lane, Hale, Cheshire

WINSTANLEY, Hon Nicholas Clayton Platt; s of Baron Winstanley and his 1 w, Nancey, *née* Perrey; *b* 1945; *Style*— The Hon Nicholas Winstanley

WINSTANLEY, Hon Stephen Woodhouse; s of Baron Winstanley and his 2 w, Joyce, *née* Woodhouse; *b* 1957; *Style*— The Hon Stephen Winstanley

WINSTON, Clive Noel; s of George Winston (d 1947), of London, and Alida Celia Winston (d 1964); *b* 20 April 1925; *Educ* Highgate Sch, Trinity Hall Cambridge (BA); *m* 2 April 1952, Beatrice Jeanette, da of Mark Lawton; 2 da (Celia Penelope b 16 Jan 1953, Clair Wendy b 26 Jan 1957); *Career* Capt (emergency cmmn) Royal Berks attached 15 Punjab Regt 1945-47; dep slr Met Police 1982-85, asst dir Fedn Against Copyright Theft 1985-88; union chm Lib and Progressive Synagogues 1981-85; *Recreations* golf, gardening; *Clubs* Bush Hill Park GC; *Style*— Clive Winston, Esq; 2 Bournwell Close, Cockfosters, Herts EN4 0JX (☎ 01 449 5693)

WINSTON, Malcolm John; s of John Winston (d 1982), of Bexhill, and Sarah, *née* Bates; *b* 8 Nov 1930; *Educ* Stationers' Co Sch; *m* 16 June 1962, Cynthia Mary Boorne, da of Hugh Napier Goodchild; 1 s (Mark Jonathan Napier b 1964), 1 da (Sarah Catherine Louise b 1967); *Career* Bank of England 1950-75, seconded Central TSB 1973, asst gen mangr Central TSB 1975 (sr asst gen mangr 1981), joined TSB England & Wales upon merger with Central TSB 1986; fndr Assoc of Int Savings Banks in London 1980: (chm 1983-84, pres 1985-); Freeman City of London 1952, Liveryman Worshipful Co of Makers of Playing Cards 1979; fell Assoc of Corporate Treasurers 1979; *Recreations* beagling, tennis; *Clubs* Overseas Bankers'; *Style*— Malcolm Winston, Esq; Maze Pond, Wadhurst, East Sussex (☎ 0892 882 074); St Mary's Ct, 100 Lower Thomas St, London EC3R 6AQ (☎ 01 623 6000, telex 8811829)

WINTELER, John Fridolin; s of Fridolin Henry Winteler, formerly of Nairobi Kenya (d 1966), and Margaret Mary, *née* Bairstow; *b* 21 August 1946; *Educ* Duke of York sch Nairobi, Pembroke Coll Cambridge (MA); *m* 10 July 1971, Candida Mary Valerie, da of Jack Donald Theodore Pickering, of Woking;, 2 s (James b 1974, David b 1976), 2 da (Anne b 1979, Alison b 1983); *Career* called to the Bar Inner Temple 1969, practised NE circuit 1970-; *Recreations* preaching, walking, gardening; *Style*— John Winteler, Esq; Barristers, Chambers, 6 Park Square East, Leeds, W Yorks LS1 2LW (☎ 0532 459763, fax 0532 424395)

WINTER, The Rev David Brian; s of Walter George Winter (d 1952), of London, and Winifred Ella, *née* Oughton (d 1972); *b* 19 Nov 1929; *Educ* Machynlleth Co Powys, Trinity GS London, Kings Coll London (BA), Inst of Educn London (PGCE), Oak Hill Theological Coll; *m* 15 April 1961, Christine Ellen, da of Bernard Martin, of Hitcham, Suffolk; 2 s (Philip b 1963, Adrian b 1969), 1 da (Rebecca b 1964); *Career* Nat Serv RAF 1948-50; sch teacher 1955-59, ed Crusade 1959-70, freelance writer and broadcaster 1970-71, prodr BBC Radio 1971-, head of religious progs BBC Radio 1982-87, hd of religious broadcasting BBC 1987-; memb Radio Acad 1985-; *Books incl* Truth in the Son (1985), Battered Bride? (1988); *Recreations* watching cricket; *Style*— The Rev David Winter; 47 Holdenhurst Ave, London N12 0JA (☎ 01 346 6969); BBC Broadcasting House, London W1A 1AA (☎ 01 927 5450)

WINTER, Frederick Thomas; CBE (1963); s of Frederick Neville Winter (d 1965), of Newmarket, and Anne Flanagan (d 1987); *b* 20 Sept 1926; *Educ* Ewell Castle; *m* 1956, Diana Ruth, da of Col T R Pearson (d 1945), of Derby; 3 da (Joana and Denise b 1957 (twins), Philippa b 1958); *Career* racehorse jockey and trainer; national hunt jockey 1947-64; champion jockey 4 times; won: grand nat twice, gold cup twice, champion hurdle 3 times; trainer 1964-; champion trainer 8 times; won: grand nat twice, Cheltenham gold cup, champion hurdle 3 times; *Recreations* golf, gardening; *Style*— Frederick Winter, Esq, CBE; Uplands, Lambourn, Newbury, Berks RG16 7QH (☎ 0488 71438)

WINTER, Prof Gerald Bernard; s of Morris Winter (d 1974), and Edith Winter (d 1984); *b* 24 Nov 1928; *Educ* Cooper's Co Sch, London Hosp Med Coll London Univ (BDS, MB, BS, DCH); *m* 24 April 1960, (Brigitte) Eva, da of Dr Hans Heinemann Fleischhacker (d 1965), of London; 1 s (Simon Michael b 1961), 1 da (Caroline Rosalind b 1965); *Career* Nat Serv RADC 1948-49; dental house surgn 1955, house surgn and house physician 1958, lectr Royal Dental Hosp 1959-62, dean and dir of studies Inst of Dental Surgery Eastman Dental Hosp London 1982- (cnslt dental surgn 1962-66, prof of children's dentistry 1966-); pres Br Paedondontic Soc 1970-71 (hon sec 1961-64), hon sec Int Assoc of Dentistry for Children 1971-79, pres Br Soc of Dentistry for the Handicappd 1976-77; FDS RCS (Eng), FFDRCSI; *Style*— Prof Gerald Winter; Inst of Dental Surgery, Eastman Dental Hospital, 256 Gray's Inn Rd, London WC1X 8LD

WINTER, John Anthony; MBE (1984); s of Frank Oliver Winter, of Norwich, and Sybil Mary, *née* Rudd (d 1976); *b* 16 May 1930; *Educ* Bishops Stortford Coll, Architectural Assoc Sch of Architecture (AA Dip), Yale Univ (MArch); *m* May 1956, Valerie Ursula, *née* Denison; 2 s (Timothy b 1960, Henry b 1963), 1 da (Martha b 1966); *Career* architect; princ of John Winter & Assocs; work inc: Morley Coll Lambeth, Housing Lucas Place Milton Keynes etc; memb Royal Fine Art Cmmn 1986-; *Books* Modern Buildings (1969), Industrial Buildings (1971), frequent contributer to architectural journals and videos; *Style*— John Winter, Esq, MBE; 81 Swains Lane, London N6 (☎ 01 340 9864); 80 Lamble St, London NW5 4AB (☎ 01 267 7567)

WINTER, William Geoffrey; s of Henry Edgar Winter, OBE, and Josephine, *née* Sims; *b* 2 July 1933; *Educ* Eton, Magdalen Coll Oxford, Heidelberg Univ; *m* 19 March 1986, Elizabeth, da of Trevor Edmondson (d 1966); 2 s (Thomas b 1977, Alexander b 1981); *Career* cmmnd 10 Royal Hussars (PWO); dir G & G Kynoch plc 1966-; *Recreations* golf, tennis; *Clubs* Royal St George's, Royal Wimbledon, IOD, Hurlingham; *Style*— William Winter, Esq; 4 Dewhurst Rd, London W14 0ET (☎ 01 602 0106); 10 Golden Square, London W1 (☎ 01 437 8822, fax 01 734 4549)

WINTERBOTHAM, Hon Mrs (Emmeline Veronica Louise); *née* Vanden-Bempde-Johnstone; er da of 5 Baron Derwent, *qv*; *b* 3 Nov 1958; *Educ* St Paul's Girls' Sch, UCL (BA); *m* 1982, James John Winterbotham, s of Richard William Consett Winterbotham, of The Hall, Wittersham, Tenterden, Kent; 1 s (Alexander William Harcourt b 1988); *Career* md The John Harris Design Partnership London; cncl memb The Franco-British Soc 1985-88, skinner of London, memb The Bach Choir; *Style*— The Hon Mrs Winterbotham; 48 Oakley Rd, London N1

WINTERBOTHAM, Gp Capt Frederick William; CBE (1942); s of Frederick Winterbotham (d 1942), and Florence Vernon, *née* Graham (d 1962, descended through Vernon (later Manners) from King Edward I); *b* 16 April 1897; *Educ* Charterhouse, Ch Ch Oxford (LLB); *m* 1, 1921, Erica Horniman (d 1946); 1 s (Jervis Anthony b 19 Nov 1927) 2 da (Pamela b 12 Aug 1924, Susan b 11 Feb 1930); m 2, 1946, Petrea Jowitt (d 1986); 1 da (Sally Petrea b 17 Nov 1956); m 3, Kathleen Price; *Career* joined Royal Gloucestershire Hussars Yeomany 1915 (aged 17, Lt), transferred to Royal Flying Corps 1916 (Capt); shot down over Passchendaele July 1917, POW 1918; farmer 1921-29; head of MI6 Air 1930; personally made contact with Hitler, Rosenberg and Hess to discover the extent of German air rearmament 1930-40; dep chief of MI6 with total responsibility for distribution and security of the 'Ultra Secret' during WWII; dir BOAC 1946-48; books include the 'Ultra Secret' (1974), The Nazi Connection (1978); *Recreations* hunting, shooting, fishing; *Clubs* RAF; *Style*— Gp Capt Frederick Winterbotham, CBE; Westwinds, Westbury Farm, Tarrant Gunville, Blandford, Dorset DT11 8JW (☎ 025 889 570)

WINTERBOTTOM, Hon Caroline Margaret Alyson; only da of Baron Winterbottom (Life Peer), and his 2 w, Ira Munk; *b* 9 Dec 1950; *Educ* Wispers Sch, Oxford Poly (Dip Pub); *Career* publishing; sales admin for Europe and the Middle E; *Recreations* creative writing; *Style*— The Hon Caroline Winterbottom; c/o The Rt Hon Lord Winterbottom, Lower Farm, Fosbury, Marlborough, Wilts SN8 3NJ (☎ 026489 269)

WINTERBOTTOM, Derek Edward; JP (1967); s of Edward Marshall Winterbottom (d 1984), and Mabel Winterbottom, (1960); *b* 29 Sept 1923; *Educ* Archbishop Halgates GS York; *m* 4 June 1949, Daphne Floris, da of Frank Brown (d 1968); 2 s (David Roy,

Michael John), 1 da (Alison Frances); *Career* CA 1949, conslt Barron & Barron York 1986 (ptnr 1953-); dep chm York Bench, sec Yorks Bldgs Preservation Tst Ltd; tres: York Georgian Soc, Fairfax House York; FCA; *Recreations* golf, skiing; *Style*— Derek E Winterbottom, Esq, JP; Skelton Croft, Skelton, York (☎ 0904 470 321); Barron & Barron, Bathurst House, Micklegate, York, YO1 2HN (☎ 0904 628 551)

WINTERBOTTOM, Hon Dudley Walter Gordon; 2 s of Baron Winterbottom (Life Peer), and his 2 w, Ira Munk; *b* 25 June 1946; *Educ* Charterhouse, Kent Univ Canterbury, Wolfson Coll Oxford; *m* 1978, Mirjana; *Career* co dir; sec Chelsea Arts Club; proprietor Cherwell Boathouse Restaurant Oxford; *Recreations* piano playing, reading, sleeping; *Style*— The Hon Dudley Winterbottom; c/o The Rt Hon Lord Winterbottom, Lower Farm, Fosbury, Marlborough, Wilts SN8 3NJ (☎ 026489 269)

WINTERBOTTOM, Hon Graham Anthony; 3 s of Baron Winterbottom (Life Peer), and his 2 w, Ira Munk; *b* 23 June 1948; *Educ* Charterhouse, RNC; *Style*— The Hon Graham Winterbottom; c/o The Rt Hon Lord Winterbottom, Lower Farm, Fosbury, Marlborough, Wilts SN8 3NJ (☎ 026489 269)

WINTERBOTTOM, Baron (Life Peer UK 1965), of Clopton, Co Northampton; Ian Winterbottom; s of George Harold Winterbottom, JP (High Sheriff Northants 1908, ld of the manor and patron of livings of Horton, Hackleton and Piddington) and his 2 w, Georgina, da of Rev Ian McLeod, of Skye; *b* 6 April 1913; *Educ* Charterhouse, Clare Coll Cambridge; *m* 1, 1939 (m dis 1944), Rosemary Mills; 1 s; m 2, 1944, Ira (Irene Eva), da of Dr Walter Munk, of Haifa; 2 s, 1 da; *Career* serv RHG 1944-46, NW Europe, Capt 1945; sits as SDP peer in House of Lords; private asst to regnl cmmr Hamburg (Sir Vaughan Berry) 1946-49, private sec to min Civil Aviation 1949, MP (Lab) Nottingham Centl 1950-55, parly under-sec MOD (RN) 1966-67, parly sec Min of Public Bldg and Works 1967-68, parly under-sec (RAF) MOD 1968-70, oppn spokesman: Def 1970-74, Trade and Indust 1976-78; lord-in-waiting to HM The Queen 1974-78 (govt whip), resigned 1978; fndr memb SDP 1981; memb: House of Lords All Pty Def Study Gp, Parly and Scientific Ctee, Cwlth Parly Assoc; chm: Venesta Int 1972-74, Centurion Housing Assoc 1980-, Collins Aircraft Co 1980-, Dynavest Ltd 1982-, Anglo Global Ltd 1983-; conslt C Z Scientific Instruments Ltd 1980-; *Recreations* music, ornithology; *Clubs* Athenaeum; *Style*— The Rt Hon the Lord Winterbottom; Lower Farm, Fosbury, Marlborough, Wilts SN8 3NJ (☎ (026489) 269)

WINTERBOTTOM, Hon John; el s of Baron Winterbottom (Life Peer) and his 1 w, Rosemary Mills; *b* 30 Sept 1940; *Educ* Charterhouse, Clare Coll Cambridge; *m* Sheila Marie Evershed; 1 s; *Style*— The Hon John Winterbottom; c/o The Rt Hon Lord Winterbottom, Lower Farm, Fosbury, Marlborough, Wilts SN8 3NJ (☎ 026489 269)

WINTERBOTTOM, Dr Michael; s of Allan Winterbottom (d 1982), of East Budleigh, Devon, and Kathleen Mary Winterbottom; *b* 22 Sept 1934; *Educ* Dulwich, Pembroke Coll Oxford (BA, MA, D Phil); *m* 31 Aug 1963 (m dis 1983), Helen, da of Harry Spencer (d 1977), of Willenhall, Staffs; m2, Nicolette Janet Streatfeild Bergel, da of Henry Shorland Gervis (d 1968), of Sherborne; 2 s (Peter, Jonathan) ; *Career* lectr in latin and greek UCL 1962-67, fell and tutor in classics Worcester Coll Oxford 1967-; Dr hc Besanon 1985; *Books* Quintilian (ed 1970), Ancient Literary Criticism (with DA Russell, 1972), Three Lives of English Saints (1972), The Elder Seneca (ed and translated, 1974), Tacitus, Opera Minora (ed with R M Ogilvie, 1975), Gildas (ed and translated 1978), Roman Declamation (1980), The Minor Declamations Ascribed to Quintilian (ed with commentary, 1984), Sopatros the Rhetor (with D C Innes 1988); *Recreations* hill walking, travel; *Style*— Dr Michael Winterbottom; 172 Walton St, Oxford, OX1 2HD (☎ 0865 515727); Worcester College, Oxford OX1 2HB (☎ 0865 278300)

WINTERBOTTOM, Sir Walter; CBE (1972, OBE 1963); s of James Winterbottom; *b* 31 Mar 1913; *Educ* Chester Coll Educn, Carnegie Coll Physical Educn; *m* 1942, Ann Richards; 1 s, 2 da; *Career* dir Coaching and mangr England Team FA 1946-62, gen sec Central Cncl Physical Educn 1963-72, dir Sports Cncl 1965-78; kt 1978; *Style*— Sir Walter Winterbottom, CBE; 15 Orchard Gdns, Cranleigh, Surrey (☎ (0483) 271593)

WINTERFLOOD, Brian Martin; s of Thomas George Winterflood (d 1978), of Slough, Bucks, and Doris Maud, *née* Waddington; *Educ* Frays Coll Uxbridge Middx; *m* 10 Oct 1966, Doreen Stella, da of Albert Frederick McCartney, of London; 2 s (Guy b 2 April 1970, Mark b 8 March 1973), 1 da (Sarah b 9 July 1974); *Career* Nat Serv 1955-57; Greener Dreyfus & Co 1953-57; Bisgood Bishop & Co: joined 1957, ptnr 1967, dir 1971 (Co incorporated) md 1981, 1986 (Co taken over by County NatWest Investmt Bank) md mkt making 1986, exec dir County NatWest Securities 1986-88, fndr and md Winterflood Securities 1988; memb Stock Exchange 1966; vice-pres REMIDI (Rehabilitation and Med Res Tst); *Recreations* family, work, travel; *Clubs* IOD; *Style*— Brian Winterflood, Esq; 5 Church Hill, Wimbledon, London SW19 7BN (☎ 01 946 4052); Winterflood Securities Ltd, Knollys House, 47 Mark Lane, London EC3R 7QH (☎ 01 621 0004, fax 01 623 9482)

WINTERSGILL, Dr William; s of Fred Wintersgill (d 1982), of School House, Darton, Barnsley, and Mary, Torkington (d 1982); *b* 20 Dec 1922; *Educ* Barnsley Holgate GS, Leeds Univ Med Sch (MB, ChB); *m* 29 March 1952, Iris May, da of William Henry Holland (d 1971), of Swedish Bungalow, Rawcliffe, Goole, Yorks; 3 da (Anne b 1953, Jane b 1956, Billie b 1964); *Career* 2 Lt Yorks and Lancs Regt 1944-46; princ in gen practice Smith 1950-66, regnl med off Miny of Health DHSS 1967-70; DHSS HQ: sr med offr 1970-72, princ med offr 1972-76, sr princ med offr 1976-83; York Health Authy: specialist community med 1983-87, med policy advsr 1987-88; memb York Med Soc, vice chm Age Concern York, fndr chm Br Assoc of Community Physicains; FFCM 1983, MRCGP 1976; *Recreations* gardening, bridge, old buildings, opera, antiques; *Style*— Dr William Wintersgill; Chandlers Cottage, Flawith, Alne, York (☎ 034 73 310)

WINTERTON, (Jane) Ann; MP (C) Congleton 1983-; da of Joseph Robert and Ellen Jane Hodgson, of Sutton Coldfield; *b* 6 Mar 1941; *Educ* Erdington GS for Girls; *m* 1960, Nicholas Raymond Winterton (C) MP, Macclesfield), *qv*, s of Norman H Winterton (d 1971), of Lysways House, Longdon Green, Staffs; 2 s, 1 da; *Career* memb Agric Select Ctee 1987-; jt master S Staffs Hunt 1959-64, memb W Midlands Cons Women's Advsy Ctee 1969-71; *Style*— Mrs Nicholas Winterton, MP; Whitehall Farm, Mow Lane, Newbold Astbury, Congleton, Cheshire

WINTERTON, Nicholas Raymond; MP ((C) Macclesfield 1971-); s of Norman H Winterton (d 1971), of Lysways House, Longdon Green, Staffs; *b* 31 Mar 1938; *Educ* Rugby; *m* 1960, Jane Ann, *qv*, da of J R Hodgson of Sutton Coldfield; 2 s, 1 da; *Career* Nat Serv 2 Lt 14/20 King's Hussars 1957-59; sales and gen mangr Stevens and Hodgson Ltd 1960-80; CC Warwickshire 1967-1972, (dep chm County Educn Ctee 1970-72, chm Co Youth Serv Sub Ctee 1969-72); contested (C) Newcastle-under-Lyme 1969 (by-election) and 1970; London; Parly advsr to: BSM Hldgs Gp Ltd, Baird Textile Hldgs Ltd, Construction Plant Hire Assoc, Paper and Bd Indust Fedn Br Paper Machinery Makers Assoc; chm Br-Namibian Parly Gp, joint vice-chm Anglo-Danish and Anglo-Swedish Parly Gp, sec Anglo-Austrian Parly Gp, jt vice-chm Br Taiwan Parly Gp, vice-chm Br-SA Parly Gp; tres: Br Bahamas Parly Gp, Br-Indonesia Parly Gp; vice-chm UK Falkland Islands Gp; memb select ctees: Social Servs 1979-, Standing Orders 1981-; memb House of Commons Chairmans' Panel; Freeman City of London, Liveryman Worshipful Co of Weavers; *Style*— Nicholas Winterton, Esq, MP; Whitehall Farm, Mow Lane, Newbold Astbury, Congleton, Cheshire

WINTERTON, 7 Earl (I 1766); Robert Chad Turnour; also Baron Winterton (I 1761) and Viscount Turnour (I 1766); s of Cecil Turnour (gs of Rev Hon Augustus Turnour, 3 s of 2 Earl Winterton); suc 3 cous once removed, 6 Earl, 1962, but has not yet established right to his Peerages; *b* 13 Sept 1915; *Educ* Nutana Coll; *m* 1, 1941, Kathleen Ella (d 1969), da of D B Whyte, of Saskatoon, Saskatchewan, Canada; m 2, 1971, Marion, da of Arthur Phillips; *Heir* nephew, (Donald) David Turnour, *qv*; *Career* Flt Sgt RCAF, serv WWII and Sardinia 1957-58; *Style*— The Rt Hon Earl Winterton; 1326 55th St, Delta, British Columbia, Canada

WINTOUR, Charles Vere; CBE (1980, MBE 1945); s of Maj-Gen FG Wintour, CB, CBE (d 1948), of Broadstairs, and Alice Jane Blanche, *née* Foster (d 1977); *b* 18 May 1917; *Educ* Oundle, Peterhouse Cambridge (BA, MA); *m* 1, 1940 (m dis 1979), Eleanor Trego, er da of Prof RJ Baker; 3 s (Gerald Jackson b 1940 (decd), James Charles b 1948, Patrick Walter b 1956), 2 da (Anna, Hilary Nora); m 2, 9 Nov 1979, Audrey Cecilia, da of Frederick George Smith, former w of WA Slaughter; *Career* Royal Norfolk Regt 1940, GSO 2 COSSAC 1944, GSO 2 SHAEF 1945 (despatches); joined Evening Standard 1946 (political editor 1952, dep editor 1959-76 and 1978-80), asst editor Sunday Express 1952-54, managing editor Daily Express 1957-59; ed: Sunday Express Magazine 1981-82, UK Press Gazette 1985-86; dir: Evening Standard Co Ltd 1959-82, Express (formerly Beaverbrook Newspapers Ltd 1964-82, TV-am (News) Ltd 1982-84, AGB Communications 1984-85, Wintour Publications 1984-85; memb Press Cncl 1978-79; Croix de Guerre (France) 1945, Croix de Guerre (Belgium) 1945, Bronze Star (US) 1945; *Books* Pressures on the Press (1972); *Recreations* theatre going; *Clubs* Garrick; *Style*— Charles Wintour, Esq, CBE; 5 Alwyne Rd, London N1 2HH (☎ 01 359 4590)

WISBECH, Archdeacon of; *see*: Fleming, Ven David

WISE, Wing Cdr Adam Nugent; LVO (1983), MBE (1976); s of Lt-Col (Alfred) Royal Wise, MBE, TD (d 1974), and Cassandra Noel Wise (d 1982); *b* 1 August 1943; *Educ* Repton, RAF Coll Cranwell, London Univ (BA); *m* 1983, Jill Amabel, da of (Cyril) Geoffrey Marmaduke Alington, of Lincolnshire; *Career* cmmnd 1965 RAF; serv Middle E, Far E, Germany; ADC to Cdr FEAF 1970-71, exchange pilot Federal German Air Force 1972-75; Equerry to HM The Queen 1980-83, OC London Univ Air Sqdn 1983-86, private sec to TRH The Duke and Duchess of York and The Prince Edward 1983-87; Hill Univ Air Sqdn 1988-; *Recreations* sailing, riding; *Clubs* RAF, Royal Ocean Racing; *Style*— Wing Cdr Adam Wise, LVO, MBE; c/o C Hoare & Co, 32 Lowndes St, London SW1

WISE, Hon Christopher John Clayton; s and h of 2 Baron Wise; *b* 19 Mar 1949; *Educ* Norwich Sch, Southampton Univ; *Style*— The Hon Christopher Wise

WISE, Prof Douglas; OBE (1981); s of Horace Watson Wise, BEM (d 1964), of Whitby, Yorks, and Doris Wise; *b* 6 Nov 1927; *Educ* King's Coll Newcastle, Durham Univ (BArch, Dip TP); *m* 8 March 1958 (m dis 1984), da of Emile Czeiler (d 1958), of Newcastle upon Tyne; 1 s ((Matthew) Gregory b 15 May 1966), 1 da (Clare Alexandra b 19 Nov 1964); *Career* Lt RE Mil Survey 1953-55; architect; prof of architecture Newcastle Univ 1968-75, dir Inst of Advanced Architectural Studies York Univ 1975; fndr Douglass Wise & Ptnrs Architects Newcastle upon Tyne 1959-; vice-chm N Housing Gp 1973-75, govr Bldg Centre Tst 1976-, tstee Interbuild Gp 1986-; FRIBA (cncl memb 1979-81); *Recreations* painting, natural history; *Style*— Prof Douglas Wise, OBE; Kings Manor, York YO1 2EW (☎ 0904 433987); Welburn, Kirkwhelpington, Newcastle upon Tyne NE19 2SA; The Institute of Advanced Architectural Studies, Kings Manor, York YO1 2EP (☎ 0904 433987, fax 0904 433 949)

WISE, Ernie; *see*: Wiseman, Ernest

WISE, Hillier Bernard Alexander; s of Emanuel Wise (d 1979), and Minnie, *née* Berg (d 1983); *b* 9 August 1928; *Educ* Kilburn GS, Bartlett Sch of Architecture UCL, Birbeck Coll London (BA), Westminster Coll Oxford (PGCE), St Catherine's Coll Oxford (MLitt); *Career* various teaching posts in primary secdy and further educn, admin offr AEB 1962; pt/t extra-mural tutor in art history Univ of London 1964-, former specia lectr Wallace Collection London, summer sch tutor Open Univ, guest lectr Swans Hellenic Art Treasures Tours, sr lectr Willesden Coll of Technol 1975-, admin offr AEB 1982; convocation senator in arts Univ of London, vice pres Univ of London Graduates Soc; memb: Nat Art Collections Fund, Friend of Tate Gallery and Royal Acad of Arts; Freeman City of London 1971, Liveryman Worshipful Co of Painter-Stainers 1971; Inter RIBA 1950, Assoc London Coll of Music 1950; memb: Soc of Architectural Historians of GB, Assoc of Art Historians, History of Educn Soc, member Oxford Univ Boat Club Tst; *Recreations* music (piano, organ, opera, ballet, concerts), travel, looking at architecture; *Clubs* Utd Oxford and Cambridge; *Style*— Hillier Wise, Esq; 8 Dicey Ave, Cricklewood, London NW2 6AT (☎ 01 452 1433); Willesden Coll of Tecnol, Denzil Rd, London NW10 2XD (☎ 01 452 6509)

WISE, 2 Baron (UK 1951); John Clayton Wise; s of 1 Baron Wise, DL (d 1968); *b* 11 June 1923; *m* 1946, Margaret, da of Frederick Snead; 2 s; *Heir* s, Hon Christopher Wise; *Career* farmer; *Style*— The Rt Hon Lord Wise; Martlets, Blakeney, Norfolk NR25 7NP

WISE, Maj Michael Henry; s of Henry Wise (d 1982), of Dolphins, Nubia Close, Cowes, IOW, and Edith Mae, *née* Parsons; *b* 9 Sept 1927; *Educ* Nautical Coll Pangbourne; *m* 5 Jan 1952, Diane, da of Sydney Cathery and May *née* Hague step da of James Grimditch; 2 da (Amanda b 1955, Nicola b 1957); *Career* cmmnd 2 Lt Gren Gds 1946, Lt 1948, Maj 1961; DAAG HQ Sthn Cnd 1969-70, GSO 2 (SO) to UKNMR SHAPE 1971-74, GSO 2 (Home Def) HQ LONDIST 1974-82; ret from Gren Gds Sept 1982; tres Household Divn funds 1982, memb Lloyds 1987; sec and tres Guards Chapel; tres: The Guards Magazine, The Guards Saddle Club, The Guards CC; *Recreations* yachting, fishing, riding; *Clubs* Household Div Yacht; *Style*— Maj Michael Wise; Cornerways, 36 Sea Lane, Middleton-on-Sea, West Sussex PO22 7RT (☎ 0243 69 2510); HQ Household Division, Horse Guards, Whitehall, London SW1A 2AX (☎

01 930 4466 ext 2499)

WISE, Prof Michael John; CBE (1979), MC (1945); s of Harry Cuthbert Wise (d 1954), of Birmingham, and Sarah Evelyn, *née* Lawton (d 1962); *b* 17 August 1918; *Educ* Saltley GS Birmingham, Univ of Birmingham (BA, DipEd, PhD); *m* 4 May 1942, Barbara Mary, da of C L Hodgetts (d 1951), of Wolverhampton; 1 s (John Charles Michael b 6 Sept 1949), 1 da ((Barbara) Janet (Mrs Meyer) b 1 June 1946); *Career* cmmnd RA 1941, serv Middle E 1942-44, Maj 1944, The Northamptonshire Regt 1944-46, serv Italy 1944-46; lectr in geography Univ of Birmingham 1946-51; LSE: lectr in geography 1951-54, Sir Ernest Cassel reader in econ geography 1954-58, prof of geography 1958-83, pro-dir 1983-85; Erskine fell Univ of Canterbury NZ 1970; chm: departmental ctee of inquiry into statutory smallholdings Miny of Agric 1964-68, Landscape Advsy ctee Dept of Tport 1981- (memb 1971-); pres: Inst of Br Geographers 1974, Geographical Assoc 1976-77, Royal Geographical Soc 1980-82, Int Geographical Union 1976-80; memb Social Sci Res Cncl 1976-82, chm of govrs Birkbeck Coll London 1983-; Fndrs Medal Royal Geographical Soc 1977, Hon DUniv Open Univ 1978, Hon DSc Birmingham 1982, Lauréat d'Honneur Int Geographical Union (1984); FRGS, FRSA; Alexander Kőrösi Csoma Medal Hungarian Geographical Soc 1980, Tokyo Geographical Soc Medal 1981, Hon Memb Geographical Socs of Paris, Poland, USSR and Mexico; *Books* Birmingham and its Regional Setting (hon ed 1950); Consultant: An Atlas of World Resources (1979), The Great Geographical Atlas (1982), Ordnance Survey Atlas of Gr Britain (1982); *Recreations* gardening, music, watching cricket; *Clubs* Athenaeum; *Style—* Prof Michael Wise, CBE, MC; 45 Oakleigh Ave, Whetstone, London N20 9JE (☎ 01 445 6057); London Sch of Econs, Houghton St, Aldwych, London WC2A 2AE (☎ 01 405 7686)

WISEMAN, David John; s of James Wiseman (d 1982), and Marjorie, *née* Ward; *b* 25 Mar 1944; *Educ* Britannia RNC Dartmouth, RNEC Manadon, Plymouth (BSc), Univ of Surrey (MSc); *Career* RN 1962-74, Lt 1967-74; asst sec DTI 1980-87, (princ 1974-80), co dir Kingsway Rowland 1987-, md Rowland Public Affrs 1988-; FIEE, CEng, MBIM; *Recreations* travel, gardening, riding, music; *Clubs* Athenaeum; *Style—* David Wiseman, Esq; Cedar Court, Haslemere, Surrey GU27 2BA; Kingsway Rowland Ltd, 67 Whitfield Street, London W1P 5RL

WISEMAN, Ernest; OBE (1976); s of Harry Wiseman and Connie, *née* Wright; *b* 27 Nov 1925; *Educ* Cncl Sch; *m* 1953, Doreen, da of Henry James William Blyth; *Career* radio, variety, TV and film actor; SFTA Awards: 1963, 1971, 1972, 1973; BAFTA Award Light Entertainment TV 1973, Silver Heart Variety Club 1964 and 1976, Water Rats 1970, Radio Indust 1971 and 1972, Sun Newspaper 1973; Royal Command Performances: 1955, 1964, 1966, 1968 and 1984; shows inc: Too Close for Comfort (TV Los Angeles 1986), The Mystery of Edwin Drood (Savoy Theatre 1987), Run for your Wife (Criterian Theatre 1988); *Recreations* boating, tennis, swimming; *Clubs* St James's, White Elephant, Ritz, Casino; *Style—* Ernie Wise, Esq, OBE; Gable End, 22 Dorney Reach Road, Dorney Reach Maidenhead, Berks SL6 0DX

WISEMAN, Joan, Lady; Joan Mary; *née* Phelps; da of Arthur Phelps, of Harrow; *m* 10 Feb 1944, as his 3 w, Sir William George Eden Wiseman, 10 Bt, CB (d 1962); 1 s (11 Bt); *Style—* Joan, Lady Wiseman

WISEMAN, Sir John William; 11 Bt (E 1628), of Canfield Hall, Essex; s of Sir William Wiseman, 10 Bt, CB, CMG (d 1962), and his 3 w, Joan, Lady Wiseman, *qv*; *b* 16 Mar 1957; *Educ* Millfield, Hartford Univ Conn USA; *m* 1980, Nancy, da of Casimer Zyla, of New Britain, Conn, USA; 1 da (Elizabeth b 1983); *Heir* fifth cous, Thomas Alan Wiseman b 8 July 1921; *Style—* Sir John Wiseman, Bt; 395 North Rd, Sudbury, Mass 01776, USA

WISEMAN, Kenneth John; s of Stephen Wiseman, of 2 Cranston Park Ave, Upminster, Essex, and Lilian Wiseman; *b* 17 Oct 1945; *Educ* Plaistow GS, NE London Poly (HNC); *m* 17 Dec 1966 (m dis 1985), Carol Ann; 1 s (Scott b 14 Aug 1971); m 2, 31 Dec 1988, Doreen; *Career* mktg dir Carless Solvents Ltd 1981, md Carless Refining of mktg Ltd 1986; MBIM, FInstPet, FInstM; *Recreations* gardening, DIY, tennis, soccer, West Ham Utd FC; *Style—* Kenneth Wiseman, Esq; Carless Refining and Mktg Ltd, St James Ho, Eastern Rd, Romford, Essex RM3 1NL (☎ 0708 755 557, fax 0708 753 890, car tel 0860 388 450, telex 261071)

WISEMAN, Prof (Timothy) Peter; s of Stephen Wiseman (d 1971), of Manchester, and Winifred Agnes Wiseman; *b* 3 Feb 1940; *Educ* Manchester GS, Balliol Coll Oxford (MA, DPhil); *m* 15 Sept 1962, (Doreen) Anne, da of Harold Williams, of Atherton, Lancs; *Career* reader in Roman history Leicester Univ 1973-76 (lectr in classics 1963-73), visiting prof in classics Univ of Toronto 1970-71, prof of classics Exeter Univ 1977-; DLitt Durham 1988; FSA 1977, FBA 1986; *Books* Catullan Questions (1969), New Men in the Roman Senate (1971), Cinna the Poet (1974), Clio's Cosmetics (1979), Catullus and His World (1985), Roman Studies (1987); *Style—* Prof Peter Wiseman; Dept of Classics, The Univ, Exeter EX4 4QH (☎ 0392 264 201, fax 0392 263 108, telex 42894 EXUNIV G)

WISEMAN, Thomas Alan; s of Thomas Edward Wiseman (d 1959, 5 in descent from Sir Thomas Wiseman, 6 Bt), and Anna Louisa, *née* Allen; hp to fifth cous, Sir John Wiseman, 11 Bt; *b* 8 July 1921; *Educ* Gravesend County Sch for Boys; *m* 11 Dec 1946, Hildemarie, da of Gustav Domnik, of Allenstein, formerly E Prussia; 1 s (Thomas, d 1947), 1 da (Susan, d 1949); *Career* Army 1941-46: Staff Quartermaster Sgt RAOC; 1946-48 English Correspondent in Brussels, 1949-75 Ships Agent, 1975-86- admin offr Forest Products Terminal, Northfleet Terminal Ltd; ret WEF 1986; *Style—* Thomas Wiseman, Esq; 14 Havisham Rd, Chalk, Gravesend, Kent DA12 4UN (☎ 0474 361375)

WISH, Timothy John; s of Charles Arnold Wish (d 1938), of Sheffield, and Kathleen Mary, *née* Bingley (d 1982); *b* 22 August 1933; *Educ* Giggleswick Sch, Sheffield Univ (BSc); *m* 29 Mar 1962, Jill Christine, da of Ferguson Bishop; 2 s (Dominic b 1963, James b 1964), 1 da (Emma b 1967); *Career* Nat Serv cmmnd Royal Signals 1955-57, TA 1957-63 (Capt); chm Abrafract Ltd 1978 (joined 1957, works mangr 1960, works dir 1962, md 1978); chm & md Abrafract Holdings Ltd 1988-; UK delegate Federation Européenne des Fabricants de Produits Abrasifs 1977- (vice pres 1988-), memb Abrasives Industs Assoc (chm tech ctee 1970-78), govr Giggleswich Sch 1986; Freeman Worshipful Co of Cutlers in Hallamshire; *Recreations* golf; *Clubs* Sickleholme Golf (Bamford), Abbeydale Park Sport's; *Style—* T Wish, Esq; Clod Hall Farm, Eastmoor, Chesterfield, S42 7DF (☎ 024 688 2148); Abrafract Holdings Ltd, Beulah Rd, Sheffield S6 2AR (☎ 0742 348971, telex 547202 ABRA G)

WISHART (Mrs R McLeod), (Margaret) Ruth; da of John Wishart (d 1960) and Margaret Smith, *née* Mitchell; *b* 27 August 1945; *Educ* Eastwood Sr Sec Sch; *m* 16 Sept 1971, Roderick McLeod, s of Roderick McLeod; *Career* Women's Ed Scottish Daily Record 1973-78; Sunday Mail 1978-82, Sunday Standard 1982-83; freelance journalist and broadcaster 1983-86, sr asst ed The Scotsman 1986-88; Columnist and broadcaster 1988-; memb: Standing Cmmn on Scottish Econ, Lothian Health Challenge, Scottish Advsy Ctee to Br Chal; dir: Wildcat Theatre Co, Assembly Theatre, Fdr dir MAYFEST; *Recreations* theatre, concerts, galleries, curling; *Style—* Ms R Wishart; Wilson Court, Wilson St, Glasgow, Advocates Close, Edinburgh (☎ 041 552 0367); The Scotsman, North Bridge, Edinburgh (☎ 031 225 2468, fax 031 225 7302, telex 72255)

WITCHELL, Nicholas N H; s of William Joseph Henshall Witchell, and Barbara Sybil Mary, *née* MacDonald; *b* 23 Sept 1953; *Educ* Epsom Coll, Leeds Univ (LLB); *Career* joined BBC TV News 1976: reporter NI 1979-81, reporter London 1982-83, Ireland corr 1984, presenter 6 O'Clock News 1984-; *Books* The Loch Ness Story (1974, 1982 and 1989); *Style—* Nicholas Witchell, Esq; BBC TV News, BBC TV Centre, London, W12 7RJ (☎ 01 743 8000)

WITHERINGTON, Giles Somerville Gwynne; s of Iltyd Gwynne Witherington (d 1962), and Gage, *née* Spicer (d 1968); *b* 7 June 1919; *Educ* Charterhouse, Oxford Univ (MA); *m* 1951, Rowena Ann Spencer, da of Lt-Col Hylton S Lynch, MC, TD (d 1976); 1 s, 3 da; *Career* Maj RA, N Africa and Italy 1939-46 (despatches); dep chm Reed Int plc 1976-82 (dir 1963-82), ret; chm Save The Children Fund 1982-87 (cncl memb SCF 1980-); cncl memb Textile Conservation Centre 1984- (chm tstees 1984-); Hon LLD Birmingham Univ 1983; *Recreations* shooting, gardening, travel; *Clubs* Arts; *Style—* Giles Witherington, Esq; Bishops, Widdington, Saffron Walden, Essex CB11 3SQ (☎ 0799 405 39)

WITHERINGTON, Paul; s of Rev Charles Townsend Witherington (d 1940), and Annie Magdalen, *née* Wright (d 1950); *b* 8 Mar 1913; *Educ* Lancing, St Edmund Hall Oxford (MSc, MA); *Career* schoolmaster: New Coll Choir Sch Oxford 1935-36, Derby Sch 1936-40, Wallasey GS 1940-46 and experimental offr chemical inspection dept MoS 1941-45, Monkton Combe Sch 1946-57, Lancing Coll 1957-79; jt ldr Jt Schools Expdns to Iceland, Shetlands, St Kilda, Outer Hebrides; *Recreations* printing, music, reading, gardening; *Style—* Paul Witherington, Esq; The Priory, Edgmond, Newport, Shropshire TF10 8HH (☎ 0952 810731)

WITHERS, Googie (Georgette) Lizette; AO (1980); da of Capt Edgar Clements Withers, CIE, CBE, RN (d 1951), and Lizette Catharina Wilhelmina, *née* Van Wageningen (d 1976); *b* 12 Mar 1917; *Educ* Fredville Park Nonnington Kent, Sch of the Holy Family London; *m* 1948, John Neil McCallum, CBE (chm & chief exec Fauna Films, Australia, also actor & prodr, as well as sometime pres Australian Film Cncl and theatre manager), s of John Neil McCallum (d 1957), of Brisbane; 1 s (Nicholas), 2 da (Joanna, Amanda); *Career* actress (as Googie Withers) since 1933, starring in 50 films including One of Our Aircraft is Missing, On Approval, It Always Rains on Sunday; plays include Deep Blue Sea, Winter Journey, Hamlet, Much Ado About Nothing, The Cherry Orchard, The Skin Game, Private Lives, The Kingfisher, The Circle, The Importance of Being Earnest, School for Scandal, Time and the Conways, The Chalk Garden; numerous tv plays including Within These Walls, Time After Time, Hotel Dulac, Northanger Abbey; Chichester Festival Theatre Hay Fever Ring Round The Moon; UK Tour Ace Award, Best Actress TV Film "Time After Time", BAFTA award best actress 1954; best actress Sun Award 1974; *Recreations* travelling, reading, interior decorating; *Clubs* Queens (Sydney); *Style—* Miss Googie Withers, AO; 1740 Pittwater Rd, Bayview, NSW 2104, Australia

WITHERS, Roy Joseph; CBE (1983); s of Joseph Withers (d 1973), and Irene Ada, *née* Jones; *b* 18 June 1924; *Educ* Tiffin Sch Kingston-upon-Thames, Trinity Coll Cambridge; *m* 20 Dec 1947, Pauline Mary Gillian, *née* Johnston; 4 s (Christopher, Stephen, Paul, Robert); *Career* sr engr ICI 1948-55; tech dir Humphreys & Glasgow 1955-63; engrg dir Davy Power Gas Corpn 1963-70 (md 1970-71), ch exec Davy Powergas 1972-73, md Davy Corpn 1973-83 (dep chm 1983-86, vice-chm 1986-), chm Vosper Thornycroft (UK) Ltd 1985-; dep chm Transmark Worldwide 1985-87 (chm 1987-); memb BOTB 1983-86, chm Overseas Projects Bd 1983-86; FEng 1983, Hon FIChemE; *Recreations* golf, painting; *Clubs* Carlton, Hampstead Golf, Bramshaw Golf; *Style—* Roy Withers Esq, CBE; 2 Clarkes Mews, Beaumont St, London W1 1RR; Davy Corporation plc, 15 Portland Place, London W1A 4PP (☎ 01 637 2821; fax, 01 637 0902; telex, 22604)

WITHERSPOON, Dr (Edward) William; s of Edward William Witherspoon (d 1982), of Liverpool, and Maude Miranda, *née* Goff (d 1987); *b* 19 Dec 1925; *Educ* King Edward's Sch Birmingham, Univ of Birmingham (MB ChB), Univ of London DTM & H, LRCP (Lond), MRCS (Eng); *m* 10 June 1954, Jean, da of John McKellar (d 1956); *Career* physician (tropical diseases/clinical pharmacology); chm BMA Pharmaceutical Physicians Gp Ctee 1986-; sr med advsr Roussel Labs 1983-; med dir: Warner Lambert/Parke Davis 1977-82, Abbott Labs 1971-77, Burroughs Wellcome 1960-71; ABPI Trade Mission Japan 1968; asst govt med offr Medico-Legal Dept Sydney 1958-60; Maj RAMC, 2 i/c 3rd Field Ambulance 4 RTR Suez Canal Zone and Cyprus 1953; FRSH 1971; author Govt and Hyperuricaemia (Wellcome Monograph 1967), Thalidomide - The Aftermath (Pharmaceut: Med: 1988); *Recreations* Nat Tst, Nat Tst for Scotland; *Clubs* Royal Soc of Medicine, Royal Cwlth, Sloane; *Style—* Dr William Witherspoon; Brook Cottage, 4 Manor Rd, Oakley, nr Aylesbury, Bucks HP18 9QD; Roussel Laboratories Ltd, Broadwater Park, N Orbital Rd, Denham, Uxbridge, Middlesex UB9 5HP (☎ 0895 834343)

WITHRINGTON, John Kenneth Brookes; s of Ronald Ernest Withrington, of 108 Priests Lane, Brentwood, Essex CM15 8HN, and Eileen Gladys, *née* Green; *b* 23 Feb 1957; *Educ* Coopers Co Sch, Jesus Coll Cambridge (BA), Leicester Univ (MA), Univ of York; *Career* int div Nat Westminster Bank 1980-83 (PA to Divnl Fin Controller 1983), p/t lectr Univ of York 1984-87; admin asst Office of Registrar Univ of Lancaster 1987-; Freeman City of London, Liveryman Worshipful Co of Coopers (1977); AUT (1987), Conference of Univ Admin (1987); *Recreations* squash, badminton, skydiving, study of later middle-english arthurian romance; *Style—* John Withrington, Esq; Office of The Registrar, Univ of Lancaster, Universtiy House, Bailrigg, Lancaster (☎ 0524 65201, fax 0524 63806, telex 65111 LANCOL G)

WITNEY, Kenneth Percy; CVO (1976); s of Rev Thomas Charles Witney (d 1952), of Church of South India Theological Coll, Nazareth, Tamil Nadu, India, and Dr Myfanwy Dyfed, *née* Rees (d 1951); *b* 19 Mar 1916; *Educ* Eltham Coll Mottingham London, Wadham Coll Oxford (BA, MA); *m* 3 April 1947, Joan Agnes, da of Harold Tait, of 76 Simonside Terr, Newcastle-on-Tyne; 1 s (Nicholas b 1949), 1 da (Jane (Mrs Witney-

Smith) b 1948); *Career* private sec to Parly Under-Sec Miny of Home Security 1942-44 (admin asst 1940-42), asst private sec to Home Sec 1945-47; princ: Home Off 1945-47, Colonial Off (police div) 1955-57; asst under-sec of state Home Off 1969-76 (asst sec 1957-69), ret 1976; special advsr to Royal Cmmn on Gambling 1976-78; memb: Tonbridge Civic Soc, Romney Marsh Res Tst; chm Kent Fedn of Amenity Socs 1982-84; fell Royal Archaeological Inst; *Books* The Jutish Forest (1976), The Kingdom of Kent (1982); *Recreations* historical research (dark age and earlly mediaeval); *Style*— Kenneth Witney, Esq, CVO

WITTICH, John Charles Bird; s of Charles Cyril Wittich (d 1976), and Minnie Amelia Victoria, *née* Daborn; *b* 18 Feb 1929; *Educ* privately (BA); *m* 10 July 1954, June Rose, da of Thomas Frederick Taylor (d 1972); 1 s (Andrew Paul b 1961), 1 da (Margaret Judith b 1957); *Career* SOAS 1951-58, AA 1966-74, Middle East Econ Digest 1977-78, EPR Partnership 1979-86; freelance writer and lectr 1986-, lectr in adult educn circles, memb Minor Order of Readers of the C of E 1980-; Freeman City of London 1971, memb Parish Clerks Co 1974, Liveryman Worshipful Co of Woolmen 1977; FRSA 1980; *Books* Off-Beat Walks in London (1969), London Curiosities (1973), London Villages (1976), London Street Names (1977), London's Inns & Taverns (1978), London's Parks & Squares (1981), Catholic London (1988), Churches, Cathedrals & Chapels (1988), Wesley's London (1989), Guide to Bayswater (1989); *Clubs* City Livery, Wig and Pen; *Style*— John Wittich, Esq

WITTY, (John) David; CBE (1985); s of Harold Witty (d 1948), of Molescroft, E Yorks, and Olive, *née* Scaife (d 1977); *b* 1 Oct 1924; *Educ* Beverley GS, Balliol Coll Oxford (MA); *m* 1955, Doreen, da of John William Hanlan (d 1952), of Hull; 1 s (Simon); *Career* served RN 1943-46; slr; chief exec Westminster City Cncl 1977-84; hon sec London Boroughs Assoc 1978-84; chm London Enterprise Pty Co 1984-85; lawyer memb London Rent Assessment Panel 1984-; dir Gt Portland Estates plc 1987-; Order of Infante D Henrique (Portugal) 1978, Order of Right Hand (Nepal) 1980, Order of King Abdul Aziz (Saudi Arabia) 1981, Order of Oman 1982, Order of Orange Nassau 1982; *Recreations* golf, motoring; *Clubs* Royal Mid Surrey Golf; *Style*— David Witty, Esq, CBE; 14 River House, The Terrace, Barnes, London SW13 0NR (☎ 01 876 0038)

WIXLEY, Gordon Robert Alexander; CBE (1979, OBE 1955), TD (1959), DL (1976); s of Walter Henry James (d 1959), and Maud Mary, *née* Neave (d 1971); *b* 22 Nov 1914; *Educ* Lindisfarne Coll; *Career* HAC 1939 RA 1939-46; 2 90 Field Regt RA (City of London) TA 1947-54, Co 1951-54; Col TA 1955-58; CA; memb Ct of Common Cncl (City of London) 1964- (chief commoner 1985), vice-chm Greater London Tavra Sch 1967-73; chm bd of govrs: Bethlem Royal and Maudsley Hosp 1980-82, City of London Freemen's Sch 1977-88; chm ctee of mgmnt Inst of Psychiatry 1984-87; vice chm Nat Biological Standards Bd 1976-89; ADC (TA) to HM The Queen 1967-73; *Recreations* travel, walking, reading; *Clubs* Bucks, Athenaeum, Army and Navy, City Livery; *Style*— Gordon Wixley, Esq, CBE, TD, DL; 947 Chelsea Cloisters, Sloane Ave London SW3 3EU (☎ 01 589 3109)

WODEHOUSE, Lady; Hon Carol Lylie; *née* Palmer; da of 3 Baron Palmer, OBE; *b* 28 Nov 1951; *Educ* St Mary's Sch Wantage, St Hugh's Coll Oxford, Ripon Coll Cuddesdon; *m* 1973, Lord Wodehouse, *qv*, s and h of 4 Earl of Kimberley; 1 s, 1 da; *Career* teacher; *Style*— The Hon Lady Wodehouse; Derry House, North End, Henley-on-Thames, Oxon RG9 6LQ

WODEHOUSE, Hon Charles James; s of 4 Earl of Kimberley (by his 4 w); *b* 1963; *Style*— The Hon Charles Wodehouse

WODEHOUSE, Hon Edward Abdy; s of 4 Earl of Kimberley (by his 3 w); *b* 1954; *Educ* Eton; *Style*— The Hon Edward Wodehouse

WODEHOUSE, The Hon Henry Wyndham; s of 4 Earl of Kimberley (by his 3 w); *b* 26 April 1956; *Educ* Millfield; *m* 1979, Sarah M, only da of J A Fleming, of Hampton, Middx; 1 s (Thomas Henry John b 1981), 1 da (Clare b 1980); *Recreations* current affairs, golf, fishing, indoor athletics, tennis, photography; *Clubs* Falmouth Shark Angling; *Style*— The Hon Henry Wodehouse

WODEHOUSE, Lord; John Armine Wodehouse; s and h of 4 Earl of Kimberley; *b* 15 Jan 1951; *Educ* Eton, E Anglia Univ (MSc); *m* 1973, Hon Carol, *qv*, da of 3 Baron Palmer; 1 s, 1 da (Hon Katherine b 1976); *Heir* s, Hon David Simon John Wodehouse b 10 Oct 1978; *Career* systems programmer with Glaxo 1979- (joined as res chemist 1974); chm UK Info Users Gp 1981-83; assoc fell Br Interplanetary Soc 1981-83 (fell 1984-); FRSA, MBCS 1988-; *Recreations* photography, computing; *Style*— Lord Wodehouse; Derry House, North End, Henley-on-Thames, Oxon RG9 6LQ; Information Systems, Glaxo Gp Res Ltd, Greenford Rd, Greenford, Middx UB6 0HE (☎ 01 422 3434)

WOLF, Colin Piers; s of Peter Wolf, of Claverdon, Nr Stratford-upon-Avon, and Gladys Mary, *née* Williams; *b* 26 Jan 1943; *Educ* Bedford Sch; *m* 8 April 1972, Jennifer Elisabeth, da of Kingsley Richard Fox, of Surbiton, Surrey; 1 s (Guy Daniel b 1976), 1 da (Jocelyn Ruth b 1975); *Career* slr 1966, ptnr Evershed & Tomkinson 1973-; memb Law Soc 1972; *Recreations* music, books, walking, cycling; *Style*— Piers Wolf, Esq; 10 Newhall St, Birmingham B3 3LX (☎ 021 233 2001, fax 021 236 1583, telex 336688 EVSHED G)

WOLF, Prof Peter Otto; s of Richard Wolf (d 1967), and Dora, *née* Bondy (d 1966); *b* 9 May 1918; *Educ* St Polten, London Univ; *m* 1, 1944, Jennie, *née* Robinson; 2 s, 1 da; m 2, 1977, Janet Elizabeth, da of T R Robertson, OBE (d 1983); *Career* chartered civil engr; Imperial Coll of Sci and Tech London Univ 1949 (reader in hydrology 1955-66), prof and head civil engrg dept City Univ London 1966-82 (conslt 1950-); pres Br Hydrological Soc 1987-89; RK Linsley Award American Inst of Hydrology; FEng, Hon D Eng; *Recreations* classical music, reading, skiing, walking; *Clubs* Athenaeum; *Style*— Prof Peter Wolf; 69 Shepherd's Hill, London N6 5RE

WOLFE, Anthony James Garnham; s of Herbert Robert Inglewood Wolfe, VRD (d 1970), and Lesley Winifred, *née* Fox; *b* 30 August 1952; *Educ* Haileybury ISC, Univ of Bristol (BSc); *m* 4 Sept 1982, Ommar Aung, da of Lionel Aung Kwa Takwali (d 1956); *Career* CA; London and Hong Kong Offs Peat Marwick Mitchell 1974-81, GT Mgmnt London and Hong Kong Offs 1981-; FCA; *Recreations* rugger, golf, travel, walking; *Clubs* Wimbledon GC; *Style*— Anthony Wolfe, Esq; 39 St Winifreds Rd, Teddington, Middx TW11 9JB

WOLFE, Richard John Russell; s of Maj John Claude Frank Wolfe, of 14 Kennel Lane, Bookham, Surrey, and Betty Doris, *née* Hopwood; *b* 15 July 1947; *Educ* Ackworth Sch, Ackworth Yorks; *m* 28 Nov 1970 (m dis 1977), Lorraine Louise Hart; 1 da (Pandora b 12 July 1976); *Career* mgmnt trainee NM Rothschild and Son Ltd 1964-68, investment dealer Br and Continental Bank 1968-72, fund mangr Hill Samuel and Co Ltd 1972-75, corporate fin offr NM Rothschild and Sons Ltd 1976-80, vice pres and head of real estate fin UK Security Pacific Nat Bank 1980; AIB 1978; *Books* Real Estate Finance (contrib 1988); *Recreations* choir singing, swimming, training, study of ancient civilisations; *Style*— Richard Wolfe, Esq; 52 Claylands Road, London SW8 1PZ (☎ 01 582 1952); Security Pacific National Bank, 4 Broadgate, London EC2M 7LE (☎ 01 374 1904, fax 374 4487)

WOLFE MURRAY, James Archibald; s of Lt-Col Malcolm Victor Alexander Wolfe Murray, DL (d 1985; ggs of James Murray, who as a Lord of Session took the title Lord Cringletie; he was gggs of Alexander Murray, 2 Bt, of Blackbarony), and his 1 w, Lady Grizel Mary Boyle (d 1942), eldest da of 8 Earl of Glasgow; *b* 25 April 1936; *Educ* Eton, Worcester Coll Oxford; *m* 1, 8 June 1963 (m dis 1976), Hon (Lady until 1963) Diana Lucy Douglas-Home, da of Lord Home of the Hirsel, KT (14 Earl of Home until 1963); 1 s (Rory James b 1965), 2 da (Fiona Grizel b 1964, Clare Elizabeth b 1969); m 2, 17 July 1978, Amanda Felicity, da of Anthony Frank Street (d 1974); 1 s (Andrew Alexander b 1978); *Career* 2 Lt Black Watch 1954-56; export dir James Buchanan & Co 1969-75, vice-chm and md: Macdonald Greenlees Ltd 1975-82, John Haig & Co 1982-87; md White Horse Distillers 1987-; *Recreations* golf, fishing, shooting, cricket; *Clubs* White's, Naval and Military, Royal St George's Golf, MCC, Hon Co Edinburgh Golfers; *Style*— James Wolfe Murray, Esq; 13 Howards Lane, London SW15 6NX (☎ 01 788 6369); United Distillers Group, Landmark House, Hammersmith Bridge Road, London W6 9DP (☎ 01 748 8580, fax 01 748 5481, telex 923484)

WOLFE-PARRY, Hon Mrs; Hon Juno Odette Denisa Palma; *née* Wynn; da of 5 Baron Newborough (d 1957); *b* 1940; *m* 1963, Philip Wolfe-Parry, LDS, RCS; 1 s; *Style*— The Hon Mrs Wolfe-Parry; 5 Braemar Avenue, Wimbledon Park, London SW19

WOLFENDALE, Prof Arnold Whittaker; s of Arnold Wolfendale (d 1963), and Doris, *née* Hoyle (d 1983); *b* 25 June 1927; *Educ* Stretford GS, Univ of Manchester (BSc, PhD, DSc); *m* 1952, Audrey, da of Arnold Darby (d 1968); 2 s (twins, Colin and David); *Career* prof of physics Univ of Durham 1965-, chm N Region Manpower Service Cmmn's Job Creation Programme 1975-78, pres Royal Astronomical Soc 1981-83; FRS, FInstP, FRAS; *Recreations* gardening, travel; *Style*— Prof Arnold Wolfendale; Ansford, Potters Bank, Durham DH1 3RR (☎ 091 384 5642); Physics Dept, University of Durham (☎ 091 374 2160)

WOLFENDEN, Hon Daniel Mark; s of Baron Wolfenden, CBE (d 1985); *b* 1942; *m* 1972, Sally Frankel; *Style*— The Hon Daniel Wolfenden; 44 Mortimer St, London W1

WOLFENDEN, Baroness; Eileen le Messurier Wolfenden; 2 da of A J Spilsbury; *m* 1932, Baron Wolfenden, CBE (d 1985; Life Peer UK 1974); 1 s, 2 da; *Style*— The Rt Hon the Lady Wolfenden; The White House, Westcott, Dorking, Surrey RH4 3NJ (☎ 0306 885475)

WOLFF *see also*: Clifford Wolff

WOLFF, Prof Heinz Siegfried; s of Oswald Wolff (d 1968), of W Germany, and Margot, *née* Saalfeld; *b* 29 April 1928; *Educ* City of Oxford Sch, UCL (BSc); *m* 21 March 1953, Joan Eleanor Mary, da of Charles Heddon Stephenson, MBE (d 1968); 2 s (Anthony b 1956, Laurence b 1961); *Career* head Div of Biomedical engrg Nat Inst for Med Res 1962-70 (joined 1954), head div of bioengineering Clinical Res Centre 1970-83; dir Brunel Inst for Bioengineering Brunel Univ 1983-; chm: Life Sci Working Gp ESA 1976-82; chm: microgravity advisory ctee ESA 1982-, microgravity panel Br Nat Spare Centre 1986-87; tv series incl: BBC TV Young Scis of the Year 1968-81, Royal Inst Christmas Lectures 1975, The Great Egg Race 1978-86, Great Experiments which Changed the World 1985-86; fell UCL 1987; FIBiol; memb Physiological Soc, Biological Engrg Soc, Ergonomics Res Soc; *Books* Biological Engineering (1969); *Recreations* working, dignified practical joking; *Style*— Prof Heinz Wolff; Brunel Institue for Bioengineering, Brunel University, Uxbridge, Middlesex UB8 3PH (☎ 0895 71206, fax 0895 74608, telex 261173)

WOLFF, Michael Gordon; s of Sergei Mikhailovich Wolff (d 1979), of London, and Mary, *née* Gordon; *b* 12 Nov 1933; *Educ* Greshams, Architectural Assoc Sch of Architecture; *m* 14 Aug 1976 (m dis 1987), Susan, da of Brig Sydney Kent; 1 da (Rebecca Rose b 27 Oct 1981); *Career* fndr and creative dir Wolff Olins 1965-83, chm Addison Design Conslts Ltd 1987-; pres Design and Art Direction Assoc (D&ADA) 1971, fndr and creative dir of the Consortium 1983-87, pres Chartered Soc of Designers (CSD) 1985-87; dir The Hunger Project (UK) 1978-83 (memb bd of tstees 1983-); FRSA, PPCSD; *Recreations* family life, seeing and walking; *Style*— Michael Wolff, Esq; Addison Design Consultants Ltd, 60 Britton Street, London EC1M 5NA (☎ 01 250 1887)

WOLFFER, Hon Mrs; Hon Naomi Anne; *née* Marks; da of 2 Baron Marks of Broughton; *b* 1952; *m* 1980, Martin Christian Wolffer; *Style*— The Hon Mrs Wolffer

WOLFSON, Sir Isaac; 1 Bt (UK 1962), of St Marylebone, London; s of Solomon Wolfson, JP (d 1941), of Glasgow, and Nellie, *née* Williamovsky (d 1943); *b* 17 Sept 1897; *Educ* Queen's Park Sch Glasgow; *m* 17 Feb 1926, Edith (d 1981), da of Ralph Specterman; 1 s; *Heir* s, Baron Wolfson, *qv*; *Career* former chm The Great Universal Stores Ltd, now hon pres Wolfson Fndn (created 1955 mainly for advancing health, educn and youth activities in UK and Cwlth); hon pres and hon fell Weizmann Inst of Science Fndn Israel; memb Grand Cncl Cancer Research Campaign; FRS; Hon: FRCP, FRCS; hon fell: St Edmund Hall and LMH Oxford, Jews' Coll; Hon DCL Oxford; Hon LLD: London, Glasgow, Cambridge, Manchester, Strathclyde, Brandeis US, Nottingham; *Style*— Sir Isaac Wolfson, Bt, FRS; c/o The Weizmann Institute of Science, PO Box 26, Rehovot 76100, Israel

WOLFSON, Baron (Life Peer UK 1985), of Marylebone in the City of Westminster; Leonard Gordon Wolfson; s and h of Sir Isaac Wolfson, 1 Bt, *qv*; *b* 11 Nov 1927; *Educ* King's Sch Worcester; *m* 14 Nov 1949, Ruth, da of Ernest A Sterling; 4 da (Hon Janet b 1952, Hon Laura b 1954, Hon Deborah b 1959, Hon Elizabeth b 1966); *Career* chm and fndr tstee Wolfson Fndn; chm: Gr Universal Stores plc, Burberrys Ltd; Hon FRCP 1977; hon fell St Catherine's Coll Oxford, Wolfson Colls Cambridge and Oxford, UCL, Worcester Coll Oxford; Hon PhD: Tel Aviv 1971, Hebrew Univ 1978; Hon DCL Oxon 1972, E Anglia 1986; Hon LLD: Strathclyde 1972, Dundee 1979, London 1982, Cambridge 1982; Hon DSc: Hull 1977, Wales 1984; Hon Dr of Hebrew Literature Bar Ilan Univ 1983; patron RCS 1976; hon fell London Sch of Hygiene and Tropical Med 1985, Queen Mary Coll 1985; memb ct of Benefactors RSM; FBA 1986; kt 1977; *Style*— The Rt Hon the Lord Wolfson; Universal House,

251 Tottenham Court Road, London W1A 1BZ (☎ 01 580 6441)

WOLFSON, Leslie; s of Aaron Wolfson (d 1964), of Glasgow, and Hannah Frank (d 1956); *b* 12 June 1929; *Educ* The High Sch Glasgow, Glasgow Univ (BL); *m* 30 Sept 1964, Alma Rosalind, da of Louis Woolfson; 3 da (Monica Natanya b 1966, Georgia b 1967, Jessica Gladys b 1972); *Career* slr; sr ptnr Leslie Wolfson & Co; dir: Heron Equities Ltd, Gander Equities Ltd; govr Tel Aviv Univ; chm: The Tel Aviv Univ Tst (Scotland), jt Israel Appeal Scotland 1982, memb Human Rights Ctee, Int Bar Assoc, memb GB - USSR Assoc, tstee Alma & Leslie Wolfson Charitable Tst; *Recreations* photography, walking, gardening; *Style*— Leslie Wolfson, Esq; Longhill, Whitecraigs, Glasgow G46 6TR; 39 Hill St, Mayfair W1X 7FF; Easdale Island, by Oban, Argyll; 19 Waterloo St, Glasgow G2 6BQ (☎ 041 226 4499, telex 779435, fax 041 221 6070)

WOLFSON, (Geoffrey) Mark; MP (C) Sevenoaks 1979-; s of Capt Vladimir Wolfson, RNVR (d 1954); *b* 7 April 1934; *Educ* Eton, Pembroke Coll Cambridge; *m* 1965, Edna Webb, *née* Hardman; 2 s; *Career* warden Brathay Hall Centre Cumbria 1962-66, head Youth Services Industrial Soc 1966-69; head of personnel 1969 dir Hambros Bank 1973- (head of personel 1969); PPS: to Adam Butler as Min State NI 1983-, as Min for Def Procurement 1984-85, to Ian Stewart as Min for the Armed Servs 1987-; *Style*— Mark Wolfson, Esq, MP; 6 Fynes St, Westminster, London SW1 (☎ 01 821 5081)

WOLLASTON, Henry Woods; s of Sir Gerald Woods Wollaston, KCB, KCVO (d 1957); *b* 14 Nov 1916; *Educ* Harrow, Cambridge Univ; *m* 1944, Daphne Margaret, *née* Clark; 1 s, 2 da; *Career* barr, princ asst legal advsr Home Office 1978-80 (joined 1946), standing counsel Gen Synod of Church of Eng 1981-83; Master Haberdasher's Co 1974-75; *Recreations* real tennis, lawn tennis; *Style*— Henry Wollaston, Esq; 2 Ashtead House, Ashtead, Surrey

WOLLEY DOD, Anthony Kirk; JP (Cheshire 1965); o s of John Cadogan Wolley Dod, JP (d 1973), of Edge Hall, Malpas, Cheshire, and his 1 w, Hilda Gertrude, *née* Elliott (d 1938); the Dods have been settled at Edge Hall since the time of Henry II (1154-89), but a connected descent can only be traced from Thomas Dod, who lived in the 14th century; The eventual heiress of the family, Frances Lucy Parker, m 1850, Rev Charles Wolley, who assumed the additional surname of Dod 1868, when his wife received the edge property from her mother; The Wolleys were of equal antiquity in Cheshire and their heiress, Mary Wolley, m 1822, Rev John Francis Thomas Hurt, who assumed the surname of Wolley in compliance with his father-in-law's will, and was mother of Rev Charles Wolley Dod above named (*see* Burke's Landed Gentry, 18 edn, Vol III, 1972); *b* 21 Dec 1918; *Educ* Rugby; *m* 29 Aug 1960, Ann Keightley, o da of Lt-Col John (Jack) Robertson, MC (d 1944), of Oxton, Birkenhead; *Career* serv in WWII as Flying Offr RAF in England, W Africa and Canada; admitted slr 1947; ptnr Batesons & Co Liverpool 1947-62; farmer at The Dairy House, Edge and Edge Hall, Malpas 1962-; High Sheriff of Cheshire 1977-78; memb: CFA, NFU, Law Soc 1947; *Recreations* fishing, shooting, forestry; *Clubs* Royal Over-Seas League; *Style*— Anthony Wolley Dod, Esq; Edge Hall, Malpas, Cheshire (☎ 094 885 530)

WOLMER, Viscount; William Lewis Palmer; s and h of 4 Earl of Selborne; *b* 1 Sept 1971; *Style*— Viscount Wolmer

WOLSELEY, Sir Charles Garnet Richard Mark; 11 Bt (E 1628), of Wolseley, Staffs; s of Capt Stephen Wolseley (ka 1944, s of Sir Edric Wolseley, 10 Bt, JP, who d 1954; the Wolseleys of Mt Wolseley, Co Carlow, who produced Sir Garnet, the Victorian general cr Visc Wolseley are a cadet branch) and Pamela, Lady Wolseley, *qv*; *b* 16 June 1944; *Educ* Ampleforth, RAC Cirencester; *m* 1, 1968 (m dis 1984), Anita, da of Hugo Fried, of Epsom; 1 s, 3 da; m 2, 1984, Mrs Imogene E Brown; *Heir* s, Stephen Garnet Hugo Charles b 1980; *Career* ptnr Smiths Gore Chartered Surveyors 1979-87 (conslt 1987-); FRICS; *Recreations* shooting, fishing, water-colour painting; *Clubs* Farmers', Shikar; *Style*— Sir Charles Wolseley, Bt; Wolseley Park, Rugeley, Staffs WS15 2TU (☎ 0889 582346)

WOLSELEY, Sir Garnet; 12 Bt (I 1745), of Mount Wolseley, Co Carlow; s of Richard Bingham Wolseley (d 1938), and kinsman of 11 Bt (d 1950); *b* 27 May 1915; *Educ* Wallasey Central Sch; *m* 1950, Lilian Mary, da of late William Bertram Ellison; *Heir* kinsman, James Douglas Wolseley b 1937; *Career* served 1939-45 with Northants Regt (Madagascar, Sicily, Italy and Germany); *Style*— Sir Garnet Wolseley, Bt; 73 Dorothy St, Brantford, Ontario, Canada

WOLSELEY, Pamela, Lady; Pamela Violette; da of Capt F Barry, of Co Cork and latterly Old Court, Whitchurch, Herefs, and Mrs W N Power; *m* 1942, Capt Stephen Wolseley, RA (ka 1944); 1 s (Sir Charles Wolseley, 11 Bt, *qv*), 1 da; *Career* granted rank of Baronet's wife 1955; *Style*— Pamela, Lady Wolseley; Wolseley Park, Rugeley, Staffs (☎ 088 94 2346)

WOLSTENHOLME, Sir Gordon Ethelbert Ward; OBE (1944); s of Ethelbert Wolstenholme (d 1940), of Sheffield; *b* 28 May 1913; *Educ* Repton, Corpus Christi Coll Cambridge, Middx Hosp Med Sch (BM, BChir); *m* 1, Mary Elizabeth, da of Rev Herbert Spackman; 1 s, 2 da; m 2, Dushanka, only da of Arthur Messinger; 2 da; *Career* WWII RAMC 1940-47, serv France, Med, Middle E; dir Ciba Fndn 1949-78, memb exec bd UK Ctee WHO 1961-70 (fndr memb 1954); memb: cncl Westfield Coll London Univ 1965-73, planning bd Univ Coll Buckingham 1969; chm Nuffield Inst for Comparative Med 1969-70, memb Gen Med Cncl 1973-83, tstee and chm academic bd St George's Univ Sch of Med 1978-, Harveian librarian RCP 1979-89, dir and chief scientific advsr Info Retrieval 1980-88, vice-pres Assoc of Special Libraries and Info Bureaux 1979-82, pres Br Soc of History of Med 1983-85, patron Fund for the Replacement of Animals in Med Experiments (FRAME), fndr and first chm Action in Int Med 1988-; hon life govr Middx Hosp 1938, hon fell Hunterian Soc (orator 1976), hon FACP, hon FRSM 1982 (hon sec 1964-70, pres library res 1968-70, chm working pty on Soc's future 1972-73, pres 1975-77 and 1978); Hon: LLD Cantab 1968, DTech Brunel 1981, MD Grenada 1983; MRCS, FRCP, FIBiol; kt 1976; *Style*— Sir Gordon Wolstenholme, OBE; 10 Wimpole Mews, London W1M 7TF (☎ 01 486 3884)

WOLTON, Harry; QC (1982); s of Harry William (d 1943), and Dorothy Beatrice, *née* Meaking (d 1982); *b* 1 Jan 1938; *Educ* King Edwards Sch Birmingham, Birmingham Univ; *m* 3 April 1971, Julie Rosina Josaphine, da of George Edward Mason (d 1985); 3 s (Matthew Harry b 1972, Andrew b 1974, Edward b 1977); *Career* called to the Bar 1969, rec Crown Ct 1985; *Style*— Harry Wolton, Esq, QC; Armscote Farm, Armscote, Stratford-upon-Avon CV37 8DQ (☎ 060 882 234); 10 St Lukes St, SW3 3RS (☎ 01 352 5056); 5 Fountain Ct, Steelhouse Lane, Birmingham B4 6DR (☎ 021 236 5771); Devereux Chambers, Temple WC2R 3JJ (☎ 01 353 7534)

WOLVERSON, Maurice Frank; s of Frank Wolverson, of 23 Meryhurst Rd, Wood Green, Wednesbury, W Mids, and (Edith Anne) Nancy, *née* Phillips (d 1973); *b* 7 June 1927; *Educ* Wednesbury Boys HS; *m* 4 June 1949, (Kathleen) Merle, da of Philip Patrick Forrester (d 1986); *Career* conscripted 1946-49, RAOC 1947-49 (demobbed Sgt); ptnr Whitehouse, Wolverson, Armston & Cox CAs (formerly Barnfield & Co) 1961-; vice chm Parklands Housing Soc Ltd 1988- (pt/t tres 1966-82, ctee memb 1982-), tres to the tstees of Crumps Almshouses, chm Walsall Family Practitioner Ctee 1983- (memb 1973-, vice chm 1975-83); memb: Walsall Health Authy 1985-, Br Acad of Gastronomy; ACA 1959, FCA 1970; Compagnon de Confrerie St Etienne D'Alsace; *Recreations* wines, music, reading, motoring; *Style*— Maurice Wolverson, Esq; 6 Greenslade Rd, Park Hall, Walsall, W Mids WS5 3QH (☎ 0922 261 33); Six Ways Ct, 24 Birmingham Rd, Walsall, W Mids WS1 2LZ (☎ 0922 721 752)

WOLVERTON, Dowager Baroness; Audrey Margaret; *née* Stubbs; da of late Richard Stubbs, of Haseley Manor, Oxford; *m* 1937, 6 Baron Wolverton, CBE (d 1988); 2 s (7 Baron, Hon Andrew), 2 da (Hon Susan (Hon Mrs Mills), Hon Joanna Caroline b 1955); The Dower House, Chute Standen, Andover, Hants

WOLVERTON, 7 Baron (UK 1869); Christopher Richard Glyn; er s of 6 Baron Wolverton, CBE (d 1988), and Dowager Baroness Wolverton, *qv*; *b* 5 Oct 1938; *Educ* Eton; *m* 1, 1961 (m dis 1967), Carolyn Jane, yr da of late Antony Noel Hunter, of 33 Brompton Square, London SW3; 2 da (Hon Sara-Jane b 1963, Hon Amanda Camilla b 1966); m 2, 1975, Mrs Frances Sarah Elisabeth Stuart Black, eldest da of Robert Worboys Skene, of 12 Kensington Gate, London W8; *Heir* bro, Hon Andrew John Glyn, *qv*; *Career* FRICS

WOMBWELL, Sir George Philip Frederick; 7 Bt (GB 1778), of Wombwell, Yorkshire; s of Maj Sir Philip Wombwell, 6 Bt, MBE (d 1977); *b* 21 May 1949; *Educ* Repton; *m* 1974, Jane, da of Thomas Wrightson, of Ulshaw Grange, Leyburn, N Yorks; 1 s, 1 da; *Heir* s, Stephen Wombwell b 12 May 1977; *Career* farmer; *Style*— Sir George Wombwell, Bt; Newburgh Priory, Coxwold, York YO6 4AS (☎ Coxwold 435)

WOMERSLEY, Sir Peter John Walter; 2 Bt (UK 1945), of Grimsby, Co Lincoln; s of late Capt John Walter Womersley (ka 1944), and gs of Rt Hon Sir Walter Womersley, 1 Bt, PC (d 1961); *b* 10 Nov 1941; *Educ* Charterhouse, RMA Sandhurst; *m* 1968, Janet Margaret, da of Alastair Grant; 2 s, 2 da; *Heir* s, John Gavin Grant Womersley b 7 Dec 1971; *Career* serv Regular Army, Offr Cadet at Sandhurst to 1962, 2 Lt King's Own Royal Border Regt 1962, Lt 1964, ret 1968; personnel offr Beecham Gp 1968-72 (personnel mangr 1972-); *Books* Collecting Stamps (with Neil Grant 1980); *Recreations* breeding rare poultry; *Style*— Sir Peter Womersley, Bt; Sunnycroft, The Street, Bramber, nr Steyning, Sussex BN4 3WE

WONTNER, Sir Hugh Walter Kingwell; GBE (1974), CVO (1969, MVO 1950); in Scotland styled Sir Hugh Wontner of Barscobe by authy of Lord Lyon King of Arms; s of Arthur Wontner, of Cherry Cross, Totnes, Devon and 3 Albert Terrace, Regent's Park, London NW1, and Rosecleer Alice Amelia Blanche Kingwell (whose stage name was Rose Pendennis), of Moat Hill House, Totnes; *b* 22 Oct 1908; *Educ* Oundle; *m* 1936, Catherine, da of Lt Thomas William Irvin, Gordon Highlanders (ka 1916), of Peterhead, Aberdeenshire; n of late Sir John Irvin, KBE, JP; 2 s, 1 da; *Career* chm Berkeley and Claridge's Hotels London, Hotel Lancaster Paris, Savoy Theatre; dir Savoy Hotel (md 1941-79, chm 1948-84), dir other cos, clerk of the Royal Kitchens 1953- (catering advsr 1938-); memb: Lloyds 1937-, London C of C 1927-33; sec Hotels and Restaurants Assoc 1933-38 (dir Savoy 1940); chllr City Univ 1973-74; pres Int Hotels Assoc 1961-64 (memb of hon 1965-); govr Univ Coll Hosp 1945-53; tstee: D'Oyly Carte Opera Tst, Coll of Arms Tst, Southwark Cathedral Devpt Tst, Morden Coll Temple Bar Tst (chm); chm: Cncl Br Hotels Restaurants and Caterers Assoc 1969-73, Historic Houses Ctee BTA 1966-77; memb: Bd of BTA 1950-69, Historic Bldgs Cncl 1968-73, Br Heritage Ctee 1977-, Barbican Centre Ctee 1979-84, Heritage of London Tst 1980-; Freeman of City 1934, one of HM Lts and JP City of London 1963-80, chief magistrate 1973-74, alderman 1963-79, Sheriff 1970-71, Lord Mayor of London 1973-74; Master Worshipful Co of Feltmakers 1962 and 1974, Master, Worshipful Co of Clockmakers 1975, Liverymen Plaisterers and Launderers, Freeman of Seychelles 1974; hon citizen St Emilion 1974, Order of Cisneros Spain 1964, Offr L'Etoile Equatoriale 1970, Ordre de l'Etoile Civique 1972, Médaille de Vermeil City of Paris 1972, KStJ 1973, Offr du Mérite Agricole 1973, Cdr Nat Order of the Leopard (Zaire) 1974, Kt Cdr Order of the Dannebrog 1974, Order of the Crown of Malaysia 1974, Kt Cdr Royal Swedish Order of the Polar Star 1980; Hon DLitt (1973); kt 1972; *Recreations* acting, collecting antiques, genealogy; *Clubs* Garrick, City Livery; *Style*— Sir Hugh Wontner, GBE, CVO; Hedsor Priory, Hedsor, nr Bourne End, Bucks (☎ 062 85 23754); Barscobe, Balmaclellan, By Castle Douglas, Kirkcudbrightshire (☎ 064 42 245); 1 Savoy Hill, London WC2 (☎ 01 836 1533)

WOOD, Anthony Hugh Boynton-; o s of Frederick Anthony Boynton-Wood (d 1939); s of Capt Albert Charles Wood, JP, of Hollin Hall, Ripon, and Gladys Gertrude, *née* Wray (Mrs Frederick Boynton-Wood, *qv*); (*see* Burke's LG 1972 edn, Boynton-Wood); ninth in descent from Dame Frances Boynton, da and co-heir of John Barnard, Mayor of Hull, who refused Charles 1 entry to the city, and was great-uncle of Anne Boldero-Barnard, Lady Carrington; ggg nephew of Rev Prof Thomas Robert Malthus, author of the celebrated 'Essay on Principle of Population'; collateral descendant of Bl Edmund Sykes (martyred 23 March 1587, beatified 22 Nov 1987), through his niece Dame Frances Boynton; *b* 1 May 1917; *Educ* privately, Leeds Univ, Hull Univ; *Career* slr 1947; landowner (manages ancestral 1,000 acre estate in family since 1719); received into Church of Rome at Ampleforth 1987; life memb: Selden Soc (8 New Sq, Lincoln's Inn), Historic Houses Assoc, Cromwell Assoc, Nat Art-Collections Fund; *Recreations* gardening, genealogy, heraldry, arts, music, theatre; *Style*— Anthony Boynton-Wood, Esq; Hollin Hall, Ripon, N Yorks (☎ 0765 2466)

WOOD, Anthony Richard; s of Rev Thomas John Wood (d 1973), and Phyllis Margaret, *née* Bold; *b* 13 Feb 1932; *Educ* St Edward's Sch Oxford, Worcester Coll Oxford (BA); *m* 1966 (m diss 1973), Sarah, *née* Drew; 1 s (Nicholas b 1969), 1 da (Lucy b 1971); *Career* Army 1950-52 TA 1952-56 Lt; Br Sch of Archaeology in Iraq, Nimrud Expedition 1956, joined HM Foreign Serv 1957; serv: Beirut 1957, Bahrain 1958, Paris 1959, Benghali 1962, Aden 1963, Basra 1966, Tehran 1970, Muscat 1980; cnsllr FCO 1984 (ret 1987); *Recreations* walking, singing; *Clubs* Army and Navy, Royal Green Jackets London; *Style*— Anthony R Wood, Esq

WOOD, David Bernard; s of Richard Edwin Wood (d 1987), and Audrey Adele Whittle, *née* Fincham; *b* 21 Feb 1944; *Educ* Chichester HS for Boys, Worcester Coll Oxford (BA); *m* 1, 1966 (m dis 1970), Sheila, *née* Ruskin; m 2, Jan 1975, Jacqueline, da of Prof Sidney William Stanbury; 2 da (Katherine b 1976, Rebecca b 1979); *Career* actor, writer, composer, theatre dir and prodr; dir: WSG Prodns Ltd 1966-, Verronmead Ltd 1982-, Westwood Theatrical Prodns Ltd 1986-; hon pres Friends of Wimbledon Theatre; many plays published by Samuel French; children's books include The Gingerbread Man (1985), The Operats of Rodent Garden (1984), The Discorats (1985), Playtheatres (1987), Sidney the Monster (1988); *Recreations* conjuring, collecting old books; *Clubs* Green Room; *Style—* David Wood, Esq; c/o Margaret Ramsay Ltd, 14A Goodwin's Court, St Martin's Lane, London WC2 (☎ 01 240 0691)

WOOD, David Frederick; s of Donald Wood (d 1983), and Deborah, *née* Kaminkovitch; *b* 19 Nov 1934; *Educ* Palmers Endowed Sch Essex; *m* 11 Dec 1960, Carole June, da of Isaac Zietman (Ka 1944); 2 s (Ivor b 1966, Roger b 1969); *Career* Nat Serv RAF 1953-55; underwriting, memb Lloyds, dir and sec Q Insur Servs plc 1988-; Freeman City of London, Liveryman Worshipful Co of Arbitrators 1988-, memb Guild of Freemen of the City of London 1986; ACII, ACIArb; *Recreations* photography, caravanning; *Style—* David Wood, Esq; 2 Archway Parade, Marsh Rd, Luton, Beds LU3 2RW (☎ 0582 490431, 0582 491045)

WOOD, David John Dargue; s of John Nöel Wood, MC (d 1976), of Sheffield, and Ruth Mary Dargue, *née* Moffitt (d 1987); *b* 17 April 1930; *Educ* King Edward VII Sch Sheffield, Wadham Coll Oxford (MA); *m* 23 March 1957, (Rosemary) Sepha, da of Lt-Col Philip Neill, TD (d 1986), of Whitby; 1 s (Justin b 1959), 1 da (Annabel b 1963); *Career* Flt Offr RAF Airfield Construction Branch Egypt and Libya 1953-54; ptnr Husband and Co, Conslt Engrs 1967-88 (jt md 1988-); pres Br section Société des Ingenieurs et Scientifiques de France 1984-85; tres Assoc of Conslting Engrs 1980-81; F Eng 1987, FICE 1964, FIWEM 1965, M Cons E 1967; *Recreations* sailing; *Clubs* Royal Cruising, Royal Ocean Racing; *Style—* David Wood, Esq; Little Crofton Cottage, Titchfield, Hants PO14 2JE (☎ 0329 47844); Husband & Co, Alliance House, 12 Caxton Street, London SW1 HOPQ (☎ 01 799 6383, fax 01 799 6386)

WOOD, Dudley Ernest; s of Ernest Edward Wood, and Ethel Louise Wood; *b* 18 May 1930; *Educ* Luton GS, St Edmund Hall Oxford (BA); *m* 1955, Mary Christine, *née* Blake, 2 s; *Career* ICI 1954-: petrochemicals and plastics div, overseas mangr 1977-82, sales and mktg mangr 1982-86; played rugby football for: Oxford Univ, Bedford, Rosslyn Pk, Waterloo, Streatham Croydon, E Mids; sec RFU 1986-; hon life memb Squash Racquets Assoc 1984; *Recreations* squash, travel, dog-breeding, Middle East affrs; *Clubs* E India, Royal Overseas League; *Style—* Dudley Wood, Esq; c/o RFU, Twickenham, Middx TW1 1DZ (☎ 01 892 8161, fax 01 892 9816)

WOOD, Hon Edward Orlando Charles; JP; s of Baron Holderness, PC, DL (Life Peer); *b* 1951; *m* 1977, Joanna H, da of John Pinches and Rosemary Pinches *qv*; 1 da (Leonora Sarah Clare b 1982); *Career* CA; *Style—* The Hon Edward Wood, JP; Flat Top House, Bishop Wilton, Yorks

WOOD, Dr Francis William; s of Harry William Wood (d 1980), and Alfreda Elizabeth Wood (d 1969); *b* 29 Jan 1930; *Educ* Wolverton GS, London Univ (BSc, PhD); *m* 30 April 1958, Christiane Elizabeth, da of Aloys Marbach (d 1965); 1 s (Robert b 1964), 1 da (Catherine b 1982); *Career* sr sci Unilever Res 1964-82; cnslt chemist, princ Gel Plan Servs; Open Univ tutor; *Recreations* music, sailing; *Style—* Dr Francis Wood, Esq; Leslie House, Kenton, Exeter EX6 8JD

WOOD, Sir Frederick Ambrose Stuart; s of Alfred Phillip Wood, of Goole, Yorks, and Patras, Greece, and Charlotte, *née* Barnes; *b* 30 May 1926; *Educ* Felsted Sch, Clare Coll Cambridge; *m* 1947, J R (Su) King; 2 s, 1 da; *Career* serv WWII Sub Lt Fleet Air Arm 1944-47; formerly chm Nat Bus Co 1972-78; chm Croda Int 1960-86 (md 1953), chm NEB 1981, NRDC 1979-81 (memb 1973) and first chm of the Br Tech Gp (after NEB and NRDC merged) 1981-83; Hon LLD Univ of Hull; kt 1977; *Style—* Sir Frederick Wood; Plaster Hill Farm, Churt, Surrey (☎ 0428 712134)

WOOD, Geoffrey Frank; s of Frank Harold Wood, (d 1959), of Rockwood, St Johns Ave, Clevedon, Avon and Elsie May Winifred, *née* Saunders (d 1944); *b* 16 Sept 1917; *Educ* Clifton, Bristol Univ (LLB); *m* 23 June 1942, Marjorie Sybil (d 1988), da of Phillip George Vowles (d 1949), of 18 Walsingham Rd, Bristol; 1 s (Jonathan b 14 Oct 1947) 1 da (Jennifer (Mrs Warner) b 15 Aug 1944); *Career* serv WWII: Capt RA 1939-45; admitted slr 1945, cmmr for oaths 1946- 82, sr ptnr Sinnolt Wood & Co Bristol 1953-82, ret 1982; chm Tickenham Parish Cncl 1975-76, formerly hon sec Old Cliftonian Soc (Bristol branch); memb: Law Soc 1946, Bristol Law Soc 1946-82; *Recreations* photography, gardening; *Style—* Geoffrey Wood, Esq; 18 The Green, Shaldon, Devon TQ14 ODN (☎ 0626 873705)

WOOD, Gladys Gertrude Boynton-; *née* Wray; yr da of Charles Frederick Wray of Hobberley House, Shadwell and The Grove, Ripon (d 1936 gs and heir of William Wray, of Castle Wray, Co Donegal, who was a direct descendant of Sir Christopher Wray, Lord Chief Justice of the Court of Queen's Bench *temp* Queen Elizabeth I), and Katrina, yr da of Robert Beacock, engr and inventor (d 1869; to whom in 1843 were apprenticed at The Round Foundry, Holbeck, Leeds, the Krupp brothers, fndrs of the world famous armaments firm at Essen); *b* 27 Feb 1888,desc Sir Christopher Wray Lord Chief Justice to Elizabeth I,; *Educ* privately, Skeffield Sch Ripon; *m* 1913, Frederick Anthony Boynton-Wood (d 1939); 1 s (Anthony Boynton-Wood, *qv*); *Recreations* gardening, theatre, portraitist in oils, miniaturist, music, theatre; *Style—* Mrs Frederick Boynton-Wood; Hollin Hall, Ripon, N Yorks

WOOD, (Francis) Gordon; s of Francis Roberts Wood (d 1953), and Florence Ada, *née* Woodcock; *b* 30 Oct 1924; *Educ* Alleyne's GS Stone Staffs; *m* 20 July 1950, Margaret Felicité, da of Albert Edward Parr (d 1944); 2 da (Hilary Christine b 1953, Dereth Margaret b 1956); *Career* RN Air Serv 1943-47; Prudential Assurance Co Ltd: dep chief gen mangr 1981-85, dir 1982-85; dir Prudential Corpn Plc 1984-; ACII 1949, FIA 1956; *Recreations* golf, walking; *Style—* Gordon Wood, Esq; Prudential Corporation Plc, 142 Holborn Bars, London, EC1N 2NH (☎ 0279 52197)

WOOD, Graham Barry; s of Anthony Philip Wood, of Hawkshead, Cumbria and Jean Wissett, *née* Snelgrove; *b* 21 June 1959; *Educ* Merchant Taylors Sch Great Crosby Liverpool, Univ of Salford Salford (BSc); *m* 6 Aug 1983 (m dis 1987) Hilene Smith da of Wilson McCloud Henry, of Thornton Crosby Liverpool; *Career* CA, ptnr Hanley & Co Cheshire 1985-; fin dir: Ebony Hldgs Plc, Ebony Devpts Ltd, Ebony Residential Properties Ltd, Stache (UK) Ltd, Brooks Owen Assocs Ltd Hanley & Co Fin Servs Ltd, Hanley & Co Accountants Ltd; memb ICAEW 1983; *Recreations* walking, squash, sailing, golf; *Style—* Graham Wood, Esq; Hanley & Co, The Polygon, Stamford Rd, Bowdon, Cheshire, WA14 3DN, (☎ 061 339 7502, car tel 0836 588436, fax 061 248 6265)

WOOD, Sir Henry Peart; CBE (1960); s of Thomas Marshall Wood (d 1968), of Bedlington Northumberland, and Margery Eleanor (d 1941), *née* Peart; *b* 30 Nov 1908; *Educ* Morpeth GS, Durham Univ (MSc), Manchester Univ (MA, MEd); *m* 1937, Isobel Mary, da of William Frederick Stamp (d 1956), of Carbis Bay, Cornwall; 1 s, 2 da; *Career* lectr Manchester Univ 1937-44, princ Jordanhill Coll of Educn Glasgow 1949-71, visiting prof Strathclyde Univ 1976-84; Hon LLD: Glasgow 1972, Strathclyde 1982; kt 1967; *Style—* Sir Henry Wood; 15A Hughenden Court, Hughenden Rd, Glasgow G12 9XP (☎ (041 334) 3647)

WOOD, Ian Clark; CBE (1982); s of John Wood (d 1986) and Margaret, *née* Clark (d 1981); *b* 21 July 1942; *Educ* Robert Gordon's Coll Aberdeen, Aberdeen Univ (BSc); *m* 1970, Helen, *née* Macrae; 3 s; *Career* chm and md John Wood Gp plc, chm J W Hldgs Ltd; memb Lloyd's; Hon LLD Aberdeen 1984; FRSA, CBIM; *Recreations* squash, family; *Style—* Ian Wood, Esq, CBE; Marchmont, 42 Rubislaw Den South, Aberdeen AB2 6BB (☎ 0224 313625); John Wood Gp plc, John Wood Hse, Greenwell Rd, East Tullos, Aberdeen AB1 4AX (☎ 0224 875464, telex 739977)

WOOD, Hon Mrs (Joan Mary); *née* Wise; da of 1 Baron Wise, DL; *b* 27 Sept 1912; *m* 1938, John Wood; 3 s (Michael v 1939, David b 1946, Roger b 1947), 1 da (Mary b 1941); *Style—* The Hon Mrs Wood; Ham Farm, Berrow, Burnham-on-Sea, Somerset

WOOD, John; CB (1989); s of Maj Thomas John Wood, IA (d 1962), of Varndean Gardens, Brighton, Sussex, and Rebecca, *née* Grand; *b* 11 Jan 1931; *Educ* King's Coll Sch Wimbledon, Law Soc Sch of Law; *m* 3 April 1958, Jean Iris, da of George Collier (d 1945), of London; 2 s (Simon b 1959, Nicholas b 1961); *Career* slr; dep dir Public Prosecutions 1985; dir Serious Fraud Off 1987; *Recreations* most sports, theatre, music; *Style—* John Wood, Esq, CB; Elm House, 10-16 Elm St, London WC1X 0BJ (☎ 01 833 7300)

WOOD, Dr John Edwin; s of John Stanley Wood (d 1974), of Darlington, and Alice Hardy (d 1968); *b* 24 July 1928; *Educ* Darlington GS, Univ of Leeds (BSc, PhD); *m* 13 June 1953 (m dis 1978), Patricia Edith Wilson, da of Alfred Sheppard (d 1956); 2 s (Jonathan (John) b 1954, Andrew b 1956), 2 da (Susan b 1961, Nicola b 1965); *Career* joined RN Scientific Serv 1959; Underwater Countermeasures and Weapons Estab 1959-76: head acoustics res div 1968, head sonar dept 1972; Admty Surface Weapons Estab: head weapons dept 1976, head communications command and control dept 1979; chief scientist (RN) and dir gen res (A) 1980; Br Aerospace (formerly Sperry Gyroscope) Bracknell 1981 (exec div Bristol div 1984-88), dir underwater engrg Br Aerospace (Dynamics) Ltd 1988-; pres Gp 12 Cncl of British Archaeology 1984-; *Books* Sun Moon and Standing Stones (second edn 1980); *Recreations* archaeology and fell walking; *Style—* Dr John Wood; 7 Pennant Hills, Havant Hants PO9 3JZ (☎ 0705 471 411); British Aerospace (Dynamics) Ltd, PO Box 5, Filton, Bristol BS12 7QW (☎ 0272 366 020, fax 0272 366 854)

WOOD, Hon Mr Justice; Hon Sir John Kember Wood; MC (1944); s of John Roskruge Wood; *b* 8 August 1922; *Educ* Shrewsbury, Magdalene Coll Cambridge; *m* 1952, Kathleen Lowe; 1 s, 1 da; *Career* serv WWII Rifle Bde; barr Lincoln's Inn 1949, QC 1969, rec Crown Ct 1975-77, High Ct judge Family Div 1977-; Judge of Employment Appeals Tbnl 1985; kt 1977; *Style—* The Hon Mr Justice Wood, MC; Royal Cts of Justice, London WC2A 2LL (☎ 01 405 7641 ext 3120)

WOOD, John Lockhart; s of George Lockhart Wood (d 1959), and Joan Wood, *née* Halsey; *b* 22 August 1935; *Educ* Eton, Trinity Coll Cambridge (MA); *m* 26 Oct 1963, (Rosemary) Sonia Despard, da of Richard Graham Hemsley Hopkins (d 1974); 1 s (Edmund b 1966), 1 da (Kirsty b 1968); *Career* Nat Serv 2 Lt 8 Kings Royal Irish Hussars; McCorquodale plc 1958-86: dir 1964-86, chief exec 1972-86, chm 1986; non exec dir: Halifax Building Soc 1986-, Bibby Line Gp Ltd 1987-, Domino Printing Scis plc 1988-; High Sheriff Hertfordshire 1988-89; *Recreations* gardening, fishing, travel; *Clubs* Cavalry and Guards'; *Style—* John Wood, Esq; The Hoo, Great Gaddesden, Hemel Hempstead, Herts HP2 6HD (☎ 0442 52689)

WOOD, John Norris; s of Wilfrid Burton Wood, MA, MD, FRCP, and Lucy Heald Sutcliffe Boston (d 1977); *b* 29 Nov 1930; *Educ* Bryanston Sch, Goldsmiths' Coll Sch of Art, Anglian Sch of Painting & Design, Royal Coll of Art (Degree with Hons/Silver medallist for zoological drawing); *m* 12 June 1962, Julie Corsellis Guyatt, da of John Nicholls (d 1968); 1 s (Wilfrid Spencer Conal b 1968), 1 da (Dinah Elizabeth Georgia b 1971); *Career* artist and author; lectr in Illustration Goldsmiths' Coll Sch of Art 1956-68; tutor Cambridge Coll of Art 1959-70; fnded Scientific, Technical, Medical Illustration Course at Hornsey Coll of Art 1965; fnded Natural History Illustration Unit Royal Coll of Art 1971 (drawing tutor to present day); Exhibited regularly at RA Summer Exhibition; consultant to BBC Life on Earth; *Recreations* conservation, natural history, art, music; *Style—* John N Wood, Esq; The Brook, Dewhurst Lane, Wadhurst, E Sussex TN5 6QE; Royal Coll of Art, Dept Natural History, 1 Darwin Building, kensington Gore, London SW1

WOOD, John Peter; s of late John Wood, and Louisa, *née* Herrington; *b* 18 June 1933; *Educ* Bradford GS, Durham Univ (BSc); *m* 28 March 1958, Valerie, da of late William Spencer; 1 s (John b 1965), 1 da (Fiona b 1963); *Career* Nat Serv; J Bibby & Sons plc: md Palethorpes Ltd 1971-76, gen mangr feeds and seeds div 1976-79, md agricultural gp 1979-84, chief exec 1984-; CBIM; *Clubs* Oriental, Farmers; *Style—* Peter Wood, Esq; 16 Stratford Place, London W1N 9AF (☎ 01 629 6243)

WOOD, John Walter; s of Prof John Walter Wood (d 1958), of New York, and Suzanne J, *née* Cort; *b* 7 July 1941; *Educ* in USA, Trinity Coll Dublin (BA), Oxford Univ (MA), LSE, Univ of California (MA); *m* Charlotte Mary Baron, da of Robert Ralph Baron Cusack-Jobson of The Old Glebe, Newcastle, Co Dublin, Ireland; 1 s (William Duncan b 12 Feb 1964); *Career* chm: Wood Brigdale Nisbet & Robinson 1969-, Trilateral Communications 1986-; dir Oxford Analytica Ltd 1982-; memb Bd of Advsrs Sch of Int Relations Univ of S California London Programme; memb: gen cncl Co-operation Ireland, cncl Regents Coll, ctee American Aid Soc; chm Republicans Abroad UK; IISS, RIIA, ISPP, APRA; *Clubs* Buck's, Caledonian, Utd Oxford and Cambridge, Union (NY); *Style—* John Wood, Esq; 35 Brompton Square, London SW3; Kent House, Market Place, London W1

WOOD, Joseph Neville (Johnnie); CBE (1978); s of Robert Hind Wood (d 1973), of Durham, and Emily Wood; *b* 25 Oct 1916; *Educ* Johnston Sch Durham, London Univ; *m* 1, 1944, Elizabeth, *née* May (d 1959); 3 da; *m* 2, 1965, Josephine Samuel, *née* Dane (d 1985); m 3, 1986, Frances, *née* Skeer; *Career* civil servant 1935, asst sec Miny Tport and Civil Aviation 1951, Far East rep 1952-55, under-sec 1961, chief highway admin Miny Tport 1967-68; memb: Baltic Exchange 1968-, Chamber of Shipping 1968, (dir 1972-75); dir-gen Gen Cncl Br Shipping 1974-78 (ret); dep chm Shipwrecked Fishermen and Mariners' Royal Benevolent Soc; memb Chichester DC 1979-;

Freeman City of London; FCIT 1976; *Recreations* gardening; *Style*— Joseph Neville Wood, Esq, CBE; Barbers Cottage, Heyshott, Midhurst, W Sussex GU29 0DE (☎ 073 081 4282)

WOOD, Kenneth Maynard; s of Frederick Cavendish Wood (d 1928), and Agnes, *née* Maynard (d 1972); *b* 4 Oct 1916; *Educ* Bromley Co Sch; *m* 1, 1944, Laurie Marion (d 1976), da of late Michael McKinlay; 2 s (Michael b 1945, Stuart b 1948), 2 da (Sally b 1949, Gillian b 1955); m 2, 15 Sept 1978, Patricia Rose, da of Herbert William Purser (d 1982); *Career* Cadet MN 1930-34, RAF then transferred for devpt of electronic equipment 1939-46; md Kenwood Gp of Cos 1946-68, chm and md Dawson-Keith Gp of Cos 1972-80, chm Hydeotech Systems Ltd 1984-87, ret; Freeman Worshipful Co of Farriers 1972; Fell Inst Ophthalmology 1967; *Recreations* golf; *Style*— Kenneth Wood, Esq; Dellwood Cottage, Wheatsheaf Enclosure, Liphook, Hampshire GU30 7EH (☎ 0428 723 108)

WOOD, Leonard George; CBE (1978); s of Leonard George Wood (d 1955), and Miriam *née* Barnes (d 1924); *Educ* Bishopshalt Sch (Hillingdon Middx), London Univ (BCom); *m* 12 Sept 1936, Christine Florence (d 1978), da of William Cooper Reason (d 1935); *Career* Flying Offr RAF 1943-46; exec dir parent bd EMI Ltd (now Thorn EMI plc) 1965-80, gp dir records and music EMI Ltd 1966-77, asst md EMI Ltd 1973-77, md EMI Records UK Ltd 1959-66 (chm 1966-78), chm: EMI Music Publishing Ltd 1972-78, Phonographic Performance Ltd 1967-80, Cncl of IFPI 1968-73 BPI 1973-80 (hon pres 1980-) Record Merchandisers Ltd 1975-80 (pres and chm of bd 1973-76), vice-pres and mem Bd of Int Fdn of Producers of Phonograms and Videograms (IFPI) 1967-82; *Recreations* gardening, music; *Style*— Leonard Wood, Esq, CBE; Lark Rise, 39 Howards Thicket Gerrards Cross, Buckinghamshire SL9 7NT (☎ 0753 884233); BPI Ltd, Roxburghe House, 273-287 Regent St, London W1R 7PB (☎ 01 629 8642)

WOOD, Rt Rev Maurice Arthur Ponsonby; DSC (1944); s of Arthur Wood, and Jane Elspeth Dalzell, *née* Piper; *b* 26 August 1916; *Educ* Monkton Combe Sch, Queens' Coll Cambridge (MA), Ridley Hall Cambridge; *m* 1, 1947, Marjorie, *née* Pennell (d 1954); 2 s, 1 da; m 2, 1955, Margaret, da of Rev E Sandford, MC, MA; 2 s, 1 da; *Career* Chaplain, Royal Navy and Royal Marine Commandos 1943-46; former rector St Ebbe's Oxford 1947-52, rural dean Islington 1952-61, princ Oak Hill Coll Southgate N14 1961-71; visitor Langley Sch, govr Monkton Combe Sch, 69th Bishop of Norwich 1971-85 (memb House of Lords 1975-85); Hon Assist Bishop Diocese of London 1985; chm Order of Christian Unity 1986-; *Books* Like a Mighty Army (1954), Your Suffering (1956), Comfort in Sorrow (1957), Christian Stability (1972), Into the Way of Peace (1982), This is Our Faith (1985); *Clubs* Royal Cwlth Soc; *Style*— The Rt Rev Maurice A P Wood; St Mark's House, Englefield, nr Reading, Berks RG7 5EN (☎ 0734 302227)

WOOD, (John) Peter; s of Walter Ralph Wood (d 1967), and Henrietta, *née* Martin (d 1944); *b* 27 Mar 1925; *Educ* Grove Park GS Wrexham, Seale Hayne Agric Coll Newton Abbott; *m* 1956, Susan Maye, da of Brig Lesley White (d 1971); 1 s (David), 1 da (Victoria); *Career* ed Amateur Gardening 1971-85, conslt ed 1985-; *Recreations* choral singing, sailing, gardening; *Style*— Peter Wood, Esq; 1 Charlton House Ct, Charlton Marshall, Blandford Forum, Dorset (☎ 0258 54653); Westover House, West Quay Rd, Poole, Dorset (☎ 0202 680586)

WOOD, Robert Eric; CBE (1972); s of Robert Wood (d 1959); *b* 6 May 1909; *Educ* Birkenhead Inst, Liverpool Univ (MSc); *m* 1935, Beatrice May (d 1983), *née* Skinner; 1 s, 1 da; *Career* princ Leicester Tech Coll 1953-69 and dir Leicester Poly 1969-73; memb: Cncl Tech Educn and Trg in Overseas Countries 1962-66, CNAA 1964-70; vice-chm Nat Advsy Cncl on Educn for Indust and Commerce 1967-72; *Recreations* voluntary serv; *Style*— Robert Wood, Esq, CBE; Gapler, Peppers Lane, Burton Lazars, Melton Mowbray, Leics (☎ 0664 64576)

WOOD, Robert Wilson; s of Peter Wilson Wood, of Whitburn, Lothian, and Elizabeth Christie, *née* Campbell; *b* 18 Oct 1948; *Educ* Bathgate Acad, Univ of Strathclyde (BSc, Dip Mgmnt); *m* 6 Aug 1971, Mary Davidson, da of James Stewart Armadale (d 1962), of Lothian; 1 s (Alastair b 5 July 1982), 1 da (Lorna b 16 May 1979); *Career* gen mangr Volvo Trucks GB Ltd 1976-80, sales and serv dir Talbot Motor Co 1980-83, md motor div Godfrey Davis Hldgs plc 1983-85, chief exec Henlys Ltd 1985-; vice-chm Elstree and Borehamwood MENCAP, govr Colnbrook Sch Watford; FBIM 1984, FInstD 1985, FIMI 1986; *Recreations* gardening, family; *Style*— Robert Wood, Esq; Henlys Ltd, 53 Theobald St, Borehamwood, Herts WD6 4RT (☎ 01 953 9953, fax 01 207 6245)

WOOD, Roger Bryan Savage; s of Frank Bryan Wood (d 1984), and Margaret Mary Wilkinson, *née* Done; *b* 11 April 1939; *Educ* Bromsgrove Sch; *m* 21 Feb 1970, Dinah, da of Henry Brian Cookson, Bradford-on-Avon, Wilts; 1 s (Alistair b 17 Feb 1972), 1 da (Philipa b 6 Jan 1974); *Career* CA 1963, Birmingham Industl Tst 1963-67, Neville Industl Securitied 1967-70, Smith Keen Cutler 1970- (ptnr 1976-, dir 1986-); sec Birmingham CA's Students Soc 1962; FCA 1973, AMSIA 1980; *Recreations* squash, golf, hockey, watersports, skiing; *Clubs* Edgbaston Priory, Edgbaston GC, Aberdovey GC, Harborne Hockey; *Style*— Roger Wood, Esq; Harkaway, 60 Harborne Rd, Edgbaston, Birmingham 15 (☎ 021 454 4913); Smith Keen Cutler Ltd, Exchange Buildings, Stephenson Place, Birmingham B2 4NN (☎ 021 643 9977)

WOOD, Roger Norman Alexander; s of Adrian Theodore Wood, of Bristol, and Doreen Mary, *née* Gordon-Harris; *b* 13 Sept 1947; *Educ* The Leys Sch Cambridge, Univ of Bistol (BSc); *m* 1971, Mary Thomasine Howard, da of Howard Reginald Thomas; 1 s (Alexander b 1973), 2 da (Emily b 1975, Joanna b 1976); *Career* gp fin dir Burmah Oil plc 1987; *Clubs* Oriental, West Hill Golf; *Style*— Roger Wood, Esq; High Leybourne, Hascombe, Godalming, Surrey GU8 4AD (☎ 048 632 559)Burmah House, Pipers Way, Swindon, Wilts, SN3 1RE (☎ 0793 30151; telex: 449221)

WOOD, Simon Richard Browne; s of Lt-Col Browne William Wood, of The Grange, Tadcaster, N Yorks, and Joan Radegunde, *née* Woollcombe; *b* 12 Dec 1947; *Educ* Eton; *m* 17 July 1970, Clare Launa, da of Lord Martin Fitzalan Howard, *qv* (bro 17 Duke of Norfolk), of Brockfield Hall, York; 1 s (Charles b 1973), 2 da (Alethea b 1975, Miranda b 1978); *Career* ptnr Sheppards and Chase 1975-80; dir Cater Allen plc 1981-; *Recreations* shooting, fishing; *Style*— Simon R B Wood, Esq; 17 Ellerby Street, London SW6 6EX (☎ 01 736 2779); 1 King William St, London EC4 N7AU (☎ 01 623 2070, fax 01 929 1641, telex 888553)

WOOD, Lady Susan Studd; da of Alfred Barclay Buxton (d 1940), and Edith Mary Crossley, *née* Studd (d 1978); *b* 19 Oct 1918; *Educ* The Manor House Surrey, London House of Citizenship (now Hartwell House Aylesbury, Dip Soc Sci); *m* 6 Nov 1943, Sir (Arthur) Michael wood, s of Arthur Henry Wood, CB; 2 s (Mark Lionel b 1945, Hugo Charles b 1948), 2 da (Janet Mary b 1946, Katrina Susan b 1951); *Career* WWII nurse Radcliffe Royal Infirmary Oxford, emigrated to Kenya 1947, mangr family farms (Kenya and Tanzania) 1951-75, fndr jewellry designer and md Kazusi Ltd (ceraics) Kenya 1975-; in E Africa helped to found: Red Cross Blood Bank, Flying Doctor Serv, African Med and Res Foundation; memb Capricorn Africa Soc during 1950's; *Books* Kenya - The Tensions of Progress (1955), A Fly in Amber (1964), A Dusty Minor, This One Thing (published privately); *Recreations* swimming; *Clubs* Sloane; *Style*— Lady Susan Wood; Mbagathi Ridge, Kareu, Nairobi, Kenya; Boc 24277, Nairobi, Kenya (☎ 254 2 882 362); Kazuri Ltd, Box 24276, Nairobi, Kenya (☎ 254 2 882 362, fax 882 723, telex 22992 HOSECS)

WOOD, Dr Timothy Campbell; s of Dr Guy E M Wood (d 1941), of Charterhouse, London EC1, and Margaret Dawson, *née* Campbell (d 1972); *b* 3 Oct 1928; *Educ* Rugby, Hertford Coll Oxford, UCH Med Sch; *m* 4 Aug 1956, (Dorothy) Ann, da of Harold Carpenter (d 1984), of Crakers Mead, Watford; 2 s (Geoffrey Campbell b 1957, Julian James b 1964), 1 da (Alison Elizabeth b 1958); *Career* 2 Lt RA 1955-57; UCH 1956-58: house physician, house surgn, res med offr; GP Watford Herts 1959-88, med offr Merchant Taylors' Sch 1966-88; hon Sec W Herts and Watford Med Soc 1970-80, memb Herts Local Med Ctee; Freeman Worshipful Co of Fishmongers; FRCGP 1982; *Recreations* sailing; *Style*— Dr Timothy Wood; 20 Grey's Close, Cavendish, Suffolk CO10 8BT (☎ 0787 281 713)

WOOD, Timothy John Rogerson; MP (C) Stevenage 1983-; *b* 1940; *Educ* King James's GS Knaresborough Yorks, Manchester Univ; *m* 1969, Elizabeth Mary Spencer; 1 s, 1 da; *Career* former proj mangr ICL Ltd, memb Bow Gp 1962- (C) memb cncl 1968-71); PPS to: Rt Hon John Stanley Min of State for NI 1987-, Min for Armed Forces 1986-87; chm Wokingham Cons Assoc 1980-83, vice-chm Thames Valley Euro Constituency Cncl 1979-83; memb: Bracknell Dist Cncl 1975-83 (ldr 1976-78), Bracknell Devpt Corpn. 1977-82; *Books* Bow Gp Pamphlets on educn, computers in Britain, and the Post Office; *Style*— Timothy Wood, Esq, MP; House of Commons, London SW1

WOOD, (René) Victor; s of Frederick Wood (d 1973); *b* 4 Oct 1925; *Educ* Jesus Coll Oxford; *m* 1950, Helen Morag, *née* Stewart; *Career* actuary; dir: Sun Life Assur Soc plc, Coalite Gp plc, Chandos Insur Co Ltd, Criterion Hldgs Ltd, Colbourne Insur Co Ltd, The Wemyss Devpt Co Ltd; *Style*— Victor Wood, Esq; Little Woodbury, Newchapel, nr Lingfield, Surrey RH7 6HR (☎ 0342 832054)

WOOD, Victoria; da of Stanely, of Bury, Lancs, and Helen *née* Mape; *b* 19 May 1953; *Educ* Bury GS, Birmingham Univ (BA, Drama and Theatre Arts); *m* 1980, Geoffrey Durham; *Career* entertainer and writer, plays: Talent 1978, (TV production won 3 Nat Drama Award 1980); Good Fun 1980; TV plays: Talent 1979, Nearly A Happy Ending 1980, Happy Since I Met You 1981; TV series Wood and Walters 1981, Victoria Wood As Seen on TV 1985 (Broadcasting Press Guilds Award, BAFTA Award), 2nd series 1986 (BAFTA Award), special 1987; West End Shows: Funny Turns 1982, Luckey Bag 1985; *Books* Lucky Bat The Victoria Wood Sketch Book (1985), Barmy The 2nd Victoria Wood Sketch Book (1987); *Style*— Miss Victoria Wood; c/o Richard Stone, 18-20 York Buildings WC2 (☎ 839 6421)

WOOD, William Henry Luke (Harry); s of Henry Sydney Wood (d 1965), of Durham, and Mary Sybil Oliver, *née* Luke; *b* 24 Oct 1934; *Educ* Oundle, Emmanuel Coll Cambridge (MA); *m* 31 Aug 1963, Margaret Elaine (Peggy), da of Harold Ashley-Biggs (d 1976), of Sussex; 2 s (Nigel b 12 Jan 1965, Robert b 8 June 1967), 1 da (Emma b 11 Nov 1971); *Career* Nat Serv 36 HAA Regt RA Malta 1953-55, Capt 324 HYAD Regt RA TA Newcastle; CA Winter Robinson Sisson & Benson (now Deloitte's) Newcastle 1958-62, md Wood & Watson Ltd (soft drinks) Durham 1962-, chm Durham Mkts Co; FCA 1973; *Recreations* gardening, DIY, walking, skiing, tennis; *Clubs* Durham Squash, Derwent Reservoir Sailing; *Style*— Harry Wood, Esq; Wood & Watson Ltd, Gilesgate, Durham DH1 1TR (☎ 091 384 8301)

WOOD, William Jeremy (Jerry); s of Maj Peter Alexander Wood, RA, of Budleigh Salterton, Devon, and Gwendoline Marion, *née* Hebron; *b* 2 June 1947; *Educ* Liverpool Coll, Univ of Manchester (BSc); *m* 17 march 1973, Judienne, da of Anthony Bridgett, of London W8; 1 da (Alexis (Lekki) b 1981); *Career* euro prod mktg mangr Avon Overseas Ltd 1973-79, conslt PE Consulting Gp 1979-82, euro strategic mktg dir Schering Plough Corpn 1983-85, bd dir Lowe Bell Fin Ltd 1986-89; *Recreations* squash, skiing, travel; *Style*— Jerry Wood, Esq; Lowe Bell Fin, 1 Red Lion Ct, London EC4A 3EB (☎ 01 353 9203); fax 01 353 7392)

WOODALL, Antony Edward; s of Col Edward Corbet Woodall, OBE (d 1972) of The Red House, Clifton, Hampden, Oxon, and Janet Inez, *née* Crawley (d 1964), *see* Crawly-Boevey Bt, 1963 Peerage edition,; *b* 18 April 1931; *Educ* Maidwell Hall Northampton, Eton; *m* 23 May 1959, Deirdre Kathleen, da of Sir John Child, 2Bt (d 1972), of Chobham Park House, Surrey; 3 s (James Henry b 1960, Andrew Hugh b 1963, Edward Antony John b 1967); *Career* stockbroker, ptnr Fielding Newson-Smith & Co 1959-83, dir Asset Mangrs plc 1986-; pres Herts Soc for the Blind, memb Cncl of mgmnt Byam Shaw Sch of Art; High Sheriff Co of Herts 1986-87; ct memb: Drapers Co 1983, Corpn of the Sons of The Clegg; *Recreations* golf, gardening; *Clubs* Brooks's, Pratt's, MCC, Royal Norfolk GC, Royal Worlington and Newmarket GC; *Style*— Antony Woodall, Esq; c/o Asset Managers plc, 4 Battle Bridge Lane, London SE1 2QE (☎ 01 378 1850)

WOODALL, Noel; s of Ernest Woodall (d 1966), and Sarah Woodhall, *née* Tromans; *b* 25 Dec 1930; *Educ* Oldbury Tech Coll, Birmingham Commercial Coll; *m* 24 July 1954, Dawn, da of Sydney Brown (d 1968); *Career* fndr memb the Cherished Numbers Dealers Assoc, memb Registration Numbers Club; *Books* Car Numbers Series (1962-88); Club Management Diploma; *Recreations* flying, photography, meeting people; *Clubs* RAF Assoc, Conservative; *Style*— Noel Woodal, Esq; 16 Boston Ave, Bispham, Blackpool FY2 9BZ (☎ 0253 55158); 122 Coronation Street, Blackpool FY1 4QQ (☎ 0253 24951)

WOODARD, Robert Nathaniel; Commodore, Royal Navy; s of Francis Alwyne Woodard (d 1974), and Catherine Mary, *née* Hayes; *b* 13 Jan 1939; *Educ* Lancing Coll Sussex; *m* 15 July 1963, Rosamund Lucia, da of Lt-Col Denis Lucius Alban Gibbs DSO and Bar (d 1984), and Lady Hilaria Agnes, *née* Edgcombe; 2 s (Rupert b 1964, Jolyon b 1969), 1 da (Melissa b 1967); *Career* 1958-75 aviator served carriers: Bulwark, Ark Royal, Eagle, Victorious; cmd: 771 and 848 Naval Air Squadron (Lt-Cdr), HMS Amazon 1978-80 (Cdr), HMS Glasgow 1983-85 (Capt), HMS Osprey 1985-86; Cdre Clyde 1988-; fell western div Woodard Schs; govr: Kings Taunton Sch, Kings Hall Sch, St Clare's Sch; FBIM 1978; *Recreations* painting, shooting, fishing and village cricket; *Clubs* Royal Cwlth; *Style*— Cdre Robert Woodard, RN; Clyde Submarine Base, Helensburgh, Dunbartonshire G84 8HL (☎ 0436 74321)

WOODBERRY, (Graham) George John; adopted; *b* 21 Sept 1938; *Educ* secdy modern sch; *m* 1962, Sheilagh Moira Eblis; 1 s (David b 1969), 2 da (Lynn, Jane); *Career* RN Submarines 1952-65; vice-chm Mint Security (Securicor Gp) 1984- (md 1979-84), dir Securicor Int 1981-, md Mint Security (Ulster) Ltd 1984-; *Style*— George Woodberry, Esq; 20 Sydenham Road, Croydon, Surrey (☎ 01 686 0123); Sutton Park House, Carlshalton Rd, Sutton, Surrey (☎ 01 770 7000)

WOODBINE PARISH, Sir David Elmer; CBE (1964); s of Walter Woodbine Parish (d 1952), and Audrey, *née* Makins; *b* 29 June 1911; *Educ* Eton, Lausanne Switzerland; *m* 1939, Mona Blair McGarel, da of Charles McGarel Johnston (d 1918), of Glynn, Co Antrim; 2 da (Vanessa b 1941, Miranda b 1944); *Career* industl conslt; dep chm Marine & General Mutual Life Assur Soc 1976-86, chm: St Thomas's Hosp Med Sch 1970-82, City and Guilds of London Inst 1967-78 (life vice-pres 1979), Bovis Ltd 1959-66, Sussex Area Royal Sch Church Music, Florence Nightingale Museu Tst 1981-86; memb bd of govrs Clothworkers Fndn 1977-, Master Worshipful Co of Clothworkers 1974-75; memb Ct Russia Co 1937-85, fell Imperial Coll; Hon FCGI, Hon LLD Leeds 1975; FCIOB, CBIM, FRSA; kt 1980; *Recreations* travel, music; *Clubs* Boodle's; *Style*— Sir David Woodbine Parish, CBE; The Glebe Barn, Pulborough, W Sussex RH20 2AF (☎ 07982 2613); 5 Lurgan Mansions, Sloane Sq, London SW1W 8BH (☎ 01 730 6512)

WOODBRIDGE, Anthony Rivers (Tony); s of John Nicholas Woodbridge, of Gerrards Cross, Bucks, and Patricia Madeleine, *née* Rebbeck; *b* 10 August 1942; *Educ* Stowe, Trinity Hall Cambridge (MA); *m* 29 Sept 1976, Lynda Anne, da of Charles Henry Nolan, of Stouffville, Ontario, Canada; 1 s (Christian b 30 March 1978); *Career* slr 1967, ptnr Woodbridge & Sons Uxbridge 1969, sr ptnr Turberville Woodbridge Uxbridge 1983; admin Uxbridge Duty Slr Scheme 1983-, chm govrs Fulmer Sch Bucks, co sec Abbeyfield Uxbridge Soc Ltd 1974-, clerk Cmmrs Income Tax 1985-; memb Law Soc 1967; *Recreations* walking, cycling, touring; *Clubs* Denham GC; *Style*— Anthony Woodbridge, Esq; Cadogan House, 39 North Park, Gerrards Cross, Bucks SL9 8JL (☎ 0753 885 442); 122 High St, Uxbridge, Middx UB8 1JT (☎ 0895 59 871, fax 0895 73 519, telex 23791)

WOODBURN, Thomas George; s of David Barkley Woodburn, CBE (d 1952), and Agnes Callender, *née* Campbell; *b* 23 June 1930; *Educ* Whitgift Sch, Christ's Coll Cambridge (BA, MA); *m* 1, 5 Sept 1959, April Janet (d 1974), da of Cecil William Picksley (d 1975); 1 s (David b 1962), 2 da (Ellen b 1960, Lucy b 1965); m 2, 12 March 1976, Rosemary, da of Cdr Gerald Alexander Llewellyn Woods, DSO, RN (d 1977); 1 s (Patrick b 1981), 1 da (Ursula b 1979); *Career* qualified slr 1955, ptnr Clifford Chance (formerly Coward Chance) 1960-, appointed slr to Univ of London 1975; chm Legal Aid Ctee Area 14; Liveryman City of London Slrs Co; memb Law Soc; *Recreations* gardening, natural history, bridge; *Clubs* Oriental; *Style*— T G Woodburn, Esq; Royex House, Aldermanbury Sq, London EC2V 7LD (☎ 01 600 0808, fax 01 726 8561, telex 8959991)

WOODCOCK, Christopher Terence; s of Maj Bernard Edward Woodcock, TD, of Norwick, and Patricia Francis Louise, *née* Mason (d 1979); *b* 3 Oct 1946; *Educ* Bredons Coll, Oratory Sch Birmingham; *m* 18 July 1968 (m dis 1986), Nora Patricia, da of Thomas McPartland, of Belfast; 2 s (Simon Edward b 1974, James Thomas b 1975); *Career* Nat Provincial Bank 1963-72, James Capel & Co 1972-76; md Kirkland Whittaker (Sterling Brokers) Ltd 1983- (jnd 1976, dir 1982); *Clubs* RAC; *Style*— Christopher Woodcock, Esq; Quince House, Briston, Melton, Constable, Norfolk; 76-80 Gt Eastern St, London EC2

WOODCOCK, Capt Graham; OBE (1980); s of Thomas Woodcock (d 1975), of Newfield, Haslingden, Rossendale, Lancs, and Beryl, *née* Duckworth (d 1957); *b* 25 July 1920; *Educ* Uppingham, St John's Coll Cambridge (BA, MA); *Career* WWII: enlisted RA 1939, active serv Gibraltar and India (seconded to Royal India Artillery) 1939-46, released with hon rank of Capt 1946; admitted slr 1949, ptnr Woodcock & Sons 1949-82 (conslt 1982-), hon legal advsr to RRF 1975-; pres: Haslingden Branch Royal Br Legion, Halingden and Dist Civil Tst, Haslingden and Helmshore Band, Haslingden and Dist Fly Fishing Assoc, Rossendale Fell Rescue Team; fndr chm Higher Mill Textile Museum Helmshore; cncllr Lancs CC 1969-81, memb fin bd Nat Union of Cons and Union Assoc 1985- (memb gen purposes and exec ctee 1985-); Guild Burgess of the Borough of Preston in the County of Lancaster since the Guild Merchant of 1922; memb Law Soc; *Recreations* travel, walking, gardening; *Clubs* Royal Over-Seas League, Cambridge Union Soc; *Style*— Capt Graham Woodcock, OBE; Heathfield, Haslingden, Rossendale, Lancs BB4 4BW (☎ 0706 214290)

WOODCOCK, HM Inspector of Constabulary John; CBE (1983), QPM (1976); s of Joseph Woodcock (d 1967), and Elizabeth May, *née* Whiteside (d 1982); *b* 14 Jan 1932; *Educ* Preston Techn Coll; *m* 4 April 1953, Kathleen Margaret, da of John Abbott; 2 s (Clive John b 1954, Aidan Edward b 1956), 1 da (Karen Belinda b 1962); *Career* police cadet, Lancs Constabulary 1947-50; Army Special Investigation Branch 1950-52; constable to Chief Inspector Lancs Constabulary 1952-65; supt and chief supt Beds and Luton Constab 1965-68; asst chief constable 1968-70, dep chief constable Gwent 1970-74; dep chief constable Devon & Cornwall 1974-78; chief constable: N Yorks Police 1978-79, S Wales Constabulary 1979-83; HM Inspector of Constabulary 1983-; Intermed Command Course Police Coll 1965, sen cmd Course 1968; Study Bavarian Police 1977; European Discussion Centre 1977; Int Police Course (lectr), Sicily, Rome 1978; FBI Nat Exec Washington 1981, Salt Lake City Utah 1986; vice-pres Welsh Assoc of Youth Clubs 1981-87; chm Wales Ctee Royal Jubilee and Prince's Tst 1983-85; memb: admin cncl Royal Jubilee Tsts 1981-85; Prince's Tst Ctee for Wales 1981-84, Govrg Body, World Coll of the Atlantic 1980-84; Hon memb Swansea Lions; O StJ 1981; Papal knighthood 1984 (KSG); *Recreations* table tennis, badminton, walking, norticulture; *Clubs* Special Forces, Cardiff Business (vice-pres); *Style*— HM Inspector of Constabulary John Woodcock, CBE, QPM; Home Office, Block A, Spur 12, Government Buildings, Whittington Rd, Worcester WR5 2PA

WOODCOCK, John Charles; s of Rev Parry John Woodcock (d 1938), and Norah Mabel, *née* Hutchinson; *b* 7 August 1926; *Educ* Dragon Sch, St Edward's Sch Oxford, Trinity Coll Oxford (MA); *Career* Manchester Guardian 1952-54; cricket corrs: The Times 1954-87, Country Life 1962-; ed Wisden Cricketers Almanack 1980-86; covered 31 Test Tours 1950-incl: Aust (15 times), S Africa, West Indies, NZ, India, Pakistan; dir The Cricketer, memb ctee of MCC, pres Cricket Writers Club; author pubns: The Ashes (1956), Barclays World of Cricket (with EW Swanton 1980, assoc ed 2 edn, conslt ed 3 edn 1986), Hockey for Oxford versus Cambridge (1946, 1947); Br Press Sportswriter of the Year 1987; *Recreations* golf, country pursuits; *Clubs* Flyfishers, Vincent's (Oxford), MCC; *Style*— John Woodcock, Esq; The Curacy, Longparish, nr Andover, Hants SP11 6PB (☎ 02647 259)

WOODCOCK, Michael (Mike); JP (1971), MP (C) Ellesmere Port and Neston 1983-; s of Herbert Eric Woodcock and Violet Irene Woodcock; *b* 10 April 1943; *Educ* Queen Elizabeth's GS Mansfield; *m* 1969, Carole Ann, da of Victor Arnold Berry; 1 s, 1 da; *Career* co dir; author and co-author; conslt; Hon DLitt 1988; *Books* Unblocking Your Organisation, People at Work, Team Development Manual, Organisation Development through Teambuilding, The Unblocked Boss, 50 Activities for Self Development, Management Development Manual, 50 Activities for Team Development; *Clubs* Farmers; *Style*— Mike Woodcock, Esq, JP, MP; Inkersall Farm, Bilsthorpe, Newark, Notts; House of Commons, London SW1

WOODCOCK, (Keith) Roy; s of Charles Roy William Woodcock, of 59 Russell Ave, March, Cambs, and Freda Margaret, *née* Smith; *b* 8 Nov 1950; *Educ* March GS; *m* 24 Sept 1977, Christine Ann, da of Ernest Barlow, of Hull; 2 s (Matthew b 9 Nov 1979, Samuel b 15 Aug 1982); *Career* features ed Hull Daily Mail 1986-88, ed Hull Star 1988-; *Style*— Roy Woodcock, Esq; 30 Southfield Dr, North Ferriby, Humberside HU14 3DX (☎ 0482 631 099); 84-86 Jameson St, Hull HU1 3DX (☎ 0482 27111 ext 232)

WOODCOCK, Thomas; s of Thomas Woodcock *qv* and Mary, *née* Woodcock, of Hurst Green, Lancs; *b* 20 May 1951; *Educ* Eton, Durham Univ (BA), Darwin Coll Cambridge (LLB); *Career* barr Inner Temple 1975; Rouge Croix Pursuivant 1978-82, Somerset Herald of Arms 1982-; *Books* Oxford Guide to Heraldry (jtly with John Martin Robinson 1988); *Clubs* Travellers'; *Style*— Thomas Woodcock, Esq; College of Arms, Queen Victoria St, London EC4 (☎ 01 236 3634)

WOODCOCK, Thomas; s of Thomas Woodcock (d 1975), of Haslington, Lancs, and Beryl, *née* Duckworth (d 1951); *b* 23 May 1918,; Family mentioned in Preston Guild Rolls since 1622; *Educ* Uppingham, Emmanuel Coll Cambridge (MA); *m* 8 July 1950, Mary, da of William Woodcock (d 1941), of Holcombe, Lancs; 1 s (Thomas *qv*), 1 da (Catherine b 1954) ; *Career* slr; snr ptnr Woodcock & Sons 1959-1984; memb Cncl of Law Soc 1969-84; Capt RA GB and Europe 1940-46; pres Bury & Dist Law Soc 1953; clerk to Gen Cmmnrs of Taxes for Div of Rochdale 1965-1988; pres Assoc of Clerks to Cmmnrs of Taxes GB 1983-87; Publications; The Expense of Time;; *Style*— Thomas Woodcock, Esq; The Old Bobbin Mill, Hurst Green, nr Blackburn, Lancashire BB6 9QB (☎ 025 486 310)

WOODD, Charles Basil; s of Rev Canon Frederick Hampden Basil Woodd (d 1986), and Emily Hornby, *née* Foss (d 1981); *b* 8 Oct 1946; *Educ* Canford Sch, Jesus Coll Cambridge (BA), LSE (Dip Social Admin); *m* 27 April 1974, Peggy Joanna, da of Rt Rev John Vernon Taylor, of Oxford; 2 s (Benjamin b 1977, Joseph b 1981), 1 da (Susannah b 1975); *Career* dir Bede House Assoc 1972-80, gen sec Voluntary Action Westminster 1980-86, dir Nat Fedn of Community Orgns 1986-; former: chm Lyndhurst Sch Assoc, sec Southwark Playgrounds Assoc, sec Advice Centre; memb: Social Responsibility Gp, St Barnabas Church Dulwich; tstee Jerusalem Tst, hon tres Nat Coalition for Neighbourhoods; Freeman City of London, Liveryman Worshipful Co of Salters 1971; *Recreations* walking, singing, DIY, cycling; *Style*— Charles Woodd, Esq; 36 Talfourd Rd, Peckham, London SE15 5NY (☎ 01 708 0540); National Federation of Community Organisations, 8/9 Upper St, London N1 OPQ (☎ 01 226 0189)

WOODD, Hugh Basil; s of Rev Canon Frederick Hampden Basil Woodd (d 1986), and Emily Hornby, *née* Foss (d 1980); *b* 13 Nov 1940; *Educ* Canford Sch Dorset, Bristol Univ (BA); *m* 21 Oct 1967, Susan (Sue) Mary, da of Norman Andrew Armitage, of Four Hedges, Woodlands, nr Wimborne, Dorset; 1 s (Christopher b 24 Nov 1968), 2 da (Rachel b 29 June 1970, Anna b 8 June 1972); *Career* CA, Mann Judd & Co London 1963-67 and 1969-88, Addis Ababa 1967-69, ptnr 1970; ptnr Touche Ross & Co (upon merger) 1979, ret 1988 to become sole practitioner in Winchester; hon tres Br Sch of Archaeology in Jerusalem; hon tres St Matthews PCC; Freeman City of London 1964, Liveryman Worshipful Co of Salters 1964; ACA 1967; *Recreations* opera, mountain walking, badminton, skiing, DIY; *Style*— Hugh Woodd, Esq; Honeywick, 17 Bereweeke Ave, Wincester, Hants SO22 6BH (☎ 0962 52924/0962 69613)

WOODFIELD, Sir Philip John; KCB (1982), CB (1974, CBE 1963); s of Ralph Woodfield; *b* 30 August 1923; *Educ* Alleyn's Sch Dulwich, King's Coll London; *m* 1958, Diana, da of Sydney Herington; 3 da; *Career* serv WWII RA; subsequently NI and Home Off; dep sec Home Off 1974-81, perm under-sec NI Off 1981-84; *Style*— Sir Philip Woodfield, KCB, CBE; c/o Lloyds Bank, 6 Pall Mall, London SW1

WOODFORD, Maj-Gen David Milner; CBE (1975); s of Maj Robert Milner Woodford, MC (d 1981), and Marion Rosa (Tessa), *née* Gregory (d 1955); *b* 26 May 1930; *Educ* Prince of Wales Sch Nairobi, Wadham Coll Oxford; *m* 1959 (m dis 1987), Ethel Mary, da of David Stanley Edwardes Jones (d 1963); *Career* CO 3 RRF 1970-72, Col Cyprus 1972-75, Cmd 3 Inf Bde 1976-77, Dep Cdr COS SE Dist 1979-80, ACGS MOD 1981-82, SDS RCDS 1982-83, Cmdt Joint Serv Def Coll 1984-86, ret 1986; *Recreations* literary, historical, golf; *Clubs* Army and Navy, NZ Golf; *Style*— Maj-Gen David Woodford, CBE; c/o Barclays Bank, Fleet, Hants;

WOODHAMS, Rev the Hon Sophie Harriet; *née* Liddell; da of Hon Cyril Arthur Liddell (d 1932), and sister of 8 Baron Ravensworth; *b* 6 July 1927; *Educ* King's Coll, Durham Univ, Cranmer Hall Theological Coll Durham; *m* 1981, Leslie Charles William Woodhams, s of Charles Woodhams, RN (d 1922); *Career* granted title, rank and precedence of a Baron's da 1951; ordained deacon in the C of E 14 March 1987; *Style*— The Rev the Hon Sophie Woodhams; 31 Hanover Close, Shaftgate Ave, Shepton Mallet, Somerset BA4 5YQ (☎ 0749 4124)

WOODHEAD, Col Michael ffolliott; OBE (1969); s of Arnold Hugh Woodhead (d 1980), of Orchard Hse, Clare Mont Park, Esher, and Vivienne Lintorn, *née* Highett (d 1962); *b* 12 May 1923; *Educ* Imperial Serv Coll Windsor, Royal Mil Coll Sandhurst; *m* 15 Jan 1955, Gillian Hazel, JP, da of Col Hugo Graham de Burgh, OBE, MC (d 1954), of Kildare, Ireland; 3 s (Nicholas ffolliot b 23 Oct 1955, Christopher Michael Anthony b 20 Feb 1957, Timothy Hugh b 28 Dec 1965), 2 da (Jane Caroline (Mrs Matthew) b 20 Feb 1959, Eleanor May (The Hon Mrs James Keith) b 25 July 1962); *Career* cmmd 9 Queen's Royal Lancers 1942, serv Middle E, N Africa, Italy and Palestine, 9/12 Royal Lancers Prince of Waller 1960, cmmnd Lt-Col 9/12 Lancers 1966-69, Col MOD 1969, Cmdt Royal Mil Sch of Music 1975-78, ret 1978, Col 9/12 Royal Lancers 1986-; Freeman City of London 1981, Liveryman Worshipful Co of Tallow Chandlers 1981;

Recreations shooting, gardening, cooking; *Clubs* Cavalry and Gds; *Style*— Col Michael Woodhead, OBE; 56 Chesilton Rd, Fulham, London SW6 5AB (☎ 01 736 1638); Tallow Chandlers Hall, 4 Dowgate Hill, London EC4R 2SH (☎ 01 248 4726)

WOODHEAD, Robin George; s of Walter Henry Woodhead (d 1976), of Zimbabwe, and Gladys Catherine Woodhead, of Johannesburg, SA; *b* 28 April 1951; *Educ* Mount Pleasant Sch Salisbury Rhodesia, Univ Coll of Rhodesia and Nyasaland (LLB); *m* 28 June 1980, Mary Fitzgerald, da of Fergus Hamilton Allen, CB, *qv*, of Berks; *Career* 1981-86: chm and dir Int Petroleum Exchange of London Ltd, md Premier Mgmnt Ltd, dir E D & F Man Int Ltd, chief exec Nat Investmt Hldgs plc 1986-, chm and chief exec Nat Investmt Gp plc 1986-; tres Contemporary Art Soc, fndr tstee Whitechapel Gallery, memb Ballet Rambert; memb Law Soc 1978; *Recreations* skiing, tennis, riding, contemporary art; *Style*— Robin Woodhead, Esq; National Investment Group plc, Salisbury House, London Wall, London EC2M 5SX (☎ 01 638 7412, fax 01 628 2634)

WOODHEAD-KEITH-DIXON, Rev James Addison; s of James Keith-Dixon (d 1967), of Lorton Hall, Cockermouth, Cumbria, and Margaret Ann, da of James Wright, of Glossop, Derbys; *b* 20 July 1925; *Educ* St Aidan's Coll Birkenhead, Liverpool Univ; *m* 1, 16 Oct 1951, Mary Constance (d 1977), da of Alfred Tindal Saul (d 1960), of Highcroft, Stanwix, Carlisle (d 1972); 1 s (Andrew James b 14 April 1953); m 2, 1 Aug 1981, Clodagh Anne, da of James Trevor Cather, of Icod, Tenerife; *Career* deacon 1948, priest 1949, curate Upperby Carlisle 1948-50, curate Dalton-in-Furness 1950-52, vicar Blawith-with-Lowick 1952-59, vicar Lorton 1959-50, chaplain of Tenerife 1980-82, team vicar of Falstone, Thorneyburn and Greystead 1982, team rector 1983, lay rector Lorton; Lord of The Manors of Lorton Brigham and Whinfell; *Recreations* shooting, fishing, heraldry and genealogy; *Style*— The Rev James Woodhead-Keith-Dixon; The Rectory, Falstone, Hexham, Northumberland NE48 1AE (☎ 0660 40213)

WOODHOUSE, Hon (Georgina) Caroline; da of 4 Baron Terrington; *b* 1 July 1946; *Educ* Downham Sch Essex, Queensgate, Villa d'Assomption Paris; *Career* interior designer; *Recreations* skiing, tennis; *Style*— The Hon Caroline Woodhouse; Flat 7, 171 Sussex Gdns, London W2 (☎ 01 723 2836); office: 62 Pimlico Rd, London SW1 (☎ 01 730 9136)

WOODHOUSE, Lady Davidema Katharine Cynthia Mary Millicent; *née* Bulwer-Lytton; da of 2 Earl of Lytton Kg, GCSI, GCIE, PC (d 1947); *b* 1909; *m* 1, 1931, 5 Earl of Erne (d 1940); 1 s (*see* 6 Earl), 2 da (*see* Lady Rosanagh Raben-Levetzau and Lady Antonia Beckwith); m 2, 1945, Col the Hon Christopher Montague Woodhouse, DSO, OBE, *qv*; 2 s (Christopher Richard James b 20 Sept 1946, Nicholas Michael John b 27 Feb 1949), 1 da (Emma Davina Mary Johnson-Gilbert b 19 April 1954); *Style*— Lady Davidema Woodhouse; Willow Cottage, Latimer, Bucks (☎ 02404 2627)

WOODHOUSE, James Stephen; s of Rt Rev John Walker Woodhouse (d 1956); *b* 21 May 1933; *Educ* St Edward's Sch Oxford, St Catharine's Coll Cambridge; *m* 1957, Sarah Maud, da of Col Hubert Blount, MC (d 1979); 3 s, 1 da; *Career* asst master Westminster Sch 1957-63, under-master and master of Queen's Scholars 1963-67; headmaster: Rugby Sch 1967-81, Lancing Coll 1981-; *Recreations* sailing, music, hill walking, natural history; *Clubs* East India, Sports and Public Sch; *Style*— James Woodhouse Esq; The Old Farmhouse, Lancing Coll, Sussex

WOODHOUSE, Hon (Christopher) Montague; DSO (1943), OBE (1944); s of 3 Baron Terrington, KBE (d 1961), and hp of bro, 4 Baron Terrington; *b* 11 May 1917; *Educ* Winchester, New Coll Oxford (MA); *m* 28 Aug 1945, Lady Davidema *qv*, wi of 5 Earl of Erne, 3 stepchildren; *Career* serv WWII organising resistance in occupied Greece; dir-gen Roy Inst of Int Affrs, and dir studies 1955-59, visiting fell Nuffield Coll Oxford 1956-64, MP (C) Oxford 1959-66 and 1970-74, parly sec Miny of Aviation 1961-62, jt under-sec state Home Office 1962-64, dir educn and trg CBI 1966-70, visiting prof King's Coll London 1978-, fellow Trinity Hall Cambridge, 1949 FRSL, corresponding memb Acad of Athens 1980, hon fellow New Coll Oxford 1982; *Books* Karamanlis, the Restorer of Greek Democracy (1982), Something Ventured (autobiography 1982), Gemistos Plethon (1986); *Style*— The Hon Montague Woodhouse; Willow Cottage, Latimer, Bucks HP5 1TW (☎ 024 04 2627)

WOODHOUSE, The Rt Hon Sir (Arthur) Owen; KBE (1981), DSC (1944), PC (1974); s of A J Woodhouse; *b* 18 July 1916; *Educ* Napier Boys' HS, Auckland Univ; *m* 1940, Margaret Leah Thorp; 4 s, 2 da; *Career* served 1939-45 War RNZNVR, Lt Cdr; asst to Naval Attaché HM Embassy Belgrade 1945; judge: Supreme Ct NZ 1961-86, Ct of Appeal 1974-86; pres Ct of Appeal 1981-86; First pres Law Cmmn 1985-; Hon LLD Victoria Univ of Wellington 1978, Hon LLD York Univ Canada 1981; kt 1974; *Style*— The Rt Hon Sir Owen Woodhouse KBE, DSC; Box 2590, Wellington, NZ

WOODHOUSE, (Bernard) Raymond; s of (Thomas) Bernard Montague Woodhouse (d 1969), of Woodcote Park Ave, Purley, Surrey, and Betty, *née* Harvey (d 1956); *b* 24 Nov 1939; *Educ* Ardingly, St Dunstans Catford, Nat Coll of Food Tech; *m* 6 Oct 1962, Judith, da of Robert Arnold Roach, of Caterham; 2 s (Richard Thomas Raymond b 5 May 1965, Martyn Bernard Robert b 26 Jan 1970); *Career* chm TSJ Woodhouse Ltd 1973- (joined 1960); life govr RNLI; Freeman City of London 1979, Liveryman Worshipful Co of Butchers 1979; *Recreations* tennis, water-skiing, boating; *Style*— Raymond Woodhouse, Esq; T S J Woodhouse Ltd, 72-98 Blundell St, London N7 9TS (☎ 01 609 2200); The Backwater, Upper Ct Rd, Woldingham, Surrey CR3 7BF

WOODHOUSE, Richard Francis; s of Wilfrid Meynell Woodhouse (d 1967), of 55 Chester Row, London SW1, and Margaret Helen, da of Frederick Kohl OBE;; *b* 23 Oct 1939; *Educ* Marlborough, Peterhouse Cambridge (MA); *m* 25 July 1964, Elizabeth Mary, da of Richard Charles Steele, OBE, of Hambledon, Surrey; 1 s (Matthew Wilfrid b 18 Sept 1969), 2 da (Alice Emma b 21 June 1967, Catherine Clare b 8 Feb 1972); *Career* called to the Bar Inner Temple 1962, SE circuit, asst rec 1982-, chm 2 Legal Aid Area 1988; sec local Archaeological Coordination Soc 1973-80, memb of cncl Reigate Soc 1975-80, ctee memb Reigate Beekeepers Assoc; *Recreations* gardening, beekeeping, country walks, classical music; *Style*— Richard Woodhouse, Esq; 6 Wray Rd, Reigate, Surrey RH2 0DD (☎ 07372 49395); 4 Kings Bench Walk, Temple, London EC4YA 7DL (☎ 01 353 8581, fax 01 583 2257)

WOODHOUSE, Ronald Michael; s of Henry Alfred Woodhouse, of Woking, Surrey (d 1961) and Phyllis *née* Gemmell (d 1983); *b* 19 August 1927; *Educ* Lancing, Queen's Coll, Oxford; *m* 15 Oct 1955, Quenilda Mary (*née* Gorton), da of Rt Rev Neville Gorton, Bishop of Coventry (1942, d 1945); 1 s (Alexander b 1961), 3 da (Harriet b 1956, Isobel b 1958, Anna b 1964); *Career* chm: The Int Paint Co Ltd 1978-84, Br Cellophane Ltd Nov 1979-86, Courtaulds Fibres 1985-86; dep chm Courtaulds plc 1986-; dir Bowater plc 1988-; *Clubs* Carlton, Oriental; *Style*— Michael Woodhouse, Esq; Tankards, Wonersh, nr Guildford, Surrey (☎ 0483 892 078); 18 Hanover Sq, London W1A 2BB (☎ 01 629 9080, Telex 28788, fax 01 629 2586)

WOODLEY, Derek George; s of George Edward Woodley (d 1957), of Romford, Essex, and Dorothy Marjorie Gwendoline Roper; *b* 28 Mar 1931; *Educ* Royal Liberty Sch (Dip Arch); *m* 9 July 1955, Thelma Joan, da of Arthur Legg (d 1971); 2 s (David b 1962, Richard b 1968), 1 da (Jacqueline b 1963); *Career* Capt RE (survey), Cyprus re-survey and other classified work; chartered arch, sr ptnr Bell & Woodley 1980-; RIBA; *Recreations* cricket, golf; *Style*— Derek Woodley, Esq; Leap House, 45 Ferry Rd, Felixstowe, Suffolk (☎ Felixstowe 284880); Bell & Woodley, 117A Hamilton Rd, Felixstowe, Suffolk (☎ Felixstowe 284550 and 284289)

WOODLEY, Ven Ronald John; s of John Owen Woodley (d 1960), and Maggie Woodley, *née* Lord (d 1973); *b* 28 Dec 1925; *Educ* Montagu Rd Sch Edmonton London, Bishops' Coll Cheshunt Herts; *m* 1959, Patricia, da of Thomas Kneeshaw (d 1979); 1 s (John), 2 da (Rachel, Elizabeth); *Career* Sgt BAOR 1944-47; ordained: deacon 1953, priest 1954; curate: St Martin Middlesbrough 1953-58, Whitby 1958-61; curate i/c the Ascension Middlesbrough 1961-66, vicar 1966-71, rector of Stokesley 1971-85, rural dean 1977-84, canon and prebendary of York 1982-, archdeacon of Cleveland 1985-; *Recreations* walking, gardening, cinema, theatre, wine-making; *Style*— The Ven the Archdeacon of Cleveland; Park House, Rosehill, Great Ayton, Middlesbrough TS9 6BH (☎ 0642 723221)

WOODROFFE, Most Rev George Cuthbert Manning; *see*: West Indies, Archbishop of

WOODROFFE, Peter Mackelcan; s of Kenneth Derry Woodroffe (d 1972), of 8 Westminster Gardens, London SW1, and Raby Alfreda Mackelcan, *née* Ryan; *b* 2 August 1927; *Educ* Mill Hill Sch ; *m* 15 June 1973, Amanda Aloysia Nicolette, da of Henry Forbes, of Chelsea Lodge, Englefield Green, nr Windsor, Berks; 2 s (Justin Mackelcan b 24 May 1977, Clifford Derry b 10 Dec 1979); *Career* enlisted 1945, cmmnd 2 Lt Royal Northumberland Fus 1946 (Lt 1947), ret 194l; admitted slr 1953; sr ptnr Woodroffes 1963- (ptnr 1956-63); sec Ct of Govrs Mill Hill Sch; memb Westminster City Cncl 1962-65; hon citizen State of Tesas USA 1967, Freeman City of London 1984; memb Law Soc 1953; *Recreations* sking, golf, tennis; *Clubs* Boodles, The Berkshire, Rye Gold, Royal Cinque Ports Golf; 13 Cadogan St, London SW3 2PP; Stonewalls, Pett Level, Nr Hastings, Sussex TN35 4EH (☎ 01 589 9339); Messrs Woodroffes, York House, 199 Westminster Bridge Rd, London SE1 7UT (☎ 01 928 6855, fax 01 633 04590

WOODROOFE, Sir Ernest George; s of Ernest Woodroofe; *b* 6 Jan 1912; *Educ* Cockburn HS, Leeds Univ (PhD); *m* 1, 1938, Margaret Downes (d 1961); 1 da; m 2, 1962, Enid Arnold; *Career* chm: Unilever 1970-74, Leverhulme Tst 1974-82; memb Br Gas Corpn 1973-82; dir: Schroders 1974-, Burton Gp 1974-83, Guthrie Corpn 1974-82; Hon DSc: Cranfield, Liverpool; Hon LLD Leeds, Hon D Univ Surrey, hon fell Univ of Manchester Inst Sci & Technol (UMIST), Hon ACT Liverpool; memb Royal Cmmn for 1851 Exhibition, 1968-84; FInstP, FIChemE; Cdr Order of Orange Nassau 1972; kt 1973; *Clubs* Athenaeum; *Style*— Sir Ernest Woodroofe; 44 The Street, Puttenham, Guildford, Surrey GU3 1AR (☎ 0483 810977)

WOODROW, David; CBE (1979); s of Sydney Melson Woodrow (d 1981), of Foston House, Foston, Leics, and Edith Constance, *née* Farmers (d 1936); *b* 16 Mar 1920; *Educ* Shrewsbury Sch, Trinity Coll Oxford (MA); *m* 1, 1 April 1950 (m dis), Marie-Armande Irène, da of Benjamin Barrios, KBE (d 1928); 2 da (Geraldine b 27 Jan 1951, Joanna b 29 June 1955); m 2, 25 Jan 1983, Mary, da of Alexander Whitamore (d 1946); *Career* enlisted 1939, cmmnd RA 1940, captured Java 1942, (POW Java and Japan 1942-45) demob 1946; slr private practice partnership 1949-84; chm: Reading & Dist Hosp Mgmnt Ctee 1966-72, Oxford Regnl Hosp Bd 1972-74, Oxford Regnl Health Authy 1974-78, Nat Staff Ctee for Admin and Clinical staff of HNS 1975-79; memb Law Soc; *Recreations* painting and drawing; *Clubs* Leander; *Style*— David Woodrow, Esq, CBE; Dobsons, Brightwell-Cum-Sotwell, Oxfordshire (☎ 0491 36170)

WOODROW, (Charles) James; s of Bernard Joseph Woodrow (d 1956), of 10 The Drive, Hartley, Plymouth, and Winifred Barbara, *née* Tregillus (d 1966); *b* 20 Mar 1918; *Educ* Plymouth Coll, Loughborough Engrg Coll (now Univ); *m* 1 Feb 1947, Elizabeth Teresa, da of Alfred Churchill Channings Jago (d 1945); 3 da (Josanne b 11 Jan 1948, Rosalind b 19 June 1950, Vanessa b 13 Oct 1953); *Career* WWII Maj REME; i/c port workshop Tobruk (during seige), staff coll Palestine, staff duties 8 Army HQ (mentioned in despatches), control cmmn Germany, demob 1946; chm: Blight & White Ltd Structural Engrs Plymouth 1964-85 (md 1947-80), Sutton Harbour Co 1964-; chm: Plymouth Guild Community Serv 1963-77, Plymouth Mfrs Gp 1982-83, Offshore Energy Plymouth, Area Bd Young Enterprise, Plymouth Barbican Assoc 1957-; memb regnl cncl CBI; JP (Plymouth Bench) 1954-88 (chm 1985-88); High Sheriff of Devon 1983-84; FRSA, CEng, FIStructE, MIProdE, MBIM; *Recreations* golf, gardening, walking; *Clubs* 7 Armoured Division Officers', Royal Western Yacht; *Style*— James Woodrow, Esq; Mount Stone, Thurlestone, Kingsbridge, Devon TQ7 3NJ (☎ 0548 560 206); Sutton Harbour Co, Plymouth PL4 0ES (☎ 0752 664 186)

WOODROW, William Robert (Bill); s of Geoffrey William Woodrow, of Chichester, W Sussex, and Doreen Mary, *née* Fasken; *b* 1 Nov 1948; *Educ* Barton Peveril GS, Winchester Sch of Art, St Martins Sch of Art, Chelsea Sch of Art (Higher Dip Fine Art); *m* 12 Nov 1970, Pauline, da of John Neville Rowley; 1 s (Harry), 1 da (Ellen); *Career* sculptor; individual exhibitions in Europe, Australia, USA and Canada 1972-; work in numerous group exhibitions inc: Br Sculpture in the 20th Century Whitechapel Art Gallery 1981, Biennale of Sydney 1982, Aperto 82 Venice 1982, XII Biennale of Paris 1982, New Art at the Tate Gallery 1983, Transformations Sao Paulo (also Riode Janeiro, Mexico City, Lisbon) 1983, Int Survey of Recent Painting and Sculpture New York 1984, Skulptur im 20 Jahrhundert Basle 1984, ROSC '84 Dublin 1984, Space Invaders toured Canada 1985, The Br Show toured Australia 1985, Carnegie Int Pittsburgh 1985, Entre el objeto y la imagen toured Spain 1986, Painting and Sculpture Today Indianapolis 1986, Br Art of the 1980's Stockholm and Tampere 1987, Documenta 8 Kassel W Germany 1987, Starlit Waters Tate Liverpool 1988, British Now Montreal 1988; work in numerous museum collections inc: Arts Cncl GB, Br Cncl, Imperial War Museum, Kunsthaus Zurich, Malmö Konsthall, Nat Gallery of Canada, Rijksmuseum Kröller-Müller, Tate Gallery; *Style*— W.R Woodrow, Esq; c/o Lisson Gallery, 67 Lisson Street, London NW1 5DA (☎ 01 724 2739)

WOODRUFF, Prof Alan Waller; CMG (1978); s of William Henry Woodruff (d 1939), of Sunderland, and Mary Margaret, *née* Thomson (d 1966); *b* 27 June 1916; *Educ* Bede Collegiate Sch Sunderland, Univ of Durham Coll of Med (MB BS, MD); *m* 21 Jan

1946, Mercia Helen, da of Leonard Henry Arnold (d 1949), of Dorking; 2 s (Arnold Henry Waller b 1951, Peter Waller Rolph b 1956), 1 da (Heather Mary Elizabeth b 1949); *Career* WWII Flt Lt (formerly Flying Offr) med branch RAF 1940-42, Sqdn Ldr med specialist 1942-46; conslt in tropical med to Army 1953-81; Wellcome prof of clinical tropical med Univ of London 1952-81 (prof emeritus 1981-), physician Hosp for Tropical Diseases (UCH) London 1952-81 (consulting physician 1981-), prof of med Univ of Juba Southern Sudan 1981-; conslt Br Airways 1959-87; pres: Durham Univ Soc 1964-75, Royal Soc of Tropical Med and Hygiene 1974-76, Med Soc of London 1976-77, history section RSM London 1977-79; chm Br Burma Soc 1969-80; cncl memb Royal Coll of Physicians 1975-79; memb: Colonial Med Res Ctee 1955-68, Tropical Med Res Bd MRC 1968-72, West African MRC 1959-62, East African MRC 1964; hon fell Royal Soc of Painters-Etchers and Engravers 1978; FRCP 1953, FRCP Edin 1961; hon fell: Burma Med Assoc 1966, Brazilian Soc of Tropical Med 1969, Belgian Soc of Tropical Med 1969, Societe de pathologie Exotique Paris 1972; *Books* Medicine in the Tropics (with S G Wright, second edn 1984), A Synopsis of Infectians and Tropical Diseases (with S Bell, third edn 1987); *Recreations* sketching and engraving, fishing; *Clubs* Athenaeum, Sunderland, Sudan (Khartoum); *Style*— Prof Alan Woodruff, CMG; 122 Ferndene Rd, London SE24 0BA; Univ of Juba, P O Box 82, Juba, Sudan

WOODRUFF, Hon Mrs; Elizabeth Trilby Charity; da of Baron Taylor (Life Peer); *b* 1943; *Educ* Sussex Univ; *m* 1, 1971 (m dis 1986), Paul Stephen Masterman; m 2, 1986, Alan George Woodruff; *Career* librarian Br Technol Gp 1981-; *Style*— The Hon Mrs Masterman; 13 Farlington Ave, Haywards Heath, W Sussex RH16 3EZ

WOODRUFF, Hon Mrs (Marie Immaculée Antoinette); *née* Lyon-Dalberg-Acton; da of 2 Baron Acton, KCVO (d 1924); 6th Bt PM of Naples during Napoleonic Wars, his s 7th Bt m heiress of Duke of Dalberg, 8th Bt Cr UK Peer 1869; *b* 1905; *m* 1933, John Douglas Woodruff, CBE (d 1978); *Career* Dame of Honour and Devotion of Sovereign O of Malta; has Cross Pro Ecclesia et Pontifice; *Style*— The Hon Mrs Woodruff; Marcham Priory, Abingdon, Oxon

WOODRUFF, William Charles (Bill); CBE (1985); s of Thomas William Woodruff (d 1943), of Ramsgate, Kent, and Caroline Elizabeth, *née* Windsor (d 1966); *b* 14 August 1921; *Educ* St George's Sch Ramsgate; *m* 1, 9 May 1946, Ethel May (d 1981), da of late Frank Miles, of Rochester, Kent; 1 s (Gerald b 1948), 1 da (Pamela b 1951); m 2, 7 April 1987, Olivia Minerva, *née* Barnes; 3 step s (John b 1946, James b 1947, David b 1949); *Career* Fl-Lt navigator/observer 1409 Flight RAF 1941-46, POW 1943-45; Miny of Civil Aviation 1945-: air trafic controller at various airports and London HQ 1946-56, air traffic controller Heathrow 1956-62, sec PATCH long-term ATC Planning Gp 1960-61, dir civil air traffic Ops 1967-69 (dep dir 1962-67), controller nat air traffic servs 1977-81 (jt field cdr 1969-74, dep controller 1974-77); master of Guild of Air Traffic Control Offrs 1956 (clerk of Guild 1952-56), aviation assesor airports pub inquiries 1981-84, specialist advsr parly select tport ctee on air traffic control safety 1988; FRAeS 1979; *Recreations* reading, gardening, crosswords; *Style*— Bill Woodruff, Esq; Great Oaks, 36 Court Rd, Ickenham, Uxbridge, Middlesex UB10 8TF (☎ 0895 639134)

WOODS, Alan Thomas De-Lima; s of Herbert De-Lima Woods (d 1970), of Chiddingfold, Surrey, and Jane Maud, *née* Ferguson (d 1975); *b* 19 Oct 1924; *Educ* Epsom Coll, London Univ (LLB); *m* 5 April 1956, Sylvia Rose, da of John Theodore Read (d 1962), of W Chiltington, Sussex; 1 s (David Jonathan b 20 Jan 1961), 1 da (Susan Elizabeth (Mrs Mitchell) b 13 June 1959); *Career* Sub-Lt RNVR 1944; slr 1947; sr ptnr Bird & Bird, chm Soc for Computers and Law 1973-78; memb Cncl of Epsom Coll 1974-; tres Royal Alexandra and Albert Sch 1982-; memb Law Soc; *Recreations* gardening; *Clubs* Naval; *Style*— Alan Woods Esq; Stourton, The Glade, Kingswood, Tadworth, Surrey KT20 6LL (☎ 0737 832480); Bird & Bird, 2 Gray's Inn Sq, London WC1 (☎ 01 242 6681)

WOODS, (Paul) Anthony John; s of Charles John Woods, of Streatham, London, and Joan Vera *née* Margetts; *b* 14 June 1945; *Educ* Dulwich Coll, New Coll Oxford (MA); *m* 9 June 1979, Louise Head, da of Jason Richard Head Palmer, of Teddington, Middx; 1 s (Richard b 1982), 1 da (Eleanor b 1980) ; *Career* slr: England and Wales 1969, NSW Australia 1973; ptnr Norton Rose 1980-; Liveryman The City of London Slrs 1981-; memb Law Soc 1969; *Recreations* theatre, reading, gardening, watching rugby union and cricket; *Clubs* MCC, Tanglin; *Style*— Anthony Woods, Esq; Kempson House, Camomile St, London EC3A 7AN (☎ 01 283 2434, fax 01 588 1181, telex 883652 NOROSE G)

WOODS, Basil Joseph Pontifex; s of Victor Jocelyn Woods (d 1966), and Marie Josephé *née* Payet (d 1971); *b* 28 August 1922; *Educ* Durban Boys' HS Natal SA, Natal Univ (BEcon), Pembroke Coll Cambridge (MA); *m* 1, 1950; 3 da (Mrs Peter Alderton b 1951, Carol Anne b 1953, Mrs Andrew Greenwood b 1956); m 2, 1971, Deborah Mary, da of Robert Charles Thomas (decd); *Career* dir Central Bank of Fedn of Rhodesia and Nyasaland, chm Allied Steel and Wire 1981-85; former dir corporate planning and econ advsr Guest Keen and Nettlefolds plc, dep md GKN plc 1981-84 (ret all GKN appts 1984); chm: European Industrial Services, Ashfield Holdings Ltd; *Recreations* cricket, golf; *Clubs* MCC; *Style*— Basil Woods, Esq; Old Roses, Upton Bishop, Ross-on-Wye, Herefs HR9 7UA; European Industrial Services Ltd, Woden Rd West, Kings Hill, Wednesbury, West Midlands WS10 7TT; Ashfield Holdings Limited, 79-81 Station Road, Sutton-in-Ashfield, Nottingham NG17 5FR

WOODS, His Hon Judge Brian; s of Edward Percival Woods, of Woodmancote, Cheltenham (d 1967), and Beulah Aileen Ruth *née* Thomas (d 1977); *b* 5 Nov 1928; *Educ* City of Leicester Boys' Sch, Nottingham Univ LLB (Hons); *m* 23 April 1957, Anne Margaret, da of Frederick James Griffiths, of Parkgate, Wirral (d 1975); 3 da (Rachel b 1962, Helen b 1965, Diana b 1969); *Career* RAF 1947-49; barr Gray's Inn 1955; memb Midland Circuit; dep chm Lincs (Lindsey) Quarter Sessions 1968; Anglican Lay Reader 1970; chancellor, Diocese of Leicester 1977-79; fell Midland Div, Woodard Corp 1978; memb cncl of Abbots Bromley Sch of St Mary & St Anne 1977-; CJ 1975; legal memb, Mental Health Review Tribunals, Trent and Northern Regions 1983-; *Recreations* music, taking photographs, avoiding complacency; *Style*— His Honour Judge Woods

WOODS, Eric Cecil; s of Cecil Vincent Edward Woods, of Rustington, Sussex, and Eileen Sybil, *née* Bays; *b* 2 Oct 1930; *Educ* Highgate Sch, LSE (LLB, LLM); *m* 24 June 1961, (Florence) Mary, da of William Gerald Edington (d 1968); 1 da (Katharine b 1962, Penelope b 1964); *Career* admitted as slr 1953, asst slr with Newport and Brighton Corpns 1953-59, asst slr and ptnr Tucker Hussey and Co London 1959-67, princ slr legal dept Midland Bank plc 1971-87 (joined 1967), memb legal ctee London Cleaning Bankers 1971-87 (chm 1980-82), chm CBI Co Law Panel 1976-83 (memb since 1974), memb CBI Ctees and Working Parties, memb Law Soc Standing Ctee on Co Law 1980-87, agent slr crown Prosecution Serv and private practice for Midland Bank 1987, conslt Stephenson Harwood 1988; memb Hertford Cons Assoc, ctee chm Cons Political Centre 1966-69, dep constituency chm 1969-71; JP Herts 1970-71, memb of panel of chm Fin Servs Tribune 1988; Freeman City of London 1962, Liveryman of Worshipful Co of Glaziers 1962; *Books* contributor articles in New Law Journal, on Housing, Kent Acts and powers of Bank of England 1964-68, also articles on banking law in Journal of Institute of Bankers; *Recreations* history, gardening, music, pedal cycling, trvel; *Style*— Eric Woods, Esq

WOODS, Maj-Gen Henry Gabriel; CB (1979), MBE (1945), DL (N Yorks 1984-); s of G S Woods (d 1961), of Bexhill-on-Sea, Sussex, and Flora, *née* MacNevin (d 1976); *b* 7 May 1924; *Educ* Highgate Sch, Trinity Coll Oxford (MA); *m* 29 April 1953, Imogen Elizabeth Birchenough Woods, da of CES Dodd (d 1975), of Bath; 2 da (Sarah b 1955, Arabella b 1958); *Career* cmmnd 5 Royal Iniskilling Dragoon Gds 1944; served NW Europe (Normandy to Baltic), 1944-45, 1945-51, 1960-62, 1967-69; Korea 1952 (Adj), served Middle East 1954 and 1964-67, Mil Asst to Vice Chief of Defence Staff 1962-64, chm 5 Royal Inniskilling Dragoon Gds 1965-67, Asst Mil Sec to C-in-C BAOR 1967-69, Cdr RAC Centre 1969-72, Cdr Br Army Staff 1972-75, Mil Attaché Br Embassy Washington USA 1972-75, GOC NE Dist 1976-80, psc 1956, jssc 1960, RCDS 1972; head Centre for Industl and Educnl Liaison W and N Yorks 1980-87, sec St William's Fndn 1987-, dir Transpennine 1988-; chm: Bradford and W Yorks BIM 1982-84, RSA (Yorks Region) 1984-, N Yorks Scout Cncl 1984-, 5 Royal Inniskilling Dragoon Gds Assoc 1979-; pres Royal Soc of St George (York and Humberside) 1986-88; memb: York Area Mental Health Appeals Ctee 1984-, TA and VR Assoc 1982-, Yorks Agric Soc 1980-; Vice Lord Lieut N Yorks 1986-; memb Merchants of the Staple of England 1982-; Hon DLitt Univ of Bradford 1988; FBIM 1980, FRSA 1981; Order of Leopold 2 Class (1966); *Books* Change and Challenge - History of the 5th, Iniskilling Dragoon Guards (with Gen Sir Cecil Blacker, 1976); *Recreations* gardening, foot follower (hunting), military history; *Clubs* Cavalry and Guards, Ends of the Earth; *Style*— Maj Gen Henry Woods, CB, MBE, MC, DL; Grafton House, Tockwith, York YO5 8PY (☎ 0423 358735); St William's Foundation, 5 College Street, York YO1 2JF (☎ 0904 642744)

WOODS, Humphrey Martin; s of Rev Howard Charles Woods, of Flat 19, Manormead, Tilford Rd, Hindhead, Surrey, and Kathleen Ailsie Clutton *née* Baker; descendant of the philosopher John Locke; *b* 23 Nov 1937; *Educ* Lancing Coll, Sussex Trinity Coll Oxford (BA); *m* 1, 4 May 1963, Dona Leslie; m 2, 25 Jan 1977, Jennifer Mary, da of Brig Edward Hayden Tinker, of 3 Ferguson Ave, Westshore, Near Napier, NZ; 2 da (Eleanor b 1977, Lucy b 1979), 3 s (Mark b 1981, Leo b 1984, Dominic b 1963); *Career* archaeologist with the Historic Bldgs & Monuments Commn for England (English Heritage formerly the Directorate of Ancient Monuments & Historic Bldgs of the Dept of the Environment) since 1974; *Publications* Excavations on the Second Site of The Dominican Priory, Oxford, in Oxoniensia Vol XLI (1976), The Despoliation of the Abbey of Sts Peter and Paul and St Augustine Between the Years 1542 and 1793, in Historical Essays in memory of James Hobbs (1980), The Completion of the Abbey Church of St Peter, St Paul and St Augustine, Canterbury, By Abbots Wido and Hugh of Fleury, in Br Archaeological Assoc Conference Transactions (1982), Excavations at Eltham Palace 1975-79, in Transactions of the London and Middlx Archaeological Soc (1982), Excavations on the Site of the Dominican Friary at Guildford in 1974 and 1978, Research Volume Number 9 of the Surrey Archaeological Soc (1984), Excavations at Wenlock Priory 1981-86, Journal Br Archaeological Assoc (1987), St Augustine's Abbey, report on excavations 1960-78, Kent Archaeological Soc Monograph Series Vol IV (1988), Romanesque West Front at The Holy Trinity Muchwenlock in transactions of Shropshire Archaeological Soc 1989; *Recreations* walking in the Quantock hills, natural history; *Style*— Humphrey Woods, Esq; 20 Wembdon Hill, Bridgwater, Somerset TA6 7PX (☎ 0278 423 955); Historic Building & Monuments Commission for England, Fortress House 23 Savile Row, London W1

WOODS, Hon Mrs; Hon Isobel Ann; *née* Byron; o child of 11 Baron Byron (d 1983), and Pauline, Baroness Byron, *qv*; *b* 23 May 1932; *Educ* St Mary's Cofe Girls' Sch; *m* 1, 1951, Robert Reford Corr (d 1980); 2 s (John b 1953, Anthony b 1956), 1 da (Helen-Jane b 1961); m 2, 1983, Norman James Woods, s of late James Park Woods, VC; *Style*— The Hon Mrs Woods; 55A Mayfair St, Mount Claremont, W Australia

WOODS, Dr John David; s of Ronald Ernest Goff Woods (d 1968), and Ethel Marjorie Woods; *b* 26 Oct 1939; *Educ* Imperial Coll Univ of London (BSc, PhD, DIC); *m* 7 April 1971, Irina Christine Alix, da of Bernd von Arnim; 1 s (Alexander Jan Roland b 1975), 1 da (Virginia Elizabeth Marina b 1980); *Career* res fell Meteorological Off 1966-72, prof of physical oceanography Univ of Southampton 1972-77, prof of oceanography Univ of Kiel and dir Institut Fuer Meereskunde Universitaet Kiel 1977-86, dir of marine sciences NERC 1986-; memb: NERC 1979-82, Robert Hooke Inst Univ of Oxford 1986-, Meteorological Res Ctee 1976-77 and 1987-; contributed papers on oceanography and meteorology to various learned jls; Hon DSc Univ of Liège 1980; ARCS 1961, FRGS 1966, FRMeteorogical Soc 1967; *Books* Underwater Science (1971), Underwater Research (1976); *Recreations* underwater swimming, history; *Style*— Dr John Woods; 30 Feilden Grove, Oxford (☎ 0865 69342); NERC, Polaris House, Swindon (☎ 0793 411637, fax 0793 411502, telex 444293 ENVRE G); Hooke Institute, Clarendon Laboratory, Oxford (☎ 0865 272 093)

WOODS, (Harold) Joseph; s of Joseph Harold Woods (d 1951), and Margaret Esther, *née* Jones (d 1952); *b* 12 Sept 1908; *Educ* Birkenhead Sch, Liverpool Univ (Dip Arch); *m* 30 Sept 1939, Dorothy Eileen, da of Roland Williams (d 1929); *Career* architect SW Regnl Hosp Bd 1963-73; major designs and contracts inc: 1st and 2nd phases Gloucester Royal Hosp, 1st and 2nd phases Barnstaple Hosp, 1st phase Derriford Hosp; pres Bristol Soc of Architects 1971; memb: Bath Preservation Tst, CPRE, Nat Tst (Bath Gp) Friends of Bristol Univ Botanic Gdn; RHS, hon assoc Landscape Inst 1983; ARIBA 1931; *Recreations* travel, gardening, horticulture, environmental education, the arts, ballet; *Style*— H Joseph Woods, Esq; Springfield Barn, Upton Cheyney, Bitton, Bristol BS15 6LY (☎ 0272 322129)

WOODS, Michael John; s of Dr L H Woods, and Margery, *née* Pickard; *Educ* Bradfield; *m* 15 Jan 1966, Carolyn Rosemary, da of William Tadman, of Tracey Hill Cottage, Roborough, nr Winkleigh, Nth Devon; 1 s (Nicholas John b 13 Aug 1967), 1

da (Jennifer Sarah Rosemary b 29 May 1969); *Career* Nat Serv 1 Bn Royal Fus (serv Suez Crisis) 1955-77; trainee exec Mecca Ltd 1957-63; dir: Silver Blades Ice Rink Ltd 1963-70, Mecca Catering 1968-, Mecca Leisure Ltd 1973-; asst md: Mecca Bingo Social Clubs 1972-80, Mecca Leisure Ltd 1979-85; chm: Ison Brothers (Newcastle) Ltd 1983-85, Pointer Motor Co 1983-85, Scottish Automatic Printing 1983-85; md Mecca Leisure Speciality Catering Div 1985-; vice-pres Variety Club of GB; co chm: Sunshine Coachers, Electric Wheelchairs; memb Confrérie de la Chaîne des Rôtisseurs; FInstD 1965; *Recreations* squash, swimming, shooting (Clay and Pheasant), fishing; *Style—* Michael Woods, Esq; Glendale, Farley Gn, Albury, Nr Guildford, Surrey (☎ 048641 2472); Mecca Leisure Ltd, 6 Hanover St, London W1 (☎ 01 491 7341, fax 01 629 4623, car 0860 524022, telex 261448)

WOODS, Rt Rev Robert (Robin) Wilmer; KCMG (1980), KCVO (1971); s of Rt Rev Edward Sydney Woods (d 1953), Bishop of Lichfield, and Clemence Rachel, 2 da of Robert Barclay, JP; *b* 15 Feb 1914; *Educ* Gresham's, Trinity Coll Cambridge; *m* 1942, Henrietta Marion, JP (1966), da of late Kenneth H Wilson, OBE, JP 2 s, 3 da; *Career* ordained priest 1939; army chaplain 1943-46; Vicar of S Wigston 1946-51; Archdeacon: Singapore 1951-58, Sheffield 1958-62; Dean of Windsor, Chaplain to HM The Queen and Register Most Noble Order of the Garter 1962-71; Bishop of Worcester 1971-81; Prelate Order of St Michael and St George 1971-89; asst bishop Diocese of Gloucester 1982; dir of Christian Aid 1969; *Books* Autobiography (1986); *Clubs* Brooks's; *Style—* The Rt Rev Robin Woods, KCMG, KCVO; Torsend House, Tirley, Glos GL19 4EU

WOODS, Robert Carr; s of Percy Charles Woods (d 1969), of Hookwood, Fittleworth, W Sussex, and Janet Woods, *née* Witney; *b* 25 Nov 1930; *Educ* Rugby, Trinity Hall Camb; *m* 20 Oct 1956, Sonia May, da of Thomas Guichard Savill (d 1984), of 20 Marine Point, Worthing, Sussex; 2 s (Richard b 1958, Nicholas b 1961) 1 da (Sally b 1963); *Career* 2 Lieut RA; 3 RHA Regt, Lieut Bucks Yeo (TA); md Woods and Maslen Ltd, dir Jardine Thompson Graham Ltd; memb of Lloyds 1955 (memb Lloyds Brokers Ctee 1983-86, chm Lloyds Brokers Motor Sub Ctee 1986; gen cmmnr of Taxes); *Recreations* bird watching, photography, art, conversation, gardening, cars; *Clubs* City of London; *Style—* Robert Woods, Esq; 19 Eastcheap, London EC3M 1HJ

WOODS, Stephen Mallon; s of Alexander Woods (d 1975), and Annie *née* Donnelly; *b* 15 Jan 1930; *Educ* St Mungo's Acad Glasgow, Glasgow Univ (BSc Pharamacy); *m* 8 Feb 1956, Margaret, da of Samuel Trousdale, of 30 Chalmers Ave, Ayr; 3 s (Mark b 1962, Paul b 1968, Alan b 1973), 3 da (Rhona b 1959, Aileen b 1960, Maureen b 1964); *Career* Ayrshire Pharmaceuticals Ltd 1961-, SM Woods (Pharmacy) Ltd 1971-, Ayrshire Off Services Ltd 1968-, Armstrongs Hawich House 1982-; ex-chm drug accounts ctee (Scotland), ex-memb Nat Pharmaceutical Advisory Ctee (Scotland); MPS (chm gen cncl 1977-80); *Recreations* golf, bridge; *Clubs* St Cuthbert Golf, Bruce Bridge; *Style—* Stephen Woods, Esq; 15 Wheatfield Rd, Ayr, Scotland; 18 Fullarton St, Ayr (☎ 0292 610032)

WOODS, Hon Mrs (Susan Lesley); eldest da of 2 Baron Gridley; *b* 1950; *m* 1, 1975 (m dis 1982), John Philip Bruce Scott; 1 s (Edward Harry Gridley b 1977), 1 da (Carrie Ann Elizabeth b 1979); m 2, Andrew Woods; *Style—* The Hon Mrs Woods; 7 West Way, Old Greenwich, Connecticut 06870, USA

WOODS, Hon Mrs; (Victoria Venetia); da of late 5 Baron Stanley of Alderley, KCMG; *b* 1917; *m* 1942, Lt-Cdr James Douglas Woods, Royal Canadian Naval VR; 2 da (Virginia b 1943, Teresa b 1946); *Style—* The Hon Mrs Woods; 31 Boswell Ave, Toronto, Ontario, Canada

WOODTHORPE, Anthony Edmund; s of Edmund Henry Woodthorpe (d 1974), of Braintree, Essex, and Olivia Constance, *née* Austin (d 1980); *b* 30 July 1935; *Educ* Brighton Coll; *m* 4 Oct 1969, Joan Deborah, da of Maj Sidney Francis Clair (d 1964), of Kingswood; 1 s (Nicholas b 1973), 1 da (Catherine b 1970); *Career* CA; sr ptnr Russell Ohly & Co Hove 1985- (ptnr 1968-85); former memb: Brighton and Hove Jr C of C, Hove Round Table; chm Royal Alexandra Hosp for Sick Children Centenary Fund Brighton, memb Rotary Club Hove (pres 1989-90), former tres Rotary Club Hove Housing Soc Ltd; Freeman City of London 1970; FCA 1964; *Recreations* golf, gardening, walking; *Clubs* Sussex YC; *Style—* Anthony Woodthorpe, Esq; Toad Hall, Buckingham Rd, Shoreham-by-Sea, W Sussex BN43 5UD (☎ 0273 461067); 94 Church Rd, Hove, E Sussex BN3 2EF (☎ 0273 778844, fax 0273 25210)

WOODWARD, Hon Mr Justice; Sir (Albert) Edward; OBE (1969); s of Lieut-Gen Sir Eric Winslow Woodward, KCMG, KCVO, CB, CBE, DSO (d 1967); *b* 6 August 1928; *Educ* Melbourne C of E GS, Melbourne Univ (LLM); *m* 1950, Lois, da of Daniel Wrixon Thorpe (d 1976); 1 s, 6 da; *Career* judge: Fed Ct of Aust 1977-, Aust Industrial Ct and Supreme Ct of ACT 1972-; Royal cmmr Aboriginal Land Rights 1973-74, dir-gen of Security 1976-81, head of Royal Cmmn into the Aust Meat Indust 1981-82; chm Cncl: Aust Defence Force Acad 1982-, Camberwell GS 1983-; kt 1982; *see Debrett's Handbook of Australia and New Zealand for further details*; *Style—* The Hon Mr Justice Woodward, OBE; 66 Tivoli Road, South Yarra, Vic 3141, Australia

WOODWARD, John Charles; s of Eric Jackson Woodward (d 1978), of Belper, Derbyshire, and Maude Woodward, *née* Adams; *b* 31 Oct 1935; *Educ* Herbert Strutt GS Belper Derbyshire, Manchester Univ (BSc); *m* 11 Sept 1962, Kathy, da of Harry Ashton (d 1982), of Hazel Grove, Cheshire; 1 s (Giles b 15 Dec 1967) 2 da (Zoë b 14 Sept 1963, Sarah b 5 Jan 1965); *Career* memb London Stock Exchange 1971-75, ptnr Colegrave & Co, investment mangr Reed Int 1975-83, chief exec BA Pensions 1984-; cncl memb Nat Assoc of Pension Funds 1982-(chm investmt ctee 1982-84, chm of Cncl 1987), investmt advsr Cleveland CC 1983-86, dir Nat Freight Corpn Tstees Ltd; FIA 1965, ASIA 1964; *Style—* John Woodward, Esq; Kershaw Hse, Great West Rd, Hounslow, Middx (☎ 01 570 7741)

WOODWARD, Adm Sir John Forster (Sandy); KCB (1982); *b* 1 May 1932; *Educ* RNC Dartmouth; *m* 1960, Charlotte Mary, *née* McMurtrie; 1 s, 1 da; *Career* RN 1946, serv HMS: Maidstone, Sheffield, Zodiac; submarine specialist 1954; served HMS: Sanguine, Porpoise, Tireless 1961-62; Lt Cdr 1962, CO HMS Grampus 1965, 1 Lt HMS Valiant to 1967; Cdr 1967, CO: qualifying course for COs 1967-69, CO HMS Warspite 1969-71; RCDS 1971-72, Capt 1972, Directorate of Naval Plans MOD 1972-74, Capt SM Sea Trg 1974-76, CO HMS Sheffield 1976-78, Dir Naval Plans MOD 1978-81, Rear-Adm 1981, Flag Offr First Flotilla 1981-83, Cmd (from HMS Hermes) S Atlantic Task Gps in Falklands War 1982, Flag Offr Submarines and NATO Cdr Submarines Eastern Atlantic 1983-85, Vice Adm 1984, Dep CDS (Commitments) MOD 1985-87, Adm 198789; C in C Naval Home Cmd 1987, Flag ADC to HM Queen 1987, awarded Seagrave Trophy for outstanding demonstration of tport possibilities by land, sea or water 1982; *Recreations* sailing, golf, bridge, skiing; *Clubs* Royal Yacht Squadron; *Style—* Adm Sir John Woodward, KCB, ADC; Commander-in-Chief Naval Home Command, HM Naval Base, Portsmouth

WOODWARD, Dr Michael Trevor; s of Trevor Woodward, of Weare Giffard Hall, Weare Giffard, N Devon, and Beryl Gladys, *née* Barker; *b* 25 Nov 1957; *Educ* Dartmouth Comprehensive Sch Sandwell, Aberdeen Univ (MA (Hons), PhD); *Career* investment mangr Ivory and Sime plc, Edinburgh 1982-, dir Ivory and Sime Int Ltd 1987-; *Recreations* squash, racketball, golf; *Clubs* Edinburgh Sports; *Style—* Dr Michael Woodward; 11 Castle Terrace, Edinburgh EH1 2DP (☎ 031 229 1229); One Charlotte Sq, Edinburgh EH2 4DZ (☎ 031 225 1357)

WOODWARD, William (Bill) Charles; QC (1985); s of Wilfred Charles Woodward, of Nottingham, and Annie Stewart, *née* Young; *b* 27 May 1940; *Educ* South County Jnr Sch, Nottingham HS, St John's Coll Oxford (BA); *m* 1965, Carolyn Edna, da of Francis Edward Doughty Johns, of Kent; 2 s (William b 1968, Fergus b 1974), 1 da (Rebecca b 1966); *Career* barr, Inner Temple 1964; memb Midland and Oxford Circuit, Marshall to late Sir Donald Finnemore; head of chambers 1987-; Nottingham Univ Law Advsy Ctee; *Recreations* sporadic cookery, swimming, gardening; *Clubs* Pre-War Austin Seven; *Style—* Bill Woodward, Esq, QC; 24 The Ropewalk, Nottingham (☎ 0602 472581)

WOOF, Richard Austin; s of Richard Woof (d 1983), of Launceston, Tasmania, Australia, and Avril Frances Chandler Hopkinson, *née* Clark (d 1984); *b* 14 June 1940; *Educ* Kings Coll Taunton; *m* 17 June 1961, Christine Julia, da of Arthur Seymour Hodgkinson (d 1978), of Devon; 1 s (Julian b 1961), 1 da (Caroline b 1972); *Career* slr, sr ptnr Debenham & Co 1974, commercial property editor The Law Soc Gazette 1975-; dir: CPV Ltd 1983-, Caribeach (St Lucia) Ltd 1985-; *Recreations* carriage driving, quarter horse racing; *Style—* Richard A Woof, Esq; Gorebridge House, Loxhill, Nr Godalming, Surrey GU8 4BH; Debenham & Co, 20 Hans Rd, Knightsbridge, London SW3 1RT (☎ 01 581 2471, telex 8954701, fax 01 584 1783)

WOOLDRIDGE, Frank Douglas; s of Frank Wooldridge (d 1956), of London, and Mary Margaret, *née* Douglas (d 1962); *b* 2 Mar 1916; *Educ* Colfes' Sch London, Coll of Estate Mgmnt; *m* 15 Nov 1941, Elizabeth Julia, da of Engr Capt John Edmund Moloney (d 1972), of Falmouth, Cornwall; 1 s (John b 1943), 1 da (Anne b 1947); *Career* jnd TA 1938; WWII 1939-46, Maj RE served India (SO Grade II Command HQ Agra 1942-45); princ in private practice joined by son 1968; conslt John Wooldridge & Ptnrs 1988-; memb of Common Cncl City of London 1988-; Freeman City of London 1965, Liveryman Worshipful Co of Cutlers 1966; ARICS 1939; *Recreations* sailing, appreciation of music; *Clubs* City Livery (asst hon sec), REYC, Medway YC; *Style—* Frank Wooldridge, Esq; 3 Harton Close, Bromley, Kent (☎ 01 290 1466); Bridge House, 181 Queen Victoria St, London EC4 (☎ 01 248 8796, fax 01 248 1106)

WOOLDRIDGE, Susan Margot; da of John De Lacy Wooldridge DSO, DFC, DFM (d 1958), and Margaretta, *née* Scott; *Educ* Convent of the Holy Child Jesus London, More House London, Central Sch of Speech and Drama London, Ecole Jacques Lecoq Paris; *Career* actress; theatre inc: Night Mother, Look Back in Anger, Ubu Roi, Dusa Fish Stas and Vi, The Cherry Orchard, School for Scandal, The Merchant of Venice, Tartuffe, Hayfever; films inc: How to Get Ahead in Advertising, Hope and Glory (BAFTA award, best supporting actress), Loyalties, Butley, The Shout, Dead Man's Folly, Frankenstein; tv inc: The Jewel in the Crown (ALVA award, best actress, also BAFTA nomination best actress), The Dark Room, The Devil's Disciple, Time and the Conways, Hay Fever, John MacNab, Ticket to Ride, The Small Assassin, Pastoral Care, The Last Place on Earth, Tickle on the Turn, The Naked Civil Servant, Rep (comedy series), The Racing Game; *Style—* Miss Susan Wooldridge; Plant and Froggatt Ltd, Julian House, 4 Windmill St, London W1 (☎ 01 636 4412)

WOOLF, David; s of Raymond Woolf, of London, and Valerie Belle, *née* Robins (d 1954); *b* 27 Jan 1945; *Educ* Clifton; *m* 19 June 1977, Vivienne Barbara, da of Lt Col David Perk, of Johanesburg; 2 s (James b 1979, John b 1982); *Career* trainee Keyser Ullman 1963-64, accountant Chalmers Imperial 1965-69, PA Corob Hldgs 1969-71, chief exec City Grove plc 1971-; FCA 1969; *Recreations* sailing, tennis, opera; *Clubs* Royal Lymington YC, Vanderbilt; *Style—* David Woolf, Esq; Citygrove plc, 77 South Audley St, London W1, (☎ 01 493 4007, fax 01 409 3515, telex 269918 CITY GG)

WOOLF, Dr Douglad Langton; s of Dr Abraham David Woolf (d 1961), and Celia, *née* Rutkowski (d 1976); *b* 20 Sept 1919; *Educ* St Aubyns Sch, Grocers Co Sch; *m* 1946, Kathorn Beth Pearce, da of Thomas Pearce (d 1948), of Melbourne; 1 s (Anthony b 1951), 1 da (Valerie b 1948); *Career* Mil Serv RAMC (capt) 1947-49; HS London Hosp 1945-46, 2nd sr Registrar (depth physical medicine-rheumatology) Middx Hosp 1949-53, cnslt physician rheumatology Willesden Gen Hosp 1952-84, conslt rheumatologist Waltham Forest Health Authy 1953-84 (hon cnslt 1984-); med dir and cnslt rheumatologist The Horder Centre for Arthritics 1982-; memb Attendance Allowance Bd Dept of Health, hon chm Arthritis Care 1982-88 (chm Welfare Ctee and memb exec ctee 1954-), vice pres League of Friends London Hosp 1986; hon memb Br Soc for Rheumatology, hon fell Hunterian Soc (pres 1979-80, Hunterian Orator 1986); FRSM FMS fell Harveian Soc fell Zoological Soc of London; Liveryman Soc of Apothecaries; *Books* guest editor Clinics in Rheumatic Diseases, author of num articles on rheumatism and arthritis, hon editor Hunterian soc transition, past ed Rheumatology and Rehabilitation; *Recreations* gardening, antiques; *Style—* Dr Douglas Woolf, Esq; 2 The Green, Woodford, Essex (☎ 01 504 8877); 2 Harley St, W1 (☎ 01 580 1199)

WOOLF, Rt Hon Lord Justice; Rt Hon Sir Harry Kenneth Woolf; PC (1986); s of Alexander Woolf and Leah, *née* Cussins; *b* 2 May 1933; *Educ* Fettes, UCL (LLB); *m* 1961, Marguerite, da of George Sassoon; 3 s; *Career* Nat Service cmmnd 15/19 Royal Hussars 1954, Capt Army Legal Service 1955; barr Inner Temple 1954, Crown Ct recorder 1972-79, jr counsel Inland Revenue 1973-74, first Treasury jr counsel Common Law 1974-79, high ct judge (Queen's Bench) 1979-86, presiding judge SE Circuit 1981-84, lord justice of appeal 1986-, memb Senate of Bar and Bench 1981-85; chm Accommodation Ctee 1981-85, chm Lord Chancellors Advisory Ctee on Legal Education, 1987-, Middx Justices Advisory Ctee 1987-, pres Management Cmmttee of Inst of Advanced Legal Studies 1986-, Law Teachers Assoc 1985-, Jt Ctee for Jewish Social Services 1988-, W London Magistrates Assoc 1987-, govr Oxford Centre for Hebrew Studies 1988-, hon memb Pub Soc of Teachers of law 1988-; fell UCL 1981; kt 1979; *Clubs* Garrick; *Style—* The Rt Hon Lord Justice Woolf; Royal Courts of Justice, Strand, London WC2 (☎ 01 936 6000)

WOOLF, Sir John; s of late Charles M Woolf, and Vera Woolf; *Educ* Institut Montana Switzerland; *m* 1955, Ann, da of late Victor Saville; 2 s; *Career* WW II, Lt Col, asst dir Army Kinematography War Office 1944-45; film and television prodr; chm: Romulus Films Ltd, British & American Film Holdings plc; dir: Anglia TV Gp plc 1958-83, First Leisure Corpn plc; tstee and memb exec cncl Cinema & TV Benevolent Fund; memb: Cinematograph Films Cncl 1969-79, bd of govrs Services Sound & Vision Corpn (formerly Services Kinema Corpn) 1974-83; awards include: British Film Acad best film of 1958 (Room at the Top), Oscar and Golden Globe best film of 1969 (Oliver!); special awards for contribution to Br Film indust: Cinematograph Exhibitors Assoc 1969, Variety Club of GB 1974; Freeman City of London; FRSA 1975; Bronze Star (USA); kt 1975; *Films include* The African Queen, Pandora and The Flying Dutchman, Moulin Rouge, I Am a Camera, Carrington VC, Room At The Top, Beat the Devil, The L-Shaped Room, Life At The Top, Oliver!, Day Of The Jackal, The Odessa File; *TV productions include* (for Anglia TV) Miss Morison's Ghosts, The Kingfisher, Edwin, Love Song, 10 series of Tales of the Unexpected; *Style*— Sir John Woolf; office: Suites 2, 3 & 4, The Chambers, Chelsea Harbour, London SW10 (telex 24479)

WOOLF, John Moss; CB (1975); s of Alfred Woolf (d 1971), and Maud Woolf (d 1979); *b* 5 June 1918; *Educ* Drayton Manor Sch; *m* 1940, Phyllis Ada Mary, da of Thomas Albert Johnson (d 1937); 1 da (Stephanie); *Career* barr 1948; rep Civil Serv Nat Whitley Cncl (Staff Side) 1953-55, exec Ctee memb Assoc of First Div Civil Servants 1950-58 and 1961-65 (chm 1955-58 and 1964-65), chm Valuation Ctee Customs Co-op Cncl Brussels 1964-65, under-sec Nat Bd for Prices and Incomes 1967 (sec 1965), asst under-sec of State Dept of Employment and Productivity 1968-70, advsr on price problems to Govt of Trinidad and Tobago 1969, cmmr HM Customs and Excise 1970 (dep chm bd 1973-78), dir gen Customs and Establishments 1973-78 (asst sec 1960, dir 1971-73); overseas advsr Central Electricity Generating Bd 1979-82; leader Review Team to examine responsibilities of the Directors of the Nat Museums and Galleries 1978-79, review of Orgn and Procedures of Chancery Div of High Ct 1979-80; Commandeur d'Honneur Ordre du Bontemps de Médoc et des Graves 1973, hon Borgenerális (Hungary) 1974; *Books* Report on Control of Prices in Trinidad and Tobago (with MM Eccleshall 1968), Report of the Review Body on the Chancery Divison of the High Court (with Lord Oliver 1981); *Recreations* gardening, wine, reading; *Clubs* Civil Service; *Style*— J M Woolf Esq, CB; West Lodge, 113 Marsh Lane, Middlesex HA7 4TH (☎ 01 952 1373)

WOOLF, (John) Nicholas; s of Adrian Jack Woolf, of Hampton, Middlesex, and Lesley Clare, *née* Freeman (d 1980); *b* 7 Sept 1946; *Educ* Hampton Sch, LSE (BSc); *m* 21 Aug 1971, Margaret Anne (d 1988), da of Edward Beal (d 1988); 1 s (Christopher b 1977), 1 da (Elizabeth b 1973); *Career* Arthur Andersen & Co 1968 (ptnr 1979); FCA 1971, FTII 1972, memb: Inst of Petroleum 1987; *Recreations* golf, squash, tennis; *Clubs* RAC; *Style*— Nicholas Woolf, Esq; 1 Surrey St, London WC2R 2PS (☎ 01 836 1200, fax 01 831 1133)

WOOLFORD, Harry Russell Halkerston; OBE (1970); s of Henry Woolford (d 1941); *b* 23 May 1905; *Educ* Roy Scottish Acad, Edinburgh Coll of Art, Carnegie Travelling Scholarship 1928; *m* 1932, Agnes Henderson, *née* Philip; 1 da; *Career* supervisor of the evacuation and conservation of The Nat Galleries of Scotland 1940, chief restorer to 1970, ret; freelance picture conservation conslt; life fell Museums Assoc, fell Int Inst for Conservation of Historic and Artistic Works, hon MA Dundee Univ 1975, hon memb Assoc of Br Picture Restorers 1970; *Clubs* Scottish Arts; *Style*— Harry Woolford Esq, OBE; Dean Park House, Golf Course Rd, Bonnyrigg, Midlothian EH19 2EV (☎ 031 663 7949)

WOOLFSON, Dr Gerald; s of late Joseph Samuel and Lilian Woolfson; *b* 25 Mar 1932; *Educ* Milton Sch Buelawayo and Zimbabwe, Capetown Univ (MB, 1954); *m* 1, 1955, Sheila Charlaff; 3 s (David b 1955, Adrian b 1965, Alexander b 1978), 1 da (Karen b 1959); m 2, 1980, Lynne Silver; *Career* consultant psychiatrist, The Hammersmith and St Marys Hosp Gp; hon sr lectr Royal Postgrad Medical Sch, London Univ; FRSM; *Recreations* chess, doodling; *Style*— Dr Gerald Woolfson, Esq; 56 Redington Rd, London NW3 (☎ (01) 794 1974); 97 Harley St, London W1 1DF (☎ (01) 794 1974)

WOOLFSON, Prof Michael Mark; s of Maurice Woolfson (d 1956), of 218 Lea View House, Springfield, London E5, and Rose, *née* Solomons; *b* 9 Jan 1927; *Educ* Wellingborough GS, Jesus Coll (BA, MA), UMIST (PhD DSc); *m* 19 July 1951, Margaret, da of Dr Mayer Frohlich; 2 s (Mark b 1954, Malcolm b 1957), 1 da (Susan b 1960); *Career* HG 7 Northants Bn 1942-44, Nat Serv cmmnd 2 Lt RE 1947-49; res asst Cavendish Laboratory Cambridge 1952-54, ICI res fell Cambridge 1954-55, reader in physics UMIST 1961-65 (lectr 1953-61), prof of theoretical physics Univ of York 1965-; pres: Yorks Philosophical Soc, York Astronomical Soc; govr York Coll of Arts and Technol; FIP, FRAS, FRS, Br Crystallographic Assoc (pres); *Books* Direct Methods in Crystallography (1961), An Introduction to X-Ray Crystallography (1970); *Recreations* gardening, winemaking; *Style*— Prof Michael Woofson; 124 Wigton Lane, Leeds, W Yorks LS17 8RZ (☎ 0532 687 890); Department of Physics, University of York, York, N Yorks Y01 5DD (☎ 0904 432230)

WOOLLAM, John Victor; s of Thomas Alfred Woollam and Edie Moss Woollam; *b* 14 August 1927; *Educ* Univ of Liverpool; *m* 1964, Lavinia Rosamond Ela, da of S R E Snow; 2 s; *Career* barr Inner Temple 1952; MP (Con) W Derby 1954-64, parly private sec to Min of Labour 1960-62; *Recreations* philately; *Style*— John Woollam Esq; Naishes Farm, Danes Hill, Dalwood, Axminster, E Devon EX13 7HB (☎ 0297 33516)

WOOLLARD, Kenneth David; s of Harry Woollard, of Clare, Suffolk and Bush Hill Park Middx, and Florence Jane, *née* Shore (d 1983); m desc of John Shore of Meersbrook Park, fdr of Shore's Bank, Sheffield; *see* Burkes Landed Gentry 1937 under Nightingale (William Shore assumed Nightingale surname and f of Florence, Order of Merit; b 20 Nov 1930; *b* 20 Nov 1980; *Educ* Tottenham Tech Coll; *m* 19 Feb 1955, Edna May, da of Frank Stallwood (d 1976), of London; 2 s (David b 1960, Peter b 1963), 1 da (Karen b 1963); *Career* Nat Serv RAOC N Africa 1948-50; commercial and mktg career elec engrg; regnl mangr, conslt and sales mangr int projects and telecommunications 1959-88; MInstM; *Recreations* sailing; *Style*— Kenneth D Woollard, Esq; 6 Langham Close, Marshalswick, St Albans, Herts AL4 9TH (☎ 0727 36861)

WOOLLCOMBE, Victor Rupert DeAmbrosis; s of Maj Frank Rupert Woollcombe MC (d 1968), of Bere Alston, Devon, and Beatrice Elena Alice Woollcombe *née* DeAmbrosis (d 1974); *b* 9 July 1921; *Educ* Sherborne Sch, Magdalene Coll, Cambridge (MA); *m* 12 June 1947, Elisabeth Hume, da of Wilson Harvey (d 1954), of Mount Hamilton, Auchincruive, by Ayr, Ayrshire; 2 s (David b 1950, John b 1959), 2 da (Rosanna b 1948, Katharine b 1954); *Career* Capt RA, N Africa and Italy (wounded); slr; sr ptnr Walker Martineau & Co, 10/11 Grays Inn Sq, London 1969-87; dir Lanhydrock Estate Co 1969, Pentewan Sands Ltd 1972, Southwick & Roche Ct Estates Co 1974, lay reader; *Style*— Rupert Woollcombe, Esq; Little Maltings, Malting Lane, Much Hadham, Herts SG10 6AW (☎ 027 984 2414); Elleric Cottage, Fasnacloich; Appin; Argyllshire PA38 4BJ (☎ 063 173 395)

WOOLLETT, Maj-Gen John Castle; CBE (1957), OBE (1955, MC 1945); o s of John Castle Woollett (d 1921), and Lily Bradley Woollett (d 1964); *b* 5 Nov 1915; *Educ* St Benedict's Sch, RMA Woolwich, St John's Coll Cambridge; *m* 1, 1941, (m dis 1957) Joan Eileen, *née* Stranks; 2 s (1 s decd); m 2, 1959, Helen Wendy, *née* Braithwaite; 2 step s; *Career* cmmnd RE 1935, served 1939-45 and Korea, Maj-Gen, chief engr BAOR 1967-70 (ret), Col Cmdt RE 1973-78, princ planning inspr DOE 1975-81; *Recreations* cruising, shooting, sailing (yacht 'Cymbeline'); *Clubs* Army & Navy, Royal Cruising, Royal Engineers Yacht, Royal Ocean Racing, Royal Lymington Yacht, Island Sailing (Cowes); *Style*— Maj-Gen John Woollett CBE, OBE, MC; 42 Rhinefield Close, Brockenhurst, Hants (☎ 0590 22417)

WOOLLEY, Hon David Jeffs; 3 s of Baron Woolley, CBE, DL (Life Peer, d 1986), and his 1 w, Martha Annie, *née* Jeffs (d 1936); bro Hans Peter, Harold Grahem *qv*; *b* 11 Jan 1934; *Educ* Dauntsey's Sch, Seale Hayne Agric Coll; *m* 26 April 1958, Freda Constance, da of late Alfred William Smith Walker, of Barrow-in-Furness; 2 s, 1 da; *Career* Captain, Air Canada; *Style*— The Hon David Woolley; Fernhill Farm, 4222 - 216 Street, RR 14, Langley, British Columbia V3A 7R2

WOOLLEY, David Rorie; s of Albert Walter Woolley, of Wallingford, Oxon, and Ethel Rorie *née* Linn; *b* 9 June 1939; *Educ* Winchester Coll, Trinity Hall Cambridge (Hons Law); *Career* barr Middle Temple 1962; QC 1980, recorder Crown Court 1983, inspector Dept of Environment Inquiry into Nat Gallery 1984; *publications* Town Hall and the Property Owner (1965); *Recreations* opera, real tennis, mountaineering; *Clubs* MCC, Oxford and Cambridge; *Style*— David Woolley, Esq; Buckland, Oxfordshire; 2 Mitre Court Building, Temple, London EC4Y 7BX (☎ 01 583 1355)

WOOLLEY, Hon (William) Graham; s of Baron Woolley, CBE, DL; *b* 27 Oct 1927,bro Hons David, Peter, Harold *qqqv*;; *Educ* Wrekin Coll; *m* 1, 1955, Joan (d 1974), da of Ralph Rowlands, of Flint; 2 s, 1 da; m 2, 1984, Shirley Ann, da of Thomas William James, LEGA, mangr Bulolo Papua New Guinea; *Style*— The Hon Graham Woolley; Hatton Hall, Hatton Heath, Cheshire CH3 9AP

WOOLLEY, Hon Harold Ewart; 2 s of Baron Woolley, CBE, DL; *b* 10 July 1929,bro Hons Peter, David Graham, *qqv*;; *Educ* Woodhouse Grove Sch Yorks, UBC; *m* 1954, Margaret, da of Alderman Thomas Bennett, JP, of Worcester; 1 s, 2 da; *Career* MD, FRCS; *Style*— The Hon Harold Woolley; 1350 Laurier Ave, Vancouver, British Columbia, Canada

WOOLLEY, Hon Peter Jeffs; 4 s of Baron Woolley, CBE, DL; *b* 11 Jan 1934,bro Hons Harold, David Graham, *qqv*;; *Educ* Dauntsey's Sch, Trinity Hall Cambridge; *m* 1960, Lois, da of Edward Chanter; 3 da; *Career* Ch A; *Style*— The Hon Peter Woolley; 2660 Queens Ave, W Vancouver, British Columbia, Canada

WOOLLEY, His Hon Judge Roy Gilbert; s of John Woolley (d 1974), and Edith Mary, *née* Holt (d 1958); *b* 28 Nov 1922; *Educ* Deeside, UCL (LLB); *m* 1953, Doreen, da of Humphrey Morris Farmer (d 1967); 2 s (Christopher, Peter), 2 da (Julie, Carolyn); *Career* served WWII Flying Offr RAF Coastal Cmd 1942-45; barr Lincoln's Inn, recorder 1975-76, circuit judge 1976-; reader dioceses of: St Asoph Chester, Lichfield 1975-; *Recreations* reading, music, art, antiques; *Style*— His Hon Judge Woolley; Henlle Hall, Gobowen, Oswestry, Shropshire SY10 7AX (☎ 0691 661257)

WOOLMER, Ken(neth) John; MP (L) Batley and Morley 1979-; s of Joseph William Woolmer (d 1979) and Gertrude May; *b* 25 April 1940; *Educ* Kettering GS, Leeds Univ; *m* 1961, Janice, *née* Chambers; 3 s; *Career* oppn front bench spokesman Trade Prices & Consumer Protection 1981-; cncllr Leeds CC 1970-78, W Yorks Metropolitan CC 1973-80, leader of opposition 1977-79; lecturer in economics Leeds Univ 1963-66 & 1968-79, 1983-; Ahmadu Bello Univ Nigeria 1966-68), previously research fellow Univ of West Indies & secondary school teacher in London; *Recreations* football, cricket, walking; *Style*— Ken Woolmer Esq, MP; House of Commons, SW1A 0AA

WOOLNOUGH, Lieut-Col George Frederick; MC (1943); s of Frederick George Woolwough (d 1934), and Caroline Noel, *née* Isles (d 1982); *b* 7 Dec 1914; *Educ* Bishop Wordsworth's Sch, Salisbury, RMC Sandhurst; *Career* cmmnd Wilts Regt 1935; served Palestine 1936-37, BEF France and Belgium 1939-40, Sicily and Italy 1943-44, Germany 1945; cmd 1 Bn Wilts Regt 1958-59 and on amalgamation 1 Bn Duke of Edinburgh's Royal Regt 1959-60; ret 1965; sec Friends of Salisbury Cathedral, area cmmr St John Ambulance Bde; *Style*— Lt-Col George F Woolnough, MC; The Cross, Middle Woodford, Salisbury, Wiltshire (☎ 072 273 304)

WOOLTON, 3 Earl of (UK 1956); Simon Frederick Marquis; also Baron Woolton (UK 1939), Viscount Woolton (UK 1952), and Viscount Walberton (UK 1956); s of 2 Earl of Woolton (d 1969, s of 1 Earl of Woolton, CH, PC, JP, DL, sometime chm of Lewis's Investmt Tst and Associated cos, min of Food 1940-43, min of Reconstruction 1943-45, lord pres of the cncl 1945 and 1951-52, Chllr of Duchy of Lancaster 1952-55, chm of Cons Pty 1946-55) by his 2 w (Cecily) Josephine, er da Sir Alastair Penrose Gordon-Cumming 5 Bt (now Countess Lloyd George of Dwyfor *qv*); *b* 24 May 1958; *Educ* Eton, St Andrews Univ (MA); *m* 30 April 1987, Hon Sophie, o da 3 Baron Birdwood *qv* merchant banker S G Warburg & Co Ltd 1982-88; *Heir* none; *Clubs* Royal and Ancient (St Andrews), New (Edinburgh), White's, Turf, Brooks's; *Style*— The Rt Hon the Earl of Woolton; Glenogil, by Forfar, Angus (☎ 03565 226)

WOOTTON, Anthony; s of Albert George Wootton, of 64, Whaddon Chase, Aylesbury, Bucks, and Marion, *née* Ibbotson (d 1973); *b* 11 August 1935; *Educ* Aylesbury GS, London Univ (external student); *Career* freelance writer, artist, photographer, lectr; author of 20 books; *Books* Discovering Garden Insects and Other Invertbrates (1975), Insects are Animals Too (1978), Spotter's Guide to Insects (1979), Insects of the World (1985), Animal Folklore, Myth and Legend (1986); *Recreations* walking, drawing, photography, reading, looking at insects and other small organisms, etymology, mystical reflection, numismatics, folklore (esp of animals); *Style*— Anthony Wootton, Esq; 40 Roundhill, Stone, nr Aylesbury, Bucks HP17 8RD (☎ 0296 748768)

WOOTTON, Frank A A; *b* 30 July 1914; *Educ* Eastbourne Coll of Art; *m* Virginia Ann; 1 s (Leigh Antony b March 1959), 1 da (Tracy Ann b Feb 1963); *Career* official war artist RAF 1939-36; artist; exhibitions: Ackermanns Gallery London 1964, Stacy-Marks Gallery Eastbourne 1965, Incurable Collector Gallery NY 1969, Horse Artists of the world Tryon Gallery London 1969, Tryon Gallery London 1974, Smithsonian Inst Nat Air and Space Museum USA 1983-84, EAA Museum Oshkosh Wisconsin; C P Robertson Trophy Air Miny 1979, Royal Aero Club Silver Medal 1985; companion Royal Aeronautical Soc 1985, Freeman Guild of Air Pilots and Air Navigators 1987, pres Guild of Aviation Artists 1970-88; *Books* How to Draw Aircraft 1940, How to Draw Cars 1949, The Aviation Art of Frank Wootton, At Home in the Sky; *Clubs* RAF; *Style—* Frank Wootton, Esq; Mayflower House, Alfriston, Sussex BN26 5QT (☎ 0323 870 343)

WOOTTON-WOOLLEY, (Charles) Derek; CBE (1971), MM; s of Henry Charles Wootton-Woolley (d 1971), of Hove, and Harriet, *née* Grisdale (d 1960); *b* 22 Jan 1921; *Educ* Haileybury; *m* 25 Aug 1944, Jacqueline Esther, da of Joseph Edmond Cattaui (d 1983), of Alexandria, Egypt; 1 s (Robin b 1949), 2 da (Jennifer b 1946, Valerie b 1949); *Career* TA 1939, 42 RTR 1939-42 served W Desert (MM 1942), Adj 46 RTR 1943-44; served as Temp Maj: N Africa, Sicily, Italy (despatches 1944), Greece; Br American Tobacco Co: China 1947-50, Brazil 1950-61, London 1962- 64; chm: Nigerian Tobacco Co 1964-71, Blackman Harvey Ltd 1972-88; ret; Freeman City of London 1972, Liveryman Worshipful Co of Basketmakers 1974; Hon LLD Lagos Univ 1969-; *Recreations* golf; *Style—* Derek Wootton-Woolley, Esq, CBE, MM; Orange Ct Farmhouse, Littleton, Guildford, GU3 1HW (☎ 0483 365 46)

WORAM, Terence Annesley; s of Victor Henry Woram (d 1940), and Helena Mary, *née* Cox; *b* 23 June 1933; *Educ* Christian Brothers Coll Kimberley SA, Univ of Capetown SA (BArch); *m* 14 Oct 1961, Patricia Eileen, da of Frederick Leslie Lawrence; 1 s (Michael Desmond b 27 Aug 1962, d 22 May 1980), 3 da (Catherine Ann b 17 Jan 1964, Frances Mary b 21 May 1965, Joanna Helen b 2 may 1967); *Career* Pallet And Price Salisbury Rhodesia SA 1953-56, Harrison and Abramovitz NY 1956-59, Trehearn Norman Preston and Ptnrs London 1960-64; ptnr: BL Adams Partnership London 1964-69, Green Lloyd and Adams London 1969-79-; architechural awards: Richmond Soc 1983, Europa Nostra 1986, Aylesbury Soc 1988; rep cricket: combined SA Univs XI 1955, USA All Stars XI v W Indies 1958; memb York House Soc; RIBA; *Recreations* cricket, travel, old Hollywood films; *Clubs* Richmond, Mddx Cricket Union; *Style—* Terence Woram, Esq; 48 Lebanon Park, Twickenham, Mddx TW1 3DG (☎ 01 892 2634); 52 Lebanon Park, Twickenham, Mddx TW1 3DG (☎ 01 891 6446)

WORCESTER; *see*: Jeffery, Very Rev Robert Martin Colquhoun

WORCESTER, Archdeacon of; *see*: Bentley, The Ven Frank William Henry **Dean of**

WORCESTER, Marquess of; Henry John Fitzroy Somerset; s and h of 11 Duke of Beaufort; *b* 22 May 1952; *Educ* Eton; *m* 13 June 1987, Tracy Louise, the actress, da Hon Peter Ward s of 3 Earl of Dudley; 1 s (Robert, Earl of Glamorgan b 20 Jan 1989); *Heir* s, Earl of Glamorgan; *Style—* Marquess of Worcester; Badminton House, Glos GL9 1DB

WORCESTER, 111 Bishop of 1982-; Rt Rev Philip Harold Ernest Goodrich; patron of sixty-six livings, of seven alternately with others and the Archdeaconries of Dudley and Worcester, and eighteen Hon Canonries. The See was founded by Ethelred of the Mercians in 679; s of Rev Canon Harold Spencer Goodrich and Gertrude Alice Goodrich; *b* 2 Nov 1929; *Educ* Stamford Sch, St John's Coll Cambridge (MA); *m* 1960, Margaret, *née* Bennett; 4 da; *Career* curate Rugby Parish Church 1954-57, chaplain St John's Coll Cambridge 1957-61, rector South Ormsby Gp of Parishes 1961-68, vicar Bromley 1968-73, bishop suffragan Tonbridge 1974-82; *Style—* The Rt Rev the Lord Bishop of Worcester; Bishop's House, Hartlebury Castle, Kidderminster, Worcs DY11 7XX

WORCESTER, Robert Milton; s of late C M Worcester of Kansas City USA and late Violet Ruth; *b* 21 Dec 1933; *Educ* Univ of Kansas (BSc); *m* 1, 1958 (m dis), Joann (*née* Ransdell); 2 s; m 2, 1982, Margaret Noel (*née* Smallbone); *Career* conslt McKinsey & Co 1962-65; controller opinion Research Corp 1965-68, past pres World Assoc for Public Opinion Research; chm and md Market & Opinion Research Int (MORI) Ltd 1973-; memb: World Wildlife Fndn (UK), Scientific Activities Ctee Int, Social Science Consul UNESCO; conslt: The Times, Sunday Times, Economist; *Books* co author: Political Communications (1982), ed Political Opinion Polling: an International Review (1983), co author: Private Opinions Public Polls (1986); *Recreations* choral music (St Bartholomews Hospital Choir), gardening, skiing; *Clubs* Reform; *Style—* Robert Worcester, Esq; 32 Old Queen Street SW1H 9HP (☎ 01 222 0232); MORI, 32 Old Queen Street, London SW1H 9HP (☎ 01 222 0232, telex 295230, fax 01 222 1653)

WORDIE, Sir John (Stewart); CBE (1975), VRD (1963); s of Sir James Mann Wordie, CBE; *b* 15 Jan 1924; *Educ* Winchester, St John's Cambridge (MA, LLM); *m* 1955, Patricia Kynoch, da of Lt-Col G B Kynoch, CBE, TD, DL; 4 s; *Career* served WW II RNVR, Cdr RNR 1967; barr Inner Temple; chm: Burnham and Pelham Cttee 1966-87, Soulbury Cttee 1966-, Wages Cncls, Nat Jt Cncl for further Education 1982-; memb: Cncl of ACAS 1986-, Ct Asst Salters' 1971- (and Master 1975); kt 1981; *Recreations* sailing, shooting, tennis; *Clubs* Travellers, RORC, Hawks, Army & Navy, Royal Tennis Ct, Clyde Corinthian Yacht; *Style—* Sir John Wordie, CBE, VRD; Shallows Cottage, Breamore, Fordingbridge, Hants (☎ Downton 22432)

WORDLEY, Ronald William; s of William Wordley and Elizabeth Anne, *née* Hackett; *b* 16 June 1928; *Educ* Barnet GS, City of London Coll, RMA Sandhurst; *m* 1953, Pamela Mary Offord; 2 s (and 1 s decd), 1 da; *Career* 2 Lt RA 1948; served: UK, Far East, Europe; liaison offr RM Commando Bde 1951, Capt; air observation post pilot 1953, Army Light Aircraft Sch 1955, seconded Army Air Corps Cadre 1957, ret 1958; Unilever (U Africa Co) 1958-59, Anglia TV Ltd 1959-1967, sales controller Harlech Consortium 1967, sales dir HTV Ltd 1971-78, md 1978-85, chm and md 1985-; dir of TV HTV Gp plc; dir: Independent TV Cos Assoc Ltd, Independent TV News Ltd, Independent TV Pubs Ltd memb Inst of Mktg; FRSA, Royal TV Soc; *Recreations* golf, swimming, music, travel; *Clubs* Crews Hill Golf, Bristol and Clifton Golf, Burnham and Berrow Golf; Clifton (Bristol); *Style—* Ron Wordley Esq; 6 Spring Leigh, Leigh Woods, Bristol, Avon; HTV Ltd, The Television Centre, Bristol BS4 3HG (☎ 0272 778366) and The Television Centre, Culverhouse Cross, Cardiff CF5 6XJ (☎ 0222 590590)

WORDSWORTH, Antony Christopher Curwen; FIAA; s of Lt Col J G Wordsworth OBE (John Gordon), of Hereford, and Doreen Blackwood, *née* Butler Henderson; ggggs of William Wordsworth, material ggs of Lords Farringdon and Clarina; *b* 24 April 1940; *Educ* Repton; *m* 3 Nov 1962, Rosamond Anne, da of Maj John David Summers, of Marsh Cottage, Old Romney, Kent; 1 s (Mark b 1965), 2 da (Lucy b 1968, Mary b 1972); *Career* Lt Irish Gds 1958-62; insurance loss adjuster; sch govr, Scout District chm, Conservative Branch chm; ptnr Tyler & Co; dir Summers Tyler Ltd 1983; *Recreations* gardening, DIY, music, dogs, horses; *Style—* Antony Wordsworth, Esq, FIAA; The Lodge, Elsenham, Bishops Stortford, Herts (☎ 0279 81 2325); 152 Commercial St, London E1 (telex, 264017, fax 01 377 6355)

WORKMAN, Hugh John; s of Hugh Workman (d 1966), and Annie Workman (d 1956); *b* 24 May 1925; *Educ* St Mungo's Acad Glasgow, Glasgow Univ (BL); *m* 15 Oct 1956, Audrey Henrietta, da of William Aylmer (d 1962), of Glasgow; *Career* slr; snr ptnr of messrs Sellar & Christie Solicitors Glasgow; dir and sec: Castle View Investmt Co (Stirling) Ltd, Commercial Catering Gp of Cos, Bridge of Allan and London, Commercial Contracting Gp of Cos Ltd London, Borthwick Blending Co Ltd, Glen Talla Blending & Broking Co Ltd, R M Stirling & Co (Contractors) Ltd; sec and tres Glasgow & District Bldg Trades Convalescent Homes Collections Ctee; *Recreations* swimming, walking, music; *Clubs* RSAC and Western Glasgow, Caledonian and Canning London; *Style—* Hugh J Workman, Esq; 11 Lockend Crescent, Bearsden, Glasgow G61 1EA; Messrs Sellar & Christie, Merchants' House, 30 George Square, Glasgow G2 1EG (☎ 041 221 4877, telex 777967 CHACOM G, fax GRP 3 041-204 0206)

WORKMAN, Timothy; s of Jonathan Gordon Russell Workman, and Eileen, *née* Dawson (d 1970); *b* 18 Oct 1943; *Educ* Ruskin GS Croydon; *m* 3 July 1971, Felicity Ann Caroline, da of John Western; 1 s (Jonathan b 1973), 1 da (Nicola b 1975); *Career* probation offr Inner London Probation Serv 1967-69, slr 1969; asst slr then ptnr C R Thomas & Son and Lloyd Howarth & Ptnrs Maidenhead 1969-86, Metropolitan Stipendary Magistrate 1986-; memb Law Soc; *Recreations* skiing; *Clubs* Medico-Legal; *Style—* Timothy Workman, Esq; Orchard House, Fleet Hill, Finchampstead, Berks RG11 4LA (☎ 0734 733 315); Marylebone Magistrates Ct, Marylebone Rd, London NW1

WORLIDGE, (Edward) John; s of Robert Leonard Worlidge (d 1960), and Kathleen Frances *née* Bonallack; *b* 31 May 1928; *Educ* Marlborough St John's Coll Cambridge (MA); *m* 8 January 1955, Margaret Elizabeth (Margot) da of John Murray (d 1965); 3 s (David b 1956, Nigel b 1960, Mark b 1963); *Career* 2 Lt RE 1946-48; dir Wiggins Teape Gp 1970, exec dir BAT Industs plc 1980, chm and chief exec Wiggins Teape Gp 1984, non exec dir Rugby Gp plc 1987, memb Thames Water Authy 1988; memb and Cncl Marlborough Coll 1988; rowing: Cambridge Univ VIII v Oxford 1951, Cambridge Univ v Harvard & Yale in USA 1951, Lady Margaret Boat Club winning VIII Grand challenge Cup Henley 1951, Leander VIII winners grand challenge Cup Menely 1952, Great Br VIII Olympics, Helsinki 1952; Liveryman Worshipful Co of Ironmongers 1985; CBIM 1982, FRSA 1986; *Recreations* sailing, golf; *Clubs* Hawks, Leander, Royal Yacht Squadron, Liphook GC; *Style—* John Worlidge, Esq; East Dene, Midhurst rd, Haslemere, Surrey, GU27 2PT

WORLIDGE, Capt (RN) Robert Alan; LVO (1977); s of Robert Leonard Worlidge (d 1960), and Kathleen Frances, *née* Bonallack; *b* 26 Oct 1933,bro John Worlidge *qv*;; *Educ* Marlborough Coll, Dartmouth, Royal Naval Engrg Coll; *m* 1, 1961 Pauline Reynolds, da of Stewart Cathie Griffith, CBE, DFC, TD; 2 da (Claire b 1964, Sarah b 1967); m 2, 1979, Agnes Margaret, (Molly) da of Maj-Gen Walter Rutherfoord Goodman, CB (d 1976), of Woodbridge, Suffolk; *Career* joined RN 1952; HMS Renown 1965-70, HMRY Britannia 1975-77; Capt HMS Sultan 1983-85; John Brown Engineers & Constructors 1986-; *Recreations* golf, cricket, sailing, theatre; *Clubs* Royal Yacht Sqdn, Royal Cinque Ports Golf, NCC; *Style—* Capt Robert Worlidge, LVO, RN; Abbey Rectory, 17 Park Lane, Bath BA1 2XH; 20 Eastbourne Terrace, London 6LE

WORLOCK, Hon Mrs; (Ann); da of Baron Edmund-Davies, PC (Life Peer); *b* 1936; *m* 1959, Frederick Cecil Worlock, MB, BChir, MRCS, LRCP; *Style—* The Hon Mrs Worlock; The Monastery, Fladbury, Pershore, Worcs

WORLOCK, David Robert; *Career* md Thomas Nelson & Son Ltd, Eurolex 1981-; *Style—* David Worlock, Esq; Thomas Nelson & Son Ltd, Lincoln Way, Windmill Rd, Sunbury, Middx (☎ 0932 76 85681)

WORMALD, Dame Ethel May; *née* Robinson; DBE (1968); da of late John Robert Robinson, a journalist, of Newcastle-on-Tyne and late Alice Fulbeck; *b* 19 Nov 1901; *Educ* Whitley Bay HS, Leeds Univ (BA, DipEd); *m* 1923, Stanley Wormald (decd), s of late Samuel Wormald, of Leeds; 2 s (Derek, Michael Robert); *Career* lectr in further educn; chm Liverpool Educn Ctee 1955-67, pres Assoc of Educn Ctees 1961-62, Lord Mayor Liverpool 1967-68; govr: Liverpool Coll Higher Educn, Burton Manor Residential Coll Further Educn; memb Ct Liverpool Univ; founder chm Ethel Wormald Coll of Higher Educn; JP Liverpool 1948, DL: Lancs 1970, Merseyside 1974; *Style—* Dame Ethel Wormald, DBE, JP, DL; 26 Princes Park Mansions, Liverpool L8 3SA (☎ 051 728 8670)

WORMELL, Peter Roydon; s of Roydon Wormell Mackay (d 1959), and Gladys Mary Barrow (d 1987); *b* 28 June 1928; *Educ* Colchester Royal GS; *m* 1, 1951 (m dis), Jean, *née* Holmes; 1 s (Stephen Peter b 1958), 1 da (Carol Elizabeth b 1956); m 2, 26 May 1979, Mary Jo Horkins (authoress Mary Lyons); *Career* landowner, author, broadcaster; ed in chief Farmers Handbook 1976-, chm Eastern Area Cons Agric Ctee 1968-; memb: Essex CC 1966-77 (chm and ldr 1973-77), Lexden and Winstree RDC 1961-67, Colchester Water Bd 1963-66, Eastern Sports Cncl 1968-71, Eastern Elec Consultative Cncl 1969-73, Ct of Univ of Essex 1968-77; chm: N Essex VSO 1968-76 (ESU 1971-75), Colchester Colne Round Table 1965 (pres 1970); Liveryman Worshipful Co of Farmers 1975-; Guild of Agric Journalists 1967; chm journal ctee Farmers Club 1975-78, Lloyds 1977; *Books* Anatomy of Agriculture (1978); *Recreations* farming, writing; *Clubs* Farmers, Royal Overseas; *Style—* Peter Wormell, Esq; The Estate Office, Langenhoe Hall, Abberton, Colchester CO5 7NA (☎ 020 635 265)

WORONIECKA, Princess Marysia Helena Gwenfra Teresa; da of Prince Krysztof Woroniecki, and Julia, *née* Jones; *b* 12 August 1956; *Educ* Sacred Heart Sch Hammersmith, Chiswick Polytechnic; *Career* proprietor of Marysia Woroniecka Publicity, one of London's premier fashion pr cos, established 1978, now handling 25 major fashion designers, shops and manufacturers; *Clubs* Chelsea Arts, Groucho's, Fred's; 44 Finborough Road, London SW10 (☎ 01 352 3144); 1 Chelsea Manor Studios, Flood Street, London SW3 5SR (☎ 01 351 7411, fax 01 352 9541, telex 918259 PANIC G)

WORSLEY, Albert; s of John Worsley (d 1986), and Ada, *née* Astell; *b* 3 Sept 1935; *Educ* Tech Coll; *m* 5 Sept 1959, Lilian Brenda, da of Albert Cross (d 1988); 1 s (Roger); *Career* Nat Serv Lancs Fus; materials controller Triplex Safety Co Ltd 1969-

74, internal audit mangr Pilkington plc 1974-83, fin dir Kitsons Insulation Ltd 1983-; 1983-: Kitson Insulation Contractors Ltd, Kitsons Insulation Products Ltd, Keith Young Insulation Ltd, Hastie Insulation (Ireland) Ltd; chm and dir Kitsons Environmental Sons Ltd 1983-; Inst of Internal Auditors: ctee memb NW branch 1980-83 (chm 1981-83), nat cncl memb; FCMA, FIIA; *Recreations* gardening; *Style—* Albert Worsley, Esq; 88 Fairholme Ave, Eccleston Park, Prescot, Merseyside (☎ 051 426 6312) Pilkington Plc, Contracting Division, Prescot Rd, St Helens Merseyside WA10 3TT (☎ 0744 69 3020, fax 0744 451035, telex 627441 PBSTH G)

WORSLEY, Hon Lady; Caroline Cicely; *née* Dewar; da of 3 Baron Forteviot, MBE; *b* 12 Feb 1934; *m* 1, 1956 (m dis 1966), 3 Duke of Fife, *qv*; 1 s, 1 da; m 2, 1980, Gen Sir Richard Edward Worsley, *qv*; *Style—* The Hon Lady Worsley

WORSLEY, Hon Mrs (Carolyn Mary Wynyard); *née* Hardinge; da of 4 Viscount Hardinge, MBE (d 1979), and Margaret Elizabeth Arnot, *née* Fleming; *b* 5 Mar 1932; *m* 1954, John Arthington Worsley, s of Col Sir William Worsley, 4 Bt (d 1973), of Hovingham Hall, York, and bro of HRH Duchess of Kent and Sir Marcus Worsley, 5 Bt, JP; 3 s (Henry b 1958, Jonathan b 1960, Dickon b 1966), 2 da (Willa b 1955, Katharine b 1968); *Style—* The Hon Mrs Worsley; RR2, Uxbridge, Ontario, Canada (☎ 416 852 6220)

WORSLEY, Lord; Charles John Pelham; s and h of 7 Earl of Yarborough, JP; *b* 5 Nov 1963; *Educ* Bristol Univ; *Style—* Lord Worsley

WORSLEY, Francis Edward (Jock); s of Francis Arthur Worsley, and Mary, *née* Diamond; *b* 15 Feb 1941; *Educ* Stonyhurst, Sorbonne; *m* 12 Sept 1962, Caroline Violet, da of James Hamilton Grey Hatherell (d 1968), of Manor Ho, Chacombe, Banbury, Oxon; 2 s (Richard, Edward), 2 da (Miranda, Joanna); *Career* CA 1964; chm The Financial Trg Co Ltd 1972-; pres ICAEW 1988-89, govr Ludgrove Sch; Freeman: City of London, CA Co; FCA 1964; *Recreations* tennis, wine, cooking; *Clubs* Carlton; *Style—* F E Worsley, Esq; ICAEW, Chartered Accountants Hall, Moorgate Place, London EC2P 2BJ (☎ 01 628 7060, fax 01 628 1874, car tel 0860 202 196, telex 884443)

WORSLEY, John Bertrand; s of Richard Samuel Lancelot Worsley (d 1937), of Broxmead, Cuckfield, Sussex, and Margaret Laura Evelyn (later Mrs Jones); *b* 7 Jan 1929; *Educ* Eton, Trinity Coll Cambridge (MA, LLB); *m* 18 July 1956, Jennifer Jane, da of Brig Sir Andrew Edmund James Clark, 3 Bt, QC, MBE, MC (d 1979); 1 s (James b 1957), 3 da (Harriet (Mrs Vernon) b 1960, Alison b 1963, Victoria b 1966); *Career* Nat Serv 2 Lt RCS 1947-49; barr Inner Temple 1954; fell Woodard Corpn, chm Inc Church Bldg Soc 1987- (gen cmmr of taxes 1974-); *Recreations* tennis, shooting, gardening, scuba diving, under water photography; *Style—* John Worsley, Esq; Furlong House, Hurstpierpoint, W Sussex BN6 9QA (☎ 0273 833320)

WORSLEY, Sir (William) Marcus John; 5 Bt (UK 1838), of Hovingham, Yorks, JP (N Yorks 1957), DL (1978); s of Col Sir William Arthington Worsley, 4 Bt (d 1973, descent from Oliver Cromwell; sis Katharine m HRH the Duke of Kent in 1961), and Joyce Morgan, *née* Brunner; *b* 6 April 1925; *Educ* Eton, New Coll Oxford; *m* 10 Dec 1955, Hon Bridget Assheton, da of 1 Baron Clitheroe, PC; 3 s (William b 1956, Giles b 1961, Peter b 1963), 1 da (Sarah b 1958); *Heir* s, William Ralph Worsley; *Career* served Green Howards, India and W Africa, WW II; MP (C): Keighley 1959-64, Chelsea 1966-74; church cmmr 1970-84, chm Nat Tst Properties Ctee 1980- dep chm Nat Tst 1986-, pres Royal Forestry Soc of England Wales and NI 1980-82; High Sheriff N Yorks 1982-83; Lord Lt N Yorks 1987; *Recreations* reading, walking, travel; *Clubs* Boodle's, Yorkshire (York); *Style—* Sir Marcus Worsley, Bt, JP; Hovingham Hall, York YO6 4LU (☎ 065 382 206)

WORSLEY, Michael Dominic; QC (1985); S of Paul Worsley, and Magdalen Teresa, *née* Pestel; *b* 9 Feb 1926; *Educ* Bedford Sch, Inns of Court School of Law; *m* 1, Oct 1962, Pamela, *née* Philpot (d 1980); 1 s (Benedict b 28 Sept 1967); m 2, 12 June 1986, Jane, da of late Percival Sharpe ; *Career* RN 1944-45; called to the Bar Inner Temple 1955, prosecuting cnsl London Sessions 1969-71, jr tres cnsl Central Criminal Ct 1971-74 (sr tres cnsl 1974-85), QC 1985-; *Recreations* music, travelling; *Clubs* Garrick, Lansdowne; *Style—* Michael Worsley, Esq, QC; 6 King's Bench Walk, Temple, London EC4Y 7DR

WORSLEY, Nicholas Jarvis; s of Edgar Taylor Worsley (d 1973), and Vida, *née* McCormick (d 1986); *b* 21 July 1943; *Educ* Clivton, Cambridge (MA,LLB); *m* 4 Nov 1967, Anna Maxine, da of Maxwell George Bekenn, of 55 West St, Stratford upon Avon; 2 da (Sophie Tamaris Worsley b 1970, Jessica Worsley b 1973); *Career* called to Bar Inner Temple 1966, chm Agricultural Tribunal 1980, rec 1984; chm: Worcester Civic Soc 1974-77, City of Worcester Building Preservation Tst 1977-; *Recreations* admiring contemporary British art; *Style—* Nicholas Worsley, Esq

WORSLEY, Paul Frederick; s of Eric Worsley, MBE, GM, and Sheila Mary, *née* Hoskin; *b* 17 Dec 1947; *Educ* Hymers Coll Hull, Mansfield Coll Oxford (MA); *m* 14 Dec 1974, Jennifer Ann Avery, JP, da of Ernest Avery; 1 s (Nicholas b 1975), 1 da (Charlotte b 1977); *Career* called to the Bar Middle Temple 1970, recorder of Crown Ct 1987-; *Recreations* spy prints, Whitby, opera, preaching; *Clubs* Yorkshire; *Style—* Paul Worsley, Esq; 10 Park Sq, Leeds (☎ 0532 455438)

WORSLEY, Gen Sir Richard Edward; GCB (1981), KCB (1976, OBE 1964); s of H Worsley of Grey Abbey, Co Down; *b* 29 May 1923; *Educ* Radley; *m* 1, 1958, Sarah Mitchell; 1 s, 1 da; m 2, 1980, Caroline, Duchess of Fife (*see* Hon Lady Worsley); *Career* served WWII (Mid East & Italy) & Malayan Emergency in Rifle Bde, Instr RMA Sandhurst and Staff Coll Camberley, CO Royal Dragoons, Cdr 7 Armoured Bde 1965-67, COS Far East Land Force 1969-71; GOC: 3 Div 1972-74, 1 Corps 1976-78; QMG 1979-82 (Vice-QMG 1974-76), ret 1982; joined Pilkington Gp 1982-87, chm Barr and Stroud, Pilkington PE, chief exec Pilkington Electro-Optical Div; *Clubs* Cavalry & Guards; *Style—* Gen Sir Richard Worsley, GCB, KCB, OBE; c/o Barclays Bank, 27 Regent St, London SW1Y 4UB

WORSLEY, William Ralph; s and h of Sir (William) Marcus John Worsley, 5 Bt, JP, of Hovingham, Yorkshire; *b* 12 Sept 1956; *Educ* Harrow, RAC; *m* 26 Sept 1987, Marie-Noelle, yr da of Bernard H Dreesmann, of Mas de la Madone, Miramar, Théole, France; 1 da (Isabella Claire b 24 Oct 1988); *Career* former Lt Queen's Own Yeomanry TAVR; chartered surveyor; ARICS; dir Graybourne Properties Ltd; conslt Humberts; *Recreations* shooting, skiing; *Clubs* Boodle's; *Style—* William Worsley, Esq; 61 Bourne St, London SW1 (☎ 01 730 0707); Fosters, Hovingham, York

WORSLEY-TAYLOR, Annette Pamela; da of Sir John Godfrey Worsley-Taylor, 3 Bt (d 1952), and Anne, *née* Paget (now Anne, Lady Jaffray, *qv*); *b* 2 July 1944; *Educ* Downham Sch Hatfield Heath Herts; *Career* fndr London Designer Collections 1975 (dir 1976-); fndr memb British Fashion Cncl 1983 (memb exec 1987-); memb BKCEC Womans Wear Exec; *Recreations* fashion, design, music, people; *Style—* Ms Annette Worsley-Taylor; 3 Ovington Gardens, London SW3 (☎ 01 584 2836); 36 Beauchamp Place, London SW3 1NU (☎ 01 581 2931, fax 01 581 9589)

WORSTHORNE, Peregrine Gerard; s of Col Alexander Koch de Gooreynd, OBE, formerly Irish Gds (d 1985), who assumed surname of Worsthorne by deed poll in 1923, but reverted to Koch de Gooreynd in 1937; *see also* er bro Simon Towneley from whose estate the Worsthorne name is derived (gd m Manuela, da of Alexandre de Laski by Joaquima, Marquesa de Souza Lisboa da of José Marques Lisboa, sometime min Plenipotentiary of Emperor of Brazil to Ct of St James), and Priscilla, now Baroness Norman, *qv*; *b* 22 Dec 1923; *Educ* Stowe, Peterhouse Cambridge (BA), Magdalen Coll Oxford; *m* 7 June 1950, Claudia Marie-Hélène, da of Victor Edouard Bertrand de Colasse, of Paris, 1 da (Dominique Elizabeth Priscilla b 18 Feb 1952); *Career* cmmnd Oxford & Bucks LI 1942, Lt Phantom GHQ Liaison Regt 1944-45; journalist and writer; formerly on editorial staff of: The Glasgow Herald 1946-48, The Times 1948-55, Daily Telegraph 1955-61; assoc ed Sunday Telegraph 1961-86, ed 1986-; *Books* The Socialist Myth (1972), Peregrinations (1980), By The Right (1987); *Recreations* tennis, reading, walking; *Clubs* Garrick, Beefsteak, Pratt's; *Style—* Peregrine Worsthorne, Esq; Westerlies, Wivenhoe, Essex (☎ 020 622 2886); 6 Kempson Rd, London SW6; The Sunday Telegraph, Peterborough Court at South Quay, 181 Marsh Wall, London E14 9SR (☎ 01 538 5000, fax 01 538 1330, telex 22874 TELLDN G)

WORTH, Brian Leslie; s of Leslie Worth of Brockenhurst, Hants (d 1988), and Grace Alice *née* Drake (d 1983); *b* 25 Jan 1938; *Educ* Haberdashers Askes Sch; *m* 28 December 1963, Gillian Mary, da of Rev Dr Victor Evelyn William Hayward of Haslemere (d 1988); 1 s (Graham 1966), 1 da (Susan 1964); *Career* Nat Serv sr Aircraftsman RAF 1960-62; chartered acct; ptnr Whitehill Marsh Jackson & Co 1964, sr ptnr Fryer Whitehill & Co 1974, mangr ptnr Clare Whitehill Chartered Accountants 1982-84, chm and chief exec Clare Whitehill Chartered Accountants 1984-, chm Clark Kenneth Leventhall & Co 1988-, main ctee memb London Soc of Chartered Accountants 1976-85 (chm 1893-84); hon tres Br Cncl of Churches 1973-78; FCA (memb cncl 1985-); *Books* Planning Your Personal Finances (1973); *Style—* B L Worth, Esq; 25 New Street Square, London EC4A 3LN (☎ 01 353 1577, 021 643 8241, fax 021 631 2270

WORTH, Prof Katharine Joyce; da of George Lorimer, and Elizabeth, *née* Jones; *b* 4 August 1922; *Educ* Univ of London (MA, PhD); *m* 30 Aug 1947, George, s of Ernest Worth; 2 s (Christopher George b 7 Nov 1952, Charles Robert Edmund b 4 July 1959), 1 da (Elizabeth Lorimer b 5 Nov 1955); *Career* prof of drama and theatre studies Royal Holloway and Bedford New Coll Univ of London (formerly Royal Holloway Coll) 1978-87 (lectr Eng lit 1964-74, reader Eng lit 1974-78); adaptor and prodr of Beckett's Company performed in Edinburgh 1987, London and New York 1988, co-ed Theatre Notebook, memb ed bd of Yeats Annual and Modern Drama, frequent lectr abroad suported by the Br Cncl and foreign universities; memb: Soc for Theatre Res 1950, Soc of Authors 1988; Friend of the Royal Academy; *Books* Revolutions in Modern English Drama (1973), Beckett the Shape Changer (ed 1975), The Irish Drama of Europe from Yeats to Beckett (1978), Oscar Wilde (1983), Maeterlinck's Plays in Performance (1985), Where There is Nothing (ed 1987); *Recreations* theatre-going, walking, travel; *Style—* Prof Katharine Worth; 48 Elmfield Ave, Teddington, Middex TW11 8BT (☎ 01 977 5778)

WORTHINGTON, (William) Anthony (Tony); MP (L) Clydebank and Milngavie 1987; s of Malcolm Thomas Henry Worthington (d 1985), and Monica, *née* Wearden; *b* 11 Oct 1941; *Educ* City Sch Lincoln, London Sch of Economics (BA, Hons), Univ of Glasgow (MEd); *m* 26 March 1966, Angela May, da of Cyril Oliver, of The Moat House, Charing, Kent; 1 s (Robert b 1972), 1 da (Jennifer b 1970); *Career* Regional Cncl Strathclyde 1974-87, chm Finance Ctee; lectr Jordanhill Coll Glasgow 1971-87; MP; *Recreations* running, gardening, reading; *Clubs* Clydebank, Athecetic; *Style—* Tony Worthington, MP; 24 Cleddans Crescent, Hardgate, Clydebank (☎ Duntocher 7315); House of Commons, London SW1 0AA (☎ 01 219 3507)

WORTHINGTON, Edgar Barton; CBE (1962); s of Edgar Worthington (d 1931), and Amy Elizabeth, *née* Beale (d 1946); *b* 13 Jan 1905; *Educ* Rugby Sch, Gonville and Caius Coll Cambridge (MA, PhD); *m* 1, 23 Aug 1930, Stella, da of Menasseh Johnson (d 1950); 3 da (Shelagh b 1932, Grizelda b 1934, Marthe 1938); m 2, 21 June 1980, Harriett, da of George Alva Stockton (d 1943), of Illinois; *Career* biologist, ecologist, environmental conslt; scientist to Lord Hailey's African Survey 1934-37, dir Freshwater Biological Assoc 1937-46, scientific advsr to Mid E Supply Cncl 1939-45, scientific sec Colonial Res Ctee 1946-, dvpt advsr Uganda Govt 1946, seconded to East Africa High Cmmn 1947-51, sec gen Scientific Cncl for Africa 1951-56, dep dir gen nature Conservancy (UK) 1956-62, scientific dir Int Biological Prog 1962-72, enviromental conslt to major dvpt cos 1973-; author; Knight of Golden Ark (Netherland 1966); *Books* reports on Fishery Surveys of African Lakes 1928-31, Inland Waters of Africa (with Stella Worthington 1933), Science in Africa (1937), Life in Lakes and Rivers (with T T Macan 1951), Science in the development of Africa (1958), The Ecological Century - a personal Appraisal (1983); *Recreations* nature conservation, field sports, farming; *Clubs* Athenaeum, Farmer's; *Style—* Barton Worthington, Esq, CBE; Colin Godmans, Furner's Green, nr Uckfield, Sussex (☎ 082 574 322)

WORTHINGTON, Air Vice-Marshal Sir Geoffrey Luis; KBE (1960), CBE (1945, CB 1957); s of Cdr H E F Worthington, RN; *b* 26 April 1903; *Educ* HMS Conway, Eastbourne Coll, RAF Coll Cranwell; *m* 1931, Margaret Joan, da of Maj-Gen A Stevenson, CB, CMG, DSO; 2 s, 1 da; *Career* WW II (despatches, CBE) AOC 40 Gp 1955-58, Air V-Marshal 1956, dir-gen Equipment Air Min 1958-61; Cdr US Legion of Merit 1955; *Style—* Air Vice-Marshal Sir Geoffrey Worthington, KBE, CB, CBE; 30 Brickwall Close, Burnham-on-Crouch, Essex (☎ Maldon 0621 782388)

WORTHINGTON, His Hon Judge George Noel; s of George Errol Worthington (d 1976), and Edith Margaret Boys Worthington *née* Stones (d 1970); *b* 22 June 1923; *Educ* Rossall Sch, Lancs; *m* 10 July 1954, Jacqueline Kemble, da of George Lionel Spencer Lightfoot (d 1972), of Carlisle; 2 s (Nicholas b 1968, Jonathan decd), 1 da (Kate b 1962); *Career* WWII 1939-45, served RAC 1941-46; adm slr 1949, recorder of the Crown Ct 1972, circuit judge 1979-; Liveryman Wax Chandlers Co; *Recreations* gardening; *Style—* His Hon Judge George N Worthington; 33 Cromwell Grove, London W6 7RQ

WORTHINGTON, Philip Michael; s of Col Lancelot Jukes Worthington, TD, JP (d

1975), and 1 w Phyllis Mary, *née* Sadler (d 1981); half-bro Stuart Worthington, *qv*; *b* 24 April 1926; *Educ* Ashby-de-la-Zouch, Univ Coll Nottingham (BSc); *m* 1, 25 June 1955, Gilliam Hazel, da of Sir William Sidney Albert Atkins, CBE, *qv*, of Cobham Place, Cobham, Surrey; 1 s (Nicholas b 1960), 1 da (Catherine b 1962); m 2, 29 July 1983, Judith Sonia May, da of Henry Peter Robson Hamlin, of Prior Lea, Upper Packington Rd, Asby-de-la-Zouch, Leics; 1 da (Miranda b 1985); *Career* conslt engr and mgmnt conslt; WS Atkins and Ptnrs 1946-78 (dir 1965-78, md 1971-78), chm AJ Worthington Hldgs plc 1972-83 (dir 1983-), md PM Worthington & Associates Ltd 1978-; exec dir Major Projects Assoc 1982-83, dir Polycast Ltd 1984-; assoc fell Templeton Coll Oxford 1982-84; CEng, FICE, CBIM, FIMC; *Publications* The Worthington Families of Medieval England; papers on engrg and economics; *Style*— P M Worthington, Esq; The Knoll House, Knossington, Oakham, Leics LE15 8LT (☎ 0664 77315)

WORTHINGTON, Stuart Gibson; s of Col Lancelot Jukes Worthington, TD, JP (d 1975), of Swainsley, Nr Leek, Staffs, and Marjorie Brown, *née* Gibson (d 1981); bro Philip Worthington *qv*; *b* 30 Oct 1940; *Educ* Winchester; *m* 2 Dec 1972, Geraldine Judith, da of Lt Col James Seth, MBE, of Las Mimomas, Guadalmina Alta, San Pedro de Alcantara, Malaga, Spain; 3 da (Melanie b 1966, Lucinda b 1969, Victoria b 1973); *Career* dir: A J Worthington (Hldgs) plc 1970-84, A J Worthington & Co (Leek) Ltd 1970-84 (chm 1974-84), princ Blore Assocs 1985-; dir: Narrow Fabrics Fedn 1969-84 (chm 1973-76), Br Man-Made Fibres Fedn 1972-77, Br Textile Confedn 1973-76; JP Co Stafford 1976, resigned 1987; Freeman City of London 1978, Liveryman Worshipful Co of Weavers 1978; *Recreations* cricket, tennis, crosswords; *Clubs* City Livery; *Style*— Stuart Worthington, Esq; The Old Rectory, Blore, Nr Ashbourne, Derby DE6 2BS (☎ 033529 287); Blore Assocs, Blore, nr Ashbourne, Derbys DE6 2BS

WORTHINGTON, Tony; MP (Clydebank and Milngate 1987); s of Malcolm Worthington (d 1985), and Monica, *née* Wearden; *b* 11 Oct 1941; *Educ* City Sch Lincoln, LSE (BA), Univ of Glasgow (MEd); *m* 26 March 1966, Angela, da of Cyril Oliver, of Moat House, Charing, Kent; 1 s (Robert b 1972), 1 da (Jennifer b 1970); *Career* lectr Jordanhill Coll Glasgow 1971-87, regnl cncllr Strathclyde 1974-87 (chm fin ctee 1986-87), memb Scottish Community Educn Cncl 1980-87, chm Strathclyde Community Business 1984-87; *Recreations* running, sailing, walking; *Clubs* Clydebank Athletic; *Style*— Tony Worthington, Esq, MP; 24 Cleddans Cres, Hardgate, Clydebank C81 5NW (☎ 0389 73195); House of Commons, London SW1A 0AA (☎ 01 219 3507)

WORTHY, David Graham; s of Marcus Gerald Worthy (d 1984), of Godalming, Surrey, and Edith Margaret, *née* Lawrence; *b* 29 Dec 1931; *Educ* Godalming GS, Balliol Coll Oxford (MA), Dip in economics; *m* 25 Nov 1967, Hon Margaret, *née* Bruce, da of 7 Lord Balfour of Burleigh (d 1967); 1 s (Henry Jonathan David Bruce b 1971); *Career* overseas civil service Kenya 1955-64: dep civil sec North Eastern Region 1955-64; exec offr Chemical Industries Assocn 1964-71, Bowaters Ltd (final post personnel dir) Bowater Bldg Products and Furniture 1971-77, dir Br Woodworking Fed 1977-79, personnel dir Br Tissues Ltd 1979-; *Recreations* walking, travel; *Clubs* Nat Liberal, Inst of Directors; *Style*— David Worthy, Esq; Keepers Cottage, Hare Warren Hollow, Merrow Downs, Guildford, Surrey GU1 2HJ (☎ 0483 69500); Lowlands House, Lowlands Rd, Harrow, Middlesex (☎ 01 864 5411)

WORTHY, Hon Mrs; Margaret; *née* Bruce; da of 7 Lord Balfour of Burleigh (d 1967); 1 Lord was Ambassador to Tuscany and Lorraine & was er Scots Peer 1607, Title Attained 1716 and reversed by Act of Parliament 1868; *b* 1934; *Educ* St Paul's Girl's Sch; *m* 1967, David Graham Worthy *qv*; 1 s; *Recreations* houses, mountains, swimming; *Style*— The Hon Mrs Worthy; Keepers Cottage, Hare Warren Hollow, Merrow Downs, Guildford, Surrey GU1 2HJ

WORTLEY, Prof Ben(jamin) Atkinson; CMG (1978), OBE (Mil 1946), QC (1969); s of John Edward Wortley (d 1940), and Mary Cicely, *née* King; *b* 16 Nov 1907; *Educ* King James's GS, Leeds Univ (LLM), Manchester Univ (LLD); *m* 1940, Kathleen Mary, *née* Prynne (d 1982); 2 s, 1 da; *Career* Instr CDR RN (temp) 1943-46; practised and taught law LSE 1931-33, Manchester Univ 1933-39, barr Gray's Inn 1947, prof of Jurisprudence and Int Law, Manchester Univ 1946-75 (now emeritus); memb: Inst of Advanced Legal Studies 1947-77, Cncl UNIDROIT 1950-75; longest standing Br memb Inst de Droit Int 1967-; sometime rep of HM Govt at Int conferences The Hague and UN; Hon. bencher Grays Inn 1989; Hon D of Rennes and Strasbourg; Hon DCL Durham; memb Netherlands Aca 1960; Kt of St Sylvester (Vatican) 1975, Commendatore (Italy) 1960, emeritus fellow Leverhulme Tst 1981-86; *Books* numerous publications in International Law and Jurisprudence; *Recreations* literature, gardening, languages; *Clubs* Athenaeum; *Style*— Prof Ben Wortley CMG, OBE, QC; 24 Gravel Lane, Wilmslow, Cheshire SK9 6LA

WOTHERSPOON, (John Munro) Iain; TD, DL (1982), WS (1950); s of Robert Wotherspoon (d 1968), of Inverness, and Jessie MacDonald, *née* Munro (d 1980); *b* 19 July 1924; *Educ* Inverness Royal Acad, Loretto Sch Musselburgh, Trinity Coll Oxford (MA), Edinburgh Univ (LLB); *m* 30 Aug 1952, Victoria Avril Jean, da of Sir Lawrie Edwards, KBE, DL (d 1968), of Newcastle-upon-Tyne; 2 s (James b 1955, Jonathan b 1957), 2 da (Ann b 1956, Victoria b 1960); *Career* Lt Royal Signals Europe & Burma 1945-46, TA 1948-78, Lt Col Cdg 51 (Highland) Div Signals 1963-67, Col Dep Cdr 13 Signals Gp 1970-72, Hon Col 32 Scottish Signal Regt 1972-78, ADC to HM The Queen 1971-76; slr and landowner, sr ptnr Macandrew & Jenkins, WS, Inverness; chm Inverness Ctee of The Royal Br Legion Housing Assoc Ltd; Dep Lt Districts of Lochaber, Inverness, Badenoch & Strathspey 1982-; clerk to the Lieutenancy 1985-; *Recreations* shooting, fishing, stalking; *Clubs* Highland, Inverness and New (Edinburgh); *Style*— Iain Wotherspoon, TD, DL; Maryfield, 62 Midmills Rd, Inverness (☎ 0463 233642); Affaric Lodge, Cannich, by Beauly (☎ Cannich 351); 5 Drummond St, Inverness IV1 1QF (☎ 0463 233001, fax 0463 230743, car phone 0035 240539)

WOYKA, Alexander Stuart; s of Alexander Graham Woyka (d 1970), of Glasgow, and Beryl Stewart, *née* Forsyth; *b* 10 May 1937; *Educ* Glenalmond Coll, CCC Cambridge (MA); *m* 22 Sept 1967, Carol Rae, da of Ronald Morton Sangster (d 1974), of Glasgow; 1 s (Scott b 1970), 2 da (Jillian b 1969, Lucy b 1972); *Career* Nat Serv, cmmnd RN, service in Eastern Med 1955-56 (GSM), ret Lt RNR 1960; md John Woyka & Co Ltd 1970-; *Recreations* golf, skiing, curling, windsurfing; *Clubs* Pollok Golf, Glasgow, Elie Golf House Fife; *Style*— Stuart Woyka, Esq; The Gables, South Ave, Paisley PA2 7SP (☎ 041 884 3573); Shieldhall Sawmills, 235 Bogmoor Rd, Glasgow G51 4JH (☎ 041 440 0060, fax 041 445 5376)

WRAGG, Prof Edward Conrad; s of George William Wragg, of 7 Errington Ave, Sheffield, and Maria, *née* Brandstetter; *b* 26 June 1938; *Educ* King Edward VII GS Sheffield, Hatfield Coll, Durham Univ (BA, DipEd); *m* 29 Dec 1960, Judith, da of Beaumont King (d 1984), of 25 Mortimer Rd, Penistone, nr Sheffield; 1 s (Christopher Beaumont b 1975), 2 da (Josephine b 1966, Caroline Maria b 1967); *Career* modern languages; master Queen Elizabeth GS Wakefield 1960-64, hd of German Wyggeston Boys' Sch 1964-66, lectr in educn Exeter Univ 1966-73, prof of educn Nottingham Univ 1973-78, prof of educn and dir of sch educn Exeter Univ 1978-; memb Devon Educn Ctee, chm Sch Broadcasting Cncl for UK (1981-86), chm Educnl Broadcasting Cncl for UK 1986-87, pres Br Educnl Res Assoc; chartered fell Coll of Preceptors 1988; DUniv Open Univ 1989; radio/TV presenter: Chalkface (Granada), Crisis in Education (BBC), Education Roadshow (BBC); *Books* Teaching Teaching (1974), Classroom Interaction (1976), Teaching Mixed Ability Groups (1976), A Handbook for School Governors (1980), Class Management and Control (1981), A Review of Research in Teacher Education (1982), Swineshead Revisited (1984), Classroom Teaching Skills (1984), The Domesday Project (1985), Education: An Action Guide for Parents (1986), Teacher Appraisal (1987), Education in the Market Place (1988), The Wragged Edge: Education in Thatcher's Britain (1988), Schools and Parents (1989); *Recreations* football watching, playing and coaching, music, running, cooking; *Style*— Prof Edward Wragg; 14 Doriam Close, Exeter EX4 4RS (☎ 0392 77052); School of Education, Exeter University EX1 2LU (☎ 0392 264877, fax 0392 411274)

WRAGG, Lawrence de Villamil; s of Arthur Donald Wragg (d 1966), of Buxton, Derbys, and Lilia Mary May, *née* Adcock; *b* 26 Nov 1943; *Educ* Rendcomb Coll Glos, Univ of Bristol (BA), Sorbonne Paris (Dip), Manchester Business Sch (MBA); *m* 23 July 1971, Aureole Margaret Willoughby, da of Lt-Col Edward Cole Willoughby Fowler (d 1985), of Chiselhurst, Kent; 1 s (David b 1979), 2 da (Isabel b 1977, Helen b 1988); *Career* systems analyst Nat Data Processing Serv 1968-69, mgmnt conslt Price Waterhouse Assocs 1969-72, exec dir Chemical Bank Int (formerly London Multinational Bank Int) 1974-82; dir: Charterhouse Japhet 1982-86, Standard Chartered Merchant Bank 1987-; chm: govrs of Duxford Sch, The Ickleton Soc; memb Ickleton PC, chm London Banks Composite Currency Ctee 1980-84, memb Assoc of MBAs 1974; *Books* Composite Currencies (ed 1984); *Recreations* music, mountaineering, skiing, gardening, aviation; *Clubs* Overseas Bankers, London Mountaineering (tres); *Style*— Lawrence Wragg, Esq; Standard Chartered Merchant Bank Ltd, 33-36 Gracechurch St, London EC3V 0AX (☎ 01 623 8711, fax 01 626 1610, telex 884689)

WRAGG, Hon Mary Ann Maud Sigrid; er da of 2 Baron Gretton; *b* 5 Jan 1939; *m* June 1986, Thomas Henry Wragg, os of late T L Wragg, of Hinckley; *Recreations* breeder and int judge of Arabian Horses; *Style*— The Hon Mary Wragg; Manor House, Stapleford, Melton Mowbray, Leics, LE14 2SF (☎ 057 284 224)

WRAIGHT, Sir John Richard; KBE (1976), CMG (1962); s of Richard George Wraight (d 1964), and Kathleen Elizabeth Mary, *née* Robinson (d 1974); *b* 4 June 1916; *Educ* Selhurst GS, London Univ; *m* 1947, Marquita, *née* Elliott; *Career* Maj HAC and RHA 1939-45; joined FO 1945, Dip Serv 1947, first sec Athens 1948, Tel Aviv 1950, Washington 1953, asst head econ rel FO 1957, commercial cnsllr Cairo 1959, Brussels and Luxembourg 1962, min and consul-gen Milan 1968-73, ambass Switzerland 1973-76, ret; co dir and co conslt 1976-; int conslt to London Stockbrokers Phillips & Drew 1976-88, pres Co Scout Cncl of Gtr London 1977-; Cdr of the Order of the Crown (Belgium) 1966, memb RIIA; *Books* The Swiss and the British (1987); *Recreations* music, gardening, birdwatching; *Style*— Sir John Wraight, KBE, CMG; c/o Lloyds Bank plc, 16 St James's St London SW1

WRANGEL, Baroness Alexis; Diana Sylvia; *née* Conolly - Carew; da of 6 Baron Carew; *b* 7 April 1940; *m* 22 May 1985, Baron Alexis Wrangel; *Style*— Baroness Alexis Wrangel; Brownstown Lodge, Navan, Co Meath

WRANGHAM, Lady Joan; *née* Boyle; Col W Boyle; *m* 1947, as his 2 w, Sir Geoffrey Walter Wrangham (d 1986); 1 s, 1 da; *Style*— Lady Wrangham; Butlesdon Hse, Low Buston, Warkworth, Morpeth, Northumberland NE65 0XY (☎ 0665 711 300)

WRATTEN, Donald Peter; s of Frederick George Wratten (d 1936), of Folkestone, Kent, and Majorie, *née* Liverton (d 1979); *b* 3 July 1925; *Educ* Harvey GS Folkestone, LSE (BSc, Econ); *m* 6 Sept 1947, Margaret Kathleen, da of Frank Marsh (d 1938), of London; 1 s (Mark b 1955), 1 da (Isobel b 1958); *Career* RAF Meteorological Wing 1943-47; PO: asst princ 1950, private sec to Asst PMG 1955-56, princ POHQ 1956-65, private sec to PMG 1965-66, head of mktg div PO Telecom 1966-67, dir E Region PO Telecom 1967-69; chief exec: Nat Girobank 1969-74, Nat Data Processing Serv 1974-75, sr dir personnel Br Telecom 1975-81, mgmnt conslt 1981-85, non exec dir Nat Counties Bldg Soc 1985-; vice chm Radlett Soc and Green Belt Assoc, chm Radlett Local History Soc, memb then chm advsy panel City Univ Business Sch 1974-80; memb: Business Educn Cncl 1975-82, of ct Cranfield Inst of Technol 1975-81; FBIM 1960, FRSA 1985, LRPS 1984; *Recreations* stereoscopic photography, social history; *Style*— Donald Wratten, Esq; 10 Homefield Rd, Radlett, Herts WD7 8PY (☎ 0923 854 500)

WRAXALL, Sir Charles Frederick Lascelles; 9 Bt (UK 1813), of Wraxall, Somerset; s of Sir Morville Wraxall, 8 Bt (d 1978); *b* 17 Sept 1961; *Educ* Archbp Tenison's GS Croydon; *m* 1983, Lesley Linda, da of William Albert Allan; 1 s; *Heir* s, William Nathaniel Lascelles b 1987; *Career* assist accountant Morgan Stanley Int 1987-; *Recreations* football, stamps, postcards; *Style*— Sir Charles Wraxall, Bt

WRAXALL, 2 Baron (UK 1928); George Richard Lawley Gibbs; DL (Avon 1974); s of 1 Baron Wraxall, TD, PC (d 1931, s of Antony Gibbs, of the banking family and 2nd cousin of 4 Baron Aldenham), and his 2 w, Hon Ursula Lawley, OBE, ARC (d 1979), el da of 6 and last Baron Wenlock, GCSI, GCIE, KCMG (for whom Queen Mary was Sponsor); *b* 16 May 1928; *Educ* Eton, Sandhurst; *Heir* bro, Hon Sir Eustace Gibbs; KCVO, CMG; *Career* Maj N Somerset and Bristol Yeo, Lt Coldstream Gds; chm N Somerset Cons Assoc 1970-74; govr: St Katherine's Comprehensive Sch 1974-81, Avon County Scout Assoc 1976-; fell Woodard Corpn and Woodard Schs (Western Div) Ltd 1980-; landowner; *Recreations* shooting; *Clubs* RAC, Cavalry and Guards, Clifton (Bristol); *Style*— The Rt Hon the Lord Wraxall, DL; Tyntesfield, Wraxall, Bristol, Avon BS19 1NU (☎ 027 583 2923; Estate Office 2021)

WRAXALL, Lady; Irmgard Wilhelmina Maria; da of Alois Larry Schnidrig, of Pratteln, Switzerland; *m* 1956, Sir Morville Wraxall, 8 Bt (d 1978); 2 s (9 Bt *qv*, Peter *qv*), 1 da (Sylvia b 1951); *Style*— Lady Wraxall

WRAXALL, Peter Edward Lascelles; s of Sir Morville Wraxall, 8 Bt; *b* 30 Mar 1967; *Style*— Peter Wraxall Esq

WRAY; *see*: Roberts-Wray

WRAY, Prof Gordon Richard; s of Joseph Wray (d 1975), of Farnworth, Bolton,

Lancs, and Letitia, *née* Jones (d 1978); *b* 30 Jan 1928; *Educ* pt/t Worsley and Bolton Tech Coll (ONC, HNC), Univ of Manchester (BSc, MSc, PhD), Loughborough Univ of Technol (DSc); *m* 20 Nov 1954, Dr Kathleen, da of Harold Greenwood Senior (d 1984), of Rastrick, Brighouse, Yorks; 1 s (Vaughan Richard b 24 Oct 1959), 1 da (Amanda Diane b 19 July 1961); *Career* engrg apprentice Bolton Lancs 1943-49, Sir Walton Preston Scholar Univ of Manchester 1949-52, devpt engr Platt Bros Ltd Manchester 1952-53, lectr mech engrg Bolton Tech Coll 1953-55, lectr in textile engrg UMIST 1955-66, reader mech engrg Loughborough Univ of Technol 1966-70, prof (later head of dept of mech engrg), Loughborough Univ of Technol 1970-88; fellowship of engrg prof in the principles of engrg design and dir Engrg Design Inst; visiting prof Univ of California (Berkeley) 1977; memb: Dept of Industs Chief Scientist's Requirement Bd 1974-75, interdisciplinary bd CEI/CSTI 1978-83, ctee on innovation SEFI Brussels 1980-82, Royal Soc Working Gp on Agric Engrg 1981-82, applied mechanics ctee SERC 1982-85, Fellowship of Engrg Working Pty on Dept of Indust Requirement Bds 1982, working pty on engrg design SERC 1983, sectional ctee 4(i) 1986-, ctee Engrg Profs Conf 1986-88, Mullard award ctee Royal Soc 1986-, Royal Soc/SERC industl fellowships panel 1987-; Royal Soc Technol Activities Ctee 1989; cncl memb Inst Mech Engrs 1964-67 (chm manip and mech handling machinery gp 1969-71); Inst Mech Engrs: Viscount Weir Prize 1959, Water Arbitration Prize 1972, James Clayton Prize 1975; Warner Medal of the Textile Inst 1976, SG Brown Prize of the Royal Soc 1978; FRS 1986, FEng 1980, FIMechE 1973, FTI 1963, FRSA 1974; Euro Engr Paris 1987; *Books* Modern Yarn Production from Man-Made Fibres (1960), Modern Developments in Weaving Machinery (1961), An Introduction to the Study of Spinning (third edn 1962); *Recreations* photography, fell-walking, theatre, music, gardening, DIY; *Style—* Prof Gordon Wray; Director, Engineering Design Instit, Lougborough Univ of Technol, Loughborough, Leics LE11 3TU (☎ 0509 223175, fax 0509 268013, telex 34319)

WREFORD-BROWN, Capt Christopher Louis; DSO (1982); s of Louis Careler Wreford-Brown, of Devon, and Anne, *née* Ridgeway; *Educ* Rugby; *m* 29 March 1969, Jenny, da of John Lawrence Pingent, of Devon; 1 s (Paul b Sept 1972), 2 da (Julia b Feb 1970, Amanda b May 1976); *Career* joined RN 1963, joined submarine service 1969, qualified as navigating offr and princ warfare offr, Lt Cdr Co HMS Opossum 1976, 2 i/c HMS Courageous, staff 2 Submarine Sqdn, Cdr 1980, Nat Def Coll 1981; Co: HMS Dreadnought, HMS Conqueror, HMS Valiant; MOD, Capt 1986, Co HMS Cornwall 1987, Capt 8 Frigate Sqdn 1988, Royal Coll of Def Studies 1989; Master Britannia Beagles; Freeman City of London 1988; FBIM 1988; *Recreations* hunting, gardening; *Style—* Capt Christopher Wreford-Brown DSO

WRENBURY, 3 Baron (UK 1915); John Burton Buckley; s of 2 Baron Wrenbury Bryan Burton Buckley (d 1940), and Helen Baroness Wrenbury (d 1981), *née* Graham; *b* 18 June 1927; *Educ* Eton, King's Coll Cambridge (MA); *m* 1, 1956 (m dis 1961), Carolyn, da of Col Ian Burn-Murdoch, OBE; m 2, 1961, Penelope, da of Edward Dimond Fort, of Dorset; 1 s, 2 da (Hon Elizabeth Margaret (Mrs Andrew Macnaughton) b 1964, Hon Katherine Lucy b 1968); *Heir* s, Hon William Edward Buckley b 19 June 1966; *Career* slr 1952, dep legal advsr Nat Tst 1955-56, ptnr: Freshfields 1956-74, Thomson Snell & Passmore 1974-; landowner (390 acres); *Clubs* Oriental; *Style—* The Rt Hon Lord Wrenbury; Oldcastle, Dallington, Heathfield, Sussex TN21 9JP (☎ 0435 0435 830400; office: 0892 510000); 3 Lonsdale Gardens, Tunbridge Wells (☎ 0892 510000); Tower House, 8-14 Southampton St, London WC2E 7HA (☎ 01 379 0921)

WREY, Sir (Castel Richard) Bourchier; 14th Bt (E 1628), of Trebitch, Cornwall; s of Edward Castell Wrey (d 1933), and n of Rev Sir Albany Bourchier Sherard Wrey, 13 Bt, JP, sometime rural dean Barnstaple (d 1948). The forename Bourchier has been used, in one position or other, by every Wrey Baronet from, 3 Bt, whose m was Lady Anne Bourchier da and co heir of 4 Earl of Bath on whose d Baronies of Fitzwarin and Daubeny fell into abeyance, 11 Bt, petitioned the House of Lords for the termination of the abeyance in 1914; *b* 27 Mar 1903; *Educ* Oundle; *m* 15 March 1947, Sybil Mabel Alice, er da of Dr George Lubke, of Durban, S Africa; 2 s; *Heir* s, George Richard Bourchier Wrey; *Career* served 1939-40 in France as 2 Lt RASC; joined RN 1940, Lt RNVR 1942; *Clubs* Natal; *Style—* Sir Bourchier Wrey, Bt; 511 Currie Road, Durban, S Africa

WREY, Lady Caroline Janet; *née* Lindesay-Bethune; only da of 15 Earl of Lindsay, of Combermere Abbey, Whitchurch, Shrops, by his 1 w, Mary Clare, *née* Douglas-Scott-Montagu (*see* Hon Mrs Horn); *b* 7 July 1957; *Educ* West Heath, Sevenoaks Kent; *m* 1 Aug 1981, George Richard Bourchier Wrey, *qv*, el s of Sir Bourchier Wrey 14 Bt *qv*; 1 s (Harry b 1984), 1 da (b 1987); *Career* qualified teacher, curtain designer; *Style—* Lady Caroline Wrey; 60 The Chase, SW4 (☎ 01 622 6625); Hollamoor Farm, Tawstock, Barnstaple, N Devon (☎ 0271 73466)

WREY, George Richard Bourchier; s and h of Sir Bourchier Wrey, 14 Bt, *qv*; *b* 2 Oct 1948; *Educ* Eton; *m* 1 Aug 1981, Lady Caroline Janet Lindesay-Bethune, da of 15 Earl of Lindsay, *qv*, 1 s (Harry b 1984); *Career* farmer; *Recreations* shooting; *Clubs* Turf; *Style—* George Wrey Esq; 60 The Chase, London SW4 0NH (☎ 01 622 6625); Hollamoor Farm, Tawstock, Barnstaple, N Devon (☎ 0271 73466)

WRIGGLESWORTH, Ian William; s of Edward Wrigglesworth, of Stockton-on-Tees; *b* 8 Dec 1939; *Educ* Stockton GS, Stockton-Billingham Tech, Coll of St Mark and St John Chelsea; *m* 1968, Patricia Susan, da of Hugh L Truscott; 2 s, 1 da; *Career* pa to Sir Ronald Gould as gen sec NUT 1966-68, head Co-Op Pty Res Dept 1968-70, press and public affrs mangr Nat Giro 1970-74; MP (Lab and Co-Op 1974-81, SDP 1981-87) Thornaby, Teesside Feb 1974-83, Stockton South 1983-87; pps to Alec Lyon when min of state Home Off 1974, to Roy Jenkins when home sec 1974-76, sec Manifesto Gp within Lab Party 1976-81, vice-chm LEFTA (Lab Econ Fin and Taxation Assoc) 1976-81, oppn spokesman Civil Service 1979-81, SDP home affrs spokesman Nov 1982-May 1983, SDP econ and industl affrs spokesman 1983-87; Alliance Trade & Indust Spokesman 1987; dep chm John Livingston & Sons Ltd, dir CIT Research Ltd, dir Medical Div, Smiths Industries plc; *Recreations* walking, music; *Clubs* IOD, Reform; *Style—* Ian Wrigglesworth, Esq; 24 Buckingham Gate, London SW1E 6LB (☎ 01 828 8323)

WRIGHT, Master Alan John; s of Rev Henry George Wright, MA (d 1963), and Winifred Annie *née* Watson; *b* 21 April 1925; *Educ* St Olave's and St Saviour's GS Southwark; Keble Coll Oxford (MA); *m* 20 Sep 1952, Alma Beatrice, da of Keith Payne Ridding (d 1961); 2 s (Keith b 1955, Matthew b 1962), 1 da (Fiona b 1958); *Career* RAF serv: India, Burma, China 1943-6; slr Shaen Roscoe and Co 1952-71; legal advsr TUC 1955-71; a Master of the Supreme Crt (Sup Crt taxing off) 1972-; *Recreations* Germanic studies, walking, travel, youth work; *Style—* Master Wright; 21 Brockley Park, Forest Hill, London SE23 (☎ 01 690 1929); Royal Courts of Justice, Strand, London WC2

WRIGHT, Hon Mrs (Alison Elizabeth); *née* Franks; da of Baron Franks (Life Peer); *b* 1945; *m* 1974, Stanley Harris Wright; *Style—* The Hon Mrs Wright; 6 Holly Place, Holly Walk, Hampstead, London NW3 (☎ 01 435 0237)

WRIGHT, (William) Allen; s of William Wright, MBE (d 1972), of Edinburgh, and Agnes Isabel May (d 1980); *b* 22 Feb 1932; *Educ* George Watson's Coll Edinburgh; *m* 9 Feb 1957, Eleanor Brunton, da of George Walker Wallace (d 1949), of Edinburgh; 3 da (Caroline b 1958, Hazel b 1960, Angela b 1962); *Career* Nat Serv RTR 1950-52; drama critic and arts ed The Scotsman 1965- (film critic 1956-65); *Books* J M Barrie: Glamour of Twilight (1979); *Recreations* golf; *Style—* Allen Wright, Esq; The Scotsman, 20 North Bridge, Edinburgh EH1 1YT (☎ 031 225 2468, fax 031 225 7302, telex 72255)

WRIGHT, Andrew Paul Kilding; s of Harold Maurice Wright (d 1983), of Walsall, and Eileen Mary, *née* Kilding; *b* 11 Feb 1947; *Educ* Queen Mary's GS Walsall, Univ of Liverpool (BArch (Hons)); *m* 10 Oct 1970, Jean Patricia, da of Alfred John Cross, of Clwyd; 1 s (Samuel b 1976), 2 da (Hannah b 1973, Sarah b 1985); *Career* associate Law & Dunbar Naismith 1979-81, ptnr Law & Dunbar Naismith Ptnrship 1981-; pres Inverness Architectural Assoc 1986- (vice-pres 1985, memb 1981); convener Festival of Architecture for N Scotland 1984; vice-pres Royal Incorporation of Architects in Scotland 1986-; RIBA; FRIAS; *Recreations* music, fishing; *Style—* Andrew P K Wright, Esq; Craiglen, Janquhar Road, Forres, Moray (☎ 0309 72749); 130 High Street, Forres, Moray (☎ 0309 73221, fax 0309 76397)

WRIGHT, Anthony Frank; s of Roger Frank Wright (d 1979), and Barbara Phyllis Wright, *née* Sutton; *b* 5 April 1945; *Educ* Repton, Staffordshire Coll of Commerce (Dip Bus Studies); *m* 20 July 1984, Lydia Hermine, da of Werner Schulz, of Leipzig, E Germany; 1 da by previous m (Amy b 1975); *Career* chm and mkd Frank Wright Ltd 1976-; chm: Frank Wright (Feed Supplements) Ltd 1975-, Frank Wright Feed (Int) Ltd 1977-, Frank Wright (Transport) Ltd 1975-, Frank Wright (Firm Sales) Ltd 1975-; *Recreations* golf, squash; *Clubs* Kedleston Park Golf; *Style—* Anthony Wright, Esq; Frank Wright Group, Blenheim House, Blenheim Rd, Ashbourne, Derbyshire

WRIGHT, Anthony John; s of Harry Wright (d 1972), and Flora Amelia, *née* Alexander; *b* 16 Feb 1939; *Educ* Merchant Taylors'; *m* 29 June 1968, Jane, da of George Hubbard Sumner (d 1962); 1 s (John b 1983), 3 da (Elizabeth b 1969, Katherine b 1971, Sarah b 1976); *Career* Nat Serv Chinese linguist RAF 1958-60; dir JH Little Metals 1960-73, Derby & Co Ltd Philip Bros Ltd 1984-86 (joined 1973), sr vice-pres Metallgesellschaft Corpn 1986-; hon ed Old Merchant Taylors' Soc News Sheet; Freeman City of London 1967, Liveryman Merchant Taylors' Co 1972; *Recreations* golf, cricket, reading, watching rugby; *Clubs* Oriental, Paesartes, Moor Park golf, Old Merchant Taylors' Soc; *Style—* Anthony Wright, Esq; The Orchard, Common Rd, Chorleywood, Herts WD3 5LT (☎ 09278 2937); Metallgesellschaft Corp, 1 Albemarle St, London W1X 3HF (☎ 01 491 1669, fax 01 491 0135, telex 262872)

WRIGHT, Brian Alfred; s of Alexander Wright (d 1947), and Elizabeth, *née* Parfitt (d 1963); *b* 6 Feb 1930; *m* 17 May 1952, Sheila Marion, da of Edward William Wood (d 1965); 2 da (Lesley b 1954, Stephanie b 1957); *Career* actuary; gen mangr Sun Alliance Insur Gp 1981 (dir 1984); dep chm LAUTRO 1986; FIA; *Recreations* golf, gardening, music; *Style—* Brian Wright, Esq; Fairways, Colley Manor Drive, Reigate, Surrey RH2 9JS (☎ 0737 222 046); Sun Alliance Insurance Gp, North St, Horsham, Sussex RH12 1BT (☎ 0403 64141, fax 0403 44750)

WRIGHT, Cdr Brian Harry; s of Lt Cdr Harry Wright, RNVR (d 1982), and Lilian, *née* James; *b* 15 July 1933; *Educ* King's Coll London (BSc, BCom); *m* 1, 4 Aug 1955 (m dis 1962), Virginia Rose Leslie, da of Col Ion David Leslie Beath, CBE, TD; 2 s (Jeremy b 1956, Peter b 1958); m 2, 12 Dec 1966, Coralie Mary (d 1988), da of Sir Frances Spencer Portal, 5 Bt, DL; 1 s (Alexander b 1968), 1 da (Rowena b 1970); *Career* Nat Serv Sub Lt RNVR 1953-55, eastern area mangr English Electric Co Ltd (mangr Bombay branch 1959, dep md India 1961), chm and md Hovair Int Ltd, chm Power Lift Ltd, chm Avia Lift Ltd; Freeman City of London 1969, Liveryman Worshipful Co Clothworkers 1972; CEng, FIEE, FIMH; *Recreations* sailing, skiing, shooting; *Clubs* Royal Yacht Sqdn, RORC Naval, RNVR Yacht; *Style—* Cdr Brian Wright, RD, RNR; Helensbourne, East St Helens, Abingdon, Oxon OX14 5EB (☎ 0235 30200); AV2-402 Anzere Valais Switzerland; Hovair Int Ltd, Ampere Rd, Newbury, Berks (☎ 0635 49525, fax 0635 37949, car 0836 217325, telex 847015 HOVAIR G)

WRIGHT, Christopher Julian; s of Lt Cdr Edward Joseph Wright, of York, and Doreen Lillian, *née* Askew; *b* 1 Jan 1947; *Educ* Ampleforth, Univ of St Andrews (MA); *m* 20 May 1972, Pamela Wendy, da of Geoffrey Denis Adamson (d 1959), of Dorset; 1 da (Alexandra b 1972); *Career* Lt, RN, serving: HMS Pembroke, HMS Fishguard, RNAS Yeovilton; slr, snr ptnr Christopher Wright & Co Slrs, N Yorks; chm mgmnt ctee Richmond CAB; *Recreations* beagling, riding, theatre, racing; *Clubs* English Speaking Union, Law Soc; *Style—* Christopher J Wright, Esq; The Georgian House, Burneston, nr Bedale, N Yorkshire (☎ 0845 567314); 22 Richmond Rd, Catterick Garrison, N Yorkshire (☎ 0748 832431)

WRIGHT, Christopher Norman; s of Walter Reginald Wright, of 3 Butts Lane, Tattersall, Lincs, and Edna May, *née* Corden; *b* 7 Sept 1944; *Educ* King Edward VI GS Louth Lincs, Manchester Univ (BA), Manchester Business Sch; *m* 15 March 1972, Carolyn Rochelle (Chelle), da of Lloyd B Nelson of California, USA; 2 s (Timothy b 1973, Thomas b 1974), 1 da (Chloe b 1978); *Career* operator university and college booking agency Manchester 1965-67, formed Ellis Wright Agency (with Terry Ellis) 1967, changed name to Chrysalis and moved into records and music publishing 1968 (became int with offs in : London, NYC, Los Angeles, Munich), chm Chrysalis (now Chrysalis plc) 1985-; *Recreations* tennis, bridge, breeding race horses,; *Clubs* Oriental; *Style—* Christopher Wright, Esq; Chrysalis Group plc, 12 Stratford Place, London W1 (☎ 01 408 2355, fax 01 495 3278, telex 21753)

WRIGHT, Claud William; CB (1969); s of Horace Vipan Wright (d 1945), of E Yorks, and Catherine Margaret Sales (d 1963); *b* 9 Jan 1917; *Educ* Charterhouse, Ch Ch Oxford (MA); *m* 1947, Alison Violet, da of John Jeffrey Readman, of Dumfries; 1 s (Crispin), 4 da (Dione, Daphne, Ianthe, Oenone); *Career* WO 1939, Private Essex Regt 1940, 2 Lt KRRC 1940, WO 1942-45, GSO 2; MOD 1947, asst under sec (Pol)

1961-66, asst under sec (P Air) 1966-68, dep under sec (Air) 1968-71, dep sec arts and libraries Dept of Educn and Sci 1971-76, res fell Wolfson Coll Oxford 1977-83, Lyell Fund 1947, RH Worth Prize 1958, Foulerton Award Geologists Assoc 1955, Phillips Medal Yorks Geological Soc 1976 Prestwich Medal 1987, Strimble Award Paleontology Soc of America 1988; *Books* Monographs on fossil crabs (with J S H Collins, 1972), ammonites of the middle chalk (with W J Kennedy, 1981, 1984) and sea-urchins (with A B Smith, 1988), numerous papers on geological, palaeontological and archaeological subjects; *Recreations* archaeology, botany, palaeontology; *Clubs* Athenaeum; *Style*— C W Wright, Esq, CB; Old Rectory, Seaborough, Beaminster, Dorset DT8 3QY (☎ 0308 68426)

WRIGHT, David John; s of John Frank Wright, of Wolverhampton; *b* 16 June 1944; *Educ* Wolverhampton GS, Peterhouse Cambridge; *m* 3 Feb 1968, Sally Ann Dodkin; 1 s (Nicholas b 1970), 1 da (Laura b 1973); *Career* HM Dip Serv: third sec 1966, third later second sec Tokyo 1966, second later first sec FCO 1972, ENA Paris 1975, first sec Paris 1976, private sec to Sec of Cabinet 1980, cnsllr (Econ) Tokyo 1982, head of personnel servs dept FCO 1985, dep private sec to HRH The Prince of Wales 1988-; *Recreations* running, cooking, military history; *Style*— David J Wright, Esq; Foreign and Commonwealth Office, King Charles Street, London SW1A 2AH

WRIGHT, David John Murray; s of Gordon Alfred Wright (d 1957), of Johannesburg, SA, and Jean Murray Wright (d 1983); *b* 23 Feb 1920; *Educ* Northampton Sch for the Deaf, Oriel Coll Oxford (MA); *m* 1, 6 Oct 1951, Phillipa (d 1985), da of George Reid (d 1964), of Grassington, NZ; m 2, 13 March 1987, Agnes Mary, *née* Swift; *Career* Gregory Fell in literature Univ of Leeds 1965-67; ed: Nimbus 1955-56, X Magazine 1959-62; author, poet and translator; FRSL 1967; *Books* Poems (1948), Moral Stories (1954), Monologue of a Deaf Man (1958), Roy Campbell (1960), Nerve Ends (1969), Deafness, a Personal Account (1969), A South African Album (1975), A View of the North (1976), To the Gods the Shades, New and Collected Poems (1981); translations: Beowulf 1957, The Canterbury Tales (prose version 1964, verse version 1985); *Style*— David Wright, Esq; c/o A D Peters Ltd, 5th Floor, The Chambers, Chelsea Harbour, Lots Rd, London SW10

WRIGHT, David William; s of William Richard Douglas Wright of Whitstable, Kent, and Doris Jane, *née* Arnold; *b* 2 May 1942; *Educ* Kent Coll Canterbury, Edinburgh Univ (MA); *m* 23 Sept 1917, Barbara Rita, da of Gerald Gardner, FCA (d 1973); 1 s (Oliver b 1971), 2 da (Annabel b 1973, Eleanor b 1978); *Career* barr Lincolns' Inn; var cos 1968-76; co sec Coates Bros plc 1979-84 First Leisure Corpn plc 1984-; chm Royal Tunbridge Wells Civic Soc, Freeman City of London 1983, Liveryman Worshipful Co of Spectaclemakers 1983, FCIS 1977; *Recreations* squash, tennis, theatre; *Style*— David Wright, Esq; Hollin House, Court Rd, Tunbridge Wells, Kent TN4 8EF (☎ 0892 32 943); 7 Soho St, London W1V 5FA (☎ 01 437 9727, fax 01 439 0088)

WRIGHT, Sir Denis Arthur Hepworth; GCMG (1971, KCMG 1961, CMG 1954); s of A E Wright (d 1949), and Margery Hepworth Chapman (d 1973); *b* 23 Mar 1911; *Educ* Brentwood Sch, St Edmund Hall Oxford; *m* 1939, Iona, da of Granville Craig, of Bolney, Sussex (d 1941); *Career* Diplomatic Serv, served in commercial and consular capacities: Romania, Turkey, Yugoslavia, USA; asst under-sec FO 1955-59, ambass Ethiopia 1959-62, asst under-sec FO 1962, ambass Iran 1963-71 (formerly cnsllr 1954-55, chargé d'affaires 1953-54); non exec dir: Shell Tport and Trading Co, Standard Chartered Bank, Mitchell Cotts Gp 1971-81; govr Overseas Serv, Farnham Castle 1971-87; pres Br Inst Persian Studies 1978-87; hon fellow: St Edmund Hall 1972, St Antony's Coll Oxford 1976; *Books* Persia (with James Morris and Roger Wood, 1968) The English Amongst the Persians (1977), The Persians Amongst the English (1985); *Clubs* Traveller; *Style*— Sir Denis Wright, GCMG; Duck Bottom, Haddenham, Aylesbury, Bucks HP17 8AL (☎ 0844 291 086)

WRIGHT, Hon Mrs (Doreen Julia); *née* Wingfield; da of 8 Viscount Powerscourt, KP, MVO (d 1947), and Sybil, *née* Pleydell-Bouverie (d 1946); *b* 29 Mar 1904; *m* 10 Jan 1928, FitzHerbert Wright (d 1975), formerly 15/19 Hussars, s of Henry FitzHerbert Wright, JP, CA, of Yeldersley Hall, Derbys; 1 s, 3 da (of whom Susan Mary m 1, Maj Ronald Ivor Ferguson, and is mother of HRH The Duchess of York *qv*); *Style*— The Hon Mrs Wright; Vern Leaze, Calne, Wiltshire SN11 0JF

WRIGHT, Edward Arnold; s of John Ernest Wright (d 1976), of Hornsey, and Alice Maud, *née* Arnold (d 1968); *b* 20 Nov 1926; *Educ* Tollington GS Muswell Hill; *Career* 52 RTR 1943-45, KDG 1945-47; 1962-70: sales dir Gothic Press Ltd, md Gothic Display Ltd, md Gothic "Studios" Ltd; chm and md Edward Wright Ltd 1970-; hon tres int cncl for Bird Preservation BR section; cncl memb: Br Tst Ornithology, Fauna and Flora Preservation Soc; Freeman City of London 1980, Liveryman Worshipful Co of Gardeners 1980; *Recreations* squash, gardening, shooting; *Clubs* MCC, City Livery; *Style*— Edward Wright, Esq; Edward Wright Ltd, 5/11 Palfrey Place, London SW8 1PB (☎ 01 735 9535, fax 01 793 0967, mobile 0860 539 806)

WRIGHT, Sir Edward Maitland; s of Maitland Turner Wright (d 1943), and Kate, *née* Owen (d 1954); *b* 13 Feb 1906; *Educ* Jesus Coll and Ch Ch Oxford, Göttingen Univ (BA, MA, DPhil); *m* 1934, Elizabeth Phyllis (d 1987), da of Harry Percy Harris, JP (d 1952); 1 s (John); *Career* Fl-Lt RAFVR, Princ Sci Offr Air Miny Intelligence 1943-45, prof mathematics Aberdeen Univ 1936-62, princ and vice-chllr 1962-76, research fell 1976-; hon fell Jesus Coll Oxford 1963, Hon DSc Strathclyde; Hon LLD: St Andrews, Pennsylvania, Aberdeen; Order of Polonia Restituta 1978; FRSE; kt 1977; *Books* (with G.H. Hardy) Theory of Numbers (1st edn 1938, 5th 1979); *Clubs* Caledonian (London); *Style*— Sir Edward Wright; 16 Primrosehill Ave, Cults, Aberdeen (☎ 0224 861185)

WRIGHT, Hon Mrs (Emily Ann); *née* Hughes; o da of Baron Cledwyn of Penrhos, CH, PC (Life Peer), *qv*; *b* 1950; *m* 1976, Peter Wright; children; *Style*— The Hon Mrs Wright

WRIGHT, Ernest George; GM (1952), CPM (1957); s of Thomas Bennet Wright (d 1966); *b* 25 July 1923; *Educ* Dame Allen's Sch Newcastle; *m* 1955, Lady Sarah Caroline, *qv*, da 12 Earl Waldegrave; 2 s (Thomas Geoffrey, David James); *Career* Fl-Lt Bomber Cmd RAF 1942-46, sr-supt Colonial Police Service (Kenya) 1947-63, fisheries and recreation mangr Bristol Water Works Co 1963-88, memb: Mendip Dist Cncl 1976-88 (chm 1984-86), Wells City Cncl 1976-88; mayor of Wells 1979-80; *Recreations* fishing, shooting; *Clubs* Flyfishers', Kenya Flyfishers', Nairobi and Mombasa; *Style*— Ernest Wright, Esq, GM, CPM; Honibere Farmhouse, Burton, Stogursey, Bridgwater TA5 1PZ (☎ 027874 300)

WRIGHT, Francis Gerald Gribble; OBE (1943); s of Gerald Goodhall Wright (d 1939), and Frances Amy Gribble; *b* 2 June 1902; *Educ* Clifton Coll, London Matriculation; *m* 6 Dec 1928, Dorothy Mary, da of Lt-Col G Fowler, FRCS, IMS (d 1939); 2 s (Francis b 1932, John b 1934), 3 da (Jennifer b 1930, Sylvia b 1939, Felicity b 1951); *Career* Indian Police Service 1921-47 (retired on transfer of power), dep Inspector Gen of Police 1948-59, dep Cmmnr of Police, Ethiopia; Indian Police Medal 1947, Order of the Star of Ethiopia 1959; 1959-67 Home Office Police Dept; memb United Soc of Artists; *Recreations* big game shooting, polo, hockey, tennis, golf, painting (exhibited London RI, RBA, UA, Paris Salon); *Clubs* Civil Service; *Style*— Francis Wright, Esq, OBE; Powerscourt, Cavendish Road, Redhill, Surrey (☎ 0737 766229)

WRIGHT, Geoffrey Norman; s of Walter Anthony Wright, MC (d 1939), of West Hartlepool, and Evelyn, *née* Blake (d 1979); *b* 14 April 1925; *Educ* West Hartlepool GS, Univ of Durham; *m* 16 July 1949, Jean, da of Charles Loy Mann (d 1941), of Bath; 3 s (Peter b 1951, Richard b 1954, David b 1957); *Career* groundcrew RAF 1944-47; sr master Bradford-on-Avon Sch Wilts 1970-76 (joined 1950, head English 1963-70), author; chm: Bradford-on-Avon Pres Soc 1964-73, Winsley Parish Cncl 1966-71, Dales Centre Nat Tst 1983-85, Herefords Marches Assoc Nat Tst 1988-; *Books* The East Riding (1976), Yorkshire Dales (1977), View of Wessex (1978), Stone Villages of Britain (1985), Roads and Trackways of Yorkshire Dales (1985), The Trackways of Wessex (1988), The Northumbrian Uplands (1989); *Recreations* walking; *Style*— Geoffrey Wright, Esq; 6 Huntington Green, Ashford Carbonel, Ludlow, Shops SY8 4DN (☎ 058 474 692)

WRIGHT, Gerald; s of William Arthur Reginald (d 1967), and Olive Annie Neal Wright, of Bexleyheath, Kent; *b* 9 Sept 1935; *Educ* Monmouth Sch, Queens' Coll Cambridge (MA); *m* 1959, Elizabeth Ann, da of Dr William Edward Harris (d 1974), of Llandaff; 3 s (Jeremy, Mathew, William); *Career* dir: Lintas London 1972-73, chm Lintas Scandinavia 1973-74, dep chm and md Lintas London 1974-80, md Thresher and Co Ltd 1980-81, mktg dir (UK) Whitbread & Co 1981-82 and chm Nat Sales Div 1982-83; returned to Lintas to be chm and chief exec Lintas London 1983; *Recreations* reading, opera, walking, jogging, rugby, cricket; *Clubs* Reform, Solus; *Style*— Gerald Wright, Esq; 25 Crown Lane, Chislehurst, Kent (☎ 01 467 7918); Lintas Worldwide-London, Lintas House, New Fetter Lane, London EC4 (☎ 01 822 8500 (DDI))

WRIGHT, Hon Glyn David; s of Baron Wright of Ashton-under-Lyne, CBE (d 1974) (Life Peer); bro of Hon Owen Wright *qv*; *b* 22 May 1940; *Educ* Ashton Tech; *m* 1965, May, da of George Frederick Alldridge; 2 da (Lisa, Stephanie); *Career* co dir; *Style*— The Hon Glyn Wright; 12 Brookfield Grove, Ashton-under-Lyne, Lancs

WRIGHT, Graham; s of Edward George Wright (d 1988), and Doris, *née* Belsham; *b* 28 Dec 1944; *Educ* Archbishop Tenison's GS, Univ of Newcastle upon Tyne (BSc); *m* 29 March 1969, Susan Mary, da of Kenneth Atkinson, of Broxbourne; 1 s (James Kenneth Graham b 7 March 1972), 2 da (Katherine b 29 July 1970, Lucy b 7 Jan 1977); *Career* computer programmer Rolls Royce 1968-71, Int Commodities Clearing House 1971-87 (exec dir 1984-87), dep chief exec Int Petroleum Exchange 1987-; LIMA; *Recreations* golf, bridge; *Clubs* Porters Park; *Style*— Graham Wright, Esq; 8 Falstaff Gdns, St Albans, Herts (☎ 0727 670 88); IPE Ltd, Int Hse, 1 St Katherine's Way, London E1 9UN (☎ 01 481 0643, 01 481 8485, 927479)

WRIGHT, Gregory Arthur; s of Ernest Arthur Wright, and Florence, *née* Swindells; *b* 1 Nov 1946; *Educ* Bournville Tech GS; *m* 21 Nov 1970, Christine, da of Stanley Allen Tongue, of 2 Pooltail Walk, Northfield, Birmingham; 2 s (Dale b 1974, Adam b 1977), 1 da (Emma b 1982); *Career* CA, Josolyn Layton-Bennett 1969, joined Ernst & Whinney Birmingham 1972 (ptnr 1980), managing ptnr Ernst & Whinney Cardiff 1985 (Edinburgh 1988); FCA 1969; *Recreations* chess, cricket, gardening; *Style*— Gregory Wright, Esq; Little Fosters, 120 Whitehouse Rd, Barnton, Edinburgh EH4 6DH (☎ 031 339 4853); Ernst & Whinney, 39 Melville St, Edinburgh EH3 7JL (☎ 031 226 4621, fax 031 226 2438, telex 727832 ERNSED)

WRIGHT, Lady; Helen; *née* Tait; *m* 1946, Sir Robert Wright, DSO, OBE, sometime Pres GMC (d 1981); 1 s, 2 da; *Style*— Lady Wright; 27 Thomson Drive, Bearsden, Glasgow (☎ 041 942 1008)

WRIGHT, Hubert (Hugh); s of Herbert Wright (d 1968), of Keighley, and Hilda May, *née* Chamberlin (d 1967); *b* 16 August 1931; *Educ* Keighley GS; *m* 18 July 1964, Sheila, da of Jim Jennings (d 1967), of Bradford, W Yorks; m 2, 4 Aug 1978, Olive May, da of Llewellyn Charles Harding, JP, of Cambs; *Career* CA in private practice, sr lectr in taxation Leed Poly; FCA; *Style*— Hugh Wright, Esq; 34 Oakwood Green, North Lane, Leeds LS8 2QU (☎ 0532 650323); work: Dept of Accountancy, Leeds Poly (☎ 0532 463833)

WRIGHT, Hugh Raymond; s of Rev Raymond Blayney Wright (d 1980), of Macclesfield, and Alys Mary, *née* Hawksworth (d 1972); *b* 24 August 1938; *Educ* Kingswood Sch Bath, The Queen's Coll Oxford (MA); *m* 7 April 1962, Jillian Mary, da of Peter McIldowie Meiklejohn (d 1959), of Bedford; 3 s (Andrew b 1963, William b 1967, James b 1970); *Career* asst master Brentwood Sch 1961-64, head classics dept and housemaster Boyne House Cheltenham 1964-79; headmaster: Stockport GS 1979-85, Greshams Sch Holt 1985-, chm community serv sub ctee HMC 1985-(chm NW dist 1983); memb: panel Admty Interview Bd 1982-, ACCM 1987-; lay reader Diocese Chester and Norwich, tres Eastern div ISIS; FRSA 1984, AMMA; *Books* Visual Publications incl Film Strips on History of Church (1980); *Recreations* walking, ornithology, music, theatre; *Clubs* East India; *Style*— Hugh Wright, Esq; Lockhart House, Gresham's Sch, Holt, Norfolk NR25 6DZ (☎ 0263 713 739); Gresham's School, Holt, Norfolk NR25 6EA (☎ 0263 713 271, fax 0263 712 028)

WRIGHT, Col Humphrey Bradshaw Mellor; s of Rev Ernest Hugh Wright (d 1939), and Violet Helen Frances, *née* Mellor (d 1917); *b* 7 Mar 1907; *Educ* Shrewsbury, RMA Woolwich; *m* 24 May 1935, Sybil Mary (d 1981), da of Maj Hon George Algernon Lascelles (d 1932), of Windleshore, Bembridge, Isle of Wight; *Career* cmmnd 2 Lt RA 1927, served UK 1927-30, Lt 1930, Egypt and Sudan 1930-38, Capt 1936, BEF 1939-40 (POW 1940-45), Staff Coll 1946, WO 1946-48, CO 56 HAA Regt Malta 1949-51, AAG Western Cmd 1951-54, Col AQ Midwest Dist 1954-57, ret 1958; *Recreations* bridge, gardening; *Clubs* Naval and Military, MCC; *Style*— Col Humphrey Wright; Conyers Place, Marnhull, Dorset (☎ 0258 820372)

WRIGHT, Ian Wheeler; s of Rev Ernest Wright (d 1961), and Emily Elizabeth, *née* Wheeler; *b* 9 Mar 1934; *Educ* Kingswood Sch Bath, Ch Ch Oxford (MA); *m* 1968, (Janet) Lydia, da of Norman Giles (d 1982); 1 s (Oliver b 1973); *Career* HM Overseas CS Kenya 1956-59; ed Elliot Lake Standard Ontario Canada 1960; joined The Guardian 1961, film critic, dep features ed 1964, special correspondent Sudan Aden 1967, Far

East correspondent, war correspondent Vietnam 1968-70, foreign ed 1970-76; managing and dep ed 1977-; dir Guardian Newspapers 1984-; *Style*— Ian Wright, Esq; The Guardian, 119 Farringdon Road, London EC1 (☎ 01 278 2332)

WRIGHT, Hon Mrs (Jane Anne Caroline); *née* Littleton; yr da of 5 Baron Hatherton (d 1969); *b* 10 Sept 1929; *m* 24 Jan 1967, Rev Charles Piachaud Wright, s of late Charles Moncrieff Piachaud Wright, of St Andrews, Fife; *Style*— The Hon Mrs Wright; 12 St Swithun St, Winchester, Hants

WRIGHT, Joe Booth; CMG (1979); s of Joe Booth Wright (d 1967), of Notts, and Annie Elizabeth, *née* Stockdale (d 1964); *b* 24 August 1920; *Educ* King Edward VI GS Retford, London Univ (BA); *m* 1, 1945, Pat, *née* Beaumont; 1 s (Christopher), 2 da (Helen, Annie); m 2, 1967, Patricia Maxine, da of Albert Nicholls (d 1965); *Career* serv in Armed Forces 1941-46; HM Diplomatic Serv 1947-79 at Jerusalem, Munich, Basrah, Formosa, Indonesia, Cyprus, Tunisia; HM consul-gen: Hanoi 1971-72, Geneva 1973-75; HM ambass: Ivory Coast, Upper Volta & Niger 1975-78, ret 1979; writer, lectr, translator; memb Inst of Linguistics and Translators Guild 1982; FRSA 1987; *Books* Francophone Black Africa Since Independence (1981), Zaire Since Independence (1983), Paris As It Was (1985); *Recreations* cricket, writing, music, cinema; *Clubs* Royal Overseas League; *Style*— Joe Wright Esq, CMG; 29 Brittany Rd, St Leonards-on-Sea, E Sussex TN38 0RD (☎ 0424 439563)

WRIGHT, John Derek; s of Leslie Thomas Wright, of Cornwall, and Ceinwen Angharad, *née* Johns (d 1984); *b* 25 June 1937; *Educ* West Bridgford GS; *m* 20 Sept 1958, Maureen Pemberton, da of Albert Edward Butler, of Truro; 2 da (Angela Elizabeth b 10 Aug 1960, Sara Jane b 19 Feb 1966); *Career* regnl dir Contractors Servs Gp 1974-78, md Lomount Construction 1978-83, chm and md Mid Cornwall Plant 1983-89; *Recreations* walking, breeding and showing pug dogs; *Clubs* Lighthouse; *Style*— John Wright, Esq; The Coppice, Trebetherick, Wadebridge, Cornwall (☎ 0208 862328); Mid Cornwall Plant Ltd, Singlerose, Stenalees, St Austell, Cornwall (☎ 0726 851133, fax 0726 850900)

WRIGHT, John Gordon Laurence; s of Rev William Henry Laurence Wright (Chaplain RAF 1939-45), of Edinburgh, and Mary Campbell, *née* Macdonald; *b* 6 June 1944; *Educ* Glenalmond, Brasenose Coll Oxford (MA); *m* 16 July 1974, (Faith) Alison, da of Dr John Allan Guy (d 1986, Capt RAMC 1939-45), of Kendal; 2 s (Thomas b 1977, Richard b 1981); *Career* Hambros Bank Ltd 1967-71, dir: Stewart Ivory and Co Ltd 1971- (formerly Stewart Fund Managers Ltd) 1972; *Recreations* photography, skiing; *Clubs* New (Edinburgh); *Style*— John Wright, Esq; 34 Greenhill Gardens, Edinburgh EH10 4BP; Stewart Ivory & Co Ltd, 45 Charlotte Sq, Edinburgh EH2 4HW

WRIGHT, John Keith; JP (Dover and E Kent 1983-); s of James Henry Wright (d 1965), and Elsie May Willis (d 1984); *b* 30 May 1928; *Educ* Tiffins, King's Coll Cambridge, Yale; *m* 1958, Thérèse Marie-Claire, da of René Aubenas (d 1977), of Paris; *Career* OEEC (Paris) 1951-56, UKAEA 1956-61, MOD 1961-66, FCO 1966-71, under-sec Overseas Dvpt Admin FCO 1971-84; econ and fin conslt; dir Sadler's Wells (Trading) 1983-; memb cncl: Queen Elizabeth Coll Univ of London 1982-85, King's Coll Univ of London 1984-; tstee Thomson Foundation 1986-, Bd of Visitors Canterbury Prison 1987; *Recreations* economic and mil history, music, amateur radio; *Clubs* Athenaeum, Beefsteak; *Style*— John Wright, Esq, JP; 47 Brunswick Gardens, London W8; Bowling Corner, Sandwich, Kent

WRIGHT, Keith Elliot; s of Wilfred Stratten Wright (d 1961), and Dorothea, *née* Elliot (d 1961); *b* 20 Nov 1920; *Educ* Giggleswick Sch Settle, Selwyn Coll Cambridge (BA); *m* 20 Feb 1954, Patricia Ann, da of Raymond Tustin Taylor (d 1985); 1 s (David b 1956), 2 da (Catherine b 1958, Sally b 1959); *Career* WWII offr Duke of Wellington Regt 1939-45; sr ptnr Slaughter & May 1976-84 (slr 1950-, ptnr 1955); chm exec ctee King Edward VII's Hosp for Offrs 1986- (memb 1979-); vice chm London Advsy Bd Salvation Army; memb: cncl Offr's Assoc, ctee of mgmnt Wilts Rural Housing Assoc; memb Law Soc 1950; *Recreations* theatre, walking, gardening; *Style*— Keith Wright, Esq; Kestrels, Oak Lane, Easterton, nr Devizes, Wilts SN10 4PD (☎ 0380 812573); King Edward VII's Hospital for Officers, Beaumont St, London WIN 2AA (☎ 01 486 4411)

WRIGHT, Col Leslie William; TD (1952, clasps 1961 and 1963), DL (Derbyshire 1983); s of Leonard Wright (d 1925), of Glossop, and Gertrude Veronica, *née* Wain (d 1938); *b* 26 June 1920; *Educ* Glossop GS, Univ of Sheffield Inst of Educ; *m* 30 Aug 1941, Kathleen, da of John Howard (d 1964), of Bakewell; 1 da (Christina Mary b 1943); *Career* enlisted 2 (N Midland) Corps Signals TA 1939, 12 Wireless section Rifle Bde (BEF) Def of Calais 1940, 4 Corps Signals, 11 Armd Divnl Signals, cmmnd RCS 1943; 77 Divnl Signals, 76 Divnl Signals; Central Med Forces 1944-46: II L of C and 8 Army Signals, Battle of Cassino 1944, Chief Signalmaster Naples 1945, memb Allied mission for observing the Greek electns Crete 1946; joined Royal Signals reconstituted TA 1947, Lt-Col cmdg 46 (N Midland) Signal Regt TA 1964-67, Bt-Col 1967; Hon Col: Univ of Sheffield OTC 1977-85, Derbys Cadet Bn Worcs and Sherwood Foresters Regt 1988-; sr lectr in history and def studies (formerly lectr) Sheffield City Poly (formerly Sheffield Coll of Technol), memb mil educn ctee Univ of Sheffield 1970-; vice chm: E Midlands TAVR Assoc 1981-84, Royal Signals Assoc 1972-84; pres Sheffield and Dist branch 1940 Dunkirk Veterans Assoc 1972-, pres Bakewell and Dist branch Royal Br Legion 1978-; chm Sheffield Def Studies Dining Club 1986-, lectr in principles and Law Br Red Cross Soc 1983; memb: W Derbys DC 1973-83, Peak Park Jt Planning Bd 1973-77; Mayor of Bakewell 1978-79; Hon MA univ of Sheffield 1986; *Recreations* music, walking, Holy Land; *Style*— Col Leslie Wright, TD, DL; Rock House, Buxton Rd, Bakewell, Derby DE4 1DA (☎ 0629 812530)

WRIGHT, Malcolm Allan; s of Frederick Thomas Wright (d 1969), and Dorothy Jessie, *née* Crossingham; *b* 25 Jan 1939; *Educ* St Dunstans Coll, Harvard Business Sch (advanced mgmnt programme); *m* 8 July 1967, Brenda Mary, da of Edward Rupert Nicholson, of Grey Wings, The Warren, Ashtead, Surrey; 2 da (Helen Gail b 1968, Elizabeth Mary b 1971, d 1976); *Career* 2 Lt RR Artillery 25 Field Regt RA 1958-60, 1 Lt (Gazetted) on Reserve 1961; fin dir Beck and Pollitzer Engrg Ltd 1961-74; Cape Industs plc 1974-84: md Cape Contracts Ltd 1979-81, gp personnel mangr 1981-86, chm Automotive Divn 1983-85; conslt 1985-86, exec dir and chief exec indust textiles divn BBA Gp plc, memb governing cncl Br Rubber Mfrs Assoc; memb Round Table 1973-79; Freeman City of London 1973, Freeman Worshipful Co of Horners 1973; ACIS 1966, FCIS 1974; *Recreations* golf, gardening, DIY (and occasional cricket), photography; *Clubs* Army and Navy; *Style*— Malcolm Wright, Esq; High Point, 58 The Mount, Fetcham, Surrey KT22 9EA (☎ 0372 376 918); Suites 45-47, The Hop Exchange, 24 Southwark St, London SE1 1TY (☎ 01 407 3461, fax 01 403 7086, car tel 0860 738 108)

WRIGHT, Malcolm Carter; s of Edward Wright (d 1977); *b* 11 April 1938; *Educ* King's Sch Macclesfield; *m* 1964, Susan Helen, *née* Winter; 2 s; *Career* jt md R Bailey & Son plc; chm Surgical Dressings Manufacturers Assoc 1980-83; memb RYA; *Recreations* yachting (yacht 'Sunchase'); *Clubs* South Caernarvon Yacht, Pwllheli Sailing, Rudyard Lake Sailing; *Style*— Malcolm Wright, Esq; 62 Longhurst Lane, Mellor, Stockport, Cheshire SK6 5AH (☎061 427 4506); office: Dysart St, Stockport, Cheshire (☎ 061 483 1133; telex 668211)

WRIGHT, (John) Michael; QC (1974); s of Prof John George Wright (d 1972), and Elsie Lloyd, *née* Razey (d 1955); *b* 26 Oct 1932; *Educ* The King's Sch Chester, Oriel Coll Oxford (BA, MA); *m* 25 July 1959, Kathleen Esther Gladys, da of Frederick Arthur Meanwell, MM (d 1945); 1 s (Timothy b 1965), 2 da (Elizabeth b 1961, Katharine b 1963); *Career* nat Serv RA 1951-53, 2 Lt 1952, Lt 1953, TA 1953-56, TARO 1956-; barr Lincoln's Inn 1957, Crown Ct Recorder 1974-, bencher 1983-, legal assessor RCVS 1984-; ldr SE Circuit 1981-83, chm Bar 1983-84 (vice chm 1982-83); *Style*— Michael Wright, Esq, QC; Old Coombe House, Sharpthorne, West Sussex; 2 Crown Office Row, Temple, London EC4Y 7HJ (☎ 01 353 9337, fax 01 583 0589, telex 8954005 TWO COR G)

WRIGHT, Michael Leslie Beaumont; s of Harold Norman Wright, of Solihull, Warks and Elsie Margaret, *née* Beaumont (d 1971); *b* 18 Oct 1922; *Educ* Wellesbourne Sch Solihull Warks; *m* 1946, Maisie Dawn, da of Dr Adam Turner (d 1926), of Stratford Road, Birmingham; 2 s (Timothy, Andrew), 2 da (Penelope, Susan); *Career* Lt (A) RNVR; chm Newman-Tonks Gp plc and other cos; *Recreations* golf, power boating; *Style*— Michael Wright Esq; Bats Hall, Knowle, Warwickshire (☎ 560 2423); c/o Newman-Tonks Group plc, Hospital St, Birmingham (☎ 021 359 3221)

WRIGHT, Miles Francis Melville; yst s of Montague Francis Melville Wright (d 1968), and Marjorie Isobel, *née* Brook (d 1968); *b* 3 Dec 1943; *Educ* Ampleforth, Ch Ch Oxford (MA); *Career* dir: American Int Underwriters (UK) Ltd 1982-84, asst md AIU (UK) Ltd 1984-87; md Polwring Underwriting Agency at Lloyds 1988-, Active Underwriter Syndicate 1098 Lloyds 1988-; memb: Worshipful Co of Glaziers, Worshipful Co of Insurers; *Recreations* cricket, tennis, shooting, gardening; *Clubs* Naval and Military, MCC, I Zingari; *Style*— Miles Wright, Esq; The Barracks, Cranbrook, Kent TN17 2LG (☎ 0580 712209); 10 Philpot Lane, London EC3M 8AA; Lloyds, 1 Lime St, London EC3 (☎ 01 626 8201/623 7100 ext 3634, fax 01 283 2381, telex 9419440)

WRIGHT, Neville Clarkson; s of Percival Albert Wright, of Petts Wood, Kent (d 1965), and Phyllis Marjorie, *née* Clarkson (d 1984); *b* 21 Feb 1929; *Educ* Aldenham, Queens' Coll Cambridge (MA); *m* 18 Apr 1959, Jennifer Margaret, da of Geoffrey William Tookey, QC, of Beckenham, Kent (d 1976); 1 s (Andrew b 1962), 2 da (Jane b 1960, Victoria b 1964); *Career* 2 Lt RA; slr in private practice; ptnr Clarkson Wright and Jakes (Orpington); Notary Public; former pres: Bromley Hockey Club, Petts Wood Operatic Soc; memb: The Law Soc, The Prov Notaries Soc; *Clubs* Hawks (Cambridge), Bromley Hockey; *Style*— Neville C Wright, Esq; Vine Cottage, Hollybush Lane, Sevenoaks, Kent TN13 3UJ; Villa San Miguel, Binisafua, Menorca; Clarkson Wright and Jakes, Valiant House, 12 Knoll Rise, Orpington, Kent BR6 0PG (☎ 0689 71621, fax 0689 78537).

WRIGHT, Sir (John) Oliver; GCMG (1981, KCMG 1974, CMG 1964), GCVO (1978), DSC (1944); s of Arthur Wright (d 1963), of Seaford; *b* 6 Mar 1921; *Educ* Solihull Sch, Christ's Coll Cambridge (MA); *m* 1942, (Lillian) Marjory, da of Hedley Vickers Osborne, of Solihull; 3 s (Nicholas b 1946, John b 1949, Christopher b 1950); *Career* RNVR WW II; joined HM Diplomatic Service 1945, served: NY, Bucharest, Singapore, Berlin, Pretoria; private sec to: Foreign Sec 1963, PM 1964-66; ambass Denmark 1966-69; seconded to Home Office, UK rep to NI Govt 1969-70; chief clerk 1970-72, dep under-sec FCO 1972-75, ambass: FRG 1975-81, ret; dir Siemens Ltd and bd memb Br Cncl 1981-82; hon fellow and master designate of Christ's Coll Cambridge, resigned July 1982; recalled from ret to be ambass Washington 1982-86; tstee Br Museum 1986-; King of Arms, Order of St Michael and St George; dir: Savoy Hotel plc 1987-, Board of the Burton Council 1986-; chm: Anglo-trust Encounter 1986-. Burton Kömgowinhu Conference Serving Committee 1986-, formerly Shakespeare Inheritance Globe Center and vice-chm of Int Council 1986-; visiting prof Univ of S Carolina 1986-; Clark Fell Cornell Univ 1987; Hon DHL Univ of Nebraska 1983, Grand Cross German Order of Merit 1978; *Recreations* theatre, opera; *Clubs* Travellers'; *Style*— Sir Oliver Wright, GCMG, GCVO, DSC; Burstow Hall, Horley, Surrey RH6 9SR (☎ 0293 783494)

WRIGHT, Hon Owen Mortimor; s of Baron Wright of Ashton-under-Lyne, CBE (d 1974) (Life Peer); bro of Hon Glyn Wright, *qv*; *b* 18 Nov 1934; *m* 1960, Barbara, da of Arthur Hudson, of Stalybridge; 1 s, 1 da; *Style*— The Hon Owen Wright; Wingthorne, Slade Rd, Newton, Swansea SA3 4UE

WRIGHT, Sir Patrick Richard Henry; KCMG (1984, CMG 1978); s of Herbert Wright (d 1977), of The Hermitage, Chetwode, Buckingham, and Rachel, *née* Green; *b* 28 June 1931; *Educ* Marlborough, Merton Coll Oxford; *m* 1958, Virginia Anne, step da of Col Samuel John Hannaford (d 1983), of Hove; 2 s (Marcus b 1959, Angus b 1964), 1 da (Olivia b 1963); *Career* Nat Service Lt RA; entered Foreign Serv 1955; served: Beirut, Washington, Cairo, Bahrain; private sec (Overseas Affrs) to PM 1974-77; ambass: Luxembourg 1977-79, Syria 1979-81; dep under-sec FCO Jan 1982-84, ambass Saudi Arabia 1984-86; perm under sec FCO and head Dip Serv 1986-; hon fell Merton Coll Oxford 1987; *Clubs* Oxford and Cambridge; *Style*— Sir Patrick Wright, KCMG; FCO, King Charles St, London SW1

WRIGHT, Sir Paul Hervé Giraud; KCMG (1975, CMG 1960, OBE (1952); s of Richard Hervé Giraud Wright (sec of White's Club), and Ellen Margaret, da of Lewis Mercier; *b* 12 May 1915; *Educ* Westminster; *m* 1942, Beatrice Frederika, MP Bodmin 1941-45, da of Frank Roland Clough and widow of Flt-Lt John Rankin Rathbone, MP, RAFVR (ka 1940; 1 da; *Career* served WWII, Maj KRRC, HQ 21 Army Gp (despatches); contested (Lib) Bethnal Green 1945; asst dir PR NCB 1946-48, pr dir Festival of Britain 1948-51; joined HM Foreign Serv 1951, Paris and NY 1951-54, FO 1954-56, The Hague 1956-57, head of Info Policy Dept FO 1957-60, Cairo 1960-61, memb UK delegn to NATO 1961-64, dir-gen Br Info Services NY 1964-68, min (info) Washington 1965-68; ambass: Congo (Kinshasa) and Republic of Burundi 1969-71, Lebanon 1971-75, ret; special rep of sec state Foreign and Cwlth Affrs 1975-78, hon sec London Celebrations Ctee for Queen's Silver Jubilee 1977, chm Irvin GB Ltd 1979-, govr Westminster Cathedral Choir Sch 1981-, chm Br American Arts Assoc

1983-, Br Lebonese Assoc 1987, pres The Elizabethan Club 1988-, memb Trusthouse Forte Cncl 1987; *Books* A Brittle Glory; *Clubs* Garrick; *Style*— Sir Paul Wright, KCMG, OBE; 62 Westminster Gardens, London SW1P 4JG

WRIGHT, Peter Robert; CBE (1985); s of Bernard Wright (d 1981), and Hilda Mary, *née* Foster (d 1973); *b* 25 Nov 1926; *Educ* Bedales, Leighton Park; *m* 1954, Sonya Hana, da of Yoshi Sueyoshi (d 1931); 1 s (Jonathan), 1 da (Poppy); *Career* dancer Ballet Jooss and Sadler's Wells Theatre Ballet 1947-55, ballet master Sadler's Wells Opera Ballet and teacher Royal Ballet Sch 1955-58, ballet master Stuttgart Ballet 1960-63, guest prodr BBC TV 1963-65, freelance choreographer and prodr 1965-69; memb Cncl of Mgmnt of Inst of Choreology, cncl memb Friends of Covent Garden, vice-pres Friends of Sadler's Wells Theatre, memb exec cncl of Royal Acad of Dancing, govr Royal Ballet Sch, govr Sadler's Wells Fndn, assoc dir Royal Ballet 1970-76, dir Sadler's Wells Royal Ballet 1976-; noted for productions of 19C classical ballets, The Sleeping Beauty, Swan Lake, Giselle, The Nutcracker, and Coppelia, for most major cos in Europe and USA, including both Royal Ballet Cos, Dutch and Canadian Nat Ballets, Stuttgart Ballet, Bavarian State Opera Ballet; own creations include The Mirror Walkers, The Great Peacock, A Blue Rose, Dance Macabre, Summertide; Standard Award for Most Outstanding Achievement in Ballet 1981; *Recreations* ceramics; *Style*— Peter Wright, Esq, CBE; 4 The Old Orchard, 4 Nassington Road, Hampstead, London NW3 2TR; Royal Opera House, Covent Garden, London WC2E 9DD

WRIGHT, Hon Sir Reginald Charles; s of John F Wright; *b* 10 July 1905; *Educ* Devonport St HS Tas, Univ of Tas (BA, LLB); *m* 1930, Evelyn, da of E A Arnett; 2 s, 4 da; *Career* barr Tas 1928, lectr in law Univ of Tas 1931-46, MHA Franklin Tas 1946-49, Lib senator for Tas 1949-78, min for Works and min assisting Min for Trade & Indust and i/c of Tourist Activities 1968-72; kt 1978; *Style*— The Hon Sir Reginald Wright; Wally's Farm, Central Castra, Tasmania, Australia

WRIGHT, Very Rev Dr Ronald (William Vernon) Selby; CVO (1968), TD (1950), JP (Edinburgh 1963); s of Vernon Oswald Wright, ARCM (d 1942), of Saxe-Coburg Place, Edinburgh, Anna Gilberta, *née* Selby; *b* 12 June 1908; *Educ* Edinburgh Acad, Melville Coll, Edinburgh Univ (MA); *Career* radio padre (HM Forces) 1942-47 and sr chaplain: 52 Lowland Div 1942-43, 10 Indian Div 1944-45; minister Canongate Edinburgh 1937-77, minister emeritus 1977-; chaplain: Edinburgh Castle 1959-, to HM The Queen 1963-78 and extra chaplain 1978- (and 1961-63), The Queen's Body Guard for Scotland (Royal Co of Archers) 1973-; moderator Church of Scotland 1972-73; extraordinary dir Edinburgh Acad 1973-; FRSE; Hon DD Edinburgh Univ 1956, CStJ 1976; Hon: Old Lorettonian, Old Fettesian, Old Cargilfield; *Clubs* Athenaeum, New (Edinburgh, hon memb); *Style*— The Very Rev Dr R Selby Wright, CVO, TD; The Queen's House, 36 Moray Place, Edinburgh EH3 6BX (☎ 031 226 5566)

WRIGHT, Sir Rowland Sydney; CBE (1970); s of Sydney Wright; *b* 4 Oct 1915; *Educ* High Pavement Sch Nottingham, Univ Coll Nottingham (BSc, London); *m* 1940, Kathleen Hodgkinson; 2 s, 1 da; *Career* joined ICI Ltd 1937, chm 1975-78 (dep chm 1971-75); chm Reorganisation Ctee Cmmn for Eggs 1967-68, dep chm AE&CI Ltd 1971-75; dir: Royal Insurance Co 1973-79, Barclays Bank plc 1977-84, Hawker Siddeley Gp 1979-, Shell Tport and Trading Co 1981-86, Blue Circle Industries plc 1983-86 (chm 1978-83); former govr London Graduate Sch Business Studies, hon pres Inst Manpower Studies 1977- (pres 1971-77); memb: Royal Inst, Ford European Advsy Cncl 1976-83, Court Sussex Univ 1983-; Hon LLD: St Andrews, Belfast, Nottingham; chllr Queen's Univ Belfast 1984-; tstee Westminster Abbey Tst 1984-, chm Blue Circle Trust: 1983-; Hon DSc Belfast 1985, CChem, FRSC, CBIM, Hon FIChemE;; *Clubs* Athenaeum; *Style*— Sir Rowland Wright, CBE; Newick Lodge, Church Rd, Newick, Lewes, E Sussex BN8 4JZ

WRIGHT, Lady Sarah Caroline; *née* Waldegrave; da of 12 Earl Waldegrave; *b* 23 Oct 1931; *m* 1955, Ernest Wright, GM, CPM, *qv*; 2 s; *Style*— Lady Sarah Wright; Honibere Farmhouse, Burton, Stogursey, Bridgewater TA5 1PZ (☎ 027874 300)

WRIGHT, Stanley Harris; s of John Charles Wright (d 1965); *b* 9 April 1930; *Educ* Bolton Sch, Merton Coll Oxford (MA); *m* 1973, Alison Elizabeth, da of Baron Franks, OM, GCMG, KCB, CBE; 1 s; *Career* Bd of Trade 1952, HM Foreign Serv 1955-57, HM Treasy 1958, first sec (financial) Br Embassy Washington DC 1964-66, HM Treasury 1972- (under-sec 1970-72), dir Lazard Bros & Co Ltd 1972-81; non exec dir: Wilkinson Match Ltd 1974, the Law Land Co Ltd 1979-81; chm: Inter Commercial Bank 1981-83, Royal Tst Bank 1984-88, Wolstenholme Rink plc since 1982-; ptnr Price Waterhouse & Ptnrs 1985-88; *Recreations* various; *Clubs* Reform, MCC; *Style*— S H Wright, Esq; 6 Holly Place, London NW3 (☎ 01 435 0237)

WRIGHT, Thomas William John; s of John William Richard Wright (d 1977), of Canterbury, Kent, and Jane Elizabeth, *née* Nash (d 1978); *b* 5 August 1928; *Educ* Kent Coll, Simon Langton Sch Canterbury, Wye Coll Univ of London (BSc); *m* 4 Jan 1956, Shirley Evelyn, da of Henry Parkinson (d 1943), of Beckenham, Kent; 2 da (Geraldine b 1959, Jane b 1962); *Career* tea plantation mangr Kenya and govt horticultural res offr UK 1953-58, mangr Nursery and Landscape Co Devon 1956-60, lectr Pershore Coll 1962-68; sr lectr in landscape horticulture Wye Coll Univ of London 1968-; vis prof Univs of Beijing and Shanghai China; garden est mgmnt conslt and int lectr; ALI (1978), FIHort (1986), HHA, RHS Int Dendrological Soc; *Books* The Gardens of Kent, Sussex and Surrey (No 4 in Batsford Series, 1978), Large Gardens and Parks, Management and Design (1982); *Recreations* travel, natural history, gardening, music; *Style*— Thomas Wright, Esq; Cumberland House, Chilham, Canterbury, Kent (☎ 0227 730 246); Wye College (Univ of London), Wye, Ashford, Kent TN25 5AH

WRIGHT, Prof Verna; s of Thomas William Wright (d 1934), and Nancy Eleanor, *née* Knight (d 1978); *b* 31 Dec 1928; *Educ* Bedford Sch, Univ of Liverpool (MB, ChB, MD); *m* 8 Aug 1952, Esther Margaret, da of John Bruce Brown (d 1962), of Kings Walden, Hertfordshire; 5 s (Stephen b 1953, Paul b 1955, Andrew b 1958, Mark b 1964, James b 1970), 4 da (Susannah b 1956, Miriam b 1959, Deborah b 1962, Philippa b 1968); *Career* res fell div of applied physiosology Johns Hopkins Hosp Baltimore 1958-59; Univ of Leeds: res asst 1956-58, lectr dept of clinical medicine 1960-64, sr lectr 1964-70, ARC prof of rheumatology 1970-; conslt physician in rheumatology Leeds W Dist and Yorkshire RHA 1970-; former pres: Heberden Soc, Br Assoc for Rheumatology and Rehabilitation, Creation Res Soc; vice pres Biblical Creation Soc; chm standing advsry ctee for rheumatology Royal Coll of Pysicians, United Beach Mission, Young Life Assoc; cncllr standing ctee on devpts in academic rheumatology Arthritis and Rheumatism Cncl; MRCP 1958, FRCP 1970; *Books* Bone and Joint Disease in the Elderly (1983), Integrated Clinical Science, Musculasketal Disease (1984), Personal Peace in a Nuclear Age (1985), Arthritis and Joint Replacement (1987); *Style*— Professor Verna Wright; Inglehurst, Park Drive, Harrogate HG2 9AY (☎ 0423 502 326); Rheumatism Research Unit, Univ of Leeds, 36, Clarendon Rd, Leeds LS2 9NZ (☎ 0532 334940)

WRIGHT, Mrs Wendy; *née* Morane-Griffith; da of Gp Capt Desmond Robert Morane-Griffith, DFC, of Majorca, and Daphne Eve, *née* Fawke; *b* 9 August 1947; *Educ* Kent Coll (Dip ISGD 1982), Mme Anita's, Villa de L'Assomption Paris, Inchbald Sch of Design (Dip ISGD 1982); *m* 1, 25 Sept 1971, Robert Sullivan Thomas; m 2, 2 June 1978, John Charles Wright, s of Sir Rowland Sidney Wright, CBE; 1 s (William Rowland Hawksworth b 1984), 1 da (Clemency Sarah b 1980); *Career* garden designer, landscape conslt, memb advsy ctee to Inchbald Sch of Design, lectr Inchbald Garden Sch and English Gardening Sch; FSLGE 1987;; *Recreations* gardening, horses, bridge; *Clubs* Hurlingham; *Style*— Mrs Wendy Wright; 29 Lurline Gardens, London SW11 4DB (☎ 091 374 3764)

WRIGHTSON, Sir (Charles) Mark Garmondsway; 4 Bt (UK 1900), of Neasham Hall, Co Durham; s of Sir John Wrightson, 3 Bt, TD, DL (d 1983), and Hon Lady Wrightson, *qv*; 1 Bt chm of Head Wrightson & Co Ltd (bridge builders) and MP (C) for Stockton-on-Tees and E Div of St Pancras; *b* 18 Feb 1951; *Educ* Eton, Queens Coll Cambridge; *m* 1975, Stella, da of late George Dean; 3 s (Barnaby, James, William); *Heir* s, Barnaby Thomas Garmondsway Wrightson b 5 Aug 1979; *Career* dir Hill Samuel and Co Ltd 1984; *Style*— Sir Mark Wrightson, Bt; 39 Westbourne Park Road, London W2

WRIGHTSON, Hon Lady (Rosemary Monica); *née* Dawson; yr da of 1 and last Viscount Dawson of Penn, GCVO, KCB, KCMG, PC (d 1945); *b* 1913; *m* 30 Nov 1939, Maj Sir John Garmondsway Wrightson, 3 Bt, TD, DL (d 1983), High Sheriff of Co Durham 1959; 1 s (Charles, 4 Bt, *qv*), 3 da (Penelope b 1940, Juliet b 1943, Elizabeth b 1946); *Style*— The Hon Lady Wrightson; Stud Yard House, Neasham, nr Darlington, Co Durham

WRIGLEY, Dr (Edward) Anthony (Tony); s of Edward Ernest Wrigley (d 1953), and Jessie Elizabeth, *née* Holloway (d 1976); *b* 17 August 1931; *Educ* King's Sch Macclesfield, Univ of Cambridge (BA, MA, PhD); *m* 2 July 1960, Maria Laura, da of Everhard Dirk Spelberg (d 1968); 1 s (Nicholas b 1963), 3 da (Marieke b 1961, Tamsin b 1966, Rebecca b 1969); *Career* William Volker res fell Univ of Chicago 1953-54, lectr in geog Cambridge Univ 1958-74; Peterhouse Cambridge; tutor 1962-64, sr bursar 1964-74, fell 1958-; co dir Cambridge Gp for the History of Population and Social Structure 1974; memb Inst for Advanced Study Princeton 1970-71, Hinkley visiting prof John Hopkins Univ 1975, Tinbergen visiting prof Erasmus Univ Rotterdam 1979, prof of population studies LSE 1979-88, sr res fell All Souls Coll Oxford 1988-; *Books* Industrial Growth and Population Change (1961), English Historical Demography (ed, 1966), Population and History (1969), Nineteenth Century Society (ed, 1972), Towns in Societies (ed with P Abrams, 1978), Population History of England (ed with R S Schofield 1981), Works of Thomas Robert Malthus (ed with D Souden 1987), People, Cities and Wealth (1987), Continuity, Chance and Change (1988); *Recreations* gardening; *Style*— Dr Tony Wrigley; 13 Sedley Taylor Rd, Cambridge CB2 2PW (☎ 0223 247614); All Souls College, Oxford OX1 4AL (☎ 0865 279287)

WRIGLEY, Dr Christopher John; s of Arthur Wrigley, of Shipton Gorge, Dorset, and Eileen Sylvia, *née* Herniman; *b* 18 August 1947; *Educ* Kingston GS, Univ of E Anglia (BA), Birkbeck Coll London (PhD); *m* 11 Sept 1987, Margaret, da of Anthony Walsh, of Wigton, Cumbria; *Career* lectr econ history Queen's Univ Belfast 1971-72; reader econ history: Loughborough Univ 1984-88 (lectr 1972-78, sr lectr 1978-84), Nottingham Univ 1988-; chm Loughborough Lab Pty 1977-79 and 1980-85 tres 1973-77), exec memb Loughborough Trades Cncl 1981-86; cllr 1981-89 and ldr of lab Gp 1986-89 Leics, borough cllr and dep ldr Lab Gp 1983-87 Charnwood; Parly candidate (Lab): Blaby 1983, Loughborough 1987; memb Historical Assoc Cncl 1980-, Econ History Soc Cncl 1983-; *Books* David Lloyd George and The British Labour Movement (1976), AJP Taylor A Complete Bibliography (1980), A History of British Industrial Relations Vol 1 1875-1914 (ed 1982) and Vol 2 1914-1939 (ed 1986), William Barnes: The Dorset Poet (1984), Warfare Diplomacy and Politics (ed 1986), Arthur Henderson (1989); *Recreations* swimming, walking; *Style*— Dr Christopher Wrigley; 2 Beacon Drive, Loughborough, Leicestershire LE11 2BD (☎ 0509 217 074); Dept of History, Nottingham University, Nottingham, Notts NG7 2RD (☎ 0602 484 848 ext 2719)

WRIGLEY, Dr Peter Francis Martyn; s of Dr Fred Wrigley, CBE (d 1982), of Hatfield, Herts, and Catherine Margaret, *née* Hogley; *b* 13 May 1939; *Educ* Alleyne's Sch, Magdalen Coll Oxford (BM BCh, UCL, BSc), St Bart's Hosp Med Coll (PhD); *m* 24 Feb 1968, Sally, da of Col George Frederick Hilton Walker, OBE, TD, of Gargrave, Yorks; 1 s (Matthew John Martyn b 1970), 1 da (Elizabeth Anne Wrigley b 1972); *Career* conslt cancer physician St Barts Hosp and Homerton Hosp 1974; Freeman City of London 1961, Liveryman Worshipful Co of Apothecaries 1965; MRCP 1967, FRCP 1979; *Style*— Dr Peter Wrigley; 3 Egbert St, Primrose Hill, London NW1 8LJ (☎ 01 586 9560); 134 Harley St, London W1N 1AH (☎ 01 487 3193)

WRIGLEY, Thomas James Borgen; s of Edmund Wrigley (d 1963), of Skipton, and Karen Olga, *née* Borgen (d 1961); *b* 31 August 1936; *Educ* Merchant Taylors Sch; *m* 1961, Catherine Ethel, da of Sq Ldr Clement James Gittins (d 1969), of Herts; 2 s (Edmund b 1967, Michael b 1970), 1 da (Sarah b 1965); *Career* CA, md: First Nat Finance Corp plc, First Nat Securities Ltd; memb Mgmnt Ctee Finance Houses Assoc; *Recreations* gold, gardening; *Style*— Thomas Wrigley; The Old Malt House, St Peter Street, Marlow, Bucks (☎ 06284 2677); First National House, Harrow, Middsx (☎ 01 861 1313; St Alphage House, London EC2 (☎ 01 638 2855)

WRIXON-BECHER, John William Michael; s and h of Sir William Wrixon-Becher, 5 Bt, MC, by his 1 w, later Countess of Glasgow (d 1984); *b* 29 Sept 1950; *Educ* Harrow, Neuchatel Univ Switzerland; *Career* Lloyds broker; *Recreations* shooting, fishing, golf; *Clubs* Whites, MCC; *Style*— John Wrixon-Becher Esq; 113A Alderney St, London SW1

WRIXON-BECHER, Maj Sir William Fane; 5 Bt (UK 1831), MC (1943); s of Sir Eustace William Windham Wrixon-Becher, 4 Bt, of Mallow, Co Cork, Ireland (d 1934), and Hon Constance Gough-Calthorpe (d 1957); *b* 7 Sept 1915; *Educ* Harrow, Magdalene Cambridge (BA); *m* 1, 1946 (m dis 1960), Hon Mrs (Ursula Vanda Maud) Bridgewater (later Countess of Glasgow, d 1984), 2 da of 4 Baron Vivian; 1 s, 1 da; m 2, 1960, Yvonne Margaret, former w of Hon Roger Lloyd-Mostyn (now 5 Baron Mostyn, *qv*), and da of A Stuart Johnson, of Henshall Hall, Congleton, Cheshire (d 1970); 1 s (John); *Heir* s, John Wrixon-Becher; *Career* Temp Maj Rifle Bde (Supp

Reserve), served West Desert, Tunisian Campaign 1940-43, (wounded, POW), Sidi Rezegh Battle NN 1941, Italian Campaign 1944, ADC to FM Lord Wilson, Supreme and Allied Cdr Mediterranean; Lloyds underwriter 1950; memb: British Boxing Bd of Control 1961-82, Nat Playing Field Assoc 1953-65; pres Wilts Branch NPFA 1950-56; played cricket Sussex 1939, capt Wiltshire 1949-53 sec of I Zingari 1953-; landowner; *Recreations* golf, cricket; *Clubs* White's, Royal Green Jackets, MCC, I Zingari; *Style*— Maj Sir William Wrixon-Becher, Bt, MC; 37 Clabon Mews, London SW1 (☎ 01 589 7780)

WROBEL, Brian John Robert Karen; s of Charles Karen Wrobel, of USA, and Marian, *née* Wiseman; *b* 4 Sept 1949; *Educ* Stowe, London Univ (LLB, LLM); *Career* barr Lincoln's Inn and Gray's Inn, also Bars State of California and US Supreme Ct; memb ctee of mgmnt of the Inst of Advanced Legal Studies Univ of London; hon assoc legal advsr to all party Br Parly Human Rights Gp; a participant in human rights fact-finding missions 1975-: Iran (before and after rev), S Korea, S Africa, USA; memb Br legal delgn Poland, USSR, China; election observer Zimbabwe 1985; govr Br Inst of Human Rights, chm Readers Int (Publishers), conslt on legal colloquia to Great Britain-USSR Assoc, dir East-West Conf and Business Forum; author various legal papers, reports and articles; *Style*— Brian Wrobel, Esq; 22 Regency House, 22 Osnaburgh Street, London NW1

WROTH, Hon Mrs (Mary Octavia); *née* Addington; da of late 6 Viscount Sidmouth; *b* 1927; *m* 1, 1953, David Christopher Leeming; 1 s; m 2, 1959, David Tilling Wroth (d 1986); *Style*— The Hon Mrs Wroth; Santiani, Moscari c/Campanet No.29, Mallorca, Spain

WROTH, (Charles) Peter; s of Dr Charles Wroth (d 1982), of Exeter, and Violet Beynon, *née* Jenour (d 1974); *b* 2 June 1929; *Educ* Marlborough, Emmanuel Coll Cambridge (BA, PhD), Brasenose Coll Oxford (DSc); *m* 11 Dec 1954, Mary Parlane (d 1988), da of Rev John Christopher Weller, MC (d 1959), of Nottingham; 2 s (Christopher Charles, Richard Peter), 2 da (Helen Margaret (Mrs Wilkins), Rachel Caroline (Mrs Andrews); *Career* Nat Snr 2Lt RA 1947-49; schoolmaster Felsted Sch Essex 1953-54, res student Univ of Cambridge 1954-58, engr G Maunsell & Ptnrs London 1958-61, reader in soil mechanics Univ of Cambridge 1975-79 (lectr in engrg 1961-75), Prof of Engrg Sci Univ of Oxford 1979-; fell: Churchill Coll Cambridge 1963-79, Brasenose Coll Oxford 1979-; Hockey Blue Univ of Cambridge 1954, capt Welsh Hockey Int 1954-58; F Eng 1983, FGS 1968, MICE 1962; *Books* Critical State Soil Mechanics (with A N Schofield, 1968); *Recreations* golf, real tennis, crosswords; *Clubs* MCC, Jesters; *Style*— Prof Peter Wroth; Dept of Engineering Science, Parks Rd, Oxford, OX1 3PJ

WROTTESLEY, 6 Baron (UK 1838); Sir Clifton Hugh Lancelot de Verdon Wrottesley; 14 Bt (E 1642); s of Hon Richard Wrottesley (d 1970), and Georgina, now Mrs J Seddon-Brown, *qv*; suc gf (5 Baron, sixteenth in descent from Sir Walter Wrottesley, a chamberlain of the Exchequer under Edward IV and himself third in descent from Sir Hugh de Wrottesley, KG (one of the original members of the Order), who fought in the Black Prince's div at Crécy) 1977; *b* 10 August 1968; *Educ* Eton; *Heir* half unc, Hon Stephen John b 21 Dec 1955; *Career* patron of three livings; *Style*— The Rt Hon the Lord Wrottesley; c/o Barclays Bank, 8 High Street, Eton, Windsor, Berks, SL4 6AU

WROTTESLEY, Baroness; Mary Ada Van Echten; da of Edgar Dryden Tudhope, of Kenilworth, Cape Province, S Africa; *m* 5 March 1955, as his 3 w, 5 Baron Wrottesley (d 1977); 2 s; *Style*— The Rt Hon Lady Wrottesley; 18 Sonnehoogte, Thomas Rd, Kenilworth, Cape Province, S Africa

WROTTESLEY, Hon Stephen John; s of 5 Baron Wrottesley (d 1977); half-uncle and h of 6 Baron; *b* 21 Dec 1955; *m* 16 Dec 1982, Mrs Roz Fletcher, *née* Taylor; 1 da (Alexandra b 11 May 1985)

WU, Kung Chao; s of Wu Kuang Hua (d 1944), of Amoy, China, and Chao Fu Kuan (d 1955); *b* 20 Nov 1922; *Educ* Anglo Chinese Coll Amoy China, LSE; *m* 10 May 1951, Daisy Chan, da of Chan Khay Gwan, of Rangoon (d 1979); 1 s (Ping 1953), 1 da (Ling b 1956); *Career* dep gen mangr Bank of China: London 1978-86, New York 1981-83; sr deputy gen mangr London 1986; dir Banque Arabe et Internationale d'Investissement, Luxembourg; memb: FCIB 1985; *Recreations* tennis, reading, travel, theatre; *Clubs* Overseas Bankers; *Style*— K C Wu, Esq; 79 Hervey Close, London N3 2HH (☎ 01 346 1827); Bank of China, 8/10 Mansion House Place, London EC4N 8BL (☎ 01 626 8301, fax 01 626 3892)

WULSTAN, David; s of Rev Norman B Jones (d 1948), and (Sarah) Margaret, *née* Simpson (d 1973); *b* 18 Jan 1937; *Educ* Royal Masonic Sch, Coll of Tech Birmingham, Magdalen Coll Oxford (BSc, ARCM, MA, BLitt); *m* 9 Oct 1965, Susan Nelson, da of Frank Nelson Graham (d 1963); 1 s (Philip Richard James b 1969); *Career* fell and lectr Magdalen Coll Oxford 1964-78, visiting prof Univ of California Berkeley USA 1978, statutory lectr Univ Coll Cork 1979-80 (prof of music 1980-83), Gregynog prof of music Univ Coll of Wales 1983-; dir The Clerkes of Oxenford 1964-; numerous recordings and appearances for TV and radio, appearance at festivals, recordings of incidental music for TV and cinema, composer of church music, etc; *Books* Gibbons Church Music (Early English Church Music) Vol 3 (1964) and vol 27 (1979), Anthology of English Church Music (1968), Play of Daniel (1976), Coverdale Chant Book (1978), Sheppard, Complete Works (1979), and many other editions, articles and reviews; *Recreations* tennis, badminton, food and drink, bemoaning the loss of the English language; *Style*— Prof David Wulstan; Ty Isaf, Llanilar, Aberystwyth SY23 4NP (☎ 09747 229); Music Dept, Univ Coll of Wales, Aberystwyth, Dyfed SY23 2AX (☎ 0970 624441)

WURTZEL, David Ira; s of Paul Bernard Wurtzel, of Los Angeles, California, and Shirley Lorraine, *née* Stein; *b* 28 Jan 1949; *Educ* Univ of California Berkeley (BA), Queen Mary Coll London (MA) Fitzwilliam Coll Cambridge (MA); *Career* barr 1976-; novelist and Free lance theatre critic, pubns incl: Thomas Lyster, A Cambridge Novel (1983), Succession (1989); memb: Laurence Olivier Awards Panel 1987; *Recreations* theatre, opera, travelling abroad, taking exercise, architecture, conservation; *Style*— David Wurtzel, Esq; 3 Dr Johnson's Building, Temple, London, ECYY 7BA, (☎ 01 353 8778)

WYATT, David Francis; s of Francis Edward Wyatt, of Newent and Enid, *née* Barrett (d 1981); *b* 3 July 1941; *Educ* Marling Sch Stroud Glos, LSE; *m* 24 Apr 1976, Rosalind Blair, da of Philip Robert Henwood John (d 1955) of Downside House, Bridge Sollers, Hereford (d 1955); 2 s (Timothy b 1980, Jeremy b 1982) 1 da (Briony b 1986); *Career* slr and Notary Public 1968 (cncl memb Notaries Soc 1977-), ptnr Treasures and Rivers Wyatt, dir TC Vermeer Ltd (agri machinery), tstee Gloucester Municipal Charities, Freemasons: past master Lodge of True Friendship No 218, past sec Royal York Lodge No 2709, asst sec and registrar prov Grand Lodge of Gloucestershire; memb Law Soc; *Books* Two Hundred Years of True Friendship (1987), Ninety Years without Slumbering (1988) (Histories of Masonic Lodges 218 and 2709); *Recreations* gardening, golf; *Clubs* Gloucester, Minchinhampton, Golf; *Style*— David Wyatt, Esq; 17 St John's Lane, Gloucester, GL1 2AZ (☎ 0452 25351, fax 0452 506735)

WYATT, Gavin Edward; CMG (1965); s of Edward Adolphus Wyatt (d 1947); *b* 12 Jan 1914; *Educ* Newton Abbot GS; *m* 1950, Mary Mackinnon, *née* MacDonald; 1 s, 1 da; *Career* chief exec offr and gen mangr Electricity Corpn of Nigeria 1957-62, md E African Power & Lighting Co Ltd 1962-64, dir projects dept Europe, Middle East and N Africa Regn World Bank 1965-76 (formerly sr engr), consIt; *Recreations* gardening; *Style*— Gavin Wyatt Esq, CMG; Holne Bridge Lodge, Ashburton, Devon (☎ 0364 52597)

WYATT, John Leslie; *Career* dir: Amalgamated Power Engrg Ltd, Belliss & Morcom Hldgs, Crossley-Premier Engines, Valtek Engrg Ltd; md NEI-A P E Ltd 1981-, memb IOD; FCA; *Style*— John Wyatt, Esq; NEI-A P E Ltd, Icknield Sq, Ladywood, Birmingham B16 0QL (☎ 021 455 7010, telex 337958)

WYATT, Hon Mrs (Margaret Agnes); *née* Blades; da (twin) of late 1 Baron Ebbisham, GBE; *b* 1908; *m* 1933, Brig Richard John Penfold Wyatt, MC, TD, DL, JP, late Royal Sussex Regt (TA) (d 1954); 2 s; *Style*— The Hon Mrs Wyatt; Hillbarn Cottage, Findon, nr Worthing, Sussex

WYATT, Robert (Bob) Laurence; s of Charles Wyatt (d 1987), and Phyliss Muriel, *née* Wheeler; *b* 20 Jan 1943; *Educ* Portsmouth Northern GS; *m* 15 May 1965, Linda Doreen, da of Alan Patrick Mullin; 2 s (James b 1968, David b 1971); *Career* with Midland Bank plc: joined Portsmouth branch 1959, seconded to Bank of Bermuda 1967, Asst Gen Mangr 1981, Gen Mangr 1984; vice chm/ chief exec Forward Trust Gp Ltd 1987; vice-chm Finance Houses Assoc 1988; AIB 1964; *Recreations* golf, gardening, ballet; *Style*— Bob Wyatt, Esq; 145 City Rd, London EC1V 1JY (☎ 01 251 9090, fax 01 251 0064)

WYATT, (Christopher) Terrel; s of Lionel Harry and Audrey Vere Wyatt; *b* 17 July 1927; *Educ* Kingston GS, Battersea Poly, Imperial College (BSc, DIC); *m* 1970, Geertruida; 4 s; *Career* RE 1946-48; Charles Brand & Son Ltd 1948-54, joined Richard Costain Ltd 1955 (dir 1970, gp chief exec 1975-80, dep chm 1979-80), chm Costain Gp plc 1980-87, WS Atkins Ltd 1987; FEng, FICE, FIStructE; *Recreations* sailing; *Style*— Terrel Wyatt Esq; Lower Hawksfold, Fernhurst, nr Haslemere, Surrey GU27 3NR (☎ 0428 54538); W S Atkins Ltd, Woodcote Grove, Ashley Rd, Epsom, Surrey KT18 5BW (☎ 03727 26140)

WYATT, (Richard) Wesley; s of James Richard Dinham Wyatt (d 1985), of Croford, Wiveliscombe, Somerset, and Elsie, *née* Reed (d 1977); *b* 16 April 1932; *Educ* Taunton Sch; *m* 11 April 1955 (m dis 1989), (Evelyn) Mary, da of Herbert George Gibbons (d 1980), of Croford, Wiveliscombe, Som; 1 s (Robert Hugh b 1958), 1 da ((Maria) Jayne b 1959); *Career* farmer; dir Rural Devpts of Portugal, chm Wiveliscombe Young Cons 1959-62, vice-pres Som Co Young Cons 1962, chm Burnham & Berrow GC 1986-88 (Capt-elect 1989), pres Old Tauntonian Assoc 1979, chm farm advsy ctee Liscombe Experimental Husbandry Farm 1985-, memb Home Grown Cereals Authy R & D ctee 1986-; memb Wiveliscombe Parish Cncl 1970-87, organist Wiveliscombe Methodist Church 1951-86; *Recreations* golf, gardening, classical music, rugby, cricket; *Clubs* Burnham & Berrow Golf; *Style*— Wesley Wyatt, Esq; The Nineteenth, Orchard Close, Westford, Wellington, Somerset TA21 ODR (☎ 0823 47 4016); Fitzhead Farms, Croford, Wiveliscombe

WYATT, (Alan) Will; s of Basil Wyatt, of Oxford, and Hettie Evelyn, *née* Hooper; *b* 7 Jan 1942; *Educ* Magdalen Coll Sch Oxford, Emmanuel Coll Cambridge (BA); *m* 2 April 1966, Jane Bridgit, da of Beauchamp Bagenal (d 1958), of Kitale, Kenya; 2 da (Hannah b 1967, Rosalind b 1970); *Career* reporter Sheffield Morning Telegraph 1964-65, sub editor BBC Radio News 1965-68; BBC TV: prodr 1968- (programmes include Robinsons Travels, B Traven A Mystery Solved, Late Night Line Up, The Book Programme), head presentation programmes 1977-80, head documentary features 1981-87, head features and documentaries gp 1987-88, asst md Network TV 1988-; chm ctee on violence in tv programmes BBC 1983 and 1987, tstee Br Video History Tst; *Books* The Man Who Was B Traven (1980); *Recreations* walking, horse racing, theatre; *Style*— Will Wyatt, Esq; 38 Abinger Rd, London W4 1EX; BBC Television, Wood Lane, London W12

WYATT OF WEEFORD, Baron (Life Peer UK 1987), of Weeford, Co Staffs; Sir Woodrow Lyle; s of Robert Harvey Lyle Wyatt (d 1932), and Ethel, *née* Morgan (d 1974); descended from Humphrey Wyatt (d 1610), the ancestor of the Wyatt architects, painters, sculptors and inventors; yr bro of Robert David Lyle, *qv*; *b* 4 July 1918; *Educ* Eastbourne Coll, Worcester Coll Oxford; *m* 1, 1939 (m dis 1944), Susan Cox; m 2, 1948 (m dis 1956), Nora Robbins; m 3, 1957 (m dis 1966), Lady Moorea Hastings (now Black), da of 15 Earl of Huntingdon by his 1 w, Cristina; 1 s (Pericles); m 4, 1966, Verushka, *née* Racz, widow of Baron Dr Lazlo Banszky von Ambroz; 1 da (Petronella); *Career* Maj WW II (despatches); journalist, jt fndr Panorama while with BBC 1955-59; MP (Lab): Aston 1945-55, Bosworth 1959-70; parly under-sec state and fin sec War Office 1951; chm: Horserace Totalisator Bd 1976-; kt 1983; *Books Incl:* The Jews at Home (1950), Turn Again Westminster (1973), The Exploits of Mr Saucy Squirrel (1976), To the Point (1981), Confessions of an Optimist (1985); *Style*— The Rt Hon Lord Wyatt of Weeford; 19 Cavendish Ave, London NW8 9JD (☎ 01 286 9020)

WYBREW, John Leonard; s of Leonard Percival Wybrew, of Radlett, Herts, and May Edith Wybrew; *b* 27 Jan 1943; *Educ* Bushey GS, Sir John Cass Coll; *m* 1967, Linda Gillian, da of Wing Cdr John James Frederick Long of Goddards Lane, Camberley; 1 s, 2 da; *Career* life mangr and actuary Time Assur Soc 1971-72, gen mangr and dir: Windsor Life Assur Co Ltd 1972-76 (md 1976-, chm 1988-), World-Wide Assur Co Ltd 1972-76 (dir 1982-); dir: Br-American Life and General Bhd 1984-, Br-American Insur Co Ltd 1986-; chm: Windsor Investmnt Mgmnt 1986-, Windsor Tst Mangrs 1986-; *Recreations* horses, sailing, reading, golf; *Clubs* IOD, Oriental; *Style*— John Wybrew Esq; 15 West Heath Rd, London NW3 7UU (☎ 01 794 1121); Windsor Life Assurance Co Ltd, Windsor House, Telford Centre, Salop TF3 4NB (☎ 0952 292929, telex 849780)

WYFOLD, 3 Baron (UK 1919); Sir Hermon Robert Fleming Hermon-Hodge; 3 Bt (UK 1902); s of 2 Baron Wyfold, DSO, MVO (d 1942), and Dorothy, da of Robert

Fleming and aunt of Peter Fleming, the travel writer, and Ian Fleming, the creator of James Bond; *b* 26 June 1915; *Educ* Eton, Le Rosey Switzerland; *Heir* none; *Career* Capt Gren Gds (reserve); dir Robert Fleming Hldgs & other cos; ret; *Recreations* gardening; *Clubs* Carlton, Pratt's, Metropolitan (New York); *Style*— The Rt Hon the Lord Wyfold; c/o Robert Fleming Holdings, 25 Copthall Avenue, London EC2R 7DR (☎ 01 638 5858)

WYKEHAM, Air Marshal Sir Peter; KCB (1965, CB 1961), DSO and bar (1943, 1944), OBE (1949), DFC and bar (1940, 1941), AFC (1951); s of Guy Vane Wykeham-Barnes; relinquished surname of Barnes 1955; *b* 13 Sept 1915; *Educ* RAF Halton; *m* 1949, Barbara Elizabeth, da of late John Boynton Priestley, OM, the writer; 2 s, 1 da; *Career* cmmnd RAF 1937, served Fighter Sqdns 73, 257 and 23 WW II; dir Jt Warfare Staff MOD 1962-64, Cdr Far East Air Force 1964-66, Dep Chief Air Staff 1967-69, ret; tech conslt 1969-; FBIM, FRAes; *Style*— Air Marshal Sir Peter Wykeham, KCB, DSO, OBE, DFC, AFC; Green Place, Stockbridge, Hampshire

WYKES, Richard James; s of Bryan Charles Browett Wykes, Luton, Beds, and Sheila Mary, *née* Johnson; *b* 5 Oct 1963; *Educ* Bedfordshire; *Career* asst archivist to Marquess of Bath 1984-86; *Recreations* tennis, walking, bidding at auctions; *Style*— Richard Wykes, Esq; The Hermitage, Nunney, nr Frome, Somerset (☎ 037 384 580); 3C Gloucester House, Combe Park, Bath

WYLDBORE-SMITH, Maj-Gen Sir (Francis) Brian; CB (1964), DSO (1943), OBE (1944); yr s of Rev William Reginald Wyldbore-Smith (d 1943, sometime domestic chaplain to the Marquess of Londonderry and ggs of Sir John Wyldbore Smith, 2 Bt); *b* 10 July 1913; *Educ* Wellington, RMA Woolwich; *m* 1944, Hon Molly Angela Cayzer, *qv*, yr da of 1 Baron Rotherwick; 1 s, 4 da; *Career* GOC 44 Div (TA) and Home Counties dist 1965-68, Maj-Gen Middle East, Far E, France, Italy, Germany; Col 15/19 Hussars 1970-77; dep constable of Dover Castle 1965-68, ret 1968; dir Cons Bd of Finance 1970-; kt 1980; *Recreations* shooting, hunting; *Clubs* Buck's, Naval and Military; *Style*— Maj-Gen Sir Brian Wyldbore-Smith, CB, DSO, OBE; Grantham House, Grantham, Lincs (☎ 0476 64705)

WYLDBORE-SMITH, Hon Lady; Molly Angela; *née* Cayzer; yr da of 1 Baron Rotherwick (d 1958); *b* 6 Sept 1917; *m* 1 April 1944, Maj-Gen Sir Brian Wyldbore-Smith, CB, DSO, OBE, *qv*; 1 s, 4 da; *Style*— The Hon Lady Wyldbore-Smith; Grantham House, Grantham, Lincs (☎ 0476 64705)

WYLDBORE-SMITH, Nicolas Hugh; s of Lt Cdr Hugh Deane Wyldbore-Smith, RN (ka 1941), and Rachel Caroline Lucy Orlebar; *b* 23 May 1938; *Educ* Wellington Coll Berks, St James Sch Maryland USA; *m* 1964, Gillian Mary, da of Leslie Boland Carman (d 1968), of Hants; 2 s (Alexander b 1969, James b 1971); *Career* joined Ind Coope Gp 1963; dir: Friary Meux Ltd 1967, Ind Coope Oxford 1971, Benskins 1975;md Design Co 1988-; cmmnd 23 Special Air Service Regt TA and Leicestershire, Derbyshire Yeomanry; *Recreations* sailing, shooting, gardening; *Style*— Nicolas Wyldbore-Smith, Esq; The Courtiers, Clifton Hampden, Abingdon, Oxon (☎ 086 730 7941)

WYLDBORE-SMITH, William Francis; s of John Henry Wyldbore-Smith (d 1982), of Scaynes Hill, Sussex, and Tighnabruaich, Argyll, and Robina, *née* Ward; *b* 15 Jan 1948; *Educ* Marlborough; *m* 27 Dec 1974, Prisca Faith, da of Rev Peter Nourse, of Leominster, Herefordshire; 1 da (Philippa b 15 April 1977); *Career* admitted slr 1972, asst slr with Theodore Goddard 1972-75, joined Osborne Clarke of Bristol 1975 (ptnr 1977-85); ptnr Wood & Awdry 1986-; chm: N Wilts Business Assoc 1985-86, N Wilts Enterprise Enterprise Agency 1986-; Under Sheriff of Wilts 1987-; Freeman of City of London, Liveryman Worshipful Co of Musicians; memb Law Soc 1972;; *Recreations* gardening, walking, shooting, reading, music; *Clubs* Brooks's; *Style*— W F Wyldbore-Smith, Esq; Wood & Awdry, 3 St Mary Street, Chippenham, Wilts (☎ 0249 444422, fax 0249 443666)

WYLIE, Alastair James Blair; TD (1946); s of Alex Wylie (d 1950), of Turnberry Ayrshire, and Hilda Gwladys, *née* Paton (d 1973); *b* 21 April 1916; *Educ* Kelvinside Acad Glasgow, Warriston Moffat, Sedbergh Yorks; *m* 1 Feb 1951, Jessie Elizabeth Kerr, da of William Walker, JP, of Foreland Island of Islay, Argyll; *Career* cmmnd Territorial Argyll and Sutherland Highlanders 1935; served RA France 1939-40, Egypt 1941, Italy 1942-45, Lt-Col 1949; Wylie's Ltd Glasgow 1935-: dir 1946, md 1949, chm 1950; dir: James Sword & Son Ltd 1964-83, Hamilton Park Racecourse Co Ltd 1978-; *Recreations* golf, shooting, fishing, racing; *Clubs* Western Glasgow, Royal Scottish Automobile, Ranfurly Castle, Western Gailes; *Style*— Alastair Wylie, Esq, TD; 17 Fotheringay Rd, Glasgow G41 (☎ 041 423 1713); The Loaning, Crawford John, Lanarks (☎ 08644-237); Wylie's Ltd, 370 Pollokshaws Rd, Glasgow G41 (☎ 041 423 6644, telex 778440)

WYLIE, Keith Francis; s of Shaun Wylie, of Cambridge, and Odette Frances, *née* Murray; *b* 29 Mar 1945; *Educ* Winchester, King's Coll Cambridge; *m* 2 July 1988, Helen Margaret, da of John Francis Cassidy of Stevenage; *Career* computer scientist Applied Res of Cambridge 1970-74, barr Grays Inn 1976-; Br Open Croquet Champion 1970 and 1971, memb GB Croquet Test Team 1974 and 1982; *Books* Expert Croquet Tactics (1985); *Recreations* skiing, gardening, wine, opera, croquet; *Style*— Keith Wylie, Esq; 17 Carlton Crescent, Southampton (☎ 0703 639001, fax 0703 339625)

WYLIE, Rt Hon Lord; Norman Russell Wylie; VRD (1961), PC (1970), QC (1964); s of William Wylie; *b* 26 Oct 1923; *Educ* Paisley GS, St Edmund Hall Oxford, Glasgow Univ, Edinburgh Univ; *m* 1963, Gillian, da of Dr Richard Verney, of Edinburgh; 3 s (Julian b 1964, Russell b 1966, Philip b 1968); *Career* Lt-Cdr RNR, served Fleet Air Arm and Russian and Atlantic Convoys; advocate 1952, standing counsel to Air Miny Scotland 1956-59, crown counsel 1959-64, solicitor-gen Scotland 1964 (April-Oct), MP (C) Edinburgh Pentlands 1964-74, lord advocate 1970-74, Scottish Lord of Session (senator of the Coll of Justice) 1974-; hon fell St Edmund Hall 1975-; *Recreations* sailing (yacht 'Niarana'), shooting; *Clubs* New, Royal Highland Yacht, RNSA; *Style*— The Rt Hon Lord Wylie, VRD, QC; 30 Lauder Rd, Edinburgh EH9 (☎ 031 667 8377)

WYLIE, Ronald James; OBE (1984); s of James Baird Wylie (d 1977), of Edinburgh, and Christina, *née* Mathieson (d 1977); *b* 31 August 1930; *Educ* Melville Coll, Edinburgh Univ (CA, JDipMA); *m* 17 Sept 1955, Brenda Margaret, da of George Paterson Wright (d 1952), of Leeds; 2 s (Roderick b 1957, Stuart b 1960); *Career* md Tullis Russell Co & Ltd 1973-81 (chief exec 1981-85); exec dir: Young Enterprise Scotland 1986-, Understanding Indust Scotland 1987-; *Recreations* sailing, photography, music; *Clubs* Burntisland Sailing (Commodore); *Style*— Ronald J Wylie, Esq, OBE; Treetops, 123 Dysart Road, Kirkcaldy KY1 2BB (☎ 0592 51 597)

WYLIE-HARRIS, William Harold; s of Richard Charles Harris (d 1947), of Priory Road, Kilburn, London, and Ellen Mabel, *née* Parsons (d 1957), assumed additional surname of Wylie by Deed Poll 1957; *b* 26 Jan 1898; *Educ* City of London Sch; *m* 26 Jan 1932, (Ada) Margaret, da of George Edwards (d 1964), of 16 Donovan Avenue, Muswell Hill, London; 4 s (Michael b 1933, d 1978, Raymond b 1933, d 1978, Clifton b 1939, Peter b 1942), 3 da (Christine b 1936, Pearl b 1942, Dawn b 1947); *Career* Wylie-Harris & Co (Export) Ltd; chm Gresham Ctee; FRSA 1971; Master Worshipful Co of Plaisterers 1966, Worshipful Co of Loriners 1982; DL Farringdon Within 1975; memb Ct of Common Cncl City of London 1957; ; *Books* Panorama of the City of London (16 booklets on the topography of City Wards 1970-75), American Links with the City of London 1977; *Style*— William Wylie-Harris, Esq; 41 Lauderdale Tower, Barbican London EC2 (☎ 01 628 9097)

WYMAN, Peter Lewis; s of John Bernard Wyman, MBE, of Sharpthorne, Sussex, and Joan Dorthea, *née* Beighton; *b* 26 Feb 1950; *Educ* Epsom Coll; *m* 16 Sept 1978, Joy Alison, da of Edward George Foster, of Horsted Keynes, Sussex; 1 s (John b 1985), 1 da (Gemma b 1988); *Career* CA, ptnr Deloitte Haskins & Sells 1978, chm London Soc of CAs 1987-88; Freeman: Worshipful Co of Chartered Accountants 1988, City of London 1988; FCA 1973, FCCA 1978, FBIM 1978; *Recreations* equestrian sports, gardening; *Style*— Peter Wyman, Esq; Reapyears Corner, Streeters Rough, Chelwood Gate, W Sussex RH17 7LL (☎ 0825 74 243); Deloitte Haskins & Sells, 128 Queen Victoria St, London EC4M 7PL (☎ 01 248 3913, fax 01 236 2367, car telephone 0860 385 900)

WYMER, Michael George Petre; s of Norman George Wymer, of Grassmere Close, Felpham, Sussex (d 1982), and Mary Jean Hamilton, *née* Kinloch; *b* 25 Nov 1936; *Educ* Sherborne; *m* 5 Sept 1964, Patricia Lorraine, da of Tom Bruce Jones, of Redcar, Blairlogie, Stirling, Scotland (d 1984); 1 s (Bruce b 1968), 2 da (Penny b 1966, Joanna b 1971); *Career* served 2 Lt Royal Signals 1955-57; joined Longman's Green 1957, gp sales dir Longman Gp Ltd 1973-82 (overseas sales mangr 1967-72); dep chief exec: Longman Holding Ltd 1983-88, Addison-Wesley-Longman Ltd 1988-; dep chm Longman Gp UK Ltd 1988-; govr Waterside Sch 1974-83; bd memb Book Devpt Cncl 1979-81; *Recreations* golf, gardening, collecting landscape paintings, watching cricket; *Style*— Michael Wymer, Esq; Old Kiln House, 79 Haymeads Lane, Bishop's Stortford, Herts CM23 5JJ (☎ 0279 54738); Longman Gp Ltd, Longman House, Burnt Mill, Harlow, Essex (☎ 0279 26721, fax 0279 31060)

WYNDHAM, Hon Harry Hugh Patrick; s of late 6 Baron Leconfield and (1) Egremont, and Pamela, *née* Wyndham-Quin, gda of 5 Earl of Dunraven and Mount Earl; bro of present Baron Egremont (and Leconfield); *b* 28 Sept 1957; *Educ* Eton, Ch Ch Oxford (BA); *m* 2 Nov 1985, Susan Fiona McLean, eldest da of Bruce Woodall, of 7 Sheffield Terrace, London W8; 1 s (Alexander Harry John Valentine b 27 Dec 1986); *Career* company dir; *Recreations* football, skiing, motor cars; *Style*— The Hon Harry Wyndham

WYNDHAM, Hon Mark Hugh; OBE, MC; s of late 5 Baron Leconfield, DSO, and Gladys, da of Fitzroy Farquhar, OBE (s of 3 Bt, decd); *b* 1921; *m* 1947 (m dis), Anne, da of Hon Reginald Winn (s of 2 Baron St Oswald); 1 s, 2 da (*see Lord Charles Spencer-Churchill*); *m 2; Patricia, da of Esmond Baring (see Baron Asburton)*; *Career* Capt 12 Royal Lancers, served Middle East and Italy (wounded twice) WW II 1939-45, chm C of E Children's Soc 1967-82, ret; *Style*— The Hon Mark Wyndham, OBE, MC; Newmans Cottage, Froxfield Green, Petersfield, Hants GU32 1DQ (☎ 0730 64333)

WYNDHAM, Hon Ursula Constance; da of 5 Baron Leconfield, DSO (d 1967), and Gladys Mary *née* Farquhar; *b* 20 Sept 1913; *Educ* private; *Books* Astride The Wall, Laughter and the Love of Friends (1989); *Recreations* travel, needlework, reading, gardening; *Style*— The Hon Ursula Wyndham; Honeyway House, Petworth, Sussex (☎ 0798 42291)

WYNDHAM, William Wadham; s of George Colville Wyndham (d 1982), of Orchard Wyndham, Somerset, and Anne Dorothy Hodder, *née* Hodder-Williams; *b* 4 August 1940; *Educ* Eton, Wadham Coll Oxford; *Career* barr 1966; Parly Counsel Off 1968-70, legal advsr: Formica Int/ De La Rue 1971-78, Esso/Exxon Chemical 1979-88; co sec and legal advsr AB Electronic Prods Gp plc 1988-89; *Recreations* natural history, forestry, theology; *Clubs* Lansdowne; *Style*— William Wyndham, Esq; Orchard Wyndham, William Taunton, Somerset TA4 4HH (☎ 09 843 2309); AB Electronic Products Group plc, Abercynon, Mid Glamorgan CF45 4SF (☎ 0443 7403 31, fax 443 7416 76)

WYNESS, James Alexander Davidson; s of Dr James Alexander Davidson Wyness (d 1984), of Dyce, Aberdeen, and Millicent Margaret, *née* Wyness; *b* 27 August 1937; *Educ* Stockport GS, Emmanuel Coll Cambridge (MA, LLB); *m* 18 June 1966, Josephine Margaret, da of Lt-Col Edward Stow Willard Worsdell, MBE, TD, of Eynsford, Kent; 3 da (Rachel b 28 July 1968, Emily b 3 Feb 1971, Jeannie b 27 Aug 1974); *Career* Nat Serv 2 Lt RA; slr; articled clerk AF & RW Tweedie 1964-66; Linklaters & Paines 1966-: ptnr 1970-87, managing ptnr 1987-; non exec dir Bowthorpe Hldgs plc 1979-; vice-pres and memb gen ctee Saracens FC RFU Middx and London Div (Capt 1962-65); memb Worshipful Co of City of London Slrs; memb Law Soc; *Recreations* visiting France, growing vegetables, rugby football, reading; *Style*— James Wyness, Esq; Linklaters & Paines, Barrington House, 59-67 Gresham St, London EC2V 7JA (☎ 01 606 7080)

WYNFORD, 8 Baron (UK 1829); Robert Samuel Best; MBE (Mil 1952), DL (Dorset 1970); s of 7 Baron Wynford (d 1942), and Evelyn (d 1929), da of Maj-Gen Sir Edward Sinclair May, KCB, CMG; *b* 5 Jan 1917; *Educ* Eton, Sandhurst; *m* 1941, Anne, da of Maj-Gen John Minshull-Ford, CB, DSO, MC (d 1948); 1 s, 2 da; *Heir* s, Hon John Best; *Career* landowner and farmer, formerly Instructor Jt Serv Staff Coll 1957-60; Croix de Guerre; *Recreations* shooting, hill climbing; *Clubs* Army and Navy; *Style*— The Rt Hon the Lord Wynford, MBE, DL; Wynford House, Wynford Eagle, Dorchester, Dorset DT2 0ER (☎ 0300 20241)

WYNN, Cdr Andrew Guy; LVO (1984); yr s of Lt-Cdr Hon Charles Wynn, RN, and Hon Hermione Willoughby, da of 11 Baron Middleton; *b* 26 Nov 1950; *Educ* Eton, Gonville and Caius Coll Cambridge (MA); *m* 1978 (m dis 1987), Susanjane, da of Selwyn Willis Fraser-Smith, CBE, MC, of Crowborough; 1 s (Alexander Charles Guy b 1980); m 2, 1988, Shelagh Jean Macsorley, yr da of Prof I K M Smith, of Welwyn Garden City; *Career* Lt Cdr RN, Equerry to HRH The Duke of Edinburgh 1982-84; Dep Supply Offr HMS Ark Royal 1984-86. Cdr RN, Officer Policy Section 1987-88; sch burser Eton 1988-; *Style*— Cdr Andrew Wynn, LVO; c/o Lloyds Bank, 6 Pall Mall, London SW1Y 5NH

WYNN, Hon Mrs Angela Hermione Ida; *née* Willoughby; da of 11 Baron Middleton,

KG, MC, TD (d 1970); *b* 5 May 1924; *m* 1947, Lt Cdr the Hon Charles Henry Romer Wynn, s of 6 Baron Newborough, OBE (d 1965); 2 s (Antony, Andrew); *Style*— The Hon Mrs Wynn; Bunkersland, Withleigh, Tiverton, Devon (☎ 0844 252444)

WYNN, Hon Charles Henry Romer; s of 6 Baron Newborough, OBE (d 1965); *b* 1923; *Educ* Canford School; *m* 1947, Hon Angela Hermione Ida Willoughby, da of 11 Baron Middleton; 2 s; *Career* Lt Cdr RN (ret); *Recreations* fishing; *Style*— Lt Cdr the Hon Charles Wynn, RN; Bunkersland, Withleigh, Tiverton, Devon

WYNN, Hon Robert Vaughan; s and h of 7 Baron Newborough, DSC, of Rhug, Corwen, N Wales, by his 1 w, Rosamund, da of late Maj Robert Barbour, of Bolesworth Castle, Tattenhall, Cheshire; *b* 11 August 1949; *Educ* Milton Abbey; *m* 1, 1981, Sheila Christine Massey; 1 da (Lucinda); m 2, 16 April 1988, Mrs Susan Hall, da of late Andrew Lloyd, of Malta; *Career* landowner and farmer; chm and md Wynn Electronics Ltd; *Recreations* skiing, sailing; *Style*— The Hon Robert Wynn; Peplow Hall, Peplow, Market Drayton, Shropshire; Wynn Electronics Ltd, Wynn House, Halesfield 20, Telford, Shropshire TF7 4QU (☎ 0952 588222; telex: 35740; fax: 0952 583510)

WYNN, Hon Mrs Rowland; Eleanor Mary Tydfil; da of late Arthur Edmund Smith-Thomas; *m* 1943, Hon Rowland Tempest Beresford Wynn, CBE (d 1977); *Style*— The Hon Mrs Rowland Wynn

WYNN-WILLIAMS, George; s of William Wynn-Williams, MRCS, LRCP (d 1948), and Jane Anderson, *née* Brymer (d 1953); *b* 19 August 1911; *Educ* Rossall, London Univ, King's Coll, Westminster Hosp Med Sch; *m* 20 Nov 1943, Lady Penelope, da of and last Earl Jowitt, PC (d 1957), Lord High Chancellor 1944-51, Lord of Appeal 1951-57; 2 s (William Jowitt Dafydd b 1947, Hugo James b 1955), 1 da (Lesley-Jane b 1944); *Career* obstetrician, gynaeologist, conslt gynaecologist Chelsea Hosp for Women 1947-76, conslt obstetrician Queen Charlotte's Hosp 1947-81; MBBS, FRCS (Eng), FRCOG, LRCP; *Books* various articles on infertility and its management and treatment; *Recreations* fishing, golf; *Clubs* Hurlingham, Royal Society of Medicine; *Style*— George Wynn-Williams, Esq; 39 Hurlingham Court, Ranelagh Gardens, London SW7 (☎ 01 736 2139)

WYNN-WILLIAMS, Lady Penelope; da of 1 and last Earl Jowitt, PC (d 1957); *m* 20 Nov 1943, George Wynn-Williams, FRCS, FRCOG; *qv* 2 s, 1 da; govnr two schools Fulham; *Recreations* tennis; *Clubs* Hurlingham; *Style*— Lady Penelope Wynn-Williams; 39 Hurlingham Court, Ranelagh Gdns, SW6 (☎ 01 736 2139)

WYNNE, David; s of Cdr Charles Edward Wynne, RNR, and Millicent, *née* Beyts; *b* 25 May 1926; *Educ* Stowe, Trinity Coll Cambridge; *m* 1958, Gillian May Leslie, da of Leslie Grant, of Argentina and Switzerland; 2 s (Edward, Roland) and 2 step children; *Career* served WWII Sub Lt RNVR; sculptor, important public works numerous over the last 36 years; *Recreations* active sports, poetry, travel; *Clubs* Garrick, Leander, Queen's, Cresta Run, Hurlingham; *Style*— David Wynne, Esq; 12 Southside, Wimbledon Common, London SW19; (☎ 01 946 1514)

WYNNE, Edward John Carleton; s of Wilfrid Edward Carleton Wynne (d 1973), of Margate, and Marjorie Frances Sibthorpe (d 1982); *b* 10 Oct 1926; *Educ* Epsom Coll, Trinity Hall, Cambridge, Middx Hosp Med Sch, (MA, MCHIR, MB, FRCS); *m* 5 Dec 1953, Erica Louise, da of Eric Ferdinando, of Barn House, Upper Basildon, Berks, 1 s (William b 1957), 1 da (Clare b 1954); *Career* conslt surgeon; *Recreations* surgery, house work; *Style*— Edward Wynne, Esq; The Mews House, Down Ampney, Cirencester , Glos GL7 5QW (☎ 0285 750400); Princess Margaret Hospital, Swindon (☎ 0793 36231)

WYNNE, Hon Mrs (Nancy Clare); *née* Eden; 3 and yst da of 6 Baron Henley (d 1962); *b* 1918; *m* 22 Nov 1941, Edmund Ernest Wynne, Lt Reconnaissance Corps, 2 s of Charles Edmund Wynne, of Blackpool; 1 s, 5 da; *Style*— The Hon Mrs Wynne

WYNNE, Thomas Meirion; s of Rev E E Wynne (d 1981), of Flint; *b* 26 April 1934; *Educ* UCW (LLB); *m* 21 June 1958, Elizabeth Gwenda; 2 s (Michael Vaughan b 1960, Gareth Dylan b 1961); *Career* slr; clerk to Justices of Dolgellau and Barmouth, supt registrar, clerk to Cmmrs of Taxes; vice-chm Gwynedd Agric Wages Ctee, memb Gwynedd Family Practitioner Ctee, former Mental Health Cmmr; FBIM; *Style*— T Meirion Wynne, Esq; Llifor, Friog, Fairbourne, Gwynedd LL38 2RX (☎ 0341 250428); J Charles Hughes & Co, Solicitors, Dolgellau, Gwynedd (☎ 0341 422464)

WYNNE-EDWARDS, Prof Vero Copner; CBE (1973); s of Rev Canon John Rosindale Wynne-Edwards, and Lilian Agnes, *née* Streatfeild; *b* 4 July 1906; *Educ* Leeds GS, Rugby, New Coll Oxford (BA, MA, DSc); *m* 19 Dec 1929, Jeannie Campbell, da of Percy Morris (d 1944), of Exeter; 1 s (Hugh b 1934), 1 da (Janet b 1931); *Career* Lt Cmdr (Spec Branch) RCNVR 1942-45; student probationer Marine Biological Assoc Plymouth 1927-29, asst/assoc prof zoology McGill Univ Montreal 1930-46; Aberdeen Univ: regius prof of nat hist 1946-74, vice princ 1972-74; expeditions to Arctic Canada: Baffin Island 1937, 1950, 1953, MacKenzie River 1943, Yukon 1944; visiting prof Univ of Louisville Kentucky 1959, Br Cncl Cwlth Interchange fell NZ 1962, Leverhulme Fell 1978-80, memb: Nature Conservancy 1954-57, Red Deer Cmmn (vice chm) 1959-68, Royal Cmmn on Environmental Pollution 1970-74; pres: Br Ornithologists Union 1965-70, Scottish Marine Biological Assoc 1967-73; Section D Br Assoc 1974; chm: Natural Environment Res Cncl 1968-71, Scientific Authy for Animals DoE 1976-77; Hon Fell Inst of Biology 1980, hon memb: Br Ecological Soc 1977, American Ornithologists Union 1959, Cooper Ornithological Soc (California) 1961; Finnish Societas Scientiarum 1965, Hon DUniv (Stirling) 1974, Hon LLD (Aberdeen) 1976; 1965, Godman-Salvin Medal BOU 1977, Neill Prize Royal Soc Edinburgh 1977, Frink Medal Zoo Soc London 1980; *Books* Animal Dispersion in relation to Social Behaviour (1962), Evolution through Group Selection (1986); FRS (1940, Canada, 1950 Edin, 1970); *Recreations* hill walking, skiing, gardening, natural history; *Style*— Prof Vero Wynne-Edwards, CBE; Ravelston, William St, Torphins, Scotland AB3 4JR

WYNNE-JONES, Baroness; Rusheen; da of Neville Preston; *m* 1972, as his 2 w, Baron Wynne-Jones (Life Peer d 1982), sometime Prof Chemistry Newcastle Univ; *Career* chm Friends of Chelsea Gp; *Style*— The Rt Hon Lady Wynne-Jones; 16 Chelsea Embankment, SW3 (☎ 01 352 8511)

WYNNE-MORGAN, David Wynne; s of Col John Wynne-Morgan, and Marjorie Mary, *née* Wynne; *b* 22 Feb 1931; *Educ* Bryanston; *m* 1 (m dis), Romaine Chevers, *née* Ferguson; m 2 (m dis), Sandra, *née* Paul; 2 s (Nicholas b 1956, Adrian b 1957); m 3, 26 June 1973, Karin Elizabeth, da of Daniel Eugene Stings; 2 s (Jamie b 1975, Harry b 1980); *Career* journalist: Daily Mail 1951-54, Daily Express 1954-57; fndr ptnr Plan PR (sold to Extel Gp 1980), chm; Hill and Knowlton 1984-; chm Mktg Gp GB 1989; played squash for Wales 1953-56; MIPR; *Books* author of: autiobiography of late Pres Gamal Abdel Nassar (serialised Sunday Times), biography of Pietro Annigoni (serialised Daily Express), I Norman Levy; *Recreations* cricket, tennis, riding, squash; *Clubs* Turf, Lords Taverners, Queen's; *Style*— David Wynne-Morgan, Esq; Hill and Knowlton, 5/11 Theobalds Rd, London WC1 (☎ 01 405 8755, car 0860 512 042)

WYNNE-PARKER, Michael; s of David Boothby Wynne-Parker (d 1955), descended from the ancient Welsh family whose records go back to 1079 and Gruffudd ap Cynan, who ranks first amoung the five ancient Royal Tribes of Wales; *b* 20 Nov 1945; *Educ* Lady Manners Sch; *m* 1975, Jennifer (who m, as her 1 husb, 1966, Marchese Giorgio Caralli-Parenzi), yr da of Joseph Guy Lubbock (direct descendant of 15 Earl of Erroll and cous of 4 Baron Avebury) and Ruth, *née* Gurney, of the Norfolk Quaker family; 2 da (Sarah Ruth Isabella b 1978, Fiona Alice Elizabeth b 1981); *Career* chm Wynne-Parker Fin Mgmnt; dir (and major shareholder) Lanke Carbons Ltd Sri Lanka, Ceylon Share Mgmnt Co Ltd, Ceylon Farms Ltd (Sri Lanka), Wynne Parker Nominees Ltd; Simkut Ltd 1985-, Saxingham Enterprises 1988-; pres Cncl ESU of S Asia 1987, vice-pres ESU of Sri Lanka, govr ESU of the Cwlth, chm ESU Eastern Region UK, memb ESU Nat Cncl for Eng and Wales; dir Utd Charities Unit Tst 1987, Mental Handicap Servs Int Ltd; chm editorial bd The Monarchist, former chm Cncl for Advancement of Arab-British Understanding in East Anglia, vice-pres Muscular Dystrophy, govr Mencap City Fndn, vice-pres Norfolk Agric Assoc, pres Knockie Stalking Club, fndr and patron Pensthorpe Tst, Wynne Parker Charitable Tst, Waterfowl Tst 1988, vice-chm Norfolk Beagles 1988, fndr and life memb Sri Lanka Friendship Assoc 1988; memb: Distressed Gentlefolks' Aid Assoc, Royal Soc for Asia Affrs, Anglo-Chilean Soc, Pan Europe Club, Royal Stuart Soc, Br Deer Soc, Salmon and Trout Assoc, Clan Hay Soc, Atlantic Salmon Tst, Nat Arts Collection Fund, Prayer Book Soc, Salisbury Gp 1983-, Keats Shelly Soc, cncl of mgmnt Norfolk Churches Tst 1988; Papal Medal Rome 1971; *Recreations* antique collecting, gardening, travelling, politics, beagling, shooting, fishing, stalking; *Clubs* English Speaking Union, Carlton, Annabel's, Puffins (Edinburgh), Orient (Colombo); *Style*— Michael Wynne-Parker Esq; The Lodge, Saxlingham Thorpe, Norfolk, NR15 1TU (☎ 0508 470 018); 15 Unthank Rd, Norwich, Norfolk (☎ 0603 612 769)

WYNNE-WILLIAMS, John Anthony; s of John Gabriel Wynne-Williams, MBE, and Mary Adele Josephine, *née* Corazza; *b* 9 Nov 1949; *Educ* Farleigh House Sch Farleigh Wallop Hants, Stonyhurst; *Career* dir D'Arcy MacManus and Masuis 1970-79; dep chm: Ryman plc 1981-87, Levelmill Ltd 1987-; dir Holland & Holland Ltd 1989-; chm appeal co ordinating ctee Royal Marsden Hosp, memb Worshipful Co of Fanmakers; *Recreations* shooting, Cresta Run, backgammon, theatre; *Clubs* Brooks's, Annabel's, Marks, RAC; *Style*— John Wynne-William, Esq; 27 St Leonards Terr, London SW3 4QG (☎ 01 730 2189); Levelmill Ltd, Omega Ho, 471 Kings Rd, London SW10 (☎ 01 375 5011, fax 01 351 5576, car tel 0860 323 493)

WYVILL, (Marmaduke) Charles Asty; lord of the manor of Constable Burton and patron of three livings; s of Marmaduke Frederick Wyvill (d 1953) (7 in descent from D'Arcy Wyvill, yr bro of Sir Marmaduke Wyvill, 5 Bt, unc of 6 Bt and great unc of 7 Bt, since whose death in 1774 the Btcy has been dormant; D'Arcy was himself 11 in descent from Richard Wyvill, one of the 25,000 supporters of Henry VI killed at the rout of Towton 1461), and May Bennet; *b* 30 August 1945; *Educ* Stowe, RAC Cirencester; *m* 1972, Margaret Ann, da of Maj Sydney Hardcastle, RA; 3 s (Marmaduke b 1975, Edward b 1977, Frederick b 1983), 1 da (Katherine b 1981); *Career* land agent; patron of the livings of Spennithorne, Fingall and Denton; ARICS; landowner (3000 acres); High Sheriff of North Yorkshire 1986; *Recreations* shooting, fishing; *Clubs* Brooks's; *Style*— Charles Wyvill, Esq; Constable Burton Hall, Leyburn, N Yorks

Y

YAFFE, Ronnie Malcolm; s of Maurice Yaffe, of Prestwich (d 1963), and Victoria, *née* Hodari (d 1978); *b* 23 Oct 1952; *Educ* Manchester GS; *m* 15 Aug 1978, Marjorie Rachel, da of Frank Lea, Whitefield; 1 s (Adam b 1984), 1 da (Vikki b 1987); *Career* dir Kingsley & Forrester plc 1984-87; md Martin Yaffe Int Ltd 1987-; *Recreations* tennis, golf; *Clubs* Whitefield Golf; *Style*— Ronnie Yaffe, Esq; Martin Yaffe International Ltd, Victoria Lane, offr Moorside Rd, Swinton, Manchester (☎ 061 794 5553, car tel 0836 294458)

YAMADA, Taro; s of Haruo Yamada, and Sayuri, *née* Haraguchi; *b* 19 Nov 1934; *Educ* Asahigaoka HS Nagota Japan, Keio Univ Tokyo; *m* 6 March 1961, Nobuko, da of Matsutaro Gotoh (d 1988); 2 s (Jun b 30 Sept 1965, Tadashi b 21 Feb 1969); *Career* joined Yamaichi Securities Co Ltd 1957, dep gen mangr foreign capital dept Yamaichi Securities Co Ltd 1975; Yamaichi Int: pres (America) 1979, gen mangr foreing capital dept 1983, gen mangr int fin dept 1985, dir and gen mangr Int Fin dept 1985, md 1987, chm (Europe) and md i/c Europe and Middle East; Japanese Securities Dealers' Assoc, registered princ Nat Assoc Dealers' Assoc; *Recreations* music; *Clubs* Les Ambassadeurs, Woburn GC; *Style*— Taro Yamada, Esq; Yamaichi Int (Europe) Ltd, Finsbury Ct, 111-117 Finsbury Pavement, London EC2A 1EQ (☎ 01 638 5599, fax 01 638 2849, telex 887414 YSCLDN G)

YAPP, Sir Stanley Graham; s of William Yapp; *m* 1; m 2 (m dis), Carol; 1 s, 1 da; m 3, 1983, Christine, da of late Ernest Horton, former Lord Mayor of Birmingham; *Career* ldr W Midlands CC 1973-77; vice-chm Local Authorities' Mgmnt Services & Computer Ctee; kt 1975; *Style*— Sir Stanley Yapp; 172 York Road, Hall Green, Birmingham B28 8LW

YARBOROUGH, 7 Earl of (UK 1837); John Edward Pelham; JP (Parts of Lindsey 1965); also Baron Yarborough (GB 1794) and Baron Worsley (UK 1837); s of 6 Earl of Yarborough, DL (d 1966, ggs of 2 Earl, Lord-Lieut and Custos Rotulorum of Lincs, who did something to recoup the outlay involved in his father's munificent hospitality as Cdr of the Royal Yacht Sqdn by offering odds of 1,000 to 1 against a 'Yarborough' turning up in a Whist hand, whereas the actual odds are 1,827 to 1; the term 'Yarborough', meaning an honourless hand, is now standard in Bridge), and Hon Pamela Douglas-Pennant, da of 3 Baron Penrhyn; *b* 2 June 1920; *Educ* Eton, Trinity Coll Cambridge; *m* 12 Dec 1957, Florence Ann Petronel, da of John Upton, JP, of Ingmire Hall, Yorks, by his 2 w (Petronel, *née* Fursdon, whose mother was da of Sir William Salusbury-Trelawny, 10 Bt, sometime Capt Roy Cornwall Rangers); 1 s, 3 da; *Heir* s, Lord Worsley; *Career* served WW II France and N W Europe, Maj Gren Gds; high sheriff Lincs 1964, vice-lord-lieut (formerly vice-lieut) 1964-; contested (C) Grimsby 1955; patron E Midlands British Legion 1974-; *Clubs* Royal Yacht Sqdn, Cavalry and Guards', Boodle's; *Style*— The Rt Hon The Earl of Yarborough, JP; Brocklesby Park, Habrough, S Humberside (☎ Roxton 60242)

YARDE-BULLER, Hon Mrs John - Guendolen; da of late Rev Charles Roots; *m* 1939, Hon Reginald Henry Yarde-Buller (d 1962); 2 s; *Style*— The Hon Mrs John Yarde-Buller; Le Vallon, Mont Felard, Jersey

YARDE-BULLER, Hon John Francis; s (by 1 m) and h of 4 Baron Churston, VRD; *b* 29 Dec 1934; *Educ* Eton; *m* 1973, Alexandra, da of Anthony Contomichalos; 1 s, 2 da; *Career* late 2 Lt RHG; *Style*— The Hon John Yarde-Buller; Yowlestone House, Puddington, Tiverton, S Devon

YARDLEY, Prof David Charles Miller; s of Geoffrey Miller Yardley (d 1987), and Doris Woodward, *née* Jones (d 1934); *b* 4 June 1929; *Educ* Ellesmere Coll, Birmingham Univ (LLB, LLD), Lincoln Coll Oxford (DPhil, MA); *m* 30 Aug 1954, Patricia Anne Tempest (Patsy), da of Lt Col Basil Harry Tempest Olver, MBE (d 1980); 2 s (Adrian b 1956, Alistair b 1962), 2 da (Heather b 1958, Briony b 1960); *Career* Nat Serv Flying Offr educn branch RAF 1949-51; barr Grays Inn 1952, emeritus fell St Edmund Hall 1974- (fell 1954-74), Barber prof of law Univ of Birmingham 1974-78, head of dept of law politics and econs Oxford Poly 1978-80, Rank Fndn prof of law Univ of Buckingham 1980-82, chm Cmmn for Local Admin in Eng 1982-; chm: rent assessment ctees, rent tbnls and nat insur local tbnls 1963-82; *Books* Introduction to British Constitutional Law (1960, seventh edn 1989), A Source Book of English Administrative Law (1963, second edn 1970), The Future of the Law (1964), Principles of Administrative Law (1981 second edn 1986), Geldarts Introduction to English Law (ed 1984), Hanbury and Yardley's English Courts of Law (1979), The Protection of Freedom (with I Stevens 1982); *Recreations* lawn tennis, squash racquets, opera, cats; *Clubs* RAF; *Style*— Prof Yardley; 9 Belbroughton Rd, Oxford OX2 6UZ (☎ 0865 54831); 21 Queen Anne's Gate, London SW1H 9BU (☎ 01 222 5622)

YARMOUTH, Earl of; Henry Jocelyn; s and h of 8 Marquess of Hertford; *b* 6 July 1958; *Career* farm manager; *Style*— Earl of Yarmouth; Ragley Hall, Alcester, Warwicks B49 5NJ

YARNOLD, Edward John; s of Edward Cabré Yarnold, MM (Sgt Queens Westminster Rifles, d 1972), of Burley-in-Wharfedale, W Yorks, and Agnes *née* Deakin; *b* 14 Jan 1926; *Educ* St Michael's Coll Leeds, Heythrop Coll, Campion Hall Oxford (MA, DD) ; *Career* entered Soc of Jesus 1943, ordained 1960; tutor in theology Campion Hall 1964- (Master 1965-72); visiting prof Univ of Notre Dame Indiana 1982-; memb Anglican-RC Int cmmn 1970-81 and 1982-; pres Catholic Theological Assoc of GB 1968-88; Cross of Order of St Augustine of Canterbury 1981; *Books* The Theology of Original Sin (1971), The Awe-Inspiring Rites of Initiation (1972), The Second Gift (1974), The Study of Liturgy (ed with C Jones and G Wainwright 1978), Seven Days with the Lord (1984), The Study of Spirituality (ed with C Jones and G Wainwright 1986); *Recreations* opera, cricket; *Style*— The Rev Edward Yarnold, SJ; Campion Hall, Oxford OX1 1QS (☎ 0865 726811, 0865 240861)

YARNOLD, Patrick; s of Leonard Francis Yarnold (d 1963), of Hassocks, Sussex, and Gladys Blanche, *née* Merry; *b* 21 Mar 1937; *Educ* Bancroft's Sch Woodford Green Essex; *m* 14 Jan 1961, Caroline, da of Andrew James Martin (d 1988), of King's Lynn, Norfolk; 2 da (Louise b 2 Feb 1962, Frances b 12 Feb 1964); *Career* Nat Serv 1955-57; joined HM For (now Dip) Serv 1957: FO 1957-60, Addis Ababa 1961-64, Belgrade 1964-66, FO (later FCO) 1966-70; 1 sec and head of chancery Bucharest 1970-73, 1 sec (commercial) Bonn 1973-76, 1 sec FCO 1976-79, cnsllr (econ and commercial) Brussels 1980-83, consul gen Zagreb 1983-85, cnsllr head of chancery and consul gen Belgrade 1985-87, cnsllr FCO 1987-; *Recreations* travel, photography, walking, genealogy, chinese cooking, local history, reading, etc; *Style*— Patrick Yarnold, Esq; c/o FCO, King Charles St, London SW1A 2AH (☎ 01 270 3000)

YARRANTON, Peter George; s of Edward John Yarranton (d 1955), of 8 Mardale Dr, London NW9, and Norah Ellen, *née* Atkins (d 1978); *b* 30 Sept 1924; *Educ* Willesden Tech Coll; *m* 10 April 1947, Mary Avena, da of Sydney Flawitt, MC (d 1957), of Farfield Manor, Granville Rd, Scarborough; 1 s (Ross b 9 Sept 1952), 1 da (Sandy (Mrs Turnbull) b 16 Oct 1950); *Career* RAF 1942-57; WWII Pilot Offr 1944, Flying Offr 1945, served Liberators Burma and SE Asia, Flt Lt 1949; post war served: Canada, USA, Bahamas, Ceylon, Malaya, India, Australia, UK; Shell Mex and BP Ltd: trg 1957-58, ops offr Reading 1958-61, UK industl relations liaison offr 1961-63, i/c industl relations 1963-66, mangr industl relations 1966-69, regnl ops mangr SE Region 1969-75; mangr plant and engrg distribution div Shell UK Oil Ltd 1975-77, gen mangr Lensbury RFC 1978-; currently vice pres and PR advsr RFU; formerly: pres Middx Co RFU, pres Wasps RFC , chm of selectors for London and Middx; former outside broadcast commentator BBC, presenter on the world's largest TV screen at Twickenham, memb editorial bd Rugby World and Post; England rugby international (5 caps); former capt: Barbarians, London, Middx, Wasps, Br Combined Servs, RAF; former capt RAF Swimmng and Water Polo Teams; chm London Regnl Cncl for Sport and Recreation 1983-, fndr dir London Docklands Arena Ltd, regnl dir Sports Aid Fndn, memb Nat Sports Cncl 1988; Freeman City of London 1977, memb Worshipful Co of Gold and Silver Wyre Drawers 1977 (Ct of Assts 1987); FBIM, FIPM, memb Recreational Mangrs Assoc; *Recreations* all sports; *Clubs* RAF, East India, Devonshire Sports and Public Schs, London River YC; *Style*— Peter Yarranton, Esq; Broom Point, Broomswater West, Teddington TW11 9QH; Sunnydale Villas, Durlston Rd, Swanage, Dorset; Lensbury Club, Broom Rd, Teddington, Middx (☎ 01 977 8821/01 943 2066, fax 01 943 4283)

YARROW, Sir Eric Grant; 3 Bt (UK 1916), of Homestead, Hindhead, Frensham, Co Surrey, MBE (1946), DL (Renfrewshire 1970); s of Sir Harold Yarrow, 2 Bt, GBE (d 1962), by his 1 w, Eleanor; *b* 23 April 1920; *Educ* Marlborough, Glasgow Univ; *m* 1, Rosemary Ann (d 1957), da of late H T Young; 1 s (Richard d 1987); m 2, 1959 (m dis 1975), Annette Elizabeth Francoise, da of late A J E Steven; 3 s (Norman, Peter (twins), Davis); m 3, 1982, Mrs Caroline Joan Rose Botting, da of late R F Masters; *Heir* gs, Ross b 1985; *Career* serv RE Burma 1939-45, Maj 1944, chm Clydesdale Bank plc, dir Standard Life Assur Co (md 1958-67, chm 1962-85, former Yarrow plc), pres exec ctee Princess Louise Scottish Hosp at Erskine; memb cncl IOD, deacon Incorpn of Hammermen of Glasgow 1961-62, prime warden of Worshipful Co of Shipwrights 1970, pres Smeatonian Soc of Civil Engrs 1983, pres Marlburian Club 1984, hon vice-pres Cncl of Royal Inst of Naval Architects; FRSE, OStJ; *Style*— Sir Eric Yarrow, Bt, MBE, DL; Cloak, Kilmacolm, Renfrewshire PA13 4SD (☎ 050 587 2067); Clydesdale Bank plc, 30 St Vincent Place, Glasgow G1 2HL (☎ 041 248 7070)

YARWOOD, Michael Edward; OBE (1976); s of Wilfred Yarwood and Bridget Yarwood (d 1983); *b* 14 June 1941; *Educ* Bredbury Sec Cheshire; *m* 1969 (m dis 1987), Sandra Jean, da of Eric Burville; 2 da (Charlotte b 1970, Clare b 1972); *Career* first tv appearance 1963; BBC TV: Three of a Kind 1967, Look - Mike Yarwood, Mike Yarwood in Persons (series) 1971-82; ATV: Will the Real Mike Yarwood Stand Up? (series) 1968; Thames: Mike Yarwood in Persons 1983-87; Mike Yarwood Christmas Show 1984-87, One For The Pot (Nat Tour) 1988; Royal Variety performances 1968, 1972, 1976, 1981, 1987; 1987 Variety Club of GB Award for BBC TV Personality of 1973, Royal Television Soc Award for outstanding creative achievement in front of camera 1978, memb Grand Order of Water Rats; *Books* And This Is Me (1974), Impressions of My Life (1986); *Recreations* golf, tennis; *Clubs* Lord's Taverners; *Style*— Michael Yarwood, Esq, OBE; c/o Billy Marsh, Billy Marsh Assoc, 19 Denmark St, London WC2H 8NA

YASS, Irving; s of Abraham Yass (d 1961), and Fanny, *née* Caplin (d 1980); *b* 20 Dec 1935; *Educ* Harrow Co GS, Balliol Coll Oxford (BA); *m* 14 Aug 1962, Marion Ruth, da of Benjamin Leighton (d 1979); 2 s (David b 1965, Michael b 1966), 1 da (Catherine b 1963); *Career* asst princ Miny of Transport and Civil Aviation 1958, private sec to jt parly sec 1960, princ HM Tresy 1967-70, asst sec DOE 1971, sec ctee of Inquiry into local govt fin 1974-76; Dept of Transport 1976-: under-sec fin 1982-86, dir Traffic Policy and London Regnl Off 1987-; *Style*— Irving Yass, Esq; Dept of Transport, 2 Marsham St, London SW1 (☎ 01 276 6089)

YASSUKOVICH, Stanislas Michael; s of Dimitri Yassukovich, and Denise Yassukovich; *b* 5 Feb 1935; *Educ* Deerfield Acad, Harvard; *m* Diana Veronica Obree, da of Ralph Obre Crofton Townsend; 2 s (Michael, Nicholas), 1 da (Tatyana); *Career* US Marine Corps 1957-61; White Weld & Co Zurich 1961 (London 1962, gen ptnr (NY) 1969, md London); md Euro Banking Co Ltd (London) 1973 (dep chm 1983-85);

chm: Merrill Lynch Europe Ltd 1985-, Merrill Lynch Int Bank Ltd; dir: Merrill Lynch, Pierce Fenner & Smith (Brokers & Dealers) Ltd, Merrill Lynch Banque (Suisse) SA, chm The Securities Assoc, dep chm The Int Stock Exchange; *Recreations* hunting, shooting, polo; *Clubs* Buck's, Turf, The Brook Union (USA), Travellers (Paris); *Style*— Stanislas Yassukovich, Esq; Merrill Lynch Europe Ltd, 25 Ropemaker St, London EC2Y 9LY (☎ 01 867 2958)

YATES, Ann Elizabeth Alice; da of Thomas Berry (d 1978), and Gwladys May, *née* Thomas; *b* 20 August 1937; *Educ* SE Essex County Tech Sch; *m* 25 March 1961 (m dis 1966), Donald Aubrey Yates; *Career* dir Learoyd Packaging Ltd 1983- (co sec 1976); memb: gen purposes ctee Burnley C of C, Burnley Enterprise Tst; advsr Young Enterprise Ltd; *Recreations* keep fit, aerobics; *Style*— Ms Ann Yates; 26 Harrogate Crescent, Burnley, Lancs BB10 2NX (☎ 0282 26089); Learoyd Packaging Ltd, Heasandford Mill, Queen Victoria Rd, Burnley, Lancs BB10 2EJ (☎ 0282 38016)

YATES, Douglas Martin; s of Albert Sidney Yates, of West Yelland, N Devon, and Lily Gertrude, *née* Jones; *b* 16 Jan 1943; *Educ* St Clement Danes GS, London Sch of Econ (BSc); *m* 1967, Gillian, da of Edward Gallimore, of Ealing, London; 1 s (Nicholas b 1972), 2 da (Lindsay b 1969, Alexandra b 1979); *Career* chartered accountant; finance dir The Rank Orgn plc 1982-; dir: A Kershaw and Sons plc 1982, Rank Xerox Ltd 1983; *Recreations* tennis, badminton, bridge, music; *Clubs* West Middlesex Lawn Tennis; *Style*— Douglas M. Yates, Esq; The Rank Organisation plc, 6 Connaught Place, London W2 2EZ (☎ 01 629 7454)

YATES, Ian Humphrey Nelson; s of James Nelson Yates (d 1954), of Carnforth, Lancs, and Martha Wyatt, *née* Nutter (d 1965); *b* 24 Jan 1931; *Educ* Lancaster Royal GS, Canford; *m* 16 June 1956, Daphne June, da of Cyril Henry Hudson (d 1985), of Sanderstead, Surrey; 3 s (David b 1958, Nicholas b 1960, Simon b 1963); *Career* nat serv cmmn Lt Royal Scots Greys Germany and Middle East 1951-53; management trainee Westminster Press Ltd 1953-58; asst gen mangr Bradford & Dist Newspapers 1960, gen mangr 1964, md 1969-75; dir: Westminster Press Planning Divn; gen mangr and chief exec Press Assoc Ltd 1975, dir and chief exec 1989-; chm Tellex Monitors Ltd 1987-; dir Universal News Services Ltd 1986-; pres: Young Newspapermens Assoc 1966, Yorks Newspaper Soc 1968; memb: Newspaper Soc Cncl 1970-75, Cncl Cwlth Press Union 1977-; pres Alliance of Euro News Agencies 1987-88; chm new media ctee of Alliance of Euro News Agencies 1984-; FRSA 1989; *Recreations* walking, reading, theatre; *Style*— Ian Yates, Esq; Woodbury, 11 Holmwood Close, East Horsley, Surrey (☎ 04865 3873); The Press Association Ltd, 85 Fleet St, London EC4P 4BE (☎ 01 353 7440, fax 01 353 5191, telex 922330 PA LDN)

YATES, Rt Rev John; *see*: Gloucester, Bishop of

YATES, Robert Eric Burton; s of Lt-Col George Dougal Yates, of Todhillwood (d 1957), of Canonbie, Dumfriesshire, and Elizabeth Reaney (d 1975); *b* 6 May 1922; *Educ* Sedbergh, St John's Coll Cambridge (MA); *m* 1 Sept 1951, Suzanne, da of Hugh Trenchard, of Swallowfield (d 1950), of Mill Hill, London; 1 da (Penelope b 1954), 2 s (George b 1957, Michael b 1961); *Career* WWII Maj 6 QEO Gurkha Rifles India Burma 1940-45; land agent Earl of Lonsdale 1949-55, asst factor Duke of Buccleuch 1955-66, chief agent Earl of Seafield 1966-74, sr land agent NW Water Authy 1975-84, FRICS; *Recreations* fishing, shooting, photography; *Clubs* Naval; *Style*— Robert Yates, Esq; Heaton Mill, Cornhill-on-Tweed, Northumberland TD12 4XQ (☎ 0890 2303)

YATES, Rodney Brooks; s of Henry Bertram Yates, of The Lawns, Schl Lane, Alvechurch, Birmingham, and Emily Barbara, *née* Wenham (d 1984); *b* 7 June 1937; *Educ* Uppingham; *m* 16 Sept 1983, Hazel, da of Leonard Brown, of Tyne Cottage, Tixover, Stamford, Lincolnshire; 1 s (Benjamin b 1986), and 2 s (Mark b 1965, Duncan b 1966), 1 da (Camilla b 1970) by previous m; *Career* dir: Akroyd & Smithers plc 1976-86, Mercury Gp Mgmnt 1986-87, Hemsley & Co Securities Ltd 1988-; md Madoff Securities Int Ltd 1987-88, chm Olliff & Ptnrs plc 1987-; FCA, memb Int Stock Exchange; *Recreations* tennis, reading; *Clubs* RAC; *Style*— Rodney Yates, Esq; The Old Rectory, Marholm, Peterborough PE6 7JA (☎ (0733) 269466); Hemsley & Co, Securities Ltd 15-18 Lime St, London EC3M 7AP (☎ 01 621 0999, 01 621 1189)

YATES, Roger Philip; s of Eric Yates, of Warrington, and Joyce Mary, *née* Brown; *b* 4 April 1957; *Educ* Boteler GS Warrington, Worcester Coll Oxford (BA), Reading Univ; *m* 7 Sept 1985, Kim Patricia, s of Anthony Gerald Gibbons, of Abinger, Surrey; 1 s (Max b 1987); *Career* joined GT Mgmnt Ltd 1981; dir: GT Mgmnt (UK) Ltd 1984, GT Mgmnt plc 1986; investment dir GT Unit Mangrs Ltd 1988; left GT 1988; dir and ch investment offr Morgan Grenfell Investment Mgmnt 1988-; *Recreations* golf, windsurfing, skiing, tennis; *Style*— Roger Yates, Esq; 51 Broxash Road, London SW11 6AD (☎ 01 223 4492); Morgan Grenfell Investment Management, 46 New Broad Street, London EC2M INB (☎ 01 256 7500, fax 01 826 0331, telex 920286 MGAM G)

YEABSLEY, Lady; Hilda Maude; da of Wilmot C M Willson; *m* 1923, Sir Richard Ernest Yeabsley, CBE (d 1983); 1 da; *Style*— Lady Yeabsley; Ingles Court Hotel, Ingles Road, Folkestone, Kent CT20 2SN

YEAMAN, Keith Ian Bentley; s of Sir Ian David Yeaman (d 1977), of The Moat House, Uckington, Glos, and Anne Doris, *née* Wood (d 1975); *b* 20 July 1931; *Educ* Cheltenham; *m* 23 Sept 1967, Caroline Clare, da of His Honour Judge Anthony Clare Bulger, of The Dower House, Forthampton, Glos; 2 da ((Katharine) Jemima b 1969, Nicola Clare b 1970); *Career* 2 Lt Gloucestershire Regt, served Kenya, Aden and Persian Gulk 1950-52, offr TA Inns of Ct Regt and Royal Gloucestershire Hussars (Major); slr 1959; memb Cncl Law Soc; sec Gloucestershire and Wilts Inc Law Soc 1964-83 (pres 1980-81); dir: Nat Centre for Disabled Youth; slrs Indemnity Fund; *Recreations* gardening, most country sports; *Clubs* East India and Sports; *Style*— Keith Yeaman, Esq; The Dower House, Forthampton, Gloucester (☎ 0684 298498); Flat 5, 65 Onslow Gardens, London SW7; Ellenborough House, Wellington Street, Cheltenham, Glos (☎ 0242 222022)

YEANDLE, Geoffrey Ernest Lascelles; s of Rev Walter Harold Yeandle (d 1952), of Bearsted Vicarage, Maidstone, Kent, and Irene Mary, *née* Snow (d 1972); *b* 12 Oct 1931; *Educ* Maidstone GS; *m* 14 Sept 1957, June Pamela, da of Nathaniel Mendess (d 1957); 2 s (Mark b 1962, Simon b 1966); *Career* Nat Serv 1950-52, cmmnd RA Lt, TA 1952-58, cmmnd Capt Kent Yeomanry; sales dir Warner Fabrics plc 1972-, chm West end Furnishing Fabrics Assoc 1980-84; vice chm Borden Parish Cncl 1981-; Freeman City of London 1980, Liveryman Worshipful Co of Weavers 1980; MIEK, FBIM, FRSA; *Recreations* shooting, cricket, photography; *Style*— Geoffrey Yeandle, Esq; The Thatched Cottage, Chestnut Wood, Borden, Sittingbourne, Kent (☎ 0795 842343); Warner Fabrics plc, 7-11 Noel St, London W1V 4AL (☎ 01 439 2411)

YEARDLEY, Brian; s of John Henry Yeardley, and Elizabeth Anne, *née* Holmes; *b* 7 May 1948; *Educ* Dinnington Tech Sch; *m* 22 Aug 1975, Sandra, da of John Whitworth Stapleton (d 1968); 1 da (Suzanne Louise b 1976), 1 steps (Dominic Rispin b 1967), 1 stepda (Fiona Large b 1965); *Career* chm and md Brian Yeardley Ltd 1975-; dir Leconfield Pk Service Stn Ltd 1985-, Kiplingcotes Stud Ltd 1987-; chm and md Brian Yeardley Continental Ltd, Int Haulage Co, 1983-; chm Road Haulage Assn Hull Area 1982-84; *Recreations* snooker, working golf, walking with dogs and wife; *Clubs* Kirkella Golf, Willerby, Kirkella Gentlemans; *Style*— Brian Yeardley, Esq; 'Goodmanham Dale', Goodmanham Wold, Market Weighton, York YO4 3NA; Brian Yeardle, Continental Ltd, Strand House, Wakefield Rd, Featherstone WF7 5BP (telex 556213, fax (0977) 791856)

YEATES, Roger; s of Charles Henry Yeates, of Basingstoke, Hants, and Elsie Victoria May Yeates; *b* 18 Sept 1945; *Educ* Queen Marys GS, Basingstoke; *m* 15 Sept 1973 (m dis 1984); 1 s (Robert David b 1971), 1 da (Ellen b 1974); *Career* CA 1967; AMF Legg 1967-71, Alexander Duckham & Co Ltd 1971-73; Lansing Bagnall Ltd 1974-; dir and sec: Alderlake Ltd, Bonser Engineering Ltd, Henley Forklift Gp Ltd, Lansing Int Fork Trucks Ltd, Millar Simpson Const Ltd, Pilebond Ltd, Videofilm Ltd and numerous others; *Recreations* gliding, stock car racing, photography, reading; *Style*— Roger Yeates, Esq; 8 Grainger Close, Basingstoke, Hants RG22 4DY; The Kaye Organisation Ltd, Hart House, Hartley Wintney, Hants RG26 8PE (☎ 025126 3773)

YEATES, W Keith; s of William Ravensbourne Yeates (d 1953), and Winifred Scott (d 1969); *b* 10 Mar 1920; *Educ* Glasgow Acad, Whitley Bay GS, Kings Coll Newcastle, Durham Univ (MD, MS); *m* 3 April 1946, Jozy McIntyre, da of Paul Fairweather (d 1949); 1 s (Rodney b 1947), 1 da (Deborah b 1949); *Career* house surgn Professorial Unit Royal Victoria Infirmary Newcastle upon Tyne 1942 (gen surgical registrar 1943-44), demonstrator in anatomy Med Sch Newcastle 1944-45, res surgical offr Tynemouth Infirmary 1945-47, asst surgn Dept of Urology Newcastle Gen Hosp 1948-49; sr registrar: St Paul's Hosp London 1950, Dept of Urology Newcastle Gen Hosp 1951-52; conslt urologist Newcastle Health Authy 1952-85; hon conslt urologist 1985-; chm: Specialist Advsy Ctee Urology RCS 1984-86, Intercollegiate Bd in Urology RCS 1984-88; conslt advsr in urology DHSS 1978-84; Univ visiting prof: Baghdad 1974 and 1978, California 1976, Texas 1976, Delhi 1977, Cairo 1978, Kuwait 1980; guest prof NY section American Urological Assoc 1977 and 1985; princ guest lectr: Urological Soc of Australia 1977, Italian Urological Assoc 1978, Yugoslavian Urological Assoc 1980, Rio de Janiero 1975; Br Jl of Urology: ed 1973-78, chm editorial ctee 1978-84, hon consulting ed 1985-90; St Peters Medal Br Assoc of Urological Surgns 1983; FRCS, FRCSE; memb: Int Soc of Urology 1958 (sr memb 1985-), Euro Assoc of Urology 1974 (sr memb 1985-); hon memb: Br Assoc of Urological Surgns 1985- (pres 1980-82), Urological Soc of Aust 1977-, Canadian Urological Assoc 1981-; *Publications* author of various papers and chapters in text books on Urology and Andrology; *Style*— W Keith Yeates, Esq; 22 Castleton Grove, Newcastle upon Tyne NE2 2HD (☎ 091 281 4030); 71 King Henry's Rd, London NW3 3QU (☎ 01 586 7633)

YEATES, William Ronald; s of Richard Henry Yeates (d 1972), of Coatbridge, Strathclyde, and Caroline McAra Barclay (d 1983); *b* 24 June 1929; *Educ* Kildonan HS Coatbridge, Cranfield Business Sch; *m* 4 Sept 1955, Jean Valentine, da of Frederick Ernest Boxall (d 1960); 2 s (Douglas b 20 Feb 1957, Colin 30 Oct 1958); 2 da (Cheryl b 23 Sept 1961, Heather b 18 Nov 1963); *Career* Nat Serv RAF July 1947-Oct 1949; J Sainsbury plc: branch managr 1964-74, dist mangr 1974-76, area dir 1976-83; md Savacentre Ltd 1983-, charitable activities: Marwell Zoological Tst, Guide Dogs for the Blind, Cancer Research, Inst of Dir 1983; *Recreations* golf; *Clubs* Ampfield GC; *Style*— Ronald Yeates, Esq; Bruma, Southdown Rd, Shawford, Winchester, Hampshire

YEATMAN, Anthony Graham; JP (1972); s of Graham N Yeatman, TD, JP, DL, of Poole, Dorset, High Sheriff Dorset, and Lilian, *née* Gruning; *b* 13 May 1936; *Educ* Blundell's, RAC Cirencester; *m* 27 May 1961, Wendy Joan, da of Edward Robert West (d 1976); 1 s (Graham Edward b 7 May 1966), 1 da (Belinda Jane b 29 Dec 1963); *Career* md Yeatman Gp of Cos; pres Poole Rotary Club 1973 (memb 1962-); memb: Poole branch Cancer Res Campaign Ctee 1962, Game Conservancy, Soc of Dorset Men; memb Poole Borough Cncl 1974-76; memb IOD; *Recreations* sailing, photography; *Clubs* Royal Motor YC; *Style*— Anthony Yeatman, Esq, JP; Ct Hse, Corfe Mullen, Wimborne, Dorset BH21 3RH (☎ 0258 857 328)

YEEND, Sir Geoffrey John; AC (1986), CBE (1976); s of Herbert John Yeend (d 1956), and Ellen Muriel, *née* Inglis (d 1981); *b* 1 May 1927; *Educ* Canberra HS, Canberra Univ Coll, Melbourne Univ (BCom); *m* 1952, Laurel Dawn, da of Leslie George Mahoney; 1 s (Timothy), 1 da (Julie); *Career* Royal Aust Eng 1945-46; PM's Dept 1950, private sec to PM 1952-55, asst sec Aust High Cmmn London 1958-61, various appts in PM's Dept 1961-76, sec to Cabinet and head PM's Dept 1978-86; dir: Amatil Ltd, Alcan Aust Ltd, Civic Advance Bank Ltd, Menzies Meml Tst; memb Archives Advsy Cncl 1985-88; pro chllr Aust Nat Univ 1988-; tstee and memb of hon Int Hockey Fedn, tstee Cricket Youth Devpt Fndn, patron Woden Valley Choir, vice patron Nat Eisteddfad Soc; kt 1979; dir Amatil Ltd; Alcan Australia Ltd; Civic Advance Bank Ltd (1986-); memb Archives Advsy Cncl 1985; *Recreations* golf, fishing; *Clubs* Royal Canberra Golf, Commonwealth; *Style*— Sir Geoffrey Yeend, AC, CBE; 1 Loftus St, Yarralumla, ACT 2600, Australia (☎ 062 81 3266)

YELLOWLEES, Dr Walter Walker; MC (1944); s of David Yellowlees (d 1966), of Elderslie, and Mary Ann Wingate, *née* Primrose (d 1978); *b* 13 April 1917; *Educ* Merchiston Castle Sch, Edinburgh Univ (MBChB); *m* 16 Sept 1950, Sonia, da of James Hamilton Doggart, MD, FRCS, of Surrey; 2 s (Robi b 1956, Michael b 1959), 1 da (Jane b 1962); *Career* GP ret; Edinburgh Univ Capt Rugby 1939, cricket 1940, pres Athletic Club 1940, county cricket team Stirling 1947, Perthshire 1947; Capt RAMC 1942-46, 220 Field Ambulance 1st Army N African campaign, 5th Bn Queens Own Cameron Highlanders, Sicily Normandy, NW Europe campaign; house sgn Sitling Royal Infirmary 1942-42 (SHO 1946), house physician Perth Royal Infirmary 1946-47, house paediatrician Western Gen Hosp Edinburgh 1947-48, GP 1948-81, fndr memb RCGP (FRCGP 1976), fndr memb McCarrison Soc (pres 1975-86), Potter 1981-; *Books* Ill Fares the Land (1979, James McKenzie Lecture), Food and Health in the Scottish Highlands (1985); *Recreations* organic gardening, skiing, trout fishing, golf; *Clubs* Edinburgh Univ Staff, Sloane, BHA Aberfeldy Rotary, Scottish Potters Assoc; *Style*— Dr Walter W Yellowlees, MC; Duiness, Aberfeldy, Perthshire PH15 2ET (☎ (0887) 20277); The Haining Pottery, Taybridge Road, Aberfeldy (☎ 20277)

YEO, Brig Colin (John Russell); CBE (1962), MC, TD, DL; s of Frank Russell Yeo

JP (d 1936), and Evelyn Mary, *née* Kateley; *b* 16 May 1915; *Educ* Rugby Sch, RMA; *m* 9 June 1945, Pamela Sherriff, da of Col G S Hussey MBE, MC (d 1971); 3 da (Susan b 1946, Annabella b 1952, Catherine (decd)); *Career* staff offr NATO (Fontainbleau) 1954-56, CO 38 Regt RA 1956-59, mil advsr High Cmmr Rhodesia 1959-62, Cdr RA 44 Home Counties Div 1962-65, Chief of Staff UN Cyprus 1964; ret 1965; *Recreations* sailing, gardening, photography; *Style*— Brigadier Colin Yeo, CBE, MC, TD, DL; Manor Cottage, Sparrows Green, Wadhurst, E Sussex (☎ 089288 2689)

YEO, Timothy Stephen Kenneth; MP (C) South Suffolk 1983-; s of Dr Kenneth John Yeo (d 1979), and Norah Margaret Yeo; *b* 20 Mar 1945; *Educ* Charterhouse, Emmanuel Coll Cambridge; *m* 1970, Diane Helen, da of Brian Harold Pickard; 1 s (Jonathan b 1970), 1 da (Emily b 1972); *Career* contested (C) Bedwellty Feb 1974; dir Worcester Engrg Co Ltd 1975-86; tres Int Voluntary Service 1975-78, dir Spastics Soc 1980-83; chm Charities VAT Reform Gp; tstee Tanzania Dvpt Tst 1980-; chm Tadworth Court Tst 1983-; jt sec: Constructive Back-Bench Fin Ctee 1984-, Social Services Select Ctee 1985-; *Publications* Public Accountability and Regulation of Charities (1983); *Recreations* skiing; *Clubs* Carlton, Royal St George's; *Style*— Timothy Yeo, Esq, MP; House of Commons, London SW1 (☎ 01 219 3000)

YEOMAN, Maj-Gen Alan; CB (1987); s of George Smith Patterson Yeoman (d 1978), and Wilhelmina Tromans Elwell (d 1944); *b* 17 Nov 1933; *Educ* Dame Allan's Sch, Newcastle upon Tyne, RMA Sandhurst; *m* 12 March 1960, Barbara Joan Davies, da of Norman Albert Davies (d 1975); 2 s (Michael b 1 April 1965, Timothy b 1 May 1961), 1 da (Sally b 29 Jan 1963); *Career* cmmnd RCS 1954; served 1954-70 Korea, Malaysia, Singapore, Cyprus, UK, BAOR, Canada 1954-70; Staff Coll 1963, CO 2 Div Signals Regt BAOR 1970-73; HQ 1 (Br) Corps 1973-74, MOD 1974-77; Col AQ HQLF Cyprus 1978-79; cmd trg gp Royal Signals and communications BAOR 1984-87, ret 1988; Hon Col 37 Wessex and Welsh Signals Regt (V) 1987-, Col Cmdt Royal Signals 1987-, dir Army Sport Control Bd; Catterick Garrison 1979-82, Brig AQ HQ 1 (Br) Corps, BAOR 1982-84;; *Recreations* golf, cricket, skiing; *Clubs* Army and Navy, MCC; *Style*— Major General A Yeoman, CB; c/o Lloyds Bank, Catterick Garrison, North Yorks

YEOMAN, Nigel Robin Edward; s of Robin Edward Ferg Yeoman (d 1985), and Ada Kate, *née* Carpenter (d 1984); *b* 14 Oct 1936; *Educ* Salisbury Cath Sch, King Sch Bruton; *m* 15 Oct 1960, Tessa Esme, da of Lt James Edward Hill, RN (ka 1944), of Poole, Dorset; 1 s (Gareth b 1961), 3 da (Joanna b 1962, Elaine b 1966, Suzanne b 1966); *Career* slr, Supreme Court of Judicature; chm Southern Rent Assessment Ctee; *Recreations* yacht racing, rugby, golf, skiing; *Clubs* Bournemouth Sports, Parkstone Yacht, Parkstone Golf; *Style*— Nigel R E Yeoman, Esq; Sea Rigs, 28 Dorset Lake Avenue, Lilliput, Poole, Dorset; 221 The Broadway, Broadstone, Dorset (☎ 0202 692308, fax 0202 601353)

YEOMAN, Capt Paul Stanley Pressick; s of William Gordon Yeoman (d 1978), of Claremont Road, Marlow, Bucks, and Fernande Lidy Susanne Georgette Margurite, *née* Gilles; *b* 30 Dec 1926; *Educ* The Nautical Coll Pangbourne; *m* 20 June 1953, Phyllis Genevieve, da of George Victor Were (d 1972), of Auckland, New Zealand; 3 s (Philip, Mark, Richard), 2 da (Sarah (Mrs Poziades), Clare (Mrs Pritchard)); *Career* cadet RNR 1940-44, jr offr Merchant Navy WWII served Europe and Far East; offr Shaw Savill Line 1946-53; joined Limehouse Paperhouse Mills Gp of Cos 1953 (dir 1960-86), chm Condor Paper Sales Ltd; Freeman: City of London 1973, Worshipful Co of Feltmakers 1973; *Clubs* Marlow RUFC; *Style*— Capt Paul Yeoman; Meadow House, Stoney Ware, Marlow, Bucks SL7 1RN (☎ 06284 4269); Condor Paper Sales Ltd, The Old School House, Station Rd, Bourne End Bucks SL8 5QD (☎ 06285 29747/8, fax 0628 810754)

YEOMANS, Joseph; s of Joseph Yeomans (d 1979), of Grange-over-Sands, and Myra Phyllis, *née* Quigley (d 1963); *b* 19 Mar 1929; *Educ* Barrow Boys GS, Univ of Nottingham (BA); *m* 7 July 1952, Jacqueline Averil, da of Cyril Arnold (d 1974), of Rhyl; 2 s (John b 1953, d 1988, Paul b 1973), 5 da (Cherry b 1954, Gay b 1956, Christine b 1958, Jacqueline 1963, Hazel 1966); *Career* Nat Serv RAF 1947-49; joined Cyril Arnold & Co CAs Rhyl 1952 (ptnr 1955-); memb: Rotary Int 1955-61, Round Table 1953-70 (chm 1962); Fell ICEAW 1958; *Style*— Joseph Yeomans, Esq; 14 Clwyd St, Rhyl, Clwyd (☎ 0745 343 476)

YEOMANS, Richard David; s of Richard James Yeomans (d 1964), of Eversley, Basingstoke, Hants, and Elsie Marian, *née* Winson; *b* 15 Feb 1943; *Educ* Hartley Wintney Co Secdy Modern Sch, Hamps Coll of Agric, Shuttleworth Coll (NDA); *m* 6 April 1968, Doreen Ann, da of William Herring, of Aldershot; 1 s (Jonathon b 24 Feb 1976), 1 da (Claire b 14 Dec 1972); *Career* with Milk Mktg Bd 1965-71; Unigate plc: area mangr tport 1971-, gen mangr (milk) 1975-, md Wincanton Tport Ltd 1978-, md Wincanton Gp Ltd 1982, appt main bd Unigate plc; tstee Nat Motor Museum Beaulieu; Liveryman Worshipful Co of Carmen; memb: bd of Groundwork Fndn 1988, econ situation CBI 1982, FBIM 1982; *Recreations* shooting, opera, gardening, photography; *Clubs* RAC; *Style*— David Yeomans, Esq; Newland, 4 Gainsborough, Milborne Port, Sherborne, Dorset, DT9 5BA (☎ 0963 250246); Wincanton Group Ltd, Station Road, Wincanton, Somerset, BA9 9EQ (☎ 0963 33933, fax 0963 32490, telex 46237)

YERBURGH, Lt-Col John Rochfort; s of Canon Oswald Rochfort Yerburgh (d 1966), and Cicely Joan, *née* Savile (d 1981); *b* 14 Sept 1931; *Educ* Marlborough Coll, RMA Sandhurst, RMCS Shrivenham; *m* 17 Aug 1963, Gillian Elizabeth, da of Derek Plint Clifford, of Hartlip Place, Sittingbourne, Kent; 1 s (Toby b 9 Oct 1965), 1 da (Sophia b 8 Jan 1967); *Career* cmmd RE 1952, cmmd RE NII 1972-74, ret 1983; memb for Swale Central Kent CC 1984, vice chm Gillingham Cons Assoc 1987; High Sheriff of Kent 1988-89; Freeman City of London 1989; *Recreations* travel, tennis; *Clubs* Turf; *Style*— Lt-Col John Yerburgh; Hartlip Place, Sittingbourne, Kent ME9 7TR (☎ 0795 842 583); West Heath, Ashgrove Road, Sevenoaks, Kent (☎ 0732 452 541)

YERBURGH, Capt Hon Robert Richard Guy; o s and h of 2 Baron Alvingham, CBE, *qv* ; *b* 10 Dec 1956; *Educ* Eton; *m* 1981, Vanessa Kelty, yr da of Capt Duncan Kinloch Kirk; 2 s (Robert William Guy b 16 Sept 1983, Edward Alexander Henry b 6 April 1986); *Career* Lt 17/21 Lancers 1978, Capt 1980, attached to Army Air Corps as pilot 1979-83, resigned 1983; *Recreations* shooting, fishing, skiing (jt services instr); *Clubs* Cavalry & Guards; *Style*— Capt the Hon Robert Yerburgh; Valley Farm House, Bix Bottom, Henley-on-Thames, Oxon (☎ (0491) 576043)

YONGE, Dame (Ida) Felicity Ann; DBE (1982); da of Cdr William Humphry Nigel Yonge, RN (d 1973), by his w Kathleen Ida Marion (d 1974); *b* 28 Feb 1921; *Educ* Covent of The Holy Child, St Leonards-on-Sea; *Career* WRNS 1940-46, 2 Offr; purser office P&OSN Co 1947-50, private sec to: chm of Cons Pty 1951-64, ldr of oppn 1964-65, Cons chief whip 1965-70 and 1974-79, ldr of House of Commons 1970-74; special advsr Govt Chief Whip's Office 1979-83; *Style*— Dame Felicity Yonge, DBE; 58 Leopold Rd, Wimbledon, London SW19 7JF (☎ 01 946 3018)

YORK, Maj Christopher; DL (1952); s of Col Edward York, TD (d 1951), of Hutton Wandesley Hall, York, and Violet Helen, *née* Milner; *b* 17 July 1909; *Educ* Eton, Sandhurst; *m* 16 Oct 1934, Pauline Rosemary, da of Lt-Col Sir Lionel Fletcher, KBE (d 1961), of Tanganika; 1 s (Edward Christopher b 22 Feb 1939), 3 da (Caroline (Lady Nuttall m dis 1970)), b 28 July 1936, Louise (Mrs Seymour) b 11 April 1942, Mary (Mrs Mallaby) b 16 Aug 1947); *Career* joined The Royal Dragoons 1930, supplementary reserve 1934-39, served 1939-45 Maj 1943; landowner & farmer 1951-, chm Hutton Wandesley Farms Co 1966-, MP (U) Ripon 1939-51, MP Harrogate 1951-54; memb Cncl RASE 1948- (hon tres 1961-78, pres 1979, tstee 1979-), hon tres RVC 1948-80; hon FRCVS 1971; QALAS 1936; *Recreations* writing; *Clubs* Carlton, Boodles Yorkshire (York); *Style*— Maj Christopher York, DL; Sth Pk, Long Marston, York YO5 8LL (☎ 090 483 357, 090 483 4620 755)

YORK, 95 Archbishop of (cr 625) 1983-; Most Rev and Rt Hon John Stapylton Habgood; patron of many livings, the Archdeaconries of York, Cleveland and the East Riding, and the Canonries in his Cathedral; the Archbishopric was founded AD 625, and the Province comprises fourteen Sees; s of Arthur Henry Habgood, DSO, MB, BCh, and Vera, da of late Richard Chetwynd-Stapylton, ggggs of 4 Viscount Chetwynd; *b* 23 June 1927; *Educ* Eton, King's Coll Cambridge, Cuddesdon Theol Coll Oxford; *m* 1961, Rosalie Mary Anne, da of Edward Lansdown Boston; 2 s, 2 da; *Career* former demonstrator in pharmacology Cambridge; ordained 1954, rector St John's Jedburgh 1962-67, princ Queen's Coll Birmingham 1967-73, hon canon of Birmingham Cathedral 1971-73, bishop of Durham 1973-83; Privy Cncl 1983; hon fell King's Coll Cambridge 1986; *Books* Religion and Science (1964), A Working Faith (1980), Church and Nation in a Secular Age (1983), Confessions of a Conservative Liberal (1988); *Recreations* DIY, painting; *Clubs* Athenaeum; *Style*— The Most Rev and Rt Hon the Lord Archbishop of York; Bishopthorpe, York YO2 1QE (☎ 0904 707021)

YORK, Michael; s of Joseph Gwynne Johnson, of Sidmouth Devon, and Florence Edith May Chown; *b* 27 Mar 1942; *Educ* Hurstpierpoint Coll, Bromley GS, UC Oxford (BA); *m* 1968, Patricia Frances, da of Richard McCallum; *Career* actor: with Nat Theatre Co; Outcry, Broadway; films: Romeo & Juliet, Cabaret, The Three Musketeers, Conduct Unbecoming, Logans Run, Jesus of Nazareth, For Those I Loved; *Style*— Michael York; c/o The William Morris Agency

YORK, Susannah Yolanda; da of William Peel Simon Fletcher, and Joan Nita Mary Howey; *b* 9 Jan 1942; *m* 2 May 1960, Michael Barry Wells; 1 s (Orlando Wells b 1973), 1 da (Sasha Wells b 1972); *Career* actress, films: 'Tunes of Glory', 'Greengage Summer', 'Tom Jones', 'A Man for All Seasons', 'The Killing of Sister George', 'They Shoot Horses, Don't They?', 'Images'; theatre: London, New York, Sydney, Paris; *Books* In Search of Unicorns, Lark's Castle; *Recreations* travelling, houses, gardens, reading; *Style*— Susannah Y York; c/o Jeremy Conway, 109 Jermyn St, London SW1Y 6HB

YORK-JOHNSON, Michael; *see*: York, Michael

YORKE, David Harry Robert; s of Harry Reginald Francis Yorke (d 1958), and Marie Christine, *née* Miller Frost; *b* 5 Dec 1931; *Educ* Dean Close Sch Cheltenham, Coll of Estate Mgmnt; *m* 23 April 1955, Patricia Gwynneth, da of Henry Arthur Fowler-Tutt (d 1975); 1 da (Sarah b 1960); *Career* Nat Serv RA 1954-56 (2 Lt 1955); chartered surveyor; Weatherall Green & Smith (UK, France, Germany, USA): ptnr London 1961-84, sr ptnr 1984-89, gp chm 1989-; memb mgmnt ctee Schroder Property Fund 1988, memb Bristol Devpt Corpn 1989, dir Br Waterways Bd 1989; pres RICS 1988-89; Freeman City of London 1978, Liveryman Worshipful Co of Chartered Surveyors 1979; ARICS 1956, FRICS 1966; *Recreations* narrow-boating, crosswords, swimming, occasional cookery; *Clubs* Bucks, East India; *Style*— David Yorke, Esq; Holford Manor, North Chailey, Sussex (☎ 044 404 277); 2 Chester Cottage's, London SW1; 22 Chancery Lane, London WC2 (☎ 01 405 6944)

YORKE, David John; s of Maj John Edward Evelyn Yorke, JP, and Eleanor, *née* Assheton, *qv*; *b* 26 Oct 1927; *Educ* Eton, Trinity Coll Cambridge (MA); *m* 1957, Susan Alexandra, da of Lt-Col Scrope Arthur Francis Sutherland Egerton, Highland LI (decd); 2 s, 1 da; *Career* late The Life Guards; FRICS; a JP and DL of Lancs; *Style*— David Yorks, Esq

YORKE, David John Napier Edward; JP (W Sussex); yr s of Hon Claud John Yorke (d 1940), and gs of 7 Earl of Hardwicke; *b* 17 Oct 1919; *Educ* Eton, Jesus Coll Cambridge; *m* 2 Feb 1950, Anne Margaret (d 1984), da of Denis George Mackail; 2 s (Charles Edward, and James Alexander Yorke); *Career* barr 1949, Lloyd's underwriter; *Recreations* walking, reading, visual arts; *Clubs* Brook's; *Style*— David Yorke, Esq; Gatewick, Steyning, Sussex

YORKE, Eleanor; *née* Assheton; CBE (1956); da of Sir Ralph Cockayne Assheton, 1 Bt (d 1955), and Mildred Estelle Sybella, CBE, JP, *née* Master (d 1949); sis of 1 Baron Clitheroe (d 1984); *b* 1907; *m* 1926, Maj John Edward Evelyn Yorke, JP; 1 s (David J Yorke, *qv*), 1 da; *Career* vice-chm Yorkshire Prov Area of Nat Union of Cons and Unionist Assoc 1952-55; *Style*— Mrs John Yorke, CBE; Halton Place, Hellifield, Skipton, Yorks

YORKE, Richard Michael; QC (1971); s of Gilbert Victor Yorke; *b* 13 July 1930; *Educ* Solihull Sch Warwickshire, Balliol Coll Oxford (MA); *Career* cmmnd 2 Lt RA 1949 (Prize of Honour Best Offr Cadet), Lt Hon Artillery Co 1951, Capt 1953; asst to sec Br Road Services 1953-56; barr Gray's Inn 1956 (Lee Prizeman), bencher 1981; joined Inner Temple 1968, barr Supreme Ct and NSW and High Ct of Aust 1972, QC NSW 1974; conslt Bodington of Yturbe Paris 1973-82; coutested (C): Durham 1966, Loughborough Feb and Oct 1974; pres Civil Aviation Review Bd 1972-75; vice-chm Senate Law Soc Jt Working Party on Banking Law 1975-83; memb Special Panel Tport Tribunal 1976-, Panel of Arbitrators Assoc 1984-, vol govr Bart's Hosp 1974; recorder Crown Ct 1972-83; gov Sadler's Wells Theatre 1986; *Recreations* flying, skiing, sailing, tennis; *Clubs* Cavalry and Guards, Roy Ocean Racing, St Stephen's Constitutional, Hurlingham, Island Sailing (Cowes); *Style*— Richard Yorke, Esq, QC; 5 Cliveden Place, London SW1W 8LA; Eden Roc, Rue de Ransou, 1936 Verbier, Switzerland (☎ (026) 76504); 4 and 5 Gray's Inn Square, Gray's Inn, London WC1R 5AY (☎ 01 404 5252, telex 895 3743 GRALAW)

YOUARD, Richard Geoffrey Atkin; s of Lt-Col Geoffrey Youard, MBE (d 1987), of

Gwernowddy Old Farmhouse, Llandrinio, Llanymynech, Powys, and Hon Mrs Rosaline Joan Youard, *née* Atkin (d 1973); *b* 27 Jan 1933; *Educ* Bradfield, Magdalen Coll Oxford (BA); *m* 31 Dec 1960, Felicity Ann, da of Kenneth Valentine Freeland Morton, CIE, of Temple End House, 27 Temple End, Great Wilbraham, Cambridge; 1 s (Andrew b 1964), 2 da (Penelope b 1961, Elizabeth b 1966); *Career* Nat Serv 1951-53, cmmnd RA 1952, Lt TA; slr 1959, Slaughter and May 1956-68 (ptnr 1968-); chm: Islington Consumers Gp 1965, Nat Fedn of Consumer Gps 1968; memb: Home Off Ctee on London Taxicab and Car Hire Trade 1967, inspr DTI 1987, clerk governing body Bradfield Coll 1968-; hon res fell Kings Coll London 1988; memb Law Soc 1968; *Books* various works on banking law and practice incl Butterworths Banking: Forms and Precedents (ed 1986); *Recreations* gardening, electronics, beekeeping, map collecting, reading; *Style—* Richard Youard, Esq; 12 Northampton Park, London N1 2PJ; (☎ 01 226 8055); Cwm Mynach Ganol, Bontddu, Dolgellau, Gwynedd; Slaughter and May, 35 Basinghall St, London EC2V 5DB (☎ 01 600 1200, fax 01 726 0038/600 0289, telex 883486/888926)

YOUDALE, Peter John Michael; s of Reginald John Youdale (d 1966), of Brighton, and Olga, *née* Baume (d 1979); *b* 21 June 1928; *Educ* Brighton Hove & Sussex GS; *m* 1 July 1950, Marie, da of G Hart (d 1939); 1 s (Richard Graham b 24 June 1953), 1 da (Wendy Anne b 3 May 1951); *Career* Nat Serv Grenadier Gds; mgmnt trainee Chubb Gp 1950-53, Salesman Dexion Gp 1953-56, div mangr Br Uralite Gp 1956-61, dir int mgmnt trg Eutectic Corpn USA 1961-63, dir sales and mktg Eutectic Ltd UK 1963-67, vice-pres mktg Mattel Toys California 1967-69, chm and chief exec Pirbic Gp Ltd 1969-; FInstM, FInstD, MBIM; *Books* Setting up an Effective Marketing Operation, Sales Management for Profit; *Recreations* swimming, painting, writing; *Clubs* RAC; *Style—* Peter Youdale, Esq; Birdingbury Hall, Birdingbury, Nr Rugby, Warwicks (☎ 073781 3955); The Pirbic Gp Ltd, Tile House, Ridgemount Rd, Sunningdale, Berks (☎ 0990 22291, fax 0990 872996, car 0836 282015)

YOUENS, Ven John Ross; CB (1970), OBE (1959), MC (1946); s of late Canon Fearnley Algernon Cyril Youens, and late Dorothy Mary, *née* Ross; *b* 4 Sept 1914; *Educ* Buxton Coll, Kelham Theol Coll; *m* 1940, Pamela Gordon Lincoln, da of Maj Alfred Lincoln Chandler (d 1948); 1 s (Richard), 2 da (Esme decd, Georgina decd); *Career* Royal Army Chaplain Dept 1940-74, chaplain gen 1966-74, archdeacon emeritus 1974, chaplain to HM The Queen 1969-84; sr tres Corpn of the Sons of the Clergy 1982-84, dep chm Keston Coll Centre for the Study of Religion and Communism; *Clubs* Cavalry & Guards; *Style—* The Ven John Youens, CB, OBE, MC; Fir Tree Cottage, Stedham, nr Midhurst, W Sussex GU29 0QN

YOUENS, Sir Peter William; CMG (1962), OBE (1960); s of Rev Canon F A C Youens (d 1968), and Dorothy Mary Ross (d 1975); *b* 29 April 1916; *Educ* King Edward VII Sch Sheffield, Wadham Coll Oxford (MA); *m* 1943, Diana Stephanie, da of Edward Hawkins; 2 da (Stephanie, Sarah); *Career* dep chief sec Nyasaland 1953-63 (asst sec 1951), sec to PM and Cabinet Malawi 1964-66 and Nyasaland 1963-64; exec dir Lonrho plc 1966-69 and 1981- (non-exec dir 1980-81), ptnr Tyzack and Ptnrs Ltd 1969-81, dir Oxford Playhouse Co (Anvil Prod Ltd) 1978-; kt 1965; *Recreations* walking, theatre; *Clubs* East India and Sports, Vincent's (Oxford); *Style—* Sir Peter Youens, CMG, OBE; The Old Parsonage, Hurstbourne Priors, Whitchurch, Hants; Lonrho plc, Cheapside House, 138 Cheapside, London EC2V 6BL (☎ 01 606 9898)

YOUNG, Sir Brian Walter Mark; er s of Sir Mark Young, GCMG (d 1974), sometime Govr of: Barbados, Tanganyika and Hong Kong; gs of Sir George Young, 2 Bt, of Formosa Place; *b* 23 August 1922; *Educ* Eton, King's Coll Cambridge; *m* 1947, Fiona Marjorie, only da of Allan Stewart, 16 of Appin; 1 s (Timothy b 1951), 2 da (Joanna b 1949, m 1974 Lt Col Peter Grant Peterkin, 1 s, 1 da; Deborah b 1953, m 1979 Geoffrey Hudson, 1 s, 1 da); *Career* serv WWII RNVR; asst master Eton 1947-52, headmaster Charterhouse 1952-64, memb Centl Advsy Cncl Educn 1956-59, dir Nuffield Fndn 1964-70 (managing tstee 1978-), dir-gen IBA (previously ITA) 1970-82, memb Arts Cncl 1983-88, chm Christian Aid 1983-; Hon DLitt Heriot-Watt Univ; Hon RNCM 1987; kt 1976; *Style—* Sir Brian Young; Hill End, Woodhill Ave, Gerrards Cross, Bucks (☎ 0753 887793)

YOUNG, Cecil Leonard Ronald; s of Ronald Harold Young (d 1942), and Agnes, *née* Denton (d 1977); *b* 27 August 1918; *Educ* Acton GS; *m* 2 April 1949, Doris Lilian, da of Howard Parkes (d 1926); *Career* WW11 Sqdn Ldr RAF 1940-48 serv SE Asia; Head of Inspection Dept Nat Westminster Bank 1973-78; Freeman City of London, Liveryman Worshipful Co of Chartered Secretaries; FCIS, ACIB; *Recreations* genealolgy, gardening; *Style—* Cecil Young, Esq; 25 Staveley Rd, Chiswick, London W4 3HU (☎ 01 994 8847)

YOUNG, His Hon Judge; Christopher Godfrey; s of Dr H G Young, MB (d 1949); *b* 9 Sept 1932; *Educ* Bedford Sch, King's Coll London (LLB); *m* 1969, Jeanetta Margaret, *née* Vaughan (d 1984); 1 s; *Career* barr Gray's Inn 1957, Midland and Oxford Circuit 1959-75, rec 1975-79, circuit judge 1980-; liaison judge with magistrates for Peterborough, Huntingdon and Toseland 1980-7, Leicestershire 1987-; *Recreations* music, natural history, gardening, foreign travel; *Style—* His Hon Judge Young; Stockshill House, Duddington, Stamford, Lincs

YOUNG, Hon Christopher Ivan; s of Baron Young of Dartington by 1 w Joan; *b* 1946; *Style—* The Hon Christopher Young

YOUNG, David Edward Michael; QC (1980); s of George Henry Edward Young and Audrey Seymour; *b* 30 Sept 1940; *Educ* Monkton Combe Sch Somerset, Oxford Univ (MA); *m* 1967, Anne, da of John Henry de Bromhead, of Ireland; 2 da (Yolanda b 1970, Francesca b 1972); *Career* barr; rec SE Circuit; *Books* Terrell on the Law of Patents (1982), Passing Off (1985); *Recreations* tennis, skiing, country pursuits; *Style—* David Young, Esq, QC; 6 Pump Ct, Temple, London EC4Y 7AR (☎ 01 353 8588)

YOUNG, David Ernest; s of Harold Ernest Young (d 1971), of Sheffield, and Jessie, *née* Turnbull; *b* 8 Mar 1942; *Educ* King Edward VII Sch Sheffield, Corpus Christi Coll Oxford (BA); *m* 8 Feb 1964, Norma, Alwyn Robinson (d 1979); 2 da (Wendy b 1965, Michele b 1968); *Career* asst princ Air Miny 1963; private sec: chief of Air Staff 1968-70, Min State of Def 1973-75; asst sec Central Policy Review Staff Cabinet Off 1975-77; John Lewis Ptnrship: joined 1982, md Peter Jones Sloane Square 1984-86, fin dir 1987-; Independent Memb Steering Bd of Companies House 1988-; RIPA 1977; *Recreations* walking, gardening, theatre; *Style—* David Young, Esq; 4 Old Cavendish Street, London W1A 1EX (☎ 01 637 3434, fax 01 493 4013)

YOUNG, Hon David Justin; 2 s of Baron Young of Dartington (Life Peer), and his 1 w Joan, *née* Lawson; *b* 1949; *Style—* The Hon David Young; 7 St Catherine's Precincts, London NW1

YOUNG, Rt Rev David Nigel de Lorentz; *see*: Ripon, Bishop of

YOUNG, Lt-Gen Sir David Tod; KBE (1980), CB (1977), DFC (1952); s of William Young (d 1930), by his w Davina Tod Young, *née* Young (d 1974); *b* 17 May 1926; *Educ* George Watson's Coll Edinburgh; *m* 1, 1950, Joyce Marian Melville (d 25 Oct 1987); 2 s; m 2, 11 June 1988, Mrs Joanna M Oyler, *née* Torin; *Career* cmmnd Royal Scots 1945, Col GS Staff Coll 1969-70, Cdr 12 Mechanised Bde 1970-72, Dep Mil Sec MOD 1972-74, Cdr Land Forces NI 1975-77, Col The Royal Scots 1975-80, dlr Infantry 1977-80; Col Cmdt Scottish Div, GOC Scotland 1980-82, govr Edinburgh Castle 1980-82, ret; chm Cairntech Ltd 1983; HM cmmr Queen Victoria Sch, Dunblane 1984; pres Army Cadet Force Assoc Scotland 1984; Col Comdt Ulster Defence Regiment 1986; Scottish Ctee Marie Curie Memorial Fndn (Memb 1983, chm 1986); govr St Columba's Hospice 1986, chm St Mary's Cathedral Workshop 1986; *Recreations* golf, shooting; *Clubs* New, Royal Scots (both Edinburgh); *Style—* Lt-Gen Sir David Young, KBE, CB, DFC; c/o Adam & Co plc, 22 Charlotte Sq, Edinburgh EH2 4DF. Cairntech Ltd, 67 Marionville Rd, Edinburgh EH7 6AJ (☎ 031 652 1108, telex 727618-G)

YOUNG, David Tyrrell; s of Tyrrell Francis Young, of 143 Cranmer Court, London, and Patricia Morrison, *née* Spicer; *b* 6 Jan 1938; *Educ* Charterhouse; *m* 11 Sept 1965, Madeline Helen Celia, da of Anthony Burton Capel Philips (d 1983)), of The Heath House, Tean, Stoke-on-Trent; 3 da (Melanie Rosamond b 1969, Annabel Katharine b 1971, Corinna Lucy b 1974); *Career* TA 1 Regt HAC 1955-67, ret Capt 1967; trainee CA Gerard Van De Linde & Son 1955-60, audit mangr James Edwards Daugerfield & Co 1961-65; Spicer & Oppeheim (formerly Spicer & Pegler): audit mangr 1965-68, ptnr 1968-82, managing ptnr 1982-88, sr ptnr and int chm 1988-; cncl memb ICEAW 1979-82; Freeman City of London, memb Ct Worshipful Co of Fishmongers; FCA; *Recreations* golf, tennis; *Clubs* Royal St Georges GC, Royal Worlington GC, City of London; *Style—* David T Young, Esq; Overhall, Ashdon, Saffron Walden, Essex CB10 2JH (☎ 0799 84 556) Friary Court, 65 Crutched Friars, London EC3N 2NP (☎01 480 7766, fax 01 480 6958, telex 884257 ESANO G)

YOUNG, David Wright; MP (Lab) Bolton SE 1983-; *Educ* Greenock Acad, Glasgow Univ, St Paul's Coll Cheltenham; *Career* former alderman Nuneaton Boro Cncl and cllr Nuneaton Dist Cncl, contested (Lab): S Worcestershire 1959, Banbury, Bath 1970; chm Coventry E Lab Pty 1964-68, MP (Lab) Bolton E Feb 1974-1983, parly ps to Sec of State Def 1977-79; memb House of Commons Public Accounts Cmmn; offr Cwlth and former Cwlth Centres; *Style—* David Young, Esq, MP; House of Commons, London SW1

YOUNG, Elizabeth; da of Benn E Glanvill, of Crescent Cottage, Aldeburgh, Suffolk, and (Beatrice) Catherine Bonn, *née* Newbald; *b* 21 Dec 1936; *Educ* Winceby House Beehill Surrey, Pensionat Belri Arosa Switzerland; *m* 16 Feb 1961, Kenneth Charles Stuart Young; 2 da (Kate b 20 Dec 1962, Miranda b 1 Dec 1964, d 8 Oct 1988); *Career* journalist Daily Telegraph 1960-86 (Staff and freelance), ed Embroidery Magazine 1980-84, freelance ed and writer books on Embroidery 1988-; as Elizabeth Benn: chm Embroiderer's Guild Hampton Ct Palace 1985-; Liveryman Worshipful Co Stationers and Newspapermakers 1977; *Recreations* golf; *Style—* Mrs Kenneth Young; Old Rectory, Buckland, nr Aylesbury, Bucks (☎ 0296 630 461); 3C St John's Wharf, Wapping High St, London E1

YOUNG, Hon Emily Tacita; da of 2 Baron Kennet; *b* 13 Mar 1951; *Educ* various, Chelsea Sch of Arts, St Martins Sch of Art; *m* 1 s (Arthur William Phoenix b 1978); *Career* Artist; *Recreations* reading, walking; *Clubs* Chelsea Arts; *Style—* The Hon Emily Young

YOUNG, Eric Alexander Irons; s of George Irons Young (d 1945), of Hall Hill, Howwood, Redfredshire, and May Litster, *née* Ingram (d 1960); *b* 27 Dec 1921; *Educ* Trinity Coll Glenalmond, Jesus Coll Cambridge; *m* 22 Aug 1948, Camilla Campbell, da of Dr Edward Milgrove, Sydney, Australia (d 1974); 2 s (Mark b 1952, Simon b 1955); *Career* XI Hussars PAO Italy and Europe 1942-45; Dept Lt of Ayr and Arran 1979; Maj in the Ayrshire ECO Yeo 1957-58; dir Ingram Bros 1946- (md 1968); chm George Ingram & Assoc Co 1969-; *Recreations* racing, shooting, golf; *Clubs* Royal Scottish Automobile; *Style—* Eric Young; Hillhouse Lodge, Fenwick, Ayrshire KA3 6BU (☎ 05606 260); George Ingram Ltd, Lawmoor Place, Glasgow G5 0YE

YOUNG, George Horatio; s and h of Sir George Young, Bt, MP; *b* 11 Oct 1966; *Educ* Windsor CFE, Christ Church Oxford; *Career* student; *Recreations* cricket, tennis, classical guitar; *Style—* George Young, Esq; Formosa Place, Cookham, Berks

YOUNG, Sir George Samuel Knatchbull; 6 Bt (UK 1813), of Formosa Place, Berks; MP (C) Ealing Acton 1974-; s of Sir George Young, 5 Bt, CMG (d 1960), by his w Elisabeth (herself er da of Sir Hugh Knatchbull-Hugessen, KCMG, who was in turn n of 1 Baron Brabourne); *b* 16 July 1941; *Educ* Eton, Christ Church Oxford; *m* 1964, Aurelia, da of Oscar Nemon and Mrs Nemon-Stuart, of Boars Hill, Oxford; 2 s, 2 da; *Heir* s, George Horatio Young; *Career* econ NEDO 1966-67, Kobler Res fell Univ of Surrey 1967-69, memb Lambeth Boro Cncl 1968-71, econ advsr Post Off Corpn 1969-74, memb GLC (Ealing) 1970-73, oppn whip 1976-79, under-sec state: DHSS 1979-81, DOE 1981-86; tstee Guinness Tst 1986; *Books* Tourism, Blessing or Blight?; *Style—* Sir George Young, Bt, MP; 91 Shakespeare Rd, London W3 (☎ 01 992 2743); Formosa Place, Cookham, Berks

YOUNG, Gerard Francis; CBE (1967); s of Smelter Joseph Young (d 1954), of Richmond Park, Sheffield, and Edith, *née* Aspinall (d 1983); *b* 5 May 1910; *Educ* Ampleforth; *m* 7 Aug 1937, Diana, da of Charles Murray MD; 2 s (Hugo b 13 Oct 1938, Charles b 29 April 1947), 3 da (Caroline b 8 June 1980, Jane b 6 March 1945, Sarah b 8 Dec 1950); *Career* The Tempered Spring Co Ltd 1930-78 (chm 1954-78); dir 1967-79 Sun Alliance and London Insur Gp (Sheffield area), Nat Vulcan Engrg Insur; chm Radio Hallam Ltd 1973-79 dir Crucible Theatre Tst Ltd dir 1967-75; memb: Nat Bd for Prices and Incomes 1965-71; Top Salaries Review Body, Armed Forces Pay Review Body 1971-74; tstee: Sheffield Town Tst (town collector 1978-81), JG Graves Charitable Tst (chm 1974-86); govr Utd Sheffield Hosps 1945-53, memb cncl Univ of Sheffield 1943-84 (pro-chllr 1951-67), gen cmmr of income tax 1947-74; J P Sheffield 1950-74, High Sheriff Allanshire 1973-74, DL West Riding Yorks 1973, Lord Lt S Yorks 1974-85, Custos Rotolorum, KStJ 1976; memb Worshipful Co of Cutlers in Allanshire (master 1961-62); hon LLD Sheffield Univ 1962; FI Mech E; GCSG (Vatican) 1974; *Recreations* gardening, 13 grandchildren; *Clubs* Sheffield; *Style—* Gerard Young, Esq, CBE, DL; Roundfield, 69 Carsick Hill Crescent, Sheffield S10 3LS (☎ 0742 302 834)

YOUNG, Gertrude, Lady; Gertrude Annie; da of John Elliott, of Braunton, N Devon; *m* 1912, Sir Cyril Young, 4 Bt; 3 s (1 - late 5 Bt - decd, also Patrick Young, *qv*), 1 da (Mrs Stanley Claremont); *Style*— Gertrude, Lady Young; Le Copacabana, Jardin des Hesperides, Palm Beach, Cannes, Alpes Maritimes, France; 66 Kensington Mans, Trebovir Rd, SW5

YOUNG, Hon Mrs Gillian Margaret; *née* Campbell; da of late 2 Baron Colgrain; *b* 1925; *m* 1951, Peter Scott Young; 2 s, 2 da; *Style*— The Hon Mrs Young; Orchard House, Broom Lane, Langton Green, Tunbridge Wells TN3 0RA

YOUNG, (John Andrew) Gordon; s of Harold James Young, of Grantown-on-Spey, and Agnes Elizabeth, *née* Wilson; *b* 19 Mar 1945; *Educ* King's Coll Sch Wimbledon ; *m* 30 Nov 1968, Jane Pamela (d 1988), da of Ronald Victor Seyd, of of W Sussex; 1 s (Angus b 17 Jan 1972), 1 da (Suzanna b 9 May 1969); *Career* with Baring Bros & Co Ltd 1970-73; N M Rothschild & Sons Ltd 1973-87, exec dir 1981-87, non-exec dir 1987-; exec dir Smith New Court plc 1987-; MICAS; *Recreations* golf, travel; *Clubs* Oriental, West Sussex Golf, Hong Kong ; *Style*— Gordon Young, Esq; Flat 9, 53 Millbank, London SW1P 4RL (☎ 01 821 5455); Smith New Court plc, Chetwynd House, 24 St Swithin's Lane, London EC4N 8AE (☎ 01 626 1544, fax 01 623 3947, telex 884410)

YOUNG, Graham Christopher McKenzie; s of Archibald Hamilton Young (d 1964), of Caterham, and Lurline, *née* Chandler; *b* 20 Dec 1935; *Educ* Culford Sch, Trinity Coll Cambridge (MA, LLM); *m* 15 Dec 1962, Pamela Frances, da of Geoffrey Frances Anthony Bisley, of Kempsford, Glos; 1 s (Jonathan Graham b 1965), 2 da (Alison b 1964, Caroline b 1968); *Career* slr 1962, ptnr Townsends Swindon 1964-; pres Swindon Lions Club 1970; NSPCC: memb Central Exec Ctee, hon sec Swindon and N Wilts branch; pres Glos and Wilts inc Law Soc 1986, memb Prospect Fndn Swindon; pt/t chm: rent assessment panels, social security appeal tbnls; Parly candidate (c) Swindon 1974; memb Law Soc; *Recreations* squash, swimming, DIY ; *Style*— Graham Young, Esq; Kempsford House, Kempsford, nr Fairford, Glos (☎ 0285 810487); Townsends, 42 Cricklade St, Swindon, Wilts (☎ 0793 35 421, fax 0793 616 294, telex 44712)

YOUNG, Hon Sir Harold William; KCMG (1983); s of Frederick Garfield James Young (d 1977), and Edith Mabel Scott Young; *b* 30 June 1923; *Educ* Prince Alfred Coll, Adelaide Univ; *m* 1952, Eileen Margaret, da of George Westwood Downing (d 1981); 2 s, 2 da; *Career* senator (Lib) for SA 1968-83, govt whip then oppn whip in Senate 1971-75, pres of the Senate 1981-83; *Style*— The Hon Sir Harold Young, KCMG; 32 Greenwood Grove, Urrbrae, SA 5064 Australia

YOUNG, Hugh Kenneth; s of John Young (d 1974), and Monica, *née* Auckland (d 1936); *b* 6 May 1936; *Educ* Edinburgh Acad; *m* 19 Sept 1962, Marjory Bruce, da of Charles Wilson (d 1987), of Edinburgh; 2 s (Hugh b 1967, Angus b 1970), 1 da (Susan b 1965); *Career* TA 1957-59, Nat Serv 2 Lt Royal Scots 1960, served Libya, TA 1961-69 (Capt 1966), joined HSF 1986; accountant and banker: dir Radio Forth Ltd 1974-75, exec dir British Linen Bank Ltd 1978-84, dir Pentland Oil Exploration Ltd 1980-86, sec and memb mgmnt bd Bank of Scotland 1984-, chm Bank of Scotland (Jersey) Ltd 1986-, dir Bank of Wales (Jersey) 1986-, dir Edinburgh Sports Club Ltd 1983-87 (chm 1984-87); FIB (Scot); *Recreations* squash, tennis, hill-waking; *Clubs* New (Edinburgh), Edinburgh Sports; *Style*— Hugh Young, Esq; 30 Braid Hills Rd, Edinburgh EH10 6HY (☎ 031 447 3101); Bank of Scotland, Head Office, PO Box No 5, The Mound, Edinburgh EH1 1YZ (☎ 031 243 5562, switchboard 031 442 7777, telex 72275, fax 031 243 5437)

YOUNG, Air Cdre Ian Matheson; MBE (1967), MID (1960); s of Gp Capt Peter Hutchinson Young (d 1967), of Devon, and Hylda, *née* Matheson; *b* 18 May 1927; *Educ* Blundell's; *m* 31 Dec 1953, Kathleen Scott, da of James William Mathewson, MD (d 1924), of Cambridgeshire; 2 da (Beverley b 1956, Lesley b 1959); *Career* RM 1946-47, RAF 1947-81 (ret as Air Cdre), provost marshal, dir Security and Chief of RAF Police, serv: Aden, Cyprus, Singapore, Germany 1978-81; dir Security Playboy Gp Co and Trident Casinos Ltd 1981-82, md Sprite Security Servs Ltd 1983-84, security conslt 1984-86, hd of Security Eurotunnel 1986-; FBIM, FIPI (princ 1985-87); *Recreations* boating swimming, spectator of sports; *Style*— Air Cdre Ian M Young; Russets, Ridgeway Rd, Dorking, Surrey RH4 3EY (☎ 0306 888844); Eurotunnel, Portland House, Stag Place, London SW1E 5BT (☎ 01 834 757, telex 915539, fax 01 821 5242)

YOUNG, Baroness (Life Peer UK 1971); Janet Mary Young; PC (1981); da of John Baker and Phyllis, *née* Hancock; *b* 23 Oct 1926; *Educ* Dragon Sch Oxford, in USA, St Anne's Coll Oxford; *m* 1950, Dr Geoffrey Tyndale Young (fellow Jesus Coll Oxford); 3 da; *Career* sits as Cons peer in House of Lords; memb Oxford City Cncl 1957-72 (alderman and ldr Cons Gp 1967-72); Baroness-in-Waiting to HM The Queen (first ever Cons woman govt whip in upper chamber) 1972-73, parly under-sec state DOE 1973-74; vice-chm Cons Pty Orgn 1975-83 (with special responsibility for women's orgns), dep chm 1977-79; min state DES 1979-81, chllr Duchy of Lancaster 1981-82, Cons ldr House of Lords Sept 1981-83, lord privy seal 1982-83, min state FCO 1983-87; dir: Nat Westminster Bank 1987-; formerly dir UK Provident; formerly memb BR Western Region Advsy Bd; dir Marks and Spencer plc 1987, vice pres W India 1987; hon fell: Inst of Civil Engrs, St Annes Coll Oxford; tstee Lucy Cavendish Coll Cambridge 1988; Hon DLL Mt Holyoake Coll USA; *Clubs* Univ Women's; *Style*— The Rt Hon the Baroness Young, PC; House of Lords, London SW1

YOUNG, John Adrian Emile; s of John Archibald Campbell Young (d 1979), of Plaxtol, Kent, and Irene Eugenie, *née* Bouvier (d 1976); *b* 28 July 1934; *Educ* Cranbrook Sch Kent, London Univ (LLB); *m* 20 June 1959, Yvonne Lalage Elizabeth, da of John Digby Hyde Bankes (d 1976), of Twitton House, Otford, Kent; 3 s (Charles b 1961, Paul b 1962, Simon b 1965), 1 da (Anna b 1963); *Career* ptnr Cameron Markby Slrs 1965-; nat chm Young Slrs Gp 1965-66, pres Association Internationale des Jeunes Avocats 1968-69, cncl memb Int Bar Assoc 1983-, sen warden City of London Slrs Co 1988-89; choirmaster/organist of local church; Liveryman City of London Slrs Co (Freeman 1967); memb Law Soc 1958 (asst sec 1958-64, cncl memb 1971-); *Recreations* music, gardening, foreign travel; *Style*— John Young, Esq; Stonewold Ho, Plaxtol, Kent (☎ 0732 810 289); Cameron Markby, Sceptre Court, 40 Tower Hill, London EC3N 4BB (☎ 01 702 2345, fax 01 702 2303, telex 925779)

YOUNG, Sir John Kenyon Roe; 6 Bt (UK 1821), of Bailieborough Castle, Co Cavan; s of Sir John William Roe Young, 5 Bt (d 1981), by his 1 w, Joan Minnie Agnes, *née* Aldous (d 1958); *b* 23 April 1947; *Educ* Hurn Ct Sch, Christchurch, Napier Coll; *m* 1977, Frances Elise, only da of W R Thompson; 1 s, 1 da (Tamara Elizabeth Eve b 9 Nov 1986); *Heir* s, Richard Christopher Roe Young, b 14 July 1983; *Career* former hydrographic surveyor; sr buyer; *Recreations* golf; *Style*— Sir John Young, Bt; Bolingey, 159 Chatham Rd, Maidstone, Kent ME14 2ND

YOUNG, Hon Mr Justice; Hon Sir John McIntosh; KCMG (1975); s of George David Young (d 1956); *b* 17 Dec 1919; *Educ* Geelong GS, BNC Oxford, Inner Temple, Melbourne Univ; *m* 1951, Elisabeth Mary, da Dr E W Twining; 1 s, 2 da; *Career* barr Victoria Aust 1949-74, QC 1961, Lt-Govr Victoria and chief justice Supreme Ct of Victoria 1974-; pres: Scout Assoc of Aust 1986-, St John Cncl Victoria 1975-82; rep Hon Col RAAC 1986-, Hon Col 4/19 Prince of Wales's Light Horse 1978-, chllr Order of St John in Aust 1982, Hon Air Cdre No 21 (City of Melbourne) Sqdn, RAAF 1986-; Hon LLD Monash 1986, KStJ 1977; *Recreations* riding, golf; *Clubs* Cavalry and Guards', Melbourne and Aust, (Melbourne); *Style*— The Hon Mr Justice Young, KCMG; Supreme Court, William St, Melbourne, Vic 3000, Australia

YOUNG, John Robert Chester; s of Robert Nisbet Young (d 1956), and Edith Mary Young (d 1981); *b* 6 Sept 1937; *Educ* Bishop Vesey's GS, St Edmund Hall Oxford; *m* 1963, Pauline Joyce, da of George Yates (d 1966); 1 s (and 1 s decd), 1 da; *Career* ptnr Simon & Coates (stockbrokers) 1965-82; memb cncl Stock Exchange 1965-82 (cncl memb 1978-82), dir of policy and planning Stock Exchange 1982-87, chief exec The Securities Assoc 1987-, vice chm exec bd The Int Stock Exchange; *Recreations* rugby football; *Clubs* Harlequin's, Vincent's; *Style*— John Young, Esq; Richmond House, Falkland Grove, Dorking, Surrey; The Stock Exchange, London EC2N 1HP (☎ 01 588 2355)

YOUNG, John Todd; s of Ian Taylor Young, of Rugby, Warwick, and Flora Leggett, *née* Todd; *b* 14 Jan 1957; *Educ* Manchester GS, Sidney Sussex Coll Cambridge (BA, MA); *m* 11 April 1981, Elizabeth Jane, da of Philip John Grattidge, of Wareham, Dorset; *Career* Lovell White Durrant (formerly Lovell White & King): articled clerk 1979-81, slr 1981-, ptnr 1987-; memb Worshipful Co of Slrs; memb Law Soc; *Recreations* mountaineering, windsurfing; *Clubs* Cannons Sailing; *Style*— John Young, Esq; 21 Holborn Viaduct, London EC1A 2DY (☎ 01 236 0066, fax 01 248 4212, telex 887122 LWD)

YOUNG, John William Garne; s of David Richard Young, of Shaftestbury, Dorset, and Pamela Mary *née* Garne; *b* 6 Jan 1945; *Educ* Shaftesbury GS; *m* 1 Jan 1971, (Eleanor) Louise, da of Abryn Walsh Sparks (d 1980), of Swinburne SA; 3 s (Michael b 1972, David b 1974, Peter b 1980); *Career* chm: Parmiter Ltd 1982- (md 1973-87), Kidd Ltd 1980-; dir Wolseley plc 1982-; chm: McConnel Ltd 1982-, Bypy Ltd 1982-, Dihurst Hldgs Ltd 1986-, Sparex Ltd 1986-, Vapormatic Ltd 1986-; pres Agn Engrs Assoc 1987-88, govr Agric Engrg Res Silsoe memb engrg advsy gp AFRC; tstee Tisbury Village Hall, govr Lackham Coll; CIAgrE; *Recreations* cricket, tennis, water sports; *Style*— John Young, Esq; The Gables, Hindon Lane, Tisbury, Wilts (☎ 0747 870756) c/o P J Parmiter & Sons Ltd, Station Works, Tisbury, Wiltshire (☎ 0747 870 821, fax 0747 871 171, telex 417 197)

YOUNG, Hon Judith Anne; yr da of Baron Young of Graffham (Life Peer); *b* 1960; *Style*— Hon Judith Young

YOUNG, (David) Junor; s of David Young (d 1974), and Margaret Mellis; *b* 23 April 1934; *Educ* Robert Gordon's Coll Aberdeen; *m* 6 Nov 1954, Kathleen, da of E Brooks, of Eastbourne; 2 da (Stephanie b 1955, Philippa b 1967), 2 s (Ashley b 1958, Jonathan b 1964); *Career* joined FO 1951, consul Stuttgart 1978-81, first sec Kampala 1981-84, consul-gen, Hamburg 1984-86, cnsllr (commercial) Br Embassy Bonn 1986-88, Br High Cmmr Honiara, Solomon Islands 1988-; *Recreations* fishing, shooting; *Clubs* Naval and Millitary; *Style*— D J Young, Esq; Pine Cottage, Hintlesham, Suffolk; British Embassy, Bonn BFPO 19 (☎ 0228 234061)

YOUNG, Sir Leslie Clarence; CBE (1980), DL; s of late Clarence James Young, and Ivy Isabel Young (d 1984); *Educ* LSE (BSc, LLD); *m* 1949, Muriel Howard Pearson; 1 s, 1 da; *Career* formerly with Courtaulds Ltd; chm: NW regnl cncl CBI 1976-78, NW Industl Devpt Bd 1978-81, J Bibby & Sons plc 1979-84, Merseyside Devpt Corpn 1981-84, Br Waterways Bd 1984-87, Natwest Bank 1986-, tstees of Nat Museum and Galleries in Merseyside 1986-, Pioneer Mutual Insur Co Ltd 1986-, SIBEC Devpts Ltd 1988-; non-exec dir Granada TV 1979-83, tstee Civic Tst for NW 1978-83; kt 1984; *Style*— Sir Leslie Young, CBE, DL; Overwood, Vicarage Lane, Burton, S Wirral L64 5TJ

YOUNG, Hon Mrs (Lilian Vida Lechmere); *née* Moncreiff; da of 4 Baron Moncreiff (d 1942); *b* 1912; *m* 1942, David Robert Young; 1 s, 1 da; *Style*— The Hon Mrs Young; Tanworth, Fossoway, Kinross-shire

YOUNG, (Clayton) Mark; s of Arnold Young, and Florence May, *née* Lambert; *b* 7 June 1929; *Educ* Pendower Tech Sch Newcastle-on-Tyne; *m* 1, 1952, Charlotte (d 1978); 2 s (Mark b 14 Aug 1962, Robin b 26 Nov 1964), 2 da (Vanessa b 16 Sept 1957, Ursula b 12 Jan 1960); m 2, 1979, Marie Therese; 1 s (Henry b 16 Sept 1981); *Career* RAF; mining and shipbuilding until 1962, head res dept Electrical Trades Union 1962 (nat offr 1963), chm Ford Trade Unions 1965-69, sec Nat Jt Cncl for Civil Air Tport 1964-74 and 1977- (chm 1975-77), gen sec Br Air Line Pilots Assoc 1974, sec Br Airways Trade Union Cncl; *Recreations* ballooning, reading; *Style*— Mark Young, Esq; 44f Sutton Ct Rd, Chiswick, London W4 (☎ 01 995 8552); Dovengill, Fell End, nr Kirby Stephen, Cumbria; British Air Line Pilots Assoc, 81 New Rd, Harlington, Hayes, Middx UB3 5BG (☎ 01 759 9331, fax 01 564 7957, telex 265871 MONREF G)

YOUNG, Dr Patrick Chisholm; s of Prof William Henry Young (d 1942) of Villa Collonge, La Conversion, Vaud, Switzerland, and Grace Emily, *née* Chisholm (d 1944); *b* 18 Mar 1908; *Educ* Baccalaureat-es-Sciences, Cambridge Univ (MA), Oxford Univ (DPhil), London Univ (post graduate Dip Chemical Engrg); Univs of: Strasbourg, Gottingen, Geneva; Middle Temple London; *m* 1 June 1950, Marjorie d of Frederick Charles Sargent (d 1968) of London; 2 s (Norman Patrick b 1955, Lionel Henry b 1955), 1 da (Janet (Mrs Bills) b 1952); *Career* chief chemist John Heathcoat & Co Ltd 1930-31, plant mangr and devpt offr ICI Plastics Ltd 1934-39, chief engr and tech mangr Jablo Propellers Ltd 1939-41, chief engr and tech advsr ME Stace Ltd and F Bender & Co Ltd 1942-43, works mangr De la Rue Plastics Ltd 1943-45, tech dir De La Rue Plastics do Brasil SA 1945-46, indust conslt UN Econ Cmmn for Asia and Far E 1948, cnsllr Head central off OEEC Technical Directorecte 1948-51, head of UNESCO Sci Co-Operation off for S Asia 1951-54, md Beecham's Gp Labs (India) Private Ltd 1956-57, Sec Gen CEN (the assoc for Euro Standards) 1970-74; involvement in local resident's assocs, participation in socs and instns concerned with Asian, Euro, S American and S African affairs; Freeman City of London 1930-,

Liveryman Worshipful Co of Fishmongers 1930-; MRAeS 1940, FICHemE 1941; *Recreations* scientific consideration of biology and human behaviour, Genealogy; *Style*— Dr Patrick Young; 14 Russell Hill, Purley, Surrey CR2 2JA (☎ 01 660 5556)

YOUNG, Sir Richard Dilworth; s of Philip Young, by his w Constance Maria Lloyd; *b* 9 April 1914; *Educ* Bromsgrove, Bristol Univ; *m* 1951, Jean Barbara Paterson, *née* Lockwood; 4 s; *Career* Boosey & Hawkes Ltd: dep chm 1978-79, chm 1979-84; dir: Tube Investmts Ltd 1958 (md 1961-64), Rugby Portland Cement Co 1968-88, Cwlth Fin Devpt Corpn 1968-83, Ingersoll Engrs Inc (USA) 1976-71; memb Central Advsy Cncl on Sci and Technol 1967-70, Cncl CBI 1967-74, Cncl Warwick Univ 1966-; FIMechE, CBIM; kt 1970; *Clubs* Athenaeum; *Style*— Sir Richard Young; Bearley Manor, Bearley, nr Stratford-on-Avon, Warwicks (☎ 0789 731 220)

YOUNG, Robert; s of Walter Horace Young (d 1963), of Wood Green, London, and Evelyn Joan, *née* Jennings; *b* 27 Mar 1944; *Educ* The Boys' GS London, Magdalen Coll Oxford (BA); *m* 18 Dec 1965, Patricia Anne, da of Robert Archibald Cowin, of Hest Bank, Lancs; 2 s (Matthew b 1969, Alec b and d 1972), 1 da (Judithy b 1974); *Career* dir Rolls-Royce Motors Diesel Div 1977-81, gp commercial dir Vickers plc 1981-83; on secondment from Vickers: memb central policy review staff Cabinet Off 1983, memb 10 Downing St Policy Unit 1983-84; md Crane Ltd 1985-88; CBI: regnl cncllr W Mids 1980-81, chm Shrops 1981; monopolies and mergers cmmn 1986-; chief exec Plastics Div McKechnie plc 1988-; FInstD 1985; *Recreations* music, photography, cats, horse-riding; *Clubs* IOD; *Style*— Robert Young, Esq; 54 Fordhook Ave, Ealing Common, London W5 3LR (☎ 01 992 2228); McKechnie plc, Leighswood Rd, Aldridge, W Midlands WS9 8DS

YOUNG, (John) Robertson; s of Francis John Young (d 1982), and Marjorie Elizabeth, *née* Imrie; *b* 21 Feb 1945; *Educ* Norwich Sch, Leicester Univ; *m* 15 July 1967, Catherine Suzanne Francoise, da of Jean Houssait (d 1945); 1 s (Jerome Robertson b 9 Jan 1971), 2 da (Isabelle b 10 April 1969, Juliette Claire b 29 Oct 1978); *Career* Foreign Serv: serv MECAS Lebanon 1968, first sec Cairo 1970, FCO 1972, Paris 1976, FCO 1981, cnsllr Damascus 1984, head of Middle E Dept FCO 1987; *Recreations* sailing, music; *Clubs* Cruising Assoc; *Style*— Rob Young, Esq; 57 Richborne Terrace, London SW8 1AT; Les Choiseaux, Artannes Sur Indre, Tours, France; c/o Foreign and Commonwealth Office, King Charles St, London SW1 (☎ 01 270 2981)

YOUNG, Roderic Neil; s of Frederick Hugh Young, OBE (d 1969), of The Gables, Woodhurst Lane, Oxted, Surrey, and Stella Mary, *née* Robinson; *b* 29 May 1933; *Educ* Eton, Trinity Coll Cambridge (MA); *m* 16 June 1962, Gillian Margaret, da of Col William Alexander Salmon, OBE, of Balcombe Place, Balcombe, W Sussex; 2 s (Peter b 1964, Rupert b 1969), 1 da (Jennifer b 1966); *Career* 2 Lt Queens Own Royal W Kent Regt 1952; dir: Murray Johnstone Ltd 1969-70, Kleinwort Benson Ltd 1972-86, Globe Investmt Tst plc 1973-, Brunner Investmt Tst plc 1975-, Merchants Tst plc 1975-85, Kleinwort Grievson Investmt Mgmnt Ltd 1986-88, Aberdeen Petroleum plc 1988-; dep chm Assoc of Investmt Tst Cos 1987-; memb advsy ctee Greenwich Hosp, almoner Christ's Hosp, Alderman and JP City of London; Liveryman and memb of Ct Worshipful Co Gunmakers, Liveryman Worshipful Co of CA's; ACA 1959, FCA 1969; *Recreations* shooting, gardening, DIY, golf, tennis; *Style*— Neil Young, Esq, JP; Pembury Hall, Pembury, Kent TN2 4AT (☎ 089 282 2971)

YOUNG, Sir Roger William; s of Charles Bowden Young (d 1963), and Dr Ruth Young, *née* Wilson (d 1983); *b* 15 Nov 1923; *Educ* Dragon Sch, Westminster, Christ Church Oxford (MA, STh, LHD); *m* 1950, Caroline Mary, da of Lt-Cdr Charles Perowne Christie, RN (d 1929); 2 s (Patrick, Christopher), 2 da (Elizabeth, Janet); *Career* Sub Lt RNVR (Navigating Offr) 1943-45; res tutor St Catharine's Cumberland Lodge Windsor Gt Park 1949-51, asst master Manchester GS 1951-58, princ George Watson's Coll Edinburgh 1958-85, chm Cheltenham Ladies Cncl 1986-, memb Public Schs Cmmn 1968-70, pres Head Teachers Assoc of Scotland 1972-74; chm Headmasters' Conf 1976, memb GBA Ctee 1986- (dep chm 1987); Scottish nat govr BBC 1979-84; FRSE 1965; kt 1983; *Books* Lines of Thought (1958), Everybody's Business (1968); *Recreations* gardening, hill-climbing, photography, knitting; *Clubs* E India; *Style*— Sir Roger Young; 11 Belgrave Terrace, Bath, Avon BA1 5JR (☎ 0225 336940)

YOUNG, Brig (Henry Lawrence) Savill; DSO (1944), DL (Somerset 1974); s of Maj George Edward Savill Young (d of wounds 1917), and Alison Jane *née* Poole (d 1957); *b* 19 Oct 1915; *Educ* Harrow, RMC Sandhurst; *m* 19 Sept 1939, Noreen De Vere, da of Thomas Brabgzon Ponsonby (d 1946), of Kilcooley Abbey Thurles, Ireland; 1 s (Savill), 1 da (Verona); *Career* Irish Gds: 2 Lt 1936, serv Egypt and Palestine 1936-38, serv WWII: Norway, N Africa, Italy, NW Europe; with 1Bn and Gds Armd Div, Cdr 1Bn 1954-57, Col cmdg Irish Gds 1957-61, Cmdt 107 Indep (Ulster) Bde Gp TA 1961-62, ret 1962-, Co Cmdt Som ACF 1973-76, sec Som T and AFA 1964-66;; *Recreations* shooting, fishing; *Clubs* Army and Navy, Pratt's; *Style*— Brig Savill Young, DSO, DL; Fulford House, Kingston St Mary, Taunton, Somerset TA2 8AJ

YOUNG, Hon Sophie Ann; da of Baron Young of Dartington by his 2 w Sasha; *b* 1961; *Style*— The Hon Sophie Young; 67 Gibson Sq, London N1

YOUNG, Sir Stephen Stewart Templeton; 3 Bt (UK 1945), of Partick, Co City of Glasgow; s of Sir Alastair Spencer Templeton Young, 2 Bt, DL (d 1963), and (Dorothy Constance) Marcelle (d 1964), widow of Lt John Hollington Grayburn, VC, and da of Lt-Col Charles Ernest Chambers; *b* 24 May 1947; *Educ* Rugby, Trinity Coll Oxford, Edinburgh Univ; *m* 1974, Viola Margaret, da of Prof Patrick Horace Nowell-Smith (whose mother was Cecil, ggda of Most Rev Hon Edward Vernon-Harcourt, sometime archbishop of York and yr bro of 3 Baron Vernon) by his 1 w, Perilla (da of Sir Richard Southwell and who m subsequently, as his 2 w, Baron Roberthall); 2 s (Charles, Alexander David b 6 Feb 1982); *Heir* s, Charles Alastair Stephen Young b 21 July 1979; *Career* advocate; Sheriff of: Glasgow and Strathkelvin March-June 1984, North Strathclyde at Greenock 1984-; *Style*— Sir Stephen Young, Bt; Glen Rowan, Shore Rd, Cove, Dunbartonshire G84 0NU

YOUNG, Hon (William Aldus) Thoby; s and h of 2 Baron Kennet; *b* 24 May 1957; *Educ* Marlborough, Dartington Hall Sch, Sussex Univ; *m* 25 April 1987, Hon Josephine Mary Keyes, 2 da of 2 Baron Keyes; 1 da (Maud Elizabeth b 8 March 1989); *Recreations* playing the trumpet, writing; *Style*— The Hon Thoby Young

YOUNG, Hon Toby Daniel Moorsom; s of Baron Young of Dartington by his 2 w Sasha; *b* 1963; *Educ* Brasenose Coll Oxford, Harvard; *Career* writer; *Recreations* swimming, windsurfing; *Clubs* Groucho; *Style*— The Hon Toby Young; 67 Gibson Sq, London N1

YOUNG, William Chalmers (Bill); s of William Henry Young (d 1967), of Reigate, Surrey, and Joan Margaret, *née* McGlashan (d 1978); *b* 8 Oct 1919; *Educ* King's Sch Canterbury, Clare Coll Cambridge (MA); *m* 12 April 1944, Elizabeth Irene, da of Maj Alfred Russel Marshall, DSO, MC; 1 s (Martin), 3 da (Jane, Francesca, Rosemary); *Career* WWII cmmnd RA 1939, Lt 1 Kent Yeo 143 Field Regt, Capt HQ RA 49 Div, Capt OC 60 Field Security Section Intelligence Corps; jt md Smith & Young Ltd (family business) 1947-80 (chm 1980-); chm: Nat Assoc Engravers and Diestampers 1957-58, Envelope Makers and Manufacturing Stationers Assoc 1963-66; pres: SE Dist London Masterprinters Assoc 1960-61, London Printing Industs Assoc 1973-74; Inst of Printing 1976-78 (cncl memb 1969-81); memb Surrey CC educn ctee 1970-74, govr (later vice chm and chm) Camberwell Sch of Arts and Crafts, hon sec (later dir) Surrey Co Playing Fields Assoc 1958-85 (Nat Playing Field Assoc Duke of Edinburgh Award), chm Surrey Play Cncl 1976-79; chm Marshall Tst (C of E charity) 1982-87, pres Old Boys Assoc Kings Sch Canterbury 1970-73, general cmmr of income tax 1973-; Worshipful Co of Stationers and Newspaper Makers: Liveryman 1952, Renter Warden, chm Livery Ctee 1969-71, Ct Asst 1982-; FIOP; memb Royal Cwlth Soc, Royal Inst of Int Affrs; *Recreations* hunting beagling, tennis, squash, jogging, music (opera, ballet); *Style*— Bill Young, Esq; Rushpond Cottage, School Lane, Winfrith Newburgh, Dorset DT2 8JX (☎ 0305 852 951); 66a Penton Place, London SE17 (☎ 01 708 5858); Smith and Young Ltd, 40 Crimscott St, London SE1 5TP (☎ 01 231 1261, fax 01 262 1512, telex 22403 SAY G)

YOUNG, Sir William Neil; 10 Bt (GB 1769), of North Dean, Buckinghamshire; s of Capt William Elliot Young (ka 1942), and gs of Sir Charles Young, 9 Bt, KCMG, MVO (d 1944); Sir Charles's w was Clara, da of Sir Francis Elliot, GCMG, GCVO (gs of 2 Earl of Minto, also Envoy Extraordinary & Min Plenipotentiary to the King of the Hellenes 1903-17); *b* 22 Jan 1941; *Educ* Wellington, RMA Sandhurst; *m* 1965, Christine Veronica, da of R B Morley, of Buenos Aires; 1 s, 1 da; *Heir* s, William Lawrence Elliot Young, b 26 May 1970; *Career* formerly Capt 16/5 Queen's Royal Lancers; stockbroker with Phillips & Drew; *Style*— Sir William Young, Bt; 41 Blenheim Gdns, Kingston upon Thames, Surrey; 20 Briantspuddle, Dorchester, Dorset

YOUNG, Hon (Alice Matelda) Zoe; da of 2 Baron Kennet; *b* 24 Jan 1969; *Style*— The Hon Zoe Young

YOUNG OF DARTINGTON, Baron (Life Peer UK 1978); Michael Young; s of Gibson Young (musician); *b* 9 August 1915; *Educ* Dartington Hall, London Univ; *m* 1, 1945, Joan Lawson; 2 s, 1 da; m 2, 1960, Sasha, da of Raisley Moorsom; 1 s, 1 da; *Career* sits as SDP peer in House of Lords; barr Gray's Inn 1939; sec Res Dept Lab Pty 1945-51, dir Inst Community Studies 1953-, fell Churchill Coll Cambridge 1961-66, fndr and chm Social Sci Res Cncl 1965-68, memb NEDC 1975-78 pres: Consumers' Assoc 1965-, Nat Extension Coll 1971-, Advsy Centre for Educn 1976-; chm: Mutual Aid Centre 1977-, Tawney Soc (SDP's Think Tank) 1982-; dep chm Dartington Hall 1980- (trustee 1942-); hon fellow LSE 1978; *Books Incl:* Family and Kinship in East London (with Peter Willmott, 1957), The Rise of the Meritocracy (1958), Learning Begins at Home (with Patrick McGeeney, 1968), The Symmetrical Family (with Peter Willmott, 1974), The Elmhirsts of Dartington - the creation of an Utopian Community (1982); *Style*— The Rt Hon the Lord Young of Dartington; 18 Victoria Pk Square, London E2 (☎ 01 980 6263)

YOUNG OF GRAFFHAM, Baron (Life Peer UK 1984); David Ivor Young; PC (1984); s of late Joseph Young and his w, Rebecca; *b* 27 Feb 1932; *Educ* Christ's Coll Finchley, Univ Coll London (LLB); *m* 1956, Lita Marianne, da of Jonas Shaw; 2 da; *Career* slr 1956; chm Eldonwall Ltd 1961-75, dir Town & City Properties 1972-75, chm: Manufacturers Hanover Property Servs 1974-84, Br Orgn for Rehabilitation by Training (ORT) 1975-80, Admin Ctee World ORT Union 1980-84, Int Cncl of Jewish Social and Welfare Servs 1981-; dir Centre for Policy Studies 1979-82 (memb mgmnt bd 1977-82), industl advsr 1979-80 and special advsr Dept of Indust 1980-81; memb: Eng Industl Estates Corpn 1980-82, Nat Econ Devpt Cncl 1982-; chm Manpower Servs Cmmn 1982-84; min without portfolio 1984-85; sec of state: for Employment 1985-87, for Trade and Indust 1987-; Hon FRPS 1981; *Clubs* Savile; *Style*— The Rt Hon Lord Young of Graffham; 88 Brook St, London W1

YOUNG-HERRIES; see Herries

YOUNGER, Hon Alexander James; 2 s of 3 Viscount Younger of Leckie, OBE, TD; *b* 5 May 1933; *Educ* Winchester, Worcester Coll Oxford; *m* 1959, Annabelle Christine, da of late Gerald Furnivall, of Bishop's Waltham, Hants; 2 s, 2 da; *Career* late Capt Argyll & Sutherland Highlanders (serv Korea 1952); dir Sir J Causton & Sons 1963-68, md Robert Maclehose & Co 1968-77, dir: Simpson Label Co Ltd (Dalkeith), Stationers Co of Glasgow 1972-77; chm sch cncl Balfron 1975-78; Dist Comm Strathblane and Dist Pony Club 1974-78; memb BHS Scottish Ctee 1974-78; Stationers Co of Glasgow 1972-77; chm School Cncl, Balfron 1975-78; Dist Comm, Strathblane and Dist Pony Club 1974-78; memb BHS Scottish Ctee 1974-78; *Recreations* golf, music, shooting; *Clubs* Highland Bde; *Style*— The Hon Alexander Younger; Wester Leckie, Kippen, Stirlingshire FK8 3JL

YOUNGER, Gp Capt Anne Rosaleen; da of Lt-Col John Logan, TD, DL (d 1987), Wester, Craigend, Stirling and Rosaleen Muriel, *née* O'Hara (d 1967); *b* 2 Jan 1939; *Educ* West Heath Sch Sevenoaks, Kent, Edinburgh Sch of Mothercraft; *m* 1 Dec 1962, (John) David Binghay, s of Maj O B Younger, MC, of The Old Rectory Etal, Cornhill-On-Tweed, Northumberland; 1 s (Mark Robert b 20 May 1972), 2 da (Sarah Juliet b 29 March 1964, Camilla Jane b 12 Dec 1966); *Career* dir Broughton Brewery Ltd 1979; JP Tweeddale Dist; memb Upper Tweed Community Cncl 1976-86; ARSH 1959; *Recreations* music, country pursuits, family; *Style*— Mrs Anne Younger, JP; Kilbucho Old Schoolhouse, Broughton, Peeblesshire ML12 6JG (☎ 0899 20276); Broughton Brewery Ltd, Broughton, Peeblesshire ML12 6HQ (☎ 08994 345)

YOUNGER, Charles Frank Johnston; DSO (1944), TD (1952); s of late Maj Charles Arthur Johnston Younger; *b* 11 Dec 1908; *Educ* RNC Dartmouth; *m* 1935, Joanna, da of late Rev John Kyrle Chatfield; 1 da; *Career* serv RN 1926-37 (resigned cmmn to enter William Younger Brewers 1937), serv WWII (despatches), RA (FD) 15 Scottish Div 1939-41, 17 Indian Light Div Burma 1942-45, cmd 129 Lowland FD Regt RA 1942-45 and 278 Lowland FD Regt RA (TA) 1946-52, Lt-Col; dir: William Younger & Co 1945-73, Scottish & Newcastle Breweries Ltd 1946-73; chm Scottish Union & Nat Insur Co 1954-57 and 1966-68 (dep chm 1968-79), dir: Bank of Scotland 1960-79, Norwich Union and Assoc Co's 1966-79 (vice-chm 1976-79); chm Socttish advsy bd Norwich Union 1976-80: vice-pres Brewers Soc 1965-73 (chm 1962-64); Freeman City of London, Liveryman Worshipful Co of Brewers; memb Royal Co of Archers (Queen's Body Gd for Scotland); *Recreations* country pursuits; *Clubs* Boodle's, Pratt's, Castaways; *Style*— Charles Younger, Esq, DSO, TD; Painsthorpe Hall, Kirby Underdale, York (☎ 075 96 342)

YOUNGER, Capt (John) David Bingham; s of Maj Oswald Bingham Younger, MC, of the Old Rectory, Etal, Cornhill-On-Tweed, Northumberland, and Dorothea Elizabeth, *née* Hobbs; *b* 20 May 1939; *Educ* Eton, RMA Sandhurst; *m* 1 Dec 1962, Anne Rosaleen, da of Lt-Col John Logan, TD, DL (d 1987), of Wester Craigend, Stirlingshire; 1 s (Mark Robert b 1972), 2 da (Sarah Juliet b 1964, Camilla Jane b 1966); *Career* Argyll and Sutherland Highlanders cmmnd 1959, Adj 1 Bn Borneo and Singapore 1965-67 (GSM Clasps Borneo and Malaysia); GSO 3 Directorate of Mil ops MOD 1967-69, ret 1969; Capt RARO (class 1) 1969-, memb Queen's Bodyguard for Scotland Royal Co of Archers 1969- Scottish & Newcastle Breweries Ltd 1969-79: sr exec London 1971-73, sr exec Glasgow 1973-76, sr exec Edinburgh (incl 8 months secondment to GEC Marconi Space and Def Systems) 1976-79; co-fndr and md Broughton Brewery Ltd 1979-; DL Borders Regn dist of Tweeddale, memb Argyll and Sutherland Highlanders Regtl Tst and Ctee; chm Tweeddale Dist Tourist Ctee, vice-chm Scottish Borders Tourist Bd, memb Tweeddale Crime Prevention Panel, chm govrs Belhaven Hill Sch Dunbar; MInst D 1984; *Recreations* country pursuits; *Clubs* MCC; *Style*— Capt David Younger; Kilbucho Old School House, Broughton, Peeblesshire ML12 6JG (☎ 0899 20276); Broughton Brewery Ltd, Broughton, Peeblesshire ML12 6HQ (☎ 08994 345)

YOUNGER, Hon Lady (Elizabeth Kirsteen); da of William Duncan Stewart, JP, of Achara, Duror, Argyll; *m* 1934, Rt Hon Sir Kenneth Younger, KBE, PC, (d 1976, sometime MP (Lab) Grimsby 1945-59 and min state For Affrs 1950-51), 2 s of 2 Viscount Younger of Leckie, DSO, TD, JP, DL; 1 s, 2 da; *Style*— The Hon Lady Younger; Dicker's Farm, Sandy Lane, E Ashling, W Sussex

YOUNGER, Rt Hon George Kenneth Hotson; TD (1964), PC (1979), DL (Stirlingshire 1968), MP (C) Ayr 1964-; s and h of 3 Viscount Younger of Leckie, OBE, TD; *b* 22 Sept 1931; *Educ* Winchester, New Coll Oxford; *m* 7 Aug 1954, Diana Rhona, er da of Capt Gerald Seymour Tuck, DSO, RN (d 1984), of Chichester; 3 s (James b 11 Nov 1955, Charles b 4 Oct 1959, Andrew b 19 Nov 1962), 1 da (Joanna b 16 Jan 1958); *Career* 2 Lt Argyll and Sutherland Highlanders 1950, with 1 Bn BAOR and Korea 1951, 7 Bn (TA) 1952-65; Hon Col 154 (Lowland) Tport Regt RCT TA & VR 1977-85; contested (C) N Lanarks 1959 and stood down from Kinross and W Perths 1963 in favour of Sir Alec Douglas-Home; govr Royal Scottish Acad of Music 1960-70, Scottish Cons whip 1965-67, dir Charrington Vintners Ltd 1966-68, dep chm Cons Pty in Scotland 1967-70 and chm 1974-75, parly under-sec state for Devpt Scottish Off 1970-74, min state Def Jan-March 1974, dir Tennant Caledonian Breweries 1977-79; sec state: Scotland May 1979- Jan 1986, Def Jan 1986-; dilivered Sir Andrew Humphrey Meml lectr on 'The Future of Air Power' 1988; pres Nat Union of Cons Assocs 1987-88; Brig Queen's Body Gd for Scotland (Royal Co of Archers); *Recreations* tennis, sailing; *Clubs* Caledonian (London), Highland Brigade; *Style*— The Rt Hon George Younger, TD, PC, DL; Easter Leckie, Gargunnock, Stirlingshire (☎ 078 686 274)

YOUNGER, Julian William Richard; s and h of Maj-Gen Sir John Younger, 3 Bt, CBE, *qv*; *b* 10 Feb 1950; *Educ* Eton, Grinnell Univ USA; *m* 3 Oct 1981, Deborah Ann Wood; 1 s (Andrew William); *Career* Govt Service; *Books* Who's Who of British Business Travel (annually since 1986, ed); *Style*— Julian Younger, Esq

YOUNGER, Maj Oswald Bingham; MC; s of Lt-Col John Henderson Younger, OBE (d 1944), of Hassendean Burn, Hawick, Roxburghshire, and Marion Frances Bingham, *née* Smith-Bingham (d 1953); *b* 20 April 1907; *Educ* Eton, RMC Sandhurst; *m* 10 June 1937, (Dorothea) Elizabeth, da of Lt-Col Charles James Willoughby Hobbs, DSO (ka Battle of the Somme 1917); 1 s ((John) David Bingham b 20 May 1939), 1 da (Susan Dorothea (Mrs Gourlay) b 16 May 1945); *Career* cmmnd Argyll and Sutherland Highlanders 1927, 2 Bn (93) IOW, Jamaica 1927-29, N China and Hong Kong 1929-31, Adj Regt Depot Stirling Castle 1932-35, Adj 7 Bn 1939, France 1940 (wounded and POW 1940); cmd Royal Guard at Balmoral Aug to Oct 1945, ret; memb Royal Co of Archers (The Queen's Body Guard for Scotland) 1959; chm Berwick-upon-Tweed Conservative Assoc 1971-73; *Recreations* cricket, fishing; *Clubs* New (Edinburgh); *Style*— Maj Oswald Younger, MC; The Old Rectory, Etal, Cornhill-on-Tweed, Northumberland TD12 4TN (☎ 089 082 223)

YOUNGER, Hon Robert Edward Gilmour; 3 s of 3 Viscount Younger of Leckie, OBE, TD, DL; bro of Rt Hon George Younger, TD, DL, MP, sec state Defence; *b* 25 Sept 1940; *Educ* Winchester, New Coll Oxford, Edinburgh Univ, Glasgow Univ; *m* 1972, Helen, da of Eric Hayes (d 1958), and Margaret, sis of Sir John Muir, 3 Bt, TD; 1 s, 2 da ; *Career* advocate 1968; Sheriff: Glasgow and Strathkelvin at Glasgow 1979-82, Tayside Central and Fife at Stirling and Falkirk 1982-87, Stirling and Alloa 1987-; *Style*— The Hon Robert Younger; Old Leckie, Gargunnock, Stirling (☎ 078 686 213)

YOUNGER, Sir William McEwan; 1 Bt (UK 1964), of Fountainbridge, Co and City of Edinburgh, DSO (1942), DL (Midlothian 1956); s of late William Younger (yr bro of 1 Viscount Younger, and er bro of 1 and last Baron Blanesburgh, GBE, PC), of Ravenswood, Melrose; *b* 6 Sept 1905; *Educ* Winchester, Balliol Coll Oxford; *m* 1, 1936 (m dis 1967), Nora Elizabeth, da of Brig Edward Balfour, CVO, DSO, OBE, MC (d 1955) and Lady Ruth Balfour (eldest da of 2 Earl of Balfour (s of Cons PM 1902-05) by his w Lady Elizabeth Lytton, da of 1 Earl of Lytton), of Balbirnie, Markinch, Fife; 1 da; m 2, 1983, June Peck; *Heir* none; *Career* serv WWII RA, Western Desert and Italy (despatches), Lt Col 1944; dir: Br Linen Bank 1955-71, Scottish Television 1964-71; chm: Scottish & Newcastle Breweries 1960-69 (md 1960-67), Second Scottish Investmt Tst Co Ltd 1965-75, Highland Tourist (Cairngorm Dvpt) Ltd 1966-78, Cons Pty in Scotland 1971-74 memb Queen's Bodyguard for Scotland (Royal Co of Archers) 1955-; *Recreations* mountaineering, fishery; *Clubs* Carlton, Caledonian, New (Edinburgh), Alpine; *Style*— Sir William Younger, Bt, DSO, DL; 27 Moray Place, Edinburgh, Scotland (☎ 031 225 8173)

YOUNGER OF LECKIE, 3 Viscount (UK 1923); Sir Edward George Younger; 3 Bt (UK 1911), OBE (1940), TD, DL; s of 2 Viscount Younger of Leckie, DSO, TD, JP, DL (d 1946), and Maud (d 1957), er da of Sir John Gilmour, 1 Bt; *b* 21 Nov 1906; *Educ* Winchester, New Coll Oxford (BA); *m* 7 June 1930, Evelyn Margaret, MBE (d 1983), da of late Alexander Logan McClure, KC, sometime Sheriff of Aberdeen, Kincardine and Banff; 3 s, 1 da; *Heir* s, Rt Hon George Younger, TD, DL, MP, *qv*; *Career* Capt A Staff, France 1940, Col Gen Staff, France 1939-40, UK 1940-45, Col Argyll and Sutherland Highlanders (TA); Ld-Lt Stirling and Falkirk 1964-79; *Clubs* New (Edinburgh); *Style*— The Rt Hon the Viscount Younger of Leckie, OBE, TD, DL; Leckie, Gargunnock, Stirling (☎ 078 686 281)

YOUNGMAN, Dr Richard; s of Arthur Henry Youngman (d 1941), of Hillside, Northam, N Devon, and Edith Mary, *née* Taylor (d 1962); *b* 15 Sept 1921; *Educ* Mill Hill, St Bart's Hosp London Univ (MB BS, MRCS, LRCP); *m* 1 Oct 1947 (seperated), Nancye Clifford, da of Dudley Clifford Christopherson (d 1962), of Lochinvar, Reigate; 1 s (Paul Dudley b 1952), 1 da (Verna (Mrs Lipinski) b 1949); *Career* RAF Med Branch: Fly offr 1946, Flt Lt 1947; orthopaedic house surgn St Barts 1945-46, sr house offr Kent & Sussex Hosp 1946, casualty surgn W Middx 1950-52, surgical registrar St Barts Hosp 1952-53, GP 1953-85; chm med ctee Iver Cottage Hosp; memb: local med ctee Bucks, Area Health Authy Bucks, Windsor Med Soc 1953 (cncl memb 1979-83); *Clubs* Old Millhillians; *Style*— Dr Richard Youngman; 64 Bicester Rd, Long Crendon, Bucks (☎ 0844 208 450)

YOUNGREN, Hon Mrs (Catherine Elizabeth); el da of 2 Baron Greenhill; *b* 1948; *Educ* (BA); *m* 1978, Kenneth Youngren, of North Vancouver; *Career* interior designer and store planner; memb: Interior Designers Inst of British Columbia, Inst of Store Planners (Seattle Washington), Interior Designers of Canada.; *Style*— The Hon Mrs Youngren; 4118 Russell Court, North Vancouver, British Columbia

YOUNGSON, Prof Alexander John; CBE (1987); s of Dr Alexander Brown (d 1954), and Helen Youngson (d 1945); *b* 28 Sept 1918; *Educ* Aberdeen GS; Aberdeen Univ (MA, DLitt), Univ of California; *m* 14 Sept 1948, Elizabeth Gisborne, da of Leonard Brown Naylor, CBE (d 1957); 1 s (Graeme b 1952), 1 da (Sheila b 1954); *Career* Lt RNVR serv 5th Atlantic, Europe 1939-45; lectr Cambridge Univ 1950-58, prof Edinburgh Univ 1958-74; dir RSSS Aust Nat Univ 1974-80; chm Royal Fine Art Cmmn for Scot 1983-; *Books* Possibilities of Economic Progress (1959), The Making of Classical Edinburgh (1966), After the '45 (1973), The Prince and the Pretender (1985); *Recreations* gardening; *Style*— Prof Alexander Youngson, CBE; Hilltop, Station Rd, Scawby, Brigg, S Humberside DN20 9DW (☎ 0652 55566); RFAC, 9 Atholl Crescent, Edinburgh EH3 8HA (☎ 031 229 1109)

YOUNIE, Edward Milne; OBE (1978); s of Rev John Milne Younie (d 1971), of The Manse, Kippen, Stirling, and Mary, *née* Dickie (d 1974); *b* 9 Feb 1926; *Educ* Fettes, Gonville and Caius Coll Cambridge (BA); *m* 1, 26 May 1952, Mary Elizabeth (d 1976), da of Alfred Groves, of Georgetown, Guyana; 2 s (Philip b 1955, Peter b 1957); m 2, 19 June 1979, Mimi Barkeley, da of Col Paul Morris, of Washington DC, USA; *Career* Colonial Serv Tanganyika 1950-61; FCO 1963-: SA 1964-66, Malawi 1966-69, Nigeria 1972-76, Kenya 1977-78, Zimbabwe 1979-81; conslt Trefoil Ptnrship 1981, chm Kippen Conrs Assoc, session clerk; Zimbabwe Medal; *Recreations* golf, shooting, music; *Clubs* Brooks; *Style*— Edward Younie, Esq, OBE; Glebe House, Kippen, Stirling (☎ 078 687 252); Trefoil Parnership Ltd, 50 Pall Mall, London SW1 (☎ 01 839 1030, fax 01 930 1816, telex 918934 DISCOSE G)

YOUNSON, Maj-Gen Eric John; OBE (1952); s of Ernest Matthew Magnus Younson (d 1974), of Jarrow, Co Durham, and Mary Edith, *née* Baker (d 1948); *b* 1 Mar 1919; *Educ* Jarrow GS, Durham Univ (BSc), RMC of Sci, Admin Staff Coll Henley; *m* 21 Dec 1946, Jean Beaumont Muriel, da of William Henry Carter (d 1968), of Broadstairs, Kent; 3 da (Hilary (Mrs Barry) b 1950, Frances b 1952, Alexandra (Mrs Heaton) b 1957); *Career* cmmnd RA 2 Lt 1940, serv WWII NW Europe (despatches), dir Staff RMCS 1952-54, Atomic Weapons Res Estab 1957-58, attaché Embassy Washington 1958-61, head Defence Science 3 MOD 1961-63, Lt-Col 1962, dep dir Artillery MOD 1964-66, Brig 1967, dir Guided Weapons Acceptance Trials and Range Facilities Miny of Technol 1967-69, Maj-Gen 1969; vice-pres Ordnance Board 1970-72, pres 1972-73, ret; sr asst dir Central Bureau for Educnl Visits 1973-74, dep dir SIMA 1974-78; clerk Worshipful Co of Scientific Instrument Makers 1976-87 (Hon Liveryman and Clerk-Emeritus 1987), Freeman City of London 1981; CEng 1969, FRAeS 1969, FBIM 1971, FIIM 1980, FRSA 1944; *Books* The Worshipful Company of Scientific Instrument Makers: A History (1989); *Recreations* photography, electronics; *Style*— Maj-Gen Eric Younson, OBE; 7 Pondwick Rd, Harpenden, Herts AL5 2HG (☎ 05827 5892)

YOXALL, George Thomas; s of George Thomas Yoxall (d 1983), of Sandbach, Cheshire, and Mary, *née* Bunn; *b* 22 Feb 1949; *Educ* Crewe Co GS, Hertford Coll Univ of Oxford (MA); *m* 10 April 1976, Barbara Elizabeth, da of Thomas Donald Gorrie, of Liverpool; 2 s (Matthew b 1980, Richard b 1982); *Career* admin sci offr Sci Res Cncl 1970-72, actuarial student Duncan C Fraser & Ptnrs 1972-73, asst to investmt mangr Nat Farmers Union Mutual Insur Soc 1973-76, UK equity mangr Airways Pension Scheme 1976-82, asst investmt mangr Central Fin Bd Methodist Church 1982-84, sr portfolio mangr Abbey Life N America 1984-86, dir investmts Abbey Life Assur Co 1989-, md Abbey Life Investmts Servs 1989-(dir N America 1986-88); hon sec Poole Hockey Club; AIA 1978; *Recreations* hockey, sailing, railways, civil aviation; *Style*— George Yoxall, Esq; Abbey Life Assur Co, 80 Holdenhurst Rd, Bournemouth BH8 8AL (☎ 0202 292 373, fax 0202 296 816, telex 41310)

YUDKIN, Prof John; s of Louis (d 1917), of London and Sarah (d 1951); *b* 8 August 1910; *Educ* Hackney Downs Sch, London Univ, Cambridge Univ (BSc, MA, PhD, MD); *m* 1933, Emily Himmelweit; 3 s (Michael, Jonathan, Jeremy); *Career* prof London Univ 1945-71, dir of med studies Christs Coll Cambridge 1935-43; *Books* author of many professional res pubns in med and nutrition, and several lay books on nutrition; *Recreations* listening to music, writing, book-collecting; *Style*— Professor John Yudkin; 20 Wellington Ct, Wellington Rd, London NW8 9TA

YUGOSLAVIA, HRH Prince Tomislav (Karadjordjević) of; 2 s of King Alexander I of Yugoslavia (reigned from 1921 to 1934, when assassinated at Marseilles) and yr bro of King Peter II; gt-gt-gs of Queen Victoria through his mother, *née* Princess Marie of Roumania; *b* 19 Jan 1928,Belgrade,; *Educ* Oundle, Clare Coll Cambridge (BA); *m* m 1, 6 June 1957 (m dis 1982), Her Grand Ducal Highness Margarita Alice Thyra Viktoria Marie Louise Scholastica, only da of HRH The Margrave (Berthold Friedrich Wilhelm Ernst August Heinrich Karl) of Baden (d 1963), and Theodora, 2 da of HRH Prince Andrew of Greece and Denmark and sis of Prince Philip, Duke of Edinburgh; 1 s (HRH Prince Nikola b 15 March 1958, is a lorry driver), 1 da (HRH Princess Katarina b 28 Nov 1959, m 5 Dec 1987, Desmond de Silva, QC, *qv*); m 2, 17 Oct 1982, Linda, da of Holbrook Van Dyke Bonney (d 1988); 2 s (HRH Prince George b 25 May 1984, HRH Prince Michael b 15 Dec 1985); *Career* ptnr in garden centre business; *Style*— HRH Prince Tomislav of Yugoslavia; Orchard Cottage, Redlands Farm, Kirdford, nr Billingshurst, W Sussex (☎ 040 388 263)

YUILL, Peter Mortley; s of Cecil Mortley Yuill, and Hilda May, *née* Fothergill; *b* 16 May 1949; *Educ* Oundle, Univ of Birmingham (BSc), Univ of Durham (MSc); *m* 12 April 1980, Margaret Helen, da of James Robinson Booth, of Hartlepool, Cleveland; 1 s (David b 9 April 1981), 2 da (Joanna b 27 Sept 1982, Alexandra b 27 Sept 1984); *Career* civil engr Laings; chm and vice-chm C M Yuill Ltd; dir: C M Yuill Ltd, C M Yuill Investmts, Eaglescliffe Prop Ltd, Mowden Park Estate Co Ltd, Owten Fens Props Ltd, Orchard Estate Ltd, Chartstrand Ltd, Yuill Devpts Ltd, Westfield Estates Ltd, C M Yuill Construction Ltd, C M Yuill Hldgs Ltd, Yuill Heritage Homes Ltd, Elco (Stockton) Ltd, Melfort Farms Ltd, Ardenstuir Ltd, J W Hobbs Ltd, Billerford Ltd, Yutec Ltd, Peaklene Ltd, Kingston Wharf Mgmnt Co Ltd, Hollin House Maintainance Co Ltd, George Howe Ltd, Blue Anchor Residents Assoc Ltd; pres Bldg Employers Confedn Northern Co's Region 1988-89; Magistrate, Sch Govr; MICE 1976; *Recreations* squash, golf, snooker, bridge; *Clubs* West Hartlepool Gentlemens, West Hartlepool RFC; *Style—* Peter Yuill, Esq; Magnolias, 8 Pk Ave, Hartlepool, Cleveland TS26 ODZ (☎ 0429 273274); Cecil M Yuill Ltd, Cecil House, Loyalty Rd, Hartlepool, Cleveland TS25 5BD (☎ 0429 266620, fax 0429231359, car 0836 239720)

Z

ZACCOUR, Makram Michel; s of Michel Zaccour (d 1937), former MP and For & Interior Min of Lebanon, and Rose, *née* Gorayeb; *b* 19 August 1935; *Educ* Berkeley Coll California Univ (BSc, Phi, BETA, KAPPA); *Career* gen mangr Industrias Textiles Ultratex (Colombia) 1964-66 (sales 1957-64), Merrill Lynch: fin cnslt ME 1967-73, mangr Beirut off 1973 Beirut and Paris 1976, London 1977-83; regnl dir Merrill Lynch Pierce Fenner & Smith Ltd 1983-; Arab Banker Assoc; Phi, BETA, KAPPA Edinburgh Univ; *Clubs* Annabel's Harry's Bar, Mark's, Les Ambassadeurs; *Style*— Makram M Zaccour, Esq; Merrill Lynch, Pierce, Fenner & Smith Ltd, Time Life Building, 153 New Bond Str, London, W1Y 0RS (☎ 01 493 7242, fax 01 629 0622, car tel 0836 280 487, telex 21262 A B MERLEAP London W1)

ZAMBONI, Richard Frederick Charles; s of Alfred Charles Zamboni (d 1957), and Frances, *née* Hosler (d 1983); descendent of a Swiss (Engiadina) family with lineage from 1465; *b* 28 July 1930; *Educ* Monkton House Sch Cardiff; *m* 2 Jan 1960, Pamela Joan, da of Laurence Brown Marshall, of Hanger Hill Weybridge, Surrey; 2 s (Edward, b 1962, Rupert b 1967), 1 da (Charlotte b 1964); *Career* CA; Br Egg Mktg Bd 1959-70, vice-chm Sun Life Assur Soc plc 1986- (md 1979-86), chm: Sun Life Investmt Mgmnt Servs Ltd 1985-, Sun Life Tst Mgmnt Ltd 1985-; *Recreations* ornithology, gardening, tennis; *Style*— Richard Zamboni, Esq ; Long Meadow, Beech Avenue, Effingham, Surrey KT24 5PH (☎ (0372) 58211); Sun Life Assurance Soc plc, 107 Cheapside, London EC2V 6DU (☎ 01 606 7788, telex 8811871 SLCOL/G, fax 01 606 7788 ext 1126)

ZAMOYSKA, Countess Betka Marya; da of Count Andrzej Zamoyski (yr bro of Count Stefan, whose children are Counts Zdzisz, *chef de famille* in UK, and Adam and Countess Marilena, *qqv*) by Priscilla, 2 da of Sir Hugh Stucley, 4 Bt, JP, DL; *b* 12 Mar 1948; *Educ* Cranborne Chase, Lady Margaret Hall Oxford; *Career* freelance journalist; *Recreations* reading, theatre, films; *Style*— Countess Betke Zamoyska; 136 Hurlingham Rd, London SW6

ZAMOYSKI, Count Adam Stefan; s of Lt-Col Count Stefan Zamoyski, OBE, VM, LLD, Order of Polonia Restituta (d 1976, fifth in descent from Andreas Zamoyski, cr Count 1778 (confirmed 1780) by Empress Maria Teresa of Austria at the time of the Partitions of Poland) by his w Princess Elizabeth Czartoryska; the Princess's gf was Prince Wladyslaw Czartoryski (s of Tsar Alexander I's Foreign Minister Prince Adam, who was also briefly head of Independent Poland 1830), while her grand mother (Wladyslaw's w) was HRH Princess Marguerite d'Orléans (da of HRH The Duc de Nemours, 2 s of Louis Philippe, King of the French); *b* 11 Jan 1949, in New York; *Educ* Downside, Queen's Coll Oxford; *Career* author, books include a biography of Chopin and a History of Poland; Knight of Honour & Devotion Sov Mil Order of Malta 1977, Kt of Justice Constantinian Order of St George (House of Bourbon Sicily) 1978, Order of Polonia Restituta 1982; *Clubs* Pratt's, Polish Hearth; *Style*— Count Adam Zamoyski; 33 Ennismore Gdns, London SW7 (☎ 01 584 9053)

ZAMOYSKI, Tomasz Józef Tadeusz Różyc; s of Tadeusz Kazimierz Juljan Różyc Zamoyski, Kt Cdr Order of Polonia Restituta, Chevalier de la Légion d'Honneur, Cdr de l'Ordre Nat du Mérite (d 1980, of the Poraj clan, the Counts Zamoyski (*qqv*) being of the Jelita clan; Tadeusz's ancestors were involved in defence of Częstochowa during the Swedish invasion of Poland 1655-56), author of Kodeks Honorowy (Code of Honour), published in Warsaw in 1924, and universally acknowledged as the authoritative handbook governing the correct procedure relating to duels in pre-war Poland; *b* 22 May 1935,Warsaw,; *Educ* Malvern, Sidney Sussex Coll Cambridge, Johann Wolfgang Goethe Univ Frankfurt, Florence Univ; *m* 1959, Nicole, da of Marcel Tranier (d 1983), of Paris; 1 s (Matthew Tomasz Tadeusz Różyc b 1972), 1 da (Arabella Halina Suzanne Różyc Zamoyska b 1974); *Career* Nat Serv 2 Lt 5 RTR; dir HZI Int Ltd; *Recreations* hunting; *Clubs* Boodle's, Lansdowne; *Style*— Tomasz Zamoyski, Esq; 132 Kensington Park Rd, London W11 (☎ 01 229 8040, office 01 242 6346)

ZAMOYSKI, Count Wojciech Michal; eld s of Count Michal Zamoyski (2 s of Count Adam Zamoyski, sometime ADC to Tsar Nicholas II, by his marriage with Countess Maria Potocka; Adam the ADC was youngest bro of Count Stefan, who was the ggf of Count Adam Stefan Zamoyski, *qv*); *b* 12 Sept 1927,Kozlowka Palace; *Educ* Poland, Angola, S Africa; *m* 1955, Isobel Zamoyska, MA, er da of William Forbes-Robertson Mutch; 2 s (Count Paul b 1957, Count Alexander b 1962), 1 da (Countess Anna Isabella Zamoyska b 1960); *Career* formerly official at Rhodesian High Cmmn and Overseas Dvpt Admin; *Recreations* Poland, the Third World, travel; *Style*— Count Wojciech Zamoyski; (☎ 01 581 0998)

ZAMOYSKI, Count Zdzisz; s of late Count (Stefan) Zamoyski, *chef de famille* in UK; er bro of Count Adam Zamoyski, *qv*; *Style*— Count Zdzisz Zamoyski; Ashfield House, The Horns, Hawkhurst, Kent

ZAMOYSKI, Count Zygmunty Ignacy Stukely; s of Count Andrzej Zamoyski (s of Count Wladislaw Zamoyski and yr bro of late Count Stefan, f of Counts Zdzisz and Adam and Countess Marelina, *qv*) by Priscilla, 2 da of Sir Hugh Stukeley, 4 Bt, JP, DL; *b* 23 Nov 1937; *Educ* Stowe, Christ Church Oxford, Imede Geneva (MBA); *Style*— Count Zygmunt Zamoyski

ZAMYATIN, Leonid Mitrofanovich; s of Mitrofan Zamyatin; *b* 9 Mar 1922; *Educ* Moscow Aviation Inst and Higher Diplomatic Sch; *m* 1946, Olga Alexeevna; 1 da (Elena); *Career* Miny of Foreign Affairs USSR 1953-: cnsllr on political questions of USSR mission to UN, soviet dep rep on preparatory ctee (later on bd of govrs), Soviet rep on IAEA 1959-60, dep head of American countries dept 1960-62, head of press dept ;1962-70, memb Collegium Miny of Foreign Affrs 1962-70, dir gen TASS News Agency 1970-78, chief dept of Int Info of Centl Ctee 1978-86, ambass to UK 1986-; Lenin Prye 1978, orders and medals of the USSR including the Order of Lenin; *Style*— His Excellency Leonid Zamyatin; 13 Kensington Palace Gardens, London (☎ 01 229 3620)

ZANDER, Prof Michael; s of Dr Walter Zander, of Crohamleigh, S Croydon, and Margaret, *née* Magnus (d 1969); *b* 16 Nov 1932; *Educ* RGS High Wycombe, Jesus Coll Cambridge (BA, LLB), Harvard Law Sch (LLM); *m* 27 Aug 1965, Elizabeth Treegar (Betsy), da of Clarence R Treegef, of NYC; 1 s (Jonathan b 1970), 1 da (Nicola b 1969); *Career* 2 Lt RA; slr 1962, Sydney Morse & Co 1962-63; LSE: asst lectr 1963, lectr 1965, sr lectr 1970, reader 1970, prof 1977, convenor law dept 1984-88; frequent broadcasts on radio and TV, legal corr The Guardian 1963-87; *Books* Lawyers and the Public Interest (1968), Legal Services for the Community (1973), The Police and Criminal Evidence Act (1984), A Bill of Rights (third edn 1985), Cases and Materials on English Legal Systems (fifth edn 1988), A Matter of Justice: The Legal System in Ferment (1988); *Recreations* learning the cello; *Style*— Prof Michael Zander; 12 Woodside Ave, London N6 4SS (☎ 01 883 6257); LSE, Houghton St, London WC2 (☎ 01 405 7686, fax 01 242 0392)

ZANKEL, Hon Mrs (Alison Victoria); *née* Poole; da of 1 Baron Poole, CBE, TD, PC; *b* 1936; *m* 1961, Dr Fitz Zankel; 2 s; *Style*— The Hon Mrs Zankel; Staudgasse 75, Vienna

ZAPHIRIOU-ZARIFI, Ari Charles; s of Prof George Aristotle Zaphiriou, of Washington DC, and Frosso, *née* Zarifi; *b* 10 Mar 1946; *Educ* Stowe, LSE (BSc); *m* 27 Dec 1973, Yana, da of Ulysses Sistovaris (d 1985); 1 s (Stefan b 1975), 1 da (Viki b 1978); *Career* Peat Marwick Mitchell 1967-70, J Henry Schroder Wagg 1970-73, chm and chief exec The Heritable and Gen Investmt Bank Ltd 1988- (dir 1975, md 1979), md Heritable Group plc 1983-, chm Alpha Gamma Gp 1983-; chm cncl King Alfred Sch; FCA 1970; *Recreations* tennis, swimming, sailing, reading, gardening; *Clubs* The Traveller's; *Style*— Ari Zaphiriou-Zarifi, Esq; 19 Willoughby Rd, London NW3 1RT (☎ 01 435 9080); Spence House, Dock Lane, Beaulieu, Hants; 52 Berkeley Sq, London W1X 6EH (☎ 01 493 6621, fax 01 629 1958, telex 291184 HERIT G)

ZATZ, Paul Simon Jonah; s of Samuel Zatz (d 1981), and Stella Rachel Morgan, *née* Levy; *b* 21 April 1938; *Educ* King William's Coll, Sidnem Sussex Coll Cambridge (MA, LLM); *m* 5 Sept 1965, Patricia Ann, da of Sidney Landau (d 1971); 1 s (Joshua b 1969), 1 da (Rachel b 1967); *Career* slr 1964; ptnr Lawrance Messer & Co 1968-81; co sec Clyde Petroleum plc 1980 (legal and corporate dir 1983); hon sec Brindex (Assoc of Br Independent Exploration Cos); *Recreations* opera, walking; *Clubs* City Univ; *Style*— Paul Zatz, Esq; Coddington Court, Coddington, Ledbury, Herefordshire HR8 1JL (☎ 0531 86811, fax 0531 86579)

ZEFFERT, Clive Lewis; s of Henry Zeffertt (sic), of Portsmouth, and Ann, *née* Levison; *b* 11 August 1938; *Educ* Portsmouth GS, Portsmouth Sch of Architecture (Dip Arch); *m* 21 April 1966, Sherry Lynn, da of Charles Weinstein, (d 1966), of Portland, Oregon, USA; 1 s (Simeon b 1977), 1 da (Sara b 1973); *Career* architect; princ Clive Zeffert Assocs 1978; dir Thames Housing Ltd 1981; dir Easefern Ltd 1984; ARIBA; *Recreations* squash, sailing; *Style*— Clive Zeffert, Esq; 32 Crouch Hall Rd, London N8 8HJ (☎ 01 341 3375, (work) 01 340 3963)

ZEIDLER, Sir David Ronald; CBE (1971); s of Otto William Zeidler (d 1958), and late Hilda Maude Hunter; *b* 18 Mar 1918; *Educ* Scotch Coll Melbourne, Melbourne Univ (MSc); *m* 1943, June Susie, da of Robert Broadhurst (d 1953); 4 da; *Career* CSIRO 1941-51; chm and md ICI Australia Ltd 1973-80, chm Metal Mfrs 1980-; dir Amatil Ltd, Westpac Banking Corpn, Australian Fndn Investmt Co; chm: Cwlth Inquiry into Electricity Generation and the Sharing of Power Resources in SE Australia 1980-81, Vic Govt Inquiry into State Electricity Cmmn of Vic 1982; FTS, FAA, FRACI, FAIM; kt 1980; *see Debrett's Handbook of Australia and New Zealand for further details*; *Style*— Sir David Zeidler, CBE; 360 Collins St, Melbourne, Vic 3000, Australia

ZELLICK, Prof Graham John; s of Reginald Hyman Zellick, of Windsor, Berks, and Beana, *née* Levey; *b* 12 August 1948; *Educ* Christ's Coll Finchley, Gonville and Caius Coll Cambridge (MA, PhD), Stanford Univ Sch of Law California; *m* 18 Sept 1975, Prof Jennifer, da of Michael Temkin, of London; 1 s (Adam b 1977), 1 da (Lara b 1980); *Career* visiting prof of law Univ of Toronto 1975 and 1978-79; QMC: lect in laws 1971-78, 1982-88, prof of public law (reader 1978-82), dean faculty of laws 1984-88, head of dept of law 1984-, Drapers prof of law 1988-; Univ of London: dean faculty of laws 1986-88, senator 1985-, dep chm academic cncl 1987-; ed: Euro Human Rights Reports 1978-82, Public Law 1981-86; memb ed bds: Br Jl of Criminology 1980-, Public Law 1981-, Howard Jl of Criminal Justice 1984-87, Civil Law Library 1987-; chm: Tel Aviv Univ Tst Lawyer's Gp 1984-1989, chm Prisoners Advice and Law Serv 1984-, legal ctee All Party Parly War Crimes Gp 1988-, Ctee of Heads of Univ Law Schs 1988-; dep chm Justice Ctee on Prisoners' Rights 1981-83, cncl memb Howard League for Penal Reform 1973-82, memb Jellicoe Ctee on Bds of Visitors of Prisons 1973-75, memb Newham Dist Ethics Ctee 1985-86; govr: Central London Poly 1973-77, Pimlico Sch 1973-77, QMC 1983-, Univ Coll Sch 1983-, N London Poly 1986-; memb: Lord Chancellor's Advsy Ctee on Legal Aid 1985-1988, Data Protection Tbnl 1985-; JP Inner London 1981-85; *Books* Justice in Prison (with Sir Brian MacKenna, 1983), The Law Commission and Law Reform (ed 1988), Prisons in Halsbury's Laws of England (4 edn, with Louis Blom-Cooper, QC); *Clubs* Reform; *Style*— Prof Graham Zellick; 14 Brookfield Park, London NW5 1ER (☎ 01 485 8219); Faculty of Laws, QMC, London E1 4NS (☎ 01 975 5139/01 980 4811, fax 01 981 7517, telex 891750)

ZEMAN, Zbynek Anthony Bohuslav; s of Jaroslav Zeman (d 1972), and Ruzena

Zemanova *née* Petnikova (d 1980); *b* 18 Oct 1928; *Educ* Prague Univ, London Univ (BA), Oxford (DPhil); *m* 1956, Anthea, da of Norman Collins; 2 s (Adam b 1957, Alexander b 1964), 1 da (Sofia b 1966); *Career* res fell St Antony's Coll Oxford 1958-61, memb editorial staff The Economist 1959-62, lectr in modern history Univ of St Andrews 1962-70, head of res Amnesty Int 1970-73, dir East-West SPRL (Brussels) and Euro Co-operation Res Gp 1974-76, prof of central and south east euro studies dir Comenius Centre Lancaster Univ 1976-82, res profess in euro history 1982, professional fell St Edmund Hall Oxford 1983-; *Books* The Break-up of the Habsburg Empire 1914-18 (1961), Nazi Propaganda, The Merchant of Revolution, A Life of Alexander Helphand, (with W B Scharlau 1964), Prague Spring (1969), A Diplomatic History of the First World War (ed jtly, 1971), International Yearbook of East-West Trade (1975), the Masaryks Selling the War: art and propaganda in the First World War (1978), Heckling Hitler: caricatures of the Third Reich (1984); Pursued by a Bear, The Making of Eastern Europe (1989); *Recreations* squash, skiing, cooking; *Style—* Prof Zbynek Zeman; St Edmund Hall, Oxford

ZERMANSKY, Victor David; s of Isaac Zermansky (d 1987), and Sarah, *née* Cowen; *b* 28 Dec 1931; *Educ* Cowper St Sch, Leeds GS, Leeds Univ (LLB); *m* 1 June 1958, Anita Ann, da of Victor Levison (d 1973); 2 da (Susan Sadot b 1959, Karin Lobetta b 1962); *Career* Nat Serv Army Legal Aid 1953-55; slr 1953-, sr ptnr Victor D Zermansky & Co 1955-, immigration appeal adjudicator 1970-78, dep circuit judge and asst rec 1976 ; formerly pres: Leeds Jewish Rep Cncl, Leeds Law Soc, Leeds Zionist Cncl, Leeds Kashrvt cmmn (Beth Din Admin), Leeds Jewish Students Assoc; memb: Law Soc, Leeds Law Soc; *Recreations* travel, books; *Style—* Victor Zermansky, Esq; 52 Alwoodley Lane, Leeds 17 (☎ 0535 673523); Victor D. Zermansky & Co, Solicitors 10 Butts Court, Leeds 1 (☎ 0532 459 766 0532 467465, telex 557826 ZEDCO G)

ZERNY, Richard Guy Frederick; s of Marcus Zerny (d 1984), and Eunice Irene Mary, *née* Diggle (d 1982); *b* 27 June 1944; *Educ* Charterhouse; *m* 11 Sept 1970, Jane Alicia, da of Albert George Steventon (d 1984); 2 s (Charles Marcus Stephen b 1972, Miles Patrick Richard b 1973), 1 da (Clare Louise b 1979); *Career* Zernys Ltd 1969-, Johnson Gp cleaners plc 1983-, Johnson Gp Properties plc 1983-, Cleaning Tokens Ltd 1986; md Joseph Harris Ltd 1983-; sec to Hull and Dist Lifeboat Branch 1975-83; ctee memb Hull and Dist Lifeboat Branch 1967-83; Liveryman Worshipful Co of Launderers 1987; Freeman City of London 1986; *Recreations* sailing, golf, squash, bridge; *Clubs* Royal Yorks Yacht, Moor Hall Gf, Sutton Coldfield Squash, Erdington Cons Assoc; *Style—* Richard G F Zerny, Esq; 23 Boultbee Road, Wylde Green, Sutton Coldfield B72 1DW (☎ 021 373 5527); Joseph Harris Ltd, Aldridge Rd, Perry Barr, Birmingham B42 2EU (☎ 021 356 4512)

ZERVUDACHI, Nolly Emmanuel; s of Maj Laky Emmanuel, of Daira Draneht, 25 Sh Talaat Harb, BP 1277, Alexandria, Egypt, and Alice, *née* Polymeris (d 1983); *b* 2 Jan 1929; *Educ* Victoria Coll Alexandria, Victoria Coll Cairo, English Sch Heliopolis Cairo, New Coll Oxford, Faculte de Droit Paris; *m* 2 July 1957, Carolyn Elinor, da of Maj John Karney Gorman, MC; 3 s (Laky b 1958, Patrick b 1960, Constantine b 1963) 1 da (Manuela (twin) b 1963); *Career* 2 Lt "E" Batty RHA RA 1948-49; md: Niarchos Hamburg GmBh 1954-60 (dir 1953-54), Hellenic Shipyards Ltd London 1960-85; special memb gen ctee Lloyd's Register of Shipping 1970-88, dir Hellenic war Risks Assoc 1971-88 (Bermuda 1971-86), md Niarchos (London) Ltd 1972-88 (dir 1958-72), dir UK Mutual Steam Ship Assur Assoc Bermuda Ltd 1972-88; memb: cncl Int Tanker Owners Assoc 1972-88, exec ctee Inter Tanko 1976-86 (vice-chm 1984-86); *Recreations* riding, skiing, sailing; *Style—* Nolly Zervudachi, Esq; 22 Holland Villas Rd, London W14 8DH (☎ 01 603 7133)

ZETTER, Paul Isaac; CBE (1981); *b* 9 July 1923; *Educ* City of London; *m* 1954, Helen Lore Morgenster;, 1 s (Adam), 1 da Carolyn); *Career* chm: Zetters Gp, Zetters Int Pools, Metagraph Ltd, Zetter Leisure plc; Sports Council, Sports Aid Foundation; Pres John Carpenter Club 1987-88; *Books* It Could Be Verse; *Recreations* walking; *Clubs* RAC; *Style—* Paul Zetter, Esq, CBE; c/o Zetters Group Ltd, 86-88 Clerkenwell Rd, London EC1 (T 01 251 4971)

ZIEGLER, Paul Oliver; s of Maj Colin Louis Ziegler DSO, DL (d 1977), and Dora, *née* Barnwell (d 1941); *b* 9 Dec 1925; *Educ* Eton; *m* 1950, Margaret Sybil, da of Sir Lionel George Archer Cust, CBE (d 1962, s of Sir Lionel Cust, KCVO, and Hon Sybil Lyttelton); 2 s (Adam Charles b 1952, William James Archer b 1956); *Career* slr, sr ptnr Moore & Blatch (Lymington); *Recreations* reading, gardening, theatre; *Style—* Paul Ziegler, Esq; Hightown Farm, Ringwood, Hants (☎ 0425 474278); Moore & Blatch, High St, Lymington, Hants (☎ 0590 72371)

ZIEGLER, Philip Sandeman; s of Maj Colin Louis Ziegler, DSO, DL (d 1977); *b* 24 Dec 1929; *Educ* Eton, New Coll Oxford; *m* 1, 1960, Sarah (decd), da of Sir William Collins (d 1976), and Lady (Priscilla) Collins, *qv*; 1 s, 1 da; m 2, 1971, Mary Clare, *née* Charrington; 1 s; *Career* HM Dip Serv 1952-67, ed dir William Collins and Sons (joined 1967); chm Soc of Authors 1988-; commissioned to write official biography of King Edward VIII, 1987; *Books* Duchess of Dino (1962), Addington (1965), The Black Death (1968), William IV (1971), Melbourne (1976), Crown and People (1978), Diana Cooper (1981), Mountbatten (1985); *Clubs* Brooks'; *Style—* Philip Ziegler, Esq; 22 Cottesmore Gardens, London W8 (☎ 01 937 1903); Picket Orchard, Ringwood, Hants (☎ 042 54 3258)

ZIELENKIEWICZ, Hon Mrs; Hon Catherine; *née* Sinclair; da of 1 Viscount Thurso, KT, CMG, PC (d 1970); *b* 25 Oct 1919; *Educ* Kensington Central Sch of Arts & Crafts London, Academie Ranson Paris, Euston Rd Sch London; *m* 1957, Kazimierz Zielenkiewicz; 1 da (Clementina b 1958); *Career* memb Soc Scottish Women Artists; exhibitions: one man shows in Edinburgh and Paris; memb: New English Art Club (London) Royal Soc of Portrait Painters; *Style—* The Hon Mrs Zielenkiewicz; The Mill House, Isle Brewers, Taunton

ZIFF, (Robert) Paul; s of Max Ziff (d 1954), by his w Annie (d 1953); *b* 20 Dec 1935; *Educ* Giggleswick Sch; *m* 29 April 1987, Lea, da of late Irving Charles Bambage, of Yorks; *Career* chm: Stylo Matchmakers Int Ltd, Public Eye Enterprises Ltd, Pentagon Prodns & Mgmnt Ltd, Whitham & Schofield Ltd; dir Well Worth Watching Prodns Ltd, vice chm Stylo plc; *Recreations* mechanical music; *Clubs* St James's, Annabel's, White Elephant; *Style—* Paul Ziff, Esq; Gallogate House, Weston, Nr Leeds; Stylo Matchmakers Int Ltd, Matchmakers House, Clayton Wood Bank, Leeds LS16 6RJ (☎ 0532 783501, telex 557369)

ZIMMER, Dr Robert Mark; s of Norman Zimmer, NY, USA, and Lenore *née* Wasserman; *Educ* Churchill Coll Cambridge, MIT (SB), dol Columbia Univ NY (MA, M Phil, PhD); *m* 23 July 1983, Joanna Elizabeth Marlow, da of Thomas Gondris, Ipswich, Suffolk; *Career* lectr: Columbia Univ 1982-85, Brunel Univ 1985-; published poetry and articles on Mathematics, Computer Sci, Electrical Engrg and 18 Century Eng Literature; *Recreations* food, books; *Clubs* Young Johnsonians; *Style—* Dr Robert Zimmer; 12 Myddleton Road, Uxbridge, Middx, UB8 2DN (☎ 0895 33308), Dept Electrical Engrg Brunel Univ, Uxbridge, Middx, UB8 3PH (☎ 0895 74000 ext 2756, fax 0895 32806, telex 261173 G)

ZINNEMANN, Fred; s of Dr Oskar Zinnemann (d 1941), and Anna (d 1942); *b* 29 April 1907; *Educ* Vienna U Law Sch (BA), Ecole Technique de Cinematographie Paris; *m* 1936, Renée, *née* Bartlett; 1 s (David); *Career* film director; *films* The Seventh Cross (1942), The Search (1947), Act of Violence (1948), The Men (1949), High Noon (1951), A Member of The Wedding (1952), From Here To Eternity (1953), Oklahoma (1955), The Nun's Story (1958), The Sundowners (1960), A Man For All Seasons (1967), The Day Of The Jackal (1973), Julia (1977), Five Days One Summer (1982); 4 motion picture Acad Awards (Oscars) for directing: 1951, 1954, 1967 (and for producing); Br Acad of Film and TV Arts Awards (BAFTA, fellow 1978): 1967, 1979; other prof Awards incl: NY Film Critics 1952, 1954, 1959 and 1967, Directors' Guild 1954 and 1967, Moscow Festival 1965, Golden Thistle (Edinburgh) 1965, D W Griffith (LA) 1970, Donatello (Florence) 1978; 2 vice-pres Directors' Guild of America 1961-64, co-founder and ex-trustee American Film Inst 1967-71, US Congressional Life Achievement Award (1987), Order of Arts and Letters (Fr) 1982, Gold Medal, City of Vienna (Austria) 1967; *Recreations* mountaineering, chamber music; *Clubs* Sierra (San Francisco); *Style—* Fred Zinnemann, Esq; 128 Mount St, London W1 (☎ 01 629 4335)

ZINS, Stefan; s of Maximilian Zins (d 1966), of Zofia, *née* Kurzman; *b* 5 June 1927; *Educ* Hammersmith Coll of Art and Architecture, London Univ Coll (Cert Town Planning); *m* 17 Aug 1959, Harriet Norah, da of Henry Frank Back (d 1968); 1 da (Deborah b 1962); *Career* architect, planning conslt; fndr and dir: Stefan Zins Ltd, PS Mgmnt; i/c numerous building schemes in SE England, for public and private sectors, inc hotels, youth hostels, old peoples' homes, etc, also commercial projects; *Recreations* tennis, skiing, swimming, wine tasting; *Clubs* Confrerie des Compagnons Haut Normands du Gouste-Vin; *Style—* Stefan Zins, Esq; 31 Valiant House, London SW11 3LU; 71 Warwick Road, London SW5 (☎ 01 370 3129, fax 373 5993)

ZITCER, Hon Mrs (Diane Susan); *née* Morris; da of 2 Baron Morris of Kenwood and Hon Ruth Joan Gertrude Rahle, *née* Janner; *b* 25 Jan 1960; *Educ* St Paul's Girls Sch, Central Sch of Drama (dip stage mgmnt); *m* 1981, Cary Haskell Zitcer, er s of Chaim Josek Zitcer; 2 da (Natasha Esther b 1986, Emily Margaret b 1988); *Career* television presenter and producer; mem: NUJ, ACTT; *Recreations* theatre, cinema, water and snow skiing, DIY, interior design, needlework; *Style—* The Hon Mrs Zitcer; 2 Sidmouth Rd, Brondesbury Park, London NW2

ZOLLINGER, Fred Edward; s of Alfred Edward Zollinger (d 1957); *b* 6 July 1922; *Educ* Queens' Coll Cambridge; *m* 1953, Flora, da of late Brig-Gen Wallace Wright, VC; *Career* chm: Imperial Continental Gas Assoc 1974-, Century Power & Light Ltd 1974-; dir: Lazard Bros & Co Ltd 1966-, Pirelli General plc 1971-, Calor Group Ltd 1974-; *Recreations* skiing; *Style—* Fred Zollinger Esq; The House of Barns, Chobham, Woking, Surrey (☎ 099 05 8815)

ZOLLNER, Stephen; s of Stephen Zollner (d 1956) and Nina, *née* Dragicevic; *b* 7 May 1946; *Educ* Charterhouse, Pembroke Coll Oxford (MA); *m* July 1982, Alison, da of Gerard Frater; 1 da (Amelia b 1982); *Career* barr Gray's Inn 1969; *Recreations* travel, photography; *Style—* Stephen Zollner, Esq; 23 Fitzjohns Ave, London NW3 5JY (☎ 01 435 9848); 15 Old Sq Lincoln's Inn, London WC2A 3UE (☎ 01 831 0801, fax 01 405 1387)

ZOLLO, Jeffrey Michael; s of Michael Joseph Zollo (d 1981), and Florence Lillian, *née* Green; *b* 4 Jan 1945; *m* 2 July 1976, Sirkka-Liisa, da of Kustaa Malm (d 1974); *Career* freelance journalist, trg Salisbury Journal and Bournemouth Times; reporter: East London News Agency (nat papers), Stockholm Sweden; foreign corr Helsinki contrib: Br, Dutch, American, Spanish, German pubns; currently writing for Br and Finnish magazines; memb: Poole Cons club, Finnish Spitz Club and Soc; memb: NUJ, Int Press Assoc, Int Fedn Journalists; *Recreations* reading; *Style—* Jeffrey Zollo, Esq; 39 Tatnam Rd, Poole, Dorset BH15 2DW (☎ 0202 677071, fax 0202 684461)

ZOUCHE, 18 Baron (E 1308); Sir James (Jimmie) Assheton Frankland; 12 Bt (E 1660); s of Hon Sir Thomas Frankland, 11 Bt (d 1944, s of Sir Frederick Frankland, 10 Bt, by his w Baroness Zouche (d 1965), 17 holder of the Peerage and descendant of Eudes La Zouche, yr bro of Sir Roger La Zouche of Ashby after whose family Ashby-de-la-Zouch is named); Lord Zouche is coheir to Baronies of St Maur and Grey of Codnor (abeyant since 1628 & 1496 respectively); *b* 23 Feb 1943; *Educ* Lycée Jacard Lausanne; *m* 1978, Sally, da of Roderic M Barton, of Brook House, Pulham St Mary, Norfolk; 1 s, 1 da; *Heir* s Hon William Thomas Assheton b 23 July 1984; *Career* Capt 15/19 King's Roy Hussars (ret 1968), ADC to Govr Tasmania 1965-68, Hon ADC to Govr Victoria 1975-; vice pres Multiple Sclerosis Soc Victoria 1973-; co dir; *Recreations* shooting; *Clubs* Cavalry & Guards, Melbourne (Australia); *Style—* The Rt Hon the Lord Zouche; 7 St Vincent's Place, Albert Park, Vic 3206, Australia

ZUCKER, Kenneth Harry; QC (1981); s of Nathaniel Zucker, of London, and Norma Zucker, *née* Mehlberg (d 1937); *b* 4 Mar 1935; *Educ* Westcliff HS, Exeter Coll Oxford; *m* 1961, Ruth Erica, da of Dr Henry Brudno (d 1967); 1 s (Jonathan), 1 da (Naomi); *Career* barr, recorder 1982; *Recreations* reading, walking, photography; *Style—* Kenneth Zucker Esq, QC; 10 Kings Bench Walk, Temple, London EC4 (☎ 01 353 2501)

ZUCKERMAN, Baroness; Lady Joan Alice Violet Rufus; *née* Isaacs; da of 2 Marquess of Reading, GCMG, CBE, TD, PC, QC, and Hon Eva Mond, CBE, JP (da of 1 Baron Melchett); *b* 19 July 1918; *m* 1939, Baron Zuckerman, *qv*; 1 s (Paul), 1 da (Stella); *Career* JP: Birmingham 1961, Norfolk 1967; amateur artist exhibiting in Norfolk and London; chm Friends of the Sainsbsury Centre for Visual Arts Norwich; *Books* Birmingham Heritage (1979); *Style—* The Rt Hon Lady Zuckerman; The Shooting Box, Burnham Thorpe, King's Lynn, Norfolk PE1 8HW

ZUCKERMAN, Hon Paul Sebastian; s of Baron Zuckerman (Life Peer), and Lady Joan Rufus Isaacs, da of 2 Marquess of Reading; *b* 1945; *Educ* Rugby, Trinity Coll Cambridge, Univ of Reading; *m* 1972 (m dis), Mrs Janette Hampel, da of R R Mather, of Stoke-by-Clare, Suffolk; Dir S G Warburg & Co Ltd; *Clubs* Brooks's; *Style—* The Hon Paul Zuckerman; The Old Rectory, Grosvenor Rd, London SW1

ZUCKERMAN, Baron (Life Peer UK 1971); Solly Zuckerman; OM (1968), KCB (1964, CB 1946); s of Moses Zuckerman; *b* 30 May 1904,Cape Town,; *Educ* Cape

Town Univ; *m* 1939, Lady Joan Alice Violet Rufus Isaacs, da of 2 Marquess of Reading; 1 s, 1 da; *Career* sits as Independent peer in House of Lords; pres: Zoological Soc London 1977-84, Fauna Preservation Soc 1974-81, British Industrial Biological Research Association 1974-; chief scientific advsr: Defence Secretary 1960-66, HM Govt 1964-71; FRS, MRCS, FRCP; kt 1956; *Books* Nuclear Illusion and Reality (1982), From Apes to Warlords (1978), Social Life of Monkeys and Apes (1932,1981), Monkeys, Men and Missiles (1988); *Clubs* Brooks's; *Style—* The Rt Hon Lord Zuckerman OM KCB; University of East Anglia, Norwich, NR4 7TJ

ZULUETA; *see*: de Zulueta

ZUTSHI, Dr Derek Wyndham Hariram; s of Lambodha Zutshi (d 1964), of Srinagar, Kashmir, and London, and Eileen Dorothy Wyndham Lord (d 1944); *b* 26 April 1930; *Educ* Epsom Coll, Univ of Bristol (MB ChB); *m* 11 May 1974, Marguerite Elizabeth, da of Edgar Montague Smith (d 1944), of Lima Peru, and Bournemouth; *Career* rheumatology conslt 1973-; med registrar MRC rheumatism res unit Canadian Red Cross Memorial Hosp Taplow 1966-68, sr registrar rheumatology and clinical tutor medicine The London Hosp 1968-73, med dir sch of physiotherapy Prince of Wales Gen Hosp 1973-77; rheumatology conslt Gen Hosps Tottenham (Prince of Wales, St Ann's) 1973-77; examiner: Chartered Soc of Physiotherapy 1974-78, Coll of Occupational Therapists 1980-; hon tres Federal Cncl of Indian Orgns 1974-, memb cncl and hon sec Br Assoc for Rheumatology and Rehabilitation 1974-78, memb cncl Med Soc of London 1977-80, Hunterian Soc 1978- (hon tres 1979-); memb: ct Univ of Bristol 1958- (memb cncl 1988-), bd of tstees The Hindu Centre London 1962-, bd of govrs Tottenham Coll of Further Educn 1974- (dep chm 1978-87, chm 1988-), med advsy panel Nat Rubella Cncl 1988-; FRSA, FRSM, MRCP; *Recreations* travel, music, reading; *Clubs* Athenaeum; *Style—* Dr Derek Zutshi; 36 Eton Court, Eton Ave, Hampstead, London NW3 3HJ; 99 Harley St, London W1N 1DF (☎ 01 486 8495)

ZVEGINTZOV, Hon Mrs (Rachel Kathleen); *née* Bailey; da of late Hon Herbert Crawshay Bailey (d 1936), 4 s of 1 Baron Glanusk; sister of 4 Baron; raised to the rank of a Baron's da 1948, and Kathleen Mary, *née* Salt (d 1948); *b* 5 June 1914; *Educ* St Pauls Girls Sch; *m* 1940, Brig Dimitry Zvegintzov, CBE (d 1984), late Border Regt (ret), s of Col Dimitry Ivan, CMG, DSO (d 1967), of Parc Gwynne, Glasbury-on-Wye; 2 s (Ivan, Paul), 1 da (Elizavietta); *Style—* The Hon Mrs Zvegintzov; The Studio, White Lodge, Hill Brow Road, Liss, Hants, GU33 7PS (☎ 0730 893866)